FOREWORD

THE EUROPA YEAR BOOK was first published in 1926. Since 1960 it has appeared in annual two-volume editions, and has become established as an authoritative reference work, providing a wealth of detailed information on the political, economic and commercial institutions of the world.

Volume I contains international organizations and the first part of the alphabetical survey of countries of the world, from Afghanistan to Jordan. Volume II contains countries from Kampuchea to Zimbabwe.

Readers are referred to our four regional books, THE MIDDLE EAST AND NORTH AFRICA, AFRICA SOUTH OF THE SAHARA, THE FAR EAST AND AUSTRALASIA and SOUTH AMERICA, CENTRAL AMERICA AND THE CARIBBEAN, for additional information on the geography, history and economy of these areas.

The information is revised annually by a variety of methods, including direct mailing to all the institutions listed. Many other sources are used, such as national statistical offices, government departments and diplomatic missions. The editors thank the innumerable individuals and organizations throughout the world whose generous co-operation in providing current information for this edition is invaluable in presenting the most accurate and up-to-date material available, and acknowledge particular indebtedness for material from the following publications: the United Nations' *Demographic Yearbook*, *Statistical Yearbook* and *Industrial Statistics Yearbook*; the Food and Agriculture Organization of the United Nations' *Production Yearbook*, *Yearbook of Fishery Statistics* and *Yearbook of Forest Products*; and *The Military Balance 1986–87*, published by the International Institute for Strategic Studies, 23 Tavistock Street, London, WC2E 7NQ.

February 1987.

CONTENTS

Abbreviations	Page xi
International Comparisons	xiv
Late Information	xix

PART ONE

International Organizations*

The United Nations	3
Members	3
Permanent Missions	4
Observers	6
Information Centres	6
Budget	8
Charter of the United Nations	9
Secretariat	17
General Assembly	18
Security Council	19
Economic and Social Council—ECOSOC	19
Trusteeship Council	20
International Court of Justice	21
United Nations Regional Economic Commissions	23
Economic Commission for Europe—ECE	23
Economic and Social Commission for Asia and the Pacific—ESCAP	24
Economic Commission for Latin America and the Caribbean—ECLAC	27
Economic Commission for Africa—ECA	28
Economic and Social Commission for Western Asia—ESCWA	32
Other United Nations Bodies	33
International Atomic Energy Agency—IAEA	33
International Sea-Bed Authority	35
Office of the United Nations Disaster Relief Co-Ordinator—UNDRO	36
United Nations Centre for Human Settlements—UNCHS (Habitat)	37
United Nations Children's Fund—UNICEF	38
United Nations Conference on Trade and Development—UNCTAD	39
United Nations Development Programme—UNDP	40
United Nations Environment Programme—UNEP	42
United Nations Fund for Population Activities—UNFPA	44
United Nations High Commissioner for Refugees—UNHCR	45
United Nations Institute for Training and Research—UNITAR	47

	Page
United Nations Observer Mission and Peace-keeping Forces in the Middle East	48
United Nations Relief and Works Agency for Palestine Refugees in the Near East—UNRWA	49
United Nations Research Institute for Social Development—UNRISD	51
World Food Council—WFC	51
World Food Programme—WFP	52
Membership of the United Nations and its Specialized Agencies	53
Specialized Agencies within the UN System	56
Food and Agriculture Organization—FAO	56
General Agreement on Tariffs and Trade—GATT	59
International Bank for Reconstruction and Development—IBRD (World Bank)	60
International Development Association—IDA	66
International Finance Corporation—IFC	67
International Civil Aviation Organization—ICAO	68
International Fund for Agricultural Development—IFAD	69
International Labour Organisation—ILO	70
International Maritime Organization—IMO	72
International Monetary Fund—IMF	73
International Telecommunication Union—ITU	77
United Nations Educational, Scientific and Cultural Organization—UNESCO	79
United Nations Industrial Development Organization—UNIDO	82
Universal Postal Union—UPU	83
World Health Organization—WHO	84
World Intellectual Property Organization—WIPO	86
World Meteorological Organization—WMO	87
African Development Bank—ADB	90
Andean Group	92
ANZUS	94
Arab Bank for Economic Development in Africa—BADEA	95
Arab Fund for Economic and Social Development—AFESD	97
Arab Monetary Fund	98
Asian Development Bank—ADB	100
Association of South East Asian Nations—ASEAN	103
Bank for International Settlements—BIS	106
Caribbean Community and Common Market—CARICOM	108
Central American Common Market—CACM	110
The Colombo Plan for Co-operative Economic and Social Development in Asia and the Pacific	112
The Commonwealth	114

* A complete Index of International Organizations is to be found on p. 1603.

CONTENTS

	Page
Communauté Économique de l'Afrique de l'Ouest—CEAO	121
Conseil de l'Entente	123
Co-operation Council for the Arab States of the Gulf	124
Council for Mutual Economic Assistance—CMEA	126
Council of Arab Economic Unity	128
Council of Europe	130
Economic Community of West African States—ECOWAS	133
The European Communities	135
European Free Trade Association—EFTA	153
The Franc Zone	155
Inter-American Development Bank—IDB	157
International Bank for Economic Co-operation—IBEC	159
International Chamber of Commerce—ICC	160
International Confederation of Free Trade Unions—ICFTU	162
International Investment Bank	164
International Olympic Committee	165
International Red Cross	166
International Committee of the Red Cross	166
League of Red Cross and Red Crescent Societies	167
Islamic Development Bank	168
Latin American Integration Association—LAIA	170
League of Arab States	171
Nordic Council	176
Nordic Council of Ministers	177
North Atlantic Treaty Organisation—NATO	179
Organisation for Economic Co-operation and Development—OECD	182
International Energy Agency	184
OECD Nuclear Energy Agency—NEA	184
Organization of African Unity—OAU	186
Organization of American States—OAS	189
Organization of Arab Petroleum Exporting Countries—OAPEC	192
Organization of the Islamic Conference—OIC	193
Organization of the Petroleum Exporting Countries—OPEC	195
OPEC Fund for International Development	198
South Pacific Commission—SPC	200
South Pacific Forum	202
South Pacific Bureau for Economic Co-operation—SPEC	202
Southern African Development Co-ordination Conference—SADCC	204
Warsaw Treaty of Friendship, Co-operation and Mutual Assistance—The Warsaw Pact	206
Western European Union—WEU	207
World Confederation of Labour—WCL	208
World Council of Churches—WCC	209
World Federation of Trade Unions—WFTU	210
Other International Organizations	211

PART TWO

Afghanistan–Jordan

Afghanistan	Page 281
Albania	295
Algeria	307
Andorra	323
Angola	326
Antarctica	340
Antigua and Barbuda	342
Argentina	348
Australia	372
Australian External Territories:	399
Christmas Island	399
Cocos (Keeling) Islands	399
Norfolk Island	400
Other Territories	401
Austria	402
The Bahamas	425
Bahrain	432
Bangladesh	441
Barbados	460
Belgium	468
Belize	492
Benin	499
Bhutan	511
Bolivia	519
Botswana	535
Brazil	547
Brunei	575
Bulgaria	582
Burkina Faso	600
Burma	612
Burundi	626
Cameroon	636
Canada	651
Cape Verde	684
The Central African Republic	690
Chad	701
Chile	712
China, People's Republic	731
China (Taiwan)	761
Colombia	775
The Comoros	794
The Congo	799
Costa Rica	811
Côte d'Ivoire—see Ivory Coast	
Cuba	825
Cyprus	842
Czechoslovakia	857
Denmark	879
Danish External Territories:	903
Faeroe Islands	903
Greenland	905
Djibouti	907
Dominica	913

CONTENTS

The Dominican Republic	Page	920
Ecuador		934
Egypt		951
El Salvador		975
Equatorial Guinea		990
Ethiopia		995
Fiji		1009
Finland		1017
France		1040
French Overseas Possessions:		1088
Overseas Departments:		1088
French Guiana		1088
Guadeloupe		1091
Martinique		1095
Réunion		1099
Overseas Collectivités Territoriales:		1103
Mayotte		1103
Saint Pierre and Miquelon		1104
Overseas Territories:		1107
French Polynesia		1107
French Southern and Antarctic Territories		1111
New Caledonia		1112
Wallis and Futuna Islands		1117
Gabon		1119
The Gambia		1132
German Democratic Republic		1140
Federal Republic of Germany	Page	1164
Ghana		1209
Greece		1225
Grenada		1246
Guatemala		1252
Guinea		1267
Guinea-Bissau		1277
Guyana		1282
Haiti		1292
Honduras		1302
Hungary		1317
Iceland		1339
India		1348
Indonesia		1387
Iran		1409
Iraq		1429
Ireland		1447
Israel		1467
Italy		1491
The Ivory Coast		1525
Jamaica		1539
Japan		1553
Jordan		1587

Index of International Organizations   1603

An Index of Territories is to be found at the end of Volume II.

ABBREVIATIONS

AB	Aktiebolag (joint stock company)
Acad.	Academician; Academy
ACT	Australian Capital Territory
ADB	African Development Bank; Asian Development Bank
Adm.	Admiral
admin.	administration
AG	Aktiengesellschaft (Joint Stock Company)
a.i.	ad interim
AID	(US) Agency for International Development
AIDS	Acquired Immunodeficiency Syndrome
Al.	Aleja (alley, avenue)
Ala	Alabama
ALADI	Asociación Latino-Americana de Integración
Alt.	Alternate
Alta	Alberta
AM	Amplitude Modulation
amalg.	amalgamated
AP	Andhra Pradesh
apdo	apartado (Post Box)
approx.	approximately
Apt	Apartment
Ariz	Arizona
Ark	Arkansas
A/S	Aktieselskab (Joint Stock Company)
ASEAN	Association of South East Asian Nations
asscn	association
assoc.	associate
asst	assistant
Aug.	August
auth.	authorized
Ave	Avenue
Avda	Avenida (Avenue)
BC	British Columbia
Bd	Board
Bd, Bld, Blv., Blvd	Boulevard
b/d	barrels per day
Bhd	Berhad (Public Limited Company)
Bldg	Building
BP	Boîte postale (Post Box)
br.(s)	branch(es)
Brig.	Brigadier
Bt	Baronet
bte	boîte (box)
bul.	bulvar (boulevard)
C	Centigrade
c.	circa; cuadra(s) (block(s))
CACM	Central American Common Market
Cad.	Caddesi (street)
Calif	California
cap.	capital
Capt.	Captain
CARICOM	Caribbean Community
CB	Companion of (the Order of) the Bath
CBE	Commander of (the Order of) the British Empire
CCL	Caribbean Congress of Labour
Cdre	Commodore
Cen.	Central
CEO	Chief Executive Officer
CFA	Communauté Financière Africaine, Co-opération Financière en Afrique centrale
CH	Companion of Honour
Chair.	Chairman
CI	Channel Islands
Cia	Companhia
Cía	Compañía
Cie	Compagnie
c.i.f.	cost, insurance and freight
C-in-C	Commander-in-Chief
circ.	circulation
cm	centimetre(s)
CMEA	Council for Mutual Economic Assistance
Cnr	Corner
Co	Company; County
Col	Colonel
Col.	Colonia
Colo	Colorado
COMECON	Council for Mutual Economic Assistance (CMEA)
Comm.	Commission; Commendatore
Commdr	Commander
Commdt	Commandant
Commr	Commissioner
Confed.	Confederation
Conn	Connecticut
Corpn	Corporation
CP	Case Postale; Caixa Postal; Casella Postale (Post Box); Communist Party
CPSU	Communist Party of the Soviet Union
Cres.	Crescent
CSTAL	Confederación Sindical de los Trabajadores de América Latina
CTCA	Confederación de Trabajadores Centro-americanos
Cttee	Committee
cu	cubic
cwt	hundredweight
DC	District of Columbia; Distrito Central
DDR	Deutsche Democratische Republik (German Democratic Republic)
DE	Departamento Estatal
Dec.	December
Del	Delaware
Del.	Delegación
Dem.	Democratic; Democrat
Dep.	Deputy
dep.	deposits
Dept	Department
devt	development
DF	Distrito Federal
Diag.	Diagonal
Dir	Director
Div.	Division(al)
DM	Deutsche Mark
DN	Distrito Nacional
Doc.	Docent
Dott.	Dottore
Dr	Doctor
Dra	Doctora
dr.(e)	drachma(e)
Drs	Doctorandus
dwt	dead weight tons
E	East; Eastern
ECA	(United Nations) Economic Commission for Africa
ECE	(United Nations) Economic Commission for Europe
ECLAC	(United Nations) Economic Commission for Latin America and the Caribbean
Econ.	Economist; Economics
ECOSOC	(United Nations) Economic and Social Council
ECOWAS	Economic Community of West African States
ECU	European Currency Unit
ECWA	(United Nations) Economic Commission for Western Asia
Edif.	Edificio (Building)
edn	edition
EEC	European Economic Community
EFTA	European Free Trade Association
e.g.	exempli gratia (for example)
eKv	electron kilovolt
eMv	electron megavolt
Eng.	Engineer; Engineering

ABBREVIATIONS

Esc.	Escuela; Escudos; Escritorio
ESCAP	(United Nations) Economic and Social Commission for Asia and the Pacific
esq.	esquina (corner)
est.	established; estimate; estimated
etc.	et cetera
EUA	European Unit of Account
eV	eingetragener Verein
excl.	excluding
exec.	executive
Ext.	Extension
F	Fahrenheit
f.	founded
FAO	Food and Agriculture Organization
Feb.	February
Fed.	Federation; Federal
Fla	Florida
FM	frequency modulation
fmrly	formerly
f.o.b.	free on board
Fr	Father
Fr.	Franc
FRG	Federal Republic of Germany
Fri.	Friday
ft	foot (feet)
g	gram(s)
Ga	Georgia
GATT	General Agreement on Tariffs and Trade
GBE	Knight (or Dame) Grand Cross of (the Order of) the British Empire
GCMG	Knight Grand Cross of (the Order of) St Michael and St George
GDP	gross domestic product
GDR	German Democratic Republic
Gen.	General
GeV	giga electron volts
GmbH	Gesellschaft mit beschränkter Haftung (Limited Liability Company)
GNP	gross national product
Gov.	Governor
Govt	Government
grt	gross registered tons
GWh	gigawatt hours
ha	hectares
HE	His (or Her) Eminence; His (or Her) Excellency
hf	hlutafelag (Company Limited)
hl	hectolitre(s)
HM	His (or Her) Majesty
Hon.	Honorary (or Honourable)
hp	horsepower
HQ	Headquarters
HRH	His (or Her) Royal Highness
IBRD	International Bank for Reconstruction and Development (World Bank)
ICC	International Chamber of Commerce
ICFTU	International Confederation of Free Trade Unions
IDA	International Development Association
IDB	Inter-American Development Bank
i.e.	id est (that is to say)
Ill	Illinois
ILO	International Labour Organisation
IMF	International Monetary Fund
in (ins)	inch (inches)
Inc, Incorp., Incd	Incorporated
incl.	including
Ind	Indiana
Ind.	Independent
Ing.	Engineer
Insp.	Inspector
Int.	International
Inž.	Engineer
irreg.	irregular
Is	Islands
ISIC	International Standard Industrial Classification
Jan.	January
Jnr	Junior
Jr	Jonkheer (Netherlands); Junior
Jt	Joint
Kans	Kansas
KBE	Knight Commander of (the Order of) the British Empire
KCMG	Knight Commander of (the Order of) St Michael and St George
kg	kilogram(s)
KG	Knight of (the Order of) the Garter; Kommandit Gesellschaft (Limited Partnership)
kHz	kilohertz
KK	Kaien Kaisha (Limited Company)
km	kilometre(s)
kv.	kvartal (apartment block)
kW	kilowatt(s)
kWh	kilowatt hours
Ky	Kentucky
La	Louisiana
lb	pound(s)
Lic.	Licenciado
Licda	Licenciada
LNG	liquefied natural gas
LPG	liquefied petroleum gas
Lt, Lieut	Lieutenant
Ltd	Limited
m	metre(s)
m.	million
Maj.	Major
Man	Manitoba
Man.	Manager; managing
March.	Marchese
Mass	Massachusetts
MBE	Member of (the Order of) the British Empire
mbH	mit beschränkter Haftung (with limited liability)
Mc/s	megacycles per second
Md	Maryland
Me	Maine
mem.	member
MEP	Member of the European Parliament
MEV	mega electron volts
mfrs	manufacturers
Mgr	Monseigneur; Monsignor
MHz	megahertz
Mich	Michigan
Minn	Minnesota
Miss	Mississippi
Mlle	Mademoiselle
mm	millimetre(s)
Mme	Madame
Mo	Missouri
Mon.	Monday
Mont	Montana
MP	Member of Parliament; Madhya Pradesh
MSS	Manuscripts
MW	megawatt(s); medium wave
MWh	megawatt hour(s)
N	North; Northern
n.a.	not available
nab.	naberezhnaya (embankment, quai)
nám.	náměstí (square)
Nat.	National
NATO	North Atlantic Treaty Organization
NB	New Brunswick
NC	North Carolina
NCO	Non-Commissioned Officer
ND	North Dakota
Neb	Nebraska
Nev	Nevada
Nfld	Newfoundland
NH	New Hampshire
NJ	New Jersey
NM	New Mexico
NMP	net material product
no	número (number)
no.	number
Nov.	November
nr	near
nrt	net registered tons
NS	Nova Scotia
NSW	New South Wales
NV	Naamloze Vennootschap (Limited Company)

ABBREVIATIONS

NY	New York
NZ	New Zealand
OAPEC	Organization of Arab Petroleum Exporting Countries
OAS	Organization of American States
OAU	Organization of African Unity
OBE	Officer of (the Order of) the British Empire
OCAM	Organisation Commune Africaine et Mauricienne
Oct.	October
OECD	Organisation for Economic Co-operation and Development
OECS	Organization of East Caribbean States
Of.	Oficina
OIC	Organization of the Islamic Conference
Okla	Oklahoma
Ont	Ontario
OPEC	Organization of Petroleum Exporting Countries
opp.	opposite
Ore	Oregon
Org.	Organization
ORIT	Organización Regional Interamericana de Trabajadores
p.	page
p.a.	per annum
Pa	Pennsylvania
Parl.	Parliament(ary)
PC	Privy Counsellor
per.	pereulok (lane, alley)
Perm. Rep.	Permanent Representative
PK	Post Box (Turkish)
pl.	platz; place; ploshchad (square)
PLC	Public Limited Company
PMB	Private Mail Bag
POB	Post Office Box
Pr.	prospekt (avenue)
Pres.	President
Prin.	Principal
Prof.	Professor
Propr	Proprietor
Prov.	Province; Provincial; Provinciale (Dutch)
PT	Perseroan Tarbates (Limited Company)
Pte	Private
Pty	Proprietary
p.u.	paid up
publ.	publication; published
Publr	Publisher
Pvt.	Private
QC	Queen's Counsel
Qld	Queensland
Que	Quebec
q.v.	quod vide (to which refer)
Rd	Road
R(s)	rupee(s)
reg., regd	register; registered
reorg.	reorganized
Rep.	Republic; Republican; Representative
Repub.	Republic
res	reserve(s)
retd	retired
Rev.	Reverend
RI	Rhode Island
RJ	Rio de Janeiro
Rm	Room
Rp.(s)	rupiah(s)
RSFSR	Russian Soviet Federative Socialist Republic
RSR	Republica Socialistă Romănia (Socialist Republic of Romania)
Rt	Right
S	South; Southern; San
SA	Société Anonyme, Sociedad Anónima (limited company); South Australia
SARL	Sociedade Anônima de Responsabilidade Limitada (Joint Stock Company of Limited Liability)
Sask	Saskatchewan
Sat.	Saturday
SC	South Carolina
SD	South Dakota
Sdn Bhd	Sendirian Berhad (Private Limited Company)
SDR(s)	Special Drawing Right(s)
Sec.	Secretary
Sen.	Senior; Senator
Sept.	September
SER	Sua Eccellenza Reverendissima (His Eminence)
SFRY	Socialist Federal Republic of Yugoslavia
SITC	Standard International Trade Classification
SJ	Society of Jesus
Soc.	Society
Sok.	Sokak (street)
SP	São Paulo
SpA	Società per Azioni (Joint Stock Company)
Sq.	Square
sq	square (in measurements)
Sr	Senior; Señor
Sra	Señora
SrL	Società a Responsabilità Limitata (Limited Company)
SSR	Soviet Socialist Republic
St	Saint; Street
Sta	Santa
Ste	Sainte
subs.	subscriptions; subscribed
Sun.	Sunday
Supt	Superintendent
Tas	Tasmania
TD	Teachta Dála (Member of Parliament)
tech., techn.	technical
tel.	telephone
Tenn	Tennessee
Tex	Texas
Thur.	Thursday
Treas.	Treasurer
Tue.	Tuesday
TV	television
t/yr	tons per year
u.	utca (street)
u/a	unit of account
UDEAC	Union Douanière et Economique de l'Afrique Centrale
UK	United Kingdom
ul.	ulitsa (street)
UN	United Nations
UNCTAD	United Nations Conference on Trade and Development
UNDP	United Nations Development Programme
UNESCO	United Nations Educational, Scientific and Cultural Organization
UNHCR	United Nations High Commissioner for Refugees
Univ.	University
UNRWA	United Nations Relief and Works Agency for Palestine Refugees in the Near East
UP	Uttar Pradesh
USA	United States of America
USAID	United States Agency for International Development
USSR	Union of Soviet Socialist Republics
Va	Virginia
VAT	Value Added Tax
VEB	Volkseigener Betrieb (Public Company)
VHF	Very High Frequency
Vic	Victoria
viz.	videlicet (namely)
Vn	Veien (street)
vol.(s)	volume(s)
Vt	Vermont
W	West; Western
WA	Western Australia
Wash	Washington (state)
WCL	World Confederation of Labour
Wed.	Wednesday
WFTU	World Federation of Trade Unions
WHO	World Health Organization
Wis	Wisconsin
W Va	West Virginia
Wy	Wyoming
yr	year

INTERNATIONAL COMPARISONS

The following table provides a general comparison of area, population, life expectancy and gross national product for every independent state (excluding the Vatican City) and every other territory with more than 25,000 inhabitants (excluding the Gaza Strip). An attempt has been made to provide comparable information under each heading, and the figures in the table refer to the latest period for which uniform data are available in each category.

Area figures refer to total area, including inland water. Unless otherwise indicated, population figures are mid-year estimates. Most of the data refer to *de facto* population (persons actually present in the area), though some are estimates of *de jure* population (persons normally resident). Figures for life expectancy are estimates, prepared in the Population Division of the United Nations, of the average number of years of life remaining to a new-born child if subject to the mortality conditions (recorded or assumed) of the period 1975–80. It should be stressed that the figures refer to the average life expectancy *at birth* for both sexes. In many developing countries mortality rates are high during the first few years of life, but persons who survive infancy have a life expectancy much greater than the average at birth. It is also noteworthy that in all developed countries the life expectancy of females is greater than that of males.

Figures for gross national product (GNP) may be taken as indicators of the comparative sizes of the various national economies, while data on GNP per head facilitate international comparisons of average levels of economic activity. Owing to variations in price levels and the unequal distribution of income, a figure for GNP per head is only an approximate measure of a country's wealth or poverty, and should not be regarded as a reliable indicator of the relative standard of living in each country. Sources are quoted at the end of the tables, but it must be stressed that the data on total GNP and on GNP per head are, to a considerable extent, estimates, and may be used only as a general guide. In particular, a wide margin of error may be expected in estimates for centrally planned economies, and in figures for GNP per head of less than $300, where the subsistence sector is unusually important and the degree of precision tends to decrease as the ratio of subsistence production to total GNP increases. Figures refer to GNP at market prices, converted to US dollars, with totals usually rounded to the nearest 10 of the unit employed. The conversion factor from national currencies to US dollars is the average of exchange rates for three consecutive years, e.g. for 1984 the base period is 1982–84. Data on GNP per head are based on World Bank figures for population, which may differ from figures shown elsewhere in the tables.

Country	Area (sq km)	Mid-1984 population ('000)	Mid-1984 population density (per sq km)	Average population increase, 1980–84 (% per year)	Life expectancy at birth, 1975–80 (years)	1984 Gross national product ($ million)	1984 GNP per head ($)
Afghanistan[1,2]	647,497	17,672	27	2.6	37.0	2,290	160
Albania[2]	28,748	2,901	101	2.1	69.7	1,930	740
Algeria[3,4]	2,381,741	20,500	8.6	3.3	55.3	50,680	2,380
American Samoa[4,5]	197	35	178	1.9	n.a.	160	4,690
Andorra[6,7]	467	40	86	6.0	n.a.	n.a.	n.a.
Angola[8]	1,246,700	8,540*	6.9	2.5	40.0	3,320	470
Antigua and Barbuda	440	79	180	1.3	n.a.	150	1,830
Argentina	2,766,889	30,097	11	1.6	68.7	67,150	2,230
Aruba[3,9]	193	67	347	n.a.	n.a.	n.a.	n.a.
Australia[10]	7,686,848	15,556	2.0	1.4	73.5	184,980	11,890
Austria	83,855	7,552	90	0.0	72.0	68,800	9,140
Bahamas[5]	13,935	226	16	1.8	n.a.	960	4,260
Bahrain[11]	622	400	643	4.1	66.1	4,260	10,480
Bangladesh	143,998	96,730	672	2.2	46.6	12,360	130
Barbados	431	252	585	0.3	70.0	1,100	4,340
Belgium[4,12]	30,519	9,853	323	0.0	72.3	83,070	8,430
Belize[13,14]	22,965	166	7.2	3.0	n.a.	180	1,150
Benin	112,622	3,825	34	2.8	40.5	1,060	270
Bermuda[5,15,16]	53	68	1,279	1.5	n.a.	920	15,810
Bhutan[17,18]	1,165	1,165	25	n.a.	43.9	110	80
Bolivia	1,098,581	6,253	5.7	2.8	48.6	2,560	410
Botswana	581,730	1,046	1.8	n.a.	52.5	940	910
Brazil[19]	8,511,965	132,580	16	2.3	61.8	227,280	1,710
Brunei[5,20,21]	5,765	216	37	3.9	n.a.	4,270	20,520
Bulgaria[8]	110,912	8,961	81	0.3	71.5	37,390	4,150
Burkina Faso[22]	274,200	7,920	29	n.a.	40.0	1,040	160
Burma[11]	676,552	37,614	56	2.3	52.5	6,620	180
Burundi	27,834	4,537	163	2.4	42.0	1,010	220
Cameroon	475,442	9,542	20	n.a.	46.0	8,000	810
Canada	9,976,139	25,150*	2.5	1.1	74.2	330,870	13,140
Cape Verde	4,033	319*	79	1.5	54.6	100	320
Central African Republic[13,14]	622,984	2,608	4.2	2.2	41.0	680	270
Chad[23]	1,284,000	4,902*	3.8	2.3	41.0	360	80
Channel Islands	195	130	668	0.2	n.a.	1,340	10,300
Chile	756,945	11,878	16	1.7	65.7	20,340	1,710
China, People's Republic[24,25]	9,571,300	1,034,750	108	1.2	64.5	318,310	310
China (Taiwan)[20,26,27]	36,000	18,873	524	1.7	68.2	56,919	3,016
Colombia[28]	1,138,914	26,526	23	1.4	62.2	38,410	1,370
Comoros[3,23,29]	2,171	421	194	n.a.	48.0	120	340
Congo	342,000	1,695*	5.0	2.6	44.5	2,060	1,120
Costa Rica[30,31]	50,700	2,417	48	2.3	71.4	2,930	1,210

See notes on page xvii

(continued opposite)

xiv

INTERNATIONAL COMPARISONS

(continued)

Country	Area (sq km)	Mid-1984 population ('000)	Mid-1984 population density (per sq km)	Average population increase, 1980–84 (% per year)	Life expectancy at birth, 1975–80 (years)	1984 Gross national product ($ million)	1984 GNP per head ($)
Cuba[2]	110,861	9,992	90	0.7	72.8	12,330	1,270
Cyprus	9,251	657	71	1.2	73.7	2,390	3,590
Czechoslovakia[8]	127,903	15,459	121	0.2	70.5	89,260	5,820
Denmark	43,092	5,112	119	−0.1	74.2	57,700	11,290
Djibouti[18]	22,000	405	18	n.a.	n.a.	180	480
Dominica[32, 33, 34]	751	74	98	0.4	67.4	80	1,080
Dominican Republic	48,734	6,102	125	n.a.	60.3	6,040	990
East Timor[35, 36, 37]	14,874	593	40	1.8	31.2	100	150
Ecuador[38]	283,561	9,115	32	2.9	60.0	10,340	1,220
Egypt	1,001,449	47,191	47	2.8	54.7	33,340	720
El Salvador	21,041	4,780	227	1.5	62.2	3,820	710
Equatorial Guinea[18, 39]	28,051	300	11	n.a.	42.0	62	180
Ethiopia	1,221,900	42,441*	35	2.5	40.9	4,780	110
Faeroe Islands[40]	1,399	45	32	0.9	73.9	500	11,030
Fiji	18,274	686	38	2.0	71.3	1,250	1,840
Finland	338,145	4,882	14	0.5	72.2	53,090	10,830
France	543,965	54,947	101	0.6	73.0	542,960	9,860
French Guiana[12, 23, 41]	91,000	78	0.9	3.9	n.a.	210	3,230
French Polynesia[20, 42, 43, 44]	4,000	167	42	3.0	56.7	1,300	8,190
Gabon	267,667	1,131*	4.2	1.6	47.0	2,830	3,480
Gambia[45, 46]	11,295	696	62	3.5	33.5	180	260
German Democratic Republic[8]	108,333	16,671	154	−0.1	71.6	120,940	7,180
Germany, Federal Republic[47]	248,717	61,181	246	−0.2	72.3	678,880	11,090
Ghana[48, 49]	238,537	12,206	51	2.6	50.0	4,730	350
Gibraltar[4, 24]	5.5	28	5,153	−1.1	n.a.	130	4,240
Greece	131,957	9,896	75	0.7	73.1	36,940	3,740
Greenland[5]	2,175,600	53	0.02	1.2	n.a.	380	7,190
Grenada[33, 34, 50]	344	89	259	−0.5	67.4	80	880
Guadeloupe[23]	1,779	331	186	0.3	69.1	1,370	4,330
Guam[51]	549	120	219	2.9	60.2	760	6,580
Guatemala	108,889	7,740	71	2.9	57.8	9,110	1,120
Guinea[52]	245,857	5,781	24	n.a.	38.2	1,810	300
Guinea-Bissau[53]	36,125	810	22	n.a.	41.0	160	180
Guyana[13, 14]	214,969	790	3.7	0.8	66.4	470	580
Haiti[54]	27,750	5,185	187	1.4	50.7	1,710	320
Honduras	112,088	4,232	38	3.5	57.1	2,980	700
Hong Kong[20]	1,045	5,364	5,133	1.6	72.0	33,970	6,300
Hungary[55]	93,033	10,668	115	−0.1	69.9	21,950	2,050
Iceland	103,000	239	2.3	1.2	76.3	2,250	9,380
India[13, 56]	3,287,590	750,900	228	n.a.	50.6	197,210	260
Indonesia[35]	1,904,569	159,302	84	2.2	50.0	85,400	540
Iran[57]	1,648,000	43,414	26	3.2	58.2	69,170	2,060
Iraq[8, 58, 59]	434,924	14,110	32	3.2	59.0	39,500	3,020
Ireland	70,283	3,535	50	1.0	72.0	17,500	4,950
Isle of Man	572	64	112	0.4	n.a.	390	5,600
Israel[60]	20,770	4,159	200	1.8	73.1	21,290	5,100
Italy	301,277	56,983	189	0.3	73.6	367,040	6,440
Ivory Coast[3, 61]	322,463	9,300	29	4.1	45.0	6,030	610
Jamaica[24, 62]	10,991	2,190	199	1.0	69.0	2,480	1,080
Japan	377,708	120,018	318	0.7	75.6	1,248,090	10,390
Jordan[63]	97,740	3,380*	35	3.7	60.1	4,340	1,710
Kampuchea[36, 64]	181,035	7,058*	39	2.5	31.2	570	70
Kenya	582,646	19,536	34	4.1	50.5	5,950	300
Kiribati[20, 51]	861	62	72	1.7	60.2	30	460
Korea, Democratic People's Republic[2]	120,538	19,896*	165	2.5	62.5	17,040	1,000
Korea, Republic	98,484	40,578	412	1.6	65.5	84,860	2,090
Kuwait	17,818	1,636	92	4.5	69.2	27,570	15,410
Laos[18, 65]	236,800	3,585	15	n.a.	47.5	290	80
Lebanon[36, 66]	10,400	2,644*	254	−0.2	65.0	3,290	1,070
Lesotho	30,355	1,470	48	2.4	47.3	790	530
Liberia	111,369	2,109	19	3.4	47.0	990	470
Libya	1,759,540	3,624	2.1	4.5	55.4	29,790	8,230
Liechtenstein[4, 67]	160	27	169	1.1	n.a.	n.a.	n.a.
Luxembourg	2,586	366	142	0.1	71.9	4,980	13,650
Macau[23]	16	359	22,438	n.a.	n.a.	810	2,710
Madagascar[13, 68]	587,041	9,985	17	2.8	47.7	2,600	270
Malawi	118,484	6,839	58	3.1	43.0	1,430	210
Malaysia[69]	329,749	13,183	40	n.a.	65.3	30,280	1,990
Maldives[5, 8, 70, 71]	298	181	609	3.4	n.a.	40	260
Mali	1,240,000	7,973	6.4	2.9	40.0	1,060	140
Malta[6, 7]	316	360	1,139	1.3	70.6	1,210	3,370

See notes on page xvii *(continued overleaf)*

INTERNATIONAL COMPARISONS

(continued)

Country	Area (sq km)	Mid-1984 population ('000)	Mid-1984 population density (per sq km)	Average population increase, 1980–84 (% per year)	Life expectancy at birth, 1975–80 (years)	1984 Gross national product ($ million)	1984 GNP per head ($)
Martinique[21]	1,102	327	297	0.1	69.7	1,320	4,260
Mauritania[72,73]	1,030,700	1,420	1.4	n.a.	42.0	750	450
Mauritius	2,045	1,011	494	1.4	64.9	1,100	1,100
Mexico	1,972,547	76,792	39	2.6	64.1	158,310	2,060
Monaco[7,74]	1.8	27	14,952	1.1	n.a.	n.a.	n.a.
Mongolia[2]	1,565,000	1,843	1.2	2.6	62.5	1,100	700
Morocco[72]	446,550	21,408*	48	n.a.	55.4	14,340	670
Mozambique[8,75]	801,590	12,615	16	n.a.	47.4	2,810	270
Namibia[76]	824,292	1,507*	1.8	2.8	46.2	1,660	1,470
Nauru[51,77]	21	7	345	n.a.	60.2	n.a.	n.a.
Nepal[68,78]	140,797	16,625	118	2.6	43.9	2,630	160
Netherlands	40,844	14,420	353	0.5	75.3	135,830	9,430
Netherlands Antilles[5,9,23,79]	800	172	215	n.a.	n.a.	1,370	5,430
New Caledonia[20,44,80,81]	19,058	145	7.6	1.3	65.9	920	6,240
New Zealand	268,676	3,233	12	0.9	72.4	23,530	7,240
Nicaragua[3,4]	130,000	3,058	24	3.8	56.3	2,700	870
Niger[53]	1,267,000	5,686	4.5	n.a.	40.5	1,190	190
Nigeria[82]	923,768	92,037*	100	3.4	46.5	74,120	770
Norway	323,883	4,140	13	0.3	75.3	57,080	13,750
Oman	212,457	1,193*	5.6	5.0	47.3	7,380	6,230
Pacific Islands (Trust Territory)[3,4,51]	1,779	142	80	2.2	60.2	160	1,100
Pakistan[83]	796,095	93,286	117	3.1	48.0	35,420	380
Panama	77,082	2,134	28	2.2	69.2	4,210	2,100
Papua New Guinea[13,68]	461,691	3,329	7.2	2.6	50.3	2,480	760
Paraguay	406,752	3,278	8.1	n.a.	64.1	4,120	1,250
Peru[19]	1,285,216	19,198	15	2.6	56.9	17,960	980
Philippines	300,000	53,170	177	2.4	62.5	35,040	660
Poland[8]	312,683	36,914	118	0.9	70.9	139,780	3,900
Portugal	92,072	10,090	110	0.8	69.4	20,050	1,970
Puerto Rico	8,897	3,270	368	0.5	73.8	14,000	4,200
Qatar[58]	11,000	257	23	n.a.	69.1	6,020	20,600
Réunion[4,12]	2,510	532	212	2.3	64.8	1,950	3,690
Romania[18,55]	237,500	22,625	95	0.5	69.8	57,030	2,540
Rwanda[3,4]	26,338	5,757	219	3.7	47.5	1,610	270
Saint Christopher and Nevis[6,7]	262	45	172	−0.9	n.a.	60	1,390
Saint Lucia[34]	616	134	218	4.1	67.4	150	1,130
Saint Vincent and the Grenadines[15,16,34]	388	98	252	1.1	67.4	100	900
San Marino[4]	61	22	364	0.9	n.a.	n.a.	n.a.
São Tomé and Príncipe[13]	964	108	112	n.a.	n.a.	30	320
Saudi Arabia	2,149,690	11,093*	5.2	4.3	53.0	116,380	10,740
Senegal	196,192	6,397	33	2.9	41.3	2,440	380
Seychelles[5,21]	308	65	211	0.6	n.a.	160	2,430
Sierra Leone[84]	71,740	3,700	52	n.a.	32.0	1,120	300
Singapore	581	2,529	4,353	1.2	70.8	18,390	7,260
Solomon Islands[20,44,85,86]	28,446	221	7.8	3.9	41.1	170	680
Somalia	637,657	4,539*	7.1	3.1	40.9	1,360	260
South Africa[76]	1,221,037	31,586*	26	2.5	51.5	73,970	2,260
Spain[87]	504,782	38,390	76	0.6	73.5	172,360	4,470
Spanish North Africa[33,36,37,87,88]	32	129	4,041	−0.2	n.a.	90	720
Sri Lanka	65,610	15,599	238	1.4	65.0	5,660	360
Sudan[89]	2,505,813	20,564	8.2	n.a.	45.1	7,360	340
Suriname[24]	163,265	389	2.4	2.2	67.8	1,350	3,520
Swaziland	17,363	626	36	3.4	46.2	590	890
Sweden	449,964	8,337	19	0.1	75.2	99,060	11,880
Switzerland	41,293	6,442	156	0.5	75.2	105,060	15,990
Syria	185,180	9,934	54	3.4	64.4	18,540	1,870
Tanzania[90]	945,087	21,062	22	3.2	49.0	4,460	210
Thailand	514,000	50,396	98	2.1	61.2	42,760	850
Togo[6]	56,785	2,747	48	n.a.	46.6	730	250
Tonga[13,23,44,91]	699	97	139	0.9	55.2	70	740
Trinidad and Tobago[3,4]	5,130	1,149	224	1.6	68.7	8,350	7,140
Tunisia[92,93]	163,610	6,975	43	2.6	58.1	8,840	1,250
Turkey	779,452	48,265	62	2.1	60.5	57,810	1,200
Tuvalu[18,51,94]	25	7	292	n.a.	60.2	5	680
Uganda[1,85,86]	236,036	13,225	56	3.4	50.0	3,290	230
USSR[8]	22,402,200	275,066	12	0.9	69.6	1,212,030	4,550
United Arab Emirates[3,4]	83,600	1,206	14	5.9	69.1	28,480	22,300
United Kingdom	244,103	56,488	231	0.1	72.8	480,680	8,530
USA	9,372,614	236,681	25	1.0	73.2	3,670,490	15,490
US Virgin Islands	342	108	316	2.5	n.a.	900	8,800
Uruguay[95,96]	176,215	2,931	17	0.5	69.6	5,900	1,970

See notes on opposite page

(continued opposite)

INTERNATIONAL COMPARISONS

(continued)

Country	Area (sq km)	Mid-1984 population ('000)	Mid-1984 population density (per sq km)	Average population increase, 1980–84 (% per year)	Life expectancy at birth, 1975–80 (years)	1984 Gross national product ($ million)	1984 GNP per head ($)
Vanuatu[18,44]	14,763	128	8.7	2.7	44.6	40	350
Venezuela[19]	912,050	16,851	18	2.9	66.2	57,360	3,220
Viet-Nam[57]	332,559	58,567*	176	2.0	55.8	7,750	160
Western Sahara[72,85,86]	266,000	165	0.6	8.9	n.a.	n.a.	n.a.
Western Samoa[5,57]	2,842	159	56	0.5	n.a.	50	350
Yemen Arab Republic[97]	195,000	9,274	48	n.a.	41.3	3,940	510
Yemen, People's Democratic Republic	332,968	2,225	6.7	3.1	44.0	1,130	560
Yugoslavia	255,804	22,963	90	0.7	70.1	48,690	2,120
Zaire	2,345,409	29,671	13	n.a.	48.0	4,220	140
Zambia[3]	752,614	6,242	8.3	n.a.	49.3	3,020	470
Zimbabwe	390,580	7,980	20	2.8	53.4	6,040	740

* United Nations estimate.

[1] Figures for population and increase rate assume stable growth and take no account of emigration.

[2] Figures for GNP refer to 1978 and are estimated on a 1977–79 base period.

[3] Figures for population and density refer to mid-1983.

[4] The population increase rate refers to 1980–83.

[5] Although no estimates are available of 1975–80 life expectancy for both sexes, the UN *Demographic Yearbook* includes separate figures of life expectancy for males and females at another date.

[6] Figures for population and density refer to mid-1982.

[7] The population increase rate refers to 1975–82.

[8] Figures for GNP are provisional data for 1980 and are estimated on a 1978–80 base period.

[9] Aruba, listed separately, was part of the Netherlands Antilles prior to 1 January 1986. Data relating to life expectancy and GNP for the Netherlands Antilles include Aruba.

[10] Figure for life expectancy includes Australian dependencies: Christmas Island, the Cocos (Keeling) Islands and Norfolk Island.

[11] The population increase rate refers to 1981–84.

[12] Figures for population and density refer to 1 January 1984.

[13] Figures for population and density refer to mid-1985.

[14] The population increase rate refers to 1980–85.

[15] Figures for population and density refer to the census of 12 May 1980.

[16] The population increase rate refers to 1970–80.

[17] Figures for population and density refer to mid-1980.

[18] Figures for GNP refer to 1981 and are estimated on a 1979–81 base period.

[19] Population figures exclude Indian jungle inhabitants.

[20] Figures for GNP refer to gross domestic product.

[21] Figures for GNP refer to 1983 and are estimated on a 1981–83 base period.

[22] Figures for population and density refer to the census of December 1985.

[23] Figures for GNP refer to 1982 and are estimated on a 1980–82 base period.

[24] Figures for population and density refer to 31 December 1984.

[25] The figure for life expectancy refers to the whole of China, including Taiwan.

[26] The estimate of life expectancy refers to 1965–70.

[27] Figures for GNP are in terms of current 1984 prices, rather than on a 1982–84 base period.

[28] Figures for population and density refer to the census of 15 October 1985, and the population increase rate refers to 1973–85.

[29] Except for GNP, figures include the island of Mayotte, which has remained under French administration since the Comoros became independent in July 1975.

[30] Figures for population and density refer to the census of 10 June 1984.

[31] The population increase rate refers to 1973–84.

[32] Figures for population and density refer to the census of 7 April 1981.

[33] The population increase rate refers to 1970–81.

[34] The figure for life expectancy is the average for the Windward Islands (Dominica, Grenada, Saint Lucia and Saint Vincent and the Grenadines).

[35] East (formerly Portuguese) Timor, listed separately, was incorporated into Indonesia on 17 July 1976. Figures for Indonesia, except the data on GNP, exclude East Timor.

[36] Figures for GNP refer to 1974.

[37] Figures for GNP are estimated on a 1973–75 base period.

[38] Population figures exclude nomadic Indian tribes.

[39] Figures for population and density refer to 1 January 1983.

[40] The figure for life expectancy is the 1965–70 average for the Faeroe Islands and Iceland.

[41] The population increase rate refers to 1974–82.

[42] Figures for population and density refer to the census of 15 October 1983.

[43] The population increase rate refers to 1977–83.

[44] The estimate of life expectancy refers to 1965.

[45] Figures for population and density refer to the census of 24 April 1983.

[46] The population increase rate refers to 1973–83.

[47] Figures include data for West Berlin.

[48] Figures for population and density refer to the census of 18 March 1984.

[49] The population increase rate refers to 1970–84.

[50] Figures for population and density refer to the census of 30 April 1981.

[51] The figure for life expectancy is the average for Micronesia.

[52] Figures for population and density refer to the census of 4–17 February 1983.

[53] Figures for population and density refer to mid-1981.

[54] The population increase rate refers to 1971–82.

[55] Figures for GNP are not comparable with those of other centrally planned economies.

[56] Figures include the Indian-held part of the disputed territory of Jammu and Kashmir.

[57] Figures for GNP refer to 1976 and are estimated on a 1975–77 base period.

[58] Figures for population and density refer to October 1982.

[59] The population increase rate refers to 1979–82.

[60] Including East Jerusalem, annexed from Jordan in 1967. Population figures also include Israeli residents in other territories under military occupation.

[61] The population increase rate refers to 1979–83.

[62] The population increase rate refers to 1970–82.

[63] Figures for GNP relate to the East Bank region only.

[64] Figures for GNP are estimated on a 1972–74 base period.

[65] Figures for population and density refer to the census of 1 March 1985.

INTERNATIONAL COMPARISONS

[66] Figures for GNP are estimated on a 1974–76 base period.
[67] Figures for population and density refer to 31 December 1983.
[68] The population increase rate refers to 1981–85.
[69] Figures for population and density refer to the census of 10 June 1980.
[70] Figures for population and density refer to the census of 25–28 March 1985.
[71] The population increase rate refers to 1977–85.
[72] Western (formerly Spanish) Sahara, listed separately, was partitioned in 1976 between Mauritania and Morocco. Mauritania withdrew in August 1979, when Morocco annexed the former Mauritanian area. Figures for the area, life expectancy and GNP of these countries exclude their respective portions of the territory.
[73] Figures for population and density refer to the census of 22 December 1976.
[74] Figures for population and density refer to the census of 4 March 1982.
[75] Figures for population and density refer to 31 December 1981.
[76] The area and population of Walvis Bay, an integral part of South Africa, are included with Namibia.
[77] Figures for population and density refer to the census of 22 January 1977.
[78] Figures for population and density refer to 22 June 1985.
[79] Figures for population and density refer to the census of 1 February 1981.
[80] Figures for population and density refer to the census of April 1983.
[81] The population increase rate refers to 1976–83.
[82] Population estimates are UN projections which assume stable growth and take no account of the effect of civil disturbances.
[83] Figures exclude the disputed territory of Jammu and Kashmir (total area 222,802 sq km, of which 83,807 sq km is held by Pakistan).
[84] Figures for population and density refer to the census of 15 December 1985, including an adjustment for underenumeration.
[85] Figures for population and density refer to mid-1979.
[86] The population increase rate refers to 1975–79.
[87] Data for Spanish North Africa (Ceuta and Melilla) are also included with the figures for Spain.
[88] Figures for population and density refer to the census of 1 March 1981.
[89] Figures for population and density refer to the census of 1 February 1983.
[90] Figures for GNP refer to mainland Tanzania only, excluding Zanzibar (population 555,000 at mid-1984).
[91] The population increase rate refers to 1976–85.
[92] Figures for population and density refer to the census of 30 March 1984.
[93] The population increase rate refers to 1975–84.
[94] Figures for population and density refer to the census of May 1979.
[95] Figures for population and density refer to the census of 23 October 1985.
[96] The population increase rate refers to 1975–85.
[97] Figures for population and density refer to the census of 1 February 1986, including nationals living abroad.

Principal Sources: Population estimates taken from the United Nations *Population and Vital Statistics Report* (quarterly) and *World Population Prospects: Estimates and Projections as Assessed in 1982* (Population Studies, No. 86); figures for area taken from the United Nations *Demographic Yearbook 1984*; data on life expectancy taken mainly from *World Population Prospects*; estimates of gross national product and GNP per head taken from *The World Bank Atlas* (International Bank for Reconstruction and Development, 1986).

LATE INFORMATION

UNITED NATIONS ECONOMIC COMMISSION FOR EUROPE (p. 23)

Executive Secretary: GERALD HINTEREGGER (Austria) (from 15 March 1987).

UNITED NATIONS FUND FOR POPULATION ACTIVITIES—UNFPA (p. 44)

The Executive Director, RAFAEL M. SALAS, died on 4 March 1987.

INTERNATIONAL MONETARY FUND (p. 73)

Managing Director: MICHEL CAMDESSUS (France) (from 16 January 1987).

EUROPEAN PARLIAMENT (p. 142)

President: Sir HENRY PLUMB (United Kingdom) (elected 20 January 1987).

AFGHANISTAN (p. 291)

Government Changes
(December 1986)

President of the Revolutionary Council: Maj.-Gen. NAJIB (NAJIBULLAH), (took office 23 December 1986).

Full Members of the Politburo of the Central Committee of the People's Democratic Party of Afghanistan: ABDOL WAKIL, ABDUZZOHUR RAZMJO.

(January 1987)

Minister-Adviser: NAMATULLAH PAZHWAK.

ALBANIA (p. 303)

Government and other Changes
(February 1987)

Presidium of the People's Assembly

The President, Vice-President and Secretary were re-elected, as were seven members. IBRAHIM GJEVORI, NIK PRENG SHYTI and ELMAZ PUTO were replaced by SOTIR KOÇOLLARI, TEREZINA MARUBI and KRISTAQ RAMA.

Council of Ministers
Chairman: ADIL ÇARÇANI.
Deputy Chairman: BESNIK BEKTESHI.
Deputy Chairman and Minister of Home Affairs: HEKURAN ISAI.
Deputy Chairman: MANUSH MYFTIU.
Deputy Chairman: VANGJEL ÇERRAVA.
Minister of Foreign Affairs: REIS MALILE.
Minister of People's Defence: PROKOP MURRA.
Chairman of the State Planning Commission: NIKO GJYZARI.
Chairman of the State Control Commission: ENVER HALILI.
Minister of Finance: ANDREA NAKO.
Minister of Industry and Mining: LLAMBI GEGPRIFTI.
Minister of Energy: LAVDOSH HAMETAJ.
Minister of Light Industry: VITO KAPO.
Minister of the Foodstuff Industry: JOVAN BARDHI.
Minister of Agriculture: THEMIE THOMAI.
Minister of Construction: FARUDIN HOXHA.
Minister of Transport: LUAN BABAMETO.
Minister of Home Trade: OSMAN MURATI.
Minister of Foreign Trade: SHANE KORBECI.
Minister of Public Services: XHEMAL TAFAJ.
Minister of Education: SKENDA GJINUSHI.
Minister of Health Service: AHMET KAMBERI.

Kuvënd Popullore
(People's Assembly)

President: PETRO DODE.
Vice-Presidents: IBRAHIM HANZA, VITORIA CURRI.
Secretary: SALI SHIJAKU.

Partia e Punës te Shqipërisë (Party of Labour of Albania)

VANGJEL ÇERRAVA was replaced as Secretary of the Central Committee by HAJREDIN ÇELIKU.

ANTIGUA AND BARBUDA (p. 345)

Government Changes
(January 1987)

Minister of Agriculture, Fisheries, Lands and Housing: HILLROY HUMPHRIES.
Minister of Health and Labour: ADOLPHUS ELEAZER FREELAND.
Minister of Home Affairs: CHRISTOPHER MANASSEH O'MARD.
Minister of Public Utilities and Aviation: ROBIN YEARWOOD.
Minister of Public Works and Communications: VERE BIRD, Jr.

AUSTRIA (p. 414)

New Government
(January 1987)

Following lengthy negotiations after the general election of 23 November 1986, a coalition government was formed between the Socialist Party (SPÖ) and the Austrian People's Party (ÖVP). A new Council of Ministers was sworn in on 21 January 1987.

Federal Chancellor: Dr FRANZ VRANITZKY (SPÖ).
Vice-Chancellor and Minister of Foreign Affairs: Dr ALOIS MOCK (ÖVP).
Minister of Finance: Dkfm. FERDINAND LACINA (SPÖ).
Minister of the Public Sector and Transport: Dipl.-Ing. Dr RUDOLF STREICHER (SPÖ).
Minister of the Interior: KARL BLECHA (SPÖ).
Minister of Social Affairs: ALFRED DALLINGER (SPÖ).
Minister of Education, the Arts and Sport: HILDE HAWLICEK (SPÖ).
Minister of National Defence: ROBERT LICHAL (ÖVP).
Minister of Agriculture and Forestry: JOSEF RIEGLER (ÖVP).
Minister of Trade: ROBERT GRAF (ÖVP).
Minister of Family Affairs, Youth and Environment: MARILIES FLEMMING (ÖVP).
Minister of Science: HANS TUPPY (ÖVP).
Minister of Justice: EGMONT FOREGGER (Independent).
Ministers of the Federal Chancellery: FRANZ LÖSCHNAK (SPÖ), JOHANNES DITZ (ÖVP).
Secretary of State for Women's Affairs: JOHANNA DOHNAL (SPÖ).
Secretary of State to the Federal Chancellery: HEINRICH NEISSER (ÖVP.

BENIN (p. 507)

Government Changes
(February 1987)

Minister Delegate to the Presidency in Charge of Planning and Statistics: IBRAHIM SOURADJOU.
Minister of Rural Development and Co-operative Action: MARTIN DOHOU AZONHIHO.
Minister of Equipment and Transport: SOULE DANKORO.
Minister of Finance and Economy: BARNABÉ BIDOUZO.
Minister of Trade, Crafts and Tourism: GADO GIRIGISSOU.

LATE INFORMATION

Minister of Foreign Affairs and Co-operation: GUY LANDRY HAZOUMÉ.
Minister of Justice and Inspection of Parastatal Enterprises: SALIOU ABOUDOU.

BOLIVIA (p. 528)
Government Changes
(February 1987)

Minister of Labour: ALFREDO FRANCO GUACHALLA.
Minister of the Interior and Justice: JUAN CARLOS DURÁN.
Minister of Industry, Commerce and Tourism: FERNANDO MOSCOSO.
Minister of Rural Affairs: JOSÉ GUILLERMO JUSTINIANO.
Minister of Aviation: Gen. JAIME HURTADO.
Secretary-General of the Presidency: WALTER ZULETA RONCAL.

BURUNDI (p. 633)
Government Change
(January 1987)

Minister of Finance: ISAAC BUDABUDA.

CAMEROON (p. 645)
Government Changes
(January 1987)

Minister of Foreign Affairs: PHILIPPE MATAGA.
Minister of Labour and Welfare: ADOLPHE MOUDIKI.

CANADA (p. 662)
Government Changes
(February 1987)

Minister of State: (vacant).
Minister of State (Transport): (vacant).
Minister of Consumer and Corporate Affairs with responsibility for Canada Post: HARVIE ANDRE.
Minister of Regional Industrial Expansion: MICHEL CÔTÉ.

CENTRAL AFRICAN REPUBLIC (p. 698)
The Constitution

The creation of a one-party state, with the Rassemblement démocratique centrafricaine as the sole legal and ruling political party, was officially announced in February 1987. A 44-member provisional council was to be created to oversee party activities until a special convention could be held to elect the ruling board.

ETHIOPIA (p. 1004)
New Constitution

It was announced on 22 February 1987 that 81% of voters in the national referendum of 1 February had approved the new constitution, which therefore went into force immediately.

FRENCH POLYNESIA (p. 1109)
Government Changes
(February 1987)

Council of Ministers
President: JACQUES TEUIRA.
Vice-President and Minister for Education, Culture and Relations with the South Pacific Commission: JACQUES TEHEIRUA.
Minister for the Economy, Tourism and Maritime Affairs: ALEXANDRE LÉONTIEFF.
Minister for Youth, Sport and Housing: MICHEL BUILLARD.
Minister for Social Affairs and Unity: Mme HUGUETTE HONG-KIOU.
Minister for Development of the Archipelagos, Transport, Posts and Telecommunications: GEFFRY SALMON.
Minister for Agriculture and Traditional Crafts: GEORGES KELLY.
Minister for Equipment, Development, Energy and Mines: GASTON TONG-SANG.
Minister for Health and the Environment: LYSIS LAVIGNE.
Minister for Finance and Internal Affairs: MANATE VIVISH.
Minister for Employment, Public Offices and Vocational Education: TERII SANFORD.

FEDERAL REPUBLIC OF GERMANY (p. 1182)
Hesse Landtag Elections

Following the collapse of the SPD-Green coalition in the Hesse Landtag in February 1987, it was announced that new regional elections would take place on 5 April 1987. The Minister-President of Hesse, Holger Börner, also resigned in February.

GRENADA (p. 1249–1250)
Government Changes
(February 1987)

Prime Minister and Minister of Finance, Trade, Industry, Planning, Carriacou and Petit Martinique Affairs, Security, Information and Energy: HERBERT BLAIZE.
Minister of External Affairs, Tourism, Agriculture, Land and Forestry: BEN JONES.
Minister of Education, Culture, Co-operatives and Fisheries: GEORGE BRIZAN.
Attorney-General and Minister of Legal Affairs and Labour: Dr FRANCIS ALEXIS.
Minister of Local Government, Civil Aviation, Social Security, Youth Affairs and Sports: GEORGE McGUIRE.
Minister of Communications, Works, Public Utilities and Community Development: Dr KEITH MITCHELL.
Minister of Health, Housing, Women's Affairs and Physical Planning: DANNY WILLIAMS.

HAITI (p. 1299)

The 61-member Constituent Assembly approved a new constitution in March 1987.

IRELAND (p. 1457)
New Cabinet
(March 1987)

A new government, consisting entirely of Fianna Fáil members, was formed on 10 March 1987.

Taoiseach (Prime Minister) and Minister for the Gaeltacht: CHARLES HAUGHEY.
Tánaiste (Deputy Prime Minister) and Minister of Foreign Affairs: BRIAN LENIHAN.
Minister of Finance and Minister of the Public Service: RAYMOND MACSHARRY.
Minister of Justice: GERARD COLLINS.
Minister of Agriculture: MICHAEL O'KENNEDY.
Minister of Social Welfare: Dr MICHAEL WOODS.
Minister of Industry and Commerce: ALBERT REYNOLDS.
Minister of Energy: RAY BURKE.
Minister of Tourism and Minister of Fisheries and Forestry: BRENDAN DALY.
Minister of the Environment: PADRAIG FLYNN.
Minister of Labour: BERTIE AHERNE.
Minister of Health: Dr ROY O'HANLON.
Minister of Defence: MICHAEL J. NOONAN.
Minister of Education: MARY O'ROURKE.
Minister of Communications: JOHN WILSON.

Attorney-General (not in the Cabinet): JOHN MURRAY.

PART ONE
International Organizations

THE UNITED NATIONS

Address: United Nations Plaza, New York, NY 10017, USA.
Telephone: (212) 754-1234.

The United Nations was founded in 1945 to maintain international peace and security and to develop international co-operation in economic, social, cultural and humanitarian problems.

ORIGIN

The United Nations was a name devised by President Franklin D. Roosevelt of the United States. It was first used in the Declaration by United Nations of 1 January 1942, when representatives of 26 nations pledged their governments to continue fighting together against the Axis powers.

The United Nations Charter (see p. 9) was drawn up by the representatives of 50 countries at the United Nations Conference on International Organization, which met at San Francisco from 25 April to 26 June 1945. The representatives deliberated on the basis of proposals worked out by representatives of China, the USSR, the United Kingdom and the United States at Dumbarton Oaks in August–October 1944. The Charter was signed on 26 June 1945. Poland, not represented at the Conference, signed it later but nevertheless became one of the original 51 members.

The United Nations officially came into existence on 24 October 1945, when the Charter had been ratified by China, France, the USSR, the United Kingdom and the United States, and by a majority of other signatories. United Nations Day is now celebrated annually on 24 October.

MEMBERS

(with assessments for percentage contributions to the UN budget for 1986, 1987 and 1988, and year of admission)

Country	Assessment	Year
Afghanistan	0.01	1946
Albania	0.01	1955
Algeria	0.14	1962
Angola	0.01	1976
Antigua and Barbuda	0.01	1981
Argentina	0.62	1945
Australia	1.66	1945
Austria	0.74	1955
Bahamas	0.01	1973
Bahrain	0.02	1971
Bangladesh	0.02	1974
Barbados	0.01	1966
Belgium	1.18	1945
Belize	0.01	1981
Benin	0.01	1960
Bhutan	0.01	1971
Bolivia	0.01	1945
Botswana	0.01	1966
Brazil	1.40	1945
Brunei	0.4	1984
Bulgaria	0.16	1955
Burkina Faso	0.01	1960
Burma	0.01	1948
Burundi	0.01	1962
Byelorussian SSR[1]	0.34	1945
Cameroon	0.01	1960
Canada	3.06	1945
Cape Verde	0.01	1975
Central African Republic	0.01	1960
Chad	0.01	1960
Chile	0.07	1945
China, People's Republic[2]	0.79	1945
Colombia	0.13	1945
Comoros	0.01	1975
Congo	0.01	1960
Costa Rica	0.02	1945
Cuba	0.09	1945
Cyprus	0.02	1960
Czechoslovakia	0.70	1945
Denmark	0.72	1945
Djibouti	0.01	1977
Dominica	0.01	1978
Dominican Republic	0.03	1945
Ecuador	0.03	1945
Egypt	0.07	1945
El Salvador	0.01	1945
Equatorial Guinea	0.01	1968
Ethiopia	0.01	1945
Fiji	0.01	1970
Finland	0.50	1955
France	6.37	1945
Gabon	0.03	1960
The Gambia	0.01	1965
German Democratic Republic	1.33	1973
Germany, Federal Republic	8.26	1973
Ghana	0.01	1957
Greece	0.44	1945
Grenada	0.01	1974
Guatemala	0.02	1945
Guinea	0.01	1958
Guinea-Bissau	0.01	1974
Guyana	0.01	1966
Haiti	0.01	1945
Honduras	0.01	1945
Hungary	0.22	1955
Iceland	0.03	1946
India	0.35	1945
Indonesia	0.14	1950
Iran	0.63	1945
Iraq	0.12	1945
Ireland	0.18	1955
Israel	0.22	1949
Italy	3.79	1955
Ivory Coast	0.02	1960
Jamaica	0.02	1962
Japan	10.84	1956
Jordan	0.01	1955
Kampuchea	0.01	1955
Kenya	0.01	1963
Kuwait	0.29	1963
Laos	0.01	1955
Lebanon	0.01	1945
Lesotho	0.01	1966
Liberia	0.01	1945
Libya	0.26	1955
Luxembourg	0.05	1945
Madagascar	0.01	1960
Malawi	0.01	1964
Malaysia	0.10	1957
Maldives	0.01	1965
Mali	0.01	1960
Malta	0.01	1964
Mauritania	0.01	1961
Mauritius	0.01	1968
Mexico	0.89	1945
Mongolia	0.01	1961
Morocco	0.05	1956
Mozambique	0.01	1975
Nepal	0.01	1955
Netherlands	1.74	1945
New Zealand	0.24	1945
Nicaragua	0.01	1945
Niger	0.01	1960
Nigeria	0.19	1960
Norway	0.54	1945
Oman	0.02	1971
Pakistan	0.06	1947
Panama	0.02	1945
Papua New Guinea	0.01	1975
Paraguay	0.02	1945
Peru	0.07	1945
Philippines	0.10	1945
Poland	0.64	1945
Portugal	0.18	1955
Qatar	0.04	1971
Romania	0.19	1955
Rwanda	0.01	1962

INTERNATIONAL ORGANIZATIONS

United Nations

Saint Christopher and Nevis	0.01	1983
Saint Lucia	0.01	1979
Saint Vincent and the Grenadines	0.01	1980
São Tomé and Príncipe	0.01	1975
Saudi Arabia	0.97	1945
Senegal	0.01	1960
Seychelles	0.01	1976
Sierra Leone	0.01	1961
Singapore	0.10	1965
Solomon Islands	0.01	1978
Somalia	0.01	1960
South Africa	0.44	1945
Spain	2.03	1955
Sri Lanka	0.01	1955
Sudan	0.01	1956
Suriname	0.01	1975
Swaziland	0.01	1968
Sweden	1.25	1946
Syria	0.04	1945
Tanzania[3]	0.01	1961
Thailand	0.09	1946
Togo	0.01	1960
Trinidad and Tobago	0.04	1962
Tunisia	0.03	1956
Turkey	0.34	1945
Uganda	0.01	1962
Ukrainian SSR[1]	1.28	1945
USSR	10.20	1945
United Arab Emirates	0.18	1971
United Kingdom	4.86	1945
USA	25.00	1945
Uruguay	0.04	1945
Vanuatu	0.01	1981
Venezuela	0.60	1945
Viet-Nam	0.01	1977
Western Samoa	0.01	1976
Yemen Arab Republic	0.01	1947
Yemen, People's Democratic Republic	0.01	1967
Yugoslavia	0.46	1945
Zaire	0.01	1960
Zambia	0.01	1964
Zimbabwe	0.02	1980

Total Membership: 159 (October 1986)

[1] The Byelorussian SSR and the Ukrainian SSR are integral parts of the USSR and not independent countries, but they have separate UN membership.

[2] From 1945 until 1971 the Chinese seat was occupied by the Republic of China (confined to Taiwan since 1949).

[3] Tanganyika was a member of the United Nations from December 1961 and Zanzibar was a member from December 1963. From April 1964, the United Republic of Tanganyika and Zanzibar continued as a single member, changing its name to United Republic of Tanzania in November 1964.

SOVEREIGN COUNTRIES NOT IN THE UNITED NATIONS
(October 1986)

Andorra
China (Taiwan)
Kiribati
Democratic People's Republic of Korea
Republic of Korea
Liechtenstein
Monaco
Nauru
San Marino
Switzerland
Tonga
Tuvalu
Vatican City (Holy See)

PERMANENT MISSIONS TO THE UNITED NATIONS
(with Permanent Representatives—October 1986)

Afghanistan: 866 United Nations Plaza, Suite 520, New York, NY 10017; tel. (212) 754-1191; MOHAMMAD FARID ZARIF.

Albania: 320 East 79th St, New York, NY 10021; tel. (212) 249-2059; BASHKIM PITARKA.

Algeria: 15 East 47th St, New York, NY 10017; tel. (212) 750-1960; HOCINE DJOUDI.

Angola: 747 Third Ave, 18th Floor, New York, NY 10017; tel. (212) 752-4612; ELÍSIO DE FIGUEIREDO.

Antigua and Barbuda: 610 Fifth Ave, Suite 311, New York, NY 10020; tel. (212) 541-4117; LLOYDSTONE JACOBS.

Argentina: 1 United Nations Plaza, 25th Floor, New York, NY 10017; tel. (212) 688-6300; Dr MARCELO DELPECH.

Australia: 1 Dag Hammarskjöld Plaza, 885 Second Ave, 16th Floor, New York, NY 10017; tel. (212) 421-6910; RICHARD A. WOOLCOTT.

Austria: 809 United Nations Plaza, 7th Floor, New York, NY 10017; tel. (212) 949-1840; Dr KARL FISCHER.

Bahamas: 767 Third Ave, 9th Floor, New York, NY 10017; tel. (212) 421-6925; Dr DAVIDSON L. HEPBURN.

Bahrain: 2 United Nations Plaza, 25th Floor, New York, NY 10017; tel. (212) 223-6200; HUSSEIN RASHID AL-SABBAGH.

Bangladesh: 821 United Nations Plaza, 8th Floor, New York, NY 10017; tel. (212) 867-3434; B. A. SIDDIKY.

Barbados: 800 Second Ave, 18th Floor, New York, NY 10017; tel. (212) 867-8431; Dame NITA BARROW.

Belgium: 809 United Nations Plaza, 2nd Floor, New York, NY 10017; tel. (212) 599-5250; Mlle EDMONDE DEVER.

Belize: 801 Second Ave, Suite 401-02, New York, NY 10017; tel. (212) 599-0233; KENNETH E. TILLETT.

Benin: 4 East 73rd St, New York, NY 10021; tel. (212) 249-6014; SIMON IFÉDÉ OGOUMA.

Bhutan: 2 United Nations Plaza, 27th Floor, New York, NY 10017; tel. (212) 826-1919.

Bolivia: 211 East 43rd St, 8th Floor (Room 802), New York, NY 10017; tel. (212) 682-8132; Dr JORGE GUMUCIO GRANIER.

Botswana: 2 Dag Hammarskjöld Plaza, 866 Second Ave, 2nd Floor, New York, NY 10017; tel. (212) 759-6587; LEGWAILA JOSEPH LEGWAILA.

Brazil: 747 Third Ave, 9th Floor, New York, NY 10017; tel. (212) 832-6868; GEORGE A. MACIEL.

Brunei: 866 United Nations Plaza, 2nd Floor, Room 248, New York, NY 10017; tel. (212) 838-1600; AWANG AHMAD BIN Haji MOHD YUSSOF.

Bulgaria: 11 East 84th St, New York, NY 10028; tel. (212) 737-4790; BORIS ATANASOV TSVETKOV.

Burkina Faso: 115 East 73rd St, New York, NY 10021; tel. (212) 288-7515.

Burma: 10 East 77th St, New York, NY 10021; tel. (212) 535-1310; MAUNG MAUNG GYI.

Burundi: 201 East 42nd St, 28th Floor, New York, NY 10017; tel. (212) 687-1180; MELCHIOR BWAKIRA.

Byelorussian Soviet Socialist Republic: 136 East 67th St, New York, NY 10021; tel. (212) 535-3420; LEV I. MAKSIMOV.

Cameroon: 22 East 73rd St, New York, NY 10021; tel. (212) 794-2295; PAUL BAMELA ENGO.

Canada: 866 United Nations Plaza, Suite 250, New York, NY 10017; tel. (212) 751-5600; STEPHEN LEWIS.

Cape Verde: 27 East 69th St, New York, NY 10021; tel. (212) 472-0333; Dr CORENTINO VIRGÍLIO SANTOS.

Central African Republic: 386 Park Ave South, Room 1614, New York, NY 10016; tel. (212) 689-6195; MICHEL GBEZERA-BRIA.

Chad: 211 East 43rd St, Suite 1703, New York, NY 10017; tel. (212) 986-0980; MAHAMAT ALI ADOUM.

Chile: 809 United Nations Plaza, 4th Floor, New York, NY 10017; tel. (212) 687-7547; PEDRO DAZA.

China, People's Republic: 155 West 66th St, New York, NY 10023; tel. (212) 787-3838; LI LUYE.

Colombia: 140 East 57th St, 5th Floor, New York, NY 10022; tel. (212) 355-7776; Dr CARLOS ALBAN-HOLGUÍN.

Congo: 14 East 65th St, New York, NY 10021; tel. (212) 744-7840; Dr MARTIN ADOUKI.

Costa Rica: 211 East 43rd St, Room 903, New York, NY 10017; tel. (212) 986-6373; Dr CARLOS JOSÉ GUTIÉRREZ.

Cuba: 315 Lexington Ave and 38th St, New York, NY 10016; tel. (212) 689-7215; OSCAR ORAMAS-OLIVA.

Cyprus: 13 East 40th St, New York, NY 10016; tel. (212) 686-6016; CONSTANTINE MOUSHOUTAS.

Czechoslovakia: 1109–1111 Madison Ave, New York, NY 10023; tel. (212) 535-8814; JAROSLAV CÉSAR.

Democratic Kampuchea: (see Kampuchea).

Democratic Yemen: (see Yemen, People's Democratic Republic).

Denmark: 2 United Nations Plaza, 26th Floor, New York, NY 10017; tel. (212) 308-7009; OLE BIERRING.

Djibouti: 866 United Nations Plaza, Suite 4011, New York, NY 10017; tel. (212) 753-3163; SALEH Haji FARAH DIRIR.

INTERNATIONAL ORGANIZATIONS

Dominica: 41 East 42nd St, Suite 315, New York, NY 10017; tel. (212) 949-9077; FRANKLIN ANDREW BARON.

Dominican Republic: 144 East 44th St, 4th Floor, New York, NY 10017; tel. (212) 867-0833; Dr ELADIO KNIPPING-VICTORIA.

Ecuador: 820 Second Ave, 15th Floor, New York, NY 10017; tel. (212) 986-6670; CARLOS TOBAR-ZALDUMBIDE.

Egypt: 36 East 67th St, New York, NY 10021; tel. (212) 879-6300; ABDEL HADIM BADAWI.

El Salvador: 46 Park Ave, New York, NY 10016; tel. (212) 679-1616; ROBERTO MEZA.

Equatorial Guinea: 801 Second Ave, Room 1403, New York, NY 10017; tel. (212) 599-1523; FLORENCIO MAYE ELA.

Ethiopia: 866 United Nations Plaza, Room 560, New York, NY 10017; tel. (212) 421-1830; TESFAYE TADESSE.

Fiji: 1 United Nations Plaza, 26th Floor, New York, NY 10017; tel. (212) 355-7316; WINSTON THOMPSON.

Finland: 866 United Nations Plaza, 2nd Floor, New York, NY 10017; tel. (212) 355-2100; Dr KEIJO KORHONEN.

France: 1 Dag Hammarskjöld Plaza, 245 East 47th St, New York, NY 10017; tel. (212) 308-5700; CLAUDE DE KÉMOULARIA.

Gabon: 820 Second Ave, Room 902, New York, NY 10017; tel. (212) 867-3100; JEAN FÉLIX OYOUÉ.

The Gambia: 19 East 47th St, New York, NY 10017; tel. (212) 752-6213.

German Democratic Republic: 58 Park Ave, New York, NY 10016; tel. (212) 686-2596; HARRY OTT.

Germany, Federal Republic: 600 Third Ave, 41st Floor, New York, NY 10016; tel. (212) 949-9200; Dr HANS WERNER LAUTENSCHLAGER.

Ghana: 19 East 47th St, New York, NY 10017; tel. (212) 832-1300; JAMES VICTOR GBEHO.

Greece: 733 Third Ave, 23rd Floor, New York, NY 10017; tel. (212) 490-6060; MIHALIS DOUNTAS.

Grenada: 820 Second Ave, New York, NY 10017; tel. (212) 599-0301; Dr LAMUEL A. STANISLAUS.

Guatemala: 57 Park Ave, New York, NY 10016; tel. (212) 679-4760; FERNANDO ANDRADE-DÍAZ DURÁN.

Guinea: 1 United Nations Plaza, 26th Floor, New York, NY 10017; tel. (212) 486-9170.

Guinea-Bissau: 211 East 43rd St, Room 604, New York, NY 10017; tel. (212) 661-3977; ALFREDO LOPES CABRAL.

Guyana: 622 Third Ave, 35th Floor, New York, NY 10017; tel. (212) 953-0930; NOEL G. SINCLAIR.

Haiti: 801 Second Ave, Room 300, New York, NY 10017; tel. (212) 370-4840; SERGE ELIE CHARLES.

Honduras: 866 United Nations Plaza, Suite 509, NY 10017; tel. (212) 752-3370; Dr ROBERTO MARTÍNEZ ORDÓÑEZ.

Hungary: 10 East 75th St, New York, NY 10021; tel. (212) 535-8660; FERENC ESZTERGALYOS.

Iceland: 370 Lexington Ave, 5th Floor, New York, NY 10017; tel. (212) 686-4100.

India: 750 Third Ave, 21st Floor, New York, NY 10017; tel. (212) 661-8020; NATARAJAN KRISHNAN.

Indonesia: 325 East 38th St, New York, NY 10016; tel. (212) 972-8333; ALI ALATAS.

Iran: 622 Third Ave, 34th Floor, New York, NY 10017; tel. (212) 687-2020; Dr SAID RAJAIE-KHORASSANI.

Iraq: 14 East 79th St, New York, NY 10021; tel. (212) 737-4434; ISMAT TAHA KITTANI.

Ireland: 1 Dag Hammarskjöld Plaza, 885 Second Ave, 19th Floor, New York, NY 10017; tel. (212) 421-6934; ROBERT MCDONAGH.

Israel: 800 Second Ave, New York, NY 10017; tel. (212) 697-5500; BENJAMIN NETANYAHU.

Italy: 2 United Nations Plaza, 24th Floor, New York, NY 10017; tel. (212) 486-9191; MAURIZIO BUCCI.

Ivory Coast: 46 East 74th St, New York, NY 10021; tel. (212) 988-3930; AMARA ESSY.

Jamaica: 866 Second Ave, 15th Floor, 2 Dag Hammarskjöld Plaza, New York, NY 10017; tel. (212) 688-7040; LLOYD M. H. BARNETT.

Japan: 866 United Nations Plaza, 2nd Floor, New York, NY 10017; tel. (212) 223-4300; KIYOAKI KIKUCHI.

Jordan: 866 United Nations Plaza, Room 550–552, New York, NY 10017; tel. (212) 752-0135; ABDULLAH SALAH.

Kampuchea: 747 Third Ave, 8th Floor, New York, NY 10017; tel. (212) 888-6646; PRASITH THIOUNN.*

Kenya: 866 United Nations Plaza, Room 486, New York, NY 10017; tel. (212) 421-4740; RAPHAEL MULI KIILU.

Kuwait: 321 East 44th St, New York, NY 10017; tel. (212) 973-4300; MOHAMMAD A. ABULHASAN.

Laos: 820 Second Ave, Suite 400, New York, NY 10017; tel. (212) 986-0227; Dr KITHONG VONGSAY.

Lebanon: 866 United Nations Plaza, Room 531–533, New York, NY 10017; tel. (212) 355-5460; RACHID FAKHOURY.

Lesotho: 866 United Nations Plaza, Suite 580, New York, NY 10017; tel. (212) 421-7543; THABO MAKEKA.

Liberia: 820 Second Ave, 4th Floor, New York, NY 10017; tel. (212) 687-1033; SYLVESTER JARRETT.

Libya: 309-315 East 48th St, New York, NY 10017; tel. (212) 752-5775; Dr ALI A. TREIKI.

Luxembourg: 801 Second Ave, New York, NY 10017; tel. (212) 370-9850; ANDRÉ PHILIPPE.

Madagascar: 801 Second Ave, Suite 404, New York, NY 10017; tel. (212) 986-9491; BLAISE RABETAFIKA.

Malawi: 767 Third Ave, 8th Floor, New York, NY 10017; tel. (212) 755-8470; TIMON SAM MANGWAZU.

Malaysia: 140 East 45th St, 43rd Floor, New York, NY 10017; tel. (212) 986-6310; YUSOF M. HITAM.

Maldives: 820 Second Ave, Suite 800C, New York, NY 10017; tel. (212) 599-6195; MOHAMED MUSTHAFA HUSSAIN.

Mali: 111 East 69th St, New York, NY 10021; tel. (212) 737-4150; SEYDOU NIARE.

Malta: 249 East 35th St, New York, NY 10016; tel. (212) 725-2345; GEORGE AGIUS.

Mauritania: 9 East 77th St, New York, NY 10021; tel. (212) 737-7780; MOHAMED MAHJOUB OULD BOYE.

Mauritius: 211 East 43rd St, New York, NY 10017; tel. (212) 949-0190; RAMESHCHAND SEEREEKISSOON.

Mexico: 2 United Nations Plaza, 28th Floor, New York, NY 10017; tel. (212) 752-0220; MARIO MOYA-PALENCIA.

Mongolia: 6 East 77th St, New York, NY 10021; tel. (212) 861-9460; GENDENGIIN NYAMDOO.

Morocco: 767 Third Ave, 30th Floor, New York, NY 10017; tel. (212) 421-1580; DRISS SLAOUI.

Mozambique: 70 East 79th St, New York, NY 10021; tel. (212) 517-4550; MANUEL DOS SANTOS.

Nepal: 820 Second Ave, Suite 1200, New York, NY 10017; tel. (212) 370-4188; JAI PRATAP RANA.

Netherlands: 711 Third Ave, 9th Floor, New York, NY 10017; tel. (212) 697-5547; ADRIAAN JACOBOVITS DE SZEGED.

New Zealand: 1 United Nations Plaza, 25th Floor, New York, NY 10017; tel. (212) 826-1960; DAVID KEITH MCDOWELL.

Nicaragua: 820 Second Ave, 8th Floor, New York, NY 10017; tel. (212) 490-7997; NORA ASTORGA-GADEA.

Niger: 417 East 50th St, New York, NY 10022; tel. (212) 421-3260; JOSEPH DIATTA.

Nigeria: 733 Third Ave, 15th Floor, New York, NY 10017; tel. (212) 953-9130; Maj.-Gen. JOSEPH GARBA.

Norway: 825 Third Ave, 18th Floor, New York, NY 10022; tel. (212) 421-0280; TOM ERIC VRAALSEN.

Oman: 866 United Nations Plaza, Suite 540, New York, NY 10017; tel. (212) 355-3505; SAOUD BIN SALIM BIN HASSAN AL-ANSI.

Pakistan: 8 East 65th St, New York, NY 10021; tel. (212) 879-8600; S. SHAH NAWAZ.

Panama: 866 United Nations Plaza, Room 544–545, New York, NY 10017; tel. (212) 421-5420; DAVID SAMUDIO.

Papua New Guinea: 100 East 42nd St, Room 1005, New York, NY 10017; tel. (212) 682-6447; KIATRO ABISINITO.

Paraguay: 211 East 43rd St, Room 1206, New York, NY 10017; tel. (212) 687-3490; ALFREDO CAÑETE.

Peru: 820 Second Ave, Suite 1600, New York, NY 10017; tel. (212) 687-3336; CARLOS ALZAMORA.

Philippines: 556 Fifth Ave, 5th Floor, New York, NY 10036; tel. (212) 764-1300; SALVADOR P. LOPEZ.

Poland: 9 East 66th St, New York, NY 10021; tel. (212) 744-2506; EUGENIUSZ NOWORYTA.

Portugal: 777 Third Ave, 27th Floor, New York, NY 10017; tel. (212) 759-9444; JOÃO UVA DE MATOS PROENÇA.

INTERNATIONAL ORGANIZATIONS

United Nations

Qatar: 747 Third Ave, 22nd Floor, New York, NY 10017; tel. (212) 486-9335; Hamad Abdelaziz al-Kawari.

Romania: 573–577 Third Ave, New York, NY 10016; tel. (212) 682-3273; Teodor Marinescu.

Rwanda: 124 East 39th St, New York, NY 10016; tel. (212) 696-0644; Célestin Kabanda.

Saint Christopher and Nevis: 412–414 East 75th St, 5th Floor, New York, NY 10021; tel. (212) 535-1234; Dr William Herbert.

Saint Lucia: 41 East 42nd St, Suite 315, New York, NY 10017; tel. (212) 697-9360; Dr Joseph Edsel Edmunds.

Saint Vincent and the Grenadines: 801 Second Ave, 21st Floor, New York, NY 10017; tel. (212) 687-4490.

São Tomé and Príncipe: 801 Second Ave, Suite 1504, New York, NY 10017; tel. (212) 697-4211; Joaquim Rafael Branco.

Saudi Arabia: 405 Lexington Ave, 56th Floor, New York, NY 10017; tel. (212) 697-4830; Samir Shihabi.

Senegal: 228 East 68th St, New York, NY 10021; tel. (212) 517-9030; Massamba Sarre.

Seychelles: 820 Second Ave, Suite 203, New York, NY 10017; tel. (212) 687-9766; Dr Giovinella Gonthier.

Sierra Leone: 57 East 64th St, New York, NY 10021; tel. (212) 570-0030; Sahr Matturi.

Singapore: 2 United Nations Plaza, 25th Floor, New York, NY 10017; tel. (212) 826-0840; Kishore Mahbubani.

Solomon Islands: 820 Second Ave, Suite 800A, New York, NY 10017; tel. (212) 599-6193; Francis Joseph Saemala.

Somalia: 711 Third Ave, 12th Floor, New York, NY 10017; tel. (212) 687-9877; Abdillahi Said Osman.

South Africa: 326 East 48th St, New York, NY 10017; tel. (212) 371-8154; Kurt Robert Samuel von Schirnding.

Spain: 809 United Nations Plaza, 6th Floor, New York, NY 10017; tel. (212) 661-1050; Fernando Morán.

Sri Lanka: 630 Third Ave, 20th Floor, New York, NY 10017; tel. (212) 986-7040; Nissanka Wijewardane.

Sudan: 210 East 49th St, New York, NY 10017; tel. (212) 421-2680; Amin M. Abdoun.

Suriname: 1 United Nations Plaza, 26th Floor, New York, NY 10017; tel. (212) 826-0660.

Swaziland: 866 United Nations Plaza, Suite 420, New York, NY 10017; tel. (212) 371-8910; Dr Timothy L. L. Dlamini.

Sweden: 825 Third Ave, 39th Floor, New York, NY 10022; tel. (212) 751-5900; Anders Ferm.

Syria: 820 Second Ave, 10th Floor, New York, NY 10017; tel. (212) 661-1313.

Tanzania: 205 East 42nd St, 13th Floor, New York, NY 10017; tel. (212) 972-9160; Dr Wilbert K. Chagula.

Thailand: 628 Second Ave, New York, NY 10016; tel. (212) 689-1004; Birabhongse Kasemsri.

Togo: 112 East 40th St, New York, NY 10016; tel. (212) 490-3455; Dr Kwam Kouassi.

Trinidad and Tobago: 801 Second Ave, 8th Floor, New York, NY 10017; tel. (212) 697-7620; D. H. N. Alleyne.

Tunisia: 405 Lexington Ave, 65th Floor, New York, NY 10174; tel. (212) 557-3344; Nejib Bouziri.

Turkey: 821 United Nations Plaza, 11th Floor, New York, NY 10017; tel. (212) 949-0150; İlter Türkmen.

Uganda: 336 East 45th St, New York, NY 10017; tel. (212) 949-0110; Wanume Kibedi.

Ukrainian Soviet Socialist Republic: 136 East 67th St, New York, NY 10021; tel. (212) 535-3418; Guennadi I. Oudovenko.

USSR: 136 East 67th St, New York, NY 10021; tel. (212) 861-4900; Aleksandr Belonogov.

United Arab Emirates: 747 Third Ave, 36th Floor, New York, NY 10017; tel. (212) 371-0480; Muhammad Hussain al-Shaali.

United Kingdom: 845 Third Ave, 10th Floor, New York, NY 10022; tel. (212) 752-8586; Sir John Thomson.

United Republic of Tanzania: (see Tanzania).

USA: 799 United Nations Plaza, New York, NY 10017; tel. (212) 415-4000; Vernon A. Walters.

Uruguay: 747 Third Ave, 37th Floor, New York, NY 10017; tel. (212) 752-8240; Dr Julio César Lupinacci.

Vanuatu: 411 West 148th St, New York, NY 10031; tel. (212) 926-5762; Nikenike Vurobaravu.

Venezuela: 231 East 46th St, New York, NY 10017; tel. (212) 838-2800; Dr Andrés Aguilar.

Viet-Nam: 20 Waterside Plaza (Lobby), New York, NY 10010; tel. (212) 679-3779.

Western Samoa: 820 Second Ave, Suite 800D, 8th Floor, New York, NY 10017; tel. (212) 599-6196; Maiava Iulai Toma.

Yemen Arab Republic: 747 Third Ave, 8th Floor, New York, NY 10017; tel. (212) 355-1730; Salem Basendwah.

Yemen, People's Democratic Republic: 413 East 51st St, New York, NY 10022; tel. (212) 752-3066; Abdalla Saleh al-Ashtal.

Yugoslavia: 854 Fifth Ave, New York, NY 10021; tel. (212) 879-8700; Ignac Golob.

Zaire: 767 Third Ave, 25th Floor, New York, NY 10017; tel. (212) 754-1966; Bagbeni Adeito Nzengeya.

Zambia: 237 East 52nd St, New York, NY 10022; tel. (212) 758-1110; Peter Dingiswayo Zuze.

Zimbabwe: 19 East 47th St, New York, NY 10017; tel. (212) 980-9511; Dr Isack S. G. Mudenge.

* Representing the government of Democratic Kampuchea, overthrown in January 1979. The People's Republic of Kampuchea, which succeeded the deposed regime, has not been recognized by the United Nations.

OBSERVERS

Non-member states, inter-governmental and other organizations which have received an invitation to participate in the sessions and the work of the General Assembly as Observers, maintaining permanent offices at the UN.

Non-member states

Holy See: 20 East 72nd St, New York, NY 10021; tel. (212) 734-2900; The Most Rev. Mgr Giovanni Cheli.

Korea, Democratic People's Republic: 225 East 86th St, New York, NY 10028; tel. (212) 722-3589; Pak Gil Yon.

Korea, Republic: 866 United Nations Plaza, Suite 300, New York, NY 10017; tel. (212) 371-1280; Dr Kun Park.

Monaco: 845 Third Ave, 2nd Floor, New York, NY 10022; tel. (212) 880-4842; John Dubé.

Switzerland: 757 Third Ave, 21st Floor, New York, NY 10017; tel. (212) 421-1480; Mme Francesca Pometta.

Inter-governmental organizations*

Asian-African Legal Consultative Committee: 404 East 66th St, New York, NY 10021; tel. (212) 734-7608; K. Bhagwat-Singh.

European Community: 3 Dag Hammarskjöld Plaza, 12th Floor, 305 East 47th St, New York, NY 10017; tel. (212) 371-3804; the Observer is the Permanent Representative to the UN of the country currently exercising the Presidency of the Council of Ministers of the Community.

League of Arab States: 747 Third Ave, 35th Floor, New York, NY 10017; tel. (212) 838-8700; Dr Clovis Maksoud.

Organization of African Unity: 346 East 50th St, New York, NY 10022; tel. (212) 319-5490; Oumara Garba Youssoufou.

Organization of the Islamic Conference: 130 East 40th St, 5th Floor, New York, NY 10016; tel. (212) 883-0140.

Sistema Económica Latinoamericana: 250 East 63rd St, New York, NY 10021; tel. (212) 755-8129.

* The following inter-governmental organizations have a standing invitation to participate as Observers, but do not maintain permanent offices at the United Nations:
Agency for Cultural and Technical Co-operation.
Commonwealth Secretariat.
Organization of American States.
The Council for Mutual Economic Assistance (CMEA–COMECON) is represented by the Permanent Mission of the country currently holding the Presidency of the CMEA.

Other organizations

Palestine Liberation Organization: 115 East 65th St, New York, NY 10021; tel. (212) 288-8500; Zehdi Labib Terzi.

South West Africa People's Organisation of Namibia: 801 Second Ave, Room 1401, New York, NY 10017; tel. (212) 557-2450; Helmut Angula.

INFORMATION CENTRES

Afghanistan: POB 5; Shah Mahmoud Ghazi Watt, Kabul.

Algeria: 19 ave Chahid el-Ouali Mustapha Sayed, Algiers.

INTERNATIONAL ORGANIZATIONS — *United Nations*

Argentina: Junín 1940, 1° piso, 1113 Buenos Aires (also covers Uruguay).
Australia: GPO Box 4045; 44 Market St, Sydney, NSW 2001 (also covers Fiji, Kiribati, Nauru, New Zealand, Tonga, Tuvalu, Vanuatu and Western Samoa).
Austria: POB 500; Vienna International Centre, Wagramerstrasse 5, 1220 Vienna (also covers the Federal Republic of Germany).
Bahrain: POB 26004: King Faisal Rd, Gufool, Manama (also covers Qatar and the United Arab Emirates).
Bangladesh: POB 3658; House 12, Rd 6, Dhanmandi, Dhaka.
Belgium: 108 rue d'Arlon, 1040 Brussels (also covers Luxembourg and the Netherlands).
Bolivia: POB 686; Edif. Naciones Unidas, Plaza Isabel la Católica, Ex-Clinica Santa Isabel, Planta Baja, La Paz.
Brazil: Rua Cruz Lima 19, Grupo 201, 22230 Rio de Janeiro.
Burkina Faso: POB 135; 218 rue de la Gare, Ouagadougou (also covers Chad, Mali and Niger).
Burma: POB 230; 28A Manawhari Rd, Rangoon.
Burundi: POB 2160; ave de la Poste 7, place de l'Indépendance, Bujumbura.
Cameroon: POB 836; Immeuble Kamden, rue Joseph Clère, Yaoundé (also covers the Central African Republic and Gabon).
Chile: Edif. Naciones Unidas, Avda Dag Hammarskjöld, Casilla 179-D, Santiago.
Colombia: Apdo Aéreo 058964; Calle 72, No. 12–65, Piso 2, Bogotá 2 (also covers Ecuador and Venezuela).
Congo: POB 465; S.22 Ave Pointe-Hollandaise, Mpila, Brazzaville.
Czechoslovakia: Panská 5, 110 00 Prague 1 (also covers the German Democratic Republic).
Denmark: 37 H. C. Andersen Blvd, 1553 Copenhagen V (also covers Finland, Iceland, Norway and Sweden).
Egypt: POB 262; 1 Osiris St, Tagher Bldg, Garden City, Cairo (also covers Saudi Arabia and the Yemen Arab Republic).
El Salvador: Apdo 2157; 87 Avda Norte, Colonia Escalón, San Salvador (also covers Costa Rica, Guatemala and Honduras).
Ethiopia: POB 3001; Africa Hall, Addis Ababa.
France: 4 et 6 ave de Saxe, 75700 Paris.
Ghana: POB 2339; Liberia and Nassar Rds, Accra (also covers Sierra Leone).
Greece: 36 Amalia Ave, 105 58 Athens (also covers Cyprus and Israel).
India: 55 Lodi Estate, New Delhi 110003 (also covers Bhutan).
Indonesia: Gedung Dewan Pers, 5th Floor, 32–34 Jalan Kebon Sirih, Jakarta.
Iran: POB 1555; Gandhi Ave, 43 St No. 3, Teheran.
Iraq: POB 27; Amiriya, Airport St, Baghdad.
Italy: Palazzetto Venezia, Piazza San Marco 50, Rome (also covers the Holy See and Malta).
Japan: Shin Aoyama Bldg Nishikan, 22nd Floor, 1-1 Minami Aoyama 1-chome, Minato-ku, Tokyo 107 (also covers the Trust Territory of the Pacific Islands).
Kenya: POB 30218; Electricity House, 11th Floor, Harambee Ave, Nairobi (also covers Seychelles and Uganda).
Lebanon: POB 4656; Apt No 1, Fakhoury Bldg, Montée Bain Militaire, Beirut (also covers Jordan, Kuwait and Syria).
Lesotho: POB 301; Corner Kingsway and Hilton Rds, opposite Sanlam Centre, Maseru 100.
Liberia: POB 274; LBDI Bldg, Tubman Blvd, Monrovia.
Libya: POB 286; Muzaffar Al Aftas St, Hay El-Andalous, Tripoli.
Madagascar: POB 1348; 22 rue Rainitovo, Antsahavola, Antananarivo.
Mexico: Presidente Mazaryk 29, 7° piso, México 11570, DF (also covers Cuba and the Dominican Republic).
Morocco: 'Casier ONU', Angle Charia Ibnouzaid et Zankat Roundanat No. 6, Rabat.
Nepal: POB 107; Pulchowk, Patan, Kathmandu.
Nicaragua: POB 3260; Bolonia, de Plaza España, 2 cuadros abajo, Managua, DN.
Nigeria: POB 1068; 17 Kingsway Rd, Ikoyi, Lagos.
Pakistan: POB 1107; House No. 26, 88th St, Ramna 6/3, Islamabad.
Panama: POB 6-9083, El Dorado; Urbanización Obarrio, Calle 54 y Avda Tercera Sur, Casa No. 17, Panama City.
Papua New Guinea: POB 472; Credit House, Third Floor, Musgrave St, Ela Beach, Port Moresby (also covers Solomon Islands).
Paraguay: Casilla de Correo 1107, Asunción.
Peru: Apdo 11199; Mariscal Blas Cerdeña 450, San Isidro, Lima.
Philippines: POB 7285 (ADC); NEDA Bldg, Ground Floor, 106 Amorsolo St, Legaspi Village, Makati, Metro Manila (also covers Papua New Guinea and Solomon Islands).
Portugal: Rua Latina Coelho No. 1, Edif. Aviz, Bloco A1, 10°, 1000 Lisbon.
Romania: POB 1-701; 16 Aurel Vlaicu St, Bucharest.
Senegal: POB 154; 9 allées Robert Delmas, Dakar (also covers Cape Verde, The Gambia, Guinea, Guinea-Bissau, the Ivory Coast and Mauritania).
Sri Lanka: POB 1505; 202–204 Bauddhaloka Mawatha, Colombo 7 (also covers Maldives).
Sudan: POB 1992; Al Qasr Ave, St No. 15, Block No. 3, House No 3, Khartoum East (also covers Somalia).
Switzerland: Palais des Nations, 1211 Geneva 10 (also covers Bulgaria, Hungary, Poland and Spain).
Tanzania: POB 9224; Matasalamat Bldg, Samora Machel Ave, Dar es Salaam.
Thailand: United Nations Bldg, Rajadamnern Ave, Bangkok 10200 (also covers Kampuchea, Laos, Malaysia, Singapore and Viet-Nam).
Togo: POB 911; 107 blvd Circulaire, Lomé (also covers Benin).
Trinidad and Tobago: POB 130; 15 Keate St, Port of Spain (also covers Antigua and Barbuda, the Bahamas, Barbados, Belize, Dominica, Grenada, Guyana, Jamaica, the Netherlands Antilles, Saint Christopher and Nevis, Saint Lucia, Saint Vincent and the Grenadines and Suriname).
Tunisia: POB 863; 61 blvd Bab Benat, Tunis.
Turkey: PK 407; 197 Atatürk Bulvarı, Ankara.
USSR: 4/16 Ulitsa Lunacharskogo, Moscow 121002 (also covers the Byelorussian SSR and the Ukrainian SSR).
United Kingdom: 20 Buckingham Gate, London, SW1E 6LB (also covers Ireland).
USA: 1889 F St, NW (Ground Floor), Washington, DC 20006.
Yugoslavia: POB 157; Svetozara Markovica 58, Belgrade (also covers Albania).
Zaire: POB 7248: Bâtiment Deuxième République, blvd du 30 juin, Kinshasa.
Zambia: POB 32905, Lusaka (also covers Botswana, Malawi and Swaziland).
Zimbabwe: POB 4408; Dolphin House, 23 Moffat St/Union Ave, Harare.

INTERNATIONAL ORGANIZATIONS
United Nations

TWO-YEAR BUDGET OF THE UNITED NATIONS (US dollars)

	1984–85*	1986–87†
Overall policy-making, direction and co-ordination	40,173,400	45,090,200
Political and Security Council affairs, peace-keeping activities	91,584,400	93,640,100
Political affairs, trusteeship and decolonization	28,696,500	25,606,800
Policy-making organs (economic and social activities)	3,936,000	2,526,100
Office of the Director-General for Development and International Economic Co-operation	3,772,200	3,814,000
Centre for Science and Technology for Development	3,995,200	4,230,300
Regional Commissions Liaison Office	620,900	665,100
Department of International Economic and Social Affairs	50,056,800	54,160,700
Department of Technical Co-operation for Development	18,100,400	20,218,300
Office of Secretariat Services for Economic and Social Matters	3,926,600	4,387,700
Transnational corporations	9,783,500	10,078,000
Economic Commission for Europe	22,784,800	26,767,900
Economic and Social Commission for Asia and the Pacific	34,998,000	34,818,400
Economic Commission for Latin America and the Caribbean	43,210,300	45,293,700
Economic Commission for Africa	46,358,100	48,166,300
Economic and Social Commission for Western Asia	27,302,800	33,707,500
United Nations Conference on Trade and Development	51,577,500	60,135,300
International Trade Centre	7,892,300	8,041,300
United Nations Industrial Development Organization‡	74,323,300	—
United Nations Environment Programme	9,976,300	10,142,400
United Nations Centre for Human Settlements (Habitat)	8,816,900	8,610,400
International drug control	5,451,600	6,291,200
Office of the United Nations High Commissioner for Refugees	28,484,400	34,485,200
Office of the United Nations Disaster Relief Co-ordinator	4,794,000	5,708,300
Human rights	10,310,000	11,675,400
Regular programme of technical co-operation	32,932,900	29,277,200
International Court of Justice	9,049,700	10,500,800
Legal activities	15,040,700	15,896,500
Public information	70,170,600	75,668,900
Administration and management	303,456,500	321,993,400
Conference and library services	266,603,700	288,823,600
United Nations bond issue	16,769,100	16,758,600
Staff assessment	244,735,600	275,416,800
Construction, alteration, improvement and major maintenance of premises	20,366,200	30,145,100
Grant to United Nations Institute for Training and Research	1,500,000	600,000
Grand total	**1,611,551,200**	**1,663,341,500**

* Budget approved December 1983 and revised December 1984.
† Budget approved December 1985.
‡ Became a UN Specialized Agency in 1986.

Charter of the United Nations

We the peoples of the United Nations determined

to save succeeding generations from the scourge of war, which twice in our lifetime has brought untold sorrow to mankind, and

to reaffirm faith in fundamental human rights, in the dignity and worth of the human person, in the equal rights of men and women and of nations large and small, and

to establish conditions under which justice and respect for the obligations arising from treaties and other sources of international law can be maintained, and

to promote social progress and better standards of life in larger freedom,

And for these ends

to practise tolerance and live together in peace with one another as good neighbours, and

to unite our strength to maintain international peace and security, and

to ensure, by the acceptance of principles and the institution of methods, that armed force shall not be used, save in the common interest, and

to employ international machinery for the promotion of the economic and social advancement of all peoples,

Have resolved to combine our efforts to accomplish these aims.

Accordingly, our respective Governments, through representatives assembled in the city of San Francisco, who have exhibited their full powers found to be in good and due form, have agreed to the present Charter of the United Nations and do hereby establish an international organization to be known as the United Nations.

I. PURPOSES AND PRINCIPLES

Article 1

The Purposes of the United Nations are:

1. To maintain international peace and security, and to that end: to take effective collective measures for the prevention and removal of threats to the peace, and for the suppression of acts of aggression or other breaches of the peace, and to bring about by peaceful means, and in conformity with the principles of justice and international law, adjustment or settlement of international disputes or situations which might lead to a breach of the peace:

2. To develop friendly relations among nations based on respect for the principle of equal rights and self-determination of peoples, and to take other appropriate measures to strengthen universal peace;

3. To achieve international co-operation in solving international problems of an economic, social, cultural, or humanitarian character, and in promoting and encouraging respect for human rights and for fundamental freedoms for all without distinction as to race, sex, language, or religion; and

4. To be a centre for harmonizing the accusations of nations in the attainment of these common ends.

Article 2

The Organization and its Members, in pursuit of the Purposes stated in Article 1, shall act in accordance with the following Principles.

1. The Organization is based on the principle of the sovereign equality of all its Members.

2. All Members, in order to ensure to all of them the rights and benefits resulting from membership, shall fulfil in good faith the obligations assumed by them in accordance with the present Charter.

3. All Members shall settle their international disputes by peaceful means in such a manner that international peace and security, and justice, are not endangered.

4. All Members shall refrain in their international relations from the threat or use of force against the territorial integrity or political independence of any state, or in any manner inconsistent with the Purposes of the United Nations.

5. All Members shall give the United Nations every assistance in any action it takes in accordance with the present Charter, and shall refrain from giving assistance to any state against which the United Nations is taking preventive or enforcement action.

6. The Organization shall ensure that states which are not Members of the United Nations act in accordance with these Principles so far as may be necessary for the maintenance of international peace and security.

7. Nothing contained in the present Charter shall authorize the United Nations to intervene in matters which are essentially within the domestic jurisdiction of any state or shall require the Members to submit such matters to settlement under the present Charter; but this principle shall not prejudice the application of enforcement measures under Chapter VII.

II. MEMBERSHIP

Article 3

The original Members of the United Nations shall be the states which, having participated in the United Nations Conference on International Organization at San Francisco, or having previously signed the Declaration by United Nations of January 1, 1942, sign the present Charter and ratify it in accordance with Article 110.

Article 4

1. Membership in the United Nations is open to all other peace-loving states which accept the obligations contained in the present Charter and, in the judgement of the Organization, are able and willing to carry out these obligations.

2. The admission of any such state to membership in the United Nations will be effected by a decision of the General Assembly upon the recommendation of the Security Council.

Article 5

A member of the United Nations against which preventive or enforcement action has been taken by the Security Council may be suspended from the exercise of the rights and privileges of membership by the General Assembly upon the recommendation of the Security Council. The exercise of these rights and privileges may be restored by the Security Council.

Article 6

A Member of the United Nations which has persistently violated the Principles contained in the present Charter may be expelled from the Organization by the General Assembly upon the recommendation of the Security Council.

III. ORGANS

Article 7

1. There are established as the principal organs of the United Nations: a General Assembly, a Security Council, an Economic and Social Council, a Trusteeship Council, an International Court of Justice, and a Secretariat.

2. Such subsidiary organs as may be found necessary may be established in accordance with the present Charter.

Article 8

The United Nations shall place no restrictions on the eligibility of men and women to participate in any capacity and under conditions of equality in its principal and subsidiary organs.

IV. THE GENERAL ASSEMBLY

Composition

Article 9

1. The General Assembly shall consist of all the Members of the United Nations.

2. Each Member shall have not more than five representatives in the General Assembly.

Functions and Powers

Article 10

The General Assembly may discuss any questions or any matters within the scope of the present Charter or relating to the powers and functions of any organs provided for in the present Charter, and, except as provided in Article 12, may make recommendations to the Members of the United Nations or to the Security Council or to both on any such questions or matters.

Article 11

1. The General Assembly may consider the general principles of co-operation in the maintenance of international peace and security, including the principles governing disarmament and the regulation of armaments, and may make recommendations with regard to such principles to the Members or to the Security Council or to both.

2. The General Assembly may discuss any questions relating to the maintenance of international peace and security brought before it by any Member of the United Nations, or by the Security Council, or by a state which is not a Member of the United Nations in accordance with Article 35, paragraph 2, and, except as provided in Article 12, may make recommendations with regard to any such question to the state or states concerned or to the Security Council or both. Any such question on which action is necessary shall be referred to the Security Council by the General Assembly either before or after discussion.

3. The General Assembly may call the attention of the Security Council to situations which are likely to endanger international peace and security.

4. The powers of the General Assembly set forth in this Article shall not limit the general scope of Article 10.

Article 12

1. While the Security Council is exercising in respect of any dispute or situation the functions assigned to it in the present Charter, the General Assembly shall not make any recommendations with regard to that dispute or situation unless the Security Council so requests.

2. The Secretary-General, with the consent of the Security Council, shall notify the General Assembly at each session of any matters relative to the maintenance of international peace and security which are being dealt with by the Security Council and shall similarly notify the General Assembly, or the Members of the United Nations if the General Assembly is not in session, immediately the Security Council ceases to deal with such matters.

Article 13

1. The General Assembly shall initiate studies and make recommendations for the purpose of:

(a) promoting international co-operation in the political field and encouraging the progressive development of international law and its codification;

(b) promoting international co-operation in the economic, social, cultural, educational, and health fields, and assisting in the realization of human rights and fundamental freedoms for all without distinction as to race, sex, language, or religion.

2. The further responsibilities, functions and powers of the General Assembly with respect to matters mentioned in paragraph 1(b) above are set forth in Chapters IX and X.

Article 14

Subject to the provision of Article 12, the General Assembly may recommend measures for the peaceful adjustment of any situation, regardless of origin, which it deems likely to impair the general welfare or friendly relations among nations, including situations resulting from a violation of the provisions of the present Charter setting forth the Purposes and Principles of the United Nations.

Article 15

1. The General Assembly shall receive and consider annual and special reports from the Security Council; these reports shall include an account of the measures that the Security Council has decided upon or taken to maintain international peace and security.

2. The General Assembly shall receive and consider reports from the other organs of the United Nations.

Article 16

The General Assembly shall perform such functions with respect to the international trusteeship system as are assigned to it under Chapters XII and XIII, including the approval of the trusteeship agreements for areas not designated as strategic.

Article 17

1. The General Assembly shall consider and approve the budget of the Organization.

2. The expenses of the Organization shall be borne by the Members as apportioned by the General Assembly.

3. The General Assembly shall consider and approve any financial and budgetary arrangements with specialized agencies referred to in Article 57 and shall examine the administrative budgets of such specialized agencies with a view to making recommendations to the agencies concerned.

Voting

Article 18

1. Each Member of the General Assembly shall have one vote.

2. Decisions of the General Assembly on important questions shall be made by a two-thirds majority of the members present and voting. These questions shall include: recommendations with respect to the maintenance of international peace and security, the election of the non-permanent Members of the Security Council, the election of the Members of the Economic and Social Council, the election of Members of the Trusteeship Council in accordance with paragraph 1(c) of Article 86, the admission of new Members to the United Nations, the suspension of the rights and privileges of membership, the expulsion of Members, questions relating to the operation of the trusteeship system, and budgetary questions.

3. Decisions on other questions, including the determination of additional categories of questions to be decided by a two-thirds majority, shall be made by a majority of the members present and voting.

Article 19

A Member of the United Nations which is in arrears in the payment of its financial contributions to the Organization shall have no vote in the General Assembly if the amount of its arrears equals or exceeds the amount of the contributions due from it for the preceding two full years. The General Assembly may, nevertheless, permit such a Member to vote if it is satisfied that the failure to pay is due to conditions beyond the control of the Member.

Procedure

Article 20

The General Assembly shall meet in regular annual sessions and in such special sessions as occasion may require. Special sessions shall be convoked by the Secretary-General at the request of the Security Council or of a majority of the members of the United Nations.

Article 21

The General Assembly shall adopt its own rules of procedure. It shall elect its President for each session.

Article 22

The General Assembly may establish such subsidiary organs as it deems necessary for the performance of its functions.

V. THE SECURITY COUNCIL

Composition

Article 23

1. The Security Council shall consist of 11 Members of the United Nations. The Republic of China, France, the Union of Soviet Socialist Republics, the United Kingdom of Great Britain and Northern Ireland, and the United States of America shall be permanent members of the Security Council. The General Assembly shall elect six other Members of the United Nations to be non-permanent members of the Security Council, due regard being specially paid, in the first instance to the contribution of Members of the United Nations to the maintenance of international peace and security and to the other purposes of the Organization, and also to equitable geographical distribution.

2. The non-permanent members of the Security Council shall be elected for a term of two years. In the first election of the non-permanent members, however, three shall be chosen for a term of one year. A retiring member shall not be eligible for immediate re-election.

3. Each member of the Security Council shall have one representative.

Functions and Powers

Article 24

1. In order to ensure prompt and effective action by the United Nations, its Members confer on the Security Council primary responsibility for the maintenance of international peace and security, and agree that in carrying out its duties under this responsibility the Security Council acts on their behalf.

2. In discharging these duties the Security Council shall act in accordance with the Purposes and Principles of the United Nations. The specific powers granted to the Security Council for the discharge of these duties are laid down in Chapters VI, VII, VIII and XII.

3. The Security Council shall submit annual and, when necessary, special reports to the General Assembly for its consideration.

Article 25

The Members of the United Nations agree to accept and carry out the decisions of the Security Council in accordance with the present Charter.

Article 26

In order to promote the establishment and maintenance of international peace and security with the least diversion for armaments of the world's human and economic resources, the Security Council shall be responsible for formulating, with the assistance of the Military Staff Committee referred to in Article 47, plans to be submitted to the Members of the United Nations for the establishment of a system for the regulation of armaments.

Voting

Article 27

1. Each member of the Security Council shall have one vote.

2. Decisions of the Security Council on procedural matters shall be made by an affirmative vote of seven members.

3. Decisions of the Security Council on all other matters shall be made by an affirmative vote of seven members including the concurring votes of the permanent members; provided that, in decisions under Chapter VI, and under paragraph 3 of Article 52, a party to a dispute shall abstain from voting.

Procedure

Article 28

1. The Security Council shall be so organized as to be able to function continuously. Each member of the Security Council shall for this purpose be represented at all times at the seat of the Organization.

2. The Security Council shall hold periodic meetings at which each of its members may, if it so desires, be represented by a member of the government or by some other specially designated representative.

3. The Security Council may hold meetings at such places other than the seat of the Organization as in its judgment will best facilitate its work.

Article 29

The Security Council may establish such subsidiary organs as it deems necessary for the performance of its functions.

Article 30

The Security Council shall adopt its own rules of procedure, including the method of selecting its President.

Article 31

Any Member of the United Nations which is not a member of the Security Council may participate, without vote, in the discussion of any question brought before the Security Council whenever the latter considers that the interests of that Member are specially affected.

Article 32

Any Member of the United Nations which is not a member of the Security Council or any state which is not a Member of the United Nations, if it is a party to a dispute under consideration by the Security Council, shall be invited to participate, without vote, in the discussion relating to the dispute. The Security Council shall lay down such conditions as it deems just for the participation of a state which is not a Member of the United Nations.

VI. PACIFIC SETTLEMENT OF DISPUTES

Article 33

1. The parties to any dispute, the continuance of which is likely to endanger the maintenance of international peace and security, shall, first of all, seek a solution by negotiation, enquiry, mediation, conciliation, arbitration, judicial settlement, resort to regional agencies or arrangements, or other peaceful means of their own choice.

2. The Security Council shall, when it deems necessary, call upon the parties to settle their disputes by such means.

Article 34

The Security Council may investigate any dispute, or any situation which might lead to international friction or give rise to a dispute, in order to determine whether the continuance of the dispute or situation is likely to endanger the maintenance of international peace and security.

Article 35

1. Any Member of the United Nations may bring any dispute, or any situation of the nature referred to in Article 34, to the attention of the Security Council or of the General Assembly.

2. A state which is not a Member of the United Nations may bring to the attention of the Security Council or of the General Assembly any dispute to which it is a party if it accepts in advance, for the purposes of the dispute, the obligations of pacific settlement provided in the present Charter.

3. The proceedings of the General Assembly in respect of matters brought to its attention under this Article will be subject to the provisions of Articles 11 and 12.

Article 36

1. The Security Council may, at any stage of a dispute of the nature referred to in Article 33 or of a situation of like nature, recommend appropriate procedures or methods of adjustment.

2. The Security Council should take into consideration any procedures for the settlement of the dispute which have already been adopted by the parties.

3. In making recommendations under this Article the Security Council should also take into consideration that legal disputes should as a general rule be referred by the parties to the International Court of Justice in accordance with the provisions of the statute of the Court.

Article 37

1. Should the parties to a dispute of the nature referred to in Article 33, fail to settle it by the means indicated in that Article, they shall refer it to the Security Council.

2. If the Security Council deems that the continuance of the dispute is in fact likely to endanger the maintenance of international peace and security, it shall decide whether to take action under Article 36 or to recommend such terms of settlement as it may consider appropriate.

Article 38

Without prejudice to the provisions of Articles 33 to 37, the Security Council may, if all the parties to any dispute so request, make recommendations to the parties with a view to a pacific settlement of the dispute.

VII. ACTION WITH RESPECT TO THREATS TO THE PEACE, BREACHES OF THE PEACE, AND ACTS OF AGGRESSION

Article 39

The Security Council shall determine the existence of any threat to the peace, breach of the peace, or act of aggression and shall make recommendations, or decide what measures shall be taken in accordance with Articles 41 and 42, to maintain or restore international peace and security.

Article 40

In order to prevent an aggravation of the situation, the Security Council may, before making the recommendations or deciding upon the measures provided for in Article 39, call upon the parties concerned to comply with such provisional measures as it deems necessary or desirable. Such provisional measures shall be without prejudice to the rights, claims, or position of the parties concerned. The Security Council shall duly take account of failure to comply with such provisional measures.

Article 41

The Security Council may decide what measures not involving the use of armed force are to be employed to give effect to its decisions, and it may call upon the Members of the United Nations to apply such measures. These may include complete or partial interruption of economic relations and of rail, sea, air, postal, telegraphic, radio, and other means of communication, and the severance of diplomatic relations.

Article 42

Should the Security Council consider that measures provided for in Article 41 would be inadequate or have proved to be inadequate, it may take such action by air, sea, or land forces as may be necessary to maintain or restore international peace and security. Such action may include demonstrations, blockade, and other operations by air, sea, or land forces of Members of the United Nations.

Article 43

1. All Members of the United Nations, in order to contribute to the maintenance of international peace and security, undertake to make available to the Security Council, on its call and in accordance with a special agreement or agreements, armed forces, assistance, and facilities, including rights of passage, necessary for the purpose of maintaining international peace and security.

2. Such agreement or agreements shall govern the numbers and types of forces, their degree of readiness and general location, and the nature of the facilities and assistance to be provided.

3. The agreement or agreements shall be negotiated as soon as possible on the initiative of the Security Council. They shall be concluded between the Security Council and Members or between the Security Council and groups of Members and shall be subject to ratification by the signatory states in accordance with their respective constitutional processes.

Article 44

When the Security Council has decided to use force it shall, before calling upon a Member not represented on it to provide armed forces in fulfilment of the obligations assumed under Article 43, invite that Member, if the Member so desires, to participate in the decisions of the Security Council concerning the employment of contingents of that Member's armed forces.

Article 45

In order to enable the United Nations to take urgent military measures, Members shall hold immediately available national air-force contingents for combined international enforcement action. The strength and degree of readiness of these contingents and plans for their combined action shall be determined, within the limits laid down in the special agreement and agreements referred to in Article 43, by the Security Council with the assistance of the Military Staff Committee.

Article 46

Plans for the application of armed force shall be made by the Security Council with the assistance of the Military Staff Committee.

Article 47

1. There shall be established a Military Staff Committee to advise and assist the Security Council on all questions relating to the Security Council's military requirements for the maintenance of international peace and security, the employment and command of forces placed at its disposal, the regulation of armaments, and possible disarmament.

2. The Military Staff Committee shall consist of the Chiefs of Staff of the permanent members of the Security Council or their representatives. Any Member of the United Nations not permanently represented on the Committee shall be invited by the Committee to be associated with it when the efficient discharge of the Committee's responsibilities requires the participation of that Member in its work.

3. The Military Staff Committee shall be responsible under the Security Council for the strategic direction of any armed forces placed at the disposal of the Security Council. Questions relating to the command of such forces shall be worked out subsequently.

4. The Military Staff Committee, with the authorization of the Security Council and after consultation with appropriate regional agencies, may establish regional sub-committees.

Article 48

1. The action required to carry out the decisions of the Security Council for the maintenance of international peace and security shall be taken by all the Members of the United Nations or by some of them, as the Security Council may determine.

2. Such decisions shall be carried out by the Members of the United Nations directly and through their action in the appropriate international agencies of which they are members.

Article 49

The Members of the United Nations shall join in affording mutual assistance in carrying out the measures decided upon by the Security Council.

Article 50

If preventive or enforcement measures against any state are taken by the Security Council, any other state, whether a Member of the United Nations or not, which finds itself confronted with special economic problems arising from the carrying out of those measures shall have the right to consult the Security Council with regard to a solution of those problems.

Article 51

Nothing in the present Charter shall impair the inherent right of individual or collective self-defence if an armed attack occurs against a Member of the United Nations, until the Security Council has taken measures necessary to maintain international peace and security. Measures taken by Members in the exercise of this right of self-defence shall be immediately reported to the Security Council and shall not in any way affect the authority and responsibility of the Security Council under the present Charter to take at any time such action as it deems necessary in order to maintain or restore international peace and security.

VIII. REGIONAL ARRANGEMENTS

Article 52

1. Nothing in the present Charter precludes the existence of regional arrangements or agencies for dealing with such matters relating to the maintenance of international peace and security as are appropriate for regional action, provided that such arrangements or agencies and their activities are consistent with the Purposes and Principles of the United Nations.

2. The Members of the United Nations entering into such arrangements or constituting such agencies shall make every effort to achieve pacific settlement of local disputes through such regional agencies before referring them to the Security Council.

3. The Security Council shall encourage the development of pacific settlement of local disputes through such regional arrangements or by such regional agencies either on the initiative of the states concerned or by reference from the Security Council.

4. This Article in no way impairs the application of Articles 34 and 35.

Article 53

1. The Security Council shall, where appropriate, utilize such regional arrangements or agencies for enforcement action under its authority. But no enforcement action shall be taken under regional arrangements or by regional agencies without the authorization of the Security Council, with the exception of measures against any enemy state, as defined in paragraph 2 of this Article, provided for pursuant to Article 107 or in regional arrangements directed against renewal of aggressive policy on the part of any such state, until such time as the Organization may, on request of the Governments concerned, be charged with the responsibility for preventing further aggression by such a state.

2. The term enemy state as used in paragraph 1 of this Article applies to any state which during the Second World War has been an enemy of any signatory of the present Charter.

Article 54

The Security Council shall at all times be kept fully informed of activities undertaken or in contemplation under regional arrangements or by regional agencies for the maintenance of international peace and security.

IX. INTERNATIONAL ECONOMIC AND SOCIAL CO-OPERATION

Article 55

With a view to the creation of conditions of stability and well-being which are necessary for peaceful and friendly relations among nations based on respect for the principle of equal rights and self-determination of peoples, the United Nations shall promote:

(a) higher standards of living, full employment, and conditions of economic and social progress and development;

(b) solutions of international economic, social, health, and related problems; and international cultural and educational co-operation; and

(c) universal respect for, and observance of, human rights and fundamental freedoms for all without distinction as to race, sex, language, or religion.

Article 56

All Members pledge themselves to take joint and separate action in co-operation with the Organization for the achievement of the purposes set forth in Article 55.

Article 57

1. The various specialized agencies, established by intergovernmental agreement and having wide international responsibilities,

as defined in their basic instruments, in economic, social, cultural, educational, health, and related fields, shall be brought into relationship with the United Nations in accordance with the provisions of Article 63.

2. Such agencies thus brought into relationship with the United Nations are hereinafter referred to as specialized agencies.

Article 58

The Organization shall make recommendations for the co-ordination of the policies and activities of the specialized agencies.

Article 59

The Organization shall, where appropriate, initiate negotiations among the states concerned for the creation of any new specialized agencies required for the accomplishment of the purposes set forth in Article 55.

Article 60

Responsibility for the discharge of the functions of the Organization set forth in this Chapter shall be vested in the General Assembly and, under the authority of the General Assembly, in the Economic and Social Council, which shall have for this purpose the powers set forth in Chapter X.

X. THE ECONOMIC AND SOCIAL COUNCIL

Composition

Article 61

1. The Economic and Social Council shall consist of 18 Members of the United Nations elected by the General Assembly.

2. Subject to the provisions of paragraph 3, six members of the Economic and Social Council shall be elected each year for a term of three years. A retiring member shall be eligible for immediate re-election.

3. At the first election, 18 members of the Economic and Social Council shall be chosen. The term of office of six members so chosen shall expire at the end of one year, and of six other members at the end of two years, in accordance with arrangements made by the General Assembly.

4. Each member of the Economic and Social Council shall have one representative.

Functions and Powers

Article 62

1. The Economic and Social Council may make or initiate studies and reports with respect to international economic, social, cultural, educational, health, and related matters and may make recommendations with respect to any such matters to the General Assembly, to the Members of the United Nations, and to the specialized agencies concerned.

2. It may make recommendations for the purpose of promoting respect for, and observance of, human rights and fundamental freedoms for all.

3. It may prepare draft conventions for submission to the General Assembly, with respect to matters falling within its competence.

4. It may call, in accordance with the rules prescribed by the United Nations, international conferences on matters falling within its competence.

Article 63

1. The Economic and Social Council may enter into agreements with any of the agencies referred to in Article 57, defining the terms on which the agency concerned shall be brought into relationship with the United Nations. Such agreements shall be subject to approval by the General Assembly.

2. It may co-ordinate the activities of the specialized agencies through consultation with and recommendations to such agencies and through recommendations to the General Assembly and to the Members of the United Nations.

Article 64

1. The Economic and Social Council may take appropriate steps to obtain regular reports from the specialized agencies. It may make arrangements with the Members of the United Nations and with specialized agencies to obtain reports on the steps taken to give effect to its own recommendations and to recommendations on matters falling within its competence made by the General Assembly.

2. It may communicate its observations on these reports to the General Assembly.

Article 65

The Economic and Social Council may furnish information to the Security Council and shall assist the Security Council upon its request.

Article 66

1. The Economic and Social Council shall perform such functions as fall within its competence in connection with the carrying out of the recommendations of the General Assembly.

2. It may, with the approval of the General Assembly, perform services at the request of Members of the United Nations and at the request of specialized agencies.

3. It shall perform such other functions as are specified elsewhere in the present Charter or as may be assigned to it by the General Assembly.

Voting

Article 67

1. Each member of the Economic and Social Council shall have one vote.

2. Decisions of the Economic and Social Council shall be made by a majority of the members present and voting.

Procedure

Article 68

The Economic and Social Council shall set up commissions in economic and social fields and for the promotion of human rights, and such other commissions as may be required for the performance of its functions.

Article 69

The Economic and Social Council shall invite any Member of the United Nations to participate, without vote, in its deliberations on any matter of particular concern to that Member.

Article 70

The Economic and Social Council may make arrangements for representatives of the specialized agencies to participate, without vote, in its deliberations and in those of the commissions established by it, and for its representatives to participate in the deliberations of the specialized agencies.

Article 71

The Economic and Social Council may make suitable arrangements for consultation with non-governmental organizations which are concerned with matters within its competence. Such arrangements may be made with international organizations and, where appropriate, with national organizations after consultation with the Member of the United Nations concerned.

Article 72

1. The Economic and Social Council shall adopt its own rules of procedure, including the method of selecting its President.

2. The Economic and Social Council shall meet as required in accordance with its rules, which shall include provision for the convening of meetings on the request of a majority of its members.

XI. NON-SELF-GOVERNING TERRITORIES

Article 73

Members of the United Nations which have or assume responsibilities for the administration of territories whose peoples have not yet attained a full measure of self-government recognize the principle that the interests of the inhabitants of these territories are paramount, and accept as a sacred trust the obligation to promote to the utmost, within the system of international peace and security established by the present Charter, the well-being of the inhabitants of these territories, and, to this end:

(a) to ensure, with due respect for the culture of the peoples concerned, their political, economic, social, and educational advancement, their just treatment, and their protection against abuses;

(b) to develop self-government, to take due account of the political aspirations of the peoples, and to assist them in the progressive development of their free political institutions, according to the particular circumstances of each territory and its peoples and their varying stages of advancement;

(c) to further international peace and security;

(d) to promote constructive measures of development, to encourage research, and to co-operate with one another and, when and where appropriate, with specialized international bodies with a view to the practical achievement of the social, economic, and scientific purposes set forth in this Article; and

(e) to transmit regularly to the Secretary-General for information purposes, subject to such limitations as security and constitutional considerations may require, statistical and other information, of a technical nature relating to economic, social, and educational conditions in the territories for which they are respectively responsible other than those territories to which Chapters XII and XIII apply.

Article 74

Members of the United Nations also agree that their policy in respect of the territories to which this Chapter applies, no less than in respect of their metropolitan areas, must be based on the general principles of good-neighbourliness, due account being taken of the interests and well-being of the rest of the world, in social, economic, and commercial matters.

XII. INTERNATIONAL TRUSTEESHIP SYSTEM

Article 75

The United Nations shall establish under its authority an international trusteeship system for the administration and supervision of such territories as may be placed thereunder by subsequent individual agreements. These territories are hereinafter referred to as trust territories.

Article 76

The basic objectives of the trusteeship system, in accordance with the Purposes of the United Nations laid down in Article 1 of the present Charter, shall be:

(a) to further international peace and security;

(b) to promote the political, economic, social, and educational advancement of the inhabitants of the trust territories, and their progressive development towards self-government or independence as may be appropriate to the particular circumstances of each territory and its peoples and the freely expressed wishes of the peoples concerned, and as may be provided by the terms of each trusteeship agreement;

(c) to encourage respect for human rights and for fundamental freedoms for all without distinction as to race, sex, language, or religion, and to encourage recognition of the interdependence of the peoples of the world; and

(d) to ensure equal treatment in social, economic, and commercial matters for all Members of the United Nations and their nationals, and also equal treatment for the latter in the administration of justice, without prejudice to the attainment of the foregoing objectives and subject to the provisions of Article 80.

Article 77

1. The trusteeship system shall apply to such territories in the following categories as may be placed thereunder by means of trusteeship agreements.

(a) territories now held under mandate;

(b) territories which may be detached from enemy states as a result of the Second World War; and

(c) territories voluntarily placed under the system by states responsible for their administration.

2. It will be a matter for subsequent agreement as to which territories in the foregoing categories will be brought under the trusteeship system and upon what terms.

Article 78

The trusteeship system shall not apply to territories which have become Members of the United Nations, relationship among which shall be based on respect for the principle of sovereign equality.

Article 79

The terms of trusteeship for each territory to be placed under the trusteeship system, including any alteration or amendment, shall be agreed upon by the states directly concerned, including the mandatory power in the case of territories held under mandate by a Member of the United Nations, and shall be approved as provided for in Articles 83 and 85.

Article 80

1. Except as may be agreed upon in individual trusteeship agreements, made under Articles 77, 79, and 81, placing each territory under the trusteeship system, and until such agreements have been concluded, nothing in this Chapter shall be construed in or of itself to alter in any manner the rights whatsoever of any states or any peoples or the terms of existing international instruments to which Members of the United Nations may respectively be parties.

2. Paragraph 1 of this Article shall not be interpreted as giving grounds for delay or postponement of the negotiation and conclusion of agreements for placing mandated and other territories under the trusteeship system as provided for in Article 77.

Article 81

The trusteeship agreement shall in each case include the terms under which the trust territory will be administered and designate the authority which will exercise the administration of the trust territory. Such authority, hereinafter called the administering authority, may be one or more states or the Organization itself.

Article 82

There may be designated, in any trusteeship agreement, a strategic area or areas which may include part or all of the trust territory to which the agreement applies, without prejudice to any special agreement or agreements made under Article 43.

Article 83

1. All functions of the United Nations relating to strategic areas, including the approval of the terms of the trusteeship agreements and of their alteration or amendment, shall be exercised by the Security Council.

2. The basic objectives set forth in Article 76 shall be applicable to the people of each strategic area.

3. The Security Council shall, subject to the provisions of the trusteeship agreements and without prejudice to security considerations, avail itself of the assistance of the Trusteeship Council to perform those functions of the United Nations under the trusteeship system relating to political, economic, social, and educational matters in the strategic areas.

Article 84

It shall be the duty of the administering authority to ensure that the trust territory shall play its part in the maintenance of international peace and security. To this end the administering authority may make use of volunteer forces, facilities, and assistance from the trust territory in carrying out the obligations towards the Security Council undertaken in this regard by the administering authority, as well as for local defence and the maintenance of law and order within the trust territory.

Article 85

1. The functions of the United Nations with regard to trusteeship agreements for all areas not designated as strategic, including the approval of the terms of the trusteeship agreements and of their alteration or amendment, shall be exercised by the General Assembly.

2. The Trusteeship Council, operating under the authority of the General Assembly, shall assist the General Assembly in carrying out these functions.

XIII. THE TRUSTEESHIP COUNCIL

Composition

Article 86

1. The Trusteeship Council shall consist of the following Members of the United Nations:

(a) those Members administering trust territories:

(b) such of those Members mentioned by name in Article 23 as are not administering trust territories; and

(c) as many other Members elected for three-year terms by the General Assembly as may be necessary to ensure that the total number of members of the Trusteeship Council is equally divided between those Members of the United Nations which administer trust territories and those which do not.

2. Each member of the Trusteeship Council shall designate one specially qualified person to represent it therein.

Functions and Powers

Article 87

The General Assembly and, under its authority, the Trusteeship Council, in carrying out their functions, may:

(a) consider reports submitted by the administering authority;

(b) accept petitions and examine them in consultation with the administering authority;

(c) provide for periodic visits to the respective trust territories at times agreed upon with the administering authority; and

(d) take these and other actions in conformity with the terms of the trusteeship agreements.

Article 88

The Trusteeship Council shall formulate a questionnaire on the political, economic, social, and educational advancement of the inhabitants of each trust territory, and the administering authority for each trust territory within the competence of the General Assembly shall make an annual report to the General Assembly upon the basis of such questionnaire.

Voting

Article 89

1. Each member of the Trusteeship Council shall have one vote.

2. Decisions of the Trusteeship Council shall be made by a majority of the members present and voting.

Procedure

Article 90

1. The Trusteeship Council shall adopt its own rules of procedure, including the method of selecting its President.

2. The Trusteeship Council shall meet as required in accordance with its rules, which shall include provision for the convening of meetings on the request of a majority of its members.

Article 91

The Trusteeship Council shall, when appropriate, avail itself of the assistance of the Economic and Social Council and of the specialized agencies in regard to matters with which they are respectively concerned.

XIV. THE INTERNATIONAL COURT OF JUSTICE

Article 92

The International Court of Justice shall be the principal judicial organ of the United Nations. It shall function in accordance with the annexed Statute, which is based upon the Statute of the Permanent Court of International Justice and forms an integral part of the present Charter.

Article 93

1. All Members of the United Nations are *ipso facto* parties to the Statute of the International Court of Justice.

2. A state which is not a Member of the United Nations may become a party to the Statute of the International Court of Justice on condition to be determined in each case by the General Assembly upon the recommendation of the Security Council.

Article 94

1. Each Member of the United Nations undertakes to comply with the decision of the International Court of Justice in any case to which it is a party.

2. If any party to a case fails to perform the obligations incumbent upon it under a judgment rendered by the Court, the other party may have recourse to the Security Council, which may, if it deems necessary, make recommendations or decide upon measures to be taken to give effect to the judgment.

Article 95

Nothing in the present Charter shall prevent Members of the United Nations from entrusting the solution of their differences to other tribunals by virtue of agreements already in existence or which may be concluded in the future.

Article 96

1. The General Assembly or the Security Council may request the International Court of Justice to give an advisory opinion on any legal question.

2. Other organs of the United Nations and specialized agencies, which may at any time be so authorized by the General Assembly, may also request advisory opinions of the Court on legal questions arising within the scope of their activities.

XV. THE SECRETARIAT

Article 97

The Secretariat shall comprise a Secretary-General and such staff as the Organization may require. The Secretary-General shall be appointed by the General Assembly upon the recommendation of the Security Council. He shall be the chief administrative officer of the Organization.

Article 98

The Secretary-General shall act in that capacity in all meetings of the General Assembly, of the Security Council, of the Economic and Social Council, and of the Trusteeship Council, and shall perform such other functions as are entrusted to him by these organs. The Secretary-General shall make an annual report to the General Assembly on the work of the Organization.

Article 99

The Secretary-General may bring to the attention of the Security Council any matter which in his opinion may threaten the maintenance of international peace and security.

Article 100

1. In the performance of their duties the Secretary-General and the staff shall not seek or receive instructions from any government or from any other authority external to the Organization. They shall refrain from any action which might reflect on their position as international officials responsible only to the Organization.

2. Each Member of the United Nations undertakes to respect the exclusively international character of the responsibilities of the Secretary-General and the staff and not to seek to influence them in the discharge of their responsibilities.

Article 101

1. The staff shall be appointed by the Secretary-General under regulations established by the General Assembly.

2. Appropriate staffs shall be permanently assigned to the Economic and Social Council, the Trusteeship Council, and, as required, to other organs of the United Nations. These staffs shall form a part of the Secretariat.

3. The paramount consideration in the employment of the staff and in the determination of the conditions of service shall be the necessity of securing the highest standards of efficiency, competence, and integrity. Due regard shall be paid to the importance of recruiting the staff on as wide a geographical basis as possible.

XVI. MISCELLANEOUS PROVISIONS

Article 102

1. Every treaty and every international agreement entered into by any Member of the United Nations after the present Charter comes into force shall as soon as possible be registered with the Secretariat and published by it.

2. No party to any such treaty or international agreement which has not been registered in accordance with the provisions of paragraph 1 of this Article may invoke that treaty or agreement before any organ of the United Nartions.

Article 103

In the event of a conflict between the obligations of the Members of the United Nations under the present Charter and their obligations under any other international agreement, their obligations under the present Charter shall prevail.

Article 104

The Organization shall enjoy in the territory of each of its Members such legal capacity as may be necessary for the exercise of its functions and the fulfilment of its purposes.

Article 105

1. The Organization shall enjoy in the territory of each of its Members such privileges and immunities as are necessary for the fulfilment of its purposes.

2. Representatives of the Members of the United Nations and officials of the Organization shall similarly enjoy such privileges and immunities as are necessary for the independent exercise of their functions in connection with the Organization.

3. The General Assembly may make recommendations with a view to determining the details of the application of paragraphs 1 and 2 of this Article or may propose conventions to the Members of the United Nations for this purpose.

XVII. TRANSITIONAL SECURITY ARRANGEMENTS

Article 106

Pending the coming into force of such special agreements referred to in Article 43 as in the opinion of the Security Council enable it to begin the exercise of its responsibilities under Article 42, the parties to the Four-Nation Declaration signed at Moscow, October 30, 1943, and France, shall, in accordance with the provisions of paragraph 5 of that Declaration, consult with one another and as occasion requires with other Members of the United Nations with a view to such joint action on behalf of the Organization as may be necessary for the purpose of maintaining international peace and security.

Article 107

Nothing in the present Charter shall invalidate or preclude action, in relation to any state which during the Second World War has been an enemy of any signatory to the present Charter, taken or authorized as a result of that war by the Governments having responsibility for such action.

XVIII. AMENDMENTS

Article 108

Amendments to the present Charter shall come into force for all Members of the United Nations when they have been adopted by a vote of two-thirds of the members of the General Assembly and ratified in accordance with their respective constitutional processes by two-thirds of the Members of the United Nations, including all the permanent members of the Security Council.

Article 109

1. A General Conference of the Members of the United Nations for the purpose of reviewing the present Charter may be held at a date and place to be fixed by a two-thirds vote of the members of the General Assembly and by a vote of any seven members of the Security Council. Each Member of the United Nations shall have one vote in the conference.

2. Any alteration of the present Charter recommended by a two-thirds vote of the conference shall take effect when ratified in accordance with their respective constitutional processes by two-thirds of the Members of the United Nations including all the permanent members of the Security Council.

3. If such a conference has not been held before the tenth annual session of the General Assembly following the coming into force of the present Charter, the proposal to call such a conference shall be placed on the agenda of that session of the General Assembly, and the conference shall be held if so decided by a majority vote of the members of the General Assembly and by a vote of any seven members of the Security Council.

XIX. RATIFICATION AND SIGNATURE

Article 110

1. The present Charter shall be ratified by the signatory states in accordance with their respective constitutional processes.

2. The ratifications shall be deposited with the Government of the United States of America, which shall notify all the signatory states of each deposit as well as the Secretary-General of the Organization when he has been appointed.

3. The present Charter shall come into force upon the deposit of ratifications by the Republic of China, France, the Union of Soviet Socialist Republics, the United Kingdom of Great Britain and Northern Ireland, and the United States of America, and by a majority of the other signatory states. A protocol of the ratifications deposited shall thereupon be drawn up by the Government of the United States of America which shall communicate copies thereof to all the signatory states.

4. The states signatory to the present Charter which ratify it after it has come into force will become original Members of the United Nations on the date of the deposit of their respective ratifications.

Article 111

The present Charter, of which the Chinese, French, Russian, English, and Spanish texts are equally authentic, shall remain deposited in the archives of the Government of the United States of America. Duly certified copies thereof shall be transmitted by that Government to the Governments of the other signatory states.

IN FAITH WHEREOF the representatives of the Governments of the United Nations have signed the present Charter.

DONE at the city of San Francisco the twenty-sixth day of June, one thousand nine hundred and forty-five.

Amendments

The following amendments to Articles 23 and 27 of the Charter came into force in August 1965.

Article 23

1. The Security Council shall consist of 15 Members of the United Nations. The Republic of China, France, the Union of Soviet Socialist Republics, the United Kingdom of Great Britain and Northern Ireland, and the United States of America shall be permanent members of the Security Council. The General Assembly shall elect 10 other Members of the United Nations to be non-permanent members of the Security Council, due regard being specially paid, in the first instance to the contribution of Members of the United Nations to the maintenance of international peace and security and to the other purposes of the Organization, and also to equitable geographical distribution.

2. The non-permanent members of the Security Council shall be elected for a term of two years. In the first election of the non-permanent members after the increase of the membership of the Security Council from 11 to 15, two of the four additional members shall be chosen for a term of one year. A retiring member shall not be eligible for immediate re-election.

3. Each member of the Security Council shall have one representative.

Article 27

1. Each member of the Security Council shall have one vote.

2. Decisions of the Security Council on procedural matters shall be made by an affirmative vote of nine members.

3. Decisions of the Security Council on all other matters shall be made by an affirmative vote of nine members including the concurring votes of the permanent members; provided that, in decisions under Chapter VI and under paragraph 3 of Article 52, a party to a dispute shall abstain from voting.

The following amendments to Article 61 of the Charter came into force in September 1973.

Article 61

1. The Economic and Social Council shall consist of 54 Members of the United Nations elected by the General Assembly.

2. Subject to the provisions of paragraph 3, 18 members of the Economic and Social Council shall be elected each year for a term of three years. A retiring member shall be eligible for immediate re-election.

3. At the first election after the increase in the membership of the Economic and Social Council from 27 to 54 members, in addition to the members elected in place of the nine members whose term of office expires at the end of that year, 27 additional members shall be elected. Of these 27 additional members, the term of office of nine members so elected shall expire at the end of one year, and of nine other members at the end of two years, in accordance with arrangements made by the General Assembly.

4. Each member of the Economic and Social Council shall have one representative.

The following amendment to Paragraph 1 of Article 109 of the Charter came into force in June 1968.

Article 109

1. A General Conference of the Members of the United Nations for the purpose of reviewing the present Charter may be held at a date and place to be fixed by a two-thirds vote of the members of the General Assembly and by a vote of any nine members of the Security Council. Each Member of the United Nations shall have one vote in the conference.

INTERNATIONAL ORGANIZATIONS — United Nations

Secretariat

SECRETARY-GENERAL

The Secretary-General is the UN's chief administrative officer, elected for a five-year term by the General Assembly on the recommendation of the Security Council. He acts in that capacity at all meetings of the General Assembly, the Security Council, the Economic and Social Council, and the Trusteeship Council, and performs such other functions as are entrusted to him by those organs. He is required to submit an annual report to the General Assembly and may bring to the attention of the Security Council any matter which in his opinion may threaten international peace. (See Charter, p. 15.)

Secretary-General: Javier Pérez de Cuéllar (Peru) (1987–91).

HEADQUARTERS STAFF
(October 1986)

Office of the Director-General for Development and International Economic Co-operation
Director-General: Jean L. Ripert (France).

Executive Office of the Secretary-General
Chef de Cabinet: Virendra Dayal (India).

Office of the Under-Secretaries-General for Special Political Affairs
Under-Secretaries-General: Diego Cordóvez (Ecuador), Marrack I. Golding (United Kingdom).

Office for Field Operational and External Support Activities
Assistant Secretary-General: James O. C. Jonah (Sierra Leone).

Office for Special Political Questions
Under-Secretary-General and Co-ordinator, Special Economic Assistance Programmes: Abdulrahim A. Farah (Somalia).

Office of the Under-Secretary-General for Political and General Assembly Affairs
Under-Secretary-General: William B. Buffum (USA).

Office of Secretariat Services for Economic and Social Matters
Assistant Secretary-General: Sotirios Mousouris (Greece).

Office of Legal Affairs
Under-Secretary-General, The Legal Counsel: Carl-August Fleischhauer (FRG).

Department of Political and Security Council Affairs
Under-Secretary-General: Viacheslav A. Ustinov (USSR).

Department for Disarmament Affairs
Under-Secretary-General: Jan Martenson (Sweden).

Department of Political Affairs, Trusteeship and Decolonization
Under-Secretary-General: Rafeeuddin Ahmed (Pakistan).

Department of International Economic and Social Affairs
Under-Secretary-General: Shuaib Uthman Yolah (Nigeria).

Department of Technical Co-operation for Development
Under-Secretary-General: Xie Qimei (People's Republic of China).

Department of Administration and Management
Under-Secretary-General: Patricio Ruedas (Spain).

Office of Financial Services
Assistant Secretary-General, Controller: J. Richard Foran (Canada).

Office of Personnel Services
Assistant Secretary-General: Louis-Pascal Nègre (Mali).

Office of General Services
Assistant Secretary-General: Alice E. Weil (USA).

Department of Conference Services
Under-Secretary-General: Eugeniusz Wyzner (Poland).

Department of Public Information
Under-Secretary-General: Yasushi Akashi (Japan).

Office of the United Nations Commissioner for Namibia
Assistant Secretary-General, Commissioner for Namibia: Brajesh Chandra Mishra (India).

Office of the Special Representative of the Secretary-General for Nambia
Under-Secretary-General: Martti Ahtisaari (Finland).

Office of the Special Representative of the Secretary-General for the Law of the Sea
Assistant Secretary-General, Special Representative: Satya N. Nandan (Fiji).

The chief administrative staff of the UN Regional Commissions and of all the subsidiary organs of the UN (not including the International Atomic Energy Agency) are also members of the Secretariat staff and are listed in the appropriate chapters on pp. 23–52. The Secretariat staff also includes a number of special missions and special appointments, including some of senior rank.

On 31 December 1985 the total number of staff of the Secretariat holding appointments continuing for a year or more was 15,701, including those serving away from the headquarters. This comprised 4,342 professional and higher-level staff and 10,014 in the General Service, Field Service and other categories.

On 31 December 1985 the total number of staff in the whole United Nations system (including the specialized agencies) was 27,304. This comprised 9,275 professional and higher-level staff and 18,029 in the General Service and other categories.

GENEVA OFFICE

Address: Palais des Nations, 1211 Geneva 10, Switzerland.
Telephone: (022) 310211.
Director-General: Under-Sec.-Gen. Erik Suy (Belgium)
Deputy Director-General: Wahid Tarzi.
Chef de Cabinet: André Varchaver.

VIENNA OFFICE

Address: Vienna International Centre, POB 500, 1400 Vienna, Austria.
Director-General: Asst Sec.-Gen. Mowaffak Allaf (Syria).

UN CONFERENCES, 1986–87

UN Conference on Conditions for Registration of Ships: Geneva, January–February 1986.
Conference on the Law of Treaties between States and International Organizations or between International Organizations: Vienna, February–March 1986.
World Conference on Sanctions against Racist South Africa: Paris, June 1986.
International Conference for the Immediate Independence of Namibia: Vienna, July 1986.
Second Review Conference of the States Parties to the Convention on the Prohibition of the Development, Production and Stockpiling of Bacteriological (Biological) and Toxin Weapons and on Their Destruction: Geneva, September 1986.
UN Conference for the Promotion of International Co-operation in the Peaceful Uses of Nuclear Energy: Geneva, March–April 1987.
International Conference on Drug Abuse and Illicit Trafficking: Vienna, June 1987.
International Conference on the Relationship Between Disarmament and Development: Paris, 1987.

INTERNATIONAL ORGANIZATIONS   *United Nations*

General Assembly

The General Assembly was established as a principal organ under the United Nations Charter; first met 10 January 1946. It is the main deliberative organ of the United Nations. (See Charter, p. 9.) Each delegation consists of not more than five representatives and five alternates with as many advisers, technical advisers and experts as may be required. The Assembly meets regularly for three months each year, but special sessions may also be held. It has the power to adopt recommendations only, not binding decisions. Important questions are decided by a two-thirds majority. Each nation has one vote and each vote is equal.

President of 41st Session (from September 1986): HUMAYUN RASHEED CHOUDHURY (Bangladesh).

MAIN COMMITTEES

There are seven Main Committees, on which all members have a right to be represented. The first six were appointed in 1946. An *ad hoc* Political Committee was first established in November 1948 and re-established annually until November 1956, when it was made permanent and renamed Special Political Committee.

First Committee: Disarmament and Related International Security Questions.
Special Political Committee.
Second Committee: Economic and Financial.
Third Committee: Social, Humanitarian and Cultural.
Fourth Committee: Decolonization.
Fifth Committee: Administrative and Budgetary.
Sixth Committee: Legal.

OTHER SESSIONAL COMMITTEES

General Committee: f. 1946; composed of 29 members, including the Assembly President, the 21 Vice-Presidents and the Chairmen of the seven Main Committees.
Credentials Committee: f. 1946; composed of nine members elected at each Assembly session.

POLITICAL AND SECURITY

Special Committee on Peace-keeping Operations: f. 1965; 33 appointed members.
Disarmament Commission: f. 1978 (replacing body f. 1952); composed of all UN members.
UN Scientific Committee on the Effects of Atomic Radiation: f. 1955; 20 members.
UN Scientific Advisory Committee: f. 1954 under different title; seven members.
Committee on the Peaceful Uses of Outer Space: f. 1959; 53 members; has a Legal Sub-Committee and a Scientific and Technical Sub-Committee.
Special Committee against Apartheid: f. 1962; 18 members.
Committee of Trustees of the UN Trust Fund for South Africa: f. 1965; five members.
Ad Hoc Committee on the Indian Ocean: f. 1972; 48 members.
Ad Hoc Committee on the Implementation of the Collective Security Provisions of the Charter of the United Nations: f. 1983.
Committee on the Exercise of the Inalienable Rights of the Palestinian People: f. 1975; 23 members.

TRUST TERRITORY AND COLONIAL QUESTIONS

UN Council for Namibia: f. 1967 as UN Council for South West Africa; changed name in 1968; 31 members.
Special Committee on the Implementation of the Declaration on Decolonization: f. 1961; 24 members.
Advisory Committee on the UN Educational and Training Programme for Southern Africa: f. 1968; 13 members.

DEVELOPMENT

Intergovernmental Committee on Science and Technology for Development: f. 1980; open to all states.
Committee on the Development and Utilization of New and Renewable Sources of Energy: f. 1983; open to all states.

LEGAL QUESTIONS

International Law Commission: f. 1947; 34 members elected for a five-year term; originally established in 1946 as the Committee on the Progressive Development of International Law and its Codification.
Advisory Committee on the UN Programme of Assistance in Teaching, Study, Dissemination and Wider Appreciation of International Law: f. 1965; 13 members.
UN Commission on International Trade Law: f. 1966; 36 members.
Special Committee on the Charter of the United Nations and on the Strengthening of the Role of the Organization: f. 1975; 47 members.
Special Committee on Enhancing the Effectiveness of the Principle of Non-Use of Force in International Relations: f. 1977; 35 members.

ADMINISTRATIVE AND FINANCIAL QUESTIONS

Advisory Committee on Administrative and Budgetary Questions: f. 1946; 16 members appointed for three-year terms.
Committee on Contributions: f. 1946; 18 members appointed for three-year terms.
International Civil Service Commission: f. 1948; 15 members appointed for four-year terms.
Committee on Information: f. 1978, formerly the Committee to review UN Policies and Activities; 69 members.

There is also a Board of Auditors, Investments Committee, UN Administrative Tribunal, Committee on Applications for Review of Administrative Tribunal Judgments, UN Joint Staff Pension Board, Joint Inspection Unit, UN Staff Pension Committee and Committee on Conferences.

HIGHER EDUCATION

Council of the United Nations University (see p. 81).

INTERNATIONAL ORGANIZATIONS — United Nations

Security Council

The Security Council was established as a principal organ under the United Nations Charter; its first meeting was held on 17 January 1946. Its task is to promote international peace and security in all parts of the world. (See Charter, p. 10.)

MEMBERS
Permanent members:
People's Republic of China, France, USSR, United Kingdom, USA.
The remaining 10 members are normally elected by the General Assembly for two-year periods (five countries from Africa and Asia, two from Latin America, one from socialist Eastern Europe, and two from Western Europe and others).

ORGANIZATION
The Security Council has the right to investigate any dispute or situation which might lead to friction between two or more countries, and such disputes or situations may be brought to the Council's attention either by one of its members, by any member state, by the General Assembly, by the Secretary-General or even, under certain conditions, by a state which is not a member of the United Nations.

The Council has the right to recommend ways and means of peaceful settlement and, in certain circumstances, the actual terms of settlement. In the event of a threat to or breach of international peace or an act of aggression, the Council has powers to take 'enforcement' measures in order to restore international peace and security. These include severance of communications and of economic and diplomatic relations and, if required, action by air, land and sea forces.

All members of the United Nations are pledged by the Charter to make available to the Security Council, on its call and in accordance with special agreements, the armed forces, assistance and facilities necessary to maintain international peace and security. These agreements, however, have not yet been concluded.

The Council is organized to be able to function continuously. The Presidency of the Council is held monthly in turn by the member states in English alphabetical order. Each member of the Council has one vote. On procedural matters decisions are made by the affirmative vote of any nine members. For decisions on other matters the required nine affirmative votes must include the votes of the five permanent members. This is the rule of 'great power unanimity' popularly known as the 'veto' privilege. In practice, an abstention by one of the permanent members is not regarded as a veto. Any member, whether permanent or non-permanent, must abstain from voting in any decision concerning the pacific settlement of a dispute to which it is a party.

The Council held 74 meetings in 1985. Of these, 20 were devoted to South Africa, 19 to the Middle East, 17 to Namibia, seven to complaints by Nicaragua against the USA, two to the UN Peace-keeping Force in Cyprus and one each to a complaint by Chad against Libya, the consideration of prisoners of war in the Iran-Iraq conflict, a complaint by Iran concerning the use of chemical weapons by Iraq, the 'hijacking' of the ship *Achille Lauro* by Palestinians and the question of hostage-taking and abduction. One was a 40th anniversary commemorative meeting, one was held to elect members to the ICJ and two were held in private to adopt the Council's report to the General Assembly.

SUBSIDIARY BODIES
Military Staff Committee: Consists of the Chiefs of Staff (or their representatives) of the five permanent members of the Security Council: assists the Council on all military questions.
(See also UN Peace-keeping Missions in the Middle East, p. 48.)

STANDING COMMITTEES
There are three standing committees, each composed of representatives of all Council members: Committee of Experts (to examine provisional rules of procedure and other matters); Committee on Council Meetings Away from Headquarters; Committee on the Admission of New Members.

Economic and Social Council—ECOSOC

ECOSOC promotes world co-operation on economic, social, cultural and humanitarian problems. (See Charter, p. 13.)

MEMBERS
Fifty-four members are elected by the General Assembly for three-year terms: 18 are elected each year. Membership is allotted by regions as follows: Africa 14 members, Western Europe and others 13, Asia 11, Latin America 10, Eastern Europe 6.

ORGANIZATION
The Council, normally meeting twice a year in New York and Geneva, is mainly a central policy-making and co-ordinating organ. It has a co-ordinating function between the UN and the specialized agencies, and also makes consultative arrangements with approved voluntary or non-governmental organizations which work within the sphere of its activities. The Council has functional and regional commissions to carry out much of its detailed work.

SESSIONAL COMMITTEES
Each sessional committee comprises the 54 members of the Council: there is a First (Economic) Committee, a Second (Social) Committee and a Third (Programme and Co-ordination) Committee.

FUNCTIONAL COMMISSIONS
Statistical Commission: Standardizes terminology and procedure in statistics and promotes the development of national statistics; 24 members.
Population Commission: Advises the Council on population matters and their relation to socio-economic conditions; 27 members.
Commission for Social Development: Plans social development programmes; 32 members.
Commission on Human Rights: Seeks greater respect for the basic rights of man, the prevention of discrimination and the protection of minorities; reviews specific instances of human rights violation, provides policy guidance; works on declarations, conventions and other instruments of international law; 43 members. There is a Sub-Commission on Prevention of Discrimination and Protection of Minorities.
Commission on the Status of Women: Aims at equality of political, economic and social rights for women; 32 members.
Commission on Narcotic Drugs: Mainly concerned in combating illicit traffic; 40 members. There is a Sub-Commission on Illicit Drug Traffic and Related Matters in the Near and Middle East.

COMMITTEES AND SUBSIDIARY BODIES
Committee for Programme and Co-ordination: f. 1962.
Committee on Non-Governmental Organizations: f. 1946.
Committee on Negotiations with Intergovernmental Agencies: f. 1946.
Committee for Development Planning: f. 1965.
Committee on Natural Resources: f. 1970.
Committee on Crime Prevention and Control: f. 1972.
Commission on Transnational Corporations: f. 1974.
Commission on Human Settlements: f. 1977. (See Habitat, p. 37.)

INTERNATIONAL ORGANIZATIONS *United Nations*

REGIONAL COMMISSIONS
(see pp. 23–32)

Economic Commission for Europe—ECE.
Economic and Social Commission for Asia and the Pacific—ESCAP.
Economic Commission for Latin America and the Caribbean—ECLAC.
Economic Commission for Africa—ECA.
Economic and Social Commission for Western Asia—ESCWA.

RELATED BODIES

UNICEF Executive Board: 41 members, elected by ECOSOC (see p. 38).
UNHCR Executive Committee: 41 members, elected by ECOSOC (see p. 45).
UNDP Governing Council: 48 members, elected by ECOSOC (see p. 40).
Committee on Food Aid Policies and Programmes: one-half of the 30 members are elected by ECOSOC, one-half by FAO; governing body of the World Food Programme (see p. 52).
International Narcotics Control Board: f. 1964; 13 members.
Board of Trustees of the International Research and Training Institute for Women (INSTRAW): 11 members.

The Trusteeship Council

The Trusteeship Council has supervised United Nations' Trust Territories through the administering authorities to promote the political, economic, social and educational advancement of the inhabitants towards self-government or independence. (See Charter, p. 14.)

MEMBERS

The Council consists of member states administering Trust Territories, permanent members of the Security Council which do not administer Trust Territories, and other non-administering countires elected by the Assembly for three-year terms.

Administering Country:	Other Countries:
United States	China, People's Republic*
	France
	USSR
	United Kingdom

* China does not participate in the work of the Council.

ORGANIZATION

The Council meets once a year, generally in May–June. Each member has one vote, and decisions are made by a simple majority of the members present and voting. A new President is elected at the beginning of the Council's regular session each year.

The only territory remaining under United Nations trusteeship is the Trust Territory of the Pacific Islands, which consists of the Caroline Islands and the Marshall Islands, island groups in Micronesia. The Northern Mariana Islands, formerly the Marianas District of the Trust Territory, became a Commonwealth territory of the USA in January 1978, although it remains legally part of the area covered by the Trusteeship Agreement. The Trust Territory of the Pacific Islands has been designated a strategic area, and the supervisory functions of the United Nations are, in its case, exercised by the Trusteeship Council under the authority of the Security Council.

The Constitution of the Marshall Islands entered into force on 1 May 1979. The Constitution of the Federated States of Micronesia, four districts of the Caroline Islands, entered into force on 10 May 1979. A referendum held in July 1979 in the Palau district approved a proposed local constitution, and in January 1981 it became the Republic of Palau. With the entries into force of the Constitutions, the High Commissioner, the chief executive of the Trust Territory, retained only the authority necessary to carry out the obligations of the USA under the Trusteeship and other agreements. In October and November 1980 agreements were initialled providing for the future self-government of the islands under compacts of 'free association' with the USA, subject to approval by the US Congress and by plebiscite in the islands (conducted in the Marshall Islands and the Federated States of Micronesia in 1983, and in Palau in 1986), after which the agreements were to be submitted to the UN for formal termination of the trusteeship agreements.

In May 1986, the USA requested termination of the Trusteeship. The Trusteeship Council stated that it considered that the USA had satisfactorily discharged its obligations under the Trusteeship Agreement and that it was appropriate for that Agreement to be terminated upon entry into force of the Compact of Free Association for the Federated States of Micronesia, the Marshall Islands and Palau, and the Commonwealth Covenant in respect of the Northern Mariana Islands. Because it is a 'strategic area', any alteration of the status of Micronesia must be exercised by the Security Council.

High Commissioner: JANET MCCOY.

INTERNATIONAL ORGANIZATIONS
United Nations

International Court of Justice

Address: Peace Palace, 2517 KJ The Hague, Netherlands.
Telephone: (070) 92-44-41.
Telex: 32323.

Set up in 1945, the Court is the principal judicial organ of the UN. All members of the UN, and also Switzerland, Liechtenstein and San Marino, are parties to the Statute of the Court. (See Charter, p. 15.)

THE JUDGES
(September 1986; in order of precedence)

	Term Ends*
President: NAGENDRA SINGH (India)	1991
Vice-President: GUY LADREIT DE LACHARRIÈRE (France)	1991
Judges:	
MANFRED LACHS (Poland)	1994
JOSÉ-MARIA RUDA (Argentina)	1991
TASLIM OLAWALE ELIAS (Nigeria)	1994
SHIGERU ODA (Japan)	1994
ROBERTO AGO (Italy)	1988
JOSÉ SETTE-CAMARA (Brazil)	1988
STEPHEN M. SCHWEBEL (USA)	1988
Sir ROBERT JENNINGS (United Kingdom)	1991
KÉBA MBAYE (Senegal)	1991
MOHAMMED BEDJAOUI (Algeria)	1988
NI ZHENGYU (People's Republic of China)	1994
JENS EVENSEN (Norway)	1994
NIKOLAI K. TARASSOV (USSR)	1988

* Each term ends on 5 February of the year indicated.

The Court is composed of 15 judges, each of a different nationality, elected with an absolute majority by both the General Assembly and the Security Council. Representation of the main forms of civilization and the different legal systems of the world are borne in mind in their election. Candidates are nominated by national panels of jurists.

The judges are elected for nine years and may be re-elected; elections for five seats are held every three years. The Court elects its President and Vice-President for each three-year period. Members may not have any political, administrative, or other professional occupation, and may not sit in any case with which they have been otherwise connected than as a judge of the Court. For the purposes of a case, each side—consisting of one or more States—may, unless the Bench already includes a judge with a corresponding nationality, choose a person from outside the Court to sit as a judge on terms of equality with the Members. Judicial decisions are taken by a majority of the judges present, subject to a quorum of nine Members. The President has a casting vote.

FUNCTIONS

The International Court of Justice operates in accordance with a Statute which is an integral part of the UN Charter. Only States may be parties in cases before the Court; those not parties to the Statute may have access in certain circumstances and under conditions laid down by the Security Council.

The Jurisdiction of the Court comprises:

1. All cases which the parties refer to it jointly by special agreement (there have been nine such, indicated in the list below by a stroke between the names of the parties).

2. All matters concerning which a treaty or convention in force provides for reference to the Court. About 700 bilateral or multilateral agreements make such provision. Among the more noteworthy: Treaty of Peace with Japan (1951), European Convention for Peaceful Settlement of Disputes (1957), Single Convention on Narcotic Drugs (1961), Protocol relating to the Status of Refugees (1967), Hague Convention on the Suppression of the Unlawful Seizure of Aircraft (1970).

3. Legal disputes between States which have recognized the jurisdiction of the Court as compulsory for specified classes of dispute. Declarations by the following 46 States accepting the compulsory jurisdiction of the Court are in force: Australia, Austria, Barbados, Belgium, Botswana, Canada, Colombia, Costa Rica, Denmark, the Dominican Republic, Egypt, El Salvador, Finland, The Gambia, Haiti, Honduras, India, Japan, Kampuchea, Kenya, Liberia, Liechtenstein, Luxembourg, Malawi, Malta, Mauritius, Mexico, the Netherlands, New Zealand, Nicaragua, Nigeria, Norway, Pakistan, Panama, the Philippines, Portugal, Senegal, Somalia, Sudan, Swaziland, Sweden, Switzerland, Togo, Uganda, the United Kingdom and Uruguay.

Disputes as to whether the Court has jurisdiction are settled by the Court.

Judgments are without appeal, but are binding only for the particular case and between the parties. States appearing before the Court undertake to comply with its Judgment. If a party to a case fails to do so, the other party may apply to the Security Council, which may make recommendations or decide upon measures to give effect to the Judgment.

Advisory opinions on legal questions may be requested by the General Assembly, the Security Council or, if so authorized by the Assembly, other United Nations organs or specialized agencies.

Rules of Court governing procedure are made by the Court under a power conferred by the Statute.

CONSIDERED CASES

Judgments

By September 1986 55 cases had been referred to the Court by States. Some were removed from the list as a result of settlement or discontinuance, or on the grounds of a lack of basis for jurisdiction. Cases which have been the subject of a Judgment by the Court include: Corfu Channel (United Kingdom v. Albania); Fisheries (United Kingdom v. Norway); Asylum (Colombia/Peru), Haya de la Torre (Colombia v. Peru); Rights of Nationals of the United States of America in Morocco (France v. United States); Ambatielos (Greece v. United Kingdom); Anglo-Iranian Oil Co. (United Kingdom v. Iran); Minquiers and Ecrehos (France/United Kingdom); Nottebohm (Liechtenstein v. Guatemala); Monetary Gold Removed from Rome in 1943 (Italy v. France, United Kingdom and United States); Certain Norwegian Loans (France v. Norway); Right of Passage over Indian Territory (Portugal v. India); Application of the Convention of 1902 Governing the Guardianship of Infants (Netherlands v. Sweden); Interhandel (Switzerland v. United States); Sovereignty over Certain Frontier Land (Belgium/Netherlands); Arbitral Award made by the King of Spain on 23 December 1906 (Honduras v. Nicaragua); Temple of Preah Vihear (Cambodia v. Thailand); South West Africa (Ethiopia and Liberia v. South Africa); Northern Cameroons (Cameroon v. United Kingdom); Barcelona Traction, Light and Power Co, Ltd (New Application: 1962) (Belgium v. Spain); North Sea Continental Shelf (Federal Republic of Germany/Denmark and Netherlands); Appeal relating to the Jurisdiction of the ICAO Council (India v. Pakistan); Fisheries Jurisdiction (United Kingdom v. Iceland; Federal Republic of Germany v. Iceland); Nuclear Tests (Australia v. France; New Zealand v. France); Aegean Sea Continental Shelf (Greece v. Turkey); United States Diplomatic and Consular Staff in Teheran (USA v. Iran); Continental Shelf (Tunisia/Libya); Delimitation of the Maritime Boundary in the Gulf of Maine Area (Canada/USA); Continental Shelf (Libya/Malta); Application for revision and interpretation of the Judgment of 24 February 1982 in the case concerning the Continental Shelf (Tunisia v. Libya); Military and Paramilitary Activities in and against Nicaragua (Nicaragua v. USA).

The cases under consideration in 1986 concerned: Frontier Dispute (Burkina Faso/Mali); Border and Transborder Armed Actions (Nicaragua v. Costa Rica); Border and Transborder Armed Actions (Nicaragua v. Honduras).

Advisory Opinions

Advisory Opinions on the following matters have been given by the Court at the request of the United Nations General Assembly or an organ thereof: Condition of Admission of a State to Membership in the United Nations; Competence of the General Assembly for the Admission of a State to the United Nations; Reparation for

Injuries Suffered in the Service of the United Nations; Interpretation of the Peace Treaties with Bulgaria, Hungary and Romania; International Status of South West Africa; Voting Procedure on Questions relating to Reports and Petitions concerning the Territory of South West Africa; Admissibility of Hearings of Petitioners by the Committee on South West Africa; Reservations to the Convention on the Prevention and Punishment of the Crime of Genocide; Effect of Awards of Compensation Made by the United Nations Administrative Tribunal (UNAT); Certain Expenses of the United Nations; Western Sahara; Application for Review of UNAT Judgment No. 158; Application for Review of UNAT Judgment No. 273. Pending before the Court in 1986 was a request for advisory opinion on an Application for Review of UNAT Judgment No. 333.

One Advisory Opinion has been given at the request of the Security Council: Legal Consequences for States of the continued presence of South Africa in Namibia (South West Africa) notwithstanding Security Council resolution 276 (1970).

The Court has also, at the request of UNESCO, given an Advisory Opinion on Judgments of the Administrative Tribunal of the ILO upon Complaints made against UNESCO and, at the request of IMCO, on the Constitution of the Maritime Safety Committee of the Inter-Governmental Maritime Consultative Organization.

In December 1980 the Court gave the World Health Organization an advisory opinion concerning the Interpretation of the Agreement of 25 March 1951 between the WHO and Egypt.

FINANCE

The budget for the two years 1986–87 amounted to US $10,500,800, financed entirely by the United Nations.

PUBLICATIONS

Reports (Judgments, Opinions and Orders): series.

Pleadings (Written Pleadings and Statements, Oral Proceedings, Correspondence): series.

Yearbook (published in 3rd quarter each year).

Bibliography (annually).

Catalogue (irregular).

Acts and Documents, No. 4 (contains Statute and Rules of the Court, the Resolution concerning its internal judicial practice and other documents).

UNITED NATIONS REGIONAL ECONOMIC COMMISSIONS

Economic Commission for Europe—ECE

Address: Palais des Nations, 1211 Geneva 10, Switzerland.
Telephone: (022) 346011.
Telex: 289696.

The UN Economic Commission for Europe was established in 1947. Representatives of all European countries (including Cyprus and Turkey) and of the USA and Canada study the economic and technological problems of the region and recommend courses of action.

MEMBERS

Albania	Italy
Austria	Luxembourg
Belgium	Malta
Bulgaria	Netherlands
Byelorussian SSR	Norway
Canada	Poland
Cyprus	Portugal
Czechoslovakia	Romania
Denmark	Spain
Finland	Sweden
France	Switzerland
German Democratic Republic	Turkey
Federal Republic of Germany	Ukrainian SSR
Greece	USSR
Hungary	United Kingdom
Iceland	USA
Ireland	Yugoslavia

Organization
(October 1986)

COMMISSION

ECE, with ECAFE (now ESCAP), was the earliest of the five regional economic commissions set up by the UN Economic and Social Council. The Commission holds an annual plenary session and brief meetings of subsidiary bodies are convened throughout the year. Specialists seek agreements for later government approval, collect statistics and exchange technical information, both at meetings and through distribution of reports and special papers.
President: STEFAN MURI (Czechoslovakia).

SECRETARIAT

The Secretariat services the meetings of the Commission and its subsidiary bodies and publishes periodic surveys and reviews, including a number of specialized statistical bulletins on coal, timber, steel, chemicals, housing and building, electric power, gas, general energy and transport (see list of publications below). It maintains close and regular liaison with the United Nations Secretariat in New York, with the secretariats of the other UN regional commissions, and with the UN Specialized Agencies.
Executive Secretary: KLAUS AKSEL SAHLGREN (Finland).

Activities

Energy questions account for more than one-quarter of the total projects in the ECE's work programme. Other important topics include improvement of the environment; scientific and technical co-operation; transport policies; trade and industrial co-operation between eastern and western Europe; and economic projections. Work is carried out by the subsidiary bodies listed below, advised by groups of experts.

Committee on Agricultural Problems: Keeps market conditions under review, examines problems arising from mechanization and rationalization of agriculture, and drafts standard clauses for the international sale of certain agricultural products (cereals and citrus fruits). There are groups of experts to discuss the standardization of fresh fruit and vegetables, dried fruit, poultry meat, eggs and perishable products. Joint working groups are held with the FAO on agricultural mechanization and rationalization.

Timber Committee: Regularly reviews the market in sawn softwood, small-sized roundwood and hardwood, watches trends in the use of wood and its products and of wood waste, and drafts standard clauses for the international sale of certain categories of timber. Joint working groups are held with the FAO on technology, training and statistics.

Coal Committee: Concentrates on problems of production (underground and open-cast), upgrading, conversion, trade (including world trade) and use; studies related research and development activities; analyses market developments; exchanges information on policies; undertakes demand projections.

Committee on Electric Power: Analyses the electric power situation and its prospects, studies the planning and operation of large power systems, as well as particular aspects of hydroelectric, thermal and nuclear generation, international interconnections, rural electrification, the efficient use of electricity, and the relation between electricity and the environment.

Committee on Gas: Deals with gas resources, the economic and technical aspects of the production, transport and utilization of gas, natural and manufactured as well as liquefied petroleum gases, monitors trade in gas, and forecasts demand.

Committee on Housing, Building and Planning: Reviews trends and progress, with special reference to industrialization of construction, building costs and standardization. Studies land use and prices, urban renewal and physical planning. Housing problems of southern Europe receive special consideration.

Inland Transport Committee: Covers road, rail and inland water transport, customs, contracts, transport of dangerous and perishable goods, equipment, statistics, tariffs, river law, road transport regime and road traffic accidents, construction of vehicles and passenger transport services by road. A number of international agreements are in force following their adoption through ECE.

Steel Committee: Annually reviews trends in the European and world markets, changes in price policy, growth of capacity supply factors and future prospects. Also studies long-term economic and technological problems.

Committee on the Development of Trade: Examines intra-European trade, especially east/west trade. Organizes facilities in arbitration, trade fairs and technical shows, standardization of general conditions of sale of goods, insurance, simplification and standardization of export documents, payments arrangements, including multilateral compensation procedures, and consultations.

Conference of European Statisticians: Promotes improvement of national statistics and their international comparability in economic, social and demographic fields; facilitates exchange of information between European countries. A joint study group is held with the FAO on food and agriculture statistics.

Senior Economic Advisers to ECE Governments: Brings together high-level governmental experts for an exchange of views and experience on selected problems of governmental economic policy; organizes groups of experts, joint research projects and seminars on methodological problems relating to medium- and long-term planning and projections.

Committee on Water Problems: Reviews major trends and policies with regard to the conservation and development of water resources, particularly where international co-operation is required. Studies problems relating to the methodology of surveying water resources and needs including the establishment of relevant balances and statistics. Also studies selected problems of water pollution control and of governmental policy related to the formulation and administration of water management plans.

Chemical Industry Committee: Regularly reviews the market of chemical products and their raw materials in Europe, USA and elsewhere. Compiles annual statistics on production of and trade in chemical products. Carries out studies on special problems arising in connection with the development of the chemical industry.

INTERNATIONAL ORGANIZATIONS

Senior Advisers to ECE Governments on Science and Technology: Keeps under review developments in the sphere of science and technology in the ECE region and makes proposals to promote international co-operation. Priority activities are: review and analysis of problems of scientific and technological policy; technological forecasting; transfer of technology; dissemination of scientific and technological information; co-operative research; co-operation with other subsidiary bodies of the Commission and other international organizations.

Senior Advisers to ECE Governments on Environmental Problems: Exchanges experience and information on environmental problems of common concern; surveys and assesses the state of the environment in the ECE countries; considers national policies, institutions, and legislation and the international implications of environmental policies, with emphasis on socio-economic questions. There are working groups on air pollution, on low-pollution industrial techniques and on the recycling of waste.

Senior Advisers to ECE Governments on Energy: Exchanges information on general energy problems, including energy resources and national policies; work programme comprises programmes, policies and prospects; demand and supply; trade and co-operation; conservation.

BUDGET

ECE's budget for the two years 1986–87 was US $26.8m.

United Nations (Regional Economic Commissions)

PUBLICATIONS

ECE Annual Report.
Economic Bulletin for Europe.
Economic Survey of Europe.
Prices of Agricultural Products and Selected Inputs in Europe and North America—Annual ECE/FAO Price Review.
Agricultural Trade in Europe.
Review of the Agricultural Situation in Europe.
Timber Bulletin for Europe.
ECE Timber Committee Yearbook.
Annual Forest Products Market Review.
Annual Review of the Chemical Industry.
Annual Review of Engineering Industries and Automation.
Annual Bulletin of Coal Statistics for Europe.
Annual Bulletin of Electrical Energy Statistics for Europe.
Annual Bulletin of General Energy Statistics for Europe.
Annual Bulletin of Gas Statistics for Europe.
Annual Bulletin of Housing and Building Statistics for Europe.
Annual Bulletin of Steel Statistics for Europe.
Annual Bulletin of Transport Statistics for Europe.
Statistics of Road Traffic Accidents in Europe.
Bulletin of Statistics on World Trade in Engineering Products.
Reports, proceedings of meetings, technical documents, etc.

Economic and Social Commission for Asia and the Pacific—ESCAP

Address: United Nations Bldg, Rajadamnern Ave, Bangkok 2, Thailand.
Telephone: 2829161.
Telex: 82392.

The Commission was founded in 1947 to encourage the economic and social development of Asia and the Far East; it was originally known as the Economic Commission for Asia and the Far East (ECAFE). The title ESCAP, which replaced ECAFE, was adopted after a reorganization in 1974.

MEMBERS

Afghanistan	Japan	Philippines
Australia	Kampuchea	Singapore
Bangladesh	Korea, Republic	Solomon Islands
Bhutan	Laos	Sri Lanka
Brunei	Malaysia	Thailand
Burma	Maldives	Tonga
China, People's Republic	Mongolia	Tuvalu
	Nauru	USSR
Fiji	Nepal	United Kingdom
France	Netherlands	USA
India	New Zealand	Vanuatu
Indonesia	Pakistan	Viet-Nam
Iran	Papua New Guinea	Western Samoa

ASSOCIATE MEMBERS

Cook Islands	Hong Kong	Trust Territory of the Pacific Islands
Guam	Kiribati	
	Niue	

Organization

(October 1986)

COMMISSION

The Commission meets annually at ministerial level to examine the region's problems, to review progress, to establish priorities and to launch new projects.

Committees of officials dealing with the specific areas of work listed below meet annually or every two years; *ad hoc* conferences may also be held on subjects not otherwise covered.

SECRETARIAT

Executive Secretary: S. A. M. S. KIBRIA (Bangladesh).
Deputy Executive Secretary: KOJI NAKAGAWA.
Chief, Programme Co-ordination and Monitoring Office: SEIKO TAKAHASHI.

The secretariat includes the Programme Co-ordination and Monitoring Office, the Information Service and three specialized units: the ESCAP/CTC Joint Unit on Transnational Corporations (working with the UN Centre for Transnational Corporations), the Inter-agency Committee and Task Force on Integrated Rural Development (comprising specialists from ESCAP and nine UN agencies), and the Environmental Co-ordinating Unit (run jointly with the UN Environment Programme). ESCAP's work is covered by 12 Divisions: Administration; Agriculture; Development Planning; Industry, Human Settlements and Technology; International Trade; Natural Resources; Population; Shipping, Ports and Inland Waterways; Social Development; Statistics; Transport, Communications and Tourism; and Technical Co-operation.

PACIFIC OFFICE

Pacific Operations Centre: Port Vila, Vanuatu; f. 1984 by merging the ESCAP Pacific Liaison Office (Nauru) and the UN Development Advisory Team (Fiji).

Activities

ESCAP acts as a UN regional centre, providing the only intergovernmental forum for the whole of Asia and the Pacific, and executing a wide range of development programmes through technical assistance, advisory services to governments, research, training and information.

AGRICULTURE

ESCAP helps to analyse and formulate regional and national policies that lead to increased agricultural production. It conducts training courses and visits by planners to successful existing projects, disseminates information through a quarterly bulletin, and provides consultancy services for regional farm radio broadcasting. Training in the safe use of pesticides is given, and a Fertilizer Advisory, Development and Information Network for Asia and the

Pacific is run in co-operation with UNIDO and FAO. ESCAP also monitors the effects of weather on certain crops, enabling prediction of food shortages.

Regional Co-ordination Centre for Research and Development of Coarse Grains, Pulses, Roots and Tuber Crops: Jalan Merdeka 99, Bogor, Indonesia; tel. (0251) 26290; telex 48369; f. 1981 to provide technical services for research on the production of and trade in these crops in the humid tropics of Asia and the Pacific. Dir SHIRO OKABE.

Regional Network for Agricultural Machinery: c/o UNDP, POB 7285 ADC, Pasay City, Metro Manila, Philippines; tel. 3470; telex 72222250; f. 1977 to supplement and co-ordinate the efforts of national institutes designated by participating governments to design, develop and manufacture simple farm machinery to meet the needs of small farmers; provides prototypes of selected machinery; organizes training facilities, study tours and international symposia. Project Man. Dr Z. U. RAHMAN.

DEVELOPMENT PLANNING

This division provides comprehensive general information on regional planning. It reviews progress and publishes studies on specific development issues, together with an annual Economic and Social Survey of the region. Projects under way in 1983/84 included: studies of economic interdependence in the Pacific; comparative analyses of economic policy in the South Pacific islands; studies on the promotion of co-operation in southern Asia; a review of tax planning; and a project to assist member governments in economic forecasting. In 1982 a separate section was established within the Division to undertake activities connected with the least-developed countries of the region (Afghanistan, Bangladesh, Bhutan, Laos, Maldives and Western Samoa).

Asian and Pacific Development Centre: POB 12224, Kuala Lumpur, Malaysia; tel. 03-2548088; telex 30676; f. 1980 by the integration of four former regional training and research institutions (Asian and Pacific Development Institute, Asian and Pacific Development Administration Centre, Asian and Pacific Centre for Women and Development, Social Welfare and Development Centre). Dir Dr M. A. J. SHAHARI. Publs Newsletter (3 a year), studies, reports.

INDUSTRY, HUMAN SETTLEMENTS AND TECHNOLOGY

In co-operation with the UN Industrial Development Organization (UNIDO), ESCAP provides support for industrial development, particularly agriculture-based industry, through studies, advisory services, information and training. It carries out feasibility studies for the establishment of industries away from metropolitan areas, and promotes 'catalyst' industries in the least-developed countries of the region: during 1984, for example, ESCAP assisted the establishment of leather-tanning and the processing of medicinal herbs in Bangladesh. It encourages foreign investment and provides tax advice. A Unit on Transnational Corporations was established in 1977, jointly with the UN Centre on Transnational Corporations, to support governments in dealing with such corporations.

The 40th session of ESCAP in 1984 adopted a series of measures aimed at accelerating technological progress. ESCAP's work covers both the harnessing of traditional technology and the introduction of new technology, such as micro-electronics. Training, technical assistance and advisory services are provided.

Asian and Pacific Centre for Transfer of Technology: 49 Palace Rd, POB 115, Bangalore 560052, India; tel. 76931; telex 0845-719; f. 1977 to assist countries of the ESCAP region in technology development and transfer. Dir M. NAWAZ SHARIF. Publs *Asia Pacific Tech Monitor* (every 2 months), monographs, proceedings.

INTERNATIONAL TRADE

The ESCAP Trade Promotion Centre provides information on trade, and training and advisory services in export promotion and market development. ESCAP has helped to establish a number of regional groups linking producers of coconuts, jute, rubber and other commodities. Technical assistance is given to land-locked and remote island countries of the region for the improvement of transport facilities.

Asian and Pacific Coconut Community: POB 343, 3rd Floor, Wisma Bakrie Bldg, Jalan H. R. Rasuna Said Kav. Bl., Kuningan, Jak-Selatan 10002, Indonesia; tel. 510192; telex 44916; f. 1969 to promote, co-ordinate, and harmonize all activities of the coconut industry towards better production, processing, marketing and research. Mems: India, Indonesia, Malaysia, Papua New Guinea, the Philippines, Solomon Islands, Sri Lanka, Thailand, Vanuatu, Western Samoa; assoc. mems: Federated States of Micronesia, Palau. Dir P. G. PUNCHIHEWA.

Asian Clearing Union—ACU: c/o Central Bank of the Islamic Republic of Iran, Teheran, Iran; tel. 311321; telex 312120; f. 1974 to provide clearing arrangements to economize on the use of foreign exchange and promote the use of domestic currencies in trade transactions among developing countries; part of ESCAP's Asian trade expansion programme; the Central Bank of Iran is the Union's agent; mems: Bangladesh, Burma, India, Iran, Nepal, Pakistan, Sri Lanka. Gen.-Man. HASSAN GOLRIZ. Publs *Annual Report, Newsletter* (monthly).

Asian Free Trade Zone: f. 1976 by the Bangkok Agreement; provides for the reduction and eventual elimination of tariff and non-tariff barriers in trade; co-operation in commodities, industrial and other goods; and preferences for the least developed countries; mems: Bangladesh, India, the Republic of Korea, Laos, Sri Lanka.

Asian Reinsurance Corporation: 6th Floor, Sinthon Bldg, 132 Wireless Rd, Lumpini, Bangkok 10500, Thailand; tel. 250-1476; telex 87231; f. 1979 by ESCAP with UNCTAD, to operate as a professional reinsurer, giving priority in retrocessions to national insurance and reinsurance markets of member countries, and as a development organization providing technical assistance to national markets; cap. (authorized) US $15m., (paid-up) US $4.5m. Mems: Afghanistan, Bangladesh, Bhutan, the People's Republic of China, India, the Republic of Korea, the Philippines, Sri Lanka, Thailand. Gen. Man. C. N. S. SHASTRI.

International Pepper Community: 3rd Floor, Wisma Bakrie, Jalan H. R. Rasuna Said, Kav. B1, Kuningan, Jakarta, Indonesia; tel. 510192; telex 62218; f. 1972 for joint action among producing countries on the standards, supplies, marketing and promotion of pepper; mems: Brazil, India, Indonesia, Malaysia. Dir A. G. NASUTION.

NATURAL RESOURCES

ESCAP assists the countries of the region to benefit from their mineral resources, by promoting interdisciplinary research, sponsoring technical co-operation, and stressing the environmental impact of the exploitation of these resources.

ESCAP sponsors the investigation of new and renewable energy sources in the region. A computer information centre on solar, wind and biomass energy was established in Bangkok in 1983.

ESCAP's Regional Remote Sensing Programme promotes advanced techniques in compiling and analysing remote-sensing data, gathered by aircraft and satellites, for use in agriculture, forestry, and exploration for mineral and water resources. Special training was to be provided during the period 1984–86 for about 50 trainees annually.

The development of water resources through national water plans (covering irrigation, drinking-water supply and sanitation, hydro-electric power, and control of flood and storm damage) also forms part of the work of this division.

Committee for Co-ordination of Investigations of the Lower Mekong Basin: Pibultham Villa, Kasatsuk Bridge, Rama I Rd, Bangkok 10500, Thailand; tel. 223-7422; telex 21322; f. 1957 to develop the resources of the lower Mekong River basin; since 1978 an Interim Committee, formed by Laos, Thailand and Viet-Nam, has supervised work until Kampuchea (formerly a member) resumes participation. Activities are covered by six programmes: hydrology and meteorology (at the end of 1985 there were 404 hydrological stations and 337 meteorological stations gathering data); basin planning, including the compilation of maps, satellite surveys, economic, social and environmental studies, and the formation of a data bank; land and water resources development, including flood control, irrigation and hydroelectric power; navigation improvement; development of agriculture and fisheries; and power, industry and minerals. The Nam Ngum hydroelectric project (Laos), providing total generating capacity of 150 MW, was completed in 1984; pre-feasibility studies for a similar project in the Nam Theun basin (Laos) were begun in March 1984. By 1985 13 dams had been built on tributaries of the Mekong, and six more were under construction. Contributions pledged at the end of 1985 amounted to US $591.5m., of which $239.6m. was from the 25 co-operating countries, $208.4m. from mem. states, and the rest from UNDP and other UN agencies and international organizations. Exec. Agent C. J. KAMP.

Committee for Co-ordination of Joint Prospecting for Mineral Resources in Asian Offshore Areas—CCOP/East Asia: 2nd Floor, Omo Bldg, 110/2 Sathorn Nua Rd, Bangrak, Bangkok 10500, Thailand; tel. 2343578; telex 82392; f. 1966 to

INTERNATIONAL ORGANIZATIONS

reduce the cost of advanced mineral surveying and prospecting to member nations by a co-ordinated regional approach involving the pooling of expertise and resources such as ships, aircraft and expensive scientific equipment; works in partnership with developed nations which have provided geologists and geophysicists as technical advisers; receives aid from UNDP and other sources; mems: People's Republic of China, Indonesia, Japan, Kampuchea, the Republic of Korea, Malaysia, Papua New Guinea, the Philippines, Singapore, Thailand and Viet-Nam. Dir SERMSAKDI KULVANICH.

Committee for Co-ordination of Joint Prospecting for Mineral Resources in the South Pacific Area—CCOP/SOPAC: c/o Mineral Resources Dept, Private Mail Bag, GPO, Suva, Fiji; receives support from UNDP; undertakes prospecting for petroleum, manganese and other minerals; mems: Cook Islands, Fiji, Kiribati, New Zealand, Papua New Guinea, Solomon Islands, Tonga, the Trust Territory of the Pacific Islands, Tuvalu, Vanuatu, Western Samoa. Man. CRUZ A. MATOS.

ESCAP/WMO Typhoon Committee: c/o UNDP, POB 7285 ADC, Pasay City, Metro Manila, Philippines; tel. 986-767; f. 1968; an intergovernmental body sponsored by ESCAP and WMO for mitigation of typhoon damage. It aims at establishing efficient typhoon and flood warning systems through improved meteorological and telecommunication facilities. Other activities include promotion of disaster preparedness, training of personnel and co-ordination of research. The committee's programme is supported from national resources and also by UNDP and other international and bilateral assistance. Mems: People's Republic of China, Hong Kong, Japan, Kampuchea, Republic of Korea, Laos, the Philippines, Thailand, Viet-Nam. Co-ordinator of Secretariat: Dr ROMAN L. KINTANAR.

Regional Energy Development Programme: (for Asia) c/o ESCAP, UN Bldg, Rajadamnern Ave, Bangkok 10200, Thailand; tel. 282-9161; telex 82392; f. 1982 to encourage co-operation in the planning and management of energy programmes, efficient use of energy and development of new energy sources, with special emphasis on augmenting rural energy supplies. Senior Co-ordinator FILINO HARAHAP.

Regional Mineral Resources Development Centre: Jalan Jenderal Sudirman 623, Bandung, Indonesia; tel. 022-614168; telex 28279; f. 1973 to provide advisory services on mineral development in Asia; organizes workshops and training courses and promotes research; Governing Council mems: Bangladesh, India, Indonesia, Japan, the Republic of Korea, Malaysia, the Philippines, Solomon Islands and Thailand. Co-ordinator JAMES MCDIVITT. Publ. *Newsletter*.

South-East Asia Tin Research and Development Centre: Tiger Lane, Ipoh, Malaysia; tel. 05-559366; telex 44380; f. 1977 by Indonesia, Malaysia and Thailand, which produce about two-thirds of the world's output of tin. The Centre aims at developing methods of locating new primary ore deposits, efficient mining, ore beneficiation and smelting. Dir Prof. CHADAP PADMASUTA. Publs *SEATRAD Bulletin* (quarterly), technical publs, proceedings of seminars, reports.

WMO/ESCAP Panel on Tropical Cyclones: Technical Support Unit, c/o Dept of Meteorology, Colombo, Sri Lanka; tel. 93943; f. 1973 to mitigate damage caused by tropical cyclones in the Bay of Bengal and the Arabian Sea; mems: Bangladesh, Burma, India, Maldives, Pakistan, Sri Lanka, Thailand.

POPULATION

The region's high rate of population growth, estimated at 1.75% per year in 1982, means that population control has an important place in development planning. ESCAP makes comparative demographic studies of individual member countries, and in 1984 a study was under way on the efficiency of national family-planning programmes. A data bank on population information was established in 1982, and in 1983 17 member governments received advice on demography and family planning. Much of ESCAP's work in this field is funded by the UN Fund for Population Activities (UNFPA).

SHIPPING, PORTS AND INLAND WATERWAYS

ESCAP aims to help developing maritime members to adopt up-to-date technology in ship design and cargo handling, and to cope with the increased cost of ships' fuel. It organizes meetings of chief executives of national shippers' and shipowners' organizations; makes surveys on maritime manpower requirements, and provides training for shipping management personnel; provides statistical information; and prepares guidelines for drawing up maritime legislation. Studies on container transport and port management have been made, and ESCAP assists member countries in setting up freight study units to analyse export and import freight bills. In 1984 a project was under way to develop energy-saving measures in shipping. Training in inland waterways management and dredging technology has also been given.

SOCIAL DEVELOPMENT

ESCAP's social development programme aims to encourage participation in development by disadvantaged groups, namely the disabled, women, the young and the old. In 1983 it convened a regional meeting to prepare for the International Youth Year (1985), studying problems of access to education, training and employment. ESCAP attempts to increase the self-reliance of rural women by bringing groups together for the sharing of expertise, and provides advice for policy-makers in the area of women's participation in development. Health programmes cover basic community health services; health planning as part of overall development schemes; analysis of the pharmaceuticals industry; and children's health. Training courses on primary health care and on planning, development and health are provided. ESCAP also undertakes comparative studies and prepares planning manuals.

STATISTICS

Recognizing the importance of statistical data in drawing up and evaluating development programmes, ESCAP undertakes periodical reviews of national statistical systems, provides training and advisory services, organizes conferences, and issues publications. Particular emphasis is placed on household surveys as a means of compiling demographic information. ESCAP is also involved in developing methods of compiling regional statistics on energy, the environment, transport and consumer prices.

Statistical Institute for Asia and the Pacific: Akasaka POB 13, Tokyo 107-91, Japan; tel. (03) 357-8351; telex 32217; f. 1970; trains professional statisticians; prepares teaching materials, provides facilities for special studies and research of a statistical nature, assists in the development of statistical education and training at all levels in national and sub-regional centres. Dir T. A. MIJARES.

TRANSPORT AND COMMUNICATIONS

At the 40th session of ESCAP, delegates agreed to designate the period 1985–94 as the Transport Decade for Asia and the Pacific, owing to the vital part played by transport improvements in the process of development.

Intergovernmental meetings of road experts are regularly held by ESCAP to discuss road transport. The Asian Highway Network Project comprises a network of 65,000 km of roads in 15 countries; ESCAP publishes maps of the network and reports on its development. In 1983 a study of potential standardization of vehicle safety requirements in the countries of the network was undertaken. ESCAP publishes manuals on labour-intensive rural road construction and maintenance, and conducts training courses for officials in charge of roadworks.

ESCAP gives technical assistance to member countries for modernizing railways. An Asia-Pacific Railway Co-operation Group was established by transport ministers in 1983. Studies have been made by ESCAP on container transport by rail in selected countries, and on the feasibility of the electrification of railways in Thailand.

Asia-Pacific Telecommunity: Office Compound of the Communications Authority of Thailand, Bangkok 10500, Thailand; tel. 233-2334; telex 84198; f. 1979 to cover all matters relating to telecommunications in the region. Mems: Afghanistan, Australia, Bangladesh, Burma, the People's Republic of China, India, Indonesia, Iran, Japan, the Republic of Korea, Malaysia, Maldives, Nauru, Nepal, Pakistan, the Philippines, Singapore, Sri Lanka, Thailand, Viet-Nam; assoc. mems: Hong Kong, Brunei; two affiliated mems in the Republic of Korea, two in Hong Kong, two in Japan, and five in the Philippines. Exec. Dir BOONCHOO PHIENPANIJ.

FINANCE

For the two-year period 1986–87 ESCAP's estimated regular budget, an appropriation from the UN budget, was US $35m. The regular budget is supplemented annually by funds from various sources for technical assistance.

PUBLICATIONS

Economic and Social Survey of Asia and the Pacific (annually).
ESCAP Today.
Agricultural Information Development Bulletin (quarterly).

INTERNATIONAL ORGANIZATIONS

Agro-chemicals News in Brief (quarterly).
Fertilizer Trade Information (monthly).
Economic Bulletin (2 a year).
Development Papers (occasional).
ESCAP Atlas of Stratigraphy.
Energy Newsletter.

Electric Power in Asia and the Pacific (2 a year).
Water Resources Journal.
Confluence (water resources newsletter).
Regional Remote Sensing Newsletter.
Sample Surveys in the ESCAP Region (annually).
Manuals, maps, studies and reports.

Economic Commission for Latin America and the Caribbean—ECLAC

Address: Edificio Naciones Unidas, Avenida Dag Hammarskjöld, Casilla 179D, Santiago, Chile.
Telephone: 485051.
Telex: 340925.

The UN Economic Commission for Latin America was founded in 1948 to co-ordinate policies for the promotion of economic development in the Latin American region. In 1984 the title 'Economic Commission for Latin America and the Caribbean' was adopted.

MEMBERS

Antigua and Barbuda	El Salvador	Portugal
Argentina	France	Saint Christopher and Nevis
Bahamas	Grenada	
Barbados	Guatemala	Saint Lucia
Belize	Guyana	Saint Vincent and the Grenadines
Bolivia	Haiti	
Brazil	Honduras	Spain
Canada	Jamaica	Suriname
Chile	Mexico	Trinidad and Tobago
Colombia	Netherlands	
Costa Rica	Nicaragua	United Kingdom
Cuba	Panama	USA
Dominica	Paraguay	Uruguay
Dominican Republic	Peru	Venezuela
Ecuador		

ASSOCIATE MEMBERS

British Virgin Islands	Netherlands Antilles	United States Virgin Islands
Montserrat		

Organization
(October 1986)

COMMISSION

The Commission normally meets every two years in one of the Latin American capitals. It has established permanent bodies with various sub-committees:

Central American Economic Co-operation Committee: sub-committees on trade; statistical co-ordination; transport; housing, building and planning; electric power; industrial initiatives; and agricultural development.
Trade Committee.
Caribbean Development and Co-operation Committee.

SECRETARIAT

The Executive Secretariat comprises the Executive Secretary; Deputy Executive Secretaries for Economic and Social Development and for Co-operation and Support Services; the Programme Planning and Co-ordination Office; the Secretary of the Commission, with a conference service unit; and the UN Information Service.
There are divisions as follows:
Economic development.
Social development (including a unit for the integration of women in development).
International trade and development.
Statistics and quantitative analysis.

United Nations (Regional Economic Commissions)

Natural resources and energy (including a water resources unit).
Transport and communications.
Joint ECLAC/FAO agriculture division.
Joint ECLAC/UNIDO industry and technology division (including a science and technology unit).
Joint ECLAC/CTC unit on transnational corporations.
Joint ECLAC/UNEP development and environment unit.
Latin American Economic and Social Documentation Centre (see below).
Operations.
Documents and publications services.
Library.
Computer centre.

There is a Sub-regional Office in Mexico, a Sub-regional Headquarters for the Caribbean, and offices in Bogotá, Brasília, Buenos Aires, Montevideo and Washington.

Executive Secretary: NORBERTO GONZÁLEZ (Argentina).

Activities

ECLAC collaborates with regional governments in the investigation and analysis of regional and national economic problems, and provides guidance in the formulation of development plans. Many of its activities are undertaken in co-operation with other UN agencies.

The 20th session of the Commission was held in Lima, Peru, from 29 March to 6 April 1984. The meeting discussed the prospects of Latin America and the Caribbean for the rest of the decade in the light of the current economic crisis, and internal adjustment policies and the renegotiation of the external debt. Four sessional committees examined the topics of water, human settlements, co-operation among developing countries and regions, and population (in preparation for the International Conference on Population, held in Mexico in August 1984). The Secretariat was requested to carry out studies on domestic adjustment processes; policies leading to increased production and employment levels; suitable formulae for determining the extent to which export income could be committed to the service of the external debt; and the problems faced by the countries of the region in gaining access to the markets of the developed countries.

In collaboration with SELA (q.v.) the Latin American Economic Conference was held in Quito, Ecuador, in January 1984, discussing in particular the problem of external debt. In May 1985 ECLAC organized a meeting of regional governmental experts to discuss the effects of the economic recession and possible solutions to the serious problems resulting from it, both in the short and long term. ECLAC publications (see below) include a comprehensive annual survey of the region's economy.

Instituto Latinoamericano de Planificación Económica y Social—ILPES (Latin American Institute for Economic and Social Planning): Edificio Naciones Unidas, Avenida Dag Hammarskjöld, Casilla 179D, Santiago, Chile; founded by ECLA in 1962; undertakes research and provides training and advisory services; encourages co-operation among the planning services of the region. Dir ALFREDO COSTA-FILHO.

Centro Latinoamericano de Demografía—CELADE (Latin American Demographic Centre): Alonso de Córdova 3107, Casilla 91, Santiago, Chile; f. 1957, became an integral part of the Commission in 1975; assists governments in forming population policies; provides demographic estimates and projections, documentation, data processing and training.

INTERNATIONAL ORGANIZATIONS

BUDGET

ECLAC's share of the UN budget for the two years 1986–87 was US $45.3m. In addition, voluntary extrabudgetary contributions are received.

PUBLICATIONS

Revista de la CEPALC (Spanish and English, 3 a year).
Economic Survey of Latin America (Spanish and English, annually).
Boletín de planificación (2–3 a year).
Temas de planificación (3 a year).
PLANINDEX (2 a year).
Boletín demográfico (2 a year).
DOCPAL Resúmenes (population studies, 2 a year).
Notas de Población (3 a year).
Boletín del Banco de Datos (annually).
Statistical Yearbook for Latin America (Spanish and English, annually).
CEPALCINDEX (2 a year).
Studies, reports, bibliographical bulletins.

Economic Commission for Africa—ECA

Address: Africa Hall, POB 3001, Addis Ababa, Ethiopia.
Telephone: 447200.
Telex: 976 21029.

The UN Economic Commission for Africa was founded in 1958 by a resolution of ECOSOC to initiate and take part in measures for facilitating Africa's economic development.

MEMBERS

Algeria	Madagascar
Angola	Malawi
Benin	Mali
Botswana	Mauritania
Burkina Faso	Mauritius
Burundi	Morocco
Cameroon	Mozambique
Cape Verde	Niger
Central African Republic	Nigeria
Chad	Rwanda
Comoros	São Tomé and Príncipe
Congo	Senegal
Djibouti	Seychelles
Egypt	Sierra Leone
Equatorial Guinea	Somalia
Ethiopia	South Africa*
Gabon	Sudan
The Gambia	Swaziland
Ghana	Tanzania
Guinea	Togo
Guinea-Bissau	Tunisia
Ivory Coast	Uganda
Kenya	Zaire
Lesotho	Zambia
Liberia	Zimbabwe
Libya	

* Suspended since 1963.

Organization
(October 1986)

COMMISSION

The Commission may only act with the agreement of the government of the country concerned. It is also empowered to make recommendations on any matter within its competence directly to the government of the member or associate member concerned, to governments admitted in a consultative capacity, and to the UN Specialized Agencies. The Commission is required to submit for prior consideration by ECOSOC any of its proposals for actions that would be likely to have important effects on the international economy.

CONFERENCE OF MINISTERS

The Conference is attended by Ministers responsible for economic or financial affairs, planning and development of governments of Member States, and is the main deliberative body of the Commission. It meets annually. A Technical Preparatory Committee of the Whole, representing all Member States, was established in 1979 to deal with matters submitted for the consideration of the Conference.

The Commission's responsibility to promote concerted action for the economic and social development of Africa is vested primarily in the Conference, which considers matters of general policy and the priorities to be assigned to the Commission's programmes, considers inter-African and international economic policy and makes recommendations to Member States in connection with such matters. It reviews the course of programmes being implemented in the preceding year and examines and approves the programmes proposed for the next.

OTHER POLICY-MAKING BODIES

Conference of African Ministers of Industry.
Conference of African Ministers of Social Affairs.
Conference of African Ministers of Trade.
Conference of African Ministers of Transport, Communications and Planning.
Conference of Ministers Responsible for Human Resources Planning Development and Utilization.
ECA/FAO Regional Conference of Ministers of Agriculture.
Councils of Ministers of the MULPOCs (see below).

SECRETARIAT

The Secretariat provides the services necessary for the meeting of the Conference of Ministers and the meetings of the Commission's subsidiary bodies, carries out the resolutions and implements the programmes adopted there.

The Headquarters of the Secretariat is in Addis Ababa, Ethiopia. It comprises a Cabinet Office and 11 Divisions.

Cabinet Office of the Executive Secretary:
    Administration and Conference Services Division
    Policy and Programme Co-ordination Office
    Economic Co-operation Office
    Office of the Secretary of the Commission
    Technical Assistance Co-ordination and Operations Office
    Information Service
    Pan-African Documentation and Information Service (PADIS)
    African Training and Research Centre for Women
    Security and Safety Unit

Divisions:
    Socio-Economic Research and Planning
    International Trade and Finance
    Joint ECA/FAO Agriculture
    Joint ECA/UNIDO Industry
    Social Development, Environment and Human Settlements
    Natural Resources
    Transport, Communications and Tourism
    Public Administration, Management and Manpower
    Statistics
    Population
    Administration and Conference Services

Executive Secretary: ADEBAYO ADEDEJI (Nigeria).

Subsidiary Bodies
Joint Conference of African Planners, Statisticians and Demographers.
Intergovernmental Committee of Experts for Science and Technology Development.

INTERNATIONAL ORGANIZATIONS

Intergovernmental Regional Committee on Human Settlements and Environment.
Follow-up Committee on Industrialization in Africa.
Intergovernmental Committee of Experts of African Least-Developed Countries.
Conference of Ministers of African Least-Developed Countries.

Regional Operational Centres
Multinational Programming and Operational Centres (MULPOCs) act as 'field agents' for the implementation of regional development programmes. The Centres are located in Yaoundé, Cameroon (serving central Africa), Gisenyi, Rwanda (Great Lakes Community), Lusaka, Zambia (east and southern Africa), Niamey, Niger (west Africa) and Tangier, Morocco (north Africa). Each centre holds regular ministerial meetings.

Activities

The Commission's 1984–89 work programme is largely derived from the 'Development Strategy for Africa for the United Nations' Third Development Decade', which was drawn up by the ECA Conference of Ministers and approved by the OAU summit conference in 1979. The plan for the implementation of this strategy, known as the Lagos Plan of Action, was adopted by the OAU in 1980: its aim is the economic integration of the continent (an 'African Common Market') by the end of the century.

SOCIO-ECONOMIC RESEARCH AND PLANNING
Monitoring economic and social trends in the African region and studying the development problems concerning it are among the fundamental tasks of the Commission. The annual Survey of Economic and Social Conditions in Africa analyses past trends and prospects. Studies of specific issues are also carried out at the request of member States of the Commission.

The Commission gives assistance to governments in general economic analysis, in fiscal, financial and monetary issues and in planning. Studies on planning are carried out in the Secretariat in order to provide African planning departments with better tools. A current project is to develop short-term forecasting techniques suitable to the needs and means of African countries, particularly for least-developed, land-locked and island countries which have a much lower income level than other countries and which are faced with heavier constraints than others.

The Conference of African Planners, Statisticians and Demographers, which is held every two years, provides an important opportunity for African governments to exchange views and experiences, to obtain information on new techniques and to discuss the most appropriate approaches to development problems.

POLICY AND PROGRAMME CO-ORDINATION
The Policy and Programme Co-ordination Office assists the Executive Secretary in directing the Commission's work programme. It submits proposals on African development to the policy-making bodies of the UN and OAU, and co-ordinates the ECA side of the ECA/OAU Intersecretariat Committee and other inter-agency committees. It services the annual conference of ministers, and attempts to ensure that policy decisions are reflected in the planning of ECA activities. It prepares reports for the evaluation of programme performance.

STATISTICS
The Statistics Division of ECA, which comprises four sections (General Economic Statistics, Demographic and Social Statistics, Censuses and Surveys Advisory Service and International Trade and Related Statistics) promotes the development and co-ordination of national statistical services in the region and the improvement and comparability of statistical data. It prepares documents to assist in the improvement of statistical methodology and undertakes the collection, evaluation and dissemination of statistical information. Since 1978 ECA's efforts in the field of statistics have been concentrated in five main areas:

(a) The African Household Survey Capability Programme (AHSCP), which aims at helping African countries in the collection and analysis of integrated demographic, social and economic data on households and household members on a continuing basis.
(b) The Statistical Training Programme for Africa (STPA), which aims to make the region self-sufficient in statistical personnel at all levels.

United Nations (Regional Economic Commissions)

(c) The Statistical Data Base, part of the Pan-African Documentation and Information Service (PADIS), which provides on-line statistical information to users.
(d) The Regional Advisory Service in Demographic Statistics (RASDS), which provides technical advisory services for population censuses, demographic surveys and civil registration.
(e) The National Accounts Capability Programme (NACP), which aims at improving economic statistics generally by building up a capability in each country for the collection, processing and analysis of economic data.

POPULATION
ECA assists its member states in (a) population data collection and data processing, which is done by the Statistics Division of the Commission; (b) analysis of demographic data obtained from censuses or surveys: this assistance is given by the Population Division; (c) training demographers at the Regional Institute for Population Studies (RIPS) in Accra (Ghana) and at the Institut de formation et de recherche démographique (IFORD) in Yaoundé (Cameroon); (d) formulation of population policies and integrating population variables in development planning, through advisory missions and through the organization of national seminars on population and development; (e) dissemination of information through its *Newsletter, Demographic Handbook for Africa*, the *African Population Studies* series and other publications. The Commission conducts studies on population dynamics and their relationship to development.

The Lagos Plan of Action called for greater integration of population variables in development planning, bearing in mind the expected doubling of the African population between 1975 and 2000 and the impact of this on economic planning and development. It appealed to member states to attach importance to (a) the analysis of demographic data from censuses and demographic surveys and (b) training of nationals of ECA member states in demographic data collection and analysis.

The second African Population Conference was held in Arusha, Tanzania, in January 1984; it adopted 93 recommendations for the future management of the regional population. The Fourth Joint Conference of African Planners, Statisticians and Demographers was held in March 1986. The Population Information Network for Africa (POPIN-Africa) began operation in January 1984.

TRANSPORT AND COMMUNICATIONS
For the United Nations Transport and Communications Decade in Africa (UNTACDA), a comprehensive programme was adopted by ECA for the period 1978–88, to encourage the formation of efficient and reliable transport and communications links among all African countries.

The programme includes the construction of the following trans-African roads: Lagos–Mombasa (6,300 km, of which about 44% had been completed by February 1983); Dakar–N'Djamena (4,600 km, 60% complete in February 1983); Nouakchott–Lagos (4,600 km, 70% complete in February 1983); Cairo–Gaborone (9,027 km, 53% complete in February 1983); and Algiers–Lagos, the Trans-Saharan Highway (5,929 km, expected to be completed in 1986). Four other highways were at the planning stage in 1984 and, together with the major feeder road system, would enable linkage of all mainland African countries by road. Emphasis is being given to the removal of all physical and non-physical barriers as well as uniform regulations, signs, signals and a highway code.

The UNTACDA programme aims to enable inter-connection of some African railway networks, extension of some into the land-locked countries, modernization of track and rolling stock and the introduction of uniform operating and training procedures. Efforts will also be made to establish spare parts and component manufacturing capability in Africa.

The programme aims to strengthen international and coastal shipping in Africa through the pooling of resources on a subregional basis, the rationalization of sailing schedules, port modernization, and the establishment of joint training and repair facilities in the continent.

In the air transport subsector, the programme aims to introduce a four-zone air-route grid system covering the entire region, development of a regional air navigational plan, joint acquisition of aircraft and equipment, establishment of joint maintenance and repair facilities, establishment of regional and sub-regional training institutions and the harmonization of tariffs and charges within the region.

ECA and the International Telecommunication Union (ITU) collaborate with the OAU in assisting member states towards completion of the Pan-African Telecommunication network (PAN-

AFTEL). Projects on low-cost broadcasting systems have also been undertaken, in collaboration with UNESCO.

The Pan-African Documentation and Information Service (PADIS) was established in 1980. The main objectives of PADIS are: to provide access to numerical and other information on African social, economic, scientific and technological development issues; to assist African countries in their efforts to develop national information handling capabilities; to establish teledata-transmission linkages within and beyond Africa; and to design sound technical specifications, norms and standards to minimize technical barriers in the exchange of information.

SOCIAL DEVELOPMENT, ENVIRONMENT AND HUMAN SETTLEMENTS

The Social Development, Environment and Human Settlements Division undertakes studies, produces technical publications and organizes meetings. It provides advisory services to member states on formulating policies relating to overall social development, integrated rural development, youth and social welfare, and housing. It co-ordinates environmental activities in Africa with UNEP and other agencies.

In January 1980 the African Centre for Applied Research and Training in Social Development (ACARTSOD) was inaugurated in Tripoli, Libya, to provide training of high-level personnel required for research and development programmes, and to organize seminars and conduct research.

AGRICULTURE

Major emphasis continues to be laid on the problem of attaining self-sufficiency in food. The Regional Food Plan for Africa, prepared by ECA in collaboration with FAO, was adopted by the African ministers of agriculture in 1978. ECA has undertaken the implementation of the Regional Food Plan along with the various inter-governmental organizations working in Africa. During 1984–86 its work fell into three main categories: (i) agricultural planning, including the conservation of forest and land resources; (ii) promotion of integrated rural development, particularly institution-building, agricultural research and livestock improvement; (iii) marketing of produce, with emphasis on prevention of food losses and providing incentives for increasing food production.

INDUSTRY

The UN Industrial Development Decade for Africa covers the years 1980–90. The fifth conference of African ministers of industry (1979), sponsored jointly by the ECA, OAU and UNIDO, gave priority to five basic industries: food and agro-industry; building materials and construction; engineering; basic metals; chemicals. It initiated plans for the setting-up of African multinational corporations in these areas.

ECA is assisting member states to form inter-governmental technical committees for developing key multinational industrial projects.

The African Industrial Development Fund was established in 1979 to provide resources for pre-investment activities for developing industrial projects, especially multinational ones. A Regional Centre for Engineering Design and Manufacturing (Ibadan, Nigeria) was set up in 1983, while a Regional Centre for Consulting Engineering and Management was also planned.

SCIENCE AND TECHNOLOGY

ECA activities in this field concentrate on the development of training facilities and on promoting regional co-operation. In 1986 preparatory work was carried out on the establishment of a demonstration centre for technology suited to rural areas. The African Regional Centre for Technology (Dakar, Senegal) became operational in 1980, aiming to assist African countries in the development of indigenous technologies, the improvement of negotiating capabilities for imported technologies and related areas.

NATURAL RESOURCES

In 1986 three ground stations (in Burkina Faso, Kenya and Zaire) were being built to receive signals from US and European remote-sensing satellites and process the data received on mineral, land and water resources.

The Eastern and Southern African Mineral Resources Development Centre at Dodoma, Tanzania, provides information on the development of mineral resources, practical courses in geology and mining, advisory services, pre-feasibility studies and specialized laboratory services; in 1986 it had six member states. A similar Central African multinational centre was established in 1983 at Brazzaville, Congo, and had eight member states by 1986. The second Regional Conference on the Development and Utilization of Mineral Resources, held in 1985, adopted a programme of action including surveys of raw materials for fertilizers, small-scale mining, intra-African trade in minerals, and drawing up national and regional policies for exploitation of minerals.

Two Regional Centres, for Services in Surveying, Mapping and Remote Sensing (Nairobi, Kenya) and for Training in Aerial Surveys (Ile-Ife, Nigeria), provide specialized services for an inventory of natural resources. Standardized specifications for basic topographical mapping in Africa were drawn up in 1985.

Member states are assisted in the assessment and use of water resources, and the development of river-basins common to more than one country. A programme of activities for marine development was begun in 1983, with particular reference to the effects of the Law of the Sea.

ENERGY

Assistance is being given in the development of energy resources, in planning and efficient utilization. A study of African coal resources began in 1984. Investigations are being made on development and use of non-conventional sources of energy including solar, geothermal and biogas energy. Maps of the primary energy resources of Africa were updated and published in 1984, and work on an atlas of energy resources continued. A study on the prospects of nuclear energy in Africa was completed in 1985. A Regional Centre for Solar Energy Research and Development was to be opened in 1986 in Bujumbura, Burundi.

INTERNATIONAL TRADE AND FINANCE

In its efforts to meet its mandate and the goals set out in the Lagos Plan of Action, ECA assists African countries in expanding trade among themselves and with other regions of the world and in promoting financial and monetary co-operation. ECA attempts to ensure that African countries should participate effectively in current international negotiations. To this end, assistance has been provided to member states in negotiations under UNCTAD and GATT; in the annual conferences of the IMF and IBRD; in negotiations with the European Community; and in meetings related to economic co-operation among developing countries. Studies have been prepared on problems and prospects likely to arise for the African region from the implementation of the Common Fund Agreement; the Generalized System of Trade Preferences; the impacts of exchange rate fluctuations on the economies of African countries; and on long-term implications of different debt arrangements for African economies. Other studies have also been undertaken on prospects for expansion of African trade with Arab, Latin American and European socialist countries.

ECA was instrumental in the establishment of the Preferential Trade Area for Eastern and Southern Africa (1983) and of the Economic Community of Central African States (1985). In West Africa, assistance has been provided to harmonize the trade liberalization programmes of the Economic Community of West African States (ECOWAS), the Communauté économique de l'Afrique de l'ouest (CEAO) and the Mano River Union.

An area of importance in intra-African trade has been the work towards the establishment in 1984 of an African Regional Federation of Chambers of Commerce, based in Egypt. In 1982 experts from central banks and ministries of finance adopted draft guidelines for the establishment of an African Monetary Fund, together with draft terms of reference for a feasibility study on the establishment of the Fund. A second meeting, held in 1985, agreed that the Fund's initial authorized capital should be US $2,000m., of which $750m. should be paid during the first five years, with participation of up to $250m. by non-African members.

As part of its programme on trade expansion, the activities of ECA in the field of transnational corporations (TNCs) have included the preparation of several studies on the impact of transnational corporations in the agro-processing industries of selected countries; banking and financial institutions; balance of payments; transfer of technology; and inter-regional studies on the role of TNCs in selected export-oriented primary commodities.

PUBLIC ADMINISTRATION, MANAGEMENT AND MANPOWER

The Public Administration, Management and Manpower Division aims to assist governments and public corporations in, for example, budgeting and financial management; planning of human resources; and administration of fellowships and scholarships. It conducts studies and analyses and provides advisory services and training programmes in public administration.

The Division services the Conference of Ministers Responsible for Human Resources, Planning, Development and Utilization and

INTERNATIONAL ORGANIZATIONS

meetings of various African professional bodies, and supports the African Institute for Higher Technical Training and Research (AIHTTR), the Eastern and Southern African Management Institute in Arusha, Tanzania, and four sub-regional Graduate Schools of Management.

BUDGET

ECA's share of the UN budget for the two years 1986–87 was US $48.2m.

PUBLICATIONS

Report of the Executive Secretary (every 2 years).
African Statistical Yearbook.
Foreign Trade Statistics for Africa series.
   Series A: *Direction of Trade* (quarterly).
   Series B: *Trade by Commodity* (2 a year).
   Series C: *Summary Table* (annually).

Statistical Information Bulletin for Africa (annually).
Statistical Newsletter (2 a year).
Directory of African Statisticians (every 2 years).
African Socio-Economic Indicators (every 2 years).
Investment Africa (quarterly).
Survey of Economic Conditions in Africa (annually).
African Census Programme Newsletter (irregular).
African Directory of Demographers (irregular).
African Population Newsletter (quarterly).
African Population Studies Series (irregular).
Demographic Handbook for Africa (irregular).
African Trade (quarterly).
Bulletin of ECA-sponsored Institutions (annually).
Rural Progress (quarterly).

Economic and Social Commission for Western Asia—ESCWA

Address: Amiriyah, POB 27, Baghdad, Iraq.
Telephone: 5569400-405.
Telex: 213468.

The UN Economic Commission for Western Asia was established in 1974 by a resolution of ECOSOC (see p. 19) to provide facilities of a wider scope for those countries previously served by the UN Economic and Social Office in Beirut (UNESOB). The name 'Economic and Social Commission for Western Asia' (ESCWA) was adopted in 1985.

MEMBERS

Bahrain
Egypt
Iraq
Jordan
Kuwait
Lebanon
Oman
Palestine Liberation Organization (PLO)
Qatar
Saudi Arabia
Syria
United Arab Emirates
Yemen Arab Republic
Yemen, People's Democratic Republic

Organization

(October 1986)

COMMISSION

The annual sessions of the Commission are attended by representatives of member states, of UN bodies and specialized agencies, of regional and intergovernmental organizations, and of other states attending in a consultative capacity.

SECRETARIAT

In 1982 the Commission established its permanent headquarters in Baghdad, Iraq.

Divisions:
 Development Planning
 Joint ESCWA/FAO Agriculture
 Joint ESCWA/UNIDO Industry
 Administration
 Natural Resources, Science and Technology
 Human Settlements
 Transport, Communications and Tourism
 Social Development and Population
 Statistics
 Technical Co-operation
 Programme Planning and Co-ordination
 Environmental Co-ordination
 Information

Executive Secretary: MOHAMMED SAID NABULSI (Jordan).

Activities

ESCWA undertakes or sponsors studies of economic and technological problems of the region, collects and disseminates information, and provides advisory services.

ESCWA's development plans for the 1980s comprise the following points: making the best use of natural resources; strengthening the regional economy so as to reduce dependence on external sources, such as food imports, and to cut trade imbalances; planned use of petroleum energy; development of human resources; regulation of the movement of workers between countries; integration of women in development.

Much of ESCWA's work is carried out in co-operation with other UN bodies. It conducts industrial studies for individual countries in conjunction with UNIDO. It co-operates with FAO in regional planning, food security and management of agricultural resources; in 1983–84, for example, a joint mission was undertaken with FAO and UNDP to Egypt, Iraq, Kuwait and Saudi Arabia, to assess training needs in agricultural planning and project analysis. UNDP supports ESCWA's work on household surveys in western Asia and the Arab Planning Institute in Kuwait, and during 1984–85 negotiations continued with UNDP on the financing of an Arab Institute for Banking and Financial Studies. During 1984–85 work was also undertaken with UNFPA in population programmes, with ILO in statistical surveys on labour, with UNCTAD in development planning and maritime transport training, and with UNEP in integrating environmental considerations (particularly control of desertification) into development programmes.

The programme of work and priorities comprises studies of various technical and socio-economic problems, particularly those demanding inter-country and sub-regional co-operation. The main areas are:

 food and agriculture;
 development planning (particularly in the least-developed countries in the region);
 human settlement (particularly housing finance and city management);
 industrial development (appraisal of potential, co-ordination of policies);
 international trade (identification of intra-regional trade and integration opportunities);
 labour, management and employment (making the best use of available manpower, development of required skills);
 natural resources (energy planning, minerals and water development);
 science and technology (problems of dependence on imported technology; training of manpower);
 social development (welfare, participation in development, training and planning);
 statistics (improvement of procedures, adopting uniform standards);
 transport, communications and tourism (multinational shipping enterprises, railway networks, road construction and maintenance, and tourism development);
 transnational corporations.

BUDGET

ESCWA's share of the UN budget for the two years 1986–87 was US $33.7m.

PUBLICATIONS

Agriculture and Development (annually).
Population Bulletin (2 a year).
Studies on Development Problems in Selected Countries of the Middle East (annually).
Statistical Abstract (annually).
Survey of Economic and Social Developments in the ESCWA Region (annually).

OTHER UNITED NATIONS BODIES

International Atomic Energy Agency—IAEA

Address: POB 100, Wagramerstrasse 5, 1400 Vienna, Austria.
Telephone: (0222) 2360.
Telex: 1-12645.

The International Atomic Energy Agency (IAEA) is an intergovernmental organization, established in 1957 in accordance with a decision of the General Assembly of the United Nations. Although it is autonomous, the IAEA is administratively a member of the United Nations, and reports on its activities once a year to the UN General Assembly. Its main objectives are to enlarge the contribution of atomic energy to peace, health and prosperity throughout the world and to ensure, so far as it is able, that assistance provided by it or at its request or under its supervision or control is not used in such a way as to further any military purpose.

Organization
(October 1986)

GENERAL CONFERENCE
The Conference, comprising representatives of all 113 member states, convenes each year to participate in the general debate on the Agency's policy, budget and programme. It elects members to the Board of Governors, and approves the appointment of the Director-General; it admits new member states.

BOARD OF GOVERNORS
The Board of Governors consists of 35 member states: 22 elected by the General Conference for two-year periods and 13 designated by the rest of the Board. It is the executive body of the Agency and is responsible to the General Conference. Under its own authority, the Board approves all safeguards agreements, important projects and safety standards.

SECRETARIAT
The Secretariat, comprising about 2,000 staff, is headed by the Director-General who is assisted by five Deputy Directors-General. The Secretariat is divided into five departments: Technical Co-operation; Nuclear Energy and Safety; Research and Isotopes; Safeguards; Administration. The Director-General is also advised on scientific and technical matters by a Scientific Advisory Committee, comprising 15 distinguished scientists having a wide variety of expertise. A Standing Advisory Group on Safeguards Implementation advises the Director-General on technical aspects of safeguards.

Director-General: HANS BLIX (Sweden).

Activities

The IAEA's functions can be divided into two main categories: technical co-operation (assisting research on and practical application of atomic energy for peaceful uses); and safeguards (ensuring that special fissionable and other materials, services, equipment and information made available by the Agency or at its request or under its supervision are not used for any military purpose).

TECHNICAL ASSISTANCE AND TRAINING
In 1984 technical assistance provided by the IAEA exceeded $32m. in value. More than 80 countries received technical assistance in the form of expert services, equipment and training. A total of 825 fellows were carrying out individual field studies, and 850 persons participated in 51 group training projects: 1,675 scientists and technicians received training during 1984.

FOOD AND AGRICULTURE
In co-operation with FAO (see p. 56), the Agency conducts 30 programmes of applied research on the use of radiation and isotopes in six main fields: efficiency in the use of water and fertilizers; improvement of food crops by induced mutations; eradication or control of destructive insects by the introduction of sterilized insects; improvement of livestock nutrition and health; studies on improving efficacy and reducing residues of pesticides, and increasing utilization of agricultural wastes; and food preservation by irradiation.

LIFE SCIENCES
In co-operation with the World Health Organization (WHO, see p. 84), IAEA promotes the use of nuclear techniques in medicine, biology and health-related environmental research, provides training, and conducts research on techniques for improving the accuracy of radiation dosimetry.

The IAEA/WHO Network of Secondary Standard Dosimetry Laboratories (SSDLs) comprised 48 member laboratories in 1984. The Agency's Dosimetry Laboratory performs dose inter-comparisons for both SSDLs and radiotherapy centres. During 1984 22 co-ordinated research programmes were active at some time, including: maintenance plans for nuclear laboratories in South-East Asia and Latin America; national programmes of quality control for nuclear medicine instruments in Asia and Latin America; quality control of radioimmunoassay techniques; radiation sterilization of medical supplies; and improvement of cancer therapy.

PHYSICAL SCIENCES AND LABORATORIES
The Agency's programme in physical sciences includes industrial applications of isotopes and radiation technology; application of nuclear techniques to mineral exploration and exploitation; and hydrology, involving the use of isotope techniques for assessment of water resources. Nuclear data services are provided, and training is given for nuclear scientists from developing countries. The IAEA Laboratory at Seibersdorf, Austria, supports the Agency's research, radio-isotope and safeguards programmes, while the Safeguards Analytical Laboratory, in Vienna, analyses nuclear fuel-cycle samples collected by IAEA safeguards inspectors. The International Laboratory of Marine Radioactivity, in Monaco, studies radionuclides and other ocean pollutants. The IAEA co-ordinates international research on controlled fusion through the International Tokamak Reactor (INTOR).

NUCLEAR POWER
The Agency helps developing member states to introduce nuclear-powered electricity-generating plants through assistance with planning, feasibility studies, surveys of manpower and infrastructure, and safety measures. It publishes books on numerous aspects of nuclear power, and provides training courses on safety in nuclear power plants and other topics. An energy data bank collects and disseminates information on nuclear technology, and a power-reactor information system monitors the technical performance of nuclear power plants.

NUCLEAR SAFETY
The IAEA's nuclear safety programme encourages international co-operation in the exchange of information, promoting implementation of its safety standards and providing advisory safety services. It includes the IAEA Incident Reporting System; an emergency preparedness programme; operational safety review teams; and a safety research co-ordination programme.

The revised edition of the Basic Safety Standards for Radiation Protection (IAEA Safety Series No 9) was published in 1982. Regulations for the safe transport of radioactive materials have also been issued.

In 1983, to provide Member States with advice on achieving and maintaining a high level of safety in the operation of nuclear power plants, the Agency established operational safety review teams, which will visit a power plant on request. Co-ordinated research programmes establish risk criteria for the nuclear fuel cycle and identify cost-effective means to reduce risks in energy systems. The International Nuclear Safety Advisory Group (INSAG) met for the first time in March 1985: it comprises 13 experts from nuclear safety licensing authorities, nuclear industry and research, and aims to provide a forum for exchange of information and to identify important current safety issues.

INTERNATIONAL ORGANIZATIONS

United Nations (Other Bodies)

Following the serious accident at the Chernobyl nuclear power plant in the Ukraine, in April 1986, the IAEA convened a series of meetings to consider the implications of the disaster and ways of improving the response to such emergencies. Two conventions were drawn up, and entered into force in October: the first commits parties to provide early notification and information about nuclear accidents with possible trans-boundary effects; and the second commits parties to endeavour to provide assistance in the event of a nuclear accident.

DISSEMINATION OF INFORMATION

The International Nuclear Information System (INIS) provides a computerized indexing and abstracting service. Information on the peaceful uses of atomic energy is collected by member states and international organizations and sent to the IAEA for processing and dissemination (see list of publications below). IAEA also co-operates with the FAO in an information system for agriculture (AGRIS). The IAEA Nuclear Data Section provides cost-free data centre services and co-operates with other national and regional nuclear and atomic data centres in the systematic worldwide collection, compilation, dissemination and exchange of nuclear reaction data, nuclear structure and decay data, and atomic and molecular data for fusion.

SAFEGUARDS

The Treaty on the Non-Proliferation of Nuclear Weapons (NPT), which entered into force in 1970, requires each non-nuclear-weapon state (one which had not manufactured and exploded a nuclear weapon or other nuclear explosive device prior to 1 January 1967) Party to the Treaty to conclude a safeguards agreement with the IAEA. Under such an agreement the State undertakes to accept IAEA safeguards on all nuclear material in all its peaceful nuclear activities for the purpose of verifying that such material is not diverted to nuclear weapons or other nuclear explosive devices. By the end of 1984 121 states had ratified and acceded to the Treaty, but 39 had not yet concluded the relevant safeguards agreements with the Agency.

Two nuclear-weapon states, the United Kingdom and the USA, both Party to the NPT, concluded safeguards agreements with the Agency (in 1978 and 1980 respectively) that permit the application of IAEA safeguards to all their nuclear activities, excluding those with 'direct national significance'. A third nuclear-weapon state, France, concluded a similar agreement in 1981 under which it accepts IAEA safeguards on nuclear material in facilities to be designated by France. In February 1985 an agreement was signed by the IAEA and the USSR on the application of IAEA safeguards to certain peaceful nuclear installations in the USSR.

The Treaty for the prohibition of Nuclear Weapons in Latin America (Tlatelolco Treaty) entered into force in 1968, aiming to create a zone free of nuclear weapons in Latin America. The IAEA administers full applications of safeguards in relation to the Treaty. In addition, the IAEA applies safeguards in 10 states under agreements other than those in connection with the NPT and the Tlatelolco Treaty.

In 1985 1,980 inspections were carried out under safeguards agreements at 514 nuclear installations in 51 non-nuclear-weapon states and four nuclear-weapon states.

INTERNATIONAL CENTRE FOR THEORETICAL PHYSICS

The Centre, in Trieste, Italy, brings together scientists from the developed and the developing countries. With support from the Italian government, the Centre has been operated jointly by the IAEA and UNESCO since 1970. Each year it offers seminars followed by a research workshop, as well as short topical seminars, training courses, symposia and panels. Independent research is also carried out. The programme concentrates on solid-state physics, high-energy and elementary particle physics, physics of nuclear structure and reactions, applicable mathematics and, to a lesser extent, on physics of the earth and the environment, physics of energy, biophysics, microprocessors and physics of technology.

NUCLEAR FUEL CYCLE

The Agency promotes the exchange of information between Member States on technical, safety, environmental, and economic aspects of nuclear fuel cycle technology, including uranium prospecting and the treatment and disposal of radioactive waste; it provides assistance to Member States in the planning, implementation and operation of nuclear fuel cycle facilities and assists in the development of advanced nuclear fuel cycle technology. Every two years, in collaboration with the OECD, the Agency prepares estimates of world uranium resources, demand and production.

BUDGET

The Agency is financed by regular and voluntary contributions from member states.

The regular budget for 1986 was about US $100m., and the target for voluntary contributions to finance the IAEA technical assistance programme was $30m.

PUBLICATIONS

Annual Report.

Nuclear Safety Review (annually).

IAEA Bulletin.

Nuclear Fusion: Journal of Plasma Physics and Thermonuclear Fusion.

Technical Directories.

Panel Proceedings Series.

Safety Series.

Legal Series.

Technical Reports Series.

INIS Atomindex.

INIS Reference Series.

Publications Catalogue (annually).

International Sea-Bed Authority

The Authority is to be established one year after the United Nations Convention on the Law of the Sea, adopted in 1982, has been ratified by 60 countries. The seat of the Authority is to be in Kingston, Jamaica.

Organization
(October 1986)

ASSEMBLY
The Assembly is to be the supreme organ of the Authority, consisting of representatives of all parties to the Convention, and will establish policies, approve the budget and elect council members.

COUNCIL
The Council will be elected by the Assembly, and is to consist of 36 members, of whom 18 are to be elected from four 'major interest groups'—the four states who are the largest investors in sea-bed minerals, the four major importers of sea-bed minerals, the four major land-based exporters of the same minerals, and six developing countries representing special interests—while 18 are to be elected on a general basis, but ensuring that all regions of the world are represented. The Council is to decide on the most important questions by consensus rather than by voting.

OTHER ORGANS
The Council is to be assisted by an Economic Planning Commission, which will review supply, demand and pricing of sea-bed minerals and monitor the effects of sea-bed production on land-based mining concerns; and by a Legal and Technical Commission which will supervise sea-bed activities. Each Commission is to have 15 members, elected by the Council with regard for equitable geographical distribution and the representation of special interests. The Sea-Bed Disputes Chamber of the International Tribunal for the Law of the Sea will adjudicate on disputes with respect to activities.

PREPARATORY COMMISSION
Address: Office of the Special Representative of the United Nations Secretary-General for the Law of the Sea, United Nations Plaza, New York, NY 10017, USA.

The Preparatory Commission, which first met in 1983 and held its fourth session in March/April 1986, was formed to set up the different organs of the Authority pending the entering into force of the Convention. It is also to act as an executive body when registering the applications of pioneer investors.

The Law of the Sea Convention

The third UN Conference on the Law of the Sea (UNCLOS) began its work in 1973, with the aim of regulating maritime activities by defining zones and boundaries, ensuring fair exploitation of resources, and providing machinery for settlement of disputes. Negotiations, involving over 160 countries, continued until 1982, having been delayed in 1981 when the newly elected US Government decided to review its policy. The UN Convention of the Law of the Sea was finally adopted by UNCLOS in April 1982; 130 states voted in its favour, while the USA, Israel, Turkey and Venezuela voted against, and there were 17 abstentions including the Federal Republic of Germany, the USSR and the United Kingdom. The Convention was opened for signing in December for a two-year period: by December 1984 159 states had signed, but the USA, the United Kingdom, and the Federal Republic of Germany refused to sign, and by July 1986 only 29 states had ratified the Convention, which requires 60 ratifications before it can come into force. The main provisions of the Convention are as follows:

Coastal states are allowed sovereignty over their territorial waters of up to 12 miles in breadth; foreign vessels are to be allowed 'innocent passage' through these waters.

Ships and aircraft of all states are allowed 'transit passage' through straits used for international navigation.

Archipelagic states (composed of islands) have sovereignty over a sea area enclosed by straight lines drawn between the outermost points of the islands.

Coastal states have sovereign rights in a 200-mile exclusive economic zone with respect to natural resources and certain economic activities, and rights over the adjacent continental shelf up to 350 miles from the shore under specified circumstances.

All states have freedom of navigation, overflight, scientific research and fishing on the high seas, but must co-operate in measures to conserve living resources.

A 'parallel system' is to be established for exploiting the international sea-bed, where all activities are to be supervised by the International Sea-Bed Authority. The Authority will conduct its own mining operations and also contract with private and state ventures to give them mining rights.

States are bound to control pollution and co-operate in forming preventive rules, and incur penalties for failing to combat pollution.

Marine scientific research in the zones under national jurisdiction is subject to the prior consent of the coastal state, but consent may be denied only under specific circumstances.

States must submit disputes on the application and interpretation of the Convention to a compulsory procedure entailing decisions binding on all parties. An International Tribunal for the Law of the Sea is to be established.

The objections of the USA and other industrialized nations which have refused to support the Convention concern the provisions for exploitation of the international ocean bed, and particularly the minerals to be found there (chiefly manganese, cobalt, copper and nickel), envisaged as the 'common heritage of mankind'. It is argued that those countries which possess adequate technology for deep-sea mining would be insufficiently represented in the new Authority; the operations of private mining consortia, according to the objectors, would be unacceptably limited by the stipulations that their technology should be shared with a supranational mining enterprise, and that production should be limited in order to protect land-based producers.

Office of the United Nations Disaster Relief Co-ordinator — UNDRO

Address: Palais des Nations, 1211 Geneva 10, Switzerland.
Telephone: (022) 346011.
Telex: 28148.

UNDRO was established in 1972 to mobilize and co-ordinate international emergency relief to disaster-stricken areas, and to co-operate in promoting disaster preparedness and prevention.

Organization
(October 1986)

DISASTER RELIEF CO-ORDINATOR
In March 1972 a Disaster Relief Co-ordinator was appointed, at Under-Secretary-General level, to report directly to the UN Secretary-General. UNDRO is a separate entity within the UN Secretariat and consists of a Relief Co-ordination and Preparedness Branch and a Prevention and Support Services Branch.
Co-ordinator: M'HAMED ESSAAFI (Tunisia).

FIELD ORGANIZATION
UNDRO is represented in developing countries by the Resident Representatives of UNDP (see p. 40). UNDRO also has a Liaison Office at UN headquarters in New York.
Liaison Office: Room 2935A, United Nations, New York, NY 10017; tel. (212) 754-5704; telex 421852.

Activities

The Co-ordinator's mandate derives from a number of General Assembly resolutions on assistance in case of natural disaster and other disaster situations. The Office has four main functions: relief co-ordination; disaster preparedness; disaster prevention; and the provision of public information, data processing services and communications. UNDRO has also entered into agreements (Memoranda of Understanding) with other UN agencies, defining areas and means of co-operation, in order to strengthen the collective response of the United Nations system to disasters.

RELIEF CO-ORDINATION
The Office aims to ensure that, in case of natural or other disaster, all emergency relief activities are mobilized and co-ordinated so as to supply the needs of the disaster-stricken country in a timely and effective manner. UNDRO provides 24-hour monitoring of natural disasters and emergency situations as they occur. Once a disaster situation calling for international assistance is recognized and a request from the government of the affected country is received, the UNDP Resident Representative, often assisted by an UNDRO relief co-ordination officer, reviews the damage and the immediate relief needs with the competent local authorities, and communicates the findings to UNDRO headquarters. The extent and the compound nature of disasters often calls for an assessment by specialists in various spheres, and multi-agency missions are organized in which representatives of specialized agencies and other organizations take part. Close co-operation is maintained with the other organizations of the UN system and with other intergovernmental and non-governmental organizations. UNDRO places emphasis on obtaining and disseminating all relevant information in good time, so as to avoid waste or misuse of resources, and to determine the timing of the response. UNDRO participated in the work of the Office for Emergency Operations in Africa (OEOA), which, between December 1984 and October 1986, undertook special responsibilities to alleviate the particularly grave situation in many countries of Africa.

During the two years 1984–85, UNDRO's activities were largely dominated by the widespread and continuing emergency situation in Africa, involving some 20 countries and an estimated 30m. people out of a total population of more than 160m. In the discharge of its mandate in 1984–85, the Office was involved in 98 disaster situations. A considerable number were major disasters calling for concerted relief programmes whereby bilateral donors, the United Nations system and other agencies provide assistance to the stricken population. Such disasters included tropical storms in Bangladesh, Madagascar, Mozambique and the Philippines, armed conflict in Lebanon, epidemics in Mali and Somalia, an earthquake in Colombia, and drought in Chad, Ethiopia, Mali, Mauritania, Mozambique, Niger and Sudan.

DISASTER PREPAREDNESS AND PREVENTION
UNDRO promotes the integration of human and material resources and of different skills and disciplines into an effective national system of readiness, in order to minimize the loss of lives and the damage when a disaster strikes.

Disaster preparedness advisory missions are usually undertaken by consultants recruited by UNDRO, who advise governments on the best methods of improving their organization to deal with all kinds of disasters, and not just those which arise from natural causes. The recommendations of these missions sometimes call for specific projects to be carried out, and if these cannot be funded by the government then UNDRO may be asked to seek the necessary financing from donors. Preparedness organizations naturally need trained personnel, and UNDRO arranges or takes part in many seminars for disaster managers and others concerned in relief work, in the preparation and issue of warnings, and in the application of new technologies to disaster work generally. UNDRO is also engaged in attempts to remove obstacles to the rapid delivery of international relief, and this requires willingness by donors as well as by potential recipients to streamline procedures and to waive normal legal requirements for the movement of relief goods and personnel.

In the area of disaster prevention UNDRO is engaged in the development and application of techniques of vulnerability analysis, and in promoting the use of legislation, land-use planning and other inexpensive methods of reducing or eliminating disaster risks. UNDRO is also engaged, jointly with other UN agencies, in attempts to reduce both the hazards created by industrial activities and the effects of industrial accidents.

In 1984–85 technical assistance in disaster prevention and preparedness was given to: Afghanistan, Algeria, Argentina, the Central African Republic, Chad, Egypt, El Salvador, Fiji, Guinea, Honduras, Indonesia, Madagascar, Mali, Nepal, the Philippines, Sudan, Tunisia, Vanuatu, Viet-Nam, Yugoslavia and Zaire. In addition, activities in co-operation with regional inter-governmental organizations are carried out: for instance, in 1984–85, a regional training centre at the Asian Institute of Technology, Bangkok, was developed and established; training activities continued under UNDRO's Pan Caribbean Project; a national training project in Indonesia was initiated and collaboration continued with the Administrative Staff College of India (ASCI) in training and research activities in disaster management. Action was taken to increase and expand the capacity of the UN Supply Depot at Pisa, Italy, in order to provide a greater quantity and wider variety of relief supplies ready for immediate dispatch to affected countries.

During 1984–85 work continued on the regional project of earthquake risk reduction in the Balkan countries, and national studies relating to earthquake risk were conducted in Cyprus and Yugoslavia. Two countries, the Congo and Argentina, received specialized assistance to help to avoid or reduce the risk of catastrophic flooding. Co-operation continued with the IAEA (q.v.) in the preparation of new volumes in the Safety Series of publications, relating to preparedness for accidents at nuclear installations.

PUBLIC INFORMATION, DATA PROCESSING AND COMMUNICATIONS
As well as issuing the publications listed below, UNDRO maintains a reference library and a data processing and communications unit. It has developed a computer-based telecommunications system for processing and disseminating information before and during emergencies. There is a large and comprehensive data base of disaster-related information, also available to other organizations.

FINANCE
The amount allocated to UNDRO in the regular budget of the UN for the two years 1984-85 was US $4.8m., and UNDRO's share for

INTERNATIONAL ORGANIZATIONS

1986–87 amounted to $5.7m. This is supplemented by a voluntary Trust Fund established by the General Assembly in 1974: the Fund's total expenditure for 1984 was $7,073,936.

As a co-ordinating Office, UNDRO is not itself regarded as a principal source of relief assistance, although the Co-ordinator has the authority to make a contribution from the regular budget not exceeding US $50,000 for any one disaster (and not exceeding in total US $600,000 in one year) to meet immediate needs, e.g. for medicines, food or the transport of life-saving equipment. The Co-ordinator is also empowered to receive contributions in kind or in cash to be used for providing relief supplies. However, the greater part of the international assistance provided goes direct to the country concerned, and it is normally expected that the amount and nature of these contributions will be based upon the information given in UNDRO 'situation reports' which are sent by telex to donor sources and other interested organizations throughout the world. During the two years 1984/85 emergency relief accounted for by UNDRO exceeded $2,100m.

PUBLICATIONS

Annual Report to the UN General Assembly.
UNDRO News (6 a year).
Disaster Prevention and Mitigation: a Compendium of Current Knowledge (11 vols).
Guidelines for Disaster Prevention (3 vols).
Shelter after Disaster: Guidelines for Assistance.
Disasters and the Disabled.
Technical papers, case reports, Disaster Assessment Mission reports.

United Nations Centre for Human Settlements—UNCHS (Habitat)

Address: POB 30030, Nairobi, Kenya.
Telephone: 333930/520600.
Telex: 22996.

UNCHS (Habitat) was established in October 1978 to service the intergovernmental Commission on Human Settlements, and to serve as a focus for human settlements activities in the UN system.

Organization
(October 1986)

UN COMMISSION ON HUMAN SETTLEMENTS

The Commission (see ECOSOC, p. 19) is the governing body of UNCHS. It meets annually and has 58 members, serving for four years. Sixteen members are from Africa, 13 from Asia, six from Eastern European Socialist countries, 10 from Latin America and 13 from Western Europe and other countries.

CENTRE FOR HUMAN SETTLEMENTS

The Centre's work covers technical co-operation, research and development (incorporating settlement planning and policies, shelter and community services, construction and infrastructure), training and information (audio-visual and documentation). Other units include the Office of the Executive Director, Administration, and Secretariat for the International Year of Shelter for the Homeless (IYSH). The Habitat and Human Settlements Foundation (HHSF) serves as the financial arm of the Centre.

The Executive Director oversees the work of the Centre, which is to service the Commission on Human Settlements and to implement its resolutions; to ensure the integration and co-ordination of technical co-operation, research and the exchange and dissemination of information; and to execute human settlements projects funded by the United Nations Development Programme (UNDP), funds-in-trust or other contributions.

Executive Director: Dr ARCOT RAMACHANDRAN.

Activities

UNCHS (Habitat) assists governments in activities related to human settlements. It supports and conducts research, provides technical co-operation and disseminates information, under the eight sub-programmes listed below. At the beginning of 1986 activities included 150 technical co-operation projects in 81 countries, with project budgets totalling US $18.8m.; of these, 65 were in Africa, 31 in Latin America and the Caribbean, 33 in Asia and the Pacific, 17 in western Asia and four in Europe.

UNCHS also conducts research and training and organizes meetings of experts. Advisory services are provided to governments on building materials and methods, financing procedures, and the application of advanced technology to human settlements planning. During 1985 advisory services in data management were provided in 20 countries, and one data management 'workshop' was held. UNCHS runs an informal network of human settlements planners who use microcomputers.

UNCHS acts as the secretariat for the International Year of Shelter for the Homeless (1987), which is intended to persuade governments to adopt practical solutions to the shelter needs of disadvantaged people.

Settlement Policies and Strategies
This sub-programme aims to identify high-priority settlements policy issues and to prepare guidelines for formulating and implementing national policies.

Settlements Planning
UNCHS promotes the use of effective methods of settlements planning in both urban and rural areas. In 1986–87 the main emphasis was to be on forecasting settlements trends and prospects, and on the planning and development of rural settlements. During 1986 training courses in community participation were in operation in Bolivia, Sri Lanka and Zambia.

Shelter and Community Services
This sub-programme assists in improving conditions and services for low-income settlements in urban and rural areas, by upgrading squatter settlements, rehabilitating inner-city slums and supporting co-operative housing: community participation is seen as an essential part of this work.

Development of the Indigenous Construction Sector
Work under this sub-programme concentrates on increasing the capacity of the construction sector to meet demand. Reports being prepared during 1986 covered earth construction; planning of the construction industry using indigenous methods; reformulation of building acts, regulations and codes in African countries; and the use of selected indigenous building materials with potential for wide application in developing countries. Manuals were being prepared on lime, stone construction and earth construction.

Low-cost Infrastructure for Human Settlements
UNCHS encourages the development of appropriate infrastructure. In 1985–86 reports were published on traffic in low-income urban settlements and on low-cost vehicles, and the Centre was in the process of preparing guidelines for legislation on water supply and sanitation; a design manual on shallow sewerage; and guidelines for the operation of low-cost water supply and sanitation systems. It published reports on the use of solar energy, and on natural forces in the design of buildings, and studies on energy-efficient housing.

Land
This sub-programme promotes effective government measures for developing land for human settlements, essentially through eval-

INTERNATIONAL ORGANIZATIONS

uating regulations on land use, analysing methods of land acquisition and allocation, and collecting data on land use.

Mobilization of Finance
This sub-programme aims to mobilize financial resources for the development of human settlements. Particular emphasis is placed on monitoring the performance of human settlements finance institutions, the role of non-conventional finance mechanisms and support to community-based institutions.

Human Settlements Institutions and Management
UNCHS helps to establish or strengthen institutions and management capabilities through case studies, guidelines and training.

United Nations (Other Bodies)

FINANCE
The amount allocated to the Centre in the UN budget for 1984–85 was US $8.8m. The Centre received $8.6m. in the UN budget for 1986–87, and extra-budgetary resources were expected to amount to $35m., while contributions to the HHSF were expected to total $5m.

PUBLICATIONS
UNCHS Habitat News (3 a year).
IYSH Bulletin (8 a year).
Technical reports and studies, occasional papers, bibliographies, directories.

United Nations Children's Fund—UNICEF

Address: 866 United Nations Plaza, New York, NY 10017, USA.
Telephone: (212) 415-8000.
Telex: 62346.

UNICEF was established in 1946 by the General Assembly as the UN International Children's Emergency Fund, to meet the emergency needs of children in post-war Europe and China. In 1950 its mandate was changed to emphasize programmes giving long-term benefits to children everywhere, particularly those in developing countries who are in the greatest need.

Organization
(October 1986)

EXECUTIVE BOARD
The governing body of UNICEF meets once a year to establish policy, review programmes and commit funds. Membership comprises 41 governments from all regions, elected in rotation for a three-year term by ECOSOC.

SECRETARIAT
The Executive Director of UNICEF is appointed by the UN Secretary-General in consultation with the Executive Board. The administration of UNICEF and the appointment and direction of staff are the responsibility of the Executive Director, under policy directives laid down by the Executive Board, and under a broad authority delegated to the Executive Director by the Secretary-General. UNICEF has 87 field offices in which over three-quarters of its staff are located.
Executive Director: JAMES P. GRANT (USA).

MAJOR UNICEF OFFICES
Europe: Palais des Nations, 1211 Geneva 10, Switzerland.
Eastern and Southern Africa: POB 44145, Nairobi, Kenya.
Middle East and North Africa: POB 811721, Amman, Jordan.
Central and West Africa: BP 443, Abidjan 04, Ivory Coast.
The Americas: Apdo Aéreo 7555, Bogotá, Colombia.
East Asia and Pakistan: POB 2-154, Bangkok 10200, Thailand.
South Central Asia: 73 Lodi Estate, New Delhi 110003, India.
Australia and New Zealand: GPO Box 4045, Sydney, NSW 2001, Australia.
Japan: c/o UN Information Centre, 22nd Floor, Shin Aoyama Bldg, Nishikan, 1-1, Minami-Aoyama 1-chome, Minato-ku, Tokyo 107.

NATIONAL COMMITTEES
There are 33 National Committees, mostly in industrialized countries, whose volunteer members raise money through various activities, including the sale of greetings cards; the Committees also undertake advocacy efforts within their own societies and act as focal points of local support for governmental fund-raising.

Activities

UNICEF's efforts for the 1980s concentrate on the drastic reduction of infant mortality rates through an attack on the principal causes of preventable death and disease, using community-based health and other first-level services and drawing on a wide variety of national and community organizations for support in mobilizing the necessary human and financial resources. In 1985 UNICEF was working with the governments of 118 developing countries by assisting in the development, administration and evaluation of services benefiting children; delivery of technical supplies, equipment and other aid for extending those services; and providing funds to strengthen training of national personnel. UNICEF facilitates the exchange of programming experience among developing countries, and encourages governments to undertake a regular review of the situation of their children and to incorporate a national policy for children in their comprehensive development plans. UNICEF provides assistance on the basis of mutually agreed priorities for children in collaboration with the governments concerned. Priority is given by UNICEF to aiding children in the lower-income groups in the least-developed countries.

Community participation is the key element of the 'basic services' approach adopted by UNICEF in 1975. This approach emphasizes meeting the basic needs of children through community involvement in the planning and running of services. By mobilizing community energies, drawing on local skills through simple training, and the use of relevant and available technology, a great deal can be done to improve maternal and child care, introduce safe water supplies and sanitation, expand primary and non-formal education, including nutrition education for mothers and children, improve the household production of nutritious foods and improve the situation of women, particularly through training and support for income-generating activities.

Economic stringency in the 1980s sharpened the search for innovative, low-cost solutions to development problems. Alternative approaches to tackling such major problems of child health and nutrition as immunizable diseases, diarrhoeal dehydration and others have made possible a virtual revolution in child survival and development, with a substantial reduction of death and disease. Since 1982 UNICEF has advocated a concerted international effort to make this potential a reality, focusing on: (a) immunizable, child-killing diseases such as measles, diphtheria, tuberculosis, whooping cough, tetanus and poliomyelitis; (b) diarrhoeal disease; (c) early detection of malnutrition through growth monitoring; (d) promotion of breast-feeding and proper weaning; (e) female education; and (f) birth spacing. The new approaches depend crucially upon community participation and therefore build upon the community-based services strategy which UNICEF has been advocating and supporting since 1975. An allied dimension is social mobilization, by which community organizations and other groups and sectors of society involve themselves in broad, mutually-reinforcing efforts, often on a nation-wide basis. This approach is exemplified by a number of recent immunization campaigns, such as those undertaken by Bolivia, Brazil, Burkina Faso, Colombia, the Dominican Republic, Mozambique, Nigeria and Turkey, among others. By 1986 77 countries had committed themselves to the UN goal of universal child immunization by 1990.

In several crucial health areas, new medical technologies have substantially improved the chances of success. In particular, the development of a simple mixture of salt plus sugar or cereal starch in water (oral rehydration therapy) has revolutionized family and

INTERNATIONAL ORGANIZATIONS

community-level treatment of diarrhoeal dehydration, one of the leading causes of death for infants and young children.

UNICEF estimated that about 1.5m. child deaths were prevented in 1985 by oral rehydration therapy and immunization. Sustained efforts of this kind against the major killers of children, it was felt, could reduce child death and disability by 50% in much of the developing world over the next seven or eight years.

In emergency relief and rehabilitation, working closely with other UN agencies (as well as with numerous non-governmental organizations), UNICEF provided some $50m. worth of assistance in 1985 to 30 countries affected by disasters (of which 21 were in Africa). Aid was in the form of shelter materials, medicaments, water supply equipment, food supplements, and the support or strengthening of essential services. UNICEF has supported the initiative of the UN Secretary-General, aimed at mobilizing extra resources for the victims of drought, famine and conflict in the African continent. In Lebanon, where a significant role has been undertaken since 1974, UNICEF is continuing to co-operate in a major UN programme of rehabilitation.

FINANCE

UNICEF's work is accomplished with voluntary contributions from both governments and non-governmental sources. Total income in 1985 came to US $362m. Income from governments and intergovernmental organizations accounted for 76% of this.

UNICEF's income is divided between contributions for general resources and contributions for specific purposes. General resources are the funds available to fulfil commitments for co-operation in country programmes approved by the Executive Board, and to meet administrative and programme support expenditures. They include contributions from governments, the net income from greetings cards sales, funds contributed by the public (mainly through National Committees) and other income. These funds amounted to $236m. in 1985. Contributions for specific purposes are those sought by UNICEF from governments and intergovernmental organizations as supplementary funds to support projects for which general resources are insufficient, or for relief and rehabilitation programmes in emergency situations. Supplementary funding in 1985 amounted to $78m. (compared with $109m. in 1984).

UNICEF PROGRAMME EXPENDITURE BY SECTOR
(1985)

	Cost (US $ million)
Basic health (including family planning)	82.3
Water supply	58.5
Nutrition	16.6
Social services for children	14.5
Formal and non-formal education	32.4
Planning and project support	38.9
Emergency relief	35.4
Total	278.6

PUBLICATIONS

State of the World's Children (annually, in English, French, Spanish and Arabic).
UNICEF Annual Report (summarizes UNICEF policies and programmes; in English, French and Spanish).
Facts about UNICEF (annually, in English, French and Spanish).
UNICEF News (contains articles on UNICEF-related programmes and activities; quarterly, in English, French, Spanish and German).
Les Carnets de l'Enfance/Assignment Children (concerned with planning development for women, children and youth; in English and French).

United Nations Conference on Trade and Development—UNCTAD

Address: Palais des Nations, 1211 Geneva 10, Switzerland.
Telephone: (022) 346011.
Telex: 289696.

UNCTAD was established by the UN General Assembly as one of its permanent organs in December 1964. Its role is to promote international trade, particularly that of developing countries, with a view to accelerating economic development. With 168 member states (October 1986), it has become a principal instrument of the General Assembly for deliberation and negotiation in the field of international trade and related issues of international economic cooperation.

Organization
(October 1986)

CONFERENCE

The Conference is held every four years in different capitals of member states. Sixth session, Belgrade, Yugoslavia, June 1983.
Secretary-General: KENNETH DADZIE (Ghana).
Deputy Secretary-General, Officer-in-Charge of UNCTAD: ALISTER MCINTYRE (Grenada).
Deputy Secretary-General: YVES BERTHELOT (France).

TRADE AND DEVELOPMENT BOARD

Between Conferences, the continuing work of the organization is carried out by the Trade and Development Board together with its various committees and subsidiary bodies.

MAIN COMMITTEES

The Board has six main committees: on commodities, manufactures, invisibles and financing related to trade, shipping, technology, and economic co-operation among developing countries; there is also a special committee on preferences.

COMMODITY CONFERENCES

UNCTAD has primary responsibility within the United Nations system for the negotiation and renegotiation of international commodity agreements. For this purpose, it convenes commodity conferences as required.

Activities

UNCTAD's concern covers the entire spectrum of policies in both developed and developing countries which influence the external trade and payments and economic progress of developing countries.

UNCTAD's efforts to strengthen the commodity sector in developing countries are carried out through the Integrated Programme for Commodities (IPC), adopted by the Conference in 1976. Through international agreements by both consuming and producing countries on individual commodities (some of which already existed before the Programme's inception, e.g. agreements on cocoa, coffee, sugar, wheat, olive oil and tin), the IPC aims to stabilize prices by the use of 'buffer stocks' and/or export quotas, and to improve the productivity and competitiveness of the developing exporters. Under the IPC, three international commodity agreements have so far been concluded: on rubber (entered into force in April 1982), jute and jute products (January 1984) and tropical timber (April 1985). Renegotiation of existing agreements due for renewal also takes place under the IPC, e.g. the negotiations on sugar which took place, unsuccessfully, in 1984. (See also the section on Other International Organizations—Commodities.)

A report by the UNCTAD Secretariat in 1985, however, showed that the commodity agreements had in many respects failed to achieve their aims: although the agreements on coffee, wheat, tin and rubber had so far been relatively successful in stabilizing prices, the agreements on cocoa and sugar had virtually collapsed, and little progress had been made in the longer-term objectives of improving developing countries' export earnings and competitiveness and enabling them to cope with falls in demand. The report argued that the success of such agreements depended on a high

INTERNATIONAL ORGANIZATIONS   United Nations (Other Bodies)

degree of participation by both producers and consumers, suggesting that the cocoa agreement had failed owing to the absence of the USA and the Ivory Coast (the largest consumer and producer respectively) while the non-participation of the USA and the European Community had led to the failure of the sugar agreement. The collapse of the International Tin Agreement in October 1985 cast further doubt on the efficacy of the commodity agreements.

Another important component of the IPC is the Common Fund for Commodities, with capital of US $470m. to support buffer stocks, together with voluntary contributions of about $255m., intended for longer-term purposes such as research, market promotion and conservation of resources. The Fund's articles of agreement were adopted in 1980. For it to become operational, ratification by 90 countries, contributing at least two-thirds of the capital, was necessary: this was achieved by February 1986. During 1985 UNCTAD proposed the establishment of an additional facility to compensate for shortfalls in commodity export earnings by developing countries.

Another major concern of UNCTAD is the expansion and diversification of the export trade of developing countries in manufactured and semi-manufactured products, chiefly through the Generalized System of Preferences, under which manufactured goods that are exported by developing countries receive preferential tariff treatment by developed countries. A comprehensive review of the system was to take place in 1990. In 1980 UNCTAD adopted a set of rules for the control of restrictive business practices that adversely affect international trade: these rules were reviewed by a special conference in November 1985. UNCTAD also has a mandate to review problems of protectionism and structural adjustment, and the secretariat has established a comprehensive database on trade measures.

In the area of finance, UNCTAD is intended to give particular attention to the debt problems of developing countries, and has negotiated measures of debt relief for the poorer of these countries, together with a set of guidelines for dealing with future debt problems before they reach a critical stage.

UNCTAD also seeks to help developing countries to increase their participation in world shipping. It negotiated the Convention on a Code of Conduct for Liner Conferences, which entered into force in 1980, and in 1985 it was studying the problems of securing for developing countries a greater share in the bulk cargo sector. Another UNCTAD initiative led to the adoption in 1980 of the UN Convention on International Multimodal Transport of Goods, which establishes a single liability regime for the carriage of goods entailing more than one mode of transport. In 1984–85 UNCTAD serviced the UN Conference on Conditions for the Registration of Ships, which drew up an agreement on ownership and manning of open-registry ships (flying 'flags of convenience'). The Convention on Registration of Ships was adopted in 1986, subject to ratification by a minimum of 40 countries, representing at least one-quarter of the world's shipping.

UNCTAD's work also covers the transfer of technology to developing countries. The sixth session of the UN Conference on an International Code of Conduct on the Transfer of Technology, in June 1985, failed to reach agreement and referred the issue to the UN General Assembly.

Through technical assistance activities, studies and the arrangement of bilateral consultations, UNCTAD seeks to promote trade between developing countries and the socialist countries of eastern Europe. It also supports programmes of economic co-operation between developing countries themselves. In 1981 it serviced the UN Conference on the Least Developed Countries, which adopted the 'Substantial New Programme of Action' for the 1980s for the 36 poorest countries; a mid-term review of this programme was carried out by UNCTAD in October 1985. In its 1986 annual report, UNCTAD analysed the effect of the developed countries' deflationary policies on commodity prices and on the developing economies, and called for the developed countries to adopt co-ordinated fiscal and monetary measures in order to stimulate the world economy. UNCTAD also proposed measures (based on domestic bankruptcy legislation in the USA) to deal with the international debt crisis, allowing debtor countries to rebuild their debt-servicing capacity.

The International Trade Centre in Geneva is operated jointly by GATT and UNCTAD (see p. 59).

FINANCE

The budget approved by the UN General Assembly for the two-year period 1986–87 was US $60.1m.

PUBLICATIONS

UNCTAD Bulletin (monthly).
Trade and Development (annually).
Trade and Development Report (annually).
Handbook of International Trade and Development Statistics (annually).
Monthly Commodity Price Bulletin.
Guide to UNCTAD Publications (monthly).
Reports.

United Nations Development Programme—UNDP

Address: One United Nations Plaza, New York, NY 10017, USA.
Telephone: (212) 906-5000.

The Programme was established in 1965 by the General Assembly to help the developing countries increase the wealth-producing capabilities of their natural and human resources.

Organization
(October 1986)

The UNDP is responsible to the UN General Assembly, to which it reports through ECOSOC.

GOVERNING COUNCIL

The Council, which meets annually, is the policy-making body of UNDP, and comprises representatives of 48 countries; 27 seats are filled by developing countries and 21 by economically more advanced countries; one-third of the membership changes each year.

SECRETARIAT

Administrator: WILLIAM H. DRAPER (USA).

REGIONAL BUREAUX

Headed by assistant administrators, the regional bureaux share the responsibility for implementing the programme with the Administrator's office. Within certain limitations, large-scale projects may be approved and funding allocated by the Administrator, and smaller-scale projects by the Resident Representatives, based in 115 countries.

The four regional bureaux, all at the Secretariat in New York, cover: Africa; Asia and the Pacific; the Arab states; and Latin America and the Caribbean; there is also a Unit for Europe, and a division for global and regional projects.

FIELD OFFICES

In almost every country receiving UNDP assistance there is a Country Office, headed by the UNDP Resident Representative, who co-ordinates all UN technical assistance, advises the government on formulating the country programme, sees that the field activities are carried out, and acts as the leader of the UN team of experts working in the country. Resident Representatives are normally designated as co-ordinators for all UN operational development activities; the field offices function as the primary presence of the UN in most developing countries.

EXECUTING AGENCIES

The following act as executing agencies or otherwise participate in the work of UNDP: the UN Department of Technical Co-operation for Development, the International Trade Centre and 26 of the UN agencies and organizations, three regional development banks, five regional economic commissions and the Arab Fund for Economic and Social Development. An Inter-Agency Task Force co-ordinates the activities of participating agencies.

Activities

As the world's largest source of grant technical assistance in developing countries, UNDP works with more than 150 governments and 36 international agencies for faster economic growth and better standards of living throughout the world. Agriculture (including forestry and fisheries) is the largest component of UNDP activities, accounting for about 23% of expenditure in 1985 (see table). Most of the work is carried out in the field by the United Nations and its agencies, or by the government of the country concerned.

Project work covers five main areas: locating, assessing and activating latent natural resources and other development assets; stimulating capital investment to help realize these possibilities; support for professional and vocational training; expansion of scientific research and applied technology; and strengthening of national and regional development planning.

Countries receiving UNDP assistance are allocated an indicative planning figure (IPF) for a five-year period. The IPF represents the approximate total funding that a country can expect to receive, based on a formula taking per caput GNP and other criteria into account. In partnership with UNDP's Country Offices, governments calculate their technical assistance requirements on the basis of this formula. Activities covering more than one country are developed by UNDP's Division for Global and Inter-regional Programmes, in consultation with the relevant national and regional institutions.

In UNDP's Fourth Programming Cycle (1987-91), 80% of the resources available was to be devoted to the poorest developing countries, with per caput GNP of US $750 or less; within this group, countries with per caput GNP of less than $375 were to receive particular attention.

FINANCE

The Development Programme is financed by the voluntary contributions of members of the United Nations and the Programme's participating Agencies. Pledges by governments fell from US $716m. in 1980 to $664.2m. in 1983, when expenditure had to be limited to 55% of the amount originally programmed for that year. Pledges for 1984 rose to $687.3m., with a further $39.8m. contributed from the (now liquidated) UN Emergency Operations Trust Fund. Pledges for 1985 totalled $676.7m.

UNDP EXPENDITURE BY SECTOR (1985)

	Cost (US $ m. equivalent)	Number of projects in operation
Agriculture, forestry and fisheries	119.6	977
Transport and communications	56.8	481
Development policies	70.5	882
Natural resources	68.3	527
Industry	66.0	875
Education	23.5	324
Employment	24.6	292
Health	20.4	246
Science and technology	41.2	298
Trade and development finance	9.9	145
Human settlements, social conditions and equity	9.4	115
Total (incl. other)	510.2	5,162

UNDP PROJECTS APPROVED, BY REGION (1985)

	Number of new projects approved	UNDP contribution (US $ million)
Africa	514	127.3
Asia and the Pacific	434	157.0
Latin America	260	27.0
Arab States	155	28.6
Europe	45	3.4
Inter-regional and global	28	5.5
Total (incl. other)	1,436	348.8

PUBLICATIONS

Report and Review (annually).
Co-operation South (quarterly).
Development in Action (quarterly).

Affiliated Organizations

UNITED NATIONS CAPITAL DEVELOPMENT FUND—UNCDF

The Fund was established in 1966 and became fully operational in 1974. It assists developing countries by supplementing existing sources of capital assistance by means of grants and loans on concessionary terms. Rapid assistance is available to governments for small-scale projects directly and immediately benefiting the low-income groups who have not benefited from earlier development efforts. Assistance may be given to any of the member states of the UN system, and is not necessarily limited to specific projects. The Fund is mainly used for the benefit of the least-developed countries. Voluntary contributions pledged for 1985 amounted to US $19.9m.

Activities fall into two categories: projects to meet such basic needs as food production, storage and transport, health care, safe drinking water, housing and primary education; and projects to develop productive facilities in agriculture, energy, light industry and other key sectors.

UNITED NATIONS DEVELOPMENT FUND FOR WOMEN

This Fund (formerly the Voluntary Fund for the UN Decade for Women) was established in 1985 as an associated fund of UNDP. Its purpose is to involve women in development and to support innovative activities benefiting women in all regions.

UNITED NATIONS FINANCING SYSTEM FOR SCIENCE AND TECHNOLOGY FOR DEVELOPMENT—UNFSSTD

UNFSSTD was established in 1982 to help developing countries acquire the capacity to formulate science and technology policies linked to their development goals. During 1985 the System was supporting 81 projects. Voluntary contributions for 1984 amounted to US $277,172, while cost-sharing and sub-trust funds income received was $4,682,192. Training and the exchange of information are also undertaken.

UNITED NATIONS REVOLVING FUND FOR NATURAL RESOURCES EXPLORATION—RFNRE

The RFNRE was established in 1974 to provide risk capital to finance exploration for natural resources (particularly minerals) in developing countries and, when discoveries are made, to help to attract investment. The revolving character of the Fund, which distinguishes it from most other UN system technical co-operation programmes, lies in the undertaking of contributing governments to make replenishment contributions to the Fund when the projects it finances lead to commercial production.

Announced and anticipated pledges of US $2.1m. for 1984 brought cumulative contributions to a total of $48.1m., insufficient to meet the Fund's needs.

UNITED NATIONS SUDANO-SAHELIAN OFFICE—UNSO

UNSO's dual responsibility is to help eight countries of the Sahel region (members of the CILSS, q.v.) to carry out their medium- and long-term programmes for recovery from drought; and to assist them, along with 11 other Sudano-Sahelian countries, in implementing the Plan of Action to Combat Desertification. Activities include planting improved crop strains; setting up food storage facilities; establishing agricultural implement workshops; developing transport and communications; agrometeorological and hydrological services; forest conservation and expansion; water resources management; sand dune fixation; and the development of alternative systems for energy production and overall policy planning. Voluntary contributions pledged for 1984 to the UN Trust Fund for Sudano-Sahelian Activities amounted to US $580,082, while cost-sharing and sub-trust funds income was $17,537,540.

UN Sahelian Regional Office: BP 366, ave Dimdolobsom, Ouagadougou, Burkina Faso; tel. 367-81; telex 5262; Chief WALLY N'DOW.

INTERNATIONAL ORGANIZATIONS

UNITED NATIONS VOLUNTEERS—UNV

The United Nations Volunteers is an important source of urgently needed middle-level skills for the UN development system supplied at modest cost, particularly in the least-developed countries. Volunteers expand the scope of UNDP project activities by supplementing the work of international and host country experts and by extending the influence of projects to local community levels. One of the most important parts of its work is the support of technical co-operation within and among the developing countries by encouraging volunteers from the countries themselves and by forming regional exchange teams made up of such volunteers. UNV is also engaged in a variety of activities to increase youth participation in development and to promote the involvement of domestic development services.

In early 1985 there were 1,087 volunteers, and a further 519 were being recruited.

OTHER FUNDS

Other special funds include the Special Fund for Landlocked Developing Countries and the Energy Account, which works with the World Bank to carry out energy sector assessments in developing countries. UNDP also gives assistance to national liberation movements in southern Africa for training in technical skills, agriculture and health.

United Nations Environment Programme—UNEP

Address: POB 30552, Nairobi, Kenya.
Telephone: 333930.
Telex: 22068.

The United Nations Environment Programme was established in 1972 by the UN General Assembly following recommendations of the 1972 UN Conference on the Human Environment, in Stockholm, Sweden, to encourage international co-operation in matters relating to the human environment.

Organization

(October 1986)

GOVERNING COUNCIL

The main function of the Governing Council, which meets annually, is to provide general policy guidelines for the direction and co-ordination of environmental programmes within the UN system. It comprises representatives of 58 states, elected by the UN General Assembly on a rotating basis.

SECRETARIAT

The Secretariat serves as a focal point for environmental action within the UN system.
Executive Director: MOSTAFA K. TOLBA (Egypt).

REGIONAL OFFICES

Europe: Palais des Nations, 1211 Geneva 10, Switzerland; tel. (022) 999400; telex 28877.
Asia and the Pacific: UN Bldg, 10th Floor, Rajadamnern Ave, Bangkok 10200, Thailand; tel. 2829161; telex 82392.
Latin America: Presidente Mazaryk 29, Ap. Postal 6-718, México 5, DF, Mexico; tel. 2501555; telex 01771055.
West Asia: 1083 Road No 425, Jufair 342, Manama, Bahrain; tel. 729040; telex 8337.
Africa: UNEP Headquarters (see above).
Liaison Office: UNDC Two Bldg, Room 0803, 2 United Nations Plaza, New York, NY 10017, USA; tel. (212) 754-8139; telex 420544.

Activities

UNEP aims to maintain a constant watch on the changing state of the environment; to analyse the trends; to assess the problems using a wide range of data and techniques; and to promote projects leading to environmentally sound development. It plays a catalytic and co-ordinating role within and beyond the UN system. During 1984, 87 UNEP projects were being implemented in co-operation with other UN agencies, particularly FAO, UNESCO and WHO. About 40 intergovernmental organizations outside the UN system have official observer status on UNEP's Governing Council, and, through the Environment Liaison Centre in Nairobi, UNEP is linked to over 6,000 non-governmental bodies concerned with the environment.

ENVIRONMENT AND DEVELOPMENT

UNEP conducts studies on the integration of environmental considerations in development planning; in 1984, for example, it undertook analyses of the experience of Japan and of centrally-planned economies in this sphere. Training courses for those involved in planning are also provided. During 1984 a manual of guidelines for environmental impact assessment in developing countries was being prepared.

UNEP makes comparative assessments of the environmental impact of different energy sources. A comprehensive report on energy storage systems in developing countries was published in 1984, together with reports on harnessing renewable sources of energy in Indonesia and on the establishment of an experimental rural energy centre in Senegal.

UNEP draws up and reviews international environmental law. It administers the Convention on International Trade in Endangered Species of Wild Fauna and Flora (to which 87 states were Parties at the end of 1984). It also organizes working groups of experts to develop legal guidelines and principles on, for example (during 1984), the protection of the earth's ozone layer, management of hazardous wastes, and marine pollution. UNEP also provides technical assistance for drawing up national legislation.

ENVIRONMENTAL AWARENESS

UNEP encourages the inclusion of environmental issues in education. The joint UNEP/UNESCO International Programme in Environmental Education, launched in 1976, includes the training of teachers, publications and technical assistance to governments. UNEP also provides environmental training components for use in ILO management programmes, and joint ILO/UNEP regional meetings of employers' organizations were held in Bangkok and Nairobi in 1984 to study environmentally sound development.

UNEP provides information through its publications (see below), and press releases. During 1984 it conducted a Desertification Information Campaign, aimed at the media throughout the world. The INFOTERRA programme forms a network of national 'focal points' for the exchange of environmental information, including the annual compilation of a Directory of Sources.

ENVIRONMENTAL ASSESSMENT

UNEP's environmental assessment programme, known as Earthwatch, aims to study the interaction between man and the environment, provide early warning of potential environmental hazards, and determine the state of natural resources. The Global Environmental Monitoring System (GEMS), which began in 1975, collects data on the following topics: renewable resources; climate; health hazards; long-range transport of pollutants; and oceans. To convert the data collected into information usable by decision-makers, a global resource information data-base (GRID) was being set up in 1985.

UNEP conducts research on the 'outer limits' of tolerance of the biosphere and its subsystems to the demands made on it by human activities, and undertakes climate impact studies (e.g. assessing the effect of carbon dioxide emission on climate, and developing the use of data derived from satellites). In 1985 a study was completed on the effects of chloro-fluorocarbon emissions on the layer of ozone in the earth's atmosphere, warning that serious climatic changes were likely to result if governments did not limit such emissions.

INTERNATIONAL ORGANIZATIONS United Nations (Other Bodies)

OCEANS

UNEP co-operates with other agencies in assessing marine pollution, chiefly through its regional seas programme: by the end of 1985 action plans had been adopted in nine regions (the Mediterranean; the seas around Kuwait; the Caribbean; the West and Central African region; the East African region; the East Asian region; the Red Sea and the Gulf of Aden; the South Pacific; and the South-East Pacific), and regional conventions had been signed by member states in six of these regions. With FAO, a joint Plan of Action for the Conservation, Management and Utilization of Marine Mammals was drawn up in 1984.

WATER AND LAND ECOSYSTEMS

UNEP supports research and training in the management of inland water resources and the protection of fresh-water ecosystems. It monitors and attempts to combat topsoil erosion, the destruction of tropical forests and the misuse of agricultural pesticides. It collaborates with the International Union for the Conservation of Nature and Natural Resources (IUCN, q.v.) in the protection of endangered species and habitats, and provides a secretariat for the Ecosystem Conservation Group (consisting of UNEP, FAO, UNESCO and IUCN), which sends expert missions to help prepare national conservation strategies. UNEP co-ordinates the UN Plan of Action to Combat Desertification (begun in 1978), which is particularly active in the Sudano-Sahelian region.

HEALTH AND HUMAN SETTLEMENTS

UNEP promotes increased awareness of environmental health problems, particularly those caused by chemical contamination. It maintains the International Register of Potentially Toxic Chemicals, and provides guidance on chemical hazards and waste management. UNEP collaborates with other UN agencies, especially UNCHS, in combating deteriorating environmental standards in towns; in 1985 it was to publish three volumes of guidelines for environmental planning and management of human settlements.

FINANCE

UNEP derives its finances from the regular budget of the United Nations (from which US $9.98m. was allotted to it for the two years 1984–85), and from voluntary contributions to the Environment Fund, which amounted to about $29.5m. in 1984. Payments of contributions were slower during 1984 than in previous years, and as a result commitments for new projects amounted to $22.84m. for the year, compared with the sum of $30.97m. originally allocated for this purpose; commitments for 1983 had amounted to $24.8m. In the UN budget for 1986–87 UNEP was allocated $10.1m.

ENVIRONMENT FUND: COMMITMENTS FOR PROGRAMME ACTIVITIES, 1984

Purpose	Commitments (US dollars)
Environment and development	2,589,976
Environmental awareness	3,709,109
'Earthwatch'	3,088,379
Oceans	2,761,444
Water	477,098
Terrestrial ecosystems	2,582,074
Desertification	2,314,359
Health and human settlements	2,509,876
Arms race and the environment	115,000
Regional and technical co-operation	2,107,614
Fund programme reserve	588,348
Total	22,843,278

GEOGRAPHICAL DISTRIBUTION OF FUND COMMITMENTS, 1984

Region	Amount (US dollars)
Africa	2,721,352
Asia	1,985,771
Latin America	1,491,092
North America	37,639
Europe	360,500
Inter-regional	2,233,365
Global	14,013,559
Total	22,843,278

PUBLICATIONS

Annual Report of the Executive Director.
UNEP News (every 2 months).
Desertification Control Bulletin (2 a year).
Industry and Environment Bulletin (quarterly).
INFOterra (quarterly).
INFOterra International Directory of Sources.
IRPTC Bulletin (3 a year: on toxic chemicals).
Ozone Layer Bulletin (annually).
The Siren (quarterly, on regional seas programme).
Catalogue of Publications (annually).
Studies, reports, legal texts, technical guidelines, etc.

INTERNATIONAL ORGANIZATIONS *United Nations (Other Bodies)*

United Nations Fund for Population Activities — UNFPA

Address: 220 E. 42nd St, New York, NY 10017, USA.
Telephone: (212) 754-1234.

Created in 1967 as the Trust Fund for Population Activities. Became a Fund of the UN General Assembly in 1972 and was made a subsidiary organ of the UN General Assembly in 1979, with the UNDP Governing Council designated as its governing body.

Organization
(October 1986)

EXECUTIVE DIRECTOR

The Executive Director, who has the rank of Under-Secretary-General of the UN, is responsible for the overall direction of the Fund, working closely with governments, United Nations bodies and agencies, regional groups, and non-governmental organizations to ensure the most effective programming and use of resources in population activities.

Executive Director: RAFAEL M. SALAS (Philippines).

EXECUTING AGENCIES

In most projects assistance is extended through member organizations of the UN system; ultimate responsibility for execution of projects lies with recipient governments, using the services of the UN organizations as required. The Fund may also call on the services of non-governmental organizations in this role and sometimes it acts as its own executing agency.

FIELD ORGANIZATION

UNFPA Deputy Representatives and Senior Advisers on Population, attached to the offices of the UNDP Resident Representatives, assist governments in formulating requests for aid and co-ordinate the work of the executing agencies in any given country or area.

Activities

At the end of 1985 UNFPA was providing assistance for 2,667 projects, of which 845 were in Africa, 784 in Asia and the Pacific, 411 in Latin America and the Caribbean, 312 in the Middle East, the Mediterranean and Europe, 141 inter-regional, and 174 global. UNFPA approved 478 new projects during 1985, at a total cost of US $23.2m. Many UNFPA-supported projects are executed by other UN agencies, notably WHO, UNESCO and ILO, or by the government of the country concerned. 'Needs assessment missions' were undertaken to 16 countries to assist governments in drawing up or reviewing population programmes.

Priority programme areas are as follows:

1. Family planning. In 1985 51% of total programme expenditure allocations were for family planning, concentrating on extending acceptance of family planning and expanding the delivery of services to rural and marginal urban areas. The emphasis is on combining family planning services with maternal and child health care. UNFPA supports research into contraceptives and training in contraceptive technology.

2. Communication and education. This accounted for 14.4% of total programme allocations in 1985. UNFPA assists broadcasting, poster campaigns and itinerant drama groups which convey family planning information, and supports school education programmes.

3. Basic data collection and use. UNFPA provides assistance and training for carrying out censuses and demographic surveys, and for analysing the results. It also supports training and research in using data for policy formulation and development planning.

UNFPA also has special programmes on women, health and development, on youth, and on ageing, involving national and regional seminars and training programmes. It produces publications (see below) and audio-visual aids, promotes conferences, and encourages wider coverage of population issues in the media.

FINANCE

Total expenditure in 1985 (provisional) was $149m. (compared with $137m. in 1984): this included $91.4m. for country programmes and $32.8m. for inter-country programmes. In 1986 the US Government announced that it was to withhold some $25m. of funding from UNFPA, in protest at the Fund's support for the 'one child per family' policy of the People's Republic of China.

Allocations by Region (US $ million, 1985)

Africa south of the Sahara	28.1
Asia and the Pacific	60.7
Latin America and the Caribbean	19.0
Middle East and Mediterranean	12.2
Europe	1.9
Inter-regional	16.1
Global	3.3
Total	141.4

PUBLICATIONS

Annual Report.
State of World Population Report (annually).
Population (newsletter, monthly in Arabic, English, French and Spanish).
Population Profiles.
Populi (quarterly).
Inventory of Population Projects in Developing Countries Around the World (annually).
Policy Development Studies (series).
Reports and reference works.

United Nations High Commissioner for Refugees—UNHCR

Address: Palais des Nations, 1211 Geneva 10, Switzerland.
Telephone: (022) 310261.
Telex: 27492.

The Office of the High Commissioner was established in 1951 to provide international protection for refugees and to seek permanent solutions to their problems.

Organization
(October 1986)

HIGH COMMISSIONER

The High Commissioner is elected by the United Nations General Assembly on the nomination of the Secretary-General, and is responsible to the General Assembly and to ECOSOC.

High Commissioner: JEAN-PIERRE HOCKÉ (Switzerland).
Deputy High Commissioner: ARTHUR E. DEWEY (USA).

EXECUTIVE COMMITTEE

The Executive Committee of the High Commissioner's Programme, established by ECOSOC, gives the High Commissioner policy directives in respect of material assistance programmes and advice at his request in the field of international protection. It meets once a year, usually at Geneva. It includes representatives of 41 states, both members and non-members of the UN.

ADMINISTRATION

Headquarters includes the High Commissioner's Office, and the following divisions: External Affairs, Protection, Assistance, and Administration and Management. In January 1986 the High Commissioner had 90 Representatives and Chargés de Mission in the field, covering 126 countries.

Activities

The competence of the High Commissioner extends to any person who, owing to well-founded fear of being persecuted for reasons of race, religion, nationality or political opinion, is outside the country of his nationality and is unable or, owing to such fear or for reasons other than personal convenience, remains unwilling to avail himself of the protection of that country; or who, not having a nationality and being outside the country of his former habitual residence, is unable or, owing to such fear or for reasons other than personal convenience, is unwilling to return to it. Refugees meeting these criteria are entitled to the protection of the Office of the High Commissioner irrespective of their geographical location. Refugees who are assisted by other United Nations agencies, or who have the same rights or obligations as nationals of their country of residence, are outside the mandate of UNHCR.

INTERNATIONAL PROTECTION

As laid down in the Statute of the Office, one of the two primary functions of UNHCR is to extend international protection to refugees. In the exercise of this function, UNHCR seeks to ensure that refugees and asylum-seekers are protected against *refoulement* (forcible return), that they receive asylum, and that they are treated according to internationally recognized standards of treatment. UNHCR pursues these objectives by a variety of means which include promoting the conclusion and ratification by states of international conventions for the protection of refugees.

The most comprehensive instrument concerning refugees which has been elaborated at the international level is the 1951 United Nations Convention relating to the Status of Refugees. This Convention, the scope of which was extended by a Protocol adopted in 1967, defines the rights and duties of refugees and contains provisions dealing with a variety of matters which affect the day-to-day lives of refugees. The application of the 1951 United Nations Refugee Convention and the 1967 Protocol is supervised by UNHCR. Important provisions for the treatment of refugees are also contained in a number of instruments adopted at the regional level. These include the OAU Convention of 1969 Governing the Specific Aspects of Refugee Problems, the European Agreement on the Abolition of Visas for Refugees, and the 1969 American Convention on Human Rights.

UNHCR has actively encouraged States to accede to the 1951 United Nations Refugee Convention and the 1967 Protocol: 100 States had accepted either or both of these basic refugee instruments by July 1986. An increasing number of states have also adopted domestic legislation and/or administrative measures to implement the international instruments, particularly in the field of procedures for the determination of refugee status. Such measures provide an important guarantee that refugees will be accorded the standards of treatment which have been internationally established for their benefit.

A continuing concern of UNHCR has been to ensure that States scrupulously observe the fundamental principle of *non-refoulement* according to which no-one may be forcibly returned to a territory where he has reason to fear persecution. While this principle is now widely reflected in the practice of States, violations still occur. UNHCR has also continued to promote the adoption of liberal practices of asylum by States, so that refugees and asylum seekers are granted admission, at least on a temporary basis. Major problems have arisen in regard to violation of the physical safety of refugees as a result of piracy, abduction and armed attack. UNHCR has urged the international community to find solutions to these problems as a matter of priority. In 1981 the High Commissioner launched an anti-piracy campaign in the Gulf of Thailand, in co-operation with the Thai Government, and in June 1986 the campaign was extended for a further year, at a cost of $2.57m. UNHCR has also attempted to deal with the problem of military attacks on refugee camps in southern Africa and elsewhere, by formulating and encouraging the acceptance of a set of principles to ensure the safety of refugees.

MATERIAL ASSISTANCE TO REFUGEES

Emergency relief is provided to refugees when food supplies, medical aid or other forms of assistance are required on a large scale at short notice. Other members of the UN system, as well as inter-governmental and non-governmental organizations, co-operate closely with UNHCR in this field.

Even in the more stable refugee situations, UNHCR is often called upon to provide material assistance beyond the initial emergency phase, while permanent solutions are being sought. This assistance can take various forms, including the provision of food, shelter, medical care and essential supplies. Also covered in many instances are basic services, including education and counselling. Whenever possible, measures of this kind are accompanied by efforts to encourage maximum levels of self-reliance among the refugee population.

As far as possible, assistance is geared towards the identification and implementation of durable solutions to refugee problems—this being the second statutory responsibility of UNHCR. Such solutions generally take one of three forms: voluntary repatriation, local integration or resettlement in another country. Where voluntary repatriation is feasible, the Office assists refugees to overcome obstacles preventing their return to their country of origin. This may be done through negotiations with governments involved, or by providing funds either for the physical movement of refugees or for the rehabilitation of returnees once back in their own country.

When voluntary repatriation is not feasible, efforts are made to assist refugees to integrate locally and to become self-supporting in their countries of asylum. In Europe, this has generally been done either by granting loans to refugees, or by assisting them, through vocational training or in other ways, to learn a skill and to set themselves up in gainful occupations. One major form of assistance to help refugees re-establish themselves outside camps is the provision of housing.

In contrast to the situation in Europe, the majority of refugees in Africa, and some of those in Asia, are assisted through local settlement in agriculture. In Africa, the consolidation of refugee settlements frequently requires close co-operation between UNHCR and other members of the UN system which provide development assistance to the areas affected. The problem of needy individual refugees in search of employment or educational opportunities in urban areas of Africa, and who are mainly without agricultural skills, also claims special attention. Assistance is provided through special refugee counselling services, in some cases in co-operation with the OAU Bureau for African Refugees.

In cases where resettlement through emigration is the only viable solution to a refugee problem, UNHCR negotiates with governments in an endeavour to obtain suitable resettlement opportunities, to encourage liberalization of admission criteria and to draw up special immigration schemes.

ASIA AND THE MIDDLE EAST

Since 1975 UNHCR assistance activities in the Far East and Australasia have been dominated by the problems of refugees and displaced persons in and from the Indo-Chinese peninsula: Laotians, Kampucheans and Vietnamese, needing both immediate assistance in the countries of temporary asylum to which they had fled, and help in finding a place of permanent resettlement. Between 1975 and 1985 UNHCR provided assistance to over 570,000 refugees in Thailand, at a cost of US $376m.; in 1981, however, departures began to outnumber arrivals. The total number of refugee arrivals in South-East Asian countries of temporary asylum fell from 119,402 in 1980 to 99,168 in 1981. By March 1986 over 1.2m. Indo-Chinese refugees had been resettled, chiefly in the USA (620,223, a figure which does not include some 130,000 persons who arrived in the USA in 1975), the People's Republic of China (276,000), France (102,250), Canada (102,435) and Australia (100,781). At the end of the year 159,664 refugees still remained in camps, however, awaiting resettlement; of these about 130,400 were in Thailand, 9,400 in Hong Kong and 8,500 in Malaysia. A special programme, launched in 1980, continued to assist about 100,000 Kampucheans who had returned to their homeland from Thailand, Viet-Nam and Laos.

In May 1979 UNHCR and Viet-Nam signed a 'memorandum of understanding' on the orderly departure of persons wishing to leave: under the Orderly Departure Programme which resulted, over 99,500 persons had left Viet-Nam by the end of 1985; there were 24,940 departures during 1985.

In early 1986 there were over 10,000 refugees from Irian Jaya, Indonesia, in Papua New Guinea, where most had arrived in early 1984.

As a result of events in Afghanistan, almost 1m. refugees crossed into the North-West Frontier and Baluchistan provinces of Pakistan between January 1979 and mid-1980. By 1984 UNHCR assistance was being extended to about 2.3m. beneficiaries in 340 refugee villages, and covered immediate relief assistance, health care, education, vocational training and the promotion of income-generating and self-help programmes, in collaboration with the World Food Programme, the International Labour Organisation and the World Bank. UNHCR contributions to the Afghan refugee programme between 1979 and 1985 amounted to over $500m. in cash and kind. Projected expenditure for Pakistan in 1986 was $48m. UNCHR also assists Afghan refugees in Iran (who numbered about 1.9m. in 1985).

Between June 1982 and the end of 1984 emergency allocations for the relief of displaced persons in Lebanon (estimated to number 160,000 in October 1984) amounted to about $4.5m.

AFRICA

The total number of refugees and displaced persons in Africa (including North Africa) increased from about 1m. in 1975 to over 5m. in 1980: the main groups had fled from Ethiopia to Djibouti, Somalia and Sudan, from Chad to Cameroon and Nigeria, from Burundi to Tanzania and from Uganda to Zaire.

In 1980 the High Commissioner was requested by the Government of Zimbabwe and the Secretary-General of the UN to act as co-ordinator of a UN programme of immediate humanitarian assistance to returning refugees and displaced persons in Zimbabwe. Financial requirements under this programme, which covered some 200,000 returnees, amounted to US $110m.; they were met through co-ordination by UNHCR of multilateral and bilateral aid, with about $24m. provided directly by UNHCR.

Appeals were launched by the High Commissioner in December 1981 for the repatriation of Chad refugees ($10m.) and in April 1982 for assistance to returnees in Ethiopia ($14m.). The programme of voluntary repatriation to Chad was successfully completed in 1982, while assistance to about 126,000 spontaneous returnees in Ethiopia continued in 1983. In June 1983 the High Commissioner also launched an appeal for $6m. for a programme of organized voluntary repatriation from Djibouti to Ethiopia, concluded in December 1984 after over 13,000 refugees had been repatriated. A further appeal for $23.5m. for repatriation in Ethiopia was launched in April 1985. A programme of assistance for refugees returning from Rwanda to Uganda (who numbered 30,000 between August and November 1985) was begun in January 1986, at a cost of $1m. An appeal for $4.4m. to assist over 75,000 Ugandans returning from Sudan was launched in June.

In April 1981 the first International Conference on Assistance to Refugees in Africa (ICARA) was held, with the object of focusing public attention on the plight of refugees in Africa, mobilizing additional resources for refugee programmes there, and strengthening the economic capacity of countries affected by large influxes of refugees. A total of $566.9m. was pledged by donor governments as a result of the conference: the original target had been $1,150m. A second conference (ICARA II) was held in July 1984, with the particular aim of helping host countries, themselves poor, to cope with large numbers of refugees. During 1983 a team of UN experts visited 14 countries at the invitation of the governments, evaluating proposed projects relating to refugees and returnees, and a list of 128 projects, requiring a total of $362m., was drawn up for presentation to ICARA II. The projects include improvement of transport and energy supplies; development of agriculture; education

REFUGEES OF CONCERN TO UNHCR*
(1 January 1985)

Host Country	Number of Registered Refugees
Africa	
Algeria	167,000
Angola	92,200
Burundi	256,300
Cameroon	13,700
Central African Republic	42,000
Djibouti	16,700
Ethiopia	59,600
Lesotho	11,500
Rwanda	49,000
Somalia	700,000
Sudan	690,000†
Tanzania	179,000
Uganda	151,000
Zaire	317,000
Zambia	96,500
Zimbabwe	46,500
Asia and the Pacific	
Australia	89,000
China, People's Republic	179,800
Hong Kong	11,900
Iran	1,900,000
Malaysia	175,000
Pakistan	2,500,000
Papua New Guinea	10,900
Philippines	15,100
Thailand	128,500
Viet-Nam	21,000
Latin America	
Argentina	11,500
Costa Rica	16,800
Guatemala	70,000
Honduras	47,800
Mexico	175,000
Nicaragua	18,500
Europe and North America	
Austria	20,500
Belgium	36,400
Canada	353,000
France	167,300
Federal Republic of Germany	126,600
Italy	15,100
Netherlands	15,000
Norway	10,000
Sweden	90,600
Switzerland	31,200
United Kingdom	135,000
USA	1,000,000

* The table shows only those countries where more than 10,000 refugees were present. The figures do not include Palestine refugees, who come under the care of UNRWA (q.v.), nor non-registered refugees (e.g. Ethiopians living in Somalia outside official refugee camps), nor returnees and persons displaced within their own country (e.g. in Ethiopia, Kampuchea, Uganda, Zaire and Zimbabwe). Most figures are based on government estimates.

† At 31 March 1986 there were an estimated 852,000 refugees from Ethiopia in Sudan, of whom 405,000 were receiving UNHCR assistance.

and training; health; water supplies; and social development, such as the organization of handicrafts. By the end of the Conference one-third of the necessary funds had been pledged.

In November and December 1984 the High Commissioner launched special appeals for $24.8m., and for over 12,000 metric tons of cereals, to meet the urgent additional needs of refugees and returnees in Africa caused by drought, food shortage and other emergencies, particularly in Ethiopia, Somalia, Sudan and the Central African Republic. By February 1985 the worsening situation had caused the target for African emergency programmes in 1985 to be raised to $96.4m. In February 1986 the High Commissioner launched a further appeal for $80.7m. for emergency assistance in Africa (of which $51.9m. was for Sudan, $15.4m. for Somalia and $13.4m. for Ethiopia): it was reported that, although the situation had improved considerably in comparison with that in 1985, emergency assistance was still necessary for vulnerable groups, needing food, water and medical care, and for beginning rehabilitation schemes.

CENTRAL AMERICA

Central America has been an area of increasingly grave concern to UNHCR. By the end of 1980, 80,000 refugees from El Salvador had sought refuge in neighbouring countries. The total refugee population of the area was about 338,000 at the end of 1984: most were Salvadoreans, with increasing numbers from Guatemala and Nicaragua.

Recent UNHCR assistance has concentrated largely on emergency relief to destitute new arrivals, the consolidation of care and maintenance measures for the largely rural refugee populations living in camps in Honduras and Mexico or spontaneously settled in Costa Rica and Nicaragua, and the development of self-sufficiency through rural settlements.

EUROPE

UNHCR's material assistance activities in Europe have, in recent years, been limited in scale as assistance is, in most cases, provided by governments and private organizations. In 1977, however, a UNHCR Branch Office was opened in Portugal to assist large numbers of refugees from former Portuguese territories in Africa. Moreover, in late 1981, a large influx of Polish asylum-seekers into Austria began, prompting the High Commissioner to make an allocation from his Emergency Fund to provide for local integration measures. Assistance was also given with resettlement overseas. At the beginning of 1985 there were about 670,000 refugees in Europe.

Finance

UNHCR administrative expenditure is financed under the United Nations Regular Budget. Material assistance programmes are financed from voluntary contributions made by governments and also from non-governmental sources. Expenditure for General Programmes in 1984 amounted to US $346m., of which about 96% was for regular field operations. In addition, UNHCR undertakes a number of Special Programmes, as requested by the UN General Assembly, the Secretary-General of the UN or a member state, to assist returnees and, in some cases, displaced persons. The total requirements for both General and Special Programmes amounted to $444m. in 1984 (see table), compared with $398m. in 1983.

UNHCR Expenditure (1984)

Region	Total expenditure (US $'000)
Africa	181,154.7
Americas and Europe	60,912.6
East and South Asia and Oceania	82,696.1
Middle East and South-West Asia	104,636.9
Global and regional	29,240.4
Total	458,640.7*

* Of this total, $14,590,200 was from the UN Regular Budget, $345,954,000 was from General Programmes financing (including $9,760,787 from the Emergency Fund), and $98,096,500 from Special Programmes financing.

PUBLICATIONS

Refugees (monthly, in English and French).
Press releases, reports.

United Nations Institute for Training and Research—UNITAR

Address: 801 United Nations Plaza, New York, NY 10017, USA.
UNITAR was established in 1965 as an autonomous body within the framework of the United Nations to improve, by means of training and research, the effectiveness of the United Nations, in particular the maintenance of peace and security and the promotion of economic and social development.

Organization
(October 1986)

BOARD OF TRUSTEES

The Board comprises up to 30 members appointed by the UN Secretary-General to serve for three years. The UN Secretary-General and the Presidents of the General Assembly and ECOSOC, and the Executive Director of the Institute are ex-officio members. The Board meets usually once a year and is responsible for determining basic policies of the Institute and for reviewing and adopting the annual budget.

EXECUTIVE DIRECTOR

The Executive Director is appointed by the Secretary-General, after consultation with the Board, and is responsible for the overall organization, direction and administration of the Institute. He is assisted by the Directors of Training and Research, the Special Assistant to the Executive Director, the Secretary of the Board of Trustees and External Relations Co-ordinator, and the Administrative Officer.

Executive Director: MICHEL DOO KINGUÉ (Cameroon).

Activities

TRAINING

Training is given at various levels, with particular attention given to the needs of officials from developing countries. The Institute organizes seminars and short courses for delegates to the UN, including new delegates to the General Assembly and new members of permanent missions, and briefing seminars on issues currently before the UN, such as international economic development and international negotiations. Courses are also held for officials other than diplomats, e.g. training in the modernization of public administration, the management of public enterprises and finance. UNITAR has also organized special programmes at the request of member states, including courses on basic diplomacy and multinational co-operation.

RESEARCH

UNITAR's research is divided between those studies which focus on the short- and medium-term needs of the UN, and those dealing with longer-term trends. Since 1966 the Institute has published many studies on peace and security, international organization and development, and the first of a series of studies on the effectiveness of various parts of the UN system and aspects of regional co-operation (including case studies of the Economic and Social Council, the International Law Commission and the Law of the Sea Conference, which have been debated by the General Assembly.

The 'Project on the Future' includes studies and conferences on two broad themes: (a) policy choices related to the creation of a new international economic order, and (b) the meaning of physical limits and supply constraints in energy and natural resources. A

INTERNATIONAL ORGANIZATIONS

United Nations (Other Bodies)

major project on Technology, Domestic Distribution and North-South Relations is to prepare a new model of economic growth relevant to the social and economic circumstances of the developing countries. Conferences have been organized dealing with aspects of energy, including two on small-scale resources and two on heavy crude and tar sands.

PUBLICATIONS

UNITAR News (annually).
Important for the Future (quarterly).
UNITAR Review on World Issues (quarterly).
Over 130 titles in English and some in Arabic, French, Russian and Spanish.

United Nations Observer Mission and Peace-keeping Forces in the Middle East

Address: Office of the Under-Secretaries-General for Special Political Affairs, United Nations Plaza, New York, NY 10017, USA.

United Nations peace-keeping operations have been conceived as instruments of conflict control. Each operation has been established with a specific mandate. The UN has used these operations, with the consent of the parties involved in various conflicts, to maintain peaceful conditions, without prejudice to the parties, in order to facilitate the search for political settlements through peaceful means such as mediation and the good offices of the Secretary-General. United Nations peace-keeping operations fall into two categories: peace-keeping forces and observer missions.

Peace-keeping forces are composed of contingents of armed troops made available by member states. These forces assist in preventing the recurrence of fighting, restoring and maintaining law and order, and promoting a return to normal conditions. To this end, peace-keeping forces are authorized as necessary to undertake negotiations, persuasion, observation and fact-finding. They run patrols and interpose physically between the opposing parties. They must at all times maintain complete impartiality and avoid any action that might affect the claims or positions of the parties. Peace-keeping forces are armed but are permitted to use their weapons only in self-defence.

Military observer missions are composed of unarmed officers made available, on the Secretary-General's request, by member states. A mission's function is to observe and report to the Secretary-General (who in turn informs the UN Security Council) on the maintenance of a cease-fire, to investigate violations and to do what it can to improve the situation.

UNITED NATIONS TRUCE SUPERVISION ORGANIZATION – UNTSO

Headquarters: Government House, Jerusalem.

Set up in 1948 to supervise the truce called for by the Security Council in Palestine. The authorized strength of UNTSO in 1985 was 298 military observers from 17 countries.

Chief of Staff: Lt-Gen. E. A. ERSKINE (Ghana).

ACTIVITIES

UNTSO was established initially to supervise the truce called by the Security Council in May 1948 and has assisted in the application of the 1949 Armistice Agreements. Its activities have changed over the years in response to the development of affairs in the Middle East and in accordance with the relevant resolutions of the Security Council.

UNTSO observers assist the UN peace-keeping forces in the Middle East (see below), UNIFIL as a separate group and UNDOF as an integral part of the force. After the expiry of the mandate of UNEF (United Nations Emergency Force) on 24 July 1979, UNTSO established Observer Group Egypt to maintain a number of outposts in the Sinai.

In September 1982 the military observers assigned to the Israel-Lebanon Mixed Armistice Commission and 40 additional observers formed the Observer Group Beirut to monitor the situation in and around Beirut.

FINANCE

UNTSO expenditures are covered by the regular budget of the United Nations. For the biennial period 1984–85, a sum of US $42,786,900 was appropriated by the General Assembly.

UNITED NATIONS DISENGAGEMENT OBSERVER FORCE – UNDOF

Headquarters: Damascus, Syria.

Established for an initial period of six months by a Security Council resolution in May 1974, following the signature in Geneva of a disengagement agreement between Syrian and Israeli forces. The mandate has since been extended by successive resolutions. In May 1985 the Force comprised 1,323 troops from Austria, Canada, Finland and Poland, and eight military observers detailed from UNTSO.

Commander: Maj.-Gen. CARL-GUSTAF STAHL (Sweden).

ACTIVITIES

The initial task of the Force was to take over territory evacuated in stages by the Israeli troops, in accordance with the disengagement agreement, to hand over territory to Syrian troops, and to establish an area of separation.

UNDOF continues to man the area of separation, from which Syrian and Israeli forces are excluded; it carries out inspections of the areas of limited armaments and forces, and it uses its best efforts to maintain the ceasefire. The area of separation has been placed under Syrian civil administration.

FINANCE

The General Assembly appropriated $17.9m. for UNDOF for the period from 1 December 1984 to 31 May 1985. In addition to this appropriation, it authorized the Secretary-General to enter into commitments at a rate not to exceed $2.9m. per month for the period from 1 June to 30 November 1985.

UNITED NATIONS INTERIM FORCE IN LEBANON – UNIFIL

Headquarters: Naqoura, Lebanon.

Set up in March 1978 by Security Council resolution, for a six-month period, subsequently extended by successive resolutions. In May 1985 the Force comprised 5,822 troops from 10 countries. A group of 75 UNTSO military observers assists UNIFIL in the performance of its tasks. They form the Observer Group, Lebanon.

Commander: Maj.-Gen. GUSTAV HAGGLUND (Finland).

ACTIVITIES

The functions of the force are to confirm the withdrawal of Israeli forces, to restore international peace and security and to assist the Government of Lebanon in ensuring the return of its effective authority in southern Lebanon. In June 1982, after the invasion of Lebanon by Israel, UNIFIL was also given the interim task of extending protection and humanitarian assistance to the population of the area.

FINANCE

The General Assembly authorized the Secretary-General to enter into commitments for UNIFIL at a rate not to exceed $11.7m. per month for the period from 19 April to 18 December 1985.

INTERNATIONAL ORGANIZATIONS   United Nations (Other Bodies)

UNITED NATIONS PEACE-KEEPING FORCE IN CYPRUS — UNFICYP

Headquarters: Nicosia, Cyprus.
Set up in March 1964 by Security Council resolution, for a three-month period, subsequently extended by successive resolutions. In May 1985 the Force comprised 2,301 military personnel from seven countries, and 36 police.
Special Representative of the Secretary-General: JAMES HOLGER (Chile) (acting).
Commander: Maj.-Gen. GÜNTHER G. GREINDL (Austria).

ACTIVITIES

The purpose of the Force has been to keep the peace between the Greek and Turkish Cypriot communities pending a resolution of outstanding issues between them, to help maintain law and order, and to promote a return to normal conditions. UNFICYP now also performs functions in relation to the supervision of the ceasefire between the armed forces of Turkey and Cyprus, and in providing humanitarian assistance to refugees and to villages isolated behind military lines. The United Nations High Commissioner for Refugees (see p. 205) acts as co-ordinator of UN humanitarian assistance for Cyprus.

FINANCE

The estimated cost to the United Nations for maintaining the Force during the period from 16 December 1984 to 15 June 1985 was US $13.9m., to be covered entirely by voluntary contributions; additional costs of some $36.2m. were to be absorbed by the countries contributing troops. In February 1985 the UN Secretary-General appealed for an increase in voluntary contributions to meet an accumulated deficit of $122m.

United Nations Relief and Works Agency for Palestine Refugees in the Near East — UNRWA

Addresses: (Vienna): POB 700, 1400 Vienna, Austria; (Amman): POB 484, Amman, Jordan.
Telephone (Vienna): (0222) 26 310.
Telex (Vienna): 135310.

UNRWA began operations in 1950 to provide relief, health, education and welfare services for Palestine refugees in the Near East.

Organization
(October 1986)

UNRWA employs an international staff of 134 and 17,300 local staff, mainly Palestine refugees. The Commissioner-General is assisted by an Advisory Commission consisting of representatives of the governments of:

Belgium	Jordan	Turkey
Egypt	Lebanon	United Kingdom
France	Syria	USA
Japan		

Commissioner-General: GIORGIO GIACOMELLI (Italy).

REGIONAL OFFICES

Gaza Strip: UNRWA Field Office, POB 61, Gaza.
Jordan: UNRWA Field Office, POB 484, Amman.
West Bank: UNRWA Field Office, POB 19149, Jerusalem.
Lebanon: UNRWA Field Office, POB 947, Beirut.
Syria: UNRWA Field Office, POB 4313, Damascus.
Egypt: UNRWA Liaison Office, 2 Dar-esh-Shifa, Garden City, POB 277, Cairo.
United States: UNRWA Liaison Office, Room DC 2-0550, United Nations, New York, NY 10017.

Activities

SERVICES FOR PALESTINE REFUGEES

Since 1950, UNRWA has provided relief, health and education services for the needy among the Palestine refugees in Lebanon, Syria, Jordan, the West Bank and the Gaza Strip. For UNRWA's purposes, a Palestine refugee is one whose normal residence was in Palestine for a minimum of two years before the 1948 conflict and who, as a result of the Arab-Israeli hostilities, lost his home and means of livelihood. To be eligible for assistance, a refugee must reside in one of the 'host' countries in which UNRWA operates and be in need. A refugee's children and grandchildren who fulfil certain criteria are also eligible for UNRWA assistance. At 30 June 1986, the registered refugee population numbered 2,145,794 (about half the estimated total number of Palestinians), living in five areas administered by four governments. There were 749,235 registered refugees (plus about 40,000 unregistered) living in 61 camps, while the remaining refugees have settled in the towns and villages already existing.

UNRWA's activities fall into the categories of education and training; health services; and relief and welfare services.

Education (under the technical supervision of UNESCO) took up about 67% of UNRWA's budget in 1986. In the 1985/86 school year there were 349,224 pupils in 635 UNRWA schools (82 schools in Lebanon, 115 in Syria, 195 in Jordan, 98 on the West Bank and 145 in the Gaza Strip) and 9,930 teachers. At three-quarters of the schools, morning and afternoon shifts are held in order to accommodate more pupils. UNRWA also runs eight vocational and teacher-training centres with 5,002 places. UNRWA awarded 360 scholarships for study at Arab universities in 1985/86.

Health services accounted for 22% of UNRWA expenditure in 1986. There are 2,997 medical staff posts, 98 health units, 75 specialist clinics and 85 mother and child health clinics; over 4.8m. visits by patients are made each year to UNRWA medical units. UNRWA also runs a supplementary feeding programme, mainly for children, to combat malnutrition: there are 94 feeding centres. Technical supervision for the health programme is provided by WHO.

Relief services (which accounted for 11% of UNRWA expenditure in 1986) comprise the distribution of food rations, the provision of emergency shelter and the organization of welfare programmes for about 109,000 of the poorest refugees.

AID TO DISPLACED PERSONS

After the renewal of Arab-Israeli hostilities in the Middle East in June 1967, hundreds of thousands of people fled from the fighting and Israeli-occupied areas to east Jordan, Syria and Egypt. UNRWA provided emergency relief for displaced refugees and was additionally empowered by a UN General Assembly resolution to provide 'humanitarian assistance, as far as practicable, on an emergency basis and as a temporary measure' for those persons other than Palestine refugees who were newly displaced and in urgent need. In practice, UNRWA has lacked the funds to aid the other displaced persons and the main burden of supporting them has fallen on the Arab governments concerned. The Agency, as requested by the Government of Jordan in 1967 and on that Government's behalf, distributes rations to displaced persons in Jordan who are not registered refugees of 1948.

With the agreement of the Israeli Government, UNRWA has continued to provide assistance for registered refugees living in the Israeli-occupied territories of the West Bank and the Gaza Strip.

RECENT EMERGENCIES

Beginning with the 1975–1976 civil war, Palestine refugees and UNRWA's services have been adversely affected by the continuing disturbances in Lebanon. UNRWA launched an emergency relief programme following the Israeli invasion of the south in March 1978, which caused the temporary evacuation of most of the 60,000 refugees living there and the flight of 17,000 refugees in other parts of the country. While most of the refugees returned to their home towns and villages by the end of April 1978, the devastated economy of the south left them in continued need of extra-budgetary relief supplies and services.

In 1979 UNRWA again launched an emergency appeal for aid to southern Lebanon because of continuing Israeli and other attacks. In 1981 civil strife and Israeli attacks disrupted UNRWA activities. The education programme was hardest hit, with up to 50 school days lost in some schools during the 1980/81 school year.

The Israeli invasion of June 1982 meant that over 150,000 persons were displaced, necessitating an emergency relief programme costing US $52m. Many UNRWA schools, clinics and offices were destroyed or damaged. The emergency programme was extended to spring 1984 and an appeal for $13m. was made to provide funds for reconstruction of UNRWA facilities, refugee shelters and refugee camp infrastructure.

During the first half of 1985 UNRWA organized two emergency relief operations in Lebanon, providing food and medical care for 40,000 displaced refugees during factional fighting in the Sidon area in March and April, and emergency assistance to 35,000 displaced refugees when refugee camps in Beirut were besieged in May and June. Two similar emergency operations were also mounted in the first half of 1986. UNRWA also provides cash grants to refugees whose homes have been damaged or destroyed in the fighting.

FINANCE

For the most part, UNRWA's income is made up of voluntary contributions, almost entirely from governments, the remainder being provided by voluntary agencies, business corporations and private sources. Much of UNRWA's budget is used to pay its educational and medical staff. However, the cost of 125 international staff is funded by the UN, WHO and UNESCO, and a further nine international staff are paid from UNRWA's budget.

Contributions dropped from $190.6m. in 1980 to about $174m. in 1985, despite UNRWA's rising expenses. Planned expenditure for 1985 had to be cut by $43m., through deferral of pay and cost-of-living increases to 12,000 field staff, a cut in overhead costs and supplies and cuts in construction, maintenance and the purchase of new equipment.

STATISTICS

Refugees Registered with UNRWA (30 June 1986)

	Refugees in camps	Refugees not in camps	Total registered refugees
Jordan	204,221	618,403	822,624*
West Bank	92,445	272,870	365,315
Gaza Strip	240,046	195,432	435,478
Lebanon	140,037	131,387	271,424
Syria	72,486	178,467	250,953
Total	749,235	1,396,559	2,145,794

* Including refugees displaced from the West Bank and the Gaza Strip in 1967. These totalled 365,131 at 30 June 1986.

Displaced Persons

Apart from the Palestine refugees of 1948 who are registered with UNRWA and who are UNRWA's main concern (see table above), considerable numbers of people have, since 1967, been displaced within the UNRWA areas of operations, and others have had to leave these areas. According to government estimates, there were 210,000 displaced persons in Jordan and 125,000 in Syria in June 1986.

UNRWA Schools (1985/86)

	Number of schools	Number of teachers	Number of pupils
Jordan	195	3,683	136,202
West Bank	98	1,272	40,221
Gaza Strip	145	2,352	86,928
Lebanon	82	1,105	33,959
Syria	115	1,518	51,914
Total	635	9,930	349,224

PUBLICATIONS

Annual Report of the Commissioner-General of UNRWA.

UNRWA—a Survey of United Nations Assistance to Palestine Refugees (every 2 years).

Palestine Refugees Today—the UNRWA Newsletter (quarterly).

UNRWA Report (quarterly).

A Brief History: 1950–82.

UNRWA: Past, Present and Future. Catalogues of publications and audio-visual materials.

United Nations Research Institute for Social Development — UNRISD

Address: Palais des Nations, 1211 Geneva 10, Switzerland.
Telephone: (022) 988400.
Telex: 28 96 96.

The Institute was established in 1964 as an autonomous UN activity to conduct research into problems and policies of social development and economic development during different phases of economic growth.

Organization
(October 1986)

BOARD
The Board, which supervises the activities of the Institute, includes representatives of the Secretary-General of UN, of two of the four Specialized Agencies directly concerned (ILO, UNESCO, FAO, WHO) in rotation, and of the UN regional economic commissions, as well as the Institute's Director and seven individuals nominated by the Commission for Social Development and elected by the Economic and Social Council.
Chairman: P. M. HENRY.

PROFESSIONAL STAFF
There are seven full-time professional researchers and a number of consultants and collaborators, particularly in the developing countries.
Director: E. OTEIZA (Argentina).

Activities

The Institute focuses its research on the social implications of global questions that are a major concern of the United Nations and of governments and on what can be done, locally and nationally and by the international community, to speed the achievement of development goals. It believes, however, that this can be accomplished most effectively by first identifying and analysing the impact on different social groups of dominant social processes at the national and local levels. What must be analysed are the social structures and the social forces associated with these processes, the practical policy alternatives in each situation and the social forces that might sustain these alternatives. Studies need to be carried out in a wide variety of ecological and institutional settings. Only then can analyses and generalizations be attempted at inter-country levels. The task is further complicated by the fact that there are seldom simple relationships among different social systems and subsystems. UNRISD's research programme comprises the following long-term studies:

Food and food systems: research aiming at the improvement of food security; main projects in India and Mexico, also in the People's Republic of China, Chile and Nicaragua; and in the Ivory Coast, Senegal and Burkina Faso, with special emphasis on the changes in women's roles and conditions that accompany agricultural modernization.

People's participation in development: studies in Latin American and Asian people's movements, e.g. the success or otherwise of peasants' and workers' organizations.

Refugee settlements: case studies in Pakistan and Somalia, with possible extension to other countries, of the sociological factors influencing the settlement and integration of refugees.

Improvement of development statistics: includes a field study in southern India to obtain and analyse data at the local level on the living conditions of the people; other studies aim to improve the collection of information on children (e.g. infant mortality, nutrition, and the extent of primary education) and the reliability of conclusions drawn from statistical data.

BUDGET
Estimated income and expenditure for 1985 was US $1.5m.

PUBLICATIONS
Research Notes (annually).
List of Publications (annually).

World Food Council — WFC

Address: Via delle Terme di Caracalla, 00100 Rome, Italy.
Telephone: 57971.
Telex: 610181.

The World Food Council was created in December 1974 by the UN General Assembly, upon the specific recommendation of the World Food Conference held in November 1974. It aims to stimulate governments and the international community to adopt the necessary policies and programmes required to alleviate world hunger and improve the global food system.

Organization
(October 1986)

COUNCIL
The Council meets annually and consists of ministers representing 36 member states, elected by the UN General Assembly: one-third retire each year. Membership is drawn from regional groups in the following proportions: nine from Africa, eight from Asia, seven from Latin America, four from the socialist states of Eastern Europe, and eight from Western Europe and North America.

SECRETARIAT
With the help of various multilateral and bilateral organizations and research institutions, the Secretariat reviews the current world food situation and recommends to the Council appropriate policy changes designed to improve food production and nutritional well-being, particularly in the developing countries.
Executive Director: GERALD I. TRANT (Canada).

Activities

The Council reviews problems and recommends actions; it co-ordinates the activities of the UN in relation to food problems, and co-operates with regional bodies to formulate and follow up the approved policies.

The Council concentrates on promoting the international political consensus necessary (1) to increase food production in the developing countries, most notably in sub-Saharan Africa; (2) to improve national and international food security measures through policies that link food production, agricultural trade and nutritional concerns; (3) to assure the greater effectiveness of food aid; and (4) to reduce barriers to trade in agricultural commodities between developed and developing countries.

At the 10th session of the WFC in June 1984, ministers reviewed the period 1974–84, noting that, in spite of an overall increase in per caput world food production during the decade, the risks of food shortages were now greater for many low-income developing countries, the severest problems being faced by Africa south of the Sahara, in terms both of inadequate levels of food production and of the relative proportion of hungry and malnourished people to total population. Despite the expansion of the international food trade during the decade, the stability and predictability of agricultural markets had not improved; import restrictions and export subsidy programmes adopted by the developed countries resulted in a destabilizing effect on international markets and the food security of developing countries, while there was a lack of political will to conclude improved international commodity agreements, especially on cereals, aimed at stabilizing trade flows and world market prices. Although resource flows to the food and agriculture sector through the United Nations system increased by some 13.7% per annum in real terms during the period 1974–82, the volume of assistance remained short of agreed objectives, and the rate of increase of commitments was falling. The Executive Director recommended an increase of at least US $5,000m. in external resources over the five-year period beginning in 1986, in equal proportions for programme food aid and technical and capital assistance.

FOOD PRODUCTION

In 1979 a system of 'food strategies' was launched, whereby individual developing countries, in collaboration with a particular developed country or institution, were to prepare overall food plans so as to enable a more co-ordinated approach and the best use of aid: strategies would include consideration of such issues as the stimulation of production by price incentives; improvement of marketing and distribution infrastructure; the effect of exchange rates on production; research on higher-yielding crops; improved supply of fertilizers and pesticides; land-holding reforms; and the supply of credit to small farmers. By 1982 50 developing countries had adopted such a scheme, with assistance from eight developed countries, the World Bank, FAO, ILO, IFAD, UNDP, the African Development Bank and the Inter-American Development Bank.

At the 1984 Council meeting ministers agreed to give priority to African food problems and to undertake a review of the implementation of national food sector plans and policies in Africa. The agreed work programme also included reviews of the effectiveness of systems whereby food is delivered to the poor; of resources requirements and priorities; and of the progress made in GATT, UNCTAD and other institutions pertaining to the liberalization of international trade.

FOOD SECURITY

In July 1980 a new Food Aid Convention entered into force, increasing the guaranteed minimum level of food aid from grain-exporting countries to developing countries in need from 4.2 to 7.6m. tons a year, which was, however, still short of the 10m. minimum recommended by the WFC. The 1985 Council called for a clearer distinction between food aid and the disposal of highly subsidized surpluses, which has disruptive effects on markets and production incentives; it criticized the 'dumping' of surplus cereals by industrialized countries.

WFC sponsored the creation of a food credit facility, adopted by the International Monetary Fund in 1981 for an initial period of four years, to help developing countries finance food imports when crops fail or import prices suddenly rise. By June 1985 eight drawings by six countries, amounting to US $1,000m., had been made from the facility.

At the 1986 Council meeting, ministers discussed the international agricultural problems caused by the farm policies of the major grain exporters, such as the European Community and the USA, which subsidize both the production and export of major cereal crops. These subsidies have not only proved costly to taxpayers, but also create a major disincentive to domestic cereal producers in the developing countries because of the artificially low price of internationally-traded cereals.

World Food Programme—WFP

Address: Via delle Terme di Caracalla, 00100 Rome, Italy.
Telex: 680096.

WFP, the food aid arm of the United Nations, became operational in 1963. It aims to stimulate economic and social development through food aid and to provide emergency relief.

Organization
(October 1986)

COMMITTEE ON FOOD AID POLICIES AND PROGRAMMES (CFA)

The Committee has 30 members: 15 elected by ECOSOC (see p. 19) and 15 by FAO.

SECRETARIAT

Executive Director: JAMES INGRAM (Australia).

Activities

Member governments make voluntary contributions of commodities, cash, and services (particularly shipping) to WFP, which uses the food to support economic and social development projects in the developing countries. The food is supplied, for example, as an incentive in development self-help schemes, as part wages in labour-intensive projects of many kinds, particularly in the rural economy, but also in the industrial field, and in support of institutional feeding schemes where the emphasis is mainly on enabling the beneficiaries to have an adequate and balanced diet. One of the criteria for WFP aid to projects is that the recipient country can continue them after the aid has ceased. Priority is given to low-income, food-deficit countries and to vulnerable groups such as pregnant women and children.

WFP also provides emergency food aid for victims of natural and man-made disasters, chiefly from the International Emergency Food Reserve, which it manages; by 30 June 1986 contributions worth US $1,199.7m. had been made available to the Programme through the Reserve.

By the end of June 1986, 1,373 projects in 120 countries had been approved since the beginning of the Programme's operations, at a total cost to WFP of US $7,586.3m. In addition, 862 emergency operations had been undertaken in 96 countries at a total cost to the Programme of US $1,804.3m.

In 1985 523 projects, valued at US $5,012.6m., were operational in 93 countries. By the end of the year, pledges in food aid and cash for the two years 1985–86 amounted to $1,002.7m. or 74% of the target. A total of $642m. was committed to development projects in 1985; of this, over 85% was for low-income, food-deficit countries. Of the 55 projects approved in 1985, 77% in value terms were in the field of economic infrastructures, agricultural and rural development; the remaining 23% were for feeding of vulnerable groups, primary schools and institutional training.

In 1985 WFP committed $225.17m. to provide 733,023 tons of emergency food aid to an estimated 11m. people. Over two-thirds of this was for refugees, mainly in Pakistan and Somalia; 27% was for emergencies caused by drought and 11% was for emergency operations caused by natural disasters.

INTERNATIONAL ORGANIZATIONS   *United Nations (Membership)*

Membership of the United Nations and its Specialized Agencies

	UN	IBRD	IDA	IFC	IMF	FAO	IFAD[7]	GATT	IMO[5]	ICAO	ILO[6]	ITU[7]	UNESCO[8]	UNIDO	UPU[9]	WHO[10]	WMO[11]	WIPO
Afghanistan	x	x	x	x	x	x	x			x	x	x	x	x	x	x	x	
Albania	x					x						x	x			x	x	x
Algeria[1]	x	x	x		x	x	x	x	x	x	x	x	x	x	x	x	x	x
Angola[1]	x					x	x	x	x	x	x	x	x	x	x	x	x	x
Antigua and Barbuda	x	x			x	x	x		x	x	x					x		
Argentina	x	x	x	x	x	x	x	x	x	x	x	x	x	x	x	x	x	x
Australia	x	x	x	x	x	x	x	x	x	x	x	x	x	x	x	x	x	x
Austria	x	x	x	x	x	x	x	x	x	x	x	x	x	x	x	x	x	x
Bahamas[1]	x	x			x	x			x	x	x	x	x			x	x	x
Bahrain[1]	x	x			x	x			x	x	x	x	x		x	x	x	
Bangladesh	x	x	x	x	x	x	x	x	x	x	x	x	x	x	x	x	x	x
Barbados	x	x			x	x	x		x	x	x	x	x		x	x	x	x
Belgium	x	x	x	x	x	x	x	x	x	x	x	x	x	x	x	x	x	x
Belize[1]	x	x	x	x	x	x			x		x		x		x	x		
Benin	x	x	x		x	x	x	x		x	x	x	x	x	x	x	x	x
Bhutan	x	x	x		x	x	x					x	x	x	x	x		
Bolivia	x	x	x	x	x	x	x			x	x	x	x	x	x	x	x	
Botswana[1]	x	x	x	x	x	x	x	x		x	x	x	x	x	x	x	x	
Brazil	x	x	x	x	x	x	x		x	x	x	x	x	x	x	x	x	x
Brunei	x								x	x	x				x	x	x	
Bulgaria	x					x			x	x	x	x	x	x	x	x	x	x
Burkina Faso	x	x	x	x	x	x	x	x		x	x	x	x	x	x	x	x	x
Burma	x	x	x	x	x	x		x	x	x	x	x	x		x	x	x	
Burundi	x	x	x	x	x	x	x	x		x		x	x	x	x	x	x	x
Byelorussian SSR	x									x	x	x	x	x	x	x	x	x
Cameroon	x	x	x	x	x	x	x	x	x	x	x	x	x	x	x	x	x	x
Canada	x	x	x	x	x	x	x	x	x	x	x	x	x	x	x	x	x	x
Cape Verde[1]	x	x	x		x	x	x		x	x	x	x	x	x	x	x	x	
Central African Republic	x	x	x		x	x	x	x		x	x	x	x	x	x	x	x	x
Chad	x	x	x		x	x	x	x		x	x	x	x		x	x	x	
Chile	x	x	x	x	x	x	x	x	x	x	x	x	x	x	x	x	x	x
China, People's Republic	x	x	x	x	x	x	x		x	x	x	x	x	x	x	x	x	x
Colombia	x	x	x	x	x	x	x		x	x	x	x	x	x	x	x	x	x
Comoros	x	x	x		x	x	x			x	x	x	x	x	x	x	x	
Congo	x	x	x	x	x	x	x	x		x	x	x	x	x	x	x	x	x
Costa Rica	x	x	x	x	x	x	x		x	x	x	x	x		x	x	x	x
Cuba	x					x		x	x	x	x	x	x	x	x	x	x	x
Cyprus	x	x	x	x	x	x	x	x	x	x	x	x	x	x	x	x	x	x
Czechoslovakia	x					x		x	x	x	x	x	x	x	x	x	x	x
Denmark	x	x	x	x	x	x	x	x	x	x	x	x	x	x	x	x	x	x
Djibouti	x	x	x	x	x	x	x			x	x	x			x	x	x	
Dominica[1]	x	x	x	x	x	x			x		x		x	x	x	x		
Dominican Republic	x	x	x	x	x	x	x		x	x	x	x	x	x	x	x	x	x
Ecuador	x	x	x	x	x	x	x		x	x	x	x	x	x	x	x	x	x
Egypt	x	x	x	x	x	x	x	x	x	x	x	x	x	x	x	x	x	x
El Salvador	x	x	x	x	x	x			x	x	x	x	x	x	x	x	x	x
Equatorial Guinea[1]	x	x	x		x	x	x			x	x	x	x	x	x	x		
Ethiopia	x	x	x	x	x	x	x		x	x	x	x	x	x	x	x	x	
Fiji[1]	x	x	x	x	x	x	x		x	x	x	x	x	x	x	x		x
Finland	x	x	x	x	x	x	x	x	x	x	x	x	x	x	x	x	x	x
France	x	x	x	x	x	x	x	x	x	x	x	x	x	x	x	x	x	x
Gabon	x	x	x	x	x	x	x	x		x	x	x	x	x	x	x	x	x
The Gambia	x	x	x	x	x	x	x	x		x		x			x	x	x	
German Democratic Republic	x								x		x	x	x	x	x	x	x	x
Germany, Federal Republic	x	x	x	x	x	x	x	x	x	x	x	x	x	x	x	x	x	x
Ghana	x	x	x	x	x	x	x	x	x	x	x	x	x	x	x	x	x	x
Greece	x	x	x	x	x	x	x	x	x	x	x	x	x	x	x	x	x	x
Grenada[1]	x	x	x		x	x			x		x				x	x	x	
Guatemala	x	x	x	x	x	x	x		x	x	x	x	x	x	x	x	x	x
Guinea	x	x	x	x	x	x	x			x	x	x	x	x	x	x	x	x
Guinea-Bissau[1]	x	x	x		x	x	x		x	x	x	x	x	x	x	x	x	
Guyana	x	x	x	x	x	x	x	x	x	x	x	x	x	x	x	x	x	
Haiti	x	x	x	x	x	x	x	x		x	x	x	x	x	x	x		x
Honduras	x	x	x	x	x	x	x		x	x	x	x	x		x	x	x	x
Hungary	x	x	x	x	x	x		x	x	x	x	x	x	x	x	x	x	x
Iceland	x	x	x	x	x	x		x	x	x	x	x	x		x	x	x	
India	x	x	x	x	x	x	x	x	x	x	x	x	x	x	x	x	x	x

continued overleaf

INTERNATIONAL ORGANIZATIONS — United Nations (Membership)

	UN	IBRD	IDA	IFC	IMF	FAO	IFAD[4]	GATT	IMO[5]	ICAO	ILO[6]	ITU[7]	UNESCO[8]	UNIDO	UPU[9]	WHO[10]	WMO[11]	WIPO
Indonesia	x	x	x	x	x	x	x	x	x	x	x	x	x	x	x	x	x	x
Iran	x	x	x	x	x	x	x		x	x	x	x	x	x	x	x	x	
Iraq	x	x	x	x	x	x	x		x	x	x	x	x	x	x	x	x	x
Ireland	x	x	x	x	x	x	x	x	x	x	x	x	x	x	x	x	x	x
Israel	x	x	x	x	x	x		x	x	x	x	x	x	x	x	x	x	x
Italy	x	x	x	x	x	x	x	x	x	x	x	x	x	x	x	x	x	x
Ivory Coast	x	x	x	x	x	x	x	x	x	x	x	x	x	x	x	x	x	x
Jamaica	x	x		x	x	x	x		x	x	x	x	x	x	x	x	x	x
Japan	x	x	x	x	x	x	x	x	x	x	x	x	x	x	x	x	x	x
Jordan	x	x	x	x	x	x	x		x	x	x	x	x	x	x	x	x	x
Kampuchea[1]	x	x	x	x		x				x	x	x	x		x	x	x	
Kenya	x	x	x	x	x	x	x	x	x	x	x	x	x	x	x	x	x	x
Kiribati[1]		x							x	x					x	x		
Korea, Democratic People's Republic						x			x	x		x	x	x	x	x	x	x
Korea, Republic		x	x	x	x	x			x	x		x	x	x	x	x	x	x
Kuwait	x	x	x	x	x	x	x	x	x	x		x	x	x	x	x	x	x
Laos	x	x	x		x	x				x	x	x	x	x	x	x	x	
Lebanon	x	x	x	x	x	x			x	x	x	x	x	x	x	x	x	x
Lesotho[1]	x	x	x	x	x	x	x		x	x	x	x	x	x	x	x	x	
Liberia	x	x	x	x	x	x		x	x	x	x	x	x	x	x	x	x	
Libya	x	x	x	x	x	x	x		x	x	x	x	x	x	x	x	x	x
Liechtenstein												x		x				x
Luxembourg	x	x	x	x	x	x	x	x	x	x	x	x	x	x	x	x	x	x
Madagascar	x	x	x	x	x	x	x	x	x	x	x	x	x	x	x	x	x	x
Malawi	x	x	x	x	x	x	x	x	x	x	x	x	x	x	x	x	x	x
Malaysia	x	x	x	x	x	x		x	x	x	x	x	x	x	x	x	x	
Maldives[1]	x	x	x		x	x			x	x		x	x		x	x	x	x
Mali[1]	x	x	x	x	x	x	x		x	x	x	x	x	x	x	x	x	
Malta	x	x			x	x	x		x	x	x	x	x	x	x	x	x	x
Mauritania	x	x	x	x	x	x	x		x	x	x	x	x	x	x	x	x	
Mauritius	x	x	x	x	x	x	x	x	x	x	x	x	x	x	x	x	x	x
Mexico	x	x		x	x	x	x		x	x	x	x	x	x	x	x	x	x
Monaco									x			x	x		x	x	x	x
Mongolia	x					x					x	x	x	x	x	x	x	x
Morocco	x	x	x	x	x	x	x		x	x	x	x	x	x	x	x	x	x
Mozambique[1]	x	x	x	x	x	x	x		x	x	x	x	x	x	x	x	x	
Nauru									x			x			x			
Nepal	x	x	x	x	x	x			x	x	x	x	x	x	x	x	x	
Netherlands	x	x	x	x	x	x	x	x	x	x	x	x	x	x	x	x	x	x
New Zealand	x	x	x	x	x	x		x	x	x	x	x	x	x	x	x	x	x
Nicaragua	x	x	x	x	x	x	x	x	x	x	x	x	x	x	x	x	x	x
Niger	x	x	x	x	x	x	x	x	x	x	x	x	x	x	x	x	x	x
Nigeria	x	x	x	x	x	x	x	x	x	x	x	x	x	x	x	x	x	
Norway	x	x	x	x	x	x	x	x	x	x	x	x	x	x	x	x	x	x
Oman	x	x	x	x	x	x			x	x		x	x	x	x	x	x	
Pakistan	x	x	x	x	x	x	x	x	x	x	x	x	x	x	x	x	x	x
Panama	x	x	x	x	x	x	x		x	x	x	x	x	x	x	x	x	x
Papua New Guinea[1]	x	x	x	x	x	x			x	x	x	x	x		x	x	x	
Paraguay	x	x	x	x	x	x	x			x	x	x	x	x	x	x	x	
Peru	x	x	x	x	x	x	x		x	x	x	x	x	x	x	x	x	x
Philippines	x	x	x	x	x	x	x	x	x	x	x	x	x	x	x	x	x	x
Poland	x	x				x		x	x	x	x	x	x	x	x	x	x	x
Portugal	x	x		x	x	x		x	x	x	x	x	x	x	x	x	x	x
Qatar[1]	x	x			x	x	x		x	x		x	x	x	x	x	x	x
Romania	x	x			x	x		x	x	x	x	x	x	x	x	x	x	x
Rwanda	x	x	x	x	x	x	x			x	x	x	x	x	x	x	x	x
Saint Christopher and Nevis	x	x			x	x	x								x	x		
Saint Lucia[1]	x	x	x	x		x	x		x	x				x	x	x	x	
Saint Vincent and the Grenadines[1]	x				x	x			x	x					x	x		
San Marino													x	x	x	x		
São Tomé and Príncipe[1]	x	x	x		x	x	x			x	x	x	x		x	x	x	
Saudi Arabia	x	x	x	x	x	x	x		x	x	x	x	x	x	x	x	x	x
Senegal	x	x	x	x	x	x	x	x	x	x	x	x	x	x	x	x	x	x
Seychelles[1]	x	x	x		x	x			x	x		x	x	x	x	x	x	
Sierra Leone	x	x	x	x	x	x	x	x	x	x	x	x	x	x	x	x	x	
Singapore	x	x		x	x			x	x	x	x	x			x	x	x	
Solomon Islands[1]	x	x	x	x	x	x			x	x					x	x	x	x
Somalia	x	x	x	x	x	x	x		x	x	x	x	x	x	x	x	x	x
South Africa[2]	x	x	x	x	x			x	x	x		x			x	x	x	x
Spain	x	x	x	x	x	x	x	x	x	x	x	x	x	x	x	x	x	x
Sri Lanka	x	x	x	x	x	x	x	x	x	x	x	x	x	x	x	x	x	x
Sudan	x	x	x	x	x	x	x		x	x	x	x	x	x	x	x	x	x

continued opposite

INTERNATIONAL ORGANIZATIONS

United Nations (Membership)

	UN	IBRD	IDA	IFC	IMF	FAO	IFAD[4]	GATT	IMO[5]	ICAO	ILO[6]	ITU[7]	UNESCO[8]	UNIDO	UPU[9]	WHO[10]	WMO[11]	WIPO
Suriname	x	x			x	x		x	x	x	x		x	x	x	x	x	x
Swaziland[1]	x	x	x	x	x	x	x	x		x	x	x			x	x		
Sweden	x	x	x	x	x	x	x	x	x	x	x	x	x	x	x	x	x	x
Switzerland					x	x	x	x	x	x	x	x	x	x	x	x	x	x
Syria	x	x	x	x	x	x	x		x	x	x	x	x	x	x	x	x	
Tanzania	x	x	x	x	x	x	x	x	x	x	x	x	x	x	x	x	x	x
Thailand	x	x	x	x	x	x	x	x	x	x	x	x	x	x	x	x	x	
Togo	x	x	x	x	x	x	x	x	x	x	x	x	x	x	x	x	x	x
Tonga[1]		x			x	x	x	x		x			x	x		x	x	
Trinidad and Tobago	x	x	x	x	x	x		x	x	x	x	x	x	x	x	x	x	
Tunisia[3]	x	x	x	x	x	x	x	x	x	x	x	x	x	x	x	x	x	x
Turkey	x	x	x	x	x	x	x	x	x	x	x	x	x	x	x	x	x	x
Tuvalu[1]								x								x		
Uganda	x	x	x	x	x	x	x			x	x	x	x	x	x	x	x	x
Ukrainian SSR	x									x	x	x	x	x	x	x	x	x
USSR	x								x	x	x	x	x	x	x	x	x	x
United Arab Emirates[1]	x	x	x	x	x	x	x	x	x	x	x	x	x	x	x	x		x
United Kingdom	x	x	x	x	x	x	x	x	x	x	x	x	x	x	x	x	x	x
USA	x	x	x	x	x	x	x	x	x	x	x		x		x	x	x	x
Uruguay	x	x		x	x	x	x	x	x	x	x	x	x	x	x	x	x	x
Vanuatu	x			x	x	x			x					x	x	x		
Vatican City										x			x					x
Venezuela	x	x		x	x	x		x	x	x	x	x	x	x	x	x	x	x
Viet-Nam	x	x	x	x	x	x	x		x	x	x	x		x	x	x	x	x
Western Samoa	x	x	x	x	x	x	x									x		
Yemen Arab Republic	x	x	x	x	x	x	x			x	x	x	x	x	x	x	x	x
Yemen, People's Democratic Republic[1]	x	x	x		x	x	x	x	x	x	x	x	x	x	x	x	x	
Yugoslavia	x	x	x	x	x	x	x	x	x	x	x	x	x	x	x	x	x	x
Zaire	x	x	x	x	x	x	x	x	x	x	x	x	x	x	x	x	x	x
Zambia[1]	x	x	x	x	x	x	x			x	x	x	x	x	x	x	x	x
Zimbabwe	x	x	x	x	x	x	x			x	x	x	x	x	x	x	x	x

[1] Countries to whose territories GATT has been applied and which now, as independent states, maintain a *de facto* application of the GATT pending final decisions as to their future commercial policy.
[2] Suspended from WMO April 1975.
[3] Acceded provisionally to GATT.
[4] For a breakdown of IFAD members by category, see p. 69.
[5] Hong Kong is an associate member of IMO.
[6] Namibia (South West Africa) is a full member of ILO.
[7] Members also include British Overseas Territories, French Overseas Territories, Macau, United States Territories and Namibia (South West Africa).
[8] Namibia (South West Africa) is also a member of UNESCO.
[9] Members also include British Overseas Territories, French Overseas Territories, Macau, the Netherlands Antilles and United States Territories.
[10] The Cook Islands is a member of WHO and Namibia (South West Africa) is an associate member.
[11] Members also include British Caribbean Territories, French Polynesia, Hong Kong, the Netherlands Antilles and New Caledonia, all of which maintain their own meteorological service.

SPECIALIZED AGENCIES WITHIN THE UN SYSTEM

Food and Agriculture Organization—FAO

Address: Via delle Terme di Caracalla, 00100 Rome, Italy.
Telephone: 57971.
Telex: 610181.

FAO, the first specialized agency of the UN to be founded after World War II, was established in Quebec, Canada, in October 1945. The Organization fights malnutrition and hunger and serves as a co-ordinating agency for development programmes in the whole range of food and agriculture, including forestry and fisheries. It helps developing countries to promote educational and training facilities and institution-building.

MEMBERS
158 members: see Table on pp. 53–55.

Organization
(October 1986)

CONFERENCE
The governing body is the FAO Conference of member nations. It meets every two years, formulates policy, determines the Organization's programme and budget on a biennial basis, and elects new members. It also elects the Director-General of the Secretariat and the Independent Chairman of the Council. Every other year, FAO also holds conferences in each of its five regions (the Near East, Asia and the Pacific, Africa, Latin America and the Caribbean, and Europe).

COUNCIL
The FAO Council is composed of representatives of 49 member nations, elected by the Conference for staggered three-year terms. It is the interim governing body of FAO between sessions of the Conference. The most important standing Committees of the Council are: the Finance and Programme Committees, the Committee on Commodity Problems, the Committee on Fisheries, the Committee on Agriculture and the Committee on Forestry.

SECRETARIAT
The total number of staff at FAO headquarters at the end of 1985 was 3,459, while staff in field, regional and country offices numbered 3,492; there were also 36 associate experts at headquarters and 292 in field, regional and country offices. Work is supervised by the following Departments: Administration and Finance; General Affairs and Information; Economic and Social Policy; Agriculture; Forestry; Fisheries; and Development.

Director-General (1976–88): EDOUARD SAOUMA (Lebanon).
Deputy Director-General: DECLAN WALTON (Ireland).

REGIONAL OFFICES
Africa: UN Agency Building, North Maxwell Rd, POB 1628, Accra, Ghana; tel. 666851; telex 2139; Regional Rep. JACOB A. C. DAVIES.
Asia and the Pacific: Maliwan Mansion, Phra Atit Rd, Bangkok 2, Thailand; tel. 2817844; telex 82815; Regional Rep. SURGIT SINGH PURI.
Europe: Via delle Terme di Caracalla, 00100 Rome, Italy; tel. 57971; telex 610181; Regional Rep. ALESSANDRO BOZZINI.
Latin America and the Caribbean: Avenida Santa Maria 6700, Casilla 10095, Santiago, Chile; tel. 462061; telex 228 8056; Regional Rep. MARIO E. JALIL.
Near East: Via delle Terme di Caracalla, 00100 Rome, Italy; tel. 57971; telex 610181; Regional Rep. S. JUNIA.

LIAISON OFFICES
North America: Suite 300, 1001 22nd St, NW, Washington, DC 20437, USA; telex 64255; Dir R. A. SORENSON.
United Nations: Suite DC1-1125, 1 United Nations Plaza, New York, NY 10017, USA; tel. (212) 754-6036; telex 236350; Rep. GABRIEL S. SAAB.

Activities

FAO published its fifth World Food Survey in 1985. It showed that during the 1970s, for the first time on record, the proportion of the world's population recorded as undernourished fell (from 19% to 15%). But with increasing populations, the estimated total number of undernourished people increased by about 10m.; by the most conservative criteria, there were at least 335m. undernourished people in the world in 1980.

FAO aims to raise levels of nutrition and standards of living, by improving the production and distribution of food and other commodities derived from farms, fisheries and forests. Its work falls into four basic categories: analysis and dissemination of information; advising governments on policy and planning; promoting consultations and co-operation among member countries; and providing technical advice and assistance.

AGRICULTURE
About one third of FAO's Field Programme expenditure is devoted to increasing crop production, through demonstrating techniques that will enable small farmers to increase production, particularly of staple foods and oil crops, without high risk of failure. Governments are advised on the conservation of genetic resources, on improving the supply of seeds and on crop protection.

Cereal and food legume production continue to be a primary focus of FAO's activities, with emphasis on demonstrations at the farm level. In 1985, for example, an expert from Kenya assisted four co-operatives of small-scale farmers in Ethiopia to introduce new varieties of wheat and barley. Through the International Rice Commission, which held its 16th session in 1985 in the Philippines, FAO promotes the development of the world's most important single food crop. Particular attention is given to methods of integrating rice cultivation with other produce—allowing farmers with little land to produce more rice and, for example, fish, small animals, or mushrooms. FAO also gives considerable help to horticulture and to livestock production, with the aim of raising standards of nutrition as well as increasing the availability of staple foods. Despite the emphasis on Africa (see below), FAO programmes do not overlook the needs of the rest of the developing world. During 1985, for example, the pejibaye, a nutritious Latin American palm, was introduced into India, the Philippines, Thailand, Indonesia, Sri Lanka and Burma.

Plant protection and animal health programmes form an important part of FAO's work as farming methods become more intensive, and pests more resistant to control methods. At the FAO conference in November 1985 the member nations approved an International Code of Conduct on the Distribution and Use of Pesticides. FAO has also been developing and introducing new weed-control techniques which require less labour, and enable poor farming families to cultivate larger areas than is possible with traditional methods. In 1986 FAO set up an emergency centre for operations to counter the threat to much of Africa posed by enormous numbers of five separate species of grasshoppers and locusts.

An increasing proportion of FAO's resources is being applied to revitalizing agriculture throughout Africa. In mid-1986, FAO presented a major study *African Agriculture: the Next 25 Years*. This study examined the reasons for the widening gap between population growth and food production throughout much of that continent—highlighted by the disastrous drought years in the first half of the 1980s. It concluded that if current agricultural conditions were to continue, many countries would need to import massive quantities of food (far beyond the capacities of their economies) to feed the populations predicted for the year 2010. However, with changes in development policies and external economic conditions, food production could be raised to the level where only a handful of countries could neither grow nor import enough food, and would need to rely on food aid.

Following the study, FAO's Director-General proposed a Plan of Action for African Agriculture, which calls for changes in agricultural policies to give greater priority to food production by concentrating on measures to conserve the environment; and by providing small-scale producers with the inputs (including improved seeds,

INTERNATIONAL ORGANIZATIONS

fertilizers, pesticides, and access to credit) needed for increased production, improving incentives (for example with more favourable pricing policies), together with the development of the institutions and infrastructure required to support increased production. The plan also emphasizes the importance of increased assistance from the industrialized countries—especially making use of their vast overcapacity in many areas—and on the vital importance of creating international trade conditions that no longer hinder the economic development of African countries.

FISHERIES

In 1979 FAO began a special programme to help developing countries to adjust to the imposition of exclusive economic zones (EEZs) which extend the jurisdiction of coastal states over the waters up to 200 nautical miles (370 km) offshore. It also runs a Fisheries Law Advisory Programme, enabling neighbouring states, for example, to harmonize legislation and provide uniform conditions of access to foreign fleets. FAO's work on fisheries development concentrates on small-scale fisheries and aquaculture, such as a programme for developing artisanal fisheries in the countries with a coastline on the Bay of Bengal (1979–86). It also supports projects for improving the processing and transport of fish so as to avoid wastage. In 1984 FAO held the first World Conference on Fisheries Management and Development, which approved five 'action programmes' on planning and management, small-scale fisheries, aquaculture, trade in fish and fish products, and promoting the role of fisheries in alleviating under-nutrition.

FORESTRY

FAO emphasizes the importance of tropical forests in the provision of food, wood for energy, shelter and employment for millions of people, as well as their role in the conservation of soil and water, and attempts to prevent their destruction. Following the first comprehensive study of the world's tropical forest resources, undertaken by FAO and UNEP, the Forest Resources Information System came into operation in 1983. In 1985 FAO introduced a Tropical Forestry Action Plan, which outlines priority action in five major areas: forestry in land use; forest-based industrial development; fuelwood and energy; conservation of tropical forest ecosystems; and the development of institutions.

PROCESSING AND MARKETING

Conservative estimates suggest that at least 10% of all food harvested is lost before it can be consumed. FAO helps reduce immediate post-harvest losses, with the introduction of improved processing methods and storage systems. It also advises on the distribution and marketing of agricultural produce and on the selection and preparation of foods for optimum nutrition. Many of these activities form part of wider rural development projects. For many developing countries, agricultural products are the main source of foreign earnings, but the terms under which they are traded often favour the industrialized countries. FAO's long-standing Committee on Commodity Problems agreed at its 55th session in 1985 that all efforts should be made to eliminate export subsidies and other related practices, as well as protectionist measures which curb access to international markets.

FOOD SECURITY

FAO's food security policy aims to encourage the production of adequate food supplies, to maximize stability in the flow of supplies, and to ensure access on the part of those who need them. The Global Information and Early Warning System monitors the world food situation and identifies countries threatened by shortages to guide potential donors. The Food Security Assistance Scheme, established in 1976, aims to help developing countries in strengthening their food security by setting up food reserves and by developing national and regional early warning systems. During 1984, for example, FAO missions visited 14 African countries to identify food security training needs, and approved a scheme to establish a food security system in the Andean region.

FAO INVESTMENT CENTRE

The Investment Centre was established in 1964 to help countries prepare viable investment projects that will attract external financing. By the end of 1985 it had channelled US $28,288m. for 626 projects. The World Bank is the single most important financing institution for investment projects prepared by FAO. Joint activities with regional development banks have increased during the 1980s, along with support for national development banks and co-operation with various Arab funds.

United Nations (Specialized Agencies)

EMERGENCY RELIEF

The Office for Special Relief Operations (OSRO) was set up in 1973 to cope with the disastrous drought in the Sahel in that year. In 1975 the office was expanded to handle such emergencies globally. As well as providing emergency aid, OSRO aims to rehabilitate agricultural production following disasters. Jointly with the United Nations, FAO is responsible for the World Food Programme (q.v.) which provides emergency food supplies, and food aid in support of development projects.

INFORMATION AND RESEARCH

FAO issues regular statistical reports, commodity studies, and technical manuals in local languages (see list of publications below).

General and specialized computerized data bases co-ordinated by FAO contain information on every area of food and agriculture; the Current Agricultural Research Information System (CARIS), for example, enables over 70 countries to exchange information on current research; other systems provide information on agricultural sciences and technology (AGRIS), commodities (ICS), fisheries (ASFIS and FISHDAB) and forest resources (FORIS).

In January 1984 a new Research and Technology Development Division was established, to co-ordinate members' agricultural research. During the year missions to review and plan research were sent to 12 countries.

FAO Councils and Commissions

(Based at the Rome headquarters unless otherwise indicated.)

African Commission on Agricultural Statistics: c/o FAO Regional Office for Africa, POB 1628, Accra, Ghana: f. 1961 to advise member countries on the development and standardization of food and agricultural statistics. Mems: 37 states.

African Forestry Commission: f. 1959 to advise on the formulation of forest policy and to review and co-ordinate its implementation on a regional level; to exchange information and advise on technical problems. Mems: 41 states.

Asia and Pacific Commission on Agricultural Statistics: c/o FAO Regional Office, Maliwan Mansion, Phra Atit Rd, Bangkok 2, Thailand; f. 1962 to review the state of food and agricultural statistics in the region and to advise member countries on the development and standardization of agricultural statistics. Mems: 23 states.

Asia and Pacific Plant Protection Commission: c/o FAO Regional Office, Maliwan Mansion, Phra Atit Rd, Bangkok 2, Thailand; f. 1956 (new title 1983) to strengthen international co-operation in plant protection to prevent the introduction and spread of destructive plant diseases and pests. Mems: 27 states.

Asia-Pacific Forestry Commission: f. 1949 to advise on the formulation of forest policy, and review and co-ordinate its implementation throughout the region; to exchange information and advise on technical problems. Mems: 24 states.

Caribbean Plant Protection Commission: f. 1967 to preserve the existing plant resources of the area. Mems: 21 states.

Commission for Controlling the Desert Locust in the Eastern Region of its distribution area in South West Asia: f. 1964 to carry out all possible measures to control plagues of the desert locust in the region. Mems: Afghanistan, India, Iran, Pakistan.

Commission for Controlling the Desert Locust in the Near East: f. 1965 to carry out all possible measures to control plagues of the desert locust within the Middle East and to reduce crop damage. Mems: 14 states.

Commission for Controlling the Desert Locust in North-West Africa: f. 1971 to promote research on control of the desert locust in NW Africa. Mems: 4 states.

Commission for Inland Fisheries of Latin America: f. 1976 to promote, co-ordinate and assist national and regional fishery and limnological surveys and programmes of research and development leading to the rational utilization of inland fishery resources. Mems: 20 states.

Commission on African Animal Trypanosomiasis: f. 1979 to develop and implement programmes to combat this disease. Mems: 39 states.

Commission on Fertilizers: f. 1973 to provide guidance on the effective distribution and use of fertilizers. Mems: 83 states.

Commission on Plant Genetic Resources: f. 1983 to provide advice on programmes dealing with crop improvement through plant genetic resources. Mems: 77 states.

INTERNATIONAL ORGANIZATIONS

United Nations (Specialized Agencies)

European Commission for the Control of Foot-and-Mouth Disease: f. 1953 to promote national and international action for the control of the disease in Europe and its final eradication. Mems: 25 states.

European Commission on Agriculture: f. 1949 to encourage and facilitate action and co-operation in technological agricultural problems among member states and between international organizations concerned with agricultural technology in Europe; to make recommendations on all matters within its technical and geographical competence. Mems: 29 states.

European Forestry Commission: f. 1947 to advise on the formulation of forest policy and to review and co-ordinate its implementation on a regional level; to exchange information and to make recommendations. Mems: 28 states.

European Inland Fisheries Advisory Commission: f. 1957 to promote improvements in inland fisheries and to advise member Governments and FAO on inland fishery matters. Mems: 25 states.

FAO Regional Commission on Farm Management for Asia and the Far East: c/o FAO Regional Office, Maliwan Mansion, Phra Atit Rd, Bangkok 2, Thailand; f. 1959 to stimulate and co-ordinate farm management research and extension activities and to serve as a clearing-house for the exchange of information and experience among the member countries in the region.

FAO/WHO Codex Alimentarius Commission: f. 1962 to make proposals for the co-ordination of all international food standards work and to publish a code of international food standards. Mems: 130 states.

General Fisheries Council for the Mediterranean—GFCM: f. 1952 to develop aquatic resources, to encourage and co-ordinate research in the fishing and allied industries, to assemble and publish information, and to recommend the standardization of equipment, techniques and nomenclature. Mems: 19 states.

Indian Ocean Fishery Commission: c/o FAO Regional Office, Maliwan Mansion, Phra Atit Rd, Bangkok 2, Thailand; f. 1967 to promote national programmes, research and development activities, and to examine management problems. Mems: 41 states.

Indo-Pacific Fishery Commission: c/o FAO Regional Office, Maliwan Mansion, Phra Atit Rd, Bangkok 2, Thailand; f. 1948 to develop fisheries, encourage and co-ordinate research, disseminate information, recommend projects to governments, propose standards in technique and nomenclature. Mems: 19 states.

International Poplar Commission: f. 1947 to study scientific, technical, social and economic aspects of poplar and willow cultivation; to promote the exchange of ideas and material between research workers, producers and users; to arrange joint research programmes, congresses, study tours; to make recommendations to the FAO Conference and to National Poplar Commissions. Mems: 32 states.

International Rice Commission: f. 1948 to promote national and international action on production, conservation, distribution and consumption of rice, except matters relating to international trade. Meetings: Sessions of the IRC are held every four years and its three technical working parties every two years. Mems: 54 states.

Joint FAO/WHO/OAU Regional Food and Nutrition Commission for Africa: c/o FAO Regional Office for Africa, POB 1628, Accra, Ghana; f. 1962 to provide liaison in matters pertaining to food and nutrition, and to review food and nutrition problems in Africa. Mems: 43 states.

Latin American Forestry Commission: f. 1948 to advise on formulation of forest policy and review and co-ordinate its implementation throughout the region; to exchange information and advise on technical problems. Mems: 29 states.

Near East Forestry Commission: f. 1953 to advise on formulation of forest policy and review and co-ordinate its implementation throughout the region; to exchange information and advise on technical problems. Mems: 21 states.

Near East Regional Commission on Agriculture: f. 1983 to conduct periodic reviews of agricultural problems in the region; to promote policies and regional and national programmes for improving production of crops and livestock; to expand agricultural services and research; to promote the transfer of technology and regional technical co-operation; and to provide guidance on training and manpower development. Mems: 18 states.

Near East Regional Economic and Social Policy Commission: f. 1983 to review developments relating to food, agriculture and food security; to recommend policies on agrarian reform and rural development; to review and exchange information on food and nutrition policies and on agricultural planning; and to compile statistics. Mems: 19 states.

North American Forestry Commission: f. 1959 to advise on the formulation and co-ordination of national forest policies; to exchange information and to advise on technical problems. Mems: Canada, Mexico, USA.

Regional Animal Production and Health Commission for Asia, the Far East and the South-West Pacific: c/o FAO Regional Office, Maliwan Mansion, Phra Atit Rd, Bangkok 2, Thailand; f. 1973 to promote livestock development in general, and national and international research and action with respect to animal health and husbandry problems in the region. Mems: 14 states.

Regional Commission on Food Security for Asia and the Pacific: c/o FAO Regional Office, Maliwan Mansion, Phra Atit Rd, Bangkok 2, Thailand; f. 1982 to review regional food security; to assist member states in preparing programmes for strengthening food security and for dealing with acute food shortages; and to encourage technical co-operation. Mems: 17 states.

Regional Commission on Land and Water Use in the Near East: f. 1967 to review the current situation with regard to land and water use in the region; to identify the main problems concerning the development of land and water resources which require research and study and to consider other related matters. Mems: 22 states.

Regional Fisheries Advisory Commission for the Southwest Atlantic: f. 1961 to advise FAO on fisheries in the Southwest Atlantic area, to advise member countries on the administration and rational exploitation of marine and inland resources; to assist in the collection and dissemination of data, in training, and to promote liaison and co-operation. Mems: Argentina, Brazil, Uruguay.

Western Central Atlantic Fishery Commission: f. 1973 to assist international co-operation for the conservation, development and utilization of the living resources, especially shrimps, of the Western Central Atlantic. Mems: 28 states.

FINANCE

The Regular Programme Budget for the two years 1986–87 amounted to US $437m. The Regular Programme, which is financed by contributions from member governments, covers the cost of the FAO's Secretariat, its Technical Co-operation Programme and part of the cost of several special action programmes.

Advice and assistance in the field is provided through the Field Programme, funded largely from external sources such as the UNDP and various trust funds provided by donor governments. Owing to a reduction in funds available from UNDP, its share of FAO's Field Programme costs fell from 87% in 1972 to 40% in 1985. This fall was partly offset by an increase in financing by trust funds, which amounted to US $147.6m. in 1985 (about 52% of Field Programme costs). Total Field Programme expenditure in 1985 was $290m.

FAO FIELD PROGRAMMES BY REGION, 1985

Region	Number of projects	Number of staff	Expenditure in 1985 (US $ million)
Africa	1,052	1,282	119.7
Asia and the Pacific	629	927	67.9
Latin America and the Caribbean	361	488	27.4
Near East	358	556	58.5
Europe	71	71	2.5
Global/inter-regional	133	127	13.0
World Total	2,603	3,451	291.0

FAO PUBLICATIONS

World Food Report (annually)
Monthly Bulletin of Statistics.
Food Outlook (monthly).
Production Yearbook.
Yearbook of Fishery Statistics.
Yearbook of Forest Products.
The State of Food and Agriculture (annually).
Ceres (every 2 months).
Food and Agricultural Legislation.
World Animal Review.
Unasylva.
Commodity reviews; studies; manuals.

INTERNATIONAL ORGANIZATIONS *United Nations (Specialized Agencies)*

General Agreement on Tariffs and Trade—GATT

Address: Centre William Rappard, 154 rue de Lausanne, 1211 Geneva 21, Switzerland.
Telephone: (022) 310231.
Telex: 28 787.

GATT was established in 1948 as a multilateral treaty aiming to liberalize world trade and place it on a secure basis.

CONTRACTING PARTIES TO GATT

In October 1986 there were 92 contracting parties (including Hong Kong, which became a member in its own right in 1986); one state has acceded provisionally to GATT and a further 31 in practice apply the rules of GATT to their commercial policy: see Table on pp. 53–55.

Organization
(October 1986)

SESSIONS

The sessions of contracting parties are usually held annually, in Geneva. The session is the highest body of GATT. Decisions are generally arrived at by consensus, not by vote. On the rare occasions that voting takes place, each contracting party (member country) has one vote. Most decisions by vote are taken by simple majority; but a two-thirds majority, with the majority comprising more than half the member countries, is needed for 'waivers': authorizations, in particular cases, to depart from specific obligations under the General Agreement. Outside the sessions, votes may be taken by postal ballot.

COUNCIL OF REPRESENTATIVES

Meets as necessary (generally about 10 times a year) to deal with urgent and routine matters arising between sessions of contracting parties and to supervise the work of committees and working groups.

SECRETARIAT

The secretariat, numbering about 300 people, consists of experts in trade policy and economics and an administrative staff (including translators and interpreters). It prepares and runs the sessions of contracting parties and services the work of the Council and of the committees, working groups and panels of independent experts. It is also responsible for organizing multilateral trade negotiations held within the framework of GATT.

Director-General: ARTHUR DUNKEL (Switzerland).

COMMITTEES AND WORKING PARTIES

Standing committees or councils exist to direct GATT work on trade and development issues; to carry on trade negotiations among developing countries; to examine the situation of countries using trade restrictions to protect their balance of payments; to supervise implementation of the various Tokyo Round agreements; to supervise the Arrangement Regarding International Trade in Textiles (Multi-fibre Arrangement); and to deal with budget, financial and administrative questions.

A Consultative Group of Eighteen, consisting of high-level representatives with responsibility for trade policy in their countries, was established in 1975. It meets about three times a year.

Working parties (ad hoc committees) are set up to deal with current questions, such as requests for accession to GATT; verification that agreements concluded by member countries are in conformity with GATT; or studies of issues on which the member countries will later wish to take a joint decision. A Trade Policies Division was set up in 1983 to investigate non-tariff measures imposed to restrict imports. Panels of independent experts are often set up to investigate disputes and report their conclusions to the Council. During 1984 two new trade disputes were brought before GATT for arbitration, and several previous disputes were the subject of further consideration by the Council.

INTERNATIONAL TRADE CENTRE

Address: 54–56 rue de Montbrillant, 2102 Geneva, Switzerland.
Telephone: (022) 34 60 21.
Telex: 289052.

Established by GATT in May 1964, the Centre has been jointly operated since January 1968 by GATT and UNCTAD (see p. 39). It assists developing countries to formulate and implement trade promotion programmes, provides information and advice on export markets and marketing techniques, helps to develop export promotion and marketing institutions and services, and trains national personnel. In 1984 it became an executing agency of the UN Development Programme (UNDP, q.v.), directly responsible for carrying out UNDP-financed projects related to trade promotion.

Executive Director: GÖRAN M. ENGBLOM (Sweden).

The Agreement

GATT is based on a few fundamental principles. First, as directed in the famous 'most-favoured-nation' clause, trade must be conducted on the basis of non-discrimination: all contracting parties are bound to grant to each other treatment as favourable as they give to any country in the application and administration of import and export duties and charges. Exceptions—principally for customs unions and free trade areas and for measures in favour of and among developing countries (see Tokyo Round 'framework' agreements below)—are granted only subject to strict rules.

Second, protection should be given to domestic industry essentially through the customs tariff. The aim of this rule is to make the extent of protection clear and to make competition possible.

Third, a stable and predictable basis for trade is provided by the binding of the tariff levels negotiated among the contracting parties. These bound items are listed for each country in tariff schedules which form an integral part of the General Agreement. A return to higher tariffs is discouraged by the requirement that any increases are compensated for; consequently this provision is invoked rarely.

Consultation, to avoid damage to the trading interests of contracting parties, is another fundamental principle of GATT. Members are able to call on GATT for a fair settlement of cases in which they think their rights under the General Agreement are being withheld or compromised by other members.

There are 'waiver' procedures whereby a country may, when its economic or trade circumstances so warrant, seek a derogation from a particular GATT obligation or obligations. There are also escape provisions for emergency action against imports in certain defined circumstances.

The trade problems of developing countries receive special attention in GATT. In 1965 a new chapter on Trade and Development was added to the General Agreement; a key provision is that developing countries should not be expected to offer reciprocity in negotiations with developed countries. GATT members have also relaxed the most-favoured-nation rule to accommodate the Generalized System of Preferences by developed for developing countries and to allow an exchange of preferential tariff reductions among developing countries. (See UNCTAD, p. 39.)

Finally, GATT offers a framework within which negotiations are held for the reduction of tariffs and other barriers to trade and a structure for putting the results of such negotiations into a legal instrument.

Activities

Much of GATT's regular work consists of consultations and negotiations on specific trade problems affecting individual commodities or member countries.

From time to time, major multilateral trade negotiations also take place under GATT auspices. There have been seven rounds of such negotiations: in 1947 (in Geneva), in 1949 (Annecy, France), 1951 (Torquay, England), 1956 (Geneva), 1960–61 (Geneva, the 'Dillon Round'), 1964–67 (Geneva, the 'Kennedy Round'), and 1973–79 (Geneva, the 'Tokyo Round', so called because the negotiations were launched at a ministerial meeting in the Japanese capital in 1973). A further round, held at Punta del Este, Uruguay, began in September 1986 (see below).

Ninety-nine countries participated in the 'Tokyo Round'. In November 1979 the negotiations were concluded with agreements covering: an improved legal framework for the conduct of world trade (which includes recognition of tariff and non-tariff treatment in favour of and among developing countries as a permanent legal feature of the world trading system); non-tariff measures (subsidies and countervailing duties; technical barriers to trade; government procurement; customs valuation; import licensing procedures; and a revision of the 1967 GATT anti-dumping code); bovine meat; dairy products; tropical products; and an agreement on free trade in civil aircraft. The agreements contain provisions for special and more favourable treatment for developing countries.

Participating countries also agreed to reduce tariffs on thousands of industrial and agricultural products, for the most part by annual cuts over a period of seven years beginning on 1 January 1980. As a result of these concessions, industrialized countries will reduce the average level of their import duties on manufactures by about 34%, a cut comparable with that achieved in the Kennedy Round of 1964–67.

The agreements providing an improved framework for the conduct of world trade took effect in November 1979. The other agreements took effect on 1 January 1980, except for those covering government procurement and customs valuation, which took effect on 1 January 1981, and the concessions on tropical products which began as early as 1977. Committees were established to supervise implementation of the agreements.

A new work programme was established in November 1979, giving priority to full implementation of the Tokyo Round agreements, future trade liberalization and further efforts to assist the trade of developing countries; the Committee on Trade and Development is largely responsible for these efforts, and its role was strengthened in the work programme. Two new sub-committees were established in 1981: one to examine any new protective measures taken by developed countries against imports from developing countries, and the other to consider the trade problems of the least-developed countries.

A considerable proportion of world trade in textiles and clothing is carried out by the 51 countries participating in the Arrangement Regarding International Trade in Textiles (Multi-fibre Arrangement), which entered into force in January 1974 under GATT auspices for a period of four years. Its aim was to allow the major importers (the USA, Japan and the European Community) to reorganize their textile industries in the face of low-cost production by developing countries. Under the Arrangement all fibres, fabrics and garments are divided into categories, and within each category bilateral agreements are negotiated between suppliers and importers for every product that is likely to cause disruption in the importer's domestic textile industry. In December 1977 the signatory Governments of the Arrangement decided to extend it for four years, and at the end of 1981 the Arrangement was extended for a further period of four years and seven months, from 1 January 1982 to 31 July 1986. Although many developing countries demanded that the Arrangement should be abolished and that trade in textiles should be covered by normal GATT procedures, a new Arrangement was agreed with effect from 1 August 1986, for five years.

The 1982 session of contracting parties was held in Geneva in November and included a ministerial-level meeting (the first for nine years), attended by some 70 ministers from the GATT member countries, who adopted a joint declaration, affirming their commitment against protectionism and calling for a renewed consensus in support of the GATT. The declaration also set out a programme of work covering many aspects of trade policy, with emphasis on the following aims: to identify the means of bringing agriculture more fully into the multilateral trading system; to revise the GATT rules on emergency 'safeguard' action against imports; to identify and examine quantitative restrictions and other non-tariff barriers and to consider their possible elimination or liberalization; to review the implementation of GATT rules relating to developing countries; to examine the scope for trade liberalization in textiles and clothing; to look at problems affecting trade in certain natural resource products; and to review the operation of the Tokyo Round agreements and arrangements. Reports on much of this work were presented to the session of contracting parties in November 1984, and it was continued during 1985.

During 1985 and 1986 preparations were made for a new round of multilateral trade negotiations. Many developing countries opposed the USA's proposal that the agenda should include liberalizing trade in services (such as tourism, banking and insurance), an area not previously covered by GATT, but eventually a compromise was reached whereby negotiations on services were to be conducted by a separate committee, supervised by GATT but outside its legal framework. Proposals by the USA and others to discuss agricultural export subsidies and farm support policies were adopted, despite opposition from the European Community. The negotiations were also to cover barriers to foreign investment, and 'piracy' of intellectual property (counterfeiting and copyright violations). The 'Uruguay round' was expected to begin in December 1986 and to be completed in four years.

FINANCE

Payments are based on each member's share of the total trade between members. The budget for 1985 amounted to 57.5m. Swiss francs, and that for 1986 to 59.6m. Swiss francs.

PUBLICATIONS
(available in English, French and Spanish editions).

International Trade (annual report on the main developments in international trade).

GATT Activities (annual).

GATT Focus (monthly newsletter).

Basic Instruments and Selected Documents series. Annual supplements record the formal decisions of the Members, important committee papers, etc. Volume IV gives the current text of the General Agreement.

GATT Studies in International Trade (occasional series of staff papers).

GATT: What it is, What it does.

The Tokyo Round of Multilateral Trade Negotiations. A two-volume report by the Director-General. Copies of the multilateral agreements concluded in the Tokyo Round are also available.

International Bank for Reconstruction and Development—IBRD (World Bank)

Address: 1818 H St, NW, Washington, DC 20433, USA.
Telephone: (202) 477-1234.
Telex: 248423.

The IBRD was established on 27 December 1945. Initially it was concerned with post-war reconstruction in Europe; since then its aim has been to assist the economic development of member nations by making loans where private capital is not available on reasonable terms to finance productive investments. Loans are made either direct to governments, or to private enterprise with the guarantee of their governments. The IBRD has two affiliates, the International Development Association (IDA, q.v.) and the International Finance Corporation (IFC, q.v.). The 'World Bank', as it is commonly known, comprises the IBRD and IDA.

MEMBERS
There are 151 members: see Table on pp. 53–55. Only members of the International Monetary Fund (IMF, q.v.) may be considered for membership in the Bank. Subscriptions to the capital stock of the Bank are based on each member's quota in the IMF, which is designed to reflect the country's relative economic strength. Voting rights are related to shareholdings.

Organization
(October 1986)

Officers and staff of the IBRD serve concurrently as officers and staff in the International Development Association (IDA). The Bank has offices in New York, Paris, London, Geneva and Tokyo; regional missions in Nairobi (for eastern and southern Africa), Abidjan (for western Africa) and Bangkok; and resident missions in 35 countries.

BOARD OF GOVERNORS
The Board of Governors consists of one Governor appointed by each member nation. Typically, a Governor is the country's finance

INTERNATIONAL ORGANIZATIONS

United Nations (Specialized Agencies)

EXECUTIVE DIRECTORS AND THEIR VOTING POWER (June 1986)

Executive Director	Casting Votes of	Total Votes Bank	Total Votes IDA
Appointed:			
(vacant)	USA	138,348	975,481
Kenji Yamaguchi	Japan	41,080	437,435
Timothy P. Lankester	United Kingdom	39,197	338,259
Gerhard Boehmer	Federal Republic of Germany	34,597	367,560
Hélène Ploix	France	36,854	196,605
Elected:			
Fawzi Hamad Al-Sultan (Kuwait)	Bahrain*, Egypt, Iraq, Jordan, Kuwait, Lebanon, Maldives, Oman, Pakistan, Qatar*, Saudi Arabia†, Syria, United Arab Emirates, Yemen Arab Republic	48,803	369,275
Frank Potter (Canada)	Antigua and Barbuda*, Bahamas*, Barbados*, Belize, Canada, Dominica, Grenada, Guyana, Ireland, Jamaica*, Saint Christopher and Nevis*, Saint Lucia, Saint Vincent and the Grenadines	29,864	227,722
Jacques de Groote (Belgium)	Austria, Belgium, Hungary, Luxembourg, Turkey	30,692	173,881
C. R. Krishnaswamy Rao Sahib (India)	Bangladesh, Bhutan, India, Sri Lanka	29,609	223,487
Leonor Filardo de González (Venezuela)	Costa Rica, El Salvador, Guatemala, Honduras, Mexico, Nicaragua, Panama, Spain, Suriname*, Venezuela*	27,732	146,859
Xu Naijiong (China)	People's Republic of China	23,732	99,836
Mario Draghi (Italy)	Greece, Italy, Malta*, Portugal*	24,753	156,092
Ronald H. Dean (Australia)	Australia, Republic of Korea, New Zealand, Papua New Guinea, Solomon Islands, Vanuatu, Western Samoa	22,608	130,070
Ferdinand van Dam (Netherlands)	Cyprus, Israel, Netherlands, Romania*, Yugoslavia	21,773	160,069
Christian Ulrik Haxthausen (Denmark)	Denmark, Finland, Iceland, Norway, Sweden	25,206	255,450
Vibul Aunsnunta (Thailand)	Burma, Fiji, Indonesia, Laos, Malaysia, Nepal, Singapore*, Thailand, Viet-Nam	21,164	152,680
Edgar Gutiérrez-Castro (Colombia)	Brazil, Colombia, Dominican Republic, Ecuador, Haiti, Philippines	21,531	170,789
Astère Girukwigomba (Burundi)	Botswana, Burundi, Ethiopia, The Gambia, Guinea, Kenya, Lesotho, Liberia, Malawi, Mozambique, Nigeria, Seychelles*, Sierra Leone, Sudan, Swaziland, Tanzania, Trinidad and Tobago, Uganda, Zambia, Zimbabwe	16,584	212,389
Mourad Benachenhou (Algeria)	Afghanistan, Algeria, Ghana, Iran, Libya, Morocco, Tunisia, People's Democratic Republic of Yemen	24,112	108,854
Nicéphore Soglo (Benin)	Benin, Burkina Faso, Cameroon, Cape Verde, Central African Republic, Chad, Comoros, Congo, Djibouti, Equatorial Guinea, Gabon, Guinea-Bissau, Ivory Coast, Madagascar, Mali, Mauritania, Mauritius, Niger, Rwanda, São Tomé and Príncipe, Senegal, Somalia, Togo, Zaire	13,149	173,609
Kenneth Coates (Uruguay)	Argentina, Bolivia, Chile, Paraguay, Peru, Uruguay*	15,512	128,623

* Members of IBRD only.
† In October 1986 Saudi Arabia was given a separate seat on the Board.

Note: Democratic Kampuchea (464 votes in IBRD and 7,826 in IDA) and South Africa (7,204 votes in IBRD and 16,494 in IDA) did not participate in the 1984 election of Executive Directors. Poland (499 votes in IBRD), Tonga (527 votes in IBRD and 11,732 votes in IDA) and Kiribati (261 votes in IBRD) became members after that election.

minister, central bank governor, or a minister or an official of comparable rank. The Board normally meets once a year.

EXECUTIVE DIRECTORS

With the exception of certain powers specifically reserved to them by the Articles of Agreement, the Governors of the Bank have delegated their powers for the conduct of the general operations of the Bank to a Board of Executive Directors that performs its duties on a full-time basis at the Bank's headquarters. There are 21 Executive Directors; each Director selects an Alternate. Five Directors are appointed by the five members having the largest number of shares of capital stock, and the rest are elected by the Governors representing the other members. The President of the Bank is Chairman of the Board.

The Executive Directors fulfil dual responsibilities. First, they represent the interests of their country or groups of countries. Second, they exercise their authority as delegated by the Governors in overseeing the policies of the Bank. Since the Bank operates on the basis of consensus (formal votes are rare), this dual role involves frequent communication and consultations with governments so as to reflect accurately their views in Board discussions.

The Directors consider and decide on the loan and credit proposals made by the President. They are also responsible for presentation to the Board of Governors at its Annual Meetings of an audit of accounts, an administrative budget, the *Annual Report* on the operations and policies of the World Bank, and any other matter that, in their judgement, requires submission to the Board of Governors. Matters may be submitted to the Governors at the Annual Meetings or at any time between Annual Meetings.

OFFICERS

President and Chairman of Executive Directors: Barber B. Conable.
Senior Vice-President, Finance: Moeen A. Qureshi.
Senior Vice-President, Operations: Ernest Stern.
Vice-President: Warren C. Baum.
Vice-President, External Relations: José Botafogo Gonçalves.
Vice-President, Energy and Industry: (vacant).
Vice-President, Pension Fund: K. Georg Gabriel.

INTERNATIONAL ORGANIZATIONS

United Nations (Specialized Agencies)

Vice-President and Controller: HANS C. HITTMAIR.
Vice-President, Operations Policy: S. SHAHID HUSAIN.
Vice-President, Economics and Research: ANNE O. KRUEGER.
Vice-President, Co-financing: KUNIHIKO INAKAGE.
Vice-President, Personnel and Administration: MARTIJN J. W. M. PAIJMANS.
Vice-President and Treasurer: EUGENE H. ROTBERG.
Vice-President and General Counsel: IBRAHIM F. I. SHIHATA.
Vice-President and Secretary: TIMOTHY T. THAHANE.
Vice-President, Financial Policy, Planning and Budgeting: D. JOSEPH WOOD.
Regional Vice-President, South Asia: W. DAVID HOPPER.
Regional Vice-President, East Asia and Pacific: ATTILA KARAOSMANOGLU.
Regional Vice-President, Eastern and Southern Africa: EDWARD V. K. JAYCOX.
Regional Vice-President, Western Africa: WILFRIED P. THALWITZ.
Regional Vice-President, Europe, Middle East and North Africa: WILLI A. WAPENHANS.
Regional Vice-President, Latin America and the Caribbean: A. DAVID KNOX.
Director-General, Operations Evaluation: YVES ROVANI.

OFFICES

New York Office and World Bank Mission to the United Nations: 747 Third Ave (26th Floor), New York, NY 10017, USA; Special Rep. to UN G. DAVID LOOS.
European Office: 66 ave d'Iéna, 75116 Paris, France; Dir MAURICE P. BART.
Regional Mission in Eastern and Southern Africa: POB 30577; Reinsurance Plaza, Taifa Rd, Nairobi, Kenya; Dir JAMES W. ADAMS.
Regional Mission in Western Africa: BP 1850; Corner Booker Washington and Jacques Aka Sts, Abidjan 01, Ivory Coast; Chief JEAN-DAVID ROULET.
Regional Mission in Thailand: Udom Vidhya Bldg, 956 Rama IV Rd, Sala Daeng, Bangkok 10500, Thailand; Chief CHRISTOPHER HERMANS.

Activities

FINANCIAL OPERATIONS

IBRD loans are usually for a period of 20 years or less, with a grace period of five years. Loans are made to governments, or must be guaranteed by the government concerned, and are made for projects likely to offer a commercially viable rate of return.

The Bank's capital is derived from members' subscriptions to capital shares, the calculation of which is based on their quotas in the International Monetary Fund (see p. 75). On 30 June 1986 the total subscribed capital of the Bank was US $77,527m. of which the paid-in portion is 9%; the remainder is subject to call if required to meet the Bank's obligations. Most of the Bank's lendable funds come from its borrowing, on commercial terms, in world capital markets, and also from its retained earnings and the flow of repayments on its loans. Bank loans carry a variable interest rate, rather than a rate fixed at the time of borrowing.

The IBRD and its affiliates, IDA and IFC, made lending and investment commitments totalling $17,475m. during the year ending 30 June 1986, compared with $15,322m. in the previous year. During the year, the IBRD alone approved 131 loans to 41 countries totalling $13,179m., compared with $11,356m. in the previous year, the three largest borrowers being Brazil, India and Indonesia (which together received 34% of total commitments). Disbursements by the IBRD in the year ending 30 June 1986 amounted to $8,263m., compared with $8,645m. in the previous year.

The Bank's operations were supported by borrowings in international capital markets, which totalled $10,609m. in the year ending 30 June 1986 ($11,086m. in the previous year), chiefly (before currency swaps) in US dollars (31%), Swiss francs (18%), Japanese yen (17%), Deutsche Mark (16%) and Dutch guilders (9%). During the year ending 30 June 1986 the Bank made a record profit of $1,243m., owing largely to its low borrowing costs and the high rates of return on its liquid assets portfolio.

In July 1985 a Special Facility for Sub-Saharan Africa became effective for a three-year period, with funds of $1,250m., to finance structural adjustment, sectoral reform programmes and rehabilitation. The Facility lends on the same concessional terms as IDA (see p. 66). It provides credits mainly to co-finance projects with IDA, but also supports projects of its own. During the year ending 30 June 1986, Special Facility credits totalling $782m. were approved for 15 countries.

A draft convention establishing a Multilateral Investment Guarantee Agency (MIGA) was approved by the Board of Governors in October 1985. The Agency's objective would be to encourage the flow of investment among its members, particularly to developing member countries; it would issue guarantees against non-commercial risks and provide technical assistance. Its initial capital was to be $1,000m. Operations were to begin following ratification of the convention by 15 developing and five developed countries whose total subscriptions amounted to $360m. By the end of September 1986 45 countries had signed the convention and four had ratified it.

TECHNICAL ASSISTANCE

The provision of technical assistance to member countries has become a major component of Bank activities. The economic, sector and project analysis undertaken by the Bank in the normal course of its operations is the vehicle for considerable technical assistance. In addition, project loans and credits may include funds earmarked specifically for feasibility studies, resource surveys, management or planning advice, and training. During the calendar year 1985, technical assistance components of loans amounted to $1,345.2m. in 229 operations. In addition, 10 free-standing technical assistance loans were approved, amounting to $69.7m.

The Bank serves as an executing agency for projects financed by the UN Development Programme. At the end of 1985 the number in progress was 117, with a total allocation of $170.6m.

Technical assistance (usually reimbursable) is also extended to countries that do not need Bank financial support, e.g. for training and transfer of technology.

ECONOMIC RESEARCH AND STUDIES

About $24m. of the Bank's administrative budget was allotted to research, carried out by its own research staff, in the year ending 30 June 1986. Research is intended to provide a source of policy advice to members, and to encourage the development of indigenous research. Examples of projects being undertaken in 1986 included multi-country studies of agricultural price policy and of growth and income distribution; a study of the costs and benefits of rent control in a number of developing countries; examining the reasons for public-enterprise deficits in sub-Saharan Africa; research on the effect of government intervention in Senegalese labour markets; and a study on public-sector expenditure in the most highly-indebted countries in Latin America.

CO-OPERATION WITH OTHER ORGANIZATIONS

The Bank co-operates closely with other UN bodies through consultations, meetings, and joint activities, particularly in response to the economic crisis in Africa south of the Sahara, where co-operation with UNDP and WHO is especially important. In late 1983 the Bank agreed to administer an income-generating public works programme (at a cost of $20m., funded by UNHCR) to benefit Afghan refugees and the host population in Pakistan; a second programme was being planned in 1986. The Energy Sector Assessment Programme, run jointly with UNDP, had completed missions to 53 countries by mid-1986, helping them to develop a strategy for increasing energy production and using energy more efficiently.

The Bank conducts co-financing and aid co-ordination projects with official aid agencies, export credit institutions, and commercial banks. During the year ending 30 June 1986 a total of 113 IBRD and IDA projects involved co-financing funds amounting to $3,500m. In January 1983 the Bank announced the introduction of a set of new co-financing instruments designed to increase the participation of commercial banks in project loans. In 1985/86 commercial co-financing under these instruments amounted to $706m.

EVALUATION

The Bank's Operations Evaluation Department studies and publishes the results of projects after a loan has been fully disbursed, so as to identify problems and possible improvements in future activities. Internal auditing is also carried out, to monitor the effectiveness of the Bank's management.

INTERNATIONAL ORGANIZATIONS

United Nations (Specialized Agencies)

IBRD INSTITUTIONS

Economic Development Institute—EDI: founded in 1955. Training is provided for government officials at the middle and upper levels of responsibility who are concerned with development programmes and projects. Courses are in national economic management and project analysis. The EDI has become one of the most important of the Bank's activities in technical assistance. In its overseas courses, the aim is to build up local capability to conduct projects courses in future.

In the year ending 30 June 1986 69 courses and seminars were held, mostly abroad; there were about 3,300 participants. Dir CHRISTOPHER R. WILLOUGHBY.

Consultative Group for International Agricultural Research—CGIAR: founded in 1971 under the sponsorship of the World Bank, FAO and UNDP. The Bank is chairman of the group (which includes governments, private foundations and multilateral development agencies) and provides its secretariat. The group was formed to raise financial support for international agricultural research work for improving crops and animal production in the developing countries. In 1986 there were 13 research centres; donations for the year ending 30 June 1986 amounted to $171m. (of which the Bank provided $28m.). Exec. Sec. CURTIS FARRAR.

International Centre for Settlement of Investment Disputes—ICSID: founded in 1966 under the Convention of the Settlement of Investment Disputes between States and Nationals of Other States. The Convention was designed to encourage the growth of private foreign investment for economic development, by creating the possibility, always subject to the consent of both parties, for a Contracting State and a foreign investor who is a national of another Contracting State to settle any legal dispute that might arise out of such an investment by conciliation and/or arbitration before an impartial, international forum. The governing body of the Centre is its Administrative Council, composed of one representative of each Contracting State, all of whom have equal voting power. The President of the World Bank is ex officio the non-voting Chairman of the Administrative Council.

By the end of June 1986, 94 states had signed the Convention and 88 had deposited instruments of ratification. At mid-1986 there were eight disputes before the Centre. Sec.-Gen. IBRAHIM F. I. SHIHATA.

PUBLICATIONS

World Bank Catalog of Publications.
World Bank News (weekly).
World Bank Annual Report.
World Development Report (annually).
World Bank Research Observer.
Research News (3 a year).
World Bank Atlas (annually).
Abstracts of Current Studies: The World Bank Research Program (annually).
Annual Review of Project Performance Results.
Staff Working Papers.
ICSID Review—Foreign Investment Law Journal (2 a year).

World Bank Statistics

CUMULATIVE LENDING OPERATIONS, BY PURPOSE*
(to 30 June 1986; US $ million)

	IBRD	IDA
Agriculture and rural development	27,172.9	15,040.7
Development finance companies	11,756.7	1,029.9
Education	4,781.6	2,638.2
Energy	28,634.7	4,961.7
Industry	8,136.2	1,305.3
Non-project	7,832.4	4,132.3
Population, health and nutrition	708.8	822.5
Small-scale enterprises	2,992.3	388.0
Technical assistance	258.7	529.2
Telecommunications	1,852.7	1,134.1
Tourism	363.6	86.7
Transportation	21,834.6	5,060.4
Urban development	3,845.6	1,109.0
Water supply and sewerage	5,927.8	1,583.9
Total	**126,098.6**	**39,822.0**

CUMULATIVE LENDING OPERATIONS, BY REGION*
(to 30 June 1986; US $ million)

	IBRD	IDA
Eastern and Southern Africa	4,512.3	7,314.7
Western Africa	6,553.2	3,987.7
East Asia and Pacific	30,606.6	3,201.6
South Asia	13,177.3	22,191.6
Europe, Middle East and North Africa	31,543.2	2,301.6
Latin America and the Caribbean	39,766.0	824.7
Total	**126,098.6**	**39,822.0**

* No account is taken of cancellations and refundings subsequent to original commitment, amounting to $6,170.0m. (IBRD) and $1,088.2m. (IDA). IBRD loans of $1,817.7m. to IFC are excluded.

IBRD LOANS AND IDA CREDITS APPROVED, BY REGION (1 July 1985–30 June 1986)

	IBRD Loans[1]		IDA Credits[1]		Total[1]	
	Number[2]	US $ m.	Number[2]	US $ m.	Number[2]	US $ m.
Eastern and Southern Africa:						
Botswana	2	33.6	—	—	2	33.6
Burundi	—	—	3	37.3	3	37.3
Ethiopia	—	—	2	67.5	2	67.5
Kenya	—	—	4	75.0	4	75.0
Madagascar	—	—	4	52.3	4	52.3
Malawi	2	24.5	2	41.6	4	66.1
Mauritius	1	30.0	—	—	1	30.0
Rwanda	—	—	5	59.1	5	59.1
Somalia	—	—	2	34.3	2	34.3
Sudan	—	—	3	62.6	3	62.6
Tanzania	—	—	2	90.0	2	90.0
Zaire	1	110.0	3	107.0	4	217.0
Zambia	—	—	5	91.1	5	91.1
Total	6	198.1	35	717.8	41	915.9
Western Africa:						
Benin	—	—	1	11.9	1	11.9
Cameroon	1	30.1	—	—	1	30.1
Central African Republic	—	—	1	11.9	1	11.9
Chad	—	—	1	15.0	1	15.0
Equatorial Guinea	—	—	1	6.0	1	6.0
The Gambia	—	—	1	5.8	1	5.8
Ghana	—	—	4	96.0	4	96.0
Guinea	—	—	4	43.0	4	43.0
Ivory Coast	5	340.1	—	—	5	340.1
Mali	—	—	3	82.9	3	82.9
Mauritania	1	20.0	1	7.6	2	27.6
Niger	—	—	3	62.8	3	62.8
Nigeria	5	312.9	—	—	5	312.9
Senegal	—	—	4	66.9	4	66.9
Sierra Leone	—	—	1	5.3	1	5.3
Togo	—	—	—	6.9	0	6.9
Western Africa region	—	—	1	5.5	1	5.5
Total	12	703.1	26	427.5	38	1,130.6
East Asia and Pacific:						
China	7	687.0	4	450.0	11	1,137.0
Fiji	1	6.5	—	—	1	6.5
Indonesia	11	1,132.3	—	—	11	1,132.3
Korea, Republic of	5	626.0	—	—	5	626.0
Laos	—	—	1	3.9	1	3.9
Malaysia	5	331.1	—	—	5	331.1
Papua New Guinea	3	74.9	—	—	3	74.9
Philippines	2	151.0	—	—	2	151.0
Solomon Islands	—	—	1	5.0	1	5.0
Thailand	2	93.0	—	—	2	93.0
Vanuatu	—	—	1	2.0	1	2.0
Western Samoa	—	—	1	2.5	1	2.5
Total	36	3,101.8	8	463.4	44	3,565.2
South Asia:						
Bangladesh	—	—	6	463.0	6	463.0
Burma	—	—	1	30.0	1	30.0
India	6	1,743.2	6	625.1	12	2,368.3
Nepal	—	—	2	34.5	2	34.5
Pakistan	4	473.0	3	177.2	7	650.2
Sri Lanka	—	—	4	85.0	4	85.0
Total	10	2,216.2	22	1,414.8	32	3,631.0
Europe, Middle East and North Africa:						
Cyprus	1	20.0	—	—	1	20.0
Egypt	1	70.0	—	—	1	70.0
Hungary	3	189.0	—	—	3	189.0
Jordan	4	102.7	—	—	4	102.7
Morocco	5	538.0	—	—	5	538.0
Oman	1	30.0	—	—	1	30.0
Portugal	1	25.0	—	—	1	25.0
Syria	2	77.5	—	—	2	77.5
Tunisia	1	27.7	—	—	1	27.7
Turkey	6	1,057.0	—	—	6	1,057.0
Yemen Arab Republic	—	—	4	46.4	4	46.4
Yugoslavia	1	121.5	—	—	1	121.5
Total	26	2,258.4	4	46.4	30	2,304.8

continued opposite

INTERNATIONAL ORGANIZATIONS   United Nations (Specialized Agencies)

	IBRD Loans[1]		IDA Credits[1]		Total[1]	
	Number[2]	US $ m.	Number[2]	US $ m.	Number[2]	US $ m.
Latin America and the Caribbean:						
Argentina	3	544.5	—	—	3	544.5
Barbados	1	10.0	—	—	1	10.0
Bolivia	—	—	2	70.0	2	70.0
Brazil	11	1,620.0	—	—	1	1,620.0
Chile	4	456.0	—	—	4	456.0
Colombia	7	700.3	—	—	7	700.3
Dominican Republic	1	35.8	—	—	1	35.8
Ecuador	4	253.5	—	—	4	253.5
Guatemala	1	81.0	—	—	1	81.0
Honduras	1	37.4	—	—	1	37.4
Mexico	6	904.0	—	—	6	904.0
Peru	1	13.5	—	—	1	13.5
Uruguay	1	45.2	—	—	1	45.2
Total	41	4,701.2	2	70.0	43	4,771.2
Grand total	131	13,178.8	97	3,139.9	228	16,318.7

[1] Supplements are included in amounts, but are not counted as separate lending operations.
[2] Joint IBRD/IDA operations are counted only once, as Bank operations.

IBRD INCOME AND EXPENDITURE
(US $'000, year ending 30 June 1986)

Revenue	
Income from loans:	
Interest	4,416,750
Commitment charges	251,597
Front-end fees	1,353
Income from investments	2,121,129
Other income	24,035
Total income	**6,814,864**

Expenditure	
Interest on borrowings	5,018,178
Amortization of issuance costs	81,537
Administrative expenses	384,555
Provision for loan losses	37,200
Other financial expenses	7,212
Total	**5,528,682**
Operating income	**1,286,182**
Contributions to special programmes	42,725
Net income	**1,243,457**

IBRD OPERATIONS AND RESOURCES, 1977–86 (years ending 30 June)

	1976/77	1977/78	1978/79	1979/80	1980/81	1981/82	1982/83	1983/84	1984/85	1985/86
Amounts in US $ m.										
Loans approved*	5,759	6,098	6,989	7,644	8,809	10,330	11,138	11,947	11,356	13,179
Disbursements†	2,636	2,787	3,602	4,363	5,063	6,326	6,817	8,580	8,645	8,263
Total income	1,617	1,947	2,425	2,800	2,999	3,372	4,232	4,655	5,529	6,815
Net income	209	238	407	588	610	598	752	600	1,137	1,243
General reserve	2,026	2,245	2,498	2,893	2,859	3,124	3,134	3,450	3,727	4,918
Borrowings:										
total	4,721	3,636	5,085	5,173	5,069	8,521	10,292	9,831	11,086	10,609
net	3,258	2,171	3,235	2,382	2,347	5,692	7,349	7,175	7,138	5,758
Subscribed capital	30,869	33,045	37,429	39,959	36,614	43,165	52,089	56,011	58,846	77,526
Operations, Countries										
Operations approved	161	137	142	144	140	150	136	129	131	131
Recipient countries	54	46	44	48	50	43	43	43	44	41
Member countries	129	132	134	135	139	142	144	146	148	150
Professional staff	2,203	2,290	2,382	2,474	2,552	2,689	2,703	2,735	2,800	3,617‡

* Excludes loans to IFC of $20m. in 1976/77, $100m. in 1980/81, $390m. in 1981/82, $145m. in 1982/83, $100m. in 1983/84, $400m. in 1984/85 and $150m. in 1985/86. Includes amounts lent on Third Window terms in 1976/77.

† Excludes disbursements on loans to IFC.
‡ Increase reflects a change in job-grading structure.
Source: *World Bank Annual Report, 1986.*

International Development Association — IDA

Address: 1818 H Street, NW, Washington, DC 20433, USA.
Telephone: (202) 477-1234.

The International Development Association began operations in November 1960. Affiliated to the IBRD (see above), IDA advances capital to the poorer developing member countries on more flexible terms than those offered by the IBRD.

MEMBERS

134 members: see Table on pp. 53–55.

Organization

Officers and staff of the IBRD serve concurrently as officers and staff of IDA.

President and Chairman of Executive Directors: BARBER B. CONABLE (ex officio).

Activities

IDA assistance is aimed at the poorer developing countries (i.e. those with a per caput GNP of less than US $791 in 1983 dollars).

Under IDA lending conditions, credits can be extended to countries which, for balance of payments reasons, could not assume the burden of repayment required for IBRD loans. Terms are more favourable than those provided by the IBRD; credits are for a period of 50 years, with a grace period of 10 years, and no interest charges.

IDA's total resources, consisting of members' subscriptions and supplementary resources (additional subscriptions and contributions) amounted to US $39,177m. on 30 June 1986. Resources are replenished periodically by contributions from the more affluent member countries. Owing to a decision by the government of the USA to cut its annual contributions by 20% to $750m., a total of $9,000m. was made available for the seventh replenishment (covering the period 1984–87), compared with the IDA target figure of $16,000m., and the previous three-year replenishment amounting to $12,000m. Supplementary funding of $1,200m. was provided by developed countries (excluding the USA). Negotiations on an eighth replenishment of between $10,500m. and $12,500m. began in 1986.

During the year ending 30 June 1986, 32% of IDA assistance approved was for agriculture and rural development and 12% for energy. Over 45% of assistance was for southern Asia (chiefly India and Bangladesh) and 36% for Africa (see tables on pp. 64–65).

IDA OPERATIONS AND RESOURCES, 1977–86 (years ending 30 June)

	1976/77	1977/78	1978/79	1979/80	1980/81	1981/82	1982/83	1983/84	1984/85	1985/86
Amounts in US $ m.										
Credit amounts	1,308	2,313	3,022	3,838	3,482	2,686	3,341	3,575	3,028	3,140
Disbursements	1,298	1,062	1,222	1,411	1,878	2,067	2,596	2,524	2,491	3,155
Usable resources, cumulative	11,789	18,062	19,661	20,773	22,331	25,280	27,967	30,910	33,295	39,177
Operations, Countries										
Operations approved*	67	99	105	103	106	97	107	106	105	97
Recipient countries	36	42	43	40	40	42	44	43	45	37
Member countries	117	120	121	121	125	130	131	131	133	134

*Joint IBRD/IDA operations are counted only once, as IBRD operations.

International Finance Corporation—IFC

Address: 1818 H Street, NW, Washington, DC 20433, USA.
Telephone: (202) 477-1234.
Telex: 440098.

IFC was founded in 1956 as an affiliate of the World Bank to encourage the growth of productive private enterprise in its member countries, particularly in the less-developed areas.

MEMBERS

128 members: see Table on pp. 53–55.

Organization
(October 1986)

IFC is a separate legal entity in the World Bank Group. Executive Directors of the World Bank also serve as Directors of IFC. The President of the World Bank is ex-officio Chairman of the IFC Board of Directors, which has appointed him President of IFC. Subject to his overall supervision, the day-to-day operations of IFC are conducted by its staff under the direction of the Executive Vice-President.

PRINCIPAL OFFICERS

President: Barber B. Conable.
Executive Vice-President: Sir William Ryrie.

REGIONAL MISSIONS

East Asia: c/o Central Bank of the Philippines, Manila, Philippines: tel. 59-99-35; telex 742 40541; Dir V. K. Chaudhry.
Eastern Africa: Reinsurance Plaza, 5th Floor, Taifa Rd, POB 30577, Nairobi, Kenya; tel. 24726; telex 22022; Dir V. S. Raghavan.
Middle East: 3 Elbergas St, Garden City, Cairo, Egypt; tel. 3543923; telex 93110; Dir C. Hassan.
Western Africa: BP 1850, Corner of Booker Washington and Jacques Aka Sts, Abidjan 01, Ivory Coast; tel. 32-90-61; telex 28132; Dir J. O. Fraisse.

There are also offices in India, Indonesia, Japan and Turkey.

Activities

IFC functions as follows:

1. In association with private investors, invests without government guarantee in productive private enterprises of economic priority in member countries where sufficient private capital is not available on reasonable terms.
2. Stimulates the international flow of private capital to developing countries.
3. Encourages the development of local capital markets.
4. Invests in and gives technical help to development finance companies, and assists other institutions which also support economic development and follow policies generally consistent with those of IFC.
5. Commits limited amounts of funds for promotional purposes, to help bring development enterprises into being.
6. Revolves its portfolio by sales of its investments to other investors.

IFC's authorized capital is US $1,300m., following the authorization of $650m. in new shares in 1985. At 30 June 1986 paid-in capital was $602m. The World Bank is the principal source of borrowed funds, but IFC also borrowed $350m. from private capital markets in the year ending 30 June 1986.

In the financial year ending 30 June 1986 total investments approved amounted to $1,156m. for 85 projects, compared with $937m. for 75 projects in the previous year. Of the total approved, $1,070m. was for loans and $86m. for equity or equity-like investments.

Projects approved during the year were located in 39 countries (and one was world-wide in scope): 42% of investment finance went to Asia, 32% to Latin America, 16% to Europe and the Middle East, and 10% to Africa. About 39% of financing was for countries with a per caput income of less than $800. The largest proportion of investment was for fertilizers, chemicals and petrochemicals (30%), while 19% was for energy and minerals, 16% for other manufacturing, 9% for tourism, 8% for capital markets and financial services, 7% for wood, pulp and paper, 6% for agribusiness and 5% for cement and steel.

IFC also undertakes technical assistance for the creation of new enterprises and the restructuring of existing ones, often in co-operation with the UN Development Programme (UNDP). IFC acts as the executing agency of the Caribbean Project Development Facility, established by UNDP in 1981 to raise funds for new investment in the Caribbean; by June 1985 30 projects in 18 Caribbean states had been completed.

IFC's five-year programme for 1985–89 includes four major objectives: to provide technical and financial assistance to firms which, although otherwise sound, are faced with severe market and financial difficulties and must re-structure their businesses; to give increased attention to high-priority development projects in low-income countries, especially in agriculture and agro-industry; to increase investment in petroleum and gas exploration and development; and to expand its activities in Africa south of the Sahara. Real net investment was expected to expand by about 7% per year during the period. In July 1984 a change in IFC's loan policy was announced: instead of borrowing at fixed rates of interest, as hitherto enforced, companies were to have the option of borrowing at 'floating' rates, on terms designed to meet the particular needs of the borrower.

In May 1986 IFC, in co-operation with UNDP and the African Development Bank, launched the Africa Project Development Facility (APDF). IFC was to manage the Facility, which consists of two teams of experts based in Nairobi, Kenya (covering eastern and southern Africa) and in Abidjan, Ivory Coast (covering western and central Africa). The APDF aims to support the private sector of African countries by helping African entrepreneurs to develop sound investment projects and to find financing for them. The Emerging Markets Growth Fund was also launched in 1986 to invest in publicly listed shares in certain developing countries.

IFC's total operating income rose to $210.4m. in the year ending 30 June 1986, from $172.7m. the previous year. Interest from loans amounted to $141.9m. Net income of $25.4m. brought total accumulated earnings to $283.8m. The Corporation's investment portfolio held for its own account (including undisbursed balances) was $2,387.2m., and $1,053.8m. was being held and administered for participants in IFC financings.

PUBLICATION

Annual Report.

IFC OPERATIONS AND RESOURCES, 1982–86 (fiscal years ending 30 June)

	1982	1983	1984	1985	1986
Approved investments					
Number of projects	65	58	62	75	85
Number of countries	31	36	37	38	39
Amount (gross US $ million)	612	845	696	937	1,156
Total project costs* (US $ million)	2,936	2,894	2,473	2,768	3,588
Resources and income (US $ million)					
Borrowings	531	536	582	825	1,223
Paid-in capital	497	544	544	546	602
Accumulated earnings	181	204	230	258	284
Net income	21.6	23.0	26.3	28.3	25.4

* Including investment mobilized from other sources.

INTERNATIONAL ORGANIZATIONS   United Nations (Specialized Agencies)

International Civil Aviation Organization—ICAO

Address: 1000 Sherbrooke St West, Montreal, PQ H3A 2R2, Canada.
Telephone: (514) 285-8219.
Telex: 05-24513.

The Convention on International Civil Aviation was signed in Chicago in 1944. As a result ICAO was founded in 1947 to develop the techniques of international air navigation and to help in the planning and improvement of international air transport.

MEMBERS

156 members: see Table on pp. 53–55.

Organization

(October 1986)

ASSEMBLY

Composed of representatives of all member states, the Assembly is the organization's legislative body and meets at least once in three years. It reviews the work of the organization, sets out the work programme for the next three years, approves the budget and determines members' contributions.

COUNCIL

Composed of representatives of 33 member states, elected by the Assembly. It is the executive body, and establishes and supervises subsidiary technical committees and makes recommendations to member governments; meets in virtually continuous session; elects the President, appoints the Secretary-General, and administers the finances of the organization. The functions of the Council are:

to adopt international standards and recommended practices and incorporate them as annexes to the Convention on International Civil Aviation;

to arbitrate between member states on matters concerning aviation and implementation of the Convention;

to investigate any situation which presents avoidable obstacles to development of international air navigation;

to take whatever steps are necessary to maintain safety and regularity of operation of international air transport;

to provide technical assistance to the developing countries under the UN Development Programme and other assistance programmes.

President of the Council: Dr Assad Kotaite (Lebanon).
Secretary-General: Yves Lambert (France).

AIR NAVIGATION COMMISSION

The Commission comprises 15 members.
President: H. L. Bingel.

STANDING COMMITTEES

These include the Air Transport Committee, the Committee on Joint Support of Air Navigation Services, the Finance Committee, the Legal Committee, the Committee on Unlawful Interference, and the Edward Warner Award Committee.

REGIONAL OFFICES

Africa: BP 2356, Dakar, Senegal.
Eastern Africa: POB 46294, Nairobi, Kenya.
Asia and Pacific: POB 614, Bangkok, Thailand.
Europe: 3 bis, Villa Emile-Bergerat, 92522 Neuilly-sur-Seine Cedex, France.
Middle East: 16 Hassan Sabri, Zamalek, Cairo, Egypt.
North America and Caribbean: Apartado Postal 5-377, CP 11590, México 5, DF, Mexico.
South America: Apartado 4127, Lima 100, Peru.

Activities

ICAO aims to ensure the safe and orderly growth of civil aviation; to encourage skills in aircraft design and operation; to improve airways, airports and air navigation; to prevent the waste of resources in unreasonable competition; to safeguard the rights of each contracting party to operate international air transport; and to prevent discriminatory practices.

ICAO SPECIFICATIONS

These are contained in annexes to the Chicago Convention, and in three sets of Procedures for Air Navigation Services (PANS Documents). The specifications are periodically revised in keeping with developments in technology and changing requirements. The 18 annexes to the Convention include personnel licensing, rules relating to the conduct of flights, meteorological services, aeronautical charts, air-ground communications, safety specifications, identification, air traffic control, rescue services, environmental protection, security and the transporting of dangerous goods. Technical Manuals and Circulars are issued to facilitate implementation.

ICAO REGIONAL PLANS

These set out the technical requirements for air navigation facilities in the nine ICAO regions; Regional Offices offer assistance (see addresses above). Because of growth in air traffic and changes in the pattern of air routes, the Plans are periodically amended.

EUROPEAN AIR NAVIGATION PLANNING GROUP

Reviews current problems and the need for changes in the air navigation facilities in the European Region.

ICAO PROJECTS

Studies of current problems aiming to apply new technology, including: airworthiness of aircraft, all-weather navigation, aircraft separation, obstacle clearances, noise abatement, operation of aircraft and carriage by air of dangerous goods, automated data interchange systems, aviation security and use of space technology in air navigation.

ENVIRONMENT

International standards and guidelines for noise certification of aircraft and international provisions for the regulation of aircraft engine emissions have been adopted and published in Annex 16 to the Chicago Convention.

AIR TRANSPORT

Continuing functions include preparation of regional air transport development studies; studies on international air transport fares and rates; review of the economic situation of airports and route facilities; development of guidance material on civil aviation forecasting and planning; collection and publication of statistics; facilitation of passenger and freight clearance formalities; and multilateral financing of certain air navigation facilities.

TECHNICAL ASSISTANCE BUREAU

The Bureau assists developing countries in the execution of various projects. At least US $52m. was to be spent on assistance in 1986.

LEGAL COMMITTEE

The general work programme of the Committee in 1986 included the following subjects: the UN Convention on the Law of the Sea and its implications for the application of the Chicago Convention, its annexes and other international air law instruments; the liability of air traffic control agencies; study of the status of the instruments of the 'Warsaw System'; and preparation of a draft instrument on the interception of civil aircraft.

INTERNATIONAL ORGANIZATIONS

United Nations (Specialized Agencies)

FINANCE

Total ICAO net budget appropriations for 1985 were US $30.5m., and for 1986 were $32.3m.

PUBLICATIONS

Catalogue of ICAO Publications.
ICAO Bulletin (monthly, in English, French and Spanish; quarterly digest in Russian).
Digest of Statistics.
Minutes and Documents of the Legal Committee.
Lexicon of terms.
The 18 Annexes to the Convention.
Procedures for Air Navigation Services.
ICAO Training Manual.
Regional Air Navigation Plans.
Aircraft Accident Digest.

International Fund for Agricultural Development—IFAD

Address: (provisional) Via del Serafico 107, 00142 Rome, Italy.
Telephone: 54591.
Telex: 614160/2.

Following a decision by the 1974 UN World Food Conference, IFAD was established in 1976 to fund rural development programmes specifically aimed at the poorest of the world's people. It began operations in December 1977.

MEMBERS

141 members: see Table on pp. 53–55.

Category I	Category II	Category III
Australia	Algeria	109 developing countries
Austria	Gabon	
Belgium	Indonesia	
Canada	Iran	
Denmark	Iraq	
Finland	Kuwait	
France	Libya	
Germany, Federal Republic	Nigeria	
	Qatar	
Ireland	Saudi Arabia	
Italy	United Arab Emirates	
Japan	Venezuela	
Luxembourg		
Netherlands		
New Zealand		
Norway		
Spain		
Sweden		
Switzerland		
United Kingdom		
USA		

Organization

(October 1986)

GOVERNING COUNCIL

Each member state is represented in the Governing Council by a Governor and an Alternate. There are three categories of members: industrialized countries (OECD members) forming Category I; petroleum-exporting developing countries (OPEC members) forming Category II; recipient developing countries (Category III). Categories I and II *shall* contribute to the resources of the Fund while Category III *may* do so. All the powers of the Fund are vested in the Governing Council. It may, however, delegate certain powers to the Executive Board. Sessions are held annually with special sessions as required. The Governing Council elects the President of the Fund by a two-thirds majority for a three-year term. He is eligible for re-election. The President is also the Chairman of the Executive Board.

EXECUTIVE BOARD

Consists of 18 members and 17 alternates, elected by the Governing Council, one-third by each category of membership. Members serve for three years. The Executive Board is responsible for the conduct and general operation of IFAD and approves loans and grants for projects; it meets three or four times a year.

The total number of votes in the Governing Council and the Executive Board is 1,800, distributed equally between the three categories of membership. Thus two-thirds of the votes lie with the developing countries (Categories II and III) which will therefore have a major influence on the investment decisions of the Fund. At the same time two-thirds of the votes are held by donor countries (Categories I and II).

President and Chairman of Executive Board: IDRISS JAZAIRY.

DEPARTMENTS

IFAD has three main administrative departments: the Economic and Planning Department (with Divisions for Planning and Economic Analysis, Policy Review, and Monitoring and Evaluation); the Project Management Department (with four regional Divisions and a Loan Implementation Unit); and the General Affairs Department. At the end of 1984 regular staff numbered 165, of whom 71 were in executive or technical positions.

Activities

The Fund's objective is to mobilize additional resources to be made available on concessional terms for agricultural development in developing member states. IFAD provides financing primarily for projects designed to improve food production systems and to strengthen related policies and institutions within the framework of national priorities and strategies. In allocating resources IFAD is guided by: the need to increase food production in the poorest food-deficit countries; the potential for increasing food production in other developing countries; and the importance of improving the nutritional level of the poorest populations in developing countries and the conditions of their lives. Particular emphasis is placed on assistance to rural women.

IFAD is empowered to make both grants and loans. Under its Agreement, grants are limited to 12.5% of the resources committed in any one financial year. There are three kinds of loan: highly concessional loans, which carry no interest but have an annual service charge of 1% and a maturity period of 50 years, including a grace period of 10 years; intermediate term loans, which have an annual interest rate of 4% and a maturity period of 20 years, including a grace period of five years; and ordinary term loans which have an interest rate of 8% and a maturity period of 15–18 years, including a grace period of three years. During 1978–84 67.6% of loans were on highly concessional terms. To avoid duplication of work, the administration of loans, for the purposes of disbursements and supervision of project implementation, is entrusted to competent international financial institutions, with the Fund retaining an active interest.

Between 1978 and the end of 1984 the Fund approved loans for 160 projects in 84 countries, at a cost of about US $1,968m. from its own resources, representing 28.5% of total project costs, while 36.7% was provided by other external donors and 34.8% by domestic sources. In addition, the Fund provided technical assistance grants amounting to $90.4m.

During 1984 IFAD approved 25 loans amounting to $196m., of which 34% was for Africa, 30% for Asia, 21% for the Near East and North Africa, and 15% for Latin America and the Caribbean. Technical assistance grants of $14m. were also made, bringing the total financial assistance provided to $210m., compared with $279m. in 1983 and $339m. in 1982. Commitments for 1985 were further reduced (about $160m.) as a result of the delay in reaching agreement on the Fund's second replenishment (see Finance, below). Disbursements during 1984 amounted to $195m. in loans and $17m. in technical assistance grants.

IFAD's development projects usually include a number of components, such as infrastructure (e.g. improvement of water supplies, irrigation and road construction); input supply (e.g. improved seeds, fertilizers and pesticides); institutional support (e.g. research, training and extension services); and producer incentives (e.g. pricing and marketing improvements). IFAD also attempts to enable the landless to acquire income-generating assets: by increasing the supply of loanable funds for the rural poor, it seeks to free them from dependence on the unorganized and exploitative capital market and to generate productive activities. An example is IFAD's support for the Grameen Bank in Bangladesh, which by October 1983 had given small loans to more than 50,000 landless people (with a credit recovery rate of 96%).

In addition to its regular efforts to identify projects and programmes, IFAD organizes special programming missions to certain selected countries to undertake a comprehensive review of the constraints affecting the rural poor, and to help countries to design strategies for the removal of these constraints. Based on the recommendations of these missions, a number of projects have been identified or prepared. In general, these projects tend to focus on institutional improvements at the national and local level to direct inputs and services to small farmers and the landless rural poor.

In 1985 IFAD launched a Special Programme for Africa south of the Sahara, aiming to spend $300m. over the next three years on improving food production and water conservation in Africa.

LOANS APPROVED BY IFAD IN 1984

Region and Country	Loan Amount (US $m.)
Africa south of the Sahara	
Central African Republic	3.3
Comoros	3.3
The Gambia	5.0
Ivory Coast	2.85
Liberia	5.8
Malawi	13.6
Rwanda	3.8
São Tomé and Príncipe	2.13
Sierra Leone	5.4
Somalia	7.0
Sudan	6.0
Uganda	14.5
Zaire	6.5
Asia and the Pacific	
Bangladesh	23.6
China, People's Republic	25.0
Pakistan	8.6
Solomon Islands	1.5
Latin America	
Bolivia	12.0
El Salvador	5.0
Guatemala	5.0
Paraguay	7.0
Near East and North Africa	
Cyprus	4.9
Egypt	10.2
Turkey	10.0
Yemen Arab Republic	4.0

FINANCE

The total initial resources pledged by members, valued as at 31 December 1981, amounted to US $1,015m.

In order to assure continuity in the operations of the Fund, the Governing Council periodically reviews the adequacy of the available resources as stipulated in the Agreement establishing IFAD. The first such review took place three years after the beginning of operations. At the Third Session of the IFAD Governing Council, in January 1980, a resolution calling for the replenishment of IFAD's resources was adopted by the Fund's member states. At its Fifth Session, in January 1982, the Council reached final agreement on the level of replenishment. Member countries offered to provide contributions totalling about US $1,100m. for the period 1981–83 (later extended to 1984). This comprised $620m. (56%) from the developed (Category I) countries, $450m. (41%) from petroleum-exporting developing (Category II) countries and $30m. (3%) from other developing (Category III) countries. Together with the carrying-over of available resources, this would have enabled the Fund to undertake an operational programme of about $1,350m. during 1981–84. However, actual payments (particularly those of the USA) were slower than expected. As a result, the size of IFAD's lending operations decreased from 1982 onwards. Talks on a second replenishment for 1985–87 began in July 1983, and continued until January 1986, when members finally agreed on a replenishment of $500m. This was to be supplemented by an extra $300m. for the Special Programme for sub-Saharan African countries.

PUBLICATION

Annual Report.

International Labour Organisation—ILO

Address: 4 route des Morillons, 1211 Geneva 22, Switzerland.
Telephone: (022) 996111.
Telex: 22 271.

ILO was founded in 1919 to work for social justice as a basis for lasting peace. It carries out this mandate by promoting decent living standards, satisfactory conditions of work and pay and adequate employment opportunities. Methods of action include the creation of international labour standards; the provision of technical co-operation services; and research and publications on social and labour matters. In 1946, the Organisation became a specialized agency associated with the UN. It was awarded the Nobel Peace Prize in 1969.

MEMBERS

150 members: see Table on pp. 53–55.

Organization

(October 1986)

INTERNATIONAL LABOUR CONFERENCE

The supreme deliberative body of ILO, the Conference normally meets annually in Geneva, with a session devoted to maritime questions when necessary; it is attended by about 2,000 delegates, advisers and observers. National delegations are composed of two government delegates, one employers' delegate and one workers' delegate. Non-governmental delegates can speak and vote independently of the views of their government. Conference elects the Governing Body and adopts the Budget and International Labour Conventions and Recommendations.

INTERNATIONAL ORGANIZATIONS   United Nations (Specialized Agencies)

The President and Vice-Presidents hold office for the term of the Conference only.

GOVERNING BODY

ILO's executive council; normally meets three or four times a year in Geneva to decide policy and programmes. Composed of 28 Government members, 14 employers' members and 14 workers' members. Ten seats are reserved for 'states of chief industrial importance': Brazil, the People's Republic of China, France, the Federal Republic of Germany, India, Italy, Japan, the USSR, the United Kingdom and the USA. The remaining 18 are elected from other countries every three years. Employers' and workers' members are elected as individuals, not as national candidates.

Chairman (1986/87): W. R. B. ROBINSON (United Kingdom).

Employers' Vice-Chairman: JEAN-JACQUES OECHSLIN (France).

Workers' Vice-Chairman: GERD MUHR (Federal Republic of Germany).

INTERNATIONAL LABOUR OFFICE

The International Labour Office is the Organisation's secretariat, operational headquarters and publishing house. It is staffed in Geneva and in the field by about 1,900 people of some 110 nationalities. Operations are decentralized to regional, area and branch offices in nearly 40 countries.

Director-General: FRANCIS BLANCHARD (France).

REGIONAL OFFICES

Regional Office for Africa: POB 2788, Addis Ababa, Ethiopia.

Regional Office for the Americas: Apdo Postal 3638, Lima 1, Peru.

Regional Office for Arab States: ILO, 4 route des Morillons, 1211 Geneva 22, Switzerland.

Regional Office for Asia and the Pacific: POB 1759, Bangkok 2, Thailand.

Activities

INTERNATIONAL LABOUR CONFERENCE

70th session: June 1984. Adopted an International Labour Recommendation on employment policy, and held first discussions on occupational health services and the revision of convention no. 63 (on statistics of wages and hours of work) with a view to the adoption of new instruments in these fields in 1985. Also evaluated the ILO's International Programme for the Improvement of Working Conditions and Environment.

71st session: June 1985. Adopted a Convention and Recommendation on occupational health services and a Convention and Recommendation on statistics of wages and hours of work. A first discussion was held with a view to the adoption of standards of safety in the use of asbestos.

72nd session: June 1986. Adopted a Convention and Recommendation on safety in the use of asbestos. General discussions were held on youth and unemployment, and on the promotion of small- and medium-sized enterprises. The session also adopted amendments to the Constitution, reforming the structure of ILO.

INTERNATIONAL LABOUR STANDARDS

One of the ILO's primary functions is the adoption by the International Labour Conference of Conventions and Recommendations setting minimum labour standards. Through ratification by member states, Conventions create binding obligations to put their provisions into effect. Recommendations provide guidance as to policy and practice. A total of 162 Conventions and 172 Recommendations have been adopted, ranging over a wide field of social and labour matters, including basic human rights such as freedom of association, abolition of forced labour and elimination of discrimination in employment. Together they form the International Labour Code. By July 1986 over 5,200 ratifications of the Conventions had been registered by member states.

TECHNICAL CO-OPERATION

Technical co-operation continues to be a major ILO activity. About US $90.3m. from all sources, including the United Nations Development Programme, was spent in 1985 for the promotion of employment, the development of human resources and social institutions, and the improvement of living and working conditions. Of the total figure, $38.9m. was provided by UNDP, $35.5m. by bilateral aid agencies in trust fund arrangements, and $5.3m. by the UN Fund for Population Activities, the ILO regular budget contributing $10.6m.

WORLD EMPLOYMENT PROGRAMME

The employment objective has been incorporated by the United Nations as a key policy factor in the Second United Nations Development Decade. The ILO has the role of catalyst in bringing employment considerations to the fore in the activities of all agencies within the UN system, and for this purpose launched the World Employment Programme.

The aim of the programme is to assist decision makers in identifying and putting into effect specific employment-promoting development policies. This is accomplished through comprehensive employment strategy missions and exploratory country employment missions; through regional employment teams for Africa, Asia and Latin America and the Caribbean; and through country employment teams.

The programme also includes research activities which cover eight major project areas: technology and employment, income distribution and employment, population and employment, education and training and employment, rural employment, promotion, urbanization and employment, trade expansion and employment, and emergency employment schemes.

MEETINGS

Among meetings held during 1986, in addition to the International Labour Conference and Governing Body sessions, were the 12th Conference of American States Members of ILO (Montreal), the Petroleum Committee (10th session), and the Preparatory Technical Maritime Conference. A meeting on the settlement of labour disputes in the public service, and the 11th session of the Iron and Steel Committee, were due to be held later in the year.

INTERNATIONAL INSTITUTE FOR LABOUR STUDIES

Established in 1960 and based at the ILO's Geneva headquarters, the Institute is an advanced educational and research institution dealing with social and labour policy, and brings together international experts representing employers, management, workers and government interests. Activities include international and regional study courses, and are financed by grants and an Endowment Fund to which governments and other bodies contribute.

INTERNATIONAL CENTRE FOR ADVANCED TECHNICAL AND VOCATIONAL TRAINING

Address: Via Ventimiglia 201, 10127 Turin, Italy.

The Centre became operational in 1965. It provides programmes for directors in charge of technical and vocational institutions, training officers, senior and middle-level managers in private and public enterprises, trade union leaders, and technicians, primarily from the developing regions of the world. The ILO Director-General is Chairman of the Board of the Centre.

Director: JULIO GALER (Argentina).

FINANCE

The net expenditure budget for 1986–87 was US $253m.

PUBLICATIONS

(in English, French and Spanish unless otherwise indicated)

International Labour Review (6 a year).

Official Bulletin (3 a year).

Legislative Series (selected labour and social security laws and regulations; 2 a year).

Bulletin of Labour Statistics (quarterly).

Social and Labour Bulletin (quarterly).

Year Book of Labour Statistics.

International studies, surveys, works of practical guidance or reference on questions of social policy, manpower, industrial relations, working conditions, social security, training, management development, etc.

Training and Development Abstracts (a service providing digests of articles, laws, reports on vocational guidance and training and management development).

Reports for the annual sessions of the International Labour Conference, etc. (in English, French, German, Russian, Spanish).

ILO-Information (bulletin issued in Arabic, Danish, English, Finnish, French, German, Japanese, Norwegian, Russian, Spanish, Swedish and Urdu).

INTERNATIONAL ORGANIZATIONS — United Nations (Specialized Agencies)

International Maritime Organization—IMO

Address: 4 Albert Embankment, London, SE1 7SR, England.
Telephone: (01) 735-7611.
Telex: 23588.

The Inter-Governmental Maritime Consultative Organization (IMCO) began operations in 1959, as a specialized agency of the UN to facilitate co-operation among governments on technical matters affecting international shipping. Its main functions are the achievement of safe and efficient navigation, and the control of pollution caused by ships and craft operating in the marine environment. IMCO became IMO in 1982.

MEMBERS
129 members and one associate member: see Table on pp. 53–55.

Organization
(October 1986)

ASSEMBLY
The Assembly consists of delegates from all member countries, who each have one vote. Associate members and observers from other governments and the international agencies are also present. Regular sessions are held every two years. The Assembly is responsible for the election of members to the Council and to the Maritime Safety Committee. It considers reports from all subsidiary bodies and decides the action to be taken on them; it votes the agency's budget and determines the work programme and financial policy.

The Assembly also recommends to members measures to promote maritime safety and to prevent and control maritime pollution from ships.

COUNCIL
The Council is the governing body of the Organization between the biennial sessions of the Assembly. Its members, representatives of 32 states, are elected by the Assembly for a term of two years. The Council appoints the Secretary-General; transmits reports by the subsidiary bodies, including the Maritime Safety Committee, to the Assembly and reports on the work of the Organization generally; submits budget estimates and financial statements with comments and recommendations to the Assembly. The Council normally meets twice a year.
Chairman: W. A. O'Neil (Canada).

Facilitation Committee: Constituted by the Council in May 1972 as a subsidiary body, this Committee deals with measures to facilitate maritime travel and transport and matters arising from the 1965 Facilitation Convention. Membership open to all IMO member states.

MARITIME SAFETY COMMITTEE
The Maritime Safety Committee is open to all IMO members. The Committee meets at least once a year and submits proposals to the Assembly on technical matters affecting shipping, including prevention of marine pollution.

Sub-Committees:

Bulk Chemicals.
Cargoes and Containers.
Carriage of Dangerous Goods.
Fire Protection.
Life-Saving Appliances.
Radiocommunications.
Safety of Navigation.
Standards of Training and Watchkeeping.
Ship Design and Equipment.
Stability and Load Lines and Fishing Vessel Safety.

LEGAL COMMITTEE
Established by the Council in June 1967 to deal initially with problems connected with the loss of the tanker *Torrey Canyon*, and subsequently with any legal problems laid before IMO. Membership open to all IMO Member States.

MARINE ENVIRONMENT PROTECTION COMMITTEE
Established by the eighth Assembly (1973) to co-ordinate IMO's work on the prevention and control of marine pollution from ships, and to assist IMO in its consultations with other UN bodies, and with international organizations and expert bodies in the field of marine pollution. Membership is open to all IMO members.

TECHNICAL CO-OPERATION COMMITTEE
Constituted by the Council in May 1972, this Committee evaluates the implementation of UN Development Programme projects for which IMO is executing agency and generally reviews IMO's technical assistance programmes. Its membership is open to all IMO member states.

SECRETARIAT
The Secretariat consists of the Secretary-General and a staff appointed by the Secretary-General and recruited on as wide a geographical basis as possible.
Secretary-General: C. P. Srivastava (India).
Divisions of the Secretariat:

Maritime Safety
Navigation (Sub-Division)
Technology (Sub-Division)
Marine Environment
Legal Affairs and External Relations
Administrative
Conference
Technical Co-operation

Activities

In addition to the work of its committees and sub-committees, the organization works in connection with the following Conventions, of which it is the depository:

International Convention for the Prevention of Pollution of the Sea by Oil, 1954. IMO has taken over administration from the United Kingdom.

Convention on Facilitation of International Maritime Traffic, 1965. Came into force in March 1967.

International Convention on Load Lines, 1966. Came into force in July 1968.

International Convention on Tonnage Measurement of Ships, 1969. Convention embodies a universal system for measuring ships' tonnage. Came into force in 1982.

International Convention relating to Intervention on the High Seas in Cases of Oil Pollution Casualties, 1969. Came into force in May 1975.

International Convention on Civil Liability for Oil Pollution Damage, 1969. Came into force in June 1975.

Intenational Convention on the Establishment of an International Fund for Compensation for Oil Pollution Damage, 1971. Came into force in October 1978.

Convention on the International Regulations for Preventing Collisions at Sea, 1972. Came into force in July 1977.

International Convention for Safe Containers, 1972. Came into force in September 1977.

International Convention on the Prevention of Pollution from Ships, 1973 (as modified by the Protocol of 1978). Came into force in October 1983.

International Convention for Safety of Life at Sea, 1974. Came into force in May 1980. A Protocol drawn up in 1978 came into force in May 1981.

Athens Convention relating to the Carriage of Passengers and their Luggage by Sea, 1974. Will come into force 90 days after 10 states have either signed it or have deposited the required instruments of ratification, acceptance, approval or accession.

Convention on the International Maritime Satellite Organization, 1976. Came into force in July 1979.

Convention on Limitation of Liability for Maritime Claims, 1976. Will come into force one year after acceptance by 12 states.

INTERNATIONAL ORGANIZATIONS

United Nations (Specialized Agencies)

International Convention for the Safety of Fishing Vessels, Torremolinos, 1977. Will come into force 12 months after 15 countries whose combined fishing fleets constitute 50% of world fishing fleets of 24 metres in length and over have become parties.

International Convention on Standards of Training, Certification and Watchkeeping for Seafarers, 1978. Came into force in April 1984.

International Convention on Maritime Search and Rescue, 1979. Came into force in June 1985.

BUDGET

Contributions are received from the member states. The budget appropriation for 1986–87 was US $30m.

PUBLICATIONS

IMO News (quarterly, English and French).

Numerous specialized publications, including international conventions of which IMO is depositary.

International Monetary Fund — IMF

Address: 700 19th St, NW, Washington, DC 20431, USA.
Telephone: (202) 477-7000.

The IMF was established at the same time as the World Bank in December 1945, to promote international monetary co-operation, to facilitate the expansion and balanced growth of international trade and to promote stability in foreign exchange.

MEMBERS

151 members: see Table on pp. 53–55.

Organization
(October 1986)

Managing Director: Jacques de Larosière de Champfeu (France) (to end of 1986).
Deputy Managing Director: Richard D. Erb (USA).

BOARD OF GOVERNORS

The highest authority of the Fund is exercised by the Board of Governors, on which each member country is represented by a Governor and an Alternate Governor. Normally the Board of Governors meets once a year, but the Governors may take votes by mail or other means between annual meetings. The Board of Governors has delegated many of its powers to the Executive Directors. However, the conditions governing the admission of new members, adjustment of quotas, election of Executive Directors, as well as certain other important powers remain the sole responsibility of the Board of Governors. The voting power of each member in the Board of Governors is related to its quota in the Fund (see p. 75).

The Interim Committee of the Board of Governors, established in 1974, usually meets twice a year. It comprises 22 members, representing the same countries or groups of countries as those on the Board of Executive Directors (see below). It reviews the international monetary system and advises the Board of Governors.

The Development Committee (the Joint Ministerial Committee of the Boards of Governors of the World Bank and the IMF on the Transfer of Real Resources to Developing Countries) was also set up in 1974, with a structure similar to that of the Interim Committee, to review development policy issues and financing requirements.

BOARD OF EXECUTIVE DIRECTORS
(see Table overleaf)

The 22-member Board of Executive Directors, responsible for the day-to-day operations of the Fund, is in continuous session in Washington, under the chairmanship of the Fund's Managing Director. The USA, the United Kingdom, the Federal Republic of Germany, France, Japan and Saudi Arabia each appoint one Executive Director, while 15 of the remaining Executive Directors are elected by groups of member countries with similar interests; there is also a Director from the People's Republic of China. As in the Board of Governors, the voting power of each member is related to its quota in the Fund, but in practice the Executive Directors operate by consensus.

The Managing Director of the Fund serves as head of its staff, which is organized into departments by function and area. On 30 April 1985 the Fund staff comprised 1,661 people from 97 countries.

Activities

The purposes of the IMF, as set out in the Articles of Agreement, are:

(i) To promote international monetary co-operation through a permanent institution which provides the machinery for consultation and collaboration on monetary problems.

(ii) To facilitate the expansion and balanced growth of international trade, and to contribute thereby to the promotion and maintenance of high levels of employment and real income and to the development of members' productive resources.

(iii) To promote exchange stability, to maintain orderly exchange arrangements among members, and to avoid competitive exchange depreciation.

(iv) To assist in the establishment of a multilateral system of payments in respect of current transactions between members and in the elimination of foreign exchange restrictions which hamper the growth of trade.

(v) To give confidence to members by making the general resources of the Fund temporarily available to them, under adequate safeguards, thus providing them with the opportunity to correct maladjustments in their balance of payments, without resorting to measures destructive of national or international prosperity.

(vi) In accordance with the above, to shorten the duration of and lessen the degree of disequilibrium in the international balances of payments of members.

In joining the Fund, each country agrees to co-operate with the above objectives, and the Fund monitors members' compliance by holding an annual consultation with each country, in order to survey the country's exchange rate policies and determine its need for assistance.

SPECIAL DRAWING RIGHTS

The special drawing right (SDR) was introduced in 1970 as a substitute for gold in international payments: it is intended eventually to become the principal reserve asset in the international monetary system. SDRs are allocated to members in proportion to their quotas. Originally SDR 9,300m. were allocated, and further allocations of approximately SDR 4,000m. each were made in 1979, 1980 and 1981, bringing the total of SDRs in existence to SDR 21,300m. or about 5% of international non-gold reserves.

From 1974 to 1980 the SDR was valued on the basis of the market exchange rate for a basket of 16 currencies, belonging to the members with the largest exports of goods and services; since 1981 it has been based on the currencies of the five largest exporters (France, the Federal Republic of Germany, Japan, the United Kingdom and the USA). The value of the SDR on 30 June 1986 was US $1.17757.

The Second Amendment to the Articles of Agreement (1978) altered and expanded the possible uses of the SDR in transactions with other participants. In the year ending 30 April 1985 the volume of transactions by agreement in SDRs decreased to SDR 2,706m. from SDR 3,175m. in 1983/84. Transactions with designation (those in which certain participants are designated by the Fund to receive specified amounts of SDRs from other participants in exchange for an equivalent amount of freely usable currencies) came to SDR 2,152m. 'Other holders' of the SDRs have the same degree of freedom as Fund members to buy and sell SDRs and to receive or use them in loans, pledges, swaps, donations or settlement of financial obligations. In September 1986 there were 16 'other holders': the African Development Bank and the African Development

BOARD OF EXECUTIVE DIRECTORS (November 1986)

Director	Casting Votes of	Total Votes	%
Appointed:			
Charles H. Dallara	USA	179,433	19.14
Timothy P. Lankester	United Kingdom	62,190	6.63
Günter Grosche	Federal Republic of Germany	54,287	5.79
Hélène Ploix	France	45,078	4.81
Hirotake Fujino	Japan	42,483	4.53
Yusuf A. Nimatallah	Saudi Arabia	32,274	3.44
Elected:			
Guillermo Ortiz (Mexico)	Costa Rica, El Salvador, Guatemala, Honduras, Mexico, Nicaragua, Spain, Venezuela	44,401	4.74
G. A. Posthumus (Netherlands)	Cyprus, Israel, Netherlands, Romania, Yugoslavia	40,425	4.31
Jacques de Groote (Belgium)	Austria, Belgium, Hungary, Luxembourg, Turkey	40,178	4.29
Marcel Massé (Canada)	Antigua and Barbuda, Bahamas, Barbados, Belize, Canada, Dominica, Grenada, Ireland, Jamaica, Saint Christopher and Nevis, Saint Lucia, Saint Vincent and the Grenadines	38,709	4.13
Salvatore Zecchini (Italy)	Greece, Italy, Malta, Portugal	38,307	4.09
Mohamed Finaish (Libya)	Bahrain, Iraq, Jordan, Kuwait, Lebanon, Libya, Maldives, Oman, Pakistan, Qatar, Somalia, Syria, United Arab Emirates, Yemen Arab Republic, People's Democratic Republic of Yemen	34,642	3.69
C. R. Rye (Australia)	Australia, Republic of Korea, New Zealand, Papua New Guinea, Philippines, Seychelles, Solomon Islands, Vanuatu, Western Samoa	32,979	3.52
Hans Lundström (Sweden)	Denmark, Finland, Iceland, Norway, Sweden	32,338	3.45
Arjun K. Sengupta (India)	Bangladesh, Bhutan, India, Sri Lanka	28,208	3.01
Alexandre Kafka (Brazil)	Brazil, Colombia, Dominican Republic, Ecuador, Guyana, Haiti, Panama, Suriname, Trinidad and Tobago	27,582	2.94
A. Abdallah (Kenya)	Botswana, Burundi, Ethiopia, The Gambia, Guinea, Kenya, Lesotho, Liberia, Malawi, Mozambique, Nigeria, Sierra Leone, Sudan, Swaziland, Tanzania, Uganda, Zambia, Zimbabwe	27,567	2.94
Julius Emmanuel Ismael (Indonesia)	Burma, Fiji, Indonesia, Laos, Malaysia, Nepal, Singapore, Thailand, Viet-Nam	26,812	2.86
Dai Qianding	People's Republic of China	24,159	2.58
Alvaro Donoso (Chile)	Argentina, Bolivia, Chile, Paraguay, Peru, Uruguay	23,373	2.49
Ghassem Salehkhou (Iran)	Afghanistan, Algeria, Ghana, Iran, Morocco, Tunisia	21,691	2.31
Mawakani Samba (Zaire)	Benin, Burkina Faso, Cameroon, Cape Verde, Central African Republic, Chad, Comoros, Congo, Djibouti, Equatorial Guinea, Gabon, Guinea-Bissau, Ivory Coast, Madagascar, Mali, Mauritania, Mauritius, Niger, Rwanda, São Tomé and Príncipe, Senegal, Togo, Zaire	18,111	1.93

Note: Votes in the General Department and the SDR Department total 937,625, including the votes of Egypt, Kampuchea, Kiribati, Poland, South Africa and Tonga. The number of votes in the Executive Board is 915,227.

Fund, the Andean Reserve Fund, the Arab Monetary Fund, the Asian Development Bank, the Bank of Central African States, the Bank for International Settlements, the Central Bank of West African States, the East African Development Bank, the Eastern Caribbean Central Bank, the Islamic Development Bank, the International Bank for Reconstruction and Development and the International Development Association, the International Fund for Agricultural Development, the Nordic Investment Bank and the Swiss National Bank.

QUOTAS

Each member is assigned a quota related to its national income, monetary reserves, trade balance and other economic indicators. A member's subscription is equal to its quota and is payable partly in SDRs and partly in its own currency. The quota approximately determines a member's voting power, the amount of foreign exchange it may purchase from the Fund, and its allocation of SDRs.

Quotas are reviewed at intervals of not more than five years, to take into account the state of the world economy and members' different rates of development. General increases were made in 1959, 1966, 1970, 1978 and 1980, while special increases were made for the People's Republic of China in April 1980, for a group of 11 members in December 1980, and for Saudi Arabia in April 1981. The eighth general review of quotas resulted in March 1983 in an agreement to raise quotas by 47.5% to SDR 90,035m., subject to approval by national legislatures. The early review (two years ahead of schedule) was considered necessary in view of the debt crisis afflicting some member states. By April 1984 all of the 142 members that had consented to increases in quotas had completed payments of their subscriptions, raising the total of IMF quotas to SDR 89,236.3m. At 31 July 1986 total quotas in the Fund amounted to SDR 89,987.6m. (see table below).

RESOURCES

Members' subscriptions form the basic resource of the IMF. They are supplemented by borrowing: during 1981/82, for the first time, IMF commitments involved a higher proportion of borrowed resources (amounting to about SDR 6,000m.) than of ordinary resources (SDR 4,500m.). In 1981 Saudi Arabia agreed to lend the Fund SDR 8,000m. over two years, and a further SDR 1,300m. was lent by other countries, partly under a borrowing agreement with the Bank for International Settlements (BIS). These loans were regarded as a bridging operation until the next general increase in members' subscriptions.

Under the General Arrangements to Borrow (GAB), established in 1962, the 'Group of Ten' industrialized nations (Belgium, Canada, France, the Federal Republic of Germany, Italy, Japan, the Netherlands, Sweden, the United Kingdom and the USA) and Switzerland (not a member of the IMF, but a full participant in the GAB from April 1984) undertake to lend the Fund up to SDR 17,000m. in their own currencies, so as to help meet the balance-of-payments requirements of any member of the group, or to meet requests to the Fund from countries with balance-of-payments problems that

INTERNATIONAL ORGANIZATIONS

United Nations (Specialized Agencies)

could threaten the stability of the international monetary system. In July 1983 the Fund entered into an agreement with Saudi Arabia, in association with the GAB, making available SDR 1,500m., and other borrowing arrangements were completed in 1984 with the BIS, the Saudi Arabian Monetary Agency, Belgium and Japan, making available a further SDR 6,000m.

As part of the effort to reduce the monetary role of gold, a third of the Fund's gold holdings was sold between 1976 and 1980: one-half of this amount was sold at public auction for the benefit of developing member states. Of the resulting US $4,640m., part was allotted to the 104 eligible members according to their quotas, and part was put into a Trust Fund making low-interest loans. By the time the Trust Fund was wound up in April 1981 it had disbursed $3,560m. Repayments of Trust Fund loans are used to make further concessionary loans, for example under the structural adjustment facility described below.

DRAWING ARRANGEMENTS

Exchange transactions within the Fund take the form of members' purchases (i.e. drawings) from the Fund of the currencies of other members for the equivalent amounts of their own currencies. Fund resources are available to eligible members on an essentially short-term and revolving basis to provide members with temporary assistance to contribute to the solution of their payments problems. Before making a purchase, a member must show that its balance of payments or reserve position make the purchase necessary. Apart from this requirement, reserve-tranche purchases (i.e. purchases that do not bring the Fund's holdings of the member's currency to a level above its quota) are permitted unconditionally.

With further purchases, however, the Fund's policy of 'conditionality' means that a member requesting assistance must agree to adjust its economic policies, as stipulated by the IMF. All requests other than for use of the reserve tranche are examined by the Executive Board to determine whether the proposed use would be consistent with the Fund's policies, and a member must discuss its proposed adjustment programme (including fiscal, monetary, exchange and trade policies) with IMF staff. Purchases outside the reserve tranche are made in four credit tranches, each equivalent to 25% of the member's quota; a member must reverse the transaction by repurchasing its own currency (with SDRs or currencies specified by the Fund) within three to five years. Under the Fund's extended facility, a country with more serious difficulties may obtain assistance for longer periods (between four and 10 years) and in amounts larger in relation to its quota (up to 140%) than under the credit tranche policies.

In addition, there are special-purpose arrangements, all of which are subject to the member's co-operation with the Fund to find an appropriate solution to its difficulties. The compensatory financing facility (established in 1963) assists countries which have balance of payments difficulties caused by a temporary fall in export earnings (owing to natural disasters or low commodity prices) or excessive cereal import requirements. Members may draw up to 83% of their quota for export shortfall and cereal import compensation respectively, or up to 105% for the two together. The buffer stock financing facility (established in 1969) enables members to pay their contributions to the buffer stocks which are intended to stabilize primary commodity markets. Members may draw up to 45% of their quota for this purpose. In March 1986 the Fund established a structural adjustment facility (SAF) to provide balance of payments assistance on concessional terms to low-income developing countries. The facility was to be funded with about SDR 2,700m., expected to become available during 1985–91 from repayments of Trust Fund loans. The member concerned may draw up to 47% of its quota, and must develop a medium-term adjustment programme (with assistance given jointly by staff of the Fund and of the World Bank) to restore sustainable economic growth.

During the year ending 30 April 1985, purchases in the credit tranches fell to SDR 2,768m. from the record total of SDR 4,164m. in the previous year. Purchases under the Fund's extended facility amounted to SDR 2,044m., compared with SDR 4,718m. in the previous year: they were made by three members, Brazil (SDR 1,122m.), Malawi (SDR 19m.) and Mexico (SDR 903m.). Purchases under the compensatory financing facility totalled SDR 1,250m. (compared with SDR 1,180m. in 1983/84) (see table below).

There are also temporary financing facilities to meet special emergencies, such as the oil facility, which enabled members to draw SDR 6,900m. to meet balance-of-payments requirements arising from higher petroleum prices in 1974–75. A supplementary financing facility, using borrowed resources of SDR 7,784m., acted in 1979–81 to help members facing serious payments imbalances that were large in relation to their quotas. A similar arrangement followed, the policy on enlarged access, under which a member may draw up to a limit of between 102% and 125% annually, for up to three years. By 31 August 1985 borrowing arrangements totalling SDR 15,300m. had been concluded for this purpose.

TECHNICAL ASSISTANCE

This is provided by special missions or resident representatives who advise members on every aspect of economic management. The Central Banking Department and the Fiscal Affairs Department are particularly involved in technical assistance. The IMF Institute, founded in 1964, trains officials from member countries in financial analysis and policy, balance of payments methodology and public finance: it also gives assistance to national and regional training centres.

PUBLICATIONS

Annual Report.
Annual Report on Exchange Arrangements and Exchange Restrictions.
International Financial Statistics (monthly and annually).
Balance of Payments Statistics (monthly and annually).
Government Finance Statistics Yearbook.
Direction of Trade Statistics (monthly and annually).
IMF Survey (2 a month).
Finance and Development (quarterly, published jointly with the World Bank).
Staff Papers (quarterly economic journal).
International Capital Markets (annually).
World Economic Outlook (annually).
Occasional papers, publications brochure.

Statistics

QUOTAS

	Quotas (31 July 1986; million SDRs)	% of total
Afghanistan	86.7	0.10
Algeria	623.1	0.69
Antigua and Barbuda	5.0	0.01
Argentina	1,113.0	1.24
Australia	1,619.2	1.80
Austria	775.6	0.86
Bahamas	66.4	0.07
Bahrain	48.9	0.05
Bangladesh	287.5	0.32
Barbados	34.1	0.04
Belgium	2,080.4	2.31
Belize	9.5	0.01
Benin	31.3	0.03
Bhutan	2.5	0.002
Bolivia	90.7	0.10
Botswana	22.1	0.02
Brazil	1,461.3	1.62
Burkina Faso	31.6	0.04
Burma	137.0	0.15
Burundi	42.7	0.05
Cameroon	92.7	0.10
Canada	2,941.0	3.27
Cape Verde	4.5	0.01
Central African Republic	30.4	0.03
Chad	30.6	0.03
Chile	440.5	0.49
China, People's Republic	2,390.9	2.66
Colombia	394.2	0.44
Comoros	4.5	0.01
Congo	37.3	0.04
Costa Rica	84.1	0.09
Cyprus	69.7	0.08
Denmark	711.0	0.79
Djibouti	8.0	0.01
Dominica	4.0	0.004
Dominican Republic	112.1	0.12
Ecuador	150.7	0.17

continued overleaf

INTERNATIONAL ORGANIZATIONS — United Nations (Specialized Agencies)

	Quotas (31 July 1986; million SDRs)	% of total
Egypt	463.4	0.51
El Salvador	89.0	0.10
Equatorial Guinea	18.4	0.02
Ethiopia	70.6	0.08
Fiji	36.5	0.04
Finland	574.9	0.64
France	4,482.8	4.98
Gabon	73.1	0.08
The Gambia	17.1	0.02
Germany, Federal Republic	5,403.7	6.00
Ghana	204.5	0.23
Greece	399.9	0.44
Grenada	6.0	0.01
Guatemala	108.0	0.12
Guinea	57.9	0.06
Guinea-Bissau	7.5	0.01
Guyana	49.2	0.05
Haiti	44.1	0.05
Honduras	67.8	0.08
Hungary	530.7	0.59
Iceland	59.6	0.07
India	2,207.7	2.45
Indonesia	1,009.7	1.12
Iran	660.0	0.73
Iraq	504.0	0.56
Ireland	343.4	0.38
Israel	446.6	0.50
Italy	2,909.1	3.23
Ivory Coast	165.5	0.16
Jamaica	145.5	0.16
Japan	4,223.3	4.69
Jordan	73.9	0.08
Kampuchea	25.0	0.03
Kenya	142.0	0.16
Kiribati	2.5	0.002
Korea, Republic	462.8	0.51
Kuwait	635.3	0.71
Laos	29.3	0.03
Lebanon	78.7	0.09
Lesotho	15.1	0.02
Liberia	71.3	0.08
Libya	515.7	0.57
Luxembourg	77.0	0.09
Madagascar	66.4	0.07
Malawi	37.2	0.04
Malaysia	550.6	0.61
Maldives	2.0	0.002
Mali	50.8	0.06
Malta	45.1	0.05
Mauritania	33.9	0.04
Mauritius	53.6	0.06
Mexico	1,165.5	1.30
Morocco	306.6	0.34
Mozambique	61.0	0.07
Nepal	37.3	0.04
Netherlands	2,264.8	2.52
New Zealand	461.6	0.51
Nicaragua	68.2	0.08
Niger	33.7	0.04
Nigeria	849.5	0.94
Norway	699.0	0.78
Oman	63.1	0.07
Pakistan	546.3	0.61
Panama	102.2	0.11
Papua New Guinea	65.9	0.07
Paraguay	48.4	0.05
Peru	330.9	0.37
Philippines	440.4	0.49
Poland	680.0	0.76
Portugal	376.6	0.42
Qatar	114.9	0.13
Romania	523.4	0.58
Rwanda	43.8	0.05
Saint Christopher and Nevis	4.5	0.01
Saint Lucia	7.5	0.01
Saint Vincent and the Grenadines	4.0	0.004
São Tomé and Príncipe	4.0	0.004
Saudi Arabia	3,202.4	3.56
Senegal	85.1	0.09
Seychelles	3.0	0.003
Sierra Leone	57.9	0.06
Singapore	92.4	0.10
Solomon Islands	5.0	0.01
Somalia	44.2	0.05
South Africa	915.7	1.02
Spain	1,286.0	1.43
Sri Lanka	223.1	0.25
Sudan	169.7	0.19
Suriname	49.3	0.05
Swaziland	24.7	0.03
Sweden	1,064.3	1.18
Syria	139.1	0.15
Tanzania	107.0	0.12
Thailand	386.6	0.43
Togo	38.4	0.04
Tonga	3.25	0.003
Trinidad and Tobago	170.1	0.19
Tunisia	138.2	0.15
Turkey	429.1	0.48
Uganda	99.6	0.11
United Arab Emirates	202.6	0.23
United Kingdom	6,194.0	6.88
USA	17,918.3	19.91
Uruguay	163.8	0.18
Vanuatu	9.0	0.01
Venezuela	1,371.5	1.52
Viet-Nam	176.8	0.20
Western Samoa	6.0	0.01
Yemen Arab Republic	43.3	0.05
Yemen, People's Democratic Republic	77.2	0.09
Yugoslavia	613.0	0.68
Zaire	291.0	0.32
Zambia	270.3	0.30
Zimbabwe	191.0	0.21
Total	89,987.55	100.0*

* The sum of the individual percentage shares differs from 100.0 because of rounding.

TRANSACTIONS (million SDRs, years ending 30 April)

	1984	1985	1986
Total purchases	11,518	6,289	4,101
Reserve tranche	1,354	229	160
Credit tranches	4,164	2,768	2,841
Buffer stock facility	102	—	—
Compensatory financing	1,180	1,248	601
Extended facility	4,718	2,044	498
Total repurchases	2,018	2,730	4,298

BALANCE SHEETS ('000 SDRs at 30 April)
General Resources Account

Assets	1984	1985
Currencies and securities	93,574,681	95,994,219
Special drawing rights	6,436,730	4,615,747
Gold with depositories	3,620,396	3,620,396
Borrowed resources held in suspense	601,642	203,407
Charges receivable and accrued	786,931	932,071
Accrued interest on SDR holdings	224,704	97,116
Other assets	20,873	23,489
Total	**105,265,957**	**105,486,445**

Quotas, Reserves and Liabilities	1984	1985
Quotas: Subscriptions of members	89,236,300	89,301,800
Reserves	1,073,774	1,043,919
Borrowing	13,791,229	14,202,990
Remuneration payable to members	667,752	413,789
Interest payable and accrued	435,258	397,076
Other liabilities	61,644	126,871
Total	**105,265,957**	**105,486,445**

Special Drawing Rights Department
('000 SDRs at 30 April)

Allocations	1984	1985
Net cumulative allocations of special drawing rights to participants	21,433,330	21,433,330
Charges due but not paid	1,038	5,348
Total	**21,434,368**	**21,438,678**

Holdings	1984	1985
Participants		
With holdings above allocations		
Allocations	8,424,789	9,881,074
Net receipt of SDRs	2,114,823	3,490,643
Total	10,539,612	13,371,717
With holdings below allocations		
Allocations	13,008,541	11,552,256
Net use of SDRs	8,587,585	8,118,755
Total	4,420,956	3,433,501
Total holdings by participants	14,960,568	16,805,218
General Resources Account	6,436,730	4,615,747
Prescribed holders	37,070	17,713
Grand total	**21,434,368**	**21,438,678**

International Telecommunication Union—ITU

Address: Place des Nations, 1211 Geneva 20, Switzerland.
Telephone: (022) 995111.
Telex: 421 000.

Founded in 1865, ITU became a Specialized Agency of the UN in 1947. It acts to encourage world co-operation in the use of telecommunication, to promote technical development and to harmonize national policies in the field.

MEMBERS
160 members: see Table on pp. 53–55.

Organization
(October 1986)

PLENIPOTENTIARY CONFERENCE
The supreme organ of ITU; meets about every five years. Each member has one vote at the Conference, whose main tasks are to approve budget policy and accounts, to negotiate with other international organizations, and generally direct policy. The 1982 Conference (September–November) was held in Nairobi, Kenya.

WORLD ADMINISTRATIVE CONFERENCES
The Administrative Telegraph and Telephone Conference revises telegraph and telephone regulations. The World Administrative Radio Conference revises radio regulations and reviews the activities of the International Frequency Registration Board. World Administrative Conferences meet at irregular intervals according to technical needs, and there may also be regional Administrative Conferences held *ad hoc*.

ADMINISTRATIVE COUNCIL
The Administrative Council meets annually in Geneva and is composed of 41 members elected by the Plenipotentiary Conference.
The Council helps the implementation of the Convention's provisions, and executes the decisions of the Plenipotentiary Conference and, where appropriate, the decisions of the conferences and meetings of the Union. It conducts relations with other international organizations, and approves the annual budget.

GENERAL SECRETARIAT
The Secretary-General is elected by the Plenipotentiary Conference, and is responsible to it for the General Secretariat's work, and for the Union's administrative and financial services. The General Secretariat's staff totals 425; the working languages are English, French and Spanish.
Secretary-General: RICHARD E. BUTLER (Australia).

Convention
The International Telecommunication Convention is the definitive convention of the Union, member countries being those who signed it in 1932 or acceded to it later. Since 1932 it has been superseded by new versions at successive plenipotentiary conferences.
The Convention deals with the structure of the Union, the application of its own provisions and regulations, relations with the United Nations and other organizations, and special rules for radio.

TELEGRAPH AND TELEPHONE REGULATIONS
The Telegraph and Telephone Regulations were adopted during the 1973 Geneva Telegraph and Telephone Conference. They deal

INTERNATIONAL ORGANIZATIONS

United Nations (Specialized Agencies)

with problems of telegraph and telephone rates and tariffs among ITU member countries. These two Regulations lay down the general principles to be observed in the international telegraph and telephone service. Their provisions are applied to both wire and wireless telegraph and telephone communications in so far as the Radio Regulations and the Additional Radio Regulations do not provide otherwise.

RADIO REGULATIONS

The Radio Regulations include general rules for the assignment and use of frequencies and—the most important part of the Regulations—a Table of Frequency Allocations between 10 kHz and 275 GHz to the various radio services: broadcasting, television, radio astronomy, navigation aid, point-to-point service, maritime mobile, amateur, etc. Chapter III deals with the duties of the International Frequency Registration Board. The Regulations governing measures against interference follow. Subsequently, there are administrative provisions for stations (secrecy, licences, identification, service documents, inspection of mobile stations).

Chapters VI and VII are concerned with personnel and working conditions in the mobile services, and Chapter VIII with radio assistance in life saving. The last two chapters deal with radiotelegrams and radiotelephone calls and miscellaneous stations and services. Partial revisions of the Radio Regulations are in force for Space Services (1965 and 1973), the Aeronautical Mobile Services (1967 and 1978), the Maritime Mobile Service (1969 and 1974), Broadcasting (1975), and Broadcasting—Satellite Service (1977).

A 10-week World Administrative Radio Conference (WARC) was held in 1979 to undertake the most complete revision of the radio spectrum allocation to be made since 1959. The results of this conference were expected to govern the planning and operation of radio communication services (radio navigation, broadcasting, mobile radio and satellites) for the rest of the century. Partial revisions were also made subsequently by regional administrative radio conferences. The 1984 WARC agreed on a plan to make more high-frequency broadcasting channels available through the use of 'single sideband' transmissions, although developing member countries opposed this method because it requires new equipment. The Conference also agreed to monitor the deliberate 'jamming' of broadcasts.

The first session of the WARC on the use of the geostationary-satellite orbit and the planning of space services using it opened in August 1985. The objective of the Conference was to guarantee in practice, for all countries, equitable access to the geostationary-satellite orbit and to the frequency bands allocated to the space services using it.

Activities

INTERNATIONAL FREQUENCY REGISTRATION BOARD—IFRB

IFRB records assignments of radio frequencies and provides technical advice to enable members of the Union to operate as many radio channels as possible in overcrowded parts of the radio spectrum. It also investigates cases of harmful interference and makes recommendations for their solution.

Chairman: V. Kozlov (USSR).

INTERNATIONAL TELEGRAPH AND TELEPHONE CONSULTATIVE COMMITTEE—CCITT

CCITT is currently organizing 18 study groups covering transmission problems, operation and tariffs, maintenance, electromagnetic dangers, protection of equipment, definitions, vocabulary and symbols, apparatus, local connecting lines, facsimile and photo-telegraphy, quality of transmission, specifications, telegraph and telex switching, telephone signalling and switching and planning the development of an international network. It has its own telephony laboratory.

Director: T. Irmer (Federal Republic of Germany).

INTERNATIONAL RADIO CONSULTATIVE COMMITTEE—CCIR

The work of CCIR is done by 11 study groups covering spectrum utilization and monitoring; space research and radio astronomy services; fixed services below about 30 MHz; fixed services using satellites; propagation in non-ionized media; ionospheric propagation; standard frequency and time-signal services; mobile services; fixed services using radio-relay systems; sound broadcasting service; television broadcasting service. The television study group is working on the following matters: television recording, television standards for both black and white and colour transmission, ratio of the wanted to unwanted signal in television, reduction of band width, conversion of a television signal from one standard to another, estimates of the quality of television pictures, etc.

Director: Richard C. Kirby (USA).

PLAN COMMITTEES

The Plan Committees are joint CCIR/CCITT committees responsible for preparing plans setting out circuit and routing requirements for international telecommunications and for giving estimates of the growth of international traffic. They comprise a World Plan Committee and four regional committees, for Africa, for Latin America, for Asia and Oceania and for Europe and the Mediterranean Basin.

TECHNICAL CO-OPERATION

ITU's programme of technical co-operation in developing countries is carried out within the framework of UNDP (q.v.). In 1985, 584 experts were on mission, 834 fellows were undergoing training abroad and US $7.2m. worth of equipment was delivered. The total cost of this assistance amounted to $26.2m.

The three main objectives of ITU's activity in the field of technical co-operation are: (*a*) promoting the development of regional telecommunication networks in Africa, Asia and Latin America; (*b*) strengthening telecommunications technical and administrative services in developing countries; and (*c*) developing the human resources required for telecommunications. A Center for Telecommunications Development was established in Geneva in 1986.

Assistance is also provided by ITU in the specialized fields of telephony, telegraphy, radio-communications, frequency management, satellite communications, planning, organization, administration and management.

FINANCE

The total 1986 budget amounted to 101m. Swiss francs (compared with 122m. the previous year).

… United Nations (Specialized Agencies)

United Nations Educational, Scientific and Cultural Organization—UNESCO

Address: 7 place de Fontenoy, 75700 Paris.
Telephone: (1) 45-77-16-10.
Telex: 204461.

UNESCO was established in 1946 'for the purpose of advancing, through the educational, scientific and cultural relations of the peoples of the world, the objectives of international peace and the common welfare of mankind'.

MEMBERS

160 members and one associate member: see Table on pp. 53–55.

Organization

(October 1986)

GENERAL CONFERENCE

The supreme governing body of the Organization, the Conference meets in ordinary session once in two years and is composed of representatives of the member states.

EXECUTIVE BOARD

The Board, comprising 50 members, prepares the programme to be submitted to the Conference and supervises its execution; it meets twice or sometimes three times a year.

SECRETARIAT

In March 1984 the Secretariat employed about 3,380 staff, of whom about 950 were engaged in missions to member countries.
Director-General: AMADOU MAHTAR M'BOW (Senegal).
Director of the Executive Office: CHIKH BEKRI (Algeria).

CO-OPERATING BODIES

In accordance with UNESCO's Constitution, national Commissions have been set up in most member states. These help to integrate work within the member states and the work of UNESCO.

UNESCO LIAISON OFFICES

Office for Liaison with the United Nations: Room 2401, United Nations, New York, NY 10017, USA.
UNESCO Liaison Office in Geneva: Bureau Bocage 4, Palais des Nations, 1211 Geneva, Switzerland.
UNESCO Liaison Office in Washington: 918 16th St, NW, Suite 201, Washington, DC 20006, USA.

UNESCO REGIONAL EDUCATION AND CULTURAL OFFICES

Regional Office for Education in Latin America and the Caribbean: POB 3187, Santiago, Chile.
Regional Office for Education in Asia (including the Asian Centre for Educational Innovation for Development): 920 Sukhumvit Rd, POB 1425, Bangkok 11, Thailand.
Regional Office for Education in Africa: BP 3311, Dakar, Senegal.
Regional Office for Education in the Arab States: 7 place de Fontenoy, 75700 Paris, France.
Arab States Regional Centre for Functional Literacy in Rural Areas: Sirs-El-Layan, Menoufia, Egypt.
European Centre for Higher Education (CEPES): Palatul Kretulescu, Stirbei St 39, Voda, Bucharest, Romania.
Office for the Pacific States: Apia, Western Samoa; tel. 24276; telex 209; Dir F. L. HIGGINSON.
Regional Centre for Higher Education in Latin America and the Caribbean (CRESALC): Altos de Sebucan, Avda Los Chorros/Cruce, Calle Acueducto, Edificio Asovincar, Apdo 62090, Caracas 1060, Venezuela.
Regional Office for Culture in Latin America and the Caribbean: Calzada 551, esq. a D, Vedado, Apdo 4158, Havana, Cuba; tel. 32-7741; telex 51-2154.

Regional Office for Book Development in Asia and the Pacific: POB 8950, Karachi 29, Pakistan; tel. 416428; telex 25044.

UNESCO SCIENCE AND TECHNOLOGY OFFICES

Regional Office for Science and Technology for Africa: POB 30592, Nairobi, Kenya; tel. 333930; telex 22275; Dir Dr M. S. NTAMILA.
Regional Office for Science and Technology for Latin America and the Caribbean: 1320 Bulevar Artigas, Casilla 859, Montevideo, Uruguay; tel. 41.18.07; telex 22340; Dir Dr GUSTAVO MALEK.
Regional Office for Science and Technology in the Arab States: c/o UNESCO Secretariat, 7 place de Fontenoy, 75700 Paris, France.
Regional Office for Science and Technology for South and Central Asia: UNESCO House, 15 Jor Bagh, New Delhi 110003, India; tel. 618092; telex 31-65896; Dir Dr M. P. DERKATCH.
Regional Office for Science and Technology for South-East Asia: UN Building (2nd Floor), Jl. Thamrin 14, Tromol Pos 273/JKT, Jakarta, Indonesia; tel. 321308; telex 44178.

Activities

UNESCO's activities, which take three main forms as outlined below, are funded through a regular budget provided by member states and also through other sources, particularly the UNDP. UNESCO co-operates with many other UN agencies, and the conference of international non-governmental organizations co-operating with UNESCO, held in June 1984, was attended by 60 organizations.

International Intellectual Co-operation: UNESCO assists the interchange of experience, knowledge and ideas through a world network of specialists. Apart from the work of its professional staff, UNESCO co-operates regularly with the national associations and international federations of scientists, artists, writers and educators, some of which it helped to establish. UNESCO convenes conferences and meetings, and co-ordinates international scientific efforts; it helps to standardize procedures of documentation and provides clearing house services; it offers fellowships; and it publishes a wide range of specialized works, including source books and works of reference. UNESCO promotes various international agreements, including the International Copyright Convention, which member states are invited to accept.

Operational Assistance: UNESCO has established missions which advise governments, particularly in the developing member countries, in the planning of projects; and it appoints experts to assist in carrying them out. The projects are concerned with the teaching of functional literacy to workers in development undertakings; teacher training; establishing of libraries and documentation centres; provision of training for journalists, radio, television and film workers; improvement of scientific and technical education; training of planners in cultural development; and the international exchange of persons and information.

Promotion of Peace: UNESCO organizes various research efforts on racial problems, and is particularly concerned with prevention of discrimination in education, and improving access for women to education. It also promotes studies and research on conflicts and peace, violence and obstacles to disarmament, and the role of international law and organizations in building peace. It is stressed that human rights, peace and disarmament cannot be dealt with separately, as the observance of human rights is a prerequisite to peace and vice versa.

In 1984 the government of the USA (which had been due to provide about 25% of UNESCO's budget for the two years 1984–85) withdrew from the organization, alleging inefficiency, financial mismanagement and political bias against Western countries. The United Kingdom gave notice that it, too, would withdraw by the end of 1985 if reforms were not carried out, and criticisms were also voiced by other European countries and Japan. In response, a 13-member committee was formed to investigate the allegations and to recommend reforms. A seven-week meeting of the Executive Board, ending in June 1985, reached consensus on some economies to compensate for the withdrawal of the USA's financial support,

INTERNATIONAL ORGANIZATIONS
United Nations (Specialized Agencies)

and agreed on a rearrangement of budget priorities in favour of UNESCO's educational and scientific activities rather than its more politically controversial ones (subject to approval by the General Conference in October). The United Kingdom and Singapore nevertheless withdrew from UNESCO at the end of 1985. In October 1986 the Director-General, Amadou Mahtar M'Bow, announced that he would not be standing for a third six-year term of office when his present term expired in 1987.

EDUCATION

UNESCO's most important activities are in the sphere of education, particularly the spread of literacy. It places special emphasis on the attainment of education by women and the handicapped, and on literacy as an integral part of rural development. During 1981–83 this sector was allocated US $105.8m. from the organization's regular budget, while contributions from other sources brought the total education budget to $280m. for the period.

Each year expert missions are sent to member states on request to advise on all matters concerning education. During 1981–83 UNESCO provided almost 3,000 fellowships and study grants. In these forms of assistance priority is given to the rural regions of developing member countries.

Examples of activities being undertaken during 1984 included: co-operation with UNRWA (see p. 49) to provide schooling for Palestinian refugee children; a four-year project (1982–85) for improving access to education in the remote far west of Nepal; a project for improving science teaching in Indonesian secondary schools; preparation of a major scheme to eradicate illiteracy in Latin America and the Caribbean by the year 2000; a feasibility study on the establishment of regional industries in the Middle East to provide educational equipment; and about 90 teacher-training schemes. The International Institute for Educational Planning and the International Bureau of Education (see p. 81) carry out training, research and the exchange of information on aspects of education.

NATURAL SCIENCES AND TECHNOLOGY

While the main emphasis in UNESCO's work in science and technology is on harnessing these to development, and above all on meeting the needs of developing countries, the Organization is also active in promoting and fostering collaborative international projects among the highly industrialized countries. UNESCO's activities can be divided into three levels: international, regional and sub-regional, and national.

At the international level, UNESCO has over the years set up various forms of intergovernmental co-operation concerned with the environmental sciences and research on natural resources. Examples of these are the Man and Biosphere Programme (MAB) which in 1982 had 1,000 projects under way in 78 countries, using an inter-disciplinary approach to solving practical problems of environmental resource management in such areas as arid lands, humid tropical zones, mountain ecosystems, urban systems, etc.; the International Geological Correlation Programme (IGCP), run jointly with the International Union of Geological Sciences (q.v.); the International Hydrological Programme (IHP), dealing with the scientific aspects of water resources assessment and management; and the Intergovernmental Oceanographic Commission (q.v.) which promotes scientific investigation into the nature and resources of the oceans through the concerted action of its member states. Another programme, UNISIST, ensures worldwide co-operation in the field of scientific and technological information. In the basic sciences, UNESCO helps promote international and regional co-operation in close collaboration with the world scientific communities, with which it maintains close co-operative links particularly through its support to ICSU and member unions. Major disciplinary programmes are promoted in the fields of physics (including support to the International Centre for Theoretical Physics), the chemical sciences, life sciences, including applied microbiology, mathematics, informatics and new sources of energy.

At the regional and sub-regional level, UNESCO develops co-operative scientific and technological research programmes through organization and support of scientific meetings and contacts with research institutions, and the establishment or strengthening of co-operative networks; the African Network of Scientific and Technological Institutions, for example, was launched in 1980 at UNESCO's Nairobi Regional Office, to encourage collaboration among these institutions, and in 1982 a regional network of engineering institutions was established in the Middle East. Periodically, regional ministerial conferences are organized on science and technology policy and on the application of science and technology to development. More specialized regional and sub-regional meetings are also organized.

At the national level, UNESCO assists member states, upon request, in policy-making and planning in the field of science and technology generally, and by organizing training and research programmes in basic sciences, engineering sciences and environmental sciences, particularly work relevant to development, such as projects concerning the use of small-scale energy sources for rural and dispersed populations. In 1983 a two-year programme was set up to assist the teaching of the natural sciences in universities in the developing countries, through grants for the production of low-cost laboratory equipment and teaching materials, and training courses for university teachers and laboratory technicians.

SOCIAL SCIENCES

The social sciences programme aims to encourage the development of the social sciences throughout the world by strengthening national and regional institutions, the conceptual development of the social sciences, training, the exchange and diffusion of information, and co-operation with international non-governmental organizations.

The activities concerning human rights and peace include three major projects: first, definition of human rights norms and action and study of socio-economic and cultural conditions for the promotion of human rights; second, development of human rights teaching; third, peace research, concentrating on obstacles to disarmament.

The programme on the application of social sciences to mankind's development problems relates to environmental and population issues, and it lays stress upon the study of the socio-cultural bases for the establishment of a new international economic order.

Activities related to women in societies correspond to the three objectives set for the UN Decade for Women, namely: promotion of equality, women's participation in development and their contribution to peace. Youth programmes are also under way in co-operation with member states and international non-governmental organizations.

CULTURE

UNESCO's World Heritage Programme, launched in 1978, aims to protect landmarks of outstanding universal value, in accordance with the 1972 UNESCO Convention Concerning the Protection of the World Cultural and Natural Heritage, by providing financial aid for restoration, technical assistance, training and management planning. By 1984 the 'World Heritage List' comprised 165 sites. UNESCO has participated in the restoration of the Buddhist temple at Borobudur, Indonesia (1973–83), the re-siting of the temples of Abu Simbel, Egypt, preliminary work on preserving the ancient city of Moenjodaro, Pakistan, and many other conservation projects.

The International Fund for the Promotion of Culture, set up in 1974, had given assistance worth over $2m. to more than 100 projects by 1984, including the translation of literary works, the recording of traditional music, dancing and theatre, book promotion exhibitions, and the training of specialists in cultural development.

The fourth volume of an eight-volume history of Africa was published in 1984, and a programme to promote the study of African languages and oral traditions, and to encourage the teaching of these subjects, was under way.

COMMUNICATION

UNESCO's programme aims at fostering a free flow and a wider and better balanced exchange of information among individuals, communities and countries, and focuses on the role of the mass media in furthering international understanding and peace. The international movement of persons and circulation of materials are promoted through measures for the reduction of obstacles of a legislative, administrative or economic nature.

Assistance is provided to member states in the formulation of national communication policies, and a series of regional intergovernmental conferences on this subject has been organized since 1976. UNESCO also promotes research in the field of communication, and for this purpose has been instrumental in setting up an International Network of Documentation Centres on Communication Research and Policies.

UNESCO co-operates with member states, particularly in the developing countries, in strengthening and expanding their communication systems, and for this purpose executes a number of programmes both in individual countries and at the regional and sub-regional levels, to provide advisory services and help advance professional training in communication skills.

In 1977 UNESCO set up a 16-member International Commission for the Study of Communication Problems whose final report was

INTERNATIONAL ORGANIZATIONS

published in June 1980. At the General Conference in October 1980 a 'New World Information and Communication Order' (NWICO) (including plans for an international code of journalistic ethics and for the 'licensing' of journalists) was approved, in spite of objections from the United Kingdom and USA; those in favour of NWICO argued that established agencies and commercial interests had too much control over news and information, while their opponents maintained that the new proposals infringed press freedom. Following the approval of NWICO, the Intergovernmental Programme for the Development of Communication (IPDC) was established and held its first council meeting with representatives of 35 states in June 1981. In January 1982 the IPDC voted funds for two international and 15 regional projects. A sum of US $910,000 was earmarked for 1982 and a further $2,190,000 for 1983–84. Projects included the Pan-African News Agency, a regional training centre for the Arab states, a Latin American information service and, in Asia, a network of information exchange and a 'bank' of films and television programmes. The two international projects are a study on the role of satellites in the exchange of information, and a project on rural communications.

FINANCE

UNESCO's budget for the two years 1984–85 was US $374.4m.

PUBLICATIONS

(in English, French and Spanish unless otherwise indicated)

UNESCO Courier (monthly in 27 languages).
UNESCO News (monthly, giving official information, records of meetings, reports, and articles on UNESCO's programme, etc.; English, French, Arabic and Spanish).
Copyright Bulletin (quarterly, in English, French, Spanish and Russian).
Museum (quarterly, English and French).
Impact of Science on Society (quarterly, in English, French, Spanish, Russian, Arabic and Chinese).
International Social Science Journal (quarterly).
Nature and Resources (quarterly review on environment and conservation; official bulletin of the Man and Biosphere Programme, the International Hydrological Programme and the International Geological Correlation Programme, in English, French, Spanish and Russian).
Prospects (quarterly review on educational planning, in English, French, Spanish, Russian and Arabic).
Cultures (quarterly, in English, French, Spanish, Russian and Arabic).
International Marine Science Newsletter (quarterly, issued on behalf of the Intergovernmental Oceanographic Commission and UN Specialized Agencies with interests in the marine field).

INTERNATIONAL INSTITUTE FOR EDUCATIONAL PLANNING – IIEP

Address: 7-9 rue Eugène Delacroix, 75016 Paris, France.
Telephone: (1) 45-04-28-22.
Telex: 620074.

The Institute was established by UNESCO in 1963 to serve as a world centre for advanced training and research in educational planning. Its purpose is to help all member states of UNESCO in their social and economic development efforts, by enlarging the fund of knowledge about educational planning and the supply of competent experts in this field.

Legally and administratively a part of UNESCO, the Institute enjoys intellectual autonomy, and its policies and programme are controlled by its own Governing Board, under special statutes voted by the General Conference of UNESCO.

Chairman of Governing Board: Prof. MALCOLM S. ADISESHIAH.
Director: SYLVAIN LOURIÉ.

United Nations (Specialized Agencies)

INTERNATIONAL BUREAU OF EDUCATION – IBE

Address: POB 199, 1211 Geneva 20, Switzerland.
Telephone: (022) 981455.
Telex: 22644.

Founded in 1925, the IBE became an intergovernmental organization in July 1929 and was incorporated into UNESCO in January 1969. Through its International Educational Reporting Service (IERS) the Bureau provides information on developments and innovations in education; it has a library of 90,000 volumes, with 212,500 research reports on microfiche. It publishes a quarterly bulletin, surveys on comparative education and innovations, and other reference works. The Council of the IBE is composed of representatives of 24 Member States designated by the General Conference of UNESCO. The International Conference on Education is held every two years: its 39th session (1984) discussed primary education as an introduction to science and technology, and the 1986 session was to discuss the improvement of secondary education.

Director: C. BEKRI.

INTERGOVERNMENTAL COMMITTEE FOR PHYSICAL EDUCATION AND SPORT – ICPES

Address: 7 place de Fontenoy, 75700 Paris.

Established by UNESCO in 1978 to serve as a permanent intergovernmental body in the field of physical education and sport.

The Committee is composed of 30 member states of UNESCO, elected by the General Conference at its ordinary sessions.

Among its many activities aimed at further development of physical education and sport throughout the world, the Committee is responsible for supervising the planning and implementation of UNESCO's programme of activities in physical education and sport, promoting international co-operation in this area and facilitating the adoption and implementation of an International Charter of physical education and sport.

UNITED NATIONS UNIVERSITY

Address: Toho Seimei Building, 15-1, Shibuya 2-chome, Shibuya-ku, Tokyo 150, Japan.
Telephone: (81) (3) 499-2811.
Telex: 25442.

The University is sponsored jointly by the UN and UNESCO. It is an autonomous institution within the UN framework, guaranteed academic freedom by a charter approved by the General Assembly in 1973. The University is not traditional in the sense of having students or awarding degrees, but works through networks of collaborating institutions and individuals. It had 39 Associated Institutions in 1986. Initially, the University's activities were concentrated in the areas of hunger, human and social development, and use and management of natural resources. For the period 1982–87 projects were established in the following areas of study: Peace, Security, Conflict Resolution, and Global Transformation; Global Economy; Hunger, Poverty, Resources and the Environment; Human and Social Development and Co-existence of Peoples, Cultures and Social Systems; Science and Technology and their Social and Ethical Implications. There are three Divisions to plan and co-ordinate research, postgraduate training and knowledge-dissemination activities: Development Studies (country-specific research); Regional and Global Studies (international and cross-cultural dimensions); Global Learning (dissemination and use of knowledge). In 1984 the UNU established the World Institute for Development Economics Research in Helsinki, Finland. The University awarded 108 fellowships in 1984.

Rector: SOEDJATMOKO.
Chairman of Council: Dr VICTOR URQUIDI.

United Nations Industrial Development Organization—UNIDO

Address: POB 300, 1400 Vienna, Austria.
Telephone: (0222) 26 310.
Telex: 135612.

UNIDO began operations in 1967, as an autonomous organization within the UN Secretariat, and became a specialized agency of the UN on 1 January 1986. Its objective is to promote industrial development in developing countries, so as to help in the establishment of a new international economic order.

MEMBERS
142 members: see Table on pp. 53–55.

Organization
(October 1986)

GENERAL CONFERENCE
The General Conference meets every two years and consists of representatives of all member states. It is the chief policy-making body of the Organization.

INDUSTRIAL DEVELOPMENT BOARD
The Board consists of 53 members elected by the General Conference for a three-year period: 33 members are from developing countries, 15 from developed market-economy countries, and five from countries with centrally-planned economies.

PROGRAMME AND BUDGET COMMITTEE
The Committee consists of 27 members, elected by the General Conference for a two-year term.

SECRETARIAT
At the beginning of 1986 there were 1,454 staff members in the UNIDO Secretariat. The Secretariat comprises the office of the Director-General and five departments, each headed by a Deputy Director-General: Programme and Project Development; Industrial Operations; Industrial Promotion, Consultations and Technology; External Relations, Public Information, Language and Documentation Services; and Administration.
Director-General: Domingo L. Siazon.

FIELD REPRESENTATION
UNIDO's Senior Industrial Development Field Advisers work in developing countries, in collaboration with the Resident Representatives of UNDP. In 1985 there were 29 such advisers, and 65 Junior Professional Officers. A total of 1,132 experts were engaged in field work.

Activities

Activities cover macro-economic and micro-economic aspects of industrial development. At macro-economic level, questions are considered concerning the formulation of industrial development policies, planning, programming, surveys, infrastructure and structure, and institutional services to industry. At micro-economic level, assistance is provided in problems of pre-feasibility and feasibility of industry or plant, investment and financing, production and productivity, product development and design, technology and techniques, management, marketing, quality and research.

Technical assistance is provided on request to developing countries through governments, industries or other bodies. Such assistance usually consists of expert services, but can also include supply of equipment or fellowships for training in management or production.

The Secretariat provides contacts between industrialized and developing countries and identifies possibilities for the solution of specific problems in developing countries. The Industrial and Technological Information Bank provides information on technologies developed or adapted for developing countries.

There are Investment Promotion Offices in Cologne, Milan, New York, Paris, Tokyo, Vienna, Warsaw and Zürich to publicize investment opportunities and provide information to investors. UNIDO also co-sponsors (with the governments concerned) investment promotion meetings in a particular country or region, identifying projects and bringing together potential investors.

The system of consultations, introduced in 1977, is designed to help developing countries increase their share of total world production as much as possible, as recommended in the Lima Declaration and Plan of Action on Industrial Development and Co-operation (see below). During 1983 and 1984 consultations were held on the iron and steel industry, industrial financing, wood and wood products, agricultural machinery, the pharmaceutical industry, fertilizers, leather and leather products, and the food-processing industry. These meetings are attended by representatives of government, labour, industry, consumer interests and financial institutions, who examine prospects and targets for the growth of production of the commodity concerned until the year 2000 in both developed and developing countries. At all meetings the need is stressed to harmonize expansion plans to maintain a reasonable balance between world demand and supply, and to make contractual arrangements for industrial co-operation among developing countries.

In 1981 UNIDO convened a meeting of scientists to explore possible applications of genetic engineering in developing countries. This led to an agreement, adopted in April 1984, on the establishment of an International Centre for Genetic Engineering and Biotechnology, to be based in Trieste (Italy) and New Delhi (India), linked with national centres.

During 1984 UNIDO awarded 1,278 fellowships (1,220 in 1983). A total of 96 group training programmes were carried out, and training was provided for 1,764 nationals of developing countries through fellowships, group training programmes and workshops in factories, study tours and as counterparts attached to field projects.

In 1985 UNIDO carried out 1,694 projects at a cost of $94.5m., of which 47% was for expert personnel, 24% for equipment and 14% for training and fellowships.

UNIDO project expenditure by sector and programme (1985)

Purpose	Amount (US $ million)
Chemical industries	24.5
Engineering industries	13.9
Agro-industries	9.9
Metallurgical industries	7.2
Institutional infrastructure	9.8
Training	5.8
Feasibility studies	5.3
Industrial planning	7.3
Factory establishment	3.9
Other	6.9

FINANCE
In December 1976 the UN General Assembly decided to establish a United Nations Industrial Development Fund (UNIDF) to enable UNIDO to meet, more promptly and flexibly, the needs of the developing countries. The amount pledged by donor countries for 1984 was $12.9m. (at the end of December 1984) compared with the annual funding level of $50m. recommended by the Industrial Development Board. UNDP, for which UNIDO is an executing agency, provided 67% of funds for project costs in 1985. Total project costs for 1985 were $94.5m.

PUBLICATIONS
UNIDO Newsletter (monthly).
Industrial Development Survey (annually).

INTERNATIONAL ORGANIZATIONS

United Nations (Specialized Agencies)

Guide to Information Sources (about 6 a year).
Transfer of Technology Series (6 to 8 a year).
Guide to Training Opportunities for Industrial Development (annually).
Annual Report of the Executive Director.
Industry and Development Series.

Industrial Development Abstracts.
Manual for the Preparation of Industrial Feasibility Studies (10 languages).
Bulletin of the Industrial Development Decade for Africa.
Numerous working papers and reports (listed in *UNIDO Newsletter* as they appear).

Universal Postal Union—UPU

Address: 3000 Berne 15, Switzerland.
Telephone: (031) 432211.
Telex: 912761.

The General Postal Union was founded by the Treaty of Berne (1874), beginning operations in July 1875. Three years later its name was changed to the Universal Postal Union. In 1948 UPU became a Specialized Agency of the UN.

MEMBERS
168 members: see Table on pp. 53–55.

Organization
(October 1986)

CONGRESS
The supreme body of the Union is Congress, which meets every five years. Its duties are legislative and consist mainly of revision of the Acts (see below). The 19th Congress was held in Hamburg, Federal Republic of Germany, in 1984, and the 20th was to be held in Washington, DC, USA, in 1989.

EXECUTIVE COUNCIL
Between Congresses, an Executive Council, created by the Paris Congress, 1947, meets annually at Berne. It is composed of 40 member countries of the Union elected by Congress on the basis of an equitable geographical distribution. It ensures continuity of the Union's work in the interval between Congresses, supervises the activities of the International Bureau, undertakes studies, draws up proposals, and makes recommendations to the Congress. It is responsible for encouraging, supervising and co-ordinating international co-operation in the form of postal technical assistance and vocational training.

CONSULTATIVE COUNCIL FOR POSTAL STUDIES
At the Ottawa Congress, 1957, a Consultative Committee for Postal Studies was established, which, at the Tokyo Congress, 1969, became the Consultative Council for Postal Studies (CCPS). Its 35 member countries meet annually, generally at Berne. It is responsible for organizing studies of major problems affecting postal administrations in all UPU member countries, in the technical operations and economic fields and in the sphere of technical co-operation. The CCPS also provides information and opinions on these matters, and examines teaching and training problems arising in the new and developing countries.

INTERNATIONAL BUREAU
The day-to-day administrative work of UPU is executed through the International Bureau, stationed at Berne. It serves as an instrument of liaison, information and consultation for the postal administration of the member countries, provides secretarial services for UPU bodies, promotes technical assistance and organizes conferences.

Director-General of the International Bureau: A. C. BOTTO DE BARROS (Brazil).

Activities

The essential principles of the Union are the following:
1. Formation of one single postal territory.
2. Unification of postal charges and weight steps.
3. Non-sharing of postage paid for ordinary letters between the sender country and the country of destination.
4. Guarantee of freedom of transit.
5. Settlement of disputes by arbitration.
6. Establishment of a central office under the name of the International Bureau paid for by all members.
7. Periodical meeting of Congress.
8. Promotion of the development of international postal services and postal technical assistance to Union members.

The common rules applicable to the international postal service and to the letter-post provisions are contained in the Universal Postal Convention and its Detailed Regulations. Owing to their importance in the postal field and their historical value, these two Acts, together with the Constitution and the General Regulations, constitute the compulsory Acts of the Union. It is therefore not possible to be a member country of the Union without being a party to these Acts and applying their provisions.

The activities of the international postal service, other than letter mail, are governed by Special Agreements. These are binding only for the countries which have acceded to them. There are eight such Agreements:
1. Agreement concerning Insured Letters and Boxes.
2. Agreement concerning Postal Parcels.
3. Agreement concerning Postal Money Orders and Postal Travellers' Cheques.
4. Agreement concerning Giro Transfers.
5. Agreement concerning Cash on Delivery Items.
6. Agreement concerning the Collection of Bills.
7. Agreement concerning the International Savings Bank Service.
8. Agreement concerning Subscriptions to Newspapers and Periodicals.

FINANCE
The Executive Council fixed 24.7m. Swiss francs as the maximum figure for annual gross expenditure in the year 1986 (compared with 24m. the previous year). Members are listed in eight classes setting out the proportion they should pay.

PUBLICATIONS
Union Postale (every 2 months, in French, German, English, Arabic, Chinese, Spanish and Russian).
Other UPU publications are listed in *Liste des publications du Bureau international*; all are in French, some also in English, Arabic and Spanish.

World Health Organization—WHO

Address: Avenue Appia, 1211 Geneva 27, Switzerland.
Telephone: (022) 912111.
Telex: 27821.

WHO was established in 1948 as the central agency directing international health work. Of its many activities, the most important single aspect is technical co-operation with national health administrations, particularly in the developing countries.

MEMBERS

166 members: see Table on pp. 53–55.

Organization
(October 1986)

WORLD HEALTH ASSEMBLY

The Assembly usually meets in Geneva, once a year; it is responsible for policy making, and the biennial programme and budget; appoints the Director-General, admits new members and reviews budget contributions.

EXECUTIVE BOARD

The Board is composed of 31 health experts designated by, but not representing, their governments; they serve for three years, and the World Health Assembly elects 10 or 11 member states each year to the Board. It meets at least twice a year to review the Director-General's programme, which it forwards to the Assembly with any recommendations that seem necessary. It advises on questions referred to it by the Assembly and is responsible for putting into effect the decisions and policies of the Assembly. It is also empowered to take emergency measures in case of epidemics or disasters.

SECRETARIAT

Director-General: Dr HALFDAN MAHLER (Denmark).
Deputy Director-General: Dr ADEOYE T. LAMBO (Nigeria).
Assistant Directors-General: Dr LU RUSHAN (People's Republic of China), WARREN W. FURTH (USA), Dr SERGEY K. LITVINOV (USSR), Dr JACQUES HAMON (France), Dr FAROUK PARTOW (Iraq).

Administrative Divisions:
Environmental Health.
Epidemiological Surveillance & Health Situation and Trend Assessment.
Public Information and Education for Health.
Family Health.
Health Manpower Development.
Strengthening of Health Services.
Mental Health.
Non-communicable Diseases.
Diagnostic, Therapeutic and Rehabilitative Technology.
Communicable Diseases.
Vector Biology and Control.
Information Systems Support.
Personnel and General Services.
Budget and Finance.

REGIONAL OFFICES

Each of WHO's six geographical regions has its own organization consisting of a regional committee representing the member states and associate members in the region concerned, and a regional office staffed by experts in various fields of health.

Africa: POB 6, Brazzaville, Congo; Prof. GOTTLIEB LOBE MONEKOSSO.
Americas: Pan-American Sanitary Bureau, 525 23rd St, NW, Washington, DC 20037, USA; Dir Dr CARLYLE GUERRA DE MACEDO.
Eastern Mediterranean: POB 1517, Alexandria, Egypt; Dir Dr HUSSEIN ABDUL-RAZZZAQ GEZAIRY.
Europe: 8 Scherfigsvej, 2100 Copenhagen Ø, Denmark; Dir Dr JO ERIK ASVALL.
South-East Asia: Indraprastha Estate, Mahatma Gandhi Rd, New Delhi 110002, India; Dir Dr U KO KO.
Western Pacific: POB 2932, 12115 Manila, Philippines; Dir Dr HIROSHI NAKAJIMA.

Activities

WHO's objective is stated in the constitution as 'the attainment by all peoples of the highest possible level of health'.

It acts as the central authority directing international health work, and establishes relations with professional groups and government health authorities on that basis.

It supports, on request from member states, programmes to control or eradicate disease, train health workers best suited to local needs and strengthen national health systems. Aid is provided in emergencies and natural disasters.

A global programme of collaborative research and exchange of scientific information is carried out in co-operation with leading national institutions. Particular stress is laid on the widespread communicable diseases of the tropics, and the countries directly concerned are assisted in developing their research capabilities.

It keeps communicable diseases under constant surveillance, promotes the exchange of prompt and accurate information, and administers the International Health Regulations. It sets standards for the quality control of drugs, vaccines and other substances affecting health.

It collects and disseminates health data and carries out statistical analyses and comparative studies in such diseases as cancer, heart disease and mental illness.

It receives reports on drugs observed to have shown adverse reactions in any country, and transmits the information to other member states. All available information on effects on human health of the pollutants in the environment is critically reviewed and published.

Co-operation among scientists and professional groups is encouraged, and the organization may propose international conventions and agreements. It assists in developing an informed public opinion on matters of health.

HEALTH FOR ALL

In May 1981 the 34th World Health Assembly adopted a Global Strategy in support of 'Health for all by the year 2000', or the attainment by all citizens of the world of a level of health that will permit them to lead a socially and economically productive life. Almost all members indicated a high level of commitment to this goal, and guiding principles for national, regional and global plans of action were prepared, in response to the UN General Assembly resolution concerning health as an integral part of development. Primary health care is seen as the key to 'Health for all', with the following as minimum requirements:

Safe water in the home or within 15 minutes' walking distance, and adequate sanitary facilities in the home or immediate vicinity;

Immunization against diphtheria, pertussis, tetanus, poliomyelitis, measles and tuberculosis;

Local health care, including availability of at least 20 essential drugs, within one hour's travel;

Trained personnel to attend childbirth, and to care for pregnant mothers and children up to at least one year old.

The Seventh General Programme of Work for the period 1984–89, approved in 1982, comprised activities supporting the 'Health for All' strategy outlined above.

DISEASE CONTROL

WHO's Expanded Programme on Immunization (EPI), launched in 1974, aims to provide immunization for all children by 1990 against six diseases which constitute a major cause of death and disability in the developing countries: diphtheria, pertussis (whooping cough), tetanus, poliomyelitis, measles and tuberculosis. The programme costs WHO some US $8m. annually. An essential requirement is the 'cold chain' providing special containers and refrigerators for the transport of vaccines in tropical climates; WHO has developed appropriate equipment and training manuals for this purpose, and by 1985 about 18,000 health workers had attended its special training courses.

In 1984 a new vaccine development programme was launched to complement the EPI, by co-ordinating research on new vaccines and improving vaccine distribution systems, technical support and the transfer of technology.

Since 1960 WHO's Division of Vector Biology and Control has maintained a programme for the control of vector-borne diseases such as malaria, African trypanosomiasis (sleeping-sickness),

INTERNATIONAL ORGANIZATIONS

United Nations (Specialized Agencies)

American trypanosomiasis (Chagas disease), onchocerciasis (river-blindness), filiariases, dengue and dengue haemorrhagic fever—all of which are transmitted by insects—and schistosomiasis (bilharzia), transmitted by a water-snail. WHO evaluates the insecticides developed to control these vectors, and also conducts research on biological control, using the natural enemies of the vectors, such as larva-eating fish. It also encourages the environmental management of potential breeding-grounds for vectors. The programme aims to establish, by 1989, national vector control strategies in at least 50% of the countries affected. A special programme for research and training in tropical diseases, sponsored jointly by WHO, UNDP and the World Bank, was set up in 1975, and by 1986 it comprised a worldwide network of about 4,000 scientists, working on the development of vaccines, new drugs, diagnostic kits, non-chemical insecticides and other methods of control. The programme aims to strengthen research institutions in developing countries, and to encourage participation by scientists from the countries most affected.

WHO helped in preparations for the UN International Drinking Water Supply and Sanitation Decade (1981–90) by participating in regional and national meetings to plan strategies for the Decade and by drawing up new guidelines for drinking water quality. In 1986 a review of progress showed that despite some major achievements (e.g. extension of water supply to 36m. rural and 20m. urban residents in Africa since 1981), by 1990 there were likely to be more people without access to clean water and sanitation than at the beginning of the decade, particularly in rural areas. WHO's Diarrhoeal Diseases Control Programme encourages national programmes based on improved hygienic practices and the use of simple oral rehydration therapy to prevent infant deaths.

During 1985 and 1986 WHO monitored the spread of Acquired Immunodeficiency Syndrome (AIDS), drew up guidelines for its prevention, and initiated a programme of research, surveillance, education and training to attempt to deal with the disease.

NUTRITION

WHO collaborates with FAO, the World Food Programme and other UN agencies to ensure that health needs are included in their nutrition programmes. A joint WHO/UNICEF Nutrition Support Programme was active in 17 countries in 1985, assisting long-term national nutrition plans.

In May 1981 the International Code of Marketing of Breastmilk Substitutes was adopted by the World Health Assembly, aiming to provide safe and adequate nutrition for infants by promoting breast-feeding and by ensuring the proper use of breastmilk substitutes, when necessary, with controls on production, storage and advertising.

DRUGS

The WHO Action Programme on Essential Drugs and Vaccines aims to prevent the inappropriate and excessive prescription of drugs and to ensure the availability of a selected number of safe and effective drugs and vaccines of acceptable quality and at low cost, in support of primary health care. A meeting of experts was held in 1985 to discuss methods of ensuring the rational use of drugs, ways of improving access to information, and the marketing practices adopted by the pharmaceutical companies, particularly in developing countries.

WHO is also active in monitoring and controlling drug abuse. During 1986 it was preparing guidelines for member states on the assessment of drug abuse problems, and a manual for primary health care workers in drug dependence and alcohol-related problems.

DISASTER RELIEF

Who acts as the 'health arm' of disaster relief carried out within the UN system, particularly by UNDP, UNDRO and UNICEF (q.v.). It works in close co-operation with the UN High Commissioner for Refugees, appointing joint health co-ordinators and providing technical advice, for example in listing essential drugs needed for refugee camps.

During 1984, in addition to its normal programmes, WHO provided about $3.5m. in emergency aid (of which one-third was financed by other sources) for victims of drought and famine in 26 African countries; in particular, it provided medical supplies and vaccines for cholera, yellow fever and diarrhoeal diseases, and collaborated with other UN agencies to ensure that health needs were covered in their relief and nutrition programmes.

WORLD HEALTH DAY

World Health Day is held on 7 April every year, and is used to promote awareness of a particular health topic. In 1985 the theme was 'Healthy Youth—Our Best Resource', and in 1986 it was 'Healthy Living—Everyone a Winner'.

ASSOCIATED AGENCY

International Agency for Research on Cancer: 150 Cours Albert Thomas, 69372 Lyon Cedex 08, France. Established in 1965 as a self-governing body within the framework of WHO, the Agency organizes international research on cancer. It has its own laboratories and runs a programme of research on the environmental factors causing cancer. Members: Australia, Belgium, Canada, France, Federal Republic of Germany, Italy, Japan, Netherlands, Sweden, USSR, United Kingdom, USA.
Director: Dr LORENZO TOMATIS (Italy).

FINANCE

WHO's regular budget is provided by assessment of member states and associate members. An additional fund for specific projects is provided by voluntary contributions from members and other sources. Funds are received from the UN Development Programme for particular projects and from UNFPA for appropriate programmes.

WHO Budget appropriations by region, 1986–87

Region	Amount (US dollars)	% of total budget
Africa	101,164,000	18.26
Americas	58,076,000	10.48
South-East Asia	69,873,000	12.62
Europe	36,503,000	6.59
Eastern Mediterranean	62,405,000	11.26
Western Pacific	51,288,000	9.26
Global and inter-regional	167,689,100	30.27
World Health Assembly & Executive Board	7,001,900	1.26
Total	554,000,000	100.00

Budget appropriations by purpose, 1986–87

Purpose	Amount (US dollars)	% of total budget
Direction, co-ordination and management	64,450,700	11.63
Health system infrastructure	180,705,500	32.62
Health science and technology—health promotion and care	102,513,300	18.51
Health science and technology—disease prevention and control	85,377,400	15.41
Programme support	120,953,100	21.83
Total	554,000,000	100.00

PUBLICATIONS

Full catalogue of publications supplied free on request.
World Health (10 a year).
Technical Report Series.
Public Health Papers.
Monograph Series (technical guides on specific subjects serving as textbooks for the postgraduate worker).
Bulletin of WHO (6 a year).
Official Records.
Weekly Epidemiological Record.
World Health Statistics Report (quarterly).
World Health Statistics Annual.
International Digest of Health Legislation (quarterly).
Reports on the World Health Situation: (approximately every 6 years) the sixth report (January 1981) covers the period 1973–77.
World Health Forum (quarterly, in Arabic, Chinese, French, Russian and Spanish).

World Intellectual Property Organization—WIPO

Address: 34 chemin des Colombettes, 1211 Geneva 20, Switzerland.
Telephone: (022) 999111.
Telex: 22376.

WIPO was established by a Convention signed in Stockholm in 1967, which came into force in 1970. It became a specialized agency of the UN in December 1974.

MEMBERS

115 members: see Table on pp. 53–55.

Organization
(October 1986)

INTERNATIONAL BUREAU

The secretariat of WIPO and the Unions which it administers (see below). It is controlled by the member states in the General Assembly and Conference of WIPO, and in the separate Assemblies and Conferences of Representatives held by its constituent Unions. The Paris and Berne Unions elect Executive Committees from among their members and the joint membership of these two Committees constitutes the Co-ordination Committee of WIPO.

The International Bureau prepares the meetings of the various bodies of WIPO and the Unions, mainly through the provision of reports and working documents. It organizes the meetings, and sees that the decisions are communicated to all concerned, and, as far as possible, that they are carried out.

The International Bureau carries out projects and initiates new ones to promote international co-operation in the field of intellectual property. It acts as an information service and publishes reviews. It is also the depositary of most of the treaties administered by WIPO.

Director-General: Dr Arpad Bogsch (USA).
Deputy Directors-General: Marino Porzio, Lev Kostikov.

Activities

WIPO aims to promote the protection of intellectual property throughout the world through co-operation among states and, where appropriate, with other international organizations. It also centralizes the administration of the Unions which deal with legal and technical aspects of intellectual property. Each Union is founded on a multilateral treaty.

Intellectual property comprises two main branches: industrial property, chiefly patents and other rights in technological inventions, trademarks, industrial designs and appellations of origin; and copyright, chiefly in literary, musical, artistic, photographic and cinematographic works.

Under its agreement with the UN, WIPO is recognized as a specialized agency responsible for promoting creative intellectual activity and for facilitating the transfer of technology to the developing countries.

CO-OPERATION WITH DEVELOPING COUNTRIES

In the field of industrial property, the main objectives of WIPO's co-operation with developing countries are: to encourage and increase, in quantity and quality, the creation of patentable inventions by their own nationals and in their own enterprises, and thereby to increase the degree of their technological self-reliance; to improve the conditions of acquisition of foreign patented technology; to increase the competitiveness of developing countries in international trade through better protection of the trademarks and service marks of relevance in such trade; and to facilitate access by developing countries to the technological information contained in patent documents. In order to achieve these objectives, most developing countries need to create or modernize domestic legislation and governmental institutions; to accede to international treaties; to employ more specialists in government, in industry and in the legal professions; and to acquire more patent documents and better methods of analysing their contents.

These activities are supervised by the WIPO Permanent Committee for Development Co-operation Related to Industrial Property, membership of which is voluntary and carries no financial obligation with it. By September 1986, 92 States were members of the Permanent Committee.

In the field of copyright, the main objectives of WIPO's co-operation with developing countries are: to encourage and increase the creation of literary and artistic works by their own nationals, and thereby to maintain their national culture in their own languages and/or corresponding to their own ethnic and social traditions and aspirations; and to improve the conditions of acquisition of the right to use or enjoy the literary and artistic works in which copyright is owned by foreigners. In order to achieve these objectives, most developing countries are in need of creating or modernizing domestic legislation and institutions, acceding to international treaties and having more specialists, all in the field of copyright.

Most of these development co-operation activities are kept under review by the WIPO Permanent Committee for Development Co-operation Related to Copyright and Neighbouring Rights, membership of which is voluntary and carries no financial obligation with it. By September 1986, this Committee had 77 States as members.

In both industrial property and copyright, WIPO's co-operation consists mainly of advice, training and the furnishing of documents and equipment. The advice is given by the staff of WIPO, experts chosen by WIPO or international meetings called by WIPO. The training is individual (on-the-job) or collective (courses, seminars and workshops).

LEGAL AND TECHNICAL

Revision of treaties; revision of classifications of goods and services; preparation for entry into force of new treaties, and for other possible new international instruments.

WIPO Permanent Committee on Patent Information: composed of representatives of 68 states; encourages co-operation between national and regional industrial property offices in all matters concerning patent information.

International Patent Documentation Centre—INPADOC: Vienna, Austria; f. 1972; computer storage of bibliographic data on patent documents; access to the data is given to patent offices, industry and research and development institutions.

SERVICES

International registration of trademarks: operating since 1893; by September 1986 over 580,000 registrations and renewals of trademarks had been made, of which 13,696 were made during 1986; publ. *Les Marques internationales* (monthly).

International deposit of industrial designs: operating since 1928; by August 1986 over 82,000 deposits had been made, of which about 1,800 were made during 1985; publ. *International Designs Bulletin* (monthly).

International registration of appellations of origin: operating since 1966; by September 1986 over 720 appellations had been registered; publ. *Les Appellations d'origine* (irreg.).

International applications for patents: operating since 1978; by September 1986 over 33,000 record copies of international applications for patents under the Patent Co-operation Treaty (PCT) had been received.

THE UNIONS

International Union for the Protection of Industrial Property (Paris Convention): the treaty was signed in Paris in 1883; there were 97 member states in September 1986. Member states must accord to nationals and residents of other member states the same advantages under their laws relating to the protection of inventions, trademarks and other subjects of industrial property as they accord to their own nationals.

The treaty contains provisions concerning the conditions under which a state may license the use of a patent in its territory; for example, that the owner of the patent does not exploit it to unfair advantage in that country.

A conference was held in February 1980, and continued in 1981, 1982 and 1984, for the revision of the Paris Convention, with the particular aim of meeting the needs of developing countries.

International Union for the Protection of Literary and Artistic Works (Berne Union): the treaty was signed in Berne in 1886 and last revised in 1971; there were 76 member states in

INTERNATIONAL ORGANIZATIONS

United Nations (Specialized Agencies)

September 1986. Member states must accord the same protection to the copyright of nationals of other member states as to their own. The treaty also prescribes minimum standards of protection, for example, that copyright protection generally continues throughout the author's life and for 50 years after. It includes special provision for the developing countries.

OTHER AGREEMENTS

Signatories of the agreements form unions similar to those described above.

International Protection of Industrial Property:
Madrid agreement of 14 April 1891, for the repression of false or deceptive indications of source of goods.
Madrid Agreement of 14 April 1891, concerning the international registration of marks.
The Hague Agreement of 6 November 1925, concerning the international deposit of industrial designs.
Nice Agreement of 15 June 1957, concerning the international classification of goods and services for the purposes of the registration of marks.
Lisbon Agreement of 31 October 1958, for the protection of appellations of origin and their international registration.
Locarno Agreement of 8 October 1968, establishing an international classification for industrial designs.
Patent Co-operation Treaty of 19 June 1970 (PCT).
Strasbourg Agreement of 24 March 1971, concerning international patent classification (IPC).
Vienna Agreement of 12 June 1973, concerning the classification of the figurative elements of trademarks.
Budapest Treaty of 28 April 1977, on the international recognition of the deposit of micro-organisms for the purposes of patent procedure.
Nairobi Treaty of 26 September 1981, on the Protection of the Olympic Symbol.

International Protection of Literary and Artistic Property (Copyright):
Rome convention, 26 October 1961, for the protection of performers, producers of phonograms and broadcasting organizations.
Geneva convention, 29 October 1971, for the protection of producers of phonograms against unauthorized duplication of their phonograms.
Brussels convention, 21 May 1974, relating to the distribution of programme-carrying signals transmitted by satellite.

FINANCE

The budget for 1986–87 was about 100m. Swiss francs.

PUBLICATIONS

Copyright (monthly in English and French).
Industrial Property (monthly in English and French).
International Designs Bulletin (monthly in English and French).
Les marques internationales (monthly in French).
Newsletter (irregular in Arabic, English, French, Portuguese, Russian and Spanish).
PCT Gazette (fortnightly in English and French).
Les appellations d'origine (irregular in French).

World Meteorological Organization—WMO

Address: Case postale 5, 1211 Geneva 20, Switzerland.
Telephone: (022) 346400.
Telex: 23260.

The WMO started activities and was recognized as a Specialized Agency of the UN in 1951, aiming to improve the exchange of weather information and its applications.

MEMBERS

159 members, of which one is suspended; see Table on pp. 53–55.

Organization
(October 1986)

WORLD METEOROLOGICAL CONGRESS

The supreme organ of the Organization, the Congress is convened every four years and represents all members; it adopts regulations, approves policy, programme and budget. Ninth session: May 1983.

EXECUTIVE COMMITTEE

The Committee has 36 members and meets at least yearly to prepare studies and recommendations for the Congress; it supervises the implementation of Congress resolutions and regulations, informs members on technical matters and offers advice.
President: R. L. KINTANAR (Philippines).

SECRETARIAT

The secretariat acts as an administrative, documentary and information centre; undertakes special technical studies; produces publications; organizes meetings of WMO constituent bodies; acts as a link between the meteorological and hydrometeorological services of the world, and provides information for the general public. In December 1985 there were 295 staff members in Geneva and in two regional offices, together with 52 experts and 37 local staff employed in Technical Assistance projects in 32 countries.
Secretary-General: Prof. G. O. P. OBASI (Nigeria).
Deputy Secretary-General: D. K. SMITH (Canada).

REGIONAL ASSOCIATIONS

Members are grouped in six Regional Associations (Africa, Asia, Europe, North and Central America, South America and South-West Pacific), whose task is to co-ordinate meteorological activity within their regions and to examine questions referred to them by the Executive Committee. Sessions are held at least once every four years.

TECHNICAL COMMISSIONS

The Technical Commissions are composed of experts nominated by the members of the Organization. Sessions are held at least once every four years. The Commissions cover the following areas:
Basic Systems
Climatology
Instruments and Methods of Observation
Atmospheric Sciences
Aeronautical Meteorology
Agricultural Meteorology
Hydrology
Marine Meteorology

Activities

WORLD WEATHER WATCH PROGRAMME

Combining facilities and services provided by the members, the Programme's primary purpose is to make available meteorological and related geophysical and environmental information enabling them to maintain efficient meteorological services. Facilities in regions outside any national territory (outer space, ocean areas and Antarctica) are maintained by members on a voluntary basis.

Global Observing System: Simultaneous observations are made by 9,500 land stations. Meteorological information is also received from 3,000 aircraft, 7,000 ships and a number of polar orbiting and geostationary meteorological satellites. About 150 members operate some 300 ground stations equipped to receive picture transmissions from the satellites.

INTERNATIONAL ORGANIZATIONS

Global Data Processing System: consists of world meteorological centres (WMCs) at Melbourne (Australia), Moscow (USSR) and Washington, DC (USA), 26 regional meteorological centres (RMCs) and national meteorological centres. The WMCs and RMCs make analyses, forecasts and warnings for exchange on the Global Telecommunications System. These analyses and forecasts are designed to assist the members in making local and specialized forecasts.

Global Telecommunication System: consists of (a) the Main Telecommunication Network (MTN), (b) the regional telecommunication networks, and (c) the national telecommunication networks. The system operates through 150 national meteorological centres, 30 Regional Telecommunications Hubs and three World Meteorological Centres.

Executive Council Working Group on Antarctic Meteorology: The Executive Council Working Group on Antarctic Meteorology co-ordinates WMO activities related to the Antarctic, in particular the surface and upper-air observing programme, plans the regular exchange of observational data and products needed for operational and research purposes, studies problems related to instruments and methods of observation peculiar to the Antarctic and develops appropriate regional coding practices. It maintains active contacts with scientific bodies dealing with Antarctic research and co-operates with relevant WMO constituent bodies with regard to aspects of Antarctic meteorology.

Executive Council Panel of Experts on Satellites: co-ordinates WMO's satellite-related activities, examines and records plans for new satellites and satellite operations in member countries and promotes the use of satellite data in WMO programmes. It makes appropriate recommendations to WMO bodies and considers ways in which the processing and distribution of information from satellites may best meet the needs of the members.

Tropical Cyclone Programme: established in response to UN General Assembly Resolution 2733 (XXV), aims at the development of national and regionally co-ordinated systems to ensure that the loss of life and damage caused by tropical cyclones are reduced to a minimum. The programme operates through general and regional components, the latter conducted principally by four regional tropical cyclone bodies, to improve warning systems and for collaboration with other international organizations in activities related to disaster preparedness.

WORLD CLIMATE PROGRAMME

Adopted by the Eighth World Meteorological Congress (1979), the World Climate Programme (WCP) comprises the following components: World Climate Data Programme (WCDP), World Climate Applications Programme (WCAP), World Climate Impact Studies Programme (WCIP), World Climate Research Programme (WCRP). The objectives of the WCP are: to use existing climate information to improve economic and social planning; to improve the understanding of climate processes through research, so as to determine the predictability of climate and the extent of man's influence on it; and to detect and warn governments of impending climate variations or changes, either natural or man-made, which may significantly affect critical human activities.

Co-ordination of the overall Programme is the responsibility of the WMO, along with direct management of the WCDP and WCAP. The UN Environment Programme (q.v.) has accepted responsibility for the WCIP, while the WCRP is a joint effort between WMO and the International Council of Scientific Unions (ICSU, q.v.). Other organizations involved in the Programme include UNESCO, FAO, WHO, IFAD and the Consultative Group of International Agricultural Research Centres.

World Climate Data Programme: aims to make available reliable climate data, through three main projects: the World Climate Data Information Service; transfer of technology in the use of computer-based climate data; and the World Climate Monitoring System.

World Climate Applications Programme: promotes applications of climate knowledge in the areas of food production, water, energy (especially solar and wind energy), urban planning and building, and human health.

World Climate Research Programme: organized jointly with the International Council of Scientific Unions, to determine to what extent climate can be predicted, and the extent of man's influence on climate. Its three specific objectives are: establishing the physical basis for weather predictions over time ranges of one to two months; understanding the variability of the global climate over periods of several years; and studying the long-term variations and the response of climate to natural or man-made influence over periods of several decades. Studies include: the effect of cloudiness on the radiation balance; the effect of ground water storage and vegetation on evaporation; and the effects of oceanic circulation changes on the global atmosphere.

World Climate Impact Studies Programme: aims to make reliable estimates of the socio-economic impact of climate changes, and to assist in forming national policies accordingly. It concentrates on: study of the impact of climate variations on national food systems; assessment of the impact of man's activities on the climate, especially through increasing the amount of carbon dioxide and other radiatively active gases in the atmosphere; developing methodology of climate impact assessments.

RESEARCH AND DEVELOPMENT PROGRAMME

This major programme aims to help members to implement research projects; to disseminate relevant scientific information; to draw the attention of members to outstanding research problems of major importance; and to encourage and help members to incorporate the results of research into operational forecasting or other appropriate techniques, particularly when such changes of procedure require international co-ordination and agreement.

Weather Prediction Research Programmes: the Programme on Short- and Medium-Range Weather Prediction Research aims at strengthening members' research in short- and medium-range weather forecasting, including local forecasting techniques, with particular emphasis on exploiting the results of the various Global Atmospheric Research Programme (GARP) experiments, in order to improve weather forecasting services. The main objective of the Programme on Long-Range Forecasting Research is to improve the level of members' capabilities in monthly and seasonal weather forecasting.

Programme on Tropical Meteorology: aims at the promotion and co-ordination of members' research efforts into such important problems as monsoons, tropical cyclones, droughts in the arid zones of the tropics, and rain-producing tropical weather systems, and assists in the establishment of Numerical Weather Prediction Centres for tropical regions.

Weather Modification Programme: encourages scientific research on the potential for modifying weather by economically viable means, particularly rain-making and hail suppression. It provides information and guidance in the design and evaluation of experiments.

Environmental Pollution Monitoring and Research Programme: The projects under this programme deal mainly with the organization of global, standardized observations of substances and parameters (e.g. carbon dioxide, precipitation chemistry, and aerosols) which have or may have a long-term effect on the state of the environment and on climate. The Background Air Pollution Monitoring Network involves 91 countries. WMO is responsible for the meteorological part of the ECE Co-operative Programme for the Monitoring and Evaluation of the Long-range Transmission of Air Pollutants in Europe, and has organized two Meteorological Synthesizing Centres. It implements the Global Ozone Research and Monitoring Project.

The programme also includes atmospheric chemistry studies (e.g. on ozone and acidifying deposition) and the furthering of integrated environmental monitoring. The UN Environment Programme has been providing support to many projects under this programme.

APPLICATIONS OF METEOROLOGY PROGRAMME

Services to ocean activities: Supervised by the Commission for Marine Meteorology, international arrangements are made for the provision of marine meteorological and other related geophysical information, including sea ice and wave information, to shipping, fishing operations and other marine activities; the preparation of marine climatological information is also arranged internationally for multiple applications. Close collaboration is maintained with the Intergovernmental Oceanographic Commission to undertake joint programmes in ocean services and oceanic research.

Applications to aviation: to contribute to the safety and efficiency of civil aviation, the Commission for Aeronautical Meteorology supervises the applications projects; close collaboration is maintained with ICAO (q.v.), particularly in the development of joint regulatory material.

Applications to agriculture: the study of weather and climate as they affect agriculture, the selection of crops and their protection from disease and deterioration in storage, soil conservation, phenology and physiology of crops and farm animals; the Commission for Agricultural Meteorology supervises the applications projects and also advises the Secretary-General in his efforts to co-ordinate activities in support of food production. There are also special activities in agrometeorology to monitor and combat drought and desertification and to apply climate information in agricultural planning; close co-operation is maintained with the UN Environment Programme.

HYDROLOGY AND WATER RESOURCES PROGRAMME

This major programme concentrates on promoting world-wide co-operation in the evaluation of water resources and the development of hydrological networks and services, including data collection and processing, hydrological forecasting and warnings and the supply of meteorological and hydrological data for design purposes. The three components of the programme are:

Operational Hydrology Programme: Planned and executed under the auspices of the Commission of Hydrology, this Programme deals with all aspects of hydrological data, including instruments, methods of observation and transmission, systems of forecasting and their application to water resources projects. The regional implementation of this Programme is the responsibility of the WMO Regional Associations.

Hydrological Operational Multipurpose Subprogramme: consists of the organized transfer of hydrological technology used in network design, observations, collection, processing and storage of data and hydrological modelling. Manuals of procedures and general guidance, descriptions of equipment and computer software are produced.

Applications and Services to Water Resources: directed towards achieving the targets of various water-dependent sectors, it also contributes to WMO projects which have important hydrological aspects, such as those in the Tropical Cyclone and World Climate programmes.

Co-operation with Water-Related Programmes of other International Organizations: includes participation in the International Hydrological Programme of UNESCO, joint activities with other UN agencies, and participation in regional projects concerned with large international river basins such as the Rhine and the Danube.

EDUCATION AND TRAINING PROGRAMME

Activities include surveys of personnel training requirements, the development of appropriate training programmes, the establishment and improvement of regional training centres, the organization of training courses, seminars and conferences and the preparation of training materials. The Programme also arranges individual training programmes and the provision of fellowships. There are about 500 trainees in any one year. About 230 fellowships are awarded annually. Advice is given on training facilities, and there is a library of training materials for meteorological and related instruction. The focal point of WMO's education and training activities is the Panel of Experts on Education and Training set up by the Executive Council.

TECHNICAL CO-OPERATION PROGRAMME

United Nations Development Programme: WMO provides assistance in the development of national meteorological and hydrological services, in the application of meteorological and hydrological data to national economic development and in the training of personnel. Assistance in the form of expert missions, fellowships and equipment was provided to 89 countries in 1985 at a cost of US $13.5m., financed by the UNDP.

Voluntary Co-operation Programme: WMO assists members in implementing the World Weather Watch Programme to develop an integrated observing and forecasting system. Member governments contribute equipment, services and fellowships for training. In 1985, 23 projects were completed and a further 89 were in progress under this programme.

WMO also carries out assistance projects under Trust-Fund arrangements, financed by national authorities, either for activities in their own country or in a beneficiary country. Six such projects, at a cost of US $1.6m., were in progress in 1985.

CO-OPERATION WITH OTHER BODIES

As a Specialized Agency of the UN, WMO is actively involved in the activities of the UN system. In addition, WMO has concluded a number of formal agreements and working arrangements with international organizations both within and outside the UN system, at the inter-governmental and non-governmental level. As a result, WMO participates in major international conferences convened under the auspices of the United Nations or other organizations.

FINANCE

WMO is financed by contributions from members on a proportional scale of assessment. The budget for 1984–87 was US $77,516,400. Outside this budget, WMO implements a number of projects as executing agency for the UNDP or else under trust-fund arrangements.

PUBLICATIONS

Annual Report.
WMO Bulletin (quarterly in English, French, Russian and Spanish).
Reports, technical notes and training publications.

AFRICAN DEVELOPMENT BANK—ADB

Address: 01 BP 1387, Abidjan 01, Ivory Coast.
Telephone: 32-07-11.
Telex: 23717.
Established in August 1963, the Bank began operations in July 1966.

AFRICAN MEMBERS

Algeria	Libya
Angola	Madagascar
Benin	Malawi
Botswana	Mali
Burkina Faso	Mauritania
Burundi	Mauritius
Cameroon	Morocco
Cape Verde	Mozambique
Central African Republic	Niger
Chad	Nigeria
Comoros	Rwanda
Congo	São Tomé and Príncipe
Djibouti	Senegal
Egypt	Seychelles
Equatorial Guinea	Sierra Leone
Ethiopia	Somalia
Gabon	Sudan
The Gambia	Swaziland
Ghana	Tanzania
Guinea	Togo
Guinea-Bissau	Tunisia
Ivory Coast	Uganda
Kenya	Zaire
Lesotho	Zambia
Liberia	Zimbabwe

There are also 25 non-African members.

Organization
(October 1986)

BOARD OF GOVERNORS

The highest policy-making body of the Bank. Each member country nominates one Governor, usually its Minister of Finance and Economic Affairs, and an alternate Governor. The Board meets once a year. It elects the Board of Directors and the President.

BOARD OF DIRECTORS

The Board consists of 18 members (of whom six are non-African and hold 36.57% of the voting power) elected by the Board of Governors for a term of three years; it is responsible for the general operations of the Bank. It holds ordinary meetings twice a month.

PRESIDENT

Responsible for the organization and the day-to-day operations of the Bank under guidance of the Board of Directors. The President is elected for a five-year term and serves as the Chairman of the Board of Directors. He is assisted by five Vice-Presidents, elected for a three-year term by the Board of Directors on his recommendation.
Executive President and Chairman of Board of Directors: BABACAR N' DIAYE (Senegal).

FINANCIAL STRUCTURE

The Bank uses a unit of account (UA) which is equivalent to one United States dollar before the devaluation of 1971.
The capital stock of the Bank was at first exclusively open for subscription by African countries, with each member's subscription consisting of an equal number of paid-up and callable shares. In 1978, however, the Governors agreed to open the capital stock of the Bank to subscription by non-regional states on the basis of nine principles aimed at maintaining the African character of the institution. The decision was finally ratified in May 1982, and the participation of non-regional countries became effective on 30 December. It was agreed that African members should still hold two-thirds of the share capital, that all loan operations should be restricted to African members, and that the Bank's President should always be an African national. In 1986 a committee was established to study a proposed increase in the ADB Group's authorized capital from $6,200m. to $18,400m. (with paid-up capital as a proportion of the whole to be reduced from 25% to 12½%).

Activities

The ADB Group of development financing institutions comprises the African Development Fund (ADF) and the Nigeria Trust Fund (NTF), which provide concessionary loans, and the African Development Bank itself.
At the end of 1985 total loan approvals by the ADB Group since the beginning of its operations amounted to US $6,800m. In 1985 the Group approved loans of $1,154m., compared with $879.3m. in 1984. Of this total, the largest share (36.7%) was for agriculture, and the next largest (26.7%) was for transport projects (see table). Co-financing amounting to $763.6m. (of which the Group's share was $451.9m.) was arranged with a number of other organizations and governments. Disbursement of loans during 1985 totalled $531m., compared with $288m. in 1984: this increase was attributed to efforts made during the year to strengthen dialogue with borrowers, and especially with officials responsible for the execution of projects.
During 1985 important policy decisions by the Board of Directors included: increased use of agricultural lines of credit; help for countries affected by drought; and guidelines for including environmental considerations in its operations. Priority was given to rehabilitation projects in all sectors.

Bank Group lending approvals, by sector, 1985

Sector	Amount (US $ million)	% of total
Agriculture (incl. lines of credit)	423.895	36.73
Transport	307.807	26.67
Public utilities	221.154	19.16
Industry (incl. lines of credit)	65.327	5.66
Education and health	135.879	11.78
Total	**1,154.062**	**100.00**

The Bank also provides technical assistance in the form of experts' services, pre-investment studies, and staff training; much of this assistance is financed through bilateral aid funds contributed by developed member states.

AFRICAN DEVELOPMENT BANK (ADB)

The Bank makes loans at an annual interest rate of 9.86%, plus commission and commitment fees of 1% each. In 1985 the Bank approved 28 loans amounting to $709m. (compared with $494m. in 1984). Disbursements came to $302m. (compared with $168m. in 1984).

AFRICAN DEVELOPMENT FUND (ADF)

The Fund commenced operations in 1973. It grants interest-free loans to African countries for projects with repayment over 50 years (including a 10-year grace period) and with a service charge of 0.75% per annum. Loans for project feasibility studies carry a similar service charge and a repayment period of 10 years (after a three-year grace period). Priority is given to the poorest African countries.
In 1984 a replenishment was negotiated for the period 1985–87, amounting to $1,470m., contributed by 26 countries; the USA contributed 15% and Japan 14%. In 1985 68 loans amounting to

$439m. (compared with $369m. the previous year) were approved by the Fund. Disbursements in that year came to $216m. (compared with $112.7m. in the previous year).

NIGERIA TRUST FUND (NTF)

The Agreement establishing the Nigeria Trust Fund was signed in February 1976 by the Bank and the Government of Nigeria. It came into force in April. The Fund is administered by the Bank and its loans are granted for up to 25 years, including grace periods of up to five years, and carry 0.75% commitment charges and 4% interest charges. The loans are intended to provide financing for projects in co-operation with other lending institutions.

By the end of 1985 the Fund had approved 29 loans, amounting to $127m., of which 34% was for transport projects. During 1985 only one loan was approved, amounting to $5.5m. (compared with three loans totalling $15.6m. in 1984).

ASSOCIATED INSTITUTIONS

The ADB actively participated in the setting-up of four associated institutions:

Société internationale financière pour les investissements et le développement en Afrique—SIFIDA: 8C ave de Champel, BP 396, 1211 Geneva 12, Switzerland; tel. (022) 476000; telex 422047; f. 1970; holding company which aims to promote the establishment and growth of productive enterprises in Africa. It finances industrial projects, organizes syndicated loans, project identification and development, and export finance. At the end of 1985 SIFIDA was engaged in 87 operations in 28 African countries. Its shareholders include the ADB, IFC and about 130 financial, industrial and commercial institutions in the USA, Europe and Asia. Initial authorized share capital was US $50m., subscribed capital $18.7m. Chair. DEREK C. PEY; Man. Dir PHILIPPE SÉCHAUD.

Africa Reinsurance Corporation—Africa-Re: 60/52 Broad St, PMB 12765, Lagos, Nigeria; f. 1977; started operations in 1978; its purpose is to foster the development of the insurance and reinsurance industry in Africa and to promote the growth of national and regional underwriting capacities. Africa-Re has an authorized capital of US $15m., of which the African Development Bank holds 10%. There are nine Directors, one appointed by the Bank.

Shelter-Afrique (Société pour l'habitat et le logement territorial en Afrique): POB 41479, Mamlaka Rd, Nairobi, Kenya; tel. 722305; telex 25355; f. 1982 to finance housing for low-income groups in ADB member countries. Share capital is US $40m., of which the ADB provided $10m. Dir EBENEZER OLUSEYI LUFADEJU.

Association of African Development Finance Institutions—AADFI: c/o ADB, 01 BP 1387, Abidjan 01, Ivory Coast; tel. 32-07-11; telex 23717; f. 1975; aims to promote co-operation among the development banks of the region in matters relating to development ideas, project design and financing. Mems: 130 institutions. Exec. Pres. JOHN BENTUM WILLIAM.

PUBLICATIONS

Annual Report.
ADB News (monthly).
Quarterly Statement.
Basic Information (2 a year).
Statistical Handbook (annually).
Summaries of operations in each member country.

ANDEAN GROUP
(ACUERDO DE CARTAGENA)

Address: Av. Paseo de la República 3895, Casilla de Correo 18-1177, Lima 27, Peru.
Telephone: 414212.
Telex: 20104.

The organization, officially known as the Acuerdo de Cartagena (from the Cartagena Agreement which established it in 1969) and also known as the Grupo Andino (Andean Group) or the Pacto Andino (Andean Pact), aims to accelerate the harmonious development of the member states through economic and social integration. The group covers an area of 4,710,000 sq km, with about 80m. inhabitants.

MEMBERS

Bolivia   Colombia   Ecuador   Peru   Venezuela
Chile withdrew from the Group in January 1977.

Organization
(October 1986)

COMMISSION

This is the supreme authority of the Group, consisting of a plenipotentiary representative from each member country. Each country has the presidency in turn. The Commission is assisted by two Consultative Councils, each comprising four representatives from each country, elected respectively by national employers' organizations and by trades unions.

ANDEAN COUNCIL

The Council consists of the ministers of foreign affairs of the member countries, meeting annually or whenever it is considered necessary, to formulate a common external policy and to co-ordinate the process of integration.

JUNTA

Technical body which ensures that the Agreement is implemented and that the Commission's decisions are complied with. It submits proposals to the Commission for facilitating the fulfilment of the Agreement. Members are appointed for a three-year term. They supervise technical officials assigned to the following Departments: External Relations, Agricultural Development, Press Office, Economic Policy, Physical Integration, Programme of Assistance to Bolivia, Industrial Development, Programme Planning, Legal Affairs, Technology.
Members: JAIME SALAZAR MONTOYA (Colombia), JOSÉ GUILLERMO JUSTINIANO SANDÓVAL (Bolivia), PEDRO LUIS ECHEVERRÍA MONAGAS (Venezuela).

PARLIAMENT

Parlamento Andino: Sede del Congreso Nacional, Bogotá, Colombia; f. 1979; comprises five members from each country, and meets in each capital city in turn; makes recommendations on regional policy. Exec. Sec. MILOS ALCALAY.

COURT OF JUSTICE

Tribunal de Justicia del Acuerdo de Cartagena: Calle Roca 450, Casilla Postal 9054, Suc. 7, Quito, Ecuador; f. 1979, began operating in 1984; its function is to resolve disputes and interpret legislation. It comprises five judges, one from each member country, appointed for a renewable period of six years. The Presidency is assumed by each judge in turn, by alphabetical order of country. Pres. HUGO POPPE (Bolivia); other judges: LUIS CARLOS SÁCHICA (Colombia), ESTUARDO HURTADO (Ecuador), NICOLÁS DE PIEROLA Y BALTA (Peru), JOSÉ GUILLERMO ANDUEZA (Venezuela).

RESERVE FUND

Fondo Andina de Reservas: Carrera 5, 15-80 P. 26, Bogotá, Colombia; tel. 285811; f. 1977 to support the balance of payments of member countries, provide credit, guarantee loans, and contribute to the harmonization of monetary and financial policies. In 1984 it began operating in the foreign exchange market. It is administered by an Assembly of the ministers of finance and economy of the member countries, and a Board of Directors comprising the presidents of the central banks of member states. In October 1985 it was decided that the Fund's capital should be expanded from US $100m. to $500m., and the admission of other Latin American countries was discussed. Assets (30 June 1986): $650m. Exec. Pres. GUILLERMO CASTAÑEDA (Peru).

DEVELOPMENT CORPORATION

Corporación Andina de Fomento: Torre Central, Avda Luis Roche, Altamira, Pisos 5 al 10, Apdo de Correos 5086, Caracas, Venezuela; tel. 284 2221; telex 22587; f. 1968, began operations in 1970; aims to encourage the integration of the Andean countries by specialization and an equitable distribution of investments. It conducts research to identify investment opportunities, and prepares the resulting investment projects; gives technical and financial assistance; and attracts internal and external credit. Authorized capital: US $1,000m., subscribed by the member states; shares worth about $200m. were to be offered to non-regional countries in 1986. The Board of Directors comprises representatives of each country at ministerial level. Exec. Pres. JOSÉ C. CARDENAS (Ecuador).

Activities

At a three-day summit meeting held at Cartagena, Colombia, in May 1979, the Presidents of the five member countries signed the 'Mandate of Cartagena', which called for greater economic and political co-operation in the 1980s, including the establishment of more sub-regional development programmes (especially in industry).

The operations of the Group have frequently been hindered by political problems: Bolivia threatened to withdraw in September 1980 following criticism of its Government by other members of the group, while Ecuador suspended its membership temporarily at the beginning of 1981, following border disputes with Peru. In 1983 the Presidents of the five member states reaffirmed their commitment to regional integration, particularly in agriculture, trade, industry, finance, science and technology, physical integration, and aid to Bolivia and Ecuador.

TRADE

Trade between members amounted to US $1,400m. in 1980, or about 4.5% of their foreign trade, compared with $111m. (2.5%) between the same countries in 1970. Trade within the group increased by about 37% annually between 1978 and 1980. Tariff reduction on manufactured goods traded between Colombia, Peru and Venezuela was almost complete by 1980, although agreement on a common external tariff had not yet been made. A council for customs affairs met for the first time in January 1982, aiming to harmonize national legislation within the group. Owing to the world recession trade within the group fell by some 40% during 1983. In response the Junta undertook schemes to promote exports and to establish a barter system.

In December 1983 an agreement was signed with the European Community, to eliminate obstacles in trade between the two regions and to develop co-operation programmes.

In December 1984 the member states launched a new common currency, the Andean peso, aiming to reduce dependence on the US dollar and to increase regional trade. The new currency was to be backed by special contributions to the Fondo Andina de Reservas amounting to $80m., and was to be 'pegged' to the US dollar, taking the form of financial drafts rather than notes and coins.

INDUSTRY

Negotiations began in 1970 for the formulation of joint industrial programmes, particularly in the petrochemicals, metal-working and motor vehicle industries, but disagreements over the allocation of different plants, and the choice of foreign manufacturers for co-operation, prevented progress and by 1984 the more ambitious schemes had been abandoned. Instead, emphasis was to be placed on assisting small- and medium-sized industries, particularly in the agro-industrial and electronics sectors, in co-operation with national industrial organizations.

Since 1971, in accordance with a Commission directive (Decision 24), foreign investors are required to transfer 51% of their shares to local investors within 15 years, in order to qualify for the preferential trade arrangements. Transfers were to be completed by 1989 for Colombia, Peru and Venezuela, and by 1994 for Bolivia and Ecuador. Foreign-owned companies were not to repatriate dividends of more than 14% (later raised to 20%), except with approval of the Commission, on pain of disqualification from preferential tariffs. In addition, foreign investors were forbidden to participate in transport undertakings, public utilities, banking and insurance, and were not to engage in activities already adequately covered by existing national enterprises. In early 1985 individual Pact members began to liberalize these laws, recognizing that the Group's policy, by deterring foreign investors, had contributed to its collective foreign debt of some US $70,000m., and in February 1986 ministers discussed a relaxation of the 'Decision 24' rules for foreign investors. In May a new formula for trade among member countries was agreed, in order to restrict the number of products exempted from trade liberalization measures: under the new agreement each country could retain trade restrictions on up to 40 'sensitive' products.

A further directive (Decision 169) in force since 1982, covers the formation of 'Empresas Multinacionales Andinas' (multinational enterprises) with capital from two or more member countries and non-member countries. At the end of 1985 there were 11 such enterprises (six in industry and the rest in agro-industry, trade, transport and construction).

AGRICULTURE

The Andean Agricultural Development Programme was formulated at a meeting of the Ministers of Agriculture held in Quito, Ecuador, in 1976. Twenty-two resolutions aimed at integrating the Andean agricultural sector were approved there. In 1984 the Andean Food Security System was created to develop the agrarian sector, replace imports progressively with local produce, and improve rural living conditions.

TRANSPORT AND COMMUNICATIONS

The first meeting of Andean Group transport ministers was held in March 1982, and adopted a plan of action for improving road and maritime transport. In 1983 the Commission drew up a plan to assist Bolivia by giving attention to its problems as a landlocked country, particularly through improving roads connecting it with the rest of the region and with the Pacific. Studies on the improvement of regional posts and telecommunications were under way in 1984, and a scheme for attracting tourists to the region was drawn up.

Asociación de Empresas Estatales de Telecomunicaciones: Calle San Ignacio 969 y Jonás Guerrero, Casilla 6042, Quito, Ecuador; tel. 549-855; undertakes improvements of the postal and telecommunications systems in the region. Sec.-Gen. JAIME AGUILERA BLANCO.

SOCIAL DEVELOPMENT

Three Secretariats co-ordinate activities in social development and welfare:

Health: Av. Salaverry 2960, San Isidro, Casilla 5170, Lima 100, Peru; tel. 625433; Exec. Sec. ARCADIO ANDRADE DUQUE.

Labour Affairs: Luis Felipe Borja y Ponce s/n, Edificio Géminis, Piso 9, Casilla Postal 601 A, Quito, Ecuador; tel. 545 374; Exec. Sec. WASHINGTON BARRIGA LÓPEZ.

Education, Science and Culture: Carrera 19, No 80-64, Apdo Aéreo 53465, Bogotá, Colombia; tel. 256-0221. Exec. Sec. HERNANDO OCHOA NÚÑEZ.

ANZUS

Address: c/o Dept of Foreign Affairs, Canberra, ACT 2600, Australia.

The ANZUS Security Treaty was signed in San Francisco in September 1951 and ratified in April 1952 to co-ordinate partners' efforts for collective defence for the preservation of peace and security in the Pacific area.

MEMBERS

| Australia | New Zealand | USA |

Organization
(October 1986)

ANZUS COUNCIL

The ANZUS Council is the main consultative organ of the ANZUS Treaty, consisting of the Foreign Ministers, or their deputies, of the three signatory powers. Meetings are held annually, rotating between the three capitals. Talks between officials, and other forms of practical co-operation, are held more frequently.

The Council meetings are also attended by a military officer representing each country. These officers also meet separately, and it is their function to advise the Council on military co-operation.

The organization has no permanent staff or secretariat, and costs are borne by the Government in whose territory the meeting is held.

The instruments of ratification are deposited with the Government of Australia in Canberra.

Activities

Military co-operation among the ANZUS partners includes the exchange of strategic intelligence; scientific and technical collaboration in defence matters; the supply of defence equipment to ensure the modernization of forces; combined ground, air and naval exercises; visits by military aircraft and naval vessels; and training programmes. The ANZUS partners also arrange defence co-operation programmes on a bilateral basis with other countries of the region.

At its annual meeting the ANZUS Council reviews the state of the partnership and discusses world and regional affairs. The 33rd meeting of the Council, held in Wellington, New Zealand, on 16–17 July 1984, discussed arms control and disarmament issues, including the proposed formation of a South Pacific Nuclear-Free Zone; political and economic developments in the Pacific and the reinforcement of regional security; relations with Japan and the People's Republic of China; the situation in Kampuchea and Afghanistan; and other world affairs, including the economic situation.

Following the election of a Labour Government in New Zealand in July 1984, New Zealand refused to allow visits by US naval vessels carrying nuclear weapons, and this led to the cancellation of joint ANZUS military exercises planned for March and October 1985. Instead of the annual ANZUS Council meetings, bilateral talks were held between Australia and the USA in 1985 and 1986.

Security Treaty

The treaty itself is brief, containing only 11 articles. Like the NATO treaty upon which it was based, the ANZUS Treaty is largely a declaratory document which is not drafted in precise and detailed legal terms.

In the words of the preamble to the treaty, the purposes of the signatory powers are: 'to strengthen the fabric of peace in the Pacific Area'; 'to declare publicly and formally their sense of unity, so that no potential aggressor could be under the illusion that any of them stand alone in the Pacific Area'; 'to co-ordinate further their efforts for collective defence for the preservation of peace and security pending the development of a more comprehensive system of regional security in the Pacific Area'.

The Parties to the treaty undertake to 'consult together whenever in the opinion of any of them, the territorial integrity, political independence or security of any of the parties is threatened in the Pacific' (Article 3). Each Party is bound to act to meet the common danger according to its constitutional processes, since each Party recognizes that an armed attack on any of the Parties would be dangerous to its own peace and safety (Article 4).

An armed attack in the terms of the treaty includes an armed attack on the metropolitan territory of any of the Parties, or on the island territories under its jurisdiction in the Pacific, or on its armed forces, public vessels or aircraft in the Pacific.

Any armed attack and all measures taken as a result thereof shall be immediately reported to the Security Council of the UN. These measures are to be terminated when the Security Council has taken the measures necessary to restore and maintain international peace and security (Article 4).

ARAB BANK FOR ECONOMIC DEVELOPMENT IN AFRICA
(BANQUE ARABE POUR LE DÉVELOPPEMENT ÉCONOMIQUE EN AFRIQUE – BADEA)

Address: Sayed Abdel Rahman El-Mahdi Ave, POB 2640, Khartoum, Sudan.
Telephone: 73646, 70498, 73709.
Telex: 22248, 22739.

The Bank was created by the Arab League at the Sixth Arab Summit Conference in Algiers, November 1973. Operations began in early 1975. The purpose of the Bank is to contribute to Africa's economic development by providing all or part of the financing required for development projects and by supplying technical assistance to African countries.

MEMBERS

Subscribing countries: all members of the Arab League except Djibouti, Somalia, the Yemen Arab Republic and the People's Democratic Republic of Yemen. Egypt's membership was suspended in April 1979.

Recipient countries: all member countries of the Organization of African Unity except the member countries of the Arab League. A total of 41 countries are eligible for BADEA aid.

Organization
(October 1986)

BOARD OF GOVERNORS

The Board of Governors, the highest authority of the Bank, is composed of finance ministers of Arab League member states; it meets annually, examines the Bank's activities in the preceding past year and provides the resources required for the tasks assigned to it in the coming year. Only the Board of Governors has the power to increase the Bank's capital.

BOARD OF DIRECTORS

The Board meets three times a year to make recommendations concerning policy to the Board of Governors and supervises the implementation of their decisions; performs all the executive functions of the Bank. The Board comprises a chairman, appointed by the Board of Governors for a five-year term, and 11 other members. Countries with 200 or more shares each have a permanent seat on the Board (Algeria, Iraq, Kuwait, Libya, Qatar, Saudi Arabia and the United Arab Emirates); appointments to the remaining four seats are made by the Governors for a four-year term.

President of the Bank and Chairman: Dr CHEDLI AYARI (Tunisia).

SUBSCRIPTIONS TO CAPITAL STOCK
(US $ million at 31 December 1985)

Algeria	42.6	Oman	15.6
Bahrain	2.1	Palestine	2.1
Egypt	2.1	Qatar	85.2
Iraq	149.1	Saudi Arabia	255.6
Jordan	2.1	Sudan	2.1
Kuwait	156.2	Syria	1.4
Lebanon	7.1	Tunisia	8.9
Libya	170.4	United Arab Emirates	127.8
Mauritania	2.1		
Morocco	15.6	**Total**	1,048.3

Paid-up capital: US $1,045.5m.

Activities

BADEA aid consists mainly of loans on concessional terms for development projects, not exceeding US $10m. (exceptionally $15m.) or 40% of the total cost of each project (80% for loans of under $5m.). Technical assistance (e.g. pre-investment studies, training and assistance for institutions) is also provided, and Arab investment in Africa is encouraged.

The Special Arab Assistance Fund for Africa (SAAFA), established in 1972 as the Arab Loan Fund for Africa, was integrated with BADEA in 1977 after disbursing aid to the total of $214,244,000 to 32 African countries.

By December 1985 BADEA had approved loans and grants amounting to US $741.093m. (or $955.337m. when SAAFA operations are included) involving 97 projects, seven lines of credit, 26 grants for technical assistance and 14 special emergency aid operations, for a total of 39 African countries. Most projects are co-financed with other organizations or countries, chiefly Arab or predominantly Arab aid organizations (including the OPEC Fund and the Islamic Development Bank), western industrialized countries, the World Bank and the African Development Bank. Total disbursements to the end of 1985 (including SAAFA loans) amounted to $567.9m., or about 59% of total commitments. In regional terms, $399.9m. of total aid (up to the end of 1985) went to West Africa and $337.1m. to East Africa.

The sectoral distribution of aid is determined by development priorities adopted by the African countries themselves. The average distribution has been weighted in favour of projects for infrastructural development, which received 48.8% of total aid up to the end of 1985. Commitments in this sector, however, declined between 1975, when about 59% of aid financed infrastructure, and 1977,

TOTAL COMMITMENTS BY REGION

	West Africa		East Africa		Total	
	US $ million	%	US $ million	%	US $ million	%
1975	51.600	72.1	20.000	27.9	71.600	100
1976	27.124	44.4	37.974	55.6	61.098	100
1977	39.983	60.9	25.626	39.1	65.609	100
1978	32.563	60.2	21.432	39.6	54.104*	100
1979	33.573	76.3	10.422	23.7	43.995	100
1980	27.500	43.1	36.321	56.9	63.821	100
1981	32.746	53.9	28.000	46.1	60.746	100
1982	29.000	38.7	46.000	61.3	75.000	100
1983	46.350	55.5	37.185	44.5	83.535	100
1984	39.200	44.6	48.100	54.8	87.795*	100
1985	40.240	54.5	30.050	40.7	73.790*	100
1975–85	399.879	54.0	337.110	45.5	741.093*	100

* Including $0.109m. in 1978, $0.495m. in 1984 and $3.5m. in 1985, unspecified by region.

INTERNATIONAL ORGANIZATIONS

Arab Bank for Economic Development in Africa

when its share was about 20%. The commitments to agriculture, industrial and energy development projects in 1975–85 were 22.9%, 15.3% and 10.4% respectively.

In 1985 $73.790m. was allocated for 10 projects, one line of credit, three studies, three technical assistance operations and one exceptional aid allocation. Projects for which loans were approved in 1985 were: road-building in Benin ($8m.), Kenya ($6.82m.) and Rwanda ($7.6m.); a rubber plantation in the Congo ($8.5m.); artisanal fisheries in Guinea ($10m.); a power station in Guinea-Bissau ($4.7m.); an oil-palm complex in Madagascar ($3.53m.); livestock development in Niger ($4m.); urban electrification in Senegal ($4m.); and grain silos in Zimbabwe ($6m.). Exceptional aid of $3m. was granted to Sudan, and a line of credit of $6m. was extended to the Uganda Development Bank.

LOANS APPROVED BY BADEA*
(US $ million cumulative to 31 December 1985)

Country	Amount	Country	Amount
Angola	33.4	Madagascar	32.9
Benin	38.7	Mali	39.7
Botswana	33.8	Mauritius	20.7
Burkina Faso	18.1	Mozambique	47.0
Burundi	30.0	Niger	35.8
Cameroon	31.9	Rwanda	28.6
Cape Verde	24.3	São Tomé and Príncipe	14.7
Central African Republic	12.9	Senegal	36.2
Chad	10.8	Seychelles	6.1
Comoros	26.2	Sierra Leone	25.1
Congo	33.8	Swaziland	4.2
Equatorial Guinea	8.0	Tanzania	34.2
Ethiopia	14.7	Togo	8.6
The Gambia	9.1	Uganda	38.2
Ghana	31.7	Zaire	22.4
Guinea	30.7	Zambia	47.7
Guinea-Bissau	16.0	Zimbabwe	34.1
Ivory Coast	3.3	Unspecified	15.2
Kenya	30.4	**Total**	**955.3**
Lesotho	15.7		
Liberia	10.7		

Grants totalling US $4,135m. were made for a telecommunications study (1983), technical assistance (1984), and exceptional aid to Sudan (1985). A line of credit of $5m. was opened for the Banque des états de l'Afrique centrale (1978), and another for the Banque ouest-africaine de développement (1984), to help finance small and medium-sized industries.

* Including grants made by the Special Arab Assistance Fund for Africa before 1977, totalling $214.2m.

TOTAL BADEA COMMITMENTS BY SECTOR
(US $ million)

Sector	1985	1975–85
Infrastructure	22.67	362.05
Transport and communications	22.67	315.85
Dams, bridges and public services	—	32.20
Water supply and drainage	—	14.00
Agriculture	32.63	169.36
Rural development	0.30	50.40
Food production	6.30	32.25
Livestock and fishing	14.00	50.53
Agro-industry	12.03	28.18
Forestry development	—	8.00
Industry	6.00	113.53
Building materials industry	—	51.68
Chemical industry	—	20.00
Small and medium-sized industry	6.00	37.15
Textiles industry	—	4.70
Energy infrastructure and electric power	8.70	77.32
Special programme (emergency aid)	3.00	17.60
Technical assistance	0.79	1.24
Total	**73.79**	**741.09**

PUBLICATION

Annual Report.

ARAB FUND FOR ECONOMIC AND SOCIAL DEVELOPMENT — AFESD

Address: POB 21923, Safat, 13080 Kuwait.
Telephone: 451580.
Telex: 22153.

Established in 1968 by the Economic Council of the Arab League, the Fund began its operations in 1973. It participates in the financing of economic and social development projects in the Arab states.

MEMBERSHIP

Twenty-one countries and the Palestine Liberation Organization (see table of subscriptions below).

Organization
(October 1986)

BOARD OF GOVERNORS

The Board of Governors consists of a Governor and an Alternate Governor appointed by each member of the Fund. The Board of Governors is considered as the General Assembly of the Fund, and has all powers.

BOARD OF DIRECTORS

The Board of Directors is composed of six full-time Directors elected by the Board of Governors from among Arab citizens of recognized experience and competence. They are elected for a renewable term of two years.

The Board of Directors is charged with all the activities of the Fund and exercises the powers delegated to it by the Board of Governors.

Director-General and Chairman of the Board of Directors: ABDELATIF YOUSEF AL-HAMAD.

FINANCIAL STRUCTURE

The authorized capital at commencement of operations in April 1973 was 100m. Kuwaiti dinars (KD). In 1982 the capital was increased to KD 800m., divided into 80,000 shares having a value of KD 10,000 each. At the end of 1985 subscribed capital was KD 750.10m. (see table below), and paid-up capital was KD 581.09m.

SUBSCRIPTIONS (KD million)*

Country	Amount	Country	Amount
Algeria	64.78	Palestine Liberation Organization	1.10
Bahrain	2.16	Qatar	9.0
Djibouti	0.20	Saudi Arabia	159.07
Egypt†	40.5	Somalia	0.21
Iraq	63.52	Sudan	12.64
Jordan	17.30	Syria	24.0
Kuwait	169.70	Tunisia	6.16
Lebanon	2.0	United Arab Emirates	43.20
Libya	96.12	Yemen Arab Republic	4.32
Mauritania	0.82	Yemen, People's Democratic Republic	0.20
Morocco	16.0	**Total**	**750.10**
Oman	17.28		

* 100 Kuwaiti dinars = US $345.72 (December 1985).
† In April 1979 all aid to and economic relations with Egypt were suspended, but finance for projects already in progress continued.

Activities

The Fund participates in the financing of economic and social development projects in the Arab states and countries by:

1. Financing economic projects of an investment character by means of loans granted on easy terms to governments, and to public or private organizations and institutions, giving preference to economic projects of interest specifically to Arab peoples, and to joint Arab projects.

2. Encouraging, directly or indirectly, the investment of public and private capital in such a manner as to ensure the development and growth of the Arab economy.

3. Providing technical expertise and assistance in the various fields of economic development.

The Fund co-operates with other Arab organizations such as the Arab Monetary Fund, the League of Arab States and OAPEC in preparing regional studies and conferences, and acts as the secretariat of the Co-ordination Group of Arab National and Regional Development Institutions.

By the end of 1985 the Fund had made 171 loans for 131 projects in 17 countries, since the beginning of its operations. The total value of these loans was KD 716.843m. Disbursements amounted to KD 348.339m. by the end of 1985.

During 1985 the Fund approved 15 loans totalling KD 90m. for 15 projects (see table below). Agricultural projects received by far the largest share of lending (83%). Disbursements of loans during the year amounted to KD 44.5m.

Technical assistance grants reached KD 10m. by the end of 1985. During 1985 14 new grants were approved, totalling KD 1,357m., of which seven were for feasibility studies on inter-Arab industrial projects; other grants were for feasibility studies in individual countries, agricultural research, training in planning and statistics, and conferences.

LOANS BY SECTOR, 1985

Sector	Amount (KD million)	%
Agriculture (incl. fisheries)	74.7	83.0
Transport and telecommunications	1.9	2.1
Electrical power	10.4	11.6
Water and sewerage	3.0	3.3
Total	**90.0**	**100.0**

LOANS BY COUNTRY, 1985

Country	Project	Amount (KD million)
Algeria	Irrigation	6.5
Djibouti	Telecommunications cable	1.9
Iraq	Deep freeze storage	8.9
Jordan	River-basin development	5.0
Mauritania	Oases development	3.4
Morocco	Dam for irrigation and power	15.0
Oman	Fisheries development	3.0
Palestine*	Irrigation	3.0
Sudan	Agricultural rehabilitation	4.4
Syria	Power station extension	4.5
	Water supply	3.0
Tunisia	Integrated rural development	14.0
Yemen Arab Republic	Grain silos	8.0
Yemen, People's Democratic Republic	Agriculture	3.5
	Electrification	5.9

* Allocated to Wadi Fara'a Irrigation Committee.

ARAB MONETARY FUND

Address: POB 2818, Abu Dhabi, United Arab Emirates.
Telephone: 328500.
Telex: 22989.

The Agreement establishing the Arab Monetary Fund was approved by the Economic Council of Arab States in Rabat, Morocco, in April 1976 and entered into force on 2 February 1977.

MEMBERS

Algeria	Palestine Liberation Organization
Bahrain	Qatar
Egypt*	Saudi Arabia
Iraq	Somalia
Jordan	Sudan
Kuwait	Syria
Lebanon	Tunisia
Libya	United Arab Emirates
Mauritania	Yemen Arab Republic
Morocco	Yemen, People's Democratic Republic
Oman	

* Egypt's membership was suspended in April 1979.

Organization
(October 1986)

BOARD OF GOVERNORS

The Board of Governors is the highest authority of the Arab Monetary Fund. It formulates policies on Arab economic integration and liberalization of trade among member states. With certain exceptions, it may delegate to the Board of Executive Directors any of its powers. The Board of Governors is composed of a governor and a deputy governor appointed by each member state for a term of five years. It meets at least once a year; meetings may also be convened at the request of half the members, or of members holding half of the total voting power.

BOARD OF EXECUTIVE DIRECTORS

The Board of Executive Directors exercises all powers vested in it by the Board of Governors and may delegate to the President such powers as it deems fit. It is composed of the President and eight non-resident directors elected by the Board of Governors. Each director holds office for three years and may be re-elected.

PRESIDENT

The President of the Fund is appointed by the Board of Governors for a renewable five-year term, and serves as Chairman of the Board of Executive Directors and as Managing Director of the Fund.

The President supervises a Committee on Loans and a Committee on Investments to make recommendations on loan and investment policies to the Board of Executive Directors, and is required to submit an Annual Report to the Board of Governors.

President (1982–86): SAEED AHMAD GHOBASH (United Arab Emirates).

FINANCE

The Arab Accounting Dinar (AAD) is a unit of account equivalent to 3 IMF Special Drawing Rights (SDR 1 = US $1.09842 at 31 December 1985).

Each member paid, in convertible currencies, 5% of the value of its shares at the time of its ratification of the Agreement and another 20% when the Agreement entered into force. In addition, each member paid 2% of the value of its shares in its national currency regardless of whether it is convertible. The second 25% of the capital was to be subscribed by the end of September 1979, bringing the total paid-up capital in convertible currencies to AAD 131.5m. (SDR 394.5m.). An increase in requests for loans led to a resolution by the Board of Governors in April 1981, giving members the option of paying the balance of their subscribed capital. This payment became obligatory in July 1981, when total approved loans exceeded 50% of the already paid-up capital in convertible currencies. In April 1983 the authorized capital of the Fund was increased from AAD 288m. to AAD 600m. The new capital stock comprised 12,000 shares, each having the value of AAD 50,000. The increase was to be paid over five years by annual instalments, equally divided. At the end of 1985 total paid-up capital was AAD 295,390,000 (SDR 886.2m.).

CAPITAL SUBSCRIPTIONS
(million Arab Accounting Dinars, 31 December 1985)

Member	Authorized capital	Paid-up capital	Shares
Algeria	60.00	38.00	1,200
Bahrain	9.00	5.00	180
Egypt	60.00	6.75	1,200
Iraq	60.00	38.00	1,200
Jordan	11.00	6.80	220
Kuwait	60.00	32.00	1,200
Lebanon	13.00	5.00	260
Libya	30.00	13.44	600
Mauritania	9.00	4.00	180
Morocco	35.00	15.00	700
Oman	9.00	5.00	180
Palestine Liberation Organization	4.00	—	80
Qatar	24.00	10.00	480
Saudi Arabia	90.00	58.80	1,800
Somalia	9.00	4.00	180
Sudan	25.00	10.00	500
Syria	20.00	4.00	400
Tunisia	15.00	5.00	300
United Arab Emirates	36.00	19.20	720
Yemen Arab Republic	12.00	10.40	240
Yemen, People's Democratic Republic	9.00	5.00	180
Total	**600.00**	**268.25**	**12,000**

Activities

The creation of the Arab Monetary Fund was seen as a step towards the goal of Arab economic integration. It assists member states in balance of payments difficulties, and also has a broad range of aims.

The Articles of Agreement define the Fund's aims as follows:

(a) to correct disequilibria in the balance of payments of member states;

(b) to promote the stability of exchange rates among Arab currencies, the realization of their mutual convertibility, and the removal of restrictions on current payments between member states;

(c) to establish policies and modes of monetary co-operation to speed up Arab economic integration and economic development in the member states;

(d) to tender advice on the investment of member states' financial resources in foreign markets, whenever called upon to do so;

(e) to promote the development of Arab financial markets;

(f) to promote the use of the Arab dinar as a unit of account and to pave the way for the creation of a unified Arab currency;

(g) to co-ordinate the positions of member states in dealing with international monetary and economic problems; and

(h) to provide a mechanism for the settlement of current payments between member states in order to promote trade among them.

INTERNATIONAL ORGANIZATIONS

Arab Monetary Fund

The Arab Monetary Fund functions both as a fund and a bank. It is empowered:

(a) to provide short- and medium-term loans to finance balance of payments deficits of member states;

(b) to issue guarantees to member states to strengthen their borrowing capabilities;

(c) to act as intermediary in the issuance of loans in Arab and international markets for the account of member states and under their guarantees;

(d) to co-ordinate the monetary policies of member states;

(e) to manage any funds placed under its charge by member states;

(f) to hold periodic consultations with member states on their economic conditions; and

(g) to provide technical assistance to banking and monetary institutions in member states.

Loans are intended to finance an overall balance of payments deficit and a member may draw up to 75% of its paid-up subscription, in convertible currencies, for this purpose unconditionally (automatic loans). A member may, however, obtain loans in excess of this limit, subject to agreement with the Fund on a programme aimed at reducing its balance of payments deficit (ordinary and extended loans, equivalent to 175% and 225% of its quota respectively). A country receiving no extended loans is entitled to a loan under the Inter-Arab Trade Facility (introduced in 1981) of up to 100% of its quota. In addition, a member has the right to borrow up to 100% of its paid-up capital in order to cope with an unexpected deficit in its balance of payments resulting from a decrease in its exports of goods and services or a large increase in its imports of agricultural products following a poor harvest (compensatory loans). Over the period 1978–85, such loans were extended to six member countries.

Automatic and compensatory loans are repayable within three years, while ordinary and extended loans are repayable within five and seven years respectively, and trade facility loans within four years. Loans are granted at concessionary and uniform rates of interest which increase with the length of the period of the loan.

The Fund has granted loans to 10 members: Egypt, Iraq, Jordan, Mauritania, Morocco, Somalia, Sudan, Syria, the Yemen Arab Republic and the People's Democratic Republic of Yemen. At the end of 1985 total approved loans amounted to AAD 299.013m.

In 1985, following a two-year inquiry, charges were brought in the United Arab Emirates against Jawad Hashim, the former President of the Fund (1977–82), in connection with losses incurred by the Fund during his presidency.

The Fund's lending declined from AAD 85m. in 1983 to AAD 18.5m. in 1984, but increased to AAD 51m. in 1985, comprising nine loans to five member states (see below).

LOANS APPROVED, 1985

Type of loan	Borrower	Amount (AAD '000)
Automatic loans	Iraq	27,930
	Jordan	1,050
	Mauritania	2,190
	Morocco (two)	7,350
	Yemen Arab Republic	3,975
Compensatory loans	Jordan	2,660
	Yemen Arab Republic	5,100
Inter-Arab Trade Facility	Jordan	700
Total		50,955

LOANS APPROVED, 1977–85

Type of loan	Number of loans	Amount (AAD '000)
Automatic	32	127,853
Extended	6	75,580
Ordinary	3	22,820
Compensatory	7	58,280
Inter-Arab Trade Facility	5	14,480
Total	53	299,013

The Fund also undertakes studies and surveys on inter-Arab trade; provides technical assistance, in the form of training courses or placements for trainees, seminars, and expert advisory services; and co-operates with other regional organizations by participating in meetings.

PUBLICATIONS

Annual Report.
Arab Countries: Selected Economic Indicators.
Cross Rates of Currencies of Arab Countries.
Foreign Trade of Arab Countries.
Foreign Trade of Members of the Arab Common Market.
Foreign Trade of Members of the Arab Gulf Co-operation Council.
Joint Arab Economic Report (annually).
Money and Credit in Arab Countries.
National Accounts of Arab Countries.
Balance of Payments Statistics for Arab Countries.
Reports on commodity structure (by value and quantity) of member countries' imports from and exports to other Arab countries.

ASIAN DEVELOPMENT BANK—ADB

Address: 2330 Roxas Blvd, Metro Manila, Philippines; POB 789, Manila, Philippines 2800.
Telephone: 8344444; (632) 7113851 (international calls).
Telex: 23103.

The Bank commenced operations in December 1966; its aims are to raise funds from private and public sources for development purposes in the region, to assist member states in co-ordinating economic policies, and to give technical assistance in development projects.

MEMBERS
There are 32 member countries within the ESCAP region and 15 others (see list of subscriptions below).

Organization
(October 1986)

BOARD OF GOVERNORS
All powers of the Bank are vested in the Board which may delegate its powers to the Board of Directors except in such matters as admission of new members, changes in the Bank's authorized capital stock, election of Directors and President, amendment of the Charter. One Governor and one Alternate Governor are appointed by each member country. The Board meets at least once a year.

BOARD OF DIRECTORS
The Board of Directors is responsible for general direction of operations and exercises all powers delegated by the Board of Governors, which elects it. Of the 12 Directors, eight represent member countries within the ESCAP region and four represent the rest of the member countries. Each Director serves for two years and may be re-elected. The President of the Bank, though not a Director, is Chairman of the Board.
Chairman of Board of Directors and President: MASAO FUJIOKA (Japan).
Vice-Presidents: M. NARASIMHAM (India); S. STANLEY KATZ (USA); GÜNTHER SCHULZ (Federal Republic of Germany).

ADMINISTRATION
There were 1,553 Bank staff from 36 countries on 31 December 1985.
Departments: Country, Agriculture, Irrigation and Rural Development, Infrastructure, Industry and Development Banks, Budget, Personnel and Management Systems, Controller's, Treasurer's.
Offices: President, Secretary, General Counsel, Development Policy, Central Projects Services, Administrative Services, Special Projects, Economics, Information, Computer Services, Internal Auditor, Post-Evaluation, Bangladesh Resident Office and Regional Office for the South Pacific.
Secretary: ARUN B. ADARKAR (India).
General Counsel: CHUN PYO JHONG (Republic of Korea).
Bangladesh Resident Office: Bangladesh Steel House, Old Airport Rd, Karwan Bazar Commercial Area, Dhaka, Bangladesh; tel. 325001; telex 642736.
South Pacific Regional Office: Pilioko House, Kumul Highway, POB 127, Port Vila, Vanuatu; tel. 3300; telex 1082.

FINANCIAL STRUCTURE
The Bank's ordinary capital resources (which are used for loans to the more advanced developing countries in the region) are held and used entirely separately from its Special Funds resources (see below). A third General Capital Increase, of 105%, was authorized in April 1983.
At 31 March 1986 the position of subscriptions to the capital stock was as follows: Authorized US $18,107.7m.; Subscribed $17,876.5m.; Paid-in $2,166.2m.

The Bank has also borrowed funds from the world capital markets. Total borrowings during 1985 amounted to the equivalent of $792m.
In July 1986 the Bank abolished the system of fixed lending rates, under which ordinary operations loans had carried interest rates fixed at the time of loan commitment for the entire life of the loan. Under the new system the lending rate is adjusted every six

SUBSCRIPTIONS AND VOTING POWER
(31 December 1985)*

Country	Subscriptions to Capital Stock (US $'000)	Voting Power (% of Total)
Regional:		
Afghanistan	13,126	0.510
Australia	1,124,452	6.077
Bangladesh	198,419	1.438
Bhutan	1,208	0.450
Burma	105,833	0.975
Cook Islands	516	0.447
Fiji	13,214	0.511
Hong Kong	51,626	0.703
India	1,230,285	6.607
Indonesia	1,058,328	5.746
Japan	2,645,819	13.698
Kampuchea	9,611	0.493
Kiribati	780	0.448
Korea, Republic	978,945	5.348
Laos	2,702	0.458
Malaysia	529,164	3.095
Maldives	780	0.448
Nepal	28,570	0.588
New Zealand	298,441	1.939
Pakistan	423,331	2.565
Papua New Guinea	18,234	0.536
Philippines	463,006	2.764
Singapore	66,125	0.776
Solomon Islands	637	0.448
Sri Lanka	112,698	1.009
Taiwan	211,665	1.505
Thailand	264,576	1.770
Tonga	780	0.448
Vanuatu	1,296	0.451
Viet-Nam	66,323	0.777
Western Samoa	637	0.448
Sub-total	9,921,127	63.476
Non-regional:		
Austria	66,125	0.776
Belgium	66,125	0.776
Canada	1,016,511	5.537
Denmark	66,125	0.776
Finland	26,450	0.577
France	330,712	2.101
Germany, Fed. Repub.	840,665	4.655
Italy	264,576	1.770
Netherlands	145,508	1.173
Norway	66,125	0.776
Sweden	26,450	0.577
Switzerland	90,894	0.900
United Kingdom	396,870	2.432
USA	2,645,819	13.698
Sub-total	6,048,955	36.524
Total	15,970,082	100.000

* Spain became a member of the Bank in February 1986 (subscription to capital stock: $70m.) and the People's Republic of China joined in March (subscription: $1,317.7m.).

INTERNATIONAL ORGANIZATIONS

Asian Development Bank

months, to take into account changing conditions in international financial markets.

SPECIAL FUNDS

The Asian Development Fund (ADF) was established in June 1974 in order to provide a systematic mechanism for mobilizing and administering resources for the Bank to lend on concessionary terms to the least-developed member countries. Administration of the earlier Special Funds—the Multi-Purpose Special Fund (MPSF) and the Agricultural Special Fund (ASF)—had been complicated by the fact that contributions of individual donors had been made voluntarily at the initiative of the countries concerned and were frequently tied to procurement in those countries. Under the restructuring proposals, the ASF was wound up in the first half of 1973 and its resources consolidated with those of the MPSF. By the end of 1980 all the resources of the MPSF had been transferred to the ASF.

The initial mobilization of ADF resources (ADF I) was intended to finance the Bank's concessionary lending programme for the three-year period ending 31 December 1975. Contributions to ADF I totalling $486.1m. were received from 14 countries. At the end of 1975 the Board of Governors authorized a replenishment of the resources of the ADF (ADF II), intended to finance the Bank's concessionary lending programme over the period 1976-78. The amount initially authorized was $830m., but this was subsequently reduced to $809m. In 1978 the ADF was replenished a second time (ADF III) to finance the Bank's concessionary lending programme until 1982. The amount authorized was $2,150m.

Discussions of a proposed third replenishment (ADF IV) of $4,100m. were held in 1981 for the period 1983-86, but owing to restrictions on US aid policy, this figure was cut to $3,214m. Negotiations on ADF IV were concluded in 1982, and the replenishment became effective in April 1983. Total contributed resources of the ADF stood at $5,822.61m. on 31 December 1985. A further replenishment (ADF V) was approved in 1986, providing $3,600m. for the four years 1987-90.

The Bank provides technical assistance grants from its Technical Assistance Special Fund. By the end of 1985, contributions to this fund amounted to $76m., of which $67.7m. had been used by the Bank.

A special emergency financing facility was created in 1983 to enable the completion of existing projects financed by the Bank but held up by shortages of domestic currency. The Bank made US $125m. available for this purpose.

Activities

Loans by the Bank are usually aimed at specific projects, resulting in the creation of real physical assets: it does not provide balance-of-payments support of the type given by the IMF. In responding to requests from member governments for loans, the Bank's staff assesses the financial and economic viability of projects and the way in which they fit into the economic framework and priorities of development of the country concerned.

In 1985 the Bank approved 46 loans, amounting to US $1,908.1m., (14.6% lower than the 1984 figure of $2,234m.). Loans from ordinary capital resources fell by 18% to $1,271m., while loans from the ADF fell by 6.8% to $637m. Disbursements during 1985 totalled $620.3m. (ordinary loans) and $389.8m. (ADF). Co-financing by other institutions fell by 45% to $640m.

During 1985 agriculture and agro-industry received 29% of loans approved, for irrigation improvement in several countries, livestock development in Bangladesh and Nepal, forestry in Indonesia and Nepal, and three integrated agricultural development projects in Malaysia.

Social infrastructure received 28.5% of loans, for urban improvements, housing and sanitation projects in a number of countries (notably the Bandung urban development project in Indonesia, improving water supply, drainage and sewerage with a Bank loan of $132.4m.); education (including improvement of science education facilities in Pakistan); and health and population projects.

The energy sector's share of loans fell from 34% in 1984 to 12.8% in 1985. Transport and communications accounted for 16.3%, and development banks for 11.9%.

Loans and grants for technical assistance (e.g. project preparation, consultant services and training) amounted to $175.3m. for 110 projects in 1985. The Bank's Post-Evaluation Office prepared 33 reports on completed projects, in order to assess achievements and problems.

In 1985 the Bank decided to expand its assistance to the private sector. It was decided that a government guarantee would no longer be necessary for providing loans to private enterprises, and that the Bank would increase its support for financial institutions and capital markets and, where appropriate, give assistance for the privatization of public sector enterprises.

The Bank co-operates with other international organizations active in the region, particularly the World Bank group and UNDP, and participates in meetings of aid donors for developing member countries.

LENDING ACTIVITIES BY COUNTRY (US $ million)

Country	Loans approved in 1985 Ordinary Capital	ADF	Total	Cumulative 1968-85 Ordinary Capital	ADF	Total	%
Afghanistan	—	—	—	—	95.10	95.10	0.54
Bangladesh	—	212.30	212.30	11.40	1,827.23	1,838.63	10.51
Bhutan	—	3.48	3.48	—	15.88	15.88	0.09
Burma	—	—	—	6.60	489.26	495.86	2.83
Cook Islands	—	—	—	—	2.50	2.50	0.01
Fiji	7.00	—	7.00	56.10	—	56.10	0.32
Hong Kong	—	—	—	101.50	—	101.50	0.58
Indonesia	500.70	—	500.70	3,291.70	162.28	3,453.98	19.75
Kampuchea (Cambodia)	—	—	—	—	1.67	1.67	0.01
Kiribati	—	—	—	—	2.30	2.30	0.01
Korea, Republic	167.00	—	167.00	2,112.83	3.70	2,116.53	12.10
Laos	—	—	—	—	60.14	60.14	0.34
Malaysia	132.38	—	132.38	1,174.11	3.30	1,177.41	6.73
Maldives	—	—	—	—	3.38	3.38	0.02
Nepal	—	58.00	58.00	2.00	496.32	498.32	2.85
Pakistan	278.80	292.80	571.60	1,155.17	1,528.95	2,684.12	15.35
Papua New Guinea	16.40	8.50	24.90	103.60	119.44	223.04	1.28
Philippines	—	—	—	2,031.74	79.30	2,111.04	12.07
Singapore	—	—	—	178.08	3.00	181.08	1.04
Solomon Islands	—	—	—	—	24.60	24.60	0.14
Sri Lanka	—	54.40	54.40	14.13	452.03	466.16	2.67
Taiwan	—	—	—	100.39	—	100.39	0.57
Thailand	168.90	—	168.90	1,605.28	72.10	1,677.38	9.59
Tonga	—	—	—	—	8.25	8.25	0.05
Vanuatu	—	3.00	3.00	—	5.10	5.10	0.03
Viet-Nam	—	—	—	3.93	40.67	44.60	0.26
Western Samoa	—	4.40	4.40	—	44.98	44.98	0.26
Total	**1,271.18**	**636.88**	**1,908.06**	**11,948.56**	**5,541.48**	**17,490.04**	**100.00**

Source: ADB Annual Report 1985.

INTERNATIONAL ORGANIZATIONS　　　　　　　　　　　　　　　　　　　　　　　　　　　　　　　　*Asian Development Bank*

BANK ACTIVITIES BY SECTOR (to December 1985)

Sector	1968–85 Amount	%	1984 Amount	%	1985 Amount	%
Agriculture and agro-industry	5,333.18	30.49	758.00	33.93	559.46	29.32
Energy	4,372.29	25.00	766.70	34.31	244.70	12.82
Industry and non-fuel minerals	2,447.84	14.00	54.00	2.42	242.80	12.73
Transport and communications	2,367.85	13.54	381.20	17.06	310.00	16.25
Social infrastructure	2,856.67	16.33	239.60	10.72	543.70	28.49
Multi-sector	112.21	0.64	34.78	1.56	7.40	0.39
Total	17,490.04	100.00	2,234.28	100.00	1,908.06	100.00

Loan Approvals (US $ million)

BUDGET

Internal administrative expenses amounted to US $89.3m. in the 1986 budget. Services to member countries financed from the Bank's own resources (e.g. project preparation and advisory services) were expected to come to $24m. in 1985.

PUBLICATIONS

Annual Report.
ADB Quarterly Review.
Summary of Proceedings (Annual Meeting of the Board of Governors).
Regional Studies and Reports, Occasional Papers, Sector Papers, Economic Staff Papers.
Key Indicators of Developing Member Countries of ADB (2 a year).
Asian Development Review (2 a year).
Operational Information on Proposed Projects (monthly).
Project Profiles for Potential Co-financing (quarterly).

ASSOCIATION OF SOUTH EAST ASIAN NATIONS—ASEAN

Address: Jalan Sisingamangaraja, POB 2072, Jakarta, Indonesia.
Telephone: 712272.
Telex: 47214.

ASEAN was established in August 1967 at Bangkok, Thailand, to accelerate economic progress and to increase the stability of the South-East Asian region.

MEMBERS

Brunei
Indonesia
Malaysia
Philippines
Singapore
Thailand

Observer: Papua New Guinea.

Organization
(October 1986)

SUMMIT MEETING

The highest authority of ASEAN, bringing together the Heads of Government of member countries. The first meeting was held in Bali in February 1976; the second in Kuala Lumpur in August 1977. A third summit meeting was to be held in December 1987.

MINISTERIAL CONFERENCES

The ministers of foreign affairs of member states meet annually in each member country in turn. Ministers of economic affairs also meet about once a year, to direct ASEAN economic co-operation, and other ministers meet when necessary. Ministerial meetings are serviced by the committees described below.

STANDING COMMITTEE

The Standing Committee meets when necessary between ministerial meetings for consultations in one of the five countries in annual rotation. It consists of the minister of foreign affairs of the host country and ambassadors of the other four.

SECRETARIATS

A permanent secretariat was established in Jakarta, Indonesia, in 1976 to form a central co-ordinating body. The post of Secretary-General rotates among the member countries in alphabetical order every three years. In each member country day-to-day work is co-ordinated by an ASEAN national secretariat.

Secretary-General: RODERICK YONG YIN FATT (Brunei).

COMMITTEES

Economic co-operation is directed by ministers of economic affairs through five Committees, on Food, Agriculture and Forestry; Finance and Banking; Industry, Minerals and Energy; Transport and Communications; and Trade and Tourism.

Other ministerial meetings are serviced by the following three Committees: Culture and Information; Science and Technology; and Social Development.

These committees are serviced by a network of subsidiary technical bodies comprising sub-committees, expert groups, ad-hoc working groups, working parties, etc.

To support the conduct of relations with other countries and international organizations, ASEAN committees (composed of heads of diplomatic missions) have been established in 10 foreign capitals: those of Australia, Belgium, Canada, France, the Federal Republic of Germany, Japan, New Zealand, Switzerland, the United Kingdom and the USA.

Activities

ASEAN was established in 1967 with the signing of the ASEAN Declaration, otherwise known as the Bangkok Declaration, by the ministers of foreign affairs of Indonesia, Malaysia, the Philippines, Singapore and Thailand. Brunei joined the organization in January 1984, shortly after attaining independence. The ASEAN Declaration sets out the objectives of the organization as follows:

To accelerate economic growth, social progress and cultural development in the region through joint endeavours in the spirit of equality and partnership in order to strengthen the foundation for a prosperous and peaceful community of South East Asian nations.

To promote regional peace and stability through abiding respect for justice and the rule of law in the relationship among countries of the region and adherence to the principles of the United Nations Charter.

To promote active collaboration and mutual assistance on matters of common interest in the economic, social, cultural, technical, scientific and administrative fields.

To provide assistance to each other in the form of training and research facilities in the educational, professional, technical and administrative spheres.

To collaborate more effectively for the greater utilization of their agriculture and industries, the expansion of their trade, including the study of the problems of international commodity trade, the improvement of their transportation and communication facilities and the raising of the living standards of their people.

To promote South-East Asian studies.

To maintain close and beneficial co-operation with existing international and regional organizations with similar aims and purposes, and explore all avenues for even closer co-operation among themselves.

ASEAN's first summit meeting was held at Denpasar, Bali, Indonesia, in February 1976. Two major documents were signed:

Treaty of Amity and Co-operation, laying down principles of mutual respect for the independence and sovereignty of all nations; non-interference in the internal affairs of one another; settlement of disputes by peaceful means; and effective co-operation among the five countries.

Declaration of Concord, giving guidelines for action in economic, social and cultural relations, including: the maintenance of political stability; the establishment of a 'Zone of Peace, Freedom and Stability'; the promotion of social justice and improvement of living standards; mutual assistance in the event of natural disasters; and co-operation in economic development.

EXTERNAL RELATIONS

The European Community: A joint Study Group was set up by ASEAN and the EEC Commission in 1975 to discuss the possibilities for economic co-operation between the two regions, and to act as a forum for contacts with European officials and companies. The principal achievement in the ASEAN countries' negotiations with the EEC Commission was a reduction of duties under the EEC's Generalized System of Preferences in favour of ASEAN countries. In March 1980 a five-year co-operation agreement was signed between ASEAN and the EEC, following a joint ministerial conference. The agreement, which entered into force on 1 October, provides for the strengthening of existing trade links and increased co-operation in the scientific and agricultural spheres. A joint co-operation committee met in Manila in November; it drew up a programme of scientific and technological co-operation, approved measures to promote contracts between industrialists from the two regions, and agreed on the financing of ASEAN regional projects by the Community. An ASEAN-EEC Business Council was launched in December 1983 to provide a forum for businessmen from the two regions and to identify joint projects. The first meeting of ministers of economic affairs from ASEAN and EEC member countries took place in October 1985, and agreed to encourage European investment in the ASEAN region (currently estimated at 13% of total foreign investment, compared with 28% for Japanese investment and 17% for the USA). A second joint ASEAN-EEC industrial conference was held in November, on the processing of agricultural products.

Japan: The ASEAN-Japan Forum was established in 1977 to discuss matters of mutual concern in trade, investment, technology transfer and development assistance; the eighth meeting of the Forum was held in 1986. In 1978 Japan promised US $1,000m. for implementing industrial projects. In January 1981 the Japanese

Prime Minister made a tour of ASEAN countries, declaring support for their opposition to the Vietnamese over Kampuchea (see below), and announcing the approval of yen-based credits worth $870m. for Indonesia, Malaysia, the Philippines and Thailand. Further support was offered in 1983 in the form of increased financial aid for Indonesia, Malaysia and Thailand and a scheme for renovating industrial installations originally built with Japanese assistance. Discussions were also held concerning Japanese restrictions on imports of ASEAN agricultural produce: Thailand and the Philippines in particular expressed concern over their trade deficit with Japan. Tariff cuts on certain ASEAN exports were made by Japan in 1985, but in 1985 and 1986 ASEAN members continued to criticize Japan's attitude and called for Japan to import more manufactured products rather than raw materials.

Indo-China: The question of relations with the new communist governments in Indo-China was prominent at the Bali summit in February 1976. The documents signed at the summit made clear that ASEAN countries wished to form a zone of peace, freedom and neutrality, a concept adopted by ASEAN in 1971, and would respect the independence and sovereignty of all nations. ASEAN was to be an economic and diplomatic forum, with no question of a military alliance. Diplomatic relations with the communist governments were established in 1976. In 1978 the hostilities between Viet-Nam, Kampuchea and the People's Republic of China caused both Viet-Nam and China to seek closer ties with ASEAN and to negotiate with ASEAN as a group, not in bilateral terms. Fears of Viet-Nam's military ambitions, stirred by the invasion of Kampuchea in December 1978, and the severe strain placed on the ASEAN countries by the exodus of refugees from Viet-Nam, however, caused ASEAN to reassess its relations with Viet-Nam, which it accused of trying to destabilize South-East Asia, and to seek new ways of establishing peace. At the 12th meeting of ministers of foreign affairs in June 1979 grave concern was expressed over the thousands of displaced persons from Indo-China, and the delegates deplored the fact that Viet-Nam had not taken effective measures to stop the exodus. The ASEAN Foreign Ministers also reiterated their support for the right of the Kampuchean people to self-determination. In July 1981 the United Nations held a conference on Kampuchea, sponsored by ASEAN: the ASEAN countries proposed a coalition of the three main factions in Kampuchea, the withdrawal of Vietnamese troops, and elections supervised by the UN (see chapter on Viet-Nam). ASEAN made it clear that it would not, as a group, supply arms to any faction.

In September 1983 ASEAN issued an 'Appeal for Kampuchean Independence', in which it called for phased withdrawals of Vietnamese troops, supervised by a peace-keeping force, and for safe areas to be established for Kampuchean refugee camps; these actions were seen as the first steps in a comprehensive political settlement. This appeal was rejected by Viet-Nam in October.

In February 1985 a meeting of ASEAN ministers of foreign affairs, repeating their previous demands for Vietnamese withdrawal from Kampuchea, also called for military aid from foreign countries to the anti-Vietnamese coalition in Kampuchea. In July ASEAN proposed 'proximity' talks to be held (through an intermediary) between Viet-Nam and the Kampuchean coalition, but Viet-Nam refused to take part.

Other countries: ASEAN holds regular discussions on trade and other matters with a number of countries, and receives assistance for various development projects. The tenth ASEAN-Australia Forum was held in February 1986 between Australian and ASEAN senior officials, to discuss trade and co-operation. Under the ASEAN-Australia Economic Co-operation Programme, Australia gives financial support (amounting to $A 93.5m. by February 1985) for ASEAN activities, including energy and food technology projects. A joint Business Council was set up in 1980. The sixth ASEAN-New Zealand Dialogue was held in 1983; New Zealand has given technical and financial assistance in livestock development projects and a major forestry scheme in the Philippines. The seventh ASEAN-US Dialogue was held in May 1986: the USA gives assistance for the development of small and medium-sized businesses and other projects, and supports a Center for Technology Exchange. The ASEAN-Canada Joint Co-operation Committee met for the third time in October 1985; ASEAN-Canada co-operation projects include fisheries technology, a joint programme to reduce post-harvest crop losses, and a forest seed centre; a working group was also set up to examine ASEAN's trade with Canada.

INDUSTRY

A meeting of Economic Ministers in Kuala Lumpur in March 1976 agreed to set up five equity-sharing medium-sized industries; a 60% share of each was to be owned by the host country, and the remaining 40% by the other four members. The projects originally comprised the manufacture of diesel engines in Singapore, urea for fertilizers in Indonesia and Malaysia, superphosphates in the Philippines, and soda ash in Thailand. In 1978 the text of the Basic Agreement on ASEAN Industrial Projects was agreed. By 1982, however, only the urea projects in Indonesia and Malaysia were ready to be implemented. The Indonesian project had its ASEAN company incorporated in March 1979 and was inaugurated in January 1984, with an annual production capacity of 570,000 metric tons. The Malaysian project, with an annual production capacity of 530,000 tons of urea and 360,000 tons of ammonia, began operations in 1985. The Singapore diesel engine project was abandoned and an alternative scheme, the establishment of a hepatitis vaccine plant, was not decided on until 1984. The Thai soda ash project was also abandoned in 1985 owing to falling demand.

In July 1980 ASEAN representatives agreed to set up their first joint private banking institution, the ASEAN Finance Corporation, to provide financing for industrial projects of benefit to the region. The Corporation had an initial capital of $47m.

The ASEAN Industrial Complementation programme, begun in 1981, encourages member countries to produce complementary products in specific industrial sectors for preferential exchange among themselves, for example components to be used in the automobile industry. The establishment of ASEAN Industrial Joint Ventures was approved in 1983. This scheme, initiated by ASEAN chambers of commerce and industry, aims to set up projects with at least 51% participation by private sector companies from two or more ASEAN member states; the resultant products would receive preferential treatment (tariff reductions of 75%) from the participating countries, and, after four years, preferential treatment from other member states. By August 1986 five joint projects had been approved, including the manufacture of car components and security paper (for banknotes), production of potash, feldspar and quartz, and meat processing. The ASEAN Finance Corporation (see above) plays an important part in evaluating and financing such projects.

TRADE

Meeting in Manila in January 1977 the Economic Ministers concluded a Basic Agreement on the Establishment of ASEAN Preferential Trade Arrangements. This was not intended to lead directly to the formation of a free trade zone. The Philippines, Thailand and Singapore have been in favour of trade liberalization, and early in 1977 they concluded bilateral agreements for 10% tariff cuts on a wide range of items traded between themselves. Indonesia, on the other hand, has been opposed to trade liberalization, taking the view that its own economy is of a type that would be bound to suffer under free trade. The ASEAN agreement therefore provides for negotiations to lead to the introduction of preferences product by product.

Under the agreement, the five countries were to accord priority to buying and selling their products to each other at preferential rates during gluts or shortages, as from January 1978. At their sixth meeting in Jakarta in June, the Economic Ministers agreed that in each future round of negotiations on trade preferences, to take place every three months, each country will make offers of at least 100 items. In July 1980 it was decided that all imports with trade values of less than US $50,000 (as recorded in the trade statistics for 1978) should have the existing tariff reduced by 20%, bringing the number of items under the preferential trading arrangements to over 6,000. By June 1982 8,563 items were included. A system of 'across-the-board' tariff cuts of 20%–25% was adopted in 1982 to replace the 'product-by-product' approach. An import value ceiling of US $1m. for these cuts, imposed in January, was raised to $2.5m. in May and to $10m. in November. Tariff cuts of 50% were approved in November for certain non-food products. By mid-1984 18,000 items were included. In February 1985 the 'across-the-board' tariff cut was raised to 25% (instead of 20%–25% as previously). In spite of these measures, however, intra-ASEAN trade accounted for less than 20% of ASEAN's total trade in 1984.

In 1986 the annual meeting of ministers of foreign affairs deplored ASEAN's lack of progress in economic co-operation, and called on the meeting of heads of government, to be held in 1987, to consider new initiatives to improve the situation.

A customs code of conduct was signed in March 1983 by the heads of national customs authorities, aiming to harmonize customs procedures and classification of goods.

AGRICULTURE

The ASEAN Agricultural Development Planning Centre was set up in 1981 to conduct research and training and to draw up regional production plans. An Agricultural Research Co-ordination Board has also been established.

An emergency grain reserve agreement was signed in 1979. During the year an emergency reserve of 50,000 tons of rice was established, available to any member country at three days' notice. Other areas of co-operation include: a Regional Seed Technology Programme; an ASEAN Food-Handling Bureau; a Plant Quarantine Training Institute; an Agricultural Development Planning Centre; a Forest Tree Seed Centre; and programmes on animal diseases.

In October 1983 a ministerial agreement on fisheries co-operation was concluded, providing for the joint management of fish resources, the sharing of technology, and co-operation in marketing.

The first ASEAN Forestry Congress was held in October 1983 to discuss the state of the regional timber industry and the problems of forest depletion. In January 1985 it was announced that an ASEAN Institute for Forest Management was to be set up in Malaysia, with assistance from Canada.

MINERALS AND ENERGY

Under the ASEAN Minerals Co-operation Plan, formulated in 1981, projects have been established on mining safety and technology, minerals exploration, and the exploitation of kaolin and barite.

A meeting on energy co-operation was held by economic ministers in March 1983, resulting in the formation of a Committee on Energy Co-operation, the commissioning of a study on coal power development (to be completed in 1985 with technical assistance from the Asian Development Bank), a scheme for petroleum sharing, and 10 co-operative projects. In 1986 member states signed an agreement on regional sharing of petroleum supplies in the event of an emergency.

TRANSPORT AND COMMUNICATIONS

By 1984 over 100 joint projects in this field had been identified, including: harmonization of shipping and ports procedures; marine pollution control; the possible establishment of an ASEAN Liner Service; co-operation in the development of roads, railways and inland waterways; ASEAN countries' participatory rights on international air routes; joint use of satellites; and the ASEAN Submarine Cable Project, of which three-quarters was completed in 1984.

JOINT RESEARCH AND TECHNOLOGY

The ASEAN Committee on Science and Technology has co-ordinated the Protein Project, investigating low-cost alternative sources of protein; research in food technology and the management of food waste materials; completion of a Climatic Atlas and Regional Compendium of Climatic Statistics; a nature conservation scheme; and non-conventional energy research. An energy exploration programme was planned for 1981-85 at a cost of $33,100m. The ASEAN-US Center for Technology Exchange (based in New York, with a regional office in Kuala Lumpur, Malaysia) was opened in November 1984. The first ASEAN Science and Technology Week was held in 1986

EDUCATION

Under the ASEAN Development Education Programme five projects (financed by Australia) have been set up: Special Education; Education Management Information System; Teacher Education Reform; Work-oriented Education; Test Development. A National Agency of Development Education has been set up in each country.

SOCIAL DEVELOPMENT

Programmes include a Population Programme to promote family planning; co-operation against drug abuse; mutual assistance in natural disasters; collaboration in health and nutrition programmes; and co-operation in labour administration and vocational training.

TOURISM

Visits of up to 14 days may be made to other member countries without a visa; tourists may also obtain ASEAN Common Collective Travel Documents for package tours and may use these in lieu of a passport within the member countries. In August 1986 ASEAN ministers of foreign affairs approved the establishment of a Tourism Promotion Centre, to be situated in Kuala Lumpur, Malaysia.

CULTURE

Activities include tours by theatrical and dance groups, holding of art exhibitions and exchange of radio and television programmes, films and visual aids. A film festival and a Youth Music Workshop are held annually. Cultural exchanges are also arranged. In 1978 it was agreed to establish an ASEAN Cultural Fund to promote regional cultural development, with Japanese support.

PUBLICATIONS

Annual Report of the ASEAN Standing Committee.

ASEAN Newsletter (every 2 months).

ASEAN Journal on Science and Technology for Development (2 a year).

Information Series and *Documents Series.*

BANK FOR INTERNATIONAL SETTLEMENTS—BIS

Address: Centralbahnplatz 2, 4002 Basel, Switzerland.
The Bank for International Settlements was founded in 1930 to promote co-operation among national central banks and to provide additional facilities for international financial operations.

Organization
(October 1986)

GENERAL MEETING
The General Meeting is held annually. The right of representation and of voting is exercised, in proportion to the number of shares subscribed in each country, by the central banks (or the financial institutions acting in their stead) of the following countries: Australia, Austria, Belgium, Bulgaria, Canada, Czechoslovakia, Denmark, Finland, France, the Federal Republic of Germany, Greece, Hungary, Iceland, Ireland, Italy, Japan, the Netherlands, Norway, Poland, Portugal, Romania, South Africa, Spain, Sweden, Switzerland, Turkey, the United Kingdom, the USA and Yugoslavia (i.e. 24 European countries and five others).

BOARD OF DIRECTORS
The Board of Directors is responsible for the conduct of the Bank's operations at the highest level, and comprises the Governors in office of the central banks of Belgium, France, the Federal Republic of Germany, Italy and the United Kingdom, each of whom appoints another member of the same nationality. The USA does not occupy the two seats to which it is entitled. Other members may be co-opted.
Chairman of the Board and President of the Bank: JEAN GODEAUX (Belgium).
Vice-Chairman: Lord RICHARDSON OF DUNTISBOURNE (United Kingdom).

CHIEF EXECUTIVE OFFICER
General Manager: Prof. ALEXANDRE LAMFALUSSY (Belgium).
The Bank has a staff of about 300 employees.

Activities

The BIS is a financial institution whose special role is to promote the co-operation of central banks, and to fulfil the function of a 'central banks' bank'. Although it has the legal form of a company limited by shares, it is an international organization governed by international law, and enjoys special privileges and immunities in keeping with its role. The participating central banks were originally given the option of subscribing to the shares themselves or arranging for their subscription in their own countries: thus the BIS also has some private shareholders, but they have no right of participation in the General Meeting and 85% of the total share capital is in the hands of central banks.

FINANCE
The authorized capital of the Bank is 1,500m. gold francs, divided into 600,000 shares of 2,500 gold francs each.

Statement of Account*
(In gold francs; units of 0.29032258 . . . gram of fine gold—Art. 4 of the Statutes; 30 June 1986)

Assets		%
Gold	5,033,424,221	18.8
Cash on hand and on sight a/c with banks	9,594,157	0.0
Treasury bills	341,001,526	1.3
Time deposits and advances	18,707,039,930	70.0
Securities at term	2,615,895,852	9.8
Miscellaneous	14,192,145	0.1
Total	26,721,147,831	100.0

Liabilities		%
Authorized cap.: 1,500,000,000		
Issued cap.: 1,182,812,500		
viz. 473,125 shares of which 25% paid up	295,703,125	1.1
Reserves	908,483,397	3.4
Deposits (gold)	4,441,809,067	16.6
Deposits (currencies)	20,289,753,464	75.9
Miscellaneous	766,226,972	2.9
Dividend payable on 1 July 1986	19,171,806	0.1
Total	26,721,147,831	100.0

* Assets and liabilities in US dollars are converted at US $208 per fine ounce of gold (equivalent to 1 gold franc = US $1.94149 . . .) and all other items in currencies on the basis of market rates against the US dollar.

BANKING OPERATIONS
The BIS assists central banks in managing and investing their monetary reserves: in 1985 about 80 central banks from all over the world had deposits with the BIS, which managed almost 10% of world foreign exchange reserves.

The BIS uses the funds deposited with it partly for lending to central banks. Its credit transactions may take the form of swaps against gold; covered credits secured by means of a pledge of gold or marketable short-term securities; credits against gold or currency deposits of the same amount and for the same duration held with the BIS; unsecured credits in the form of advances or deposits; or standby credits, which in individual instances are backed by guarantees given by member central banks.

In late 1982, faced with the increasingly critical debt situation of some Latin American countries and the resultant threat to the viability of the international financial system, the BIS granted comparatively large-scale loans to central banks that did not number among its shareholders: the central banks of Argentina, Brazil and Mexico were granted bridging loans pending the disbursement of balance-of-payments credits extended by the IMF. These facilities amounted to almost US $3,000m., all of which had been repaid by the end of 1983.

The BIS also engages in traditional types of investment: funds not required for lending to central banks are placed in the market as deposits with commercial banks and purchases of short-term negotiable paper, including Treasury bills. Such operations constitute a major part of the Bank's business.

Because the central banks' monetary reserves must be available at short notice, they can only be placed with the BIS at short term, for fixed periods and with clearly defined repayment terms. The BIS has to match its assets to the maturity structure and nature of its commitments, and must therefore conduct its business with special regard to maintaining a high degree of liquidity.

The Bank's operations must be in conformity with the monetary policy of the central banks of the countries concerned. It is not permitted to make advances to governments or to open current accounts in their name. Real estate transactions are also excluded.

INTERNATIONAL MONETARY CO-OPERATION
Governors of central banks meet for regular discussions at the BIS to co-ordinate international monetary policy and ensure orderly conditions on the international financial markets. There is close co-operation with the IMF and, since its membership includes central banks of eastern European countries, the BIS also provides a forum for contacts between East and West.

The BIS plays an important part in the European Monetary System by acting as Agent for the European Monetary Co-operation Fund (EMCF: see p. 152). It also provides the secretariat for the Committee of Governors of the EEC Central Banks and for the Board of Governors of the EMCF.

A Euro-currency Standing Committee was set up at the BIS in 1971 to provide the central bank Governors of the 'Group of Ten' industrialized countries (see p. 74) and Switzerland with information concerning the monetary policy aspects of the Euro-currency markets. Since 1982 it has provided a regular critical survey of the entire international credit system.

The BIS was expected to become the central clearing agent in an international clearing system for bank deposits denominated in European Currency Units (ECUs), due to enter into operation by the beginning of 1987.

In 1974 the Governors of central banks of the Group of Ten and Switzerland set up the Committee on Banking Regulations and Supervisory Practices (whose secretariat is provided by the BIS) to co-ordinate banking supervision at the international level. The Committee pools information on banking supervisory regulations and surveillance systems, including the supervision of banks' foreign currency business, identifies possible danger areas and proposes measures to safeguard the banks' solvency and liquidity.

The Bank also organizes and provides the secretariat for periodic meetings of experts, such as the Group of Computer Experts, the Group of Experts on Payment Systems and the Group of Experts on Monetary and Economic Data Bank Questions.

Research is conducted by the Bank's Monetary and Economic Department, whose most important publication is the BIS Annual Report, highly regarded as an independent analysis of monetary and economic developments. Statistics on international banking are also published regularly.

CARIBBEAN COMMUNITY AND COMMON MARKET—CARICOM

Address: Bank of Guyana Building, POB 10827, Georgetown, Guyana.
Telephone: 02-69281.
Telex: 2263.

CARICOM was formed by the Treaty of Chaguaramas in 1973 as a movement towards unity in the Caribbean; it replaced the Caribbean Free Trade Association (CARIFTA), founded in 1965.

MEMBERS

Antigua and Barbuda	Jamaica
Bahamas	Montserrat
Barbados	Saint Christopher and Nevis
Belize	Saint Lucia
Dominica	Saint Vincent and the Grenadines
Grenada	Trinidad and Tobago
Guyana	

OBSERVERS

Dominican Republic	Suriname
Haiti	

Organization
(October 1986)

HEADS OF GOVERNMENT CONFERENCE

The Conference is the final authority of the Community and determines policy. It is responsible for the conclusion of treaties on behalf of the Community and for entering into relationships between the Community and international organizations and states. The Conference is also responsible for making the financial arrangements to meet the expenses of the Community, but has delegated this function to the Common Market Council. Decisions of the Conference are generally taken unanimously, but in 1984 the Conference instructed the Secretariat to examine the introduction of a voting procedure other than by unanimous vote. Heads of Government met in November 1982 (the first meeting for seven years) and thereafter annually.

COMMON MARKET COUNCIL

The principal organ of the Common Market, the Council consists of a Minister of Government designated by each member state. It is responsible for the development and smooth running of the Common Market, and for the settlement of any problems arising out of its functioning. However, the Conference may issue directives to the Council. The Council generally takes decisions unanimously.

INSTITUTIONS

There are several institutions of the Caribbean Community responsible for formulating policies and supervising co-operation in services such as education, health, labour matters and foreign policy. Each member state is represented on each institution by a Minister of Government. These institutions are the Conference of Ministers Responsible for Health and the Standing Committees of Ministers Responsible (respectively) for Education; Labour; Foreign Affairs; Finance; Agriculture; Industry; Transport; Energy, Mines and Natural Resources; and Science and Technology.

SECRETARIAT

The Secretariat is organized into five divisions: Trade and Agriculture; Economics and Industry; Functional Co-operation; General Services and Administration; Legal. At the end of 1983 there were 159 permanent staff and 48 project staff. The functions of the Secretariat are: to service meetings of the Community and of its Institutions or Committees; to take appropriate follow-up action on decisions made at such meetings; to carry out studies on questions of economic and functional co-operation relating to the region as a whole; to provide services to member states at their request in respect of matters relating to the achievement of the objectives of the Community.

Secretary-General: Roderick Rainford (Jamaica).
Deputy Secretary-General: Louis A. Wiltshire (Trinidad and Tobago).

Activities

ECONOMIC CO-OPERATION

The Caribbean Community's main field of activity is economic integration by means of a Caribbean Common Market which replaced the former Caribbean Free Trade Association (CARIFTA). However, the economic difficulties of member states have hindered the development of intra-regional trade, which accounted for 9.3% of imports in 1981, falling to 6% in 1983. The value of Community trade fell from US $555m. in 1982 to $481m. in 1983, and to $433m. in 1984, and was estimated to have fallen by a further 10% in 1985. Among the reasons for this decline were currency fluctuations within the region, import-licensing measures taken by individual members (notably Trinidad and Tobago), and the collapse in 1983 of the Community's trade payments facility, the Multilateral Clearing Facility (MCF) after it had exceeded its credit limit. Another problem is the difficulty of applying the CARICOM Rules of Origin which attempt to verify that imported goods genuinely come from within the community; the garment industry is particularly affected by illegal imports.

The Secretariat and the Caribbean Development Bank carry out research on the best means of facing economic difficulties, and meetings of the Chief Executives of commercial banks and of central bank officials are also held with the aim of strengthening regional co-operation.

In July 1984 the Conference of Heads of Government agreed to establish a common external tariff on certain products, such as steel, cement and fertilizers. They also issued the 'Nassau Understanding' calling for structural adjustment in the economies of the region, including measures to expand production and reduce imports. The common external tariff was to be implemented by 1 January 1985, but the target date was postponed until 31 August, and several members had still not implemented the measures by mid-1986. In July 1986 the Conference agreed to establish a trade credit facility (TCF) to replace the defunct MCF. The TCF was to be made up of US $15m. in equity (to be subscribed by the participating countries) and $60m. in loans from outside sources. It was to become operational in 1987, providing pre-shipment financing for a maximum of two years, and post-shipment financing for up to five years, and covering most of the region's exports, except for well-established ones such as sugar, bananas and bauxite.

INDUSTRY AND ENERGY

The CARICOM industrial programme aims to promote the development of exporting industries through an 'Enterprise Regime' (subject to ratification by member governments). Work on an Investors' Guide for each member state was undertaken in 1983. CARICOM's Export Promotion Project (financed by the European Development Fund) gives training and consultancy services to regional manufacturers, and there is also a trade information unit and a sellers' and buyers' data bank at the Secretariat. The first regional manufacturers' exhibition (CARIMEX) was held in 1985.

The Secretariat is active in setting up a National Standards Bureau in each member country to harmonize technical standards, and supervises the metrication of weights and measures: in 1983 a metrication expert was engaged for a year (through the Commonwealth Fund for Technical Co-operation) to provide technical assistance to each member country during conversion to the metric system.

The CARICOM Alternative Energy Systems Project provides training, assesses energy needs and conducts energy audits.

TRANSPORT

The West Indies Shipping Corporation (WISCO) forms the official carrier in the region, and in 1983 a special CARICOM committee was formed to encourage co-operation between WISCO and the national shipping lines. A survey was carried out on improving navigational aids, and training in maritime safety was given, while studies and inventories of small vessel shipping were completed with financial assistance from the UNDP. An agreement on co-ordination of regional air transport services (including fuel purchase, maintenance, cargo storage and schedules) had been ratified by nine countries by the end of 1985.

AGRICULTURE

In 1983 the Agricultural Marketing Protocol, a mechanism for promoting trade in agricultural products, was abolished and alternative arrangements were being considered. The Secretariat also worked on plans for a regional nutrition strategy; the establishment of a regional information system on animal diseases and of a regional Aquaculture Centre (in collaboration with the FAO); and the development of the coconut industry. Fisheries training was also provided.

The Caribbean Agricultural Research and Development Institute (CARDI) was founded in 1975; its work concentrates on the problems of small farmers producing for local consumption, for example projects aimed at increasing productivity of yams and groundnuts. A regional food and nutrition strategy, approved in 1982, aims to improve standards of nutrition, increase production and establish food reserves, largely through the Caribbean Food Corporation, which attracts investments for agricultural projects and food marketing. In 1983 ministers of agriculture approved an investment programme of 19 projects to be implemented by 1985.

EDUCATION AND HEALTH

With assistance from UNESCO the Secretariat provided workshops on literacy teaching in 1984, and prepared a constitution for the Caribbean Council for Adult Education. It also sponsored meetings on technical education, and awarded 57 individual training grants in 1983.

In 1983 the Secretariat prepared plans of action on food safety and on community health education, and assumed responsibility for management of the Pan-Caribbean Disaster Preparedness and Prevention Project.

ASSOCIATE INSTITUTIONS

Caribbean Development Bank: POB 408, Wildey, St Michael, Barbados; tel. (809) 42 61152; telex 2287; f. 1969 to stimulate regional economic growth through support for agriculture, industry, transport, tourism and education; cap. US $281.6m. (Nov. 1983) of which $57.2m. is paid-up. In 1985 loan approvals amounted to $41m. for 13 projects. Mems: CARICOM states, plus Canada, Colombia, Mexico, Venezuela, the United Kingdom, Anguilla, the British Virgin Islands, the Cayman Islands, and the Turks and Caicos Islands. Pres. WILLIAM DEMAS.

Organisation of Eastern Caribbean States—OECS: POB 179, The Morne, Castries, Saint Lucia; tel. 3185; f. 1981 by the seven states which formerly belonged to the West Indies Associated States (f. 1966). Principal institutions are: the Authority of Heads of Government (the supreme policy-making body), the Foreign Affairs Committee, the Defence and Security Committee, and the Economic Affairs Committee. A treaty forming the Eastern Caribbean Development Bank was signed by the seven members in July 1983. Following a military coup in Grenada in October 1983, the OECS acted jointly in requesting US military aid to invade the island. Mems: Antigua and Barbuda, Dominica, Grenada, Montserrat, Saint Christopher and Nevis, Saint Lucia and Saint Vincent and the Grenadines; assoc. mem.: the British Virgin Islands. Dir Dr VAUGHAN A. LEWIS.

Other Associate Institutions of CARICOM, in accordance with its constitution, are: the Caribbean Examinations Council, the Caribbean Meteorological Institute, the Council of Legal Education, the West Indies Shipping Corporation, the University of Guyana and the University of the West Indies.

CENTRAL AMERICAN COMMON MARKET—CACM

(MERCADO COMÚN CENTROAMERICANO)

Address: 4a Avenida 10-25 Zona 14, Apdo postal 1237, Guatemala City, Guatemala.
Telephone: 682151.
Telex: 5676.

CACM was established by the Organization of Central American States (ODECA, q.v.) under the General Treaty of Central American Economic Integration (Tratado General de Integración Económica Centroamericana) signed in Managua on 15 December 1960. It was ratified by all countries by September 1963.

MEMBERS

Costa Rica	El Salvador	Nicaragua
Guatemala	Honduras	

Organization

(October 1986)

MINISTERIAL MEETINGS

The organization's policy is formulated by regular meetings of Ministers and Vice-Ministers of Central American Integration; meetings of other ministers, and of Presidents of Central Banks, also play an important part.

PERMANENT SECRETARIAT

Secretaría Permanente del Tratado General de Integración Económica Centroamericana—SIECA: supervises the correct implementation of the legal instruments of economic integration, carries out relevant studies at the request of the Common Market authorities, and arranges the meetings of the main bodies. There are departments of: industry; agriculture; taxes and tariffs; physical integration; commercial policy; statistics; economic and social programmes; finance and administration; and science and technology.
Secretary-General: RAÚL SIERRA FRANCO.

Activities

The General Treaty envisaged the eventual liberalization of intra-regional trade and the establishment of a free-trade area and a customs union. Economic integration in the region, however, has been hampered by ideological differences between governments, difficulties in internal supply, protectionist measures by overseas markets, external and intra-regional debts, adverse rates of exchange and high interest rates.

By 1969, 95% of customs items had been awarded free-trade status; the remaining 5% consisted of goods covered by international agreements and other special arrangements. In 1970, however, following a dispute with El Salvador, Honduras reintroduced duties on imports from other CACM countries; trade between El Salvador and Honduras was not resumed until 1982, and Honduras' trade with the other members continued to be governed by bilateral agreements. Regular meetings of senior customs officials aim to increase co-operation, to develop a uniform terminology, and to recommend revisions of customs legislation. CACM member-countries also aim to pursue a common policy in respect of international trade agreements on commodities, raw materials and staples. SIECA participates in meetings with other regional organizations (such as SELA and ECLAC, q.v.) and represents the region at meetings of international organizations, such as UNCTAD.

Little headway has been made in industrial integration, mainly because of the continuing heavy external dependence of the region's economies. Under the Convention for Fiscal Incentives for Industrial Development, which came into operation in 1969, a wide range of tax benefits are applied to various categories of industries in the region, to encourage productivity. SIECA carries out studies on the industrial sector, compiles statistics, and provides information to member governments. It also analyses energy consumption in the region and gives assistance to governments in drawing up energy plans, aiming to reduce dependence on imported petroleum.

A co-ordinating commission supervises the marketing of four basic crops (maize, rice, beans and sorghum), recording and forecasting production figures and recommending minimum guarantee prices. Information on other crops is also compiled. A permanent commission for agricultural research and extension services monitors and co-ordinates regional projects in this field.

SIECA gives technical assistance to governments in improving their transport systems. In March 1983 regional Ministers of Transport agreed to establish in each country, in collaboration with existing bodies, a mechanism for encouraging regional co-operation in transport and related matters.

An agreement to establish a Central American Monetary Union was signed in 1964, with the eventual aim of establishing a common currency (the Central American peso, at par with the US dollar) and aligning foreign exchange and monetary policies. The Central American Monetary Council, comprising the Presidents of the member states' Central Banks, meets regularly to consider monetary policy and financial affairs. A Fund for Monetary Stabilization, founded in 1969 by the Central Banks of member states, provides short-term financial assistance to members facing temporary balance-of-payments difficulties.

In 1971 the Secretariat began work on a new integration model for the region and a draft treaty for a Central American Economic and Social Community was finalized in March 1976. It provided for the establishment of new top-level administrative organizations and a number of regional institutions, for a free-trade area, a customs union, and common industrial policies similar to those contained in the 1960 General Treaty. It also called for the harmonization of fiscal and financial policies, the establishment of a monetary union and the enactment of common programmes for social and economic development. Member states' legislatures, however, failed to ratify the new treaty, and CACM's achievements remained limited.

Trade within the region increased in value from US $33m. in 1960 to $1,129m. in 1980, but subsequently diminished every year, amounting to less than $600m. in 1985. This decline was due to a number of factors: low prices for the region's main export commodities, and heavy external debts, both resulting in a severe shortage of foreign exchange; and intra-regional trade 'freezes' provoked by trade debts amounting to $700m. at mid-1986 (Guatemala and Costa Rica being the chief creditors, and Nicaragua and El Salvador the main debtors). In January 1986 a new CACM tariff and customs agreement came into effect, imposing standard import duties for the whole region (aimed at discouraging the import of non-essential goods from outside the region), and a uniform tariff nomenclature. Honduras, however, continued to insist on bilateral tariff agreements with other member countries. In July CACM members agreed on a new payments mechanism for mutual trade, based on the Derecho de Importación Centroamericano (DICA—Central American Import Right), a voucher issued by central banks and used as currency to avoid using scarce US dollars.

An agreement with the Europan Community was signed in November 1985, providing for economic co-operation and EEC aid for the region.

PUBLICATIONS

Carta Informativa (monthly).
Anuario Estadístico Centroamericano de Comercio Exterior.
Cuadernos de la SIECA (2 a year).

Institutions

FINANCE

Banco Centroamericano de Integración Económica—BCIE (Central American Bank for Economic Integration): Apdo Postal 772, Tegucigalpa, Honduras; tel. 222805; f. 1960 to promote the economic integration and balanced economic development of member countries; finances public and private development projects, particularly those related to industrialization and infrastructure. By June 1982 cumulative lending amounted to US $1,731m., mainly for roads, hydroelectricity projects, housing and telecommunications. Authorized capital was increased from $200m. to $600m. in January 1982. Exec. Pres. DANTE GABRIEL RAMÍREZ. Publs *Annual Report, Revista de la Integración.*

Consejo Monetario Centroamericano: Apdo Postal 5438, San José, Costa Rica; formed by the presidents of CACM central banks, to co-ordinate monetary policies. Sec.-Gen. OLIVIER CASTRO. Publs *Boletín Estadístico* (annualy), *Balanza de Pagos* (annually).

TRADE AND INDUSTRY

Federación de Cámaras de Comercio del Istmo Centroamericano (Federation of Central American Chambers of Commerce): Av. Ecuador y Av. Cuba, Apdo Postal 74, Panamá 1, Panama; tel. 25-0833; telex 2434; f. 1961; for planning and co-ordinating industrial and commercial interchanges. Pres. GILBERT MALLOL.

Federación de Cámaras y Asociaciones Industriales Centroamericanas—FECAICA (Federation of Industrial Chambers and Associations in Central America): Edificio Cámara de Industria de Guatemala, Ruta 6 No. 9-21, Zona 4, POB 214, Guatemala; established in 1959 by the Chambers of Commerce and Industry of the CACM countries to promote commerce and industry, principally by interchange of information.

Instituto Centroamericano de Investigación y Tecnología Industrial (Central American Research Institute for Industry): Apdo Postal 1552, Avda La Reforma 4-47, Zona 10, Guatemala C.A.; tel. 310631; telex 5312; f. 1956 by the five Central American Republics, with assistance from the United Nations, to provide technical advisory services to regional governments and private enterprise. Dir FRANCISCO AGUIRRE BATRES (Guatemala); Deputy Dir W. LUDWIG INGRAM (Nicaragua).

Instituto Centroamericano de Administración de Empresas (Central American Institute for Business Administration): Apdo Postal 2485, Managua, Nicaragua; tel. 58403; telex 2360; Apdo 960, 4050 Alajuela, Costa Rica; tel. 41 22 55; telex 7040; f. 1964; provides postgraduate programme in business administration; executive training programmes; management research and consulting; library of 28,000 vols. Rector Dr MARC LINDENBERG; Librarian THOMAS BLOCH.

PUBLIC ADMINISTRATION

Instituto Centroamericano de Administración Pública (Central American Institute of Public Administration): Apdo Postal 10.025, San José, Costa Rica; tel. 223133; telex 2180; f. 1954 by the five Central American Republics and the United Nations, with later participation by Panama. The Institute aims to train the region's public servants, provide technical assistance and carry out research leading to reforms in public administration. Dir CARLOS CORDERO D'AUBUISSON.

EDUCATION AND HEALTH

Confederación Universitaria Centroamericana (Central American University Confederation): Apdo 37, Universidad de Costa Rica, San José, Costa Rica; tel. 252744; telex 3011; f. 1948 to guarantee academic, administrative and economic autonomy for universities and to encourage regional integration of higher education; Council of 14 mems. Mems.: seven universities, in Costa Rica (two), El Salvador, Guatemala, Honduras, Nicaragua and Panama. Sec.-Gen. Dr RODRIGO FERNÁNDEZ (Costa Rica). Publs *Estudios Sociales Centroamericanas* (quarterly), *Estadísticas Universitarias* (2 a year), *Cuadernos de Investigación* (monthly), *Carta Informativa de la Secretaría General* (monthly).

Instituto de Nutrición de Centro América y Panamá—INCAP (Institute of Nutrition of Central America and Panama): Apdo Postal 1188, Carretera Roosevelt, Zona 11, Guatemala City, Guatemala; tel. 723762; telex 5696; f. 1949 to promote and encourage the development of nutritional science in member countries; conducts research in food chemistry, biochemistry, food technology, animal nutrition and clinical nutrition; provides training and technical assistance for nutrition education and planning; maintains library (including 400 periodicals). Administered by the Pan-American Health Organization (PAHO). Mems: CACM mems and Panama. Dir Dr LUIS OCTAVIO ANGEL.

TRANSPORT AND COMMUNICATIONS

Corporación Centroamericana de Servicios de Navegación Aérea—COCESNA (Central American Air Navigation Service Corporation): Apdo Postal 660, Tegucigalpa, Honduras; tel. 33-1141; telex 1411; f. 1960; Gen. Man. FERNANDO A. CASTILLO R.

Comisión Técnica de las Telecomunicaciones de Centroamerica—COMTELCA (Technical Commission for Telecommunications in Central America): Apdo 1793, Tegucigalpa, Honduras; tel. 32-9527; telex 1235.

THE COLOMBO PLAN FOR CO-OPERATIVE ECONOMIC AND SOCIAL DEVELOPMENT IN ASIA AND THE PACIFIC

Address: 12 Melbourne Ave, POB 596, Colombo 4, Sri Lanka.
Telephone: 581813.

Founded by seven Commonwealth countries in 1950 (as the Colombo Plan for Co-operative Economic Development in South and South-East Asia), the Colombo Plan was subsequently joined by more countries in Asia and the Pacific as well as the USA and Japan.

MEMBERS

Afghanistan	Iran	Pakistan
Australia	Japan	Papua New Guinea
Bangladesh	Kampuchea	Philippines
Bhutan	Korea, Republic	Singapore
Burma	Laos	Sri Lanka
Canada	Malaysia	Thailand
Fiji	Maldives	United Kingdom
India	Nepal	USA
Indonesia	New Zealand	

Organization
(October 1986)

CONSULTATIVE COMMITTEE

The highest deliberative body of the Colombo Plan, consisting of ministers representing member governments. It meets every two years in a member country. The ministers' meeting is preceded by a meeting of senior officials who are directly concerned with the operation of the Plan in their respective countries, to identify issues for discussion by the ministers.

COLOMBO PLAN COUNCIL

The Council meets three or four times a year in Colombo to review the economic and social development of the region and promote co-operation among member countries. Its executive arm is the Colombo Plan Bureau.

COLOMBO PLAN BUREAU

The only permanent institution of the Plan, with its headquarters in Colombo, the Bureau serves the Council, carries out research, conducts seminars and workshops, records the flow of bilateral assistance and disseminates information on the Colombo Plan as a whole. It also provides assistance to the host government for the holding of Consultative Committee Meetings. The Bureau represents the Colombo Plan at meetings where such representation is necessary.

The operating costs of the Bureau are met by equal contributions from member states.

Director: GILBERT H. SHEINBAUM (USA).

Activities

The basic principles and policies governing assistance under the Plan are agreed upon by ministers at the meetings of the Consultative Committee. Specific aid programmes are then negotiated bilaterally on a government-to-government basis, within the framework of the policies adopted. There is no centralized programming, nor a common fund to finance national development projects.

CAPITAL AID

Capital aid under the Plan takes the form of grants and loans for national projects, mainly from six developed countries to the developing member countries of the Plan. It covers almost all aspects of social and economic development, including projects in agriculture, communications, energy and education.

From 1950 to 1984 total amounts of assistance from the major donors were as follows:

Country	US $ million
Australia	5,429.5
Canada	4,264.4
India	800.1
Japan	16,525.3
New Zealand	257.4
United Kingdom	6,249.4
USA	42,142.1
Total	75,668.2

TECHNICAL CO-OPERATION

Under the Technical Co-operation programme experts are provided, training fellowships are awarded and equipment for training and research is supplied, to assist recipient countries in agriculture, fisheries, industry, planning, education, health, and many other aspects of economic and social development. Examples of projects being undertaken in 1983 included the following (the donor country is indicated in parentheses): drilling of 4,000 tube-wells in Bangladesh (Australia); forestry research in Nepal (United Kingdom); training courses in water works, sewage works and bridge engineering (Japan); soil studies in Fiji (New Zealand); and rural electrification in Bangladesh (USA).

During 1984, 20,566 students and trainees received training, and 8,178 experts and 1,149 volunteers were engaged under technical assistance programmes. The total value of technical co-operation activities from the inception of the Plan to December 1984 was $5,900m.; disbursements in 1984 totalled $587m.

Japan provided 8,663 fellowship awards in 1984; other leading donors were the United Kingdom and Australia, which provided 4,302 and 3,056 awards respectively. Among recipients, Indonesia was the chief beneficiary, receiving 3,250 awards; the other main recipients were India, Thailand, Malaysia, the Philippines, the Republic of Korea and Bangladesh.

Of the total of 8,178 experts financed in 1984, Japan provided 5,519, Australia 1,151, the USA 841, the United Kingdom 397, Canada 179 and New Zealand 159. Indonesia received the largest number of experts (2,200), and the other main recipients were Thailand, the Philippines and Malaysia.

DRUG ADVISORY PROGRAMME

The programme was launched in 1973 to help develop co-operative schemes to eliminate the causes and ameliorate the effects of drug abuse in member states. The programme is supplementary in nature and does not duplicate the efforts of other agencies involved. Its activities are directed towards the promotion of effective national, regional and sub-regional efforts in tackling problems and identifying areas in which bilateral and multilateral assistance and international co-operation under the Colombo Plan would be useful.

Seminars are held in member countries to inform governments and the public and to help organize remedial measures. Assistance is given in training narcotics officials in all aspects of drug abuse prevention by means of exchanges, fellowships, study, training and observation. Bilateral and multilateral talks among member countries are held.

Member countries are helped in establishing narcotics control offices or boards, revising legislation on narcotics, improving law enforcement, treatment, rehabilitation and prevention education, and in improving public understanding of these matters by the use of mass media, workshops and seminars.

Drug Adviser: PIO A. ABARRO (Philippines).

DISBURSEMENTS OF BILATERAL TECHNICAL ASSISTANCE
Disbursements by donor and sector, 1984 (US $ million)

Donor	Students and Trainees	Experts and Volunteers	Equipment	Other*	Total
Australia	54.2	32.5	0.1	18.0	104.8
Canada	—	—	—	9.7	9.7
India	1.8	0.4	0.1	0.1	2.4
Japan	60.7	100.9	24.0	13.8	199.4
Korea, Republic	2.6	0.2	—	—	2.8
Malaysia	0.4	—	—	—	0.4
New Zealand	—	—	—	4.4	4.4
Pakistan	0.1	—	—	—	0.1
Singapore	0.2	—	—	—	0.2
Thailand	0.2	—	—	—	0.2
United Kingdom	21.2	11.5	4.6	20.3	57.6
USA	—	—	—	205.0	205.0
Other donors	—	—	—	0.3	0.3
Total	141.4	145.5	28.8	271.6	587.3

* Total disbursements are shown under 'Other' against countries for which breakdown by type is not available.

TRAINING COLLEGE

Colombo Plan Staff College for Technician Education: Tanglin POB 187, Singapore 9124; tel. 2356055; telex 39713; f. 1974 as a specialized institution of the Colombo Plan, funded by contributions from member governments; trains staff for the education of technicians, conducts conferences and research, and provides advisory services. Dir Dr ROBERT MCCAIG (Australia). Publs *Annual Report, Newsletter* (quarterly).

PUBLICATIONS

The Colombo Plan Newsletter (quarterly).

Proceedings and Conclusions of the Consultative Committee (every 2 years).

Annual Report of the Colombo Plan Council.

The Colombo Plan: What It Is, How It Works (revised April 1983).

Development Perspectives: Country Issues, Papers by Member Governments to the Consultative Committee (every 2 years).

THE COMMONWEALTH

Address: Marlborough House, Pall Mall, London, SW1Y 5HX, England.
Telephone: (01) 839-3411.
Telex: 27678.

The Commonwealth is a voluntary association of 49 independent states, comprising about one-quarter of the world's population. It includes the United Kingdom and most of its former dependencies, and former dependencies of Australia and New Zealand (themselves Commonwealth countries).

The evolution of the Commonwealth began with the introduction of self-government in Canada in the 1840s; Australia, New Zealand and South Africa became independent before the first world war. At the Imperial Conference of 1926 the United Kingdom and the four Dominions, as they were then called, were described as 'autonomous communities within the British Empire, equal in status', and this change was enacted into law by the Statute of Westminster, in 1931.

The modern Commonwealth began with the entry of India and Pakistan in 1947, and of Sri Lanka (then Ceylon) in 1948. In 1950 India became a republic, and the Commonwealth Heads of Government then decided that allegiance to the same monarch need not be a condition of membership. This was a precedent for a number of other members (see Heads of State and Heads of Government, below).

MEMBERS*

Antigua and Barbuda
Australia
Bahamas
Bangladesh
Barbados
Belize
Botswana
Brunei
Canada
Cyprus
Dominica
Fiji
The Gambia
Ghana
Grenada
Guyana
India
Jamaica
Kenya
Kiribati
Lesotho
Malawi
Malaysia
Maldives
Malta
Mauritius
Nauru†
New Zealand
Nigeria
Papua New Guinea
Saint Christopher and Nevis
Saint Lucia
Saint Vincent and the Grenadines
Seychelles
Sierra Leone
Singapore
Solomon Islands
Sri Lanka
Swaziland
Tanzania
Tonga
Trinidad and Tobago
Tuvalu†
Uganda
United Kingdom
Vanuatu
Western Samoa
Zambia
Zimbabwe

* Ireland, South Africa and Pakistan withdrew from the Commonwealth in 1949, 1961 and 1972 respectively.
† Nauru and Tuvalu are special members of the Commonwealth; they have the right to participate in functional activities but are not represented at Meetings of Commonwealth Heads of Government.

Dependencies and Associated States

Australia:
  Australian Antarctic Territory
  Christmas Island
  Cocos (Keeling) Islands
  Coral Sea Islands Territory
  Heard and McDonald Islands
  Norfolk Island
New Zealand:
  Cook Islands
  Niue
  Ross Dependency
  Tokelau
United Kingdom:
  Anguilla
  Bermuda
  British Antarctic Territory
  British Indian Ocean Territory
  British Virgin Islands
  Cayman Islands
  Channel Islands
  Falkland Islands
  Gibraltar
  Hong Kong
  Isle of Man
  Montserrat
  Pitcairn Islands
  St Helena
  Ascension
  Tristan da Cunha
  South Georgia and South Sandwich Islands
  Turks and Caicos Islands

HEADS OF STATE AND HEADS OF GOVERNMENT

In November 1986, 23 member countries were monarchies and 26 were republics. All Commonwealth countries accept Queen Elizabeth II as the symbol of the free association of the independent member nations and as such the Head of the Commonwealth. Of the 26 republics, the offices of Head of State and Head of Government were combined in 18: Bangladesh, Botswana, Cyprus, The Gambia, Ghana, Guyana, Kenya, Kiribati, Malawi, Maldives, Nauru, Nigeria, Seychelles, Sierra Leone, Sri Lanka, Tanzania, Uganda and Zambia. The two offices were separated in the remaining eight: Dominica, India, Malta, Singapore, Trinidad and Tobago, Vanuatu, Western Samoa and Zimbabwe.

Of the monarchies, the Queen is Head of State of the United Kingdom and of 17 others, in each of which she is represented by a Governor-General: Antigua and Barbuda, Australia, the Bahamas, Barbados, Belize, Canada, Fiji, Grenada, Jamaica, Mauritius, New Zealand, Papua New Guinea, Saint Christopher and Nevis, Saint Lucia, Saint Vincent and the Grenadines, Solomon Islands and Tuvalu. Brunei, Lesotho, Malaysia, Swaziland and Tonga are also monarchies, where the traditional monarch is Head of State.

The Governors-General are appointed by the Queen on the advice of the ministers of the country concerned. They are wholly independent of the Government of the United Kingdom.

HIGH COMMISSIONERS

Governments of member countries are represented in other Commonwealth countries by High Commissioners, who have a status equivalent to that of Ambassadors.

Organization
(October 1986)

The Commonwealth is not a federation: there is no central government nor are there any rigid contractual obligations such as bind members of the United Nations.

The Commonwealth has no written constitution but its members subscribe to the ideals of the Declaration of Commonwealth Principles (see p. 120) unanimously approved by a meeting of Heads of Government in Singapore in 1971. Members also approved the 1977 statement on apartheid in sport (the Gleneagles Agreement); the 1979 Lusaka Declaration on Racism and Racial Prejudice; the 1981 Melbourne Declaration on relations between developed and developing countries; the 1983 New Delhi Statement on Economic Action; the 1983 Goa Declaration on International Security; and the 1985 Nassau Declaration on World Order.

MEETINGS OF HEADS OF GOVERNMENT

Meetings are private and informal and operate not by voting but by consensus. The emphasis is on consultation and exchange of views for co-operation. A communiqué is issued at the end of every meeting. Meetings are held every two years in different capitals in the Commonwealth. The 1985 meeting was held in Nassau, Bahamas; the 1987 meeting was to be held in Canada.

OTHER CONSULTATIONS

Meetings at ministerial and official level are also held regularly. Since 1959 Finance Ministers have met in a Commonwealth country in the week prior to the annual meetings of the IMF and the World Bank. Education Ministers, Health Ministers and Law Ministers usually meet about every three years. Ministers of Food and Agriculture and of Employment and Labour held their first full meetings in 1981 and 1982 respectively. The Commonwealth Youth Affairs Council, at ministerial level, meets every two years. Ministers of Industry met in 1984, and a meeting of ministers responsible for women and development was held in 1985.

INTERNATIONAL ORGANIZATIONS

The Commonwealth

Senior officials—Cabinet Secretaries, Permanent Secretaries to Heads of Government and others—meet regularly in the year between meetings of Heads of Government to provide continuity and to exchange views on various developments.

COMMONWEALTH SECRETARIAT

The Secretariat, established by Commonwealth Heads of Government in 1965, operates as an international organization at the service of all Commonwealth countries. It organizes consultations between governments and runs programmes of co-operation. Meetings of heads of government, ministers and senior officials decide these programmes and provide overall direction.

The Secretariat is headed by a Secretary-General (elected by Heads of Government), with two Deputy Secretaries-General and two Assistant Secretaries-General. One Deputy is responsible for political affairs (divisions of international affairs, legal affairs, information, and administration and conference services), the other for economic affairs (divisions of economic affairs, export market development, and food production and rural development). One Assistant Secretary-General is responsible for the Human Resource Development Group (education, training, management, medical, women's and youth programmes) and the science division, the other for the Commonwealth Fund for Technical Co-operation (CFTC).

Secretary-General: Sir SHRIDATH S. RAMPHAL (Guyana).

Deputy Secretary-General (Political): Chief EMEKA C. ANYAOKU (Nigeria).

Deputy Secretary-General (Economic): Sir PETER MARSHALL (UK).

Assistant Secretaries-General: ROBERT MCLAREN (Canada), MANMOHAN MALHOUTRA (India).

Director, Administration Division: Tunku ABDUL AZIZ (Malaysia).

Director, Information Division: CHARLES A. GUNAWARDENA (Sri Lanka).

BUDGET

The Secretariat's budget for 1986/87 was £6,297,705. Member governments meet the cost of the Secretariat through subscriptions on a scale related to income and population, similar to the scale for contributions to the United Nations.

Activities

INTERNATIONAL AFFAIRS

The most publicized achievement of the 1979 Lusaka meeting of Heads of Government was the nine-point plan to help bring Zimbabwe-Rhodesia to legal independence, worked out by a group of leaders—from Australia, Jamaica, Nigeria, Tanzania, the United Kingdom and Zambia, together with the Commonwealth Secretary-General—and endorsed at a special session of all delegation heads. The leaders issued the Lusaka Declaration on Racism and Racial Prejudice as a formal expression of their abhorrence of all forms of racist policy. A proposal for a Commonwealth role in upholding human rights was welcomed in principle and was to be further studied.

At their 1981 meeting in Melbourne, the Heads of Government issued the Melbourne Declaration in which they asserted that the current 'gross inequality of wealth and opportunity' was a 'fundamental source of tension and instability in the world', and declared their common resolve 'to end the present impasse; to advance the dialogue between developing and developed countries; to infuse an increased sense of urgency and direction into the resolution of these common problems of mankind'. The meeting confirmed the Commonwealth's commitment to independence for Namibia, and condemned South Africa's attempts to destabilize neighbouring states.

In November 1983 the Heads of Government, meeting in New Delhi, issued the Goa Declaration on International Security 'in the context of heightened tensions and a continuing build-up of nuclear arsenals' threatening the future of civilization. The leaders called for 'a concerted effort... to restore constructive dialogue to the conduct of East-West relations', for the cessation of the nuclear arms race, and for funds released by disarmament to be used in world development. More specifically, the leaders expressed concern at the vulnerability of small states to external attack and interference in their affairs, and requested the Secretary-General to undertake a study of the special needs of such states. The Secretary-General subsequently established a Commonwealth Consultative Group for this purpose, to report to the 1985 meeting of Heads of Government. The New Delhi meeting also decided that the Commonwealth (in co-operation with the United Nations) should undertake to disseminate accurate information about South African apartheid.

In October 1985 Heads of Government, meeting at Nassau, Bahamas, issued the Nassau Declaration on World Order, reaffirming Commonwealth commitment to the United Nations, to international co-operation for development and to the eventual elimination of nuclear weapons. The same meeting issued the Commonwealth Accord on Southern Africa, calling on the South African authorities to dismantle apartheid and open dialogue with a view to establishing a representative government. The meeting also established a Commonwealth 'Eminent Persons Group'. It visited South Africa in February and March 1986 and attempted unsuccessfully to establish a dialogue between the South African Government and opposition leaders. In August the heads of government of seven Commonwealth countries (Australia, the Bahamas, Canada, India, the United Kingdom, Zambia and Zimbabwe) met to consider the Group's report, and (with the exception of the United Kingdom) agreed to adopt a series of measures to exert economic pressure on the South African Government, and to encourage other countries to adopt such measures. These included bans on the following: air links with South Africa; new investment or reinvestment of profits earned in South Africa; imports of agricultural produce from South Africa; government assistance to, investment in, and trade with, South Africa; government contracts with majority-owned South African companies; promotion of tourist visits to South Africa; new bank loans to South Africa; imports of uranium, coal, iron and steel from South Africa.

International Affairs Division: promotes consultation among member governments on international and Commonwealth matters of common interest. In association with host governments, it organizes the meetings of Heads of Government and senior officials. Since 1978 the Division has organized and serviced Commonwealth regional Heads of Government meetings for the Asia-Pacific region (CHOGRM): these meetings discuss regional political trends and establish programmes of co-operation in trade, energy, industry, agriculture and maritime issues. The Division services committees and special groups set up by Heads of Government dealing with political matters, such as the Commonwealth Committee on Southern Africa through which governments have worked to help Zimbabwe to independence and continue to do so for Namibia. It serviced the Commonwealth observer groups at the pre-independence elections in Zimbabwe and the 1980 elections in Uganda. The Secretariat has observer status at the UN; the Division monitors international progress on such matters as the Law of the Sea, and reports back to governments. A Unit for the Promotion of Human Rights in the Commonwealth was established within the Division in 1985.

Director: HUGH CRAFT (Australia).

LAW

Legal Division: services the meetings of law ministers and attorneys-general. It runs a Commonwealth commercial crime service, administers training programmes for legislative draftsmen, and assists co-operation and exchange of information on law reform, taxation policy, extradition, the reciprocal enforcement of judgments and other legal matters. It liaises with the Commonwealth Magistrates' Association, the Commonwealth Legal Education Association, the Commonwealth Lawyers' Association, the Commonwealth Association of Legislative Counsel, and with other international organizations. It also provides in-house legal advice for the Secretariat, and helps to prepare the triennial Commonwealth Law Conference for the practising profession. The 1986 Conference, involving about 2,000 delegates, was held in Jamaica. The quarterly *Commonwealth Law Bulletin* reports on legal developments in and beyond the Commonwealth.

Director: JEREMY D. POPE (New Zealand).

ECONOMIC CO-OPERATION

Economic Affairs Division: forms the focus for Secretariat activities in the economic sphere; it services the regular meetings of Commonwealth Finance Ministers, and Labour and Employment Ministers, and prepares papers for these meetings and for meetings of Heads of Government; undertakes studies on economic issues of interest to member governments and publishes regular bulletins on commodities, international development policies, capital markets, regional co-operation and on basic statistics of small countries. It also services expert groups commissioned by Heads of Government or Ministers to make proposals towards the resolution of global economic problems. Such groups have reported on, among other things, protectionism; obstacles to the North-South negotiating process; reform of the international financial and trading system; the debt crisis; management of technological change; and the special needs of small states. There is also a programme to assist consultations between government officials and the financial community on access to international capital markets.

Director: Dr B. PERSAUD (Barbados).

Export Market Development Division: assists governments to improve foreign exchange earnings through expert assistance and by organizing major trade promotion events such as export business intensification programmes, buyer-seller meetings and contact promotion programmes. It gives advice on setting up export institutions, product adaptation and integrated marketing programmes. The division is financed by the CFTC.

Director: A. G. BARVE (Kenya).

Food Production and Rural Development Division: responds to needs expressed at meetings of ministers of agriculture, giving attention to agricultural and irrigation management, planning of development projects, land-use planning, dry land farming, credit and organizations of smallholders, smallholder livestock development and fisheries. Particular attention has been given to African countries in their attempts to alleviate famine and economic crisis. The division is financed by the CFTC.

Director: M. MOKAMMEL HAQUE (Bangladesh).

HUMAN RESOURCES

Human Resource Development Group (HRDG): set up in 1983, brings together six previously separate programmes (see below) whose primary purpose is the development of human resources in Commonwealth countries. The group encourages increased inter-programme collaboration and more multi-disciplinary activity, with greater emphasis on operational projects in the field. The group aims to assist member countries in a number of important areas of human resource development and the upgrading of professional skills.

Assistant Secretary-General, HRDG: MANMOHAN MALHOUTRA (India).

The **Education Programme** arranges specialist seminars and co-operative projects and commissions studies in areas identified by education ministers, whose three-yearly meetings it also services. Its present areas of emphasis include Commonwealth student mobility and co-operation in higher education, distance teaching and non-formal education, the cost-effective use of educational resources, and youth unemployment.

The **Fellowships and Training Programme** (financed by the CFTC) provides awards and finds training places and work attachments; it supported about 1,800 trainees in 1984/85. The majority of trainees are at middle management and technician level and most training is provided in developing countries.

The **Management Development Programme** (financed by the CFTC) assists governments in improving public management systems and practice, through seminars, training programmes, consultations, project studies and publications; it provides opportunities for policy-makers to share their experience, and acts as a clearing-house for information. A *Directory of Commonwealth Training in Public Administration* is published.

The **Medical Programme,** guided by the meetings of Commonwealth health ministers, assists governments to strengthen their health services. It supports the work of regional health organizations, undertakes training, seminars and studies and provides advisory services at the request of governments.

The **Women and Development Programme** supports the efforts of governments to enhance women's participation in and benefits from development through training, policy analysis, research, and consultancies on issues such as employment and income, health, agriculture, education and violence against women.

The **Commonwealth Youth Programme,** funded through separate contributions from governments, seeks to promote the involvement of young people in the economic and social development of their countries. It provides policy advice for governments and operates regional training programmes for youth workers through its centres in Africa, Asia, the Caribbean and Pacific. It conducts a Youth Study Fellowship scheme, a Youth Projects Fund and a Youth Service Awards Scheme, carries out research and disseminates information. A conference of young people from 50 Commonwealth countries was held in Ottawa, Canada in June 1985, with the theme 'Participation, Development and Peace'.

SCIENCE

Science Division: provides the secretariat of the Commonwealth Science Council of 33 governments; organizes regional and global programmes to enhance the scientific and technological capabilities of member countries, through co-operative research, training and the exchange of information. Work is carried out in the areas of energy, mineral resources, renewable natural resources, environmental planning, agriculture, industrial support, and science management and organization.

Science Adviser: Prof. JOSÉ I. FURTADO (Singapore).

TECHNICAL CO-OPERATION

Commonwealth Fund for Technical Co-operation: financed by voluntary subscriptions from all member governments, provides technical assistance to developing Commonwealth countries. It provides consultancy and advisory services, assigns experts to work in member countries, and finances specialized training. The CFTC also funds training organized by the Secretariat. Expenditure during the year ending 30 June 1986 was expected to be £27m., an increase of 19% over the previous year's figure. The number of experts on long-term assignments was 255 in April 1986, with a further 50 experts on assignments of less than six months' duration.

The **General Technical Assistance Division** of the CFTC supplies experts and consultants and undertakes feasibility studies. Each year it provides governments with some 500 specialists in law, finance, planning, agriculture, industry, communications, education and other areas.

The CFTC's **Technical Assistance Group** is an in-house consultancy providing governments with assistance (including financial, legal and policy advice) in negotiations on natural resources and other investment projects, maritime boundary delimitation and fisheries, macroeconomic policies and financial management.

The **Industrial Development Unit** of the CFTC assists governments in the development and implementation of industrial projects. During the period 1982–85 237 projects were assisted, chiefly in the agro-industrial sector: two-thirds of the projects involve the reactivation and up-grading of existing industries, and most are in the least-developed countries in the Commonwealth.

CFTC Managing Director: ROBERT MCLAREN (Canada).

SELECTED PUBLICATIONS

Publications Catalogue.
The Commonwealth Factbook.
Report of the Commonwealth Secretary-General (every 2 years).
Commonwealth Currents (every 2 months).
Commonwealth Organisations (directory).
Notes on the Commonwealth (series of reference leaflets).
Commonwealth Youth Programme Youth News Service (quarterly).
International Development Policies (quarterly).
Meat and Dairy Products (2 a year).
Fruit and Tropical Products (2 a year).
Hides and Skins (2 a year).
Tobacco Quarterly.
Wool Quarterly.
Wool Statistics (annually).
Numerous reports, studies and papers.

Commonwealth Organizations

(In England, unless otherwise stated)

AGRICULTURE AND FORESTRY

CAB International (CABI): Farnham House, Farnham Royal, Slough, SL2 3BN, England; tel. (02814) 2281; telex 847964; f. 1929; formerly Commonwealth Agricultural Bureaux; consists of four Institutes and 10 Bureaux under the control of an Executive Council comprising representatives of the Commonwealth countries which contribute to its funds. The functions of the CABI are to provide:

1. a world information service for agricultural scientists and other professional workers in the same and allied fields;
2. a biological control service;
3. a pest and disease identification service.

Each Institute and Bureau is concerned with its own particular branch of agricultural science and acts as an effective clearing house for the collection, collation and dissemination of information of value to research workers. The information, compiled from world-wide literature is published in 26 main journals, 17 specialist journals and several serial publications which have a monthly circulation of 32,000 in 150 countries.

Annotated bibliographies provide information on specific topics, and review articles, books, maps and monographs are also issued. The CABI Abstracts database is accessible online through the following retrieval services: DIALOG (USA), CAN/OLE (Canada), ESA-IRS (Italy), DIMDI (Federal Republic of Germany), BRS and JICST; many organizations provide SDI services from CABI tapes.

In addition, Institutes of Entomology, Mycology and Parasitology provide identification and taxonomic services and the Institute of Biological Control undertakes field work in biological control throughout the world. Dir-Gen. D. MENTZ.

CAB International Institute of Entomology: 56 Queen's Gate, London, SW7 5JR; tel. (01) 584-0067; telex 265871; f. 1913 for the collection, co-ordination and dissemination of all information concerning injurious and useful insects and other arthropods; undertakes identifications; organizes international training courses and workshops on applied taxonomy of insects and mites. Dir K. M. HARRIS. Publs *Bulletin of Entomological Research* (quarterly), *Review of Applied Entomology; Series A—Agricultural; Series B—Medical and Veterinary* (both monthly); *Distribution Maps of Pests* (18 a year), bibliographies and monographs.

CAB International Institute of Parasitology: 395A Hatfield Rd, St Albans, Herts, AL4 0XU; tel. (0727) 33151; f. 1929; collates world research literature on helminth parasites of animals, on nematode parasites of plants and on parasitic protozoans with reference particularly to those of economic importance; also provides advisory services and conducts identification and taxonomic research. Dir R. MULLER. Publs *Helminthological Abstracts: Series A—Animal and Human Helminthology* (monthly); *Series B—Plant Nematology* (quarterly); *Protozoological Abstracts* (monthly).

CAB International Mycological Institute: Ferry Lane, Kew, Surrey, TW9 3AF; tel. (01) 940-4086; telex 265871; f. 1920 for the collection and dissemination of information on the fungal, bacterial, virus and physiological disorders of plants; on fungal diseases of man and animals; and on the taxonomy of fungi; undertakes identifications of micro-fungi and plant pathogenic bacteria from all over the world; runs national collection of fungus cultures and a biodeterioration centre; consultancy services, especially in industrial mycology and surveys on plant disease; holds training courses. Dir D. L. HAWKSWORTH. Publs *Review of Plant Pathology* (monthly), *International Biodeterioration* (quarterly), *Distribution Maps of Plant Diseases* (42 a year), *Index of Fungi* (2 a year), *Review of Medical and Veterinary Mycology* (quarterly), *Mycological Papers* (irregular), *Phytopathological Papers* (irregular), *Descriptions of Pathogenic Fungi and Bacteria* (4 sets a year), *Bibliography of Systematic Mycology* (2 a year), *Annotated Bibliographies* (irregular), books on mycology and plant pathology.

Commonwealth Bureau of Agricultural Economics: Dartington House, Little Clarendon St, Oxford, OX1 2HH; tel. (0865) 59829; f. 1966; provides an information service on agricultural economics and business, rural sociology, rural development in low-income countries, rural extension, education and training, tourism, leisure and recreation. Officer-in-charge MARGOT BELLAMY. Publs *World Agricultural Economics and Rural Sociology Abstracts* (monthly), *Rural Development Abstracts* (quarterly), *Rural Extension, Education and Training Abstracts* (quarterly), *Leisure, Recreation and Tourism Abstracts* (quarterly), *LRTA Word List*, bibliographies and articles.

Commonwealth Bureau of Animal Breeding and Genetics: Animal Breeding Research Organisation, The King's Bldgs, West Mains Rd, Edinburgh, EH9 3JX, Scotland; tel. (031) 667-6901; f. 1929 for the collection and abstracting of the world's literature on the breeding and the genetics of animals, and for the dissemination of this information throughout the world. Dir J. D. TURTON. Publs *Animal Breeding Abstracts* (monthly), *Poultry Abstracts* (monthly).

Commonwealth Bureau of Dairy Science and Technology: Lane End House, Shinfield, Reading, Berks, RG2 9BB; tel. (0734) 883895; telex 847204; f. 1938 for the collection, collation, and distribution of scientific and technological information on dairy husbandry, milk and milk products, and the economics, physiology, microbiology, chemistry and physics of dairying for the benefit of research workers, teachers, advisory officers, etc. Dir J. M. DAVIES. Publ. *Dairy Science Abstracts* (monthly), *Pig News and Information* (quarterly).

Commonwealth Bureau of Horticulture and Plantation Crops: East Malling Research Station, near Maidstone, Kent, ME19 6BJ; tel. (0732) 843833; f. 1929. Dir D. O'D. BOURKE. Publs *Horticultural Abstracts, Ornamental Horticulture, Cotton and Tropical Fibres Abstracts, Sorghum and Millets Abstracts, Tropical Oil Seeds Abstracts* (all monthly).

Commonwealth Bureau of Nutrition: Rowett Research Institute, Bucksburn, Aberdeen, AB2 9SB, Scotland; tel. (0224) 712162; f. 1929 to collect and abstract the world's literature in the field of human and animal nutrition, and to disseminate this information world-wide. Dir D. J. FLEMING. Publs *Nutrition Abstracts and Reviews: Series A—Human and Experimental* (monthly), *Series B—Livestock Feeds and Feeding* (monthly).

Commonwealth Bureau of Pastures and Field Crops: Hurley, Maidenhead, Berks, SL6 5LR; tel. (062882) 3457; f. 1929; publishes abstracts compiled from the world's scientific literature on grasses and grasslands, herbage plants, rangelands and annual field crops, weeds and weed control, and produces annotated bibliographies on selected subjects within its scope. Officer-in-Charge P. WIGHTMAN. Publs *Herbage Abstracts, Field Crop Abstracts, Weed Abstracts, Crop Physiology Abstracts, Plant Growth Regulator Abstracts, Potato Abstracts, Rice Abstracts, Seed Abstracts, Soyabean Abstracts* (all monthly), *Faba Bean Abstracts* (quarterly), *Lentil Abstracts* (annually), and occasional publications.

Commonwealth Bureau of Plant Breeding and Genetics: Department of Applied Biology, Pembroke St, Cambridge, CB2 3DX; tel. (0223) 334422; f. 1929 to abstract and review current world literature on the breeding and genetics of plants of economic importance and to maintain an information service on all these subjects. Dir O. HOLBEK. Publs *Plant Breeding Abstracts* (monthly), *Maize Abstracts* (every 2 months), *Wheat, Barley and Triticale Abstracts* (every 2 months).

Commonwealth Bureau of Soils: Rothamsted Experimental Station, Harpenden, Herts, AL5 2JQ; tel. (05827) 63133; f. 1929 for the collection and dissemination of information from the world scientific literature on all aspects of soils, the use of fertilizers, and the relationship between plants and soils, particularly plant nutrition. Dir B. BUTTERS. Publs *Soils and Fertilizers* (monthly), *Irrigation and Drainage Abstracts* (quarterly), series of Technical Communications (occasional).

Commonwealth Forestry Bureau: c/o Oxford Forestry Institute, South Parks Rd, Oxford, OX1 3RD; tel. (0865) 57185; telex 847964; f. 1938 for the collection and abstracting of the world's literature on forestry, forest products and their utilization, and for the dissemination of this information throughout the world. Publs *Forestry Abstracts* (monthly), *Forest Products Abstracts* (monthly), *COM Catalogue* (quarterly, cumulative), *Annotated Bibliography* (occasional), textbooks.

Commonwealth Institute of Biological Control: Imperial College, Silwood Park, Ascot, Berks, SL5 7PY; tel. (0990) 28426; telex 847964; f. 1927 as the Farnham House Laboratory of the Imperial Institute of Entomology; transferred to Canada 1940 and to Trinidad 1962; since 1983 its main research and administrative centre has been in the United Kingdom; its purpose is the biological control of injurious insects and noxious weeds, and the collection and distribution throughout the world of beneficial organisms with which to attack the pests. Dir D. J. GREATHEAD. Publs *A Catalogue of the Parasites and Predators of Insect Pests, Technical Communications, Biocontrol News and Information* (quarterly).

Commonwealth Forestry Association: c/o Oxford Forestry Institute, South Parks Rd, Oxford, OX1 3RD; tel. (0865) 510156; f. 1921; produces, collects and circulates information relating to forestry and the commercial utilization of forest products and provides a means of communications in the Commonwealth and other interested countries. Mems: 1,500. Chair. Dr M. E. D. POORE. Publs *Commonwealth Forestry Review* (quarterly), *Commonwealth Forestry Handbook*.

Standing Committee on Commonwealth Forestry: Forestry Commission, 231 Corstorphine Rd, Edinburgh, EH12 7AT, Scotland; tel. (031) 334-0303; telex 727879; f. 1923 to provide continuity between one Conference and another, and to provide a forum for discussion on any forestry matters of common interest to member governments which may be brought to the Committee's notice by any member country or organization; mems about 50. Sec. R. N. BURGESS. Publs *Newsletter,* reports and papers.

INTERNATIONAL ORGANIZATIONS   The Commonwealth

COMMONWEALTH STUDIES

Institute of Commonwealth Studies: 27–28 Russell Sq., London, WC1B 5DS; tel. (01) 580-5876; f. 1949 to promote advanced study of the Commonwealth; provides a library and meeting place for postgraduate students and academic staff engaged in research in this field. Incorporates the Australian Studies Centre. Dir SHULA MARKS; Sec. P. H. LYON. Publs *Annual Report, Commonwealth Papers* (series), *Collected Seminar Papers*.

COMMUNICATIONS

Commonwealth Air Transport Council: 2 Marsham St, London, SW1P 3EB; tel. (01) 212-5594; telex 22221; f. 1945 to keep under review the development of Commonwealth civil air transport. Meetings every three years. Mems: governments of Commonwealth Countries and British Dependent Territories. Sec. P. BRAUNTON. Publs *Commonwealth Air Transport Review* (3 a year), *Commonwealth Air Transport Electronics News* (2 a year), *Selected R & D Abstracts* (2 a year), *Civil Aviation Training Facilities in Commonwealth Countries* (every 3 years).

Commonwealth Telecommunications Organization: 28 Haymarket, London SW1Y 4SR; tel. (01) 930-5511; telex 27328; f. 1967 to enhance the development of international telecommunications in Commonwealth countries through financial and technical collaborative arrangements. Gen. Sec. GRAHAM H. CUNNOLD.

EDUCATION

Association of Commonwealth Universities: John Foster House, 36 Gordon Sq., London, WC1H 0PF; tel. (01) 387-8572; f. 1913; holds quinquennial Congresses and other meetings in intervening years; publishes factual information about universities and access to them; acts as a general information centre and provides an advisory service for the filling of university teaching staff appointments overseas; supplies secretariats for the Commonwealth Scholarship Commission in the United Kingdom and the Marshall Aid Commemoration Commission; administers Senior Travelling Fellowships for academics with administrative roles, Administrative Travelling Fellowships for registrars, etc., the Third World Academic Exchange Programme, the THES Third World Academic Exchange Fellowship and (for medical students) the Commonwealth Foundation, Edward Boyle and Lennox-Boyd electives bursaries schemes. Mems: 306 universities in 31 countries. Sec.-Gen. Dr A. CHRISTODOULOU. Publs include *Commonwealth Universities Yearbook, ACU Bulletin of Current Documentation, British Universities' Guide to Graduate Study, Compendium of University Entrance Requirements for First Degree Courses in the United Kingdom, Awards for Commonwealth University Academic Staff, Scholarships Guide for Commonwealth Postgraduate Students, Financial Aid for First Degree Study at Commonwealth Universities, Grants for Study Visits by University Administrators and Librarians, Research Opportunities in Commonwealth Developing Countries.*

Commonwealth Association of Science, Technology and Mathematics Educators—CASTME: c/o Education Programme, HRDG, Commonwealth Secretariat, Marlborough House, Pall Mall, London, SW1Y 5HX; tel. (01) 839-3411; telex 27678; f. 1974; special emphasis is given to the social significance of education in these subjects. Organizes an Awards Scheme to promote effective teaching and learning in these subjects, and biennial regional seminars. Pres. Dr MAURICE GOLDSMITH; Hon. Sec. E. APEA. Publ. *CASTME Journal* (quarterly).

Commonwealth Council for Educational Administration: c/o Faculty of Education, University of New England, Armidale, NSW, Australia 2351; tel. (067) 732543; telex 66050; f. 1970; aims to foster links among educational administrators; holds annual national conferences and biennial regional conferences, as well as visits and seminars. Mems: 23 affiliated groups representing 5,000 persons. Exec. Dir BASIL W. KINGS. Publs *Newsletter* (quarterly), *Studies in Educational Administration* (quarterly), *Directory of Courses*, reports.

League for the Exchange of Commonwealth Teachers: Seymour Mews House, 26-37 Seymour Mews, London W1H 9PE; tel. (01) 486-2849; f. 1901; promotes educational exchanges for a period of one year between teachers in Australia, the Bahamas, Barbados, Bermuda, Canada, India, Jamaica, Kenya, New Zealand and Trinidad and Tobago. Exec. Sec. PATRICIA SWAIN. Publ. *Annual Report*.

HEALTH

Commonwealth Medical Association: c/o BMA House, Tavistock Sq., London WC1H 9JP; tel. (01) 387-4499; f. 1962 to promote within the Commonwealth the interests of the medical and allied sciences; meetings of its Council are held every two years. Mems: Medical Associations in 31 countries. Dir J. A. BYRNE (UK). Publ. *Bulletin* (quarterly).

Commonwealth Pharmaceutical Association: 1 Lambeth High St, London, SE1 7JN; tel. (01) 735-9141: f. 1971 to promote the interests of pharmaceutical sciences and the profession of pharmacy in the Commonwealth; to maintain high professional standards, encourage links between members and the creation of national associations; and to facilitate the dissemination of information. Holds conferences (every five years) and regional meetings. Mems: 35 pharmaceutical associations. Sec. RAYMOND DICKINSON (UK). Publ. *Quarterly Newsletter*.

Commonwealth Society for the Deaf: 105 Gower St, London, WC1E 6AH; tel. (01) 387-8033; promotes the health, education and general welfare of the deaf in developing Commonwealth countries; encourages and assists the development of educational facilities, the training of teachers of the deaf, and the provision of support for parents of deaf children; assists volunteer workers to find posts abroad; provides audiological equipment and encourages the establishment of maintenance services for such equipment; conducts research into the causes and prevention of deafness. Admin. Sec. Miss E. LUBIENSKA (UK). Publs *Annual Report*, seminar and research report, *Newsletter*.

Royal Commonwealth Society for the Blind: Commonwealth House, Haywards Heath, Sussex, RH16 3AZ; tel. (0444) 412424; telex 87167; f. 1950 to prevent blindness and to promote the education, employment and welfare of the 15m. blind people in the Commonwealth countries of Africa, Asia, the Caribbean, and the Pacific. The Society conducts the largest non-governmental international programme of its kind for the restoration of sight. Chair. Sir FRANK MILLS; Dir A. W. JOHNS. Publs *Annual Report, Horizons* (newsletter).

INFORMATION AND THE MEDIA

Commonwealth Broadcasting Association: Broadcasting House, London, W1A 1AA; tel. (01) 580-4468, ext. 6023; telex 265781; f. 1945; General Conferences are held every two years. Mems: 56 national public service broadcasting organizations in 51 Commonwealth countries. Sec.-Gen. ALVA CLARKE. Publs *COMBROAD* (quarterly), *CBA Handbook* (updated every 2 years).

Commonwealth Institute: Kensington High St, London, W8 6NQ; tel. (01) 603-4535; f. 1887 as the Imperial Institute; a centre for public information and educational services, the Institute houses a permanent exhibition designed to express countries of the modern Commonwealth in visual terms, art galleries showing contemporary works of art, a library and resource centre of more than 40,000 vols and audiovisual materials, and an Arts Centre with a continuous programme of dance, drama, music and films. Dir JAMES PORTER.

Commonwealth Institute, Scotland: 8 Rutland Sq., Edinburgh, EH1 2AS, Scotland; tel. (031) 229-6668. Dir C. G. CARROL.

Commonwealth Journalists' Association: 3rd Floor, UPI Bldg, 8 Bouverie St, London, EC4Y 8BB; tel. (01) 583-0618; f. 1978 to improve standards of journalism, maintain a free flow of news, and provide training; first conference Nicosia, Cyprus, April 1983. Pres. DEREK INGRAM; Sec. LAWRIE BREEN.

Commonwealth Press Union: Studio House, Hen and Chickens Court, 184 Fleet St, London, EC4A 2DU; tel. (01) 242-1056; f. 1909 to promote the welfare of the Commonwealth press and to give effect to the opinion of members on all matters affecting the freedom and interests of the press, by opposing measures likely to affect the freedom of the press, by seeking improved reporting and telecommunications facilities and by promoting training; organizes conferences. Mems: over 800 newspapers, news agencies, periodicals in 32 countries. Pres. Lord ROTHERMERE; Chair. of Council LYLE TURNBULL; Dir Lt-Col T. PIERCE-GOULDING. Publs *CPU Quarterly, Annual Report*.

LAW

Commonwealth Lawyers' Association: c/o The Law Society, 113 Chancery Lane, London, WC2A 1PL; tel. (01) 242-1222; telex 261203; f. 1983 (formerly the Commonwealth Legal Bureau); seeks to maintain and promote the rule of law throughout the Commonwealth, by ensuring that the people of the Commonwealth are served by an independent and efficient legal profession; assists in organizing the triennial Commonwealth law conferences. Hon. Sec. H. C. ADAMSON. Publ. *Commonwealth Lawyer* (2 or 3 a year).

Commonwealth Legal Advisory Service: c/o British Institute of International and Comparative Law, Charles Clore House, 17 Russell Sq., London, WC1B 5DR; tel. (01) 636-5802; financed by the British Institute and by contributions from the Commonwealth

Governments; besides operating the advisory service, the British Institute prepares surveys and organizes lectures, study courses and conferences. Dir HENRY STEEL. Publ. *ICLQ, Bulletin of Legal Developments.*

Commonwealth Legal Education Association: Legal Division, Commonwealth Secretariat, Marlborough House, Pall Mall, London, SW1Y 5HX; tel. (01) 839-3411; f. 1971; to promote contacts and exchanges; to provide information. Hon. Sec. JEREMY POPE. Publs *Commonwealth Legal Education Newsletter, List of Schools of Law in the Commonwealth* (every 2 years), *Compendium of Post-Graduate Law Courses in the Commonwealth,* occasional papers and reports.

Commonwealth Magistrates' Association: 28 Fitzroy Sq., London W1P 6DD; tel. (01) 387-4889; telex 896616; f. 1970 to advance the administration of the law by promoting the independence of the judiciary, to further education in law and crime prevention and to disseminate information; conferences and study tours; corporate membership for associations of the judiciary or courts of limited jurisdiction; associate membership for individuals. Pres. ANDREAS LOIZOU; Sec. Dr J. S. BUCHANAN. Publs *Commonwealth Judicial Journal* (2 a year), Reports.

PARLIAMENTARY AFFAIRS

Commonwealth Parliamentary Association: 7 Old Palace Yard, London, SW1P 3JY; tel. (01) 219-4666; telex 911569; f. 1911 to promote understanding and co-operation between Commonwealth parliamentarians; organization: Executive Committee of 25 Members of Parliament responsible to annual General Assembly; 110 branches throughout the Commonwealth; holds annual Commonwealth Parliamentary Conferences and seminars, and also regional conferences and seminars; 31st Conference, Saskatchewan, Canada, 1985. Sec.-Gen. Sir ROBIN VANDERFELT. Publs *The Parliamentarian* (quarterly), monographs on parliamentary subjects.

PROFESSIONS

Commonwealth Association of Architects: The Building Centre, 26 Store St, London, WC1E 7BT; tel. (01) 636-8276; telex 22914; f. 1964; an association of 29 societies of architects in various Commonwealth countries. Objects: to facilitate the reciprocal recognition of professional qualifications through a Commonwealth Board of Architectural Education; to provide a clearing house for information on architectural practice, and to encourage collaboration. Plenary Conferences every two years; regional Conferences have also been held. Sec. GORDON MATTEY. Publs *Handbook* (every 2 years), *List of Recognised Schools of Architecture,* Conference Reports, low cost textbooks, slide-tape programmes and manuals.

Commonwealth Foundation: Marlborough House, Pall Mall, London, SW1Y 5HY; tel. (01) 930-3783; f. 1965 to administer a fund to promote closer professional co-operation within the Commonwealth. The Foundation is an autonomous body assisting professionals from Commonwealth countries to visit other Commonwealth countries to attend conferences and undertake advisory and study visits and training attachments. Also supports the Commonwealth Professional Associations and Professional Centres; runs short-term fellowship and bursary schemes and a senior visiting practitioner scheme; encourages exchange of information. Funds are provided by 42 Commonwealth governments on an agreed basis. Dir INOKE FALETAU (Tonga).

SCIENCE AND TECHNOLOGY

Commonwealth Advisory Aeronautical Research Council: Room 9145, St Christopher House, Southwark St, London, SE1 0TD; tel. (01) 921-1355; f. 1946; encourages and co-ordinates aeronautical research throughout the Commonwealth. Sec. R. D. HILLARY.

Commonwealth Engineers' Council: c/o Institution of Civil Engineers, 1–7 Great George St, London, SW1 3AA; tel. (01) 222-7722; telex 935637; f. 1946; the Conference meets periodically to provide an opportunity for Presidents and Secretaries of Engineering Institutions of Commonwealth countries to exchange views on collaboration; organizes seminars on related topics; last meeting held in Sri Lanka, 1985. Sec. J. C. MCKENZIE.

Commonwealth Geological Surveys Consultative Group: c/o Commonwealth Science Council, CSC Earth Services Programme, Marlborough House, Pall Mall, London, SW1Y 5HX; f. 1948 (as the Commonwealth Committee on Mineral Resources and Geology) to promote collaboration in geochemical, geophysical and remote sensing techniques and the exchange of information. Publ. *Earth Sciences Newsletter.*

SPORT

Commonwealth Games Federation: 20 Essex St, London, WC2; tel. (01) 240-1671; telex 24213; the Games were first held in 1930 and are now held every four years; participation is limited to amateur teams representing the member countries of the Commonwealth; held in Edinburgh, Scotland, in 1986, and to be held in Auckland, New Zealand, in 1990. Mems: 64 affiliated bodies. Hon. Sec. DAVID DIXON.

YOUTH

Commonwealth Youth Exchange Council: 18 Fleet St, London, EC4Y 1AA; tel. (01) 353-3901; f. 1970; promotes contact between groups of young people of the United Kingdom and other Commonwealth countries by means of educational exchange visits, provides information for organizers and allocates grants; 168 member organizations. Exec. Sec. R. F. GRAY. Publs *Contact* (handbook), *Exchange* (newsletter).

Duke of Edinburgh's Award Scheme: 5 Prince of Wales Terrace, London, W8 5PG; tel. (01) 937-5205; telex 923753; f. 1956; offers a programme of leisure-time activities for young people, operating in over 40 countries (not confined to the Commonwealth). The programme comprises service, expeditions, sport and skills. Dir ROBERT HERON; International Sec. DAVID NEWING. Publs *Award Journal, Award News, Award World* (3 a year), handbooks and guides.

MISCELLANEOUS

British Commonwealth Ex-services League: 48 Pall Mall, London, SW1Y 5JG; tel. (01) 930-8131, ext. 39; links the ex-service organizations in the Commonwealth, assists ex-servicemen of the Crown and their dependants; holds triennial conferences. Sec.-Gen. Col G. STOCKER. Publ. *Triennial Report.*

Commonwealth Countries League: 14 Thistleworth Close, Isleworth, Middx, TW7 4QQ; tel. (01) 568-9868; f. 1925 to secure equal opportunities and status between men and women in the Commonwealth, and the social and political education of women, to act as a link between Commonwealth women's organizations, and to promote and finance secondary education of disadvantaged girls of high ability in their own countries, through the CCL Educational Fund; holds meetings with speakers and an annual Conference, organizes the annual Commonwealth Fair for fundraising; individual mems and affiliated socs in the Commonwealth. Sec.-Gen. SHEILA O'REILLY. Publ. *CCL Newsletter* (3 a year).

Commonwealth War Graves Commission: 2 Marlow Rd, Maidenhead, Berks, SL6 7DX; tel. (0628) 34221; f. 1917 (as Imperial War Graves Commission); provides for the marking and permanent care of the graves of members of the Commonwealth Forces who died during 1914–18 and 1939–45 wars; maintains over 1m. graves in some 140 countries and commemorates by name on memorials more than 750,000 who have no known grave or who were cremated; mems: United Kingdom, Canada, Australia, New Zealand, South Africa, India; the Commission's work is directed from the Head Office in Maidenhead, to which Area Offices are responsible; a number of agencies have been established by agreement with the governments of certain Commonwealth countries and South Africa. Pres. HRH The Duke of KENT; Dir-Gen. Sir ARTHUR HOCKADAY.

Joint Commonwealth Societies' Council: c/o Victoria League for Commonwealth Friendship, 18 Northumberland Ave, London, WC2N 5BJ; tel. (01) 930-1671; co-ordinates the activities of recognized societies promoting mutual understanding in the Commonwealth; mems: 13 unofficial Commonwealth organizations and four official bodies. Secs Mrs SYLVIA BARNETT, Sir MICHAEL SCOTT.

Royal Commonwealth Society: 18 Northumberland Ave, London, WC2N 5BJ; tel. (01) 930-6733; to promote knowledge and understanding among the people of the Commonwealth; branches in principal Commonwealth countries; has full residential club facilities, lecture programmes and library. Sec.-Gen. Sir MICHAEL SCOTT. Publ. *Newsletter* (3 a year), library notes, conference reports.

Royal Over-Seas League: Over-Seas House, Park Place, St James's St, London, SW1A 1LR; tel. (01) 408-0214; telex 261426; f. 1910 to promote friendship and understanding in the Commonwealth; membership is open to all British subjects and Commonwealth citizens. Dir-Gen. Capt. J. B. RUMBLE. Publ. *Overseas* (quarterly).

Victoria League for Commonwealth Friendship: 18 Northumberland Ave, London, WC2N 5BJ; tel. (01) 930-1671; f. 1901 to further personal friendship among Commonwealth peoples; about 41,000 mems. Pres. HRH Princess MARGARET; Chair. Lord MACLEHOSE; Sec. Mrs SYLVIA BARNETT.

Declaration of Commonwealth Principles

Agreed by the Commonwealth Heads of Government Meeting at Singapore, 22 January 1971.

The Commonwealth of Nations is a voluntary association of independent sovereign states, each responsible for its own policies, consulting and co-operating in the common interests of their peoples and in the promotion of international understanding and world peace.

Members of the Commonwealth come from territories in the six continents and five oceans, include peoples of different races, languages and religions, and display every stage of economic development from poor developing nations to wealthy industrialized nations. They encompass a rich variety of cultures, traditions and institutions.

Membership of the Commonwealth is compatible with the freedom of member-governments to be non-aligned or to belong to any other grouping, association or alliance. Within this diversity all members of the Commonwealth hold certain principles in common. It is by pursuing these principles that the Commonwealth can continue to influence international society for the benefit of mankind.

We believe that international peace and order are essential to the security and prosperity of mankind; we therefore support the United Nations and seek to strengthen its influence for peace in the world, and its efforts to remove the causes of tension between nations.

We believe in the liberty of the individual, in equal rights for all citizens regardless of race, colour, creed or political belief, and in their inalienable right to participate by means of free and democratic political processes in framing the society in which they live. We therefore strive to promote in each of our countries those representative institutions and guarantees for personal freedom under the law that are our common heritage.

We recognize racial prejudice as a dangerous sickness threatening the healthy development of the human race and racial discrimination as an unmitigated evil of society. Each of us will vigorously combat this evil within our own nation.

No country will afford to regimes which practise racial discrimination assistance which in its own judgment directly contributes to the pursuit or consolidation of this evil policy. We oppose all forms of colonial domination and racial oppression and are committed to the principles of human dignity and equality.

We will therefore use all our efforts to foster human equality and dignity everywhere, and to further the principles of self-determination and non-racialism.

We believe that the wide disparities in wealth now existing between different sections of mankind are too great to be tolerated. They also create world tensions. Our aim is their progressive removal. We therefore seek to use our efforts to overcome poverty, ignorance and disease, in raising standards of life and achieving a more equitable international society.

To this end our aim is to achieve the freest possible flow of international trade on terms fair and equitable to all, taking into account the special requirements of the developing countries, and to encourage the flow of adequate resources, including governmental and private resources, to the developing countries, bearing in mind the importance of doing this in a true spirit of partnership and of establishing for this purpose in the developing countries conditions which are conducive to sustained investment and growth.

We believe that international co-operation is essential to remove the causes of war, promote tolerance, combat injustice, and secure development among the peoples of the world. We are convinced that the Commonwealth is one of the most fruitful associations for these purposes.

In pursuing these principles the members of the Commonwealth believe that they can provide a constructive example of the multi-national approach which is vital to peace and progress in the modern world. The association is based on consultation, discussion and co-operation.

In rejecting coercion as an instrument of policy they recognize that the security of each member state from external aggression is a matter of concern to all members. It provides many channels for continuing exchanges of knowledge and views on professional, cultural, economic, legal and political issues among member states.

These relationships we intend to foster and extend, for we believe that our multi-national association can expand human understanding and understanding among nations, assist in the elimination of discrimination based on differences of race, colour or creed, maintain and strengthen personal liberty, contribute to the enrichment of life for all, and provide a powerful influence for peace among nations.

COMMUNAUTÉ ÉCONOMIQUE DE L'AFRIQUE DE L'OUEST — CEAO

(WEST AFRICAN ECONOMIC COMMUNITY)

Address: BP 643, Ouagadougou, Burkina Faso.
Telex: 5212.
Replacing the West African Customs Union (UDEAO), the Economic Community came into being in January 1974.

MEMBERS

Benin	Mali	Niger
Burkina Faso	Mauritania	Senegal
Ivory Coast		

Observers: Guinea, Togo.

Organization
(October 1986)

CONFERENCE OF HEADS OF STATE
The Conference of Heads of State is the supreme organ of the Community. It is held at least once a year in one of the member states, and its President is the Head of State of the host country. Decisions of the Conference must be unanimous. It appoints the officers of the Community. Eleventh conference: Ouagadougou, Burkina Faso, March 1986.

COUNCIL OF MINISTERS
The Council of Ministers meets at least twice a year, usually at the seat of the Community. Each member state is represented by its Minister of Finance or a member of government, according to the subject under discussion. Decisions are taken unanimously.

GENERAL SECRETARIAT
The Secretariat is responsible for carrying out decisions of the Conference of Heads of State and the Council of Ministers. It comprises four main departments: trade; rural development; industrial development; administration and finance. The Secretary-General is appointed for a four-year term.
Secretary-General: MAMADOU HAIDARA (Mali).

Activities

The Community has three main areas of activity: trade, regional economic co-operation and economic integration through Community projects.

TRADE
Three categories of produce are traded within the Community:
Non-manufactured, crude products may be imported and exported within the Community without internal taxes.
Traditional handicrafts are to be exempted from internal taxes, according to an agreement in June 1979.
Industrial products of member states, when exported to other member states, may benefit from the special preferential system based on the Regional Co-operation Tax (see below), which replaces the import taxes of the separate states. Certain products remain subject to special agreements.
In 1981 total community imports from non-member countries amounted to 1,200,000m. francs CFA, while intra-community trade was worth 90,000m. francs CFA, of which 29% was subject to preferential agreements (chiefly textiles, food products and chemicals).
In 1984 a three-year programme was begun, aiming to harmonize customs procedure and the codification of merchandise, and to establish a common tariff for imports from outside the community.

Other projects included the improvement of statistical data; commercial training (through, for example, regional seminars on marketing and exporting); and the establishment of a Centre Régional d'Information et de Documentation Commerciale. In 1984 the Conference of Heads of State adopted a convention harmonizing rates of taxation for nationals of member states, and in 1985 the first part of a common investment code was completed.

RURAL AND INDUSTRIAL DEVELOPMENT
Proposals for regional rural development projects approved in 1984 and under way in 1985 comprised the establishment of a seed-production centre in Baguinéda, Mali, of an agricultural training centre in Ouagadougou, Burkina Faso, and of rural savings banks. Studies were also being made for a programme of industrial co-operation (particularly in the production of fertilizers, glass and metals); the harmonization of national investment laws; co-operation in traditional medicine; development of regional tourism; setting up a community shipping line; a regional transport plan; and a programme of agricultural and veterinary research.

ECONOMIC INTEGRATION
In 1978, 1982 and 1983 the conferences of Heads of State approved the formation of common programmes and institutions, at a cost of over 60,000m. francs CFA, to be financed by a number of donors (notably the African Development Bank and African Development Fund, BADEA, the Islamic Development Bank, the World Bank, the OPEC Fund, France, the Federal Republic of Germany and Kuwait). The projects comprised: a rural water programme throughout the region, to provide 2,634 village wells at a cost of some 23,000m. francs CFA; a regional solar energy centre in Bamako, Mali, to be completed in late 1986 (8,146m. francs CFA); a corporation for the manufacture of railway rolling-stock, to be based in Burkina Faso and Senegal; a centre for higher studies in management, opened in Dakar, Senegal in 1985 (2,217m. francs CFA); a college of geology and mining, to be constructed in Niamey, Niger, by 1987 (11,046m. francs CFA); a college for textile studies in Ségou, Mali, to be completed in 1987 (5,002m. francs CFA); a community fisheries company, based in Mauritania (17,136m. francs CFA); and two centres for research and training in fisheries, in Mauritania and Ivory Coast.
In 1983 a total of 800m. francs CFA was allotted to member states affected by drought, and in 1984 a second rural waterworks programme was approved, to provide a further 500 village wells and boreholes in each of the member states.

REGIONAL CO-OPERATION TAX
Industrial products manufactured in the West African Economic Community may benefit from a special preferential system when exported to the other member states. This system involves the substitution for customs duties and taxes of a sole tax called Regional Co-operation Tax. The main purpose of the tax is to encourage exchanges within the Community; it is always lower than the ones payable in the member states. The tax came into force on 1 January 1976: by mid-1985 it had been applied to 428 products or groups of products from 253 enterprises, of which 127 were from the Ivory Coast and 75 from Senegal. Trade in these products increased sevenfold from 4,500m. francs CFA in 1976 to 32,000m. in 1984.

COMMUNITY DEVELOPMENT FUND—FCD
The Fund is financed by member states according to their respective shares in the trade of industrial products within the Community. The sum is decided annually, at the Conference of Heads of State, in relation to the revenue from the Community Tax. It compensates for certain types of trade loss and finances economic development projects. The Fund's budget for 1985 amounted to 10,571m. francs CFA. Members' difficulties in paying their subscriptions, however,

INTERNATIONAL ORGANIZATIONS

have severely hampered the Fund's activities: by June 1985 overdue contributions amounted to 15,333m. francs CFA.

SOLIDARITY AND INTERVENTION FUND—FOSIDEC

FOSIDEC was established in 1977 to contribute to regional equilibrium by granting and guaranteeing loans, financing studies and granting subsidies. The Fund's initial capital was 5,000m. francs CFA. By June 1985 the Fund's total interventions amounted to 26,267.6m. francs CFA, of which 49.5% was for industrial projects, 32.3% for water development and 14.4% for agriculture and agro-industry. In November 1984 the Fund's director was dismissed, and in April 1986 he was convicted (together with a former secretary-general of the CEAO) of the embezzlement of 6,400m. francs CFA.

Communauté Economique de l'Afrique de l'Ouest

CO-OPERATION AGREEMENTS

An agreement of non-aggression and mutual co-operation was signed by the member countries in June 1977, and an agreement on free circulation and the right to establish residence was signed in October 1978. Agreements to exchange information on economic development, to co-ordinate general studies and finance joint projects had been signed with 19 other international and regional organizations by the end of 1985.

PUBLICATIONS

Rapport annuel (annually).
Intégration africaine (2 a year).

CONSEIL DE L'ENTENTE
(ENTENTE COUNCIL)

Address: Fonds d'Entraide et de Garantie des Emprunts, 01 BP 3734, Abidjan 01, Ivory Coast.
Telephone: 33-28-35.
Telex: 23558.

The Conseil de l'Entente, founded in 1959, is a political and economic association of four states which were formerly part of French West Africa, and Togo, which joined in 1966. In recent years it has given priority to economic co-ordination in member states.

MEMBERS

Benin   Burkina Faso   Ivory Coast   Niger   Togo

Organization
(October 1986)

THE COUNCIL

The Council consists of the Heads of State and the ministers concerned with the items on the agenda of particular meetings.

The Council meets annually, the place rotating each year between the member states, and is chaired by the President of the host country. Secretariat services are provided by the Secretariat of the Mutual Aid and Guarantee Fund. Extraordinary meetings may be held at the request of two or more members.

FONDS D'ENTRAIDE ET DE GARANTIE DES EMPRUNTS

The Mutual Aid and Loan Guarantee Fund is responsible for carrying out the economic projects decided on by the Council. Its Management Committee, comprising three representatives of each member state, meets twice a year, and a small group of professional advisers assists development institutions in member countries in the preparation of projects and the presentation of requests for aid. Financial resources comprise annual contributions from member states, subsidies and grants, and investment returns and commissions from guarantee operations. At the end of 1985 the Fund's capital amounted to 12,449m. francs CFA.

Administrative Secretary: PAUL KAYA.

Activities

The Entente Council, through the Mutual Aid and Loan Guarantee Fund, aims to promote economic development in the region; to assist in preparing specific projects and to mobilize funds from other sources; to act as a guarantee fund to encourage investments in the region; and to encourage trade and investment between the member states. It is empowered to finance the reduction of interest rates and the extension of maturity periods of foreign loans to member countries.

During 1984 the Fund was engaged in supporting eight agricultural projects (for improving and rehabilitating crops) in the five member countries; these projects were initiated between 1978 and 1980, and the total cost of the programme was 9,000m. francs CFA, of which member states provided 2,000m. francs and the rest was contributed by France, the USA and the World Bank. There were seven projects for the development of livestock, again initiated between 1978 and 1980, at a total cost of 3,000m. francs CFA, of which two-thirds was provided by external donors. In 1983 the Fund undertook the construction of over 1,700 village wells, at a cost of 6,330m. francs CFA, mainly financed by loans from France; a second programme, for the building of 2,000 more wells, was to be undertaken in 1986 at a cost of 9,000m. francs CFA.

The Fund's programme of assistance to industry, begun in 1973 with financial aid from the USA, had led to the creation of 662 small and medium-sized enterprises by the end of 1983. In 1983 two special funds were created to provide conditional credit, funds for feasibility studies, and technical assistance; a fund for financing feasibility studies was also created, but was abolished in 1984. During 1985 the special funds for conditional credit and technical assistance spent 43.5m. francs CFA on 26 enterprises. Three projects on industrial standardization were undertaken in 1985, with aid from France: they comprised training for industrial inspectors, the creation of a standards bureau (particularly for food products and building materials) and a system for standardizing electrical equipment.

In 1979 preliminary work began on a major programme for producing geological maps of member states: by 1981 maps of areas of Benin and Togo had been completed, and surveying in other areas was to take place in 1985. Other projects include the training of motor mechanics and drivers of heavy goods vehicles; research into new sources of energy (particularly the exploitation of biogas and the use of vegetable waste as fuel); the building of hotels and encouragement of tourism; and support for national schools of administration and technical training.

Loans guaranteed by the Fund included assistance for extension of the port of Lomé, Togo, in 1981 (1,276m. francs CFA), for building a telecommunications station in Benin in 1982 (1,000m. francs CFA), for the development of coffee and cotton cultivation in Togo in 1983 (6,750m. francs CFA), and for a hydro-electric scheme to benefit Benin and Togo (4,300m. francs CFA).

Expenditure in 1985 amounted to 1,355m. francs CFA (compared with 1,451m. francs CFA in 1984).

PUBLICATIONS

Entente Africaine (quarterly).
Rapport d'activité (annually).

ASSOCIATED ORGANIZATION

Communauté économique du bétail et de la viande du Conseil de l'Entente (Livestock and Meat Economic Community of the Entente Council): BP 638, Ouagadougou, Burkina Faso; f. 1970 to promote the production, processing and marketing of livestock and meat; negotiates between members and with third countries on technical and financial co-operation and co-ordinated legislation; attempts to co-ordinate measures to combat drought and cattle disease. Mems: states belonging to the Conseil de l'Entente. Sec. Dr ALOUA MOUSSA.

CO-OPERATION COUNCIL FOR THE ARAB STATES OF THE GULF

Address: POB 7153, Riyadh 11462, Saudi Arabia.
Telephone: 4760000.
Telex: 203635.

More generally known as the Gulf Co-operation Council (GCC), the organization was established on 25 May 1981 by six Arab states.

MEMBERS

Bahrain	Oman	Saudi Arabia
Kuwait	Qatar	United Arab Emirates

Organization

(October 1986)

SUPREME COUNCIL

The Supreme Council comprises the heads of member states, meeting annually in ordinary session, and in emergency session if demanded by two or more members. The Presidency of the Council is undertaken by each state in turn, in alphabetical order. The Supreme Council draws up the overall policy of the organization; it discusses recommendations and laws presented to it by the Ministerial Council and the Secretariat General in preparation for endorsement. A body for resolving disputes is also to be attached to and formed by the Supreme Council.

MINISTERIAL COUNCIL

The Ministerial Council consists of the foreign ministers of member states, meeting every three months, and in emergency session if demanded by two or more members. It prepares for the meetings of the Supreme Council, and draws up policies, recommendations, studies and projects aimed at developing co-operation and co-ordination among member states in various spheres.

SECRETARIAT GENERAL

The Secretariat assists member states in implementing recommendations by the Supreme and Ministerial Councils, and prepares reports and studies, budgets and accounts. The Secretary-General is appointed by the Supreme Council, upon the recommendation of the Ministerial Council, for a renewable three-year term. All member states contribute in equal proportions towards the budget of the Secretariat, which amounted to US $27m. for 1985/86.

Secretary-General: ABDULLA YACOUB BISHARA (Kuwait).
Assistant Secretary-General for Political Affairs: IBRAHIM HAMUD AS-SUBHI (Oman).
Assistant Secretary-General for Economic Affairs: Dr ABDULLAH I. AL-KUWAIZ (Saudi Arabia).

Activities

The Council was set up following a series of meetings of foreign ministers of the states concerned, culminating in an agreement on the basic details of its constitution on 10 March 1981. The Constitution was signed by the six heads of state on 25 May. It describes the organization as providing 'the means for realizing co-ordination, integration and co-operation' in all economic, social and cultural affairs. A series of ministerial meetings subsequently began to put the proposals into effect.

ECONOMIC CO-OPERATION

In June 1981 Gulf finance ministers drew up an economic co-operation agreement covering investment, petroleum, the abolition of customs duties, harmonization of banking regulations and the eventual formation of a common currency. In November 1982 Heads of State approved the formation of a Gulf Investment Corporation with capital of US $2,100m., to be based in Kuwait (see below). Customs duties on domestic products of the Gulf states were abolished in March 1983, and new regulations allowing free movement of workers and vehicles between member states were also introduced. A common minimum customs levy on foreign imports was imposed from September 1983. In 1985 unified patent legislation was discussed, to deal with the increasing problem of counterfeit goods in the region.

INDUSTRY

In October 1981 ministers of industry met to discuss the protection of domestic products, and set up a committee to prepare a system for exchanging industrial information. The establishment of a joint body for standardizing industrial specifications and measures was approved in November 1982. A feasibility study for the establishment of a joint industrial spare parts centre was undertaken in 1983.

AGRICULTURE

In January 1983 ministers of agriculture met to draw up a unified agricultural policy, which was endorsed by the Supreme Council in November 1985. Between 1983 and 1985 ministers also approved proposals for harmonizing legislation relating to water conservation, veterinary vaccines, insecticides, fertilizers and fisheries. Joint poultry and seed-production companies were established during this period, and in January 1986 ministers examined proposals for a factory to produce agricultural equipment (mainly for poultry and dairy farms). Studies on the establishment of two joint veterinary laboratories (for diagnosis of virus diseases and for production of vaccines) have also been undertaken.

TRANSPORT AND COMMUNICATIONS

During 1985 feasibility studies were being undertaken on new rail and road links between member states, and on the establishment of a joint coastal transport company. In December it was announced that implementation of a scheme to build a 1,700-km railway to link all the member states and Iraq (and thereby the European railway network) had been postponed, owing to its high cost (estimated at US $4,000m.). In January 1986 ministers agreed to establish a joint telecommunications network.

ENERGY

In 1982 a ministerial committee was established to co-ordinate hydrocarbons policies and prices. Sub-committees were also formed to exchange information on marketing and prices; to discuss the development of the hydrocarbons refining industry; to examine domestic energy consumption and subsidies; to co-ordinate training by national oil companies; and to co-ordinate exploration for minerals. Specific studies were undertaken on the expansion of hydrocarbons refining in Oman, and on the building of a pipeline from the Gulf oilfields to the coast of Oman, which would mean that petroleum no longer had to be carried by sea through the Strait of Hormuz. In 1982 ministers also adopted a petroleum security plan to safeguard individual members against a halt in their production, to form a stockpile of petroleum products, and to organize a boycott of any non-member country when appropriate. A unified policy on the acquisition of technology was also approved. Feasibility studies on the integration of member states' electricity networks to form a regional power grid were commissioned in March 1983, and the scheme was approved by ministers of energy in September 1986. Unified water and electricity charges were to be introduced in member states from October 1985.

REGIONAL SECURITY

Although no mention of defence or security was made in the original constitution, the summit meeting which ratified the constitution also issued a statement rejecting any foreign military presence in the region. The Supreme Council meeting in November 1981 agreed to include defence co-operation in the activities of the organization: as a result, defence ministers met in January 1982 to discuss a common security policy, including a joint air defence system and standardization of weapons. Ground forces of the member states held a joint military exercise in October 1983, followed by naval and air exercises in 1984. In November 1984 member states agreed to form a joint defence force for rapid deployment against external

INTERNATIONAL ORGANIZATIONS

aggression, comprising units from the armed forces of each country under a central command.

In 1981 the Council jointly endorsed the Saudi Arabian 'Fahd Plan' (see under Arab League) for peace in the Middle East. Between 1982 and 1986 the Council made repeated offers to mediate in the war between Iraq (supported by the member states individually) and Iran.

EXTERNAL RELATIONS

In 1984 and 1985 representatives of the GCC and the European Community discussed access to European markets by GCC petrochemicals (with reference to the tariff of 13.5% that was imposed on Saudi Arabian methanol by the EEC in June 1984). More comprehensive discussions were also held on the possibility of a wider agreement with the EEC, to cover industrial and technical co-operation. Talks with Japan and the USA on the entry of GCC petrochemicals into their markets were also expected to be held in 1986.

INVESTMENT CORPORATION

Gulf Investment Corporation: Kuwait; f. 1983 by the six member states of the GCC, each contributing US $350m. of the total capital of $2,100m.; investment chiefly in the Gulf region, financing energy and transport projects (see above). Chair. AHMAD HAMID AT-TA'IR (United Arab Emirates); Chief Exec. Dr KHALED AL-FAYEZ.

COUNCIL FOR MUTUAL ECONOMIC ASSISTANCE—CMEA

Address: Prospekt Kalinina 56, Moscow 121205, USSR.
Telex: 411141.

The CMEA (sometimes known as COMECON) was founded in 1949 to assist the economic development of its member states through the sharing of resources and the co-ordination of efforts.

MEMBERS

Bulgaria	German Democratic Republic	Poland
Cuba	Hungary	Romania
Czechoslovakia	Mongolia	USSR
		Viet-Nam

Albania ceased to participate in the activities of the Council at the end of 1961. The Mongolian People's Republic was admitted in 1962, the Republic of Cuba in 1972 and the Socialist Republic of Viet-Nam in 1978.

OBSERVERS

In accordance with Article XI of the Charter, the Council may invite participation of non-member countries in the work of its organs, or in spheres agreed by arrangement with the relevant countries. Afghanistan, Angola, Ethiopia, Laos, Mozambique, Nicaragua and the People's Democratic Republic of Yemen sent observers to the session of the Council held in Warsaw in June 1985.

In 1964 an agreement was concluded whereby Yugoslavia can participate in certain defined spheres of the Council's activity, where a mutual interest with member countries prevails. The agreement also envisaged Yugoslavia attending meetings of the Council's standing commissions and other organs where matters of mutual interest are discussed.

Organization
(October 1986)

MEETING OF HEADS OF STATE

A summit meeting of heads of state of member countries (the first since 1969) was held in June 1984.

COUNCIL

The Council meets once a year in the capital of each member state in turn, all members being represented, usually by heads of government. It examines the reports of the Executive Committee, discusses economic, scientific and technical co-operation and determines the main directions of activities.

EXECUTIVE COMMITTEE

The Executive Committee, the chief executive organ of the CMEA, is composed of the representatives of the member states at the level of deputy heads of government. It meets at least once every three months to examine proposals from member states, the Permanent Commissions and the Secretariat. It guides all co-ordinating work, in agreement with the decisions of the Session of the Council. The Chair is taken in turn by representatives of each country.

COMMITTEES

CMEA Committee on Co-operation in Planning.
CMEA Committee on Scientific and Technical Co-operation.
CMEA Committee on Co-operation in Material and Technical Supplies.
CMEA Committee on Co-operation in Engineering.

PERMANENT COMMISSIONS

The Permanent Commissions organize multilateral economic, scientific and technological co-operation in particular economic areas, namely: the chemical industry; iron and steel; non-ferrous metallurgy; the oil and gas industry; the coal industry; electric power; peaceful uses of nuclear energy; radio engineering; the electronics industry; the food industry; agriculture; transport; civil aviation; standardization; geology; posts and telecommunications; statistics; foreign trade; monetary and financial relations; construction; public health; light industry; and development of new materials and technologies.

CONFERENCES

Certain conferences are established in the CMEA structure as permanent representative bodies. These include conferences of heads of water management bodies; ministers of internal trade; legal experts; heads of pricing agencies; heads of state labour organizations; representatives of freight organizations and shipowners' organizations.

SECRETARIAT

Secretary of Council: Vyacheslav Vladimirovich Sychev (USSR).
Deputy Secretaries: A. Chaushev (Bulgaria), I. Rățoi (Romania), B. Kádár (Hungary), Z. Kurowski (Poland), V. Liebig (German Democratic Republic), L. Šupka (Czechoslovakia).

Activities

The CMEA aims to unite and co-ordinate the efforts of the member countries in order to improve the development of socialist economic integration; to achieve more rapid economic and technical progress in these countries, and particularly a higher level of industrialization in countries where this is lacking; to achieve a steady growth of labour productivity; to work gradually towards a balanced level of development in the different regions, and a steady increase in standards of living in the member states.

Trade is one of the most important forms of economic co-operation between member states of CMEA. Trade between member states was planned by yearly agreements until 1951 and thereafter by long-term bilateral and multilateral trade agreements linked to the development plans of the member countries. In 1956 the Permanent Commission for Foreign Trade was set up. In 1985 trade between member countries comprised about 60% of their foreign trade, which is wholly state-controlled.

In 1971 the Council adopted the 'Comprehensive Programme for Further Extension and Improvement of Co-operation and the Development of Socialist Economic Integration among CMEA Countries'. Reviewing the first 10 years of this programme in 1981, the Council noted that CMEA industrial production had increased by 84% during the period, and trade among members by over 300%. In 1979 the Council adopted long-term specific programmes for energy, fuel, raw materials, agriculture, food production, machine-building and transport for the period up to 1990.

The national five-year economic plans of member states are co-ordinated by the CMEA secretariat, in consultation with national planning offices. The original emphasis on mutual trade has shifted to co-operation in production, involving specialization, joint ventures and the standardization of equipment and components, supervised by the various Permanent Commissions listed above.

The CMEA's long-term programme on fuels and energy provides for joint power engineering projects and supply networks, with particular emphasis on the development of nuclear and solar power and the reduction of petroleum consumption.

In industry, the programme for the 1980s gives special attention to the electronics industry and the standardization of electronic components. A major plan for the introduction of robots in industry was agreed in 1982. Member countries also co-operate in attempts to protect the environment from pollution caused by industry (especially the chemicals industry). In December 1985 the Council adopted a 'Comprehensive Programme for the Scientific and Technical Progress of the CMEA Countries to the Year 2000', covering electronics, industrial automation (robotics), development of new industrial materials and computer technology, biotechnology, and nuclear energy. A new organization, Interrobot, was established to co-ordinate industrial automation.

Agricultural co-operation emphasizes the improved availability and nutritional quality of food supplies, through higher-yielding crop varieties, more extensive use of fertilizers, and collaboration in producing up-to-date equipment for processing foodstuffs.

Problems in co-operation have included the lack of a convertible currency for trade between member nations, and the cumbersome procedures of state trading organizations. There were disagreements over the pricing of food and petroleum during 1983 and 1984: although the USSR agreed to raise the prices it pays for imports of food from other members, chiefly Bulgaria, Hungary and Romania (the first increase for 10 years), this was offset by the high price of petroleum exports to them from the USSR. The USSR also expressed dissatisfaction with the quality of goods imported from its partners.

The CMEA has co-operation agreements with Finland (signed in 1973), Iraq (1975), Mexico (1975) and Nicaragua (1983). Special commissions meet regularly to discuss and organize co-operation with each of these countries. At the beginning of 1984 there were over 300 industrial co-operation projects in developing countries, particularly India. The CMEA has observer status at the United Nations, and co-operates with numerous UN and other international bodies. In June 1985 CMEA leaders agreed to propose the establishment of official links with the European Community, and exploratory talks were held by EEC and CMEA officials in September 1986.

TRADE TOTALS WITHIN CMEA (million roubles)

	1950	1960	1970	1980
Bulgaria	199	872	2,570	9,623
Cuba	n.a.	192	1,355	5,541
Czechoslovakia	695	2,150	4,329	13,252
German Democratic Republic	570	2,679	5,709	16,122
Hungary	356	1,037	2,669	10,303
Mongolia	64	127	176	616
Poland	685	1,437	4,067	13,211
Romania	342	821	1,689	5,714
USSR	1,679	5,343	12,284	45,777
Total	4,525	14,338	33,493	120,159

International Economic Bodies established by CMEA member countries

INDUSTRIAL ORGANIZATIONS

Assofoto: 2 Smolenskii per. 1/4, Moscow, USSR; f. 1973; photochemical industry; joint planning; co-operation in all stages of the reproduction process. Mems: German Democratic Republic, USSR.

Central Control Administration of the United Power Grids of European CMEA Member Countries (CCA): Jungmannova 29, 111 32 Prague 1, Czechoslovakia; f. 1962. Mems: seven countries.

Computers: ul. Chaikovskogo 11, Moscow, USSR; f. 1969; computer engineering, establishment of standardized computer technology; joint planning of international industrial complex. Mems: nine countries.

Interatomenergo: ul. Kitaiskii proezd 7, Moscow, USSR; f. 1973; nuclear power plant construction; co-ordination of research, development and production; specialization and co-operation of production; mutual support in planning and training. Mems: eight countries.

Interatominstrument: ul. Chocimska 28, 00-791 Warsaw, Poland; nuclear-technical apparatus construction; co-operation in research, production and sales, industrial co-ordination. Mems: six countries.

Interchim: Thälmannplatz 5, Halle, German Democratic Republic; f. 1970; branches of chemical industry. Specialization and co-operation in production; co-ordination of production plans. Mems: nine countries.

Interchimvolokno: Piaţa Rosetti, Sector 1, Bucharest, Romania; f. 1974; organizes and co-ordinates research and production in the chemical fibres industry, promotes the development of trade and co-ordinates the supply of raw materials and equipment.

Interelektro: ul. 1 Smolenskaya 7, Moscow, USSR; f.1973; selected branches of electrotechnology; joint planning and prognostics; specialization and co-operation of production; scientific and technical co-operation; co-ordination of mutual goods supplies. Mems: eight countries.

Intermetall: Cházár András ul. 9, 1146 Budapest, Hungary; f. 1964; ferrous metallurgy; specialization and co-operation in production; assortment exchange. Mems: six countries.

Interrobot: f. 1985; for co-ordination of industrial automation. Mems: six countries.

Intertextilmash: ul. Shchepkina 49, Moscow, USSR; f. 1973; selected branches of textile machinery construction; co-ordination of research, development and production; specialization and co-operation in production, research, development, construction, sales and service. Mems: seven countries.

Organization for Co-operation in the Roller-Bearings Industry: ul. Senatorska 13/15, Warsaw, Poland; tel. 261546; telex 813489; f. 1964; co-ordinates production of anti-friction roller-bearings for use in engineering; carries out research into improvements in design and equipment. Mems: eight countries.

JOINT RESEARCH INSTITUTES AND ASSOCIATIONS

Interetalonpribor: Ezdakov per, Moscow, USSR; f. 1972; measurement technology, joint research, development and production of measuring apparatus. Mems: seven countries.

Interkosmos: Leninskii prospekt 14, Moscow, USSR; f. 1970; research. Mems: 10 countries.

International Centre for Scientific and Technological Information: ul. Kuusinena 21b, Moscow, USSR; f. 1969; develops methods and technical aspects of information work, provides an information service for participating countries. Mems: 10 countries.

TRANSPORT ORGANIZATIONS

International Shipowners Association: Sieroszewskiego 7, 81-376 Gdynia, Poland; tel. 210974; telex. 054 250; f. 1970; members co-operate in technical, operational, documentary and legal matters concerning maritime traffic. Mems: four national associations and six companies from nine countries. Pres. J. Ivović; Sec.-Gen. V. A. Vassiliev.

Interport: 70-464 Szczecin, ul. Armii Czerwonej 37, Poland; f. 1973; co-ordination and rationalization of seaport capacities. Mems: German Democratic Republic, Poland.

OPW: ul. Italska 37, Prague, Czechoslovakia; f. 1963; railway freight transport. Mems: seven countries.

Ship-chartering Co-ordination Bureau: Prospekt Kalinina 56, Moscow, USSR; f. 1952; co-operation in rationalizing maritime freight. Mems: nine countries.

CURRENCY AND CREDIT ORGANIZATIONS

See chapters on the International Bank for Economic Co-operation and the International Investment Bank.

PUBLICATIONS

Statistical Yearbook.
Survey of CMEA Activities (annually).
Economic Co-operation of the CMEA Member Countries (monthly in Russian; quarterly in English and Spanish).
Press Bulletin.
International Agricultural Journal.
Books (between 10 and 15 a year) and press releases.

COUNCIL OF ARAB ECONOMIC UNITY

Address: POB 925100, Amman, Jordan.
Telephone: 664326-9.
Telex: 21900.
The first meeting of the Council was held in 1964.

MEMBERS

Egypt*
Iraq
Jordan
Kuwait
Libya
Mauritania
Palestine Liberation Organization
Somalia
Sudan
Syria
United Arab Emirates
Yemen Arab Republic
Yemen, People's Democratic Republic

* Egypt's membership is suspended.

Organization
(October 1986)

COUNCIL
The Council consists of representatives of member states, usually ministers of economy, finance and trade. It meets twice a year; meetings are chaired by the representative of each country for one year.

GENERAL SECRETARIAT
Entrusted with the implementation and follow-up of the Council's decisions and with proposing work plans, including efforts to encourage participation by member states in the Arab Economic Unity Agreement. The Secretariat also conducts research and publishes studies on Arab economic problems and on the effects of major world economic trends.

Secretary-General: MAHDI M. AL-OBAIDI.
Assistant Secretaries-General: MUHAMMAD ASH-SHARIF, NASOUH BARGHOUTI.

Activities

A five-year work plan for the General Secretariat in 1981–85 was approved in November 1980. It included the co-ordination of the development plans of individual Arab countries; formulation of measures leading to a customs union subject to a unified administration; market and commodity studies; unification of statistical terminology and methods of data collection; studies for the formation of new joint Arab companies and federations; formulation of specific programmes for agricultural and industrial co-ordination and for improving road and railway networks.

In June 1985 an agreement was concluded with the Council for Mutual Economic Assistance for co-operation and the exchange of expertise in scientific and technical matters, particularly in industry, agriculture and the environment.

ARAB COMMON MARKET
Members: Iraq, Jordan, Libya, Mauritania, Syria and the People's Democratic Republic of Yemen (Egypt's membership is suspended).

Based on a resolution passed by the Council in August 1964; its implementation is supervised by the Council and does not constitute a separate organization. Customs duties and other taxes on trade between the member countries were eliminated in annual stages, the process being completed in 1971. The second stage was to be the adoption of a full customs union, and ultimately all restrictions on trade between the member countries, including quotas, and residence, employment and transport restrictions, were to be abolished. In practice, however, the trading of national products has not been freed from all monetary, quantitative and administrative restrictions.

Between 1978 and 1981, the following measures were undertaken by the Council for the development of the Arab Common Market:

Introduction of flexible membership conditions for the least developed Arab states (Mauritania, Somalia, Sudan, People's Democratic Republic of Yemen, Yemen Arab Republic).

Approval in principle of a fund to compensate the least developed countries for financial losses incurred as a result of joining the Arab Common Market.

Approval of legal, technical and administrative preparations for unification of tariffs levied on products imported from non-member countries.

Formation of a committee of ministerial deputies to deal with problems in the application of market rulings and to promote the organization's activities.

MULTILATERAL AGREEMENTS
The Council has initiated the following multilateral agreements aimed at achieving economic unity:

Agreement on Basic Levels of Social Insurance.
Agreement on Reciprocity in Social Insurance Systems.
Agreement on Labour Mobility.
Agreement on Organization of Transit Trade.
Agreement on Avoidance of Double Taxation and Elimination of Tax Evasion.
Agreement on Co-operation in Collection of Taxes.
Agreement on Capital Investment and Mobility.
Agreement on Settlement of Investment Disputes between Host Arab Countries and Citizens of Other Countries.

JOINT VENTURES
A number of multilateral organizations in industry and agriculture have been formed on the principle that faster development and economies of scale may be achieved by combining the efforts of member states. In industries that are new to the member countries, Arab Joint Companies are formed, while existing industries are co-ordinated by the setting up of Arab Specialized Unions. The unions are for closer co-operation on problems of production and marketing, and to help companies deal as a group in international markets. The companies are intended to be self-supporting on a purely commercial basis; they may issue shares to citizens of the participating countries. The joint ventures are:

Arab Joint Companies (cap. = capital; figures in Kuwaiti dinars unless otherwise stated):

Arab Company for Drug Industries and Medical Appliances: PO Box 925161, Amman, Jordan; cap. 60m.

Arab Company for Industrial Investment: PO Box 2154, Baghdad, Iraq; cap. 150m.

Arab Company for Livestock Development: PO Box 5305, Damascus, Syria; tel. 66 60 37; telex 11376; cap. 60m.

Arab Mining Company: PO Box 20198, Amman, Jordan; telex 21169; cap. 120m.

Specialized Arab Unions and Federations:

Arab Federation for Cement and Building Materials: PO Box 9015, Damascus, Syria.

Arab Federation of Chemical Fertilizers Producers: PO Box 23696, Kuwait.

Arab Federation of Engineering Industries: PO Box 509, Baghdad, Iraq; tel. 776 11 01; telex 2724.

Arab Federation of Leather Industries: PO Box 2188, Damascus, Syria.

Arab Federation of Paper Industries: PO Box 5456, Baghdad, Iraq.

Arab Federation of Shipping Industries: PO Box 1161, Baghdad, Iraq.

INTERNATIONAL ORGANIZATIONS

Arab Federation of Textile Industries: PO Box 620, Damascus, Syria.

Arab Seaports Federation: Basrah, Iraq.

Arab Sugar Federation: PO Box 195, Khartoum, Sudan.

Arab Union of Fish Producers: PO Box 15064, Baghdad, Iraq; tel. 55 11 261.

Arab Union of Food Industries: PO Box 13025, Baghdad, Iraq.

Arab Union of Land Transport: PO Box 926324, Amman, Jordan.

Arab Union of Railways: POB 6599, Aleppo, Syria; tel. 220302; telex 331009.

PUBLICATION

Arab Economic Unity.

THE COUNCIL OF EUROPE

Address: BP 431, R6-67006 Strasbourg Cedex, France.
Telephone: (88) 61-49-61.
Telex: 870943.

The Council was founded in May 1949 to achieve a greater unity between its members, to facilitate their economic and social progress and to uphold the principles of parliamentary democracy. Membership has risen from the original 10 to 21.

MEMBERS

Austria	Liechtenstein
Belgium	Luxembourg
Cyprus	Malta
Denmark	Netherlands
France	Norway
Federal Republic of Germany	Portugal
	Spain
Greece	Sweden
Iceland	Switzerland
Ireland	Turkey
Italy	United Kingdom

Organization
(October 1986)

COMMITTEE OF MINISTERS

The Committee consists of the Ministers of Foreign Affairs of all member states; it decides with binding effect all matters of internal organization, makes recommendations to governments and may also draw up conventions and agreements; it also discusses matters of political concern, such as East-West relations, United Nations activities, and the protection of human rights. It usually meets in May and November.

CONFERENCES OF SPECIALIZED MINISTERS

There are 18 Conferences of specialized ministers, meeting regularly for intergovernmental co-operation in various fields.

MINISTERS' DEPUTIES

Senior diplomats are accredited to the Council as permanent representatives of their governments, and deal with most of the routine work at monthly meetings. Any decision reached by the Deputies has the same force as one adopted by the Ministers.

PARLIAMENTARY ASSEMBLY

President: Louis Jung (France).
Chairman of the Socialist Group: Lucien Pignion (France).
Chairman of the Christian Democratic Group: Wolfgang Blenk (Austria).
Chairman of the European Democratic (Conservative) Group: Anders Björk (Sweden).
Chairman of the Liberal Democratic and Reformers' Group: Bjørn Elmquist (Denmark).
Chairman of the Group of Communists and Allies: Gérard Bordu (France).

Members are elected or appointed by their national parliaments from among the members thereof; political parties in each delegation follow the proportion of their strength in the national parliament. Members do not represent their governments; they are spokesmen for public opinion. The Assembly has 170 members: 18 each for France, the Federal Republic of Germany, Italy and the United Kingdom; 12 each for Spain and Turkey; seven each for Belgium, Greece, the Netherlands and Portugal; six each for Austria, Sweden and Switzerland; five each for Denmark and Norway; four for Ireland; three each for Cyprus, Iceland, Luxembourg and Malta; and two for Liechtenstein.

The Assembly meets in ordinary session once a year for not more than a month. The session is usually divided into three parts held in January–February, April–May and September–October. The Assembly may submit recommendations to the Committee of Ministers, pass resolutions, discuss reports and any matters of common European interest. It is also a consultative body to the Committee of Ministers, and elects the Secretary-General, the Deputy Secretary-General, the Clerk of the Assembly and the members of the European Court of Human Rights.

Standing Committee: Represents the Assembly when it is not in session, and may adopt Recommendations to the Committee of Ministers and Resolutions on behalf of the Assembly. Consists of the President, Vice-Presidents, Chairmen of the Ordinary Committees and a number of ordinary members. Meets at least three times a year (once in 'mini' session).

Ordinary Committees: political, economic and development, social and health, legal, culture and education, science and technology, environment, regional planning and local authorities, rules of procedure, agriculture, relations with European non-member countries, parliamentary and public relations, migration, refugees and demography, budget and intergovernmental work programme.

SECRETARIAT

Secretary-General: Marcelino Oreja Aguirre (Spain).
Deputy Secretary-General: Gaetano Adinolfi (Italy).
Clerk of the Parliamentary Assembly: Heinrich Klebes (FRG) (from 1 January 1987).

Activities

In an effort to harmonize national laws, to put the citizens of member countries on an equal footing and to pool certain resources and facilities, the Council has concluded a number of Conventions and Agreements covering particular aspects of European co-operation. By June 1986 a total of 124 treaties had been concluded, of which 22 had not yet come into force.

HUMAN RIGHTS

The promotion and development of human rights is one of the major tasks of the Council of Europe. All member states are parties to the European Convention for the Protection of Human Rights and Fundamental Freedoms of 1950. A steering committee for human rights prepares new protocols to the Convention, and declarations of the Committee of Ministers; it also conducts a human rights education and information programme. The first ministerial conference on human rights was held in March 1985.

European Commission of Human Rights

The Commission has 21 members. It is competent to examine complaints made either by a contracting party, or in certain cases, by an individual, non-governmental organization or group of individuals, that the European Convention for the Protection of Human Rights and Fundamental Freedoms has been violated by one or more of the contracting parties. If the Commission decides to admit the application, it then ascertains the full facts of the case and places itself at the disposal of the parties in order to try and reach a friendly settlement. If no settlement is reached, the Commission sends a report to the Committee of Ministers in which it states an opinion as to whether there has been a violation of the Convention. It is then for the Committee of Ministers or, if the case is referred to it, the Court to decide whether or not a violation has taken place. By the end of 1985 over 11,800 human rights applications had been lodged.

President: Prof. Karl Aage Nørgaard (Denmark).
First Vice-President: Prof. Giuseppe Sperduti (Italy).
Second Vice-President: Prof. Dr Jochen A. Frowein (FRG).
Secretary: Hans-Christian Krüger (FRG).

European Court of Human Rights

The Court comprises 21 judges. It may deal with a case only after the Commission has acknowledged the failure of efforts for a friendly settlement. The following may bring a case before the Court, provided that the High Contracting Party or Parties concerned have accepted its compulsory jurisdiction or, failing that, with the consent of the High Contracting Party or Parties concerned: the Commission, a High Contracting Party whose national is alleged to be a victim, a High Contracting Party which referred the case to the Commission, and a High Contracting Party against which the complaint has been lodged. In the event of dispute as to whether the Court has jurisdiction, the matter is settled by the Court. The judgment of the Court is final. The Court may, in certain circumstances, give advisory opinions at the request of the Committee of Ministers.

President: ROLV RYSSDAL (Norway).
Vice-President: JOHN J. CREMONA (Malta).
Registrar: MARC-ANDRÉ EISSEN (France).

MASS MEDIA

In 1982 the Committee of Ministers adopted a Declaration on the freedom of expression and information. The activities in this field are carried out by a steering committee of governmental experts and cover political and legal aspects of current developments relating to broadcasting and the press, as well as the promotion of European programme production.

SOCIAL WELFARE

The European Social Charter, in force since 1965, is now applied in Austria, Cyprus, Denmark, France, the Federal Republic of Germany, Greece, Iceland, Ireland, Italy, the Netherlands, Norway, Spain, Sweden and the United Kingdom; it lays down the rights and principles which are the basis of the Council's social policy, and guarantees a number of social and economic rights to the citizen, including the right to work, the right to form workers' organizations, the right to social security and social assistance, the right of the family to protection and the right of migrant workers to protection and assistance.

The European Code of Social Security and its Protocol entered into force in 1968; by 1986 the Code and Protocol had been ratified by Belgium, the Federal Republic of Germany, Luxembourg, the Netherlands, Norway, Portugal and Sweden, while the Code alone had been ratified by Denmark, France, Greece, Ireland, Italy, Switzerland, Turkey and the United Kingdom. These instruments set minimum standards for medical care and the following benefits: sickness, old-age, unemployment, employment injury, family, maternity, invalidity and survivor's benefit. In 1986 a revision of these instruments was being carried out, aiming to provide higher standards and greater flexibility.

The European Convention on Social Security, in force since 1977, now applies in Austria, Belgium, Luxembourg, the Netherlands, Portugal, Spain and Turkey; most of the provisions apply automatically, while others are subject to the conclusion of additional multilateral or bilateral agreements. The Convention is concerned with establishing equality of treatment for nationals of member states and with ensuring the granting and maintenance of social security rights by such means as the adding together of insurance periods completed in more than one state; two interim agreements are also in force, which will progressively be superseded by the Convention.

A number of resolutions passed by the Committee of Ministers give guidance for intergovernmental action on particular aspects of social policy, welfare or labour law. Eight states are co-operating in drawing up common standards on the protection of safety and health at work.

The Council of Europe operates a fellowships scheme for the benefit of personnel in the social services drawn from the member countries, and an annual research fellowships programme, in which a group of specialists investigates a subject chosen by the Social Committee.

HEALTH

Through a series of expert committees, the Council aims at ensuring constant co-operation in Europe in a variety of health-related fields: e.g., promotion of education for health, evaluation of programmes for the prevention of diseases, assessment and implementation of new methods of treatment and techniques, adaptation of training curricula for health personnel. It strives to formulate cost-effective policies in order to contain the rising costs of health care in member States.

A programme of Medical Fellowships enables members of the health professions to study new techniques and participate in co-ordinated research programmes. Availability of blood and blood products (also of very rare groups) has been ensured through European Agreements and a network of co-operating transfusion centres. Advances in this field and in histocompatibility are continuously assessed by expert committees.

Eleven states co-operate in drawing up common standards on the proper use of pharmaceuticals and veterinary medicaments, the health control of foodstuffs, the correct use of pesticides and on cosmetic products. Study projects carried out by the said states include: congenital anomalies, epidemiological patterns, the safe conducting of clinical trials, and microbiological problems.

Twelve states co-operate in elaborating a common conception of rehabilitation of the disabled as a process of social integration by drawing up common standards with regard to medical and functional treatment, educational training, occupational and vocational work, social rehabilitation and integration, training of rehabilitation staff, health education and information.

In the co-operation group to combat drug abuse and illicit drug trafficking (Pompidou Group), states work together at ministerial level to counteract drug abuse. The Group follows a multidisciplinary approach embracing in particular legislation, law enforcement, prevention, treatment, rehabilitation and data collection.

The European Agreement on the restriction of the use of certain detergents in washing and cleaning products entered into force in September 1968 (amended by a protocol, November 1984). There are 10 parties to the Agreement.

The Convention on the Elaboration of a European Pharmacopoeia (establishing standards for medicinal substances) entered into force in May 1974: 17 states are parties to the Convention and two observer states and the EEC participate in the meetings. Publication of a second edition began in 1980: it covered about 500 substances by 1986.

POPULATION

The steering committee on population, an intergovernmental committee of experts responsible to the Committee of Ministers, monitors and analyses population trends in member states and informs governments and the public of implications for policy. It compiles an annual review of demographic developments and publishes the results of studies of particular aspects of population, for example the implications of low fertility, changing marriage and family patterns, and migration. Seminars and conferences are held.

MIGRANT WORKERS AND REFUGEES

In May 1977 the Committee of Ministers adopted the European Convention on the Legal Status of Migrant Workers. The Committee also made a number of recommendations to governments on the reunion of migrant workers' families; clandestine immigration; social and economic repercussions on migrant workers of economic recessions and crises; migrant women; integration of migrant workers returning to their countries of origin.

Language classes for migrant workers and special experimental classes for their children are sponsored. Vocational training grants are awarded to student-instructors and instructor-trainees.

The Council of Europe Resettlement Fund was created in 1956 to make loans for the resettlement of refugees or those made homeless by natural disasters. In 1985 19 countries were members of the Fund and the loans granted amounted to about US $500m. in that year.

LEGAL MATTERS

The European Committee on Legal Co-operation supervises the work programme for international, administrative, civil and commercial law. Specialized committees of legal experts work under its direction. Its work has resulted in numerous conventions on matters which include: foreign liabilities; information on foreign law; consular functions; bearer securities; state immunity; motorists' liability; legal status of children of unmarried parents; product liability; mutual aid in administrative matters; custody of children; data protection.

Conferences of Ministers of Justice of Member States, although not formally under the Council of Europe, make proposals for the Council's work programme.

CRIME

The European Committee on Crime Problems has prepared conventions on such matters as extradition, mutual assistance in procedural matters, the international validity of criminal judgements, the transfer of proceedings, the suppression of terrorism, the transfer of prisoners and the compensation to be paid to victims of violent crime. A number of resolutions on various questions relating to penal law, penology and criminology have been adopted by the Committee of Ministers.

The Criminological Scientific Council is composed of specialists in law, psychology, sociology and related sciences. Advises the

European Committee on Crime Problems and the conferences of directors of criminological research institutes.

Penological items are examined by the Directors of Prison Administrations whose resolutions and conclusions serve as guidelines to the member States for the penal policy to be adopted.

EDUCATION AND CULTURE

The Council for Cultural Co-operation (CCC) implements the educational and cultural programme which gives priority to primary education, education and cultural development of migrants, modern language teaching, reform and development of tertiary education, adult education and community development, cultural development in towns, cultural development policies at regional and local level, promotion of creativity, taking into account the development of cultural industries. It administers the Cultural Fund which was established to promote and finance educational and cultural activities in accordance with the statute of the Council of Europe. Mems: member states and other signatories of the Cultural Convention, namely Finland, the Holy See and San Marino. The Parliamentary Assembly is also represented. Activities include co-operation in research, Europe in the school curriculum, the European Schools Day Competition, and the management of the European Documentation and Information System in Education (EUDISED).

The Council also organizes: Council of Europe Higher Education scholarships, teacher-training courses and bursaries, and European Art Exhibitions.

Secretariat services are provided by the Council of Europe for the Standing Conference of European Ministers of Education. Sessions are held every two years. The Conference of European Ministers responsible for Cultural Affairs is held usually every three years.

YOUTH

The European Youth Centre (EYC) is equipped with audio-visual workshops, reading and conference rooms; provides about 40 residential courses a year for youth leaders, on European affairs, problems of modern society, the role of youth, and techniques of leading and organizing youth movements. About 1,500 people can be accommodated annually. A notable feature of the EYC, which it shares with the European Youth Foundation, is its decision-making structure, by which decisions on its programme and general policy matters are taken by a Governing Board composed of an equal number of youth organizations and government representatives. A European Youth Week was organized by the EYC in 1985, involving more than 600 young people.

The European Youth Foundation (EYF) aims to provide financial assistance to European activities of non-governmental youth organizations and began operations in 1973. Since that time more than 100 organizations have received financial aid for carrying out international activities held in all member countries of the Council of Europe. The total number of young people taking part in meetings supported by the Foundation amounts to about 40,000, coming from more than 30 countries. More than 50m. French francs have been distributed.

The Ad hoc Committee of Experts on Youth Questions, set up in 1981, focuses on the study of national policies and solutions to common problems involving young people (unemployment, youth participation, mobility, etc.). It is also called upon to advise the Committee of Ministers on ways of assuring follow-up to suggestions arising from the programmes of the EYC and EYF. In 1985 it prepared the first Conference of European Ministers responsible for youth.

SPORT

The Committee for the Development of Sport, founded in November 1977, has the same membership as the Council for Cultural Co-operation (see above) and administers the Sports Fund. Its activities concentrate on the implementation of the European Sport for All Charter (1975); the role of sport in society (e.g. medical, political, educational aspects); the practice of sport (activities, special projects, etc.); the diffusion of sports information and co-ordination of sports research. The Committee is also responsible for preparing the Conference of European Ministers responsible for Sport.

In June 1985 the conference adopted a Convention containing measures to prevent violence at sporting events, particularly at football matches.

ENVIRONMENT

The European Committee for the Conservation of Nature and Natural Resources, founded in 1962, prepares policy recommendations and promotes co-operation in all environmental questions. It introduced a European Water Charter in 1968, a Soil Charter in 1974 and a Charter on Invertebrates in 1986. The Committee awards the European Diploma for protection of areas of European significance, supervises a network of biogenetic reserves, and maintains 'red lists' of threatened animals and plants.

The fourth Ministerial Conference on the Environment was held in 1984, and discussed the problems of coastal areas, river banks and lake shores, their planning and management in compatibility with the ecological balance. Sixteen member states, one non-member and the European Community have signed a Convention on the Conservation of European Wildlife and Natural Habitats, which entered into force in June 1982 and gives total protection to 119 species of plants, 55 mammals, 294 birds, 34 reptiles, 17 amphibians and their habitats. The Convention is also open to non-member states. A European Campaign for the Countryside was to be undertaken in 1987–88, attempting to reconcile development with conservation.

LOCAL GOVERNMENT AND REGIONAL PLANNING

The Standing Conference of Local and Regional Authorities in Europe was created in 1956 as a representative assembly of regions and municipalities of the member States of the Council of Europe; since April 1976 annual sessions have been chiefly concerned with local government matters, regional planning, regional policy of the European Communities, protection of the environment, town planning and social and cultural affairs. Ad hoc conferences and public hearings are also held.

The Steering Committee on Regional and Municipal Matters was set up in 1970 as a forum for senior officials from ministries of local government, for the exchange of experience between national governments, and for a common approach to the development of the national structures and legislature. The committee has stressed the value of strengthening local government, and adapting it to changing requirements, as well as to the increasing contacts between all European countries. It publishes an information bulletin and studies on local and regional authorities.

Secretariat services for the Conference of European Ministers responsible for Local Government are provided by the Council of Europe. The seventh conference was held in 1986, discussing local finance and foreign workers. The seventh Conference of Ministers responsible for Regional Planning was held in 1985.

MONUMENTS AND SITES

The Steering Committee for Urban Policies and Architectural Heritage maintains contact between authorities in charge of historic buildings and encourages public interest. A second conference of ministers responsible for conservation of the architectural heritage was held in 1985.

The European Campaign for Urban Renaissance (1980/81) was the first step in a programme of urban policies for the period 1981–86.

EXTERNAL RELATIONS

Agreements providing for co-operation and exchange of documents and observers have been concluded with the United Nations and its Agencies, and with most of the European inter-governmental organizations and the Organization of American States. Particularly close relations exist with the European Community, OECD, EFTA and Western European Union.

Israel and San Marino are represented in the Consultative Assembly by observers, and certain European non-member countries have been invited to participate in or send observers to certain meetings of technical committees and specialized conferences.

Relations with non-member states, other organizations and non-governmental organizations are co-ordinated within the Secretariat by the Directorate of Political Affairs inside which an external relations division was established in 1972, and a political research and study unit in 1980.

FINANCE

The ordinary budget for 1986 was 363m. French francs, of which France, the Federal Republic of Germany, Italy and the United Kingdom each contributed 16.73%; other states make smaller contributions.

PUBLICATIONS

Forum (quarterly, in English, French, German and Italian).
Catalogue of Publications (annually).

ECONOMIC COMMUNITY OF WEST AFRICAN STATES—ECOWAS

Address: 6 King George V Rd, PMB 12745, Lagos, Nigeria.
Telephone: 636841.
Telex: 22633.

The Treaty of Lagos, establishing ECOWAS, was signed in May 1975 by 15 states, with the object of promoting trade, co-operation and self-reliance in West Africa. Outstanding protocols bringing certain key features of the Treaty into effect were ratified in November 1976. Cape Verde joined in 1977.

MEMBERS

Benin
Burkina Faso
Cape Verde
The Gambia
Ghana
Guinea
Guinea-Bissau
Ivory Coast
Liberia
Mali
Mauritania
Niger
Nigeria
Senegal
Sierra Leone
Togo

Organization
(October 1986)

AUTHORITY OF HEADS OF STATE AND GOVERNMENT

The Authority meets once a year. The Chairman is drawn from the member states in turn.

COUNCIL OF MINISTERS

The Council consists of two representatives from each country; a chairman is drawn from each country in turn. It meets twice a year, and is responsible for the running of the Community.

TRIBUNAL

The treaty provides for a Community Tribunal, whose composition and competence are determined by the Authority of Heads of State and Government; it interprets the provisions of the treaty and settles disputes between member states that are referred to it.

EXECUTIVE SECRETARIAT

The Headquarters of the Executive Secretariat is in Lagos. There was a staff of about 200 in 1986. The Executive Secretary is elected for a four-year term, which may be renewed once only. The Secretariat's operational budget for 1986 was US $5.8m.
Executive Secretary: MOMODU MUNU (Sierra Leone).

SPECIALIZED COMMISSIONS

There are four commissions:
(a) Trade, Customs, Immigration, Monetary and Payments;
(b) Industry, Agriculture and Natural Resources;
(c) Transport, Communications and Energy;
(d) Social and Cultural Affairs.

FUND FOR CO-OPERATION, COMPENSATION AND DEVELOPMENT

Address: ave du 24 janvier, Lomé, Togo.
Telex: 5339.

The Fund is administered by a Board of Directors. The chief executive of the Fund is the Managing Director, who holds office for a renewable term of four years. There is a staff of 50. The authorized capital of the Fund was raised from US $90m. to $360m. in 1986. The Fund's first loan was approved in November 1982, amounting to $12.5m. for the initial phase of a telecommunications improvement scheme involving seven member states (see below). By the end of 1985 loans (totalling $6m.) had also been approved for the construction of bridges in Benin and a major highway in Liberia; grants amounting to $665,221 had been approved for Liberia, Mali and Togo, for feasibility studies on the proposed Trans-West African Highway. Grants were also made to finance studies by the Secretariat on energy and monetary affairs. The Fund's investment budget for 1986 amounted to $25.7m.
Managing Director: MAHANTA FALL (Senegal).

Activities

ECOWAS aims to promote co-operation and development in economic, social and cultural activity, particularly in the fields for which specialized commissions (see above) are appointed, to raise the standard of living of the people of the member countries, increase and maintain economic stability, improve relations among member countries and contribute to the progress and development of Africa.

The treaty provides for compensation for states whose import duties are reduced through trade liberalization and contains a clause permitting safeguard measures in favour of any country affected by economic disturbances through the application of the treaty.

The treaty also contains a commitment to abolish all obstacles to the free movement of people, services and capital, and to promote: harmonization of agricultural policies; common projects in marketing, research and the agriculturally based industries; joint development of economic and industrial policies and elimination of disparities in levels of development; and common monetary policies.

Lack of success in many of ECOWAS' aims has been attributed to the existence of numerous other intergovernmental organizations in the region (such as the CEAO and the Mano River Union, q.v.), and to member governments' lack of commitment, shown by their reluctance to implement policies at the national level, their failure to provide the agreed financial resources, and the absence of national links with the Secretariat.

CUSTOMS UNION

Elimination of tariffs and other obstructions to trade among member states, and the establishment of a common external tariff, are planned over a transitional period of 15 years. At the 1978 Conference of Heads of State and Government it was decided that from 28 May 1979 no member state might increase its customs tariff on goods from another member. This was regarded as the first step towards the abolition of customs duties within the Community. During the first two years import duties on intra-community trade were to be maintained, and then eliminated in phases over the next eight years. Quotas and other restrictions of equivalent effect were to be abolished in the first 10 years. In the remaining five years all differences between external customs tariffs were to be abolished.

The 1980 Conference of Heads of State and Government decided to establish a free trade area for unprocessed agricultural products and handicrafts from May 1981. Tariffs on industrial products made by specified community enterprises were also to be abolished from that date, but implementation was delayed by difficulties in defining the enterprises. An eight-year timetable for liberalizing trade in industrial products was established: the more developed members (Ghana, Ivory Coast, Nigeria and Senegal) were to eliminate barriers more quickly than the less developed. A compensation procedure for loss of revenue among the less advanced states resulting from trade liberalization was also adopted.

The 1983 Conference of Heads of State and Government decided to initiate studies on the formation of a single ECOWAS monetary zone. The Governors of member states' central banks met in September to examine the project. In the same year a programme was approved for the establishment of a computer unit in Lomé, to process customs and trade statistics and to calculate the loss of revenue resulting from the liberalization of intra-community trade.

TRAVEL, TRANSPORT AND COMMUNICATIONS

At the 1979 Conference of Heads of State a Protocol was signed relating to free circulation of the region's citizens and to rights of residence and establishment. The first provision (the right of entry without a visa) came into force in July 1980, following ratification by eight members. The second phase, allowing unlimited rights of residence, came into effect in 1986, although Nigeria indicated that unskilled workers and certain categories of professionals would not be allowed to stay for an indefinite period.

The Conference also adopted a programme for the improvement and extension of the internal and interstate telecommunications network, 'Intelcom', estimated to cost US $60m. In June 1983 equipment supply contracts were awarded to French and Federal German companies for the first phase of the programme, comprising the construction of microwave telephone, telex and television links between Ghana and Burkina Faso, Benin and Burkina Faso, Nigeria and Niger, and Mali and the Ivory Coast. Contracts for part of the second phase, financed by the European Investment Bank, were awarded in 1985.

A programme for the development of regional transport was adopted by the 1980 Conference. It includes the harmonization of road signs and laws and the construction of new road and rail links between member states. A regional motor insurance ('Brown Card') scheme was launched in July 1984, and a revised regional road map was being drawn up in collaboration with the UN Economic Commission for Africa. A feasibility study on the establishment of an ECOWAS shipping line was completed in 1984, and a programme on air traffic safety was begun with the co-operation of the International Civil Aviation Organization. In 1986 a data bank was established to monitor traffic in West African ports, with the aim of improving efficiency.

ECONOMIC DEVELOPMENT

ECOWAS undertook a critical appraisal of economic conditions in member states in 1979 and 1980 to provide information for development planning. The Nigerian Institute of Social and Economic Research co-ordinated the survey, and other institutions and universities were called upon to take part. In September 1978 a meeting of Customs and Statistics Experts was convened in Lagos to consider the problem of different standards and measures in the region; this led to the adoption of a common customs and statistical nomenclature and a code of standards and definitions.

Pre-feasibility studies on the establishment of a private regional investment bank were undertaken by the ECOWAS Secretariat in 1984. The creation of the bank (to be known as Ecobank, based in Lomé, Togo) was approved by heads of state and government in November. It began operations in late 1985, with capital of US $100m.

The West African Industrial Forum, sponsored by ECOWAS, is held every two years to promote regional industrial investment. The sixth Forum was held in Dakar, Senegal, in December 1984, with assistance from the European Community and UNIDO. During 1984–85 the Secretariat identified several possible industrial enterprises to be undertaken as part of a regional industrialization scheme.

DEFENCE

At the third Conference of Heads of State and Government a protocol of non-aggression was signed. Thirteen members signed a protocol on mutual defence assistance at the 1981 Conference. A mutual defence force and defence council were planned.

ENERGY

The 1981 Conference agreed on a work programme for energy development, involving a regional analysis of energy use and plans for increasing efficiency and finding alternative sources. The creation of an Energy Resources Development Fund was approved in 1982. In October 1983 it was announced that (in co-operation with UNESCO) a regional information centre and data base was to be set up in Dakar, Senegal, to disseminate information on renewable energy. A seminar on energy co-operation, held in November, called for more logical distribution of petroleum resources among members, and also for joint anti-pollution activities.

AGRICULTURE

An Agricultural Development Strategy was adopted in 1982, aiming at sub-regional self-sufficiency by the year 2000. The strategy included plans for selecting seeds and cattle species, and called for solidarity among member states during international commodity negotiations. Seven seed selection and multiplication centres and eight livestock-breeding centres were designated in 1984.

The years 1983–93 were designated as an ECOWAS tree-planting decade by the 1982 Conference.

SOCIAL PROGRAMME

Four organizations have been established within ECOWAS by the Executive Secretariat: the Organization of Trade Unions of West Africa, which held its first meeting in 1984; the West African Youth Association; the West African Universities' Association; and the West Africa Women's Association. Regional sports competitions are held annually.

THE EUROPEAN COMMUNITIES

No final decision has been made on a headquarters for the Communities. Meetings of the principal organs take place in Brussels, Luxembourg and Strasbourg.

The European Coal and Steel Community (ECSC) was created by a treaty signed in Paris on 18 April 1951 (effective from 25 July 1952) to pool the coal and steel production of the six original members (see below). It was seen as a first step towards a united Europe. The European Economic Community (EEC) and European Atomic Energy Community (Euratom) were established by separate treaties signed in Rome on 25 March 1957 (effective from 1 January 1958), the former to create a Common Market and to approximate economic policies, the latter to promote growth in nuclear industries. The common institutions of the three Communities were established by a treaty signed in Brussels on 8 April 1965 (effective from 1 July 1967). Political union is regarded as the ultimate aim of the Communities. Increasingly the three institutions are being regarded as a single entity, the European Community, and since 1967 they have been supervised by a single Commission (see p. 140).

MEMBERS

Belgium*	Greece	Netherlands*
Denmark	Ireland	Portugal
France*	Italy*	Spain
Federal Republic of Germany*	Luxembourg*	United Kingdom

* Original members. Denmark, Ireland and the United Kingdom joined on 1 January 1973, and Greece on 1 January 1981. In a referendum held in February 1982, the inhabitants of Greenland voted to end their membership of the Community, entered into when under full Danish rule. Greenland's withdrawal took effect from 1 February 1985. Portugal and Spain became members on 1 January 1986.

PERMANENT REPRESENTATIVES OF MEMBER STATES

Belgium: 62 Belliardstraat, 1040 Brussels; tel. (02) 230-99-00; P. NOTERDAEME.
Denmark: 73 rue d'Arlon, 1040 Brussels; tel. (02) 230-41-80; JAKOB E. LARSEN.
France: 37–40 blvd du Régent, 1000 Brussels; tel. (02) 513-64-45; telex 21265; FRANÇOIS SCHEER.
Federal Republic of Germany: 64 rue Royale, 1000 Brussels; tel. (02) 513-45-00; telex 21745; WERNER UNGERER.
Greece: 71 ave de Cortenberg, 1040 Brussels; tel. (02) 735-80-85; CONSTANTINOS LYBEROPOULOS.
Ireland: 5 ave Galilée, bte 22, 1030 Brussels; tel. (02) 218-06-05; telex 26730; JOHN CAMPBELL.
Italy: 74 rue de la Loi, 1040 Brussels; tel. (02) 230-81-70; telex 01121462; PIETRO CALAMIA.
Luxembourg: 73 ave de Cortenberg, 1040 Brussels; tel. (02) 735-20-60; telex 21707; JOSEPH WEYLAND.
Netherlands: 46 ave des Arts, 1040 Brussels; tel. (02) 513-77-75; telex 26125; M. H. J. C. RUTTEN.
Portugal: 66 blvd de l'Impératrice, 1000 Brussels; tel. (02) 513-25-78; telex 25170; LEONARDO C. DE ZAFFIRI DUARTE MATHIAS.
Spain: 53 rue d'Arlon, 1040 Brussels; tel. (02) 230-30-90; CARLOS WESTENDORP Y CABEZA.
United Kingdom: 6 rond-point Robert Schumann, 1040 Brussels; tel. (02) 230-62-05; telex 24312; DAVID HANNAY.

PERMANENT MISSIONS TO THE EUROPEAN COMMUNITIES, WITH AMBASSADORS
(October 1986)

Afghanistan: 32 ave Raphaël, 75016 Paris, France; tel. (1) 45-27-66-09; Chargé d'affaires: ABDULLAH KESHTMAND.
Algeria: 209 ave Molière, 1060 Brussels; tel. (02) 343-50-78; AHMED GHOZALI.
Angola: 182 rue Franz Merjay, 1180 Brussels; tel. (02) 344-49-80; NOÉMIA G. DE ALMEIDA TAVIRA.
Antigua and Barbuda: 15 Thayer St, London, W1, England; tel. (01) 486-7073; telex 8814503; RONALD SANDERS.
Argentina: 225 ave Louise (7e étage), 1050 Brussels; tel. (02) 648-93-71; telex 23079; LUIS RAMIRO ALFONSÍN.
Australia: 6/8 rue Guimard, 1040 Brussels; tel. (02) 231-05-00; telex 21834; HAROLD DAVID ANDERSON.
Austria: 35–36 ave des Klauwaerts, 1050 Brussels; tel. (02) 649-00-83; telex 21407; MANFRED SCHEICH.
Bangladesh: 29–31 rue Jacques Jordaens, 1050 Brussels; tel. (02) 640-55-00; telex 63189; MOHAMMED MOHSIN.
Barbados: 14 ave Lloyd George, 1050 Brussels; tel. (02) 648-12-28; telex 63926; RUALL C. HARRIS.
Belize: 15 Thayer St, London, W1, England; tel. (01) 486-8381; telex 8814503.
Benin: 5 ave de l'Observatoire, 1180 Brussels; tel. (02) 374-91-91; telex 24568; SALIOU ABOUDOU.
Bhutan: 17–19 chemin Champs-d'Amier, 1209 Geneva, Switzerland; TOBGYE S. DORJI.
Bolivia: 5 rue de la Presse, 1000 Brussels; tel. (02) 217-35-54; telex 26962; AUGUSTO CUADROS SÁNCHEZ.
Botswana: 169 ave de Tervuren, 1040 Brussels; tel. (02) 735-61-10; telex 22849.
Brazil: 350 ave Louise (6e étage), 1050 Brussels; tel. (02) 640-20-40.
Burkina Faso: 16 place Guy d'Arezzo, 1060 Brussels; tel. (02) 345-99-11; AMADÉ OUEDRAOGO.
Burma: 5300 Bonn, Schumannstrasse 112, Federal Republic of Germany; tel. (0228) 21 00 91; telex 8869560; U MAUNG MAUNG THAN TUN.
Burundi: 46 square Marie-Louise, 1040 Brussels; tel. (02) 230-45-35; telex 23572; EGIDE NKURYINGOMA.
Cameroon: 131 ave Brugmann, 1060 Brussels; tel. (02) 345-18-70; telex 24117; ZACHÉE MONGO SO'O.
Canada: 6 rue de Loxum (5e étage), 1000 Brussels; tel. (02) 513-06-00.
Cape Verde: 96 Koninginnegracht, 2514 AK The Hague, Netherlands; tel. (070) 60-79-30; telex 34321; HUMBERTO BETTENCOURT SANTOS.
Central African Republic: 416 blvd Lambermont, 1030 Brussels; tel. (02) 242-28-80; telex 0222 493; CYRIAQUE SAMBA-PANZA.
Chad: 52 blvd Lambermont, 1030 Brussels; tel. (02) 215-19-75.
Chile: 326 ave Louise, Boîte 22 (5e étage), 1050 Brussels; tel. (02) 649-94-83; MANUEL TRUCCO.
China, People's Republic: 19 blvd Général Jacques, 1050 Brussels; tel. (02) 649-67-73; LIU SHAN.
Colombia: 44 rue Van Eyck (2e étage), 1050 Brussels; tel. (02) 649-56-79.
Comoros: 15 rue de la Néva, 75008 Paris, France; tel. (1) 47-63-81-78; telex 642390; ALI MLAHAILI.
Congo: 16 ave F. D. Roosevelt, 1050 Brussels: tel. (02) 648-38-56; telex 23677.
Costa Rica: 437 ave Louise (6 étage), 1050 Brussels; tel. (02) 640-55-41.
Cyprus: 83–85 rue de la Loi, 1040 Brussels; tel. (02) 230-12-95; ANGELOS ANGELIDES.
Djibouti: 26 rue Emile Ménier, 75116 Paris, France; tel. (1) 47-27-49-22; AHMED IBRAHIM ABDI.
Dominica: 12 rue des Bollandistes, 1040 Brussels; tel. (02) 733-43-28; CHARLES SAVARIN.
Dominican Republic: 2 rue Georges-Ville, 75116 Paris, France; tel. (1) 45-01-88-81; MILTON LEONIDAS RAY GUEVARA.
Ecuador: 70 chaussée de Charleroi, 1060 Brussels; tel. (02) 537-91-30.

Egypt: 44 ave Leo Errera, 1180 Brussels; tel. (02) 345-52-53; FAWZI MOHAMED EL IBRACHY.

El Salvador: 3 blvd Saint-Michel, 1040 Brussels; tel. (02) 733-04-85; FRANCISCO A. SOLER.

Equatorial Guinea: 6 rue Alfred de Vigny, 75008 Paris, France; tel. 766-44-33; JESÚS ELA ABEME.

Ethiopia: 32 blvd Saint-Michel, 1040 Brussels; tel. (02) 733-49-29; Dr GHEBRAY BERHANE.

Fiji: 66 ave de Cortenberg (7e étage, boîte 7), 1040 Brussels; tel. (02) 736-90-50; telex 26934; POSECI BUNE.

Finland: 489 ave Louise, 1050 Brussels; tel. (02) 648-84-84; telex 23099; LEIF BLOMQVIST.

Gabon: 112 ave Winston Churchill, 1180 Brussels; tel. (02) 343-00-55; ANDRÉ MANGONGO-NZAMBI.

The Gambia: 126 ave F. D. Roosevelt, 1050 Brussels; tel. (02) 640-10-49; telex 24344; ABDULLAH M. K. BOJANG.

Ghana: 44 rue Gachard, 1050 Brussels; tel. (02) 649-01-63; JOSEPH AHWA LARYEA.

Grenada: 24 ave des Arts, 1040 Brussels; tel. (02) 230-62-65; telex 64015; OSWALD M. GIBBS.

Guatemala: 3 blvd Saint-Michel, 1040 Brussels; tel. (02) 736-03-40; telex 25130.

Guinea: 75 ave Roger Vandendriessche, 1150 Brussels; tel. (02) 771-01-90; IBRAHIM SYLLA.

Guinea-Bissau: 70 ave F. D. Roosevelt, 1050 Brussels; tel. (02) 647-08-90; telex 63631; BUBACAR TURÉ.

Guyana: 21–22 ave des Arts, 1040 Brussels; tel. (02) 230-60-65; telex 26180; HAROLD SAHADEO.

Haiti: 3 rue Joseph II, 1040 Brussels; tel. (02) 230-96-75; PIERRE POMPÉE.

Holy See: 5–9 ave des Franciscains, 1150 Brussels; tel. (02) 762-20-05; Apostolic Nuncio: Mgr ANGELO PEDRONI.

Honduras: 3 ave des Gaulois (5e étage), 1040 Brussels; tel. (02) 734-00-00; MANUEL LÓPEZ LUNA.

Iceland: 19 ave des Lauriers, 1150 Brussels; tel. (02) 215-10-35; telex 23763; TÓMAS A. TÓMASSON.

India: 217 chaussée de Vleurgat, 1050 Brussels; tel. (02) 640-91-40.

Indonesia: 294 ave de Tervuren, 1150 Brussels; tel. (02) 771-20-12.

Iran: 415 ave de Tervuren, 1150 Brussels; tel. (02) 762-37-45; ALIREZA SALARI.

Iraq: 131 ave de la Floride, 1180 Brussels; tel. (02) 374-59-91; Dr ZAID HWAISHAN HAIDAR.

Israel: 40 ave de l'Observatoire, 1180 Brussels; tel. (02) 374-90-80; JOSEPH HADASS.

Ivory Coast: 234 ave F. D. Roosevelt, 1050 Brussels; tel. (02) 672-23-54; CHARLES VALY TUHO.

Jamaica: 83–85 rue de la Loi, 1040 Brussels: tel. (02) 230-11-70; CARMEN YVONNE PARRIS.

Japan: 58 ave des Arts (7e étage), 1040 Brussels; tel. (02) 513-92-00; HIDEO KAGAMI.

Jordan: 104 ave F. D. Roosevelt, 1050 Brussels; tel. (02) 640-77-55; telex 62513; HASAN ABU NIMAH.

Kenya: 1–5 ave de la Joyeuse Entrée, 1040 Brussels; tel. (02) 230-30-65; JOSEPH W. N. NYAGAH.

Korea, Republic: 3 ave Hamoir, 1180 Brussels; tel. (02) 375-39-80; telex 24668; CHUNG SUP SHIN.

Kuwait: 15 rue de la Loi, 1040 Brussels; tel. (02) 231-15-75; ABDULMOHSEN N. A. EL-JEAAN.

Lebanon: 2 rue Guillaume Stocq, 1050 Brussels; tel. (02) 649-94-60; telex 22547; SAID AL-ASSAAD.

Lesotho: 66 ave de Cortenberg, 1040 Brussels; tel. (02) 736-39-76.

Liberia: 55 ave F. D. Roosevelt, 1050 Brussels; tel. (02) 640-84-46; telex 61384; RUDOLPH JOHNSON.

Libya: 28 ave Victoria, 1050 Brussels; tel. (02) 649-21-12; telex 23398.

Madagascar: 276 ave de Tervuren, 1150 Brussels; tel. (02) 770-17-26; CHRISTIAN RÉMI RICHARD.

Malawi: 13–17 rue de la Charité, 1040 Brussels; tel. (02) 217-43-70; STEVENS ERASMUS MAPUNDA.

Malaysia: 414A ave de Tervuren, 1150 Brussels; tel. (02) 762-67-67; telex 26396; Datuk MOHD MUSTAPHA bin Datuk MAHMUD.

Maldives: 212 East 47th St, New York, NY 10017, USA; tel. (212) 688-07-76; telex 960945; MOHAMED MUSTHAFA HUSSAIN.

Mali: 487 ave Molière, 1060 Brussels; tel. (02) 345-74-32; telex 22508.

Malta: 44 rue Jules Lejeune, 1060 Brussels; tel. (02) 343-01-95; telex 26616; Dr PAUL FARRUGIA.

Mauritania: 1 rue Paul Lauters, 1050 Brussels; tel. (02) 640-76-75; telex 26034; ELY OULD ALLAF.

Mauritius: 68 rue des Bollandistes, 1040 Brussels; tel. (02) 733-99-88; RAYMOND CHASLE.

Mexico: 6 rue Paul Emile Janson, 1050 Brussels; tel. (02) 648-26-71; telex 22355; LUIS WECKMANN-MUÑOZ.

Morocco: 98 ave F. D. Roosevelt, 1050 Brussels; tel. (02) 647-34-52; ABDELMALEK CHERKAOUI.

Mozambique: 97 blvd St Michel, 1040 Brussels; tel. (02) 736-25-64; FRANCES VITORIA VELHO RODRIGUES.

Nepal: 53 Bonn-Bad Godesberg, Im Hag 15, Federal Republic of Germany; tel. (0228) 34-30-97; SIMHA PRATAP SHAH.

New Zealand: 47–48 blvd du Régent, 1000 Brussels; tel. (02) 512-10-40; telex 22025; GERARD FRANCIS THOMPSON.

Nicaragua: 255 chaussée de Vleurgat, 1050 Brussels; tel. (02) 345-19-25; telex 63553; GIOVANNI DELGADO CAMPOS.

Niger: 78 ave F. D. Roosevelt, 1050 Brussels; tel. (02) 648-61-40; telex 22857; YACOUBA SANDI.

Nigeria: 288 bis ave de Tervuren, 1150 Brussels; tel. (02) 762-52-00; telex 22435; JOSHUA O. B. IROHA.

Norway: 17 rue Archimède, 1040 Brussels; tel. (02) 230-78-65; telex 21071; CHRISTIAN BERG-NIELSEN.

Oman: 50 ave d'Iéna, 75116 Paris, France; tel. (1) 47-23-01-63; telex 613765; MOHAMMED HASSAN ALI.

Pakistan: 57 ave Delleurs, 1170 Brussels; tel. (02) 673-80-07; telex 61816; MAHDI MASUD.

Panama: 23 rue Crolle, 1328 Ohain; tel. 633-23-90; ANGEL ERNESTO RIERA DÍAZ.

Papua New Guinea: 327 ave Louise, 1050 Brussels; tel. (02) 640-34-95; PETER IPU PEIPUL.

Paraguay: 42 ave de Saturne, 1180 Brussels; tel. (02) 374-87-48; telex 26535; DIDO FLORENTIN-BAGADO.

Peru: 179 ave de Tervuren, 1150 Brussels; tel. (02) 733-33-19; JULIO EGO-AGUIRRE-ALVAREZ.

Philippines: 299 ave Molière, 1060 Brussels; tel. (02) 343-68-32; Mme ROSARIO G. MANALO.

Qatar: 37 ave F. D. Roosevelt, 1050 Brussels; tel. (02) 640-29-00; telex 63754.

Rwanda: 1 ave des Fleurs, 1150 Brussels; tel. (02) 763-07-21; telex 26653; ILDÉPHONSE MUNYESHYAKA.

Saint Lucia: 10 Kensington Court, London, W8, England; tel. (01) 937-9522; Dr CLAUDIUS C. THOMAS.

San Marino: 44 ave Brugmann, 1060 Brussels; tel. (02) 344-60-67.

São Tomé and Príncipe: 42 ave Brugmann, 1060 Brussels; tel. (02) 347-53-75; telex 65313; GUILHERME POSSER DA COSTA.

Saudi Arabia: 45 ave F. D. Roosevelt, 1050 Brussels; tel. (02) 649-57-25; IBRAHIM SALEH BAKR.

Senegal: 196 ave F. D. Roosevelt, 1050 Brussels; tel. (02) 672-90-51; SEYDINA OUMAR SY.

Sierra Leone: 410 ave de Tervuren, 1150 Brussels; tel. (02) 771-00-52; telex 63624; ABDUL KOROMA.

Singapore: 198 ave F. D. Roosevelt, 1050 Brussels; tel. (02) 660-30-98.

Somalia: 66 ave F. D. Roosevelt, 1050 Brussels; tel. (02) 640-16-69; telex 24807; MOHAMED OMAR GIAMA.

South Africa: 14A rue de Luxembourg, 1040 Brussels; tel. (02) 513-28-10; ROBERT ABRAHAM DU PLOOY.

Sri Lanka: 21–22 ave des Arts, 1040 Brussels; tel. (02) 230-48-90; ANTHONY WIRATUNGA.

Sudan: 124 ave F. D. Roosevelt, 1050 Brussels; tel. (02) 647-51-59; OSMAN ABDULLAHI AL-SAMMAHOUNI.

Suriname: 379 ave Louise, 1050 Brussels: tel. (02) 640-11-72.

Swaziland: 71 rue Joseph II (5e étage), 1040 Brussels; tel. (02) 230-00-44; SIPHO PETER NKAMBULE.

Sweden: 6 rond-point Robert Schumann, 1040 Brussels; tel. (02) 230-72-60; telex 26126; STIG BRATTSTRÖM.

Switzerland: 53 rue d'Arlon, 1040 Brussels; tel. (02) 230-14-90; telex 21660; CARLO JAGMETTI.

Syria: 3 ave F. D. Roosevelt, 1050 Brussels; tel. (02) 648-01-35.

INTERNATIONAL ORGANIZATIONS

Tanzania: 363 ave Louise, 1050 Brussels; tel. (02) 640-65-00; telex 63616; SIMON M. M. MBILINYI.

Thailand: 2 square du Val de la Cambre, 1050 Brussels; tel. (02) 640-68-10; telex 63510; VITTHYA VEJJAJIVA.

Togo: 264 ave de Tervuren, 1150 Brussels; tel. (02) 770-17-91; EKOUÉ ASSIONGBON.

Tonga: c/o Fijian Embassy, 66 ave de Cortenberg, 1040 Brussels; tel. (02) 736-90-50; SIAOSI TAIMANI'AHO.

Trinidad and Tobago: 14 ave de la Faisanderie, 1150 Brussels; tel. (02) 762-94-00; telex 23539; MAURICE O. ST JOHN.

Tunisia: 278 ave de Tervuren, 1150 Brussels; tel. (02) 771-73-94; MOHAMED MEGDICHE.

Turkey: 4 rue Montoyer, 1040 Brussels; tel. (02) 513-28-34; PULAT TACAR.

Uganda: 317 ave de Tervuren, 1150 Brussels; tel. (02) 762-58-25; telex 62814; AGGREY SIRYOY AWORI.

United Arab Emirates: 73 ave F. D. Roosevelt, 1050 Brussels; tel. (02) 640-60-00; ISSA KHALFAN AL-HURAIMEL.

USA: 40 blvd du Régent, 1000 Brussels; tel. (02) 513-44-50; JOHN W. MIDDENDORF, II.

Uruguay: 437 ave Louise, 1050 Brussels; tel. (02) 649-46-26; telex 24663; MIGUEL J. BERTHET.

Venezuela: 5 square Vergote, 1200 Brussels; tel. (02) 736-10-23; telex 61742; ROMÁN ROJAS-CABOT.

Western Samoa: 95 ave F. D. Roosevelt, 1050 Brussels; tel. (02) 660-84-54; telex 25657; FEESAGO SIAOSI FEPULEA'I.

Yemen Arab Republic: 41 Noordeinde, 2514 GC The Hague, Netherlands; tel. (070) 65-39-36; MOHAMMED ABDUL REHMAN AL-ROBAEE.

Yugoslavia: 11 ave Emille de Mot, 1050 Brussels; tel. (02) 649-83-49; JOZEF KOROSEC.

Zaire: 30 rue Marie de Bourgogne, 1040 Brussels; tel. (02) 513-66-10; EKILA LIYONDA.

Zambia: 469 ave Molière, 1060 Brussels; tel. (02) 343-56-49; telex 63102; BITWELL ROBINSON KUWANI.

Zimbabwe: 21–22 ave des Arts, 1040 Brussels; tel. (02) 230-85-35; SOLOMON MAHAKA.

Source: Directorate-General for External Relations.

Summary of the Treaty establishing the European Economic Community (Treaty of Rome)

(effective from 1 January 1958)

PART I. PRINCIPLES

The aim of the Community is, by establishing a Common Market and progressively approximating the economic policies of the member states, to promote throughout the Community a harmonious development of economic activities, a continuous and balanced expansion, an increased stability, an accelerated raising of the standard of living and closer relations between its member states. With these aims in view, the activities of the Community will include:

(a) the elimination between member states of customs duties and of quantitative restrictions in regard to the importation and exportation of goods, as well as of all other measures with equivalent effect;

(b) the establishment of a common customs tariff and a common commercial policy towards third countries;

(c) the abolition between member states of the obstacles to the free movement of persons, services and capital;

(d) the inauguration of a common agricultural policy;

(e) the inauguration of a common transport policy;

(f) the establishment of a system ensuring that competition shall not be distorted in the Common Market;

(g) the application of procedures that will make it possible to co-ordinate the economic policies of member states and to remedy disequilibria in their balance of payments;

(h) the approximation of their respective municipal law to the extent necessary for the functioning of the Common Market;

(i) the creation of a European Social Fund in order to improve the possibilities of employment for workers and to contribute to the raising of their standard of living;

(j) the establishment of a European Investment Bank intended to facilitate the economic expansion of the Community through the creation of new resources; and

(k) the association of overseas countries and territories with the Community with a view to increasing trade and to pursuing jointly their effort toward economic and social development.

Member states, acting in close collaboration with the institutions of the Community, shall co-ordinate their respective economic policies to the extent that is necessary to attain the objectives of the Treaty; the institutions of the Community shall take care not to prejudice the internal and external financial stability of the member states. Within the field of application of the Treaty and without prejudice to certain special provisions which it contains, any discrimination on the grounds of nationality shall be hereby prohibited.

The Common Market shall be progressively established in the course of a transitional period of 12 years. This transitional period shall be divided into three stages of four years each.

PART II. BASES OF THE COMMUNITY

Free Movement of Goods

Member states shall refrain from introducing between themselves any new import or export customs duties, or charges with equivalent effect, and from increasing such duties or charges as they apply in their commercial relations with each other. Member states shall progressively abolish between themselves all import and export customs duties, charges with an equivalent effect, and also customs duties of a fiscal nature. Independently of these provisions, any member state may, in the course of the transitional period, suspend in whole or in part the collection of import duties applied by it to products imported from other member states, or may carry out the foreseen reductions more rapidly than laid down in the Treaty if its general economic situation and the situation of the sector so concerned permit.

A common customs tariff shall be established, which, subject to certain conditions (especially with regard to the Italian tariff), shall be at the level of the arithmetical average of the duties applied in the four customs territories (i.e. France, Germany, Italy and Benelux) covered by the Community. This customs tariff shall be applied in its entirety not later than at the date of the expiry of the transitional period. Member states may follow an independent accelerating process similar to that allowed for reduction of inter-Community customs duties.

Member states shall refrain from introducing between themselves any new quantitative restrictions or measures with equivalent effect, and existing restrictions and measures shall be abolished not later than at the end of the first stage of the transitional period. These provisions shall not be an obstacle to prohibitions or restrictions in respect of importation, exportation or transit which are justified on grounds of public morality, health or safety, the protection of human or animal life or health, the preservation of plant life, the protection of national treasures of artistic, historic or archaeological value or the protection of industrial and commercial property. Such prohibitions or restrictions shall not, however, constitute either a means of arbitrary discrimination or a disguised restriction on trade between member states. Member states shall progressively adjust any state monopolies of a commercial character in such a manner as will ensure the exclusion, at the end of the transitional period, of all discrimination between the nationals of member states in regard to conditions of supply and marketing of goods. These provisions shall apply to any body by means of which a member state shall *de jure* or *de facto* either directly or indirectly, control or appreciably influence importation or exportation between member states, and also to monopolies assigned by the state. In the case of a commercial monopoly which is accompanied by regulations designed to facilitate the marketing or the valorisation of agricultural products, it should be ensured that in the application of these provisions equivalent guarantees are provided in respect of the employment and standard of living of the producers concerned.

The obligations incumbent on member states shall be binding only to such extent as they are compatible with existing international agreements.

Agriculture

The Common Market shall extend to agriculture and trade in agricultural products. The common agricultural policy shall have as its objectives:

(a) the increase of agricultural productivity by developing technical progress and by ensuring the rational development of agricultural production and the optimum utilization of the factors of production, particularly labour;

(b) the ensurance thereby of a fair standard of living for the agricultural population;

(c) the stabilization of markets;

(d) regular supplies;

(e) reasonable prices in supplies to consumers.

Due account must be taken of the particular character of agricultural activities, arising from the social structure of agriculture and from structural and natural disparities between the various agricultural regions; of the need to make the appropriate adjustments gradually; and of the fact that in member states agriculture constitutes a sector which is closely linked with the economy as a whole. With a view to developing a common agricultural policy during the transitional period and the establishment of it not later than at the end of the period, a common organization of agricultural markets shall be effected.

Free Movement of Persons, Services and Capital

Workers: The free movement of workers shall be ensured within the Community not later than at the date of the expiry of the transitional period, involving the abolition of any discrimination based on nationality between workers of the member states as regards employment, remuneration and other working conditions. This shall include the right to accept offers of employment actually made, to move about freely for this purpose within the territory of the member states, to stay in any member state in order to carry on an employment in conformity with the legislative and administrative provisions governing the employment of the workers of that state, and to live, on conditions which shall be the subject of implementing regulations laid down by the Commission, in the territory of a member state after having been employed there. (These provisions do not apply to employment in the public administration.)

In the field of social security, the Council shall adopt the measures necessary to effect the free movement of workers, in particular, by introducing a system which permits an assurance to be given to migrant workers and their beneficiaries that, for the purposes of qualifying for and retaining the rights to benefits and of the calculation of these benefits, all periods taken into consideration by the respective municipal law of the countries concerned shall be added together, and that these benefits will be paid to persons resident in the territories of the member states.

Right of Establishment: Restrictions on the freedom of establishment of nationals of a member state in the territory of another member state shall be progressively abolished during the transitional period, nor may any new restrictions of a similar character be introduced. Such progressive abolition shall also extend to restrictions on the setting up of agencies, branches or subsidiaries. Freedom of establishment shall include the right to engage in and carry on non-wage-earning activities and also to set up and manage enterprises and companies under the conditions laid down by the law of the country of establishment for its own nationals, subject to the provisions of this Treaty relating to capital.

Services: Restrictions on the free supply of services within the Community shall be progressively abolished in the course of the transitional period in respect of nationals of member states who are established in a state of the Community other than that of the person to whom the services are supplied; no new restrictions of a similar character may be introduced. The Council, acting by a unanimous vote on a proposal of the Commission, may extend the benefit of these provisions to cover services supplied by nationals of any third country who are established within the Community.

Particular services involved are activities of an industrial or artisan character and those of the liberal professions.

Capital: Member states shall during the transitional period progressively abolish between themselves restrictions on the movement of capital belonging to persons resident in the member states, and also any discriminatory treatment based on the nationality or place of residence of the parties or on the place in which such capital is invested. Current payments connected with movements of capital between member states shall be freed from all restrictions not later than at the end of the first stage of the transitional period.

Member states shall endeavour to avoid introducing within the Community any new exchange restrictions which affect the movement of capital and current payments connected with such movements, and making existing rules more restrictive.

Transport

With a view to establishing a common transport policy, the Council of Ministers shall, acting on a proposal of the Commission and after consulting the Economic and Social Committee and the European Parliament, lay down common rules applicable to international transport effected from or to the territory of a member state or crossing the territory of one or more member states, conditions for the admission of non-resident carriers to national transport services within a member state and any other appropriate provisions. Until these have been enacted and unless the Council of Ministers gives its unanimous consent, no member state shall apply the various provisions governing this subject at the date of the entry into force of this Treaty in such a way as to make them less favourable, in their direct or indirect effect, for carriers of other member states by comparison with its own national carriers.

Any discrimination which consists in the application by a carrier, in respect of the same goods conveyed in the same circumstances, of transport rates and conditions which differ on the ground of the country of origin or destination of the goods carried, shall be abolished in the traffic of the Community not later than at the end of the second stage of the transitional period.

A Committee with consultative status, composed of experts appointed by the governments of the member states, shall be established and attached to the Commission, without prejudice to the competence of the transport section of the Economic and Social Committee.

PART III. POLICY OF THE COMMUNITY

Common Rules

Enterprises: The following practices by enterprises are prohibited: the direct or indirect fixing of purchase or selling prices or of any other trading conditions; the limitation of control of production, markets, technical development of investment; market-sharing or the sharing of sources of supply; the application to parties to transactions of unequal terms in respect of equivalent supplies, thereby placing them at a competitive disadvantage; the subjection of the conclusion of a contract to the acceptance by a party of additional supplies which, either by their nature or according to commercial usage, have no connection with the subject of such contract. The provisions may be declared inapplicable if the agreements neither impose on the enterprises concerned any restrictions not indispensable to the attainment of improved production, distribution or technical progress, nor enable enterprises to eliminate competition in respect of a substantial proportion of the goods concerned.

Dumping: If, in the course of the transitional period, the Commission, at the request of a member state or of any other interested party, finds that dumping practices exist within the Common Market, it shall issue recommendations to the originator of such practices with a view to bringing them to an end. Where such practices continue, the Commission shall authorise the member state injured to take protective measures of which the Commission shall determine the conditions and particulars.

Re-importation within the Community shall be free of all customs duties, quantitative restrictions or measures with equivalent effect.

Aid granted by States: Any aid granted by a member state or granted by means of state resources which is contrary to the purposes of the treaty is forbidden. The following shall be deemed to be compatible with the Common Market:

(a) aids of a social character granted without discrimination to individual consumers;

(b) aids intended to remedy damage caused by natural calamities or other extraordinary events;

(c) aids granted to the economy of certain regions of the Federal German Republic affected by the division of Germany, to the extent that they are necessary to compensate for the economic disadvantages caused by the division.

The following may be deemed to be compatible with the Common Market:

(a) aids intended to promote the economic development of regions where the standard of living is abnormally low or where there exists serious under-employment;

(b) aids intended to promote the execution of important projects of common European interest or to remedy a serious economic disturbance of the economy of a member state;

(c) aids intended to facilitate the development of certain activities or of certain economic regions, provided that such aids do not change trading conditions to such a degree as would be contrary to the common interest;

(d) such other categories of aids as may be specified by a decision of the Council of Ministers acting on a proposal of the Commission.

The Commission is charged to examine constantly all systems of aids existing in the member states, and may require any member state to abolish or modify any aid which it finds to be in conflict with the principles of the Common Market.

Fiscal Provisions: A member state shall not impose, directly or indirectly, on the products of other member states, any internal charges of any kind in excess of those applied directly or indirectly to like domestic products. Furthermore, a member state shall not impose on the product of other member states any internal charges of such a nature as to afford indirect protection to other productions. Member states shall, not later than at the beginning of the second stage of the transitional period, abolish or amend any provisions existing at the date of the entry into force of the Treaty which are contrary to these rules. Products exported to any member state may not benefit from any drawback on internal charges in excess of those charges imposed directly or indirectly on them. Subject to these conditions, any member states which levy a turnover tax calculated by a cumulative multi-stage system may, in the case of internal charges imposed by them on imported products or of drawbacks granted by them on exported products, establish average rates for specific products or groups of products.

Approximation of Laws: The Council, acting by means of a unanimous vote on a proposal of the Commission, shall issue directives for the approximation of such legislative and administrative provisions of the member states as have a direct incidence on the establishment or functioning of the Common Market. The European Parliament and the Economic and Social Committee shall be consulted concerning any directives whose implementation in one or more of the member states would involve amendment of legislative provisions.

Economic Policy

Balance of Payments: Member states are charged to co-ordinate their economic policies in order that each may ensure the equilibrium of their overall balances of payments and maintain confidence in their currency, together with a high level of employment and stability of prices. In order to promote this co-ordination a Monetary Committee is established.

Each member state engages itself to treat its policy with regard to exchange rates as a matter of common interest. Where a member state is in difficulties or seriously threatened with difficulties as regards its balance of payments as a result either of overall disequilibrium of the balance of payments or of the kinds of currency at its disposal, and where such difficulties are likely, in particular, to prejudice the functioning of the Common Market or the progressive establishment of the common commercial policy, the Commission shall examine the situation and indicate the measures which it recommends to the state concerned to adopt; if this action proves insufficient to overcome the difficulties, the Commission shall, after consulting the Monetary Committee, recommend to the Council of Ministers the granting of mutual assistance. This mutual assistance may take the form of:

(a) concerted action in regard to any other international organization to which the member states may have recourse;

(b) any measures necessary to avoid diversions of commercial traffic where the state in difficulty maintains or re-establishes quantitative restrictions with regard to third countries;

(c) the granting of limited credits by other member states, subject to their agreement.

Furthermore, during the transitional period, mutual assistance may also take the form of special reductions in customs duties or enlargements of quotas. If the mutual assistance recommended by the Commission is not granted by the Council, or if the mutual assistance granted and the measures taken prove insufficient, the Commission shall authorise the state in difficulties to take measures of safeguard, of which the Commission shall determine the conditions and particulars. In the case of a sudden balance-of-payments crisis, any member state may take immediate provisional measures of safeguard, which must be submitted to the consideration of the Commission as soon as possible. On the basis of an opinion of the Commission and after consulting the Monetary Committee, the Council may decide that the state concerned shall amend, suspend or abolish such measures.

Commercial Policy: Member states shall co-ordinate their commercial relations with third countries in such a way as to bring about, not later than at the expiry of the transitional period, the conditions necessary to the implementation of a common policy in the matter of external trade. After the expiry of the transitional period, the common commercial policy shall be based on uniform principles, particularly in regard to tariff amendments, the conclusion of tariff or trade agreements, the alignment of measures of liberalisation, export policy and protective commercial measures, including measures to be taken in cases of dumping or subsidies. The Commission will be authorised to conduct negotiations with third countries. As from the end of the transitional period, member states shall, in respect of all matters of particular interest in regard to the Common Market, within the framework of any international organizations of an economic character, only proceed by way of common action. The Commission shall for this purpose submit to the Council of Ministers proposals concerning the scope and implementation of such common action. During the transitional period, member states shall consult with each other with a view to concerting their action and, as far as possible, adopting a uniform attitude.

Social Policy

Social Provisions: Without prejudice to the other provisions of the Treaty and in conformity with its general objectives, it shall be the aim of the Commission to promote close collaboration between member states in the social field, particularly in matters relating to employment, labour legislation and working conditions, occupational and continuation training, social security, protection against occupational accidents and diseases, industrial hygiene, the law as to trade unions and collective bargaining between employers and workers.

Each member state shall in the course of the first stage of the transitional period ensure and subsequently maintain the application of the principle of equal pay for men and women.

The European Social Fund: See p. 152.

The European Investment Bank: See p. 143.

PART IV. OVERSEAS COUNTRIES AND TERRITORIES

The member states agree to bring into association with the Community the non-European countries and territories which have special relations with Belgium, France, Italy and the Netherlands in order to promote the economic and social development of these countries and territories and to establish close economic relations between them and the Community as a whole.

Member states shall, in their commercial exchanges with the countries and territories, apply the same rules which they apply among themselves pursuant to the Treaty. Each country or territory shall apply to its commercial exchanges with member states and with other countries and territories the same rules which it applied in respect of the European state with which it has special relations. Member states shall contribute to the investments required by the progressive development of these countries and territories.

Customs duties on trade between member states and the countries and territories are to be progressively abolished according to the same timetable as for trade between the member states themselves. The countries and territories may, however, levy customs duties which correspond to the needs of their development and to the requirements of their industrialisation or which, being of a fiscal nature, have the object of contributing to their budgets.

(The Convention implementing these provisions is concluded for a period of five years only from the date of entry into force of the Treaty.)

PART V. INSTITUTIONS OF THE COMMUNITY

Provisions Governing Institutions

For the achievement of their aims and under the conditions provided for in the Treaty, the Council and the Commission shall adopt regulations and directives, make decisions and formulate recommendations or opinions. Regulations shall have a general application and shall be binding in every respect and directly applicable in each member state. Directives shall bind any member state to which they are addressed, as to the result to be achieved, while leaving to domestic agencies a competence as to form and means. Decisions shall be binding in every respect for the addressees named therein. Recommendations and opinions shall have no binding force.

Financial Provisions

Estimates shall be drawn up for each financial year for all revenues and expenditures of the Community and shall be shown in the budget.

The revenues of the budget shall comprise the financial contributions of member states assessed by reference to a fixed scale.

The Commission shall implement the budget on its own responsibility and within the limits of the appropriations made. The Council of Ministers shall:

INTERNATIONAL ORGANIZATIONS — European Communities

(a) lay down the financial regulations specifying, in particular, the procedure to be adopted for establishing and implementing the budget, and for rendering and auditing accounts;

(b) determine the methods and procedure whereby the contributions by member states shall be made available to the Commission; and

(c) establish rules concerning the responsibility of pay-commissioners and accountants and arrange for the relevant supervision.

PART VI. GENERAL AND FINAL PROVISIONS

Member states shall, in so far as is necessary, engage in negotiations with each other with a view to ensuring for the benefit of their nationals:

(a) the protection of persons as well as the enjoyment and protection of rights under the conditions granted by each state to its own nationals;

(b) the elimination of double taxation within the Community;

(c) the mutual recognition of companies, the maintenance of their legal personality in cases where the registered office is transferred from one country to another, and the possibility for companies subject to the municipal law of different member states to form mergers; and

(d) the simplification of the formalities governing the reciprocal recognition and execution of judicial decisions and arbitral awards.

Within a period of three years after the date of the entry into force of the Treaty, member states shall treat nationals of other member states in the same manner, as regards financial participation by such nationals in the capital of companies, as they treat their own nationals, without prejudice to the application of the other provisions of the Treaty.

The Treaty shall in no way prejudice the system existing in member states in respect of property.

The provisions of the Treaty shall not detract from the following rules:

(a) no member state shall be obliged to supply information the disclosure of which it considers contrary to the essential interests of its security.

(b) any member state may take the measures which it considers necessary for the protection of the essential interests of its security, and which are connected with the production of or the trade in arms, ammunition and war material; such measures shall not, however, prejudice conditions of competition in the Common Market in respect of products not intended for specifically military purposes.

The list of products to which (b) applies shall be determined by the Council in the course of the first year after the date of entry into force of the Treaty. The list may be subsequently amended by the unanimous vote of the Council on a proposal of the Commission.

Member states shall consult one another for the purpose of enacting in common the necessary provisions to prevent the functioning of the Common Market from being affected by measures which a member state may be called upon to take in case of serious internal disturbances affecting public order, in case of war or in order to carry out undertakings into which it has entered for the purpose of maintaining peace and international security.

In the course of the transitional period, where there are serious difficulties which are likely to persist in any sector of economic activity or difficulties which may seriously impair the economic situation in any region, any member state may ask for authorization to take measures of safeguard in order to restore the situation and adapt the sector concerned to the Common Market economy.

The provisions of the Treaty shall not affect those of the Treaty establishing the European Coal and Steel Community, nor those of the Treaty establishing the European Atomic Energy Community; nor shall they be an obstacle to the existence or completion of regional unions between Belgium and Luxembourg, and between Belgium, Luxembourg and the Netherlands, in so far as the objectives of these regional unions are not achieved by the application of this Treaty.

The government of any member state of the Commission may submit to the Council proposals for the revision of the Treaty.

Any European state may apply to become a member of the Community.

The Community may conclude with a third country, a union of states or an international organization agreements creating an association embodying reciprocal rights and obligations, joint actions and special procedures.

The Treaty is concluded for an unlimited period.

OTHER TREATIES

The following additional treaties have been signed by the members of the European Communities:

Treaty Instituting a Single Council and a Single Commission of the European Communities: signed in Brussels on 8 April 1965 by the six original members.

Treaty Modifying Certain Budgetary Arrangements of the European Communities and of the Treaty Instituting a Single Council and a Single Commission of the European Communities: signed in Luxembourg on 22 April 1970 by the six original members.

Treaty Concerning the Accession of the Kingdom of Denmark, Ireland, the Kingdom of Norway and the United Kingdom of Great Britain to the European Economic Community and the European Atomic Energy Community: signed in Brussels on 22 January 1972 (amended on 1 January 1973, owing to the non-accession of Norway).

Treaty of Accession of the Hellenic Republic to the European Economic Community and to the European Atomic Energy Community: signed in Athens on 28 May 1979.

Treaty of Accession of the Portuguese Republic and the Kingdom of Spain to the European Economic Community and to the European Atomic Energy Community: signed in Lisbon and Madrid on 12 June 1985.

(Accession of new members to the European Coal and Steel Community is enacted separately, by a Decision of the Council of the European Communities.)

Community Institutions

Originally each of the Communities had its own Commission (High Authority in the case of the ECSC) and Council, but a treaty transferring the powers of these bodies to a single Commission and a single Council came into effect in 1967.

COMMISSION OF THE EUROPEAN COMMUNITIES

Address: 200 rue de la Loi, 1049 Brussels, Belgium.
Telephone: (02) 235-11-11.
Telex: 21877.

MEMBERS OF THE COMMISSION
(with their responsibilities: October 1986)

President: Jacques Delors (France): Secretariat-General; Legal Service; Spokesman's Service; Joint Interpreting and Conference Service; Security Office; Monetary Affairs.

Vice-Presidents:

Lorenzo Natali (Italy): Co-operation and Development.

Karl-Heinz Narjes (Federal Republic of Germany): Industrial Affairs; Information Technology; Science and Research; Joint Research Centre.

Frans Andriessen (Netherlands): Agriculture; Forestry.

Lord Francis Cockfield (United Kingdom): Internal Market; Customs Union; Taxation; Financial Institutions.

Henning Christophersen (Denmark): Budget; Financial Control; Personnel and Administration.

Manuel Marín (Spain): Social Affairs and Employment; Education and Training.

Other members:

Claude Cheysson (France): Mediterranean Policy and North-South Relations.

Alois Pfeiffer (Federal Republic of Germany): Economic Affairs; Regional Policy; Statistical Office.

Grigoris Varfis (Greece): Co-ordination of Structural Funds; Consumer Protection.

Willy de Clercq (Belgium): External Relations and Trade Policy.

Nicolas Mosar (Luxembourg): Energy; Euratom Supply Agency; Publications Office.

Stanley Clinton Davis (United Kingdom): Environment; Nuclear Safety; Transport.

INTERNATIONAL ORGANIZATIONS

Carlo Ripa de Meana (Italy): Institutional Questions; Matters concerning a Citizen's Europe; Information and Communication; Culture; Tourism.

Peter D. Sutherland (Ireland): Competition; Relations with European Parliament.

António Cardoso e Cunha (Portugal): Fisheries.

Abel Matutes (Spain): Credit; Investments; Financial Instruments; Small and Medium-Sized Businesses.

The functions of the Commission are fourfold: to ensure the application of the provisions of the Treaties and of the provisions enacted by the institutions of the Communities in pursuance thereof; to formulate recommendations or opinions in matters which are the subject of the Treaties, where the latter expressly so provides or where the Commission considers it necessary; to dispose, under the conditions laid down in the Treaties, of a power of decision of its own and to participate in the preparation of acts of the Council of Ministers and of the European Parliament; and to exercise the competence conferred on it by the Council of Ministers for the implementation of the rules laid down by the latter.

The Commission may not include more than two members having the nationality of the same state; the number of members of the Commission may be amended by a unanimous vote of the Council of Ministers. In the performance of their duties, the members of the Commission are forbidden to seek or accept instructions from any Government or other body, or to engage in any other paid or unpaid professional activity.

The members of the Commission are appointed by the Governments of the member states acting in common agreement for a renewable term of four years; the President and Vice-Presidents are appointed for renewable terms of two years. Any member of the Commission, if he no longer fulfils the conditions required for the performance of his duties, or if he commits a serious offence, may be declared removed from office by the Court of Justice. The Court may furthermore, on the petition of the Council of Ministers or of the Commission itself, provisionally suspend any member of the Commission from his duties.

ADMINISTRATION

Offices are at the address of the European Commission: 200 rue de la Loi, 1049 Brussels, Belgium; tel. (02) 235-11-11; telex 21877 (unless otherwise stated).

Secretariat-General of the Commission: Sec.-Gen. Emile Noël.

Legal Service: Dir-Gen. Claus-Dieter Ehlermann.

Spokesman's Service: Spokesman Hugo Paemen.

Joint Interpreting and Conference Service: Dir-Gen. Renée Van Hoof.

Statistical Office: Bâtiment Jean Monnet, rue Alcide de Gasperi, 2920 Luxembourg; tel. 430-11; telex 3423; Dir-Gen. Silvio Ronchetti (acting).

Customs Union Service: Dir-Gen. Friedrich Klein.

Directorates-General:

I (**External Relations**): Dir-Gen. Leslie Fielding.

II (**Economic and Financial Affairs**): Dir-Gen. Massimo Russo.

III (**Internal Market and Industrial Affairs**): Dir-Gen. Fernand Braun.

IV (**Competition**): Dir-Gen. Manfred Caspari.

V (**Employment, Social Affairs and Education**): Dir-Gen. Jean Degimbe.

VI (**Agriculture**): Dir-Gen. Guy Legras.

VII (**Transport**): Dir-Gen. Eduardo Peña Abizanda.

VIII (**Development**): Dir-Gen. Dieter Frisch.

IX (**Personnel and Administration**): Dir-Gen. Richard Hay.

X (**Information, Communication and Culture**): Dir-Gen. Franz Froschmaier.

XI (**Environment, Consumer Protection and Nuclear Safety**): Dir-Gen. A. J. Fairclough.

XII (**Science, Research and Development**): Dir-Gen. Paolo Fasella.

   Joint Research Centre: Dir-Gen. Jean-Pierre Contzen.

XIII (**Telecommunications, Information and Innovation**): Bâtiment Jean Monnet, rue Alcide de Gasperi, 2920 Luxembourg-Kirchberg; tel. 430-11; telex 2752; Dir-Gen. Michel Carpentier.

XIV (**Fisheries**): Dir-Gen. Eamonn Gallagher.

XV (**Financial Institutions and Company Law**): Dir-Gen. Geoffrey Fitchew.

XVI (**Regional Policy**): Dir-Gen. Eneko Landaburu.

XVII (**Energy**): Dir-Gen. Alberto Hasson (acting).

XVIII (**Credit and Investments**): Bâtiment Jean Monnet, rue Alcide de Gasperi, 2920 Luxembourg-Kirchberg; tel. 430-11; telex 3423; Dir-Gen. Enrico Cioffi.

XIX (**Budgets**): Dir-Gen. Jean-Claude Morel.

XX (**Financial Control**): Dir-Gen. Carlo Facini.

XXI (**Customs Union and Indirect Taxation**): Dir-Gen. Emilio Rui Vilar.

XXII (**Co-ordination of Structural Instruments**): Dir-Gen. Kaj Barlebo-Larsen.

Euratom Supply Agency: Dir-Gen. Georg von Klitzing.

Security Office: Dir Peter de Haan.

THE EUROPEAN COUNCIL

The Heads of State or of Government of the member countries meet twice a year, in the capital of the member state which currently exercises the presidency of the Council of Ministers, or in Brussels. Until 1975 summit meetings were held at rather less frequent intervals and were often required to take decisions which came to be regarded as the major guidelines for the development of the Community.

In answer to the evident need for more frequent consultation at the highest level it was decided at the summit meeting in Paris in December 1974 to hold the meetings on a regular basis. The Council discusses matters relating to the Community and matters handled by the 'Political Co-operation' system (under which the Foreign Ministers of the member states meet at least four times a year to co-ordinate foreign policy).

COUNCIL OF MINISTERS OF THE EUROPEAN COMMUNITIES

Address: 170 rue de la Loi, 1049 Brussels, Belgium.

The Council of Ministers has the double responsibility of ensuring the co-ordination of the general economic policies of the member states and of taking the decisions necessary for carrying out the Treaties.

The Council is composed of representatives of the member states, each Government delegating to it one of its members, according to the subject to be discussed. The Councils of foreign affairs, economics and finance and agriculture normally meet once a month. About 60 Council sessions are held each year. The office of President is exercised for a term of six months by each member of the Council in rotation according to the alphabetical order of the member states. Meetings of the Council are called by the President acting on his or her own initiative or at the request of a member or of the Commission.

The Treaty of Rome prescribed three types of voting: simple majority, qualified majority and unanimity. Where conclusions require a qualified majority, the votes of its members are weighted as follows: France, Federal Republic of Germany, Italy and the United Kingdom 10; Spain 8; Belgium, Greece, the Netherlands and Portugal 5; Denmark and Ireland 3; Luxembourg 2 (Total 76). Majorities are required for the adoption of any conclusions as follows: 54 votes in cases where the Treaty requires a previous proposal of the Commission, or 54 votes including a favourable vote by more than half the members in all other cases. Abstentions by members present or represented do not prevent the adoption by the Council of conclusions requiring unanimity. It was declared at a meeting of the Council of Ministers in January 1966 that when decisions affecting very important national interests are at stake, discussions should be continued for a reasonable length of time, so that mutually acceptable solutions can be found, giving each member what amounted to a right of veto. The effect of this 'Luxembourg compromise' has been that the Council of Ministers has seldom taken decisions by majority voting except on budgetary and agricultural management affairs. However, pressure to agree is exerted not only by the Commission but also by the presidency, which has gained in importance since the period of the 'Luxembourg compromise'. Amendments to the Treaty of Rome adopted in February 1986 (subject to ratification by national legislatures) restricted the right of 'veto', and were expected to speed up the development of a genuine common market: they allowed proposals relating to the

INTERNATIONAL ORGANIZATIONS

dismantling of barriers to the free movement of goods, persons, services and capital to be approved by a majority vote in the Council, rather than by a unanimous vote. Unanimity would still be required, however, for certain areas, including harmonization of indirect taxes, legislation on health and safety, veterinary controls, and environmental protection; individual states would also retain control over immigration rules, prevention of terrorism and drug-trafficking.

When the Council acts on a proposal of the Commission, it must, where the amendment of such a proposal is involved, act only by means of a unanimous vote; as long as the Council has not so acted, the Commission may amend its original proposal, particularly in cases where the European Parliament has been consulted. The Council may request the Commission to undertake any studies which the Council considers desirable for the achievement of the common objectives, and to submit to it any appropriate proposals.

PERMANENT REPRESENTATIVES

Preparation and co-ordination of the Council's work is entrusted to a Committee of Permanent Representatives (COREPER), meeting in Brussels, consisting of the ambassadors of the member countries to the Communities, and aided by committees of national civil servants.

SECRETARIAT

The General Secretariat of the Council has a staff of about 1,600, who service the Council and COREPER.

Secretary-General: NIELS ERSBØLL (Denmark).

EUROPEAN PARLIAMENT

Address: Centre Européen, Plateau de Kirchberg, BP 1601, Luxembourg.

Telephone: 43001.

PRESIDENT AND MEMBERS
(October 1986)

President: PIERRE PFLIMLIN (France).

Members: 518 members, apportioned as follows: France, the Federal Republic of Germany, Italy and the United Kingdom 81 members each; Spain 60; the Netherlands 25; Belgium, Greece and Portugal 24 each; Denmark 16; Ireland 15; Luxembourg 6. Members are elected by direct universal suffrage by the citizens of the member states. When Portugal and Spain joined the Community in January 1986, their national legislatures nominated members of the European Parliament, pending elections to be held in these two countries before 1989. Members sit in the Chamber in political, not national, groups.

Political Groupings

	Distribution of seats following accession of Portugal and Spain, 1986
Socialist Group	172
European People's Party (Christian-Democratic Group)	119
European Democratic Group	63
Communist and Allies Group	46
Liberal and Democratic Reformist Group	41
European Renewal and Democratic Alliance*	34
Rainbow Group	20
Group of the European Right	16
Non-affiliated	7
Total	**518**

* Formerly Group of European Progressive Democrats.

The tasks of the European Parliament are: advising on legislation, scrutinizing the Community budget and exercising a measure of democratic control over the executive organs of the European Communities, the Commission and the Council. It has the power to dismiss the Commission by a vote of censure. A small increase in parliamentary powers was brought about by the amendments to the Treaty of Rome adopted in 1986, allowing Parliament to modify Community legislation by making amendments which could only be rejected by a unanimous decision of the Council of Ministers.

European Communities

This fell far short of demands by members of Parliament for full powers of joint decision-making.

Parliament has an annual session, divided into about 12 one-week meetings, normally held in Strasbourg. The session opens with the March meeting. Committees normally meet in Brussels.

The budgetary powers of Parliament (which, with the Council, forms the Budgetary Authority of the Communities) were increased to their present status by a treaty of 22 July 1975. Under this treaty, it can amend non-agricultural spending and reject the draft budget, acting by a majority of its members and two-thirds of the votes cast.

The Parliament is run by a Bureau comprising the President, and 14 vice-presidents elected from its members by secret ballot to serve for 2½ years. Parliament has 18 specialized committees, which deliberate on proposals for legislation put forward by the Commission before Parliament's final opinion is delivered by a resolution in plenary session.

There are Standing Committees on Political Affairs; Agriculture, Fisheries and Food; Budgets; Budgetary Control; Economic and Monetary Affairs and Industrial Policy; Energy, Research and Technology; External Economic Relations; Legal Affairs and Citizens' Rights; Social Affairs and Employment; Regional Policy and Planning; Transport; Environment, Public Health and Consumer Protection; Youth, Culture, Education, Information and Sport; Development and Co-operation; Rules of Procedure and Petitions; Verification of Credentials; Institutional Affairs; Women's Rights.

The first direct elections to the European Parliament took place in June 1979. The directly elected Parliament met for the first time in July 1979. The second elections were held from 14–17 June 1984.

COURT OF JUSTICE OF THE EUROPEAN COMMUNITIES

Address: 2925 Luxembourg.

Telephone: 4303-1.

Telex: 2510.

The task of the Court of Justice is to ensure the observance of law in the interpretation and application of the Treaties setting up the three Communities, and in implementing regulations issued by the Council or the Commission. The 13 Judges and the six Advocates General are appointed for renewable six-year terms by the Governments of the member states. The President of the Court is elected by the Judges from among their members for a renewable term of three years. The majority of cases, including all those of major importance, are dealt with by a full bench of 13 judges. The remainder are dealt with by one of the six chambers, each of which consists of a President of Chamber and two or four judges. The Court has jurisdiction to award penalties. It may review the legality of acts (other than recommendations or opinions) of the Council or the Commission and is competent to give judgment on actions by a member state, the Council or the Commission on grounds of lack of competence, of infringement of an essential procedural requirement, of infringement of a Treaty or of any legal rule relating to its application, or of misuse of power. Any natural or legal person may, under the same conditions, appeal against a decision addressed to him or against a decision which, although in the form of a regulation or decision addressed to another person, is of direct and specific concern to him.

The Court is also empowered to hear certain other cases concerning the contractual and non-contractual liability of the Communities and disputes between member states in connection with the objects of the Treaties. It also gives preliminary rulings at the request of national courts on the interpretation of the Treaties, of Community legislation, and of the Brussels Convention on Jurisdiction and the Enforcement of Judgments in Civil and Commercial Matters. During 1985 433 new cases were brought before the Court, of which 139 were cases referred to it for preliminary rulings by the national courts of the member states. In the same period 211 judgments and interim orders were delivered.

Composition of the Court (in order of precedence, October 1986)

Lord MACKENZIE STUART, President.

Judge Y. GALMOT (President of the Third and Fifth Chambers).

Judge C. N. KAKOURIS (President of the Fourth and Sixth Chambers).

First Advocate General C. O. LENZ.

Judge T. F. O'HIGGINS (President of the Second Chamber).

Judge F. A. SCHOCKWEILER (President of the First Chamber).

INTERNATIONAL ORGANIZATIONS *European Communities*

Judge G. Bosco.
Judge T. Koopmans.
Judge O. Due.
Judge U. Everling.
Advocate General Sir Gordon Slynn.
Judge K. Bahlmann.
Advocate General G. F. Mancini.
Advocate General M. Darmon.
Judge R. Joliet.
Advocate General J. Mischo.
Judge J. C. de Carvalho Moitinho de Almeida.
Advocate General J. L. da Cruz Vilaça.
Judge G. C. Rodríguez Iglesias.
P. E. Heim (Registrar).

COURT OF AUDITORS OF THE EUROPEAN COMMUNITIES

Address: 29 rue Aldringen, 1118 Luxembourg.

Telephone: 47731.

The Court of Auditors was created by a Treaty which came into force on 22 July 1975. It is the body responsible for the external audit of the resources managed by the three Communities. It consists of 12 Members who are appointed for six-year terms by unanimous decision of the Council of Ministers, after consultation with the European Parliament. The Members elect the President from among their number for a term of three years.

The Court is organized and acts as a corporate body. It adopts its decisions by a majority of its Members. Each Member, however, has a direct responsibility to audit certain Community sectors.

The Court examines the accounts of all expenditure and revenue of the European Communities and of any body created by them in so far as the relevant constituent instrument does not preclude such examination. It examines whether all revenue has been received and all expenditure incurred in a lawful and regular manner and whether the financial management has been sound. The audit is based on records, and if necessary is performed on the spot in the institutions of the Communities and in the member states. In the member states the audit is carried out in liaison with the national audit bodies. The Court draws up an annual report after the close of each financial year. It may also, at any time, submit observations on specific questions and deliver opinions at the request of one of the institutions of the Communities. It assists the Assembly and the Council in exercising their powers of control over the implementation of the budget, and gives its prior opinion on the financial regulations, on the methods and procedure whereby the budgetary revenue is made available to the Commission, and on the laying-down of rules concerning the responsibility of authorizing officers and accounting officers and concerning appropriate arrangements for inspection.

President: Marcel Mart (Luxembourg).

First Group: Richie Ryan (Ireland), Josep Subirats Pinana (Spain), Charles J. Carey (United Kingdom), Keld Brixtofte (Denmark).

Second Group: Paul Gaudy (Belgium), Aldo Angioi (Italy), Pierre Lelong (France), André J. Middelhoek (Netherlands).

Third Group: Marcel Mart (Luxembourg), Lothar Haase (Federal Republic of Germany), Stergios Vallas (Greece), Carlos Manuel Botelheiro Moreno (Portugal).

EUROPEAN INVESTMENT BANK

Address: 100 blvd Konrad Adenauer, 2950 Luxembourg.

Telephone: 4379-1.

Telex: 3530.

Board of Governors: One Minister (usually the Finance Minister) from each member state.

Board of Directors: France, the Federal Republic of Germany, Italy and the United Kingdom each nominate three directors and two alternates; Spain nominates two directors and, jointly with Portugal, one alternate; Portugal nominates one director; Belgium, Luxembourg and the Netherlands each nominate one director and, jointly, one alternate; Denmark, Greece and Ireland each nominate one director and, jointly, one alternate, and the Commission nominates one director and one alternate.

Management Committee:

President: Ernst-Günther Bröder (FRG).

Vice-Presidents: C. Richard Ross (UK), Arie Pais (Netherlands), Lucio Izzo (Italy), Noel Whelan (Ireland), Alain Prate (France), M. Arnedo Orbañanos (Spain).

The European Investment Bank (EIB) is the European Community's bank for long-term finance. It was created in 1958 under the Treaty of Rome. Its principal task is laid down in Article 130 of the Treaty: working on a non-profit-making basis, the Bank makes or guarantees loans for investment projects, principally in industry, energy and infrastructure, which further balanced regional development, a common interest of several Member Countries or the Community as a whole, or industrial modernization and conversion. Capital is subscribed by member states (see table). In June 1985 the Board of Governors decided to double the Bank's subscribed capital: from 1 January 1986, subscriptions of the 10 existing

CAPITAL STRUCTURE
(as from 1 January 1986, in ECUs)

	Subscribed	Paid-in	%
France	5,508,725,000	497,529,375	19.127
Federal Republic of Germany	5,508,725,000	497,529,375	19.127
Italy	5,508,725,000	497,529,375	19.127
United Kingdom	5,508,725,000	497,529,375	19.127
Spain	2,024,928,000	181,333,940	7.031
Belgium	1,526,980,000	136,742,250	5.302
Netherlands	1,526,980,000	136,742,250	5.302
Denmark	773,154,000	69,236,550	2.684
Greece	414,190,000	37,091,750	1.438
Portugal	266,922,000	23,903,086	0.927
Ireland	193,288,000	17,309,100	0.671
Luxembourg	38,658,000	3,461,850	0.134
Total	28,800,000,000	2,595,938,276	100.000

FINANCING PROVIDED (million ECUs)

	1985 Amount	%	1981–85 Amount	%
Recipient				
Belgium	77.8	1.1	353.4	1.3
Denmark	332.5	4.8	1,439.7	5.4
France	1,247.4	18.4	4,070.6	15.2
Federal Republic of Germany	91.4	1.3	690.7	2.6
Greece	423.7	6.2	1,820.2	6.8
Ireland	174.5	2.6	1,403.6	5.2
Italy	2,978.0	43.9	12,362.4	46.3
Luxembourg	—	—	16.4	0.1
Netherlands	69.1	1.0	69.1	0.3
Portugal	100.0	1.5	424.0	1.6
Spain	160.0	2.4	550.0	2.0
United Kingdom	1,130.0	16.6	3,490.1	13.1
Non-member countries[1]	—	—	22.8	0.1
Sub-total	6,784.4	100.0	26,713.0[2]	100.0
Outside the Community				
from the Bank's own resources	324.3	81.0	1,454.8	80.7
from budgetary resources	75.9	19.0	347.7	19.3
Sub-total	400.2	100.0	1,802.5	100.0
Total	7,184.6	—	28,515.5	—

[1] Loans granted for energy projects in Austria, Norway and Tunisia but of direct importance to the Community.
[2] Including loans granted from the resources of the New Community Instrument for borrowing and lending, i.e. a total of 4,596m. ECUs in 1981–85, of which 2,434.6m. was for investments in Italy, 1,008.2m. for France, 392.2m. for Denmark, 301.5m. for Greece, 247.7m. for Ireland and 211.7m. for the United Kingdom.

members increased from 14,400m. ECUs to 26,500m., while a further 2,300m. was subscribed by Portugal and Spain. Paid-in capital amounts to 9.01% of subscribed capital. The bulk of resources, however, comes from borrowings, principally public or private bond issues on capital markets inside and outside the Community. Borrowings between 1961 and 1985 amounted to 32,254.4m. ECUs. During 1985 borrowings came to 5,709m. ECUs, compared with 4,360m. in 1984.

Lending within the Community (excluding pre-accession finance for Portugal and Spain) amounted to 6,524m. ECUs in 1985; between 1958 and 1985 the total amount was 40,535m. ECUs. Priority is given to regional development in less-favoured regions, such as southern Italy and Ireland, with particular emphasis on small and medium-sized investments. The EIB also finances projects of common interest, particularly those which meet the Community's energy objectives, and gives support to regional or sectoral modernization and conversion.

The EIB also plays a major part in development finance outside the Community. Between 1963 and 1985 it made available 5,157.5m. ECUs for 12 countries in the Mediterranean region and 66 African, Caribbean and Pacific (ACP) countries, signatories to the Lomé Convention (see p. 149). During 1985 it made available 425m. ECUs in the Mediterranean countries (including pre-accession financial co-operation worth 160m. ECUs for Spain and 100m. for Portugal) and 165m. ECUs for the ACP states.

CONSULTATIVE BODIES

ECONOMIC AND SOCIAL COMMITTEE—ECOSOC

Address: 2 rue Ravenstein, 1000 Brussels.
Telephone: (02) 512-39-20.
Telex: 25 983.

The Committee is advisory and is consulted by the Council of Ministers or by the Commission of the European Communities, particularly with regard to agriculture, free movement of workers, harmonization of laws and transport, as well as legislation adopted under the Euratom Treaty. In addition, the Committee has the power to deliver opinions on its own initiative.

The Committee has 189 members representing economic and social fields, 24 each from France, the Federal Republic of Germany, Italy and the United Kingdom, 21 from Spain, 12 each from Belgium, Greece, the Netherlands and Portugal, nine from Denmark and Ireland, and six from Luxembourg. One-third represent each side of industry and one-third the general economic interest. The Committee is appointed for a renewable term of four years by the unanimous vote of the Council of Ministers of the European Communities. Members are appointed in their personal capacity and are not bound by any mandatory instructions.

Chairman: GERD MUHR.

ECSC CONSULTATIVE COMMITTEE

The Committee is advisory and is attached to the Commission. Its members are appointed by the Council of Ministers for two years and are not bound by any mandate from the organizations that designated them in the first place.

There are 84 members representing, in equal proportions, producers, workers and consumers and dealers in the coal and steel industries.

AGRICULTURAL ADVISORY COMMITTEES

There is one Committee for the organization of the market of each sector; two for dealing with social questions in agriculture; and one for structures.

In addition to the consultative bodies listed above there are several hundred special interest groups representing every type of interest within the Community. All these hold unofficial talks with the Commission.

Activities of the Community

AGRICULTURE

Co-operation in the Community is at its most highly-organized in the area of agriculture. The objectives of the Common Agricultural Policy (CAP) are described in the Treaty of Rome (see p. 137). The markets for agricultural products have been progressively organized following three basic principles: (i) unity of the market (products must be able to circulate freely within the Community and markets must be organized according to common rules); (ii) Community preference (products must be protected from low-cost imports and from fluctuations on the world market); (iii) common financial responsibility (the European Agricultural Guidance and Guarantee Fund, described on p. 151, finances, through its Guarantee Section, all public expenditure intervention, storage costs, marketing subsidies and export rebates, and, through its Guidance Section, the improvement of farms and facilities).

Monetary compensation amounts (MCAs) are added or deducted in agricultural exchanges between member states to take account of fluctuations between the reference rate of exchange (the 'green' currencies) and the real rate. Thus a subsidy is paid to the supplier in a country whose currency has appreciated against a reference rate of exchange, and a tax is paid by the supplier where the currency has depreciated or not appreciated as much. In practice, however, the MCA system has led to wide variations in prices within the Community, and has proved disadvantageous to any country which is a net food exporter with a weak currency. In 1984 it was decided that the system should be phased out by 1987, thereby restoring a single market.

Agricultural prices are, in theory, fixed each year at a common level for the community as a whole. For 1982/83 the average price increase was 10.4%, while for 1983/84, owing to the reduced rate of inflation, the increase dropped to 4.2%. As a measure to discourage surplus production, smaller increases were allotted to milk, cereals, sugar, colza (rape-seed) and tomatoes, while higher levels were allowed for products in which the Community was not self-sufficient, e.g. Mediterranean vegetables and oil-seeds. For 1984/85 the average increase was fixed at only 0.8%, with a price 'freeze' on some products. For 1985/86 the Commission proposed a virtual price 'freeze' for most products and a cut of 3.5% in cereal prices, following the record grain harvest of 1984. Prolonged negotiations brought the proposed price cut down to 1.8%, but even this was rejected by the Federal Republic of Germany in June 1985, using an unprecedented formal veto in the Council of Ministers, although the Commission was still empowered to undertake market management which would, in practice, involve a price cut of a similar amount. In April 1986 ministers of agriculture agreed on what amounted to a price 'freeze' on most products for 1986/87 (alleviated by the devaluation in April of 'green' currency rates for all members except the Federal Republic of Germany and the Netherlands). A 3% 'co-responsibility levy' was imposed on cereal production to finance the export subsidies needed to sell the surplus. Export subsidies are paid to enable farmers to sell produce at the lower world market prices without loss. These subsidies account for some 50% of agricultural spending, and have attracted criticism from other producers, particularly the USA.

An intervention price has been established for sugar, certain cereals, dairy produce, beef, veal and sheep-meat: when market prices fall below this level the Community intervenes, and buys a certain quantity which is then stored until prices recover. Expanding production has led to food surpluses, costly to maintain, particularly in dairy produce, beef, cereals and wine. In May 1982 the Community's ministers of agriculture agreed to extend production thresholds, already existing for sugar, to dairy products, cereals, colza and processed tomatoes: once these thresholds are passed, producers do not receive the full guaranteed EEC prices, and have to share the cost of disposing of surpluses. The accession of Spain and Portugal to the Community in 1986 was expected to lead to further problems by creating a surplus of Mediterranean produce such as wine and olive oil. The Community's Mediterranean aid programme, launched in February 1983, aims to increase farming efficiency and diversify production in the region.

Agriculture is by far the largest item on the Community budget, accounting for over two-thirds of annual expenditure, mainly for supporting prices. In 1983 and 1984 agricultural spending exceeded the original predictions, so that supplementary budgets had to be adopted (see Finance, p. 150). In July 1983 the Commission submitted proposals for adapting the CAP so as to limit the burden on the Community budget and make the agricultural sector more responsive to the level of supply and demand. Some of these reforms were finally adopted by ministers of agriculture in April 1984. They agreed to eliminate the system of MCAs, in phases, over a period of three years (see above). Lower milk production quotas were to be imposed in most countries, with a drop in the total production of some 7% to 99.5m. metric tons a year (although this would still exceed annual consumption of about 88m. tons): production in excess of the quota would be subject to a levy. As a result, production decreased slightly, but consumption also fell, and by 1986 surplus dairy produce had reached record levels, despite the Community's efforts to dispose of surplus butter by selling it cheaply within and outside Europe, and to use skimmed milk powder as animal feed. The chief reason for the failure to reduce the surplus was thought to be the system of inter-regional offsetting, whereby over-production in one area of a country was allowed to offset under-production in another; farmers were also permitted to 'lease' quotas to one another. The imposition of quotas thus failed to deter individuals or regions from over-producing milk. In 1986 ministers of agriculture agreed to impose a further cut of 3% in milk production quotas over the next three years.

In 1985 the Commission proposed more radical reforms for the CAP, with a shift of emphasis away from price support and the resultant massive expenditure on buying up surplus produce, towards income aid for the poorer farmers. The probability that such a shift would mean increased unemployment in the agricultural sector, however, made it unlikely that it would be politically acceptable to member states.

FISHERIES

The Common Fisheries Policy (CFP) came into effect in January 1983 after seven years of negotiations, particularly over the problem of access to fishing-grounds. In 1973 a 10-year agreement had been reached, whereby member states could have exclusive access to waters up to six nautical miles (11.1 km) or in some cases 12 miles from their shores; 'historic rights' were reserved in certain cases for foreign fishermen who had traditionally fished within a country's waters. In 1977 the Community set up a 200-mile (370-km) fishing zone around its coastline (excluding the Mediterranean) within which all members would have access to fishing. The 1983 agreement confirmed the 200-mile zone and allowed exclusive national zones of six miles with access between six and 12 miles from the shore for other countries according to specified 'historic rights'. Rules furthering conservation (e.g. standards for fishing tackle) are imposed under the policy, with checks by a Community fisheries inspectorate. Total allowable catches are fixed annually by species, divided into national quotas. Full implementation of the fisheries policy was delayed during 1983 by repeated failures to agree on national quotas of herring to be caught in the North Sea, but a long-term agreement was finally reached in December. During 1985 negotiations on fishing quotas for Portugal and Spain were successfully concluded, enabling them to participate in the CFP after their accession to the Community in January 1986.

The organization of fish marketing involves common rules on quality and packing, and a system of guide prices established annually by the Council of Ministers. Fish are withdrawn from the market if prices fall too far below the guide price, and compensation may then be paid to the fishermen. As with agricultural produce, export subsidies are paid to enable the export of fish onto the lower-priced world market, and import levies are imposed to prevent competition from low-priced imports.

The Community supports re-structuring of the fishing industry by offering grants for equipment and building. A three-year plan, beginning in 1983 and involving expenditure of 250m. ECUs, supported capacity reduction (scrapping or laying-up of fishing-vessels), the exploration and development of new grounds and the modernization of existing facilities.

Agreements have been signed with other countries (Norway, Sweden, Canada and the USA) allowing reciprocal fishing rights and other advantages, and with some West African countries which receive assistance in building up their fishing industries in return for allowing EEC boats to fish in their waters. Following the withdrawal of Greenland from the Community in February 1985, Community vessels retained fishing rights in Greenland waters, in exchange for financial compensation under a 10-year agreement.

SCIENCE AND TECHNOLOGY

In September 1981 the Commission brought together under a single Directorate-General all the departments responsible for scientific research, and proposed the formation of a common research and development policy, aiming to make the most of national potential, with emphasis on industrial and agricultural applications. In July 1983 the Council approved a programme for scientific research and technological development during the period 1984–87, involving total expenditure originally estimated at 3,750m. ECUs, and covering: promotion of industrial and agricultural competitiveness; improving the management of raw materials (including recycling and substitution); improving management of energy resources and reducing energy dependence; reinforcing development aid; improving living and working conditions; and improving the efficacy of the Community's scientific and technical potential. In 1986 the Commission drew up a new programme for 1988–91, with an original budget of 10,300m. ECUs (including a reserve), although it was expected that, in view of the Community's budgetary problems, member governments would insist on a reduction in this amount. The programme covered: health and environment; information technology; advanced telecommunications; 'technology transfusion' to traditional industries; energy; biotechnology; exploitation of the sea-bed and marine resources; promoting the mobility of research workers and encouraging cross-frontier and inter-disciplinary co-operation. The Commission pointed out the need for a 'European Technology Community' in view of the enormous technological advances being made elsewhere, particularly in Japan and the USA. In amendments to the Treaty of Rome approved in 1986 a section on research and technology was included for the first time, defining the extent of Community co-operation and introducing new decision-making structures.

Of the planned expenditure on scientific and technical research for the 1984–87 period, over 47% was allotted to energy research (see separate section below). The Community's Joint Research Centre (JRC) has establishments at Ispra (Italy), Geel (Belgium), Karlsruhe (Federal Republic of Germany) and Petten (Netherlands). Its 1984–87 work programme (with a budget of 700m. ECUs and a staff complement of 2,260) comprised joint research activities chiefly in energy (nuclear fusion, fission and non-nuclear energy sources) and also in industrial technologies and environmental problems.

Another major area of research is information technology: in November 1982 the Council approved a series of pilot projects preparing for the 10-year European Strategic Research Programme in Information Technology (ESPRIT), which concentrates on five key areas: advanced micro-electronics; software technology; advanced information processing; office automation; and computer integrated manufacturing. The programme is financed half by the EEC and half by research institutes, universities and industrial companies. The programme was launched in 1984, at an estimated cost to the Community of 750m. ECUs over the next five years. At the end of 1985 there were 468 organizations taking part in ESPRIT projects, involving some 2,000 research workers.

The Community also supports biotechnological research, aiming to promote the use of modern biology in agriculture and industry. A five-year programme (1982–86) in biomolecular engineering supported more than 100 projects (e.g. in animal vaccines, dairy micro-organisms and crop genetics), and in 1984 a further five-year programme was approved, with an appropriation of 55m. ECUs.

In June 1985 ministers agreed in principle on a joint programme for research and development in advanced communications technology in Europe (RACE), aiming to establish an integrated broad-band telecommunications network.

A second research project on forecasting and assessment in science and technology (FAST) took place in 1983–87, with a budget of 8.5m. ECUs: its work covers the effects of new technology on work and employment; the development of renewable natural resources; technological change in the service industries; and new industrial systems, particularly in the communications and food industries.

An experimental project was approved by the Council in June 1983 to encourage joint scientific research, for example in pharmaco-biology, solid state physics, optics, combustion, photometry/photoacoustics, interface phenomena and climatology. The means of stimulating joint research include grants, twinning laboratories in different countries, developing specific multinational projects and encouraging the mobility of research workers. The project proved successful and led to a four-year programme (1985–88) for stimulating joint research, with an appropriation of 60m. ECUs. The Community also co-operates with non-member countries in specific research projects, for example (in 1985) on wood as a renewable raw material (Switzerland), on metals and mineral substances (Norway) and on hearing impairment, thrombosis and nutrition (Sweden). In 1985 the Commission and 18 European countries (including the members of the Community as individuals) adopted the draft charter for the EUREKA programme of research in advanced technology.

The Direct Information Access Network (Euronet DIANE), inaugurated in 1980, comprised 600 data bases and banks by the end of 1984, managed by national posts and telecommunications administrations and easily accessible to individuals or organizations seeking information on thousands of scientific, medical, technological or economic topics.

ENERGY

The treaty setting up the European Atomic Energy Community (Euratom) came into force on 1 January 1958, to encourage the growth of the nuclear energy industry in the Community through conducting research, providing access to information, supplying nuclear fuels, building reactors, and establishing common laws and procedures for the nuclear industry. A common market for nuclear materials was introduced in 1959, and there is a common insurance scheme against nuclear risks. The Commission is empowered to make loans on behalf of Euratom to finance investment in nuclear power stations and the enrichment of fissile materials. Loans made during 1985 amounted to 229m. ECUs for five firms, bringing the total since 1977 (when such operations began) to 1,974m. ECUs. An agreement with the International Atomic Energy Authority entered into force in 1977, to facilitate co-operation in research on nuclear safeguards and controls.

Activities are also undertaken in other fields of energy, and the Commission has consistently urged the formation of an effective overall energy policy. Energy objectives for the decade to 1995 were proposed by the Commission and discussed by the Council in 1986; they included co-ordination of external energy relations, development of a common energy market (e.g. through interconnections between electricity and gas grids), realistic energy-pricing policies, environmental protection and innovative technology. The proposals envisaged an increase in the proportion of electricity generated by solid fuel and nuclear power.

In July 1979 a second four-year energy research programme was approved, covering the following main areas of research: energy conservation; improved production of indigenous fossil fuels; development of nuclear fission; development of new energy sources such as wind, solar power and nuclear fusion; coal conversion as a substitute for crude petroleum; development of substitutes for electricity as an energy vector (mainly hydrogen). Between 1978 and 1984 grants totalling 435m. ECUs were awarded for research in energy-saving techniques and alternative sources of energy.

The Joint Research Centre's 1984–87 programme included research on nuclear fusion, fission and non-nuclear energy resources. In 1985 the Council adopted a programme of research in non-nuclear energy for 1985–88, with funding of 175m. ECUs.

The Joint European Torus (JET) is an experimental thermonuclear machine designed to pioneer new processes of nuclear fusion, using the 'Tokamak' system of magnetic confinement to heat gases to very high temperatures and bring about the fusion of tritium and deuterium nuclei. Sweden and Switzerland are also members of the JET project. Since 1974 work has been proceeding at Culham in the United Kingdom, and the project was formally inaugurated in April 1984. In 1982 a five-year programme of research in the field of controlled thermonuclear fusion was established (revised and continued for the period 1985–89 when the Commission's financial contribution was set at 690m. ECUs). The programme also includes preparation of the Next European Torus (NET), the intermediate stage in the development of a demonstration reactor: work on possible alternative methods of nuclear fusion is also being undertaken.

INDUSTRY

Industrial co-operation was the earliest activity of the Community, or more accurately of the European Coal and Steel Community (ECSC). The treaty establishing the ECSC came into force in July 1952, and by the end of 1954 nearly all barriers to trade in coal, coke, steel, pig-iron and scrap iron had been removed. The Community fixes prices and supervises production levels, and assists investment and redevelopment programmes by granting loans, from funds raised on the capital market (see below).

In other sectors the Community has less influence, although the European Commission has to approve state aid to industry by Community members, and forbids measures which might result in unfair competition. Community aid is given to certain sectors. Steel, textiles and shipbuilding have been given particular attention as areas with special difficulties.

'Anti-crisis' measures for the steel industry, first adopted in 1977 in the face of a fall in world demand and a 50% price slump between 1974 and 1977, were renewed in December 1979, mainly consisting of minimum price rules, guide prices and arrangements with 17 major steel-exporting countries. In October 1980 the Council agreed to proclaim a state of 'manifest crisis' in the steel industry, enabling compulsory production quotas to be imposed so as to maintain price levels. In 1981 a new aids code for the steel industry was introduced, ensuring that assistance is granted only to firms implementing a restructuring programme which will reduce their capacity and restore their competitiveness and financial viability. By late 1985 the industry had lost 30m. metric tons of annual production capacity. In July ministers of industry agreed to phase out state aids to steel and production quotas by the end of 1988. Stricter controls on state aid to the coal industry were also envisaged over the same period.

Through redeployment loans and non-reimbursable aid for retraining, the Community has attempted to compensate for the loss of about 350,000 jobs in the steel industry between 1974 and 1984. During 1985 the Community made loans of 1,010.5m. ECUs to the coal and steel industries for investment in job-creation projects (62%), conversion in areas affected by the restructuring of the steel industry (36%) and subsidized housing (2%).

In 1982 a three-year Arrangement was agreed with the USA to limit Community steel exports to the USA by about 9%, after the American steel industry had filed anti-subsidy and anti-dumping suits.

The European textile and clothing industry has been affected by overseas competition: 15% of the Community's textile firms closed between 1973 and 1980, with an average loss of 115,000 jobs per year during that period. The Community participates in the Multi-fibre Arrangement (see GATT, p. 60), to limit imports from low-cost suppliers overseas. The European Regional Development Fund gives particular support to regions where textiles formerly provided a large proportion of industrial employment, while the European Social Fund also assists in retraining workers. An Information Centre on Textiles and Clothing was set up in 1981 to provide economic and statistical details of production levels, stocks and consumption.

In the Community's shipyards, production fell by 50% in 1976–80, while the workforce was reduced by 40%. In 1981 the Council adopted the Fifth Directive on aid to shipbuilding, providing a framework for aid in reorganizing the industry and increasing efficiency, while discouraging any increase in capacity; this Directive was extended until the end of 1986, after which the Commission proposed that a Sixth Directive, involving rigorous curbs on state aids to ship-building, would come into force.

The Commission has made a number of proposals on a joint strategy for developing the information technology industry in Europe, particularly in view of the superiority of Japan and the USA in the market for advanced electronic circuits. The ESPRIT research programme (see above) aims to build the technological foundations for a fully competitive European industry. In 1985 the Council adopted a programme of basic research in industrial technologies (BRITE), with Community funding of 125m. ECUs for 1985–88, aiming to develop new methods for the benefit of existing industries, such as aeronautics, chemicals, textiles and metalworking.

Harmonization of national company law to form a common legal structure is continuing: by the end of 1985 nine Directives (concerning disclosure of information, company capital, internal mergers, company and group accounts, division of companies and the qualification of auditors) had been adopted, and another on cross-frontier mergers of public limited liability companies was still being considered. The Community Patent Convention, providing for the issue of a Community patent valid for all members was signed in 1975, subject to ratification by all member states. Proposals for a Community Trade Mark Office were made by the Commission in November 1980, and were still being studied in 1986. By the end of 1983 the Council had adopted 158 Directives on the removal of technical barriers to trade with regard to industrial products.

The Business Co-operation Centre, created by the Commission in 1973, supplies information to businesses and introduces businesses from different countries wishing to co-operate or form links. It gives particular attention to small and medium-sized concerns, and to companies in applicant countries wishing to acquaint themselves with the Community market. In 1986 the Commission proposed an action programme for small and medium-sized enterprises, including simplified tax procedures and easier access to capital.

TRANSPORT

The establishment of a common transport policy is stipulated in the EEC Treaty (see p. 138), with the aim of gradually standardizing national regulations which hinder the free movement of traffic within the Community, such as the varying safety and licensing rules, diverse restrictions on the size of lorries, and frontier-crossing formalities. Although some progress has been made (for example in identifying bottlenecks, observing transport markets, fixing rates for carriage of goods between states, harmonizing safety regulations such as the control of hours worked by drivers, standardizing the beginning of 'summer time', and reducing frontier delays) large-scale co-operation has not come about, and in January 1983 the President of the European Parliament brought an action against the Council before the European Court of Justice for failure to implement the common transport policy: at this time over 40 Commission proposals on transport were still before the Council. In May 1985 the Court ruled that the Council had indeed failed to carry out its obligations: no penalty, however, could be imposed by the Court, and it emphasized that member states must agree on a common policy according to their own timetable.

A Communication from the Commission to the Council on progress towards a common policy for inland transport, issued in

INTERNATIONAL ORGANIZATIONS

European Communities

February 1983, offered revised proposals, including: co-operation in removing physical and legislative obstacles to a unified railway network; creation of Community authorizations for specific types of road transport; adjustment of national taxation systems for commercial vehicles; a permanent pricing system for international road haulage; harmonization of national scrapping schemes to reduce surplus capacity on inland waterways; negotiations with non-member countries such as Yugoslavia and Austria on transit and combined services; and the establishment of a Community system for paying infrastructure costs. In 1986 transport ministers agreed on a system of Community-wide permits for commercial vehicles, to allow easier crossing of frontiers.

In 1984 and 1985 the Commission also made proposals on the development of a Community air transport policy (to apply only to flights within the Community and aiming to produce a more flexible system, with greater scope for competition and more moderate fares). In April 1986 the European Court of Justice confirmed that the Community's rules on competition applied to air transport, and the Commission subsequently threatened to begin legal proceedings against European airlines operating a price-fixing 'cartel'. During 1985 and 1986 the Council of transport ministers also discussed the Commission's proposals for maritime transport (including co-ordinated action against restrictive practices by other countries, preventing EEC vessels from having free access to cargoes; and freedom for any company to provide sea transport services throughout the Community).

EDUCATION AND CULTURE

The postgraduate European University Institute was founded in Florence in 1972, with departments of history and civilization, economics, law, and political and social sciences; it had about 180 students in 1986. In June 1980 the Council approved the following recommendations by the Commission: intensification of modern language teaching; promotion of the study of the European Community in schools; development of a common policy on the admission of higher-education students from other member states; equality of education and vocational training for girls.

In September 1980 an educational information network known as EURYDICE began operations, with a central unit in Brussels and national units providing data on the widely varying systems of education within member states. During 1985 the Commission awarded 380 grants to teachers and administrative staff to study higher education teaching systems in other member states. In 1985 the Commission proposed a European Action Scheme for the Mobility of University Students (ERASMUS), which aimed to make grants enabling 44,000 university students to spend a study period in another Community country during 1987–89.

In 1985 the Council approved a programme of education and training for technology (COMETT), comprising a network of university/industry training partnerships and exchange schemes, to be undertaken in 1986–92 with Community support of about 80m. ECUs.

Although it has no common cultural policy as such, the Community has given practical help for cultural activities. Grants are given to young musicians and cultural workers, and to conservation and restoration centres. A programme of sponsoring translations of works from member states began in 1982 with 20 titles. In 1985 the Community sponsored a 'European Music Year' jointly with the Council of Europe. Under the Community's programme for conserving the European architectural heritage, 12 projects had been approved by the end of 1985.

SOCIAL POLICY

Persistent unemployment (estimated to affect an average of 12% of the Community's labour force in 1986, with considerable regional variations) has given most concern in this field. Funds are allotted to areas most affected by unemployment, to aid redeployment of workers and early retirement schemes. Priority has also been given to the problems of migrant workers from within and outside the Community (numbering about 6m. in 1980), women, the handicapped and the young unemployed. In December 1983 the Council approved a resolution on the promotion of youth employment through reorganization of working time, recruitment subsidies, community work schemes and assistance to young people in establishing new enterprises. The European Social Fund (see p. 152) is the main channel for resources.

Three Community Directives had been adopted by 1979 on equal rights for women in pay, access to employment and social security, and the Commission has undertaken legal proceedings against several member states before the European Court of Justice for infringements. In 1982 the Council adopted the Community Action Programme on the Promotion of Equal Opportunities for Women (1982–85), involving concrete action by national governments (including positive discrimination where necessary) in combating unemployment among women; bringing about equal treatment for men and women in occupational social schemes (e.g. sick pay and pensions) and in self-employed occupations, including agriculture; and legislation on parental leave. A second programme (1986–90) was proposed by the Commission in 1986 to encourage more effective action by member states.

CONSUMER PROTECTION

The Community's second five-year Consumer Protection Programme was approved by the Council in 1981, based on the same principles as those of the first programme (protection of health and safety, with procedures for withdrawal of goods from the market; standardization of rules for food additives and packaging; rules for machines and equipment; authorization procedures for new products). The second programme also includes measures for monitoring the quality and durability of products, improving after-sale service, legal remedies for unsatisfactory goods and services, and the encouragement of consumer associations. The Consumers' Consultative Committee, established in 1973, has 33 members representing European consumers' organizations, and gives opinions on consumer matters. In 1983 the Council approved a proposal for a Community system for the rapid exchange of information whenever a particular consumer product is found to present an immediate risk to consumers. In 1984 and 1985 it adopted directives to protect consumers from misleading advertising and from 'doorstep selling'; on manufacturers' liability for defective products; and on analysis of cosmetics.

ENVIRONMENT POLICY

The second environment Action Programme (1977–81) laid down the following principles for action: reduction of pollution and nuisance, protection of natural resources, organization of relevant research and participation in international efforts to improve the environment. A third Action Programme (1982–86) drawn up in 1981 and approved by the Council in December 1982, laid greater emphasis on prevention, and included the introduction of environmental impact assessment in all forms of planning, improved monitoring techniques and co-operation with developing countries. A fourth Action Programme (1987–92) was proposed by the Commission in 1986, aiming to make environmental protection an integral part of economic and social policies.

By 1985 over 60 directives had been adopted, obliging member states to make regulations on air and water pollution (e.g. 'acid rain' and lead levels in the air), the transport of toxic waste, waste treatment, noise abatement and the protection of natural resources. In 1985 ministers agreed on stricter rules controlling exhaust fumes emitted by cars.

In 1981 the Council adopted a five-year programme (1981–85) for environmental research done on a shared-cost basis by various scientific institutions; the programme included measurements of pollutants, development of 'clean technologies', and climatology. Community expenditure on the programme was expected to amount to 42m. ECUs.

ECONOMIC AND MONETARY UNION

The following objectives for the end of 1973 were agreed by the Council in 1971, as the first of three stages towards union:

the narrowing of exchange rate margins to 2.25%;

creation of a medium-term pool of reserves;

co-ordination of short- and medium-term economic and budgetary policies;

a joint position on international monetary issues;

harmonization of taxes;

creation of the European Monetary Co-operation Fund;

creation of the Regional Development Fund.

The narrowing of exchange margins (the 'snake') came into effect in 1972; but Denmark, France, Ireland, Italy and the United Kingdom later floated their currencies, with only Denmark permanently returning to the arrangement. Sweden and Norway also linked their currencies to the 'snake'; but Sweden withdrew from the arrangement in August 1977, and Norway withdrew in December 1978.

The European Monetary System (EMS) came into force in March 1979, with the aim of creating closer monetary co-operation leading to a zone of monetary stability in Europe. All the Community members except the United Kingdom joined the EMS; Greece did not join on acceding to the Community in 1981, but did so in July 1985, though without participating in the exchange rate mechanism described below. The system works by fixing for each currency a

INTERNATIONAL ORGANIZATIONS
European Communities

central rate in European Currency Units (ECUs, see p. 150), which are based on a 'basket' of national currencies identical to those used to calculate the European unit of account (EUA). A reference rate in relation to other currencies is fixed for each currency, with established fluctuation margins (6% for the Italian lira, 2.25% for others); Central Banks of the participating states intervene when the agreed margin is likely to be exceeded. Each member places 20% of its gold reserves and dollar reserves respectively into the European Monetary Co-operation Fund (see p. 152), and receives a supply of ECUs to regulate Central Bank interventions. Short- and medium-term credit facilities are given to support the balance of payments of member countries. The EMS is put under strain by the wide fluctuations in the exchange rates of non-Community currencies and by the differences in economic development among members, which led to nine realignments of currencies between the system's inception and April 1986. The absence of the pound sterling from the exchange rate mechanism is regarded by the Commission as hindering the EMS from achieving its full potential. In June 1985 measures were adopted by the governors of the Community's central banks, aiming to strengthen the EMS by expanding the use of the ECU, e.g. by allowing international monetary institutions and the central banks of non-member countries to become 'other holders' of ECUs.

A report on the economic situation is presented annually by the Commission, analysing recent developments and short- and medium-term prospects. Economic policy guidelines for the following year are adopted annually by the Council.

External Relations

Although there is as yet no single Community institution dealing with foreign affairs, the Community acts as a single entity in many aspects of international affairs. It has diplomatic relations in its own right with over 100 countries (see p. 135), and with international organizations, and participates as a body in international conferences on trade and development and the 'North-South dialogue'. It has observer status at the United Nations.

In amendments to the Treaty of Rome adopted in 1986 it was laid down that member states should inform and consult each other on foreign policy matters (as was already often the case) and that a secretariat was to be established to co-ordinate foreign policy. During 1986 Community ministers of foreign affairs held a number of urgent consultations, on the alleged involvement of Libya and Syria in international terrorism, and on economic sanctions against South Africa.

Agreements have been signed with numerous countries and groups of countries, allowing for co-operation in trade and other matters. The Community is also a party to 37 International Conventions (in 17 of these to the exclusion of the individual member states).

EUROPE

Association agreements, intended to lead to customs union or possible accession, were signed between the Community and Greece (1961), Turkey (1963), Malta (1970) and Cyprus (1972). The agreements established free access to the Community market for most industrial products and tariff reductions for most agricultural products. Annexed are financial protocols under which the Community provides concessional finance to these countries. Aid to Turkey (which had originally been allocated 600m. ECUs for the period 1981–86) was suspended owing to the violation of human rights there following the coup in 1980.

Trade negotiations with the CMEA (mainly Eastern European) countries were proposed by the Community in 1974, but progress has been confined to a non-preferential agreement with Romania on trade in industrial goods, and an agreement on setting up a Joint Committee with Romania, both concluded in 1980, and to sectoral agreements on textiles, steel and certain agricultural products with Bulgaria, Czechoslovakia, Hungary, Poland and Romania (some of which were in the process of renewal during 1985). A proposal for talks leading to closer co-operation with the Community was made by the CMEA in June 1985; in 1986 there were exchanges of correspondence with the European CMEA countries, and discussions were opened with several of these countries and with the CMEA itself on the normalization of relations and the possibility of more far-reaching agreements.

A co-operation agreement was also signed with Yugoslavia in 1980 (but not ratified until April 1983), allowing tariff-free imports (with 'ceilings' for a number of sensitive items) and Community loans of 200m. ECUs over five years.

The members of EFTA (Austria, Finland, Iceland, Norway, Sweden and Switzerland) each have bilateral Free Trade Agreements with the EEC and the ECSC. The agreements mainly concern the industrial sector. Free trade was introduced by the immediate abolition of quantitative restrictions and the elimination of tariffs in stages. For certain sensitive industrial products, which could have had a disruptive effect on the Community market, the transition period was longer. Customs duties for the majority of products were abolished in July 1977. On 1 January 1984 the last tariff barriers were eliminated, thus establishing full free trade for industrial products.

In 1975 Greece applied for full membership: the Treaty of Accession was signed in May 1979 and came into force on 1 January 1981. Portugal and Spain applied to join the Community in 1977, and the signature of the accession treaties for the two countries took place in June 1985, taking effect in January 1986 following ratification by all the members.

THE MIDDLE EAST

Co-operation agreements came into force with Israel in 1975, with the Maghreb countries (Algeria, Morocco and Tunisia) in 1976 and with the Mashreq countries (Egypt, Jordan, Lebanon and Syria) in 1977, covering free access to the Community market for industrial products, customs preferences for certain agricultural products, and financial aid in the form of grants and loans from the European Investment Bank. A non-preferential co-operation agreement was negotiated with the Yemen Arab Republic in 1984.

In 1984 discussions began with the Gulf Co-operation Council on the possibility of concluding a comprehensive co-operation agreement covering trade, energy and industrial matters. During 1984–86 talks took place in particular on access to European markets for GCC refined petroleum products, after tariffs were imposed by the EEC in 1984 on certain petrochemicals from the region. Contacts with the Arab world in general take place within the framework of the 'Euro-Arab Dialogue', established in 1973 to provide a forum for discussion of economic issues through working groups on specific topics.

LATIN AMERICA

A non-preferential trade agreement was signed with Uruguay in 1974 and economic and commercial co-operation agreements with Mexico in 1975, Brazil in 1980, and the Andean Group in 1983. Negotiations on a five-year co-operation agreement with the members of the Central American Common Market and with Panama were concluded in 1985.

ASIA AND AUSTRALASIA

Non-preferential co-operation agreements were signed with the EEC by India (1973 and 1981), Bangladesh (1976), Sri Lanka (1975) and Pakistan (1976 and 1986). A trade agreement was signed with the People's Republic of China in 1978, and renewed and expanded in May 1985. A co-operation agreement was signed with the countries of the Association of South East Asian Nations (ASEAN) in 1980.

Under the Multi-fibre Arrangement (see GATT, p. 60) the Community negotiates periodically with a number of Asian countries on their textile exports to Europe, allotting quotas to the largest producers (notably Hong Kong and the Republic of Korea).

Numerous discussions have been held since 1981 on the Community's increasing trade deficit with Japan. The Community has requested in particular a greater opening of the Japanese market to European goods and moderation in Japanese exports of certain sensitive products. Between 1981 and 1985 the Japanese Government announced seven series of external economic measures in order to improve access to the Japanese market. Moderation of exports of certain products to the Community was exercised between 1983 and 1985, but in June 1985 European heads of government repeated their concern at the continuing trade deficit with Japan, amounting to some US $12,000m. per year, and at the slow opening of the Japanese market.

Regular consultations are held with Australia at ministerial level. Australia has repeatedly criticized the Community's agricultural export subsidies and their effect on Australia's own agriculture. In 1986 Australia received assurances that the Community would not extend its export subsidies to markets in the Far East, and talks were to be held on improving access to the European market for Australian beef. An agreement was also reached in 1986 on maintaining the Community's imports of butter from New Zealand, despite the surplus of dairy produce within the Community.

CANADA AND THE USA

A framework agreement for commercial and economic co-operation between the Community and Canada was signed in Ottawa in July

INTERNATIONAL ORGANIZATIONS

European Communities

1976, the Community's first non-preferential co-operation agreement concerned not only with trade promotion but also with wide-ranging economic co-operation. It is also the Community's only economic co-operation agreement with an advanced industrial country.

A number of specific agreements have been concluded between the Community and the USA: a co-operation agreement on the peaceful use of atomic energy entered into force in 1959, and agreements on environmental matters and on fisheries came into force in 1974 and 1984 respectively.

The USA has frequently criticized Community policy, in particular the Common Agricultural Policy, which it sees as creating unfair competition for American exports by its system of export refunds and preferential agreements: in 1985, for example, the USA raised its import duties on European pasta products, as a retaliatory measure, alleging that Community agreements with Mediterranean producers of citrus fruit discriminated against US citrus exports. A provisional settlement of the so-called 'pasta war' was reached in August 1986. A similar criticism has been levelled at Community subsidies to the steel industry. In October 1982 the Community and the USA concluded an Arrangement relating to the export of steel products to the USA, but disputes continued over certain categories of steel products of which Community exports to the USA trebled between 1981 and 1984. In October 1985 an agreement was reached on Community exports of steel to the USA for the period to September 1989, covering carbon steels, speciality steel and pipes and tubes. In September 1986 the agreement was extended to cover Community exports of semi-finished steel products.

GENERALIZED PREFERENCES

In July 1971 the Community introduced a scheme of generalized preferences (GSP) in favour of developing countries: in 1986 the list of beneficiaries covered 128 independent states and 22 dependent territories. In line with objectives agreed by UNCTAD (see p. 39), the scheme provides for duty-free entry of all otherwise dutiable manufactured and semi-manufactured industrial products, including textiles—but subject in certain circumstances to preferential limits. Preferences, usually in the form of a tariff reduction, are also offered on some 360 agricultural products. In 1980 the Council agreed to the extension of the scheme for a second decade (1981–90): at the same time it adopted an operational framework for industrial products, which gives individual preferential limits based on the degree of competitiveness of the developing country concerned. Since 1977 the Community has progressively liberalized GSP access for the least-developed countries (numbering 38 in 1986, under the United Nations definition) by according them duty-free entry on all products and by exempting them from virtually all preferential limits.

OVERSEAS AID

The main channel for Community aid to developing countries is the Lomé Convention (see below), but technical and financial aid (about 268m. ECUs in 1985) is also given to about 30 non-associated countries, mainly in Asia and Latin America. To assist victims of the African famine, emergency aid of 143m. ECUs (including food aid worth about 85m. ECUs) was granted to the region during 1984. In November 1985 a rehabilitation plan for the African countries most affected by drought was approved by Community ministers of development, involving grants of 108m. ECUs for the following year.

THE LOMÉ CONVENTION

The First Lomé Convention (Lomé I), which came into force on 1 April 1976, replaced the Yaoundé Conventions and the Arusha Agreement (under which some of the former overseas possessions of France and the United Kingdom retained privileged access to the European market, together with financial assistance). Lomé I was designed to provide a new framework of co-operation, taking into account the varying needs of developing countries. The Second Lomé Convention came into force on 1 January 1981. The Third Lomé Convention was signed in December 1984, and came into force on 1 March 1985. In October 1986 66 African, Caribbean and Pacific (ACP) states were parties to the Convention.

ACP–EEC INSTITUTIONS

Council of Ministers: one Minister from each signatory state; one Co-chairman from each of the two groups; meets annually.

Committee of Ambassadors: one Ambassador from each signatory state; Chairmanship alternates between the two groups; meets at least every six months.

Joint Assembly: EEC and ACP are equally represented; attended by delegates of the ACP countries and members of the European Parliament; one Co-chairman from each of the two groups; meets twice a year.

Centre for the Development of Industry: 28 rue de l'Industrie, 1040 Brussels, Belgium; tel. 513-41-00; telex 61427; f. 1977 to encourage investment in the ACP states by providing contracts and advice, holding promotion meetings, and helping to finance feasibility studies; Dir Dr ISAAC ADEDAYO AKINRELE.

Technical Centre for Agricultural and Rural Co-operation: De Rietkampen Galvinistraat 19, Ede, Netherlands; Dir ASSOUMOU MBA.

ACP INSTITUTIONS

ACP Council of Ministers.

ACP Committee of Ambassadors.

ACP Secretariat: ACP House, ave Georges Henri, Brussels, Belgium; Sec.-Gen. EDWIN W. CARRINGTON.

THE ACP STATES

Angola	Madagascar
Antigua and Barbuda	Malawi
Bahamas	Mali
Barbados	Mauritania
Belize	Mauritius
Benin	Mozambique
Botswana	Niger
Burkina Faso	Nigeria
Burundi	Papua New Guinea
Cameroon	Rwanda
Cape Verde	Saint Christopher and Nevis
Central African Republic	Saint Lucia
Chad	Saint Vincent and the Grenadines
Comoros	São Tomé and Príncipe
Congo	Senegal
Djibouti	Seychelles
Dominica	Sierra Leone
Equatorial Guinea	Solomon Islands
Ethiopia	Somalia
Fiji	Sudan
Gabon	Suriname
The Gambia	Swaziland
Ghana	Tanzania
Grenada	Togo
Guinea	Tonga
Guinea-Bissau	Trinidad and Tobago
Guyana	Tuvalu
Ivory Coast	Uganda
Jamaica	Vanuatu
Kenya	Western Samoa
Kiribati	Zaire
Lesotho	Zambia
Liberia	Zimbabwe

FUNCTIONS

In the First Lomé Convention the Community committed about 3,500m. ECUs for aid and investment in developing countries. Provision was made for over 99% of ACP (mainly agricultural) exports to enter the EEC market duty free, while certain products which compete directly with Community agriculture, such as sugar, were given preferential treatment but not free access. The Stabex (Stabilization of Export Earnings) scheme was designed to help developing countries to withstand fluctuations in the price of their agricultural products, by paying compensation for lost export earnings. The Convention also provided for Community funds to help finance projects in ACP countries through the European Development Fund and the European Investment Bank.

The Second Lomé Convention, which came into force on 1 January 1981, to run until 28 February 1985, envisaged Community expenditure of 5,530m. ECUs: it extended some of the provisions of Lomé I, and introduced new fields of co-operation. One of the most important innovations was a scheme (Sysmin), similar to Stabex, to safeguard exports of mineral products. Other chapters concerned new rules on investment protection, migrant labour, fishing, sea transport, co-operation in energy policy and agricultural development, and procedures to speed the administration of aid.

INTERNATIONAL ORGANIZATIONS — European Communities

Negotiations for a Third Lomé Convention began in October 1983. The ACP states expressed dissatisfaction with the current arrangements, particularly the inadequacy of Stabex funds (which had been unable to cover more than 50% of the amounts requested during 1979–83) and the presence of non-tariff barriers which restricted their access to European markets.

The Third Lomé Convention, which came into force on 1 March 1985 for a five-year period (to expire on 28 February 1990), made commitments of 8,500m. ECUs, including loans of 1,100m. ECUs from the European Investment Bank. Innovations included an emphasis on agriculture and fisheries, and measures to combat desertification; assistance for rehabilitating existing industries or sectoral improvements, rather than new individual capital projects; improvements in the efficiency of the Stabex system (now covering a list of 48 agricultural products) and of Sysmin; simplification of the rules of origin of products exported to the EEC; an undertaking to promote private investment; co-operation in transport and communications, particularly shipping; and cultural and social co-operation.

COMMITMENTS MADE UNDER THE LOMÉ CONVENTION (million ECUs)*

	1985	1976–85
Development of production	486.7	2,845
Industrialization	231.4	1,179
Tourism	5.6	30
Rural production	249.7	1,636
Economic infrastructure, transport and communications	78.9	1,354
Social development	84.1	962
Education and training	33.7	491
Health	14.0	136
Hydraulics, environment	36.4	335
Trade promotion	8.2	82
Emergency aid	82.6	311
Stabex	32.0	1,011
Other	19.6	20
Total	792.1	6,585

* Estimated.
Source: Directorate-General for Development.

Finance

THE COMMUNITY BUDGET

Until 1970 the Community's revenue was derived from financial contributions by member states, based on their gross national product (GNP). In 1970 the Commission was empowered to begin raising money from 'own resources': member states were to collect on the Community's behalf levies on the imports of agricultural produce, and customs duties on products covered by the common customs tariff. A proportion (not to exceed 1%) of revenue gained from value-added tax (VAT) on goods and services was to be transferred to the Community.

The replacement of financial contributions by revenue from own resources did not take place on 1 January 1975, as planned, and only in 1980 did all members transfer VAT own resources to the Community budget. Between 1981 and 1986 Greece was allowed to defer application of the common VAT system and to pay a financial contribution based on GNP. Portugal was to be allowed to do the same for three years from 1 January 1986, while Spain was to pay VAT own resources from that date.

Under the system of financial contributions, there was, theoretically at least, no limit on the size of the budget. Under the own resources system expenditure is limited by the revenue available. Indeed, the revenue from the different own resources does not necessarily grow from one year to another in the same way as needs for expenditure. It therefore proved even more necessary than before to ensure accuracy in estimating revenue and expenditure and efficiency in implementing the budget. The creation of new own resources requires approval by the national legislatures.

Under this system it is possible for an unfair proportion of the budget to be paid by certain countries, particularly since over 60% is allocated to agriculture, to the disadvantage of those countries with a relatively small agricultural sector, such as the United Kingdom. In 1980 the Council adopted a three-year plan to reduce the British contribution to the budget by making refunds in the form of special investments to benefit disadvantaged areas.

Measures for the reform of the Community budget became urgently necessary in 1983, when a supplementary budget for 1983 and the preliminary draft budget for 1984 envisaged the exhaustion of almost all the available own resources. In June 1984, after a number of unsuccessful attempts, the European Council reached the 'Fontainebleau Agreement' on the amount of compensation to be granted to the United Kingdom, to reduce its contribution to the Community budget: a lump-sum of 1,000m. ECUs was to be paid in 1985, while in subsequent years the United Kingdom was to receive 66% of the difference between what it pays in VAT and what it receives from the Community budget. Agreement was also reached on the creation of new resources by raising the VAT 'ceiling' from 1% to 1.4% (with a possible further increase to 1.6% in 1988), and on future budgetary and financial discipline (including curbs on agricultural spending). A supplementary budget for 1984 increased appropriations for payments by 1,887m. ECUs, of which 1,003m. was to be financed by 'reimbursable advances' from member states. Most of this extra financing was for the agricultural sector. It brought total appropriations for payments in 1984 to 27,248.63m. ECUs.

The draft budget for 1985 (giving appropriations of 28,307m. ECUs for commitments and 26,133m. ECUs for payments, and envisaging supplementary funding from October if necessary) was rejected in December 1984 by the European Parliament, on the grounds that it was not sufficient for a 12-month period. As a result, expenditure during the first half of 1985 had to be calculated in 'provisional twelfths'—monthly payments each equivalent to one-twelfth of the previous year's expenditure. A budget for 1985 was finally approved by Parliament in June, with appropriations for commitments of 30,616m. ECUs and appropriations for payments of 28,433m. ECUs. The difference between revenue and expenditure was to be met by another 'one-off' payment of some 2,300m. ECUs by member states.

It was hoped that the raising of the VAT 'ceiling' to 1.4%, with effect from 1 January 1986 (subject to ratification by all the national legislatures), would increase revenue sufficiently to avoid a recurrence of the budget crises of previous years. In the event, however, the 1986 budget was the subject of a complex dispute. In December 1985 the European Parliament rejected the budget approved by the Council of Ministers, on the grounds that it failed to meet legal commitments to the Community's regional and social funds and to the new members, Portugal and Spain: Parliament approved a budget of 35,121m. ECUs for commitments and 33,315m. ECUs for payments, which was then adopted by the Commission. In July, however, the European Court of Justice declared this budget illegal, ruling that Parliament had exceeded its powers by approving a budget without the approval of the Council of Ministers. A new budget for 1986 was then drawn up urgently, and approved by both the Council and Parliament: it comprised commitments of 36,267m. ECUs and payments of 35,125m. ECUs—considerably more than the amounts previously disputed. This increase had become necessary for three principal reasons: the ever-increasing cost of the Common Agricultural Policy, particularly the growth in export subsidies as a result of the falling value of the US dollar against the ECU; the backlog of commitments to the social and regional funds; and the budget rebate owed to the United Kingdom, which was higher than originally calculated. The same problems were expected to affect negotiations for the 1987 budget, which began in July 1986: technological research and overseas aid were expected to be the principal targets for spending cuts, and, as in 1986, agricultural market support was likely to absorb over 60% of expenditure.

PROPOSED REVENUE (ECUs)

	1987*
Agricultural levies	2,078,400,000
Sugar/isoglucose levies	1,218,700,000
Customs duties	9,761,500,000
Value-added taxes	23,132,495,880
Financial contributions	209,108,576
Miscellaneous revenue	277,201,808
Total	36,677,406,264

* Preliminary draft budget.

INTERNATIONAL ORGANIZATIONS

European Communities

PROPOSED EXPENDITURE BY SECTOR (ECUs)

	Appropriations for commitments 1986*	Appropriations for commitments 1987 preliminary draft	Appropriations for payments 1986*	Appropriations for payments 1987 preliminary draft
Support for agricultural markets				
EAGGF Guarantee	21,927,254,929	22,960,800,000	21,927,254,929	22,960,800,000
Structural policies				
EAGGF Guidance	894,530,721	1,000,000,000	838,708,260	895,000,000
Specific agricultural measures	69,397,818	73,229,000	66,097,818	71,182,000
Fisheries	243,354,654	260,000,000	192,124,654	221,000,000
Regional Fund	3,176,500,000	3,319,000,000	2,373,000,000	2,495,000,000
Mediterranean programme	260,000,000	245,000,000	133,000,000	240,000,000
Miscellaneous regional measures	32,176,500	29,814,000	44,876,500	35,771,000
Transport	75,840,000	33,300,000	57,840,000	34,000,000
Social Fund	2,370,500,000	2,592,000,000	2,533,000,000	2,589,000,000
Miscellaneous social measures	66,520,463	70,628,400	63,050,463	68,894,720
Education and culture	36,454,125	82,661,000	36,454,125	80,661,000
Environment and consumers	24,450,325	34,600,000	21,750,325	35,105,000
Total	7,249,724,606	7,740,232,400	6,359,902,145	6,765,613,720
Research, energy and industry				
Energy	160,307,000	124,240,000	45,920,000	87,640,000
Research and investment	664,374,250	1,134,140,000	628,656,250	822,000,000
Information and innovation	17,536,250	21,000,000	18,786,250	25,000,000
Industry and internal market	75,051,500	180,050,000	65,438,500	120,000,000
Total	917,269,000	1,459,430,000	758,801,000	1,054,750,000
Refunds and reserves				
Refunds to the Member States	1,239,920,000	1,305,860,000	1,239,920,000	1,305,860,000
VAT/GNP refunds	1,809,081,437	1,279,000,274	1,809,081,437	1,279,000,274
1984 advances	250,854,655	250,854,655	250,854,655	250,854,655
Reserves	5,000,000	700,000,000	5,000,000	35,000,000
Total	3,304,856,092	2,905,714,929	3,304,856,092	2,870,714,929
Development co-operation and non-member countries				
Food aid	698,610,000	545,700,000	553,277,100	620,400,000
Co-operation with non-associated developing countries	297,930,750	272,620,000	223,495,250	289,020,000
Specific and exceptional measures	118,735,050	116,050,000	89,235,050	112,550,000
Co-operation with Mediterranean countries	81,446,000	211,700,000	238,035,800	162,000,000
Miscellaneous co-operation measures	67,500,000	75,700,000	67,500,000	75,700,000
Total	1,246,221,800	1,221,770,000	1,171,543,200	1,259,670,000
Staff and administrative appropriations				
Commission	1,047,926,425	1,163,812,805	1,047,926,425	1,163,812,805
Other institutions	555,266,888	602,044,810	555,266,888	602,044,810
Total	1,603,193,313	1,765,857,615	1,603,193,313	1,765,857,615
Grand total	36,266,519,740	38,053,804,944	35,125,550,679	36,677,406,264

* Including supplementary and amending budget (July 1986).

THE EUROPEAN CURRENCY UNIT

With the creation of the European Monetary System (EMS) (see p. 147) a new monetary unit, the European Currency Unit (ECU) was adopted. Its value and composition were identical to those of the European Unit of Account (EUA) already used in the administrative fields of the Community. The ECU is a composite monetary unit, in which the relative value of each currency is determined by the gross national product and the volume of trade of each country. In September 1984 the Greek drachma was incorporated for the first time, and the amounts of other currencies were altered. The composition of the ECU thus became (with previous amounts in brackets):

- 3.71 Belgian francs (3.66)
- 0.219 Danish krone (0.217)
- 1.31 French francs (1.15)
- 0.719 Deutsche Mark (0.828)
- 1.15 Greek drachmae
- 0.00871 Irish pound (0.00759)
- 140 Italian lire (109)
- 0.14 Luxembourg franc (0.14)
- 0.256 Netherlands guilder (0.286)
- 0.0878 pound sterling (0.0885)

The rate of the ECU in terms of any currency is equal to the sum of the equivalents in that currency of the amounts of each of the above currencies.

The ECU, which has been assigned the function of the unit of account used by the European Monetary Co-operation Fund, is also used:

- as the denominator for the exchange rate mechanism;
- as the basis for the divergence indicator;
- as the denominator for operations in both the intervention and the credit mechanisms;
- as a means of settlement between monetary authorities of the European Community.

From April 1979 onwards the ECU has also been used as the unit of account for the purposes of the common agricultural policy. Since 1981 it has replaced the EUA in the general budget of the Community; the activities of the European Development Fund under the Lomé Convention; the balance sheets and loan operations of the European Investment Bank; and the activities of the European Coal and Steel Community. It is now the only unit of account used in the Community.

The ECU's value in national currencies is calculated and published daily. Its value on 30 September 1986 was US $1.02959.

SPECIAL FUNDS

The European Agricultural Guidance and Guarantee Fund, the European Regional Development Fund and the European Social

INTERNATIONAL ORGANIZATIONS

European Communities

Fund are part of the General Budget and are financed by the Community's own resources.

EUROPEAN AGRICULTURAL FUND

Created in 1962, the European Agricultural Guidance and Guarantee Fund (or FEOGA as it is known after its French initials) is administered by the Commission. The Guidance Section contributes credits towards the structural reform of agriculture. Proposed appropriations for this section in the 1987 preliminary draft budget amounted to 1,000m. ECUs. The Guarantee Section, under which a large proportion of the Community's budget is spent, intervenes to regularize the internal market, and provides export refunds which compensate for the difference between Community and world market prices. Guarantee appropriations for 1985 amounted to 19,883m. ECUs of which about 33% was for dairy products, 16% for fruit and vegetables (including wine and tobacco), and 12% for cereals. The proposed amount for guarantee appropriations in 1986 was 21,053m. ECUs and in the preliminary draft budget for 1987 the amount was 22,961m. ECUs.

EUROPEAN REGIONAL DEVELOPMENT FUND

Payments began in autumn 1975. The Fund is intended to compensate for the unequal rate of development in different regions of the Community, by encouraging investment and improving infrastructure in 'problem regions'. Initially, funds were spent entirely according to a system of national quotas, but in 1979 an additional non-quota section was adopted, allowing the financing of specific Community measures to aid, for example, frontier areas or different areas affected by the same problem. In 1984 agreement was reached on a revision of the Fund, whereby a larger proportion (up to 15%) could be allocated to supra-national programmes, initiated by the Commission but subject to a veto by the governments concerned. In addition, more flexible national quotas were drawn up, with upper and lower limits. In 1986 Italy had the highest quota (between 21.62% and 28.79%), followed by Spain (17.97%–23.93%), the United Kingdom (14.50%–19.31%), Portugal (10.66%–14.20%) and Greece (8.36%–10.64%). During 1985 grants of 2,321.4m. ECUs were made for investment projects under the national quota section, and special programmes under the non-quota section received 171.8m. ECUs.

EUROPEAN SOCIAL FUND

The Fund was established in 1960, with the aim of improving employment opportunities by assisting training and workers' mobility. From 1972 there was a new emphasis on job creation schemes as well as on training. Under new rules approved in 1983 the Fund was to increase its aid for the employment of young people, reserving 75% of its resources for this purpose, while a guaranteed minimum of 40% was to be spent in the Community's poorest regions (Greece, the French Overseas Departments, Ireland, southern Italy, and Northern Ireland). Areas of high unemployment and industrial decline were also to be given priority, while about 5% of aid was to be used for pilot projects experimenting with new training methods, job creation schemes, or job-sharing projects.

Appropriations committed by the Fund in 1985 amounted to 2,188m. ECUs, of which about 27% was for Italy, 24% for the United Kingdom, 17% for France and 12% for Ireland. Eligible applications exceeded available resources by over 99%, and from 1986 stricter rules were to be applied for selection of suitable schemes.

EUROPEAN DEVELOPMENT FUND

This fund administers the Community's overseas financial aid, under the terms of the Lomé Conventions (see p. 149). Under the Third Convention, EDF funds are allotted under five headings: grants, special loans, risk capital formation aid, the Stabex scheme (guaranteeing minimum export earnings) and a special scheme for protecting mineral producers (Sysmin).

NEW COMMUNITY INSTRUMENT FOR BORROWING AND LENDING

In October 1978 a borrowing and lending instrument was set up to raise funds for financing structural investment projects to reflect the Community's priorities, particularly for energy, industrial conversion and infrastructure. Funds are deposited with the European Investment Bank, which makes loans on the Community's behalf (see table, p. 143). Loans under the NCI totalling 883.7m. ECUs were signed in 1985; of this amount, infrastructure projects accounted for 26% and the development of small and medium-sized businesses for 71%. Total loans granted since 1979 came to 4,960m. ECUs, of which Italy was the largest recipient with 54%.

EUROPEAN MONETARY CO-OPERATION FUND

The Fund was created in 1973 to administer the Community's special narrow margin currency system (the 'snake'), which was replaced by the European Monetary System (EMS) in March 1979. The Fund still has the function of keeping account of the short-term borrowings made by national Central Banks to support currencies. It is also intended, under the EMS, to administer the pooling of the Community's gold and dollar reserves, and eventually to become a European Monetary Fund.

PUBLICATIONS*

General Report on the Activities of the European Communities (annually).

Bulletin of the European Communities (11 a year).

The Courier (every 2 months, on ACP-EEC affairs).

European Economy (3 a year, with supplements).

Information sheets, background reports and statistical documents.

* Most publications are available in all the official languages of the Community. They are obtainable from the Office for Official Publications of the European Communities, 5 rue du Commerce, 2985 Luxembourg; tel. 49 00 81; telex 1324.

EUROPEAN FREE TRADE ASSOCIATION—EFTA

Address: 9-11 rue de Varembé, 1211 Geneva 20, Switzerland.
Telephone: (022) 349000.
Telex: 22660.

Established in 1960, EFTA aims to bring about free trade between member and other countries in industrial goods and an expansion of trade in agricultural goods.

MEMBERS

Austria
Finland*
Iceland
Norway
Sweden
Switzerland

* Finland, formerly an associate member of EFTA, became a full member on 1 January 1986. Portugal left EFTA when it joined the European Community on 1 January 1986.

Organization

(October 1986)

COUNCIL

Council delegations are led by Ministers (normally twice a year) or by the Heads of National Delegations (usually every other week). The Chair is held for six months by each country in turn.

Heads of Permanent Delegations:
Austria: G. REISCH
Finland: O. MENNANDER
Iceland: H. HAFSTEIN
Norway: M. HUSLID
Sweden: L. ANELL
Switzerland: P.-L. GIRARD

EFTA STANDING COMMITTEES

Committee of Trade Experts.
Committee of Origin and Customs Experts.
Committee on Technical Barriers to Trade.
Economic Committee.
Consultative Committee.
Committee of Members of Parliament of the EFTA Countries.
Budget Committee.
Economic Development Committee.
Committee on Agriculture and Fisheries.

SECRETARIAT

Secretary-General: PER KLEPPE (Norway).
Deputy Secretary-General: NORBERT FAUSTENHAMMER (Austria).

Activities

EFTA unites in one free trade area the markets of its member countries, as a means of working towards a sustained growth in economic activity and a continuous improvement in living standards in EFTA countries, and of contributing to the growth of world trade.

The creation of a single market including all the countries in Western Europe was the ultimate objective of EFTA when it was created in 1960. Its first target, the creation of free trade in industrial goods between its members, was achieved by the end of 1966.

Each of the members is also linked with the European Communities, through agreements which established free trade in most industrial goods between them from 1 July 1977. The last restrictions on free industrial trade were abolished from 1 January 1984.

In 1976, while Portugal was a member, EFTA set up the Industrial Development Fund for Portugal to assist the development of the Portuguese economy and in particular the modernization or creation of small and medium-sized industries. Although Portugal left EFTA at the end of 1985 to join the European Community, it was decided to maintain the Fund in operation to the end of the 25-year period originally foreseen. The Joint EFTA-Yugoslavia Committee, established in 1978, aims to expand trade and industrial co-operation with Yugoslavia.

EFTA's main tasks are to ensure the efficient working of free trade between its members, and to use the framework of EFTA for consultations or co-ordination between members on matters connected with their free trade agreements with the European Community, which to a large extent are identical. It also encourages co-operation between its members, not only in trade matters but also in other economic questions, particularly those which are dealt with by large international organizations: EFTA countries, each of them relatively small, often have similar interests which can be furthered by their mutual support.

EFTA TRADE, 1985
Imports, c.i.f. (US $ million)

	EFTA	EEC	USA	Japan	Eastern Europe	World*
Importing Country:						
Austria	1,576.4	12,942.7	776.0	683.9	2,212.2	20,829.6
Finland	2,268.9	5,112.5	714.8	699.5	3,111.0	13,233.4
Iceland	178.6	476.8	61.5	39.2	79.3	904.1
Norway	3,578.6	7,137.1	1,043.9	893.6	403.6	14,523.0
Sweden	4,482.9	15,974.6	2,402.8	1,404.2	1,482.8	28,547.7
Switzerland	1,985.1	21,729.1	1,808.3	1,216.3	859.6	30,728.6
Total EFTA	14,070.4	63,372.7	6,807.3	4,936.8	8,148.5	108,776.3

* Including OPEC member countries (total $3,017.4m.), newly-industrializing countries (total $4,116.6m.) and others (total $2,961.9m.)

INTERNATIONAL ORGANIZATIONS — European Free Trade Association

Exports, f.o.b. (US $ million)

	EFTA	EEC	USA	Japan	Eastern Europe	World*
Exporting Country:						
Austria	1,796.6	9,596.7	798.8	161.6	1,884.9	17,107.7
Finland	2,658.9	4,949.6	847.5	195.3	3,159.2	13,616.9
Iceland	69.8	397.5	219.9	40.3	63.8	813.8
Norway	2,249.6	12,966.4	956.1	236.3	162.0	18,666.2
Sweden	5,858.0	14,839.3	3,566.0	411.0	776.0	30,467.1
Switzerland	2,064.0	14,433.7	2,843.0	874.3	861.0	27,446.8
Total EFTA	14,696.9	57,183.3	9,231.2	1,918.9	6,906.9	108,118.6

* Including OPEC member countries (total $4,363.0m.), newly-industrializing countries (total $4,783.4m.), and others (total $6,235.6m.).

INTRA-EFTA TRADE, 1985
Total Exports, f.o.b. (US $ million)

	Austria	Finland	Iceland	Norway	Sweden	Switzerland	Total EFTA
Exporting Country:							
Austria	—	148.4	4.2	172.7	317.2	1,154.1	1,796.6
Finland	95.3	—	19.9	568.5	1,781.3	193.9	2,658.9
Iceland	0.8	16.4	—	17.3	9.3	26.1	69.8
Norway	117.8	294.6	66.2	—	1,640.9	130.0	2,249.6
Sweden	337.0	1,719.3	69.4	3,188.5	—	543.8	5,858.0
Switzerland	1,063.9	218.3	8.4	230.7	542.7	—	2,064.0
Total EFTA	1,614.9	2,397.0	168.1	4,177.6	4,291.4	2,047.9	14,696.9

FINANCE

Net budget for 1986/87: 12.2m. Swiss francs. The basis for contributions, determined by reference to the GNP at factor cost of the EFTA countries, was as follows: Austria 17.00%, Finland 13.20%, Iceland 1.65%, Norway 14.35%, Sweden 25.25%, Switzerland 28.55%.

PUBLICATIONS

EFTA Bulletin (4 a year).
EFTA Trade (annually).
EFTA Annual Report.
Annual Report of EFTA Industrial Development Fund for Portugal.

THE FRANC ZONE

Address: Direction Générale des Services Etrangers (Service des Relations avec la Zone Franc), Banque de France, 39 rue Croix-des-Petits-Champs, BP 140-01, Paris Cedex 01, France.
Telephone: (1) 42-92-31-46.
Telex: 220932.

MEMBERS

Benin	French Republic*
Burkina Faso	Gabon
Cameroon	Ivory Coast
Central African Republic	Mali
Chad	Niger
Comoros	Senegal
Congo	Togo
Equatorial Guinea	

* Metropolitan France, Mayotte, St Pierre and Miquelon and the Overseas Departments and Territories.

The Franc Zone embraces all those countries and groups of countries whose currencies are linked with the French franc at a fixed rate of exchange and who agree to hold their reserves mainly in the form of French francs and to effect their exchange on the Paris market. Each of these countries or groups of countries has its own central issuing Bank and its currency is freely convertible into French francs. This monetary union is based on agreements concluded between France and each country or group of countries.

Apart from Guinea and Mauritania, all of the countries that formerly comprised French West and Equatorial Africa are members of the Franc Zone. The former West and Equatorial African territories are still grouped within the currency areas that existed before independence, each group having its own currency issued by a central bank.

Mali withdrew from the Franc Zone in 1962, setting up its own currency, the Mali franc, and its own issuing Bank. Mali rejoined the Franc Zone in 1968, and the Mali franc returned to full convertibility with the French franc: agreement was reached on the establishment of a central issuing bank, jointly administered by France and Mali, until Mali rejoined UMOA (see below) in 1984.

A number of states left the Franc Zone during the period 1958–73: Guinea, Tunisia, Morocco, Algeria, Mauritania and Madagascar.

The Comoros, formerly a French Overseas Territory, did not join the Franc Zone on achieving independence in 1975. However, francs CFA were used as the currency of the new state and the Institut d'émission des Comores continued to function as a Franc Zone organization. In 1976 the Comoros formally assumed membership. In July 1981 the Banque centrale des Comores replaced the Institut d'émission des Comores, establishing its own currency, the Comoros franc.

Equatorial Guinea, a former Spanish colony, joined the Franc Zone in January 1985.

WEST AFRICA

Union monétaire ouest-africaine—UMOA (West African Monetary Union): established by Treaty of November 1973, entered into force 1974; comprises Benin, Burkina Faso, Ivory Coast, Niger, Senegal (all parts of former French West Africa) and Togo; Mali, which left the Union in 1962 after creating its own currency, rejoined in June 1984.

Banque centrale des états de l'Afrique de l'ouest—BCEAO: ave du Barachois, BP 3108, Dakar, Senegal; tel. 21 16 15; telex 3154; f. 1955 under the title 'Institut d'émission de l'AOF et du Togo' and re-created under present title by a treaty between the West African states and a convention with France in 1962, both of which were modified in 1973; central issuing bank for the members of UMOA. Gov. ABDOULAYE FADIGA (Ivory Coast); Dep. Gov. BOUBACAR AMADOU HAMA (Burkina Faso); Sec.-Gen. JACQUES DIOUF. Publs *Annual Report, Notes d'Information et Statistiques* (monthly).

Banque ouest-africaine de développement—BOAD: BP 1172, Lomé, Togo; tel. 21-42-44; telex 5289; f. 1973 by heads of member states of UMOA, to promote the balanced development of member states and the economic integration of West Africa; capital (authorized) 100,000m. francs CFA, (subscribed) 73,500m. francs CFA. Mems: Benin, Burkina Faso, Ivory Coast, Mali, Niger, Senegal, Togo. Pres. ABOU BAKAR BABA-MOUSSA; Vice-Pres. HAROUNA BEMBELLO; Sec.-Gen. (vacant). Publ. *Rapport Annuel.*

CENTRAL AFRICA

Union douanière et économique de l'Afrique centrale—UDEAC (Customs and Economic Union of Central Africa): BP 969, Bangui, Central African Republic; tel. 61-09-22; telex 5254; established by the Brazzaville Treaty in 1964 (revised in 1974); comprises: Cameroon, Central African Republic, Congo, Equatorial Guinea and Gabon; Chad left the Union in 1968, retaining observer status until it rejoined in December 1984. As well as forming a customs union, with free trade between members and a common external tariff for imports from other countries, UDEAC has a common code for investment policy and a Solidarity Fund to counteract regional disparities of wealth and economic development. Plans for four community industrial projects were drawn up in 1977: a petrochemicals complex in Gabon, a chemical complex in Congo, a pharmaceuticals laboratory and watchmaking factory in the Central African Republic, and an aluminium plant in Cameroon, none of which was under way by early 1985. UDEAC sponsored the first Central African Industrial Forum, to be held in December 1985, aiming to promote industrial investment by the European Community and other industrialized nations. Budget (1985) 2,432m. francs CFA. Sec.-Gen. AMBROISE FOALEM (Cameroon).

At the summit meeting in December 1981, UDEAC leaders agreed in principle to form an economic community of Central African states (Communauté économique des états d'Afrique centrale—CEEAC), to include UDEAC members and Burundi, Rwanda, São Tomé and Príncipe and Zaire. CEEAC began operations in 1985 (see p. 217).

Banque des états de l'Afrique centrale: BP 1917, Yaoundé, Cameroon; f. 1973 as the central bank of issue of Cameroon, the Central African Republic, Chad, Congo, Equatorial Guinea and Gabon. Gov. CASIMIR OYE MBA (Gabon); Vice-Gov. JEAN-EDOUARD SATHOUD (Congo). Publs *Rapport annuel, Etudes et statistiques* (monthly).

Banque de développement des états de l'Afrique centrale: BP 1177, Brazzaville, Congo; tel. 81 02 12; telex 5306; f. 1976; capital 41,880m. francs CFA (from Nov. 1983); non-African shareholders comprise France, the Federal Republic of Germany and Kuwait; Dir-Gen. CÉLESTIN LEROY GAOMBALET.

CENTRAL ISSUING BANKS

Banque des états de l'Afrique centrale: see above.
Banque centrale des états de l'Afrique de l'ouest: see above.
Banque centrale des Comores: BP 405, Moroni, Comoros; tel. 73-10-02; telex 213; f. 1981; Dir-Gen. MOHAMED HALIFA.
Institut d'émission des départements d'outre-mer: Cité du Retiro, 35/37 rue Boissy d'Anglas, 75379 Paris Cedex 08, France; tel. 42-66-93-45; issuing authority for the French Overseas Departments and the French Overseas Collectivité Territoriale of St Pierre and Miquelon; Pres. JACQUES WAITZENEGGER; Dir-Gen. YVES ROLAND-BILLECART.
Institut d'émission d'outre-mer: Cité du Retiro, 35/37 rue Boissy d'Anglas, 75379 Paris Cedex 08, France; tel. 42-66-93-45; issuing authority for the French Overseas Territories and the French Overseas Collectivité Territoriale of Mayotte; Pres. JACQUES WAITZENEGGER; Dir-Gen. YVES ROLAND-BILLECART.
Banque de France: 1 rue de la Vrillière, Paris, France; f. 1800; issuing authority for Metropolitan France; Gov. MICHEL CAMDESSUS; Dep. Govs JACQUES WAITZENEGGER, PHILIPPE LAGAYETTE.

EXCHANGE REGULATIONS

Currencies of the Franc Zone are freely convertible into the French franc at a fixed rate, through 'Operations Accounts' established by agreements concluded between the French Treasury and the individual issuing Banks. It is backed fully by the French Treasury, which also provides the issuing Banks with overdraft facilities.

INTERNATIONAL ORGANIZATIONS

The monetary reserves of the CFA countries are normally held in French francs in the French Treasury. However, the Banque centrale des états de l'Afrique de l'ouest and the Banque des états de l'Afrique centrale are authorized to hold up to 35% of their foreign exchange holdings in currencies other than the franc. Exchange is effected on the Paris market. Part of the reserves earned by richer members can be used to offset the deficits incurred by poorer countries.

Regulations drawn up in 1967 provided for the free convertibility of currency with that of countries outside the Franc Zone. Restrictions were removed on the import and export of CFA banknotes, although some capital transfers are subject to approval by the governments concerned.

When the French government instituted exchange control to protect the French franc following the May 1968 crisis, other Franc Zone countries were obliged to take similar action in order to maintain free convertibility within the Franc Zone. The franc CFA was devalued following devaluation of the French franc in August 1969. Since March 1973 the French authorities have ceased to maintain the franc–US dollar rate within previously agreed margins, and, as a result, the value of the franc CFA has fluctuated on foreign exchange markets in line with the French franc.

CURRENCIES OF THE FRANC ZONE

French franc (= 100 centimes): used in Metropolitan France, in the Overseas Departments of Guadeloupe, French Guiana, Martinique, Réunion, and in the Overseas Collectivités Territoriales of St Pierre and Miquelon and Mayotte.

1 franc CFA=2 French centimes. CFA stands for Communauté financière africaine in the West African area and for Coopération financière en Afrique centrale in the Central African area. Used in the monetary areas of West and Central Africa respectively.

1 Comoros franc=2 French centimes. Used in the Comoros, where it replaced the franc CFA in 1981.

1 franc CFP=5.5 French centimes. Used in New Caledonia, French Polynesia and the Wallis and Futuna Islands.

French Economic Aid

France's ties with the African Franc Zone countries involve not only monetary arrangements, but also include comprehensive French assistance in the forms of budget support, foreign aid, technical assistance and subsidies on commodity exports.

Official French financial aid and technical assistance to developing countries is administered by the following agencies:

Fonds d'aide et de coopération—FAC: 20 rue Monsieur, 75007 Paris, France; in 1959 FAC took over from FIDES (Fonds d'investissement pour le développement économique et social) the administration of subsidies and loans from the French government to the former French African states. FAC is administered by the Ministry of Co-operation, which allocates budgetary funds to it.

Caisse centrale de coopération économique—CCCE: Cité du Retiro, 35/37 rue Boissy d'Anglas, 75379 Paris Cedex 08, France; tel. (1) 42-66-93-66; telex 212632; f. 1941, and given present name in 1958. French development bank which lends money to member states and former member states of the Franc Zone and several other states, and executes the financial operations of the FAC. Loans approved in 1985 totalled US $675m. Dir-Gen. Yves Roland-Billecart.

Bureau de liaison des agents de coopération technique: 19 rue Barbet de Jouy, 75007 Paris, France.

INTER-AMERICAN DEVELOPMENT BANK—IDB

Address: 1300 New York Ave, NW, Washington, DC 20577, USA.

The Bank was founded in 1959 to promote the individual and collective development of regional developing member countries through the financing of economic and social development projects and the provision of technical assistance; helps to implement the objectives of the Inter-American system. Membership was increased in 1976 and 1977 to include countries in other world regions.

MEMBERS

Argentina	Finland	Norway
Austria	France	Panama
Bahamas	Germany, Federal	Paraguay
Barbados	Republic	Peru
Belgium	Guatemala	Portugal
Bolivia	Guyana	Spain
Brazil	Haiti	Suriname
Canada	Honduras	Sweden
Chile	Israel	Switzerland
Colombia	Italy	Trinidad and Tobago
Costa Rica	Jamaica	United Kingdom
Denmark	Japan	USA
Dominican Republic	Mexico	Uruguay
Ecuador	Netherlands	Venezuela
El Salvador	Nicaragua	Yugoslavia

Organization
(October 1986)

BOARD OF GOVERNORS

All the powers of the Bank are vested in a Board of Governors, consisting of one Governor and one alternate appointed by each member country. The Board meets annually, with special meetings when necessary.

BOARD OF EXECUTIVE DIRECTORS

There are 12 executive directors and 12 alternates. Each Director is elected by a group of two or more countries, except the Directors representing Canada and the USA. The USA holds 35% of votes on the Board.

ADMINISTRATION

The Bank has eight departments: operations; finance; economic and social development; project analysis; legal affairs; plans and programmes; administrative; and secretariat. There is also an External Review and Evaluation Office, and field offices in 23 countries. At the end of 1985 there were 2,013 Bank staff, of whom 591 were serving in field offices.

President: ANTONIO ORTIZ MENA (Mexico).

Executive Vice-President: MICHAEL E. CURTIN (USA).

Activities

Loans are made to governments, and to public and private entities for specific economic and social development projects. These loans are repayable in the currencies lent and their terms range from 15 to 40 years. Total lending by the Bank at the end of 1985 amounted to US $31,520m. During 1985 the Bank approved 78 loans, totalling $3,061m., compared with 75 loans totalling $3,567m. in 1984. Disbursements during the year came to $2,343m. Total loans of $13,000m. were envisaged for the 1983–86 period.

The subscribed capital stock, including both the ordinary capital and the inter-regional capital, totalled $26,714m. at the beginning of 1986, of which $2,323m. is paid-in and $24,391m. is callable. The callable capital constitutes, in effect, a guarantee of the securities which the Bank issues in the capital markets in order to increase its resources available for lending. Replenishments are made every four years: the Sixth Replenishment, agreed in 1983, raised the authorized capital to $35,000m. During 1985 54 loans were made from capital resources, amounting to $2,766m., bringing the net cumulative total of such loans to $21,056m. (671 loans) at the end of the year.

The Fund for Special Operations enables the Bank to make concessional loans for economic and social projects where circumstances call for special treatment, such as lower interest rates and longer repayment terms than those applied to loans from the ordinary resources, and possibility of repayments in whole or in part in local currency. Under the Sixth Replenishment (1983) the Fund received only $703m., compared with $1,750m. four years previously. During 1985 the Fund made 22 loans totalling $251m., bringing the net cumulative total to $9,150m. (671 loans) at the end of the year.

Several donor countries have placed sums under the Bank's administration for assistance to Latin America, outside the framework of the Ordinary Resources and the Bank's Special Operations. These include the United States Social Progress Trust Fund (set up in 1961), which had made 121 loans amounting to $533m. by the end of 1985; the Venezuelan Trust Fund (set up in 1975), which had made 41 loans totalling $684m. by the end of 1985; and other funds administered on behalf of Argentina, Canada, Norway, Sweden, Switzerland, the United Kingdom and the Vatican. Total cumulative lending from all these funds amounted to $1,314m. at the end of 1985.

The industry and mining sector accounted for the largest share ($995.5m.) of loans approved in 1985, of which nearly one-half was dedicated to industrial recovery projects in six countries; another $355m. was authorized for credit organizations supporting industrial investment, and two direct loans were approved for a steel plant in Argentina and a new bauxite mine in Venezuela. Lending for projects in the energy sector amounted to $826.1m. (27% of total loans). A total of $384.8m. was granted for the expansion of electricity transmission and distribution systems in Brazil, Colombia and Guyana; loans were also approved for hydroelectric plants in Chile, Colombia and Guatemala and for a gas pipeline in Argentina. The Bank approved loans of $361.6m. (11.8% of total loans) for transport and communications, chiefly for road improvements.

A special programme provides financing for small projects run by, for example, co-operatives or local producers' associations, which would normally fail to obtain credit from conventional sources: the beneficiaries are low-income farmers, small-scale entrepreneurs and craftsmen. During 1985 18 projects were financed at a cost of $6.7m.

The Bank provides technical co-operation in the form of short-term advisory missions (78 in 1984) and grants for the transfer of technical assistance between the countries of the region. Such assistance amounted to $40.8m. in 1985.

In March 1986 the charter of the Inter-American Investment Corporation (IIC), an affiliate of the Bank, entered into force, with the aim of promoting private-sector investment in the region (particularly in small- and medium-sized industries). Its initial capital stock was to be US $200m., of which 55% was to be contributed by developing member nations, 25.50% by the USA, and the remainder by non-regional members.

Outstanding borrowings (US $ million, 31 December 1985)

Source	Total	Ordinary capital	Inter-regional capital
Austria	52.5	17.3	35.2
Belgium	0.8	0.8	—
France	12.2	12.2	—
Germany, Federal Republic	1,573.4	374.2	1,199.2
Italy	2.5	2.5	—
Japan	2,139.3	574.7	1,564.6
Netherlands	604.2	181.8	422.4
Switzerland	1,685.5	395.9	1,389.6
Trinidad and Tobago	5.5	5.5	—
United Kingdom	480.5	360.9	119.6
USA	2,718.2	1,272.0	1,446.2
Venezuela	2.0	2.0	—
Others	88.8	88.8	—
Total	9,365.4	3,188.6	6,176.8

INTERNATIONAL ORGANIZATIONS — Inter-American Development Bank

Distribution of loans (US $ million)

Sector	1985	%	1961–85	%
Productive Sectors				
Agriculture	320.5	10.5	6,670.9	21.2
Industry and mining	995.5	32.5	5,545.6	17.6
Tourism	46.5	1.5	362.6	1.2
Physical Infrastructure				
Energy	826.1	27.0	8,510.6	27.0
Transportation and communications	361.6	11.8	3,986.4	12.6
Social Infrastructure				
Environmental and public health	181.9	5.9	2,679.2	8.5
Education, science and technology	125.9	4.1	1,390.9	4.4
Urban development	54.1	1.8	1,149.6	3.6
Other				
Export financing	75.9	2.5	658.1	2.0
Preinvestment	73.1	2.4	422.9	1.4
Other	—	—	142.9	0.5
Total	3,061.1	100.0	31,519.7	100.0

Total loans by country (US $ million)

Country	1983	1984	1985
Argentina	80.1	458.8	108.9
Barbados	5.0	36.5	21.7
Bolivia	58.9	78.0	—
Brazil	441.0	393.7	395.3
Chile	548.0	293.3	522.5
Colombia	405.9	405.0	413.3
Costa Rica	41.8	92.6	6.0
Dominican Republic	96.2	205.5	146.2
Ecuador	83.3	306.4	274.4
El Salvador	25.0	110.2	26.2
Guatemala	167.9	13.9	192.0
Guyana	—	40.7	58.5
Haiti	18.8	0.4	24.7
Honduras	130.2	42.0	69.8
Jamaica	120.2	10.0	30.1
Mexico	286.4	229.8	401.5
Nicaragua	30.8	—	—
Panama	112.0	8.4	52.8
Paraguay	48.6	37.5	—
Peru	264.9	195.8	14.5
Suriname	—	—	8.0
Trinidad and Tobago	—	—	25.6
Uruguay	50.0	119.8	21.6
Venezuela	30.0	448.3	238.0
Regional	—	40.0	9.6
Total	3,045.0	3,566.6	3,061.2

Cumulative lending, 1961–85 (US $ million; net of cancellations and exchange adjustments)

Country	Total amount	Ordinary capital	Inter-regional capital	Fund for special operations	Funds in administration
Argentina	3,291.0	1,379.1	1,339.4	524.7	47.8
Bahamas	4.9	—	2.9	—	2.0
Barbados	122.9	52.7	10.7	43.5	16.0
Bolivia	997.1	139.8	173.6	640.6	43.1
Brazil	5,204.7	2,232.6	1,685.3	1,147.2	139.6
Chile	2,451.4	583.5	1,622.0	203.3	42.6
Colombia	2,987.8	806.2	1,473.2	646.7	61.7
Costa Rica	773.5	165.9	175.6	361.4	70.6
Dominican Republic	1,078.6	155.0	301.1	554.9	67.6
Ecuador	1,704.8	602.0	317.4	694.6	90.8
El Salvador	745.0	196.8	52.6	389.9	105.7
Guatemala	992.8	195.8	260.6	474.2	62.2
Guyana	217.9	54.5	44.1	113.3	6.0
Haiti	243.2	—	—	233.2	10.0
Honduras	781.8	47.9	160.7	507.8	65.4
Jamaica	445.1	117.3	99.2	169.9	58.7
Mexico	3,787.0	1,550.8	1,638.3	562.9	35.0
Nicaragua	462.7	88.9	—	317.6	56.2
Panama	699.9	125.3	245.2	290.9	38.5
Paraguay	547.7	64.6	81.4	389.9	11.8
Peru	1,621.0	540.3	462.6	464.0	154.1
Suriname	8.0	—	6.5	1.5	—
Trinidad and Tobago	44.5	25.0	—	18.5	1.0
Uruguay	540.9	242.7	157.1	102.6	38.5
Venezuela	1,024.6	292.3	558.0	101.4	72.9
Regional	740.9	483.7	45.8	195.8	15.6
Total	31,519.7	10,142.7	10,913.3	9,150.3	1,313.4

AFFILIATED INSTITUTE

Instituto para la Integración de América Latina (Institute for Latin American Integration): Esmeralda 130, pisos 16, 17 y 18 (Casilla de Correo 39, Sucursal 1), Buenos Aires, Argentina; f.1964 as a permanent department of the Inter-American Development Bank. Its functions are: to study the regional integration process; to carry out research into problems which the integration movement poses for individual countries; to organize training courses and seminars; to conduct, at the request of member countries, preliminary studies on joint development schemes and on economic integration alternatives available to individual countries; to provide advisory services to the Bank and to other public and private institutions; to offer courses on the economic, political, social, institutional, legal, scientific and technological aspects of regional integration. Dir JUAN MARIO VACCHINO.

PUBLICATIONS

Integración Latinoamericana (monthly).

Annual Report (annually, in English and Spanish).

The Process of Integration in Latin America (monthly, in English and Spanish).

INTERNATIONAL BANK FOR ECONOMIC CO-OPERATION—IBEC

Address: 15 Kuznetski Most, 103031 Moscow, USSR.
Telephone: 925-16-88.
Telex: 411391.

The Bank was founded in October 1963 with eight member countries, and commenced operations in January 1964 to assist in the economic co-operation and development of member countries (see also CMEA, p. 126, and International Investment Bank, p. 164).

MEMBERS

Bulgaria	German Democratic Republic	Poland
Cuba*	Hungary	Romania
Czechoslovakia	Mongolia	USSR
		Viet-Nam*

* Cuba joined the Bank in 1974, and Viet-Nam in 1977.

Organization

(October 1986)

THE COUNCIL

The Council is composed of representatives of all member countries. Each country has one vote irrespective of its share in the capital of the Bank. The Council considers and decides questions of policy, determining the general policy of the Bank and the orientation of the development of its activities. It meets about twice a year. Representatives of the central banks of Afghanistan, Ethiopia, Finland, Laos, Mozambique, the People's Democratic Republic of Yemen and Yugoslavia attend spring meetings (at which the Annual Report and balance sheet are approved) as observers.

THE BOARD

The Board is the executive body subordinate to the Council; there is one permanent representative from each of the member states.
Chairman: Vaja G. Djindjikhadze (USSR).

Activities

The Bank acts as the central institution of the CMEA member countries for credit and settlements. Its main purpose is to effect multilateral settlements in the collective currency of its members, the transferable rouble (TR), and to grant credits in TRs to the authorized banks of the member countries and to international economic organizations. Favourable credit conditions are granted to Cuba, Mongolia and Viet-Nam, with interest rates of between 0.5% and 2%. Settlements in the collective currency include trade-related and non-commercial payments. The Bank also carries out credit and other transactions in convertible currencies with members and non-member countries.

In 1985 the total transactions of the Bank in transferable roubles amounted to 543,900m. TR, while transactions in convertible currencies were worth 325,000m. TR. The volume of mutual settlements of member countries increased by 7.7% over the previous year to 211,000m. TR. Credits in transferable roubles granted to the banks of member countries grew by 12.3% to 15,300m. TR, of which 75% was trade-related. The balance of credits in transferable roubles outstanding at the end of 1985 amounted to 4,400m. TR.

CAPITAL (31 December 1985; million transferable roubles)

	Authorized	Paid-up
Bulgaria	17.0	10.6
Cuba	4.4	2.8
Czechoslovakia	45.0	28.1
German Democratic Republic	55.0	34.4
Hungary	21.0	13.1
Mongolia	3.0	1.4
Poland	27.0	16.9
Romania	16.0	10.0
USSR	116.0	72.5
Viet-Nam	0.9	0.5
Total	**305.3**	**190.3**

BALANCE SHEET (31 December; transferable roubles)

Assets	1984	1985
Monetary funds	1,399,951,597	1,301,254,662
Current accounts and cash on hand	36,654,685	9,170,966
Time deposits	1,363,296,912	1,292,083,696
Credits granted	4,819,550,350	4,914,259,201
Property of the Bank	765,161	824,539
Other assets	47,914,705	40,508,961
Total	**6,268,181,813**	**6,256,847,363**

Liabilities	1984	1985
Capital funds of the Bank	381,281,887	394,481,672
Capital paid up	190,316,160	190,316,160
Reserve capital	190,965,727	204,165,512
Deposits	5,327,408,102	5,250,283,077
Current accounts	580,866,162	954,334,596
Time deposits	4,746,541,940	4,295,948,481
Credits received	392,916,551	454,118,934
Other liabilities	132,084,326	135,203,360
Net profit	34,490,947	22,760,320
Total	**6,268,181,813**	**6,256,847,363**

INTERNATIONAL CHAMBER OF COMMERCE—ICC

Address: 38 Cours Albert 1er, 75008 Paris, France.
Telephone: 45-62-34-56.
Telex: 650770.

The ICC was founded in 1919 to promote free trade and private enterprise, provide practical services and represent business interests at governmental and inter-governmental levels.

MEMBERS

At the end of 1984 membership consisted of 5,281 individual corporations and 1,570 organizations (mainly trade and industrial organizations and chambers of commerce). In the following 58 countries National Committees or Councils have been formed to co-ordinate certain functions at the national level, while the ICC is also represented in 50 other countries and territories.

Argentina
Australia
Austria
Belgium
Brazil
Burkina Faso
Cameroon
Canada
China (Taiwan)
Colombia
Cyprus
Denmark
Egypt
Finland
France
Gabon
Federal Republic of Germany
Greece
Iceland
India
Indonesia
Iran
Ireland
Israel
Italy
Ivory Coast
Japan
Jordan
Republic of Korea
Kuwait
Lebanon
Luxembourg
Madagascar
Mexico
Morocco
Netherlands
Nigeria
Norway
Pakistan
Portugal
Saudi Arabia
Senegal
Singapore
South Africa
Spain
Sri Lanka
Sweden
Switzerland
Thailand
Togo
Tunisia
Turkey
United Kingdom
USA
Uruguay
Venezuela
Yugoslavia
Zaire

Organization
(October 1986)

COUNCIL

The Council is the governing body of the organization. It is composed of members nominated by the National Committees and Councils who consider, co-ordinate, amend and approve reports and activities of the Technical Commissions. It meets twice a year.

EXECUTIVE BOARD

The Executive Board consists of 15 members appointed by the Council on the recommendation of the President and four ex-officio members. Members serve for a three-year term, one-third of the members retiring at the end of each year. It ensures close direction of ICC activities and meets four times a year.

INTERNATIONAL SECRETARIAT

The ICC secretariat is based at International Headquarters in Paris, with additional offices maintained in Geneva and New York principally for liaison with the United Nations and its agencies.
Secretary-General: Hans König.
First Director: Marie C. Psimènos.

NATIONAL COMMITTEES AND COUNCILS

Each Committee or Council is composed of leading business organizations and individual companies. It has its own secretariat, and draws public and government attention to ICC policies.

CONGRESS

The ICC's supreme assembly, to which all member companies and organizations are invited to send senior representatives. Congresses are held every three years, in a different place on each occasion, with up to 2,000 participants. The 29th Congress was to be held in New Delhi, India, in February 1987.

CONFERENCE

Conferences with about 250 participants take place in non-Congress years. The seventh Conference was held in Barcelona, Spain, in May 1986.

Activities

The various Commissions of the ICC (listed below) are composed of practising businessmen and experts from all sectors of economic life, nominated by National Committees and Councils. Many are further divided into special working parties on particular topics. They produce a wide array of specific codes and guidelines of direct use to the world business community, draw up statements and initiatives for presentation to governments and international bodies, and comment constructively and in detail on proposed actions by intergovernmental organizations that are likely to affect business.

ICC works closely with the United Nations and its various organizations. The ICC-UN, GATT Economic Consultative Committee, for example, brings together ICC members and the heads of UN economic organizations and the OECD for annual discussions on the world economy. The Commission on International Trade Policy campaigns against protectionism in world trade and in support of the General Agreement on Tariffs and Trade (GATT), and ensures that ICC views are represented in the multilateral trade negotiations which take place under GATT auspices (see p. 59). The ICC also works closely with the European Community, commenting on EEC directives and making recommendations on, for example, tax harmonization and laws relating to competition.

ICC plays a part in combating international crime connected with commerce. The International Maritime Bureau attempts to deal with maritime fraud, for example insurance fraud and the theft of cargoes. The Counterfeiting Intelligence Bureau was established in 1985 to investigate counterfeiting in trade-marked goods, copyrights and industrial designs. Commercial disputes are submitted to the ICC Court of Arbitration: during 1985 339 new cases were registered and 89 final arbitral awards were made.

Policy and Technical Commissions:
Commission on International Trade Policy
Commission on International Monetary Relations
Commission on Multinational Enterprises and International Investments
Commission on Industrial Property
Commission on Taxation
Commission on Law and Practices Relating to Competition
Commission on Insurance
Commission on Marketing
Commission on Energy
Commission on Environment
Commission on Computing, Telecommunications and Information Policy
Commission on Sea Transport
Commission on Air Transport
International Bureau of Transport Users
Commission on Trade Regulations and Procedures
Commission on International Commercial Practice
Commission on Banking Technique and Practice
Commission on International Arbitration

Bodies for the Settlement of Disputes:
Court of Arbitration
International Centre for Technical Expertise

INTERNATIONAL ORGANIZATIONS

International Maritime Arbitration Organization
Committee on Regulation of Contractual Relations
International Council on Marketing Practice

Other Bodies:
ICC-UN, GATT Economic Consultative Committee
East-West Committee
International Bureau of Chambers of Commerce
International Maritime Bureau
Counterfeiting Intelligence Bureau
Centre for Maritime Co-operation
Institute of International Business Law and Practice
International Environment Bureau.

International Chamber of Commerce

FINANCE

The International Chamber of Commerce is a private organization financed partly by contributions from National Committees and other members, according to the economic importance of the country which each represents, and partly by revenue from fees for various services and from sales of publications. The operating budget for 1986 was about 55m. French francs.

PUBLICATIONS

ICC Business World (quarterly).
Annual Report.
Handbook.
Numerous publications on general and technical subjects.

INTERNATIONAL CONFEDERATION OF FREE TRADE UNIONS—ICFTU

Address: 37-41 rue Montagne aux Herbes Potagères, 1000 Brussels, Belgium.
Telephone: (02) 217-80-85.
Telex: 26785.

ICFTU was founded in 1949 by trade union federations which had withdrawn from the World Federation of Trade Unions (see p. 210). It aims to promote the interests of working people and to secure recognition of workers' organizations as free bargaining agents; to reduce the gap between rich and poor; and to defend fundamental human and trade union rights. See also the World Confederation of Labour (p. 208).

MEMBERS
144 organizations in 99 countries with 82m. members (May 1986).

Organization
(October 1986)

WORLD CONGRESS
The Congress, the highest authority of ICFTU, normally meets every four years. Thirteenth Congress: Oslo, Norway, June 1983.

Delegations from national federations vary in size according to membership. The Congress examines past activities, maps out future plans, elects the Executive Board and the General Secretary, considers the functioning of the regional machinery, examines financial reports and social, economic and political situations. It works through plenary sessions and through technical committees which report to the plenary sessions.

EXECUTIVE BOARD
The Board meets twice a year, for about three days, usually at Brussels, or at the Congress venue; consists of 37 members elected by Congress and nominated by areas of the world. The General Secretary is an ex officio member. After each Congress the Board elects a President and at least seven Vice-Presidents.

The Board considers administrative questions; hears reports from field representatives, missions, regional organizations and affiliates, and makes resultant decisions; and discusses finances, applications for affiliation, and problems affecting world labour. It elects a sub-committee of nine to deal with urgent matters between Board meetings.
President: P. P. NARAYANAN (Malaysia).

PERMANENT COMMITTEES
Finance and General Purposes Committee. Administers the General Fund made up of affiliation fees and the International Solidarity Fund constituting additional voluntary contributions.
Economic and Social Committee.
Education Policy Committee.
Women's Committee.
ICFTU/ITS Working Group on Young Workers' Questions.
ICFTU/ITS Working Party on Multinational Corporations.
Working Group on International Trade and Monetary Questions.

SECRETARIAT
The headquarters staff numbers 84, comprising some 25 different nationalities.

The six departments are: Economic and Social Policy; Education; Administration; Finance; Press, Publications and Communications; Programme Administration and Co-ordination. There are also Regional Desks and a Women's Bureau.
General Secretary: JOHN VANDERVEKEN.

BRANCH OFFICES
ICFTU Geneva Office: 27–29 rue de la Coulouvrenière, 1204 Geneva, Switzerland.
ICFTU United Nations Office: Suite 705, 104 East 40th St, New York, NY 10016, USA.

There are also Permanent Representatives accredited to FAO (Rome) and to UNIDO (Vienna).

REGIONAL ORGANIZATIONS
ICFTU African Regional Organization—AFRO: c/o Liberia Federation of Labour Unions, POB 415, Monrovia, Liberia; Pres. S. ALLOUCHE; Sec. AMOS N. GRAY.
Inter-American Regional Organization of Workers—ORIT: Edificio de la CTM, Vallarta No 8, 3° piso, México DF, CP 06470, Mexico; tel. 566-7024; telex 1771699; Pres. A. MADARIAGA; Gen. Sec. L. ANDERSON.
ICFTU Asian and Pacific Regional Organization—APRO: P-20 Green Park Extension, New Delhi 110016, India; Pres. T. USAMI; Gen. Sec. V. S. MATHUR.

ICFTU-APRO Programme and Education Bureau: Trade Union House, Shenton Way, Singapore 0106; tel. 2226555; telex 24543.

There is a Liaison Office in Indonesia and Field Representatives in Brazil, Kenya, Lesotho, Thailand and Papua New Guinea. In addition, a number of Project Planners for development co-operation travel in different countries.

FINANCE
Affiliated federations pay a standard fee of 4,655 Belgian francs (1986), or its equivalent in other currencies, per 1,000 members per annum, which covers the establishment and routine activities of the ICFTU headquarters in Brussels.

An International Solidarity Fund was set up in 1956 to assist unions in developing countries, and workers and trade unionists victimized by repressive political measures. It provides legal assistance and supports educational activities. In cases of major natural disasters affecting workers token relief aid is granted.

PUBLICATIONS
Free Labour World (official journal, fortnightly).
Economic and Social Bulletin (quarterly).
World Economic Review (annually).
Survey of Violations of Trade Union Rights (annually).

All these periodicals are issued in English, French, German and Spanish. In addition Congress reports and numerous other publications on labour, economic and trade union training have been published in various languages.

Associated International Trade Secretariats

International Federation of Building and Woodworkers: 27–29 rue de la Coulouvrenière, 1204 Geneva; tel. (022) 211611; telex 428577; f. 1934. Mems: national unions with a membership of 3m. workers. Organization: Congress, Executive Committee. Pres. KONRAD CARL (FRG); Sec.-Gen. J. LÖFBLAD (Sweden). Publs *Bulletin* (quarterly).

International Federation of Chemical, Energy and General Workers' Unions: 109 ave Emile de Béco, 1050 Brussels, Belgium; tel. (02) 647-02-35; telex 6484316; f. 1907. Mems: 200 national unions covering 7m. people in 78 countries. Organization: Congress (every four years), Executive Committee (meets twice a year), Management Committee. Pres. NILS KRISTOFFERSON (Sweden); Sec.-Gen. MICHAEL BOGGS. Publs *Bulletin* (quarterly), reports.

INTERNATIONAL ORGANIZATIONS

International Federation of Commercial, Clerical, Professional and Technical Employees—FIET: 15 ave de Balexert, 1219 Châtelaine-Geneva, Switzerland; tel. (022) 962733; telex 418736; f. 1904. Mems: 250 national unions of non-manual workers comprising 8,287,132 workers in 93 countries. Organization: World Congresses (every four years), Executive Committees, five trade sections (for bank workers, insurance workers, workers in social insurance and health care, commercial workers and salaried employees in industry), regional organizations for Europe, Western Hemisphere, Asia and Africa. Pres. THOMAS G. WHALEY (USA); Sec.-Gen. HERIBERT MAIER (Austria). Publs *Newsletter* (monthly in English, French, German and Spanish), Press service, *Studies*.

International Federation of Free Teachers' Unions: Herengracht 54–56, 1015 BN Amsterdam, Netherlands; tel. (020) 24 90 72; telex 17118; f. 1951. Mems: 75 national organizations of teachers' trade unions covering 6,100,000 members in 57 countries. Organization: Congress (every four years), Executive Committee (meets annually), Secretariat. Pres. A. SHANKER (USA); Gen. Sec. FRED VAN LEEUWEN (Netherlands). Publs *Fortnightly Bulletin*, *Workers in Education* (4–6 a year in English, French and Spanish).

International Federation of Journalists: IPC, blvd Charlemagne 1, Bte 5, 1041 Brussels, Belgium; tel. (02) 230-62-15; telex 61275; f. 1952 to link national unions of professional journalists dedicated to the freedom of the press, to defend the rights of journalists, and to raise professional standards; it conducts surveys, assists in training programmes, organizes seminars and provides information; it arranges fact-finding missions in countries where press freedom is under pressure, and issues protests against the persecution and detention of journalists and the censorship of the mass media. Mems: 37 unions in 32 countries, comprising 125,000 individuals. Pres. MIA DOORNAERT (Belgium); Gen. Sec. HANS LARSEN (Denmark).

International Federation of Plantation, Agricultural and Allied Workers: 17 rue Necker, 1201 Geneva, Switzerland; tel. (022) 313105; f. 1959. Mems: unions covering approx. 6m. workers. Organization: Congress (every six years), Executive Committee, Central Secretariat. Pres. BÖRJE SVENSSON (Sweden); Gen. Sec. D. F. HODSDON. Publ. *News* (monthly).

International Graphical Federation: Monbijoustrasse 73, 3007 Berne, Switzerland; tel. (31) 45-99-20; f. 1949. Mems: 45 national organizations in 37 countries, covering 790,000 individuals. Organization: Congress (every three years), Executive Committee and working parties. Pres. ERWIN FERLEMANN (FRG); Gen. Sec. ALFRED KAUFMANN (Switzerland). Publs *Journal of the IGF* (2 a year), reports.

International Metalworkers' Federation: Route des Acacias 54 bis, 1227 Geneva, Switzerland; tel. (022) 436150; telex 423298; f. 1893. Mems: national organizations covering 14m. workers in 70 countries. Organization: Congress (every four years), Central Committee (meets annually), Executive Committee; seven regional offices; six industrial departments; World Company Councils for unions in multinational corporations. Pres. H. MAYR (FRG); Gen. Sec. HERMAN REBHAN (USA). Publ. *IMF News* (every 2 weeks, seven languages).

International Secretariat for Arts, Mass Media and Entertainment Trade Unions: 15 ave de Balexert, 1219 Châtelaine-Geneva, Switzerland; tel. (022) 962733; telex 28468; f. 1965; Pres. WALTER BACHER; Sec. IRENE ROBADEY.

International Textile, Garment and Leather Workers' Federation: rue Joseph Stevens 8, 1000 Brussels, Belgium; tel. (02) 512-28-33; f. 1970. Mems: 145 national federations covering over 5m. workers in 69 countries. Organization: Congress, Executive Committee of 31. Pres. K. E. PERSSON (Sweden); Gen. Sec. CHARLES FORD (UK).

International Transport Workers' Federation: 133–135 Great Suffolk St, London, SE1 1PD, England; tel. (01) 403-2733; telex 8811397; f. 1896. Mems: national trade unions covering 4,500,000 workers in 90 countries. Organization: Congress (every four years), General Council, Executive Board, Management Committee, Secretariat, eight Industrial Sections. Pres. JIM HUNTER (Canada); Gen. Sec. HAROLD LEWIS (UK). Publ. *ITF Newsletter* (monthly).

International Union of Food and Allied Workers' Associations: 8 rampe du Pont-Rouge, 1213 Petit-Lancy, Switzerland; tel. (022) 93-22-33; telex 429292; f. 1920. Mems: national organizations covering about 2,200,000 workers in 62 countries. Organization: Congress (every four years), Executive Committee of 27, Administrative Committee of four. Pres. G. DÖDING (FRG); Gen. Sec. DAN GALLIN (Switzerland). Publs monthly bulletins, reports, brochures.

Miners' International Federation: 8 rue Joseph Stevens, 1000 Brussels, Belgium; tel. (02) 511-35-43; f. 1890. Mems: 39 national unions covering over 1m. miners in 36 countries. Organization: Congress (every four years), Executive Committee, Bureau, Regional Conferences. Pres. A. STENDALEN (Sweden); Gen. Sec. J. OLYSLAEGERS (Belgium).

Postal, Telegraph and Telephone International: 36 ave du Lignon, 1219 Geneva, Switzerland; tel. (022) 96-83-11; f. 1920. Mems: national trade unions covering 3,924,319 workers in 93 countries. Organization: Congress (every four years), Executive Committee. Pres. AKIRA YAMAGISHI (Japan); Gen. Sec. S. NEDZYNSKI. Publs *PTTI News* (six languages, monthly), *PTTI Studies* (four languages, quarterly).

Public Services International: 45 ave Voltaire, 01210 Ferney-Voltaire, France; tel. (50) 40-64-64; telex 380559; f. 1907; Mems: 250 unions and professional associations covering over 11m. workers in 80 countries. Organization: Congress (every four years), Regional Conferences, vocational meetings, Executive Committee, Management Committee, Secretariat. Pres. VICTOR GOTBAUM (USA); Gen. Sec. HANS ENGELBERTS (Netherlands). Publs *INFO* (10 a year), specialized reports.

Universal Alliance of Diamond Workers: Lange Kievitstraat 57 (Bus 1), 2018 Antwerp, Belgium; tel. (03) 232-91-51; f. 1905. Mems: 10,800 in six countries; annual Executive committee meetings. Pres. J. MEIJNIKMAN (Netherlands); Gen. Sec. C. DENISSE (Belgium).

INTERNATIONAL INVESTMENT BANK

Address: 17 Presnensky Val, Moscow 123557, USSR.
Telex: 7558.

Established by an intergovernmental Agreement of the members of the Council for Mutual Economic Assistance (see p. 126) in 1970, the Bank commenced operations on 1 January 1971.

MEMBERS

Bulgaria	German Democratic	Poland
Cuba	Republic	Romania
Czechoslovakia	Hungary	USSR
	Mongolia	Viet-Nam

Organization
(October 1986)

COUNCIL
The Council of the Bank is the highest authority and consists of representatives of all the member countries. Each member country, irrespective of the amount of its quota, has one vote in the Council. Major decisions require a unanimous vote. The Council meets as often as necessary but not less than twice a year.

BOARD
The Board is the executive body of the Bank and consists of a Chairman and three Deputies appointed by the Council. Its task is to supervise the Bank's activities in accordance with the Agreement, the Statutes of the Bank and the decisions of the Council.

Chairman: ALBERT N. BELICHENKO (USSR).

Activities

Under Article II of the Agreement on the Establishment of the International Investment Bank the fundamental task of the Bank is to grant long-term and medium-term credits for projects connected with the international socialist division of labour, specialization and co-operation in production, expenditure for expansion of raw materials and fuel resources in the members' collective interest, for the construction of enterprises of mutual concern to member countries in other branches of the economy, for the construction of projects for the development of the national economies of member countries and for other purposes established by the Council. Credits may be granted to:

(i) banks, economic organizations and enterprises of member countries;

(ii) international economic organizations and enterprises of member countries;

(iii) banks and economic organizations of other countries.

The Bank may:

(i) form reserve capital and create its own special funds;

(ii) attract funds in collective currency (transferable roubles), in national currencies of interested countries and in convertible currency;

(iii) issue interest-bearing bond loans placed on international capital markets;

(iv) place surplus funds with other banks, buy and sell currency, gold and securities, grant guarantees and conduct other banking operations;

(v) co-operate with the Council for Mutual Economic Assistance, the International Bank for Economic Co-operation (see p. 159) and other economic organizations of the member countries of the Bank;

(vi) make contact and establish business relations with international and other financial and credit institutions as well as with banks;

(vii) conclude international agreements and the like, as well as making business transactions within its competence.

In 1974, a Special Fund was formed for financing programmes of economic and technical assistance to developing countries.

By the end of 1985 the Bank had authorized credits for 94 projects, with a total estimated value of about 11,000m. transferable roubles. The largest proportion of credits granted between 1971 and the end of 1985 was for the energy and fuel sector (62%), while 24% was for machine-building and metal-working (including electrical engineering and electronics). Credits granted during 1985 included assistance for the following: industrial robots in Bulgaria; modernization and extension of machine-tools production in the German Democratic Republic; and construction of a plant for producing organic dyes in Czechoslovakia.

AUTHORIZED CAPITAL
(million transferable roubles as at 1 January 1986)

Country	Amount
Bulgaria	85.1
Cuba	15.7
Czechoslovakia	129.9
German Democratic Republic	176.1
Hungary	83.7
Mongolia	4.5
Poland	121.4
Romania	52.6
USSR	399.3
Viet-Nam	3.0
Total	**1,071.3**

STATEMENT OF ACCOUNT (transferable roubles)

Assets	As at 1 January 1986
Cash, balance on current accounts and time deposits with banks	763,191,551
Credits disbursed	1,527,443,966
Bank building and other property	15,139,479
Other assets	49,067,979
Total	**2,354,842,975**

Liabilities	As at 1 January 1986
Authorized capital	1,071,300,000
Paid-up portion	374,970,000
Reserve capital	155,713,495
Special Fund	32,837,689
Credits and time deposits received	1,668,805,298
Bank premises construction fund and amortization	15,503,619
Other liabilities	83,966,059
Net income	23,046,815
Total	**2,354,842,975**

INTERNATIONAL OLYMPIC COMMITTEE

Address: Château de Vidy, 1007 Lausanne, Switzerland.
Telephone: 253271.
Telex: 24024.

The International Olympic Committee was founded in 1894 to ensure the regular celebration of the Olympic Games.

Organization
(October 1986)

INTERNATIONAL OLYMPIC COMMITTEE

The International Olympic Committee unites 160 National Olympic Committees. The 92 members of the International Olympic Committee are chosen as individuals, not as national representatives. At the meeting of the Committee in September 1981 athletes were represented for the first time.

EXECUTIVE BOARD

The Executive Board takes decisions affecting the management of the International Olympic Committee, and assigns duties connected with its current affairs to the general secretariat in Lausanne.

President: JUAN ANTONIO SAMARANCH (Spain).
First Vice-President: ASHWINI KUMAR (India).
Second Vice-President: BERTHOLD BEITZ (FRG).
Third Vice-President: Prince ALEXANDRE DE MÉRODE (Belgium).
Members of the Board:
RICHARD W. POUND (Canada).
Judge KÉBA MBAYE (Senegal).
Major SYLVIO DE MAGALHÃES PADILHA (Brazil).
MARC HODLER (Switzerland).
HE ZHENLIANG (People's Republic of China).
VITALY SMIRNOV (USSR).
RICHARD K. GOSPER (Australia).
Director: RAYMOND GAFNER.
General Secretary: FRANÇOISE ZWEIFEL.

Activities

According to Rule 1 of the Olympic Charter, the aims of the Olympic movement are:

to promote the development of those physical and moral qualities which are the basis of sport,

to educate young people through sport in a spirit of better understanding between each other and of friendship, thereby helping to build a better and more peaceful world,

to spread the Olympic principles throughout the world, thereby creating international goodwill,

to bring together the athletes of the world in the great four-yearly sport festival, the Olympic Games.

THE GAMES

1896	Athens	1952	Helsinki
1900	Paris	1956	Melbourne
1904	St Louis	1960	Rome
1908	London	1964	Tokyo
1912	Stockholm	1968	Mexico City
1920	Antwerp	1972	Munich
1924	Paris	1976	Montreal
1928	Amsterdam	1980	Moscow
1932	Los Angeles	1984	Los Angeles
1936	Berlin	1988	Seoul
1948	London	1992	Barcelona

The programme of the Games comprises the following sports: archery, athletics, basketball, boxing, canoeing, cycling, equestrian sports, fencing, football, gymnastics, handball, field hockey, judo, modern pentathlon, rowing, shooting, swimming, table tennis, tennis, volleyball, water polo, weight-lifting, wrestling, yachting.

WINTER GAMES

1924	Chamonix	1964	Innsbruck
1928	St Moritz	1968	Grenoble
1932	Lake Placid	1972	Sapporo
1936	Garmisch-Partenkirchen	1976	Innsbruck
1948	St Moritz	1980	Lake Placid
1952	Oslo	1984	Sarajevo
1956	Cortina d'Ampezzo	1988	Calgary
1960	Squaw Valley	1992	Albertville

The Winter Games may include skiing, skating, ice hockey, bobsleigh, luge, biathlon and curling.

THE INTERNATIONAL RED CROSS

The International Red Cross is a world-wide independent humanitarian organization, comprising two bodies working at an international level: one in time of armed conflict, the International Committee of the Red Cross (ICRC), founded in 1863; and the other in peace time, the League of Red Cross and Red Crescent Societies (LRCS), founded in 1919, and 137 National Red Cross and Red Crescent Societies working mainly at national level.

Organization

INTERNATIONAL CONFERENCE

The supreme deliberative body of the International Red Cross, the Conference comprises delegations from the ICRC, the League and the National Societies, and of representatives of States Parties to the Geneva Conventions (see below). The Conference's function is to determine the general policy of the Red Cross movement and to ensure unity in the work of the various bodies. It usually meets every four years, and is hosted by the National Society of the country in which it is held.

STANDING COMMISSION

The Commission meets twice a year in ordinary session, to coordinate the work of the ICRC and the League, and to prepare for the next International Conference. It is formed of two members from the ICRC, two from the League, and five elected by the Conference.

OTHER MEETINGS

The three Presidents of the Standing Commission, the ICRC and the League meet as a rule every six months, or as necessary. At least once a month a meeting is held between representatives of the ICRC and of the League.

Principles of the Red Cross

Humanity. The Red Cross endeavours to prevent and alleviate human suffering wherever it may be found, to protect life and health and to ensure respect for the human being.

Impartiality. It makes no discrimination as to nationality, race, religious beliefs, class or political opinions.

Neutrality. The Red Cross may not take sides in hostilities or engage in controversies of a political, racial, religious or ideological nature.

Independence. The National Societies, while auxiliaries in the humanitarian services of their governments and subject to national laws, must retain their autonomy so that they may always be able to act in accordance with Red Cross principles.

Voluntary Service. The Red Cross is a voluntary relief organization, not prompted by desire for gain.

Unity. There must be only one Red Cross Society in any one country, open to all.

Universality. The Red Cross is a world-wide organization in which all National Societies have equal status and share equal responsibilities and duties.

International Committee of the Red Cross—ICRC

Address: 17 avenue de la Paix, 1202 Geneva, Switzerland.
Telephone: (022) 346001.
Telex: 22269.

Organization
(October 1986)

INTERNATIONAL COMMITTEE

The ICRC is an independent institution of a private character. It is exclusively composed of Swiss nationals. Members are co-opted, and their total number may not exceed 25. The international character of the ICRC is based on its mission and not on its composition.
President: ALEXANDRE HAY.
President-Elect: CORNELIO SOMMARUGA (to take office in 1987).
Vice-Presidents: MAURICE AUBERT, VICTOR H. UMBRICHT.

EXECUTIVE COUNCIL

President: ALEXANDRE HAY.
Members: MAURICE AUBERT, RICHARD PESTALOZZI, ATHOS GALLINO, RUDOLF JÄCKLI, OLIVIER LONG, PIERRE KELLER.

Activities

The International Committee of the Red Cross was founded in 1863, in Geneva, by Henry Dunant and four of his friends. The original purpose of the Committee was to assist wounded soldiers on the battlefield. The present activities of the ICRC consist in giving legal protection and material assistance to military and civilian victims of wars (international wars, internal strife and disturbances).

The ICRC promoted the foundation in each country of the world of National Committees of the Red Cross, which later became the National Societies of the Red Cross (and National Societies of the Red Crescent in Islamic countries).

As well as providing medical aid and emergency food supplies in many countries, the ICRC plays an important part in inspecting prison conditions and in tracing missing persons. Examples of its recent activities include the following:

Africa: assistance for detainees and their families in southern Africa; food and medical aid in Angola, Chad, Ethiopia and other countries; programmes for the rehabilitation of the disabled in several countries.

Latin America: relief activities, medical aid, visits to detainees, and a campaign to disseminate humanitarian principles in an attempt to protect non-combatants from violence.

Asia: medical assistance in Kampuchea and Thailand, visits to detainees in Indonesia, Malaysia, the Philippines and Thailand; dealing with enquiries about missing relatives among refugees from Viet-Nam and Kampuchea; medical assistance programme for Afghan refugees in Pakistan; assistance in Timor.

Middle East: emergency action in Lebanon, providing medical supplies and evacuating the wounded and refugees; visits to prisoner-of-war camps in Iran and Iraq; exchanges of war-wounded.

THE GENEVA CONVENTIONS

In 1864, one year after its foundation, the ICRC submitted to the states called to a Diplomatic Conference in Geneva a draft international treaty for 'the Amelioration of the Condition of the Wounded in Armies in the Field'. This treaty was adopted and signed by twelve states, which thereby bind themselves to respect as neutral wounded soldiers and those assisting them. This was the first Geneva Convention.

INTERNATIONAL ORGANIZATIONS

With the development of technology and weapons, the introduction of new means of waging war, and the manifestation of certain phenomena (the great number of prisoners of war during World War I; the enormous number of displaced persons and refugees during World War II; the internationalization of internal conflicts in recent years) the necessity was felt of having other international treaties to protect new categories of war victims. The ICRC, for over 120 years now, has been the leader of a movement to improve and complement international humanitarian law.

There are now four Geneva Conventions, adopted on 12 August 1949: I—to protect wounded and sick in armed forces on land, as well as medical personnel; II—to protect the same categories of people at sea, as well as the shipwrecked; III—concerning the treatment of prisoners of war; IV—for the protection of civilians in time of war; and there are two Additional Protocols of 8 June 1977, for the protection of victims in international armed conflicts (Protocol I) and in non-international armed conflicts (Protocol II).

As at 31 August 1986, 164 states were parties to the Geneva Conventions; 60 were parties to Protocol I and 53 to Protocol II.

FINANCE

The ICRC's work is financed by a voluntary annual grant from governments parties to the Geneva Conventions, voluntary contributions from National Red Cross Societies and by gifts and legacies from private people.

PERIODICALS AND PUBLICATIONS

International Review of the Red Cross (every 2 months, French, English and Spanish editions; short edition *Extracts* in German).
ICRC Bulletin (monthly, French, English, Spanish and German editions).
Annual Report (editions in Arabic, English, French, German and Spanish).
The Geneva Conventions: texts and commentaries.
The Protocols Additional.
Various publications on humanitarian law and subjects of Red Cross interest.

League of Red Cross and Red Crescent Societies—LRCS

Address: 17 Chemin des Crêts, Petit-Saconnex, Case Postale 372, 1211 Geneva 19, Switzerland.
Telephone: (022) 345580.
Telex: 22555.

The League was founded in 1919. It is the world federation of all Red Cross and Red Crescent Societies. The general aim of the League is to inspire, encourage, facilitate and promote at all times all forms of humanitarian activities by the National Societies, with a view to the prevention and alleviation of human suffering, and thereby contribute to the maintenance and promotion of peace in the world.

MEMBERS

National Red Cross and Red Crescent Societies in 137 countries in October 1986, with an aggregate youth and adult membership of over 250m.

Organization
(October 1986)

GENERAL ASSEMBLY

The General Assembly is the highest authority of the League and meets every two years in commission sessions (commissions for development, disaster relief, health and community services, and youth) and plenary sessions. It is composed of representatives from all National Societies that are members of the League.
President: D. Enrique de la Mata Gorostizaga.

EXECUTIVE COUNCIL

The Council, which meets every six months, is composed of the President of the League, nine Vice-Presidents and 16 National Societies elected by the Assembly. Its functions include the implementation of decisions of the General Assembly; it also has emergency powers to act between meetings of the Assembly.

ASSEMBLY AND FINANCE COMMISSIONS

Development Commission.
Disaster Relief Commission.
Health and Community Services Commission.
Youth Commision.
Finance Commission.
Permanent Scale of Contributions Commission.

The Advisory Commissions meet, in principle, once every two years, at the same time as the General Assembly. Members are elected by the Assembly under a system that ensures each Society a seat on one Commission. The Finance Commission, which has seven members, meets twice a year, and the Permanent Scale of Contributions Commission, also with seven members, meets annually.

SECRETARIAT
Secretary General: Hans Høegh (Norway).
Treasurer-General: al-Mehdi Bennouna (Morocco).

Activities

RELIEF

The Secretariat assumes the statutory responsibilities of the League in the field of relief to victims of natural disasters, refugees and civilian populations who may be displaced or exposed to abnormal hardship. This activity has three main aspects:

(i) Relief Operations: for the co-ordination of relief operations on the international level and execution by the National Society of the stricken country or by the League itself;

(ii) Supply, Logistics and Warehouses: for the co-ordination and purchase, transport and warehousing of relief supplies;

(iii) Disaster Preparedness: for co-ordination of assistance to National Societies situated in disaster-prone areas in the study and execution of practical measures calculated to prevent disasters and diminish their effects.

SERVICES TO NATIONAL SOCIETIES

The Secretariat promotes and co-ordinates assistance to National Societies in developing their basic structure and their services to the community. The Secretariat is equipped to advise Societies in the fields of health, social welfare, information, nursing, first aid and training; and the operation of blood programmes. It also promotes the establishment and development of educational and service programmes for children and youth.

The League maintains close relations with many inter-governmental organizations, the United Nations and its Specialized Agencies, and with non-governmental organizations, and represents member Societies in the international field.

FINANCE

The permanent secretariat of the League is financed by the contributions of Member Societies on a pro-rata basis. Each relief action is financed by separate, voluntary contributions, and development programme projects are also financed on a voluntary basis.

PUBLICATIONS

Annual Review.
The League (quarterly).
Secretariat (monthly).
Weekly News.
Transfusion International (quarterly).
Nursing News (2 a year).

ISLAMIC DEVELOPMENT BANK

Address: POB 5925, Jeddah 21432, Saudi Arabia.
Telephone: 6361400.
Telex: 401137.

An international financial institution established following a conference of finance ministers of member countries of the Organization of the Islamic Conference (see p. 193), held in Jeddah in December 1973. Its aim is to encourage economic development and social progress of member countries and Muslim communities, in accordance with the principles of the Islamic Shari'ah (sacred law). The Bank formally opened in October 1975.

MEMBERS
There are 43 members (see table of subscriptions below).

Organization
(October 1986)

BOARD OF GOVERNORS
Each member country is represented by a governor, usually its Finance Minister or his alternate. The Board of Governors is the Supreme Authority of the Bank, and meets annually.
President of the Bank and Chairman of the Board of Executive Directors: Dr AHMAD MUHAMMAD ALI (Saudi Arabia).

BOARD OF EXECUTIVE DIRECTORS
Consists of 11 members, five of whom are appointed by the four largest subscribers to the capital stock of the Bank; the remaining six are elected by Governors representing the other subscribers. Members of the Board of Executive Directors are elected for three-year terms. Responsible for the direction of the general operations of the Bank.

FINANCIAL STRUCTURE
The authorized capital of the Bank is 2,000m. Islamic Dinars divided into 200,000 shares having a value of 10,000 Islamic Dinars each. The Islamic Dinar (ID) is the Bank's unit of account and is equivalent to the value of one Special Drawing Right of the IMF (US $1.0594 at 30 September 1985).
The subscribed capital stood at ID 1,952.07m. in June 1985.

SUBSCRIPTIONS (million Islamic Dinars, as at 30 June 1985)

Afghanistan	2.5	Morocco	12.6
Algeria	63.1	Niger	6.3
Bahrain	7.0	Oman	7.0
Bangladesh	25.0	Pakistan	63.1
Benin	2.5	Palestine Liberation Organization	5.0
Burkina Faso	6.3		
Cameroon	6.3		
Chad	2.5	Qatar	50.0
Comoros	2.5	Saudi Arabia	506.37
Djibouti	2.5	Senegal	6.3
Egypt	25.0	Sierra Leone	2.5
Gabon	7.5	Somalia	2.5
The Gambia	2.5	Sudan	25.2
Guinea	6.3	Syria	2.5
Guinea-Bissau	6.3	Tunisia	5.0
Indonesia	63.1	Turkey	160.0
Iraq	25.2	Uganda	6.3
Jordan	10.1	United Arab Emirates	194.7
Kuwait	252.2		
Lebanon	2.5	Yemen Arab Republic	6.3
Libya	315.3		
Malaysia	40.4	Yemen, People's Democratic Republic	6.3
Maldives	2.5		
Mali	2.5		
Mauritania	2.5	**Total**	**1,952.07**

Activities

The Bank adheres to the Islamic principle forbidding usury, and does not grant loans or credits for interest. Instead, its methods of financing are: provision of interest-free loans (with a service fee) mainly for infrastructural projects which are expected to have a marked impact on long-term socio-economic development; provision of technical assistance (e.g. for feasibility studies); equity participation in industrial and agro-industrial projects; leasing operations, involving the leasing of equipment such as ships; and profit-sharing operations. Funds not immediately needed for projects are used for foreign trade financing, particularly for importing commodities to be used in development (i.e. raw materials rather than consumer goods); priority is given to the import of goods from other member countries (see table). In addition, the Special Assistance Account provides emergency aid and other assistance, with particular emphasis on education in Islamic communities in non-member countries.

By September 1985 the Bank had approved a total of ID 1,321.5m. for project financing and technical assistance, and a total of ID 3,373.55m. for foreign trade financing. During the year ending 16 September 1985, the Bank approved a total of ID 940.36m. for 87 operations: of this amount 29% was for ordinary operations and 71% for foreign trade financing (see table).

The Bank approved 12 interest-free loans in the year to 16 September 1985, amounting to ID 98.62m. These loans supported the following projects: flood control drainage and irrigation works in Bangladesh and Pakistan; integrated rural development projects in Benin, Cameroon and Tunisia; water supply schemes in Algeria and Guinea; airport and seaport construction in the Comoros and Mali; rice cultivation schemes in Chad and Uganda; rehabilitation of higher education institutes in Tunisia and the Yemen Arab Republic; a fisheries infrastructure development in Indonesia; and the acquisition of electric cables for Bahrain.

Lease financing has become the most important method of project financing, accounting for 34.56% in the year ending 16 September 1985, when ID 92.1m. was approved for nine leasing operations.

Thirteen technical assistance operations were approved during the year at a cost of ID 6.63m.: these included feasibility and design studies for road projects in Mali, Mauritania, Senegal and Sierra Leone, and forestry and land development studies for Burkina Faso, Guinea, Djibouti and Mali.

Twenty-one IDB members are among the world's least-developed countries, and the Bank's policy is to give them a major share of its concessional financing: 51% of loans and 28% of total project financing approved in the year ending 25 September 1984 was for these countries.

Foreign trade financing approved during the year ending 16 September 1985 amounted to ID 667.25m. for 39 operations in 13 member countries; of this amount 57% was for imports of crude petroleum and refined petroleum products, 15% for intermediate industrial goods and 11% for vegetable oil.

The Bank's Special Assistance Account financed 11 operations during the year, amounting to ID 63.9m., including a special programme of emergency assistance for member countries in the Sahel region, to alleviate the effects of chronic drought.

Disbursements during the year ending 16 September 1985 amounted to ID 784m., of which ID 43.73m. was for project financing and technical assistance, ID 726.5m. was for foreign trade financing and ID 13.77m. was financed from the Special Assistance Account.

RESEARCH AND TRAINING INSTITUTE
Islamic Research and Training Institute: POB 9201, Jeddah 21413, Saudi Arabia; tel. 6361400; telex 401407; f. 1982 for research enabling economic, financial and banking activities to conform to Islamic law, and to provide training for staff involved in development activities in the Bank's member countries.

PUBLICATION
Annual Report.

INTERNATIONAL ORGANIZATIONS

Islamic Development Bank

Operations approved, October 1984–September 1985

Type of operation	Number of operations	Total amount (milllion Islamic Dinars)
Ordinary operations	48	273.11
Project financing	35	266.48
Loan	15	98.62
Equity	4	9.87
Leasing	9	92.10
Profit-sharing	—	—
Technical assistance	13	6.63
Foreign trade financing	39	667.25
Operations financed from the Special Assistance Account	11	63.90

Project financing by sector, October 1984–September 1985

Sector	Amount (million Islamic Dinars)	%
Agriculture	91.71	35.6
Industry and mining	65.47	24.0
Transport and communications	7.23	2.7
Utilities	79.84	29.2
Social services	26.48	9.7
Others	2.33	0.8
Total	273.11	100.0

LATIN AMERICAN INTEGRATION ASSOCIATION—LAIA

(ASOCIACIÓN LATINOAMERICANA DE INTEGRACIÓN – ALADI)

Address: Cebollatí 1461, Casilla de Correo 577, Montevideo, Uruguay.
Telephone: 40 11 21-28.
Telex: 32 6944.

The Latin American Integration Association was established in August 1980 to replace the Latin American Free Trade Association, set up in February 1960.

MEMBERS

Argentina	Colombia	Peru
Bolivia	Ecuador	Uruguay
Brazil	Mexico	Venezuela
Chile	Paraguay	

Organization
(October 1986)

COUNCIL OF MINISTERS

The Council of Ministers of Foreign Affairs is responsible for the adoption of the Association's policies. It meets when convened by the Committee of Representatives.

COMMITTEE OF REPRESENTATIVES

The Committee, the permanent political body of the Association, comprises a permanent and a deputy representative from each member country, and, by mid-1986, 10 permanent observers representing Cuba, the Dominican Republic, El Salvador, Guatemala, Honduras, Portugal, Spain, the UN Economic Commission for Latin America and the Caribbean (ECLAC), the Inter-American Development Bank and the Organization of American States. Its task is to ensure the correct implementation of the Treaty and its supplementary regulations. There are four auxiliary bodies:

Council for Financial and Monetary Affairs: comprises the Presidents of member states' central banks, who examine all aspects of financial, monetary and exchange co-operation.

Technical Assistance and Co-operation Commission: advises the Committee on technical assistance programmes.

Advisory Commission on Financial and Monetary Affairs.

Meeting of Directors of National Customs Administrations.

EVALUATION AND CONVERGENCE CONFERENCE

The Conference, comprising plenipotentiaries of the member governments, assesses the Association's progress and encourages negotiations between members. It meets when convened by the Committee of Representatives.

SECRETARIAT

The Secretariat is the technical body of the Association; it submits proposals for action, carries out research and follows the progress of activities. The Secretary-General is appointed for a three-year term.

Secretary-General: JUAN JOSÉ REAL (Uruguay).
Deputy Secretaries-General: FRANKLIN BUITRÓN AGUILAR (Ecuador), ROBERTO GATICA SUÁREZ (Mexico).

Activities

The Latin American Free Trade Association (LAFTA) was an intergovernmental organization, created by the Treaty of Montevideo in February 1960 with the object of increasing trade between the Contracting Parties and of promoting regional integration, thus contributing to the economic and social development of the member countries. The Treaty provided for the gradual establishment of a free trade area, which would form the basis for a Latin American Common Market. Reduction of tariff and other trade barriers was to be carried out gradually up to 1980.

This scheme, however, made little progress. By 1980 only 14% of annual trade among members could be attributed to LAFTA agreements, and it was the richest states which were receiving most benefit. In June 1980 it was decided that LAFTA should be replaced by a less ambitious and more flexible organization, the Latin American Integration Association (LAIA), established by the 1980 Montevideo Treaty, which came into force in March 1981, and was fully ratified in March 1982. Instead of across-the-board tariff cuts, the Treaty envisaged an area of economic preferences, comprising a regional tariff preference for goods originating in member states (in effect from 1 July 1984) and regional and partial scope agreements (on economic complementation, trade promotion, trade in agricultural goods, scientific and technical co-operation, the environment, tourism, and other matters), taking into account the different stages of development of the members, and with no definite timetable for the establishment of a full common market.

The members of LAIA are divided into three categories: most developed (Argentina, Brazil and Mexico); intermediate (Chile, Colombia, Peru, Uruguay and Venezuela); and least developed (Bolivia, Ecuador and Paraguay), enjoying a special preferential system. By the end of 1983 the transition from LAFTA to LAIA had been completed with the renegotiation of over 22,000 tariff cuts granted among the partners from 1962 onwards. During 1982 the value of exports within LAIA accounted for 12% of member countries' total exports; the proportion fell to 8.5% in 1983, and stood at 8.9% in 1984 and 8.3% in 1985.

Certain LAFTA institutions were retained and adapted by LAIA, e.g. the Reciprocal Payments and Credits Agreement (1965, modified in 1982) and the Multilateral Credit Agreement to Alleviate Temporary Shortages of Liquidity, known as the Santo Domingo Agreement (1969, extended in 1981 to include mechanisms for counteracting global balance-of-payments difficulties and for assisting in times of natural disaster).

A feature of LAIA is its 'outward' projection, allowing for multilateral links or agreements with Latin American non-member countries or integration organizations. Likewise, the Treaty contemplates partial agreements with other developing countries or economic groups outside the continent.

By mid-1986 LAIA members had signed 40 renegotiation agreements (concerning the former LAFTA tariff cuts); 27 trade agreements (mostly on the basis of former LAFTA industrial complementation pacts); five economic complementation agreements; two economic co-operation agreements in favour of Bolivia; one agricultural agreement; 15 agreements with Latin American non-member countries; three regional market-opening agreements in favour of the least developed members; and an agreement on the regional tariff preference. A new system of tariff nomenclature was adopted from 1 May 1986 as a basis for common trade negotiations.

In 1984-85 the Secretariat's work included studies on safeguards mechanisms for regional trade; counter-trade; food export financing; the pharmaceuticals industry in Latin America; and potential import substitution of certain capital goods (boilers; food-processing equipment; agricultural and construction machinery; and pumps and compressors). The Secretariat convenes meetings of entrepreneurs in various private industrial sectors, to encourage regional trade and co-operation. There were 26 such meetings in 1985, and nearly 30 were planned for 1986.

A regional round of negotiations was launched by LAIA members in April 1986, aiming to develop a renewed preferential trade and payments system in the region, open to the participation of Latin American non-member countries. The agenda comprised four main fields of negotiation: trade expansion and regulation; co-operation and economic complementarity; payments and export financing; and preferential measures for the less-developed members. Between meetings of high-level government officials, permanent committees, based at LAIA headquarters in Montevideo, were to conduct specific negotiations.

PUBLICATIONS

Síntesis ALADI (monthly).

Ambito Empresarial (monthly for entrepreneurs, in Portuguese and Spanish).

Newsletter (every 2 months).

Reports, studies, texts of agreements, and trade statistics.

LEAGUE OF ARAB STATES

Address: 37 avenue Khereddine Pacha, Tunis, Tunisia.
Telephone: 890 100.
Telex: 13241.

The League of Arab States (more generally known as the Arab League) is a voluntary association of sovereign Arab states designed to strengthen the close ties linking them and to co-ordinate their policies and activities and direct them towards the common good of all the Arab countries. It was founded in March 1945 (see Pact of the League, p. 174).

MEMBERS

Algeria	Palestine†
Bahrain	Qatar
Djibouti	Saudi Arabia
Egypt*	Somalia
Iraq	Sudan
Jordan	Syria
Kuwait	Tunisia
Lebanon	United Arab Emirates
Libya	Yemen Arab Republic
Mauritania	Yemen, People's Democratic
Morocco	Republic
Oman	

* In March 1979 Egypt's membership of the Arab League was suspended, and it was decided to make Tunis the temporary headquarters of the League, its Secretariat and its permanent committees.
† Palestine is considered an independent state, as explained in the Charter Annex on Palestine, and therefore a full member of the League.

Organization
(October 1986)

COUNCIL

The supreme organ of the Arab League. Consists of representatives of the 21 member states, each of which has one vote, and a representative for Palestine. Unanimous decisions of the Council shall be binding upon all member states of the League; majority decisions shall be binding only on those states which have accepted them.

The Council may, if necessary, hold an extraordinary session at the request of two member states. Invitations to all sessions are extended by the Secretary-General. The ordinary sessions are presided over by representatives of the member states in turn.

Sixteen committees are attached to the Council:

Political Committee: studies political questions and reports to the Council meetings concerned with them. All member states are members of the Committee. It represents the Council in dealing with critical political matters when the Council is meeting. Usually composed of the foreign ministers.

Cultural Committee: in charge of following up the activities of the Cultural Department and the cultural affairs within the scope of the secretariat; co-ordinates the activities of the general secretariat and the various cultural bodies in member states.

Economic Committee: complemented by the Economic Council since 1953.

Communications Committee: supervises land, sea and air communications, together with weather forecasts and postal matters.

Social Committee: supports co-operation in such matters as family and child welfare.

Legal Committee: an extension of the Nationality and Passports Committee abolished in 1947; studies and legally formulates draft agreements, bills, regulations and official documents.

Arab Oil Experts Committee: for study of oil affairs; also investigates methods to prevent the smuggling of Arab oil into Israel; and for co-ordination of oil policies in general.

Information Committee: studies information projects, suggests plans and carries out the policies decided by the Council of Information Ministers.

Health Committee: for co-operation in health affairs.

Human Rights Committee: studies subjects concerning human rights, particularly violations by Israel; collaborates with the Information and Cultural Committees.

Permanent Committee for Administrative and Financial Affairs.

Permanent Committee for Meteorology.

Committee of Arab Experts on Co-operation.

Arab Women's Committee.

Organization of Youth Welfare.

Conference of Liaison Officers: co-ordinates trade activities among commercial attachés of various Arab embassies abroad.

The Arab League maintains a permanent office at the United Nations in New York, and has observer status at the UN General Assembly.

GENERAL SECRETARIAT

The administrative and financial offices of the League. The Secretariat carries out the decisions of the Council, and provides financial and administrative services for the personnel of the League. There are a number of departments: economic, political, legal, cultural, social and labour affairs, petroleum, finance, Palestine, health, information, communications, protocol. The most recently formed department deals with African affairs.

The Secretary-General is appointed by the League Council by a two-thirds majority of the member states, for a five-year term. He appoints the assistant secretaries and principal officials, with the approval of the Council. He has the rank of ambassador, and the assistant secretaries have the rank of ministers plenipotentiary.

Secretary General: CHEDLI KLIBI (Tunisia).

Assistant Secretaries-General:
  Arab Affairs: ASAAD AL-ASSAAD (Lebanon).
  Economic Affairs: Dr ABDUL-HASSAN ZALZALAH (Iraq).
  Legal Affairs: MUHAMMAD BEN SALAMAH (Tunisia).
  Political Affairs: ADNAN OMRAN (Syria).
  Palestine Affairs: Dr MUHAMMAD AL-FARRA (Jordan).
  Information Affairs: LAKHDAR AL-IBRAHIMI (Algeria).
  Technical Assistance Fund: MAHDHI MOSTAPHA AL-HADI (Sudan).
  Social Affairs: IBRAHIM AS-SAAD AL-IBRAHIM (Saudi Arabia).

DEFENCE AND ECONOMIC CO-OPERATION

Groups established under the Treaty of Joint Defence and Economic Co-operation, concluded in 1950 to complement the Charter of the League.

Arab Unified Military Command: f. 1964 to co-ordinate military policies for the liberation of Palestine.

Economic Council: to compare and co-ordinate the economic policies of the member states; the Council is composed of ministers of economic affairs or their deputies. Decisions are taken by majority vote. The first meeting was held in 1953.

Joint Defence Council: supervises implementation of those aspects of the treaty concerned with common defence. Composed of foreign and defence ministers; decisions by a two-thirds majority vote of members are binding on all.

Permanent Military Commission: established 1950; composed of representatives of army general staffs; main purpose: to draw up plans of joint defence for submission to the Joint Defence Council.

ARAB DETERRENT FORCE

Set up in June 1976 by the Arab League Council to supervise successive attempts to cease hostilities in Lebanon, and afterwards to maintain the peace. The mandate of the Force has been successively renewed. The Arab League Summit Conference in October 1976 agreed that costs were to be paid in the following percentage contributions: Saudi Arabia and Kuwait 20% each, United Arab Emirates 15%, Qatar 10% and other Arab states 35%.

OTHER INSTITUTIONS OF THE COUNCIL

Other bodies established by resolutions adopted by the Council of the League:

Academy of Arab Music: POB 6150, Baghdad, Iraq; tel. 552 15 37; Sec.-Gen. MUNIR BASHIR.

Administrative Tribunal of the Arab League: f. 1964; began operations 1966.

Special Bureau for Boycotting Israel: POB 437, Damascus, Syria.

SPECIALIZED ORGANIZATIONS

All member states of the Arab League are also members of the Specialized Agencies, which constitute an integral part of the Arab League. (See also chapters on the Arab Bank for Economic Development in Africa, the Arab Fund for Economic and Social Development, the Arab Monetary Fund, the Council of Arab Economic Unity and the Organization of Arab Petroleum Exporting Countries.)

Arab Academy of Maritime Transport: POB 1552, Sharjah, United Arab Emirates; tel. 358866; telex 68167; f. 1975. Dir-Gen. MOUSTAPHA WAJIH TAYARA.

Arab Centre for the Study of Arid Zones and Dry Lands (ACSAD): POB 2440, Damascus, Syria; tel. 755713; telex 412697; f. 1971 to conduct regional research and development programmes related to water and soil resources, plant and animal production, agro-meteorology, and socio-economic studies of arid zones. The Centre holds conferences and training courses and encourages the exchange of information by Arab scientists. Dir-Gen. MUHAMMAD EL-KHASH.

Arab Civil Aviation Council: POB 4410, 17 Al-Nasr St, Rabat, Morocco; tel. 74178; telex 32817; created 1965, began operations 1967; aims to develop the principles, techniques and economics of air transport in the Arab world; to co-operate with the International Civil Aviation Organization and to attempt to standardize laws and technical terms; also deals with Arab air rates. Pres. N. AL-KHANI. Publs *Air Transport Activities in Arab Countries, Lexicon of Civil Aviation Terminology* (Arabic); *Unified Air Law for Arab States* (Arabic and English).

Arab Fund for Technical Assistance to African and Arab Countries—AFTAAAC: 37 ave Khereddine Pacha, Tunis, Tunisia; tel. 890 100; telex 13242; f. 1975 to provide technical assistance for development projects by providing African and Arab experts, grants for scholarships and training, and finance for technical studies. Exec. Sec. MAHDI MUSTAFA AL-HADI.

Arab Industrial Development Organization: POB 3156, Al-Sa'adoun, Baghdad, Iraq; tel. 7184655; telex 2823; f. 1980; conducts sectoral studies on the situation and prospects of Arab industry, assists national industrial surveys, and provides consultation and training services. Dir-Gen. HATEM ABDUR-RASHEED. Publs *Bulletin, Journal of Arab Industrial Development* (in Arabic), reports and studies.

Arab Labour Organization: Sa'adoun Ave, POB 3237, Baghdad, Iraq; tel. 96191; telex 212746; established in 1965 for co-operation between member states in labour problems; unification of labour legislation and general conditions of work wherever possible; research; technical assistance; social insurance; training, etc.; the organization has a tripartite structure: governments, employers and workers. Dir-Gen. HASHEMI AL-BANANI. Publs *Bulletin* (monthly), *Arab Labour Review* (quarterly).

Arab League Educational, Cultural and Scientific Organization—ALECSO: ave Mohamed V, Tunis, Tunisia; tel. 784-466; f. 1970 to promote and co-ordinate educational, cultural and scientific activities in the Arab region. Dir-Gen. Dr MOHIEDDINE SABER. Publs *Arab Journal of Language Studies, Arab Journal of Information, Arab Journal of Educational Research, Arab Journal of Culture, Arab Journal of Science*.

Arab Organization of Administrative Sciences: POB 17159, Amman, Jordan; tel. 812118; telex 21594; f. 1969 to improve Arab administrative systems, develop Arab administrative organizations and enhance the capabilities of Arab civil servants, through training, research and documentation. Dir-Gen. Dr NASSIR AS-SAIGH. Publs *Arab Journal of Administration*, research series.

Arab Organization for Agricultural Development: 4 El Jamea St, POB 474, Khartoum, Sudan; tel. 78760; telex 22554; f. 1970 to contribute to co-operation in agricultural activities, and in the development of natural and human resources for agriculture; compiles data, conducts studies, training and food security programmes; has regional offices in five countries; includes Arab Forestry and Pastures Institute, Syria. Dir-Gen. Dr HASSAN FAHMI JUMHA.

Arab Organization for Social Defence Against Crime: POB 1341, Hassan II St, Rabat, Morocco; tel. 22218; telex 32914; f. 1960 to study causes and remedies for crime and the treatment of criminals and to reinforce co-operation in legal, judicial and correctional fields. Sec.-Gen. Dr MUHAMMAD CHEDDADI; the organization consists of three bureaux:

Arab Bureau for Narcotics: POB 17225, Amman, Jordan; tel. 813012; telex 21020; f. 1961 to supervise anti-drug campaigns and co-ordinate efforts to prevent the illegal production and smuggling of drugs.

Arab Bureau for Prevention of Crime: POB 5687, Baghdad, Iraq.

Arab Bureau of Criminal Police: Immeuble Union Sportive, ave Mayssaloume, Damascus, Syria.

Arab Organization for Standardization and Metrology: POB 926161, Amman, Jordan; tel. 663834; telex 22463; began activity in 1968 to unify technical terms and standard specifications for products; has 33 technical committees; runs an Arab Centre for Information and Documentation; assists in the establishment of national bodies and collaborates with international standards activities. Sec.-Gen. Dr MAHDI H. HNOOSH. Publs *Annual Report* (French and English), *Standardization* (10 a year, Arabic, English and French) and information pamphlets.

Arab Postal Union: POB 7999, Dubai, United Arab Emirates; tel. 66 05 08; telex 46284; f. 1954; aims to establish more strict postal relations between the Arab countries than those laid down by the Universal Postal Union, to pursue the development and modernization of postal services in member countries. Sec.-Gen. HUSSEIN AL-HANADAN. Publs *Bulletin* (monthly), *Review* (quarterly), *News* (annually) and occasional studies.

Arab Satellite Communication Organization—ASCO: POB 1038, Riyadh, Saudi Arabia; tel. 464 6666; telex 201300; plans ARABSAT project, under which the first satellite was launched in February 1985, for the improvement of telephone, telex, data transmission and radio and television in Arab countries. Dir-Gen. ABDELKADER BAIRI.

Arab States Broadcasting Union—ASBU: POB 65, 17 rue El Mensoura, El Mensah 4, Tunis 1014, Tunisia; tel. 238 818; telex 13398; f. 1969 to promote Arab fraternity, co-ordinate and study broadcasting subjects, to exchange expertise and technical co-operation in broadcasting; conducts training and audience research. Mems: 21 Arab radio and TV stations and six foreign associates. Sec.-Gen. ABDALLAH CHAKROUN. Publ. *ASBU Review* (every 2 months).

Arab Telecommunications Union: POB 28015, Baghdad, Iraq; tel. 5550630; telex 212007; f. 1953 to co-ordinate and develop telecommunications between the 21 member countries; to exchange technical aid and encourage research. Sec.-Gen. SALEM KALAF IBRAHIM AL-ANI. Publs *Economic and Technical Studies; Arab Telecommunications Union Journal* (quarterly).

Inter-Arab Investment Guarantee Corporation: POB 23568, Safat, Kuwait.

External Relations

ARAB LEAGUE OFFICES AND INFORMATION CENTRES ABROAD

Set up by the Arab League to co-ordinate work at all levels among Arab embassies abroad.

Argentina: Avda 3 de Febrero 1358, 1426 Buenos Aires.
Austria: Grimmelshausengasse 12, 1030 Vienna.
Belgium: 106 ave Franklin D. Roosevelt, 1050 Brussels.
Brazil: Shis-Qi 15, Conj. 7, Casa 23, 71600 Brasília, DF.
Canada: 170 Laurier Ave West, Suite 709, Ottawa K1P 5VP.
Ethiopia: POB 5768, Addis Ababa.
France: 114 blvd Malesherbes, 75017 Paris.
Federal Republic of Germany: Friedrich Wilhelm Str. 2A, 5300 Bonn 1.
Greece: 10 Antheon St, Palaio Psychico, Athens.
India: 61 Golf Links, New Delhi 110003.
Italy: Piazzale delle Belle Arti 6, 00196 Rome.

INTERNATIONAL ORGANIZATIONS — League of Arab States

Japan: 1-1-12 Moto Asabu, Minato-ku, Tokyo 106.
Kenya: POB 30770, Nairobi.
Mexico: Monte Altai 524, Lomas de Chapultepec, 11000 México, DF.
Netherlands: Lange Voorhout 12, 2514 ED The Hague.
Senegal: 41 rue El Hadji Amadou, Assane Ndoye, Dakar.
Switzerland: 9 rue du Valais, 1202 Geneva.
United Kingdom: 52 Green St, London W1Y 3RH.
USA: 747 Third Ave, New York, NY 10017; 1100 17th St, NW, Suite 901, Washington, DC 20036; and in Chicago, Dallas and San Francisco.

Record of Events

1945 Pact of the Arab League signed, March.
1946 Cultural Treaty signed.
1950 Joint Defence and Economic Co-operation Treaty.
1952 Agreements on extradition, writs and letters of request, nationality of Arabs outside their country of origin.
1953 Formation of Economic Council.
      Convention on the privileges and immunities of the League.
1954 Nationality Agreement.
1956 Agreement on the adoption of a Common Tariff Nomenclature.
      Sudan joined Arab League.
1961 Kuwait joined League.
      Syrian Arab Republic rejoined League as independent member.
1962 Arab Economic Unity Agreement.
1964 First Summit Conference of Arab kings and presidents, Cairo, January.
      First session of the Council of Arab information ministers, Cairo, March.
      First meeting of Economic Unity Council, June. Arab Common Market approved by Arab Economic Unity Council, August.
      Second Summit Conference welcomed establishment of Palestine Liberation Organization (PLO), September.
      First Conference of Arab ministers of communications, Beirut, November.
1965 Arab Common Market established, January.
1969 Fifth Summit Conference, Rabat. Call for mobilization of all Arab Nations against Israel.
1971 Bahrain, Qatar and Oman admitted to Arab League, September.
1973 Mauritania admitted to Arab League, December.
1974 Somalia admitted to Arab League, February.
1977 Djibouti admitted to membership, September.
      Tripoli Declaration, December. Decision of Algeria, Iraq, Libya and Yemen PDR to boycott League meetings in Egypt in response to President Sadat's visit to Israel.
1978 69th meeting of Arab League Council in Cairo, March, boycotted by 'rejectionist' states. Resolutions calling for an emergency summit to settle differences within the League and for the establishment of an Arab Solidarity Committee to be chaired by President Nimeri of Sudan. All members except Egypt were present at a Council meeting in Baghdad in November. A number of resolutions were adopted to be taken should Egypt sign a peace treaty with Israel of which the three principal ones were: diplomatic rupture with Egypt, transfer of the League's headquarters from Cairo, and the economic boycott of Sadat's Government.
1979 Council meeting in Baghdad, March: various resolutions were adopted of which the main points were: to withdraw Arab ambassadors from Egypt; to recommend severance of political and diplomatic relations with Egypt; to suspend Egypt's membership of the League on the date of the signing of the peace treaty with Israel; to make the city of Tunis the temporary HQ of the League, its Secretariat, ministerial councils and permanent technical committees; to condemn United States' policy regarding its role in concluding the Camp David agreements and the peace treaty; to halt all bank loans, deposits, guarantees or facilities, as well as all financial or technical contributions and aid to Egypt; to prohibit trade exchanges with the Egyptian state and with private establishments dealing with Israel.
1980 Meeting of Arab foreign and economic ministers (as the Arab Economic and Social Council), Amman, July. An Iraqi plan for investment of at least $10,000m. over 10 years, to aid development in poorer Arab states (particularly Djibouti, Mauritania, Somalia, Sudan and the two Yemens), was discussed. The November Summit Conference in Amman was boycotted by the Palestine Liberation Organization, Algeria, Lebanon, Libya, Syria and the People's Democratic Republic of Yemen, maintaining that the conference should have been postponed because of the serious differences in the Arab world over the Iran–Iraq war and the approach to negotiations on Israel. The Summit Conference agreed to set up a $5,000m. fund for the benefit of poorer Arab states, with Iraq, Kuwait, Qatar, Saudi Arabia and the United Arab Emirates as donors: assistance was to take the form of 20-year development loans, and the fund was to be administered by the Arab Fund for Social and Economic Development (q.v.). The conference also approved a wider 'Strategy for Joint Arab Economic Action', covering pan-Arab development planning up to the year 2000.
1981 In March the Council of Ministers set up a conciliation mission to try to improve relations between Morocco and Mauritania.
      Extraordinary meeting of Arab foreign ministers in May (on Lebanon), and June (following the Israeli attack on an Iraqi nuclear reactor).
      Twelfth Summit Conference, Fez, Morocco, November. The meeting was suspended after a few hours, following disagreement over a Saudi Arabian proposal known as the Fahd Plan, which includes not only the Arab demands on behalf of the Palestinians, as approved by the UN General Assembly, but also an implied *de facto* recognition of Israel.
1982 In February the conference of Arab ministers set up a ministerial commission to consider retaliatory measures against states supporting Israel.
      Second Arab Energy Conference held in Qatar, March.
      Twelfth Summit Conference reconvened, Fez, September: peace plan, similar to the Fahd Plan mentioned above, adopted. The plan demanded Israel's withdrawal from territories occupied in 1967, and removal of Israeli settlements in these areas; freedom of worship for all religions in the sacred places; the right of the Palestinian people to self-determination, under the leadership of the Palestine Liberation Organization; temporary UN supervision for the West Bank and the Gaza Strip; the creation of an independent Palestinian state, with Jerusalem as its capital; and a guarantee of peace for all the states of the region by the UN Security Council. An Arab League delegation, led by King Hussein of Jordan, subsequently visited Washington, Paris, Moscow and Beijing seeking support for the peace plan.
1983 The summit meeting due to be held in November was postponed owing to members' differences of opinion concerning Syria's opposition to Yasser Arafat's chairmanship of the PLO, and Syrian support of Iran in the war against Iraq.
1984 In March an emergency meeting established an Arab League committee to encourage international efforts to bring about a negotiated settlement of the Iran–Iraq war. In May ministers of foreign affairs adopted a resolution calling on Iran to stop attacking non-belligerent ships and installations in the Gulf region: similar attacks by Iraq were not mentioned.
1985 The Third Arab Energy Conference, sponsored by the Arab League and OAPEC, was held in Algeria in May. In August an emergency Summit Conference was boycotted by Algeria, Lebanon, Libya, Syria and the People's Democratic Republic of Yemen, while of the other 16 members only nine were represented by their heads of state. The conference reaffirmed its support for the peace plan adopted in 1982 (see above), but was non-committal on proposals made by Jordan and the Palestine Liberation Organization, envisaging eventual talks with Israel on Palestinian rights. Two commissions were set up to mediate in disagreements between Arab states (between Jordan and Syria, Iraq and Syria, Iraq and Libya, and Libya and the PLO).
1986 Proposals to hold an emergency summit meeting in May, in response to the US bombing of Libyan cities in April, were unsuccessful. In July King Hassan of Morocco announced that he was resigning as chairman of the next League Summit Conference (for which no date had yet been fixed), after criticism by several Arab leaders of his meeting with the Israeli Prime Minister earlier that month.

PUBLICATIONS

Sh'oun Arabiyya (*Journal of Arab Affairs,* monthly).
Information Bulletin (Arabic and English).
Bulletins of treaties and agreements concluded among the member states.
New York Office: *Arab World* (monthly), and *News and Views.*
Geneva Office: *Le Monde Arabe* (monthly), and *Nouvelles du Monde Arabe* (weekly).
Buenos Aires Office: *Arabia Review* (monthly).
Paris Office: *Actualités Arabes* (fortnightly).
Brasília Office: *Oriente Arabe* (monthly).
Rome Office: *Rassegna del Mondo Arabo* (monthly).
London Office: *The Arab* (monthly).
New Delhi Office: *Al Arab* (monthly).
Bonn Office: *Arabische Korrespondenz* (fortnightly).
Ottawa Office: *Spotlight on the Arab World* (fortnightly), *The Arab Case* (monthly).

The Pact of the League of Arab States
(22 March 1945)

Article 1. The League of Arab States is composed of the independent Arab States which have signed this Pact.

Any independent Arab state has the right to become a member of the League. If it desires to do so, it shall submit a request which will be deposited with the Permanent Secretariat-General and submitted to the Council at the first meeting held after submission of the request.

Article 2. The League has as its purpose the strengthening of the relations between the member states; the co-ordination of their policies in order to achieve co-operation between them and to safeguard their independence and sovereignty; and a general concern with the affairs and interests of the Arab countries. It has also as its purpose the close co-operation of the member states, with due regard to the organization and circumstances of each state, on the following matters:

(*a*) Economic and financial affairs, including commercial relations, customs, currency, and questions of agriculture and industry.

(*b*) Communications: this includes railways, roads, aviation, navigation, telegraphs and posts.

(*c*) Cultural affairs.

(*d*) Nationality, passports, visas, execution of judgments, and extradition of criminals.

(*e*) Social affairs.

(*f*) Health problems.

Article 3. The League shall possess a Council composed of the representatives of the member states of the League; each state shall have a single vote, irrespective of the number of its representatives.

It shall be the task of the Council to achieve the realization of the objectives of the League and to supervise the execution of agreements which the member states have concluded on the questions enumerated in the preceding article, or on any other questions.

It likewise shall be the Council's task to decide upon the means by which the League is to co-operate with the international bodies to be created in the future in order to guarantee security and peace and regulate economic and social relations.

Article 4. For each of the questions listed in Article 2 there shall be set up a special committee in which the member states of the League shall be represented. These committees shall be charged with the task of laying down the principles and extent of co-operation. Such principles shall be formulated as draft agreements, to be presented to the Council for examination preparatory to their submission to the aforesaid states.

Representatives of the other Arab countries may take part in the work of the aforesaid committees. The Council shall determine the conditions under which these representatives may be permitted to participate and the rules governing such representation.

Article 5. Any resort to force in order to resolve disputes arising between two or more member states of the League is prohibited. If there should rise among them a difference which does not concern a state's independence, sovereignty, or territorial integrity, and if the parties to the dispute have recourse to the Council for the settlement of this difference, the decision of the Council shall then be enforceable and obligatory.

In such a case, the states between whom the difference has arisen shall not participate in the deliberations and decisions of the Council.

The Council shall mediate in all differences which threaten to lead to war between two member states, or a member state and a third state, with a view to bringing about their reconciliation.

Decisions of arbitration and mediation shall be taken by majority vote.

Article 6. In case of aggression or threat of aggression by one state against a member state, the state which has been attacked or threatened with aggression may demand the immediate convocation of the Council.

The Council shall by unanimous decision determine the measures necessary to repulse the aggression. If the aggressor is a member state, its vote shall not be counted in determining unanimity.

If, as a result of the attack, the government of the state attacked finds itself unable to communicate with the Council, that state's representative in the Council shall have the right to request the convocation of the Council for the purpose indicated in the foregoing paragraph. In the event that this representative is unable to communicate with the Council, any member state of the League shall have the right to request the convocation of the Council.

Article 7. Unanimous decisions of the Council shall be binding upon all member states of the League; majority decisions shall be binding only upon those states which have accepted them.

In either case the decisions of the Council shall be enforced in each member state according to its respective basic laws.

Article 8. Each member state shall respect the systems of government established in the other member states and regard them as exclusive concerns of those states. Each shall pledge to abstain from any action calculated to change established systems of government.

Article 9. States of the League which desire to establish closer co-operation and stronger bonds than are provided by this Pact may conclude agreements to that end.

Treaties and agreements already concluded or to be concluded in the future between a member state and another state shall not be binding or restrictive upon other members.

Article 10. The permanent seat of the League of Arab States is established in Cairo. The Council may, however, assemble at any other place it may designate.

Article 11. The Council of the League shall convene in ordinary session twice a year, in March and in September. It shall convene in extraordinary session upon the request of two member states of the League whenever the need arises.

Article 12. The League shall have a permanent Secretariat-General which shall consist of a Secretary-General, Assistant Secretaries, and an appropriate number of officials.

The Council of the League shall appoint the Secretary-General by a majority of two-thirds of the states of the League. The Secretary-General, with the approval of the Council, shall appoint the Assistant Secretaries and the principal officials of the League.

The Council of the League shall establish an administrative regulation for the functions of the Secretariat-General and matters relating to the Staff.

The Secretary-General shall have the rank of Ambassador and the Assistant Secretaries that of Ministers Plenipotentiary.

Article 13. The Secretary-General shall prepare the draft of the budget of the League and shall submit it to the Council for approval before the beginning of each fiscal year.

The Council shall fix the share of the expenses to be borne by each state of the League. This share may be reconsidered if necessary.

Article 14. The members of the Council of the League as well as the members of the committees and the officials who are to be designated in the administrative regulation shall enjoy diplomatic privileges and immunity when engaged in the exercise of their functions.

The building occupied by the organs of the League shall be inviolable.

Article 15. The first meeting of the Council shall be convened at the invitation of the head of the Egyptian Government. Thereafter it shall be convened at the invitation of the Secretary-General.

The representatives of the member states of the League shall alternately assume the presidency of the Council at each of its ordinary sessions.

Article 16. Except in cases specifically indicated in this Pact, a majority vote of the Council shall be sufficient to make enforceable decisions on the following matters:

(*a*) Matters relating to personnel.

(*b*) Adoption of the budget of the League.

(*c*) Establishment of the administrative regulations for the Council, the Committees, and the Secretariat-General.

(*d*) Decisions to adjourn the sessions.

Article 17. Each member state of the League shall deposit with the Secretariat-General one copy of every treaty or agreement concluded or to be concluded in the future between itself and another member state of the League or a third state.

Article 18. (deals with withdrawal).

Article 19. (deals with amendment).

Article 20. (deals with ratification).

ANNEX REGARDING PALESTINE

Since the termination of the last great war the rule of the Ottoman Empire over the Arab countries, among them Palestine, which has become detached from that Empire, has come to an end. She has come to be autonomous, not subordinate to any other state.

The Treaty of Lausanne proclaimed that her future was to be settled by the parties concerned.

However, even though she was as yet unable to control her own affairs, the Covenant of the League (of Nations) in 1919 made provision for a regime based upon recognition of her independence.

Her international existence and independence in the legal sense cannot, therefore, be questioned, any more than could the independence of the Arab countries.

Although the outward manifestations of this independence have remained obscured for reasons beyond her control, this should not be allowed to interfere with her participation in the work of the Council of the League.

The states signatory to the Pact of the Arab League are therefore of the opinion that, considering the special circumstances of Palestine and until that country can effectively exercise its independence, the Council of the League should take charge of the selection of an Arab representative from Palestine to take part in its work.

ANNEX REGARDING CO-OPERATION WITH COUNTRIES WHICH ARE NOT MEMBERS OF THE COUNCIL OF THE LEAGUE

Whereas the member states of the League will have to deal in the Council as well as in the committees with matters which will benefit and affect the Arab world at large;

And whereas the Council has to take into account the aspirations of the Arab countries which are not members of the Council and has to work toward their realization;

Now therefore, it particularly behoves the states signatory to the Pact of the Arab League to enjoin the Council of the League, when considering the admission of those countries to participation in the committees referred to in the Pact, that it should do its utmost to co-operate with them, and furthermore, that it should spare no effort to learn their needs and understand their aspirations and hopes; and that it should work thenceforth for their best interests and the safeguarding of the future with all the political means at its disposal.

NORDIC COUNCIL

Address: Tyrgatan 7, Box 19506, 10432 Stockholm, Sweden.
Telephone: (08) 14-34-20.
Telex: 12 867.

The Nordic Council was founded in 1952 for co-operation between the Nordic parliaments and governments. The four original members were Denmark, Iceland, Norway and Sweden; Finland joined in 1955, and the Faeroe Islands and Åland were granted representation in 1970 within the Danish and Finnish delegations respectively. Greenland had separate representation within the Danish delegation from 1984.

MEMBERS

Denmark (with the Faeroe Islands and Greenland)
Finland (with Åland)
Iceland
Norway
Sweden

Organization
(October 1986)

COUNCIL

The Council convenes annually in a plenary session of about one week's duration. Following an introductory general debate, the Session considers proposals put forward by Council members, by the Council of Ministers (q.v.) or national governments. The Session also follows up the outcome of past decisions and the work of the various Nordic institutions.

The Council comprises 87 members, elected annually by and from the parliaments of the respective countries (Denmark 16 members; Faeroes 2; Greenland 2; Finland 18; Åland 2; Iceland 7; Norway 20; Sweden 20). The various parties are proportionately represented in accordance with their representation in the national parliaments.

The Council initiates and follows up co-operative efforts among the Nordic countries. It does this by issuing recommendations and statements of position to the Council of Ministers and the respective governments. The recommendations of the Council, which express political judgements and opinions with solid foundations in the Nordic parliaments, generally result in the taking of measures on the part of Councils of Ministers of the national governments in question.

STANDING COMMITTEES

Council members are assigned to six Standing Committees (Economic; Legal; Communications; Cultural; Social and Environmental; and Budget and Control Committees). The Committees prepare business to be put before the Council during the annual Session.

PRESIDIUM

The Presidium of the Council, in which all five countries have two parliamentary representatives, is the supreme executive body of the Council.

President (1986/1987): ANKER JØRGENSEN (Denmark).

SECRETARIATS

Each delegation to the Nordic Council has a secretariat at its national parliament. The secretaries of the five standing committees are attached to the secretariat of the Presidium in Stockholm.

Secretary of the Presidium: ILKKA-CHRISTIAN BJÖRKLUND (Finland) (to be replaced by GERHARD AF SCHULTEN).

FINANCE

Budget contributions are calculated according to a formula based on the countries' respective gross national products; approximately 40% is paid by Sweden and 20% each by Denmark, Finland and Norway.

PUBLICATIONS

Yearbook of Nordic Statistics (in English and Swedish).

Nordiska Samarbetsorgan (list of all Nordic institutions, with their names in English).

NU-Series (reports of policy and fact-finding research committees; summaries available in English).

Nordisk Kontakt.

NORDIC COUNCIL OF MINISTERS

Address: Store Strandstraede 18, 1255 Copenhagen K, Denmark.
Telephone: (01) 11-47-11.
Telex: 15544.

The Governments of Denmark, Finland, Iceland, Norway and Sweden co-operate through the Nordic Council of Ministers. This co-operation is regulated by the revised Treaty of Co-operation between Denmark, Finland, Iceland, Norway and Sweden of 1972 and 1974 (revised Treaty of Helsinki) and the Treaty between Denmark, Finland, Iceland, Norway and Sweden concerning cultural co-operation of 1971. Unanimous decisions taken by the Nordic Council of Ministers are binding on the member states, when not subject to parliamentary approval in the national assemblies. The Prime Ministers and the Ministers of Defence and Foreign Affairs do not meet within the Nordic Council of Ministers.

MEMBERS

Denmark	Iceland	Norway
Finland		Sweden

Organization
(October 1986)

COUNCIL OF MINISTERS

The Nordic Council of Ministers holds formal and informal meetings and is attended by ministers with responsibility for the subject under discussion. Each member state also appoints a minister in its own cabinet as Minister for Nordic Co-operation.

Formal decisions must be taken unanimously, and are binding on the member governments, except in certain cases where ratification in the parliaments is required.

Meetings are concerned with: agreements and treaties, guidelines for national legislation, recommendations from the Nordic Council, financing joint studies, setting up Nordic institutions.

The Council of Ministers reports each year to the Nordic Council on progress in all co-operation between member states as well as on future plans.

SECRETARIAT

There are Divisions for:
1. Co-ordination, administration, budget and legislative questions;
2. Cultural and educational co-operation;
3. Research, advanced education, computer technology. protection of the environment, energy;
4. Labour market questions, occupational environment, social policy and health care, equality;
5. Finance and monetary policy, industry, co-operation in the building sector, trade and development aid;
6. Regional policy, transport, communications, tourism, farming, forestry, fishing and consumer questions;
7. Information.

Secretary-General: Fridtjov Clemet.

COMMITTEES

Committee of Ministers' Deputies: for final preparation of material for the meetings of Ministers of Nordic Co-operation.

Committees of Senior Civil Servants: prepare the meetings of the Council of Ministers and conduct research at its request. There are a number of sub-committees. The Committees of Senior Civil Servants cover the subjects listed under the Secretariat (above).

Activities

ECONOMIC CO-OPERATION

Nordic Investment Bank: founded under an agreement of December 1975 to provide finance and guarantees for the implementation of investment projects and exports; authorized and subscribed capital 800m. IMF Special Drawing Rights. The main sectors of the Bank's activities are energy, metal and wood-processing industries (including petroleum extraction) and manufacturing. By December 1985 the Bank had granted 341 loans totalling 1,713m. SDRs. In 1982 a scheme for financing investments in developing countries was established.

Nordic Industrial Fund: f. 1973 with a capital of 10m. Swedish kronor, to be increased in stages to 50m. Makes grants, subsidies and loans for industrial research and development projects of interest to more than one member country. The budget for 1984 was 35.2m. Swedish kronor.

Nordic Economic Research Council: f. 1980 to promote research and analysis on Nordic economic interdependence particularly with regard to economic stabilization policies.

NORDTEST: f. 1973 as an inter-Nordic agency for technical testing and standardization; collaborates with the Nordic Committee on Building Regulations.

Nordic Project Fund: f. 1982 to strengthen the international competitiveness of Nordic exporting companies, and to promote industrial co-operation.

The national administrations for overseas development have carried out several projects as a group, and consult with one another frequently.

COMMUNICATIONS AND TRANSPORT

A Nordic agreement for transport and communications entered into force in 1973. The main areas of co-operation have been road research, urban transport, transport in sparsely populated areas, transport for the disabled and road safety. Earlier agreements cover co-operation in post and telecommunications. Passports are not required for travel by Nordic citizens within the region.

LABOUR MARKET

Since 1954 a free labour market has been in force between Denmark, Finland, Norway and Sweden. By 1980 more than one million people had moved across the frontiers in Scandinavia. There is a joint centre for labour market training at Övertorneå in Sweden.

ENVIRONMENT

The Nordic Convention on the protection of the environment was signed in 1974, entering into force in October 1976. The member states undertake to harmonize regulations for protecting the environment, and to assess certain measures affecting neighbouring countries.

The coastal states have also signed a Convention on the Marine Environment of the Baltic, which entered into force in May 1980; special agreements have been concluded between Denmark and Sweden on pollution in the Öresund, and between Finland and Sweden on pollution in the Gulf of Bothnia.

NORDFORSK (Scandinavian Council for Applied Research) has a special secretariat for environmental research in Helsinki.

The Nordic Institute for Advanced Studies on Occupational Environment was established in 1982.

ENERGY

Co-operation within the sector includes studies of energy saving, the use of coal, the introduction of new and renewable sources of energy, and the use of petroleum and gas. There is a special committee for atomic energy. A common authority for electricity supply (NORDEL) was set up in 1963.

CONSUMER AFFAIRS

The main areas of co-operation are in consumer legislation, information on goods and services, consumer education and general questions of consumer policy.

LAW

The five countries have similar legal systems and tend towards uniformity in legislation and interpretation of law. Much of the preparatory committee work within the national administrations on new legislation involves consultation with the neighbour countries.

Citizens of one Nordic country working in another are in many respects given the status of nationals. In all the Nordic countries they already have the right to vote in local elections in the country of residence. The changing of citizenship from one Nordic country to another has been simplified.

There are special extradition facilities between the countries and further stages towards co-operation between the police and the courts have been recommended.

There is a permanent Council for Criminology, a Nordic Institute for Maritime Law in Oslo and a permanent committee for Penalty Law.

REGIONAL POLICY

Under a joint programme agreed in 1986, regional policy gives priority to cross-border co-operation for development in nine areas, with most financial support allotted to the 'Northern Cap' area (the northern provinces of Finland, Norway and Sweden) and the Western Nordic area (Greenland, the Faeroes and Iceland).

SOCIAL WELFARE AND HEALTH

Under the Convention on Social Security, 1955 (renewed in 1981), Nordic citizens have the same rights, benefits and obligations in each Nordic country. In 1974 a new agreement was made on arrangements for sickness, pregnancy and childbirth when temporarily in another Nordic country. Uniform provisions exist concerning basic pension and supplementary pension benefits when moving from one Nordic country to another.

In 1981 an agreement was concluded for doctors, dentists, nurses and pharmacists on the standards of competence required for obtaining work in other Nordic countries.

Institutions:
Nordic School of Public Health, Gothenburg, Sweden;
Scandinavian Institute of Dental Materials, Oslo;
Nordic Council on Medicines, Uppsala, Sweden;
Nordic Council on Alcohol and Drug Research, Helsinki;
Nordic Committee on Disability, Stockholm.

Other Permanent Bodies:
Scandiatransplant, under Nordic Committee on Kidney Transplantation, Århus, Denmark;
Nordic Medico-Statistical Committee, Copenhagen;
Nordic Committee of Social Security Statistics, Helsinki.

CULTURAL AND SCIENTIFIC CO-OPERATION

Nordic Cultural Fund: The Fund receives applications within the fields of research, education and general cultural activities. The Fund is part governmental, part parliamentary. The Fund board consists of a member of parliament and a senior civil servant from each of the member states. The Nordic Cultural Fund is located within and administered by the Secretariat of the Nordic Council of Ministers in Copenhagen. In 1985 it was allotted 10.3m. Danish kroner.

Education: Nordic co-operation in the educational field includes the objective content and means of education, the structure of the educational system and pedagogical development work.

Priority is given to:

1. Secondary education, adult education and vocational training.
2. Projects relevant for all levels of the educational system such as the teaching of Nordic languages and pedagogical research and development.

Joint projects include:
Nordic Co-operation in Adult Education
Nordic Educational Courses
Nordic Folk Academy
Nordic School of Journalism
Nordic Language Secretariat
Nordic Language and Information Centre
Nordic Federation for Medical Education
Nordic School of Nutritional and Textile Sciences
Nordic School Co-operation

Research: Nordic co-operation in research comprises information on research activities and research findings, joint research projects, joint research institutions, the methods and means in research policy, the organizational structure of research and a co-ordination of the national research programmes.

Much of the research co-operation activities at the more permanent joint research institutions consists of establishing science contacts in the Nordic areas by means of grants, visiting lecturers, courses and symposia.

The research institutions and research bodies listed below receive continuous financial support via the Nordic cultural budget. In many cases, these joint Nordic institutions ensure a high international standard that would otherwise have been difficult to maintain at a purely national level.

Nordic Accelerator Committee
Nordic Council for Arctic Medical Research
Scandinavian Institute of Asian Studies
Nordic Documentation Centre for Mass Communication Research
Nordic Committee on East European Studies
Nordic Council for Ecology
Nordic Institute of Folklore
Nordic Geoexcursions to Iceland
Nordic Co-operation Committee for International Politics
Nordic Council for Marine Biology
Scandinavian Institute of Maritime Law
Nordic Council for Physical Oceanography
Nordic Institute for Studies in Urban and Regional Planning
Nordic Research Courses
Nordic Research Grants
Nordic Research Symposia
Nordic Association for Research on Latin America
Nordic Council for Scientific Information and Research Libraries
Nordic Summer University
Nordic Institute for Theoretical Atomic Physics
Nordic Volcanological Institute
Nordic Council for Co-operation in Silvicultural Research
Nordic Gene Bank
Nordic Research Policy Council

Cultural activities: Cultural co-operation is concerned with artistic and other cultural exchange between the Nordic countries; activities relating to libraries, museums, radio, television, and film; promotion of activities within organizations with general cultural aims, including youth and sports organizations; the improvement of conditions for the creative and performing arts; and encouragement for artists and cultural workers.

Joint projects include:
Nordic Co-operation among Adult Education Organizations
Nordic Amateur Theatre Council
Nordic Art Association
Nordic Arts Centre
Nordic Co-operation in Athletics
Nordic Council Literature Prize
Nordic Council Music Prize
Nordic Film Seminars
Nordic House in Reykjavík
Nordic House in the Faeroe Islands
Nordic Music Co-operation
Nordic Sami Institute
Nordic Theatre Committee
Nordic Writers' Courses
Nordic Youth Co-operation Committee
Nordic Literature Committee

FINANCE

Joint expenses are divided according to an agreed scale in proportion to the relative national product of the member countries. The 1987 budget of the Nordic Council of Ministers amounted to 537m. Danish kroner, of which Sweden was to contribute 37.1%, Norway 21.5%, Denmark 20.5%, Finland 20.0% and Iceland 0.9%. Various forms of co-operation are financed directly from the national budgets.

NORTH ATLANTIC TREATY ORGANISATION—NATO

Address: 1110 Brussels, Belgium.
Telephone: (02) 241-00-40.
Telex: 23867.

NATO was founded in 1949 by the North Atlantic Treaty as an international collective defence organization linking a group of European states with the USA and Canada. Member countries agree to treat an armed attack on any one of them as an attack against all.

MEMBERS*

Belgium
Canada
Denmark
France
Federal Republic of Germany
Greece
Iceland
Italy
Luxembourg
Netherlands
Norway
Portugal
Spain
Turkey
United Kingdom
USA

* France withdrew from the integrated military structure of NATO in 1966 although remaining a member of the Atlantic Alliance. Following the Turkish invasion of Cyprus in 1974, Greece also announced a partial withdrawal from the integrated military structure of NATO; it re-joined in October 1980. Spain joined NATO in May 1982.

Organization
(October 1986)

NORTH ATLANTIC COUNCIL

The highest authority of the alliance, composed of representatives of the 16 member states. It meets at the level of Ministers or Permanent Representatives. Ministerial meetings, attended by Ministers of Foreign Affairs, are held at least twice a year. At the level of Permanent Representatives it meets at least once a week.

The Secretary-General of NATO is chairman of the Council. Annually, the Foreign Minister of a member state is nominated honorary President, following the English alphabetical order of countries.

Decisions are taken by common consent and not by majority vote. The Council is a forum for wide consultation between member governments on major issues, including political, military, economic and other subjects. It also gives political guidance to the military authorities.

PERMANENT REPRESENTATIVES

Belgium: JUAN CASSIERS
Canada: GORDON SCOTT SMITH
Denmark: OTTO ROSE BORCH
France: GILLES CURIEN
Federal Republic of Germany: NIELS HANSEN
Greece: CHRISTOS ZACHARAKIS
Iceland: TÓMAS TÓMASSON
Italy: FRANCESCO PAOLO FULCI
Luxembourg: GUY DE MUYSER
Netherlands: J. G. N. DE HOOP SCHEFFER
Norway: EIVINN BERG
Portugal: ANTÓNIO VAZ PEREIRA
Spain: JAIME DE OJEDA
Turkey: OSMAN OLÇAY
United Kingdom: MICHAEL ALEXANDER
USA: DAVID M. ABSHIRE

DEFENCE PLANNING COMMITTEE

The Committee, in which decisions are taken on matters relating specifically to defence, comprises representatives of all the member countries except France. It is the highest forum for discussion of military policy. Like the Council it meets in both Ministerial and Permanent Representative sessions.

NUCLEAR PLANNING GROUP

The Group meets regularly at the level of Permanent Representatives, and twice yearly with Defence Ministers; 14 countries participate.

OTHER COMMITTEES

There are also committees for political affairs, economics, armaments, defence review, science, infrastructure, logistics, communications, civil emergency planning, information and cultural relations, and civil and military budgets. The Committee on the Challenges of Modern Society examines methods of improving allied co-operation in creating a better environment. In addition other committees deal with specialized subjects such as NATO pipelines, European air space co-ordination, etc.

INTERNATIONAL SECRETARIAT

The Secretary-General is Chairman of the North Atlantic Council, the Defence Planning Committee, the Nuclear Planning Group, and the Committee on the Challenges of Modern Society. He is the head of the International Secretariat, with staff drawn from the member countries. He proposes items for NATO consultation and is generally responsible for promoting consultation. He is empowered to offer his help informally in cases of disputes between member countries, to facilitate procedures for settlement.

Secretary-General: Lord CARRINGTON (UK).
Deputy Secretary-General: MARCELLO GUIDI (Italy).

There is an Assistant Secretary-General for each of the divisions listed below.

PRINCIPAL DIVISIONS

Division of Political Affairs: maintains political liaison with national delegations and international organizations. Prepares reports on political subjects for the Secretary-General and the Council. Asst Sec.-Gen. Dr FREDO DANNENBRING (FRG).

Division of Defence Planning and Policy: studies all matters concerning the defence of the Alliance, especially any with political or economic effect on defence problems, and also the overall financial aspects of defence by country. Asst Sec.-Gen. JAMES MORAY STEWART (UK).

Division of Defence Support: promotes the most efficient use of the Allies' resources in the production of military equipment and studies its standardization. Asst Sec.-Gen. ROBIN L. BEARD (USA).

Division of Infrastructure, Logistics and Council Operations: supervises the technical and financial aspects of the infrastructure programme. Co-ordinates the operational aspects of the Council's activities, crisis management plans and arrangements. Provides guidance co-ordination and support to the activities of all NATO committees or bodies active in the field of consumer logistics. Asst Sec.-Gen. C. M. E. DE LAAT DE KANTER (Netherlands).

Division of Scientific and Environmental Affairs: advises the Secretary-General on scientific matters of interest to NATO. Responsible for the exchange of scientific information between the civil and military authorities of NATO and the international organizations concerned. Asst Sec.-Gen. HENRY DURAND (France).

Military Organization

MILITARY COMMITTEE

Composed of the allied Chiefs-of-Staff, or their representatives, of member countries except France: the highest military authority in NATO. Meets at least twice a year at Chiefs-of-Staff level and remains in permanent session with Permanent Military Representatives. It is responsible for making recommendations to the Council and Defence Planning Committee on military matters and for supplying guidance on military questions to Supreme Allied Commanders and subordinate military authorities.

Although France is not a member there is a French Military Mission to the Military Committee for regular consultation.

President: Admiral W. J. CROWE (USA).
Chairman: Gen. WOLFGANG ALTENBURG (FRG).
Deputy Chairman: Lt-Gen. PAUL S. WILLIAMS (USA).

INTERNATIONAL ORGANIZATIONS

INTERNATIONAL MILITARY STAFF
Director: Lt-Gen. A. MORIAU (Belgium).

COMMANDS
European Command: Casteau, Belgium—Supreme Headquarters Allied Powers Europe—SHAPE. Supreme Allied Commander Europe—SACEUR: Gen. BERNARD W. ROGERS (USA).

Atlantic Ocean Command: Norfolk, Virginia, USA. Supreme Allied Commander Atlantic—SACLANT: Admiral LEE BAGGETT (USA).

Channel Command: Northwood, England. Allied Commander-in-Chief Channel—CINCHAN: Admiral Sir NICHOLAS HUNT (UK).

Activities

The NATO Alliance maintains military preparedness with the aim of preventing war. It provides for consultation on all political problems relevant to its members, draws up joint defence plans, organizes the necessary infrastructure and arranges for joint training and exercises.

NATO attempts to maintain sufficient forces to preserve the military balance with the countries of the Warsaw Pact (q.v.) and to provide a credible deterrent. NATO forces comprise three elements: conventional forces; intermediate and short-range nuclear forces; and the strategic nuclear forces of the United Kingdom and USA to provide the 'ultimate deterrent'.

Each year member countries take part in a Defence Review designed to assess their contribution to the common defence in relation to their respective capabilities and constraints. Allied defence policy is reviewed periodically by defence ministers.

Political consultations on other matters are an important feature of the Alliance, particularly discussion of East-West relations and of arms reduction. The North Atlantic Council takes part in such consultations and is directly involved in a decision-making capacity in the negotiations on Mutual and Balanced Force Reductions which began in 1973.

Co-operation in science and technology is undertaken under the Science Fellowships Programme, the Advanced Study Institutes Programme and the Research Grants Programme. A Science for Stability Programme was established in 1980 to help Greece, Portugal and Turkey develop their scientific and technological capabilities.

NATO AGENCIES
1. Civilian production and logistics organizations responsible to the Council:

Central European Operating Agency—CEOA: Versailles, France; f. 1957 to supervise the integrated military pipeline network in Central Europe; eight member nations.

Nato Airborne Early Warning and Control Programme Management Organisation—NAPMO: Brunssum, Netherlands; f. 1978 to manage the procurement aspects of the NATO Airborne Early Warning and Control System.

NATO HAWK Production and Logistics Organisation —NHPLO: Rueil-Malmaison, France; f. 1959 to supervise the multinational production of the HAWK surface-to-air missile system in Europe; now gives logistic support to HAWK units and has started a European Limited Improvement Programme; seven nations participate.

NATO Maintenance and Supply Organisation—NAMSO: Luxembourg; f. 1958; supplies spare parts and logistic support for a number of jointly-used weapon systems, missiles and electronic systems; all member nations except Iceland participate.

NATO MRCA Development and Production Management Organisation—NAMMO: Munich, Federal Republic of Germany; f. 1969 to supervise development and production of the Multi-Role Combat Aircraft project; mems: Federal Republic of Germany, Italy, UK.

NATO Communications and Information Systems Organisation—NACISO: Brussels, Belgium; f. 1985 by expansion of NATO Integrated Communications System Organisation; supervises planning and implementation of an integrated voice, telegraph and data communications system, to improve the Alliance's capability for crisis management and for the command and control of NATO forces.

2. Responsible to the Military Committee:

Advisory Group for Aerospace Research and Development—AGARD: Neuilly-sur-Seine, France; f. 1952; brings together aerospace scientists from member countries for exchange of information and research co-operation; provides scientific and technical advice for the Military Committee, for other NATO bodies and for member nations.

Allied Communications Security Agency—ACSA: Brussels, Belgium; f. 1953.

Allied Data Systems Interoperability Agency—ADSIA: Brussels, Belgium; f. 1979 to improve interoperability within the NATO Command, Control and Information Systems.

Allied Long Lines Agency—ALLA: Brussels, Belgium; f. 1951 to formulate policies to meet the long lines communications requirements of NATO.

Allied Naval Communications Agency—ANCA: London, England; f. 1951 to establish reliable communications for maritime operations.

Allied Radio Frequency Agency—ARFA: Brussels, Belgium; f. 1951 to establish policies concerned with military use of the radio frequency spectrum.

Allied Tactical Communications Agency—ATCA: Brussels, Belgium; f. 1972 to establish policies concerned with tactical communications for land and air operations.

Military Agency for Standardization—MAS: Brussels, Belgium; f. 1951 to improve military standardization of equipment for NATO forces.

NATO Defence College—NADEFCOL: Rome, Italy; f. 1951 to train officials for posts in NATO organizations or in national ministries.

3. Responsible to Supreme Allied Commander Atlantic (SACLANT):

SACLANT Anti-submarine Warfare Research Centre —SACLANTCEN: La Spezia, Italy; f. 1962 for research in submarine detection and oceanographic problems.

4. Responsible to Supreme Allied Commander Europe (SACEUR):

SHAPE Technical Centre—STC: The Hague, Netherlands; f. 1960 to provide scientific and technical advice, originally on the formation of an integrated air defence system, subsequently on a broader programme covering force capability and structure; command and control; communications.

FINANCE
As NATO is an international, not a supra-national, organization, its member countries themselves decide the amount to be devoted to their defence effort and the form which the latter will assume. Thus, the aim of NATO's defence planning is to develop realistic military plans for the defence of the alliance at reasonable cost.

TOTAL DEFENCE EXPENDITURE (Current Prices)

	Unit (million)	1983	1984	1985 (forecast)
Belgium	B. Francs	136,853	141,676	155,668
Canada	Can. $	8,086	9,320	10,263
Denmark	D. Kroner	12,574	13,045	13,750
France	Francs	165,029	176,638	186,242
Germany, Federal Republic[1]	DM	56,496	57,274	59,737
Greece	Drachmae	193,340	271,922	321,722
Italy	'000 Lire	14,400	16,433	18,059
Luxembourg	L. Francs	2,104	2,234	2,317
Netherlands	Guilders	12,149	12,765	12,885
Norway	N. Kroner	12,395	12,688	15,431
Portugal	Escudos	76,765	92,009	111,522
Turkey	Liras	556,738	803,044	1,198,125
United Kingdom	£ Sterling	15,952	16,923	18,572
USA	US $	217,198	237,052	266,642
Total Europe[2]	US $	92,866	86,818	83,559
Total North America	US $	223,759	244,248	274,181
Total NATO[2]	US $	316,625	331,066	357,740

Figures are based on NATO definitions of defence expenditure. Data for Spain are not available.

[1] Excluding expenditure for Berlin, forecast to be 15,116m. DM in 1985.

[2] Totals based on currency exchange rates in force during the years concerned.

Under the annual Defence Planning review, the political, military and economic factors are considered in relation to strategy, force requirements and available resources. The procedure for the co-ordination of military plans and defence expenditures rests on the detailed and comparative analysis of the capabilities of member countries. All installations for the use of international forces are financed under a common-funded infrastructure programme.

PUBLICATIONS

(in English and French, with some editions in other languages)

NATO Review (6 a year in English, French, Dutch, German, Italian and Spanish; quarterly editions in Danish, Greek, Portuguese and Turkish; annual editions in Icelandic and Norwegian).

NATO Facts and Figures. A major reference book giving a detailed description of the historical, operational and structural aspects of NATO.

NATO Basic Documents.

NATO Final Communiqués.

NATO and the Warsaw Pact Force Comparisons.

NATO Handbook.

Economic and scientific publications.

ORGANISATION FOR ECONOMIC CO-OPERATION AND DEVELOPMENT — OECD

Address: 2 rue André-Pascal, 75775 Paris Cedex 16, France.
Telephone: (1) 45-24-82-00.

OECD was founded in 1961, replacing the Organisation for European Economic Co-operation (OEEC) which had been set up in 1948 in connection with the Marshall Plan. It constitutes a forum where representatives of the governments of the industrialized democracies attempt to co-ordinate their economic and social policies.

MEMBERS

Australia	Greece	Norway
Austria	Iceland	Portugal
Belgium	Ireland	Spain
Canada	Italy	Sweden
Denmark	Japan	Switzerland
Finland	Luxembourg	Turkey
France	Netherlands	United Kingdom
Federal Republic of Germany	New Zealand	USA

Yugoslavia participates in the work of OECD with a special status. The Commission of the European Communities also takes part in the Organisation's work.

Organization
(October 1986)

COUNCIL

The governing body of OECD is the Council on which each member country is represented. The Council meets from time to time (usually once a year) at the level of government ministers, and regularly at official level, when it comprises the heads of Permanent Delegations to OECD (diplomatic missions headed by ambassadors). It is responsible for all questions of general policy and may establish subsidiary bodies as required to achieve the aims of the Organisation. Decisions and recommendations of the Council are adopted by mutual agreement of all its members. The Chairman of the Council at ministerial level is a member of government from the country elected to the chairmanship for that year. The Chairman of the Council at official level is the Secretary-General.

Heads of Permanent Delegations (with ambassadorial rank):
Australia: ALEXANDER MCGOLDRICK
Austria: GEORG LENNKH
Belgium: GUY STUYCK
Canada: WILLIAM J. JENKINS
Denmark: HENRIK NETTERSTRØM
Finland: WILHELM BREITENSTEIN
France: EMILE CAZIMAJOU
Germany, Federal Republic: KLAUS MEYER
Greece: DIMITRIS KOULOURIANOS
Iceland: HARALDUR KRÖYER
Ireland: ANDREW O'ROURKE
Italy: GIUSEPPE JACOANGELI
Japan: HIROMU FUKADA
Luxembourg: PIERRE WURTH
Netherlands: A. G. O. SMITSENDONK
New Zealand: JOHN G. MCARTHUR
Norway: THORVALD MOE
Portugal: PEDRO M. CRUZ ROSETTA
Spain: JOSÉ-VICENTE TORRENTE SECORÚN
Sweden: BO KJELLEN
Switzerland: JEAN ZWAHLEN
Turkey: TANSUG BLEDA
United Kingdom: NICOLAS BAYNE
USA: EDWARD J. STREATOR

Yugoslavia: TOMISLAV JANKOVIĆ
Commission of the European Communities: PIERRE DUCHATEAU

EXECUTIVE COMMITTEE

Each year the Council designates 14 of its members to form the Executive Committee which prepares the work of the Council. It is also called upon to carry out specific tasks where necessary. Apart from its regular meetings, the Committee meets occasionally in special sessions attended by senior government officials.

SECRETARIAT

The Council, the committees and other bodies in OECD are assisted by an independent international secretariat headed by the Secretary-General.
Secretary-General: JEAN-CLAUDE PAYE (France).
Deputy Secretaries-General: JACOB M. MYERSON (USA), PIERRE VINDE (Sweden).

AUTONOMOUS AND SEMI-AUTONOMOUS BODIES

International Energy Agency (see p. 184).
Nuclear Energy Agency (see p. 184).
Development Centre: f. 1962; includes all member countries except New Zealand. Pres. LOUIS EMMERIJ (see also under Development Co-operation, p. 183).
Centre for Educational Research and Innovation: includes all member countries and Yugoslavia. Dir J. R. GASS (UK) (see also under Manpower, Social Affairs and Education, p. 183).

Activities

The greater part of the work of OECD, which covers all aspects of economic and social policy, is prepared and carried out in about 200 specialized bodies (Committees, Working Parties, etc.); all members are normally represented on these bodies, except on those of a restricted nature. Participants are usually civil servants coming either from the capitals of member states or from the Permanent Delegations to OECD. The main bodies are:

Economic Policy Committee
Economic and Development Review Committee
Environment Committee
Group on Urban Affairs
Development Assistance Committee
Technical Co-operation Committee
Trade Committee
Payments Committee
Committee on Capital Movements and Invisible Transactions
Committee on International Investment and Multinational Enterprises
Committee on Financial Markets
Committee on Fiscal Affairs
Committee of Experts on Restrictive Business Practices
Tourism Committee
Maritime Transport Committee
Committee on Consumer Policy
Committee for Agriculture
Fisheries Committee
Committee for Scientific and Technological Policy
Committee for Information, Computer and Communications Policy
Education Committee
Industry Committee
Steel Committee
Committee for Energy Policy
Manpower and Social Affairs Committee
Steering Committee of the Programme of Co-operation in the Field of Road Research
Steering Committee of the Programme on Educational Building
High Level Group on Commodities
Group on North-South Economic Issues

ECONOMIC POLICY

The main organ for the consideration and direction of economic policy among the member countries is the Economic Policy Committee, which comprises governments' chief economic advisors and central bankers, and meets two or three times a year to review the economic and financial situation and policies of member countries. It has several working parties and groups, the most important of which are Working Party No. 1 on Macro-Economic and Structural Policy Analysis, Working Party No. 3 on Policies for the Promotion of a Better International Payments Equilibrium and the Working Group on Short-Term Economic Prospects.

The Economic and Development Review Committee is responsible for the annual examination of the economic situation of each member country. Usually, a report is issued each year on each country, after an examination carried out by a panel of representatives of a number of other member countries; this process of mutual examination, has been extended also to other branches of the Organisation's work (agriculture, manpower and social affairs, scientific policy and development aid efforts).

ENERGY

Work in the field of energy includes co-ordination of members' energy policies, assessment of short-, medium- and long-term energy prospects; a long-term programme of energy conservation, development of alternative energy sources and energy research and development; a system of information on the international oil and energy markets; and improvement of relations between oil-producing and oil-consuming countries. This work is carried out in OECD's International Energy Agency (IEA: see below), an autonomous body in which 21 member countries of OECD and the Commission of the European Communities participate, as well as within the context of OECD as a whole under the Committee for Energy Policy. Co-operation in the development of nuclear power is undertaken by the Nuclear Energy Agency (see below).

DEVELOPMENT CO-OPERATION

The Development Assistance Committee (DAC) consists of representatives of the main OECD capital-exporting countries; it discusses methods for making national resources available for assisting countries and areas in the process of economic development anywhere in the world, and for expanding and improving the flow of development assistance and other long-term funds.

The Group on North-South Economic Issues deals with the wide range of subjects involved in economic relationships between OECD countries and developing countries. It is particularly concerned with the treatment of these issues in the various fora of international economic discussion, such as UNCTAD.

A Technical Co-operation Committee has the task of drawing up and supervising the programmes of technical assistance arranged for the benefit of member countries, or areas of member countries, in the process of development.

The OECD Development Centre (a semi-autonomous body) was set up in 1962 for the collection and dissemination of information in the field of economic development, research into development problems and the training of specialists both from the industrialized and developing countries.

INTERNATIONAL TRADE

The activities of the Trade Committee are aimed at maintaining the degree of trade liberalization achieved, avoiding the emergence of new trade barriers, and improving further the liberalization of trade on a multilateral and non-discriminatory basis. These activities include examination of issues concerning trade relations among member countries as well as relations with non-member countries, in particular developing countries. The existing procedures allow, inter alia, any member country to obtain prompt consideration and discussions by the Trade Committee of trade measures taken by another member country which adversely affect its own interests.

The task of the High-Level Group on Commodities is to find a more active and broader approach to commodity problems, notably with a view to contributing to a greater stability in the markets.

FINANCIAL AND FISCAL AFFAIRS

The progressive abolition of obstacles to the international flow of services and capital is the responsibility of various OECD Committees. The Committee on Capital Movements and Invisible Transactions watches over the implementation of the Codes of Liberalization of Invisible Transactions and of Capital Movements. The Committee on International Investment and Multinational Enterprises prepared a Code of Behaviour (called 'Guidelines') for multinational enterprises, recommended to them by all member governments; the Committee is to follow up the implementation of these guidelines in order to improve the effectiveness of co-operation among member countries in international investment and multi-national enterprises. Other specialized committees have been set up to deal with financial markets, fiscal matters, restrictive business practices, tourism, maritime transport, consumer policy, etc.

FOOD, AGRICULTURE AND FISHERIES

The Committee for Agriculture reviews major developments in agricultural policies, deals with the adaptation of agriculture to changing economic conditions, elaborates forecasts of production and market prospects, holds consultations on import and export practices and assesses implications of world developments in food and agriculture for member countries' policies. A separate Fisheries Committee carries out similar tasks in its own sector.

ENVIRONMENT

The Environment Committee is responsible for the economic and policy aspects of OECD's work in this field. The Committee is assisted by various Sector Groups. Its work has led to agreements adopted by member countries setting out guiding principles on the international trade aspects of environment policies (e.g. the 'Polluter pays' principle), and on trans-frontier movements of hazardous waste. A special Chemicals Programme promotes co-operation and mutual assistance in controlling the 80,000 chemicals on the commercial market. The Committee also deals with policies for air and water management, noise abatement, trans-frontier pollution, etc.

Urban problems in OECD countries are dealt with by a Group on Urban Affairs, covering economic, social and administrative issues in cities, as well as ecological aspects of the built-up environment.

SCIENCE, TECHNOLOGY AND INDUSTRY

The Committee for Scientific and Technological Policy is responsible for encouraging co-operation among member countries in scientific and technological policies with a view to contributing to the achievement of their economic and social aims.

The Committee for Information, Computer and Communications Policy is to examine policy issues arising from the development and application of technologies in the field of information, computer and communications systems and services, including the impact of such issues on the economy and on society in general.

The Steel Committee, enables governments, consistent with general economic policies, to act promptly to cope with crisis situations, to keep steel trade as unrestricted and undistorted as possible and to facilitate the necessary structural adjustment of the industry.

The Industry Committee has overall responsibility for all aspects of the Organisation's work in the field of industry which require co-operation and confrontation among member governments.

MANPOWER, SOCIAL AFFAIRS AND EDUCATION

The Manpower and Social Affairs Committee is concerned with the development of manpower and selective employment policies to ensure the utilization of manpower at the highest possible level and to improve the quality and flexibility of working life as well as the integration of social policies. Its work includes such aspects as the role of women in the economy, industrial relations, intra-European migration movements and the development of social indicators.

The Committee for Education relates educational planning to educational policy and evaluates the implications of policy for the allocation and use of resources. The Committee reviews educational trends, develops statistics and indicators and analyses policies for greater equality of educational opportunity, new options for youth and learning opportunities for adults. Together, the Manpower and Education Committees seek to provide for greater integration of manpower and educational policy.

The OECD's Centre for Educational Research and Innovation (CERI) promotes the development of research activities in education together with experiments of an advanced nature designed to test innovations in educational systems and to stimulate research and development. Yugoslavia is also a member.

RELATIONS WITH OTHER INTERNATIONAL ORGANIZATIONS

The Commission of the European Communities generally takes part in the work of OECD under a Protocol signed at the same time as the OECD Convention. EFTA may also send representatives to attend all OECD meetings. Official relations exist with 11 UN agencies and with about 20 other intergovernmental organizations.

International non-governmental organizations which are deemed to be widely representative in general economic matters or in a specific economy sector are granted a consultative status enabling them to discuss subjects of common interest with a Liaison Committee chaired by the Secretary-General, and to be consulted in a

INTERNATIONAL ORGANIZATIONS — OECD

particular field by the relevant OECD Committee or its Officers. So far, this status has been granted to: the Business and Industry Advisory Committee to OECD (BIAC); the Trade Union Advisory Committee to OECD (TUAC); the International Association of Crafts and Small and Medium Sized Enterprises; the International Federation of Agricultural Producers; and the European Confederation of Agriculture.

PUBLICATIONS

Activities of OECD (Secretary-General's Annual Report).
OECD (a general interest booklet).
News from OECD (monthly).
OECD Employment Outlook (annually).
The OECD Observer (every 2 months).
The OECD Economic Outlook (2 a year).
Economic Surveys by OECD (annually for each country).
Development Assistance Efforts and Policies (annually).
Foreign Trade Statistics Bulletin (monthly).
Main Economic Indicators (monthly).
OECD Convention and Report of Preparatory Committee.
Numerous specialized reports, books and statistics on economic and social subjects (about 350 titles a year) are also published.

International Energy Agency

Address: 2 rue André Pascal, 75775 Paris Cedex 16, France.

The Agency was set up by the Council of OECD in 1974 to develop co-operation on energy questions among participating countries.

MEMBERS

Australia
Austria
Belgium
Canada
Denmark
Federal Republic of Germany
Greece
Ireland
Italy
Japan
Luxembourg
Netherlands
New Zealand
Norway
Portugal
Spain
Sweden
Switzerland
Turkey
United Kingdom
USA

The Commission of the European Communities is represented.

Activities

The Agreement on an International Energy Programme was signed in November 1974 and formally entered into force in January 1976. The Programme commits the participating countries of the International Energy Agency to share oil in emergencies, to strengthen their long-term co-operation in order to reduce dependence on oil imports, to increase the availability of information on the oil market and to develop relations with the oil-producing and other oil-consuming countries.

The emergency oil-sharing plan has been established and the IEA ensures that the necessary technical information and facilities are in place so that it can be readily used in the event of a reduction in oil supplies.

The IEA Long-Term Co-operation Programme is designed to strengthen the security of energy supplies and promote stability in world energy markets. It provides for co-operative efforts to conserve energy, to accelerate the development of alternative energy sources by means of both specific and general measures, to step up research and development of new energy technologies and to remove legislative and administrative obstacles to increased energy supplies. Regular reviews of member countries' efforts in the fields of energy conservation and accelerated development of alternative energy sources assess the effectiveness of national programmes in relation to the objectives of the Agency.

The Agency has developed an extensive system of information and consultation on the oil market with a view to obtaining a better idea of probable future developments in the oil market. Another function of the Agency is to develop a long-term co-operative relationship among oil-producing and consuming countries.

GOVERNING BOARD

Composed of ministers or senior officials of the member governments. Decisions may be taken by a weighted majority on a number of specified subjects, particularly concerning emergency measures and the emergency reserve commitment; a simple weighted majority is required for procedural decisions and decisions implementing specific obligations in the agreement. Unanimity is required only if new obligations, not already specified in the agreement, are to be undertaken.

The Governing Board is assisted by four Standing Groups and a high-level Committee, dealing respectively with emergency questions; long-term co-operation; oil market; relations with producer and other consumer countries; and energy research and development.

There is also a Coal and an Oil Industry Advisory Board, composed of industrial executives.

SECRETARIAT

Executive Director: Helga Steeg (FRG).
Deputy Executive Director: J. Wallace Hopkins (USA).

OECD Nuclear Energy Agency — NEA

Address: 38 boulevard Suchet, 75016 Paris, France.
Telephone: (1) 45-24-82-00.
Telex: 630668.

The NEA was established in 1958 to further the peaceful uses of nuclear energy. Originally a European agency, it has since admitted four of the five OECD members outside Europe.

MEMBERS

All members of OECD except New Zealand.

Organization

(October 1986)

STEERING COMMITTEE FOR NUCLEAR ENERGY
Chairman: Richard Kennedy (USA).

SECRETARIAT

Director-General: Howard Shapar (USA).
Deputy Director-General: Pierre Strohl (France).
Deputy Director (Science and Development): Sumio Horiuchi.
Deputy Director (Safety and Regulation): Klaus Stadie.

MAIN COMMITTEES

Committee for Technical and Economic Studies on Nuclear Energy Development and the Fuel Cycle;
Committee on the Safety of Nuclear Installations;
Committee on Radiation Protection and Public Health;
Radioactive Waste Management Committee;
NEA Nuclear Data Committee (NEANDC);
NEA Committee on Reactor Physics (NEACRP);
Group of Governmental Experts on Third Party Liability in the Field of Nuclear Energy.

Activities

The main purpose of the Agency is to promote international co-operation within the OECD area for the development and application of nuclear power for peaceful purposes through international research and development projects and exchange of scientific and technical experience and information. The Agency also maintains a continual survey with the co-operation of other organizations, notably the International Atomic Energy Agency (IAEA, see p. 33), of world uranium resources, production and demand, and of economic and technical aspects of the nuclear fuel cycle.

A major part of the Agency's work is devoted to the safety and regulation of nuclear power, including co-operative studies and projects related to the prevention of nuclear accidents and the long-term safety of radioactive waste disposal systems.

JOINT PROJECTS

Halden Project: Halden, Norway; experimental boiling heavy water reactor, which became an OECD project in 1958. From 1964, under successive agreements with participating countries, the reactor has been used for long-term testing of water reactor fuels and for research into automatic computer-based control of nuclear power stations. Nuclear energy research institutions and authorities in 10 countries support the project.

OECD Loft Project: this international safety research programme, launched in 1983, is designed to provide data for developing and verifying nuclear safety computer programmes, for identifying important reactor accident phenomena experimentally, and for providing information on the operator/plant interface, using the Loss-of-Fluid Test Facility at the Idaho National Engineering Laboratory in the USA. Ten countries are members of this project.

International Stripa Project: set up in early 1980, this project is conducting experiments in an abandoned iron mine in Sweden, on the use of hard crystalline rock for isolating nuclear waste. Nine countries participate in the project.

Incident Reporting System: introduced in 1980 to exchange experience in operating nuclear power plants in OECD member countries and to improve nuclear safety by facilitating feedback of this experience to nuclear regulatory authorities, utilities and manufacturers.

Chemical Thermodynamic Data Base: the objective of this project, set up in 1983, is to compile fundamental chemical thermodynamic data which permit the quantification of mass transfers in chemical reactions occurring in ground water and in water-rock reactions. Such data can be used in geochemical modelling of waste disposal systems performance assessments to predict the concentration of radioelements under various conditions.

Decommissioning of Nuclear Installations: this co-operative programme, set up in 1985, provides for an exchange of scientific and technical information to develop the operational experience and data base needed for the future decommissioning of large nuclear power plants. Nine countries are participating in this programme.

COMMON SERVICE

NEA Data Bank: Saclay, France; set up in 1978 in succession to the Computer Programme Library and the Neutron Data Compilation Centre, the Data Bank allows the 17 participating countries to share large computer programmes used in reactor calculations, and nuclear data applications. It also operates as one of a worldwide network of four nuclear data centres.

FINANCE

The Agency's budget for 1985 amounted to 50.4m. French francs.

PUBLICATIONS

Annual Report.
NEA Newsletter (2 a year).
Nuclear Law Bulletin (2 a year).
Summary of Nuclear Power and Fuel Cycle Data for the OECD area (annually).
Reports and proceedings.

ORGANIZATION OF AFRICAN UNITY—OAU

Address: POB 3243, Addis Ababa, Ethiopia.
Telephone: 4 74 80.

The Organization was founded in 1963 to promote unity and solidarity among African states.

FORMATION

There were various attempts at establishing an inter-African organization before the OAU Charter was drawn up. In November 1958 Ghana and Guinea (later joined by Mali) drafted a Charter which was to form the basis of a Union of African States. In January 1961 a conference was held at Casablanca, attended by the Heads of State of Ghana, Guinea, Mali, Morocco, and representatives of Libya and of the provisional government of the Algerian Republic (GPRA). Tunisia, Nigeria, Liberia and Togo declined the invitation to attend. An African Charter was adopted and it was decided to set up an African Military Command and an African Common Market.

Between October 1960 and March 1961 three conferences were held by French-speaking African countries, at Abidjan, Brazzaville and Yaoundé. None of the 12 countries which attended these meetings had been present at the Casablanca Conference. These conferences led eventually to the signing in September 1961, at Tananarive, of a charter establishing the Union africaine et malgache, later the Organisation commune africaine et mauricienne (OCAM, q.v.).

In May 1961 a conference was held at Monrovia, Liberia, attended by the Heads of State or representatives of 19 countries: Cameroon, Central African Republic, Chad, Congo Republic (ex-French), Dahomey, Ethiopia, Gabon, Ivory Coast, Liberia, Madagascar, Mauritania, Niger, Nigeria, Senegal, Sierra Leone, Somalia, Togo, Tunisia and Upper Volta. They met again (with the exception of Tunisia and with the addition of the ex-Belgian Congo Republic) in January 1962 at Lagos, Nigeria, and set up a permanent secretariat and a standing committee of finance ministers, and accepted a draft charter for an Organization of Inter-African and Malagasy States.

It was the Conference of Addis Ababa, held in 1963, which finally brought together African states despite the regional, political and linguistic differences which divided them. The Foreign Ministers of 32 African states attended the Preparatory Meeting held in May: Algeria, Burundi, Cameroon, Central African Republic, Chad, Congo (Brazzaville) (now the Congo), Congo (Léopoldville) (now Zaire), Dahomey (now Benin), Ethiopia, Gabon, Ghana, Guinea, Ivory Coast, Liberia, Libya, Madagascar, Mali, Mauritania, Morocco, Niger, Nigeria, Rwanda, Senegal, Sierra Leone, Somalia, Sudan, Tanganyika (now Tanzania), Togo, Tunisia, Uganda, United Arab Republic, Upper Volta (now Burkina Faso).

The topics discussed by the meeting were: (i) creation of the Organization of African States; (ii) co-operation among African states in the following fields: economic and social; education, culture and science; collective defence; (iii) decolonization; (iv) apartheid and racial discrimination; (v) effects of economic grouping on the economic development of Africa; (vi) disarmament; (vii) creation of a Permanent Conciliation Commission; and (viii) Africa and the United Nations.

The Heads of State Conference which opened on 23 May drew up the Charter of the Organization of African Unity, which was then signed by the heads of 30 states on 25 May 1963. The Charter was essentially functional and reflected a compromise between the concept of a loose association of states favoured by the Monrovia Group and the federal idea supported by the Casablanca Group, and in particular by Ghana.

SUMMARY OF OAU CHARTER

Article I. Establishment of the Organization of African Unity. The Organization to include continental African states, Madagascar, and other islands surrounding Africa.

Article II. Aims of the OAU:

1. To promote unity and solidarity among African states.

2. To intensify and co-ordinate efforts to improve living standards in Africa.

3. To defend sovereignty, territorial integrity and independence of African states.

4. To eradicate all forms of colonialism from Africa.

5. To promote international co-operation in keeping with the Charter of the United Nations.

Article III. Member states adhere to the principles of sovereignty, non-interference in internal affairs of member states, respect for territorial integrity, peaceful settlement of disputes, condemnation of political subversion, dedication to the emancipation of dependent African territories, and international non-alignment.

Article IV. Each independent sovereign African state shall be entitled to become a member of the Organization.

Article V. All member states shall have equal rights and duties.

Article VI. All member states shall observe scrupulously the principles laid down in Article III.

Article VII. Establishment of the Assembly of Heads of State and Government, the Council of Ministers, the General Secretariat, and the Commission of Mediation, Conciliation and Arbitration.

Articles VIII–XI. The Assembly of Heads of State and Government co-ordinates policies and reviews the structure of the Organization.

Articles XII–XV. The Council of Ministers shall prepare conferences of the Assembly, and co-ordinate inter-African co-operation. All resolutions shall be by simple majority.

Articles XVI–XVIII. The General Secretariat. The Administrative Secretary-General and his staff shall not seek or receive instructions from any government or other authority external to the Organization. They are international officials responsible only to the Organization.

Article XIX. Commission of Mediation, Conciliation and Arbitration. A separate protocol concerning the composition and nature of this Commission shall be regarded as an integral part of the Charter.

Articles XX–XXII. Specialized Commissions shall be established, composed of Ministers or other officials designated by Member Governments. Their regulations shall be laid down by the Council of Ministers.

Article XXIII. The Budget shall be prepared by the Secretary-General and approved by the Council of Ministers. Contributions shall be in accordance with the scale of assessment of the United Nations. No Member shall pay more than 20% of the total yearly amount.

Article XXIV. Texts of the Charter in African languages, English and French shall be equally authentic. Instruments of ratification shall be deposited with the Government of Ethiopia.

Article XXV. The Charter shall come into force on receipt by the Government of Ethiopia of the instruments of ratification of two-thirds of the signatory states.

Article XXVI. The Charter shall be registered with the Secretariat of the United Nations.

Article XXVII. Questions of interpretation shall be settled by a two-thirds majority vote in the Assembly of Heads of State and Government.

Article XXVIII. Admission of new independent African states to the Organization shall be decided by a simple majority of the Member States.

Articles XXIX–XXXIII. The working languages of the Organization shall be African languages, English and French. The Secretary-General may accept gifts and bequests to the Organization, subject to the approval of the Council of Ministers. The Council of Ministers shall establish privileges and immunities to be accorded to the personnel of the Secretariat in the territories of Member States. A State wishing to withdraw from the Organization must give a year's written notice to the Secretariat. The Charter may only be amended after consideration by all Member States and by a two-thirds majority vote of the Assembly of Heads of State and Government. Such amendments will come into force one year after submission.

INTERNATIONAL ORGANIZATIONS   *Organization of African Unity*

MEMBERS*

Algeria	Libya
Angola	Madagascar
Benin	Malawi
Botswana	Mali
Burkina Faso	Mauritania
Burundi	Mauritius
Cameroon	Mozambique
Cape Verde	Niger
Central African Republic	Nigeria
Chad	Rwanda
Comoros	São Tomé and Príncipe
Congo	Senegal
Djibouti	Seychelles
Egypt	Sierra Leone
Equatorial Guinea	Somalia
Ethiopia	Sudan
Gabon	Swaziland
The Gambia	Tanzania
Ghana	Togo
Guinea	Tunisia
Guinea-Bissau	Uganda
Ivory Coast	Zaire
Kenya	Zambia
Lesotho	Zimbabwe
Liberia	

* The Sahrawi Arab Democratic Republic (Western Sahara) was admitted to the OAU in February 1982, following recognition by 26 of the 50 members, but its membership was disputed by Morocco and other states which claimed that a two-thirds majority was needed to admit a state whose existence was in question. Morocco withdrew from the OAU with effect from November 1985.

Organization
(October 1986)

ASSEMBLY OF HEADS OF STATE
The Assembly of Heads of State and Government meets annually to co-ordinate policies of African states. Resolutions are passed by a two-thirds majority, procedural matters by a simple majority. A chairman is elected at each meeting from among the members, to hold office for one year.

Chairman (1986/87): Col DENIS SASSOU-NGUESSO (Congo).

COUNCIL OF MINISTERS
Consists of Foreign and/or other Ministers and meets twice a year, with provision for extraordinary sessions. Each session elects its own Chairman. Prepares meetings of, and is responsible to, the Assembly of Heads of State.

GENERAL SECRETARIAT
The permanent headquarters of the organization. It carries out functions assigned to it in the Charter of the OAU and by other agreements and treaties made between member states. Departments: Political; Finance; Education, Science, Culture and Social Affairs; Economic Development and Co-operation; Administration and Conferences. The Secretary-General is elected for a four-year term by the Assembly of Heads of State.

Secretary-General: IDE OUMAROU (Niger).

ARBITRATION COMMISSION
Commission of Mediation, Conciliation and Arbitration: Addis Ababa; f. 1964; consists of 21 members elected by the Assembly of Heads of State for a five-year term; no state may have more than one member; has a Bureau consisting of a President and two Vice-Presidents, who shall not be eligible for re-election. Its task is to hear and settle disputes between member states by peaceful means.

SPECIALIZED COMMISSIONS
There are specialized commissions for economic, social, transport and communications affairs; education, science, culture and health; defence; and labour.

LIBERATION COMMITTEE
Co-ordinating Committee for the Liberation Movements of Africa: Dar es Salaam, Tanzania; f. 1963; to provide financial and military aid to nationalist movements in dependent countries; regional offices in Maputo, Mozambique, Lusaka, Zambia, and Luanda, Angola.

Executive Secretary: Col HASHIM MBITA (Tanzania).

BUDGET
Member states contribute in accordance with their United Nations assessment. No member state is assessed for an amount exceeding 20% of the yearly regular budget of the Organization. The 1986/87 budget amounted to US $25.3m.

Principal Events, 1980-86

1980

May — An economic summit meeting resolved to take steps towards establishment of an African Common Market by year 2000; adopted 'Lagos Plan of Action' to this end.

July — The 17th Assembly of Heads of State postponed a decision on admitting the Sahrawi Arab Democratic Republic (SADR), proclaimed by the Polisario Front in Western Sahara (the former Spanish Sahara, claimed by Morocco), after Morocco threatened to leave the OAU if admission was granted.

Sept. — The OAU committee on Western Sahara announced a six-point ceasefire plan, to include a referendum organized by the OAU with assistance from the UN.

1981

Jan. — A conference on Chad and Libya condemned the proposed merger of the two countries, demanded the withdrawal of all foreign forces from Chad and decided to send an African force to maintain peace there and supervise elections. A meeting of Ministers of Justice approved an African Charter on Human and People's Rights which (subject to ratification by a majority of OAU members) would establish a Commission to investigate violations of human rights.

Feb. — Ministers of foreign affairs supported proposals for an intensified guerrilla war in Namibia and mandatory economic sanctions against South Africa to persuade the South African Government to negotiate on Namibian independence.

June — At the 18th Assembly of Heads of State, Morocco agreed to hold a referendum in Western Sahara. A ministerial committee was created to investigate the Nigeria-Cameroon border dispute.

Nov. — The first members of the OAU peace-keeping force (from Nigeria, Senegal and Zaire) arrived in Chad to replace the Libyan troops previously supporting the Government against opposition forces.

1982

Feb. — The committee on Chad established a timetable for ceasefire, negotiations, a provisional constitution and elections in Chad, and announced that the OAU peace-keeping force's mandate would cease at the end of June. The committee on Western Sahara empowered Pres. Moi of Kenya to conduct negotiations for a ceasefire between Morocco and the Polisario Front. At a meeting of Ministers of Foreign Affairs, the admission of a representative of the SADR led to a walk-out by 19 countries.

March–April — Ordinary OAU business was disrupted because boycotts by opponents and supporters of Polisario meant that three ministerial meetings were without a quorum of members. Discussions by a special group representing nine countries failed to solve the deadlock.

Aug. — The 19th Assembly of Heads of State, due to be held in Tripoli, Libya, failed to achieve a quorum when 19 states boycotted the meeting owing to the dispute over the admission of the SADR. A five-member committee was set up to try to convene another summit before the end of the year.

Nov. — A second attempt to hold the 19th Assembly of Heads of State in Tripoli was abandoned after a dispute over the representation of Chad: the Libyan leader, Col Gaddafi, and others opposed the presence of Pres. Hissène Habré in favour of the former Pres. Goukouni Oueddei, leading to a boycott by representatives of 14 moderate states.

INTERNATIONAL ORGANIZATIONS

Organization of African Unity

1983

June — The 19th Assembly of Heads of State met in Addis Ababa: SADR representatives agreed not to attend, in order to avoid a boycott of the meeting by their opponents. The Assembly again called for a referendum in Western Sahara and for direct negotiations between Morocco and the SADR.

1984

Jan. — The OAU-sponsored talks between the rival factions in Chad, held in Addis Ababa, broke down without result, chiefly owing to the refusal of Pres. Habré to attend.

March — The council of ministers of foreign affairs discussed cumulative budgetary arrears amounting to over US $34m.: less than one-third of contributions due for the 1983/84 period had been paid. The SADR delegation again agreed not to attend the meeting, but declared that they would be present at the next Assembly of Heads of State.

May — The 20th Assembly, due to be held in Guinea in May, was postponed following the death in March of Pres. Sekou Touré.

Nov. — The 20th Assembly was held in Addis Ababa. Nigeria became the 30th OAU member to recognize the Sahrawi Arab Democratic Republic. A delegation from the SADR was admitted to the Assembly, and Morocco immediately announced its resignation from the OAU (to take effect after one year); only Zaire supported Morocco by withdrawing from the meeting. The Assembly concentrated on economic matters, discussing Africa's balance-of-payments problems, debts and the drought affecting many countries. An emergency fund was set up to combat the effects of drought, with initial contributions of US $10m. each from Algeria and Libya.

1985

July — The 21st Assembly of Heads of State was held in Addis Ababa, and again discussed mainly economic issues. It resulted in the Addis Ababa Declaration, in which member countries reiterated their commitment to the Lagos Plan of Action (see under 1980) and adopted a priority programme for the next five years, emphasizing the rehabilitation of African agriculture: they agreed to increase agriculture's share of public investment to between 20% and 25% by the year 1989. The meeting also expressed concern at Africa's heavy external debt (expected to total over US $170,000m. by the end of 1985) and called for a special conference of creditors and borrowers to seek a solution to the problem, and for an increase in concessional financial resources. The Assembly also agreed on the appointment of a new Secretary-General.

1986

May — At a special session of the UN General Assembly on the economic problems of Africa, the OAU (represented by its Chairman) presented a programme, prepared jointly with the UN Economic Commission for Africa, calling for debt relief and an increase in assistance for agricultural investment.

July — The 22nd Assembly of Heads of State called for comprehensive economic sanctions against South Africa, and strongly criticized the governments of the United Kingdom and the USA for opposing sanctions. Among other resolutions the Assembly condemned outside interference in Angola; called upon France to return the island of Mayotte to the Comoros; and resolved to continue efforts (led by the OAU Chairman) to bring about reconciliation in Chad. A council of 'wise men', comprising former African heads of state, was established to mediate, when necessary, in disputes between member countries. The Assembly reiterated its call for an international conference on Africa's foreign debt.

Specialized Agencies

African Civil Aviation Commission—AFCAC: BP 2356, Dakar, Senegal; f. 1969 to provide mems with a framework for co-ordination and co-operation in all civil aviation activities; to promote co-ordination and better utilization and development of African air transport systems and to encourage the application of ICAO standards and recommendations. Membership open to all mems of ECA or OAU. Pres. J. KAHUKI (Kenya); Sec. E. LOMBOLOU.

Inter-African Bureau of Languages: POB 7284, Kampala, Uganda; tel. 56619; telex 61100; f. 1966 to encourage the use of indigenous African languages for education, commerce and communications through training interpreters and translators, arranging meetings, and producing bilingual manuals and books in indigenous languages. Dir Dr K. MATEENE. Publ. *OAU Linguistic Bulletin.*

Organization of African Trade Union Unity—OATUU: POB M386, Accra, Ghana; tel. 74531; f. 1973 as a single continental trade union organization, independent of international trade union organizations; has affiliates from all African trade unions. Congress, composed of four delegates from all affiliated trade union centres, meets at least every four years as supreme policy-making body; General Council, composed of one representative from all affiliated trade unions, meets annually to implement Congress decisions and to approve annual budget. Mems: trade union movements in 50 independent African countries, including trade unions within the liberation movements; in February 1986, however, 28 countries formed a separate group, alleging financial mismanagement by OATUU officials. Sec.-Gen. HASSAN SUNMONU (Nigeria). Publ. *Voice of African Workers.*

Pan-African News Agency—PANA: BP 4056, Dakar, Senegal; tel. 22 61 20; telex 3261 3307; regional headquarters in Khartoum, Sudan; Lusaka, Zambia; Kinshasa, Zaire; Lagos, Nigeria; Tripoli, Libya; began operations in May 1983; receives information from national news agencies and circulates news in English and French. Dir AUGUSTE MPASSI-MUBA.

Pan-African Postal Union: POB 6026, Arusha, Tanzania; tel. 3910; telex 42096; f. 1980, subject to ratification; Admin. Council to consist of 16 countries elected on regional basis. Sec.-Gen. COMLANVI AMOUSSOU (Togo) (see entry below).

Pan-African Telecommunications Union (PATU): BP 8634, Kinshasa, Zaire; telex 21049; f. 1977 for co-ordination of telecommunications development. Sec.-Gen. RAJABU MABULA YUSUF. In July 1986 the OAU Assembly of Heads of State resolved that PATU should be merged with the Pan-African Postal Union to form a single post and telecommunications organization.

Scientific, Technical and Research Commission (STRC): Nigerian Ports Authority Bldg, PMB 2359, Marina, Lagos, Nigeria; f. 1965 to succeed the Commission for Technical Co-operation in Africa (f. 1954). Supervises the Inter-African Bureau for Animal Resources (Nairobi, Kenya), the Inter-African Bureau for Soils (Bangui, Central African Republic) and the Inter-African Phytosanitary Commission (Yaoundé, Cameroon) and several joint research projects; provides training in agricultural management, and conducts pest control programmes. Exec. Sec. Prof. A. OLUFEMI WILLIAMS.

Supreme Council for Sports in Africa: BP 1363, Yaoundé, Cameroon; tel. 22-27-11; telex 8295. Sec.-Gen. AMADOU LAMINE BA.

Union of African Railways: BP 687, Kinshasa, Zaire; tel. 23861; telex 21258 ZR; f. 1972 to standardize, expand, co-ordinate and improve members' railway services; the ultimate aim is to link all systems; main organs: General Assembly, Executive Board, General Secretariat, five technical cttees. Mems in 30 African countries. Pres. TOM MMARI; Sec.-Gen. ADAMA DIAGNE.

ORGANIZATION OF AMERICAN STATES—OAS

Address: 1889 F St, NW, Washington, DC 20006, USA.
Telex: 440118.

The OAS was founded at Bogotá, Colombia, in 1948 (succeeding the International Union of American Republics, founded in 1890) to foster peace, security, mutual understanding and co-operation among the nations of the Western Hemisphere.

MEMBERS

Antigua and Barbuda	Haiti
Argentina	Honduras
The Bahamas	Jamaica
Barbados	Mexico
Bolivia	Nicaragua
Brazil	Panama
Chile	Paraguay
Colombia	Peru
Costa Rica	Saint Christopher and Nevis
Cuba*	Saint Lucia
Dominica	Saint Vincent and the Grenadines
Dominican Republic	Suriname
Ecuador	Trinidad and Tobago
El Salvador	USA
Grenada	Uruguay
Guatemala	Venezuela

Austria, Belgium, Canada, Cyprus, Egypt, France, the Federal Republic of Germany, Greece, Guyana, the Holy See, Israel, Italy, Japan, the Republic of Korea, Morocco, the Netherlands, Portugal, Saudi Arabia, Spain and Switzerland are Permanent Observers.

* The Cuban Government was suspended from OAS activities in 1962.

Organization
(October 1986)

GENERAL ASSEMBLY

The Assembly meets annually and can also hold special sessions when convoked by the Permanent Council. Supreme organ of the OAS, it decides general action and policy.

MEETINGS OF CONSULTATION OF MINISTERS OF FOREIGN AFFAIRS

Meetings are held to consider problems of an urgent nature and of common interest to member states; they may be held at the request of any member state.

PERMANENT COUNCIL

The Council meets regularly throughout the year at OAS headquarters. It is composed of one representative of each member state with the rank of ambassador; each government may accredit alternate representatives and advisers and when necessary appoint an interim representative. The office of Chairman is held in turn by each of the representatives, following alphabetical order according to the names of the countries in Spanish. The Vice-Chairman is determined in the same way, following reverse alphabetical order. Their terms of office are three months.

The Council acts as an Organ of Consultation and oversees the maintenance of friendly relations between members. It supervises the work of the OAS and promotes co-operation with a variety of other international bodies including the United Nations. The official languages are English, French, Portuguese and Spanish.

INTER-AMERICAN ECONOMIC AND SOCIAL COUNCIL

The Council holds annual meetings of expert representatives and of ministers of finance and economy. Its aim is to promote co-operation among the countries of the region, in order to accelerate economic and social development. The permanent executive committee of the Council provides technical assistance.
Executive Secretary: Jesús Alberto Fernández (Venezuela).

INTER-AMERICAN COUNCIL FOR EDUCATION, SCIENCE AND CULTURE

The Council is composed of one representative from each member state, appointed by the respective governments; it meets annually at the level of ministers of education. Its principal purpose is to promote friendly relations and mutual understanding between the peoples of the Americas through educational, scientific and cultural co-operation and exchange between member states.

The council has a permanent executive committee and three committees in charge of carrying out regional development programmes in the fields of education, science and technology, and culture.
Executive Secretary: Enrique Martín del Campo (Mexico).

INTER-AMERICAN JURIDICAL COMMITTEE

Address: Rua Senador Vergueiro 81, Rio de Janeiro, RJ, Brazil; tel. 225-1361. Composed of 11 jurists, nationals of different member states, elected for a period of four years with the possibility of re-election once. Equitable geographical distribution is sought as far as possible, and a proportion of members are replaced each year. The Committee's purpose is to serve as an advisory body to the Organization on juridical matters; to promote the progressive development and codification of international law and to study juridical problems related to the integration of the developing countries in the hemisphere, and in so far as may appear desirable, the possibility of attaining uniformity in legislation. Meetings are held twice a year for about four weeks. Special meetings can also be called. The Committee has prepared numerous studies, reports and draft conventions on legal topics.

INTER-AMERICAN COMMISSION ON HUMAN RIGHTS

The Commission was established in 1960 and comprises seven members. It promotes the observance and protection of human rights in the member states of the OAS; it examines and reports on the human rights situation in member countries, and provides consultative services.

INTER-AMERICAN COURT OF HUMAN RIGHTS

Based in San José, Costa Rica, the Court was established in 1978, as an autonomous judicial institution whose purpose is to apply and interpret the American Convention on Human Rights (which entered into force in 1978 and had been ratified by 19 OAS member states by the end of June 1985). The Court comprises seven jurists from OAS member states.

GENERAL SECRETARIAT

The central and permanent organ of the Organization, carries out the duties entrusted to it by the General Assembly, Meeting of Consultation of Ministers of Foreign Affairs and the Councils.
Secretary-General: João Clemente Baena Soares (Brazil).
Assistant Secretary-General: Val McComie (Barbados).

Record of Events

1826	First Congress of American States, convened by Simón Bolívar at Panama City. The Treaty of Perpetual Union, League and Confederation was signed by Colombia, the United Provinces of Central America, Peru, and Mexico.
1889–90	First International Conference of American States (Washington) founded the International Union of American Republics and established a central office, the Commercial Bureau, the purpose of which was the 'prompt collection and distribution of commercial information'.
1910	Fourth Conference (Buenos Aires) changed the organization's name to Union of American Republics. The name of its principal organ was changed from Commercial Bureau to Pan American Union.

INTERNATIONAL ORGANIZATIONS
Organization of American States

1923	Fifth Conference (Santiago, Chile) changed the title to Union of Republics of the American Continent, with the Pan American Union as its permanent organ.
1928	Sixth Conference (Havana): the Governing Board and Pan American Union were prohibited from exercising political functions.
1945	Inter-American Conference on Problems of War and Peace: Mexico City. The Act of Chapultepec established a system of Continental Security for the American States.
1947	The Inter-American Treaty of Reciprocal Assistance set up a joint security pact for the defence of the Western Hemisphere against attack from outside and for internal security.
1948	Ninth Conference (Bogotá). Member Governments signed the Charter of the Organization of American States.
1954	OAS adopted the Declaration of Solidarity for the Preservation of the Political Integrity of the American States against the Intervention of International Communism.
1959	An Act was passed by 21 American States to establish the Inter-American Development Bank (see p. 157).
1960	A committee was established to co-ordinate the activities of OAS, the Inter-American Development Bank and the UN Economic Commission for Latin America (ECLA).
1962	Cuba was suspended from OAS, which supported the USA in its demand for the removal of missile bases in Cuba.
1964	OAS mediated in dispute between USA and Panama, and voted for sanctions against Cuba by 15 votes to 4 (Bolivia, Chile, Mexico and Uruguay).
1965	An Inter-American Peace Force was created in reaction to events in the Dominican Republic.
1967	A treaty for the establishment of a Latin American nuclear-free zone was signed in Mexico City. In April a regional summit conference agreed to create a Latin American Common Market based on existing integration systems LAFTA and CACM.
1969	El Salvador and Honduras called on OAS to investigate alleged violation of human rights of Salvadoreans in Honduras. A committee was sent to investigate after fighting broke out. Observers from OAS member nations supervised cease-fire and exchange of prisoners.
1970	Entry into force of the Protocol of Buenos Aires, establishing the General Assembly as the highest body of OAS, replacing the Inter-American Conferences, and the three Councils as its main organs. The General Assembly held two special sessions to establish the new system and to discuss other current problems, in particular kidnapping and extortion.
1971	First regular Session of the General Assembly of OAS at San José, Costa Rica, in April.
1976	Sixth General Assembly; chief resolutions concerned human rights, the US Trade Act of 1974 and transnational enterprises. It also resolved to hold a Special Assembly to review matters concerning inter-American co-operation for development. The Assembly proclaimed a Decade of Women 1976–85: Equality, Development and Peace. Honduras and El Salvador signed the Act of Managua to end a series of border incidents between them.
1977	The Seventh General Assembly was held in Grenada, a new member state. The delegations adopted four resolutions on human rights and a resolution condemning terrorist activities in the hemisphere and in the world. The financial problems of many of the countries, caused by the energy crisis and their less-than-satisfactory positions in international trade, was a matter of continuing concern. 1978 was declared Inter-American Rural Youth Year.
1978	The Eighth General Assembly was held in Washington, DC; resolutions included one calling for member states to co-operate with the Inter-American Commission on Human Rights in on-site inspections, and another recommending the establishment of an Inter-American Court of Human Rights in San José, Costa Rica. In view of the USA's announced intention to reduce its quota, the Permanent Council received a mandate to develop a new formula to finance the OAS programme budget. Funds were authorized for purchase of new OAS headquarters under construction in Washington, DC.
1979	The Inter-American Court of Human Rights was formally established in San José, Costa Rica, its members installed, and the statutes governing its operation were adopted.
1980	The Permanent Council met in July and passed a resolution condemning the military coup in Bolivia and deploring the interruption of the return to democracy there. In November the Tenth General Assembly named Argentina, Chile, El Salvador, Haiti, Paraguay and Uruguay as countries of special concern with regard to human rights violations (but avoided condemning them outright after Argentina threatened to withdraw from the organization if this was done).
1981	In February Ministers of Foreign Affairs called on Ecuador and Peru to stop military operations in their border area: both countries agreed to a cease-fire monitored by a committee composed of representatives of Argentina, Brazil, Chile and the USA.
1982	In May the Ministers of Foreign Affairs called on Argentina and the United Kingdom to cease hostilities over the Falkland (Malvinas) Islands and to resume negotiations for a peaceful settlement of the conflict, taking into account Argentina's 'rights of sovereignty' and the interests of the islanders.
1984	In November the General Assembly discussed the political crisis in Central America and the increasing foreign debts incurred by Latin American countries; it agreed to attempt to 'revitalize' the OAS during the next year, so that the Organization could play a more effective part in solving regional problems.
1985	In December amendments to the OAS Charter were adopted by the General Assembly (subject to ratification by two-thirds of the member states, which was expected to take several years). The amendments increased the executive powers of the OAS Secretary-General, who would henceforth be allowed to take the initiative in bringing before the Permanent Council matters that 'might threaten the peace and security of the hemisphere or the development of the member states', something which previously only a member country had been permitted to do. The OAS also gained greater powers of mediation through an amendment allowing the Permanent Council to try to resolve a dispute between members, whether or not all the parties concerned had (as previously stipulated) agreed to take the matter before the OAS.

FINANCE

The total funds managed by the OAS at the end of 1984 amounted to US $214m., of which $129m. comprised quotas and contributions of the member states, $67m. was in counterpart contributions from them, and $18m. was in contributions from other organizations. Serious arrears in members' payments were reported in 1986.

PUBLICATIONS
(in English and Spanish)

Catalog of Publications (annually).

Américas (6 a year).

Annual Report.

Ciencia Interamericana (quarterly).

La Educación (quarterly).

Statistical Bulletin (quarterly).

Numerous cultural, legal and scientific reports and studies.

SPECIALIZED ORGANIZATIONS OF THE OAS

Inter-American Children's Institute: Avenida 8 de Octubre 2904, Montevideo, Uruguay; tel. 80 14 12; f. 1927 to achieve better health, education, social legislation, social service and statistics. Dir-Gen. Dr RODRIGO CRESPO T. (Ecuador). Publ. *Boletín*.

Inter-American Commission of Women: General Secretariat of the OAS, 1889 F St, NW, Washington, DC 20006, USA; tel. (202) 789-6084; f. 1928 for the extension of civil, political, economic, social and cultural rights for women. Chair. PRINCESS LAWES (Jamaica).

Inter-American Indian Institute: Av. Insurgentes Sur 1690, Colonia Florida, México 01030, DF, Mexico; tel. 660-0007; f. 1940 to direct research for the better understanding of Indian groups and the solution of their educational, economic and social problems; provides technical assistance for programmes of Indian community development and trains personnel. Dir Oscar Arze Quintanilla (Bolivia). Publs *América Indígena* (quarterly), *Anuario Indigenista*, *News of the Americas*, *Noticias Indigenistas de América* (quarterly).

Inter-American Institute for Co-operation on Agriculture: Apdo 55–2200 Coronado, San José, Costa Rica; tel. 290222; telex 21441; f. 1942 (as the Inter-American Institute of Agricultural Sciences: new name 1980); supports the efforts of member states to improve agricultural development and rural well-being; encourages co-operation between regional organizations, and provides a forum for the exchange of experience. Dir Dr Martín E. Piñeiro (Argentina).

Pan American Health Organization: 525 23rd St, NW, Washington, DC 20037, USA; tel. (202) 861-3200; co-ordinates regional efforts to improve health; maintains close relations with national health organizations and serves as a regional agency of the World Health Organization. Dir Dr Carlyle Guerra de Macedo (Brazil).

Pan-American Institute of Geography and History: Ex-Arzobispado 29, México 18, DF, Mexico; tel. 2775888; encourages and co-ordinates cartographical, geographical, historical and geophysical studies; provides training and promotes co-operation among interested organizations. Sec.-Gen. Leopoldo Rodríguez (Argentina).

ASSOCIATED ORGANIZATIONS

Inter-American Defense Board: 2600 16th St, NW, Washington, DC 20441, USA; tel. (202) 939-6600; works in liaison with member governments to plan the common defence of the western hemisphere; operates the Inter-American Defense College. Chair. Lieut-Gen. John L. Ballantyne (USA).

Inter-American Nuclear Energy Commission: General Secretariat of the OAS, 17th St and Constitution Ave, NW, Washington, DC 20006, USA; f. 1959 to assist member countries in developing and co-ordinating nuclear energy research; organizes periodic conferences and gives fellowships and financial assistance to research institutions. Exec. Sec. (vacant).

Inter-American Statistical Institute: 1889 F St, NW, Washington, DC 20006, USA; tel. (202) 789-3753; telex 64128; f. 1940; seeks to stimulate improvement of both governmental and non-governmental statistics and to offer a medium for collaboration among statisticians; organizes seminars, workshops and meetings. Mems: 476 individuals, 49 institutions. Sec.-Gen. Evelio O. Fabbroni (Argentina).

ORGANIZATION OF ARAB PETROLEUM EXPORTING COUNTRIES—OAPEC

Address: POB 20501, Safat, 13066 Kuwait City, Kuwait.
Telephone: 2448200.
Telex: 22166.

OAPEC was established in 1968 to safeguard the interests of members and to determine ways and means for their co-operation in various forms of economic activity in the petroleum industry.

MEMBERS

Algeria	Kuwait	Syria
Bahrain	Libya	Tunisia
Egypt*	Qatar	United Arab Emirates
Iraq	Saudi Arabia	

* Egypt's membership was suspended from 17 April 1979.

Organization
(October 1986)

COUNCIL OF MINISTERS

The Council consists normally of the ministers of petroleum of the member states, and forms the supreme authority of the Organization, responsible for drawing up its general policy, directing its activities and laying down its governing rules. It meets twice yearly as a minimum requirement and may hold extraordinary sessions. Chairmanship is on an annual rotation basis.

EXECUTIVE BUREAU

Assists the Council to direct the management of the Organization, approves staff regulations, reviews the budget, and refers it to the Council, considers matters relating to the Organization's agreements and activities and draws up the agenda for the Council. The Bureau consists of senior officials from each member state. Chairmanship is by rotation. The Bureau convenes twice a year before meetings of the Council of Ministers, and may convene on two other occasions.

SECRETARIAT

Secretary-General: Dr ALI AHMAD ATTIGA (Libya).
Assistant Secretary-General: ABDEL-AZIZ AL-WATTARI.

Besides the Office of the Secretary-General, which assists the Secretary-General in following up resolutions and recommendations of the Council, there are seven departments: Financial and Administrative Affairs, Legal, Information and International Relations, Petroleum Projects, Library and Documentation. The Arab Centre for Energy Studies, established in 1983, comprises the Energy Resources and Economics Departments. There is also a training unit.

JUDICIAL TRIBUNAL

The Tribunal comprises nine judges from Arab countries. Its task is to settle differences in interpretation and application of the OAPEC Agreement, arising between members and also between OAPEC and its affiliates; disputes among member countries on oil activities falling within OAPEC's jurisdiction and not under the sovereignty of member countries; and disputes that the Council of Ministers decides to submit to the Tribunal.
President: FARES AL-WEGEYAN.

Activities

OAPEC co-ordinates different aspects of the Arab petroleum industry through the joint undertakings described below. It co-operates with the League of Arab States and other Arab organizations, and attempts to link petroleum research institutes in the Arab states. It organizes or participates in conferences and seminars, many of which are held in co-operation with non-Arab organizations; examples include the Sixth Industrial Development Conference for Arab States (October 1984); a UNIDO meeting on co-operation in the petrochemicals industries of the region (October 1984); a workshop on energy data held in conjunction with the European Economic Community (October 1984); an Arab-Japan Conference of Energy Industries (December 1984); a symposium on the use of solar energy (December 1984); the Fifth Arab Conference on Mineral Resources (February 1985); the third triennial Arab Energy Conference (May 1985); and seminars on new techniques in petroleum production (October 1985), on the integration of the Arab petrochemical industry (January 1986) and on financing petroleum projects (February 1986).

OAPEC provides training in technical matters and in documentation and information. In January 1985 it held its Ninth Training Programme on the Fundamentals of the Oil and Gas Industry, for 67 trainees at middle management level from 14 Arab countries. The General Secretariat also conducts technical and feasibility studies and carries out market reviews. It provides information through a library, data base and the publications listed below.

JOINT UNDERTAKINGS

Arab Engineering Company—AREC: POB 898, Abu Dhabi; f. 1981 to give support to national engineering firms by providing Arab experts, organizing a common operational base and supervising the training of Arab engineers. Authorized capital $20m.; subscribed capital $12m. Chair. MAHMOUD HAMRA KROUHA; Gen.-Man. AZIZ AMARA KORBA.

Arab Maritime Petroleum Transport Company—AMPTC: POB 22525, Safat, Kuwait; tel. 2411815; telex 23175; f. 1973 to undertake transport of crude oil, gas, refined products and petrochemicals, and thus to increase Arab participation in the tanker transport industry; capital (authorized and subscribed) $500m. Mems: Algeria, Bahrain, Iraq, Kuwait, Libya, Qatar, Saudi Arabia, United Arab Emirates. Chair. RASHED AWEIDAH AL-THANI; Man.-Dir SULEIMAN AL-BASSAM.

Arab Petroleum Investments Corporation—APICORP: POB 448, Dhahran Airport, Saudi Arabia; f. 1975 to finance petroleum investments in the Arab world and build up a regionally integrated petroleum sector. Projects financed include gas liquefaction plants, petrochemicals, tankers, oil refineries and fertilizers. Authorized capital: US $1,200m.; subscribed capital: $400m. Chair. JAMAL HASSAN JAWA; Gen.-Man. Dr NUREDDIN FARRAG.

Arab Petroleum Services Company—APSC: POB 12925, Tripoli, Libya; f. 1977 to provide petroleum services through the establishment of one or more companies specializing in various activities. Also concerned with training of specialized personnel. Authorized capital: 100m. Libyan dinars; subscribed capital: 15m. Libyan dinars. Chair. AYYAD AL-DALY; Gen.-Man. RAFID ABDUL-HALIM JASSIM.

   Arab Drilling and Workover Company: Tripoli, Libya; established 1977 as a subsidiary of APSC.

   Arab Logging Company: Basra, Iraq; f. 1982 to test stratigraphic measuring instruments.

Arab Petroleum Training Institute: POB 6037, Al-Mansour, Baghdad, Iraq; f. 1979; Dir BARRAK SAID YEHYA.

Arab Shipbuilding and Repair Yard Company: POB 50110, Manama, Bahrain; tel. 671111; telex 8455; f. 1974 to undertake all activities related to repairs, service and eventually construction of vessels for the transport of hydrocarbons; operates a dry dock in Bahrain. Capital (authorized and subscribed) $340m. Chair. Sheikh DAIJ BIN KHALIFAH AL-KHALIFAH; Gen.-Man. ANTÓNIO MACHADO LOPES.

PUBLICATIONS

Annual Report of the Secretary-General.
Annual Statistical Report.
Oil and Arab Cooperation (quarterly).
OAPEC Bulletin (monthly).
Oil and Arab Development (2 a month).
Energy Resources Monitor (quarterly).
Papers, conference proceedings.

ORGANIZATION OF THE ISLAMIC CONFERENCE—OIC

Address: Kilo 6, Mecca Rd, POB 178, Jeddah, Saudi Arabia.
Telephone: 6873880.
Telex: 401366.

The Organization was established in May 1971, following a summit meeting of Muslim heads of state at Rabat, Morocco, in September 1969, and the Islamic Foreign Ministers' Conference in Jeddah in March 1970, and in Karachi, Pakistan in December 1970.

MEMBERS

Afghanistan*	Maldives
Algeria	Mali
Bahrain	Mauritania
Bangladesh	Morocco
Benin	Niger
Brunei	Nigeria
Burkina Faso	Oman
Cameroon	Pakistan
Chad	Palestine Liberation
The Comoros	Organization
Djibouti	Qatar
Egypt*	Saudi Arabia
Gabon	Senegal
The Gambia	Sierra Leone
Guinea	Somalia
Guinea-Bissau	Sudan
Indonesia	Syria
Iran	Tunisia
Iraq	Turkey
Jordan	Uganda
Kuwait	United Arab Emirates
Lebanon	Yemen Arab Republic
Libya	Yemen, People's Democratic
Malaysia	Republic

* Egypt's membership was suspended in May 1979 and restored in March 1984. Afghanistan's membership was suspended in January 1980.

Note: Observer status has been granted to the 'Turkish Federated State of Cyprus' (which declared independence as the 'Turkish Republic of Northern Cyprus' in November 1983).

Organization
(October 1986)

SUMMIT CONFERENCES

The supreme body of the Organization is the Conference of Heads of State, which met in 1969 at Rabat, Morocco, in 1974 at Lahore, Pakistan, and in January 1981 at Mecca, Saudi Arabia, when it was decided that summit conferences would be held every three years in future. Fourth Conference: Casablanca, Morocco, January 1984.

CONFERENCES OF FOREIGN MINISTERS

Conferences take place annually, to consider the means for implementing the general policy of the Organization. An extraordinary session was held for the first time in January 1980 to discuss the situation in Afghanistan: further extraordinary sessions were held in July, September and October.

SECRETARIAT

The executive organ of the Organization, headed by a Secretary-General and four Assistant Secretaries-General.
Secretary-General: SAYED SHARIFUDDIN PIRZADA.

SPECIALIZED COMMITTEES

Al-Quds Committee: f. 1975 to implement the resolutions of the Islamic Conference on the status of Jerusalem (Al-Quds); since 1979 it has met at the level of foreign ministers, under the chairmanship of King Hassan II of Morocco.

Islamic Commission for Economic, Cultural and Social Affairs: f. 1976.

Permanent Finance Committee.

Standing Committee for Scientific and Technical Co-operation: f. 1981.

Standing Committee for Economic and Trade Co-operation: f. 1981.

Standing Committee for Information and Cultural Affairs: f. 1981.

Activities

The Organization's aims, as set out in the Charter adopted in 1972 are:

1. To promote Islamic solidarity among member states;

2. To consolidate co-operation among member states in the economic, social, cultural, scientific and other vital fields, and to arrange consultations among member states belonging to international organizations;

3. To endeavour to eliminate racial segregation and discrimination and to eradicate colonialism in all its forms;

4. To take necessary measures to support international peace and security founded on justice;

5. To co-ordinate all efforts for the safeguard of the Holy Places and support of the struggle of the people of Palestine, and help them to regain their rights and liberate their land;

6. To strengthen the struggle of all Muslim people with a view to safeguarding their dignity, independence and national rights; and

7. To create a suitable atmosphere for the promotion of co-operation and understanding among member states and other countries.

The first summit conference of Islamic leaders (representing 24 states) took place in 1969 following the burning of the Al Aqsa Mosque in Jerusalem. At this conference it was decided that Islamic governments should 'consult together with a view to promoting close co-operation and mutual assistance in the economic, scientific, cultural and spiritual fields, inspired by the immortal teachings of Islam'. Thereafter the foreign ministers of the countries concerned met annually, and adopted the Charter of the Organization of the Islamic Conference in 1972.

At the second Islamic summit conference (Lahore, Pakistan, 1974), the Islamic Solidarity Fund was established, together with a committee of representatives which later evolved into the Islamic Commission for Economic, Social and Cultural Affairs. Subsequently, numerous other subsidiary bodies have been set up (see below).

ECONOMIC CO-OPERATION

A general agreement for economic, technical and commercial co-operation came into force in 1981, providing for the establishment of joint investment projects and trade co-ordination. This was followed by an agreement on promotion, protection and guarantee of investments among member states. A plan of action to strengthen economic co-operation was adopted at the third Islamic summit conference in 1981, aiming to promote collective self-reliance and the development of joint ventures in all sectors. In April 1983 the Islamic Reinsurance Corporation was launched by the OIC with authorized capital of US $200m.

A meeting of ministers of industry was held in February 1982, and agreed to promote industrial co-operation, including joint ventures in agricultural machinery, engineering and other basic industries.

CULTURAL CO-OPERATION

The Organization supports education in Muslim communities throughout the world, and, through the Islamic Solidarity Fund, has helped to establish Islamic universities in Niger, Uganda and Malaysia. It organizes seminars on various aspects of Islam, and encourages dialogue with the other monotheistic religions. Support is given to publications on Islam both in Muslim and Western countries.

HUMANITARIAN ASSISTANCE

Assistance is given to Muslim communities affected by wars and natural disasters, in co-operation with UN organizations, particularly UNHCR. The countries of the Sahel region (Burkina Faso, Cape Verde, Chad, The Gambia, Guinea, Guinea-Bissau, Mali, Mauritania, Niger and Senegal) receive particular attention as victims of drought.

POLITICAL CO-OPERATION

The Organization is also active at a political level. From the beginning it called for vacation of Arab territories by Israel, recognition of the rights of Palestinians and of the Palestine Liberation Organization as their sole legitimate representative, and the restoration of Jerusalem to Arab rule. The 1981 summit conference called for a *jihad* (holy war—though not necessarily in a military sense) 'for the liberation of Jerusalem and the occupied territories'; this was to include an Islamic economic boycott of Israel.

The first extraordinary Conference of Foreign Ministers was held in Islamabad, Pakistan, in January 1980. The member states called for the immediate and unconditional withdrawal of Soviet troops from Afghanistan and suspended Afghanistan's membership of the organization. The Conference also reaffirmed the importance of the Iranian Islamic Republic's sovereignty, territorial integrity and political independence, and adopted a resolution opposing any foreign pressures exerted on Islamic countries in general and Iran in particular. The Conference further asked members not to participate in the 1980 Olympics unless the Soviet troops had withdrawn from Afghanistan; and adopted a resolution condemning armed aggression against Somalia and denouncing the presence of military forces of the USSR and some of its allies in the Horn of Africa.

In May 1980 a special committee was set up to conduct consultations on Afghanistan. Mediation in the Gulf war between Iran and Iraq was also attempted: an Islamic Peace Committee, headed by the Secretary-General of the Organization, was established in September 1980 and suggested a cease-fire supervised by an observer force of troops drawn from Islamic countries, but the terms were rejected by the protagonists.

The third Islamic summit conference (Mecca, Saudi Arabia, January 1981) repeated the demand for Soviet withdrawal from Afghanistan and affirmed Afghanistan's political independence. It also decided to continue attempts at mediation between Iran and Iraq.

In 1982 Islamic foreign ministers decided to set up Islamic offices for boycotting Israel and for military co-operation with the Palestine Liberation Organization. The OIC endorsed the peace plan proposed by the League of Arab States.

The 1984 summit conference agreed to reinstate Egypt as a member of the Organization, although the resolution was opposed by seven states.

SUBSIDIARY ORGANS

Al-Quds Fund: f. 1976.

International Commission for the Islamic Heritage: f. 1980.

International Islamic Law Commission: f. 1982.

Islamic Centre for the Development of Trade: Complexe Commerciale des Habous, BP 13545, ave des FAR, Casablanca, Morocco; tel. 31 49 74; telex 22026; opened 1983 to encourage regular commercial contacts, harmonize policies and promote investments among OIC members.

Islamic Centre for Technical and Vocational Training and Research: KB Bazar, Joydebpur, Gazipur Dist., Dhaka, Bangladesh; tel. 390154; telex 642739; f. 1979 to provide skilled technicians and instructors in mechanical, electrical, electronic and chemical technology, and to conduct research; expected to begin operations in 1986, with 650 students, later to increase to 1,150. Dir Dr RAFIQUDDIN AHMAD.

Islamic Civil Aviation Council: Tunis, Tunisia; f. 1982.

Islamic Commission for the International Crescent: f. 1980.

Islamic Foundation for Science, Technology and Development—IFSTAD: POB 9833, Jeddah, Saudi Arabia; tel. 6322273; telex 404081; f. 1981 to promote co-operation in science and technology within the Islamic world. Dir-Gen. Dr ALI KETTANI.

Islamic Jurisprudence Academy: f. 1982.

Islamic Solidarity Fund: c/o OIC Secretariat, POB 178, Jeddah, Saudi Arabia; f. 1974 to meet the needs of Islamic communities by providing emergency aid and the wherewithal to build mosques, Islamic centres, hospitals, schools and universities. Sec.-Gen. SHEIKH AHMAD AL-MOUBARAK.

Research Centre for Islamic History, Art and Culture: Istanbul, Turkey; f. 1976.

Statistical, Economic and Social Research and Training Centre for the Islamic Countries: Ankara, Turkey; f. 1977.

OTHER INSTITUTIONS WITHIN THE OIC SYSTEM

International Islamic News Agency: POB 5054, Prince Fahd St, Jeddah, Saudi Arabia; f. 1972. Dir-Gen. SAFDAR ALI QURESHI; Editor-in-Charge SHAH ALAM.

Islamic Capitals Organization: c/o Mayor of Mecca, Mecca, Saudi Arabia; f. 1978.

Islamic Chamber of Commerce, Industry and Commodity Exchange: NBP Bldg, Kahkashan, Clifton Road, Karachi, Pakistan; f. 1979. Pres. Sheikh ISMAIL ABUDAWOOD; Sec.-Gen. SAMI CANSEN ONARAN.

Islamic Development Bank (q.v.).

Islamic Educational, Scientific and Cultural Organization: BP 755, Rabat, Morocco; f. 1982. Dir-Gen. ABDELHADI BOUTALEB.

Islamic Shipowners' Association: Jeddah, Saudi Arabia; f. 1981.

Islamic States Broadcasting Organization: c/o Pakistan Broadcasting Corpn, Broadcasting House, Islamabad, Pakistan; tel. 829021; telex 5816; f. 1975. Sec.-Gen. AHMAD FARRAJ.

At the summit conference in January 1981 it was decided that an Islamic Court of Justice should be established to adjudicate in disputes between Muslim countries. Experts met in January 1983 to draw up a constitution for the court.

ORGANIZATION OF THE PETROLEUM EXPORTING COUNTRIES—OPEC

Address: Obere Donaustrasse 93, 1020 Vienna, Austria.
Telephone: (0222) 26-55-11.
Telex: 134474.

OPEC was established in 1960 to link countries whose main source of export earnings is petroleum; it aims to unify and co-ordinate members' petroleum policies and to safeguard their interests generally. The OPEC Fund for International Development is described on p. 198.

MEMBERS*

Algeria	Iraq	Saudi Arabia
Ecuador	Kuwait	United Arab
Gabon	Libya	Emirates
Indonesia	Nigeria	Venezuela
Iran	Qatar	

* OPEC's share of world petroleum production was 31.9% in 1984, decreasing from 32.6% in 1983 (compared with 45% in 1980 and a peak of 55.5% in 1973). At the end of 1984 OPEC members were estimated to possess 68.4% of the world's known reserves of crude petroleum, and 33.7% of known reserves of natural gas.

Organization
(October 1986)

CONFERENCE

The Conference is the supreme authority of the Organization, responsible for the formulation of its general policy. It consists of representatives of member countries, who examine reports and recommendations submitted by the Board of Governors. It approves the appointment of Governors from each country and elects the Chairman of the Board of Governors. It works on the unanimity principle, and meets at least twice a year.

THE BOARD OF GOVERNORS

The Board directs the management of the Organization; it implements resolutions of the Conference and draws up an annual budget. It consists of one governor for each member country, and meets at least twice a year.

THE ECONOMIC COMMISSION

A specialized body operating within the framework of the Secretariat, with a view to assisting the Organization in promoting stability in international oil prices at equitable levels; consists of a board, national representatives and a commission staff; the Board meets at least twice a year.

SECRETARIAT

Office of the Secretary-General: Provides the Secretary-General with executive assistance in carrying out contacts with governments, organizations and delegations, in matters of protocol and in the preparation for and co-ordination of meetings.
Secretary-General: (vacant).
Deputy Secretary-General (acting as Secretary-General): Dr FADHIL J. ASH-SHALABI (Iraq).
Energy Studies Department: Conducts a continuous programme for research in energy and related matters; monitors, forecasts and analyses developments in the energy and petrochemical industries; and the evaluation of hydrocarbons and products and their non-energy uses.
Economics and Finance Department: Analyses economic and financial issues of significant interest; in particular those related to international financial and monetary matters, and to the international petroleum industry.
Data Services Department:
  Computer Section: Maintains and expands information services to support the research activities of the Secretariat and those of member countries.
  Statistics Section: Collects, collates and analyses statistical information from both primary and secondary sources.
Personnel and Administration Department: Responsible for all organization methods, provision of administrative services for all meetings, personnel matters, budgets accounting and internal control.
Public Information Department: Responsible for a central public relations programme; production and distribution of publications, films, slides and tapes; and communication of OPEC objectives and decisions to the world at large.
Legal Office: Undertakes special and other in-house legal studies and reports to ascertain where the best interests of the Organization and member countries lie.

OPEC NEWS AGENCY

Founded 1980 to provide information on OPEC to about 77 countries and counteract inaccurate reporting by some other sources: covers member countries' petroleum and energy issues; activities of the OPEC Secretariat; co-operation with other developing countries; news on oil companies; technical and policy information on the upstream and downstream sectors of the industry; energy supply and demand; and economic and social development in member countries.

Record of Events

1960   The first OPEC Conference was held in Baghdad in September, attended by representatives from Iran, Iraq, Kuwait, Saudi Arabia and Venezuela.

1961   Second Conference, Caracas, January. Qatar was admitted to membership; a Board of Governors was formed and statutes agreed.

1962   Fourth Conference, Geneva, April and June. Protests were addressed to oil companies against price cuts introduced in August 1960. Indonesia and Libya were admitted to membership.

1965   In July the Conference reached agreement on a two-year joint production programme, implemented from 1965 to 1967, to limit annual growth in output to secure adequate prices.

1967   Abu Dhabi was admitted to membership.

1968   Fifteenth Conference (extraordinary), Beirut, January. OPEC accepted an offer of elimination of discounts submitted by oil companies following negotiations in November 1967.

1969   Algeria was admitted to membership.

1970   Twenty-first Conference, Caracas, December. Tax on income of oil companies was raised to 55%.

1971   A five-year agreement was concluded in February between the six producing countries in the Gulf and 23 international oil companies (Teheran Agreement).
Twenty-fourth Conference, Vienna, July. Nigeria was admitted to membership.

1972   In January oil companies agreed to adjust oil revenues of the largest producers after changes in currency exchange rates (Geneva Agreement).

1973   Agreement with companies was reached under which posted prices of crude oil were raised by 11.9% and a mechanism was installed to make monthly adjustments to prices in future (Second Geneva Agreement).
Negotiations with oil companies on revision of the Teheran Agreement broke down in October and the Gulf states unilaterally declared 70% increases in posted prices, from $3.01 to $5.11 per barrel.
Thirty-sixth Conference, Teheran, December. The posted price was to increase by nearly 130%, from $5.11 to $11.65 per barrel, from 1 January 1974. Ecuador was admitted to full membership and Gabon became an associate member.

INTERNATIONAL ORGANIZATIONS

Organization of the Petroleum Exporting Countries

1974 As a result of Saudi opposition to the December price increase, prices were held at current level for first quarter (and subsequently for the remainder of 1974). Abu Dhabi's membership was transferred to the United Arab Emirates.
A meeting in June increased royalties charged to oil companies from 12.5% to 14.5% in all member states except Saudi Arabia.
A meeting in September increased governmental take by about 3.5% through further increases in royalties on equity crude to 16.67% and in taxes to 65.65%, except in Saudi Arabia.

1975 OPEC's first summit conference was held in Algiers in March. Gabon was admitted to full membership.
A ministerial meeting in September agreed to raise prices by 10% for the period until June 1976.

1976 The OPEC Special Fund for International Development was created in May.
In December, a general 15% rise in basic prices was proposed and supported by 11 member states. This was to take place in two stages: a 10% rise as of 1 January 1977, and a further 5% rise as of 1 July 1977. However, Saudi Arabia and the United Arab Emirates decided to raise their prices by 5% only.

1977 Following an earlier waiver by nine members of the 5% second stage of the price rise agreed at Doha, Saudi Arabia and the United Arab Emirates announced in July that they would both raise their prices by 5%. As a result, a single level of prices throughout the organization was restored.
Because of continued disagreements between the 'moderates', led by Saudi Arabia and Iran, and the 'radicals', led by Algeria, Libya and Iraq, the year's second Conference at Caracas, December, was unable to settle on an increase in prices.

1978 In May a ministerial committee from six member states was established to draw up long-term pricing and production strategy. Production ceilings of members were lowered.
Fifty-first Conference, Geneva, June. Price levels were to remain stable until the end of 1978. A committee of experts, chaired by Kuwait, met in July to consider ways of compensating for the effects of the depreciation of the US dollar.
In December 1978 it was decided to raise prices by instalments of 5%, 3.8%, 2.3% and 2.7%. These would bring a rise of 14.5% over nine months, but an average increase of 10% for 1979.

1979 At an extraordinary meeting in Geneva at the end of March it was decided to raise prices by 9%. Many members maintained surcharges they had imposed in February after Iranian exports were halted.
In June the Conference agreed minimum and maximum prices which seemed likely to add between 15% and 20% to import bills of consumer countries.
The December Conference recommended replenishment of the OPEC Fund and agreed in principle to convert the Fund into a development agency with its own legal personality. An OPEC News Agency was to be set up, based at the Secretariat.

1980 In June the Conference decided to set the price for a marker crude at US $32.00 per barrel, and that the value differentials which could be added above this ceiling (on account of quality and geographical location) should not exceed $5.00 per barrel.
It was decided to begin studies on the feasibility of an OPEC Institute of Higher Education, for technological research and training.
The planned OPEC summit meeting in Baghdad in November was postponed indefinitely because of the Iran–Iraq war, but the scheduled price-fixing meeting of petroleum ministers went ahead in Bali in December, with both Iranians and Iraqis present. A ceiling price of US $41.00 per barrel was fixed for premium crudes.

1981 In May attempts to achieve price reunification were made, but Saudi Arabia refused to increase its $32.00 per barrel price unless the higher prices charged by other countries were lowered. Most of the other OPEC countries agreed to cut production by 10% so as to reduce the surplus. An emergency meeting in Geneva in August again failed to unify prices, although Saudi Arabia agreed to reduce production by 1m. barrels per day, with the level of output to be reviewed monthly.
In October OPEC countries agreed to increase the Saudi marker price by 6% to $34 per barrel, with a ceiling price of $38 per barrel. This price structure was intended to remain in force until the end of 1982. Saudi Arabia also announced that it would keep its production below 8.5m.b/d.

1982 The continuing world oil glut (resulting from a fall in demand to a predicted 46m. b/d in 1982, compared with 52m. in 1979) forced prices below the official mark of $34 per barrel in some producer countries. In March an emergency meeting of petroleum ministers was held in Vienna and agreed (for the first time in OPEC's history) to defend the Organization's price structure by imposing an overall production ceiling of 18m. b/d, effectively 17.5m. b/d with Saudi Arabia's separate announcement of a cut to 7m. b/d in its own production. Measures were taken to support Nigerian prices following a slump in production.
In December the Conference agreed to limit OPEC production to 18.5m. b/d in 1983 (representing about one-third of total world production) but postponed the allocation of national quotas pending consultations among the respective governments.

1983 In January an emergency meeting of petroleum ministers, fearing a collapse in world oil prices, decided to reduce the production ceiling to 17.5m. b/d (itself several million b/d above actual current output) but failed to agree on individual production quotas or on adjustments to the differentials in prices charged for the high-quality crude petroleum produced by Algeria, Libya and Nigeria compared with that produced by the Gulf States.
In February Nigeria cut its prices to $30 per barrel, following a collapse in its production. To avoid a 'price war' OPEC set the official price of marker crude at $29 per barrel, and agreed to maintain existing differentials among the various OPEC crudes at the level agreed on in March 1982, with the temporary exception that the differentials for Nigerian crudes should be $1 more than the price of the marker crude. It also agreed to maintain the production ceiling of 17.5m. b/d and allocated quotas for each member country except Saudi Arabia, which was to act as a 'swing producer' to supply the balancing quantities to meet market requirements. It called on member countries to avoid giving discounts in any form, and to refrain from 'dumping' petroleum products into the world oil market at prices which would endanger the crude oil pricing structure. The official marker price and production ceiling were maintained throughout the year, although actual production by members was believed to be in excess of 18m. b/d at the end of the year. Despite demands for revised quotas by some countries, and Iran's attempt to restore the marker price to $34 per barrel, the meeting agreed to maintain the existing production and pricing agreement as the policy most likely to restore stability to the world petroleum market.

1984 The production ceiling of 17.5m. b/d and the official price of $29 per barrel were maintained until October, when the production ceiling was lowered to 16m. b/d. In December price differentials for light (more expensive) and heavy (cheaper) crudes were slightly altered in an attempt to counteract price-cutting by non-OPEC producers, particularly Norway and the United Kingdom. An auditing commission was set up to monitor members' adherence to production limits.

1985 In January members (except Algeria, Iran and Libya) effectively abandoned the marker price system: the price of Arabian light crude (the former marker price) was lowered to $28 per barrel, and price differentials between the cheapest and most expensive grades were cut from $4 to $2.40; this system was also adopted by Iran in February.
During the year production in excess of quotas by OPEC members, unofficial discounts and barter deals by members, and price cuts by non-members (such as Mexico, which had hitherto kept its prices in line with those of OPEC) contributed to a weakening of the market. Saudi Arabia indicated that it was not prepared to continue cutting its own output, to make up for others' increases, in an attempt to support world prices. In July, 10 members agreed to small price cuts of $0.50 and $0.20 per barrel respectively for heavy and medium crudes. Ecuador, Gabon and Iraq demanded larger production quotas, and when, in October, discussion of the redistribution of quotas was postponed, Ecuador announced that it was 'temporarily' leaving OPEC, the first member country to do so. In December ministers of petroleum of OPEC member states resolved to 'secure and defend for OPEC a fair share in the world market consistent with the income necessary for member countries' development'. A

special committee was established to determine what OPEC's share of the world market should be, and how it should be defended in the face of falling prices and the steady production levels maintained by some non-members.

1986 During the first half of the year prices dropped to below $10 per barrel. In April ministers from 10 member states agreed to set OPEC production at 16.7m. b/d for the third quarter of 1986 and at 17.3m. b/d for the fourth quarter. Algeria, Iran and Libya dissented, arguing that production should be reduced to 14.5m. b/d and 16.8m. b/d respectively for those periods, in order to restore prices. Discussions were also held with non-member countries (Angola, Egypt, Malaysia, Mexico and Oman), which agreed to co-operate in limiting production. However, requests by OPEC that the United Kingdom should reduce its petroleum production levels continued to be rejected by the British Government. In August members agreed upon a return to production quotas (for all members except Iraq), with the aim of cutting production to 14.8m. b/d (about 16.8m. b/d including Iraq's production) for the ensuing two months. This measure resulted in an increase in prices to about $15 per barrel, and in October the agreement was extended until the end of the year, with a slight increase in collective output to 15m. b/d (excluding Iraq's production).

FINANCE

1986 budget: 232.3m. Austrian schillings.

PUBLICATIONS

OPEC Bulletin (monthly).
OPEC Review (quarterly).
Annual Report.
Basic Oil Industry Information.
Selected Documents of the International Petroleum Industry.
Annual Statistical Bulletin.
Facts and Figures.
OPEC Information Booklet.
OPEC at a Glance.
OPEC Official Resolutions and Press Releases.

OPEC FUND FOR INTERNATIONAL DEVELOPMENT

Address: POB 995, 1011 Vienna, Austria.
Telephone: (0222) 51-56-40.
Telex: 1-31734.
The Fund was established by OPEC member countries in 1976.

MEMBERS
Member countries of OPEC (see p. 195).

Organization
(October 1986)

ADMINISTRATION
The Fund is administered by a Ministerial Council and a Governing Board composed of one representative of each member country.
Chairman, Ministerial Council: HECTOR HURTADO (Venezuela).
Chairman, Governing Board: OSAMAH FAQUIH (Saudi Arabia).
Director-General of the Fund: Y. SEYYID ABDULAI (Nigeria).

FINANCIAL STRUCTURE
The resources of the Fund, whose unit of account is the US dollar, consist of contributions by OPEC member countries, and income received from operations or otherwise accruing to the Fund.

The initial endowment of the Fund amounted to US $800m. Its resources have been replenished three times, and have been further increased by the profits accruing to seven OPEC member countries through the sales of gold held by the International Monetary Fund. The pledged contributions to the OPEC Fund amounted to US $3,435m. at the end of 1985, and paid-in contributions totalled $2,579m.

Activities

The OPEC Fund for International Development is a multilateral agency for financial co-operation and assistance. Its objective is to reinforce financial co-operation between OPEC member countries and other developing countries through the provision of financial support to the latter on appropriate terms, to assist them in their economic and social development. The Fund was conceived as a collective financial facility which would consolidate the assistance extended by its member countries; its resources are additional to those already made available through other bilateral and multilateral aid agencies of OPEC members. It is empowered to:

(a) Provide concessional loans for balance-of-payments support;
(b) Provide concessional loans for the implementation of development projects and programmes;
(c) Make contributions and/or provide loans to eligible international agencies; and
(d) Finance technical assistance activities.

The eligible beneficiaries of the Fund's assistance are the governments of developing countries other than OPEC member countries, and international development agencies whose beneficiaries are developing countries. The Fund gives priority to the countries with the lowest income.

The Fund may undertake technical, economic and financial appraisal of a project submitted to it, or entrust such an appraisal to an appropriate international development agency, the executing national agency of a member country, or any other qualified agency. Most projects financed by the Fund have been co-financed by other development finance agencies. In each such case, one of the co-financing agencies may be appointed to administer the Fund's loan in association with its own. This practice has enabled the Fund to extend its lending activities to 83 countries over a short period of time and in a simple way, avoiding duplication and complications. As its experience grew, the Fund increasingly resorted to parallel, rather than joint financing, taking up separate project components to be financed according to its rules and policies. In addition, it has started to finance some projects completely on its own. These new trends necessitated the issuance in 1982 of guidelines for the procurement of goods and services under the Fund's loans, allowing for a margin of preference for goods and services of local origin or originating in other developing countries: competitive bidding, for example, may be limited to contractors from a given developing country or countries, if such countries agree to participate with the Fund in co-financing a project on concessional terms.

Since its inception the Fund has implemented six lending programmes; the seventh lending programme, covering the period 1986–87, was approved in 1985. Besides extending loans for project and programme financing and balance of payments support, the Fund has also undertaken other operations, including grants in support of technical assistance and other activities (mainly research), and financial contributions to other international institutions.

By the end of August 1986 the number of loans extended by the Fund was 392, totalling US $1,944m., of which 207 loans were for project financing, 176 for balance-of-payments support and nine for programme financing. Over 77% of the amount committed had been disbursed.

Direct loans are supplemented by grants to support technical assistance, food aid and research. By the end of December 1985 160 grants, amounting to US $151m., had been extended, including $29.86m. to cover the subscriptions of 28 low-income developing countries to the Common Fund for Commodities, and a special contribution of $20m. to the International Fund for Agricultural Development (IFAD). In addition, the Fund had contributed $971.9m. to other international institutions by the end of 1985. It has met OPEC members' contributions to the resources of IFAD, and made irrevocable transfers in the name of its members to the IMF Trust Fund.

During the year ending 31 December 1985, the Fund's total commitments were $117.5m.; total lending commitments amounted to $113.5m., of which 92% was for project financing. The largest proportion of project loans ($31.5m., or 30.1% of total project financing) was for the education sector, for which eight loans were provided. Five of these loans financed primary and basic education projects in Benin, Burkina Faso, the Central African Republic, Ethiopia and Senegal; the remaining three loans were allocated to two technical projects, one in Mali and one in Nepal, and a science education project in Pakistan. Agriculture and agro-industry pro-

OPEC FUND COMMITMENTS AND DISBURSEMENTS
(cumulative to 31 December 1985, US $ million).

	Commitments	Disbursements
Lending operations:	1,968.224	1,417.415
Project financing	1,205.694	680.533
Balance of payments support	698.430	687.700
Programme financing	64.100	49.181
Grant Programme	150.989	105.367
Technical assistance	69.488	54.002
Food aid	5.000	5.000
World Food Programme	25.000	25.000
Special contribution to IFAD	20.000	20.000
Research and other intellectual activities	1.641	1.365
Common Fund for Commodities	29.860	—
IFAD	861.142	731.989
IMF Trust Fund	110.721	110.721
Total	3,091.076	2,365.492

jects accounted for 20.1% (flood control, credit services and market roads in Bolivia; agro-industry in Ghana; rice production in Kenya; livestock in Mauritania; dairying in Niger; and shrimp culture in Thailand). Transport projects received 20% of loans (for rehabilitation of roads, railways and ports in Burma, the Central African Republic, the Dominican Republic, Mozambique and the People's Democratic Republic of Yemen). The energy sector received 13.4% of loans for a thermal power project in Bangladesh and a petroleum products storage and distribution project in the Yemen Arab Republic. National development banks in Bangladesh, Guyana and Mali received 10.7% of loans. Grants, totalling $4.05m. during the year, included $3.81m. for 18 technical assistance projects and $234,400 for research and similar activities.

PUBLICATIONS

Annual Report.
OPEC Fund Newsletter (quarterly).
OPEC Aid and OPEC Aid Institutions—A Profile (annually).
Occasional books and papers.

SOUTH PACIFIC COMMISSION — SPC

Address: BP D5, Nouméa Cedex, New Caledonia.
Telephone: 26-20-00.
Telex: 139.

The Commission was established by an agreement signed in Canberra, Australia, by the governments of Australia, France, the Netherlands, New Zealand, the United Kingdom and the USA, in February 1947, effective from July 1948. (The Netherlands withdrew from the Commission in 1962, when it ceased to administer the former colony of Dutch New Guinea, now Irian Jaya, part of Indonesia.) The Commission allows the discussion of regional issues, and gives training and assistance in economic, social and cultural development to the countries of the region. It serves a population of about 5m. people, scattered over some 30m. sq km., over 98% of which is sea.

MEMBERS

American Samoa	Northern Mariana Islands
Australia	Palau
Cook Islands	Papua New Guinea
Federated States of Micronesia	Pitcairn Islands
Fiji	Solomon Islands
France	Tokelau
French Polynesia	Tonga
Guam	Tuvalu
Kiribati	United Kingdom
Marshall Islands	USA
Nauru	Vanuatu
New Caledonia	Wallis and Futuna Islands
New Zealand	Western Samoa
Niue	

Organization
(October 1986)

SOUTH PACIFIC CONFERENCE

The Conference is held annually and since 1974 has combined the former South Pacific Conference, attended by delegates from the countries and territories within the Commission's area of action, and the former Commission Session, attended by representatives of the participating governments. Each government and territorial administration has the right to send a representative and alternates to the Conference and each representative (or in his absence an alternate) has the right to cast one vote on behalf of the government or territorial administration which he represents.

The Conference is the supreme decision-making body of the Commission; it examines and adopts the Commission's work programme and budget for the coming year, and discusses any other matters within the competence of the Commission.

COMMITTEE OF REPRESENTATIVES OF GOVERNMENTS AND ADMINISTRATIONS

This Committee comprises representatives of all 27 member states and territories, having equal voting rights, and was formed in 1983 to replace the former Committee of Representatives (of only 13 members) and the Planning and Evaluation Committee. It meets annually, before the annual South Pacific Conference: it recommends the administrative budget, evaluates the effectiveness of the past year's work programme, examines the draft budget and work programme presented by the Secretary-General, and nominates the principal officers of the Commission.

SECRETARIAT

Since November 1976 the Secretariat has had a Management Committee which has a supervisory and advisory role over all Commission activities. Committee members are the Principal Officers of the Commission. The Secretary-General is the chief executive officer of the Commission.
Secretary-General: Palauni Tuiasosopo (American Samoa).
Director of Programmes: Tamarii Pierre (Cook Islands).
Deputy Director of Programmes: F. Vitolio Lui (Western Samoa).

Activities

Each territory has its own programme of development activities. The Commission's role is advisory and consultative: it assists these programmes by bringing people together for discussion and study, by research into some of the problems common to the region, by providing expert advice and assistance and by disseminating technical information.

The 16th South Pacific Conference adopted a recommendation by the 1976 Review Committee that the Commission should carry out the following specific activities:

(a) rural development
(b) youth and community development
(c) ad hoc expert consultancies
(d) cultural exchanges (in arts, sports and education)
(e) training facilitation
(f) assessment and development of marine resources and research;

and that special consideration should be given to projects and grants-in-aid which do not necessarily fall within these specific activities, but which respond to pressing regional or sub-regional needs or to the expressed needs of the smaller Pacific countries. The work programme subsequently adopted by the South Pacific Conference was developed in response to these guidelines, and gives priority to projects in the following areas:

FOOD AND MATERIALS

Agricultural activities in 1985 concentrated on the Family-level Food Crops and Home Economics Project. The Commission also provides a regional Plant Protection Service to conduct research and give advice on the control of pests and diseases and the preservation of crops; training courses and workshops are held and publications issued. The Tropical Agriculturalist and the Plant Protection Officer travel in the region providing information and advice.

MARINE RESOURCES

SPC fisheries advisers and a specialist in fish-handling and processing travel in the region to provide advice and training for local fishing projects. A 23-week Pacific Island Fisheries Training Course is held annually in Nelson, New Zealand, and training courses in refrigeration techniques and fish-processing were held in 1985 and 1986. The Deep Sea Fisheries Development Project, supervised by three Master Fishermen, tests techniques and compiles data on deep sea fishing. Statistics are gathered on commercial fishing for tunas and billfishes in the region, and research on the biology of tunas and billfishes is conducted for the purpose of stock assessment.

RURAL MANAGEMENT AND TECHNOLOGY

The Action Plan for Managing the Natural Resources and Environment of the South Pacific Region was adopted in 1982, giving guidance to the South Pacific Region for the sustainable management of land, sea and air resources. To implement the Plan, the South Pacific Regional Environment Programme (SPREP) undertakes research, monitoring, education and the provision of information. Consultative meetings are held annually with the research and training institutions of the region to determine environmental research to be carried out under SPREP: such research has included studies of water quality, marine pollution, pesticides and oceanography. An Association of Environmental Institutions of the Pacific was formed at the 1986 consultative meeting. There are three Pollution Monitoring and Advisory Centres in the region. A four-year environmental radio project was begun in 1983, to provide training in the broadcasting of programmes related to the environment. In September 1984 a third meeting of experts was held to draw up a Convention for the Protection and Development of the

Natural Resources and Environment of the South Pacific Region: the meeting agreed on provisions concerning co-operation in combating pollution emergencies and the prevention of ocean dumping. The third South Pacific National Parks and Reserves Conference was held in Western Samoa in June 1985, to discuss the establishment and management of protected areas in the region.

Four SPC volunteer water technicians give assistance in water supply and sanitation projects, for example building rainwater catchment systems and installing water-seal latrines. Under the SPC Renewable Energies Programme two photovoltaic electricity supply projects (using solar energy) had been completed by March 1984, while four more were in preparation. The Commission's project on Rural Employment and Development co-operates with planners to draw up and implement rural development programmes in the region.

COMMUNITY SERVICES

The Commission employs a Health Education Officer, a Nutritionist and an Epidemiologist, who travel in the region, visiting health and community institutions, helping to organize surveys and analyse data, and giving advice on possible improvements. Educational materials, such as leaflets on nutritious foods, are published. The sixth regional training course in drug identification and drug concealment methods was held in June 1986.

The SPC Community Education Training Centre at Narere, Fiji, provides training in the form of 10-month courses for about 30 community-work students annually. Mobile training units also provide short courses in community development and youth work. A regional seminar on Pacific youth was held in February 1986, and a directory of youth organizations in the region was being compiled in 1986. The Pacific Women's Resource Bureau aims to link regional and national women's organizations and develop programmes for the benefit of women. A directory of women's groups and a directory of skilled women were being compiled in 1986.

SOCIO-ECONOMIC STATISTICAL SERVICES

The Statistics Section provides statistical training and information, and organizes regular regional conferences of statisticians. SPC training courses on statistical operations and procedures, at basic and intermediate levels, are held regularly in different places. The Population Section assists in conducting censuses and population surveys, and in the analysis and application of population data. Training in demographic data collection and application is also given. The Third Regional Meeting of Population Census Planners was held in 1985. A project on Migration, Employment and Development in the South Pacific was begun in 1981 in collaboration with the International Labour Organisation (ILO), to collect and analyse data. An SPC/ILO regional training course on population mobility, employment and development planning was to be held in 1987.

The Economic Section provides advisory services of a technical nature in economic development planning, marketing and price stabilization, and holds annual or biennial training courses on planning techniques, project analysis and farm management. The Section also compiles and publishes relevant economic data. A Regional Conference of Development Planners is held every two years.

EDUCATION SERVICES

Consultant services are provided on English as a second language, and the Commission maintains a primary school programme consisting of a comprehensive range of materials for the development of oral and written English (under revision in 1985).

CULTURAL CONSERVATION AND EXCHANGE

The Commission supports cultural development and conservation. It organizes meetings of the Council of Pacific Arts and provides assistance for the Festival of Pacific Arts: the fourth Festival was held in Tahiti (French Polynesia) in December 1984, and the fifth was to be held in 1988.

FINANCE

Contributions to the regular budget of the Commission are made by member governments and administrations, according to a formula based on per caput income. The total regular budget for 1984 was 404m. francs CFP, and the proposed budget for 1985 was 471m. francs CFP (of which 427.3m. francs CFP consisted of contributions by governments and administrations, in the following proportions: Australia 33.3%, USA 16.8%, New Zealand 16.1%, France 13.9%, United Kingdom 12.2%, others 7.7%). In addition to projects funded from the regular budget, the Commission carries out activities funded by special voluntary contributions from governments, international organizations and other sources. In 1984 extra-budgetary funding amounted to 377.4m. francs CFP, or 48% of total expenditure.

PUBLICATIONS

SPC Publications Catalogue.
Library Accessions List.
Annual Report.
Report of the South Pacific Conference.
Monthly News of Activities.
SPELT News.
Fisheries Newsletter.
Youthlink.
Women's Newsletter.
Cultural Newsletter.
Technical publications, statistical bulletins, advisory leaflets and reports.

SOUTH PACIFIC FORUM

c/o SPEC (see below)

MEMBERS

Australia
Cook Islands
Fiji
Kiribati
Federated States of
  Micronesia (observer)
Nauru
New Zealand
Niue
Papua New Guinea
Solomon Islands
Tonga
Tuvalu
Vanuatu
Western Samoa

The South Pacific Forum is the gathering of Heads of Government of the independent and self-governing states of the South Pacific. Its first meeting was held on 5 August 1971, in Wellington, New Zealand. It provides an opportunity for informal discussions to be held on a wide range of common issues and problems and meets annually or when issues require urgent attention. The Forum has no written constitution or international agreement governing its activities nor any formal rules relating to its purpose, membership or conduct of meeting. Decisions are always reached by consensus, it never having been found necessary or desirable to vote formally on issues.

The 14th Forum was held in August 1983 in Canberra, Australia. It adopted a resolution calling on France to grant greater political and administrative autonomy to the French Overseas Territory of New Caledonia, and to establish a timetable for the territory's independence. The Forum reiterated that it would continue to condemn nuclear testing by France or by any other country in the South Pacific region, and to oppose the dumping of nuclear waste there; it commended the Australian initiative in reviving the concept of a nuclear-free zone in the region and undertook to continue consultations on the matter. The Forum discussed the establishment of a single regional organization combining the South Pacific Commission and SPEC (q.v.) and appointed a committee of four Ministers of Foreign Affairs to consult the governments concerned, as well as the governments of France, the United Kingdom and the USA. A programme was adopted for the long-term development of rural and inter-island telecommunications, aiming to provide a regional co-operative approach and a framework for co-ordinating external assistance. The viability of the Pacific Forum Line was also discussed.

The 15th Forum, held in August 1984 in Tuvalu, commissioned a group of experts to draw up a treaty for establishing a nuclear-free zone, to be presented at the next year's meeting. It also discussed the question of independence for New Caledonia, and agreed that there was a risk of serious violence in the territory if France refused to grant it independence before 1989; the Forum decided, however, not to bring the matter before the United Nations Special Committee on Decolonization, as requested by the government of Vanuatu.

The 16th Forum was held in August 1985 in Rarotonga, Cook Islands. It adopted a treaty declaring a nuclear-free zone in the South Pacific and prohibiting the possession, testing and use of nuclear weapons in the region (which would come into force following ratification by eight member states); France, the United Kingdom, the USA, the People's Republic of China and the USSR were to be invited to sign protocols committing them to support the treaty. The Forum also reaffirmed its support for self-determination in New Caledonia, and set up a group to observe developments there. The SPARTECA agreement (see below) was discussed, and its scope was widened.

The 17th Forum, held in August 1986 in Suva, Fiji, agreed unanimously to bring the question of New Caledonia before the UN Special Committee on Decolonization, on the grounds that the French Government which had taken office earlier that year appeared to be committed to retaining New Caledonia as a French territory. Five countries declared that they were ready to ratify the 1985 treaty on a nuclear-free zone, which had so far been ratified by only four members. The Forum also approved an amendment in the protocols to be offered to the non-regional powers for signature: this would allow the signatories to withdraw if unforeseen circumstances made it necessary for their national interest. The meeting expressed concern over the lack of progress in negotiations with the USA over fishing rights in the South Pacific region.

South Pacific Bureau for Economic Co-operation—SPEC

Address: GPO Box 856, Suva, Fiji.
Telephone: 312600.
Telex: 2229.

SPEC was established by an agreement signed on 17 April 1973, at the third meeting of the South Pacific Forum in Apia, Western Samoa.

Organization

(October 1986)

COMMITTEE

The Committee is the Bureau's executive board. It comprises representatives and senior officials from all member countries. It meets twice a year, immediately before the meetings of the South Pacific Forum and at the end of the year, to discuss in detail the Bureau's work programme and annual budget.

SECRETARIAT

The Secretariat carries out the day-to-day activities of the Bureau. It is headed by a Director, with an executive staff of 25 drawn from the member countries. In 1975 the Bureau became the official secretariat of the South Pacific Forum and its secretariat is responsible for the administration of the Forum.

Director: HENRY FAATI NAISALI.
Deputy Director: TREVOR SOFIELD.

Pacific Regional Advisory Service—PRAS: c/o SPEC Secretariat; aims to maintain register of local skills and to co-ordinate and support the transfer of these skills from one member to another.

Activities

The Bureau was set up as a result of proposals for establishing a 'Trade Bureau' which were put forward at the second meeting of the South Pacific Forum in 1972. Its aim is to facilitate continuing co-operation and consultation between members on trade, economic development, transport, tourism and other related matters. In 1974 the Bureau absorbed the functions of the Pacific Islands Producers' Association (PIPA).

SPEC's trade activities cover trade promotion, the identification and development of export-oriented industries, and the negotiation of export opportunities. Following a study of trade relations and industrial development in the South Pacific, SPEC co-ordinated and assisted island countries in negotiating the South Pacific Regional Trade and Economic Co-operation Agreement (SPARTECA) which came into force in 1981, aiming to redress the trade deficit of the South Pacific countries with Australia and New Zealand. It is a non-reciprocal trade agreement under which Australia and New Zealand offer duty-free and unrestricted access or concessional access for specified products originating from the developing island member countries of the Forum. In August 1985 Australia agreed to further liberalization of trade by abolishing (from the beginning of 1987) duties and quotas on all Pacific products except steel, cars, sugar, footwear and garments. SPEC has also undertaken an investigation into the prospects for closer economic co-operation between members, market surveys in Japan and the USA, and surveys on regional industry, the harmonization of industrial incentives, possibilities of bulk purchasing and regional crop insurance. It provides support for national trade promotion and trade information services, and in 1984 presided over the formation of the Pacific Islands Association of Chambers of Commerce, to promote contacts between organizations in the private sector.

Regional transport forms an important part of SPEC's activities. A Regional Shipping Council was set up by the Forum in 1974, and a Regional Civil Aviation Council and Advisory Committee in 1976. In 1984 these bodies undertook a regional transport survey, to compile a comprehensive data base on transport in the region. SPEC established the Pacific Forum Line and the Association of South Pacific Airlines (see below), and is involved in formulating regional maritime standards and in supervising wage rates and working conditions for seamen. Since 1973 SPEC has acted as the co-ordinating agency for telecommunications work undertaken in the region by UNDP and other agencies. In 1983 the 14th South Pacific Forum approved the establishment of the South Pacific Telecommunications Development Programme, to be conducted over the next decade.

In 1981 the Forum decided that SPEC should assume the role of overall regional energy co-ordinator, and a SPEC Energy Unit was formed in 1982: its work includes research on alternative energy sources, financed by the European Community.

Since 1981 SPEC has acted as the secretariat to the Pacific Group Council of ACP states receiving assistance from the European Community under the Lomé Convention (see p. 149). It also manages a regional disaster relief fund and a Fellowship Scheme to provide in-service training in island member countries for two candidates per country per year, financed by Australia, New Zealand and the Commonwealth Fund for Technical Co-operation. With funds from UNDP, SPEC recruits specialists to carry out short-term advisory services in the islands of the region. A Pacific Regional Advisory Service (see above) was established in 1981. SPEC participates in the South Pacific Regional Environment Programme (SPREP) with the South Pacific Commission. A Regional Disaster Adviser assists disaster preparedness and relief within the region.

BUDGET

The Governments of Australia and New Zealand each contribute one-third of the annual budget and the remaining third is equally shared by the other member Governments. Total estimated revenue for 1985 was $F 1,063,730, an increase of about 13% over the 1984 budget of $F 940,956. Extra-budgetary funding during the 12 months to June 1984 amounted to $F 2,558,000.

Associated and Affiliated Organizations

Association of South Pacific Airlines—ASPA: POB 9817, Nadi Airport, Nadi, Fiji; tel. 72066; telex 5394; f. 1979 at a meeting of airlines in the South Pacific convened by the SPEC to promote co-operation among the member airlines for the development of regular, safe and economical commercial aviation within, to and from the South Pacific. Mems: 18 regional airlines, three associates. Chair. JOHN SCHAAP; Sec.-Gen. GEORGE FAKTAUFON.

Pacific Forum Line: POB 655, Apia, Western Samoa; f. 1977 as a joint venture by 10 South Pacific countries, to provide shipping services to meet the special requirements of the region; operates three container vessels and one general cargo vessel. In 1983 Australia, claiming that the line was proving non-viable, refused to provide further financial assistance, but the European Community agreed to provide a grant of $A1m. and a loan of $A5m., so that the line could buy its own containers instead of hiring them; the line recorded a profit of US $1.6m. for 1985. Chair. D. TUFUI; Chief Exec. W. J. MACLENNAN.

South Pacific Forum Fisheries Agency—FFA: POB 629, Honiara, Solomon Islands; tel. (677) 21-124; telex 66336; f. 1978 by the South Pacific Forum to facilitate, promote and co-ordinate co-operation and mutual assistance among coastal states in the region in the matter of fisheries; polices an Exclusive Economic Zone within 370 km (200 nautical miles) of the coastlines of member states; signed agreement with the USA in November 1986, allowing fishing rights to the US fishing fleet in exchange for payments amounting to US $60m. Dir D. A. MULLER.

South Pacific Trade Commission: 225 Clarence St, Sydney, NSW 2000, Australia; tel. 290-2833; telex 70342; opened 1979 to identify and develop markets in Australia for exports from the Pacific islands; funded by the Australian Government. Trade Commissioner: WILLIAM T. MCCABE.

PUBLICATIONS

Annual Report.
SPEC Activities (monthly).
Trade and Industry Scene (monthly).
SPARTECA (guide for Pacific island exporters).
SPEC Series for Trade and Investment in the South Pacific.
Reports of Forum and Bureau meetings.

SOUTHERN AFRICAN DEVELOPMENT CO-ORDINATION CONFERENCE—SADCC

Address: Private Bag 0095, Gaborone, Botswana.
Telephone: 51863.
Telex: 2555.

The first Conference was held at Arusha, Tanzania, in July 1979, to harmonize development plans and to reduce the region's economic dependence on South Africa.

MEMBERS

Angola	Malawi	Tanzania
Botswana	Mozambique	Zambia
Lesotho	Swaziland	Zimbabwe

Organization
(October 1986)

SUMMIT MEETING
The Meeting is held annually and is attended by heads of state and government or their representatives.

COUNCIL OF MINISTERS
Representatives of SADCC member countries at ministerial level meet at least twice a year; in addition, special meetings are held to co-ordinate regional policy in a particular field by, for example, ministers of energy and ministers of transport.

CONFERENCES ON CO-OPERATION
A conference with SADCC's 'international co-operating partners' (donor governments and international agencies) is held annually to review progress in the various sectors of the SADCC programme and to present new projects requiring assistance.

SECRETARIAT
Executive Secretary: Dr SIMBARASHE MAKONI (Zimbabwe).

SECTORAL CO-ORDINATION OFFICES

Southern Africa Transport and Communications Commission (SATCC): c/o Dr S. Bhatt, CP 2677, Maputo, Mozambique; tel. 20246; telex 6597.

Energy Sector Technical and Administrative Unit: c/o Carvalho Simões, CP 172, Luanda, Angola; tel. 23382; telex 3170.

Agricultural Research and Animal Disease Control: c/o M. Mokone, Ministry of Agriculture, Private Bag 003, Gaborone, Botswana; tel. 51171; telex 2414.

Tourism: Lesotho Tourist Board, POB 1378, Maseru, Lesotho; tel. 323760; telex 4820.

Soil and Water Conservation and Utilisation: c/o B. Leleka, Ministry of Agriculture and Marketing, POB 24, Maseru 100, Lesotho; tel. 22741; telex 4330.

Fisheries, Wildlife and Forestry: c/o A. J. Mathotho, Ministry of Forestry and Natural Resources, Private Bag 350, Lilongwe 3, Malawi; tel. 731322; telex 4465.

Manpower Development: c/o V. E. Sikhondze, Dept of Economic Planning and Statistics, POB 602, Mbabane, Swaziland; tel. 43765; telex 2109.

Industrial Co-ordination Division: c/o A. T. Pallangyo, Ministry of Industries, POB 9503, Dar es Salaam, Tanzania; tel. 22775; telex 41686.

Mining: c/o K. Nyirenda, Ministry of Mines, POB 31969, Lusaka, Zambia; tel. 211220; telex 45970.

Food Security Technical and Administrative Unit: c/o S. Marume, Ministry of Agriculture, Private Bag 7701, Causeway, Harare, Zimbabwe; tel. 706081; telex 2455.

Activities

In July 1979 the first Southern African Development Co-ordination Conference was attended by delegations from Angola, Botswana, Mozambique, Tanzania and Zambia, with representatives from donor governments and international agencies; the group was later joined by Lesotho, Malawi, Swaziland and Zimbabwe. In April 1980 a regional economic summit conference was held in Lusaka, Zambia, and the Lusaka Declaration, a statement of strategy entitled 'Southern Africa: Towards Economic Liberation', was approved, together with a programme of action allotting specific studies and tasks to member governments (see list of co-ordinating offices, above). The members aimed to reduce their dependence on South Africa for rail and air links and port facilities, imports of raw materials and manufactured goods, and the supply of electric power. In 1985, however, an SADCC report noted that since 1980 the region had become still more dependent on South Africa for its trade outlets, and the 1986 summit meeting, although it recommended the adoption of economic sanctions against South Africa, failed to adopt a timetable for doing so.

TRANSPORT AND COMMUNICATIONS

Transport is seen as the most important area to be developed, on the grounds that, as the Lusaka Declaration noted, 'The dominance of the Republic of South Africa has been reinforced by its transport system. Without the establishment of an adequate regional transport and communications system, other areas of co-operation become impractical'. Priority was to be given to the improvement of road and railway services into Mozambique, so that the landlocked countries of the region could transport their goods through Mozambican ports instead of South African ones. Rehabilitation of the railway between Malawi and Beira on the coast of Mozambique was under way in 1982, while work on the line from Malawi to the port of Nacala in Mozambique began in 1983. Other proposed railway projects include improvement of lines and equipment in Angola and Botswana, between Mozambique and Swaziland, and between Tanzania and Zambia. Port facilities are to be improved at Luanda in Angola, Beira, Maputo and Nacala in Mozambique, and Dar es Salaam, Tanzania. There are plans for the rehabilitation and upgrading of roads throughout the region, and, in particular, work on the main roads connecting Mozambique with Swaziland (to begin in 1986) and with Zimbabwe, and on the road between Tanzania and Zambia. Civil aviation projects include a new airport at Maseru, Lesotho, under way in 1984, and improvements of major airports in Mozambique, Swaziland, Zambia and Zimbabwe, together with studies on the joint use of maintenance facilities, on regional airworthiness certification and aviation legislation, and on navigational aids. Work on a satellite earth station in Swaziland had been completed by 1984, while two more, in Angola and Zimbabwe, were being constructed, and microwave communications links are planned throughout the region.

The total cost of the 116 projects planned for this sector amounts to US $3,100m. By July 1985 $729m. (22% of the total) had been made available by donors, with financing fully secured for 36 projects and partly secured for 22 more, while a further $689m. was under negotiation.

ENERGY

The energy programme consists of 56 projects, with total funding requirements of $181m. By July 1985 three projects had been completed, and complete or partial funding had been secured for 38 others. The main areas of work comprised: a study on regional self-sufficiency in the supply of petroleum products; exploitation of the region's coal resources; development of hydroelectric power, and the linking of national electricity grids (Botswana-Zimbabwe, Botswana-Zambia, Mozambique-Swaziland and Zimbabwe-Mozambique); and new and renewable sources of energy, including pilot projects in solar energy and wind-power and the developing of integrated energy systems for villages.

INDUSTRY AND MINING

In the industry sector 85 projects are planned, of which 30 are feasibility studies (most of which had been completed or were under

INTERNATIONAL ORGANIZATIONS

way by July 1985). Funding amounting to $221m. had been secured by July 1985, while a further $231m. was being negotiated. Projects include production of textiles, salt, pesticides, cement, machine tools, mining equipment, farming equipment, railway rolling-stock, pharmaceuticals and baby-foods. During 1985 a group of experts was established to co-ordinate standardization and quality control. An investment guide was to be issued in that year, to encourage the mobilization of capital from private and public sources.

During 1985 seven project studies in the mining sector were being undertaken, covering the manufacture and repair of mining machinery, production of explosives, small-scale mining, a manpower survey and an inventory of mineral resources. Other studies approved in 1985 aimed to assess demand and examine the feasibility of producing salt, soda ash, lime, diamond tools, copper sheet and bauxite.

AGRICULTURE AND FOOD SECURITY

By July 1985 financing of $110m. had been secured for this sector, of a total requirement of $368m. Priority is given to regional food security and to self-sufficiency in basic foods. In 1985 programmes were under way for the establishment of a regional early-warning system (to predict food shortages and crop failure), an inventory of agricultural resources, and a Post-Production and Food Industry Advisory Unit. Studies were undertaken on food marketing, agricultural staff recruitment, the production and supply of seeds, and irrigation management. The Southern African Centre for Co-operation in Agricultural Research (SACCAR), in Gaborone, Botswana, began operations in 1985. It co-ordinates national research systems and operates a small research grants programme. Its three initial programmes covered sorghum and millet improvement, grain legume improvement, and land and water management. Other agricultural projects undertaken by SADCC include animal disease control, inland fisheries, wildlife protection, and forestry.

Southern African Development Co-ordination Conference

SADCC PROJECT FINANCING BY SECTOR (US $'000, July 1985)

Sector	Total cost	Funding secured	Funding under negotiation
Agriculture	367,834	109,932	162,776
Agricultural research	51,400	27,400	24,000
Animal disease control	94,319	37,815	21,245
Fisheries	7,748	4,230	3,452
Food security	177,325	37,072	93,099
Forestry	32,800	2,000	20,900
Soil and water conservation and land utilization	1,662	1,415	—
Wildlife	2,580	—	80
Energy	181,196	41,155	59,893
Industry	1,134,075	220,802	230,940
Manpower development	34,332	3,149	14,566
Mining	2,097	661	1,186
Tourism	145	145	—
Transport and communications	3,107,350	729,170	689,400
Total	4,827,029	1,104,869	1,158,761

PUBLICATIONS

Annual Progress Report.
SADCC Energy Bulletin.
SACCAR Newsletter.
Soil and Water Conservation and Land Utilization Newsletter.

THE WARSAW TREATY OF FRIENDSHIP, CO-OPERATION AND MUTUAL ASSISTANCE— THE WARSAW PACT

Headquarters of the Joint Command: Moscow, USSR.

The Warsaw Treaty of Friendship, Co-operation and Mutual Assistance (The Warsaw Pact) was signed in Warsaw in May 1955. It was automatically extended for a further 10 years in June 1975, and renewed, before its expiry, for a further period of 20 years (with an option to extend it for a further 10 years) in April 1985: the terms of the treaty were unchanged. The treaty is supplemented by an interlocking system of treaties between the member countries. Albania, an original signatory, ceased to participate in 1961 and formally withdrew from the Treaty in 1968.

MEMBERS

Bulgaria
Czechoslovakia
German Democratic Republic
Hungary
Poland
Romania
USSR

Organization
(October 1986)

POLITICAL CONSULTATIVE COMMITTEE (PCC)

The PCC was intended to meet not less than twice a year but, in fact, there have been fewer meetings; since 1972 meetings have usually taken place in alternate years. Following the renewal of the Warsaw Treaty in April 1985, the PCC met in October 1985 and June 1986. The venue rotates among the member countries and individual sessions are chaired by the leaders of the delegations in turn. Delegations of member states are normally led by the General Secretary of the Party, supported by the Head of Government, Ministers for Foreign Affairs and Defence and others. Meetings are normally attended by the Commander-in-Chief, Warsaw Pact Joint Armed Forces. Summit meetings of heads of government of Pact countries (not formally described as PCC meetings) also take place from time to time.

COMMITTEE OF DEFENCE MINISTERS

The Committee was established by the PCC in 1969, as part of a reorganization of the Treaty's military structure; it meets annually. Each member country provides the Chairman and the venue in turn. Meetings receive a report from the Commander-in-Chief of the Armed Forces.

MILITARY COUNCIL

Established by the PCC in 1969, the Council comprises national Chiefs of Staff or Deputy Ministers of Defence, with status of Deputy Commanders-in-Chief of the Warsaw Pact Joint Armed Forces. It normally meets twice a year, in each member country in turn, under the Chairmanship of the Commander-in-Chief of the Joint Armed Forces. The autumn meeting of the Military Council is usually combined with a general conference of national Force Commanders.

TECHNICAL COMMITTEE OF THE JOINT ARMED FORCES

The Technical Committee was established in 1969.
Chairman: Col-Gen. I. A. FABRIKOV.

COMMITTEE OF FOREIGN MINISTERS

The Committee was established by the PCC in 1976 as a permanent organ parallel to the Committee of Defence Ministers. It meets in each member country in turn.

JOINT SECRETARIAT

The Secretariat was formally established in Moscow in 1956, and reinstituted in 1976, after a period of inactivity.

JOINT COMMAND OF THE ARMED FORCES

Set up in 1955 under the general supervision of the PCC.
Commander-in-Chief: Marshal VIKTOR G. KULIKOV (USSR).
Chief of Staff and First Deputy Commander-in-Chief: Army Gen. ANATOLY I. GRIBKOV (USSR).
Deputy Commanders-in-Chief: The members of the Military Council.

COMBINED GENERAL STAFF

Composed of representatives of the seven member states with headquarters in Moscow. Services meetings of the Committee of Defence Ministers and of the Military Council. Plans and evaluates manoeuvres and exercises of Warsaw Pact Joint Armed Forces.

WARSAW PACT FORCES (July 1986)

	Army	Navy	Air Force	Strategic Nuclear Forces	Air Defence Force	Total regular forces
Bulgaria	105,000	8,500	35,000	—	—	148,500
Czechoslovakia	145,000	—	56,000	—	—	201,000
German Democratic Republic	123,000	16,000	40,000	—	—	179,000
Hungary	83,500	—	22,000	—	—	105,000
Poland	295,000	19,000	88,000	—	—	402,000
Romania	150,000	7,700	32,000	—	—	189,700
USSR	1,991,000	451,000	453,000	298,000	371,000	5,130,000*

* This total includes about 1,471,000 railway construction and labour troops, command and general support troops, not listed elsewhere, but excludes paramilitary forces, numbering 570,000 (border troops, internal security forces, etc.).

Source: International Institute of Strategic Studies, *The Military Balance 1986–1987*.

WESTERN EUROPEAN UNION—WEU

Address: 9 Grosvenor Place, London, SW1X 7HL, England.
Telephone: (01) 235-5351.

Based on the Brussels Treaty of 1948, Western European Union was set up in 1955. Member States seek to harmonize their views on security and defence questions.

MEMBERS

Belgium
France
Federal Republic of Germany
Italy
Luxembourg
Netherlands
United Kingdom

Organization
(October 1986)

COUNCIL

The Council of Western European Union consists of the ministers of foreign affairs and of defence of the seven member countries, or the Ambassadors resident in London and an Under-Secretary of the British Foreign and Commonwealth Office. As supreme authority of WEU, it is responsible for formulating policy and issuing directives to the Secretary-General and the Agencies for Security Questions (see below). The Council meets twice a year at ministerial level, and at permanent (ambassadorial) level as often as required (usually twice a month). Each country holds the Presidency of the Council for one year, beginning on 1 July.

SECRETARIAT-GENERAL

Secretary-General: ALFRED CAHEN (Belgium).
Deputy Secretary-General: H. HOLZHEIMER (FRG).

AGENCIES FOR SECURITY QUESTIONS

Address: 43 ave du Président Wilson, 75775 Paris Cedex 16, France.
Agency for the Study of Arms Control and Disarmament Questions: Dir Lt-Gen. E. RAMBALDI.
Agency for the Study of Security and Defence Questions: Dir I. DAWSON.
Agency for the Development of Co-operation in the Field of Armaments: Dir M. E. HINTERMANN.

ASSEMBLY

Address: 43 ave du Président Wilson, 75775 Paris Cedex 16, France.

The Assembly of Western European Union consists of the delegates of the member countries to the Parliamentary Assembly of the Council of Europe. It meets twice a year in Paris. The Assembly considers defence policy in Western Europe, besides other matters concerning member states in common, and may make recommendations or transmit opinions to the Council, to national parliaments, governments and international organizations. An annual report is presented to the Assembly by the Council.

President: JEAN-MARIE CARO (France).
Clerk: GEORGES MOULIAS.

PERMANENT COMMITTEES OF THE ASSEMBLY

There are permanent committees on: Defence Questions and Armaments; General Affairs; Scientific Questions; Budgetary Affairs and Administration; Rules of Procedure and Privileges; and Parliamentary and Public Relations.

Activities

The Brussels Treaty was signed in 1948 by Belgium, France, Luxembourg, the Netherlands and the United Kingdom. It foresaw the potential for international co-operation in Western Europe and provided for collective defence and collaboration in economic, social and cultural activities. Within this framework, NATO and the Council of Europe (see chapters) were formed in 1949.

On the collapse in 1954 of plans for a European Defence Community, a nine-power conference was convened in London to try to reach a new agreement. This conference's decisions were embodied in a series of formal agreements drawn up by a ministerial conference held in Paris in October 1954. The agreements entailed: arrangements for the Brussels Treaty to be strengthened and modified to include the Federal Republic of Germany and Italy, the ending of the occupation regime in the Federal Republic of Germany, and the invitation to the latter to join NATO. These agreements were ratified on 6 May 1955, on which date the seven-power Western European Union came into being.

The new organization was given the task of settling the future of the Saar region. Under a Franco-German agreement of October 1954, the Saar was to have a European statute within the framework of WEU, subject to approval by referendum. In October 1955 the Saar population voted against the statute and expressed the wish for incorporation in the Federal Republic of Germany. Political and economic incorporation were achieved in January 1957 and July 1959 respectively.

The modified Brussels Treaty provided for a system of co-operation in social and cultural affairs, and these activities were transferred in June 1960 to the Council of Europe.

Between 1963 and 1970, while negotiations for the United Kingdom's accession to the EEC were suspended, the WEU Council invited the Commission of the EEC to participate in meetings on European economic affairs. These were discontinued in 1970 on the re-opening of negotiations which led to the Treaty of Accession in January 1972.

A meeting of ministers of defence and of foreign affairs, held in Rome in October 1984, agreed to 'reactivate' WEU by restructuring its organization and by holding more frequent ministerial meetings, in order to harmonize members' views on defence questions, arms control and disarmament, developments in East-West relations, Europe's contribution to the Atlantic alliance, and European armaments co-operation.

FINANCE

The total budget for 1985 amounted to £1,111,210 for the London office, and 44,775,030 French francs for the Paris office, financed by contributions from member states. Each member contributes one-fifth of the budget (Belgium, Luxembourg and the Netherlands provide one-fifth between them).

PUBLICATIONS

Assembly of Western European Union: Texts adopted and Brief Account of the Session (2 a year).
Annual Report of the Council.
Assembly documents and reports.

WORLD CONFEDERATION OF LABOUR—WCL

Address: 33 rue de Trèves, 1040 Brussels, Belgium.
Telephone: (02) 230-62-95.
Telex: 26966.

Founded in 1920 as the International Federation of Christian Trade Unions (IFCTU); reconstituted under present title in 1968. (See also the International Confederation of Free Trade Unions, p. 162, and the World Federation of Trade Unions, p. 210.)

MEMBERS

Affiliated national federations and trade union internationals; about 15,000,000 members in 78 countries.

Organization
(October 1986)

CONGRESS

The supreme and legislative authority. The most recent meeting was held in November 1981 in Manila, Philippines. Congress consists of delegates from national confederations and trade internationals. Delegates have votes according to the size of their organization. Congress receives official reports, elects the Executive Board, considers the future programme and any proposals.

CONFEDERAL BOARD

The Board meets annually, and consists of at least 36 members (including eight representatives of national confederations and six representatives of trade internationals) elected by Congress from among its members for four-year terms. It issues executive directions and instructions to the Secretariat.
President: Juan C. Tan (Philippines).

SECRETARIAT-GENERAL
Secretary-General: J. Kulakowski (Belgium).

REGIONAL OFFICES
Latin America: Latin-American Confederation of Trade Unions, Apdo 6681, Caracas 101, Venezuela. Sec.-Gen. E. Maspero.
Asia: BATU, POB 163, Manila, Philippines. Pres. J. Tan.
North America: CSN, 1601 rue Delorimier, Montreal, Canada. Pres. G. Larose; Sec.-Gen. M. Gauthier.

INTERNATIONAL INSTITUTES OF TRADE UNION STUDIES
Africa: Fondation panafricaine pour le développement économique, social et culturel (Fopadesc), Lomé, Togo.
Asia: Batu Social Institute, Manila, Philippines.
Latin America:
Instituto Centro-Americano de Estudios Sociales (ICAES), San José, Costa Rica.
Instituto Latino Americano de Estudios Sociales (ILATES), Caracas, Venezuela.
Instituto del Cono Sur (INCASUR), Buenos Aires, Argentina.
Universidad de Trabajadores de América Latina (UTAL).

FINANCE
Income is derived from affiliation dues, contributions, donations and capital interest.

PUBLICATIONS
Labor Press and Information Bulletin (every 2 months; in English, French, German, Dutch and Spanish).
Flash (in English, French, German, Dutch and Spanish).
Reports of Congresses; Study Documents.

International Trade Union Federations

European Federation of Christian Miners' Unions: Oudergemselaan 26-32, 1040 Brussels, Belgium; tel. (02) 231-00-90; f. 1901. Mems: national federations grouping 231,000 miners in 11 countries. Organization: Congress, Bureau, Secretariat. Pres. R. Mourer (France); Sec. A. Daemen (Belgium).

European Federation of Trade Unions of Non-Manual Workers—EFTUNMW: 1 Beggaardenstraat, 2000 Antwerp, Belgium; f. 1921. Mems: national federations of unions and professional associations covering 400,000 workers in 11 countries. Organization: Congress (every 2 years), Council, Executive Bureau, Secretariat. Sec.-Gen. M. Geerts (Belgium). Publ. *Revue* (every 2 years).

Graphical International Federation: Valeriusplein 30, 1075 BJ Amsterdam, Netherlands; tel. (020) 71-32-79; telex 18695; f. 1925. Mems: national federations in 10 countries, covering 100,000 workers. Pres. M. Van Onsem (Belgium); Sec.-Gen. B. van Marle (Netherlands).

International Federation of Textile and Clothing Workers: 27 Koning Albertlaan, Ghent, Belgium; f. 1901. Mems: unions covering 400,000 workers in 19 countries. Organization: Congress (every two years), Bureau, Secretariat. Pres. L. Fruru (Belgium); Sec. C. Pauwels (Belgium). Publ. *Intervetex* (quarterly).

International Federation of Trade Unions of Employees in Public Service—INFEDOP: 33 rue de Trèves, 1040 Brussels, Belgium; tel. (02) 230-60-90; f. 1922. Mems: national federations of workers in public service, covering 4m. workers. Organization: World Congress (at least every five years), World Confederal Board (meets every year), six Trade Groups, Secretariat. Pres. A. Hengchen (Belgium); Sec.-Gen. C. Damen (Netherlands). Publ. *Labor Professional Action* (6 a year).

INFEDOP has four regional organizations:
EUROFEDOP: 33 rue de Trèves, 1040 Brussels, Belgium.
CLASEP: Apartado 6681, Caracas 101, Venezuela.
CLTC: Apartado 4456, Caracas 101, Venezuela.
ASIAFEDOP: POB 163, Manila, Philippines.

International Federation of Trade Unions of Transport Workers—FIOST: 31 rue de Trèves, 1040 Brussels, Belgium; tel. (02) 230-60-90; telex 26966; f. 1921. Mems: national federations in 28 countries covering 600,000 workers. Organization: Congress (every four years), Committee (meets twice a year), Executive Board. Pres. B. de Smet (Belgium). Publ. *Trade Action* (6 a year).

World Confederation of Teachers: 33 rue de Trèves, 1040 Brussels, Belgium; f. 1963. Mems: national federations of unions concerned with teaching. Organization: Congress (every four years), Council (at least once a year), Steering Committee. Pres. L. van Beneden; Sec.-Gen. C. Damen (Netherlands).

World Federation of Trade Unions for Energy, Chemical and Miscellaneous Industries—ECI: Oudergemselaan 26-32, 1040 Brussels, Belgium; tel. (02) 231-00-90; f. 1920. Mems: 150,000. Pres. C. de Schryver (Belgium); Sec.-Gen. J. van Hoof (Belgium). Publ. *Bulletin d'Information* (quarterly).

World Federation of Agriculture and Food Workers: 31 rue de Trèves, 1040 Brussels, Belgium; tel. (02) 230-60-90; f. 1982 (merger of former World Federation of Agricultural Workers and World Federation of Workers in the Food, Drink, Tobacco and Hotel Industries). Mems: national federations covering 2,800,000 workers in 38 countries. Organization: Congress (every five years), World Board, Daily Management Board. Pres. O. Semerel (Netherlands Antilles); Sec. E. Vervliet (Belgium). Publ. *Labor Trade Action.*

World Federation of Building and Woodworkers Unions: 31 rue de Trèves, 1040 Brussels, Belgium; f. 1936. Mems: national federations covering 2,438,000 workers in several countries. Organization: Congress, Bureau, Permanent Secretariat. Pres. R. Maris (Belgium); Sec. G. de Lange (Netherlands). Publ. *Bulletin.*

WORLD COUNCIL OF CHURCHES — WCC

Address: 150 route de Ferney, POB 66, 1211 Geneva 20, Switzerland.
Telephone: (022) 916111.
Telex: 23423.

The Council was founded in 1948 to promote co-operation between Christian Churches and to prepare for a clearer manifestation of the unity of the Church.

MEMBERS

There are 305 member Churches in over 90 countries, of which 30 are associate members. Chief denominations: Anglican, Baptist, Congregational, Lutheran, Methodist, Moravian, Old Catholic, Orthodox, Presbyterian, Reformed and Society of Friends. The Roman Catholic Church is not a member but sends official observers to meetings.

Organization
(October 1986)

ASSEMBLY

The governing body of the World Council, consisting of delegates of the member Churches, it meets every six or seven years to frame policy and consider some main theme. The sixth Assembly was held at Vancouver, Canada, in 1983.
Presidium: Dame R. Nita Barrow (Barbados), Dr Marga Buehrig (Switzerland), Metropolitan Paulos Mar Gregorios (India), Bishop Johannes Hempel (GDR), Patriarch Ignatios IV (Syria), Most Rev. W. P. Khotso Makhulu (Botswana), Very Rev. Dr Lois Wilson (Canada).

CENTRAL COMMITTEE

Appointed by the Assembly to carry out its policies and decisions, the Committee consists of 150 members chosen from Assembly delegates. It meets annually.
Moderator: Rev. Dr Heinz Joachim Held (FRG).
Vice-Moderators: Metropolitan Chrystostomos of Myra (Turkey), Dr Sylvia Talbot (USA).

EXECUTIVE COMMITTEE

Consists of the Presidents, the Officers and 16 members chosen by the Central Committee from its membership to prepare its agenda, expedite its decisions and supervise the work of the Council between meetings of the Central Committee. Meets every six months.

GENERAL SECRETARIAT

The General Secretariat implements the policies laid down by the WCC, and co-ordinates the work programme units described below. It includes a Communication Department, a Finance Department and a Library, and supervises the work of the Ecumenical Institute at Bossey, Switzerland, which provides training in ecumenical leadership.
General Secretary: Rev. Dr Emilio Castro (Uruguay).

Activities

The work of the WCC is carried out by three programme units:

FAITH AND WITNESS

This unit studies the theological questions which divide the churches (producing, for example, recent statements on baptism, the Eucharist and the ministry) and the problems facing the Church in the modern world; it assists the Christian community in sharing information and resources for mission and evangelism; and conducts dialogues with people of non-Christian faiths.

JUSTICE AND SERVICE

The WCC's Inter-Church Aid, Refugee and World Service provides a joint response to those in need, as indicated by local churches: it channels about US $48m. annually in financial and material assistance, while the Ecumenical Development Fund aims to encourage people's participation in development. The unit aims to provide an instrument for Christian witness in international affairs, particularly in cases of conflict and the violation of human rights. The WCC's Programme to Combat Racism, established in 1969, had provided over $6.8m. for victims of racial oppression by the end of 1985. The Christian Medical Commission encourages community health care and provides a link between church hospitals and state health services.

EDUCATION AND RENEWAL

This unit aims to increase participation by women, young people and lay people generally in the activities of the Church and of society; to serve theological education institutions and stimulate new developments in Christian education; and to help make the ecumenical movement a reality at parish level.

FINANCE

The WCC's budget for 1986 amounted to 38.8m. Swiss francs. The main contributors are the churches and their agencies, with funds for certain projects contributed by other organizations. Of total income, about 47% is allotted to the Justice and Service Unit, 14.4% to the Faith and Witness Unit, and 16% to the Educational and Renewal Unit; the General Secretariat, Communication Department, Governing Bodies, administrative services and Library together account for 17%; and an allocation to the Ecumenical Institute, Bossey, 5.6%.

PUBLICATIONS

Catalogue of periodicals, books and audio-visuals.
One World (monthly).
Ecumenical Review (quarterly).
International Review of Mission (quarterly).
Ecumenical Press Service (weekly).

WORLD FEDERATION OF TRADE UNIONS—WFTU

Address: Vinohradská 10, 12147 Prague 2, Czechoslovakia.
Telephone: 243741-9.
Telex: 121525.

The Federation was founded in 1945, on a world-wide basis. A number of members withdrew from the Federation in 1949 to set up the International Confederation of Free Trade Unions (see p. 162). (See also the World Confederation of Labour, p. 208.)

MEMBERS

There are 94 affiliated national federations, with 214m. members.

Organization
(October 1986)

WORLD TRADE UNION CONGRESS

Congress meets every four years. The size of the delegations is based on the total membership of national federations. The 11th Congress, held in East Berlin in September 1986, was attended by 1,014 delegates, observers and guests.

The Congress reviews WFTU's work, endorses reports from the executives, and elects the General Council and Bureau.

GENERAL COUNCIL

The General Council meets once a year and comprises 105 members and 105 deputies, representing 81 countries and 11 Trade Unions Internationals, and elected by Congress from nominees of national federations. Every affiliated organization has one member and one deputy member.

The Council receives reports from the Bureau, approves the budget, plans the Congress agenda, and elects the General Secretary and Secretariat officers.

BUREAU

President: SÁNDOR GASPAR (Hungary).
Vice-Presidents: ERNEST BOATSWAIN (Australia), INDRAJIT GUPTA (India), ELIAS EL-HABR (Lebanon), KAREL HOFFMANN (Czechoslovakia), HENRI KRASUCKI (France), B. LUVSATSEREN (Mongolia), IZZEDINE NASSER (Syria), VALENTIN PACHO (Peru), STEPAN A. SHALAYEV (USSR), TADESSE TAMERAT (Ethiopia), ROBERTO VEIGA (Cuba), ROMAIN VILON GUEZO (Benin), ANDREAS ZIARTIDES (Cyprus).

The Bureau, which has 40 members, meets twice a year and conducts most of the executive work of WFTU.

SECRETARIAT

The Secretariat consists of the General Secretary and eight secretaries. It is appointed by the General Council and is responsible for economic and social affairs, national trade union liaison, press and information, the Trade Unions Internationals, women's affairs, solidarity activities, education, administration and finance.
General Secretary: IBRAHIM ZAKARIA.

BUDGET

Income is derived from affiliation dues, which are based on the number of members in each trade union federation.

PUBLICATIONS

World Trade Union Movement (monthly; published in 10 languages).
Flashes from the Trade Unions (weekly; published in five languages).

Trade Unions Internationals

The following autonomous Trade Unions Internationals are affiliated to WFTU:

Trade Unions International of Agricultural, Forestry and Plantation Workers: Opletalova 57, 110 00 Prague 1, Czechoslovakia; f. 1949. Mems: 104 unions grouping over 70m. workers in 62 countries. Pres. A. KYRIACOU (Cyprus); Sec.-Gen. RENÉ DIGNE (France). Publ. *Bulletin* (every 2 months in Arabic, French, Spanish, English and Russian).

Trade Unions International of Workers of the Building, Wood and Building Materials Industries: Box 281, Helsinki 10, Finland; f. 1949. Mems: 73 unions in 57 countries, grouping 17m. workers. Pres. LOTHAR LINDNER (GDR); Sec.-Gen. MAURI PERÄ (Finland). Publ. bulletin in seven languages.

Trade Unions International of Chemical, Oil and Allied Workers (ICPS): 1415 Budapest, Hungary; f. 1950. Mems: about 13m., grouped in 100 unions in 54 countries; Industrial Commissions for Oil, Chemicals, Rubber, Paper-board and Glass/Pottery. Pres. FERENC DAJKA (Hungary); Gen. Sec. ALAIN COVET (France). Publs *Information Bulletin, Information Sheet* (French, English, Spanish, Russian, German, Arabic, Japanese).

Trade Unions International of Food, Tobacco, Hotel and Allied Industries Workers: 6th September St 4, Sofia 1000, Bulgaria; tel. 88-02-51; telex 23410; f. 1949. Mems: 94 unions grouping 21m. individuals in 54 countries. Pres. BERTRAND PAGE (France); Gen. Sec. LUIS MARTELL ROSA (Cuba). Publ. *News Bulletin.*

Trade Unions International of Textile, Clothing, Leather and Fur Workers: Opletalova 57, 110 00 Prague 1, Czechoslovakia; f. 1949. Mems: 12m. workers in 71 organizations in 58 countries. Pres. GILBERTO MORALES (Colombia); Sec.-Gen. JAN KŘIZ (Czechoslovakia). Publ. *Information Courier.*

Trade Unions International of Metal and Engineering Workers: POB 158, Pouchkinskaya 5/6, Moscow 109003, USSR; tel. (095) 292-52-02; telex 411370; f. 1949. Mems: 62 unions grouping 22.5m. workers from 43 countries. Pres. REINHARD SOMMER (GDR); Sec.-Gen. ALAIN STERN (France). Publ. *Informations, Bulletin.*

Trade Unions International of Workers in Energy: 36/40 ul. Kopernika, 00-924 Warsaw, Poland; tel. 264316; telex 816913; f. 1949. Mems: 26 unions with 7.2m. mems. in 25 countries. Pres. FRANÇOIS DUTEIL (France); Gen. Sec. MIECZYSŁAW JUREK (Poland). Publ. *Information Bulletin.*

Trade Unions International of Public and Allied Employees: 1086 Berlin, Französische Str. 47, German Democratic Republic; tel. 2992662; f. 1949. Mems: 35.6m. in 116 unions in 46 countries. Branch Commissions: State, Municipal, Postal and Telecommunications, Health, Banks and Insurance. Pres. ALAIN POUCHOL (France); Gen. Sec. JOCHEN MEINEL (GDR). Publs *Public Services* (in English, French and Spanish), *Information Bulletin* (in seven languages).

World Federation of Teachers' Unions: 1110 Berlin, Wilhelm-Wolff-Str. 21, Postfach 176, German Democratic Republic; tel. 4800591; telex 115037; f. 1946. Mems: 132 national unions of teachers and educational and scientific workers in 85 countries, representing over 25m. individuals. Pres. LESTURUGE ARIYAWANSA (Sri Lanka); Gen. Sec. DANIEL RETUREAU (France). Publs *Teachers of the World* (quarterly, in English, French, German and Spanish), *International Teachers' News* (8 a year, in seven languages), reports and papers.

Trade Unions International of Workers in Commerce: Opletalova 57, 110 00 Prague I, Czechoslovakia; f. 1959. Mems: 70 national federations in 61 countries, grouping 23m. members. Pres. JANOS VAS (Hungary); Sec.-Gen. ILLIE FRUNZA (Romania).

Trade Unions International of Transport Workers: Váci u. 69-79, 1139 Budapest, Hungary; tel. 209-601; telex 225861; f. 1949. Mems: 145 unions grouping 18m. workers from 72 countries. Pres. G. LANOUE (France); Gen. Sec. K. C. MATHEW. Publs *Bulletin* (monthly, in English, French, Russian and Spanish), *Journal* (quarterly, in English, French and Spanish).

OTHER INTERNATIONAL ORGANIZATIONS

Agriculture, Food, Forestry and Fisheries	*page* 213	Religion	*page* 246
Aid and Development	216	Science	249
Arts and Culture	219	Social Sciences and Humanistic Studies	255
Commodities	221	Social Welfare	258
Economics and Finance	223	Sport and Recreations	262
Education	225	Technology	264
Government and Politics	229	Tourism	267
Industrial and Professional Relations	232	Trade and Industry	268
Law	234	Transport	273
Medicine and Health	236	Youth and Students	275
Posts and Telecommunications	244		
Press, Radio and Television	244	**Index at end of volume**	

OTHER INTERNATIONAL ORGANIZATIONS

Agriculture, Food, Forestry and Fisheries

(For organizations concerned with agricultural commodities see Commodities, p. 221)

African Timber Organization: BP 1077, Libreville, Gabon; tel. (241) 732928; telex 5620; f. 1976 to enable members to study and co-ordinate ways of influencing prices of wood and wood products by ensuring a continuous flow of information on forestry matters; to harmonize commercial policies and carry out industrial and technical research. Mems: Angola, Cameroon, Central African Republic, Congo, Equatorial Guinea, Gabon, Ghana, Ivory Coast, Liberia, Madagascar, Tanzania, São Tomé and Príncipe, Zaire. Sec.-Gen. GAHURANYI TANGANIKA.

Asian Vegetable Research and Development Center: POB 42, Shanhua, Tainan 741, Taiwan 74199; tel. (06) 5837801; telex 73560; f. 1971 to improve diet and standard of living of rural populations in the Asian tropics by increased production of vegetable crops through the breeding of better varieties and the development of improved cultural methods; research programme includes plant breeding, plant pathology, plant physiology, soil science, entomology and chemistry; the Centre has an experimental farm, laboratories, greenhouses, library and weather station and provides training for research and production specialists in tropical vegetables. Mems: Federal Republic of Germany, Japan, the Republic of Korea, the Philippines, Taiwan, Thailand and the USA. Dir-Gen. Dr G. A. MARLOWE; Deputy Dir-Gen. PAUL M. H. SUN. Publs *Annual Report, Newsletter, Technical Bulletin, CENTERPOINT,* crop research reports, scientific papers.

Association for the Advancement of Agricultural Science in Africa—AAASA: POB 30087, Addis Ababa, Ethiopia; f. 1968 to promote the development and application of agricultural sciences and the exchange of ideas; to encourage Africans to enter training; holds several seminars each year in different African countries. Mems: individual agronomists, research institutes, organizations in the agricultural sciences in Africa. Sec.-Gen. Prof. M. EL-FOULY (acting). Publs *Journal* (2 a year), *Newsletter* (quarterly), proceedings of seminars and workshops (in English and French).

Caribbean Food and Nutrition Institute: Jamaica Centre, UWI Campus, POB 140, Kingston 7, Jamaica; tel. 92 78338; Trinidad Centre, UWI Campus, St. Augustine, Trinidad; tel. 66 31544; f. 1967 to serve the governments and people of the region and to act as a catalyst among persons and organizations concerned with food and nutrition through research and field investigations, training in nutrition, dissemination of information, advisory services and production of educational material. Mems: all English-speaking Caribbean territories, including the mainland countries of Belize and Guyana. Dir Dr ADELINE WYNANTE PATTERSON. Publs *Cajanus* (quarterly), *Nyam News* (monthly), educational material.

Collaborative International Pesticides Analytical Council Ltd.—CIPAC: c/o Plantenziektenkundige Dienst, Postbus 9102, 6700 HC Wageningen, Netherlands; tel. 8370 96420; telex 45163; f. 1957 to organize international collaborative work on methods of analysis for pesticides used in crop protection. Mems: individuals in 15 countries and corresponding mems. in 19 countries. Chair. Dr H. P. BOSSHARDT (Switzerland); Sec. Dr A. MARTIJN (Netherlands). Publs handbooks and monographs.

Common Organization for the Control of Desert Locust and Bird Pests—OCLALAV: BP 1066, Dakar, Senegal; f. 1965 to destroy insect pests, in particular the desert locust, and grain-eating birds, in particular the quelea-quelea, and to sponsor related research projects; co-operates with the International African Migratory Locust Organization (see below). Mems: Benin, Burkina Faso, Cameroon, Chad, The Gambia, Ivory Coast, Mali, Mauritania, Niger, Senegal. Dir-Gen. ABDULLAHI OULD SOUEÏD AHMED.

Dairy Society International—DSI: 7185 Ruritan Drive, Chambersburg, Pa 17201, USA; tel. (717) 375-4392; f. 1946 to foster the extension of dairy and dairy industrial enterprise internationally through an interchange and dissemination of scientific, technological, economic, dietary and other relevant information; organizer and sponsor of the first World Congress for Milk Utilization. Mems: in 50 countries. Pres. JAMES E. CLICK (USA); Man. Dir G. W. WEIGOLD (USA). Publs *DSI Report to Members, DSI Bulletin, Market Frontier News, Dairy Situation Review.*

Desert Locust Control Organization for Eastern Africa: POB 4255, Addis Ababa, Ethiopia; tel. 18 14 75; f. 1962 to promote most effective control of desert locust in the region and to carry out research into the locust's environment and behaviour, and pesticides residue analysis; assists member states in the monitoring and extermination of other migratory pests such as the quelea-quelea (grain-eating birds), the army worm and the tsetse fly; bases at Asmara and Dire Dawa (Ethiopia), Mogadishu and Hargeisa (Somalia), Nairobi (Kenya), Khartoum (Sudan), Arusha (Tanzania) and Djibouti. Mems: Djibouti, Ethiopia, Kenya, Somalia, Sudan, Tanzania and Uganda. Dir-Gen. D. M. WAKO (Kenya). Publs *Desert Locust Situation Reports* (monthly), *Annual Report, Technical Reports.*

European and Mediterranean Plant Protection Organization: 1 rue Le Nôtre, 75016 Paris, France; tel. (1) 45-20-77-94; telex 614148; f. 1951, present name adopted in 1955; aims to promote international co-operation in plant protection research and in preventing the introduction and spread of pests and diseases of plants and plant products. Mems: governments of 34 countries and territories. Chair. H. PAG; Dir-Gen. I. M. SMITH. Publs *EPPO Bulletin, Data Sheets on Quarantine Organisms, Guidelines for the Biological Evaluation of Pesticides, Crop Growth Stage Keys, Summary of the Phytosanitary Regulations of EPPO Member Countries, Reporting Service.*

European Association for Animal Production (Fédération européenne de zootechnie): Corso Trieste 67, 00198 Rome, Italy; tel. (06) 860785; f. 1949 to help improve the conditions of animal production and meet consumer demand; holds annual meetings; Mems: associations in 30 member countries. Pres. A. ROOS (Sweden); Sec.-Gen. Prof. Dr J. BOYAZOGLU.

European Association for Research on Plant Breeding—EUCARPIA: c/o POB 128, 6700 AC Wageningen, Netherlands; f. 1956 to promote scientific and technical co-operation in the plant breeding field. Mems: 1,008 individuals, 77 corporate mems; 12 sections and several working groups. Pres. Prof. Dr G. RÖBBELEN (Federal Republic of Germany); Sec. I. M. MESKEN. Publs *Bulletin,* Proceedings of Congress and section meetings.

European Confederation of Agriculture: CP 87, 5200 Brugg, Aargau, Switzerland; tel. (056) 413177; telex 825110; f. 1889 as International Confederation, re-formed in 1948 as European Confederation; represents the interests of European agriculture in the international field; social security for independent farmers and foresters in the member countries. Mems: 436 ordinary and 43 advisory mems. from 20 countries. Pres. HEINRICH ORSINI-ROSENBERG (Austria); Gen. Sec. WILLY STRAUB. Publs *CEA Dialog, Rapport sur le marché international du lait et des produits laitiers* (quarterly); publs on current technical, economic, social and cultural problems affecting European agriculture, annual report on the General Assembly.

European Grassland Federation: c/o Dr W. H. Prins, POB 30003, 9750 RA Haren, Netherlands; tel. (050) 346541; telex 53990; f. 1963 to facilitate and maintain liaison between European grassland organizations and to promote the interchange of scientific and practical knowledge and experience; a general meeting is held every two or three years (1986 in Portugal; 1988 in Ireland) and symposia at other times. Mems: 20 organizations and four individuals from 24 countries. Pres. Dr A. CONWAY; Federation Sec. Dr W. H. PRINS. Publs proceedings of meetings.

European Livestock and Meat Trade Union: 81a rue de la Loi, 1040 Brussels, Belgium; tel. (02) 230-46-03; telex 64685; f. 1952 to study problems of the European livestock and meat trade and inform members of all legislation affecting it, and to act as an international arbitration commission; conducts research on agricultural markets, quality of livestock, and veterinary regulations. Mems: national organizations in Austria, Belgium, Denmark, France, Federal Republic of Germany, Greece, Ireland, Italy, Luxembourg, Netherlands, Portugal, Spain, Sweden and Switzerland; and the European Association of Livestock Markets. Pres. F. BERTOLAZZI; Sec.-Gen. J.-L. MERIAUX.

Inter-American Association of Agricultural Librarians and Documentalists (Asociación Interamericana de Bibliotecarios y Documentalistas Agrícolas—AIBDA): CP 7170, Turrialba, Costa Rica; tel. 566431; telex 8005; f. 1953 to promote professional improvement of its members through technical publications and meetings, and to promote improvement of library services in agricultural sciences. Mems: about 700 in 30 countries. Pres. ORFILA MÁRQUEZ; Exec. Sec. ANA MARÍA PAZ DE ERICKSON. Publs *Boletín Informativo* (quarterly), *Boletín Especial* (irregular), *Proceedings of Inter-American Meetings of AIBDA* (every 3 years), *Revista AIBDA* (2 a year), *Páginas de Contenido: Ciencias de la Información* (quarterly), *AIBDA Actualidades* (quarterly).

Inter-American Tropical Tuna Commission—IATTC: c/o Scripps Institution of Oceanography, La Jolla, Calif 92093, USA; tel. (619) 453-2820; telex 697115; f. 1950; investigates the biology, ecology and population dynamics of the tropical tunas of the eastern Pacific Ocean to determine the effects of fishing and natural factors on stocks; recommends appropriate conservation measures to maintain stocks at levels which will afford maximum sustainable catches. Mems: France, Japan, Nicaragua, Panama, USA. Dir JAMES JOSEPH. Publs *Bulletin* (irregular), *Annual Report*.

International African Migratory Locust Organization —OICMA: BP 136, Bamako, Mali; Technical Centre, Kara-Macina, Mali; f. 1955 to destroy the African migratory locust in its breeding areas and to conduct research on locust swarms. Mems: governments of 18 countries. Dir-Gen. H. S. ALOMENU (Ghana); Pres. of Exec. Cttee JOSEPH KABORE (Burkina Faso). Publs *Locusta, Bulletin mensuel d'information,* annual reports.

International Association for Cereal Science and Technology: Wiener Strasse 22A, POB 77, 2320 Schwechat, Austria; tel. (0222) 77-72-02; telex 133316; f. 1955 (as the International Association for Cereal Chemistry; name changed 1984) to standardize the methods of testing and analysing cereals and cereal products. Mems: 33 member states. Pres. (1984–86) Dipl. Ing. KJELL M. FJELL (Norway); Sec.-Gen. Dr Dipl. Ing. H. GLATTES (Austria).

International Association for Vegetation Science: 3400 Göttingen, Wilhelm-Weber-Str. 2, Federal Republic of Germany; tel. (0551) 395700; f. 1938. Mems: 540 from 39 countries. Chair. Prof. Dr S. PIGNATTI; Sec. Prof. Dr H. DIERSCHKE. Publs *Phytocoenologia, Berichte über die Internationalen Symposien in Stolzenau/Weser* (1959–64), *in Rinteln* (1965–), *Vegetatio*.

International Association of Agricultural Economists: 1211 West 22nd St, Oak Brook, Ill 60521, USA; f. 1929 to foster development of the sciences of agricultural economics and further the application of the results of economic investigation in agricultural processes and the improvement of economic and social conditions relating to agricultural and rural life. Mems: 2,359 from 89 countries. Pres. MICHEL PETIT (France); Sec. and Treas. R. J. HILDRETH (USA). Publs Proceedings of Conferences, occasional papers.

International Association of Agricultural Librarians and Documentalists: Collingham, 3 Burlescombe Leas, Thorpe Bay, Southend-on-Sea, Essex, SS1 3QF, England; f. 1955 to promote agricultural library science and documentation, and the professional interests of agricultural librarians and documentalists; affiliated to the International Federation of Library Associations and to the Fédération Internationale de Documentation. Mems: 600 in 80 countries. Pres. E. MANN (UK); Sec.-Treas. P. J. WORTLEY (UK). Publs *Quarterly Bulletin, Current Agricultural Serials* (2 vols.), *Primer for Agricultural Libraries, IAALD News*.

International Association of Horticultural Producers: Bezuidenhoutseweg 153, POB 93099, 2509 AB The Hague, Netherlands; tel. (70) 8104631; telex 31 406; f. 1948; represents the common interests of commercial horticultural producers in the international field by frequent meetings, regular publications, press-notices, resolutions and addresses to governments and international authorities; authorizes international horticultural exhibitions. Mems: national associations in 20 countries. Pres. R. MATHIS; First Vice-Pres. H. OBERSCHELP; Gen. Sec. J. B. M. ROTTEVEEL. Publs *Economic Report on Horticulture* (annually), annual statistics, documentation of production costs and wages (every 3 years), list of professional associations and institutes in member countries, works on organization and methods of publicity.

International Bee Research Association: Hill House, Gerrards Cross, Bucks., SL9 0NR, England; tel. (0753) 885011; telex 23152; f. 1949 to further and co-ordinate research on bees, etc. (including pollination) in all countries. Mems: 1,500 in 103 countries. Dir Dr MARGARET ADEY. Publs *Bee World* (quarterly), *Apicultural Abstracts* (quarterly), *Journal of Apicultural Research* (quarterly), also books, pamphlets, bibliographies, multilingual dictionaries of beekeeping terms.

International Centre for Advanced Mediterranean Agronomic Studies: 11 rue Newton, 75116 Paris, France; postgraduate centre provides a supplementary technical, economic and social education for graduates of agriculture, forestry, veterinary sciences and economics in Mediterranean countries; examines the international problems posed by agricultural development; participates in research; attached agronomic institutes in Valenzano (Italy), Montpellier (France) and Zaragoza (Spain). Mems: France, Greece, Italy, Portugal, Spain, Turkey, Yugoslavia; associate mems: Egypt, Lebanon, Tunisia. Sec.-Gen. RAYMOND LIGNON.

International Centre for Agricultural Education—CIEA: Federal Office of Agriculture, Mattenhofstrasse 5, 3003 Berne, Switzerland; tel. (31) 612619; f. 1958; organizes international courses on vocational education and teaching in agriculture every two years for teachers of agriculture.

International Centre for Tropical Agriculture (Centro Internacional de Agricultura Tropical): Apdo Aéreo 6713, Cali, Colombia; tel. 57-3-680111; telex 05769; f. 1969 to accelerate agricultural and economic development and to increase agricultural productivity in the tropics; research and training focuses on production problems of the lowland tropics concentrating on field beans, cassava, rice and tropical pastures. Dir-Gen. Dr JOHN L. NICKEL. Publs *Annual Report*, catalogue of publications.

International Commission for Agricultural and Food Industries: 35 rue du Général Foy, 75008 Paris, France; tel. (1) 42-93-19-24; f. 1934 to study scientific, technical and economic questions related to the food and agricultural industries in various countries, to co-ordinate investigations in these areas and to assemble and distribute relevant documentation for these industries (the information centre is managed by CDIUPA, Le Noyer Lambert, 91305 Massy, France); to organize yearly international congresses for agricultural and food industries. Pres. JUAN JOSÉ GUITIAN; Gen. Sec. GUY DARDENNE (France). Publs *Comptes Rendus des Congrès Internationaux des Industries Agricoles*, Reports of Symposia, Calendar of international meetings related to food industries, List of international organizations associated with food industries.

International Commission for the Conservation of Atlantic Tunas: Calle Príncipe de Vergara 17, 28001 Madrid, Spain; tel. 431 03 29; telex 46330; f. 1969 to promote the conservation and rational exploitation of tuna resources in the Atlantic Ocean and adjacent seas.

International Commission for the Southeast Atlantic Fisheries: Paseo de la Habana 65, 28036 Madrid, Spain; tel. 458 8766; telex 45533; f. 1971 under the Convention for the Conservation of the Living Resources of the Southeast Atlantic; monitors fish stocks and determines quotas. Mems: 17 countries. Chair. P. KRUGER (South Africa); Exec. Sec. R. LAGARDE.

International Commission of Sugar Technology: 1 Aandorenstraat, 3300 Tienen, Belgium; f. 1948 to organize meetings with a view to discussing past investigations and promoting scientific and technical research work. Pres. of Scientific Cttee. G. MANTOVANI (Italy); Gen. Sec. R. PIECK (Belgium).

International Committee for Recording the Productivity of Milk Animals: Corso Trieste 67, 00198 Rome, Italy; tel. (06) 860785; f. 1951 to extend and improve the work of milk recording, standardize methods; 24th session, Södertälje, Sweden, June 1984. Mems: in 23 countries. Pres. P. CATTIN-VIDAL (France); Sec.-Gen. Prof. Dr J. BOYAZOGLU.

International Committee on Veterinary Gross Anatomical Nomenclature—ICVGAN: Dept of Veterinary Anatomy, Cornell University, Ithaca, NY 14853, USA; tel. (607) 256-5454; f. 1957. Chair. Prof. ROBERT E. HABEL (USA); Sec. Prof. JOSEF FREWEIN (Switzerland). Publs Reports, *Nomina Anatomica Veterinaria* (3rd edn, 1983).

International Crops Research Institute for the Semi-Arid Tropics—ICRISAT: Patancheru Post Office, Andhra Pradesh 502 324, India; tel. 224016; telex 0152 203; f. 1972 as world centre for genetic improvement of sorghum, pearl millet, pigeonpea, chickpea and groundnut, and for development of improved farming systems for the world's semi-arid tropics; research covers all physical and socio-economic aspects of improving farming systems on unirrigated land. Dir LESLIE D. SWINDALE (New Zealand). Publs *Annual Report, Research Highlights, ICRISAT Newsletter* (quarterly), *Sorghum and Millet Information Center Newsletter* (3 a year), *International Chickpea Newsletter* (2 a year), *International Pigeonpea Newsletter* (occasional), information and research bulletins, conference proceedings, bibliographies.

International Dairy Federation: 41 Square Vergote, 1040 Brussels, Belgium; tel. (02) 733-98-88; telex 63818; f. 1903 to link all dairy associations in order to encourage the solution of scientific, technical and economic problems affecting the dairy industry. Mems: national committees in 35 countries. Sec.-Gen. P. F. J. STAAL (Netherlands). Publs *Annual Bulletin, IDF News, Mastitis Newsletter, Packaging News.*

International Federation of Agricultural Producers—IFAP: 21 rue Chaptal, 75009 Paris, France; tel. (1) 45-26-05-53; telex 281210; f. 1946 to represent, in the international field, the interests of agricultural producers, by laying the co-ordinated views of the national member organizations before any appropriate international body; to exchange information and ideas and help develop understanding of world problems and their effects upon agricultural producers; to encourage efficiency of production, processing, and marketing of agricultural commodities. National farmers' organizations and agricultural co-operatives of 51 countries are represented in the Federation. Pres. GLEN FLATEN (Canada); Sec.-Gen. J. H. FEINGOLD (Kenya). Publs *World Agriculture/IFAP News, Farming for Development* (quarterly), *IFAP Tropical Commodity Newsletter* (monthly), *Proceedings of General Conferences.*

International Federation of Beekeepers' Associations—APIMONDIA: Corso Vittorio Emanuele 101, 00186 Rome, Italy; tel. (6) 65121; telex 612533; f. 1949; collects and brings up to date documentation concerning international beekeeping; studies the particular problems of beekeeping through its permanent committees; organizes international congresses, seminars, symposia and meetings; stimulates research into new techniques for more economical results; co-operates with other international organizations interested in beekeeping, in particular with FAO. Mems: 80 associations from 68 countries. Pres. BORNECK RAYMOND; Sec.-Gen. Dr SILVESTRO CANNAMELA. Publs *Apiacta* (every 3 months, in English, French, German, Russian and Spanish), Proceedings of International Beekeeping Congresses and Symposia, and many publications relating to beekeeping.

International Hop Growers' Convention: c/o Institut za hmeljarstvo in pivovarstvo, 63310 Žalec, Yugoslavia; tel. (063) 711221; telex 33 514; f. 1950 to act as a centre for the collection of data on hop production, and to conduct scientific, technical and economic commissions. Mems: national associations in Australia, Belgium, Czechoslovakia, France, German Democratic Republic, Federal Republic of Germany, Hungary, Poland, Spain, United Kingdom, USA and Yugoslavia. Pres. GEORGE W. SIGNOROTTI (USA); Gen. Sec. ALOJZ ČETINA (Yugoslavia). Publ. *Hopfen-Rundschau* (fortnightly).

International Institute for Sugar Beet Research: 47 rue Montoyer, 1040 Brussels, Belgium; tel. (02) 512-65-06; telex 21287; f. 1931 to promote research and exchange of information, by organizing meetings and study groups. Mems: 517 in 33 countries. Pres. of the Admin. Council H. J. VON LÖBBECKE; Sec.-Gen. L. WEICKMANS. Publ. *IIRB Winter Congress Proceedings.*

International Institute of Tropical Agriculture—IITA: Oyo Rd, PMB 5320, Ibadan, Nigeria; tel. 413048; telex 31417; f. 1967; principal financing arranged by the Consultative Group on International Agricultural Research (CGIAR), co-ordinated by the IBRD. The four main research programmes comprise farming systems, grain legume improvement, cereal improvement and root and tuber improvement; training programme for researchers in tropical agriculture; library of 35,000 vols. Dir LAURENCE D. STIFEL. Publs *Annual Report,* technical bulletins, research reports and proceedings.

International Laboratory for Research on Animal Diseases—ILRAD: POB 30709, Nairobi, Kenya; tel. 592311; telex 22040; f. 1973, became operational 1976; support provided by 14 countries, UNDP, the EEC, the Rockefeller Foundation and the World Bank; research programmes on the development of control procedures for trypanosomiasis and theileriosis; training programme for researchers in animal disease control as well as technical and other staff; regular seminars, conferences; specialized library. Dir-Gen. Dr A. R. GRAY. Publs *Annual Report, ILRAD Report,* scientific papers.

International Livestock Centre for Africa—ILCA: POB 5689, Addis Ababa, Ethiopia; tel. 183215; telex 21207; f. 1974; an international research centre supported by and financed largely through the Consultative Group on International Agricultural Research of the IBRD; a multidisciplinary research, information and training institute concerned with livestock and agricultural production systems, particularly the productivity of ruminants and the pastoral resources of Africa, and the interdependence of crop and livestock production; also stimulates and reinforces national research programmes. Dir-Gen. PETER J. BRUMBY. Publs *ILCA Bulletin, ILCA Newsletter,* research reports, bibliographies.

International Maize and Wheat Improvement Centre—CIMMYT: Apdo. Postal 6-641, México 6, DF, Mexico; tel. (905) 585 43 55; telex 177 2023; to develop varieties and techniques for improved production of maize, wheat, triticale and barley in the developing countries. Dir-Gen. ROBERT D. HAVENER.

International North Pacific Fisheries Commission: 6640 N.W. Marine Drive, Vancouver, British Columbia, V6T 1X2, Canada; tel. (604) 228-1128; f. 1953. Mems: Canada, Japan and USA. Publs *Annual Report, Bulletin and Statistical Yearbook.*

International Organization for Biological Control of Noxious Animals and Plants: Institut für Phytomedizin, Swiss Federal Institute of Technology (ETH), 8092 Zürich, Switzerland; f. 1955 to promote and co-ordinate research on the more effective biological control of harmful insects and plants; re-organized in 1971 as a central council with world-wide affiliations and largely autonomous regional sections in different parts of the world: the West Palaearctic (Europe, North Africa, the Middle East), the Western Hemisphere, South-East Asia, Pacific Region and Tropical Africa. Pres. Dr V. DELUCCHI (Switzerland); Sec.-Gen. Dr J.-P. AESCHLIMANN (Switzerland).

International Organization of Citrus Virologists: c/o Dr H. D. Ohr, Dept of Plant Pathology, University of California, Riverside, Calif 92521, USA; tel. (714) 787-4140; f. 1957 to promote research on citrus virus diseases at international level by standardizing diagnostic techniques and exchanging information relating to these diseases and their control. Mems: 250. Chair. Dr ARY A. SALIBE; Sec.-Treas. Dr H. D. OHR.

International Red Locust Control Organization for Central and Southern Africa: POB 37, Mbala, Zambia; f. 1971 as successor to International Red Locust Control Service, to control red locust populations in recognized outbreak areas. Mems: 10 countries. Chair. W. R. MESWELE (Botswana); Dir Dr M. E. A. MATERU. Publs *Annual Report, Quarterly Report* and scientific reports.

International Regional Organization of Plant Protection and Animal Health (Organismo Internacional Regional de Sanidad Agropecuaria—OIRSA): Edif. Carbonell 2, Pasaje Carbonell, Col. Roma, San Salvador, El Salvador; tel. 232391; telex (0373) 20746; f. 1953 for the prevention of the introduction of animal and plant pests and diseases unknown in the region; research, control and eradication programmes of the principal pests present in agriculture; technical assistance and advice to the Ministries of Agriculture and Livestock of member countries; education and qualification of personnel. Mems: Costa Rica, El Salvador, Guatemala, Honduras, Mexico, Nicaragua, Panama. Exec. Dir Ing. RAFAEL GARCÍA BESNÉ (acting). Publs Reports.

International Rice Research Institute—IRRI: POB 933, Manila, Philippines; tel. 88-48-69; telex 45365; f. 1960; conducts a comprehensive basic research programme on the rice plant and its management with the objective of increasing the quantity and quality of rice; maintains a library to collect and provide access to the world's technical rice literature; publishes and disseminates research results; conducts regional rice research projects in co-operation with scientists in rice-producing countries; offers a resident training programme in rice research methods and techniques for staff members of organizations concerned with rice; organizes international conferences and symposia. Dir-Gen. M. S. SWAMINATHAN. Publs *Annual Report, Technical Bulletins, Technical Papers, The IRRI Reporter, The International Bibliography of Rice Research, International Rice Research Newsletter, IRRI Research Paper Series, Research Highlights, International Bibliography on Cropping Systems.*

International Seed Testing Association: Reckenholz, POB 412, 8046 Zürich, Switzerland; tel. (01) 573133; f. 1906 (reconstituted 1924) to promote uniformity and accurate methods of seed testing and evaluation in order to facilitate efficiency in production, processing, distribution and utilization of seeds; organizes triennial conventions, meetings, workshops, symposia and training courses. Mems: 60 countries. Pres. A. B. EDNIE (Canada); Hon. Sec. Treas. Dr C. ANSELME (France). Publs *Seed Science and Technology* (3 a year), *ISTA News Bulletin* (quarterly).

International Sericultural Commission: 25 quai Jean-Jacques Rousseau, 69350 La Mulatière, France; tel. 78-50-41-98; f. 1948 to encourage the development of silk production. Library of 8,000 vols. Mems: governments of Algeria, Brazil, Egypt, France, India, Japan, Lebanon, Madagascar, Mauritius, Philippines, Romania, Thailand, Tunisia. Sec.-Gen. Dr H. BOUVIER (France). Publ. *Sericologia* (quarterly).

International Service for National Agricultural Research—ISNAR: POB 93375, 2509 AJ The Hague, Netherlands; tel. (070) 472991; telex 33746; f. 1980 by the Consultative Group on International Agricultural Research (q.v.) to strengthen national agricultural research systems in developing countries; to link these systems to sources of technical assistance and co-operation. Chair. HENRI CARSALADE; Dir-Gen. ALEXANDER VON DER OSTEN.

International Society for Horticultural Science: De Dreijen 6, 6703 BC Wageningen, Netherlands; tel. (08370) 21747; telex 45760; f. 1959 to co-operate in the research field. Mems: 50 member-countries, 265 organizations, 2,800 individual members. Pres. Prof. Dr F. SCARAMUZZI (Italy); Sec.-Gen. and Treas. Ir. H. H. VAN DER BORG (Netherlands). Publs *Chronica Horticulturae* (4 a year), *Acta Horticulturae, Scientia Horticulturae* (monthly), *Horticultural Research International.*

International Society for Soilless Culture—ISOSC: POB 52, 6700 AB Wageningen, Netherlands; tel. (08370) 13809; f. 1955 as International Working Group on Soilless Culture, to promote world-wide distribution and co-ordination of research, advisory services, and practical application of soilless culture; international congress held every four years. Mems: 512 from 64 countries. Pres. Prof. Dr FRANZ PENNINGSFELD; Sec.-Gen. Ing. Agr. ABRAM A. STEINER. Publ. *Proceedings, Bibliography on Hydroponics, Soilless Culture* (2 a year).

International Society of Soil Science: c/o POB 353, 6700 AJ Wageningen, Netherlands; tel. (08370) 19063; telex 45888; f. 1924. Mems: 8,000 individuals and associations in 135 countries. Pres. Dr K. H. HARTGE (FRG); Sec.-Gen. Dr W. G. SOMBROEK (Netherlands). Publ. *Bulletin* (2 a year).

International Union of Forestry Research Organizations—IUFRO: 1131 Vienna, Schönbrunn-Tirolergarten, Austria; tel. (222) 82-01-51; f. 1890/92. Mems: 600 organizations in 100 countries, more than 10,000 individual mems. Pres. Prof. Dr DUŠAN MLINŠEK (Yugoslavia); Sec. OTMAR BEIN (Austria). Publs *Annual Report, IUFRO News* (quarterly), Congress Proceedings, scientific papers.

International Veterinary Association of Animal Production: c/o Sociedad Veterinaria de Zootecnia, Isabel la Católica 12, 4° izq., 28013 Madrid, Spain; tel. 2471838; holds world congresses on livestock genetics, animal feeding and zootechnology. Mems: about 8,000 veterinary specialists from 52 countries. Pres of Exec. Cttee Prof. A. DE VUYST (Belgium); Sec.-Gen. Prof. Dr CARLOS LUIS DE CUENCA (Spain). Publs *Zootechnia* (4 a year), *Proceedings.*

North Pacific Fur Seal Commission: c/o National Oceanic and Atmospheric Administration, National Marine Fisheries Service, Washington, DC 20235, USA; f. 1958 to co-ordinate research and make recommendations concerning the objective of the 1957 Interim Convention on Conservation of North Pacific Fur Seals—'achieving maximum sustainable productivity of the fur seal resources of the North Pacific Ocean . . . with due regard to their relation to the productivity of other living marine resources of the area'. Signatories: governments of Canada, Japan, USSR and USA. Sec. JACK GEHRINGER. Publs *Proceedings, Reports.*

Northwest Atlantic Fisheries Organization: POB 638, Dartmouth, Nova Scotia, B2Y 3Y9, Canada; tel. 469-9105; telex 019-31475; f. 1979 (formerly International Commission for the Northwest Atlantic Fisheries); aims at optimum use, management and conservation of resources, promotes research and compiles statistics. Pres. H. SCHMIEGELOW; Exec. Sec. J. C. E. CARDOSO. Publs *Annual Report, Statistical Bulletin, Journal of Northwest Atlantic Fishery Science, Scientific Council Reports, Scientific Council Studies, Sampling Yearbook, Proceedings, List of Fishing Vessels.*

Permanent Inter-State Committee on Drought Control in the Sahel—CILSS: POB 7049, Ouagadougou, Burkina Faso; f. 1973; works in co-operation with UN Sudano-Sahelian Office (UNSO, q.v.); aims to combat the effects of chronic drought in the Sahel region, by improving irrigation and food production, halting deforestation and creating food reserves. Mems: Burkina Faso, Cape Verde, Chad, The Gambia, Guinea-Bissau, Mali, Mauritania, Niger, Senegal. Exec. Sec. BRAH MAHAMANE (Niger).

World Association for Animal Production: Corso Trieste 67, 00198 Rome, Italy; tel. (06) 860785; f. 1965; holds world conference on animal production every five years; encourages, sponsors and participates in regional meetings, seminars and symposia. Pres. Prof. Dr E. P. CUNNINGHAM (Ireland); Sec.-Gen. Dr K. KÁLLAY. Publ. *News Items* (2 a year).

World Association of Veterinary Food-Hygienists: Institut für Veterinärmedizin des Bundesgesundheitsamtes, Postfach 330013, 1000 Berlin 33, Federal Republic of Germany; f. 1955 to promote hygienic food control and discuss research. Mems: 34 member countries. Pres. Prof. Dr D. GROSSKLAUS (FRG); Sec. Treas. Dr P. TEUFEL. Publs Reports from symposia and conferences.

World Association of Veterinary Microbiologists, Immunologists and Specialists in Infectious Diseases: Ecole Nationale Vétérinaire d'Alfort, 7 ave du Général de Gaulle, 94704 Maisons-Alfort Cedex, France; f. 1967 to facilitate international contacts in the fields of microbiology, immunology and animal infectious diseases. Pres. Prof. CH. PILET (France). Publs *Comparative Immunology, Microbiology and Infectious Diseases.*

World Ploughing Organization—WPO: Whiteclose, Longtown, Carlisle, Cumbria, CA6 5TY, England; tel. (0228) 791153; f. 1952 to promote World Ploughing Contest in a different country each year, to improve techniques and promote better understanding of soil cultivation practices through research and practical demonstrations. Affiliates in 26 countries. Gen. Sec. ALFRED HALL. Publs *WPO Handbook* (annual), *WPO Bulletin of News and Information* (irregular).

World's Poultry Science Association: Institut für Kleintierzucht, 3100 Celle, Dörnbergstr. 25/27, Federal Republic of Germany; tel. (05141) 31031; f. 1912 to exchange knowledge in the industry, to encourage research and teaching, to publish information relating to production and marketing problems; to promote World Poultry Congresses and co-operate with governments. Mems: individuals in 95 countries, branches in 40 countries. Pres. KRISTER EKLUND (Finland); Sec. Prof. ROSE-MARIE WEGNER (FRG). Publ. *The World Poultry Science Journal* (3 a year).

World Veterinary Association: c/o Prof. Dr C. L. De Cuenca, Isabel la Católica 12, 28013 Madrid, Spain; tel. 247 18 38; telex 22762; f. 1959 as a continuation of the International Veterinary Congresses; first Congress 1863. Mems: organizations in 69 countries and 15 organizations of veterinary specialists as associate members. Pres. Dr J. F. FIGUEROA (Peru); Sec.-Treas. Prof. Dr CARLOS L. DE CUENCA. Publs *WVA Informative Bulletin, World Catalogue of Veterinary Films.*

Aid and Development

African Training and Research Centre in Administration for Development (Centre africain de formation et de recherches administratives pour le développement—CAFRAD): 19 rue Abou al Alae al Maari, BP 310, Tangier, Morocco; tel. 36601; telex 33664; f. 1964 by agreement between Morocco and UNESCO; research into administrative problems in Africa, documentation of results, provision of a consultative service for governments and organizations; holds frequent seminars; aided by UNDP and other national and international organizations. Mems: 29 African countries. Pres. S. E. ABDERRAHIM; Dir-Gen. Dr MOSTAFA RHOMARI. Publs *Cahiers Africains d'Administration Publique/African Administrative Studies* (2 a year), *CAFRAD News* (quarterly), case studies and other documents.

Afro-Asian Housing Organization—AAHO: POB 523, 30 26th July St, Cairo, Egypt; tel. 752-757; f. 1965 to promote co-operation between African and Asian countries in housing, reconstruction, physical planning and related matters. Sec.-Gen. HASSAN M. HASSAN (Egypt).

Afro-Asian Rural Reconstruction Organization—AARRO: C/117-118, Defence Colony, New Delhi 110024, India; tel. 621175; f. 1962 to act as a catalyst for co-operative restructuring of rural life in Africa and Asia; to explore collectively opportunities for co-ordination of efforts for promoting welfare and eradicating hunger, thirst, disease, illiteracy and poverty amongst the rural people; and to assist the formation of organizations of farmers and other rural people. Through its technical programme, AARRO promotes collaborative research on development issues, training, conferences, and the exchange of information; awards 100 training and study fellowships at six institutes in Egypt, India, the Republic of Korea and Taiwan. Mems: 12 African, 14 Asian countries and the Institute of Rural Development, Kenya (assoc. mem.). Sec.-Gen. B. C. GANGOPADHYAY. Publ. *Rural Reconstruction* (2 a year).

Agence de coopération culturelle et technique: 13 quai André Citroën, 75015 Paris, France: tel. (1) 45-75-62-41; telex 2011916; f. 1970, Niamey, Niger, to exchange knowledge of the cultures of French-speaking countries, to provide technical assistance, to assist relations between member countries. Technical and financial assistance has been given to projects in every member country, mainly to aid rural people. Mems: 30 countries, mainly African; associates: Cameroon, Egypt, Guinea-Bissau, Laos, Mauritania, Morocco; participants: Saint Lucia and the Canadian provinces of Quebec and New Brunswick. Sec.-Gen. PAUL OKUMBA D'OKOUATSEGUE (Gabon). Publ. *Agecoop Liaison* (monthly).

Arab Authority for Agricultural Investment and Development—AAAID: POB 2102, Khartoum, Sudan; tel. 41423; telex 24041; f. 1976 to accelerate agricultural development in the Arab world and to ensure food security; activities began in Sudan owing to its great unexplored agricultural potential; by the end of 1985

OTHER INTERNATIONAL ORGANIZATIONS
Aid and Development

seven companies had been launched in Sudan, covering dairy products, vegetable oils, starch and glucose, poultry, fruit and vegetables, sugar, sesame, sorghum and soya beans; capital US $525m. (Dec. 1985), of which $334m. was paid-in. Mems: Algeria, Egypt, Iraq, Kuwait, Mauritania, Morocco, Qatar, Saudi Arabia, Somalia, Sudan, Syria, United Arab Emirates. Pres. Dr HUSSAIN YOUSIF AL-ANI.

Arab Gulf Programme for the United Nations Development Organizations—AGFUND: POB 18371, Riyadh 11415, Saudi Arabia; tel. 4416240; telex 204071; f. 1981 to provide grants for projects carried out by United Nations organizations and co-ordinate assistance by the nations of the Gulf; between 1981 and May 1985 AGFUND committed a total of US $133m. for the benefit of 112 countries. Contributions to AGFUND stood at $167m. in May 1985. Pres. HRH Prince TALAL IBN ABDUL AZIZ AL-SAUD.

Association of Development Financing Institutions in Asia and the Pacific: c/o Private Development Corporation of the Philippines, PDCP Building, Ayala Ave, Makati, Manila, Philippines; tel. 816-16-72; telex 45022; f. 1977 to promote the interest and economic development of the respective countries of its member-institutions, and the Asia-Pacific region as a whole, through development financing. Mems: 49 ordinary (national), five special (national and international) mems and 13 associate (regional) mems. Chair. Management Cttee. JOHN W. FLETCHER (Australia).

BAM International (Frères des Hommes): 20 rue du Refuge, 78000 Versailles, France; tel. (1) 39-50-69-75; f. 1965 to support local partners helping the under-privileged to have more control of their own development, to recruit qualified European volunteers to work on development and health projects in Asia, Africa and South America, and to increase public awareness of the Third World in Europe. Affiliated organizations in Belgium, Italy, Luxembourg and the United Kingdom. Mems: approx. 1,000. Pres. JEAN ALLAIN. Publ. *Newsletter* (4 a year).

Caritas Internationalis (International Confederation of Catholic Organizations for charitable and social action): Piazza San Calisto 16, 00153 Rome, Italy; tel. 6987197; telex 504/2014; f. 1950 to study problems arising from poverty, their causes and possible solutions; national member organizations undertake assistance and development activities. The Confederation co-ordinates emergency relief and development projects, and represents members at international level. Mems: 115 national organizations. Pres. Cardinal ALEXANDRE DO NASCIMENTO (Angola); Sec.-Gen. Dr GERHARD MEIER (Switzerland). Publs *Intercaritas* (quarterly), leaflets, monographs.

Club of Dakar: 4 ave Hoche, 75008 Paris, France; f. 1974 for private discussion on questions of development and co-operation; identifies development problems and formulates proposals for their solution. Mems: 200 administrators, industrial executives, scientists and bankers from many industrialized and developing countries. Pres. ERIC GUILLON.

Communauté Economique des Etats de l'Afrique Centrale—CEEAC (Economic Community of Central African States): BP 2112, Libreville, Gabon; f. 1983; operational 1 January 1985; aims to promote co-operation between member states by abolishing trade restrictions, establishing a common external customs tariff, and setting up a development fund, over a period of 12 years. Membership comprises the states belonging to UDEAC (q.v.) and five others: Burundi, Cameroon, Central African Republic, Chad, Congo, Equatorial Guinea, Gabon, Rwanda, São Tomé and Príncipe and Zaire; Angola has observer status. Sec.-Gen. Dr LUNDA-BULULU.

Conference of Regions in North-West Europe: POB 107, 8000 Bruges 1, Belgium; f. 1955 to co-ordinate regional studies with a view to planned development in the area between the North Sea, the Ruhr, Rhine Valley and Boulogne; also compiles cartographical documents. Mems: individual scholars and representatives of planning offices in Belgium, France, Federal Republic of Germany, Luxembourg, Netherlands and the United Kingdom. Pres. Ir. À. PETERS (Netherlands); Sec.-Gen. Prof. I. B. F. KORMOSS (Belgium).

Council of American Development Foundations—SOLIDARIOS: Feliz Miranda 21, POB 620, Santo Domingo, Dominican Republic; tel. (809) 567-7725; telex 0597; f. 1972; exchanges information and experience, arranges technical assistance, raises funds to organize training programmes and scholarships; administers development fund to finance programmes carried out by members; the foundations provide technical and financial assistance to low-income groups for rural, housing and handicraft projects. Mems: 25 institutional mems in 14 Latin American and Caribbean countries. Pres. WALTER BRUSA; Sec.-Gen. ENRIQUE A. FERNÁNDEZ P. Publ. *Solidarios* (quarterly), *Annual Report*.

Economic Co-operation Organization—ECO: 5 Hejab Ave, Blvd Keshavarz, POB 11365-8396, Teheran, Iran; tel. 658614; telex 213774; f. 1964 (as Regional Co-operation for Development), a tripartite arrangement aiming at closer economic, technical and cultural co-operation; members aim to co-operate in certain industrial projects and standards, trade, tourism, transport (including the building of road and rail links), communications and cultural affairs; a meeting of officials was held in July 1984 to revive the organization. Mems: Iran, Pakistan, Turkey. Sec.-Gen. BEHCET TUREMAN (Turkey).

Food Aid Committee: c/o International Wheat Council, Haymarket House, 28 Haymarket, London, SW1Y 4SS, England; tel. (01) 930-4128; telex 916128; f. 1967; responsible for administration of the Food Aid Convention (1986), a constituent element of the International Wheat Agreement. The 23 donor members are pledged to supply 7m. tons of grain annually to developing countries, mostly as gifts. In 1984/85 shipments reached a peak of almost 12m. tons. Publ. *Report on shipments* (annually).

Foundation for the Peoples of the South Pacific—FSP: Pacific House, POB 727, 2–12 West Park Ave, Long Beach, NY 11561, USA; tel. (516) 432-3563; telex 62895; f. 1965 to promote the growth and welfare of the Pacific Islanders through development research in the fields of economics, anthropology, medicine and community development, planning, fund-raising and liaison services; operates a nine-nation maternal and infant nutrition programme, and country programmes in Fiji, Kiribati, Papua New Guinea, Solomon Islands, Tonga and Vanuatu. Pres. ELIZABETH SILVERSTEIN; Exec. Dir Rev. STANLEY W. HOSIE. Publ. *Annual Report*, technical reports.

Gambia River Basin Development Organization—OMVG: BP 2353, Région du Cap Vert, Dakar, Senegal; tel. 21-16-48; f. 1978 by Senegal and The Gambia; Guinea joined in 1981 and Guinea-Bissau in 1983. Plans include the construction of dams on the 1,100-km river at Balingho, The Gambia, and Kekreti, Senegal, to provide irrigation and hydroelectricity, at a cost of about US $270m.; feasibility studies were undertaken in 1984, and a meeting of heads of state in January 1985 agreed to seek funding for the project. High Commissioner MALICK JOHN.

Indian Ocean Commission—IOC: f. 1982 to promote regional co-operation, particularly in economic development; proposed schemes include tuna-fishing development and the formation of a regional shipping line, with assistance from the European Community; tariff reduction is also envisaged. Liaison offices are to be established in each member country. Mems: Comoros, France (representing the French Overseas Department of Réunion), Madagascar, Mauritius and Seychelles.

Institute of Economic Growth, Asian Research Centre: University Enclave, Delhi 110007, India; tel. 222221; f. 1967 to bring the resources of social science to bear upon the solution of problems connected with social and economic development in South and South East Asia; specialized library and documentation services. Dir Prof. L. K. KRISHNAMURTY; Head of Centre Prof. T. N. MADAN. Publs *Asian Social Science Bibliography* (annually), *Contributions to Indian Sociology: New Series* (annually), *Studies in Asian Social Development* (occasional).

Inter-American Planning Society (Sociedad Interamericana de Planificación—SIAP): Apdo postal 27-716, 06140 México DF, Mexico; f. 1956 to promote development of comprehensive planning as a continuous and co-ordinated process at all levels. Mems: 55 institutions and 2,460 individuals in 25 countries. Pres. Arq. GUILLERMO GEISSE (Chile); Exec. Sec. LUIS E. CAMACHO (Colombia). Publs *Correo Informativo* (quarterly), *Inter-American Journal of Planning* (quarterly), *Congress Proceedings*, special studies, pamphlets, books on Development and Planning (SIAP's editions) (all in Spanish and some in English).

Intergovernmental Authority on Drought and Development—IGADD: c/o Ministry of Foreign Affairs and Co-operation, Djibouti; f. 1986 by six drought-affected states to co-ordinate measures to combat the effects of drought and desertification. Mems: Djibouti, Ethiopia, Kenya, Somalia, Sudan, Uganda. Exec. Sec. MEKONEN KIBRET (Ethiopia).

Intermediate Technology Development Group: Myson House, Railway Terrace, Rugby, CV21 3HT, England; tel. (0788) 60631; telex 317466; f. 1965 to investigate ways of applying the most appropriate technologies to development; studies the range of technologies and seeks to distribute their use more widely; special emphasis is given to low-cost, labour-intensive methods of production. The Group is a limited company registered as a charity and has four subsidiary companies and three associate companies. Research, development and demonstration programmes are undertaken in collaboration with institutions in many developing countries. Chair. DENNIS STEVENSON; Company Sec. NIGEL SINKER. Publs

Appropriate Technology (quarterly), *Waterlines* (quarterly), and over 100 manuals, bibliographies and buyers' guides to small-scale equipment.

International Co-operation for Socio-Economic Development—CIDSE: 1-2 ave des Arts, 1040 Brussels, Belgium; tel. (02) 219-00-80; telex 64208; f. 1965 to study the means of rendering more effective the co-operation amongst member organizations in the field of socio-economic development aid; to promote the creation of new organizations in both developed and developing countries, the co-ordination of its members, development aid projects and programmes by means of a computerized central registration of all development projects introduced to the affiliated organizations. Mems: Catholic agencies in 13 countries. Pres. JACQUES CHAMPAGNE (Canada); Sec.-Gen. PATRICE ROBINEAU.

Lake Chad Basin Commission: BP 727, N'Djamena, Chad; tel. 30 34; telex 5250; f. 1964 to encourage co-operation in developing the Lake Chad region by attracting financial and technical assistance for research; the 1986–91 programme emphasizes anti-desertification measures and improvements in road and railway links between member countries. Mems: Cameroon, Chad, Niger and Nigeria.

Latin American Association of Development Financing Institutions (Asociación Latinoamericana de Instituciones Financieros de Desarrollo—ALIDE): POB 3988, Lima, Peru; tel. 422400; telex 21037; f. 1968 to promote co-operation among regional development financing bodies. Mems: about 190 financing institutions and development organizations in 27 countries. Pres. Dr GUSTAVO PETRICIOLI; Sec.-Gen. CARLOS GARATEA YORI. Publs *Memoria anual, Directorio Latinoamericano de Instituciones Financieras de Desarrollo, Boletín Informativo.*

Liptako-Gourma Integrated Development Authority: POB 619, route de Fada, N'Gourma, Burkina Faso; f. 1972 for regional development, particularly in transport and water resources. Mems: Burkina Faso, Mali, Niger. Sec.-Gen. SILIMANE GANOU (Niger).

Mano River Union: Private Post Bag 113, Freetown, Sierra Leone; f. 1973 to establish a customs and economic union between member states to improve living standards. A common external tariff was instituted in April 1977. Intra-union free trade was officially introduced in May 1981, as the first stage in progress towards a customs union. An industrial development unit was set up in 1980 to identify projects and encourage investment. Construction of a Freetown–Monrovia road and other road projects are planned. Feasibility studies for a hydroelectric scheme were completed in 1983. Joint institutes have been set up to provide training in posts and telecommunications, forestry, marine activities and customs, excise and trade. Decisions are taken at meetings of a Joint Ministerial Cttee formed by the economic and finance ministers of member states. Mems: Guinea, Liberia, Sierra Leone. Sec.-Gen. Dr AUGUSTUS CAINE (Liberia).

Niger Basin Authority (Autorité du bassin du Niger): BP 729, Niamey, Niger; f. 1964 (as River Niger Commission; name changed 1980) to harmonize national programmes concerned with the River Niger Basin and to execute an integrated development plan; activities comprise: statistics; navigation regulation; hydrological forecasting; environmental control; infrastructure and agro-pastoral development; and arranging assistance for these projects. Mems: Benin, Burkina Faso, Cameroon, Chad, Ivory Coast, Mali, Niger, Nigeria. Exec. Sec. IBRAHIM SORY BALDE (Guinea). Publs *Bulletin, Bibliographical Index.*

Organization for the Development of the Senegal River (Organisation pour la Mise en Valeur du Fleuve Sénégal—OMVS): 46 rue Carnot, BP 3152, Dakar, Senegal; tel. 22-36-79; telex 670; f. 1972; Heads of State meet as necessary, and Council of Ministers meets at least once a year, deciding on policy and projects, which include hydroelectric dams and the improvement of ports; later mining, industrial and agricultural projects are planned. A 40-year plan requiring about 800,000m. CFA francs investment has been formed; the first phase, due to be completed by 1990, involves the construction of two dams, at Djama and Manantali. Mems: Mali, Mauritania, Senegal. High Commr MOKHTAR OULD HAIBA (Mauritania); Sec.-Gen. FOUNÉKÉ KEITA (Mali).

Organization for the Management and Development of the Kagera River Basin (Organisation pour l'aménagement et le développement du bassin de la rivière Kagera): BP 297, Kigali, Rwanda; tel. 2172; telex 567; f. 1978; for joint development and management of resources, including the construction of an 80-MW hydroelectric dam at Rusumo Falls, on the Rwanda-Tanzania border (for which final engineering studies were under way in 1986), and a 2,000-km railway network between the four member countries (for which the final study was completed in 1983); a telecommunications network, to be financed mainly by the African Development Bank, is also planned. Mems: Burundi, Rwanda, Tanzania and Uganda. Exec. Sec. Dr DAVID S. O. WACHA.

Pacific Basin Economic Council: Industry House, Barton, Canberra, Australia; f. 1967; a businessmen's organization composed of the representatives of business circles of Australia, Canada, Japan, Republic of Korea, New Zealand, Taiwan, USA and the countries of the Pacific Basin, which co-operates with government and international institutions in the overall economic development of the Pacific Area and the advancement of the livelihood of the population; promotes economic collaboration among the member countries and co-operates with the developing countries in their effort to achieve self-sustaining economic growth; holds annual International General Meeting. Chair. R. W. B. REID (Australia); Exec. Dir-Gen. M. J. OVERLAND.

Pan-African Institute for Development—PAID: BP 4056, Douala, Cameroon; tel. 42-43-35; telex 6048; f. 1964 to train rural development officers from Africa at intermediate and senior levels; emphasis in education is given to: involvement of local populations in development; staff training for national centres; preparation of projects for regional co-operation; consultation, applied research, local project support and specialized training. There are four regional institutes: Central Africa (Douala), Sahel (Ouagadougou) (French-speaking), West Africa (Buea), Eastern and Southern Africa (Kabwe) (English-speaking). Sec.-Gen. Prof. A. C. MONDJANAGNI.

Pan American Development Foundation—PADF: 1889 F St, NW, Washington, DC 20006, USA; tel. (202) 789-6153; telex 64128; f. 1962 to improve the quality of life of low-income groups in Latin America and the Caribbean through providing low-interest credit for small-scale entrepreneurs, vocational training, improved health care, agricultural development and reforestation, and to strengthen the ability of the private sector in the region to participate in development activities; provides emergency disaster relief and reconstruction assistance. Chair. JOÃO CLEMENTE BAENA SOARES; Pres. LEVEO V. SÁNCHEZ; Exec. Vice-Pres. EDWARD MARASCIULO. Publ. *PADF Newsletter* (3 a year).

Population Council: 1 Dag Hammarskjöld Plaza, New York, NY 10017, USA; tel. (212) 644-1300; telex 234722; f. 1952; conducts research in human reproductive biomedicine, the development of contraceptive methods, and social science useful to the understanding of public policy issues; disseminates information and publications. Three regional offices, in Mexico City, Bangkok and Cairo. Chair. ROBERT H. EBERT; Pres. GEORGE ZEIDENSTEIN; Sec. JAMES J. BAUSCH. Publs *Studies in Family Planning* (monthly), *Population and Development Review* (quarterly), monographs, brochures.

Preferential Trade Area for Eastern and Southern African States: POB 30051, Lusaka, Zambia; tel. 219880; telex 40127; f. 1981 with the aim of improving commercial and economic co-operation in the region, and ultimately to form a common market and economic community; began operations in July 1984 with the announcement of tariff reductions for six categories of goods traded between members; the Reserve Bank of Zimbabwe acts as a clearing house for transactions for goods and services within the PTA, enabling member states to conduct multilateral trade in their own currencies. A PTA development bank (based in Bujumbura, Burundi) was to begin operations in 1986, with initial capital of US $400m. Mems: Burundi, the Comoros, Djibouti, Ethiopia, Kenya, Lesotho, Malawi, Mauritius, Rwanda, Somalia, Swaziland, Tanzania, Uganda, Zambia, Zimbabwe. Sec.-Gen. BAX NOMVETE.

Sistema Económico Latinoamericano—SELA (Latin American Economic System): Apdo 17035, El Conde, Caracas 1010, Venezuela; telex 24615; f. 1975 to allow regional consultation and co-operation in economic and social progress, chiefly through the creation of regional enterprises (in fertilizers, fish products, handicrafts, housing, tourism and technology). Mems: 26 Caribbean and Latin American states. Sec. SEBASTIÁN ALEGRETT (Venezuela).

Society for International Development: Palazzo Civiltà del Lavoro, EUR, 00144 Rome, Italy; telex 612339; f. 1957 to provide a forum for an exchange of ideas, facts and experience among persons concerned with the problems of economic and social development in both developed and developing countries. Mems: 9,500. Pres. EDGARD PISANI; Sec.-Gen. MAURICE WILLIAMS. Publs *Development* (quarterly), *Compass* (quarterly).

South Asian Association for Regional Co-operation—SAARC: expected to be based in Kathmandu, Nepal; f. 1985 by the leaders of seven South Asian nations, to improve regional co-operation, particularly in economic development. The 1985 summit meeting agreed on 11 programmes of co-operation: agriculture; rural development; health and population; telecommunications; postal services; science and technology; transport; meteorology; sports, arts and culture; action against drug-trafficking; and countering terrorism. The SAARC charter stipulates that decisions should be made unanimously, and that 'bilateral and contentious issues' should not be discussed; meetings of heads of governments are to be held annually, and ministers of foreign affairs are to meet at least twice a year. Mems: Bangladesh, Bhutan, India, Maldives, Nepal, Pakistan and Sri Lanka.

United Methodist Committee on Relief: 475 Riverside Drive, Room 1374, New York, NY 10115, USA; tel. (212) 870-3600; f. 1940 to represent the United Methodist Church in the field of relief, refugee resettlement and rehabilitation, and in efforts to alleviate root causes of hunger, in 80 countries (including within the United States), to assist the workers and members of United Methodist churches outside the USA and co-operate with ecumenical agencies in this same field of endeavour. Chair. Bishop ROY CLARK; Assoc. Gen. Sec. NORMA J. KEHRBERG. Publ. *Inasmuch* (3 a year).

Vienna Institute for Development (Wiener Institut für Entwicklungsfragen): Vienna 1010, Kärntner Str. 25, Austria; f. 1964 to publicize problems and achievements of developing countries, to encourage industrialized countries to increase aid; research programmes. Mems from 20 countries. Pres. BRUNO KREISKY (Austria).

World University Service—WUS: 5 chemin des Iris, 1216 Geneva, Switzerland; tel. (022) 988711; telex 27273; f. 1920; links students, faculty and administrators in post-secondary institutions concerned with economic and social development; seeks to extend technical, personal and financial resources of post-secondary institutions to under-developed areas and communities; provides scholarships at university level for refugees from South Africa, Namibia and Latin America; the principle is to assist people to improve and develop their own communities. WUS is independent and is governed by an assembly of national committees. Pres. HARUNUR RASHID (Bangladesh); Gen. Sec. NIGEL HARTLEY (UK). Publs *WUS Action, WUS News, Annual Report,* Reports on conferences and research.

Arts and Culture

Europa Nostra: 9 Buckingham Gate, London, SW1E 6JP, England; tel. (01) 821-1171; f. 1963 as an international federation of non-governmental associations for the protection of Europe's natural and cultural heritage; has consultative status with the Council of Europe. Mems: c. 2,000 organizations. Hon. Pres. Rt. Hon. Lord DUNCAN-SANDYS (UK); Pres. HENRI J. DE KOSTER (Netherlands); Hon. Sec.-Gen. Dr MAURICE LINDSAY (UK).

European Association of Conservatoires, Music Academies and Music High Schools: Place Neuve, 1204 Geneva, Switzerland; f. 1953 to establish and foster contacts and exchanges between members. Mems: 95. Sec.-Gen. CLAUDE VIALA.

European Cultural Centre (Centre Européen de la Culture): Villa Moynier, 122 rue de Lausanne, 1211 Geneva 21, Switzerland; tel. (022) 322803; f. 1950 to contribute to the unity of Europe by encouraging cultural pursuits, providing a meeting place, and conducting research in the various fields of European Studies; holds conferences on European subjects, European documentation and archives. Groups the Secretariats of the European Association of Music Festivals and the Association of Institutes of European Studies. Pres. JACQUES FREYMOND (Switzerland); Admin. RAYMOND RACINE. Publ. *Cadmos* (quarterly).

European Society of Culture: S. Marco 2516, 30124 Venice, Italy; tel. (041) 5230210; f. 1950 to unite artists, poets, scientists, philosophers and others through mutual interests and friendship in order to safeguard and improve the conditions required for creative activity; library of 10,000 volumes. Mems: 2,000. Pres. Prof. GIUSEPPE GALASSO (Italy); International Sec. Dott. MICHELLE CAMPAGNOLO-BOUVIER.

Inter-American Music Council (Consejo Interamericano de Música—CIDEM): 1889 F St, NW, 510-B, Washington, DC 20006, USA; tel. (202) 789-3706; telex 64128; f. 1956 to promote the exchange of works, performances and information in all fields of music, to study problems relative to music education, to encourage activity in the field of musicology, to promote folklore research and music creation, to establish distribution centres for music material of the composers of the Americas, etc. Mems: national music societies of 30 American countries. Sec.-Gen. EFRAIN PAESKY.

Interfilm (International Interchurch Film Centre): POB 515, 1200 AM Hilversum, Netherlands; tel. (035) 17645; f. 1955 to promote film criticism and film education; ecumenical, associated with the World Council of Churches; makes awards and recommendations at international film festivals, holds study conferences. Mems: organizations in 40 countries. Pres. Dr AMAL DIBO (Lebanon); Gen. Sec. Dr JAN HES (Netherlands). Publ. *Interfilm Information* (quarterly).

International Association of Art (Painting-Sculpture-Graphic Art) (Association internationale des arts plastiques—Peinture, Sculpture, Arts Graphiques): Maison de l'UNESCO, 1 rue Miollis, 75015 Paris, France; f. 1954. Mems: 81 national committees. Sec.-Gen. DUNBAR MARSHALL-MALAGOLA (UK).

International Association of Art Critics: 11 rue Berryer, 75008 Paris, France; f. 1949 to increase co-operation in plastic arts, promote international cultural exchanges and protect the interests of members. Mems: 2,000 individuals, 50 national sections. Pres. DAN HAULICA (Romania); Sec.-Gen. RAOUL-JEAN MOULIN (France).

International Association of Bibliophiles: Bibliothèque nationale, 58 rue Richelieu, 75084 Paris Cedex 02, France; f. 1963 to create contacts between bibliophiles and to encourage book-collecting in different countries; to organize or encourage congresses, meetings, exhibitions, the award of scholarships, the publication of a bulletin, yearbooks, and works of reference or bibliography. Mems: 500. Pres. ANTHONY R. A. HOBSON (UK); Sec.-Gen. ANTOINE CORON (France). Publ. *Le Bulletin du Bibliophile.*

International Association of Museums of Arms and Military History—IAMAM: Bayerisches Armeemuseum, 8070 Ingolstadt, Neues Schloss, Paradeplatz 4, Federal Republic of Germany; f. 1957; links museums and other scientific institutions with public collections of arms and armour and military equipment, uniforms, etc.; triennial conferences and occasional specialist symposia. Mems: 245 institutions in 49 countries. Pres. W. REID (UK); Sec.-Gen. Dr ERNST AICHNER (FRG). Publs *Repertory of Museums of Arms and Military History, Triennial Report, Glossarium Armorum,* reports on symposia.

International Board on Books for Young People—IBBY: Leonhardsgraben 38A, 4051 Basel, Switzerland; tel. (061) 253404; f. 1953 to support and unify bodies in all countries connected with children's book work; to encourage the distribution of good children's books; to promote scientific investigation into problems of juvenile books; to organize educational aid for developing countries; to present the Hans Christian Andersen Medal every two years to a living author and a living illustrator whose work is an outstanding contribution to juvenile literature; sponsors International Children's Book Day (2 April). Mems: national sections in 60 countries, and individuals. Pres. MIGUEL AZAOLA (Spain); Sec. LEENA MAISSEN. Publs *Bookbird* (quarterly, in English), *Congress Papers, IBBY Honour List* (every 2 years); special bibliographies.

International Cello Centre: Edrom House, Duns, Berwickshire, TD11 3PX, Scotland; f. 1953 to foster musical culture in the spirit of Pablo Casals's teaching and philosophy. Mems: approx. 400 in 14 countries. Dirs JANE COWAN, JOHN GWILT. Publ. *Diary of Events* (3 a year).

International Centre for the Study of the Preservation and Restoration of Cultural Property—ICCROM: Via di San Michele 13, 00153 Rome, Italy; tel. 580 9021; telex 613114; f. 1959; assembles documents on preservation and restoration of cultural property; stimulates research and proffers advice in this domain; organizes missions of experts; undertakes training of specialists and organizes regular courses on (i) Architectural Conservation; (ii) Conservation of Mural Paintings; (iii) Scientific Principles of Conservation; (iv) Preventive Conservation in Museums; (v) Conservation of Paper. Mems: 71 countries. Dir Dr CEVAT ERDER (Turkey); Asst Dir Dr GIORGIO TORRACA. Publ. *Newsletter* (annually, English and French).

International Centre of Films for Children and Young People—ICFCYP: 111 rue Notre Dame des Champs, 75006 Paris, France; f. 1957; a clearing house of information about: entertainment films (cinema and television) for children and young people, influence of films on the young, and regulations in force for the protection and education of young people; promotes production and distribution of suitable films and their appreciation; to this end it encourages the setting up of National Centres. Mems: 32 full mems (National Centres), 23 assoc. mems (International Organizations). Pres. PREDRAG GOLUBOVIĆ (Yugoslavia). Publ. *Young Cinema International.*

International Committee for the Diffusion of Arts and Literature through the Cinema (Comité international pour la diffusion des arts et des lettres par le cinéma—CIDALC): 24 blvd Poissonnière, 75009 Paris, France; tel. (1) 42-46-65-36; f. 1930 to promote the creation and release of educational, cultural and documentary films and other films of educational value in order to contribute to closer understanding between peoples; awards medals and prizes for films of exceptional merit. Mems: national committees in 25 countries. Pres. HENRI PIALAT (France); Sec.-Gen. MARIO VERDONE (Italy). Publ. *Annuaire CIDALC.*

International Comparative Literature Association: c/o Dept Literatuurwetenschap, 21 Blijde Inkomststraat, 3000 Leuven, Belgium; f. 1954 to work for the development of the comparative study of literature in modern languages. Member societies and individuals in over 60 countries. Mems: 2,500. Pres. DOUWE FOKKEMA (Netherlands); Secs JOSÉ LAMBERT (Belgium), ULRICH WEISSTEIN (USA). Publ. *ICLA Bulletin.*

International Confederation of Societies of Authors and Composers—World Congress of Authors and Composers: 11 rue Keppler, 75116 Paris, France; f. 1926 to protect the rights of authors and composers; documentation centre. Mems: 120 member societies from 56 countries. Pres. EDGAR FAURE (France); Sec.-Gen. JEAN-ALEXIS ZIEGLER.

International Council of Museums—ICOM: Maison de l'UNESCO, 1 rue Miollis, 75732 Paris Cedex 15, France; tel. (1) 47-34-05-00; f. 1946 to further international co-operation among museums and to advance museum interests; maintains with UNESCO the most extensive museum documentation centre in the world. Mems: over 7,000. Pres. G. LEWIS (UK); Sec.-Gen. P. CARDON (USA). Publ. *ICOM News—Nouvelles de l'ICOM* (quarterly).

International Council on Monuments and Sites—ICOMOS: 75 rue du Temple, 75003 Paris, France; tel. (1) 42-77-35-76; telex 240918; f. 1965 to promote the study and preservation of monuments and sites; to arouse and cultivate the interest of public authorities, and people of every country in their monuments and sites and in their cultural heritage; to liaise between public authorities, departments, institutions and individuals interested in the preservation and study of monuments and sites; to disseminate the results of research into the problems, technical, social and administrative, connected with the conservation of the architectural heritage, and of centres of historic interest. Mems: 3,500; 13 International Committees, 66 National Committees. Pres. MICHEL PARENT (France); Sec.-Gen. A. DAOULATLI (Tunisia). Publ. *ICOMOS Information* (quarterly).

International Federation for Theatre Research: 14 Woronzow Rd, London, NW8 6QE, England; f. 1955 by 21 countries at the International Conference on Theatre History, London. Chair. Prof. WILLIAM GREEN; Joint Secs-Gen. ROSE-MARIE MOUDOUES, ERIC ALEXANDER. Publ. *Theatre Research International* (in association with Oxford University Press) (3 a year).

International Federation of Film Archives: c/o B. van der Elst, 70 Coudenberg, 1000 Brussels, Belgium; tel. (02) 511-13-90; telex 64783; f. 1938 to encourage the creation of archives in all countries for the collection and conservation of the film heritage of each land; to facilitate co-operation and exchanges between these film archives; to promote public interest in the art of the cinema; to aid research in this field and to compile new documentation; conducts research; publishes manuals, etc.; holds annual congresses. Mems in 55 countries. Pres. ANNA-LENA WIBOM (Sweden); Sec.-Gen. GUIDO CINCOTTI (Italy).

International Federation of Film Producers' Associations: 33 ave des Champs-Elysées, 75008 Paris, France; tel. (1) 42-25-62-14; f. 1933 to represent film production internationally, to defend its general interests and promote its development, to study all cultural, legal, economic, technical and social problems of interest to the activity of film production. Mems: national associations in 21 countries. Pres. FRANCO CRISTALDI (Italy); Sec.-Gen. ALPHONSE BRISSON (France). Publ. Information Circulars.

International Institute for Children's Literature and Reading Research (Internationales Institut für Jugendliteratur und Leseforschung): 1040 Vienna, Mayerhofgasse 6, Austria; tel. (022) 65-03-59; f. 1965 as an international documentation, research and advisory centre of juvenile literature and reading; maintains specialized library; arranges conferences and exhibitions; compiles recommendation lists. Mems: individual and group members in 28 countries. Pres. Dr HERMANN LEIN; Dir Dr LUCIA BINDER. Publs *Bookbird* (quarterly in co-operation with the International Board on Books for Young People), *Jugend und Buch* (quarterly in co-operation with the Austrian Children's Book Club), *Schriften zur Jugendlektüre, PA-Kontakte* (published irregularly).

International Institute for Conservation of Historic and Artistic Works: 6 Buckingham St., London, WC2N 6BA, England; tel. (01) 839-5975; f. 1950. Mems: 2,800 individual, 400 institutional members. Pres. S. P. SACK; Sec.-Gen. N. S. BROMMELLE. Publs *Studies in Conservation* (quarterly), *Art and Archaeology Technical Abstracts—IIC* (2 a year).

International Institute of Iberoamerican Literature: 1312 C.L., University of Pittsburgh, Pa 15260, USA; f. 1938 to advance the study of Iberoamerican literature, and intensify cultural relations among the peoples of the Americas. Mems: scholars and artists in 35 countries. Exec. Dir ALFREDO ROGGIANO. Publs *Revista Iberoamericana, Memorias.*

International Liaison Centre for Cinema and Television Schools (Centre international de liaison des écoles de cinéma et de télévision): 8 rue Thérésienne, 1000 Brussels, Belgium; tel. (02) 512-32-36; f. 1955 to co-ordinate teaching standards and to develop plans for creation of cultural, artistic, teaching and technical relations between mems. Pres. COLIN YOUNG (UK); Sec.-Gen. RAYMOND RAVAR (Belgium).

International Music Council—IMC: Maison de l'UNESCO, 1 rue Miollis, 75732 Paris Cedex 15, France; tel. (1) 45-68-25-50; telex 204461; f. 1949 to foster the exchange of musicians, music (written and recorded), and information between countries and cultures; to support contemporary composers and young professional musicians. Mems: 18 international non-governmental organizations, national committees in 60 countries. Pres. M. NOBRE; Sec.-Gen. VLADIMIR STEPANEK.

Members of IMC include:

European Association of Music Festivals: 122 rue de Lausanne, 1211 Geneva 21, Switzerland; tel. (022) 322803; telex 289917; f. 1951; aims to maintain high artistic standards and the representative character of music festivals; holds annual General Assembly. Mems: 43 regularly-held music festivals in 18 European countries, Israel and Japan. Pres. TASSILO NEKOLA (Austria). Publs *Season* (annually), *Festivals* (annually).

Federation of International Music Competitions: 12 rue Hôtel de Ville, 1204 Geneva, Switzerland; tel. (022) 213620; f. 1957 to co-ordinate the arrangements for affiliated competitions, to exchange experience, etc.; a General Assembly is held every April. Mems: 76. Pres. PIERRE COLOMBO; Sec.-Gen. Mme ALINE VERNET. Publs brochure (every December), list of First Prize winners (every spring).

International Association of Music Libraries, Archives and Documentation Centres—IAML: c/o Music Library/Hornbake Library, University of Maryland, College Park, MD 20742, USA; tel. (301) 454-6903; telex 908787; f. 1951. Mems: 1,830 institutions and individuals in 38 countries. Pres. ANDERS LÖNN (Sweden); Sec.-Gen. NEIL RATLIFF (USA). Publ. *Fontes artis musicae* (every 4 months).

International Council for Traditional Music: Dept of Music, Columbia University, New York, NY 10027; tel. (212) 678-0332; telex 220094; f. 1947 (as International Folk Music Council) to further the study, practice, documentation, preservation and dissemination of traditional music of all countries; conferences held every two years. Mems: 1,100. Pres. Dr ERICH STOCKMANN (German Democratic Republic); Sec.-Gen. Prof. DIETER CHRISTENSEN (USA). Publs *Yearbook for Traditional Music, Bulletin* (2 a year).

International Federation of 'Jeunesses Musicales': Palais des Beaux-Arts, 10 rue Royale, 1000 Brussels, Belgium; tel. (02) 513-97-74; telex 61825; f. 1945 to promote the development of musical appreciation among young people, to encourage the creation of new societies and to ensure co-operation between national societies. Mems: organizations in 35 countries. Sec.-Gen. ALEXANDER SCHISCHLIK.

International Federation of Musicians: Hofackerstrasse 7, 8032 Zürich, Switzerland; tel. (01) 556611; f. 1948 to promote and protect the interests of musicians in affiliated unions; promotes international exchange of musicians; has agreements with European Broadcasting Union and International Federation of the Phonographic Industry. Mems: 34 unions totalling 331,765 individuals in 34 countries. Pres. JOHN MORTON (UK); Gen. Sec. YVONNE BURCKHARDT (Switzerland).

International Institute for Comparative Music Studies and Documentation (Internationales Institut für Vergleichende Musikstudien und Dokumentation); 1000 Berlin 33, Winklerstrasse 20; tel. (030) 8262853; telex 182875; f. 1963; supported by the City of Berlin to study practical means of integrating the musical achievements of extra-European cultures into world culture and of helping the preservation of authentic traditional music; the Institute works in close co-operation with the International Music Council and UNESCO. There is a sister institution, Istituto Internazionale di Musica Comparata, in Venice. Mems from 20 countries. Gen. Sec. MICHAEL JENNE. Publs *Unesco Anthology of the Orient, Unesco Anthology of African Music, Musical Sources, Musical Atlas* (record series), books, etc., *The World of Music* (quarterly), in asscn with the International Music Council and UNESCO).

OTHER INTERNATIONAL ORGANIZATIONS

Arts and Culture, Commodities

International Jazz Federation: 13 Foulser Rd., London, SW17 8UE, England; tel. (01) 767-2213; f. 1969 to promote the knowledge and appreciation of jazz throughout the world; arranges jazz education conferences and competitions for young jazz groups; encourages co-operation among national societies. Mems: 16 national organizations. Pres. CHARLES ALEXANDER (UK). Publ. *Jazz Forum* (6 a year).

International Music Centre (Internationales Musikzentrum—IMZ): 1030 Vienna, Lothringerstr. 20, Austria; tel. (0222) 72-57-95; telex 133663; f. 1961 for the study and dissemination of music through the technical media (film, television, radio, gramophone); co-operates with other international organizations such as EBU and OIRT; organizes congresses, seminars and screenings on music in the audio-visual media; courses and competitions to strengthen the relationship between performing artists and the audio-visual media; exhibitions of scores, manuscripts, records and books. Mems: 79 ordinary mems and 29 associate mems in 33 countries, including 50 broadcasting organizations. Pres. RUDOLF SAILER (FRG); Sec.-Gen. WILFRIED SCHEIB (Austria); Exec. Sec. ERIC MARINITSCH. Publs *IMZ Report, UNESCO Catalogue, IMZ Bulletin* (10 a year in English, French and German) and seminar reports.

International Society for Contemporary Music: Postfach 3, 1015 Vienna, Austria; tel. (0222) 65-86-95; telex 111397; f. 1922 to promote the development of contemporary music and to organize annual World Music Days. Member organizations in 33 countries. Pres. Prof. SIEGFRIED PALM (FRG); Sec.-Gen. TRYGVE NORDWALL.

International PEN (A World Association of Writers): 38 King St, London, WC2E 8JT, England; f. 1921 to promote co-operation between writers. There are 87 centres throughout the world, with total membership about 8,000. International Pres. FRANCES KING; International Sec. ALEXANDRE BLOKH. Publs *The Survival and Encouragement of Literature,* International PEN anthologies, *PEN International* (in English and French, with the assistance of UNESCO).

International Theatre Institute—ITI: Maison de l'UNESCO, 1 rue Miollis, 75015 Paris, France; tel. (1) 45-68-26-50; f. 1948 to facilitate cultural exchanges and international understanding in the domain of the theatre; conferences, publications, etc. Mems: 64 member nations, each with an ITI national centre. Pres. WOLE SOYINKA (Nigeria); Sec.-Gen. ANDRÉ-LOUIS PERINETTI.

International Typographic Association: 4142 Münchenstein, Gutenbergstrasse 1, Switzerland; f. 1957 to co-ordinate the ideas of those whose profession or interests have to do with the art of typography and to obtain effective international legislation to protect type designs. Mems: 320. Pres. MARTIN FEHLE. Publs *Typographic Opportunities in the Computer Age, Interpressgrafik.*

Royal Asiatic Society of Great Britain and Ireland: 56 Queen Anne St, London, W1M 9LA, England; tel. (01) 935-8944; f. 1823 for the study of history and cultures of the East. Mems: c. 1,000, branch societies in Asia. Pres. Prof. Sir CYRIL PHILIPS; Dir D. J. DUNCANSON; Sec. Miss E. V. GIBSON. Publ. *Journal* (2 a year).

Society of African Culture: 18 rue des Ecoles, 75005 Paris, France; tel. (1) 43-54-57-69; telex 200891; f. 1956 to create unity and friendship among scholars in Africa for the encouragement of their own cultures and the development of a universal culture. Mems: from 45 countries. Pres. AIMÉ CÉSAIRE; Sec.-Gen. CHRISTIANE ALIOUNE DIOP. Publ. *Présence Africaine* (quarterly).

United Towns Organization: 2 rue de Logelbach, 75017 Paris, France; tel. (1) 47-66-75-10; telex 660569; f. 1957 by Le Monde Bilingue (f. 1951); since 1960 has specialized in twinning towns in developed areas with those in less developed areas; aims to set up permanent links between towns throughout the world, leading to social, cultural, economic and other exchanges favouring world peace, understanding and development; encourages the spread of bilingualism. The Organization has consultative status with the UN, UNESCO, UNICEF and the Council of Europe. Mems: 3,500 towns throughout the world. World Pres. PIERRE MAUROY; Sec.-Gen. HUBERT LESIRE-OGREL. Publs *Cités Unies* (quarterly, French and English), *United Towns Newsletter* (quarterly, English), *Cités Unies Informations* (monthly), *Notiziario* (quarterly), *Mitteilungsblatt* (quarterly), quarterly newsletter in Arabic, *Index of International Relations of Towns of World* (annually), special studies on bilingual education, international co-operation, the environment and youth questions.

World Union of French Speakers (Union mondiale des voix françaises): BP 56-05, 75222 Paris Cedex 05, France; f. 1960; cultural exchange in the French language by records, tape recordings, etc. Mems: 1,000. Pres. B. LABONDE; Sec.-Gen. A. REGUS. Publ. *Via Vox Contact.*

Commodities

African Groundnut Council: Badagry Expressway Km 15, POB 3025, Lagos, Nigeria; tel. 880982; telex 21366; European office: 66 ave de Cortenberg, 1040 Brussels, Belgium; tel. (02) 736-54-82; telex 25562; f. 1964 to advise producing countries on marketing policies. Mems: The Gambia, Mali, Niger, Nigeria, Senegal, Sudan. Chair. Alhaji U. B. DANFULANI (Nigeria); Exec. Sec. MOUR MAMADOU SAMB (Senegal).

Association of European Jute Industries: 3 ave du Président Wilson, 75116 Paris, France; f. 1954 to study questions of common interest, disseminate information and represent the industry at international level; conducts technical, statistical and economic research. Mems: national associations in Belgium, France, Federal Republic of Germany, Italy, Netherlands, Portugal, Spain, Sweden, United Kingdom. Pres. REMBERT VAN DELDEN (FRG); Sec.-Gen. P. TOMMY-MARTIN (France). Publs. *Statistiques de production* (2 a year), *Statistiques du commerce extérieur* (quarterly), *Annuaire statistique.*

Association of Iron Ore Exporting Countries—APEF: Le Château, 14 chemin Auguste Vilbert, 1218 Grand Saconnex, Geneva, Switzerland; tel. (022) 982955; telex 289443; f. 1975 to co-ordinate policies of the exporting countries. Mems: nine countries. Sec.-Gen. I. ARCAYA (Venezuela).

Association of Natural Rubber Producing Countries—ANRPC: Natural Rubber Bldg, 148 Jalan Ampang, Kuala Lumpur, Malaysia; tel. 481735; f. 1970 to co-ordinate the production and marketing of natural rubber, to promote technical co-operation amongst members and to bring about fair and stable prices for natural rubber. Structure: Assembly, Executive Committee, Committee of Experts, Secretariat. A joint regional marketing system has been agreed in principle. Seminars and meetings on technical and statistical subjects are held. Mems: India, Indonesia, Malaysia, Papua New Guinea, Singapore, Sri Lanka and Thailand. Sec.-Gen. (vacant). Publs *Quarterly Statistical Bulletin,* proceedings, technical papers.

Cadmium Association: 34 Berkeley Square, London, W1X 6AJ, England; tel. (01) 499-8425; telex 261286; f. 1976; covers all aspects of the use of cadmium; an affiliate of the Zinc Development Association (q.v.); includes almost all companies concerned with the production of cadmium except in North America, where close liaison is kept with the Cadmium Council. Chair. K. A. HEWITT (UK); Chief Exec. F. D. WARD (UK).

Cocoa Producers' Alliance: POB 1718, Western House, 8–10 Broad St, Lagos, Nigeria; tel. 635506; telex 21311; f. 1962 to exchange technical and scientific information; to discuss problems of mutual concern to producers; to ensure adequate supplies at remunerative prices; to promote consumption. Mems: Brazil, Cameroon, Ecuador, Gabon, Ghana, Ivory Coast, Mexico, Nigeria, São Tomé and Príncipe, Togo and Trinidad and Tobago. Sec.-Gen. DJEUMO SILAS KAMGA.

European Aluminium Association: 4000 Dusseldorf 1, Königsallee 30, POB 1207, Federal Republic of Germany; tel. (0211) 80871; telex 8587407; f. 1981 to encourage studies, research and technical co-operation, to make representations to international bodies and to assist national associations in dealing with national authorities. Mems: individual producers of primary aluminium, 14 national groups for wrought producers, the Organization of European Aluminium Smelters, representing producers of secondary aluminium and the European Aluminium Foil Association, representing foil rollers and converters. Chair. G. Y. KERVERN (France); Sec.-Gen. Dr LENORE ERNST.

European Association for the Trade in Jute Products: Adriaan Goekooplaan 5, 2517 JX The Hague, Netherlands; tel. (070) 5460111; telex 31440; f. 1970 to maintain contacts between national associations and carry out scientific research; to exchange information and to represent the interests of the trade. Mems: enterprises in Belgium, Denmark, France, Federal Republic of Germany, Greece, Netherlands, Portugal, Spain, Switzerland, United Kingdom. Sec.-Gen. L. ANTONINI (Netherlands).

European Committee of Sugar Manufacturers: 45 ave Montaigne, 75008 Paris, France; tel. (1) 47-23-68-25; telex 280401; f. 1954 to collect statistics and information, conduct research and promote co-operation between national organizations. Mems: national associations in Austria, Belgium, Denmark, Finland, France, Federal Republic of Germany, Greece, Ireland, Italy, Netherlands, Spain, Sweden, Switzerland, United Kingdom. Pres. O. ADRIAENSEN; Dir-Gen. M. DE LA FOREST DIVONNE.

Group of Latin American and Caribbean Sugar Exporting Countries—GEPLACEA: Ejército Nacional 373, Piso 1, Col.

Granada, ZC 11520, México, DF, Mexico; tel. 250-75-66; telex 1771042; f. 1974 to serve as a forum of consultation on the production and sale of sugar; to contribute to the adoption of agreed positions at international meetings on sugar; to exchange scientific and technical knowledge on agriculture and the sugar industry; to consider the co-ordination of the various branches of sugar processing; to co-ordinate policies of action in order to achieve fair and remunerative prices. Mems: 21 Latin American and Caribbean countries and the Philippines. Exec. Sec. EDUARDO LATORRE (Dominican Republic).

Inter-African Coffee Organization—IACO: BP V210, Abidjan, Ivory Coast; tel. 32 61 31; telex 22406; f. 1960. Mems: 25 coffee-producing countries in Africa. Pres. Dr DENIS BRA KANON (Ivory Coast); Sec.-Gen. AREGA WORKU (Ethiopia). Publs *African Coffee* (quarterly), *Directory of African Exporters* (annually).

Intergovernmental Council of Copper Exporting Countries (Conseil intergouvernemental des pays exportateurs du cuivre—CIPEC): 39 rue de la Bienfaisance, 75008 Paris, France; tel. (1) 42-25-00-24; telex 649077; f. 1967 to co-ordinate research and information policies among the members. Mems: Chile, Peru, Zaire, Zambia. Assoc. mems: Australia, Indonesia, Papua New Guinea and Yugoslavia. Sec.-Gen. MOSSO ANGBOLI MBENGO. Publ. *CIPEC Quarterly Review*.

International Bauxite Association: 67 Knutsford Blvd, POB 551, Kingston 5, Jamaica; tel. 92-64535; telex 2428; f. 1974 to promote the development of the bauxite industry, to co-ordinate policies of the producing countries and to ensure a fair price for exports of bauxite. Mems: Australia, Dominican Republic, Ghana, Guinea, Guyana, India, Indonesia, Jamaica, Sierra Leone, Suriname, Yugoslavia. Sec.-Gen. HENRY O. BOVELL (Guyana). Publs *Quarterly Review, IBA Newsletter* (monthly).

International Cocoa Organization—ICCO: 22 Berners St, London, W1P 3DB, England; tel. (01) 637-3211; telex 28173; f. 1973 under the first International Cocoa Agreement, 1972 (renewed in 1975 and 1980; the fourth agreement was adopted in 1986). ICCO supervises the implementation of the agreement, and provides member governments with conference facilities and up-to-date information on the world cocoa economy and the operation of the agreement. Mems: 18 exporting countries which account for over 72% of world cocoa exports, and 23 importing countries which account for over 67% of world cocoa imports. (The USA is not a member.) Chair. ORLANDO CARBONAR (Brazil); Exec. Dir K. G. ERBYNN (Ghana); Buffer Stock Manager J. PLAMBECK (FRG). Publs *Quarterly Bulletin of Cocoa Statistics, Annual Report*, studies on the world cocoa economy.

International Coffee Organization: 22 Berners St, London, W1P 4DD, England; tel. (01) 580-8591; telex 267659; f. 1963 under the International Coffee Agreement, 1962, which was renegotiated in 1968, 1976 and 1983; aims to achieve a reasonable balance between supply and demand on a basis which will assure adequate supplies at fair prices to consumers and expanding markets at remunerative prices to producers. Mems: 50 exporting countries accounting for over 99% of world coffee exports, and 25 importing countries accounting for approximately 90% of world imports. Chair. of Council W. ODONGO OMAMO (Kenya); Exec. Dir ALEXANDRE F. BELTRÃO.

International Confederation of European Sugar Beet Growers: 29 rue du Général Foy, 75008 Paris, France; tel. (1) 42-94-41-00; telex 640241; f. 1925 to act as a centre for the co-ordination and dissemination of information about beet sugar production and the industry; to represent the interests of sugar beet growers at an international level. Member associations in Austria, Belgium, Denmark, Finland, France, Federal Republic of Germany, Greece, Ireland, Italy, Netherlands, Spain, Sweden, Switzerland, United Kingdom. Pres. M. E. GARROD (UK); Sec.-Gen. H. CHAVANES (France).

International Cotton Advisory Committee: 1225 19th St, NW, Suite 650, Washington, DC 20036, USA; tel. (202) 463-6660; telex 701517; f. 1939 to keep in touch with developments affecting the world cotton situation; to collect and disseminate statistics; to suggest to the governments represented any measures for the furtherance of international collaboration in maintaining and developing a sound world cotton economy. Mems: 45 countries. Exec. Dir J. C. SANTLEY. Publs *Cotton—Review of the World Situation, Cotton—World Statistics*.

International Institute for Cotton: 10 rue du Commerce, 1040 Brussels, Belgium; tel. (02) 513-83-10; telex 23135; f. 1966 to increase world consumption of raw cotton and cotton products through utilization research, market research, sales promotion, education and public relations; to form a link between cotton exporting countries and the main importers. Mems: 10 countries. Pres. PAUL BOMANI (Tanzania); Exec. Dir PETER PEREIRA (UK); Sec. HARPAL LUTHER (India).

International Jute Organization: 95A Rd No 4, Banani, POB 6073, Gulshan, Dhaka, Bangladesh; tel. 412146; telex 642792; agreement made by 48 producing and consuming countries in October 1982 under the auspices of UNCTAD; the organization was formally established in January 1984; aims to improve the jute economy by research and development projects, market promotion and cost reduction. Mems: five exporting and 23 importing countries.

International Lead and Zinc Study Group: Metro House, 58 St James's St, London, SW1A 1LD, England; tel. (01) 499-9373; telex 299819; f. 1959, first meeting 1960; provides opportunities for intergovernmental consultation on world trade in lead and zinc; conducts studies and provides information on trends in supply and demand. Standing committee usually meets in spring in London, and the study group and all committees in October in Geneva. Mems: 34 countries. Chair. B. F. MEERE (Australia); Sec.-Gen. R. W. BOEHNKE. Publs *Lead and Zinc Statistics* (monthly), reports of studies.

International Natural Rubber Organization—INRO: 12th Floor, MUI Plaza, Jalan P. Ramlee, POB 10374, 50712 Kuala Lumpur, Malaysia; tel. 486466; telex 31570; f. 1980 to stabilize natural rubber prices by operating a buffer stock, and to seek to ensure an adequate supply, under the International Natural Rubber Agreement (1979), which entered into force in April 1982, and was extended for two years in 1985. Mems: 26 importing countries (including the European Community) and seven exporting countries. Exec. Dir PANG SOEPARTO.

International Office of Cocoa, Chocolate and Confectionery: 172 ave de Cortenbergh, 1040 Brussels, Belgium; tel. (02) 735-81-70; telex 26246; f. 1930, present title adopted in 1934. Aims to conduct research on all questions concerning the cocoa, chocolate and confectionery industry, to collect and disseminate information, and to keep member associations informed of results of research; maintains a documentation and abstracting service. Mems: national associations in 24 countries. Sec.-Gen. A. M. VAN TULDER.

International Olive Federation: Via del Governo Vecchio 3, 00186 Rome, Italy; f. 1934 to promote the interests of olive growers and to effect international co-ordination of efforts to improve methods of growing and manufacturing and to promote the use of olive oil. Mems: organizations and government departments in Algeria, Argentina, France, Greece, Israel, Italy, Lebanon, Libya, Morocco, Portugal, Spain, Syria, Tunisia.

International Olive Oil Council: Juan Bravo 10, 2°–3°, 28006 Madrid, Spain; tel. 2759506; telex 48197; f. 1959; entrusted with the administration of the International Olive Oil Agreement, the objectives of which are as follows: to promote international co-operation in connection with world olive oil problems; to prevent the occurrence of any unfair competition in the world olive oil trade; to put into operation, or to facilitate the application of, measures designed to extend the production and consumption of, and international trade in, olive oil; to reduce the disadvantages due to fluctuations of supplies on the market; to examine the possibility of taking necessary action with regard to other products of the olive tree. Mems: of the 1979 Agreement (Third Agreement): five mainly producing members, two mainly importing members and the European Economic Community. Dir GABRIELE LUZI; Deputy Dir HEDI GUERBAA. Publs *Survey of the International Olive Oil Council* (fortnightly, French and Spanish), *OLIVAE* (every 2 months, in English, French, Italian and Spanish), *National Olive Oil Policies* (annually).

International Rubber Study Group: Brettenham House, 5-6 Lancaster Place, London, WC2E 7ET; tel. (01) 836-6811; telex 8951293; f. 1944 to provide a forum for the discussion of problems affecting rubber and to provide statistical and other general information on rubber. Mems: 27 governments. Sec.-Gen. J. CARR. Publs *Rubber Statistical Bulletin* (monthly), *International Rubber Digest* (monthly), *Proceedings of Group Meetings and Assemblies, Records of International Rubber Forums* (annually).

International Silk Association: 20 rue Joseph Serlin, 69001 Lyon, France; tel. 78-39-18-41; telex 330949; f. 1949 to promote closer collaboration between all branches of the silk industry and trade, develop the consumption of silk and foster scientific research; collects and disseminates information and statistics relating to the trade and industry; organizes triennial Congresses. Mems: employers' and technical organizations in 34 countries. Pres. MARIO BOSELLI (Italy); Gen. Sec. R. CURRIE. Publs monthly newsletter, standard method of testing and classifying raw silk, international trade rules for Far-Eastern raw silk, dictionary of silk waste, etc.

International Sugar Organization: 28 Haymarket, London, SW1Y 4SP, England; tel. (01) 930-3666; administers the International Sugar Agreement negotiated in 1984 by the United Nations Sugar Conference. Mems: 43 exporting countries and 12 importing countries. Sec. C. POLITOFF. Publs *Pocket Sugar Year Book, Monthly Statistical Bulletin, Annual Report, World Sugar Economy, Structure and Policies.*

International Tea Committee: Sir John Lyon House, 5 High Timber St, London, EC4V 3NH, England; tel. (01) 248-4672; telex 887911; f. 1933 to administer the International Tea Agreement; now serves as a statistical and information centre; in 1979 membership was extended to include consuming countries. Producer Mems: national tea boards of Bangladesh, India, Indonesia, Kenya, Malawi, Mozambique, Sri Lanka, Zimbabwe; Consumer Mems: United Kingdom Tea Association, Tea Association of the USA Inc., Comité Européen du Thé, The Australian Tea and Coffee Traders' Association and the Tea Council of Canada; Assoc. Mem: Ministry of Agriculture, Fisheries and Food, London. Chair. A. C. DAVIES; Vice-Chair. W. J. EDGE; Sec. Mrs N. C. CARNEGIE-BROWN. Publs *Bulletin of Statistics* (annually), *Statistical Summary* (monthly).

International Tea Promotion Association: POB 30007, Coolsingel 58, 3011 AE Rotterdam, Netherlands; tel. (010) 12-08-53; telex 24499; f. 1979. Mems: eight countries (Bangladesh, Indonesia, Kenya, Malawi, Mauritius, Mozambique, Tanzania, and Uganda), accounting for about 80% of world exports of black tea. Liaison Officer NGOIMA WA MWAURA. Publ. *International Tea Journal* (4 a year).

International Tin Council: Haymarket House, 1 Oxendon St, London, SW1Y 4EQ, England; tel. (01) 930-0451; telex 918939; f. 1956; the Sixth International Tin Agreement (1982–87) was intended to achieve a long-term balance between world production and consumption of tin and to prevent excessive fluctuations in the price of tin. Under the Agreement the Council was to set floor and ceiling prices, operate a buffer stock and regulate tin exports from producing members. In 1985 a crisis arose in the tin market when the world production (including that by non-members of the ITC, notably Brazil and the People's Republic of China) greatly exceeded demand, and the ITC was obliged to protect the price of tin by buying up the surplus, thereby incurring heavy debts. In October the ITC was no longer able to buy surplus stocks, and trading in tin on the London Metal Exchange was suspended. Negotiations with creditors continued during 1986, and legal proceedings were undertaken by a number of creditors, owing to the refusal of some member governments to meet the ITC's debts. Mems: governments of 23 countries (of which six are producers), and the EEC. Exec. Chair. PETER LAI; Sec. N. L. PHELPS.

International Tropical Timber Organization: to be based in Yokohama, Japan; f. 1985 under the International Tropical Timber Agreement; aims to assist timber-producing countries in forest management, replenishment and timber processing, to gather information and promote research; no provision is made for price stabilization. Mems: 16 producer countries and 19 consumer countries. Exec. Dir FREEZAILAH BIN CHE YEOM (Malaysia).

International Vine and Wine Office: 11 rue Roquépine, 75008 Paris, France; f. 1924 to study all the scientific, technical, economic and human problems concerning the vine and its products; to spread knowledge by means of its publications; to assist contacts between researchers and establish international research programmes. Mems: 31 countries. Dir GILBERT CONSTANT. Publs *Bulletin de l'OIV* (monthly), *Lexique de la Vigne et du Vin, Recueil des méthodes internationales d'analyse des vins, Code international des Pratiques oenologiques, Codex oenologique international.*

International Wheat Council: Haymarket House, 28 Haymarket, London, SW1Y 4SS, England; tel. (01) 930-4128; telex 916128; f. 1949; responsible for the administration of the Wheat Trade Convention of the International Wheat Agreement, 1986; aims to further international co-operation in wheat problems, to promote international trade in wheat and wheat flour, and to contribute to the stability of the international wheat market; acts as forum for consultations between members, and provides comprehensive information on the international grain market and factors affecting it. Mems: 46 countries and the EEC. Exec. Sec. J. H. PAROTTE. Publs *World Wheat Statistics* (annually), *Record of Operations* (annually), *Market Report* (monthly), *Annual Report, Secretariat Papers* (occasional).

International Wool Secretariat: Wool House, 6 Carlton Gardens, London, SW1Y 5AE; tel. (01) 930-7300; telex 263926; f. 1937 to expand the use and usefulness of wool through promotion and research. Financed by Australia, South Africa, New Zealand, Uruguay and Brazil, it has an international policy of promoting wool irrespective of the country of origin. A non-trading organization, the IWS has branches in 34 countries and Technical Offices in Italy, Japan, Netherlands, United Kingdom and the USA. Man. Dir J. MCPHEE.

International Wool Study Group: Ashdown House, 123 Victoria St, London, SW1E 6RB, England; tel. (01) 212-7676; telex 8813148; f. 1946 to collect and collate statistics relating to world supply of and demand for wool; to review developments and to consider possible solutions to problems and difficulties unlikely to be resolved in the ordinary course of world trade in wool. Mems: 14 countries. Sec.-Gen. D. V. ZIMMER.

Lead Development Association: 34 Berkeley Square, London, W1X 6AJ, England; tel. (01) 499-8422; telex 261286; f. 1954; provides authoritative information on the use of lead and its compounds; maintains a library and abstracting service in collaboration with the Zinc Development Association (see below). Financed by lead producers and users in the United Kingdom, Europe and elsewhere. Chair. J. MILLS (UK); Chief Exec. F. D. WARD (UK).

Mutual Assistance of the Latin American Government Oil Companies (Asistencia Recíproca Petrolera Estatal Latinoamericana—ARPEL): Javier de Viana 2345, Montevideo, Uruguay; tel. 406993; telex 6430; f. 1965 to study and recommend the implementation of mutually beneficial agreements among members in order to promote technical and economic development; to further Latin-American integration; to promote the interchange of technical assistance and information; to plan congresses, lectures, and meetings concerning the oil industry. Mems: State enterprises in Argentina, Bolivia, Brazil, Chile, Colombia, Costa Rica, Ecuador, Jamaica, Mexico, Paraguay, Peru, Suriname, Uruguay, Venezuela. Sec.-Gen. HÉCTOR J. FIORIOLI. Publs *Boletín Informativo, Boletín Técnico ARPEL.*

Primary Tungsten Association: 280 Earls Court Rd, London, SW5 9AS, England; tel. (01) 373-7413; telex 889077; f. 1975; 15 mems, one observer (People's Republic of China). Pres. K. ROCHE; Sec. M. R. P. MABY.

Sugar Association of the Caribbean (Inc.): 80 Abercromby St, Port of Spain, Trinidad; f. 1942. Mems: five associations. Chair. H. B. DAVIS; Sec. M. Y. KHAN. Publs *SAC Handbook, SAC Annual Report, Proceedings of Meetings of WI Sugar Technologists.*

Union of Banana-Exporting Countries—UPEB: Apdo. 4273, Panama 5, Panama; tel. 636766; telex 2568; f. 1974 as an intergovernmental agency to further the banana industry; mems: Colombia, Costa Rica, Dominican Republic, Guatemala, Honduras, Nicaragua, Panama, Venezuela. Exec. Dir ABELARDO CARLES. Publs *Informe Mensual UPEB, Boletín Mensual de Estadísticas, BIBLIOBAN* (annually), bibliographies.

West African Rice Development Association—WARDA: POB 1019, Monrovia, Liberia; tel. 221466; telex 44333; f. 1970, aiming to make West Africa self-sufficient in rice; has regional research programme, assists in rural development projects and operates regional training centre in Liberia and courses in member countries; budget (1984) US $12.5m.; funded by member countries, UN agencies, the EEC and other organizations. Mems: Belgium, Benin, Burkina Faso, Chad, Federal Republic of Germany, The Gambia, Ghana, Guinea, Guinea-Bissau, Italy, Ivory Coast, Japan, Liberia, Mali, Mauritania, the Netherlands, Niger, Nigeria, Senegal, Sierra Leone, Switzerland, Togo. Exec. Sec. ALIEU M. B. JAGNE (The Gambia) (acting). Publs technical reports.

West Indian Sea Island Cotton Association (Inc.): c/o Barbados Agricultural Society, 'The Grotto', Beckles Rd, St Michael, Barbados. Pres. E. LEROY WARD; Sec. MICHAEL I. EDGHILL.

World Federation of Diamond Bourses: 62 Pelikaansstraat, 2018 Antwerp, Belgium; tel. (03) 232-76-55; telex 73314; f. 1947 to protect the interests of affiliated organizations and their individual members and to settle or arbitrate in disputes. Mems: 19 in 11 countries. Pres. E. GOLDSTEIN (UK); Sec.-Gen. PH. BLONDIN (Belgium).

Zinc Development Association: 34 Berkeley Square, London, W1X 6AJ, England; tel. (01) 499-6636; telex 261286; provides authoritative advice on the uses of zinc, its alloys and its compounds; maintains a library and abstracting service in collaboration with the Lead Development Association (q.v.). Affiliates are: Zinc Alloy Die Casters Association, Galvanizers' Association and Zinc Pigment Development Association. Financed by zinc producers and users in the United Kingdom, Europe and elsewhere. Chair. O. BLOMBERG (Norway); Chief Exec. F. D. WARD (UK).

Economics and Finance

African Centre for Monetary Studies: 15 blvd Franklin Roosevelt, BP 1791, Dakar, Senegal; tel. 21-38-21; telex 3256; began operations 1978; aims to promote better understanding of banking

OTHER INTERNATIONAL ORGANIZATIONS
Economics and Finance

and monetary matters; to study monetary problems of African countries and the effect on them of international monetary developments; seeks to enable African countries to co-ordinate strategies in international monetary affairs. Established as an organ of the Association of African Central Banks (AACB) as a result of a decision by the OAU Heads of State and Government. Mems: all mems of AACB (q.v.).

Arab Bankers Association: 1/2 Hanover St, London, W1R 9WB; tel. (01) 629-5423; telex 297338; f. 1980 to co-ordinate interests of Arab bankers, improve relations with other countries, prepare studies for development projects in the Arab world, administer a code for arbitration between financial institutions, and provide training for Arab bankers. Chair. HIKMAT NASHASHIBI.

Association of African Central Banks: 15 blvd Franklin Roosevelt, BP 1791, Dakar, Senegal; tel. 21-38-21; telex 3256; f. 1968 to promote contacts in the monetary and financial sphere in order to increase co-operation and trade among member states; to strengthen monetary and financial stability on the African continent. Mems: 34 African central banks representing 43 states.

Association of African Tax Administrators: c/o ECA, POB 3001, Addis Ababa, Ethiopia; f. 1980 to promote co-operation in the field of taxation policy, legislation and administration among African countries. Mems: 22 states. Chair. FAROUK MOURSY METWALLY (Egypt).

Association of European Institutes of Economic Research (Association d'instituts européens de conjoncture économique): 3 place Montesquieu, BP 4, 1348 Louvain-la-Neuve, Belgium; tel. (10) 43-41-52; f. 1955; provides a means of contact between member institutes; organizes two meetings yearly, in the spring and autumn, at which discussions are held, on the economic situation and on a special theoretical subject. Mems: 40 Institutes in 20 European countries. Admin. Sec. PAUL OLBRECHTS.

Association of International Bond Dealers: Postfach, 8033 Zürich, Switzerland; f. 1969 for discussion of questions relating to the international securities markets, to issue rules governing their functions, and to maintain a close liaison between the primary and secondary markets. Mems: 793 banks and major financial institutions in 39 countries. Chair. ARTHUR SCHMIEGELOW (Denmark); Sec.-Gen. JOHN WOLTERS (Switzerland). Publs *International Bond Manual*, daily Eurobond listing, electronic price information, weekly Eurobond guide, yield book, reports, etc.

Benelux Economic Union: 39 rue de la Régence, 1000 Brussels, Belgium; tel. (02) 519-38-11; telex 61540; f. 1960 to bring about the economic union of Belgium, Luxembourg and the Netherlands; structure comprises: the Committee of Ministers; the Council, consisting of one chairman from each country and the presidents of the eight Committees, on foreign economic relations, monetary and financial matters, industry and commerce, agriculture, food and fisheries, customs and taxation, transport, social affairs and movement of persons; the Court of Justice; the Consultative Inter-Parliamentary Council; the Economic and Social Advisory Council; and the Secretariat-General. Sec.-Gen. Drs E. D. J. KRUIJTBOSCH (Netherlands), C. RIJMENANS (Belgium), M. R. WORMERINGER-BERNA (Luxembourg). Publs *Benelux-Info* (monthly), *Benelux Periodical* (quarterly), *Benelux Textes de Base*.

Centre for Latin American Monetary Studies (Centro de Estudios Monetarios Latinoamericanos): Durango 54, Col. Roma, Delegación Cuauhtémoc, 06700 México, DF, Mexico; tel. 533-03-00; telex 1771229; f. 1952; organizes technical training programmes on monetary policy, development finance, etc., applied research programmes on monetary and central banking policies and procedures, regional meetings of banking officials. Mems: 29 associated members (Central Banks of Latin America and the Caribbean), 21 co-operating members (development agencies, regional financial agencies and non-Latin American Central Banks). Dir JORGE GONZALEZ DEL VALLE. Publs *Bulletin* (every 2 months), *Monetaria* (quarterly), proceedings of meetings and seminars.

Econometric Society: Dept of Economics, Northwestern University, Evanston, Ill 60201, USA; tel. (312) 491-3615; f. 1930 to promote studies that aim at a unification of the theoretical-quantitative and the empirical-quantitative approach to economic problems. Mems: 6,000. Sec. JULIE P. GORDON. Publ. *Econometrica* (6 a year).

Economic Community of the Great Lakes Countries (Communauté économique des pays des Grands Lacs—CEPGL): POB 58, Gisenyi, Rwanda; telex 602; f. 1976; main organs: annual Conference of Heads of State, Council of Ministers of Foreign Affairs, Permanent Executive Secretariat, Consultative Commission, three Specialized Technical Commissions. There are four specialized agencies: a development bank, the Banque de Développement des Etats des Grands Lacs (BDEGL) at Goma, Zaire; an energy centre at Bujumbura, Burundi; the Institute of Agronomic and Zootechnical Research, Gitega, Burundi; and a regional electricity company at Bukavu, Zaire. Mems: Burundi, Rwanda, Zaire. Exec. Sec. ANTOINE NDUWAYO (Burundi). Publs *Grands Lacs* (quarterly review), and an annual journal.

Eurofinas: 267 ave de Tervuren, bte 10, 1150 Brussels, Belgium; tel. (02) 771-21-07; f. 1959 to study the development of instalment credit financing in Europe, to collate and publish instalment credit statistics, to promote research into instalment credit practice; mems: finance houses and professional associations in Austria, Belgium, Finland, France, Federal Republic of Germany, Ireland, Italy, Netherlands, Norway, Spain, Sweden, Switzerland and United Kingdom. Chair. H. R. TACKE (FRG); Sec.-Gen. FLORENT DE CUYPER. Publs *Eurofinas Newsletter* (monthly), *Study Reports, Proceedings of Annual Conferences*.

European Federation of Financial Analysts Societies: c/o SAFE, 45 rue des Petits Champs, 75001 Paris, France; tel. (1) 42-98-02-00; telex 210041; f. 1962 to co-ordinate the activities of all European associations of financial analysts. Mems: 5,283 in 12 societies. Pres. A. LAVIOLETTE; Sec.-Gen. J.-G. DE WAEL. Publs Reports of Conferences, standing commissions and working groups.

European Financial Marketing Association: 7 rue Royale, 75008 Paris, France; tel. (1) 742-52-72; telex 280288; f. 1971 to link financial institutions by organizing seminars, conferences and training sessions and an annual World Convention, and by providing documentation services. Mems: over 700 European financial institutions. Pres. ROBERT AMOS; Sec.-Gen. LOUIS LENGRAND. Publ. *Newsletter*.

European Insurance Committee: 3 rue Meyerbeer, 75009 Paris, France; tel. (1) 42-47-94-64; telex 641901; f. 1953. Mems: national insurance associations of 18 western European countries. Pres. M. R. SLOAN (UK); Sec.-Gen. H. FAVRE (France).

Inter-American Institute of Capital Markets: Apdo 1766, Caracas 1010-A, Venezuela; f. 1977 under the joint sponsorship of the OAS and the Venezuelan Government, to assist member countries in the development of their capital markets; organizes international conferences. Mems: 28 countries. Pres. BERNARDO PAUL. Publ. *Boletín Bibliográfico*.

International Accounting Standards Committee—IASC: 41 Kingsway, London, WC2B 6YU, England; tel. (01) 240-8781; telex 295177; f. 1973 to formulate and publish in the public interest standards to be observed in the presentation of financial statements and to promote worldwide acceptance and observance, and to work for the improvement and harmonization of regulations, accounting standards and procedures relating to the presentation of financial statements. Mems: over 90 accounting bodies representing 900,000 accountants in 70 countries. Chair. J. L. KIRKPATRICK; Sec.-Gen. DAVID H. CAIRNS. Publs *Statements of International Accounting Standards, Exposure Drafts, IASC News* (6 a year), *Discussion Papers*.

International Association for Research in Income and Wealth: POB 1962, Yale Station, New Haven, Conn 06520, USA; tel. (203) 436-8583; f. 1947 to further research in the general field of national income and wealth and related topics by the organization of periodic conferences and by other means. Mems: approx. 350. Chair. LENNART FASTBOM (Sweden); Exec. Sec. NANCY D. RUGGLES (USA). Publ. *Review of Income and Wealth* (quarterly).

International Association of Islamic Banks: POB 4992, Jeddah, Saudi Arabia; branches in Cairo, Egypt (POB 2838), and Karachi, Pakistan (POB 541); f. 1977 to link Islamic banks, which do not deal at interest but work on the principle of participation: activities include training and research. Chair. Prince MOHAMED AL-FAISAL AL-SAUD; Sec.-Gen. Dr AHMED AL-NAGGAR.

International Bureau of Fiscal Documentation: 'Muiderpoort', Sarphatistraat 124, POB 20237, 1000 HE Amsterdam, Netherlands; tel. (020) 267726; telex 13217; f. 1938 to supply information on fiscal law and its application; specialized library on international taxation. Pres. A. NOOTEBOOM; Man. Dir H. M. A. L. HAMAEKERS. Publs *Bulletin for International Fiscal Documentation* (monthly), *European Taxation* (monthly), *Supplementary Service to European Taxation* (monthly), *Tax News Service* (fortnightly); various loose-leaf services (in English and French editions), studies and other publications on aspects of taxation in Africa, Asia, Europe, the Middle East and Latin America.

International Centre for Local Credit: Koninginnegracht 2, 2514 AA The Hague, Netherlands; f. 1958 to promote local authority credit by gathering, exchanging and distributing information and advice on member institutions and on local authority credit and related subjects; studies important subjects in the field of local authority credit. Mems: 22 financial institutions in 16 countries.

Pres. F. Narmon (Belgium); Sec.-Gen. W. Griffioen (The Netherlands). Publs *Bulletin, Newsletter*, special reports.

International Economic Association: 23 rue Campagne Première, 75014 Paris, France; tel. (1) 43-27-91-44; telex 240 918; f. 1949 to promote international collaboration for the advancement of economic knowledge and develop personal contacts between economists, and to encourage provision of means for the dissemination of economic knowledge. Member associations in 58 countries. Pres. Prof. K. J. Arrow (USA); Sec.-Gen. Prof. Jean-Paul Fitoussi (France).

International Federation of Accountants: 540 Madison Ave, New York, NY 10022, USA; tel. (212) 486-2446; telex 640428; f. 1977 to develop a co-ordinated worldwide accounting profession with harmonized standards. Mems: 93 accountancy bodies in 68 countries. Pres. Robert L. May (USA); Exec. Dir Robert Sempier (USA).

International Federation of Stock Exchanges: 22 blvd de Courcelles, 75017 Paris, France; tel. (1) 47-63-17-60; telex 642720; f. 1961 to promote among its members a co-operation that is not detrimental to the traditional relations which some of them may maintain with stock exchanges of third countries; represents its members at international organizations. Mems: 15 European and 16 other stock exchanges. Pres. Sir Nicholas P. Goodison; Sec.-Gen. Mrs Jeanne Abbey.

International Fiscal Association: c/o Erasmus University, Woudestein, POB 1738, Burg. Oudlaan 50, 3000 DR Rotterdam, Netherlands; tel. (010) 452-59-57; telex 24421; f. 1938 to study international and comparative public finance and fiscal law, especially taxation; holds annual congresses. Mems in over 80 countries and national branches in 35 countries. Pres. Richard M. Hammer (USA); Sec.-Gen. Prof. Dr J. H. Christiaanse (Netherlands). Publs *Cahiers de Droit Fiscal International, Yearbook of the International Fiscal Association, IFA Congress Seminar Series*.

International Institute of Banking Studies (Institut international d'études bancaires): c/o Kredietbank NV, 7 rue d' Arenberg, Brussels, Belgium; f. 1951. Mems: 55 in 18 countries. Chair. Jan Ekman; Sec.-Gen. L. Wauters.

International Institute of Public Finance: University of the Saar, 66 Saarbrücken, Federal Republic of Germany; f. 1937; a private scientific organization aiming to establish contacts between people of every nationality, whose main or supplementary activity consists in the study of public finance; holds one meeting a year devoted to a certain scientific subject. Acting Pres. Prof. K. W. Roskamp (USA).

International Savings Banks Institute: 1–3 rue Albert Gos, 1206 Geneva, Switzerland; tel. (022) 477466; telex 428702; f. 1925 to act as an intelligence and liaison centre for savings banks. Mems: 120 savings banks and savings banks associations in 78 countries. Pres. J. J. Sancho Dronda (Spain); Gen. Man. J. M. Pesant (France). Publs (in English, French and German) *Savings Banks International* (quarterly), *International Information* (monthly), *International Savings Banks Directory, Savings Banks Foreign Business Directory*, Congress reports, special publications on education, automation and marketing.

International Union for Land-Value Taxation and Free Trade: 177 Vauxhall Bridge Rd, London, SW1V 1EU, England; tel. (01) 834-4266; f. 1923; based on the writings of Henry George, the Union advocates the raising of public revenues by taxes and rates upon the value of land apart from improvements in order to secure the economic rent for the community and the abolition of taxes, tariffs, or imposts that interfere with the free production and exchange of wealth. International conferences are held every two or three years. Mems: approx. 1,000. Pres. Richard Noyes; Gen. Sec. Mrs B. P. Sobrielo. Publ. *The Georgist Journal* (quarterly).

International Union of Building Societies and Savings Associations: 20 North Wacker Drive, Chicago, Ill 60606, USA; f. 1914 to foster world-wide interest in thrift and home-ownership and co-operation among members; to encourage comparative study of methods and practice; to encourage initiation and promotion of legislation and other methods designed to safeguard and expand the movement. Sec.-Gen. Norman Strunk. Publs *Union Newsletter* (quarterly), *Directory* (every 3 years), *Congress Proceedings* (every 3 years), *International Insights*.

Latin American Banking Federation (Federación Latinoamericana de Bancos—FELABAN): Apartado Aéreo 091959, Bogotá, DE1, Colombia; tel. 2560875; telex 45548; f. 1965 to co-ordinate efforts towards a wide and accelerated economic development in Latin American countries. Mems: 18 Latin American national banking associations. Pres. of Board José Díaz Seixas; Sec.-Gen. Maricielo Glende Tobón (Colombia).

Organisation Commune Africaine et Mauricienne—OCAM: BP 965, Bangui, Central African Republic; f. 1965 as the Organisation commune africaine et malgache, in succession to the Union africaine et malgache de coopération économique (which evolved from the 'Brazzaville Group' of 12 newly-independent francophone states, formed in 1960). The original objectives included a customs union, common trade and investment policies, and a fund to support commodity prices. Mauritania withdrew from the group in 1965, Congo and Zaire in 1973, Cameroon, Chad and Madagascar in 1974, Gabon in 1976, Seychelles in 1978 and Mauritius in 1983. Following a conference of heads of state and government, held in March 1985 (when membership comprised Benin, Burkina Faso, Central African Republic, Ivory Coast, Niger, Rwanda, Senegal and Togo), it was announced that OCAM was to be dissolved, and a ministerial committee was appointed to supervise the dissolution.

West African Clearing House: PMB 218, Freetown, Sierra Leone; tel. 24485; telex 3368; f. 1975; handles transactions between its nine member central banks in order to promote local trade and currency transactions. Mems: Banque Centrale des Etats de l'Afrique de l'Ouest (serving Benin, Burkina Faso, Ivory Coast, Mali, Niger, Senegal, Togo) and the central banks of The Gambia, Ghana, Guinea, Guinea-Bissau, Liberia, Mauritania, Nigeria and Sierra Leone. Exec. Sec. Chris E. Nemedia (Nigeria); Deputy Exec. Sec. Sounkoutou Sissoko (Mali).

World Council of Credit Unions—WOCCU: POB 391, 5810 Mineral Point Rd, Madison, WI 53701, USA; tel. (608) 231-7130; telex 467918; f. 1970 to link credit unions and similar co-operative financial institutions and assist them in expanding and improving their services; provides technical and financial assistance to credit union associations in developing countries. Mems: 43,000 credit unions in 76 countries. Pres. G. A. Charbonneau. Publs *WOCCU Statistical Report and Directory* (annually), *World Reporter* (quarterly), *Credit Union Technical Reporter* (quarterly).

Education

African Association for Literacy and Adult Education: POB 72511/50768, Old East Bldg, 4th Floor, Tom Mboya St, Nairobi, Kenya; tel. 331512; telex 22261; f. 1984, combining the former African Adult Education Association and the AFROLIT Society (both f. 1968); aims to promote adult education and literacy in Africa, to study the problems involved, and to allow the exchange of information; holds Conference every three years. Mems: 19 national education associations, 167 institutions, and 700 individuals from 50 countries. Chair. Prof. James Ogunlade (Nigeria); Exec. Dir. Paul Wangoola (Uganda). Publs *AALAE Newsletter* (2 a year, French and English), *Regional Conference Report* (every 3 years), *Journal* (2 a year).

Association for Childhood Education International: 11141 Georgia Ave, Suite 200, Wheaton, MD 20902, USA; tel. (301) 942-2443; f. 1892 to work for the education of children (from infancy through early adolescence) by promoting desirable conditions in schools, raising the standard of teaching, co-operating with all groups concerned with children, informing the public of the needs of children. Mems: 12,000. Pres. Diane Pitmon; Exec. Dir James S. Packer. Publs *Childhood Education* (5 a year), *ACEI Exchange Newsletter* (10 a year), *Journal of Research in Childhood Education* (2 a year), leaflets on current educational subjects (3 a year).

Association of African Universities: POB 5744, Accra North, Ghana; tel. 63670; telex 2284; f. 1967 to promote exchanges, contact and co-operation among African university institutions and to collect and disseminate information on research and higher education in Africa. Mems: 88 university institutions. Pres. Prof. R. Haroubia (Algeria); Sec.-Gen. Prof. L. MaKany (Congo). Publs *AAU Newsletter* (quarterly); *Staff Vacancies in African Universities* (monthly); *Directory of African Universities* (every 2 years); specialized reports and conference reports.

Association of Arab Universities: POB 401, Jubeyha, Amman, Jordan; tel. 845131; telex 23855; f. 1964. Mems: 55 universities. Sec.-Gen. Dr Mohammad F. Doghaim. Publs *Bulletin* (annually in Arabic and English), *Directory of Arab Universities, Directory of Teaching Staff of Arab Universities, Proceedings of Seminars*.

Association of Caribbean Universities and Research Institutes: POB 11532, Caparra Heights Station, San Juan, Puerto Rico 00922; tel. (809) 789-4388; f. 1968 to foster contact and collaboration between member universities and institutes; conferences, meetings, seminars, etc.; circulation of information through newsletters, bulletins; facilitates co-operation and the pooling of resources in research; encourages exchange of staff and students.

Mems: 46. Sec.-Gen. Dr THOMAS MATHEWS. Publ. *Caribbean Educational Bulletin* (quarterly).

Association of Institutes for European Studies (Association des Instituts d'Etudes Européennes—AIEE): 122 rue de Lausanne, 1202 Geneva, Switzerland; tel. (022) 322803; f. 1951, to co-ordinate activities of member institutes in teaching and research, exchange information, provide a centre for documentation. Mems: 32 institutes in nine countries. Pres. Prof. E. CEREXHE (Belgium); Sec.-Gen. Prof. DUSAN SIDJANSKI. Publ. *Bulletin intérieur* (2 a month).

Association of Partially or Wholly French-Language Universities (Association des universités partiellement ou entièrement de langue française—AUPELF): Université de Montréal, BP 6128, Montreal H3C 3J7, Canada; tel. (514) 343-6630; telex 055-60955; f. 1961; aims: documentation, co-ordination, co-operation, exchange. Mems: 140, and 351 assoc. mems. Pres. MICHEL GUILLOU; Sec.-Gen. MAURICE-ETIENNE BEUTLER. Publs *Perspectives universitaires* (2 a year), *Idées* (irregular), *Universités* (quarterly).

Association of South-East Asian Institutions of Higher Learning—ASAIHL: Secretariat, Ratasastra Bldg, Chulalongkorn University, Henri Dunant St, Bangkok 5, Thailand; tel. 251 6966; f. 1956 to promote the economic, cultural and social welfare of the people of South-East Asia by means of educational co-operation and research programmes. Mems: 90 university institutions in 10 countries. Pres. Dr NAYAN ARIFFIN (Malaysia); Exec. Sec. Dr NINNAT OLANVORAVUTH.

Catholic International Education Office: 60 rue des Eburons, 1040 Brussels, Belgium; tel. (02) 230-72-52; f. 1952 for the study of the problems of Catholic education throughout the world; co-ordination of the activities of members; and representation of Catholic education at international bodies. Mems: 84 countries, 16 assoc. mems, 13 collaborating mems, 5 corresponding mems. Pres. Mgr J. MEYERS (acting); Sec.-Gen. PAULUS ADAMS, FSC. Publs *OIEC Bulletin* (every 2 months in English, French and Spanish), Proceedings of congresses and conferences, special studies, *L'éducation sociale des jeunes à l'école* (French and Spanish), Proceedings of the General Assembly, *Aujourd'hui l'école et l'audiovisuel, Les organisations internationales catholiques d'enseignement, Education in values for societies in the year 2000* (in English, French and Spanish).

Catholic International Federation for Physical and Sports Education: 5 rue Cernuschi, 75017 Paris, France; tel. (1) 47-66-03-23; f. 1911 to group Catholic associations for physical education and sport of different countries and to develop the principles and precepts of Christian morality by fostering meetings, study and international co-operation. Mems: 14 affiliated national federations representing about 2.5m. members. Pres. Dr J. FINDER (Austria); Sec.-Gen. ROBERT PRINGARBE (France).

Centre for Research and Documentation on International Language Problems: Nieuwe Binnenweg 176, 3015 BJ Rotterdam, Netherlands; tel. (010) 436-10-44; f. 1952 by Universala Esperanto-Asocio (renamed 1969); encourages and disseminates information about research on language problems in international relations; sponsors seminars on Esperanto studies. Dirs D. BLANKE, P. DASGUPTO, B. GOLDEN, U. LINS, J. POOL, B. SHERWOOD, E. SYMOENS, H. TONKIN. Publ. *Newsletter* (irregular).

Comparative Education Society in Europe: 51 rue de la Concorde, 1050 Brussels, Belgium; f. 1961 to promote teaching and research in comparative and international education; the Society organizes conferences and promotes literature. Mems in 39 countries. Pres. Prof. J.-L. GARCÍA GARRIDO (Spain); Sec.-Treas. Prof. H. VAN DAELE (Belgium). Publs *Proceedings, Newsletter* (quarterly).

European Association of Teachers: AEDE, 1049 Bournens, Switzerland; tel. (022) 447750; f. 1956 to develop understanding of European civilization and of European problems and to instruct students in this understanding. Mems in Austria, Belgium, France, Federal Republic of Germany, Greece, Italy, Luxembourg, Portugal, Spain, Switzerland, United Kingdom. Pres. P. VANBERGEN (Belgium); Sec.-Gen. S. MOSER (Switzerland). Publs *Documents pour l'enseignement, Education for Europe*, 9 national newsletters.

European Bureau of Adult Education: Nieuweweg 4, POB 367, 3800 AJ Amersfoort, Netherlands; tel. (33) 631114; f. 1953 as a clearing-house and centre of co-operation for all groups concerned with adult education in Europe. Mems: 150 in 18 countries. Pres. A. K. STOCK (UK); Sec., Dir W. BAX. Publs *Conference Reports, Directory of Adult Education Organisations in Europe, Newsletter, Survey of Adult Education Legislation, Glossary of Terms.*

European Council for Education by Correspondence: 18 Prof. Baekelandstraat, 9000 Ghent, Belgium; f. 1962 to make known the applications, achievements, and possibilities of education by correspondence; to co-operate with educational and official bodies; to develop improved teaching methods and materials; to promote higher ethical standards in correspondence education throughout Europe; to exchange knowledge, experience, and publications among member schools. Mems: 38 European Correspondence Schools in 11 countries. Pres. T. ONKEN (Switzerland); Sec.-Gen. T. VAN DER SALM. Publs *Yearbook* and occasional papers.

European Cultural Foundation: Jan van Goyenkade 5, 1075 HN Amsterdam, Netherlands; tel. (20) 760222; telex 18710; f. 1954 as a non-governmental organization, supported by private sources, to promote activities of mutual interest to European countries, concerning basic values, culture, education, environment, international affairs, communications media, social issues, or the problems of European society in general (excluding strictly scientific or medical subjects); national committees in 15 countries; has established a transnational network of seven institutes and centres: European Institute of Education and Social Policy, Paris (with Office for Co-operation in Education, Brussels); Institute for European Environmental Policy, Bonn (branch offices in London and Paris); European Co-operation Fund, Brussels; European Centre for Environmental Communication, Paris; European Centre for Work and Society, Maastricht; EURYDICE Central Unit (the Education Information Network of the European Community), Brussels; European Institute for the Media, Manchester. A grants programme, for projects involving at least three European countries, is also conducted. Pres. HRH Princess MARGRIET of the Netherlands; Sec.-Gen. R. GEORIS; Dir A. N. VAN DER WIEL. Publs *Annual Report, Newsletter* (3 a year), information brochures, *List of Grants,* Essay Series, etc.

European Federation for Catholic Adult Education: Kapuzinerstrasse 84, 4020 Linz, Austria; tel. (0732) 274441; f. 1963 to strengthen international contact between members, to assist international research and practical projects in adult education; to help communications between its members and other international bodies; holds annual conferences. Pres. Dr WALTER SUK (Austria).

European Foundation for Management Development: 40 rue Washington, 1050 Brussels, Belgium; tel. (02) 648-03-85; telex 65080; f. 1971 through merger of European Association of Management Training Centres and International University Contact for Management Education; aims to help improve the quality of management development within the economic, social and cultural context of Europe and in harmony with its overall needs. Mems: more than 550 institutions and individuals. Pres. Baron ANTOINE BEKAERT; Dir-Gen. R. SYBREN TIJMSTRA. Publs *International Management Development* (quarterly), *IMD Bulletin* (every 2 months), *Documentation on Books, Cases and other teaching Material in Management* (every 2 months).

European Union of Arabic and Islamic Scholars: Juan XXIII 5, 28040 Madrid, Spain; tel. 2535300; f. 1960 to organize congresses of Arabic and Islamic Studies; congresses are held every two years. Mems: about 200. Sec. Dr MANUELA MARIN (Spain).

Graduate Institute of International Studies (Institut universitaire de hautes études internationales): POB 36, 132 rue de Lausanne, Geneva, Switzerland; tel. (022) 311730; telex 412151; f. 1927 to establish a centre for advanced studies in international relations of the present day, juridical, historical, political, economic and social. Library of 120,000 vols. Dir Prof. LUCIUS CAFLISCH; Sec.-Gen. J.-C. FRAICHEBOURG.

Inter-American Centre for Research and Documentation on Vocational Training (Centro Interamericano de Investigación y Documentación sobre Formación Profesional—CINTERFOR): Avda Uruguay 1238, Casilla de correo 1761, Montevideo, Uruguay; tel. 98 65 71; telex 6521; f. 1964 by the International Labour Organisation (q.v.) for mutual help among the Latin American and Caribbean countries; a technical committee of government representatives meets once a year to consider the programme of work and budget; the Centre assists the members in planning vocational training; services are provided in documentation, research, exchange of experience; holds seminars and courses. The director is appointed by the Director-General of ILO. Dir JOÃO CARLOS ALEXIM. Publs *Bulletin* (4 a year), *Documentation* (2 a year), *Bibliographical Series, Studies, Monographs and Abstracts.*

Inter-American Confederation for Catholic Education (Confederación Interamericana de Educación Católica): Calle 78 No 12–16 (ofna 101), Apdo Aéreo 90036, Bogotá 8 DE, Colombia; f. 1945 to defend and extend the principles and rules of Catholic education, freedom of education, and human rights; organizes congress every three years. Pres. CÉSAR BLONDET SABROSO; Exec. Sec. MARIO IANTORNO. Publs *Colección CENTRAL, Colección RADIAR, Colección Textos.*

International Association for Educational and Vocational Guidance—IAEVG: Dept of Economic Development, Netherleigh, Massey Ave, Belfast, BT4 2JP, Northern Ireland; tel. 63244; f. 1951 to contribute to the development of vocational guidance and promote contact between persons associated with it. Mems: 40,000 from 40 countries. Pres. JEAN LONG (France); Sec.-Gen. K. M. V. HALL (UK). Publ. *Bulletin AIOSP*.

International Association for Educational and Vocational Information: 20 rue de l'Estrapade, 75005 Paris, France; f. 1956 to facilitate co-operation between national organizations concerned with supplying information to university and college students and secondary pupils and their parents. Mems: national organizations in 50 countries. Pres. C. VIMONT (France); Sec.-Gen. J. L. C. BOUVIER (Belgium); Dir L. TODOROV. Publ. *Informations universitaires et professionnelles internationales* (quarterly).

International Association for the Development of Documentation, Libraries and Archives in Africa: BP 375, Dakar, Senegal; f. 1957 to organize and develop documentation and archives in all African countries. Sec.-Gen. ZACHEUS SUNDAY ALI (Nigeria).

International Association of Papyrologists: Fondation Egyptologique Reine Elisabeth, Parc du Cinquantenaire 10, 1040 Brussels, Belgium; f. 1947; Mems: about 500. Pres. Prof. ORSOLINA MONTEVECCHI (Italy); Sec. Prof. JEAN BINGEN (Belgium).

International Association of Colleges of Physical Education: Institut Supérieur d'Education Physique, Université de Liège au Sart Tilman, 4000 Liège, Belgium; tel. (041) 56-18-90; f. 1962; organizes congresses, exchanges, and research in physical education. Mems: institutions in 43 countries. Gen. Sec. MAURICE PIERON.

International Association of Universities—IAU: 1 rue Miollis, 75732 Paris Cedex 15, France; tel. (1) 45-68-25-45; f. 1950 to promote practical academic co-operation and to assist university institutions throughout the world; the secretariat provides information and maintains a reference library; research and studies are carried out, closely related to the themes of the General Conference. A joint research programme in higher education is carried out with UNESCO. Organization: General Conference, at least every 5 years, Administrative Board, Secretariat. Ninth General Conference, University of Helsinki, Finland, 1990. Budget: approximately $560,000 each year. Mems: 870 universities and institutions of higher education in 121 countries; assoc. mems: eight international university organizations. Pres. JUSTIN THORENS; Sec.-Gen. FRANZ EBERHARD. Publs *Bulletin of the International Association of Universities* (quarterly), *International Handbook of Universities* (every 2 years), *World List of Universities* (every 2 years), *Papers and Reports*.

International Association of University Professors and Lecturers—IAUPL: 18 rue du Docteur Roux, 75015 Paris, France; f. 1945 for the development of academic fraternity amongst university teachers and research workers; the protection of independence and freedom of teaching and research; the furtherance of the interests of all university teachers; and the consideration of academic problems. Mems: 186,000 in 35 countries. Hon. Sec.-Gen. Dr L. P. LAPRÉVOTE. Publ. *Communication*.

International Baccalaureate Office—IBO: Route des Morillons 15, Grand Saconnex 1218, Geneva, Switzerland; tel. (022) 910274; telex 265871; f. 1967 to plan curricula and an international university entrance examination, the International Baccalaureate, recognized by major universities in Europe, North and South America, Africa, Middle East and Australia; provides international board of examiners. Mems: 350 participating schools. Chair. of Council Dr PIET GATHIER (Netherlands); Dir-Gen. ROGER M. PEEL.

International Congress of Africanists: c/o Yusuf Fadhil Hassan, Vice-Chancellor, University of Khartoum, POB 321, Khartoum, Sudan; tel. 75100; f. 1900 to encourage co-operation and research in African studies. Sec.-Gen. Prof. HURREIZ. Publ. *Proceedings*.

International Council for Adult Education: 29 Prince Arthur Ave, Toronto, Ontario M5R 1B2, Canada; tel. (416) 924-6607; f. 1973 to promote adult education and thereby further economic and social development; undertakes research and training; organizes seminars, the exchange of information, and co-operative publishing; General Assembly meets every three years. Mems: six regional organizations and national associations in 71 countries. Pres. Dame NITA BARROW; Sec.-Gen. BUDD HALL. Publ. *Convergence*.

International Federation for Parent Education: 1 ave Léon Journault, 92310 Sèvres, France; tel. (1) 45-34-75-27; f. 1964 to gather in congresses and colloquia experts from different scientific fields and those responsible for family education in their own countries and to encourage the establishment of family education where it does not exist. Mems: 153. Pres. JEAN AUBA (France); Vice-Pres. MANGA BEKOMBO (Cameroon), ALZIRA LOPES (Brazil). Publs *Quarterly Bulletin, Child International Review*.

International Federation of Catholic Universities: 78A rue de Sèvres, 75341 Paris Cedex 07, France; tel. (1) 42-73-36-25; f. 1948; to ensure a strong bond of mutual assistance among all Catholic universities in the search for truth; to help to solve problems of growth and development, and to co-operate with other international organizations. Mems: 165 in 35 countries. Pres. M. MICHEL FALISE (France); Sec.-Gen. LUCIEN MICHAUD (Canada). Publs *Quarterly Newsletter, Proceedings*, monographs, studies in population and human development, technology and the third world.

International Federation of 'Ecole Moderne' Movements: 35 ave Jottrand, 1030 Brussels, Belgium; f. 1957 to bring into contact associations devoted to the improvement of school organization and to work for the adoption of techniques advocated by C. Freinet; conducts courses for teachers, promotes interschool exchange of correspondence and magazines. Mems: associations of teachers in 38 countries. Pres. HENRY LANDROIT. Publs *L'Educateur* (2 a month), *Art Enfantin* (bi-monthly), *Bibliothèque de Travail Sonore, Bibliothèque de l'Ecole Moderne, Bibliothèque de Travail* (bi-monthly), *Bibliothèque de Travail Junior* (monthly), *Bibliothèque de Travail Second degré, La Multilettre*.

International Federation of Library Associations and Institutions—IFLA: c/o Royal Library, POB 95312, 2509 CH The Hague, Netherlands; tel. (70) 140884; telex 34402; f. 1927 to promote international co-operation in librarianship and bibliography. Mems: 181 associations, representing 123 countries, 1,040 institutions and individual members. Pres. Dr HANS-PETER GEH; Sec.-Gen. Dr MARGREET WIJNSTROOM. Publs *IFLA Annual, IFLA Directory, IFLA Journal, International Cataloguing* (quarterly), *IFLA Professional Reports*.

International Federation of Organisations for School Correspondence and Exchange: 29 rue d'Ulm, 75230 Paris Cedex 05, France; tel. (1) 43-45-37-21; f. 1929 to contribute to the knowledge of foreign languages and civilizations and to bring together young people of all nations by furthering international scholastic exchanges including correspondence, individual and group visits to foreign countries, individual accommodation with families, placements in international holiday camps, etc. Mems: comprises 78 national bureaux of scholastic correspondence and exchange in 36 countries. Pres. J. PLATT (UK); Gen. Sec. A. ELMARY (France).

International Federation of Physical Education: 4 Cleevecroft Ave, Bishops Cleeve, Cheltenham, GL52 4JZ, England; f. 1923; studies physical education on scientific, pedagogic and aesthetic bases in order to stimulate health, harmonious development or preservation, healthy recreation, and the best adaptation of the individual to the general needs of social life; organizes international congresses and courses. Mems: from 100 countries. Pres. JOHN C. ANDREWS. Publ. *Bulletin* (quarterly in Arabic, French, English, Portuguese and Spanish).

International Federation of Secondary Teachers: 7 rue de Villersexel, 75007 Paris, France; tel. (1) 45-55-14-00; f. 1912 to contribute to the progress of secondary education. Mems: 47 associations with 850,000 members in 30 countries. Gen. Sec. LOUIS WEBER. Publ. *Bulletin* (3 a year).

International Federation of Teachers' Associations: 3 rue de La Rochefoucauld, 75009 Paris, France; tel. (1) 48-74-58-44; f. 1926 to raise the level of popular education and improve teaching methods; to protect interests of teachers; to promote international understanding. Mems: 33 national associations. Pres. JEAN-JACQUES MASPERO (Switzerland); Sec.-Gen. JEAN-BERNARD GICQUEL (France). Publs *Feuilles d'Informations, FIAI-IFTA-Informations* (3 or 4 a year).

International Federation of Teachers of Modern Languages: Seestrasse 247, 8038 Zürich, Switzerland; tel. (01) 4825040; telex 815250; f. 1931; holds meetings on every aspect of foreign-language teaching; has consultative status with UNESCO. Mems: 33 national and regional language associations and six international unilingual associations (teachers of English, French, German, Italian and Spanish). Pres. EDWARD M. BATLEY; Sec.-Gen. JOHN McNAIR. Publ. *FIPLV World News* (quarterly in English, French and Spanish).

International Federation of University Women: 37 Quai Wilson, 1201 Geneva, Switzerland; f. 1919 to promote understanding and friendship among university women of the world; to encourage international co-operation; to further the development of education; to represent university women in international organizations; to encourage the full application of members' skills to the problems which arise at all levels of public life. Affiliates: 53 national associations with over 230,000 mems. Pres. Dr HELEN S. DUNSMORE (UK);

Exec. Sec. A. PAQUIER (Switzerland). Publs *The Newsletter* (once a year), *Communiqué* (annually), triennial report.

International Federation of Workers' Educational Associations: Temple House, 9 Upper Berkeley St, London, W1H 8BY, England; tel. (01) 402-5608; f. 1947 to promote co-operation between national non-governmental bodies concerned with workers' education, through clearing-house services, exchange of information, publications, international seminars, conferences, summer schools, etc. Pres. Prof. KURT PROKOP (Austria); Sec.-Gen. JACK TAYLOR (UK).

International Institute for Adult Literacy Methods: POB 13145-654, Teheran, Iran; f. 1968 by UNESCO and the government of Iran; a clearing-house for information on activities concerning literacy in various countries; carries out comparative studies of the methods, media and techniques used in literacy programmes; maintains documentation service and library on literacy; arranges seminars. Dir Dr S. MAKNOON.

International Institute of Philosophy—IIP (Institut international de philosophie—IIP): 8 rue Jean-Calvin, 75005 Paris, France; tel. (1) 43-36-39-11; f. 1937 to clarify fundamental issues of contemporary philosophy in annual meetings and to promote mutual understanding among thinkers of different backgrounds and traditions; a maximum of 115 members are elected, chosen from all countries and representing different tendencies. Mems: 108 in 36 countries. Pres. JERZY PELC (Poland); Sec.-Gen. Y. BELAVAL (France). Publs *Bibliography of Philosophy* (quarterly), *Proceedings* of annual meetings, *Chroniques, Philosophy and World Community* (series).

International Institute of Public Administration: 2 ave de l'Observatoire, Paris 6e; tel. (1) 43-20-12-60; telex 270229; f. 1967; trains high-ranking civil servants for all the countries which want to co-operate with the institute; administrative, economic, financial and diplomatic programmes; Africa, Latin America, Asia, Europe and Near East departments; research department, library of 80,000 vols; Documentation Centre. Dir J. P. PUISSOCHET. Publs *Revue française d'administration publique* (quarterly), *Administration* (annually).

International Montessori Association: Koninginneweg 161, 1075 CN Amsterdam, Netherlands; tel. (20) 798932; f. 1929 to propagate the ideals and educational methods of Dr Maria Montessori, co-operate with organizations which strive to affirm human rights, betterment of systems of education and furtherance of peace; organizes training courses for teachers, and international congresses connected with education, creation of new training centres and new national Montessori Associations. Pres. G. J. PORTIELJE; Organizing Sec. H. VAN SON.

International Reading Association: 800 Barksdale Rd, POB 8139, Newark, Del 19714-8139, USA; tel. (302) 731-1600; telex 5106002813; f. 1956 to improve the quality of reading instruction at all levels, to promote the habit of lifelong reading, and to develop every reader's proficiency. Mems: 60,000 in 85 countries. Pres. ROSELMINA INDRISANO. Publs *The Reading Teacher* (9 a year), *Journal of Reading* (8 a year), *Reading Research Quarterly, Lectura y Vida* (quarterly in Spanish), *Reading Today* (6 a year); books on reading and related topics (about 10 a year).

International Schools Association—ISA: CIC CASE 20, 1211 Geneva 20, Switzerland; f. 1951 to co-ordinate work in international schools and promote their development; merged in 1968 with the Conference of Internationally-minded Schools; member schools maintain the highest standards and accept pupils of all nationalities, irrespective of race and creed. ISA carries out curriculum research; convenes annual conferences on problems of curriculum and educational reform; organizes occasional teachers' training workshops and specialist seminars; has consultative status with UNESCO, UNEP, UNICEF and ECOSOC. Mems: 80 schools throughout the world. Pres. ROBERT BELLE-ISLE. Publs *Education Bulletin* (4 a year), *ISA Magazine* (annually), *Conference Report* (annually), curriculum studies (occasional).

International Society for Business Education: Bureau Permanent, Rédaction de la Revue Félix Schmidt, 1052 Le Mont sur Lausanne, Switzerland; f. 1901 to organize international courses and congresses on business education; c. 2,500 mems, national organizations and individuals in 15 countries. Pres. SUZANNE ROTH (Canada); Dir Prof. FELIX SCHMID (Switzerland). Publ. *International Review for Business Education*.

International Society for Education through Art: c/o NSEAD, 7A High St, Corsham, Wilts, SN13 0ES, England; tel. (0249) 714825; f. 1951 to unite art teachers throughout the world, to exchange information and to co-ordinate research into art education; organizes international congresses and exhibitions of children's art. Pres. MARIE-FRANÇOISE CHAVANNE (France); Sec. JOHN STEERS. Publ. *INSEA News*.

International Society for Music Education: 14 Bedford Sq., London, WC1B 3JG; tel. (01) 636-5400; f. 1953 to organize international conferences, seminars and publications on matters pertaining to music education; acts as advisory body to UNESCO in matters of music education. Mems: national committees and individuals in 58 countries. Rector ELLEN URHO (Finland); Sec.-Gen. RONALD SMITH (UK). Publ. *ISME Yearbook*.

International Society for the Study of Medieval Philosophy: Collège Thomas More (SH3), 1348 Louvain-la-Neuve, Belgium; tel. (010) 43-48-07; f. 1958 to promote the study of medieval thought and the collaboration between individuals and institutions concerned in this field; organizes international congresses. Mems: 486. Pres. Prof. JOHN E. MURDOCH (USA); Sec. Prof. Dr CHRISTIAN WENIN (Belgium). Publ. *Bulletin de Philosophie Médiévale* (annually).

International Youth Library (Internationale Jugendbibliothek): 8000 Munich 60, Schloss Blutenburg, Federal Republic of Germany; tel. (089) 8112028; f. 1948, since 1953 an associated project of UNESCO, to promote the international exchange of children's literature and to provide study opportunities for specialists in children's books. Maintains a library of over 400,000 volumes in about 110 languages. Dir of the Library Board Dr ANDREAS BODE. Publs *The White Ravens, IJB Bulletin, IJB Report*, catalogues, etc.

League of European Research Libraries—LIBER: Universitätsbibliothek Graz, 8010 Graz, Universitätsplatz 3, Austria; tel. (0316) 380-3101; telex 03-1662; f. 1971 to establish close collaboration between the general research libraries of Europe, and national and university libraries in particular; and to help in finding practical ways of improving the quality of the services these libraries provide. Mems: 170. Pres. FRANZ KROLLER. Publs *LIBER Bulletin* (2 a year), *LIBER News Sheet* (2 or 3 a year).

Organization of Ibero-American States for Education, Science and Culture (Organización de Estados Iberoamericanos para la Educación, la Ciencia y la Cultura): Ciudad Universitaría, 28040 Madrid, Spain; tel. 449 69 54; telex 48422; f. 1949 (as the Ibero-American Bureau of Education); provides information on education, science and culture; encourages exchanges and organizes training courses; the General Assembly (at ministerial level) meets every four years. Mems: governments of 20 countries. Sec.-Gen. MIGUEL ANGEL ESCOTET ALVAREZ. Publs *Educación—Noticias de Educación, Ciencia y Cultura Iberoamericana* (every 2 months), *Sumarios de Revistas de Educación* (2 a year), *Becas y Cursos de Educación*, monographs.

Organization of the Catholic Universities of Latin America (Organización de Universidades Católicas de América Latina—ODUCAL): c/o Mgr Dr O. Derisi, Rector, Pontificia Universidad Católica Argentina, Juncal 1912, Buenos Aires, Argentina; f. 1953 to assist the social, economic and cultural development of Latin America through the promotion of Catholic higher education in the continent. Mems: 24 Catholic universities in Argentina, Brazil, Chile, Colombia, Dominican Republic, Ecuador, Mexico, Nicaragua, Paraguay, Peru, Puerto Rico and Venezuela. Pres. Mgr Dr OCTAVIO N. DERISI (Argentina); Sec.-Gen. Lic. JUAN ROBERTO COURREGES. Publs *Anuario; Sapientia; Universitas*.

Organization for Museums, Monuments and Sites in Africa: POB 3343, Accra, Ghana; f. 1975 to foster the collection, study and conservation of the natural and cultural heritage of Africa; co-operation between member countries through seminars, workshops, conferences, etc., exchange of personnel, training facilities. Mems from 30 countries. Pres. Dr J. M. ESSOMBA (Cameroon); Sec.-Gen. K. A. MYLES (Ghana).

Regional Centre for Adult Education and Functional Literacy in Latin America (Centro Regional de Educaçio de Adultos y Alfabetización Funcional para América Latina): Quinta Eréndira s/n, Pátzcuaro, Michoacán, Mexico; tel. 21740; f. 1951 by UNESCO and OAS to encourage literacy and rural development through adult education and co-operative research; library of 60,000 vols. Dir Dr TOMAS MIKLOS. Publ. *Retablos de Papel, Cuadernos del CREFAL*.

Southeast Asian Ministers of Education Organization —SEAMEO: Darakarn Bldg, 920 Sukhumvit Rd, Bangkok 10110, Thailand; tel. 391 0144; f. 1965 to promote co-operation among the Southeast Asian nations through education, science and culture, and to advance the mutual knowledge and understanding of the peoples in Southeast Asia. Mems: Brunei, Indonesia, Kampuchea, Laos, Malaysia, the Philippines, Singapore and Thailand; Assoc. mems: Australia, France and New Zealand; Affiliate mem.: Asscn of Canadian Community Colleges. Pres. ABDUL AZIZ UMAR (Brunei);

Dir Prof. Dr ADUL WICHIENCHAROEN. Publs *SEAMEO Quarterly*, Reports of Conferences and Seminars, Journals and Newsletters of SEAMEO Regional Centres/Projects.

Standing Conference of Rectors and Vice-Chancellors of the European Universities (Conférence permanente des recteurs, présidents et vice-chanceliers des universités européennes—CRE): 10 rue du Conseil Général, 1211 Geneva 4, Switzerland; tel. (022) 292644; telex 428380; f. 1959; holds two conferences a year, a General Assembly every five years and ad hoc seminars. Mems: 360 university heads in 23 countries. Pres. Prof. CARMINE ROMANZI; Sec.-Gen. Dr ANDRIS BARBLAN; Asst Sec.-Gen. ALISON M. DE PUYMÈGE. Publ. *CRE-Information* (4 a year).

Union of Latin American Universities (Unión de Universidades de América Latina—UDUAL): Edificio UDUAL, Apdo postal 70-232, Ciudad Universitaria, 04510 México, Mexico; tel. 548-9786; telex 1777429; f. 1949 to further the improvement of university association, to organize the interchange of professors, students, research fellows and graduates and generally encourage good relations between the Latin American universities; arranges conferences, conducts statistical research; centre for university documentation. Mems: 155 universities. Pres. Dr JORGE CARPIZO (Mexico); Sec.-Gen. Dr JOSÉ LUIS SOBERANES. Publs reports and proceedings of conferences, *Universidades* (annually), *Gaceta UDUAL* (quarterly), *Censo* (every 2 years).

United Schools International: USO House, 6 Special Institutional Area, New Delhi 110067, India; tel. 661103; f. 1961 to promote teaching in the schools of the world about the various aspects of the UN and the UN specialized agencies, to create support for the UN in furthering international peace and co-operation among nations and to encourage the free exchange of views, information and correspondence between school children. Mems in 34 countries. Pres. M. VIJAYAVARDHANA (Sri Lanka); Sec.-Gen. JIYA LAL JAIN (India). Publ. *World Informo* (monthly), *Workshop of Peace* (every 2 months).

Universal Esperanto Association: Nieuwe Binnenweg 176, 3015 BJ Rotterdam, Netherlands; tel. (010) 4361044; telex 23721; f. 1908 to assist the spread of the international language, Esperanto, and to facilitate the practical use of the language. Mems: 45 affiliated national associations and 39,556 individuals in 98 countries. Pres. GRÉGOIRE MAERTENS (Belgium); Gen. Sec. Dr FLORÁ SZABÓ-FELSÖ (Hungary). Publs *Esperanto* (monthly, except August), *Kontakto* (every 2 months), *Jarlibro* (yearbook), *Esperanto Documents*.

World Association for Educational Research: Rijksuniversiteit Gent, Pedagogisch Laboratorium, 1 Henri Dunantlaan, 9000 Ghent, Belgium; tel. (91) 25-41-00; f. 1953, present title adopted 1977; aims to encourage research in educational sciences by organizing congress, issuing publications, the exchange of information, etc. Member societies and individual members in 50 countries. Pres. Prof. Dr ARTURO DE LA ORDÉN (Spain); Gen. Sec. Prof. Dr M.-L. VAN HERREWEGHE (Belgium). Publ. *Communicationes* (2 a year).

World Confederation of Organizations of the Teaching Profession: 5 ave du Moulin, 1110 Morges, Vaud, Switzerland; tel. (021) 717467; telex 458 219; f. 1952 to foster a conception of education directed toward the promotion of international understanding and goodwill; to improve teaching methods, educational organization and the training of teachers to equip them better to serve the interests of youth; to defend the rights and the material and moral interests of the teaching profession; to promote closer relationships between teachers in different countries. Mems: 152 national teachers' associations in 101 countries. Pres. JOSEPH O. ITOTOH; Sec.-Gen. NORMAN M. GOBLE. Publs *WCOTP Reports* (in English, French, Spanish), *Echo* (quarterly, in English, French, Spanish, Japanese, Chinese and German).

World Education Fellowship: 33 Kinnaird Ave, London, W4 3SH, England; tel. (01) 994-7258; f. 1921 to promote education for international understanding, and the exchange and practice of ideas together with research into progressive educational theories and methods. Sections and groups in 20 countries. Pres. Mrs MADHURI R. SHAH; Chair. Prof. NORMAN GRAVES; Sec. Mrs R. CROMMELIN. Publ. *The New Era* (4 a year).

World Union of Catholic Teachers (Union Mondiale des Enseignants Catholiques—UMEC): Piazza San Calisto 16, Rome, Italy; f. 1951. Objects: (1) on the national level, the Union encourages the grouping of Catholic teachers for the greater effectiveness of the Catholic school, distributes documentation on Catholic doctrine with regard to education, and facilitates personal contacts through congresses, seminars, etc.; (2) on the international level, the Union is a member of the Conference of International Catholic Organizations, and has consultative status with UNESCO, ECOSOC, IBE, ILO and with a number of non-governmental organizations. Mems: 45 organizations in 35 countries. Pres. OSVALDO BRIVIO; Sec.-Gen. BRUNO VOTA. Publ. *Nouvelles de l'UMEC*.

Government and Politics

African Association for Public Administration and Management: POB 60087, Addis Ababa, Ethiopia; tel. 150389; telex 21029; f. 1971 to provide senior officials with opportunities for exchanging ideas and experience, to promote the study of professional techniques and encourage research in particular African administrative problems. Mems: over 500 corporate and individual. Pres WILLIAM N. WAMALWA; Sec.-Gen. CORNELIUS K. DZAKPASU. Publs *Newsletter* (quarterly), *Annual Seminar Report*, studies.

Afro-Asian Peoples' Solidarity Organization—AAPSO: 89 Abdel Aziz Al-Saoud St, Manial, Cairo, Egypt; tel. 845495; telex 92627; f. 1957; acts among and for the peoples of Africa and Asia in their struggle for genuine independence, sovereignty, socio-economic development, peace and disarmament; sixth Congress held in 1984 (the first since 1972); has consultative status with ECOSOC (UN), UNCTAD, UNESCO and UNIDO, observer status with the Non-aligned Movement. Mems: 82 national committees from African and Asian countries, and 10 European organizations as associate mems. Sec.-Gen. NOURI ABDEL RAZZAK (Iraq). Publs Afro-Asian Publications series, *Socio-Economic Development and Progress* (quarterly).

Agency for the Prohibition of Nuclear Weapons in Latin America (Organismo para la Proscripción de las Armas Nucleares en la América Latina—OPANAL): Temístocles 78, Col. Polanco, CP 011560, México, DF, Mexico; tel. 250-62-22; f. 1969 to administer the Treaty for the Prohibition of Nuclear Weapons in Latin America (Treaty of Tlatelolco), 1967; to ensure the absence of all nuclear weapons in the application zone of the Treaty; to provide protection against possible nuclear attacks on the zone; to contribute to the movement against proliferation of nuclear weapons; to promote general and complete disarmament; to prohibit all testing, use, manufacture, acquisition, storage, installation and any form of possession, by any means, of nuclear weapons. Mems: 23 states which have fully ratified the Treaty. The Treaty has two additional Protocols; the first signed and ratified by the UK, the Netherlands and the USA, and signed by France; the second signed and ratified by China, the USA, France, the UK and the USSR. Sec.-Gen. Dr ANTONIO STEMPEL PARÍS (Venezuela).

Association of Secretaries General of Parliaments: c/o Table Office, House of Commons, London, SW1, England; f. 1938; studies the law, practice and working methods of different Parliaments and proposes measures for improving those methods and for securing co-operation between the services of different Parliaments; operates as a consultative body to the Inter-Parliamentary Union (q.v.), and assists the Union on subjects within the scope of the Association. Mems: about 125, representing about 60 countries. Pres. W. KOOPS (Netherlands); Vice-Pres. K. BRADSHAW (UK), H. HAYATOU (Cameroon). Publ. *Constitutional and Parliamentary Information* (quarterly).

Atlantic Institute for International Affairs (Institut atlantique des affaires internationales): 9 ave Hoche, 75008 Paris, France; tel. (1) 42-25-58-17; f. 1961; aims to provide timely, reasoned analysis, to promote informed discussion and to make practical recommendations on problems common to the advanced industrial countries of the world in their relations with each other and with developing and Communist countries; 22 countries are represented on the Board of Governors and leading firms in these countries are participating members. Chair. WILFRIED GUTH; Dir-Gen. RICHARD D. VINE. Publs *The Atlantic Papers* (English), *Research Volumes* (English).

Atlantic Treaty Association: 185 rue de la Pompe, 75116 Paris, France; tel. (1) 45-53-28-80; f. 1954 to inform public opinion on the North Atlantic Alliance and to promote the solidarity of the peoples of the North Atlantic; holds annual assemblies, seminars, study conferences for teachers and young politicians. Mems: national associations in the 16 NATO countries (see p. 179). Chair. FRANCIS PYM; Sec.-Gen. JEAN BELIARD (France).

Celtic League: 24 St Germains Place, Peel, Isle of Man; f. 1961 to foster co-operation between the six Celtic nations (Ireland, Scotland, Man, Wales, Cornwall and Brittany), especially those who are actively working for political autonomy by non-violent means. Mems: approx. 1,500 individuals in the Celtic communities and elsewhere. Chair. MICHEAL MAC AONGHUSA (Ireland); Gen. Sec. BERNARD MOFFATT (Isle of Man). Publ. *Carn* (quarterly).

Christian Democratic World Union: Via del Plebiscito 107, 00186 Rome, Italy; tel. 06-6782064; telex 611356; f. 1961 (as the World Union of Christian Democratic Parties, Movements and International Organizations) to serve as a platform for the co-operation of political parties of Christian Social inspiration. Mems: 53 parties in four continents. Pres. ANDRÉS ZALDIVAR (Chile); Sec.-Gen. ANGELO BERNASSOLA (Italy). Publ. *IDC-News* (monthly, in five languages).

Confederation of Socialist Parties of the European Community: 3 blvd de l'Empéreur, 1000 Brussels, Belgium; tel. (02) 512-51-21; telex 62184; f. 1974; affiliated to the Socialist International (q.v.). Mems: 14 parties (including those of Portugal and Spain). Chair. JOOP DEN UYL (Netherlands); Sec.-Gen. MAURO GIALLOMBARDO.

Contadora Group: c/o Secretariat for Foreign Affairs, México, DF, Mexico; comprises representatives of Colombia, Mexico, Panama and Venezuela, with a 'support group' representing Argentina, Brazil, Peru and Uruguay; first met January 1983 on the island of Contadora, Panama, to seek a peaceful solution to conflict in the countries of Central America (Costa Rica, El Salvador, Guatemala, Honduras and Nicaragua) through negotiating the withdrawal of external and irregular military forces and the holding of democratic elections. In September 1984 the Group submitted a draft agreement, the 'Acta de Contadora para la paz y la cooperación en Centroamérica', to the Central American countries. Subsequent discussion failed to resolve questions of arms control and demilitarization in the region, and in 1986 the June deadline for signing a regional peace treaty passed without agreement, although a summit meeting of Central American leaders, held in May, agreed to establish a Central American parliament. In November Costa Rica announced that it would not participate in future Contadora meetings while proceedings instituted by Nicaragua against Costa Rica in the International Court of Justice were under way. (See chapters on the countries concerned.)

Eastern Regional Organization for Public Administration—EROPA: Rizal Hall, Padre Faura St, Manila, Philippines; f. 1960 to promote regional co-operation in improving knowledge, systems and practices of governmental administration to help accelerate economic and social development; organizes regional conferences, seminars, special studies, surveys and training programmes. There are three regional centres: Training Centre (New Delhi), Local Government Centre (Tokyo), Organization and Management Centre (Seoul). Mems: 11 countries, 57 organizations, 159 individuals. Chair. Dr SONDANG P. SIAGIAN (Indonesia); Sec.-Gen. RAUL P. DE GUZMAN (Philippines).

European Movement: 47-49 rue de Toulouse, 1040 Brussels, Belgium; tel. (02) 230-08-51; f. 1947 by a liaison committee of representatives from European organizations, to study the political, economic and technical problems of a European Union and suggest how they can be solved; to inform and lead public opinion in the promotion of integration. Consists of a Federal Council, an Executive Committee and a Directive Committee, all composed of representatives of national councils and member organizations. Conferences have led to the creation of the Council of Europe, College of Europe, etc. Mems: European movements and national councils in Austria, Belgium, Denmark, France, Federal Republic of Germany, Greece, Ireland, Italy, Luxembourg, Malta, Netherlands, Norway, Spain, Sweden, Switzerland, United Kingdom and several international social and economic organizations. Pres. GASTON THORN (Luxembourg); Sec.-Gen. LUIGI VITTORIO MAJOCCHI (Italy).

EUROGROUP: f. 1968; an informal grouping of European countries within the NATO alliance, aiming to ensure that the European contribution to the common defence is as cohesive and effective as possible; defence ministers meet annually; sub-groups deal with collaboration in procurement of defence equipment, communications, military medicine, logistics and training. Mems: 11 NATO countries (see p. 179).

European Union of Women—EUW: Nymphenburger Str 64, 8000 Munich, Federal Republic of Germany; f. 1955 to increase the influence of women in the political and civic life of their country and of Europe. Mems: 16 member countries. Chair. URSULA SCHLEICHER. Publ. *Bulletin* (biennial).

European Young Christian Democrats—EYCD: 2 place de l'Albertine, 1000 Brussels, Belgium; tel. (02) 512-56-98; telex 63885; f. 1947; holds monthly seminars and meetings for young political leaders; conducts training in international political matters. Mems: 20 organizations in 18 European countries, Pres. ANDREA DE GUTTRY (Italy); Sec.-Gen. FILIPPO LOMBARDI (Switzerland). Publ. *Newsletter* (monthly).

Hansard Society for Parliamentary Government: 16 Gower St, London, WC1E 6DP, England; tel. (01) 323-1131; f. 1944 to promote political education and research and the informed discussion of all aspects of modern parliamentary government. Gen. Sec. MARY GOUDIE. Publ. *Parliamentary Affairs—A Journal of Comparative Politics* (quarterly), reports and teaching aids.

Inter-African Socialist Organization (Interafricaine socialiste): c/o Parti Socialiste Destourien, blvd 9 avril 55, Tunis, Tunisia; f. 1981. Mems: 13 parties in Chad, Comoros, Djibouti, Egypt, The Gambia, Mauritius, Morocco, Senegal, Somalia and Tunisia. Chair. LÉOPOLD SENGHOR (Senegal); Sec.-Gen. HEDI BACCOUCHE (Tunisia).

Inter-Parliamentary Union: place du Petit-Saconnex, CP 438, 1211 Geneva 19, Switzerland; tel. (022) 344150; telex 289784; f. 1889 to promote personal contacts among the members of the world's parliaments, with a view to the firm establishment and development of representative institutions and to advancing international peace and co-operation; holds two conferences annually, bringing together national groups of members of parliament to study political, economic, social and cultural problems of international significance; there are four Committees comprising representatives of all national groups. The Union operates an International Centre for Parliamentary Documentation, and co-ordinates a technical co-operation programme to help strengthen the infrastructures of legislatures in developing countries. Budget (1986): 5.3m. Swiss francs. Mems: 105 Inter-Parliamentary Groups. Pres. of Inter-Parliamentary Council H. STERCKEN (FRG); Sec.-Gen. PIO-CARLO TERENZIO (Italy). Publs. *Inter-Parliamentary Bulletin* (quarterly), *World Directory of Parliaments* (annually), *Chronicle of Parliamentary Elections and Developments* (annually), *Parliaments of the World: A Reference Compendium*, reports, conference proceedings.

International Alliance of Women: 1st Floor, Jeb Wing, Regent's College, Inner Circle, Regent's Park, London, NW1 9NS, England; tel. (01) 935-6592; f. 1904 to obtain equality for women in all fields and to encourage women to take up their responsibilities; to join in international activities. Mems: 75 national affiliates in 65 countries. Pres. Mrs OLIVE BLOOMER. Publ. *International Women's News* (quarterly).

International Association of Educators for World Peace: POB 3282, Mastin Lake Station, Huntsville, Alabama 35810, USA; tel. (205) 534-5501; f. 1969 to develop the kind of education which will contribute to the promotion of peaceful relations at personal, community and international levels, to communicate and clarify controversial views in order to achieve maximum understanding and to help put into practice the Universal Declaration of Human Rights. Mems: 17,500 in 52 countries. Pres. Dr P. ACHAVA AMRUNG (Thailand); Vice-Pres. Dr CHARLES MERCIECA (USA); Sec.-Gen. Dr GEORGE VAIDEANU (Romania). Publs *Peace Progress* (annually), *IAEWP Newsletter* (quarterly), *Peace Education* (2 a year).

International Commission for the History of Representative and Parliamentary Institutions: c/o M. Scorciulo, Via Q. Baldassarri 25, 00139 Rome, Italy; tel. (06) 8125156; f. 1936. Mems: 300 individuals in 31 countries. Pres. S. MASTELLONE (Italy); Sec. M. SCORCIULO (Italy). Publs *Parliaments, Estates and Representation*; many monographs.

International Federation of Resistance Movements: 1021 Vienna II, Alliiertenstrasse 2-4/5, Austria; tel. (022) 247135; f. 1951; supports the medical and social welfare of former victims of fascism; works for peace, disarmament and human rights, against fascism and neo-fascism; has consultative status at UN Economic and Social Council and UNESCO. Mems: 68 national organizations in 25 European countries and in Israel. Pres. ARIALDO BANFI (Italy); Sec.-Gen. ALIX LHOTE (France). Publs *Résistance Unie—Service d'Information* (in French and German; monthly), *Cahier d'informations médicales, sociales et juridiques* (in French and German).

International Institute for Peace: 1040 Vienna, Mollwaldplatz 4, Austria; f. 1957; studies the possibilities, principles and forms of peaceful co-existence and co-operation between the two social world systems. Mems: individuals and corporate bodies invited by the executive board. Pres. Dr GEORG FUCHS (Austria); Vice-Pres. Prof. Dr RAIMO VÄYRYNEN (Finland), Prof. Dr OLEG BYKOV (USSR). Publ. *Peace and the Sciences* (in English and German).

International Institute for Strategic Studies: 23 Tavistock St, London, WC2E 7NQ, England; tel. (01) 379-7676; f. 1958; concerned with the study of the role of force in international relations, including problems of international strategy, disarmament and arms control, peace-keeping and intervention, defence economics, etc.; is independent of any government. Mems: 2,500. Dir Dr ROBERT O'NEILL. Publs *Survival* (every 2 months), *The*

Military Balance (annually), *Strategic Survey* (annually), *Adelphi Papers* (10 a year), *Studies in International Security* (occasional), IISS paperbacks (occasional).

International League for Human Rights: 432 Park Avenue South, 11th Floor, New York, NY 10016, USA; tel. (212) 684-1221; f. 1942 to implement political, civil, social, economic and cultural rights contained in the Universal Declaration of Human Rights adopted by the United Nations and to support and protect defenders of human rights world-wide. Maintains consultative relations with UN, ILO, UNESCO and the Council of Europe. Mems: individuals, national affiliates and correspondents throughout the world. Pres. JEROME J. SHESTACK; Hon. Pres. ANDREI D. SAKHAROV (USSR); Exec. Dir FELICE D. GAER. Publs *Review, Human Rights Bulletin*, human rights reports.

International Peace Bureau: 41 rue de Zürich, 1200 Geneva, Switzerland; f. 1892; promotes international co-operation for general and complete disarmament and the non-violent solution of international conflicts; the Bureau was awarded the Nobel Peace Prize in 1910. Mems: international organizations, national peace councils or other federations co-ordinating peace movements in their respective countries, national and local organizations, totalling 35 organizations with a total affiliated membership of about 30 million. Pres. SÉAN MACBRIDE; Chair. Venerable G. N. SATO; Sec.-Gen. GERD GREUNE; Treas. LOTHAR BELCK. Publ. *Co-operation for Disarmament* (monthly).

International Political Science Association: c/o University of Ottawa, Ottawa, Ontario K1N 6N5, Canada; tel. (613) 564-5818; telex 053-3338; f. 1949; aims to promote the development of political science. Mems: 38 national associations, 90 institutions, 1,000 individual mems. Pres. KINHIDE MUSHAKOJI (Japan); Sec.-Gen. JOHN E. TRENT (University of Ottawa, Ottawa, Ont. K1N 6N5, Canada). Publs *Newsletter* (3 a year), *Information Supplement* (annually), *International Political Science Abstracts* (bi-monthly), *International Political Science Review* (quarterly).

International Union of Local Authorities: Wassenaarseweg 41, 2596 CG The Hague, Netherlands; tel. (070) 244032; telex 32504; f. 1913 to promote local government, improve local administration and encourage popular participation in public affairs. Functions include organization of conferences, seminars, and biennial international congress; servicing of specialized committees (municipal insurance, wholesale markets, European affairs, technical); research projects; comparative courses for local government officials, primarily from developing countries; development of intermunicipal relations to provide a link between local authorities of all countries; maintenance of a permanent office for the collection and distribution of information on municipal affairs. Members in over 65 countries. Pres. LARS ERIC ERICSSON (Sweden); Sec.-Gen. J. G. VAN PUTTEN. Publs *Local Government* (monthly newsletter), *Bibliographia* (bi-monthly), *Planning and Administration* (2 a year), preparatory reports and proceedings of conferences, reports of study groups.

International Union of Young Christian Democrats—IUYCD: Via del Plebiscito 107, 00186 Rome, Italy; f. 1962. Mems: 51 national organizations. Pres. MILOS ALCALAY (Venezuela); Sec.-Gen. GIANFRANCO ASTORI (Italy). Publs *Information* (monthly), *Documents* (quarterly).

Inuit Circumpolar Conference: Box 204, Godthåb, Greenland; tel. 23632; telex 90671; f. 1977 to protect the indigenous culture, environment and rights of the Inuit people (Eskimoes), and to encourage co-operation among the Inuit; conferences held every three years. Mems: Inuit communities in Canada, Greenland and Alaska. Pres. HANS-PAVIA ROSING.

Jewish Agency for Israel: POB 92, Jerusalem, Israel; f. 1929 as an instrument through which world Jewry could build up a national home. It is now the executive arm of the World Zionist Organization. Mems: Zionist federations in 61 countries. Exec. Chair. LEON DULZIN; Chair. of Board of Govs JEROLD C. HOFFBERGER; Dir-Gen. SHLOMO TADMOR; Sec.-Gen. HARRY M. ROSEN. Publs *Israel Digest* (weekly), *Economic Horizons* (monthly in USA), *Folk and Zion* (monthly in Yiddish).

Latin American Parliament (Parlamento Latinoamericano): Carrera 7a, No. 12-25 P. 7, Bogotá, Colombia; f. 1965; permanent democratic institution, representative of all existing political trends within the national legislative bodies of Latin America; aims to promote the movement towards economic, political and cultural integration of the Latin American republics, and to uphold human rights, peace and security. Pres. GILBERTO AVILA BOTTIA (Colombia); Sec.-Gen. ANDRÉS TOWNSEND EZCURRA (Peru). Publs *Acuerdos, Resoluciones de las Asambleas Ordinarias* (annually), *Revista del Parlamento Latinoamericano* (annually); statements and agreements.

Liberal International: 1 Whitehall Place, London, SW1A 2HE, England; tel. (01) 839-5905; telex 8956551; f. 1947 to bring together people of liberal ideas and principles (not necessarily directly engaged in politics) all over the world and to secure international co-operation amongst the political parties which accept the Manifesto (1947), the Liberal Declaration of Oxford (1967) and the Appeal of Rome (1981), and are affiliated to the International. Pres. Senator GIOVANNI MALAGODI (Italy); Exec. Vice-Pres. URS SCHÖTTLI (Switzerland). Publs general political literature, including *Experiment in Internationalism*.

Non-aligned Movement: Co-ordination Bureau, ul. Kneza Miloša 24, 11000 Belgrade, Yugoslavia; f. 1961 by a meeting of 25 Heads of State, aiming to link countries which refuse to adhere to the main East-West military and political blocs; co-ordination bureau established in 1973; works for the establishment of a new international economic order, and especially for better terms for countries producing raw materials; maintains special funds for agricultural development, improvement of food production and the financing of buffer stocks. Eighth summit conference: Harare, Zimbabwe, September 1986. Mems: 102 countries.

North Atlantic Assembly: 3 place du Petit Sablon, Brussels, Belgium; tel. (02) 513-28-65; telex 24809; f. 1955 as the NATO Parliamentarians' Conference; name changed 1966; the inter-parliamentary assembly of the North Atlantic Alliance; holds two plenary sessions a year and meetings of committees (Political, Military, Economic, Scientific and Technical, Civilian Affairs, Special Committee on Nuclear Strategy and Arms Control) where North Americans and Europeans examine the problems confronting the Alliance. Pres. T. FRINKING (Netherlands); Sec.-Gen. PHILIPPE DESHORMES (Belgium). Publs *Annual Report*, committee reports, *North Atlantic Assembly News, Bulletin of the Committee on Civilian Affairs*.

Open Door International (for the Economic Emancipation of the Woman Worker); 16 rue Américaine, 1050 Brussels, Belgium; tel. (02) 537-67-61; f. 1929 to obtain equal rights and opportunities for women in the whole field of work. Mems in 10 countries. Pres. ESTHER HODGE (UK); Hon. Sec. ADÈLE HAUWEL (Belgium). Publs Reports, Circular Letters.

Organization of Central American States (Organización de Estados Centroamericanos—ODECA): Oficina Centroamericana, Pino Alto, Paseo Escalón, San Salvador, El Salvador; f. 1951 to strengthen unity in Central America, settle disputes, provide mutual assistance and promote economic, social and cultural development through joint action. Mems: Costa Rica, El Salvador, Guatemala, Honduras, Nicaragua. Gen. Sec. RICARDO JUÁREZ MÁRQUEZ (Guatemala).

Organization of the Cooperatives of America (Organización de las Cooperativas de América): Carrera 10A, No 15-22, Of. 103, Apdo Postal 241263, Bogotá, DE, Colombia; tel. 2867626; telex 45103; f. 1963 for improving socio-economic, cultural and moral conditions through the use of the co-operatives system; works in every country of the continent; regional offices sponsor plans of activities based on the most pressing needs and special conditions of individual countries. Mems: 7,000. Pres. Dr ARMANDO TOVAR PARADA; Exec. Sec. CARLOS JULIO PINEDA. Publ. *Cooperative America* (every 4 months, in Spanish).

Organization of Solidarity of the Peoples of Africa, Asia and Latin America (Organización de Solidaridad de los Pueblos de Africa, Asia y América Latina—OSPAAAL): Apdo 4224, Havana, Cuba; tel. 30-5520; telex 512259; f. 1966 at the first Conference of Solidarity of the Peoples of Africa, Asia and Latin America, to unite, co-ordinate and encourage national liberation movements in the three continents, to oppose foreign intervention in the affairs of sovereign states, and to fight against racialism and all forms of racial discrimination. Mems: revolutionary organizations in 82 countries. Sec.-Gen. Dr RENÉ ANILLO CAPOTE. Publ. *Tricontinental* (every 2 months, in English, French and Spanish).

Pan-European Union: 1 place de la Louve, 1003 Lausanne, Switzerland; f. 1923; aims to establish the United States of Europe with common trade, economic, foreign and defence policies, based on European patriotism respecting all national cultures having their own personality as a free, united and independent world power. First Congress, Vienna, Austria, 1926; 12th Congress, Aachen, Federal Republic of Germany, 1976. Mems: 17 organizations in 12 countries. Pres. HRH Archduke OTTO VON HABSBURG; Vice-Pres. PIERRE GRÉGOIRE (Luxembourg), JOACHIM VON MERKATZ (FRG), ROGER CHINAUD (France); Gen. Sec. Dr VITTORIO PONS. Publ. *Paneuropa* (monthly).

Parliamentary Association for Euro-Arab Co-operation: 20 rue Tournon, 75006 Paris, France; tel. (1) 43-26-44-20; f. 1974 to work for peace with justice in the Middle East and to improve relations between Europe and the Arab world; holds annual meeting alternately in an Arab and a European capital; holds Euro-Arab working groups between members of the European Parliament and Arab ambassadors accredited to the European Community; participates in international conferences. Mems: 650 mems from national parliaments of countries which belong to the Council of Europe, and from the European Parliament. Chair. MICHAEL LANIGAN (Ireland), RAFAEL ESTRELLA (Spain); Sec.-Gen. ROBERT SWANN.

Socialist International: Maritime House, Old Town, Clapham, London, SW4 0JW, England; tel. (01) 627-4449; telex 261735; f. 1864; the world's oldest and largest association of political parties, grouping democratic socialist, labour and social democratic parties from every continent; provides a forum for political action, policy discussion and the exchange of ideas; works with many international organizations and trades unions (particularly members of ICFTU, q.v.); holds Congress every two years; the Bureau meets twice a year, and regular conferences and meetings of party leaders are also held; committees and councils on a variety of subjects and in different regions meet frequently. Mems: 49 full member parties and 17 consultative parties in 59 countries. There are three fraternal organizations (see below) and eight associated organizations, including: the Asia-Pacific Socialist Organization; the Confederation of Socialist Parties of the European Community (q.v.); and the International Federation of the Socialist and Democratic Press (q.v.). Pres. WILLY BRANDT (FRG); Gen. Sec. PENTTI VAANANEN; Asst ROBIN V. SEARS; Sec. for Latin America and the Caribbean LUIS AYALA. Publ. *Socialist Affairs* (quarterly).

International Falcon Movement—Socialist Educational International: 13 place du Samedi, 1000 Brussels, Belgium; tel. (02) 217-97-86; f. 1924 to promote international understanding, develop a sense of social responsibility and to prepare children and adolescents for democratic life. The Movement has consultative status with ECOSOC, UNESCO and Council of Europe and co-operates with several institutions concerned with children, youth and education. Mems: about 1m.; 62 co-operating organizations in all countries. Pres. NIC NILLSON (Sweden); Sec.-Gen. JACQUI COTTYN (Belgium). Publs *IFM-SEI Bulletin* (quarterly in English, French, German, Spanish, Finnish and Swedish), *IFM-SEI Documents* (in the same languages).

International Union of Socialist Youth: 1070 Vienna, Neustiftgasse 3, Austria; f. 1946 to educate young people in the principles of free and democratic socialism and further the co-operation of democratic socialist youth organizations; conducts international meetings, symposia, etc. Mems: 64 youth and student organizations in 47 countries. Pres. JOAN CALABUIG; Gen. Sec. DIRK DRIJBOOMS. Publ. *IUSY Bulletin*.

Socialist International Women: Maritime House, Old Town, Clapham, London, SW4 0JW, England; tel. (01) 627-4449; telex 261735; f. 1955 to strengthen relations between its members, to exchange experience and views, to promote the understanding among women of the aims of democratic socialism, to promote programmes to oppose any discrimination in society and to work for human rights in general and for development and peace. Mems: 57 organizations. Pres. ANITA GRADIN; Gen. Sec. MARÍA RODRÍGUEZ-JONAS. Publ. *Bulletin* (quarterly).

Stockholm International Peace Research Institute—SIPRI: Pipers väg 28, 171 73 Solna, Sweden; tel. 46 8 559700; f. 1966; particular attention is given to disarmament and arms control. About 55 staff mems, half of whom are research workers. Dir Dr WALTHER STÜTZLE (FRG); Chair. ERNST MICHANEK (Sweden). Publs *SIPRI Yearbook, Monographs,* and research reports.

Trilateral Commission: 345 East 46th St, New York, NY 10017, USA; tel. (212) 661-1180; telex 424787; (also offices in Paris and Tokyo); f. 1973 by private citizens of Western Europe, Japan and North America, to encourage closer co-operation among these regions on matters of common concern; by analysis of major issues the Commission seeks to improve public understanding of such problems, to develop and support proposals for handling them jointly, and to nurture the habit of working together in the 'trilateral' area. The Commission issues 'task force' reports on such subjects as monetary affairs, political co-operation, trade issues, the energy crisis and reform of international institutions. Mems: about 300 individuals eminent in academic life, industry, finance, labour, etc.; top government officials are excluded. Chairmen DAVID ROCKEFELLER, GEORGES BERTHOIN, TAKESHI WATANABE; Dirs CHARLES B. HECK, PAUL REVAY, TADASHI YAMAMOTO. Publs Task Force Reports.

Union of European Federalists: 49 rue de Toulouse, 1040 Brussels, Belgium; tel. (02) 230-04-16; f. 1946 to promote the creation of a European federation exercising limited powers through a federal government, an elected assembly, a federal senate and a court of justice. Mems: individuals in 10 countries. Pres. JOHN PINDER; Sec.-Gen. CATERINA CHIZZOLA.

War Resisters' International: 55 Dawes St, London, SE17 1EL, England; tel. (01) 703-7189; f. 1921; encourages refusal to participate in or support wars or military service, collaborates with peace and non-violent social change movements. Mems: approx. 200,000. Chair. DAVID MCREYNOLDS; Sec. HOWARD CLARK. Publs *Newsletter* (6 a year in English) and occasional pamphlets.

Women's International Democratic Federation: 1080 Berlin, Unter den Linden 13, German Democratic Republic; f. 1945 to unite women regardless of nationality, race, religion and political opinion, so that they may work together to win and defend their rights as citizens, mothers and workers, to protect children and to ensure peace and progress, democracy and national independence. Structure: Congress, Council, Bureau, Secretariat and Finance Control Commission. Mems: 135 organizations in 117 countries as well as individual mems. Pres. FREDA BROWN (Australia); Sec.-Gen. MIRJAM VIRE-TUOMINEN (Finland). Publs *Women of the Whole World* (quarterly in 6 languages), *Documents and Information, News in Brief, Women in Action* (4 languages).

World Association of World Federalists: Leliegracht 21, 1016 GR Amsterdam, Netherlands; tel. (020) 227502; f. 1947 to achieve a just world order through a strengthened United Nations; to acquire for the UN the authority to make and enforce laws for peaceful settlement of disputes, to govern the high seas and outer space, and to raise revenue under limited taxing powers; to establish better international co-operation in areas of environment, development and disarmament. Congresses have been held in many cities. Mems: 25,000 in 20 countries. Pres. HERMOD LANNUNG; Exec. Dir RON J. RUTHERGLEN. Publs *World Federalist News* (quarterly).

World Council of Indigenous Peoples: 555 King Edward Ave, Ottawa, Ontario K1N 6N5, Canada; tel. (613) 230-9030; telex 0533338; f. 1975 to strengthen the political and cultural organizations of indigenous peoples and combat racism. Mems in 26 countries.

World Disarmament Campaign: 45–47 Blythe St, London, E2 6LX, England; tel. (01) 729-2523; f. 1980 to encourage governments to take positive and decisive action to end the arms race, acting on the four main commitments called for in the Final Document of the UN's First Special Session on Disarmament; aims to mobilize people of every country in a demand for multilateral disarmament, and to encourage consideration of alternatives to the nuclear deterrent for ensuring world security. Pres. Lord (FENNER) BROCKWAY; Chair. Dr FRANK BARNABY, Dr TONY HART.

World Federation of United Nations Associations—WFUNA: c/o Palais des Nations, 1211 Geneva 10, Switzerland; tel. (022) 330730; telex 289696; f. 1946 to encourage popular interest and participation in United Nations programmes, discussion of the role and future of the UN, and education for international understanding. Plenary Assembly meets every two years, supreme organ of WFUNA; Exec. Committee of 17 representatives responsible for execution of policy decisions, administration and finance; Secretariat responsible for administration. WFUNA founded International Youth and Student Movement for the United Nations (see p. 276); has consultative status with ECOSOC and UNESCO and consultative relations with other Specialized Agencies. Pres. Dr DAVIDSON NICOL (Sierra Leone); Chair. Exec. Cttee Prof. Dr KLAUS HÜFNER (FRG); Sec.-Gen. Dr MAREK HAGMAJER (Poland). Publ. *WFUNA Bulletin* (quarterly).

World Peace Council: Lönnrotinkatu 25A/VI, SF 00180 Helsinki 18, Finland; tel. 649004; telex 121680; f. 1950 at the Second World Peace Congress, Warsaw. Principles: the prevention of nuclear war; the peaceful co-existence of the various socio-economic systems in the world; settlement of differences between nations by negotiation and agreement; complete disarmament; elimination of colonialism and racial discrimination; respect for the right of peoples to sovereignty and independence; status as a non-governmental organization with UN, UNESCO, UNCTAD, UNIDO, ILO. Mems: Representatives of c. 2,500 political parties and national organizations from 141 countries, and of 30 international organizations; Presidential Committee of 228 mems elected by the Council. Pres. ROMESH CHANDRA. Publs *New Perspectives* (every 2 months), *Peace Courier* (monthly) and pamphlets in four languages.

Industrial and Professional Relations

See also the chapters on ICFTU, WCL and WFTU.

Alliance Graphique Internationale—AGI: Sonnhaldenstr. 3, 8032 Zürich, Switzerland; f. 1949. Mems: national organizations of graphic designers in 24 countries. Pres. MASSIMO VIGNELLI (USA); Gen. Sec. FRITZ GOTTSCHALK (Switzerland). Publ. *Bulletin.*

Arab Federation of Petroleum, Mining and Chemicals Workers: 5 Zaki St, Cairo, Egypt; tel. 52257; f. 1961; runs the Arab Petroleum Institute for Labour Studies, Cairo. Mems: 18 affiliated unions in 12 countries. Sec.-Gen. ANWAR ASHMAWI MOHAMED (Egypt). Publs *Arab Petroleum* (monthly), specialized publications and statistics.

Association for Systems Management: 24587 Bagley Rd, Cleveland, Ohio 44138, USA; tel. (216) 243-6900; f. 1947; an international professional organization for the advancement and self-renewal of management information systems analysis throughout business and industry. Mems: 10,000 in 35 countries. Pres. JAMES T. HERLIKY; Exec. Dir RICHARD L. IRWIN. Publ. *Journal of Systems Management.*

Caribbean Congress of Labour: Room 405, Norman Centre, Broad St, Bridgetown, Barbados; tel. 429-5517; f. 1960 to fight for the recognition of trade union organizations; to build and strengthen the ties between the Free Trade Unions of the Caribbean and the rest of the world; to support the work of ICFTU (q.v.); to encourage the formation of national groupings and centres. Mems: 26 in 17 countries. Pres. LEONARD ARCHER (Bahamas); Sec.-Treas. KERTIST AUGUSTUS (Dominica).

Council of the Professional Photographers of Europe—EUROPHOT: 40 rue Washington, 1050 Brussels, Belgium; f. 1954 to widen the exchange of experience at international level, to publicize the photography of the best professional photographers and publish the results of tests on equipment, to create a Europhot copyright, a European basic tariff and an international information centre, and to collaborate with the press and with the photography industry. Mems: 20,000 in 15 countries. Pres. HEINZ BINDSEIL (FRG); Sec.-Gen. VICTOR COUCKE (Belgium). Publ. *Europhot Bulletin* (quarterly).

European Association for Personnel Management: 4000 Düsseldorf 30, Kaiserswerther Str. 137, Federal Republic of Germany; f. 1962 to disseminate knowledge and information concerning the personnel function of management, to establish and maintain professional standards, to define the specific nature of personnel management within industry, commerce and the public services, to establish an organization representative of personnel management in Europe and to assist in the development of national associations. Mems: 15 national associations. Pres. DE MOL VAN OTTERLOO (Netherlands); Sec. Dr FRIEDRICHS (FRG).

European Civil Service Federation: 200 rue de la Loi, 1049 Brussels, Belgium; tel. (02) 235-11-11; telex 21877; f. 1962 to foster the idea of a European civil service of staff of international organizations operating in Western Europe or pursuing regional objectives; upholds the interests of civil service members. Pres. HELMUT MUELLERS; Sec. MARINA IJDENBERG. Publ. *Eurechos.*

European Federation of Conference Towns: 40 rue Washington, 1050 Brussels, Belgium; tel. (02) 452-98-30; telex 65080; lays down standards for conference towns; provides advice and assistance to its members and other organizations holding conferences in Europe; undertakes publicity and propaganda for promotional purposes; helps conference towns to set up national centres. Perm. Sec. RITA DE LANDTSHEER.

European Industrial Research Management Association—EIRMA: 38 cours Albert 1, 75008 Paris, France; tel. (1) 42-25-60-44; telex 643 908; f. 1966 under auspices of the OECD (q.v.); a permanent body in which European science-based firms meet to discuss and study industrial research policy and management and take joint action in trying to solve problems in this field. Mems: 150 in 15 countries. Pres. J.-P. CAUSSE; Gen. Sec. Dr R. SCHULZ. Publs *Annual Report, Conference Reports, Working Group Reports.*

European Trade Union Confederation: 37–41 rue Montagne aux Herbes Potagères, 1000 Brussels, Belgium; tel. (02) 219-10-90; f. 1973; comprises 35 national trade union confederations in 21 western European countries, representing over 43m. workers; holds congress every three years. Gen. Sec. MATHIAS HINTERSCHEID.

European Union of Veterinary Surgeons: c/o Union Syndicale Vétérinaire Belge, 41 ave Fosny, 1070 Brussels, Belgium; f. 1970 to gain representation in international organizations and co-ordinate the work of veterinary surgeons throughout Europe. Mems: 13 associations in 12 countries. Pres. Dr P. RONSSE; Sec.-Gen. Dr H. STEVENS.

Federation of International Civil Servants' Associations: Palais des Nations, 1211 Geneva 10, Switzerland; tel. (022) 988400; f. 1952 to co-ordinate policies and activities of member associations, to represent staff interests before inter-agency and legislative organs of the UN and to promote the development of an international civil service. Mems: 26 associations consisting of staff of UN organizations, 16 consultative associations and five inter-organizational Federations with observer status. Pres. MARJORY DAM. Publs *Annual Report, FICSA News, Focus on FICSA.*

International Association of Conference Interpreters: 10 ave de Sécheron, 1202 Geneva, Switzerland; tel. (022) 313323; f. 1953 to represent professional conference interpreters, ensure the highest possible standards and protect the legitimate interests of members. Establishes criteria designed to improve the standards of training and recognizes schools meeting the required standards. Has consultative status with the UN, UNESCO, ILO, ISO and WIPO. Mems: 1,800 in 53 countries. Pres. GISELA SIEBOURG (FRG); Sec.-Gen. JEAN-DANIEL KATZ (Switzerland). Publs *Code of Professional Conduct, Yearbook* (listing interpreters), etc.

International Association of Conference Translators: 15 route des Morillons, 1218 Le Grand-Saconnex, Geneva, Switzerland; tel. (022) 910666; f. 1962; aims to examine problems of revisers, translators, précis writers and editors working for international conferences and organizations, to protect the interests of those in the profession and help maintain high standards; establishes links with international organizations and conference organizers. Mems: 460 in 17 countries. Pres. JEAN-PIERRE LERAY (France). Publ. *Directory.*

International Association of Crafts and Small and Medium-Sized Enterprises—IACME: Schwarztorstrasse 26, 3007 Berne, Switzerland; tel. (031) 257785; f. 1947 to defend undertakings and the freedom of enterprise within private economy, to develop training, to encourage the creation of national organizations of independent enterprises and promote international collaboration, to represent the common interests of members and to institute exchange of ideas and information. Mems: organizations in 26 countries which also belong to one of the international organic federations composing the IACME: International Federation of Master Craftsmen (IFC), International Federation of Small and Medium-Sized Industrial Enterprises (IFSMI) and International Federation of Small and Medium-Sized Commercial Enterprises (IFSMC). Chair. PAUL SCHNITKER; Gen. Sec. BALZ HORBER.

International Association of Medical Laboratory Technologists: c/o Mast House, Derby Road, Bootle, Merseyside, L20 1EA, England; tel. (051) 933-6072; telex 628178; f. 1954 to afford opportunities for meetings and communication between medical laboratory technologists, to raise training standards and to standardize training in different countries in order to facilitate free exchange of labour; holds international congress every second year. Last congress Perth, Australia, 1984. Mems: 105,000 in 38 societies in 35 countries. Pres. SHIRLEY POHL (USA); Exec. Dir ALEX MCMINN. Publ. *MedTecInternational* (2 a year).

International Association of Mutual Insurance Companies: 114 rue La Boétie, 75008 Paris, France; tel. (1) 42-25-84-86; f. 1964 for the establishment of good relations between its members and the protection of the general interests of private insurance based on the principle of mutuality. Mems: over 250 in 25 countries. Pres. A. TORP-PEDERSEN (Denmark); Sec.-Gen. A. CHOIMET (France). Publs *Mutuality* (2 a year), *AISAM dictionary.*

International Confederation of Executive and Professional Staffs (Confédération internationale des cadres): 30 rue de Gramont, 75002 Paris, France; f. 1950 to improve the material and moral status of executive staffs. Mems: national organizations in Belgium, Denmark, France, Federal Republic of Germany, Italy, Luxembourg, Monaco, Netherlands, UK, and international professional federations for chemistry and allied industries (FICCIA), mines (FICM), transport (FICT), metallurgical industries (FIEM), agriculture (FIDCA) and insurance (AECA). Pres. Dr FAUSTO D'ELIA (Italy); Sec.-Gen. JEAN DE SANTIS (France). Publ. *Cadres.*

International Confederation of Professional and Intellectual Workers: 1 rue de Courcelles, 75008 Paris, France; f. 1923 to defend the rights of all intellectual workers, promote their well-being and encourage their international co-operation; consultative status with ECOSOC, UNESCO, ILO and the Council of Europe. Mems: over 2,200,000 in eight countries, and five international organizations. Pres. MAURICE LETULLE (France); Vice-Pres. GIUSEPPE MARTUCCI (Italy); Sec.-Gen. GEORGES POULLE (France).

International European Construction Federation: 9 rue La Pérouse, 75116 Paris, France; tel. (1) 47-20-10-20; telex 613456; f. 1905. Mems: 25 national employers' organizations in 18 countries. Pres. PAUL WILLEMEN (Belgium); Sec.-Gen. ERIC LEPAGE (France). Publ. *L'Entreprise Européenne* (quarterly).

International Federation of Actors: 31A Thayer St, London, W1M 5LH, England; tel. (01) 487-4699; f. 1952. Mems: actors' unions totalling 200,000 individuals in 43 countries. Pres. PETER HEINZ KERSTEN (Austria); Sec.-Gen. ROLF REMBE.

International Federation of Air Line Pilots' Associations: Interpilot House, 116 High St, Egham, Surrey, TW20 9HQ, England; tel. (0784) 37361; telex 8951918; f. 1948 to aid in the establishment of fair conditions of employment; to contribute towards safety within the industry; to provide an international basis for rapid and accurate evaluation of technical and industrial aspects of the profession. Mems: 66 associations, 57,000 pilots. Pres. Capt. R. H. J. SMITH; Exec. Administrator T. V. MIDDLETON.

International Federation of Business and Professional Women: Buchanan House, 24/30 Holborn, London, EC1N 2HS, England; tel. (01) 242-1601; f. 1930 to promote interests of business and professional women and secure combined action by them. Mems: national federations and associate clubs totalling more than 200,000 mems in 67 countries. Pres. ROSAMARIE MICHEL (Switzerland); Gen. Sec. HILDA TREW. Publ. *Widening Horizons* (quarterly).

International Industrial Relations Association: c/o International Labour Office, 1211 Geneva 22, Switzerland; tel. (022) 996841; telex 22271; f. 1966 to encourage development of national associations of specialists, facilitate the spread of information, organize conferences, and to promote internationally planned research, through study groups and regional meetings. Mems: 26 associations, 39 institutions and 650 individuals. Pres. Prof. Dr ROGER BLAUPAIN; Sec. Dr A. GLADSTONE. Publs *IIRA Bulletin* (2 or 3 a year), World Congress papers and proceedings and membership directory.

International Organization of Employers—IOE: 28 chemin de Joinville, 1216 Cointrin/Geneva, Switzerland; tel. (022) 981616; telex 28 92 95; f. 1920, reorganized 1948; aims to represent the interests of private employers, to defend free enterprise, to maintain contacts in labour matters; has consultative status with the UN Economic and Social Council and the International Labour Organisation. General Council meets annually; there is an Executive Committee and a General Secretariat. Mems: 99 federations in 95 countries. Pres. (1985/86) ROGER DECOSTERD (Switzerland); Sec.-Gen. RAPHAEL LAGASSE (Belgium). Publ. *Information Bulletin* (monthly).

International Organization of Experts—ORDINEX: 163 rue Saint-Honoré, 75001 Paris, France; tel. (1) 42-60-54-41; f. 1961 to establish co-operation between experts on an international level. Mems: 2,400. Pres.-Gen. ROBERT MAZIN (France). Publ. *General Yearbook*.

International Public Relations Association—IPRA: Case Postale 126, 1211 Geneva 20, Switzerland; tel. (022) 292821; telex 428380; f. 1955 to provide for an exchange of ideas, technical knowledge and professional experience among those engaged in international public relations, and to foster the highest standards of professional competence. Mems: over 800 in 60 countries. Pres. PAUL KOOP (Pres.-Elect ALAIN MODOUX); Sec.-Gen. ANTHONY J. MURDOCH. Publs *Newsletter* (6 a year), *International Public Relations Review* (4 a year).

International Society of City and Regional Planners—ISoCaRP: Mauritskade 23, 2514 HD The Hague, Netherlands; tel. (70) 46 26 54; f. 1965 to promote better planning practice through the exchange of knowledge. Mems: 387 in 48 countries. Pres. M. L. DA COSTA LOBO (Portugal); Sec.-Gen. CH. DELFANTE (France).

International Union of Architects: 51 rue Raynouard, 75016 Paris, France; tel. 4524-36-88; telex 614 855; f. 1948; 16th Congress: Brighton, 1987. Mems: 81 countries. Pres. GEORGI STOILOV; Sec.-Gen. NILS CARLSON. Publ. *Bulletin d'informations* (monthly).

International Union of Long-Distance Lorry-Drivers (Union internationale des chauffeurs routiers): 6 rue de l'Isly, 75008 Paris, France; tel. (1) 43-87-61-68; telex 280 521; f. 1957 for the defence, mutual assistance and security of long-distance lorry-drivers. Mems: 1,500,000 in 15 member countries. Pres. FRANÇOIS DE SAULIEU; Sec.-Gen. JEAN CLAUDE PECHIN. Publs *Information UICR*, *Les Routiers* (both newspapers).

Latin American Farmworkers Federation (Federación Campesina Latinoamericana): Apdo 114B, Edif. La Línea, Avda Libertador, Caracas 101, Venezuela; f. 1961 to represent the interests of farmworkers in Latin America and to fight for their active participation in the social, economic, cultural, technical and scientific aspects of life in that area. Mems: 1,800,000. Sec.-Gen. JOSÉ RAMÓN RANGEL PARRA. Publs *Bulletins, Constitution*.

Nordic Federation of Factory Workers' Unions (Nordiska Fabriksarbetarefederationen): Box 1114, 111 81 Stockholm, Sweden; f. 1901 to promote collaboration between affiliates in Denmark, Finland, Iceland, Norway and Sweden; supports sister unions economically and in other ways in labour market conflicts. Mems: 400,000 in 13 unions. Pres. UNO EKBERG (Sweden); Sec. NILS KRISTOFFERSON (Sweden).

World Federation of Scientific Workers: 6 Endsleigh St, London, WC1H 0DX, England; tel. (01) 387-5096; f. 1946 to improve the position of science and scientists, to assist in promoting international scientific co-operation and to promote the use of science for beneficial ends; studies and publicizes problems of general, nuclear, biological and chemical disarmament; surveys the position and activities of scientists. Member organizations in 35 countries, totalling over 300,000 mems. Sec.-Gen. R. A. BIRD (UK). Publ. *Scientific World* (quarterly in English, Esperanto, German and Russian).

World Movement of Christian Workers—WMCW: 90 rue des Palais, 1210 Brussels, Belgium; tel. (02) 216-56-96; f. 1961 to unite national movements which advance the spiritual and collective well-being of workers; general assembly every four years. Mems: 42 affiliated movements in 36 countries. Sec.-Gen. LUC VOS. Publ. *Infor-WMCW*.

Law

Asian-African Legal Consultative Committee: 27 Ring Rd, Lajpat Nagar-IV, New Delhi 110024, India; tel. 6415280; f. 1956 to consider legal problems referred to it by member countries and to be a forum for Afro-Asian co-operation in international law and economic relations; provides background material for conferences, prepares standard/model contract forms suited to the needs of the region; promotes arbitration as a means of settling international commercial disputes; trains officers of member states; has permanent UN observer status. Mems: 40 states. Pres. D. LUBUVA (Tanzania); Sec.-Gen. B. SEN (India).

Consultative Committee of the Bars and Law Societies of the European Community—CCBE: 40 rue Washington, 1050 Brussels, Belgium; tel. (02) 640-42-74; telex 65080; f. 1960 to ensure liaison between the bars and law societies of the member countries as between these and the European Community authorities (Parliament, Economic and Social Committee, Court and Commission). Mems: 12 delegations and observers from Austria, Norway, Sweden and Switzerland. Pres. JØRGEN GRØNBORG (Denmark); Sec.-Gen. JEAN-RÉGNIER THYS (Belgium).

Hague Conference on Private International Law: Javastraat 2C, 2585 AM The Hague, Netherlands; tel (070) 633303; telex 33383; f. 1893 to work for the unification of the rules of private international law, Permanent Bureau f. 1955. Mems: 22 European and 12 other countries. Sec.-Gen. Dr G. A. L. DROZ. Publs *Actes* and *Documents* relating to each Session; various printed and mimeographed documents.

Institute of International Law (Institut de droit international): 22 ave William Favre, 1207 Geneva, Switzerland; tel. (022) 360772; f. 1873 to promote the development of international law by endeavouring to formulate general principles in accordance with civilized ethical standards, and by giving assistance to genuine attempts at the gradual and progressive codification of international law. Mems: limited to 132 members and associates from all over the world. Pres. Prof. BOUTROS BOUTROS-GHALI (Egypt) (acting); Sec.-Gen. NICOLAS VALTICOS (Greece). Publs *Annuaire de l'Institut de Droit international*, 61 vols, *Tableau général des Résolutions* (1873–1956).

Inter-American Bar Association: 1889 F St, NW, Suite 450, Washington, DC 20006–4499, USA; tel. (202) 789-2747; telex 64128; f. 1940 to promote the rule of law and to establish and maintain relations between associations and organizations of lawyers in the Americas. Mems: 90 associations and 3,500 individuals in 27 countries. Sec.-Gen. JOHN O. DAHLGREN (USA). Publs *Newsletter* (quarterly), *Conference Proceedings*.

Intergovernmental Copyright Committee: Copyright Division, UNESCO, 7 place de Fontenoy, 75700 Paris, France; established to study the problems concerning the application and operation of the Universal Copyright Convention and to make preparations for periodic revisions of this Convention. Mems: 18 states. Chair. R. DITTRICH.

International Association for the Protection of Industrial Property: Bleicherweg 58, Postfach, 8027 Zürich 27, Switzerland; f. 1897 to encourage legislation regarding the international protection of industrial property and the development and extension of international conventions, and to make comparative studies of existing legislation with a view to its improvement and unification. Mems: 5,700 (national and regional groups and individual mems) in 89 countries. Pres. EDWARD ARMITAGE (UK); Exec. Pres. DONALD VINCENT (UK); Sec.-Gen. ALFRED BRINER (Switzerland).

International Association of Democratic Lawyers: 263 ave Albert, 1180 Brussels, Belgium; f. 1946 to facilitate contacts and exchange between lawyers, to encourage study of legal science and international law and support the democratic principles favourable to maintenance of peace and co-operation between nations; conducts research on banning atomic weapons, on labour law, private international law, agrarian law, etc.; consultative status with ECOSOC and UNESCO. Mems: in 90 countries. Pres. JOË NORDMANN (France); Sec.-Gen. AMAR BENTOUMI (Algeria). Publs *International Review of Contemporary Law*, in French, English and Spanish (every 6 months).

International Association of Juvenile and Family Court Magistrates: Tribunal pour Enfants, Palais de Justice, 75055 Paris, France; f. 1928 to consider questions concerning child welfare legislation and to encourage research in the field of juvenile courts and delinquency. Activities: international congress, study groups and regional meetings. Pres. A. DUNANT (Switzerland); Gen.-Sec. J. P. PEIGNE (France).

International Association of Law Libraries: c/o The Law School Library, University of Chicago, 1121 East 60th St, Chicago, Ill 60637, USA; tel. (312) 962-9599; f. 1959 to encourage and facilitate the work of librarians and others concerned with the bibliographic processing and administration of legal materials. Mems: 600 from more than 50 countries (personal and institutional). Pres. ADOLF SPRUDZS (USA); Sec. TIMOTHY KEARLEY (USA). Publ. *International Journal of Legal Information* (6 a year), *The IALL Messenger* (irregular).

International Association of Legal Sciences (Association internationale des sciences juridiques): c/o CISS, 1 rue Miollis, 75015 Paris, France; tel. (1) 45-68-25-59; f. 1950 to promote the mutual knowledge and understanding of nations and the increase of learning by encouraging throughout the world the study of foreign legal systems and the use of the comparative method in legal science. Governed by a president and an executive bureau of 10 members known as the International Committee of Comparative Law. National committees in 47 countries. Sponsored by UNESCO. Pres. Prof. A. TUNC (France); Sec.-Gen. Dr S. FRIEDMAN (France).

International Bar Association: 2 Harewood Place, Hanover Sq., London, W1R 9HB, England; tel. (01) 629-1206; telex 8812664; f. 1947; a non-political federation of national bar associations and law societies; aims to discuss problems of professional organization and status; to advance the science of jurisprudence; to promote uniformity and definition in appropriate fields of law; to promote administration of justice under law among peoples of the world; to promote in their legal aspects the principles and aims of UN; to co-operate with international juridical organizations having similar purposes. Mems: 99 member organizations in 59 countries, 10,000 individual members in 117 countries. Pres. R. K. P. SHANKARDASS (India); Exec. Dir Mrs MADELEINE MAY (UK); Sec.-Gen. IDOWU SOFOLA (Nigeria). Publs *International Business Lawyer* (11 a year), *International Bar News* (6 a year), *International Legal Practitioner* (quarterly), *Journal of Energy and Natural Resources Law* (quarterly).

International Commission of Jurists: POB 120, 109 route de Chêne, 1224 Chêne-Bougeries, Geneva, Switzerland; f. 1952 to strengthen the Rule of Law in its practical manifestations and to defend it by mobilizing world legal opinion; has consultative status with UN, UNESCO, Council of Europe, and is on ILO's Special List of non-governmental organizations. There are 59 sections in 49 countries. Pres. ANDRÉS AGUILAR MAWDSLEY (Venezuela); Sec.-Gen. NIALL MACDERMOT. Publs *The Rule of Law and Human Rights, The Review, ICJ Newsletter, Bulletin of the Centre for the Independence of Judges and Lawyers (CIJL)*, special reports.

International Commission on Civil Status: Faculté de Droit et des Sciences politiques, place d'Athènes, 67084 Strasbourg Cedex, France; f. 1950 for the establishment and presentation of legislative documentation relating to the rights of individuals, and research on means of simplifying the judicial and technical administration concerning civil status. Mems: governments of Austria, Belgium, France, the Federal Republic of Germany, Greece, Italy, Luxembourg, Netherlands, Portugal, Spain, Switzerland, Turkey. Pres. D. ESPÍN CANOVAS (Spain); Sec.-Gen. J. M. BISCHOFF (France).

International Copyright Society: 8000 Munich 2, Herzog-Wilhelm-Strasse 28, Federal Republic of Germany; tel. (089) 55991; telex 523220; f. 1954 to enquire scientifically into the natural rights of the author and to put the knowledge obtained to practical application all over the world, in particular in the field of legislation. Mems: 435 individuals and 52 corresponding organizations and personalities. Pres. Prof. Dr ERICH SCHULZE. Publs *Schriftenreihe* (61 vols), *Yearbook*.

International Council of Environmental Law: 5300 Bonn, Adenauerallee 214, Federal Republic of Germany; tel. (0228) 2692-240; f. 1969 to exchange information and expertise on legal, administrative and policy-making aspects of environmental questions. Exec. Governors Dr WOLFGANG BURHENNE, Dr NAGENDRA SINGH. Publs *Directory, References, Environmental Policy and Law*.

International Criminal Police Organization—INTERPOL: POB 205, 92210 Saint Cloud, France; tel. 46-02-55-50; telex 270658; f. 1923, reconstituted 1946; aims to promote and ensure the widest possible mutual assistance between police forces within the limits of laws existing in different countries, to establish and develop all institutions likely to contribute to the prevention and suppression of ordinary law crimes; co-ordinates activities of police authorities of member states in international affairs, centralizes records and information regarding international criminals; operates a radio network of 70 stations. The General Assembly is held annually. Mems: official bodies of 138 countries. Pres. JOHN SIMPSON (USA); Sec.-Gen. R. E. KENDALL. Publs *International Criminal Police Review* (6 a year), *Counterfeits and Forgeries, International Crime Statistics*.

International Customs Tariffs Bureau: 38 rue de l'Association, 1000 Brussels, Belgium; tel. (02) 516-87-74; the executive instrument of the International Union for the Publication of Customs Tariffs; f. 1890, to translate and publish all customs tariffs in five languages—English, French, German, Italian, Spanish. Mems: 76. Pres. F. ROELANTS (Belgium); Dir BERNARD DENNE. Publs *International Customs Journal, Annual Report*.

International Development Law Institute: Via Paolo Frisi 23, 00197 Rome, Italy; tel. 872008; telex 622381; f. 1983 to strengthen the lawyer's role in solving development problems, and to offer training and technical assistance to legal advisers and contract negotiators from developing countries; the 1987 training programme includes seminars on international business transactions and courses for development lawyers; provides documentation services. Dir L. MICHAEL HAGER.

International Federation for European Law—FIDE: POB 760, 3000 DK Rotterdam, Netherlands; f. 1961 to advance studies on European law among members of the European Community by co-ordinating activities of member societies and by organizing regular colloquies on topical problems of European law. Mems: 10 national associations. Pres. T. KOOPMANS; Sec. D. BUIJS.

International Federation of Senior Police Officers: 4400 Münster, Feldkamp 4, Postfach 480 164, Federal Republic of Germany; tel. (02501) 7171; f. 1950 to unite policemen of different nationalities, adopting the general principle that prevention should prevail over repression, and that the citizen should be convinced of the protective role of the police; seeks to develop methods, and studies problems of traffic police. Set up International Centre of Crime and Accident Prevention, 1976. Mems: 16 national groups and individuals of 48 different nationalities. Pres. HERMAN BERGER (Norway); Vice-Pres. Dr HUBERT HOLLER (Austria), Col WARICHET (Belgium); Sec.-Gen. G. KRATZ (FRG). Publ. *International Police Information* (every 3 months, French, German and English).

International Institute for the Unification of Private Law—UNIDROIT: Via Panisperna 28, 00184 Rome, Italy; tel. (06) 6783189; f. 1926 to undertake studies of comparative law, to prepare for the establishment of uniform legislation, to prepare drafts of international agreements on private law and to organize conferences and publish works on such subjects. Drafts of various uniform laws and drafts of international Conventions have been presented to diplomatic conferences, the United Nations, the Council of Europe and IMO; holds international congresses on private law and meetings of organizations concerned with the unification of law; library of 215,000 vols. Mems: governments of 52 countries. Pres. RICCARDO MONACO (Italy); Sec.-Gen. MALCOLM EVANS (UK). Publs *Uniform Law Review* (2 a year), *Digest of Legal Activities of International Organizations, News Bulletin* (quarterly), etc.

International Institute of Space Law—IISL: 3–5 rue Mario Nikis, 75015 Paris, France; f. 1960 at the XI Congress of the International Astronautical Federation; organizes annual Space Law colloquium; studies juridical and sociological aspects of astronautics and makes awards. Mems: individuals from many countries elected for life. Hon. Pres. E. PÉPIN (France); Pres. I. DIEDERICKS-VERSCHOOR (Netherlands); Sec. PRIYATNA ABDURRASYID (Indonesia); Publs *Proceedings of Annual Colloquium on Space Law, Survey of Teaching of Space Law in the World*.

International Juridical Institute: Permanent Office for the Supply of International Legal Information, 't Hoenstraat 5, 2596 HX The Hague, Netherlands; tel. (070) 460974; telex 32419; f. 1918 to supply information in connection with any matter of international interest, not being of a secret nature, respecting international, municipal and foreign law and the application thereof. Pres. C. D. VAN BOESCHOTEN; Sec. C. J. VAN RIJN VAN ALKEMADE; Dir A. L. G. A. STILLE.

International Law Association: 3 Paper Buildings, The Temple, London, EC4Y 7EU, England; tel. (01) 353-2904; f. 1873 for the study and advancement of international law, public and private; the promotion of international understanding and goodwill. Mems: 4,000 in 35 regional branches. Pres. Dr THOK-KYU LIMB (Republic of Korea); Chair. Exec. Council Prof. C. J. OLMSTEAD (USA); Sec. R. C. H. BRIGGS. Publs Reports of biennial conferences, *Index of Conference Reports* (1873–1972).

International Maritime Committee (Comité Maritime International): 17 Borzestraat, 2000 Antwerp, Belgium; tel. (03) 232-24-71; telex 31653; f. 1897 to contribute to the unification of maritime law by means of conferences, publications, etc. and to encourage the creation of national associations to the same end; work includes drafting of conventions on collisions at sea, salvage and assistance at sea, limitation of shipowners' liability, maritime mortgages, etc. Mems: national associations in 44 countries. Pres. FRANCESCO BERLINGIERI (Italy); Secs-Gen. JAN RAMBERG (Exec.), HENRI VOET (Admin. and Treas.). Publs *CMI Newsletter, Year Book*.

International Nuclear Law Association: 29 sq. de Meeûs, 1040 Brussels, Belgium; f. 1972 to promote international studies of legal problems related to the peaceful use of nuclear energy, particularly the protection of man and the environment; holds conference every two years. Mems: 430 in 30 countries. Pres. F. VANDENABELLE (Belgium); Sec.-Gen. FERNAND LACROIX (Belgium). Publ. proceedings of conferences.

International Penal and Penitentiary Foundation: c/o Dr K. Hobe, Bundesministerium der Justiz, Postfach 20 06 50, 5300 Bonn 2, Federal Republic of Germany; tel. (0228) 584226; f. 1951 to encourage studies in the field of prevention of crime and treatment of delinquents. Mems in 20 countries (membership limited to three people from each country) and corresponding mems. Pres. HELGE RÖSTAD (Norway); Sec.-Gen. KONRAD HOBE (FRG). Publs reports of operations and meetings.

International Penal Law Association: Günterstalstrasse 73, 7800 Freiburg i. Br., Federal Republic of Germany; f. 1924 to establish collaboration between those from different countries who are working in penal law, studying criminology, and promoting the theoretical and practical development of an international penal law. Mems: 1,500. Pres. H.-H. JESCHECK. Publ. *Revue Internationale de Droit Pénal* (bi-annual).

International Police Association—IPA: County Police HQ, Sutton Rd, Maidstone, Kent, ME15 9BZ, England; tel. (0622) 685785; f. 1950 to establish the exchange of professional information, create ties of friendship between all sections of police service, organize group travel, studies, etc. Mems: 210,000. Pres. H. V. D. HALLETT; CEO K. H. ROBINSON. Publs *Police World* (quarterly), *International Bibliography of the Police, Annual Scholarship Report, Youth Gatherings, Police and Public, Police Participation in the Council of Europe*.

International Society for Labour Law and Social Security: ILO, Case 500, 1211 Geneva 22, Switzerland; f. 1958 to encourage collaboration between specialists; holds World Congress every three years as well as irregular regional congresses (Europe, Asia and Americas). Mems: 1,000 in 54 countries. Pres. Prof. B. AARON (USA); Sec.-Gen. JOHANNES SCHREGLE (FRG).

International Union of Latin Notaries (Unión Internacional del Notariado Latino): Callao 1542, Buenos Aires, Argentina; f. 1948 to study and standardize notarial legislation and promote the progress and stability and advancement of the Latin notarial system. Mems: organizations and individuals in 37 countries. Pres. CARLOS ENRIQUE PERALTA MÉNDEZ. Publs *Revista Internacional del Notariado, Boletín Informativo de la presidencia*.

International Union of Lawyers: 60 rue Pierre Charron, 75008 Paris, France; f. 1927 to promote the independence and freedom of lawyers, and defend their ethical and material interests on an international level; to contribute to the development of international order based on law. Mems: 84 groups, 1,700 corresponding mems. Pres. ERNEST ARENDT (Luxembourg). Publs *Bulletin* (quarterly), *Notes rapides*.

Law Association for Asia and the Western Pacific—Lawasia: 10th Floor, 170 Phillip St, Sydney, NSW 2000, Australia; tel. (02) 221-2970; telex 10101; f. 1966 to promote the administration of justice, the protection of human rights and the maintenance of the rule of law within the region, to advance the standard of legal education, to promote uniformity within the region in appropriate fields of law and to advance the interests of the legal profession.

Mems: 48 asscns in 18 countries; 2,000 individual mems. Pres. FALI S. NARIMAN (India); Sec.-Gen. Dr D. H. GEDDES. Publs *Lawasia* (annual journal), *Lawasia Human Rights Bulletin, Lawasia Newsletter, Lawasia Human Rights Newsletter*, proceedings of conference, research reports.

Permanent Court of Arbitration: Carnegieplein 2, 2517 KJ The Hague, Netherlands; tel. (070) 469680; f. by the Convention for the Pacific Settlement of International Disputes (1899, 1907) to enable immediate recourse to be made to arbitration for international disputes which cannot be settled by diplomacy, to facilitate the solution of disputes by international inquiry and conciliation commissions. Mems: governments of 75 countries. Sec.-Gen. JACOB VAREKAMP (Netherlands).

Society of Comparative Legislation: 28 rue Saint-Guillaume, 75007 Paris, France; tel. (1) 45-44-44-67; f. 1869 to study and compare laws of different countries as well as to investigate practical means of improving the various branches of legislation. Mems: 1,700 in 48 countries. Pres. SIMONE ROZES (France); Sec.-Gen. XAVIER BLANC-JOUVAN (France). Publs *Revue Internationale de Droit Comparé* (quarterly), *Journées de la Société de Legislation comparée* (annually).

Union of Arab Jurists: POB 6026, Al-Mansour, Baghdad, Iraq; tel. 5375820; telex 2-2661; f. 1975 to facilitate contacts between Arab lawyers, to safeguard and develop legislative and judicial language, and to restore the study of Muslim law; consultative status with ECOSOC. Mems: 16 Bar Asscns in 16 countries and individual mems. Sec.-Gen. SHEBIB LAZIM AL-MALIKI. Publs *Al-Haak*, documents and studies.

Union of International Associations: 40 rue Washington, 1050 Brussels, Belgium; tel. (02) 640-41-09; telex 65080; f. 1907, present title adopted 1910. Aims: to serve as a documentation centre on international organizations, to undertake and promote research into the phenomenon of 'organization' and into the legal, administrative and technical problems common to international organizations, to publicize their work and to encourage mutual contacts. Mems: 200 in 54 countries. Pres. F. A. CASADIO (Italy); Sec.-Gen. R. FENAUX (Belgium). Publs *Transnational Associations* (6 a year), *International Congress Calendar* (quarterly), *Yearbook of International Organizations, International Organization Participation* (annually), *Global Action Network* (annually), *Encyclopedia of World Problems and Human Potential, Documents for the Study of International Non-Governmental Relations, International Congress Science Series*.

World Peace through Law Center—WPTLC: Suite 800, 1000 Connecticut Ave, NW, Washington, DC 20036, USA; f. 1963; promotes the continued development of international law and legal maintenance of world order; holds biennial world conferences, World Law Day, demonstration trials; organizes research programmes. Mems: lawyers, jurists and legal scholars in 156 countries. World Pres. CHARLES S. RHYNE (USA); Sec.-Gen. WILLIAM S. THOMPSON (USA); Exec. Dir MARGARETHA M. HENNEBERRY (USA). Publs *The World Jurist* (English, bi-monthly), Research Reports, *Law and Judicial Systems of Nations*, 3rd revised edn (directory), *World Legal Directory* (biennial), *Law and Computer Technology* (quarterly), *World Law Review* Vols I–V (World Conference Proceedings), *The Chief Justices and Judges of the Supreme Courts of Nations* (directory), etc.

World Association of Center Associates: f. 1979. Pres. GERTRUDE BRUMMUND (USA).

World Association of Judges—WAJ: f. 1966 to advance the administration of judicial justice through co-operation and communication among ranking jurists of all countries. World Pres. Hon. Dr T. O. ELIAS (Nigeria); Sec.-Gen. Dr jur. KARL-GEORG ZIERLEIN (FRG).

World Association of Law Professors—WALP: f. 1975 to improve scholarship and education in dealing with matters related to international law. Co-Chair. ZIVOJIN ALEKSIĆ (Yugoslavia), JOHN N. HAZARD (USA); Exec. Sec. MARGARETHA M. HENNEBERRY (USA).

World Association of Lawyers—WAL: f. 1975 to develop international law and improve lawyers' effectiveness in dealing with it; 70 cttees. World Pres. CURT FREIHERR VON STACKELBERG (FRG).

Medicine and Health

Council for International Organisations of Medical Sciences—CIOMS: c/o WHO, ave Appia, 1211 Geneva 27, Switzerland; tel. (022) 913406; telex 27821; f. 1949; general assembly every three years. Mems: 99 organizations. Pres. Dr M. BELCHIOR (Brazil); Exec. Sec. Dr Z. BANKOWSKI. Publs *Calendar of International and Regional Congresses* (annual), *Proceedings of CIOMS, Round Table Conferences, International Nomenclature of Diseases*.

MEMBERS OF CIOMS

Members of CIOMS include the following:

International Academy of Legal and Social Medicine: c/o Prof. E. Leibhardt, Munich, 7A Frauenlobstrasse, Federal Republic of Germany; f. 1938; holds an international Congress and General Assembly every three years. Pres. L. ROCHE (France); Sec.-Gen. Prof. ERICH LEIBHARDT.

International Agency for the Prevention of Blindness: c/o Carl Kupfer, National Eye Institute, Bldg 31, Room 6AO3, Bethesda, Md 20892, USA; tel. (301) 496-2234; f. 1975 to collaborate with the World Health Organization and other UN organizations in promoting and co-ordinating global action for the prevention of blindness, with emphasis on the major blinding diseases of the developing world. Operates through national committees in 57 countries and regional organizations in eight areas. Pres. CARL KUPFER.

International Association for the Study of the Liver: c/o J. Bircher, 3400 Göttingen, Robert-Koch-Str. 40, Federal Republic of Germany; f. 1958; Pres. V. DESMET; Sec. J. BIRCHER.

International Association of Allergology and Clinical Immunology: 611 East Wells St, Milwaukee, WI 53202, USA; tel. (414) 276-6445; f. 1945 to further work in the educational, research and practical medical aspects of allergy diseases. Next Congress: Montreux, Switzerland, 1988. Mems: 40 national societies. Pres. Prof. Dr A. L. DE WECK (Switzerland); Sec.-Gen. Dr O. L. FRICK (USA); Exec. Sec. D. L. MCNEIL.

International Association of Gerontology: Duke University Medical Center, Box 2948, Durham, NC 27710, USA; f. 1950 to promote research and training in all fields of gerontology and to protect interests of gerontologic societies and institutions. Mems: 45 national societies and groups in 40 countries. Pres. Dr E. W. BUSSE (USA); Sec. Prof. Dr G. MADDOX (USA).

International College of Surgeons: 1516 N. Lake Shore Drive, Chicago, Ill. 60610, USA; tel. (312) 642-3555; telex 324629; f. 1935, as a world-wide institution for the advancement of the art and science of surgery, to create a common bond among the surgeons of all nations and promote the highest standards of surgery without regard to nationality, creed, or colour; sends teams of surgeons to developing countries to teach local surgeons; organizes research and scholarship programme and International Surgical Congresses; maintains the International Museum of Surgical Science in Chicago. Mems: about 15,000 in 100 countries. Pres. Prof. GIUSEPPE PEZZUOLI; Corporate Sec. Dr ANDREW G. SHARF; International Sec.-Gen. Dr F. C. OTTATI. Publ. *International Surgery* (quarterly), *International Newsletter* (annually).

International Dental Federation: 64 Wimpole St, London, W1M 8AL, England; f. 1900. Mems: 78 national dental associations in 72 countries and 13 affiliates. Pres. Dr A. O. GÓMEZ (Argentina); Exec. Dir Dr J. E. AHLBERG (Sweden). Publs *International Dental Journal* (quarterly) and *Newsletter* (every 2 months).

International Diabetes Federation: 40 rue Washington, 1050 Brussels, Belgium; tel. (02) 647-44-14; telex 65080; f. 1949 to help in the collection and dissemination of information regarding diabetes and to improve the welfare of people suffering from that disease. Mems: 88 mem. associations. Pres. Prof J. S. BAJAJ (India); Sec. N. STIELS (Belgium). Publ. *IDF Bulletin* (3 a year).

International Epidemiological Association—IEA: c/o Prof. W. M. Garraway, Dept of Community Medicine, University Usher Institute, Warrender Park Rd, Edinburgh, EH9 1DW, Scotland; tel. (031) 229-6207; f. 1954. Mems: 1,685. Pres. and Chair. Dr JOHANNES MOSBECH (Denmark); Sec. Prof. W. M. GARRAWAY. Publ. *International Journal of Epidemiology* (quarterly).

International Federation of Oto-Rhino-Laryngological Societies: 91-12 Fruithoflaan, 2600 Berchem, Belgium; tel. (32-3) 440-20-21; f. 1965; Congresses every four years; last Congress: Miami, Florida, 1985. Pres. J. R. CHANDLER (USA); Exec. Dir Prof. J. MARQUET (Belgium). Publ. *IFOS Newsletter* (monthly).

International Federation of Physical Medicine and Rehabilitation: 1000 N 92 St, Milwaukee, Wisconsin 53226, USA; tel. (414) 259-1414; f. 1952 to link national societies, organize conferences and disseminate information to developing countries. Last conference: Israel, 1984. Pres. Dr J. CHACO; Sec. Dr J. MELVIN (USA).

International Federation of Societies for Electroencephalography and Clinical Neurophysiology: c/o Dr B. W. Ongerboer de Visser, Department of Clincal Neurophysiology, Academic Medical Centre, Meibergdreef 9, 1105 AZ Amsterdam, Netherlands; tel. (020) 5663415; f. 1949 to attain the highest level of knowledge in the field of electro-encephalography and clinical neurophysiology in all the countries of the world. Mems: 43 organizations. Pres. Prof. J. E. DESMEDT (Belgium); Sec. Dr B. W. ONGERBOER DE VISSER (Netherlands). Publ. *The EEG Journal* (monthly).

International League Against Rheumatism: Hôpital Cochin, 27 rue du Faubourg, St Jacques, 75014 Paris, France; f. 1927 to promote international co-operation for the study and control of rheumatic diseases; to encourage the foundation of national leagues against rheumatism; to organize regular international congresses and to act as a connecting link between national leagues and international organizations. Sec. Prof. C. J. MENKES (France). Publs *Annals of the Rheumatic Diseases* (in England), *Revue du Rhumatisme* (in France), *Reumatismo* (in Italy), *Arthritis and Rheumatism* (USA), etc.

International Leprosy Association: 5 Amrita Shergill Marg, New Delhi 110003, India; tel. 386920; telex 31-4495; f. 1931 to promote international co-operation in work on leprosy, from which about 15m. people in the world are suffering. Thirteenth Congress, The Hague, 1988. Pres. Prof. M. F. LECHAT (Belgium); Sec. Dr R. H. THANGARAJ (India). Publ. *International Journal of Leprosy and Other Mycobacterial Diseases* (quarterly).

International Pediatric Association: Château de Longchamp, Carrefour de Longchamp, Bois de Boulogne, 75016 Paris, France; tel. (1) 47-72-15-90; telex 610584; f. 1912; holds triennial congresses and regional meetings. Mems: 100 national paediatric societies, associations or academies in 96 countries. Pres. Prof. NÜLO HALLMAN (Finland); Exec. Dir Prof. IHSAN DOGRAMACI (Turkey). Publ. *Bulletin* (quarterly).

International Rhinologic Society: c/o Dr Drumheller, 1515 Pacific Ave, Everett, Washington 98201, USA. Pres. T. AZUARA; Sec. Dr G. DRUMHELLER.

International Society and Federation of Cardiology: CP 117, 1211 Geneva 12, Switzerland; tel. (022) 464157; f. 1978 through merger of the International Society of Cardiology and the International Cardiology Federation; aims to promote the study, prevention and relief of the cardiovascular diseases through scientific and public education programme and the exchange of materials between its affiliated societies and foundations and with other agencies having related interests. Official relations with WHO. Organizes World Congresses every four years. Pres. Dr CH. KAWAI (Japan); Sec. Dr E. G. OLSEN; Exec. Sec. M. B. DE FIGUEIREDO. Publ. *Heartbeat* (quarterly).

International Society of Audiology: 330–332 Gray's Inn Rd, London, WC1, England; tel. (01) 837-8855, ext. 4321; f. 1962. Mems: 300 individuals. Gen. Sec. R. HINCHCLIFFE. Publ. *Audiology* (bi-monthly).

International Society of Criminology: 4 rue de Mondovi, 75001 Paris, France; tel. (1) 42-61-80-22; f. 1934 to promote the development of the sciences in their application to the criminal phenomenon. Mems: 800. Pres. GIACOMO CANEPA (Italy). Publ. *Annales internationales de Criminologie* (2 a year).

International Society of Geographical Pathology—ISGP: c/o Dr R. Cooke, Pathology Dept, Herston Rd, Brisbane 4029, Australia; tel. (07) 253 8030; telex 40871; f. 1931 to study the relations between diseases and the geographical environments in which they occur. Mems: national and regional committees in 42 countries. Sec.-Gen. Dr ROBIN A. COOKE. Publ. Transactions of the Conferences (published every third year).

International Society of Internal Medicine: Dept. of Medicine, Regionalspital, 4900 Langenthal, Switzerland; f. 1948 to encourage research and education in internal medicine. Mems: 35 national societies, 3,000 individuals in 57 countries. Congresses: Bogotá 1986, Brussels 1988. Pres. Prof. M. SANGIORGI (Italy); Sec. Dr ROLF A. STREULI (Switzerland).

International Society of Psychosomatic Obstetrics and Gynaecology: c/o Prof. E. V. van Hall, Dept of Obstetrics and Gynaecology, University Hospital, Rijnsburgerweg 10, 2333 AA Leiden, Netherlands; tel. (071) 263332. Pres. Dr LORRAINE DENNERSTEIN (Australia); Sec.-Gen. Prof. EYLARD VAN HALL (Netherlands).

International Society of the History of Medicine: 22 rue François Villeneuve, 34000 Montpellier, France; f. 1921. International congresses are organized. Sec.-Gen. Dr L. DULIEU. Publ. *Actes des congrès*.

OTHER INTERNATIONAL ORGANIZATIONS

International Union against Cancer: 3 rue du Conseil Général, 1205 Geneva, Switzerland; tel. (022) 201811; telex 429724; f. 1933 to promote on an international level the campaign against cancer in its research, therapeutic and preventive aspects; administers the American Cancer Society Eleanor Roosevelt International Cancer Fellowships, the International Cancer Research Technology Transfer Project and the Yamagiwa-Yoshida Memorial International Cancer Study Grants. Mems: voluntary national organizations, private or public cancer research and treatment organizations and institutes and governmental agencies in 84 countries. Pres. Dr C. G. SCHMIDT (FRG); Sec.-Gen. Dr G. P. MURPHY (USA); Exec. Dir Dr P. SELBY (Switzerland). Publs *International Cancer News* (quarterly), *International Journal of Cancer* (monthly), *International Calendar of Meetings on Cancer*, technical reports and monographs.

International Union against Tuberculosis: 199 rue des Pyrénées, 75020 Paris, France; f. 1920 to co-ordinate the efforts of anti-tuberculosis and respiratory disease associations, to mobilize public interest, to assist control programmes and research around the world, to collaborate with governments and the WHO, to promote conferences. Mems: associations in 118 countries, numerous individual mems. Pres. Dr N. C. SEN-GUPTA; Chair. Exec. Cttee Dr M. A. BLEIKER; Exec. Dir Dr ANNIK ROUILLON. Publ. *Bulletin* (in English, French and Spanish; incl. conference proceedings).

International Union for Health Education: 9 rue Newton, 75116 Paris, France; tel. (1) 47-20-97-93; f. 1951 to stimulate and facilitate health education activities by providing an international clearing house for the exchange of practical information on developments in health education; promoting research into effective methods and techniques in health education and encouraging professional training in health education for health workers, teachers, social workers and others, by means of standing committees, international conferences and regional seminars. Mems: in 75 countries. Pres. Dr HENRY CRAWLEY (Ireland); Sec.-Gen. Dr JEAN-MARTIN COHEN-SOLAL (France). Publ. *HYGIE-International Journal of Health Education* (quarterly).

International Union of Angiology: Via Bonifacio Lupi 11, Florence, Italy; f. 1958. Mems: 24 national societies. Pres. Prof. P. BALAS (Greece); Sec.-Gen. Prof. M. TESI (Italy). Publ. *Angéiologie* (8 a year).

International Union of Therapeutics: c/o Prof. J. Dry, Hôpital Rothschild, 33 blvd de Picpus, 75571 Paris Cedex 12, France; tel. (1) 43-41-72-72; f. 1934; international congresses every other year. Mems: 500 from 22 countries. Pres. Prof. J. DRY; Gen. Sec. A. PRADALIER.

Latin American Association of National Academies of Medicine: Calle 60A, No-5-29, Bogotá 2, Colombia; tel. 2-493122; f. 1967. Mems: nine national Academies. Pres. Dr CARLOS LANFRANCO LA HOZ (Peru); Sec. Dr ALBERTO CÁRDENAS-ESCOVAR (Colombia).

Medical Women's International Association: 5000 Cologne 41, Herbert-Levin-Strasse 1, Federal Republic of Germany; tel. (221) 4004235; telex 08882161; f. 1919 to facilitate contacts between medical women and to encourage their co-operation in matters connected with international health problems. Mems: national associations in 38 countries and individuals. Pres. BEVERLEY L. TAMBOLINE (Canada); Hon. Sec. CAROLYN MOTZEL (FRG).

World Association of Societies of (Anatomic and Clinical) Pathology—WASP: Postfach 10-08-44, 5090 Leverkusen, Federal Republic of Germany; f. 1947 to initiate permanent co-operation between the national associations of Anatomic and Clinical Pathology of the member countries or groups of countries; to co-ordinate their scientific and technical means of action; and to promote the development of Anatomic and Clinical Pathology in every aspect of its field of interest, especially by convening conferences, congresses and meetings, and by the interchange of publications and personnel. Membership: 45 national associations. Pres. Dr. H. LOMMEL (FRG); Sec. Prof. T. KAWAI. Publ. *News Bulletin* (quarterly).

World Federation of Associations of Clinical Toxicology Centres and Poison Control Centres: c/o Prof. L. Roche, 150 cours Albert-Thomas, 69372 Lyon Cedex 2, France. Pres. Dr M. GOVAERTS (Belgium); Sec. Prof. L. ROCHE.

World Federation of Associations of Paediatric Surgeons: c/o Prof. J. Boix-Ochoa, Clinica Infantil 'Vall d'Hebrón', Departamento de Cirugía Pediátrica, Valle de Hebrón, s/n, Barcelona 08035, Spain; f. 1974. Mems: 42 associations. Pres. Prof. MARCEL BETTEX; Sec. Prof. J. BOIX-OCHOA.

World Federation of Neurology: Dept of Neurology, Bowman Gray School of Medicine, Winston-Salem, NC 27103, USA; tel. (919) 748-2336; telex 806449; f. 1955 as International Neurological Congress, present title adopted 1957. Aims to assemble at the same time and place members of various congresses associated with neurology, and organize co-operation of neurological researchers. Organizes Congress every four years. Mems: 12,000 in 68 countries. Pres. RICHARD L. MASLAND (USA); Sec.-Treas. JAMES F. TOOLE (USA). Publs *Journal of the Neurological Sciences, Acta Neuropathologica*.

World Federation of Societies of Anaesthesiologists—WFSA: Frenchay Hospital, Bristol, BS16 1LE, England; tel. (0272) 565656; f. 1955 to make available the highest standards of anaesthesia to all peoples of the world. Mems: 77 national societies. Pres. Dr CARLOS PARSLOE (Brazil); Sec. Dr JOHN S. M. ZORAB (UK). Publ. *Newsletter* (2 a year), *Annual Report, Lectures in Anaesthesiology* (2 a year), *Obstetric analgesia and anaesthesia, Cardiopulmonary Resuscitation, Anaesthesiology—A Career Guide*.

World Medical Association: 28 ave des Alpes, 01210 Ferney-Voltaire, France; tel. (50) 40-75-75; telex 385755; f. 1947 to achieve the highest international standards in all aspects of medical practice, to promote closer ties among doctors and national medical associations by personal contact and all other means, to study problems confronting the medical profession and to present its views to appropriate bodies. Structure: annual General Assembly and Council (meets twice a year). Mems: national medical associations in 42 countries. Sec.-Gen. Dr ANDRÉ WYNEN (Belgium). Publ. *The World Medical Journal* (6 a year).

World Organization of Gastroenterology: Department of Medicine, Royal Infirmary, Edinburgh EH3 9YW, Scotland; f. 1935. Mems in 56 countries. Sec.-Gen. Prof. IAN A. D. BOUCHIER (UK).

World Psychiatric Association: Dept of Psychiatry, Kommunehospitalet, 1399 Copenhagen K, Denmark; tel. (1) 158500, ext. 3390; f. 1961 at the third World Congress of Psychiatry in Montreal. Aims at the exchange of information concerning the problems of mental illness; the strengthening of relations between psychiatrists in all countries; the establishment of working relations with WHO, UNESCO and other international organizations; the organization of World Psychiatric Congresses and of regional and inter-regional scientific meetings. Mems: 72 societies totalling 65,000 psychiatrists. Sec.-Gen. Prof. FINI SCHULSINGER (Denmark).

ASSOCIATE MEMBERS OF CIOMS

Asia Pacific Academy of Ophthalmology: Dept of Ophthalmology, Juntendo University School of Medicine, 3-1-3 Hongo Bunkyo-ku, Tokyo, Japan; tel. 03-813-3111 (ext. 3354); telex 2723270. Pres. Dr R. PARARAJASEGARAM; Sec.-Gen. Dr AKIRA NAKAJIMA (Japan).

Association for Paediatric Education in Europe: Paediatric Dept, University Hospital, Leyden, Netherlands; f. 1970 to encourage improvements and promote research in paediatric education. Mems: 70 in 20 European countries. Pres. Prof. A. TH. SCHWEIZER (Netherlands); Sec. Dr M. PECHEVIS (France).

International Association of Hydatid Disease: Florida 460, 1005 Buenos Aires, Argentina; tel. 392-3431; f. 1941. Mems: 830. Pres. Dra. DINORAH CASTIGLIONI TULA (Venezuela); Sec.-Gen. Prof. Dr RAUL MARTIN MENDY (Argentina). Publ. *Archivos Internacionales de la Hidatidosis* (every 4 years), *Boletín de Hidatidosis* (quarterly).

International Association of Medicine and Biology of the Environment: c/o 115 rue de la Pompe, 75116 Paris, France; tel. (1) 45-53-45-04; telex 614584; f. 1972 with assistance from the UN Environment Programme; aims to contribute to the solution of problems caused by human influence on the environment; structure consists of President, 40 Vice-Presidents, 4 administrative and 13 technical commissions. Mems: individuals and organizations in 59 countries. Hon. Pres. Prof. R. DUBOS; Pres. Dr R. ABBOU.

International Committee of Military Medicine and Pharmacy: 79 rue Saint-Laurent, 4000 Liège, Belgium; tel. (41) 22-21-83; f. 1921. Mems: official delegates from 90 countries. Pres. Col Maj. Dr BEN BOUMEHDI (Morocco); Sec.-Gen. Lt.-Col Dr M. COOLS (Belgium). Publ. *Revue Internationale des Services de Santé des Forces Armées*.

International Congress on Tropical Medicine and Malaria: c/o Prof. M. Miller, Faculty of Medicine, University of Calgary, Calgary T2N 1N4, Canada; to work towards the solution of the problems concerning malaria and tropical diseases. Sec. Prof. MAX MILLER.

International Council for Laboratory Animal Science: c/o G. J. R. Hovell, Dept of Physiology, Parks Rd, Oxford, England. Pres. Prof. H. C. ROWSELL (Canada); Sec. G. J. R. HOVELL (UK).

OTHER INTERNATIONAL ORGANIZATIONS

International Federation of Clinical Chemistry: c/o Prof. Dr M. M. Müller, 2nd Dept of Surgery, Division of Clinical Biochemistry, University of Vienna, Spitalgasse 23, 1090 Vienna, Austria; tel. (0222) 4800-2339; f. 1952. Mems: 47 national societies (about 20,000 individuals). Pres. DDr D. S. YOUNG (USA); Vice-Pres. DDr A. KALLNER (Sweden); Sec. Dr M. M. MÜLLER (Austria). Publs *News* (3 a year), *Annual Report*.

International Medical Society of Paraplegia: National Spinal Injuries Centre, Stoke Mandeville Hospital, Aylesbury, Bucks, HP21 8AL, England. Pres. Dr A. ROSSIER (Switzerland); Sec. Dr H. L. FRANKEL.

International Society of Neuropathology: c/o Dr S. Ludwin, Dept of Pathology, Queen's University, Kingston, Ontario K7L 3N6, Canada. Pres. Dr H. deF. WEBSTER; Sec.-Gen. Dr S. LUDWIN.

Transplantation Society: c/o Dr Mary Wood, New England Deaconess Hospital, 185 Pilgrim Rd, Boston, Mass 02215, USA. Pres. Dr A. P. MONACO; Secs Prof. R. F. M. WOOD, Dr MARY L. WOOD (USA).

OTHER ORGANIZATIONS

Aerospace Medical Association: National Airport, Washington, DC 20001, USA; tel. (703) 892-2240; f. 1929 as Aero Medical Association; to advance the science and art of aviation and space medicine; to establish and maintain co-operation between medical and allied sciences concerned with aerospace medicine; to promote, protect, and maintain safety in aviation and astronautics. Mems: individual, constituent and corporate in 75 countries. Pres. ROBERT W. FASSOLD (Canada); Exec. Vice-Pres. RUFUS R. HESSBERG (USA). Publ. *Aviation Space and Environmental Medicine* (monthly).

Asian-Pacific Dental Federation: 165-A Jalan SS 2/24, Petaling Jaya, Malaysia; f. 1955 to establish closer relationship among dental associations in Asian and Pacific countries and to encourage research, with particular emphasis on dental health in rural areas. Asian Pacific Regional Organization of the International Dental Federation. Congress: Bangkok, December 1985. Mems: 13 national associations. Pres. Dr WILLIAM W. WONG (Hong Kong); Sec.-Gen. Dr. LOW TEONG (Malaysia). Publ. *APDF/APRO Newsletter* (3 a year).

Association of National European and Mediterranean Societies of Gastro-enterology—ASNEMGE: Lange Lozanastraat 222, 2018 Antwerp, Belgium; tel. (03) 238-01-85; f. 1947 to facilitate the exchange of ideas between gastro-enterologists and disseminate knowledge; organizes International Congress of Gastroenterology every four years. Mems in 30 countries, national societies and sections of national medical societies. Pres. Prof. Dr J. M. CARRILHO-RIBEIRO (Portugal); Sec. Dr L. O. STANDAERT (Belgium).

Balkan Medical Union: 1 rue Gabriel Peri, 70148 Bucharest, Romania; tel. 16-78-46; f. 1932; studies medical problems, particularly ailments specific to the Balkan region, to promote a regional programme of public health; serves as a clearing house for information and knowledge between doctors in the region; organizes research programmes and congresses. Mems: doctors and specialists from Albania, Bulgaria, Cyprus, Greece, Romania, Turkey and Yugoslavia. Pres. Dr M. POPESCU BUZEU (Romania); Sec.-Gen. Dr A. KARASSI (Romania). Publs *Archives de l'union médicale Balkanique* (6 a year), *Bulletin de l'union médicale Balkanique* (6 a year), *Annuaire, Bulletin de l'Entente Médicale Méditerranéenne* (annually).

European Association for Cancer Research: c/o Dr M. R. Price, Cancer Research Campaign Laboratories, University of Nottingham, University Park, Nottingham, NG7 2RD, UK; tel. (0602) 506101 (ext. 3401); f. 1968 to facilitate contact between cancer research workers and to organize scientific meetings in Europe. Mems: 1,050 in 40 countries in and outside Europe. Pres. Dr J. KIELER (Denmark); Sec. Dr M. R. PRICE (UK).

European Association for the Study of Diabetes: 10 Queen Anne St, London, W1M 0BD, England; tel. (01) 637-3644; f. 1965 to encourage and support research in the field of diabetes, to promote the rapid diffusion of acquired knowledge and to facilitate its application; holds annual scientific meetings within Europe. Mems: 1,650 in 50 countries not confined to Europe. Pres. Prof. D. ANDREANI (Italy); Exec. Dir JAMES G. L. JACKSON. Publ. *Diabetologia* (12 a year).

European Association of Internal Medicine: Clinique Médicale B, 1 place de l'Hôpital, 67091 Strasbourg, France; tel. 88-36-71-11; f. 1969 to promote internal medicine from the ethical, scientific and professional points of view; to bring together European internists; to organize meetings, etc. Mems: 400 in 20 European countries. Pres. Prof. E. COCHE (Belgium); Sec. Dr J. F. BLICKLE (France).

European Association of Programmes in Health Services Studies: 1 Carlton Villas, Shelbourne Rd, Dublin 4, Ireland; tel. 689642; f. 1966 to promote collaboration between European countries in the organization and development of training programmes in hospital and health services administration; to encourage studies and research. Mems: 74 (corporate) in 21 countries, and 28 associate mems. Pres. Dr R. J. MAXWELL; Dir PHILIP C. BERMAN; Publ. *Newsletter* (quarterly), *Directory* (every 2 years).

European Association of Radiology: c/o P. Delorme, Hôpital Pellegrin, Place Amélie Raba-Léon, 33076 Bordeaux, France; tel. (56) 96-83-83; f. 1962 to develop and co-ordinate the efforts of radiologists in Europe by promoting radiology in both biology and medicine, studying its problems, developing professional training and establishing contact between radiologists and professional, scientific and industrial organizations. Mems: national associations in 25 countries. Sec.-Gen. Pr. G. DELORME.

European Association of Social Medicine: Via dei Mille 34, 10123 Turin, Italy; f. 1953 to provide co-operation between national associations of preventive medicine and public health. Mems: associations in 10 countries. Pres. Prof. Dr FERNANDO LUIGI PETRILLI (Italy); Sec.-Gen. Prof. Dr ENRICO BELLI (Italy).

European Brain and Behaviour Society: c/o Dr F. D. Rose, Dept of Psychology, University of London: Goldsmiths' College, London, SE14 6WW, England. Pres. Prof. P. KARLI; Sec. Dr F. D. ROSE.

European Committee for the Protection of the Population against the Hazards of Chronic Toxicity—EUROTOX: Faculté des Sciences Pharmaceutiques et Biologiques, Laboratoire de Toxicologie et d'Hygiène Industrielle, 4 ave de l'Observatoire, Paris 6e, France; f. 1957; studies risks of long-term build-up of toxicity. Gen. Sec. Prof. R. TRUHAUT (France). Publ. *Reports of Meetings*.

European Dialysis and Transplant Association/European Renal Association: c/o Dr S. T. Boen, Dept of Nephrology, Sint Lucas Hospital, Jan Tooropstraat 164, 1061 AE Amsterdam, Netherlands; f. 1965 to encourage and to report advances in the field of haemodialysis, peritoneal dialysis, renal transplantation, nephrology and related subjects. Mems: 1,300. Pres. Prof. V. ANDREUCCI (Italy); Sec.-Treas. Dr S. T. BOEN. Publ. *Proceedings* (annual).

European League against Rheumatism: c/o E. Munthe, Oslo City Dept of Rheumatology, Diakonhjemmets Hospital, POB 23, Vinderen, Oslo 3, Norway; f. 1947 to co-ordinate research and treatment of rheumatic complaints, conducted by national societies. Mems in 33 countries. Sec. EIMAR MUNTHE.

European Organization for Caries Research—ORCA: c/o Dr G. S. Ingram, Unilever Research, Port Sunlight Laboratory, Bebington, Wirral, Merseyside, L63 3JW, England; tel. (051) 645-2000; f. 1953 to promote and undertake research on dental health, encourage international contacts, and make the public aware of the importance of care of the teeth. Mems: research workers in 23 countries. Pres. Prof. R. Z. M. TRILLER (France); Sec.-Gen. Dr G. S. INGRAM (UK).

European Orthodontic Society: 64 Wimpole St, London, W1M 8AL, England; tel. (01) 935-2795; f. 1907 to advance the science of orthodontics and its relations with the collateral arts and sciences. Mems: 1,475 in 46 countries. Sec. Prof. J. MOSS. Publ. *European Journal of Orthodontics* (quarterly).

European Society for Comparative Endocrinology: c/o Prof. A. de Loof, Zoologisch Instituut, 59 Naamsestraat, 3000 Leuven, Belgium; tel. (16) 22-23-19; f. 1965 to promote interdisciplinary exchange between scientists engaged in various aspects of comparative endocrinology; sponsors a conference every two years. Mems: 320 in 30 countries. Pres. Prof. Dr P. G. W. VAN OORDT; Sec. Prof. A. DE LOOF. Publs abstracts of papers presented at conferences in General & Comparative Endocrinology.

European Society of Cardiology: POB 23410, 3001 KK Rotterdam, Netherlands; f. 1950 to promote scientific co-operation and contacts between European cardiologists, encourage the development of cardiology and organize scientific meetings. Mems in 31 countries. Pres. P. G. HUGENHOLTZ; Sec. Prof. H. E. KULBERTUS.

European Union of Medical Specialists: 20 ave de la Couronne, Brussels 1050, Belgium; tel. (02) 649-21-47; f. 1958 to safeguard the interests of medical specialists. Mems: two representatives each from Belgium, Denmark, France, Federal Republic of Germany, Greece, Ireland, Italy, Luxembourg, Netherlands, Portugal, Spain and UK. Pres. Prof. M. FANFANI (Italy); Sec.-Gen. Dr G. DES MAREZ (Belgium).

Eurotransplant Foundation: c/o University Hospital, Leiden 2333 AA, Netherlands; tel. (071) 263807; telex 39266; f. 1967; co-ordinates the exchange of organs for transplants in the Federal

Republic of Germany, Austria, Belgium, the Netherlands; keeps register of almost 6,500 patients with all necessary information for matching with suitable donors in the shortest possible time; organizes transport of the organ and the transplantation; collaboration with similar organizations in Western and Eastern Europe. Chair. Prof. Dr J. J. van Rood; Dir Dr B. Cohen.

Federation of French-Language Obstetricians and Gynaecologists (Fédération des gynécologues et obstetriciens de langue française): Clinique Baudelocque, 123 blvd de Port-Royal, 75674 Paris Cedex 14, France; tel. (1) 42-34-11-40; f. 1920 for the scientific study of phenomena having reference to obstetrics, gynaecology and reproduction in general. Mems: 1,500 in 50 countries. Pres. Prof. C. Sureau (France); Gen. Sec. Prof. J. R. Zorn (France). Publ. *Journal de Gynécologie Obstétrique et Biologie de la Reproduction* (8 a year).

Federation of the European Dental Industry: 5000 Cologne 1, Pipinstrasse 16, Federal Republic of Germany; tel. (0221) 215993; telex 8882226; f. 1957 to promote the interests of the dental industry. Mems: national associations in Austria, France, the Federal Republic of Germany, Italy, the Netherlands, Sweden, Switzerland and the United Kingdom. Pres. and Chair. M. J. d'Hollosy (Netherlands); Vice-Pres. (vacant).

Federation of World Health Foundations: Ave Appia, 1211 Geneva 27, Switzerland; f. 1967 to co-ordinate the work of the members and to maintain relations between them and the World Health Organization. The General Council of representatives of the member foundations is assisted by a steering committee. The Federation examines projects to be considered by the foundations, seeks to establish new foundations, advice and training. Mems: 10 national health foundations which have entered into formal agreement with WHO, in Canada, Hong Kong, Indonesia, Ireland, Philippines, Sri Lanka, Switzerland, USA. Pres., CEO Milton P. Siegel.

General Association of Municipal Health and Technical Experts: 9 rue de Phalsbourg, 75017 Paris, France; tel. (1) 42-27-38-91; f. 1905 to study all questions related to urban and rural health—the control of preventable diseases, disinfection, distribution and purification of drinking water, construction of drains, sewage, collection and disposal of household refuse, etc. Mems in 35 countries. Pres. F. Ozanne (France); Sec.-Gen. M. Brès (France). Publ. *TSM-Techniques, Sciences, Méthodes* (monthly).

Inter-American Association of Sanitary and Environmental Engineering: Av. Beira-Mar 216, 13° andar, 20021 Rio de Janeiro, RJ Brazil; tel. 220 3422; telex 021 31902; f. 1946 to establish uniform health standards. Mems: 22 countries.

Inter-American Society of Cardiology (Sociedad Interamericana de Cardiología): Instituto Nacional de Cardiología Ignacio Chávez de México, Juan Badiano 1, Tlalpan, DF, Mexico 14080; tel. (905) 573-29-11; f. 1944 to stimulate the development of cardiology. Mems: 22,000 in 23 countries. Pres. (1985–89) Dr Bernardo Boskis; Sec.-Treas. Dr Eduardo Salazar.

International Academy of Aviation and Space Medicine: 9350 rue de Lagauchetière W, Montreal, PQ H3C 3N4, Canada; f. 1955; to facilitate international co-operation in research and teaching in the fields of aviation and space medicine. Mems: 146 in 32 countries. Pres. Dr Ch. A. Berry (USA); Sec.-Gen. Dr Peter Vaughan.

International Academy of Cytology: 1050 chemin Ste-Foy, Québec, Que., Canada G1S 4L8; f. 1957 to foster and facilitate international exchange of knowledge and information on specialized problems of clinical cytology and to stimulate research in clinical cytology; to standardize terminology. Mems: 1,975. Pres. Alexander Meisels; Sec.-Treas. Claude Gompel. Publ. *Acta Cytologica*.

International Anatomical Congress: Prof. J. A. Didio, Dept of Anatomy, Medical College of Ohio, CS 10008 Toledo, OH 43699, USA; f. 1905; runs congresses for anatomists from all over the world to discuss research, teaching methods and terminology in the fields of gross and microscopical anatomy, histology, cytology, etc. Pres. Prof. Sir Richard Harrison (UK); Sec.-Gen. Prof. A. Delmas (France).

International Association for Child and Adolescent Psychiatry and Allied Professions: c/o Dr Philippe Jeammet, Hôpital de l'Université de Paris, 42 blvd Jourdan, 75014 Paris, France; f. 1948 to promote scientific research in the field of child psychiatry by collaboration with allied professions. Mems: national associations and individuals in 33 countries. Pres. Prof. Colette Chiland; Sec.-Gen. Dr Philippe Jeammet.

International Association for Dental Research: 1111 14th St, NW, Suite 1000, Washington, DC 20005, USA; tel. (202) 898-1050; f. 1920 to encourage research in dentistry and related fields, and to further the communication of the results of such research by publication and by annual meetings; triennial conferences and divisional meetings are also held. Pres. Ivar A. Mjör; Exec. Dir Dr J. A. Gray.

International Association of Agricultural Medicine and Rural Health: Saku Central Hôspital, 197 Usuda-machi, Minamisaku-Gun, Nagano 384-03, Japan; f. 1961 to study the problems of medicine in agriculture in all countries and to prevent the diseases caused by the conditions of work in agriculture. Mems: 405. Pres. Prof. Pavel Macuch (Czechoslovakia); Sec.-Gen. Prof. Toshikazu Wakatsuki (Japan).

International Association of Applied Psychology: Montessorilaan 3, Nijmegen 6500 HE, Netherlands; f. 1920, present title adopted in 1955; aims to establish contacts between those carrying out scientific work on applied psychology, to promote research and the adoption of measures contributing to this work. Mems: 3,000 in 90 countries. Pres. Prof. C. Levy-Leboyer (France); Sec.-Gen. and Treas. Prof. Ch. J. de Wolff (Netherlands). Publ. *International Review of Applied Psychology* (quarterly).

International Association of Asthmology—INTERASMA: c/o Prof. Dr A. Palma-Carlos, R. Sampaio e Pina 16-4°, 1000 Lisbon, Portugal; f. 1954 to advance medical knowledge of bronchial asthma and allied disorders. Mems: 1,100 in 54 countries. Pres. Prof. A. Oehling (Spain); Sec.-Gen. Prof. A. Palma-Carlos (Portugal). Publ. *Allergologia et Immunopathologia* (every 2 months).

International Association of Group Psychotherapy: POB 327, Three Bridges, NJ 08822, USA; f. 1954; holds congresses every three years. Mems: 500 individuals in 30 countries; 20 organizations in 10 countries. Pres. Jay W. Fidler (USA); Sec.-Treas. Rollin Ives (USA). Publ. *Newsletter*.

International Association of Logopedics and Phoniatrics: 6 ave de la Gare, 1003 Lausanne, Switzerland; f. 1924 to promote standards of training and research in human communication disorders in all countries, to establish information centres and communicate with kindred organizations. Mems: 400 individuals and 50 societies from 31 countries. Pres. K. G. Butler (USA); Gen. Sec. Dr André Muller. Publ. *Folia Phoniatrica* (6 a year).

International Association of Oral and Maxillofacial Surgeons: c/o Dept of Oral and Maxillofacial Surgery, Guy's Hospital, London, SE1 9RT, England; tel. (01) 378-6918; f. 1963 to advance the science and art of oral surgery. Mems: 2,000. Pres. Prof. Dr W. Schilli (FRG); Sec.-Gen. Prof. D. E. Poswillo (UK). Publs *International Journal of Oral Surgery* (bi-monthly), *Transactions of International Conferences on Oral and Maxillofacial Surgery*, *Newsletter* (every 6 months).

International Brain Research Organization—IBRO: 51 blvd de Montmorency, 75016 Paris, France; f. 1958 to further all aspects of brain research. Mems: 35 corporate and 18,000 individual. Pres. Prof. D. P. Purpura (USA); Sec.-Gen. Dr D. Ottoson. Publs *IBRO News, Neuroscience* (bi-monthly), *IBRO Monograph Series*, handbooks.

International Bronchoesophagological Society: 3401 North Broad St, Philadelphia, Pa 19140, USA; f. 1951 to promote by all means the progress of bronchoesophagology and to provide a forum for discussion among broncho-esophagologists of various specialities. Mems: 450 in 45 countries. Pres. Dr Eric Carlens; Exec. Sec. Dr Gabriel Tucker.

International Bureau for Epilepsy: c/o Dr R. H. E. Grant, David Lewis Centre for Epilepsy, near Alderley Edge, Cheshire, SK9 7UD, England; tel. Mobberly 2613; f. 1961; the 27 national branches of the International League against Epilepsy (q.v.) are members of the Bureau; to collect and disseminate information about social and medical care for epileptics, to organize international and regional meetings; to advise and answer questions on social aspects of epilepsy. Mems: 48 organizations and 150 individuals in 38 countries. Pres. F. Castellano (Italy); Sec.-Gen. Dr R. H. E. Grant (UK). Publ. *Newsletter* (quarterly).

International Catholic Confederation of Hospitals (Confédération internationale catholique des institutions hospitalières): Linnaeusdreef 60, Breukelen, Netherlands; f. 1951; organizes regular international and regional congresses. Mems: 16 national organizations; corresponding mems: 9 national organizations. Pres. Mgr. W. Mühlenbrock (FRG); Sec.-Gen. G. Stulemeyer (Netherlands).

International Cell Research Organization: c/o UNESCO, 7 place de Fontenoy, 75700 Paris, France; f. 1962 to create, encourage and promote co-operation between scientists of different disciplines throughout the world for the advancement of fundamental knowledge of the cell, normal and abnormal; organizes every year four to six international laboratory courses on modern topics of cell and molecular biology for young research scientists in important research centres all over the world; sponsors exchange of scientists. Mems: 650. Chair. Dr R. P. PERRY (USA); Exec. Sec. Dr G. BUTTIN (France).

International Center of Information on Antibiotics: c/o Prof. Welsch, Institut de Pathologie, Université de Liège, Sart-Tilman, 4000 Liège, Belgium; f. 1961 to gather information on antibiotics and strains producing them; to establish contact with discoverers of antibiotics with a view to obtaining samples and filing information; to establish contact with the curators of culture collections in order to publish a catalogue of the producing strains, and with research workers in order to avoid duplication of investigations and confusion in the scientific literature. Dir Prof. M. WELSCH; Senior Scientist in Charge Dr L. DELCAMBE.

International Chiropractors' Association: 1901 L St, NW, Suite 800, Washington, DC, USA; f. 1926 to promote advancement of the art and science of chiropractic. Mems: 9,000 individuals in addition to affiliated associations. Pres. MICHAEL D. PEDIGO, DC; Sec.-Treas. ANDREW WYMORE. Publs *International Review of Chiropractic* (quarterly), *ICA Today* (every 2 months).

International Commission for Optics: Physics Dept, University of Technology, Lorentzweg 1, 2628 CJ Delft, Netherlands; tel. (015) 785309; telex 38151; f. 1948 to contribute to the progress of theoretical and instrumental optics, to assist in research and to promote international agreement on specifications; Gen. Assembly every three years (last meeting, Sapporo, 1984). Mems: national committees from 32 countries. Pres. S. LOWENTHAL (France); Sec.-Gen. Prof. H. J. FRANKENA (Netherlands). Publs *ICO Newsletter*.

International Commission on Occupational Health: 10 ave Jules-Crosnier, 1206 Geneva, Switzerland; tel. (022) 476184; f. 1906 (present name 1985) to study and prevent pathological conditions arising from industrial work; arranges congresses on occupational medicine and the protection of workers' health; provides information for public authorities and learned societies. Mems: 1,200 from 75 countries. Pres. Dr ROBERT MURRAY (UK); Sec.-Treas. Prof. LUIGI PARMEGGIANI (Italy). Publ. *Newsletter* (quarterly).

International Commission on Radiological Protection—ICRP: Clifton Ave, Sutton, Surrey, SM2 5PU, England; tel. (01) 642-4680; telex 895 1244; f. 1928 to provide technical guidance and promote international co-operation in the field of radiation protection; committees on Radiation Effects, Secondary Limits, Protection in Medicine, and the application of recommendations. Mems: about 70. Chair. Dr D. BENINSON (Argentina); Scientific Sec. Dr M. C. THORNE (UK). Publ. *Annals of the ICRP*.

International Committee of Aesthetics and Cosmetology (Comité internationale d'Esthétique et de Cosmétologie—CIDESCO): Zeltweg 50, 8023 Zürich, Switzerland; f. 1946 to improve beauticians' training and to promote aesthetics and beauty care wherever possible. Mems: in 26 countries. Pres. KRISTINA PELTOMAA (Finland); Gen. Sec. HEDY DETTWILER (Switzerland).

International Committee of Catholic Nurses: Palazzo San Calisto, Piazza San Calisto 16, 00153 Rome, Italy; f. 1933 to group professional catholic nursing associations; to represent Christian thought in the general professional field at international level; to co-operate in the general development of the profession and to promote social welfare. Mems: 49 full, 20 corresponding mems. Pres. KATHLEEN KEANE; Gen. Sec. LILIANA FIORI. Publs *Nouvelles/News/Nachrichten* (every 4 months).

International Council for Physical Fitness Research—ICPFR: Department of Anthropology, Southern Methodist University, Dallas, Texas 75275, USA; f. 1964 to construct international standardized physical fitness tests, to obtain information on world standards of physical fitness, to promote comparative studies and to encourage health and physical fitness in all countries through the exchange of scientific knowledge. Mems: 122 in 38 countries. Pres. Prof. O. BAR-OR; Sec. Dr DIRK VAN GERVEN (Belgium).

International Council of Nurses—ICN: 3 place Jean-Marteau, 1201 Geneva, Switzerland; tel. (022) 312960; f. 1899 to provide a medium through which national associations of nurses may share their common interests, working together to develop the contribution of nursing to the promotion of the health of people and the care of the sick. Quadrennial congresses are held in different countries. Mems: 97 national nurses' associations. Pres. NELLY GARZÓN (Colombia); Exec. Dir CONSTANCE HOLLERAN. Publ. *The International Nursing Review* (6 a year, in English).

International Cystic Fibrosis Association: 3567 East 49th St, Cleveland, Ohio 44105, USA; tel. (216) 271-1100; f. 1964 to disseminate current information on cystic fibrosis in those areas of the world where the disease occurs and to stimulate the work of scientific and medical researchers attempting to discover its cure. Conducts annual medical symposia. Mems: 30 national organizations. Pres. R. D. MCCREERY; Sec. ROBERT JOHNSON (UK).

International Federation for Hygiene, Preventive Medicine and Social Medicine: Via Salaria 237, 00199 Rome, Italy; tel. 8457928; f. 1951. Eleventh Conference: Madrid, Spain, September 1986. Mems: national associations and individual members in 74 countries. Pres. Prof. Dr G. A. CANAPERIA (Italy); Sec.-Gen. Dr ERNST MUSIL (Austria). Publ. *Bulletin*.

International Federation for Medical and Biological Engineering: National Research Council of Canada, Bldg M-50, Ottawa, Ont. K1A 0R8, Canada; tel. (613) 993-1686; telex 053-4134; f. 1959. Mems: national associations in 30 countries. Sec.-Gen. OREST Z. ROY (Canada).

International Federation for Medical Psychotherapy: Box 26, Vinderen, Oslo 3, Norway; tel. (02) 146190; f. 1946 to further research and teaching of psychotherapy, to organize international congresses. Mems: 3,200 psychotherapists from 24 countries, 36 societies. Pres. Dr FINN MAGNUSSEN (Norway); Sec.-Gen. Dr TRULS-EIRIK MOGSTAD (Norway). Publ. *Psychotherapy and Psychosomatics*.

International Federation of Fertility Societies: Hegewischstrasse 4, 2300 Kiel 1, Federal Republic of Germany; tel. (0431) 5972040. Vice-Pres. Prof. Dr KURT SEMM.

International Federation of Gynecology and Obstetrics: 27 Sussex Place, Regent's Park, London, NW1 4RG, England; tel. (01) 723-2951; f. 1954; assists and contributes to research in gynaecology and obstetrics; aims to facilitate the exchange of information and perfect methods of teaching; organizes international congresses. Membership: national societies in 86 countries. Pres. of Bureau Prof. S. RATNAM (Singapore); Sec.-Gen. Prof. D. V. I. FAIRWEATHER (UK). Publ. *Journal*.

International Federation of Multiple Sclerosis Societies: 3/9 Heddon St, London, W1R 7LE, England; f. 1965 to co-ordinate and further the work of 31 national multiple sclerosis organizations throughout the world, to stimulate and encourage scientific research in this and related neurological diseases, to aid member societies in helping individuals who are in any way disabled as a result of these diseases, to collect and disseminate information and to provide counsel and active help in furthering the development of voluntary national multiple sclerosis organizations. Pres. WILLIAM P. BENTON; Sec.-Gen. JOSEPH M. AGUAYO. Publs *Federation Update* (quarterly), *Annual Report*.

International Federation of Ophthalmological Societies: c/o Prof. A. Deutman, Institute of Ophthalmology, University of Nijmegen, 16 Philips van Leijden laan, 6525 EX Nijmegen, Netherlands; tel. (080) 513138; f. 1953; holds international congress every four years. Pres. Prof. A. E. MAUMENEE (USA); Sec. Prof. A. DEUTMAN.

International Federation of Pharmaceutical Manufacturers Associations—IFPMA: 67 rue St Jean, 1211 Geneva 11, Switzerland; f. 1968 for the exchange of information and international co-operation in all questions of interest to the pharmaceutical industry, particularly in the field of health legislation, science and research in order to contribute to the advancement of the health and welfare of the peoples of the world; development of ethical principles and practices and co-operation with national and international organizations, governmental and non-governmental. Mems: the pharmaceutical manufacturers associations of the EEC, EFTA, Latin America, Australia, Canada, Hong Kong, India, Israel, Japan, Republic of Korea, Malaysia, New Zealand, Pakistan, the Philippines, Singapore, South Africa, Spain, Sri Lanka, Turkey and the USA. Pres. P. CUNLIFFE; Exec. Vice-Pres. Dr RICHARD B. ARNOLD.

International Federation of Surgical Colleges: c/o Prof. W. A. L. MacGowan, Royal College of Surgeons in Ireland, 123 St Stephen's Green, Dublin 2, Ireland; tel. 780200; telex 30795; f. 1958 to encourage high standards of surgery and surgical training; co-operates closely with the World Health Organization in compiling standard lists of surgical requirements in developing countries and evaluating surgical manpower. Mems: colleges or associations in 37 countries, and 88 individual associates. Pres. Prof. W. P. LONGMIRE (USA); Sec. Prof. W. A. L. MACGOWAN (Ireland).

International Federation of Thermalism and Climatism: Centre Thermal, POB 143, 1400 Yverdon-les-Bains, Switzerland; tel. (024) 214456; f. 1947. Mems in 26 countries. Pres. Dr G. EBRARD; Gen. Sec. C. OGAY.

International Guild of Dispensing Opticians: 40 Portland Place, London, W1N 4BA, England; tel. (01) 637-2507; f. 1951 to promote the science of, and to maintain and advance standards and effect co-operation in optical dispensing. Sec. A. P. D. WESTHEAD (UK).

International Hospital Federation: 2 St Andrew's Place, London, NW1 4LB, England; tel. (01) 935-9487; f. 1947 to maintain an information bureau on matters connected with hospital work and health service; to sponsor projects and study groups; to organize international congresses, seminars and study tours; to sponsor training courses for senior administrators. Mems in five categories: national hospital and health service organizations, professional associations, regional organizations and individual hospitals; individual mems; professional and industrial mems; honorary mems. Pres. Dr G. FAJARDO ORTIZ (Mexico); Dir-Gen. M. C. HARDIE. Publ. *Yearbook, World Hospitals* (quarterly; English with French and Spanish supplements).

International League against Epilepsy: c/o Dr F. E. Dreifuss, University of Virginia Medical Center, Charlottesville, Va 22903, USA; tel. (804) 924-5669; f. 1910 to link national professional associations and to encourage research, including classification and anti-epileptic drugs; collaborates with the International Bureau for Epilepsy (q.v.) and with WHO. Mems: 33 associations. Pres. F. E. DREIFUSS (USA); Sec.-Gen. H. MEINARDI (Netherlands).

International Medical Association for the Study of Living Conditions and Health: Institute of Nutrition, blvd D. Nestorov 15, 1431 Sofia, Bulgaria; tel. 58 101 707; f. 1951 to co-ordinate research in a wide range of subjects relating to living, working and environmental conditions which favour man's healthy physical and moral development; holds international congresses. Mems: doctors in 35 countries. Pres. Prof. T. TASHEV (Bulgaria). Publ. *Acta Medica et Sociologica,* congress and conference reports.

International Narcotics Control Board—INCB: 1400 Vienna, POB 500, Austria; tel. 26310; telex 135612; f. 1961 to supervise the implementation of the Drug Control Treaties by governments. Mems: 13 individuals. Pres. BETTY GOUGH (USA); Sec. ABDELAZIZ BAHI (Tunisia). Publ. *Annual Report* (with four statistical supplements).

International Optometric and Optical League: 10 Knaresborough Place, London, SW5 0TG, England; tel. (01) 370-4765; f. 1927 to co-ordinate efforts to provide a good standard of ophthalmic optical (optometric) care throughout the world; the League is active in providing a forum for exchange of ideas between different countries; a large part of its work is concerned with optometric education, and advice upon standards of qualification. The League also interests itself in legislation in relation to optometry throughout the world. Mems: 50 optometric organizations in 37 countries. Pres. G. B. HOLMES (UK). Publs *Interoptics* (6 a year).

International Organization for Medical Physics: c/o Dr B. Stedeford, Dept of Radiation Physics, Churchill Hospital, Headington, Oxford, OX3 7LJ, England; tel. (0865) 64841 (ext. 7158); telex 83147; f. 1963 to organize international co-operation in medical physics, to promote communication between the various branches of medical physics and allied subjects, to contribute to the advancement of medical physics in all its aspects and to advise on the formation of national organizations for medical physics in those countries where no such organization exists. Mems: national organizations of medical physics in 30 countries. Pres. Prof. LAWRENCE LANZL (USA); Sec.-Gen. Dr BRIAN STEDEFORD (UK).

International Pharmaceutical Federation: Alexanderstraat 11, 2514 JL The Hague, Netherlands; tel. (70) 631925; telex 32781; f. 1912 to promote the development of pharmacy both as a profession and as an applied science. Meetings of the Bureau and Council annually since 1956; Assembly of Pharmacists every two years, International Congress every year. Mems: 65 national pharmaceutical organizations in 53 countries are ordinary members, and approx. 4,000 individual pharmacists are associate members. Pres. L. A. BÉDAT (Switzerland); Sec. J. H. M. A. MARTENS (Netherlands), Prof. D. D. BREIMER (Netherlands); Dir L. FÉLIX-FAURE. Publ. *Pharmacy International* (monthly).

International Psycho-Analytical Association: Broomhills, Woodside Lane, London, N12 8UD, England; tel. (01) 446-8324; f. 1908 to hold meetings to define and promulgate the theory and teaching of psychoanalysis, to act as a forum for scientific discussions, to control and regulate training and to contribute to the interdisciplinary area which is common to the behavioural sciences. Mems: 6,500. Pres. ROBERT S. WALLERSTEIN (USA); Sec. EDWARD M. WEINSHEL (USA). Publs *Bulletin, Newsletter. Monograph, Roster.*

International Rehabilitation Medicine Association: c/o Prof. M. Grabois, Dept of Physical Medicine, Baylor College of Medicine, 1333 Moursund Ave, Houston, Texas 77030, USA; tel. (713) 799-5090; f. 1968. Mems: 1,160 in 59 countries. Pres. TYRONE REYES (Philippines); Sec. Prof. M. GRABOIS (USA). Publ. *Journal of International Rehabilitation Medicine* (quarterly).

International Scientific Council for Trypanosomiasis Research and Control: Joint Secretariat, OAU/STRC, PM Bag 2359, Lagos, Nigeria; f. 1949 to review the work on tsetse and trypanosomiasis problems carried out by organizations and workers concerned in laboratories and in the field; to stimulate further research and discussion and to promote co-ordination between research workers and organizations in the different countries in Africa, and to provide a regular opportunity for the discussion of particular problems and for the exposition of new experiments and discoveries. Publ. Proceedings of ISCTR Conferences.

International Society for Cardiovascular Surgery: 13 Elm St, POB 1565, Manchester, MA 01944-0865, USA; tel. (617) 927-8330; telex 940103; f. 1950 to stimulate research in the diagnosis and therapy of cardiovascular diseases and to exchange ideas on an international basis. Pres. ADIB D. JATENE (Brazil); Sec.-Gen. JOHN L. OCHSNER (USA). Publ. *Journal of Cardiovascular Surgery.*

International Society for Clinical and Experimental Hypnosis—ISCEH: Psychiatric Clinic, Charles University, Pha 2, Ke Karlova 11, Prague 2, Czechoslovakia; f. 1958 as an affiliate of the World Federation for Mental Health, to stimulate and improve professional research, discussion and publications pertinent to the scientific study of hypnosis; to encourage co-operative relations among scientific disciplines with regard to the study and application of hypnosis; to bring together persons using hypnosis and set up standards for professional training and adequacy. Pres. Prof. JEAN LASSNER, MD (130 rue de la Pompe, Paris 16e, France); Exec. Sec. Dr IVAN HORVAI (Czechoslovakia); Treas. Dr A. S. PATERSON. Publ. *International Journal of Clinical and Experimental Hypnosis.*

International Society for Mental Imagery Techniques: 6 rue des Ursulines, 75005 Paris, France; tel. (1) 43-26-98-92; f. 1968; a group of research workers, technicians and psychotherapists using oneirism techniques under waking conditions, with the belief that a healing action cannot be dissociated from the restoration of creativity. Mems: in 17 countries. Pres. Dr ANDRÉ VIREL (France); Vice-Pres ODILE DRECK-DORKEL (France), SERENELLA RIGO (Italy).

International Society for Research on Civilization Diseases and Environment: 61 rue E. Bouilliot, Bte 11, 1060 Brussels, Belgium; tel. (02) 343-97-48; f. 1972 to study environmental conditions, non-transmissive diseases and occupational medicine; holds annual congress and one or two workshops a year. Mems: associations and individuals in 61 countries. Pres. Dr S. KLEIN (Belgium); Dirs of Scientific Council Prof. M. CLOAREC (France), Prof. H. WRBA (Austria).

International Society of Art and Psychopathology: Centre Hospitalier St Anne, 100 rue de la Santé, 75014 Paris, France; tel. (1) 45-89-55-21; f. 1959 to bring together the various specialists interested in the problems of expression and artistic activities in connection with psychiatric, sociological and psychological research, as well as in the use of methods applied to other fields than that of mental illness. Mems: 625. Pres. Prof. VOLMAT (France); Sec.-Gen. Dr C. WIART (France).

International Society of Blood Transfusion: 6 rue Alexandre Cabanel, 75739 Paris Cedex 15, France; tel. (1) 69-07-20-40; telex 603218; f. 1937. Mems: about 1,500 in 89 countries. Pres. L. BARKER (USA); Sec.-Gen. M. GARRETTA. Publ. *Vox Sanguinis.*

International Society of Cybernetic Medicine: Via Roma 348, 80134 Naples, Italy; f. 1958 to promote international co-operation in the use of cybernetic methods in the biological and medical sciences; organizes congresses; individual and collective members in various countries. Pres. Prof. A. MASTURZO (Italy); Sec. Dr P. BATTARRA (Italy). Publ. *Cybernetic Medicine* (quarterly).

International Society of Developmental Biologists: Department of Biology, University of Southampton, Medical and Biological Sciences Bldg, Bassett Crescent East, Southampton, SO9 3TU, England; f. 1911 as International Institute of Embryology. Objects: to promote the study of developmental biology and to promote international co-operation among the investigators in this field; the Hubrecht Laboratory is an International Research Laboratory for descriptive and experimental embryology, and has a Central Embryological Library and Collection of slides and material. Mems: 850. Pres. Prof. T. S. OKADA (Japan); Int. Sec. Prof. J. R. COLEMAN (USA); Sec.-Treas. Dr F. S. BILLETT (UK).

International Society of Lymphology: 7800 Freiburg, Tullastr. 72, Federal Republic of Germany; f. 1966 to further progress in lymphology through personal contact and exchange of ideas among members. Mems: 400 in 43 countries. Pres. MARLYS WITTE (USA); Sec.-Gen. M. FOELDI (FRG). Publ. *Lymphology* (quarterly).

OTHER INTERNATIONAL ORGANIZATIONS

International Society of Orthopaedic Surgery and Traumatology: 40 rue Washington, 1050 Brussels, Belgium; tel. (02) 648-68-23; telex 65080; f. 1929; congresses are convened every three years. Mems: 74 countries, 2,500 individuals. Pres. R. DE MARNEFFE (Belgium); Sec.-Gen. J. WAGNER (Belgium). Publ. *International Orthopaedics.*

International Society of Radiology: Dept of Diagnostic Radiology, University Hospital, 3010 Berne, Switzerland; tel. (031) 642435; f. 1953 to promote diagnostic radiology and radiation oncology through its International Commissions on Radiation Units and Measurements, on Radiation Protection, on Radiological Education and on Rules and Regulations; organizes quadrennial International Congress of Radiology; collaborates with the World Health Organization. Mems: 63 national radiological societies. Sec. W. A. FUCHS.

International Society of Dermatology: Tropical, Geographic and Ecologic: Mayo Clinic, Rochester, Minn 55905, USA; f. 1960. Mems: about 2,800 in 80 countries. Pres. Dr FRANCISCO KERDEL-VEGAS (Venezuela); Sec.-Gen. Prof. SIGFRID A. MULLER (USA). Publ. *International Journal of Dermatology* (10 a year).

International Society of Urology: 9 blvd du Temple, 75003 Paris, France; f. 1921; congress every three years. Mems: 2,400 in 61 countries. Pres. WILLY GREGOIR (Belgium); Sec.-Gen. ALAIN JARDIN (France).

League against Trachoma (Ligue contre le trachome): Hôpital du Val-de-Grâce, 1 place Alphonse Laveran, 75230 Paris Cedex 05, France; f. 1923. Mems: 2,000. Pres. Prof. G. CORNAND (France). Publ. *Revue Internationale du Trachome* (in French and English, quarterly).

Middle East Neurosurgical Society: c/o Dr Fuad S. Haddad, Neurosurgical Department, American University Medical Centre, POB 113-6044, Beirut, Lebanon; tel. 347348; telex 20801; f. 1958 to promote clinical advances and scientific research among its members and to spread knowledge of neurosurgery and related fields among all members of the medical profession in the Middle East. Mems: 324 in nine countries. Pres. Dr OSMAN SROUR; Hon. Sec. Dr FUAD S. HADDAD.

Odontological Federation of Central America and Panama (Federación Odontológica de Centro America y Panama): Apdo Postal 6406, Zona 5, Panama; f. 1957 to link national odontological societies and institutions in Central America and Panama. Mems: 6 national societies and 2 colleges in 6 countries. Pres. Dr RODRIGO EISENMANN; Sec. Dr HERNÁN RAMOS. Publ. *Congresses.*

Organization for Co-ordination and Co-operation in the Fight against Endemic Diseases (Organisation de coordination et de coopération pour la lutte contre les grandes endémies—OCCGE): BP 153, Bobo-Dioulasso, Burkina Faso; tel. 98-28-75; f. 1960. Mems: governments of Benin, Burkina Faso, Ivory Coast, Mali, Mauritania, Niger, Senegal, Togo; assoc. mem: France. Sec.-Gen. Dr EMMANUEL AKINOCHO. Publs *Rapport Technique, Revue d'épidémiologie et de santé publique* (3 a year).

Research centres:
  Centre de Recherches sur les Méningites et les Schistosomiases: BP 10 887, Niamey, Niger.
  Centre Muraz: BP 153, Bobo-Dioulasso, Burkina Faso; tel. 98-18-72; telex 8208; f. 1939; Dir CHARLES DOUCHET.
  Institut Marchoux de Léprologie: BP 251, Bamako, Mali; tel. 22 51 31; telex 466; Dir MAX NEBOUT.
  Institut d'Ophtalmologie Tropicale Africaine: BP 248, Bamako, Mali; Dir PIERRE VINGTAIN.
  Institut de Recherches sur les Trypanosomiases et l'Onchocercose: BP 1500, Bouake, Ivory Coast; Dir DANIEL QUILLEVERE.
  Office de Recherches sur l'Alimentation et la Nutrition Africaine: BP 2089, Dakar, Senegal; tel. 22-58-92; Dir Dr MAKHTAR N'DIAYE.

Offices are also based in Cotonou, Benin, (entomology), Lomé, Togo (nutrition), Nouakchott, Mauritania (tuberculosis), and Bafoulabé, Mali (onchocerciasis).

Organization for Co-ordination in the Fight against Endemic Diseases in Central Africa (Organisation de coordination pour la lutte contre les endémies en Afrique Centrale—OCEAC): BP 288, Yaoundé, Cameroon; tel. 23-22-37; telex 8411; f. 1965 to standardize methods of fighting endemic diseases, to co-ordinate national action, and to negotiate programmes of assistance and training on a regional scale. Mems: Cameroon, Central African Republic, Chad, Congo, Equatorial Guinea, Gabon. Pres. Dr JEAN-PIERRE OKIAS; Sec.-Gen. Dr DANIEL KOUKA BEMBA. Publs *EPI—Notes* (quarterly), *Rapports Finals des Conférences Techniques* (every 3 years), *Bulletin Liaison Documentation* (quarterly).

Pan-American Association of Ophthalmology: 267 Miller Ave, Suite 2, Mill Valley, Calif 94941, USA; f. 1940 to promote friendship and dissemination of scientific information among the profession throughout the Western Hemisphere. Mems: national opthalmological societies in 22 countries. Pres. Dr BENJAMIN BOYD (Panama); Exec. Dir Dr FRANCISCO CONTRERAS (Peru).

Pan-American Medical Association (Asociación Médica Panamericana): 745 Fifth Ave, New York, NY 10022, USA; f. 1925; holds inter-American congresses, conducts seminars and grants post-graduate scholarships. Mems: 15,000 doctors in 24 countries. Dir-Gen. JOSEPH J. ELLER.

Pan-Pacific Surgical Association: POB 553, Honolulu, Hawaii 96809, USA; f. 1929 to bring together surgeons to exchange scientific knowledge relating to surgery and medicine; congresses are held every two years; 19th Congress, Honolulu, Jan. 1988. Mems: 2,716 regular, associate and senior mems from 44 countries. Chair. WILLIAM J. YARBROUGH.

Rehabilitation International: 25 East 21st St, New York, NY 10010, USA; tel. (212) 420-1500; telex 66125; f. 1922 to advance the welfare of the disabled through the exchange of information and research on equipment and methods of assistance; organizes international conferences and co-operates with UNDP, UNICEF, UNESCO and other international organizations. Mems: national organizations in 80 countries. Pres. OTTO GEIECKER; Sec.-Gen. SUSAN R. HAMMERMAN. Publs *International Rehabilitation Review* (3 a year), *International Journal of Rehabilitation Research* (quarterly), *Rehabilitación* (2 a year).

Scandinavian Neurosurgical Society (Nordisk Neurokirurgisk Forening): c/o J. Haase, Neurokirurgisk afdeling, Aalborg Sygehus, POB 365, 9100 Aalborg, Denmark; tel. (08) 131111; f. 1946. Mems: 300 including hon., corresp. and assoc. mems in 23 countries. Pres. HELGE NORNES (Norway); Sec. J. HAASE (Denmark). Publ. Abstracts: *Acta Neurochirurgica* (Vienna).

Society of French-speaking Neuro-Surgeons (Société de neuro-chirurgie de langue française): 60 blvd Latour-Maubourg, 75007 Paris, France; tel. (1) 45-21-24-17; f. 1949. Mems: 600 in numerous countries. Pres. M. HURTH (France); Sec. G. FISCHER (France). Publ. *Neuro-Chirurgie* (16 a year).

Society of Ski Traumatology: Clinique Saint-Joseph, square Massalaz, 73000 Chambéry, France; f. 1956 to exchange experiences in treating injuries caused by winter sports and mountain accidents; discussion of questions relating to sports medicine in mountains. Mems: doctors from Austria, Federal Republic of Germany, France, Italy and Switzerland. Pres. Prof. Dr H. U. BUFF; Sec. Dr PIERRE TRUCHET. Publ. Congress reports (every 2 years).

Transnational Association of Acupuncture and Taoist Medicine: 48 ave Kléber, 75116 Paris, France; tel. (1) 47-27-05-95; f. 1963 to develop and promote knowledge of acupuncture in the world. Mems: national societies and individuals in 70 countries. Pres. Dr J.C. DE TYMOWSKI; Sec.-Gen. Dr CASSARD. Publ. *Ecomédecine* (monthly).

World Confederation for Physical Therapy: 16–19 Eastcastle St, London, W1N 7PA, England; tel. (01) 637-2104; f. 1951 to encourage improved standards of physical therapy in training and practice; to promote exchange of information between nations; to assist the development of informed public opinion regarding physical therapy. Mems: 44 organizations. Sec.-Gen. Miss M. H. O'HARE. Publs *Newsletter* (2 a year), *Programmes of Physical Therapy Education, Proceedings of Congresses.*

World Federation for Cancer Care: 28 Belgrave Sq., London, SW1X 8QG, England; tel. (01) 235-9438; f. 1982 to advance scientific, medical, nursing and social welfare knowledge in cancer care throughout the world; gives advice and information to the general public and to cancer associations; surveys the availability of cancer care services and collaborates with other relevant organizations. Mems: 50 societies. Pres. RONALD RAVEN (UK); Exec. Dir CYNTHIA YONKO.

World Federation for Mental Health: 1021 Prince St, Alexandria, Va 22314, USA; tel. (703) 684-7722; f. 1948 to promote among all people and nations the highest possible standard of mental health in the broadest biological, medical, educational, and social aspects; to work with ECOSOC, UNESCO, the World Health Organization, and other agencies of the United Nations, in so far as they promote mental health; to help other voluntary associations in the improvement of mental health services; and to further the establishment of better human relations. Mems: 88 associations in 41 countries and five trans-national associations. Pres. EDITH MORGAN (UK); Dir-Gen. Dr EUGENE B. BRODY; Deputy Sec.-Gen. RICHARD HUNTER. Publs *Newsletter* (5 a year).

OTHER INTERNATIONAL ORGANIZATIONS

World Federation of Neurosurgical Societies: c/o Dr H. A. D. Walder, St. Radboud Academic Hospital, 6500 HB Nijmegen, Netherlands; tel. (80) 513477; telex 48232; f. 1957 to assist the development of neurosurgery and to help the formation of associations; to assist the exchange of information and to encourage research. Mems: 53 societies representing 56 countries. Pres. Prof. W. KEMP CLARK; Sec. Dr H. ALPHONS D. WALDER.

World Federation of Occupational Therapists: University of Western Ontario, Occupational Therapy Dept, Health Sciences Bldg, London, Ontario, Canada N6A 5C1; f. 1952 to further the rehabilitation of the physically and mentally disabled by promoting the development of occupational therapy in all countries; to facilitate the exchange of information and publications; to promote research in occupational therapy. National Professional Associations of occupational therapists in 36 countries are members of the Federation; they have a total membership of approximately 36,000; international congresses are held every four years. Pres. JOANNA BARKER (Australia)); Hon. Sec.-Treas. BARBARA POSTHUMA (Canada). Publs *Bulletin* (2 a year), *Requirements for Employment of Occupational Therapists*, proceedings of international congresses, studies and bibliography of occupational therapy.

World Federation of Public Health Associations: c/o Dr Susi Kessler, Director of International Health Programs, American Public Health Assen, 1015 15th St, NW, Washington, DC 20005, USA; f. 1967. Mems: 36 national public health associations. Pres. Dr YOUSIF OSMAN (Sudan); Exec. Sec. Dr SUSI KESSLER (USA). Publs *Salubritas* (newsletter in English, French and Spanish), *WFPHA News* (in English), and occasional technical papers.

Posts and Telecommunications

African Posts and Telecommunications Union: ave Patrice Lumumba, BP 44, Brazzaville, Congo; tel. 812778; telex 5212; f. 1961 to improve postal and telecommunication services between member administrations. Mems: 12 countries. Sec.-Gen. M. SIMPORE.

Asian-Pacific Postal Union: Post Office Bldg, Manila, Philippines 2801; tel. 47-07-60; f. 1962 to extend, facilitate and improve the postal relations between the member countries and to promote co-operation in the field of postal services. Mems: 20 countries. Dir ANGELITO T. BANAYO. Publs *Annual Report, Exchange Program of Postal Officials, Newsletter*.

European Conference of Postal and Telecommunications Administrations: Post and Telegraphs Office, 1530 Copenhagen V, Denmark; tel. (01) 15-66-10; telex 911-1845; f. 1959 to strengthen relations between member administrations and to harmonize and improve their technical services; set up Eurodata Foundation, for research and publishing. Mems: 26 countries. Publ. *Bulletin*.

International Maritime Satellite Organization—INMARSAT: 40 Melton St, London, NW1 2EQ, England; tel. (01) 387-9089; telex 297201; f. 1979 to provide (from February 1982) global communications for shipping via satellites on a commercial basis; satellites in geo-stationary orbit over the Atlantic, Indian and Pacific Oceans provide telephone, telex, facsimile, telegram, low to high speed data services and distress and safety communications for ships of all nations and structures such as oil rigs; in 1985 the operating agreement was amended to include aeronautical communications. Organs: Assembly of all Parties to the Convention (every 2 years); council of representatives of 22 national telecommunications administrations; executive Directorate. Mems: 43 countries. Chair. of Council J. T. FENELEY (Canada); Dir-Gen. OLOF LUNDBERG (Sweden). Publ. *Ocean Voice* (quarterly), *Aeronautical Satellite News* (quarterly).

International Telecommunications Satellite Organization—INTELSAT: 3400 International Drive, NW, Washington, DC 20008-3098, USA; tel. (202) 944-6800; telex 892707; f. 1964 to establish a global commercial satellite communications system. Assembly of Parties attended by representatives of member governments, meets every two years to consider policy and long-term aims and matters of interest to members as sovereign states. Meeting of Signatories to the Operating Agreement held annually; Board of Governors of 27 members representing 90 signatories meets four times a year. Sixteen INTELSAT satellites in synchronous orbit provide a global communications service; there are 212 earth stations carrying international commercial traffic and 14 facilities for performing specialized tracking, telemetry, command and monitoring (TTC & M). INTELSAT provides two-thirds of the world's overseas traffic through 70,000 units. Mems: 110 governments. Dir-Gen. RICHARD R. COLINO (suspended Nov. 1986).

Medicine and Health, Posts and Telecommunications, etc.

Pacific Telecommunications Council: 1110 University Ave, Suite 308, Honolulu, HI 96826; tel. (808) 941-3789; telex 7430550; non-governmental organization aiming to promote the development, understanding and beneficial use of telecommunications throughout the Pacific region; provides forum for users and providers of communications services; sponsors annual conference and seminars. Exec. Dir RICHARD J. BARBER. Publs conference proceedings, documents on communications development.

Postal Union of the Americas and Spain (Unión Postal de las Américas y España): Calle Cebollatí 1468/70, Casilla de Correos 20.042, Montevideo, Uruguay; tel. 400070; telex 22073; f. 1911 to extend, facilitate and study the postal relationships of member countries. Mems: 23 countries. Sec.-Gen. Ing. PEDRO MIGUEL CABERO (Argentina).

Press, Radio and Television

Asia-Pacific Broadcasting Union—ABU: POB 1164, Jalan Pantai Bharu, 59700 Kuala Lumpur, Malaysia; tel. 2743592; telex 32227; f. 1964 to assist in the development of radio and television in the Asian/Pacific area, particularly in its use for educational purposes. Mems: 35 full, 12 additional and 25 assoc. countries. Pres. Dato' ABDULLAH MOHAMAD (Malaysia); Sec.-Gen. HUGH LEONARD (Fiji). Publs *ABU Newsletter* (every 2 months in English), *ABU Technical Review* (every 2 months in English).

Association for the Promotion of the International Circulation of the Press—DISTRIPRESS: 8002 Zürich, Beethovenstrasse 20, Switzerland; tel. (01) 2024121; telex 815591; f. 1955 to assist in the promotion of the freedom of the press throughout the world, supporting and aiding UNESCO in promoting the free flow of ideas. Organizes meetings of publishers and distributors of newspapers, periodicals and paperback books, to promote the exchange of information and experience among members. Mems: 441. Pres. ALAN Y. PARDO (USA); Man. Dr ARNOLD E. KAULICH (Switzerland). Publs *Distripress News, Distripress Letter*.

Association of European Journalists: Chopinlaan 26, Voorschoten, Netherlands 2253 BV; tel. (01717) 3888; f. 1963 to participate actively in the development of a European consciousness; to promote deeper knowledge of European problems and secure appreciation by the general public of the work of European institutions; and to facilitate members' access to sources of European information. Mems: 1,000 individuals and national associations in 12 countries. Sec.-Gen. FRANS WILBERS.

Association of French-Language Television Services (Communauté des télévisions francophones): c/o Radio-Télévision Suisse Romande, 20 quai Ernest Ansermet, 1211 Geneva 8, Switzerland; f. 1964 to promote programme exchanges, joint ventures, exchange of information relating to television production and programming. Mems: French-language television organizations in France, Belgium, Switzerland, Monaco, Luxembourg and Canada. Pres. PIERRE DESROCHES (Canada); Gen. Sec. HENRI BUJARD (Switzerland).

Broadcasting Organizations of Non-aligned Countries—BONAC: c/o SLBS, New England, Freetown, Sierra Leone; tel. 40311; f. 1977 to ensure an equitable, objective and comprehensive flow of information through broadcasting; General Conference held every three years; Secretariat moves to the broadcasting organization of host country. Mems: 95 countries. Sec.-Gen. SAMA LENGOR (Sierra Leone).

Community of French-Language Radio Broadcasters (Communauté des radios publiques de langue française): c/o Société Nationale de Radiodiffusion, 116 ave Président Kennedy, 75016 Paris, France; tel. (1) 42-30-27-41; telex 200002; f. 1955 for the diffusion of French culture through the co-operation of Programme Directors in France, Belgium, Switzerland and Canada; holds annual competition. Gen. Sec. M. GÉRALD CAZAUBON (France).

Confederation of ASEAN Journalists: Gedung Dewan Pers, Lantai 4, Jalan Kebonsirih 34, Jakarta, 10110 Indonesia; f. 1975 for journalists of South-East Asia. Exec. Sec. DIA'FAR H. ASSEGAFF. Publs *CAJ Newsletter* (quarterly), *CAJ Year Book*.

European Alliance of Press Agencies: c/o ANSA, Via della Dataria 94, 00187 Rome; tel. 67741; telex 610242; f. 1957 to assist co-operation among members and to study and protect their common interests; annual assembly. Mems in 23 countries. Sec.-Gen. ARRIGO ACCORNERO.

European Broadcasting Union—EBU: Ancienne-Route 17A, CP 67, 1218 Grand-Saconnex, Geneva, Switzerland; tel. (022) 987766; telex 415700; f. 1950 in succession to the International Broadcasting Union; a professional association of broadcasting

OTHER INTERNATIONAL ORGANIZATIONS — Press, Radio and Television

organizations, supporting the interests of members and assisting the development of broadcasting in all its forms; activities include the Eurovision news and programme exchanges. General Assembly meets annually, Admin. Council composed of 15 members meets twice a year; there are four standing committees (Legal, Technical, Television Programme and Radio Programme). Mems: 102 active (European) and associate in 74 countries. Pres. (1987–88) ALBERT SCHARF (FRG); Sec.-Gen. Dr R. DE KALBERMATTEN (Switzerland). Publs *EBU Review* (monthly in English and French), in two editions: Geneva (Programmes, Administration, Law) and Brussels (Technical).

Technical Centre: 32 ave Albert Lancaster, 1180 Brussels, Belgium; tel. (02) 375-59-90; telex 21230; comprises the Technical Directorate of the EBU, the Eurovision Control Centre, the Receiving and Measuring Centre and the Technical Committee Secretariat. Dir GEORGE T. WATERS (Ireland).

Eurovision: f. 1954; a permanent sound and vision network covering Europe and North Africa; 33 television services in 26 countries are linked. Cyprus, Israel and Jordan are connected by satellite. The technical aspects are organized at the Technical Centre, in Brussels. An important application is in the exchange of television news.

Federation of European Industrial Editors Associations: c/o John Hartvig, Kemp and Lauritzen, 12 Roskildevej, 2620 Albertslund, Denmark; f. 1955 to raise the standard of industrial journals, and of industrial communications as a whole. Mems: 12 national associations. Sec.-Gen. JOHN HARTVIG.

Inca-Fiej Research Association: Washingtonplatz 1, 6100 Darmstadt, Federal Republic of Germany; tel. (6151) 76057; telex 0419273; f. 1961 to develop methods, machines and techniques for the newspaper industry; to evaluate standard specifications for raw materials for use in newspaper production; to investigate economy and quality improvements for newspaper printing and publishing. Mems: 651 newspapers, 57 trade asscns. Pres. JACQUES ST CRICQ (France); Man. Dir Dr F. W. BURKHARDT. Publ. *Newspaper Techniques* (in English, French and German), *Boletín del Centro Técnico* (monthly, in Spanish).

Inter-American Press Association (Sociedad Interamericana de Prensa): 2911 NW 39th St, Miami, Fla 33142, USA; tel. (305) 634-2465; telex 522873; f. 1942 to guard the freedom of the press in the Americas; to promote and maintain the dignity, rights and responsibilities of the profession of journalism; to foster a wider knowledge and greater interchange among the peoples of the Americas. Mems: 1,400. Exec. Dir W. P. WILLIAMSON, Jr. Publ. *IAPA News* (monthly in English and Spanish).

International Alliance of Distribution by Cable: President Rooseveltlaan 1, 9000 Ghent, Belgium; tel. (091) 25-58-31; telex 11473; f. 1955 to encourage the development of distribution by cable and defend its interests; to ensure exchange of documentation and carry out research on relevant technical and legal questions. Mems: 16 organizations in 10 countries. Pres. M. DE SUTTER; Sec.-Gen. G. MOREAU.

International Association of Broadcasting (Asociación Internacional de Radiodifusión—AIR): Calle Yi 1264, Montevideo, Uruguay; tel. (2) 98-5408; telex 843; f. 1946 to preserve free and private radio broadcasting; to promote co-operation between the corporations and public authorities; to defend freedom of expression. Mems: national associations of broadcasters. Pres. LUIZ EDUARDO BORGERTH; Dir-Gen. Dr LUIS ALBERTO SOLÉ. Publ. *La Gaceta de AIR* (every 2 months).

International Association of Sound Archives: c/o H. Harrison, Media Library, Open University Library, Walton Hall, Milton Keynes, MK7 6AA, England; tel. (0908) 653530; telex 826739; f. 1969; involved in the preservation and exchange of sound recordings, and in developing recording techniques; holds annual conference. Mems: institutions in 36 countries, and 10 international and regional organizations. Pres. ULF SCHARLAU (FRG); Sec.-Gen. HELEN HARRISON (UK). Publ. *Phonographic Bulletin* (3 a year).

International Catholic Union of the Press (Union catholique internationale de la presse—UCIP): Case Postale 197, 1211 Geneva 20, Switzerland; f. 1927 to link all Catholics who influence public opinion through the press, to inspire a high standard of professional conscience and to represent the interest of the Catholic press at international organizations. Mems: Federation of Catholic Press Agencies, International Federation of Catholic Journalists, International Federation of Catholic Dailies and Periodicals, International Catholic Association of Teachers in the Sciences and Information, International Federation of Church Press Associations, UCIP Africa, UCIP Asia, UCIP Latin America. Pres. Dr HANS SASSMANN (Austria); Sec.-Gen. Father PIERRE CHEVALIER (Switzerland). Publ. *UCIP-Informations.*

International Council of French-speaking Radio and Television Organizations: (Conseil international des radios-télévisions d'expression française): 20 quai Ernest-Ansermet, POB 234, 1211 Geneva 8, Switzerland; tel. (022) 281211; telex 428274; f. 1978 to establish links between French-speaking radio and television organizations. Mems: 41 organizations. Pres. JACQUES GIRARD (Canada); Sec.-Gen. RENÉ SCHENKER (Switzerland).

International Federation of Newspaper Publishers—FIEJ: 6 rue du Faubourg Poissonnière, 75010 Paris, France; tel. (1) 45-23-38-88; telex 290513; f. 1948 to defend the freedom of the press, to safeguard the ethical and economic interests of newspapers and to study all questions of interest to newspapers at international level. Mems: national organizations in 27 countries. Pres. GORDON LINACRE (UK); Sec.-Gen. GIOVANNI GIOVANNINI (Italy).

International Federation of Press Cutting Agencies: Streulistrasse 19, POB 8030 Zürich, Switzerland; tel. (01) 2524937; telex 816543; f. 1953 to improve the standing of the profession, prevent infringements, illegal practices and unfair competition; and to develop business and friendly relations among press cuttings agencies throughout the world. Mems: 62 agencies. Pres. GÖRAN TAMM (Sweden); Gen. Sec. Dr DIETER HENNE (Switzerland). Publ. *Newsletter* (twice yearly).

International Federation of the Cinematographic Press—FIPRESCI: 24 rue Falguière, 75015 Paris, France; tel. (1) 43-20-25-72; f. 1930 to develop the cinematographic press and promote cinema as an art; organizes international meetings and juries in film festivals. Mems: national organizations or corresponding members in 45 countries. Pres. ERWIN GYERTYAN (Hungary); Sec.-Gen. MARCEL MARTIN (France).

International Federation of the Periodical Press: Suite 19, Grosvenor Gardens House, 35–37 Grosvenor Gardens, London, SW1W 0BS, England; tel. (01) 828-1366; telex 24224; f. 1925 to protect and promote the material and moral interests of the periodical press, facilitate contacts between members and develop the free exchange of ideas and information. Mems: 104 national associations and publishing companies in 31 countries. Pres. P. CHOPIN (France); Dir R. WHARMBY (UK).

International Federation of the Socialist and Democratic Press: Foro Bonaparte 24, 20121 Milan, Italy; tel. (02) 806319; f. 1953 to promote co-operation between editors and publishers of socialist newspapers; affiliated to the Socialist International (q.v.). Mems: about 100. Sec. UMBERTO GIOVINE.

International Film and Television Council: 1 rue Miollis, 75732 Paris Cedex 15, France; f. 1958 to arrange meetings and co-operation generally. Mems: full: 39 international film and television organizations; associate: 25 national bodies of international scope. Pres. Prof. ENRICO FULCHIGNONI; Dir MARIO VERDONE. Publ. *Letter of Information* (monthly, in English, French and Spanish).

International Institute of Communications: Tavistock House South, Tavistock Sq., London, WC1H 9LF, England; tel. (01) 388-0671; telex 24578; f. 1969 (as the International Broadcast Institute) to link all working in the field of communications, including policy makers, broadcasters, industrialists and engineers; holds local, regional and international meetings, undertakes and sponsors research and gathers information. Mems: over 80 corporate and institutional. Pres. THOMAS P. HARDIMAN (Ireland); Exec. Dir JOHN HAWKINS.

International Maritime Radio Committee: Southbank House, Black Prince Rd, London, SE1 7SJ, England; tel. (01) 582-6300; telex 295555; f. 1928 to study and develop means of improving marine wireless communications and radio aids to marine navigation. Mems: 52 organizations and companies operating wireless stations on vessels of the Merchant Marine and fishing boats of practically all the maritime nations of the world. Pres. R. BRYSSINCK (Belgium); Sec.-Gen. and Chair. of Technical Cttee Commdr C. C. WAKE-WALKER (UK); Admin. Sec. Miss J. CASTANHETA (Belgium).

International Organization of Journalists: Pařížská 9, 110 01 Prague 1, Czechoslovakia; tel. 2316412; telex 122631; f. 1946 to defend the freedom of the press and of journalists and to promote their material welfare. Activities include the maintenance of international training centres and international recreation centres for journalists. Consultative status with ECOSOC and UNESCO. Mems: national organizations and individuals in 114 countries. Chair. KAARLE NORDENSTRENG (Finland); Sec.-Gen. JIŘI KUBKA (Czechoslovakia). Publs *The Democratic Journalist* (monthly in English, French, Russian and Spanish), *Interpressgrafik* (quarterly), *Interpressmagazin* (every 2 months), *IOJ Newsletter* (2 a month, in English, French, German and Spanish; monthly in Arabic).

International Press Institute—IPI: Dilke House, Malet St, London, WC1E 7JA, England; tel. (01) 636-0703; telex 25950; f. 1951 as a non-governmental association of editors, publishers and news broadcasters who support the principles of a free and responsible press; activities: defence of press freedom, regional meetings of members, programme to train staff of Asian newspapers, research and library and press centre; annual general assembly. Mems: 1,700 from 62 countries. Pres. JUAN LUIS CEBRIÁN (Spain); Dir PETER GALLINER (UK). Publ. *IPI Report* (monthly).

International Press Telecommunications Council: Studio House, 184 Fleet St, London, EC4, England; tel. (01) 405-2608; f. 1965 to safeguard and promote the interests of the Press on all matters relating to telecommunications; keeps its members informed of current and future telecommunications developments. The Council meets once a year and maintains five committees. Mems: 26 press associations, newspapers and news agencies. Chair. JOSEPH P. RAWLEY; Dir OLIVER G. ROBINSON. Publ. *IPTC News* (3 a year).

International Radio and Television Organization (OIRT): ul. Skokanská 169 56 Prague 6, Czechoslovakia; tel. 341371; telex 122144; f. 1946 as the International Broadcasting Organization in succession to Union internationale de radiodiffusion; present name adopted 1959; links broadcasting and television services in member countries and exchanges information on technical developments and programmes; includes Technical Commission (with five study groups), Radio Programme Commission (with six specialized groups), Television Programme Commission and Intervision Council; Technical Centre; Intervision network to link members' television services; holds general assembly every two years. Mems: broadcasting organizations from Afghanistan, Algeria, Bulgaria, Byelorussian SSR, Cuba, Czechoslovakia, Egypt, Estonian SSR, Finland, German Democratic Republic, Hungary, Iraq, Kampuchea, Democratic People's Republic of Korea, Laos, Latvian SSR, Lithuanian SSR, Mali, Moldavian SSR, Mongolia, Nicaragua, Poland, Romania, Sudan, Ukrainian SSR, USSR, Viet-Nam, People's Democratic Republic of Yemen. Sec.-Gen. Dr GENNADIJ CODR.

Latin-American Catholic Press Union: CP 90023, 25600 Petropolis, Brazil; tel. (0242) 435112; f. 1959 to co-ordinate, promote and improve the Catholic press in Latin America. Mems: national groups and local associations in Latin America. Pres. CLARENCIO NEOTTI (Brazil); Sec. PEDRO GILBERTO GOMES (Brazil).

Organization of Asia-Pacific News Agencies—OANA: c/o Press Trust of India, 4 Parliament St, New Delhi 110001, India; tel. 385848; telex 031-66400; f. 1961 to promote co-operation in professional matters and mutual exchange of news, features, etc. among the news agencies of Asia and the Pacific via the Asia-Pacific News Network (ANN). Mems: Anadolu Ajansi (Turkey), Antara (Indonesia), APP (Pakistan), Bakhtar Information Agency (Afghanistan), BERNAMA (Malaysia), BSS (Bangladesh), ENA (Bangladesh), Hindustan Samachar (India), IRNA (Iran), KCNA (Korea, Democratic People's Republic), KPL (Laos), Kyodo (Japan), Lankapuvath (Sri Lanka), Montsame (Mongolia), PNA (Philippines), PPI (Pakistan), PTI (India), RSS (Nepal), Samachar Bharati (India), TASS (USSR), TNA (Thailand), UNI (India), Viet-Nam News Agency, Yonhap (Republic of Korea), Xinhua (People's Republic of China). Pres. P. UNNIKRISHNAN (India); Sec.-Gen. P. K. BANDYOPADHYAY (India).

Press Foundation of Asia: POB 1843, Manila, Philippines; tel. 598633; telex 27674; f. 1967; an independent, non-profit making organization governed by its newspaper members; acts as a professional forum for about 200 newspapers in Asia; aims to reduce cost of newspapers to potential readers, to improve editorial and management techniques through research and training programmes and to encourage the growth of the Asian press; operates *Depthnews* feature service. Mems: 200 newspapers. Chair. KIM SANG MAN (Republic of Korea); Dir-Gen. MOCHTAR LUBIS (Indonesia). Publ. *Pressasia* (quarterly), *Asian Women and Children* (quarterly), *Environment Folio* (quarterly).

Union of African News Agencies—UANA: Algérie Presse Service, 7 blvd de la République, Algiers; f. 1963; meets annually. Mems: 50 agencies (incl. nine European and Asian associates).

Union of National Radio and Television Organizations of Africa—URTNA: 101 rue Carnot, BP 3237, Dakar, Senegal; tel. 21-16-25; telex 650; f. 1962; co-ordinates radio and television services, including monitoring and frequency allocation, the exchange of information and coverage of national and international events among African countries; maintains programme exchange centre (Nairobi, Kenya), technical centre (Bamako, Mali) and a centre for rural radio studies (Ouagadougou, Burkina Faso). Mems: 43 organizations and nine associate members. Sec.-Gen. FRANÇOIS ITOUA (Congo). Publs *URTNA Review* (English and French, 2 a year), *Family Health and Communication Bulletin* (monthly), reports.

World Association for Christian Communication—WACC: 122 King's Rd, London, SW3 4TR, England; tel. (01) 589-1484; telex 8812669; f. 1975; works among churches, church-related organizations and individuals to promote more effective use of all forms of media (including radio, television, newspapers, books, film, cassettes, dance, drama etc.) for proclaiming the Christian gospel, particularly with reference to ethical and social issues. Mems in 61 countries. Pres. WILLIAM F. FORE; Gen.-Sec. CARLOS A. VALLE. Publs *Action* newsletter (10 a year), *Media Development* (quarterly).

Religion

Agudath Israel World Organisation: Hacherut Sq, POB 326, Jerusalem 91002, Israel; tel. 223357; f. 1912 to help solve the problems facing Jewish people all over the world in the spirit of the Jewish tradition; holds World Rabbinical Council (every five years), and an annual Central Council comprising 100 mems nominated by affiliated organizations; has consultative status with ECOSOC and UNESCO. Mems: over 500,000 in 25 countries. Sec.-Gen. A. HIRSCH (Jerusalem). Publs *Hamodia* (Jerusalem daily newspaper), *Jewish Tribune* (London, weekly), *Jewish Observer* (New York, monthly), *La Voz Judia* (Buenos Aires, monthly), *Jüdische Stimme* (Zürich, monthly).

All Africa Conference of Churches—AACC: Waiyaki Way, POB 14205, Nairobi, Kenya; tel. 61166; telex 22175; f. 1958; an organ of co-operation and continuing fellowship among Protestant, Orthodox and Independent churches and Christian Councils in Africa. Assemblies in Kampala, Uganda (1963), Abidjan, Ivory Coast (1969), Lusaka, Zambia (1974) and Nairobi, Kenya (1981). Mems: 123 churches and Christian councils in 33 African countries. Pres. Archbishop WALTER KHOTSO MAKHULU (Botswana); Gen. Sec. Rev. VICTORY MAXIME RAFRANSOA (Madagascar). Publ. *AACC Magazine* (quarterly).

Alliance Israélite Universelle; 45 rue La Bruyère, 75009 Paris, France; f. 1860 to work for the emancipation and moral progress of the Jews; maintains 39 schools in the Mediterranean area; library of 100,000 vols. Mems: 12,000 in 20 countries. Pres. ADY STEG; Dir JACQUES LEVY (France). Publs *Cahiers de l'Alliance Israélite Universelle* (2 a year) in French, *The Alliance Review* in English, *Les Nouveaux Cahiers* (quarterly) in French.

Bahá'í International Community: Bahá'í World Centre, POB 155, 31 001 Haifa, Israel; tel. (04) 672433; telex 46626; f. 1844 in Persia to promote the unity of mankind and world peace through the teachings of the Bahá'í religion, including the equality of men and women and the elimination of all forms of prejudice; maintains schools for children and adults worldwide, and maintains educational and cultural radio stations in the USA and Latin America; has 27 publishing trusts throughout the world; consultative status with the UN (ECOSOC) and UNICEF. Governing body: Universal House of Justice (nine mems elected by 148 National Spiritual Assemblies). Mems: in 111,577 centres (166 countries). Sec.-Gen. DONALD M. BARRETT (USA); Dir-Gen. DOUGLAS MARTIN (Canada). Publs *Bahá'í World, La Pensée Bahá'ie* (quarterly), *World Order* (quarterly), *Opinioni Bahá'í* (quarterly).

Baptist World Alliance: 6733 Curran St, McLean, Va 22101, USA; tel. (703) 790-8980; f. 1905 as an association of national Baptist conventions and unions; 15th World Congress, Los Angeles, 1985. Mems in 144 countries. Pres. Dr G. NOEL VOSE (Australia); Gen. Sec. Dr GERHARD CLAAS. Publ. *The Baptist World* (11 a year).

Christian Conference of Asia: 10 New Industrial Rd, 05-00 Singapore 1953; tel. 2861511; telex 33733; f. 1959 to promote co-operation and joint study in matters of common concern among the Churches of the region and to encourage interaction with other regional Conferences and the World Council of Churches. Mems: 15 national Christian Councils and 92 churches in 17 countries: Australia, Bangladesh, Burma, Hong Kong, India, Indonesia, Japan, Republic of Korea, Laos, Malaysia, New Zealand, Pakistan, Philippines, Singapore, Sri Lanka, Taiwan and Thailand. Gen. Sec. Rev. PARK SANG JUNG. Publs *Directory, CCA News* (monthly), and various other books and pamphlets.

Christian Peace Conference: 111 21 Prague 1, Jungmannova 9, Czechoslovakia; tel. 243338; telex 123363; f. 1958 as an international movement of theologians, clergy and laymen, and growing from their conviction of faith in a time of rising international tension: it aims to bring Christendom to recognize its share of guilt in both world wars and to dedicate itself to the service of friendship, reconciliation and peaceful co-operation of nations, to concentrate on united action for peace, and to co-ordinate peace groups in individual churches and facilitate their effective participation in the peaceful development of society. It works through regional committees and member churches in many countries. Pres. Bishop Dr KÁROLY TÓTH (Reformed Church of Hungary); Gen. Sec. Rev. LUBOMÍR MIŘEJOVSKÝ (Evangelical Church of Czech Brethren). Publs *Christian Peace Conference* (quarterly in English and German), *CPC News Bulletin* (2 a month in English and German), occasional *Study Volume* and *Summary of Information* (in French and Spanish), *News from the UN* (monthly, in English).

Conference of European Churches—CEC: 150 route de Ferney, 1211 Geneva 20, Switzerland; tel. (022) 916111; telex 23423; f. 1957 to provide a meeting-place for European churches from East and West and for members and non-members of the World Council of Churches; conferences every few years (latest: Stirling, 1986). Mems: 116 Protestant, Anglican and Orthodox churches in 26 European countries. Pres. (vacant); Gen. Sec. JEAN FISCHER. Publs. Occasional Papers, Information Bulletins and Study Documentation Service.

Conference of International Catholic Organizations: 37-39 rue de Vermont, Geneva, Switzerland; f. 1927 to encourage collaboration and agreement between the different Catholic international organizations in their common interests, and to contribute to international understanding; organizes international assemblies and meetings to study specific problems. Permanent commissions deal with human rights, the new international economic order, social problems, the family health, education, etc. Mems: 46 Catholic international organizations. Administrator RUDI RUEGG (Switzerland).

Consultative Council of Jewish Organizations—CCJO: Woburn House, Upper Woburn Place, London, WC1H 0EP, England; f. 1946 to co-operate and consult with the UN and other international bodies directly concerned with human rights and to defend the cultural, political and religious rights of Jews throughout the world. The CCJO has consultative status with the UN, UNESCO, UNICEF and the Council of Europe. Mems: Jewish organizations with over 46,000 mems. Co-Chairmen HARRY BATSHAW, JULES BRAUNSCHVIG, Dr BASIL BARD, CBE; Sec.-Gen. MOSES MOSKOWITZ (USA).

European Baptist Federation: Laerdalsgade 7, 2300 Copenhagen S, Denmark; tel. (01) 590904; f. 1949 to promote fellowship and co-operation among Baptists in Europe; to further the aims and objects of the Baptist World Alliance; to stimulate and co-ordinate evangelism in Europe; to provide for consultation and planning of missionary work in Europe and stimulate and co-ordinate missionary work of European Baptists elsewhere in the world. Mems: Baptist Unions in 23 European countries. Pres Dr PIERO BENSI; Sec.-Treas. Dr KNUD WÜMPELMANN.

Evangelical Alliance: 186 Kennington Park Rd, London, SE11 4BT, England; tel. (01) 582-0228; f. 1846 to promote Christian unity and co-operation, religious freedom and evangelization; affiliated to the European Evangelical Alliance and the World Evangelical Fellowship. Gen. Sec. CLIVE CALVER. Publs *Idea* (quarterly).

Friends (Quakers) World Committee for Consultation: Drayton House, 30 Gordon St, London, WC1H 0AX, England; tel. (01) 388-0497; f. 1937 to encourage and strengthen the spiritual life within the Religious Society of Friends; to help Friends to a better understanding of their vocation in the world; to promote consultation among Friends of all countries; representation at the United Nations as a non-governmental organization. Mems: appointed representatives and individuals from 56 countries. Gen. Sec. VAL FERGUSON. Publs *Friends World News* (2 a year), *Calendar of Yearly Meetings* (annually), *Finding Friends around the World* (handbook, eighth edition 1982), *Quaker Information Network* (6 a year).

General Anthroposophical Society: The Goetheanum, 4143 Dornach, Switzerland; f. 1923 by Rudolf Steiner to study spiritual science and its application to art, education, medicine, agriculture, and other spheres of life. There are branches in practically all countries. Pres MANFRED SCHMIDT-BRABANT; Lending Library: Rudolf Steiner Library, 38 Museum St, London, WC1, England. Publ. *Das Goetheanum* (weekly).

International Association for Religious Freedom—IARF: 6000 Frankfurt 70, Dreieichstr. 59, Federal Republic of Germany; tel. (69) 617367; f. 1900 as a world community of religions, subscribing to the principle of openness; conducts intercultural encounters, inter-religious dialogues, a social service network and development programme. Regional conferences and triennial congress. Mems: 50 groups in 21 countries. Pres. Dr ROY SMITH (UK); Gen. Sec. Rev. DIETHER GEHRMANN (FRG). Publ. *IARF News* (2 a year), Congress/Conference Proceedings and occasional papers.

International Association of Buddhist Studies: c/o Prof. Lewis Lancaster, Dept of Oriental Languages, University of California, Berkeley, Calif 94720, USA; tel. (415) 642-3547; f. 1976; holds international conference every two years; supports studies of Buddhist literature. Gen. Sec. LUIS GOMEZ. Publ. *Journal* (2 a year).

International Bible Reading Association; Robert Denholm House, Nutfield, Redhill, Surrey, RH1 4HW, England; tel. (073) 782-2411; f. 1882 to encourage reading and study of the Bible. Total membership over 250,000. Gen. Sec. Rev. SIMON OXLEY. Publs Bible readings and notes, prayer-books.

International Council of Jewish Women: 15 East 26th St, New York, NY 10010, USA; f. 1912 to promote friendly relations and understanding among Jewish women throughout the world; exchanges information on community welfare activities, promotes volunteer leadership, sponsors field work in social welfare and fosters Jewish education. It has consultative status with UN, ECOSOC, UNICEF, UNESCO and Council of Europe. Mems: affiliates totalling over 1 million members in 31 countries. Pres. LEILA SEIGEL (Switzerland); Sec. THEA HACKER (Switzerland). Publ. *Newsletter* (2 a year, English and Spanish).

International Fellowship of Reconciliation: Hof van Sonoy 15-17, 1811 LD Alkmaar, Netherlands; tel. (72) 123014; f. 1919; a transnational inter-religious movement committed to non-violence as a principle of life and to forming a world community of peace and liberation. Branches in 30 countries. Pres. DIANA FRANCIS (UK); Gen. Sec. JAMES H. FOREST. Publs national magazines and *IFOR Report* (5 a year).

International Humanist and Ethical Union: Oudkerkof 11, 3512 Utrecht, Netherlands; tel. (30) 31-21-55; f. 1952 to bring into association all those interested in promoting ethical and scientific humanism. Mems: national organizations and individuals in 51 countries. Pres Prof. Dr P. KURTZ (USA), Prof. Dr S. STOJANOVIĆ (Yugoslavia), Dr R. A. P. TIELMAN (Netherlands). Publ. *International Humanist* (quarterly).

International Organization for the Study of the Old Testament: c/o 34 Gough Way, Cambridge, CB3 9LN, England; f. 1950. Holds triennial congresses (next congress: Leuven, 1989). Pres. C. BREKELMANS (Belgium); Sec. Prof. J. A. EMERTON (UK). Publ. *Vetus Testamentum* (quarterly).

Islamic Council of Europe: 16 Grosvenor Crescent, London, SW1, England; tel. (01) 235-9832; telex 894240; f. 1973 as a co-ordinating body for Islamic centres and organizations in Europe; an autonomous Council collaborating with the Islamic Secretariat and other Islamic organizations; aims to develop a better understanding of Islam and Muslim culture in the West. Sec.-Gen. SALEM AZZAM.

Latin American Episcopal Council: Apartado Aéreo 5278, Bogotá, Colombia; tel. 2357044; telex 41388; f. 1955 to study the problems of the Church in Latin America; to co-ordinate Church activities. Mems: the Episcopal Conferences of Central and South America and the Caribbean. Pres. Most Rev. ANTONIO QUARRACINO (Argentina); Gen. Sec. Most Rev. DARÍO CASTRILLÓN (Colombia).

Lutheran World Federation: 150 route de Ferney, 1211 Geneva 20, Switzerland; tel. (022) 916111; f. 1947; confederation of 99 Lutheran Churches of 87 countries. Current activities: inter-church aid; relief work in various areas of the globe; service to refugees including resettlement; aid to missions; theological research, conferences and exchanges; scholarship aid in various fields of church life; inter-confessional dialogue with Roman Catholic, Reformed, Anglican and Orthodox churches; religious communications projects and international news and information services; seventh Assembly, Budapest, Hungary, 1984. Pres. Bishop Dr ZOLTÁN KÁLDY (Hungary); Gen. Sec. Rev. Dr GUNNAR JOHAN STAALSETT (Norway). Publs *Lutheran World Information* (English and German, weekly and monthly editions), *LWF Report* and *LWF Documentation* (English and German, 6 a year).

Muslim World League (Rabitat al-Alam al-Islami): POB 537, Mecca al-Mukarramah, Mecca, Saudia Arabia; tel. 025 363995; f. 1962 to advance Islamic unity and solidarity; provides financial assistance for Islamic education, medical care and relief work; has 30 offices throughout the world. Sec.-Gen. Dr ABDULLAH OMAR NASSEEF. Publs *Majalla Rabitat al-Alam al Islami* (monthly, Arabic), *Akhbar al-Alam al Islami* (weekly, Arabic), *Journal* (monthly, English).

Opus Dei (Prelature of the Holy Cross and Opus Dei): Viale Bruno Buozzi 73, 00197 Rome, Italy; tel. 870562; f. 1928 by Mgr Escrivá de Balaguer to spread, at every level of society, a profound awakening of consciences to the universal calling to sanctity and apostolate in the course of members' own professional work. Mems; 73,000 laymen and 1,200 priests. Prelate Mgr ALVARO DEL PORTILLO.

OTHER INTERNATIONAL ORGANIZATIONS

Pax Romana International Catholic Movement for Intellectual and Cultural Affairs—ICMICA; and International Movement of Catholic Students—IMCS: 1 route de Jura, BP 1062, 1701 Fribourg, Switzerland; tel. (037) 262649; f. 1921 (IMCS), 1947 (ICMICA), to encourage in members an awareness of their responsibilities as men and Christians in the student and intellectual milieux; to promote contacts between students and graduates throughout the world and co-ordinate the contribution of Catholic intellectual circles to international life. Mems: 80 student and 60 intellectual organizations in 80 countries. ICMICA—Pres. Manuela Silva (Portugal); Gen. Sec. R. J. Rajkumar (India); IMCS—Pres. Carles Torner; Sec.-Gen. Etienne Bisimwa. Publ. *Convergence* (every 2 months).

Salvation Army: International HQ, 101 Queen Victoria St, London, EC4P 4EP, England; tel. (01) 236-5222; telex 8954847; f. 1865 to spread the Christian gospel; emphasis is placed on the need for personal discipleship, and to make its evangelism effective it adopts a quasi-military form of organization. Social, medical and educational work is also performed in the 85 countries where the Army operates. Gen. Jarl Wahlstrom; Chief of Staff Commissioner Caughey Gauntlett; Chancellor Commissioner David Durman. Publs: 116 periodicals in various languages with a total circulation of 1,800,000. United Kingdom publs include *The War Cry, The Young Soldier* and *The Musician*.

Soroptimist International: 87 Glisson Rd, Cambridge, CB1 2HG, England; tel. (0223) 311833; f. 1921 to maintain high ethical standards in business and professional life; to strive for human rights for all people and, in particular, to advance the status of women; to develop friendship and unity among Soroptimists of all countries; to contribute to international understanding and universal friendship. Mems: 77,000 members in 2,450 clubs. International Pres. Sadun Katipoglu (Turkey); Sec. Doreen Astley (UK). Publ. *Soroptimist International Newsletter* (quarterly).

Theosophical Society: Adyar, Madras 600 020, India; tel. (044) 412815; f. 1875; aims at universal brotherhood, without distinction of race, creed, sex, caste or colour; study of comparative religion, philosophy and science; investigation of unexplained laws of nature and powers latent in man. Mems: 34,000 in 65 countries. Pres. Radha S. Burnier; Sec. Norma Y. Sastry. Publs *The Theosophist* (monthly), *Adyar News Letter* (quarterly), *Brahmavidya* (annually).

Toc H: 1 Forest Close, Wendover, Bucks., HP22 6BT, England; tel. (0296) 623911; f. 1915 to practise fellowship and service and encourage members to seek God and carry out His will, to encourage service in all sections of society and foster a sense of responsibility for the well-being of others. Mems: approx. 11,000. Gen. Sec. Dr J. M. A. Kilburn. Publ. *Point Three* (monthly).

United Bible Societies: 7000 Stuttgart 80, POB 81 03 40, Federal Republic of Germany; tel. (0711) 71810; telex 7255299; f. 1946. Mems: 70 Bible Societies and 31 Bible Society Offices at work throughout the world. Pres. Rev. Dr Oswald C. J. Hoffmann (USA); Gen. Sec. Rev. Dr Ulrich Fick. Publs *United Bible Societies Bulletin, Technical and Practical Papers on Translation* (both quarterly), *Prayer Booklet* (annually), *World Report* (monthly).

United Lodge of Theosophists: Theosophy Hall, 40 New Marine Lines, Bombay 400020, India; tel. 299024; f. 1929 to form the nucleus of a Universal Brotherhood of Humanity, without distinction of race, creed, sex, caste or colour; Mems: 24 lodges in nine countries. Publs *Theosophy, The Theosophical Movement* (monthly), *The Aryan Path* (bi-monthly), *Bulletin* (quarterly).

Watch Tower Bible and Tract Society: 25 Columbia Heights, Brooklyn, New York, NY 11201, USA; tel. (718) 625-3600; f. 1881; 95 branches; serves as legal agency for Jehovah's Witnesses, whose membership is 3m. Pres. Frederick W. Franz; Sec. and Treas. Lyman Swingle. Publs *The Watchtower* (2 a month, in 103 languages), *Awake!* (2 a month, in 53 languages).

World Alliance of Reformed Churches (Presbyterian and Congregational): 150 route de Ferney, 1211 Geneva 20, Switzerland; tel. (022) 916111; telex 23423; f. 1970 by merger of WARC (Presbyterian) (f. 1875) with International Congregational Council (f. 1891) to promote fellowship among Reformed, Presbyterian and Congregational churches. Mems: 159 Churches in 80 countries. Gen. Sec. Rev. Dr Edmond Perret. Publs *Reformed World* (quarterly), *Reformed Perspectives* (monthly, in four languages).

World Assembly for Moral Rearmament: Mountain House, Caux, 1824 Vaud, Switzerland; tel. (021) 634821; other international centres at Panchgani, India and Petropolis, Brazil; f. 1921; aims: a new social order for better human relations and the elimination of political, industrial and racial antagonism. Legally incorporated bodies in 20 countries. Pres. Daniel Mottu; Sec. Heinrich Karrer. Publs *Changer* (monthly), *New World News* (fortnightly), *Caux Information* (German, monthly), other publs in Dutch, Japanese, Norwegian and Swedish.

World Confederation of Jewish Community Centres: J. D. C. Hill, Jerusalem, Israel; tel. (02) 661261; telex 26212; f. 1977 to foster the unity of the Jewish Community Centres and of the Jewish people throughout the world. Mems: national bodies in 20 countries. Pres. Esther Leah Ritz; Exec. Dir Haim Zipori.

World Conference on Religion and Peace: 14 chemin Auguste-Vilbert, 1218 Grand Saconnex, Geneva, Switzerland; tel. (022) 985162; f. 1970 to co-ordinate education and action of various world religions for world peace and justice. Mems: religious organizations and individuals in 50 countries. Pres. Dr Inamullah Khan; Sec.-Gen. Dr John B. Taylor. Publ. *Religion for Peace* (quarterly newsletter).

World Congress of Faiths: 28 Powis Gdns, London, W11 1JG, England; f. 1936 to promote a spirit of fellowship among mankind through religion, to bring together people of all nationalities, backgrounds and creeds, to encourage the study and undertaking of world faiths, and to promote welfare and peace. Mems: about 500. Pres. Very Rev. E. Carpenter, Dean of Westminster; Chair. Rev. Marcus Braybrooke. Publ. *World Faiths Insight* (2 a year).

World Federation of Christian Life Communities: Borgo S. Spirito 8, Casella Postale 6139, 00195 Rome, Italy; tel. 6568079; f. 1953 as World Federation of the Sodalities of our Lady (first group founded 1563) as a lay movement (based on the teachings of Ignatius Loyola) to integrate Christian faith and daily living. Mems: groups in 55 countries representing 45,000 individuals. Pres. Brendan McLoughlin (Ireland); Exec. Sec. José Reyes (Chile). Publ. *Progressio* (every 2 months in English, French, Spanish).

World Fellowship of Buddhists: 33 Sukhumvit Rd, (between Soi 1 and Soi 3), Bangkok 10110, Thailand; f. 1950 to promote practice, teaching and philosophy of Buddhism; holds annual General Congress. Regional centres in 36 countries. Pres. Sanya Dharmasakti; Hon. Gen. Sec. Prasert Ruangskul. Publ. *WFB Review* (quarterly).

World Jewish Congress: 1 Park Ave, Suite 418, New York, NY 10016, USA; tel. (212) 679-6000; telex 236129; f. 1936; a voluntary association of representative Jewish bodies, communities and organizations throughout the world, aiming to foster the unity of the Jewish people and to ensure the continuity and development of their heritage. Mems: Jewish communities in 63 countries. Pres. Edgar M. Bronfman; Sec.-Gen. Israel Singer. Publs *Patterns of Prejudice* (quarterly, London), *Gesher* (Hebrew quarterly, Israel), *Christian Jewish Relations* (quarterly, London), *Boletín Informativo OJI* (fortnightly, Buenos Aires).

World Methodist Council: International Headquarters, POB 518, Lake Junaluska, NC 28745, USA; tel. (704) 456-9432; f. 1881 to deepen the fellowship of the Methodist peoples, to encourage evangelism, to foster Methodist participation in the ecumenical movement, and to promote the unity of Methodist witness and service. Mems: 64 Church bodies in 90 countries, comprising 23.7m. individuals. Chair. Bishop Lawi Imathiu (Kenya); Gen. Sec. Joe Hale (USA). Publ. *World Parish* (6 a year).

World Sephardi Federation: 13 rue Marignac, 1206 Geneva, Switzerland; tel. (022) 473313; telex 427569; f. 1951 to strengthen the unity of Jewry and Judaism among Sephardi and Oriental Jews, to defend and foster religious and cultural activities of all Sephardi and Oriental Jewish communities and preserve their spiritual heritage, to provide moral and material assistance where necessary and to co-operate with other similar organizations. Mems: 50 communities and organizations in 30 countries. Pres. Nessim D. Gaon.

World Student Christian Federation: 27 chemin des Crêts de Pregny, 1218 Grand-Saconnex, Geneva, Switzerland; tel. (022) 988953; f. 1895 to proclaim Jesus Christ as Lord and Saviour in the academic community, and to present students with the claims of the Christian faith over their whole life. Gen. Assembly every four years. Mems: 67 national Student Christian Movements, and 34 national correspondents. Chair. Bishop Poulose Mar Poulose (India); Sec.-Gen. Christine Ledger (Australia), Manuel Quintero (Cuba).

World Union for Progressive Judaism: 13 King David St, Jerusalem, Israel; North American Board, 838 Fifth Ave, New York, NY 10021, USA; f. 1926; promotes and co-ordinates efforts of Reform, Liberal and Progressive congregations throughout the world; supports new congregations; assigns and employs rabbis; sponsors seminaries and schools; organizes international conferences; maintains a youth section. Mems: organizations and individuals in 25 countries. Pres. Gerard Daniel (USA); Exec. Dir Rabbi Richard G. Hirsch (Israel). Publs *AMMI* (quarterly), *Telem* (monthly in Hebrew), *International Conference Reports, European Judaism* (bi-annual).

World Union of Catholic Women's Organisations: 20 rue Notre-Dame-des-Champs, 75006 Paris, France; tel. (1) 45-44-27-65; f. 1910 to promote and co-ordinate the contribution of Catholic women in international life, in social, civic, cultural and religious matters. Mems: 30,000,000. Pres.-Gen. Mrs E. E. AITKEN (Canada); Sec.-Gen. GERALDINE MACCARTHY. Publ. *Newsletter* (bi-monthly in four languages).

Science

International Council of Scientific Unions—ICSU: 51 blvd de Montmorency, 75016 Paris, France; tel. (1) 45-25-03-29; telex 630 553; f. 1919 as International Research Council; present name adopted 1931; new statutes adopted 1984; to co-ordinate international co-operation in theoretical and applied sciences and to promote national scientific research through the intermediary of affiliated national organizations; General Assembly of representatives of national and scientific members meets every two years to formulate policy. The following committees have been established: Scientific Cttee on Antarctic Research, Scientific Cttee on Oceanic Research, Cttee on Space Research, ICSU-UATI Co-ordinating Cttee on Water Research, Scientific Cttee on Solar-Terrestrial Physics, Cttee on Science and Technology in Developing Countries, Cttee on Data for Science and Technology, Cttee on the Teaching of Science, Scientific Cttee on Problems of the Environment, Cttee on Genetic Experimentation and Special Cttee on Toxic Waste Disposal. The following services and Inter-Union Committees and Commissions have been established: Federation of Astronomical and Geophysical Services, Inter-Union Commission on Frequency Allocations for Radio Astronomy and Space Science, Inter-Union Commission on Radio Meteorology, Inter-Union Commission on Spectroscopy, Inter-Union Commission on Lithosphere and Inter-Union Commission on the Application of Science to Agriculture, Fisheries and Aquaculture. Budget prepared annually by Finance Committee, presented to Assembly, which determines contributions for members. National mems: academies or research councils in 71 countries; Scientific mems and assocs: 20 international unions (see below) and 21 scientific associates. Pres. Sir JOHN KENDREW (UK); Sec.-Gen. L. ERNSTER (Sweden); Exec. Sec. F. W. G. BAKER (UK). Publs *ICSU Yearbook, ICSU Newsletter* (quarterly).

UNIONS FEDERATED TO THE ICSU

International Astronomical Union: 61 ave de l'Observatoire, 75014 Paris, France; tel. (1) 43-25-83-58; telex 205671; f. 1919 to facilitate co-operation between the astronomers of various countries and to further the study of astronomy in all its branches; last General Assembly was held in 1985 in Delhi, India. Mems: 50 countries are affiliated; there are 5,200 individual mems. Pres. J. SAHADE (Argentina); Gen. Sec. Dr J.-P. SWINGS (Belgium). Publs *Transactions*.

International Geographical Union—IGU: Dept of Geography, University of Alberta, Edmonton, Alberta, T6G 2H4, Canada; tel. (403) 432-3329; telex 037-2979; f. 1922 to encourage the study of problems relating to geography, to promote and co-ordinate research requiring international co-operation, and to organize international congresses and commissions. Mems: 80 regular mem. countries, 10 associates. Pres. Prof. PETER SCOTT (Australia); Sec.-Gen. Prof. L. A. KOSINSKI (Canada). Publs *IGU Bulletin* (1–2 a year), Circular Letter, congress proceedings.

International Mathematical Union: c/o Dept of Mathematics, Hallituskatu 15, 00100 Helsinki, Finland; tel. (3580) 191-2883; telex 124690; f. 1952 to support and assist the International Congress of Mathematicians and other international scientific meetings or conferences; to encourage and support other international mathematical activities considered likely to contribute to the development of mathematical science—pure, applied or educational. Mems: 53 countries. Pres. Prof. L. FADDEEV; Sec.-Gen. Prof. O. LEHTO.

International Union for Pure and Applied Biophysics: Institute of Biophysics, Medical University, 7643 Pécs, Hungary; tel. (72) 14017; telex 12311; f. 1961 to organize international co-operation in biophysics and promote communication between biophysics and allied subjects, to encourage national co-operation between biophysical societies, and to contribute to the advancement of biophysical knowledge. Mems: 36 adhering bodies. Pres. Prof. B. PULLMAN (France); Sec.-Gen. Prof. J. TIGYI (Hungary). Publ. *Quarterly Reviews of Biophysics*.

International Union of Biochemistry: Dept of Biochemistry, Duke University Medical Center, POB 3711, Durham, NC 27710, USA; tel. (919) 684-5326; telex 802829; f. 1955 (a) to sponsor the International Congresses of Biochemistry, (b) to co-ordinate research and discussion, (c) to organize co-operation between the societies of biochemistry, (d) to promote high standards of biochemistry throughout the world and (e) to contribute to the advancement of biochemistry in all its international aspects. Mems: 51 bodies. Pres. Dr M. GRUNBERG-MANAGO (France); Sec.-Gen. Dr R. L. HILL (USA).

International Union of Biological Sciences: 51 blvd de Montmorency, 75016 Paris, France; tel. (1) 45-25-00-09; telex 630553; f. 1919. Mems: 67 scientific bodies. Exec. Sec. Dr T. YOUNES. Publ. *Biology International* (2 a year, plus special issues), proceedings.

International Union of Crystallography: c/o Dr J. N. King, 5 Abbey Sq., Chester, CH1 2HU, England; tel. 42878; f. 1947 to facilitate international standardization of methods, of units, of nomenclature and of symbols used in crystallography; and to form a focus for the relations of crystallography to other sciences. Mems in 34 countries. Pres. Prof. T. HAHN (FRG); Gen. Sec. Prof. K. KURKI-SUONIO (Finland); Exec. Sec. Dr J. N. KING. Publs *Acta Crystallographica, Journal of Applied Crystallography* (bi-monthly), *Structure Reports* (2 volumes a year), *International Tables for Crystallography, Molecular Structures and Dimensions, World Directory of Crystallographers, Fifty Years of X-ray Diffraction, Fifty Years of Electron Diffraction, Early Papers on Diffraction of X-rays by Crystals, Symmetry Aspects of M. C. Escher's Periodic Drawings, Index of Crystallographic Supplies, Crystallographic Book List, Bibliographies, World List of Crystallographic Computer Programs*.

International Union of Geodesy and Geophysics—IUGG: Observatoire Royal de Belgique, 3 ave Circulaire, 1180 Brussels, Belgium; tel. (02) 375-24-84; telex 21565; f. 1919; federation of seven associations representing Geodesy, Seismology and Physics of the Earth's Interior, Physical Sciences of the Ocean, Volcanology and Chemistry of the Earth's Interior, Scientific Hydrology, Meteorology and Atmospheric Physics, Geomagnetism and Aeronomy, which meet at the General Assemblies of the Union. In addition, there are Joint Committees of the various associations either among themselves or with other unions. The Union organizes scientific meetings and also sponsors various permanent services, the object of which is to collect, analyse and publish geophysical data. Mems: in 78 countries. Pres. Prof. D. LAL (India); Gen. Sec. Prof. P. MELCHIOR (Belgium). Publs *IUGG Chronicle* (monthly), *Geodetic Bulletin* (quarterly), *International Bibliography of Geodesy* (irregular), *International Seismological Summary* (yearly), *Bulletin Volcanologique* (2 a year), *Bulletin mensuel du Bureau Central Sismologique* (monthly), *Bulletin de l'Association Internationale d'Hydrologie Scientifique* (quarterly), *International Bibliography of Hydrology, Catalogue des Volcans Actifs* (both irregular), texts of communications, *IUGG Monographs* (irregular).

International Union of Geological Sciences—IUGS: Leiv Erikssons vei 39, POB 3006, 7001 Trondheim, Norway; tel. (7) 92-15-00; telex 55417; f. 1961 to encourage the study of geoscientific problems, facilitate international and inter-disciplinary co-operation in geology and related sciences, and support the quadrennial International Geological Congress. IUGS organizes international meetings and co-sponsors joint programmes, including the International Geological Correlation Programme (with UNESCO). Mems from 95 countries. Pres. Dr W. W. HUTCHINSON (Canada); Sec.-Gen. Prof. R. SINDING-LARSEN (Norway).

International Union of Immunological Societies: 9650 Rockville Pike, Bethesda, Md 20814, USA; tel. (301) 530-7178; holds triennial international congress. Mems: national societies in 37 countries. Pres. G. V. NOSSAL (Australia); Sec.-Gen. H. METZGER (USA). Publ. *Proceedings*.

International Union of Microbiological Societies—IUMS: Dept of Genetics, University of Newcastle, Ridley Bldg, Claremont Place, Newcastle-upon-Tyne, NE1 7RU, England; tel. (091) 232-8511; telex 53654; f. 1930. Mems: 71 national microbiological societies. Pres. Prof. P. GERHARDT (USA); Sec.-Gen. Prof. S. W. GLOVER. Publs *Microbiological Sciences* (monthly), *International Journal of Systematic Bacteriology* (quarterly), *Intervirology* (monthly), *International Journal of Food Microbiology* (every 2 months), *Advances in Microbial Ecology* (annually), *Journal of Biological Standardization* (quarterly).

International Union of Nutritional Sciences: c/o Dept of Human Nutrition, Agricultural University, De Dreijen 12, 6703 BC Wageningen, Netherlands; tel. (08370) 82589; telex 45015; f. 1946 to promote international co-operation in the scientific study of nutrition and its applications, to encourage research and exchange of scientific information by holding international congresses and publications. Mems: organizations in 56 countries. Sec.-Gen. Prof. J. G. A. J. HAUTVAST (Netherlands). Publs *IUNS Directory* and *Newsletter*.

International Union of Pharmacology: c/o Vice-Chancellor's Office, The University of Buckingham, Buckingham, MK18 1EG, England; tel. (0280) 814080, ext. 207; f. 1963 to promote international co-ordination of research, discussion and publication in the field of pharmacology, including clinical pharmacology, drug metabolism and toxicology; co-operates with WHO in all matters concerning drugs and drug research; holds international congresses. Mems: national and regional societies in 43 countries. Pres. P. LECHAT (France); Sec.-Gen. A. M. BARRETT (UK). Publ. *TIPS (Trends in Pharmacological Sciences)*.

International Union of Physiological Sciences: c/o Prof. R. Naquet, Laboratoire de Physiologie Nerveuse, CNRS, ave de la Terrasse, 91190 Gif-sur-Yvette, France; tel. 69-07-78-28; f. 1955. Mems: 48 national and four assoc. mems. Pres. Sir ANDREW HUXLEY (UK); Sec.-Gen. Prof. R. NAQUET.

International Union of Psychological Science: c/o Prof. K. Pawlik, Psychologisches Institut I, Von-Melle-Park II, 2000 Hamburg 13, Federal Republic of Germany; f. 1951 to contribute to the development of intellectual exchange and scienific relations between psychologists of different countries. Mems: national societies in 47 countries. Pres. Prof. WAYNE H. HOLTZMAN (USA); Sec.-Gen. Prof. KURT PAWLIK (FRG). Publs *International Journal of Psychology* (quarterly), *International Directory of Psychologists* (irregular).

International Union of Pure and Applied Chemistry—IUPAC: Bank Court Chambers, 2–3 Pound Way, Cowley Centre, Oxford, OX4 3YF, England; tel. (0865) 717744; telex 83147; f. 1919 to organize permanent co-operation between chemical associations in the member countries, to study topics of international importance requiring regulation, standardization or codification, to co-operate with other international organizations in the field of chemistry and to contribute to the advancement of all aspects of chemistry. Biennial General Assembly. Mems: in 42 countries. Pres. Prof. C. N. R. RAO (India); Sec.-Gen. Prof. T. S. WEST (UK). Publs *Chemistry International* (bi-monthly), *Pure and Applied Chemistry* (monthly).

International Union of Pure and Applied Physics: Chalmers University of Technology, 412 96 Göteborg, Sweden; tel. (031) 81-01-00; telex 2369; f. 1922 to promote and encourage international co-operation in physics. Mems: in 45 countries. Pres. Prof. D. A. BROMLEY; Sec.-Gen. JAN S. NILSSON (Sweden).

International Union of Radio Science: 32 ave A. Lancaster, 1180 Brussels, Belgium; tel. (02) 374-13-08; f. 1919 to encourage and organize scientific research in radio science, particularly where international co-operation is required, and to stimulate the discussion and publication of the results of such research; and to promote the development of uniform methods of measurement and standardized measuring instruments on an international basis, to stimulate and co-ordinate studies of the scientific aspects of telecommunications using electro-magnetic waves, guided and unguided. There are 40 national committees. Sec.-Gen. Prof. J. VAN BLADEL (Belgium). Publs *Proceedings of General Assemblies of the URSI*, *URSI Information Bulletin*, *Review of Radio Science*.

International Union of the History and Philosophy of Science: Division of the History of Science: Dept of Philosophy, McGill University, 855 Sherbrooke West, Montreal H3A 2T7, Canada; tel. (514) 392-4517; telex 05268510; Division of the History of Logic, Methodology and Philosophy of Science: Dept of Philosophy, University of Turku, 20500 Turku 50, Finland; f. 1954 to promote research into the history and philosophy of science. There are 34 national committees. DHS Council (Montreal): Pres. Prof. P. GALLUZZI (Italy); Sec. W. SHEA (Canada). DLMPS Council: Pres. Prof. D. SCOTT (USA); Sec. R. HILPINEN (Finland).

International Union of Theoretical and Applied Mechanics: Institute B of Mechanics, University of Stuttgart, 7000 Stuttgart 80, Federal Republic of Germany; telex 7255445; f. 1947 to form a link beween persons and organizations engaged in scientific work (theoretical or experimental) in mechanics or in related sciences; to organize international congresses of theoretical and applied mechanics, through a standing Congress Committee, and to organize other international meetings for subjects falling within this field; and to engage in other activities meant to promote the development of mechanics as a science. The Union is directed by its General Assembly, which is composed of representatives of the organizations adhering to and affiliated to the Union and of elected members. Mems: from 37 countries. Pres. Sir JAMES LIGHTHILL (UK); Sec. Prof. W. SCHIEHLEN (FRG). Publ. *Annual Report*.

OTHER ORGANIZATIONS

Association for the Taxonomic Study of the Flora of Tropical Africa: Institut für Allgemeine Botanik und Botanischer Garten, 2000 Hamburg 52, Ohnhorstr. 18, Federal Republic of Germany; tel. (040) 8222397; telex 214732; f. 1950 to facilitate cooperation and liaison between botanists engaged in the study of the flora of Tropical Africa; maintains a library in Brussels. Mems: about 600 botanists in 70 countries. Sec.-Gen. Prof. Dr₁ H.-D. IHLENFELDT. Publs *Bulletin* (annual), *Proceedings*.

Association of African Geological Surveys: 103 rue de Lille, 75007 Paris, France; tel. (1) 45-50-32-22; f. 1929 to synthesize the geological knowledge of Africa and neighbouring countries and encourage research in geological and allied scientific knowledge; affiliated to the International Union of Geological Sciences (q.v.). Mems: about 60 (Official Geological Surveys, public and private organizations). Pres. A. AZZOUZ (Tunisia); Sec.-Gen. M. BENSAÏD (Morocco). Publs *Information and Liaison Bulletin Géologie Africaine*, maps and studies.

Association of European Atomic Forums—FORATOM: 1 St Alban's St, London, SW1Y 4SL, England; tel. (01) 930-6888; telex 264476; f. 1960; holds periodical conferences. Mems: atomic 'forums' in Austria, Belgium, Denmark, Finland, France, Federal Republic of Germany, Italy, Luxembourg, Netherlands, Norway, Spain, Sweden, Switzerland, United Kingdom. Pres. Sir JOHN HILL; Sec. Gen. JIM CORNER.

Association of Geoscientists for International Development—AGID: c/o Asian Institute of Technology, POB 2754, Bangkok 10501, Thailand; tel. 529-0100-13, ext. 2528; telex 84276; f. 1974 to encourage communication between those interested in the application of the geosciences to international development; to give priority to the developing countries in these matters; to organize meetings and publish information; affiliated to the International Union of Geological Sciences (q.v.). Mems: 1,600 individuals and 633 organizations in 107 countries. Pres. Prof. P. G. COORAY (Saudi Arabia); Sec.-Treas. Dr THEERAPONGS THANASUTHIPITAK (Thailand).

Biometric Society: Dept of Applied Statistics, University of Reading, Whiteknights, POB 217, Reading, RG6 2AN, England; tel. (0734) 875123, ext. 450; telex 847813; f. 1947 for the advancement of quantitative biological science through the development of quantitative theories and the application, development and dissemination of effective mathematical and statistical techniques; the Society has 14 regional organizations and 5 national groups, is affiliated with the International Statistical Institute and the World Health Organization, and constitutes the Section of Biometry of the International Union of Biological Sciences (q.v.). Mems: over 6,000 in more than 60 countries. Pres. Prof. G. H. FREEMAN (UK); Sec. Prof. R. MEAD (UK). Publ. *Biometrics* (quarterly).

Charles Darwin Foundation for the Galapagos Isles: c/o Juan Black, Casilla 38–91, Quito, Ecuador; f. 1959 to support and administer research at a station authorized by the Government of Ecuador, with primary emphasis on ecology and conservation; to protect the wildlife of the Galapagos Islands; and to encourage scientific education. Pres. Dr CRAIG MACFARLAND (USA); Sec.-Gen. JUAN BLACK. Publs *Noticias de Galapágos* (twice a year), *Annual Report*.

Council for the International Congresses of Entomology: c/o British Museum (Natural History), Cromwell Rd, London, SW7, England; f. 1910 to act as a link between quadrennial congresses and to arrange the venue for each congress; the committee is also the entomology section of the International Union of Biological Sciences (q.v.). Chair. Prof. R. F. SMITH (USA); Sec. Dr L. A. MOUND (UK). Publ. *Proceedings* (after each Congress).

European Association for the Exchange of Technical Literature in the Field of Metallurgy: BP 443, Luxembourg; f. 1959 to promote translation and exchange of technical literature in metallurgy especially from the USSR and the Far East for the benefit of industry, research institutes, etc., in the European Community. Mems: institutes in six countries. Pres. C. PAGLIUCCI (Italy). Publs Lists of translations (monthly), bibliographical index-cards.

European Association of Exploration Geophysicists: Wassenaarseweg 22, 2596 CH The Hague, Netherlands; tel. (70) 45-36-88; telex 31414; f. 1951 to facilitate contacts between exploration geophysicists, disseminate information to members, arrange annual meetings, technical exhibitions, and courses. Mems 4,000, and 1,150 subscribers in 82 countries throughout the world. Treas./Sec. D. G. CANE (UK). Publs *Geophysical Prospecting* (8 a year), *First Break* (monthly).

European Association of Veterinary Anatomists: 3000 Hannover 1, Bischofsholer Damm 15, Federal Republic of Germany; f.

1964 to provide opportunities for meetings for the advancement of studies in veterinary anatomy. Mems: 195 in 30 countries. Pres. Prof. A. KING (UK); Gen. Sec. Prof. R. SCHWARZ (FRG).

European Atomic Energy Society: c/o Institute for Energy Technology, PB 40, 2007 Kjeller, Norway; f. 1954 to encourage co-operation in atomic energy research. Mems: national atomic energy commissions in Austria, Belgium, Denmark, Finland, France, Federal Republic of Germany, Greece, Italy, Netherlands, Norway, Portugal, Spain, Sweden, Switzerland, United Kingdom. Pres. Prof. P. JAUHO (Finland); Exec. Vice-Pres. N. G. AAMODT (Norway).

European Molecular Biology Organization—EMBO: 6900 Heidelberg 1, Postfach 1022.40, Federal Republic of Germany; tel. (6221) 383031; f. 1964 to promote collaboration in the field of molecular biology; to establish fellowships for training and research; to establish a European Laboratory of Molecular Biology where a majority of the disciplines comprising the subject will be represented. Mems: approximately 640. Chair. Prof. G. TOCCHINI-VALENTINI (Italy); Sec.-Gen. Prof. G. SCHATZ (Switzerland); Exec. Sec. Dr J. TOOZE (FRG).

European Organization for Nuclear Research—CERN: European Laboratory for Particle Physics, 1211 Geneva 23, Switzerland; tel. (022) 836111; telex 41900; f. 1954 to provide for collaboration among European states in nuclear research of a pure scientific and fundamental character; the work of CERN as defined by its convention is for peaceful purposes only and concerns subnuclear, high-energy and elementary particle physics; it is not concerned with the development of nuclear reactors or fusion devices. Council, composed of two representatives of each member state, a Cttee of the Council and Cttees on Scientific Policy, Finance and the major experimental facilities: Synchro-Cyclotron (of 600 MeV), Proton Synchrotron (of 25–28 GeV), and Super Proton Synchrotron (of 450 GeV). A large electron-positron ring (LEP) is to be completed in 1988. Budget (1986): 755.3m. Swiss francs. Mems: Austria, Belgium, Denmark, France, Federal Republic of Germany, Greece, Italy, Netherlands, Norway, Portugal, Spain, Sweden, Switzerland, United Kingdom; Observers: Poland, Turkey, Yugoslavia. Pres. of Council Prof. W. KUMMER; Dir-Gen. Prof. H. SCHOPPER (FRG). Publs *CERN Courier* (monthly), *Annual Report*, *Scientific Reports*.

European Space Agency—ESA: 8–10 rue Mario Nikis, 75738 Paris Cedex 15, France; tel. (1) 42-73-76-54; telex 202746; f. 1975 to promote co-operation among European states in space research and technology and their application for peaceful purposes; replaced the European Space Research Organization (ESRO) and the European Organization for the Development and Construction of Space Vehicle Launchers (ELDO). Council composed of representatives of member states is the governing body. The Agency runs ESTEC (European Space Research and Technology Centre), ESOC (European Space Operations Centre) and ESRIN (Space Documentation Centre). Mems: Austria, Belgium, Denmark, Finland, France, Federal Republic of Germany, Ireland, Italy, Netherlands, Norway, Spain, Sweden, Switzerland, United Kingdom; observer: Canada. Chair. Dr H. H. ATKINSON (UK); Dir-Gen. REIMAR LÜST. Publs *Annual Report*, *ESA Bulletin*, *ESA Journal*.

European-Mediterranean Seismological Centre: 5 rue René Descartes, 67084 Strasbourg Cedex, France; tel. (88) 61-48-20, ext. 307; telex 890 826; f. 1976 for rapid determination of seismic hypocentres in the region. Sec.-Gen. J. BONNIN. Publ. monthly list of preliminary hypocentral determinations.

Federation of Arab Scientific Research Councils: POB 13027, Baghdad, Iraq; tel. 5381090; telex 212466; f. 1976 to encourage co-operation in scientific research, to promote the establishment of new institutions and plan joint regional research projects. Mems: national science bodies in 15 countries. Sec.-Gen. MOHAMMED O. KHIDIR. Publs *Journal*, *Newsletter*.

Federation of Asian Scientific Academies and Societies —FASAS: c/o Indian National Science Academy, Bahadur Shah Zafar Marg, New Delhi 110002, India; tel. 331-0717; telex 3161835; f. 1984 by 11 Asian learned societies, to stimulate regional co-operation and promote national and regional self-reliance in science and technology, by organizing meetings, training and research programmes and encouraging the exchange of scientists and of scientific information. Mems: national scientific academies and societies from Afghanistan, Bangladesh, the People's Republic of China, India, Malaysia, Nepal, Pakistan, the Philippines, Singapore, Sri Lanka and Thailand. Pres. Prof. A. K. SHARMA (India); Sec. Dr M. K. RAJAKUMAR (Malaysia).

Federation of European Biochemical Societies: c/o Prof. G. Dirheimer, 15 rue René-Descartes, 67084 Strasbourg Cedex, France; tel. 88-61-02-02; telex 870260; f. 1964 to promote the science of biochemistry by arranging and encouraging meetings of European biochemists, by giving short-term fellowships and organizing advanced courses, by disseminating information about meetings, lectures, fellowships, etc., by engaging in publication on a regular or occasional basis. Mems: 26,000 in 27 societies. Chair. Prof. K. DECKER; Sec.-Gen. Prof. G. DIRHEIMER. Publs *European Journal of Biochemistry*, *FEBS Letters*, *FEBS Bulletin*, *Symposia*, abstracts of meetings.

Foundation for International Scientific Co-ordination (Fondation 'Pour la science', Centre international de synthèse): 12 rue Colbert, 75002 Paris, France; tel. (1) 42-97-50-68; f. 1924. Dir JACQUES ROGER; Asst Dirs ERNEST COUMET, JEAN-CLAUDE PERROT. Publs *Revue de Synthèse*, *Revue d'Histoire des Sciences*, *Semaines de Synthèse*, *L'Évolution de l'Humanité*.

Intergovernmental Oceanographic Commission: UNESCO, 7 place de Fontenoy, 75700 Paris, France; tel. (1) 45-68-39-83; telex 204461; f. 1960 to promote scientific investigation with a view to learning more about the nature and resources of the oceans through the concerted action of its members. Mems: 114 governments. Chair. Prof. I. A. RONQUILLO (Philippines); Sec. MARIO RUIVO. Publs Summary Reports of Assembly sessions (every 2 years) and Executive Council sessions (annually), Biennial Reports of Activities, *IOC Technical series* (irregular), *IOC Manuals* and *Guides* (irregular).

International Academy of Astronautics—IAA: 3–5 rue Mario-Nikis, 75015 Paris, France; tel. (1) 45-67-49-66; f. 1960 at the XI Congress of the International Astronautical Federation; holds scientific meetings and makes scientific studies and reports, awards and prizes; maintains committees on numerous aspects of space science and Scientific-Legal Liaison Committees. Mems: 515 mems and 284 corresponding mems from 44 countries. Pres. GEORGE E. MUELLER; Dir Dr THEODORE VON KARMAN. Publs *Acta Astronautica* (monthly), *Proceedings of Symposia*.

International Association for Earthquake Engineering: Kenchiku Kaikan, 3rd Floor, 5-26-20, Shiba, Minato-ku, Tokyo 108, Japan; f. 1963 to promote international co-operation among scientists and engineers in the field of earthquake engineering through exchange of knowledge, ideas and results of research and practical experience. Mems: 36 countries. Pres. HAJIME UMEMURA (USA).

International Association for Ecology—INTECOL: Institute of Ecology, University of Georgia, Athens, GA 30602, USA; tel. (404) 542-2968; f. 1967 to provide opportunities for communication between ecologists, to co-operate with organizations and individuals having related aims and interests; to encourage studies in the different fields of ecology; affiliated to the International Union of Biological Sciences (q.v.). Mems: 35 national and international ecological societies, and 1,000 individuals. Pres. F. BOURLIÈRE (France); Sec.-Gen. F. GOLLEY (USA).

International Association for Mathematical Geology: US Geological Society, National Center 920, Reston, Va 22092, USA; f. 1968 for the preparation and elaboration of mathematical models of geological processes; the introduction of mathematical methods in geological sciences and technology; assistance in the development of mathematical investigation in geological sciences; the organization of international collaboration in mathematical geology through various forums and publications; educational programmes for mathematical geology; affiliated to the International Union of Geological Sciences (q.v.). Mems: c. 800. Pres. Prof. J. C. DAVIS (USA); Sec.-Gen. Dr R. B. MCCAMMON (USA). Publs *Journal of the International Association for Mathematical Geology* (8 a year), *Computers and Geosciences* (4 a year), *Newsletter* (quarterly).

International Association for Mathematics and Computers in Simulation: c/o Institut Montefiore, Bâtiment B28, Sart Tilman, 4000 Liège, Belgium; tel. (41) 56-17-10; f. 1955 to further the study of mathematical tools and computer software and hardware, analogue, digital or hybrid computers for simulation of soft or hard systems. Mems: 1,100 and 27 assoc. mems. Pres. R. VICHNEVETSKY (USA); Sec. J. ROBERT (Belgium). Publs *Proceedings of International Computation Meetings*, *Mathematics and Computers in Simulation* (6 a year), *IMACS News* (6 a year).

International Association for the Physical Sciences of the Ocean—IAPSO: La Fond Oceanic Consultants, POB 7325, San Diego, Calif 91207, USA; f. 1919 to promote the study of scientific problems relating to the oceans and interactions occurring at its boundaries, chiefly in so far as such study may be carried out by the aid of mathematics, physics and chemistry; to initiate, facilitate and co-ordinate research; to provide for discussion, comparison and publication; affiliated to the International Union of Geodesy and Geophysics (q.v.). Mems: 75 member states. Pres. Prof. WOLFGANG KRAUSS (FRG); Sec.-Gen. Dr E. C. LA FOND (USA). Publs *Publi-*

cations *Scientifiques* (irregular), *Procès-Verbaux* of General Assemblies (every fourth year).

International Association for Plant Physiology—IAPP: c/o Dr D. Graham, Plant Physiology Group, Food Research Laboratories, CSIRO, POB 52, North Ryde, NSW, Australia 2113; tel. (02) 887-8333; telex 23407; f. 1955 to promote the development of plant physiology at the international level through congresses, symposia and workshops, by maintaining communication with national societies and by encouraging interaction between plant physiologists in developing and developed countries; affiliated to the International Union of Biological Sciences (q.v.). Pres. Prof. Dr H. ZIEGLER; Sec.-Treas. Dr D. GRAHAM.

International Association for Plant Taxonomy: Bureau for Plant Taxonomy and Nomenclature, Room 1904, Tweede Transitorium, Uithof, POB 010102, 35001 TC Utrecht, Netherlands; tel. (30) 531830; f. 1950 to promote the development of plant taxonomy and encourage contacts between people and institutes interested in this work; affiliated to the International Union of Biological Sciences (q.v.). Mems: institutes and individuals in 85 countries. Pres. S. W. GREENE (UK); Sec.-Gen. F. A. STAFLEU (Netherlands). Publs *Taxon* (quarterly), *Regnum vegetabile* (irregular).

International Association of Biological Standardization: Biostandards, CP 229, 1211 Geneva 4, Switzerland; telex 421859; f. 1955 to connect producers and controllers of immunological products (sera, vaccines, etc.) for the study and the development of methods of standardization; supports international organizations (WHO, IOE, FAO, etc.) in their efforts to solve problems of standardization. Mems: 650. Pres. IRENE BATTY (UK); Sec.-Gen. D. GAUDRY (France). Publs *Quarterly Newsletter, Journal of Biological Standardization,* Minutes of the Cell Culture Committee, *Development in Biological Standardization.*

International Association of Botanic Gardens: Botanical Garden, c/o Dr B. Morley, Botanical Garden of Adelaide, North Terrace, Adelaide, SA 5000, Australia; f. 1954 to promote co-operation between scientific collections of living plants, including the exchange of information and specimens; to promote the study of the taxonomy of cultivated plants; and to encourage the conservation of rare plants and their habitats; affiliated to the International Union of Biological Sciences (q.v.). Pres. Prof. KAI LARSEN (Denmark); Sec. Dr BRIAN D. MORLEY (Australia).

International Association of Geodesy: 140 rue de Grenelle, 75700 Paris, France; tel. (1) 4354-19-21; telex 204989; f. 1922 to promote the study of all scientific problems of geodesy and encourage geodetic research; to promote and co-ordinate international co-operation in this field; to publish results; affiliated to the International Union of Geodesy and Geophysics (q.v.). Mems: national committees in 73 countries. Pres. P. V. ANGUS-LEPPAN (Australia); Sec.-Gen. M. LOUIS (France); Asst. Sec.-Gen. C. BOUCHER (France). Publs *Bulletin géodésique, Travaux de l'AIG, Bibliographie géodésique internationale.*

International Association of Geomagnetism and Aeronomy—IAGA: Natural Philosophy Dept, Aberdeen University, Aberdeen, AB9 2UE, Scotland; tel. (0224) 640074; telex 73458; f. 1919 for the study of questions relating to geomagnetism and aeronomy and the encouragement of research; affiliated to the International Union of Geodesy and Geophysics (q.v.). Mems: the countries which adhere to the International Union of Geodesy and Geophysics (q.v.) are eligible as members. Pres. D. I. GOUGH (Canada); Sec.-Gen. M. GADSDEN (UK). Publs *Transactions of the General Assemblies* (every 4 years), *Transactions of the Scientific Assemblies* (every 4 years), *IAGA Bulletin* (including annual *Geomagnetic Data* and other monographs), *IAGA News* (annually).

International Association of Hydrological Sciences: Institute of Hydrology, Maclean Bldg, Crowmarsh Gifford, Wallingford, OX10 8BB, England; tel. (0491) 38800; telex 849365; f. 1922 to promote co-operation in the study of hydrology and water resources. Pres. GYÖRGY KOVÁCS (Hungary); Sec.-Gen. JOHN C. RODDA (UK). Publs *Journal,* proceedings of symposia.

International Association of Meteorology and Atmospheric Physics—IAMAP: NCAR, POB 3000, Boulder, Colo 80307, USA; tel. (303) 497-8998; telex 45694; f. 1919; permanent commissions on atmospheric ozone, radiation, atmospheric chemistry and global pollution, dynamic meteorology, polar meteorology, cloud physics, climate, atmospheric electricity, planetary atmospheres and their evolution, and meteorology of the upper atmosphere; general assemblies held once every four years; special assemblies held once between general assemblies; affiliated to the International Union of Geodesy and Geophysics (q.v.). Pres. Prof. H. J. BOLLE (Austria); Sec. S. RUTTENBERG (USA). Publs Proceedings of General Assembly, Proceedings of Special Assembly, *IAMAP News Bulletin.*

International Association of Photobiology: c/o Rex M. Tyrrell, Institut Suisse de Recherches Expérimentales sur le Cancer, 1066 Epalinges, Lausanne, Switzerland; tel. (021) 333061; f. 1928; stimulation of scientific research concerning the physics, chemistry and climatology of non-ionizing radiations (ultra-violet, visible and infra-red) in relation to their biological efffects and their applications in biology and medicine; 18 national committees represented; affiliated to the International Union of Biological Sciences (q.v.). International Congresses held every four years. Pres. Prof. K. K. ROHATGI-MUKHERJEE; Sec.-Gen. Dr R. M. TYRRELL (Switzerland); Publ. *Congress Proceedings.*

International Association of Sedimentologists: c/o Dr C. L. V. Monty, Laboratoire de Biosédimentologie, Université de Liège, 7 place du 20 Août, Liège 4000, Belgium; tel. 42-00-80; f. 1952; affiliated to the International Union of Geological Sciences (q.v.). Mems: 2,100. Pres. Prof. H. READING (UK); Gen. Sec. Dr C. L. V. MONTY (Belgium). Publ. *Sedimentology,* newsletters (bimonthly), books on particular sedimentological topics.

International Association of Theoretical and Applied Limnology (Societas Internationalis Limnologiae): Dept of Biology, University of Michigan, Ann Arbor, Mich. 48109, USA; f. 1922; study of physical, chemical and biological phenomena of lakes and rivers; affiliated to the International Union of Biological Sciences (q.v.). Mems: about 3,200. Pres. H. LÖFFLER (Austria); Gen. Sec. and Treas. ROBERT G. WETZEL (USA). Publs *Verhandlungen, Mitteilungen.*

International Association of Volcanology and Chemistry of the Earth's Interior—IAVCEI: c/o Institut Mineralogie, Ruhr Universität Bochum, 4630 Bochum, Federal Republic of Germany; tel. (0234) 7003520; telex 0825-860; f. 1919 to examine scientifically all aspects of volcanology; affiliated to the International Union of Geodesy and Geophysics (q.v.). Pres. M. GASS; Sec. H.-U. SCHMINKE (FRG). Publs *Bulletin of Volcanology, Catalogue of the Active Volcanoes of the World, Newsletter.*

International Association of Wood Anatomists: c/o Institute of Systematic Botany, University of Utrecht, Netherlands; tel. 030-532643; f. 1931 for the purpose of study, documentation and exchange of information on the structure of wood. Mems: 500 in 61 countries. Exec. Sec. B. J. H. TER WELLE. Publ. *IAWA Bulletin.*

International Association on Water Pollution Research and Control: 1 Queen Anne's Gate, London, SW1H 9BT, England; tel. (01) 222-3848; telex 918518; f. 1965 to encourage international communication, co-operative effort, and a maximum exchange of information on water quality management; to sponsor conferences every two years; to provide a scientific medium for the publication of research reports. Mems: 32 national, 225 corporate and 1,450 individuals. Pres. Prof. P. HARREMOES; Exec. Dir A. MILBURN. Publs *Water Research* (monthly), *Water Science and Technology* (12 a year), *Water Quality International* (quarterly).

International Astronautical Federation—IAF: 3–5 rue Mario-Nikis, 75015 Paris, France; tel. (1) 45-67-42-60; telex 205917; f. 1950 to foster the development of astronautics for peaceful purposes at national and international levels. The IAF has created the International Academy of Astronautics (IAA) and the International Institute of Space Law (IISL). Mems: 80 national astronautical societies in 37 countries. Pres. J. GREY (USA); Exec. Sec. M. CLAUDIN. Publ. *Proceedings of Annual Congresses and Symposia.*

International Botanical Congress: c/o Prof. W. Greuter, Botanischer Garten, Königin-Luise-Str. 6–8, 1000 Berlin (West) 33, Federal Republic of Germany; tel. (030) 8316010; f. 1864 to inform botanists of recent progress in the plant sciences; the Nomenclature Section of the Congress attempts to provide a uniform terminology and methodology for the naming of plants; other Divisions deal with developmental, metabolic, structural, systematic and evolutionary, ecological botany; genetics and plant breeding; next Congress: Berlin, 1987; affiliated to the International Union of Biological Sciences (q.v.). Mems: about 3,000 persons attended the 13th Congress in Sydney in 1981.

International Bureau of Weights and Measures: Pavillon de Breteuil, 92312 Sèvres Cedex, France; tel. 45-34-00-51; telex 201067; f. 1875 for the international unification of physical measures; establishment of fundamental standards and of scales of the principal physical dimensions; preservation of the international prototypes; determination of national standards; precision measurements in physics. Mems: 47 states. Pres. D. KIND (FRG); Sec. J. DE BOER (Netherlands); Dir PIERRE GIACOMO (France). Publs *Procès-Verbaux* (annually), *Proceedings of the Comités Consultatifs* (every few years), *Comptes Rendus de la Conférence Générale* (every 6 years or less), *Recueil de Travaux.*

OTHER INTERNATIONAL ORGANIZATIONS

International Cartographic Association: 24 Strickland Rd, Mt Pleasant, Western Australia 6153, Australia; tel. (09) 364-5380; telex 95791; f. 1959 for the advancement, instigation and co-ordination of cartographic research involving co-operation between different nations. Particularly concerned with furtherance of training in cartography, study of source material, compilation, graphic design, drawing, scribing and reproduction techniques of maps; organizes international conferences, symposia, meetings, exhibitions. Mems: 64 nations. Pres. (1984–87) Dr JOEL M. MORRISON (USA); Sec.-Treas. DON PEARCE (Australia). Publs *ICA Newsletter* (2 a year), technical books.

International Centre of Insect Physiology and Ecology: POB 30772, Nairobi, Kenya; f. 1970 to increase food production by undertaking research on pests of major crops, vectors of livestock diseases, and insect carriers of human diseases critical to tropical rural health; and to increase the capacity of developing countries in pest management research and its application, by training scientists and technologists; field stations in Kenya and the Philippines. Dir Prof. THOMAS R. ODHIAMBO (Kenya). Publs *Insect Science and its Application* (quarterly), *Annual Report*, *DUDU* (quarterly), technical reports.

International Commission for Bee Botany: c/o Dr S. N. Holm, Royal Veterinary and Agricultural University, Department of Crop Husbandry, Experimental Station, Hajbakkegaard, 2630 Taastrup, Denmark; f. 1950 to promote research and its application in the field of bee botany, and collect and spread information; to organize meetings, etc., and collaborate with scientific organizations; affiliated to the International Union of Biological Sciences (q.v.). Mems: 175 in 34 countries. Pres. Dr S. N. HOLM; Sec. J. N. TASEI.

International Commission for Physics Education: c/o Dept of Physics, Ohio State University, 174 West 18th Ave, Columbus, OH 43210-1106, USA; tel. (614) 422-6959; telex 810482 1715; f. 1960 to encourage and develop international collaboration in the improvement and extension of the methods and scope of physics education at all levels; collaborates with UNESCO and organizes international conferences. Mems: appointed triennially by the International Union of Pure and Applied Physics. Chair. Prof. R. U. SEXL (Austria); Sec. E. L. JOSSEM (USA).

International Commission for the Scientific Exploration of the Mediterranean Sea (Commission internationale pour l'exploration scientifique de la mer Méditerranée—CIESM): 16 blvd de Suisse, 98030 Monaco Cedex; tel. (93) 30-38-79; f. 1919 for scientific exploration of the Mediterranean Sea; includes 12 scientific committees. Mems: 1,500 scientists, 17 member countries. Pres. SAS The Prince RAINIER III of MONACO; Sec.-Gen. Cdt. J. Y. COUSTEAU (France). Publ. *Rapports et Procès-Verbaux des réunions de la CIESM*.

International Commission on Glass: c/o Institut National du Verre, 10 blvd Defontaine, 6000 Charleroi, Belgium; tel. (071) 31-00-41; telex 51430; f. 1950 to organize and co-ordinate research in glass and allied products and to promote scientific co-operation through exchange of information and the holding of congresses. Mems: 24 organizations. Treas. F. HUBERT.

International Commission on Radiation Units and Measurements—ICRU: 7910 Woodmont Ave, Suite 1016, Bethesda, Md 20814, USA; tel. (301) 657-2652; f. 1925 at the First International Congress of Radiology (London), to develop internationally acceptable recommendations regarding: (1) quantities and units of radiation and radioactivity, (2) procedures suitable for the measurement and application of these quantities in clinical radiology and radiobiology, (3) physical data needed in the application of these procedures. Makes recommendations on quantities and units for radiation protection (see below, International Radiation Protection Association). Mems: from about 18 countries. Chair. A. ALLISY; Sec. R. S. CASWELL; Exec. Sec. W. R. NEY. Publs *Reports*.

International Commission on Zoological Nomenclature: c/o British Museum (Natural History), Cromwell Rd, London, SW7 5BD, England; tel. (01) 589-6323, ext. 387; f. 1895; has judicial powers to determine all matters relating to the interpretation of the International Code of Zoological Nomenclature and also plenary powers to suspend the operation of the Code where the strict application of the Code would lead to confusion and instability of nomenclature; the Commission is responsible also for maintaining and developing the Official Lists and Official Indexes of Names in Zoology; affiliated to the International Union of Biological Sciences (q.v.). Pres. W. D. L. RIDE (Australia); Exec. Sec. Dr P. K. TUBBS (UK). Publs *International Code of Zoological Nomenclature*, *Bulletin of Zoological Nomenclature*, *Opinions and Declarations rendered by the International Commission on Zoological Nomenclature*, *Copenhagen Decisions on Zoological Nomenclature*, 1953.

International Council for Bird Preservation: 219c Huntingdon Rd, Cambridge, CB3 0DL, England; tel. (0223) 277318; telex 817036; f. 1922; determines status of bird species throughout the world and compiles data on all endangered species; identifies conservation problems and priorities; initiates and co-ordinates conservation projects and international conventions. Representatives in 42 countries; national sections in 63 countries. Pres. Dr R. W. PETERSON (USA); Dir Dr CHRISTOPH IMBODEN (UK). Publs *Bulletin*, *ICBP Newsletter*, *ICBP/IUCN Bird Red Data Book*, *World Birdwatch*, technical publications, study reports.

International Council for the Exploration of the Sea —ICES: Palaegade 2–4, 1261, Copenhagen K, Denmark; tel. (01) 15-42-25; telex 22498; f. 1902 to encourage concerted biological and hydrographical investigations for the promotion of a planned exploitation of the resources of the Atlantic Ocean and its adjacent seas, and primarily the North Atlantic; library of 15,000 vols. Membership: governments of 18 countries. Gen. Sec. B. B. PARRISH. Publs *Journal du Conseil*, *Rapports et Procès-Verbaux*, *Bulletin Statistique*, *ICES Oceanographic Data Lists and Inventories*, *Annales Biologiques*, *Co-operative Research Reports*, *Fiches d'Identification du Plancton*, *Fiches d'Identification des Maladies et Parasites des Poissons, Crustacés et Mollusques*.

International Council of Psychologists: 4805 Regent St, Madison, WI 53705, USA; tel. (608) 238-5373; f. 1959 to advance psychology and the application of its findings throughout the world; holds annual conventions. Mems: 1,800 qualified psychologists. Sec.-Gen. PATRICIA CAUTLEY. Publs *International Psychologist* (quarterly), abstracts of convention papers.

International Council of the Aeronautical Sciences: Godesberger Allee 70, 5300 Bonn 2, Federal Republic of Germany; f.1957 to encourage free interchange of information on all phases of mechanical flight; holds biennial Congresses. Mems: national associations in 28 countries. Pres. J. SINGER (Israel); Exec. Sec. R. W. STAUFENBIEL (FRG).

International Federation of Cell Biology: c/o Dr A. Zimmerman, Dept of Zoology, University of Toronto, 25 Harbord St, Toronto M5S 1A1, Canada; f. 1972 to foster international co-operation, and organize conferences. Sec.-Gen. Dr A. ZIMMERMAN. Publs *Cell Biology International* (monthly), reports.

International Federation of Operational Research Societies: c/o IMSOR, Bldg 321, Technical University of Denmark, 2800 Lyngby, Denmark; tel. (2) 881433; telex 37529; f. 1959 for development of operational research as a unified science and its advancement in all nations of the world. Mems: about 30,000 individuals, 35 national societies, 6 kindred societies. Pres. Prof. JACQUES LESOURNE (France); Sec. Mrs HELLE WELLING. Publs *International Abstracts in Operational Research*, *Proceedings of Triennial International Conferences on Operational Research*, *IFORS Bulletin*.

International Federation of Societies for Electron Microscopy: Hearst Mining Bldg, University of California, Berkeley, Calif 94720, USA; f. 1955. Mems: representative organizations of 40 countries. Pres. Prof. H. HASHIMOTO (Japan); Gen.-Sec. Prof. GARETH THOMAS.

International Food Information Service: Editorial Office, Lane End House, Shinfield, Reading, RG2 9BB, England; tel. (0734) 883895; telex 847204; f. 1968 by the Gesellschaft für Information und Dokumentation (Frankfurt), the Institute of Food Technologists (Chicago), the Commonwealth Agricultural Bureaux and the Centrum voor Landbouwpublikaties en Landbouwdocumentaties for the collection and dissemination of scientific and technological information on foods and their processing. Joint Man. Dirs E. J. MANN, Dr U. SCHÜTZSACK. Publ. *Food Science and Technology Abstracts* (monthly).

International Foundation of the High-Altitude Research Stations Jungfraujoch and Gornergrat: Sidlerstrasse 5, 3012 Berne, Switzerland; tel. (031) 654052; telex 32320; f. 1931; international research centre which enables scientists from many scientific fields to carry out experiments at high altitudes. Eight countries contribute to support the station: Austria, Belgium, France, Federal Republic of Germany, Holland, Italy, Switzerland, United Kingdom. Pres. Prof. H. DEBRUNNER.

International Glaciological Society: Lensfield Rd, Cambridge, CB2 1ER, England; tel. (0223) 355974; f. 1936 to stimulate interest in and encourage research into the scientific and technical problems of snow and ice in all countries. Mems: 850 in 33 countries. Pres. Dr H. RÖTHLISBERGER (Switzerland); Gen. Sec. H. RICHARDSON. Publs *Journal of Glaciology* (3 a year), *Ice* (News Bulletin—3 a year), *Annals of Glaciology*, Conference Proceedings.

International Group of Scientific, Technical and Medical Publishers: Keizersgracht 462, 1016 GE Amsterdam, Netherlands;

tel. (020) 225214; f. 1969 to deal with problems of international copyright protection and assist publishers and authors in disseminating scientific information by both conventional and advanced methods; holds seminars and study groups. Sec. PAUL NIJHOFF ASSER. Publs *STM Newsletter, STM Copyright Bulletin, STM Innovations Bulletin*.

International Hydrographic Organization: ave Président J. F. Kennedy, BP 445, Monte Carlo, 98011 Monaco Cedex; tel. (93) 50-65-87; telex 479164; f. 1921 to link the hydrographic offices of its member governments and co-ordinate their work with a view to rendering navigation easier and safer on all the seas of the world; to obtain as far as possible uniformity in charts and hydrographic documents; to encourage the adoption of the best methods of conducting hydrographic surveys and improvements in the theory and practice of the science of hydrography, and to encourage surveying in those parts of the world where accurate charts are lacking; to extend and facilitate the application of oceanographic knowledge for the benefit of navigators and specialists in marine sciences; to render advice and assistance to developing countries upon request, facilitating their application for financial aid from the UNDP for creation or extension of their hydrographic capabilities; to fulfil the role of world data centre for bathymetry; provides computerized Tidal Constituent Data Bank. Next conference: 1987. Mems: 54 states. Directing Committee: Pres. Rear Adml F. L. FRASER, AVSM (India); Dirs Vice-Adml O. A. A. AFFONSO (Brazil), Capt. J. E. AYRES (USA). Publs *International Hydrographic Review* (2 a year), *International Hydrographic Bulletin* (monthly), *IHO Yearbook, Reports of Proceedings of I.H. Conferences, Repertory of Technical Resolutions*, special publications on various technical subjects, all in English and French, *General Bathymetric Chart of the Oceans* (in 24 sheets).

International Hibernation Society: 300 Dean Drive, Rockville, Md 20851, USA; f. 1960 for exchange of information on mammalian hibernation. Mems: 147 in 14 countries. Exec. Sec. RICHARD C. SIMMONDS (USA). Publ. *Newsletter* (fortnightly).

International Institute of Refrigeration: 177 blvd Malesherbes, 75017 Paris, France; tel. (1) 42-27-32-35; telex 643269; f. 1920 to further the development of the science and practice of refrigeration on a world-wide scale; to investigate, discuss and recommend any aspects leading to improvements and energy-saving in the field of refrigeration. Mems: 57 countries and 950 associates. Dir A. GAC (France). Publs *Bulletin* (bi-monthly), *International Journal of Refrigeration* (bi-monthly), Proceedings of Meetings, International Recommendations, etc.

International Mineralogical Association: Institute of Mineralogy, University of Marburg, 3550 Marburg, Federal Republic of Germany; f. 1958 to further international co-operation in the science of mineralogy; affiliated to the International Union of Geological Sciences (q.v.). Mems: national societies in 31 countries. Sec. Prof. S. S. HAFNER.

International Organisation of Legal Metrology: 11 rue Turgot, 75009 Paris, France; f. 1955 to serve as documentation and information centre on the verification, checking, construction and use of measuring instruments, to determine characteristics and standards to which measuring instruments must conform for their use to be recommended internationally, and to determine the general principles of legal metrology. Mems: governments of 48 countries. Pres. K. BIRKELAND (Norway); Dir B. ATHANÉ (France). Publ. *Bulletin* (quarterly).

International Palaeontological Association: US Geological Survey, E-305 Natural History Museum, Smithsonian Institution, Washington, DC 20560, USA; tel. (202) 343-3523; telex 264729; f. 1933; affiliated to the International Union of Geological Sciences and the International Union of Biological Sciences (q.v.). Pres. Prof. A. J. BOUCOT (USA); Sec.-Gen. Dr W. A. OLIVER, Jr (USA).

International Peat Society: Unioninkatu 40B, 00170 Helsinki, Finland; tel. 358-0-1924340; f. 1968 to encourage co-operation in the study and use of mires, peatlands, peat and related material, through international meetings, research groups and the exchange of information. Mems: 14 National Cttees, 225 research institutes and other organizations, and 500 individuals from 41 countries. Pres. Dr Y. PESSI (Finland); Sec.-Gen. Dr I. DAVYDIK (USSR). Publs *IPS Bulletin* (annually), *International Peat Journal* (annually), proceedings of congresses and symposia.

International Phonetic Association—IPA: Dept of Linguistics and Phonetics, University of Leeds, LS2 9JT, England; f. 1886 to promote the scientific study of phonetics and its applications. Mems: 800. Sec. P. J. ROACH (UK). Publ. *Journal* (2 a year).

International Phycological Society: c/o Dept of Botany, Duke University, Durham, NC 27706, USA; tel (919) 684-3375; f. 1961 to promote the study of algae, the distribution of information, and international co-operation in this field. Mems: about 1,000. Sec. RICHARD SEARLES (USA). Publ. *Phycologia* (quarterly).

International Polar Motion Service: International Latitude Observatory of Mizusawa, Mizusawa, Iwate-ken, Japan; f. 1962 to replace the International Latitude Service (f. 1899), to make observations in latitude and time stations all over the world for the study of all problems relating to the earth's rotation; central bureau of the service collects astronomical observations, determines polar motion and distributes the data and results. Dir Dr K. YOKOYAMA. Publs *Monthly Notes, Annual Reports*.

International Primatological Society: c/o Dr G. Epple, Deutsches Primatenzentrum, 34 Göttingen, Kellnerweg 4, Federal Republic of Germany; f. 1964 to promote primatological science in all fields. Mems: about 900. Pres. Dr JOHN P. HEARN (UK); Sec.-Gen. Dr GISELA EPPLE (FRG).

International Radiation Protection Association—IRPA: 1030 Vienna, Gartnergasse 15-1/27, Austria; f. 1966 to unite in an international scientific society, individuals and societies throughout the world concerned with protection against ionizing radiations and allied effects, and to be representative of doctors, health physicists, radiological protection officers and others engaged in radiological protection, radiation safety, nuclear safety, legal, medical and veterinary aspects and in radiation research and other allied activities. Mems: approx. 6,400 individual founding members and associates from 23 associate societies.

International Scientific Film Library: 29 rue Vautier, 1040 Brussels, Belgium; f. 1961; created under the patronage of the International Scientific Film Association and the Belgian Ministry of National Education and Culture; to preserve the most outstanding scientific and technical films and also to promote the knowledge, study, widest possible dissemination and the rationalization of the production of scientific films. Mems: 49. Pres. Prof. JAN JACOBY (Poland); Dir-Curator P. BORMANS (Belgium). Publs. Catalogue of Films Deposited, *The Pioneers of the Scientific Cinema* (series).

International Society for General Semantics: POB 2469, San Francisco, Calif 94126, USA; f. 1943 to advance knowledge of and inquiry into non-Aristotelian systems and general semantics. Mems: 3,000 individuals in 28 countries. Pres. MARY MORAIN (USA); Exec. Dir RUSSELL JOYNER (USA).

International Society for Human and Animal Mycology—ISHAM: c/o D. W. R. Mackenzie, Mycological Reference Library, Central Public Health Laboratory, 61 Colindale Ave, London, NW9 5HT, England; tel. (01) 200-4400; f. 1954 to pursue the study of fungi pathogenic for man and animals; holds congresses every 3 years. Mems: 800 from 68 countries. Pres. H. URABE (Japan); Gen. Sec. D. W. R. MACKENZIE (UK). Publs *Sabouraudia* (6 a year), *Newsletter*.

International Society for Rock Mechanics: c/o Laboratório Nacional de Engenharia Civil, 101 Av. do Brasil, 1799 Lisboa Codex, Portugal; tel. (1) 882131; telex 16760; f. 1962 to encourage and co-ordinate international co-operation in the science of rock mechanics; to assist individuals and local organizations to form national bodies primarily interested in rock mechanics; to maintain liaison with other organizations that represent sciences of interest to the Society, including geology, geophysics, soil mechanics, mining engineering, petroleum engineering and civil engineering. The Society organizes international meetings and encourages the publication of the results of research in rock mechanics. Mems: c. 6,000. Pres. Prof. E. T. BROWN; Sec.-Gen. NUNO F. GROSSMANN. Publ. *News* (quarterly).

International Society for Stereology: c/o Luis Cruz-Orive, Institute of Anatomy, Buhlstr. 26, Postfach 139, 3000 Berne, Switzerland; tel. (031) 658433; f. 1961; an interdisciplinary society gathering scientists from metallurgy, geology, mineralogy and biology to exchange ideas on three-dimensional interpretation of two-dimensional samples (sections, projections) of their material by means of stereological principles; sixth Congress, Gainsville, Florida, USA, Oct. 1983. Mems: 450. Pres. ROGER MILES; Sec. LUIS CRUZ-ORIVE.

International Society for Tropical Ecology: c/o Botany Dept, Banaras Hindu University, Varanasi, 221005 India; f. 1956 to promote and develop the science of ecology in the tropics in the service of man; to publish a journal to aid ecologists in the tropics in communication of their findings; and to hold symposia from time to time to summarize the state of knowledge in particular or general fields of tropical ecology. Mems: 500. Sec. Dr K. C. MISRA (India); Editor Prof. J. S. SINGH. Publ. *Tropical Ecology* (2 a year).

International Society of Biometeorology: 446 Witikonerstrasse, 8053 Zürich, Switzerland; f. 1956 to unite all biometeorologists working in the fields of agricultural, botanical, cosmic, entomological, forest, human, medical, veterinarian, zoological and other branches of biometeorology. Mems: 450 individuals, nationals of 46 countries. Pres. Prof. H. M. KIKUCHI (Japan); Sec. Dr B. P. PRIMAULT (Switzerland). Publ. *International Journal of Biometeorology* (quarterly).

International Society of Electrochemistry—ISE: Institut für Technische Elektrochemie, 1060 Vienna, 9 Getreidemarkt, Austria; f. 1949. Mems: 800 in 36 countries. Chair. Prof. J. KORYTA; Sec.-Gen. Prof. M. W. BREITER. Publ. *Electrochimica Acta* (monthly).

International Time Bureau: Pavillon de Breteuil, 92310 Sèvres, France; tel. (1) 45-34-00-51; telex 201067; f. 1912 to determine Universal Time and the co-ordinates of the terrestrial pole; to maintain international atomic time; to co-ordinate time signals emissions. Mems: observatories and laboratories of standards in 32 countries. Dir Prof. B. GUINOT. Publs *Annual Report, Circulars.*

International Translations Centre: 101 Doelenstraat, 2611 NS Delft, The Netherlands; tel. (015) 142242; telex 38104; f. 1961 as the European Translations Centre, by the OECD; an international clearing house for scientific and technical translations prepared from all languages into Western languages; over 200 organizations regularly send notifications of translations to the Centre, or deposit a copy; through the World Transindex over 900,000 translations are made available. Chair. Dr S. SCHWARZ (Sweden); Dir M. RISSEEUW (Netherlands). Publs *World Transindex* (10 a year, annual cumulative edition and nine-year cumulation 1977–1985), *WTI Database, Journals in Translation* (irregular).

International Union for Conservation of Nature and Natural Resources—IUCN: 1196 Gland, Switzerland; tel. (022) 647181; telex 22618; f. 1948 to promote the conservation of natural resources by the scientific monitoring of their conditions, by determining scientific priorities for conservation, mobilizing the scientific and professional resources to investigate the most serious conservation problems and recommend solutions to them, developing programmes to protect and sustain the most important and threatened species and eco-systems and assisting governments to devise and carry out conservation projects; maintains a conservation library and documentation centre and units for monitoring traffic in wildlife. Mems: governments of 58 countries, 125 government agencies, 333 national and 26 international non-governmental organizations and 15 affiliates. Pres. Dr MONKUMBU K. SWAMINATHAN (India); Dir-Gen. Dr KENTON R. MILLER (USA). Publs *IUCN Bulletin* (every 3 months) incl. annual report, *Red Data Book* (on mammals, plants, invertebrates, amphibians and reptiles), *World Conservation Strategy, United Nations List of National Parks and Protected Areas,* Environmental Policy and Law Papers.

International Union for Quaternary Research—INQUA: Institute of Foundation Engineering, ETH-Hönggerberg, 8093 Zürich, Switzerland; tel. (01) 3772521; telex 823474; f. 1928 to co-ordinate research on the quaternary geological era throughout the world. Pres. H. FAURE (France); Sec.-Treas. C. SCHLÜCHTER (Switzerland).

International Union for the Study of Social Insects: Dept of Zoology, The University, Southampton, England; f. 1951; affiliated to the International Union of Biological Sciences (q.v.). Mems: about 700 of almost all nationalities. Pres. Prof. C. D. MICHENER; Sec. Dr P. E. HOWSE. Publs *Insectes sociaux,* Congress, Symposia proceedings.

International Union of Food Science and Technology: CSIRO Division of Food Research, POB 52, North Ryde, NSW 2113, Australia; tel. (02) 887-8333; telex 23407; f. 1970; sponsors international symposia and congresses. Mems; 46 national groups. Pres. R. L. HALL (USA); Sec.-Gen. J. F. KEFFORD. Publ. *IUFOST Newsletter* (2 a year).

International Waterfowl Research Bureau: Slimbridge, Glos, GL2 7BX, England; tel. (045 389) 333; telex 437145; f. 1954 to stimulate and co-ordinate research on and conservation of waterfowl and their wetland habitats, particularly through the Ramsar Convention. Mems: 36 countries. Dir Prof. G. V. T. MATTHEWS. Publs *Bulletin* and special volumes.

International Weed Science Society: c/o IPPC, Oregon State University, Corvallis, OR 97331, USA; tel. (503) 754-3541; f. 1975 to encourage co-operation in the study and control of weeds, through special symposia, liaison with relevant national and international organizations, and assistance for training in weed science and technology. Mems: about 600 individuals and six regional societies. Sec. L. C. BURRILL. Publs *IWSS Newsletter, Bibliography.*

Joint Institute for Nuclear Research: POB 79, 101000 Moscow, USSR; f. 1956 to promote the development of nuclear research among member countries; Committee of Government Plenipotentiaries meets annually to determine future policy and finance; Institute includes research laboratories for: Nuclear Problems, High Energies, Theoretical Physics, Neutron Physics, Nuclear Reactions, Computing and Automation, New Methods of Acceleration. Mems: Bulgaria, Cuba, Czechoslovakia, German Democratic Republic, Hungary, Democratic People's Republic of Korea, Mongolia, Poland, Romania, USSR, Viet-Nam. Chair. Scientific Council and Dir Academician N. N. BOGOLUBOV (USSR); Admin. Dir V. L. KARPOVSKY.

Nordic Institute for Theoretical Atomic Physics—NORDITA: Blegdamsvej 17, 2100 Copenhagen Ø, Denmark; tel. (1) 42-16-16; telex 15216; f. 1957 to promote scientific research and co-operation in theoretical atomic physics among the Nordic countries and to provide advanced training for younger physicists. Mems: Denmark, Finland, Iceland, Norway, Sweden. Dir Prof. A. MACKINTOSH; Chair. of Board Prof. A. KALLIO.

Nordic Society for Cell Biology (Nordisk Forening for Celleforskning): c/o Prof. Nils Björkman, Dept of Anatomy, Royal Veterinary and Agricultural College, Bülowsvej 13, 1870 Frederiksberg C, Denmark; tel. (01) 351788; f. 1960 to promote contact between cell biologists through symposia and a congress every two years. Mems: 150 in Denmark, Finland, Iceland, Norway, Sweden. Chair. Prof. BJÖRN AFZELIUS (Sweden); Sec. Prof. NILS BJÖRKMAN (Denmark). Publs abstracts of papers presented at congresses in *Experimental Cell Research* and *Norwegian Journal of Zoology, Proceedings of Congress.*

Oceanographic Institute: 195 rue Saint-Jacques, 75005 Paris, France; f. 1906. Dir Prof. P. BOUGIS; Sec. J. F. COLLINET. Publs *Annales, Océanis.*

Pacific Science Association: POB 17801, Honolulu, Hawaii 96817; tel. (808) 847-3511; f. 1920 to promote co-operation in the study of scientific problems relating to the Pacific region, more particularly those affecting the prosperity and well-being of Pacific peoples; sponsors Pacific Science Congresses and Inter-Congresses. Mems: institutional representatives from 35 areas, scientific societies, individual scientists. Sixth Inter-Congress, Chile, 1989; 16th Congress, Seoul, 1987. Pres. Dr TAI WHAN SHIN; Gen. Sec. BRENDA BISHOP. Publs *Congress and Inter-Congress Record of Proceedings, Information Bulletin* (6 a year).

Pugwash Conferences on Science and World Affairs: 60 Great Russell St, London, WC1; f. 1957 to organize international conferences of scientists to discuss problems arising from development of science, particularly the dangers to mankind from weapons of mass destruction. Mems: national Pugwash groups in 30 countries. Pres. DOROTHY HODGKIN (UK); Sec.-Gen. Prof. J. ROTBLAT (UK). Publs *Pugwash Newsletter* (quarterly), conference proceedings (annually).

Unitas Malacologica (Malacological Union): Dr E. Gittenberger, Rijksmuseum van Natuurlijke Historie, Raamsteeg 2, 2311 PL Leiden, Netherlands; f. 1962 to further the study of molluscs; affiliated to the International Union of Biological Sciences (q.v.). Mems: 200 in 20 European and 10 non-European countries. Pres. Dr DAVID HEPPELL (UK); Sec. Dr E. GITTENBERGER. Publ. *Proceedings* of congresses (every 3 years).

World Organization of General Systems and Cybernetics —WOGSC: c/o Prof. J. Rose, 5 Margate Rd, Lytham St Annes, Lancs., FY8 3EG, England; tel. (0253) 725114; f. 1969 to act as clearing-house for all societies concerned with cybernetics and allied subjects, to aim for the recognition of cybernetics as a fundamental science, to organize and sponsor international exhibitions of automation and computer equipment, congresses and symposia, and to promote and co-ordinate research in general systems and cybernetics. Mems: national and international societies in 42 countries. Dir-Gen. Prof. J. ROSE (UK); Dir Ext. Affairs Prof. T. C. HELVEY (USA). Publs abstracts of papers, *Proceedings of the Congresses of Cybernetics and General Systems, Newsletters, International Journal of Cybernetics and Systems (Kybernetes), International Journal of Information, Education and Research (Robotica), Monographs.*

World Wildlife Fund—WWF: World Conservation Centre, 1196 Gland, Switzerland; tel. (022) 647181; telex 28183; f. 1961 to conserve the world's flora, fauna and natural resources and environment. Mems: 24 national organizations. Pres. HRH The Prince PHILIP, Duke of EDINBURGH; Dir-Gen. CH. DE HAES. Publs *Conservation Review* (2 a year), *Monthly Report, WWF News* (every 2 months).

Social Sciences and Humanistic Studies

International Council for Philosophy and Humanistic Studies—ICPHS: Maison de l'UNESCO, 1 rue Miollis, 75732

Paris Cedex 15, France; f. 1949 under the auspices of UNESCO to encourage respect for cultural autonomy by the comparative study of civilization and to contribute towards international understanding through a better knowledge of man; to develop international co-operation in philosophy, humanistic and kindred studies and to encourage the setting up of international organizations; to promote the dissemination of information in these fields; to sponsor works of learning, etc. The Council is composed of the international non-governmental organizations listed below: these organizations represent 143 countries. Pres. J. BIAŁOSTOCKI(Poland); Sec.-Gen. J. D'ORMESSON (France). Publs *Bulletin of Information* (biennially), *Diogenes* (quarterly).

UNIONS FEDERATED TO THE ICPHS

International Academic Union: Palais des Academies, 1 rue Ducale, 1000 Brussels, Belgium; tel. (02) 512-60-79; f. 1919 to promote international co-operation through collective research in philology, archaeology, history and social sciences. Mems: academic institutions in 35 countries. Pres. S. A. WURM (Australia). Publs dictionaries and catalogues.

International Association for the History of Religions: c/o Philipps-Universität, FG Religionswissenschaft, Liebigstrasse 37, 3550 Marburg, Federal Republic of Germany; f. 1950 to promote international collaboration of scholars, to organize congresses and to stimulate the production of works. Mems: 24 countries. Pres. A. SCHIMMEL; Sec.-Gen. MICHAEL PYE.

International Committee for Historical Sciences: 17 rue de la Sorbonne, 75005 Paris, France; tel. (1) 43-29-12-13; f. 1926 to work for the advancement of historical sciences by means of international co-ordination; 10 internal commissions; an international congress is held every five years. Mems: 47 national committees and 24 affiliated international organizations. Sec.-Gen. HÉLÈNE AHRWEILER. Publs *Bulletin d'Information du CISH, Bibliographie internationale des sciences historiques*, congress reports and studies.

International Committee on the History of Art: Palais Universitaire, 67084 Strasbourg Cedex, France; f. 1900 by the 12th International Congress on the History of Art, for collaboration in the scientific study of the history of art. International congress every five years, and two colloquia between congresses. Mems: National Committees in 31 countries. Pres. Prof. IRVING LAVIN (USA); Sec. Prof. A. A. SCHMID (Switzerland). Publs *Répertoire d'Art et d'Archéologie* (quarterly), *Corpus international des vitraux, Bulletin du CIHA*.

International Federation of Modern Languages and Literatures: c/o D. A. Wells, Dept of German, Queen's University of Belfast, Belfast, BT7 1NN, Northern Ireland; tel. (0232) 245133; telex 74487; f. 1928 to establish permanent contact between historians of literature, to develop or perfect facilities for their work and to promote the study of the history of modern literature. Congress every three years. Mems: 21 associations, with individual mems in 98 countries. Sec.-Gen. D. A. WELLS (UK). Publ. *Acta of the Triennial Congresses*.

International Federation of Philosophical Societies: c/o E. Agazzi, Séminaire de Philosophie, Université, 1700 Fribourg, Switzerland; f. 1948 under the auspices of UNESCO, to encourage international co-operation in the field of philosophy, and to promote congresses, symposia and publications. Mems: 84 societies from 46 countries; 20 international societies. Pres. VENANT GAUCHY (Canada); Sec.-Gen. EVANDRO AGAZZI. Publs *International Bibliography of Philosophy, Chroniques de Philosophie, Proceedings of the World Congress of Philosophy* (every 5 years), series of books *Philosophers on Their Own Work*.

International Federation of Societies of Classical Studies: c/o Prof. F. Paschoud, 26 rue de Vermont, 1202 Geneva, Switzerland; f. 1948 under the auspices of UNESCO. Mems: 60 societies in 34 countries. Pres. Prof. E. GABBA (Italy); Sec. Prof. F. PASCHOUD (Switzerland). Publs *L'Année Philologique*, other bibliographies, dictionaries, reference works, *Thesaurus linguae Latinae*.

International Union for Oriental and Asian Studies: Institut d'Etudes Turques, 13 rue de Santeuil, 75231 Paris Cedex 05, France; f. 1951 by the 22nd International Congress of Orientalists under the auspices of UNESCO, to promote contacts between orientalists throughout the world, and to organize congresses, research and publications. Mems: in 64 countries. Pres. R. N. DANDEKAR; Sec.-Gen. LOUIS BAZIN (France). Publs Four oriental bibliographies, *Philologiae Turcicae Fundamenta, Materialien zum Sumerischen Lexikon, Sanskrit Dictionary, Corpus Inscriptionum Iranicarum, Linguistic Atlas of Iran, Matériels des parlers iraniens, Turcica*.

International Union of Anthropological and Ethnological Sciences: c/o Prof. E. Sunderland, University College of North Wales, Bangor, Gwynedd, LL57 2DG, Wales; tel. (0248) 351151, ext. 482; telex 61100; f. 1948 under the auspices of UNESCO; has 14 international research commissions. Mems: institutions and individuals in 100 countries. Pres. Prof. H. MAVER (Yugoslavia); Sec.-Gen. Prof. E. SUNDERLAND (UK). Publs *IUAES Newsletter* (3 a year), *Anthropological Index* (4 a year), research newsletters, books.

International Union of Prehistoric and Protohistoric Sciences: c/o Prof. J. Nenquin, Séminaire d'archéologie de l'Université de Gand, Blandijnberg 2, 9000 Ghent, Belgium; tel. (91) 25-75-71; f. 1931 to promote congresses and scientific work in the fields of pre- and proto-history. Mems: 120 countries. Pres. H. K. BÖHNER (FRG); Sec.-Gen. J. NENQUIN (Belgium).

Permanent International Committee of Linguists: Dr Kuyperlaan 11, 2215 NE Voorhout, Netherlands; tel. (02522) 11852; f. 1928 to further linguistic research, to co-ordinate activities undertaken for the advancement of linguistics, and to make the results of linguistic research known internationally. Mems in 44 countries and two international linguistic organizations. Pres. R. H. ROBINS (UK); Sec.-Gen. E. M. UHLENBECK (Netherlands). Publs *Linguistic Bibliography* (annually), *Dictionaries of Linguistic Terminology, Proceedings of Congresses* (every 5 years), etc.

OTHER ORGANIZATIONS

Arab Towns Organization: PO Box 4954, Safat, Kuwait; tel. 2435540; telex 46390; f. 1967 to help Arab towns in solving problems, preserving the natural environment and cultural heritage; runs a fund to provide loans on concessional terms for needy members, and an Institute for Urban Development (AUDI) based in Riyadh, Saudi Arabia; provides training courses for officials of Arab municipalities and holds seminars on urban development and other relevant subjects. Mems: 325 municipalities. Dir-Gen. TALEB T. AL-TAHER; Sec.-Gen. ABDUL AZIZ Y. AL-ADASANI. Publ. *Al-Madinah Al-Arabiah* (quarterly).

Association for the Study of the World Refugee Problem—AWR: POB 75, 9490 Vaduz, Liechtenstein; tel. 22424; f. 1961 to promote and co-ordinate scholarly research on refugee problems. Mems: 475 in 19 countries. Pres. FRANCO FOSCHI (Italy); Sec.-Gen. ALDO CLEMENTE (Italy). Publ. *AWR Bulletin* (quarterly) in English, French, Italian and German; treatises on refugee problems (17 vols).

Council for the Development of Economic and Social Research in Africa: BP 3304, Dakar, Senegal; tel. 230211; telex 3339; f. 1973; provides conferences, working groups and information services. Mems: research institutes and university faculties in all African countries. Publs *Africa Development* (quarterly), *Newsletter* (every 2 months), studies, occasional and working papers, directories.

Eastern Regional Organisation for Planning and Housing: Kuala Lumpur, Malaysia; f. 1958 to promote and co-ordinate the study and practice of housing and regional town and country planning. Sub-regional offices at Tokyo (JASOPH) and at Bandung (Regional Housing Centre). Mems: 72 organizations and 145 individuals in 13 countries. Pres. Prof. CESAR H. CONCIO (Philippines); Sec.-Gen. C. S. CHANDRASEKHARA (India). Publs *EAROPH News and Notes* (monthly), *Town and Country Planning* (bibliography), conference and congress reports.

English-Speaking Union of the Commonwealth: Dartmouth House, 37 Charles St, Berkeley Square, London, W1X 8AB, England; f. 1918 to promote international understanding between Britain, the Commonwealth, the United States and Europe, in conjunction with the ESU of the USA. Mems: 70,000 (incl. USA). Chair. Sir DONALD TEBBIT; Dir-Gen. ALAN LEE WILLIAMS, OBE. Publ. *Concord* (3 a year).

European Association for Population Studies: POB 11676, 2502 AR The Hague, Netherlands; tel. (070) 469482; telex 31130; f. 1953 to conduct research and provide information on European population problems; organizes conferences, seminars and workshops. Mems: demographers from 29 countries. Sec.-Treas. Prof. GUILLAUME WUNSCH. Publ. *European Journal of Population/Revue Européenne de Démographie* (quarterly).

European Co-ordination Centre for Research and Documentation in Social Sciences: POB 974, 1011 Vienna, Grünangergasse 2, Austria; tel. (0222) 52-43-33; telex 112035; f. 1963 for promotion of contacts between East and West European countries in all areas of social sciences. Activities include co-ordination of international comparative research projects; training of social scientists in problems of international research; organization of conferences; exchange of information and documentation; administered by a Board of Directors (21 social scientists from East and West) and a permanent secretariat in Vienna. Pres. PIERRE FELDHEIM (Belgium); Dir F. CHARVAT (Czechoslovakia). Publs *Vienna Centre Newsletter, ECSSID Bulletin,* bibliographies, directories, registers, books on research, papers.

European Society for Rural Sociology: Department of Sociology, Hollandseweg 1, 6706 KN Wageningen, Netherlands; f. 1957 to further research in, and co-ordination of, rural sociology and provide a centre for documentation of information. Mems: 360 individuals, institutions and associations in 21 European countries and 16 countries outside Europe. Chair. Dr A. T. J. NOOIJ (Netherlands); Sec. Dr E. P. HARSCHE (FRG). Publ. *Sociologia Ruralis* (quarterly).

Experiment in International Living: POB 595, Putney, Vermont 05346, USA; tel. (802) 387-4210; telex 6817462; a non-profit educational and cultural exchange institution; f. 1932 to create mutual understanding and respect among people of different nations, as a means of furthering peace. Mems: over 100,000; national offices in 52 countries. Sec.-Gen. PETER DE JONG.

Institute for International Sociological Research: 35 Am Urbacher Wall (90), POB 100705, 5000 Cologne 1, Federal Republic of Germany; tel. (0221) 486019; f. 1964; diplomatic and international affairs, social and political sciences, moral and behavioural sciences, arts and literature. Mems: 132 Life Fellows, 44 Assoc. Fellows; 14 research centres; affiliated institutes: Academy of Diplomacy and International Affairs, International Academy of Social and Moral Sciences, Arts and Letters. Pres., Chair. Exec. Cttee and Dir-Gen. Consul Dr EDUARD S. ELLENBERG. Publs *Diplomatic Observer* (monthly), *Newsletter, Bulletin* (quarterly), *Annual Report,* etc.

International African Institute: 10 Portugal St, London, WC2A 2HD, England; tel. (01) 831-3068; f. 1926 to promote the study of African peoples, their languages, cultures and social life in their traditional and modern settings; international seminar programme brings together scholars from Africa and elsewhere; links scholars so as to facilitate research projects, especially in the social sciences. Mems: 1,500 in 97 countries. Chair. Prof. J. F. ADE AJAYI; Dir Prof. I. M. LEWIS. Publs *Africa, Ethnographic Survey, International African Library* (monograph series), *International African Seminar Series.*

International Association for Mass Communication Research: c/o Prof. J. D. Halloran, Centre for Mass Communication Research, Univ. of Leicester, 104 Regent Rd, Leicester, LE1 7LT, UK; tel. (0533) 555557; f. 1957 to stimulate interest in mass communication research and the dissemination of information about research and research needs, to seek to bring about improvements in communication practice, policy and research and in the training for journalism, to provide a forum for researchers and others involved in mass communication to meet and exchange information. Mems: over 1,000 in 65 countries. Pres. JAMES D. HALLORAN; Sec.-Gen. T. SZECSKO (Hungary).

International Association of Applied Linguistics: c/o Prof. Dr A. Valdman, Creole Institute, Indiana University, Ballantine Hall 602, Bloomington, Ind 47405, USA; tel. (812) 335-0097; f. 1964; organizes seminars on applied linguistics, and a World Congress every three years (1987 Congress: Sydney, Australia). Mems: associations in 31 countries. Pres. Prof. Dr J. NIVETTE (Belgium); Sec.-Gen. Prof. Dr A. VALDMAN (USA). Publs. *AILA Review* (annually), *AILA News* (quarterly).

International Association of Documentalists and Information Officers—IAD: 74 rue des Saints-Pères, Paris 7e, France; f. 1962 to serve the professional interests of documentalists and to work on the problems of documentation at an international level. Mems: approx. 700. Gen. Sec. Dr JACQUES SAMAIN. Publ. *Monthly News.*

International Association of Metropolitan City Libraries —INTAMEL: Dienstopenbare Bibliotheek, Bilderdijkstraat 1-3, 2513 CM The Hague, Netherlands; tel. (070) 469235; f. 1967. Pres. C. B. COOKE (USA); Sec. W. M. RENES (Netherlands).

International Association of Technological University Libraries: c/o Radcliffe Science Library, University of Oxford, Parks Rd, Oxford, OX1 3QP, England; tel. (0865) 244675; telex 83656; f. 1955 to promote co-operation between member libraries and stimulate research on library problems. Mems: about 133 university libraries in 34 countries. Pres. Dr D. F. SHAW (UK); Sec. Dr N. FJÄLLBRANT (Sweden). Publ. *IATUL Quarterly.*

International Committee for Social Sciences Information and Documentation: 27 rue Saint-Guillaume, 75007 Paris, France; tel. (1) 42-60-39-60; telex 201002; f. 1950 to collect and disseminate information on documentation services in social sciences, help improve documentation, advise societies on problems of documentation and to draw up rules likely to improve the presentation of all documents. Members from international associations specializing in social sciences or in documentation, and from other specialized fields. Sec.-Gen. JEAN MEYRIAT (France). Publs *International Bibliography of the Social Sciences* (annually), *Confluence* (surveys of research; irregular), occasional reports, etc.

International Council on Archives: 60 rue des Francs-Bourgeois, 75003 Paris, France; tel. (1) 42-77-11-30; f. 1948. Mems: 720 from 125 countries. Pres. HANS BOOMS (FRG); Exec. Sec. CHARLES KECSKEMETI (France). Publs *Archivum* (annually), *ICA Bulletin* (2 a year).

International Ergonomics Association: c/o I. Kuorinka, Institute of Occupational Health, Haartmanink. 1, 00290 Helsinki, Finland; tel. 47471; telex 121394; f. 1957 to bring together organizations and persons interested in the scientific study of human work and its environment; to establish international contacts among those specializing in this field, promote the knowledge of these sciences, co-operate with employers' associations and trade unions in order to encourage the practical application of ergonomic sciences in industries, and promote scientific research by qualified persons in this field. Mems: 16 federated societies. Pres. HARRY L. DAVIS (USA); Sec.-Gen. ILKKA KUORINKA (Finland). Publ. *Ergonomics* (monthly).

International Federation for Housing and Planning: Wassenaarseweg 43, 2596 CG The Hague, Netherlands; f. 1913 to study and promote the improvement of housing, the theory and practice of town planning inclusive of the creation of new agglomerations and the planning of territories at regional, national and international levels. Mems: 400 organizations and 500 individuals in 65 countries. Pres. Prof. R. RADOVIĆ (Yugoslavia); Sec.-Gen. J. H. LÉONS (Netherlands). Publs *News Sheet* (7 a year), Congress and Seminar Reports, and occasional special publications.

International Federation of Institutes for Socio-religious Research: 1/21 place Montesquieu, 1348 Louvain-la-neuve, Belgium; f. 1958; federates centres engaged in undertaking scientific research in order to analyse and discover the social and religious phenomena at work in contemporary society. Mems: institutes in 26 countries. Pres. V. COSMAO (France); Vice-Pres. Canon Fr. HOUTART (Belgium); Sec.-Gen. F. DASSETTO (Italy). Publ. *Social Compass (International Review of Sociology of Religion)* (4 a year, in English and French).

International Federation of Social Science Organizations: Forskningssekretariatet, Holmens Kanal 7, 1060 Copenhagen, Denmark; f. 1979 to succeed the Conference of National Social Science Councils and Analogous Bodies (f. 1975) to further the exchange of information, experience and ideas among its member organizations, to contribute to the more effective organizations of research and teaching and to institution-building in the social sciences, and to facilitate co-operation and enlist mutual assistance in the planning and evaluation of programmes of major importance to members. Mems: 31 organizations. Pres. Prof. N. AMSTRUP; Sec.-Gen. Dr J. R. B. LOPES. Publs *Newsletter, International Directory of Social Science Organizations.*

International Federation of Vexillological Associations: 3 Edgehill Rd, Winchester, Mass 01890, USA; tel. (617) 729-9410; f. 1967 to promote through its member organizations the scientific study of the history and symbolism of flags, and especially to hold International Congresses every two years and sanction international standards for scientific flag study. Mems: 25 associations in 19 countries. Pres. Rev. HUGH BOUDIN (Belgium); Sec.-Gen. Dr WHITNEY SMITH (USA). Publs *Recueil* (every 2 years), *The Flag Bulletin* (every 2 months), *Archivum Heraldicum* (quarterly).

International Institute for Ligurian Studies: Museo Bicknell, via Romana 89 bis, 18012 Bordighera, Italy; f. 1947 to conduct research on ancient monuments and regional traditions in the north-west arc of the Mediterranean (France and Italy). Library of 55,000 vols. Mems: in France, Italy, Spain, Switzerland. Pres. Avv. COSIMO COSTA (Italy), PAUL-ALBERT FÉVRIER (France), Prof. MARTIN ALMAGRO GORBEA (Spain); Dir Dott FRANCISCA PALLARÉS (Italy).

International Institute of Administrative Sciences: 1 rue Defacqz, Bte 11, 1050 Brussels, Belgium; tel. (02) 538-90-77; telex 65933; f. 1930 for comparative examination of administrative experience in the various countries; research and programmes for improving administrative law and practices and for technical assistance; library of 10,000 vols; consultative status with UN and UNESCO; international congresses; special programme for schools and institutes of public administration; working groups on history of administration, on international civil service administration, and on integrated budgeting systems; standing committees on law and science of public administration, administrative structures and management, personnel administration, planning and forecasting, public enterprise. Mems: 48 mem. states, 30 national sections, 21 corporate and individual members. Pres. JOSEPH H. KAISER (FRG); Dir.-Gen. MICHEL LESAGE (France). Publs *International Review of Administrative Sciences* (quarterly), *Interadmin* (3 a year), *Infoadmin* (annually), reports, readers, bibliographies.

International Institute of Sociology: Piazzale Aldo Moro 5, 00185 Rome, Italy; f. 1893 to enable sociologists to meet and study sociological questions. Mems: 300, representing 45 countries. Pres. EDGAR BORGATTA (USA); Gen. Sec. Prof. GIOACCHINO (Italy). Publ. *Revue de l'Institut Internationale de Sociologie*.

International Peace Academy: 777 United Nations Plaza, New York, NY 10017, USA; tel. (212) 949-8480; f. 1967 to teach and educate government officials in the procedures needed for conflict resolution, peace-keeping, mediation and negotiation, through international training seminars, curriculum development and publication; off-the-record meetings are also conducted to gain complete understanding of a specific conflict. Chair. Ambassador KARL I. R. FISCHER (Austria); Pres. Maj.-Gen. INDAR JIT RIKHYE (retd) (India); Exec. Vice-Pres. THOMAS WEISS. Publs *Coping with Conflict* (2 a year), quarterly newsletter, special reports and studies.

International Peace Research Association: Mershon Center, Ohio State University, 199 West 10th Ave, Columbus, OH 43201, USA; tel. (614) 422-1681; telex 245334; f. 1964 to increase research on world peace and to ensure its scientific quality; to promote the establishment of new research institutions and develop contacts and co-operation between scholars from different parts of the world and different disciplines interested in peace research. Mems: 67 corporate mems in 27 countries, four scientific associations, and 569 individuals in 57 countries. Sec.-Gen. CHADWICK F. ALGER (USA). Publs *International Peace Research Newsletter* (4 a year), Proceedings of International Peace Research Association (bi-annually).

International Phenomenological Society: Box 1947, Brown University, Providence, RI 02912, USA; f. 1939 to encourage the study and development of E. Husserl's philosophy. Mems: individuals in 73 countries. Publ. *Philosophy and Phenomenological Research* (quarterly).

International Social Science Council—ISSC: Maison de l'UNESCO, 1 rue Miollis, Paris 75015, France; tel. (1) 45-68-25-58; f. 1952; since 1973 a federation of the organizations listed below. Aims: the advancement of the social sciences throughout the world and their application to the major problems of the world; the spread of co-operation at an international level between specialists in the social sciences. ISSC has a Standing Committee for Conceptual and Terminological Analysis (COCTA, established in co-operation with IPSA and ISA); and Issue Groups on Peace and on Technological Change; also created the European Co-ordination Centre for Research and Documentation in the Social Sciences, in Vienna. Pres. C. MENDES (Brazil); Sec.-Gen. L. I. RAMALLO (Spain). Publs *Social Science Information* (6 a year), *Newsletter* (3 a year).

Associations Federated to the ISSC

(details of these organizations will be found under their appropriate category elsewhere in the International Organizations section)

International Association of Legal Sciences (p. 235).
International Economic Association (p. 225).
International Federation of Social Science Organizations (p. 257).
International Geographical Union (p. 249).
International Institute of Administrative Sciences (p. 257).
International Law Association (p. 236).
International Peace Research Association (p. 258).
International Political Science Association (p. 231).
International Sociological Association (p. 258).
International Union for the Scientific Study of Population (p. 258).
International Union of Anthropological and Ethnological Sciences (p. 256).
International Union of Psychological Science (p. 250).
World Association for Public Opinion Research (p. 258).
World Federation for Mental Health (p. 243).

International Society for Ethnology and Folklore—SIEF: c/o Institute of Ethnography and Folklore, Str. N. Beloiannis 25, Bucharest, Romania; f. 1964 to establish and maintain collaboration between specialists in folklore and ethnology; organizes commissions, symposia, congresses, etc.; affiliated to Union internationale des sciences anthropologiques et ethnologiques and Conseil international de philosophie et des sciences humaines, links with International Council for Traditional Music and International Council of Museums. Mems: 400. Pres. Prof. MIHAI POP (Romania). Publ. *Bulletin d'Informations SIEF* (annually).

International Society of Social Defence: 28 rue Saint-Guillaume, 75007 Paris, France; f. 1945 to combat crime, to protect society and to prevent citizens from being tempted to commit criminal action. Mems in 34 countries. Pres. SIMONE ROZES (France); Sec.-Gen. A. BERIA DI ARGENTINE (Italy). Publs *Cahiers de défense sociale, Bulletin de la Société internationale de défense sociale* (annually).

International Sociological Association: Oude Hoogstraat 24, 1012 CE Amsterdam, Netherlands; tel. 5253584; f. 1949 to promote sociological knowledge, facilitate contacts between sociologists, encourage the dissemination and exchange of information and facilities and stimulate research; has 38 research committees on various aspects of sociology; holds World Congresses every four years (11th Congress: New Delhi, India, August 1986). Pres. FERNANDO CARDOSO (Brazil); Exec. Sec. R. FELIX GEYER. Publs *Current Sociology* (3 a year), *International Sociology, Sage Studies in International Sociology* (based on World Congress).

International Statistical Institute: Prinses Beatrixlaan 428, 2270 AZ Voorburg, Netherlands; tel. (70) 694341; telex 32260; f. 1885; devoted to the development and improvement of statistical methods and their application throughout the world; administers among others a statistical education centre in Calcutta in co-operation with UNESCO and the Indian Statistical Institute; executes international research programmes through the International Statistical Research Centre. Mems: 1,351 ordinary mems; 168 ex-officio mems; 41 affiliated organizations. Pres. S. MORIGUTI;; Dir Permanent Office E. LUNENBERG. Publs *Bulletin of the International Statistical Institute* (proceedings of biennial sessions), *International Statistical Review* (3 a year), *Statistical Education Newsletter* (3 a year), *Short Book Reviews* (3 a year), *Statistical Theory and Method Abstracts* (quarterly), *International Statistical Information* (newsletter, 3 a year), *Directories* (annually).

International Union for the Scientific Study of Population: 34 rue des Augustins, 4000 Liège, Belgium; tel. (041) 22-40-80; f. 1928 to advance the progress of quantitative and qualitative demography as a science. Mems: 1,800 in 112 countries. Pres. W. BRASS (UK); Sec.-Gen. G. TAPINOS (France). Publs. *IUSSP Newsletter*, proceedings of conferences and seminars, papers.

Mensa International: 50/52 Great Eastern St, London, EC2A 3EP, England; tel. (01) 729-6576; f. 1946, for social contact between members, and to provide a control group for research workers in psychology and social science; encourages identification and fostering of intelligence for the benefit of humanity. Members are individuals who score in a recognized intelligence test higher than 98% of people in general: there are 75,000 mems world-wide. Pres. Chair. HYMAN BROOK (Canada); Exec. Dir E. J. VINCENT (UK). Publ. *Mensa Journal International* (monthly).

World Association for Public Opinion Research: c/o Dr D. R. Deluca, The Roper Centre, Yale University, POB 1732, New Haven, Conn 06520, USA; f. 1947 to establish and promote contacts between persons in the field of survey research on opinions, attitudes and behaviour of people in the various countries of the world; to further the use of objective, scientific survey research in national and international affairs. Mems: 315 from 57 countries. Pres. HANS ZETTERBERG (Sweden); Exec. Sec. Dr DONALD R. DELUCA. Publ. *WAPOR Newsletter* (quarterly).

World Society of Ekistics: c/o Athens Centre of Ekistics, 24 Strat. Syndesmou St, 106 73 Athens, Greece; tel. 3623-216; telex 215227; f. 1965; aims to promote knowledge and ideas concerning ekistics through research, publications and conferences; to recognize the benefits and necessity of an inter-disciplinary approach to the needs of human settlements; to stimulate world-wide interest in ekistics. Pres. CHARLES M. HAAR; Sec.-Gen. P. PSOMOPOULOS.

World Union of Catholic Philosophical Societies: Catholic University of America, Washington, DC 20064, USA; tel. (202) 635-5636; f. 1948. Mems: about 1,500 persons from about 20 countries. Pres. Prof. JEAN LADRIÈRE (Belgium); Sec.-Gen. R. P. G. MCLEAN (USA). Publ. *Circulaires* (1 or 2 issues a year).

Social Welfare

Aid to Displaced Persons and its European Villages: 35 rue du Marché, 5200 Huy, Belgium; tel. (085) 21-34-81; f. 1957 to carry on and develop work begun by the Belgian association Aid to

Displaced Persons; aims to provide material and moral aid for refugees; European Villages established at Aachen, Bregenz, Augsburg, Berchem-Ste-Agathe, Spiesen, Euskirchen, Wuppertal as centres for refugees. Pres. J. EECKHOUT (Belgium); Vice-Pres. Mrs T. ERNST (FRG).

Amnesty International: 1 Easton St, London, WC1X 8DJ, England; tel. (01) 833-1771; telex 28502; f. 1961; an independent worldwide movement working impartially for the release of all prisoners of conscience, fair and prompt trials for all political prisoners, and the abolition of torture and the death penalty; financed by donations. Mems: organized sections in 45 countries and territories; over 3,000 local groups; over 500,000 individuals in 150 countries. Chair. WOLFGANG HEINZ (Austria); Gen. Sec. IAN MARTIN (UK). Publs *Newsletter* (monthly), *Annual Report*, Reports on political imprisonment, torture and executions around the world.

Anti-Slavery Society for the Protection of Human Rights: 180 Brixton Rd, London, SW9 6AT, England; tel. (01) 582-4040; f. 1839 to eradicate slavery and forced labour in all their forms, to promote the well-being of indigenous peoples, and to protect human rights in accordance with the Universal Declaration of Human Rights, 1948. Mems: 900 members in 30 countries. Chair. JEREMY SWIFT; Dir R. P.H. DAVIES. Publs *Annual Report, Anti-Slavery Reporter* (annually) and special reports of research.

Associated Country Women of the World: Vincent House, Vincent Square, London, SW1P 2NB; tel. (01) 834-8635; f. 1930 to aid the economic and social development of countrywomen and home-makers of all nations; to promote study of an interest in home-making, housing, health, education, and aspects of food and agriculture. Mems: approx. 9m. Pres. Dr E. McLEAN; Gen. Sec. JENNIFER PEARCE. Publ. *The Countrywoman* (quarterly).

Association of Social Work Education in Africa: Dept of Applied Sociology, Addis Ababa University, POB 1176, Addis Ababa, Ethiopia; tel. 126827; f. 1971 to promote teaching and research in social development, to improve standards of institutions in this field, to exchange information and experience. Mems: schools of social work, community development training centres, other institutions and centres; 53 training institutions and 140 social work educators in 32 African countries, 22 non-African assoc. mems. in Europe and North America. Exec. Sec. AREGA YIMAN. Publs *Journal for Social Work Education in Africa*; professional documents and seminar proceedings.

Aviation sans frontières—ASF: Orly Sud 130, 94541 Orly Aérogare Cedex, France; tel. (1) 48-84-44-56; f. 1980 to make available the resources of the aviation industry to humanitarian organizations, for carrying supplies and equipment at minimum cost, both on long-distance flights and locally. Mems: about 800 pilots and other airline staff.

Catholic International Union for Social Service: 111 rue de la Poste, 1030 Brussels, Belgium; f. 1925 to develop social service on the basis of Christian doctrine; to unite Catholic social schools and social workers' associations in all countries to promote their foundation; to represent at the international level the Catholic viewpoint as it affects social service. Mems: 172 schools of social service, 26 associations of social workers, 52 individual members. Exec. Sec. A. .M. GELEYNS. Publs *Service Social dans le monde* (quarterly), *News Bulletin, Bulletin de Liaison, Boletín de Noticias* (quarterly), and reports of seminars.

Co-ordinating Committee for International Voluntary Service—CCIVS: Maison de l'UNESCO, 1 rue Miollis, 75015 Paris, France; tel. (1) 45-68-27-31; f. 1948; acts as an information centre and co-ordinating body for voluntary service organizations all over the world. Affiliated mems: 110 organizations. Dir C. BARBE. Publs *News from CCIVS* (4 a year), books, lists of organizations.

Council of World Organizations Interested in the Handicapped: c/o Rehabilitation International, 25 East 21st St, New York, NY 10010, USA; tel. (212) 420-1500; telex 66125; f. 1953 to assist the UN and its specialized agencies to develop a well coordinated international programme for rehabilitation of the handicapped. Mems: 50 organizations in consultative status with ECOSOC and/or WHO, ILO, UNESCO, UNICEF. Chair. NORMAN ACTON.

EIRENE—International Christian Service for Peace: 5450 Neuwied 1, Engerser Str. 74B, Federal Republic of Germany; f. 1957; works in North Africa, Asia and Latin America (professional training, apprenticeship programmes, agricultural work and co-operatives), Europe and the USA (volunteer programmes in co-operation with peace groups). Gen. Sec. JEAN-LUC TISSOT. Publ. circular letter.

European Federation for the Welfare of the Elderly—EURAG: 8010 Graz, Schmiedg. 26 (Amtshaus), Austria; tel. (0316) 76431-485; f. 1962 for the exchange of experience among member associations; practical co-operation among member organizations to achieve their objectives in the field of ageing; representation of the interests of members before international organizations; promotion of understanding and co-operation in matters of social welfare; to draw attention to the problems of old age. Mems: organizations in 25 countries. Pres. ROBERT PRIGENT (France); Sec.-Gen. EDUARD PUMPERNIG (Austria). Publs. (in English, French, German and Italian) *EURAG Newsletter* (quarterly), *EURAG Information* (monthly).

Federation of Asian Women's Associations—FAWA: Escoda Memorial 1501, San Marcelino, Philippines; f. 1959 to provide closer relations, and bring about joint efforts among Asians, particularly among the women, through mutual appreciation of cultural, moral and socio-economic values. Mems: 415,000. Pres. Dr H. SJAMSINOOR ADNOES; Sec. Mrs NICOLASA J. TRIA TIRONA (Philippines). Publ. *FAWA News Bulletin* (every 3 months).

Inter-American Conference on Social Security (Comité Permanente Interamericano de Seguridad Social): Apdo postal 99089, CP 10100 México 20, DF, Mexico; tel. 595-01-07; telex 1775793; f. 1942 to facilitate and develop co-operation between social security administrations and institutions in the American states; 14th General Assembly, 1986. Mems: governments and social security institutions in 20 countries. Pres. Lic. RICARDO GARCÍA SAINZ (Mexico); Sec.-Gen. and Treas. Dr GASTÓN NOVELO (Mexico). Publs *Seguridad Social, Boletín Informativo*.

Intergovernmental Committee for Migration—ICM: 17 route des Morillons, POB 71, 1211 Geneva 19, Switzerland; tel. (022) 980066; telex 22155; f. 1951 to effect the orderly migration of Europeans who could not migrate without international assistance, to help the resettlement of refugees in countries of permanent asylum and to sponsor immigration into less-developed countries in accordance with their economic needs; later included non-Europeans. Since its inception, it has helped over 3.6m. refugees and migrants to resettle overseas; since 1965 26,900 Europeans have been placed in Latin America under a Selective Migration Programme to ensure the transfer of technology to Latin America through the migration of highly qualified Europeans, and 6,900 Latin Americans have returned to their countries of origin under the Return of Talent programme. Budget (1986): US $103.5m. Mems: 32 states and 16 observer states. Dir JAMES L. CARLIN (USA); Deputy Dir G. MASELLI (Italy). Publs *International Migration* (quarterly), *Monthly Dispatch, Review of Achievements* (annually).

International Abolitionist Federation: 47 rue de Rivoli, 75001 Paris, France; tel. (1) 45-08-97-52; f. 1875 for the abolition of the organization and exploitation of the prostitution of others and the regulation of prostitution by public authorities; consultative status with ECOSOC (UN). Affiliated organizations in 21 countries. Corresponding mems in 60 countries. Pres. ANIMA BASAK (Austria); Gen. Sec. MARIE-RENÉE JAMET (France). Publs *Revue abolitionniste* (2 a year), *General Assembly* (every year), *International Congress* (every 3 years).

International Association against Noise: Hirschenplatz 7, 6004 Lucerne, Switzerland; tel. (041) 513013; f. 1959 to promote noise-control at an international level; to promote co-operation and the exchange of experience and prepare supranational measures; issues information, carries out research, organizes conferences, and assists national anti-noise associations. Mems: 17, and three associate mems. Pres. JOCHEN BERG (FRG); Sec. Dr WILLY AECHERLI (Switzerland). Publ. *Reports of Congresses*.

International Association for Children's International Summer Villages: Mea House, Ellison Place, Newcastle upon Tyne, England; f. 1950 to conduct International Camps for children and young people between the ages of 11 and 18. Mems: c. 15,000. International Pres. RUTH LUND; Sec.-Gen. JOSEPH G. BANKS. Publ. *CISV News* (3 a year).

International Association for Mutual Benefit Societies: 8–10 rue de Hesse, 1204 Geneva, Switzerland; tel. (022) 214528; f. 1947 to propagate and develop mutual benefits funds in all countries. Mems: national and regional institutions in 14 countries. Pres. ROBERT VAN DEN HEUVEL (Belgium); Sec.-Gen. W. J. BOUVIER (Switzerland).

International Association for Suicide Prevention: 1811 Trousdale Drive, Burlingame, Calif 94010, USA; tel. (415) 877-5604; f. 1960 to establish an organization where individuals and agencies of various disciplines and professions from different countries can find a common platform for interchange of acquired experience, literature and information about suicide; disseminates information; arranges special training; encourages and carries out research; organizes the Biannual International Congress for Suicide Prevention. Mems: 730 individuals and societies, in 42 countries of all continents. Vice-Pres. CHARLOTTE P. ROSS (USA). Publ. *Crisis* (2 a year).

International Association for Education to a Life without Drugs (Internationaler Verband für Erziehung zu suchtmittelfreiem Leben—IVES): Lyshoj 6, 6300 Graasten, Denmark; f. 1954 (as the International Association for Temperance Education) to promote international co-operation in education on the dangers of alcohol and drugs; collection and distribution of information on drugs; maintains regular contact with national and international organizations active in these fields; holds conferences. Mems: 17,000 in seven countries. Pres. WILLY STUBER; Sec. JÜRGEN KLAHN.

International Association of Schools of Social Work: 1210 Vienna, Freytaggasse 32, Austria; tel. (0222) 38-74-79; f. 1929 to provide international leadership and encourage high standards in social work education. Mems: 500 schools of social work in 70 countries, and 23 associations of schools. Pres. HEINRICH SCHILLER (FRG); Sec.-Gen. VERA MEHTA (India). Publs *International Social Work* (quarterly), *Directory of Members, IASSW News*.

International Association of Workers for Maladjusted Children: 66 chaussée d'Antin, 75009 Paris, France; f. 1951 to promote the profession of specialized social workers for maladjusted children; to provide a centre of information about child welfare and encourage co-operation between the members; next Congress Israel, 1986. Mems: national associations from 19 countries and individual members in many other countries. Pres. DANIEL DUPIED (France); Sec.-Gen. BRUNO NEFF (France). Publs Reports on Congresses, Chronicle in each issue of *International Review for Child Welfare* (quarterly).

International Catholic Migration Commission: CP 96, 37–39 rue de Vermont, 1211 Geneva 20, Switzerland; tel. (022) 334150; telex 28100; f. 1951; offers migration aid programmes to those who are not in a position to secure by themselves their resettlement elsewhere; grants interest-free travel loans; assists refugees on a worldwide basis, helping with all social and technical problems. Sub-committees dealing with Europe and Latin America. Mems: in 58 countries. Pres. JOHN E. MCCARTHY (USA); Sec.-Gen. Dr ELIZABETH WINKLER (Austria). Publs *Migrations, Migration News, Menschen Unterwegs, ICMC Newsletter*.

International Children's Centre (Centre international de l'enfance): Château de Longchamp, carrefour de Longchamp, Bois de Boulogne, 75016 Paris, France; tel. (1) 45-06-79-92; telex 610584; f. 1949 to improve the health and well-being of children and families, especially in developing countries; financed by the French Government and other sources; three departments: Education and Training (organizing courses, seminars and working groups all over the world), Communicable Diseases and Immunization (developing immunization techniques); Information (documentation centre, publications and bibliographical data base), and External Relations Office. Pres. of Admin Council Prof. PIERRE ROYER; Dir-Gen. CLAUDE JOLIF. Publs *Children in the Tropics* (6 a year, French, English and occasionally Spanish), *Reports, Bibliographical Bulletins* and *Technical Reviews*.

International Christian Federation for the Prevention of Alcoholism and Drug Addiction: 27 Tavistock Sq., London, WC1H 9HH, England; tel. (01) 387-8413; f. 1960, reconstituted 1980 to promote worldwide education and remedial work through the churches, to co-ordinate Christian concern about alcohol and drug abuse, in co-operation with WHO. Chair. Bishop JAMES K. MATHEWS (USA); Gen. Sec. Rev. J. KENNETH LAWTON (UK); Publ. occasional bulletins.

International Civil Defence Organisation: 10–12 chemin Surville, 1213 Petit-Lancy/Geneva, Switzerland; telex 423786; f. 1931, present statutes 1966; aims to intensify and co-ordinate on a world-wide scale the development and improvement of organization, means and techniques for preventing and reducing the consequences of natural disasters in peacetime or of the use of weapons in time of conflict. Sec.-Gen. Dr MILAN M. BODI (Switzerland). Publs *International Civil Defence* (monthly in English, French, Spanish, German and Arabic), *Monographs* (occasional), training manuals, information booklets, meetings reports.

International Commission for the Prevention of Alcoholism and Drug Dependence: 6830 Laurel St, NW, Washington, DC 20012, USA; tel. (202) 722-6729; telex 440186; f. 1953 to encourage scientific research on intoxication by alcohol, its physiological, mental and moral effects on the individual, and its effect on the community; seventh World Congress, Brisbane, Australia, 1988. Mems: individuals in 90 countries. Exec. Dir ERNEST H. J. STEED. Publ. *ICPA Quarterly*.

International Commission for the Protection of the Rhine against Pollution: 5400 Koblenz, Kaiserin-Augusta-Anlagen 15, POB 309, Federal Republic of Germany; tel. (0261) 33623; telex 862499; f. 1950 and institutionalized 1963 to prepare and commission research to establish the nature of the pollution of the Rhine; to propose measures of protection to the signatory governments. Mems: 23 delegates from France, Federal Republic of Germany, Luxembourg, the Netherlands, Switzerland and the EEC. Pres. Baron D. W. VAN LYNDEN; Sec. J. M. GOPPEL. Publ. annual report.

International Council of Voluntary Agencies: 13 rue Gautier, 1201 Geneva, Switzerland; tel. (022) 316602; telex 22891; f. 1962 to provide a forum for voluntary humanitarian and development agencies. Mems: 79 non-governmental organizations. Chair. FRANK JUDD; Exec. Dir ANTHONY J. KOZLOWSKI. Publs *ICVA News* (6 a year, English, French and Spanish), *NGO Management* (quarterly in English and French), Information papers on humanitarian and developmental situations and activities (to members).

International Council of Women: c/o 13 rue Caumartin, 75009 Paris, France; tel. (1) 47-42-19-40; f. 1888 to bring together in international affiliation National Councils of Women from all continents for consultation and joint action in order to promote equal rights for men and women and the integration of women in development and in decision-making; has consultative status with ECOSOC (UN); 13 standing committees. Mems: 75 national councils. Pres. Dr SOOKJA HONG; Sec.-Gen. Mrs JACQUELINE BARBET-MASSIN.

International Council on Alcohol and Addictions: CP 189, 1001 Lausanne, Switzerland; tel. (021) 209865; telex 26666; f. 1907; consultative status with the UN Economic and Social Council; official relations with the World Health Organization and International Labour Office; co-operative relations with the Council of Europe, the League of Arab States and the Colombo Plan; organizes training courses, congresses, symposia and seminars in different countries. Mems: affiliated organizations in 60 countries, as well as individual members. Pres. DAVID ARCHIBALD (Canada); Dir ARCHER TONGUE (UK). Publs *ICAA News* (quarterly), *Alcoholism* (2 a year), *Legal Issues Newsletter* (irregular), *Drug and Alcohol Dependence* (bi-monthly), *Proceedings of Conferences*, monographs.

International Council on Jewish Social and Welfare Services: 75 rue de Lyon, 1211 Geneva 13, Switzerland; tel. (022) 449000; telex 23163; f. 1961; functions include the exchange of views and information among member agencies concerning the problems of Jewish social and welfare services including medical care, old age, welfare, child care, rehabilitation, technical assistance, vocational training, agricultural and other resettlement, economic assistance, refugees, migration, integration and related problems; representation of views to governments and international organizations. Mems: six national and international organizations. Pres. K. D. RUBENS; Exec. Sec. L. LEIBERG.

International Council on Social Welfare: 1060 Vienna, Koestlergasse 1/29, Austria; tel. (022) 587-81-64; f. 1928 to provide an international forum for the discussion of social work and related issues; to promote interest in social welfare; documentation and information services. Mems: 68 countries, 23 international organizations. Pres. N. PRÉFONTAINE (Canada); Sec.-Gen. INGRID GELINEK (Austria). Publs *Conference Proceedings* (biennially), *International Social Work* (quarterly), *ICSW Newsletter* (quarterly), National Committee Bulletins.

International Dachau Committee: 65 rue de Haerne, 1040 Brussels, Belgium; f. 1958 to perpetuate the memory of the political prisoners of Dachau; to manifest the friendship and solidarity of former prisoners whatever their beliefs or nationality; to maintain the ideals of their resistance, liberty, tolerance and respect for persons and nations; and to maintain the former concentration camp at Dachau as a museum and international memorial. Pres. Dr A. GUERISSE; Sec.-Gen. GEORGES-VALÉRY WALRAEVE. Publ. *Bulletin Officiel du Comité International de Dachau* (2 a year).

International Federation of Blue Cross Societies: Kermely 10, 1206 Geneva, Switzerland; tel. (022) 472088; telex 428639; f. 1877 to aid the victims of intemperance and drug addicts; and to take part in the general movement against alcoholism. Pres. JEAN-PAUL A. WIDMER (Switzerland); Gen. Sec. DANIEL ROCHAT (Switzerland). Publ. report (every 4 years).

International Federation of Educative Communities: c/o Prof. Dr Othmar Roden, 1030 Vienna, Dapontegasse 3/7, Austria; f. 1948 under the auspices of UNESCO; consultative status with ECOSOC and UNESCO. Objects: to co-ordinate the work of national associations, and to promote children's communities particularly by technical aid to underdeveloped countries. Mems: national associations from Algeria, Austria, Belgium, Czechoslovakia, Denmark, France, German Democratic Republic, Federal Republic of Germany, Hungary, India, Ireland, Israel, Italy, Jamaica, Luxembourg, Netherlands, Poland, Sweden, Switzerland,

Tunisia, United Kingdom, USA, Yugoslavia. Pres. Prof. Dr HEINRICH TUGGENER (Switzerland); Gen. Sec. Prof. Dr OTHMAR RODEN (Austria). Publs *Etudes Pédagogiques, Documents, Recherches et Témoignages.*

International Federation of Disabled Workers and Civilian Handicapped: c/o Reichsbund, 5300 Bonn 2, Beethovenallee 56–58, Federal Republic of Germany; tel. (0228) 363071; telex 885557; f. 1953 to bring together representatives of the disabled and handicapped into an international non-political organization under the guidance of the disabled themselves; to promote greater opportunities for the disabled; to create rehabilitation centres; to act as a co-ordinating body for all similar national organizations. Consultative member of ECOSOC, official relations with ILO, WHO and UNESCO. Mems: national groups from Austria, Czechoslovakia, Denmark, Finland, France, German Federal Republic, Hungary, Iceland, Italy, Netherlands, Norway, Poland, Spain, Sweden, Switzerland, Yugoslavia. Pres. HERMANN MEYER (FRG); Gen. Sec. MARIJA ŠTIGLIC (FRG). Publs *Bulletin, Nouvelles.*

International Federation of Social Workers—IFSW: 33 rue de l'Athénée, 1206 Geneva, Switzerland; tel. (022) 471236; f. 1928 as International Permanent Secretariat of Social Workers; present name adopted 1950; aims to promote social work as a profession through international co-operation concerning standards, training, ethics and working conditions; represents the profession at international meetings; assists in welfare programmes sponsored by international organizatons. Mems: national associations in 44 countries. Pres. JANIE THOMAS (UK); Sec.-Gen. ANDREW M. APOSTOL (Switzerland).

International Fellowship of Former Scouts and Guides—IFOFSAG: 9 rue du Champ de Mars, bte 14, 1050 Brussels, Belgium; tel. (02) 511-96-45; f. 1953 to help former scouts and guides to keep alive the spirit of the Scout and Guide Promise and Laws in their own lives; to bring that spirit into the communities in which they live and work; to establish liaison and co-operation between national organizations for former scouts and guides; to encourage the founding of an organization in any country where no such organization exists; to promote friendship amongst former scouts and guides throughout the world. Mems: 54,000 in 34 member states. Chair. of Council ALAN K. B. BEAVIS; Sec.-Gen. SUZANNE PRITT. Publ. *The Fellowship Bulletin* (quarterly).

International League of Societies for Persons with Mental Handicap: 248 ave Louise, bte 17, 1050 Brussels, Belgium; tel. (02) 647-61-80; f. 1960 to promote the interests of the mentally handicapped without regard to nationality, race or creed, furthers co-operation between national bodies, organizes congresses. Consultative status with UNESCO, UNICEF, official relations with WHO, ILO, ECOSOC, the Council of Europe and the Inter-American Children's Institute. Mems: 105 in 68 countries (incl. 47 national associations and 58 affiliates) and four associate (regional) mems. Pres. P. MITTLER (UK); Sec.-Gen. V. WAHLSTRÖM (Sweden). Publs Proceedings of Conferences, Symposia, etc., brochures and pamphlets.

International Lifeboat Conference: c/o Royal National Lifeboat Institution, West Quay Rd, Poole, Dorset, BH15 1HZ, England; tel. (0202) 671133; telex 41328; f. 1924; conferences held at four-yearly intervals; next Conference: Spain, 1987. Sec. Lieut-Commdr BRIAN MILES. Publs Conference reports, *Lifeboat International* (technical articles).

International Planned Parenthood Federation—IPPF: 18–20 Lower Regent St, London, SW1Y 4PW, England; tel. (01) 839-2911; telex 919573; f. 1952; aims to initiate and support family planning services throughout the world, and to increase understanding of population problems; offers technical assistance and training; collaborates with other international organizations and provides information on all aspects of family planning; annual budget of US $47m. (1985). Mems: independent family planning associations in 120 countries. Pres. Mrs AVABAI WADIA; Sec.-Gen. BRADMAN WEERAKOON. Publs *People* (quarterly, in English and French), *Medical Bulletin* (every 2 months, in English, French and Spanish), *Research in Reproduction* (quarterly), publications list.

International Prisoners Aid Association: Department of Sociology, University of Louisville, Louisville, Ky 40208, USA; f. 1950; to improve prisoners' aid services for rehabilitation of the individual and protection of society. Mems: 28 National Federations in 27 countries and three individual member agencies in Canada, one in Australia, one in Austria, one in Egypt and one in Malaysia. Pres. Dr WOLFGANG DOLEISCH (Austria); Exec. Dir Dr BADR-EL-DIN ALI. Publ. *Newsletter* (3 a year).

International Social Security Association: Case Postale No. 1, 1211 Geneva 22, Switzerland; telex 22271; f. 1927 to promote the development of social security through the improvement of techniques and administration. Mems: 313 institutions in 128 countries. Pres. JÉRÔME DEJARDIN (Belgium); Sec.-Gen. VLADIMIR RYS (UK). Publs *International Social Security Review* (quarterly, English, French, German, Spanish), *Estudios de la Seguridad Social* (irregular), *World Bibliography of Social Security* (2 a year, English, French, Spanish, German), *African News Sheet* (English and French), *Asian News Sheet, Caribbean News Sheet, Social Security Documentation* (African, Asian, European and American series), *Current Research in Social Security* (2 a year, English, French, German and Spanish), *Automatic Data Processing Information Bulletin* (2 a year), *ISSA News* (2 a year).

International Social Service: 32 quai du Seujet, 1201 Geneva, Switzerland; tel. (022) 317454; telex 289283; f. 1921 to aid families and individuals whose problems require services beyond the boundaries of the country in which they live and where the solution of these problems depends upon co-ordinated action on the part of social workers in two or more countries; to study from an international standpoint the conditions and consequences of emigration in their effect on individual, family, and social life. Operates on a non-sectarian and non-political basis. Mems: branches in 14 countries, two affiliated offices, and correspondents in some 100 other countries. Pres. Sir CLIVE BOSSOM (UK); Sec.-Gen. MARCELLE L. BRISSON (Canada).

International Union for Moral and Social Action—UIAMS: 4700 Hamm 1, Jägerallee 5, Federal Republic of Germany; tel. (02381) 8768; f. 1951 to co-ordinate efforts being made in different countries to maintain a high standard of public morals, and in that endeavour to oppose everything which might injure or attack a sound and healthy public life. This is based on the Universal Declaration of Human Rights as defined by the United Nations. Congresses are held every three years. Mems: in 22 countries. Pres. RICHARD GATZWEILER (Federal Republic of Germany). Publs *Bulletin* (quarterly).

International Union of Family Organisations: 28 place Saint-Georges, 75009 Paris, France; tel. (1) 48-78-07-59; f. 1947 to bring together all organizations throughout the world which are working for family welfare; conducts permanent commissions on standards of living, housing, marriage guidance, work groups on family movements, rural families, etc.; there are five regional organizations: the Pan-African Family Organisation (Dakar, Senegal), the Arab Family Organisation (Tunis, Tunisia), the Asian Union of Family Organisations (New Delhi, India), the European regional organization (Vienna, Austria) and the Latin American Secretariat (Bogotá, Colombia). Mems: national associations, groups and governmental departments in 55 countries. Pres. MARIA TERESA DA COSTA MACEDO (Portugal); Sec.-Gen. ANDRÉ RAUGET (France).

International Union of Societies for the Aid of Mental Health: Croix Marine, 39 rue Charles Monselet, 33000 Bordeaux, France; tel. 56-81-60-05; f. 1964 to group national societies and committees whose aim is to help mentally handicapped or maladjusted people. Gen. Pres Mme DELAUNAY, Prof. CARAVEDO; Gen. Sec. Dr DEMANGEAT.

International Union of Tenants: Box 7514, 10392 Stockholm, Sweden; tel. (08) 24-63-50; f. 1955 to achieve a fruitful measure of collaboration which will help safeguard the interests of tenants. Mems: national tenant organizations in Denmark, Finland, France, Federal Republic of Germany, Greece, Italy, Norway, Sweden, Switzerland and the United Kingdom. Chair. LARS ANDERSTIG; Sec. NIC NILSSON. Publ. *IUT International Information* (quarterly).

International Workers' Aid: 5300 Bonn, Oppelner Strasse 130, Federal Republic of Germany; f. 1950 to assist refugees and displaced persons and to take action as a relief organization in cases of catastrophes or political disturbances. Members in Austria, Belgium, Denmark, France, Federal Republic of Germany, Israel, Italy, Norway, Portugal, Spain, Switzerland. Pres. KURT PARTZSCH (FRG); Vice-Pres. KÅRE WERNER (Norway). Publ. *Information Bulletin.*

Inter-University European Institute on Social Welfare—IEISW: 179 rue de Débarcadene, 6001 Marcinelle, Belgium; tel. (71) 36-62-73; f. 1970 to promote, carry out and publicize scientific research on social welfare; since 1976 IEISW has taken over the European Regional Clearing House for Community Work; consists of a Board of Directors, Scientific Committee and Executive Board. Chair. Board of Dirs JACQUES HOCHEPIED (Belgium); Gen. Sec. P. ROZEN (Belgium). Publ. *COMM.*

Lions Clubs International: 300 West 22nd St, Oak Brook, Ill 60570-0001, USA; tel. (312) 986-1700; telex 297236; f. 1917 to foster understanding among people of the world; to promote principles of good government and citizenship; and an interest in civic, cultural, social and moral welfare; to encourage service-minded men to serve their community without financial reward. Mems: 1.35m. with over

37,000 clubs in 161 countries and geographic areas. Exec. Admin. ROY SCHAETZEL. Publ. *The Lion* (10 a year, in 18 languages).

Médecins sans frontières—MSF: 68 blvd St Marcel, 75005 Paris, France; tel. (1) 47-07-29-29; telex 201720; f. 1971; composed of physicians and other members of the medical profession; aims to provide medical assistance to victims of war and natural disasters. Mems: 3,000 in France, groups in other European countries. Pres. Dr RONY BRAUMAN; Dir-Gen. Dr FRANCIS CHARHON.

Pan-Pacific and South East Asia Women's Association —PPSEAWA: 4-1-13 Kitamachi, Kichijoji, Musashino-shi, Tokyo 180, Japan; tel. 0422-51-7220; f. 1928 to strengthen the bonds of peace by fostering better understanding and friendship among women of all Pacific and South-East Asian areas, and to promote co-operation among women of these regions for the study and improvement of social conditions. Pres. Dr RINKO YAMAZAKI. Publs *International Bulletin* (2 a year), Reports of Conference Proceedings (every 3 years).

Rotary International: 1600 Ridge Ave, Evanston, Illinois, USA; tel. (312) 328-0100; telex 724465; f. 1905 to foster the ideal of service as a basis of worthy enterprise, to promote high ethical standards in business and professions and to further international understanding, goodwill and peace. Mems: over 985,000 members of 21,800 Rotary Clubs in 159 countries and regions. Pres. EDWARD F. CADMAN; Gen. Sec. H. A. PIGMAN (USA). Publs *The Rotarian* (monthly, English), *Revista Rotaria* (bi-monthly, Spanish).

Service Civil International—SCI: 783 10th Main, 4th Block, Jayanagar, Bangalore 560011, India; tel. 91-812-42-025; f. 1920 to promote peace and understanding through voluntary service projects (work-camps, local groups, long-term community development projects and education). Mems: 10,000 in 22 countries; projects in over 50 countries. Pres. NIGEL WATT. Publ. *Action* (every 2 months).

Society of Saint Vincent de Paul: 5 rue du Pré-aux-Clercs, Paris 7e, France; tel. (1) 42-61-50-25; telex 240918; f. 1833 to conduct charitable activities such as child care, youth work, work with immigrants, adult literacy programmes, residential care for the sick, handicapped and elderly, social counselling and work with prisoners and the unemployed—all conducted through personal contact. Mems: over 800,000 in 108 countries. Pres. AMIN A. DE TARRAZI; Sec.-Gen. COLETTE GLANDIÈRES, FRANCIS DARDOT. Publ. *Vincenpaul* (monthly, in French, English and Spanish).

Women's International Zionist Organization: Box 33159, 38 David Hemelech Blvd, Tel-Aviv, Israel; tel. 03-257321; telex 98151; f. 1920 to provide constructive social welfare and education facilities for women, children and senior citizens in Israel. Represented on UNICEF and ECOSOC at the UN. Mems: 260,000 in 50 countries. Pres. Mrs RAYA JAGLOM; Chair. MICHAL MODAI. Publs *WIZO Review* (every 2 months), *Bamat Haisha* (every 2 months), *Menorah* (annually), *Report of the World WIZO Executive* (every 4 years), leaflets, booklets, cultural publications.

World Blind Union: 58 ave Bosquet, 75007 Paris, France; tel. (1) 45-55-67-54; telex 206471; f. 1984 (amalgamating the World Council for the Welfare of the Blind and the International Federation of the Blind) to work for the prevention of blindness and the welfare of blind and visually-impaired people; encourages development of braille, talking book programmes and other media for the blind; rehabilitation, training and employment; prevention and cure of blindness in co-operation with the International Agency for the Prevention of Blindness; co-ordinates aid to the blind in developing countries; conducts studies on technical, social and educational matters, maintains the Louis Braille birth-place as an international museum. Mems in 71 countries. Pres. A. M. AL-GHANIM (Saudi Arabia); Hon. Sec.-Gen. (vacant). Publs *World Blind* (quarterly, in English, French, Spanish), General Assembly Reports, etc.

World Federation of the Deaf—WFD: 120 via Gregorio VII, 00165, Rome, Italy; tel. (06) 6377041; f. 1951 for the social rehabilitation of the deaf and the fight against deafness; aims to promote and exchange information; to facilitate the union and federation of national associations; organize international meetings and protect the rights of the deaf. Mems: 72 member countries. Pres. Dr Y. ANDERSSON; Sec.-Gen. Dr C. MAGAROTTO (Italy). Publ. *The Voice of Silence* (quarterly).

World ORT Union: ORT House, Sumpter Close, Finchley Rd, POB 346, London, NW3 5HR, England; tel. (01) 431-1333; telex 8953281; f. 1880 for the development of industrial, agricultural and artisan work among the Jews, training and generally improving the economic situation; conducts vocational training programmes for adolescents and adults, including instructors' and teachers' education and apprentice training in 30 countries, including technical assistance programmes in co-operation with interested governments. Mems: committees in 29 countries. Dir-Gen. JOSEPH HARMATZ. Publs *Annual Report, Yearbook, Technical and Pedagogical Bulletin, ORT data, ORT Magazine*.

World Society for the Protection of Animals: 106 Jermyn St, London, SW1Y 6EE, England; tel. (01) 839-3026; f. 1981, incorporating the World Federation for the Protection of Animals (f. 1950) and the International Society for the Protection of Animals (f. 1959); promotes animal welfare and conservation by humane education; disseminates literature to encourage humane management and slaughter of food animals, control of domestic and wild animal communities. Dir-Gen. T. H. SCOTT (UK).

World Veterans Federation: 16 rue Hamelin, 75116 Paris, France; tel. (1) 47-04-33-00; telex 643253; f. 1950 to maintain international peace and security by the application of the San Francisco Charter and helping to implement the Universal Declaration of Human Rights and related international conventions, to defend the spiritual and material interests of war veterans and war victims. It promotes practical international co-operation in fields of disarmament, human rights problems, economic development, rehabilitation of the handicapped, accessibility of the manmade environment, legislation concerning war veterans and war victims; has regional committees for Africa, Asia and the Pacific, and Europe; consultative status with UN ECOSOC, with several UN specialized agencies and the Council of Europe. Mems: national organizations in 52 countries, representing more than 20,000,000 war veterans and war victims. Pres. W. Ch. J. M. VAN LANSCHOT (Netherlands); Sec.-Gen. SERGE WOURGAFT (France). Publs special studies (disarmament, human rights, rehabilitation).

Zonta International: 35 E. Wacker Drive, Chicago, Ill. 60601, USA; f. 1919; executive women's service organization; international and community service projects, educational and cultural needs. Mems: 33,000 in 47 countries. Pres. ANNIKKI MAKINEN (Finland); Exec. Dir VALERIE LEVITAN. Publ. *The Zontian* (every 2 months).

Sport and Recreations

Arab Sports Confederation: POB 6040, Riyadh, Saudi Arabia; tel. 33628; telex 201081; f. 1976 to encourage regional co-operation by linking 19 Olympic Committees. Sec.-Gen. OTHMAN M. AL-SAAD.

Fédération Aéronautique Internationale (International Aeronautical Federation): 6 rue Galilee, 75782 Paris Cedex 16, France; tel. (1) 47-20-91-85; telex 611580; f. 1905 to encourage all aeronautical sports; organizes world championships and makes rules through technical committees. Mems: in 73 countries. Pres. CENEK KEPAK. Publ. *Annual Bulletin*.

General Association of International Sports Federations: 7 blvd de Suisse, Monte Carlo, Monaco; tel. 50-74-13; telex 479459; f. 1967 to act as a forum for the exchange of ideas and discussion of common problems in sport; to collect and circulate information; to provide secretarial and translation services; and to co-ordinate the main international competitions. Mems: 66 international sports organizations (27 Olympic Federations, 39 other federations and organizations). Sec.-Gen. LUC NIGGLI (Monaco). Publs *Calendar of International Sports Competitions* (2 a year), *GAISF News* (monthly, in English and French).

International Amateur Athletic Federation: 3 Hans Crescent, Knightsbridge, London, SW1X 0LN, England; tel. (01) 581-8771; telex 296859; f. 1912 to ensure co-operation and fairness among members, and to combat discrimination in athletics; to affiliate national governing bodies, to compile athletic competition rules and to organize championships at all levels; to settle disputes between members, and to conduct a programme of development for members who need coaching, judging courses, etc., and to frame regulations for the establishment of World, Olympic and other athletic records. Mems: 170 countries. Pres. P. NEBIOLO (Italy); Gen. Sec. J. B. HOLT (UK). Publs *IAAF Handbook* (English and French editions; biennial); *IAAF Bulletin* (4 a year); scoring tables, record lists, athletic arena layout charts, coaching and judges' books.

International Amateur Boxing Association: 135 Westervelt Place, Cresskill, NJ 07626, USA; tel. (201) 567-1339; telex 642806; f. 1946 as the world body controlling amateur boxing for the Olympic Games, continental, regional and inter-nation championships and tournaments in every part of the world. Mems: 137 nations. Pres. Col DON HULL (USA); Sec.-Gen. Prof. A. CHOWDHRY (Pakistan). Publ. *World Amateur Boxing* (quarterly).

International Amateur Radio Union: POB AAA, Newington, CT 06111, USA; tel. (203) 666-1541; telex 643958; f. 1925 to link national amateur radio societies and represent the interests of two-way amateur radio communication. Mems: 121 national amateur radio societies. Pres. RICHARD L. BALDWIN; Sec. DAVID SUMNER.

OTHER INTERNATIONAL ORGANIZATIONS

Sport and Recreations

International Amateur Swimming Federation (Fédération internationale de natation amateur—FINA): 208-3540 West 41st Ave, Vancouver, BC, V6N 3E6, Canada; tel. (604) 263-4144; telex 04508534; f. 1908 to promote amateur swimming and swimming sports internationally; to administer rules for swimming sports, for competitions and for establishing records; to arbitrate in disputes between members; to secure guarantees that members travelling to FINA international events will not be denied visas by the countries concerned. Mems: 120 countries. Pres. ROBERT H. HELMICK (USA); Sec. E. ALLAN HARVEY (Canada). Publs *Handbook* (every 4 years), *FINA News* (monthly).

International Amateur Wrestling Federation: 3 ave Ruchonnet, 1003 Lausanne, Switzerland; tel. (021) 228426; telex 25958; f. 1912 to encourage the development of amateur wrestling and promote the sport in countries where it is not yet practised; to further friendly relations between all members; to oppose any form of political, racial or religious discrimination. Mems: 103 federations. Pres. MILAN ERCEGAN; Sec.-Gen. (vacant). Publs *News Bulletin, Theory and Practice of Wrestling.*

International Council on Health, Physical Education, and Recreation: 1900 Association Drive, Reston, VA 22091, USA; f. 1958 by the World Confederation of Organizations of the Teaching Profession; f. as separate organization in 1959 to encourage the development of programmes in health, physical education, and recreation throughout the world.

International Cricket Conference: Lord's Cricket Ground, London, NW8 8QN, England; f. 1909 (as Imperial Cricket Conference; name changed 1965) to discuss aspects of the game at the international level. Annual conference; seven full and 18 associate mems. Sec. J. A. BAILEY.

International Cycling Union: 6 rue Amat, 1202 Geneva, Switzerland; tel. (022) 322914; telex 27196; f. 1900 to develop, regulate and control all forms of cycling as a sport. Mems: 128 federations. Pres. LUIS PUIG; Gen. Sec. MICHAL JEKIEL. Publs *Le Monde Cycliste Magazine* (4 a year), *International Calendar* (annually).

International Federation of Association Football (Fédération internationale de football association—FIFA): Hitzigweg 11, POB 85, 8030 Zürich, Switzerland; tel. (01) 555400; telex 55678; f. 1904 to promote the game of Association Football and foster friendly relations among players and National Associations; to control football and uphold the laws of the game as laid down by the International Football Association Board; to prevent discrimination of any kind between players; and to provide arbitration in any disputes between National Associations. Pres. Dr JOÃO HAVELANGE (Brazil); Gen. Sec. J. S. BLATTER (Switzerland). Publs. *FIFA News, FIFA Magazine* (quarterly) (both in English, French, Spanish and German).

International Federation of Park and Recreation Administration—IFPRA: The Grotto, Lower Basildon, Reading, Berkshire, RG8 9NE, England; tel. (0491) 873558; f. 1957 to provide a world centre where members of government departments, local authorities, and all organizations concerned with recreational services can discuss relevant matters. Mems: 225 in 34 countries. Pres. G. J. BRADBOURNE (New Zealand); Gen. Sec. J. S. THORNTON.

International Gymnastic Federation: CP 405, 3250 Lyss, Switzerland; tel. (032) 841960; telex 934961; f. 1881 to promote the exchange of official documents and publications on gymnastics; to set up a procedure for invitations among members; and to organize international competitions. Associations pursuing political or religious aims are not recognized, and professionals are banned from competitions. Mems: 100 affiliated federations. Pres. YURI TITOV (USSR); Gen. Sec. MAX BANGERTER (Switzerland). Publ. *Bulletin* (4 a year).

International Hockey Federation: Boîte 5, 1 ave des Arts, 1040 Brussels, Belgium; tel. (02) 219-45-37; telex 63393; f. 1924 to fix the rules of outdoor and indoor hockey for all affiliated national associations; to control the game of hockey and indoor hockey; to control the organization of international tournaments, such as the Olympic Games and the World Cup. Mems: 101 national associations. Pres. ETIENNE GLICHITCH (France); Sec.-Gen. JUAN ANGEL CALZADO DE CASTRO. Publ. *World Hockey* (quarterly).

International Judo Federation: Kasumigaseki Bldg 33F, 3-2-5, Kasumigaseki, Chiyoda-ku, Tokyo, Japan; tel. (3) 581-6665; telex 27762; f. 1949 to promote cordial and friendly relations between members; to protect the interests of Judo throughout the world; to organize the separate Senior, Junior and Women's World Championships every two years and organize the Judo events of the Olympic Games; to develop and spread the techniques and spirit of Judo throughout the world. Pres. Dr SHIGEYOSHI MATSUMAE; Sec.-Gen. HEINZ KEMPA.

International Philatelic Federation: Zollikerstrasse 128, 8008 Zürich, Switzerland; tel. (01) 553839; f. 1926 to promote philately internationally. Pres. L. DVORACEK; Sec.-Gen. M. L. HEIRI.

International Rowing Federation (Fédération internationale des Sociétés d'Aviron—FISA): POB 352, 2001 Neuchâtel, Switzerland; tel. (38) 257121; telex 931102; f. 1892 to establish contacts between oarsmen in all countries and to draw up racing rules. Mems: national organizations in 65 countries. Sec.-Gen. DENIS OSWALD.

International Shooting Union: 8000 Munich 2, Bavariaring 21, Federal Republic of Germany; tel. (089) 531012; telex 5216792; f. 1907 to promote and guide the development of the amateur shooting sports; to organize World Championships; to control the organization of continental and regional championships; to supervise the shooting events of the Olympic and Continental Games under the auspices of the International Olympic Committee. Mems: in 113 countries. Pres. OLEGARIO VÁZQUEZ-RAÑA (Mexico); Sec.-Gen. HORST G. SCHREIBER (FRG). Publ. *International Shooting Sport* (6 a year).

International Skating Union: Hofstrasse 13, 7270 Davos-Platz, Switzerland; tel. (083) 37577; telex 74613; f. 1892; holds regular conferences. Mems: 41 skating organizations in 34 countries. Pres. OLAF POULSEN; Sec.-Gen. BEAT HÄSLER.

International Ski Federation: Worbstrasse 210, Guemligen bei Bern, Switzerland; tel. (31) 525815; telex 911109; f. 1924 to further the sport of skiing, to create and maintain friendly relations between the member associations; to prevent discrimination in skiing matters on racial, religious or political grounds; to organize World Ski Championships and regional championships and, as supreme international skiing authority, to establish the international competition calendar and rules for all ski competitions approved by the FIS, and to arbitrate in any disputes. Mems: 54 national ski associations. Pres. MARC HODLER (Switzerland); Sec.-Gen. GIAN-FRANCO KASPER (Switzerland). Publ. *FIS Bulletin* (4 times a year).

International Table Tennis Federation: 53 London Rd, St Leonards-on-Sea, East Sussex, TN37 6AY, England; tel. (0424) 430971; telex 896691. Pres. H. ROY EVANS; Sec.-Gen. TONY BROOKS.

International Tennis Federation: Church Rd, Wimbledon, London, SW19 5TF, England; tel. (01) 946-5587; telex 919253; f. 1913 to govern the game of tennis throughout the world and promote its teaching; to preserve its independence of outside authority; to produce the Rules of Tennis, to promote the Davis Cup Competition for men, the Federation Cup for women, the Dubler Cup for veterans and the World Youth Cup for players of 16 years old and under; to organize tournaments. Mems: 84 full mems and 45 associate mems. Pres. PHILIPPE CHATRIER (France); Sec.-Gen. SHIRLEY WOODHEAD. Publs *Rules of the ITF* (annually), *Rules of Tennis* (annually), *Regulations for the Davis Cup* (annually), *Regulations for the Federation Cup* (annually), *Regulations for the Dubler Cup, World of Tennis* (annually), *President's Newsletter* (monthly), *ITF News* (quarterly).

International Weightlifting Federation: PF 614, 1374 Budapest, Hungary; tel. 311162; telex 227553; f. 1920 to control international weightlifting; to set up technical rules and to train referees; to supervise World Championships, Olympic Games, regional games and international contests of all kinds; to supervise the activities of national and continental federations; to register world records. Mems: in 124 countries. Pres. GOTTFRIED SCHÖDL (Austria); Gen. Sec. TAMÁS AJAN (Hungary). Publs *IWF Constitution and Rules* (every 4 years), *World Weightlifting* (quarterly).

International Yacht Racing Union: 60 Knightsbridge, London, SW1X 7JX, England; tel. (01) 235-6221; telex 915487; f. 1907; establishes and amends international yacht racing rules, organizes the Olympic Yachting Regatta and other championships. Mems: 76 national yachting authorities. Pres. (vacant); Sec.-Gen. NIGEL HACKING.

World Bridge Federation: c/o American Contract Bridge League, 2200 Democrat Rd, POB 161192, Memphis, Tenn 38116, USA; f. 1958 to promote the game of contract bridge throughout the world, federate national bridge associations in all countries, conduct bridge associations in all countries, conduct world championships competitions, establish standard bridge laws. Mems: 63 countries. Pres. JAIME ORTIZ-PATINO (Switzerland); Sec. RICHARD L. GOLDBERG (USA). Publ. *World Bridge News* (every 2 months).

World Chess Federation: Abendweg 1, 6006 Lucerne, Switzerland; tel. (041) 513378; telex 862845; f. 1924; controls chess competitions of world importance and awards international chess titles. Pres. FLORENCIO CAMPOMANES (Philippines); Gen. Sec. LIM KOK-ANN (Singapore).

OTHER INTERNATIONAL ORGANIZATIONS

World Underwater Federation: 34 rue du Colisée, 75008 Paris, France; tel. (1) 42-25-60-42; telex 641078; f. 1959 to develop underwater activities; to form bodies to instruct in the techniques of underwater diving; to perfect existing equipment and encourage inventions and to experiment with newly marketed products, suggesting possible improvements; to organize international competitions. Mems: 68 countries. Pres. PIERRE PERRAUD (France); Gen. Sec. MARCEL BIBAS (France). Publs *International Year Book of CMAS, Bulletin News* (every 3 months).

Technology

Union of International Technical Associations (Union des associations techniques internationales—UATI): UNESCO House, Room S1.60, 1 rue Miollis, 75015 Paris, France; tel. (1) 45-66-94-10; telex 204461; f. 1951 under the auspices of UNESCO to co-ordinate activities of member organizations and represent their interests; helps to arrange international congresses and the publication of technical material. Mems: 30 organizations. Chair. ROGER GINOCCHIO (France); Sec.-Gen. MAURICE REMILLIEUX (France). Publ. *Bulletin* (quarterly).

MEMBER ORGANIZATIONS

Members of UATI include the following:

International Association for Hydraulic Research: c/o Delft Hydraulics Laboratory, Rotterdamseweg 185, POB 177, 2600 MH Delft, Netherlands; tel. (015) 569353; f. 1935; holds biennial congresses. Mems: 2,300 individual, 280 corporate. Sec. J. E. PRINS (Netherlands). Publs *Directory of Hydraulic Research Institutes and Laboratories, Journal of Hydraulic Research, Proceedings of Congresses and Symposia, List of Papers*.

International Association of Lighthouse Authorities: 13 rue Yvon Villarceau, 75116 Paris, France; tel. (1) 45-00-38-60; telex 610 480; f. 1957; holds technical conference every five years; working groups study special problems and formulate technical recommendations, guidelines and manuals. Mems in 80 countries. Sec.-Gen. J. PRUNIERAS (France). Publs *Bulletin* (quarterly), technical dictionary (in English, French, German and Spanish).

International Bridge, Tunnel and Turnpike Association: 2120 L St, NW, Suite 305, Washington, DC 20037, USA; tel. (202) 659-4620. Pres. J.-L. CERON; Exec. Dir J. J. HASSETT.

International Commission of Agricultural Engineering: 17–21 rue de Javel, 75015 Paris, France; tel. (1) 45-77-75-78; f. 1930. Mems: associations from 26 countries, individual mems from six countries. Pres. Prof. LEHOCZKY (Hungary); Sec.-Gen. M. CARLIER (France). Publs *Yearbook*, technical reports.

International Commission on Irrigation and Drainage: 48 Nyaya Marg, Chanakyapuri, New Delhi 110021, India; tel. (11) 301 68 37; telex 031-65920; f. 1950; holds triennial congresses. Mems: 70 national committees. Pres. Dr M. E. JENSEN (USA); Sec.-Gen. K. K. FRAMJI (India). Publs *Bulletin, Bibliography* (annually), *World Irrigation, Multilingual Technical Dictionary, World Flood Control*, technical books.

International Commission on Large Dams: 151 blvd Haussmann, 75008 Paris, France; tel. (1) 47-64-67-33; telex 641320; f. 1928; holds triennial congresses. Mems in 77 countries. Pres. G. LOMBARDI (Switzerland); Sec.-Gen. J. COTILLON. Publs *Technical Bulletin, World Register of Dams, World Register of Mine and Industrial Wastes, Technical Dictionary on Dams*, studies.

International Committee of Foundry Technical Associations: Walchestrasse 27, Case Postale 7190, 8023 Zürich, Switzerland; tel. (01) 3613060; telex 56669. Pres. J. A. FERREIRINHA; Sec. M. J. GERSTER.

International Congress on Fracture: c/o Prof. Takeo Yokobori, Research Institute for Strength and Fracture of Materials, Tohoku University, Aramaki-Aza-Aoba, Sendai, Japan; tel. (0222) 22 18 00, ext. 31 38; f. 1965 to foster research in the mechanics and phenomena of fracture, fatigue and strength of materials for the development of better failure-resistant materials, to promote international and inter-disciplinary co-operation, and to publish the results of research. Mems: 28 national delegations, 31 affiliated organizations. Pres. D. FRANÇOIS; Sec.-Gen. Prof. TAKEO YOKOBORI (Japan). Publ. *Proceedings*.

International Federation for the Theory of Machines and Mechanisms: BME.MM.I, Pf. 91.15.21, Budapest, Hungary; tel. 664-011. Pres. G. BIANCHI; Sec.-Gen. E. FILEMON.

International Federation of Automatic Control—IFAC: 2361 Laxenburg, Schlossplatz 12, Austria; tel. (02236) 71447; telex 79248; f. 1957. Mems: 41. Pres. M. THOMA; Sec. G. HENCSEY. Publs *Automatica* (bi-monthly), *Newsletter*.

International Federation of Industrial Energy Consumers: Rhône-Poulenc SA, 25 quai Paul-Doumer, 92408 Courbevoie Cedex, France; tel. (1) 47-68-16-98. Pres. ETIENNE DAVIGNON; Sec.-Gen. A. MONGON.

International Fertilizer Industry Association: 28 rue Marboeuf, 75008 Paris, France; tel. (1) 42-25-27-07. Pres. A. B. AL-NOURI; Sec.-Gen. K. L. C. WINDRIDGE.

International Gas Union: 62 rue de Courcelles, 75008 Paris, France; tel. (1) 47-54-34-34; telex 642621; f. 1931 to study all aspects and problems of the gas industry with a view to promoting international co-operation and the general improvement of the industry. Mems: national organizations in 44 countries. Pres. J. KEAN (USA); Sec.-Gen. B. GOUDAL.

International Institute of Welding: 54 Princes Gate, Exhibition Rd, London, SW7 2PL, England; tel. (01) 584-8556; telex 81183; f. 1948. Mems: 48 societies in 35 countries. Pres. F. WALLNER (Austria); Sec.-Gen. P. D. BOYD (UK). Publs *Welding in the World* (6 a year), etc.

International Institution for Production Engineering Research: 10 rue Mansart, 75009 Paris, France; tel. (1) 45-26-21-80; f. 1951 to promote by scientific research the study of the mechanical processing of all solid materials including checks on efficiency and quality of work. Mems: 136 active, 127 associate, 74 corresponding, in 36 countries. Pres. J. G. BOLLINGER; Sec.-Gen. R. GESLOT. Publ. *Annals*.

International Measurement Confederation: POB 457, 1371 Budapest, Hungary; tel. (36 1) 531 562; telex 225792. Pres. G. TOUMANOFF; Sec.-Gen. T. KEMENY.

International Society for Soil Mechanics and Foundation Engineering: Engineering Dept, Trumpington St, Cambridge, CB2 1PZ, England; tel. (0223) 355020; telex 81239; f. 1936 to promote international co-operation among scientists and engineers in the field of geotechnics and its engineering applications; maintains 24 technical committees; holds quadrennial international conference, and regional conferences. Mems: 16,000 individuals, 57 national societies. Pres. Prof. B. B. BROMS; Gen. Sec. Dr R. PARRY. Publs *Newsletter* (quarterly), *Conference Proceedings* (every 2 years), *Lexicon of Soil Mechanics Terms* (in eight languages).

International Solid Wastes and Public Cleansing Association: 9 rue de Phalsbourg, 75017 Paris, France; tel. (1) 42-27-38-91. Pres. J. DEFECHE; Sec.-Gen. M. BRES.

International Union for Electro-heat: Tour Atlantique, 92080 Paris-la-Défense Cedex 6; tel. (1) 47-78-99-34; telex 615739; f. 1953, present title adopted 1957. Aims to study all questions relative to electro-heat, except commercial questions, and to maintain liaisons between national groups and to organize international Congresses on Electro-heat. Mems: 16 countries and associate members. Pres. M. SETTERWALL (Sweden); Gen. Sec. A. DAILLIET (Belgium).

International Union of Air Pollution Prevention Associations: 136 North St, Brighton, BN1 1RG, England; tel. (0273) 26313. Pres. K. M. SULLIVAN; Sec.-Gen. P. G. SHARP.

International Union of Producers and Distributors of Electrical Energy: 39 ave de Friedland, Paris 8e, France; f. 1925 for study of all questions relating to the production, transmission and distribution of electrical energy. Mems: 34 countries. Pres. RUDOLF GUCK (FRG); Sec.-Gen. GEORGES LUCENET (France). Publs reports on periodical congresses, periodical circulars on statistical matters.

International Union of Testing and Research Laboratories for Materials and Structures: 12 rue Brancion, 75015 Paris, France; tel. (1) 45-39-22-33; telex 250071; f. 1947 for the exchange of information and the promotion of co-operation on experimental research concerning structures and materials, for the study of research methods with a view to improvement and standardization. Mems: laboratories and individuals in 73 countries. Pres. J. R. WRIGHT (USA); Sec.-Gen. M. FICKELSON (France). Publ. *Materials and Structures—Testing and Research* (bi-monthly).

Permanent International Association of Navigation Congresses—PIANC: 155 rue de la Loi, 1040 Brussels, Belgium; tel. (02) 733-96-70; f. 1885, present form adopted 1902; aims to promote the maintenance and operation of both inland and ocean navigation by fostering and encouraging progress in the design, construction, improvement, maintenance and operation of inland and maritime waterways, of inland and maritime ports and of coastal areas; assembles and publishes information in this field, undertakes studies, organizes international and national meetings. Congresses are held every four years. Mems: 40 governments, 2,786 others. Pres. Ir. R. DE PAEPE; Sec.-Gen. H. VANDERVELDEN. Publs *Papers and*

Proceedings of Congresses, Bulletin (quarterly), *Illustrated Technical Dictionary* (in 6 languages), final reports of international study commissions and working groups.

Permanent International Association of Road Congresses: 27 rue Guénégaud, 75006 Paris, France; tel. (1) 46-33-71-90; f. 1909 to promote the construction, improvement, maintenance, use and economic development of roads; organizes technical committees and study sessions. Mems: governments, public bodies, organizations and private individuals in 61 countries. Pres. M. E. BALAGUER (Spain); Sec.-Gen. M. B. FAUVEAU (France). Publs *Bulletin, Technical Dictionary, Reports and Proceedings of Congresses, Reports of Technical Committees.*

World Energy Conference: 34 St James's St, London, SW1A 1HD, England; tel. (01) 930-3966; telex 264707; f. 1924 to link all branches of energy and resources technology and maintain liaison between world experts; holds congresses every three years. Mems: 79 committees. Pres. M. BOITEUX (France); Sec.-Gen. I. D. LINDSAY (UK). Publs energy supply and demand projections, fuel surveys, technical assessments, reports.

OTHER ORGANIZATIONS

African Association of Cartography: BP 102, Hussein Dey, Algiers, Algeria; tel. 77 40 02; telex 52635; f. 1976 to encourage the development of cartography, organize conferences and other meetings, promote establishment of training institutions; the ECA has set up two centres, one in Kenya for cartographic services and one in Nigeria for training. Mems: principal cartographic services of 29 African countries; 14 associate mems (of which seven are non-African). Chair. SERIGNE M'BAYE THIAM (Senegal); Sec.-Gen. FEZZANI CHEDLY.

Bureau International de la Récupération: 13 place du Samedi, 1000 Brussels, Belgium; tel. (02) 217-82-51; telex 61965; f. 1948 as the world federation of the reclamation and recycling industries, to promote international trade in scrap iron and steel, non-ferrous metals, paper, textiles, plastics and rubber. Mems: 56 associations and 502 individuals in 46 countries.

European Builders of Internal Combustion Engines and Electric Locomotives: 12 rue Bixio, 75007 Paris, France; tel. (1) 47-05-36-62; telex 270105; f. 1953 as an information centre on economic and technical matters relating to the production, distribution and consumption of locomotives throughout the world. Mems: 29 full, 12 associates in 13 countries. Chair. Dipl.-Ing. E. KOCHER; Gen. Del. J.-L. BURCKHARDT.

European Computer Manufacturers Association—ECMA: 114 rue de Rhône, 1204 Geneva, Switzerland; tel. (022) 353634; telex 22288; f. 1961 to study and develop, in co-operation with the appropriate national and international organizations, as a scientific endeavour and in the general interest, methods and procedures in order to facilitate and standardize the use of data processing systems; and to promulgate various standards applicable to the functional design and use of data processing equipment. Mems: 30 ordinary and 12 associate. Sec.-Gen. D. HEKIMI. Publ. *ECMA Standards.*

European Convention for Constructional Steelwork: 326 ave Louise, bte 52, 1050 Brussels, Belgium; f. 1955 for the consideration of problems involved in metallic construction. Member organizations in Austria, Belgium, Denmark, Finland, France, Federal Republic of Germany, Italy, Japan, Luxembourg, Netherlands, Norway, Sweden, Switzerland, United Kingdom, USA, Yugoslavia.

European Federation of Chemical Engineering: c/o Institution of Chemical Engineers, Geo. E. Davis Bldg, 165–171 Railway Terrace, Rugby, Warwickshire, CV21 3HQ, England; tel. (0788) 78214; telex 311780; f. 1953 to encourage co-operation in Europe between non-profit-making scientific and technical societies for the advancement of chemical engineering and its application in the process industries. Mems: 56 societies in 22 European countries; 12 corresponding societies in other countries.

European Federation of Corrosion: 14 Belgrave Sq., London, SW1X 8PS, England; tel. (01) 235-3681; f. 1955 to encourage co-operation in research on corrosion and methods of combating it. Member societies in 20 countries. Hon. Secs R. MAS (France), DIETER BEHRENS (FRG), P. P. KING (UK).

European Federation of National Associations of Engineers: 4 rue de la Mission Marchand, 75016 Paris, France; tel. (1) 42-24-91-43; f. 1951 to strengthen cultural and professional links and exchange information among members; to study problems of training engineers and recognizing and protecting their status; and to organize periodical congresses. Mems: 830,000 in 20 national engineers' associations. Pres. M. GOLLING; Sec.-Gen. M. GUERIN (France). Publ. *FEANI-INFO* (quarterly).

European Organization for Civil Aviation Electronics —EUROCAE: 11 rue Hamelin, 75783 Paris Cedex 16, France; f. 1963; studies and advises on problems related to the application of electronics and electronic equipment to aeronautics and assists international bodies in the establishment of international standards. Mems: 61. Pres. A. CARNELL; Chair. H. POPP.

Eurospace: 16 bis ave Bosquet, 75007 Paris, France; tel. (1) 45-55-83-53; telex 270716; f. 1961; an association of European aerospace industrial companies, banks, press organizations and national associations for promoting space activity in the fields of telecommunication, television, aeronautical, maritime, meteorological, educational and press usage satellites, as well as launchers (conventional and recoverable). The Association carries out studies on the legal, economic, technical and financial aspects. It enjoys consultative status with UNESCO and the Council of Europe; acts as an industrial adviser to the European Space Agency. Mems (direct or associate) in the following countries: Belgium, Denmark, Finland, France, Federal Republic of Germany, Italy, Netherlands, Norway, Spain, Sweden, Switzerland, United Kingdom. Pres. JEAN DELORME; Sec.-Gen. YVES DEMERLIAC; Tech. Sec. REX TURNER.

Inter-African Committee for Hydraulic Studies—CIEH: BP 369, Ouagadougou, Burkina Faso; f. 1960 to ensure co-operation in hydrology, hydrogeology, climatology, urban sanitation and other water sciences, through exchange of information and co-ordination of research and other projects. Mems: 13 African countries. Sec.-Gen. ABDOU HASSANE. Publs *Bulletin de Liaison technique* (quarterly), research studies.

Intergovernmental Bureau for Informatics: POB 10253, Viale Civiltà del Lavoro, 00144 Rome, Italy; tel. (396) 5916041; telex 612065; f. 1969, replacing the International Computation Centre; present title adopted in 1974; the only international organization in the field of informatics with intergovernmental status; aims to promote the development and knowledge of informatics; an advisory body, helping member countries to establish national policies in informatics and to execute technical projects. Structure: General Assembly (every two years) and Executive Council. Mems: 36 countries. Dir-Gen. Prof. F. A. BERNASCONI. Publs *Agora* (quarterly), *IBI Newsletter* (every 2 months).

International Association for Bridge and Structural Engineering: ETH—Hönggerberg, 8093 Zürich, Switzerland; tel. (01) 3772647; telex 822 186; f. 1929 to promote the interchange of knowledge and research work results concerning bridge and structural engineering and to foster co-operation among those connected with this work. Mems: 3,000 government departments, local authorities, universities, institutes, firms and individuals in 70 countries. Pres. Prof. H. VON GUNTEN (Switzerland); Exec. Dir A. GOLAY. Publs *IABSE Periodica* (quarterly), *Congress Report, IABSE Report, Structural Engineering Documents.*

International Association for Cybernetics: 2 rue Sergent Vrithoff, 5000 Namur, Belgium; tel. (081) 22-22-09; f. 1957 to ensure liaison between research workers engaged in various sectors of cybernetics, to promote the development of the science and of its applications and to disseminate information about it. Mems: firms and individuals in 32 countries. Man. Dir J. RAMAEKERS; Gen. Sec. A. NELIS. Publs *Cybernetica* (quarterly), *Cybernetics—Works in Progress* (series), *Proceedings of International Congresses.*

International Association of Rolling Stock Builders: 12 rue Bixio, 75007 Paris, France; tel. (1) 47-05-36-62; telex 270105; f. 1934; an information centre on economic and technical questions relating to the production, distribution and consumption of railway rolling stock throughout the world. Mems: 46 firms in 12 countries. Chair. O. J. BRONCHART; Gen. Del. J.-L. BURCKHARDT.

International Cargo Handling Co-ordination Association—ICHCA: 1 Walcott St, London, SW1P 2NY, England; tel. (01) 828-3611; telex 261106; f. 1952. Mems: in 90 countries. Pres. H. ROOTLIEP (Netherlands); Sec.-Gen. JOHN T. WARBURTON. Publs *Cargo Systems International* (monthly), *Cargo Handling Abstracts* (quarterly), *Biennial Report, Who's Who in Cargo Handling* (annually), *International Cargo Handling* (annual buyers' guide), technical studies and bibliographies (lists on request).

International Colour Association: c/o Dr J. J. Vos, Institute for Perception TNO, Kampweg 5, Postbus 23, Soesterberg, Netherlands; f. 1967 to encourage research in colour in all its aspects, disseminate the knowledge gained from this research and promote its application to the solution of problems in the fields of science, art and industry; holds international congresses and symposia. Mems: organizations in 17 countries. Pres. Dr H. TERSTIEGE (FRG); Sec. Dr J. WALRAVEN (Netherlands). Publ. Proceedings of congresses and symposia.

International Commission on Illumination: 52 blvd Malesherbes, 75008 Paris, France; tel. (1) 49-93-25-04; telex 053-4322; f.

1900 as International Commission on Photometry, present name 1913; aims to provide an international forum for all matters relating to the science and art of light and lighting; to exchange information; to develop and publish international standards, and to provide guidance in their application. Mems: 35 national committees and four individuals. Exec. Sec. W. BUDDE (Canada). Publs standards, technical reports, *CIE Journal*.

International Committee on Aeronautical Fatigue—ICAF: c/o Prof. J. Schijve, Dept of Aerospace Engineering, THD, Kluyverweg 1, 2629 HS Delft, Netherlands; tel. (15) 781341; telex 38151; f. 1951 for collaboration on fatigue of aeronautical structures among aeronautical bodies and laboratories by means of exchange of documents and by organizing periodical conferences. Mems: national centres in 13 countries. Sec. Prof. J. SCHIJVE (Netherlands). Publs *Minutes of Conferences (every 2 years) Proceedings of Symposia* (every 2 years), *ICAF—Documents*.

International Conference on Large High-Voltage Electric Systems: 112 blvd Haussmann, 75008 Paris, France; tel. (1) 45-22-65-12; telex 650445; f. 1921 to facilitate and promote the exchange of technical knowledge and information between all countries in the general field of electrical generation and transmission at high voltages; holds general sessions (every two years), symposia. Mems: 3,500 in 79 countries. Pres. W. S. WHITE, Jr (USA); Sec.-Gen. G. LEROY (France). Publs *Proceedings of the Biennial Sessions, Electra* (every 2 months).

International Copper Research Association, Inc: 708 Third Ave, New York, NY 10017, USA; f. 1960; non-profit association financed by the copper mining industry; sponsors and directs research at laboratories, institutes and universities throughout the world. Mems: companies in 11 countries. Pres. WILLIAM H. DRESHER. Publs reports.

International Council for Building Research, Studies and Documentation—CIB: POB 20704, Weena 704, 3001 JA Rotterdam, Netherlands; tel. (010) 411-02-40; telex 22530; f. 1953 to encourage and facilitate co-operation in building research, studies and documentation in all aspects. Mems: governmental and industrial organizations and qualified individuals in 70 countries. Pres. P. CHEMILLIER (France); Gen. Sec. GY. SEBESTYEN. Publs *Information Bulletin* (bi-monthly), *Building Research and Practice* (bi-monthly), *Directory of Building Research Information and Development Organizations, Congress and Symposia Proceedings*, technical reports and recommendations, etc.

International Electrotechnical Commission—IEC: 3 rue de Varembé, POB 131, 1211 Geneva 20, Switzerland; tel. (022) 340150; telex 28872; f. 1906 as the authority for world standards for electrical and electronic engineering: its standards are used as the basis for regional and national standards, and are used in preparing specifications for international trade. Mems: national cttees representing all branches of electrical and electronic activities in 42 countries. Gen.-Sec. C. J. STANFORD. Publs *International Standards and Reports, IEC Bulletin, Annual Report, Report on Activities, Catalogue of Publications*.

International Special Committee on Radio Interference: British Electrotechnical Committee, British Standards Institution, 2 Park St, London, W1A 2BS, England; tel. (01) 629-9000; telex 266933; f. 1934; special committee of the IEC to promote international agreement on the protection of radio reception from interference by equipment other than authorized transmitters; recommends limits of such interference and specifies equipment and methods of measurement; determines requirements for immunity of sound and TV broadcasting receivers from interference and the impact of safety regulations on interference suppression. Mems: the 42 national committees of IEC and seven other international organizations. Sec. P. DE LUSIGNAN.

International Federation for Documentation: Prins Willem-Alexanderhof 5, The Hague, Netherlands; tel. (070) 14-06-71; f. 1895 to promote, through international co-operation, research in and development of documentation; study committees for: universal decimal classification; research on the theoretical basis of information; classification research; linguistics in documentation; information for industry; education and training; terminology of information and documentation; patent information and documentation; social sciences documentation; Broad system of ordering; informetrics; information systems and network design and management; study of user needs; regional commissions for Latin America, Asia and Oceania. Mems: 69 national, one international, some 270 affiliates. Pres. M. W. HILL; Sec.-Gen. STELLA KEENAN. Publs *International Forum on Information and Documentation* (quarterly), *FID News Bulletin* (monthly), *R & D Projects in Documentation and Librarianship* (bi-monthly), *FID/ET Newsletter on Education and Training Programmes for Information Personnel* (quarterly), monographs.

International Federation for Information Processing: 3 rue du Marché, 1204 Geneva, Switzerland; tel. (022) 282649; telex 428472; f. 1960 to promote information science and technology; to stimulate research, development and application of information processing in science and human activities; to further the dissemination and exchange of information on information processing; to encourage education in information processing; to advance international co-operation in the field of information processing. Mems: 43 national organizations representing 57 countries. Pres. K. ANDO (Japan); Sec. J. FOUROT (France).

International Federation of Airworthiness—IFA: 58 Whiteheath Ave, Ruislip, Middx, HA4 7PW, England; tel. (0895) 672504; telex 8951771; f. 1964 to provide a forum for the exchange of international experience in maintenance, design and operations; holds annual conference; awards international aviation scholarship annually. Mems: 83, comprising 12 aircraft engineering and allied organizations, 30 airlines, 13 airworthiness authorities, 18 aerospace manufacturing companies, seven professional societies of aeronautical engineers, and the Flight Safety Foundation (USA). Pres. J. CORNELIS (Netherlands); Exec. Dir K. J. ANDERSON (UK). Publ. *IFA News* (quarterly).

International Federation of Automobile Engineers' Associations: Steinacherstrasse 59, 8308 Ober-Illnau, Zürich, Switzerland; f. 1947 to promote the technical development of automobile engineering and research; congresses every two years. Mems: national asscns. in 22 countries. Sec.-Gen. W. LEMMENMEYER. Publ. *Bulletin*.

International Federation of Consulting Engineers: 13C ave du Temple, POB 86, 1000 Lausanne 12, Switzerland; tel. (021) 335003; telex 24698; f. 1913 to encourage international co-operation and the setting up of standards for consulting engineers. Mems: National Associations in 44 countries, comprising some 26,000 individual members. Pres. J. G. ELDRIDGE (UK); Publs conditions of contract, model forms, rules and guides.

International Federation of Hospital Engineering: 1A Quarry School Place, Headington Quarry, Oxford, OX3 8LH, England; tel. (0865) 61922; f. 1970 to promote internationally the standards of hospital engineering and to provide for the interchange of knowledge and ideas. Mems: 50. Gen. Sec. BASIL HERMON.

International Information Management Congress: POB 34404, Bethesda, Md 20817, USA; tel. (301) 983-0604; telex 904100; f. 1962 (as the International Micrographic Congress) to promote co-operation in document-based information management; to provide an international clearing-house for information, exchange publications and encourage the establishment of international standards; to promote international product exhibitions, seminars and conventions. Mems: 36 associations, 116 regular and 600 affiliate mems from 64 countries. Pres. M. A. H. VAN DEN AKKER (Netherlands); Exec. Dir DON M. AVEDON (USA). Publ. *IMC Journal* (every 2 months).

International Institute of Seismology and Earthquake Engineering: Building Research Institute, Ministry of Construction, 1 Tatehara, Oho-machi, Tsukuba-gun, Ibaraki Pref., Japan; tel. 0298 64-2151; telex 3652560; f. 1962 to work on seismology and earthquake engineering for the purpose of reducing earthquake damage in the world. The main activities are to train the seismologists and earthquake engineers from the seismic countries and to undertake survey, research, guidance and analysis of information on earthquakes and their related matters. Mems: 50 countries. Dir S. HATTORI.

International Iron and Steel Institute—IISI: 120 rue Col Bourg, 1140 Brussels, Belgium; tel. (02) 375-39-20; telex 22639; f. 1967 to promote the welfare and interest of the world's steel industries; to undertake research in all aspects of steel industries; to serve as a forum for exchange of knowledge and discussion of problems relating to steel industries; to collect, disseminate and maintain statistics and information; to serve as a liaison body between international and national steel organizations. Mems: in 43 countries. Chair. J. D. HOOGLANDT; Sec.-Gen. LENHARD J. HOLSCHUH. Publs *Conference Proceedings, Members' Directory, Bulletins*, statistical, economic, and technical reports.

International Organization for Standardization: POB 56, 1 rue de Varembé, 1211 Geneva 20, Switzerland; tel. (022) 341240; telex 23887; f. 1947 to reach international agreement on industrial and commercial standards. Mems: national standards institutions of 90 countries. Pres. I. YAMASHITA; Sec.-Gen. LAWRENCE D. EICHER. Publs *ISO International Standards, ISO Memento* (annually), *ISO Catalogue* (annually), *ISO Bulletin* (monthly).

OTHER INTERNATIONAL ORGANIZATIONS — Technology, Tourism

International Research Group on Wood Preservation: Drottning Kristinas väg 47C, 114 28 Stockholm, Sweden; tel. (08) 10 14 53; telex 14375; f. 1965 as Wood Preservation Group by OECD; independent since 1969; consists of five working groups and 14 sub-groups, plenary annual meeting, executive council, secretariat; there is an IRG Foundation Fund (Sweden) and Friends of IRG (IRG Conference Awards) (UK and Sweden). Mems: 398 in 66 countries. Pres. Prof. Dr Björn Henningsson (Sweden); Sec.-Gen. Ron Cockcroft (Sweden). Publs technical documents and books, *Annual Report*.

International Rubber Research and Development Board—IRRDB: Chapel Building, Brickendonbury, Hertford, SG13 8NP, England; tel. (0992) 54966; telex 817449; f. 1937. Mems: 15 research institutes. Sec. P. W. Allen.

International Society for Photogrammetry and Remote Sensing: c/o Department of Photogrammetry, Royal Institute of Technology, 10044 Stockholm, Sweden; tel. (8) 787-73-44; telex 10389; f. 1910; holds congress every four years, and technical symposia. Mems: 74 countries. Pres. G. Konecny (FRG); Sec.-Gen. K. Torlegård (Sweden). Publs *International Archives of Photogrammetry and Remote Sensing, Photogrammetria*.

International Solar Energy Society: POB 52, National Science Centre, 191 Royal Parade, Parkville, Melbourne, Victoria 3052, Australia; tel. (03) 556-2242; telex 37130; f. 1954 to foster science and technology relating to the applications of solar energy, to encourage research and development, to promote education and to gather, compile and disseminate information in this field; holds international conferences. Mems: 4,000 in 95 countries. Pres. W. A. Beckman (USA); Sec.-Treas. W. R. Read (Australia). Publs *Journal* (monthly), *Newsletter* (quarterly), *Sunworld* (quarterly).

International Tin Research Council: Kingston Lane, Uxbridge, Middx, UB8 3PJ, England; tel. (0895) 72406; f. 1932 to develop world consumption of tin; engages in scientific research, technical development and aims to spread knowledge of tin throughout the world by publishing research articles, issuing handbooks, giving lectures and demonstrations, and taking part in exhibitions and trade fairs. Dir B. T. K. Barry. Publs *Annual Report, Tin and its Uses* (quarterly, in English, French, German, Japanese, Italian and Spanish), various studies and reports.

International Union for Vacuum Science, Technique and Applications: Boltzmanngasse 5, 1090 Vienna, Austria; tel. (0222) 34-52-32; telex 116222; f. 1958; collaborates with the International Standards Organization in defining and adopting technical standards; co-ordinates the programme of major international conferences; promotes the triennial International Vacuum Congress and International Conference on Solid Surfaces; regulates the Welch Foundation for postgraduate research in vacuum science and technology; scientific interests for surface science, thin film physics, vacuum science, electronic materials, fusion technology and vacuum metallurgy. Mems: organizations in 24 countries. Pres. Prof. Dr J. Antal (Hungary); Sec.-Gen. Prof. Dr M. J. Higatsberger (Austria). Publs *News Bulletin* (every 2 months), supporting edition of *Surface and Vacuum Physics Index (Zentralstelle für Atomenergie-Dokumentation*, monthly), *Visual aids for instruction in vacuum technology and applications* (5 series).

International Union of Heat Distributors: Bahnhofplatz 3, 8023 Zürich, Switzerland; tel. (01) 2115191; telex 814002; f. 1954 to study the various problems concerning the development and distribution of heat for all purposes by means of pipes laid underground. The Union assembles the results of research and tests and puts statistical information at the disposal of the members. It maintains relations with national and international organizations for the study of economical, technical, scientific questions of interest to its members. Mems: 114 companies in 14 countries. Pres. Dr G. Deuster (FRG); Sec. Dr E. Keppler (Switzerland). Publ. *Bulletin* (quarterly).

International Union of Metal: Seestrasse 105, 8002 Zürich, Switzerland; tel. (01) 2017376; telex 57644; f. 1954 for liaison between national bodies to exchange documentation and study common problems. Mems: national federations from Austria, Belgium, Federal Republic of Germany, Luxembourg, Netherlands, Sweden, Switzerland. Pres. Adriaan de Ruyter (Netherlands); Sec. Hans-Jörg Federer (Switzerland).

International Water Resources Association: 208 North Romine St, Urbana, Ill 61801 USA; tel. (217) 333-0536; telex 5101011969; f. 1972 to promote collaboration in and support for international water resources programmes; holds conferences; conducts training in water resources management. Pres. Peter J. Reynolds (Canada); Sec.-Gen. Glenn E. Stout (USA). Publs *Water International* (quarterly), *Frontiers in Hydrology, Proceedings*.

International Water Supply Association: 1 Queen Anne's Gate, London, SW1H 9BT, England; tel. (01) 222-8111; telex 918518; f. 1947 to co-ordinate technical, legal and administrative aspects of public water supply; congresses held every two years. Mems: national organizations, water authorities and individuals in 90 countries. Pres. J. Dirickx (Belgium); Sec.-Gen. L. R. Bays (UK). Publs *Aqua* (6 a year), *Water Supply* (quarterly), *Proceedings of the Congresses, Reports on Corrosion and Protection of Underground Pipelines*.

Latin-American Energy Organization (Organización Latino-americana de Energía–OLADE): Av. Occidental, OLADE Bldg, Sector San Carlos, POB 6413 CCI, Quito, Ecuador; tel. 538-122; f. 1973 to act as an instrument of co-operation in using and conserving the energy resources of the region. Mems: 26 Latin-American and Caribbean countries. Exec. Sec. Marcio Nunes (Brazil). Publ. *Revista Energética*.

Latin-American Iron and Steel Institute: Dario Urzua 1994, Casilla 16065, Santiago 9, Chile; tel. 2237581; telex 340348; f. 1959 to help achieve the harmonious development of iron and steel production, manufacture and marketing in Latin America; conducts economic surveys on the steel sector; organizes technical conventions and meetings; disseminates industrial processes suited to regional conditions; prepares and maintains statistics on production, end uses, prices, etc., of raw materials and steel products within this area. Mems: 91, and 96 associate mems. Chair. César Mendoza O.; Sec.-Gen. Aníbal Gómez. Publs *Siderurgia Latinoamericana* (monthly), *Statistical Year Book, Directory of Latin American Iron and Steel Companies* (every 2 years), various technical and economic studies and reports.

Regional Centre for Services in Surveying, Mapping and Remote Sensing: POB 18118, Nairobi, Kenya; tel. 803320; telex 25285; f. 1975 to provide services in the professional techniques of map-making, and the application of satellites and remote sensing in resource analysis and development planning; to undertake research and provide advisory services to African governments. Mems: 10 signatory and 12 non-signatory governments. Dir-Gen. B. A. Sikilo.

Regional Centre for Training in Aerial Surveys: PMB 5545, Ile-Ife, Nigeria; f. 1972 for training, research and advisory services; administered by the ECA; bilingual in English and French. Mems: eight governments. Dir Dr S. O. Ihemadu.

World Association of Industrial and Technological Research Organizations—WAITRO: Engelbrektsgatan 29, 114 32 Stockholm, Sweden; tel. (08) 21-22-89; f. 1970 by the UN Industrial Development Organization to encourage co-operation in industrial and technological research, through financial assistance for training and joint activities, arranging international seminars, and allowing the exchange of information; has consultative status with the UN and co-operates closely with UNIDO, UNDP and UNESCO. Mems: about 70 research institutes in 43 countries. Publs *Communique* (quarterly), reports, proceedings of meetings, and handbooks.

World Bureau of Metal Statistics: 41 Doughty St, London, WC1N 2LF, England; f. 1949; statistics of production, consumption, stocks, prices and international trade in copper, lead, zinc, tin, nickel, aluminium and several other minor metals. Gen. Man. J. L. T. Davies. Publs *World Metal Statistics* (monthly bulletin), and annual studies in world trade in metals; occasional surveys of minor metals.

World Federation of Engineering Organizations—WFEO: c/o C. Herselin, 19 rue Blanche, 75009 Paris, France; f. 1968 to advance engineering as a profession in the interests of the world community; to foster co-operation between engineering organizations throughout the world; to undertake special projects through co-operation between members and in co-operation with other international bodies. Mems: 80 national, five international. Pres. S. Ben Jemaa (Tunisia); Sec.-Gen. C. Herselin (France).

World Petroleum Congresses: 61 New Cavendish St, London, W1M 8AR, England; tel. (01) 636-1004; telex 264380; f. 1933 to provide an international congress every four years where oil scientists and technologists can meet and discuss advances in knowledge; executive board represents 16 member countries. Pres. Dr W. von Ilsemann (FRG); Sec.-Gen. D. C. Payne (UK). Publ. *Proceedings of Congress*.

Tourism

Alliance Internationale de Tourisme: 2 quai Gustave Ador, 1207 Geneva, Switzerland; tel. (022) 352727; telex 413103; f. 1898, present title adopted 1919; aims to study all questions relating to

Tourism, Trade and Industry

international touring and to suggest reforms, to encourage the development of tourism and all matters concerning the motorist, traffic management, road safety, consumer protection and to defend the interests of touring associations. Mems: 134 associations totalling over 67m. members in 87 countries. Pres. B. R. LUNN (Australia); Sec.-Gen. J. WARD (UK).

Arab Tourism Union: POB 2354, Amman, Jordan; f. 1954; seven members form the executive committee for a term of two years. Mems: national tourist organizations of 21 Arab countries, and four associate members in the private sector. Pres. FA'UD BEN SHA'ABAN (Libya); Sec.-Gen. Dr ABDUL RAHMAN ABU RABAH (Jordan). Publs *Arab Tourism Magazine* (bi-monthly), and Research Supplements.

Caribbean Tourism Association—CTA: 20 East 46th St, New York, NY 10017, USA; tel. (212) 682-0435; telex 666916; f. 1951 to encourage and assist development in the Caribbean region through tourism. Mems: 26 Caribbean governments and 400 allied mems. Dir-Gen. AUDREY PALMER HAWKS.

East Asia Travel Association: c/o Japan National Tourist Organization, 2-10-1 Yurakucho, Chiyoda-ku, Tokyo, Japan; tel. (03) 216-2905; telex 24132; f. 1966 to promote tourism in the East Asian region, encourage and facilitate the flow of tourists to that region from other parts of the world, and to develop regional tourist industries by close collaboration among members. Mems: six national tourist organizations, seven airlines and two travel associations. Pres. DAE DON HA (Republic of Korea); Sec.-Gen. TETSUYA SATO (Japan).

European Motel Federation—EMF: Diepenveenseweg 6, 7413 AP Deventer, Netherlands; tel. (05700) 35444; telex 49601; f. 1956 to represent the interests of European motel-owners. Mems: 100. Sec. H. J. KLOOSTERHUIS (Netherlands).

European Travel Commission: Confederation House, Kildare St, Dublin 2, Ireland; tel. (01) 714487; telex 93502; f. 1948 to promote tourism in and to Europe, particularly from the United States, Canada, Japan, Australia and Latin America, to foster co-operation and the exchange of information, to organize research. Mems: national tourist organizations of 23 European countries. Exec. Dir T. J. O'DRISCOLL (Ireland); Sec. E. P. KEARNEY.

International Academy of Tourism: 4 rue des Iris, 98000 Monte-Carlo, Monaco; tel. 93-30-97-68; f. 1951 to develop the cultural and humanistic aspects of international tourism and to establish an accepted vocabulary for tourism. Mems: 117. Pres. TIMOTHY O'DRISCOLL; Chancellor LOUIS NAGEL. Publs *Revue, Dictionnaire Touristique International*.

International Association of Scientific Experts in Tourism: Varnbüelstrasse 19, 9000 St Gallen, Switzerland; tel. (071) 235511; telex 77425; f. 1949 to encourage scientific activity by its members; to support tourist institutions of a scientific nature; to organize conventions. Mems: 339 from 48 countries. Pres. Prof. Dr CLAUDE KASPAR (Switzerland); Gen. Sec. Dr HANSPETER SCHMIDHAUSER (Switzerland). Publ. *The Tourist Review* (quarterly).

International Congress and Convention Association: J. W. Brouwersplein 27, POB 5343, 1007 AH Amsterdam, Netherlands; tel. (020) 64-74-21; telex 11629; f. 1963 to establish worldwide co-operation between all involved in organizing congresses, conventions and exhibitions (including travel agents, airlines, hotels, congress centres and professional congress organizers). Mems: 380 in 64 countries. Exec. Dir JOHN E. MOREU. Publ. *TW/ICCA News* (every 2 months).

International Federation of Popular Travel Organizations: Tour Maine Montparnasse, 33 ave du Maine, 75755 Paris Cedex 15, France; tel. (1) 45-38-28-28; telex 260938; f. 1950. Mems: 23 organizations. Pres. ANDRÉ GUIGNAND (France); Sec.-Gen. FLORENCE FOUQUIER (France).

International Federation of Tourist Centres: c/o Landes-Fremdenverkehrsamt, 4010 Linz, Schillerstrasse 50, Austria; f. 1949. Mems: Austria, Belgium, France, Federal Republic of Germany, Italy, Liechtenstein, Netherlands, Norway, Sweden, Switzerland, United Kingdom. Pres. Dr ALDO DEBENE (Austria); Sec.-Gen. KONRAD BERTHOLD (Liechtenstein).

International Ho-Re-Ca: Gotthardstrasse 61, 8027 Zürich, Switzerland; tel. (01) 2012611; f. 1949 to bring together national associations of hotel, restaurant and café proprietors to further the interests of the trade, international tourism, etc. Mems: 29 national organizations. Pres. JOCHEN KOEPP (FRG); Gen. Sec. Dr XAVER FREI (Switzerland).

International Hotel Association: 80 rue de la Roquette, 75011 Paris, France; tel. (1) 47-00-84-57; telex 216410; f. 1946 to link internationally national hotel associations and hotels active in international tourism; to consider all questions of interest to the international hotel industry; to assist in the employment of qualified hotel staff and the exchange of students; to distribute information. Mems: 90 national hotel associations, 220 restaurants, 240 affiliate mems, 95 national and international chains, and 3,600 hotels. Pres. JENS P. LUND (Denmark); Gen. Sec. RAYMOND K. FENELON (UK). Publs *Hotels and Restaurants International* (monthly), *International Hotel Guide* (annually), *Directory of Travel Agencies* (annually), *Opportunities Newsletter* (6 a year), *IHA Bulletin* (every 2 months).

Latin-American Confederation of Tourist Organizations: Viamonte 640, 8° piso, 1053 Buenos Aires, Argentina; f. 1957 to link Latin American national associations of travel agents and their members with other tourist bodies around the world. Mems: in 19 countries and affiliate mems in 70 countries. Pres. ROBERTO R. REZZIO; Sec.-Gen. VICENTE LINES. Publs *Revista COTAL* (monthly), *Aqui-Cotal Newsletter*.

Pacific Asia Travel Association—PATA: 228 Grant Ave, San Francisco, Calif 94108, USA; telex 170685; f. 1951 for the promotion of travel to and between the countries and islands of the Pacific; regional offices in Manila and Sydney. Mems: over 2,500 in 68 countries. Exec. Vice-Pres. KENNETH L. CHAMBERLAIN. Publs *Pacific Travel News*.

Universal Federation of Travel Agents' Associations—UFTAA: 1 rue Defacqz, 1050 Brussels, Belgium; tel. (02) 537-03-20; telex 61808; f. 1966 to unite travel agents associations, to represent the interests of travel agents at the international level, to help in international legal differences; issues literature on travel, etc. Mems: national associations of travel agencies in 81 countries. Sec.-Gen. J. DE WACHTER (Belgium).

World Association of Travel Agencies: 37 Quai Wilson, Geneva, Switzerland; tel. (022) 314760; telex 22447; f. 1949 to foster the development of tourism, to help the rational organization of tourism in all countries, to collect and disseminate information and to participate in all commercial and financial operations which will foster the development of tourism. Individual travel agencies may use the services of the world-wide network of 250 members. Pres. INDER SHARMA (India); Sec.-Gen. HERVÉ CHOISY (Switzerland).

World Tourism Organization: Calle Capitan Haya 42, 28020 Madrid, Spain; tel. 279-28-04; telex 42188; f. 1975 to link national organizations and study general problems; to facilitate and improve travel between and within member countries; and to develop tourism with a view to contributing to economic expansion and international understanding; compiles statistics and technical information; there are six regional commissions and a General Assembly is held every two years. Mems: governments of 105 countries; also three associate members, one observer, and 155 affiliated tourism organizations. Sec.-Gen. WILLIBALD PAHR. Publs *World Tourism Statistics*, *World Travel/Tourisme Mondial* (every 2 months, *Tourist Bibliography* (annually), *Travel Abroad* (annually), manuals, studies.

Trade and Industry

African Regional Organization for Standardization: POB 57363, Nairobi, Kenya; tel. 24561; telex 33082; f. 1977 to promote standardization, quality control, certification and metrology in the African region, formulate regional standards, and co-ordinate participation in international standardization activities. Mems: 23 states. Sec.-Gen. ZAWDU FELLEKE.

Arab Iron and Steel Union—AISU: BP 4, Cheraga, Algiers, Algeria; tel. 78 15 78; telex 52553; f. 1972 to develop commercial and technical aspects of Arab steel production by helping member associations to commercialize their production in Arab markets, guaranteeing them high quality materials and intermediary products, informing them of recent developments in the industry and organizing training sessions. Mems: 71 producers, whose production is worth not less than £1 million per year, in 14 Arab countries. Gen. Sec. MOHAMED LAID LACHGAR. Publs *Arab Steel Review* (monthly), *Information Bulletin* (2 a month), *Directory* (annually).

Asian Productivity Organization: 8-4-14 Akasaka, Minato-ku, Tokyo 107, Japan; tel. (03) 4087221; f. 1961 to strengthen the productivity movement in the Asian region and disseminate technical knowledge. Mems: 17 countries. Sec.-Gen. HIROSHI YOKOTA. Publs *APO News* (monthly), *Annual Report*, reports of surveys and symposia, monographs, etc.

Association of African Trade Promotion Organizations—AATPO: BP 23, Tangier, Morocco; tel. 41687; telex 33695; f. 1975 under the auspices of the OAU and the ECA to foster regular contact between African states in trade matters and to assist in the harmonization of their commercial policies in order to promote intra-African trade; conducts research and training; organizes meetings and trade information missions. Mems: 26 states. Sec.-Gen. Dr FAROUK SHAKWEER. Publs *FLASH: African Trade* (monthly), *Directory of Trade Information Sources in Africa, Directory of State Trading Organizations, Directory of Importers and Exporters of Food Products in Africa,* bibliographies, calendars of events, studies on markets in member countries.

Association of European Chambers of Commerce (EUROCHAMBERS): 30 sq. Ambiorix, Box 57, 1040 Brussels, Belgium; tel. (02) 735-10-92; telex 25315; f. 1958 to promote the exchange of experience and information among its members and to bring their joint opinions to the attention of the institutions of the European Community; conducts studies and seminars. Mems: associations in the EEC member states; seven associate and corresponding mems; Pres. H. PATTBERG (FRG); Sec.-Gen. H. J. VON BÜLOW (FRG).

Committee for European Construction Equipment—CECE: 22–26 Dingwall Rd, Croydon, Surrey, CR9 2PL, England; tel. (01) 688-4422; telex 9419625; f. 1959 to further contact between manufacturers, to improve market conditions and productivity and to conduct research into techniques. Mems: representatives from Belgium, Finland, France, Federal Republic of Germany, Italy, Sweden, United Kingdom. Pres. G. JOHNSTON (UK); Sec.-Gen. D. BARRELL (UK).

Committee of European Foundry Associations: 2 rue de Bassano, 75783 Paris Cedex 16, France; tel. (1) 47-23-55-50; telex 620617; f. 1953 to safeguard the common interests of European foundry industries; to collect and exchange information. Mems: associations in 13 countries. Pres. M. MÖLLMANN (FRG); Sec.-Gen. J. P. BURDEAU.

Confederation of Asia-Pacific Chambers of Commerce and Industry: 10th Floor, 122 Tunhua North Rd, Taipei 10590, Taiwan; tel. 7163016; telex 11144; f. 1966; holds biennial conferences to examine regional co-operation; undertakes liaison with governments in the promotion of laws conducive to regional co-operation; serves as a centre for compiling and disseminating trade and business information; encourages contacts between businesses; conducts training and research. Mems: national chambers of commerce and industry of Australia, Hong Kong, India, Indonesia, Japan, Republic of Korea, New Zealand, the Philippines, Sri Lanka and Taiwan; also affiliate, associate and special mems. Dir-Gen. PAUL T. M. KING.

Confederation of European Soft Drinks Associations—CESDA: 51 ave Général de Gaulle, 1050 Brussels, Belgium; tel. (02) 649-12-86; f. 1961 to promote co-operation among the national associations of soft drinks manufacturers on all industrial and commercial matters, to stimulate the sales and consumption of soft drinks, to deal with matters of interest to all member-associations and to represent the common interests of member-associations and authorities; holds a congress every two years. Pres. R. DELVILLE; Gen. Sec. P. E. FOSSEPREZ.

Confederation of International Contractors' Associations: 9 rue Lapérouse, 75116 Paris, France; tel. (1) 47-20-10-20; telex 613456; f. 1974 to promote co-operation and the exchange of information among building contractors' federations. Mems: four international associations (Europe, Asia and the Western Pacific, North America and Latin America). Pres. JULIO PICCINI-MARTÍN; Sec.-Gen. ERIC LEPAGE.

Customs Co-operation Council: 26–38 rue de l'Industrie, 1040 Brussels, Belgium; tel. (02) 513-99-00; telex 61597; f. 1950 to study all questions relating to co-operation in customs matters, and examine technical aspects, bearing in mind economic factors, of customs systems with a view to attaining uniformity; preparation of conventions and recommendations; ensuring uniform interpretation and application of customs conventions (e.g. on valuation and tariff nomenclature), and conciliatory action in case of dispute; circulation of information and advice regarding Customs regulations and procedures and co-operation with other international organizations. Mems: governments of 96 countries. Chair. J. UITTO (Finland); Sec.-Gen. G. R. DICKERSON (USA). Publs relating to: Nomenclature of the Customs Co-operation Council, Harmonized Commodity Description and Coding System, Brussels Definition of Value, GATT Valuation Agreement, Customs techniques, *Bulletin* (annually), *CCC News*.

Economic Research Committee of the Gas Industry: 4 ave Palmerston, 1040 Brussels, Belgium. Mem. organizations: Austria, Belgium, Denmark, Federal Republic of Germany, France, Ireland, Italy, Netherlands, Spain, Sweden, Switzerland, United Kingdom. Pres. R. GRUBER (Austria); Gen. Sec. L. BLOM (Belgium).

European Association of Advertising Agencies: 28 ave du Barbeau, 1160 Brussels, Belgium; f. 1960 to maintain and to raise the standards of service to advertisers of all European advertising agencies, and to strive towards uniformity in fields where this would be of benefit; to serve the interests of all agency members in Europe. Mems: 15 national advertising agency associations and 17 multinational agency groups. Pres. ARMAND DE MALHERBE; Sec.-Gen. RONALD BEATSON. Publs *Bulletins* and other documentation.

European Association of Manufacturers of Radiators—EURORAD: Walchestrasse 27, 8023 Zürich, Switzerland; f. 1966 to represent the national associations of manufacturers of radiators made of steel and cast iron, intended to be attached to central heating plants and which convey heat by natural convection and radiation without the need for casing. Mems: 12 countries. Pres. J. DE PALÉZIEUX (Switzerland); Gen. Sec. K. EGLI (Switzerland).

European Association of National Productivity Centres: 60 rue de la Concorde, 1050 Brussels, Belgium; tel. (02) 511-71-00; f. 1966 to enable members to pool knowledge about their changing policies and individual activities, specifically as regards the relative importance of various productivity factors, and the ensuing economic and social consequences; co-operation with the OECD, UN bodies and Asian productivity centres. Mems: 18 European, North American and Australasian productivity and quality of working life centres. Pres. ZOLTAN ROMAN; Sec.-Gen. A. C. HUBERT. Publs *EPI* (quarterly), *EUROproductivity* (monthly), *Annual Report*.

European Brewery Convention: POB 510, 2380 BB Zoeterwoude, Netherlands; tel. (071) 814047; telex 39390; f. 1947, present name adopted 1948; aims to promote scientific co-ordination in brewing. Mems: national associations in Austria, Belgium, Denmark, Finland, France, Federal Republic of Germany, Italy, Luxembourg, Netherlands, Norway, Portugal, Spain, Sweden, Switzerland, United Kingdom. Pres. T. M. ENARI (Finland); Sec.-Gen. Mrs M. VAN WIJNGAARDEN (Netherlands).

European Ceramic Association: 44 rue Copernic, 75116 Paris, France; tel. (1) 45-00-18-56; telex 611913; f. 1948 to improve techniques of the industry and promote use of all types of ceramics. Mems: national organizations in Austria, Belgium, Denmark, Finland, France, Federal Republic of Germany, Greece, Italy, Luxembourg, Netherlands, Norway, Portugal, Spain, Sweden, Switzerland, United Kingdom. Pres. HELMUT LEHMANN (FRG); Sec. ROBERT BOUCHET (France).

European Committee for Standardization: 2 rue Bréderode, 1000 Brussels, Belgium; tel. (02) 513-55-64; telex 26257; f. 1961 to promote European standardization and provide the CEN conformity certification marking system and the CEN system of mutual recognition of test and inspection results, so as to eliminate obstacles caused by technical requirements in order to facilitate the exchange of goods and services. Mems: 16 national standards bodies. Sec.-Gen. EVANGELOS VARDAKAS.

European Committee of Associations of Manufacturers of Agricultural Machinery: 19 rue Jacques Bingen, 75017 Paris, France; tel. (1) 47-66-02-20; telex 640362; f. 1959 to study economic and technical problems, to protect members' interests and to disseminate information. Mems: Austria, Belgium, Denmark, Finland, France, Federal Republic of Germany, Italy, Netherlands, Spain, Sweden, Switzerland, United Kingdom. Pres. C. SONNE-SCHMIDT (Denmark); Sec.-Gen. R. PICARD (France).

European Committee of Manufacturers of Domestic Heating and Cooking Appliances: 21 rue des Drapiers, 1050 Brussels, Belgium; f. 1951 to study all questions affecting member organizations and to encourage liaison between them; conducts statistical research, comparison of standards. Mems: national organizations in Belgium, France, Federal Republic of Germany, Netherlands, Switzerland, United Kingdom. Sec. L. DE VOCHT.

European Committee of Paint, Printing Ink and Artists' Colours Manufacturers' Associations: 49 square Marie Louise, 1040 Brussels, Belgium; tel. (02) 230-78-09; telex 23167; f. 1951 to study questions relating to paint and printing ink industries, to take or recommend measures for their development and interests, to exchange information. Mems: national associations in 16 European countries. Pres. B. BENEDINI (Italy); Gen. Sec. H.-A. LENTZE (Belgium).

European Committee of Textile Machinery Manufacturers: Kirchenweg 4, Postfach, 8032 Zürich, Switzerland; telex 816519; f. 1952; organizes international textile machinery exhibitions. Mems: organizations in Belgium, France, Federal Republic of Germany, Italy, Netherlands, Spain, Switzerland, United Kingdom. Pres. E. G. SMALLEY (UK); Sec. Dr J. MERMOD (Switzerland).

European Confederation of Iron and Steel Industries—EUROFER: 5 square de Meeûs, 1040 Brussels, Belgium; tel. (02) 512-98-30; telex 62112; f. 1976 as a confederation of national federations or companies in the steel industries of member states of the European Coal and Steel Community to foster co-operation between the member federations and to represent their common interests to the EEC and other international organizations. Mems: Belgium, Denmark, France, Federal Republic of Germany, Ireland, Italy, Luxembourg, Netherlands, Portugal, Spain, United Kingdom. Dir-Gen. H.-G. VORWERK.

European Confederation of Woodworking Industries: 109–111 rue Royale, 1000 Brussels, Belgium; tel. (02) 217-63-65; telex 61983; f. 1952 to act as a liaison between national organizations, to undertake research and to defend the interests of the trade. Mems: national federations in 13 European countries and European sectoral organizations in woodworking. Pres. M. ROUGIER (France); Sec.-Gen. E. RONSÉ.

European Council of Chemical Manufacturers' Federations: 250 ave Louise, bte 71, 1050 Brussels, Belgium; tel. (02) 640-20-95; telex 62444; represents and defends the interests of the chemical industry relating to legal and trade policy, internal market, environmental and technical matters; liaises with intergovernmental organizations. Mems: 15 national associations. Dir.-Gen. Drs H. H. LEVER.

European Dehydrators Association: 5 quai Voltaire, 75007 Paris, France; tel. (1) 42-61-72-94; f. 1960 to promote co-operation between the companies, to encourage the study of national laws, prices and markets relating to dried products and to enlarge the use of dried green crops. Mems: nine national asscns. Pres. GÉRARD DEMAZURE (France); Sec. CHRISTIAN DE CORBIAC (France).

European Federation of Associations of Engineers and Heads of Industrial Safety Services: c/o Institution of Industrial Safety Officers, 222 Uppingham Rd, Leicester, England; f. 1952 to prevent industrial accidents and conduct studies on industrial safety and hygiene. Mems: associations in Austria, Belgium, France, Federal Republic of Germany, Italy, Sweden, United Kingdom, and five observers. Pres. C. BAUDET (France); Sec. LUTIER (France). Publ. *Chronicle of the FEAICS* (irregular).

European Federation of Associations of Insulation Enterprises: 10 rue du Débarcadère, 75852 Paris Cedex 17, France; tel. (1) 45-74-99-42; telex 660044; f. 1970; groups the organizations in Europe representing insulation firms including thermal insulation, sound-proofing and fire-proofing insulation; aims to facilitate contacts between member associations, to study any problems of interest to the profession, to safeguard the interests of the profession and represent it in international forums. Mems: professional organizations in 15 European countries. Chair. W. B. MACMILLAN; Vice-Chair. L. P. CHARBONNEL, T. WREDE.

European Federation of Fibreboard Manufacturers—FEROPA: 6300 Giessen, Wilhelmstrasse 25, Federal Republic of Germany; tel. (06 41) 71596; telex 4 828 77; f. 1954 to organize joint research, facilitate contacts and represent the industry at the international level. Mems: in 12 European countries. Chair. JOSÉ ALVAREZ-NOVOA (Spain); Sec.-Gen. A. KRIER.

European Federation of Handling Industries: POB 179, Kirchenweg 4, 8032 Zürich, Switzerland; tel. (01) 478400; telex 816519; f. 1953 to facilitate contact between members of the profession, conduct research, standardize methods of calculation and construction and promote standardized safety regulations. Mems: organizations in 14 European countries. Pres. Dr H. MÖLLER (FRG); Sec. E. HORAT (Switzerland).

European Federation of Management Consultants' Associations: 3 rue Léon Bonnat, 75016 Paris, France; tel. (1) 45-24-43-53; telex 612938; f. 1960 to bring management consultants together and promote a high standard of professional competence in all European countries concerned, by encouraging open discussions of, and co-operative research into, problems of common professional interest. Mems: 16 associations. Gen. Sec. E. LABOUREAU.

European Federation of Particle Board Manufacturers: 63 Giessen, Postfach 5423, Wilhelmstrasse 25, Federal Republic of Germany; f. 1958 to develop and encourage international co-operation in the particle board industry. Mems: 12 countries and one associate. Pres. T. BOJSEN-MØLLER (Denmark); Sec.-Gen. A. KRIER (FRG). Publs *Annual Report*, technical documents.

European Federation of Plywood Industry: 30 ave Marceau, 75008 Paris, France; f. 1957 to organize joint research between members of the industry at international level. Mems: associations in eight European countries. Pres. B. HAUSMANN (FRG); Sec.-Gen. PIERRE LAPEYRE.

European Federation of Productivity Services: c/o Sveriges Rationaliseringsförbund SRF, Tjärhovsgatan 8A, 11621 Stockholm, Sweden; tel. (8) 249225; telex 12442; f. 1961 to promote throughout Europe the application of productivity services; to promote and support the development of the practice and techniques of industrial and commercial productivity and efficiency; and to provide a contact network for the exchange of information and ideas. Mems: 12, and three corresponding organizations. Pres. W. HELMS; Exec. Sec. K. HELMRICH.

European Federation of Tile and Brick Manufacturers: Obstgartenstrasse 28, 8035 Zürich, Switzerland; f. 1952 to co-ordinate research between members of the industry, improve technical knowledge, encourage professional training. Mems: associations in Austria, Belgium, Denmark, Finland, France, Federal Republic of Germany, Ireland, Italy, Netherlands, Norway, Spain, Sweden, Switzerland, United Kingdom. Chair. A. PALOHEIMO.

European Federation of Unions of Joinery Manufacturers: 6000 Frankfurt 1, Bockenheimer Anlage 13, Federal Republic of Germany; tel. (69) 550060; telex 0416547; f. 1957 to facilitate contacts between members of the industry, promote research and represent its members at international level. Mems: associations in Belgium, France, Federal Republic of Germany, Italy, Netherlands, United Kingdom, Scandinavia. Pres. M. ALBERS; Sec.-Gen. K. H. HERBERT (FRG).

European Furniture Manufacturers Federation: 15 rue de l'Association, 1000 Brussels; tel. (02) 218-18-59; telex 61933; f. 1950 to determine and support general interests of the European furniture industry, facilitate contacts between members of the industry, and to support the Federation's decisions internally and internationally. Mems: organizations in Belgium, Denmark, France, Federal Republic of Germany, Italy, Norway, Spain, Sweden, Switzerland, United Kingdom, Yugoslavia. Pres. R. RODRÍGUEZ; Sec.-Gen. E. RONSÉ.

European General Galvanizers Association: c/o Zinc Development Association, 34 Berkeley Square, London, W1X 6AJ, England; tel. (01) 499-6636; telex 261286; f. 1955 to promote co-operation between members of the industry, especially in improving processes and finding new uses for galvanized products; maintains a film and photographic section and library. Mems: associations in Belgium, Denmark, Finland, France, Federal Republic of Germany, Italy, Netherlands, Norway, Portugal, Spain, Sweden, Switzerland, United Kingdom and individual firms in Austria. Pres. K. SEPPELER (FRG).

European Glass Container Manufacturers' Committee: 19 Portland Place, London, W1N 4BH, England; tel. (01) 580-6952; telex 27470; f. 1951 to facilitate contacts between members of the industry, inform them of legislation regarding it. Mems: representatives from 15 European countries. Sec. OLIVER C. T. R. NORMANDALE (UK).

European Organization for Quality Control—EOQC: POB 2613, 3001 Berne, Switzerland; tel. (031) 216111; telex 912110; f. 1956 to encourage the use and application of quality control with the intent to improve quality, reduce costs and increase productivity; organizes annual congresses for the exchange of information, documentation, etc. Member organizations in all European countries. Pres. Dr H. D. SEGHEZZI (Switzerland); Sec. M. CONRAD (Switzerland). Publs *Quality* (quarterly), *Glossary, Sampling Books, Specifications Guide, Quality Survey in Automotive Industry, Conference Proceedings, Reliability Book*.

European Packaging Federation: c/o Nederlandse Verpakkings-centrum, Postbus 835, 2501 CV The Hague, Netherlands; tel. (070) 654953; telex 32412; f. 1953 to encourage the exchange of information between national packaging institutes and to promote technical and economic progress. Mems: organizations in Austria, Belgium, Denmark, Finland, France, Federal Republic of Germany, Hungary, Ireland, Italy, Netherlands, Poland, Portugal, Romania, Spain, Sweden, Switzerland, United Kingdom. Pres. J. P. A. GROENHUIJSEN (Netherlands); Sec.-Gen. ALICE VERHAGE (Netherlands).

European Patent Office—EPO: 8000 Munich 2, Erhardtstrasse 27, Federal Republic of Germany; tel. (089) 2399; telex 523656; f. 1977 to grant European patents according to the Munich convention of 1973; conducts searches and examination of patent applications. Mems: Austria, Belgium, France, Federal Republic of Germany, Greece, Italy, Liechtenstein, Luxembourg, Netherlands, Spain, Sweden, Switzerland, United Kingdom. Pres. P. BRAENDLI (Switzerland); Chair. Admin. Council Prof. O. LEBERL (Austria). Publs *Annual Report, Official Journal* (monthly), *European Patent Bulletin, European Patent Applications, Granted Patents*.

European Society for Opinion and Marketing Research—ESOMAR: J. J. Viottastraat 29, 1071 JP Amsterdam, Netherlands; tel. (020) 64-21-41; telex 18535; f. 1948 to further professional interests and encourage high technical standards. Mems: about 2,100 in 45 countries. Pres. BRYAN A. BATES (UK); Dir FERNANDA MONTI (Netherlands). Publs *European Research* (4 a year), *Newsbrief* (6 a year), *Marketing Research in Europe* (annual handbook), codes of practice, congress papers and seminar proceedings, monographs.

OTHER INTERNATIONAL ORGANIZATIONS

Trade and Industry

European Union of Coachbuilders: 46 Woluwedal, bte 14, 1200 Brussels, Belgium; tel. (02) 771-17-42; f. 1948 to promote research on questions affecting the industry, exchange information, and establish a common policy for the industry. Mems: national federations in Belgium, France, Federal Republic of Germany, Italy, Luxembourg, Netherlands, Switzerland, United Kingdom. Pres. G. BAETEN (Belgium); Sec.-Gen. KRIS BOSTOEN (Belgium).

General Union of Chambers of Commerce, Industry and Agriculture for Arab Countries: POB 11-2837, Beirut, Lebanon; tel. 814269; telex 20347; f. 1951 to foster Arab economic collaboration, to increase and improve production and to facilitate the exchange of technical information in Arab countries. Mems: Chambers of Commerce, Industry and Agriculture in 22 Arab countries. Pres. (vacant); Gen. Sec. BURHAN DAJANI. Publ. *Arab Economic Report* (Arabic and English).

Gulf Organization for Industrial Consulting: POB 5114, Doha, Qatar; tel. 831234; telex 4619; f. 1976 by seven Gulf Arab states to pool industrial expertise and encourage joint development of projects. Sec.-Gen. Dr ABDULLAH AL-MOAJIL (Saudi Arabia). Publs *Industrial Co-operation in the Arabian Gulf* (quarterly, Arabic and English), *Annual Report*, *Bulletin* (monthly), *Gulf Industrial Focus* (every 2 months), occasional studies and pamphlets.

Inter-American Commercial Arbitration Commission: CP 06048, Paseo de la Reforma 42, México, DF, Mexico; tel. 592-26-77; telex 1777262; f. 1934 to establish an inter-American system of arbitration for the settlement of commercial disputes by means of tribunals. Mems: national committees, commercial firms and individuals in 21 countries. Pres. IGNACIO ARMIDA MORÁN; Dir-Gen. ANGEL DOMÍNGUEZ ROJO.

International Advertising Association Inc.: 475 Fifth Ave, New York, NY 10017, USA; tel. (212) 684-1583; telex 237969; f. 1938 to raise the general level of advertising and marketing efficiency throughout the world; to promote the concept of freer trade and facilitate the interchange of ideas, experience and information. Mems: 2,400. Pres. A. E. PITCHER (UK); Exec. Dir JOSEPH NOVAS (USA). Publs *IAA Membership Directory and Annual Report*, *IAA Airletter* (6 a year), *Intelligence Summary* (6 a year), *United Nations Report for Advertising and Marketing* (6 a year), reports and studies.

International Association for Business Research and Corporate Development: Gainsford House, 115 Station Rd, West Wickham, Kent, BR4 0PX, England; tel. (01) 777-9200; f. 1965 to facilitate contacts between researchers; holds annual conferences and seminars; main specialist divisions: European chemical marketing research; European technological forecasting; paper and related industries; industrial materials; automotive; textiles; methodology. Mems: 700. Pres. PHILIP D. WILMOT (UK); Gen. Sec. A. L. WADDAMS.

International Association of Bicycle and Motorcycle Trading and Repair: 4800 Bielefeld, Danziger Str. 1, Federal Republic of Germany; tel. (0521) 200136; f. 1956 for the exchange of ideas and information between members. Mems: eight in seven countries. Pres. ANTON PAULSEN (FRG); Sec. HERMANN FÖSTE (FRG).

International Association of Chain Stores: 61 quai d'Orsay, Paris 7e, France; tel. (1) 47-05-48-43; telex 206387; f. 1953; links general merchandise and food retail companies and their suppliers; organizes annual congress and symposia to exchange ideas on trends, techniques and practices, and to improve professional standards and consumer service. Mems: 500 companies in 25 countries. Chair. DAVID SILVERBERG; CEO ETIENNE LAURENT. Publ. *Quarterly Review*.

International Association of Congress Centres (Association internationale des palais de Congrès—AIPC): c/o Muzejski prostor, Jezuitski trg 4, POB 19, 41000 Zagreb, Yugoslavia; tel. (041) 433-722; telex 22398; f. 1958 to unite conference centres fulfilling certain criteria, to study the administration and technical problems of international conferences, to promote a common commercial policy and co-ordinate all elements of conferences. Mems: 73 from 29 countries. Pres. MATTHIAS FUCHS; Sec.-Gen. RADOVAN VOLMUT (Yugoslavia). Publ. list of principal conferences of the world (3 a year).

International Association of Department Stores: 72 blvd Haussmann, 75008 Paris, France; tel. (1) 43-87-25-80; f. 1928 to conduct research, exchange information and statistics on management, organization and technical problems; centre of documentation; library of 5,000 volumes. Mems: large-scale retail enterprises in Andorra, Belgium, Denmark, Finland, France, Federal Republic of Germany, Italy, Netherlands, Norway, Spain, Sweden, Switzerland, United Kingdom; associate mem. in Japan. Pres. Dr R. BITTERLI (Switzerland); Gen. Sec. E. KALDEREN (Sweden). Publ. *Retail News Letter* (monthly).

International Association of Electrical Contractors: 5 rue Hamelin, 75116 Paris, France; tel. (1) 47-27-97-49; telex 620 993. Pres. FRANCO GEMMO (Italy).

International Association of Scholarly Publishers: c/o Edvard Aslaksen, Universitetsforlaget, POB 2959 Toyen, 0608 Oslo 6, Norway; tel. (2) 276060; telex 71896; f. 1972 for the exchange of information and experience on scholarly and academic publishing by universities and others; assists in the transfer of publishing skills to developing countries. Mems: 139 in 40 countries. Pres. EDVARD ASLAKSEN (Norway); Sec.-Gen. DOROTHY J. ANTHONY (USA). Publs *IASP Newsletter* (every 2 months), *International Directory of Scholarly Publishers*.

International Association of Textile Dyers and Printers: 272 Royal Exchange, Manchester, M2 7ED, England; tel. (061) 834-7871; telex 666737; f. 1967 to defend and promote the interests of members in international affairs and to provide a forum for discussion of matters of mutual interest. Mems: national trade associations representing dyers and printers in nine countries. Pres. Dr ANDREAS RHOMBERG (Austria); Sec.-Gen. BARRY G. HAZEL (UK).

International Booksellers Federation—IBF: 1010 Vienna, Grünangergasse 4, Austria; tel. (0222) 512-15-35; f. 1956 to promote the booktrade and the exchange of information and to protect the interests of booksellers when dealing with other international organizations; special committees deal with questions of postage, resale price maintenance, book market research, advertising, customs and tariffs, the problems of young booksellers, etc.; consultative relationship with UNESCO. Mems: 200 in 24 countries. Pres. PETER MEILI; Sec.-Gen. Dr GERHARD PROSSER. Publs *IBF-bulletin* (4 a year), *Booksellers International*.

International Bureau for the Standardization of Man-Made Fibres: Lautengartenstrasse 12, 4010 Basel, Switzerland; tel. 236250; telex 64331; f. 1928 to examine and establish rules for the standardization, classification and naming of various categories of man-made fibres. Mems: 62. Sec.-Gen. Dr H. L. SARASIN.

International Bureau of Insurance and Reinsurance Producers: c/o G. Oranovsky, rue Jéliotte, 64400 Oloron Ste Marie, France; tel. (59) 39-18-78; telex 570 820; f. 1937. Mems: 37 associations from 29 countries, representing approx. 250,000 brokers and agents. Pres. OSWALD HUEBENER; Sec.-Gen. GEORGES ORANOVSKY. Publ. *Tribune Internationale* (irregular).

International Confederation for Printing and Allied Industries—INTERGRAF: 18 square Marie-Louise, bte 25, 1040 Brussels, Belgium; tel. (02) 230-86-46; telex 64393; f. 1983 (formerly EUROGRAF, f. 1975) to defend the common interests of the printing and allied interests in member countries. Mems: federations in 15 countries. Pres. SØREN BRUHN; Sec.-Gen. GEOFFREY WILSON.

International Confederation of Art Dealers: 32 rue Ernest Allard, 1000 Brussels, Belgium; f. 1936 to co-ordinate the work of associations of dealers in works of art and paintings and to contribute to artistic and economic expansion. Mems: associations in 14 countries. Pres. GÜNTHER ABELS (FRG).

International Confederation of the Butchers' and Delicatessen Trade: Steinwiesstrasse 59, 8028 Zürich, Switzerland; f. 1946. Sec.-Gen. Dr H. GERBER.

International Co-operative Alliance—ICA: 15 route des Morillons, 1218 Grand-Saconnex, Geneva, Switzerland; tel. (022) 984121; telex 27935; f. 1895 to link individual mems. and affiliated organizations in the pursuit of co-operative aims; regional offices in India, Tanzania and Ivory Coast; Congress meets every four years; 13 auxiliary committees exist for the sharing of technical expertise by co-operative organizations in the following fields: agriculture, banking, fisheries, consumer affairs, wholesale distribution, housing, insurance, women's participation and industrial and artisanal co-operatives; annual budget about £500,000 obtained from subscriptions. Mems: 500m. individuals in 705,640 co-operative societies. Pres. LARS MARCUS (Sweden); Dir R. BEASLEY (USA). Publs *Review of International Co-operation* (quarterly, in English, French and Spanish), studies, reports.

International Council of Shopping Centres: 665 Fifth Ave, New York, NY 10022, USA; tel. (212) 421-8181; telex 128185; f. 1957 as a trade association for the shopping centre industry, to promote professional standards of performance in the development, construction, financing, leasing and management of shopping centres throughout the world; organizes training courses; gives awards for new centres. Exec. Vice-Pres. JOHN T. RIORDAN.

International Council of Societies of Industrial Design—ICSID: 45 ave Legrand, 1050 Brussels, Belgium; tel. (02) 648-

OTHER INTERNATIONAL ORGANIZATIONS

Trade and Industry

59-79; f. 1957 to encourage the development of high standards in the practice of industrial design; to improve and expand the contribution of industrial design throughout the world. Mems: 67 societies in 36 countries. Pres. L. VAN DER SANDE (Netherlands); Sec.-Gen. PETER J. LORD (UK). Publs *Reports of Seminars on the Education of Industrial Designers, ICSID News* (every 2 months), *International Design Competitions, Design for Disaster Relief*, Regulations governing conduct.

International Council of Tanners: 192 High St, Lewes, East Sussex, BN7 2NP, England; tel. (0273) 472149; telex 21505; f. 1926 to study all questions relating to the leather industry and maintain contact with national associations. Mems: national tanners' organizations in 35 countries. Pres. PERTTI HELLEMAA (Finland); Sec. G. G. REAKS (UK).

International Exhibitions Bureau: 56 ave Victor Hugo, Paris 16e, France; tel. (1) 45-00-38-63; f. 1928, revised by Protocol 1972, for the authorization and registration of international exhibitions falling under the 1928 Convention. Mems: 47 states. Pres. JACQUES SOL-ROLLAND; Sec.-Gen. MARIE-HÉLÈNE DEFRENE.

International Federation for Household Maintenance Products: 49 sq. Marie-Louise, 1040 Brussels, Belgium; tel. (02) 230-40-90; telex 23167; f. 1967 to promote in all fields the manufacture and use of a wide range of cleaning products, polishes, bleaches, disinfectants and insecticides, to develop the exchange of statistical information and to study technical, scientific, economic and social problems of interest to its members. Mems: in 10 countries. Pres. G. F. VERRI; Sec. P. COSTA (Belgium).

International Federation of Associations of Textile Chemists and Colourists—IFATCC: 4133 Pratteln, Postfach 93, Switzerland; f. 1930 to encourage the development and maintenance of friendly relations between the various member associations; the creation of permanent liaison on professional matters between members; and the furtherance of scientific and technical collaboration in the development of the textile finishing industry and the colouring of materials. Mems: in 12 countries. Pres. Prof. J. SUNDQUIST (Finland); Sec. Dr H. HERZOG (Switzerland).

International Federation of Buying Societies: Neumarkt 14, 5 Cologne 1, Federal Republic of Germany; f. 1951 to promote contact between members and exchange information. Mems: 60 buying groups in 12 European countries. Pres. Drs DE LANGEN (Netherlands); Sec. Dr GÜNTER OLESCH. Publ. *IVE—Handbuch*.

International Federation of Grocers' Associations—IFGA: Falkenplatz 1, 3001 Berne, Switzerland; tel. (031) 237646; f. 1927; initiates special studies and works to further the interests of members having special regard to new conditions resulting from European integration and developments in consuming and distribution. Mems: 500,000. Sec.-Gen. PETER SCHUETZ (Switzerland); Publs studies, codes of practice, etc.

International Federation of Phonogram and Videogram Producers: 54 Regent St, London, W1R 5PJ, England; tel. (01) 434-3521; telex 919044; f. 1933; association of the worldwide sound and video recording industry, making representations to governments and international bodies and generally defending the interests of its members. Mems: 630 in 64 countries. Pres. NESUHI ERTEGUN; Dir-Gen. I. D. THOMAS.

International Fragrance Association—IFRA: 8 rue Charles-Humbert, 1205 Geneva, Switzerland; tel. (022) 213548; telex 428354; f. 1973 to collect and study scientific data on fragrance materials and to make recommendations on their safe use. Mems: national Associations in 14 countries. Pres. R. G. SHELDRAKE; Scientific Adviser F. GRUNDSCHOBER. Publs *Code of Practice, Guidelines*.

International Fur Trade Federation: 69 Cannon St, London, EC4N 5AB, England; tel. (01) 248-4444; telex 888941; f. 1949 to promote and organize joint action by fur trade organizations for promoting, developing and protecting trade in furskins and/or processing thereof. Mems: 32 organizations in 29 countries. Pres. J. E. POSER (USA); Sec. J. KRAUSE.

International Group of National Associations of Agrochemical Manufacturers: 12 ave Hamoir, 1180 Brussels, Belgium; tel. (02) 374-59-81; telex 62120; f. 1967 to encourage the rational use of chemicals in agriculture, the harmonization of national and international legislation, and the respect of industrial property rights; encourages research on chemical residues and toxicology. Mems: associations in 29 countries. Dir-Gen. JACQUES COSSE; Technical Dir RON G. GARDINER.

International Group of Users of Information Systems—IGIS: Enschedepad 41-43, 1324 GB Almere-Stad, Netherlands. Pres. S. J. BOGAERTS (Belgium); Sec. P. FLAPPER (Netherlands). Publs *Information and Management* (6 a year), *IGIS Newsletter* (6 a year).

International Master Printers' Association—IMPA: 18 sq. Marie-Louise, BP 25, 1040 Brussels, Belgium; f. 1930 to supply affiliated associations of employers with information about conditions relating to the printing, binding, and allied trades in other countries, and to organize conferences for members of these associations. Mems: 24 associations of employers engaged in the printing, binding, and allied trades in 17 countries. Pres. S. BRUHN (Denmark). Publ. *IMPA Newsletter* (monthly).

International Organization for Motor Trades and Repairs: Veraartlaan 12, 2288 GM Rijswijk, Netherlands; tel. (70) 907222; telex 31296; f. 1947 to collect and disseminate information about all aspects of the trade; to hold meetings and congresses. Mems: 35 associations in 25 countries. Pres. F. HABERL (FRG); Gen. Sec. J. A. HOEKZEMA (Netherlands). Publ. *Newsletter*.

International Organization of Consumers' Unions—IOCU: Emmastraat 9, 2595 EG The Hague, Netherlands; tel. (070) 47-63-31; telex 33561; f. 1960; links consumer groups worldwide through information networks and international seminars; supports new consumer groups and represents consumers' interests at the international level. Mems: 140 national associations in 52 countries. Dir LARS BROCH. Publs *IOCU Newsletter* (10 a year), *Consumer Currents* (10 a year).

International Organization of Motor Manufacturers: 4 rue de Berri, 75008 Paris; tel. (1) 43-59-00-13; telex 290012; f. 1919 to co-ordinate and further the interests of the automobile industry, to promote the study of economic and other matters affecting automobile construction; to control automobile manufacturers' participation in international exhibitions in Europe. Full mems: manufacturers' associations of 15 European countries, Japan and the USA. Assoc. mems: three importers' associations. Corresponding mems: five automobile associations. Pres. A. FRASER (UK); Gen. Sec. J. M. MULLER. Publ. *Répertoire International de l'Industrie Automobile*.

International Organization of the Flavour Industry—IOFI: 8 rue Charles-Humbert, 1205 Geneva, Switzerland; tel. (022) 213548; telex 428354; f. 1969 to support and promote the flavour industry; active in the fields of safety evaluation and regulation of flavouring substances. Mems: national associations in 21 countries. Pres. F. RIJKENS; Scientific Adviser F. GRUNDSCHOBER. Publs *Documentation Bulletin* (monthly), *Information letters, Code of Practice*.

International Publishers' Association: 3 ave de Miremont, 1206 Geneva, Switzerland; tel. (022) 463018; telex 421883; f. 1896 to defend the freedom of publishers, promote their interests and foster international co-operation; helps the international trade in books and music, works on international copyright, and translation rights. Mems: 48 professional book publishers' organizations in 43 countries and music publishers' associations in 20 countries. Pres. JOHAN SOMERWIL; Sec.-Gen. J. ALEXIS KOUTCHOUMOW.

International Rayon and Synthetic Fibres Committee: 29 rue de Courcelles, Paris 8e, France; tel. (1) 45-63-87-10; telex 650931; f. 1950 to improve the quality and use of rayon and manmade fibres and of products made from fibres. Mems: national associations and individual producers in 24 countries. Pres. N. S. WOODING. (UK); Dir-Gen. Prof. J. L. JUVET.

International Shopfitting Organisation: Zuidzijde 92, 2977 XC Goudriaan, Netherlands; tel. (01838) 1396; f. 1959 to promote friendship and interchange of ideas between individuals and firms concerned with the common interests of shopfitting. Mems: companies in 16 countries. Pres. P. MEYER; Sec. H. J. SIPS. Publs circular letters, technical papers, etc.

International Textile Care and Rental Association—ITCRA: Reitseplein 1, 5037 AA Tilburg, Netherlands; tel. (013) 654441; telex 52384; f. 1950; functions include consultation relating to all matters of common interest, promotion of development of the industry, international exchange and co-operation, maintenance of libraries, organizations of conferences and congresses, encouragement of technical education in the industry. Mems: 10. Pres. W. M. GIEZEMAN (Netherlands); Dir Dr J. C. VAN ZUNDERT (Netherlands). Publs *News Bulletins, Press Releases* (3-4 a year).

International Textile Manufacturers Federation—ITMF: Am Schanzengraben 29, Postfach, 8039 Zürich, Switzerland; tel. (01) 2017080; telex 56798; f. 1904, present title adopted 1978. Aims to protect and promote the interests of its members, to disseminate information, and encourage co-operation. Mems: national textile trade associations in 42 countries. Pres. BERNARD CRONE-RAWE (FRG); Dir Dr HERWIG STROLZ (Austria). Publs *Newsletter, State of Trade Report* (quarterly), *International Cotton System Fibre Consumptions Statistics* (annually), *International Cotton Industry Statistics* (annually), *International Textile Machinery Ship-*

ment Statistics (annually), *International Textile Manufacturing* (annually), etc.

International Union of Marine Insurance: Stadthausquai 5, 8001 Zürich, Switzerland; f. 1873 to collect and distribute information on marine insurance on a world-wide basis. Mems: 50 associations. Pres. ENRICO ORLANDO (Italy); Gen. Sec. Dr PETER ALTHER (Switzerland).

International Whaling Commission: The Red House, Station Rd, Histon, Cambridge, CB4 4NP, England; tel. (022 023) 3971; telex 817960; f. 1946 under the International Convention for the Regulation of Whaling signed in Washington to provide for the conservation of the world whale stocks for the common good and to review, and if necessary amend, the regulations covering the operations of whaling; to encourage research relating to whales and whaling, to collect and analyse statistical information and to study and disseminate information concerning methods of increasing whale stocks; a ban on commercial whaling was passed by the Commission in July 1982, to take effect three years subsequently (although, in some cases, a phased reduction of commercial operations was not to be completed until 1988). Mems: governments of 41 countries. Chair. I. L. G. STEWART (New Zealand); Sec. Dr R. GAMBELL. Publs *Annual Report, Report and Papers of the Scientific Committee of the Commission, Schedule to the International Convention for the Regulation of Whaling* 1946, special scientific reports (irregular).

International Wool Textile Organisation: 19–21 rue de Luxembourg, 1040 Brussels, Belgium; f. 1929 to maintain a connection between the wool textile organizations in member-countries and represent their interests. Mems: 26 countries. Pres. G. J. TEN BROEKE (Netherlands); Sec.-Gen. W. H. LAKIN (UK).

International Wrought Copper Council: 6 Bathurst St, Sussex Sq., London, W2 2SD, England; tel. (01) 723-7465; telex 23556; f. 1953 to bind together and represent the copper fabricating industries in the member countries, and to represent the views of copper consumers to raw material producers; organizes specialist activities on technical work, development of copper and uses, accident prevention. Mems: 16 national groups representing non-ferrous metals industries in all West European countries and Japan. Chair. L. GUSTAFSSON; Sec. S. N. PAYTON.

Liaison Organization of the European Engineering Industries: 99 rue de Stassart, 1050 Brussels, Belgium; tel. (02) 511-34-84; telex 21078; f. 1954 to provide a permanent liaison between the mechanical, electrical and electronic engineering, and metalworking industries of member countries. Mems: 24 trade associations in 15 West European countries. Pres. HELMUT LOHR (FRG); Sec.-Gen. TREVOR GAY.

Union of Industries of the European Community: 6 rue de Loxum, 1000 Brussels, Belgium; tel. (02) 512-67-80; telex 26013; an association of central industrial and employers' federations of the EEC member countries and western Europe; aims to ensure that Community policy-making takes account of the views of industry; committees and working groups work out joint positions in the various fields of interest to industry and submit them to the Community institutions concerned. The Council of Presidents (of member federations) lays down general policy; the Executive Committee (of Directors-General of member federations) is the managing body; and the Committee of Permanent Delegates, consisting of federation representatives in Brussels, ensures permanent liaison with members. Mems: 14 industrial federations from the EEC member states, and 16 federations from non-Community countries. Pres. KARL-GUSTAF RATJEN; Sec.-Gen. ZYGMUNT TYSZKIEWICZ. Publs *Monthly Report*.

Union of International Fairs: 35 bis, rue Jouffroy, 75017 Paris, France; tel. (1) 42-67-99-12; telex 660097; f. 1925 to increase co-operation between international fairs, safeguard their interests and extend their operations; annual congress determines the programme of work and decides on applications for membership; a steering committee carries out the decisions of the congress, and supervises the commissions and technical committees. The Union has defined the conditions to be fulfilled to qualify as an international fair, and is concerned with the standards of the fairs. It studies improvements which could be made in the conditions of the fairs and organizes training seminars. Mems: 137 organizers, 65 general fairs and 322 specialized exhibitions. Pres. Prof. CARLO G. BERTOLOTTI (Italy); Sec.-Gen. GERDA MARQUARDT (France).

World Council of Management—CIOS: c/o RKW, 6236 Eschborn, POB 5867, Federal Republic of Germany; f. 1926 to promote the understanding of the principles and the practice of the methods of modern management; to organize conferences, congresses and seminars on management; to exchange information on management techniques; to promote training programmes. Mems: national organizations in 41 countries. Pres. W. PIAZZA T. (Peru); Acting Sec. L. BOUWENS. Publ. *Newsletter* (for members, in English and French).

World Federation of Advertisers: 54 rue des Colonies, Bte 13, 1000 Brussels; tel. (02) 219-06-98; telex 63801; f. 1953; promotes and studies advertising and its related problems. Mems: associations in 26 countries and 21 international companies. Dir P. P. DE WIN.

World Packaging Organisation: 42 ave de Versailles, 75016 Paris, France; tel. (1) 43-80-92-77; telex 649167; f. 1967 to provide a forum for the exchange of knowledge of packaging technology and, in general, to create conditions for the conservation, preservation and distribution of world food production; to contribute to the development of world-wide trade. Mems: Asian Packaging Federation, North American Packaging Federation, Latin American Packaging Union, European Packaging Federation. Pres. PIERRE SCHMIT (France); Gen. Sec. PIERRE J. LOUIS (France).

World Trade Centers Association: One World Trade Center, 63 West, New York, NY 10048, USA; tel. (212) 466-8380; f. 1968 to promote trade through the establishment of world trade centres, including education facilities, information services and exhibition facilities. Mems: trade centres, chambers of commerce and other organizations in 42 countries. Pres. GUY F. TOZZOLI; Sec. TADAYOSHI YAMADA. Publs *WTCA News* (monthly), *World Traders* (quarterly).

Transport

African Airlines Association: POB 20116, Nairobi, Kenya; f. 1968 to give African air companies expert advice in technical, financial, juridical and market matters; to improve communications in Africa; to represent the mem. airlines; and to develop manpower resources. Mems: 36 national carriers. Sec.-Gen. Col SEMRET MEDHANE (Ethiopia).

Arab Air Carriers' Organization—AACO: Zakaria Nsouli Bldg, 10th and 11th Floors, Anis Nsouli St, Verdun, POB 130468, Chouran, Beirut, Lebanon; tel. 861294; telex 22370; f. 1965 to co-ordinate and promote co-operation in the activities of Arab airline companies. Mems: 18 Arab air carriers. Pres. MUHAMMAD AL-HAIMY; Sec.-Gen. SALIM A. SALAAM; Dir-Gen. AMER A. SHARIF. Publs Monthly statistical bulletins and research documents on aviation in the Arab world.

Arab Union of Railways: POB 6599, Aleppo, Syria; tel. 220302; telex 331009; f. 1979 to stimulate co-operation between railways in Arab countries, and to co-ordinate the interconnection of Arab railways with each other and with international railways; holds Symposium every two years. Mems: 16, comprising railways of Algeria, Iraq, Jordan, Lebanon, Morocco, Sudan, Syria, Tunisia; construction companies in Morocco, Tunisia and Syria; the Arab Union of Land Transport; and the Palestine Liberation Organization. Gen. Sec. MOURHAF SABOUNI. Publs *Al Sikak Al Arabie* (Arab Railways, quarterly), *Statistics of Arab Railways* (annually), *Glossary of Railway Terms* (Arabic, English, French and German).

Association of European Airlines: 350 ave Louise, Bte 4, 1050 Brussels, Belgium; tel. (02) 640-31-75; telex 22918; f. 1954 to carry out research on political, commercial, economic and technical aspects of air transport; maintains statistical data bank. Mems: 20 airlines. Sec.-Gen. KARL-HEINZ NEUMEISTER.

Baltic and International Maritime Council—BIMCO: 19 Kristianiagade, 2100 Copenhagen, Denmark; tel. (01) 26-30-00; telex 19086; f. 1905 to unite shipowners and other persons and organizations connected with the industry. Mems: in 100 countries representing nearly 50% of world merchant tonnage. Pres. ATLE JEBSEN; Sec.-Gen. TORBEN C. SKAANILD. Publs bulletins and weekly circulars, etc.

Central Commission for the Navigation of the Rhine: Palais du Rhin, Strasbourg, France; tel. (88) 32-35-84; f. 1815 to ensure free movement of traffic and standard river facilities to ships of all nations; draws up navigational rules, standardizes customs regulations, arbitrates in disputes involving river traffic, approves plans for river maintenance work; there is an administrative centre for social security for boatmen, and a tripartite commission for labour conditions. Mems: Belgium, France, Federal Republic of Germany, Netherlands, Switzerland, United Kingdom. Pres. M. RIPHAGEN; Sec.-Gen. R. DOERFLINGER (France).

Central Office for International Carriage by Rail: Thunplaz, Bern, Switzerland; tel. (031) 431762; telex 912063; f. 1893 as General Secretariat of the Union of States adhering to the international conventions regulating the carriage of goods, passengers, and baggage by rail (CIM and CIV), as subsequently revised;

maintains and publishes lists of lines on which international carriage is undertaken; circulates communications from the contracting States and railways to other States and railways; publishes information on behalf of international transport services; undertakes conciliation, gives an advisory opinion or assists in arbitration on disputes arising between railways; examines requests for the amendment of the conventions and convenes conferences. Mems: 33 states. Dir-Gen. PETER TRACHSEL. Publ. *Bulletin des Transports Internationaux par Chemins de Fer* (every 2 months, in French and German).

Danube Commission: Benczúr utca 25, 1068 Budapest, Hungary; tel. 228-083; f. 1948 to supervise facilities for shipping on the Danube; holds annual sessions; approves projects for river maintenance, supervises a uniform system of traffic regulations on the whole navigable portion of the Danube. Mems: seven countries on the Danube. Pres. B. I. STOUKALINE (USSR); Sec. O. DUREJ (Czechoslovakia). Publs *Basic Regulations for Navigation on the Danube, Hydrological Yearbook, Statistical Yearbook*, documentation.

European Civil Aviation Conference—ECAC: 3 bis Villa Emile-Bergerat, 92522 Neuilly-sur-Seine Cedex, France; tel. (1) 46-37-96-96; telex 610075; f. 1955 to review the development of European air transport with the object of promoting the co-ordination, the better utilization, and the orderly development of such air transport, and to consider any special problem that might arise in this field. Mems: 22 European states. Pres. ROLF KÜNZI; Sec. EDWARD HUDSON.

European Conference of Ministers of Transport—ECMT: 19 rue Franqueville, 75775 Paris Cedex 16, France; tel. (1) 45-24-82-00; telex 611040; f. 1953 to achieve the maximum use and most rational development of European inland transport. Council of Ministers of Transport meets twice yearly; Committee of Deputy Ministers meets six times a year and is assisted by Subsidiary Bodies concerned with; General Transport Policy, Railways, Roads, Inland Waterways, Investment, Road and Traffic Signs and Signals, Urban Safety and Economic Research. Mems: 19 European countries; Associate Mems: Australia, Canada, Japan, USA. Chair. JOHAN J. JAKOBSEN (Norway); Sec.-Gen. Dr J.-C. TERLOUW.

European Organisation for the Safety of Air Navigation—EUROCONTROL: 72 rue de la Loi, 1040 Brussels, Belgium; tel. (02) 233-02-11; telex 21173; f. 1963 to strengthen co-operation among member states in matters of air navigation and in particular to provide for the common organization of air traffic services in the upper airspace. Permanent Commission is governing body, consisting of two representatives from each member state, who are the Ministers responsible for civil and military aviation; there are four Directorates: Operations, Engineering, Personnel and Finance, and General Secretariat. The EUROCONTROL External Services comprise the Eurocontrol Experimental Centre, the EUROCONTROL Institute of Air Navigation Services, the Central Route Charges Office and the Upper Area Control Centre at Maastricht, Netherlands. Budget (1986) EUA 142m., including EUA 33.1m. for the joint financing of the operating costs of traffic control services for the upper airspace of the Benelux/Federal Republic of Germany region. Mems: Belgium, France, Federal Republic of Germany, Ireland, Luxembourg, Netherlands, Portugal, United Kingdom. Pres. Perm. Commission HERMAN DE CROO (Belgium); Pres. Cttee of Management J. V. FEEHAN (Ireland); Dir-Gen. HORST FLENTJE (FRG).

European Passenger Train Time-Table Conference: Direction générale des chemins de fer fédéraux suisses, Hochschulstrasse 6, 3030 Berne, Switzerland; tel. (031) 601111; telex 991121; f. 1923 to arrange international passenger connections by rail and water and to help obtain easing of customs and passport control at frontier stations. Mems: rail and steamship companies and administrations, representatives of governments and other organizations in 25 countries. Administered by the Directorate of the Swiss Federal Railways.

European Railway Wagon Pool—EUROP: SNCB, Direction Exploitation, 85 rue de France, 1070 Brussels, Belgium; tel. (02) 525-21-30; telex 21526; f. 1953 for the common use of wagons put into the pool by member railways. Mems: nine national railway administrations. Managing railway: Belgian Railways. Pres. J. DEKEMPENEER.

Institute of Air Transport: 103 rue La Boétie, 75008 Paris, France; tel. (1) 43-59-38-68; telex 642584; f. 1945 to serve as an international centre of research on economic, technical and policy aspects of air transport, and on the economy and sociology of transport and tourism; acts as economic and technical consultant in carrying out research requested by members on specific subjects; maintains a data bank, a library and a consultation and advice service; organizes training courses on air transport economics.

Mems: organizations involved in air transport, production and equipment, universities, banks, insurance companies, private individuals and government agencies in 79 different countries. Pres. JEAN-MICHEL AMIRAULT; Dir-Gen. JACQUES PAVAUX. Publs in French and English, *Studies* (about 6 a year), *ITA Magazine* (monthly), *ITA Newsletter* (monthly).

International Air Transport Association—IATA: POB 160, 26 chemin de Joinville, 1216 Cointrin-Geneva, Switzerland; tel. (022) 983366; telex 23391; f. 1945 to promote safe, regular and economic air transport, to foster air commerce and to provide a means of international air transport collaboration. Fields of activity: finance (through IATA Clearing House for international accounts), technical problems, air traffic fares and documentation, international law on conditions of contract and carriage, documentation and information research and international co-operation. Exec. Cttee of 25 members, assisted by Financial, Legal, Technical and Traffic Cttees; Tariff Co-ordinating Conferences on fares and rates meet regularly; there are Traffic Service Offices in Montreal and Singapore; Regional Technical Offices for Africa in Nairobi and Dakar, Europe in Geneva, Middle East, North Atlantic/North America in London, South America/Caribbean in Rio de Janeiro and South East Asia/Pacific in Bangkok. Mems: 137 companies. Pres. MOHAMMED MEKOUAR (Morocco); Dir-Gen. GÜNTER ESER; Corporate Sec. Mrs H. AUBRY.

International Association for the Rhine Vessels Register—IVR: Koningin Emmaplein 6, 3016 AA Rotterdam (POB 23210, 3001 KE Rotterdam), Netherlands; tel. (010) 4361133; telex 22600; f. 1947 for the classification of Rhine ships, the organization and publication of a Rhine ships register and for the unification of general average rules, etc. Mems: shipowners and associations, insurers and associations, shipbuilding engineers, average adjusters and others interested in Rhine traffic. Dir J. W. THISSEN.

International Association of Ports and Harbors: Kotohira-Kaikan Bldg, 2-8 Toranomon 1-chome, Minato-ku, Tokyo 105, Japan; tel. (03) 591-4261; telex 02222516; f. 1955 to increase the efficiency of ports and harbours through the dissemination of information relative to the fields of port organization, management, administration, operation, development and promotion; to encourage the growth of water-borne commerce. Mems: 359 in 78 states. Pres. J. DEN TOOM (Netherlands); Sec.-Gen. Dr HAJIME SATO (Japan). Publs *Ports and Harbors* (10 a year), *Membership Directory* (annually), *Proceedings of Conference*.

International Automobile Federation: 8 place de la Concorde, 75008 Paris, France; tel. (1) 42-65-34-70; telex 290442; f. 1904 to develop international automobile sport and motor touring. Represented at ECOSOC (UN), Council of Europe and EEC. Mems: 106 national automobile clubs or associations in 93 countries. Pres. JEAN-MARIE BALESTRE; Sec.-Gen. J. J. FREVILLE.

International Chamber of Shipping: 30/32 St. Mary Axe, London, EC3A 8ET, England; tel. (01) 283-2922; telex 884008; f. 1921 to promote the interests of its members, primarily in the technical and legal fields of shipping operations. Mems: national associations representative of free enterprise shipowners in 35 countries, covering two-thirds of merchant shipping from the non-communist countries. Sec.-Gen. J. C. S. HORROCKS. Publs various technical publications on safety, pollution and operational questions.

International Civil Airports Association—ICAA: Bâtiment 226, Orly Sud 103, 94396 Orly Aérogare Cedex, France; tel. (1) 48-84-59-88; telex 261120; f. 1962 to develop relations and co-operation among civil airports throughout the world and promote the interests of air transport in general. Mems: 240 from 86 countries and territories. Pres. CLIFTON A. MOORE (USA); Dir-Gen. JACQUES BLOCK (France). Publs *ICAA Weekly, ICAA News*.

International Container Bureau: 14 rue Jean Rey, 75015 Paris, France; tel. (1) 47-34-68-13; telex 270835; f. 1933 to group representatives of all means of transport and activities concerning containers, to promote combined door-to-door transport by the successive use of several means of transport; to examine and bring into effect administrative, technical and customs advances and to centralize data on behalf of its members. Mems: 800. Pres. C. SEIDELMANN. Publs *Containers* (quarterly), *Container Bulletin*.

International Federation of Freight Forwarders' Associations: 29 Brauerstrasse, POB 177, 8026 Zürich, Switzerland; f. 1926 to protect and represent its members at international level. Mems: 60 organizations and 1,400 associate members in 130 countries. Pres. A. N. PARIKH; Sec.-Gen. Dr F. GYSSENS; Dir-Gen. W. ZEILBECK. Publ. *FIATA News* (quarterly).

International Rail Transport Committee: Direction générale des chemins de fer fédéraux suisses, Service juridique, 43 Mittelstrasse, 3030 Berne, Switzerland; tel. (031) 602565; telex 691212; f.

OTHER INTERNATIONAL ORGANIZATIONS

Transport, Youth and Students

1902 for the development of international law relating to railway transport on the basis of the Convention concerning International Carriage by Rail and its Appendices, and for the adoption of standard rules on other questions relating to international transport law. Mems: 300 transport undertakings in 33 countries Pres. M. LATSCHA (Switzerland); Sec. M. BERTHERIN (Switzerland).

International Railway Congress Association: 85 rue de France, 1070 Brussels, Belgium; tel. (02) 522-62-83; f. 1885 to facilitate the progress and development of railways by the holding of periodical congresses and by means of publications. Mems: governments, railway administrations and national or international organizations. Pres. E. FLACHET; Sec.-Gen. L. VERBERCKT. Publs *Rail International* (monthly in French, German, Russian and English), *Selection of International Railway Documentation* (in French, German, English and Spanish).

International Road Federation—IRF: 525 School St, SW, Washington, DC 20024, USA; f. 1948 to encourage the development and improvement of highways and highway transportation; organizes World Highway Conferences. Mems: 68 national road associations and 500 individual firms and industrial associations. *Geneva:* Chair. JEAN CLOUET; Dir-Gen. Count F. ARCO; *Washington:* Chair. DANA E. LOW; Pres. W. J. WILSON. Publs *World Road Statistics* (annually, Geneva), *Routes du Monde* (8 a year), *World Highways* (9 a year), *IRF Directory of World Road Administrators* (Geneva/Washington).

International Road Safety: 75 rue de Mamer, 8081 Luxembourg-Bertrange; tel. 31 83 41; telex 2338; f. 1959 for exchange of ideas and material on road safety; organizes international action; assists non-member countries; consultative status at UN and Council of Europe. Mems: 58 national organizations. Pres. L. NILLES. Publ. quarterly liaison bulletin.

International Road Transport Union—IRU: Centre International, 3 rue de Varembé, BP 44, 1202 Geneva, Switzerland; tel. (022) 341330; telex 27107; f. 1948 to study all problems of road transport, to promote unification and simplification of regulations relating to road transport, and to develop the use of road transport for passengers and goods. Mems: 113 national federations for road transport and interested groups, in 52 countries. Sec.-Gen. P. GROENENDIJK.

International Shipping Federation Ltd: 30/32 St Mary Axe, London, EC3A 8ET, England; tel. (01) 283-2922; telex 884008; f. 1909 to consider all personnel questions affecting the interests of shipowners; responsible for Shipowners' Group at conferences of the International Labour Organisation. Mems: national shipowners' organizations in 28 countries. Pres. W. N. MENZIES-WILSON (UK); Dir F. J. WHITWORTH; Sec. D. A. DEARSLEY.

International Union for Inland Navigation: 1 place de Lattre, 67000 Strasbourg, France; tel. (88) 36-01-80; telex 87005; f. 1952 to promote the interests of inland waterways carriers before all international organizations. Mems: national waterways organizations of Belgium, France, Federal Republic of Germany, Italy, Luxembourg, Netherlands, Switzerland, United Kingdom. Pres. D. GALLI (Switzerland); Sec. H. MULLENBACH (France). Publs annual and occasional reports.

International Union of Public Transport: 19 ave de l'Uruguay, 1050 Brussels, Belgium; tel. (02) 673-04-66; telex 63916; f. 1885 to study all problems connected with the urban and regional public passenger transport industry. Mems: 350 public transport systems in 63 countries, 250 contractors and services and 1,500 personal members. Pres. I. BÄCKSTRÖM (Sweden); Sec.-Gen. PIERRE LACONTE. Publs *Review* (quarterly), Congress reports and proceedings, *Biblio-Index* (quarterly), Compendium of Statistics.

International Union of Railways: 14 rue Jean-Rey, 75015 Paris, France; tel. (1) 42-73-01-20; telex 270835; f. 1922 for the harmonization of railway operations; collects and makes available material concerning economic, legal, social and technical aspects of railways. Mems: 85 railways. Chair. R. GOHLKE; Sec.-Gen. J. BOULEY. Publs *Rail International,* jointly with the International Railway Congress Association (IRCA) (monthly, in English, French and German), *Selection of International Railway Documentation,* jointly with the IRCA (10 a year, in English, French, German and Spanish), *International Railway Statistics* (annually, in English, French and German), *Annual Report,* lexicons and technical handbooks.

Northern Shipowners' Defence Club (Nordisk Skibsrederforening): Kristinelundv. 22, POB 3033 El., 0207 Oslo 2, Norway; f. 1889 to assist members in disputes over contracts, taking the necessary legal steps on behalf of members and bearing the cost of such claims. Members are mainly Finnish, Swedish and Norwegian and some non-Scandinavian shipowners, representing about 1,500 ships and drilling rigs with gross tonnage of about 37 million. Man.

Dir NICHOLAS HAMBRO; Chair. FRIDTJOF LORENTZEN. Publ. *A Law Report of Scandinavian Maritime Cases* (annually), and a quarterly members' periodical.

Organisation for the Collaboration of Railways: Hożà 63–67, Warsaw, Poland; tel. 21 61 54; f. 1956 for the development of international traffic and technical and scientific co-operation in the sphere of railway and road traffic. Conference of Ministers of member countries meets annually. Mems: railway and road traffic administrations of the People's Republic of China, Cuba, Democratic People's Republic of Korea, Mongolia, Viet-Nam, Albania, Bulgaria, Czechoslovakia, German Democratic Republic, Hungary, Poland, Romania and USSR. Chair. Dr RYSZARD STAWROWSKI (Poland). Publ. *O.S.SH.D. Journal* (bi-monthly; in Chinese, German and Russian).

Orient Airlines Association: 5th Floor, Standard Bldg, 151 Paseo de Roxas Ave, Manila, Philippines; tel. 8190151; f. 1967; member carriers exchange information and plan the development of the industry within the region by means of research, technical, security, data processing and marketing committees. Mems: Air Viet-Nam (inactive), Cathay Pacific Airways Ltd, China Airlines, Japan Air Lines, Korean Air Lines, Malaysian Airline System, Philippine Airlines, Qantas Airways Ltd, Singapore Airlines, Royal Brunei Airlines and Thai Airways International. Sec.-Gen. HIDEO MITSUHASHI. Publs *MIC Monthly Bulletin, Annual Report, Operating Manual.*

Pan American Railway Congress Association (Asociación del Congreso Panamericano de Ferrocarriles): Av. 9 de Julio 1925, Piso 13, 1332 Buenos Aires, Argentina; tel. 38 4625; telex 0122507; f. 1907; present title adopted 1941; aims to promote the development and progress of railways in the American continent; structure: Congresses (held every three years in capital cities of the member states; 16th Congress, Washington, DC, 1984), Permanent Commission, Executive Committee, national commissions. Mems: government representatives, railway enterprises and individuals in 26 countries. Pres. JUAN CARLOS DE MARCHI (Argentina); Gen. Sec. CAYETANO MARLETTA RAINIERI (Argentina). Publ. *Technical Bulletin* (every 2 months).

Trans-Sahara Liaison Committee: c/o Ministère des Travaux Publiques, 135 rue Didouche Mourade, Algiers, Algeria; f. 1964 to study and build a Trans-Saharan Road and to obtain the necessary finance; the Algerian section as far as Tamanrasset was opened in June 1978, and work then began on the next section, running into Niger; with UNDP backing a feasibility study was made and an international consortium was engaged for designing the project; estimated cost for the road, 7 metres wide and 2,800 km in total length, is US $300m. Mems: Algeria, Mali, Niger, Nigeria and Tunisia.

Union of European Railway Industries: 12 rue Bixio, 75007 Paris, France; tel. (1) 47-05-36-62; telex 270105; f. 1975 as a union of associations which represent companies concerned in the manufacture of railway equipment in Europe, in order to represent their collective interests towards all European and international organizations concerned. Chair. M. O. J. BRONCHART; Sec.-Gen. J. L. BURCKHARDT.

Union of European Railway Road Services: Direction générale de la Société Nationale des Chemins de Fer Français (SNCF), 88 rue Saint-Lazare, 75436 Paris, France; f. 1950/1951; runs the EUROPABUS international railway road services, an international network of scheduled coach services covering 100,000 km. Mems: railway administrations in Austria, Belgium, Denmark, France, Federal Republic of Germany, Greece, Hungary, Italy, Luxembourg, Netherlands, Norway, Portugal, Spain, Sweden, Switzerland and the United Kingdom. Pres. LOUIS LACOSTE (France); Sec.-Gen. (vacant).

World Airlines Clubs Association: c/o IATA, Suite 3050, 2000 Peel St, Montreal, Quebec, Canada H3A 2R4; f. 1966; holds a General Assembly annually, regional meetings, international events and sports tournaments. Mems: 98 clubs in 42 countries. Pres. DAVID LARKIN (UK); Man. JOSEPH LEDWOS. Publs *WACA World, WACA Contact, WACA World News,* annual report.

Youth and Students

Asian Students' Association: 511 Nathan Rd, 1/F, Kowloon, Hong Kong; tel. 3-311234; telex 66347; f. 1969 to help in the solution of local and regional problems; to assist in promotion of an Asian identity; to promote programmes of common benefit to member organizations; since 1972 the organization has opposed all forms of colonialism or foreign intervention in Asia; activities: Conference,

OTHER INTERNATIONAL ORGANIZATIONS — Youth and Students

Seminars, Workshops. There are four Student Commissions for Economics, Education, Students' Rights and Women's Affairs. Mems: 13 national or regional student unions, five assoc. mems. Sec.-Gen. EMMANUEL CALONZO. Publ. *Asian Student News.*

Council of European National Youth Committees—CENYC: 120 rue du Cornet, 1040 Brussels, Belgium; f. 1963 to further the consciousness of European youth and to represent the European National Co-ordinating Committees of youth work vis-à-vis European institutions. Activities include research on youth problems in Europe; projects, seminars, study groups, study tours; the Council provides a forum for the exchange of information, experiences and ideas between members, and represents European youth organizations in relations with other regions; has observer status with the Council of Europe and UNESCO. Mems: national committees in 17 countries. Sec.-Gen. ALAN CHRISTIE (UK). Publs *CENYC Information* (quarterly), *CENYC Newsletter* (2 a year).

Council on International Educational Exchange: 205 East 42nd St, New York, NY 10017, USA; tel. (212) 661-1414; f. 1947; issues International Student Identity Card entitling holders to discounts and to accommodation in student hostels and restaurants; arranges passage on intra-European student flights and trans-Atlantic transport; offers students short-term unskilled jobs in Europe and New Zealand for full-time US university students, and similar work programmes in the USA for students from participating countries in Europe and New Zealand; provides low-cost accommodation in New York City; co-ordinates summer programmes in the USA for foreign students and teachers; sponsors conferences on educational exchange; publications list overseas programmes for high school and college students, sources of information on independent student travel abroad and describe transport and student travel services. Mems: 186 student organizations. Exec. Dir JACK EGLE. Publs include *Annual Report, Whole World Handbook, Campus Update* (monthly).

International Association for the Exchange of Students for Technical Experience—IAESTE: Instituto Superior Técnico, Av. Rovisco Pais, 1096 Lisbon Codex, Portugal; tel. 890844; telex 63423; f. 1948. Mems: 49 national committees. Gen. Sec. Prof. BERNARDO J. HEROLD. Publ. *Annual Report.*

International Association of Dental Students: c/o Mr Lynn Walters, Medical Protection Society Ltd, 50 Hallam St, London, W1N 6DE, England; f. 1951 to represent dental students and their opinions internationally, to promote dental student exchanges and international congresses. Mems: 10,000 students in 14 countries. Pres. S. HAMEED (Singapore); Sec.-Gen. S. SMITH (UK). Publ. *IADS Newsletter* (3 a year).

International Association of Students in Economics and Business Management: 40 rue Washington, POB 10, 1050 Brussels, Belgium; tel. (02) 648-88-03; telex 65080; f. 1948 to promote understanding between members and practical management experience, through international education programmes, e.g. trainee exchanges, seminars, conferences and study tours. Mems: 40,000 from 532 universities in 62 countries. Pres. MARTIN BEAN. Publs *Compendium, Annual Report, Linkletter, Programmes Manual,* etc.

International Federation of Medical Students Associations: 1090 Vienna, Liechtensteinstr. 13, Austria; tel. (022) 31-55-66; telex 116706; f. 1951 to study and promote the professional interests of medical students throughout the world; improve medical education, medical student health and arrange international exchanges. Mems: national associations in 46 countries, corresponding mems in 50 countries. Sec.-Gen. FEDERICO MAHRER. Publs *Medical Students—How to go Abroad, Intermedica, IFMSA Information Service, Introducing IFMSA, IFMSA Internal Information.*

International Pharmaceutical Students' Federation: 4 Hachartzit St, Kiryat Rishon, Rishon Lezion 75100, Israel; tel. (03) 9612597; telex 35855; f. 1949 to study and promote the interests of pharmaceutical students and to encourage international co-operation. Mems: 27 national organizations and 17 local associations. Pres. RUI DOS SANTOS IVO; Sec.-Gen. ILAN KREISER. Publ. *IPSF News Bulletin* (3 a year).

International Union of Students: POB 58, 17 November St, 110 01 Prague 01, Czechoslovakia; tel. 231 28 12; telex 122858; f. 1946 to defend the rights and interests of students and strive for peace, disarmament, the eradication of illiteracy and of all forms of discrimination; activities include conferences, meetings, solidarity campaigns, relief projects, award of 300 scholarships, travel and exchange, sports events, cultural projects. Mems: 109 organizations from 105 countries. Pres. MIROSLAV ŠTĚPÁN (Czechoslovakia); Gen. Sec. GIORGOS MICHAELIDES (Cyprus). Publs *World Student News* (monthly), *News Service* (fortnightly), *Young Cinema and Theatre* (quarterly), *DE—Democratization of Education* (quarterly), regional bulletins and newsletters.

International Young Christian Workers: 11 rue Plantin, 1070 Brussels, Belgium; tel. (02) 521-69-83; f. 1945, on the inspiration of the Priest-Cardinal Joseph Cardijin; aims to educate young workers to take on present and future responsibilities in their commitment to the working class, and to confront all the situations which prevent them from fulfilling themselves. Pres. JUANITO PENEQUITO (Philippines); Sec.-Gen. SAGRARIO GUERRERO (Spain).

International Youth and Student Movement for the United Nations—ISMUN: Palais des Nations, 1211 Geneva 10, Switzerland; tel. (022) 330861; f. 1948 by the World Federation of United Nations Associations, independent since 1949; an international non-governmental organization of students and young people dedicated especially to supporting the principles embodied in the United Nations Charter and Universal Declaration of Human Rights. The Movement encourages constructive action in building economic, social and cultural equality and in working for national independence, social justice and human rights on a worldwide scale; regional offices in Austria, France, Ghana, Panama and the USA. Mems: associations in 53 countries. Sec.-Gen. JUAN CARLOS GIACOSA. Publs *ISMUN Newsletter* (monthly), documents on human rights, disarmament and economic and social development; seminar reports and background papers.

International Youth Hostel Federation: Midland Bank Chambers, Howardsgate, Welwyn Garden City, Herts., AL8 6BT, England; tel. (0707) 324170; telex 298784; f. 1932; facilitates international travel by members of the various youth hostel associations and advises and helps in the formation of youth hostel associations in all countries where no such organizations exist; records over 33m. overnight stays annually in 5,000 youth hostels. Mems: 56 national associations with 4m. individual members; 18 associated national organizations. Pres. OTTO WIRTHENSOHN (FRG); Sec.-Gen. DENNIS LEWIS (Canada). Publs *Annual Report, Handbook* (annually), *Manual, Monthly News Bulletin, Phrase Book.*

Jaycees International: 400 University Drive (POB 140-577), Coral Gables, Fla 33134-0577, USA; tel. (305) 446-7608; telex 441084; f. 1944 to encourage and advance international understanding and goodwill. Jaycee organizations throughout the world provide young people with opportunities for leadership training, promoting goodwill through international fellowship, solving civic problems by arousing civic consciousness and discussing social, economic and cultural questions. Mems: national organizations in 83 countries grouping more than 450,000 persons. Pres. MONCEF BAROUNI; Sec.-Gen. W. DANIEL LAMEY. Publs *Leader* (annually, in English, Spanish, French, Japanese, Korean and Chinese), handbooks.

Latin American Confederation of Young Men's Christian Associations (Confederación Latinoamericana de Asociaciones Cristianas de Jóvenes): Casilla 172, Montevideo, Uruguay; tel. 49-71-94; telex 23106; f. 1914 to unite the Young Men's Christian Associations of the continent; to secure the more effective accomplishment of its aims, which are the moral, spiritual, intellectual, social and physical development of young men; to strengthen the work of the Associations and to sponsor the establishment of new Associations. Mems: affiliated YMCAs in 14 countries, with over 500,000 individuals. Pres. FRANCISCO SALES DIAS HORTA (Brazil); Gen. Sec. EDGARDO CROVETTO (Peru). Publs *Articulos Técnicos, Revista Trimestral, Informes Internacionales.*

Pan-African Youth Movement (Mouvement pan-africain de la jeunesse): 19 rue Debbih Chérif, Algiers, Algeria; tel. 57-19-78; telex 61244; f. 1962; promotes political independence and the economic, social and cultural development of Africa; serves as the voice of African youth in regional and international forums. Mems: over 40 organizations. Sec.-Gen. HAMADOUN IBRAHIM ISSEBERE. Publ. *MPJ News* (quarterly).

World Alliance of Young Men's Christian Associations: 37 quai Wilson, 1201 Geneva; tel. (022) 323100; telex 27332; f. 1855 to unite the National Alliances of Young Men's Christian Associations throughout the world. Mems: national alliances and related associations in 90 countries. Pres. JAMES R. BELLATTI; Sec.-Gen. LEE SOO-MIN. Publ. *World Communique* (quarterly).

World Association of Girl Guides and Girl Scouts: Olave Centre, 12C Lyndhurst Rd, London, NW3 5PQ, England; tel. (01) 794-1181; f. 1928 to promote unity of purpose and common understanding in the fundamental principles of the Girl Guide and Girl Scout Movement throughout the world and to encourage friendship amongst girls of all nations within frontiers and beyond. The supreme body of the World Association is the World Conference. The World Committee, consisting of 12 members, meeting at least once a year, acts on behalf of the World Conference between its triennial meetings. Mems: about 8m. individuals in 81 organizations and 27 associate member-organizations. Chair. World Cttee DORIS STOCKMANN; Dir World Bureau ELLEN CLARK; Publs *Triennial Report, Trefoil Round the World, Newsletter,* reference books, booklets, etc.

World Council of Young Men's Service Clubs: c/o John Weatherall, Kamloops, Maple Ave, Bishops Stortford, Herts., CM 23 2RP England; f. 1946 to provide a means of exchange of information and news for furthering international understanding and co-operation, to facilitate the extension of young men's service clubs, and to create in young men a sense of civic responsibility. Mems: 3,982 clubs and 96,000 members in 37 Associations in 65 countries. Pres. JOSEPH ZAMMIT TABONA (Malta).

World Federalist Youth/Youth Movement for a New International Order—WFY/NIO Youth: Leliegracht 21, 1016 GR Amsterdam, Netherlands; tel. (020) 261993; works for a new international order fulfilling the conditions for responsible use and fair distribution of the world's resources, full realization of human rights, and decentralization of decision-making; seminars and daily political work on the problems of the Third World (development, liberation), East-West relations (détente) and important problems dealt with by the UN and specialized agencies (food, population, law of the seas, etc.). Mems: 37 organizations. Chair. POUL HVILSTED. Publs *Transnational Perspectives* (quarterly), *Progress Report* (bi-monthly), *LLDCs—Campaign Newsletter* (quarterly).

World Federation of Catholic Youth: 31 ave de l'Hôpital Français, 1080 Brussels, Belgium; f. 1968 to bring together organizations of Catholic youth in order to promote Christian engagement of young people in church and world. 84 affiliated organizations and 32 corresponding centres in five continents representing about 10m. members. Pres. MARIETTE THILL (Luxembourg); Sec.-Gen. LEO VERSWIJVEL. Publ. *Informations/Informaciones* (English, French and Spanish).

World Federation of Democratic Youth—WFDY: POB 147, 1389 Budapest, Hungary; tel. 154-095; telex 22-7197; f. 1945 to strive for peace and disarmament and joint action by democratic and progressive youth movements in support of national independence, democracy, social progress and youth rights; to support liberation struggles in Asia, Africa and Latin America; and to work for a new and more just international economic order; 12th Assembly, Budapest, Hungary, November 1986. Mems: 270 organizations in 115 countries. Pres. WALID MASRI (Lebanon); Gen. Sec. VILMOS CSERVENY (Hungary). Publs *WFDY News* (fortnightly, in English, French and Spanish), *World Youth* (monthly, in English, French and Spanish).

World Organization of the Scout Movement: Case Postale 78, 1211 Geneva 4, Switzerland; tel. (022) 204233; telex 428139; f. 1920 to promote unity and understanding of scouting throughout the world; to develop good citizenship among young people by forming their characters for service, co-operation and leadership; to provide aid and advice to members and potential member associations; acts as the Secretariat of the World Scout Conference; Regional Offices in Costa Rica, Egypt, Kenya, the Philippines and Switzerland. Mems: over 16m. in 150 countries and territories. Sec.-Gen. Dr L. NAGY (Switzerland). Publs *World Scouting Newsletter* (monthly), *Biennial Report,* regional and departmental bulletins, handbooks.

World Union of Jewish Students: POB 7914, 91077 Jerusalem, Israel; f. 1924; organization for national student bodies concerned with educational and political matters where possible in co-operation with non-Jewish student organizations, UNESCO, etc.; divided into six regions; organizes Congress every three years. Mems: 35 national unions representing over 700,000 students. Chair. DAVID MAKOVSKY (USA); Exec. Dir DANIEL YOSSEF (UK). Publs *Shofar, WUJS Report.*

World Young Women's Christian Association—World YWCA: 37 quai Wilson, 1201 Geneva, Switzerland; tel. (022) 323100; f. 1894 for the linking together of national YWCAs in 83 countries for their mutual help and development and the initiation of work in countries where the Association does not yet exist; works for international understanding, for improved social and economic conditions and for basic human rights for all people. Pres. ANN NORTHCOTE; Gen. Sec. ELAINE H. GREIF. Publs *Annual Report, Programme of International Co-operation, Programme Material, Common Concern.*

PART TWO
Afghanistan–Jordan

AFGHANISTAN

Introductory Survey

Location, Climate, Language, Religion, Flag, Capital

The Democratic Republic of Afghanistan is a land-locked country in south-western Asia. Its neighbours are the USSR to the north, Iran to the west, China to the north-east and Pakistan to the east and south. The climate varies sharply between the highlands and lowlands; the temperature in the south-west in summer reaches 48.8°C (120°F), but in the winter, in the Hindu Kush mountains of the north-east, it falls to −26°C (−15°F). Of the many languages spoken in Afghanistan, the principal two are Pashtu and Dari (a dialect of Persian). The majority of Afghans are Muslims of the Sunni sect; there are also minority groups of Hindus, Sikhs and Jews. The national flag has three equal horizontal stripes, of red, black and green, with a superimposed emblem of an open book under a candle, surrounded by stylized heads of grain. The capital is Kabul.

Recent History

The last King of Afghanistan, Zahir Shah, reigned from 1933 to 1973. His country was neutral during both World Wars and became a staunch advocate of non-alignment. In 1953 the King's cousin, Lt-Gen. Sardar Mohammad Daud Khan, became Prime Minister and, securing aid from the USSR, initiated a series of economic plans for the modernization of the country. In 1963 Gen. Daud resigned and Dr Mohammad Yusuf became the first Prime Minister not of royal birth. He introduced a new democratic constitution which combined western ideas with Islamic religious and political beliefs, but the King never allowed political parties to operate. Afghanistan made little progress under the succeeding Prime Ministers.

In July 1973, while King Zahir was in Italy, the monarchy was overthrown by a coup, in which the main figure was the former Prime Minister, Gen. Daud. The 1964 constitution was abolished and Afghanistan was declared a republic. Daud renounced his royal titles and took office as Head of State, Prime Minister and Minister of Foreign Affairs and Defence.

A Loya Jirgah (National Assembly), appointed from among notable elders by provincial governors, was convened in January 1977 and adopted a new constitution, providing for presidential government and a one-party state. Daud was elected to continue as President for six years and the Assembly was then dissolved. In March 1977 President Daud formed a new civilian government, nominally ending military rule. However, during 1977 there was growing discontent with Daud, especially within the armed forces, and in April 1978 a coup, known (from the month) as the 'Saur Revolution', ousted the President, who was killed with several members of his family.

Nur Mohammad Taraki, imprisoned leader of the formerly banned People's Democratic Party of Afghanistan (PDPA), was released and installed as President of the Revolutionary Council and Prime Minister. The country was renamed the Democratic Republic of Afghanistan, the year-old constitution was abolished and no political parties other than the communist PDPA were allowed to function. Afghanistan's already close relations with the USSR were further strengthened. However, opposition to the new regime led to armed insurrection, particularly by Islamic groups, in almost all provinces, and the flight of thousands of refugees to Pakistan and Iran. In spite of purges of the army and civil service, Taraki's position became increasingly insecure, and in September 1979 he was ousted by Hafizullah Amin, who had been Deputy Prime Minister and Minister of Foreign Affairs since March. Amin's imposition of rigorous communist policies was unsuccessful and unpopular. In December 1979 he was removed and killed in a coup that was supported by the entry into Afghanistan of about 80,000 combat troops from the USSR. This incursion by Soviet armed forces into a traditionally non-aligned neighbouring country aroused world-wide condemnation. Babrak Karmal, a former Deputy Prime Minister under Taraki, was installed as the new Head of State, having been flown into Kabul by a Soviet aircraft from virtual exile in Eastern Europe.

Riots, strikes and inter-factional strife and purges continued into 1980 and 1981. President Karmal centralized his authority by reorganizing government departments within the Prime Minister's Office in July 1980. Sultan Ali Keshtmand took over from Karmal as Prime Minister in June 1981: In the hope of strengthening the position of Karmal's Parcham ('Flag') faction of the PDPA over the Khalq ('Masses') faction of the party, the Revolutionary Council and the Politburo were enlarged. In the same month the regime launched the long-awaited National Fatherland Front, incorporating the PDPA and other organizations, with the aim of promoting national unity. Neither measure appeared to achieve its aim and the Council of Ministers was reshuffled again in August and September 1982 to strengthen Karmal's Parcham faction further. At its 12th plenum in July 1983, the PDPA Central Committee elected 10 new full members and 16 new alternate members, nearly all of them Parcham supporters.

However, throughout 1984 and 1985, the PDPA regime continued to fail to win widespread popular support. As a result, the Government made a series of moves in an attempt to broaden the base of its support: in April 1985 it summoned a Loya Jirgah (National Assembly), comprising indirectly elected tribal elders, who ratified a new constitution for Afghanistan (see Government, below); a non-PDPA member was appointed chairman of the National Fatherland Front in May 1985; elections were held between August 1985 and March/April 1986 for new local government organs (it was claimed that 60% of those elected were non-party members), and several non-party members were appointed to high-ranking government posts between December 1985 and February 1986.

In May 1986, however, Maj.-Gen. Najib (Najibullah, the former head of the state security service, KHAD) succeeded Karmal as General Secretary of the PDPA. Karmal was allowed to retain the lesser post of President of the Revolutionary Council. In the same month Maj.-Gen. Najib (like Karmal, a member of the Parcham faction) announced the formation of a collective leadership comprising himself, Karmal and Prime Minister Keshtmand. In November 1986, however, Karmal was relieved of all party and government posts. Muhammad Chamkani, formerly Deputy President (and a non-PDPA member), became Acting President of the Revolutionary Council, pending the introduction of a new constitution and the establishment of a permanent legislature.

Fighting between fiercely traditionalist Muslim rebel tribesmen (Mujaheddin) and Afghan army units had begun in the eastern provinces after the 1978 coup and was aggravated by the implementation of social and economic reforms by the new administrations. The Afghan army relied heavily upon Soviet military aid in the form of weapons, equipment and expertise, but morale and resources were severely affected by defections to the rebels' ranks: numbers fell from about 80,000 men in 1978 to about 40,000 in 1985. A vigorous recruitment drive and stricter conscription regulations, implemented by Najib in June 1986, failed to increase the size of the Afghan army by any great extent, and the defections continued. In July 1986 an estimated 115,000 Soviet troops were still in Afghanistan to help the regime to keep order. It is also suspected that, in 1985, the USSR sent into Afghanistan special purpose forces ('spetsnaz'), trained to carry out ambushes, assassinations and infiltration. Between 1980 and 1985, government forces mounted a series of major campaigns in the Panjsher Valley, about 130 km north of Kabul, through which runs the main road between the capital and the border with the USSR, and which has been the scene of some of the most obstinate resistance to successive Soviet-supported regimes; the results, however, were inconclusive. By 1986 it was estimated that more than 10,000 Soviet troops had been killed or wounded in Afghanistan.

AFGHANISTAN

In 1984–86 the guerrilla groups, which had been poorly armed at first, received ever-increasing support (both military and financial) from abroad, notably from the USA (which began to supply them with sophisticated anti-aircraft weapons in 1986) and the People's Republic of China. Despite the Government's decision to seal the border with Pakistan, announced in September 1985, and the strong presence of Soviet forces there, foreign weapons continued to reach the guerrillas via Pakistan. Many of the guerrillas are now based in Pakistan (notably in Peshawar). A major effort has been made to enlist the support of border tribes by offering important concessions, financial inducements and guns in return for their support. A frontier tribal jirgah (assembly), held in September 1985, decided to establish anti-Mujaheddin militias on both sides of the Pakistan border. Throughout 1985 and 1986, the fighting intensified, especially in areas close to the border between Afghanistan and Pakistan. The general pattern of the war, however, remained the same: the regime held the main towns and a few strategic bases, and relied on bombing of both military and civilian targets, and occasional attacks in force, together with conciliatory measures such as the provision of funds for local development, while the rebel forces still dominated rural areas and were capable of causing serious disruption, even in the major towns.

With the civil war came famine in parts of Afghanistan, and there was a mass movement of population from the countryside to Kabul (whose population increased from about 750,000 in 1978 to more than 2m. in 1985), and of refugees to Pakistan and Iran. Relations with Pakistan remained strained because of violations of airspace by Afghan aircraft, the seeking of refuge over the border by rebel tribesmen and Pakistan's refusal to recognize the Soviet-backed Afghan Government. In August 1986 a UNHCR estimate assessed the number of Afghan refugees in Pakistan at 2.5m.–3m. (living in about 380 camps), and the number in Iran at 1.5m.–2m.

Since 1980, extensive international negotiations have taken place to try to bring about complete withdrawal of Soviet forces. The UN General Assembly demanded the withdrawal of foreign troops in eight successive resolutions between 1980 and 1986. In 1980 the Organization of the Islamic Conference, having refused to recognize the Kabul regime until Soviet forces withdrew, established a special committee to negotiate a solution to the problem, but little progress was made. During 1981 further initiatives were proposed by the UN, the EEC and by individual governments, and several attempts were made to begin talks between the Governments of Afghanistan, Pakistan and Iran, with the UN Secretary-General's representative acting as mediator. In August 1981 the Afghan Government expressed its willingness to participate in the trilateral talks, but Pakistan's refusal to recognize the regime, and Iran's insistence that the rebel forces should be included in the negotiations, prevented any progress. Between June 1982 and May 1986, seven rounds of indirect talks took place between the Afghan and Pakistani Ministers of Foreign Affairs in Geneva, under the auspices of the UN. As a result of these talks, agreement was finally reached on three documents relating to the questions of non-interference in each other's affairs, international guarantees of Afghan neutrality (with the USA and the USSR as prospective guarantors), and the safe return of refugees from Pakistan and Iran. Differences continued, however, over the fourth document, which concerned the proposed timetable for the completion of Soviet troop withdrawals and the cessation of external interference, and the talks were suspended indefinitely in August.

In October 1986 the withdrawal from Afghanistan of six Soviet regiments (6,000–8,000 men), including three anti-aircraft regiments, began. Many observers (including the USA and the People's Republic of China, as well as the guerrillas) viewed this withdrawal as a 'token' gesture, timed to coincide with the summit meeting in Iceland between the US President, Ronald Reagan, and the Soviet leader, Mikhail Gorbachev. It was also widely claimed that the withdrawal would have little impact on the conflict, as it involved a relatively small percentage of the total Soviet troops in Afghanistan, and some sources suggested that other troops from the USSR were being drafted into Afghanistan; also, as the guerrillas possessed no aircraft, the withdrawal of anti-aircraft personnel was believed by some to be of limited significance. By November 1986, the USSR, with the agreement of the Afghan Government, had offered a complete withdrawal over four to five years, conditional upon the prior signing of an accord that would deny further foreign support to the guerrillas. Pakistan, however, insisted upon a complete withdrawal within four to five months.

Government

The April 1978 coup brought to power the People's Democratic Party of Afghanistan (PDPA), and no other political party is allowed to function. After the 1978 coup, a Revolutionary Council was established as the principal organ of government. It abrogated the 1977 constitution and assumed legislative functions. Following the coup of December 1979, a new Presidium of the 57-member Council was announced. In April 1980 the Revolutionary Council ratified a declaration of 'Basic Principles', an interim constitution which gave the Council power to rule by decree. In April 1985 a Loya Jirgah (National Assembly), comprising indirectly elected tribal elders, approved a new constitution, closely modelled on the 'Basic Principles'. In January 1986 the Revolutionary Council was expanded to 165 members. To direct their policies, the Central Committee of the PDPA and the Revolutionary Council elect, respectively, a Politburo (with 14 members in December 1986) and a Presidium (to which 18 members were elected in January 1986). Members of the Council of Ministers are nominated by the Central Committee, and their appointments are approved by the Revolutionary Council. The 28 provinces of Afghanistan are each administered by an appointed governor.

Defence

Every able-bodied Afghan male (excepting religious scholars and preachers) between the ages of 15 and 55 years has to serve three years in the army, which was estimated to number 45,000 men in July 1986, but conscription is difficult to enforce and desertions are frequent. Equipment and training are provided largely by the USSR, which, according to Western estimates, in July 1986 had 115,000 troops stationed in Afghanistan. The Afghan air force, which numbered 5,000, is equipped with supersonic jet aircraft. Paramilitary forces include a gendarmerie of 35,000 and numerous regional militias; police security forces come under the Ministry of the Interior.

Economic Affairs

Afghanistan is essentially a tribal society, and in 1982 about 2.6m. of its people were nomadic. Agriculture, which provided employment for an estimated 78% of the settled labour force in 1980, is the mainstay of the economy and accounted for 50% of export earnings and for 63% of gross domestic product (GDP) in 1981/82. Principal agricultural exports include livestock, wool and cotton, fresh and dried fruits, processed hides and skins and medicinal herbs. A programme of land reform was implemented in the first six months of 1979, each landowner receiving no more than 6 ha of redistributed land. In August 1981, however, owing to the unpopularity of this measure, steps were taken effectively to reverse the programme, and by October 1983 the Government had abandoned it in an attempt to improve the regime's popularity. The formation of farm co-operatives was encouraged, and, according to the Government, they numbered nearly 1,300 by 1984. Afghanistan is self-sufficient in food in years of normal output, but in 1979 the country had to import wheat because of reduced production, caused by the agrarian reforms, inadequate rainfall and civil unrest. According to government figures, Afghanistan's annual production of wheat reached 2.8m. metric tons in 1980/81 and 2.9m. tons in 1981/82, 1982/83 and 1983/84. However, shortages of food became a serious problem in 1981 and 1982, as Soviet troops destroyed crops in their efforts to curb the activities of anti-government rebels, who themselves were engaged in fighting rather than farming.

The country is well-endowed with minerals: natural gas (with estimated reserves of over 100,000m. cu m), coal, salt, lapis lazuli, barite and talc are extracted. In May 1980 a new complex for the extraction and purification of gas became operational at Jarquduq, with an annual capacity of 2,000m. cu m. Gas exports to the USSR totalled 2,400m. cu m in 1983/84, according to government figures, and remained at a similar level in 1985/86. The most promising recent discovery is that of 1,700m.

metric tons of high-grade iron ore at Hajigak, although the high altitude of the site was expected to cause problems in exploiting the deposit. According to official plans, other mineral deposits, such as petroleum and copper (estimated total reserves 4.7m. tons), are to be exploited with the help of foreign aid. A copper mining and smelting project has been initiated near Kabul; when completed, this could give Afghanistan a 2% share of world copper production. Energy plans include the development of two small oilfields in the north of the country, which, when fully operational, should satisfy Afghanistan's total needs for petroleum products. Such products have been imported at special low prices from Iran and the USSR, but it is planned to increase internal sources of energy by establishing hydro- and thermal electric power stations. Hydroelectricity constitutes about 80% of energy resources. The first hydroelectric power station to be built since 1978 began operating in October 1983 at Asadabad.

Afghanistan's major manufacturing industries include cotton textiles, chemical fertilizers, leather and plastic goods. The output of cotton textiles in 1980/81, however, was 43.3m. metres, which was insufficient to satisfy domestic demand, and by 1981/82 it had fallen to 26.5m. metres, but in 1982/83 it rose to 38.6m. metres. Cotton exports declined from US $47m. in 1979 to less than $9m. in 1984. The 1979–84 five-year plan proposed a total investment of Afs 105,000m., of which 25% was to be allocated to agriculture in an attempt to triple output. Investment in industry (which employed only 12% of the working population in 1979) and mining was to amount to Afs 43,654m. Compared with 1980, industrial output in 1985 was reported to have risen by 25%, while gross production in the agriculture and forestry sector increased by 5%. During 1981–85 the annual rate of inflation remained at about 20%. In January 1986 the Government announced a Five-Year Economic and Social Development Plan (March 1986–91), involving proposed expenditure of Afs 115,000m. ($2,300m.). The main emphasis of the Plan was on improving the infrastructure and on increasing investment in industry. Of the few Plan objectives to be announced, the extraction of gas condensate was to rise to 6,000 tons annually, and coal output was to double to 370,000 tons per year by 1991; a new petroleum refinery was to be constructed in Jawzjan Province; a unified banking system was to be established, and private businessmen and local merchants were to be encouraged under a government-sponsored system of 'state capitalism'. (Traders account for 45% of foreign trade and 80% of domestic business in Afghanistan.) The economy, which, according to government figures, had expanded by less than 2% annually since 1980, was projected to grow by 25% over the Plan period. Gross industrial production was scheduled to increase by 38% between 1986 and 1991, and agricultural production by 14%–16%. In May 1986 the Economic Consultative Council, the body responsible for economic planning, was restructured.

As well as carpets and rugs, Afghanistan exports fruit and vegetables to Pakistan and India, natural gas and ginned cotton to the USSR (its principal trading partner), oil-cake to Iran and Pakistan and karakul to the European fur markets. Imports include wheat, buses, machinery and petroleum products from the USSR. According to government figures, the two main exporters to Afghanistan in 1982/83 were the USSR (67.1%) and Japan (8.6%); principal importers of Afghanistan goods in 1982/83 were the USSR (50.2%, compared with 35.1% in 1978/79) and Pakistan (8.8%). In 1984/85, according to government figures, the USSR accounted for 56% of Afghanistan's exports (worth $370m.) and 57% of imports (worth $515m.). Foreign trade turnover (imports plus exports) was about $1,400m. in 1985/86, compared with $1,600m. in the previous year. Eastern bloc countries accounted for 71.5% of the total in 1985/86, compared with 61% in 1984/85. In 1985/86 total exports were worth $565m., and imports amounted to $848m. The trade deficit thus widened to $283m., compared with $124m. in 1984/85.

Owing to the backwardness of the economy and continuing civil strife, the Government has had difficulty in raising revenue. About 50% of domestic revenue comes from indirect taxes and only 10% from direct taxes. Revenue from natural gas is the next largest contributor, totalling 21% in 1979 and 34% in 1980. In the 1979–84 plan, socialist countries were to contribute 66% of the foreign aid necessary for basic projects. Aid from Western countries and OPEC members declined from about US $100m. per year in the late 1970s to $23.2m. in 1981. Since 1980 Afghanistan has received foreign aid chiefly from the USSR. Project aid from the USSR in the year to March 1986 totalled US $110m., 73.3% of the total. In 1981 the two countries concluded a mutual trade agreement for the period 1981–85, whereby Afghanistan was to supply the USSR with raw materials, natural gas and food products in return for industrial equipment and machinery. During this period, Soviet trade with Afghanistan was reported to have increased by almost 300%. A further five-year agreement, under which bilateral trade was to expand by 30%, was signed in 1986.

Social Welfare

Workers and employees are entitled to free hospital treatment. Most private companies have their own doctor and hospitals. Disabled people are looked after in social welfare centres in the provincial capitals. In 1977 Afghanistan had 58 hospital establishments, with a total of 3,084 beds. In 1978 there were 906 physicians working in the government health service. Serious damage was reported to have been caused to hospital facilities by the disturbances from 1980 onwards. The estimated average life expectancy at birth in 1980 had fallen by two years from the 1970 figure to 36 years, the lowest in Asia. Between 1975 and 1980, according to UN estimates, there were 205 deaths of children under 12 months old for every 1,000 live births, the highest infant mortality rate in Asia. In 1980 only 20% of the urban population and 3% of the rural population had access to safe water supplies. The average daily intake of calories per person had fallen to 1,775, also the lowest in Asia, although this had risen to 2,280 in 1982, according to government figures. In 1982/83 estimated expenditure on social services was Afs 2,315m., about 20% of the ordinary budget.

Education

It is estimated that the proportion of children aged six to 11 years receiving primary education rose from 9% in 1960 to 23% in 1980. Only 7% of girls in this age-group were enrolled and only 8% of all children aged 12 to 16 attended secondary schools. In 1979 the Government announced the introduction of free and compulsory primary education for children between the ages of seven and 10 years. The 1979–84 five-year plan provided for a literacy campaign and a restructuring of the education system to dilute the Islamic influence. Afghanistan's estimated adult literacy rate of 20% in 1982 was the third lowest in Asia, above only Bhutan and Nepal. In September 1982 the Government announced a plan to eradicate illiteracy by 1990, with 570 schools to be opened in 1982 and with all children attending school by 1987. Basic and secondary education has already been shortened from 12 to 10 years. According to the Government, 1,500 schools have been destroyed, but by 1986 many had been rebuilt. More than 700,000 pupils were being taught by 22,000 teachers at 1,223 schools. Since 1979 higher education has been disrupted by the departure of many teaching staff from Afghanistan. In 1986 many Afghan students and trainees were receiving education at establishments in the USSR. The University of Kabul has 13 faculties, and in 1986 had 6,000 students.

Tourism

Afghanistan's potential attractions for the foreign visitor include: Bamian, with its high statue of Buddha and thousands of painted caves; Bandi Amir, with its suspended lakes; the Blue Mosque of Mazar; Herat, with its Grand Mosque and minarets; the towns of Qandahar and Girishk; Balkh (ancient Bactria), 'Mother of Cities', in the north; Bagram, Hadda and Surkh Kotal (of interest to archaeologists); and the high mountains of the Hindu Kush. However, travel outside Kabul is not generally permitted for foreigners.

Tourism was formerly an important contributor to Afghanistan's foreign currency reserves, raising US $28m. in 1978, but, with the change of regime and internal unrest, the number of visitors declined from over 118,000 in 1977 to only 6,623 in 1980, when income from tourism was $1m. There were 9,200 visitors (including 4,700 from the USSR) in 1981, and about the same number in 1982.

AFGHANISTAN

Public Holidays

The Afghan year 1366 runs from 21 March 1987 to 20 March 1988, and the year 1367 runs from 21 March 1988 to 20 March 1989.

1987: 21 March (Nau-roz: New Year's Day, Iranian calendar), 27 April (Revolution Day), 30 April* (first day of Ramadan), 1 May (Workers' Day), 30 May* (Id al-Fitr, end of Ramadan), 6 August* (Id al-Adha, Feast of the Sacrifice), 18 August (Independence Day), 4 September* (Ashura, Martyrdom of Iman Husayn), 4 November* (Roze-Maulud, Birth of Prophet Muhammad).

1988: 21 March (Nau-roz: New Year's Day, Iranian calendar), 18 April* (first day of Ramadan), 27 April (Revolution Day), 1 May (Workers' Day), 18 May* (Id al-Fitr, end of Ramadan), 25 July* (Id al-Adha, Feast of the Sacrifice), 18 August (Independence Day), 23 August* (Ashura, Martyrdom of Iman Husayn), 23 October* (Roze-Maulud, Birth of Prophet Muhammad).

* These holidays are dependent on the Islamic lunar calendar and may vary by one or two days from the dates given.

Weights and Measures

The metric system has been officially adopted but traditional weights are still used. One 'seer' equals 16 lb (7.3 kg).

Currency and Exchange Rates

100 puls = 2 krans = 1 afghani (Af).

Exchange rates (30 September 1986):
 £1 sterling = 73.22 afghanis;
 US $1 = 50.60 afghanis.

AFGHANISTAN

Statistical Survey

Source (unless otherwise stated): Central Statistics Office, Kabul.

Area and Population

AREA, POPULATION AND DENSITY

Area (sq km)	652,225*
Population (census results) 23 June 1979†	
Males	6,712,377
Females	6,338,981
Total	13,051,358
Population (official estimates at mid-year)‡	
1983	17,222,000
1984	17,672,000
1985	18,136,000
Density (per sq km) at mid-1985	27.8

* 251,773 sq miles.
† Figures exclude nomadic population, estimated to total 2,500,000. The census data also exclude an adjustment for underenumeration, estimated to have been 5% for the urban population and 10% for the rural population.
‡ These data include estimates for nomadic population (2,734,000 in 1983), but take no account of emigration by refugees. Assuming an average net outflow of 319,000 persons per year in 1980–85, the UN Population Division has estimated Afghanistan's total mid-year population (in '000) as: 14,228 in 1983; 14,292 in 1984; 14,636 in 1985 (Source: UN, *World Population Prospects: Estimates and Projections as Assessed in 1982*). In 1986, according to other estimates, the total Afghan refugee population numbered more than 5m., of whom more than 3m. were living in Pakistan.

PRINCIPAL TOWNS (estimated population at March 1982)

Kabul (capital)	1,036,407	Kunduz	57,112
Qandahar	191,345	Baghlan	41,240
Herat	150,497	Maymana	40,212
Mazar-i-Sharif	110,367	Pul-i-Khomri	32,695
Jalalabad	57,824	Ghazni	31,985

BIRTHS AND DEATHS

1979 (demographic survey): Live births 627,619 (birth rate 48.1 per 1,000); Deaths 290,974 (death rate 22.3 per 1,000).

PROVINCES (estimates, March 1982)*

	Area (sq km)	Population	Density (per sq km)	Capital (with population)
Kabul	4,585	1,517,909	331.1	Kabul (1,036,407)
Kapesa†	1,871	262,039	140.1	Mahmudraki (1,262)
Parwan	9,399	527,987	56.2	Sharikar (25,117)
Wardag†	9,023	300,796	33.3	Maidanshar (2,153)
Loghar†	4,652	226,234	48.6	Baraiki Barak (1,164)
Ghazni	23,378	676,416	28.9	Ghazni (31,985)
Paktia	9,581	506,264	52.8	Gardiz (10,040)
Nangarhar	7,616	781,619	102.6	Jalalabad (57,824)
Laghman	7,210	325,010	45.0	Mehterlam (4,191)
Kunar	10,479	261,604	25.0	Asadabad (2,196)
Badakhshan	47,403	520,620	10.9	Faizabad (9,564)
Takhar	12,376	543,818	43.9	Talukan (20,947)
Baghlan	17,109	516,921	30.2	Baghlan (41,240)
Kunduz	7,827	582,600	74.4	Kunduz (57,112)
Samangan	15,465	273,864	17.7	Aibak (5,191)
Balkh	12,593	609,590	48.4	Mazar-i-Sharif (110,367)
Jawzjan	25,553	615,877	24.1	Shiberghan (19,969)
Fariab	22,279	609,703	27.3	Maymana (40,212)
Badghis	21,858	244,346	11.2	Kalainow (5,614)
Herat	61,315	808,224	13.2	Herat (150,497)
Farah	47,788	245,474	5.1	Farah (19,761)
Neemroze	41,356	108,418	2.6	Zarang (6,809)
Helmand	61,829	541,508	8.8	Lashkargha (22,707)
Qandahar	47,676	597,954	12.5	Qandahar (191,345)
Zabul	17,293	187,612	10.8	Qalat (6,251)
Uruzgan	29,295	464,556	15.5	Terincot (3,534)
Ghor	38,666	353,494	9.1	Cheghcheran (3,126)
Bamian	17,414	280,859	16.1	Bamyan (7,732)
Paktika	19,336	256,470	13.3	Sheran (1,469)
Total	**652,225**	**13,747,786**	**21.1**	

* Population figures refer to settled inhabitants only, excluding kuchies (nomads), estimated at 2,600,000 for the whole country.
† Formed in 1981.

AFGHANISTAN

Statistical Survey

ECONOMICALLY ACTIVE POPULATION* (ISIC Major Divisions, persons aged 8 years and over, 1979 census)

	Males	Females	Total
Agriculture, hunting, forestry and fishing	2,358,821	10,660	2,369,481
Mining and quarrying	57,492	1,847	59,339
Manufacturing	170,908	252,465	423,373
Electricity, gas and water	11,078	276	11,354
Construction	50,670	416	51,086
Wholesale and retail trade	135,242	2,618	137,860
Transport, storage and communications	65,376	867	66,243
Other services	716,511	32,834	749,345
Total	3,566,098	301,983	3,868,081

* Figures refer to settled population only and exclude 77,510 persons seeking work for the first time (66,057 males; 11,453 females).

Agriculture

PRINCIPAL CROPS ('000 metric tons, year ending 20 March)

	1980/81	1981/82	1982/83*
Wheat	2,750	2,850	2,860*
Maize	797	798	800
Rice (paddy)	461	475	473
Barley	321	330	329
Cotton (lint)	23	14	45
Sugar beet	35	20	20
Sugar cane	70	70	72
Vegetables	828	865	912
Fruits	891	913	920
Oil seeds	43	44	45

* Provisional.

LIVESTOCK ('000 head, year ending 20 March)

	1980/81	1981/82	1982/83*
Cattle	3,170	3,750	3,740
Sheep	18,700	18,900	18,900
Goats	2,850	2,900	2,900
Horses, Asses, Mules	1,730	1,750	1,750
Camels	265	265	265
Poultry	6,400	6,600	6,600

* Provisional.

LIVESTOCK PRODUCTS
('000 metric tons, year ending 20 March)

	1979/80	1980/81	1981/82
Beef	71	74	76
Sheep and goat meat	137	134	138
Poultry meat	9	10	11
Cows' milk	550	554	570
Sheep's and goats' milk	262	276	283
Hen eggs (million)	480	488	515
Wool (greasy)	22	22.4	22.7
Sheep skins ('000 units)	1,546	1,750	1,500

Forestry

ROUNDWOOD REMOVALS
(FAO estimates, '000 cu m, excluding bark)

	1982	1983	1984
Sawlogs, veneer logs and logs for sleepers*	856	856	856
Other industrial wood	591	586	590
Fuel wood	4,269	4,233	4,253
Total	5,716	5,675	5,699

* Assumed to be unchanged from 1976.
Source: FAO, *Yearbook of Forest Products*.

SAWNWOOD PRODUCTION (FAO estimates, '000 cu m)

	1974	1975	1976
Total (incl. boxboards)	410	330	400

1977–84: Annual production as in 1976 (FAO estimates).
Source: FAO, *Yearbook of Forest Products*.

Fishing

1964–84: Total catch 1,500 metric tons each year (FAO estimate).

Mining

(year ending 20 March)

	1980/81	1981/82*	1982/83*
Hard coal ('000 metric tons)	118.7	125.0	145.4
Salt (unrefined) ('000 metric tons)	37.1	30.4	45.1
Natural gas (million cu m)	2,790.3	2,674.6	2,583

* Provisional.

Industry

SELECTED PRODUCTS (year ending 20 March)

		1980/81	1981/82	1982/83*
Margarine	'000 metric tons	6.5	4.5	2.8
Cotton fabrics	million metres	43.3	26.5	38.6
Woollen fabrics[1]	'000 metres	405.3	244.8	0.2[4]
Rayon fabrics	'000 metres	14,800.0	9,640.0	6.7[4]
Cement	'000 metric tons	87.2	77.1	107.8
Electric energy[2]	million kWh	956.2	1,018.3	976.0
Wheat flour	'000 metric tons	113.1	122.9	123.9
Refined sugar	'000 metric tons	2.7	1.83	1.1
Vegetable oil	'000 metric tons	6.5	4.5	2.8
Nitrogenous fertilizers[3]	'000 metric tons	48.9	48.3	48.3

* Provisional.
[1] Including blankets.
[2] Production for public use, excluding industrial establishments generating electricity for their own use.
[3] Production in terms of nitrogen.
[4] Million square metres.

Finance

CURRENCY AND EXCHANGE RATES

Monetary Units
100 puls (puli) = 2 krans = 1 afghani (Af.).

Denominations
Coins: 25 and 50 puls: 1, 2, and 5 afghanis.
Notes: 10, 20, 50, 100, 500 and 1,000 afghanis.

Sterling and Dollar Equivalents (30 September 1986)
£1 sterling = 73.22 afghanis;
US $1 = 50.60 afghanis;
1,000 afghanis = £13.66 = $19.76.

Exchange Rate
Fixed at US $1 = 50.60 afghanis since September 1981.

BANK OF AFGHANISTAN RESERVES*
(US $ million at December)

	1983	1984	1985
IMF special drawing rights	10.44	13.23	13.64
Reserve position in IMF	5.03	4.71	5.29
Foreign exchange	198.70	210.76	276.27
Total	214.16	228.71	295.21

* Figures exclude gold reserves, totalling 965,000 troy ounces since 1980. Assuming a gold price of 12,850 afghanis per ounce, these reserves were officially valued at US $245.04 million in December 1983, and at $245.05 million in December 1984.
Source: IMF, *International Financial Statistics*.

BUDGET (million afghanis, year ending 21 September)

Revenue	1977/78	1978/79	1979/80
Direct taxes	2,428	2,535	2,461
Indirect taxes	6,830	6,913	4,794
Revenue from monopolies and other enterprises	1,316	1,192	1,407
Natural gas revenue	1,510	2,637	3,874
Revenue from other property and services	2,357	1,954	2,456
Other revenue	480	1,224	796
Total revenue	14,921	16,455	15,788

Expenditure	1977/78	1978/79	1979/80
Administration	1,255	1,690	4,218
Defence, security	2,656	3,007	6,294
Social services	2,538	3,186	3,279
Economic services	870	985	1,092
Total ministries	7,319	8,868	14,883
Foreign debt service	2,087	2,493	1,029
Subsidies (exchange, etc.)	2,532	1,024	870
Total ordinary	11,938	12,385	16,782
Development budget	5,200	6,845	5,374

1980/81 (estimates in million afghanis): Revenue: internal sources 23,478, grants-in-aid from USSR 1,735, loans and project assistance 8,546, total revenue 33,759; Expenditure: ministries' allocation 19,213, development budget 14,546, total expenditure 33,759.

AFGHANISTAN

Statistical Survey

COST OF LIVING
(year ending 20 March. Base: 1979/80 = 100)

	1979/80*	1980/81	1981/82
Cereals	113.2	105.1	117.3
Meat	100.8	123.3	162.0
Fruits	118.2	109.1	131.6
Vegetables	122.5	99.3	134.3
Total (incl. others)	111.2	109.6	128.4

* Base: 1978/79 = 100.

NATIONAL ACCOUNTS
('000 million afghanis at 1978 prices, year ending 20 March)
Net Material Product*

	1980/81	1981/82	1982/83
Agriculture, hunting, forestry and fishing	63.1	64.3	64.7
Mining and quarrying } Manufacturing } Electricity, gas and water	13.7	12.8	13.0
Construction	2.8	2.9	3.0
Trade, restaurants and hotels	8.2	8.4	8.6
Transport, storage and communications	2.9	3.3	3.3
Other services	1.4	1.5	1.5
Total	92.1	93.2	94.0

* Defined as the total net value of goods and 'productive' services, including turnover taxes, produced by the economy. This excludes economic activities not contributing directly to material production, such as public administration, defence and personal and professional services.

MONEY SUPPLY (million afghanis at 21 December)

	1982	1983	1984
Currency outside banks	46,674	53,782	58,716
Private sector deposits at Bank of Afghanistan	3,628	4,534	5,561
Demand deposits at commercial banks	1,850	2,612	2,946

Source: IMF, *International Financial Statistics*.

BALANCE OF PAYMENTS
(US $ million, year ending 20 March)

	1977/78	1978/79	1979/80
Merchandise exports f.o.b.	326.7	336.7	481.2
Merchandise imports c.i.f.	−521.3	−638.6	−681.1
Trade balance	−194.6	−301.9	−199.9
Travel (net)	38.0	28.0	7.0
Service component of project aid	−18.9	−17.1	—
Official loans and grants: project	198.1	204.3	264.5
other	20.3	31.5	52.6
External public debt service	−50.8	−58.0	−18.0
Other transactions (net)*	163.4	212.0	17.5
Changes in reserves, etc	155.5	98.8	60.7

* Including errors and omissions.

External Trade

PRINCIPAL COMMODITIES
(US $ '000, year ending 20 March)

Imports c.i.f.	1979/80	1980/81	1981/82
Wheat	14,460	798	18,100
Sugar	17,828	40,833	50,328
Tea	25,799	28,369	n.a.
Cigarettes	5,067	5,114	7,219
Vegetable oil	24,905	17,320	26,332
Drugs	6,055	4,497	4,195
Soaps	7,186	9,991	17,256
Tyres and tubes	11,001	16,766	12,764
Textile yarn and thread	12,026	16,800	24,586
Cotton fabrics	1,214	873	6,319
Rayon fabrics	4,890	6,879	9,498
Other textile goods	32,341	52,546	49,036
Vehicles and spare parts	33,512	89,852	141,062
Petroleum products	65,186	124,000	112,093
Footwear (new)	3,316	2,058	5,275
Bicycles	2,872	2,042	488
Matches	1,553	1,171	1,542
Sewing machines	844	140	285
Electric and non-electric machines	2,557	2,333	765
Chemical materials	7,546	7,464	6,636
Agricultural tractors	55	1	8,280
Fertilizers	14,926	8,325	3,300
Used clothes	2,293	2,523	1,875
Television receivers	5,370	5,391	3,241
Other items	122,661	106,662	92,307
Total	425,464	551,748	622,416

Exports f.o.b.	1979/80	1980/81	1981/82
Fresh fruit	31,337	39,762	50,544
Dried fruit	177,056	169,478	174,933
Hides and skins	15,427	14,491	11,711
Karakul fur skins	24,916	33,299	18,845
Oil-seeds	1,769	6,412	2,031
Wool and other animal hair	10,945	12,308	23,364
Cotton	36,770	39,650	22,566
Casings	4,274	5,369	4,617
Medicinal herbs	4,944	4,206	11,511
Natural gas	102,857	233,128	272,589
Carpets and rugs	57,154	103,590	72,680
Other commodities	26,241	43,551	28,901
Total	493,690	705,244	694,292

AFGHANISTAN *Statistical Survey*

PRINCIPAL TRADING PARTNERS (US $ '000)

Imports	1979/80	1980/81	1981/82
Germany, Federal Republic	14,569	16,959	16,779
Hong Kong	19,686	18,586	27,386
India	21,580	20,572	17,024
Japan	71,389	98,207	76,670
Pakistan	13,730	14,895	11,737
USSR	195,526	290,496	365,000
USA	20,287	14,216	7,156
Total (incl. others)	425,462	551,748	622,416

Exports	1979/80	1980/81	1981/82
Czechoslovakia	6,018	14,585	12,088
Germany, Federal Republic	33,326	51,513	41,801
India	42,156	54,746	43,212
Pakistan	54,552	52,101	61,249
Saudi Arabia	14,609	21,188	19,214
USSR	254,399	417,872	412,635
United Kingdom	32,195	51,844	36,340
Total (incl. others)	493,690	705,244	694,292

Transport

CIVIL AVIATION (year ending 20 March)

	1979/80	1980/81	1981/82
Kilometres flown ('000)	3,765	3,012	2,071
Passengers carried	104,000	86,199	69,364
Passenger-km ('000)	238,068	173,855	164,455
Freight ton-km ('000)	19,084	21,366	21,032
Cargo and mail	6,000	7,070	7,752

ROAD TRAFFIC (motor vehicles in use)

	1979/80	1980/81	1981/82
Passenger cars	34,192	34,080	34,908
Commercial vehicles	27,555	28,714	30,800

Tourism

INTERNATIONAL TOURIST ARRIVALS BY COUNTRY

	1978	1979	1980
Australia	3,070	967	28
France	4,781	1,153	234
Germany, Federal Republic	7,496	1,817	258
India	9,744	4,350	992
Pakistan	23,663	10,126	2,466
United Kingdom	9,102	1,850	128
USA	6,389	1,039	79
Others	27,744	8,902	2,438
Total	91,989	30,204	6,623

Receipts from tourism (US $ million): 28 in 1978; 7 in 1979; 1 in 1980.

Communications Media

Telephones in use: 23,680 in 1979/80. Radio receivers in use: 135,000 in 1984. Television receivers in use: 12,600 in 1984.

Education

(1981/82)

	Institutions	Teachers	Students
Elementary	3,824	35,364	1,115,993
Secondary	447	6,170	124,488
Vocational	42	1,053	13,201
Technical	3	261	1,230
Teacher training	14	343	4,427
Higher education	5	1,226	12,868

Directory

The Constitution

Immediately after the coup of 27 April 1978 (the Saur Revolution), the 1977 Constitution was abolished. Both Nur Muhammad Taraki (Head of State from April 1978 to September 1979) and his successor, Hafizullah Amin (September–December 1979), promised to introduce new constitutions, but these leaders were removed from power before any drafts had been prepared by special commissions which they had appointed. On 21 April 1980 the Revolutionary Council ratified the Basic Principles of the Democratic Republic of Afghanistan. These were superseded when a new constitution was ratified by a meeting of the Loya Jirgah (National Assembly), held on 23–25 April 1985. The following is a summary of the Constitution:

GENERAL PROVISIONS

The role of the state is to serve the well-being and prosperity of the people, to safeguard their peaceful life and to protect their rights.

The People's Democratic Party of Afghanistan, the party of the workers and the working class, is the country's guiding force. It aims to realize the ideals of the Great Saur Revolution for the creation of a new, just society.

Muslims are free to practise religious rites, as are members of other religions provided they pose no threat to Afghan society.

All nationalities, tribes and ethnic groups are equal.

Foreign policy is based on the principle of peaceful co-existence and active and positive non-alignment. Friendship and co-operation is to be strengthened with the USSR as it will be with all countries of the socialist community. Afghanistan abides by the UN Charter, professes its desire for peace between neighbouring countries of the region and supports the struggle against colonialism, imperialism, Zionism, racism and fascism. Afghanistan favours disarmament and the prevention of proliferation of nuclear weapons. War propaganda is prohibited.

The state protects private ownership and guarantees the law of inheritance of private ownership. Banks, mines, institutes, insurance, heavy industries, radio and television are state-owned. The establishment of agricultural and industrial co-operatives is encouraged.

One of the state's major duties is to provide adequate housing for the workers. Family, mother and child are given special protection by the state.

The capital is Kabul.

RIGHTS AND DUTIES OF THE PEOPLES

All subjects of Afghanistan are equal before the law. The following rights are guaranteed: the right to life and security, to observe the religious rites of Islam and of other religions, to work, to protection of health and social welfare, to education, to scientific, technical, cultural and artistic activities, to freedom of speech and thought, to security of residence and privacy of correspondence and to complain to the appropriate government organs.

In crime, the accused is considered innocent until guilt is recognized by the court. Nobody may be arrested, detained or punished except in accordance with the law.

The defence of the homeland and of the achievements of the Saur Revolution, loyalty to its aims and ideals and services to the people are the responsibilities of every subject.

LOYA JIRGAH

This is the highest organ of state power. Its composition and the election of its representatives will be regulated by law. Elections to the Loya Jirgah will be based on a general, secret, free, direct and equal vote. (The Loya Jirgah, comprising indirectly elected tribal elders, ratified the Constitution during the session of 23–25 April 1985.)

THE REVOLUTIONARY COUNCIL

The highest organ of state power until the necessary conditions for elections to the Loya Jirgah are met.

The number and election or selection of new members is proposed by the Presidium of the Revolutionary Council and ratified by the Revolutionary Council. It is empowered to ratify laws, decrees, state economic and social development plans and to form the Presidium and the Council of Ministers. It also has the authority to call elections for the Loya Jirgah and to declare war. Laws and decrees are ratified by a majority vote of the members and are enforced after their publication in the official gazette. Sessions of the Revolutionary Council are held twice a year and they require a minimum attendance of two-thirds of the members.

The permanent organ of the Revolutionary Council is the Presidium. The Revolutionary Council elects the Presidium from amongst its members. The President of the Revolutionary Council is the President of the Presidium. The Presidium's responsibilities include the interpretation and enforcement of laws, the granting of amnesty and the commuting of punishment. Between sessions all responsibilities of the Revolutionary Council are transferred to the Presidium.

THE COUNCIL OF MINISTERS

The supreme executive organ of state power, responsible to the Revolutionary Council and to the Presidium when the Revolutionary Council is in recess. It is vested with the authority to implement domestic and foreign policy and to submit draft laws to the Revolutionary Council (or Presidium) for consideration and ratification. It comprises the President of the Council of Ministers (also known as the Prime Minister), his deputy or deputies and ministers.

LOCAL ADMINISTRATIVE ORGANS

Local committees and councils are to be formed in the provinces, cities, sub-districts and villages for the solution of all questions relating to the locality. All matters of election and representation will be regulated by law. Local executive committees of state power are to be established too. Besides taking decisions within the limits of their authority, these local organs are authorized to implement the decisions of higher organs.

THE JUDICIARY

(See Section on the Judicial System.)

THE PUBLIC PROSECUTION DEPARTMENT

The Attorney-General guides the activities of the country's prosecution organs. The Department consists of the Prosecutor-General and the prosecution department of the provinces, cities, districts and sub-districts. These organs are independent of local organs, answerable only to the Prosecutor-General. The Attorney-General, who is responsible to the Revolutionary Council, and the prosecutors supervise the implementation and observance of all laws.

FINAL ORDERS

Any alteration of the Constitution may be implemented on the proposal of the Presidium and the ratification by two-thirds of the members of the Revolutionary Council. Decrees, laws and other documents issued prior to the enforcement of the Basic Principles remain valid provided they are not contradictory to the Basic Principles.

Note: In January 1986 a 74-member commission was established to draft a new constitution, which was to incorporate the principle that 'all state power belongs to the people'.

The Government

HEAD OF STATE

President of the Revolutionary Council: MUHAMMAD CHAMKANI (took office as Acting President, 20 November 1986).

PRESIDIUM OF THE REVOLUTIONARY COUNCIL

President: MUHAMMAD CHAMKANI (acting).
Vice-Presidents: Gen. ABDUL QADIR, Maj.-Gen. GUL AQA.
Secretary: MUHAMMAD ANWAR FARZAN.
Members: Dr ANAHITA RATEBZAD, KHODAYNUR BAWAR, SAYED MANSUR KAYHANI, SHAH ALI AKBAR SHAHRESTANI, ABDURRAHIM OWRAZ, ABDURRAHIM HATIF, MAWLAWI ABDURRA'UF, ABDUSSATAR PORDELI, FARID AHMAD MAZDAK, MUHAMMAD ASEF KESBGAR, MUHAMMAD A'ZAM SYSTANI, NASER DEHQAN, NAJMUDDIN KAWIANI, NASRULLAH WAZIRI.

AFGHANISTAN

COUNCIL OF MINISTERS
(December 1986)

President of the Revolutionary Council: MUHAMMAD CHAMKANI (acting).
Prime Minister and Chairman of the Council of Ministers: SULTAN ALI KESHTMAND.
Deputy Chairman of the Council of Ministers and President of the State Planning Committee: Eng. MUHAMMAD AZIZ.
Deputy Chairman of the Council of Ministers and Minister of Defence: Brig.-Gen. MUHAMMAD RAFI.
Deputy Chairmen of the Council of Ministers: SAYED ANAMUDDIN AMIN, SAYED MUHAMMAD NASIM MAYHANPARAST, MUHAMMAD HAKIM, Lt-Gen. NAZAR MUHAMMAD.
Deputy Prime Ministers of the Council of Ministers (without portfolio): Prof. ABDUL MAJID SARBULAND, POHANMAL GULDAD.
Minister of State Security: Maj.-Gen. GHULAM FARUQ YAQUBI.
Minister of Justice: MUHAMMAD BASHIR BAGHLANI.
Minister of Foreign Affairs: ABDOL WAKIL.
Minister of the Interior: Brig. SAYED MUHAMMAD GULABZOI.
Minister of Communications: Lt-Col MUHAMMAD ASLAM WATANJAR.
Minister of Education: ABDUL SAMAD QAYUMI.
Minister of Nationalities and Tribal Affairs: SULIEMAN LAEQ.
Minister of Agriculture and Land Reform: Dr ABDUL GHAFFAR LAKANWAL.
Minister of Higher and Vocational Education: BORHANUDDIN GHAISI.
Minister of Finance: Dr MUHAMMAD KABIR.
Minister of Commerce: MUHAMMAD KHAN JALALAR.
Minister of Mines and Industry: NAJIBULLAH MASSER.
Minister of Transport: Lt-Col SHERJAN MAZDOORYAR.
Minister of Power and of Public Works: Prof. RAS MUHAMMAD PAKTIN.
Minister of Irrigation: Eng. AHMAD SHAH SORKHABI.
Minister of Public Health: Dr MUHAMMAD NABI KAMYAR.
Minister without Portfolio: FAQIR MUHAMMAD YAQUBI.
Minister of Light Industries and Foodstuffs: LMAR AHMAD LMAR.
Minister of Islamic Affairs: MAWLAWI ABDOL JAMIL ZARIFI.
Minister of Civil Aviation: MUHAMMAD AZIZ NEGAHBAN.
Minister of State for Nationalities and Tribal Affairs: SARGANG KHAN ZAZAY.
Minister of State for Social and Cultural Affairs: Dr ABDUL WAHED SORABI.
Minster of State for Islamic Affairs: ABDUL GHAFUR BAHER.
Minister of State for Financial and Economic Affairs: FAZL HAQ KHAZEQIAR.
Minister of State for Foreign Affairs: SHAH MUHAMMAD DOST.

MINISTRIES

Office of the Council of Ministers: Kabul; tel. (93) 26926.
Office of the Prime Minister: Shar Rahi Sedarat, Kabul; tel. (93) 24954.
Ministry of Agriculture and Land Reform: Jamal Mina, Kabul; tel. (93) 40841.
Ministry of Civil Aviation and Tourism: Ansari Watt, Kabul.
Ministry of Commerce: Darulaman Watt, Kabul; tel. (93) 41041.
Ministry of Communications: Puli Bagh-i-Omomi, Kabul; tel. (93) 21456.
Ministry of Defence: Kabul; tel. (93) 41232.
Ministry of Education: Shar Rahi Malek Asghar, Kabul; tel. (93) 25251.
Ministry of Energy: Kabul; tel. (93) 25109.
Ministry of Finance: Shar Rahi Pashtoonistan, Kabul; tel. (93) 26041.
Ministry of Foreign Affairs: Shar-i-Nau, Kabul; tel. (93) 25341.
Ministry of Higher and Vocational Education: Jamal Mina, Kabul; tel. (93) 20194.
Ministry of Information and Culture: Puli Bagh-i-Omomi, Kabul.
Ministry of the Interior: Shar-i-Nan, Kabul; tel. (93) 21417.
Ministry of Justice: Darulaman Watt, Kabul; tel. (93) 26041.
Ministry of Mines and Industries: Kabul; tel. (93) 25841.
Ministry of Public Health: Micro-Rayon, Kabul; tel. (93) 20841.
Ministry of Public Works: Micro-Rayon, Kabul; tel. (93) 20345.
Ministry of Radio and Television: Ansari Watt, Kabul.
Ministry of State Security: Kabul.
Ministry of Transport: Kabul; tel. (93) 25541.
Ministry of Tribal Affairs: Kabul; tel. (93) 21793.
Ministry of Water: Micro-Rayon, Kabul; tel. (93) 40743.
State Planning Committee: Shar-i-Nan, Kabul; tel. (93) 23218.

POLITBURO OF THE CENTRAL COMMITTEE OF THE PEOPLE'S DEMOCRATIC PARTY OF AFGHANISTAN

General Secretary: Maj.-Gen. NAJIB (NAJIBULLAH).
Full Members: Dr ANAHITA RATEBZAD, SULTAN ALI KESHTMAND, Dr SALEH MUHAMMAD ZIRAY, NUR AHMAD NUR, Brig.-Gen MUHAMMAD RAFI, Lt-Gen. MUHAMMAD ASLAM WATANYAR, Maj.-Gen. GHULAM FARUQ YAQUBI.
Alternate Members: MAHMUD BARIALAY, ABDUZZOHUR RAZMJO, Lt-Gen. NAZAR MUHAMMAD, SULIEMAN LAEQ, Brig. SAYED MUHAMMAD GULABZOI, FARID AHMAD MAZDAK.

Legislature

LOYA JIRGAH
(National Assembly)

The Loya Jirgah is the supreme tribal assembly of Afghanistan. Its most recent session took place on 23–25 April 1985. The members of the assembly are indirectly elected tribal elders.

Note: A new constitution was being drawn up in 1986. This envisaged the formation of a bicameral legislature, comprising a Council of Representatives of the People and a Council of Nationalities.

Political Organizations

National Fatherland Front: f. 1981 as union of PDPA representatives, nat. and tribal groups; aims to promote nat. unity under the leadership of the PDPA; Exec. Board of 23 mems; Chair. Nat. Cttee ABDURRAHIM HATIF; Vice-Chair. SULIEMAN LAEQ, SAYED AFGHANI, NEJMUDDIN KAWYANI, SAYED EKRAM PAYGIR.

People's Democratic Party of Afghanistan (PDPA): Kabul; f. 1965, split 1967; refounded 1976, when the Khalq (Masses) Party and its splinter Parcham (Flag) Party reunited and absorbed the Musawat Party; communist; Secretariat of Cen. Cttee Maj.-Gen. NAJIB (NAJIBULLAH), Dr SALEH MUHAMMAD ZIRAY, NUR AHMAD NUR, MAHMUD BARIALAY, NEYAZ MOHD MOHMAND, SAHEB KARWAL, MUHAMMAD YASIN SADEQI; c. 120,000 mems.

No other political parties are allowed to function. There are many insurgent groups of Mujaheddin fighting against the Government in Afghanistan. The principal ones (each with headquarters in Pakistan) are the Islamic fundamentalist alliance of the two factions of **Hizb-i Islami** (Leaders: GULBUDDIN HIKMATYAR and YUNUS KHALIS), **Jamiat-i Islami** (Leader: Prof. BURHANEDDIN RABBANI), and **Harakat-i Inqilab-i-Islami** (Movement for Islamic Revolution of Afghanistan; Leader: MUHAMMAD NABI MUHAMMADI); the **Shora-ye-melli Inqilab-i-Islami** (the National Islamic Front; Leader: SAYED AHMAD GAILANI) and **Nejat-e-Melli Afghanistan** (the National Liberation Front; Leader: Prof. SIBGHATULLAH MOJADDEDI). The different groups co-operate to varying degrees; the last three groups joined forces in June 1981 to form the **Islamic Unity of Mujaheddin of Afghanistan** (Chair. Prof. SIBGHATULLAH MOJADDEDI) but the alliance has been strained by rivalry and feuding. A grand alliance of the six major groups was formed in 1982; Chair. Prof. ABDURRASSUL SAYYAF. In May 1985 the major factions joined with the moderate National Islamic Front and the fundamentalist Islamic Party to form a further alliance, called the **Ittehad-i-Islami Afghan Mujaheddin.**

Diplomatic Representation

EMBASSIES IN AFGHANISTAN*

Bangladesh: House no. 19, Sarak 'H', Wazir Akbar Khan Mena, POB 510, Kabul; tel. (93) 62783; Chargé d'affaires a.i.: AHMED RAHIM.

AFGHANISTAN

Bulgaria: Wazir Akbar Khan Mena, Kabul; tel. (93) 22996; Ambassador: PETAR VALKANOV.

China, People's Republic: Shah Mahmoud Ghazi Wat, Kabul; tel. (93) 20446; Chargé d'affaires a.i.: HONG XICHENG.

Cuba: Shar Rahi Haji Yaqub, opp. Shar-i-Nau Park, Kabul; tel. (93) 30863; Ambassador: MANUEL PENADO CASANOVA.

Czechoslovakia: Taimani Wat, Kala-i-Fatullah, Kabul; tel. (93) 32080; Ambassador: Dr VÁCLAV KOUBA.

France: Djadeh Solh (E), tel. (93) 23631; Kabul; Chargé d'affaires a.i.: ROLAND BARRAUX.

German Democratic Republic: Ghazi Ayub Khan Wat, Shar-i-Nau, Kabul; tel. (93) 20782; telex 249; Ambassador: KRAFT BUMBEL.

Germany, Federal Republic: POB 83, Wazir Akbar Khan Mena, Kabul; tel. (93) 22432; Chargé d'affaires a.i.: DIETER WOLTMANN.

Hungary: Sin 306–308, Wazir Akbar Khan Mena, POB 830, Kabul; tel. (93) 20469; Ambassador: Dr GYÖRGY VARGA.

India: Malalai Wat, Shar-i-Nau, Kabul; tel. (93) 30557; Ambassador: INDER PAL KHOLSA.

Indonesia: POB 532, Wazir Akbar Khan Mena, Kabul; tel. (93) 61334; telex 239; Chargé d'affaires a.i.: ABDULLAH FUAD RACHMAN.

Iran: Malekyar Wat, Kabul; tel. (93) 26255; Chargé d'affaires a.i.: MUHAMMAD MUHAMMADI.

Iraq: POB 523, Wazir Akbar Khan Mena, Kabul; tel. (93) 24797; Ambassador: BURHAN KHALIL GHAZAL.

Italy: POB 606, Khoja Abdullah Ansari Wat, Kabul; tel. (93) 24624; telex 55; Chargé d'affaires a.i.: Dr PIETRO BALLERO.

Japan: POB 80, Wazir Akbar Khan Mena, Kabul; tel. (93) 26844; telex 216; Chargé d'affaires a.i.: AKIRA WATANABE.

Korea, Democratic People's Republic: Wazir Akbar Khan Mena, Kabul; tel. (93) 22161; Ambassador: KANG HUI-SUN.

Libya: 103 Wazir Akbar Khan Mena, Kabul; tel. (93) 24947; Secretary: SALEM A. EL-HUNI.

Mongolia: Wazir Akbar Khan Mena, Kabul; tel. (93) 22138; Ambassador: KHAYANGIIN BANZRAGEH.

Pakistan: Zarghouna Wat, Kabul; tel. (93) 21374; Chargé d'affaires a.i.: S. FIDA YUNAS.

Poland: Gozargah St, Kabul; tel. (93) 42461; Ambassador: EDWARD PORADKO.

Turkey: Shah Mahmoud Ghazi Wat, Kabul; tel. (93) 20072; Chargé d'affaires a.i.: SALIH ZEKI KARACA.

USSR: Dar-ul-Aman Wat, Kabul; tel. (93) 41541; Ambassador: PAVEL PETROVICH MOZHAYEV.

United Kingdom: Karte Parwan, Kabul; tel. (93) 30511; Chargé d'affaires a.i.: CHARLES DRACE-FRANCIS.

USA: Khwaja Abdullah Ansari Wat, Kabul; tel. (93) 62230; Chargé d'affaires a.i.: EDWARD HURWITZ.

Viet-Nam: No. 27 Peace St, Shar-i-Nua, Kabul; tel. (93) 26596; Ambassador: VAN BA KIEM.

Yugoslavia: No. 923 Main Rd, Wazir Akbar Khan Mena, Kabul; tel. (93) 23671; Ambassador: (vacant).

* Not all of the above-mentioned countries recognize the Soviet-backed administration as the legitimate government of Afghanistan.

Judicial System

The functions and structure of the judiciary are established in Articles 54–58 of the Constitution ratified by the Loya Jirgah in April 1985.

Judgment is made by the courts on the basis of democratic principles. The courts implement the laws of the Democratic Republic of Afghanistan and, in cases of ambivalence, will judge in accordance with the rules of Shari'ah (Islamic religious law). Trials are held in open session except when circumstances defined by law deem the trial to be held in closed session. Trials are conducted in Pashtu and Dari or in the language of the majority of the inhabitants of the locality. The right to speak in court in one's mother tongue is guaranteed to the two sides of the lawsuit.

The judiciary comprises the Supreme Court, provincial, city and district courts, the courts of the armed forces and other such special courts as are formed in accordance with the directives of the law.

The supreme judicial organ is the Supreme Court, which consists of a President, Vice-Presidents and other members. It supervises the judicial activities of the courts and ensures the uniformity of law enforcement and interpretation by those courts.

The Presidium of the Revolutionary Council appoints all judges. Death sentences are carried out after ratification by the Presidium.

President of the Supreme Court: NEZAMUDDIN TAHZIB.

Prosecutor-General: MUHAMMAD OSMAN RASEKH.

Religion

The official religion of Afghanistan is Islam. Muslims comprise 99% of the population, approximately 80% of them of the Sunni and the remainder of the Shi'ite sect. There are small minority groups of Hindus, Sikhs and Jews.

The Press

The newspapers and periodicals marked * were reported to be the only ones appearing regularly in July 1986.

PRINCIPAL DAILIES

*Anis: (Friendship): Kabul; f. 1927; evening; independent; Dari and Pashtu; news and literary articles; state-owned; Chief Editor MOHAMMAH S. KHARNIKASH; circ. 25,000.

Badakhshan: Faizabad; f. 1945; Dari and Pashtu; Chief Editor HADI ROSTAQI; circ. 3,000.

Bedar: Mazar-i-Sharif; f. 1920; Dari and Pashtu; Chief Editor ROZEQ FANI; circ. 2,500.

Ettehadi-Baghlan: Baghlan; f. 1930; Dari and Pashtu; Chief Editor SHAFIQULLAH MOSHFEQ; circ. 1,200.

*Haqiqat Enqelab Saur (Truth of the April Revolution): Kabul; f. 1980; Dari; organ of the PDPA; Editor GHULAM SEDIQ KAWUN; circ. 50,000.

*Hewad: Kabul; f. 1959; Dari and Pashtu; Editor-in-Chief ABDULLAH BAKHTIANAE; circ. 12,200.

Jawzjan: Jawzjan; f. 1942; Dari and Pashtu; Chief Editor A. RAHEM HAMRO; circ. 1,500.

*Kabul New Times: Ansari Wat, Kabul; tel. (93) 26848; f. 1962 as Kabul Times, renamed 1980; English; state-owned; Editor-in-Chief DANESHYOR; circ. 5,000.

Nangarhor: Jalalabad; f. 1919; Pashtu; Chief Editor MORAD SANGARMAL; circ. 1,500.

Sanae: Parwan; f. 1953; Dari and Pashtu; Chief Editor G. SAKHI ESHANZADA; circ. 1,700.

Tulu-i-Afghan: Qandahar; f. 1924; Pashtu; Chief Editor TAHER SHAFEQ; circ. 1,500.

Wolanga: Paktia; f. 1943; Pashtu; Chief Editor M. ANWAR; circ. 1,500.

PERIODICALS

*Afghanistan: Historical Society of Afghanistan, Kabul; tel. (93) 30370; f. 1948; quarterly; English and French; historical and cultural; Editor MALIHA ZAFAR.

*Aryana: Historical Society of Afghanistan, Kabul; tel. (93) 30370; f. 1943; quarterly; Pashtu and Dari; cultural and historical; Editor FAQIR MUHAMMAD KHAIRKHAH.

*Awaz: Kabul; f. 1940; 2 a month; Pashtu and Dari; radio and television programmes; Editor NASIR TOHORI; circ. 20,000.

*Eqtesad (Economics): Afghan Chambers of Commerce and Industry, Mohd Jan Khan Wat, Kabul; tel. (93) 26796; telex 45; f. 1922; weekly; Dari and Pashtu; Editor FAQIR MUHAMMAD.

*Erfan: Ministry of Education, Mohd Jan Khan Wat, Kabul; f. 1923; monthly; Dari and Pashtu; Chief Editor KUBRA MAZHARI MALORAW; circ. 2,500.

Geography: Kabul; f. 1965; monthly; Pashtu and Dari; Editor-in-Chief STANAMIR ZAHER; circ. 2,500.

Gorash: Ministry of Information and Culture, Mohd Jan Khan Wat, Kabul; f. 1979; weekly; Turkmani; Chief Editor S. MISEDIQ AMINI; circ. 1,000.

*Haqiqat-e-Sarbaz: Ministry of National Defence, Kabul; f. 1980; 3 a week; Dari and Pashtu; Chief Editor MER JAMALUDIN FAKHR; circ. 18,370.

Helmand: Bost; f. 1954; weekly; Pashtu; Editor-in-Chief M. OMER FARHAT BALEGH; circ. 1,700.

Herat: Ministry of Information and Culture, Mohd Jan Khan Wat, Kabul; f. 1923; monthly; Dari and Pashtu; Chief Editor JALIL SHABGER FOLADYON.

AFGHANISTAN

*Kabul:** Academy of Sciences, Scientific Research Centre for Languages and Literature, Kabul; f. 1931; monthly; Pashtu; literature and language research; Editor N. M. SAHEEM.
Mojala-e-Ariana (Light): Kabul; f. 1978; monthly; Dari and Pashtu; Editor-in-Chief RASHID ASHTI; circ. 1,000.
*Muhasel-e-Emroz** (Today's Student): Kabul; f. 1986; monthly; state-owned; juvenile; circ. 5,000.
Nengarhar: Kabul; f. 1919; weekly; Pashtu; Editor-in-Chief KARIM HASHIMI; circ. 1,500.
*Pamir:** Micro-Rayon, Kabul; tel. (93) 20585; f. 1952; fortnightly; Dari and Pashtu; combined organ of the Kabul Cttee and Municipality; Chief Editor ENAYET POZHOHAN GURDANI; circ. 30,000.
Payam-e-Haq: Kabul; f. 1953; monthly; Dari and Pashtu; Editor-in-Chief FARAH SHAH MOHIBI; circ. 1,000.
Samangon: Aibak; f. 1978; weekly; Dari; Editor-in-Chief M. MOHSEN HASSAN; circ. 1,500.
Sawad (Literacy): Kabul; f. 1954; monthly; Dari and Pashtu; Editor-in-Chief MALEM GOL ZADRON; circ. 1,000.
Seistan: Farah; f. 1947; weekly; Dari and Pashtu; Editor-in-Chief M. ANWAR MAHAL; circ. 1,800.
*Seramiasht:** Afghan Red Crescent Society, Puli-Hartel, Kabul; tel. (93) 26152; telex 318; f. 1958; 2 a month; Dari and Pashtu; Editor H. R. JADIR; circ. 2,000.
Sob: Kabul; tel. (93) 25240; f. 1979; weekly; Balochi; Editor-in-Chief WALIMUHAMMAD ROKHSHONI; circ. 1,000.
Talim wa Tarbia (Education): Kabul; f. 1954; monthly; publ. by Institute of Education.
Urdu (Military): Kabul; f. 1922; quarterly; Dari and Pashtu; military journal; issued by the Ministry of National Defence; Chief Editor KHALILULAH AKBARI; circ. 500.
*Yulduz** (Star): Ministry of Information and Culture, Mohd Jan Khan Wat, Kabul; f. 1979; weekly; Uzbek; Chief Editor EKHAN BAYONI; circ. 2,000.
Zeray: Academy of Sciences, Scientific Research Centre for Languages and Literature, Kabul; f. 1938; weekly; Pashtu; Pashtu folklore, literature and language; Editor A. W. WAJID; circ. 1,000.
*Zhwandoon** (Life): Kabul; tel. (93) 26849; f. 1944; weekly; Pashtu and Dari; illustrated; Editor ROHELA ROSEKH KHORAMI; circ. 1,400.

NEWS AGENCIES

Bakhtar News Agency: Ministry of Information and Culture, Mohd Jan Khan Wat, Kabul; tel. (93) 24089; f. 1939; Pres. MUHAMMAD DAVID KAYAIAN; Dir ABDULQUDDUS TANDER.

Foreign Bureaux

The following foreign agencies are represented in Kabul: APN (USSR), ČTK (Czechoslovakia) and Tanjug (Yugoslavia).

PRESS ASSOCIATION

Union of Journalists of Afghanistan: Wazir Akbar Khan Mena, St No. 13, Kabul; Sec. MAHMUD HABIBI.

Publishers

Afghan Book: POB 206, Kabul; f. 1969; books on various subjects, translations of foreign works on Afghanistan, books in English on Afghanistan and Dari language textbooks for foreigners; Man. Dir JAMILA AHANG.
Afghanistan Publicity Department: c/o Kabul New Times, Ansari Wat, Kabul; tel. (93) 26848; publicity materials; answers enquiries about Afghanistan.
Balhaqi Book Publishing and Importing Institute: POB 2025, Kabul; tel. (93) 26818; f. 1971 by co-operation of the Government Printing House, Bakhtar News Agency and leading newspapers; publishers and importers of books; Pres. MUHAMMAD ANWAR NUMYALAI.
Book Publishing Institute: Herat; f. 1970 by co-operation of Government Printing House and citizens of Herat; books on literature, history and religion.
Book Publishing Institute: Qandahar; f. 1970; supervised by Government Printing House; mainly books in Pashtu language.
Educational Publications: Ministry of Education, Shar Rahi Malek Asghar, Kabul; tel. (93) 21716; textbooks for primary and secondary schools in the Pashtu and Dari languages; also three monthly magazines in Pashtu and in Dari.
Historical Society of Afghanistan: Kabul; tel. (93) 30370; f. 1931; mainly historical and cultural works and two quarterly magazines: *Afghanistan* (English and French), *Aryana* (Dari and Pashtu); Pres. AHMAD ALI MOTAMEDI.
Institute of Geography: Kabul University, Kabul; geographical and related works.
Kabul University Press: Kabul; tel. (93) 42433; f. 1950; textbooks; two quarterly scientific journals in Dari and in English, etc.
Pashtu Tolana (Pashtu Academy): Shar Alikhan St, Kabul; tel. (93) 20350; f. 1937 by the Dept of Press and Information; research works on Pashtu language and literature; Pres. POHAND RSHTEENE; publs *Zeray* (weekly), *Kabul* (monthly).

Government Publishing House

Government Printing House: Kabul; tel. (93) 26851; f. 1870 under supervision of the Ministry of Information and Culture; four daily newspapers in Kabul, one in English; weekly, fortnightly and monthly magazines, one of them in English; books on Afghan history and literature, as well as textbooks for the Ministry of Education; 13 daily newspapers in 13 provincial centres and one journal and also magazines in three provincial centres; Dir MUHAMMAD AYAN AYAN.

Radio and Television

In 1986 there were an estimated 135,000 radio receivers and 12,800 television receivers in use. Television broadcasting in colour began in August 1978 with a transmission range of 50 km. In March 1985 new radio stations were commissioned in Qandahar, Herat, Jalalabad, Ghazni and Asadabad, in addition to existing main stations in the provinces of Kabul and Nangarhar. Further radio stations were to be established in the provinces of Paktia, Farah and Badakhshan.

People's Radio and TV Afghanistan POB 544, Ansari Wat, Kabul; tel. (93) 25241; under the supervision of the Ministry of Communications; home service in Dari, Pashtu, Pashai, Nuristani, Uzbeki, Turkmani and Balochi; foreign service in Urdu, Arabic, English, Russian, German, Dari and Pashtu; Pres. (Radio) ABDUL LATIF NAZEMI; Pres. (Television) ABDULLAH SHADAN.

Finance

(cap. = capital; auth. = authorized; p.u. = paid up; res = reserves; m. = million; brs = branches; amounts in afghanis)

BANKING

In June 1975 all banks were nationalized. There are no foreign banks operating in Afghanistan.

Da Afghanistan Bank (Central Bank of Afghanistan): Ibne Sina Wat, Kabul; tel. (93) 24075; telex 223; f. 1939; main functions: banknote issue, foreign exchange regulation, credit extensions to banks and leading enterprises and companies, govt and private depository, govt fiscal agency; cap. 4,000m., res 5,299m., dep. 15,008m. (1985); Pres. ABDUL BASHIR RANJBAR; 72 brs.
Agricultural Development Bank of Afghanistan: POB 414, Kabul; tel. (93) 22530; f. 1955; makes available credits for farmers, co-operatives and agro-business; aid provided by IBRD and UNDP; auth. share cap. 1,000m.; Pres. AMANUDDIN AMIRPUR (acting); Gen. Man. G. N. RAHIMI (acting).
Banke Milli Afghan (Afghan National Bank): Jada Ibn Sina, Kabul; tel. (93) 25451; telex 31; f. 1932; brs throughout Afghanistan; cap. 500m.; total resources 3,807m. (1980); Pres. MUHAMMAD AKRAM KHALIL; Chair. H. E. ABDUL WAKIL.
Export Promotion Bank of Afghanistan: 24 Mohammad Jan Khan Wat, Kabul; tel. (93) 24447; telex 02; f. 1976; provides financing for exports and export-oriented investments; cap. and res 308m.; dep. 819m. (March 1984); Pres. GHULAM MUHAMMAD YEILAQI.
Industrial Development Bank of Afghanistan: POB 14, Kabul; tel. (93) 35259; f. 1973; provides financing for industrial development; total financial resources including cap. 879m.; Pres. H. K. AZIZI; Projects Man. W. M. RAHEN.
Mortgage and Construction Bank: 2 Jade' Maiwand, Kabul; tel. (93) 23341; f. 1955 to provide short- and long-term building loans; cap. 100m.; Pres. FAIZ MUHAMMAD.

AFGHANISTAN

Pashtany Tejaraty Bank (Afghan Commercial Bank): Mohd Jan Khan Wat, Kabul; tel. (93) 26551; telex 243; f. 1954 to provide short-term credits, forwarding facilities, opening letters of credit, purchase and sale of foreign exchange; cap. p.u. 1,000m., dep. 4,710m., total assets 7,480m. (1984); Pres. and CEO ZIR GUL WARDAK; Vice-Pres. A. Q. FAZLY; 18 brs in Afghanistan and abroad.

INSURANCE

There is one national insurance company:

Afghan National Insurance Co: POB 329, Pamir Bldg, 1st Jade Maiwand, Kabul; tel. (93) 26816; telex 231; f. 1964; mem. of Asian Reinsurance Corpn; marine, aviation, fire, motor and accident insurance; cap. 175m.; Pres. M. Y. DEEN; Vice-Pres. ABDUL RAZAQUE.

No foreign insurance companies are permitted to operate in Afghanistan.

Trade and Industry

CHAMBER OF COMMERCE

Federation of Afghan Chambers of Commerce and Industry: Mohd Jan Khan Wat, Kabul; tel. (93) 26796; telex 45; f. 1923; includes chambers of commerce and industry in Ghazni, Qandahar, Herat, Mazar-i-Sharif, Fariab, Jawzjan, Kunduz, Jalalabad and Andkhoy; Pres. MEHAR CHAND VERMA.

TRADING CORPORATIONS

Afghan Carpet Exporters' Guild: POB 3159, Darul Aman Rd, Kabul; tel. (93) 41765; telex 234; f. 1968; a non-profit making asscn for carpet manufacturers and exporters; Pres. AHMAD J. RATEB; 861 mems.

Afghan Raisins Export Promotion Institute: POB 3034, Kabul; tel. (93) 42362; exporters of dried fruit.

Afghanistan Karakul Institute: POB 506, Muhammad Jan Khan Wat, Kabul; tel. (93) 21239; exporters of furs.

TRADE UNIONS

Central Council of Afghanistan Trade Unions: POB 756, Kabul; tel. (93) 23040; f. 1978 to establish and develop the trade union movement, including the setting up of councils and organizational cttees in the provinces; 285,000 mems; Pres. ABDUL SATAR PORDELY; Vice-Pres. HAZRAT HAMGAR.

Transport

RAILWAYS

In 1977 the government approved plans for the creation of a railway system. The proposed line (of 1,815 km) was to connect Kabul to Qandahar and Herat, linking with the Iranian State Railways at Islam Quala and Tarakun, and with Pakistan Railways at Chaman. By 1986 work had not yet begun on the proposed railway.

A combined road and rail bridge was completed across the Amu-Dar'ya (Oxus) river in 1982, linking the Afghan port of Hairatan with the Soviet port of Termez. There are plans for a 200-km railway line from Hairatan to Pul-i-Khomri, 160 km north of Kabul, but work had not begun by 1986. It has been reported that Afghan personnel are receiving training in the USSR.

ROADS

Ministry of Communications and **Ministry of Public Works:** Kabul; in 1978 there were 2,812 km of paved roads out of a total distance of 18,752 km. All-weather highways now link Kabul with Qandahar and Herat in the south and west, Jalalabad in the east and Mazar-i-Sharif and the Amu-Dar'ya river in the north.

Land Transport Company: Khoshal Mena, Kabul; tel. (93) 20345; f. 1943; commercial transport within Afghanistan.

Afghan International Transport Company: Wazir Akbar Khan Mena, behind US Embassy, POB 768, Kabul.

The Millie Bus Enterprise: Ministry of Transport, Kabul; state-owned and run; Pres. Eng. AZIZ NAGHABAN.

INLAND WATERWAYS

River ports on the Amu-Dar'ya are linked by road to Kabul.

CIVIL AVIATION

There are international airports at Kabul and Qandahar and there are plans to rebuild Kabul airport and construct six airports in the north-east, with Soviet help. There are 29 local airports.

Civil Aviation and Tourism Authority: Ansari Wat, POB 165, Kabul; tel. (93) 26541; Dir-Gen. of Air Operations ABDUL WASEH HAIDARI.

National Airlines

Ariana Afghan Airlines Co Ltd: POB 76, Ansari Wat, Kabul; tel. (93) 24731; telex 28; f. 1955; 100% government-owned; Bakhtar Afghan Airlines took control of the company's operations in 1985; internal services to Qandahar and Mazar; services to Dubai, India, the USSR and Czechoslovakia; services to the remainder of Europe, Iran, Turkey and Pakistan have been suspended since 1982; Pres. ABDUL QAYUM BASHARYAR; Comptroller S. G. HAZRAT; fleet of 1 Boeing 727-100C.

Bakhtar Afghan Airlines: Ansari Wat, POB 3058, Kabul; tel. (93) 24043; f. 1968; internal services between Kabul and 18 regional locations; external services to the USSR, Czechoslovakia, India and the UAE; Pres. NIAZ MUHAMMAD; Dir of Operations Capt. R. NAWRUZ; Gen. Dir Lt-Col ABDUL LATIF; fleet of 2 Boeing 727, 3 Antonov-26, 2 Antonov-24, 2 YAK-40, 1 DHC-6 Twin Otter.

Tourism

Afghan Tour: Shar-i-Nau, Ansari Wat, Kabul; tel. (93) 31320; official travel agency supervised by ATO.

Afghan Tourist Organization (ATO): Shar-i-Nau, Ansari Wat, Kabul; tel. (93) 30323; f. 1958; Pres. M. OMAR KARIMZADA.

Atomic Energy

Atomic Energy Commission: Faculty of Science, Kabul University, Kabul; Pres. of Comm. and Dean of Faculty Dr MUHAMMAD RASUL.

ALBANIA

Introductory Survey

Location, Climate, Language, Religion, Flag, Capital

The People's Socialist Republic of Albania lies in south-eastern Europe. It is bordered by Yugoslavia to the north and east, by Greece to the south and by the Adriatic and Ionian Seas (parts of the Mediterranean Sea) to the west. The climate is Mediterranean throughout most of the country. The sea plays a moderating role, although frequent cyclones in the winter months make the weather unstable. The average temperature is 14°C (57°F) in the north-east and 18°C (64°F) in the south-west. The language is Albanian, the principal dialects being Gheg (north of the Shkumbini river) and Tosk (in the south). The literary language is being formed on the basis of a strong fusion of the two dialects, with the phonetic and morphological structure of Tosk prevailing. The State recognizes no religion and supports atheist propaganda. All religious institutions have been closed. Before 1946 Islam was the predominant faith, and there were small groups of Christians (mainly Roman Catholic in the north and Eastern Orthodox in the south). The national flag (proportions 7 by 5) is red, with a two-headed black eagle, above which is a gold-edged, five-pointed red star, in the centre. The capital is Tirana (Tiranë).

Recent History

On 28 November 1912, after more than 400 years of Turkish rule, Albania declared its independence under a provisional government. The country was occupied by Italy in 1914 but its independence was re-established in 1920. A republic was proclaimed in 1925 and Ahmet Beg Zogu was elected President. He was proclaimed King Zog in 1928 and reigned until the occupation of Albania by Italy in April 1939, after which Albania was united with the Italian crown for four years. Albania was occupied by German forces in 1943, but they withdrew after a year. A provisional government was formed in October 1944.

The Communist-led National Liberation Front (NLF), established with help from Yugoslav Communists in 1941, was the most successful wartime resistance group and took power on 29 November 1944. Elections in December 1945 were based on a single list of candidates, sponsored by the Communists. The new regime was led by Enver Hoxha, head of the Albanian Communist Party since 1943. King Zog was deposed and the People's Republic of Albania was proclaimed on 11 January 1946. The Communist Party was renamed the Party of Labour of Albania (PLA) in 1948.

The NLF regime had close links with Yugoslavia, including a monetary and customs union, until the latter's expulsion from the Cominform in 1948. Albania's leaders, fearing Yugoslav expansionism, quickly turned against their former mentors. Albania became a close ally of the USSR and joined the Moscow-based Council for Mutual Economic Assistance (CMEA) in 1949. Albania's adherence to the Eastern bloc was weakened by the relaxation of Soviet policy towards Yugoslavia after the death of Marshal Stalin, the Soviet leader, in 1953.

Hoxha resigned as Head of Government in 1954 but retained effective national leadership as First Secretary of the PLA. Albania joined the Warsaw Pact in 1955 but relations with the USSR deteriorated when Soviet leaders attempted a *rapprochement* with Yugoslavia. Albania supported Beijing in the Sino-Soviet ideological dispute. The USSR denounced Albania and broke off relations in 1961. Albania turned increasingly to the People's Republic of China for support, ended participation in the CMEA in 1962 and withdrew from the Warsaw Pact in 1968. However, following the improvement of relations between China and the USA after 1972, Albania became disenchanted with its alliance with Beijing. Sino-Albanian relations deteriorated further upon the death of Mao Zedong, the Chinese leader, in 1976. A new constitution was adopted in December 1976, declaring Albania a People's Socialist Republic, and reaffirming its policy of self-reliance.

In 1974 the Minister of Defence, Gen. Beqir Balluku, was dismissed, but it was not until 1978 that the Government chose to reveal that he had been involved in a plot against it on behalf of China, and that he had been executed in 1975. In 1978 Albania announced its full support of Viet-Nam in its dispute with Beijing, and China formally terminated all economic and military co-operation with Albania. Albania recognized the Vietnamese-backed government of Kampuchea in 1983.

In September 1979 Hysni Kapo, a member of the PLA's Politburo and one of Hoxha's closest collaborators, died. A government reshuffle took place in April 1980, and Mehmet Shehu, Chairman of the Council of Ministers since 1954, was relieved of his concurrent post of Minister of Defence. In December 1981 Shehu died as a result of a shooting incident. It was officially reported that he had committed suicide, but other sources suggested his involvement in a leadership struggle with Hoxha. (A year later Hoxha claimed that Shehu had been the leader of a plot to assassinate him, and in March 1985, amidst suggestions that Shehu had in fact been executed—which were subsequently denied by the Government—allegations that Shehu had worked as a secret agent, successively for the USA, the USSR and Yugoslavia, were repeated.) Following the death of Shehu, a new government was formed under Adil Çarçani, hitherto First Deputy Chairman. Feçor Shehu, Minister of the Interior and nephew of Mehmet Shehu, was not reappointed.

In September 1982 a group of armed Albanian exiles landed on the coast, but were promptly disposed of by the authorities. The Pretender to the throne of Albania, Leka I, while not directly involved, admitted his acquaintance with the rebels' leader. In November Ramiz Alia replaced Haxhi Lleshi as President of the Presidium of the People's Assembly (Head of State), and the Council of Ministers was reshuffled. A number of former state and Party officials, including Feçor Shehu and two other former Ministers, were reportedly executed in September 1983. In February 1984 Qirjako Mihali was appointed as an additional Deputy Chairman of the Council of Ministers.

Enver Hoxha died in April 1985. No foreign delegations were permitted to attend the funeral, and a Soviet message of condolence was rejected. Ramiz Alia replaced Hoxha as First Secretary of the PLA, and pledged that he would uphold the independent policies of his predecessor. In mid-1985 the Chairman of the State Planning Commission and the Minister of Finance were replaced. To celebrate the 40th anniversary of the proclamation of the Republic, in January 1986 an amnesty for certain categories of prisoners was announced. In March 1986 Nexhmije Hoxha, widow of Enver Hoxha, was elected to the chair of the General Council of the Democratic Front of Albania. The Ninth PLA Congress was held in November 1986.

Albania has diplomatic relations with over 100 countries. Albania remains hostile to the USSR, and Soviet attempts to renew links have been repeatedly rebuffed. In November 1985 Albania reiterated its determination not to have any relations with the USSR or the USA. Since the rift with Beijing, Albania has shown an interest in emerging from its isolation and in improving relations with Western Europe. Two separate border incidents during 1984, in which a Frenchman employed on the Greek island of Corfu and a Greek citizen were shot dead by Albanian frontier guards, created only temporary setbacks. In 1985 delegations from the Italian Ministry of Foreign Affairs and from the French Ministry of External Relations visited Tirana, and it was reported that secret talks were taking place between Albania and the United Kingdom with a view to re-establishing diplomatic relations (severed as a result of the sinking of two British warships in the Corfu channel in 1946). In October 1985 the Albanian Minister of Foreign Trade, Shane Korbeci, visited Italy and was received by the Italian Prime Minister, Bettino Craxi. Relations between the two countries were subsequently strained, however, following an incident involving six Albanian citizens who entered the Italian embassy in Tirana in December 1985 in search of political asylum. Diplomatic relations with Spain were established in September 1986. Negotiations between Albania and Greece took place in Athens in 1984, and in December the visit to Tirana by the Greek Minister of State for Foreign Affairs resulted in the signing of several co-operation agreements. In January 1985 the Albanian/Greek border crossing at Kakavija was reopened. Ideological differences have prevented friendly relations with Yugoslavia. The question of the status of the Albanian minority in Yugoslavia, and also of the Greek minority in Albania, remain sensitive issues. The visit to Yugoslavia by Albania's Minister of Foreign Trade in July 1980 led to closer economic co-operation, but since 1981 relations have been strained following riots in the Yugoslav province of Kosovo by ethnic Albanians demanding better conditions. During 1985, however, talks on trade and transport between Albania and Yugoslavia were successful.

Albania was not represented at the 1984 Stockholm Conference on Security and Co-operation in Europe, and did not attend the Athens Conference on Balkan Co-operation and the creation of a nuclear-free zone. A report released in December 1984 by the human rights organization, Amnesty International, was highly critical of Albania's detention of thousands of political and religious dissidents.

Government
Nominally the supreme organ of government is the People's Assembly, a single-chamber legislature of 250 deputies. In practice the Assembly meets for only a few days each year to ratify actions taken in its name by the Presidium of the Assembly, whose President is Head of State. Executive authority is held by the Council of Ministers, whose Chairman is Head of Government. The Council is elected by the Assembly.

Real power is held by leaders of the (Communist) Party of Labour of Albania, or Workers' Party, the only political party in the country. The Party has a political monopoly; it controls the entire functioning of government, and all the country's leaders are members. The Party Congress, convened every five years, elects the Central Committee (85 full members and 46 candidate members were elected in November 1986), which, in turn, elects the Political Bureau (Politburo).

Elections to the People's Assembly, held every four years, are based on a single list of candidates standing for the Communist-led Democratic Front of Albania.

For local government, Albania is divided into 26 districts, each under a People's Council elected every three years.

Defence
Defence in Albania is conducted under the auspices of the People's Army, which was founded in 1943. Military service lasts for two years in the Army, and three years in the Air Force, Navy and paramilitary units. In July 1986, according to Western estimates, the total strength of the armed forces was 42,000 (including 22,400 conscripts), comprising Army 31,500, Air Force 7,200 and Navy 3,300. The internal security forces number 5,000 and the frontier force 7,000. Defence expenditure in 1986 was estimated at 2,300m. lekë.

Economic Affairs
In material terms, Albania is the poorest country in Europe. The World Bank's estimate of GNP per caput in 1981 was only US $820. There are, however, considerable mineral resources, and Albania is self-sufficient in grain. The economy operates on the principles of public ownership of the means of production. Long-term planning began in 1951, and by 1965 the semi-feudal society had been replaced by the state-run agrarian-industrial system. The fifth Five-Year Plan (1971–75) aimed to develop production through extensive capital investments and large industrial building projects. During the sixth Five-Year Plan (1976–80) the annual growth in net material product (NMP) averaged 5%. Industrial output increased by an average annual rate of 6.8%. Agricultural production rose by 21.4% over the previous five-year period. Exports increased by 33%, with processed and semi-processed goods accounting for 70% of the total. The seventh Five-Year Plan (1981–85) envisaged an increase of 35–37% in NMP, but growth of only 16% was achieved. Industrial production was expected to rise by 36–38%, but went up by only 27%. Agricultural output increased by 13%, compared with a target of 30–32%. Exports were planned to increase by 58–60% but rose by only 29%.

The eighth Five-Year Plan (1986–90) continued to stress the development of energy and mineral resources. Compared with 1985, the 'global social product' (gross output of goods and material services) was to increase by 31–33% and NMP was to rise by 35–37%. The volume of industrial production was to grow by 29–31%. Compared with the 1981–85 period, average annual agricultural output during the 1986–90 Plan was to go up by 35–37%. The volume of foreign trade was due to expand by 34–36% during the 1986–90 period, with exports alone increasing by 44–46%. Real income per head in 1990 was to rise by 7–9% over 1985. Basic investment during the 1986–90 Plan was to be 11–13% higher than during the 1981–85 Plan, with about 25,000m. lekë to be invested in the country's socio-economic development. State budget expenditure in 1986 was estimated at 9,250m. lekë.

Albania's hydroelectric potential is being expanded rapidly, and accounts for over 80% of total electricity production. Compared with the previous five-year period, the total output of electricity rose by 46% in 1981–85. In late 1984, however, electricity shortages were reported, owing to drought. The largest hydroelectric project is the Enver Hoxha station at Koman (planned eventually to be capable of producing 2,000m. kWh annually), the third phase of the Drini River system in northern Albania. Its first two turbines were installed by early 1986, and the third and fourth turbines were due to be in operation later in the year. A major project of the 1986–90 Five-Year Plan is the construction of a new hydroelectric power and irrigation complex at Bënjë, in Gramsh District, which will generate 250m. kWh per year. The Light of the Party hydropower station in Fierza has a generating capacity of 500,000 kW. Albania has its own reserves of petroleum, producing an estimated 3.5m. metric tons in 1983, and its own refining facilities. Albania is the world's second largest producer and exporter of chromite (chromium ore), with an estimated output of 258,000 metric tons (chromium content) in 1983. Production was scheduled to increase by 34–36% between 1986 and 1990. Todo Manço mine, at Bulqize in Dibër District, accounted for 44% of all chromium extracted in Albania in 1982. Output of coal rose by 48% in the 1981–85 period. One of the most important coal mines is that of Memaliaj in Tepelenë District. Other important minerals include copper, nickel, bitumen and pyrite. Copper smelting and processing plants are located at Rubik, Kukës, Shkodër and Laç. Production of blister copper increased by 25% in 1981–85, and output of copper wires and cables was almost double that of the previous Five-Year Plan. Under the 1986–90 Plan, a total of 1,100m. lekë was to be invested in the chrome and copper industries. An iron and steel plant opened at Elbasan in 1976, and a second blast furnace began production in 1981. Output of rolled steels went up by 44% in 1981–85.

Industrial production represents about 70% of total social product, and agricultural production about 30%. Industry is based on the processing of agricultural raw materials and the production of machinery and equipment, chemicals, fertilizers, building materials and textiles, the latter accounting for 65% of total light industrial output. In 1984 foodstuffs accounted for 25% of total industrial output, light industry for 16.1% and engineering for 15.4%. The chemical and fertilizer industries have expanded rapidly since the mid-1960s. In the 1981–85 period production of phosphatic fertilizers doubled, and that of sulphuric acid rose by 160%. It was envisaged that output of the chemical industry in 1990 would be 38–40% higher than in 1985. The light and foodstuffs industries meet over 85% of domestic needs, with the 125 enterprises and combines employing some 100,000 people. The 1986–90 Plan emphasized increased output in light industry, especially the production of consumer goods. Major industrial projects to be commissioned in 1986 included the lubricant oils plant in Ballsh, extension of the existing superphosphate factory and the building of a new sulphuric acid factory at Laç, and a new urea factory at Fier.

Agriculture was transformed after 1945 by land reclamation and mechanization, and complete collectivization was achieved in 1967. Albania became self-sufficient in bread grain in 1976. Besides wheat and maize, other important crops are rice, potatoes, dry beans, olives, citrus fruits and grapes. Industrial crops include tobacco, cotton, sunflowers and sugar beet. With the expansion of the planted area by 34%, tobacco production in 1986 was to increase by 50% over 1985. In 1983 709,800 ha were under cultivation. In 1981–85 42,000 ha were brought under irrigation and 11,000 ha of existing irrigated land underwent improvements. By 1985 56.5% of arable land was under irrigation. When completed in 1990, at a cost of 570m. lekë, the Bënjë irrigation system will provide 120m. cu m of water for agricultural purposes. In 1983 the 421 co-operatives accounted for 73.6% of total agricultural production. The severe weather of early 1985 led to the loss of large numbers of livestock. Compared with 1984, agricultural output rose by 2.2% in 1985. About 35% of Albania is forested, and investment in afforestation was increased under the 1981–85 Plan. About 40,000 ha are afforested and improved annually.

Albania's principal exports, other than chromite, include ferro-nickel ore, coal, copper wire, bitumen, tobacco and cigarettes, timber and furniture, textiles, canned foods, wine, fruit and vegetables, and handicrafts. In 1982 fuels made up 27.1% of total exports, minerals and metals 26.2%, and electricity 13.2%. Of total imports, fuels, minerals and metals accounted for 33.3%, machinery and equipment for 22.2%, and chemical and rubber products for 16.6%; foodstuffs accounted for only 5.2%. The export of electricity to neighbouring countries is of increasing significance. In 1982 Albania and Greece concluded an agreement for the construction of a power line linking their respective grids, and the construction of a 220-km line between a new Albanian hydroelectric station and the Yugoslav grid was scheduled for completion in the mid-1980s.

The Constitution forbids the acceptance of foreign credits, and the principle of self-reliance was reiterated in 1985. Economic growth has been hindered by the Government's inflexible trading policies and by the ending of all agreements with the People's Republic of China which, until 1978, accounted for about one-half of Albania's foreign trade. A *rapprochement* began in 1983, however, when a Chinese trade delegation visited Albania, resulting in trade accords worth US $5m.–7m. Commercial relations with both Western and Eastern European countries are also improving steadily. In 1984 Albania's trade with CMEA member countries was worth an estimated US $300m., or 40% of total foreign trade, while trade with Western European countries also accounted for 40% of the total. Albanian trade delegations visited Greece, Italy, the Netherlands and Finland in 1985. The signing of an exchange agreement with Greece in January 1986 was expected to lead to a further increase in mutual trade. Albania's main trading partner is Yugoslavia, followed by Italy, trade with these countries in 1984 totalling an estimated US $88m. and $60m. respectively. A goods exchange agreement for 1986–90 was signed with Yugoslavia in 1985, setting the total value of their bilateral trade at $680m. Similar five-year agreements were also concluded with most CMEA member countries (except the USSR and Mongolia) and with Algeria, Austria, the People's Republic of China and Finland. A three-year agreement (1986–88) was signed with Turkey. In November 1985 the first visit to Albania by an economic delegation from the Federal Republic of Germany was made, and in May 1986 a French trade delegation visited Tirana.

Social Welfare
In Albania all medical services are free of charge, and medicines are supplied free to children up to one year of age. The 1983 state budget allocated 441m. lekë to the health service, and 901m. lekë to social care and social insurance. There are hospitals, clinics and maternity homes throughout the country. In 1983 the number of health institutions exceeded 5,165, and there were 17,600 beds available. There were 4,957 doctors and dentists, or one for every 573 persons. Kindergartens and nursery schools receive large subsidies. Women are entitled to 180 days' maternity leave, receiving 80% of salary. There is a non-contributory state social insurance system for all workers, with 70–100% of salary being paid during sick leave, and a pension system for the old and disabled. Retirement pensions represent 70% of the average monthly salary. Men retire between the ages of 50 and 60, and women between 45 and 55. Income tax has been abolished, government expenditure being met by surpluses earned by state enterprises.

Education
Education in Albania is provided free at primary and secondary level. Students in higher education pay a fee in accordance with the family income. The state budget allocated 891m. lekë to education and culture in 1983. Children in the age group of three to six years may attend nursery school (kopshte). Children between the ages of seven and 15 years attend an 'eight-grade school' which is compulsory. Secondary schools in Albania may be divided into three main categories, namely '12-year schools' (shkollat 12-vjeçare) giving four-year courses, secondary technical-professional schools (shkollat e mesme tekniko-profesionale) which combine vocational training with a general education, and lower vocational schools (shkollat e ulte profesionale) which train workers in the fields of agriculture and industry. The school-year in secondary schools lasts six and a half months. All secondary-school graduates are required to spend a year working in factories or on collective farms.

In the 1985/86 school year a total of 744,000 pupils and students enrolled at educational institutes. The Enver Hoxha University at Tirana has eight faculties and had 12,500 full- and part-time students in 1986/87. Students at higher education institutes spend seven months of every year at the institute, two months in production or construction work, one month in physical culture and military training, and two months on vacation. Since 1979 a number of Albanian students have been permitted to attend training courses in the West.

Tourism
All aspects of tourism in Albania are handled by Albturist, the state tourist department. Only a few thousand foreign visitors, mostly from France, Italy, the Federal Republic of Germany and Scandinavia, are permitted to enter Albania each year. There are few recognized resorts apart from Durrës. The Roman amphitheatre at Durrës is one of the largest in Europe. Great potential exists in the beauty spots on the coast and in the scenery of the interior. Of historic interest are the castles of Berat, Krujë and Kuculla (in Gjirokastër).

Public Holidays
1987: 1 January (New Year's Day), 11 January (Proclamation of the Republic), 1 May (May Day), 7 November (Victory of the October Socialist Revolution), 28 November (Proclamation of Independence), 29 November (Liberation Day 1944).

1988: 1 January (New Year's Day), 11 January (Proclamation of the Republic), 1 May (May Day), 7 November (Victory of the October Socialist Revolution), 28 November (Proclamation of Independence), 29 November (Liberation Day 1944).

Weights and Measures
The metric system is in force.

Currency and Exchange Rates
100 qindarka = 1 new lek.

Exchange rates (30 September 1986):
 £1 sterling = 10.13 lekë;
 US $1 = 7.00 lekë.

Statistical Survey

Area and Population

AREA, POPULATION AND DENSITY

Area (sq km)	
Land	27,398
Inland water	1,350
Total	28,748*
Population (census result)	
January 1979	2,591,000
Population (official estimates at mid-year)	
1983	2,841,300
Males	1,466,000
Females	1,375,300
1984	2,900,700
1985	2,962,000
Density (per sq km) at mid-1985	103.0

* 11,100 sq miles.

DISTRICTS (1983)

	Area (sq km)	Population (mid-year)	Density (per sq km)
Berat	1,027	157,300	153.2
Dibër	1,568	137,800	87.9
Durrës	848	220,600	250.1
Elbasan	1,481	213,200	144.0
Fier	1,175	216,400	184.2
Gramsh	695	39,300	56.5
Gjirokastër	1,137	61,200	53.8
Kolonjë	805	22,500	28.0
Korçë	2,181	201,300	92.3
Krujë	607	94,600	155.8
Kukës	1,330	88,400	66.5
Lezhë	479	54,200	113.1
Librazhd	1,013	64,100	63.3
Lushnjë	712	117,800	165.4
Mat	1,028	68,700	66.8
Mirditë	867	45,800	52.8
Përmet	929	37,100	39.9
Pogradec	725	62,700	86.5
Pukë	1,034	46,100	44.6
Sarandë	1,097	78,200	71.3
Shkodër	775	42,500	54.8
Skrapar	2,528	210,200	83.1
Tepelenë	817	46,100	56.4
Tiranë	1,238	316,100	255.3
Tropojë	1,043	40,900	39.2
Vlorë	1,609	158,200	98.3
Total	28,748	2,841,300	98.8

Source: *40 Years of Socialist Albania*.

PRINCIPAL TOWNS (population at mid-1983)

Tiranë (Tirana, the capital)	206,100
Durrës (Durazzo)	72,400
Shkodër (Scutari)	71,200
Elbasan	69,900
Vlorë (Vlonë or Valona)	61,100
Korçë (Koritsa)	57,100
Fier	37,000
Berat	36,600
Lushnjë	24,200
Kavajë	22,500
Gjirokastër	21,400

Source: *40 Years of Socialist Albania*.

BIRTHS, MARRIAGES AND DEATHS

	Registered live births		Registered marriages		Registered deaths	
	Number	Rate (per 1,000)	Number	Rate (per 1,000)	Number	Rate (per 1,000)
1980	70,680	26.5	21,729	8.1	16,981	6.2
1981	72,180	26.5	23,301	8.3	18,001	6.4
1982	77,232	27.8	25,157	8.8	16,521	5.8
1983	73,762	26.0	25,607	9.0	17,416	6.1
1985*	77,535	26.2	n.a.	n.a.	17,179	5.8

* Provisional. Figures for 1984 are not available.

Average Life Expectation (1982/83): 70.4 years (Males 67.9 years, Females 72.9 years).

Source: *40 Years of Socialist Albania* and UN, *Demographic Yearbook*.

ECONOMICALLY ACTIVE POPULATION
(ILO estimates, '000 persons at mid-1980)

	Males	Females	Total
Agriculture, etc.	338	339	677
Industry	237	74	311
Services	144	79	223
Total	719	492	1,211

Source: ILO, *Economically Active Population Estimates and Projections, 1950–2025*.

Mid-1984 (estimates in '000): Agriculture, etc. 743; Total 1,286 (Source: FAO, *Production Yearbook*).

EMPLOYMENT IN THE 'SOCIALIZED' SECTOR
(excluding agricultural co-operatives)

	1980	1983
Industry	225,300	252,700
Construction	73,600	80,700
Agriculture	136,900	152,400
Transport and communications	27,200	33,400
Trade	47,700	53,900
Education and culture	48,900	52,800
Health service	32,500	34,400
Others	30,200	37,500
Total	622,300	697,800

Source: *40 Years of Socialist Albania*.

Agriculture

PRINCIPAL CROPS ('000 metric tons)

	1982	1983	1984
Wheat and spelt	524	583	600*
Rice (paddy)	12	13	13*
Barley*	25	30	34
Maize	342	366	400*
Rye	8	10	10*
Oats*	30	30	30
Sorghum*	30	35	35
Potatoes	101	136	137*
Dry beans*	16	17	18
Sunflower seed	33	53	53*
Seed cotton	21	16	16*
Cotton seed*	14	10	10
Olives	18	45	25*
Vegetables*	182	184	188
Grapes	80	82	83*
Sugar beet	319	320	320*
Apples*	13	14	15
Plums*	12	13	13
Oranges*	11	11	12
Tobacco (leaves)	18	18	18*
Cotton (lint)*	7	6	6

* FAO estimate.
Source: FAO, *Production Yearbook*.

LIVESTOCK (FAO estimates, year ending September)

	1982	1983	1984
Horses	43,000	43,000	43,000
Mules	22,000	22,000	22,000
Asses	52,000	52,000	52,000
Cattle	580,000	600,000	600,000
Pigs	205,000	200,000	200,000
Sheep	1,180,000	1,200,000	1,200,000
Goats	680,000	700,000	700,000

Poultry (FAO estimates, million): 4 in 1982; 5 in 1983; 5 in 1984.
Source: FAO, *Production Yearbook*.

LIVESTOCK PRODUCTS (FAO estimates, metric tons)

	1982	1983	1984
Beef and veal	26,000	27,000	28,000
Mutton and lamb	18,000	18,000	18,000
Goats' meat	8,000	8,000	8,000
Pig meat	9,000	9,000	9,000
Poultry meat	12,000	12,000	13,000
Cows' milk	330,000	337,000	352,000
Sheep's milk	40,000	41,000	41,000
Goats' milk	28,000	28,000	29,000
Cheese*	12,200	12,453	12,955
Butter	3,600	3,690	3,700
Hen eggs	12,000	12,000	12,723
Wool:			
greasy	3,100	3,100	3,202
scoured (clean)	1,600	1,650	1,685
Cattle hides	4,312	4,466	4,598
Sheep and lamb skins	2,325	2,375	2,387
Goat and kid skins	664	664	665

* Cheese from whole or partly skimmed milk of cows or buffaloes.
Source: FAO, *Production Yearbook*.

Forestry

ROUNDWOOD REMOVALS ('000 cubic metres)
Annual total 2,330 (Industrial wood 722, Fuel wood 1,608) in 1971 (official estimates) and in 1972–84 (FAO estimates).

SAWNWOOD PRODUCTION ('000 cubic metres)
Annual total 200 (coniferous 105, broadleaved 95) in 1966–71 (official estimates) and in 1972–84 (FAO estimates).
Source: FAO, *Yearbook of Forest Products*.

Fishing

Annual catch 4,000 metric tons (FAO estimate).

Mining

PRODUCTION (estimates, '000 metric tons)

	1981	1982	1983
Brown coal (incl. lignite)	1,600	1,600	1,700
Crude petroleum	2,200	3,500	3,500
Natural gas (terajoules)	15,000	16,000	16,000
Copper*†	11.5	14.0	15.0
Nickel*†	8.8	9.0	9.0
Chromium*‡	244	251	258

* Figures relate to the metal content of ores.
† Estimated by Metallgesellschaft Aktiengesellschaft (Frankfurt).
‡ Estimated by the US Bureau of Mines.
Source: UN, *Industrial Statistics Yearbook*.

Industry

SELECTED PRODUCTS

		1981	1982	1983
Olive oil[1]	metric tons	3,000	2,000	7,000
Raw sugar[2]	metric tons	25,000	25,000	20,000
Wine[1]	hectolitres	210,000	210,000	220,000
Cigarettes[3]	million	6,200	6,200	6,100
Nitrogenous fertilizers (a)[4]	metric tons	73,000	70,800	73,000
Phosphate fertilizers (b)[4]	metric tons	6,000	22,800	25,000
Motor spirit (Petrol)	metric tons	155,000	250,000	250,000
Kerosene	metric tons	65,000	80,000	80,000
Distillate fuel oils	metric tons	250,000	350,000	350,000
Bitumen (Asphalt)	metric tons	1,200,000	1,400,000	1,500,000
Cement[5]	metric tons	1,088,000	1,088,000	1,088,000
Copper (unrefined)[6]	metric tons	10,000	12,000	12,500
Electric energy	million kWh	2,500	2,600	2,725

[1] Estimated by the FAO.
[2] Estimated by the International Sugar Organization (London).
[3] Estimated by the US Department of Agriculture.
[4] Figures for fertilizer production are unofficial estimates quoted by the FAO. Output is measured in terms of (a) nitrogen or (b) phosphoric acid.
[5] Estimated by the US Bureau of Mines.
[6] Estimated by Metallgesellschaft Aktiengesellschaft (Frankfurt).

Source: mainly UN, *Industrial Statistics Yearbook*.

1984: Electric energy 3,800 million kWh (Source: *40 Years of Socialist Albania*); Olive oil 3,000 metric tons (FAO estimate); Nitrogenous fertilizers 75,000 metric tons (estimate); Phosphate fertilizers 18,000 metric tons (estimate).

Finance

CURRENCY AND EXCHANGE RATES

Monetary Units
100 qindarka (qintars) = 1 new lek.

Denominations
Coins: 5, 10, 20 and 50 qintars; 1 lek.
Notes: 1, 3, 5, 10, 25, 50 and 100 lekë.

Sterling and Dollar Equivalents (30 September 1986)
£1 sterling = 10.13 lekë;
US $1 = 7.00 lekë (non-commercial rates);
1,000 lekë = £98.73 = $142.86.

Exchange Rate
The non-commercial rate, applicable to tourism, has been fixed at US $1 = 7.000 lekë since June 1979.

STATE BUDGET

1984 (million lekë, final): Revenue 8,753.8; Expenditure 8,739.4.

1985 (million lekë, provisional): Revenue 9,250; Expenditure 9,200 (National economy 4,831, Socio-cultural measures 2,460, Defence 1,700, Administration 138).

1986 (million lekë, provisional): Revenue 9,300 (National economy 8,962, Non-productive sector and other income from the socialist sector 338); Expenditure 9,250 (National economy 4,612, Socio-cultural measures 2,565, Defence 978, Administration 141).

Source: Albanian Telegraphic Agency.

INVESTMENT

Investment in socio-economic development during the 1986–90 Five-Year Plan was estimated at about 25,000 million lekë.

Source: Albanian Telegraphic Agency.

External Trade

No figures are available for the total value of trade since 1964, when imports totalled 4,906.4m. old lekë and exports 2,996.2m. old lekë. The old lek was replaced in August 1965 by the new lek (1 new lek=10 old lekë). Prior to this change the official rate of exchange was US $1=50 old lekë.

TRADE WITH OECD COUNTRIES* (US $ million)

Imports†	1979	1980
Austria	4.3	6.8
Belgium/Luxembourg	1.0	—
Canada	—	0.1
Denmark	0.3	0.3
Finland	0.5	0.1
France	7.5	5.1
Germany, Federal Republic	—	20.5
Greece	13.0	28.8
Italy	20.6	23.1
Japan	4.0	2.0
Netherlands	6.0	4.2
Sweden	2.5	2.0
Switzerland	2.5	3.0
United Kingdom	1.3	3.0
USA	10.0	7.0

* Compiled from data of partner countries.
† OECD exports to Albania.

Exports‡	1979	1980
Austria	9.1	7.0
Belgium/Luxembourg	0.5	2.0
Denmark	0.5	0.3
Finland	—	1.0
France	0.2	9.5
Germany, Federal Republic	—	9.1
Greece	9.0	9.0
Italy	31.4	42.0
Japan	4.0	—
Netherlands	5.6	5.6
Norway	0.8	—
Spain	4.5	4.0
Sweden	18.2	7.0
Switzerland	1.4	2.0
United Kingdom	—	0.3
USA	10.8	12.0

‡ OECD imports from Albania.

Transport

ROADS AND RAILWAYS

(1978): Total freight 57,434,000 metric tons; Total passengers 132,917,000. Source: Albanian Telegraphic Agency.

INTERNATIONAL SEA-BORNE SHIPPING

(estimated freight traffic, '000 metric tons)

	1981	1982	1983
Goods loaded	1,180	1,165	1,150
Goods unloaded	551	631	631

Source: UN, *Monthly Bulletin of Statistics*.

Communications Media

	1981	1982	1983
Book production:			
Titles*	1,043	1,149	997
Copies ('000)*	6,600	4,607	6,224
Daily newspapers:			
Number	n.a.	2	n.a.
Average circulation	n.a.	145,000	n.a.
Radio receivers in use	n.a.	n.a.	476,000
Television receivers in use	n.a.	n.a.	196,000

* Figures include pamphlets (151 titles and 1,211,000 copies in 1981; 112 titles and 319,000 copies in 1982; 130 titles and 419,000 copies in 1983).
Source: UNESCO, *Statistical Yearbook*.

Education

(1983)

	Institutions*	Teachers	Pupils
Pre-primary	2,931	4,600*	103,034*
Primary (8-year)	1,621	27,100†	531,520†
Secondary:			
general	20	1,370†	24,313†
vocational	313	4,020†	69,354†
Higher	8	1,360†	19,670†

* Source: *40 Years of Socialist Albania*.
† Source: UNESCO, *Statistical Yearbook*.

Directory

The Constitution

A new Constitution was adopted on 27 December 1976. The following is a summary of its main provisions:

THE SOCIAL ORDER

The Political Order

Articles 1–15. Albania is a People's Socialist Republic, based on the dictatorship of the proletariat. The Party of Labour of Albania (Workers' Party) is the sole leading political force of the State and society. Marxism-Leninism is the ruling ideology.

The representative bodies are the People's Assembly and the People's Councils, elected by the people through universal suffrage by equal, direct and secret ballot. Officials serve the people and render account to them. They also participate directly in production work, in order to prevent the creation of a privileged stratum.

In the construction of socialism, Albania relies primarily on its own efforts.

The Economic Order

Articles 16–31. The economy is a socialist economy, which relies on the socialist ownership of the means of production. Socialist property is inviolable and state property belongs to all the people. The State works to narrow the differences between the countryside and the cities. The personal property of the citizens is recognized and protected by the State.

Foreign trade is a state monopoly.

The granting of concessions to, and the creation of foreign or joint economic or financial institutions with, capitalist, bourgeois and revisionist monopolies and States, as well as the acceptance of credits from them, is prohibited.

Citizens pay no levies or taxes whatsoever.

Education, Science and Culture

Articles 32–37. The State carries out broad ideological and cultural activity for the communist education of the working people. Education is organized by the State and is free of charge.

The State organizes the development of science and technology.

The State recognizes no religion and supports and carries out atheist propaganda.

THE FUNDAMENTAL RIGHTS AND DUTIES OF CITIZENS

Articles 38–65. The rights and duties of citizens are founded on the reconciliation of the interests of the individual with those of the socialist society.

All citizens are equal before the law. Women enjoy the same rights as men.

Citizens reaching the age of 18 have the right to take part in voting for, and to be elected to, all organs of state power.

Citizens enjoy the right to work and to recreation. Workers are guaranteed the necessary material means for life in old age and sickness.

Marriage and the family are under the care and protection of the State and society. Marriage is contracted before the competent state organs.

Citizens enjoy freedom of speech.

The creation of all organizations of a fascist, anti-democratic, religious or anti-socialist nature is prohibited.

SUPREME BODIES OF STATE POWER

The People's Assembly

Articles 66–74. The People's Assembly is the supreme body of state power and sole law-making body. It defines the main directions of the domestic and foreign policy of the State. It elects, appoints and dismisses the Presidium of the People's Assembly, the Council of Ministers, the Supreme Court, the Attorney-General and his deputies.

The People's Assembly is composed of 250 deputies, elected for a period of four years, and meets in regular session twice a year.

The Presidium of the People's Assembly

Articles 75–79. The Presidium of the People's Assembly is the supreme body of state power, with permanent activity, and is composed of a President, three Vice-Presidents, a Secretary and 10 members. It convenes the sessions of the People's Assembly and, between sessions, supervises the implementation of the laws and decisions of the People's Assembly, and controls all state organs.

The Presidium directs and controls the activity of the People's Councils.

The Supreme Organs of State Administration

Articles 80–86. The Council of Ministers is the supreme executive and order-issuing body, and is composed of the Chairman, Vice-Chairmen and ministers. It directs activity for the realization of the domestic and foreign policies of the State. It directs and controls the activity of the ministries, other central organs of the state administration and the executive committees of the People's Councils.

The Chairman and Vice-Chairmen of the Council of Ministers constitute the Presidium of the Council of Ministers.

The Country's Defence and the Armed Forces

Articles 87–91. The State protects the victories of the people's revolution and of socialist construction, and defends the freedom, national independence and territorial integrity of the country.

The armed forces are led by the Party of Labour of Albania. The First Secretary of the Central Committee of the Party of Labour of Albania is the Supreme Commander of the armed forces and Chairman of the Defence Council. The stationing of foreign bases and military forces in Albania is not permitted.

LOCAL ORGANS OF STATE POWER AND STATE ADMINISTRATION

Articles 92–100. The People's Councils are organs of state power, which carry out the administration in the respective administrative-territorial units with the broad participation of the working masses. The People's Councils are elected for a term of three years.

A Higher People's Council may dissolve a lower People's Council. Executive committees are an executive and order-issuing organ of the People's Councils.

THE PEOPLE'S COURTS

Articles 101–103. The People's Courts are bodies which administer justice. At the head of the organs of justice stands the Supreme Court, which directs and controls the activity of the courts. The Supreme Court is elected at the first session of the People's Assembly. The other People's Courts are elected by the people.

THE ATTORNEY-GENERAL'S OFFICE

Articles 104–106. It is the duty of the Attorney-General's Office to supervise the implementation of the laws. The Attorney-General and his deputies are appointed at the first session of the People's Assembly. Attorneys are appointed by the Presidium of the Assembly.

THE EMBLEM, THE FLAG, THE CAPITAL

Articles 107–109. The emblem of the People's Socialist Republic of Albania consists of a black double-headed eagle, encircled by two sheaves of wheat with a five-pointed red star at the top and tied at the bottom by a red ribbon bearing the inscription '24th May 1944'.

The state flag has a red background with a black double-headed eagle in the middle and a red five-pointed star outlined in gold at the top.

The capital is Tirana.

FINAL PROVISIONS

Articles 110–112. The Constitution is the fundamental law of the State. Drafts for amendments may be presented by the Presidium of the People's Assembly, the Council of Ministers or two-fifths of the deputies. The approval of the Constitution and amendments to it requires a two-thirds majority of all deputies.

The Government
(December 1986)

HEAD OF STATE
President of the Presidium of the People's Assembly: Ramiz Alia (elected 22 November 1982).

PRESIDIUM OF THE PEOPLE'S ASSEMBLY
President: Ramiz Alia.
Vice-Presidents: Rita Marko, Xhafer Spahiu, Emine Guri.
Secretary: Sihat Tozaj.
Members:

Simon Ballabani	Nik Preng Shyti
Faik Çinaj	Elmaz Puto
Petrit Gaçe	Stefan Qirjako
Ibrahim Gjevori	Lumturi Rexha
Rahman Hanku	Eleni Selenica

COUNCIL OF MINISTERS
Chairman: Adil Çarçani.
Deputy Chairmen: Besnik Bekteshi, Qirjako Mihali, Manush Myftiu.
Chairman of State Planning Commission: Niko Gjyzari.
Minister of Agriculture: Mrs Themie Thomai.
Minister of Foreign Trade: Shane Korbeci.
Minister of Internal Trade: Osman Murati.
Minister of Communal Economy: Kudret Arapi.
Minister of Communications: Luan Babameto.
Minister of Construction: Farudin Hoxha.
Minister of Education and Culture: Mrs Tefta Çami.
Minister of Finance: Andrea Nako.
Minister of Foreign Affairs: Reis Malile.
Minister of Heavy Industry and Mining: Hajredin Çeliku.
Minister of Energy: Lavdosh Hametaj.
Minister of the Interior: Hekuran Isai.
Minister of Light and Food Industry: Mrs Vito Kapo.
Minister of National Defence: Prokop Murra.
Minister of Public Health: Ajli Alushani.

MINISTRIES
All Ministries are in Tirana.

Ministry of Foreign Affairs: Ministria e Punëvet të Jashtme, Tirana; telex 2164.
Ministry of Foreign Trade: Ministria e Tregetisë të Jashtme, Tirana; telex 2152.

POLITBURO OF THE CENTRAL COMMITTEE OF THE PARTY OF LABOUR OF ALBANIA
First Secretary: Ramiz Alia.

Other Members:

Muho Asllani	Hekuran Isai
Besnik Bekteshi	Rita Marko
Foto Çami	Pali Miska
Adil Çarçani	Prokop Murra
Hajredin Çeliku	Manush Myftiu
Lenka Çuko	Simon Stefani

Candidate Members:

Vangjel Çerrava	Qirjako Mihali
Llambi Gegprifti	Kiço Mustaqi
Pirro Kondi	

Legislature

KUVËND POPULLORE
(People's Assembly)

President: Pali Miska.
Vice-Presidents: Jashar Menzelxhiu, Mrs Vitori Curri.
Secretary: Jakup Shiqerukaj.

The Assembly has 250 members, elected (unopposed) for a four-year term. At the general election held on 14 November 1982, it was reported that 1,627,968 votes were cast in favour of the 250 candidates, with one vote against and eight invalid. A new People's Assembly was due to be elected in February 1987.

Political Organizations

Partia e Punës te Shqipërisë (Party of Labour of Albania, PLA): Tirana; f. 1941; the Communist Party of Albania, which adopted its present name in 1948; also known as the Workers' Party; the country's only permitted political party; Marxist-Leninist; 128,000 members, 15,300 candidate members (Jan. 1986); First Sec. of Central Cttee Ramiz Alia; Secs Foto Çami, Vangjel Çerrava, Lenka Çuko, Simon Stefani.

Frontit Demokratik te Shqipërisë (Democratic Front of Albania): Tirana; tel. 79-57; f. 1942; serves as the main link between the people and the PLA and the people's state power in the struggle for the construction of socialism and in the defence of the homeland; the Front is responsible for the enlightenment and education of the working people, according to the party line, and serves as a powerful means for the active participation of the broad working masses in the solution of major social and state problems; nominates all candidates in elections; Gen. Council has 25-mem. Presidency; Chair. of Gen. Council Nexhmije Hoxha.

Bashkimi i Rinisë së Punës i Shqipërisë (Union of Albanian Working Youth): Tirana; tel. 78-18; f. 1941; political organization for young people, sponsored by the Party of Labour of Albania, playing an important role in the political, economic, social, educational and cultural life of the country; at the 8th Congress, held in October 1982, 171 mems were elected to the Central Cttee; First Sec. of the Central Cttee Mehmet Elezi.

Bashkimi të Grave të Shqipërisë (Women's Union of Albania): Tirana; tel. 79-59; f. 1943 for the ideological, political and social education of women, aiming to achieve their complete emancipation, to help build a socialist society, and to consolidate the international solidarity of women; at the 9th Congress, held in June 1983, a General Council of 167 mems, a Presidium of 27 and a Secretariat of 5 were elected; Pres. of General Council Lumturi Rexha; Sec.-Gen. Leonora Çaro.

Diplomatic Representation

EMBASSIES IN ALBANIA

Bulgaria: Rruga Skënderbeu 12, Tirana; tel. 26-72; Chargé d'affaires: Marko Markov.
China, People's Republic: Rruga Skënderbeu 57, Tirana; tel. 26-00; telex 2148; Ambassador: Fan Chengzuo.
Cuba: Rruga Kongresi i Përmetit, Tirana; tel. 51-77; telex 2155; Ambassador: Carlos Alonso Moreno.
Czechoslovakia: Rruga Skënderbeu 10, Tirana; telex 2162; Chargé d'affaires: Otto Jaček.
Egypt: Rruga Skënderbeu 43, Tirana; tel. 30-13; telex 2156; Ambassador: Yusuf Umar Hindi.
France: Rruga Skënderbeu 14, Tirana; tel. 28-04; Ambassador: Philippe Legrain.
German Democratic Republic: Rruga Asim Zeneli, Tirana; tel. 23-01; telex 2161; Chargé d'affaires: Dieter Kulitzka.
Greece: Rruga Frederick Shiroka 3, Tirana; tel. 68-50; Ambassador: (vacant).
Hungary: Rruga Skënderbeu 16, Tirana; tel. 20-14; telex 2169; Chargé d'affaires: István Kádár.
Italy: Rruga Labinoti 103, Tirana; tel. 28-00; telex 2166; Ambassador: Francesco Carlo Gentile.
Korea, Democratic People's Republic: Rruga Skënderbeu 55, Tirana; tel. 22-58; Ambassador: Pak Yong-Si.
Poland: Rruga Kongresi i Përmetit 123, Tirana; Chargé d'affaires: Jan Siuchniński.
Romania: Rruga Themistokli Gërmenji 2, Tirana; tel. 22-59; Ambassador: Gheorghe Pop.
Turkey: Rruga Konferenca e Pezës 31, Tirana; tel. 24-49; Ambassador: Bilal Shimshir.
Viet-Nam: Rruga Lek Dukagjini, Tirana; tel. 25-56; Ambassador: Le Ngoc Thanh.
Yugoslavia: Rruga Kongresi i Përmetit 192–196, Tirana; tel. 30-42; telex 2167; Ambassador: Novak Pribicević.

ALBANIA							Directory

Judicial System

Justice is administered under the Constitution by the Supreme Court, and by District, Village, City and City Quarter Courts created by a special law in October 1968 as links of the judicial system which functions within the ranks of the people. Military Tribunals are held at the Supreme and District Courts. Courts of Justice are independent in the exercise of their functions, and are separated from the administration.

Until March 1966 the judicial system was supervised by a Minister of Justice and his officials. This department now no longer exists and its principal responsibilities are discharged by the Supreme Court. A revised Penal Code came into effect in October 1977, together with a Code of Penal Procedure (1980), a Labour Code (1980), a Code of Civil Procedure (1982) and a Family Code (1982). Trials are normally held in public. The accused is assured the right of defence, and the principle of presumption of innocence is sanctioned by the Code of Penal Procedure. For first-degree cases, the Supreme Court and the District Courts are made up of a professional judge and an Assistant Judge. Trials in the Village, City and City Quarter Courts are held before an Assistant Judge from the District Court and two social activists. Second-degree cases are held in the Supreme Court or the District Courts, before three Judges and two Assistant Judges. The verdicts of the lower courts may be altered, within the law, by the higher courts, and judges may be recalled before the expiration of their term by their electors or the organ which has elected them.

The Supreme Court is elected for a four-year term by the People's Assembly; between sessions of the Assembly, individual members of the Court are elected by the Presidium of the People's Assembly. The District Courts are elected for a three-year term by a secret ballot of all voting citizens. The Attorney-General and his deputies are appointed by the People's Assembly, and District Attorneys by the Presidium of the People's Assembly.

President of the Supreme Court: Aranit Çela.

Attorney-General: Rrapo Mino.

Religion

There is no formal practice of the previously predominant Muslim religion, although certain social traditions persist. All religious institutions were closed by the Government in 1967. Article 37 of the 1976 Constitution states that Albania recognizes no religion and supports and carries out atheist propaganda. All of the old mosques have now been shut down and are preserved as centres of cultural interest. Formerly the population was approximately 70% Muslim, 10% Roman Catholic (in the north) and 20% Greek Orthodox (in the south).

CHRISTIANITY
The Roman Catholic Church

Albania formally comprises the archdioceses of Durrës (directly responsible to the Holy See) and Shkodrë (Shkodër), three dioceses, one territorial abbacy and Southern Albania (previously the responsibility of an Apostolic Administrator). There are no longer any resident prelates holding office in the country.

Apostolic Administrator of Durrës and Lezhë: Nicola Troshani, Titular Bishop of Cisamo.

Apostolic Administrator of Shkodrë: Ernesto Çoba, Titular Bishop of Mideo.

The Press

The Albanian press recognizes itself as a powerful medium of educational and organizational propaganda with a profound Marxist-Leninist ideological content. It expresses party doctrine probably more forcefully than any other European communist press. There are numerous local newspapers, generally the organs of the regional party committees.

In 1985 the 23 newspapers and 77 magazines had a total circulation of 64m. copies. The most important publications are the Party of Labour daily, *Zëri i Popullit*, and *Bashkimi*, the organ of the Democratic Front, published twice a week. In 1984 there were 14 district newspapers.

The Albanian Telegraphic Agency (ATA), has a monopoly of news distribution in Albania.

PRINCIPAL DAILIES

Zëri i Popullit (The Voice of the People): Bulevardi Stalin, Tirana; tel. 78-13; f. 1942; publ. by the Central Committee of the Party of Labour; Editor-in-Chief Arshin Xhezo; circ. 105,000.

Bashkimi (Unity): Bulevardi Stalin, Tirana; tel. 81-10; f. 1943; publ. by the Democratic Front; Editor-in-Chief Hamit Boriçi; circ. 30,000.

PERIODICALS
Tirana

Bibliografi Kombëtare e RPSSH, Libri Shqip (National Bibliography of the PSRA, Albanian Books): Tirana; quarterly; published by the National Library of Albania.

Bibliografi Kombëtare e RPSSH Periodikeve Shqip (National Bibliography of the PSRA, Albanian periodicals): Tirana; monthly; published by the National Library of Albania.

Bujqësia Socialiste (Socialist Agriculture): Tirana; monthly; publ. by the Ministry of Agriculture; Editor Faik Labinoti.

Buletini i Shkencave Bujqësore (Agricultural Sciences Bulletin): Tirana; quarterly; summaries in French; publ. by the Agricultural Scientific Research Institute; Editor-in-Chief Lefter Veshi.

Buletini i Shkencave të Natyrës (Natural Sciences Bulletin): Tirana; f. 1957; quarterly; summaries in French; publ. by the Enver Hoxha University of Tirana; Editor-in-Chief Muharrem Frasheri.

Buletini i Shkencave Mjekësore (Medical Sciences Bulletin): Tirana; quarterly; summaries in French; publ. by the Enver Hoxha University of Tirana; Editor-in-Chief Ylvi Vehbiu.

Buletini i Shkencave Teknike (Technical Sciences Bulletin): Tirana; quarterly; summaries in French; publ. by the Enver Hoxha University of Tirana.

Buletini i Studimeve Gjeologjike (Bulletin of Geological Studies): Tirana; quarterly; publ. by Ministry of Industry and Mining.

Drejtësia Popullore (People's Law): Tirana; quarterly; publ. of Supreme Court and Attorney-General's Office.

Drita (The Light): Baboci 37z, Tirana; f. 1960; weekly; publ. by Union of Writers and Artists of Albania; Chief Editor Zija Çela.

Estrada (Variety Shows): Tirana; every 2 months; publ. by the Central House of Popular Creativity.

Fatosi (The Valiant): Tirana; fortnightly; publ. by Cen. Cttee of Union of Working Youth.

Gazeta Zyrtare e RPS Të Shqipërisë (Official Gazette of the PSR of Albania): Tirana; occasional government review.

Gjuha Jonë (Our Language): Tirana; 3 a year; organ of the Institute of Language and Literature at the Academy of Sciences; Editor Ali Dhrimo.

Horizonti (Horizon): Tirana; fortnightly; publ. by Cen. Cttee of Union of Working Youth.

Hosteni (The Goad): Tirana; f. 1945; fortnightly; political review of humour and satire; publ. by the Union of Journalists; Editor-in-Chief Niko Nikolla.

Iliria (Illyria): Qendra e Kërkimeve Arkeologjike, Tirana; 2 a year; summaries in French; publ. by Archaeological Centre at Academy of Sciences.

Kënga Jonë (Our Song): Tirana; f. 1960; every 2 months; publ. by the Central House of Popular Creativity.

Kultura Popullore (Popular Culture): Tirana; 2 a year; annually in French; publ. by the Institute of Folk Culture at the Academy of Sciences; Editor-in-Chief Alfred Uçi.

Laiko Vima (People's Step): Tirana; f. 1945; 2 a week; in Greek; publ. by the Democratic Front for the Greek minority of Gjirokastër; Editor-in-Chief Vasil Çami.

Les Lettres Albanaises: Rruga Konferenca e Pezës, Tirana; tel. 26-91; quarterly; in French; literary and artistic review; publ. by Union of Writers and Artists of Albania; Editor-in-Chief Ismail Kadare.

Luftëtari (The Fighter): Tirana; f. 1945; 2 a week; publ. by the Ministry of National Defence; Editor-in-Chief Demokrat Anastasi.

Mbrëmje Tematike (Evening Parties): Tirana; publ. by the Central House of Popular Creativity.

Mësuesi (The Teacher): Tirana; f. 1961; weekly; publ. by the Ministry of Education and Culture; Editor-in-Chief Thoma Qendro.

Monumentet (Monuments): Tirana; f. 1971; 2 a year; summaries in French; publ. by the Institute of Monuments and Culture; Editor-in-Chief Sotir Kosta.

ALBANIA

Ndërtuesi (The Builder): Tirana; quarterly; publ. by the Ministry of Construction.

Në shërbim të popullit (In the Service of the People): Tirana; f. 1955; Editor-in-Chief Thoma Naqe.

Në skenën e fëmijëve (On the Children's Stage): Tirana; published by the Central House of Popular Creativity.

Nëna dhe Fëmija (Mother and Child): Tirana; 3 a year; publ. by Ministry of Public Health.

Nëntori (November): Baboci 37z, Tirana; f. 1954; monthly; publ. by the Union of Writers and Artists of Albania; Chief Editor Valentina Leskaj.

Për Mbrojtjen e Atdheut (For the Defence of the Fatherland): Tirana; publ. of the Ministry of National Defence; Editor-in-Chief Bege Tena.

Përmbledhje Studimesh (Collection of Studies): Tirana; quarterly; summaries in French; bulletin of the Ministry of Industry and Mining.

Pionieri (The Pioneer): Tirana; f. 1944; fortnightly; publ. by the Cen. Cttee of the Union of Working Youth; Editor-in-Chief Skender Hasko; circ. 38,000.

Probleme Ekonomike: Tirana; quarterly; organ of Institute for Economic Studies.

Puna (Labour): Bulevardi Dëshmorët e Kombit, Tirana; f. 1945; 2 a week; also quarterly in French; organ of the Central Council of Albanian Trade Unions; Editor-in-Chief Namik Dokle.

Radio Përhapja: Tirana; fortnightly; organ of Albanian Radio and Television.

Revista Mjekësore (Medical Review): Tirana; every 2 months; publ. by Ministry of Health.

Revista Pedagogjike: Tirana; quarterly; organ of the Institute of Pedagogical Studies; Editor Sotir Temo.

Rruga e Partisë (The Party's Road): Tirana; f. 1954; monthly; publ. by Cen. Cttee of the Party of Labour; Editor Stefi Kotmilo; circ. 9,000.

Shëndeti (Health): Tirana; f. 1949; monthly; publ. by the Ministry of Public Health; Editor-in-Chief Roza Theohari.

Shkenca dhe Jeta (Science and Life): Tirana; every 2 months; organ of the Central Committee of the Union of Working Youth; Editor-in-Chief Kudret Isai.

Shqipëria e Re (New Albania): Rruga Themistokli Gërmenji 6, Tirana; f. 1947; published monthly in Albanian; every 2 months in Arabic, English, French, German, Italian, Russian and Spanish; organ of the Committee for Foreign Cultural Relations; illustrated political and social magazine; Editor Ymer Minxhozi; circ. 170,000.

Shqipëria Sot (Albania Today): Tirana; every 2 months; published in English, French, German, Italian and Spanish; political, cultural and social review; Editor-in-Chief Dhimiter Verli.

Shqiptarja e Re (The New Albanian Woman): Tirana; f. 1943; monthly; publ. by the Women's Union of Albania; political and socio-cultural review; Editor-in-Chief Drita Siliqi.

Skena dhe Ekrani (Stage and Screen): Tirana; quarterly; publ. by the Committee for Culture and Arts.

Sporti Popullor (People's Sport): Tirana; f. 1945; weekly; publ. by the Ministry of Education and Culture; Editor Besnik Dizdari; circ. 60,000.

Studenti (The Student): Tirana; weekly; publ. by the Committee of the University Working Youth Union.

Studia Albanica: Tirana; f. 1964; 2 a year; history and philology; in French; publ. by the Albanian Academy of Sciences; Editor-in-Chief Luan Omari.

Studime Filologjike (Philological Studies): Tirana; f. 1964; quaterly; summaries in French; publ. by the Institute of Language and Literature at the Albanian Academy of Sciences; Editor-in-Chief Androkli Kostallari.

Studime Historike (Historical Studies): Tirana; f. 1964; quarterly; summaries in French; publ. by the Institute of History at the Albanian Academy of Sciences; historical sciences; Editor-in-Chief Stefanaq Pollo.

Teknika (Technology): Tirana; f. 1954; quarterly; publ. by the Ministry of Industry and Mining; Editor Natasha Varfi.

Teatri (Theatre): Tirana; f. 1960; every 2 months; publ. by the Central House of Popular Creativity.

Tregtia e Jashtme Popullore (Albanian Foreign Trade): Rruga Konferenca e Pezës 6, Tirana; tel. 29-34; telex 2179; f. 1961; every 2 months; in English and French; organ of the Albanian Chamber of Commerce; Editor Agim Korbi.

Tribuna e Gazetarit (The Journalist's Tribune): Tirana; every 2 months; publ. by the Union of Journalists of Albania; Editor Adriatik Kanani.

Vatra e Kulturës (Field of Culture): Tirana; publ. by the Central House of Popular Creativity.

Ylli (The Star): Tirana; f. 1951; monthly; socio-political and literary review; Editor-in-Chief Nevruz Turhani.

Yllkat (Little Stars): Tirana; monthly; publ. by Institute of Pedagogical Studies.

Zëri i Rinisë (The Voice of the Youth): Tirana; 2 a week; publ. by Cen. Cttee of the Union of Albanian Working Youth; Editor-in-Chief Remzi Lani; circ. 53,000.

10 Korriku (10 July): Tirana; f. 1946; monthly; publ. by the Ministry of National Defence; Editor-in-Chief Selami Vehbiu.

Other Towns

Adriatiku (Adriatic): Durrës; 2 a week.

Drapër e Çekan (Hammer and Sickle): Fier; 2 a week.

Fitorjë (Victory): Sarandë; f. 1971; 2 a week; Editor-in-Chief Belul Korkuti.

Jehona e Skraparit: Skrapar; 2 a week.

Jeta e Re (New Life): Shkodër; 2 a week.

Kastrioti: Krujë; f. 1971; 2 a week.

Kukësi i Ri (New Kukës): Kukës; 2 a week.

Kushtrimi (Clarion Call): Berat; 2 a week.

Pararoja (Vanguard): Gjirokastër; 2 a week.

Përpara (Forward): Korçë; f. 1967; 2 a week; publ. by the Cttee of the Korçë Workers' Party; Editor-in-Chief Strati Marko; circ. 4,000.

Shkëndija (The Spark): Lushnjë; f. 1971; 2 a week.

Shkumbimi: Elbasan; 2 a week; Editor-in-Chief Mefail Pupuleku.

Ushtimi e Maleve (Echo of the Mountains): Peshkopi; 2 a week.

Zëri i Vlorës (The Voice of Vlorë): Vlorë; 2 a week.

NEWS AGENCY

Albanian Telegraphic Agency (ATA): Bulevardi Marcel Cachin 23, Tirana; tel. 44-12; telex 2142; f. 1945; domestic and foreign news; branches in provincial towns; Dir Taqo Zoto.

Foreign Bureau

Xinhua (New China) News Agency (People's Republic of China): Rruga Skënderbeu 57, Tirana; tel. 2600; telex 2148; Bureau Chief Wang Hongqi.

PRESS ASSOCIATION

Bashkimi i Gazetarëve të Shqipërisë (Union of Journalists of Albania): Tirana; tel. 79-77; f. 1949; Chair. Marash Hajati; Sec.-Gen. Ymer Minxhozi.

Publishers

In 1983 a total of 997 book titles were published.

Drejtoria Qëndrore e Përhapjes dhe e Propagandimit të Librit (Central Administration for the Dissemination and Propagation of the Book): Tirana; tel. 78-41; directed by the Ministry of Education and Culture.

Naim Frashëri State Publishing House: Tirana; tel. 79-06; publishes books in foreign languages; Dir Thanes Leci.

Ndërmarja e botimeve ushtarake: Tirana; military, technology.

8 Nëntori Publishing House; Tirana; books and journals on Albania; Dir Pavllo Gjidede.

Government Publishing House

N.I.SH. Shtypshkronjave Mihal Duri (Mihal Duri State Printing House): Tirana; government publications, politics, law, education; Dir Hajri Hoxha.

WRITERS' UNION

Lidhja e Shkrimtarëve dhe e Artistëve të Shqipërisë (Union of Writers and Artists of Albania): Baboci 37z, Tirana; tel. 79-89; f. 1945; 1,750 mems; Chair. Dritëro Agolli; Secs Llazar Siliqi, Feim Ibrahimi, Kujtim Buza.

ALBANIA   *Directory*

Radio and Television

It was estimated that there would be about 500,000 radio receivers and 300,000 television sets in use by 1987.

Radiotelevisioni Shqiptar: Rruga Ismail Qemali, Tirana; tel. 81-34; f. 1944; Dir-Gen. MARASH HAJATI.

RADIO

Radio Tirana: home programmes are broadcast daily from Tirana for 18 hours; regional stations in Berat, Fier, Gjirokastër, Korçë, Kükes, Pukë, Rogozhina, Sarandë and Shkodër; wire-relay service in Tirana and in factories, mines and clubs all over the country.

External Service: broadcasts for 83 hours daily in Albanian, Arabic, Bulgarian, Chinese, Czech, English, French, German, Greek, Hungarian, Indonesian, Italian, Persian, Polish, Portuguese, Romanian, Russian, Serbo-Croat, Spanish, Swedish and Turkish; Dir AGIM PAPAPROKO.

TELEVISION

There are stations at Tirana, Berat, Elbasan, Gjirokastër, Kükes, Peshkopi and Pogradec. Programmes are broadcast in colour in Tirana only and in black and white elsewhere for 5 hours daily (8 hours on Sundays).

Finance

Banka e Shtëtit Shqiptar (Albanian State Bank): Head Office: Sheshi Skënderbeu 1, Tirana; tel. 24-35; telex 2153; f. 1945; sole credit institution; branches in 34 towns; Gen. Man. KOSTAQ PASTOLI.

State Agricultural Bank: Tirana; tel. 77-38; f. 1970; gives short- and long-term credits to agricultural co-operatives and enterprises; Dir S. KUCI.

Drejtoria e Përgjithshme e Kursimeve dhe Sigurimeve (Directorate of Savings and Insurance): Tirana; tel. 25-42; f. 1949; Dir SEIT BUSHATI.

In 1984 there were 115 savings offices and 3,600 agencies.

Trade and Industry

CHAMBER OF COMMERCE

Dhoma e Tregtisë e Republikës Popullore të Shqipërisë (Chamber of Commerce of the People's Republic of Albania): Rruga Konferenca e Pezës 6, Tirana; tel. 42-46; telex 2179; f. 1958; Chair. LIGOR DHAMO.

SUPERVISORY ORGANIZATION

Albkontroll: Bul. Enver Hoxha 45, Durrës; tel. 23-54; telex 2181; brs throughout Albania; independent control body for inspection of goods, means of transport, etc.; Dir H. MINGA.

FOREIGN TRADE ORGANIZATIONS

Agroeksport: Rruga 4 Shkurti 6, Tirana; tel. 52-27; telex 2137; export of vegetables, fruit, canned fish, wine, tobacco, etc.; Gen. Dir FERDINAND KITA.

Albimport: Rruga 4 Shkurti 6, Tirana; tel. 27-11; telex 2112; textiles, paper, photographic equipment, chemicals, etc.; Dir J. BORODNI.

Albkoop: Rruga 4 Shkurti 6, Tirana; tel. 41-79; f. 1986; import and export of consumer goods.

Industrialimpeks: Rruga 4 Shkurti 6, Tirana; tel. 45-40; telex 2140; export of textiles, kitchenware, paper, clothing, etc.; import of cotton, wool, paper, etc.; Gen. Dir HAZBI GJIKONDI.

Makinaimport: Rruga 4 Shkurti 6, Tirana; tel. 52-20; telex 2127; import of factory installations and machine parts.

Metalimport: Rruga 4 Shkurti 6, Tirana; tel. 38-48; telex 2116; imports ferrous and non-ferrous metals, electrodes, oil lubricants, minerals, etc.; Dir T. BORODNI.

Mineralimpeks: Rruga 4 Shkurti 6, Tirana; tel. 33-70; telex 2123; import and export of chromium ore, ferro-nickel ore, electricity, etc.; Gen. Dir NIQIFOR ALIKAJ.

Transshqip: Rruga 4 Shkurti 6, Tirana; tel. 30-76; telex 2131; transport of foreign trade goods by sea and road; agents in the Enver Hoxha Port of Durrës, Vlorë and Sarandë; Gen. Dir GIOLEKË ZENELI.

CO-OPERATIVE ORGANIZATIONS

Centrocoop: Sheshi Skënderbeu, Tirana; co-operative import and export organization.

Bashkimi Qëndror i Kooperativave të Artizanatit (Central Union of Handicraft Workers' Co-operatives): Tirana; Pres. KRISTO THEMELKO.

Bashkimi Qëndror i Kooperativave Tregtare (Central Union of Commercial Co-operatives): Tirana.

Bashkimi Qëndror i Kooperativave të Shit-Blerjes (Central Union of Buying and Selling Co-operatives): Tirana.

TRADE UNIONS

The principal function of Albanian trade unions is to mobilize the working class to carry out the task of socialist construction. In every work and production centre there is a trade union grass-root organization which elects the trade union committee, while in each ward and district there is a ward committee and a district council.

Këshilli Qëndror i Bashkimeve Profesionale të Shqipërisë (Central Council of Albanian Trade Unions): Tirana; f. 1945; 610,000 mems; a 171-member Central Council, a 21-member Presidium and six secretaries were elected at the 1982 Congress; Pres. of Gen. Council SOTIR KOÇOLLARI.

Transport

RAILWAYS

In 1984 there were 408 km of railway track, with lines linking Tirana–Vorë–Sukth–Durrës, Durrës–Kavajë–Rrogozhinë–Elbasan–Librazhd–Prenjas–Pogradec, Rrogozhinë–Lushnje–Fier–Ballsh, Vorë–Laç–Lezhë–Shkodër and Selenicë–Vlorë. A standard-guage line is being built between Fier and Selenicë. A new 35-km line between Fier and Vlorë was opened in 1985. In March 1986 work began on the Milot–Rrëshen–Klos railway, to comprise 63 km of main line and 32 km of secondary lines.

In 1979 Albania and Yugoslavia agreed to construct a 50-km line between Shkodër and Titograd. Construction of the 35-km extension from Laç to Shkodër was completed in 1981, and the Shkodër–Hani i Hotit link (35.5 km) was completed in 1984. Work on the Yugoslav section was completed in late 1985. The Shkodër–Titograd line opened to international freight traffic in September 1986. There were also plans to link the Enver Hoxha Port of Durrës with the Bulgarian Black Sea ports, via the Yugoslav cities of Skopje and Kumanovo.

Drejtoria e Hekurudhave: Tirana; railways administration.

ROADS

All regions are linked by the road network, but many roads in mountainous districts are unsuitable for motor transport. Private cars are banned in Albania. Bicycles and mules are widely used.

SHIPPING

Albania's merchant fleet had an estimated total displacement of 56,000 grt in 1982. The chief ports are the Enver Hoxha Port of Durrës, Vlorë, Sarandë and Shëngjiu. Durrës harbour has been dredged to allow for bigger ships. In 1980 construction of a new port near Vlorë began. When completed, the port will have a cargo-handling capacity of more than 4m. tons per year. A ferry service for the transport of freight between the Enver Hoxha Port of Durrës and Trieste (Italy) was inaugurated in November 1983.

Drejtoria e Agjensisë së Vaporave: Enver Hoxha Port of Durrës; shipping administration.

CIVIL AVIATION

Albania has air links with Athens, Belgrade, Bucharest, Budapest, East Berlin, Rome, and Vienna and Zürich in summer. An agreement to establish air links between Albania and Turkey was signed in February 1984. There is a small but modern airport at Rinas, 28 km from Tirana. There is no regular internal air service.

Albtransport: Rruga Kongresi i Përmetit 202, Tirana; tel. 30-26; telex 2124; air agency.

Tourism

Albturist: Bulevardi Dëshmorët e Kombit 6, Tirana; tel. 38-60; telex 2148; Dir VASO PANO.

ALGERIA

Introductory Survey

Location, Climate, Language, Religion, Flag, Capital

The Democratic and Popular Republic of Algeria lies in north Africa, with the Mediterranean Sea to the north, Mali and Niger to the south, Tunisia and Libya to the east, and Morocco and Mauritania to the west. The climate on the Mediterranean coast is temperate, becoming more extreme in the Atlas mountains immediately to the south. Further south is part of the Sahara, a hot and arid desert. Temperatures in Algiers, on the coast, are generally between 9°C (48°F) and 29°C (84°F), while in the interior they may exceed 50°C (122°F). Arabic is the official language but French is still widely used. There is a considerable Berber-speaking minority. Islam is the state religion, and almost all Algerians are Muslims. The national flag (proportions 3 by 2) has two equal vertical stripes, of green and white, with a red crescent moon and a five-pointed red star superimposed in the centre. The capital is Algiers (El Djezaïr).

Recent History

Algeria was conquered by French forces in the 1830s and annexed by France in 1842. For most of the colonial period, official policy was to colonize the territory with French settlers. Many French citizens were attracted to settle in Algeria and became permanent residents. Unlike most of France's overseas possessions, Algeria was not formally a colony but was 'attached' to metropolitan France. However, political and economic power within Algeria was largely held by the white settler minority, as the indigenous Muslim majority did not have equal rights.

On 1 November 1954 the major Algerian nationalist movement, the Front de libération nationale (FLN), began a war for national independence, in which about 1m. Muslims were killed or wounded. Despite resistance from the Europeans in Algeria, the French Government agreed to a cease-fire in March 1962 and independence was declared on 3 July 1962. In August the Algerian provisional government transferred its functions to the Political Bureau of the FLN, and in September a National Constituent Assembly was elected (from a single list of FLN candidates) and the Republic proclaimed. A new government was formed, with Ahmed Ben Bella, founder of the FLN, as Prime Minister. As a result of the nationalist victory, about 1m. French settlers emigrated from Algeria.

A draft constitution, providing for a presidential regime with the FLN as the sole party, was adopted by the Constituent Assembly in August 1963. In September the Constitution was approved by popular referendum and Ben Bella was elected President. Under his leadership, economic reconstruction was begun and the foundation was laid for a single-party socialist state. However, the failure of the FLN to function as an active political force left real power with the bureaucracy and the army. In June 1965 the Minister of Defence, Col Houari Boumedienne, deposed Ben Bella in a bloodless coup and took control of the state as President of a Revolutionary Council of 26 members, chiefly army officers.

Boumedienne faced considerable opposition from left-wing members of the FLN, but by 1971 the Government felt strong enough to adopt a more active social policy. French petroleum interests were nationalized and an agrarian reform programme was initiated. In June 1975 Boumedienne announced a series of measures to consolidate the regime and his personal power, including the drawing up of a National Charter and a new constitution, and the holding of elections for a President and National Assembly. These actions provoked a resurgence of opposition which had been dormant since the 1960s. However, after the publication in April 1976 of the National Charter, which formulated the principles and plans for creating a socialist system and maintaining Islam as the state religion, the administration encouraged public discussion and responded to criticisms by amending the Charter. In a referendum in June the Charter was adopted by 98.5% of the electorate. In November a new constitution (see below) was approved by another referendum, and in December Boumedienne was elected President unopposed, winning more than 99% of the votes cast. The new formal structure of power was completed in February 1977 by the election of FLN members to the National Assembly.

In December 1978 President Boumedienne died, and the Council of the Revolution (now consisting of only eight members) took over the government. An FLN Congress in January 1979 adopted a new party structure, electing a Central Committee which was envisaged as the highest policy-making body both of the party and of the nation as a whole: this Committee was to choose a party leader who would automatically become the sole presidential candidate. Their choice of Col Bendjedid Chadli, commander of Oran military district, was upheld by a national referendum in February, and was seen as representing a compromise between liberal and radical contenders. Unlike Boumedienne, Chadli appointed a Prime Minister, Col Mohamed Abdelghani, anticipating constitutional changes which were approved by the National Assembly in June and which included the obligatory appointment of a Prime Minister. Further changes in the party structure of the FLN were made in June 1980, when the FLN authorized Chadli to form a smaller Political Bureau of seven members (increased to 10 in July 1981) with more limited responsibilities, thereby increasing the power of the President. Membership of the National Assembly was increased to 281 in the legislative elections of March 1982, when the electorate was offered a choice of three candidates per seat. Of the successful candidates, 55 were FLN party officials and 142 were government officials, so executive control of the Assembly was expected to increase.

At the fifth conference of the FLN, held in December 1983, Chadli was re-elected to the post of secretary-general of the party, and became the sole candidate for the presidential election, which was held on 12 January 1984. His candidature was endorsed by 95.4% of the electorate, and he was therefore returned to office for another five years. Immediately after his re-election, President Chadli effected a major government reshuffle and named a new Prime Minister, Abdelhamid Brahimi, the former Minister of Planning. Throughout 1985, Boumedienne's National Charter of 1976 was the subject of a public debate (initiated by Chadli), which resulted in the adoption of a new National Charter at a special congress of the FLN in December. The revised Charter sought a balance between socialism and Islam as the state ideology, and aimed to encourage the private sector. At a referendum in January 1986, 98.37% of the votes cast (with 95.92% of the electorate participating) favoured the adoption of the new Charter. In February Chadli carried out a series of minor ministerial reshuffles, intended to maintain party unity.

In recent years the Government has faced criticism and violent protests from students, who have condemned the slowness of the authorities in replacing French with Arabic as the official language, and also from the Berbers of the Kabyle region, who felt that their culture and language were being suppressed. Another serious problem is the gradual emergence in Algeria of Muslim fundamentalists, who have caused several disturbances since 1981. In December 1985 Ahmed Ben Bella, the former President, and Dr Hocine Aït Ahmed, an FLN founder and Berber activist, announced from London the formation of a united democratic front to oppose the Government of President Chadli. In the same month 18 alleged supporters of Ben Bella were sentenced to terms of imprisonment, following their conviction on charges of threatening state security. In a separate trial, a total of 22 human rights and Berber cultural activists were found guilty of membership of illegal organizations, and received short prison sentences.

Since independence, Algeria has been one of the most prominent non-aligned states and, as such, played an important part in the release of the American hostages in Iran in January 1981.

The Algerian Government has supported various liberation movements in Africa and the Middle East, providing military, financial and diplomatic aid for the Polisario Front in the Western Sahara (see chapter on Morocco). The protracted Sahara struggle embittered Algeria's relations with France, which supported the claims of Morocco and Mauritania. Algeria also criticized French military intervention elsewhere in Africa, while further grievances were the heavy trade surplus in France's favour, and France's determination to reduce the number of Algerians resident in France. Relations improved, however, with the advent of a socialist government in France in May 1981, and in December 1982 President Chadli made the first official visit to France by an Algerian head of state since independence. In September 1986 the French Prime Minister, Jacques Chirac, visited Algiers to discuss bilateral trade and foreign policy, although the impact of his visit was decreased by the announcement of proposals to introduce visa requirements for visitors from non-EEC countries to France, following a series of bombings in Paris. In October Algeria retaliated by introducing similar requirements for French visitors. In the early 1980s there was a noticeable improvement in relations with the USA, culminating, in April 1985, in a meeting between the US and Algerian presidents in Washington. As a result of this visit, Chadli succeeded in having Algeria removed from the list of countries that the US Government had declared 'ineligible' to purchase US military equipment. In March 1986 President Chadli paid an official visit to Moscow, in a bid to improve relations with the USSR.

During 1983 relations between the Maghreb countries (Algeria, Morocco, Mauritania and Tunisia) improved considerably, following a series of meetings between the various heads of state. As a result, Algeria partially opened its frontier with Morocco in February, and signed the Maghreb Fraternity and Co-operation Treaty, which normalized relations with Tunisia, in March. It was hoped that this treaty would eventually form the basis of the long-discussed Greater Maghreb Union. It was therefore left open for other countries to sign; Mauritania did so in December 1983. However, the *rapprochement* with Morocco was hindered by Algeria's continuing support of the Polisario Front, and, despite calls for definite steps to be taken towards the formation of a political union in the Maghreb, closer links seemed impossible as long as the situation in the Western Sahara remained unresolved.

In 1985–86 relations with Morocco continued to deteriorate: in July 1985 the Moroccan Minister of the Interior accused Algeria of training Moroccan terrorists for operations against his Government. Meanwhile, relations with Libya improved, following President Chadli's meetings with Dr Ali Abdel-Salim Treiki, the Libyan Secretary for Foreign Liaison, in November 1985, and with Col Gaddafi, the Libyan leader, in January 1986. Both countries reiterated their commitment to the Maghreb, and agreed that the people of the Western Sahara should have the right to self-determination. In April 1986, following the US attack on Libya, Algeria unsuccessfully appealed for the convening of an emergency meeting of Arab nations.

Government

Under the 1976 Constitution (with modifications adopted by the National Assembly in June 1979), Algeria is a socialist single-party state. The Head of State is the President of the Republic, who is nominated by a Congress of the FLN (the only authorized party) and is elected for a five-year term by universal adult suffrage. The President presides over a Council of Ministers, appointed by himself, and a High Security Council. The President may appoint Vice-Presidents and must appoint a Prime Minister, but executive power is essentially concentrated in his own hands. The President shares legislative power with a unicameral National People's Assembly, with 281 members, elected by universal adult suffrage for a five-year term. The President may dissolve the Assembly at any time and is empowered to legislate by decree when it is not in session. The country is divided into 48 departments (wilayaat), sub-divided into communes. Each wilaya and commune has an elected assembly. All candidates for election, whether to local or national assemblies or to the Presidency of the Republic, are nominated by the FLN, but the electorate may be offered a choice of candidates.

Defence

In July 1986 the estimated strength of the armed forces was 169,000, comprising an army of 150,000, a navy of 7,000 and an air force of 12,000. The 1986 defence budget was estimated at 5,459m. dinars. The USSR provides military equipment and training. Military service is compulsory for six months, and there is a gendarmerie of 30,000.

Economic Affairs

Following Algeria's long war of independence, and the consequent departure of French personnel, the economy was severely disrupted and suffered from a shortage of skilled workers. In the period following independence, the Government assumed a dominant role in the economy through the nationalization of large agricultural estates, important manufacturing enterprises and banks. The main sector of the economy, the extraction and processing of hydrocarbons (petroleum and natural gas), was brought under state control in 1971. Assisted by the sharp rises in petroleum prices after 1973, Algeria experienced rapid economic expansion and industrialization, with a consequent decline in the importance of agriculture. Despite a high rate of population growth, average incomes have risen steadily. In 1984, according to estimates by the World Bank, Algeria's gross national product (GNP) per head, measured at average 1982–84 prices, was US $2,410, the fourth highest level among African countries. It was estimated that GNP per head increased, in real terms, at an average rate of 3.6% per year between 1965 and 1984. The average rate of inflation fell from 6.7% in 1982 to 4.6% in 1983, but rose again to 6.6% in 1984 and to an estimated 12% in 1985.

Only about 10% of Algeria's land can be used for agriculture, which accounts for around 7% of gross domestic product (GDP), and employed 45.4% of the working population in 1984. Land reforms have led to the establishment of large co-operatives, but about one-half of the cultivated land is still under private ownership. Depopulation of rural areas is a serious problem. In an attempt to reduce food imports and boost employment, the Government's Development Plan for 1980–84 increased investment in agriculture, particularly irrigation, to 11.8% of the total. To improve efficiency, co-operatives were to be split into smaller units, and the private sector was to be encouraged by a state lending programme and by the relaxation of price controls, allowing farmers to sell directly to markets or, more controversially, to traders. The 1985–89 Plan continued to stress the importance of the agricultural sector, and investment was to be further increased. Algeria's major agricultural products are cereals, wine and citrus fruits. However, the country produces only 35% of domestic cereal requirements, and large quantities of foodstuffs (dairy produce, vegetable oils and sugar, as well as cereals) have to be imported. In 1985 imports of food accounted for about 20% of total imports, in spite of a record cereal harvest of over 3m. metric tons. The 1986 budget allocated 2,000m. dinars to food subsidies. About 25% of Algeria's imports were supplied by France in 1984.

Algeria is rich in minerals, notably iron ore, phosphates, petroleum and natural gas. It is a relatively small petroleum producer: annual output declined from 54m. metric tons in 1978 to 28.3m. tons in 1984. Algeria is a member of OPEC. With reserves estimated at 9,000m. barrels, under the OPEC agreement of October 1986 Algeria's production quota was raised to 669,000 barrels per day. Algeria's proven recoverable reserves of natural gas, estimated at 2,674,000m. cu m in 1981, are the world's fourth largest. Production of natural gas totalled 69,800m. cu m in 1983 and 81,550m. cu m in 1985, of which nearly 40,000m. cu m is exported annually. The hydrocarbons industry contributed about 26% of GDP in 1984 and 97.5% of export revenues in 1985. Hydrocarbon exports totalled $12,800m. in 1985, of which crude petroleum represented 26% and liquefied natural gas (LNG) 24%. In view of the rapid decline in oil prices, however, export revenues were expected to fall sharply in 1986. Recent development programmes have included the construction of gas plants at Arzew and Skikda, which have a joint capacity of 31,500m. cu m of LNG per year, and the completion, in 1983, of a 2,500-km gas pipeline linking Algeria with Italy, via Tunisia. A contract for the doubling of the Algerian section of the pipeline, to allow exports of up to 16,000m. cu m per year, was agreed in 1984. Algeria is aiming at self-sufficiency in cement, iron and steel, plastics, chemicals and fertilizers, although in 1985 many plants were still working below their full potential. Commerce and industry are dominated by state-controlled enterprises. Socialist management of companies by their workers was introduced in 1974.

During the period of the 1970–73 Four-Year Plan, GDP rose by about 10% annually. After the large increases in the price of petroleum in 1973–74, the Government decided on a more intensive investment programme, using increased revenue to expand the economy even faster. In 1974, for the first time, Algeria achieved a large export surplus. Subsequently, however, petroleum production fell and natural gas production was slow to expand, and trade deficits occurred over the next four years. Increased earnings from gas and petroleum exports, however, led to a trade surplus from 1979. The surplus reached US $4,056m. in 1980, falling to $3,226m. in 1983, and rising to an estimated $4,223m. in 1985. In 1984 the current account registered a surplus of $74m., which rose to an estimated $1,015m. in 1985. Revenues from the hydrocarbons sector led to a rapid growth in GDP during the 1970s, reaching a peak of 16.3% growth in 1980. However, the world recession, decreased petroleum production and loss of gas revenues (owing to pricing disagreements and voluntary conservation of reserves) meant that real GDP rose by only 1.2% in 1981, by 3.4% in 1982 and by an estimated 3.5% in 1983. Annual GDP growth was estimated at 6% in 1984 and 1985, but was expected to decline in 1986. At the end of 1985 Algeria's external debt was estimated at $17,000m. The cost of servicing the debt in 1986 was expected to total $3,800m., with interest accounting for $1,200m.

Algeria's development has so far been concentrated in heavy industry along the northern coastal strip, emphasizing capital-intensive production for export. Reliance on the existing infrastructure, together with an annual population growth rate of 6.5% in the cities, has caused a general decline in urban living standards. About 160,000 jobs were created in 1985, insufficient to offset an overall population increase of more than 3% per year, and in 1984 16.9% of the workforce were unemployed. Nearly 1m. Algerians work abroad, and in 1985 remittances from overseas workers totalled an estimated US $373.2m. In December 1979 the FLN Central Committee indicated a shift of emphasis by condemning the country's dependence on the export of hydrocarbons, persistent regional imbalances and insufficient use of human resources. Policies were initiated to conserve hydrocarbon reserves, to split the giant state industrial concerns into less cumbersome units, and to decentralize industry away from Algiers. Exports of crude oil were to be reduced in order to increase sales of refined products. The 1980–84 Development Plan aimed to complete the large-scale projects which had already been started, but to encourage smaller industrial units and the private sector. Emphasis was to switch from heavy industry to previously neglected social areas and infrastructure. There was to be considerable investment in light industry. New codes relating to foreign investment and joint ventures were introduced in 1982, and modified in 1986. In an attempt to solve the chronic housing shortage, a major construction programme was launched, with a target of 450,000 new homes to be built in 1980–84.

The 1985–89 Development Plan, approved in July 1984, envisaged total investment of 550,000m. dinars, and GDP growth of 6.5% annually. The Plan continued to emphasize the agricultural sector and the importance of increasing the share of export revenue coming from non-hydrocarbons; there was also to be considerable investment in the country's infrastructure, particularly in the railway network and in housing, which was to take 16% of the total investment. In 1986 the Government announced measures to encourage tourism as an alternative means of earning foreign exchange, following the decline in the hydrocarbon sector. In March 1986 various austerity measures were adopted, and in April the 1986 budget was revised to take account of the decline in petroleum revenues: total planned investment was reduced from 61,000m. dinars to 45,000m., with expenditure on new projects being severely curtailed.

Social Welfare

Since 1974, all Algerian citizens have had the right to free medical attention. In 1979 Algeria had 367 hospital establishments, with a total of 47,116 beds, and there were 6,881 physicians working in the country. In 1984 a new health plan was launched. In 1986 the revised investment budget allocated 2,575m. dinars to expenditure on health and social services. Under the 1984 plan, several new health centres and clinics were to be built, an institution for training health care administrators was to be founded, and vaccinations were to be made more readily available.

Education

Education is officially compulsory for nine years between six and 15 years of age. Primary education begins at the age of six and lasts for six years. Secondary education begins at 12 years of age and lasts for up to seven years (a first cycle of four years and a second of three years). In 1983 the total enrolment at primary and secondary schools was equivalent to 69% of the school-age population (79% of boys; 59% of girls). Enrolment at primary schools in 1983 included an estimated 83% of children in the relevant age-group (92% of boys; 74% of girls). Nearly 19% of planned expenditure in the 1981 administrative budget was allocated to education. In accordance with the National Charter, the various primary and secondary schools were unified in 1976, private education was abolished and a nine-year 'enseignement fondamental' was introduced. Priority is being given to teacher-training, to the development of technical and scientific teaching programmes, and to adult literacy and training schemes. In 1982 there were four established universities and eight newer ones, with a total of 80,000 students; a programme was under way to establish a 'Centre universitaire' in every wilaya. In 1985, according to UNESCO estimates, the average rate of adult illiteracy was 50.4% (males 37%; females 63%).

Tourism

The principal attractions for tourists are the Mediterranean coast, the Atlas mountains, boar-hunting reserves, thermal springs and the desert. There were about 230,000 tourist visits in 1983. Receipts from tourism totalled US $157m. in 1981, declining to about US $60m. per year in 1982 and 1983. During 1984–1986 160 private projects were approved, to provide a further 12,000 hotel beds.

Public Holidays

1987: 1 January (New Year), 1 May (Labour Day), 30 May* (Id al-Fitr, end of Ramadan), 19 June (Ben Bella's Overthrow), 5 July (Independence), 6 August* (Id al-Adha, Feast of the Sacrifice), 26 August* (Islamic New Year), 4 September* (Ashoura), 1 November (Anniversary of the Revolution), 4 November* (Mouloud, Birth of Muhammad).

1988: 1 January (New Year), 1 May (Labour Day), 18 May* (Id al-Fitr, end of Ramadan), 19 June (Ben Bella's Overthrow), 5 July (Independence), 25 July* (Id al-Adha, Feast of the Sacrifice), 14 August* (Islamic New Year), 23 August* (Ashoura), 1 November (Anniversary of the Revolution), 23 October* (Mouloud, Birth of Muhammad).

* Religious holidays, which are dependent on the Islamic lunar calendar, may differ by one or two days from the dates given.

Weights and Measures

The metric system is in force.

Currency and Exchange Rates

100 centimes = 1 Algerian dinar.

Exchange rates (30 September 1986):
 £1 sterling = 6.760 dinars;
 US $1 = 4.672 dinars.

Statistical Survey

Source (unless otherwise stated): Office National des Statistiques, Ministère de la Planification et de l'Aménagement du Territoire, 8 rue des Moussebiline, BP 55, Algiers; tel. 64-77-90; telex 52620.

Area and Population

AREA, POPULATION AND DENSITY

Area (sq km)	2,381,741*
Population (census results)†	
4 April 1966	11,821,679
12 February 1977‡	16,948,000
Population (official estimates at mid-year)†	
1981	19,246,000
1982	19,857,006§
1983	20,499,277
Density (per sq km) at mid-1983	8.6

* 919,595 sq miles.
† Excluding Algerian nationals residing abroad, numbering 268,868 at the 1966 census and an estimated 828,000 at 1 January 1978.
‡ Provisional.
§ Comprising 9,893,262 males and 9,963,744 females.

Population: 20,841,000 (official estimate) at 1 January 1984.

PRINCIPAL TOWNS
(estimated population at 1 January 1983)

Algiers (El-Djezaïr, capital)	1,721,607	Tlemcen (Tilimsen)	146,089
Oran (Ouahran)	663,504	Skikda	141,159
Constantine (Qacentina)	448,578	Béjaia	124,122
Annaba	348,322	Batna	122,788
Blida (El-Boulaïda)	191,314	El-Asnam (Ech-Cheliff)	118,996
Sétif (Stif)	186,978	Boufarik	112,000*
Sidi-Bel-Abbès	146,653	Tizi-Ouzou	100,749
		Médéa (Lemdiyya)	84,292

* 1977 figure.

EMPLOYMENT
(estimate, '000 employees at 31 December 1983)*

Agriculture, forestry and fishing	960
Mining and quarrying }	475
Manufacturing }	
Construction and public works	609
Wholesale and retail trade }	158
Transport and communications }	
Administrative and community services	797
Other services }	568
Unstated }	
Total	3,567

* Excluding nomads, students and members of the armed forces.

AREA AND POPULATION BY WILAYAS (DEPARTMENTS)*

	Area (sq km)	Population (estimates at 1 Jan. 1984)†
Adrar	422,498.0	161,936
El-Asnam (Ech-Cheliff)	8,676.7	1,040,563
Laghouat	112,052.0	391,817
Oum El-Bouaghi (Oum el-Bouagul)	8,123.0	464,806
Batna	14,881.5	691,079
Béjaia	3,442.2	659,040
Biskra (Beskra)	109,728.0	662,778
Béchar	306,000.0	184,069
Blida (El-Boulaïda)	3,703.8	1,126,303
Bouira	4,517.1	454,805
Tamanrasset (Tamenghest)	556,000.0	62,680
Tébessa (Tbessa)	16,574.5	439,638
Tlemcen (Tilimsen)	9,283.7	678,025
Tiaret (Tihert)	23,455.6	731,542
Tizi-Ouzou	3,756.3	1,028,864
Algiers (El-Djezaïr)	785.7	2,442,303
Djelfa (El-Djelfa)	22,904.8	403,500
Jijel	3,704.5	604,319
Sétif (Stif)	10,350.4	1,776,673
Saida	106,777.4	450,594
Skikda	4,748.3	597,530
Sidi-Bel-Abbès	11,648.2	604,773
Annaba	3,489.3	650,096
Guelma	8,624.4	633,733
Constantine (Qacentina)	3,561.7	807,245
Médéa (Lemdiyya)	6,704.1	575,305
Mostaganem (Mestghanem)	7,023.6	396,765
M'Sila	19,824.6	540,013
Mascara (Mouaskar)	5,845.6	526,644
Ouargla (Wargla)	559,234.0	261,760
Oran (Ouahran)	1,820.0	889,800
Total	**2,381,741.0**	**20,841,000**

* In December 1983 an administrative reorganization created 17 new wilayas, bringing the total number to 48.
† Excluding Algerian nationals abroad, estimated to total 828,000 at 1 January 1978.

BIRTHS AND DEATHS
Average annual birth rate 48.8 per 1,000 in 1970–75, 47.0 per 1,000 in 1975–80; death rate 15.4 per 1,000 in 1970–75, 13.4 per 1,000 in 1975–80 (UN estimates).

ALGERIA   Statistical Survey

Agriculture

PRINCIPAL CROPS ('000 metric tons)

	1982	1983	1984
Wheat	977	790	1,200
Barley	483	447	588
Oats	60	49	69
Potatoes	415	491	600*
Pulses	70	71	81
Sugar beets†	72	75	110
Onions (dry)	113	121	130*
Tomatoes	246	252	298*
Grapes	255	315	360*
Olives	135	160*	100*
Oranges	201	162	228†
Tangerines and mandarins	109	81	112†
Dates	207	182	207†
Water-melons	193	207	230*
Tobacco†	4	4	5

* FAO estimate.   † Unofficial figure.
Source: FAO, *Production Yearbook*.

LIVESTOCK ('000 head, year ending September)

	1982	1983	1984
Sheep†	14,111	14,500	14,700
Goats†	2,857	2,970	3,000
Cattle	1,408†	1,440†	1,450*
Horses†	168	165	170
Mules†	168	170	210
Asses*	540	550	570
Camels†	156	160	164

Chickens (FAO estimates, million): 19 in 1982; 20 in 1983; 25 in 1984.
* FAO estimate.   † Unofficial figure.
Source: FAO, *Production Yearbook*.

LIVESTOCK PRODUCTS (FAO estimates, '000 metric tons)

	1982	1983	1984
Beef and veal	43	43	45
Mutton and lamb	67	70	72
Goat's meat	13	13	14
Poultry meat	48	49	50
Other Meat	10	11	11
Cows' milk	530	540	550
Sheep's milk	166	170	180
Goats' milk	140	150	160
Hen eggs	20.3	21.0	23.0
Wool:			
greasy	21.0	22.0	23.0
clean	10.5	10.8	12.0
Cattle hides	7.4	7.6	7.8
Sheep skins	10.5	10.8	11.0
Goat skins	2.4	2.6	2.8

Source: FAO, *Production Yearbook*.

Forestry

ROUNDWOOD REMOVALS
(FAO estimates, '000 cu m, excluding bark)

	1982	1983	1984
Sawlogs, veneer logs and logs for sleepers*	20	20	20
Other industrial wood	193	199	207
Fuel wood†	1,461	1,461	1,461
Total	1,674	1,680	1,688

* Assumed to be unchanged since 1975.
† Assumed to be unchanged since 1981.
Source: FAO, *Yearbook of Forest Products*.

Fishing

(FAO estimates, '000 metric tons, live weight)

	1982	1983	1984
European sardine (pilchard)	35.8	38.9	41.7
Other marine fishes	25.8	28.0	30.0
Marine crustaceans	2.9	3.1	3.4
Total catch	64.5	70.0	75.0

Source: FAO, *Yearbook of Fishery Statistics*.

Mining

	1981	1982	1983
Coal ('000 metric tons)	7	7	7
Iron ore:			
gross weight ('000 metric tons)	3,423	3,705	3,648
metal content ('000 metric tons)	897	1,059	1,113
Salt ('000 metric tons)*	170	175	180
Lead ore ('000 metric tons)†	4.9	4.9	4.6
Zinc ore ('000 metric tons)†	20.0	20.8	20.9
Copper ore ('000 metric tons)†	0.6	0.6	0.6
Mercury ('000 metric tons)	0.9	0.4	0.8
Phosphate rock ('000 metric tons)	915.0	968.8	876.0
Crude petroleum ('000 metric tons)	39,530	43,670	31,790
Natural gas (million cu metres)	45,700	63,061	70,736

* Estimates by the US Bureau of Mines.
† Figures refer to the gross weight of concentrates. The estimated metal content (in '000 metric tons) was: Lead 3.3 in 1981, 3.2 in 1982; Zinc 10.9 in 1981, 11.3 in 1982; Copper 0.2 in 1981, 0.2 in 1982.

Crude petroleum ('000 metric tons): 28,300 in 1984; 29,770 in 1985.

Industry

SELECTED PRODUCTS

		1981	1982	1983
Olive oil (crude)	'000 metric tons	20	20	24*
Margarine	'000 metric tons	14.6	14.1	13.4*
Flour	'000 metric tons	694	769	650*
Raw sugar	'000 metric tons	4*	4*	5*
Wine	'000 hectolitres	2,669	1,510	1,880
Beer	'000 hectolitres	497	470	n.a.
Cigarettes	metric tons	16,178*	17,542	17,500
Cotton yarn (pure and mixed)	'000 metric tons	21.4	19.9	n.a.
Woven cotton fabrics	million sq metres	109	102	105*
Footwear (excl. rubber)	'000 pairs	22,183	n.a.	n.a.
Nitrogenous fertilizers (a)†	'000 metric tons	23.8	23.7	51.0
Phosphate fertilizers (b)†	'000 metric tons	30.8	22.7	48.0
Naphtha	'000 metric tons	2,557	4,011	3,940
Motor spirit (petrol)	'000 metric tons	1,469	1,417	1,400
Kerosene	'000 metric tons	50	100	110
Jet fuel	'000 metric tons	514	530	520
Distillate fuel oils	'000 metric tons	4,670	7,088	7,090
Residual fuel oils	'000 metric tons	3,765	5,392	5,180
Liquefied petroleum gas	'000 metric tons	921	1,373	1,470*
Cement	'000 metric tons	4,457	3,743	4,776*
Pig-iron	'000 metric tons	897	1,059	900*
Crude steel	'000 metric tons	557	868	600*
Television receivers	'000	150	174	n.a.
Buses and coaches (assembled)	number	577	663	700
Lorries (assembled)	number	5,625	5,543	6,500
Electric energy	million kWh	8,149	8,448	8,520

* Provisional or estimated figure.
† Production, in terms of (a) nitrogen or (b) phosphoric acid, during 12 months ending 30 June of year stated. Phosphate fertilizers include ground rock phosphate.
Source: mainly UN, *Industrial Statistics Yearbook*.

1984: Olive oil 14,000 metric tons (FAO estimate); Wine 2,150,000 hectolitres (FAO estimate); Nitrogenous fertilizers 47,000 metric tons; Phosphate fertilizers 53,000 metric tons.

1985: Olive oil 24,000 metric tons (FAO estimate); Wine 2,200,000 hectolitres (FAO estimate); Nitrogenous fertilizers 65,000 metric tons (provisional); Phosphate fertilizers 77,460 metric tons.

Finance

CURRENCY AND EXCHANGE RATES

Monetary Units
100 centimes = 1 Algerian dinar (AD).

Denominations
Coins: 1, 2, 5, 10, 20 and 50 centimes; 1 and 5 dinars.
Notes: 5, 10 and 100 dinars.

Sterling and Dollar Equivalents (30 September 1986)
£1 sterling = 6.760 dinars;
US $1 = 4.672 dinars;
100 Algerian dinars = £14.79 = $21.41.

Average Exchange Rate (dinars per US $)
1983   4.7888
1984   4.9834
1985   5.0278

MONEY SUPPLY (million AD at 31 December)

	1982	1983	1984
Currency outside banks	49,159	60,067	67,645
Demand deposits at deposit money banks	61,991	76,878	95,281
Checking deposits at post office	12,279	14,065	15,952
Private sector demand deposits at treasury	1,871	1,796	1,739
Total money	125,300	152,806	180,617

Source: IMF, *International Financial Statistics*.

ALGERIA

Statistical Survey

ADMINISTRATIVE BUDGET (estimates, million AD)

Expenditure	1985	1986*
Presidency	611.8	640.0
National defence	4,793.1	5,459.0
Foreign affairs	583.5	619.3
Light industry	137.6	149.5
Housing and construction	359.4	460.9
Finance	1,252.4	1,446.1
Home affairs	n.a.	3,543.0
Commerce	130.6	146.8
Youth and sport	403.6	446.6
Information	350.8	384.8
Ex-servicemen	2,984.5	3,289.0
Culture and tourism	218.3	258.2
Agriculture and fishing	766.0	838.1
Health	2,720.6	3,518.3
Transport	373.7	414.0
Justice	477.4	556.4
Professional training	1,397.9	1,539.8
Religious affairs	363.7	403.1
Public works	690.8	784.1
Education	11,026.7	13,626.7
Higher education and scientific research	2,764.4	2,931.6
Heavy industry	94.6	108.3
Water, environment and forests	798.3	866.0
Energy and petrochemicals industries	201.5	220.9
Planning and land development	n.a.	165.9
Social protection	476.7	530.1
Extra expenditure	25,197.5	23,384.4
Total (incl. others)	62,200.0	67,000.0

* As announced in November 1985. A revised administrative budget, announced in April 1986, projected total expenditure of 59,500 million AD.

INVESTMENT BUDGET (estimates, million AD)

Expenditure	1986*
Industry (incl. rural electrification)	2,700
Agriculture	1,300
Water	6,280
Tourism	70
Fisheries	30
Forests	1,050
Railway infrastructure	3,000
Urban development	1,200
Storage and distribution	15
Education	7,470
Training	2,557
Social affairs	4,490
Housing	1,640
Administrative structure	2,710
Communications (incl. telecommunications)	4,680
Completion works	140
Computers	168
Total (incl. others)	61,000

* As announced in November 1985. A revised investment budget, announced in April 1986, projected total expenditure of 45,000 million AD.

CENTRAL BANK RESERVES
(US $ million at 31 December)

	1982	1983	1984
Gold*	216	205	192
IMF special drawing rights	154	107	111
Reserve position in IMF	139	180	162
Foreign exchange	2,129	1,593	1,191
Total	2,638	2,085	1,656

* Valued at 35 SDRs per troy ounce.

Source: IMF, *International Financial Statistics*.

COST OF LIVING (Retail Price Index, Algiers—average of monthly figures. Base: 1980 = 100)

	1981	1982	1983
Food	118.3	100.5	103.3
Clothing	110.9	149.1	158.4
Water, gas and electricity	103.9	103.8	110.2
All items (incl. others)	114.6	112.7	117.8

1984: Food 109.5; All items 138.7.

Source: ILO, mainly *Year Book of Labour Statistics*.

NATIONAL ACCOUNTS
('000 million AD at current prices)

	1981	1982	1983
Gross domestic product	191.8	208.7	231.9

Source: IMF, *International Financial Statistics*.

BALANCE OF PAYMENTS (US $ million)

	1982	1983	1984
Merchandise exports f.o.b.	13,509	12,742	12,792
Merchandise imports f.o.b.	−9,889	−9,516	−9,235
Trade balance	3,620	3,226	3,557
Exports of services	856	866	778
Imports of services	−4,989	−4,415	−4,442
Balance on goods and services	−513	−323	−107
Private unrequited transfers (net)	347	237	186
Government unrequited transfers (net)	−18	1	−5
Current balance	−183	−85	74
Long-term capital (net)	−956	−848	−404
Short-term capital (net)	157	319	193
Net errors and omissions	−88	193	−197
Total (net monetary movements)	−1,070	−421	−333
Valuation changes (net)	−204	−101	−45
Changes in reserves	−1,273	−522	−379

Source: IMF, *International Financial Statistics*.

ALGERIA

External Trade

PRINCIPAL COMMODITIES (million AD)

Imports c.i.f.	1982	1983	1984
Foodstuffs and tobacco	8,745	9,200	8,815
Energy and lubricants	317	881	1,053
Primary products and raw materials	1,273	1,557	3,174
Semi-finished products	15,984	16,136	15,208
Capital goods	11,983	12,854	15,130
Consumer goods	3,760	3,959	7,242
Total (incl. others)	49,384	49,782	51,257

Exports f.o.b.	1982	1983	1984
Foodstuffs and tobacco	324	178	239
Energy and lubricants	59,391	59,824	57,646
Primary products and raw materials	756	702	976
Total (incl. others)	60,478	60,722	59,106

PRINCIPAL TRADING PARTNERS (million AD)*

Imports	1981	1982	1984†
Belgium-Luxembourg	1,855	1,965	2,170
Brazil	1,385	823	1,407
Canada	3,936	1,974	1,985
France	9,016	10,360	12,063
Germany, Federal Republic	6,631	6,841	5,478
Italy	6,417	3,335	4,501
Japan	2,527	3,607	n.a.
Netherlands	1,240	1,205	1,296
Romania	207	368	n.a.
Spain	3,106	3,746	2,252
Sweden	534	547	n.a.
Switzerland	794	531	n.a.
USSR	303	363	n.a.
United Kingdom	1,733	1,730	n.a.
USA	1,677	3,746	2,894
Total (incl. others)	48,780	49,384	51,257

Exports	1981	1982	1984†
Belgium-Luxembourg	238	665	454
Brazil	1,181	907	410
France	11,383	19,172	16,806
Germany, Federal Republic	7,578	3,205	1,777
Italy	5,952	8,588	10,715
Japan	3,251	2,038	n.a.
Netherlands	4,569	7,536	7,085
Romania	2	91	n.a.
Spain	2,569	3,332	2,034
Sweden	448	121	n.a.
USSR	541	878	n.a.
United Kingdom	782	907	852
USA	19,149	9,199	12,809
Total (incl. others)	62,837	60,478	59,106

* Imports by country of production; exports by country of consignment.
† No data are available for 1983.
Source: Ministère du Commerce, Algiers.

Transport

RAILWAYS (traffic)

	1981	1982	1983
Passengers carried ('000)	23,557	24,842	34,043
Freight carried ('000 metric tons)	10,750	11,355	11,437
Passenger-km (million)	2,158	1,774	1,804
Freight ton-km (million)	2,703	2,765	2,671

ROAD TRAFFIC (motor vehicles in use at 31 December)

	1977	1978	1981
Passenger cars	355,125	411,894	573,573
Lorries and vans	174,801	186,169	248,258
Coaches and buses	5,484	6,401	8,417
Motorcycles	16,637	16,812	17,608

Source: Ministère de la Planification et de l'Aménagement du Territoire, Algiers; and (1981) International Road Federation. Figures for 1979 and 1980 are not available.

INTERNATIONAL SEA-BORNE SHIPPING

	Goods loaded ('000 metric tons)		Goods unloaded ('000 metric tons)	
	1981	1982	1981	1982
Algiers	1,443.3	1,209.4	4,605.7	4,961.0
Annaba	2,517.5	2,399.7	3,305.5	3,647.9
Arzew	21,660.6	22,467.0	401.8	440.8
Béjaia	7,302.3	5,862.1	1,308.7	1,338.4
Oran	150.3	183.5	1,663.4	2,688.7
Total (inc. others)	47,165.4	51,599.3	14,566.8	17,785.8

CIVIL AVIATION (traffic on scheduled services)

	1980	1981	1982
Kilometres flown ('000)	27,900	28,800	29,800
Passengers carried ('000)	2,950	3,000	3,150
Passenger-km (million)	2,300	2,400	2,610
Freight ton-km ('000)	12,900	14,200	15,900
Mail ton-km ('000)	1,600	1,700	1,800
Total ton-km ('000)	220,000	232,000	253,000

Source: UN, *Statistical Yearbook*.

Tourism

FOREIGN VISITORS BY COUNTRY OF ORIGIN

	1983	1984	1985
France	148,238	167,811	108,278
Germany, Federal Republic	22,578	27,568	19,720
Italy	29,588	30,844	23,318
Morocco	1,239	1,537	821
Tunisia	6,930	9,233	8,203
United Kingdom	9,497	9,684	7,969
USA	4,023	4,070	3,279
Total (incl. others)	222,093	250,747	171,588

Hotel Capacity (1985): 170 hotels; 30,314 beds.
Source: Ministère de la Culture et du Tourisme, Algiers.

Communications Media

	1981	1982	1983
Radio receivers ('000 in use)	4,000	4,200	4,400
Television receivers ('000 in use)	1,190	n.a.	1,325
Book production: titles	n.a.	504	n.a.
Daily newspapers:			
Number	n.a.	4	n.a.
Average circulation ('000 copies)	n.a.	445	n.a.
Non-daily newspapers:			
Number	n.a.	15	n.a.
Average circulation ('000 copies)	n.a.	309	n.a.
Other periodicals:			
Number	n.a.	27	n.a.
Average circulation ('000 copies)	n.a.	476	n.a.

Source: UNESCO, *Statistical Yearbook*.
Telephones: 485,000 in use (1980).

Education

(state institutions only, 1983)

	Institutions	Pupils	Teachers
Primary	10,453	3,336,536	109,173
Middle and Secondary			
General	1,250*	1,420,303	61,961
Teacher training	40†	20,664	1,311*
Technical	174*	32,086	1,168*
Higher (Universities, etc.)*	13	95,867	11,601

* 1981/82 figures.
† 1978/79 figures.

Source: mainly UNESCO, *Statistical Yearbook*.

Directory

The Constitution

A new constitution for the Democratic and Popular Republic of Algeria, approved by popular referendum on 19 November 1976, was promulgated on 22 November 1976. The Constitution was amended by the National People's Assembly on 30 June 1979. The main provisions of the Constitution, as amended, are summarized below:

The preamble recalls that Algeria owes its independence to a war of liberation which will go down in history as one of the epic struggles in the resurrection of the peoples of the Third World. It emphasizes that the institutions which have been established since June 1965 are intended to transform the progressive ideas of the revolution into real achievements, affecting daily life, and to develop the content of the revolution by thought and action towards a definitive commitment to socialism.

FUNDAMENTAL PRINCIPLES OF THE ORGANIZATION OF ALGERIAN SOCIETY

The Republic
The State is socialist. Islam is the state religion and Arabic is the official national language. National sovereignty resides in the people. The National Charter is the fundamental source of national policy and law. It is to be referred to on ideological questions and for the interpretation of the Constitution. The popular assemblies are the basic institution of the State.

Socialism
The irreversible option of socialism is the only path to complete national independence. The individual ownership of property for personal or family use is guaranteed. Non-exploitative private property is an integral part of the new social system. The cultural, agrarian and industrial revolutions and socialist management of enterprises are the bases for the building of socialism.

The State
The State is exclusively at the service of the people. Those holding positions of responsibility must live solely on their salaries and may not, directly or by the agency of others, engage in any remunerative activity.

Fundamental Freedoms and the Rights of Man and the Citizen
Fundamental rights and freedoms are guaranteed. All discrimination on grounds of sex, race or occupation is forbidden. Law cannot operate retrospectively and a person is presumed innocent until proved guilty. Victims of judicial error shall receive compensation from the State.

The State guarantees the inviolability of the home, of private life and of the person. The State also guarantees the secrecy of correspondence, the freedom of conscience and opinion, freedom of intellectual, artistic and scientific creation, and freedom of expression and assembly.

ALGERIA

The State guarantees the right to join a trade union, the right to work, to protection, to security, to health, to leisure, to education, etc. It also guarantees the right to leave the national territory, within the limits set by law. The law lays down the conditions under which the fundamental rights and freedoms may be withdrawn from anyone who uses them to attack the Constitution, the essential interests of the nation, the unity of the people and of the national territory, the internal and external security of the State, and the socialist revolution.

Duties of citizens
Every citizen must protect public property and safeguard national independence. The law sanctions the duty of parents to educate and protect their children, as well as the duty of children to help and support their parents. Women must participate fully in the building of socialism and national development.

The National Popular Army
The Army safeguards national independence and sovereignty. It participates in the development of the country and the building of socialism.

Principles of foreign policy
Algeria subscribes to the objectives of the UN, the OAU and the League of Arab States. It supports Arab, Maghreb and African unity, on a basis of popular liberation. It is non-aligned and advocates peace and non-interference in the internal affairs of states. It fights against colonialism, imperialism and racial discrimination and supports the peoples of Africa, Asia and Latin America in their liberation struggles.

POWER AND ITS ORGANIZATION

Political power
The Algerian institutional system rests on the principle of the single-party state. The Front de Libération Nationale (FLN) is a vanguard force, guiding and organizing the people for the building of socialism. Party and state organs work in different frameworks and with different means to attain the same objectives. The decisive posts in the state organization are held by members of the party leadership.

The Executive
The President of the Republic is Head of State, Head of the Armed Forces and responsible for national defence. He must be of Algerian origin, a Muslim and more than 40 years old. He is nominated by the FLN Congress and elected by universal, secret, direct suffrage. His mandate is for five years, and is indefinitely renewable. The President embodies the unity of the political leadership of the party and the state. The President presides over joint meetings of the party and the executive. Ministers are appointed by the President. The President presides over meetings of the Council of Ministers. He may appoint one or more vice-presidents, to whom he may delegate some of his powers, and must appoint a Prime Minister, who will co-ordinate government activity. Should the Presidency fall vacant, the President of the National People's Assembly temporarily assumes the office (subject to the approval of two-thirds majorities in the FLN Central Committee and the National Assembly) and organizes presidential elections within 45 days. He may not himself be a candidate in the election. The President presides over a High Security Council which advises on all matters affecting national security.

The Legislature
The National People's Assembly prepares and votes the law. Its members are nominated by the party leadership and elected by universal, direct, secret suffrage for a five-year term. The deputies enjoy parliamentary immunity. The Assembly sits for two ordinary sessions per year, each of not more than three months' duration. The commissions of the Assembly are in permanent session. Both the President and the Assembly may initiate legislation. The Assembly may legislate in all areas except national defence. In the periods between sessions of the Assembly the President may legislate by decree, but all such legislation must be submitted to the Assembly in the following session.

The Head of State is empowered to dissolve the Assembly or call premature elections, having consulted a joint meeting of the party leadership and the Government.

The Judiciary
Judges obey only the law. They defend the socialist revolution. The right of the accused to a defence is guaranteed. The Supreme Court regulates the activities of courts and tribunals. The Higher Court of the Magistrature is presided over by the President of the Republic; the Minister of Justice is Vice-President of the Court. All magistrates are answerable to the Higher Court for the manner in which they fulfil their functions.

Constitutional revision
The Constitution can be revised on the initiative of the President of the Republic by a two-thirds majority of the National Assembly. The basic principles of the Constitution may not be revised.

The Government

HEAD OF STATE
President: BENDJEDID CHADLI (elected 7 February 1979; re-elected 12 January 1984).

COUNCIL OF MINISTERS
(October 1986)

President and Minister of Defence: BENDJEDID CHADLI.
Prime Minister: ABDEL-HAMID BRAHIMI.
Minister of the Interior and Local Communities: MUHAMMAD YALA.
Minister of Foreign Affairs: AHMED TALEB IBRAHIMI.
Minister of Agriculture and Fisheries: KASDI MERBAH.
Minister of Public Works: AHMED BENFREHA.
Minister of Energy and Petrochemical Industries: BELKACEM NABI.
Minister of Light Industry: ZITOUNI MESSAOUDI.
Minister of Heavy Industry: FAYCAL BOUDRAA.
Minister of Finance: ABDEL-AZIZ KHELLEF.
Minister of Planning and Regional Development: ALI OUBOUZART.
Minister of Health: DJAMEL EDDINE HOUHOU.
Minister of Higher Education: ABDEL-HAQ BREHRI.
Minister of Basic and Secondary Education: Mme ZHOR OUNISSI.
Minister of Labour and of Vocational Training: BOUBAKAR BELKAID.
Minister of Commerce: MOSTEFA BENAMMAR.
Minister of Posts and Telecommunications: MOSTEFA BENZAZA.
Minister of Housing, Town Planning and Construction: ABDEL-MALEK NOURANI.
Minister of War Veterans: MUHAMMAD DJEGHABA.
Minister of Religious Affairs: BOUALEM BAKI.
Minister of Youth and Sport: KAMAL BOUCHAMA.
Minister of Transport: RACHID BENYELLES.
Minister of Justice: MUHAMMAD CHERIF KHARROUBI.
Minister of Culture and of Tourism: BOUALEM BESSAIEH.
Minister of Information: BACHIR ROUIS.
Minister of Hydraulics, Environment and Forestry: MUHAMMAD ROUIGH.
Minister of Social Affairs: MUHAMMAD NABI.
Minister-Counsellor to the Presidency: MOHAMED BEN AHMED ABDEL-GHANI.

MINISTRIES

Office of the President: Présidence de la République, El-Mouradia, Algiers; tel. 60-03-60; telex 53761.
Office of the Prime Minister: Palais du Gouvernement, Algiers; tel. 60-23-40; telex 52073.
Ministry of Agriculture and Fisheries: 12 blvd Col Amirouche, Algiers; tel. 63-89-50; telex 52984.
Ministry of Basic and Secondary Education: 8 ave de Pékin, El-Mouradia, Algiers; tel. 60-54-41; telex 52443.
Ministry of Commerce: 44 rue Muhammad Belouizdad, Algiers; tel. 63-33-66; telex 52768.
Ministry of Culture and Tourism: Palais de la Culture, Algiers; tel. 58-91-10; telex 52555.
Ministry of Defence: ave des Tagarins, Algiers; tel. 61-15-15; telex 52627.
Ministry of Energy and Petrochemical Industries: 80 rue Ahmed Ghermoul, Algiers; tel. 66-33-00; telex 52790.

ALGERIA

Ministry of Finance: Palais du Gouvernement, Algiers; tel. 63-23-40; telex 52062.

Ministry of Foreign Affairs: 6 rue 16n- Batran, El-Mouradia, Algiers; tel. 60-47-44; telex 52794.

Ministry of Health: 25 blvd Laala Abderrahmane, El-Madania, Algiers; tel. 66-33-15; telex 51263.

Ministry of Heavy Industry: 6 rue Ahmed Bey, Immeuble le Colisée, Algiers; tel. 60-11-14; telex 52707.

Ministry of Higher Education: 1 rue Bachir Attar, Palace du 1er Mai, Algiers; tel. 66-33-61; telex 52720.

Ministry of Housing, Town Planning and Construction: route des 4 Canons, Tagarins, Algiers; tel. 61-20-14; telex 53880.

Ministry of Hydraulics, Environment and Forestry: le Grand Seminaire, Kouba, Algiers; tel. 58-95-00; telex 62560.

Ministry of Information: 11 chemin Doudon Mokhtar Ben-Aknoun, Algiers; tel. 79-23-23; telex 52469.

Ministry of the Interior: Palais du Government, Algiers; tel. 63-23-40; telex 52073.

Ministry of Justice: 8 rue de Khartoum, El-Biar, Algiers; tel. 78-20-90; telex 52761.

Ministry of Labour and Vocational Training: rue Farid Zouieoueche, Kouba Algiers; tel. 77-91-33; telex 53447.

Ministry of Light Industry: 3 rue Ahmed Bey, Algiers; tel. 60-11-44; telex 52707.

Ministry of Planning and Regional Development: chemin Ibn Badis, El-Mouiz, El-Biar, Algiers; tel. 78-03-23; telex 52560.

Ministry of Posts and Telecommunications: 4 blvd Salah Bouakouir, Algiers; tel. 61-12-20; telex 52020.

Ministry of Public Works: 135 rue Didouche Mourad, Algiers; tel. 59-00-29; telex 52713.

Ministry of Religious Affairs: 2 ave Timgad, Hydra, Algiers; tel. 60-85-55; telex 52648.

Ministry of Social Affairs: rue Boudjadit Muhammad, Kouba, Algiers; tel. 77-30-55; telex 53984.

Ministry of Transport: chemin Abdel-Kader Gadouche, Hydra, Algiers; tel. 60-60-33; telex 52775.

Ministry of War Veterans (Moudjahidine): 2 rue Lt Benafa, Château-Neuf, Algiers; tel. 78-23-55; telex 52011.

Ministry of Youth and Sport: 3 place du 1er Mai, Algiers; tel. 66-33-70; telex 52110.

Legislature

ASSEMBLÉE NATIONALE POPULAIRE

The National People's Assembly comprises 281 deputies, elected by universal suffrage for a five-year term. The most recent elections took place on 5 March 1982. A single-party list of candidates was presented by the FLN, but the electorate was offered a choice of three candidates per seat. Electoral participation was 72.7%.

President of the National Assembly: RABAH BITAT.

Political Organizations

Front de Libération Nationale (FLN): place Emir Abdelkader, Algiers; telex 53931; f. 1954; sole legal party; socialist in outlook, the party is organized into a Secretariat, a Central Committee, a Political Bureau, Federations, Kasmas and cells; according to party statutes adopted at the FLN Congress in January 1979, the Central Committee (elected by Congress and consisting of 120–160 full members and 30–40 alternate members, meeting twice annually) chooses a party Secretary-General who automatically becomes the candidate for the Presidency of the Republic. Members of the Political Bureau (between seven and 11, meeting monthly) are chosen by the Secretary-General and endorsed by the Central Committee; Sec.-Gen. Col BENDJEDID CHADLI; Head of Secretariat MUHAMMAD CHERIF MESSAADIA.

Political Bureau: BENDJEDID CHADLI (President), RABAH BITAT, ABDALLAH BELHOUCHET, MUHAMMAD BEN AHMED ABDEL-GHANI, MUHAMMAD CHERIF MESSAADIA, AHMED TALEB IBRAHIMI, BOUALEM BAKI, MUHAMMAD HADJ YALA, BOUALEM BENHAMOUDA. Deputy Members: ABDEL-HAMID BRAHIMI, RACHID BENYELLES, BACHIR ROUIS, MOSTEFA BELLOUCIF, ABDELLAH KHALEF.

Under the aegis of the FLN there exists a number of mass political organizations, including the Union Nationale de la Jeunesse Algérienne (UNJA) and the Union Nationale des Femmes Algériennes (UNFA).

There are several small opposition groups: all are officially proscribed and in exile in France or in other Arab countries. These include:

Parti de l'avant-garde socialiste: successor to the Algerian Communist Party.

Mouvement pour la Démocratie en Algérie (MDA): f. 1984 in Paris; seeks pluralist democratic system of government; Pres. AHMED BEN BELLA.

In December 1985 AHMED BEN BELLA and Dr HOCINE AIT AHMED announced the formation of a united democratic front.

Diplomatic Representation

EMBASSIES IN ALGERIA

Albania: 50 rue Oukil Muhammad, Birmandréis, Algiers; Ambassador: NESIP KACI.

Angola: 34 chemin Abdelkader, El-Mouradia, Algiers; tel. 56-15-24; telex 62204; Ambassador: JOÃO ARNALDO SARAIVA DE CARVALHO.

Argentina: 7 rue Hamani, Algiers; telex 53964; Chargé d'affaires a.i.: EDUARDO MARIO MENDIZABAL.

Australia: 12 ave Emile Marquis, Djenane-El-Malik, Hydra, Algiers; telex 52600; Ambassador: CHARLES O'HANLON.

Austria: Les Vergers, rue 2, Lot 9, DZ-16300 Bir Mourad Rais, Algiers; tel. 56-26-99; telex 62302; Ambassador: GERFRIED BUCHAUER.

Bangladesh: 141 blvd Salah Bouakouir, Algiers; telex 52565; Ambassador: REAZ RAHMAN.

Belgium: 22 chemin Youcef Tayebi, El-Biar, Algiers; telex 52525; Ambassador: ROBERT GUILLOT-PINGUE.

Benin: rue 3, Villa no. 4, Beaulieu, El-Harrach, Algiers; telex 52447; Ambassador: ANTOINE LALEYE.

Brazil: 48 blvd Muhammad V, Algiers; telex 52470; Ambassador: RONALD L. M. SMALL.

Bulgaria: 13 blvd Col Bougara, Algiers; Ambassador: GRIGOR TODOROV KRUCHMARSKI.

Burundi: 116 bis blvd des Martyrs, Algiers; telex 53501; Ambassador: ANDRÉ NADAYIRAGE.

Cameroon: 26 chemin Cheikh Bachir Ibrahimi, El-Biar, Algiers; telex 52421; Ambassador: SIMON NKO'O ETOUNGOU.

Canada: 25 rue d'Anjou, Hydra, Algiers; tel. 60-66-11; telex 52036; Ambassador: PAUL E. LABERGE.

Cape Verde: 3 rue Wiasse, Algiers; Ambassador: ADELINO NUNES CORREIA (also representing Guinea-Bissau).

Chad: 6 rue Sylvain Fourastier, Le Golf, Algiers; telex 52642; Ambassador: MBAILAOU NAIMBAYE LOSSIMIAN.

China, People's Republic: 34 blvd des Martyrs, Algiers; telex 53233; Ambassador: JIN SEN.

Congo: 13 rue Rabah Noël, Algiers; telex 52069; Ambassador: BENJAMIN BOUNKOULOU.

Cuba: 22 rue Larbi Alik, Hydra, Algiers; telex 52963; Ambassador: CLAUDIO RAMOS BORREGO.

Czechoslovakia: Villa Malika, 7 chemin Ziryab, BP 999, Algiers; Ambassador: JAN ŽIŽKA.

Denmark: 29 blvd Zirout Youcef, BP 500 Alger Gare, Algiers; tel. 63-88-71; telex 67328; Ambassador: PREBEN HANSEN.

Finland: 4 blvd Muhammad V, Algiers; telex 52215; Ambassador: ERKKI PAJARI.

France: 6 rue Larbi Alik, Hydra, Algiers; telex 52644; Ambassador: BERNARD BOCHET.

Gabon: 136 bis blvd Salah Bouakouir au 80 rue Allili, BP 85, Algiers; tel. 72-02-64; telex 52242; Ambassador: YVES ONGOLLO.

German Democratic Republic: 16 rue Payen, Hydra, Algiers; tel. 56-19-18; telex 62374; Ambassador: MANFRED THIEDE.

Germany, Federal Republic: 165 chemin Sfindja, BP 664, Algiers; tel. 63-48-45; telex 67343; Ambassador: Dr HEINZ DRÖGE.

Ghana: 5 rue Commandant Rouibah, Hydra, Algiers; Ambassador: GEORGE AVI ENYONAM SEPENU.

Greece: 31 rue A, les Crêtes Hydra, Algiers; tel. 60-08-55; telex 66071; Ambassador: EVANGELOS FRANGOULIS.

Guinea: 43 blvd Central Said Hamdine, Hydra, Algiers; telex 53451; Ambassador: FODE BERETE.

ALGERIA

Guinea-Bissau: 3 rue Wiasse, Algiers; Ambassador: ADELINO NUNES CORREIA (also representing Cape Verde).
Holy See: 1 rue de la Basilique, Algiers; tel. 62-34-30; Pro-Nuncio: Dr GABRIEL MONTALVO.
Hungary: 18 ave des Frères Oughlis, Algiers; tel. 56-21-95; telex 52957; Ambassador: Dr BÉLA HAVASI.
India: 119 ter rue Didouche Mourad, Algiers; tel. 59-46-00; telex 66138; Ambassador: V. K. NAMBIAR.
Indonesia: 6 rue Etienne Baïlac, BP 62, El-Mouradia, Algiers; tel. 56-01-02; telex 52710; Ambassador: ILEN SURIANEGARA.
Iran: 60 rue Didouche Mourad, Algiers; telex 52880; Ambassador: KAZEM CHIVA.
Iraq: 4 rue Arezki Abri, Hydra, Algiers; telex 53067; Ambassador: IBRAHIM SHUJAA SULTAN.
Italy: 37 chemin Cheikh Bachir Ibrahimi, El-Biar, Algiers; tel. 78-33-99; telex 52468; Ambassador: MICHELANGELO JACOBUCCI.
Ivory Coast: Immeuble 'Le Bosquet', Le Paradou, Hydra, Algiers; telex 52881; Ambassador: LAMBERT AMON TANOH.
Japan: 1 chemin Macklay, El-Biar, Algiers; tel. 78-62-00; telex 61389; Ambassador: MUNEOKI DATE.
Jordan: 6 rue du Chenoua, Algiers; telex 52464; Ambassador: YASIN ISTANBULI.
Korea, Democratic People's Republic: 49 rue Hamlia, Bologtrine, Algiers; telex 53929; Ambassador: LI MAN-SOK.
Kuwait: 1 ter rue Didouche Mourad, Algiers; telex 52267; Ambassador: ABDEL-LATIF HAMAD AL-SALIH.
Lebanon: 9 rue Kaïd Ahmed, El-Biar, Algiers; telex 52416; Ambassador: SALHAD NASRI.
Libya: 15 chemin Cheikh Bachir Ibrahimi, Algiers; telex 52700; Ambassador: ABDEL-FATTAH NAAS.
Madagascar: 22 rue Abdel-Kader Aouis Bologhine, Algiers; tel. 62-31-96; telex 61156; Ambassador: SAMUEL LAHADY.
Mali: Villa no. 15, Cité DNC/ANP, chemin du Kaddous, Algiers; telex 52631; Ambassador: BOUBACAR KASSE.
Mauritania: BP 276, El-Mouradia, Algiers; telex 53437; Ambassador: OULD MUHAMMAD MAHMOUD MUHAMMADOU.
Mexico: 103 rue Didouche Mourad, Algiers; telex 52474; Ambassador: OSCAR GONZALES CEZAR.
Mongolia: 4 rue Belkacem Amani, Hydra, Algiers; Ambassador: TSEBEENGOMBYN DEMIDDAGBA.
Netherlands: 23 chemin Cheikh Bachir Ibrahimi, BP 72, El-Biar, Algiers; tel. 78-28-29; telex 52524; Ambassador: JAN TONNY WARMENHOVEN.
Niger: 54 rue Vercors Rostamia Bouzareah, Algiers; telex 52625; Ambassador: Prof. DJIBO HABI.
Nigeria: 27 bis rue Blaise Pascal, BP 629, Algiers; tel. 60-60-50; telex 52523; Ambassador: B. A. OKI.
Oman: 126 rue Didouche Mourad, Algiers; telex 52223; Ambassador: SALEM ISMAIL SUWAID.
Pakistan: 14 ave Souidani Boudjemâa, Algiers; tel. 60-57-81; Ambassador: MUHAMMAD YAMIN.
Philippines: Hôtel St George, Algiers; Ambassador: PACIFICO CASTRO.
Poland: 37 ave Mustafa Ali Khodja, El-Biar, Algiers; telex 52562; Ambassador: STANISŁAW PICHLA.
Portugal: 67 chemin Muhammad Gacem, Algiers; tel. 56-61-95; telex 62202; Ambassador: PEDRO BENITO GARCIA.
Qatar: BP 118, 25 bis allée Centrale, Clairval, Algiers; tel. 79-80-56; telex 52224; Ambassador: KHALIFA SULTAN AL-ASSIRY.
Romania: 24 rue Si Arezki, Hydra, Algiers; telex 52915; Ambassador: (vacant).
Saudi Arabia: 4 rue Arezki Abri, Hydra, Algiers; telex 53039; Ambassador: HASAN FAQQI.
Senegal: 1 rue Arago, Algiers; tel. 60-32-85; telex 52133; Ambassador: YOUSSOUPH BARO.
Somalia: 11 impasse Tarting, blvd des Martyrs, Algiers; telex 52140; Ambassador: ABDELHAMID ALI YOUCEF.
Spain: 10 rue Azil Ali, Algiers; telex 52806; Ambassador: JOSÉ MARÍA ULLRICH Y ROJAS.
Sweden: BP 23, place Allendé, Bir-Mourad-Rais B, Algiers; tel. 59-42-90; telex 66069; Ambassador: JEAN-CHRISTOPHE ÖBERG.
Switzerland: 27 blvd Zirout Youcef, Algiers; telex 52859; Ambassador: O. UHL.
Syria: Domaine Tamzali, chemin A. Gadouche, Hydra, Algiers; telex 52572; Ambassador: AHMAD MADANIYA.
Tunisia: 11 rue du Bois de Boulogne, Hydra, Algiers; telex 52968; Ambassador: M'HEDI BACCOUCHE.
Turkey: Villa dar el Ouard, chemin de la Rochelle, blvd Col Bougara, Algiers; tel. 60-12-59; telex 53806; Ambassador: SENCER ASENA.
USSR: impasse Boukhandoura, El-Biar, Algiers; telex 52511; Ambassador: VASILIY TARATUTA.
United Arab Emirates: 26 rue Aouis Mokrane, POB 454, El-Mouradia, Algiers; tel. 56-46-47; telex 62208; Ambassador: MUHAMMAD I. AL-JOWAIED.
United Kingdom: 7 chemin des Glycines, BP 43, Algiers; tel. 60-56-01; telex 66151; Ambassador: ALAN MUNRO.
USA: 4 chemin Cheikh Bachir Ibrahimi, Algiers; tel. 60-14-25; telex 52064; Ambassador: CRAIG JOHNSTONE.
Venezuela: 38 rue Jean Jaurès, El-Mouradia, Algiers; telex 52695; Ambassador: FRANCISCO SALAZAR MARTÍNEZ.
Viet-Nam: 30 rue de Chenoua, Hydra, Algiers; telex 52147; Ambassador: VO TOAN.
Yemen Arab Republic: 74 rue Bouraba, Algiers; telex 53582; Ambassador: HAMOD MOHAMED BAYDER.
Yemen, People's Democratic Republic: 12 ave Chahid El Wali Mustapha Sayed, Algiers; Ambassador: ABDEL-WAKIL ISMAIL ESSAROURI.
Yugoslavia: 7 rue des Frères Benhafid, BP 662, Hydra, Algiers; tel. 60-47-04; telex 66076; Ambassador: BORIS MILOŠEVIĆ.
Zaire: 12 rue A, Les Crêtes, Hydra, Algiers; telex 52749; Ambassador: IKOLO BOLELAMA W'OKONDOLA.
Zimbabwe: 24 rue Arab Si Ahmad, Birkhadem, Algiers; Ambassador: SOLOMON RAKOBE NKOMO.

Judicial System

The highest court of justice is the Supreme Court (Cour suprême) in Algiers. Justice is exercised through 183 courts (tribunaux) and 31 appeal courts (cours d'appel), grouped on a regional basis. Three special Criminal Courts were set up in Oran, Constantine and Algiers in 1966 to deal with economic crimes against the State. From these there is no appeal. In April 1975 a Cour de sûreté de l'état, composed of magistrates and high-ranking army officers, was established to try all cases involving state security. The Cour des comptes was established in the same year. A new penal code was adopted in January 1982, retaining the death penalty.

President of Supreme Court: A. MEDJHOUDA.
Procurator-General: Y. BEKKOUCHE.

Religion

ISLAM

Islam is the official religion, and the whole Algerian population, with a few rare exceptions, is Muslim.

President of the Superior Islamic Council: AHMED HAMANI; place Cheik Abdel-Hamid ibn Badis, Algiers.

CHRISTIANITY

The Europeans, and a few Arabs, are Christians, mostly Roman Catholics.

The Roman Catholic Church

Algeria comprises one archdiocese and three dioceses (including one directly responsible to the Holy See). At 31 December 1984 there were an estimated 60,000 adherents in the country.

Bishops' Conference: Conférence Episcopale Régionale du Nord de l'Afrique, 13 rue Khélifa-Boukhalfa, Algiers; tel. 63-42-44; f. 1985; Pres. Mgr HENRI TEISSIER, Coadjutor-Archbishop of Algiers.

Archbishop of Algiers: HE Cardinal LÉON-ETIENNE DUVAL, Archevêché, 13 rue Khélifa-Boukhalfa, Algiers; tel. 63-42-44.

Protestant Church

Protestant Church of Algeria: 31 rue Reda Houhou, Algiers; tel. 66-22-16; three parishes; 1,000 mems; Pastor (Algiers) Dr HUGH G. JOHNSON.

The Press

DAILIES

Ach-Cha'ab (The People): 1 place Maurice Audin, Algiers; f. 1962; national information journal in Arabic; Dir MUHAMMAD BOUARROUDJ; circ. 80,000.

Horizons 2000: Algiers; f. 1985; evening; French; circ. 100,000.

Al-Joumhouria (The Republic): 6 rue Bencenoussi Hamida, Oran; f. 1963; Arabic language; Editor AÏSSA ADJINA; circ. 70,000.

El-Massa: Algiers; f. 1985; evening; Arabic; circ. 100,000.

El-Moudjahid (The Fighter): 20 rue de la Liberté, Algiers; f. 1965; FLN journal in French and Arabic; Dir ABDEL-AZIZ MORSLI; circ. 360,000.

An-Nasr (The Victory): 100 rue Larbi Ben M'Hidi, Constantine; f. 1963; Arabic language; Editor-in-Chief EL-HADI BENYAKHLEF; circ. 60,000.

WEEKLIES

Algérie Actualité: 20 rue de la Liberté, Algiers; tel. 63-70-30; telex 53505; f. 1965; French language weekly; Dir KAMEL BELKACEM; circ. 200,000.

El-Hadef (The Goal): 100 rue Larbi Ben M'Hidi, Constantine; f. 1972; sports; in French; Editor-in-Chief MOSTEFA MANCERI; circ. 110,000.

Révolution Africaine: 7 rue du Stade, Hydra, Algiers; FLN journal in French; socialist; circ. 15,000.

OTHER PERIODICALS

Al-Acala: rue Timgad, Hydra, Algiers; f. 1970; published by the Ministry of Religious Affairs.

Algérie Médicale: 3 blvd Zirout Youcef, Algiers; f. 1964; publ. of Union médicale algérienne; 2 a year; circ. 3,000.

Alouan (Colours): 119 rue Didouche Mourad, Algiers; f. 1973; cultural review published by the Ministry of Culture; monthly; Arabic.

Bibliographie de l'Algérie: Bibliothèque Nationale, 1 ave Docteur Fanon, Algiers 16000; tel. 63-06-32; f. 1964; lists books, theses, pamphlets and periodicals published in Algeria; 2 a year; Arabic and French.

Ach-Cha'ab ath-Thakafi (Cultural People): Algiers; f. 1972; cultural monthly; Arabic.

Ech-Chabab (Youth): 2 rue Khélifa Boukhalfa; journal of the UNJA; bi-monthly; French and Arabic.

El-Djeza'ir Réalités (Algeria Today): BP 95–96, Bouzareah, Algiers; f. 1972; organ of the Popular Assembly of the Wilaya of Algiers; monthly; French and Arabic.

El-Djeza'iria (Algerian Woman): Villa Joly, 24 ave Franklin Roosevelt, Algiers; f. 1970; organ of the UNFA; monthly; French and Arabic.

El-Djeich (The Army): Office de l'Armée Nationale Populaire, 3 chemin de Gascogne, Algiers; f. 1963; monthly; Algerian army review; Arabic and French; circ. 10,000.

Economie: 7 blvd Ché Guévara, Algiers; tel. 62-10-00; telex 66380; f. 1963; monthly; summary of items issued by state news agency; Dir AHCENE DJABALLAH BELKACEM, Editor-in-Chief BRAHIMI MOKHTAR.

Journal Officiel de la République Algérienne Démocratique et Populaire: 7, 9 and 13 ave A. Benbarek; f. 1962; French and Arabic.

Al-Kitab (The Book): 3 blvd Zirout Youcef, Algiers; f. 1972; bulletin of SNED; every 2 months; French and Arabic.

Libyca: 3 blvd Zirout Youcef, Algiers; f. 1953; anthropology and ethnography; irregular; French; Dir MOULOUD MAMMERI.

Nouvelles Economiques: 6 blvd Amilcar Cabral, Algiers; f. 1969; publ. of Institut Algérien du Commerce Extérieur; monthly; French and Arabic.

Révolution et Travail: 48 rue Khellifa Boukhalfa, Algiers; journal of UGTA (central trade union) with Arabic and French editions; monthly; Editor-in-Chief ZIANE FARRAH.

Revue Algérienne du Travail: 28 rue Hassiba Benbouali, Algiers; f. 1964; Ministry of Labour publication; quarterly; French.

Revue d'Histoire et de Civilisation du Maghreb: 3 blvd Zirout Youcef, Algiers; f. 1966; history and civilization; irregular; French and Arabic; circ. 4,000; Dir M. KADDACHE.

Ath-Thakafa (Culture): 2 place Cheikh Ben Badis, BP 96, Algiers; tel. 62-20-73; f. 1971; published by the Ministry of Culture; cultural review; circ. 10,000; Editor-in-Chief CHEBOUB OTHMANE.

NEWS AGENCIES

Algérie Presse Service (APS): 7 blvd Ché Guévara, Algiers; tel. 62-10-00; telex 66445; f. 1961; Dir-Gen. BELKACEM AHCENE DJABALLAH.

Foreign Bureaux

Agence France-Presse (AFP): 6 rue Abdel-Karim El-Khettabi, Algiers; tel. 63-62-01; telex 67427; Chief JEAN-FRANÇOIS RICHARD.

Agencia EFE (Spain): 4 ave Pasteur, Algiers; tel. 61-64-16; telex 53402; Chief MIGUEL ANGEL AGEA.

Agentstvo Pechati Novosti (APN) (USSR): BP 24, El-Mouradia, Algiers; Chief Officer YURI S. BAGDASAROV.

Agenzia Nazionale Stampa Associata (ANSA) (Italy): 4 ave Pasteur, Algiers; tel. 63-73-14; telex 66467; Chief CESARE RIZZOLI.

Allgemeiner Deutscher Nachrichtendienst (ADN) (German Democratic Republic): 38 rue Larbi Alik, Hydra, Algiers; tel. 60-07-14; telex 52997; Chief MICHAEL KLAUSS.

Associated Press (AP) (USA): 4 ave Pasteur, BP 769, Algiers; tel. 63-59-41; telex 52971; Chief MICHAEL GOLDSMITH.

Bulgarian Telegraph Agency (BTA): Zaatcha 5, El-Mouradia, Algiers; Chief GORAN GOTEV.

Middle East News Agency (Egypt): 10 ave Pasteur, BP 800, Algiers.

Prensa Latina (Cuba): 26 rue Claude Debussy; tel. 61-39-49; telex 52972; Bureau Chief JULIO HERNÁNDEZ.

Reuters (UK); 4 ave Pasteur, Algiers.

Telegrafnoye Agentstvo Sovetskovo Soyuza (TASS) (USSR): 21 rue de Boulogne, Algiers; Chief KONSTANTIN DUDAREV.

Xinhua (New China) News Agency (People's Republic of China): 32 rue de Carthage, Hydra, Algiers; tel. 60-76-85; telex 66204; Chief BAI GUORUI.

Wikalat al-Maghreb al-Arabi (Morocco) is also represented.

Publishers

Entreprise Nationale du Livre (ENAL): 3 blvd Zirout Youcef, BP 49, Algiers; tel. 63-97-12; telex 53845; f. 1966 as Société Nationale d'Edition et de Diffusion, name changed 1983; publishes books of all types, and is sole importer, exporter and distributor of all printed material, stationery, school and office supplies; also holds state monopoly for commercial advertising; Dir-Gen. SEGHIR BENAMAR.

Office des Publications Universitaires: 1 place Centrale de Ben, Aknoun, Algiers; tel. 78-87-18; telex 61396; controlled by Ministry of Higher Education; publishes university textbooks.

Radio and Television

In 1983 there were an estimated 4.4m. radio receivers and 1,325,000 television receivers in use.

Radiodiffusion Télévision Algérienne (RTA): Immeuble RTA, 21 blvd des Martyrs, Algiers; tel. 60-23-00; telex 52042; government-controlled; Dir of RTA LAZHARI CHERIET; Dir of Radio M. A. BOUREGHEDA; Dir of TV M. HAOUES.

RADIO

Arabic Network: transmitters at Aïn Beïda, Algiers, Batna, Béchar, Oran, Touggourt and Souk-Ahras.

French Network: transmitters at Algiers, Constantine, Oran and Tipaza.

Kabyle Network: transmitters at Algiers and Michelet.

TELEVISION

The principal transmitters are at Algiers, Batna, Sidi-Bel-Abbès, Constantine, Souk-Ahras and Tlemcen. The national network was completed during 1970. Television is taking a major part in the national education programme.

ALGERIA

Finance

(cap. = capital; dep. = deposits; res = reserves; m. = million; AD = Algerian dinars; Fr. = French francs; brs = branches)

BANKING
Central Bank

Banque Centrale d'Algérie: 8 blvd Zirout Youcef, 16000 Algiers; tel. 64-75-00; telex 66500; f. 1963; cap. 40m. AD; central bank of issue; Gov. BADER-EDDINE NOUIOUA; Gen. Man. AHMED HANIFI.

Nationalized Banks

From November 1967 only the following nationalized banks were authorized to conduct exchange transactions and to deal with banks abroad, and by May 1972 these three banks had absorbed all foreign and private banks. It was announced in June 1982 that the banking system was to be restructured. The existing institutions were to change some of their functions and a new bank for industry, manufacturing and services was to be created.

Banque Extérieure d'Algérie (BEA): 11 blvd Col Amirouche, Algiers; tel. 61-12-52; telex 52057; f. 1967; cap. 1,000m. AD, res 1,600.8m. AD (Dec. 1984); chiefly concerned with energy and maritime transport sectors; Pres. and Gen. Man. MOURAD KHELLAF; 26 brs.

Banque Nationale d'Algérie (BNA): 8 blvd Ché Guévara, Algiers; tel. 62-05-44; telex 52788; f. 1966; cap. 1,000m. AD, res 1,592m. AD (1981); specializes in heavy industry and transport sectors; Chair. and Pres. MUHAMMAD THAMINY; Gen. Man. FAOUZI BENMALEK; 186 brs.

Crédit Populaire d'Algérie (CPA): 2 blvd Col Amirouche, Algiers; tel. 63-28-55; telex 52512; f. 1966; cap. 320m. AD (1984); bank for tourism; Gen. Man. MAHFOUD ZERROUTA; 73 brs.

Development Banks

Banque de l'Agriculture et du Développement Rural: 12 blvd Col Amirouche, Algiers; tel. 63-80-47; telex 52487; f. 1982; finance for the agricultural sector; Man. Dir MOSTEFA ACHOUR.

Banque Algérienne de Développement (BAD): Villa Jolly, 38 ave Franklin Roosevelt, Algiers; tel. 60-10-44; telex 52529; f. 1963; a public establishment with fiscal sovereignty, to contribute to Algerian economic development through long-term investment programmes; Pres. and Dir-Gen. HABIB HAKIKI.

Banque de Développement Local (BDL): 5 rue Gaci Amar, Staoueli, (W. Tipaza); tel. 81-58-00; telex 63171; regional development bank; Dir BENHOUDA BENHALIMA.

Caisse Nationale d'Epargne et de Prévoyance (CNEP): 40–42 rue Larbi Ben M'Hidi, Algiers; tel. 63-25-10; telex 52037; savings and housing bank; Man. Dir HABIB DJAFARI.

INSURANCE

Insurance is a state monopoly.

Caisse Algérienne d'Assurance et de Réassurance: 48 rue Didouche Mourad, Algiers; tel. 63-11-95; telex 52894; f. 1963 as a public corporation; Dir ABDEL-KADER BELHADJ.

Caisse Nationale de Mutualité Agricole: 24 blvd Victor Hugo, Algiers; tel. 63-76-82; telex 52815; Dir O. LARFAOUI.

Compagnie Centrale de Réassurance: 21 blvd Zirout Youcef, Algiers; tel. 63-72-88; telex 62150; f. 1973; general; Chair. and Gen. Man. FAROUK LAZRI.

Société Algérienne d'Assurances: 5 blvd Ché Guévara, Algiers; tel. 62-29-44; telex 52716; f. 1963; state-sponsored company; Chair. MAHFOUD BATTATA.

Trade and Industry

EXPORT INSTITUTE

Centre National Algérien du Commerce Extérieur—CNCE: 24 Bordj El-Kiffan, BP 571, Algiers; tel. 62-70-44; telex 52763; f. 1982; Dir-Gen. ZAHIR ABDER-RAHIM.

DEVELOPMENT

Entreprise Nationale d'Engineering et de Développement des Industries Légères (EDIL): 50 rue Khélifa Boukhalfa, BP

Directory

1140, Algiers; tel. 66-33-90; telex 52883; f. 1982; Dir-Gen. MISSOUM ABDEL-HAKIM.

Société Centrale pour l'Equipement du Territoire (SCET) International: 8 rue Sergent Addoun, Algiers; Dir A. GAMBRELLE.

NATIONALIZED INDUSTRIES

A large part of Algerian industry is nationalized. The following are some of the most important nationalized industries, each controlled by the appropriate Ministry.

Entreprise Nationale de Commerce: 6–9 rue Belhaffat-Ghazali, Hussein Dey, Algiers; tel. 77-43-20; telex 52063; monopoly of imports and distribution of materials and equipment; Dir-Gen. MUHAMMAD LAÏD BELARBIA.

Entreprise Nationale de Développement et de Coordination des Industries Alimentaires (ENIAL): 2 rue Ahmed Ait Muhammad-El-Harrach, Algiers; tel. 76-51-42; telex 54-031; f. 1965; semolina, pasta, flour and couscous; Dir-Gen. MOSTEFA MOKRAOUI.

Entreprise Nationale des Pêches (ENAPECHES): Quai d'Aigues Mortes, Port d'Alger; tel. 62-01-00; telex 52279; f. 1979 to replace (with ECOREP which deals with fishing equipment) former Office Algérien des Pêches; fish importers and exporters; Man. Dir ZOUAOUI REGGAM.

Office Régional des Produits Oléicoles du Centre (ORECPO): Appartement 9, Bâtiment 3, Cité des 280 Logements, Draâel-Bordj, Bouira; tel. 52-92-11; telex 77098; production and marketing of olives and olive oil.

Pharmacie Centrale Algérienne: 2 rue Bichat, Algiers; tel. 65-18-27; telex 52993; f. 1969; pharmaceutical products; Man. Dir M. MORSLI.

Secrétariat d'Etat aux Forêts et au Reboisement: Immeuble des Forêts, Bois du Petit Atlas, El-Mouradia, Algiers; tel. 60-43-00; telex 52854; f. 1971; production of timber, care of forests; Man. Dir DANIEL BELBACHIR.

Société de Gestion et de Développement des Industries Alimentaires (SOGEDIA): 13 ave Claude Debussy, Algiers; tel. 64-38-01; telex 52837; food industry; Dir-Gen. M. AICHOUR.

Société Nationale de l'Artisanat Traditionnel (SNAT): 1 blvd du Front de Mer, Bab El-Oued, Algiers; tel. 62-68-02; telex 53093; traditional crafts; Man. Dir SAÏD AMRANI.

Société Nationale de Constructions Mécaniques (SONACOME): 1 route Nationale, BP 8, Birkhadem, Algiers; tel. 65-93-92; telex 52800; f. 1967; to be reorganized into 11 smaller companies, most of which will specialize in manufacture or distribution of one of SONACOME's products; Dir DAOUD AKROUF.

Société Nationale de Constructions Métalliques (SN METAL): 38 rue Didouche Mourad, BP 8, Algiers; tel. 63-29-30; telex 52889; f. 1968; production of metal goods; Chair. HACHEM MALIK; Man. Dir ABDEL-KADER MAIZA.

Société Nationale des Eaux Minérales Algériennes (SNEMA): 21 rue Bellouchat Mouloud, Hussein Dey, Algiers; tel. 77-17-91; telex 52310; mineral water; Man. Dir TAHAR KHENEL.

Société Nationale de l'Electricité et du Gaz (SONELGAZ): 2 blvd Salah Bouakouir, Algiers; tel. 64-82-60; telex 52898; monopoly of production, distribution and transportation of electricity and gas; Man. Dir MOSTEFA HARRATI.

Société Nationale de Fabrication et de Montage du Matériel Electrique (SONELEC): 4 & 6 blvd Muhammad V, Algiers; tel. 63-70-82; telex 52867; electrical equipment.

Société Nationale des Industries de la Cellulose (SONIC): BP 72, 63 rue Ali Haddad, El-Mouradia, Algiers; tel. 65-38-00; telex 52933; Pres. SALAH LOUANCHI; Man. Dir BENBOUALI ABDENOUR.

Société Nationale des Industries Chimiques (SNIC): 4–6 blvd Muhammad V, BP 641, Algiers; tel. 64-07-73; telex 52802; production and distribution of chemical products; Dir-Gen. RACHID BENIDDIR.

Société Nationale des Industries des Lièges et du Bois (SNLB): 1 rue Kaddour Rahim, BP 61, Hussein Dey, Algiers; tel. 77-99-99; telex 52726; f. 1973; production of cork and wooden goods; Chair. MALEK BELLANI.

Société Nationale des Industries des Peaux et Cuirs (SONIPEC): 100 rue de Tripoli, BP 113, Hussein Dey, Algiers; tel. 77-66-00; telex 52832; f. 1967; hides and skins; Chair. and Man. Dir MUHAMMAD CHERIF AZI; Man. Dir HASSAN BEN YOUNES.

Société Nationale des Industries Textiles (SONITEX): 4–6 rue Patrice Lumumba, BP 41, Algiers; tel. 63-41-35; telex 52929;

ALGERIA

f. 1966; split in 1982 into separate cotton, wool, industrial textiles, silk, clothing and distribution companies; 22,000 employees; Man. Dir MUHAMMAD AREZKI ISLI.

Société Nationale des Matériaux de Construction (SNMC): 90 rue Didouche Mourad, Algiers; tel. 64-35-13; telex 52204; f. 1968; production and import monopoly of building materials; Man. Dir ABDEL-KADER MAIZI.

Société Nationale de Recherches et d'Exploitations Minières (SONAREM): BP 860, 127 blvd Salah Bouakouiz, Algiers; tel. 63-15-55; telex 52910; f. 1967; mining and prospecting; Dir-Gen. OUBRAHAM FERHAT.

Société Nationale pour la Recherche, la Production, le Transport, la Transformation et la Commercialisation des Hydrocarbures (SONATRACH): 10 rue du Sahara, Hydra, Algiers; tel. 56-18-56; telex 62103; f. 1963; State-owned organization for exploration, exploitation, transport and marketing of petroleum, natural gas and their products; Dir-Gen. YOUCEF YOUSFI.

In May 1980 it was announced that SONATRACH was to be split up and its functions divided between 12 companies (including SONATRACH itself). The other 11 were:

Entreprise Nationale de Canalisation (ENAC): Ouargla; piping.

Entreprise Nationale d'Engineering (ENE): Skikda; engineering.

Entreprise Nationale de Forage (ENAFOR): 1 place Biz Hakeim, El-Biar, Algiers; tel. 78-46-23; telex 52512; drilling; Dir-Gen. ABDER-RACHID ROUABAH.

Entreprise Nationale de Génie Civil et Bâtiments (ENGCB): route de Corso, Boudouaou, Algiers; civil engineering.

Entreprise Nationale de Géophysique (ENAGEO): rue Muhammad Oudir, Amelial, El-Biar, Algiers; tel. 59-33-40; telex 52849; geophysics; Dir-Gen. ALI OUARTSI.

Entreprise Nationale des Grands Travaux Pétroliers (ENGTP): zone industriel, BP 09, Reghaïa; tel. 80-06-80; telex 52747; major industrial projects; Dir-Gen. FAROUK HOUHOU; Asst Dir-Gen. Mr BENAMEUR.

Entreprise Nationale de Pétrochimie et d'Engrais (ENPE): route des Dunes, Chéraga, Algiers; tel. 81-09-69; telex 53876; petrochemicals and fertilizers.

Entreprise Nationale des Plastiques et de Caoutchouc (ENPC): route de Batna Ain Trick, BP 452, Sétif; tel. 90-32-40; telex 86040; production and marketing of rubber and plastics; Dir-Gen. BOUALEM BENAISSA.

Entreprise Nationale de Raffinage et de Distribution des Produits Pétroliers (ENRDP): 46 blvd Muhammad V, BP 161, Chéraga, Algiers; tel. 61-12-24; telex 53034; refining, export and internal distribution of products; Dir-Gen. ABDEL-MADJID KAZI-TANI.

Entreprise Nationale de Service aux Puits (ENSP): 1 blvd Anatole France, Hassi Messaoud; oil-well servicing; Dir-Gen. AMMAR BENALI.

Entreprise Nationale des Travaux aux Puits (ENTP): 2 rue du Capitaine Azzoug, Côte Rouge, Hussein Dey, Algiers; tel. 77-84-44; telex 52380; oil-well construction; Dir-Gen. ABDEL-AZIZ KRISSAT.

Société Nationale de la Sidérurgie (SNS): Ravin de Sidi-Yahia, Algiers; tel. 64-75-60; telex 52887; f. 1964; steel, cast iron, zinc and products; Chair. LAKHDAR BENTEBBAL; Man. Dir RESKI HOCINE.

Société Nationale des Tabacs et Alumettes (SNTA): 40 rue Hocine-Nourredine, Algiers; tel. 66-18-68; telex 52780; monopoly of manufacture and trade in tobacco, cigarettes and matches; Dir-Gen. MUHAMMAD TAHAB BOUZEGHOUB.

STATE TRADING ORGANIZATIONS

Since 1972 all international trading has been carried out by state organizations, of which the following are the most important:

Entreprise Nationale d'Approvisionnements en Produits Alimentaires (ENAPAL): 29 rue Larbi Ben M'hidi, Algiers; tel. 64-02-75; telex 52991; f. 1983; monopoly of import, export and bulk trade in basic foodstuffs; brs in more than 40 towns; Chair. LAID SABRI; Man. Dir FAROUK MILOUD CADI.

Entreprise Nationale d'Approvisionnement et de Régulation en Fruits et Légumes (ENAFLA): 12 ave des 3 Frères Bouadou, BP 42, Birmandreis, Algiers; tel. 56-54-41; telex 52884; f. 1983; division of the Ministry of Commerce; fruit and vegetable marketing, production and export; Man. Dir ALI BENSEGUENI.

Office Algérien Interprofessionel des Céréales (OAIC): 5 rue Ferhat Boussaad, Algiers; tel. 66-38-14; telex 52121; f. 1962; monopoly of trade in wheat, rice, maize, barley and products derived from these cereals; Man. Dir HADJ MOKHTAR LOUHIBI.

Office National de la Commercialisation des Produits Viti-Vinicoles (ONCV): 112 Quai-Sud, Algiers; tel. 63-09-40; telex 52964; f. 1968; monopoly of importing and exporting products of the wine industry; Chair. BOURHANE EDDINE KAHLI; Man. Dir B. DOUAOURIA.

TRADE FAIR

Foire Internationale d'Alger: Palais des Expositions, Pins Maritimes, BP 656, Algiers; tel. 76-31-00; telex 54061.

PRINCIPAL TRADE UNIONS

Union Générale des Travailleurs Algériens (UGTA): Maison du Peuple, place du 1er mai, Algiers; tel. 66-89-47; telex 52066; f. 1956; 1,000,000 mems; Sec.-Gen. TAYEB BELAKHDAR.

Affiliates

In 1982 the affiliated federations were replaced by eight national 'professional sectors'.

Secteur Alimentation, Commerce et Tourisme (Food, Commerce and Tourist Industry Workers): Maison du Peuple, place du 1er mai, Algiers; Gen. Sec. GHRIBLI ABDEL-KADER.

Secteur Bois, Bâtiments et Travaux Publics (Building Trades Workers): Maison du Peuple, place du 1er mai, Algiers; Gen. Sec. LATRECHE LAIFA.

Secteur Education et Culture (Teachers): Maison du Peuple, place du 1er mai, Algiers; Gen. Sec. BENGANA SAIDI.

Secteur de l'Energie, Chimie et Mines (Energy, Chemical and Mine Workers): Maison du Peuple, place du 1er mai, Algiers; telex 53577; Gen. Sec. BELHOUCHET ALI.

Secteur Finances, Plan et Collectivités Locales (Financial, Planning and Municipal Workers): Maison du Peuple du 1er mai, Algiers; Gen. Sec. ZAAF MUHAMMAD.

Secteur Métallurgie, Cuirs et Textiles (Metallurgy, Leather and Textile Industries Workers): Maison du Peuple, place du 1er mai, Algiers; telex 53574; Gen. Sec. MALKI ABDEL-KADER.

Secteur Santé et Sécurite Sociale (Health and Social Security Workers): Maison du Peuple, place du 1er mai, Algiers; Gen. Sec. DJEFFAL ABDEL-AZIZ.

Secteur Transports et Télécommunications (Transport and Telecommunications Workers): Maison du Peuple, place du 1er mai, Algiers; Gen. Sec. BENMOUHOUB EL-HACHEMI.

Union Nationale des Paysans Algériens—UNPA: f. 1973; 700,000 mems; Sec.-Gen. NEDJEM AÏSSA.

Transport

RAILWAYS

Under the 1980–84 Development Plan, US $1,250m. was allocated to extending and improving the rail network, and in 1982 plans were announced for the investment of $11,000m. in constructing new railways by 1990. Studies were carried out in 1982 for an underground railway in Algiers, which is eventually to cover a 64-km network. The contract was awarded to the Parisian Metro Authority, RATP, and work started in 1983. The system was originally scheduled to become operational by 1986 but the first construction contracts were not due to be awarded until the end of 1985.

Société Nationale des Transports Ferroviaires (SNTF): 21–23 blvd Muhammad V, Algiers; tel. 61-15-10; telex 52455; f. 1976 to replace Société Nationale des Chemins de Fer Algériens; 3,912 km of track, of which 299 km are electrified and 1,263 km are narrow gauge; daily passenger services from Algiers to the principal provincial cities and a service to Tunis; Chair. AMMAR BOUSBAH; Gen. Man. SASSEK BENMEHDJOUBA.

ROADS

There are about 82,000 km of roads and tracks, of which 24,000 km are main roads and 19,000 km are secondary roads. The total is made up of 55,000 km in the north, including 24,000 km of good roads, and 27,000 km in the south, including 3,200 km with asphalt

ALGERIA

surface. The French administration built a good road system, partly for military purposes, which since independence has been allowed to deteriorate in parts, and only a small percentage of roads are surfaced. New roads have been built linking the Sahara oil fields with the coast, and the trans-Sahara highway is a major project. Algeria is a member of the Trans-Sahara Road Committee, organizing the building of this road, now renamed the 'Road of African Unity'. The first 360-km stretch, from Hassi Marroket to Aïn Salah, was opened in April 1973, and the next section, ending at Tamanrasset, was opened in June 1978.

Société Nationale des Transports Routiers (SNTR): 27 rue des 3 Frères Bouadou, Birmandreis, Algiers; tel. 56-21-21; telex 52962; f. 1967; holds a monopoly of goods transport by road; Chair. Haoussine el-Hadj; Dir-Gen. Benaouda Benelhadj Djelloul.

Société Nationale des Transports des Voyageurs (SNTV): 19 rue Rabah Midat, Algiers; tel. 66-00-52; telex 52603; f. 1967; holds monopoly of long-distance passenger transport by road; Man. Dir M. Dib.

SHIPPING

Algiers is the main port, with anchorage of between 23 m and 29 m in the Bay of Algiers, and anchorage for the largest vessels in Agha Bay. The port has a total quay length of 8,380 m. There are also important ports at Annaba, Arzew, Béjaia, Djidjelli, Ghazaouet, Mostaganem, Oran and Skikda. The contract for a new port for steel at Djenden was awarded to an Italian firm in 1984. Petroleum and liquefied gas are exported through Arzew, Béjaia and Skikda. Algerian crude petroleum is also exported through the Tunisian port of La Skhirra.

Compagnie Algéro-Libyenne de Transports Maritimes (CALTRAM): 31 blvd Muhammad V, Birmandreis, Algiers; tel. 56-54-78; telex 52685; Chair. M. O. Das; Man. Dir A. Hasmin.

NAFTAL Direction Aviation Maritime: Aéroport Houari Boumedienne, Dar-el-Beida, BP 717, Algiers; tel. 75-73-75; telex 64346; Dir Z. Ben Merabet.

Office National des Ports (ONP): quai d'Arcachon, BP 830, Algiers-Port; tel. 62-57-48; telex 52738; f. 1971; responsible for management and growth of port facilities and sea pilotage; Man. Dir M. Harrati.

Société Nationale de Manutention (SONAMA): 6 rue de Béziers, Algiers; tel. 64-65-61; telex 52339; monopoly of port handling; Man. Dir Amos Belalem.

Société Nationale de Transportes Maritimes et Compagnie Nationale Algérienne de Navigation (SNTM-CNAN): 2 quai d'Ajaccio, Nouvelle Gare Maritime, BP 280, Algiers; tel. 63-74-13; telex 52980; f. 1964; state-owned company which has the monopoly of conveyance, freight, chartering and transit facilities in all Algerian ports; operates fleet of freight and passenger ships; office in Marseilles and reps. in Paris, all French ports and the principal ports in many other countries. In October 1980 it was announced that CNAN was to be split into three units, dealing with hydrocarbons, general freight and passenger transport; Chair. Muhammad Guendouz; Man. Dir Ammar Bousbah.

Société Nationale de Transportes Maritimes des Hydrocarbures et des Produits Chimiques (SNTM-HYPROC): BP 60, Arzew; telex 12097.

CIVIL AVIATION

Algeria's main airport, Dar-el-Beïda, 20 km from Algiers, is a class A airport of international standing. At Constantine, Annaba, Tlemcen and Oran there are also airports which meet international requirements. All five were to be substantially improved during the 1980–84 Development Plan. There are also 65 aerodromes of which 20 are public, and a further 135 airstrips connected with the oil industry.

Air Algérie (Entreprise Nationale d'Exploitation des Services Aériens Internationaux de Transport Public) and **Inter-Air Services (Entreprise Nationale d'Exploitation des Services Aériens de Transport Intérieur et Travail Aériens):** 1 place Maurice Audin, BP 858, Algiers; telex 52436; Air Algérie f. 1953 by merger; state-owned from 1972; divided into Inter-Air Services (internal flights) and Air Algérie (external flights) 1983; internal services and extensive services to Europe, North, Central and West Africa, the Middle East and Asia; Man. Dir Slimane Bendjedid; Dir-Gen. International Operations Bahri el Fejir; Dir-Gen. Domestic Operations Omar Belkhodma; fleet of 2 Airbus A310-200, 11 Boeing 727, 15 Boeing 737, 1 Boeing 737-200C, 3 Lockheed L-100-30, 14 Grumman AG-CAT, 8 Fokker F27, 6 Beechcraft, 1 Alouette 2.

Tourism

Office National Algérien de l'Animation de la Promotion et de l'Information Touristique (ONAT): 25–27 rue Khélifa-Boukhalfa, Algiers; tel. 61-29-86; telex 66339; Dir-Gen. Maarif Rachid.

Atomic Energy

Commissariat aux Energies Nouvelles (CEN): BP 1017, Algiers-Gare; tel. 61-14-18; telex 52245; f. 1983; formerly Centre des Sciences et de la Technologie Nucléaires; government-funded; research and development in the field of renewable sources of energy, including atomic, solar, wind and geothermal energy.

Subsidiary organizations include:

Energy Conversion Centre: reactor physics and technology, nuclear and process instrumentation, turbo-machinery, heat-transfer technology.

Centre for Nuclear and Solar Studies: basic and applied research, nuclear physics, gamma irradiation technology, training.

ANDORRA

Introductory Survey

Location, Climate, Language, Religion, Flag, Capital
The Valleys of Andorra form an autonomous principality in western Europe. The country lies in the eastern Pyrenees, bounded by France and Spain, and is situated roughly midway between Barcelona and Toulouse. The climate is alpine, with much snow in winter and a warm summer. The official language is Catalan, but French and Spanish are also widely spoken. Most of the inhabitants are Christians, mainly Roman Catholics. The flag (proportions 3 by 2) has three equal vertical stripes, of blue, yellow and red, with the state coat of arms (a quartered shield above the motto *Virtus unita fortior*) in the centre of the yellow stripe. The capital is Andorra la Vella.

Recent History
Owing to the lack of distinction between the competence of the General Council of Andorra and the co-princes who have ruled the country since 1278, the Andorrans have encountered many difficulties during recent years in their attempts to gain international status for their country and control over its essential services.

Until 1970 the franchise was granted only to third-generation Andorran males who were more than 25 years of age. Thereafter, women, persons aged between 21 and 25, and second-generation Andorrans were allowed to vote in elections to the General Council. In 1977 the franchise was extended to include all first-generation Andorrans of foreign parentage who were aged 28 and over. The electorate remained small, however, when compared with the size of the population, and Andorra's foreign residents (who comprise 70% of the total population) increased their demands for political and nationality rights. Immigration is on a quota system, being restricted to French and Spanish nationals intending to work in Andorra.

Political parties are not directly represented in the General Council, but there are loose groupings with liberal and conservative sympathies. The country's only political organization, the Partit Democràtic d'Andorra, is technically illegal, and in the 1981 elections to the General Council the party urged its supporters to cast blank votes.

During discussions on institutional reform, held in 1980, representatives of the co-princes and the General Council agreed that an executive council should be formed, and that a referendum should be held on changes in the electoral system. In January 1981 the co-princes formally requested the General Council to prepare plans for reform, in accordance with these proposals. After elections to the General Council in December 1981, the new Council elected Oscar Ribas Reig as Head of Government. He then appointed an executive of six ministers who expressed their determination to give Andorra a full constitution, to defend local industry and to encourage private investment.

Severe storm damage in November 1982, and the general effects of the world recession, led to a controversial vote by the General Council, in August 1983, in favour of the introduction of income tax, to help to alleviate Andorra's budgetary deficit of 840m. pesetas, and to provide the Government with extra revenue to pursue development projects. Subsequent government proposals for an indirect tax on bank deposits, hotel rooms and property sales encountered strong opposition from financial and tourism concerns, and prompted the resignation of the Government in April 1984. Josep Pintat Solens, a local businessman, was elected unopposed by the General Council as Head of Government in May. In August, however, the Ministers of Finance, and Industry, Commerce and Agriculture resigned from their posts over disagreements concerning the failure to implement economic reforms. Major extensions of citizenship rights were proposed in August 1985.

In December 1985 a general election was held for the General Council, which later re-elected Francesc Cerqueda i Pascuet to the post of First Syndic. The electorate was increased by about 27% as a result of the newly-introduced lower minimum voting age of 18 years. The Council also re-elected Josep Pintat Solens as President of Government in January 1986, when he won the support of 27 of its 28 members.

Government
Andorra has no proper constitution, and its peculiar autonomy is a legacy of feudal conditions; the country, although administratively independent, has no clear international status. Andorra is a co-principality, under the suzerainty of the President of France and the Spanish Bishop of Urgel. The valleys pay a nominal biannual tax, the *questia*, to France and to the Bishop of Urgel. The French President is represented in Andorra by the Veguer de França, and the Bishop by the Veguer Episcopal. Each co-ruler has set up a permanent delegation for Andorran affairs. The Permanent Delegates are, respectively, the prefect of the French department of Pyrénées-Orientales and one of the vicars general of the Urgel diocese.

The General Council of the Valleys submits motions and proposals to the permanent delegation. The 28 members of the Council (four from each of the seven parishes) are elected by Andorran citizens for a term of four years, one-half of the Council being renewed every two years until December 1981, when an election was held for the whole Council. The Council elects as its head, for a three-year term, the First Syndic (Syndic Procurador General), who until 1982 also acted as chief executive, and the Second Syndic, who cease to be members of the Council on their election. The General Council appointed an Executive Council for the first time in January 1982. This entails the separation of powers between an executive and a legislature and represents an important step towards institutional reform.

In a 'popular consultation' on electoral reform, held in May 1982, some 30% of votes supported the existing majority vote system, while 42% called for a new system of proportional representation; approval of such a reform, however, still depended on the consent of the co-princes.

Economic Affairs
Andorra's products are mainly agricultural, with potatoes and tobacco being the principal crops; in 1981 production was 472 and 264 metric tons respectively. Livestock is raised and in 1982 there were approximately 9,000 sheep and 1,115 cattle. Iron, lead, alum, stone and timber are produced. Since the Second World War, Andorra has become a market for numerous European and overseas goods, owing to favourable excise conditions, and consequently the economy has expanded rapidly. However, Spain's accession to membership of the EEC on 1 January 1986, and the consequent removal of Spanish tariff barriers, threatened this lucrative trade in duty-free consumer goods. The Government hopes to negotiate a trade agreement with the EEC, giving the country a special status within the Community and thereby preserving the principality's economic livelihood. Concern within Andorra over the social implications of rapid development has led to demands for a curb on economic expansion, although the authorities, as yet, have had little real control over managing this development. Tourism is an important source of revenue, both in winter and summer, and is much encouraged. There are an estimated 250 hotels in Andorra.

French and Spanish currencies are in use. The absence of income tax or other forms of direct taxation has favoured the development of Andorra as a tax haven. The Government derives its revenue from a small levy on imports, indirect taxes on petrol and other items, stamp duty and the sale of postage stamps. The failure to balance revenue and expenditure has produced an increasing budget deficit, financed by borrowing. There is minimal company law or property registration within the principality, and land speculation has led to a rapid growth

ANDORRA

in construction. Banking is an important sector of the economy, although an informal agreement limits the number of banks operating within the country to five.

In August 1986 part of the Teruel power station, which belongs to the National Electricity Company, was closed down, owing to the low water-level of the Río Guadalope. It was believed that, if the river did not regain its previous high water-level by September, another part of the 350 MW station would have to be closed down, adversely affecting the Teruel coalfield, which provides fuel for the station.

Education

Education is provided by both French- and Spanish-language schools. Instruction in Catalan has only recently become available, at a school under the control of the local Roman Catholic Church. In 1983 there were a total of 8,356 pupils attending the 18 schools. The total number of teaching staff in 1982 was 305.

Tourism

Andorra has attractive mountain scenery, with winter sports facilities available at five skiing centres. In 1982 about 10m. foreign tourists entered Andorra, most of them visitors in transit.

Public Holidays

1987: 1 January (New Year's Day), 8 September (National Holiday), 25 December (Christmas).

1988: 1 January (New Year's Day), 8 September (National Holiday), 25 December (Christmas).

Each Parish also holds its own annual festival, which is taken as a public holiday, usually lasting for three days, in July, August or September.

Weights and Measures

The metric system is in force.

Statistical Survey

AREA AND POPULATION

Area: 467 sq km (180 sq miles).

Population: 42,000 (estimate, 1983), comprising 11,219 Andorrans, 24,095 Spanish, 2,723 French and 3,963 others. *Capital:* Andorra la Vella, population 16,200. Source: Conselleria de Treball i Benestar Social.

Births, Marriages and Deaths (1983): 563 live births; 138 marriages; 157 deaths.

FINANCE

Currency and Exchange Rates: French and Spanish currencies are both in use. *French currency:* 100 centimes = 1 franc. *Coins:* 1, 5, 10, 20 and 50 centimes; 1, 2, 5 and 10 francs. *Notes:* 10, 20, 50, 100 and 500 francs. *Sterling and Dollar Equivalents* (30 September 1986): £1 sterling = 9.6125 francs; US $1 = 6.6425 francs; 1,000 French francs = £104.03 = $150.55. *Average Exchange Rate* (francs per US dollar): 7.621 in 1983; 8.739 in 1984; 8.985 in 1985. *Spanish currency:* 100 céntimos = 1 peseta. *Coins:* 50 céntimos; 1, 5, 25, 50 and 100 pesetas. *Notes:* 100, 500, 1,000 and 5,000 pesetas. *Sterling and Dollar Equivalents* (30 September 1986): £1 sterling = 192.96 pesetas; US $1 = 133.50 pesetas; 1,000 Spanish pesetas = £5.182 = $7.491. *Average Exchange Rate* (pesetas per US dollar): 143.43 in 1983; 160.76 in 1984; 170.04 in 1985.

Budget (million pesetas, 1983): Expenditure 3,683.4; Revenue 3,719.7.

EXTERNAL TRADE

Imports (1977): from France 681,838,000 francs; from Spain 5,102,726,000 pesetas. *Exports* (1977): to France 18,870,000 francs; to Spain 155,000,000 pesetas (estimate).

TOURISM

Tourist Arrivals (1977): via France 2,200,000; via Spain 4,500,000; Total 6,700,000. Source: data supplied by French and Spanish Customs.

COMMUNICATIONS MEDIA

Radio Receivers (1984): 8,000 in use.

Television Receivers (1984): 5,000 in use.

EDUCATION

Enrolment (1983): 3- to 6-year-olds 1,978; 7- to 15-year-olds 5,508; 15 and over 1,050; Total 8,356.

Directory

The Government

(October 1986)

Episcopal Co-Prince: Dr JOAN MARTÍ ALANIS, Bishop of Urgel.
French Co-Prince: FRANÇOIS MITTERRAND.
Permanent Episcopal Delegate: Mgr RAMÓN VILARDELL MITJANETA.
Permanent French Delegate: JOAN KELLER.
Veguer Episcopal: FRANCESC BADIA-BATALLA.
Veguer de França: ENRIC BENOÎT DE COIGNAC.

EXECUTIVE COUNCIL

President of Government: JOSEP PINTAT SOLENS.
Minister of Finance: BONAVENTURA RIBERAYGUA MIQUEL.
Minister of Commerce, Industry and Agriculture: FRANCESC FORNE MOLNE.
Minister of Public Services: PERE VILA FONT.
Minister of Education and Culture: ROC ROSSELL DOLCET.
Minister of Tourism and Sport: JOAN SAMARRA VILA.

Legislature

CONSELL GENERAL DE LAS VALLS D'ANDORRÀ
(General Council of the Valleys)

First Syndic: FRANCESC CERQUEDA I PASCUET.
Second Syndic: JOSEP MARIA MAS I PONS.

There are 28 members (four from each of the seven parishes), directly elected for a term of four years. The most recent general election was held on 12 December 1985.

Judicial System

In Civil Law judicial power is exercised in civil matters in the first instance by four judges (Battles), two appointed by the French Veguer and two by the Veguer Episcopal. There is a Judge of Appeal appointed alternately by France and Spain, and in the third instance (Tercera Sala) cases are heard in the Supreme Court of Andorra at Perpignan or in the court at Urgel.

Criminal Law is administered by the Tribunal des Corts, consisting of the two Veguers, the Judge of Appeal, the two Battles and two members of the General Council (Parladors).

The Press

Poble Andorra: Avinguda Meritxell 112, Andorra la Vella; tel. (078) 22500; f. 1974; weekly; Publr Antoni Cornella Serra; circ. 3,000.

Radio and Television

In 1984 there were an estimated 8,000 radio receivers and 5,000 television receivers in use.

Radio Andorra: BPI, Andorra la Vella; f. 1984 as an Andorran-owned commercial public broadcasting service, to replace two stations which closed in 1981 after the expiry of their contracts with French and Spanish companies; Dir Gualberto Ossorio.

Sud Radio: 7 Avinguda Meritxell, Andorra la Vella; tel. (078) 20260; commercial radio station, broadcasting in Catalan, French and Spanish; Dir-Gen. Thierry Bernard.

Finance

(cap. = capital; res = reserves; dep. = deposits; m. = million; brs = branches; amounts in Spanish pesetas)

PRINCIPAL BANKS

Banc Agricol i Comercial d'Andorra: Carrer Mossèn Cinto Verdaguer 6, Andorra la Vella; tel. (078) 21333; telex 201; f. 1930; cap. 600m., res 4,889m., dep. 53,760m. (Dec. 1984); brs at Les Escaldes, Pas de la Casa and Sant Julià de Lòria; Pres. and Man. Dir Manuel Cerqueda-Escaler.

Banca Cassany SA: Avinguda Meritxell 39–41, Andorra la Vella; tel. (078) 20138; f. 1958; Dir Alain Frechu; Sec. J. Pierre Canturri.

Banc Internacional: Avinguda Meritxell 32, Andorra la Vella; tel. (078) 20037; telex 206; f. 1958; affiliated to Banco de Bilbao, Spain; cap. 882m., res 3,581m., dep. 71,494m. (Dec. 1984); Chair. Jordi Aristot Mora; Gen. Man. Pere Forch Soler; 4 brs.

Banca Mora: Plaça Coprinceps 2, Les Escaldes; tel. (078) 20913; telex 222; f. 1952; affiliated to Banc Internacional; cap. 504m., res 1,949m., dep. 63,467m. (Dec. 1984); Chair. F. Mora Font; Gen. Man. Pere Forch Soler; 7 brs.

Banca Reig: Sant Julià de Lòria; tel. (078) 41074; telex 240; Chair. J. Reig.

Crèdit Andorrà: Avinguda Príncep Benlloch 19, Andorra la Vella; tel. (078) 20326; telex 200; f. 1955; cap. 2,500m., res 924m., dep. 70,540m. (Dec. 1983); Chair. Narcís Casal i Vall; Man. Dir P. Roquet; 8 brs.

Transport

RAILWAYS

There are no railways in Andorra, but the nearest stations are Ax-les-Thermes, Hospitalet and La Tour de Carol, in France (with trains from Toulouse and Perpignan), and Puigcerdà, in Spain, on the line from Barcelona. There is a connecting bus service from all four stations to Andorra.

ROADS

Roads are maintained by the General Council of Andorra. A good road connects the Spanish and French frontiers, passing through Andorra la Vella. There are about 25,000 motor vehicles in current use.

CIVIL AVIATION

There is an airport at Seo de Urgel in Spain, 20 km from Andorra la Vella, with three flights daily from Barcelona. A bus service connects to Andorra.

Tourism

Consellería de Turisme i Esport: Casa de la Vall, Andorra la Vella; tel. (078) 21234; telex 309.

Sindicat d'Initiativa de las Valls d'Andorra: Carrer Dr Vilanova, Andorra la Vella; tel. (078) 20214.

ANGOLA

Introductory Survey

Location, Climate, Language, Religion, Flag, Capital

The People's Republic of Angola lies on the west coast of Africa. The Cabinda district is separated from the rest of the country by the estuary of the River Congo and Zairian territory, with the Congo lying to its north. Angola is bordered by Zaire to the north, Zambia to the east and Namibia to the south. The climate is tropical, locally tempered by altitude. There are two distinct seasons (wet and dry) but little seasonal variation in temperature. It is very hot and rainy in the coastal lowlands but temperatures fall inland. The official language is Portuguese, but African languages (mainly Ovimbundu, Kimbundu, Bakongo and Chokwe) are also in common use. Much of the population follows traditional beliefs, although there is a large minority of Christians, mainly Roman Catholics. The flag (proportions 3 by 2) has two equal horizontal stripes, of red and black; superimposed in the centre, in gold, are a five-pointed star, half a cog-wheel and a machete. The capital is Luanda.

Recent History

Formerly a Portuguese colony, Angola became an overseas province in 1951. Small nationalist groups began to form in the 1950s. There was an unsuccessful nationalist rebellion in 1961. Severe repression followed and there was a lull in nationalist activity until 1966. After a new wave of fighting, nationalist guerrilla groups were able to establish military and political control in large parts of eastern Angola and to press westward. Three major nationalist organizations were formed: the Movimento Popular de Libertação de Angola (MPLA) in 1956, the Frente Nacional de Libertação de Angola (FNLA) in 1962 and the União Nacional para a Independência Total de Angola (UNITA) in 1966. A movement calling for the secession of the Cabinda district, the Frente de Libertação do Enclave de Cabinda (FLEC), was formed in 1963.

Following the April 1974 coup d'état in Portugal, Angola's right to independence was recognized, and negotiations between the Portuguese Government and the nationalist groups began in September. After the formation of a common front by these groups, it was agreed that Angola would become independent in November 1975.

In January 1975 a transitional government was established, comprising representatives of the MPLA, the FNLA, UNITA and the Portuguese Government. However, violent clashes between the MPLA and the FNLA occurred in March, as a result of the groups' political differences, and continued throughout the country. By the second half of 1975 control of Angola was effectively divided between the three major nationalist groups, each aided by foreign powers. The MPLA (which held the capital) was supported by the USSR and Cuba, the FNLA by Zaire and Western powers (including the USA), while UNITA was backed by South African forces. The FNLA and UNITA formed a united front to fight the MPLA.

The Portuguese Government proclaimed Angola independent from 11 November 1975, transferring sovereignty to 'the Angolan people' rather than to any of the liberation movements. The MPLA proclaimed the People's Republic of Angola and the establishment of a government in Luanda under the presidency of the movement's leader, Dr Agostinho Neto. The FNLA and UNITA proclaimed the People's Democratic Republic of Angola and a coalition government, based in Nova Lisboa (renamed Huambo). The involvement of South African and Cuban troops caused an international furore.

By the end of February 1976, however, the MPLA, aided by Cuban technical and military expertise, had effectively gained control of the whole country. South African troops were withdrawn from Angola in March, but Cuban troops remained to assist the MPLA regime in countering guerrilla activity by the remnants of the defeated UNITA forces.

In May 1977 an abortive coup, led by Nito Alves, a former minister, resulted in the deaths of about 200 people. The task of national reconstruction was severely hampered by subsequent arrests and a purge of state and party officials. In December 1977 the MPLA was restructured as a political party, the Movimento Popular de Libertação de Angola—Partido de Trabalho (MPLA—PT), but further divisions were evident in December 1978, when President Neto abolished the post of Prime Minister and ousted several other ministers.

President Neto died in September 1979, and José Eduardo dos Santos, then Minister of Planning, was unanimously elected party leader and President by the MPLA—PT Central Committee. President dos Santos has continued to encourage strong links with the Soviet bloc, and has led campaigns to eliminate corruption and inefficiency. Elections to the National People's Assembly were first held in 1980. Fresh elections, due to be held in 1983, were postponed for three years, owing to political and military problems.

The MPLA Government's recovery programme has been continually hindered by security problems. Although the FNLA rebel movement reportedly surrendered to the Government in 1984, UNITA has, with considerable material aid from South Africa, conducted sustained and disruptive guerrilla activities, mainly in southern and central Angola. The South Africans themselves have also mounted numerous armed incursions over the Angolan border with Namibia, ostensibly in pursuit of guerrilla forces belonging to the South West Africa People's Organisation (SWAPO), who have bases within Angola. In response to the deteriorating security situation, the Angolan Government formed regional military councils in the provinces affected by the fighting, and a new Defence and Security Council. Although the Government's military campaign against the rebels appeared to be increasingly successful during 1985, UNITA's position was strengthened in April 1986, when US military aid began to arrive. In addition, UNITA appeared to enjoy greater support from South African forces, as part of a general escalation of the South African policy of destabilization in the southern Africa region from May 1986.

Angola, along with the other 'front-line' states, supports independence in Namibia following a UN-supervised cease-fire and elections. However, South Africa and the USA have insisted since 1982 that any withdrawal of South African troops from Namibia must be preceded, or at least accompanied, by the withdrawal of Cuban troops from Angola. During 1982 and 1983 this stipulation was considered by the Angolan Government to be unacceptable, and, subsequently, meetings between Angolan and South African government officials made no progress towards a settlement of the Namibia issue. However, in December 1983, soon after launching its invasion of southern Angola, South Africa proposed a complete withdrawal of its forces from Angola, on condition that the Angolan Government undertook to prevent SWAPO and Cuban forces from entering the areas vacated by the South African troops. Angola eventually accepted this proposal, and a cease-fire was established in the occupied area in early 1984. In February, as part of the settlement (which came to be known as the Lusaka agreement), Angola and South Africa established a Joint Monitoring Commission (JMC) to supervise the progress of the South African disengagement. Although some South African forces remained about 40 km inside Angolan territory in early 1985, the cease-fire was maintained, and in September and October 1984, in talks held with US delegates, President dos Santos proposed a peace plan for Namibia involving a phased withdrawal of most of the Cuban forces in Angola. Under the plan, the Cuban withdrawal would be conditional on the withdrawal of the remaining South African forces from Angola, and would begin only after the implementation of Namibian independence was under way and the number of South African troops in Namibia had been reduced to 1,500. The peace proposals were conveyed to South Africa by the USA in November, but differences between South Africa and Angola concerning the timetable for (and the extent of) the Cuban withdrawal have prevented the conclusion of an agreement, although in April 1985 South Africa officially 'withdrew' virtually all of its remaining troops from Angola, and in May the JMC was dissolved. Since that time, however, South Africa has periodically deployed military forces in Angola and mounted 'hot-pursuit' operations, ostensibly to curb continued activity by guerrillas of SWAPO, and the African National Congress (a banned South African opposition movement). In April 1985 two South African Defence Force commandos were killed by Angolan forces in Cabinda, some 1,350 km from the Angola/Namibia border, while involved in what Angola claimed was a mission to sabotage a petroleum refinery. In June 1985 South African troops launched another raid into Angola, followed in September by a further invasion which South Africa claimed to be necessary to forestall SWAPO assaults on Namibia, but which Angola alleged to be an attempt to aid UNITA during a major military offensive by the MPLA Government's forces. Shortly after launching a three-pronged attack on Botswana, Zambia and Zimbabwe in May 1986, South Africa was allegedly responsible for a further raid on the port of Namibe, in southern Angola, seriously damaging fuel storage tanks and cargo ships. South Africa denied any involvement in the raid, and refused to comment on accusations by Angola that South African forces had launched attacks on MPLA Government forces during an offensive against UNITA, mounted later in 1986.

Progress towards a settlement of the Namibian independence issue was also hampered by a concurrent deterioration in Angolan relations with the USA, largely as a result of the reverse in US policy towards UNITA. In July 1985 the Clark Amendment, which had prohibited US military support for UNITA since 1976, was repealed by the US Congress. Angola subsequently suspended all contacts with the USA, although the Angolan proposals of 1984, concerning the Cuban withdrawal, remained valid. Following a visit by Jonas Savimbi, the President of UNITA, to the USA in January 1986, the Reagan administration announced its decision, endorsed by the US Congress in September 1986, to grant $15m. in covert military aid to UNITA. In response, the Angolan Government complained to the UN and requested that the UN should replace the US Government as primary mediator in negotiations concerning Namibia. Angola also implied in June 1986 that it no longer considered the Cuban withdrawal necessarily relevant to Namibian independence. As a result of Angola's deteriorating relations with the USA and with South Africa, exacerbated by Pretoria's installation of an 'interim government' in Namibia in June 1985, the prospects for a Namibian agreement became increasingly remote. In August 1986, however, the Angolan Government requested a meeting with the US Government, with a view to improving relations.

The USA has hitherto made the withdrawal of Cuban forces a precondition for diplomatic recognition of the Angolan Government, which has been withheld since independence. Angola has diplomatic and economic links with most other countries, both Eastern and Western. In January 1982 a major co-operation agreement was signed with the USSR, under which Soviet assistance, worth about US $2,000m., was to be given for the construction of dams and a second petroleum refinery. Agreements on economic and technical co-operation were also signed with Portugal and Cuba in that year. In 1983 diplomatic relations were established with the People's Republic of China, which had supported the MPLA's opponents in the civil war. In February 1985 Angola and Zaire signed a defence and security agreement which reportedly included an undertaking that neither country would allow its territory to be used as a base for attacks against the other. The efficacy of this agreement was brought into question in March 1986, when it appeared that a UNITA raid on the diamond-mining town of Andrada in northern Angola, in which 178 foreign workers were taken hostage, had been launched from Zaire. However, the two countries reaffirmed the terms of the 1985 agreement at talks held in July 1986. In May 1986 it was announced that diplomatic relations with India were to be established.

Government

According to the 1975 constitution (amended in October 1976 and September 1980), the MPLA is responsible for the country's political, economic and social leadership. At its first congress, in December 1977, the MPLA was renamed the MPLA—Partido de Trabalho (Workers' Party) or MPLA—PT, and transformed into a Marxist-Leninist vanguard party. No other political parties are permitted. The MPLA—PT's supreme organ is the Congress, which normally meets every four years. The party held its first extraordinary congress in December 1980. The Congress elected the MPLA—PT's President and 75-member Central Committee to supervise the movement's work. In March 1981 the Committee elected a nine-member Secretariat to recommend policies to the Council of Ministers. A new eight-member Secretariat and a new 90-member Central Committee were elected at the second Party Congress, held in December 1985. In addition, the Central Committee appointed a new 13-member Political Bureau, which is the principal policy-making body of the MPLA—PT, and is effectively senior to the Central Committee Secretariat.

The Council of the Revolution was the supreme organ of state until the installation in November 1980 of the National People's Assembly, comprising 223 members, of whom 203 were chosen by electoral colleges (composed of representatives elected by 'loyal citizens') and 20 were nominated by the Central Committee of the MPLA—PT. The Assembly's term of office is normally three years, but the 1983 elections were postponed for three years. The Head of State is the President of the Republic, who is also President of the MPLA—PT, Commander-in-Chief of the armed forces, Chairman of the Political Bureau of the MPLA—PT and Chairman of the Council of Ministers. The President appoints the Council of Ministers to exercise executive authority.

Defence

Military service is by compulsory conscription. In July 1986 the armed forces, FAPLA (Forças Armadas Populares de Libertação de Angola), had an estimated total strength of 49,500: 46,000 serving in the army, 1,500 in the navy and 2,000 in the air force. The Directorate of People's Defence and Territorial Troops (formerly the People's Defence Organisation), a people's militia, has about 50,000 members. The People's Vigilance Brigades, an unarmed civilian militia organization, was created in 1984 and had some 320,000 members in 1985. In addition, there were an estimated 27,000 Cuban troops stationed in Angola in 1986, as well as Portuguese, East German and Soviet, advisers and technicians. The defence budget for 1986 was 32,730m. kwanza.

Economic Affairs

Following the protracted guerrilla campaign for independence, and the consequent departure of Portuguese personnel, Angola's economy was severely disrupted and suffered from a shortage of skilled workers. Angola has ample natural resources and considerable potential. However, continuing civil strife and incursions by South African troops have hampered recovery. In 1981, according to estimates by the World Bank, Angola's gross national product per head (at average 1979–81 prices) was about US $800. According to estimates by the UN Economic Commission for Africa, Angola's gross domestic product (GDP) increased, in real terms, at an average rate of 3.6% per year between 1976 and 1980, but declined by 2.3% in 1981, and by a further 5% in 1982.

Agriculture is the largest sector of the economy, employing more than 70% of the working population, although only about 2% of Angola's arable land is cultivated. The principal subsistence crops are maize, cassava, sweet potatoes and bananas. The major commercial crops are coffee (normally the third largest export commodity), sugar cane, cotton and sisal. Livestock herds were reduced as a result of the civil war and drought in 1981, but they subsequently increased. Much of Angola's territory is covered by forests, but commercial forestry has been developed only in the Cabinda and Moxico districts. The illegal export of timber by UNITA disrupts the forestry industry. Fishing was formerly an important industry but catches were drastically reduced by the withdrawal of most European-owned fleets in 1975–76. Measures to restore the industry were taken in 1981, when the Government formed a fisheries enterprise, and Angola was granted a loan of US $10m. from BADEA for the rehabilitation of fisheries facilities. A further grant of ECU 6.76m. ($4.9m.) was made to the sector by the EEC in

1984. The total catch was 168,114 metric tons in 1983, considerably lower than the projected total of 224,000 tons.

All aspects of the economy were severely affected by the exodus in 1975 of more than 300,000 Portuguese, who had held virtually all key positions in agricultural and industrial activity, and by the effects of the two-year civil war. Subsequently, the continuing war against UNITA and incursions by South African forces have prevented economic recovery. The widespread disruption of transport routes, the devastation of land, and the displacement of large numbers of the population (in early 1986 it was estimated that there were 1m. displaced people in Angola) ensuing from the strife have caused a deterioration in the economy as a whole, which has been exacerbated by drought and the severe lack of skilled workers and administrators. With restrictions on the import of items that peasant producers would wish to buy, the susequent lack of incentive to earn money and the re-emergence of a barter economy have also affected production levels adversely. Angola is now receiving financial and technical aid from several Soviet bloc and West European countries, including Portugal. However, in the period 1970–80 GDP registered an average annual rate of decline of more than 9%, and a further drop of 4% occurred in 1981/82.

The agricultural sector, in particular, continues to decline. Coffee is the principal cash crop and Angola was formerly the world's principal supplier of robusta coffee. Annual production of green coffee was more than 200,000 metric tons before independence, but the coffee crop was reduced by more than half in 1975–76, and then subsequently declined even further, owing to neglect of coffee plantations, to drought and to the continuing civil strife. Production slumped to 24,000 tons in 1981. The production target for 1982 was 35,000 tons, but preliminary figures assessed actual output at about 17,000 tons. There has since been only a slight improvement in production, to 22,000 tons in 1983 and 27,000 tons in 1984. In June 1983 the Government established a new company, Cafangol, to purchase and market coffee. The area of production under state control has declined in recent years, owing to labour shortages, induced by the lack of incentive to earn money. The widespread return by peasant coffee producers to subsistence farming has similarly reduced production in the private sector. The UN World Food Programme plans to spend $14.25m. on a food-for-work project to alleviate this problem, which affects the whole of the agricultural sector, and the Government is committed, in principle, to policy changes, such as the devaluation of Angola's currency, the kwanza, initially by about 40%. It was estimated that coffee provided some $55m. in export earnings in 1985 (2.7% of total exports).

Production of raw sugar was 82,000 metric tons in 1973 but only 27,000 tons in 1980. Cuban technicians are assisting with the rehabilitation of sugar estates, and production rose to 30,000 tons in 1983/84, and to 34,400 tons in 1984/85. The staple diet of most inhabitants is cassava, and production was estimated at 1.95m. tons in 1984. An estimated 320,000 tons of maize was produced in 1980, but subsequent harvests suffered as a result of prolonged drought: maize production was estimated at 275,000 tons in 1983 when total cereal production was estimated to be some 350,000 tons, little more than one-half of the annual pre-independence levels of about 600,000 tons. The total cereal import requirement for 1983/84 was estimated at 290,000 tons, and that for 1984/85 at about 217,000 tons. Before independence, Angola was a net exporter of food, but the country now imports at least 50% of its needs: marketing of home-produced food fell by 26% in 1981. The 1984 annual economic plan aimed to raise overall food production by 16.8%.

Angola is very rich in minerals, especially petroleum, diamonds and iron ore, and there are also deposits of copper, manganese, phosphates and salt. In 1975 deposits of uranium were discovered on the border with Namibia. Petroleum is the major source of foreign exchange, accounting for nearly 50% of export earnings in 1974, rising to about 95% in 1985. Petroleum officially provided 35% of GDP and 40% of state revenues in 1985. Angola's proven reserves of petroleum were estimated at about 252m. tons at the beginning of 1985. Between 75% and 80% of production comes from offshore fields in Cabinda, where production reached between 165,000 and 170,000 barrels per day (b/d) in 1984. The Cabinda Gulf Oil Company (Cabgoc), in association with Sonangol (the state oil company), increased production from these fields alone to about 200,000 b/d in early 1986. While capital expenditure in the Cabinda enclave from 1983 to 1986 was projected at US $645m., other fields, both onshore and offshore, are of increasing importance, and the total annual investment in the hydrocarbons sector was expected to be $606m. in 1984 and $650m. in 1985. Angola's overall petroleum production reached 190,000 b/d in 1983, making Angola the second largest petroleum producer in sub-Saharan Africa. Angola's overall production reached 220,000 b/d in 1984, and 231,000 b/d in 1985, as further fields came into production. It is forecast that by 1991 total petroleum production will be 550,000 b/d. Petroleum earnings reached about $1,800m. in 1984, and were estimated at some $2,000m. in 1985. Owing to the instability of international petroleum prices from late 1985, earnings from this sector were expected to reach only about $900m. in 1986. Angola's sole refinery, at Luanda, is operated by the state-owned Petrangol, and currently processes about 1.35m. metric tons of petroleum per year. Domestic oil consumption was only 42,000 b/d in 1984, however, and most of Angola's oil output is exported in its crude form, although long-term plans to increase the refinery's capacity to 2m. tons, or to build a second refinery, are being considered. Sonangol has trade and technical co-operation agreements with several major international oil companies, and prospects for the petroleum sector are excellent, with further exploration currently under way and several new fields due to come 'on stream' during the period 1986–88. In 1986, however, the collapse of the oil price, and increasing pressure from the US administration on US oil companies to withdraw from Angola, prompted the Angolan Government to stress the need to develop other sectors of the economy, such as agriculture.

Diamonds are the country's second largest foreign exchange earner, and between 5% and 8% of world diamond production is normally accounted for by Angola. The output of Angolan diamonds (of which a high proportion are of gem quality) was 1,960,000 carats in 1974, but fell to only 353,000 carats in 1977. Recorded output rose to 1.5m. carats in 1980, but declined thereafter, owing to the worsening security situation, caused by UNITA attacks, and to extensive diamond smuggling. Production fell to some 920,000 carats in 1984, and to 714,000 carats in 1985. Earnings from diamond sales fell from $234m. in 1980 to $94m. in 1983, and to only $58m. in 1984. In a major reorganization of the diamond industry, the diamond mining company, Diamang (in which the state enterprise, Endiama, held 77% of the shares), was dissolved in July 1986. Endiama then instigated a new national diamond policy, whereby diamond mining is to be divided into blocks, to be exploited under production-sharing agreements with foreign concessionaires.

The other principal mineral is iron ore, the production of which reached 5.6m. metric tons (60% to 65% iron) in 1974. Angola is thought to have high-grade iron ore reserves of over 1,000m. metric tons, but production was halted in August 1975, when the Cassinga mines in southern Angola were partially destroyed. Mining was expected to recommence in late 1985, following delays in the rehabilitation work, caused by the South African raids of December 1983. The cost of rehabilitating the mines is estimated at between $25m. and $28m. Export of pre-independence stocks started in 1981. The state-owned Empresa Nacional de Ferro Angola (Ferrangol), founded in 1981, plans to extend iron mining to other known deposits, and development of the Cassala deposits, north of the Cuanza River, should benefit from the Kapanda dam and hydroelectricity project, to be carried out with Soviet and Brazilian assistance. This project, the largest construction scheme ever undertaken in Angola, will cost about $900m. Construction work on the dam began in 1983 and is scheduled for completion in 1989–92. The project will have a generating capacity of 520 MW and will provide both irrigation for farming and electricity for the industrial sector. Angola has a massive hydroelectricity potential, and there are plans to increase the capacity of the existing Cambambe dam. Exploratory drilling in the Cassala and Quitungo areas revealed aggregate reserves of iron and magnetite of about 200m. tons, which could eventually be mined to produce an output of 5m.–6m. tons per year, but the development of these resources is expected to depend on how the market develops in the near future. Mining of phosphate rock started in the north in 1981, with annual production capacity of 15,000 metric tons. Research work, completed on a deposit in Cabinda province in 1984, revealed that between 400,000 and 600,000 metric tons of phosphates could be extracted annually. Important deposits of feldspar have been found in Huíla province.

Angola's traditional surplus on trade and current payments ended in 1981, when there was a trade deficit of US $243m., owing to a combination of low prices for the three major export commodities (petroleum, diamonds and coffee) and continuing security problems. However, as a result of the thriving petroleum industry, Angola's trade balance recovered in 1983 and 1984, when it registered small surpluses. Angola has a good record in repayment of foreign debts, and a foreign investment law of June 1979, which made arrangements for royalties, taxes and the repatriation of capital in the event of nationalization, also aimed to make the country attractive to foreign investors. None the less, it is unlikely that many large investments will be made in the near future, except in the fields of hydroelectricity and petroleum. Angola's economic development remains limited by internal security problems, and the Government's ability to import vital raw materials and machinery is restricted by the need to spend about 50% of foreign exchange earnings on defence, and a further 25% on food imports. Export earnings were around US $1,600m. in 1982, rising to about $1,990m. in 1984 when the total expenditure on imports (excepting capital goods) was to be restricted to some $818m. Private enterprise is permitted in some sectors of the economy, but more than 80% of industry and commerce was state-owned in 1981.

The targets of the 1981-85 national economic plan had to be scaled down because of falling commodity prices and the worsening economic and military situation in the country. The national plan was transformed into a General Emergency Plan in 1983, resulting in further economic stringency. This continued under the 1984 annual economic plan, which placed a stress on defence, increased food production and restrictions on expenditure of foreign exchange, in order to limit external debt. The disbursed medium- and long-term external debt grew to only $2,5000m. by the end of 1985, while the cost of debt servicing in that year was $324m. In the absence of rescheduling, debt service costs for 1986 were expected to rise to $540m., owing to the decline in petroleum prices. However, the USSR, which is owed over 62% of the total debt, has reportedly agreed to reschedule payment for two years. The 1986-90 plan, adopted at the second Party Congress (held in December 1985), again placed the emphasis on defence, and on the need to stimulate internal production and to restrict foreign exchange expenditure.

Angola's decision to become a party to the Lomé convention (see p. 149), which it formally signed in April 1985, will make the country eligible for increased aid from the EEC and for preferential trade tariffs. Angola participates fully in the affairs of the Southern African Development Co-ordination Conference (SADCC, see p. 204), in which it has special responsibility for the co-ordination of energy development and conservation.

Social Welfare

Medical care is provided free of charge, but its availability is limited by a shortage of trained personnel and medicines. At independence there were 24 hospitals in Angola (eight of them in Luanda), but these were left without trained staff. In 1981 there were 460 foreign physicians in the country, mainly from Cuba, and a major training programme produces about 1,000 Angolan paramedics per year, and helps to spread basic medical knowledge to village communities. In 1977 a major vaccination programme was launched, and by 1981 about 3m. children had been immunized against poliomyelitis. An agreement with the USSR, signed in 1984, provided for the completion and equipment of hospitals in Lubango, Luanda and Malanje. In the same year Spain approved a loan of $3m. to Angola for the construction of a medical school. War veterans are cared for by the Ministry of Defence.

Education

Education is officially compulsory for children aged seven to 15, but the Government's target of free universal education has not yet been reached. Free primary education is provided for four years, beginning at the age of seven. Secondary education begins at the age of 11 and lasts for up to six years. In 1973, under Portuguese rule, primary school pupils numbered only 300,000; by 1982 there were 1,178,467. Secondary school numbers increased from 4,000 to 136,466 between 1973 and 1981. Higher education is also being encouraged, and there were 2,674 students at the University of Angola in 1982. Much education now uses national languages rather than Portuguese.

At independence the estimated adult illiteracy rate was over 85%. A national literacy campaign was launched in 1976, and the average rate of adult illiteracy in 1985 was officially estimated at 59% (males 51%). Angola's independent economic development is severely hampered by the widespread lack of basic skills.

Public Holidays

1987: 1 January (New Year's Day), 4 February (Anniversary of the outbreak of the armed struggle against Portuguese colonialism), 27 March (Victory Day), 14 April (Youth Day)*, 1 May (Workers' Day), 1 August (Armed Forces' Day)*, 17 September (National Hero's Day, birthday of Dr Agostinho Neto), 11 November (Independence Day), 1 December (Pioneers' Day)*, 10 December (Anniversary of the Foundation of the MPLA), 25 December (Family Day).

1988: 1 January (New Year's Day), 4 February (Anniversary of the outbreak of the armed struggle against Portuguese colonialism), 27 March (Victory Day), 14 April (Youth Day)*, 1 May (Workers' Day), 1 August (Armed Forces' Day)*, 17 September (National Hero's Day, birthday of Dr Agostinho Neto), 11 November (Independence Day), 1 December (Pioneers' Day)*, 10 December (Anniversary of the Foundation of the MPLA), 25 December (Family Day).

* Although not officially recognized as public holidays, these days are popularly treated as such.

Weights and Measures

The metric system is in force.

Currency and Exchange Rates

100 lwei = 1 kwanza (K).

Exchange rates (30 September 1986):
 £1 sterling = 42.86 kwanza;
 US $1 = 29.62 kwanza.

Statistical Survey

Sources (unless otherwise stated): Direcção dos Serviços de Estatística, Luanda.

Area and Population

AREA, POPULATION AND DENSITY

Area (sq km)	1,246,700*
Population (census results)	
30 December 1960	4,480,719
15 December 1970	
Males	2,943,974
Females	2,702,192
Total	5,646,166
Population (UN estimates at mid-year)	
1982	8,142,000
1983	8,339,000
1984	8,540,000
Density (per sq km) at mid-1984	6.9

* 481,354 sq miles.

1985: Population 8,573,493 (official estimate).

BIRTHS AND DEATHS

Average annual birth rate 48.0 per 1,000 in 1970–75, 47.5 per 1,000 in 1975–80; death rate 25.4 per 1,000 in 1970–75, 23.6 per 1,000 in 1975–80 (UN estimates).

ECONOMICALLY ACTIVE POPULATION
(ILO estimates, '000 persons at mid-1980)

	Males	Females	Total
Agriculture, etc.	1,281	1,237	2,518
Industry	304	22	326
Services	442	128	569
Total	2,027	1,386	3,414

Source: ILO, *Economically Active Population Estimates and Projections, 1950–2025*.

DISTRIBUTION OF POPULATION BY DISTRICT*
(Census of 15 December 1970)

	Area (sq km)	Population†	Density (per sq km)
Cabinda	7,270	81,265	11.17
Zaire	40,130	40,365	1.00
Uíge	55,818	386,709	6.92
Luanda	33,789	569,113	16.84
Cuanza Norte	27,106	304,565	11.23
Cuanza Sul	59,269	462,968	7.81
Malanje	101,028	558,630	5.52
Lunda	167,786	302,538	1.80
Benguela	37,808	474,897	12.56
Huambo	30,667	837,627	27.31
Bié	71,870	650,337	9.04
Moxico	199,786	189,885	0.95
Cuando-Cubango	192,079	113,562	0.59
Namibe	55,946	52,179	0.93
Huíla	166,348	644,864	3.87
Total	1,246,700	5,669,504	4.54

* Subsequent administrative reorganization has altered the area of most districts, created three new ones, Cunene, Lunda Norte and Bengo, and redesignated all districts as provinces.

† Provisional figures. The revised total is 5,646,166.

PRINCIPAL TOWNS (population at 1970 census)

Luanda (capital)	480,613*	Benguela	40,996
Huambo (Nova Lisboa)	61,885	Lubango (Sá de Bandeira)	31,674
Lobito	59,258	Malanje	31,559

* 1982 estimate: 1,200,000.

Agriculture

PRINCIPAL CROPS (FAO estimates, '000 metric tons)

	1982	1983	1984
Wheat	10	10	10
Rice (paddy)	20	22	22
Maize	250	275	260
Millet and sorghum	50	50	50
Potatoes	40	40	40
Sweet potatoes	180	180	180
Cassava (Manioc)	1,950	1,950	1,950
Dry beans	40	40	40
Groundnuts (in shell)	20	20	20
Sunflower seed	10	10	10
Seed cotton	33	33	33
Cottonseed	22	22	22

	1982	1983	1984
Cotton (lint)	11	11	11
Palm kernels	12	12	12
Palm oil	40	40	40
Vegetables	227	227	227
Citrus fruit	80	80	80
Pineapples	35	35	35
Bananas	280	280	280
Sugar cane	250	350	360
Coffee (green)*	17	22	27
Tobacco	3	3	3
Sisal	20	20	20

* Unofficial estimates.

Source: FAO, *Production Yearbook*.

ANGOLA

LIVESTOCK
(FAO estimates, '000 head, year ending September)

	1982	1983	1984
Cattle	3,250	3,300	3,350
Pigs	440	450	460
Sheep	235	240	245
Goats	945	950	955

Poultry (FAO estimates, million): 6 in 1982; 6 in 1983; 6 in 1984.
Source: FAO, *Production Yearbook*.

LIVESTOCK PRODUCTS (FAO estimates, '000 metric tons)

	1982	1983	1984
Beef and veal	52	53	53
Goats' meat	3	3	3
Pig meat	14	15	15
Poultry meat	7	7	7
Other meat	6	5	6
Cows' milk	148	148	148
Butter	0.8	0.8	0.8
Cheese	2.5	2.5	2.5
Hen eggs	3.8	3.8	3.9
Cattle hides	7.3	7.5	7.7

Honey: 15,000 metric tons per year (FAO estimate).
Source: FAO, *Production Yearbook*.

Forestry

ROUNDWOOD REMOVALS
(FAO estimates, '000 cubic metres, excluding bark)

	1982	1983	1984
Sawlogs, veneer logs and logs for sleepers*	556	556	556
Pulpwood*	140	140	140
Other industrial wood	685	702	719
Fuel wood†	7,663	7,663	7,663
Total	9,044	9,061	9,078

* Assumed to be unchanged since 1973.
† Assumed to be unchanged since 1981.
Source: FAO, *Yearbook of Forest Products*.

SAWNWOOD PRODUCTION ('000 cubic metres)

	1978	1979	1980
Total (incl. boxboards)	40	20	10

Source: FAO, *Yearbook of Forest Products*.
1981–84: Annual production as in 1980.

Fishing

('000 metric tons, live weight)

	1980	1981	1982
Freshwater fishes*	8.0	8.0	8.0
Cunene horse mackerel	36.9	49.7	49.1
Round and shortbody sardinellas	22.8	49.4	27.7
Skipjack tuna	3.5	2.5	2.3
Large-head hairtail	3.8	6.9	4.9
Others (incl. unspecified)	10.7	14.9	20.1
Total catch	85.6	131.5	112.0

* Assumed to be unchanged since 1973.
1983 ('000 metric tons): Total catch 110.8 (FAO estimates).
1984 ('000 metric tons): Total catch 70.7 (FAO estimates).
Source: FAO, *Yearbook of Fishery Statistics*.

Mining

	1981	1982	1983
Crude petroleum ('000 metric tons)*	7,158	6,410	8,304
Natural gas (terajoules)*	49,000	48,000	50,000
Salt (unrefined) ('000 metric tons)*†	50	50	41
Diamonds ('000 carats)†	1,400	1,325*	1,200*
Gypsum (crude) ('000 metric tons)*†	200	200	200

* Estimates. † Source: US Bureau of Mines.
Source: UN, *Industrial Statistics Yearbook*.
1984: Crude petroleum 10,280,000 metric tons.
1985: Crude petroleum 11,420,000 metric tons.

Industry

SELECTED PRODUCTS

		1981	1982	1983
Raw sugar†	'000 metric tons	50	35	60
Cigarettes‡	million	2,400	2,400	2,400
Jet fuels	'000 metric tons	62	60	70
Motor spirit	'000 metric tons	60	65	70
Distillate fuel oils	'000 metric tons	215	210	250
Residual fuel oils	'000 metric tons	560	525	600
Cement	'000 metric tons	250*	300§	300§
Crude steel§	'000 metric tons	10	10	10
Electric energy	million kWh.	1,500	1,600	1,740

* Estimates.   † Estimates by International Sugar Organization.
‡ Estimates by US Department of Agriculture.   § Estimates by US Bureau of Mines.
Source: UN, *Industrial Statistics Yearbook*.

Finance

CURRENCY AND EXCHANGE RATES

Monetary Units
100 lwei = 1 kwanza (K).

Denominations
Coins: 50 lwei; 1, 2, 5, 10 and 20 kwanza.
Notes: 20, 50, 100, 500 and 1,000 kwanza.

Sterling and Dollar Equivalents (30 September 1986)
£1 sterling = 42.86 kwanza;
US $1 = 29.62 kwanza;
1,000 kwanza = £23.33 = $33.76.

Exchange Rate
Since 1976 the official rate has been fixed at US $1 = 29.62 kwanza.

BUDGET (million kwanza)

Revenue	1983	1984
State enterprises	10,126	10,420
Taxes	38,669	54,372
Other	6,796	9,764
Total	55,591	74,556

Expenditure	1983	1984
Economic development	17,907	21,961
Social services	14,838	17,254
Defence and security	23,295	29,426
Administration	9,159	9,487
Other	2,378	4,174
Total	67,577	82,302

Source: Instituto Nacional de Estatística, Angola.

BALANCE OF PAYMENTS (million kwanza)

	1982	1983	1984
Trade balance	11,021	17,785	20,850
Services (net)	−19,007	−19,792	−23,613
Unrequited transfers	794	986	1,047
Current balance	−7,192	−1,021	−1,716
Long-term capital (net)	3,026	1,628	6,103
Short-term capital, errors and omissions	3,901	−466	−2,557
Changes in reserves	−265	141	1,830

Source: Banco Nacional de Angola.

NATIONAL ACCOUNTS (estimates, million kwanza at current prices)
Expenditure on the Gross Domestic Product

	1980	1981	1982
Government final consumption expenditure	40,100	44,330	50,090
Private final consumption expenditure	91,140	100,040	109,590
Increase in stocks / Gross fixed capital formation	16,300	17,140	17,950
Total domestic expenditure	147,540	161,510	177,630
Exports of goods and services	97,250	102,830	96,630
Less Imports of goods and services	56,100	64,810	72,290
GDP in purchasers' values	188,690	199,530	201,970
GDP at constant 1970 prices	31,419	30,695	29,157

Gross Domestic Product by Economic Activity

	1980	1981	1982
Agriculture, hunting, forestry and fishing	65,430	68,380	77,200
Mining and quarrying	38,170	41,000	31,160
Manufacturing	3,910	4,190	4,690
Electricity, gas and water	680	730	810
Construction	3,050	3,280	3,310
Trade, restaurants and hotels	8,380	8,870	8,490
Transport, storage and communications	7,890	8,350	7,990
Finance, insurance, real estate and business services	610	640	620
Public administration and defence	18,480	20,430	23,580
Other services	5,060	5,350	5,110
GDP at factor cost	151,660	161,220	162,960
Indirect taxes, *less* subsidies	37,030	38,310	39,010
GDP in purchasers' values	188,690	199,530	201,970

Source: UN Economic Commission for Africa, *African Statistical Yearbook*.

External Trade

PRINCIPAL COMMODITIES

Imports (US $'000)*	1982	1983	1984
Fresh, chilled or frozen meat	11,916	10,045	4,396
Milk and cream	26,065	24,501	23,312
Wheat and meslin (unmilled)	10,249	9,450	12,425
Wheat flour	11,946	15,690	13,587
Refined petroleum products	50,274	12,529	2,913
Soya bean oil	14,414	12,214	4,739
Medicinal and pharmaceutical products	12,057	19,035	13,336
Woven cotton fabrics	716	10,405	56
Iron and steel tubes and pipes	37,823	8,612	22,509
Metal structures and parts	19,168	10,227	5,179
Rotating electric plant	4,986	2,985	11,876
Civil engineering equipment	108,339	49,475	35,448
Telecommunications and sound equipment	14,900	5,024	14,207
Road motor vehicles for goods transport	33,846	17,045	14,632
Spare parts for road vehicles	15,267	10,315	16,961
Ships, boats and floating structures	26,837	25,450	2,907

* Source: Organisation for Economic Co-operation and Development, microfilms.

Exports (million kwanza)	1978	1979
Crude petroleum	16,507.1	26,746.0
Petroleum derivatives	1,102.7	2,497.1
Coffee	6,732.1	5,699.9
Diamonds	2,996.6	4,219.0
Cement	89.7	59.1
Sisal	82.4	164.6
Fish meal	59.6	39.7
Total (incl. others)	27,739.0	39,530.8

ANGOLA

Statistical Survey

SELECTED TRADING PARTNERS (US $ million)

Imports	1977	1978
Belgium and Luxembourg	23.4	38.7
Denmark	1.2	4.6
France	33.1	28.3
Germany, Federal Republic	4.4	80.0
Italy	19.6	28.7
Japan	37.9	36.0
Netherlands	20.3	11.7
Portugal	63.3	64.8
Sweden	42.1	26.3
United Kingdom	18.3	38.8
USA	38.4	92.4

Exports	1977	1978
Belgium and Luxembourg	3.1	6.2
Denmark	0.1	0.0
France	9.8	4.9
Germany, Federal Republic	11.4	5.8
Italy	1.1	0.6
Japan	10.3	6.6
Netherlands	11.7	37.5
Portugal	24.2	6.6
Sweden	1.2	1.1
United Kingdom	9.6	10.9
USA	309.0	325.0

Source: Ministério do Plan, Luanda, *Angola 78*.

Note: The total value of Angola's external trade (in US $ million) was: Imports (c.i.f.) 733 in 1977, 604 in 1978, 680 in 1979, 636 in 1984; Exports (f.o.b.) 657 in 1977, 661 in 1978, 666 in 1979, 2,029 in 1984.

Transport

GOODS TRANSPORT ('000 metric tons)

	1981	1982	1983
Road	1,000.8	733.6	691.5
Railway	725.0	655.3	399.2
Shipping (inshore and offshore)	520.1	446.5	401.3
Air	27.1	20.3	21.5
Total	2,273.0	1,855.7	1,513.5

PASSENGER TRANSPORT ('000 journeys)

	1981	1982	1983
Road	100,335.5	119,767.1	75,956.5
Railway	7,622.3	8,398.7	8,007.6
Air	822.9	899.6	959.3
Shipping	77.1	—	—
Total	108,857.8	129,065.4	84,923.4

Sources: Instituto Nacional de Estatística, Angola; Ministry of Transport and Communications, Luanda.

INTERNATIONAL SEA-BORNE SHIPPING
(estimated freight traffic, '000 metric tons)

	1981	1982	1983
Goods loaded	6,361	5,936	8,301
Goods unloaded	936	888	940

Source: UN, *Monthly Bulletin of Statistics*.

CIVIL AVIATION (traffic on scheduled services)

	1980	1981	1982
Kilometres flown (million)	8.4	11.0	11.4
Passengers carried ('000)	635	801	891
Passenger-km (million)	553	691	858
Freight ton-km (million)	20.9	33.2	20.8

Source: UN, *Statistical Yearbook*.

Communications Media

	1981	1982	1983
Radio receivers ('000 in use)	138	150	162
Television receivers ('000 in use)	31	32	33
Telephones ('000 in use)	40	n.a.	n.a.

Book production (1979): 57 titles (books 33, pamphlets 24); 430,000 copies (books 239,000, pamphlets 191,000).
Daily newspapers: 1 (estimated circulation 50,000) in 1982.
Source: UNESCO, *Statistical Yearbook*; UN, *Statistical Yearbook*.

Education

1981

	Teachers	Pupils
Pre-primary*	} 40,027 {	342,316
Primary		1,258,858
Secondary:		
general	3,870	134,578
teacher training	} 410 {	2,564
vocational		2,642
Higher	374	2,666

* Initiation classes in which pupils learn Portuguese.

1982 (pupils): Pre-primary 292,457; Primary 1,178,430; Secondary: general 124,858; teacher training 3,141; vocational 3,919; Higher 2,674.

Source: UNESCO, *Statistical Yearbook*.

Directory

The Constitution

The MPLA regime adopted an independence constitution for Angola in November 1975. It was amended in October 1976 and September 1980. The main provisions of the constitution are summarized below:

BASIC PRINCIPLES

The People's Republic of Angola shall be a sovereign, independent and democratic state. All sovereignty shall be vested in the Angolan people. The Movimento Popular de Libertação de Angola—Partido de Trabalho (MPLA—PT), their legitimate representative, shall be responsible for the political, economic and social leadership of the nation. The people shall be guaranteed broad effective participation in the exercise of political power through the development of people's power organizations.

The People's Republic of Angola shall be a unitary and indivisible State. Economic, social and cultural solidarity shall be promoted between all the Republic's regions for the common development of the entire nation and the elimination of regionalism and tribalism.

Defence

Under the leadership of the MPLA—PT and with its President as Commander-in-Chief, the People's Armed Forces for the Liberation of Angola (FAPLA) shall be institutionalized as the national army of the Republic. It shall be the responsibility of FAPLA to defend the country and to participate alongside the people in production and hence in national reconstruction. The Commander-in-Chief of FAPLA shall appoint and dismiss high-ranking officers.

Religion

The Republic shall be a secular state and there shall be complete separation of the State and religious institutions. All religions shall be respected.

The Economy

Agriculture shall be regarded as the base and industry as the decisive factor in the Republic's development. The Republic shall promote the establishment of just social relations in all sectors of production, furthering and developing the public sector and fostering co-operatives. It shall recognize, protect and guarantee private activities and property, including that of foreigners, provided that they are useful to the country's economy and in the interests of the Angolan people. The fiscal system shall be guided by the principle of graduated direct taxation.

Education

The Republic shall vigorously combat illiteracy and obscurantism and shall promote the development of education and of a true national culture.

FUNDAMENTAL RIGHTS AND DUTIES

The State shall respect and protect the human person and human dignity. All citizens shall be equal before the law. They shall be subject to the same duties, without any distinction based on colour, race, ethnic group, sex, place of birth, religion, level of education, or economic or social status.

It shall be the right and duty of every citizen to participate in the defence of the country and to defend and extend the revolution. All citizens over the age of 18 shall have the right and duty to take an active part in public life, to vote and be elected or appointed to any State organ. All elected citizens shall be accountable to the electorate, which shall at any given time have the right to revoke the mandate given.

There shall be freedom of expression, assembly and association provided that the basic objectives of the Republic are adhered to. Every citizen has the right to a defence. Individual freedoms are guaranteed. Freedom of conscience and belief shall be inviolable. Work shall be the right and duty of all citizens. The State guarantees medical and health care and the right to assistance in childhood, motherhood, disability, old age, etc. It also guarantees access to education and culture.

STATE ORGANS

President of the Republic

The President of the Republic shall be the President of the MPLA—PT. As Head of State the President shall represent the Angolan nation and shall have the following specific functions:

- to swear in the government appointed by the People's Assembly on the recommendation of the MPLA—PT;
- to preside over the Council of Ministers;
- to declare war and make peace, following authorization by the People's Assembly;
- to nominate, swear in and dismiss the Provincial Commissioners;
- to sign, promulgate and publish the laws of the People's Assembly, government decrees and statutory decrees;
- to direct national defence;
- to decree a state of siege or state of emergency;
- to pardon and commute sentences;
- to indicate from among the members of the Political Bureau who shall deputize when the President is absent or temporarily prevented from exercising presidential functions;
- to discharge all the other functions conferred on the President by the People's Assembly.

In the case of the death, resignation or permanent incapacity of the president, the Central Committee shall designate from among its members the person who shall provisionally exercise the duties of the president of the Republic.

People's Assembly

The People's Assembly is the supreme State body, to which the government is responsible. Members are elected by colleges composed of representatives chosen by all loyal citizens over 18 years old in their work- or living-places. Elections are held every three years.

Government

The government shall comprise the president of the Republic, the ministers and the secretaries of state, and other members whom the law shall indicate, and shall have the following functions:

- to guarantee the safety of persons and property;
- to draw up and implement the general state budget once it is approved by the People's Assembly;
- to follow guidelines laid down by the People's Assembly.

The government may exercise by decree the legislative functions delegated to it by the People's Assembly.

Judiciary

The organization, composition and competence of the courts shall be established by law. Judges shall be independent in the discharge of their functions.

Local Administration

The People's Republic of Angola shall be administratively divided into provinces (províncias), municipalities (municípios), communes (comunas), neighbourhoods (bairros) and villages (povoações).

Local administration shall be guided by the combined principles of unity, decentralization and local initiative.

In a province, the provincial commissioner shall be the direct representative of the government. The government shall be represented in the district by the local commissioner, and in the commune by the commune commissioner, who shall be appointed on the recommendation of the MPLA—PT. The administrative bodies of the district, commune, neighbourhood and village shall be, respectively, the local commission, the commune commission, and the people's neighbourhood or village commission.

Eighteen provincial assemblies of 55–85 deputies are elected every three years by all loyal citizens over 18 years old.

The local authorities shall have legal personality and shall enjoy administrative and financial autonomy. The structure and jurisdiction of the administrative bodies and other organs of local administration shall be established by law.

FINAL PROVISIONS

An amendment to the Constitution is made by the People's Assembly. Laws and regulations may be repealed or amended if they conflict with the spirit of the present law or the Angolan revolutionary process.

The Government

HEAD OF STATE

President: José Eduardo dos Santos (assumed office 21 September 1979).

COUNCIL OF MINISTERS
(December 1986)

Chairman of the Council of Ministers: José Eduardo dos Santos.
Minister of External Relations: Afonso Van-Dúnem (Mbinda).
Minister of Planning: António Henriques da Silva.
Minister of Defence: Col Pedro Maria Tonha (Pedalé).
Minister of Justice: Fernando José França Van-Dúnem.
Minister of Health: António José Ferreira Neto.
Minister of the Interior: Manuel Alexandre Duarte Rodrigues (Kito).
Minister of State for Inspection and Control: Kundi Paihama.
Minister of State for the Productive Sphere, Minister of Petroleum and Energy: Lt-Col Pedro de Castro dos Santos Van-Dúnem (Loy).
Minister of State for the Economic and Social Sphere: Maria Mambo Café.
Minister of Education: Augusto Lopes Teixeira (Tutu).
Minister of Finance: Augusto Teixeira de Matos.
Minister of Labour and Social Security: Diogo Jorge de Jesus.
Minister of Domestic Trade: Adriano Pereira dos Santos Junior.
Minister of Foreign Trade: Ismael Gaspar Martins.
Minister of Construction and Housing: João Garcia Branco.
Minister of Industry: Henrique de Carvalho Santos (Onambwe).
Minister of Transport and Communications: Manuel Bernardo de Sousa.
Minister of Fisheries: Emilio Guerra de Carvalho.
Minister of Agriculture: Evaristo Domingos Kimba.
Minister of State Security: (vacant).

MINISTRIES

Office of the President: Luanda; telex 3072.
Ministry of Agriculture and Forestry: Avda Norton de Matos 2, Luanda; telex 3322.
Ministry of Construction: Predio da Mutamba, Luanda; telex 3067.
Ministry of Defence: Rua Silva Carvalho ex Quartel General, Luanda; telex 3259.
Ministry of Domestic Trade: Avda 4 de Fevereiro, Luanda; telex 3010.
Ministry of Education and Culture: Avda Comte. Jika, Luanda.
Ministry of Energy: Luanda.
Ministry of Finance: Avda 4 de Fevereiro, Luanda; tel. 44628; telex 3363.
Ministry of Fisheries: Ilha do Cabo Cais do Carvão, Luanda; telex 3273.
Ministry of Foreign Affairs: Avda Comte. Jika, Luanda; telex 3127.
Ministry of Foreign Trade: Largo Kinaxixi, Luanda; telex 3282.
Ministry of Health: Rua Diogo Cão, Luanda.
Ministry of Industry: Prédio Gomes Irmãos, Luanda; telex 3373.
Ministry of the Interior: Avda 4 de Fevereiro, Luanda.
Ministry of Justice: Largo do Palácio, Luanda.
Ministry of Labour and Social Security: Largo do Palácio, Luanda.
Ministry of Petroleum: Avda 4 de Fevereiro, Luanda.
Ministry of Planning: Largo do Palácio, Luanda; telex 3082.
Ministry of Provincial Co-ordination: Luanda.
Ministry of State Security: Luanda.
Ministry of Transport and Communications: Avda 4 de Fevereiro 42, Luanda; telex 3108.

PROVINCIAL COMMISSIONERS*

Bengo: Manuel Lopes Maria (Xi-Mutu).
Benguela: Maj. João Manuel Gonçalves Lourenço.
Bié: Marcolino José Carlos (Moco).
Cabinda: Jorge Barros Tchimpuati.
Cunene: Pedro Mutinde.
Huambo: Marques Monakapui (Bassovava).
Huíla: Lopo Fortunato Ferreira do Nascimento.
Kuando-Kubango: Manuel Francisco Tuta (Batalha de Angola).
Kwanza Norte: Paulo Teixeira Jorge.
Kwanza-Sul: Francisco Ramos da Cruz.
Luanda: (vacant).
Lunda Norte: Noberto Fernado dos Santos.
Lunda Sul: Rafael Sapilinha (Sambalanga).
Malanje: João Ernesto dos Santos (Liberdade).
Moxico: Jaime Baptista Ndonge.
Namibe: Fernando Faustino Muteka.
Uije: Zeferino Estevão Juliana.
Zaire: Artur Vidal Gomes.

*All Provincial Commissioners are ex-officio members of the Government.

Legislature

NATIONAL PEOPLE'S ASSEMBLY

The People's Assembly, established in November 1980, is the legislative body, and has 223 members, of whom 20 are nominated by the Central Committee of the MPLA—PT. The remaining 203 members are chosen for a three-year term by electoral colleges, composed of representatives elected by all 'loyal' citizens. The 1983 elections were postponed for three years.

Political Organization

Movimento Popular de Libertação de Angola—Partido de Trabalho (MPLA—PT) (People's Movement for the Liberation of Angola—Workers' Party): Luanda; telex 3369; f. 1956; in 1961–74, as MPLA, waged guerrilla war against the Portuguese armed forces; became party of government in 1975; restructured, as MPLA—PT, into a Marxist-Leninist political party in December 1977; 31,000 mems (1980); Chair. José Eduardo dos Santos.

The MPLA—PT held its first extraordinary congress in December 1980, at which it was decided that the role in party affairs of the JMPLA (MPLA Youth), the OMA (Organization of Angolan Women) and UNTA (National Union of Angolan Workers) should be strengthened. In March 1981 the 75-member Central Committee of the MPLA—PT held an extraordinary meeting at which a nine-member Central Committee Secretariat was elected. The Secretariat draws up policies for implementation by the executive, the Council of Ministers.

The second national congress of the MPLA-PT, held in December 1985, elected a new 90-member Central Committee and a new Central Committee Secretariat. In addition, a new 13-member Political Bureau, under the chairmanship of President dos Santos, was elected by the Central Committee. The Political Bureau is the overall policy-making body of the MPLA-PT, and is effectively senior to the Central Committee Secretariat. The two alternate members of the Political Bureau have no vote in the decisions taken by the Bureau.

ANGOLA

Political Bureau

Members:
José Eduardo dos Santos (President).
Afonso Van-Dúnem (Mbinda).
Col António dos Santos França (Ndalu).
Lt-Col Francisco Magalhães Paiva (Nvunda).
Col Julião Mateus Paulo (Dino Matross).
Kundi Payama.
Manuel Alexandre Duarte Rodrigues (Kito).
Pascoal Luvualu.
Lt-Col Pedro de Castro dos Santos Van-Dúnem (Loy).
Col Pedro Maria Tonha (Pedalé).
Maj. Roberto António Francisco Victor de Almeida.

Alternate Members:
António Jacinto do Amaral Martins.
Maria Mambo Café.

Central Committee Secretariat

Secretary for Cadres and Organization: José Eduardo dos Santos.
Secretary for Information and Propaganda: Maj. Roberto António Francisco Victor de Almeida.
Secretary for State and Judicial Bodies: Col Julião Mateus Paulo (Dino Matross).
Secretary for Youth, Mass and Social Organization: Paulo Miguel Júnior.
Secretary for Economic and Social Affairs and Production: Maria Mambo Café.
Secretary for Agrarian Policy: Santana André Pitra (Petroff).
Secretary for Foreign Relations: Afonso Van-Dúnem (Mbinda).
Secretary for Administration and Finance: Jacinto Venancio (Tchipopa).

The following groupings oppose the MPLA—PT government:

Frente de Libertação do Enclave de Cabinda (FLEC) (Front for the Liberation of the Enclave of Cabinda): f. 1963; divided into several factions; has operated a guerrilla campaign for the secession of Cabinda province; Pres. Francisco Xavier Lubota.

União Nacional para a Independência Total de Angola (UNITA) (National Union for the Total Independence of Angola): f. 1966 to fight for independence from Portugal; later received Portuguese support to counter MPLA; UNITA and the Frente Nacional de Libertação de Angola (FNLA, f. 1962 but inactive since 1984) fought the MPLA govt with aid of some Western nations, 1975–76, and of South Africa until 1984; US military aid was reported to have arrived in April 1986; operates as guerrilla force in southern Angola, with an estimated strength of 15,000; Pres. Dr Jonas Savimbi; Sec.-Gen. Miguel N'zau Puna.

Diplomatic Representation

EMBASSIES IN ANGOLA

Algeria: Luanda; Ambassador: Hanafi Oussedik.
Belgium: Luanda; Ambassador: Emile Massa.
Brazil: CP 5428, Luanda; tel. 43275; telex 3365; Ambassador: Paulo Dyrceu Pinheiro.
Bulgaria: Luanda; telex 3375; Ambassador: Boyan Mihaylov.
Cape Verde: Luanda; telex 3247; Ambassador: Corsino Fortes.
China, People's Republic: Luanda; Ambassador: Zhao Zhenkui.
Congo: Luanda; Ambassador: Anatole Khondo.
Cuba: Luanda; telex 3236; Ambassador: Rodolfo Puente Ferro.
Czechoslovakia: Rua Amílcar Cabral 5, Luanda; Ambassador: Miloslav Polansky.
Denmark: Avda 4 de Fevereiro 42, CP 1402, Luanda; tel. 70420; telex 3233; Chargé d'affaires a.i.: Mogens Prehn.
Egypt: Luanda; telex 3380; Ambassador: Ahmed Nabil el-Salawy.
France: Luanda; Ambassador: Jacques Gasseau.
Gabon: Avda 4 de Fevereiro 95, Luanda; tel. 72614; telex 3263; Ambassador: Raphaël Nkassa-Nzogho.
German Democratic Republic: Rua Reverendo Agastinho Pedro Neto 31, CP 3182, Luanda; Ambassador: Johannes Schöche.

Directory

Germany, Federal Republic: CP 1295, Luanda; tel. 34516; telex 3372; Ambassador: Dr Karl Wand.
Ghana: Luanda; telex 3331; Ambassador: (vacant).
Holy See: Rua Luther King 123, CP 1030, Luanda; tel. 30532; Apostolic Delegate: Fortunato Baldelli.
Hungary: Rua Vereador Jaime de Amorim 22–28, Alvalade, CP 2977, Luanda; telex 3084; Ambassador: András Gulyas.
Italy: Luanda; Ambassador: Francesco de Courten.
Ivory Coast: Rua Karl Marx 43, Luanda; Ambassador: Jean-Marie Kacou Gervais.
Korea, Democratic People's Republic: Luanda; Ambassador: Kim Chung Nam.
Netherlands: CP 3624, Luanda; telex 3051; Ambassador: Cornelis de Sroot.
Nigeria: CP 479, Luanda; tel. 40084; telex 3014; Ambassador: Victor N. Chibundu.
Poland: Luanda; telex 3222; Ambassador: Jan Bojko.
Portugal: Rua Karl Marx 50, CP 1346, Luanda; tel. 33027; telex 3370; Ambassador: António d'Oliveira Pinto da França.
Romania: Rua 5 de Outubro 68, Luanda; tel. 36757; telex 3022; Ambassador: Marin Iliescu.
São Tomé and Príncipe: Luanda; Ambassador: Ariosto Castelo David.
Spain: CP 3061, Luanda; tel. 71952; telex 3526; Ambassador: Miguel Angel Fernández de Mazarambroz.
Sweden: Luanda; telex 3126; Ambassador: Sten Rylander.
Switzerland: CP 3163, Luanda; tel. 38314; telex 3172; Chargé d'affaires: Fermo Geroso.
Tanzania: Luanda; Ambassador: Crispin Mbadila.
USSR: CP 3141, Luanda; tel. 45028; Ambassador: Arnold Ivanovich Kalinin.
United Kingdom: Rua Diogo Cão 4, CP 1244, Luanda; tel. 34582; telex 3130; Ambassador: P. S. Fairweather.
Viet-Nam: Luanda; telex 3226; Ambassador: Nguyen Huy Loi.
Yugoslavia: Luanda; telex 3234; Ambassador: Ivo Kustrak.
Zaire: Luanda; Ambassador: Ilangwa-e-Yoka.
Zambia: CP 1496, Luanda; tel. 31145; telex 3439; Ambassador: Boniface Zulu.

Judicial System

There is a Supreme Court and Court of Appeal in Luanda. There are also civil, criminal, military and revolutionary people's courts.

Religion

Much of the population follows traditional beliefs.

CHRISTIANITY

The Roman Catholic Church

Angola comprises three archdioceses and 11 dioceses. At 31 December 1984 there were an estimated 4,450,000 adherents in the country.

Bishops' Conference: Conferência Episcopal de Angola e São Tomé, CP 10, Huambo; tel. 2371; f. 1981; Pres. Manuel Franklin da Costa, Archbishop of Huambo.

Archbishop of Huambo: Manuel Franklin da Costa, Arcebispado, CP 10, Huambo; tel. 2371.

Archbishop of Luanda: (vacant), Arcebispado, CP 87, 1230-C, Luanda; tel. 34640.

Archbishop of Lubango: Cardinal Alexandre do Nascimento, Arcebispado, CP 231, Lubango; tel. 20405.

Other Christian Churches

Angolan Council of Evangelical Churches (CAIE): CP 1659, Luanda; tel. 30402; telex 3172; Gen. Sec. Rev. José Belo Chipenda.

There are about 800,000 Protestants. The Baptist and Methodist Churches operate a number of missionary stations.

The Press

The press was nationalized in 1976.

ANGOLA

DAILIES

O Jornal de Angola: CP 1312, Luanda; tel. 31623; telex 3341; f. 1923; Dir-Gen. Mário Lopes Guerra; mornings and Sunday; circ. 41,000.

Diário da República: CP 1306, Luanda; official govt news sheet.

Newspapers are also published in several regional towns.

PERIODICALS

A Célula: Luanda; political journal of MPLA—PT.

Lavra & Oficina: CP 2767-C, Luanda; tel. 22155; f. 1975; journal of the Union of Angolan Writers; monthly; circ. 5,000.

Novembro: CP 3947, Luanda; tel. 31660; monthly; Dir Roberto de Almeida.

A Voz do Trabalhador: CP 28, Luanda; journal of União Nacional de Trabalhadores Angolanos (National Union of Angolan Workers); monthly.

NEWS AGENCIES

ANGOP: Rua Rei Katyavala 1–120, Luanda; tel. 34595; telex 4162; Dir-Gen. and Editor-in-Chief Raimundo Sotto-Maior.

Foreign Bureaux

Agence France-Presse (AFP): Prédio Mutamba, CP 2357, Luanda; tel. 34939; telex 3334; Bureau Chief Manuela Teixeira.

Agentstvo Pechati Novosti (APN) (USSR): Luanda; Chief Officer Vladislav Z. Komarov.

Allgemeiner Deutscher Nachrichtendienst (ADN) (German Democratic Republic): CP 3193, Luanda; telex 3323; Bureau Chief Wolfgang Schmidt.

Inter Press Service (IPS) (Italy): Rua Alberto Lemos 34, CP 3593, Luanda; tel. 38724; telex 3304; Correspondent Juan Pezzuto.

Prensa Latina (Cuba): Rua D. Miguel de Melo 92-2, Luanda; tel. 36804; telex 3253; Chief Correspondent Eloy Concepción.

Telegrafnoye Agentstvo Sovetskovo Soyuza (TASS) (USSR): Rua Marecha Tito 75, Luanda; telex 3244; Correspondent Nikolai Semyonov.

Xinhua (New China) News Agency (People's Republic of China): Rua Karl Marx 57-3 Andar E, Bairro das Ingombotas, Zona 4, Luanda CP; tel. 32415; telex 4054; Correspondent Zhao Xiaozhong.

Publishers

Empresa Distribuidora Livreira (EDIL), UEE: Rua da Missão 107, CP 1245, Luanda; tel. 34034.

Neográfica, SARL: CP 6518, Luanda; publ. *Novembro.*

Nova Editorial Angolana, SARL: CP 1225, Luanda; f. 1935; general and educational; Man. Dir Pombo Fernandes.

Offsetográfica Gráfica Industrial Lda: CP 911, Benguela; tel. 2568.

Government Publishing House

Imprensa Nacional, UEE: CP 1306, Luanda; f. 1845; Gen. Man. Dr António Duarte de Almeida e Carmo.

Radio and Television

In 1982 it was announced that radio and television were to be reorganized into one body. In 1983 there were an estimated 162,000 radio receivers and 33,000 television receivers in use.

RADIO

Rádio Nacional de Angola: Rua Comandante Jika, CP 1329, Luanda; tel. 80499; telex 03066; broadcasts in Portuguese, English, French, Spanish and vernacular languages (Chokwe, Kigongo, Kimbunda, Kwanyama, Lingala, Luvale, Songu, Umbondu); Dir-Gen. Guilherme Mogas.

TELEVISION

Televisão Popular de Angola (TPA): Rua Ho Chi Min, CP 2604, Luanda; tel. 35697; telex 3238; f. 1975; parastatal company; Dir Carlos Garcia.

Directory

Finance

(cap. = capital; dep. = deposits; res = reserves; m. = million; brs = branches; amounts in kwanza)

BANKING

All banks were nationalized in 1975.

Central Bank

Banco Nacional de Angola: Avda 4 de Fevereiro 151, CP 1298, Luanda; tel. 39141; telex 3005; central bank and bank of issue; f. 1976 to supersede Banco de Angola; cap. 1,000m.; dep. 111,975m.; res 6,657m. (1983); 55 brs and agencies; Gov. (vacant); Vice-Gov. António da Silva Inácio (acting Gov.).

Commercial Banks

Banco de Crédito Comercial e Industrial: CP 1395, Luanda.

Banco Popular de Angola: Avda 4 de Fevereiro; tel. 36598; commercial bank with brs throughout the country; dep. 17,102m. (1983); Dir-Gen. João Abel das Neves.

In 1985 Banque Paribas (France) became the first foreign bank to open a representative office in Angola.

INSURANCE

Empresa Nacional de Seguros e Resseguros de Angola (ENSA), UEE: Avda 4 de Fevereiro 93, CP 5778, Luanda; tel. 70169; telex 3087.

Trade and Industry

SUPERVISORY BODIES

National Planning Committee: Ministry of Planning, CP 1205, Luanda; tel. 39052; telex 3082; f. 1977; responsible for drafting and supervising the implementation of the National Plan and for co-ordinating economic policies and decisions; Chair. Minister of Planning.

National Supplies Commission: Luanda; f. 1977 to combat sabotage and negligence.

STATE TRADING ORGANIZATIONS

Angomedica, UEE: Rua Rainha Ginga 178–2° Dto, CP 2698, Luanda; tel. 34281; telex 4195; f. 1981 to import pharmaceutical goods.

Direcção dos Serviços de Comércio (Dept of Trade): Largo Diogo Cão, CP 1337, Luanda; f. 1970; brs throughout Angola.

Epmel, UEE: Rua Karl Marx 35–37, Luanda; tel. 30943; industrial agricultural machinery.

Exportang, UEE: Rua dos Enganos 1a, CP 1000, Luanda; tel. 32363; telex 3318; co-ordinates exports.

Importang, UEE: Calçada do Municipio 10, CP 1003, Luanda; tel. 37994; telex 3169; f. 1977; co-ordinates majority of imports; Dir-Gen. Lourenço M. Neto.

Maquimport, UEE: Rua Rainha Ginga 152, CP 2975, Luanda; tel. 39044; telex 4175; f. 1981 to import office equipment.

Mecanang, UEE: Rua dos Enganos, 1°–7° Andar, CP 1347, Luanda; tel. 90644; telex 4021; f. 1981 to import agricultural and construction machinery.

STATE INDUSTRIAL ENTERPRISES

Companhia do Açúcar de Angola: 77 Rua Direita, Luanda; production of sugar.

Companhia Geral dos Algodões de Angola (COTONANG): Avda da Boavista, Luanda; production of cotton textiles.

Empresa Abastecimento Técnico Material (EMATEC), UEE: Largo Rainha Ginga 3, CP 2952, Luanda; tel. 38891; telex 3349; technical and material suppliers to the Ministry of Defence.

Empresa Açucareira Centro (OSUKA), UEE: Rua Estrada Principal Lobito, CP 037, Lobito; tel. 91459; telex 08268; sugar industry.

Empresa Açucareira Norte (ACUNOR), UEE: Rua Robert Shilds, CP 225, Caxito, Bengo; tel. 71720; sugar production.

Empresa Angolana de Embalagens (METANGOL), UEE: Rua Estrada do Cacuaco, CP 151, Luanda; tel. 70680; production of non-specified metal goods.

ANGOLA

Empresa de Cimento de Angola (CIMANGOLA): Avda 4 de Fevereiro 42, Luanda; 53% state-owned; cement production; exports to several African countries.

Empresa de Construção de Edificações (CONSTROI), UEE: Rua Alexandre Peres, CP 2566, Luanda; tel. 33930; telex 3165; construction.

Empresa de Pesca de Angola (PESCANGOLA), UEE: Luanda; f. 1981; state fishing enterprise, responsible to Ministry of Fisheries.

Empresa de Rebenefício e Exportação do Café de Angola (CAFANGOL), UEE: Avda 4 de Fevereiro 107, CP 342, Luanda; tel. 73452-37916; telex 3274-3011; f. 1983; national coffee processing and trade organization.

Empresa de Tecidos de Angola (TEXTANG), UEE: Avda N'gola Kiluanji-Kazenga, CP 5404, Luanda; tel. 80723; telex 3146; production of textiles.

Empresa Nacional de Cimento (ENCIME), UEE: CP 157, Lobito; tel. 2325; cement production.

Empresa Nacional de Comercialização e Distribuição de Produtos Agrícolas (ENCODIPA): Luanda; central marketing agency for agricultural produce; numerous brs throughout Angola.

Empresa Nacional de Construções Electricas (ENCEL), UEE: Rua Comandante Che Guevara 0191 RC 187, Luanda; tel. 31411; electric energy.

Empresa Nacional de Diamantes de Angola (ENDIAMA), UEE: Luanda; assumed control of diamond mining, following the dissolution of the Companhia de Diamantes de Angola (DIAMANG) in July 1986.

Empresa Nacional de Electricidade (ENE), UEE: Edifício Geominas 6°–7°, CP 772, Luanda; tel. 21499; telex 3170; distribution of electricity.

Empresa Nacional de Ferro de Angola (FERRANGOL): Rua João de Barros 26, CP 2692, Luanda; tel. 73800; state-owned; iron production; Dir Armando de Sousa (Machadinho).

Empresa Nacional de Manutenção (MANUTECNICA), UEE: Rua 7ª Avda do Cazenga 10-L, CP 3508, Luanda; tel. 83646; assembly of machines and specialized equipment for industry.

Empresa Publica de Telecomunicações (EPTEL), UEE: Rua I Congresso 0026 02 022, CP 625, Luanda; tel. 131040; telex 3012; telecommunications.

Empresa Texteis de Angola (ENTEX), UEE: Avda Comandante Kima Kienda, CP 5720, Luanda; tel. 36182; telex 3086; weaving and tissue finishing.

Fina Petróleos de Angola (PETRANGOL): CP 1320, Luanda; petroleum production and exploration; operates Luanda oil refinery with capacity of 35,000 b/d; also operates Quinfuquena terminal; Man. Dir J. G. Rebelo.

Siderurgia Nacional, UEE: Rua Luís Mota Fêo 18-1°, Luanda; tel. 73028; f. 1963, nationalized 1980; steelworks and rolling mill plant.

Sociedade Nacional de Combustíveis de Angola (SONANGOL): Rua I Congresso do MPLA, CP 1318, Luanda; tel. 31690; telex 3148; f. 1976 for exploration, production and refining of crude oil, and marketing and distribution of petroleum products; sole concessionair in Angola, supervises foreign oil companies working onshore and offshore; majority shareholding in jt ventures with Cabinda Gulf Oil Co, PETRANGOL and Texaco Petróleos de Angola; Dir-Gen. Hermínio Escórcio.

   Cabinda Gulf Oil Company: CP 2950, Luanda; tel. 92646; telex 3167; mining of petroleum in Cabinda province; subsidiary of Chevron Corpn; 51% owned by SONANGOL (see above); Gen. Man. Wil Lewis.

Sociedade Unificada de Tabacos de Angola (SUT): Rua Deolinda Rodrigues 537, CP 1263, Luanda; tel. 60170; telex 3237; f. 1919; tobacco products; Gen. Man. A. Campos.

TRADE UNION

União Nacional de Trabalhadores Angolanos (UNTA) (National Union of Angolan Workers): Avda 4 de Fevereiro 210, CP 28, Luanda; telex 3387; f. 1960; Sec.-Gen. Pascoal Luvualu; Asst Sec.-Gen. Galvão Branco; 600,000 mems.

Transport

RAILWAYS

The total length of track operated was 2,952 km in 1985. There are plans to extend the Namibe line beyond Menongue and to construct north–south rail links.

Caminhos de Ferro de Angola: CP 1250-C, Luanda; tel. 70061; telex 3108; national network operating four fmrly independent systems; Nat. Dir A. de S. E. Silva; Dep. Dir (Tech.) Eng. R. M. da C. Junior.

   Amboim Railway: Porto Amboim; f. 1945; 123 km of track; Dir A. V. Ferreira.

   Benguela Railway (Companhia do Caminho de Ferro de Benguela): Rua Praça 11 Novembro 3, CP 32, Lobito; tel. 2645; telex 8253; f. 1903; operates railway from the port of Lobito across Angola, via Huambo and Luena, to the Zaire border, where it connects with the Société Nationale des Chemins de Fer Zaïrois system, which in turn links with Zambia Railways, thus providing the shortest west coast route for central African trade; 1,394 km of track; privately owned, with 51% govt holding; local traffic operating despite sabotage, but international operations remain severely restricted; Propr Tanks Consolidated Investments PLC; Vice-Pres. F. G. de Magalhães Falcão; Dir-Gen. F. de Melo de Sampaio.

   Luanda Railway (Empresa de Caminho de Ferro de Luanda, UEE): CP 1250-C, Luanda; tel. 70061; telex 3108; f. 1886; serves an iron, cotton and sisal-producing region between Luanda and Malanje; 536 km of track; Dir J. M. Ferreira do Nascimento.

   Namibe Railway: Moçâmedes; f. 1905; main line from Namibe (formerly Moçâmedes) to Menongue, via Lubango, with branches to Chibia and iron ore mines at Cassinga; 899 km of track; Dir L. da M. G. Cipriano.

ROADS

In 1984 Angola had 72,300 km of roads, of which 18,600 km were main roads and 28,700 km were secondary roads. A total of 180 bridges and pontoons that were destroyed in the civil war had been rebuilt by the end of 1979.

SHIPPING

The main harbours are at Lobito, Luanda and Namibe; the commercial port of Porto Amboim, in Kwanza-Sul province, has been closed for repairs since July 1984. The expansion of port facilities in Cabinda was planned. In May 1983 a regular shipping service began to operate between Luanda and Maputo (Mozambique).

Angonave—Linhas Marítimas de Angola: Rua Cerqueira Lukoki 21, CP 5953, Luanda; tel. 30144; telex 3313; national shipping line; receives Cuban assistance in training crews; operates 8 vessels; Dir-Gen. Francisco Venâncio.

Cabotang-Cabotagem Nacional Angolana: Rua 4 de Fevereiro 83, Luanda; tel. 73133; telex 3007; operates 12 vessels off the Angolan coast and off the coast of Mozambique; Dir-Gen. João Octavio Van-Dunen.

Empresa Portuaria do Lobito: Rua Avda da Independencia, CP 16, Lobito; tel. 2711; telex 8233; long-range sea transport.

Empresa Portuaria de Moçâmedes—Namibe, UEE: Rua Pedro Benje 10-A and 10-C, CP 49, Namibe; tel. 60643; long-range sea transport; Dir Humberto de Ataide Dias.

CIVIL AVIATION

TAAG—Linhas Aéreas de Angola: Rua Luís de Camões 123-6°, CP 79, Luanda; tel. 3285; telex 3442; f. 1939; internal services, and services from Luanda to the Congo, Guinea-Bissau, Mozambique, Nigeria, São Tomé, Zaire, Zambia, Cuba, France, Italy, Portugal, the German Democratic Republic, and the USSR; Dir-Gen. José Fernandes; fleet of 1 Boeing 707-320B, 5 Boeing 707-320C, 3 Boeing 737-200, 1 Boeing 737-200C, 2 Lockheed L100-20, 3 Antonov An-26, 1 Fokker F27-400M, 1 Fokker F27-500, 3 Fokker F27-600, 3 Yakovlev Yak-40.

ANTARCTICA

Source: British Antarctic Survey, High Cross, Madingley Rd, Cambridge, CB3 0ET, England; tel. (0223) 61188; telex 817725.

The Continent of Antarctica is estimated to cover 13,900,000 sq km. There are no indigenous inhabitants, but since 1944 a number of permanent research stations have been established.

Major Stations

(The following list includes major stations south of latitude 60° occupied during 1986.)

	Latitude	Longitude
ARGENTINA		
Belgrano II	77° 51' S	34° 33' W
Esperanza	63° 24' S	56° 59' W
Jubany	62° 14' S	58° 38' W
Marambio	64° 14' S	56° 38' W
Orcadas	60° 45' S	44° 43' W
San Martín	68° 06' S	67° 08' W
AUSTRALIA		
Casey	66° 17' S	110° 32' E
Davis	68° 35' E	77° 58' E
Mawson	67° 37' S	62° 52' E
BRAZIL		
Comandante Ferraz	62° 05' S	58° 23' W
CHILE		
Arturo Prat	62° 30' S	59° 41' W
Bernardo O'Higgins	63° 19' S	57° 54' W
Rodolfo Marsh	62° 12' S	58° 54' W
PEOPLE'S REPUBLIC OF CHINA		
Great Wall	60° 13' S	58° 58' W
FRANCE		
Dumont d'Urville	66° 40' S	140° 01' E
FEDERAL REPUBLIC OF GERMANY		
Georg von Neumayer	70° 37' S	8° 22' W
INDIA		
Dakshin Gangotri	70° 05' S	12° 00' E
JAPAN		
Mizuho	70° 42' S	44° 20' E
Syowa	69° 00' S	39° 35' E
NEW ZEALAND		
Scott	77° 51' S	166° 46' E
POLAND		
Arctowski	62° 09' S	58° 28' W
SOUTH AFRICA		
Sanae	70° 19' S	2° 24' W
USSR		
Bellingshausen	62° 12' S	58° 54' W
Leningradskaya	69° 30' S	159° 23' E
Mirny	66° 33' S	93° 01' E
Molodezhnaya	67° 40' S	45° 51' E
Novolazarevskaya	70° 46' S	11° 50' E
Russkaya	74° 46' S	136° 52' W
Vostok	78° 27' S	106° 51' E
UNITED KINGDOM		
Faraday	65° 15' S	64° 16' W
Halley	75° 36' S	26° 41' W
Rothera	67° 34' S	68° 08' W
Signy	60° 43' S	45° 36' W
USA		
South Pole	South Pole	
McMurdo	77° 51' S	166° 40' W
Palmer	64° 46' S	64° 03' W
Siple	75° 56' S	84° 15' W
URUGUAY		
Artigas	62° 11' S	58° 53' W

Territorial Claims

Territory	Claimant State
Antártida Argentina	Argentina
Antártida Chilena	Chile
Australian Antarctic Territory	Australia
British Antarctic Territory	United Kingdom
Dronning Maud Land	Norway
Ross Dependency	New Zealand
Terre Adélie	France

These claims are not recognized by the USA or the USSR. No formal claims have been made in the sector of Antarctica between 90° W and 150° W.

See also Article 4 of the Antarctic Treaty below.

Research

Scientific Committee on Antarctic Research (SCAR) of the **International Council of Scientific Union (ICSU):** Secretariat: Scott Polar Research Institute, Lensfield Rd, Cambridge, CB2 1ER, England; tel. (0223) 66499; f. 1958 to further the co-ordination of scientific activity in Antarctica, with a view to framing a scientific programme of circumpolar scope and significance; mems 17 countries.

President: Dr C. Lorius (France).
Vice-Presidents: Prof. Dr G. Hempel (Federal Republic of Germany), Prof. E. S. Korotkevich (USSR).
Secretary: Dr A. C. Rocha Campos (Brazil).

The Antarctic Treaty

The Treaty (summarized below) was signed in Washington, DC, on 1 December 1959 by the 12 nations co-operating in the Antarctic during the International Geophysical Year, and entered into force on 23 June 1961.

Article 1. Antarctica shall be used for peaceful purposes only.

Article 2. On freedom of scientific investigation and co-operation.

Article 3. On exchange of information and personnel.

Article 4. i. Nothing contained in the present Treaty shall be interpreted as:

(a) a renunciation by any Contracting Party of previously asserted rights of or claims to territorial sovereignty in Antarctica;

(b) a renunciation or diminution by any Contracting Party of any basis of claim to territorial sovereignty in Antarctica which it may have whether as a result of its activities or those of its nationals in Antarctica, or otherwise;

(c) prejudicing the position of any Contracting Party as regards its recognition or non-recognition of any other State's right of or claim or basis of claim to territorial sovereignty in Antarctica.

ii. No acts or activities taking place while the present Treaty is in force shall constitute a basis for asserting, supporting or denying a claim to territorial sovereignty in Antarctica or create any rights of sovereignty in Antarctica. No new claim, or enlargement of an existing claim, to territorial sovereignty in Antarctica shall be asserted while the present Treaty is in force.

Article 5. Any nuclear explosions in Antarctica and the disposal there of radioactive waste material shall be prohibited.

Article 6. On geographical limits and rights on high seas.

Article 7. On designation of observers and notification of stations and expeditions.

Article 8. On jurisdiction over observers and scientists.

Article 9. On consultative meetings.

Articles 10–14. On upholding, interpreting, amending, notifying and depositing the Treaty.

SIGNATORIES

Argentina	France	South Africa
Australia	Japan	USSR
Belgium	New Zealand	United Kingdom
Chile	Norway	USA

ACCEDING STATES

Brazil, Bulgaria, the People's Republic of China, Cuba, Czechoslovakia, Denmark, Finland, the German Democratic Republic, the Federal Republic of Germany, Hungary, India, Italy, the Netherlands, Papua New Guinea, Peru, Poland, Romania, Spain, Sweden, Uruguay.

Brazil, the People's Republic of China, the Federal Republic of Germany, India, Poland and Uruguay have been granted consultative status under the Treaty, by virtue of their scientific activity in Antarctica.

ANTARCTIC TREATY CONSULTATIVE MEETINGS

Meetings of representatives from all the original signatory nations of the Antarctic Treaty and acceding nations accorded consultative status are held from time to time to discuss scientific and political matters. The 12th meeting was held in Canberra in September 1983, and the 13th was held in Brussels in October 1985. The representatives elect a Chairman and Secretary. Committees and Working Groups are established as required.

Among the numerous measures which have been agreed and implemented by the Consultative Parties are several designed to protect the Antarctic environment and wildlife. These include Agreed Measures for the Conservation of Antarctic Flora and Fauna, the designation of Specially Protected Areas and Sites of Special Scientific Interest, and a Convention for the Conservation of Antarctic Seals. A Convention on the Conservation of Antarctic Marine Living Resources, concluded at a diplomatic conference in May 1980, entered into force in April 1982. A number of meetings have been held to discuss the terms of a similar agreement to regulate any future mineral exploration and exploitation in Antarctica.

ANTIGUA AND BARBUDA

Introductory Survey

Location, Climate, Language, Religion, Flag, Capital

The country comprises three islands: Antigua (280 sq km), Barbuda (160 sq km) and the uninhabited rocky islet of Redonda (1.6 sq km). They lie along the outer edge of the Leeward Islands chain in the West Indies. Barbuda is the most northerly (40 km north of Antigua), and Redonda is 40 km south-west of Antigua. The climate is tropical, although tempered by constant sea breezes and the trade winds, and the mean annual rainfall of 1,000mm (40 inches) is slight for the region. The temperature averages 27°C (81°F) but can rise to 33°C (93°F) during the hot season between May and October. English is the official language but an English patois is commonly used. The majority of the inhabitants profess Christianity, and are mainly adherents of the Anglican Communion. The national flag consists of an inverted triangle centred on a red ground and divided horizontally into three bands, of black, blue and white, with the black stripe bearing a symbol of the rising sun in gold. The capital is St John's, on Antigua.

Recent History

Antigua was colonized by the British in the 17th century. The island of Barbuda, formerly a slave stud farm for the Codrington family, was annexed to the territory in 1860. Until December 1959 Antigua and other nearby British territories were administered, under a federal system, as the Leeward Islands. The first elections under universal adult suffrage were held in 1951. The colony participated in the West Indies Federation, which was formed in January 1958 but dissolved in May 1962.

Attempts to form a smaller East Caribbean Federation failed, and most of the eligible colonies subsequently became Associated States in an arrangement which gave them full internal self-government while the United Kingdom retained responsibility for defence and foreign affairs. Antigua attained associated status in February 1967. The Legislative Council was replaced by a House of Representatives, the Administrator became Governor and the Chief Minister was restyled Premier.

In the first general election under associated status, held in February 1971, the Progressive Labour Movement (PLM) ousted the Antigua Labour Party (ALP), which had held power since 1946, by winning 13 of the 17 seats in the House of Representatives. George Walter, leader of the PLM, replaced Vere C. Bird, Sr as Premier. However, a general election in February 1976 was won by the ALP, with 11 seats, while the seat representing Barbuda was won by an independent. Vere Bird, the ALP's leader, again became Premier, while Lester Bird, one of his sons, became Deputy Premier.

In 1975 the Associated States agreed that they would seek independence separately. In the 1976 elections the PLM campaigned for early independence while the ALP stood against it. In September 1978, however, the ALP Government declared that the economic foundation for independence had been laid. To enable the Government to obtain a mandate for proceeding to independence, a premature general election was held in April 1980, when the ALP won 13 of the 17 seats, but strong opposition from the inhabitants of Barbuda to independence as part of Antigua delayed the convening of a constitutional conference until December 1980. At local elections in March 1981 the Barbuda People's Movement (BPM), which continued to campaign for secession from Antigua, won all the seats on the Barbuda Council. The territory finally became independent, as Antigua and Barbuda, on 1 November 1981, remaining within the Commonwealth, with the grievances of the Barbudans concerning control of land and devolution of power still unresolved, although the ALP Government had made concessions, yielding a certain degree of internal autonomy to the Barbuda Council. The Governor became Governor-General, while the Premier, Vere Bird, became the country's first Prime Minister.

In February 1979 the former Premier, George Walter, was convicted of mishandling state finances during his period of office, but in April 1980 his appeal against this conviction was upheld by the West Indies Associated States Appeal Court. After subsequent disagreements within the PLM, Walter formed his own political party, the United People's Movement (UPM), in 1982. The first general election since independence was held in April 1984. The failure of the opposition parties to agree on the formation of a united front allowed the ALP to win convincingly in all of the 16 seats that it contested. The remaining seat, representing Barbuda, was retained by an independent, who was returned unopposed. In March 1985 the Organization for National Reconstruction (ONR), a Barbuda-based party advocating co-operation with the ALP Government in Antigua, won a majority on the Barbuda Council in local elections. A new opposition party, the National Democratic Party (NDP), was formed in Antigua in 1985. In April 1986 it merged with the UPM to form the United National Democratic Party (UNDP). George Walter declined to play any significant public role in the UNDP, and Dr Ivor Heath, who had led the NDP, was elected leader of the new party.

In foreign relations, the ALP Government follows a policy of non-alignment, although the country has strong links with the USA, and actively assisted in the US military intervention in Grenada in October 1983 as a member of the Organization of Eastern Caribbean States (OECS, see p. 109). Since 1982, Antigua has intensified its programme of foreign relations, strengthening its diplomatic representation in Canada and consolidating relations with the People's Republic of China, the Republic of Korea, Brazil and Venezuela, in return for economic assistance. It also plans to accredit ambassadors to several Latin American countries.

Government

Antigua and Barbuda is a constitutional monarchy. Executive power is vested in the British sovereign, as Head of State, and exercised by the Governor-General, who represents the sovereign locally and is appointed on the advice of the Antiguan Prime Minister. Legislative power is vested in Parliament, comprising the sovereign, a 17-member Senate and a 17-member House of Representatives. Members of the House are elected from single-member constituencies for up to five years by universal adult suffrage. The Senate is composed of 11 members (of whom one must be an inhabitant of Barbuda) appointed on the advice of the Prime Minister, four appointed on the advice of the Leader of the Opposition, one appointed at the discretion of the Governor-General and one appointed on the advice of the Barbuda Council. Government is effectively by the Cabinet. The Governor-General appoints the Prime Minister and, on the latter's recommendation, selects the other Ministers. The Prime Minister must be able to command the support of a majority of the House, to which the Cabinet is responsible.

Defence

There is a small defence force of about 700 men. In 1984 the USA provided a patrol boat for the newly-formed coastguard service.

Economic Affairs

Since the mid-1960s, economic growth has not kept pace with the increase in the islands' population. In 1984, according to estimates by the World Bank, Antigua and Barbuda's gross national product (GNP) per head, measured at average 1982–84 prices, was US $1,860. Between 1965 and 1984, however, it is estimated that GNP per head declined, in real terms, at an average rate of 0.1% per year.

Tourism is the main economic activity. Antigua was one of the first Caribbean states actively to encourage tourism in the early 1960s, and by 1981 the industry accounted for approximately 25% of employment and made a direct contribution to the gross domestic product (GDP) of 12% and an estimated 40% contribution indirectly through services. After a period of stagnation during 1981 and 1982, owing to the world recession, the tourist industry began to expand again in 1983. Tourist arrivals increased by 28% in 1984, with the largest increase being derived from the USA. During 1985 stop-over arrivals increased by a more moderate 8.2%, but there was a 51.8% increase in the number of cruise ship visitors. It was estimated that in 1985 tourism accounted for nearly 60% of GDP. The Government plans a major expansion of tourist facilities, aiming to double the number of hotel rooms available from 3,000 in 1986 to 6,000 by 1991.

Fears of over-reliance on winter tourism have led the Government towards a policy of diversification, encouraging manufacturing, agriculture and fishing. Agriculture, including livestock, forestry and fishing, contributed about 12% of GDP in 1985. Local agriculture has been encouraged in order to lessen the country's dependence on imported food, much of it consumed by the tourism industry. In 1985 the FAO approved assistance of EC $270,000 for the country's agricultural sector. A wide variety of vegetables and the speciality 'Antigua Black' pineapple are cultivated, and in 1985 the Government embarked on a four-year livestock development programme, aimed at making the country self-sufficient in meat. As a result of increased investment and improved conditions for farmers, some increases in output were achieved in 1983, but the effects of prolonged drought contributed to a decline of 8.7% in agricultural and livestock production during 1984. Emergency aid was obtained from the EEC, enabling Antigua to purchase water from neighbouring Guadeloupe and Dominica. Agricultural output increased sufficiently during 1985 to reduce imports of fresh vegetables by two-thirds.

The sugar industry, which had collapsed in 1972, was revived in 1981 with the refurbishment of the sugar factory at Gunthropes, to supply the local market and to provide molasses for rum production. Continuing financial deficits, however, led to the factory's closure in 1985. It has been estimated that up to 4,000 tons of fish per year could be yielded from the deep-sea fishing grounds, but in 1984 only about one-half of this figure was caught, despite the use of new ships, which increased catches. The Government is also hoping to increase the area currently under sea island cotton, which was formerly Antigua's principal export crop. One of the main problems confronting all economic sectors is the lack of available water, aggravated during 1983 and 1984 by low rainfall. A new desalinization plant, intended to increase Antigua's water supply by 2m. gallons per day, is under construction at Crabb's Point, and was due to be completed in 1987.

There are a number of light industries manufacturing rum, garments and household appliances, and assembling electronic components for export. The output of manufacturing industry has been adversely affected by the contraction of regional markets and by the lack of an established private industrial sector within Antigua and Barbuda. The West Indies Oil Refinery near St John's, which is partly government-owned, was reopened in 1982, after an eight-year closure, but it incurred a financial loss of EC $16m. in the first half of 1983 and was closed at the end of the year. To provide an additional source of revenue, the establishment of offshore banks in Antigua and Barbuda has been encouraged. Legislation which was approved in December 1982 allowed the foundation of offshore institutions which would bring in up to EC $4m.

Two major sources of government revenue are the annual rental of EC $4.1m. for the two military bases on Antigua, paid by the US government, and the 40% company tax which brought in EC $12.5m. in 1984. Income tax was abolished in 1977. The combination of increased government expenditure and declining economic growth produced rising budget deficits (EC $24m. in 1982). However, the strong recovery in the tourist industry, and the introduction of fiscal adjustment measures by the Government, reduced the budget deficit to EC $16.7m. in 1984. With the aim of reducing expenditure, the Government announced that no further workers would be engaged in the public sector during 1986. For the first time in 15 years, the projected recurrent budget deficit was below EC $1m. for 1986. Antigua and Barbuda also has one of the highest debt-servicing commitments in the Eastern Caribbean, and it was estimated that in 1985 16% of recurrent revenue would be devoted to repayments on the country's external debt, which stood at EC $162m. in 1983. The trade deficit, which stood at EC $178.2m. in 1983, increased to EC $263.5m. in 1984, as a consequence of declining exports and a large increase in imported goods. Antigua receives aid for development projects, capital investment and skills training from a number of governmental and international organizations. In 1984 the country began to benefit from an agricultural and educational assistance programme by the People's Republic of China.

Between 1977 and 1979 growth in GDP averaged 7.5% annually, falling to 4% in 1981 and only 2.5% in 1982. GDP was estimated to have grown by 6.4% in 1983 and by 6.5% in 1984. The average annual rate of inflation declined from 19% in 1980 to 11.5% in 1981, 4.2% in 1982 and to only 2.3% in 1983. The rate was 3.9% in 1984. An estimated 20% of the labour force were unemployed in 1983 and 1984.

Social Welfare

There are two state welfare schemes providing free health care, and a range of pensions, benefits, and grants. Antigua has a 215-bed general hospital and several health centres. In 1984 there were 33 physicians working in the islands.

Education

Education is compulsory for 11 years between five and 16 years of age. Primary education begins at the age of five and normally lasts for six years. Secondary education, beginning at 11 years of age, lasts for five years, comprising a first cycle of three years and a second cycle of two years. In 1983 there were 85 schools providing pre-primary, primary and secondary education; the majority of schools are administered by the government. Teacher training and technical training are available at the State Island College. An extra-mural department of the University of the West Indies offers several foundation courses leading to higher study at branches elsewhere.

Tourism

With a pleasant climate, reputedly 365 beaches and excellent facilities for sailing and water sports, Antigua and Barbuda draw an increasing number of tourists from the USA, the United Kingdom and Canada, and from other Caribbean countries. The annual international sailing regatta and Carnival week are major attractions. A development scheme is planned for the major tourist attraction, 'Nelson's Dockyard' in English Harbour, designated a national park in 1985. A scheme is also planned for the redevelopment of the capital, St John's, as a commercial duty-free centre. There were 139,726 tourists (excluding cruise ship visitors) in 1985, compared with 56,398 in 1976.

Public Holidays

1987: 1 January (New Year's Day), 17 April (Good Friday), 20 April (Easter Monday), 4 May (Labour Day), 8 June (Whit Monday and Queen's Official Birthday), 3 August (for Emancipation Day), 2 November (for Independence Day), 25–26 December (Christmas).

1988: 1 January (New Year's Day), 1 April (Good Friday), 4 April (Easter Monday), 2 May (Labour Day), 23 May (Whit Monday), 6 June (Queen's Official Birthday), 1 August (Emancipation Day), 7 November (for Independence Day), 25–26 December (Christmas).

Weights and Measures

The imperial system is in use but a metrication programme is being introduced.

Currency and Exchange Rates

100 cents = 1 East Caribbean dollar (EC $).

Exchange rates (30 September 1986):
 £1 sterling = EC $3.907;
 US $1 = EC $2.700.

Statistical Survey

Source (unless otherwise stated): Ministry of Finance, Redcliffe St, St John's.

AREA AND POPULATION

Area: 441.6 sq km (170.5 sq miles).

Population: 65,525 (males 31,054, females 34,471) at census of 7 April 1970; 79,269 (estimate, mid-1984).

Density (1984): 179.5 per sq km.

Principal Town: St John's (capital), population 36,000.

Births, Marriages and Deaths (1984): Live births 1,126 (birth rate 14.2 per 1,000); Marriages 203 (marriage rate 2.6 per 1,000); Deaths 386 (death rate 4.2 per 1,000).

Economically Active Population (estimates, mid-1984): Employed 24,910 (males 14,218; females 10,692); Unemployed 6,617 (males 4,795, females 1,822); Total labour force 31,527.

AGRICULTURE, ETC.

Principal Crops (metric tons, 1984): Sweet Potatoes 112.7, Pineapples 182.4, Carrots 147.4, Limes 142.9; Mangoes ('000) 375.

Livestock (FAO estimates, '000 head, year ending September 1984): Cattle 16, Pigs 7, Sheep 12, Goats 12. Source: FAO, *Production Yearbook*.

Fishing (metric tons, 1983): Fish 2,227, Lobsters 19. Source: FAO, *Yearbook of Fishery Statistics*.

INDUSTRY

Production (estimates, 1984): Rum and alcohol 6,780 hectolitres; Wines and vodka 374 hectolitres; Electric energy 68.9m. kWh.

FINANCE

Currency and Exchange Rates: 100 cents = 1 East Caribbean dollar (EC $). *Coins*: 1, 2, 5, 10, 25 and 50 cents, 1 dollar. *Notes*: 1, 5, 20 and 100 dollars. *Sterling and US Dollar equivalents* (30 September 1986): £1 sterling = EC $3.907; US $1 = EC $2.700; EC $100 = £25.60 = US $37.04. Exchange rate: Fixed at US $1 = EC $2.700 since July 1976.

Budget (estimates, EC $'000, 1984): Expenditure 138,000; Revenue 129,000.

International Reserves (US $ million at 31 December 1985): Foreign exchange 16.58; Total 16.58. Source: IMF, *International Financial Statistics*.

Money Supply (EC $ million at 31 December 1984): Currency outside banks 23.97; Demand deposits at deposit money banks 34.44; Total money 58.40. Source: IMF, *International Financial Statistics*.

Cost of Living (Consumer Price Index; base: 1 January 1969 = 100): 434.7 in 1982; 444.9 in 1983; 462.9 in 1984.

Gross Domestic Product (EC $ million at current prices): 357.3 in 1982; 398.9 in 1983; 419.3 in 1984.

Balance of Payments (US $ million, 1984): Merchandise exports f.o.b. 41.0; Merchandise imports f.o.b. −133.53; *Trade balance* −92.53; Exports of services 107.4; Imports of services −32.57; *Balance on goods and services* −17.7; Private unrequited transfers (net) 12.5; Government unrequited transfers (net) 2.0; *Current balance* −3.2; Direct capital investment (net) 10.1; Other long-term capital (net) −4.03; Other short-term capital (net) 0.04; Net errors and omissions 0.83; *Total (net monetary movements)* 2.09; Exceptional financing (net) 3.63; *Changes in reserves* 5.71. Source: IMF, *International Financial Statistics*.

EXTERNAL TRADE

Principal Commodities (EC $ million, 1983): *Imports:* Food and live animals 54.8; Beverages and tobacco 10.1; Chemicals 19.7; Basic manufactures 39.3; Machinery and transport equipment 54.4; Miscellaneous manufactured articles 37.9; Total (incl. others) 227.9. *Exports:* Chemicals 2.2; Basic manufactures 4.8; Machinery and transport equipment 17.4; Miscellaneous manufactured articles 22.0; Total (incl. others) 49.7.

Principal Trading Partners (EC $ million): *Imports* (1983): Canada 12.6; United Kingdom 29.9; USA 113.1; Venezuela 11.4; Total (incl. others) 227.9. *Exports* (1978): Saint Lucia 3.6; Trinidad and Tobago 7.0; United Kingdom 2.6; USA 11.9; Total (incl. others) 33.8.

TRANSPORT

Road Traffic (registered vehicles, 1984): Passenger motor cars 8,661; Motor cycles 707, Commercial lorries (incl. jeeps) 1,065.

Shipping (freight traffic, '000 metric tons, 1983): Goods loaded 12.7; Goods unloaded 198.4.

TOURISM

Foreign Tourist Arrivals (1984): 129,149 visitors by air; 66,418 cruise ship passengers.

COMMUNICATIONS MEDIA

Radio Receivers (1983): 19,000 in use.
Television Receivers (1983): 16,500 in use.
Telephones (1984): 5,782 in use.

EDUCATION

Pre-primary (1983): 21 schools; 23 teachers; 677 pupils.
Primary (1983): 48 schools; 426 teachers; 9,933 students.
Secondary (1983): 16 schools; 331 teachers; 4,197 students.

Directory

The Constitution

The constitution, which came into force at the independence of Antigua and Barbuda on 1 November 1981, states that Antigua and Barbuda is a 'unitary sovereign democratic state'. The main provisions of the constitution are summarized below:

FUNDAMENTAL RIGHTS AND FREEDOMS

Regardless of race, place of origin, political opinion, colour, creed or sex, but subject to respect for the rights and freedoms of others and for the public interest, every person in Antigua and Barbuda is entitled to the rights of life, liberty, security of the person, the enjoyment of property and the protection of the law. Freedom of movement, of conscience, of expression (including freedom of the press), of peaceful assembly and association is guaranteed and the inviolability of family life, personal privacy, home and other property is maintained. Protection is afforded from discrimination on the grounds of race, sex, etc., and from slavery, forced labour, torture and inhuman treatment.

THE GOVERNOR-GENERAL

The Queen, as Head of State, is represented in Antigua and Barbuda by a Governor-General of local citizenship.

PARLIAMENT

Parliament consists of the Queen, a 17-member Senate and the House of Representatives composed of 17 elected members. Senators are appointed by the Governor-General: 11 on the advice of the Prime Minister (one of whom must be an inhabitant of Barbuda), four on the advice of the Leader of the Opposition, one at his own discretion and one on the advice of the Barbuda Council. The Barbuda Council is the principal organ of local government in

ANTIGUA AND BARBUDA

that island, whose membership and functions are determined by Parliament. The life of Parliament is five years.

Each constituency returns one Representative to the House who is directly elected in accordance with the Constitution.

The Attorney-General, if not otherwise a member of the House, is an ex-officio member but does not have the right to vote.

Every citizen over the age of 18 is eligible to vote.

Parliament may alter any of the provisions of the Constitution.

THE EXECUTIVE

Executive authority is vested in the Queen and exercisable by the Governor-General. The Governor-General appoints as Prime Minister that member of the House who, in the Governor-General's view, is best able to command the support of the majority of the members of the House, and other Ministers on the advice of the Prime Minister. The Governor-General may remove the Prime Minister from office if a resolution of no confidence is passed by the House and the Prime Minister does not either resign or advise the Governor-General to dissolve Parliament within seven days.

The Cabinet consists of the Prime Minister and other Ministers and the Attorney-General.

The Leader of the Opposition is appointed by the Governor-General as that member of the House who, in the Governor-General's view, is best able to command the support of a majority of members of the House who do not support the Government.

CITIZENSHIP

All persons born in Antigua and Barbuda before independence who, immediately prior to independence, were citizens of the United Kingdom and Colonies automatically become citizens of Antigua and Barbuda. All persons born outside the country with a parent or grandparent possessing citizenship of Antigua and Barbuda automatically acquire citizenship as do those born in the country after independence. Provision is made for the acquisition of citizenship by those to whom it would not automatically be granted.

The Government

Head of State: HM Queen Elizabeth II.

Governor-General: Sir Wilfred Ebenezer Jacobs (took office 1 November 1981).

CABINET
(October 1986)

Prime Minister: Vere C. Bird, Sr.

Deputy Prime Minister and Minister of Economic Development, Foreign Affairs, Tourism and Energy: Lester Bryant Bird.

Minister of Finance: John E. St Luce.

Attorney-General and Minister of Legal Affairs: Keith B. Ford.

Minister of Public Utilities and Communications: Vere Bird, Jr.

Minister of Agriculture, Fisheries and Lands: Robin Yearwood.

Minister of Health: Christopher Manasseh O'Mard.

Minister of Education, Culture, Youth Affairs and Sport: Reuben H. Harris.

Minister of Labour, Housing and Social Security: Adolphus Eleazer Freeland.

Minister of Public Works: Hillroy Humphries.

Ministers without Portfolio: Donald Christian, Hugh Marshall, Eustace Cochrane, Henderson Simon, Molwyn Joseph.

MINISTRIES

Office of the Prime Minister: Factory Rd, St John's; tel. 20260; telex 2127.

Ministry of Agriculture, Fisheries and Lands: Long St, St John's; tel. 21007.

Ministry of Education, Culture and Youth Affairs: Church St, St John's; tel. 20192.

Ministry of Economic Development, Foreign Affairs, Tourism and Energy: Queen Elizabeth Highway, St John's; tel. 20092; telex 2122.

Ministry of Finance: Redcliffe St, St John's; tel. 21199.

Ministry of Health: St John's St, St John's; tel. 21060.

Ministry of Labour: St John's; tel. 20011.

Ministry of Legal Affairs: Hadeed Bldg, Redcliffe St, St John's; tel. 20017.

Ministry of Public Works: St John's St, St John's; tel. 20894.

Legislature

PARLIAMENT

Senate

President: Bradley Carrot.

There are 17 nominated members.

House of Representatives

Speaker: Casford Murray.

Ex-Officio Member: The Attorney-General.

Clerk: L. Dowe.

General Election, 17 April 1984

Party	Seats
Antigua Labour Party	16
Progressive Labour Movement	—
United People's Movement	—
Independent	1

Political Organizations

Antigua Caribbean Liberation Movement (ACLM): POB 493, St John's; f. 1979; left-wing; Chair. Tim Hector.

Antigua Labour Party (ALP): St Mary's St, St John's; tel. 21059; f. 1968; Leader Vere C. Bird, Sr; Chair. Lester Bryant Bird; Sec. J. E. St Luce.

Organization for National Reconstruction (ONR): Codrington; f. 1983; to promote the economic development of Barbuda by co-operating with central government; Pres. Arthur Nibbs.

Progressive Labour Movement (PLM): St John's; f. 1970; Leader Robert Hall.

United National Democratic Party (UNDP): St John's; f. 1986 by merger of the United People's Movement (f. 1982) and the National Democratic Party (f. 1985); Chair. Dr Ivor Heath.

Diplomatic Representation

EMBASSY AND HIGH COMMISSION IN ANTIGUA AND BARBUDA

United Kingdom: British High Commissioner's Office, 38 St Mary's Street, POB 483, St John's; tel. 20008; telex 2113 (High Commissioner resident in Barbados).

USA: Queen Elizabeth Highway, St John's; tel. 23505; telex 2140 (Ambassador resident in Barbados).

Judicial System

Justice is administered by the Eastern Caribbean Supreme Court, based in Saint Lucia, which consists of a High Court of Justice and a Court of Appeal. One of the Court's Puisne Judges is responsible for Antigua and Barbuda, and presides over the Court of Summary Jurisdiction on the islands. There are also Magistrate's Courts for lesser cases.

Religion

CHRISTIANITY

The Anglican Communion

The Diocese of Antigua is made up of 12 islands: Antigua, Saint Christopher (St Kitts), Nevis, Anguilla, Barbuda, Montserrat, Dominica, Saba, St Maarten, Aruba, St Bartholomew and St Eustatius; the total number of Anglicans is about 60,000. The See City is St John's.

ANTIGUA AND BARBUDA

Bishop of Antigua and Archbishop of the West Indies: Rt Rev. ORLAND LINDSAY, Bishop's Lodge, POB 23, St John's; tel. 20151.

The Roman Catholic Church

The diocese of St John's-Basseterre, suffragan to the archdiocese of Castries (Saint Lucia), includes Anguilla, Antigua and Barbuda, the British Virgin Islands, Montserrat and Saint Christopher and Nevis. The Bishop participates in the Antilles Episcopal Conference (based in Jamaica).

Bishop of St John's-Basseterre: Rt Rev. DONALD J. REECE; Catholic Offices, POB 836, St John's; tel. 21135.

Other Christian Churches

Antigua Baptist Association: POB 277, St John's; tel. 21254; Pres. IVOR CHARLES.

Evangelical Lutheran Church: POB 968, St John's; tel. 22896; Pastors R. SEEGER, L. ZESSIN.

There are also Methodist, Pentecostal, Seventh-day Adventist, Moravian, Nazarene and Wesleyan Holiness places of worship.

The Press

The Herald: 2nd Floor, Redcliffe House, Cross 8, Redcliffe Street, St John's; Editor EVERTON BARNES.

The Nation's Voice: Public Information Division, POB 590, Church St and Independence Ave, St John's; Editor BARRYMORE STEVENS.

The Outlet: Cross St and Tanner St, POB 493, St John's; f. 1975; weekly; publ. by the Antigua Caribbean Liberation Movement (ACLM); Editor JAMES KNIGHT; circ. 5,500.

The Worker's Voice: 46 North St, POB 1281, St John's; f. 1943; 2 a week; official organ of the Antigua Labour Party and the Antigua Trades and Labour Union; Editor LESLIE JOHN; circ. 3,000.

Radio and Television

In 1984 there were an estimated 20,000 radio receivers and 16,600 television receivers in use.

Antigua Government Public Information Division: Office of the Prime Minister, Factory Rd, St John's; tel. 20260; comprises:

Antigua and Barbuda Broadcasting Service (Radio): POB 590, St John's; tel. 20112; f. 1956.

Antigua and Barbuda Broadcasting Services (Television): POB 1280, St John's; f. 1964.

Caribbean Radio Lighthouse: Box 1057, St John's; tel. 21454; religious broadcasts; Dir R. CORNELIUS.

Radio ZDK: Greenville Radio Ltd, POB 1100, St John's; tel. 21100; f. 1970; Man. IVOR BIRD.

CTV cable television transmits 12 channels of US television 24 hours a day to subscribers.

Finance

(cap. = capital; brs = branches)

BANKING

Antigua Commercial Bank: corner of St Mary's and Thames Sts, POB 95, St John's; tel. 21217; telex 2175; f. 1955; auth. cap. $5m.; Man. C. W. DICKSON; 2 brs.

Antigua and Barbuda Development Bank: 27 St Mary's St, POB 1279, St John's; tel. 20838; f. 1974; Man. BERNARD S. PERCIVAL.

Bank of Antigua: POB 315, corner of High and Thames Sts, St John's; tel. 24282; telex 2180.

First National Bank of Barbuda: Long St, St John's; tel. 24318; telex 2080; f. 1984; cap. EC $1m.; development bank for Barbuda.

Foreign Banks

Bank of Nova Scotia (Canada): High St, POB 342, St John's; tel. 21104; telex 2118; Man. L. J. NELSON.

Barclays Bank (UK): High St, POB 225, St John's; tel. 20334; telex 2135; Man. K. H. L. MARSHALL; 2 brs.

Canadian Imperial Bank of Commerce: 28 High St, POB 28, St John's; tel. 20836; telex 2150; Man. G. R. HILTS.

Directory

Royal Bank of Canada: High St and Market St, POB 252, St John's; tel. 20325; telex 2120; offers a trustee service.

Swiss American Bank: Redcliffe St, POB 1302, St John's; tel. 24460; telex 2181.

INSURANCE

Several foreign companies have offices in Antigua. Local insurance companies include the following:

Diamond Insurance Co Ltd: POB 489, Camacho's Ave, St John's; tel. 23474; telex 2173.

General Insurance Co Ltd: Redcliffe St, St John's; tel. 22346.

Sentinel Insurance Co Ltd: POB 207, Antigua Mill Hotel, St John's; tel. 20808.

State Insurance Co Ltd: POB 290, Kentish Rd, St John's; tel. 20110; telex 2177.

United Security Life Assurance Co Ltd: Corner of Long St and Cutter Lane, POB 817, St John's; tel. 20857.

Trade and Industry

Antigua Chamber of Commerce Ltd: Redcliffe St, St John's; tel. 20743; telex 2105; f. 1944; 90 mems; Pres. STEPHEN SHOUL; Exec. Dir LIONEL BOULOS.

Antigua Cotton Growers' Association: Dunbars, St John's; Chair. H. A. L. FRANCIS; Sec. VINCENT L. R. BELLE.

Antigua Employers' Federation: 7 Redcliffe Quay, Redcliffe St, St John's; tel. 20449; f. 1950; 94 mems; Chair. PETER WILLIAMS; Sec. HENDERSON BASS.

Antigua Fisheries Corpn: St John's; partly funded by the Antigua and Barbuda Development Bank; aims to help local fishermen.

Antigua Manufacturers' Association: POB 1158, St John's; tel. 23231; Chair. P. HARKER; Exec. Sec. B. STUART YOUNG.

DEVELOPMENT AGENCIES

Barbuda Development Agency: St John's; economic development projects for Barbuda; Chair. HAKIM AKBAR.

Industrial Development Board: Newgate St, St John's; tel. 21038; f. 1984 to stimulate investment in local industries.

TRADE UNIONS

Antigua and Barbuda Public Service Association (ABPSA): POB 1285, St John's; Pres. LINDBERG DOWE; Gen. Sec. ELLOY DE FREITAS; 300 mems.

Antigua Trades and Labour Union (ATLU): 46 North St, St John's; tel. 20090; f. 1939; affiliated to the Antigua Labour Party; Pres. WILLIAM ROBINSON; about 10,000 mems.

Antigua Workers' Union: Freedom Hall, Newgate St, St John's; tel. 22005; f. 1967 after a split with ATLU; affiliated to the Progressive Labour Movement; Pres. M. DANIEL; Gen. Sec. KEITHLYN SMITH; 10,000 mems.

National Assembly of Workers: Cross St, St John's; affiliated to the Antigua Caribbean Liberation Movement.

Transport

ROADS

There are 240 km (150 miles) of main roads and 725 km (450 miles) of secondary dry-weather roads. In early 1986 it was announced that Antigua and Barbuda was to receive US $3.5m. from the EEC to finance the first phase of a major road rehabilitation programme.

SHIPPING

The main harbour is the St John's Deep Water Harbour. There are two tugs for the berthing of ships, and modern cargo handling equipment. The harbour can also accommodate three large cruise ships, and is used by a number of foreign shipping lines.

CIVIL AVIATION

Antigua's Vere Bird (formerly Coolidge) Airport, 7 km north-east of St John's, is modern and accommodates jet-engined aircraft. In 1986 a US $11.1m. loan for the redevelopment of the airport was agreed with a consortium of five banks. There is a small airstrip at Codrington on Barbuda.

ANTIGUA AND BARBUDA

LIAT (1974): Vere Cornwall Bird International Airport, Antigua; tel. 20700; telex 2124; f. 1956 as Leeward Islands Air Transport Services; shares are held by the governments of Antigua and Barbuda, Montserrat, Grenada, Barbados, Trinidad and Tobago, Jamaica, Guyana, Dominica, Saint Lucia, Saint Vincent and the Grenadines and Saint Christopher and Nevis; scheduled passenger and cargo services to 22 islands in the West Indies; charter flights are also undertaken; Chair. PETER BERGASSE; Man. Dir ARTHUR FOSTER; fleet of 4 Super 748, 5 Dash 8, 4 Twin Otter, (6 Britten Norman Islander operated by subsidiaries).

Four Island Air Services Ltd: wholly-owned subsidiary of LIAT; runs scheduled services between Antigua, Barbuda and Saint Christopher and Nevis.

Inter Island Air Services Ltd: wholly-owned subsidiary of LIAT; runs scheduled services between Saint Vincent and the Grenadines, Grenada and Saint Lucia.

Tourism

Tourism is the main industry. In 1985 there were 139,726 visitors (excluding cruise ship passengers), most of whom came from the USA, Canada, the United Kingdom and from other Caribbean countries. There were 36 hotels with a total of 3,368 beds in 1984. A modern luxury 500-room hotel with conference facilities was due to be opened at Deep Bay in 1987.

Antigua Department of Tourism: Long and Thames Sts, POB 363, St John's; tel. 20029; Man. EDIE HILL-THIBOU.

Antigua Hotels and Tourist Association (AHTA): POB 454; St John's; tel. 20374; telex 2172; Chair. BRIAN GONSALVES.

ARGENTINA

Introductory Survey

Location, Climate, Language, Religion, Flag, Capital

The Argentine Republic occupies almost the whole of South America south of the Tropic of Capricorn and east of the Andes. It has a long Atlantic coastline stretching from Uruguay and the River Plate to Tierra del Fuego. To the west lie Chile and the Andes mountains, while to the north are Bolivia, Paraguay and Brazil. Argentina also claims the Falkland Islands (known in Argentina as the Islas Malvinas), South Georgia, the South Sandwich Islands and part of Antarctica. The climate varies from sub-tropical in the Chaco region of the north to sub-arctic in Patagonia, generally with moderate summer rainfall. Temperatures in Buenos Aires are generally between 5°C (41°F) and 29°C (84°F). The language is Spanish. The great majority of the population profess Christianity: more than 90% are Roman Catholics and about 2% Protestants. The national flag (proportions 2 by 1) has three equal horizontal stripes, of light blue, white and light blue. The state flag (proportions 3 by 2) has the same design with, in addition, a gold 'Sun of May' in the centre of the white stripe. The capital is Buenos Aires.

Recent History

In 1916 Hipólito Yrigoyen, a member of the reformist Unión Cívica Radical (UCR), became Argentina's first President to be freely elected by direct popular vote. He remained in office until 1922, when another UCR politician became President. In 1928 Yrigoyen was elected for a second term, but in 1930 he was overthrown by an army coup, and the country's first military regime was established. Civilian rule was restored in 1932. Conservative politicians and landowners held power from then until June 1943, when another coup took place. Military rule was imposed until 1946.

A leading figure in the military regime was Col (later Lt-Gen.) Juan Domingo Perón Sosa, who became Secretary for Labour and Social Welfare in November 1943. In this post, he promoted labour reforms and encouraged unionization. Subsequently, Col Perón became also Vice-President and Minister of War, but in October 1945 he was forced to resign all his posts. This led to popular protests and demonstrations. Perón won a presidential election in February 1946, and took office in June. The new Government extended the franchise to women in 1947. President Perón founded the Peronista party in 1948, and was re-elected in November 1951. His position was greatly enhanced by the popularity, particularly among industrial workers and their families, of his second wife, Eva ('Evita') Duarte de Perón, who died, aged 33, in July 1952. As President, Gen. Perón pursued a policy of extreme nationalism and social improvement. In 1954, however, his measures of secularization and the legalization of divorce brought him into conflict with the Roman Catholic Church. In September 1955 President Perón was deposed by a revolt of the armed forces. He went into exile, eventually settling in Spain, from where he continued to direct the Peronist movement.

Following the overthrow of Gen. Perón, Argentina entered a lengthy period of political instability. The provisional government that took power after the coup was replaced in November 1955 by a military junta, with Gen. Pedro Aramburu, the Chief of the General Staff, as President. Congressional and presidential elections were held in February 1958. The presidential election was won by Dr Arturo Frondizi, a left-wing Radical, who took office in May. His party, the UCR Intransigente (UCRI), won large majorities in both chambers of Congress. In March 1962, following Peronist successes in national and provincial elections, President Frondizi was deposed by a military coup. He was replaced by Dr José María Guido, hitherto the President of the Senate, who resigned from the UCRI as a result of criticism from party members. The next presidential election was won by another Radical, Dr Arturo Illía, who took office in October. However, President Illía was overthrown by a coup in June 1966. Power was assumed by a military junta, led by Lt-Gen. Juan Carlos Onganía, a former Commander-in-Chief of the Army. The legislature was closed, and political parties were banned. In May 1970 Gen. Aramburu, the former President, was abducted by members of the Montoneros, a guerrilla group of left-wing Peronists. In June he was killed by his captors. Later that month, President Onganía was deposed by his military colleagues, and a junta of the three armed forces' leaders took power. The junta appointed Brig.-Gen. Roberto Levingston, a former Minister of Defence, to be President. In March 1971, however, President Levingston was overthrown by the junta, which nominated one of its members, Lt-Gen. Alejandro Lanusse (Commander-in-Chief of the Army since October 1968), to be President. Urban guerrilla groups intensified their activities in 1971 and 1972.

Congressional and presidential elections were held in March 1973. The Frente Justicialista de Liberación, a Peronist coalition, won control of the National Congress, while the presidential election was won by the party's candidate, Dr Héctor Cámpora, who took office in May. However, President Cámpora resigned in July, to enable the holding of a fresh presidential election which Gen. Perón, who had returned to Argentina in June (after nearly 18 years in exile), would be eligible to contest. This election, in September 1973, returned the former President to power, with more than 60% of the votes. He took office in October, with his third wife, María Estela ('Isabelita') Martínez de Perón, as Vice-President.

General Perón died in July 1974 and was succeeded as President by his widow. The Government's economic austerity programme and the soaring rate of inflation caused widespread strikes and dissension among industrial workers. This increasingly chaotic situation resulted in demands for the resignation of President Perón. In March 1976 the armed forces, led by Lt-Gen. Jorge Videla (Commander of the Army), overthrew the President and installed a three-man junta: Gen. Videla was sworn in as President. The junta made substantial alterations to the Constitution, dissolved Congress, suspended all political and trade union activity and removed most government officials from their posts. Several hundred people were arrested, while Señora Perón was placed in preventive detention and later went into exile.

The new military regime launched a successful, although ferocious, offensive against left-wing guerrillas and opposition forces, and reintroduced the death penalty for abduction, subversion and terrorism. The imprisonment, torture and murder of many people who were suspected of left-wing political activity by the armed forces provoked protests over violations of human rights, from within Argentina and from abroad. The number of people who 'disappeared' after the coup was estimated to be between 6,000 and 15,000. Repression eased in 1978, after all armed opposition had been eliminated.

In May 1978 the junta confirmed President Videla in office until March 1981. In August 1978 he retired from the army and ceased to be part of the junta. In March 1981 Gen. Roberto Viola, a former member of the junta, succeeded President Videla and promised to extend the dialogue with the political parties as a prelude to an eventual return to democracy. After suffering a heart attack, he was replaced in December by Lt-Gen. Leopoldo Galtieri, the Commander-in-Chief of the Army, who attempted to cultivate popular support by continuing the process of political liberalization which had been begun by his predecessor. Political activity increased, and a coalition of five political parties, the Multipartidaria (which had been created in July 1981), began to urge that a general election be held. The free-market policies which had been followed since 1976, combined with excessive foreign borrowing, high-level corruption and military spending, resulted in a severe economic crisis, which caused increasing labour unrest. Demonstrations, the largest since 1976, were violently suppressed.

To distract attention from the unstable domestic situation,

and following unsuccessful negotiations with the United Kingdom in February over Argentina's long-standing sovereignty claim, President Galtieri ordered the invasion of the Falkland Islands (Islas Malvinas) in April 1982 (see chapter on the Falkland Islands, Vol. II). The United Kingdom recovered the islands after a short war during which about 750 Argentine lives were lost. Argentine forces surrendered in June 1982 but no formal cessation of hostilities was signed. After the war, Argentina increased its military activity around Antarctica, where it has made several claims of sovereignty. US support for the United Kingdom during the war damaged Argentina's relations with the USA and brought about improved relations with Cuba, Nicaragua and the Non-Aligned Movement.

Popular support for the Falklands war, fed by government propaganda, was voiced in patriotic demonstrations which gave politicians an opportunity to demand the end of the military dictatorship. The defeat brought about the final humiliation of the armed forces: Galtieri was forced to resign, and the rest of the junta were replaced. The army, under the control of Lt-Gen. Cristino Nicolaides, installed a retired general, Reynaldo Bignone, as President in July 1982. The armed forces were held responsible for the disastrous economic situation, and, unable to resolve the crisis, were forced to move rapidly towards the transfer of power to a civilian government. In 1982 and 1983, general strikes, demanding higher wages and protesting against the Government, brought out over 90% of the country's workers, and mass demonstrations were held. New regulations for party political activity were approved in August 1982, and the ban on public meetings and trade union activity was lifted in October. At the same time, however, press censorship was tightened, and arrests were made for criticism of the Government.

In 1983 continuing public demands for an inquiry into Argentina's failure in the Falklands war and for an explanation regarding the 'disappeared' caused recriminations and divisions within the armed forces. A Military Commission of Inquiry into the war, established in November 1982, presented its report in September 1983. The commission concluded that the main responsibility for Argentina's defeat lay with members of the former junta, who were recommended for trial. Galtieri was given a prison sentence, while several other officers were put on trial for corruption, murder and insulting the honour of the armed forces. Meanwhile, in August 1983 the regime approved the Ley de Pacificación Nacional, an amnesty law which granted retrospective immunity to the police, the armed forces and others for political crimes that had been committed over the previous 10 years.

In February 1983 the Government had announced that general and presidential elections would be held on 30 October. In April the ban on 'Isabelita' Perón and 25 former government and trade union officials was lifted. Señora Perón was retained as titular head of the Peronist party, the Partido Justicialista, but remained in Spain. The other main party, the UCR, which was supported by some socialist and some conservative groups, announced its candidate, Dr Raúl Alfonsín, in July. The programme of both parties was similar and included the reversal of the prevailing free-market economic policies. At the elections, the UCR succeeded in attracting the votes of many former Peronist supporters. It won 317 of the 600 seats in the presidential electoral college, and 129 of the 254 seats in the Chamber of Deputies, although the Peronists won a narrow majority of provincial governorships. The military Government relinquished power seven weeks earlier than originally planned, and Dr Alfonsín took office as President on 10 December.

Shortly after taking office, President Alfonsín announced a radical reform of the armed forces, which led to the immediate retirement of more than one-half of the military high command. In addition, he repealed the Ley de Pacificación Nacional and ordered the court martial of the first three military juntas to rule Argentina after the coup of 1976, for offences including abduction, torture and murder. The majority of cases that were brought against the armed forces were to be tried by military courts. Public opposition to the former military regime was strengthened by the discovery and exhumation of hundreds of unmarked graves throughout the country. It was believed that between 15,000 and 30,000 people had disappeared during the so-called 'dirty war' between the former military regime and its opponents from 1976 until 1983. In December the Government announced the formation of the National Commission on the Disappearance of Persons (CONADEP) to investigate the events of the 'dirty war'. There was, however, mounting public criticism of the Government's attempts to avoid a full-scale prosecution of military personnel. The failure of the Supreme Military Tribunal to complete the court martial of the nine former military leaders by the September 1984 deadline, coupled with its ruling that the former leaders were not directly responsible for any violations of human rights, resulted in a public outcry. A large rally in Buenos Aires by human rights organizations placed further pressure on the Government to extend and hasten investigations into the crimes committed under military rule. A report by CONADEP, published in September, gave details of 8,960 people who had disappeared during the 'dirty war' and implicated 1,300 officers of the armed forces in the campaign of repression and violence. In October President Alfonsín announced that the court martial of the former leaders would be transferred to the civilian Federal Court of Appeal.

In March 1985, prior to the start of the court martial, President Alfonsín ordered a reshuffle of the military hierarchy, which resulted in the promotion of officers who were regarded as loyal to the Government and its policies. In April the trial of the former leaders began in an atmosphere of political tension, following the Government's denunciation of a plot by extreme right-wing groups to destabilize the civilian administration. In the course of the trial, the testimonies of the several hundred prosecution witnesses revealed the systematic atrocities and the campaign of terror which had been perpetrated by the former military leaders. The verdicts on the nine accused officers were announced in December 1985. Four of the accused were acquitted, but sentences were passed on the remaining five, including sentences of life imprisonment for two former junta members, Gen. Videla and Adm. Eduardo Massera. The public response to the verdicts was generally one of dissatisfaction; many people believed that the sentences were too lenient. Furthermore, there remained for the Government the problem of its policy towards the several hundred lower-ranking officers who were also under suspicion of violations of human rights. In April 1986 the Government requested that state and military prosecutors should accelerate trials involving members of the armed forces. In June the Federal Court of Appeal ruled that the Armed Forces Supreme Council should transfer to civilian jurisdiction some 300 cases of alleged abuses of human rights by military personnel. Despite public support for the Government's actions, continuing hostility within the armed forces towards President Alfonsín was demonstrated in May 1986 by the discovery of a bomb at a military base in Córdoba, which was timed to coincide with a visit to the base by the President.

The court martial of the members of the junta which had held power during the Falklands war was conducted concurrently with the trial of the former military leaders. In May 1986 all three members of that junta were found guilty of negligence and received prison sentences, including a term of 12 years for Galtieri.

Throughout 1984 the Government faced considerable opposition from the Peronists and the powerful trade union, the Confederación General de Trabajo (CGT), over its economic policy and its plans for trade union reform. In March the Government's draft legislation for union reform was defeated in the Senate by the Peronist majority, and in April the Minister of Labour, Antonio Mucci, resigned after criticism of his handling of the issue. In May the Government opened talks with opposition parties, with the aim of reaching a broad accord on economic and political strategy. Señora Perón returned from Spain to participate in the talks, and indicated her party's willingness to co-operate fully with the Government. The rapprochement between the two major parties was demonstrated by the signing of an accord in June.

The continuing deterioration of the Argentine economy in 1985 rendered the Government's relations with the CGT increasingly difficult. However, the Government did enjoy some measure of success in dealing with political opposition to its policies and with industrial protests. This success was partly attributable to internal disarray within the Peronist party. In June the Government's announcement of drastic austerity measures, including a 'freeze' on wages, brought immediate condemnation from the CGT and the Peronists, but met with a generally positive response from the public, and President Alfonsín's reputation was thought to have been enhanced by his Government's decisive action. Public approval of the Government's policies was reflected in the results of the national and local elections in November. At the elections for one-half of the seats in the Chamber of Deputies, the UCR received 43.5% of the votes and increased its strength by one seat. In October, prior to the elections, President Alfonsín had declared a state of siege, in order to curb a campaign of bombings and threats by right-wing groups.

In January 1986 President Alfonsín announced the formation of an 18-member advisory body, the Consejo para la Consolidación de la Democracia, which was expected to be instrumental in the proposed reform of the Constitution. In May the President announced plans to transfer the capital of Argentina from Buenos Aires to the twin towns of Viedma-Carmen de Patagones, about 750 km south of the present capital. The announcement aroused considerable controversy, principally because such a move was expected to cost in excess of US $3,000m. Throughout 1986 the Government faced consistent opposition to its economic policies from the CGT. A further conflict was envisaged with the Roman Catholic Church over the administration's plans to legalize divorce, which had been overwhelmingly approved by the Chamber of Deputies in August.

For many years, Argentina had a territorial dispute with Chile over three small islands in the Beagle Channel, south of Tierra del Fuego. In January 1979 the two countries agreed to accept an offer of mediation from the Pope. The Vatican proposals of December 1980, which awarded the disputed islands to Chile, were rejected in March 1981 by the Argentine Government, which continued to threaten military action in 1983. The civilian government which came to power in December 1983 was in favour of accepting the proposals, and signed a declaration of peace and friendship with Chile in January 1984, pending a more detailed settlement of the dispute. In October it was announced that the two countries had reached a broad agreement which guaranteed Argentine rights over deposits of petroleum and other minerals in the disputed waters in the South Atlantic. In November the treaty was approved by a national referendum and by the Senate. In May 1985 the treaty was formally ratified by representatives of the Argentine and Chilean Governments.

Government

Argentina comprises a Federal District, 23 provinces and the National Territory of Tierra del Fuego.

Legislative power is vested in the bicameral Congress: the Chamber of Deputies has 254 members, elected by universal adult suffrage for a term of four years (with one-half of the seats renewable every two years), while the Senate has 46 members, nominated by provincial legislatures for a term of nine years (with one-third of the seats renewable every three years). Executive power is vested in the President, elected by an electoral college for a six-year term. Each province has its own elected Governor and legislature, concerned with all matters not delegated to the Federal Government.

Defence

A period of national service is compulsory for men between the ages of 18 and 45 years. The length of service is 12 months in the army or air force and 14 months in the navy. The total strength of the regular armed forces in July 1986 was 73,000 (including 35,000 conscripts), of which the army had 40,000 with a further 250,000 trained reservists, the navy had 18,000 and the air force 15,000 men. There were also paramilitary forces numbering 22,000 men. Defence expenditure for 1986 was estimated to be 1,088m. australes.

Economic Affairs

Argentina is rich in natural resources. The agricultural sector (including livestock and fishing) expanded its output by 5.5% in 1982 and accounted for 60% of export revenue and 15% of gross domestic product (GDP) in 1983. The principal crops are wheat, maize, oilseeds, sorghum, soybeans and sugar. Record grain crops were recorded in 1981 and 1982, partly as a result of the introduction of high-yielding varieties. A record soybean harvest of 5.5m. metric tons was recorded in 1983, an increase of 37.5% from the previous year. The Government planned to increase the annual output of grain crops by 30% between 1984 and 1989 by introducing a programme of pesticides, new machinery, fertilizers and new crop species. The grain crop was 44.3m. tons in 1985, but was expected to fall to 36m. tons in 1986. Argentina is one of the world's major exporters of wheat and other cereals. In recent years, however, falling world prices and increased competition from sales of subsidized grain by other countries have caused the sector to decline. Between 1984 and 1986 Argentina lost US $2,100m. in export earnings as a result of falling grain prices. In 1980 the USSR signed an agreement to import a minimum of 4.5m. metric tons of grain and 60,000 metric tons of beef annually until 1985. In 1986 the USSR agreed to the renewal of (substantially reduced) imports of Argentine wheat for five years. Flooding in late 1985 caused extensive damage to crops; the 1986 wheat crop was expected to fall to 8.5m. tons, and further declines were expected in the production of linseed, soybeans and sorghum. Gross agricultural production fell by 3.4% in 1985. Argentina's beef exports decreased by 50% between 1970 and 1983, and the number of cattle fell by 10m. in the six years to 1983. In 1983 beef production fell by 5% from the 1982 level, to 2.44m. metric tons. The sector continued to decline in 1984 and exports decreased by 38%. Intense competition from West European producers has been particularly damaging to the sector. Other agricultural exports include dairy produce, cotton and wool. The EEC's share of total exports declined from 50% to 20% between 1971 and 1981. In 1985 the Government announced plans for increased investment in the agricultural sector over the following five years. In 1986 the World Bank agreed to lend $350m. to Argentina to facilitate the reform of the agricultural sector by reducing agricultural taxes, in order to increase exports and to reduce costs for producers. In July 1986 Argentina signed a two-year fishing agreement with the USSR and Bulgaria, whereby the Soviet and Bulgarian fleets obtained access to Argentine territorial waters, including the disputed waters around the Falkland Islands. In October, however, the British Government announced plans unilaterally to extend its fishing limits around the Falkland Islands to 150 nautical miles (278 km) from February 1987, a decision that was expected to jeopardize Argentina's newly-signed fishing agreement and lead to further conflict between Argentina and the United Kingdom.

Industry has been one of the sectors most severely affected by the recession. Employment in manufacturing contracted by 36.4% between 1974 and 1983, while production was affected by a shortage of raw materials and by debts, together with a sharp drop in domestic demand. The level of unemployment, which stood at 3% in 1978, reached 15% of the labour force in 1984. Real wages were estimated to have declined by 30% in 1983, and by 21% in 1985. However, certain sectors, such as chemicals, textiles, pulp and paper, began to increase production in 1983, as a result of cuts in imports. The output of motor cars, which had shrunk from 218,600 in 1980 to 106,890 in 1982, continued to decline. In 1985 output was expected to fall as a result of lay-offs and deteriorating labour relations. Gross industrial production fell by 10.4% in 1985, and spare industrial capacity was 25%.

In 1978, for the first time, foreign oil companies were allowed to drill for petroleum in Argentina. Despite a drop of 2% in domestic output, to 27.9m. cubic metres, a surplus on trade in petroleum was recorded in 1982, owing to a fall in domestic consumption. By 1982 the state oil company, Yacimientos Petrolíferos Fiscales (YPF), had extended its operations as far south as Tierra del Fuego and to the west central provinces from Mendoza to Neuquén. Argentina's petroleum refining capacity in 1983 was 700,000 barrels per day (b/d), of which 430,000 b/d was under YPF's control. The major refining installations are at La Plata and Lujan de Cujo. Argentina's proven reserves of petroleum amount to 2,428m. barrels. In 1985 production averaged 400,000 b/d, less than 40% of national petroleum consumption. In 1985 the Government announced plans to encourage foreign investment in the sector, in order to increase production by 30%. Although foreign investors were thought to have been deterred by the decline in world petroleum prices, in August 1986 YPF agreed terms on an exploration project with a consortium of foreign companies, including Esso and Chevron. It has been estimated that US $30,000m. must be invested in the sector from 1985 until 2000 if Argentina is to remain self-sufficient in petroleum and generate exports.

In 1984 the YPF announced plans to construct a gas pipeline in Neuquén, where there are proven reserves of 700,000m. cu m of natural gas: production averaged 19,000m. cu m per year in 1986. The share of thermal energy in total energy production was down to 46.6% by 1982. Coal output rose by 3.5% in 1982, to 515,000 metric tons, providing 40% of domestic requirements, but fell to 509,800 tons in 1984. The Alfonsín Government has undertaken a programme of development in the mining industry, which recorded a growth rate of only 0.4% between 1979 and 1983. In December 1983 work began on the Yacyretá hydroelectric project on the Paraná, jointly undertaken with Paraguay, which is expected to cost US $10,000m. Yacyretá is scheduled to have a generating capacity of 2,700 MW, and should be the second largest hydroelectric scheme in the world when it becomes operational in 1992–93. In 1985 a hydroelectric complex with a capacity of 2,100 MW was under construction at Piedra del Aguila, on the Limay river, and was expected to contribute 9% of Argentina's energy requirements. In 1985 hydroelectric power provided 45% of Argentina's electricity requirements.

Argentina is the leading nuclear power in Latin America. There are proven reserves of 30,000 metric tons of uranium concentrates. The Atucha I nuclear power station (capacity 640 MW) came into operation in 1974, and the Embalse Rio Tercero 600 MW reactor in Córdoba went 'on stream' in March 1983. Atucha II (capacity 690 MW) was under construction in 1986, and two more reactors were planned. In 1984 the Government announced spending cuts in the nuclear power sector, which have led to delays in construction and a decline in development. Argentina has so far resisted strong international pressure, principally from the USA, to sign the Treaty on the Non-Proliferation of Nuclear Weapons and to ratify the Treaty of Tlatelolco (see p. 34).

When the military leaders assumed power in 1976, the economy was in a state of crisis, with an annual inflation rate of 444%. The Government attempted to return to a strict orthodox monetarist economic policy, consisting of stringent control on credit, a 10% reduction in public spending and a contraction of the state sector. Financial sanctions, imposed during the war with the United Kingdom in April–June 1982, caused an acute monetary crisis and undermined all plans for a cohesive economic programme.

In March 1983 the Government imposed controls on the prices of about 1,000 items in an attempt to control inflation, which averaged 104.5% in 1981, 164.8% in 1982 and 343.8% in 1983. Argentina's mounting inflation, the highest in the world in 1982 and 1983, was matched by continuing frequent devaluations of currency: between mid-1976 and mid-1983 its cumulative depreciation was 99.8%. In June 1983 a new unit of currency, the peso argentino (worth 10,000 former pesos), was introduced. However, the new peso was devalued daily to reduce the gap between the official and the 'black market' rates against the dollar. In 1983 the flight of capital from Argentina was estimated to be approaching US $2,000m. per year. Controls on foreign exchange and imports had to be imposed, to safeguard reserves of foreign currency, and six years of open monetarism came to an end. Argentina's GDP, measured in constant prices, fell by 5.9% in 1981 and by 5.7% in 1982. The country's external debt increased from US $10,000m. in 1976 to $39,000m. in 1983.

On taking office in December 1983, the civilian Government inherited a major economic crisis from the military regime. Inflation had reached 433.7% and Argentina's total foreign debt was estimated to be $43,600m., with outstanding interest payments of $2,700m. dating from the last quarter of 1983. The Government immediately introduced a series of price controls and made a commitment to lowering unemployment and to raising real wages by between 6% and 8%. In January 1984 Argentina announced a virtual unilateral moratorium on payments and renegotiations of its foreign debt. By March, however, the Government was under pressure to make an immediate repayment of $500m. if it was to avoid a default. In order to avert an international crisis, the US Government and commercial banks arranged a bridging loan for Argentina of $500m. The Government began negotiations with the IMF on conditions for further aid, but talks were hampered by President Alfonsín's reluctance to introduce austerity measures, similar to those adopted by other Latin American countries, and, in particular, to abandon his commitment to increases in real wages. The negotiations took place against a background of growing industrial unrest in Argentina, as trade unions sought greater increases in wages. Following the collapse of talks in June, Argentina issued its own unilateral letter of intent, which was rejected by the IMF.

In September the disclosure that inflation had reached 615.5% in the year ending July 1984, coupled with the prospect of repayments of debt principal and interest amounting to $1,650m. (due in September), prompted the Government to devalue the peso by 3.9% and to agree to a memorandum of understanding with the IMF, which committed Argentina to an austerity programme of further devaluations, a reduction in wage increases, cuts in public spending and a reduction in the budget deficit. Under the terms of the agreement, Argentina was allocated a loan of $1,400m. from the IMF. In December Argentina reached a preliminary agreement with its commercial bank creditors on a new loan and the rescheduling of private and public sector debt.

In January 1985 the Government revealed details of its five-year economic plan, which based its strategy for Argentina's economic recovery on an increase in exports. In spite of the plan's commitment to fiscal and financial reform and to a reduction in public spending (policies which formed part of the existing agreement between the IMF and Argentina), the IMF announced the suspension of its aid programme to Argentina in March. The Fund's action had been prompted by the Government's failure to control inflation and by its reluctance to use foreign reserves to reduce arrears on the foreign debt of $48,400m. A consequence of the IMF's decision was the suspension of Argentina's agreement with its creditor banks on a new loan and the rescheduling of the foreign debt.

In an attempt to reach a new agreement with the IMF, President Alfonsín announced further austerity measures in May, as part of the Government's 'war economy' policy. Public spending was to be reduced by 12% in 1985, and extensive tax and financial reforms were introduced. The banking sector was particularly affected by the reforms. Ten banks, including the important Banco de Italia y Río de la Plata, closed down as a result of new legislation, and the Government was forced to impose a 120-day 'freeze' on US dollar accounts in order to avert a 'run' on foreign reserves.

In June the Government, under pressure to reach an agreement with the IMF and alarmed at the rise in the annual rate of inflation to 1,128.9%, announced a new and much stricter austerity programme, known as the Austral Plan, which marked a radical departure from the administration's hitherto restrained approach. The programme's aims were to reduce inflation, to increase revenues and to cut public expenditure. A new unit of currency, the austral (equivalent to 1,000 pesos argentinos), was introduced, and a 90-day 'freeze' on prices and wages was imposed. All new employment in the public sector was suspended. In spite of opposition to the programme from the Peronists and the CGT, the Government was able to claim some measure of success: preliminary figures indicated that the monthly rate of inflation declined from 30% in June to 6.2% in July and to 3.1% in August. The annual rate of inflation declined from 688% in 1984 to 385% in 1985.

In February 1986 the Government announced the introduction of the second phase of the Austral Plan, which emphasized the administration's commitment to the modernization of the economy and to the attainment of economic growth. One controversial aspect of the new phase was the proposed 'privatization' of some of the 353 state-owned manufacturing companies, principally in the steel and petrochemical sectors. The Government hoped that privatization would reduce Argentina's foreign debt of more than US $50,000m. by eliminating a proportion of the $11,000m. owed by public sector companies.

Further amendments to the Austral Plan were announced in April 1986, including a 3.75% devaluation of the austral (to be followed by further small devaluations) and salary increases of between 18% and 25% for workers in the private and public sectors. The CGT remained critical of the Government's economic policy and convened a series of one-day general strikes (in January, March and June) in protest, but by July 1986 more than 50% of private-sector employees had agreed wage settlements in accordance with the Austral Plan. However, increases in the monthly rate of inflation in July and August, to 6.8% and 9% respectively, represented a serious set-back for the

ARGENTINA

Government. In September the administration authorized a further 3% devaluation of the austral, and new restrictions on increases in wages and industrial prices. The resurgence of inflation was expected to place substantial pressure on the Austral Plan, and a deterioration in the Government's relations with the CGT was also anticipated.

In August 1985 the Government concluded the agreement with its creditor banks on a new loan of $4,200m. and the rescheduling of $13,400m. of private and public sector debt. In 1986 Argentina successfully obtained two 180-day postponements of payment of $10,000m. in outstanding debts to its commercial bank creditors. However, the Government's agreement with the IMF and its rescheduling settlement with its creditor banks were placed in jeopardy by Argentina's continuing failure to meet the economic targets that had been established as part of the Austral Plan.

Argentina's balance of payments has recently been characterized by a growing trade surplus, rising from US $712m. in 1981 to $3,982m. in 1984. However, because of a large deficit on services (including interest payments), the current deficit in 1984 was $2,495m. Preliminary figures for 1985 indicated a trade surplus of $4,580m.

In August 1986 Argentina and Brazil signed a trade pact which was expected to have significant economic and political implications for trade integration in the region. Under the terms of the agreement, economic links between the two countries were to be founded on extensive co-operation in the development of high-technology industries; energy, communications and transport links were to be improved, and trading between the countries was to be on a balanced basis, with preferential treatment for industrial and agricultural products from each country. Specific projects included the formation of a customs union, the purchase by Brazil of 1.3m. tons of Argentine wheat annually over the following five years and the construction of a jointly-financed hydroelectric plant at Garabi on the River Uruguay.

Social Welfare

Social welfare benefits fall into three categories: retirement, disability and survivors' pensions; family allowances; and health insurance. The first is administered by the Subsecretaría de Seguridad Social (part of the Ministry of Social Welfare) and funded by compulsory contributions from all workers, employed and self-employed, over 18 years of age. The second is supervised by the Subsecretaría and funded by employers. The third is administered by means of public funds and may be provided only by authorized public institutions. Work insurance is the responsibility of the employer. Expenditure by the central government on social security and welfare represented 30% of total government spending in 1983, while expenditure on health services accounted for a further 1.2%.

In 1975 there were 48,693 physicians working in Argentina, equivalent to one for every 530 inhabitants: the best doctor-patient ratio of any country in Latin America.

Education

Education from pre-school to university level is available free of charge. Education is officially compulsory for all children at primary level, between the ages of six and 14 years. Secondary education lasts for between four and six years, depending on the type of course: the normal certificate of education (bachillerato) course lasts for five years, whereas a course leading to a commercial bachillerato may last for four or five years, and one leading to a technical or agricultural bachillerato lasts for six years. Non-university higher education, usually leading to a teaching qualification, is for three or four years, while university courses last for four years or more. There are 29 state universities and 23 private universities.

According to census results, the average rate of adult illiteracy declined from 7.4% in 1970 to only 6.1% (males 5.7%, females 6.4%) in 1980. According to estimates by UNESCO, the illiteracy rate in 1985 was only 4.5%. The total enrolment at primary and secondary schools in 1983 was equivalent to 89% of the school-age population.

Tourism

Argentina has yet to exploit fully its superb tourist attractions. The principal ones are the Andes mountains, the lake district centred on Bariloche (where there is a National Park), Patagonia and the Perito Moreno glacier, the Atlantic beaches and Mar del Plata, the Iguazú falls (located in the National Park of Iguazú), the Pampas, the city of Buenos Aires and Tierra del Fuego. The number of foreign tourist arrivals increased from 1,145,000 in 1981 to 1,608,207 in 1984.

Public Holidays

1987: 1 January (New Year's Day), 17 April (Good Friday), 1 May (Labour Day), 25 May (Anniversary of the 1810 Revolution), 10 June (Occupation of the Islas Malvinas), 20 June (Flag Day), 9 July (Independence Day), 17 August (Death of Gen. José de San Martín), 8 December (Immaculate Conception), 25 December (Christmas).

1988: 1 January (New Year's Day), 1 April (Good Friday), 1 May (Labour Day), 25 May (Anniversary of the 1810 Revolution), 10 June (Occupation of the Islas Malvinas), 20 June (Flag Day), 9 July (Independence Day), 17 August (Death of Gen. José de San Martín), 8 December (Immaculate Conception), 25 December (Christmas).

Weights and Measures

The metric system is in force.

Currency and Exchange Rates

100 centavos = 1 austral (₳).

Exchange rates (30 September 1986):
  £1 sterling = 1.535 australes;
  US $1 = 1.0605 australes.

ARGENTINA

Statistical Survey

Statistical Survey

Sources (unless otherwise stated): Instituto Nacional de Estadística y Censos, Hipólito Yrigoyen 250, 12°, Of. 1210, 1310 Buenos Aires; tel. (1) 33-7872; telex 21952; and Banco Central de la República Argentina, Reconquista 266, 1003 Buenos Aires; tel. (1) 40-0161; telex 1137.

Area and Population

AREA, POPULATION AND DENSITY

Area (sq km)	2,766,889*
Population (census results)†	
30 September 1970	23,362,204
22 October 1980	
Males	13,755,983
Females	14,191,463
Total	27,947,446
Population (official estimates at mid-year)	
1984	30,096,918
1985	30,563,833
1986	31,029,694
Density (per sq km) at mid-1986	11.2

* 1,068,302 sq miles. The figure excludes the Falkland Islands (Islas Malvinas) and Antarctic territory claimed by Argentina.
† Figures exclude adjustment for underenumeration, estimated to have been 1% at the 1980 census.

PROVINCES (census of 22 October 1980)

	Population	Capital
Buenos Aires—Federal District	2,922,829	
Buenos Aires—Province	10,865,408	La Plata
Catamarca	207,717	Catamarca
Córdoba	2,407,754	Córdoba
Corrientes	661,454	Corrientes
Chaco	701,392	Resistencia
Chubut	263,116	Rawson
Entre Ríos	908,313	Paraná
Formosa	295,887	Formosa
Jujuy	410,008	Jujuy
La Pampa	208,260	Santa Rosa
La Rioja	164,217	La Rioja
Mendoza	1,196,228	Mendoza
Misiones	588,977	Posadas
Neuquén	243,850	Neuquén
Río Negro	383,354	Viedma
Salta	662,870	Salta
San Juan	465,976	San Juan
San Luis	214,416	San Luis
Santa Cruz	114,941	Río Gallegos
Santa Fé	2,465,546	Santa Fé
Santiago del Estero	594,920	Santiago del Estero
Tucumán	972,655	Tucumán
Territory		
Tierra del Fuego	27,358	Ushuaia

PRINCIPAL TOWNS (population at 1980 census)

Buenos Aires (capital)	2,922,829*	Mar del Plata	414,696
Córdoba	983,969	Santa Fé	291,966
Rosario	957,301	San Juan	291,707
Mendoza	605,623	Salta	260,744
La Plata	564,750	Bahía Blanca	223,818
San Miguel de		Resistencia	220,104
Tucumán	498,579	Corrientes	180,612
		Paraná	161,638

* The population of the metropolitan area was 9,969,826.

BIRTHS AND DEATHS

	Registered live births		Registered deaths	
	Number	Rate (per 1,000)	Number	Rate (per 1,000)
1978	665,000	24.3	233,482	8.5
1979	647,864	23.3	234,926	8.5
1980	697,775	24.7	241,125	8.5
1981	680,236	23.7	241,898	8.4

1982: Deaths 234,926 (death rate 8.1 per 1,000).
1983: Births 706,979 (birth rate 23.9 per 1,000).
Marriages: 161,422 (marriage rate 5.6 per 1,000) in 1981; 177,010 (marriage rate 6.0 per 1,000) in 1983.

ECONOMICALLY ACTIVE POPULATION*
(persons aged 14 years and over, census of 22 October 1980)

	Males	Females	Total
Agriculture, hunting, forestry and fishing	1,123,138	77,854	1,200,992
Mining and quarrying	44,194	2,977	47,171
Manufacturing	1,566,028	429,967	1,985,995
Electricity, gas and water	94,789	8,467	103,256
Construction	981,251	21,924	1,003,175
Wholesale and retail trade, restaurants and hotels	1,221,063	481,017	1,702,080
Transport, storage and communication	424,671	35,805	460,476
Finance, insurance, real estate and business services	265,475	130,229	395,704
Community, social and personal services	1,044,416	1,354,623	2,399,039
Activities not adequately described	494,678	196,624	691,302
Total labour force	7,249,703	2,739,487	9,989,190

* Figures exclude persons seeking work for the first time, totalling 44,608 (males 28,331; females 16,277).
Source: ILO, *Year Book of Labour Statistics*.
Mid-1985 (official estimates): Total labour force 11,467,983 (males 8,375,912; females 3,092,071).

Agriculture

PRINCIPAL CROPS ('000 metric tons)

	1982/83	1983/84	1984/85
Wheat	15,000	13,000	13,300
Rice (paddy)	277	476	400
Barley	180	140	210
Maize	9,000	9,500	12,600
Rye	148	130	140
Oats	637	593	610
Millet	179	136	140
Sorghum	8,100	6,900	6,200
Potatoes	2,013	2,118	n.a.
Sweet potatoes	310	325	n.a.
Cassava (Manioc)	139	n.a.	n.a.
Soybeans	4,000	7,000	6,500
Groundnuts (shelled)	165	230	160
Sunflower seed	2,400	2,200	3,200
Linseed	730	660	550
Seed cotton*	373	593	556
Tomatoes	611	592	n.a.
Onions (dry)	297	n.a.	n.a.
Grapes	3,547	2,746	n.a.
Sugar cane	15,070	15,468	n.a.
Tea (green)	176	178	n.a.
Tobacco (leaves)	74	75	n.a.

* Including cotton lint ('000 metric tons): 111 in 1982/83; 174 in 1983/84.

Sources: Secretaría de Agricultura, Ganadería y Pesca, Comisión Reguladora de la Producción y Comercio de la Yerba Mate.

LIVESTOCK ('000 head)

	1982	1983	1984
Horses	3,000*	3,050†	3,050†
Cattle	52,717	53,200	53,500†
Pigs	3,900*	3,800*	3,800*
Sheep	30,401	30,000	30,000†
Goats	3,000†	2,900†	3,098†

Chickens (million): 42 in 1982; 43† in 1983; 44† in 1984.
Ducks (million): 2 in 1982; 2† in 1983; 2† in 1984.
Turkeys (million): 2 in 1982; 3† in 1983; 3† in 1984.
* Estimate.   † FAO estimate.

LIVESTOCK PRODUCTS ('000 metric tons)

	1982	1983*	1984*
Beef and veal	2,578	2,441	2,570†
Mutton and lamb	113	110	103†
Goats' meat	6†	6‡	6‡
Pig meat	240	207	240†
Horse meat	60	50‡	50‡
Poultry meat	465	440	466‡
Cows' milk	5,613	5,300†	5,200†
Butter	33	34	31†
Cheese	240	248	210†
Hen eggs	299	272	280‡
Wool:			
greasy	153	155†	155‡
scoured	102	104‡	104‡
Cattle hides (fresh)	323	343‡	369‡

* Source: FAO, *Production Yearbook*.
† Unofficial figure.   ‡ FAO estimate.

Forestry

ROUNDWOOD REMOVALS
('000 cubic metres, excl. bark)

	1982	1983	1984
Sawlogs, veneer logs and logs for sleepers	2,275	2,365	2,365
Pulpwood	1,951	2,167	2,167*
Other industrial wood	529	435	435
Fuel wood	6,433	8,354	8,408*
Total	11,188	13,321	13,375

* FAO estimate.
Source: FAO, *Yearbook of Forest Products*.

SAWNWOOD PRODUCTION
('000 cubic metres, incl. boxboards)

	1981	1982	1983
Coniferous (soft wood)	180	269	304
Broadleaved (hard wood)	800	856	866
Total	980	1,125	1,170

Railway sleepers: 67,000 cubic metres in 1981.
1984: Production as in 1983 (FAO estimates).
Source: FAO, *Yearbook of Forest Products*.

Fishing

('000 metric tons, live weight)

	1982*	1983*	1984†
Freshwater fishes	15.3	14.6	9.3
Argentine hake	281.9	257.1	183.2
Other marine fishes	129.4	93.4	66.5
Crustaceans	8.1	19.6	23.4
Argentine shortfin squid	38.8	28.7	29.0
Other molluscs	1.5	3.0	3.4
Total catch	475.0	416.3	314.8

* Source: FAO, *Yearbook of Fishery Statistics*.
† Estimate (Source: Secretaría de Intereses Marítimos).

Mining

	1981	1982	1983
Hard coal ('000 metric tons)	497.6	514.9	485.8
Crude petroleum ('000 cu metres)	28,852	28,470	28,474
Natural gas ('000 terajoules)*	474	539	597
Iron ore ('000 metric tons)*†	249	389	390
Lead ore ('000 metric tons)*†	32.7	32.8	31.7
Zinc ore ('000 metric tons)*†	35.1	36.6	36.6
Tin concentrates (metric tons)*	413	342	291
Silver ore (metric tons)*	78	83	78
Uranium ore (metric tons)*†	123	155	200‡

* Source: UN, *Industrial Statistics Yearbook*.
† Figures refer to the metal content of ores and concentrates.
‡ Estimate.

1984: Hard coal ('000 metric tons) 509.8; Crude petroleum ('000 cu metres) 27,838; Tin concentrates (metric tons) 274.

Industry

SELECTED PRODUCTS

		1982	1983	1984
Edible vegetable oils	'000 metric tons	787.1	1,110.0	1,185.2
Wheat flour	'000 metric tons	2,550.2	2,678.5	2,753.6
Sugar	'000 metric tons	1,485	1,459	1,411.6
Beer and malt	'000 litres	223,805	315,909	407,926
Cigarettes	metric tons	26,930	28,241	30,843
Paper	'000 metric tons	614	675	764
Mechanical wood pulp	'000 metric tons	95	119	121
Chemical and semi-chemical pulp	'000 metric tons	254	432	439
Quebracho extract	'000 metric tons	111	85	66
Rayon and acetate continuous filaments	metric tons	1,609	1,732	2,127
Non-cellulosic continuous filaments	metric tons	19,263	26,833	30,159
Non-cellulosic discontinuous fibres	metric tons	11,987	16,164	20,868
Sulphuric acid	metric tons	250,137	262,238	253,566
Rubber tyres	metric tons	59,363	76,681	86,166
Portland cement	'000 metric tons	5,646	5,683	5,096
Crude steel	'000 metric tons	2,602	2,599	2,671
Ferro-alloys	'000 metric tons	57	59	61
Diesel oil	'000 cu metres	1,161	1,178	1,098
Fuel oil	'000 cu metres	7,362	6,502	6,229
Gas oil	'000 cu metres	7,753	7,759	7,844
Kerosene	'000 cu metres	538	650	566
Passenger motor vehicles	number	109,829	130,647	138,595
Commercial motor vehicles	number	23,857	29,585	28,367
Domestic sewing machines	number	23,414	37,096	41,496
Refrigerators and washing machines	number	312,463	394,983	431,654
Television receivers	number	447,819	335,490	430,090
Plastic footwear	'000 pairs	776	1,370	1,570

ARGENTINA — Statistical Survey

Finance

CURRENCY AND EXCHANGE RATES

Monetary Units:
100 centavos = 1 austral (₳).

Sterling and Dollar Equivalents (30 September 1986)
£1 sterling = 1.535 australes;
US $1 = 1.0605 australes;
100 australes = £65.14 = $94.30.

Average Exchange Rate (australes per US $)
1983   0.01053
1984   0.06765
1985   0.60181

Note: The austral was introduced on 15 June 1985, replacing the peso argentino at the rate of 1 austral = 1,000 pesos argentinos. The peso argentino, equal to 10,000 former pesos, had itself been introduced on 1 June 1983. Some figures in this survey are in terms of pesos argentinos or old pesos.

CENTRAL BANK RESERVES*
(US $ million at 31 December)

	1982	1983	1984
IMF special drawing rights	—	—	1
Reserve position in IMF	100	—	—
Foreign exchange	2,406	1,172	1,242
Total	2,506	1,172	1,243

* Figures exclude reserves of gold, totalling 4,372,000 troy ounces in each year. Based on the former official price of $42.22 per ounce, these reserves were valued at $185 million in 1982.

Source: IMF, *International Financial Statistics*.

BUDGET (million pesos argentinos)*

Revenue	1981	1982	1983
Taxation	7,442	18,890	92,855
Taxes on income, profits, etc.	503	1,292	4,581
Social security contributions	1,455	3,178	17,983
Taxes on property	221	811	3,436
Value-added tax	1,617	4,475	13,822
Excises	2,205	5,354	25,621
Other domestic taxes on goods and services	233	581	1,481
Import duties, etc.	769	1,495	6,726
Export duties	105	1,039	9,504
Foreign exchange conversion tax	95	235	935
Stamp duties	157	369	380
Other tax revenue	82	61	8,386
Operating surpluses of departmental enterprises	176	628	—
Property income	324	763	1,273
Administrative fees and charges, etc.	381	966	2,064
Other current revenue	861	1,961	10,072
Capital revenue	2	13	57
Total revenue	9,186	23,221	106,321

Expenditure†	1981	1982	1983
General public services	1,090	2,420	13,040
Defence	1,403	3,360	13,531
Education	897	1,904	11,369
Health	167	328	2,039
Social security and welfare	4,153	8,714	49,646
Housing	42	176	867
Other community and social services	61	162	702
Economic services	2,201	5,365	33,847
General administration, regulation and research	585	1,078	5,530
Agriculture, forestry and fishing	101	238	1,300
Electricity, gas, steam and water	460	1,391	10,286
Roads	350	881	4,686
Inland and coastal waterways	61	147	882
Other transport and communications	501	1,127	9,997
Other purposes	2,376	6,996	40,623
Interest payments	1,785	6,645	16,566
Sub-total	12,390	29,425	165,664
Adjustment to cash basis	−123	1,063	−16,872
Total expenditure	12,267	30,488	148,792
Current	10,313	26,499	133,623
Capital	1,954	3,989	15,169

Source: IMF, *Government Finance Statistics Yearbook*.

* Figures refer to the consolidated accounts of the central government, including special accounts, government agencies and the national social security system. The budgets of provincial and municipal governments are excluded.

† Excluding net lending (million pesos argentinos): 1,382 in 1981; 3,291 in 1982; 44,524 in 1983.

1984 (estimate, million pesos argentinos): Expenditure 904,719 (current 759,285; capital 145,434).
Source: Secretariat of Foreign Trade.
1985 (estimate, million australes): Revenue 6,778.6; Expenditure 8,611.7.
1986 (estimate, million australes): Revenue 11,674.7; Expenditure 14,312.9.

ARGENTINA

MONEY SUPPLY
(million australes at 31 December)

	1982	1983	1984
Currency outside banks	8.7	46.3	313.4
Demand deposits at commercial banks	6.1	23.6	121.4

Source: IMF, *International Financial Statistics*.

COST OF LIVING
(Consumer Price Index for Buenos Aires. Base: 1974 = 100)

	1982	1983	1984
All items	315,806.5	1,401,577.4	10,185,567.2

NATIONAL ACCOUNTS
Gross Domestic Product by Economic Activity (million old pesos at 1970 prices)

	1982	1983	1984
Agriculture, forestry and fishing	13,579	13,820	14,287
Mining and quarrying	2,458	2,541	2,499
Manufacturing	19,726	21,852	22,747
Construction	4,508	4,202	3,327
Electricity, gas and water	3,381	3,868	4,075
Transport and communications	9,873	10,263	10,682
Trade, restaurants and hotels	11,221	11,584	12,134
Finance	7,463	6,915	7,059
Other services	15,025	15,307	15,550
Total	87,735	90,352	92,360

BALANCE OF PAYMENTS (US $ million)

	1982	1983	1984
Merchandise exports f.o.b.	7,623	7,835	8,100
Merchandise imports f.o.b.	−4,859	−4,119	−4,118
Trade balance	2,764	3,716	3,982
Exports of services	2,132	1,929	1,809
Imports of services	−7,283	−8,097	−8,288
Balance of goods and services	−2,387	−2,452	−2,497
Unrequited transfers (net)	34	16	2
Current balance	−2,353	−2,436	−2,495
Direct capital investment (net)	257	183	268
Other long-term capital (net)	1,808	−757	−1,502
Short-term capital (net)	−4,652	−1,430	1,303
Net errors and omissions	−401	−447	−55
Total (net monetary movements)	−5,341	−4,887	−2,481
Valuation changes	−89	30	−150
Exceptional financing (net)	4,710	2,581	2,453
Official financing (net)	−38	−151	194
Changes in reserves	−758	−2,427	16

Source: IMF, *International Financial Statistics*.

External Trade

PRINCIPAL COMMODITIES (distribution by BTN, US $ '000)

Imports c.i.f.	1982	1983	1984*
Vegetable products	153,138	115,399	136,052
Coffee, tea, maté, etc.	85,577	64,971	64,282
Mineral products	815,550	585,739	613,160
Metallurgical minerals, slag and cinder	91,690	73,756	77,107
Mineral fuels and oils, bituminous substances, etc.	687,864	470,055	490,076
Chemical products	920,163	942,080	1,001,067
Inorganic chemicals, compounds of precious metals, etc.	158,907	126,276	159,154
Organic chemicals and products	402,260	439,085	436,957
Artificial resins and plastics, natural and synthetic rubber, etc.	271,367	298,567	275,339
Artificial resins and plastics, cellulose, etc.	186,342	185,356	178,735
Paper-making material, paper and manufactures	198,228	139,040	90,297
Paper and paper products	99,020	95,374	57,037
Basic metals and manufactures	538,320	486,785	514,171
Iron and steel, and manufactures	375,664	356,089	370,378
Machinery and apparatus, incl. electrical	1,478,263	1,114,594	1,061,103
Boilers, machinery and mechanical appliances	903,059	738,681	668,450
Electrical machinery	575,204	375,913	392,653
Transport equipment	329,554	289,943	349,225
Land vehicles	214,855	198,978	256,215
Sea and river vehicles	31,521	25,450	1,618
Scientific and precision instruments, audiovisual equipment, etc.	196,194	171,995	156,841
Total (incl. others)	5,336,914	4,504,156	4,584,706

* Provisional figures.

Exports f.o.b.	1982	1983	1984*
Live animals and animal products	882,186	679,572	459,992
Meat and edible offal	598,786	430,084	257,012
Vegetable products	2,611,932	3,540,295	3,474,893
Edible fruits	182,455	134,009	106,420
Cereals	1,822,180	2,894,058	2,239,846
Oilseeds and nuts	459,665	365,740	952,472
Animal and vegetable fats and oils	429,326	538,157	930,482
Prepared foodstuffs, beverages and tobacco	884,478	1,148,737	1,114,117
Meat and fish preparations	207,557	173,638	148,487
Sugar and preserves	64,434	186,304	107,508
Residues and waste from food industry; prepared animal fodder	438,617	644,337	723,701
Chemical products	348,944	297,567	270,393
Hides, skins, furs, etc.	364,055	300,057	331,000
Hides and skins	298,290	264,330	304,884
Paper-making material, paper and manufactures	46,967	38,907	42,547
Textiles and manufactures	338,439	224,452	307,328
Wool and other animal hair	233,667	188,007	216,442
Cotton	91,006	25,880	79,077
Base metals and manufactures	514,100	318,358	316,324
Iron and steel and manufactures	351,332	207,201	202,457
Machinery and apparatus, incl. electrical	295,250	180,679	210,889
Boilers, machinery and mechanical appliances	250,371	152,248	177,777
Transport equipment	215,984	92,222	168,207
Land vehicles	112,242	68,351	91,765
Total (incl. others)	7,624,936	7,836,063	8,107,413

* Provisional figures.

ARGENTINA

Statistical Survey

PRINCIPAL TRADING PARTNERS (US $ '000)

Imports c.i.f.	1980	1981	1982
Australia	83,703	123,174	53,904
Belgium/Luxembourg	160,819	105,663	74,965
Bolivia	252,421	343,457	395,678
Brazil	1,072,444	893,237	687,730
Canada	109,772	144,752	55,502
Chile	254,740	189,501	146,602
France	374,419	353,135	196,779
Germany, Federal Republic	984,728	904,771	478,881
Hong Kong	110,997	95,867	17,749
Iraq	127,526	0	—
Italy	576,875	487,970	230,746
Japan	977,265	965,298	429,620
Netherlands	232,629	211,602	97,013
Saudi Arabia	338,712	280,798	153,460
Spain	397,931	319,840	181,433
Sweden	139,887	131,461	76,859
Switzerland	216,184	173,003	132,736
United Kingdom	343,377	322,166	68,531
USA	2,362,523	2,072,614	1,160,436
Uruguay	147,867	120,631	89,852
Total (incl. others)	10,540,603	9,430,226	5,336,914

Exports f.o.b.	1980	1981	1982
Algeria	56,306	41,019	136,583
Bolivia	133,429	125,887	113,933
Brazil	765,018	595,117	567,724
Chile	217,634	188,938	164,064
China, People's Republic	188,792	92,151	136,596
France	186,139	145,190	141,502
Germany, Federal Republic	407,402	354,701	335,904
Iran	86,300	30,829	134,402
Iraq	11,516	36,722	115,499
Italy	520,265	376,407	289,753
Japan	210,849	166,473	283,065
Mexico	121,275	275,317	111,795
Netherlands	716,316	696,750	603,967
Paraguay	189,393	169,246	145,847
Peru	116,522	89,080	109,773
Spain	172,394	194,276	207,943
USSR	1,614,167	2,963,194	1,586,344
United Kingdom	203,438	217,796	73,741
USA	695,998	843,439	1,006,719
Uruguay	182,292	128,119	115,519
Total (incl. others)	8,021,418	9,143,044	7,623,727

Transport

RAILWAYS (traffic)

	1983	1984	1985
Passengers carried (million)	290	291	300
Freight carried ('000 tons)	22,509	19,502	34,436
Passenger-km (million)	10,387	10,469	10,544
Freight ton-km (million)	13,364	11,207	18,981

Source: Ministerio de Obras y Servicios Públicos

ROAD TRAFFIC (motor vehicles in use at 31 December)

	1983	1984	1985
Passenger cars	3,540,000	3,744,000	3,833,000
Commercial vehicles	1,360,000	1,420,000	1,428,000

Source: Asociación de Fábricas de Automotores.

SHIPPING (vessels entering Argentine ports)

	1983	1984	1985
Displacement ('000 net reg. tons)	35,190	33,618	35,605

Source: Ministerio de Obras y Servicios Públicos.

CIVIL AVIATION (traffic)

	1983	1984	1985
Passengers carried ('000)	4,434	4,307	4,724
Freight carried (tons)	44,822	47,286	58,849
Kilometres flown ('000)	73,480	75,400	73,923

Source: Ministerio de Obras y Servicios Públicos.

Tourism

FOREIGN VISITORS BY ORIGIN

	1982	1983	1984
North and South America	1,111,026	1,114,047	1,412,968
Europe	153,243	143,878	147,108
Asia, Africa and Oceania	31,975	55,027	48,131
Total	1,296,244	1,312,952	1,608,207

Source: Dirección Nacional de Migraciones.

Communications Media

	1981	1982	1983
Radio receivers ('000 in use)	n.a.	n.a.	16,000
Television receivers ('000 in use)	5,540	n.a.	5,910
Telephones ('000 in use)	2,767	n.a.	n.a.
Book production*:			
Titles	4,251	4,962	4,216
Copies ('000)	14,190	14,763	13,526
Daily newspapers	n.a.	191	n.a.

* Including pamphlets.
Source: mainly UNESCO, *Statistical Yearbook*.

Education

(1984—provisional)

	Institutions	Students	Teachers
Pre-primary	7,659	654,645	32,785
Primary	23,649	4,631,367	240,398
Secondary	5,104	1,562,276	206,183
Universities*	426	507,994	39,296
Colleges of higher education*	825	169,541	24,934
Other	3,819	430,859	26,766

Source: Ministerio de Educación y Justicia.

Directory

The Constitution

The return to civilian rule in 1983 represented a return to the principles of the 1853 Constitution, with some changes in electoral details. The Constitution is summarized below:

DECLARATIONS, RIGHTS AND GUARANTEES

Each province has the right to exercise its own administration of justice, municipal system and primary education. The Roman Catholic religion, being the faith of the majority of the nation, shall enjoy State protection; freedom of religious belief is guaranteed to all other denominations. All the inhabitants of the country have the right to work and exercise any legal trade; to petition the authorities; to leave or enter the Argentine territory; to use or dispose of their properties; to associate for a peaceable or useful purpose; to teach and acquire education, and to express freely their opinion in the press without censorship. The State does not admit any prerogative of blood, birth, privilege or titles of nobility. Equality is the basis of all duties and public offices. No citizens may be detained, except for reasons and in the manner prescribed by the law; or sentenced other than by virtue of a law existing prior to the offence and by decision of the competent tribunal after the hearing and defence of the person concerned. Private residence, property and correspondence are inviolable. No one may enter the home of a citizen or carry out any search in it without his consent, unless by a warrant from the competent authority; no one may suffer expropriation, except in case of public necessity and provided that the appropriate compensation has been paid in accordance with the provisions of the laws. In no case may the penalty of confiscation of property be imposed.

LEGISLATIVE POWER

Legislative power is vested in the bicameral Congress, comprising the Chamber of Deputies and the Senate. The Chamber of Deputies has 254 directly-elected members, chosen for four years and eligible for re-election; one-half of the membership of the Chamber shall be renewed every two years. The Senate has 46 members, chosen by provincial legislatures for a nine-year term, with one-third of the seats being renewed every three years.

The powers of Congress include regulating foreign trade; fixing import and export duties; levying taxes for a specified time whenever the defence, common safety or general welfare of the State so require; contracting loans on the nation's credit; regulating the internal and external debt and the currency system of the country; fixing the budget and providing for whatever is conducive to the prosperity and welfare of the nation. Congress also approves or rejects treaties, authorizes the Executive to declare war or make peace, and establishes the strength of the armed forces in peace and war.

EXECUTIVE POWER

Executive power is vested in the President, who is the supreme chief of the nation and handles the general administration of the country. The President issues the instructions and rulings necessary for the execution of the laws of the country, and himself takes part in drawing up and promulgating those laws. The President appoints, with the approval of the Senate, the judges of the Supreme Court and all other competent tribunals, ambassadors, civil servants, members of the judiciary and senior officers of the armed forces and bishops. The President may also appoint and remove, without reference to another body, his cabinet ministers. The President is Commander-in-Chief of all the armed forces.

JUDICIAL POWER

Judicial power is exercised by the Supreme Court and all other competent tribunals. The Supreme Court is responsible for the internal administration of all tribunals.

PROVINCIAL GOVERNMENT

The 22 States retain all the power not delegated to the Federal Government. They are governed by their own institutions and elect their own governors, legislators and officials.

The Government

HEAD OF STATE

President of the Republic: Dr RAÚL RICARDO ALFONSÍN FOULKES (took office 10 December 1983).
Vice-President: Dr VÍCTOR MARTÍNEZ.

MINISTERS
(October 1986)

Minister of the Interior: Dr ANTONIO TRÓCCOLI.
Minister of Foreign Affairs and Worship: Lic. DANTE CAPUTO.
Minister of Education and Justice: JULIO RAÚL RAJNERI.
Minister of National Defence: HORACIO JUAN JUANARENA.
Minister of the Economy: JUAN VITAL SOURROUILLE.
Minister of Labour and Social Security: HUGO BARRIONUEVO.
Minister of Public Health and Welfare: CONRADO STORANI.
Minister of Public Works and Services: PEDRO AGUSTÍN TRUCCO.
Secretary-General to the Presidency: CARLOS BECERRA.

MINISTRIES

General Secretariat to the Presidency: Balcarce 50, 1064 Buenos Aires; tel. (1) 46-9841.
Ministry of the Economy: Hipólito Yrigoyen 250, 1310 Buenos Aires; tel. (1) 34-6411; telex 21952.
Ministry of Education and Justice: Pizzurno 935, 1020 Buenos Aires; tel. 42-4551; telex 22646.
Ministry of Foreign Affairs and Worship: Reconquista 1088, 1003 Buenos Aires; tel. (1) 311-0071; telex 21194.

ARGENTINA

Ministry of the Interior: Balcarce 24, 1064 Buenos Aires; tel. (1) 46-9841.
Ministry of Labour and Social Security: Avda Julio A. Roca 609, 1067 Buenos Aires; tel. (1) 33-7888; telex 18007.
Ministry of National Defence: Avda Paseo Colón 255, 1063 Buenos Aires; tel. (1) 30-1561; telex 22200.
Ministry of Public Health and Welfare: Defensa 120, 1345 Buenos Aires; tel. (1) 30-4322; telex 25064.
Ministry of Public Works and Services: Avda 9 de Julio 1925, 1332 Buenos Aires; tel. (1) 37-1339; telex 22577.

President and Legislature

PRESIDENT

Election, 30 October 1983*

Candidates	Votes	%	Seats in electoral college
Dr Raúl Alfonsín Foulkes (Unión Cívica Radical)	7,659,530	51.8	317
Dr Italo Luder (Partido Justicialista—Peronists)	5,936,556	40.2	259
Oscar Alende (Partido Intransigente)	344,434	2.3	2
Others	838,719	5.7	22
Total	14,779,239	100.0	600

* The election on 30 October was for a 600-member presidential electoral college, which met on 30 November to elect the President.

CONGRESS

Cámara de Diputados
(Chamber of Deputies)

President: Dr Juan Carlos Pugliese.
Vice-President: Roberto Pascual Silva.

The Chamber has 254 members, who hold office for a four-year term, with one-half of the seats renewable every two years.

General Election, 3 November 1985*

	Seats
Unión Cívica Radical	130
Partido Justicialista	103
Partido Intransigente	6
Unión del Centro Democrático	3
Others	12
Total	254

* The table indicates the distribution of the total number of seats, following the election for one-half of the membership.

Senado
(Senate)

President: Dr Edison Otero.

The 46 members of the Senate are nominated by the legislative bodies of each province (two Senators for each), with the exception of Buenos Aires, which elects its Senators by means of a special Electoral College. The Senate's term of office is nine years, with one-third of the seats renewable every three years.

Political Organizations

Alianza Federal: Buenos Aires; f. 1983; right-wing; Pres. Francisco Manrique.
Frente de Izquierda Popular: Buenos Aires; left-wing; Leader Jorge Abelardo Ramos.
* Movimiento de Integración y Desarrollo (MID): Buenos Aires; f. 1963; Leader Arturo Frondizi; Vice-Pres. Rogelio Frigerio; 145,000 mems.
Movimiento al Socialismo (MAS): Leaders Rubén Visconti, Luis Zamora; 55,000 mems.

Partido Comunista: Buenos Aires; f.1918; Pres. Athos Fava; Sec.-Gen. Patricio Etchegaray; 76,000 mems.
Partido Demócrata Cristiano (PDC): Buenos Aires; f. 1954; Leader Carlos Auyero; 68,000 mems.
Partido Demócrata Progresista (PDP): Buenos Aires; Leader Rafael Martínez Raymonda; 53,000 mems.
Partido Intransigente: Buenos Aires; f. 1957; left-wing; Leaders Dr Oscar Alende, Lisandro Viale; Sec. Mariano Lorences; 90,000 mems.
* Partido Justicialista: Buenos Aires; Peronist Party; f. 1945; 3m. mems; Pres. Vicente Leónidas Saadi; two factions within party:
   Frente Renovador, Justicia, Democracia y Participación—Frejudepa: f. 1985; reformist wing; Leaders Carlos Saúl Menem, Antonio Cafiero, Carlos Grosso.
   Oficialistas: Leaders José María Vernet, Lorenzo Miguel.
Partido Nacional de Centro: Buenos Aires; f. July 1980; conservative; Leader Raúl Rivanera Carles.
Partido Obrero: Ayacucho 444, Buenos Aires; tel. (1) 46-8463; f. 1982; Trotskyist; Leaders Gregorio Flores, Catalina R. de Guagnini; 61,000 mems.
Partido Popular Cristiano: Leader José Antonio Allende.
Partido Socialista Democrático: Rivadavia 2307, 1034 Buenos Aires; Leader Américo Ghioldi; 39,000 mems.
Partido Socialista Popular: f. 1982; Leaders Guillermo Estévez Boero, Edgardo Rossi; 60,500 mems.
Unión del Centro Democrático (UCD): Buenos Aires; f. Aug. 1980 as coalition of eight minor political organizations to challenge the 'domestic monopoly' of the populist movements; Leader Alvaro Alsogaray.
Unión Cívica Radical (UCR): Buenos Aires; tel. (1) 49-0036; telex 21326; moderate; f. 1890; Leader Dr Raúl Alfonsín Foulkes; First Vice-Pres. César Jaroslavsky; 1,410,000 mems.
Unión para la Nueva Mayoría: Buenos Aires; f. 1986; centre-right; Leader José Antonio Romero Feris.

Other parties include: Alianza Socialista, Confederación Socialista Argentina, Movimiento Línea Popular, Movimiento Popular Neuquino, Partido Bloquista de San Juan, Partido Conservador Popular, Partido Obrero Comunista Marxista-Leninista, Partido Socialista Auténtico and Partido Socialista Unificado.

* In 1985 the Partido Justicialista formed an electoral alliance with the MID and several extra-parliamentary groups known as the **Frente Justicialista de Liberación—Frejuli**.

The following political parties and guerrilla groups are illegal:

Intransigencia y Movilización Peronista: Peronist faction; Leader Nilda Garres.
Partido Peronista Auténtico (PPA): f. 1975; Leaders Mario Firmenich, Óscar Bidegain, Ricardo Obregón Cano (in prison).
Partido Revolucionario de Trabajadores: political wing of the **Ejército Revolucionario del Pueblo (ERP)**; Leader Luis Mattini.
Triple A—Alianza Anticomunista Argentina: extreme right-wing; Leader Aníbal Gordon (in prison).

The dissolution of the Movimiento Peronista Montonero (MPM) was announced in December 1983. Mario Firmenich, the former leader of the MPM, was arrested in Brazil in 1983 and was transferred into the custody of the Argentine authorities in 1984.

Diplomatic Representation

EMBASSIES IN ARGENTINA

Albania: 3 Febrero 1365, 1426 Buenos Aires; tel. (1) 783-2888; telex 22658; Ambassador: Piro Andoni.
Algeria: Montevideo 1889, 1021 Buenos Aires; tel. (1) 22-1271; telex 22467; Ambassador: Abdelmadjid Aouchiche.
Australia: Avda Santa Fé 846, 8°, 1059 Buenos Aires; tel. (1) 312-6841; telex 21946; Ambassador: Keith Douglas-Scott.
Austria: French 3671, 1425 Buenos Aires; tel. (1) 802-7195; telex 18853; Ambassador: Dr Albert Rohan.
Belgium: Defensa 113, 8°, 1065 Buenos Aires; tel. (1) 33-0066; telex 22070; Ambassador: Luc Steyaert.
Bolivia: Corrientes 545, 2°, 1043 Buenos Aires; tel. (1) 45-0082; telex 24362; Ambassador: Eufronio Padilla Caero.

ARGENTINA

Brazil: Arroyo 1142, 1007 Buenos Aires; tel. (1) 44-0035; telex 21158; Ambassador: Carlos F. Duarte Gonçalves da Rocha.

Bulgaria: Manuel Obarrio 2967, 1425 Buenos Aires; tel. (1) 83-7458; telex 21314; Ambassador: Purvan Nikolov Chernev.

Canada: Edif. Brunetta 25°, Suipacha 1111, Casilla 1598, 1368 Buenos Aires; tel. (1) 312-9081; telex 21383; Ambassador: Louise Frechette.

Chile: Tagle 2762, 1425 Buenos Aires; tel. (1) 802-7020; telex 21669; Ambassador: Arturo Fontaine Aldunate.

China, People's Republic: Republiquetas 5349, 1431 Buenos Aires; tel. (1) 52-0084; telex 22871; Ambassador: Shen Yunao.

Colombia: Avda Santa Fé 782, 1°, 1059 Buenos Aires; tel. (1) 312-5538; telex 22254; Ambassador: Vicente Borrego Restrepo.

Costa Rica: Esmeralda 135, 6°, 1035 Buenos Aires; tel. (1) 45-8427; telex 21394; Ambassador: Roberto Morales Valle.

Cuba: Virrey del Pino 1810, 1426 Buenos Aires; tel. (1) 782-9049; telex 22433; Ambassador: Dr Fernando López Muiño.

Czechoslovakia: Figueroa Alcorta 3240, 1425 Buenos Aires; tel. (1) 801-3804; telex 22748; Ambassador: Ján Jurista.

Denmark: Avda Leandro N. Alem 1074, 9°, 1001 Buenos Aires; tel. (1) 312-7680; telex 22173; Ambassador: F. Aasberg-Petersen.

Dominican Republic: Avda Santa Fé 1206, 2°, 1059 Buenos Aires; tel. (1) 41-4669; Ambassador: Cirilio José Castellanos.

Egypt: Callao 1033, 2°, 1023 Buenos Aires; tel. (1) 41-5455; Ambassador: Mustafa Mohamed Tawfik.

El Salvador: Florida 868, 12°, 1005 Buenos Aires; tel. (1) 312-3444; Ambassador: Carlos Humberto Figueroa.

Finland: Avda Santa Fé 846, 5°, 1059 Buenos Aires; tel. (1) 312-0600; telex 21702; Ambassador: Esko Rajakoski.

France: Cerrito 1399, 1010 Buenos Aires; tel. (1) 393-1071; telex 24300; Ambassador: Antoine Blanca.

Gabon: Avda Figueroa Alcorta 3221, 1425 Buenos Aires; tel. (1) 801-9840; telex 18577; Ambassador: J.-B. Eyi-Nkoumou.

German Democratic Republic: Olazábal 2201-51, 1428 Buenos Aires; tel. (1) 781-2002; telex 21786; Ambassador: Horst Neumann.

Germany, Federal Republic: Villanueva 1055, 1426 Buenos Aires; tel. (1) 771-5054; telex 21668; Ambassador: Hans Werner Graf Finck von Finckenstein.

Greece: Avda Roque Sáenz Peña 547, 4°, 1352 Buenos Aires; tel. (1) 34-4958; telex 22426; Ambassador: Dimitri Manolatos.

Guatemala: Lavalle 1759, 6° B, 1048 Buenos Aires; tel. (1) 46-4647; Ambassador: Prof. Carlos Humberto Pacay y Pacay.

Haiti: Esmeralda 626, 3° A, 1405 Buenos Aires; tel. (1) 392-1868; Ambassador: Ives François.

Holy See: Avda Alvear 1605, 1014 Buenos Aires; tel. (1) 42-9697; telex 17406; Apostolic Nuncio: Monsignor Ubaldo Calabresi.

Honduras: Avda Roque Sáenz Peña 336, 2°, 1020 Buenos Aires; tel. (1) 40-0484; telex 18008; Ambassador: Carlos Villanueva Doblado.

Hungary: Coronel Díaz 1874, 1425 Buenos Aires; tel. (1) 824-5845; telex 22843; Ambassador: Marton Klein.

India: Paraguay 580, 3°, 1057 Buenos Aires; tel. (1) 31-3020; telex 23413; Ambassador: Mrs Soonu Kochar.

Indonesia: M. Ramón Castilla 2901, 1425 Buenos Aires; tel. (1) 801-6622; telex 21781; Ambassador: Anak Agung Gede Oke Djelantik.

Iran: Avda Libertador 2257, 1425 Buenos Aires; tel. (1) 802-1468; Ambassador: Seyed Abbas Salary.

Iraq: La Pampa 3330, 1430 Buenos Aires; tel. (1) 552-6565; telex 17134; Chargé d'affaires: Adel Ahmed Zaidan.

Ireland: Avda Santa Fé 1391, 4°, 1059 Buenos Aires; tel. (1) 44-9987; telex 17654 Ambassador: Patrick A. Walshe.

Israel: Arroyo 916, 1007 Buenos Aires; tel. (1) 392-4481; telex 17106; Ambassador: Dov. B. Schmorak.

Italy: Avda San Martín 2100, Buenos Aires; tel. (1) 83-00-71; telex 21961; Ambassador: Uberto Bozzini.

Japan: Azcuénaga 1035, Casilla 4595, 1115 Buenos Aires; tel. (1) 83-1031; telex 22516; Ambassador: Senkuro Saiki.

Korea, Republic: Coronel Díaz 2860, 1425 Buenos Aires; tel. (1) 802-2737; Ambassador: Soo Woo Ryee.

Lebanon: Avda Libertador 2354, 1425 Buenos Aires; tel. (1) 802-4493; telex 22866; Ambassador: Edmond Khayat.

Libya: Posadas 1650, 3°, 1112 Buenos Aires; tel. (1) 41-1620; telex 22682; Chargé d'affaires: (vacant).

Mexico: Larrea 1230, 1117 Buenos Aires; tel. (1) 826-2161; telex 21869; Ambassador: Ignacio Ovalle Fernández.

Morocco: Calle Mariscal Ramón Castilla No. 2952, CP 1425, Buenos Aires; tel. (1) 801-8154; telex 18161; Ambassador: (vacant).

Netherlands: Edif. Holanda 2°, Maipú 66, 1084 Buenos Aires; tel. (1) 33-6066; telex 21824; Ambassador: Eduard O. van Suchtelen.

Nicaragua: Montevideo 373, 6°, 1019 Buenos Aires; tel. (1) 45-0732; telex 23481; Ambassador: Ernesto Mejía Sánchez.

Nigeria: 3 de febrero 1365, 1462 Buenos Aires; tel. (1) 783-288; telex 23565; Ambassador: J. A. Fakayode.

Norway: Esmeralda 909, 3°, Casilla 2286, 1000 Buenos Aires; tel. (1) 312-2204; Ambassador: Arne Kapstö.

Pakistan: Avda Alvear 1402, Buenos Aires; tel. (1) 22-0355; Ambassador: Raja Tridiv Roy.

Panama: Montevideo 373, 6°, 1019 Buenos Aires; tel. (1) 49-2621; Ambassador: Roberto Puello Araúz.

Paraguay: Las Heras 2545, 1425 Buenos Aires; tel. (1) 802-4948; telex 21687; Ambassador: Dr Antonio Masulli Fuster.

Peru: Avda Libertador 1720, 1425 Buenos Aires; tel. (1) 802-6427; telex 17807; Ambassador: Alfonso Grados Bertorini.

Philippines: Juramento 1945, 1428 Buenos Aires; tel. (1) 781-4170; Ambassador: (vacant).

Poland: Alejandro María de Aguado 2870, 1425 Buenos Aires; tel. (1) 802-9681; Ambassador: Jan Janiszewski.

Portugal: Córdoba 315, 3°, 1054 Buenos Aires; tel. (1) 31-2586; telex 22736; Ambassador: (vacant).

Romania: Arroyo 962, 1007 Buenos Aires; tel. (1) 393-0883; telex 24301; Ambassador: Gheorghe Apostol.

Saudi Arabia: Alejandro María de Aguado 2881, 1425 Buenos Aires; tel. (1) 802-4735; telex 23291; Ambassador: Fuad A. Nazir.

South Africa: Marcelo T. de Alvear 590, 8°, 1058 Buenos Aires; tel. (1) 311-8991; telex 24549; (diplomatic relations broken off May 1986).

Spain: Mariscal Ramón Castilla 2720, 1425 Buenos Aires; tel. (1) 802-6031; telex 21660; Ambassador: José Luis Messía.

Sweden: Corrientes 330, 3°, 1378 Buenos Aires; tel. (1) 311-3088; telex 21340; Ambassador: Ethel Wiklund.

Switzerland: Avda Santa Fé 846, 12°, 1059 Buenos Aires; tel. (1) 311-6491; telex 22418; Ambassador: Jean-Pierre Keusch.

Syria: Calloa 956, 1023 Buenos Aires; tel. (1) 42-2113; Ambassador: Abdel Salam Akil.

Thailand: Virrey del Pino 2458, 6°, 1426 Buenos Aires; tel. (1) 785-6504; Ambassador: Sirajaya Buddhi-Baedya.

Turkey: Avda Roque Sáenz Peña 852, 1035 Buenos Aires; tel. (1) 46-8779; telex 21135; Ambassador: Gündüz Tunçbilek.

USSR: Avda Roque Sáenz Peña 1741, 1021 Buenos Aires; tel. (1) 42-1552; telex 22147; Ambassador: Oleg Kvasov.

USA: Avda Colombia 4300, Palermo, 1425 Buenos Aires; tel. (1) 774-7611; telex 18156; Ambassador: Theodore E. Gildred.

Uruguay: Avda Las Heras 1907, 1127 Buenos Aires; tel. (1) 821-6032; telex 25526; Ambassador: Luis Barrios Tassano.

Venezuela: Avda Santa Fé 1461, 7°, 1060 Buenos Aires; tel. (1) 42-0033; telex 21089; Ambassador: Jorge Dager.

Yugoslavia: Marcelo T. de Alvear 1705, 1060 Buenos Aires; tel. (1) 41-2860; telex 21479; Ambassador: Filip Matić.

Zaire: Villanueva 1356, 2°, Casilla 5589, 1426 Buenos Aires; tel. (1) 771-0075; telex 22324; Ambassador: Kamanda Ngongo.

Judicial System

SUPREME COURT

Corte Suprema: Talcahuano 550, 4°, 1013 Buenos Aires; tel. (1) 40-1540.

All members of the Supreme Court are appointed by the Executive, with the agreement of the Senate. Members are dismissed by impeachment.

President: Dr José Severo Caballero.

Justices: Enrique Santiago Petracchi, Carlos Santiago Fayt, Augusto César Belluscio.

Attorney-General: Juan Octavio Gauna.

ARGENTINA   Directory

OTHER COURTS

Judges of the lower, national or further lower courts are appointed by the President, with the agreement of the Senate, and are dismissed by impeachment.

The Federal Court of Appeal in Buenos Aires has three courts: civil and commercial, criminal, and administrative. There are six other courts of appeal in Buenos Aires: civil, commercial, criminal, peace, labour, and penal-economic. There are also federal appeal courts in: La Plata, Bahía Blanca, Paraná, Rosario, Córdoba, Mendoza, Tucumán and Resistencia.

The provincial courts each have their own Supreme Court and a system of subsidiary courts. They deal with cases originating within and confined to the provinces.

Religion

CHRISTIANITY

More than 90% of the population are Roman Catholics and about 2% are Protestants.

The Roman Catholic Church

Argentina comprises 13 archdioceses, 44 dioceses (including one for Catholics of the Ukrainian rite) and three territorial prelatures. The Archbishop of Buenos Aires is also the Ordinary for Catholics of Oriental rites.

Bishops' Conference: Conferencia Episcopal Argentina, Calle Paraguay 1867, 1121 Buenos Aires; tel. (1) 42-5708; f. 1973; Pres. Cardinal RAÚL FRANCISCO PRIMATESTA, Archbishop of Córdoba.

Armenian Rite

Apostolic Exarch of Latin America: VARTAN WALDIR BOGHOSSIAN (Titular Bishop of Mardin), Exarcado Apostólico Armenia, Charcas 3529, 1425 Buenos Aires; tel. (1) 824-1613.

Latin Rite

Archbishop of Bahía Blanca: JORGE MAYER, Avda Colón 164, 8000 Bahía Blanca; tel. (091) 22-070.

Archbishop of Buenos Aires: Cardinal JUAN CARLOS ARAMBURU, Arzobispado, Rivadavia 415, 1002 Buenos Aires; tel. (1) 30-3408.

Archbishop of Córdoba: Cardinal RAÚL FRANCISCO PRIMATESTA, Hipólito Yrigoyen 98, 500 Córdoba; tel. (051) 38-942.

Archbishop of Corrientes: FORTUNATO ANTONIO ROSSI, 9 de Julio 1543, 3400 Corrientes; tel. (0783) 22-436.

Archbishop of La Plata: ANTONIO JOSÉ PLAZA, Calle 14, No 1009, 1900 La Plata; tel. (021) 21-8286.

Archbishop of Mendoza: CÁNDIDO GENARO RUBIOLO, Catamarca 98, 5500 Mendoza; tel. (061) 233-862.

Archbishop of Paraná: ADOLFO SERVANDO TORTOLO, Monte Caseros 77, 3100 Paraná; tel. (043) 211-440.

Archbishop of Resistencia: JUAN JOSÉ IRIARTE, Bartolomé Mitre 363, Casilla 35, 3500 Resistencia; tel. (0711) 26867.

Archbishop of Rosario: JORGE MANUEL LÓPEZ, Córdoba 1677, 2000 Rosario; tel. (041) 21-5175.

Archbishop of Salta: MOISÉS JULIO BLANCHOUD, España 596, 4400 Salta; tel. (087) 214-306.

Archbishop of San Juan de Cuyo: ITALO SEVERINO DI STEFANO, Bartolomé Mitre 240, Oeste, 5400 San Juan de Cuyo; tel. (064) 22-6261.

Archbishop of Santa Fé: EDGARDO GABRIEL STORNI, Avda General López 2720, 3000 Santa Fé; tel. (042) 35-791.

Archbishop of Tucumán: HORACIO ALBERTO BÓZZOLI, Avda Sarmiento 895, 4000 Tucumán; tel. (081) 22-6345.

Ukrainian Rite

Bishop of Santa María del Patrocinio en Buenos Aires: ANDRÉS SAPELAK, Ramón L. Falcón 3350, Casilla 28, 1407 Buenos Aires; tel. (1) 67-4192.

Protestant Churches

Federación Argentina de Iglesias Evangélicas (Argentine Federation of Evangelical Churches): Tucumán 358-6L, Buenos Aires; f. 1958; 41 denominations; Chair. Rev. LUIS P. BUCAFUSCO.

Baptist Evangelical Convention: Rivadavia 3476, 1203 Buenos Aires; tel. (1) 88-8924; Pres. Rev. Dr CARLOS CARAMUTTI.

Iglesia Evangélica Congregacionalista (Evangelical Congregational Church): Calle F. Soler 525, 3100 Paraná; f. 1924; 98 congregations, 9,500 mems, 24,000 adherents; Supt Rev. GERARDO ARNDT.

Iglesia Evangélica Luterana Argentina: Concordia 3095, 1417 Buenos Aires; tel. (1) 53-3480; 25,479 mems; Pres. LEOPOLDO GROS.

Iglesia Evangélica del Río de la Plata: Esmeralda 162, 1035 Buenos Aires; tel. (1) 45-7520; f. 1899; 60,000 mems; Pres. RODOLFO R. REINICH.

Iglesia Evangélica Metodista Argentina (Methodist Church of Argentina): Rivadavia 4044, 1205 Buenos Aires; tel. (1) 982-3712; f. 1836; 7,454 mems; 40,000 adherents; seven regional superintendents; Bishop FEDERICO J. PAGURA; Admin. HUMBERTO SHIKIYA; Chair. Gen. Board of Life and Mission Rev. PABLO ANDIÑACH.

JUDAISM

Delegación de Asociaciones Israelitas Argentinas—DAIA (Delegation of Argentine Jewish Associations): Pasteur 633, 5°, Buenos Aires; f. 1935; there are about 400,000 Jews, mostly in Buenos Aires; Pres. Dr DAVID GOLDBERG; Sec.-Gen. Lic. EDGARDO A. GORENBER.

BAHÁ'Í FAITH

National Spiritual Assembly: Otamendi 215, 2°, 1405 Buenos Aires; tel. (1) 90-1078; telex 9900; mems resident in 330 localities.

The Press

Under military rule, the press was subjected to unofficial censorship. However, following the election of President Raúl Alfonsín and the appointment of a civilian government in December 1983, press freedom was fully restored.

PRINCIPAL DAILIES

Buenos Aires

Ambito Financiero: Carabelas 241, 3°, 1009 Buenos Aires; tel. (1) 35-1621; f. 1976; morning (Mon.–Fri.); business; Dir JULIO A. RAMOS.

Buenos Aires Herald: Azopardo 455, 1107 Buenos Aires; tel. (1) 34-8477; f. 1876; English; morning; independent; Man. Editor DAN NEWLAND; circ. 20,000.

Boletín Oficial de la República Argentina: Suipacha 767, 1008 Buenos Aires; tel. (1) 392-4485; f. 1893; morning (Mon.–Fri.); official records publication; Dir EDUARDO MASCHWITZ.

Clarín: Piedras 1743, 1140 Buenos Aires; tel. (1) 27-0061; f. 1945; morning; independent; Dir Sra ERNESTINA LAURA HERRERA DE NOBLE; circ. 480,000 (daily), 750,000 (Sunday).

Crónica: Garay 130, 1063 Buenos Aires; tel. (1) 361-1001; f. 1963; morning and evening; Dir MARIO ALBERTO FERNÁNDEZ (morning), RICARDO GANGEME (evening); circ. 330,000 (morning), 190,000 (evening), 450,000 (Sunday).

El Cronista Comercial: Alsina 547, 1087 Buenos Aires; tel. (1) 33-3015; f. 1908; morning; Editor DANIEL DELLA COSTA; circ. 100,000.

Diario Popular: Beguerestain 182, 1870 Avellaneda, Buenos Aires; tel. (1) 204-6056; f. 1974; morning; Dir ALBERTO ALBERTENGO; circ. 145,000.

La Gaceta: Beguerestain 182, Avellaneda, Buenos Aires; Dir RICARDO WEST OCAMPO; circ. 35,000.

La Nación: Bouchard 557, 1106 Buenos Aires; tel. (1) 313-1003; telex 18558; f. 1870; morning; independent; Dir BARTOLOMÉ MITRE; circ. 210,648.

La Prensa: Avda de Mayo 567, 1319 Buenos Aires; tel. (1) 33-1001; f. 1869; by José C. Paz; morning; independent; Dir MÁXIMO GAINZA; circ. 65,000.

La Razón: Gral Hornos 690, 1272 Buenos Aires; tel. (1) 26-9051; f. 1905; morning and evening; Exec. Dir PATRICIO PERALTA RAMOS; circ. 180,000.

The Southern Cross: Medrano 107, 1178 Buenos Aires; tel. (1) 983-1371; f. 1875; Dir P. FEDERICO RICHARDS.

Tiempo Argentino: Lafayette 1910, 1286 Buenos Aires; tel. (1) 28-1929; telex 22276; Editor Dr TOMÁS LEONA; circ. 75,000.

La Voz: Tabaré 1641, 1437 Buenos Aires; tel. (1) 922-3800; Dir VICENTE LEÓNIDAS SAADI.

PRINCIPAL PROVINCIAL DAILIES

Bahía Blanca

La Nueva Provincia: Sarmiento 60, 8000 Bahía Blanca, Provincia de Buenos Aires; tel. 20201; telex 81826; f. 1898; morning;

ARGENTINA

independent; Dir Diana Julio de Massot; circ. 38,000 (weekdays), 58,000 (Sunday).

Catamarca
El Sol: Esquiú 551, 4700 San Francisco del Valle de Catamarca; tel. 23844; f. 1973; morning; Dir Tomás Nicolás Alvarez Saavedra.

Comodoro Rivadavia
Crónica: Namuncurá 122, 9000 Comodoro Rivadavia, Provincia del Chubut; tel. 26015; telex 86996; f. 1962; morning; Dir Dr Diego Joaquín Zamit; circ. 10,000.

Concordia
El Heraldo: Quintana 46, 3200 Concordia; tel. (045) 215304; telex 46508; f. 1915; evening; Editor Dr Carlos Liebermann; circ. 8,500.

Córdoba
Comercio y Justicia: Mariano Moreno 378, 5000 Córdoba; tel. 33788; telex 51563; f. 1939; morning; economic and legal news; Editor Jorge Raúl Eguía; circ. 10,000.

Córdoba: Santa Rosa 167, 5000 Córdoba; tel. (051) 22072; f. 1928; evening; Dir Gustavo Alonso Obieta; circ. 25,000.

La Voz del Interior: Avda Colón 37/39, 5000 Córdoba; tel. (051) 28836; f. 1904; morning; independent; Dir Prof. Adelmo R. Montenegro; circ. 87,530.

Corrientes
El Liberal: 25 de Mayo 1345, 3400 Corrientes; tel. (0783) 22069; f. 1909; evening; Dir Juan Francisco Torrent.

El Litoral: H. Yrigoyen 990, 3400 Corrientes; tel. (0783) 22264; f. 1960; morning; Dir Gabriel Feris; circ. 25,000.

La Plata
El Día: Avda Ameghino Diagonal 80, No 817/21, 1900 La Plata, Provincia de Buenos Aires; tel. 21-0101; f. 1884; morning; independent; Dir Raúl E. Kraiselburd; circ. 54,868.

Gaceta: Calle 46, No 423, 1900 La Plata; tel. 21-6477; f. 1963; evening; Dir Juan Carlos Mohamed.

Mar del Plata
El Atlántico: Bolívar 2975, 7600 Mar del Plata, Provincia de Buenos Aires; tel. 3-5462; f. 1938; morning; Dir Oscar Alberto Gastiarena; circ. 20,000.

La Capital: Avda Champagnat 2551, 7600 Mar del Plata, Provincia de Buenos Aires; tel. 77-1164; telex 39884; f. 1905; Dir Tomás R. Stegagnini; circ. 32,000.

Mendoza
Los Andes: San Martín 1049, 5500 Mendoza; tel. (061) 2-44500; f. 1882; morning; independent; Dir Elcira V. Schiappa de Azevedo; circ. 60,662.

Mendoza: San Martín 947, 5500 Mendoza; tel. (061) 2-41064; f. 1969; Dir Alfredo Ortiz Barili; circ. 6,670.

Paraná
El Diario: Buenos Aires y Urquiza, 3100 Paraná, Entre Ríos; tel. 21-0082; f. 1914; morning; democratic; Dir Luis F. Etchevehere; circ. 18,000.

Quilmes, B.A.
El Sol: H. Yrigoyen 122, Quilmes 1878; tel. 253-4595; f. 1927; Dir José María Ghisani; circ. 25,000.

Resistencia
El Territorio: Casilla 320, Carlos Pellegrini 211/231, 3500 Resistencia; f. 1919; morning; Dir Raúl Andrés Aguirre; circ. 15,000.

La Rioja
El Sol: 25 de Mayo 76, 5300 La Rioja; tel. 32-4762; f. 1972; evening; Dir Jose Ricardo Furey.

Río Negro
Río Negro: Gral Roca (8332), Río Negro; tel. (0941) 22021; f. 1912; morning; Editor James Neilson.

Rosario
La Capital: Sarmiento 763, 2000 Rosario, Santa Fé; tel. 392-2193; f. 1867; morning; independent; Dir Carlos Ovidio Lagos; circ. 93,920.

Salta
El Tribuno: Ruta 68 1592, 4400 Salta; tel. 22-1199; telex 65126; f. 1949; morning; Dir Juan Carlos Romero; circ. 37,773.

San Juan
Diario de Cuyo: Mendoza 380 Sur, 5400 San Juan; tel. 29680; f. 1947; morning; independent; Dir Francisco Montes; circ. 25,000.

Tribuna de la Tarde: Mitre 85 Oeste, 5400 San Juan; tel. 40-0923; f. 1931; evening; Dir Dante Américo Montes.

Santa Fé
Hoy: 1° de Mayo 2820, 3000 Santa Fé; f. 1986; Dir Andrés Saavedra; circ. 30,000.

El Litoral: San Martín 2651-59, 3000 Santa Fé; tel. (041) 20101; f. 1918; morning; independent; Dir Enzo Vittori; circ. 40,000.

Santiago del Estero
El Liberal: Libertad 263, 4200 Santiago del Estero; tel. 21-4202; f. 1898; morning; Editor Dr Antonio Castiglione; circ. 24,766.

Tucumán
La Gaceta: Mendoza 654, 4000 San Miguel de Tucumán; tel. 219260; telex 61208; f. 1912; morning; independent; Dir Eduardo García Hamilton; circ. 80,552.

La Tarde: Mendoza 654, San Miguel de Tucumán 4000; tel. 219260; telex 61208; f. 1981; evening; Dir Enrique R. García Hamilton.

PERIODICALS

Aeroespacio: Casilla 37, Sucursal 12B, 1412 Buenos Aires; tel. (1) 392-2753; telex 21763; f. 1931; bi-monthly; aeronautics; Dir José Cándido D'Odorico; circ. 29,000.

ARS, Revista de Arte: Rodríguez Peña 339, 9°A, Buenos Aires; annually; art magazine; Dir Dr I. I. Schlagman.

Billiken: Azopardo 579, 1307 Buenos Aires; tel. (1) 30-7040; telex 21163; f. 1919; weekly; children's magazine; Dir Carlos Silveyra; circ. 240,000.

Canal TV: Azopardo 579, 1307 Buenos Aires; weekly; television guide.

Casas y Jardines (Houses and Gardens): Sarmiento 643, 1382 Buenos Aires; tel. (1) 45-1793; f. 1932; every 2 months; publ. by Editorial Contémpora SRL; Dir Norberto M. Muzio.

Chacra & Campo Moderno: Editorial Atlántida SA, Azopardo 579, 1307 Buenos Aires; tel. (1) 33-4591; telex 121163; f. 1930; monthly; farm and country magazine; Dir Constancio C. Vigil; circ. 35,000.

Claudia: Avda Leandro N. Alem 896, 1001 Buenos Aires; tel. (1) 312-6010; telex 9229; f. 1957; monthly; women's magazine; Dir Mercedes Marques; circ. 17,100.

El Derecho: Tucumán 1436, 1050 Buenos Aires; tel. (1) 45-3302; law.

Desarrollo Económico-Revista de Ciencias Sociales: Güemes 3950, 1425 Buenos Aires; tel. (1) 71-3738; publication of Instituto de Desarrollo Económico y Social; circ. 2,500.

El Economista: Avda Córdoba 632, 1054 Buenos Aires; tel. (1) 392-3308; f. 1951; weekly; financial; Dir Dr D. Radonjic; circ. 33,000.

Gente: Azopardo 579, 3°, 1307 Buenos Aires; tel. (1) 33-4591; telex 21163; f. 1965; weekly; general; Dir Jorge de Luján Gutiérrez; circ. 133,000.

El Gráfico: Azopardo 579, 1307 Buenos Aires; tel. (1) 33-4591; f. 1919; weekly; sport; Dir Constancio C. Vigil; circ. 127,000.

Humor: Salta 258, 1074 Buenos Aires; tel. (1) 38-2223; telex 21976; f. 1978; every 2 weeks; satirical revue; Editor Andrés Casciolli; circ. 79,000.

Jurisprudencia Argentina: Talcahuano 636, 1013 Buenos Aires; tel. (1) 40-7850; f. 1918; weekly; law; Dir Ricardo Estévez Boero; circ. 10,000.

Legislación Argentina: Talcahuano 650, 1013 Buenos Aires; tel. (1) 40-0528; f. 1958; Dir Ricardo Estévez Boero; circ. 15,000.

Mercado: Perú 263, 2°, 1067 Buenos Aires; tel. (1) 34-6713; f. 1969; weekly; commerce; Dir Alberto Borrini.

Mundo Israelita: Lavalle 2615, 1°, 1052 Buenos Aires; tel. (1) 47-7999; f. 1923; weekly; Editor Lic. Eftaj Tregerman; circ. 26,000.

Nuestra Arquitectura (Our Architecture): Sarmiento 643, 5°, 1382 Buenos Aires; tel. (1) 45-1793; f. 1929; every 2 months; publ. by Editorial Contémpora SRL; Dir Norberto M. Muzio.

Nueva Presencia: Castelli 330, 1032 Buenos Aires; tel. (1) 89-2727; weekly; Editor Herman Schiller.

Para Ti: Azopardo 579, 1307 Buenos Aires; tel. (1) 33-4591; f. 1922; weekly; women's interest; Dir Aníbal C. Vigil; circ. 104,000.

Pensamiento Económico: Avda Leandro N. Alem 36, 1003

ARGENTINA

Buenos Aires; tel. (1) 33-8051; f. 1925; every 3 months; review of Cámara Argentina de Comercio; Dir Lic. PEDRO NAÓN ARGERICH.

Perfil: Sarmiento 1113, 1041 Buenos Aires; tel. (1) 35-2552; telex 18213; Editor DANIEL PLINER.

La Prensa Médica Argentina: Junín 845, 1113 Buenos Aires; tel. (1) 83-9796; f. 1914; every 2 weeks; medical; Editor Dr P. A. LÓPEZ; circ. 8,000.

Prensa Obrera: Ayacucho 444, Buenos Aires; tel. (1) 46-8463; weekly; publication of Partido Obrero; circ. 16,000.

Review of the River Plate: Austria 1828, 1425 Buenos Aires; tel. (1) 982-4961; f. 1891; 3 a month; agricultural, financial, economic and shipping news and comment; Dir ARCHIBALD B. NORMAN; circ. 3,500.

Satiricon: Buenos Aires; satirical review; circ. 28,000.

La Semana: Sarmiento 1113, 1041 Buenos Aires; tel. (1) 35-2552; telex 18213; general; Editor DANIEL PLINER.

La Semana Médica: Arenales 3574, 1425 Buenos Aires; tel. (1) 824-5673; f. 1894; weekly; Dir Prof. Dr GUILLERMO R. JÁUREGUI; circ. 7,500.

Siete Días: Avda Leandro N. Alem 896, 1001 Buenos Aires; tel. (1) 32-6010; f. 1967; weekly; general; Dir RICARDO CÁMARA.

Somos: Azopardo 579, 1307 Buenos Aires; tel. (1) 33-4591; f. 1976; weekly; general; anti-Peronist; Dir ANÍBAL C. VIGIL; circ. 21,000.

Técnica e Industria (Technology and Industry): Rodríguez Peña 486, 10°, 1020 Buenos Aires; tel. (1) 49-0572; f. 1922; monthly; Dir E. R. FEDELE; circ. 5,000.

Visión: Montevideo 496, 6°, 1019 Buenos Aires; tel. (1) 49-3652; telex 21926; f. 1950; every 2 weeks; Latin American affairs, politics; Dir Dr MARIANO GRONDONA.

Vosotras: Avda Leandro N. Alem 896, 3°, 1001 Buenos Aires; tel. (1) 32-6010; f. 1935; women's weekly; Dir ABEL ZANOTTO; circ. 33,000. Monthly supplements: **Labores:** circ. 130,000; **Modas:** circ. 70,000.

NEWS AGENCIES

Agencia TELAM SA: Bolívar 531, 1066 Buenos Aires; tel. (1) 34-2162; telex 21077; Editor-in-Chief MARIO R. MONTEVERDE.

Diarios y Noticias (DYN): Chacabuco 314, 6°, 1069 Buenos Aires; tel. (1) 33-3971; telex 23058; Dir JORGE CARLOS BRINSEK.

Noticias Argentinas SA (NA): Chacabuco 314, 8°, 1069 Buenos Aires; tel. (1) 33-8688; telex 18363; f. 1973; Dir RAÚL EDUARDO GARCÍA.

Foreign Bureaux

Agence France-Presse (AFP): Avda Corrientes 456, 6°, Of. 61/62, 1366 Buenos Aires; tel. (1) 394-0371; telex 24349; Bureau Chief JEAN-PIERRE GALLOIS.

Agencia EFE (Spain): Guido 1770, 1016 Buenos Aires; tel. (1) 41-0666; telex 17568; Bureau Chief JESÚS FONSECA ESCARTÍN.

Agenzia Nazionale Stampa Associata (ANSA) (Italy): Calle San Martín 320, 6°, 1004 Buenos Aires; tel. (1) 394-7582; telex 24214; Bureau Chief VINCENZO FIASCHITELLO.

Associated Press (AP) (USA): Bouchard 551, 5°, Casilla 1296, 1106 Buenos Aires; tel. (1) 311-0081; telex 121053; Bureau Chief WILLIAM H. HEATH.

Deutsche Presse-Agentur (dpa) (Federal Republic of Germany): Avda Corrientes 456, 10°, Of. 104, 1366 Buenos Aires; tel. (1) 394-0990; Bureau Chief GERD REUTER.

Inter Press Service (IPS) (Italy): Perú 590, 10°, Of. C, 1068 Buenos Aires; tel. (1) 34-7124; telex 24712; Correspondent GUSTAVO CAPDEVILLA.

Prensa Latina (Cuba): Corrientes 456, 2°, Of. 27, Buenos Aires; tel. (1) 394-0565; telex 24410; Correspondent ELMER RODRÍGUEZ MENÉNDEZ.

Reuters (UK): Avda Eduardo Madero 940, 25°, 1106 Buenos Aires; tel. (1) 394-0561; Chief Correspondent J. REICHERTZ.

Telegrafnoye Agentstvo Sovetskovo Soyuza (TASS) (USSR): Avda Córdoba 652, 11°'E', 1054 Buenos Aires; tel. (1) 392-2044; Dir ISIDORO GILBERT.

United Press International (UPI) (USA): Casilla 796, Correo Central 1000, Avda Belgrano 271, 1092 Buenos Aires; tel. (1) 34-5501; telex 350-1225; Dir ALBERTO J. SCHAZÍN.

Xinhua News Agency (People's Republic of China): Calle Tucumán 540, 14°, Apto D, 1049 Buenos Aires; tel. (1) 313-9755; telex 23643; Bureau Chief JU QINGDONG.

The following are also represented: Central News Agency (Taiwan), Interpress (Poland), Jiji Press (Japan).

Directory

PRESS ASSOCIATION

Asociación de Entidades Periodísticas Argentinas: Esmeralda 356, 1035 Buenos Aires.

Publishers

Editorial Abril, SA: Avda Belgrano 1580, 4°, 1093 Buenos Aires; tel. (1) 37-7355; telex 22630; f. 1961; fiction, non-fiction, children's books, textbooks; Dir ADOLFO F. NERPITI.

Editorial Acme SA: Santa Magdalena 632, 1277 Buenos Aires; tel. (1) 28-2014; f. 1949; general fiction, children's books, agriculture, textbooks; Man. Dir EDUARDO A. EDERRA.

Editorial Alfa Argentina SA: Defensa 599, 3°, 1065 Buenos Aires; tel. (1) 33-1199; f. 1971; general fiction, literature, philosophy, psychology; textbooks; Man. Dir LEONARDO MILLA.

Aguilar Argentina SA de Ediciones: Balcarce 363, 1064 Buenos Aires; tel. (1) 30-1197; f. 1946; general non-fiction; Man. Dir MANUEL RODRÍGUEZ.

Editorial Albatros, SACI: Hipólito Yrigoyen 3920, 1208 Buenos Aires; tel. (1) 981-1161; f. 1967; technical, non-fiction, social sciences, medicine and agriculture; Man. GUSTAVO GABRIEL CANEVARO.

Amorrortu Editores, SA: Paraguay 1225, 7°, 1057 Buenos Aires; tel. (1) 393-8812; f. 1967; anthropology, religion, economics, sociology, etc.; Man. Dir HORACIO DE AMORRORTU.

Angel Estrada y Cía, SA: Bolívar 462, 1066 Buenos Aires; tel. (1) 33-6521; telex 17990; f. 1869; textbooks, children's books; Pres. PATRICIA DE ESTRADA.

El Ateneo, Librería—Editorial: Patagones 2463, 1282 Buenos Aires; tel. (1) 942-9002; f. 1912; medicine, engineering, economics and general; Dirs PEDRO GARCÍA RUEDA, EUSTASIO A. GARCÍA.

Editorial Atlántida, SA: Florida 643, 1005 Buenos Aires; tel. (1) 311-2261; telex 21163; f. 1918; fiction and non-fiction, children's books; Founder CONSTANCIO C. VIGIL; Man. Dir ALFREDO J. VERCELLI.

Ediciones La Aurora: Deán Funes 1823/25, 1244 Buenos Aires; tel. (1) 941-8940; f. 1926; general, religion, philosophy, psychology, history, semiology, linguistics; Dir Dr HUGO O. ORTEGA.

Editorial Bell, SA: Buenos Aires; tel. (1) 90-1076; f. 1927; scientific, sport and technical books; Man. Dir HUGO O. VARELA.

Editorial Bruguera: Avalos 365, 1427 Buenos Aires; tel. (1) 58-8122; Man. Dir JORGE MERLINI.

Centro Editor de América Latina, SA: Juan D. Perón 1228, 1038 Buenos Aires; tel. (1) 35-9449; f. 1967; literature, history; Man. Dir JOSÉ B. SPIVACOW.

Centro Nacional de Información, Documentación y Tecnología Educativa: Ministerio de Educación y Justicia, Paraguay 1657, 1°, 1062 Buenos Aires; tel. (1) 41-5420; education, bibliography, directories, etc.; Dir LAUREANO GARCÍA ELORRIO.

Editorial Ciordia, SRL: Belgrano 2271, 1094 Buenos Aires; tel. (1) 48-1681; f. 1938; general educational and fiction; Man. Dir EDUARDO B. CIORDIA.

Editorial Claretiana: Lima 1360, 1138 Buenos Aires; tel. (1) 27-9250; f. 1956; Catholic religion; Dir P. ANDRÉS BERASAIN.

Editorial Claridad, SA: San José 1627, Buenos Aires; tel. (1) 23-5573; f. 1922; literature, biographies, social science, medicine, politics; Dir Dr ELIO M. A. COLLE.

Club de Lectores: Avda de Mayo 624, 1084 Buenos Aires; tel. (1) 34-3955; f. 1938; non-fiction; Dir JUAN MANUEL FONTENLA.

Club de Poetas: Casilla 189, 1401 Buenos Aires; f. 1975; poetry and literature; Exec. Dir JUAN MANUEL FONTENLA.

Editorial Columba, SA: Sarmiento 1889, 5°, 1044 Buenos Aires; tel. (1) 45-4297; f. 1953; classics in translation, 20th century; Man. Dir CLAUDIO A. COLUMBA.

Editorial Contémpora, SRL: Sarmiento 643, 1382 Buenos Aires; tel. (1) 45-1793; architecture, town-planning, interior decoration and gardening; Dir NORBERTO M. MUZIO.

Cosmopolita, SRL: Piedras 744, 1070 Buenos Aires; tel. (1) 361-8049; f. 1940; science and technology; Man. Dir RUTH F. DE RAPP.

Ediciones Depalma SRL: Talcahuano 494, 1013 Buenos Aires; tel. (1) 46-1815; f. 1944; law, politics, sociology, philosophy, history and economics; Man. Dir ROQUE DEPALMA.

Editorial Difusión, SA: Sarandi 1065-67, Buenos Aires; tel. (1) 941-0118; f. 1937; literature, philosophy, religion, education, textbooks, children's books; Dir DOMINGO PALOMBELLA.

ARGENTINA

Emecé Editores, SA: Carlos Pellegrini 1069, 9°, 1009 Buenos Aires; tel. (1) 311-4710; telex 17736; f. 1939; fiction, non-fiction, biographies, history, art, poetry, essays; Pres. BONIFACIO DEL CARRIL; Editors JORGE NAVEIRO, BONIFACIO P. DEL CARRIL.

Espasa Calpe Argentina, SA: Tacuarí 328, 1071 Buenos Aires; tel. (1) 34-0073; f. 1937; literature, science, dictionaries; publ. *Colección Austral*; Dir RAFAEL OLARRA JIMÉNEZ.

EUDEBA—Editorial Universitaria de Buenos Aires: Rivadavia 1573, 1033 Buenos Aires; tel. (1) 37-2202; f. 1959; fiction and non-fiction; Gen. Man. LUIS GREGORICH.

Fabril Editora, SA: California 2098, 1289 Buenos Aires; tel. (1) 21-3601; f. 1958; non-fiction, science, arts, education and reference; Editorial Man. ANDRÉS ALFONSO BRAVO; Business Man. RÓMULO AYERZA.

Editorial Glem, SACIF: Avda Caseros 2056, 1264 Buenos Aires; tel. (1) 26-6641; f. 1933; psychology, technology; Pres. JOSÉ ALFREDO TUCCI.

Editorial Guadalupe: Julián Alvarez 2215, 1425 Buenos Aires; tel. (1) 84-6066; f. 1895; social sciences, religion, anthropology, children's books, and pedagogy; Man. Dir P. LUIS O. LIBERTI.

Editorial Hachette, SA: Rivadavia 739, 1002 Buenos Aires; tel. (1) 34-8481; telex 17479; f. 1931; general non-fiction; Man. Dir J. A. MUSSET.

Editorial Hemisferio Sur, SA: Pasteur 743, 1028 Buenos Aires; tel. (1) 48-9825; telex 18522; f. 1966; agriculture, science; Man. Dirs JUAN ÁNGEL PERI, ADOLFO LUIS PEÑA.

Editorial Hispano-Americana, SA (HASA): Alsina 731, 1087 Buenos Aires; tel. (1) 33-5051; f. 1942; science and technology; Pres. Prof. HÉCTOR O. ALGARRA.

Editorial Inter-Médica, SAICI: Junín 917, 1°, Casilla 4625, Buenos Aires; tel. (1) 83-3234; f. 1959; science, medicine, dentistry, psychology, odontology; Pres. JORGE MODYEIEVSKY.

Editorial Kapelusz, SA: Moreno 372, 1091 Buenos Aires; tel. (1) 34-6451; telex 18342; f. 1905; textbooks, psychology, pedagogy, children's books; Man. Dir RICARDO PASCUAL ROBLES.

Editorial Kier, SACFI: Santa Fé 1260, 1059 Buenos Aires; tel. (1) 41-0507; f. 1907; religions, astrology, occultism, medicine; Pres. JOSÉ GRIGNA.

Editorial Labor Argentina, SA (Spain): Venezuela 613, 1095 Buenos Aires; tel. (1) 33-4135; f. 1924; technology, science, art; Man. Dir PEDRO CLOTAS CIERCO.

Editorial Víctor Lerú, SA: Don Bosco 3834, Casilla 2793, 1000 Buenos Aires; tel. (1) 981-6098; f. 1944; art and architecture, music, history, technology, school books; Man. Dir VICTOR NEP.

Carlos Lohlé, SA: Tacuarí 1516, Casilla 3097, 1000 Buenos Aires; tel. (1) 27-9969; f. 1953; philosophy, religion, belles-lettres; Pres. CARLOS F. P. LOHLÉ; Dir FRANCISCO M. LOHLÉ.

Editorial Losada, SA: Moreno 3362/64, 1209 Buenos Aires; tel. (1) 88-8608; f. 1938; general; Pres. GONZALO PEDRO LOSADA.

Ediciones Macchi, SA: Alsina 1535 PB, 1088 Buenos Aires; tel. (1) 46-0594; f. 1947; economic sciences; Man. Dir RAÚL LUIS MACCHI.

Editorial Médica Panamericana, SA: Junín 831, 1113 Buenos Aires; tel. (1) 83-8819; telex 17666; f. 1962; medicine, dentistry, nursing, rehabilitation; Pres. ROBERTO BRIK.

Editorial Nova, SACI: Buenos Aires; tel. (1) 34-8698; f. 1945; arts, philosophy, religion, medicine, textbooks, science and technology; Dir HORACIO D. ROLANDO.

Ediciones Nueva Visión, SAIC: Tucumán 3748, 1189 Buenos Aires; tel. (1) 89-5050; f. 1954; psychology, art, social sciences, architecture; Man. Dir JORGE J. GRISETTI.

Editorial Paidós: Defensa 599, 1°, 1065 Buenos Aires; tel. (1) 33-2275; f. 1945; social sciences, medicine, philosophy, religion, history, literature, textbooks; Man. Dir ENRIQUE BUTELMAN.

Plaza y Janés, SA: Lambaré 893, Buenos Aires; tel. (1) 86-6769; popular fiction and non-fiction; Man. Dir JORGE PÉREZ.

Editorial Plus Ultra, SAI & C: Viamonte 1775, 1055 Buenos Aires; tel. (1) 44-6605; f. 1964; literature, history, textbooks, law, economics, politics, sociology, pedagogy, children's books; Man. Editor CARLOS ALBERTO LOPRETE.

Editorial Rodolfo Alonso, SRL: Juncal 2990, 1°, 1425 Buenos Aires; tel. (1) 821-2878; f. 1968; general literature, fiction, non-fiction, linguistics, psychology, social science; Man. Dir RODOLFO ALONSO.

Schapire Editor, SRL: Uruguay 1249, 1016 Buenos Aires; tel. (1) 44-0765; f. 1941; music, art, theatre, sociology, history, fiction; Dir MIGUEL SCHAPIRE DALMAT.

Ediciones Siglo XX, SACI: Maza 177, 1206 Buenos Aires; tel. (1) 88-2758; f. 1943; fiction and non-fiction; Gen. Man. ISIDORO WAINER.

Editorial Sigmar, SACI: Belgrano 1580, 1093 Buenos Aires; tel. (1) 38-2844; f. 1941; children's books; Man. Dir SIGFRIDO CHWAT.

Editorial Sopena Argentina, SACI e I: Moreno 957, 7°, Of. 2, Casilla 1075, 1091 Buenos Aires; tel. (1) 38-7182; f. 1918; dictionaries, classics, chess, health, politics, history, children's books; Exec. Pres. DANIEL CARLOS OLSEN.

Editorial Stella: Viamonte 1984, 1056 Buenos Aires; tel. (1) 46-0346; Prop. Asociación Educacionista Argentina; general non-fiction and textbooks.

Editorial Sudamericana, SA: Humberto 531, 1°, 1103 Buenos Aires; tel. (1) 362-2128; f. 1939; general fiction and non-fiction; Gen. Man. JAIME RODRIGUÉ.

Editorial Troquel, SA: Garay 1454, 1153 Buenos Aires; tel. (1) 23-0771; f. 1954; general literature, technology and textbooks; Pres. MARÍA A. C. DE RESSIA; Dir Prof. JOSÉ E. ENCINAS.

PUBLISHERS' ASSOCIATIONS

Cámara Argentina de Editores de Libros: Buenos Aires; tel. (1) 45-1322; Pres. HÉCTOR OSCAR TUCCI.

Cámara Argentina de Publicaciones: Reconquista 1011, 6°, 1003 Buenos Aires; tel. (1) 311-6855; f. 1970; Pres. Dr MANUEL RODRÍGUEZ; Man. LUIS FRANCISCO HOULIN.

Cámara Argentina del Libro: Buenos Aires; tel. (1) 31-2368; Pres. MODESTO EDERRA.

Radio and Television

Following the appointment of a civilian government in December 1983, censorship of radio and television was relaxed and control of the broadcasting services was transferred to non-military personnel.

In 1983 there were an estimated 16m. radio receivers in use, and in 1985 there were about 6,500,000 television receivers in use.

Secretaría de Comunicaciones: Sarmiento 151, 4°, 1000 Buenos Aires; tel. (1) 312-1283; telex 21706; co-ordinates 30 stations and the international service; Sec. Ing. JUAN HIGINIO CIMINARI.

Subsecretaría de Planificación y Gestión Tecnológica: Sarmiento 151, 4°, 1000 Buenos Aires; tel. 311-5909; telex 21706; Under-Sec. Ing. LEONARDO JOSÉ LEIBSON.

Subsecretaría de Radiodifusión: Sarmiento 151, 4°, 1000 Buenos Aires; tel. (1) 311-5909; telex 21706; Under-Sec. Dr ROBERTO HORACIO TEZÓN.

Subsecretaría de Telecomunicaciones: Sarmiento 151, 4°, 1000 Buenos Aires; tel. (1) 311-5909; telex 21706; Under-Sec. JUAN MANUEL MAGLANO.

Comité Federal de Radiodifusión (COMFER): Suipacha 765, 1008 Buenos Aires; controls various technical aspects of broadcasting and transmission of programmes.

RADIO

There are three privately-owned stations in Buenos Aires and 72 in the interior. There are also 37 state-controlled stations, four provincial, three municipal and three university stations. The principal ones are Radio El Mundo, Radio del Plata, Radio Nacional, Radio Rivadavia, Radio Belgrano, Radio Argentina, Radio Continental, Radio Mitre, Radio Antartida, Radio Excelsior, Radio Ciudad de Buenos Aires and Radio Splendid, all in Buenos Aires.

Servicio Oficial de Radiodifusión (SOR): Sarmiento 151, 1000 Buenos Aires; tel. (1) 30-2121; Dir FLORENCINO RODRÍGUEZ CROSS; runs:

Cadena Argentina de Radiodifusión (CAR): Avda Entre Ríos 149, 3°, 1079 Buenos Aires; tel. (1) 45-2113; groups all national state-owned commercial stations which are operated directly by the Subsecretaría Operativa.

Radio Nacional Buenos Aires: Ayacucho 1556, 1112 Buenos Aires; tel. (1) 84-2021; Dir MANUEL ENRIQUE FENTANES.

Radiodifusión Argentina al Exterior (RAE): Ayacucho 1556, 1112 Buenos Aires; tel. (1) 84-2021; broadcasts in 8 languages to all areas of the world.

Asociación de Radiodifusoras Privadas Argentinas (ARPA): Juan D. Perón 1561, 8°, 1037 Buenos Aires; tel. (1) 35-4412; f. 1958; Pres. EVARISTO R. E. ALONSO.

ARGENTINA

TELEVISION

There are four television channels in the federal capital of Buenos Aires, 26 in the province of Buenos Aires, 41 in the interior, and 117 relay stations. There are 19 private television channels, nine provincial, two university and eight privately-supervised stations. The national television network is controlled by the Ministry of Education and Justice.

The following are some of the more important television stations in Argentina: Argentina Televisora Color LS82 Canal 7, LS83 Canal 9, LS84 Canal 11, LS85 Canal 13, Telenueva, Teledifusora Bahiense, Telecor, Dicor Difusión Córdoba, TV Universidad Nacional Córdoba, and TV Mar del Plata.

Asociación de Teleradiodifusoras Argentinas (ATA): Córdoba 323, 6°, 1054 Buenos Aires; tel. (1) 32-4219; telex 17253; association of private television stations; Pres. EDUARDO OSCAR FARLEY.

ATC—Argentina Televisora Color LS82 TV Canal 7: Avda Figueroa Alcorta 2977, 1425 Buenos Aires; tel. (1) 802-6001; state-controlled channel; Dir MARIO SÁBATO.

LS83 TV Canal 9: Gelly 3378, 1425 Buenos Aires; tel. (1) 801-3065; Dir Col D. CLODOVEO ANTONIO BATTESTI.

LS84 Canal 11: Pavón 2444, 1248 Buenos Aires; tel. (1) 941-0091; Dir-Gen. Commdr (retd) A. GUSTAVO MASSA.

LS85 TV Canal 13: San Juan 1170, 1147 Buenos Aires; tel. (1) 27-3661; telex 21762; f. 1960; Supervisor GUILLERMO MEQUE.

Finance

(cap. = capital; p.u. = paid up; res = reserves; dep. = deposits; m. = million; amounts in pesos argentinos and australes—₳)

BANKING

In 1986 there were 25 government-owned provincial banks, five government-owned municipal banks, 38 private commercial banks in the city of Buenos Aires and 90 private commercial banks in the rest of Argentina. There were also 31 foreign-owned banks operating in Argentina. In March 1984 the civilian Government disclosed plans to reform the banking sector. Fourteen financial institutions were to be liquidated and six others were to be placed under government control. In October 1986 the Government announced a reform of banking regulations, under which reserve requirements on deposits in Argentine banks were substantially reduced.

Central Bank

Banco Central de la República Argentina: Reconquista 266, 1003 Buenos Aires; tel. (1) 394-8411; telex 1137; f. 1935 as a central reserve bank; it has the right of note issue; all capital is held by the state; cap. and res 745,018m. (Dec. 1983); Pres. JOSÉ LUIS MACHINEA; Vice-Pres. MARCELO KIGUEL.

Government-Owned Commercial Banks

Banco de la Ciudad de Buenos Aires: Florida 302, 1313 Buenos Aires; tel. (1) 45-0726; telex 22365; municipal bank; f. 1878; cap. and res ₳54m., dep. ₳420.3m. (March 1986); Pres. Dr GUILLERMO MORENO HUEYO; 37 brs.

Banco de Entre Ríos: 25 de Mayo y Monte Caseros, 3100 Paraná; tel. (042) 27-0000; f. 1935; provincial bank; cap. and res ₳16.5m., dep. ₳107.2m. (March 1986); Pres. Ing. ROQUE HUMBERTO RUBIO; 7 brs.

Banco de Mendoza: Gutiérrez 51, POB 19, 5500 Mendoza; tel. (061) 25-1200; telex 55204; f. 1934; provincial bank; cap. and res ₳25m., dep. ₳111.7m. (March 1986); Pres. ROBERTO E. PISI; 77 brs.

Banco de la Nación Argentina: Bartolomé Mitre 326, 1039 Buenos Aires; tel. (1) 30-1011; telex 21407; f. 1891; national bank; cap. and res ₳871.3m., dep. ₳2,141.5m. (March 1986); Pres. MARIO LUIS KENNY; Gen. Man. GUIDO OSCAR ROMERO; 577 brs.

Banco de la Provincia de Buenos Aires: Avda San Martín 137, 1004 Buenos Aires; tel. (1) 33-2561; telex 18276; f. 1822; provincial bank; cap. and res ₳311.1m., dep. ₳772.4m. (March 1986); Pres. ALDO FERRER; Gen. Man. ANTONIO CASTELLO; 322 brs.

Banco del Chaco: Güemes 102, 3500 Resistencia; tel. (0722) 21077; telex 71214; f. 1958; provincial bank; cap. and res ₳21.8m., dep. ₳62.6m. (March 1986); Pres. Dr MANUEL WALDEMAR AGUIRRE; Gen. Man. RUBÉN ABEL MARCÓN; 26 brs.

Banco de la Provincia de Córdoba: San Jerónimo 166, 5000 Córdoba; tel. 051-42001; telex 51610; f. 1873; provincial bank; cap. and res ₳72.9m., dep. ₳297.9m. (March 1986); Pres. Dr JOAQUÍN CENDOYA; 157 brs.

Banco de la Provincia de Corrientes: 9 de Julio y San Juan, 3400 Corrientes; tel. (0783) 23601; telex 74106; cap. and res ₳27.4m., dep. ₳107.8m. (March 1986); Pres. JORGE FÉLIX GÓMEZ; 30 brs.

Banco de la Provincia de Neuquén: Argentina 41/45, Neuquén; tel. 31-459; telex 84128; cap. and res ₳17.8m., dep. ₳66.9m. (March 1986); Pres. OMAR SANTIAGO NEGRETTI; 21 brs.

Banco Provincial de Santa Fé: San Martín 715, 2000 Rosario, Santa Fé; tel. (041) 21-1370; telex 41751; f. 1874; provincial bank; cap. and res ₳32.5m., dep. ₳247.8m. (March 1986); Pres. JORGE DOMÍNGUEZ.

Private Commercial Banks

Banco Alas: Sarmiento 528/32, 1041 Buenos Aires; tel. (1) 313-3400; telex 9127; cap. and res ₳16.3m., dep. ₳57.5m. (March 1986); Pres. CARMELO A. STANCATO; 55 brs.

Banco Comercial del Norte: Corrientes 415, 1043 Buenos Aires; tel. (1) 394-0042; telex 23879; f. 1912; cap. and res ₳37.5m., dep. ₳113.5m. (March 1986); Pres. FEDERICO J. L. ZORRAQUÍN; Gen. Man. N. POZZOLI; 75 brs.

Banco de Crédito Argentino, SA: Reconquista 2, Buenos Aires; tel. (1) 30-9561; telex 18077; f. 1887; cap. and res ₳39.3m., dep. ₳124.8m. (March 1986); Pres. Dr SALVADOR GORODISCH; Gen. Man. OSVALDO CORTESI; 65 brs.

Banco de Crédito Rural Argentina SA: Florida 200, 1005 Buenos Aires; tel. (1) 46-0221; telex 17229; f. 1925; cap. and res US $26.6m., dep. $75.8m. (July 1986); Chair. Dr ALEJANDRO CARLOS ANTUÑA.

Banco Español del Río de la Plata Ltdo: Juan D. Perón 402, 1003 Buenos Aires; tel. (1) 33-2951; telex 21562; f. 1886; cap. ₳44.6m., dep. ₳111.2m. (March 1986); Pres. Dr PABLO TERÁN NOUGUES; 65 brs.

Banco Financiero Argentino: Sarmiento 400, 1041 Buenos Aires; tel. (1) 33-1209; telex 17055; cap. and res ₳20m., dep. ₳73m. (March 1986); Pres. Dr SALVADOR GORODISCH; 56 brs.

Banco Francés del Río de la Plata: Reconquista 165, 1003 Buenos Aires; tel. (1) 33-7071; telex 9119; f. 1886; cap. and res ₳29.1m., dep. ₳92.5m. (March 1986); Pres. Dr LUIS M. OTERO MONSEGUR; 26 brs.

Banco de Galicia y Buenos Aires: Juan D. Perón 407, Casilla 86, 1038 Buenos Aires; tel. (1) 394-7080; telex 23805; f. 1905; cap. and res ₳54.3m., dep. ₳273.9m. (March 1986); Pres. ROBERTO J. BULLRICH; 129 brs.

Banco Ganadero Argentino: Defensa 113, 1065 Buenos Aires; tel. (1) 34-4061; telex 9128; f. 1962; cap. and res ₳32.8m., dep. ₳77.8m. (March 1986); Pres. Dr NARCISO E. OCAMPO; 42 brs.

Banco de Italia y Río de la Plata, SA: Reconquista 100, 1003 Buenos Aires; tel. (1) 33-1061; telex 18120; f. 1872; cap. and res 3,129m. (1983); closed down May 1985; reopened in June 1985 under government supervision; Government Administrator ARMANDO VÍCTOR REY; 88 brs.

Banco Mercantil Argentino: Avda Corrientes 629, 1324 Buenos Aires; tel. (1) 393-0073; telex 9122; f. 1923; cap. and res ₳15.6m., dep. ₳37.4m. (March 1986); Pres. NOEL WERTHEIN; 45 brs.

Banco del Oeste: San Martín 128, 1004 Buenos Aires; tel. (1) 34-0201; telex 23189; cap. and res ₳13.7m., dep. ₳55.5m. (March 1986); Pres. Dr GUIDO F. GUELAR; 53 brs.

Banco Quilmes, SA: Juan D. Perón 564, 2°, 1038 Buenos Aires; tel. (1) 33-8110; telex 17895; f. 1907; cap. and res ₳24.5m., dep. ₳134m. (March 1986); Pres. Dr PEDRO O. FIORITO; 58 brs.

Banco Río de la Plata, SA: Bartolomé Mitre 480, 1004 Buenos Aires; tel. (1) 33-8361; telex 9215; f. 1908; cap. and res ₳115m., dep. ₳229.1m. (March 1986); Chair. J. GREGORIO PÉREZ COMPANC; 84 brs.

Banco Shaw, SA: Sarmiento 355, 1041 Buenos Aires; tel. (1) 311-6271; telex 21226; f. 1959; cap. and res ₳18.7m., dep. ₳78.9m. (March 1986); Pres. Dr ALEJANDRO SHAW; 30 brs.

Other National Banks

Banco Hipotecario Nacional: Defensa 192, 1065 Buenos Aires; tel. (1) 34-2001; f. 1886; mortgage bank; cap. and res ₳184.2m., dep. ₳699.5m. (March 1986); Pres. Dr LUIS ANÍBAL REYNALDO.

Banco Nacional de Desarrollo: 25 de Mayo 145, 1002 Buenos Aires; tel. (1) 33-2091; telex 9179; f. 1944; development bank; cap. and res ₳174.7m., dep. ₳173.4m. (March 1986); Pres. (vacant).

Caja Nacional de Ahorro y Seguro: Hipólito Yrigoyen 1770, 1089 Buenos Aires; tel. (1) 45-5861; f. 1915; savings bank and insurance institution; cap. and res ₳21.8m., dep. ₳286.8m. (March 1986); Pres. Dr CARLOS AUGUSTO FONTE; Gen. Man. Dr RAFAEL ORDÓÑEZ; 61 brs.

ARGENTINA

Foreign Banks

Banco do Brasil, SA: Sarmiento 487, 1041 Buenos Aires; tel. (1) 394-9861; f. 1960; cap. and res ₳15.9m., dep. ₳3m. (March 1986); Gen. Man. ERNANI SCHMITT.

Banco Europeo para América Latina, SA: Juan D. Perón 338, 1038 Buenos Aires; tel. (1) 33-6544; telex 9152; f. 1914; cap. and res ₳10.6m., dep. ₳38.8m. (March 1986); Man. Ing. JEAN JACQUES VERDICKT.

Banco Holandés Unido (Netherlands): Florida 361, 1005 Buenos Aires; tel. (1) 394-1022; telex 9160; f. 1914; cap. and res ₳9.7m. dep. ₳27.3m. (March 1986); Regional Man. (Argentina, Paraguay and Uruguay) F. T. BRILL; Man. (Argentina) P. C. VAN DIJK.

Banco di Napoli (Italy): Bartolomé Mitre 699, 1036 Buenos Aires; tel. (1) 30-5648; f. 1930; cap. and res ₳17.1m., dep. ₳11.1 (March 1986); Gen. Man. MASSIMO FRIGIONE.

Banco Popular Argentino: Florida 201 esq. Juan D. Perón, Casilla 3650, 1005 Buenos Aires; tel. (1) 33-6075; telex 9220; f. 1887; cap. and res ₳18.2m., dep. ₳55.2m. (March 1986); Pres. RICARDO TEJERO MAGRO; 27 brs.

Banco de Santander, SA (Spain): Bartolomé Mitre 575, 1036 Buenos Aires; tel. (1) 33-0014; f. 1964; cap. and res ₳6.8m., dep. ₳37.7m. (March 1986); Pres. EMILIO BOTÍN, Gen. Man. A. MARIANO MARTÍNEZ PÉREZ.

Banco Sudameris: Juan D. Perón 500, 1038 Buenos Aires; tel.(1) 33-4061; telex 9186; f. 1910; cap. and res ₳14m., dep. ₳57.7m. (March 1986); Man. PATRICK DE VILLEMANDY.

Banco Supervielle Société Générale SA: Reconquista 330, 1003 Buenos Aires; tel. (1) 394-4051; telex 24024; f. 1887; cap. and res ₳19.8m., dep. ₳71.4m. (March 1986); Chair. FRANCISCO SÉNECA.

Banco Tornquist, SA: Bartolomé Mitre 559, 1039 Buenos Aires; tel. (1) 30-7841; telex 9193; f. 1960; cap. and res ₳27.2m., dep. ₳64.2m. (March 1986); Pres. BERNARD THIOLON; Vice-Pres. DANIEL CHOQUART; 32 brs.

Bank of America NT & SA (USA): Juan D. Perón 525, 1038 Buenos Aires; tel. (1) 394-3266; f. 1940; cap. and res ₳20.6m., dep. ₳80.7m. (March 1986); Vice-Pres. and Gen. Man. RODOLFO MON.

Bank of London and South America (UK): Reconquista 101-51, Casilla 128, 1003 Buenos Aires; tel. (1) 33-0920; telex 21558; f. 1862; part of Lloyd's Bank Group; cap. and res ₳26.2m., dep. ₳100.5m. (March 1986); Dir-Gen. Gen. A. G. G. MCWILLIAM; 41 brs.

Bank of Tokyo Ltd (Japan): Corrientes 420, 1043 Buenos Aires; tel. (1) 393-8097; f. 1956; cap. and res ₳12.5m., dep. ₳19.3m. (March 1986); Man. HIROYOSHI KASAI.

Banque Nationale de Paris (France): 25 de Mayo 471, 1002 Buenos Aires; tel. (1) 311-4490; telex 23285; f. 1981; cap. and res ₳14.1m., dep. ₳14.4m. (March 1986); Gen. Man. ROGER MARTIN.

Barclays Bank International Ltd (UK): Juan D. Perón 655, 1038 Buenos Aires; tel. (1) 49-1001; telex 22080; f. 1979; cap. and res ₳5.4m., dep. ₳3.1m.; Chief Man. J. GRAHAM POYNTON.

Chase Manhattan Bank, N.A. (USA): 25 de Mayo 140, 1002 Buenos Aires; tel. (1) 30-1135; telex 9138; f. 1904; cap. and res ₳17.2m., dep. ₳33.4m. (March 1986); Gen. Man. HARRY TETHER.

Citibank, NA (USA): Bartolomé Mitre 530, 1036 Buenos Aires; tel. (1) 33-4041; f. 1914; cap. and res ₳33.4m., dep. ₳119.8m. (March 1986); Vice-Pres. RICHARD HANDLEY; 16 brs.

Deutsche Bank AG (Federal Republic of Germany): Reconquista 134, 1003 Buenos Aires; tel. (1) 30-2510; telex 9115; f. 1960; cap. and res ₳18.2m., dep. ₳62.4m. (March 1986); Dirs RAÚL G. STOCKER, KARL OSTENRIEDER, JÜRGEN REBOUILLON, REINHARD SCHEELE; 14 brs.

First National Bank of Boston (USA): Florida 99, 1005 Buenos Aires; tel. (1) 34-3051; f. 1784; cap. and res ₳49.3m., dep. ₳212.1m. (March 1986); Vice-Pres. and Gen. Man Ing. MANUEL SACERDOTE; 22 brs.

Royal Bank of Canada: Florida 202, 1005 Buenos Aires; tel. (1) 46-9851; f. 1869; cap. and res ₳7.5m., dep. ₳17.2m. (March 1986); Gen. Man. EGON WILHELM TEGTMEYER; 2 brs.

Bankers' Associations

Asociación de Bancos Argentinos (ADEBA): San Martín 229, 10°, 1004 Buenos Aires; tel. (1) 394-1430; telex 23704; Pres. ROQUE MACCARONE; Exec. Dir Dr NORBERTO C. PERUZZOTTI; 29 mems.

Asociación de Bancos de la República Argentina (ABRA): Reconquista 458, 2°, 1358 Buenos Aires; tel. (1) 394-1871; f. 1919; Pres. JULIO J. GÓMEZ; Exec. Sec. Dr FRANCISCO RODRÍGUEZ LÓPEZ; 45 mems.

Asociación de Bancos de Provincia de la República Argentina (ABAPRA): Florida 470, 1°, 1005 Buenos Aires; tel. 392-6321; f. 1959; Pres. RENÉ SANTIAGO GIORGIS; Man. EDUARDO R. D'AMATO; 31 mems.

Asociación de Bancos del Interior de la República Argentina (ABIRA): Corrientes 538, 4°, 1043 Buenos Aires; tel. (1) 394-5671; telex 24058; f. 1956; Pres. Dr JORGE F. CHRISTENSEN; Dir IGNACIO J. C. PRÉMOLI; 40 mems.

Federación de Bancos Cooperativos de la República Argentina (FEBANCOOP): Maipú 374, 9°/10°, 1006 Buenos Aires; tel. (1) 394-9949; telex 23650; f. 1973; Pres. RAÚL MEILÁN SALGADO; Exec. Dir Lic. SAMUEL GLEMBOCKI; 37 mems.

STOCK EXCHANGES

Mercado de Valores de Buenos Aires, SA: 25 de Mayo 367, 9°, Buenos Aires; tel. (1) 313-4522; telex 17445; Pres. ALFREDO B. PANERO.

There are also stock exchanges at Córdoba, San Juan, Rosario, Mendoza and Mar del Plata.

INSURANCE

Superintendencia de Seguros de la Nación: Avda Julio A. Roca 721, 1067 Buenos Aires; tel. (1) 30-6653; f. 1938; Superintendent Lic. DIEGO PEDRO PELUFFO.

In June 1985 it was announced that all existing companies should have a minimum capital of ₳279,090 (australes) for all classes of insurance.

In June 1983 there were nearly 260 insurance companies operating in Argentina, of which 14 were foreign. The following is a list of those offering all classes or a specialized service.

La Agrícola, SA: Corrientes 447, Buenos Aires; tel. (1) 394-5031; f. 1905; associated company La Regional; all classes; Pres. LUIS R. MARCO; First Vice-Pres. JUSTO J. DE CORRAL.

Aseguradora de Créditos y Garantías, SA: San Martín 379, 6°, 1004 Buenos Aires; tel. (1) 394-1018; telex 24334; f. 1965; Pres. ALEJANDRO E. FRERS; Man. CARLOS GUSTAVO KRIEGER.

Aseguradora de Río Negro y Neuquén: Villegas 316, Cipolletti, Río Negro; f. 1960; all classes; Gen. Man. ERNESTO LÓPEZ.

Aseguradores de Cauciones SA: Paraguay 580, 1057 Buenos Aires; tel. (1) 312-5321; telex 17321; f. 1969; all classes; Pres. Dr AGUSTÍN DE VEDIA.

Aseguradores Industriales SA: Juan D. Perón 650, 6°, 1038 Buenos Aires; tel. (1) 46-5425; f. 1961; all classes; Exec. Pres. VICTORIO MIGUEL GONNELLI.

La Austral: Juncal 1319, 1062 Buenos Aires; tel. (1) 42-9881; telex 121078; f. 1942; all classes; Pres. RODOLFO H. TAYLOR.

Colón, Cía de Seguros Generales SA: San Martín 548-550, 1004 Buenos Aires; tel. (1) 393-5069; telex 23923; f. 1962; all classes; Gen. Man. L. D. STÜCK.

Columbia, SA: Juan D. Perón 690, 1038 Buenos Aires; tel. (1) 46-1240; f. 1918; all classes; Pres. EUGENIO M. BLANCO.

El Comercio, Compañía de Seguros a prima fija SA: Maipú 53, 1084 Buenos Aires; tel. (1) 34-2181; f. 1889; all classes; Pres. FELIPE JOSÉ LUIS M. GAMBA; Man. PABLO DOMINGO F. LONGO.

Compañía Argentina de Seguro de Crédito a la Exportación SA: Sarmiento 440, 4°, 1347 Buenos Aires; tel. (1) 394-7979; telex 24207; f. 1967; covers credit and extraordinary and political risks for Argentine exports; Pres. LUIS ORCOYEN.

Compañía Aseguradora Argentina SA: Casilla 3398, Avda Roque S. Peña 555, 1035 Buenos Aires; tel. (1) 30-1571; telex 012-2876; f. 1918; all classes; Man. GUIDO LUTTINI; Vice-Pres. ALBERTO O. ARGENTO.

La Continental, SA: Corrientes 655, 1043 Buenos Aires; tel. (1) 393-8051; telex 121832; f. 1912; all classes; Pres. RAÚL MASCARENHAS.

La Franco-Argentina, SA: Hipólito Yrigoyen 476, 1086 Buenos Aires; tel. (1) 30-3091; telex 17291; f. 1896; all classes; Pres. Dr GUILLERMO MORENO HUEYO; Gen. Man. Dra HAYDÉE GUZIAN DE RAMÍREZ.

Hermes, SA: Edif. Hermes, Bartolomé Mitre 754/60, 1034 Buenos Aires; tel. (1) 34-8441; f. 1926; all classes; Pres. CARLOS ANÍBAL PERALTA; Gen. Man. DIONISIO KATOPODIS.

Iguazú, SA: San Martín 442, 1004 Buenos Aires; tel. (1) 394-6661; f. 1947; all classes; Pres. RAMÓN SANTAMARINA.

India, SA: Avda Roque S. Peña 730, 1035 Buenos Aires; tel. (1) 30-6001; f. 1950; all classes; Pres. CARLOS DE ALZAGA; Vice-Pres. MATILDE DÍAZ VÉLEZ.

ARGENTINA

Instituto Italo-Argentino de Seguros Generales, SA: Avda Roque S. Peña 890, 1035 Buenos Aires; tel. (1) 45-5814; f. 1920; all classes; Pres. LUIS GOTTHEIL.

La Meridonal, SA: Juan D. Perón 646, 1038 Buenos Aires; tel. (1) 33-0941; f. 1949; life and general; Pres. G. G. LASCANO.

El Mundo, SA: Juan D. Perón 555, 1°, 1038 Buenos Aires; tel. (1) 394-1801; f. 1946; general; Pres. FEDERICO V. SÁNCHEZ BARTON; Vice-Pres. ALFREDO A. ANNUNZIATTA.

Plus Ultra, Cía Argentina de Seguros SA: San Martín 548–50, 1004 Buenos Aires; tel. (1) 393-5069; telex 23923; f. 1956; all classes; Gen. Man. L. D. STÜCK.

La Primera, SA: Blvd Villegas y Oro, Trenque Lauquén, Prov. Buenos Aires; tel. (1) 393-8125; all classes; Pres. ENRIQUE RAÚL U. BOTTINI; Man. Dr RODOLFO RAÚL D'ONOFRIO.

La Rectora, SA: Corrientes 848, 1043 Buenos Aires; tel. (1) 394-6081; f. 1951; all classes; Pres. PEDRO PASCUAL MEGNA; Gen. Man. ANTONIO LÓPEZ BUENO.

La República, SA: San Martín 627/29, 1374 Buenos Aires; tel. (1) 393-9901; f. 1928; group life and general; Pres. ARTURO EDBROOKE; Man. RODNEY C. SMITH.

Sud América Terrestre y Marítima Cía de Seguros Generales SA: Avda Pdte R. S. Peña 530, 1035 Buenos Aires; tel. (1) 30-8570; telex 24256; f. 1919; all classes; Mans ALAIN HOMBREUX, JORGE O. SALVIDIO.

La Unión Gremial, SA: Casilla 300, General Mitre 665/99, 2000 Rosario, Santa Fé; tel. 47071; f. 1908; general; Pres. GERARDO J. HERFARTH; Gen. Man. DICTINO MÉNDEZ.

La Universal: Juncal 1319, 1062 Buenos Aires; tel. (1) 42-9881; telex 1078; f. 1905; all classes; Pres. Dr E. MAYER.

Reinsurance

Instituto Nacional de Reaseguros: Avda Julio A. Roca 694, 1067 Buenos Aires; tel. (1) 34-0084; telex 1170; f. 1947; reinsurance in all branches except credit; Pres. and Man. FELICIANO SALVIA.

Insurance Associations

Asociación Argentina de Compañías de Seguros: 25 de Mayo 565, 1002 Buenos Aires; tel. (1) 313-6974; telex 23837; f. 1894; 144 mems; Pres. HERMES H. PINNEL.

Asociación de Aseguradores Extranjeros en la Argentina: San Martín 201, 7°, 1004 Buenos Aires; tel. (1) 394-3881; f. 1875; association of 13 foreign insurance companies operating in Argentina; Pres. CARLOS ALBERTO PARADISO; Sec. RICHARD MACGRATH.

Trade and Industry

CHAMBERS OF COMMERCE

Cámara Argentina de Comercio: Avda Leandro N. Alem 36, 1003 Buenos Aires; tel. (1) 33-8051; telex 18542; f. 1924; Pres. Dr ERNESTO E. GRETHER.

Cámara de Comercio, Industria y Producción de la República Argentina: Florida 1, 4°, 1005 Buenos Aires; tel. (1) 33-0813; telex 18693; f. 1913; Pres. JOSÉ CHEDIEK; Vice-Pres. Dr FAUSTINO S. DIÉGUEZ, Dr JORGE M. MAZALAN; 1,500 mems.

Cámara de Comercio Exterior de la Federación Gremial del Comercio e Industria: Avda Córdoba 1868, Rosario, Santa Fé; tel. 213896; f. 1958; deals with import-export; Pres. EDUARDO C. SALVATIERRA; Vice-Pres. OMIL FALCONE; 120 mems.

Cámara de Exportadores de la República Argentina: Diag. Roque Sáenz Peña 740, 1°, 1035 Buenos Aires; f. 1943 to promote exports; Pres. Ing. DANIEL BRUNELLA; Vice-Pres. Ing. ALEJANDRO ACHAVAL; 700 mems.

Similar chambers are located in most of the larger centres and there are many foreign chambers of commerce.

GOVERNMENT REGULATORY AND SUPERVISORY BODIES

Consejo Federal de Inversiones: San Martín 871, 1004 Buenos Aires; tel. (1) 313-2034; federal board to regulate domestic and foreign investment; Sec.-Gen. Ing. JUAN JOSÉ CIACERA.

Consejo Nacional Económico y Social: Maipú 972, 1006 Buenos Aires; tel. (1) 312-7649; national economic and social council.

Instituto de Desarrollo Económico y Social (IDES): Güemes 3950, 1425 Buenos Aires; tel. (1) 71-3738; f. 1961; 700 mems; Pres. TORCUATO S. DITELLA; Sec. Dr CATALINA WAINERMAN.

Instituto Forestal Nacional (Ifona): Avda Pueyrredón 2446, 1119 Buenos Aires; tel. (1) 826-8562; national forestry commission; f. 1940; Dir HUGO H. KUGLER.

Junta Nacional de Carnes: San Martín 459, 1004 Buenos Aires; tel. (1) 394-5161; telex 24210; national meat board; in 1978 was granted a new national autonomous organic structure and was charged with the promotion and control of livestock and meat sales; Pres. Dr ALFREDO BEGATTI.

Junta Nacional de Granos: Paseo Colón 359, Buenos Aires; tel. (1) 30-0641; telex 21793; national grain board; supervises commercial practices and organizes the construction of farm silos and port elevators; Pres. JORGE CORT.

DEVELOPMENT ORGANIZATIONS

Consejo Nacional de Desarrollo: Hipólito Yrigoyen 250, 8°, Buenos Aires; tel. (1) 33-1722; f. 1986; co-ordinates the formulation, implementation and evaluation of development plans; Head Dr BERNARDO GRINSPUN.

Instituto Argentino del Petróleo: Maipú 645, Buenos Aires; tel. (1) 392-3244; established to promote the development of petroleum exploration and exploitation.

Secretaría de Planificación: Hipólito Yrigoyen 250, 8°, Buenos Aires; tel. (1) 33-1722; f. 1961 to formulate national long-term development plans; Sec. Dr BERNARDO GRINSPUN.

Sociedad Rural Argentina: Florida 460, 1005 Buenos Aires; tel. (1) 392-2030; telex 23414; f. 1866; private organization to promote the development of agriculture; Pres. Dr GUILLERMO E. ALCHOURON; 9,400 mems.

STATE ENTERPRISES

Sindicatura General de Empresas Públicas: Lavalle 1429, 1048 Buenos Aires; tel. (1) 45-6081; f. 1978 to replace the Corporación de Empresas Nacionales; to exercise external control over wholly- or partly-owned public enterprises; Pres. Lic. JAIME ALBERTO SUJOY.

Agua y Energía Eléctrica Sociedad del Estado (AyEE): Avda Leandro N. Alem 1134, 1001 Buenos Aires; tel. (1) 311-6364; telex 21889; f. 1947; state water and electricity board; Pres. Lic. ALBERTO ENRIQUE DEVOTO.

Empresa Nacional de Correos y Telégrafos (ENCOTEL): Sarmiento 151, 1000 Buenos Aires; tel. (1) 311-5031; telex 22045; f. 1972; postal services; Gen. Administrator Dr JUAN IGNACIO YMAZ, Jr.

Empresa Nacional de Telecomunicaciones (Entel): Defensa 143, 1065 Buenos Aires; tel. (1) 49-9684; telex 18003; f. 1949; state telecommunications corporation; Gen. Administrator Dr JOSÉ ALBERTO GUERRA.

Gas del Estado: Alsina 1169, 1088 Buenos Aires; tel. (1) 37-2091; f. 1946; state gas corporation; Pres. Ing. CARLOS M. BECHELLI.

Hidroeléctrica Norpatagónica SA (Hidronor): Avda Leandro N. Alem 1074, 1001 Buenos Aires; tel. (1) 311-4990; telex 18097; f. 1967; state hydroelectric corporation; Pres. Dr CÉSAR GARCÍA PUENTE.

Obras Sanitarias de la Nación: Marcelo T. de Alvear 1840, Buenos Aires; tel. (1) 41-1081; f. 1973; sanitation; Administrator Ing. JORGE LÓPEZ RAGGI.

Petroquímica General Mosconi SAI y C: Perú 103, 1067 Buenos Aires; tel. (1) 33-5964; telex 22850; f. 1970; state petrochemical industry; Pres. Ing. HÉCTOR ENRIQUE FORMICA.

Servicios Eléctricos del Gran Buenos Aires SA (SEGBA): Balcarce 184, Buenos Aires; tel. (1) 33-1901; f. 1958; state electricity enterprise; Pres. Dr JUAN JOSÉ VALDETTARO.

Yacimientos Carboníferos Fiscales: Avda Roque S. Peña 1190, Buenos Aires; f. 1958; state coal mining enterprise; Gen. Administrator Ing. VIRGILIO BARBOSA.

Yacimientos Mineros de Agua de Dionisio: Avda Julio A. Roca 710, Buenos Aires; tel. (1) 34-8024; f. 1958; state mining enterprise; Pres. Lic. PABLO ENRIQUE CHISTIK.

Yacimientos Petrolíferos Fiscales Sociedad del Estado (YPF): Avda Roque S. Peña 777, 1364 Buenos Aires; tel. (1) 46-7270; telex 21999; f. 1922; public corporation authorized to formulate national petroleum policy and to develop, process and market hydrocarbon resources; Pres. RODOLFO OTERO; Vice-Pres. Ing. JORGE ENRICH BALADA.

TRADE ASSOCIATIONS

Asociación de Importadores y Exportadores de la República Argentina: Sarmiento 767, 1°, Buenos Aires; tel. (1)

49-5928; telex 21680; f. 1966; Pres. Lic. FERNANDO A. RAIMONDO; Man. ARIEL LIEBSTEIN.

Asociación de Industriales Textiles Argentinos: Uruguay 291, 4°, 1015 Buenos Aires; tel. (1) 49-2256; f. 1945; textile industry; Pres. MANUEL CYWIN; 250 mems.

Asociación de Industrias Argentinas de Carnes: Avda Córdoba 991, 1° A, 1054 Buenos Aires; tel. (1) 392-0587; telex 17304; meat industry; refrigerated and canned beef and mutton; Pres. JORGE BORSELLA.

Asociación Vitivinícola Argentina: Güemes 4464, 1425 Buenos Aires; tel. (1) 774-3370; f. 1904; wine industry; Pres. LUCIANO COLUMACCIO; Man. Ing. DANTE F. MARSICO.

Cámara de Sociedades Anónimas: Sarmiento 299, Buenos Aires; tel. (1) 312-7434; Pres. FERNANDO F. A. MASJUAN; Man. Dr ADALBERTO ZELMAR BARBOSA.

Centro de Exportadores de Cereales: Bouchard 454, 7°, 1106 Buenos Aires; tel. (1) 311-1697; telex 18644; f. 1943; grain exporters; Pres. EDUARDO M. E. BLUM.

Confederación de Productores y Exportadores de la República Argentina: Bartolomé Mitre 2241, 1039 Buenos Aires; tel. (1) 48-6010; Pres. JACOBO RAIES.

Confederaciones Rurales Argentinas: México 682, 2°, 1097 Buenos Aires; tel. (1) 261-1501; Pres. Dr RAÚL ROMERO FERIS.

Federación Lanera Argentina: Paseo Colón 823, 5°, 1063 Buenos Aires; tel. (1) 361-4604; telex 22021; f. 1929; wool industry; Pres. RICARDO GRAVENHORST; Sec. PEDRO LAMBLOT; 115 mems.

EMPLOYERS' ORGANIZATION

Unión Industrial Argentina (UIA): Avda Leandro N. Alem 1067, 11°, 1001 Buenos Aires; tel. (1) 313-2762; telex 21749; f. 1887; Argentine association of manufacturers; re-established in 1974 with the fusion of the Confederación Industrial Argentina (CINA) and the Confederación General de la Industria; following the dissolution of the CINA in 1977, the UIA was formed in 1979; Pres. Ing. ROBERTO FAVELEVIC; Exec. Sec. Dr JORGE PRINA.

TRADE UNIONS

Trade union activity, suspended since March 1976, recommenced towards the end of 1981 and was not suppressed. Dialogue between trade union leaders and the government took place in August 1982 and the right to belong to a trade union was re-established in September 1982. The ban on strikes was lifted in 1983.

Confederación General del Trabajo—CGT (General Confederation of Labour): Buenos Aires; f. 1984; Peronist; Sec.-Gen. SAÚL EDOLVER UBALDINI; represents approximately 90% of Argentina's 1,100 trade unions and consists of four groups:

CGT: Buenos Aires.

Independientes: Buenos Aires.

Ex 25: Buenos Aires.

Verticalistas: Buenos Aires.

Transport

Ministerio de Obras y Servicios Públicos: Avda 9 de Julio 1925, 1332 Buenos Aires; tel. (1) 37-1339; telex 22577; controls:

Secretaría de Transportes: Avda 9 de Julio 1925, 14°, 1332 Buenos Aires; tel. (1) 38-1435; Sec. HORACIO DÍAZ HERMELO.

Subsecretaría de Transporte: Avda 9 de Julio 1925, 8°, 1332 Buenos Aires; tel. (1) 38-5838, ext. 407; Under-Sec. RODOLFO F. HUICI.

Subsecretaría de Planificación del Transporte: Avda 9 de Julio 1925, 11°, 1332 Buenos Aires; tel. (1) 37-2571, ext. 465; Under-Sec. JOSÉ DOMINGO VILLADEAMGIO.

Subsecretaría de Marina Mercante: Julio A. Roca 735, 1067 Buenos Aires; tel. (1) 30-6785; telex 21091; Under-Sec. LUIS ALBERTO SIQUOT FERRE.

Dirección Nacional de Transporte Aerocomercial: Avda 9 de Julio 1925, 22°, 1332 Buenos Aires; tel. (1) 37-8365; Dir ALDO LUIS DEPETRIS.

RAILWAYS

Lines: General Belgrano (narrow gauge), General Roca, General Bartolomé Mitre, General San Martín, Domingo Faustino Sarmiento (all wide gauge) and General Urquiza (medium gauge). The Línea Metropolitana, controlling the railways of Buenos Aires and its suburbs, was under construction in 1986. There are direct rail links with the Bolivian Railways network to Santa Cruz de la Sierra and La Paz; with Chile, through the Las Cuevas–Caracoles tunnel (across the Andes) and between Salta and Antofagasta; with Brazil, across the Paso de los Libres and Uruguayana bridge; with Paraguay (between Posadas and Encarnación by ferry-boat) and with Uruguay (between Concordia and Salto). In August 1983 there were 34,509 km of tracks. In the Buenos Aires commuter area 270.4 km of wide gauge track and 52 km of medium gauge track are electrified.

Ferrocarriles Argentinos (FA): Avda Ramos Mejía 1302, 1104 Buenos Aires; tel. (1) 312-4713; telex 22507; f. 1948 with the nationalization of all foreign property; autonomous body but policies are established by the Ministry of Public Works and Services through the Secretaría de Transportes; Pres. JOSÉ LUIS SALMERÓN.

Cámara de Industriales Ferroviarios: Alsina 1607, 1°, 1088 Buenos Aires; tel.(1) 40-5571; private organization to promote the development of Argentine railway industries; Pres. GUILLERMO NOTTAGE.

Buenos Aires has an underground railway system:

Subterráneos de Buenos Aires: Bartolomé Mitre 3342, 1312 Buenos Aires; tel. (1) 89-6816; telex 18979; f. 1952; became completely state-owned in 1978; controlled by the Municipalidad de la Ciudad de Buenos Aires; five underground lines totalling 36 km; Pres. NICOLÁS VICENTE GALLO.

ROADS

In 1985 there were 211,341 km of roads, of which 378 km were motorways, 36,900 km were other main roads and 174,063 km were secondary roads. In 1983 the network carried about 80% of all freight tonnage and 85% of all medium- and long-distance passengers. Four branches of the Pan-American highway run from Buenos Aires to the borders of Chile, Bolivia, Paraguay and Brazil.

Dirección Nacional de Vialidad: Comodoro Py 2002, 1104 Buenos Aires; tel. (1) 312-9021; telex 17879; controlled by the Secretaría de Transportes; Gen. Man. Ing. JOSÉ MARCO ADJIMAN.

Asociación Argentina Empresarios Transporte Automotor (AAETA): Bernardo de Yrigoyen 330, 6°, 1072 Buenos Aires; Pres. LUIS CARRAL.

Federación Argentina de Entidades Empresarias de Autotransporte de Cargas (FADEAC): Avda de Mayo 1370, 3°, 1372 Buenos Aires; tel. (1) 37-3635; Pres. ROGELIO CAVALIERI IRIBARNE.

There are several international passenger and freight services including:

Autobuses Sudamericanos SA: Bernardo de Yrigoyen 1370, 1°, 1401 Buenos Aires; tel. (1) 27-6591; telex 9900; f. 1928; international bus services; car and bus rentals; charter bus services; Pres. ARMANDO SAMUEL SCHLEKER.

INLAND WATERWAYS

There is considerable traffic in coastal and river shipping, mainly carrying petroleum and its derivatives. In 1983 the total displacement of vessels entering Argentine ports for such transport was 28.2m. nrt.

Dirección Nacional de Construcciones Portuarias y Vías Navegables: Avda España 221, 4°, Buenos Aires; tel. (1) 361-5964; responsible for the maintenance and improvement of waterways and dredging operations; Dir Ing. ENRIQUE CASALS DE ALBA.

Flota Fluvial del Estado Argentino: Corrientes 389, 3°, 1043 Buenos Aires; tel. (1) 312-5651; f. 1958; passengers and cargo services on the Plate, Paraná, Paraguay and Uruguay rivers; Gen. Administrator Dr LUIS SUÁREZ HERTER.

SHIPPING

There are over 100 ports, of which the most important are Buenos Aires, La Plata, Rosario and Bahía Blanca. There are specialized terminals at Ensenada, Comodoro Rivadavia, San Lorenzo and Campana (petroleum); Bahía Blanca, Rosario, Santa Fé, Villa Concepción, Mar del Plata and Quequén (cereals); and San Nicolás and San Fernando/San Isidro (raw and construction materials). A deep-water port was to be constructed at Bahía Blanca. Argentina's merchant fleet totalled 2,066,661 grt in 1985; it comprised 64 cargo vessels, 26 bulk carriers, 58 tankers and 41 miscellaneous vessels.

Administración General de Puertos: Avda Julio A. Roca 734/42, 1067 Buenos Aires; tel. (1) 34-5621; telex 21879; f. 1956; state enterprise for exploitation and conservation of all national sea and river ports; Gen. Administrator Capt. PEDRO TARAMASCO.

Capitanía General del Puerto: Avda Julio A. Roca 734, 2°,

ARGENTINA

1067 Buenos Aires; tel. (1) 34-9784; f. 1967; co-ordination of port operations; Port Captain Capt. PEDRO TARAMASCO.

The chief state-owned organizations are:

Empresa Líneas Marítimas Argentinas SA (ELMA): Avda Corrientes 389, 1327 Buenos Aires; tel. (1) 312-8111; telex 21807; f. 1941; state line operating 50 vessels of 474,445 grt to Northern Europe, Scandinavia, the Mediterranean, West and East Coasts of Canada and the USA, Gulf of Mexico, Caribbean ports, Brazil, Pacific ports of Central and South America, Far East, North and South Africa and the Near East; Pres. Ing. LUIS A. OLAIZOLA; Vice-Pres. Dr LUIS SUÁREZ HERTER; fleet of 497,944 grt.

Yacimientos Petrolíferos Fiscales (YPF): Avda Roque S. Peña 777, 1364 Buenos Aires; tel. (1) 46-7271; telex 21792; Pres. Ing. RODOLFO OTERO; fleet of 338,048 grt of cargo, tankers and tanker craft and motor launches.

Private shipping companies operating on coastal and overseas routes include:

Astra Compañia Argentina de Petróleo, SA: Leandro N. Alem 621, Buenos Aires; tel. (1) 311-0091; telex 17478; Pres. Dr RICARDO GRUNEISEN; fleet of 48,506 grt of tankers and tanker craft.

Bottachi, SA de Navegación: Avda Madero 940, 17°, 1106 Buenos Aires; tel. (1) 313-0252; telex 17269; fleet of 117,494 grt of tankers and cargo craft.

Compañia Argentina de Transportes Marítimos, SA: Avda Corrientes 327, 3°, 1043 Buenos Aires; tel. (1) 311-6300; telex 24454; Pres. J. L. MARTÍN; Vice-Pres. R. E. VÁSQUEZ; fleet of 78,222 grt.

CIVIL AVIATION

Argentina has 10 international airports (Aeroparque Jorge Newbery, Córdoba, Corrientes, El Plumerillo, Ezeiza, Jujuy, Resistencia, Río Gallegos, Salta and San Carlos de Bariloche). Ezeiza, 35 km from Buenos Aires, is one of the most important air terminals in Latin America. All aviation companies, with the exception of LADE, are controlled by the Dirección Nacional de Transporte Aerocomercial.

Aerolíneas Argentinas: Paseo Colón 185, 1063 Buenos Aires; tel. (1) 30-2071; telex 22517; f. 1950; nationalized industry; services to New York, Los Angeles, Miami, Mexico, Montreal and Europe. Its South American services link Argentina with Bolivia, Chile, Colombia, Ecuador, Uruguay, Brazil, Peru, Venezuela and Paraguay. The internal network covers the whole country. Passengers, mail and freight are carried. Pres. Dr HORACIO DOMINGORENA; Vice-Pres. JOSÉ CHALEN; fleet comprises 5 Boeing 747-200B, 1 747SP, 1 707-320B, 2 707-320C, 8 727-200, 10 737-200, 2 737-200c, 3 Fokker F.28-1000, 1 F.28-4000.

Austral Líneas Aéreas (ALA): Corrientes 485, 1398 Buenos Aires; tel. (1) 313-3777; telex 22098; f. 1971; taken over by the state in 1980 to prevent financial collapse; to be 'privatized' in 1986; domestic flights linking 27 cities in Argentina; Pres. Lic. MAURICIO JARAS; fleet comprises 8 BAC 1-11 series 500, 3 DC-9-80.

Líneas Aéreas del Estado (LADE): Perú 710, Buenos Aires; tel. (1) 361-7174; telex 22040; f. 1940; controlled by the Air Ministry and operates through the Argentine Air Force. LADE operates from El Palomar Air Base, Buenos Aires, to 31 domestic points, all south of the capital; Cdre ROBERTO J. NOE; fleet comprises 1 Fokker F.28-1000C, 2 F.27-600, 2 Twin Otter.

Tourism

Dirección General de Turismo: Calle Suipacha 1111, 21°, 1368 Buenos Aires; tel. (1) 312-5621; Dir CÉSAR CRENZEL.

Asociación Argentina de Agencias de Viajes y Turismo (AAAVYT): Viamonte 640, 10°, 1053 Buenos Aires; tel. (1) 392-2804; telex 25449; f. 1951; Pres. SABET ABD EL JALIL; Gen. Man. HÉCTOR J. TESTONI.

Atomic Energy

Comisión Nacional de Energía Atómica (CNEA): Avda del Libertador 8250, 1429 Buenos Aires; telex 21388; f. 1950; Pres. Ing. ALBERTO CONSTANTINI.

Argentina's first nuclear reactor, with a capacity of 640 MW, at Atucha, on the River Paraná de las Palmas, began to operate in 1974. A second plant at Embalse (Córdoba), with an estimated capacity of 644 MW, came into operation in March 1983. A third plant, Atucha II, with an estimated capacity of 690 MW, was under construction in 1986, and was expected to begin operating in 1992. Argentina's first nuclear fuel production plant opened in April 1982 and a plutonium processing plant is expected to begin operating in early 1987. A small uranium enrichment plant situated at Pilcaniyeu in Río Negro province was to become fully operational by the end of 1986. In recent years the development of the atomic energy sector has been severely hindered by lack of funds. In 1985 nuclear power supplied 11.5% of Argentina's total energy requirements.

Research reactors: The following research reactors are in operation:
RA-1 Centro Atómico Constituyentes: maximum capacity 150 kW.
RA-2 Centro Atómico Constituyentes: maximum capacity 30 MW.
RA-3 Centro Atómico Ezeiza: maximum capacity 8 MW.

AUSTRALIA

Introductory Survey

Location, Climate, Language, Religion, Flag, Capital

The Commonwealth of Australia occupies the whole of the island continent of Australia, lying between the Indian and Pacific Oceans, and its offshore islands, principally Tasmania to the south-east. Australia's nearest neighbour is Papua New Guinea, to the north. In the summer there are tropical monsoons in the northern part of the continent (except for the Queensland coast), but the winters are dry. Both the north-west and north-east coasts are liable to experience tropical cyclones between December and April. In the southern half of the country, winter is the wet season; rainfall decreases rapidly inland. Very high temperatures, sometimes exceeding 50°C (122°F), are experienced during the summer months over the arid interior and for some distance to the south, as well as during the pre-monsoon months in the north. The official language is English. In 1966 more than 88% of the population professed Christianity. The national flag (proportions 2 by 1) is blue, with a representation of the United Kingdom flag in the upper hoist, a large seven-pointed white star in the lower hoist and five smaller white stars, in the form of the Southern Cross constellation, in the fly. The capital, Canberra, lies in one of two enclaves of federal territory known as the Australian Capital Territory (ACT).

Recent History

Since the Second World War, Australia has taken an important place in Asian affairs and has strengthened its political and economic ties with India, South-East Asia and Japan. The country co-operates more closely than formerly with the USA (see ANZUS, p. 94), and contributed troops to the war in Viet-Nam until 1972. As a founder-member of the Colombo Plan (p. 112), Australia has given much aid in money, materials and training to Asian countries. Australia also plays an important part in Pacific affairs, and is a member of the South Pacific Commission (p. 200) and of the South Pacific Bureau for Economic Co-operation (p. 202).

In January 1966 Sir Robert Menzies resigned after 16 years as Prime Minister, and was succeeded by Harold Holt, who was returned to office at elections later that year. However, Holt died in a swimming accident in December 1967. His successor, Senator John Gorton, took office in January 1968 but resigned, after losing a vote of confidence, in March 1971. William McMahon was Prime Minister from March 1971 until December 1972, when, after 23 years in office, the Liberal-Country Party coalition was defeated at a general election for the House of Representatives. The Australian Labor Party (ALP), led by Gough Whitlam, received almost 50% of the total votes and won 67 of the 125 seats in the House. Following a conflict between the Whitlam Government and the Senate, both Houses of Parliament were dissolved in April 1974, and general elections were held in May. The ALP was returned to power, although with a reduced majority in the House of Representatives. However, the Government failed to gain a majority in the Senate, and in October 1975 the Opposition in the Senate blocked budget bills concerning money supply. The Government was not willing to consent to a general election over the issue but in November 1975, the Governor-General, Sir John Kerr, intervened and took the unprecedented step of dismissing the Government. A caretaker ministry was installed under Malcolm Fraser, the Liberal leader, who formed a coalition government with the National Country Party. This coalition gained large majorities in both Houses of Parliament at general elections in December 1975, but the majorities were progressively reduced at general elections in December 1977 and October 1980.

Fraser's coalition government was defeated by the ALP at federal elections in March 1983. Robert Hawke, who had replaced William Hayden as Labor leader in the previous month, became the new Prime Minister and immediately honoured one of the party's main election promises by organizing a meeting of representatives of government, employers and trade unions to reach agreement on a prices and incomes policy which would allow economic recovery and the creation of many more jobs. Hawke called a general election for December 1984, 15 months earlier than necessary, and the ALP was returned to power with a reduced majority of seats in the House of Representatives.

Hawke opposed the ALP's pledge to prevent the development of new projects to mine and export uranium, but a compromise was reached in July 1984, when the party's national conference voted to endorse the development of the large Roxby Downs mine in South Australia. The various safeguards that were retained on the use and destination of uranium included a ban on sales to France, owing to Australian opposition to French test explosions of nuclear weapons at Mururoa Atoll in the South Pacific Ocean. However, in August 1986 the Government announced its decision to resume exports of uranium to France, claiming that the sanction had been ineffective and that the lifting of the ban—which provoked strong opposition among Labor MPs—would increase government revenue by $A66m., through the repayment of compensation that had been awarded to the mining industry. The sensitive issue of Aboriginal land rights was tackled by the Government in July 1983, when it warned land-holding companies that failure to settle outstanding land claims by traditional owners within three months would lead to government intervention. In August 1985 the Government adopted proposals for legislation that would give Aborigines inalienable freehold title to national parks, vacant Crown land and former Aboriginal reserves, in spite of widespread opposition from state governments (which had formerly been responsible for their own land policies), from mining companies and from the Aborigines themselves, who were angered by the Government's withdrawal of its earlier support for the Aboriginal right to veto mineral exploitation. In October 1985 Ayers Rock, in the Northern Territory, was officially transferred to the Mutijulu Aboriginal community, on condition that continuing access to the rock, which is Australia's principal inland tourist attraction, be guaranteed. In 1986, however, the Government abandoned its pledge to impose such federal legislation on unwilling state governments, and this led to further protests from Aboriginal leaders, who threatened to retaliate by staging demonstrations to disrupt subsequent national events.

In its foreign policy, the Hawke Government began by placing greater emphasis on its dealings with South-East Asia than the previous government had done. Australian relations with Indonesia, which had been strained since the Indonesian annexation of the former Portuguese colony of East Timor in 1976, improved in August 1985, when Robert Hawke made a statement recognizing Indonesian sovereignty over the territory, but subsequently deteriorated, following the publication in a Sydney newspaper, in April 1986, of an article containing allegations of corruption against the Indonesian President, Gen. Suharto. In August 1985 the Australian Government announced the imposition of limited trading sanctions against South Africa, on the principle that insufficient progress had been made towards disbanding the system of racial apartheid that was in force in that country. In the following year the Government introduced a series of more rigorous commercial measures against South Africa, which was to include the closure of the South African Trade Commission and Tourist Commission in Australia, the imposition of a ban on imports of agricultural products and some minerals from South Africa, the termination of South African Airways' landing rights in Australia and the restriction of Australia's consular facilities in South Africa.

The viability of the ANZUS military pact, linking Australia, New Zealand and the USA, was disputed by the US Government after the New Zealand Government of David Lange had declared, in July 1984, that vessels which were believed to be powered by nuclear energy, or to be carrying nuclear weapons, would not be allowed to enter the country's ports. Hawke did not support the New Zealand initiative, and Australia continued to participate with the USA in joint military exercises from which New Zealand had been excluded. However, the Hawke Government declined directly to endorse US retaliation against New Zealand, and in 1986 issued an official statement to the effect that Australia regarded its 'obligations to New Zealand as constant and undiminishing'. In the same year the Australian Government was proposing to adopt the recommendations of a government-commissioned report advocating a comprehensive restructuring of the country's military forces, on the basis of a more self-reliant defence strategy. Relations between Australia and the USA had suffered a reverse, following the latter's decision, earlier in 1986, to export grain at subsidized prices, notably to the USSR, a practice that was condemned by Hawke as an encroachment on Australia's markets.

In March 1986 the last vestiges of Australia's constitutional links with the United Kingdom were finally severed by the Australia Act, which abolished the UK Parliament's residual legislative, executive and judicial controls over Australian state law.

Government

Australia comprises six States and two Territories. Executive power is vested in the British monarch and exercised by the monarch's appointed representative, the Governor-General, who normally acts on the advice of the Federal Executive Council (the Cabinet), led by the Prime Minister. The Governor-General appoints the Prime Minister and, on the latter's recommendation, other Ministers.

Legislative power is vested in the Federal Parliament. This consists of the monarch, represented by the Governor-General, and two chambers elected by universal adult suffrage (voting is compulsory). The Senate has 76 members (12 from each State and two from each of the Territories), who are elected by a system of proportional representation for six years when representing a State, with half the seats renewable every three years, and for a term of three years when representing a Territory. The House of Representatives has 148 members, elected for three years (subject to dissolution) from single-member constituencies. The Federal Executive Council is responsible to Parliament.

Each State has a Governor, representing the monarch, and its own legislative, executive and judicial system. The State Governments are essentially autonomous, but certain powers are placed under the jurisdiction of the Federal Government. All except the Northern Territory, which acceded to self-governing status in 1978, and Queensland have an Upper House, the Legislative Council, and a Lower House, the Legislative Assembly or House of Assembly. The chief ministers of the States are known as Premiers, as distinct from the Federal Prime Minister.

Defence

Australia's defence policy is based on collective security and it is a member of the British Commonwealth Strategic Reserve and ANZUS, with New Zealand and the USA. In July 1986 Australia's armed forces numbered 70,456 (army 32,116, navy 15,553, air force 22,787). The defence budget for 1986/87 was $A6,929m. Service in the armed forces is voluntary.

Economic Affairs

Australia has a diversified economy, with a generally high level of material prosperity. In 1984, according to estimates by the World Bank, Australia's gross national product (GNP) per head, measured at average 1982–84 prices, was US $11,740, comparable to the average levels in industrialized West European countries. It was estimated that Australia's GNP per head increased, in real terms, at an average rate of 1.7% per year between 1965 and 1984. The average annual real growth of overall gross domestic product (GDP) was 5.6% in 1965–73, slowing to 2.4% in 1973–83.

Greatly-accelerated development of mineral and energy resources followed net increases in foreign capital inflow from $A1,806m. in 1979/80 to $A9,130m. in 1981/82, though foreign investment fell to $A7,550m. in 1983/84, following a decision in December 1983 to 'float' the Australian dollar and to abolish most foreign exchange controls. Australia has vast reserves of coal, petroleum, natural gas, nickel, iron ore and bauxite, and there is a major diamond field in the Kimberley Mountains of Western Australia, which by 1986 was producing at a rate that would yield 25m. carats of mainly industrial-quality diamonds per year, equivalent to almost 40% of 1984 world output. In addition, the Government lifted the ban on uranium exports in 1977, subject to stringent nuclear safeguards, and sales abroad were worth $A360m. in 1982/83. Uranium production totalled an estimated 3,850 metric tons in 1984. Gold, silver, lead, zinc and copper are also exploited. In 1985 gold production totalled 57,000 kg, and lead production 491,000 metric tons. The Olympic Dam project in South Australia is expected to yield large amounts of gold, copper and uranium, although their exploitation was unlikely to begin before 1987. About 70% of Australia's petroleum requirements are now met by domestic sources, but it is estimated that, in the absence of major new discoveries, self-sufficiency will fall to 42% by 1993/94. Petroleum production averaged 650,000 b/d in 1985. Coal is Australia's principal source of foreign exchange earnings, and production is being raised, both for export and to fuel the domestic aluminium smelting industry. The production of saleable coal increased from 99.6m. metric tons in 1982/83 to 105m. tons in 1983/84, and exports of coal reached a record 84m. tons in 1984/85. Work on a project to produce liquefied natural gas on the North-West Shelf, costing $A14,000m., resulted in 1984 in the first deliveries of unprocessed natural gas for domestic use, and in 1985 Japanese customers contracted to buy large quantities of gas, beginning in 1989. In 1983/84 the output of natural gas from Bass Strait, and from new fields in South and Western Australia, totalled 12.1m. cu m. In 1985 agreement was being sought with the People's Republic of China on a joint venture to exploit a rich outcrop of iron ore at Mount Channar, in the Pilbara region of Western Australia. The production of iron ore reached a record 100m. metric tons (64% iron) in 1985, and the output of nickel in the same year totalled 85,000 tons. In 1986 an important platinum deposit, which was judged to have export potential, was discovered in the Northern Territory, and it was hoped that exploitation of this reserve would end Australia's dependence on South Africa for the mineral.

In 1983/84 minerals accounted for about 38% of export revenue and contributed about 5% of GDP, although mining employed only 1.5% of the working population. Many of Australia's minerals are being exploited as raw materials for Japan's industries. The pattern of Australia's dependence on foreign trade has thus undergone a change, with Japan overtaking Western countries as the major market, taking 26.5% of Australian exports in 1983/84, and as the major source of imports, providing 22.3% of the total in 1983/84, marginally ahead of the USA, which supplied 21.6%; ASEAN countries together accounted for about 20% of exports and 17% of imports, while EEC member-states together took about 13% of exports and provided 21% of imports. Australia's trade deficit increased from $A600m. in 1984/85, when the value of exports totalled $A29,531m. and that of imports $A30,131m., to $A3,362m. in 1985/86 (exports $A32,254m., imports $A35,616m.). Relations with the EEC have been strained since 1980, owing to the fact that the subsidized prices of certain EEC products, particularly meat and sugar, make Australian goods uncompetitive in their traditional markets, but in February 1985 Australia secured an assurance that EEC subsidies on exports of beef to the Far East would not be extended. In November 1982 agreement was reached with New Zealand on the progressive reduction of tariffs affecting trade between the two countries.

Manufacturing, which in 1984/85 contributed about 18% of GDP and employed about 18% of the labour force, mainly in the iron and steel and engineering sectors, has become very diversified under the protection of tariffs, which in 1986 ranged from 4% for mineral manufactures to 66% for clothing. Other important industries are food processing, machinery, motor vehicles, chemicals, electrical goods and electronic equipment. The Government has consistently rejected calls to reduce the high level of protection afforded to manufacturing industry because it fears that such a reduction would lead to a sharp increase in unemployment.

Australia's traditional reliance on the agricultural sector has been eroded by the phenomenal mineral discoveries of recent years. However, although it contributed only 6% of GDP in

AUSTRALIA

1982/83 (falling to 5% in 1984/85), agricultural produce earned 43% of Australia's export income in that year. Severe drought affected agricultural production in 1979–83, with the important wheat crop decreasing from 16.3m. metric tons in 1981/82 to 8.8m. tons in 1982/83; the drought ended in April 1983 and crop production subsequently increased considerably, again reaching 16.3m. tons in 1985/86. Wool, wheat, meat, sugar and dairy products are major export items; as a source of foreign exchange earnings, wool is second in importance only to coal, accounting for export earnings of $A3,100m. in 1985/86.

The Labor Government that took office in March 1983 immediately devalued the Australian currency by 10% in an attempt to reverse an outflow of capital from the country and to encourage exports. In May the Government sought agreement with employers and trade unions on a policy for controlling prices and incomes, after wages had risen by about 17% per year in 1981–83, compared with an annual rate of inflation of about 11%. A mini-budget in May and a highly expansionary budget in August 1983 had as principal objectives an expansion of the public housing programme and the creation of 70,000 jobs, but budgets in May and August 1985 sought to restrain the growth of government spending, and the budget deficit decreased from $A6,750m. in 1984/85 to $A5,730m. in 1985/86. In mid-1986 the Government secured support from trade-union leaders for further wage restraint, as part of a programme of economic austerity measures, aimed at reducing the budget deficit still further. A stringent budget, announced in August 1986, sought to curb the rise in interest rates and to halt the rapid depreciation of the Australian dollar, which had been 'floated' in December 1983 and had declined in value by 54% against the Japanese yen, and by 25% against the US dollar, between January 1985 and July 1986. Public expenditure in the year 1986/87 was to be cut by $A2,800m., while the budget deficit was to be reduced to $A3,500m. and the public sector borrowing requirement was to fall by more than $A2,500m., to $A9,800m. Projected revenue of $A71,300m. was to be obtained partly through increased excise and indirect taxes on fuel, alcohol and luxury goods, and was to include $A1,400m. in new taxes. After a fall of 0.6% in 1982/83, GDP grew by 4.9% in 1983/84, by 4.6% in 1984/85 and by 3.7% in 1985/86, and was expected to increase by 2.3% in 1986/87. The annual rate of inflation declined to 4.3% in the year 1984/85, owing largely to a restraint in wage settlements, arising from the Government's tripartite agreement with employers and trade unions. However, the rise in import prices resulting from the depreciation of the Australian dollar was expected to fuel inflation; inflation in the year to the end of June 1986 was 8.4%. The seasonally adjusted unemployment rate in Australia was 8.2% of the labour force in July 1985, showing a very small decline from the figure a year earlier. Wide-ranging measures to deregulate the banking system were announced in 1984, and trading licences were granted to 16 foreign banks in February 1985.

Social Welfare

Australia provides old-age, invalid and widows' pensions, unemployment, sickness and supporting parents' benefits, family allowances and other welfare benefits and allowances. Reciprocal welfare agreements operate between Australia and New Zealand and the United Kingdom, and negotiations have taken place with several other European countries. About 30% of federal budget expenditure is allocated to welfare and 8% to health. In 1984 Australia had 3,535 hospital establishments, including nursing homes, with a total of 166,237 beds, equivalent to one for every 66 inhabitants. In 1984 there were 35,000 physicians registered in the country. The desert interior is served by the Royal Flying Doctor Service. In February 1984 the Government introduced a system of universal health insurance, known as Medicare, under which every Australian is protected against the costs of medical and hospital care. Where medical expenses are incurred, Medicare covers patients for 85% of the Government-approved Schedule Fee for any service provided by a doctor in private practice. A similar benefit is payable for eye tests by optometrists. For hospital care, Medicare pays the full cost of shared-ward accommodation in public hospitals when treatment is provided by doctors employed by the hospital. Out-patient treatment is also free. Private health insurance is available to cover private hospital accommodation and the choice of doctor in a public hospital. The Medicare scheme is financed in part by a 1% levy on taxable incomes above a certain level.

Education

Education is the responsibility of each of the States and the Federal Government. It is free and compulsory for all children from the ages of six to 15 years. Primary education generally begins at six years of age and lasts for six years. Secondary education, beginning at the age of 12, usually lasts for five years. As a proportion of children in the relevant age-groups, the enrolment ratios in 1982 were 100% in primary schools and 82% in secondary schools. In 1983 there were 2,281,022 children enrolled in government primary and secondary schools, and 734,784 attending private schools. Special services have been developed to meet the needs of children living in the remote 'outback' areas, notably Schools of the Air, using two-way receiver sets. A system of one-teacher schools and correspondence schools also helps meet these needs. Australia has 19 universities, with (in 1983) 169,350 students.

Tourism

Australian tourism is developing, along with quicker and cheaper international air transport. The main attractions are swimming and surfing on the Pacific beaches, sailing from Sydney and other harbours, skin-diving along the Great Barrier Reef, winter sports in the Australian Alps, notably the Snowy Mountains, and summer sports in the Blue Mountains. The town of Alice Springs and the sandstone monolith of Ayers Rock are among the attractions of the desert interior. Much of the country's wildlife is unique to Australia. The number of foreign tourist visitors to Australia was 943,900 in 1983.

Public Holidays

1987: 1 January (New Year's Day), 26 January (Australia Day), 17–20 April (Easter), 25 April (Anzac Day), 8 June* (Queen's Official Birthday), 25 December (Christmas Day), 26 December (Boxing Day)†.

1988: 1 January (New Year's Day), 26 January (Australia Day), 1–4 April (Easter), 25 April (Anzac Day), 7 June* (Queen's Official Birthday), 25 December (Christmas Day), 26 December (Boxing Day)†.

* In Western Australia this holiday will be held on 28 September in 1987 and 27 September in 1988.

† Boxing Day is not a public holiday in South Australia.

There are also numerous state holidays.

Weights and Measures

The metric system is in force.

Currency and Exchange Rates

100 cents = 1 Australian dollar ($A).

Exchange rates (30 September 1986):
 £1 sterling = $A2.303;
 US $1 = $A1.592.

AUSTRALIA   *Statistical Survey*

Statistical Survey

Source (unless otherwise stated): Australian Bureau of Statistics, POB 10, Belconnen, ACT 2616; tel. (062) 526627; telex 62020.

Area and Population

AREA, POPULATION AND DENSITY

Area (sq km)	7,682,300*
Population (census results)†	
30 June 1976	14,033,100
30 June 1981	
Males	7,448,300
Females	7,475,000
Total	14,923,300
Population (official estimates at mid-year)†	
1983	15,378,600
1984	15,556,000
1985	15,752,000
Density (per sq km) at mid-1985	2.1

* 2,966,151 sq miles.
† Figures include Australian residents temporarily overseas. Census results also include an adjustment for underenumeration.

STATES AND TERRITORIES (30 June 1984)

	Area (sq km)	Population*	Density (per sq km)
New South Wales (NSW)	801,600	5,406,900	6.7
Victoria	227,600	4,075,500	17.9
Queensland	1,727,200	2,505,300	1.5
South Australia	984,000	1,352,900	1.4
Western Australia	2,525,500	1,382,500	0.5
Tasmania	67,800	437,300	6.4
Northern Territory	1,346,200	138,800	0.1
Australian Capital Territory	2,400	244,500	101.9
Total	7,682,300	15,543,600	2.0

* Figures are provisional. The revised total is 15,556,000.

PRINCIPAL CITIES (estimated population at 30 June 1984)*

Canberra (national capital)	264,300
Sydney (capital of NSW)	3,355,300
Melbourne (capital of Victoria)	2,888,400
Brisbane (capital of Queensland)	1,145,400
Perth (capital of W Australia)	982,700
Adelaide (capital of S Australia)	978,900
Newcastle	418,500
Wollongong	235,800
Gold Coast	198,200
Hobart (capital of Tasmania)	175,700
Geelong	145,200
Darwin (capital of Northern Territory)	66,100

* Figures refer to metropolitan areas, each of which normally comprises a municipality and contiguous urban areas.

BIRTHS, MARRIAGES AND DEATHS*

	Registered live births		Registered marriages		Registered deaths	
	Number	Rate (per 1,000)	Number	Rate (per 1,000)	Number	Rate (per 1,000)
1977	226,291	16.1	104,918	7.5	108,790	7.7
1978	224,181	15.7	102,958	7.2	108,425	7.6
1979	223,129	15.5	104,396	7.2	106,568	7.4
1980	225,527	15.3	109,240	7.3	108,695	7.4
1981	235,842	15.8	113,905	7.6	109,003	7.3
1982	239,903	15.8	117,275	7.7	114,771	7.6
1983	242,570	15.8	114,960	7.4	110,084	7.3
1984	234,034	15.0	115,376†	7.4†	109,914	7.1

* Data are tabulated by year of registration rather than by year of occurrence.
† Provisional.

PERMANENT AND LONG-TERM MIGRATION*

	1981	1982	1983
Arrivals			
Males	113,038	103,539	80,730
Females	99,651	91,663	72,850
Total	212,689	195,202	153,580
Departures			
Males	45,616	49,836	59,870
Females	39,996	42,505	40,640
Total	85,612	92,342	100,510
Net Increase	127,077	102,860	53,070

* i.e. intending to stay for more than one year.

EMPLOYMENT ('000 persons at August)*

	1982	1983	1984
Agriculture and services to agriculture	382.8	384.2	373.1
Forestry, logging, fishing and hunting	27.4	27.4	27.1
Mining	91.2	94.3	93.2
Manufacturing	1,196.3	1,132.0	1,141.4
Electricity, gas and water	128.8	136.0	147.9
Construction	466.7	388.0	423.2
Transport and storage	375.2	365.2	354.1
Wholesale and retail trade	1,248.5	1,217.1	1,271.4
Communications	129.6	140.3	131.6
Finance, property and business services	587.0	574.5	619.3
Public administration and defence	286.6	314.0	321.7
Community services	1,056.8	1,077.3	1,138.4
Recreational, personal and other services	402.5	390.8	420.0
Total	6,379.3	6,241.1	6,462.3
Males	4,024.3	3,903.6	4,012.4
Females	2,355.0	2,337.4	2,449.9

* Estimates refer to all employed persons and are derived from a monthly population survey.

Agriculture

PRINCIPAL CROPS
('000 metric tons, year ending 31 March)

	1981/82	1982/83	1983/84
Wheat for grain	16,360	8,876	21,764
Oats for grain	1,617	848	2,296
Barley for grain	3,450	1,939	4,890
Maize for grain	212	139	238
Sorghum for grain	1,317	958	1,885
Sugar cane for crushing	25,094	24,817	24,191
Apples	294	301	267
Apricots	27	27	24
Bananas	130	140	146
Oranges	376	410	392
Peaches	64	63	48
Pears	109	119	122
Plums and prunes	16	21	20

1984/85 ('000 metric tons, provisional): Wheat for grain 18,699; Oats for grain 1,313; Barley for grain 5,834; Sugar cane for crushing 25,472.

LIVESTOCK ('000 head at 31 March)

	1983	1984	1985*
Cattle	22,478	22,161	23,026
Sheep	133,237	139,242	150,763
Pigs	2,490	2,527	2,370
Horses	449	429	n.a.

* Provisional.

DAIRY PRODUCE (year ending 30 June)

	1981/82	1982/83	1983/84
Whole milk (intake by factories, million litres)	5,268	5,524	5,923
Factory butter ('000 metric tons)	76	84	111
Factory cheese ('000 metric tons)	153	143	161
Market milk sales by factories (million litres)	1,552	1,572	1,572

OTHER LIVESTOCK PRODUCTS
('000 metric tons, year ending 30 June)

	1981/82	1982/83	1983/84
Beef and veal	1,576	1,543	1,338
Mutton	234	250	164
Lamb	277	280	292
Pig meat	228	239	253
Poultry meat	286	313	298
Hen eggs	199	204	206
Wool:			
greasy	717	702	732
clean	436	422	446

1984/85 ('000 metric tons, provisional): Wool (greasy) 773; Wool (clean) 471.

Forestry

ROUNDWOOD REMOVALS
('000 cubic metres, year ending 30 June)

	1981/82	1982/83	1983/84
Sawlogs, veneer logs and logs for sleepers	8,478	6,983	7,358
Pitprops	167	135	145
Pulpwood	5,774	6,149	7,332
Other industrial wood	453	392	449
Fuel wood	1,900	2,300	2,800
Total	16,772	15,959	18,084

Source: Bureau of Agricultural Economics, Canberra, ACT.

SAWNWOOD PRODUCTION
('000 cubic metres, year ending 30 June)

	1981/82	1982/83	1983/84
Coniferous sawnwood	1,181	1,042	1,144
Broadleaved sawnwood	1,976	1,556	1,706
Sub-total	3,157	2,598	2,850
Railway sleepers	207	198	174
Total	3,364	2,794	3,024

Source: Bureau of Agricultural Economics, Canberra, ACT.

Fishing

('000 metric tons, live weight, year ending 30 June)

	1980/81	1981/82	1982/83
Inland waters	1.2	n.a.	n.a.
Indian Ocean	75.5	101.1	109.0
Pacific Ocean	69.8	65.7*	59.5*
Total catch	146.5	166.8†	168.6†

* FAO estimate.   † Marine catch only.
Source: FAO, *Yearbook of Fishery Statistics*.

AUSTRALIA

Mining*

(year ending 30 June)

		1980/81	1981/82	1982/83
Coal (black)	'000 metric tons	96,074	99,560	107,760
Coal, brown (lignite)[1]	'000 metric tons	32,103	37,562	34,998
Coal, brown (briquettes)	'000 metric tons	1,081	993	760
Bauxite	'000 metric tons	25,450	24,690	22,865
Zircon[2]	metric tons	306,079	299,201	226,565
Iron	'000 metric tons	59,064	54,886	50,540
Lead	'000 metric tons	381.4	454.8	457.9
Zinc	'000 metric tons	581.9	623.9	678.3
Copper	'000 metric tons	246.4	259.7	235.3
Titanium[3]	'000 metric tons	1,008	941	n.a.
Tin	metric tons	12,690	12,750	10,692
Crude petroleum[4]	million litres	23,052	22,378	22,069
Natural gas	million cu m	10,435	11,550	11,654
Gold	kg	15,991	22,328	25,825
Silver	kg	759,290	887,569	n.a.
Nickel	metric tons	73,367	81,424	82,945

* Figures for metallic minerals represent metal contents based on chemical assay, except figures for bauxite, which are in terms of gross quantities produced.
[1] Excludes coal used in making briquettes.
[2] In terms of zircon (ZrO$_2$) contained in zircon and rutile concentrates.
[3] In terms of TiO$_2$ contained in bauxite and mineral sands.
[4] Including condensate.

Industry

SELECTED PRODUCTS (year ending 30 June)

		1981/82	1982/83	1983/84
Steel (ingots)	'000 metric tons	7,260	5,306	6,161
Electric motors (under 720 watts)	'000	3,460	2,305	2,358
Clay bricks	million	2,234	1,655	1,702*
Sulphuric acid	'000 metric tons	2,039	1,782	1,726
Nitric acid	metric tons	193,337	189,371	189,167
Television receivers	'000	377	235	260
Motor vehicles	'000	414	357	368
Cotton yarn	'000 metric tons	22	17	20
Cotton cloth	'000 sq m	27,349	32,707	35,452
Tinplate	'000 metric tons	404	335	340
Electricity	million kWh	104,975	105,933	111,696
Cement	'000 metric tons	6,136	5,076	5,130

* For structural purposes only.

AUSTRALIA

Statistical Survey

Finance

CURRENCY AND EXCHANGE RATES

Monetary Units
100 cents = 1 Australian dollar ($A).

Denominations
Coins: 1, 2, 5, 10, 20 and 50 cents; 1 dollar.
Notes: 2, 5, 10, 20, 50 and 100 dollars.

Sterling and US Dollar Equivalents (30 September 1986)
£1 sterling = $A2.303;
US $1 = $A1.592;
$A100 = £43.42 = US $62.80.

Average Exchange Rate (US $ per Australian dollar)
1983   0.9024
1984   0.8796
1985   0.7008

GENERAL GOVERNMENT BUDGET*
($A million, year ending 30 June)

Revenue	1981/82	1982/83	1983/84
Income from public enterprises	2,241	2,798	3,972
Interest, etc.	1,831	2,119	2,216
Indirect taxes	19,533	22,386	25,484
Direct taxes (paid) on income	26,447	28,017	29,563
Other direct taxes, fees, fines, etc.	942	976	1,033
Total	50,994	56,296	62,268

Expenditure	1981/82	1982/83	1983/84
Final consumption	25,356	29,080	32,092
Subsidies	1,095	1,243	1,398
Interest, etc.	5,002	6,236	7,682
Personal benefits to residents	13,349	16,281	19,119
Unfunded employee retirement benefits	252	291	330
Transfers overseas	733	803	874
Total	45,787	53,934	61,495

* Consolidated accounts of Commonwealth, State and local authorities, excluding public financial enterprises. This account shows current transactions only.

STATE GOVERNMENT FINANCES*
($A million, year ending 30 June)

	Receipts 1982/83	Receipts 1983/84	Expenditure 1982/83	Expenditure 1983/84
New South Wales	9,971	11,363	10,838	12,147
Victoria	7,728	8,569	9,407	10,202
Queensland	4,465	5,188	5,653	6,082
South Australia	2,580	2,945	2,957	3,224
Western Australia	2,872	3,323	3,532	3,989
Tasmania	980	1,173	1,206	1,353
Northern Territory	760	892	848	1,026

* Includes all State Government Authorities.

OFFICIAL RESERVE ASSETS ($A million at 30 June)

	1982	1983	1984
Gold	2,444	3,744	3,478
SDRs	8	105	166
IMF reserve position	—	—	162
Foreign exchange	4,065	6,900	8,611
Total	6,517	10,748	12,417

MONEY SUPPLY ($A million at 30 June)

	1982	1983	1984
Notes in circulation	5,837.5	6,362.2	7,204.5

COST OF LIVING (Consumer Price Index*. Base: 1970 = 100)

	1982	1983	1984
Food	319.1	351.3	370.4
Fuel and light	344.9	392.3	414.1
Clothing	320.1	340.0	360.6
Rent	306.4	333.9	357.9
All items	328.1	361.3	375.4

* Weighted average of six state capitals.

NATIONAL ACCOUNTS ($A million at current prices, year ending 30 June)

	1981/82	1982/83	1983/84
Gross domestic product	150,683	165,499	187,405
Indirect taxes less subsidies	17,580	20,053	23,118
Gross domestic product at factor cost	133,103	145,446	164,287
Consumption of fixed capital	10,902	12,444	13,593
Domestic factor incomes	122,201	133,002	150,694
Indirect taxes less subsidies	17,580	20,053	23,118
Net income paid overseas	2,544	3,286	4,118
National income (at market prices)	137,237	149,769	169,694
Expenditure on gross domestic product	150,683	165,499	187,405
of which:			
Private final consumption expenditure	91,234	103,051	113,988
Government final consumption expenditure	24,716	28,303	31,343
Gross fixed capital formation	38,780	38,571	40,515
Increase in stocks	1,499	−2,603	1,509
Statistical discrepancy	358	1,785	2,613
Export of goods and services	22,656	24,485	27,788
Less import of goods and services	28,560	28,093	30,351

BALANCE OF PAYMENTS ($A million, year ending 30 June)

	1982/83 Credit	1982/83 Debit	1982/83 Balance	1983/84 Credit	1983/84 Debit	1983/84 Balance
Goods and services:						
Merchandise	20,656	21,705	−1,049	23,669	23,497	172
Transportation	2,185	3,663	−1,478	2,273	3,846	−1,573
Travel	1,113	1,857	−744	1,277	2,053	−776
Investment income	1,145	3,328	−2,183	1,496	5,642	−4,146
Government n.e.s.	194	371	−177	207	387	−180
Other services	322	492	−170	362	611	−249
Total	25,615	31,416	−5,801	29,284	36,036	−6,752
Transfer payments						
Private	948	600	348	970	635	335
Central government	—	803	−803	—	874	−874
Total	948	1,403	−455	970	1,509	−539
Current balance	—	—	−6,256	—	—	−7,291
Capital and monetary Gold:						
Non-monetary:						
Government transactions (net)	813	—	813	606	—	606
Private investment	8,534	1,455	7,079	8,674	1,738	6,936
Trade credit n.e.s.	27	328	−301	224	205	19
Total	9,374	1,783	7,591	9,504	1,943	7,561
Monetary:						
Changes in official reserve assets	—	2,460	−2,460	—	1,855	−1,855
Allocation of special drawing rights	—	—	—	—	—	—
Other official monetary institutions' transactions	24	—	24	5	—	5
Other	661	—	661	—	201	−201
Total	685	2,460	−1,775	5	2,056	−2,051
Balancing item	439	—	439	1,379	—	1,379
Capital balance	—	—	6,255	—	—	6,889

Note: Any discrepancies between total and sums of components in the above table are due to rounding.

AUSTRALIA

FOREIGN INVESTMENT ($A million, year ending 30 June)

Inflow	1981/82	1982/83	1983/84
EEC—United Kingdom	2,654	2,558	2,606
—Other	609	943	1,103
Switzerland	782	214	126
USA	1,497	969	1,568
Canada	57	28	96
Japan	1,515	2,759	1,507
ASEAN*	1,717	1,093	2,055
Other countries	1,098	945	802
Total	9,923	9,503	9,858

Outflow	1981/82	1982/83	1983/84
EEC—United Kingdom	186	118	103
—Other	18	22	19
New Zealand	188	162	96
USA	441	708	1,270
Papua New Guinea	37	−11	63
ASEAN*	63	163	92
Other countries	94	298	98
Total	1,026	1,460	1,739

* Indonesia, Malaysia, the Philippines, Singapore and Thailand; also Brunei from 1 January 1984.

FOREIGN AID EXTENDED BY AUSTRALIA*
($A million, year ending 30 June)

	1982/83	1983/84	1984/85
Aid payments:			
Bilateral:			
Papua New Guinea	275	302	320
Other	272	395	438
Multilateral	184	216	235
Administration	14	19†	18†
Total	745	932	1,011

* Official only; excludes transfers by private persons and organizations to overseas recipients.
† Includes the cost of administration of overseas students by other government agencies.
Source: Statistical summary, Australian Official Development Assistance to Developing Countries.

External Trade

PRINCIPAL COMMODITIES
($A million, year ending 30 June)

Imports	1981/82	1982/83	1983/84
Food and live animals	732.2	835.5	1,015.2
Beverages and tobacco	173.0	183.8	196.1
Crude materials (inedible) except fuels	769.5	648.4	762.2
Mineral fuels, lubricants, etc.	3,002.6	3,098.4	2,218.7
Animal and vegetable oils, fats and waxes	80.0	81.5	111.1
Chemicals and related products	1,827.6	1,776.1	2,151.0
Basic manufactures	3,856.0	3,445.7	3,984.4
Paper, paperboard and manufactures	556.8	484.1	615.5
Textile yarns, fabrics, etc.	1,095.2	1,011.4	1,302.4
Machinery and transport equipment	9,356.5	8,022.2	9,317.7
Machinery	6,109.8	5,681.4	6,264.2
Transport equipment	3,246.7	2,340.9	3,053.4
Miscellaneous manufactured articles	2,680.8	2,733.8	3,119.2
Other commodities and transactions	288.3	390.1	674.2
Total merchandise	22,766.5	21,215.6	23,549.7
Non-merchandise trade	238.2	590.4	511.3
Total	23,004.7	21,806.0	24,061.0

Exports	1981/82	1982/83	1983/84
Food and live animals	5,802.8	5,457.5	6,147.0
Meat and meat preparations	1,380.9	1,677.6	1,394.0
Dairy products and birds' eggs	301.1	329.4	367.6
Cereals and cereal preparations	2,495.8	1,918.4	2,704.1
Sugar, sugar preparations and honey	793.7	581.1	648.0
Beverages and tobacco	50.0	66.7	73.3
Crude materials (inedible) except fuels	5,822.4	6,263.1	6,848.2
Wool and other animal hair*	1,763.8	1,721.1	1,900.3
Hides, skins and fur-skins (raw)	217.5	232.4	268.8
Metalliferous ores and metal scrap	3,375.8	3,753.3	4,102.8
Mineral fuels, lubricants, etc.†	3,163.5	4,575.8	5,198.3
Animal and vegetable oils, fats and waxes	95.3	87.1	105.4
Chemicals and related products	402.3	457.9	501.6
Basic manufactures	1,809.5	2,292.5	2,583.9
Machinery and transport equipment	1,099.4	1,133.1	1,336.8
Machinery	668.7	770.8	886.7
Transport equipment	430.7	362.3	450.1
Miscellaneous manufactured articles	401.3	476.1	510.3
Other commodities and transactions‡	472.7	645.7	709.4
Total merchandise	19,293.7	21,456.0	24,014.3
Non-merchandise trade	281.5	667.5	752.4
Total	19,575.2	22,123.1	24,766.6

* Excluding wool tops.
† Excluding natural and manufactured gas.
‡ Including natural and manufactured gas.

AUSTRALIA   Statistical Survey

PRINCIPAL TRADING PARTNERS
($A '000, year ending 30 June)

Imports	1982/83	1983/84
Bahrain	40,138	90,440
Belgium/Luxembourg	124,792	161,677
Brazil	154,735	177,204
Canada	434,643	459,688
China, People's Republic	278,891	311,629
Denmark	77,619	101,158
Finland	108,428	149,515
France	454,765	514,201
Germany, Federal Republic	1,298,605	1,385,079
Hong Kong	485,322	552,228
India	142,288	119,313
Indonesia	561,376	299,590
Ireland	97,179	99,258
Italy	538,320	747,986
Japan	4,506,327	5,366,669
Korea, Republic	292,856	382,722
Kuwait	354,386	435,610
Malaysia	214,502	257,044
Netherlands	303,285	336,061
New Zealand	694,278	921,512
Papua New Guinea	69,042	76,679
Philippines	84,118	92,066
Saudi Arabia	976,780	679,829
Singapore	599,843	470,224
South Africa	84,944	132,365
Sweden	277,859	343,032
Switzerland	197,395	229,154
Taiwan	649,597	854,174
Thailand	89,399	122,071
United Arab Emirates	394,027	267,205
United Kingdom	1,466,930	1,739,474
USA	4,766,424	5,188,507
Other countries	986,922	999,633
Total	21,806,015	24,062,997

Exports	1982/83	1983/84
Bangladesh	17,180	108,210
Belgium/Luxembourg	165,651	163,666
Canada	285,892	315,240
China, People's Republic	643,792	609,098
Egypt	385,243	390,267
Fiji	175,853	188,170
France	495,284	482,431
Germany, Federal Republic	548,615	720,719
Hong Kong	349,703	609,667
India	210,845	140,753
Indonesia	406,857	379,205
Iran	231,945	293,731
Iraq	108,516	174,528
Italy	368,378	482,452
Japan	5,975,673	6,534,466
Korea, Republic	829,566	936,793
Kuwait	131,947	123,555
Malaysia	482,381	467,231
Netherlands	297,477	318,775
New Zealand	1,155,458	1,422,027
Papua New Guinea	508,235	493,825
Philippines	194,623	153,630
Poland	69,624	117,803
Saudi Arabia	352,958	387,881
Singapore	733,579	947,825
South Africa	144,533	281,734
Taiwan	550,632	703,840
Thailand	179,303	208,623
USSR	506,952	583,199
United Arab Emirates	141,846	157,428
United Kingdom	1,181,251	1,139,257
USA	2,241,147	2,702,790
Other countries	2,052,162	2,027,820
Total	22,123,101	24,766,639

Transport

		1981/82	1982/83	1983/84
Railways:				
Route kilometres*	number	38,943	39,065	n.a.
Passengers	'000	411,956	412,847	n.a.
Goods and livestock	'000 metric tons	127,333	124,093	n.a.
Road traffic:				
Motor vehicles registered*	'000	8,358	8,590	8,833
Overseas shipping:				
Vessels entered†	'000 tons	232,370	223,817	n.a.
Vessels cleared†	'000 tons	235,635	230,385	n.a.
Air transport, internal services:				
Kilometres flown	'000	136,769	127,952	126,087
Passengers carried		11,396,510	10,332,934	10,597,651
Freight	metric tons	136,250	141,853	149,879
Mail	metric tons	16,841	16,767	17,571
Air transport, overseas services‡:				
Kilometres flown	'000	61,052	64,898	65,670
Passengers carried		2,020,107	2,101,788	2,189,669
Freight	metric tons	66,036	75,375	84,844
Mail	metric tons	4,344	4,219	4,410

* Figures as at end of period.
† Figures are for deadweight tonnage of vessels.
‡ Refers only to services operated by Qantas Airways Ltd.

Tourism

	1981	1982	1983
Number of visitors (arrivals)*	936,727	954,674	943,900

* i.e. intending to stay less than one year.

Communications Media

	1982	1983	1984
Telephones in use ('000 at 30 June)	8,055	8,267	8,329

Radio receivers (1982): 17,600,000 in use (estimate).
Television receivers (1982): 6,500,000 in use (estimate).
Books (1982): 2,358 titles (including 599 pamphlets) produced.
Newspapers (1979): 63 dailies (combined circulation 4,851,000); 470 non-dailies (circulation 8,930,000).

Education

(1983)

	Institutions	Teaching staff*	Students
Government schools	7,546	145,908	2,281,022‡
Non-government schools	2,362	41,589	734,784‡
Universities	19	11,437	169,350
Colleges of advanced education	45§	10,430‖	179,893‖
Technical education† (1982)	209¶	22,002	1,027,052

* Full-time staff plus full-time equivalents of part-time staff. Technical education staff are shown in units of 1,000 hours.
† Includes stream 6. Source: Commonwealth Tertiary Education Commission, *Selected TAFE Statistics*.
‡ Excludes all pre-primary education undertaken on a sessional basis or in a recognized pre-school class, and includes only students attending schools on a full-time basis.
§ Figure refers to the number of Colleges of Advanced Education.
‖ Figure refers to all advanced education activity carried out both at Colleges of Advanced Education and at other institutions.
¶ Figure refers to major institutions only.

Directory

The Constitution

The Federal Constitution was adopted on 9 July 1900 and came into force on 1 January 1901. Its main provisions are summarized below:

PARLIAMENT

The legislative power of the Commonwealth of Australia is vested in a Federal Parliament, consisting of HM the Queen (represented by the Governor-General), a Senate, and a House of Representatives. The Governor-General may appoint such times for holding the sessions of the Parliament as he or she thinks fit, and may also from time to time, by proclamation or otherwise, prorogue the Parliament, and may in like manner dissolve the House of Representatives. By convention, these powers are exercised on the advice of the Prime Minister. After any general election Parliament must be summoned to meet not later than 30 days after the day appointed for the return of the writs.

THE SENATE

The Senate is composed of 12 senators from each State, two senators representing the Australian Capital Territory and two representing the Northern Territory. The senators are directly chosen by the people of the State or Territory, voting in each case as one electorate, and are elected by proportional representation. Senators representing a State have a six-year term and retire by rotation, one-half from each State on 30 June of each third year. The term of a senator representing a Territory is limited to three years. In the case of a State, if a senator vacates his or her seat before the expiration of the term of service, the Houses of Parliament of the State for which the senator was chosen shall, in joint session, choose a person to hold the place until the expiration of the term or until the election of a successor. If the State Parliament is not in session, the Governor of the State, acting on the advice of the State's Executive Council, may appoint a senator to hold office until Parliament reassembles, or until a new senator is elected.

The Senate may proceed to the dispatch of business notwithstanding the failure of any State to provide for its representation in the Senate.

THE HOUSE OF REPRESENTATIVES

In accordance with the Australian Constitution, the total number of members of the House of Representatives must be as nearly as practicable double that of the Senate. The number in each State is in proportion to population, but under the Constitution must be at least five. The House of Representatives is composed of 148 members, including two members for the Australian Capital Territory and one member for the Northern Territory.

Members are elected by universal adult suffrage and voting is compulsory. Only Australian citizens are eligible to vote in Australian elections. British subjects, if they are not Australian citizens or already on the rolls, have to take out Australian citizenship before thay can enrol and before they can vote.

Members are chosen by the electors of their respective electorates by the preferential voting system.

The duration of the Parliament is limited to three years.

To be nominated for election to the House of Representatives, a candidate must be 18 years of age or over, an Australian citizen, and entitled to vote at the election or qualified to become an elector.

THE EXECUTIVE GOVERNMENT

The executive power of the Federal Government is vested in the Queen, and is exercisable by the Governor-General, advised by an Executive Council of Ministers of State, known as the Federal Executive Council. These ministers are, or must become within three months, members of the Federal Parliament.

The Australian Constitution is construed as subject to the principles of responsible government and the Governor-General acts on the advice of the ministers in relation to most matters.

THE JUDICIAL POWER

See Judicial System, p. 386.

THE STATES

The Australian Constitution safeguards the Constitution of each State by providing that it shall continue as at the establishment of the Commonwealth, except as altered in accordance with its own provisions. The legislative power of the Federal Parliament is limited in the main to those matters that are listed in section 51 of the Constitution, while the States possess, as well as concurrent powers in those matters, residual legislative powers enabling them to legislate in any way for 'the peace, order and good Government' of their respective territories. When a state law is inconsistent with a law of the Commonwealth, the latter prevails, and the former is invalid to the extent of the inconsistency.

The States may not, without the consent of the Commonwealth, raise or maintain naval or military forces, or impose taxes on any property belonging to the Commonwealth of Australia, nor may the Commonwealth tax State property. The States may not coin money.

AUSTRALIA

The Federal Parliament may not enact any law for establishing any religion or for prohibiting the exercise of any religion, and no religious test may be imposed as a qualification for any office under the Commonwealth.

The Commonwealth of Australia is charged with protecting every State against invasion, and, on the application of a State Executive Government, against domestic violence.

Provision is made under the Constitution for the admission of new States and for the establishment of new States within the Commonwealth of Australia.

ALTERATION OF THE CONSTITUTION

Proposed laws for the amendment of the Constitution must be passed by an absolute majority in both Houses of the Federal Parliament, and not less than two or more than six months after its passage through both Houses the proposed law must be submitted in each State to the qualified electors.

In the event of one House twice refusing to pass a proposed amendment that has already received an absolute majority in the other House, the Governor-General may, notwithstanding such refusal, submit the proposed amendment to the electors. By convention, the Governor-General acts on the advice of the Prime Minister. If in a majority of the States a majority of the electors voting approve the proposed law and if a majority of all the electors voting also approve, it shall be presented to the Governor-General for Royal Assent.

No alteration diminishing the proportionate representation of any State in either House of the Federal Parliament, or the minimum number of representatives of a State in the House of Representatives, or increasing, diminishing or altering the limits of the State, or in any way affecting the provisions of the Constitution in relation thereto, shall become law unless the majority of the electors voting in that State approve the proposed law.

STATES AND TERRITORIES

New South Wales

The State's executive power is vested in the Governor, appointed by the Crown, who is assisted by a Cabinet.

The State's legislative power is vested in a bicameral Parliament, the Legislative Council and the Legislative Assembly. The Legislative Council, formerly consisting of 60 members, began, in late 1978, a process of reconstitution at the end of which it was to consist of 45 members directly elected for the duration of three parliaments, 15 members retiring every four years. The Legislative Assembly consists of 99 members and sits for four years.

Victoria

The State's legislative power is vested in a bicameral Parliament: the Upper House, or Legislative Council, of 44 members, elected for six years, and the Lower House, or Legislative Assembly, of 88 members, elected for four years. One-half of the members of the Council retires every three years.

In the exercise of the executive power the Governor is assisted by a Cabinet of responsible ministers. Not more than five members of the Council and not more than 13 members of the Assembly may occupy salaried office at any one time.

The State has 88 electoral districts, each returning one member, and 22 electoral provinces, each returning two Council members.

Queensland

The State's legislative power is vested in a unicameral Parliament composed of 82 members who are elected from 82 districts for a term of three years.

South Australia

The State's Constitution vests the legislative power in a Parliament elected by the people and consisting of a Legislative Council and a House of Assembly. The Council is composed of 22 members, one-half of whom retires every three years. Their places are filled by new members elected under a system of proportional representation, with the whole State as a single electorate. The executive has no authority to dissolve this body, except in circumstances warranting a double dissolution.

The 47 members of the House of Assembly are elected for three years from 47 electoral districts.

The executive power is vested in a Governor, appointed by the Crown, and an Executive Council consisting of 13 responsible ministers.

Western Australia

The State's administration is vested in the Governor, a Legislative Council and a Legislative Assembly.

The Legislative Council consists of 34 members, each of the 17 provinces returning two members. Election is for a term of six years, one-half of the members retiring every three years.

The Legislative Assembly consists of 57 members, elected for three years, each representing one electorate.

Tasmania

The State's executive authority is vested in a Governor, appointed by the Crown, who acts upon the advice of his premier and ministers, who are elected members of either the Legislative Council or the House of Assembly. The Council consists of 19 members who sit for six years, retiring in rotation. The House of Assembly has 35 members elected for four years.

Northern Territory

On 1 July 1978, the Northern Territory was established as a body politic with executive authority for specified functions of government. Most functions of the government were transferred to the Territory Government in 1978 and 1979, major exceptions being Aboriginal affairs and uranium mining.

The Territory Parliament consists of a single house, the Legislative Assembly, with 25 members. The first parliament stayed in office for three years, but as from the election held in August 1980 members are elected for a term of four years.

The office of Administrator continues. The Northern Territory (Self-Government) Act provides for the appointment of an Administrator by the Governor-General charged with the duty of administering the Territory. In respect of matters transferred to the Territory Government, the Administrator acts with the advice of the Territory Executive Council; in respect of matters retained by the Commonwealth, the Administrator acts on Commonwealth advice.

Australian Capital Territory

The Australian Capital Territory, within which the Federal Seat of Government is situated, is administered by the Federal Government. Under legislation passed by the Parliament the Governor-General is given power to make ordinances for the peace, order and good government of the Territory. There is established in the Territory an elected House of Assembly, consisting of 18 elected members, which may advise the Government on matters affecting the Territory.

The Government

Head of State: HM Queen ELIZABETH II.

Governor-General: Sir NINIAN MARTIN STEPHEN (took office 29 July 1982).

FEDERAL EXECUTIVE COUNCIL
(November 1986)

Inner Cabinet

Prime Minister: ROBERT J. L. HAWKE.

Deputy Prime Minister, Attorney-General, Minister Assisting the Prime Minister for Commonwealth–State Relations, and Vice-President of the Executive Council: LIONEL BOWEN.

Minister for Industry, Technology and Commerce: Senator JOHN BUTTON.

Minister for Community Services: Senator DONALD GRIMES.

Minister for Employment and Industrial Relations and Minister Assisting the Prime Minister for Public Service Industrial Matters: RALPH WILLIS.

Treasurer: PAUL J. KEATING.

Special Minister of State: MICHAEL J. YOUNG.

Minister for Finance and Minister Assisting the Prime Minister for Public Service Matters: Senator PETER WALSH.

Minister for Foreign Affairs: WILLIAM HAYDEN.

Minister for Education and Minister Assisting the Prime Minister on the Status of Women: Senator SUSAN RYAN.

Minister for Resources and Energy, Minister Assisting the Prime Minister and Minister Assisting the Minister for Foreign Affairs: Senator GARETH EVANS.

Minister for Trade and Minister Assisting the Prime Minister for Youth Affairs: JOHN S. DAWKINS.

Minister for Primary Industry: JOHN KERIN.

Minister for Housing and Construction: STEWART WEST.

AUSTRALIA

Minister for Defence: Kim C. Beazley.
Minister for Immigration and Ethnic Affairs and Minister Assisting the Treasurer: Christopher Hurford.
Minister for Social Security: Brian Howe.

Other Ministers

Minister for Transport and Minister for Aviation: Peter Morris.
Minister for Sport, Recreation and Tourism and Minister Assisting the Minister for Defence: John Brown.
Minister for Health: Dr Neal Blewett.
Minister for Science and Minister Assisting the Minister for Industry, Technology and Commerce: Barry O. Jones.
Minister for Territories: Gordon Scholes.
Minister for Communications and Minister Assisting the Minister for Defence: Michael Duffy.
Minister for Arts, Heritage and Environment and Minister Assisting the Prime Minister for the Bicentenary: Barry Cohen.
Minister for Aboriginal Affairs: A. Clyde Holding.
Minister for Veterans' Affairs: Senator Arthur T. Gietzelt.
Minister for Local Government and Administrative Services: Tom Uren.

MINISTRIES

Department of the Prime Minister and Cabinet: Edmund Barton Bldg, Macquarie St, Barton, ACT 2600; tel. (062) 723955; telex 61616.
Department of Aboriginal Affairs: MLC Tower, Woden Town Centre, Phillip, ACT 2606; tel. (062) 891222; telex 62471.
Department of Arts, Heritage and Environment: Tasman House, Marcus Clarke St, Canberra City, ACT 2601; tel. (062) 467211; telex 62960.
Attorney-General's Department: Robert Garran Offices, Barton, ACT 2600; tel. (062) 719111; telex 62002.
Department of Aviation: Civic Advance Bank Bldg, Allara St, Canberra City, ACT 2601; tel. (062) 684111; telex 62221.
Department of Communications: Bldg 7, Benjamin Offices, Belconnen, ACT 2617; tel. (062) 641177; telex 62025.
Department of Community Services: POB 646, Woden, ACT 2606; tel. (062) 836111; telex 61210.
Department of Defence: Russell Offices, Canberra, ACT 2600; tel. (062) 659111; telex 62625.
Department of Education: MLC Tower, Keltie St, Phillip, ACT 2606; tel. (062) 837777; telex 62116.
Department of Employment and Industrial Relations: 1 Farrell Place, Canberra City, ACT 2601; tel. (062) 437333; telex 62210.
Department of Finance: Newlands St, Parkes, ACT 2600; tel. (062) 632222; telex 62639.
Department of Foreign Affairs: Administrative Bldg, Parkes, ACT 2600; tel. (062) 619111; telex 62007.
Department of Health: Alexander Bldg, Furzer St, Phillip, Canberra, ACT 2606; tel. (062) 891555; telex 62149.
Department of Housing and Construction: DHC House, 470 Northbourne Ave, Dickson, ACT 2602; tel. (062) 436111; telex 62441.
Department of Immigration and Ethnic Affairs: Benjamin Offices, Chan St, Belconnen, ACT 2617; tel. (062) 641111; telex 62037.
Department of Industry, Technology and Commerce: Edmund Barton Bldg, Kings Ave, Barton, ACT 2600; tel. (062) 723944; telex 62654.
Department of Local Government and Administrative Services: Canberra House, Marcus Clarke St, POB 1920, Canberra City, ACT 2601; tel. (062) 434811.
Department of Primary Industry: Edmund Barton Bldg, Broughton St, Barton, ACT 2600; tel. (062) 723933; telex 62188.
Department of Resources and Energy: Jolimont Centre, 65–67 Northbourne Ave, Canberra City, ACT 2600; tel. (062) 458211; telex 62101.
Department of Science: Entrance 5, Benjamin Offices, Belconnen, ACT 2617; tel. (062) 641155; telex 62484.
Department of Social Security: Juliana House, Bowes St, Phillip, ACT 2606; tel. (062) 844844; telex 62143.

Department of the Special Minister of State: West Block, Canberra, ACT 2600; Locked Bag No. 2, Queen Victoria Terrace, Canberra, ACT 2600; tel. (062) 702211; telex 62538.
Department of Sport, Recreation and Tourism: Silverton Centre, Moore St, Canberra City, ACT 2601; tel. (062) 689411; telex 61716.
Department of Territories: Electricity House, POB 158, Canberra City, ACT 2601; tel. (062) 462211; telex 61737.
Department of Trade: Edmund Barton Bldg, Kings Ave, Barton, ACT 2600; tel. (062) 723911; telex 62193.
Department of Transport: cnr Northbourne Ave and Cooyong St, Canberra, ACT 2600; POB 594, Canberra, ACT 2601; tel. (062) 687111; telex 61680.
Department of the Treasury: Parkes Place, Parkes, ACT 2600; tel. (062) 632111; telex 62372.
Department of Veterans' Affairs: MLC Tower, Keltie St, Phillip, ACT 2606; tel. (062) 891111; telex 62706.

ADMINISTRATORS OF TERRITORIES

Northern Territory: Cdre E. E. Johnston.
Norfolk Island: Cdre J. A. Matthew.
Cocos (Keeling) Islands: Carolyn Stuart.
Christmas Island: T. F. Paterson.

Legislature

FEDERAL PARLIAMENT

Elections to the House of Representatives and the Senate were held on 1 December 1984.

Senate

President: Senator Douglas McClelland (Lab.).
Chairman of Committees: Senator David Hamer (Lib.).
Leader of the Government in the Senate: Senator John Button (Lab.).
Leader of the Opposition in the Senate: Senator Frederick Michael Chaney (Lib.).

Party	Seats
Labor Party	34
Liberal Party	28
Australian Democrats	7
National Party	5
Independents	2
Total	76

House of Representatives

Speaker: Joan Child (Lab.).
Chairman of Committees: Leo McLeay (Lab.).
Leader of the House: Michael Young (Lab.).
Leader of the Opposition: John Howard (Lib.).

Party	Seats
Labor Party	82
Liberal Party	45
National Party	21
Total	148

State Governments

NEW SOUTH WALES

Governor: Air Marshal Sir James Rowland.

Labor Ministry
(November 1986)

Premier: Barrie Unsworth.

Legislature

Legislative Council: Pres. John Richard Johnson; Chair. of Cttees Clive Healey.

AUSTRALIA
Directory

Legislative Assembly: Speaker LAWRENCE BORTHWICK KELLY; Chair. of Cttees JACK RICHARD FACE.

VICTORIA
Governor: Rev. Dr DAVIS MCCAUGHEY.

Labor Ministry
(November 1986)

Premier: JOHN CAIN.

Legislature
Legislative Council: Pres. RODERICK ALEXANDER MACKENZIE; Chair. of Cttees GIOVANNI ANTONIO SGRO; Clerk of the Council ROBERT KEEGAN EVANS.
Legislative Assembly: Speaker CYRIL THOMAS EDMUNDS; Chair. of Cttees WILLIAM FRANCIS FOGARTY; Clerk of the Assembly RAYMOND KEITH BOYES.

QUEENSLAND
Governor: Sir WALTER CAMPBELL.

National Party Ministry
(November 1986)

Premier: Sir JOH(ANNES) BJELKE-PETERSEN.

Legislature
Legislative Assembly: Speaker J. H. WARNER; Chair. of Cttees E. C. ROW; Clerk A. R. WOODWARD.

SOUTH AUSTRALIA
Governor: Lt-Gen. Sir DONALD BEAUMONT DUNSTAN.

Labor Ministry
(November 1986)

Premier: JOHN CHARLES BANNON.

Legislature
Legislative Council: Pres. and Chair. of Cttees ANNE LEVY; Clerk of the Council J. M. DAVIS (acting).
House of Assembly: Speaker J. P. TRAINER; Chair. of Cttees D. M. FERGUSON; Clerk of the House G. D. MITCHELL.

WESTERN AUSTRALIA
Governor: Prof. GORDON REID.

Labor Ministry
(November 1986)

Premier: BRIAN THOMAS BURKE.

Legislature
Legislative Council: Pres. CLIVE EDWARD GRIFFITHS; Chair. of Cttees DAVID JOHN WORDSWORTH; Clerk of the Council LAURENCE BERNHARD MARQUET.
Legislative Assembly: Speaker MICHAEL BARNETT; Chair. of Cttees GRAHAM JOHN BURKETT; Clerk of the Assembly BRUCE LEFROY OKELY.

TASMANIA
Governor: Sir JAMES PLIMSOLL.

Liberal Ministry
(November 1986)

Premier: ROBIN TREVOR GRAY.

Legislature
Legislative Council: Pres. ALBERT JAMES BROADBY; Chair. of Cttees R. T. HOPE; Clerk of the Council ADRIAN JACK SHAW.
House of Assembly: Speaker MAX BUSHBY; Chair. of Cttees JOHN BEATTIE; Clerk of the House PAUL TREVOR MCKAY.

NORTHERN TERRITORY
Administrator: Cdre E. E. JOHNSTON.

Country-Liberal Party Ministry
(November 1986)

Chief Minister: STEVE HATTON.

Legislature
Legislative Assembly: Speaker R. M. STEELE.

Political Organizations

Australian Democratic Labor Party: 155–159 Castlereagh St, Sydney, NSW; f. 1956 following a split in the Australian Labor Party; Pres. P. J. KEOGH; Gen. Sec. JOHN KANE.

Australian Democrats Party: 400 Flinders St, Melbourne, Vic 3000; tel. (03) 622521; telex 39117; f. 1977; comprises the fmr Liberal Movement and the Australia Party; Leader Senator DONALD L. CHIPP.

Australian Labor Party: John Curtin House, 22 Brisbane Ave, Barton, ACT 2600; f. 1891; supports the democratic socialization of industry, production, distribution and exchange, with the declared aim of eliminating exploitation and other anti-social features in these fields; Fed. Parl. Leader ROBERT J. L. HAWKE; Nat. Pres. MICHAEL YOUNG; Nat. Sec. BOB MCMULLAN.

Communist Party of Australia: 4 Dixon St, Sydney, NSW 2000; tel. (02) 264-2161; telex 71460 (domestic), 11005 (international); f. 1920; independent of both Soviet and Chinese influence; Nat. Exec. B. AARONS, R. DURBRIDGE, P. RANALD, K. WICKS, L. CONNOR, W. NEILLEY, C. SHUTE, J. STEVENS.

Communist Party of Australia (Marxist-Leninist): f. 1967 following a split in Communist Party of Australia; Maoist; Chair. E. F. HILL.

Liberal Party of Australia: Federal Secretariat, cnr Blackall and Macquarie Sts, Barton, ACT 2600; tel. (062) 732564; telex 62630; f. 1944; advocates private enterprise, social justice, individual liberty and initiative; committed to Australia's development, prosperity and security; Fed. Pres. J. H. VALDER; Parl. Leader JOHN HOWARD.

National Party of Australia: John McEwen House, National Circuit, Barton, ACT 2600; tel. (062) 733822; telex 62543; f. 1916 as the Country Party of Australia; changed name to National Party of Australia in 1982; advocates balanced national development based on free enterprise, with special emphasis on the needs of people outside the major metropolitan areas; Fed. Pres. Mrs SHIRLEY MCKERROW; Fed. Parl. Leader IAN SINCLAIR; Fed. Dir PAUL DAVEY.

Socialist Party of Australia: 65 Campbell St, Surry Hills, NSW 2010; tel. (02) 212-6855; telex 10101; f. 1971; seeks to build a socialist society through public ownership of the means of production and working-class political power, and to build a united front of workers; Pres. J. MCPHILLIPS; Gen. Sec. P. SYMON.

Other political parties include the Farm and Town Party and the Nuclear Disarmament Party (f. 1984).

Diplomatic Representation

EMBASSIES AND HIGH COMMISSIONS IN AUSTRALIA

Argentina: 1st Floor, Suite 102, MLC Tower, Woden, ACT 2606; POB 262, Woden, ACT 2606; tel. (062) 824855; telex 62195; Ambassador: RAFAEL GOWLAND.

Austria: 107 Endeavour St, Red Hill, ACT 2603; POB 375, Manuka, ACT 2603; tel. (062) 951533; telex 62726; Ambassador: Dr JAMES PREUSCHEN.

Bangladesh: 11 Molineaux Place, Farrer, ACT 2607; POB 197, Mawson, ACT 2607; tel. (062) 863907; telex 61729; High Commissioner: Maj.-Gen. (retd) QUAZI GOLAM DASTGIR.

Belgium: 19 Arkana St, Yarralumla, ACT 2600; tel. (062) 732501; telex 62601; Ambassador: ANDRÉAS DOMUS.

Brazil: 19 Forster Crescent, Yarralumla, ACT; POB 1540, Canberra, ACT 2601; tel. (062) 732372; telex 62327; Ambassador: MARCOS HENRIQUE CAMILLO CÔRTES.

Burma: 85 Mugga Way, Red Hill, ACT 2603; tel. (062) 950045; telex 62614; Ambassador: U MAUNG MAUNG SOE TINT.

Canada: Commonwealth Ave, Canberra, ACT 2600; tel. (062) 733844; telex 62017; High Commissioner: EDWARD M. SCHREYER.

Chile: 93 Endeavour St, Red Hill, ACT 2603; POB 69, Monaro Crescent, ACT 2603; tel. (062) 959192; telex 62685; Ambassador: JORGE BERGUÑO.

China, People's Republic: 14 Federal Highway, Watson, Canberra, ACT 2602; tel. (062) 412446; telex 62489; Ambassador: ZHANG ZAI.

Cyprus: 37 Endeavour St, Red Hill, ACT 2603; tel. (062) 953713; telex 62499; High Commissioner: Dr PROKOPIS VANEZIS.

AUSTRALIA

Denmark: 15 Hunter St, Yarralumla, ACT 2600; tel. (062) 732195; telex 62661; Ambassador: BIRGER ABRAHAMSON.

Egypt: 125 Monaro Crescent, Red Hill, ACT 2603; tel. (062) 950394; telex 62497; Ambassador Dr MAHMOUD SAMIR AHMAD.

Fiji: 9 Beagle St, Red Hill, ACT 2603; POB E159, Queen Victoria Terrace, ACT 2600; tel. (062) 959148; telex 62345; High Commissioner: EPELI V. KACIMAIWAI.

Finland: 10 Darwin Ave, Yarralumla, ACT 2600; tel. (062) 733800; telex 62713; Ambassador: OSMO JUHANI LARES.

France: 6 Perth Ave, Yarralumla, ACT 2600; tel. (062) 951267; telex 62141; Ambassador: BERNARD FOLLIN.

German Democratic Republic: 8 Dalman Crescent, O'Malley, ACT 2606; tel. (062) 862300; telex 62496; Ambassador: JOACHIM ELM.

Germany, Federal Republic: 119 Empire Circuit, Yarralumla, ACT 2600; tel. (062) 733177; telex 62035; Ambassador: Dr HANS SCHAUER.

Ghana: 44 Endeavour St, Red Hill, ACT 2603; tel. (062) 951122; High Commissioner: A. K. ANDREWS (acting).

Greece: 9 Turrana St, Yarralumla, ACT 2600; tel. (062) 733011; telex 62724; Ambassador: EFTHYMIOS TZAPHERIS.

Holy See: 2 Vancouver St, Red Hill, ACT 2603; tel. (062) 953876; Chargé d'affaires a.i.: Dr DIEGO CAUSERO.

Hungary: 79 Hopetoun Circuit, Yarralumla, ACT 2600; tel. (062) 823226; telex 62737; Chargé d'affaires a.i.: PÁL IPPER.

India: 3–5 Moonah Place, Yarralumla, ACT 2600; tel. (062) 733999; telex 62362; High Commissioner: MUHAMMAD HAMID ANSARI.

Indonesia: 8 Darwin Ave, Yarralumla, ACT 2600; tel. (062) 733222; Ambassador: AUGUST MARPAUNG.

Iran: 14 Torres St, Red Hill, ACT 2603; POB 219, Manuka, ACT 2603; tel. (062) 952544; telex 62490; Ambassador: AHMAD ATTARI.

Iraq: 48 Culgoa Circuit, O'Malley, ACT 2606; tel. (062) 861333; telex 61520; Ambassador: ANWAR A. K. AL-HADITHI.

Ireland: 20 Arkana St, Yarralumla, ACT 2600; tel. (062) 733022; telex 62720; Ambassador: JOSEPH SMALL.

Israel: 6 Turrana St, Yarralumla, ACT 2600; tel. (062) 731309; telex 62224; Ambassador: YISSAKHAR BEN-YAACOV.

Italy: 12 Grey St, Deakin, ACT 2600; POB 360, Canberra City, ACT 2601; tel. (062) 733333; telex 62028; Ambassador: Dr ERIC DA RIN.

Japan: 112 Empire Circuit, Yarralumla, ACT 2600; tel. (062) 733244; telex 62034; Ambassador: TOSHIJIRO NAKAJIMA.

Jordan: 20 Roebuck St, Red Hill, ACT 2603; tel. (062) 959951; telex 62551; Ambassador: SULEIMAN DAJANI.

Kenya: 6th Floor, Amdahl House, 33–35 Ainslie Ave, Canberra, ACT; POB 1990, Canberra, ACT 2601; tel. (062) 744788; telex 61929; High Commissioner: JOHN ZAKAYO KAMENCU.

Korea, Republic: 113 Empire Circuit, Yarralumla, ACT 2600; tel. (062) 733044; Ambassador: DONG WON LIM.

Laos: 113 Kitchener St, Garran, ACT 2605; tel. (062) 816622; telex 61627; Chargé d'affaires a.i.: OUAN PHOMMACHACK.

Lebanon: 73 Endeavour St, Red Hill, ACT 2603; tel. (062) 957378; telex 61762; Ambassador: LATIF ABUL-HUSN.

Libya: 50 Culgoa Circuit, O'Malley, ACT 2606; tel. (062) 862966; Secretary of the People's Committee: SHABAN F. GASHUT.

Malaysia: 7 Perth Ave, Yarralumla, ACT 2600; tel. (062) 731543; High Commissioner: Tan Sri Datuk ZAKARIA BIN Haji MUHAMMAD ALI.

Malta: 261 La Perouse St, Red Hill, ACT 2603; tel. (062) 950273; telex 62817; High Commissioner: NICHOLAS BONELLO.

Mauritius: 43 Hampton Circuit, Yarralumla, ACT 2600; tel. (062) 811203; telex 62863; High Commissioner: JEAN-CLAUDE BIBI.

Mexico: 14 Perth Ave, Yarralumla, ACT 2600; tel. (062) 733905; telex 62329; Ambassador: JESÚS FRANCISCO DOMENE VÁSQUEZ.

Netherlands: 120 Empire Circuit, Yarralumla, ACT 2600; tel. (062) 733111; telex 62047; Ambassador: J. M. VOS.

New Zealand: Commonwealth Ave, Canberra, ACT 2600; tel. (062) 733611; High Commissioner: GRAHAM K. ANSELL.

Nigeria: 27 State Circle, Deakin, ACT 2600; tel. (062) 731028; High Commissioner: M. S. UTO.

Norway: 17 Hunter St, Yarralumla, ACT 2600; tel. (062) 733444; telex 62569; Ambassador: PER HAUGESTAD.

Pakistan: 59 Franklin St, Forrest, ACT 2603; POB 198, Manuka, ACT 2603; tel. (062) 950021; Chargé d'affaires a.i.: SAJJAD ASHRAF.

Papua New Guinea: Forster Crescent, Yarralumla, ACT 2600; POB 572, Manuka, ACT 2603; tel. (062) 733322; telex 62592; High Commissioner: JAMES WINARE.

Peru: 111 Monaro Crescent, Red Hill, ACT 2603; POB 508, Manuka, ACT 2603; tel. (062) 951016; telex 61664; Ambassador: GONZALO BEDOYA DELBOY.

Philippines: 1 Moonah Place, Yarralumla, ACT 2600; POB 297, Manuka, ACT 2603; tel. (062) 732535; telex 62665; Ambassador: ROMUALDO A. ONG.

Poland: 7 Turrana St, Yarralumla, ACT 2600; tel. (062) 731208; telex 62584; Ambassador: IRENEUSZ KOSSAKOWSKI.

Portugal: 8 Astrolabe St, Red Hill, ACT 2603; POB 539, Manuka, ACT 2603; tel. (062) 959992; telex 62649; Ambassador: Dr I. J. REBELLO DE ANDRADE.

Saudi Arabia: 12 Culgoa Circuit, O'Malley, ACT 2606; POB 63, Garran, ACT 2605; tel. (062) 862099; telex 61454; Ambassador: A. RAHMAN N. ALOHALY.

Singapore: 17 Forster Crescent, Yarralumla, ACT 2600; tel. (062) 733944; High Commissioner: LOW CHOON MING.

South Africa: cnr State Circle and Rhodes Place, Yarralumla, ACT 2600; tel. (062) 732424; Ambassador: C. A. BASTIAANSE.

Spain: 15 Arkana St, Yarralumla, ACT 2600; POB 76, Deakin, ACT 2600; tel. (062) 733555; telex 62485; Ambassador: FRANCISCO UTRAY.

Sri Lanka: 35 Empire Circuit, Forrest, ACT 2603; tel. (062) 953521; telex 61620; High Commissioner: Dr WICKREMA SENA WEERASOORIA.

Sweden: 5 Turrana St, Yarralumla, ACT 2600; tel. (062) 733033; telex 62303; Ambassador: HANS BJÖRK.

Switzerland: 7 Melbourne Ave, Forrest, ACT 2603; tel. (062) 733977; telex 62275; Ambassador: ALFRED R. GLESTI.

Thailand: 111 Empire Circuit, Yarralumla, ACT 2600; tel. (062) 731149; telex 62533; Ambassador: JETN SUCHARITKUL.

Turkey: 60 Mugga Way, Red Hill, ACT 2603; tel. (062) 950227; telex 62764; Ambassador: FARUK SAHINBAS.

Uganda: Suite 3, 2nd Floor, AMI House, 216 Northbourne Ave, Braddon, ACT 2602; tel. (062) 472235; telex 61663; High Commissioner: Prof. EMMANUEL SSENDAULA.

USSR: 78 Canberra Ave, Griffith, ACT 2603; tel. (062) 959033; telex 62239; Ambassador: YEVGENI SAMOTEIKIN.

United Kingdom: Commonwealth Ave, Canberra, ACT 2600; tel. (062) 730422; telex 62222; High Commissioner: Sir JOHN LEAHY.

USA: Chancery, Yarralumla, ACT 2600; tel. (062) 705000; Ambassador: LAURENCE WILLIAM LANE.

Uruguay: Suite 5, Bonner House, Woden, ACT 2606; POB 318, Woden, ACT 2606; tel. (062) 824418; telex 61486; Chargé d'affaires a.i.: LUIS A. CARRESSE.

Venezuela: Suite 106, 1st Floor, MLC Tower, Woden, ACT 2606; POB 37, Woden, ACT 2606; tel. (062) 824827; telex 62110; Ambassador: Dr RAMÓN DELGADO.

Viet-Nam: 6 Timbarra Crescent, O'Malley, ACT 2606; tel. (062) 866059; telex 62756; Chargé d'affaires a.i.: LUU DOAN HUYNH.

Yugoslavia: 11 Nuyts St, Red Hill, ACT 2603; POB 161, Manuka, ACT 2603; tel. (062) 951458; telex 62317; Ambassador: SVETOZAR STARČEVIĆ.

Zambia: 3rd Floor, Amdahl Bldg, 33 Ainslie Ave, Canberra City, ACT 2608; tel. 472088; telex 61796; High Commissioner: JASON C. MFULA.

Judicial System

The judicial power of the Commonwealth of Australia is vested in the High Court of Australia, in such other Federal Courts as the Federal Parliament creates, and in such other courts as it invests with Federal jurisdiction.

The High Court consists of a Chief Justice and six other Justices, each of whom is appointed by the Governor-General in Council, and has both original and appellate jurisdiction.

The High Court's original jurisdiction extends to all matters arising under any treaty, affecting representatives of other countries, in which the Commonwealth of Australia or its representative is a party, between States or between residents of different States or between a State and a resident of another State, and in which a writ of mandamus, or prohibition, or an injunction is sought against an officer of the Commonwealth of Australia. It also extends to matters arising under the Australian Constitution or involving its interpretation, and to many matters arising under Commonwealth laws.

The High Court's appellate jurisdiction has, since June 1984, been discretionary. Appeals from the Federal Court, the Family Court and the Supreme Courts of the States and of the Territories may now be brought only if special leave is granted, in the event of a legal question that is of general public importance being involved, or of there being differences of opinion between intermediate appellate courts as to the state of the law.

Legislation enacted by the Federal Parliament in 1976 substantially changed the exercise of Federal and Territory judicial power, and, by creating the Federal Court of Australia in February 1977, enabled the High Court of Australia to give greater attention to its primary function as interpreter of the Australian Constitution. The Federal Court of Australia has assumed, in two divisions, the jurisdiction previously exercised by the Australian Industrial Court and the Federal Court of Bankruptcy and has additionally been given jurisdiction in trade practices and in the developing field of administrative law. Jurisdiction has also been conferred on the Federal Court of Australia, subject to a number of exceptions, in matters in which a writ of mandamus, or prohibition, or an injunction is sought against an officer of the Commonwealth of Australia. The Court also hears appeals from the Court constituted by a single Judge, from the Supreme Courts of the Territories, and in certain specific matters from State Courts, other than a Full Court of the Supreme Court of a State, exercising Federal jurisdiction. The Federal Court is composed of a Chief Judge and 29 other Judges.

In March 1986 all remaining categories of appeal from Australian courts to the Queen's Privy Council in the UK were abolished by the Australia Act.

FEDERAL COURTS
High Court of Australia
POB E435, Queen Victoria Terrace, ACT 2600; tel. (062) 706811; telex 61430.
Chief Justice: Sir HARRY TALBOT GIBBS.
Justices:
Sir ANTHONY FRANK MASON, Sir RONALD DARLING WILSON, Sir FRANCIS GERARD BRENNAN, Sir WILLIAM PATRICK DEANE, Sir DARYL MICHAEL DAWSON.

Federal Court of Australia
Chief Judge: Sir NIGEL HUBERT BOWEN.
There are 29 other Judges.

Family Court of Australia
Chief Judge: ELIZABETH ANDREAS EVATT.
There are 44 other Judges.

NEW SOUTH WALES
Supreme Court
Chief Justice: Sir LAURENCE WHISTLER STREET.
President of the Court of Appeal: MICHAEL DONALD KIRBY.
Chief Judge in Equity: MICHAEL MANIFOLD HELSHAM.
Chief Judge of Common Law: JOHN PATRICK SLATTERY.
Masters: G. S. SHARPE, C. R. ALLEN, J. HOGAN, T. GREENWOOD, DENIS GRESSIER.

VICTORIA
Supreme Court
Chief Justice: Sir JOHN MCINTOSH YOUNG.
Masters: P. A. BARKER, G. S. BRETT, V. M. GAWNE, T. P. BRUCE.

QUEENSLAND
Supreme Court
Southern District (Brisbane)
Chief Justice: D. G. ANDREWS.
Senior Puisne Judge: J. KELLY.

Central District (Rockhampton)
Puisne Judge: A. G. DEMACK.

Northern District (Townsville)
Puisne Judge: Sir GEORGE KNEIPP.

SOUTH AUSTRALIA
Supreme Court
Chief Justice: LEONARD JAMES KING.

WESTERN AUSTRALIA
Supreme Court
Chief Justice: Sir FRANCIS BURT.
Master: G. T. STAPLES.

TASMANIA
Supreme Court
Chief Justice: Sir GUY STEPHEN MONTAGUE GREEN.
Master: RICHARD CARTER SOUTHEY.

AUSTRALIAN CAPITAL TERRITORY
Supreme Court
Chief Justice: JEFFREY ALLAN MILES.

NORTHERN TERRITORY
Supreme Court
Chief Justice: Mr JUSTICE O'LEARY.
Master: P. LEFEVRE.

Religion
CHRISTIANITY
The Anglican Church of Australia
National Office: General Synod Office, POB Q190, Queen Victoria PO, Sydney, NSW 2000; tel. (02) 265-1525; telex 24183; c. 3.75m. mems; Gen. Sec. J. G. DENTON.
Primate of Australia, Archbishop of Brisbane and Metropolitan of Queensland: Most Rev. JOHN B. R. GRINDROD.
Archbishop of Adelaide and Metropolitan of South Australia: Most Rev. KEITH RAYNER.
Archbishop of Melbourne and Metropolitan of Victoria: Most Rev. DAVID J. PENMAN.
Archbishop of Perth and Metropolitan of Western Australia: Most Rev. PETER F. CARNLEY.
Archbishop of Sydney and Metropolitan of New South Wales: Most Rev. DONALD W. B. ROBINSON.

The Roman Catholic Church
In 1984 there were 28 dioceses with c. 4m. mems.
Archbishop of Adelaide: Most Rev. LEONARD A. FAULKNER.
Archbishop of Brisbane: Most Rev. FRANCIS R. RUSH.
Archbishop of Canberra and Goulburn: Most Rev. F. CARROLL.
Archbishop of Hobart: Most Rev. GUILFORD C. YOUNG.
Archbishop of Melbourne: Most Rev. THOMAS F. LITTLE.
Archbishop of Perth: Most Rev. WILLIAM J. FOLEY.
Archbishop of Sydney: Most Rev. EDWARD B. CLANCY, Archdiocesan Chancery, 13th Floor, Polding House, 276 Pitt St, Sydney, NSW 2000; tel. (02) 264-7211.

Greek Orthodox Church
Greek Orthodox Archdiocese: 242 Cleveland St, Redfern, Sydney, NSW 2016; tel. (02) 699-5811; f. 1924; 700,000 mems; offices in Melbourne, Adelaide and Perth; leader in Australia Archbishop STYLIANOS.

Other Christian Churches
Baptist Union of Australia: POB 273, Hawthorn, Vic 3122; tel. (03) 819-2683; f. 1926; 58,000 mems; 721 churches; Pres.-Gen. Rev. Dr E. G. GIBSON; Sec. O. C. ABBOTT.
Lutheran Church of Australia: Lutheran Church House, 58 O'Connell St, North Adelaide, SA 5006; tel. (08) 267-4922; telex 89684; f. 1966; 114,000 mems; Pres. Rev. Dr L. B. GROPE; Sec. Rev. K. J. SCHMIDT.
Uniting Church in Australia: Box C103, Clarence St PO, Sydney, NSW 2000; tel. (02) 290-9611; f. 1977 with the union of Methodist, Presbyterian and Congregational Churches; 1.5m. mems; Pres. Rev. IAN TANNER; Sec. Rev. DAVID GILL.

JUDAISM
Great Synagogue: Elizabeth St, Sydney, NSW; tel. (02) 267-2477; f. 1828; Sr Minister Rabbi RAYMOND APPLE.

AUSTRALIA

The Press

Australia's legislation relating to the Press varies in different States.

Under the law concerning contempt of court, to publish names or photographs before proceedings begin may draw heavy penalties. Though accurate reporting of a case while it is being tried is privileged, a judge is empowered to ban all reports until the conclusion of the case.

Each State has its legislation against obscene publications, which is particularly severe in the State of Queensland, whose broadly defined Objectionable Literature Act of 1954 covers a wide range of offences.

The libel law covers a range of offences, from seditious libel for matter liable to cause a breach of the peace, or for excessive abuse of government officials, to defamatory libel. Certain government agencies have privilege. A journalist, if prosecuted, is obliged to justify every material part of an allegedly defamatory statement, and this has led to a marked tendency not to publish outspoken comment where there is a risk of prosecution. In all States the author, editor, owner, publisher, printer and, to some extent, the distributor of a publication are liable for damages to the person defamed.

The total circulation of Australia's daily newspapers is very high but in the remoter parts of the country weekly papers are even more popular. Most of Australia's newspapers are published in sparsely populated rural areas where the demand for local news is strong. The only newspapers that may fairly claim a national circulation are the dailies *The Australian* and *Australian Financial Review*, and the weeklies *The Bulletin*, the *National Times* and the *Nation Review*, the circulation of most newspapers being almost entirely confined to the State in which each is produced.

All newspapers in the state capitals are owned by limited companies. The trend towards concentration of ownership has led to the development of three principal groups of newspapers. Economic conditions have necessitated the extension of the activities of newspaper companies into magazine and book publishing, radio and television, etc. The principal groups are as follows:

Consolidated Press Holdings Ltd: 54 Park St, Sydney, NSW 2000; tel. (02) 268-0666; telex 20514; publishes *The Australian Women's Weekly, The Bulletin, Australian Business, Cleo* and other magazines; holds a controlling interest in several country and suburban newspapers; also has radio and television interests.

The John Fairfax Group: 235 Jones St, Broadway, POB 506, Sydney, NSW 2001; f. 1841; Chair. J. O. FAIRFAX; controls *The Sydney Morning Herald, The Sun, National Times, Australian Financial Review* and the *Sun-Herald* (Sydney), *The Age* (Melbourne), *The Canberra Times* (Canberra), *Illawarra Mercury* (Wollongong), *The Newcastle Herald* (Newcastle) and *The Spectator* (London); also has radio and television interests.

The Herald and Weekly Times Ltd Group: 44 Flinders St, Melbourne, Vic 3000; Chair. JOHN C. DAHLSEN; pubs include *The Herald, The Sun News-Pictorial, The Bendigo Advertiser* and *The Geelong Advertiser* (Melbourne), *The West Australian, Daily News* (Perth), *Kalgoorlie Miner, Papua New Guinea Post-Courier, Fiji Times*, and also has holdings in several magazines and interests in radio and television.

News Ltd: 2 Holt St, Surry Hills, Sydney, NSW 2010; tel. (02) 288-3000; telex 20124; Chair. R. H. SEARBY; CEO K. RUPERT MURDOCH; controls *Adelaide News* (Adelaide), *The Australian, Daily Mirror* (Sydney), *The Northern Territory News* (Darwin), *Sunday Times* (Perth), *Daily Sun, Sunday Sun* (Brisbane), *Daily Telegraph* and *Sunday Telegraph* (Sydney), *Northern Daily Leader* (Tamworth), *The Townsville Bulletin* (Townsville), Progress Press (Melbourne). Assoc. publs: *New Idea* and *TV Week* (Melbourne), *The Sun, News of the World, The Times* and *The Sunday Times* (London), *New York Post* (New York), *Sun-Times* (Chicago), *Boston Herald* (Boston), *Express-News* (San Antonio, Texas); also has television interests.

David Syme & Co Ltd: 250 Spencer St, Melbourne, Vic; tel. (03) 600421; telex 30449; wholly-owned by John Fairfax Group (see above); publishes *The Age* and other newspapers and magazines in Victoria.

NEWSPAPERS

Australian Capital Territory

The Canberra Times: 18 Mort St, Braddon, Canberra 2601; tel. (062) 480066; telex 62069; f. 1926; daily and Sun.; morning; Editor-in-Chief I. R. MATHEWS; circ. 45,000.

Directory

New South Wales
Dailies

The Australian: News Ltd, 2 Holt St, Surry Hills, NSW 2010, POB 4245; tel. 288-3000; telex 20124; f. 1964; edited in Sydney, simultaneous edns in Sydney, Melbourne, Perth and Brisbane; Propr K. RUPERT MURDOCH; Editor-in-Chief G. LESLIE HOLLINGS; circ. 128,000.

Australian Financial Review: 235 Jones St, Broadway, POB 506, Sydney 2001; tel. (02) 282-2512; telex 21717; f. 1951; Mon.–Fri.; distributed nationally; Editor-in-Chief P. P. MCGUINNESS; circ. 63,000.

Daily Commercial News: POB 1552, Sydney 2001; tel. (02) 211-4055; telex 121874; f. 1891; Gen. Man. C. S. WYNDHAM.

Daily Mirror: 2 Holt St, Surry Hills 2010; tel. (02) 288-3000; telex 20124; f. 1941; evening; CEO K. RUPERT MURDOCH; Editor ROY MILLER; circ. 291,496.

Daily Telegraph: 2 Holt St, Surry Hills 2010; tel. 288-3000; telex 20124; f. 1879; morning; Editor L. HOFFMAN; circ. 326,000.

The Manly Daily: 26 Sydney Rd, Manly 2095; tel. (02) 977-3333; f. 1906; Tues.–Sat.; Gen. Man. M. C. G. UTTING; circ. 77,000.

The Newcastle Herald: 28–30 Bolton St, Newcastle 2300; tel. 263222; telex 28269; f. 1858; morning; 6 a week; Editor J. A. ALLAN; circ. 56,000.

The Sun: 235 Jones St, Broadway, POB 506, Sydney 2001; tel. (02) 20944; telex 21717; f. 1910; evening; Editor-in-Chief G. R. FORD; circ. 350,000.

The Sydney Morning Herald: 235 Jones St, Broadway, POB 506, Sydney 2001; tel. (02) 282-2822; telex 20121; f. 1831; morning; Editor-in-Chief C. J. ANDERSON; circ. 266,000 (Mon.–Fri.), 400,000 (Sat.).

Weeklies

The Advertiser: 142 Macquarie St, Parramatta 2150; Wed. and Sat.; Man. Editor S. JACKSON; circ. 102,000.

Bankstown Canterbury Torch: 47 Allingham St, Bankstown 2200; tel. 709-3433; f. 1920; Wed.; Publr J. P. ENGISCH; circ. 78,000.

National Times: 235 Jones St, Broadway, Sydney 2001; tel. (02) 282-2822; telex 20121; f. 1971; weekly; edns in each state capital; Man. Editor JEFFERSON PENBERTHY; circ. 96,000.

Northern District Times: 116 Rowe St, Eastwood 2122; tel. 635-0355; f. 1921; Wed.; Man. S. HOGAN; Editor D. MORGAN; circ. 68,000.

Parramatta and District Mercury: 1st Floor, 38 George St, Parramatta 2150; f. 1977; Tues.; circ. 102,000.

St George and Sutherland Shire Leader: 172 Forest Rd, Hurstville 2220; tel. 579-5033; f. 1960; Tues. and Thurs.; Gen. Man. J. HOGAN; Editor M. WHITE; circ. 124,000.

Sun-Herald: 235 Jones St, Broadway, POB 506, Sydney 2001; tel. (02) 282-2822; telex 20121; f. 1953; Sunday; Editor P. SMARK; circ. 671,000.

Sunday Telegraph: 2 Holt St, Surry Hills 2010; tel. 288-3000; telex 20124; f. 1938; Editor IAN MOORE; circ. 665,000.

Northern Territory
Daily

Northern Territory News: Printers Place, POB 1300, Darwin 5794; tel. (089) 828200; telex 85574; f. 1952; Mon. to Sat.; Man. Editor J. HOGAN; circ. 19,000.

Weekly

The Darwin Star: 31 Bishop St, POB 39330 Winnellie, Darwin 5789; f. 1976; Thurs.; Man. Editor PATRICK CUSICK; circ. 13,000.

Sunday Territorian: Printers Place, POB 1300, Darwin 5794; tel. (089) 828200; telex 85574; Sun.; Editor G. SHIPWAY; circ. 18,000.

Queensland
Dailies

Courier-Mail: Campbell St, Bowen Hills, Brisbane 4006; tel. (07) 526011; telex 40101; f. 1933; morning; Editor D. C. SMITH; circ. 218,000.

Telegraph: Campbell St, Bowen Hills, Brisbane 4006; tel. (07) 526011; telex 40101; f. 1872; evening; Editor D. W. FLAHERTY; circ. 126,000.

Weeklies

The Suburban: 10 Aspinall St, Nundah; POB 10, Nundah 4012; tel. 266-6666; five suburban edns; Publr Mrs HEATHER JEFFERY; combined circ. 117,000.

AUSTRALIA

Sunday Mail: Campbell St, Bowen Hills, Brisbane 4006; tel. (07) 526011; telex 40110; f. 1923; Editor N. F. WISEMAN; circ. 341,500.

Sunday Sun: cnr Brunswick and McLachlan Sts, Fortitude Valley, Brisbane 4000; tel. (07) 528050; f. 1971; Man. Editor R. RICHARDS; circ. 371,000.

South Australia
Dailies

Advertiser: 121 King William St, Adelaide 5001; tel. (08) 218-9218; telex 82101; f. 1858; morning; Editor I. F. MEIKLE; circ. 216,000.

News: 112 North Terrace, Adelaide 5000, POB 1771, GPO Adelaide 5001; tel. (08) 510351; f. 1923; evening; Mon.–Fri.; Editor ROGER HOLDEN; circ. 167,000.

Weekly

Sunday Mail: 116–120 North Terrace, Adelaide 5000; f. 1912; Editor REX JORY; circ. 250,000.

Victoria
Dailies

The Age: 250 Spencer St (cnr Lonsdale St), Melbourne 3000; tel. (03) 600421; telex 30449; f. 1854; independent; morning; Man. Dir G. J. TAYLOR; Editor CREIGHTON BURNS; circ. 236,000.

The Herald: 44–74 Flinders St, Melbourne 3000; tel. (03) 652-1111; telex 30104; f. 1840; evening; Editor N. MITCHELL; circ. 280,000.

Sun News-Pictorial: 44–74 Flinders St, Melbourne 3000; tel. (03) 630211; telex 30104; f. 1922; morning; Editor ROBERT CRONIN; circ. 560,000.

Weeklies

Regional Chadstone Progress: 160 Whitehorse Rd, Blackburn 3130; tel. 877-6655; f. 1960; Wed.; Editor GREG BURCHALL; circ. 98,000.

Sporting Globe: 44 Flinders St, Melbourne 3000; tel. (03) 652-1111; telex 30104; f. 1922; Mon.; Editor NEVILLE WILLMOTT.

Sunday Observer: 46–49 Porter St, Prahran 3181; tel. 520-5555; telex 30880; f. 1971; Editor JIM LAWRENCE; circ. 135,000.

Sunday Press: 61 Flinders Lane, Melbourne 3000; tel. (03) 652-1111; telex 30104; f. 1973; Editor COLIN DUCK; circ. 145,000.

Truth: 272 Rosslyn St, West Melbourne 3003; tel. (03) 329-0277; telex 30562; f. 1890; Mon. and Thurs.; Editor G. HAWTHORNE; circ. 240,000.

Tasmania
Dailies

Advocate: POB 63, Burnie 7320; tel. 301409; telex 59049; f. 1890; morning; Editor D. J. CHERRY; circ. 27,000.

Examiner: 71–75 Paterson St, POB 99A, Launceston 7250; tel. (003) 315111; telex 58511; f. 1842; morning; independent; Editor M. C. P. COURTNEY; circ. 39,000.

Mercury: 91–93 Macquarie St, Hobart 7000; tel. (002) 300622; telex 58104; f. 1854; morning; Exec. Editor J. S. S. BURNS; Editor B. J. DARGAVILLE; circ. 56,700.

Weeklies

Advocate Weekender: POB 63, Burnie 7320; tel. 301409; telex 59049; f. 1968; Saturday; Editor D. J. CHERRY; circ. 15,000.

Sunday Examiner: 71–75 Paterson St, Launceston 7250; tel. (003) 315111; telex 58511; f. 1924; Editor M. C. P. COURTNEY; circ. 39,000.

Sunday Tasmanian: 91–93 Macquarie St, Hobart 7000; tel. (002) 300622; f. 1984; morning; Exec. Editor J. S. S. BURNS; circ. 42,000.

The Tasmanian Mail: 130 Collins St, Hobart 7000; tel. (002) 211211; telex 57150; f. 1978; Man. Editor W. A. J. HASWELL; circ. 131,000.

Western Australia
Dailies

Daily News: 125 St George's Terrace, POB D162, GPO Perth 6001; tel. (09) 321-0161; f. 1882; evening, Mon.–Fri.; Editor R. A. BARRATT; circ. 110,000.

West Australian: 125 St George's Terrace, POB D162, GPO Perth 6001; tel. (09) 321-0161; f. 1833; morning; Editor D. B. SMITH; circ. 247,000.

Weeklies

The Countryman: 125 St George's Terrace, POB D162, Perth 6001; tel. (09) 321-0161; f. 1885; Thurs.; farming; Editor G. A. BOYLEN; circ. 13,000.

Sunday Independent: 48 Stirling St, Perth 6000; POB N1083, Perth 6001; tel. (09) 326-8326; telex 95509; f. 1969; Sunday; Editor STEPHEN FOX; circ. 78,000.

Sunday Times: 34–36 Stirling St, Perth 6000; tel. (09) 326-8326; f. 1897; Man. Dir D. THOMPSON; Editor-in-Chief D. WEBB; circ. 265,000.

PRINCIPAL PERIODICALS
Weeklies and Fortnightlies

The Advocate: 143 a'Beckett St, Melbourne, Vic; f. 1868; Thurs.; Roman Catholic; Editor NEVILLE WEERERATNE; circ. 19,000.

Australasian Post: 61 Flinders Lane, Melbourne, Vic 3000; tel. (03) 652-1111; telex 30124; f. 1946; factual, general interest, Australiana; Fri.; Editor MARTIN THOMAS; circ. 230,000.

The Bulletin: 54 Park St, Sydney, NSW 2000; tel. (02) 268-0666; telex 120514; f. 1880; Wed.; Editor DAVID ARMSTRONG.

The Medical Journal of Australia: 77–79 Arundel St, Glebe, NSW 2037; tel. (02) 660-6055; telex 24814; f. 1914; fortnightly; Editor Dr KATHLEEN KING; circ. 23,000.

New Idea: 32 Walsh St, Melbourne, Vic; tel. (03) 320-7000; weekly; women's; Editor D. BOLING.

News Weekly: POB 66A, GPO Melbourne, Vic 3001; tel. (03) 602-1133; telex 38578 (domestic), 10104 (overseas); f. 1943; publ. by National Civic Council; Wed.; political and trade union affairs; international, particularly regional affairs; Editor PETER WESTMORE; circ. 17,000.

People Magazine: 140 Joynton Ave, Waterloo, NSW 2017; tel. (02)662-8888; telex 25027; weekly; Editor DAVID NAYLOR; circ. 230,000.

Queensland Country Life: 432 Queen St, Brisbane, Qld; telex 42523; f. 1935; Thurs.; Editor-in-Chief PETER OWEN; circ. 35,305.

Scene: 61 Flinders Lane, Melbourne, Vic 3000; tel. (03) 652-1111; telex 30104; f. 1925; Wed.; Editor GARRY MANSFIELD; circ. 80,000.

The South Sea Digest: 76 Clarence St, Sydney, NSW 2000; tel. (02) 20231; telex 21242; f. 1981; fortnightly; business and politics in South Pacific; Editor JOHN CARTER.

Stock and Land: POB 82, North Melbourne, Vic 3051; tel. (03) 329-7300; telex 35668; f. 1914; weekly; livestock, land and wool market journal; Man. Editor C. T. DEB. GRIFFITH; circ. 24,000.

TV Week: 32 Walsh St, Melbourne, Vic; tel. (03) 320-7000; telex 31824; f. 1957; Mon.; colour national; Editor-in-Chief JOHN HALL; circ. 850,000.

Weekly Times: Box 751F, GPO Melbourne, Vic 3001; tel. (03) 652-1111; telex 30104; f. 1869; farming, gardening, country life and sport; Wed.; Editor KEVIN BOYLE; circ. 110,000.

Woman's Day: 140 Joynton Ave, POB 600, Waterloo, NSW 2017; tel. (02) 662-8888; telex 25027; weekly; circulates throughout Australia and NZ; Editor HENRY PLOCIENNIK; circ. 580,000.

Monthlies and Others

Archaeology in Oceania: University of Sydney, NSW 2006; tel. (02) 692-2666; f. 1966; 3 a year; archaeology and physical anthropology; Editor J. PETER WHITE.

Architecture Australia: Publishing and Marketing Australia, POB 6324, Melbourne, Vic 3004; tel. (03) 267-3611; telex 33770; f. 1904; 8 a year; Editor TOM HEATH; circ. 10,000.

Australian Forest Research: CSIRO, 314 Albert St, East Melbourne, Vic 3002; tel. (03) 418-7333; telex 30236; quarterly; Editor J. J. LENAGHAN.

Australian Hi-Fi Magazine: POB 341, Mona Vale, NSW 2103; tel. (02) 997-1188; f. 1970; monthly; Editor GREG BORROWMAN; circ. 25,000.

Australian Home Beautiful: 44–74 Flinders St, Melbourne, Vic 3000; tel. (03) 652-1612; telex 30104; f. 1925; monthly; Editor A. J. HITCHIN.

Australian House and Garden: 168 Castlereagh St, Sydney, NSW 2000; tel. (02) 268-0666; telex 20514; monthly; building, furnishing, decorating, handicrafts, gardening, entertaining; Editor BERYL CLARKE MARCHI.

Australian Journal of Agricultural Research: CSIRO, 314 Albert St, East Melbourne, Vic 3002; tel. (03) 418-7333; telex 30236; f. 1950; quarterly; Man. Editor G. A. FORSTER.

Australian Journal of Biological Sciences: CSIRO, 314 Albert St, East Melbourne, Vic 3002; tel. (03) 418-7333; telex 30236; f. 1953; quarterly; Man. Editor L. A. BENNETT.

Australian Journal of Botany: CSIRO, 314 Albert St, East Melbourne, Vic 3002; tel. (03) 418-7333; telex 30236; f. 1953; 6 a year; Man. Editor L. W. MARTINELLI.

AUSTRALIA

Australian Journal of Chemistry: CSIRO, 314 Albert St, East Melbourne, Vic 3002; tel. (03) 418-7333; telex 30236; f. 1953; monthly; Man. Editor J. R. ZDYSIEWICZ.

Australian Journal of Experimental Agriculture: CSIRO, 314 Albert St, East Melbourne, Vic 3002; tel. (03) 418-7333; telex 30236; f. 1961; 6 a year; Man. Editor R. D. HOOLEY.

Australian Journal of Marine and Freshwater Research: CSIRO, 314 Albert St, East Melbourne, Vic 3002; tel. (03) 418-7333; telex 30236; f. 1950; 6 a year; Man. Editor L. A. BENNETT.

Australian Journal of Pharmacy: 35 Walsh St, West Melbourne, Vic 3003; tel. (03) 329-5799; f. 1886; monthly; journal of the associated pharmaceutical orgs; Editor S. L. DICKSON; Man. I. G. LLOYD; circ. 8,000.

Australian Journal of Physics: CSIRO, 314 Albert St, East Melbourne, Vic 3002; tel. (03) 418-7333; telex 30236; f. 1953; 6 a year; Man. Editor R. P. ROBERTSON.

Australian Journal of Plant Physiology: CSIRO, 314 Albert St, East Melbourne, Vic 3002; tel. (03) 418-7333; telex 30236; f. 1974; 6 a year; Man. Editor L. W. MARTINELLI.

Australian Journal of Politics and History: University of Queensland, St Lucia, Qld 4067; tel. 377-2265; f. 1955; 3 a year; Editor J. A. MOSES; circ. 1,000.

Australian Journal of Soil Research: CSIRO, 314 Albert St, East Melbourne, Vic 3002; tel. (03) 418-7333; telex 30236; f. 1963; quarterly; Man. Editor G. A. FORSTER.

Australian Journal of Zoology: CSIRO, 314 Albert St, East Melbourne, Vic 3002; tel. (03) 418-7333; telex 30236; f. 1953; 6 a year; Man. Editor SUSAN E. INGHAM.

Australian Law Journal: 44–50 Waterloo Rd, North Ryde, NSW 2113; tel. 887-0177; telex 27995; f. 1927; monthly; General Editor J. G. STARKE QC; Asst Editor C. A. SWEENEY.

Australian Left Review: POB A247, South Sydney PO, NSW 2000; f. 1966; 5 a year.

Australian Photography: POB 606, Sydney, NSW 2001; tel. (02) 699-7861; telex 121887; monthly; journal of the Australian Photographic Soc.; Editor LAWRY COHEN.

Australian Quarterly: 2nd Floor, 149 Castlereagh St, Sydney, NSW 2000; tel. (02) 264-8923; f. 1929; quarterly; Editors HUGH PRICHARD, ELAINE THOMPSON; circ. 3,000.

Australian Wildlife Research: CSIRO, 314 Albert St, East Melbourne, Vic 3002; tel. (03) 418-7333; telex 30236; f. 1974; quarterly; Man. Editor SUSAN E. INGHAM.

Australian Women's Weekly: 54 Park St, Sydney, NSW 2000; telex 20514; f. 1933; monthly; Editor LANA WELLS; circ. 1,150,000.

The Australian Worker incorporating The Worker: 321 Pitt St, Sydney, NSW 2000; f. 1891; monthly; journal of the Australian Workers' Union; circ. 105,000.

Brunonia: CSIRO, 314 Albert St, East Melbourne, Vic. 3002; tel. (03) 418-7333; telex 30236; f. 1978; 2 a year; Man. Editor L. W. MARTINELLI.

Cleo: 54 Park St, Sydney, NSW 2000; POB 4088, Sydney, NSW 2001; tel. (02) 282-8000; telex 20514; women's monthly; Editor LISA WILKINSON.

Current Affairs Bulletin: University of Sydney, Sydney, NSW 2006; tel. (02) 692-2584; f. 1947; monthly; Exec. Editors G. WILSON, W. KENNEDY; circ. 7,000.

Economic Record: Centre of Policy Studies, Monash University, Clayton, Vic 3168; tel. (03) 541-0811; f. 1925; quarterly; journal of Economic Soc. of Australia; Jt Editors Prof. J. W. FREEBAIRN, Dr R. G. GREGORY.

Ecos: CSIRO, POB 225, Dickson, ACT 2602; tel. (062) 484584; telex 62003; f. 1974; quarterly; reports of CSIRO environmental research findings for the non-specialist reader; Editor ROBERT LEHANE; circ. 8,000.

Electronics Australia: POB 227, Waterloo, NSW 2017; tel. (02) 693-6666; telex 74488; f. 1939; monthly; technical, radio, television, microcomputers, hi-fi and electronics; Man. Editor LEO SIMPSON; Editor GREG SWAIN.

Historical Studies: Dept of History, University of Melbourne, Parkville, Vic 3052; tel. (03) 344-4000; telex 35185; f. 1940; 2 a year; Editor STUART MACINTYRE; circ. 1,500.

Industrial and Commercial Photography: POB 606, Sydney, NSW 2001; tel. (02) 699-7861; telex 121887; every 2 months; journal of the Professional Photographers Asscn of Australia, Australian Cinematographers Soc., Australian Inst. of Medical and Biological Illustration and Photographic Industrial Marketing Asscn of Australia; Editor LAWRY COHEN.

Journal of Pacific History: Australian National University, POB 4, Canberra, ACT 2601; f. 1966; 3 a year; Editors DONALD DENOON, PETER HEMPENSTALL.

Manufacturers' Monthly: 72 Clarence St, Sydney, NSW 2000; tel. (02) 290-1888; telex 71827; f. 1961; circ. 12,000.

The Mathematical Scientist: Australian Mathematical Society, c/o Dept of Mathematics, University of Queensland, St Lucia, Qld 4067; tel. (07) 377-2673; f. 1976; 2 a year; Editors B. C. RENNIE, J. GANI.

Modern Boating: The Federal Publishing Co Pty Ltd, 180 Bourke Rd, Alexandria, NSW 2015; tel. (02) 693-6666; telex 74488; f. 1965; monthly; Editors JEFF MELLEFONT, BARRY TRANTER.

Modern Motor: 54–58 Park St, Sydney, NSW 2000; tel. (02) 282-8350; telex 120514; f. 1954; monthly; Editor BARRY LAKE; circ. 50,000.

Nation Review: POB 186, Glen Iris, Vic 3146; tel. (03) 256456; telex 38225; f. 1958; independent, progressive monthly; Editor-in-Chief GEOFFREY M. GOLD; circ. 46,000.

New Horizons in Education: c/o Dept of Education, University of Queensland, St Lucia, Qld 4067; f. 1938; 2 a year; Editor Dr L. MILLER.

Oceania: The University of Sydney, Sydney, NSW 2006; tel. (02) 692-2666; telex 20056; f. 1930; quarterly; social anthropology; Editors J. R. BECKETT, L. R. HIATT.

Open Road: 151 Clarence St, Sydney, NSW; f. 1927; every 2 months; journal of National Roads and Motorists' Asscn (NRMA); Editor B. GIULIANO; circ. 1,300,000.

Overland: POB 249, Mt Eliza, Vic 3930; tel. (03) 787-1545; f. 1954; quarterly; literary, social, political; Editor S. MURRAY-SMITH; circ. 3,000.

Pacific Islands Monthly: 76 Clarence St, Sydney, NSW 2000; tel. (02) 20231; telex 21242; f. 1930; political, economic and cultural affairs in the Pacific Islands; Editor RUSSELL HUNTER.

Photoworld Magazine: POB 341, Mona Vale, NSW 2103; tel. (02) 997-1188; f. 1978; monthly; photographic equipment; Editor NEIL SUDBURY; circ. 18,000.

POL: ADC House, 77 Pacific Highway, North Sydney, NSW 2060; monthly; women's; Editor ROBIN INGRAM.

Publishing and Marketing Australia: 3rd Floor, 480 St Kilda Rd, Melbourne, Vic 3004; tel. (03) 267-3611; telex 33770; f. 1904; 8 a year; Editor TOM HEATH; circ. 10,000.

Queensland Countrywoman: 89–95 Gregory Terrace, Brisbane, Qld; f. 1929; monthly; journal of the Qld Country Women's Asscn; Editor Mrs RAE PENNYCUICK.

Reader's Digest: POB 4353, Sydney, NSW 2001; tel. (02) 699-0111; telex 120260; monthly; Editor DENIS WALLIS; circ. 517,000.

Robotic Age: POB 186, Glen Iris, Vic 3146; tel. (03) 256456; telex 38225; f. 1983; quarterly; Editor GEOFFREY M. GOLD; circ. 7,500.

Rural Research: CSIRO, POB 225, Dickson, ACT 2602; tel. (062) 484584; telex 62003; f. 1952; quarterly; reports of CSIRO agricultural and biological research findings for the non-specialist reader; Editor ROBERT LEHANE; circ. 10,000.

Search—The Journal of Science in Australia and New Zealand: POB 873, Sydney, NSW 2001; tel. (02) 231-4827; telex 26296; f. 1970; 6 a year; journal of Australia and NZ Asscn for the Advancement of Science; Exec. Editor Dr P. L. HEWITT; circ. 5,000.

Stereo Buyer's Guide: POB 341, Mona Vale, NSW 2103; tel. (02) 997-1188; f. 1971; 6 a year; Editor DON NORRIS; circ. 18,000.

Video: POB 163, Chippendale, NSW 2008; tel. 699-3622; telex 25027; f. 1982; monthly; Editor STEWART FIST.

Videoworld Magazine: POB 341, Mona Vale, NSW 2103; tel. (02) 997-1188; f. 1982; monthly; Editor GREG BORROWMAN; circ. 16,000.

What's on Video and Cinema: POB 186, Glen Iris, Vic 3146; tel. (03) 256456; telex 38225; f. 1981; monthly; Editor GEOFFREY M. GOLD; circ. 117,500.

Wildlife in Australia: 8 Clifton St, Petrie Terrace, Brisbane, Qld 4000; quarterly; journal of the Wildlife Preservation Soc. of Qld; Editor VINCENT SERVENTY.

World Review: c/o Australian Institute of International Affairs, POB E181, Queen Victoria Terrace, Canberra, ACT 2600; tel. (062) 515500; f. 1962; quarterly; Editor Dr GLEN ST J. BARCLAY.

Your Computer: 706 Military Rd, Mosman, NSW 2088; telex 60469; circ. 30,000.

Your Garden: 61 Flinders Lane, Melbourne, Vic 3000; tel. (03) 652-1111; monthly; Editor G. PURDY; circ. 90,000.

AUSTRALIA

NEWS AGENCIES

Australian Associated Press: 364 Sussex St, Sydney, NSW; tel. (02) 236-8800; telex 20975; f. 1935; owned by major daily newspapers of Australia; Chair. M. V. SUICH; CEO C. L. CASEY.

Foreign Bureaux

Agence France-Presse (AFP): POB K389, Haymarket, NSW 2000; tel. (02) 264-1822; telex 176518; Bureau Chief DAVID DAVIES.

Agencia EFE (Spain): 5 Erldunda Circuit, Hawker, Canberra, ACT 2614; tel. (062) 543732; Correspondent ANTONIO-JOSÉ ARJONILLA.

Agenzia Nazionale Stampa Associata (ANSA) (Italy): Angus and Coote House, 500 George St, Sydney, NSW 2000; tel. (02) 264-8348; telex 71770; Bureau Chief EVASIO COSTANZO.

Associated Press (AP) (USA): 4th Floor, 364 Sussex St, Sydney, NSW 2000; tel. (02) 267-2122; telex 21181; Bureau Chief PETER O'LOUGHLIN.

Deutsche Presse-Agentur (dpa) (Federal Republic of Germany): 67 Kipling Ave, Mooroolbark, Melbourne, Vic 3138; tel. (03) 726-5551; telex 33131; Bureau Chief BORIS B. BEHRSING.

Jiji Tsushin-Sha (Japan): Suite 1, 1st Floor, Wynyard House, 291 George St, Sydney, NSW 2000; tel. (02) 291229; telex 75974; Bureau Chief IKUHIRO KISHIDA.

Kyodo Tsushin (Japan): 364 Sussex St, Sydney, NSW 2000; tel. (02) 264-7390; telex 75851; Bureau Chief HIROSHI TAMAKI.

Reuters Australia Pty Ltd: POB K342, Haymarket, Sydney, NSW 2000; tel. (02) 264-5083; telex 72835.

Telegrafnoye Agentstvo Sovetskovo Soyuza (TASS) (USSR): 8 Elliott St, Campbell, Canberra, ACT 2601; Correspondent SERGEI SOLOVEV.

United Press International (UPI) (USA): 3rd Floor, News House, 2 Holt St, Sydney, NSW 2010; tel. (02) 212-3899; Man. BRIAN DEWHURST.

Xinhua (New China) News Agency (People's Republic of China): 50 Russell St, Hackett, Canberra, ACT 2602; tel. (062) 486369; telex 61507; Correspondent JIN MINGYUAN.

The Central News Agency (Taiwan) and the New Zealand Press Association are represented in Sydney, and Antara (Indonesia) is represented in Canberra.

PRESS ASSOCIATIONS

Australian Newspapers Council: 44–74 Flinders St, Melbourne, Vic 3000; tel. (03) 652-1111; telex 30104; f. 1958; 6 mems, confined to metropolitan daily or Sunday papers; Pres. B. L. SALLIS; Sec. J. D. RILEY.

Country Press Association of New South Wales Inc: POB C599, Clarence St, Sydney, NSW 2000; tel. (02) 294658; f. 1900; Exec. Dir I. D. DAVIDSON; 75 mems.

Country Press Association of South Australia Incorporated: 130 Franklin St, Adelaide, SA 5000; tel. (08) 512626; f. 1912; represents South Australian country newspapers; Pres. I. T. TILBROOK; Sec. M. R. TOWNSEND.

Country Press Australia: POB C599, Clarence St, Sydney, NSW 2000; f. 1906; Exec. Dir I. D. DAVIDSON; 250 mems.

Queensland Country Press Association: POB 103, Paddington, Qld 4064; tel. (07) 369-6088; telex 43972; Pres. MARK HODGSON; Sec. G. P. W. WILLCOCKS.

Regional Dailies of Australia Ltd: 247 Collins St, Melbourne, Vic 3000; tel. (03) 654-2022; f. 1936; Chair. B. J. McKENDRICK; CEO R. W. SINCLAIR; 36 mems.

Tasmanian Press Association Pty Ltd: 71–75 Paterson St, Launceston, Tas; tel. (003) 315111; telex 58511; Sec. B. J. McKENDRICK.

Victoria Country Press Association Ltd: 33 Rathdowne St, Carlton, Vic 3053; tel. (03) 662-3244; f. 1910; Pres. R. L. J. BEKS; Exec. Dir R. C. McDIARMID; 103 mems.

Publishers

Addison-Wesley Publishing Co: Unit 1A, 6–8 Byfield St, North Ryde, NSW 2113; tel. (02) 888-2733; telex 71919; educational, scientific, technical, juvenile; Gen. Man. DEREK HALL.

George Allen and Unwin: 11th Floor, NCR House, 8 Napier St, POB 764, North Sydney, NSW 2060; educational, general non-fiction; Chair. M. S. UNWIN; Man. Dir P. A. GALLAGHER.

Angus and Robertson Publishers: 4 Eden Park, 31 Waterloo Rd, POB 290, North Ryde, NSW 2113; tel. (02) 887-2233; telex 26452; f. 1886; fiction, general and children's; CEO TERRY HUGHES.

Edward Arnold (Australia) Pty Ltd: 80 Waverley Rd, POB 234, Caulfield East, Vic 3145; tel. (03) 572-2211; telex 35974; f. 1974; educational; Chair. E. A. HAMILTON; Man. Dir T. M. COYLE.

Ashton Scholastic: Railway Crescent, Lisarow, Gosford, NSW 2250; tel. (043) 283555; telex 24881; f. 1968; educational, children's paperbacks; Chair. M. SINCLAIR; Man. Dir KEN JOLLY.

Australasian Medical Publishing Co Ltd: 77–79 Arundel St, Glebe, NSW 2037; tel. 660-6055; telex 24814; f. 1913; scientific, medical and educational; Man. GEOFFREY F. HILL.

The Australasian Publishing Co Pty Ltd: cnr Bridge Rd and Jersey St, Hornsby, NSW 2077; tel. 476-2000; telex 23274; f. 1937; general; Man. Dir G. A. RUTHERFORD.

Australia and New Zealand Book Co Pty Ltd: POB 459, Brookvale, NSW 2100; tel. (02) 452-4411; telex 70727; f. 1964; medical, general non-fiction, technical, scientific, arts and crafts, computers; Chair. GEOFFREY M. KING.

Australian National University Press: 19A Boundary St, Rushcutters Bay, Sydney, NSW 2011; tel. (02) 331-5211; telex 27458; scholarly; a division of Pergamon Press (Australia) Pty Ltd; Man. Dir J. MAYER.

S. John Bacon Pty Ltd: 13 Windsor Ave, POB 345, Mt Waverley, Melbourne, Vic 3149; tel. (03) 277-3944; telex 151218; f. 1938; theology and Christian education, educational; Chair. Mrs M. BACON; Man. Dir A. R. TOSTEVIN.

Butterworths Pty Ltd: 271–273 Lane Cove Rd, North Ryde, NSW 2113; tel. (02) 887-3444; telex 122033; f. 1910; law, medical, scientific and commercial; Chair. W. G. GRAHAM; Man. Dir D. J. JACKSON.

Cambridge University Press (Australia): 10 Stamford Road, Oakleigh, Melbourne, Vic 3166; tel. (03) 568-0322; scholarly and educational; Dir KIM W. HARRIS.

CBS Publishing Australia Pty Ltd: 9 Waltham St, Artarmon, NSW 2064; tel. (02) 439-3633; telex 121217; general; Man. Dir PATRICIA EVANS.

Century Hutchinson Australia Pty Ltd: 16–22 Church St, Hawthorn, Vic 3122; tel. (03) 862-3311; telex 37972; general; Man. Dir E. F. MASON.

Collins, Wm. Pty Ltd: 55 Clarence St, Sydney, NSW 2000; tel. (02) 290-2066; telex 26292; fiction, general non-fiction, children's and Australiana; Man. Dir T. KITSON.

Commonwealth Scientific and Industrial Research Organization (CSIRO): 314 Albert St, East Melbourne, Vic 3002; f. 1948; scientific journals, books and indices; Editor-in-Chief B. J. WALBY.

Doubleday Australia Pty Ltd: 14 Mars Rd, Lane Cove, NSW 2066; general; Man. Dir P. MADGWICK.

Encyclopaedia Britannica (Australia) Inc: 22 Lambs Rd, Artarmon, NSW 2064; tel. (02) 438-4544; telex 23044; reference, education, art, science and commerce; Pres. H. W. DE WEESE.

Golden Press Pty Ltd: 501 Henry Lawson Business Centre, Birkenhead Point, Drummoyne, NSW 2047; tel.(02) 819-9111; telex 26070; children's, general non-fiction, education; Gen. Man. ROSS ALEXANDER.

Gordon and Gotch Ltd: 114 William St, POB 767G, Melbourne, Vic 3001; tel. (03) 679901; telex 32099; Man. Dir C. J. B. SCOTT.

Harcourt Brace Jovanovich Group (Australia) Pty Ltd: Centrecourt, 25–27 Paul St, North Ryde, NSW 2113; tel. (02) 888-3655; telex 23394; educational, technical, scientific, medical; Man. Dir BARRY DINGLEY.

Harper and Row (Australasia) Pty Ltd: Unit 3B, Artarmon Industrial Estate, cnr Reserve Rd and Frederick St, POB 226, Artarmon, NSW 2064; tel. (02) 439-6155; telex 72598; reference, educational, medical, trade, paperbacks; Man. Dir B. D. WILDER.

Heinemann Publishers Australia Pty Ltd: 81–85 Abinger St, Richmond, Melbourne, Vic 3121; tel. (03) 429-3622; telex 35347; educational and general; Man. Dir SANDY GRANT.

Hodder and Stoughton (Australia) Pty Ltd: 2 Apollo Place, Lane Cove, NSW 2066; tel. (02) 428-1022; telex 24858; fiction, general, educational, technical, children's; Man. Dir E. COFFEY.

Horwitz Grahame Books Pty Ltd: 506 Miller St, POB 306, Cammeray, NSW 2062; tel. (02) 929-6144; telex 27833; fiction, reference, educational, Australiana, general; Man. Dir L. J. MOORE.

Hyland House Publishing Pty Ltd: 23 Bray St, South Yarra, Vic 3141; tel. (03) 241-6336; trade, general; Rep. AL KNIGHT.

AUSTRALIA

Jacaranda Wiley Ltd: 65 Park Rd, Milton, Qld 4064; POB 859, Brisbane, Qld 4001; tel. (07) 369-9755; telex 41845; f. 1954; educational, technical and cartographic; Man. Dir JOHN COLLINS.

Lansdowne-Rigby: 176 South Creek Rd, POB 60, Dee Why, NSW 2099; tel. (02) 981-0444; telex 121546; general non-fiction, literature, maps, guides and directories; CEO KEVIN WELDON.

Longman Cheshire Pty Ltd: Kings Gardens, 95 Coventry St, South Melbourne, Vic 3205; tel. (03) 697-0666; telex 33501; f. 1957; mainly educational, some general; Man. Dir N. J. RYAN.

Thomas C. Lothian Pty Ltd: 11 Munro St, Port Melbourne, Vic 3207; tel. (03) 645-1544; telex 39476; f. 1888; general, gardening, health, juvenile; Dirs LOUIS A. LOTHIAN, K. A. LOTHIAN, PETER H. LOTHIAN.

McGraw-Hill Book Co Australia Pty Ltd: 4 Barcoo St, East Roseville, Sydney, NSW 2069; tel. (02) 406-4288; telex 120849; educational and technical; Man. Dir D. J. PEGREM.

Macmillan Company of Australia Pty Ltd: 107 Moray St, South Melbourne, Vic 3205; tel. (03) 699-8922; telex 34454; f. 1967; general and educational; Man. Dir BRIAN STONIER.

McPhee Gribble Publishers Pty Ltd: 66 Cecil St, Fitzroy, Vic 3065; tel. (03) 419-9010; telex 31494; f. 1975; general fiction and non-fiction; Man. Dirs HILARY MCPHEE, DIANA GRIBBLE.

Majura Press: POB 25, Hackett, ACT 2602; tel. (062) 413329; f. 1984; non-fiction; Man. D. FRENCH.

Melbourne University Press: 268 Drummond St, Carlton South, Vic 3053; tel. (03) 347-3455; telex 35185; f. 1923; academic, educational, Australiana, general except fiction and children's; Chair. Prof. J. R. POYNTER; Dir P. A. RYAN.

Methuen LBC Ltd: 44–50 Waterloo Road, North Ryde, NSW 2113; tel. (02) 887-0177; telex 27995; legal, educational, general, non-fiction, juvenile; Chair. K. T. FELLEW; Man. Dir W. J. MACKARELL.

National Library of Australia: Canberra, ACT 2600; tel. (062) 621111; telex 62100; national bibliographical publs, facsimiles of materials in the library's collections; Dir-Gen. W. M. HORTON.

Thomas Nelson Australia: 480 La Trobe St, Melbourne, Vic 3000; tel. (03) 329-5199; telex 33088; educational, vocational and general; Man. Dir B. J. RIVERS.

New South Wales University Press Ltd: POB 1, Kensington, NSW 2033; tel. (02) 697-3403; telex 26054; f. 1961; general and educational; Gen. Man. DOUGLAS HOWIE.

Oxford University Press: POB 2784Y, Melbourne, Vic 3001; tel. (03) 267-7466; telex 35330; f. 1908; general non-fiction and educational; Man. Dir D. C. CUNNINGHAM.

Penguin Books Australia Ltd: 487/493 Maroondah Highway, Ringwood, Vic 3134; tel. (03) 871-2400; telex 32458; f. 1946; general; Man. Dir T. D. GLOVER; Publishing Dir BRIAN JOHNS.

Pergamon Press (Australia) Pty Ltd: 19A Boundary St, Rushcutter's Bay, NSW 2011; tel. (02) 331-5211; telex 27458; f. 1949; educational, general, scientific; Chair. I. R. MAXWELL; Man. Dir J. MAYER.

Pitman Publishing Pty Ltd: Kings Gardens, 91–97 Coventry St, South Melbourne, Vic 3053; tel. (03) 699-5400; telex 30107; f. 1968; educational, technical and general; Chair. NEIL RYAN; Man. Dir TUDOR N. DAY.

Prentice-Hall of Australia Pty Ltd: 7 Grosvenor Place, POB 151, Brookvale, NSW 2100; tel. (02) 939-1333; telex 74010; educational, trade, reference and general; Man. Dir P. F. GLEESON.

Reader's Digest Services Pty Ltd: 26–32 Waterloo St, Surry Hills, NSW 2010; POB 4353, Sydney, NSW; general; Man. Dir M. MATON.

Reed Books Pty Ltd: 2 Aquatic Drive, French's Forest, Sydney, NSW 2086; tel. (02) 451-8122; telex 27212; f. 1964; Australiana, general non-fiction; Gen. Man. D. A. MACLELLAN.

Rigby Education: 484 St Kilda Rd, Melbourne, Vic 3004; tel. (03) 269-4760; telex 36521; educational; CEO JOHN GILDER.

Rigby Publishers: POB 71, Burnside, SA 5066; tel. (08) 311344; telex 88090; f. 1859; general; Gen. Man. FRANK W. THOMPSON.

Schwartz and Wilkinson: 45 Flinders Lane, Melbourne, Vic 3000; tel. (03) 654-2800; telex 30625; fiction, non-fiction; Dir MORRY SCHWARTZ.

Science Research Associates Pty Ltd: 84 Waterloo Rd, North Ryde, NSW 2113; tel. (02) 888-7833; telex 70185; educational; Chair. and Man. Dir R. J. BARTON.

Simon and Schuster (Australia): 7 Grosvenor Place, POB 151, Brookvale, NSW 2100; tel. (02) 939-1333; telex 74010; educational, reference, trade and general; CEO P. F. GLEESON.

Sydney University Press: Press Bldg, University of Sydney, Sydney, NSW 2006; tel. (02) 660-4997; f. 1964; scholarly, academic and general; Dir DAVID NEW.

Thames and Hudson (Australia) Pty Ltd: 86 Stanley St, West Melbourne, Vic 3003; tel. (03) 329-8454; art and general; Man. Dir RICHARD M. GILMOUR.

D. W. Thorpe Pty Ltd: 20–24 Stokes St, POB 146, Port Melbourne, Vic 3207; tel. (03) 645-1511; telex 39476; biographies, trade, paperbacks; Chair. J. NICHOLSON; Man. Dir M. WEBSTER.

Time Life Books (Australia) Pty Ltd: 7th Floor, Philips Building, 15 Blue St, North Sydney, NSW 2060; tel. (02) 929-0933; telex 20659; Man. Dir BONNIE BOELEMAN.

Transworld Publishers (Aust.) Pty Ltd: 13–15 Helles Ave, Moorebank, NSW 2170; tel. (02) 601-7122; telex 71471; general, fiction, juvenile, education; Man. Dir G. S. RUMPF.

University of Queensland Press: POB 42, St Lucia, Qld 4067; tel. (07) 377-2127; telex 40315; f. 1948; scholarly and general cultural interest; Gen. Man. LAURIE MULLER.

University of Western Australia Press: Tuart House, cnr Mounts Bay Rd and Crawley Ave, Nedlands, WA 6009; tel. 380-3182; f. 1954; educational, secondary and university, technical, scientific, scholarly, humanities; Man. V. S. GREAVES.

Government Publishing House

Australian Government Publishing Service: POB 84, Canberra, ACT 2601; tel. (062) 954411; telex 62013; f. 1970; Dir of Publishing F. W. THOMPSON.

PUBLISHERS' ASSOCIATION

Australian Book Publishers Association: 161 Clarence St, Sydney, NSW 2000; tel. (02) 295422; telex 121822; f. 1949; c. 150 mems; Pres. TREVOR GLOVER; Dir JAN NOBLE.

Radio and Television

The programmes for the National Broadcasting Service and National Television are provided by the non-commercial statutory corporation, the Australian Broadcasting Corporation (ABC).

The Corporation operates 95 medium-wave stations, 25 FM, 5 domestic and 10 overseas (Radio Australia) short-wave stations broadcasting in English, French, Indonesian, Japanese, Standard Chinese, Cantonese, Neo-Melanesian, Thai and Vietnamese. In 1983 the Government agreed to provide funds to establish a second regional radio network for the ABC, due to be completed by 1990.

There is one national television network of 10 stations with studios, 85 transmitters and 181 translator stations.

Commercial radio and television services are provided by stations operated by companies under licences granted and renewed by the Australian Broadcasting Tribunal. They rely for their income on the broadcasting of advertisements. On 1 January 1983, there were 136 commercial radio stations in operation, and in August 1982 there were 50 commercial television stations.

In 1982 there were an estimated 17.6m. radio receivers and 6.5m. television receivers in use.

Australian Broadcasting Corporation (ABC): 145–153 Elizabeth St, POB 9994, Sydney, NSW 2001; tel. (02) 339-0211 (radio), (02) 437-8000 (television); telex 26506; f. 1932 as Australian Broadcasting Commission; Chair. DAVID HILL; Man. Dir GEOFFREY WHITEHEAD.

RADIO

Federation of Australian Radio Broadcasters: POB 294, Milson's Point, NSW 2061; tel. (02) 929-4866; telex 25161; asscn of privately-owned stations; Fed. Dir D. L. FOSTER; Dep. Fed. Dir J. M. RUSHTON; Fed. Sec. J. H. FINLAYSON.

Major Commercial Broadcasting Station Licensees

Advertiser Broadcasting Network Pty Ltd: 121 King William St, Adelaide, SA 5000; tel. (08) 211-7666; operates three stations; Gen. Man. SAM GALEA.

Amalgamated Wireless (Australasia) Ltd: 47 York St, Sydney, NSW; tel. (02) 20233; telex 121515; f. 1913; operates eight stations; Chair. and CEO J. A. L. HOOKE.

Associated Broadcasting Services Ltd: Walker St, Ballarat, Vic 3350; tel. (053) 313166; telex 39155; f. 1957; operates two television and two radio stations; Chair. W. H. HEINZ; CEO JAMES MALONE.

AUSTRALIA

Broadcast Investments Pty Ltd: 237 Miller St, North Sydney, NSW 2060; tel. (02) 922-9950; telex 20421; operates three stations; Group Gen. Man. S. J. WILLMOTT.

Broadcasting Station 2SM Pty Ltd: 186 Blues Point Rd, North Sydney, NSW 2060; tel. (02) 922-1270; telex 25350; operates five stations; CEO G. W. RUTHERFORD.

Commonwealth Broadcasting Network: 9 Rangers Rd, POB 1107, Neutral Bay, NSW 2089; tel. (02) 908-1900; telex 22797; operates six stations; CEO B. E. BYRNE.

Consolidated Broadcasting System (WA) Pty Ltd: 283 Rokeby Rd, Subiaco, WA; operates four stations; CEO K. A. GANNAWAY, R. BIGUM.

Macquarie Broadcasting Holdings Ltd: cnr Liverpool and Sussex Sts, Sydney, NSW 2000; POB 4290, Sydney, NSW 2001; tel. (02) 269-0646; telex 21502; operates more than 26 stations; Group Gen. Man. R. A. JOHNSON.

6IX Radio Network Pty Ltd: POB 77, Tuart Hill, WA 6060; tel. (09) 349-7777; telex 94273; operates three stations; Gen. Man. BRENDAN SHEEDY.

South Australian Broadcasting Network: 43 Franklin St, Adelaide, SA; tel. (08) 515511; telex 82540; operates one station.

Southern Cross Communications Ltd: Lily St, POB 888, Bendigo, Vic 3550; tel. (054) 439677; telex 32885; operates one station; CEO IAN MÜLLER.

Tamworth Radio Development Company Pty Ltd: POB 497, Tamworth, NSW 2340; tel. (067) 657055; telex 63166; operates five stations; Man. E. C. WILKINSON.

Wesgo Communications Pty Ltd: 2 Leabons Lane, Seven Hills, NSW 2147; tel. (02) 671-2411; telex 23614; operates seven stations; Man. Dir and CEO R. D. SCOTT.

TELEVISION

Federation of Australian Commercial Television Stations: 447 Kent St, Sydney, NSW 2000; tel. (02) 264-5577; telex 121542; f. 1960; represents 50 commercial television stations; Chair. L. A. MAUGER; Fed. Dir DAVID MORGAN.

Commercial Television Station Licensees

Amalgamated Television Services Pty Ltd: TV Centre, Epping, NSW 2121; tel. 858-7777; telex 20250; f. 1956; operates one station; Gen. Man. E. F. THOMAS.

Austarama Television Pty Ltd: POB 42, Hawthorn Rd, Nunawading, Vic 3131; tel. (03) 234-1010; telex 30628; f. 1964; operates one station at Melbourne; Man. Dir W. McKENZIE.

Australian Capital Television Pty Ltd: POB 777, Dickson, ACT 2602; tel. (062) 411000; telex 62046; f. 1962; operates one station; CEO W. G. RAYNER.

Ballarat and Western Victoria Television Ltd: POB 464, Ballarat, Vic 3350; tel. (053) 313166; telex 32011; f. 1962; operates five stations; Chair. W. H. HEINZ; Gen. Man. M. J. FAULKNER.

Brisbane TV Ltd: POB 604, Brisbane, Qld 4001; tel. (07) 369-7777; telex 41653; f. 1959; operates one station; Man. Dir D. BLACK.

Broadcast Operations Pty Ltd: Remembrance Driveway, Griffith, NSW 2680; tel. (069) 624500; telex 69991; f. 1965; operates one station; Man. Dir W. R. GAMBLE; Gen. Man. B. MEADLEY.

Broken Hill Television Ltd: POB 472, Broken Hill, NSW 2880; tel. (080) 6013; telex 80874; f. 1968; operates one station; Chair. P. MARTIN; Man. Dir J. M. STURROCK.

Country Television Services Ltd: POB 465, Orange, NSW 2800; tel. (063) 622288; telex 163012; f. 1962; operates four stations; Man. Dirs E. YELF, I. RIDLEY.

Darling Downs TV Ltd: POB 670, Toowoomba, Qld 4350; tel. (076) 322288; telex 140058; f. 1962; operates three stations; Gen. Man. L. R. BURROWS; Station Man. R. W. BALL.

Far Northern Television Ltd: POB 596, Cairns, Qld 4870; tel. (070) 516322; telex 48401; f. 1966; operates one station; Chair. JACK GLEESON; Gen. Man. DAVID ASTLEY.

General Television Corporation Pty Ltd: 22–46 Bendigo St, POB 100, Richmond, Vic 3121; tel. (03) 420-3111; telex 30189; f. 1957; operates one station; Pres. G. RICE; Gen. Man. I. J. JOHNSON.

Geraldton Telecasters Pty Ltd: 7 Fore St, Perth, WA 6000; tel. (09) 328-9833; telex 94382; f. 1977; operates one station; Gen. Man. BRIAN HOPWOOD.

Golden West Network Ltd: POB 112, Bunbury, WA 6230; tel. (097) 214466; telex 92305; f. 1967; operates eight stations; Gen. Man. TOM DREWELL.

Goulburn-Murray Television Ltd: POB 666, Shepparton, Vic 3630; tel. (058) 215666; telex 30742; f. 1961; operates one station; Chair. W. H. HEINZ; Gen. Man. TONY KENISON.

Herald-Sun TV Pty Ltd: POB 215D, GPO Melbourne, Vic 3001; tel. (03) 697-7777; telex 30707; f. 1956; operates one station; Chair. R. H. SAMPSON; Gen. Man. R. P. CASEY.

Mackay Television Ltd: POB 496, PO Mackay, Qld 4740; tel. (079) 576333; telex 48152; f. 1968; operates one station; Gen. Man. RAY COX.

Mid-Western Television Pty Ltd: 96 Wanneroo Rd, Tuart Hill, WA 6060; tel. (090) 213888; telex 95354; operates eight stations; Man. Dir J. H. M. DORSEY.

Mt Isa Television Pty Ltd: 110 Camooweal St, Mt Isa, Qld 4825; tel. (077) 438888; telex 49947; f. 1971; operates one station; Man. Dir Sir A. JOEL; Gen. Man. B. HILLIER.

NBN Ltd: Mosbri Crescent, POB 750L, Newcastle, NSW 2300; tel. (049) 20321; telex 28039; f. 1962; operates one station; CEO JOE SWEENEY.

Northern Rivers Television Ltd: Peterson Rd, POB 920, Coffs Harbour, NSW 2450; tel. (066) 522777; telex 66961; f. 1965; operates two stations; Gen. Man. CHRIS O'CONNELL.

Northern Television (TNT9) Pty Ltd: Watchorn St, Launceston, Tas 7250; tel. (003) 440202; telex 58512; f. 1962; operates one station; Gen. Man. D. M. McQUESTIN.

Queensland Television Ltd: POB 72, GPO Brisbane, Qld 4001; tel. (07) 369-9999; telex 42347; f. 1959; operates one station; Exec. Dir D. ASPINALL; Gen. Man. V. LOTHRINGER.

Regional Television Australia Pty Ltd: 82–84 Sydenham Rd, Marrickville, NSW 2204; POB 285, Sydney, NSW 2001; tel. (02) 516-1233; telex 72198; CEO K. STONE.

Riverina and North East Victoria TV Pty Ltd: POB 2, Kooringal via Wagga, NSW 2650; tel. (069) 211222; telex 69022; f. 1964; operates two stations; Gen. Man. N. BROWN.

Riverland Television Pty Ltd: Murray Bridge Rd, POB 471, Loxton, SA 5333; tel. (085) 847248; telex 80313; f. 1976; operates one station; Exec. Chair. E. H. URLWIN; Gen. Man. WENDY FOLEY.

Rockhampton Television Ltd: Dean St, POB 568 Rockhampton, Qld 4700; tel. (079) 285222; telex 49008; f. 1963; Man. Dir B. SAUNDERS.

South Australian Telecasters Ltd: 45–49 Park Terrace, Gilberton, SA 5081; tel. (08) 269-5522; telex 82084; f. 1965; operates one station; Gen. Man. D. EARL.

South East Telecasters Ltd: POB 821, Mount Gambier, SA 5290; tel. (087) 256366; telex 80013; f. 1966; operates one station; Chair. G. T. BARNFIELD; Man. Dir G. J. GILBERTSON.

Southern Cross Communications Ltd: Lily St, POB 888, Bendigo, Vic 3550; tel. (054) 439677; telex 32885; f. 1961; operates seven stations; CEO IAN R. MÜLLER.

Southern Television Corporation Ltd: 202 Tynte St, North Adelaide, SA; tel. (08) 267-0111; telex 82238; f. 1958; operates one station; Gen. Man. TYRRELL TALBOT.

Spencer Gulf Telecasters Ltd: POB 305, 4 Port Pirie, SA 5540; tel. (086) 322555; telex 80320; f. 1968; operates three stations; Studio Man. R. M. DAVIS.

Sunraysia Television Ltd: 18 Deakin Ave, Mildura, Vic 3500; tel. (050) 230204; telex 55304; f. 1965; Chair F. A. McMANUS; Man. A. D. SHARPE; CEO E. G. PRESSER.

Swan Television and Radio Broadcasters Ltd: POB 99, Tuart Hill, WA 6060; tel. (09) 349-9999; telex 92142; f. 1965; operates one station; Man. Dir D. R. ASPINALL.

Tasmanian Television Ltd: 52 New Town Rd, Hobart, Tas; tel. (002) 780666; telex 58019; f. 1959; operates one station; Gen. Man. P. HOGAN.

TCN Channel Nine Pty Ltd: 24 Artarmon Rd, POB 27, Willoughby, NSW 2068; tel. (02) 430-0444; telex 20689; f. 1956; operates one station; Chair. K. F. B. PACKER; Man. Dir S. H. CHISHOLM.

Telecasters North Queensland Ltd: 12 The Strand, POB 1016, Townsville, Qld 4810; tel. (077) 723377; telex 47023; f. 1962; operates one station; Chair. J. F. GLEESON; Gen. Man. DAVID ASTLEY.

Television New England Ltd: Radio Centre, Calala, POB 317, Tamworth, NSW 2340; tel. (067) 657006; telex 63238; f. 1965; operates two stations; Chair. H. JOSEPH; Gen. Man. M. M. MORONEY.

Television Wollongong Transmissions Ltd: Fort Drummond, Mt St Thomas, POB 1800, Wollongong, NSW 2500; tel. (042) 285444; telex 29029; f. 1962; Chair. W. LEAN; Gen. Man. J. RUSHTON.

AUSTRALIA
                                                                                                                                  Directory

Territory Television Pty Ltd: Blake St, Gardens Hill, POB 1764, Darwin, NT 5794; tel. (089) 818888; telex 85138; f. 1971; operates one station; Gen. Man. PETER DOOLEY.

TV Broadcasters Ltd: 125 Strangways Terrace, North Adelaide, SA 5006; tel. (08) 267-0777; telex 82141; f. 1959; operates one station; Gen. Man. J. S. DOHERTY.

TVW Enterprises Ltd: POB 77, Tuart Hill, WA 6060; tel. (09) 349-7777; telex 92235; f. 1959; operates two stations; Chair. and CEO M. R. H. HOLMES A'COURT; Gen. Man. J. REYNOLDS.

United Telecasters Sydney Ltd: Epping and Pittwater Rds, North Ryde, NSW 2113; tel. (02) 887-0222; telex 21767; f. 1965; operates one station; Man. Dir GEORGE BROWN.

Universal Telecasters Qld Ltd: POB 751, GPO Brisbane, Qld 4001; tel. (07) 369-0000; telex 40354; f. 1965; operates one station; Gen. Man. R. CAMPBELL.

Wide Bay-Burnett Television Ltd: 187-189 Cambridge St, POB 30, Granville, Qld 4650; tel. (071) 222288; telex 49702; f. 1965; Gen. Man. A. M. DANIEL.

Finance

(cap. = capital; p.u. = paid up; res = reserves; dep. = deposits; m. = million; brs = branches; amounts in Australian dollars)

BANKING

Central Bank

Reserve Bank of Australia: 65 Martin Place, POB 3947, Sydney, NSW 2001; tel. (02) 234-9333; telex 20106; f. 1911; bank of issue; cap. and res 6,176.5m., dep. and other accounts 5,373.6m. (June 1985); Gov. R. A. JOHNSTON; Dep. Gov. D. N. SANDERS.

Commonwealth Banks

Commonwealth Bank of Australia: Pitt St and Martin Place, Sydney, NSW 2000; tel. (02) 227-7111; telex 120345; f. 1912; cap. 611m., res 1,228m., dep. 22,974m. (1985); Man. Dir V. T. CHRISTIE; more than 1,300 brs worldwide.

Commonwealth Development Bank of Australia: Prudential Bldg, 39 Martin Place, Sydney, NSW 2000; POB 2719, Sydney, NSW 2001; tel. (02) 227-7111; telex 120345; f. 1960; loans, advances and bills discounted 1,026m. (1985); Gen. Man. J. W. FLETCHER.

Development Bank

Australian Resources Development Bank Ltd: 379 Collins St, Melbourne, Vic 3000; tel. (03) 616-2800; telex 32078; f. 1967 by major Australian trading banks, with support of Reserve Bank of Australia, to marshal funds from local and overseas sources for the financing of Australian participation in projects of national importance; acquired Australian Banks' Export Re-Finance Corpn in 1980; cap. p.u. 11.1m., dep. 924.7m. (Sept. 1985); Chair. W. H. HODGSON; Gen. Man. A. LOCKE.

Trading Banks

Australia and New Zealand Banking Group Ltd: Collins Place, 55 Collins St, Melbourne, Vic 3000; tel. (03) 658-2955; telex 39920; f. 1970; cap. 336.0m., res 1,875.3m., dep. 30,087.8m. (1985); over 1,650 points of representation in Australia, New Zealand, UK, USA, Canada, Japan, Hong Kong, Singapore and Federal Republic of Germany; Chair. Sir WILLIAM VINES; Man. Dir W. J. BAILEY.

Australian Bank Ltd: 17 O'Connell St, Sydney, NSW 2000; tel. (02) 264-8000; telex 72253; f. 1981; cap. p.u. 58m. (1986); CEO DICK MORATH.

Bank of Queensland Ltd: 229 Elizabeth St, Brisbane, Qld; tel. (07) 310421; telex 41565; f. 1874; cap. p.u. 8.17m., dep. 87m. (1984); Chair. JOHN R. NOSWORTHY; Gen. Man. N. H. BLUNT.

National Australia Bank Ltd: 500 Bourke St, Melbourne, Vic 3001; tel. (03) 605-3500; telex 30241; f. 1981 by merger of Commercial Banking Co of Sydney with National Bank of Australasia; cap. p.u. 344m., dep. 18,334m. (Sept. 1985); Chair. Sir ROBERT LAW-SMITH; Man. Dir N. R. CLARK; 1,240 brs.

Rural and Industries Bank of Western Australia: 54-58 Barrack St, POB E237, Perth, WA 6001; tel. (09) 320-6206; telex 92417; f. 1945; WA govt bank; cap. and res 178m., dep. 2,737m. (1985); Chair. DAVID P. FISCHER; Gen. Man. ANDREW J. GORDON; 89 brs.

State Bank of New South Wales: 52 Martin Place, Sydney, NSW 2001; tel. (02) 226-8000; telex 121550; f. 1933; cap. 386.28m., dep. 4,893.93m. (1986); Chair. R. F. W. WATSON; Man. Dir N. WHITLAM; 262 brs in Australia.

State Bank of South Australia: 97 King William St, Adelaide, SA 5000; tel. (08) 210-4411; telex 82082; f. 1984 by merger of The State Bank of South Australia with The Savings Bank of South Australia; cap. 44.0m., dep. 2,286m. (July 1985); Chair. L. BARRETT; Man. Dir T. MARCUS CLARK.

Westpac Banking Corporation: 60 Martin Place, Sydney, NSW 2001; tel. (02) 226-3311; telex 20122; f. 1982 by merger of the Bank of New South Wales and The Commercial Bank of Australia; cap. p.u. 505.7m., dep. 27,063m. (1985); Chair. Sir NOEL FOLEY; Man. Dir R. J. WHITE.

Savings Banks

The Savings Bank of Tasmania (The Hobart Savings Bank): 39 Murray St, Hobart, Tas; tel. (002) 304777; telex 58296; f. 1845; Chair. ROBERT MATHER; Gen. Man. H. A. PARKER.

State Bank of Victoria: 385 Bourke St, Melbourne, Vic 3000; tel. (03) 604-7000; telex 32910; f. 1842; dep. 8,601m., total resources 10,589m. (June 1986); Chair. J. ARNOLD HANCOCK; CEO L. G. C. MOYLE; 526 brs.

Westpac Savings Bank Ltd: 60 Martin Place, Sydney, NSW 2001; tel. (02) 226-3311; telex 20122; f. 1956; cap. p.u. 90m., dep. 6,622m. (1985); Chair. Sir JAMES FOOTS; Man. Dir R. J. WHITE.

Foreign Banks

Many of the major foreign banks maintain representative offices in Australia. In February 1985 full trading-bank licences were granted to the following 16 banks: Bankers' Trust Company (USA), Bank of America (USA), Bank of Tokyo Ltd (Japan), Barclays Bank PLC (UK), Chase Manhattan Bank NA (USA), Citibank NA (USA), Deutsche Bank (Federal Republic of Germany), Hongkong and Shanghai Banking Corporation (Hong Kong), Mitsubishi Bank Ltd (Japan), J.P. Morgan and Co (USA), National Bank of New Zealand Ltd (New Zealand), National Westminster Bank PLC (UK), Nippon Kogyo Ginko (Japan), Oversea-Chinese Banking Corpn Ltd (Singapore), The Royal Bank of Canada (Canada), Standard Chartered Bank PLC (UK). The Banque Nationale de Paris has established full branches. In September 1984 permission was being sought by the Bank of China (People's Republic of China) to open a branch in Australia.

Banque Nationale de Paris (France): 12 Castlereagh St, Sydney, NSW; tel. (02) 232-8733; telex 20132; 6 brs.

STOCK EXCHANGES

Australian Associated Stock Exchanges: King George Tower, 388 George St, Sydney, NSW 2000; f. 1937; mems: stock exchanges in the six capital cities; Exec. Dir RONALD L. COPPEL.

The Brisbane Stock Exchange Ltd: 123 Eagle St, Brisbane, Qld 4000; tel. (07) 832-4114; telex 40264; f. 1884; 39 mems; Chair. P. H. TYNAN; Man. G. P. CHAPMAN.

Hobart Stock Exchange: 86 Collins St, Hobart, Tas; tel. (002) 347333; telex 58111; f. 1891.

Stock Exchange of Adelaide Ltd: 55 Exchange Place, Adelaide, SA; tel. (08) 212-3702; telex 82186; f. 1887; 51 mems; Chair. A. R. LAMPHEE; Gen. Man. A. S. CUNNINGHAM.

Stock Exchange of Melbourne Ltd: 351 Collins St, Melbourne, Vic; tel. (03) 617-8611; telex 30550; f. 1884, inc. 1970; 252 mems; Chair. L. IAN ROACH; Gen. Man. R. B. LEE.

Stock Exchange of Perth Ltd: Exchange House, 68 St George's Terrace, Perth, WA 6001; tel. (09) 322-5066; telex 92159; f. 1889; 43 mems; Chair. P. C. HAWKINS; CEO JOHN G. THOMPSON.

Sydney Stock Exchange: 20 Bond St, POB H224, Australia Sq., Sydney, NSW 2000; tel. (02) 225-6600; telex 20630; f. 1871; 245 mems; Chair. J. K. BAIN; Man. Dir P. W. MARSHMAN.

PRINCIPAL INSURANCE COMPANIES

AGC (Insurances) Ltd: AGC House, 130 Phillip St, Sydney, NSW 2000; tel. (02) 234-1122; telex 26612; f. 1938; Chair. E. C. TAIT; Gen. Man. D. D. CRISP.

AMP Fire & General Insurance Co Ltd: 8 Loftus St, Sydney Cove, NSW 2000; telex 177001; f. 1958; Chair. J. W. UTZ; Man. Dir J. K. STAVELEY.

Australian Natives' Association Insurance Co Ltd: 114-124 Albert Road, South Melbourne, Vic 3205; f. 1948; Chair. G. D. WEARNE; Man. B. O. FENTON.

Australian Reinsurance Co Ltd: 31 Queen St, Melbourne, Vic 3000; tel. (03) 616-9200; telex 34201; f. 1962; reinsurance; Chair. S. C. G. MACINDOE; Man. Dir J. H. WINTER; Gen. Man. P. C. HEFFERNAN.

AUSTRALIA

Capita Financial Group Ltd: 60–66 Hunter St, Sydney, NSW 2000; tel. (02) 221-1788; telex 24086; f. 1878 as the City Mutual Life Assurance Society Ltd; present name adopted in 1986; Chair. GERALD WELLS; Man. Dir D. S. GREATOREX.

Catholic Church Insurances Ltd: 387 St Kilda Rd, Melbourne, Vic 3004; tel. (03) 267-5900; f. 1911; Chair. Mgr P. H. JONES; Gen. Man. C. R. O'MALLEY.

The Chamber of Manufactures Insurance Ltd: 368–374 St Kilda Rd, Melbourne, Vic 3004; tel. (03) 699-4211; telex 39482; f. 1914; Chair. W. D. MCPHERSON; Man. Dir C. L. HARWOOD; Gen. Man. T. R. LONGES.

The City Mutual General Insurance Ltd: 60 Hunter St, POB 505, Sydney, NSW 2001; f.1889; Chair. JOHN CLONEY; Gen. Man. GORDON TAYLOR.

Colonial Mutual General Insurance Co Ltd: 330 Collins St, Melbourne, Vic 3000; tel. (03) 607-6111; telex 34059; f. 1958; Chair. P. C. TRUMBLE; Gen. Man. G. D. C. SWANTON.

The Colonial Mutual Life Assurance Society Ltd: 330 Collins St, Melbourne, Vic 3000; tel. (03) 607-6111; telex 34059; f. 1873; Chair. P. C. TRUMBLE; Chief Gen. Man. JOHN MILBURN-PYLE.

Commercial Union Assurance Co of Australia Ltd: Temple Court, 428 Collins St, Melbourne, Vic; tel. (03) 605-8222; telex 33100; f. 1960; fire, accident, marine; Chair. J. A. HANCOCK; Man. Dir W. S. MANSFIELD.

Copenhagen Reinsurance Co (Aust.) Ltd: 60 Margaret St, Sydney, NSW 2000; tel. (02) 277266; telex 26721; f. 1961; reinsurance; Chair. DAVID BROWN; Gen. Man. PAUL ALLISON.

Farmers Grazcos Co-operative Ltd: 3 Spring St, Sydney, NSW 2000; tel. (02) 279284; f. 1980; Gen. Man. F. D. LUXFORD.

The Federation Insurance Ltd: 342–348 Flinders St, Melbourne, Vic 3000; tel. (03) 620101; telex 30847; f. 1926; Chair. R. L. M. SUMMERBELL; Gen. Man. A. J. KELL.

GRE Insurance Ltd: 604 St Kilda Rd, Melbourne, Vic 3004; tel. (03) 520-6233; fire, marine, accident; Man. Dir W. DIGBY.

Manufacturers' Mutual Insurance Ltd: 60–62 York St, Sydney, NSW 2000; tel. (02) 290-6222; telex 126666; f. 1914; workers' compensation; fire, general accident, motor and marine; Chair. C. W. LOVE; Man. Dir A. T. C. VENNING.

Mercantile & General Life Reinsurance Group of Australia Ltd: Royal Exchange Bldg, 56 Pitt St, Sydney, NSW 2000; tel. (02) 278651; telex 120318; f. 1956; reinsurance; Chair. G. T. KRYGER; Gen. Man. S. R. B. FRANCE.

Mercantile Mutual Holdings Ltd: 55 Clarence St, Sydney, NSW; tel. (02) 234-8111; telex 27526; f. 1878; Chair. Sir HAROLD KNIGHT; Man. Dir P. R. SHIRRIFF.

MLC Insurance Ltd: 44 Martin Place, Sydney, NSW 2000; tel. (02) 957-8000; telex 74679; f. 1958; Chair. R. C. GARROWAY; Gen. Man. D. A. WHIPP.

MLC Life Ltd: 105–153 Miller St, POB 200, North Sydney, NSW 2060; tel. (02) 957-8000; telex 121290; f. 1886; Chair. V. E. MARTIN; Man. Dir J. P. MORSCHEL.

National & General Insurance Co Ltd: 10 Bond St, Sydney, NSW; f. 1954; fire, marine, general; Chair. Sir PETER FINLEY; Gen. Man. B. I. J. CLARK.

The National Mutual Life Association of Australasia Ltd: 447 Collins St, Melbourne, Vic 3000; tel. (03) 616-3911; telex 35654; f. 1869; Chair. G. M. NIALL; Man. Dir E. A. MAYER.

NRMA Insurance Ltd: 151 Clarence St, Sydney, NSW 2000; tel. (02) 260-9222; telex 22348; f. 1926; associated with National Roads and Motorists' Asscn; Gen. Man. R. J. LAMBLE.

NZI Life Ltd: 118 Mount St, North Sydney, NSW; tel. (02) 925-1999; Chair. J. H. G. BAKER; Gen. Man. P. G. CASHMAN.

QBE Insurance Group Ltd: 82 Pitt St, Sydney, NSW 2000; tel. (02) 235-4444; telex 26914; f. 1886; general insurance; Chair. J. D. O. BURNS; Man. Dir E. J. CLONEY.

Reinsurance Co of Australasia Ltd: 1 York St, Sydney, NSW 2000; tel. (02) 221-2144; f. 1961; reinsurance, fire, accident, marine; Chair. M. T. SANDOW; Man. Dir P. J. MILLER.

South British United Life Assurance Co Ltd: 118 Mount St, North Sydney, NSW; tel. 922-1022; f. 1921; Gen. Man. PAUL G. CASHMAN.

Southern Pacific Insurance Co Ltd: 80 Alfred St, Milson's Point, NSW 2061; f. 1935; fire, accident, marine; Chair. C. H. V. CARPENTER; Chief Gen. Man. B. A. SELF.

Sun Alliance Insurance Ltd: Sun Alliance Bldg, 22 Bridge St, Sydney, NSW 2000; fire, accident and marine insurance; Man. Dir N. GREENWOOD.

Traders Prudent Insurance Co Ltd: FAI Insurance Group, 185 Macquarie St, Sydney, NSW 2000; f. 1956; Chair. J. L. ADLER; Gen. Man. Dr G. WEIPPERT.

Wesfarmers Insurance Ltd: 184 Railway Parade, Bassendean, WA 6054; tel. (09) 279-0333; telex 96159; Man. T. I. CORNFORD.

Westpac Life Insurance Services Ltd: 60 Martin Place, Sydney, NSW 2001; tel. (02) 226-2888; f. 1986; CEO MONTY HILKOWITZ.

Insurance Associations

Australian Insurance Association: 19th Floor, General Bldg, 8–18 Bent St, POB 4471, Sydney, NSW 2000; tel. (02) 233-1638; telex 75233; f. 1968; Pres. G. C. BOND; Exec. Dir I. J. FREW.

Australian Insurance Institute: 31 Queen St, Melbourne, Vic 3000; tel. (03) 624021; telex 139668; f. 1919; Pres. G. W. WEIGHTMAN; CEO A. V. SMYTHE; 6,300 mems.

Insurance Council of Australia Ltd: 31 Queen St, Melbourne, Vic 3000; tel. (03) 614-1077; telex 37334; f. 1975; CEO R. G. A. SMITH.

Life Insurance Federation of Australia: 31 Queen St, Melbourne, Vic 3000; tel. (03) 625751; f. 1979; Chair. E. A. MAYER; Exec. Dir (vacant); 44 mems.

Trade and Industry

CHAMBERS OF COMMERCE

International Chamber of Commerce: POB E118, Queen Victoria Terrace, Canberra, ACT 2600; tel. (062) 732381; telex 62507; f. 1927; 65 mems; Chair. B. C. MAKINS.

Australian Chamber of Commerce: Brisbane Ave, Barton, ACT 2600; tel. (062) 732381; telex 62507; f. 1901; mems include Chambers of Commerce in Sydney, Melbourne, Canberra, Brisbane, Adelaide, Perth, Hobart, Newcastle, Darwin, Gove, Tamworth, Cairns, Norfolk Island, and State Feds of Chambers of Commerce in Vic, Qld and WA; Pres. C. S. CULLEN; Exec. Dir Dr G. R. WEBB.

Brisbane Chamber of Commerce Inc: 243 Edward St (cnr Adelaide St), Brisbane, Qld 4000; tel. (07) 221-1766; telex 145636; f. 1868; Dir P. ROUBICEK.

Chamber of Commerce and Industry, SA, Inc: 135 Greenhill Road, Unley, SA 5061; tel. (08) 373-1422; telex 88370; 3,100 mems; Gen. Man. L. M. THOMPSON.

Hobart Chamber of Commerce: 65 Murray St, Hobart, Tas 7000; POB 969K, Hobart, Tas 7001; tel. (002) 344325; telex 346034; f. 1851; Dir V. J. BARRON.

Launceston Chamber of Commerce: 99 George St, Launceston, Tas 7250; POB 780, Launceston, Tas 7250; tel. (003) 318988; f. 1849; Sec. A. G. HART.

Melbourne Chamber of Commerce: Commerce House, World Trade Centre, cnr Flinders and Spencer Sts, Melbourne, Vic 3005; tel. (03) 611-2239; telex 31255; f. 1851; Exec. Dir D. C. JONES.

State Chamber of Commerce and Industry: 93 York St, POB 4280, GPO Sydney, NSW 2001; tel. (02) 299-7888; telex 27113; f. 1826; Dir DAVID ABBA.

Western Australian Chamber of Commerce and Industry (Inc): 14 Parliament Place, West Perth, WA 6005; tel. (09) 322-2688; telex 93609; f. 1890; 4,000 mems; Dir C. BARNETT.

AGRICULTURAL AND INDUSTRIAL ORGANIZATIONS

The Australian Agricultural Council: Dept of Primary Industry, Barton, Canberra, ACT 2600; tel. (062) 725220; telex 62188; f. 1934 to provide means for consultation between individual States and the Commonwealth on agricultural production and marketing (excluding forestry and fisheries), to promote the welfare and standards of Australian agricultural industries and to foster the adoption of national policies in regard to these industries; eight mems comprising the agricultural Ministers of the six States and the Northern Territory and the Commonwealth Minister for Primary Industry; Sec. I. R. COTTINGHAM.

   Standing Committee on Agriculture: f. 1927; an advisory body to the Australian Agricultural Council; implements co-ordination of agricultural research and of quarantine measures relating to pests and diseases of plants and animals; comprises the State and Northern Territory Dirs of Agriculture and reps of Commonwealth Depts with an interest in agriculture; Sec. I. R. COTTINGHAM.

Australian Dairy Corporation: Dairy Industry House, 576 St Kilda Rd, Melbourne, Vic 3004; promotes local consumption and

AUSTRALIA

controls the export of dairy produce; Chair. M. L. VAWSER; Gen. Man. B. A. NORWOOD.

Australian Industry Development Corporation: 212 Northbourne Ave, Canberra, ACT 2601; tel. (062) 479411; telex 62307; f. 1970; a Commonwealth statutory corpn providing finance and financial services, including the arrangement of project finance and equity participations, to promote the development of Australian industries and assist Australian participation in the ownership and control of industries and resources; brs in Sydney, Melbourne, Perth, Adelaide and Brisbane; cap. p.u. $A87.5m., total assets $A1,511.5m. (1985); Chair. Sir GORDON JACKSON; CEO J. ROBERT THOMAS.

Australian Meat and Livestock Corporation: POB 4129, Sydney, NSW 2001; tel. (02) 260-3111; telex 22887; statutory federal govt authority assisting the Australian meat and livestock industries in domestic and international trade; Chair. R. AUSTEN.

Australian Trade Development Council: c/o Dept of Trade, Canberra, ACT 2600; f. 1958; advises the Minister for Trade on all aspects of the development of overseas trade; Chair. Dr B. W. SCOTT.

Australian Wheat Board: Ceres House, 528 Lonsdale St, Melbourne, Vic 3000; tel. (03) 605-1555; telex 30196; f. 1939; has sole responsibility for marketing wheat on the domestic and export markets; 11 mems; Chair. CLINTON CONDON.

Australian Wool Corporation: Wool House, 369 Royal Parade, Parkville, Vic 3052; tel. 341-9111; f. 1973; responsible for wool marketing and research; board of 10 mems (chair., four wool growers, four from commerce, one govt mem.); Chair. DAVID ASIMUS.

Department of Resources and Energy: Jolimont Centre, 65-67 Northbourne Ave, Canberra, ACT 2600; POB 858, Canberra, ACT 2601; tel. (062) 458211; telex 62101; responsible for: national resources and energy policy, including planning, research, exploration, assessment and commercial development of minerals, fuels, solar energy and other forms of energy; radioactive waste management; water resources and electricity; geodesy and mapping; Chair. Minister for Resources and Energy; Sec. ALAN J. WOODS.

Wool Council of Australia: POB E10, Queen Victoria Terrace, Canberra, ACT 2600; tel. (062) 732531; telex 62683; comprises 20 reps from six State mem. orgs; participates in selection and nomination of Australian Wool Corpn mems and advises the Minister for Primary Industry on wool industry policy; Pres. H. S. BEGGS; Exec. Dir D. M. MOORE.

EMPLOYERS' ORGANIZATIONS

Confederation of Australian Industry: POB E14, Queen Victoria Terrace, Canberra, ACT 2600; tel. (062) 732311; telex 62733; f. 1977 by merger of Associated Chambers of Manufacturers of Australia and the Australian Council of Employers' Feds; mems: over 30 nat. asscns representing over 50,000 firms; CEO D. S. GEORGE; Sec. M. J. OVERLAND.

Dairy Farmers Co-operative Ltd: 700 Harris St, Ultimo, NSW 2007; tel. 20934; telex 21438; f. 1900; Gen. Man. M. MEAD; Sec. D. S. KINNERSLEY.

The Livestock and Grain Producers' Association of New South Wales: POB 1068, GPO Sydney, NSW 2001; f. 1978; 56 Young St, Sydney, NSW 2000.

The Master Builders' Association of New South Wales: PB 9, Broadway, NSW 2007; tel. 660-7188; telex 27308; f. 1873; Exec. Dir R. L. ROCHER; 4,500 mems.

Meat and Allied Trades Federation of Australia: POB R199, Royal Exchange, Sydney, NSW 2000; tel. (02) 275605; telex 22480; f. 1928; Pres. J. H. MEDWAY; Nat. Dir R. H. J. NOBLE.

Metal Trades Industry Association of Australia: 51 Walker St, North Sydney, NSW 2060; tel. (02) 929-5566; telex 121257; f. 1873; Nat. Pres. J. M. DOWRIE; Nat. Dir and CEO A. C. EVANS; 7,000 mems.

New South Wales Flour Millers' Council: BNZ House, 333 George St, POB 2125, Sydney, NSW 2001; Sec. K. G. WILLIAMS.

Screen Production Association of Australia: Suites 3 and 4, 33 Albany St, Crows Nest, NSW 2065; tel. (02) 436-4077; telex 10101; Pres. ROSS DIMSEY; Exec. Dir JOHN DANIELL.

Timber Trade Industrial Association: 155 Castlereagh St, Sydney, NSW 2000; f. 1940; 530 mems; Man. H. J. MCCARTHY.

MANUFACTURERS' ORGANIZATIONS

The Australian Chamber of Manufactures: Industry House, 370 St Kilda Rd, POB 1469N, GPO Melbourne, Vic 3001; tel. (03) 698-4111; telex 32596; f. 1877; 6,200 mems; CEO B. H. B. POWELL.

Australian Manufacturers' Export Council: Industry House, POB E14, Queen Victoria Terrace, Canberra, ACT 2600; tel. (062) 732311; telex 62733; f. 1955; Exec. Officer L. A. KING.

Business Council of Australia: 10 Queen's Rd, Melbourne, Vic 3004; POB 387D, Melbourne, Vic 3001; tel. (03) 267-6288; telex 36733; public policy research and advocacy; governing council comprises chief execs of Australia's major cos; Pres. Sir RODERICK CARNEGIE; Exec. Dir G. D. ALLEN.

Chamber of Manufactures of New South Wales: POB 3968, GPO Sydney, NSW 2001; tel. (02) 290-0700; telex 22050; f. 1885; CEO W. J. HENDERSON.

Confederation of Western Australian Industry, Inc: POB 6209, Hay St East, Perth, WA 6000; tel. (09) 325-0111; telex 94124; Exec. Dir W. J. BROWN.

Queensland Confederation of Industry: Industry House, 375 Wickham Terrace, Brisbane, Qld 4000; tel. (07) 831-1699; telex 41369; f. 1976; 2,500 mems; CEO G. B. SIEBENHAUSEN.

Tasmanian Chamber of Industries: 242 Liverpool St, Hobart, Tas 7000; tel. (002) 345933; telex 57210; f. 1898; Exec. Dir E. C. ILES.

PRINCIPAL TRADE UNIONS

Australian Council of Trade Unions (ACTU): 393–397 Swanston St, Melbourne, Vic 3000; tel. (03) 663-5266; telex 33943; f. 1927; br. in each State, generally known as a Trades and Labour Council; 163 affiliated trade unions; Pres. S. CREAN; Sec. W. J. KELTY.

Administrative and Clerical Officers' Association: 245 Castlereagh St, Sydney, NSW 2000; tel. (02) 267-3000; telex 26021; Nat. Sec. P. ROBSON; 54,000 mems.

Amalgamated Metal Workers' Union: 136 Chalmers St, Surry Hills, NSW 2010; tel. 690-1411; telex 23763; 155,730 mems.

Australasian Meat Industry Employees' Union: 377 Sussex St, Sydney, NSW 2000; 38,158 mems.

Australian Building Construction Employees' and Builders Labourers' Federation: Basement, Trades Hall, 54 Victoria St, Carlton South, Vic 3053; tel. (03) 662-3477; telex 33748; Gen. Sec. N. L. GALLAGHER; 45,000 mems.

Australian Postal and Telecommunications Union: 1st Floor, 139 Queensberry St, Carlton, Vic 3053; 49,000 mems.

Australian Public Service Association: 41-43 Drummond St, Carlton, Vic 3053; tel. (03) 663-5933; telex 35702; f. 1912; Pres. JOY PALMER; Sec. GARY MCMORRAN; 29,000 mems.

Australian Railways Union: 6th Floor, 377 Sussex St, Sydney, NSW 2000; tel. (02) 267-6116; telex 75362; Nat. Sec. R. C. TAYLOR; 46,720 mems.

Australian Teachers' Federation: POB 415, Carlton South, Vic 3053; tel. (03) 348-1700; telex 152486; f. 1920; Pres. GRAHAM MARSHALL; Gen. Sec. ROBERT V. BLUER; 169,377 mems.

Australian Telecommunications Employees' Association: 11th Floor, 270 Flinders St, Melbourne, Vic 3000; tel. (03) 632875; Pres. J. HALL; Sec.-Treas. C. P. COOPER; 25,200 mems.

Australian Textile Workers' Union: 132–138 Leicester St, Carlton, Vic 3053; tel. (03) 347-2766; f. 1919; Gen. Pres. J. ROUGHLEY; Gen. Sec. W. A. C. HUGHES; 30,000 mems.

Australian Workers' Union: 219/227 Elizabeth St, Sydney, NSW 2000; tel. (02) 267-9301; telex 73231; f. 1886; Pres. A. BEGG; Gen. Sec. G. A. BARR; 122,000 mems.

Building Workers' Industrial Union of Australia: 3rd floor, 490 Kent St, Sydney, NSW 2000; tel. (02) 267-3929; f. 1945; Pres. N. A. CURRIE; Gen. Sec. P. M. CLANCY; 41,260 mems.

Electrical Trades Union of Australia: National Council, 302–306 Elizabeth St, Sydney, NSW 2010; tel. (02) 211-5888; telex 73372; f. 1919; Pres. J. DEVEREUX; Nat. Sec. R. J. PERRIAM; 77,500 mems.

Federal Clerks' Union of Australia: 2nd Floor, 53 Queen St, Melbourne, Vic 3000; 100,000 mems.

Federated Ironworkers' Association of Australia: 51-65 Bathurst St, Sydney, NSW 2000; tel. (02) 264-2877; telex 176770; f. 1911; Nat. Pres. H. W. HOLOWELL; Nat. Sec. H. P. HURRELL; 69,000 mems.

The Federated Miscellaneous Workers Union of Australia: Federal Council, 1st Floor, 365 Sussex St, Sydney, NSW 2000; tel. (02) 267-9681; telex 75879; f. 1916; Gen. Sec. M. J. FERGUSON; 127,000 mems.

Federated Municipal and Shire Council Employees' Union of Australia: Suite 2, 5th Floor, Labor Council Bldg, 377 Sussex

AUSTRALIA

St, Sydney, NSW 2000; tel. (02) 264-9918; Fed. Sec. B. McCarney; 49,158 mems.

Hospital Employees' Federation: 240 Macquarie Rd, Greystanes, NSW 2145; 30,579 mems.

Printing and Kindred Industries Union: 596 Crown St, Surry Hills, NSW 2010; tel. (02) 690-1000; telex 71708; f. 1916; Sec. J. P. Cahill; 48,000 mems.

Transport Workers' Union of Australia: 17-25 Lygon St, Carlton, Vic 3053; tel. (03) 663-6399; 94,499 mems.

Vehicle Builders Employees' Federation of Australia: 57 Drummond St, Carlton South, Vic 3053; tel. (03) 419-8811; Sec. J. S. Thompson; 33,671 mems.

Waterside Workers' Federation of Australia: 365-375 Sussex St, Sydney, NSW 2000; tel. (02) 267-9134; telex 25645; f. 1902; Gen. Sec. T. I. Bull.

Transport

Australian Transport Advisory Council: POB 594, Canberra, ACT 2600; tel. (062) 687852; telex 62018; f. 1946; Mems: Federal Minister for Transport, State and Territory Ministers of Transport, Roads and Marine; Observer: the New Zealand Minister of Transport; initiates discussion, and reports as necessary, on any matter which will tend to promote a better co-ordination of transport development, while encouraging modernization and innovation; promotes research; Sec. T. Arrowsmith.

Urban Transit Authority of New South Wales: 11-31 York St, Sydney, NSW 2000; telex 25702; co-ordinates bus, rail and ferry services in Sydney, Newcastle and Wollongong; operates publicly-owned buses and ferries; exercises broad policy control over privately operated public vehicles in the above areas; Chair. G. A. Bayutti; Man. Dir K. Edgar.

RAILWAYS

Before July 1975 there were seven government-owned railway systems in Australia. In July 1975 Australian National was formed to incorporate the Commonwealth Railways, non-metropolitan South Australian Railways and the Tasmanian Government Railways. In 1984 there were 40,807 km of railway in Australia.

Australian National: 1 Richmond Rd, Keswick, SA 5035; tel. (08) 217-4111; telex 88445; f. 1978; a federal statutory authority operating 7,687 km of track (1984); Chair. L. E. Marks; Gen. Man. Dr D. G. Williams.

Queensland Railways: Railway Centre, 305 Edward St, Brisbane, Qld 4000; POB 1429, Brisbane, Qld 4001; tel. (07) 225-0211; telex 41514; operates 10,231 km of track; Commr R. T. Sheehy; Dep. Commr and Sec. R. W. Dunning.

State Rail Authority of New South Wales: 11-31 York St, Sydney, NSW 2000; POB 29, Sydney, NSW 2001; tel. (02) 219-8888; telex 25702; administers passenger and freight rail service in NSW over a network of 9,878 km; Chair. C. L. Hewitt; CEO David Hill.

State Transport Authority (South Australia): 55 King William Rd, North Adelaide, SA 5001; POB 2351, GPO Adelaide, SA 5001; tel. (08) 218-2200; telex 87115; operates 152 km of metropolitan track, and bus and tram services; Chair. J. D. Rump; Gen. Man. J. V. Brown.

State Transport Authority (Victoria): 67 Spencer St, Melbourne, Vic 3000; tel. (03) 619-1111; telex 33801; f. 1983; operates 5,809 km of track; Chair. and Man. Dir K. M. Fitzmaurice; Chief Gen. Man. J. Hearsch.

Western Australian Government Railways (Westrail): Westrail Centre, POB S1422, Perth 6001, WA; tel. (09) 326-2222; telex 92879; operates passenger and freight transport services mainly in the south of WA; 7,191 main line route km of track; Commr W. I. McCullough.

ROADS

At 31 December 1985 there were 852,986 km of roads, including 787 km of motorways, 38,728 km of other main roads and 91,777 km of secondary roads.

SHIPPING

Commonwealth of Australia, Australian National Line: (Australian Shipping Commission), 432 St Kilda Rd, Melbourne, Vic 3004; postal: POB 2238T, Melbourne, Vic 3001; tel. (03) 269-5555; telex 30584; f. 1956; services: coastal trade and coastal and overseas bulk shipping; overseas container services to Europe, Hong Kong, New Zealand, Taiwan, the Philippines, Korea, Singapore, Malaysia, Thailand, Indonesia and Japan; bulk services to Japan, India, Pakistan, Malaysia, Indonesia, New Zealand, Christmas Island and Nauru; Chair. W. Bolitho; Man. Dir M. Moore-Wilton.

The Adelaide Steamship Co Ltd: 123 Greenhill Rd, Unley, SA 5061; tel. (08) 272-3077; telex 82133; f. 1875; Man. Dir J. G. Spalvins.

Ampol Ltd: 84 Pacific Highway, North Sydney, NSW 2060; tel. (02) 929-6222; telex 121325; f. 1936; Chair. Sir Tristan Antico; Man. Dir A. E. Harris; bulk carriage of crude oil to Brisbane and Sydney, and carriage of refined products and black oils from the Brisbane refinery to Qld outports; 2 vessels.

John Burke Shipping: 14-24 Macquarie St, New Farm, POB 509, Fortitude Valley, Qld 4006; tel. 852-1701; telex 40483; f. 1887; Chair. D. J. Daly; 6 vessels; coastal services and trade with Papua New Guinea.

Burns, Philp and Co Ltd: 7 Bridge St, Sydney, NSW; POB 543, Sydney, NSW 2001; tel. (02) 20547; telex 20290; f. 1883; Chair. J. D. O. Burns; CEO Andrew Turnbull.

Holyman and Sons Pty Ltd: Remount Rd, Mowbray, POB 70, Launceston, Tas; tel. (003) 263388; telex 58517; Chair. K. C. Holyman; coastal services.

Howard Smith Industries Pty Ltd: POB N364, Grosvenor St, Sydney, NSW 2000; tel. (02) 230-1777; telex 24505; Chair. W. J. Trotter; Chief Gen. Man. J. G. Evans; ship and tug services.

McIlwraith McEacharn Ltd: Barclays House, 25 Bligh St, Sydney, NSW 2000; tel. (02) 232-1200; telex 20741; f. 1875; Chair. Sir Ian Potter; Man. Dir A. B. Lawrance; tug and launch owners and operators; shipping agents and ship management, repair and cleaning.

Mason Shipping: 26 Abbott St, POB 840, Cairns, Qld 4870; tel. (070) 516933; telex 48405; a division of Portsmith Stevedoring Co Pty Ltd; 4 vessels; Man. P. Campbell; coastal services and stevedoring.

TNT Bulkships Ltd: Tower 1, TNT Plaza, Lawson Sq., Redfern, NSW 2016; tel. (02) 698-9222; telex 27343; f. 1958; wholly owned subsidiary of Thomas Nationwide Transport Ltd; shipowner and operator; charters vessels; Man. Dir Sir Peter Abeles; Dir Roland J. Hoy.

Western Australian Coastal Shipping Commission (Stateships): Port Beach Rd, North Fremantle, WA; POB 394, Fremantle, WA; tel. (09) 430-0200; telex 92054; Chair. and Gen. Man. D. F. Wilson.

CIVIL AVIATION

In the sparsely-populated areas of central and western Australia, air transport is extremely important, and Australia has pioneered services such as the Flying Doctor Service to overcome the problems of distance. The country is also well served by international airlines.

Air New South Wales: Kingsford Smith Airport, Mascot, Sydney, NSW 2020; tel. (02) 268-1678; telex 20143; f. 1934; a division of Ansett Transport Industries (Operations) Pty Ltd; extensive services from Sydney throughout NSW and Queensland's Sunshine Coast; Chair. Sir Roden Cutler; Gen. Man. J. Hutchison; fleet includes 6 Fokker F-27-500, 3 Fokker F-28-1000.

Air Queensland: POB 1381, Cairns, Qld 4870; tel. 504222; telex 48249; f. 1951; scheduled services throughout Qld; Chair. Sir Sydney Williams; Gen. Man. P. M. Boyce; fleet of 3 F-27, 4 DC-3, 3 Cessna 310, 1 Cessna 404, 5 de Havilland Twin Otter, 1 Nomad N-24A, 2 ATR-42.

Ansett Airlines of Australia: 501 Swanston St, Melbourne, Vic 3000; telex 30085; f. 1936; a division of Ansett Transport Industries (Operations) Pty Ltd; commercial airline operators; passenger and cargo air services throughout Australia and to New Zealand; Chair. and Jt Man. Dirs K. R. Murdoch, Sir Peter Abeles; Gen. Man. E. J. B. Forrester; fleet includes 5 Boeing 767, 12 Boeing 727-200, 1 Boeing 727-200F, 12 Boeing 737-200, 5 Fokker F-27.

Ansett NT: 31 Smith St, Darwin, NT 5790; tel. (089) 819800; telex 85187; f. 1981; a division of Ansett Transport Industries (Operations) Pty Ltd; services link Darwin with Katherine, Tennant Creek, Alice Springs, Gove, Ayers Rock, Groote Eylandt and Cairns; Gen. Man. Frederick McCue; fleet includes 1 Fokker F-28-1000, 1 Fokker F-28-4000, 1 BAe 146.

Ansett WA: International House, 26 St George's Terrace, Perth, WA 6000; tel. (09) 325-0401; telex 92147; f. 1934; a division of Ansett Transport Industries (Operations) Pty Ltd; services from Perth to Darwin via north-west ports and throughout Western Australia;

AUSTRALIA

State Man. F. L. BUTCHER; Man. I. SUTTON; fleet of 4 Fokker F-28-1000, 2 Fokker F-28-4000, 2 BAe 146-200.

Australian Airlines: 50 Franklin St, POB 2806AA, Melbourne, Vic 3001; tel. (03) 665-1333; telex 30109; f. 1946 as Trans-Australia Airlines (TAA); present name adopted in 1986; operated by Australian National Airlines Comm. (Chair. NEIL A. SMITH); services to 33 points covering all States and Christchurch, New Zealand; Chair. NEIL A. SMITH; Gen. Man. JAMES A. STRONG; fleet of 5 Airbus A300, 12 Boeing 727-272, 9 Douglas DC-9-31, 3 Fokker F-27.

East-West Airlines Ltd: POB 249, Tamworth, NSW 2340; telex 63291; f. 1947; routes total 16,619 km; services to all states, the Northern Territory and Norfolk Island; Chair. R. F. STOWE; Man. Dir D. G. Howe; fleet of 4 F-28, 7 F-27.

Qantas Airways Ltd: Qantas International Centre, International Square, POB 489, Sydney, NSW 2001; tel. (02) 263-3636; telex 20113; f. 1920; govt-owned; services to 40 cities in 24 countries including destinations in the UK, Europe, the USA, Canada, Japan, People's Republic of China, South-East Asia, India, the Middle East, Africa and the South-West Pacific, including New Zealand; Chair. J. B. LESLIE; CEO J. L. MENADUE; fleet of 23 Boeing 747 and 6 Boeing 767.

Tourism

Australian Tourist Commission: 324 St Kilda Rd, Melbourne, Vic 3004; POB 73B, Melbourne, Vic 3001; tel. (03) 690-3900; telex 31911; f. 1967 for promotion of tourism; nine offices, of which seven are overseas; Chair. JOHN HADDAD; Man. Dir J. S. ROWE.

Atomic Energy

Australian Atomic Energy Commission (AAEC): Private Mail Bag, Sutherland, NSW 2232; tel. (02) 543-3111; telex 24562; f. 1953; Chair. Prof. M. H. BRENNAN; Sec. W. H. RATCLIFF; Dir of Research Establishment Dr D. G. WALKER.

The Commission is concerned with scientific research for peaceful purposes, development of practical uses of nuclear technology, radioactive waste management, environmental and health aspects of nuclear activities, the training of scientists and engineers, the production of radio-isotopes and radiopharmaceuticals. The Commission's Research Establishment was founded at Lucas Heights, near Sydney, in 1955.

HIFAR: 10 MW thermal research reactor; critical 1958; for production of radioisotopes, studies of effects of high intensity radiation on materials and of the use of neutrons to analyse crystal lattices, molecular structure, trace element concentrations and uranium in ores.

MOATA: 100 kW thermal research reactor; critical 1962; provides neutron radiography, fission and alpha track analyses, activation services and research in physical chemistry and materials.

Australian Institute of Nuclear Science and Engineering: Private Mail Bag, PO, Sutherland, NSW 2232; supports university research and training projects in all branches of nuclear science and engineering; mems comprise 18 universities, AAEC and CSIRO; Exec. Officer E. A. PALMER.

Australian School of Nuclear Technology: Private Mail Bag 1, Menai, NSW 2234; tel. (02) 543-3111; telex 24562; provides short-term, intensive courses for participants from Australia and overseas, covering radionuclides in medicine, radioisotope techniques and radiation protection; Prin. B. TONER.

The following universities have facilities for nuclear research and training: Universities of Adelaide, New South Wales, Newcastle, Melbourne, New England, Western Australia, Wollongong, Macquarie, Monash, Queensland, Sydney and Tasmania, The Australian National University, Flinders University of South Australia, James Cook University of North Queensland and La Trobe University.

AUSTRALIAN EXTERNAL TERRITORIES

CHRISTMAS ISLAND

Introduction

Christmas Island covers an area of about 135 sq km (52 sq miles) and lies 360 km (224 miles) south of Java Head in the Indian Ocean. The nearest point on the Australian coast is North West Cape, 1,408 km (875 miles) to the south-east.

Administration was transferred from Singapore to the United Kingdom on 1 January 1958, pending final transfer to Australia. It became an Australian territory on 1 October 1958. Christmas Island has no indigenous population. At 30 June 1983 the population was 3,214 (1,967 Chinese, 800 Malays, 341 Europeans and 106 others). Residents consist almost entirely of employees of the Phosphate Mining Corporation of Christmas Island and the administration and their families.

The recovery of phosphates is the sole economic activity: during the year ending 30 June 1984 about 463,000 metric tons were exported to Australia, 332,000 tons to New Zealand and 341,000 tons to other countries. It is expected, however, that reserves will be exhausted by 1991, and efforts are to be made to develop the island's considerable potential for tourism. In April 1986 initial plans were announced for a hotel and casino complex.

Directory

THE GOVERNMENT

An Administrator, appointed by the Governor-General of Australia and responsible to the Minister for Territories, is the senior government representative on the island. There is a nine-member island council.

Administrator: T. F. PATERSON.

JUDICIAL SYSTEM

The judicial system comprises a Supreme Court, a District Court, a Magistrate's Court and a Children's Court.

Supreme Court: Judge: Sir WILLIAM FORSTER; Additional Judge: J. F. GALLOP.

RADIO AND TELEVISION

There were an estimated 2,500 radio receivers in use in 1985.

Christmas Island Broadcasting: Christmas Island 6798, Indian Ocean; tel. 8216; telex 78003; f. 1967; owned and operated by the Christmas Island Services Corporation; daily broadcasting service by Radio VLU-2 on 1422 KHz, in English, Malay and Mandarin; Station Man. PETER STANDISH.

Mining Television Network: Christmas Island 6798, Indian Ocean; provides service on behalf of the Phosphate Mining Corporation of Christmas Island.

INDUSTRY

Phosphate Mining Corporation of Christmas Island (PMCI): Christmas Island 6798, Indian Ocean; tel. 8210; telex 78006; f. 1981 as the Phosphate Mining Company of Christmas Island Ltd; present name adopted in 1985; Australian govt-owned; responsible for mining, treatment and sale of Christmas Island phosphates.

TRANSPORT

Railway lines, with a total length of 24 km, serve the island's phosphate mines, and there are good roads in the developed areas. Australian government charter aircraft operate a weekly service from Perth via the Cocos (Keeling) Islands. The Australian National Line operates ships to the Australian mainland. The Phosphate Mining Corporation of Christmas Island operates a cargo-shipping service to Singapore and ships phosphate to Australia and New Zealand, and to Malaysian and other Asian ports. It also operates weekly flights from Singapore to Christmas Island.

COCOS (KEELING) ISLANDS

Introduction

The Cocos (Keeling) Islands are 27 in number and lie 2,768 km (1,720 miles) north-west of Perth, in the Indian Ocean. The islands, which have an area of 14 sq km (5.4 sq miles), form two low-lying coral atolls, densely covered with coconut palms. The population at 30 June 1984 was 584, comprising 208 residents on West Island and 376 Cocos Malays on Home Island, the only inhabited islands in the group. The Cocos Malays are descendants of the people who were brought to the islands in 1826 by Alexander Hare and of labourers who were subsequently introduced by John Clunies-Ross.

The islands were declared a British possession in 1857 and came successively under the authority of the governors of Ceylon (1878) and the Straits Settlements (1886); they were annexed to the Straits Settlements and incorporated with the Settlement (later Colony) of Singapore in 1903. Administration of the islands was transferred to the Commonwealth of Australia on 23 November 1955.

In June 1977 the Government announced new policies concerning the islands, which resulted in Australia's purchase from John Clunies-Ross of the whole of his interests in the Cocos (Keeling) Islands with the exception of his residence and associated buildings. The purchase took effect on 1 September 1978. An attempt by the Australian Government to acquire Clunies-Ross' remaining property was deemed by the Australian High Court in October 1984 to be unconstitutional.

In July 1979 the Cocos (Keeling) Islands Council was established, with a wide range of functions in the Home Island village area (which the Government has transferred to the Council on trust for the benefit of the Cocos Malay community) and, since September 1984, in the greater part of the rest of the Territory.

On 6 April 1984 a referendum to decide the future political status of the islands was held by the Australian Government, with United Nations observers present. A large majority voted in favour of integration with Australia. As a result, the islanders were to acquire the rights, privileges and obligations of all Australian citizens. The powers and functions of the Cocos (Keeling) Islands Council were to be expanded to give it greater responsibility, and the inhabitants of the Territory were to have full voting rights in elections to the Australian Parliament.

Although local fishing is good and domestic gardens provide vegetables, bananas and pawpaws, the islands are not self-sufficient, and other foodstuffs, fuels and consumer items are imported from mainland Australia. A Cocos postal service (including a philatelic bureau) came into operation in September 1979, and revenue from the service is used for the benefit of the community.

Coconuts, grown throughout the islands, are the sole cash crop: total output was an estimated 5,000 metric tons in 1984, and total exports in 1984/85 were 202 metric tons.

Primary education is provided at the schools on Home and West Islands. Secondary education is provided to the age of 16 years on West Island. A bursary scheme enables Cocos Malay children to continue their education on the Australian mainland.

AUSTRALIAN EXTERNAL TERRITORIES

Directory

THE GOVERNMENT

An Administrator, appointed by the Governor-General of Australia and responsible to the Minister for Territories, is the senior government representative in the islands.

Administrator: Carolyn Stuart.
Chairman of the Cocos (Keeling) Islands Council: Parson bin Yapat.

JUDICIAL SYSTEM

Supreme Court, Cocos (Keeling) Islands: Cocos (Keeling) Islands 6799, Indian Ocean; tel. 6660; telex 67002; Judge: Sir William Forster; Additional Judge: (vacant).
Magistrates' Court, Cocos (Keeling) Islands: Special Magistrate: Harold Bingham.

RADIO

There were an estimated 250 radio receivers in use in 1985.
Radio VKW Cocos: POB 70; tel. 6666; daily broadcasting service in Cocos Malay and English; Man. R. W. Pilsbury.

INDUSTRY

Cocos Islands Co-operative Society Ltd: Home Island, Cocos Islands, Indian Ocean; tel. 7598; telex 67001; f. 1979; conducts the business enterprises of the Cocos Islanders; activities include boat construction and repairs, copra and coconut production, sail-making, stevedoring; Chair. Medous bin Bynie.

TRANSPORT

Australian government charter aircraft from Perth provide a weekly service for passengers, supplies and mail to and from the Cocos Islands. Cargo vessels from Perth deliver supplies, at intervals of six to eight weeks.

NORFOLK ISLAND

Introduction

Norfolk Island lies off the eastern coast of Australia, about 1,400 km east of Brisbane. It is about 8 km long and 4.8 km wide. The island was discovered in 1774 by a British expedition, led by Capt. James Cook. Norfolk Island was used as a penal settlement from 1788 to 1813 and again from 1825 to 1855. It was a separate crown colony until 1897, when it became a dependency of New South Wales. In 1913 control was transferred to the Australian Government. The capital of the territory is Kingston.

Under the Norfolk Island Act 1979, Norfolk Island progressed to responsible legislative and executive government, enabling the inhabitants of the territory to control their own affairs to the greatest practicable extent. Wide powers are exercised by the nine-member Legislative Assembly (the third elections for which were held on 18 May 1983) and by an Executive Council comprising the executive members of the Legislative Assembly who have ministerial-type responsibilities. The Act preserves the Australian Government's responsibility for Norfolk Island as a territory under its authority, with the Minister for Territories as the responsible Minister. The Act indicates Parliament's intention that consideration would be given to an extension of the powers of the Legislative Assembly and the political and administrative institutions of Norfolk Island within five years.

About 400 ha are arable. The main crops are Kentia palm seed, cereals, vegetables and fruit. Some flowers and plants are grown commercially. The administration is increasing the area devoted to Norfolk Island pine and hardwoods. Seed of the Norfolk Island pine is exported. Tourism is the island's main industry.

Statistical Survey

AREA AND POPULATION

Area: 34.5 sq km (13.3 sq miles).
Population (census of 30 June 1981): 2,175 (males 1,067; females 1,108), including visitors.
Births and Deaths (1981): Live births 20 (birth rate 10.8 per 1,000); Deaths 14 (death rate 7.6 per 1,000).

FINANCE

Currency: Australian currency is used.
Budget (estimates, $A '000, year ending 30 June 1985): Revenue 4,168.2; Expenditure 4,142.4.

EXTERNAL TRADE

1983/84 (year ending 30 June): *Imports*: $A15,972,054, mainly from Australia. *Exports*: $A2,088,517.

TOURISM

Visitors (1983/84): 20,515.

Directory

The Government

The Administrator is appointed by the Governor-General of Australia and is responsible to the Minister for Territories. A form of responsible legislative and executive government was extended to the island in 1979, as outlined above.
Administrator: Cdre John A. Matthew.

Executive Council

(November 1986)

Chief Minister: David E. Buffett.
Minister for Finance: Brian G. Bates.
Minister for Social Services and Primary Industries: Alice I. Buffett.
Minister for Tourism and Lands: Phillip A. Page.
Minister for Community Services: Eleanore B. Reed.
All Ministries are in Kingston.

Legislature

ASSEMBLY

President: David E. Buffett.

Judicial System

Supreme Court of Norfolk Island: appeals lie to the Federal Court of Australia.
Judges: R. W. Fox (Chief Judge), P. G. Evatt, T. R. Morling.

The Press

Norfolk Island Government Gazette: Kingston, Norfolk Island 2899; tel. 2001; telex 30003; weekly.
Norfolk Islander: 'Greenways Press', POB 150, Norfolk Island 2889; tel. 2159; f. 1965; weekly; Co-Editors Mr and Mrs Thomas Lloyd; circ. 1,200.

Radio

There were an estimated 1,300 radio receivers in use in 1984. There is no television service.

Norfolk Island Broadcasting Service: New Cascade Rd; tel. 2137; non-commercial; broadcasts 106 hours per week; Broadcasting Officer Mrs K. M. LeCren.

Finance

BANKING

There are branches of the Commonwealth Banking Corpn (Australia) and Westpac Banking Corporation Savings Bank Ltd (Australia).

Trade

Norfolk Island Chamber of Commerce: POB 370, Norfolk Island 2899; f. 1966; affiliated to the Australian Chamber of Commerce; 80 mems; Pres. Angus Cuthbertson; Sec. Joyce Ionn.

Transport

ROADS

There are about 80 km of roads, including 53 km of sealed road.

SHIPPING

The Compagnie des Chargeurs Calédoniens operates cargo services from Sydney, Australia, and Auckland, New Zealand. A small tanker from Nouméa (New Caledonia) delivers petroleum products to the island and another from Australia delivers liquid propane gas.

CIVIL AVIATION

Norfolk Island has one airport, with two runways (of 1,900 m and 1,550 m), capable of taking medium jet aircraft.

Norfolk Airlines: 229 Elizabeth St, POB 905, Brisbane, Qld 4001, Australia; tel. 229-5872; telex 41421; f. 1973; operates regular flights from Brisbane and Sydney to Lord Howe Island (a dependency of New South Wales) and Norfolk Island, and charters throughout Australia and the South Pacific; Chair. John Brown; Gen. Man. Michael Childs; fleet of Beechcraft Super King Air 200s.

Tourism

Norfolk Island Government Tourist Bureau: Burnt Pine, POB 211, Norfolk Island 2899; tel. 2147; telex 32010; Man. Alex Lubanski.

OTHER TERRITORIES

Ashmore and Cartier Islands

Ashmore Islands (known as West, Middle and East Islands) and Cartier Island are situated in the Timor Sea, about 850 km and 790 km west of Darwin respectively. The islands are small and uninhabited, consisting of sand and coral, surrounded by shoals and reefs. Grass is the main vegetation. Maximum elevation is about 2.5 m above sea-level. The islands abound in sea-cucumbers (*bêches-de-mer*) and, seasonally, turtles.

The United Kingdom took formal possession of the Ashmore Islands in 1878, and Cartier Island was annexed in 1909. The islands were placed under the authority of the Commonwealth of Australia in 1931. They were annexed to, and deemed to form part of, the Northern Territory of Australia in 1938. On 1 July 1978 the Australian Government assumed direct responsibility for the administration of the islands, which rests with the Minister for Territories. Periodic visits are made to the islands by the Royal Australian Navy and aircraft of the Royal Australian Air Force, and the Civil Coastal Surveillance Service make aerial surveys of the islands and neighbouring waters.

The area is thought to hold good prospects for petroleum exploration. In August 1983 Ashmore Reef was declared a national nature reserve.

Australian Antarctic Territory

The Australian Antarctic Territory was established by Order in Council, proclaimed in August 1936, subsequent to the Australian Antarctic Territory Acceptance Act (1933). It consists of the portion of Antarctica (divided by the French territory of Adélie Land) lying between 45°E and 136°E, and between 142°E and 160°E. The Australian National Antarctic Research Expeditions (ANARE) maintains three permanent scientific stations, Mawson, Davis and Casey, in the territory. The area of the territory is 6,120,000 sq km (2,320,000 sq miles).

Coral Sea Islands Territory

The Coral Sea Islands became a Territory of the Commonwealth of Australia under the Coral Sea Islands Act of 1969. It comprises several islands and reefs east of Queensland between the Great Barrier Reef and longitude 156° 06'E, and between latitude 12° and 24°S. The islands have been acquired by Australia by numerous acts of sovereignty since the early years of the 20th century.

Spread over a sea area of approximately 780,000 sq km (300,000 sq miles), all the islands and reefs in the Territory are very small, totalling only a few sq km of land area. They include Cato Island, Chilcott Islet in the Coringa Group, and the Willis Group. A meteorological station, operated by the Commonwealth Bureau of Meteorology and with a staff of three, has provided a service on one of the Willis Group since 1921. The remainder of the islands are uninhabited. There are eight automatic weather stations distributed throughout the Territory.

The Act constituting the Territory did not establish an administration on the islands but provides means of controlling the activities of those who visit them. The Lihou Reef and Coringa-Herald National Nature Reserves were established in 1982 to provide protection for the wide variety of terrestrial and marine wildlife in these areas. The increasing range and scope of international fishing enterprises made desirable an administrative framework and system of law. The Governor-General of Australia is empowered to make ordinances for the peace, order and good government of the Territory and, by ordinance, the laws of the Australian Capital Territory apply. The Supreme Court and Court of Petty Sessions of Norfolk Island have jurisdiction in relation to the Territory. The Minister for Territories is responsible for matters affecting the Territory.

Heard Island and McDonald Islands

These islands are situated about 4,000 km (2,500 miles) south-west of Perth, Western Australia, and have been administered by the Australian Government since 1947, when it established a scientific research station on Heard Island (which functioned until 1955). The area is 370 sq km (143 sq miles). There are no permanent inhabitants, but Australian expeditions visit the island from time to time. Heard Island is about 44 km (27 miles) long and 20 km (12 miles) wide. The McDonald Islands, with an area of about 1 sq km (0.4 sq mile), lie approximately 40 km (25 miles) west of Heard Island.

AUSTRIA

Introductory Survey

Location, Climate, Language, Religion, Flag, Capital

The Republic of Austria lies in central Europe, bordered by Switzerland and Liechtenstein to the west, by the Federal Republic of Germany and Czechoslovakia to the north, by Hungary to the east, and by Italy and Yugoslavia to the south. The climate varies sharply, owing to great differences in elevation. The mean annual temperature lies between 7° and 9°C (45° and 48°F). The population is 99% German-speaking, with small Croat and Slovene-speaking minorities. Almost all of the inhabitants profess Christianity: about 89% are Roman Catholics, while about 6% are Protestants. The national flag (proportions 3 by 2) consists of three equal horizontal stripes, of red, white and red. The state flag has, in addition, the coat of arms (a small shield, with horizontal stripes of red separated by a white stripe, superimposed on a black eagle, wearing a golden crown and holding a sickle and a hammer in its feet, with a broken chain between the legs) in the centre. The capital is Vienna (Wien).

Recent History

Austria was formerly the centre of the Austrian (later Austro-Hungarian) Empire, which comprised a large part of central Europe. The Empire, under the Habsburg dynasty, was dissolved in 1918, at the end of the First World War, and Austria proper became a republic. The first post-war Council of Ministers was a coalition led by Dr Karl Renner, who remained Chancellor until 1920, when a new constitution introduced a federal form of government. Most of Austria's inhabitants favoured union with Germany but this was forbidden by the post-war peace treaties. In March 1938, however, Austria was occupied by Nazi Germany's armed forces and incorporated into the German Reich.

After liberation by Allied forces, a provisional government, under Dr Renner, was established in April 1945. In July, following Germany's surrender, Austria was divided into four zones, occupied by forces of the USA, the USSR, the United Kingdom and France. These four approved the first post-war elections, held in November 1945, when the conservative Austrian People's Party (Österreichische Volkspartei—ÖVP) won 85, and the Socialist Party (Sozialistische Partei Österreichs—SPÖ) 76, of the 165 seats in the Nationalrat (National Council). These two parties formed a coalition government. In December Dr Renner became the first President of the second Austrian Republic, holding office until his death in December 1950. However, it was not until May 1955 that the four powers signed a State Treaty with Austria, ending the occupation and recognizing Austrian independence, effective from 27 July. Occupation forces left in October 1955.

More than 20 years of coalition government came to an end in April 1966 with the formation of a Council of Ministers by the People's Party alone. Dr Josef Klaus, the Federal Chancellor since April 1964, remained in office. Dr Bruno Kreisky, a former Minister of Foreign Affairs, was elected leader of the Socialist Party in 1967. The SPÖ achieved a relative majority in the March 1970 general elections and formed a minority government, with Kreisky as Chancellor. In April 1971 the incumbent President, Franz Jonas of the SPÖ, was re-elected, defeating the ÖVP candidate, Dr Kurt Waldheim, a former Minister of Foreign Affairs (who subsequently served two five-year terms as UN Secretary-General, beginning in January 1972). The SPÖ won an absolute majority of seats in the Nationalrat at general elections in October 1971 and October 1975. Meanwhile, President Jonas died in April 1974. A presidential election, held in June, was won by Dr Rudolf Kirchschläger, who had been Minister of Foreign Affairs since 1970. He took office for a six-year term, and was re-elected in 1980.

In November 1978 the Government was defeated in a national referendum on whether to commission Austria's first nuclear power plant, and it was widely expected that Kreisky would resign. However, the SPÖ gave him its full support and he emerged in an apparently even stronger position. The possible use of nuclear power remains a controversial issue. At the general election in May 1979 the SPÖ increased its majority in the Nationalrat. In January 1981 Kreisky announced a government reshuffle, following the resignation of the Vice-Chancellor and Minister of Finance, Hannes Androsch, who had been criticized by both his own party and the opposition for his personal financial practices.

The general election of April 1983 marked the end of the 13-year era of one-party government, when the SPÖ lost its absolute majority in the Nationalrat, and Kreisky, unwilling to participate in a coalition government, resigned as Chancellor. The reduction in the SPÖ's representation was partly attributed to the emergence of two environmentalist 'Green' parties, both founded in 1982. The two parties together received more than 3% of the total votes, but failed to win any seats. Kreisky's successor, Dr Fred Sinowatz (the former Vice-Chancellor and Minister of Education), took office in May, leading a coalition of the SPÖ and the small liberal Freedom Party of Austria (Freiheitliche Partei Österreichs—FPÖ). The new Government continued the social welfare policy of its predecessor, also maintaining Austria's foreign policy of 'active neutrality'.

A presidential election was held in 1986, when Dr Kirchschläger retired after two six-year terms of office as Head of State. The SPÖ candidate for the election was Dr Kurt Steyrer (the Minister of Health and Environment), while Dr Waldheim, the former UN Secretary-General, stood as an independent candidate but with the support of the ÖVP. There were also two other candidates: Freda Meissner-Blau, an environmentalist, and Otto Scrinzi, a right-wing nationalist. The campaign was dominated by allegations that Waldheim, a former officer in the army of Nazi Germany, had been implicated in atrocities committed by the Nazis in the Balkans in 1942–45, provoking a bitter controversy which divided the country and brought unexpected international attention to the election. No candidate achieved the required 50% of the vote at the first ballot on 4 May (Waldheim received 49.65% of the votes cast, while Steyrer received 43.67%); a second 'run-off' ballot between the two principal candidates was therefore held on 8 June. Waldheim then won a clear victory, with 53.89% of the votes, compared with Steyrer's 46.11%. The election of Waldheim, who took office in July, drew criticism from some foreign governments, and Israel withdrew its ambassador from Vienna in protest.

After the defeat of the SPÖ presidential candidate, Chancellor Sinowatz and four of his ministers resigned. Dr Franz Vranitzky, who had been Minister of Finance, became the new Chancellor, and replaced several ministers. In September the ruling coalition collapsed, when the FPÖ elected a new leader, Jörg Haider, who represented the right wing of his party. This precipitated the end of the partnership between the SPÖ and the FPÖ, and the general election for the Nationalrat, scheduled for April 1987, was brought forward to November 1986. At the election no party won an absolute majority: the SPÖ won 80 seats, the ÖVP 77, the FPÖ 18 and the alliance of 'Green' parties 8. The preceding Government remained in power in December during protracted negotiations on the formation of a coalition.

Government

Austria is a federal republic, divided into nine provinces, each with its own provincial assembly and government. Legislative power is held by the bicameral Federal Assembly. The first chamber, the Nationalrat (National Council), has 183 members, elected by universal adult suffrage for four years (subject to dissolution) on the basis of proportional representation. The

AUSTRIA

second chamber, the Bundesrat (Federal Council), has 63 members, elected for varying terms by the provincial assemblies. The Federal President, elected by popular vote for six years, is the Head of State, and normally acts on the advice of the Council of Ministers, led by the Federal Chancellor, which is responsible to the Nationalrat.

Defence

After the ratification of the State Treaty in 1955, Austria declared its permanent neutrality. To protect its independence, the armed forces were instituted. Military service is compulsory and consists of six months' initial training, followed by a maximum of 60 days' reservist training and 30 to 90 days' specialist training for 15 years. In July 1986 the total armed forces numbered 54,700 (including 27,300 conscripts), comprising an army of 50,000 (25,000 conscripts) and an air force of 4,700 (2,300 conscripts). Austrian air units are an integral part of the army. Total reserves are 186,000, of whom 70,000 undergo refresher training each year. The defence budget for 1986 amounted to 18,768m. Schilling.

Economic Affairs

In 1984, according to estimates by the World Bank, Austria's GNP per head (at average 1982–84 prices) was US $9,140, having increased since 1965 by an average of 3.6% per year, one of the highest growth rates among industrialized countries. The Austrian economy depends mainly on manufacturing, while agriculture is of declining importance. The proportion of the labour force in agriculture and forestry dropped steadily from 17.3% in 1971 to only 8.7% in 1985. The contribution of the agricultural sector to the gross domestic product (GDP) was 3.8% in 1983, rising slightly to 4.0% in 1984 but falling to 3.5% in 1985. Austrian farms produce more than 90% of the country's food requirements, and surplus dairy products are exported.

Austria has iron ore and petroleum deposits, lignite, magnesite, lead and some copper. Hydroelectric power resources are being developed, but have proved a controversial issue; the future of several big hydroelectric and nuclear power projects is unclear, following protests by powerful environmentalist groups. Austria's electricity needs have grown considerably in recent years, and, as a result, the country is heavily dependent on imports of energy, mainly from the Eastern bloc.

After the Second World War, about one-quarter of Austrian industry was nationalized, including most of the heavy industry. The nationalized sector accounted for 22.5% of overall exports in 1984, employing 18% of the total industrial labour force. In recent years the Government has given substantial financial support to ÖIAG, the state holding company, with subsidies to the group in 1981–85 totalling 12,500m. Schilling, but in 1985 ÖIAG announced record losses of 12,500m. Schilling (of which 11,750m. Schilling was attributed to Voest-Alpine, the steel and engineering company). In 1986, faced with growing public criticism over the issue, the Government announced a major restructuring of the state sector, involving a reduction of the labour force (cutting some 10,000 jobs by 1990) and the denationalization of some sections.

Industrial relations are good, in keeping with the traditional Austrian social consensus. Manufacturing employed 28.2% of the labour force in 1985, and provided 29.1% of GDP. Older industries, such as textiles, steel and machinery, have been declining in recent years, but new industries, such as chemicals, electronics and vehicles, have become significant. Industrial output rose 4.5% in 1985.Tourism is a leading source of external revenue, and accounted for a net foreign exchange income of 45,000m. Schilling in 1985.

Austria's GDP grew by just under 3% in 1985, after an increase of 2.2% in 1984. Real GDP growth for 1986 was expected to be just under 3%. The average rate of unemployment was 4.5% in 1983–84. It reached 5% in 1985 and was expected to be around 5.3% in 1986. The Government has traditionally been committed to a policy of full employment and has established a variety of job-creation schemes, particularly in the construction industry. The inflation rate rose from 3.3% in 1983 (among the lowest in Europe), to 5.6% in 1984 owing largely to an increase in VAT. Inflation averaged 3.2% in 1985, and was expected to fall to 1.5% in 1986.

In 1985 the trade deficit increased to US $3,994m., from $3,539m. in 1984. Exports increased by 12.5% in 1985, while imports expanded by 9.9%. In 1986 Austria experienced a sharp drop in export orders, notably from the Eastern bloc and the USA, although the 1986 balance of trade was expected to benefit from the reduction in petroleum prices, as energy imports generally account for around 90% of Austria's trade deficit. The current account of the balance of payments showed a deficit of $262m. in 1985, but was expected to be $550m. in surplus in 1986, owing to a general improvement in terms of trade. By the end of 1984 Austria's foreign debt had reached 469,800m. Schilling, 12.9% higher than in 1983. The net budget deficit for 1983 reached 65,500m. Schilling, representing 5.5% of GNP. In an effort to reduce this deficit, the Government announced some cuts in expenditure, and introduced new and higher taxes. The deficit represented 4.39% of GNP in 1985, and this proportion was expected to be 4.67% in 1986.

Austria is a member of the European Free Trade Association (EFTA: see p. 153) and has a bilateral free trade agreement with the EEC, whose member-states accounted for 61.1% of Austria's imports and 54.2% of exports in 1985.

Social Welfare

The social insurance system covers all wage-earners and salaried employees, agricultural and non-agricultural self-employed and dependants, regardless of nationality. The coverage is compulsory and provides earnings-related benefits in case of old age, invalidity, death, sickness, maternity and injuries at work. About 95% of the population are protected. There are separate programmes which provide unemployment insurance, family allowance, benefits for war victims, etc. In 1981 Austria had 84,310 hospital beds (one for every 89 inhabitants), and there were 17,028 physicians working in the country. Of total expenditure by the central government in 1983, 11.5% was for health and 45.6 for social security and welfare.

Education

The central controlling body is the Federal Ministry of Education, the Arts and Sport. Higher education and research are the responsibility of the Federal Ministry of Science and Research. Provincial boards (Landesschulräte) supervise school education in each of the nine federal provinces.

Education is free and compulsory between the ages of six and 15 years. All children undergo four years' primary education at a Volksschule, after which they choose between two principal forms of secondary education. This may be a Hauptschule which, after four years, may be followed by one of a variety of schools offering technical, vocational and other specialized training, some of which provide a qualification for university. Alternatively, secondary education may be obtained in an Allgemeinbildende höhere Schule, which provides an eight-year general education covering a wide range of subjects, culminating in the Reifeprüfung or Matura. This gives access to all Austrian universities. Since 1977/78, however, all Austrian citizens over the age of 24, and with professional experience, may attend certain university courses in connection with their professional career or trade.

Opportunities for further education exist in six universities as well as 14 specialist colleges, all of which have university status, and schools of technology, art and music. Institutes of adult education (Volkshochschulen) are found in all provinces, as are other centres run by public authorities, church organizations and the Austrian Trade Union Federation.

Tourism

Austria's mountains, forests and valleys make it an ideal resort in both summer and winter. Celebrated beauty spots are the Salzkammergut Lake District, the Tyrol and Vorarlberg valleys and the Vienna woodlands. Vienna is a centre for music and art lovers and historians, with its opera houses and concert halls, art galleries and museums. In winter thousands of visitors go to Austrian skiing resorts. Festivals are held all over Austria in the summer: the Vienna Festival and the Salzburg Music Festival are internationally famous. In 1985 Austria received 15,617,830 foreign visitors.

Public Holidays

1987: 1 January (New Year's Day), 6 January (Epiphany), 20 April (Easter Monday), 1 May (Labour Day), 28 May (Ascension

Day), 8 June (Whit Monday), 18 June (Corpus Christi), 15 August (Assumption), 26 October (National Holiday), 1 November (All Saints' Day), 8 December (Immaculate Conception), 25 December (Christmas Day), 26 December (St Stephen's Day).

1988: 1 January (New Year's Day), 6 January (Epiphany), 4 April (Easter Monday), 1 May (Labour Day), 12 May (Ascension Day), 23 May (Whit Monday), 2 June (Corpus Christi), 15 August (Assumption), 26 October (National Holiday), 1 November (All Saints' Day), 8 December (Immaculate Conception), 25 December (Christmas Day), 26 December (St Stephen's Day).

Weights and Measures

The metric system is in force.

Currency and Exchange Rates

100 Groschen = 1 Schilling.

Exchange rates (30 September 1986):
   £1 sterling = 20.635 Schilling;
   US $1 = 14.275 Schilling.

Statistical Survey

Source (unless otherwise stated): Austrian Central Statistical Office, 1033 Vienna, Hintere Zollamtsstr. 2B; tel. (0222) 6628-0; telex 132600.

Area and Population

AREA, POPULATION AND DENSITY

Area (sq km)	83,855*
Population (census results)	
12 May 1971	7,491,526†
12 May 1981‡	
Males	3,572,426
Females	3,982,912
Total	7,555,338
Population (official estimates at mid-year)‡	
1983	7,548,500
1984	7,552,000
1985	7,555,000
Density (per sq km) at mid-1985	90.1

* 32,377 sq miles.
† Total includes foreign workers with families abroad.
‡ Figures include all foreign workers.

BIRTHS, MARRIAGES AND DEATHS

	Registered live births		Registered marriages		Registered deaths	
	Number	Rate (per 1,000)	Number	Rate (per 1,000)	Number	Rate (per 1,000)
1978	85,402	11.4	44,573	5.9	94,617	12.6
1979	86,388	11.5	45,445	6.1	92,012	12.3
1980	90,872	12.1	46,435	6.2	92,442	12.3
1981	93,942	12.4	47,768	6.3	92,693	12.3
1982	94,840	12.5	47,643	6.3	91,339	12.1
1983	90,118	11.9	56,171	7.4	93,041	12.3
1984	89,234	11.8	45,823	6.1	88,466	11.7
1985	87,440	11.6	44,867	5.9	89,578	11.9

Expectation of life at birth: Males 70.1 years; females 77.2 years (1984).

PRINCIPAL TOWNS (population at 1981 census)

Vienna (capital)	1,531,346	Klagenfurt		87,321
Graz	243,166	Villach		52,692
Linz	199,910	Wels		51,060
Salzburg	139,426	Sankt Pölten		50,419
Innsbruck	117,287	Steyr		38,942

ECONOMICALLY ACTIVE POPULATION
('000 persons, 1985 average*)

	Males	Females	Total
Agriculture, forestry, hunting and fishing	159	135	294
Mining and quarrying	13	1	14
Manufacturing	687	261	947
Construction	266	24	290
Electricity, gas, water and sanitary services	38	4	42
Commerce (incl. storage)	199	253	452
Transport and communications	173	39	212
Services	487	600	1,090
Other activities (not adequately described)	10	6	16
Total	**2,031**	**1,324**	**3,355**

* Yearly average based on the results of quarterly sample surveys.

PROVINCES

	Area (sq km)	Population (1985 annual average)	Density (per sq km)	Provincial Capital (with 1981 population)
Burgenland	3,965.3	267,700	67.5	Eisenstadt (10,102)
Kärnten (Carinthia)	9,533.4	540,300	56.7	Klagenfurt (87,321)
Niederösterreich (Lower Austria)	19,172.1	1,423,700	74.3	Sankt Pölten (50,419)*
Oberösterreich (Upper Austria)	11,979.6	1,286,000	107.3	Linz (199,910)
Salzburg	7,154.0	456,500	63.8	Salzburg (139,426)
Steiermark (Styria)	16,387.1	1,183,400	72.2	Graz (243,166)
Tirol (Tyrol)	12,647.1	601,600	47.6	Innsbruck (117,287)
Vorarlberg	2,601.3	309,300	118.9	Bregenz (24,561)
Wien (Vienna)*	415.0	1,489,200	3,588.4	—
Total	**83,854.9**	**7,557,700**	**90.1**	—

* Vienna, the national capital, has separate provincial status. The area and population of the city are not included in the province of Lower Austria, which is also administered from Vienna, pending the completion of provincial government buildings at Sankt Pölten, which became the provincial capital on 10 July 1986.

AUSTRIA   *Statistical Survey*

Agriculture

PRINCIPAL CROPS ('000 metric tons)

	1983	1984	1985
Wheat	1,417.4	1,501	1,562.8
Barley	1,448.9	1,517	1,521.4
Maize	1,453.7	1,542	1,726.7
Rye	347.6	381	338.7
Oats	292.2	292	283.9
Mixed grain	115.7	120	117.7
Potatoes	1,011.5	1,138	1,042.2
Sugar beet	2,020.3	2,564	2,407.4
Apples	326.5	353	293.2
Pears	151.4	151	117.9
Plums	81.7	85	76.0
Cherries	26.7	25	22.8
Currants	31.5	30	28.9

Grapes ('000 metric tons): 518 in 1983; 360 in 1984; 150 in 1985 (unofficial estimates).

LIVESTOCK ('000 head at December)

	1983	1984	1985
Horses	42.0	41.4	44.9
Cattle	2,633.3	2,669.1	2,650.6
Pigs	3,880.7	4,026.7	3,925.9
Sheep	215.8	220.2	244.9
Goats	32.1	29.9	32.6
Chickens	15,215.1	14,949.0	14,439.8
Ducks	128.1	130.4	153.1
Geese	26.2	23.6	23.4
Turkeys	244.8	253.6	243.8

LIVESTOCK PRODUCTS ('000 metric tons)

	1983	1984	1985
Milk	3,671.1	3,768.7	3,797.0
Butter	46	45	44
Cheese	101	104	102
Hen eggs*	1,722	1,720	1,798
Beef	188	203	209.5
Veal	15.5	17	16.5
Pig meats	356.5	354	364
Poultry meat	75.5	81	80

* Millions.

Forestry

ROUNDWOOD REMOVALS
('000 cubic metres, excluding bark)

	1983	1984	1985
Sawlogs, veneer logs and logs for sleepers	6,805	7,128	6,548
Pitprops (mine timber), pulpwood, and other industrial wood	2,484	2,602	2,637
Fuel wood	2,391	2,381	2,441
Total	11,680	12,111	11,626

SAWNWOOD PRODUCTION ('000 cubic metres)

	1983	1984	1985
Coniferous sawnwood*	6,006	6,041	5,743
Broadleaved sawnwood*	220	231	222
Sub-total	6,226	6,272	5,965
Railway sleepers	45	43	37
Total	6,271	6,315	6,002

* Including boxboards.

Mining

		1983	1984	1985
Brown coal (incl. lignite)	'000 metric tons	3,041.3	2,928	3,081
Crude petroleum	'000 metric tons	1,268.6	1,205	1,147
Iron ore:				
gross weight	'000 metric tons	3,540	3,600	3,270
metal content	'000 metric tons	1,107	1,138	1,019
Magnesite (crude)	'000 metric tons	1,005.8	1,180	1,255
Salt (unrefined)	'000 metric tons	530	697	734
Antimony ore*	metric tons	705	565	550
Lead ore*	metric tons	5,750	5,574	7,500
Zinc ore*	metric tons	22,688	23,797	24,259
Natural gas	million cu metres	1,273.4	1,272	1,164

* Figures refer to the metal content of ores.

AUSTRIA	Statistical Survey

Industry

SELECTED PRODUCTS

		1983	1984	1985
Wheat flour	'000 metric tons	354	354	354
Raw sugar	'000 metric tons	350	418	423
Margarine	metric tons	47,569	47,296	47,854
Wine	'000 hectolitres	3,697.9	2,518.9	1,125.7
Beer	'000 hectolitres	8,402.8	8,440	8,836
Cigarettes	million	15,625.1	14,900	16,051
Cotton yarn (pure and mixed)	metric tons	16,908	16,721	15,056
Woven cotton fabrics (pure and mixed)	metric tons	16,079	16,828	16,363
Wool yarn (pure and mixed)	metric tons	8,288	9,180	9,122
Woven woollen fabrics (pure and mixed)	metric tons	4,475	4,415	4,426
Mechanical wood pulp	'000 metric tons	191.9	180.0	197
Chemical and semi-chemical wood pulp	'000 metric tons	977.5	1,049	1,124
Newsprint	'000 metric tons	176.3	199	241
Other printing and writing paper	'000 metric tons	721.2	762	850
Other paper	'000 metric tons	593.2	634	696
Paperboard	'000 metric tons	298.6	326	340
Nitrogenous fertilizers (a)[1]	metric tons	254,800	220,000	232,500
Phosphate fertilizers (b)[1]	metric tons	95,400	110,100	112,000
Plastics and resins	'000 metric tons	549.0	613	606
Liquefied petroleum gas	'000 metric tons	124.5	76	90
Motor spirit (petrol)[2]	'000 metric tons	1,789.6	1,995	2,078
Kerosene	'000 metric tons	2.5	5.8	7
Jet fuel	'000 metric tons	137	183	180
Distillate fuel oils	'000 metric tons	2,046.6	2,082.9	2,209
Residual fuel oils	'000 metric tons	1,748.7	1,961.6	2,408
Lubricating oils	'000 metric tons	86.2	80	86
Petroleum bitumen (asphalt)	'000 metric tons	207.0	274	225
Coke-oven coke	'000 metric tons	1,725.2	1,850	1,751
Cement	'000 metric tons	4,906.6	4,900	4,560
Pig-iron (excl. ferro-alloys)	'000 metric tons	3,320.0	3,750	3,704
Crude steel	'000 metric tons	4,410.9	4,867	4,660
Aluminium (unwrought):				
primary	metric tons	94,200	95,800	94,106
secondary[3]	metric tons	70,654	77,600	79,703
Refined copper (unwrought):				
primary	metric tons	8,769	9,590	7,771
secondary	metric tons	33,131	34,200	36,141
Refined lead (unwrought):				
primary	metric tons	6,762	6,620	6,415
secondary	metric tons	11,479	13,449	13,281
Refined zinc (unwrought):				
primary	metric tons	18,774	19,400	18,973
secondary	metric tons	924	1,090	1,523
Motorcycles, etc.	'000	134.1	144.7	161
Construction: new dwellings completed	number	39,055	41,272	41,143
Electric energy	million kWh	42,625	42,382	44,534
Manufactured gas:				
from gasworks	million cu metres	35.4	36	38
from cokeries	million cu metres	646.5	737.0	702

[1] Estimated production during 12 months ending 30 June of the year stated. Figures are in terms of (a) nitrogen or (b) phosphoric acid. Source: FAO, *Monthly Bulletin of Statistics*.
[2] Including aviation gasoline.
[3] Secondary aluminium produced from old scrap and remelted aluminium.

Finance

CURRENCY AND EXCHANGE RATES

Monetary Units
100 Groschen = 1 Schilling.

Denominations
Coins: 1, 2, 5, 10 and 50 Groschen; 1, 5, 10, 25, 50, 100, 500 and 1,000 Schilling.
Notes: 20, 50, 100, 500 and 1,000 Schilling.

Sterling and Dollar Equivalents (30 September 1986)
£1 sterling = 20.635 Schilling;
US $1 = 14.275 Schilling;
1,000 Schilling = £48.46 = $70.05.

Average Exchange Rate (Schilling per US $)
1983   17.963
1984   20.009
1985   20.690

NATIONAL BANK RESERVES
(US $ million at 31 December)

	1983	1984	1985
Gold*	2,044	1,793	2,283
IMF special drawing rights	161	220	210
Reserve position in IMF	468	438	445
Foreign exchange	3,886	3,586	4,112
Total	6,559	6,037	7,050

* Valued at 60,000 Schilling per kilogram.

Source: IMF, *International Financial Statistics*.

MONEY SUPPLY ('000 million Schilling at 31 December)

	1983	1984	1985
Currency outside banks	84.1	83.9	84.5
Demand deposits at deposit money banks	86.3	92.5	97.4
Total money	170.4	176.4	181.9

Source: IMF, *International Financial Statistics*.

COST OF LIVING (Consumer Price Index. Base 1976 = 100)

	1983	1984	1985
Food	133.7	141.2	144.4
Rent (incl. maintenance and repairs)	158.1	168.5	176.1
Fuel and light	173.7	186.8	194.3
Clothing	130.7	136.0	140.8
Total (incl. others)	140.2	148.1	152.9

FEDERAL BUDGET (million Schilling)

Revenue	1983	1984	1985*
Direct taxes on income and wealth	92,975	102,933	113,852
Social security contributions—unemployment insurance	13,203	17,196	18,736
Indirect taxes	115,269	127,099	131,377
Current transfers	12,088	8,798	15,320
Sales and charges	9,716	10,558	11,230
Interest, shares of profit and other income	10,427	10,200	12,324
Sales of assets	448	725	456
Repayments of loans granted	482	529	651
Capital transfers	1,767	1,179	1,168
Borrowing	94,759	88,424	89,644
Other revenue	2,162	3,155	1,719
Total	353,297	370,796	396,477

Expenditure	1983	1984	1985*
Current expenditure on goods and services	80,357	85,151	90,948
Interest on public debt	26,356	32,558	36,775
Current transfers to:			
Regional and local authorities	27,315	28,306	31,189
Other public bodies	49,019	51,272	52,808
Households	66,235	67,823	72,421
Other	32,700	34,253	37,184
Deficits of government enterprises	5,655	4,892	5,422
Gross capital formation	12,538	12,357	11,950
Capital transfers	16,111	16,113	16,834
Acquisition of assets	3,224	3,100	3,779
Loans granted	1,163	925	974
Debt redemption	25,548	32,829	31,659
Other expenditure	3,435	2,991	6,551
Total	349,656	372,570	398,494

* Preliminary figures.

AUSTRIA

Statistical Survey

NATIONAL ACCOUNTS ('000 million Schilling at current prices)
National Income and Product

	1983	1984	1985
Compensation of employees	642.44	676.33	717.00
Operating surplus*	250.83	272.64	293.18
Domestic factor incomes	893.27	948.97	1,010.18
Consumption of fixed capital	149.24	158.19	167.53
Gross domestic product at factor cost	1,042.51	1,107.16	1,177.71
Indirect taxes	197.08	216.09	226.10
Less Subsidies	37.56	38.06	37.17
GDP in purchasers' values	1,202.03	1,285.19	1,366.64
Factor income received from abroad	47,20	58.37	66.25
Less Factor income paid abroad	56.01	66.92	73.30
Gross national product	1,193.22	1,276.64	1,359.59
Less Consumption of fixed capital	149.24	158.19	167.53
National income in market prices	1,043.98	1,118.45	1,192.06
Other current transfers from abroad	14.46	15.43	16.16
Less Other current transfers paid abroad	13.10	12.75	13.56
National disposable income	1,045.34	1,121.13	1,194.66

* Including a statistical discrepancy.

Expenditure on the Gross Domestic Product

	1983	1984	1985
Government final consumption expenditure	227.47	239.18	255.74
Private final consumption expenditure	694.66	730.79	773.66
Increase in stocks*	−2.04	32.48	30.48
Gross fixed capital formation	267.20	280.81	304.30
Total domestic expenditure	1,187.28	1,283.26	1,364.17
Exports of goods and services	448.66	497.64	550.19
Less Imports of goods and services	433.92	495.71	547.72
GDP in purchasers' values	1,202.03	1,285.19	1,366.64
GDP at 1976 prices	844.91	861.60	887.27

* Including a statistical discrepancy.

Gross Domestic Product by Economic Activity

	1983	1984	1985
Agriculture, hunting, forestry and fishing	44.14	48.70	45.45
Mining and quarrying	5.32	5.97	6.46
Manufacturing	323.24	349.67	378.59
Electricity, gas and water	39.09	38.88	42.53
Construction	87.30	87.57	90.34
Wholesale and retail trade	161.26	163.76	172.05
Restaurants and hotels	40.64	42.74	44.77
Transport, storage and communications	68.37	74.94	79.02
Owner-occupied dwellings	65.77	74.48	83.44
Finance, insurance and real estate	101.34	107.67	117.52
Public administration and defence	164.63	173.49	184.91
Other community, social and personal services	39.84	42.27	45.01
Private non-profit services to households	8.57	9.04	9.65
Domestic services of households	0.66	0.67	0.64
Sub-total	1,150.17	1,219.85	1,300.37
Value added tax	105.22	120.00	125.66
Import duties	7.71	8.63	9.07
Less Imputed bank service charges	61.06	63.30	68.46
Total	1,202.03	1,285.19	1,366.64

BALANCE OF PAYMENTS (US $ million)

	1983	1984	1985
Merchandise exports f.o.b.	15,275	15,474	16,955
Merchandise imports f.o.b.	−18,703	−19,013	−20,949
Trade balance	**−3,429**	**−3,539**	**−3,994**
Exports of services	12,526	11,130	12,603
Imports of services	−8,838	−8,265	−8,870
Balance on goods and services	**259**	**−674**	**−261**
Private unrequited transfers (net)	−38	86	37
Government unrequited transfers (net)	−44	−39	−38
Current balance	**177**	**−626**	**−262**
Direct capital investment (net)	104	66	191
Other long-term capital (net)	−1,447	−361	−304
Short-term capital (net)	1,047	994	−379
Net errors and omissions	−372	−4	745
Total (net monetary movements)	**−491**	**70**	**−9**
Monetization of gold	−28	21	30
Valuation changes (net)	−266	−363	500
Changes in reserves	**−785**	**−272**	**520**

Source: IMF, *International Financial Statistics*.

External Trade

Note: Austria's customs territory excludes Mittelberg im Kleinen Walsertal (in Vorarlberg) and Jungholz (in Tyrol). The figures also exclude trade in silver specie and monetary gold.

PRINCIPAL COMMODITIES (distribution by SITC, million Schilling)

Imports c.i.f.	1983	1984	1985
Food and live animals	19,943.1	21,751.4	23,478.6
Vegetables and fruit	6,620.8	7,250.9	8,083.1
Coffee, tea, cocoa and spices	5,094.4	5,735.7	6,401.6
Crude materials (inedible) except fuels	21,005.9	25,962.3	27,138.4
Metalliferous ores and metal scrap	4,954.2	7,563.5	7,684.2
Mineral fuels, lubricants, etc. (incl. electric current)	48,076.7	59,223.7	64,092.2
Coal, coke and briquettes	6,169.4	7,153.6	8,647.1
Petroleum, petroleum products, etc.	34,587.9	40,038.9	41,564.6
Crude petroleum oils, etc.	21,571.6	25,642.6	26,768.0
Refined petroleum products	11,652.0	12,798.3	12,996.9
Gas (natural and manufactured)	6,550.2	11,038.0	12,992.9
Petroleum gases, etc., in the gaseous state	6,117.3	10,420.5	12,227.3
Chemicals and related products	35,026.8	39,297.5	43,034.3
Organic chemicals	5,695.6	6,508.7	7,297.5
Medicinal and pharmaceutical products	5,707.2	6,224.9	7,002.3
Artificial resins, plastic materials, etc.	10,050.8	11,535.8	12,243.7
Products of polymerization, etc.	6,565.1	7,630.8	7,975.4
Basic manufactures	64,895.0	73,764.4	78,301.6
Paper, paperboard and manufactures	5,375.9	6,436.9	7,002.1
Textile yarn, fabrics, etc.	16,337.4	17,851.3	18,707.5
Non-metallic mineral manufactures	6,454.0	6,813.4	7,084.6
Iron and steel	9,456.1	11,052.7	12,107.4
Non-ferrous metals	7,597.9	9,966.1	10,365.3
Other metal manufactures	11,811.6	12,770.5	13,738.7
Machinery and transport equipment	103,645.8	109,971.5	128,610.9
Power generating machinery and equipment	5,284.8	6,375.9	7,233.9
Machinery specialized for particular industries	12,193.8	13,092.8	14,639.1
General industrial machinery, equipment and parts	15,825.9	18,068.5	20,636.2
Office machines and automatic data processing equipment	7,021.7	9,058.3	11,415.0
Telecommunications and sound equipment	6,545.4	6,960.3	6,967.8
Other electrical machinery, apparatus, etc.	18,215.1	20,609.6	23,610.9
Road vehicles and parts*	34,195.4	31,360.4	37,551.4
Passenger motor cars (excl. buses)	22,244.3	18,363.0	23,226.2
Parts and accessories for cars, buses, lorries, etc.*	5,126.2	5,427.2	6,038.3
Miscellaneous manufactured articles	51,897.1	58,018.2	61,974.7
Furniture and parts	5,451.8	6,014.0	6,214.5
Clothing and accessories (excl. footwear)	14,901.0	17,419.9	18,265.1
Professional, scientific and controlling instruments, etc.	4,821.2	5,536.3	6,481.8
Photographic apparatus, etc., optical goods, watches and clocks	4,976.8	5,467.7	5,767.4
Total (incl. others)	348,339.1	392,093.9	430,969.3

* Excluding tyres, engines and electrical parts.

Exports f.o.b.	1983	1984	1985
Food and live animals	11,093.9	12,958.2	13,480.6
Crude materials (inedible) except fuels	18,241.4	19,999.8	19,288.5
Cork and wood	9,849.0	10,310.5	9,127.2
Simply worked wood and railway sleepers	8,990.1	9,269.2	8,097.8
Simply worked coniferous wood	8,718.2	8,862.3	7,698.6
Sawn coniferous wood	8,538.3	8,657.5	7,499.6
Chemicals and related products	25,944.6	30,632.2	32,354.5
Organic chemicals	4,796.6	5,944.9	5,883.5
Artificial resins, plastic materials, etc.	8,623.5	10,298.1	10,498.9
Products of polymerization, etc.	5,774.8	7,341.4	7,459.9
Basic manufactures	94,408.4	108,185.5	119,785.8
Paper, paperboard and manufactures	14,037.8	16,823.7	19,864.3
Paper and paperboard (not cut to size or shape)	10,021.0	11,985.4	14,195.6
Printing and writing paper in bulk (incl. newsprint)	6,825.5	8,268.7	9,981.8
Textile yarn, fabrics, etc.	16,173.1	17,200.3	19,193.8
Non-metallic mineral manufactures	9,318.6	10,545.8	11,682.2
Iron and steel	24,032.5	29,651.6	31,514.5
Universals, plates and sheets	9,221.9	10,389.8	11,014.7
Tubes, pipes and fittings	4,661.9	6,357.6	7,127.6
Non-ferrous metals	6,587.3	7,848.7	8,375.5
Aluminium and aluminium alloys	4,288.7	5,407.2	5,484.4
Other metal manufactures	14,449.6	14,915.8	17,029.7
Machinery and transport equipment	83,566.4	94,165.9	110,801.8
Power generating machinery and equipment	10,679.0	12,956.2	14,246.1
Internal combustion piston engines and parts	7,402.2	9,061.5	10,641.0
Engines for road vehicles, tractors, etc.	6,482.0	8,156.9	9,381.1
Machinery specialized for particular industries	14,272.1	15,816.8	20,338.0
General industrial machinery, equipment and parts	15,659.4	16,642.5	19,550.1
Telecommunications and sound equipment	8,551.8	8,020.9	9,301.6
Other electrical machinery, apparatus, etc.	15,663.2	19,054.6	21,972.0
Road vehicles and parts (excl. tyres, engines and electrical parts)	11,801.4	12,677.0	15,010.6
Miscellaneous manufactured articles	38,185.4	41,810.9	48,713.4
Clothing and accessories (excl. footwear)	9,580.7	10,383.7	11,802.4
Footwear	5,254.5	5,500.7	6,042.9
Total (incl. others)	277,139.4	314,504.4	353,962.4

PRINCIPAL TRADING PARTNERS* (million Schilling)

Imports c.i.f.	1983	1984	1985
Algeria	3,283.3	4,268.7	3,428.7
Belgium/Luxembourg	7,233.3	8,399.9	9,156.7
Brazil	2,887.7	3,514.3	3,724.1
Czechoslovakia	7,368.9	7,863.3	8,329.0
France	14,284.4	14,536.5	15,636.4
Germany, Federal Republic	144,593.9	156,535.0	176,384.5
Hungary	5,930.1	8,110.9	8,501.9
Italy	30,969.7	33,790.1	35,466.5
Japan	12,199.4	12,793.4	14,149.9
Libya	2,698.7	4,373.2	4,511.5
Netherlands	9,574.6	10,210.7	11,401.6
Nigeria	1,633.7	3,901.6	4,555.0
Poland	3,561.6	5,035.4	4,773.4
Saudi Arabia	4,822.6	2,989.2	2,340.4
Sweden	6,138.0	7,183.1	7,781.2
Switzerland	16,538.7	17,409.2	19,435.5
USSR	14,856.0	19,625.3	19,150.9
United Kingdom	7,477.1	8,391.5	9,816.7
USA	11,718.6	13,720.7	16,044.4
Yugoslavia	3,484.1	4,409.3	4,749.4
Total (incl. others)	348,339.1	392,093.9	430,969.3

Exports f.o.b.	1983	1984	1985
Algeria	1,935.0	2,815.3	3,731.9
Belgium/Luxembourg	5,127.6	5,726.1	8,017.2
Czechoslovakia	3,586.1	3,498.4	3,888.2
Denmark	2,817.1	3,329.8	3,846.4
France	10,391.3	12,184.5	14,023.0
German Democratic Republic	6,327.8	6,807.0	4,413.9
Germany, Federal Republic	85,347.1	93,146.6	106,618.8
Hungary	6,112.2	6,959.8	9,162.2
Iran	4,931.2	3,967.1	3,602.6
Iraq	2,535.4	3,236.5	4,214.6
Italy	24,599.7	29,507.2	31,772.1
Netherlands	6,693.7	7,598.5	8,337.7
Poland	3,101.5	3,401.1	4,288.5
Saudi Arabia	5,088.8	4,418.6	3,770.6
Spain (excl. Canary Is.)	4,584.1	4,745.3	5,592.2
Sweden	5,176.8	5,964.5	6,563.3
Switzerland	18,911.9	21,730.6	23,878.7
USSR	10,782.3	14,072.9	13,409.9
United Kingdom	11,320.3	13,789.9	16,277.0
USA	8,210.5	12,911.4	16,504.2
Yugoslavia	7,202.5	7,667.8	8,249.0
Total (incl. others)	277,139.4	314,504.4	353,962.4

* Imports by country of production; exports by country of consumption.

Transport

RAILWAYS (Federal Railways only)

	1983	1984	1985
Passenger-km (millions)	7,023	7,004	7,290
Freight (net ton-km) (millions)	10,230	11,247	11,903
Freight tons carried ('000)	50,349	55,774	58,209

ROAD TRAFFIC (motor vehicles in use at 31 December)

	1983	1984	1985
Private cars	2,414,466	2,468,452	2,530,800
Buses and coaches	9,154	9,200	9,183
Goods vehicles	197,125	203,322	206,746
Motorcycles and scooters	83,409	84,480	84,640
Mopeds	555,069	561,269	563,756

SHIPPING (freight traffic in '000 metric tons)

	1983	1984	1985
Goods loaded	1,844	2,113	2,122
Goods unloaded	4,305	5,277	4,873

CIVIL AVIATION (Austrian Airlines, '000)

	1983	1984	1985
Kilometres flown	23,208	23,350	23,022
Passenger ton-km	120,420	129,576	132,021
Cargo ton-km	17,082	19,385	18,516
Mail ton-km	4,325	4,214	4,150

Tourism

FOREIGN TOURIST ARRIVALS (by country of origin)

	1983	1984	1985
Belgium-Luxembourg	344,675	350,720	339,113
France	491,816	639,070	664,933
Germany, Federal Republic	8,457,052	8,274,471	8,145,318
Italy	434,179	540,344	543,756
Netherlands	1,203,495	1,251,737	1,247,378
Switzerland	443,856	475,978	457,955
United Kingdom	755,518	821,998	785,973
USA	687,116	931,505	987,722
Total (incl. others)	14,481,531	15,110,233	15,167,830

Communications Media

	1983	1984	1985
Telephones in use	2,547,908	2,640,843	2,729,389
Radio licences issued	2,538,238	2,612,530	2,627,297
Television licences issued	2,356,024	2,418,584	2,425,920
Book titles produced	9,374	10,009	n.a.

1985: Daily newspapers 33 (average circulation 2,729,000); Non-daily newspapers 143; Other periodicals 2,348.

Education

(1985/86)

	Institutions	Staff	Students
Primary	3,411	28,305	341,867
General secondary	2,069	55,932	504,326
Compulsory vocational	1,195	22,061	366,061
Teacher training:			
second level	46	849	8,363
third level	26	1,407	7,156
Universities and other higher schools	18	10,252	160,904

Directory

The Constitution

The Austrian constitution of 1920, as amended in 1929, was restored on 1 May 1945. Its main provisions are summarized below:

Austria is a democratic republic, having a president (Bundespräsident), elected directly by the people, and a two-chamber legislature, the Federal Assembly. The republic is organized on the federal system, comprising the provinces (Länder) of Burgenland, Carinthia, Lower Austria, Upper Austria, Salzburg, Styria, Tyrol, Vorarlberg and Vienna. There is universal suffrage for men and women who are more than 19 years of age.

The Nationalrat (National Council) consists of 183 members, elected by universal direct suffrage, according to a system of proportional representation. It functions for a period of four years.

The Bundesrat (Federal Council) represents the federal provinces. Vienna sends 12 members, Lower Austria 12, Upper Austria 10, Styria 10, Carinthia 4, Tyrol 5, Salzburg 4, Burgenland and Vorarlberg 3 each, making 63 in all. The seats are divided between the parties according to the number of seats they hold in the provincial assemblies and are held during the life of the provincial government which they represent. Each province in turn provides the chairman for six months.

For certain matters of special importance the two chambers meet together; this is known as a Bundesversammlung.

The President, elected by popular vote, is the Head of State and holds office for six years. The President is eligible for re-election only once in succession. Although invested with special emergency powers, the President normally acts on the authority of the Government, and it is the Government which is responsible to the National Council for governmental policy.

The Government consists of the Chancellor, the Vice-Chancellor and the other ministers, who may vary in number. The Chancellor is chosen by the President, usually from the party with the strongest representation in the newly-elected National Council, and the other ministers are then chosen by the President on the advice of the Chancellor.

If the National Council passes an explicit vote of 'no confidence' in the Federal Government or individual members thereof, the Federal Government or the Federal Minister concerned shall be removed from office.

All new acts must be read and put to the vote in both houses. A new bill goes first to the National Council, where it usually has three readings, and secondly to the Federal Council, where it can be held up, but not vetoed.

The Constitution also provides for appeals by the Government to the electorate on specific points by means of referendum. There is further provision that if 200,000 or more electors present a petition to the Government, the Government must lay it before the National Council.

The Landtag (Provincial Assembly) exercises the same functions in each province as the National Council does in the State. The members of the Landtag elect a government (Landesregierung) consisting of a provincial governor (Landeshauptmann) and his councillors (Landesräte). They are responsible to the Landtag.

The spheres of legal and administrative competence of both national and provincial governments are clearly defined. The Constitution distinguishes four groups:

1. Law-making and administration are the responsibility of the State: e.g. foreign affairs, justice and finance.

2. Law-making is the responsibility of the State, administration is the responsibility of the provinces: e.g. elections, population matters and road traffic.

3. The State lays down the rudiments of the law, the provinces make the law and administer it: e.g. charity, rights of agricultural workers, land reform.

4. Law-making and administration are the responsibility of the provinces in all matters not expressly assigned to the State: e.g. municipal affairs, building theatres and cinemas.

The Government

HEAD OF STATE

Federal President: Dr KURT WALDHEIM (sworn in 8 July 1986).

COUNCIL OF MINISTERS
(October 1986)

A coalition of the Socialist Party of Austria (SPÖ) and the Freedom Party of Austria (FPÖ).

Federal Chancellor: Dr FRANZ VRANITZKY (SPÖ).
Vice-Chancellor and Minister of Trade, Commerce and Industry: Dr NORBERT STEGER (FPÖ).
Minister of Foreign Affairs: Dr PETER JANKOWITSCH (SPÖ).
Minister of the Interior: KARL BLECHA (SPÖ).
Minister of Agriculture and Forestry: Dr ERICH SCHMIDT (SPÖ).
Minister of the Public Sector and Transport: Dipl.-Ing. Dr RUDOLF STREICHER (SPÖ).
Minister of Justice: Dr HARALD OFNER (FPÖ).
Minister of Social Affairs: ALFRED DALLINGER (SPÖ).
Minister of Finance: Dkfm. FERDINAND LACINA (SPÖ).
Minister of National Defence: Dr HELMUT KRÜNES (FPÖ).
Minister of Construction and Engineering: Dr HEINRICH ÜBLEIS (SPÖ).
Minister of Science and Research: Dr HEINZ FISCHER (SPÖ).
Minister of Education, the Arts and Sport: Dr HERBERT MORITZ (SPÖ).
Minister of Health and Environment: FRANZ KREUZER (SPÖ).
Minister of Family Affairs: GERTRUDE FRÖHLICH-SANDNER (SPÖ).
Minister of the Federal Chancellery (Civil Service): Dr FRANZ LÖSCHNAK (SPÖ).
Secretary of State to the Federal Chancellery (Women): JOHANNA DOHNAL (SPÖ).
Secretary of State to the Ministry of Health and Environmental Protection: Dr MARIO FERRARI-BRUNNENFELD (FPÖ).
Secretary of State to the Ministry of Agriculture and Forestry: Ing. GERULF MURER (FPÖ).
Secretary of State in the Ministry of Construction and Engineering: Dr BEATRIX EYPELTAUER (SPÖ).
Secretary of State in the Ministry of Finance: Dkfm. HOLGER BAUER (FPÖ).

MINISTRIES

Office of the Federal Chancellor: 1014 Vienna, Ballhausplatz 2; tel. (0222) 66-1-50; telex 1370900.
Ministry of Agriculture and Forestry: 1010 Vienna, Stubenring 1; tel. (0222) 75-0-00.
Ministry of Construction and Engineering: 1010 Vienna, Stubenring 1; tel. (0222) 75-0-00; telex 1780.
Ministry of Education, the Arts and Sport: 1010 Vienna, Minoritenplatz 5; tel. (0222) 66-2-10.
Ministry of Family Affairs: 1010 Vienna, Himmelpfortgasse 9; tel. (0222) 53-3-30.
Ministry of Finance: 1010 Vienna, Himmelpfortgasse 2-8B; tel. (0222) 51-4-33.
Ministry of Foreign Affairs: 1014 Vienna, Ballhausplatz 2; tel. (0222) 66-1-50; telex 01371.
Ministry of Health and Environment: 1031 Vienna, Radetzkystr. 2; tel. (0222) 75-56-86.
Ministry of the Interior: 1010 Vienna, Herrengasse 7; tel. (0222) 66-2-60.
Ministry of Justice: 1070 Vienna, Museumstr. 7; tel. (0222) 96-2-20.
Ministry of National Defence: 1031 Vienna, Dampfschiffstr. 2; tel. (0222) 52-95-25; telex 112145.
Ministry of the Public Sector and Transport: 1031 Vienna, Radetzkystr. 2; tel. (0222) 75-76-31; telex 111800.
Ministry of Science and Research: 1010 Vienna, Minoritenplatz 5; tel. (0222) 66-2-10.
Ministry of Social Affairs: 1010 Vienna, Stubenring 1; tel. (0222) 75-0-00.
Ministry of Trade, Commerce and Industry: 1010 Vienna, Stubenring 1; tel. (0222) 75-0-00; telex 111780.

AUSTRIA

President and Legislature

PRESIDENT

Presidential Election, First Ballot, 4 May 1986

Candidates	Votes	%
Dr Kurt Waldheim	2,343,387	49.65
Dr Kurt Steyrer (SPÖ)	2,061,162	43.67
Freda Meissner-Blau	259,471	5.49
Otto Scrinzi	55,940	1.18

Second Ballot, 8 June 1986

Candidates	Votes	%
Dr Kurt Waldheim	2,460,203	53.89
Dr Kurt Steyrer (SPÖ)	2,105,118	46.11

NATIONALRAT

President of Nationalrat: Anton Benya.

General Election, 23 November 1986

	Votes	% of Total	Seats
Socialist Party (SPÖ)	2,092,024	43.12	80
People's Party (ÖVP)	2,003,663	41.30	77
Freedom Party (FPÖ)	472,205	9.73	18
United Green Party/Alternative List (VGO/ALÖ)	234,028	4.82	8

BUNDESRAT
(October 1986)

Chairman of Bundesrat: Reinhold Suttner (July–Dec. 1986).

Provinces	Total seats	SPÖ	ÖVP
Burgenland	3	2	1
Carinthia	4	3	1
Lower Austria	12	5	7
Upper Austria	10	4	6
Salzburg	4	2	2
Styria	10	4	6
Tyrol	5	1	4
Vorarlberg	3	1	2
Vienna	12	8	4
Total	**63**	**30**	**33**

Political Organizations

Alternative Liste Österreich (ALÖ) (Austrian Alternative List): 1050 Vienna, Margarethen-Gürtel 122-124/1/k; f. 1982; radical ecologist party, linked to the anti-nuclear Green Party in the Federal Republic of Germany; aims for an alternative energy policy; Leaders Edith Caslavsky, Werner Haslauer, Richard Krampel.

Bürgerinitiative Parlament (BIP) (Citizens' Parliamentary Initiative): Vienna; aims for the union of alternative political groups; Leaders Günther Nenning, Freda Meissner-Blau.

Freiheitliche Partei Österreichs (FPÖ) (Freedom Party of Austria): 1010 Vienna I, Kärntnerstr. 28; f. 1955; Liberal party which partially succeeds the Verband der Unabhängigen (League of Independents), dissolved in 1956, and stands for moderate social reform, for the participation of workers in management, for European co-operation and for good relations with all the countries of Free Europe; Chair. Dr Jörg Haider; Leader of Parliamentary Group Abg. Dr Friedhelm Frischenschlager.

Kommunistische Partei Österreichs (KPÖ) (Communist Party of Austria): 1201 Vienna, Höchstädtplatz 3; f. 1918; strongest in the industrial centres and trade unions; advocates a policy of strict neutrality and friendly relations with neighbouring states and with the USSR; Chair. Franz Muhri; Secs Hans Kalt, Karl Reiter, Dr. Walter Silbermayr.

Nationale Demokratische Partei (NDP) (National Democratic Party of Austria): 1030 Vienna, Landstrassergürtel 19/3; extreme right-wing party; Chair. Dr Norbert Burger.

Österreichische Volkspartei (ÖVP) (Austrian People's Party): 1010 Vienna I, Kärntnerstr. 51; f. 1945; Christian-Democratic party; the 'Salzburg programme' (1972) defines it as 'progressive centre party'; 800,000 mems; Chair. Dr Alois Mock; Sec.-Gen. Dr Michael Graff.

Sozialistische Partei Österreichs (SPÖ) (Socialist Party of Austria): 1014 Vienna I, Löwelstr. 18; tel. (0222) 63-27-31; telex 114198; founded as the Social-Democratic Party in 1889; advocates democratic socialism and Austria's permanent neutrality; 720,000 mems; Chair. Dr Fred Sinowatz; Vice-Chairs. Karl Blecha, Dr Heinz Fischer, Leopold Gratz, Hans Gross, Dr Jolanda Offenbeck, Dr Karl Grünner, Ernst Höger; Secs. Fritz Marsch, Peter Schieder, Dr Heinrich Keller.

Vereinte Grünen Österreich (VGÖ) (United Green Party of Austria): Vienna; f. 1982; conservative ecologist party; Chair. Leopold Puchner; Sec. Eva Hauk.

Diplomatic Representation

EMBASSIES IN AUSTRIA

Albania: 1030 Vienna, Jacquingasse 41; tel. (0222) 78-37-95; telex 133248; Ambassador: Idriz Bardhi.

Algeria: 1010 Vienna, Reichsratsstr. 17; tel. (0222) 43-93-73; telex 134163; Ambassador: Abdelaziz Benhassine.

Argentina: 1010 Vienna, Goldschmiedgasse 2/1; tel. (0222) 63-85-77; telex 74512; Ambassador: Juan Carlos Beltramino.

Australia: 1040 Vienna, Mattiellistr. 2-4/III; tel. (0222) 512-85-80; telex 74313; Ambassador: John Robert Kelso.

Belgium: 1040 Vienna, Operngasse 20b; tel. (0222) 56-75-79; telex 113364; Ambassador: Graf Francis de la Barre d'Erquelinnes.

Brazil: 1010 Vienna, Lugeck 1/V/15; tel. (0222) 52-06-31; telex 111925; Ambassador: Raul Henrique Castro e Silva de Vincenzi.

Bulgaria: 1040 Vienna, Schwindgasse 8; tel. (0222) 65-66-44; Ambassador: Christo Dortschev.

Canada: 1010 Vienna, Luegerring 10/IV; tel. (0222) 63-36-91; telex 75320; Ambassador: Michael Shenstone.

Chile: 1010 Vienna, Lugeck 1/III/9; tel. (0222) 512-33-70; telex 115952; Ambassador: Rafael Enrique Ortiz Navarro.

China, People's Republic: 1030 Vienna, Metternichgasse 4; tel. (0222) 75-31-49; telex 135794; Ambassador: Yang Chengxu.

Colombia: 1010 Vienna, Stadiongasse 6–8; tel. (0222) 42-42-49; telex 116798; Ambassador: Humberto Avila-Mora.

Cuba: 1130 Vienna, Eitelbergergasse 24; tel. (0222) 82-81-98; telex 131398; Ambassador: Gustavo Mazorra Hernández.

Czechoslovakia: 1140 Vienna, Penzinger Str. 11–13; tel. (0222) 82-26-29; telex 131702; Ambassador: Marek Venuta.

Denmark: 1010 Vienna, Führichgasse 6; tel. (0222) 52-79-04; telex 113261; Ambassador: Jens Christensen.

Ecuador: 1010 Vienna, Goldschmiedgasse 10/II/24; tel. (0222) 66-32-08; telex 134958; Ambassador: Dr Iván Peñaherrera Delgado.

Egypt: 1190 Vienna, Gallmeyergasse 5; tel. (0222) 36-11-34; telex 15623; Ambassador: Muhammad el-Taher Shash.

Finland: 1020 Vienna, Untere Donaustr. 13–15; tel. (0222) 24-75-21; telex 135230; Ambassador: Kaarlo Yrjö-Koskinen.

France: 1040 Vienna, Technikerstr. 2; tel. (0222) 65-47-47; Ambassador: François-Régis Bastide.

German Democratic Republic: 1130 Vienna, Frimbergergasse 6-8; tel. (0222) 82-36-54; telex 133591; Ambassador: Klaus Wolf.

Germany, Federal Republic: 1030 Vienna, Metternichgasse 3; tel. (0222) 73-65-11; telex 134261; Ambassador: Dietrich Graf von Brühl.

Greece: 1040 Vienna, Argentinierstr. 14; tel. (0222) 65-57-91; telex 133176; Ambassador: Georges Cladakis.

Guatemala: 1070 Vienna, Andreasgasse 4/2/5; tel. (0222) 93-61-00; Ambassador: Héctor Mario López Fuentes.

Holy See: 1040 Vienna, Theresianumgasse 31; tel. (0222) 65-13-27; Apostolic Nuncio: Mgr Michele Cecchini.

Hungary: 1010 Vienna, Bankgasse 4-6; tel. (0222) 63-26-31; telex 135546; Ambassador: János Nagy.

AUSTRIA

India: 1015 Vienna, Kärntner Ring 2; tel. (0222) 65-86-66; telex 113721; Ambassador: JAGDISH RUDRAYA HIREMATH.
Indonesia: 1180 Vienna, Gustav-Tschermak-Gasse 5–7; tel. (0222) 34-25-34; telex 75579; Ambassador: ARTATI SUDIRDJO.
Iran: 1030 Vienna, Jaurèsgasse 3; tel. (0222) 72-26-50; telex 131718; Ambassador: MEHDI AHARI MOSTAFAVI.
Iraq: 1010 Vienna, Johannesgasse 26; tel. (0222) 73-81-95; telex 135397; Ambassador: Dr WAHBI ABDEL RAZZAK AL-QARAGULI.
Ireland: 1030 Vienna, Hilton Centre, POB 139; tel. (0222) 75-42-46; telex 136887; Ambassador: FLORENCE O'RIORDAN.
Israel: 1180 Vienna, Anton Frank-Gasse 20; tel. (0222) 31-15-06; telex 4005; Ambassador: (vacant).
Italy: 1030 Vienna, Rennweg 27; tel. (0222) 75-51-21; telex 132620; Ambassador: GIROLAMO NISIO.
Ivory Coast: 1090 Vienna, Alser Str. 28; tel. (0222) 48-37-23; Ambassador: ADONIT MANOUAN.
Japan: 1040 Vienna, Argentinierstr. 21; tel. (0222) 65-97-71; telex 135810; Ambassador: RYOHEI MURATA.
Korea, Democratic People's Republic: 1140 Vienna, Beckmanngasse 10–12; tel. (0222) 82-92-38; telex 131750; Ambassador: CHO GI CHOL.
Korea, Republic: 1030 Vienna, Kelsenstr. 2; tel. (0222) 78-63-18; telex 131252; Ambassador: LEE SIE-YONG.
Kuwait: 1010 Vienna, Universitätsstr. 5; tel. (0222) 42-56-46; telex 135898; Ambassador: ABDUL-HAMID ABDULLAH AL-AWADHI.
Lebanon: 1010 Vienna, Schwedenplatz 2/15; tel. (0222) 63-88-21; telex 115273; Ambassador: IBRAHIM KHARMA.
Libya: 1170 Vienna, Dornbacherstr. 27; tel. (0222) 45-36-11; telex 76267; Secretary of People's Bureau: ENBEIA MANSUR WADI.
Luxembourg: 1190 Vienna, Hofzeile 27; tel. (0222) 36-21-86; telex 115276; Ambassador: EDOUARD MOLITOR.
Malaysia: 1040 Vienna, Prinz Eugen-Str. 18; tel. (0222) 65-11-42; telex 133830; Ambassador: MON JAMALUDDIN.
Mexico: 1040 Vienna, Mattiellistr. 2–4; tel. (0222) 52-99-11; telex 115660; Ambassador: ROBERTO DE ROSENZWEIG DÍAZ.
Morocco: 1020 Vienna, Untere Donaustr. 13–15; tel. (0222) 24-25-68; Ambassador: TAWFIQ KABBAJ.
Netherlands: 1020 Vienna, Untere Donaustr. 13–15/VIII; tel. (0222) 24-85-87; telex 135462; Ambassador: LODEWIJK H. J. B. VAN GORKOM.
New Zealand: 1010 Vienna, Lugeck 1; tel. (0222) 52-66-36; telex 136582; Ambassador: DONALD WALKER.
Nicaragua: 1010 Vienna, Schwedenplatz 2/7/64; tel. (0222) 63-81-13; Ambassador: IVÁN MEJÍA-SOLÍS.
Nigeria: 1030 Vienna, Rennweg 25; tel. (0222) 72-66-85; telex 131583; Ambassador: M. S. SAMBO.
Norway: 1030 Vienna, Bayerngasse 3; tel. (0222) 75-66-92; telex 132768; Ambassador: KNUT HEDEMANN.
Oman: 1090 Vienna, Währingerstr. 2–4/24–25; tel. (0222) 31-64-52; telex 116662; Chargé d'affaires: MUNIR A. MAKKI.
Pakistan: 1190 Vienna, Hofzeile 13; tel. (0222) 36-73-81; telex 135634; Ambassador: SYED AHMAD PASHA.
Panama: 1030 Vienna, Strohgasse 35; tel. (0222) 73-46-33; Ambassador: ERNESTO KOREF.
Peru: 1030 Vienna, Gottfried-Keller-Gasse 2; tel. (0222) 73-43-77; telex 135524; Ambassador: JORGE MORELLI PANDO.
Philippines: 1180 Vienna, Gregor-Mendel-Str. 48; tel. (0222) 31-59-30; Ambassador: (vacant).
Poland: 1130 Vienna, Hietzinger Hauptstr. 42c; tel. (0222) 82-74-44; Ambassador: MARIAN KRZAK.
Portugal: 1040 Vienna, Operngasse 20B; tel. (0222) 56-75-36; telex 113237; Ambassador: ANTÓNIO AUGUSTO DE MEDEIROS PATRICIO.
Qatar: 1090 Vienna, Strudlhofgasse 10; tel. (0222) 31-66-39; Ambassador: ALI ABDUL-RAHMAN AL-MUFTAH.
Romania: 1040 Vienna, Prinz Eugen-Str. 60; tel. (0222) 65-32-27; telex 133335; Ambassador: TRANDAFIR COCARLA.
Saudi Arabia: 1190 Vienna, Formanekgasse 38; tel. (0222) 36-23-16; telex 115757; Ambassador: YUSUF MUHAMMAD AHMAD AL-MOTABBAKANI.
South Africa: 1190 Vienna, Sandgasse 33; tel. (0222) 32-64-93; telex 116671; Ambassador: NAUDÉ STEYN.
Spain: 1040 Vienna, Argentinierstr. 34; tel. (0222) 65-57-80; telex 131545; Ambassador: Dr JESÚS NÚÑEZ.
Sweden: 1020 Vienna, Obere Donaustr. 49–51; tel. (0222) 33-45-45; telex 114720; Ambassador: DAG E. J. MALM.

Switzerland: 1030 Vienna, Prinz Eugen-Str. 7; tel. (0222) 78-45-21; telex 132960; Ambassador: JEAN-PIERRE RITTER.
Thailand: 1180 Vienna, Weimarer-Str. 68; tel. (0222) 34-83-61; telex 133893; Ambassador: SUCHATI CHUTHASMIT.
Tunisia: 1030 Vienna, Ghegastr. 3; tel. (0222) 78-65-53; telex 111748; Ambassador: MUHAMMAD EL-MOKHTAR ZANNAD.
Turkey: 1040 Vienna, Prinz Eugen-Str. 40; tel. (0222) 65-34-17; telex 131927; Ambassador: ERDEM ERNER.
USSR: 1030 Vienna, Reisnerstr. 45–47; tel. (0222) 73-12-15; Ambassador: GENNADI SERAFIMOVICH SHIKIN.
United Arab Emirates: 1190 Vienna, Peter-Jordan-Str. 66; tel. (0222) 36-14-55; telex 74106; Ambassador: ABDUL AZIZ AL-OWAIS.
United Kingdom: 1030 Vienna, Reisnerstr. 40; tel. (0222) 73-15-75; telex 132810; Ambassador: ROBERT O'NEILL.
USA: 1090 Vienna, Boltzmanngasse 16; tel. (0222) 31-55-11; telex 114634; Ambassador: RONALD LAUDER.
Uruguay: 1010 Vienna, Krugerstr. 3/1/4–6; tel. (0222) 513-22-40; Ambassador: JOAQUÍN COSTANZO.
Venezuela: 1030 Vienna, Marokkanergasse 22; tel. (0222) 75-32-19; telex 136219; Ambassador: Dr FRANCISCO SUCRE FIGARELLA.
Yugoslavia: 1030 Vienna, Rennweg 3; tel. (0222) 73-25-95; Ambassador: MILOŠ KRSTIĆ.
Zaire: 1130 Vienna, Auhofstr. 76; tel. (0222) 82-51-36; telex 133565; Ambassador: BINTOU' A-TSHABOLA.

Judicial System

The Austrian legal system is based on the principle of a division between legislative, administrative and judicial power. There are three supreme courts (Verfassungsgerichtshof, Verwaltungsgerichtshof and Oberster Gerichtshof). The judicial courts are organized into about 200 local courts (Bezirksgerichte), 17 provincial and district courts (Landes-und Kreisgerichte), and 4 higher provincial courts (Oberlandesgerichte) in Vienna, Graz, Innsbruck and Linz.

SUPREME ADMINISTRATIVE COURTS

Verfassungsgerichtshof (Constitutional Court): Vienna I, Judenplatz 11; f. 1919; deals with matters affecting the Constitution, examines the legality of legislation and administration; Pres. Univ. Doz. Dr LUDWIG ADAMOVICH; Vice-Pres. Prof. Dr KURT RINGHOFER.

Verwaltungsgerichtshof (Administrative Court): Vienna I, Judenplatz 11; deals with matters affecting the legality of administration; Pres. Dr VIKTOR HELLER; Vice-Pres. Dr INGRID PETRIK.

SUPREME JUDICIAL COURT

Oberster Gerichtshof: Vienna I, Museumstr. 12; Pres. Dr LEOPOLD WURZINGER; Vice-Pres. ANTON KINZEL, Dr KARL PISKA.

Religion

CHRISTIANITY

The Roman Catholic Church

The vast majority of Austrians belong to the Roman Catholic Church. Austria comprises two archdioceses, seven dioceses and the territorial abbacy of Wettingen-Mehrerau (directly responsible to the Holy See). The Archbishop of Vienna is also the Ordinary for Catholics of the Byzantine rite in Austria (totalling an estimated 3,500 at 31 December 1984).

Bishops' Conference: Österreichische Bischofskonferenz, 1010 Vienna, Rotenturmstrasse 2; tel. (0222) 52-95-11; f. 1979; Pres. D.Dr KARL BERG, Archbishop of Salzburg.

Archbishop of Salzburg: D.Dr KARL BERG, 5010 Salzburg, Kapitelplatz 2, Postfach 62; tel. (06222) 42-5-91.

Archbishop of Vienna: Fr HANS GROER, 1010 Vienna, Wollzeile 2; tel. (0222) 53-25-61.

Bishop of Eisenstadt: D.Dr STEFAN LÁSZLÓ, 7001 Eisenstadt, St Rochus-Str. 21; tel. (02682) 2525.

Bishop of Feldkirch: D.Dr BRUNO WECHNER, 6800 Feldkirch, Bahnhofstr. 13; tel. (05522) 21585.

Bishop of Graz-Seckau: JOHANN WEBER, 8010 Graz, Bischofplatz 4; tel. (0316) 714-110.

Bishop of Gurk: Dr EGON KAPELLARI, 9010 Klagenfurt, Mariannengasse 2; tel. (04222) 57-770.

AUSTRIA

Bishop of Innsbruck: Dr REINHOLD STECHER, 6021 Innsbruck, Wilhelm-Greil-Str. 7; tel. (05222) 33-621.
Bishop of Linz: D.Dr MAXIMILIAN AICHERN, 4010 Linz, Herrenstr. 19; tel. (0732) 272-676.
Bishop of Sankt Pölten: Dr FRANZ ŽAK, 3100 Sankt Pölten, Domplatz 1; tel. (02742) 2101.

Protestant Churches

Baptist Union of Austria: 1160 Vienna, Mörikeweg 16/1; tel. 94-84-465; Pres. Rev. AUGUST HIRNBÖCK.
Evangelische Kirche AB in Österreich (Protestant Church of the Augsburgian Confession): 1180 Vienna, Severin-Schreiber-Gasse 3; tel. (0222) 47-15-23; 379,496 mems; Bishop DIETER KNALL.
Evangelische Kirche HB (Helvetischen Bekenntnisses) (Protestant Church of the Helvetic Confession): 1010 Vienna, Dorotheergasse 16; tel. (0222) 512-83-93; 15,863 mems.; Landessuperintendent Pfr. Mag. PETER KARNER.

Other Christian Churches

Old Catholic: 1010 Vienna, Schottenring 17; tel. (0222) 34-83-94-0; approx. 25,000 mems; Bishop NIKOLAUS HUMMEL.

JUDAISM

There are about 7,000 Jews in Austria.
Israelitischen Kultusgemeinde (Israelite Religious Community): Vienna; Pres. IVAN HACKER.

The Press

Austria's *Wiener Zeitung*, founded in 1703, is the oldest daily paper published in the world, and Austria's press history dates back to 1605, when its first newspaper was published. Article 13 of the 1867 Constitution gave citizens of the Austro-Hungarian Empire the right to express opinions freely and stated that the Press could not be censored. Restrictions on this freedom of the Press are permissible only within the framework of Article 10 (2) of the European Convention of Human Rights.

By the 1922 Press Law, any person who had been subject to an incorrect statement in the Press was granted the right to publish a reply free of charge. This right of reply, which was unsatisfactory to the newspapers as well as to the person in question, was fundamentally reformed by the Media Law of 1982: the post of Verantwortlicher Redakteur (Responsible Editor—who had been penally liable if the newspaper refused to publish a reply) was abolished and the liability was removed. Now a newspaper may refuse to accept the reply if it is untrue.

Any person who feels himself to have been maligned by a newspaper has, in addition to the right of reply, the right to sue the author of the article. Furthermore, he may demand compensation of up to 100,000 Schilling from the publisher. This right is lost, however, if the newspaper can prove that the publication was true or that 'journalistic care' was taken.

In 1961 the Austrian Press Council (Presserat) was founded. It consists of representatives of the publishers and journalists and its principal duties are to watch over the freedom of the Press and to ascertain grievances of the Press. The political parties each have at least one newspaper, and independent papers tend to follow a political line. Although there is a strong Press in some provinces, the country's Press is centred in Vienna. The three highest circulation dailies are the *Neue Kronen-Zeitung*, the *Kurier*, and the *Kleine Zeitung* (Graz).

PRINCIPAL DAILIES

Bregenz

Neue Vorarlberger Tageszeitung: 6901 Bregenz, Kornmarktstr. 18; tel. (05574) 24-6-01; telex 05/7730; f. 1972; morning; independent; Editor WALTER ZEINER; circ. weekdays 43,000, Saturday 38,916.
Vorarlberger Nachrichten: Bregenz, Kirchstr. 35; tel. (05574) 512-0; telex 05/7710; morning; Editor Prof. Dr FRANZ ORTNER; circ. weekdays 62,018, Saturday 64,603.

Graz

Kleine Zeitung: 8011 Graz, Schönaugasse 64; tel. (0316) 70-63-0; telex 03/1782; f. 1904; independent; Editor Dr FRITZ CSOKLICH; circ. weekdays and Sunday 152,682, Friday 194,592.
Neue Zeit: 8054 Graz, Ankerstr. 4; tel. (0316) 28-08-0; telex 03/1703; f. 1945; morning; Socialist Party; Editor JOSEF RIEDLER; circ. 78,342, Friday 84,667.

Südost Tagespost: 8011 Graz, Parkstr. 1; tel. (0316) 71-4-51-0; telex 13/1375; f. 1856; morning; Austrian People's Party; Editor Dr GERFRIED SPERL; circ. weekdays 47,847, Friday 49,220.

Innsbruck

Neue Tiroler Zeitung: 6021 Innsbruck, Südtiroler Platz 6; tel. (05222) 35-1-44; f. 1945; morning; Austrian People's Party; Chief Editor HANS SCHLECHTLEITNER.
Tiroler Tageszeitung: 6020 Innsbruck, Ing.-Etzel-Str. 30; tel. (05222) 74-20; telex 54482; morning; independent; Editor JOSEPH S. MOSER; circ. weekdays 93,442, Saturday 105,754.

Klagenfurt

Kärntner Tageszeitung: 9020 Klagenfurt, Viktringer Ring 28; tel. (04222) 55-1-66; telex 422415; f. 1946; morning except Monday; Socialist; Editor Dr HELLWIG VALENTIN; circ. weekdays 64,624, Friday 67,779.
Kleine Zeitung: 9020 Klagenfurt, Funderstr. 1a; tel. (04222) 55-6-65; telex 04/2413; independent; Editor HEINZ STRITZL; circ. weekdays and Sunday 97,690, Friday 117,477.
Neue Volkszeitung: 9020 Klagenfurt, Völkermarkter Ring 25; tel. (04222) 54-4-40; telex 422430; morning; Austrian People's Party; Chief Editor KURT MARKARITZER; circ. weekdays 30,953, Saturday 34,032.

Linz

Neues Volksblatt: 4020 Linz, Hafenstr. 1–3; tel. (0732) 28-19-01; telex 02/1235; f. 1869; Austrian People's Party; Editor PETER KLAR; circ. weekdays 26,625, Friday 31,304.
Oberösterreichische Nachrichten: 4010 Linz, Promenade 23; tel. (0732) 28050; f. 1865; morning; independent; Editor Dr HERMANN POLZ; circ. weekdays 94,901, Saturday 138,804.
Oberösterreichisches Tagblatt: 4010 Linz, Anastasius-Grün-Str. 6; tel. (0732) 55-2-11; telex 02/1270; Socialist Party; Editor GERALD HÖCHTLER; circ. weekdays 27,083, Friday 30,900.

Salzburg

Salzburger Nachrichten: 5021 Salzburg, Bergstr. 14; tel. (0662) 77-5-91; telex 633583; f. 1945; morning; independent; Editor-in-Chief Prof. Dr KARL-HEINZ RITSCHEL; circ. weekdays 66,679, Saturday 106,162.
Salzburger Tagblatt: 5020 Salzburg, Auerspergstr. 42; tel. (0662) 72491; Socialist Party; Editor KARL THEMESL; circ. weekdays 11,136.
Salzburger Volkszeitung: 5020 Salzburg, Elisabethkai 58; tel. (06222) 79-49-10; telex 06/633627; Austrian People's Party; Editor WILLI SAUBERER; circ. weekdays 13,119.

Vienna

*****Kurier:** 1072 Vienna, Lindengasse 52; tel. (0222) 96-2-10; telex 132631; f. 1954; independent; Editor Dr GÜNTHER WESSIG; circ. weekdays 421,859, Saturday 623,400, Sunday 685,724.
*****Neue Arbeiter-Zeitung:** 1030 Vienna, Viehmarktgasse 4; tel. (0222) 79-02-0; f. 1889; morning; Socialist Party; Editor Dr MANFRED SCHEUCH; circ. weekdays 67,186, Friday 123,505, Saturday 67,626.
*****Neue Kronen-Zeitung:** 1190 Vienna, Muthgasse 2; tel. (0222) 3601-0; telex 114327; f. 1900; independent; Editor HANS DICHAND; circ. weekdays 922,729, Sunday 1,342,293.
*****Die Presse:** 1010 Vienna, Parkring 12A; tel. (0222) 51-4-14; telex 114110; f. 1848; morning; independent; Editor Dr THOMAS CHORHERR; circ. weekdays 59,998, Saturday 79,841.
*****Volksstimme:** 1206 Vienna, Höchstädtplatz 3; tel. 33-56-01; f. 1945; morning; Communist Party; Editor MICHAEL GRABER; circ. weekdays 39,974, Sunday 72,985.
*****Wiener Zeitung:** 1037 Vienna, Rennweg 12a; tel. (0222) 78-76-31; telex 131805; f. 1703; morning; official government paper; Editor HEINZ FAHNLER; circ. 50,000.

* National newspapers.

PRINCIPAL WEEKLIES

Agrar Post: 3430 Tulln, Königstetter Str. 132; f. 1924; independent; agriculture.
Blickpunkt: 6410 Telfs, Blickpunkt-Verlagshaus; tel. (05262) 4611; telex 05/305518; Editor NORBERT WALSER; circ. 50,900.
Die Furche: 1010 Vienna, Singerstr. 7; tel. (0222) 52-51-85; f. 1945; Catholic; Editor Dr HANNES SCHOPF; circ. 14,003.
Die ganze Woche: 1160 Vienna, Odoakergasse 34-36; tel. (0222) 46-26-91; Chief Editor FRANZ PRASSL; circ. 776,350.
Die Industrie: 1010 Vienna, Bösendorferstr. 2/16; tel. (0222) 65-72-15; Editor HERBERT KREJCI.

AUSTRIA

Kärntner Nachrichten: 9020 Klagenfurt, Dr-Arthur-Lemisch-Platz 4; tel. (04222) 51-38-69; Austrian Liberal Party; Editor KURT KNAPPINGER.

Neue Illustrierte Wochenschau: 1070 Vienna VII, Kaiserstr. 8–10; tel. (0222) 93-56-46; Editor PETER R. LANG; circ. 140,350.

Die neue IW-Internationale Wirtschaft: 1050 Vienna, Nikolsdorfer Gasse 7–11; tel. (0222) 55-55-85; economics; Editor NIKOLAUS GERSTMAYER; circ. 11,400.

NFZ—Neue Freie Zeitung: 1010 Vienna, Kärntner Str. 28; tel. (0222) 52-94-52; telex 113610; Austrian Liberal Party; Editor Dr KURT PIRINGER.

Niederösterreichische Nachrichten: 3100 St Pölten, Gutenbergstr. 12; tel. (02742) 61-5-61; telex 01/5512; Editor HANS STRÖBITZER; circ. 124,350.

Oberösterreichische Rundschau: 4010 Linz, Hafenstr. 1–3; tel. (0732) 278-1-21; telex 02/1014; circ. 112,500.

Der Österreichische Bauernbündler: 1014 Vienna, Bankgasse 1–3; tel. 63-96-76; Editor Ing. PAUL GRUBER; circ. 78,100.

Präsent: 6020 Innsbruck, Exlgasse 20; tel. (05222) 81-5-41; telex 05/33620; f. 1892; independent Catholic; Chief Editor BENEDIKT POSCH.

Tiroler Bauernzeitung: 6021 Innsbruck, Brixner Str. 1; tel. (05222) 35-5-21; telex 05/3804; published by Tiroler Bauernbund; Chief Editor NR. Dr Ing. ALOIS LEITNER; circ. 23,000.

Videňské Svobodné Listy: 1050 Vienna, Margaretenplatz 7; weekly for Czech and Slovak communities in Austria; Editor JOSEF JONÁŠ.

Vorarlberger Volksbote: 6901 Bregenz, Anton-Schneider-Str. 32; tel. (05574) 23-6-71; Editor KLAUS MORELL; circ. 21,467.

Samstag: 1081 Vienna, Strozzigasse 8; tel. (0222) 43-59-11; independent; Editor DIETMAR GRIESER; circ. 103,200.

Die Wirtschaft: 1051 Vienna, Nikolsdorfer Gasse 7-11; tel. (0222) 55-55-85; telex 111669; economics; circ. 25,500.

Wochenpost: 8011 Graz, Parkstr. 1; tel. (0316) 77-5-11; independent; illustrated; non-political; Chief Editor Dr MARGIT GRATZER; circ. 25,556.

POPULAR PERIODICALS

Austria-Ski: 6020 Innsbruck, Olympiastr. 10; tel. (05222) 22-1-43; telex 53876; 6 a year; official journal of Austrian Skiing Asscn; Editor Mag. JOSEF SCHMID.

Auto Touring: 1010 Vienna, Schubertring 3; tel. (0222) 72-99-0; telex 133907; monthly; official journal of the Austrian Automobile Organizations; Editor WALTER PRSKAWETZ; circ. 759,900.

Basta: 1050 Vienna, Krongasse 6; tel. (0222) 56-75-31; monthly; Chief Editor WOLFGANG FELLNER.

Bunte Österreich: 1190 Vienna, Muthgasse 2; tel. (0222) 3601-0; illustrated weekly; circ. 124,621.

Frauenblatt: 1081 Vienna, Strozzigasse 8; tel. (0222) 43-59-11; women's weekly; Editor TRAUDE WINKLBAUER; circ. 53,000.

Neue Frau: 1030 Vienna, Viehmarktgasse 4; tel. (0222) 79-02-0; women's weekly magazine; Editor DORIS STOISSER; circ. 79,336.

Profil: 1010 Vienna, Marc-Aurel-Str. 12; tel. (0222) 66-16-70; telex 136404; fortnightly; political general; independent; circ. 88,300.

RZ Illustrierte Romanzeitung: 1072 Vienna, Kaiser Str. 8–10; tel. (0222) 93-56-46; f. 1936; weekly illustrated; Editor HANS ADLASSNIG; circ. 35,223.

Sport und Toto: 1080 Vienna, Piaristengasse 16; tel. (0222) 43-34-63; weekly sports illustrated; Editor RALPH ZEILINGER.

Sportfunk: 1070 Vienna, Schottenfeldgasse 67; tel. (0222) 96-35-33; telex 136557; sporting weekly.

Trend: 1010 Vienna, Marc-Aurel-Str. 12; tel. (0222) 66-16-70; telex 136404; monthly; economics; circ. 72,100.

Welt der Frau: 4020 Linz, Lustenauerstr. 21; tel. (0732) 27-02-91; women's monthly magazine; circ. 80,000.

Wiener: 1060 Vienna, Lehargasse 11; tel. (0222) 56-76-77; telex 111853; monthly; Chief Editor MICHAEL HOPP.

Wochenpresse: 1070 Vienna, Lindengasse 52; tel. (0222) 96-21-0; telex 135869; f. 1946; independent; weekly news magazine; Chief Editor Dr HANS MAGENSCHAB; circ. 47,744.

SPECIALIST PERIODICALS

Acta Chirurgica Austriaca: 1130 Vienna, Gallgasse 40a; tel. (0222) 84-53-46; 6 a year; journal of the Austrian Surgical Soc.; Editor Mag. RICHARD HOLLINEK.

Acta Mechanica: Springer Verlag, 1010 Vienna, Mölkerbastei 5; tel. (0222) 63-96-14-0; f. 1965; irregular; Editors A. PHILLIPS (New Haven, Conn.), H. TROGER, F. ZIEGLER (Vienna), J. ZIEREP (Karlsruhe).

Acta Medica Austriaca: 1130 Vienna, Gallgasse 40A; tel. (0222) 84-53-46; 5 a year; journal of the Austrian Soc. for Internal Medicine and associated societies; Editor Mag. RICHARD HOLLINEK.

Computing: Springer Verlag, 1010 Vienna, Mölkerbastei 5; tel. (0222) 63-96-14-0; f. 1966; irregular; Editors R. ALBRECHT (Innsbruck), R. L. CONSTABLE (Ithaca), W. HÄNDLER (Erlangen), W. KNÖDEL (Stuttgart), W. L. MIRANKER (Yorktown Heights), H. J. STETTER (Vienna).

Forum: 1070 Vienna, Museumstr. 5; tel. 93-33-54; f. 1954; every 2 months; international monthly of Christians and Socialists for radical democracy; Editor-in-Chief MICHAEL SEEBER.

itm praktiker: 1040 Vienna, Phorusgasse 8; tel. (0222) 57-67-65; telex 12553; technical hobbies; Chief Editor GERHARD K. BUCHBERGER; circ. 18,800.

Juristische Blätter: Springer Verlag, 1010 Vienna, Mölkerbastei 5; tel. (0222) 63-96-14-0; f. 1872; fortnightly; Editors F. BYDLINSKI, H. R. KLECATSKY.

Die Landwirtschaft: 1014 Vienna, Bankgasse 1–3; tel. (0222) 63-96-76; f. 1923; monthly; agriculture and forestry; owned and published by Österreichischer Agrarverlag; Editor Ing. FRANZ GEBHART.

Literatur und Kritik: Otto Müller Verlag, 5021 Salzburg, Ernest-Thun-Str. 11; tel. (0662) 72-1-52; f. 1966; 5 a year; Austrian and East European literature and criticism; Editor KURT KLINGER.

Monatshefte für Chemie: 1010 Vienna, Mölkerbastei 5; tel. (0222) 63-96-14-0; f. 1880; monthly; chemistry; Man. Editor K. SCHLÖGL.

Monatshefte für Mathematik: Springer Verlag, 1010 Vienna, Mölkerbastei 5; tel. (0222) 63-96-14-0; f. 1890; irregular.

Österreichische Ärztezeitung: 1010 Vienna, Weihburggasse 10–12; tel. (0222) 52-44-86; f. 1945; fortnightly; organ of the Austrian Medical Board; Editor Prof. Dr GERHARD JOSEF.

Österreichische Ingenieur-und Architekten-Zeitschrift: 1010 Vienna, Mölkerbastei 5; tel. (0222) 63-96-14-0; f. 1958; monthly; Editors W. KOENNE, R. MAYR-HARTING, F. SMOLA.

Österreichische Monatshefte: 1010 Vienna, Kärntnerstr. 51; tel. (0222) 52-26-21; telex 01/1771; f. 1945; monthly; organ of Austrian People's Party; Editor Dr ALFRED GRINSCHGL.

Österreichische Musikzeitschrift: 1010 Vienna, Hegelgasse 13/22; tel. (0222) 52-68-69; f. 1946; monthly; Editors E. LAFITE, Dr M. DIEDERICHS-LAFITE.

Pädiatrie und Pädologie: Springer Verlag, 1010 Vienna, Mölkerbastei 5; f. 1965; irregular; Editor G. WEIPPL.

Reiseland Österreich: 1110 Vienna, Leberstr. 122; tel. (0222) 74-15-95; telex 13/2312; f. 1928; monthly; Editor-in-Chief GEORG KARP; circ. 35,000.

Trotzdem: 1070 Vienna, Neustiftgasse 3; tel. (0222) 93-41-23; monthly; organ of the Socialist Youth of Austria; Editor ALFRED GUSENBAUER.

Die Wacht: 1010 Vienna, Ebendorferstr. 6/V; tel. (0222) 42-54-06; monthly; Catholic; organ of Reichsbund, Verband Katholischer Männer und Jungmänner Österreichs; Editor Fr ANTON SCHWINNER.

Welt der Arbeit: 1030 Vienna, Viehmarktgasse 4; tel. (0222) 79-02-0; socialist industrial journal; Editor KURT HORAK; circ 69,516.

Wiener klinische Wochenschrift: 1010 Vienna, Mölkerbastei 5; tel. (0222) 63-96-14-0; f. 1887; medical bi-weekly; Editors O. KRAUPP, E. DEUTSCH.

Wiener Medizinische Wochenschrift: 1130 Vienna, Gallgasse 40A; tel. (0222) 84-53-46; 2 a month; journal of graduate medical education; Editor Mag. RICHARD HOLLINEK.

Die Zukunft: 1030 Vienna, Viehmarktgasse 4; tel. (0222) 79-02-0; monthly; Socialist party; Editor JOHANN SCHÜLLER.

NEWS AGENCIES

Austria Presse-Agentur (APA): Internationales Pressezentrum (IPZ), 1199 Vienna, Gunoldstr. 14; tel. (0222) 36-05-0; telex 114721; f. 1946; co-operative agency of the Austrian Newspapers and Broadcasting Co (private company); 37 mems; Man. Dir Dr WOLFGANG VYSLOZIL; Chief Editor Prof. Dr OTTO SCHÖNHERR.

AUSTRIA

Foreign Bureaux

Agence France-Presse (AFP): IPZ, 1199 Vienna, Gunoldstr. 14; tel. (0222) 36-31-87; telex 115833; Correspondent DIDIER FAUQUEUX.

Agenzia Nazionale Stampa Associata (ANSA) (Italy): IPZ, 1199 Vienna, Gunoldstr. 14; tel. (0222) 36-13-00; telex 114891; Bureau Chief LUCIANO COSSETTO.

Allgemeiner Deutscher Nachrichtendienst (ADN) (German Democratic Republic): 1030 Vienna, Reisnerstr. 18/4/18; Correspondent HEINZ SCHINDLER.

Associated Press (AP) (USA): IPZ, 1199 Vienna, Gunoldstr. 14; tel. 36-41-58; telex 115930; Bureau Chief LARRY GERBER.

Československá tisková kancelář (ČTK) (Czechoslovakia): 1080 Vienna, Auerspergstr. 15; tel (0222) 42-03-75; telex 114215.

Deutsche Presse-Agentur (dpa) (Federal Republic of Germany): IPZ, 1199 Vienna, Gunoldstr. 14; tel. 362158; telex 114633; Correspondent ALEX WACHSMUTH.

Inter Press Service (IPS) (Italy): IPZ, 1199 Vienna, Gunoldstr. 14; tel. (0222) 36-85-06; telex 136081; Dir FEDERICO NIER-FISCHER.

Kyodo Tsushin (Japan): IPZ, 1199 Vienna, Gunoldstr. 14; tel. (0222) 36-15-20; telex 135736; Bureau Chief KIYOSHI HASUMI.

Magyar Távirati Iroda (MTI) (Hungary): 1010 Vienna, Teinfaltstr. 4; tel. (0222) 63-31-38; telex 115025; Correspondent ANDRÁS HELTAI.

Novinska Agencija Tanjug (Tanjug) (Yugoslavia): IPZ, 1190 Vienna, Gunoldstr. 14.

Reuter (UK): 1010 Vienna 1, Börsegasse 11; tel. (0222) 66-36-93; telex 1-14645; Chief Correspondent D. STOREY.

Telegrafnoye Agentstvo Sovetskovo Soyuza (TASS) (USSR): 1040 Vienna, Grosse Neugasse 28; tel. (0222) 56-11-46.

United Press International (UPI) (USA): 1010 Vienna, Opernring 1/E/6; tel. (0222) 587-36-46; telex 111662.

Xinhua News Agency (People's Republic of China): 1030 Vienna, Reisnerstr. 21; tel. (0222) 73-41-40; telex 134384; Correspondent LI CHUNGUANG.

Central News Agency (CNA) (Taiwan) is also represented.

PRESS ASSOCIATIONS

Österreichischer Zeitschriftenverband (Asscn of Periodical Publishers): 1010 Vienna, Parkring 2; tel. (0222) 512-99-75; f. 1945; 162 mems; Pres. Dr RUDOLF BOHMANN.

Verband Österreichischer Zeitungsherausgeber und Zeitungsverleger (Austrian Newspaper Publishers' Asscn): 1010 Vienna, Schreyvogelgasse 3; tel. (0222) 63-61-78; telex 114223; f. 1945; all daily and most weekly papers are mems; Pres. Dir JULIUS KAINZ; Sec.-Gen. Mag. FRANZ IVAN.

Publishers

Akademische Druck- u. Verlagsanstalt: 8011 Graz, Neufeldweg 75, Postfach 598; tel. (0316) 41-1-53; telex 312234; f. 1949; scholarly reprints and new works, facsimile editions of Codices; Dir MANFRED KRAMER.

Bergland Verlag GmbH: 1051 Vienna, Spengergasse 39; tel. (0222) 55-56-41; f. 1937; belles-lettres, art, history, fiction; Owner and Dir FRIEDRICH GEYER.

Betz, Annette, Verlag: 1091 Vienna, Alserstr. 24; tel. (0222) 48-15-38; telex 114802; f. 1962; Dirs Dr OTTO MANG, Dkfm. MANFRED SETZER.

Verlag Hermann Böhlaus Nachf. GmbH: 1014 Vienna, Dr Karl Lueger-Ring 12; tel. (0222) 63-87-35; f. 1947; history, law, philology, the arts, sociology; Owner Dr DIETRICH RAUCH.

Bohmann Druck und Verlag GmbH & Co KG: 1110 Vienna, Leberstr. 122; tel. (0222) 74-15-95; telex 132312; f. 1936; trade, technical and industrial books and periodicals; Dir Dr RUDOLF BOHMANN.

Christian Brandstätter, Verlag und Edition: 1080 Vienna, Wickenburggasse 26; tel. (0222) 48-38-14.

Wilhelm Braumüller, GmbH: 1092 Vienna, Servitengasse 5; tel. (0222) 34-81-24; f. 1783; sociology, politics, history, ethnology, linguistics, psychology and philosophy; university publrs; Dir BRIGITTE KALTSCHMID.

Franz Deuticke Verlagsges. mbH: 1011 Vienna, Helferstorferstr. 4; tel. (0222) 63-43-45; f. 1878; science text books, school books; Dirs Dr SCHARETZER, KARL DONHOFER.

Ludwig Doblinger, KG: 1010 Vienna I, Dorotheergasse 10; tel. (0222) 51-5-03; telex 133008; f. 1876; music; Dir HELMUTH PANY.

Europa Verlag GmbH: 1232 Vienna, Altmannsdorfer Str. 154-156; tel. (0222) 67-26-22.

Freytag-Berndt und Artaria KG Kartographische Anstalt: 1071 Vienna VII, Schottenfeldgasse 62; tel. (0222) 93-95-01; telex 133526; f. 1879 (1770—Artaria); geography, maps and atlases; Chair. Dr WALTER PETROWITZ, HARALD HOCHENEGG.

Gerold & Co: 1011 Vienna, Graben 31; tel. (0222) 52-22-35; telex 136157; f. 1867; philology, literature, Eastern Europe, sociology and philosophy; Dirs Dr HEINRICH NEIDER, HANS NEUSSER.

Globus Zeitungs-, Druck- und Verlagsanstalt GmbH: 1206 Vienna, Höchstädtplatz 3; tel. (0222) 334501; telex 114629; f. 1945; newspapers, political science, popular sciences, fiction; Gen. Man. Dr H. ZASLAWSKI.

Herder & Co: 1011 Vienna, Wollzeile 33, Postfach 248; tel. (0222) 512-14-13; telex 01/1046; f. 1886; religion, theology, history, juvenile; Dir FRITZ WIENINGER.

Herold Druck- und Verlagsgesellschaft mbH: 1080 Vienna, Strozzigasse 8; tel. (0222) 43-15-51; telex 111760; f. 1947; art, history, politics, religion; Gen. Dir Mag. FRITZ MÜLLER.

Hölder-Pichler-Tempsky Verlag: 1096 Vienna, Frankgasse 4; tel. (0222) 43-89-93; f. 1922; school text-books; Man. Dir GUSTAV GLÖCKLER.

Brüder Hollinek: 1130 Vienna, Gallgasse 40A; tel. (0222) 84-53-46; f. 1872; science, medicine, law and administration, dictionaries; Dir Mag. RICHARD HOLLINEK.

Jugend und Volk Verlagsges. mbH: 1150 Vienna, Anschützgasse 1; tel. (0222) 87-25-15; telex 136103; f. 1921; pedagogics, art, literature, children's books; Dir Dr OTTO SCHIMPF.

Verlag Kremayr & Scheriau: 1121 Vienna, Niederhofstr. 37; tel. (0222) 83-45-01; telex 1/31405; f. 1951; non-fiction, history, children's books.

Kunstverlag Wolfrum: 1010 Vienna, Augustinerstr. 10; tel. (0222) 512-74-87-0; f. 1919; art; Dirs HUBERT WOLFRUM, MONIKA ENGEL.

Leykam Verlag: 8011 Graz, Stempfergasse 3; tel. (0316) 76-6-76-0; telex 03-2209; art, literature, academic, law; Dir Mag. K. BRUNNER.

Manz'sche Verlags- und Universitätsbuchhandlung: 1014 Vienna, Kohlmarkt 16; tel. (0222) 63-17-81; telex 113178; f. 1849; law, political and economic sciences; textbooks and schoolbooks; Exec. principals Dkfm. FRANZ STEIN, Dr ANTON C. HILSCHER.

Wilhelm Maudrich: 1097 Vienna, Lazarettgasse 1; tel. (0222) 42-47-12; telex 135177; f. 1909; medical; Dir GERHARD GROIS.

Otto Müller Verlag: 5021 Salzburg, Ernest-Thun-Str. 11; tel. (0662) 72-1-52; f. 1937; general; Man. ALEXANDER WEIGER.

Paul Neff Verlag KG: 1010 Vienna, Johannesgasse 12; tel. (0222) 513-10-31; f. 1829; fiction, biographies, etc.

R. Oldenbourg KG: 1030 Vienna, Neulinggasse 26/3; tel. (0222) 72-62-58; f. 1959; Dirs Dr KARL CORNIDES, Dr THOMAS CORNIDES.

Verlag Orac: 1010 Vienna, Graben 17; tel. (0222) 52-85-52; telex 136365; f. 1946; Dir HELMUT HANUSCH.

Österreichischer Gewerbeverlag GmbH: 1014 Vienna, Herrengasse 10; tel. (0222) 63-07-68; f. 1945; general; Man. F. SCHARETZER.

Pinguin Verlag Pawlowski KG: 6021 Innsbruck, Lindenbühelweg 2; tel. (05222) 81-8-83; illustrated books; Dirs OLAF PAWLOWSKI, HELLA PFLANZER.

Residenz Verlag GmbH: 5020 Salzburg, Gaisbergstr. 6; tel. (0662) 25-7-71; telex 6/32887; Dir Dr JOCHEN JUNG.

Anton Schroll & Co: 1051 Vienna, Spengergasse 39 (and at Munich); tel. (0222) 55-56-41; f. 1884; art books; Man. F. GEYER.

Springer-Verlag: 1010 Vienna, Mölkerbastei 5; tel. (0222) 63-96-14; telex 114506; f. 1924; medicine, science, technology, law, sociology, economics, periodicals; Dirs K. F. SPRINGER, B. SCHWEDER.

Leopold Stocker Verlag: 8011 Graz, Bürgergasse 11; tel. (0316) 71636; f. 1917; history, nature, hunting, fiction, poetry, textbooks; Dir Dr ILSE DVORAK-STOCKER.

Verlag Styria: 8011 Graz, Schönaugasse 64; tel. (0316) 77-56-10; telex 3 1782; f. 1869; literature, history, theology, philosophy, youth books; Gen. Dir Dr HANNS SASSMANN.

Verlagsanstalt Tyrolia GmbH: 6020 Innsbruck, Exlgasse 20; tel. (05222) 81-5-41; f. 1907; geography, history, science, religion, fiction; Chair. Dr GEORG SCHIEMER.

AUSTRIA   *Directory*

Carl Ueberreuter Verlag: 1091 Vienna, Alser Str. 24; tel. (0222) 48-15-38; telex 114802; popular science, children's, education, history; Proprs DKfm. Dr OTTO MANG, MICHAEL SALZER.

Universal Edition: 1015 Vienna, Postfach 3, Bösendorfer Str. 12; tel. (0222) 65-86-95; telex 11397; f. 1901; music; Dirs Dr J. JURANEK, T. NORDWALL.

Urban & Schwarzenberg, KG: 1096 Vienna, Frankgasse 4; tel. (0222) 42-27-31; f. 1866; science, medicine; Dir MICHAEL URBAN.

Paul Zsolnay Verlag GmbH: 1041 Vienna, Prinz Eugen-Str. 30 (also in Hamburg); tel. (0222) 65-76-61; telex 132279; f. 1923; fiction, poetry, general; Dir HANS W. POLAK.

Government Publishing Houses

Österreichische Staatsdruckerei (Austrian State Printing Office): 1037 Vienna, Rennweg 12A; tel. (0222) 72-61-51; f. 1804; law, art reproductions; Dir ARIBERT SCHWARZMANN.

Österreichischer Bundesverlag GmbH: 1015 Vienna, Schwarzenbergstr. 5; tel. (0222) 512-25-61; telex 131159; f. 1772 by Empress Maria Theresia; school text-books, education, educational periodicals, science, children's books, books about Austria and sports; foundation administered by the State; Dir Komm. Rat Dkfm. KURT BIAK.

PUBLISHERS' ASSOCIATION

Hauptverband des österreichischen Buchhandels (Association of Austrian Publishers and Booksellers): 1010 Vienna I, Grünangergasse 4; tel. (0222) 512-15-35; f. 1859; Pres. OTTO HAUSA; Gen. Sec. Dkfm. Dr GERHARD PROSSER; 670 mems.

Radio and Television

In December 1985 there were 596 radio transmitters in the provinces, broadcasting two national programmes (one for 18 hours and one for 24 hours), 10 local programmes and an overseas service on shortwave. In December 1985 there were 887 television transmitters. Two television channels broadcast an average of 22 hours per day. In 1986 there were 2,620,960 registered radio receivers and 2,419,851 television receivers.

Österreichischer Rundfunk (ORF) (Austrian Broadcasting Company): 1136 Vienna, Würzburggasse 30; tel. (0222) 82-91-0; f. 1955; controls all radio and television in Austria; Dir-Gen. THADDÄUS PODGORSKI; Dirs JOHANNES KUNZ, ERNST WOLFRAM MARBOE (Television Programmes), ERNST GRISSEMAN (Radio Programmes), Dipl. Ing. NORBERT WASSICZEK (Technology), Dr WALTER SKALA (Finance and Administration).

Finance

(cap. = capital; p.u. = paid up; dep. = deposits; m. = million; brs = branches; amounts in Schilling)

BANKS

Banks in Austria, apart from the National Bank, belong to one of four groups. The first group of so-called commercial banks, which operate on a national basis, includes private banks and the Austrian subsidiaries of foreign credit institutes. The two largest commercial banks which, with the Austrian National Bank, make up Austria's 'big three', are Creditanstalt Bankverein and Österreichische Länderbank AG. The second group consists of the regional banks, which mainly provide mortgage facilities. The third group comprises specialized banks concerned primarily with investment and credit facilities. In the fourth group of multi-functional banks are the Savings Banks, of which there were 130 in 1985, Raiffeisenkassen (Co-operative Banks) (890 in 1985) and the Volksbanken (119 in 1985). Both the Savings and Co-operative banks provide most retail bank services. Legislation which came into effect on 1 March 1979 further liberalized credit law and encouraged the trend towards universal banking. Banking secrecy and advantages such as the absence of a limit on foreign deposits have made Austria as attractive as Switzerland as a secure repository for foreign capital.

Central Bank

Oesterreichische Nationalbank (Austrian National Bank): 1090 Vienna, Otto Wagner-Platz 3; tel. 4360-0; telex 114669; f. 1922; Pres. Prof. Dr STEPHAN KOREN; Gen. Man. Dkfm. Dr HEINZ KIENZL; 7 brs.

Commercial Banks

AVA—Bank GmbH: 1015 Vienna, Operngasse 2; tel. (0222) 51-5-71; telex 111173; f. 1927; cap. 200m., dep. 7,929m. (1985); Gen. Man. Dr JOHANN BURGEMEISTER; 37 brs.

Bank der Österreichischen Postsparkasse AG: 1015 Vienna, Opernring 3–5; tel. (0222) 58809-0; telex 112268; cap. 120m., dep. 9,814m. (1985); Chair. and Gen-Man. Komm. Rat FREIMUT DOBRETSBERGER.

Bank für Arbeit und Wirtschaft AG: 1010 Vienna, Seitzergasse 2-4; tel. (0222) 6629-0; telex 115311; f. 1947; cap. 4,806m., dep. 154,744m. (1985); Chair. and Gen. Man. Komm. Rat WALTER FLÖTTL; 119 brs.

Bank für Wirtschaft und Freie Berufe AG: 1072 Vienna, Zieglergasse 5; tel. (0222) 96-15-46; telex 132346; f. 1914; Mans PETER SCHLADOFSKY, PETER WENINGER.

Bank Gebrüd. Gutmann Nfg AG: 1011 Vienna, Schwarzenbergplatz 16; tel. (0222) 65-76-36; telex 136506; f. 1922; cap. 16m.; Gen. Man. Dr HELMUTH E. FREY.

Bank Winter & Co AG: 1011 Vienna, Singerstr. 10; tel. (0222) 51-50-40-0; telex 112462; cap. 200m., dep. 24,600m. (1985); Chair. SIMON MOSKOVICS; 1 br.

Bankhaus Brüll & Kallmus AG: 1011 Vienna, Rotenturmstr. 5-9; tel. (0222) 663601; telex 114266; cap. 100m.; Gen. Man. PIERO ZAINO; 1 br.

Bankhaus Feichtner & Co AG: 1011 Vienna, Wipplingerstr. 1; tel. (0222) 63-16-06; telex 114260; cap. 100m., dep. 4,998m. (1985); Dir Dr WOLFGANG WIPLER.

Bankhaus Rössler AG: 1015 Vienna, Kärntner Ring 17; tel. (0222) 51-29-696; telex 131815; cap. 30m. (1985); Chair. and Man. HEINZ HIKADE.

Bankhaus Schelhammer & Schattera: 1011 Vienna, Goldschmiedgasse 3; tel. (0222) 52-06-06; telex 113206; f. 1832; private bank; Partners Komm. Rat Dipl.-Ing. JOSEF MELCHART, Dr ROBERT NORDEN; 1 br.

Bankhaus C. A. Steinhäusser: 1014 Vienna, Kohlmarkt 1/10; tel. (0222) 52-93-15; telex 133146; cap. 50m. (1985); Man. Komm. Rat Dr GERHARD SAMES.

Central Wechsel- und Creditbank AG: 1015 Vienna, Kärntner Str. 43; tel. (0222) 51-5-66-0; telex 112387; cap. 160m. (1985); Gen. Man. Dr KÁLMÁN MÉSZÁROS.

Centro Internationale Handelsbank AG: 1015 Vienna, Tegetthofstr. 1; tel. (0222) 51-5-20-0; telex 136990; cap. 250m. (1985); Exec. Bd. Dr GERHARD VOGT, JAN WOLOSZYN, CHRISTIAN SPERK.

Chase Manhattan Bank (Austria) AG: 1011 Vienna, Parkring 12A, Postfach 582; tel. (0222) 51-5-89; telex 112570; cap. 20m., total resources 3,451m. (Dec. 1985); Gen. Man. Mag. ANDREAS TREICHL.

Citibank (Austria) AG: 1015 Vienna, Lothringer Str. 7; tel. 75-65-34; telex 112105; cap. 50m.; Chair. and Gen. Man. CHRISTOPH KRAUS.

Creditanstalt-Bankverein: 1011 Vienna, Schottengasse 6; tel. (0222) 6622-0; telex 133030; f. 1855; cap. 3,000m., dep. 329,111m. (May 1986); Chair. and Gen. Man. Dkfm. Dr HANNES ANDROSCH; 161 brs.

Donau-Bank AG: 1011 Vienna, Parkring 6; tel. (0222) 5-15-35; telex 116473; f. 1974; jointly owned by the State Bank of the USSR and the Bank for Foreign Trade of the USSR; cap. 270m.; Chair. and Gen. Man. EDUARD P. GOSTEV.

Elsässische Bank AG: 1015 Vienna, Schwarzenbergplatz 1; tel. (0222) 72-51-03-0; telex 133766; wholly-owned subsidiary of Société Générale Alsacienne de Banque (France); cap. 75m.; Gen. Man. Dr ALBERT MÜRSCH.

Focobank (Austria) AG: 1011 Vienna, Rathausstr. 20, Postfach 306; tel. (0222) 43-61-61; telex 114911; cap. 45m., dep. 1,484m.; Chair and Gen. Man. Dkfm. Dr ERICH STÖGER.

Internationale Bank für Aussenhandel AG: 1011 Vienna, Neuer Markt 1; tel. (0222) 51-5-56-0; telex 113564; f. 1970; cap. 75m., dep. 6,589m. (1985); Dirs Dr WALTER KOLLER, Dkfm. HUBERT WIELEBNOWSKI.

Kathrein & Co Bankkommanditgesellschaft: 1013 Vienna, Wipplingerstr. 25; tel. 66-35-11; telex 1 14123; f. 1924; Dirs Dr FELIX ANSELMI, Mag. PETER KOHOUT, MANFRED WOLZT.

Meinl Bank GmbH: 1015 Vienna, Kärntner Ring 2; tel. (0222) 65-47-31; telex 132256; cap. 40m.; Dirs JULIUS MEINL, FRANZ MAHRINGER, ERNST WIMMER.

Mercurbank GmbH: 1015 Vienna, Kärntner Ring 8; tel. (0222) 6 5932-0; telex 131439; cap. 90m., dep. 4,358m. (1985); Mans. MANFRED KOPRIVA, Dkfm. ROBERT SCHILDER; 31 brs.

AUSTRIA

Österreichische Länderbank AG: 1011 Vienna, Am Hof 2; tel. (0222) 6624-0; telex 115561; f. 1880; cap. 1,350m., dep. 159,458m. (Dec. 1985); Gen. Man. Dkfm. GERHARD WAGNER; 132 brs.

Österreichische Verkehrskreditbank AG: 1081 Vienna, Auerspergstr. 17; tel. (0222) 42-76-48-0; telex 115965; cap. 50m. (1985); Chair. and Gen. Man. Dr OTTO ASCHENBRENNER.

Österreichisches Credit-Institut AG: 1011 Vienna, Herrengasse 12; tel. (0222) 63-56-61; telex 114821; f. 1896; cap. 275m.; Gen. Man. Dr GEROLD PIRINGER; 42 brs.

Schoeller & Co Bank AG: 1011 Vienna, Renngasse 1–3; tel. (0222) 635671; telex 114219; f. 1833; cap. 200m., dep. 15,676m. (1985); Chair. and Gen. Man. Dr HERBERT SCHOELLER; 12 brs.

Regional Banks

Bank für Handel und Industrie AG: 8011 Graz, Herrengasse 28; tel. (0316) 71-6-87; telex 31298; f. 1956; cap. 20m.; Dirs REINHARD FISCHER, Konsul ERHARD WRESSNIG; 3 brs.

Bank für Kärnten und Steiermark AG: 9010 Klagenfurt, Dr Arthur Lemisch-Platz 5; tel. (04222) 51-15-55; telex 422454; f. 1922; cap. 200m., dep. 15,278m. (1984); Gen. Man. MAXIMILIAN MERAN; Dirs Komm. Rat HERBERT KAISER,Dr HEIMO PENKER; 28 brs.

Bank für Oberösterreich und Salzburg: 4010 Linz, Hauptplatz 10-11; tel. (0732) 2802/0; telex 21802; f. 1869; cap. 500m., dep. 36,191m. (Dec. 1985); Gen. Man. Dr HERMANN BELL; 74 brs.

Bank für Tirol und Vorarlberg AG: 6021 Innsbruck, Erlerstr. 9; tel. (05222) 728-0; telex 53535; f. 1926; cap. 250m., dep. 16,688m. (1985); Gen. Man. Komm. Rat Dr GERHARD MOSER; Dir Dr OTTO KASPAR; 33 brs.

Bankhaus Daghofer & Co AG: 5010 Salzburg, Griesgasse 11; tel. (0662) 85-15-01-0; telex 633267; Chair. ARMIN HITZENBERGER; 2 brs.

Eisenstädter Bank AG: 7001 Eisenstadt, Hauptstr. 31; tel. (02682) 2501; telex 17610; cap. 35m.; Dirs FRANZ BERKI, ERNST GASSNER; 6 brs.

Salzburger Kredit- und Wechsel-Bank AG: 5024 Salzburg, Makartplatz 3; tel. (0662) 72516-0; telex 633625; f. 1921; cap. 40m.; Dir GEORG EBNER; 3 brs.

Steiermärkische Bank GmbH: 8011 Graz, Hauptplatz, Rathaus; tel. (0316) 7032; telex 311930; f. 1922; cap. 100m.; Gen. Man. Dr JAN OHMS.

Specialized Banks

Österreichische Investitionskredit AG: 1013 Vienna, Renngasse 10; tel. (0222) 6660-0; telex 114495; cap. 400m.; Chair. and Gen. Man. Dr ANTON OSOND.

Österreichische Kommunalkredit AG: 1011 Vienna, Renngasse 10; tel. (0222) 63-26-77-0; cap. 100m.

Österreichische Kontrollbank AG: 1010 Vienna, Am Hof 4; tel. (0222) 6627-0; telex 132747; f. 1946; export financing, stock exchange clearing, money market operations, etc.; cap. 100m. (Dec. 1985); Chair. and Gen. Man. Komm. Rat HELMUT H. HASCHEK.

Savings Banks

Girozentrale und Bank der österreichischen Sparkassen AG (GZ) (Central Bank of the Austrian Savings Banks): 1011 Vienna, Schubertring 5; tel. (0222) 7294-0; telex 132591; f. 1937; central institution of savings banks; cap. 1,725m., total assets 224,100m. (1985); Chair. and Gen. Man. Komm. Rat Dr KARL PALE.

Die Erste Österreichische Spar-Casse (First Austrian Savings Bank): 1010 Vienna, Graben 21; tel. (0222) 6618; telex 114012; f. 1819; cap. and reserves 3,816.6m., dep. 108,517.6m. (Dec. 1985); Chair. and CEO Dr HANS HAUMER; 110 brs.

Österreichische Postsparkasse: 1018 Vienna, Georg-Coch Platz 2; tel. (0222) 51-40-00; telex 111663; cap. 1,518m., dep. 133,123m. (1985); Gov. Dkfm. KURT NÖSSLINGER; 12 brs.

Zentralsparkasse und Kommerzialbank Wien (Z) (Savings Bank): 1030 Vienna, Vordere Zollamtsstr. 13; tel. (0222) 7292-0; telex 133615; f. 1905; cap. 3,773m., dep. 143,019m. (1984); Chair. Prof. Dr HELMUT ZILK; 165 brs.

Co-operative Banks

Genossenschaftliche Zentralbank AG (GZB-Vienna): 1011 Vienna, Herrengasse 1; tel. (0222) 6662-0; telex 136989; f. 1927; cap. 1,600m., dep. 134,449m. (June 1986); central institute of the Austrian Raiffeisen banking group; Pres. Dr KARL GRUBER; Gen. Man. Komm. Rat Dr HELLMUTH KLAUHS; 3 brs.

Österreichische Volksbanken-AG: 1090 Vienna, Peregringasse 3; tel. (0222) 3134-0; telex 134206; f. 1922; cap. 450m., dep. 48,109m. (1985); Chair. and CEO ROBERT MÄDL.

Bankers' Organization

Verband österreichischer Banken und Bankiers (Asscn of Austrian Banks and Bankers): 1013 Vienna, Börsegasse 11; tel. (0222) 66-17-71; telex 132824; f. 1945; Pres. Dr HANNES ANDROSCH; Gen. Secs Dr WILHELM HIRSCHMANN, Dr FRITZ DIWOK; 60 mems.

STOCK EXCHANGE

Wiener Börsekammer (Vienna Stock Exchange): 1011 Vienna, Wipplingerstr. 34; tel. (0222) 63-37-66; telex 132447; f. 1771; two sections: Stock Exchange, Commodity Exchange; Pres. Dkfm. GERHARD WAGNER; Gen. Sec. Dr KURT NEUTEUFEL.

INSURANCE COMPANIES

In 1986 there were 69 insurance organizations in Austria. A selection of companies is given below.

Anglo-Elementar Versicherungs-AG: 1015 Vienna, Kärntner Ring 12; tel. (0222) 65-57-67; telex 132355; Gen. Man. Dr OTTHEINRICH FRÖLICH.

Austria Österreichische Versicherungs-AG: 1021 Vienna II, Untere Donaustr. 25; tel. (0222) 24-75-11; telex 135308; f. 1936; Gen. Man. HERBERT SCHIMETSCHEK.

Donau Allgemeine Versicherungs-AG: 1010 Vienna, Schottenring 15; tel. (0222) 31-46-11; f. 1867; all classes; Gen. Man. Dr GERHARD PUSCHMANN.

Erste Allgemeine Versicherungs-AG: 1010 Vienna, Brandstätte 7–9; tel. (0222) 6338-0; telex 114085; f. 1882; Gen. Man. Dr DIETRICH KARNER.

Grazer Wechselseitige Versicherung: 8011 Graz, Herrengasse 18–20; tel. (0316) 7037-0; telex 31414; f. 1828; all classes; Gen. Man. Dr FRIEDRICH FALL.

Internationale Unfall- und Schadenversicherung AG: 1011 Vienna, Tegetthoffstr. 7; tel. (0222) 51403-0; telex 112111; cap. 200,000m. (1985); Gen. Man. Mag. Dr JOSEF CUDLIN.

Versicherungsanstalt der österreichischen Bundesländer Versicherungs-AG: 1021 Vienna, Praterstr. 1–7; tel. (0222) 2619-0; telex 134800; Gen. Man. Dr WALTER PETRAK.

Wiener Allianz Versicherungs-AG: 1131 Vienna, Hietzinger Kai 101–105; tel. (0222) 94-85-11-0; telex 134222; f. 1860; all classes except life insurance; Gen. Man. Dr ERNST BAUMGARTNER.

Wiener Städtische Wechselseitige Versicherungsanstalt (Municipal Insurance Co of the City of Vienna): 1011 Vienna I, Schottenring 30; tel. (0222) 6339-0; telex 135140; f. 1898; all classes; Chair. The Mayor of Vienna; Gen. Man. Dipl. Kfm. Dr ERICH GÖTTLICHER.

Zürich Kosmos Versicherungen AG: 1015 Vienna I, Schwarzenbergplatz 15; tel. (0222) 65-36-31-0; telex 133375; f. 1910; all classes; Gen. Man. Dr WERNER FABER.

Insurance Organization

Verband der Versicherungsunternehmungen Österreichs (Asscn of Austrian Insurance Companies): 1030 Vienna III, Schwarzenbergplatz 7; tel. (0222) 75-76-51-0; telex 133289; f. 1945; Pres. Dr ERNEST BAUMGARTNER; Gen. Sec. Dr HERBERT PFLÜGER.

Trade and Industry

CHAMBERS OF COMMERCE

All Austrian enterprises must be members of the Economic Chambers. The Federal Economic Chamber promotes international contacts and represents the economic interest of trade and industry on a federal level. Its Foreign Trade Organization includes about 90 offices abroad.

Bundeskammer der gewerblichen Wirtschaft (Federal Economic Chamber): 1045 Vienna, Wiedner Hauptstr. 63; tel. (0222) 6505; telex 111871; f. 1946; six sections: Commerce, Industry, Small-scale Production, Banking and Insurance, Transport and Tourism; these divisions are subdivided into branch associations; Local Economic Chambers with divisions and branch associations in each of the nine Austrian provinces; Pres. Abg. z. Nationalrat RUDOLF SALLINGER; Sec.-Gen. D.Dr KARL KEHRER; 253,500 mems.

INDUSTRIAL ASSOCIATIONS

Bundeskammer der gewerblichen Wirtschaft—Bundessektion Industrie: 1045 Vienna I, Wiedner Hauptstr. 63; tel. (0222) 6505; telex 11871; f. 1896 as Zentralverband der Industrie Österreichs (Central Federation of Austrian Industry), merged into present organization 1947; Chair. Dipl. Volksw. PHILIPP SCHOELLER;

Deputy Chair. Pres. Dr Christian Beurle; Dir Dr Friedrich Placek; comprises the following industrial federations:

Fachverband der Audiovisions- und Filmindustrie (Films): 1045 Vienna, Wiedner Hauptstr. 63; tel. (0222) 6505; telex 3222440; Chair. Prof. Walther K. Stoitzner, Dr Elmar A. Peterlunger; 750 mems.

Fachverband der Bauindustrie (Building): 1030 Vienna, Engelsberggasse 4; tel. (0222) 73-65-04-0; telex 135284; Chair. Dipl.-Ing. Friedrich Fellerer; Dir Dr Josef Fink.

Fachverband der Bekleidungsindustrie (Clothing): 1030 Vienna III, Schwarzenbergplatz 4; Chair. Alfons Schneider; Dir Mag. Christoph Haidinger; 470 mems.

Fachverband der Bergwerke und Eisen erzeugenden Industrie (Mining and Iron Producing): 1015 Vienna, Goethegasse 3, Postfach 300; tel. (0222) 52-46-01-0; Chair. Gen. Dir K.R. Dr Ing. Friedrich Schmollgruber; Sec. Ing. Mag. Hermann Prinz.

Fachverband der Chemischen Industrie (Chemicals): 1045 Vienna 4, Wiedner Hauptstr. 63; tel. (0222) 6505; Chair. Gen. Dir Komm. Rat Dkfm. Dr Herbert Spendul; Dir Mag. Dr Harald Strassnitzky.

Fachverband der Eisen- und Metallwarenindustrie Österreichs (Iron and Metal Goods): 1045 Vienna 4, Wiedner Hauptstr. 63, Postfach 335; tel. (0222) 6505; f. 1908; Chair. Komm. Rat Hannes Folter; Dir Dipl. Kfm. Gottfried Taurer; 800 mems.

Fachverband der Elektroindustrie (Electrical): 1010 Vienna, Rathausplatz 8; tel. (0222) 42-55-97; Dir Dr Heinz Raschka.

Fachverband der Erdölindustrie (Oil): 1031 Vienna, Erdbergstr. 72; tel. 73-23-48; telex 13 21 38; f. 1947; Gen. Dir Dr Herbert Kaes; Gen. Sec. Dr Herbert Lang; 21 mems.

Fachverband der Fahrzeugindustrie (Vehicles): 1045 Vienna 4, Wiedner Hauptstr. 63; tel. (0222) 6505; telex 613222440; Pres. Dipl.-Ing. H. Michael Malzacher; Gen. Sec. Mag. Erik Baier 160 mems.

Fachverband der Gas- und Wärmeversorgungsunternehmungen (Gas and Heating): 1010 Vienna, Schubertring 14; tel. (0222) 53-15-88; Chair. Gen. Dir Komm. Rat Dr Karl Reisinger; Dir Dkfm. Gerhard Janaczek.

Fachverband der Giessereiindustrie (Foundries): 1045 Vienna 4, Wiedner Hauptstr. 63, Postfach 339; tel. (0222) 6505-3463; telex 3222440; Chair. Komm. Rat Karl Vejskal; Dir Dr Kurt Krenkel.

Fachverband der Glasindustrie (Glass): 1045 Vienna 4, Wiedner Hauptstr. 63, Postfach 328; tel. (0222) 6505; telex 111871; Chair. Dipl. Ing. Raimund Crammer; Dir Dr Peter Schoepf; 65 mems.

Fachverband der Holzverarbeitenden Industrie (Wood Processing): 1037 Vienna III, Schwarzenbergplatz 4, Postfach 123; tel. (0222) 72-26-01; telex 134891; f. 1946; Chair. Komm. Rat Hanno Weiss; Dir Dr Georg Penka.

Fachverband der Ledererzeugenden Industrie (Leather Producing): 1045 Vienna 4, Wiedner Hauptstr. 63, Postfach 312; tel. (0222) 6505; telex 3222440; f. 1945; Chair. Ing. Helmuth Matyk; Dir Dr Heinrich Leopold; 18 mems.

Fachverband der Lederverarbeitenden Industrie (Leather Processing): 1045 Vienna 4, Wiedner Hauptstr. 63, Postfach 313; tel. (0222) 6505; telex 3222440; f. 1945; Chair. Michael von Oswald; Dir Dr Heinrich Leopold; 97 mems.

Fachverband der Maschinen- und Stahlbauindustrie (Machinery and Steel Construction): 1045 Vienna 4, Wiedner Hauptstr. 63; f. 1908; Pres. Dr Josef Bertsch; Dir Mag. Otto Neumayer; 700 mems.

Fachverband der Metallindustrie (Metals): 1045 Vienna 4, Wiedner Hauptstr. 63, Postfach 338; tel. (0222) 6505; telex 111871; f. 1946; Chair. Komm. Rat Dr Hermann Schobesberger; Dir Dr Günter Greil; 69 mems.

Fachverband der Nahrungs- und Genussmittelindustrie (Provisions): Vienna III, Zaunergasse 1-3; tel. 72-21-21; telex 131247; Chair. Ing. Martin Pecher; Dir Dr Klaus Smolka.

Fachverband der Papier und Pappe verarbeitenden Industrie (Paper and Board Processing): 1041 Vienna, Brucknerstr. 8; tel. (0222) 65-53-82; Chair. Komm. Rat Heinz Konwallin; Dir Dkfm. Dr Werner Hoschkara.

Fachverband der Papierindustrie (Paper): 1061 Vienna, Gumpendorferstr. 6; tel. (0222) 58-886-0; telex 111734; Chair. Dr Robert Launsky-Tieffenthal; Dir Dr Rudolf Steurer.

Fachverband der Sägeindustrie (Sawmills): 1011 Vienna I, Uraniastr. 4/1; tel. (0222) 75-76-25; telex 61322301; f. 1947; Chair. Dipl. Ing Herbert Kulterer; Dir Dr Gerhard Altrichter; 2,200 mems.

Fachverband der Stein- und Keramischen Industrie (Stone and Ceramics): 1045 Vienna, Wiedner Hauptstr. 63, Postfach 329; tel (0222) 6505-3531; f. 1946; Chair. Dr Carl Hennrich; Pres. Ing. Leopold Helbich; 543 mems.

Fachverband der Textilindustrie (Textiles): 1013 Vienna I, Rudolfsplatz 12; tel. (0222) 63-37-26; telex 114125; Pres. Dr Theodor Hladik; Dir Dr Helmut Huber; 400 mems.

TRADE UNIONS

The Trade Union Federation represents employees at all levels, except top managerial. By law all employees are subject to collective agreements which are negotiated annually by the Federation. About 60% of workers are members.

Österreichischer Gewerkschaftsbund (OGB) (Austrian Trade Union Federation): 1011 Vienna I, Hohenstaufengasse 10-12; tel. (0222) 63-37-11; telex 114316; non-party union organization with voluntary membership; f. 1945; organized in 15 trade unions, affiliated with ICFTU; Pres. Anton Benya; Exec. Secs F. Verzetnitsch, A. Ströer; 1,671,381 mems (1985).

Bundesfraktion Christlicher Gewerkschafter im Österreichischen Gewerkschaftsbund (Christian Trade Unionists' Section of the Austrian Trade Union Federation): 1010 Vienna I, Hohenstaufengasse 12; tel. (0222) 63-37-11; organized in Christian Trade Unionists' Sections of the following 15 trade unions; affiliated with WCL; Sec.-Gen. Günther Engelmayer.

Gewerkschaft der Bau- und Holzarbeiter (Building Workers and Woodworkers): 1082 Vienna I, Ebendorferstr. 7; tel. (0222) 42-36-47; telex 114833; Chair. Roman Rautner; 187,298 mems (1984).

Gewerkschaft der Chemiearbeiter (Chemical Workers): 1062 Vienna VI, Stumpergasse 60; tel. (0222) 57-15-01; Chair. Erwin Holzerbauer; 59,833 mems (1984).

Gewerkschaft Druck und Papier (Printing and Paper Trade Workers): 1072 Vienna, Postfach 91, Seidengasse 15–17; tel. (0222) 93-82-31; f. 1842; Chair. Herbert Bruna; 23,774 mems (1984).

Gewerkschaft der Eisenbahner (Railwaymen): 1051 Vienna V, Margaretenstr. 166; tel. (0222) 55-46-47; Chair. Fritz Prechti; 117,511 mems (1984).

Gewerkschaft der Gemeindebediensteten (Municipal Employees): 1090 Vienna IX, Maria-Theresien-Str. 11; tel. (0222) 34-36-00; Chair. Rudolf Pöder; 168,897 mems (1984).

Gewerkschaft Land-Forst-Garten (Agricultural and Forestry Workers): 1013 Vienna I, Wipplingerstr. 35; tel. (0222) 63-37-11; f. 1906; Chair. Erich Dirngrabner; 19,828 mems (1984).

Gewerkschaft Handel, Transport, Verkehr (Workers in Commerce and Transport): 1010 Vienna, Teinfaltstr. 7; tel. (0222) 63-96-61; f. 1904; Chair. Robert Zehenthofer; 37,848 mems (1984).

Gewerkschaft Hotel, Gastgewerbe, Persönlicher Dienst (Hotel and Restaurant Workers): 1043 Vienna IV, Treitlstr. 3; tel. (0222) 57-36-84; f. 1906; Chair. Florian Mück; 53,786 mems (1984).

Gewerkschaft Kunst, Medien, freie Berufe (Musicians, Actors, Artists, Journalists, etc.): 1090 Vienna IX, Maria-Theresien-Str. 11; tel. (0222) 34-36-00; f. 1945; Chair. Ing. Stefan Müller; Sec.-Gen. Walter Bacher; 17,872 mems (1986).

Gewerkschaft der Lebens- und Genussmittelarbeiter (Food, Beverage and Tobacco Workers): 1080 Vienna, Albertgasse 35; tel. (0222) 42-15-45; Chair. Dr Josef Staribacher; 42,881 mems (1985).

Gewerkschaft Metall-Bergbau-Energie (Metal Workers, Miners and Power Supply Workers): 1041 Vienna IV, Plösslgasse 15; tel. (0222) 65-46-91; f. 1890; Chair. Sepp Wille; 251,521 mems (1985).

Gewerkschaft Öffentlicher Dienst (Public Employees): 1010 Vienna I, Teinfaltstr. 7; tel. (0222) 63-96-61; telex 114402; f. 1945; Chair. Rudolf Sommer; Gen. Secs Alfred Stifter, Hanns Waas; 220,654 mems (1984).

Gewerkschaft der Post- und Fernmeldebediensteten (Postal and Telegraph Workers): 1010 Vienna I, Biberstr. 5; tel. (0222) 52-55-11; telex 112042; Chair. Norbert Tmej; 75,303 mems (1985).

AUSTRIA

Gewerkschaft der Privatangestellten (Commercial, Clerical and Technical Employees): 1013 Vienna, Deutschmeisterplatz 2; tel. (0222) 34-35-20; telex 114114; Chair. ALFRED DALLINGER; 346,126 mems (1984).

Gewerkschaft Textil, Bekleidung, Leder (Textile, Garment and Leather Workers): 1010 Vienna I, Hohenstaufengasse 10; tel. (0222) 63-37-11; f. 1945; Chair. HARALD ETTL; 50,303 mems (1984).

NATIONALIZED INDUSTRIES

After the Second World War the Nationalrat passed a law giving the State control in the sectors concerned with coal and ore mining, iron and steel, non-ferrous metals, petroleum production and processing, chemical production, electricity and engineering and shipbuilding. Nationalized industries now employ about one-fifth of industrial workers and contribute almost one-quarter of the country's industrial production. To rationalize the administration of the State's interest in these concerns and their subsidiaries, a Federal Law passed in January 1970 transferred the controlling interest to the Austrian Nationalized Industries Holding Company (ÖIAG).

Österreichische Industrieholding-Aktiengesellschaft (ÖIAG) (Austrian Nationalized Industries Holding Company): 1015 Vienna, Kantgasse 1, Postfach 99; tel. (0222) 72-36-01; telex 132047; f. 1970 to form an effective co-ordination of the nationalized enterprises on the basis of economic management and to promote research activities in the subsidiary companies; Chair. Board of Dirs Dr HUGO MICHAEL SEKYRA; Chair. Supervisory Board Dr JOSEF STARIBACHER; controls the following concerns and their subsidiaries:

Austria Metall AG: 5280 Braunau am Inn-Ranshofen; tel. (07722) 2341; telex 27745; f. 1939; aluminium production and processing, copper and copper alloy semi-finished products; Chair. Board of Dirs Dr ROBERT EHRLICH; Chair. Supervisory Board Dr FRANZ EGGL; 4,000 employees.

Bleiberger Bergwerks-Union: 9010 Klagenfurt, Radetzkystr. 2, Postfach 95; tel. (04222) 55-525; telex 422434; f. 1867; lead and zinc mining and processing; Chair. Board of Dirs Dr JULIUS STAINER; Chair. Supervisory Board Dipl. Ing. ERICH STASKA; 1,568 employees.

Chemie Linz AG: 4021 Linz, St Peter-Str. 25, Postfach 296; tel. (0732) 5910; telex 21324; f. 1939; chemical products; Chair. Board of Dirs Gen. Dir Dr RICHARD KIRCHWEGER; Chair. Supervisory Board Dkfm. Dr OSKAR GRÜNWALD; 6,400 employees.

Elin Union AG: 1140 Vienna, Penzingerstr. 76; tel. (0222) 82-900; telex 112763; f. 1892; electrical industry; Chair. Board of Dirs Dr RAINER BICHLBAUER; Chair. Supervisory Board Dkfm. HANS RUTKOWSKI; 6,639 employees.

ÖMV AG: 1091 Vienna, Otto-Wagner-Platz 5, Postfach 15; tel. (0222) 48-900; telex 114801; exploration, production, processing and distribution of crude petroleum, petroleum products and natural gas; f. 1955 as Österreichische Mineralölverwaltung; Chair. Board of Dirs, Dipl. Ing. Dr HERBERT KAES; Chair. Supervisory Board Dr OSKAR GRÜNWALD; 7,038 employees.

Simmering-Graz-Pauker AG: 1110 Vienna, Brehmstr. 16; tel. (0222) 74-69; telex 132574; f. 1831; heavy engineering; Chair. Board of Dirs Dipl. Ing. Dr KLAUS WOLTRON; Chair. Supervisory Board Dkfm. HANS RUTOWSKI; 4,128 employees.

Voest-Alpine AG: 4010 Linz, POB 2; tel. (0732) 585; telex 2207444; iron and steel works, steel processing, mechanical engineering, design and supply of industrial plants; Chair. Board of Dirs Dr HERBERT C. LEWINSKY; Chair. Supervisory Board Dr HUGO MICHAEL SEKYRA; 38,079 employees.

Wolfsegg-Traunthaler Kohlenwerks AG: 4010 Linz, Waltherstr. 22, Postfach 65; tel. (0732) 27-05-01; telex 26543; f. 1911; coal; Dirs Dr HANS SCHABEL, Dipl. Ing. FALKO PEBALL; Chair. Supervisory Board Dipl. Ing. ERICH STASKA; 776 employees.

TRADE FAIRS

Trade Fairs play an important part in the economic life of Austria. The largest are held during the spring and autumn at Vienna, but there are also a number of important fairs held in the provinces.

Dornbirner Messe GmbH: 6851 Dornbirn, Messestr. 4, Postfach 100; tel. (05572) 65-6-94; telex 059108; annually (July); average number of visitors 200,000.

Grazer Süd-Ost-Messe: 8011 Graz, Messeplatz 1, Postfach 63; f. 1906; twice yearly (May and October); exhibits of all categories, but special emphasis on agriculture, iron and steel, hotel and building equipment; average number of visitors 500,000; Dir JOSEPH STOEFFLER.

Directory

Innsbrucker Messe GmbH: 6020 Innsbruck, Falkstr. 2–4; tel. (05222) 25911; annually (April, May and September); mainly devoted to tourism and equipment for the tourist; average number of visitors 200,000.

Österreichische Holzmesse-Klagenfurter Messe (Austrian Timber Fair): Messedirektion, 9021 Klagenfurt, Postfach 79, Valentin-Leitgeb-Str. 11; annually (summer season); main emphasis on timber and articles made of wood; average number of visitors 300,000.

Rieder Messe: 4910 Ried im Innkreis, Postfach 61; tel. (07752) 4011; telex 027/720; holds International Agricultural Fair and Ried Spring Fair in alternate years; over 1m. visitors.

Vienna Fairs and Congress Ltd: 1071 Vienna, Messeplatz 1, Postfach 124; tel. (0222) 93-15-24; telex 133491; f. 1921; three annual general fairs (February, March and September), 22–26 specialized fairs per year at two sites; exhibits of all categories; average number of visitors 650,000; Pres. MANFRED MAUTNER MARKHOF; Dirs Dr REGINALD FÖLDY, GERD A. HOFFMANN.

Welser Messe: 4601 Wels, Messegelände; tel. (07242) 8-22-22; telex 25400; every 2 years; agriculture, cattle-breeding, industry, trade; average number of visitors 1,300,000.

Transport

RAILWAYS

The Austrian Federal Railways operate 90% of all the railway routes in Austria. There are approximately 5,800 km of track and all main lines are electrified.

Österreichische Bundesbahnen (ÖBB) (Austrian Federal Railways): Head Office: 1010 Vienna, Elisabethstr. 9; tel. (0222) 56-50-0; telex 112104; Dir-Gen. Dr ERNEST GOLLNER.

Innsbruck Divisional Management: 6020 Innsbruck, Claudiastr. 2; Pres. Dipl.-Ing. S. KIENPOINTNER.

Linz Divisional Management: 4020 Linz, Bahnhofstr. 3; tel. (0732) 56411; Pres. Dr GUSTAV HAMMERSCHMID.

Vienna Divisional Management: 1020 Vienna, Nordbahnstr. 50; Pres. Dr ERWIN SEMMELRATH.

Villach Divisional Management: 9500 Villach, 10.-Oktober-Str. 20; Pres. Dr RUDOLF REISP.

Other railway companies include: Achensee Railway, Graz–Köflach Railway, Györ–Sopron–Ebenfurt Railway, Montafon Railway, Salzburg-Lamprechtshausen, Stern and Hafferl Light Railways Co, Styrian Provincial Railways, Tirol Zugspitze Railway, Vienna Local Railways, Zillertal Railway (Jenbach–Mayrhofen).

ROADS

At 31 December 1985 Austria had 107,477 km of classified roads of which 1,569 km were modern motorway, 10,018 km main roads, 25,890 km secondary roads and an estimated 70,000 km communal roads.

INLAND WATERWAYS

The Danube (Donau) is Austria's only navigable river. It enters Austria from Germany at Passau and flows into Czechoslovakia near Hainburg. The length of the Austrian section of the river is 351 km. Danube barges carry up to 1,700 tons, but loading depends on the water level which varies considerably during the year. Cargoes are chiefly petroleum and derivatives, coal, coke, iron ore, iron, steel, timber and grain. A passenger service is maintained on the Upper Danube and between Vienna and the Black Sea. Passenger services are also provided on Bodensee (Lake Constance) and Wolfgangsee by Austrian Federal Railways, and on all the larger Austrian lakes.

Ministry of the Public Sector and Transport: 1010 Vienna, Elisabethstr. 9; tel. (0222) 57-56-41; responsible for the administration of inland waterways.

Erste Donau-Dampfschiffahrts-Gesellschaft (First Danube Steamship Co): 1020 Vienna, Handelskai 265; tel. (0222) 26-65-36; telex 131698; fleet consists of 8 passenger vessels, 10 towboats and pushers, 29 motor-cargoships, 107 cargo-barges and lighters, 9 motor tankships, 30 tank-barges and lighters.

CIVIL AVIATION

The main international airport is at Schwechat, near Vienna. There are also international flights from Innsbruck, Salzburg, Graz, Klagenfurt and Linz, and internal flights between these cities.

AUSTRIA

Österreichische Luftverkehrs AG (Austrian Airlines): 1107 Vienna, Fontanastr. 1; tel. (0222) 68-35-11; telex 131811; f. 1957; serves 50 cities in 35 countries of Europe, North Africa and the Middle East, covering 57,930 km; external flights from Vienna, Graz, Linz, Klagenfurt and Salzburg to Amsterdam, Athens, Baghdad, Barcelona, Beirut, Belgrade, Berlin, Brussels, Bucharest, Budapest, Cairo, Copenhagen, Damascus, Dhahran, Doha, Düsseldorf, Frankfurt, Geneva, Helsinki, Istanbul, Jeddah, Kuwait, Larnaca, London, Lyons, Madrid, Malta, Milan, Moscow, Munich, Nice, Paris, Prague, Rome, Salonika, Sofia, Stockholm, Teheran, Tel-Aviv, Tripoli, Tunis, Venice, Warsaw, Zagreb and Zürich; Chair. and Dir.-Gen. OTTO BINDER; Man. Dirs D.Dr A. HESCHGL, Dr H. PAPOUSEK; fleet of 13 MD-81 (DC-9 Super 80); on order and option: 6 MD-87, 4 Airbus A 310, 4 Fokker 50.

Tourism

Österreichische Fremdenverkehrswerbung (Austrian National Tourist Office): Vienna IV, Margaretenstr. 1; tel. (0222) 588-66; telex 115310.

Atomic Energy

Construction of Austria's first nuclear power station, at Zwentendorf on the Danube, was begun in 1971. A referendum was held in November 1978, when it was decided that the plant should not be put into operation, and public opinion remains divided on the issue. In March 1985 a formal decision to dismantle the plant was taken, in view of the high maintenance costs, and it seemed likely that parts of the installation would be sold.

Österreichisches Forschungszentrum Seibersdorf GmbH —ÖFZS (Austrian Research Centre, Seibersdorf): 2444 Seibersdorf; tel. (02254) 800; telex 014353; f. 1956; a limited company of which the capital is shared by the Austrian Government (51%), State industries (25%) and private enterprises (24%). Man. Dirs Prof. Dr PETER KOSS (Science and Technology), Prof. Dr HELMUT DETTER (Industry and Marketing); Chair. Dipl.-Ing. Dr RUDOLF STREICHER.

THE BAHAMAS

Introductory Survey

Location, Climate, Language, Religion, Flag, Capital

The Commonwealth of the Bahamas consists of about 700 islands and more than 2,000 cays and rocks, extending from off the Florida coast of the USA to just north of Cuba and Haiti, in the West Indies. The main islands are New Providence, Grand Bahama, Andros, Eleuthera and Great Abaco: a total of 29 of the islands are inhabited. The climate is mild and subtropical, with average temperatures of about 30°C (86°F) in summer and 20°C (68°F) in winter. The average annual rainfall is about 1,000 mm (39 in). The official language is English. Most of the inhabitants profess Christianity, the largest denominations being the Anglican, Baptist, Roman Catholic and Methodist churches. The national flag has three equal horizontal stripes, of blue, gold and blue, with a black triangle at the hoist, extending across one-half of the width. The capital is Nassau, on the island of New Providence.

Recent History

A former British colonial territory, the Bahamas attained internal self-government in January 1964. The first elections under universal adult suffrage were held in January 1967 for an enlarged House of Assembly. The Progressive Liberal Party (PLP), supported mainly by Bahamians of African origin and led by Lynden (later Sir Lynden) Pindling, won 18 of the 38 seats, as did the ruling United Bahamian Party (UBP), dominated by Europeans. With the support of another member, the PLP formed a government and Pindling became Premier. At the next election, in April 1968, the PLP won 29 seats and the UBP only seven.

Following a constitutional conference in September 1968, the Bahamas government was given increased responsibility for internal security, external affairs and defence in May 1969. In the elections of September 1972, which were dominated by the issue of independence, the PLP maintained its majority. Following a constitutional conference in December 1972, the Bahamas became an independent nation, within the Commonwealth, on 10 July 1973. Pindling remained Prime Minister. The PLP increased its majority in the elections of July 1977 and was again returned to power in the June 1982 elections, with 32 of the 43 seats in the House of Assembly. The remaining 11 seats were won by the Free National Movement (FNM), which had reunited for the elections after splitting into several factions over the previous five years.

Trading in illicit drugs, mainly for the US market, has become a major problem for the country, since many of the small islands and cays are being used by drug traffickers in their smuggling activities. Allegations were made in 1983 of widespread corruption, including bribery of officials and even senior ministers; it was also alleged that Bahamian laws on bank secrecy were being abused by drug financiers and US tax evaders. These claims were denied by Sir Lynden Pindling, who announced, in November 1983, the appointment of a Royal Commission to investigate thoroughly all aspects of the drug trade in the Bahamas. The Commission's hearings revealed the extent to which money deriving from the drug trade had permeated Bahamian social and economic affairs, and by November 1985 a total of 51 suspects had been indicted. In October 1984 two Cabinet ministers, implicated by the evidence presented to the Commission, resigned. The Commission also revealed that Sir Lynden had received several million dollars in gifts and loans from businessmen. Allegations of corruption were made against him, although the Commission stated that there was no evidence that the payments were drug-related. After unsuccessfully demanding Sir Lynden's resignation, the Deputy Prime Minister, Arthur Hanna, resigned, and two further ministers were dismissed. The opposition FNM staged demonstrations, demanding Pindling's resignation, but the Prime Minister refused to accept any personal responsibility for corruption by public officials, and the PLP convention at the end of October unanimously endorsed Pindling as party leader. In October 1985 the assistant police commissioner, Howard Smith, was charged with bribery and dismissed from the force.

The Bahamas' traditionally close relationship with the USA has been strained by the increasingly tough attitudes of the US Government towards the secrecy laws surrounding US offshore banks operating in the Bahamas, and towards drug smuggling in the islands. Nevertheless, the USA and the Bahamas have been collaborating increasingly in a series of operations to intercept drug smugglers, and in March 1986 the USA announced that it was to supply Nassau with aircraft, helicopters and sophisticated radio communication equipment. Relations with the Bahamas' other neighbours, Haiti and Cuba, have been strained by the influx of large numbers of illegal Haitian immigrants, and the sinking of a Bahamian patrol boat by Cuba in 1980.

Government

Legislative power is vested in the bicameral Parliament. The Senate has 16 members, of whom nine are appointed by the Governor-General on the advice of the Prime Minister, four by the Leader of the Opposition and three after consultation with the Prime Minister. The House of Assembly has 43 members, elected for five years (subject to dissolution) by universal adult suffrage. Executive power is vested in the British monarch, represented by a Governor-General, who is appointed on the Prime Minister's recommendations and who acts, in almost all matters, on the advice of the Cabinet. The Governor-General appoints the Prime Minister and, on the latter's recommendation, selects the other Ministers. The Cabinet is responsible to the House.

Defence

The paramilitary Coastguard is the only security force in the Bahamas, and numbered 496 in July 1986. The defence budget in 1985 was US $10.6m.

Economic Affairs

More than 60% of the Bahamas' inhabitants live on the island of New Providence. The remaining members of the group are known as the 'Family Islands'. In 1984, according to estimates by the World Bank, the Bahamas' gross national product (GNP) per head, measured at average 1982–84 prices, was US $6,690, the second highest level among Caribbean countries. However, it was estimated that GNP per head declined, in real terms, at an average rate of 1.6% per year between 1965 and 1984.

Tourism is the main source of income, accounting for about 60% of GNP in 1982 and employing almost 70% of the working population. The tourist industry was severely affected by the world-wide recession of 1974–75; it made a recovery during 1978–80, but the numbers of visitors fell again in 1981. In response to competition from other islands, the Government increased the budget for tourism by nearly 40% in 1982. Tourist arrivals increased by 5%, to 2.3m., in 1984, and to 2.6m. in 1985. Receipts from tourism in 1985 were estimated at US $900m. The revival of the tourist industry has encouraged foreign investment in the sector, and in 1986 the Government enhanced its Tourism Development Plan. The state-owned Bahamas Hotel Corporation plans to double the amount of tourist accommodation by 1995. In addition, improvements are being carried out at Nassau Airport and Nassau Harbour, and cruise ship facilities are being developed in several outer islands.

The Government is attempting to broaden the country's economic base by developing agriculture and fishing, which together accounted for less than 5% of gross domestic product (GDP) in 1981, and industrial activity, both for domestic and foreign markets. Approximately 80% of food supplies are imported. The reduction of these imports, which are mainly required for the tourist trade, is a primary aim of the Government's 1980–90 Master Plan to promote economic growth. The plan provides for improvements to agricultural and fisheries infrastructure, including, in 1983, a plant propagation facility, costing $0.9m., and a fish landing facility which, it was hoped, would improve efficiency. The cultivation of citrus fruit for export has been encouraged in order to take advantage of the damage caused by frost and disease to citrus fruit plantations in the southern USA. More than 20,000 acres (8,000 ha) are expected to be converted to fruit farming by 1995. In January 1986 the UN Food and Agriculture Organization (FAO) announced that it was to conduct a survey of pine forests on Andros, Abaco and Grand Bahama to assess potential for developing a lumber industry.

The Government also plans to create more jobs in the primary sector. At mid-1983 it was estimated that more than 25% of the labour force were unemployed, including a high percentage of under-25-year-olds. It was hoped that people could be encouraged to enter the agricultural and light industry sectors. About 450,000 acres (180,000 ha) of land were reserved for farmers in 1981, and improvements were made in the treatment of smallholders.

Industrial development is based on petroleum refining, although the output of salt, cement, pharmaceuticals and spirits is also expanding. The distillery at Nassau is the largest exporter of light rums in the Caribbean, selling more than 12m. litres per year, mainly to the USA, Canada and Europe. In 1986 it completed a six-year expansion programme. The Government has tried to attract light manufacturing and assembly industries through special tax incentives, but in 1982 the export of manufactured goods, which accounted for about 10% of GDP, declined in response to decreased demand in the US market. In 1985, however, Europe's largest beer-producing company, Heineken, began construction of a brewery in Nassau, in association with two Bahamian partners. When completed, the production capacity will be 1.2m. cases of beer per year. There is a large petroleum refinery on Grand Bahama, with a capacity of 500,000 barrels per day, and a government-owned transhipment terminal for oil tankers, which has a capacity of 150m. barrels per year. However, these facilities, and the economy as a whole, suffer from fluctuations in the price of, and demand for, petroleum and its derivatives. Refining operations, which had been running at a greatly reduced level, ceased in August 1985. Renewed interest was shown in 1983–84 by major oil companies in exploration for deposits of petroleum and natural gas in the Bahamas, and in 1986 a US company began drilling for offshore oil in the Great Bahama Bank area.

The Bahamas established its own shipping registry in 1976. After an initial lull, many ships have registered; the addition of 10 tankers in 1983 brought the fleet's displacement to a total of 2.5m. grt (the third largest 'open-registry' fleet in the world). By the middle of 1984 the fleet had reached 4.0m. grt.

The Government is committed to retaining the Bahamas' status as a tax haven, and the country has become a leading 'offshore' financial centre. With more than 300 banks in the Bahamas, holding at least US $100m. in deposits, at the end of 1985, banking is second only to tourism in importance.

In September 1985 the country's outstanding debt stood at $536.9m. Inflation averaged 3.9% in 1984, compared with 4.1% for the previous 12 months. The 1986 budget projected total expenditure of $529m.

Social Welfare

The health service is centralized in Nassau at the government general hospital. In the Family Islands there are 15 clinics with a resident doctor or nurse. In 1980 the Bahamas had six hospital establishments, with a total of 925 beds, and there were 197 physicians working in the country. A Flying Doctor Service supplies medical attention to islands which lack resident personnel. Flying Dental Services and nursing personnel from the Community Nursing Service are also provided. A National Insurance Scheme, established in 1972, provides a wide range of benefits, including sickness, maternity, retirement and widows' pensions as well as social assistance payments. An Industrial Injuries Scheme has been established.

Education

Education is compulsory between the ages of five and 14 years, and is provided free of charge in government schools. There is an extensive primary and secondary school system, with 101 schools in 1984. There are several private and denominational schools. Primary education begins at five years of age and lasts for six years. Secondary education, beginning at the age of 11, also lasts for six years and is divided into two equal cycles. The University of the West Indies has an extra-mural department in Nassau, and in 1979 opened a branch in the Bahamas, offering degree courses in hotel management and tourism. Technical, teacher-training and professional qualifications can be obtained at the two campuses of the College of the Bahamas, while the Universities of Miami and St John's, New York, also run degree programmes. In 1984 education received B $61.7m. of the total budgetary expenditure.

Tourism

The mild climate and beautiful beaches attract many tourists to the Bahamas, and tourism is the principal source of income. In 1985 there were 2.6m. tourist arrivals (including about 1m. cruise ship passengers), mostly from the USA, Canada and the United Kingdom.

Public Holidays

1987: 1 January (New Year's Day), 17 April (Good Friday), 20 April (Easter Monday), 6 June (Labour Day), 8 June (Whit Monday), 10 July (Independence Day), 4 August (Emancipation Day), 12 October (Discovery Day/Columbus Day), 25–26 December (Christmas).

1988: 1 January (New Year's Day), 1 April (Good Friday), 4 April (Easter Monday), 23 May (Whit Monday), 4 June (Labour Day), 10 July (Independence Day), 4 August (Emancipation Day), 12 October (Discovery Day/Columbus Day), 25–26 December (Christmas).

Weights and Measures

The imperial system is used.

Currency and Exchange Rates

100 cents = 1 Bahamian dollar (B $).
Exchange rates (30 September 1986):
 £1 sterling = B $1.447;
 US $1 = B $1.000.

Statistical Survey

Source (unless otherwise stated): Central Bank of the Bahamas, Frederick St, POB N-4868, Nassau; tel. 322-2193; telex 20115.

AREA AND POPULATION

Area: 13,939 sq km (5,382 sq miles).

Population: 175,192 at census of 7 April 1970; 209,505 (males 101,774, females 107,731) at census of 12 May 1980; 231,000 (official estimate for mid-1985). *By island* (1980): New Providence 135,437 (including the capital, Nassau); Grand Bahama 33,102; Andros 8,397; Eleuthera 8,326.

Density (1985): 16.6 per sq km.

Principal Town: Nassau (capital), estimated population 110,000 (1980).

Births and Deaths (1984): Live births 5,023 (birth rate 22.2 per 1,000); Deaths 1,139 (death rate 5.0 per 1,000).

Economically Active Population (1980 census): 87,054 (males 48,277; females 38,777).

AGRICULTURE, ETC.

Principal Crops (FAO estimates, '000 metric tons, 1984): Sugar cane 228; Tomatoes 9; Bananas 8 (Source: FAO, *Production Yearbook*).

Livestock (FAO estimates, '000 head, year ending September 1984): Cattle 4; Pigs 19; Sheep 38; Goats 18; (Source: FAO, *Production Yearbook*).

Fishing (metric tons, live weight): Total catch 4,372 in 1981; 4,686 in 1982; 5,211 in 1983 (Source: FAO, *Yearbook of Fishery Statistics*).

MINING AND INDUSTRY

Production (estimates, '000 metric tons, 1983): Unrefined salt 850; Cement 100; Motor spirit (petrol) 40; Naphthas 1,400; Jet fuels 1,075; Distillate fuel oils 1,550; Residual fuel oils 4,050; Liquefied petroleum gas 35; Electric energy 920m. kWh (Source: UN, *Industrial Statistics Yearbook*).

FINANCE

Currency and Exchange Rates: 100 cents = 1 Bahamian dollar (B $). *Coins:* 1, 5, 10, 15, 25 and 50 cents; 1, 2 and 5 dollars. *Notes:* 50 cents; 1, 3, 5, 10, 20, 50 and 100 dollars. Sterling and dollar equivalents (30 September 1985): £1 sterling = B $1.447; US $1 = B $1.000; B $100 = £69.11 = US $100.00. *Exchange rate:* Since February 1970 the official exchange rate, applicable to most transactions, has been US $1 = B $1, i.e. the Bahamian dollar has been at par with the US dollar. There is also an investment currency rate, applicable to certain transactions between residents and non-residents. The average of this exchange rate (B $ per US $) was: 1.235 in 1983; 1.195 in 1984; 1.180 in 1985.

Budget (B $ million, 1985): Revenue 423.0; Expenditure 486.9.

International Reserves (US $ million at 31 December 1985): IMF special drawing rights 0.4; Reserve position in IMF 11.0; Foreign exchange 170.2; Total 181.6.

Money Supply (B $ million at 31 December 1985): Currency outside banks 57.7; Demand deposits at commercial banks 146.2; Demand deposits at Central Bank 30.1; Total money 234.0.

Cost of Living (consumer price index for Nassau; base: 1971 = 100): 248.4 in 1984; 260.4 in 1985.

Gross Domestic Product (B $ million at current prices): 1,551.0 in 1982; 1,665.2 in 1983; 1,861.6 in 1984.

Balance of Payments (B $ million, 1982*): Merchandise exports f.o.b. 2,580.8; Merchandise imports f.o.b. −3,137.5; *Trade balance* −556.7; Exports of services 978.5; Imports of services −481.0; *Balance on goods and services* −59.2; Private unrequited transfers (net) −10.3; Government unrequited transfers (net) 17.4; *Current balance* −52.1; Direct capital investment (net) −6.0; Other long-term capital (net) 21.0; Short-term capital (net) 15.0; Net errors and omissions 62.2; *Total (net monetary movements)* −10.0.

* The figures for merchandise imports and exports include petroleum and petroleum products at export values (B $2,336 million).

EXTERNAL TRADE

Principal Commodities (B $ million, 1984): *Imports c.i.f.:* Food and live animals 148.6; Petroleum and petroleum products 3,762.4 (crude and partly refined petroleum 3,748.8, petroleum products 13.6); Chemicals 105.4; Basic manufactures 124.6; Machinery and transport equipment 157.9; Miscellaneous manufactured articles 135.4; Total (incl. others) 4,466.1. *Exports f.o.b.:* Petroleum and petroleum products 3,665.8 (crude and partly refined petroleum 16.1, petroleum products 3,649.7); Chemicals 199.9 (organic chemicals 162.7, hormones 37.2); Total (incl. others) 3,931.5.

Principal Trading Partners (B $ million 1985): *Imports:* Angola 171.0, Gabon 151.8, Indonesia 89.0, Netherlands Antilles 12.7, Nigeria 1,092, Saudi Arabia 51.7, United Kingdom 61.4, USA 842.1, Venezuela 22.2; Total (incl. others) 3,081.1. *Exports:* Belgium 23.8, Netherlands 8.5, Puerto Rico 122.5, United Kingdom 80.9, USA 2,574; Total (incl. others) 3,033.1.

TRANSPORT

Road Traffic (registered vehicles, 1983): Private motor cars 59,561, Other vehicles 5,199, Total 64,760.

Shipping: *Merchant fleet* (displacement, '000 grt at 30 June): 87 in 1980; 197 in 1981; 433 in 1982. *International sea-borne freight traffic* (estimates, '000 metric tons, 1983): Goods loaded 19,206; Goods unloaded 9,314 (Source: UN, *Monthly Bulletin of Statistics*).

TOURISM

Tourist Arrivals: 2,325,250 in 1984; 2,631,970 (by air 1,385,260; by sea 1,246,710) in 1985.

COMMUNICATIONS MEDIA

Radio Receivers (1983): 118,000 in use. Source: UNESCO, *Statistical Yearbook*).

Television Receivers (1984): 89,540 in use.

Telephones (1984): 75,207 in use.

Daily Newspapers (1983): 3 titles (total circulation 33,000 copies).

EDUCATION

Primary (1984): 73 schools, 20,713 students.

Junior High (1984): 7 schools, 6,305 students.

Junior-Senior High (1984): 13 schools, 5,711 students.

Senior High (1984): 8 schools, 6,344 students.

Special Schools (1984): 5 schools, 294 students.

In 1982 there were 3,097 students at the College of the Bahamas.

Directory

The Constitution

A new Constitution for the Commonwealth of the Bahamas came into force at independence on 10 July 1973. The main provisions of the Constitution are summarized below:

Parliament consists of a Governor-General (representing the British monarch), a nominated Senate and an elected House of Assembly. The Governor-General appoints the Prime Minister and, on the latter's recommendation, the remainder of the Cabinet. Apart from the Prime Minister, the Cabinet has not fewer than eight other ministers, of whom one is the Attorney-General. The Governor-General also appoints a Leader of the Opposition.

The Senate (upper house) consists of 16 members, of whom nine are appointed by the Governor-General on the advice of the Prime Minister, four on the advice of the Opposition Leader, and three on the Prime Minister's advice after consultation with the Opposition Leader. The House of Assembly (lower house) has 43 members. A Constituencies Commission reviews numbers and boundaries at intervals of not more than five years and can recommend alterations for approval of the House. The life of Parliament is limited to a maximum of five years.

The Constitution provides for a Supreme Court and a Court of Appeal.

The Government

Head of State: HM Queen ELIZABETH II.

Governor-General: Sir GERALD CASH (took office September 1979).

THE CABINET
(October 1986)

Prime Minister and Minister of Finance: Sir LYNDEN OSCAR PINDLING.
Deputy Prime Minister, Minister of Foreign Affairs and Tourism: CLEMENT T. MAYNARD.
Minister of National Security: A. LOFTUS ROKER.
Minister of Education and Attorney-General: PAUL L. ADDERLEY.
Minister of Economic Affairs, Agriculture, Fisheries and Co-operatives: ALFRED T. MAYCOCK.
Minister of Health: Dr NORMAN GAY.
Minister of Transport: PHILIP M. BETHEL.
Minister of Labour, Sports and Community Affairs: LIVINGSTONE N. COAKLEY.
Minister of Works: DARRELL ROLLE.

MINISTRIES

Office of the Prime Minister: Rawson Sq., POB N-7147, Nassau; tel. 322-2805.
Ministry of Agriculture and Fisheries: East Bay St, POB N-3028, Nassau; tel. 322-1277.
Ministry of Education: Shirley St, POB N-3913, Nassau; tel. 322-8140.
Ministry of Finance: Rawson Sq., POB N-3017, Nassau; tel. 322-4151; telex 20255.
Ministry of Foreign Affairs: East Hill St, POB N-3746, Nassau; tel. 322-7624; telex 20264.
Ministry of Health: Post Office Bldg, East Hill St, POB N-3730, Nassau; tel. 322-7425.
Ministry of Housing: Mosko Bldg, Hawkins Hill, POB N-275, Nassau; tel. 323-5896.
Ministry of Labour, Youth, Sports and Community Affairs: POB N-10114, Nassau; tel. 322-3140.
Ministry of National Security: Clarence Bain Bldg, Thompson Blvd, POB N-8156, Nassau; tel. 322-8163/4.
Ministry of Tourism: Bay St, POB N-3701, Nassau; tel. 322-7500; telex 20164.
Ministry of Transport: Post Office Bldg, East Hill St, POB N-3008, Nassau; tel. 322-1112; telex 20263.
Ministry of Works: J. F. Kennedy Drive, POB N-8156, Nassau; tel. 322-4830.

Legislature

SENATE
President: EDWIN COLEBY.
There are 16 nominated members.

HOUSE OF ASSEMBLY
Speaker: Sir CLIFFORD DARLING.
The House has 43 members.

General Election, 10 June 1982

Party	% of vote	Seats
Progressive Liberal Party	55.18	32
Free National Movement	42.35	11

The election was also contested by three minor parties and five independent candidates.

Political Organizations

Free National Movement (FNM): POB N-8181, Nassau; tel. 325-0637; telex 20238; f. 1972; Leader KENDAL G. L. ISAACS; Chair. CECIL WALLACE-WHITFIELD; Senate Leader JOHN HENRY BOSTWICK.
Progressive Liberal Party (PLP): Gambier House, Farrington Rd, POB N-1107, Nassau; tel. 325-2900; f. 1953; centrist party; Leader Sir LYNDEN PINDLING; Chair. SEAN MCWEENEY.
Vanguard Nationalist and Socialist Party: Nassau; f. 1971; aims to establish a socialist state free of exploitation; Chair. Dr JOHN MCCARTNEY.

Diplomatic Representation

EMBASSIES AND HIGH COMMISSIONS IN THE BAHAMAS

United Kingdom: Bitco Bldg, East St, POB N-7516, Nassau; tel. 325-7471; telex 20112; High Commissioner: COLIN MAYS.
USA: Queen St, POB N-8197, Nassau; tel. 322-4733; telex 20138; Ambassador: Mrs CAROL BOYD HALLETT.

Judicial System

The Judicial Committee of Her Majesty's Privy Council (which sits in London), the Bahamas Court of Appeal, the Supreme Court and the Magistrates' Courts are the main courts of the Bahamian judicial system.

All courts have both a criminal and civil jurisdiction. The Magistrates' Courts are presided over by professionally qualified Stipendiary and Circuit Magistrates in New Providence and Grand Bahama and by Commissioners sitting as Magistrates in the other Family Islands.

Whereas all magistrates are empowered to try offences which may be tried summarily, a Stipendiary and Circuit Magistrate may, with the consent of the accused, also try certain less serious indictable offences. However, a Stipendiary and Circuit Magistrate may in no case pass a sentence of imprisonment of more than two years for any one offence and may only in certain cases impose a fine in excess of B$1,500.

All magistrates may make maintenance orders, and, in certain circumstances, orders for separation and custody of children. Where title to land is not in dispute and the value of the land is B$142.85 or less, a magistrate may hear and determine the case.

THE BAHAMAS

A commissioner has a jurisdiction of up to B$285.71 for matters of contract or tort. The limit for a Stipendiary and Circuit Magistrate is B$572.42.

The Supreme Court consists of the Chief Justice and not more than four and not less than two justices.

Appeals in almost all matters lie from the Supreme Court to the Court of Appeal with further appeal in certain instances to the Judicial Committee of Her Majesty's Privy Council in the United Kingdom.

Justices of the Supreme Court: Prof. PHILIP TELFORD GEORGES (Chief Justice), Sir DENIS MALONE (Senior Justice), BERTRAND O. ADAMS, NEVILLE L. SMITH, JOAQUIM GONSALVES-SABOLA.

Justices of the Court of Appeal: Sir JOSEPH LUCKHOO (President), KENNETH G. SMITH, KENNETH HENRY.

Stipendiary and Circuit Magistrates: GEORGE MEERABUX, JOSEPH B. ALFRED, CLEOPATRA CHRISTIE, GEORGE VAN SERTIMA, SYLVIA BONABY, SHARON R. WILSON (acting).

Registrar of the Supreme Court: JOSEPH C. STRACHAN.

Deputy Registrar of the Supreme Court: CAROLITA D. LUCKHOO.

Religion

CHRISTIANITY

In 1980 there were approximately 38,400 Anglicans, 50,000 Baptists, 40,000 Roman Catholics, 12,000 Methodists and 10,000 Seventh-day Adventists.

The Roman Catholic Church

The Bahamas comprises the single diocese of Nassau, suffragan to the archdiocese of Kingston in Jamaica. At 31 December 1984 there were an estimated 42,524 adherents in the Bahamas. The Bishop participates in the Antilles Episcopal Conference (based in Kingston, Jamaica).

Bishop of Nassau: Most Rev. LAWRENCE A. BURKE, The Hermitage, POB N-8187, Nassau; tel. 322-8919.

The Anglican Communion

The Bahamas is part of the Province of the West Indies.

Bishop of Nassau and the Bahamas: Right Rev. MICHAEL ELDON, Addington House, POB N-7107, Nassau.

The Methodist Church

General Superintendent of the Methodist Church in the Bahamas: Rev. Dr KENNETH HUGGINS, POB N-3702, Nassau.

The Press

NEWSPAPERS

Freeport News: POB F7, Freeport; f. 1961; daily; Gen. Man. DUDLEY BYFIELD; Editor RICHARDSON CAMPBELL; circ. 4,500.

The Herald: Norfolk House, Frederick St, POB N-1914, Nassau; tel. 322-2180; f. 1844; weekly; Man. Editor MICHAEL A. SYMONETTE.

Nassau Guardian: Oakes Field, POB N-3011, Nassau; f. 1844; tel. 323-5654; daily; Publr/Gen. Man. KENNETH FRANCIS; Editor CHRISTOPHER SYMONETTE (acting); circ. 15,000.

The Tribune: Shirley St, POB N-3207, Nassau; tel. 322-1986; f. 1903; daily; Publr/Editor EILEEN DUPUCH CARRON; circ. 12,000.

PERIODICALS

The Bahamas Financial Digest: POB N-4271, Nassau; tel. 322-1149; telex 20447; f. 1973; monthly; business and investment; Publr and Editor MICHAEL A. SYMONETTE.

Bahamas Tourist News: Bayparl Bldg, Parliament St, POB N-4855, Nassau; monthly; Editor PAUL BOWER; circ. 240,000 (annually).

Bahamian Review Magazine: Collins Ave, POB N-494, Nassau; tel. 323-3075; f. 1952; monthly; Editor WILLIAM CARTWRIGHT; circ. 22,000.

Nassau: POB N-1914 Nassau; tel. 322-1149; literature, current affairs, reviews; monthly; Publr MICHAEL A. SYMONETTE.

Official Gazette: c/o Cabinet Office, POB N-7147, Nassau; tel. 322-2805; weekly; published by the Cabinet Office.

Publishers

Commonwealth Publications Ltd: POB N-4826, Nassau; tel. 322-1038; telex 20275; f. 1979; publishes *Bahamas Business Guide* (a guide to doing business in the Bahamas and the Government's economic and financial policies) and *An Economic History of the Bahamas*.

Etienne Dupuch Jr Publications Ltd: POB N-7513, Nassau; tel. 323-5665; publish *Bahamas Handbook and Businessman's Annual*, *What To Do* magazines, *Welcome Bahamas*, *Tadpole* (educational colouring book) series and *Trailblazer* maps; Dirs ETIENNE DUPUCH, JR, S. P. DUPUCH.

Radio and Television

In 1984 there were approximately 118,000 radio receivers and about 90,000 television receivers in use.

Broadcasting Corporation of the Bahamas (Radio Bahamas): POB N-1347, Nassau; tel. 322-4623; telex 20253; f. 1936; government-owned; commercial; three channels; a northern (Grand Bahama) service of Radio Bahamas was established in 1973 at Freeport; Gen. Man. CALSEY JOHNSON.

Bahamas Television: f. 1977; owned by Broadcasting Corporation of the Bahamas; transmitting power of 50,000 watts; full colour; Gen. Man. CALSEY JOHNSON.

Bahamas Television covers the Central Bahamas and the main capital of New Providence. Freeport, the second city, is covered by cable television. US television programmes can be received.

Finance

In recent years the Bahamas has developed into one of the world's foremost financial centres, and finance has become a significant feature of the economy. In 1984 there were 356 financial institutions in the Bahamas: 258 dealt with the general public while the remaining 98 were restricted, non-active or nominee institutions. There were 104 Bahamian-incorporated banks and/or trust companies; 78 were subsidiaries of foreign institutions and 29 were Bahamian-based.

There are no corporation, income, capital gains or withholding taxes or estate duty, but higher stamp, property, immigration and company registration fees were introduced for non-Bahamian companies in 1976.

BANKING

(cap. = capital; p.u. = paid up; dep. = deposits; res = reserves; m. = million; brs = branches; amounts in Bahamian dollars)

Central Bank

The Central Bank of the Bahamas: Frederick St, POB N-4868, Nassau; tel. 322-2193; telex 20115; f. 1973; bank of issue; external res B $295.5m. (June 1986); Governor W. C. ALLEN.

Development Bank

The Bahamas Development Bank: Bay St, POB N-3034, Nassau; tel. 322-8721; telex 20297; f. 1978 to fund approved projects and channel funds into appropriate investments; Chair. JAMES. H. SMITH.

Principal Bahamian-based Banks

African-Arabian Islamic Bank Ltd: POB N-10051, Nassau; f. 1981; telex 20457.

Ahlia Banking Ltd: POB N-7768, Nassau; f. 1963.

Akida Islamic Bank International Ltd: POB N-4877, Nassau; f. 1981.

Artoc Bank and Trust Ltd: Charlotte House, Charlotte St, POB N-8319, Nassau; tel. 325-1183; telex 20270; f. 1977.

Bahama Bank Ltd: POB N-272, Nassau; f. 1964.

Bank of International Trade Ltd: POB N-1372, Nassau; f. 1981.

Bank of New Providence Ltd: POB N-4723, Claughton House, Shirley and Charlotte Sts, Nassau; tel. 322-3824; telex 20464; Gen. Man. BYRD OSBORNE.

Capital Industrial Bank Ltd: POB N-4805, Nassau; f. 1973.

Commonwealth Industrial Bank Ltd: Star Plaza, Mackey St, POB SS-5541, Nassau; tel. 322-1421; f. 1960; Man. Dir VERNON G. R. BEARES; 4 brs.

THE BAHAMAS

Dominion Charter Bank Ltd: POB N-3229, Nassau; tel. 322-2754; telex 20409; f. 1980.

Equator Bank Ltd: POB SS-6273, Norfolk House, Frederick St, Nassau; f. 1974.

Fidenas International Bank Ltd: POB N-4816, Nassau; tel. 325-6052; telex 20278; f. 1979.

Finance Corporation of Bahamas Ltd: Frederick St, POB N-3038, Nassau; tel. 322-4822; f. 1953; Man. Dir ROBERT RANSON; 2 brs.

First Commercial Bank Ltd: POB N-4877, Nassau; f. 1981.

First Home Savings and Loan Ltd: POB F-2644, Queen's Highway, Freeport; tel. 352-6676; f. 1978; Man. Dir ALFRED STEWART.

First Imexco Bank Ltd: POB N-1348, Nassau; f. 1967.

Independent Bank and Trust Company Ltd: POB N-3908, 50 Shirley St, Nassau; tel. 323-8045; f. 1981.

Latin Bank and Trust Company Ltd: POB N-3239, Nassau; f. 1979.

Meridien International Bank Ltd: POB N-3902, Nassau; tel. 322-4500; telex 20111; f. 1980; Dirs P. A. D. CAVE, D. L. MONTGOMERY.

Offshore Trust Banking Corporation Ltd: POB N-7197, Nassau; telex 20111; f. 1981.

People's Penny Savings Bank: Market St, POB N-1484, Market St, Nassau; tel. 322-4140; telex 20353; f. 1952; 3 brs.

Principal Foreign Banks

In 1983 there were more than 100 foreign banks with branches in the Bahamas, including 91 from the USA.

Bank of Montreal (Bahamas and Caribbean) Ltd (Canada): Harrison Bldg, Marlborough St, POB N-7118, Nassau; tel. 322-1690; telex 20141; f. 1970; cap. B$3m., res B$2m., dep. B$139m. (Sept. 1981); Man. Dir WILLIAM HILL; 3 brs.

Bank of Nova Scotia (Canada): Rawson Sq., POB N-7518, Nassau; tel. 322-1071; telex 20187; Man. GEORGE E. MARSHALL; Deputy Man. JAMES BRAMMER; 11 brs.

Barclays Bank (UK): Bay St, POB N-8350, Nassau; tel. 322-4921; telex 20149; Man. D. B. THWAITES.

Canadian Imperial Bank of Commerce: POB N-7125, Shirley St, Nassau; tel. 322-8353; telex 20169; Area Man. TERRY HILTS; 9 brs.

Charterhouse Japhet Bank and Trust International Ltd (UK): E. D. Sassoon Bldg, Parliament St, POB N-3045, Nassau; tel. 322-4643; telex 20142; Bahamas incorporated 1950; cap. B$2m.; Chair. and CEO RENO J. BROWN; Man. IAN C. CRAIG.

Chase Manhattan Bank NA (USA): Shirley and Charlotte Sts, POB N-4921, Nassau; tel. 322-8792; telex 20140; Gen. Man. AUGUSTO CIGARRTTO; 4 brs.

Citibank, NA (USA): Thompson Blvd, Oakes Field, POB N-8158, Nassau; tel. 322-4240; telex 20153; Gen. Man. ANDREW LOWE; 2 brs.

Lloyds Bank International (Bahamas) Ltd (UK): POB N-1262, King and George Sts, Nassau; tel. 322-8711; telex 20107; Gen. Man. ENRIQUE NYBORG-ANDERSEN; Asst Man. G. L. HEFFLER; 1 br.

The Royal Bank of Canada International Ltd: Bay St, POB N-3024, Nassau; tel. 322-4980; telex 20182; Man. Dir G. A. VOYER.

Principal Bahamian Trust Companies

Bahamas International Trust Co Ltd: Bank Lane, POB N-7768, Nassau; tel. 32-21161; telex 20143; incorporated 1957; cap. B$1m.; Chair. L. B. JOHNSON; CEO JAMES M. KNOTT.

Euro-Dutch Trust Co (Bahamas) Ltd: POB N-9204, Nassau; f. 1975; telex 20303.

Guardian Trust Co Ltd: POB N-8159, Nassau; tel. 336-6233; f. 1976.

Leadenhall Trust Co Ltd: POB N-1965, Nassau; f. 1976; Man. Dir ROBERT MONTGOMERY.

Rawson Trust Co Ltd: POB N-4465, Nassau; telex 20172; f. 1969.

RoyWest Trust Corporation (Bahamas) Ltd: POB N-7788, Nassau; tel. 322-4500; telex 20111; f. 1936; Chair JOCK FINLAYSON; Deputy Chair. and Man. Dir DONALD R. KESTER.

Bankers' Organization

Association of International Banks and Trust Companies in the Bahamas: POB N-7880, Nassau; telex 20197.

INSURANCE

The leading British and a number of US and Canadian companies have agents in Nassau and Freeport. Local insurance companies include the following:

Bahamas First General Insurance Co Ltd: POB N-1216, Centreville House, Second Tce, W. Collins, Nassau; tel. 326-5439; telex 20576.

Bahamas International Assurance Co: POB SS-6201, Palmdale Ave, Nassau; tel. 322-3196.

Bahamas Pioneer Insurance Co Ltd: POB SS-6207, East Shirley and Kemp Rd, Nassau; tel. 325-7468.

International Bahamian Insurance Co: POB N-10280. Peek Bldg, New Providence; tel. 322-2504.

Trade and Industry

Bahamas Chamber of Commerce: POB N-665, Nassau; tel. 322-2145; f. 1935 to promote, foster and protect trade, industry and commerce; Pres. (vacant); Exec. Dir B. J. CLANCY-DEVEAUX; 730 mems.

Bahamas Agricultural and Industrial Corporation (BAIC): 4th Floor, Trade Winds Bldg, Bay St, POB N-4940; Nassau; tel. 322-3740; f. 1971 as Bahamas Development Corporation to promote the establishment of heavy industry and supervise agricultural development; name changed 1981; Chair. ALFRED T. MAYCOCK.

Nassau/Paradise Island Promotion Board: West Bay St, POB N-7799, Nassau; tel. 322-8381; f. 1970; Chair. MICHAEL J. WILLIAMS; Sec. MICHAEL C. RECKLEY; 36 mems.

EMPLOYERS' ASSOCIATIONS

Bahamas Association of Architects: POB N-1063, Nassau; Pres. WINSTON JONES.

Bahamas Association of Land Surveyors: POB N-7782, Nassau; tel. 322-4569; Pres. ANDREW LAVILLE; Sec. G. A. HUMES; 42 mems.

Bahamas Association of Shipping Agents: POB N-1451, Nassau.

Bahamas Boatmen's Association: f. 1974; POB ES-5212, Nassau; Pres. and Sec. FREDERICK GOMEZ.

Bahamas Employers' Confederation: POB N-166, Nassau; f. 1963; Pres. T. V. ARNETT.

Bahamas General Contractors' Association: POB SS-5513, Nassau; Pres. VERNON COLLIE.

Bahamas Hotel Employers' Association: West Bay St, POB N-7799, Nassau; tel. 322-8381; f. 1958; Pres. J. B. FARRINGTON; 26 mems.

Bahamas Institute of Chartered Accountants: POB N-7037, Nassau; Pres. WILLIAM WALLACE.

Bahamas Institute of Professional Engineers: POB N-4312, Nassau; Pres. IVERN DAVIES.

Bahamas Motor Dealers' Association: POB N-4824, Nassau; tel. 322-1149; Pres. PERCY CAMPBELL.

Bahamas Real Estate Association: POB N-8860, Bahamas Chamber Building, Nassau; Pres. FRANK CAREY.

Nassau Association of Shipping Agents: Nassau.

Soft Drink Bottlers' Association: POB N-272, Nassau.

TRADE UNIONS

The Commonwealth of the Bahamas Trade Union Congress (CBTUC): POB GT-2514, Nassau; affiliated to the Caribbean Congress of Labour; Pres. DAVID KNOWLES; 11,000 mems.

The main unions are as follows:

Airport, Airline and Allied Workers' Union: Workers House, Balfour Ave, POB N-3364, Nassau; tel. 323-5030; f. 1958; Pres. HENRY DEAN; Gen. Sec. RAMON NEWBALL; 532 mems.

Bahamas Brewery, Distillers and Allied Workers' Union: POB N-299, Nassau; f. 1968; Pres. BRADICK CLEARE; Gen. Sec. DAVID KEMP; 140 mems.

Bahamas Communication and Public Officers' Union: POB N-3190, Nassau; tel. 322-1537; f. 1973; Pres. KEITH ARCHER; Gen. Sec. ROBERT THOMPSON; 1,300 mems.

THE BAHAMAS

Bahamas Construction and Civil Engineering Union: Nassau; f. 1980; Pres. H. H. MINNIS; Gen. Sec. HERBERT WILLIAMS; 200 mems.

Bahamas Doctors' Union: POB N-3911, Nassau; Pres. Dr B. J. NOTTAGE; Gen. Sec. GEORGE SHERMAN.

Bahamas Electrical Workers' Union: Palm Beach St, POB GT-2535, Nassau; tel. 323-5545; Pres. R. S. FORBES; Gen. Sec. ALVIN SARGEANT (acting).

Bahamas Hotel Catering and Allied Workers' Union: POB GT-2514, Workers House, Balfour Ave, Nassau; tel. 323-5933; f. 1958; Pres. THOMAS BASTIAN; Gen. Sec. EDWARD GLINTON; 5,500 mems.

Bahamas Housekeepers' Union: POB 898, Nassau; f. 1973; Pres. MERLENE DECOSTA; Gen. Sec. MILLICENT MUNROE.

Bahamas Maritime Port and Allied Workers' Union: POB 10517, Nassau; Pres. JAMES BLATCH; Gen. Sec. ANTHONY WILLIAMS.

Bahamas Merchandising Workers' Union: POB N-8680, Nassau; Pres. PERRY GRANT; Gen. Sec. EUNICE PINDER.

Bahamas Musicians' and Entertainers' Union: POB N-880, Nassau Court, Nassau; f. 1958; Pres. LEROY D. HANNA; Sec. RONALD SIMMS; 410 mems.

Bahamas Oil and Fuel Services Workers' Union: POB 10597, Nassau; f. 1956; Pres. VINCENT MUNROE.

Bahamas Professional Pilots' Union: POB FH-14229, Nassau; Pres. GODFREY SYMONETTE; Gen. Sec. GODFREY ROBERTS.

Bahamas Public Services Union: POB N-4692, East St South, Nassau; tel. 325-0038; f. 1959; Pres. ARLINGTON MILLER; Sec. ERIC DARVILLE (acting); 4,247 mems.

Bahamas Taxi-Cab Union: POB N-1077, Nassau; telex 20480; Pres. OSWALD NIXON; Gen. Sec. ROSCOE WEECH.

Bahamas Transport, Agricultural, Distributive and Allied Workers' Trade Union: POB N-7821, Wulff Rd, Nassau; f. 1959; Pres. RANDOLF FAWKES; Gen. Sec. MAXWELL N. TAYLOR; 1,362 mems.

Bahamas Union of Teachers: POB N-3482, 104 Bethel Ave, Stapledon Gardens, Nassau; f. 1945; Pres. DONALD SYMONETTE; Gen. Sec. KINGSLEY BLACK; 1,800 mems.

Bahamas Utilities Services and Allied Workers' Union: POB GT-2515, Nassau; Pres. DREXEL DEAN; Gen. Sec. HERMAN ROKER.

Bahamas Workers' Council International: POB 5337 M.S., Nassau; f. 1969; Chair. DUDLEY WILLIAMS.

Commonwealth Cement and Construction Workers' Union: POB N-8680, Nassau; Pres. AUDLEY HANNA; Gen. Sec. ERMA MUNROE.

Commonwealth Electrical Workers' Union: POB F-1983, Grand Bahama; Pres. OBED PINDER Jr; Gen. Sec. CHRISTOPHER COOPER.

Commonwealth Transport Union: POB F-1983, Freeport; Pres. LEO DOUGLAS; Gen. Sec. KENITH CHRISTIE.

Commonwealth Union of Hotel Services and Allied Workers: POB F-1983, Freeport; Pres. HURIE BODIE; Gen. Sec. (vacant).

Commonwealth Wholesale, Retail and Allied Workers' Union: POB F-1983, Freeport; tel. 352-9361; Pres. MERLENE THOMAS; Gen. Sec. KIM SMITH.

Eastside Stevedores' Union: POB 1176, Nassau; f. 1972; Pres. SALATHIEL MACKEY; Gen. Sec. CURTIS TURNQUEST.

Grand Bahama Commercial, Clerical and Allied Workers' Union: POB F-839, 33A Kipling Bldg, Freeport; tel. 352-7438; Pres. NEVILLE SIMMONS; Gen. Sec. LIVINGSTONE STUART.

Grand Bahama Construction, Refinery and Maintenance Workers' Union: POB F-839, Freeport; f. 1971; Pres. JAMES TAYLOR; Gen. Sec. EPHRAIM BLACK.

Grand Bahama Entertainers' Union: POB F-2672, Freeport; Pres. CHARLES SMITH; Gen. Sec. IRMA THOMPSON.

Grand Bahama Telephone and Communications Union: POB F-2478, Freeport; Pres. NAAMAN ELLIS; Gen. Sec. DOROTHY CLARKE.

United Brotherhood of Longshoremen's Union: POB N-7317, Wulff Rd, Nassau; f. 1959; Pres. J. MCKINNEY; Gen. Sec. W. SWANN; 157 mems.

Transport

ROADS

There are about 966 km (600 miles) of roads in New Providence and 1,368 km (850 miles) in the Family Islands, mainly on Grand Bahama, Cat Island, Eleuthera, Exuma and Long Island.

SHIPPING

The Bahamas converted to free-flag status in 1976, and by 1983 possessed the world's third largest open-registry fleet. The fleet's displacement was 4.0m. grt at mid-1984.

The following are the chief shipping and cruise lines calling at Nassau: P & O, Pacific Steam Navigation Co, Tropical Shipping, Home Lines, Eastern Steamship Co, Norwegian-American Lines, Costa Lines, NCL Norwegian Caribbean Lines, Holland American Lines, and the Scandinavian World Cruises.

There is a weekly mail and passenger service to all the Family Islands.

CIVIL AVIATION

Nassau International Airport and Freeport International Airport are the main terminals for international and internal services.

Bahamasair: Windsor Field, POB N-4881, Nassau; tel. 327-8451; telex 20239; f. 1973; scheduled services between Nassau, Freeport, Miami, Fort Lauderdale, Atlanta, Tampa, Newark, Orlando, Turks and Caicos Islands, West Palm Beach and 20 locations within the Family Islands; Chair. PHILIP M. BETHEL; Gen. Man. AUBREY E. CURLING; fleet: 4 Boeing 737, 4 HS 748, 2 Shrike Commander 500 S.

Tourism

Ministry of Tourism: Bay St, POB N-3701, Nassau; tel. 322-7500; telex 20164; tourism is expanding rapidly, and there were 209 hotels in the country, with a total of 13,792 rooms, in 1983; Dir-Gen. BALTRON BETHEL.

BAHRAIN

Introductory Survey

Location, Climate, Language, Religion, Flag, Capital

The State of Bahrain consists of a group of about 35 islands, situated midway down the Persian (Arabian) Gulf, about 24 km (15 miles) from the east coast of Saudi Arabia, and 28 km (17 miles) from the west coast of Qatar. There are six principal islands in the archipelago, and the largest of these is Bahrain itself, which is about 50 km (30 miles) long and between 13 km and 25 km (8 to 15 miles) wide. To the north-east of Bahrain island, and linked to it by a causeway and motor-road, lies Muharraq island, which is approximately 6 km (4 miles) long. A causeway also links Bahrain to Sitra island. The climate is temperate from December to the end of March, with temperatures ranging between 19°C (66°F) and 25°C (77°F), but becomes very hot and humid during the summer months. In August and September temperatures can rise to 40°C (104°F). The official language is Arabic, but English is also widely spoken. Almost all Bahraini citizens are Muslims, divided into two sects: Shi'ites (almost 60%) and Sunnis (over 40%). Non-Bahrainis, who comprise more than 30% of the total population, include Muslims, Christians and adherents of other religions. The national flag (proportions 5 by 3) is scarlet, with a vertical white stripe at the hoist, the two colours being separated by a serrated line. The capital is Manama.

Recent History

Bahrain, a traditional Arab monarchy, became a British Protected State in the 19th century. Under this arrangement, government was shared between the ruling sheikh and his British adviser. Following a series of territorial disputes in the 19th century, Persia (now Iran) made renewed claims to Bahrain in 1928. This disagreement remained unresolved until May 1970, when Iran accepted the findings of a report, commissioned by the UN, which showed that the inhabitants of Bahrain overwhelmingly favoured complete independence, rather than union with Iran.

During the reign of Sheikh Sulman bin Hamad al-Khalifa, who became ruler of Bahrain in 1942, social services and public works were considerably expanded. Sheikh Sulman died in November 1961 and was succeeded by his eldest son, Sheikh Isa bin Sulman al-Khalifa. Extensive administrative and political reforms came into effect in January 1970, when a 12-member Council of State was established. The formation of this new body, which became Bahrain's supreme executive authority, represented the first formal derogation of the ruler's powers. Sheikh Khalifa bin Sulman al-Khalifa, the ruler's eldest brother, became President of the Council.

Meanwhile, in January 1968 the United Kingdom had announced its intention to withdraw British military forces from the area by 1971. In March 1968 Bahrain joined the nearby territories of Qatar and the Trucial States (now the United Arab Emirates), which were also under British protection, in a Federation of Arab Emirates. It was intended that the Federation should become fully independent, but the interests of Bahrain and Qatar proved to be incompatible with those of the smaller sheikhdoms, and both seceded from the Federation. Bahrain thus became a separate independent state on 15 August 1971, when a new treaty of friendship was signed with the United Kingdom. Sheikh Isa took the title of Amir, while the Council of State became the Cabinet, with Sheikh Khalifa as Prime Minister. A Constituent Assembly, convened in December 1972, produced a new constitution, providing for a National Assembly which would contain Cabinet ministers and 30 elected members. On 6 December 1973 the Constitution came into force, and on the following day elections were held for the new Assembly. In the absence of political parties, candidates stood in an individual capacity. In August 1975 the Prime Minister submitted his resignation, complaining of obstruction by the National Assembly. However, Sheikh Khalifa was reappointed and, at his request, the Assembly was dissolved by Amiri decree. New elections were promised, but by late 1986 there were no signs that the National Assembly would be reconvened. Without the Assembly, the ruling family has almost absolute powers.

Although major international territorial claims were brought to an end by the 1970 agreement with Iran, the Iranian revolution of 1979 led to uncertainty about possible future claims to Bahrain. There has also been evidence of tension between Shi'ite Muslims, who form a slender majority in Bahrain, and the dominant Sunni Muslims, the sect to which the ruling family belongs. In December 1981 more than 70 people, mainly Bahrainis, were arrested when a supposedly Iranian-backed plot to overthrow the Government was thwarted. In 1984 there were renewed fears of Iranian attempts to disrupt the country's stability when a cache of weapons was discovered in a Bahraini village, and in June 1985 six men were deported from the United Kingdom, following the discovery of a planned coup against the Bahraini Government.

In March 1981 Bahrain was one of the six founder-members of the Gulf Co-operation Council (GCC) (see p. 124), which by 1983 had settled agreements aimed at co-ordinating defence strategy and at freer trading and co-operative economic protection among Gulf states. In 1983 and 1984 Bahrain participated in joint military exercises, organized by the GCC, which were held as part of a strategy to develop a rapid deployment force for the region. In April 1986 the US Vice-President, George Bush, visited Bahrain to reaffirm the USA's readiness to preserve Gulf security in the event of an escalation of the Iran–Iraq war, which began in September 1980.

In recent years Bahrain has acquired focal importance in the Gulf region. Its international airport is the centre of Gulf aviation, and Bahrain is the site of a Gulf University, where the first intake of students was scheduled for April 1987. Plans to establish a stock exchange for Gulf countries in Bahrain were approved by the Cabinet in August 1986, and it was expected that the exchange would open by the end of that year. A further indication of Bahrain's growing importance within the region was the construction of a causeway linking Bahrain and Saudi Arabia, which was opened in November 1986.

In April 1986 Qatari military forces raided the island of Fasht ad-Dibal, a coral reef situated midway between Bahrain and Qatar, over which both claim sovereignty. During the raid Qatar seized 29 foreign workers (most of whom were subsequently released), who were constructing a Bahraini coastguard station on the island. Officials of the GCC met representatives from both states in an attempt to reconcile them and avoid a split within the Council. Fasht ad-Dibal became the third area of dispute between the two countries, the others being Zubara, on mainland Qatar, and Hawar island.

Government

Bahrain is ruled by an Amir through an appointed Cabinet. In August 1975 the National Assembly was dissolved.

Defence

In July 1985 the Bahrain Defence Force consisted of 2,800 men, and defence expenditure for the year was budgeted at BD 31.5m. In 1982 the GCC states pleged defence aid of some US $1,000m. for the modernization of equipment, and in 1984 this was followed by a further grant, for the same amount, to be shared between Bahrain and Oman.

Economic Affairs

During the 19th century, Bahrain's economy was dominated by pearl-diving and trade. Fishing also played an important part, while agriculture, although restricted by the harsh environment, principally involved the cultivation of dates. However, the exploitation of petroleum, first discovered in commercial quantities in 1932, has transformed the islands. The sale of refined petroleum products has become the mainstay of Bahrain's economy. In 1984, according to estimates by the World Bank, Bahrain's gross national product (GNP) per head, measured at average 1982–84 prices, was US $10,470, considerably below the level of other petroleum-producing countries in the Gulf, but comparable with European industrial countries. Between 1977 and 1983, it was estimated, Bahrain's GNP expanded, in real terms, at an average rate of 6.4% per year. Over the same period, real GNP per head increased by 1.8% per year.

Industrial pollution threatens the fishing industry: the virtual disappearance of shrimps from the Gulf forced the Bahrain Fishing Company to close in 1979. The total catch of the fishing industry declined from 6,700 metric tons in 1983 to 5,600 tons in 1984. In 1985 the Government announced an investment of BD 20,000 (US $53,200) to revive the pearling industry. Agriculture, which contributed only about 1% of Bahrain's gross domestic product (GDP) during the early 1980s, is heavily dependent on irrigation, and has been adversely affected, both by the increasing salinity of the soil and by the attraction of other sectors of the economy. In 1986 work began on a project, expected to cost BD 5.4m., to expand the Tubli sewage works and to make further use of treated effluent for irrigation purposes. This is expected to double the plant's daily production capacity to 110,000 cu m of water. By 1987 it was hoped that 16% of demand for food would be met by indigenous production. A poultry farm, which opened in 1983, met 85% of total demand for eggs in that year. By 1986 poultry production had risen to meet 51% of local demand, and egg production had risen to meet 90% of total demand. A five-year agricultural plan, announced in 1984, aimed to increase output of dairy produce, and in 1985 the Bahrain National Dairy Company was established, to concentrate on the production of milk for the domestic market.

Because Bahrain was already a well-established commercial centre, its petroleum industry developed more rapidly than that of other Gulf countries. By 1936, 16 wells were producing petroleum, which was refined at a complex in Sitra. Bahrain's annual output of crude petroleum reached a peak in 1970, with production of almost 28m. barrels, equivalent to 76,639 barrels per day (b/d). Bahrain also joined the Organization of Arab Petroleum Exporting Countries (OAPEC, see p. 192) in that year. The nation's petroleum reserves, estimated to be 150m. barrels at 1 January 1986, are small in comparison with those of other petroleum-producing countries. At 1985 levels of production, Bahrain's reserves will be exhausted by 1995. In 1968 Bahrain and Saudi Arabia signed an agreement whereby output from an oilfield to which both countries have claims, Abu Safah, is shared equally between them. By 1983 this field accounted for over 50% of Bahrain's revenues from petroleum.

In 1976 the Government made its first moves to take control of the petroleum industry, and by 1980 it had acquired all rights over petroleum production and exploration, and a 60% share in the Sitra refinery. Bahrain's output of crude petroleum averaged 42,000 b/d in 1983, but declined to 41,774 b/d in 1984. In 1985, however, production rose to 41,922 b/d.

The capacity of the Sitra refinery had been expanded to 250,000 b/d by 1983, although a decline in petroleum production and a reduction in demand limited average throughput to 174,987 b/d in that year, compared with 197,400 b/d in 1982. Throughput in 1984 rose to an average of 209,000 b/d, but in the 12 months preceding December 1985 production fell to only 75% of capacity. In 1986 the refinery was producing 243,000 b/d. A plan to upgrade the Sitra refinery, which was expected to cost US $900m., was announced in July 1986. To supplement declining reserves, exploration for further sources of petroleum is under way, and 20 new wells were to be drilled in 1986. Bahrain has substantial deposits of natural gas, with known reserves estimated at 209,000 cu m in 1985. Most of the gas is found unassociated with petroleum, and it is used as feedstock and fuel for Bahrain's indigenous industry. Bahrain's output of natural gas increased from 5,264m. cu m in 1983 to 6,332m. cu m in 1985. At 1985 rates of extraction, the country's gas reserves will be exhausted by the year 2018.

In the 1970s, in an attempt to avoid dependence upon a limited resource, Bahrain embarked upon a vigorous programme of industrial diversification. An aluminium smelter was opened in 1971, and, despite the fall in world aluminium demand which occurred in the early 1980s, production of primary aluminium rose from 171,454 metric tons in 1982 to 178,179 tons in 1984. Expansion of the plant, scheduled for completion in 1989, is expected to increase total annual capacity to 225,000 tons. Ancillary industry includes the production of atomized aluminium powder and extruded products (such as rods, sheets, windows and doors), and an aluminium rolling mill, with an annual capacity of 40,000 tons of sheet and coil aluminium, began commercial production in January 1986. An aluminium foil plant, with a capacity of 6,000 tons per year, was scheduled for completion in 1988. An iron and steel pelletization plant was opened in December 1984, but it has since faced problems of litigation and lack of orders, and has temporarily closed twice, for several months, since its opening. A dry dock for shipbuilding and repairs opened in 1977. This enterprise had failed to become profitable by 1984, but nevertheless received renewed financial support from OAPEC in that year. In 1985 the dock's occupancy was 85%, and its operating costs were $27m. In 1979 a plant for the production of liquefied petroleum gas (LPG) was opened, to process 120m. cu ft (3.4m. cu m) of associated gas per day, and to produce propane, butane and naphtha. A further plant opened in 1985 and began producing ammonia in June, and methanol in the following month. By mid-September 1986 this plant had produced a combined 840,000 tons of ammonia and methanol. Light industry, including the production of supplementary gas, asphalt, prefabricated buildings, plastics, soft drinks, air-conditioning equipment and paper products, also continued to develop during 1986.

A major reason for Bahrain's sustained prosperity has been the government decision, in 1975, to license offshore banking units (OBUs) in Bahrain. OBUs are not involved in local banking, but serve to channel money from the petroleum-producing region back into world markets. In July 1985 there were 74 OBUs, with total assets of US $57,200m., which fell to $54,270m. in the first quarter of 1986. It was hoped that the establishment of a stock exchange, plans for which were approved in 1986, would stimulate investment in Bahrain.

According to census results, Bahrain's population increased by 245% between 1959 and 1981. This rapid rise, combined with an increase of over 50% in water consumption between 1979 and 1983, has necessitated considerable expansion of power and desalination facilities. By the early 1980s Bahrain had major power stations in four towns, and in 1985 expansion work was under way on desalination units at Sitra, where it is hoped to increase capacity to 20m. gallons per day (g/d). There were also plans for a 10m. g/d reverse osmosis plant to provide water for 22% of the population. Much of the funding for development in Bahrain is supplied by its neighbours in the Gulf, on whose generosity and co-operation its relative poverty leads it to depend.

The petroleum sector accounted for about 70% of government revenues in 1982 and 1983, and an estimated 65% in 1984 and 1985. In 1983 a decline of nearly 20% in the value of exports from this sector, resulting from lower production, led to a trade deficit of BD 53.4m., and a deterioration of about 70% in the surplus on the current account of Bahrain's balance of payments. A budget deficit of BD 47m. in actual spending was recorded for 1983, compared with a budget surplus of BD 46m. for 1982. As a result, the duration of the development plan (originally scheduled to cover 1982–85) was extended for a further two years, and a reduction in capital expenditure on non-essential projects was planned. In 1984 the current account of the balance of payments went into deficit, and the trade deficit rose to BD 149m., as non-oil exports fell by 44% to BD 159.2m. In 1985 a surplus of BD 229.8m. on the current account was recorded. In that year the trade deficit declined by 18%, to BD 122.3m., as exports fell to BD 1,056.6m. Of this figure, non-oil exports accounted for BD 140.3m., and oil exports accounted for BD 916.3m., representing a 10% decline from the level of the previous year. The budget for the two years 1984–85 envisaged total expenditure of BD 1,043m., but a programme of austerity measures, introduced in 1985, was reputed to have saved about BD 24m. As a result of a shortfall in revenue (owing to the slump in petroleum prices), budgeted expenditure in 1986 was to be reduced from BD 550m. to BD 460m.–BD 475m. In 1985 GDP expanded by 1% in real terms. In September 1986 various measures to stimulate the economy were introduced,

BAHRAIN

including a 2% reduction in interest rates and the abolition of re-export fees.

Social Welfare
The state-run medical service provides comprehensive treatment for all, including expatriates. There are also physicians, dentists and opticians in private practice. In 1983 Bahrain had six hospitals, 27 health centres and 16 child welfare centres. In 1980 there were 363 physicians working in the country, and in 1985 it was announced that about BD 40m. would be spent on the provision of primary health care. A Social Security Law covers pensions, industrial accidents, sickness, unemployment, maternity and family allowances.

Education
Education is not compulsory, but state education is available free of charge. Private and religious education are also available. There are five different types of schooling: primary and religious schooling (for children aged six to 11 years), intermediate (12–14 years), secondary or commercial streaming (15–17 years). There is a technical college for students to undertake further technical training. Construction of a Gulf University, funded by seven Arab governments, was under way in the mid-1980s, with the first intake of students scheduled for April 1987. In 1985 an estimated 94% of children aged six to 11 years (94.6% of boys; 93.8% of girls) attended primary schools, 52.4% of those aged 12 to 14 were enrolled at intermediate schools, and 41% of those aged 15–17 were enrolled at secondary schools. In 1986 there were 85,867 students in 139 schools. In 1981 the average rate of adult illiteracy among the indigenous Bahraini population was 31.3% (males 21.2%; females 41.4%). In 1985, according to UNESCO estimates, the illiteracy rate among all adults was 27.3% (males 20.7%; females 35.9%).

Tourism
There are several archaeological sites of importance. Bahrain is the site of the ancient trading civilization of Dilmun. There is a wide selection of hotels and restaurants. In 1982 203,141 tourists were recorded on arrival in Bahrain, and in 1984 the number of tourists from other Gulf countries reached 154,000. In 1985 there were plans for a luxury hotel complex at Zallaq, and the construction period was estimated at three years.

Public Holidays
1987: 1 January (New Year's Day), 28 March* (Leilat al-Meiraj, Ascension of the Prophet), 30 April* (Ramadan begins), 30 May* (Id al-Fitr, end of Ramadan), 6 August* (Id al-Adha, Feast of the Sacrifice), 26 August* (Muharram, Islamic New Year), 4 September* (Ashoura), 4 November* (Mouloud, Birth of the Prophet), 16 December (National Day).

1988: 1 January (New Year's Day), 16 March* (Leilat al-Meiraj, Ascension of the Prophet), 18 April* (Ramadan begins), 18 May* (Id al-Fitr, end of Ramadan), 25 July* (Id al-Adha, Feast of the Sacrifice), 14 August* (Muharram, Islamic New Year), 23 August* (Ashoura), 23 October* (Mouloud, Birth of the Prophet), 16 December (National Day).

* These holidays are dependent on the Islamic lunar calendar and may vary by one or two days from the dates given.

Weights and Measures
The metric system is being introduced.

Currency and Exchange Rates
1,000 fils = 1 Bahrain dinar (BD).
Exchange rates (30 September 1986):
  £1 sterling = 544.1 fils;
  US $1 = 376.0 fils.

Statistical Survey

Source (unless otherwise stated): Central Statistics Organization, POB 5835, Manama; tel. 242353; telex 8853.

AREA AND POPULATION

Area: 684.9 sq km (264.4 sq miles).

Population: 216,078 at census of 3 April 1971; 350,798 (males 204,793, females 146,005), comprising 238,420 Bahraini citizens (males 119,924, females 118,496) and 112,378 aliens (males 84,869, females 27,509), at census of 5 April 1981; 417,000 (official estimate for mid-1985).

Principal Towns (population at 1981 census): Manama (capital) 121,986; Muharraq Town 61,853.

Births and Deaths (UN estimates, 1975–80): Average annual birth rate 34.4 per 1,000; Death rate 6.3 per 1,000; Life expectancy at birth 66.1 years.

Labour Force (manpower survey, 1984): Agriculture 1,496; Mining, quarrying, petroleum and gas extraction 433; Manufacturing 10,228 (petroleum, chemicals and plastics 4,533, other 5,695); Construction 27,555; Trade 11,280; Communications 1,761; Transport and storage 7,804; Financing 4,107; other non-manufacturing industries 12,308; Total 81,503. Of the total labour force, 28.2% were Bahrainis, and 71.8% non-Bahrainis.

AGRICULTURE, ETC.

Principal Crops (FAO estimates, '000 metric tons, 1984): Tomatoes 12; Other vegetables and melons 16; Dates 40 (Source: FAO, *Production Yearbook*).

Livestock (FAO estimates, '000 head, year ending September 1984): Cattle 6; Sheep 7; Goats 15 (Source: FAO, *Production Yearbook*).

Livestock Products (FAO estimates, '000 metric tons, 1984): Poultry meat 3; Cows' milk 6; Hen eggs 2.4 (Source: FAO, *Production Yearbook*).

Fishing (total catch, '000 metric tons): 6.6 in 1982; 6.7 in 1983; 5.6 in 1984 (Source: Directorate of Fisheries, Fisheries Statistical Service).

MINING

Production (1984): Crude petroleum 15,259,000 barrels; Natural gas 4,110 million cu metres.

INDUSTRY

Production ('000 barrels, 1984): Liquefied petroleum gas 500; Naphtha 11,215; Motor spirit (petrol) and aviation gasoline 17,790; Kerosene 2,374; Fuel oil 17,076; Diesel oil 80; Gas oil 21,976; Heavy lubricant distillate 1,185; Petroleum bitumen (asphalt) 1,072; Aluminium (unwrought, '000 metric tons) 177.3; Electric energy 2,187 million kWh.

FINANCE

Currency and Exchange Rates: 1,000 fils = 1 Bahrain dinar (BD). *Coins:* 1, 5, 10, 25, 50 and 100 fils. *Notes:* 500 fils; 1, 5, 10 and 20 dinars. *Sterling and Dollar Equivalents* (30 September 1986): £1 sterling = 544.1 fils; US $1 = 376.0 fils; 100 Bahrain dinars = £183.80 = $265.96. *Exchange Rate:* Fixed at US $1 = 376.0 fils (BD 1 = $2.6596) since November 1980.

Budget (two-year estimates, BD million): *Revenue:* 1,206 in 1982 and 1983; 1,120 (incl. oil receipts 732) in 1984 and 1985. *Expenditure:* 1,206 in 1982 and 1983; 1,120 (recurrent 707, capital 412) in 1984 and 1985; 1,110 in 1986 and 1987 (Source: Statistical Bureau, Ministry of Finance and National Economy).

Development Plan (proposed expenditure, BD million, 1982–87*): Infrastructure 686.6 (Electricity 219, Water and Sewerage 179, Housing 164.8, Roads 54.6, Ports and Airport 37, Other 32.2); Social Services 109.8 (Education 43.1, Health 25.2, Other 41.5); Economic Services 46.1 (Agriculture 19.5, Industry 18.5, Other 8.1); Administrative Services 76.8 (Defence and Security 53.9, Other 22.9); Other sectors 38.6; Total 957.9 (Source: Statistical Bureau, Ministry of Finance and National Economy).

* In May 1983 the Five-Year Plan was extended for a further year.

International Reserves (US $ million at 31 December 1985): Gold 6.6; IMF special drawing rights 15.0; Reserve position in IMF 27.0; Foreign exchange 1,617.7; Total 1,666.3 (Source: IMF, *International Financial Statistics*).

Money Supply (BD million at 31 December 1985): Currency outside banks 78.97; Demand deposits at commercial banks 164.17; Total money 243.14 (Source: IMF, *International Financial Statistics*).

Cost of Living (Consumer price index; base: 1976 = 100): 144.7 in 1980; 161.1 in 1981; 172.7 in 1982 (Source: Statistical Bureau, Ministry of Finance and National Economy).

Gross Domestic Product (BD million at current prices): 1,607 in 1981; 1,740.1 in 1982; 1,822.1 in 1983 (Source: Statistical Bureau, Ministry of Finance and National Economy, and British Bank of the Middle East).

Balance of Payments (US $ million, 1984): Merchandise exports f.o.b. 3,083.0; Merchandise imports f.o.b. −3,124.2; *Trade balance* −41.2; Exports of services 771.3; Imports of services −618.9; *Balance on goods and services* 111.2; Private unrequited transfers (net) −345.7; Government unrequited transfers (net) 223.9; *Current balance* −10.6; Long-term capital (net) 70.7; Short-term capital (net) −23.4; Net errors and omissions −206.4; *Total* (net monetary movements) −169.7; Valuation changes (net) 45.8; *Changes in reserves* −123.9 (Source: IMF, *International Financial Statistics*).

EXTERNAL TRADE

Principal Commodities (BD million, 1984): *Imports c.i.f.:* Crude petroleum 618.4; Total (incl. others) 1,324.9. *Exports f.o.b.:* Refined petroleum 1,019.8; Aluminium 84.0; Total (incl. others) 1,180.1 (Source: IMF, *International Financial Statistics*).

TRANSPORT

Road Traffic (registered motor vehicles, 1984): Private cars 72,253; Taxis 958; Vans and lorries 20,651; Private buses 1,952; Public buses 479; Motorcycles 1,642; Total 97,935.

Shipping (international sea-borne freight traffic, '000 dwt, 1984): *Goods loaded:* Dry cargo 385; Petroleum products 27,508,315 barrels. *Goods unloaded:* 2,117.

Civil Aviation (Bahrain International Airport, 1984): 19,327 aircraft arrived and departed.

COMMUNICATIONS MEDIA

Radio Receivers: 142,000 in use (1985).

Television Receivers: 170,000 in use (1985).

Telephones: 55,128 in use (1983).

EDUCATION

Government Institutions (1984): *Primary:* 1,454 classes; 50,936 students. *Intermediate:* 568 classes; 19,838 students. *Secondary* (general): 256 classes, 7,815 students; (commercial): 145 classes, 4,534 students; (technical): 95 classes, 2,630 students. *Religious education:* 9 classes, 114 students.

Directory

The Constitution

A 108-article Constitution was ratified in June 1973. It states that 'all citizens shall be equal before the law' and guarantees freedom of speech, of the Press, of conscience and religious beliefs. Other provisions include the outlawing of the compulsory repatriation of political refugees. The Constitution also states that the country's financial comptroller should be responsible to Parliament and not to the Government, and allows for national trade unions 'for legally justified causes and on peaceful lines'. Compulsory free primary education and free medical care are also laid down in the Constitution. The Constitution, which came into force on 6 December 1973, also provided for a National Assembly, composed of the members of the Cabinet and 30 members elected by popular vote, although this was dissolved in August 1975.

The Government

HEAD OF STATE

Amir: Sheikh ISA BIN SULMAN AL-KHALIFA (succeeded to the throne on 2 November 1961; took the title of Amir on 16 August 1971).

THE CABINET
(October 1986)

Prime Minister: Sheikh KHALIFA BIN SULMAN AL-KHALIFA.
Minister of Defence: Sheikh HAMAD BIN ISA AL-KHALIFA (Heir Apparent).
Minister of Finance and National Economy: IBRAHIM ABDEL-KARIM MUHAMMAD.
Minister of Foreign Affairs: Sheikh MUHAMMAD BIN MUBARAK BIN HAMAD AL-KHALIFA.
Minister of Education: Dr ALI MUHAMMAD FAKHRO.
Minister of Health: JAWAD SALIM AL-ARRAYEDH.
Minister of the Interior: Sheikh MUHAMMAD BIN KHALIFA BIN HAMAD AL-KHALIFA.
Minister of Information: TARIQ ABD AR-RAHMAN AL-MOAYED.
Minister of Justice and Islamic Affairs: Sheikh ABDULLAH BIN KHALID AL-KHALIFA.
Minister of Development and Industry and Acting Minister of State for Cabinet Affairs: YUSUF AHMAD ASH-SHIRAWI.
Minister of Transport: IBRAHIM MUHAMMAD HUMAIDAN.
Minister of Labour and Social Affairs: Sheikh KHALIFA BIN SULMAN BIN MUHAMMAD AL-KHALIFA.
Minister of Housing: Sheikh KHALID BIN ABDULLAH BIN KHALID AL-KHALIFA.
Minister of Public Works, Power and Water: MAJID JAWAD AL-JISHI.
Minister of Commerce and Agriculture: HABIB AHMAD QASSEM.
Minister of State for Legal Affairs: Dr HUSSAIN MUHAMMAD AL-BAHARNA.

MINISTRIES

Amiri Court: POB 555, Riffa Palace, Manama; tel. 661252; telex 8666.
Office of the Prime Minister: POB 1000, Government House, Government Rd, Manama; tel. 262266; telex 9336.
Ministry of Commerce and Agriculture: POB 5479, Bahrain Tower, Government Rd, Manama; tel. 531531; telex 9171.
Ministry of Defence: POB 245, West Rifa'a; tel. 665599; telex 8429.
Ministry of Development and Industry: POB 235, Government House, Government Rd, Manama; tel. 291511; telex 8344.
Ministry of Education: POB 43, Khalid bin Al-Walid Rd, Qudhaibiya, Manama; tel. 258400; telex 9094.
Ministry of Finance and National Economy: POB 333, Government House, Government Rd, Manama; tel. 262400; telex 8933.
Ministry of Foreign Affairs: POB 547, Government House, Government Rd, Manama; tel. 248200; telex 8228.
Ministry of Health: POB 12, Sh. Sulman Rd, Manama; tel. 250834; telex 8511.
Ministry of Housing: POB 802, Diplomatic Area, Manama; tel. 232300; telex 8599.
Ministry of Information: POB 253, Isa Town; tel. 681555; telex 8399.
Ministry of the Interior: POB 13, Police Fort Compound, Salmaniya; tel. 254021; telex 8333.
Ministry of Justice and Islamic Affairs: POB 450, Government House, Government Rd, Manama; tel. 231333.
Ministry of Labour and Social Affairs: POB 735, Sh. Isa Rd, Qudhaibiya, Manama; tel. 712891/8; telex 9062.
Ministry of Public Works, Power and Water: POB 6000, Muharraq Causeway Rd, Manama; tel. 258190; telex 8525.
Ministry of State for Cabinet Affairs: POB 1000, Government House, Government Road, Manama; tel. 262266; telex 7424.
Ministry of State for Legal Affairs: POB 790, Government House, Government Rd, Manama; tel. 253361.
Ministry of Transport: POB 325, Diplomatic Area, Manama; tel. 232023; telex 8989.

Legislature

NATIONAL ASSEMBLY

In accordance with the 1973 Constitution, elections to a national assembly took place in December 1973. About 30,000 electors elected 30 members for a four-year term. Since political parties are not allowed, all 114 candidates stood as independents but, in practice, the National Assembly was divided almost equally between conservative, moderate and more radical members. In addition to the 30 elected members, the National Assembly contained the members of the Cabinet. In August 1975 the Prime Minister resigned because, he complained, the National Assembly was preventing the Government from carrying out its functions. The Amir invited the Prime Minister to form a new Cabinet, and two days later the National Assembly was dissolved by Amiri decree. It has not been revived.

Diplomatic Representation

EMBASSIES IN BAHRAIN

Bangladesh: POB 23434, House 851, Rd 3403, Area 334, Al-Mahouz; tel. 713430; telex 7029; Chargé d'affaires: SYED TANWEER MURSHED.
Egypt: POB 818, Adiliya; tel. 712011; telex 8248.
France: POB 26134, King Faisal Rd, Diplomatic Area, Manama; tel. 291734; telex 9281; Ambassador: PIERRE JUSTINARD.
India: POB 26106, Bldg 182, Rd 2608, Qudhaibiya, Manama; tel. 712785; telex 9047; Ambassador: S. K. BHATNAGAR.
Iran: Sh. Isa Rd 2709, Manama; tel. 712151; telex 8238; Chargé d'affaires: ABBAS SHEKOUHI.
Iraq: House 261, Rd 2807, Block 328 Sughaya, Manama; tel. 250399; telex 9620; Ambassador: TAHA M. ALLAWI.
Japan: POB 23720, House 403, Rd 915, Salmaniya, Manama; tel. 243364; Ambassador: JIRO AIKO.
Jordan: POB 5242, House 1549, Rd 2733, Manama; tel. 714391; Ambassador: AMJAD AL-MAJALI.
Korea, Republic: POB 5564, King Faisal Rd, Manama; tel. 291629; telex 8736; Ambassador: HAE YUNG CHUNG.
Kuwait: POB 786, Diplomatic Area, 76 Rd 1703, Manama; tel. 242330; telex 8830; Ambassador: AHMAD AL-MUBARAKI.
New Zealand: POB 5881, Manama Centre, Government Rd, Manama; tel. 271600; telex 8748; Ambassador: J. D. L. RICHARDS.
Oman: POB 26414, Adiliya, Kuwait Rd, Manama; tel. 232606; telex 9332; Ambassador: GHALIB BIN ABDULLA BIN JUBRAN.

BAHRAIN *Directory*

Pakistan: POB 563, House 75, Rd 3403, Mahooz, Manama; tel. 712470; Ambassador: ABDEL-WAHAB KHAN.
Saudi Arabia: POB 1085, Bani-Otbah Rd, Qudhaibiya, Manama; tel. 713406; Ambassador: Dr GHAZI ABDER-RAHMAN AL-GOSAIBI.
Tunisia: Al-Mahouz, Manama; tel. 721431; Chargé d'affaires: BORHANODDINE BEN ASHORE.
United Kingdom: POB 114, 21 Government Rd, Manama; tel. 254002; telex 8213; Ambassador: FRANCIS S. E. TREW.
USA: POB 26431, Off Sh. Isa Rd, Manama; tel. 714151; telex 9398; Ambassador: SAM H. ZAKHEM.

Judicial System

Since the termination of British legal jurisdiction in 1971, intensive work has been undertaken on the legislative requirements of Bahrain. The Criminal Law is at present contained in various Codes, Ordinances and Regulations. All nationalities are subject to the jurisdiction of the Bahrain courts which guarantee equality before the law irrespective of nationality or creed.

Directorate of Courts: POB 450, Government House, Government Rd, Manama; tel. 253339.

Religion

At the April 1981 census the population was 350,798, distributed as follows: Muslims 298,140; Christians 25,611; Others 27,033; No religion 14.

ISLAM

Muslims are divided between the Sunni and Shi'ite sects. The ruling family is Sunni, although the majority of the Muslim population (almost 60%) are Shi'ite.

CHRISTIANITY
The Anglican Communion

Episcopal Church in Jerusalem and the Middle East: St Christopher's Cathedral, POB 36, Al-Mutanabi Ave, Manama; tel. 253866; Bishop in Cyprus and the Gulf: Right Rev. JOHN BROWN (resident in Cyprus).

The Press

DAILIES

Akhbar al-Bahrain (Bahrain News): POB 253, Manama; Arabic; publ. by the Ministry of Information.
Akhbar al-Khalij (Gulf News): POB 5300, Manama; tel. 291111; telex 8565; f. 1976; Arabic; circ. 14,000.
Bapco Daily News: Awali; tel. 754444; telex 8214; publ. by the Bahrain Petroleum Co BSC; English; Saturday to Wednesday inclusive; Editor BRIAN SHACKELL; circ. 1,000.
Daily News Bulletin: POB 1062, Manama; tel. 251881.
Gulf Daily News: POB 5300, Manama; tel. 290000; telex 8565; f. 1978; English; Editor GEORGE WILLIAMS; circ. 12,500.

WEEKLIES

Al-Adhwaa' Newspaper: POB 250, Manama; tel. 245251; telex 8564; f. 1965; Arabic; Chief Editor MUHAMMAD QASSIM ASH-SHIRAWI; circ. 13,000.
Akhbar Bapco (Bapco News): Bahrain Petroleum Co BSC, POB 25149, Awali; tel. 755055; telex 8214; f. 1981; Arabic; house journal; Editor KHALID MEHMAS; circ. 8,000.
Al-Bahrain al-Yawm (Bahrain Today): POB 253, Isa Town; Arabic; publ. by the Ministry of Information; Editor SALMAN TAKI; circ. 7,000 (internationally).
Gulf Weekly Mirror: POB 455, Manama; tel. 259059; telex 9006; f. 1971; English; also circulates in Kuwait, Oman, Qatar, UAE and eastern Saudi Arabia; Man. Editor GRAHAM COLE; Commercial and Admin. Man. ABDUL-KARIM ISMAIL ALI; circ. 16,000.
Al-Jaridat ar-Rasmiya (The Official Gazette): Ministry of Information, POB 253, Juffair Rd, Juffair; f. 1957; Arabic.
Al-Maseerah: Al-Maseerah Journalism, Printing and Publishing House, POB 5981, Manama; tel. 258882; telex 7421; f. 1977; Arabic; politics; Chair. and Editor-in-Chief KHALIFA HASAN KASIM.

Al-Mawakif (Situations): POB 1083, Manama; tel. 231231; f. 1973; Arabic; world news, politics, arts, religion; Editor MANSOOR RADHI; circ. 4,000.
Sada al-Usbou' (Echo of the Week): POB 549, Bahrain; tel. 290111; telex 8880; f. 1969; Arabic; Owner and Editor-in-Chief ALI SAYAR; circ. 20,000 (in various Gulf States).

OTHER PERIODICALS

Commerce Review: POB 666, Manama; tel. 233913; telex 8691; monthly; English and Arabic; publ. by Bahrain Chamber of Commerce and Industry; Editor HAFEDH ASH-SHAIKH; circ. 3,300.
Al-Hayat at-Tijariya (Commercial Life): POB 666, Manama; monthly; English and Arabic; commerce review; Editor HAFEDH ASH-SHAIKH.
Link: Al-Maseerah Printing and Publishing House, POB 5981, Manama; tel. 258882; telex 7421; f. 1986; monthly; social and cultural magazine; Chair. and Editor-in-Chief KHALIFA HASAN KASIM.
Al-Murshid (The Guide): Arabian Printing and Publishing House, POB 553, Bahrain; English and Arabic; monthly guide, including 'What's on in Bahrain'; Editor M. SOLIMAN.
This is Bahrain & What's On: POB 726, Manama; tel. 250014; telex 8494; quarterly; English; information; publ. by Gulf Advertising and Marketing; Editor GILLY TURNEY; circ. 15,000.

NEWS AGENCIES

Agence France-Press (France): POB 5890, Manama; tel. 259115; telex 8987; Correspondent NABIL JUMBERT.
Associated Press (AP) (USA): POB 11022, Manama; tel. 530101; telex 9470; Chief of Bureau ALY MAHMOUD.
Deutsche Presse-Agentur (dpa) (Federal Republic of Germany): POB 26995, 1656, Rd 3438, Al-Mahouz, Manama; tel. 727523; telex 9542; Correspondent NABIL MEGALLI.
Gulf News Agency: POB 301, Manama; tel. 687272; telex 9030.
Reuters (UK): POB 1030, Manama; tel. 255455; telex 968.
United News of India also has an office in Bahrain.

Publishers

Al-Hilal Publishing and Marketing Co: POB 224, Manama; tel. 231122; telex 8981; specialist magazines of commercial interest; Chair. A. M. ABDEL RAHMAN; Man. Dir R. MIDDLETON.
Arabcommunicators: POB 551, Manama; tel. 254258; telex 8263; publrs of annual Bahrain Business Directory; Dirs AHMAD A. FAKHRI, HAMAD A. ABUL.
Falcon Publishing WLL: POB 5028, Manama; tel. 259694; telex 8917; Group Gen. Man. RODNEY PEAKE.
Gulf Publishing Co: POB 455, Manama; tel. 259059; telex 9006; Dirs IBRAHIM ISHAQ, MUHAMMAD YOUSUF JALAL, FAROUQ K. ALMOAYYED.

Government Publishing House

Directorate of Publications: POB 121, Manama; tel. 682926; Dir SALMAN TAQI.

Radio and Television

In 1985 there were an estimated 142,000 radio receivers and 170,000 television receivers in use. English language programmes, broadcast from Saudi Arabia by the US Air Force in Dhahran and by the Arabian-American Oil Co (Aramco), can be received in Bahrain, as can the television service provided by the latter.

Bahrain Broadcasting Station: POB 253, Manama; tel. 713581; telex 9259; f. 1955; State-owned and operated enterprise; two 10 kW transmitters; programmes are in Arabic and English, and include news, plays and talks; Station Mans HASSAN SALMAN KAMAL (Arabic service), AHMAD M. SULAIMAN (English service).
Radio Bahrain: POB 702, Manama; tel. 640022; telex 8311; f. 1977; commercial radio station in English language; Man. AHMAD M. SULAIMAN.
Bahrain Television: POB 1075, Manama; tel. 681811; telex 8311; commenced colour TV broadcasting in 1973; second channel in English began broadcasting in October 1981; the station takes advertising; covers Bahrain, eastern Saudi Arabia, Qatar and UAE; Dir KHALIL ATH-THAWADI; Adviser JOHN SHAW.

Finance

(cap. = capital; p.u. = paid up; dep. = deposits; m. = millions; res = reserves; brs = branches; BD = Bahrain dinars)

BANKING

Central Bank

Bahrain Monetary Agency: POB 27, Manama; tel. 241241; telex 9144; f. 1973, in operation from January 1975; controls issue of currency, organization and control of banking system and bank credit; cap. and res BD97m. (Dec. 1983); Governor ABDULLAH HASSAN SAIF; Chair. Sheikh KHALIFA BIN SALMAN AL-KHALIFA; Deputy Chair. IBRAHIM A. KARIM MUHAMMAD.

Locally Incorporated Commercial Banks

Al-Ahli Commercial Bank BSC: POB 5941, Manama; tel. 244333; telex 9130; f. 1978; private bank; total assets BD167.3m. (Dec. 1985); Gen. Man. GREGORY KRIKORIAN.

Arlabank International EC: POB 5070, Manama Centre, Manama; tel. 232124; telex 9345; f. 1983; wholly-owned subsidiary: Arab-Latin American Bank (Banco Arabe Latinoamericano) in Peru; total assets US $1,700m. (1985); Gen. Man. CHRISTIAN RODRIGUEZ-CAMILLONI.

Bahraini Saudi Bank (BSB) BSC: POB 1159, Government Rd, Manama; tel. 263111; telex 7010; f. 1983; commenced operations in early 1985; licensed as a full Commercial Bank; total assets BD52.7m. (Dec. 1985); Chair. ABDULLAH OMRAN; Gen. Man. RICHARD F. STACKS.

Bank of Bahrain and Kuwait (BBK): POB 597, Manama; tel. 253388; telex 8919; f. 1971; total assets BD772m. (1985); Chair. RASHID ABD AR-RAHMAN AZ-ZAYANI; Gen. Man. PAUL H. FRANCIS; 16 brs.

Gulf International Bank (GIB) BSC: POB 1017, Al-Dowali Bldg, King Faisal Rd, Manama; tel. 256245; telex 8801; f. 1975; owned by governments of Bahrain, Iraq, Kuwait, Oman, Qatar, Saudi Arabia and the UAE; total assets US $7,781m. (Dec. 1985); Vice-Pres. HENRY AZZAM; Chair. ABDULLAH HASSAN SAIF; Gen. Man. GHAZI M. ABDEL-JAWAD.

National Bank of Bahrain BSC: POB 106, Government Rd, Manama; tel. 258800; telex 8242; f. 1957; commercial bank with Government of Bahrain as major shareholder; total assets BD533m. (Dec. 1985); Chair. AHMAD ALI KANOO; Gen. Man. HASSAN ALI JUMA; 19 brs.

Foreign Commercial Banks

Algemene Bank Nederland NV (Netherlands): POB 350, Manama; tel. 255420; telex 8356; Man. W. J. VAN DER MEI.

Arab Bank Ltd (Jordan): POB 395, Manama Centre, Manama; tel. 255988; telex 8232; Regional Man. Dr MAKRAM A. RAHAL; 4 brs.

Bank Melli Iran: POB 785, Government Rd, Manama; tel. 259910; telex 8266; Gen. Man. (Bahrain brs) MANOOCHEHR KHERZI; 2 brs.

Bank Saderat Iran: POB 825, Manama; tel. 250809; telex 8363; Man. BAHMAN HAJIZADEH; 2 brs.

Banque du Caire (Egypt): POB 815, Manama; tel. 254454; telex 8298; Man. MAMDOUH ABBAS ABU AL-KHAIR.

Banque Paribas FCB (France): POB 5241, Manama; tel. 259275; telex 8458; Gen. Man. F. CAZE.

British Bank of the Middle East (Hong Kong): POB 57, Manama; tel. 242555; telex 8230; Area Man. ALAN WHYTE; 6 brs.

Chase Manhattan Bank NA (USA): POB 368, Manama; tel. 251401; telex 8286; Vice-Pres. and Man. SALMAN A. ABBASI.

Citibank NA (USA): POB 548, Manama; tel. 257124; telex 8225; Sr Officer ARTHUR M. DE GRAFFENRIED III; 1 br.

Grindlays Bahrain Bank BSC: POB 793, Manama; tel. 250805; telex 8335; f. 1984 when Bahrainis took over 60% of equity held by Grindlays Bank PLC (London); cap. p.u. BD3m.; Gen. Man. R. J. WILD.

Habib Bank Ltd (Pakistan): POB 566, Manama Centre, Manama; tel. 271402; telex 9448; f. 1941; cap. US $63m.; dep. US $4,421m.; Sr Vice-Pres. and Gen. Man. ABDEL-HANNAN MIRZA.

National Bank of Abu Dhabi: POB 5247, Manama; tel. 250824; telex 8483; Man. ABDEL-AZIZ AL-ASSAR; 2 brs.

Rafidain Bank (Iraq): POB 607, Manama; tel. 255656; telex 8332; f. 1969; Man. ABBAS HADY AL-BAYATY; 2 brs.

Standard Chartered Bank (UK): POB 29, Manama; tel. 255946; telex 8229; f. in Bahrain 1920; CEO TIM NUNAN; Man. PETER RAWLINGS; 5 brs.

United Bank Ltd (Pakistan): POB 546, Government Rd, Manama; tel. 254032; telex 8247; Man. ABDEL-AZIZ KHAN; 3 brs.

Specialized Financial Institutions

Arab Banking Corpn: POB 5698, Alia Bldg, Diplomatic Area, Manama; tel. 232235; telex 9432; f. 1980 by Amiri decree; jointly owned by Kuwait Ministry of Finance, Secretariat of Treasury of Libya and Abu Dhabi Investment Authority; offers full range of commercial, merchant and investment banking services; total assets US $13,066m. (Dec. 1985); Pres. and Chief Exec. ABDULLA A. SAUDI; 6 brs.

Bahrain Islamic Bank BSC: POB 5240, Government Rd, Manama; tel. 231402; telex 9388; f. 1979; total assets BD38m. (Dec. 1984); Gen. Man. ABDEL-LATIF JANAHI.

Housing Bank: POB 5370, Diplomatic Area, Manama; tel. 233321; telex 8599; f. 1979; Chair. Sheikh KHALID BIN ABDULLAH AL-KHALIFA; Gen. Man. ISA SULTAN ATH-THAWADI.

Offshore Banking Units

Bahrain has been encouraging the establishment of Offshore Banking Units (OBUs) since October 1975. An OBU is not allowed to provide local banking services but is allowed to accept deposits from governments and large financial organizations in the area and make medium-term loans for local and regional capital projects.

Operational OBUs

Algemene Bank Nederland NV (ABN BANK): POB 350; tel. 255420; telex 8356.

Allied Banking Corporation: POB 20493; tel. 261461; telex 9349.

ALUBAF Arab International Bank EC: POB 529; tel. 276344; telex 9671.

American Express International: POB 93; tel. 231383; telex 8536.

Arab Asian Bank EC: POB 5619; tel. 233129; telex 8583.

Arab Bank Ltd: POB 813; tel. 256398; telex 8647.

Arab Banking Corporation: POB 5698; tel. 232235; telex 9432.

Arab International Bank: POB 1114; tel. 261611; telex 9489.

Arab Investment Company SAA (TAIC): POB 5559; tel. 271126; telex 8334.

Arab Malaysian Development Bank: POB 5619; tel. 257059; telex 9393.

Arab Solidarity Bank: POB 20491; tel. 230145; telex 9373.

Arlabank International EC: POB 5070; tel. 232124; telex 9345.

Al-Bahrain Arab African Bank EC (Albaab): POB 20488; tel. 230491; telex 9380.

Bahrain International Bank EC: POB 5016; tel. 274545; telex 9832.

Bahrain Middle East Bank EC: POB 797; tel. 275345; telex 9706.

Bahraini Saudi Bank: POB 1159; tel. 263111; telex 7010.

BAII (Middle East) Inc.: POB 5333; tel. 258258; telex 8542.

Banco do Brasil SA: POB 5489; tel. 250113; telex 8718.

Banco do Estado de São Paulo (BANESPA) SA: POB 26615; tel. 232241; telex 9347.

Bank Bumiputra Malaysia Berhad: POB 20392; tel. 231073; telex 8884.

Bank Negara Indonesia 1946: POB 20715; tel. 277562; telex 8208.

Bank of America NT & SA: POB 5280; tel. 245000; telex 8616.

Bank of Bahrain and Kuwait BSC: POB 597; tel. 253388; telex 8919.

Bank of Baroda: POB 1915; tel. 253681; telex 9449.

Bank of Credit and Commerce International SA: POB 569; tel. 245520; telex 8346.

Bank of Oman Ltd: POB 20654; tel. 232882; telex 9566.

Bank of Tokyo Ltd: POB 5850; tel. 246518; telex 9066.

Bank Saderat Iran: POB 825; tel. 255977; telex 8688.

Bankers' Trust Co of New York: POB 5905; tel. 259841; telex 9510.

Banque Indosuez: POB 5410; tel. 257019; telex 8976.

Banque Nationale de Paris: POB 5253; tel. 250852; telex 8595.

Banque Paribas: POB 5993; tel. 259275; telex 9078.

Barclays Bank International Ltd: POB 5120; tel. 242024; telex 8747.

British Bank of the Middle East: POB 57; tel. 255933; telex 8230.

Canadian Imperial Bank of Commerce: POB 774; tel. 250551; telex 8593.

Chase Manhattan Bank NA: POB 368; tel. 250799; telex 8286.

Chemical Bank: POB 5492; tel. 252619; telex 8562.

Citibank NA: POB 548; tel. 257124; telex 8225.

Commercial Bank of Australia: POB 5467; tel. 254792; telex 8687.

Crédit Suisse: POB 5100; tel. 232123; telex 8418.

FRAB-Bank (Middle East) EC: POB 5290; tel. 259862; telex 9024.

Grindlays Bahrain Bank: POB 5793; tel. 258610; telex 8723.

Grindlays International: POB 20324; tel. 254023; telex 9254.

Gulf International Bank BSC: POB 1017; tel. 256245; telex 8802.

Gulf Riyad Bank EC: POB 20220; tel. 232030; telex 9088.

Habib Bank Ltd: POB 566; tel. 271811; telex 9448.

BAHRAIN

Directory

Hanil Bank of South Korea: POB 1151; tel. 243503; telex 7048.
Hongkong & Shanghai Banking Corporation: POB 5497; tel. 255828; telex 8707.
Korea Exchange Bank: POB 5767; tel. 255418; telex 8846.
Kuwait Asia Bank EC: POB 20501; tel. 243645; telex 9611.
Lloyds Bank International Ltd: POB 5500; tel. 245050; telex 8641.
Manufacturers Hanover Trust Co: POB 5471; tel. 254375; telex 8556.
Massraf Faysal Al-Islami Bank of Bahrain: POB 20492; tel. 275040; telex 9270.
Midland Bank PLC: POB 5675; tel. 257100; telex 8719.
National Bank of Abu Dhabi: POB 5886; tel. 255776; telex 8982.
National Bank of Bahrain: POB 106; tel. 258800; telex 8242.
National Bank of Pakistan: POB 775; tel. 244191; telex 9221.
National Westminster Bank PLC: POB 820; tel. 255412; telex 8559.
Overseas Trust Bank Ltd: POB 5628; tel. 245145; telex 9238.
Al-Saudi Banque (Paris): POB 5820; tel 257319; telex 8969.
Saudi European Bank SA: POB 26380; tel. 232884; telex 8732.
Saudi National Commercial Bank: POB 20363; tel. 231182; telex 9298.
Scandinavian Bank Ltd: POB 5345; tel. 253341; telex 8530.
Société Générale: POB 5275; tel. 242002; telex 8568.
Standard Chartered Bank PLC: POB 29; tel. 255946; telex 8385.
State Bank of India: POB 5466; tel. 253640; telex 8804.
Swiss Bank Corporation: POB 5560; tel. 257221; telex 8814.
Union de Banques Arabes et Françaises (UBAF): POB 5595; tel. 257393; telex 8840.
United Bank of Kuwait Ltd: POB 5494; tel. 256774; telex 8649.
United Gulf Bank: POB 5964; tel. 233789; telex 9556.
Yamaichi International (Middle East) EC: POB 26894; tel. 253922; telex 9468.
Yapı Ve Kredi Bankası AS: POB 1104; tel. 270089; telex 9931.

Representative Offices

In July 1985, 60 banks maintained Representative Offices in Bahrain.

Investment Banks

Investment banks operating in Bahrain include the following: Al-Baraka Islamic Investment Bank, Arab Financial Services, Arab Multinational Investment Co (AMICO), Arabian Investment Banking Corpn (Investcorp) EC, BAII (Middle East) Corpn EC, Bahrain International Investment Centre (BIIC), Bahrain Investment Bank BSC, Bahrain Islamic Investment Co BSC, The Bahraini-Kuwaiti Investment Group (BKIG), Citicorp Investment Bank (CIB), E. F. Hutton (Middle East) Ltd, Islamic Investment Company of the Gulf EC, Merrill Lynch Int. & Co, Nomura Investment Banking (Middle East) EC, Robert Fleming Holdings Ltd, Sumitomo Finance (Middle East) EC, Trans-Arabian Investment Bank (TAIB) EC, United Gulf Investment Co, Yamaichi International (Middle East) EC.

INSURANCE

Al-Ahlia Insurance Co BSC: POB 5282, Manama; tel. 258860; telex 8761; f. 1976.

Arab Insurance Group BSC (ARIG): POB 26992, Arig House, Diplomatic Area, Manama; tel. 231110; telex 9395; f. 1980; owned by governments of Kuwait, Libya and the UAE; cap. p.u. US $150m.; all non-life reinsurance; Chair. ABDEL WAHAB A. AT-TAMMAR; Gen. Man. and CEO NOORUDDIN A. NOORUDDIN.

Atlas Assurance Co Ltd: POB 20449, Manama; tel. 254709; telex 8223; general insurance.

Bahrain Insurance Co BSC: POB 843, Suite 310, Sh. Mubarak Bldg, Government Ave, Manama; tel. 255641; telex 8463; f. 1969; all classes including life insurance; cap. BD600,000; 66.66% Bahraini-owned; 33.33% Iraqi-owned; Gen. Man. HISHAM SHUKRY BABAN; 4 brs.

Bahrain Kuwait Insurance Co BSC: POB 5483, Manama; tel. 256213; telex 8672.

National Insurance Co BSC (c): POB 1818, Unitag House, Government Rd, Manama; tel. 244181; telex 8908; f. 1982; all classes of general insurance; Chair. J. A. WAFA; Pres. W. R. MILLS.

In July 1985, 13 foreign insurance companies were represented.

Trade and Industry

CHAMBER OF COMMERCE

Bahrain Chamber of Commerce and Industry: POB 248, Manama; tel. 233913; telex 8691; f. 1939; 3,647 mems; Pres. QASIM AHMAD FAKHROO; Sec.-Gen. JASSIM MUHAMMAD ASH-SHATTI.

STATE ENTERPRISES

Aluminium Bahrain BSC (ALBA): POB 570, Manama; tel. 661751; telex 8235; f. 1971; operates a smelter owned by the governments of Bahrain (57.9%) and Saudi Arabia (20%), the remainder being held privately; by 1984 the smelter's capacity had increased to 178,179 tons per annum; Chief Exec. GUDVIN K. TOFTE; Gen. Man. AHMAD SALEH AN-NOAIMI.

Bahrain Aluminium Extrusion Co WLL (BALEXCO): POB 1053, Manama; tel. 730111; telex 8634; f. 1976; generally supplies 'unfinished' systems to the construction industry; 100% owned by the Government of Bahrain; Chair. Dr ABDEL-LATIF KANOO; Gen. Man. ABDEL-MONEM SHIRAWI.

Bahrain Atomizers International: POB 235, Manama; tel. 250232; telex 8253; f. 1973; produces atomized aluminium powder; owned by the Government of Bahrain (51%) and Breton Investments (49%); Chair. Y. SHIRAWI.

Bahrain National Gas Co BSC (BANAGAS): POB 477, Rifa'a; tel. 25005; telex 9317; f. 1979; responsible for extraction, processing and sale of hydrocarbon liquids from associated gas derived from onshore Bahrain fields; ownership is 75% Bahrain Government, 12.5% Caltex and 12.5% Arab Petroleum Investments Corporation (APICORP); produces 140,000 tons of LPG and 130,000 tons of natural gasoline per year; Chair. Sheikh IBRAHIM BIN RASHID AL-KHALIFA; Production Man. ALI A. GINDY.

Bahrain National Oil Co (BANOCO): POB 604, Manama; tel. 665048; telex 8670; f. 1976; responsible for exploration for petroleum and other hydrocarbons and involved in their refining, transport, storage, marketing and export; Dir-Gen. MUHAMMAD SALEH SHEIKH ALI.

Bahrain Petroleum Co BSC (BAPCO): Awali; tel. 754444; telex 8214; f. 1980; a refining company owned by the Government of Bahrain (60%) and Caltex Petroleum Corporation (40%); Chair. YOUSEF AHMAD ASH-SHIRAWI (Minister of Development and Industry); Chief Exec. DON F. HEPBURN.

Bahrain-Saudi Aluminium Marketing Co (BALCO): POB 20079, Manama; tel. 234164; telex 9110; f. 1976; to market ALBA products; owned by the Government of Bahrain (74.33%) and Saudi Basic Industries Corporation (25.67%); Gen. Man. MAHMOOD AS-SOUFI (acting).

Bahrain Telecommunications Co BSC (BATELCO): POB 14, Manama; tel. 270270; telex 8201; f. 1981; operates telephone and telex services; cap. BD60m.; 60% owned by Bahrain Government, 40% by Cable and Wireless PLC (United Kingdom); Chair. IBRAHIM MUHAMMAD HASSAN HUMAIDAN; Gen. Man. JOHN MUNDAY.

General Poultry Co: POB 5472, Bahrain; tel. 631001; telex 8678; fully-owned by Government of Bahrain; produces poultry feed and eggs; Chair. SIDDIQ AL-ALAWI.

Gulf Aluminium Rolling Mill Co (GARMCO): POB 20725, Manama; tel. 731000; telex 9786; f. 1980 as a joint venture between the governments of Bahrain, Saudi Arabia, Kuwait, Iraq (20% each), Oman and Qatar (10% each); initial capacity of 40,000 tons per year of aluminium sheet and coil; production commenced in January 1986.

Gulf Petrochemical Industries Co BSC (GPIC): POB 26730, Sitra; tel. 731777; telex 9897; f. 1979 as a joint venture between the governments of Bahrain, Kuwait and Saudi Arabia, each with one-third equity participation; cap. p.u. BD 60m.; a petrochemical complex at Sitra, inaugurated in 1981, began production of ammonia and methanol in 1985.

TRADE UNIONS

There are no trade unions in Bahrain.

Transport

ROADS

Most inhabited areas of Bahrain are linked by bitumen-surfaced roads, and by 1984 the number of cars on the island had risen to 90,000, compared with 20,000 in 1971. Public transport consists of taxis and privately-owned bus services. A national bus company provides public services throughout the country. A modern network of dual highways is being developed, and work on a 25-km causeway link with Saudi Arabia, expected to carry 31,000 vehicles per day, was nearing completion in January 1986, when the final section of the main framework was set in place. Work on the approach road, a three-lane dual carriageway linking the causeway to Manama, was completed in 1986. A joint Bahraini-Saudi bus company was

BAHRAIN

formed in 1986, with capital of US $266,600, to operate along the causeway.

Directorate of Roads and Sewerage: POB 5, Causeway Rd, Manama; tel. 291603; responsible for road maintenance and construction; Adviser J. K. McDade.

SHIPPING

Numerous shipping services link Bahrain and the Gulf with Europe, the USA, Pakistan, India, the Far East and Australia.

The deep-water harbour of Mina Sulman was opened in April 1962; it has 14 conventional berths, two container terminals and a roll-on/roll-off berth. In the vicinity are two slipways able to take vessels of up to 1,016 tons and 73 m in length, with services available for ship repairs afloat. The second container terminal, which has a 400-m quay (permitting two 180-m container ships to be handled simultaneously), was opened in April 1979. Further development of Mina Sulman, to allow handling of larger quantities of container cargo, began in 1983. The extension was expected to cost US $13m. During 1985 Mina Sulman handled approximately 2m. metric tons of cargo.

Directorate of Customs and Ports: POB 15, Manama; tel. 243533; telex 8642; responsible for customs activities and acts as port authority; President of Customs and Ports Sheikh Daij bin Khalifa al-Khalifa; Port Director Eid Abdullah Yusuf; Harbour Master Salih Musallam.

Arab Shipbuilding and Repair Yard Co (ASRY): POB 5110, Hidd; tel. 671111; telex 8455; f. 1974 by OAPEC members; dry dock opened 1977; cap. US $340m.; managed by Lisnave of Portugal; Chair. Sheikh Daij bin Khalifa al-Khalifa; Gen. Man. A. J. Machado Lopes.

CIVIL AVIATION

Bahrain International Airport has a first-class runway, capable of taking the largest aircraft in use, and expansion is still in progress. In 1983 a total of 2,736,000 passengers passed through the airport.

Directorate of Civil Aviation: POB 586, Bahrain International Airport, Muharraq; tel. 321332; telex 9186; Dir-Gen. Sheikh Hamad bin Abdulla al-Khalifa.

Gulf Air Co GSC (Gulf Air): POB 138, Manama; tel. (enquiries) 322200; telex 8255; f. 1950; jointly owned by the governments of Bahrain, Oman, Qatar and the UAE; network includes Abu Dhabi, Amman, Athens, Baghdad, Bahrain, Bangkok, Bombay, Cairo, Colombo, Delhi, Dhahran, Dhaka, Doha, Dubai, Hong Kong, Jeddah, Karachi, Khartoum, Kuwait, Larnaca, London, Manila, Muscat, Paris, Ras al-Khaimah, Salalah, San'a, Sharjah, Shiraz, Teheran and Tunis; Chair. of Board Abdullah bin Nasser as-Suweidi (Bahrain); Pres. and Chief Exec. Ali Ibrahim al-Malki (Qatar); fleet consists of 11 TriStar, 8 Boeing 737-200, 2 Boeing 747-200.

Tourism

Bahrain Tourism Co (BTC): POB 5831, Manama; tel. 255504; telex 8929; total assets BD1.7m. (1983).

BANGLADESH

Introductory Survey

Location, Climate, Language, Religion, Flag, Capital

The People's Republic of Bangladesh lies in southern Asia, surrounded by Indian territory except for a short south-eastern frontier with Burma and a southern coast fronting the Bay of Bengal. The country has a tropical monsoon climate and suffers from periodic cyclones. The average temperature is 19°C (67°F) from October to March, rising to 29°C (84°F) between May and September. The average annual rainfall in Dhaka is 188 cm (74 in), of which about three-quarters occurs between June and September. About 95% of the population speak Bengali, the state language, while the remainder mostly use tribal dialects. More than 85% of the people are Muslims, and there are small minorities of Hindus, Buddhists and Christians. The national flag is green, with a red disc in the centre. The capital is Dhaka (Dacca).

Recent History

Present-day Bangladesh was formerly East Pakistan, one of the five provinces into which Pakistan was divided at its initial creation, when Britain's former Indian Empire was partitioned in August 1947. East Pakistan and the four western provinces were separated by about 1,000 miles (1,600 km) of Indian territory. East Pakistan was formed from the former Indian province of East Bengal and the Sylhet district of Assam. Although the East was more populous, government was based in West Pakistan. Dissatisfaction in East Pakistan at its dependence on a remote central government flared up in 1952, when Urdu was declared Pakistan's official language. Bengali, the main language of East Pakistan, was finally admitted as the joint official language in 1954, and in 1955 Pakistan was reorganized into two wings, east and west, with equal representation in the central legislative assembly. However, discontent continued in the eastern wing, particularly as the region was under-represented in the administration and armed forces, and received a disproportionately small share of Pakistan's development expenditure. The leading political party in East Pakistan was the Awami League, led by Sheikh Mujibur Rahman, who demanded autonomy for the East. General elections in December 1970 gave the Awami League an overwhelming victory in the East, and consequently a majority in Pakistan's National Assembly, so Sheikh Mujib should have become Prime Minister. Pakistan's President, Gen. Yahya Khan, would not accept this, however, and negotiations on a possible constitutional compromise broke down in January 1971. The convening of the new National Assembly was postponed indefinitely in March, leading to violent protests in East Pakistan. The Awami League decided that the province should unilaterally secede from Pakistan, and on 26 March 1971 Mujib proclaimed the independence of the People's Republic of Bangladesh ('Bengal Nation').

Civil war immediately broke out. President Yahya Khan outlawed the Awami League and arrested its leaders. By April 1971 the Pakistan army dominated the eastern province. In August Sheikh Mujib was secretly put on trial in West Pakistan. Resistance continued, however, from the Liberation Army of East Bengal (the 'Mukhti Bahini'), a group of irregular fighters who launched a major offensive in November. As a result of the fighting, an estimated 9.5m. refugees crossed into India. On 4 December India declared war on Pakistan, with Indian forces intervening in support of the 'Mukhti Bahini'. Pakistan surrendered on 16 December and Bangladesh's independence became a reality. Pakistan was thus confined to its former western wing. In January 1972 Sheikh Mujib was freed by Pakistan's new President, Zulfiqar Ali Bhutto, and became Prime Minister of Bangladesh. Under a provisional constitution, Bangladesh was declared to be a secular state and a parliamentary democracy. The new nation quickly achieved international recognition, causing Pakistan to withdraw from the Commonwealth in January 1972. Bangladesh joined the Commonwealth in April. The members who had been elected from the former East Pakistan for the Pakistan National Assembly and the Provincial Assembly in December 1970 formed the Bangladesh Constituent Assembly. A new constitution was approved by this Assembly in November 1972 and came into effect in December. A general election for the country's first Jatiya Sangsad (Parliament) was held in March 1973. The Awami League received 73% of the total votes and won 292 of the 300 directly elective seats in the legislature. Bangladesh was finally recognized by Pakistan in February 1974. Floods in July and August 1974 led to widespread famine and an epidemic of cholera, further sapping the economy, already deeply affected by the war. Political stability was threatened by opposition groups which resorted to terrorism and included both political extremes; at the end of December a state of emergency was declared and constitutional rights suspended. In January 1975 parliamentary government was replaced by a presidential form of government. Sheikh Mujib became President, assuming absolute power, and created the Bangladesh Peasants' and Workers' Awami League. In February Bangladesh became a one-party state.

In August 1975 Sheikh Mujib and his family were assassinated in a right-wing coup, led by a group of Islamic army majors. Khandakar Mushtaq Ahmed, the former Minister of Commerce, was installed as President, declared martial law and banned political parties. A counter-coup on 3 November brought to power Brig. Khalid Musharaf, the pro-Indian commander of the Dhaka garrison, who was appointed Chief of Army Staff, but on 7 November a third coup overthrew Brig. Musharaf's four-day-old regime and power was assumed by the three service chiefs jointly, under a non-political President, Abusadet Mohammed Sayem, the Chief Justice of the Supreme Court. A neutral non-party government was formed, in which the reinstated Chief of Army Staff, Major-Gen. Ziaur Rahman (Gen. Zia), took precedence over his colleagues. Political parties were legalized again in July 1976.

An early return to representative government was promised, but in November 1976 elections were postponed indefinitely and, in a major shift of power, Gen. Zia took over the powers of Chief Martial Law Administrator from President Sayem, assuming the presidency also in April 1977. He amended the Constitution, making Islam, instead of secularism, its first basic principle. In a national referendum in May 1977, 99% of voters affirmed their confidence in President Zia's policies, and in June 1978 the country's first direct presidential election resulted in a clear victory for Zia, who formed a Council of Ministers to replace his Council of Advisers. Parliamentary elections followed in February 1979 and, in an attempt to persuade opposition parties to participate in the elections, President Zia met some of their demands by repealing 'all undemocratic provisions' of the 1974 constitutional amendment, releasing political prisoners and withdrawing press censorship. Consequently, 29 parties contested the elections, in which President Zia's Bangladesh Nationalist Party (BNP) received 49% of the total votes and won 207 of the 300 directly elective seats in the Jatiya Sangsad. A new Prime Minister was appointed in April. The lifting of martial law in April and the revocation of the state of emergency in November meant that civilian democracy had returned to Bangladesh after an absence of almost five years.

Political instability recurred, however, when Gen. Zia was assassinated on 30 May 1981 during an attempted military coup, supposedly led by Maj.-Gen. Mohammad Abdul Manzur, an army divisional commander who was himself later killed in confused circumstances. The elderly Vice-President, Justice Abdus Sattar, took over as acting President but was faced by strikes and demonstrations over the execution of several officers who had been involved in the coup, and pressure from opposition parties to have the date of the presidential election moved. As the only person acceptable to the different groups within the BNP, Sattar was nominated as the party's presidential candidate, gaining an overwhelming victory at the November election. President Sattar announced his intention of carrying on the policies of the late Gen. Zia. He found it increasingly difficult, however, to retain civilian control over the country, and in January 1982 he formed a National Security Council, which included military personnel, led by the Army Chief of Staff, Lt-Gen. Hossain Mohammad Ershad. On 24 March Gen. Ershad seized power in a bloodless coup, claiming that political corruption and economic mismanagement had become intolerable. The country was placed under martial law, with Ershad as Chief Martial Law Administrator (in October his title was changed to Prime Minister), aided by a mainly military Council of Advisers; a retired judge, Justice Abul Chowdhury, was nominated as President by Ershad. Political activities were banned. Later in the year, several former ministers were tried and imprisoned on charges of corruption.

Although the Government's economic policies (see below) met with some success and gained a measure of popular support for Ershad, there were increasing demands in 1983 for a return to democratic government. The two principal opposition groups that emerged were a 15-party alliance, headed by a faction of the Awami League under Sheikh Hasina Wazed (daughter of the late Sheikh Mujib), and a seven-party group which was led by a faction of the BNP under the former President Sattar (who died in October 1985) and Begum Khalida Zia (widow of Gen. Zia). In September 1983 the two groups formed an alliance, the Movement for the Restoration of Democracy (MRD), and jointly issued demands for an end to martial law, for the release of political prisoners and for the holding of parliamentary elections before any others. In November permission was given for the resumption of political activity, and it was announced that a series of local elections between December 1983 and March 1984 were to precede a presidential election and a parliamentary election later in the year. A new political party, the Jana Dal (People's Party), was formed in November 1983 to support Ershad as a presidential candidate. Following demonstrations demanding civilian government, the ban on political activity was reimposed at the beginning of December, only two weeks after it was lifted, and leading political figures (including, temporarily, Begum Zia and Sheikh Hasina) were detained. On 11 December Ershad declared himself President.

Bangladesh remained disturbed in 1984, with frequent strikes and political demonstrations. Local elections to *upazilla* (sub-district) councils, due to take place in March, were postponed, as the opposition objected to their being held before the presidential and parliamentary elections, on the grounds that Ershad was trying to improve his power-base. The presidential and parliamentary elections, scheduled for May, were also postponed, until December, because of persistent opposition demands for the lifting of martial law and for the formation of an interim neutral government to oversee a fair election. In October Ershad agreed to lift martial law in three stages in November and December if the opposition would participate in these elections. They responded with an appeal for a campaign of civil disobedience, which led to the announcement in October that the elections were to be indefinitely postponed.

In January 1985 it was announced that a parliamentary election would be held in April, to be preceded by a relaxation of martial law in certain respects: the Constitution was to be fully restored after the election. The announcement was followed by the formation of a new Council of Ministers, composed entirely of military officers and excluding all members of the Jana Dal, in response to demands by the opposition parties for a 'neutral' government during the pre-election period. Once more, the opposition threatened to boycott the election, as President Ershad would not relinquish power to an interim government, and in March 1985 political activity was banned again. This was immediately followed by a referendum, held in support of the presidency, in which Ershad received 94% of the total votes. Local elections for *upazilla* councils in rural areas were held in May 1985, without the participation of the opposition, and Ershad claimed that 85% of the elected council chairmen were his supporters, although not necessarily of his party. In September a new five-party political alliance, the National Front (comprising the Jana Dal, the United People's Party, the Gonotantrik Party, the Bangladesh Muslim League and a breakaway section of the Bangladesh Nationalist Party), was established to proclaim government policies.

In January 1986 the 10-month ban on political activity was lifted. The five components of the National Front formally converted themselves into a single pro-Government entity, named the Jatiya Dal (National Party). Further strikes and demonstrations were organized by opposition groups, who continued to demand the lifting of martial law before the holding of any parliamentary or presidential elections. In March President Ershad announced that parliamentary elections were to be held (under martial law) at the end of April. At first, all the opposition groups rejected this proposal, claiming that the election results would be falsified by the Government. A large demonstration under the joint leadership of the BNP and the Awami League, protesting against military rule, was held in Dhaka. In March 1986 President Ershad relaxed martial law by removing all army commanders from key civil posts and by abolishing more than 150 military courts and the martial law offices. These concessions fulfilled some of the opposition's demands and, as a result, candidates from eight parties of the Awami League alliance (including Sheikh Hasina herself), the Jamit-i-Islami and other smaller opposition parties participated in the general election for a new Jatiya Sangsad on 7 May (postponed from 26 April). However, the BNP alliance, headed by Begum Zia, boycotted the polls. Shortly before the election, President Ershad banned anti-poll activity and imposed fresh curbs on the press. Begum Zia was placed under temporary house arrest. The election was characterized by allegations of extensive fraud, violence and intimidation. According to official figures, the turn-out at the polls was 45%–50% of the total electorate. Other observers, however, suggested participation of between 10% and 30%. The Jatiya Dal won an absolute majority, securing 153 of the 300 directly-elected seats. In addition, the 30 seats reserved for women in the legislature were filled by nominees of the Jatiya Dal.

In June, when the Constitution remained suspended, the Awami League alliance again demanded the lifting of martial law, the resignation of Ershad and the restoration of a complete democratic system. At the beginning of July Ershad announced that martial law would be lifted only after a presidential election. Although the Awami League members had been sworn in as MPs, they refused to attend the inauguration of the Jatiya Sangsad. In late July the Jatiya Sangsad was prorogued for an indefinite period. A civilian Council of Ministers was sworn in. Mizanur Rahman Chowdhury, former general-secretary of the Jatiya Dal, became Prime Minister.

In order to be a candidate in the presidential election in October, Ershad stood down as Army Chief of Staff in August and appointed Maj.-Gen. M. Atiqur Raham in his place, while remaining as Chief Martial Law Administrator and Commander-in-Chief of the Armed Forces. In early September Ershad joined the Jatiya Dal, being elected as chairman of the party and nominated as its presidential candidate. Despite the banning of anti-election propaganda, the opposition alliances, headed by the BNP and the Awami League (which both boycotted the presidential poll), organized anti-election demonstrations, and Begum Zia and Sheikh Hasina were placed under house arrest. At the presidential election in mid-October, Ershad won an overwhelming victory over his 11 opponents, receiving nearly 22m. votes, according to official results. The turn-out was officially reported at more than 50%, but was generally believed to be 10%–15%. Alleged malpractice was said to be more discreet than in the May legislative elections.

In early November Ershad summoned the Jatiya Sangsad, which approved indemnity legislation, legalizing the military regime's actions since March 1982. Ershad lifted martial law and restored the 1972 Constitution. The opposition alliances criticized the indemnity law, stating that they would campaign for the dissolution of the Jatiya Sangsad and the overthrow of the Ershad Government. In December 1986, in an effort to stem increasing dissension, President Ershad reshuffled the Council of Ministers, bringing in four MPs from the Awami League. The Justice Minister, Justice A. K. M. Nurul Islam, was appointed Vice-President.

In foreign affairs, Bangladesh has maintained a policy of non-alignment. Relations with Pakistan improved in 1976: ambassadors were exchanged, and trade, postal and telecom-

BANGLADESH

munication links were resumed. Pakistan, however, refuses to accept the 300,000 Bihari Muslims (who supported Pakistan in Bangladesh's war of liberation in 1972) still remaining in refugee camps in Bangladesh, unless it does not have to bear the cost of absorbing them. Relations with India have been strained over the questions of cross-border terrorism (especially around the area of the Chittagong Hill Tracts, where Buddhist tribal rebels have been waging guerrilla warfare against the Bangladeshi police and the Bengali settlers for several years) and of a barrage that has been constructed by India on the Ganga (Ganges) river, so depriving Bangladesh of water for irrigation and river transport during the dry season. In 1986 India and Bangladesh remained in dispute over the sharing of the water. In June 1986 two Bangladeshi police stations were established in the Bangladeshi enclaves of Dahagram and Angorpota, in the Indian state of West Bengal, after several violent clashes between Indians and local residents. In August 1985 Bangladesh and Burma completed work on the demarcation of their common border, in accordance with a May 1979 agreement. In October 1986 an air service between the capitals of Bangladesh and Bhutan was inaugurated, to complement existing surface links by road and rail.

Bangladesh is a member of the South Asian Association for Regional Co-operation (SAARC, see p. 218), formally constituted in December 1985, with Bhutan, India, Maldives, Nepal, Pakistan and Sri Lanka. In December 1985 SAARC held its inaugural meeting in Dhaka, where representatives of the member states discussed, among other issues, terrorism and drug trafficking. Included in SAARC's newly-drafted charter were pledges of non-interference by members in each other's internal affairs and a joint effort to avoid 'contentious' issues whenever the association meets. The second SAARC meeting was held in Bangalore, India, in November 1986.

Government

With the ending of martial law, constitutional government was revived in November 1986 (having been suspended in March 1982).

Bangladesh is a democratic republic with a presidential form of government. The President is elected by universal suffrage for a five-year term and appoints his Council of Ministers from the 330-member Jatiya Sangsad (Parliament), 300 members of which are elected by universal suffrage. An additional 30 women members are appointed by the other members. The Jatiya Sangsad serves a five-year term.

In 1983 a system of 493 local administrative sub-districts (*upazillas*), each containing an average of 260,000 people, was established as part of a move to decentralize government. These *upazillas* are staffed by civil servants from Dhaka but headed by local chairmen, who hold office for five years. They have increased local involvement in development schemes, and development funds are allocated yearly to each of them.

Defence

Military service is voluntary. In July 1986 the armed forces numbered 91,300: an army of 81,800, a navy of 6,500 and an air force of 3,000. The paramilitary forces totalled 55,000, and included the Bangladesh Rifles (border guard) of 30,000. Budget expenditure on defence was estimated at 5,011m. taka for 1985/86.

Economic Affairs

Apart from small city-states, Bangladesh is the most densely populated country in the world, with an estimated population of 100.6m. at mid-1986, averaging 699 inhabitants per sq km. The population is increasing at about 2.0% annually, and was expected to be 157m. by the year 2000. In the year ending 30 June 1986 the expansion of domestic food production exceeded the rate of population growth, but the country was still unable to halt the increase in poverty. In terms of average income, Bangladesh is among the world's poorest countries. In 1984, according to estimates by the World Bank, the gross national product (GNP) per head, measured at average 1982–84 prices, was US $130. Between 1965 and 1984, it was estimated, Bangladesh's GNP per head increased, in real terms, at an average rate of only 0.6% per year. However, the average annual increase in overall gross domestic product (GDP), measured in constant prices, was 5.0% between 1973 and 1984. Real GDP growth was 4.9% in 1985/86, compared with 3.8% in 1984/85, 2.7% in 1983/84 and 1.4% in 1982/83. The target growth for GDP in 1986/87 was 5.2%.

Agriculture, which employs about 80% of the working population, contributed about 40% of GDP in 1984/85 and 1985/86. Agricultural output expanded by an estimated 4.9% in 1985/86. The land is fertile, but crops are often destroyed by floods, cyclone and drought. Production of rice, which is grown on about 75% of cultivated land, fell sharply after independence and did not regain former levels until 1974. Rice harvests continued to improve: output of milled rice reached 13.9m. long tons in 1982/83, 14.3m. tons in 1983/84 and 14.4m. tons in 1984/85. In 1978 the Government launched a five-year programme to double food production by bringing more arable land under irrigation (in 1979 only about 10% was irrigated), encouraging double and triple cropping, and increasing the use of fertilizers. In 1985/86 the total irrigated area in Bangladesh was 6.2m. acres (2.5m. ha), which was expected to increase to 9.2m. acres (3.7m. ha) by 1989/90. The Chittagong Urea Fertilizer Project, when completed in 1987, will produce about 561,000 metric tons of fertilizer annually. By 1985, the area producing high-yielding varieties was to increase from 3m. acres (1.2m. ha) to nearly 8m. acres (3.2m. ha) and, between 1980 and 1985, efforts were made to increase output of wheat, as it is more nutritious than rice and cheaper to produce. The Ershad government introduced a 'food for work' programme, with US aid, to boost food production and rural employment. Production of wheat rose sharply to more than 1m. long tons in 1980/81 but fell to 950,000 tons in 1981/82. Output improved to 1,080,000 tons in 1982/83, increased to 1,190,000 tons in 1983/84, and reached 1.4m. tons in 1984/85.

Three years of good harvests led to a decline in necessary food imports to 1.5m. tons in 1977/78, but the poor 1978/79 harvest, caused by a late monsoon season, meant that there was a shortfall between production and consumption, and imports returned to the former level of 2m. tons (about one-sixth of total requirements). The 1980/81 harvest produced a record total of 14.8m. tons of food grains (including rice on a milled basis), but the lack of adequate storage facilities caused severe problems. Output of food grains fell to 14.37m. tons in 1981/82, but recovered to 15.28m. tons in 1982/83, and to 15.51m. tons in 1983/84. Production was 16.08m. metric tons in 1984/85, and reached a record 16.3m. tons in 1985/86. However, despite these improvements, it was still necessary to import grain (2.65m. tons in 1984/85 and 1.5m. tons in 1985/86). The value of cereal imports increased by 132% in 1981/82 because of drought, fell slightly in 1982/83 but rose again in 1983/84 and 1984/85, as a result of the serious monsoon flooding.

Jute and tea are the main cash crops. Bangladesh supplies about 90% of world exports of raw jute. In 1986 the jute industry employed about 250,000 workers. Because of competition from synthetic substitutes for jute, general world recession and increased competition from India, Nepal and Thailand, production dropped from 7m. bales (each of 400 lb or 181.4 kg) in 1969/70 to 4m. in 1974/75, but increased world demand halted this trend and production rose steadily to 5.5m. bales in 1977/78. By 1980/81, however, estimated production had fallen to just over 4m. bales, well below the target figure of 7m. bales. In 1982/83 production rose marginally, to 4.8m. bales, but in 1983/84 floods destroyed an estimated 1m. bales, bringing production down to 4m. bales, although, because of a world shortage, jute sales earned double the average 1983 price per bale. Output of jute rose to 6m. bales in 1984/85, and the Government had to cut the export price by one-third. The reduced price did not cover the cost of production. International prices for raw jute declined by 45% in 1985/86, with no sign of immediate recovery. Accordingly, despite the high output of 7.5m. bales, the jute industry sustained a total financial loss of 2,130m. taka in 1985/86. The long-term difficulty for Bangladesh is to ensure regular and reliable supplies to satisfy demand. Jute and jute products provided 66% of export revenue in 1982/83, 57% in 1983/84 and 59% in 1984/85. Export earnings from raw jute in 1986/87 were expected to be 4,082.7m. taka, while earnings from jute goods were expected to be 9,591.5m. taka.

A programme was introduced in 1979 to improve the quality of locally-produced tea, which in that year became Bangladesh's second largest export earner. In 1982/83 exports of tea were worth 1,100.5m. taka (6.9% of total export receipts), and in

1983/84 they were worth 1,699.5m. taka (8.4% of total export receipts), but in 1984/85 tea exports fell to 1,570.4m. taka (6.3% of total export receipts). In the first four months of 1986 tea production fell to below one-half of the 1985 level (38m. kg) because of low rainfall and wastage of land. Potatoes, sugar cane, tobacco, spices and tropical fruits are also produced, while the output of cotton is being increased to lessen the burden of imports.

Mineral resources are few. There are large reserves of natural gas, estimated at 12,450m. cubic feet, and by 1985 13 gas fields had been discovered (including one off-shore). In 1986 the Government inaugurated the Second Gas Development Project, aiming to increase gas supplies from existing fields and to produce the first significant quantites of liquid hydrocarbons (kerosene and gasoline) in Bangladesh. Low-grade coal reserves of 700m. tons have also been discovered. In 1980 there were renewed hopes of on-shore petroleum discoveries, but exploration has not been successful. As part of the third Five-Year Plan (1985–90), the Government has intensified mineral exploration activities in the north of the country. The cost of petroleum imports, which in 1984/85 was US $360m., was likely to be reduced to US $300m. in 1985/86 and to US $260m. in 1986/87. In 1986 Bangladesh was importing about 1.1m. tons of crude petroleum and 500,000 tons of refined oil products annually.

Industry accounts for less than 9% of GDP. Manufactured products comprised about 45% of imports in 1982/83, and 43% in 1983/84. Between 1983 and 1986 however, the expansion of annual industrial output increased from about 6% to about 10%. About 20% of the industrial labour force are employed in jute-based industries. Other major products are cotton textiles, chemicals and sugar. Production fell in nearly all the main industries after independence in 1971, owing to war damage, the departure of the largely non-Bengali investors and managerial class and the loss of many skilled Bengali workers. Most organized industry was nationalized, and state corporations were set up for the major commodities. General Zia's Government changed industrial policy, encouraging private investment and compensating foreign investors whose assets had been nationalized in 1971, on condition that the money was reinvested in Bangladesh. Many tea plantations and state-owned industrial units were returned to the private sector during 1976 and 1977, and in 1981 the private sector was permitted to set up cotton textile spinning mills. The cotton textile industry grew rapidly during the 1980s and established itself as an important source of export earnings. Most of this has been achieved through private initiative, and in 1985/86 nearly 600 new companies (providing 150,000 new jobs) were formed. During 1984/85 the textile industry exported goods worth US $100m., which was a three-fold expansion over 1983/84. The Government planned to increase the area under cotton cultivation from 6,000 ha in 1980 to 129,090 ha by 1990. In 1986 the US Government fixed Bangladesh's annual quota of cotton textile exports to the USA at 4.2m. dozen pieces for at least the next two years.

In mid-1980 Parliament legislated for the establishment of three export-processing zones to increase trade and foreign investment, and by 1985 the first factories were in operation. In 1982, in an attempt to stimulate private investment, about one-half of the nationalized jute and textile industries returned to the private sector. In 1986 the policy of 'privatization' continued to dominate plans for economic development, and the Industrial Policy (1986) aimed to raise the contribution of the industrial sector to GDP and to achieve industrial growth, with emphasis on private-sector participation. The proportion of the country's industrial assets under government ownership was reduced from 85% in 1972 to 45% (of a considerably larger industrial base) in 1986. In 1985 the Government decided on a phased divestment of 49% of the shares of three of the four nationalized banks.

Trade patterns were disrupted by the separation from Pakistan, to which the tea crop had largely been exported before the war. In 1976, however, direct trade links were re-established with Pakistan: shipping and banking arrangements were agreed, and a joint trade committee was set up between the two countries. In 1984/85 the two-way trade between Bangladesh and Pakistan amounted to US $103.17m. Bangladesh's trade deficit, amounting to 38,027.9m. taka in 1984/85 is partly offset by remittances sent home by Bangladeshi workers abroad. Remittances from workers abroad declined from $682m. in 1982 to $525m. in 1983/84, and to $450m. in 1984/85. The 1985/86 total was estimated to have risen to $550m., but the total for 1986/87 was likely to fall to about $500m. Between 1979/80 and 1981/82, owing largely to falling jute prices, there was a 35% decline in the terms of trade (export prices relative to import costs). However, there was expected to be a 17% improvement in 1985/86, and a further improvement in 1986/87. In 1982/83 the Government imposed import restrictions and devalued the currency by 22%, and again by 20%, in relation to the US dollar. Economic policies gave priority to reducing dependence on imported food, energy and manufactures by increasing domestic production. Although Bangladesh's exports rose by 20% in volume in 1985/86, they fell in value by nearly the same percentage, owing to declines in prices for commodities such as tea and jute.

Bangladesh is heavily dependent on large amounts of foreign aid, particularly commodity aid, to meet the requirements of budget plans and development programmes, and to offset the deficit on trade in goods and services. In 1986 foreign aid accounted for over 40% of total government resources. Two major suppliers of funds are the World Bank and the USA. The US bilateral aid commitment for 1982/83 was $188m. The World Bank approved credits (in 'soft' loans from the International Development Association) totalling $393m. in 1983/84, and about $400m. in 1985/86. Total pledges of aid by the main donor countries and agencies amounted to $1,720m. in 1984/85, and to $1,680m. in 1985/86. The third Five-Year Plan (see below) projected aid disbursements, at $1,420m. per year (net), compared with $1,250m. per year over the second Five-Year Plan (1980–85). The predicted growth rate in foreign-aid disbursement, estimated at 3.3% per year, was roughly the same as in the second Plan.

The country's first Five-Year Plan (1973–78) aimed at an annual growth of 5.5% in GDP. This target was exceeded, with an average annual rate of growth of 6.7%. After an interim two-year plan for 1978–80, the second Five-Year Plan, covering 1980–85, was launched, with a total proposed outlay of 255,950m. taka, of which 201,250m. was to go to the public sector and 54,700m. to the private sector. An average annual GDP growth rate of 8.4% was projected; however, the actual rise in GDP averaged only 3.8% per year over the Plan period. GDP growth was 2.7% in 1983/84 and 3.8% in 1984/85, and 4.9% in 1985/86. A third Five-Year Plan (1985–89), launched in July 1985, envisages total investment of 284,810m. taka, average annual GDP growth of 5.4%, a reduction in the annual rate of population increase, an annual growth rate in agricultural output of 4%, an annual growth rate in industrial output of 10.1%, and a food-grain production target of 20.7m. tons per year. A greater emphasis on the promotion of small-scale and cottage industries in the rural areas was included in the third Five-Year Plan. In 1986 the co-operative movement was being fully supported by the national development policy. The aims of this movement were to shun dependence on aid and to promote policies of self-help. The proposed budget expenditure for 1986/87 totalled an estimated 91,120m. taka, of which 37,400m. taka was for recurrent expenses and 47,640m. for development spending. The overall deficit was estimated at 42,720m. taka.

Between May and August 1984, Bangladesh suffered serious floods, which affected about 25m. people, destroyed an estimated 200,000 ha of rice and jute crops, and caused damage valued at US $380m. The Government launched a rehabilitation programme, to cost $58m., and 2.4m. tons of food were imported by December to avert the threat of famine. In mid-1985 further floods and a devastating cyclone left hundreds of thousands of people homeless, and 1.5m. tons of food grain had to be imported in 1985/86.

Social Welfare

The principal medical objective after independence was to prevent epidemics and widespread malnutrition, and to treat and rehabilitate war victims. Basic health services remain relatively undeveloped: in the early 1980s about 25% of all live-born children died before reaching five years of age. Health programmes give particular priority to the popularization of birth control. In 1981 Bangladesh had 504 hospital establishments, with a total of only 19,727 beds, equivalent to one for every 4,545 inhabitants: one of the lowest levels of provision in the world. In 1981 there were 10,065 physicians working in the country. Between 1982 and 1985, the Government's annual expenditure on health rose from 899m. taka to 1,605m. taka.

In 1986 the Government adopted a policy of 'Health for All', and several programmes were incorporated in the third Five-Year Plan with the aim of achieving this objective: the number of health centres was to be increased (in 1985 a total of 355 *upazilla* health complexes were in operation), more people were to be given medical training, and the public education programme on family planning was to be expanded.

Education

Education is not compulsory but the Government provides free primary schooling for five years. Primary education begins at five years of age and lasts for five years. Secondary education, beginning at the age of 10, lasts for up to seven years, comprising a first cycle of five years and a second cycle of two further years. In 1981 an estimated 60% of children (74% of boys; 46% of girls) in the relevant age-group attended primary schools, while the comparable enrolment ratio at secondary schools was 15% (boys 24%; girls 6%). Some pilot schemes for compulsory attendance in primary schools are in progress, and there are plans to introduce universal primary education by the late 1980s. In 1984/85 there were 44,423 primary schools, with a total enrolment of 9,914,000 pupils, and 8,594 secondary schools, with 2,657,000 students. Secondary schools and colleges in the private sector vastly outnumber government institutions: in 1976 government high schools comprised only about 2% of the country's total. There are six universities (with a total of 41,215 students in 1984/85), including one for agriculture and one for engineering.

Educational reform is designed to help meet the manpower needs of the country, and most importance is given to primary, technical and vocational education. In 1986 the rate of adult illiteracy was still about 74%, despite a five-year government programme that was launched in 1980 in an attempt to eradicate illiteracy.

Government expenditure on education rose from 2,337m. taka in 1982/83 to 4,939m. taka in 1984/85.

Tourism

Tourist attractions include the cities of Dhaka and Chittagong, Cox's Bazar—which has the world's longest beach (120 km)—on the Bay of Bengal, and Teknaf, at the southernmost point of Bangladesh. The total number of tourist arrivals increased from 53,708 in 1982 to 145,634 in 1985. The majority of visitors are from India, Japan, the United Kingdom and the USA. Earnings from tourism rose from 230m. taka in 1981 to 900m. taka in 1985.

Public Holidays

1987: 1 January (New Year's Day), 21 February (National Mourning Day), 26 March (Independence Day), 17 April (Good Friday), 20 April (Easter Monday), 1 May (May Day), May* (Buddha Purinama), 30 May* (Id al-Fitr), July* (Jamat Wida), 6 August* (Id al-Adha), 26 August* (Muharram, Islamic New Year), September* (Shab-i-Bharat), September* (Durga Puja), 4 November* (Birth of the Prophet), 7 November (National Revolution Day), 16 December (National Day), 25 December (Christmas), 26 December (Boxing Day).

1988: 1 January (New Year's Day), 21 February (National Mourning Day), 26 March (Independence Day), 1 April (Good Friday), 4 April (Easter Monday), 1 May (May Day), May* (Buddha Purinama), 18 May* (Id al-Fitr), July* (Jamat Wida), 25 July* (Id al-Adha), 14 August* (Muharram, Islamic New Year), September* (Shab-i-Bharat), September* (Durga Puja), 23 October* (Birth of the Prophet), 7 November (National Revolution Day), 16 December (National Day), 25 December (Christmas), 26 December (Boxing Day).

* Dates of certain religious holidays are subject to the sighting of the moon, and there are also optional holidays for different religious groups.

Weights and Measures

The imperial system of measures is in force, pending the introduction of the metric system. The following local units of weight are also used:
  1 maund = 82.28 lb (37.29 kg).
  1 seer = 2.057 lb (932 grams).
  1 tola = 180 grains (11.66 grams).

Currency and Exchange Rates

100 poisha = 1 taka.
Exchange rates (30 September 1986):
  £1 sterling = 43.844 taka.
  US $1 = 30.300 taka.

BANGLADESH *Statistical Survey*

Statistical Survey

Source (unless otherwise stated): Bangladesh Bureau of Statistics, Dhaka; tel. (2) 409871.

Area and Population

AREA, POPULATION AND DENSITY

Area (sq km)	143,998*
Population (census results)†	
1 March 1974	76,398,000
6 March 1981	
Males	46,295,000
Females	43,617,000
Total	89,912,000
Population (official estimates at mid-year)	
1983	94,651,000
1984	96,730,000
1985	98,657,000
Density (per sq km) at mid-1985	685

* 55,598 sq miles.
† Including adjustment for net underenumeration, estimated to have been 6.9% in 1974 and 3.2% in 1981. The enumerated totals were: 71,479,071 in 1974; 87,119,965 (males 44,919,191, females 42,200,774) in 1981.

POPULATION BY DIVISIONS

	1974 Census	1981 Census
Chittagong	19,914,000	23,322,000
Dhaka	22,780,000	27,091,000
Khulna	15,177,000	17,695,000
Rajshahi	18,527,000	21,804,000
Total	76,398,000	89,912,000

PRINCIPAL TOWNS (population at 1981 census)

Dhaka (capital)	3,430,312*	Barisal	172,905
Chittagong	1,391,877	Sylhet	168,371
Khulna	646,359	Rangpur	153,174
Rajshahi	253,740	Jessore	148,927
Comilla	184,132	Saidpur	126,608

* Including Narayanganj (population 270,680 in 1974).

BIRTHS AND DEATHS*

	Registered live births Rate (per 1,000)	Registered deaths Rate (per 1,000)
1982	34.8	11.9
1983	36.0	12.3
1984	34.8	12.3
1985†	34.2	12.0

* Registration is incomplete. According to UN estimates, the average annual rates in 1980–85 were: Births 44.8 per 1,000; Deaths 17.5 per 1,000.
† Provisional.

ECONOMICALLY ACTIVE POPULATION
(1981 census, provisional results)*

Agriculture, hunting, forestry and fishing	23,789,885
Mining and quarrying	2,899
Manufacturing	1,422,512
Electricity, gas and water	11,338
Construction	49,443
Trade, restaurants and hotels	1,159,067
Transport, storage and communications	481,147
Financing, insurance, real estate and business services	83,545
Community, social and personal services	3,097,265
Activities not adequately described	3,118
Total labour force	30,100,219

* Figures exclude unemployed persons seeking work for the first time, totalling 755,742. The total labour force of 30,855,961 comprised 25,549,557 males and 5,306,404 females.

Source: ILO, *Year Book of Labour Statistics*.

Agriculture

PRINCIPAL CROPS (million long tons, year ending 30 June)

	1982/83	1983/84	1984/85
Rice (milled)	13.99	14.28	14.39
Wheat	1.08	1.19	1.44
Sugar cane	7.24	7.06	6.77
Potatoes	1.13	1.15	1.14
Sweet potatoes	0.70	0.70	0.67
Pulses	0.22	0.20	0.20
Oilseeds	0.25	0.26	0.27
Jute	0.87	0.93	0.82

Tobacco (production in '000 metric tons): 40 in 1980; 47 in 1981; 51 in 1982; 47 in 1983.

LIVESTOCK ('000 head at 30 June)

	1982/83	1983/84	1984/85
Cattle	22,174	22,490	22,811
Buffaloes	549	566	584
Sheep	520	522	524
Goats	9,711	9,942	10,178
Chickens	53,544	55,621	58,307
Ducks	21,572	23,747	26,140

BANGLADESH   Statistical Survey

LIVESTOCK PRODUCTS (year ending 30 June)

	1982/83	1983/84	1984/85
Beef and veal (metric tons)	124,074	270,735	274,580
Buffalo meat (metric tons)	2,032	4,255	4,330
Mutton and lamb (metric tons)	792	933	933
Goats' meat (metric tons)	24,689	46,398	47,480
Poultry meat (metric tons)	55,331	57,969	61,478
Edible offals (metric tons)	7,212	7,358	7,497
Cows' and buffalo milk (metric tons)	814,720	601,344	609,146
Sheep's milk (metric tons)*	16,000	16,000	17,000

	1982/83	1983/84	1984/85
Goats' milk (metric tons)*	506,000	512,000	517,000
Butter (metric tons)	610	896	933
Cheese (metric tons)	1,016	1,493	1,530
Hen eggs ('000)	842,904	693,680	839,628
Other poultry eggs ('000)	655,650	712,440	980,250
Wool:			
greasy (metric tons)*	1,296	1,308	1,320
clean (metric tons)*	790	800	810
Cattle and buffalo hides ('000)	2,811	5,138	5,211
Sheep and goat skins ('000)	5,587	5,729	5,862

* FAO estimates for 1982–84.

Forestry

ROUNDWOOD REMOVALS ('000 cubic metres)

	1982	1983	1984
Sawlogs, veneer logs and logs for sleepers	643	510	401
Pulpwood*	63	63	63
Other industrial wood*	279	287	295
Fuel wood*	24,243	24,915	25,600
Total	25,228	25,775	26,359

* FAO estimates.
Source: FAO, *Yearbook of Forest Products*.

SAWNWOOD PRODUCTION ('000 cubic metres)

	1976	1977	1978
Total (incl. boxboards)	142	159	170*

* FAO estimate.
1979–84: Annual production as in 1978 (FAO estimates).
Source: FAO, *Yearbook of Forest Products*.

Fishing

('000 long tons, year ending 30 June)

	1982/83	1983/84	1984/85
Inland	583	577	588
Marine	141	174	185
Total catch	724	751	773

Source: Directorate of Fisheries.

Mining

	1983	1984*	1985*
Natural gas (million cu ft)	72,104	83,090	92,043

* Year ending 30 June.

Industry

SELECTED PRODUCTS
(Public sector only, year ending 30 June)

	1982/83	1983/84	1984/85*
Jute textiles ('000 tons)	561	535	512
Hessian ('000 tons)	228	242	208
Sacking ('000 tons)	242	197	223
Carpet backing ('000 tons)	94	97	81
Others ('000 tons)	6	8	8
Cotton cloth (million yards)	65	64	69
Cotton yarn (million lb)	98	102	106
Newsprint ('000 tons)	27	29	46
Other paper ('000 tons)	26	28	39
Cement ('000 tons)	307	273	240
Steel ingots ('000 tons)	47	73	101
Re-rolled steel products ('000 tons)	18	7	13
Petroleum products ('000 tons)	919	1,020	943
Urea fertilizer ('000 tons)	371	728	741
Ammonium sulphate ('000 tons)	12	11	10
Chemicals ('000 tons)	17	17	19
Refined sugar ('000 tons)	178	151	88
Wine and spirits ('000 liquid proof galls)	1,107	1,142	1,104
Tea (million lb)†	84	85	94
Edible oil and vegetable ghee ('000 tons)	33	26	15
Cigarettes ('000 million)	14	15	14

* Provisional. † Including production in the private sector.

Finance

CURRENCY AND EXCHANGE RATES

Monetary Units
100 poisha = 1 taka.

Denominations
Coins: 1, 2, 5, 10, 25 and 50 poisha.
Notes: 1, 5, 10, 50, 100 taka.

Sterling and Dollar Equivalents (30 September 1986)
£1 sterling = 43.844 taka;
US $1 = 30.300 taka;
1,000 taka = £22.808 = $33.003.

Average Exchange Rate (taka per US $)
1983   24.615
1984   25.354
1985   27.995

BUDGET (estimates, million taka, year ending 30 June)

Revenue	1982/83	1983/84	1984/85*
Customs duties	10,386	14,591	11,200
Excise duties	4,985	3,238	7,050
Sales tax	2,705	2,050	4,100
Stamps	794	1,005	1,100
Motor vehicle taxes	80	68	100
Income taxes	4,324	703	3,890
Land revenue	196	228	400
Other taxes and duties	17	63	116
Interest receipts	185	7	1,400
Railways	1,505	1,444	1,680
Other revenue	3,489	891	3,734
Total	**28,666**	**24,288**	**34,770**

Expenditure	1982/83	1983/84	1984/85*
General administration	3,548	4,975	11,176
Justice and police	1,895	2,342	2,876
Defence	2,470	4,643	4,935
Scientific departments	96	68	99
Education	2,337	1,777	4,939
Health	899	1,387	1,605
Social welfare	127	255	225
Agriculture	481	632	755
Manufacturing and construction	1,944	68	99
Transport and communication	161	962	763
Railways	1,539	1,938	1,978
Other expenditure	4,722	665	1,828
Total	**20,219**	**19,712**	**31,278**

* Revised estimate.

Source: Ministry of Finance.

1985/86 (revised estimate, million taka): Revenue 40,730; Expenditure 79,756.1.
1986/87 (estimate, million taka): Revenue 48,400; Expenditure 91,120.

MONEY SUPPLY (million taka at 31 December)

	1983	1984	1985
Currency outside banks	13,444	17,250	17,672
Demand deposits at scheduled banks	18,191	25,016	28,280
Total money*	**31,636**	**42,269**	**45,956**

* Including private sector deposits held by monetary authorities.

Source: IMF, *International Financial Statistics*.

PUBLIC SECTOR DEVELOPMENT EXPENDITURE
(estimates, million taka, year ending 30 June)

	1982/83	1983/84	1984/85
Agriculture	3,946	7,479	10,315
Rural development	663	455	743
Water and flood control	4,124	3,382	6,272
Industry	1,963	2,873	2,555
Power, scientific research and natural resources	5,642	7,356	8,926
Transport	3,183	3,041	4,296
Communication	698	767	1,151
Physical planning and housing	1,088	1,074	833
Education and training	1,009	1,276	1,376
Health	719	762	887
Population planning	788	706	756
Social welfare	145	314	404
Manpower and employment	233	—	—
Miscellaneous	91	254	280
Total development expenditure	**24,292**	**29,739**	**38,794**

* Estimate.

Source: Ministry of Finance.

1985/86 (revised estimate): Total development expenditure 40,955.4m. taka.
1986/87 (estimate): Total development expenditure 47,640m. taka.

INTERNATIONAL RESERVES
(US $ million at 31 December)

	1983	1984	1985
Gold*	17.5	15.8	12.9
IMF special drawing rights	13.5	0.3	13.1
Reserve position in IMF	23.5	22.0	24.6
Foreign exchange	487.1	367.7	298.8
Total	**541.6**	**405.8**	**349.4**

* Valued at market-related prices.

Source: IMF, *International Financial Statistics*.

COST OF LIVING
(Middle-class families in Dhaka. Base: 1969/70 = 100)

	1982/83	1983/84	1984/85
Food	725	824	934
Fuel and lighting	883	894	1,057
Housing and household requisites	1,041	1,057	1,114
Clothing and footwear	793	837	926
Miscellaneous	635	713	796
All items	**758**	**833**	**931**

FOREIGN AID (US $ million, year ending 30 June)

Donor	1982/83	1983/84	1984/85
Canada	91	137	80
India	27	3	4
Japan	164	94	126
Netherlands/Belgium	54	49	61
Sweden	38	17	3
USSR	9	51	17
United Kingdom	42	44	45
USA	188	161	195
Total	**613**	**556**	**531**

Source: Ministry of Finance.

BANGLADESH

NATIONAL ACCOUNTS (million taka at current prices, year ending 30 June)
Expenditure on the Gross Domestic Product

	1982/83	1983/84	1984/85*
Government final consumption expenditure	15,906	18,978	20,876
Private final consumption expenditure	262,265	314,840	367,329
Increase in stocks	877	−1,698	−985
Gross fixed capital formation	28,832	40,327	41,678
Total domestic expenditure	307,880	372,447	428,898
Exports of goods and services	18,016	20,136	23,700
Less Imports of goods and services	37,473	42,661	54,852
GDP in purchasers' values	288,423	349,922	397,746

* Provisional.

Gross Domestic Product by Economic Activity

	1983/84	1984/85	1985/86*
Agriculture and hunting	146,550	181,403	215,079
Forestry and logging	11,876	13,716	16,267
Fishing	10,902	14,641	17,210
Mining and quarrying	4	4	4
Manufacturing	30,945	34,632	37,341
Electricity, gas and water	1,939	2,348	2,574
Construction	18,095	22,518	26,456
Wholesale and retail trade	28,513	35,280	38,092
Transport, storage and communications	26,013	27,265	28,674
Owner-occupied dwellings	24,867	27,999	31,047
Finance, insurance, real estate and business services	5,152	6,889	8,057
Public administration and defence	13,984	17,694	20,864
Other services	31,082	34,357	39,957
Total	349,922	418,746	481,622

* Provisional.

BALANCE OF PAYMENTS (US $ million)

	1983	1984	1985
Merchandise exports f.o.b.	723.9	931.7	999.5
Merchandise imports f.o.b.	−1,930.7	−2,340.0	−2,299.8
Trade balance	−1,206.8	−1,408.3	−1,300.4
Exports of services	251.8	275.6	279.7
Imports of services	−522.9	−599.9	−597.3
Balance on goods and services	−1,477.8	−1,732.6	−1,618.0
Private unrequited transfers (net)	649.6	473.3	394.8
Government unrequited transfers (net)	768.5	730.1	645.6
Current balance	−59.6	−529.2	−577.6
Long-term capital (net)	476.1	547.5	496.6
Short-term capital (net)	−51.4	12.3	−22.1
Net errors and omissions	−16.3	−47.1	−12.5
Total (net monetary movements)	348.7	−16.3	−115.5
Monetization of gold (net)	5.5	0.2	—
Valuation changes (net)	8.9	10.0	−5.0
Exceptional financing (net)	3.7	3.4	2.8
Official financing (net)	−44.7	−26.1	−4.3
Changes in reserves	322.0	−28.8	−122.0

Source: IMF, *International Financial Statistics*.

BANGLADESH   Statistical Survey

External Trade

PRINCIPAL COMMODITIES
(million taka, year ending 30 June)

Imports	1982/83	1983/84	1984/85
Food and live animals	7,652.8	8,399.8	9,846.7
Wheat	4,765.9	5,916.4	3,000.4
Rice	1,667.6	955.1	2,248.4
Beverages and tobacco	169.2	16.8	93.1
Crude materials (inedible) except fuels	2,033.6	4,671.9	4,086.5
Mineral fuels, lubricants, etc.	10,253.7	9,965.7	10,536.7
Animal and vegetable oils and fats	2,994.9	3,535.4	4,957.4
Chemicals	4,253.0	5,574.3	7,157.6
Basic manufactures	6,715.8	8,967.6	13,099.5
Machinery and transport equipment	9,608.9	8,511.1	11,835.4
Miscellaneous manufactured articles	691.1	1,018.1	1,327.2
Other commodities and transactions	91.9	112.7	93.2
Total	**45,264.9**	**50,873.5**	**63,033.3**

Exports	1982/83	1983/84	1984/85
Raw jute and jute cuttings	2,580.0	2,729.6	3,899.7
Jute goods	8,007.9	8,711.9	10,952.1
Tea	1,100.4	1,699.5	1,570.4
Hides, skins and leather goods	1,589.3	2,197.8	1,947.9
Fish and fish preparations	1,673.0	2,030.5	2,333.0
Newsprint and other paper	62.3	2.2	0.2
Spices	5.7	10.7	8.0
All other items	2,997.1	2,753.4	4,294.1
Total	**18,015.7**	**20,135.6**	**25,005.4**

PRINCIPAL TRADING PARTNERS (million taka)

Imports c.i.f.	1982/83	1983/84	1984/85
Australia	504.1	2,670.3	1,445.4
Canada	2,059.6	2,323.0	1,397.2
China, People's Republic	1,743.1	2,357.0	2,944.0
France	1,149.5	631.6	1,116.1
Germany, Federal Republic	1,596.3	1,877.8	2,347.8
Hong Kong	137.9	5,895.9	1,049.2
India	1,570.6	1,691.4	2,372.4
Japan	5,102.5	5,350.6	7,616.7
Korea, Republic	1,831.4	1,750.6	2,961.7
Malaysia	675.1	813.8	1,628.0
Netherlands	1,888.4	805.0	1,378.2
Singapore	4,940.1	4,595.7	7,659.3
USSR	593.9	910.0	1,360.3
United Kingdom	1,679.3	2,240.0	1,954.6
USA	5,704.0	5,643.5	6,503.2

Exports f.o.b.	1982/83	1983/84	1984/85
Belgium	710.2	1,122.1	1,834.0
India	423.4	143.7	734.7
Italy	805.3	1,739.8	1,220.6
Japan	1,095.1	1,544.9	1,778.4
Singapore	1,007.5	496.8	1,000.4
USSR	1,044.5	317.8	950.7
United Kingdom	835.7	1,212.5	1,357.6
USA	2,107.5	2,687.8	4,912.4

Transport

RAILWAYS (year ending 30 June)

	1982/83	1983/84	1984/85
Passenger-kilometres (million)	6,427.1	6,283.5	6,031.3
Freight ton-kilometres (million)	813.9	778.6	812.9

Source: Bangladesh Railway.

ROAD TRAFFIC (motor vehicles in use)

	1982	1983	1984
Private motor cars	23,723	24,363	25,020
Taxis	1,194	1,226	1,259
Buses and coaches	7,710	7,918	8,131
Trucks	14,486	14,738	15,132
Jeeps	7,936	8,150	8,370
Station wagons	3,808	3,911	4,016
Auto-rickshaws	12,870	13,217	13,574
Motor cycles	47,587	48,872	50,192
Others	3,848	3,952	4,059
Total	**123,162**	**126,347**	**129,753**

Source: Ministry of Communications.

INTERNATIONAL SEA-BORNE SHIPPING
(freight traffic in '000 long tons, year ending 30 June)

	1982/83	1983/84	1984/85
Chalna			
Goods loaded	803	741	555
Goods unloaded	1,099	1,087	1,821
Chittagong			
Goods loaded	454	387	341
Goods unloaded	4,963	5,591	6,829
Total goods loaded	**1,257**	**1,128**	**898**
Total goods unloaded	**6,062**	**6,678**	**8,650**

Tourism

	1983	1984	1985
Tourist arrivals	79,818	103,130	145,634

Communications Media

	1983	1984	1985
Radio receivers ('000 licensed)	636	548	587
Television receivers ('000 in use)	223	245	310
Telephones ('000 in use)	124	143	151
Book production: titles	616	708	720
Daily newspapers:			
Number of titles	62	64	54
Average circulation ('000)	582	546	554

Education

(1984/85)

	Institutions	Students
Primary schools	44,423	9,914,000
Secondary schools	8,594	2,657,000
Technical colleges and institutes (government)*	123	23,606
Universities	6	41,215

* In addition to government-owned and managed institutes, there are many privately-run vocational training centres.

Directory

The Constitution

The members who were returned from East Pakistan (now Bangladesh) for the Pakistan National Assembly and the Provincial Assembly in the December 1970 elections formed the Bangladesh Constituent Assembly. A new Constitution for the People's Republic of Bangladesh was approved by this Assembly on 4 November 1972 and came into effect on 16 December 1972. The Constitution was amended in 1973, 1974, 1975, 1977, 1979 and 1981. Following the military coup of 24 March 1982, the Constitution was suspended, and the country was placed under martial law. On 10 November 1986 martial law was lifted and the suspended Constitution was revived.

SUMMARY
Fundamental Principles of State Policy

The Constitution was initially based on the fundamental principles of nationalism, socialism, democracy and secularism, but in 1977 an amendment replaced secularism with Islam. The amendment states that the country shall be guided by 'the principles of absolute trust and faith in the Almighty Allah, nationalism, democracy and socialism'. The Constitution aims to establish a society free from exploitation in which the rule of law, fundamental human rights and freedoms, justice and equality are to be secured for all citizens. A socialist economic system is to be established to ensure the attainment of a just and egalitarian society through state and co-operative ownership as well as private ownership within limits prescribed by law. A universal, free and compulsory system of education shall be established. In foreign policy the State shall endeavour to consolidate, preserve, and strengthen fraternal relations among Muslim countries based on Islamic solidarity.

Fundamental Rights

All citizens are equal before the law and have a right to its protection. Arbitrary arrest or detention, discrimination based on race, age, sex, birth, caste or religion, and forced labour are prohibited. Subject to law, public order and morality, every citizen has freedom of movement, of assembly and of association. Freedom of conscience, of speech, of the press and of religious worship are guaranteed.

GOVERNMENT
The President

The President is the constitutional Head of State and is elected for a term of five years. He is eligible for re-election. The supreme control of the armed forces is vested in the President. He appoints the Vice-President, the Prime Minister and other Ministers as well as the Chief Justice and other judges. The President is elected by universal adult suffrage.

The Executive

Executive authority shall rest in the President and shall be exercised by him either directly or through officers subordinate to him in accordance with the Constitution.

There shall be a Council of Ministers to aid and advise the President. All ministers shall hold office during the pleasure of the President.

The Legislature

Parliament (Jatiya Sangsad) is a unicameral legislature. It comprises 300 members and an additional 30 women members elected by the other members. Members of Parliament, other than the 30 women members, are directly elected on the basis of universal adult franchise from single territorial constituencies. Persons aged 18 and over are entitled to vote. The parliamentary term lasts for five years unless Parliament is dissolved sooner by the President. War can be declared only with the assent of Parliament. In the case of actual or imminent invasion, the President may take whatever action he may consider appropriate.

THE JUDICIARY

The Judiciary comprises a Supreme Court with High Court and an Appellate Division. The Supreme Court consists of a Chief Justice and such other judges as may be appointed by the President. The High Court division has such original appellate and other jurisdiction and powers as are conferred on it by the Constitution and by

BANGLADESH

Directory

other law. The Appellate Division has jurisdiction to determine appeals from decisions of the High Court division. Subordinate courts, in addition to the Supreme Court, have been established by law.

ELECTIONS

An Election Commission supervises elections for the Presidency and for Parliament, delimits constituencies and prepares electoral rolls. It consists of a Chief Election Commissioner and other Commissioners as may be appointed by the President. The Election Commission is independent in the exercise of its functions. Subject to the Constitution, Parliament may make provision as to elections where necessary.

The Government

HEAD OF STATE

President: Lt-Gen. (retd) HOSSAIN MOHAMMAD ERSHAD (took office 11 December 1983, confirmed by referendum 21 March 1985; re-elected 15 October 1986).

COUNCIL OF MINISTERS
(December 1986)

President of the Council of Ministers and Minister of Defence: Lt-Gen. (retd) HOSSAIN MOHAMMAD ERSHAD.
Vice-President and Minister of Islam, Law and Justice: Justice A. K. M. NURUL ISLAM.
Prime Minister and Minister of Posts and Telecommunications: MIZANUR RAHMAN CHOWDHURY.
Deputy Prime Minister and Minister of Industries: MOUDUD AHMED.
Deputy Prime Minister and Minister of Ports, Shipping and Inland Water Transport: KAZI ZAFAR AHMED.
Deputy Prime Minister and Minister of Home Affairs: Prof. M. A. MATIN.
Minister of Relief and Rehabilitation: Maj.-Gen. (retd) M. SHAMSUL HUQ.
Minister of Agriculture: MUZRA RUHUL AMIN.
Minister of Works: SAWFIQUL GHANI.
Minister of Religious Affairs: MAULANA M. A. MANNAN.
Minister of Local Government, Rural Development and Co-operatives: SHAH MOAZZEM HOSSAIN.
Minister of Labour and Manpower: ABDUR RASHID ENGINEER.
Minister of Textiles: SUNIL KUMAR GUPTA.
Minister of Irrigation, Water Development and Flood Control: ANISUL ISLAM MAHMUD.
Minister of Fisheries and Livestock: SIRAJUL HOSSAIN KHAN.
Minister of Social Welfare and Women's Affairs: RABIA BHUIYAN.
Minister of Energy and Mineral Resources: ANWAR HOSSAIN.
Minister of Foreign Affairs: HUMAYUN RASHEED CHOWDHURY.
Minister of Health and Family Planning: SALAHUDDIN KADER CHOWDHURY.
Minister of Land Administration and Land Reforms: A. K. M. MAYEEDUL ISLAM.
Minister of Education: MAHBUBUR RAHMAN.
Minister of Youth and Sports: SUNIL GUPTA.
Minister of Information: ANWAR ZAHID.
Minister for Jute: Lt-Col (retd) ZAFAR IMAM.
Minister of Finance: M. SYEDUZZAMAN.
Minister of Planning: Air Vice-Marshal (retd) A. K. KHANDAKAR.
Minister of Communications: M. MATIUR RAHMAN.
Ministry of Commerce: Maj.-Gen. (retd) M. A. MUNIM.
Minister Without Portfolio: Maj.-Gen. (retd) MAHMUDUL HASAN.
Minister of State for Industries: MESBAHUDDIN AHMED BABLU.
Minister of State for Youth and Sports: Shaikh SHAHIDUL ISLAM.
Minister of State for Agriculture: Prof. ABDUS SALAM.
Minister of State for Civil Aviation and Tourism: A. SATTAR.
Minister of State for Food: SARDAR AMZAD HOSSAIN.
Minister of State for Labour and Manpower: MUSTAFA JAMAL HAIDER.
Minister of State for Mineral Resources: Maj.-Gen. (retd) IQBAL HOSSAIN CHOWDHURY.
Minister of State for Local Government, Rural Development and Co-operatives: B. K. DAWAN.
Deputy Minister for Education: GHULAM SARWAR MILAN.
Deputy Minister for Health and Family Planning: NURUL AMIN KHAN PHATAN.
Deputy Minister for Ports, Shipping and Inland Water Transport: ZIAUDDIN AHMED.
Deputy Minister for Communications: GOLAM SARWAR RAHMAN CHOWDHURY.
Deputy Minister for Commerce: Lt-Col (retd) H. M. A. GHAFFAR.
Deputy Minister for Finance: A. F. M. FAKRUL ISLAM MUNSHI.
Deputy Minister for Foreign Affairs: WAJID ALI KHAN PANNI.
Adviser for Freedom Fighters' Affairs: ZAKIR KHAN CHOWDHURY.
Adviser: M. MAHBUBUZZAMAN.

MINISTRIES

Ministry of Agriculture: Bangladesh Secretariat, Bhaban 4, 2nd Storey, Dhaka.
Ministry of Commerce and Industries: Shilpa Bhaban, Motijheel C/A, Dhaka; telex 642201.
Ministry of Communications: Bangladesh Secretariat, Bhaban 7, 1st 9-Storey Bldg, 8th Floor, Dhaka; telex 65712.
Ministry of Defence: Old High Court Bldg, Dhaka; tel. (2) 259082.
Ministry of Energy and Mineral Resources: Bangladesh Secretariat, Bhaban 6, New Bldg, 2nd Floor, Dhaka.
Ministry of Education: Bangladesh Secretariat, Bhaban 7, 2nd 9-Storey Bldg, 6th Floor, Dhaka.
Ministry of Establishment and Reorganization: Bangladesh Secretariat, Bhaban 1, Double Protected Area, 1st Floor, Dhaka.
Ministry of Finance and Planning: Bangladesh Secretariat, Bhaban 7, 1st 9-Storey Bldg, 3rd Floor, Dhaka; telex 65886.
Ministry of Foreign Affairs: Topkhana Rd, Dhaka: tel. (2) 236020; telex 642200.
Ministry of Food: Bangladesh Secretariat, Bhaban 4, 2nd 9-Storey Bldg, 3rd Floor, Dhaka; telex 65671.
Ministry of Health and Population Control: Bangladesh Secretariat, Main Bldg, 3rd Floor, Dhaka.
Ministry of Home Affairs: School Bldg, 4th Floor, Bangladesh Secretariat, Dhaka.
Ministry of Information: Bangladesh Secretariat, 2nd 9-Storey Bldg, 8th Floor, Dhaka; tel. (2) 235111.
Ministry of Irrigation, Water Development and Flood Control: Dhaka.
Ministry of Jute and Textiles: Dhaka.
Ministry of Law and Land Reforms: Bangladesh Secretariat, Bhaban 4, 2nd 9-Storey Bldg, 3rd Floor, Dhaka.
Ministry of Local Government: Bangladesh Secretariat, Bhaban 7, 1st 9-Storey Bldg, 6th Floor, Dhaka.
Ministry of Labour and Manpower: Bangladesh Secretariat, 1st 9-Storey Bldg, 4th Floor, Dhaka.
Ministry of Ports, Shipping and Inland Water Transport: Dhaka; tel. (2) 404345.
Ministry of Religious Affairs and Endowments: Dhaka.
Ministry of Social Welfare and Women's Affairs: Bangladesh Secretariat, Bhaban 6, New Bldg, Dhaka.
Ministry of Works: Bangladesh Secretariat, Main Extension Bldg, 2nd Floor, Dhaka.

President and Legislature

PRESIDENT

A total of 12 candidates contested the presidential election held on 15 October 1986. According to official results, Lt-Gen. (retd) Hossain Mohammad Ershad won 21,795,337 votes (83.5% of the votes cast). His nearest rivals were Maulana M. H. Huzur (1,510,456 votes) and Col Syed Faruk Rahman (1.17m. votes).

BANGLADESH

JATIYA SANGSAD
(Parliament)

Speaker: SHAMSUL HUDA CHOWDHURY.

General Election, 7 May 1986

	Seats
Jatiya Dal	153
Awami League	76
Jamit-i-Islami	10
Bangladesh Communist Party	5
National Awami Party—Bhashani (NAP)	5
Bangladesh Muslim League	4
Jatiya Samajtantrik Dal (R)	4
Jatiya Samajtantrik Dal (S)	3
Bangladesh Krishak Sramik	3
Bangladesh Workers Party	3
National Awami Party—Muzaffar (NAP—M)	2
Independents	32
Total	**300**

In addition to the 300 directly-elected members, a further 30 seats are reserved for women members.

Political Organizations

Since August 1975, when all political parties were banned, political activity has been prohibited intermittently. Political activity was again permitted from 1 January 1986. The following parties are among the more influential of those currently active:

Awami League (Hasina): 23 Bangabandhu Ave, Dhaka; f. 1949; socialist, pro-Soviet and pro-Indian; Chair. Sheikh HASINA WAZED; Gen. Sec. ABDUR RAZZAQ; c. 1,025,000 mems.

Awami League (Mizan): 271/4 Elephant Rd, Dhaka; f. 1978; Leader MOHAMMAD MIZANUR RAHMAN CHOUDHURY.

Bangladesh Communist Party: Dhaka; f. 1948; Leader and Gen.-Sec. MOHAMMAD FARHAD; c. 2,500 mems.

Bangladesh Jatiya League: 500A Dhanmandi R/A, Rd 7, Dhaka; f. 1970 as Pakistan National League, renamed in 1972; supports parliamentary democracy; Leader ATAUR RAHMAN KHAN; c. 50,000 mems.

***Bangladesh Jatiyatabadi Dal** (Bangladesh Nationalist Party—BNP): Sattar House No. 19A, Rd 27 (Old) and 16 (New), Dhanmandi R/A, Dhaka; f. 1978 by merger of groups supporting Ziaur Rahman, including Jatiyatabadi Gonotantrik Dal (Jagodal—Nationalist Democratic Party); supports parliamentary democracy; Chair. Begum KHALIDA ZIA; Sec.-Gen. BADRUDDOZA CHOWDHURY.

Bangladesh Khilafat Andolon: Lalbagh, Dhaka; Leader MUHAMMADULLAH HAFEZZI HUZUR.

Bangladesh Krishak Sramik (Peasants' and Workers' Party): Sonargaon Bhavan, 99 South Kamalapur, Dhaka 17; f. 1914, renamed 1953; supports parliamentary democracy and socialism; Pres. A. S. M. SULAIMAN; Gen.-Sec. S. M. K. ZAINAL ABEDIN; c. 25,000 mems.

***Bangladesh Muslim League:** 281 Rd 25, Dhanmandi R/A, Dhaka; f. 1947; conservative Islamic; Chair. TOFAZZAL ALI.

Bangladesh People's League: House 72, Dhanmandi R/A, Rd 7A, Dhaka; f. 1976; supports parliamentary democracy; Leader Dr ALIM AL-RAZEE; c. 75,000 mems.

Democratic League: 68 Jigatola, Dhaka 9; f. 1976; conservative; Leader KHANDAKAR MUSHTAQ AHMED.

Gonoazadi League: 30 Banagran Lane, Dhaka; Leader MOULANA A. R. TARKABAGISH.

***Gonotantrik Dal** (Democratic Party): Dhaka; Marxist; pro-Beijing; Leader HUSSAIN KHAN; Gen.-Sec. ANWAR ZAHID.

Islamic Democratic League: 84 Testari Bazar, Dhaka; Leader MAULANA ABDUR RAHIM.

Jamit-i-Islami: 505 Elephant Rd, Bara Maghbazar, Dhaka 17; tel. (2) 401581; f. 1941; Islamic; Pres. ABBAS ALI KHAN.

***Jatiya Dal** (National Party): Dhaka; f. 1983 as Jana Dal; reorg. 1986; advocates nationalism, democracy, Islamic ideals and progress; Chair. Lt-Gen. (retd) HOSSAIN MOHAMMAD ERSHAD; Gen.-Sec. Prof. M.A. MATIN.

Jatiya Janata Party: 6 Folder St, Wari, Dhaka 3; f. 1976; social democratic; Chair. FERDAUS AHMAD QUARISHI; Secs-Gen. A. K. MUJIBUR RAHMAN, ABDUL MATIN CHOWDHURY, YUSUF ALI; c. 25,000 mems.

Jatiya Samajtantrik Dal (R): breakaway faction of JSD; Leader A. S. RAB.

Jatiya Samajtantrik Dal (JSD—(S)) (National Socialist Party): 23 DIT Ave, Malibagh (Choudhury para), Dhaka; f. 1972; left-wing; Leader SHAJAHAN SIRAJ; c. 5,000 mems.

National Awami Party—Bhashani (NAP): 226 Outer Circular Rd, Dhaka; f. 1957; pro-Beijing; Pres. ABU NASSER KHAN BHASHANI; Gen.-Sec. ABDUS SUBHANI.

National Awami Party—Muzaffar (NAP—M): 21 Dhanmandi Hawkers' Market, 1st Floor, Dhaka 5; f. 1957, refounded 1967; socialist; pro-Soviet; Leader MUZAFFAR AHMED; Gen.-Sec. PIR HABIBUR RAHMAN; c. 500,000 mems.

Samyabadi Dal: Dhaka; secular; pro-Beijing; Leader MOHAMMAD TOAHA.

***United People's Party:** 42/43 Purana Paltan, Dhaka; f. 1974; pro-Beijing; left-wing; Leader KAZI JAFAR AHMED.

*The **National Front**, founded in September 1985, was a pro-Government five-party alliance of the Jana Dal, the United People's Party, the Gonotantrik Dal, the Bangladesh Muslim League and a breakaway section of the Bangladesh Nationalist Party, which supported an orderly resumption of constitutional government. In January 1986 the National Front formally converted itself into a single pro-Government entity, named the **Jatiya Dal**.

Diplomatic Representation

EMBASSIES AND HIGH COMMISSIONS IN BANGLADESH

Afghanistan: House CES(A)49, 96 Gulshan Ave, Gulshan Model Town, Dhaka 12; tel. (2) 603232; Chargé d'affaires: ABDUL AHAD WOLASI.

Algeria: 4 CWN(C) Gulshan Ave, Gulshan Model Town, Dhaka 12; tel. (2) 60521; Ambassador: MUHAMMAD LARBI DEMAGHLATROUS.

Australia: 184 Gulshan Ave, Gulshan Model Town, Dhaka 12; tel. (2) 600091; telex 642317; High Commissioner: Dr I. S. MITCHELL.

Belgium: House 40, Rd 21, Block B, Banani, Dhaka; tel. (2) 600138; telex 642304; Ambassador: HENRY H. VANDRECHE.

Bhutan: House 58, Rd 3A, Dhanmandi R/A, POB 3141, Dhaka; tel. (2) 505418; Ambassador: D. K. CHHETRI.

Brazil: House 12, Rd 33, Gulshan Model Town, Dhaka 12; tel. (2) 605390; telex 642334; Ambassador: ANTÔNIO CONCEIÇÃO.

Bulgaria: House 12, Rd 127, Gulshan Model Town, Dhaka 12; tel. (2) 602344; telex 642310; Chargé d'affaires a.i.: ALEKSANDUR Y. BAKALOV.

Burma: No. 89(B), Rd 4, Banani, Dhaka; tel. (2) 601915; Ambassador: U SOE MYINT.

Canada: POB 569, House 16A, Rd 48, Gulshan Model Town, Dhaka 12; tel. (2) 600181; telex 642328; High Commissioner: ANTHONY G. VINCENT.

China, People's Republic: Plot NE(L)6, Rd 83, Gulshan Model Town, Dhaka 12; tel. (2) 601037; Ambassador: ZHENG JIANYING.

Czechoslovakia: House 71, Gulshan Ave, Gulshan Model Town, Dhaka 12; tel. (2) 601673; telex 65730; Ambassador: ALEXANDER VENGLAR.

Denmark: POB 2056, House NW(1), Rd 51, Gulshan Model Town, Dhaka 12; tel. (2) 600108; telex 642320; Ambassador: ERNO OLSEN.

Egypt: House NE(N)-9, Rd 90, Gulshan Model Town, Dhaka 12; tel. (2) 600158; Ambassador: ABDUL AZIZ MOUSTAFA ELKADY.

France: POB 22, House 18, Rd 108, Gulshan Model Town, Dhaka 12; tel. (2) 600286; Ambassador: SAMUEL LE CARUYER DE BEAUVAIS.

German Democratic Republic: 32/34, Rd 74, Gulshan Model Town, Dhaka 12; tel. (2) 600202; telex 642332; Ambassador: LOTHAR NESTLER.

Germany, Federal Republic: 178 Gulshan Ave, Gulshan Model Town, POB 108, Dhaka 12; tel. (2) 600166; telex 65879; Ambassador: KLAUS MAX FRANKE.

Holy See: POB 361, Plot 1–2, Baridhara Model Town, Dhaka 12; tel. (2) 600218; Apostolic Pro-Nuncio: Most Rev. LUIGI ACCOGLI.

Hungary: POB 6012, 80 Gulshan Ave, Gulshan Model Town, Dhaka; tel. (2) 603691; telex 642314; Charge d'affaires: J. F. TOROK.

India: House 120, Rd 2, Dhanmandi R/A, Dhaka; tel. (2) 503606; High Commissioner: I. S. CHADHA.

BANGLADESH

Indonesia: 75 Gulshan Ave, Gulshan Model Town, Dhaka 12; tel. (2) 600131; telex 65639; Ambassador: Rachmat Sukartiko.
Iran: 171 Gulshan Ave, Gulshan Model Town, Dhaka 12; tel. (2) 601432; telex 65714; Ambassador: Muhammad Mahdi Akhoundzadeh Basti.
Iraq: 112 Gulshan Ave, Gulshan Model Town, Dhaka 12; tel. (2) 600298; telex 642307; Ambassador: Tariq Abdul Jabber Jawed.
Italy: House No. NWD(4), Rd 58/62, Gulshan Model Town, Dhaka 12; tel. (2) 603161; telex 642313; Ambassador: Dr Fausto Maria Pennacchio.
Japan: Plot 110, Rd 27, Block-A, Banani Model Town, Dhaka 13; tel. (2) 600053; telex 65872; Ambassador: Shunji Kobayashi.
Korea, Democratic People's Republic: Plot 157, Rd 12, Block E, Banani Model Town, Dhaka; tel. (2) 601250; Ambassador: Ko Yon-Sik.
Korea, Republic: House NW(E)17, Rd 55, Gulshan Model Town, Dhaka 12; tel. (2) 604921; Ambassador: Yoon Chu-Won.
Kuwait: 53 Gulshan Ave, Gulshan Model Town, Dhaka 12; tel. (2) 600233; telex 65600; Ambassador: Jasem Ismae'el Jumah al-Yaseen.
Libya: NE(D), 31A, Gulshan Ave (N), Gulshan Model Town, Dhaka 12; tel. (2) 600141; Secretary of People's Bureau: Muhammad Hasan el-Ayeb.
Malaysia: House 4, Rd 118, Gulshan Model Town, Dhaka 12; tel. (2) 600291; High Commissioner: Mohammad Haron.
Nepal: Lake Rd, Rd No. 2, Baridhara Model Town, Dhaka; tel. (2) 601790; Ambassador: Gehendra Bahadur Raj Bhandary.
Netherlands: House 49, Rd 90, Gulshan Model Town, Dhaka 12; tel. (2) 600278; Ambassador: H. J. du Marchie Sarvaas.
Pakistan: 22 Gulshan Ave, House SE(D)-9, Rd 140, Gulshan Model Town, Dhaka 12; tel. (2) 603064; Ambassador: Riaz H. Khokhar.
Philippines: House NE(L) 5, Rd 83, Gulshan Model Town, Dhaka 12; tel. (2) 605945; Ambassador: Reynaldo O. Arcilla.
Poland: Rd 77, Plot 11, Gulshan Model Town, Dhaka 12; tel. (2) 600371; telex 642316; Chargé d'affaires: Tadeusz Grzybowski.
Romania: House 33, Rd 74, Gulshan Model Town, Dhaka 12; tel. (2) 601467; telex 65739; Chargé d'affaires a.i.: Ion Dobobantu.
Saudi Arabia: House 5W(A)-25, Rd 10, Gulshan Ave, Dhaka 12; tel. (2) 600221; telex 642305; Ambassador: Abdul Latif Abdullah Ibrahim al-Maimanee.
Sri Lanka: House 22 (NW), Rd 56, Gulshan Model Town, Dhaka 12; tel. (2) 604009; telex 642321; High Commissioner: Edwin Tillekeratne.
Sweden: POB 304, 73 Gulshan Ave, Gulshan Model Town, Dhaka 12; tel. (2) 600161; Ambassador: Eva Heckscher.
Thailand: 21, Block B, Rd 16, Banani Residential Area, Dhaka 13; tel. (2) 601475; Ambassador: Niran Phanuphong.
Turkey: House 7, Rd 62, Gulshan Model Town, Dhaka; tel. (2) 602198; Ambassador: Halit Guvener.
USSR: NE(J) 9, Rd 79, Gulshan Model Town, Dhaka 12; tel. (2) 601050; Ambassador: Vladimir Georgievich Belyayev.
United Arab Emirates: House No. SWB(I), Rd 7, Gulshan Model Town, Dhaka 12; tel. (2) 604775; telex 642301; Ambassador: Ahmed Mohammad Ibrahim al-Tamimi.
United Kingdom: POB 6079, Abu Bakr House, Plot 7, Rd No. 84, Gulshan Model Town, Dhaka 12; tel. (2) 600133; telex 642470; High Commissioner: Terence G. Streeton.
USA: Adamjee Court, 4th and 5th Floor, 115/120 Motijheel C/A, Dhaka; tel. (2) 235093; telex 642319; Ambassador: Howard B. Schaffer.
Yugoslavia: House 10, Rd 62, Gulshan Model Town, Dhaka 12; tel. (2) 601505; Ambassador: Kalman Feher.

Judicial System

See also under Constitution.
Chief Justice: Dr F. K. M. A. Munim.
Attorney-General: M. Nurullah.

Religion

According to preliminary results of the 1981 census, 86.6% of the population were Muslims, 12.1% caste Hindus and scheduled castes, while the remainder were Buddhists, Christians and tribals.
Complete freedom of religious worship is guaranteed under the Constitution but, under the 1977 amendment to the Constitution, secularism was replaced by Islam as one of the guiding principles.

BUDDHISM
World Federation of Buddhists Regional Centre: Buddhist Monastery, Kamalapur, Dhaka 14; Leader Ven. Visuddhananda Mahathero.

CHRISTIANITY
Church of Bangladesh—Uniting Church
Bishop of Dhaka: Rt Rev. B. D. Mondal, St Thomas' Church, 54 Johnson Rd, Dhaka 1; tel. (2) 34650.

The Roman Catholic Church
Bangladesh comprises one archdiocese and three dioceses. At 31 December 1984 there were an estimated 174,000 adherents in the country.
Catholic Bishops' Conference: Archbishop's House, POB 3, Dhaka 2; tel. (2) 408879; f. 1978; Pres. Most Rev. Michael Rozario, Archbishop of Dhaka.
Archbishop of Dhaka: Most Rev. Michael Rozario, Archbishop's House, POB 3, Dhaka 2; tel. (2) 408879.

The Press

PRINCIPAL DAILIES
Bengali
Azad: 27A Dhakeswari Rd, Ramna, Dhaka 5; tel. (2) 500583; f. 1936; morning; Editor Zainul Anam Khan; circ. 12,125.
Azadi: Momin Rd, Chittagong; tel. (2) 221278; f. 1960; Editor Prof. Mohammad Khaled; circ. 13,409.
Daily Abarta: 141 Arambagh, Motijheel, Dhaka 2, POB 628; tel. (2) 254333; Editor S. M. Taufiqul Islam; circ. 4,000.
Banglar Bani: 81 Motijheel C/A, Dhaka 2; tel. (2) 235341; f. 1972, relaunched 1981; Editor Sheikh Fazlul Karim Selim; circ. 20,437.
Dainik Bangla: 1 DIT Ave, Dhaka 2; tel. (2) 235065; f. 1964; Editor Shamsur Rahman; circ. 50,210.
Dainik Barta: Natore Rd, Rajshahi; tel. (2) 3424; f. 1976; morning; govt-owned; Editor Moslem Ali Biswas; circ. 7,000.
Dainik Desh: 5 Segun Bagicha, Dhaka; tel. (2) 235161; f. 1979; newspaper of the Bangladesh Jatiyatabadi Dal (BNP) party; Editor Anwarul Islam; circ. 30,000.
Dainuk Janmabhumi: 15 Iqbalnagar Mosque Rd, Khulna; tel. (2) 21040; Editor Humayun Kabir; circ. 21,000.
Dainik Kishan: 369 Outer Circular Rd, Dhaka; tel. (2) 600360; f. 1976; Editor Kazi Abdul Qader; circ. 4,216.
Dainik Purbanchal: 38 Iqbalnagar Mosque Lane, Khulna; tel. (2) 21013; f. 1974; Editor Liaquat Ali; circ. 36,000.
Dainik Rupashi Bangla: Natun Chowdhury Para, Bagichagaon, Comilla; tel. (2) 6689; f. 1971 (a weekly until 1979); Editor Prof. Abdul Wahab.
Dainik Sangram: 423 Elephant Rd, Bara Maghbazar, Dhaka; tel. (2) 405279; Man. Dir Mohamed Shamsur Rahman; Editor Abdul Asad; circ. 18,765.
Dainik Sphulinga: POB 12, Housing Estate, P-3, S-2, Jessore; tel. (2) 6433; f. 1971; Chief Editor Mian Abdus Sattar; circ. 10,000.
Dainik Uttara: Dinajpur Town, Dinajpur; tel. (2) 3256; f. 1974; Editor Prof. Muhammad Mohsin; circ. 2,765.
Ganakantha: 24 Tipusultan Rd, Dhaka; tel. (2) 258369; f. 1979; morning; Editor-in-Chief Mirza Sultan Raza; circ. 5,000.
Ittefaq: 1 Ramkrishna Mission Rd, Dhaka 3; tel. (2) 256075; f. 1953; Editor Mainul Hosein; circ. 192,656.
Janabarta: 5 Babukhan Rd, Khulna; tel. 21075; f. 1974; Editor Syed Sohrab Ali; circ. 3,195.
Karatoa: Chandni Bazar, Bogra; tel. (2) 5238; f. 1976; Editor Mozammel Haque Lalu; circ. 2,788.
Naya Bangla: 101 Momin Rd, Chittagong; tel. (2) 202816; f. 1978; Editor Abdullah al Sagir; circ. 12,000.
Probaho: 2 Raipara Cross Rd, Khulna; tel. 23650; f. 1977; Editor Ashraful Huq; circ. 3,245.
Protidin: Ganashtola, Dinajpur; tel. (2) 4555; f. 1980; Editor Abdus Samad; circ. 2,705.

BANGLADESH

Runner: Pyari Mohan Das Rd, Jessore; tel. (2) 5129; f. 1980; Editor GULAM MAJED; circ. 2,005.

Sangbad: 263 Bangshal Rd, Dhaka 1; tel. (2) 238147; f. 1951; Editor AHMEDUL KABIR; circ. 51,950.

Swadhinata: 99A Zamal Khan Lane, Chittagong; tel. (2) 209644; f. 1972; Editor ABDULLAH-AL-HARUN; circ. 4,000.

Zamana: Kazir Dewry 2nd Lane, Chittagong; tel. (2) 205424; f. 1955; morning; Editor MOYEENUL ALAM; circ. 16,900.

English

Bangladesh Observer: Observer House, 33 Toyenbee Circular Rd, Dhaka 2; tel. (2) 235105; f. 1949; morning; Editor K. M. A. MUNIM; circ. 42,812.

Bangladesh Times: 1 DIT Ave, Dhaka 2; tel. (2) 258840; f. 1974; morning; Editor A. M. MUFAZZAL; circ. 35,000.

Daily Life: 27 Sadarghat Rd, Chittagong; tel. (2) 401198; f. 1977; Editor ANWARUL ISLAM BOBBY; circ. 10,327.

Daily News: 76A Segun Bagicha, Dhaka; tel. 413295; f. 1982; supports the government; Editor OBAIDUL HUQUE; circ. 7,610.

Daily Tribune: 38 Iqbalnagar Mosque Lane, Khulna; tel. (2) 20163; f. 1978; morning; Editor FERDOUSI ALI; circ. 15,000.

Morning Post: 280 New Eskaton Rd, Dhaka 2; tel. (2) 413256; f. 1969; Editor HABIBUL BASHAR; Gen. Man. S. M. JAMIL UDDIN; circ. 20,000.

New Nation: 1 Ram Krishna Mission Rd, Dhaka; tel. (2) 239612; f. 1981; Editor MOTHAR HOSSAIN SIDDIQUI; circ. 8,050.

People's View: 129 Panchlaish R/A, Chittagong; tel. (2) 204993; f. 1969; Editor SAIYARA ISLAM; circ. 3,215.

PERIODICALS
Bengali

Adab Sangbad: House 46A, Rd 6A, Dhanmandi R/A, Dhaka 9; tel. (2) 313318; telex 642940; f. 1974; monthly; publ. by the Asscn of Devt Agencies in Bangladesh (ADAB); Editor Dr KHAWJA SHAMSUL HUDA; circ. 7,000.

Ad-Dawat: Rajshahi Town; f. 1976; monthly; Editor MOHAMMAD ABUL QASEM.

Ahmadi: 4 Bakshi Bazar, Dhaka; f. 1925; fortnightly; Editor A. H. M. ALI ANWAR.

Ajker Samabaya: 114 Motijheel C/A, Dhaka; f. 1974; fortnightly; Editor KH. REASUL KARIM; circ. 10,000.

Amod: Comilla Town; tel. (2) 6193; f. 1955; weekly; Editor SHAMSUN NEHAR RABBI; circ. 6,900.

Begum: 66 Royal St, Dhaka 1; tel. (2) 233789; f. 1947; women's illustrated weekly; Editor NURJAHAN BEGUM; circ. 24,500.

Bichitra: 1 DIT Ave, Dhaka; tel. (2) 232084; f. 1972; weekly; Editor SHAMSUR RAHMAN; circ. 35,750.

Biplav: 5 Shegunbagicha, Dhaka 2; f. 1982; weekly; Editor SIKDER AMINUL HUQUE.

Chitrali: Observer House, 33 Toyenbee Circular Rd, Dhaka 2; tel. (2) 256029; f. 1963; film weekly; Editor AHMED ZAMAN CHOWDHURY; circ. 25,150.

Dhaka Digest: 34 Topkhana Rd, Dhaka; f. 1974; monthly; Editor RASHID CHOWDHURY; circ. 7,000.

Fashal: 28/J Toyenbee Circular Rd, Motijheel C/A, Dhaka; tel. (2) 233099; f. 1965; agricultural weekly; Chief Editor ERSHAD MAZUMDAR; circ. 30,000.

Ispat: Majampur, Kushtia; tel. (2) 3676; f. 1976; weekly; Editor WALIUR BARI CHOUDHURY; circ. 3,116.

Jahan-e-Nau: 13 Karkun Bari Lane, Dhaka; tel. (2) 252205; f. 1960; weekly; Editor MD HABIBIUR RAHMAN; circ. 8,950.

Jugabheri: Ambarkhana, Sylhet; tel. 7659; f. 1931; weekly; Editor AMINUR RASHID CHOWDHURY; circ. 6,005.

Kalantar: 87 Khanjahan Ali Rd, Khulna; tel. (2) 61424; f. 1971; weekly; Editor NOOR MOHAMMAD; circ. 1,081.

Kankan: Nawab Bari Rd, Bogra; tel. (2) 6424; f. 1974; weekly; Editor Mrs SUFIA KHATUN; circ. 6,000.

Kishore Bangla: Observer House, Motijheel C/A, Dhaka; juvenile weekly; f. 1976; Editor RAFIQUL HAQUE; circ. 5,000.

Krira Jagat: Purana Palton, Dhaka; f. 1977; fortnightly; Editor UMMESALMA RAFIQ; circ. 7,402.

Krishi Katha: 3 R.K. Mission Rd, Dhaka; f. 1957; monthly; Editor A. H. M. HALIM; circ. 6,000.

Muktibani: 70 R. K. Mission Rd, Dhaka; tel. (2) 255291; f. 1972; weekly; Editor NIZAMUDDIN AHMED; circ. 15,000.

Nayajug: 32 Purana Paltan, Dhaka; tel. (2) 283510; f. 1976; weekly; Editor KAZI ZAFAR AHMED; circ. 9,000.

Patuakhali Samachur: Patuakhali Town; f. 1970; fortnightly; Editor SHAMSUL HAQ KHAN.

Protirodh: Ministry of Home Affairs, School Bldg, 4th Floor, Bangladesh Secretariat, Dhaka; f. 1977; fortnightly; Editor AREFIN BADAL; circ. 20,000.

Purbani: 1 Ramkrishna Mission Rd, Dhaka; tel. (2) 256503; f. 1951; film weekly; Editor SHAHADAT HOSSAIN; circ. 22,310.

Reporter: 28/J Toyenbee Circular Rd, Motijheel C/A, Dhaka; tel. (2) 233099; f. 1976; news weekly; Chief Editor ERSHAD MAZUMDAR; circ. 40,000.

Robbar: 1 R. K. Mission Rd, Dhaka; tel. (2) 256071; f. 1978; weekly; Editor ABDUL HAFIZ; circ. 20,125.

Sachitra Bangladesh: Film and Publications Dept, Ministry of Information, Bangladesh Secretariat, 2nd 9-Storey Bldg, Dhaka; tel. 402129; f. 1979; weekly; Editor K. G. MUSTAFA; circ. 8,000.

Sachitra Sandhani: 41 Naya Paltan, Dhaka; tel. (2) 404680; f. 1978; weekly; Editor GAZI SAHABUDDIN AHMED; circ. 12,717.

Shishu: Shishu Academy, Old High Court Area, Dhaka; f. 1977; children's monthly; Editor JOBEDA KHANAM; circ. 5,000.

Superstar: 46/A, Razmoni Cinema Complex, Kakrail, Dhaka; tel. (2) 416079; f. 1986; socio-cultural newspaper; Editor KHONDAKER MOZAMMEL HUQ; circ. 50,000.

English

Adab News: House No. 46A, Rd No. 6A, Dhanmandi R/A, Dhaka; tel. (2) 313318; telex 642940; f. 1976; 6 a year; publ. by the Asscn of Devt Agencies in Bangladesh; Editor-in-Chief AZFAR HUSSAIN; circ. 4,000.

Bangladesh Gazette: Bangladesh Government Press, Tejgaon, Dhaka; f. 1947, name changed 1972; weekly; official publication; Editor M. HUDA.

Bangladesh Illustrated Weekly: 31/A Rankin St, Wari, Dhaka; tel. (2) 23358; Editor ATIQUZZAMAN KHAN; circ. 3,000.

Detective: Naya Paltan, Dhaka; tel. (2) 402757; f. 1960; weekly; also publ. in Bengali; Editor KAZI ZAHURUL HAQ; circ. 3,000.

Eastern Tribune: 62/1 Purana Paltan, Dhaka; tel. (2) 282258; f. 1969; weekly; Editor ABUL HOSSAIN MALLICK; circ. 3,500.

Herald: 87 Bijoy Nagar, Dhaka; tel. (2) 405043; f. 1981; weekly; Editor FAUZUL KARIM; circ. 3,910.

Holiday: 40/1 Naya Paltan, Dhaka 2; tel. (2) 403495; f. 1965; weekly; independent; Editor FAZAL KAMAL; circ. 15,000.

Karnaphuli Shipping News: 88 Ghat Farhadbag, Kazem Ali Rd, Chittagong; tel. (2) 220366; f. 1977; twice a week; Editor F. KARIM; circ. 10,000.

Motherland: Khanjahan Ali Rd, Khulna; tel. (2) 61685; f. 1974; weekly; Editor M. N. KHAN.

Saturday Post: 280 New Eskaton Rd, Dhaka 2; tel. (2) 409968; f. 1975; weekly; Editor HABIBUL BASHAR; circ. 15,000.

Sunday Star: 149/A DIT Extension Ave, Dhaka; tel. (2) 403980; f. 1981; weekly; Editor MOHIUDDIN AHMED.

Voice From the North: Dinajpur Town, Dinajpur; tel. (2) 3256; f. 1981; weekly; Editor Prof. MUHAMMAD MOHSIN; circ. 5,000.

NEWS AGENCIES

Bangladesh Sangbad Sangstha (Bangladesh News Agency): 68/2 Purana Paltan, Dhaka 2; tel. (2) 404184; telex 5526; Man. Dir. and Chief Editor A. B. M. MUSA.

Eastern News Agency (ENA): 3/3C Purana Paltan, Dhaka 2; tel. (2) 234206; telex 642410; f. 1970; Man. Dir and Chief Editor GOLAM RASUL MALLICK.

Foreign Bureaux

Reuters (UK): POB 3993, Dhaka; tel. (2) 2645083; telex 25510.

Xinhua (New China) News Agency (People's Republic of China): 22 New Eskaton Rd, Dhaka 2; tel. (2) 403167; Correspondent XUAN ZENGPEI.

PRESS ASSOCIATIONS

Bangladesh Council of Newspapers and News Agencies: Dhaka; tel. (2) 413256; Chair. RUHUL ISLAM; Gen. Sec. HABIBUL BASHAR.

Bangladesh Federal Union of Journalists: National Press Club Bldg, 18 Topkhana Rd, Dhaka 2; tel. (2) 256071; f. 1973; Pres. HABIBUR RAGMAN MILON; Sec.-Gen. SYED ZAFAR AHMED.

BANGLADESH

Bangladesh Sangbadpatra Karmachari Federation (Newspaper Employees Federation): 47/3 Toyenbee Circular Rd, Bikrampur House, Dhaka 2; tel. (2) 235065; f. 1972; Pres. JAHANGIR KABIR; Sec.-Gen. MIR MOZAMMEL HOSSAIN.

Bangladesh Sangbadpatra Press Sramik Federation (Newspaper Press Workers' Federation): 1 R.K. Mission Rd, Dhaka; f. 1960; Pres. ABDUL KARIM; Sec. FAZLE IMAM.

Overseas Correspondents' Association Bangladesh (OCAB): 18 Topkhana Rd, Dhaka 2; f. 1979; Pres. HASSAN SHAHRIAR; Gen. Sec. ALAMGIR HOSSAIN; 51 mems.

Publishers

Adyle Brothers: 60 Patuatuly, Dhaka 1.

Ahmed Publishing House: 7 Zindabahar 1st Lane, Dhaka 1; tel. (2) 36492; f. 1942; literature, history, science, religion, children's, maps and charts; Man. Dir KAMALUDDIN AHMED; Man. MESBAHUDDIN AHMED.

Ashrafia Library: 4 Hakim Habibur Rahman Rd, Chawk Bazar, Dhaka 2; Islamic religious books, texts, and reference works of Islamic institutions.

Asiatic Society of Bangladesh: 5 Old Secretariat Rd, Ramna, Dhaka; tel. (2) 239390; f. 1951; periodicals on science and humanities; Pres. A. K. M. ZAKARIA; Sec. Prof. SERAJUL.

Bangla Academy: Burdwan House, Dhaka 2; tel. (2) 500131; f. 1955; higher education textbooks in Bengali, research works in language, literature and culture, popular science, drama, children's books, translations of world classics, dictionaries; Dir-Gen. ABU HENA MOSTAFA KAMAL.

Bangladesh Book Corporation: Patuatuly, Dhaka.

Bangladesh Publishers: 45 Patuatuly, Dhaka.

Bangladesh Books International Ltd: POB 377, Ittefaq Bhavan, 1 R.K. Mission Rd, Dhaka 3; tel. (2) 256071; f. 1975; reference, academic, research, literary, children's in Bengali and English; Chair. MOINUL HOSSEIN; Man. Dir ABDUL HAFIZ.

Barnamala Prakashani: 30 Banglabazar, Dhaka.

Boi Prakashani: 38A Banglabazar, Dhaka.

Boighar: 286 Bipani Bitan, Chittagong.

Book Society: 38 Banglabazar, Dhaka.

Co-operative Book Society Ltd: Motijheel, Dhaka.

Didar Publications: 45 Johnson Rd, Dhaka.

Emdadia Library: Chawk Bazar, Dhaka.

Great Bengal Library: Islampur, Dhaka.

Habibia Library: Chawk Bazar, Dhaka.

Islamia Library: Patuatuly, Dhaka.

Islamic Foundation: Baitul Mukarram, Dhaka.

Jatiya Sahitya Prakashani: POB 3416, 51 Purana Paltan, Dhaka 2; f. 1970; Prin. Officer MOFIDUL HOQUE.

Khan Brothers & Co: 67 Pyari Das Rd, Dhaka.

Knowledge Home: Pyari Das Rd, Dhaka.

Liaquat Publications: 34 North Brook Hall Rd, Dhaka.

Model Publishing: Pyari Das Rd, Dhaka.

Modina Publications: Pyari Das Rd, Dhaka.

Mofiz Book House: 37 Banglabazar, Dhaka.

Mowla Brothers: Banglabazar, Dhaka.

Muktadhara: 74 Farashganj, Dhaka; f. 1971; educational, literary and general; Bengali and English; Man. Dir C. R. SAHA; Chief Editor S. P. LAHIRY.

Osmania Book Depot: 30–32 North Brook Rd, Dhaka 1.

Puthighar: 74 Farashganj, Dhaka; f. 1951; educational; Bengali and English; Man. Dir C. R. SAHA; Chief Editor S. P. LAHIRY.

Puthipatra: 1/6 Shirish Das Lane, Banglabazar, Dhaka 1; f. 1952.

Rangpur Publications: 13/3 Haramohan St, Amligola, Dhaka.

Royal Library: Ispahani Bldg, 31/32 P. K. Roy Rd, Banglabazar, Dhaka 1; tel. 250863.

Sahitya Kutir: Bogra.

Sahityika: 6 Banglabazar, Dhaka.

Samakal Prakashani: 36A Toyenbee Circular Rd, Dhaka 2.

Standard Publishers Ltd: Dhaka Stadium, Dhaka 1.

Student Ways: Banglabazar, Dhaka.

University Press Ltd: Red Cross Bldg, 114 Motijheel, C/A, POB 2611, Dhaka; tel. (2) 232950; f. 1975; educational, academic and general; Man. Dir. MOHIUDDIN AHMED; Editor MAHBOOB HASSAN.

Government Publishing Houses

Bangladesh Bureau of Statistics: Bldg No. 8, Room 12, Bangladesh Secretariat, Dhaka; tel. (2) 409871; f. 1971; statistical yearbooks and monthly bulletins; Publ. Officer MENHAJUDDIN AHMAD.

Bangladesh Government Press: Tejgaon, Dhaka; f. 1972.

Press Information Department: Bhavan No. 6, Bangladesh Secretariat Bldg, Dhaka; tel. (2) 400958; telex 65619.

PUBLISHERS' ASSOCIATIONS

Bangladesh Publishers' and Booksellers' Association: 3rd Floor, 3 Liaquat Ave, Dhaka 1; f. 1972; Pres. JANAB JAHANGIR MOHAMMED ADEL; 2,500 mems.

National Book Centre of Bangladesh: 5/C Bangabandhu Ave, Grantha Bhaban, Dhaka 2; f. 1963 as an autonomous body to promote the cause of 'more, better and cheaper books'; organizes book fairs, publs a monthly journal on books; Dir FAZLE RABBI.

Radio and Television

In 1985 there were 587,000 licensed radio receivers and an estimated 310,000 television receivers in use.

National Broadcasting Authority: NBA House, Shahbag Ave, Dhaka; tel. (2) 503342; telex 642228; f. 1984 by merger of Radio Bangladesh and Bangladesh Television; Chair. SAIFUL BARI.

Radio Bangladesh: f. 1971; govt-controlled; regional stations at Chittagong, Dhaka, Khulna, Rajshahi, Rangpur and Sylhet broadcast a total of 87 hours 35 minutes daily; external service broadcasts 10 programmes daily in Arabic, Bengali, English, Hindi, Nepalese and Urdu; Chair. and Dir-Gen. ENAMUL HUQ.

Bangladesh Television (BTV): POB 456, Rampura, Dhaka; tel. (2) 400131; telex 65624; f. 1971; govt-controlled; colour transmissions from 1981; daily broadcasts on one channel from Dhaka station of 6½ hours; transmissions also from stations at Chittagong, Khulna, Mymensingh, Natore, Noakhali, Rangpur, Satkhira; Sylhet, Cox's Bazar and Rangamati were opened in 1983; Dir-Gen. (vacant); Dir of Programmes KHELADA FAHMI.

Finance

(cap. = capital; p.u. = paid up; dep. = deposits; res = reserves; m. = million; brs = branches; amounts in taka)

BANKING

Central Bank

Bangladesh Bank: Motijheel C/A, POB 325, Dhaka 2; tel. (2) 252927; telex 65657; f. 1971; cap. p.u. 30m., total assets 54,278m., dep. 25,769m. (June 1986); Gov. and Chair. M. NURUL ISLAM; Dep. Govs M. A. BEG, A. K. M. KHALILUR RAHMAN; 7 brs.

Nationalized Commercial Banks

Agrani Bank: POB 531, 9-D Dilkusha C/A, Dhaka 2; tel. (2) 235170; telex 65717; f. 1972; cap. and res 82m., dep. 17,423m. (June 1986); Chair. MIR ATAUL HAQUE KHANDAKER; Man. Dir MOHAMMAD HOSSAIN; 816 brs.

Janata Bank: POB 468, 1 Dilkusha C/A, Motijheel, Dhaka 2; tel. (2) 236215; telex 65840; f. 1972; cap. and res 144.8m., dep. 20,730.7m. (June 1986); Chair. A. F. N. EHSANUL KABIR; Man. Dir A. A. QURASHI; 840 brs.

Rupali Bank: POB 719, Rupali Bhaban, 34 Dilkusha C/A, Dhaka 2; tel. (2) 256021; telex 65635; f. 1972; cap. and res 75m., dep. 9,682m. (June 1986); Chair. A. T. M. AMIN; Man. Dir M. AHSANUL HAQUE; 499 brs (incl. one in Karachi, Pakistan).

Sonali Bank: POB 3130, Motijheel C/A, Dhaka 2; tel. (2) 243210; telex 65753; f. 1972; cap. 40m., dep. 28176.7m., res 217.4m. (June 1986); Chair. M. KERAMAT ALI; Man. Dir A. A. QURESHI; 1,252 brs.

In 1985 the Government decided on a phased divestment of 49% of the shares of the Agrani, Janata and Rupali Banks. The Sonali Bank remained under the total ownership of the Government.

Private Commercial Banks

Arab Bangladesh Bank Ltd: POB 3522, Bangladesh Steel House, Karwan Bazar, Dhaka; tel. (2) 325066; telex 642520; f. 1982 as first joint-venture Bangladeshi private sector commercial bank; cap. and res 120m., dep. 1,689m. (June 1986); Chair. MORSHED KHAN; CEO A. K. M. GHAFFAR; 15 brs.

City Bank Ltd: POB 3381, 1/A Dilkusha C/A, Dhaka; tel. (2) 235071; telex 642581; f. 1983; cap. and res 64.9m., dep. 1,263.5m. (June 1986); Chair. ANWAR HOSSAIN; Man. Dir ALTAFUR RAHAMAN; 21 brs.

International Finance Investment and Commerce Bank Ltd (IFICB): POB 2229, 3rd Fl., Chamber Bldg, 122–124 Motijheel C/A, Dhaka 2; tel. (2) 238291; telex 642703; f. 1983; cap. and res 112.9m., dep. 1,586.4m. (June 1986); Chair. ZAHRUL ISLAM; Man. Dir FAZLUR RAHMAN; 12 brs.

Islamic Bank of Bangladesh (IBB): POB 233, 75 Motijheel C/A, Dhaka 2; tel. (2) 252921; telex 642525; f. 1983; cap. and res 96.7m., dep. 1,563.9m. (June 1986); interest-free banking; Chair. MOHAMMAD ABDUR RAZZAQUE LASKAR; Man. Dir M. A. KARIM; 13 brs.

National Bank Ltd: POB 3838, 18 Dilkusha C/A, Dhaka 2; tel. (2) 235056; telex 642791; f. 1983; cap. and res 126.4m., dep. 2,648.3m. (June 1986); Chair. A. R. MALLICK; Man. Dir R. A. HOWLADER; 18 brs.

Pubali Bank Ltd: POB 853, 26 Dilkusha C/A, Dhaka 2; tel. (2) 253032; telex 65844; f. 1972; cap. p.u. 149.1m., dep. 6,149.6m., res 2.9m. (June 1986); Chair. E. A. CHOUDHURY; Man. Dir AMINUL ISLAM; 376 brs.

United Commercial Bank Ltd: POB 2653, 59 Motijheel C/A, Dhaka 2; tel. (2) 235075; telex 642733; f. 1983; cap. and res 56.2m., dep. 1,464.4m. (June 1986); Chair. S. M. SAFIUL AZAM; Man. Dir M. A. YOSSUF KHAN; 24 brs.

Uttara Bank: POB 818, 94 Motijheel C/A, Dhaka 2; tel. (2) 231162; telex 65889; f. 1972; cap. and res 110.4m., dep. 3,652.6m. (June 1986); Chair. Dr SYEDA FEROZA BEGUM; Man. Dir A. M. KHAN; 182 brs.

Foreign Banks

American Express Bank Ltd (USA): POB 420, ALICO Bldg, 18–20 Motijheel C/A, Dhaka 2; tel. (2) 236125; telex 65618; f. 1966; 2 brs in Dhaka and Chittagong; First Vice-Pres. and Head (Bangladesh) PETER SCHOFIELD; 2 brs.

Bank of Credit and Commerce International (Overseas) Ltd (Cayman Islands): POB 896, Jiban Bima Bhaban, Dilkusha C/A, Dhaka 2; tel. (2) 236360; telex 65615; f. 1976; CEO M. A. RASHID; 3 brs.

Banque Indosuez (France): POB 3490, 47 Motijheel C/A, Dhaka 2; tel. (2) 238285; telex 642438; f. 1981; Man. (Bangladesh) MARC DUMETZ; Jt Gen. Man. K. T. ZAMAN; 3 brs.

Grindlays Bank PLC (UK): POB 502, 2 Dilkusha C/A, Dhaka 2; tel. (2) 230225; telex 642597; f. 1905; Gen. Man. A. J. COOPER; 9 brs.

Habib Bank Ltd (Pakistan): POB 201, 53 Motijheel C/A, Dhaka 2; tel. (2) 235091; telex 65772; f. 1976; Vice-Pres. and Man. HABIB H. MIRZA; 1 br.

Standard Chartered Bank (UK): POB 536, ALICO Bldg, 18–20 Motijheel C/A, Dhaka 2; tel. (2) 231046; telex 65859; f. 1948; also in Chittagong; Gen. Man. J. A. H. JANES; 2 brs.

State Bank of India: POB 981, 24–25 Dilkusha C/A, Dhaka 2; tel. (2) 253914; telex 642431; f. 1975; Chief Man. P. GANGULY; 1 br.

DEVELOPMENT FINANCE ORGANIZATIONS

Bangladesh House Building Finance Corporation (BHBFC): POB 805, HBFC Bldg, 22 Purana Paltan, Dhaka 2; tel. (2) 415315; f. 1973; provides credit facilities at low interest for house-building; auth. cap. and res 285.1m., dep. 127.1m. (June 1986); credit facilities exist in all urban areas; 5 zonal offices and 13 regional offices; Chair. A. K. M. MUSA; Man. Dir KHWAJA ZAHURUL HAQ; 20 brs.

Bangladesh Krishi Bank: POB 357, 83–85 Motijheel C/A, Dhaka 2; tel. (2) 255091; telex 642526; f. 1973; fmrly Bangladesh Agricultural Devt Bank; provides credit facilities for agricultural and rural devt; cap. p.u. and res 658m., dep. 3,765m. (June 1986); Chair. A. K. M. ASHAN; Man. Dir Dr S. M. AL- HUSAINY; 966 brs.

Bangladesh Samabaya Bank (BSBL): POB 505, 9-D Motijheel C/A, Dhaka 2; tel. (2) 283148; f. 1948; provides credit for agricultural co-operatives; cap. and res 170.5m., dep. 24m. (June 1986); Chair. SAADAT HUSSAIN; Man. Dir B. A. KHAN; 1 br.

Bangladesh Shilpa Bank (BSB) (Industrial Development Bank): POB 975, Shipla Bank Bhaban, 8 DIT Ave, Dhaka; tel. (2) 235150; telex 642950; f. 1972; fmrly Industrial Devt Bank; provides finance for industrial devt; cap. and res 1,401.5m., dep. 1,031.8m. (June 1986); Chair. MUSLEHUDDIN AHMED; Man. Dir MOHIUDDIN KHAN ALAMGIR; 13 brs.

Bangladesh Shilpa Rin Sangstha (BSRS) (Industrial Loan Agency): POB 473, 5–7 Floor, 141–143 BIWTA Bhavan, Motijheel C/A, Dhaka 2; tel. (2) 252016; f. 1972; cap. and res 661.4m., dep. 113.1m. (June 1986); Chair. KHORSHED ALAM; Man. Dir GHIASUDDIN AHMED; 4 brs.

Grameen Bank: 2/G Shyamoli, Dhaka 7; tel. (2) 326619; f. 1982; provides credit for the landless rural poor; cap. and res 27.8m., dep. 80m. (Oct. 1986); Chair. Prof. IQUBAL MAHMOOD; Man. Dir Prof. MUHAMMAD YUNUS; 232 brs.

Investment Corporation of Bangladesh (ICB): POB 2058, Shilpa Bank Bhaban, 8 DIT Ave, Dhaka 2; tel. (2) 254112; f. 1976; provides devt financing; cap. and res 277.1m. (June 1986); Chair. MANSURUL KARIM; Man. Dir M. SEKANDER ALI; 4 brs.

INSURANCE

Department of Insurance (attached to Ministry of Commerce): 74 Motijheel C/A, Dhaka 2; state-owned; controls activities of all insurers, home and foreign, under the Insurance Act, 1938; Controller of Insurance SHAMSUDDIN AHMAD.

In 1973 the two corporations below were formed, one for life insurance and the other for general insurance.

Jiban Bima Corporation: 24 Motijheel C/A, Dhaka 2; tel. (2) 232047; state-owned; comprises 36 national life insurance cos; life insurance; Man. Dir M. A. RAHIM.

Shadharan Bima Corporation: 33 Dilkusha C/A, Dhaka 2; tel. (2) 252026; state-owned; general insurance; Man. Dir M. SHAMSUL ALAM.

Trade and Industry

In 1972 the Government took over all cotton, jute and other major industrial enterprises and the tea estates. Management Boards were appointed by the Government. During 1976 and 1977 many tea plantations and the smaller industrial units were returned to the private sector. Further privatization, particularly in the jute and textile industries, was carried out in 1982. By 1986 the proportion of the country's industrial assets under government ownership had fallen to 45% (from 85% in 1972).

Export Promotion Bureau: 122–124 Motijheel C/A, Dhaka 2; tel. (2) 230500; telex 642204; f. 1972; under the Ministry of Commerce; regional offices in Chittagong, Khulna and Rajshahi; brs in Comilla, Sylhet, Bogra and Barisal; Vice-Chair. RUHUL AMIN MAJUMDER.

Planning Commission: Planning Commission Secretariat, G.O. Hostel, Sher-e-Bangla Nagar, Dhaka; f. 1972; govt agency responsible for all aspects of economic planning and development including the preparation of the Five-Year Plans and annual development programmes (in conjunction with appropriate govt ministries), promotion of savings and investment, compilation of statistics and evaluation of development schemes and projects.

GOVERNMENT-SPONSORED ORGANIZATIONS

Bangladesh Chemical Industries Corporation: Shilpa Bhaban, 2nd Floor, Motijheel C/A, Dhaka 2; tel. (2) 231954; telex 65847; Chair. A. K. M. MOSHARRAF HOSSAIN.

Bangladesh Export Processing Zones Authority: Jiban Bima Sadan (Ground Floor), 103 Agrabad C/A, POB 1124, Chittagong; Shilpa Bhaban, Motijheel C/A, Dhaka 2; tel. (2) 231877; telex 66319; f. 1981 to operate and control export processing zones in Bangladesh; Chair. Brig. MOHD HABIBUR RAHMAN.

Bangladesh Fisheries Development Corporation: 24/25 Dilkusha C/A, Dhaka 2; f. 1964; Chair. Dr M. B. RAHMAN.

Bangladesh Forest Industries Development Corporation: 186 Circular Rd, Motijheel C/A, Dhaka 2; Chair. M. ATIKULLAH.

Bangladesh Jute Mills Corporation: Adamjee Court, 4th Floor, Motijheel C/A, Dhaka 2; tel. (2) 238192; telex 65676; f. 1972; operates 35 jute mills with over 15,808 looms (there are also 35 mills in the private sector); Chair. SYED AHMED.

Bangladesh Mineral Exploration and Development Corporation: HBFC Bldg, 8th-9th Floors, 22 Purana Paltan, Dhaka 2; telex 65737; Chair. M. W. ALI.

Bangladesh Oil, Gas and Minerals Corporation (Petrobangla): 122–124 Motijheel C/A, Chamber Bldg, Dhaka 2; tel. (2) 253131; telex 725; Chair. SHAFIUL ALAM.

BANGLADESH

Bangladesh Small and Cottage Industries Corporation (BSCIC): 137/138 Motijheel C/A, Dhaka 2; tel. (2) 233202; f. 1957; Chair. MUHAMMAD SIRAJUDDIN.

Bangladesh Steel and Engineering Corporation: Airport Rd, Kowran Bazar, Dhaka; tel. (2) 327521; telex 65880; Chair. Dr NAZRUL ISLAM.

Bangladesh Sugar and Food Industries Corporation: Shilpa Bhaban, Motijheel C/A, Dhaka 2; tel. (2) 258084; telex 642210; f. 1972; Chair. M. NEFAUR RAHMAN.

Bangladesh Textile Mills Corporation: Shadharan Bima Bhaban, 33 Dilkusha C/A, Dhaka 2; tel. (2) 252504; telex 65703; f. 1972; Chair. M. NURUNNABI CHOWDHURY.

Trading Corporation of Bangladesh: HBFC Bldg, 22 Purana Paltan, Dhaka 2; telex 642217; f. 1972; Chair. A. K. M. AZIZUL ISLAM.

CHAMBERS OF COMMERCE

Federation of Bangladesh Chambers of Commerce and Industry: POB 2079, 60 Motijheel C/A, 4th Floor, Dhaka 2; tel. (2) 282880; telex 642418; f. 1973; Pres. M. A. SATTAR.

Agrabad Chamber of Commerce and Industry: POB 70, Chamber Bldg, Bangabandhu Rd, Chittagong; tel. (2) 501031; Pres. L. D. B. BRYCESON.

Barisal Chamber of Commerce and Industry: Asad Mansion, 1st Floor, Sadar Rd, Barisal; tel. (2) 3984; Pres. KAZI ISRAIL HOSSAIN.

Bogra Chamber of Commerce and Industry: Raja Bazar, Bogra; tel. (2) 6257; f. 1963; Pres. TAHER UDDIN CHOWDHURY.

Chittagong Chamber of Commerce and Industry: Chamber House, Agrabad C/A, POB Chittagong; tel. (2) 502325; f. 1963; 2,319 mems; Pres. SIJANDAR HUSAIN MEAH.

Comilla Chamber of Commerce and Industry: Rammala Rd, Ranir Bazar, Comilla; tel. (2) 5444; Pres. AFZAL KHAN.

Dhaka Chamber of Commerce and Industry: Dhaka Chamber Bldg, 65–66 Motijheel C/A, POB 2641, Dhaka 2; tel. (2) 234383; telex 642418; f. 1958; 4,000 mems; Pres. MAHBUBUR RAHMAN; Sr Vice-Pres. MOHD ALI HOSSAIN, Jr Vice-Pres. SAYEEDUR RAHMAN.

Dinajpur Chamber of Commerce and Industry: Jail Rd, Dinajpur; tel. (2) 3189; Pres. KHAIRUL ANAM.

Faridpur Chamber of Commerce and Industry: Chamber House, Niltuly, Faridpur; tel. (2) 3530; Pres. KHANDOKER MOHSIN ALI.

Khulna Chamber of Commerce and Industry: 6 Lower Jessore Rd, Khulna; tel. (2) 24135; f. 1934; Pres. S. K. ZAHOIUL ISLAM.

Khustia Chamber of Commerce and Industry: 15, NS Rd, Khustia; tel. (2) 3448; Pres. DIN MOHAMMAD.

Metropolitan Chamber of Commerce and Industry: Chamber Bldg (4th Floor), 122–124 Motijheel C/A, Dhaka 2; tel. (2) 282566; telex 642413; f. 1904; 216 mems; Pres. M. R. SIDDIQI; Sec. C. K. HYDER.

Noakhali Chamber of Commerce and Industry: Noakhali Pourshara Bhaban, 2nd Floor, Maiydee Court, Noakhali; tel. (2) 5229; Pres. MOHAMMAD NAZIBUR RAHMAN.

Rajshahi Chamber of Commerce and Industry: Chamber Bldg, Station Rd, Ghoramara; tel. (2) 2215; f. 1960; 48 mems; Pres. MESBAHUDDIN AHMED.

Sylhet Chamber of Commerce and Industry: Chamber Bldg, POB 97, Jail Rd, Sylhet; Admin. ABDUL KHALEQUE KHAN.

TRADE ASSOCIATIONS

Bangladeshiyo Cha Sangsad (Bangladesh Tea Association): No. 6, Jahan Bldg, 2nd Floor, 93 Agrabad C/A, POB 287, Chittagong; tel. (2) 501274; f. 1952; Chair. W. L. C. PETRIE.

Bangladesh Jute Association: BJA Bldg, 137 Bangabandhu Rd, POB 59, Narayanganj, Dhaka; tel. (2) 71455; Chair. SABETHUR RAHMAN.

Bangladesh Jute Goods Association: 3rd Floor, 150 Motijheel C/A, Dhaka; tel. (2) 253640; f. 1979; 17 mems; Chair. M. A. KASHEM, HAJI MOHAMMAD ALI.

Bangladesh Jute Mills Association: 8th Floor, Hadi Mansion, 2 Dilkusha C/A, Dhaka; tel. (2) 253279; Chair. Dr NAIMUR RAHMAN.

Bangladesh Jute Spinners Association: Chamber Bldg, 4th Floor, 122–124 Motijheel C/A, Dhaka 2; tel. (2) 282566; telex 642413; f. 1979; 29 mems; Chair. MOHAMMAD SHAMSUL HAQUE; Sec. C. K. HYDER.

Bangladesh Tea Board: 111/113 Motijheel C/A, Dhaka 2; telex 642208; Chair. QUAMRUL HUDA.

Jute Marketing and Export Corporation: 14 Topkhana Rd, Dhaka; tel. (2) 236090; Chair. MUSTAFIZUR RAHMAN.

CO-OPERATIVES

Bangladesh Co-operative Marketing Society: 9D Motijheel C/A, Dhaka 2.

Chattagram Bahini Kalyan Shamabaya Samity Ltd: 70 Agrabad C/A, Osman Court, Chittagong; f. 1972.

TRADE UNIONS

The ban on trade union activity was lifted in January 1986.

In 1986 only about 3% of the total labour force was unionized. There were 2,614 registered unions, organized mainly on a sectoral or occupational basis. There were about 17 national trade unions to represent workers at the national level.

Transport

RAILWAYS

Bangladesh Railway: Railway HQ, Chittagong; tel. (2) 500120; telex 66200; supervised by the Railway Division of the Ministry of Communications; divided into East and West zones, 1982 with HQ at Chittagong and Rajshahi (tel. 2576); total length of track 4,550.9 km (1985); Dir-Gen. (Railway Division) S. HASAN AHMAD; Gen. Man. (East Zone) M. ASJAD ALI; Gen. Man. (West Zone) M. NAZMUL HAQUE; Gen. Man. (Projects) S. A. B. M. KARIMUSHAN.

ROADS

Of the 6,240 km of road, about 3,840 km are metalled.

Bangladesh Road Transport Corporation: Paribhaban, DIT Ave, Dhaka; f. 1961; transportation services including a truck division, transports govt foodgrain; 700 vehicles (1980).

INLAND WATERWAYS

In Bangladesh there are some 8,430 km of navigable waterways, which transport 70% of total domestic and foreign cargo traffic and on which are located the main river ports of Dhaka, Narayanganj, Chandpur, Barisal and Khulna. A river steamer service connects these ports several times a week. Vessels of up to 175-m overall length can be navigated on the Karnaphuli river.

Bangladesh Inland Water Transport Corporation: 5 Dilkusha C/A, Dhaka 2; tel. (2) 257092; f. 1972; 273 vessels (1986).

SHIPPING

The chief ports are Chittagong, where the construction of a second dry-dock is planned, and Chalna. A modern seaport is being developed at Mangla.

Atlas Shipping Agencies Ltd: Jiban Bima Bhaban, S. K. Mujib Rd, Agrabad, Chittagong 2; tel. (2) 504287; telex 66213; Man. Dir S. U. CHOWDHURY; Man. M. Z. AHMED.

Bangladesh Shipping Corpn: Pine View, 100 Agrabad C/A, POB 641, Chittagong; tel. (2) 501855; telex 66277; f. 1972; maritime shipping; 21 vessels, 266,211 tons capacity (1986); Chair. M. RAHMAN; Man. Dir WALIUL ISLAM; Financial Dir S. A. M. IQBAL; Technical Dir T. A. AHMAD.

Bangladesh Steam Navigation Co Ltd: Red Cross Bldg, 87 Motijheel C/A, Dhaka 2; coastal services; Chair. A. K. KHAN; Man. Dir A. M. Z. KHAN.

Chittagong Port Authority: POB 2013, Chittagong; tel. (2) 500101; telex 66264; provides bunkering and lighterage facilities as well as provisions and drinking water supplies.

United Shipping Corpn Ltd: 4th Fl., Parachi Bldg, 54 Dilkusha C/A, POB 755, Dhaka 2; tel. (2) 24565; telex 65749.

CIVIL AVIATION

There is an international airport at Dhaka (Zia International Airport) situated at Kurmitola and opened in September 1980 which is expected to handle 5m. passengers annually, 10 times the capacity of the original Dhaka airport. There are also airports at all major towns.

Biman (Bangladesh Airlines): Biman Bhaban, Motijheel C/A, Dhaka 2; tel. (2) 255911; telex 642649; f. 1972; internal services to all major towns; international services to Abu Dhabi, Bahrain, Bhutan, Burma, Dubai, France, Greece, India, Iraq, Italy, Kuwait, Libya, Malaysia, Nepal, the Netherlands, Oman, Pakistan, Qatar, Saudi Arabia, Singapore, Thailand and the United Kingdom; Man. Dir MUHAMMAD FAIZUR RAZZAQUE; fleet of 3 F-27, 2 F-28, 1 Boeing

707 320-B, 4 707 320-C, 3 DC 10-30, 2 F-28 Fokkers and 3 F-27 Fokkers.

Tourism

Bangladesh Parjatan Corporation (National Tourist Organization): 233 Airport Rd, Tejgaon, Dhaka 15; tel. (2) 325155; telex 642206; there are two tourist information centres in Dhaka, and one each in Bogra, Chittagong, Cox's Bazar, Khulna, Rajshahi, Rangamati; Chair. Col (retd) SYED SHAHABUDDIN AHMED; Man. S. KUTUBUDDIN AHMED.

Atomic Energy

Bangladesh Atomic Energy Commission (BAEC): 7 Mymensingh Rd, POB 158, Dhaka 2; tel. (2) 505021; f. as Atomic Energy Centre of the fmr Pakistan Atomic Energy Comm. in East Pakistan in 1965, reorganized under present name in 1973; operates an atomic energy research establishment at Savar, an atomic energy centre at Dhaka, five nuclear medicine centres at Chittagong, Dhaka, Dinajpur, Rajshahi and Sylhet, a beach-sand exploitation centre at Cox's Bazar and a nuclear power project involving the exploitation of uranium and thorium; Chair. Dr ANWAR HOSSAIN; Sec. A. S. M. ENAMUL HUQ.

BARBADOS

Introductory Survey

Location, Climate, Language, Religion, Flag, Capital

Barbados is the most easterly of the Caribbean islands, lying about 320 km (200 miles) north-east of Trinidad. There is a rainy season from July to November and the climate is cool during the rest of the year. The mean annual temperature is about 26°C (78°F). The language is English. Almost all of the inhabitants profess Christianity but there are small groups of Hindus, Muslims and Jews. The majority of the population are Anglicans but about 90 other Christian denominations are represented. The national flag (proportions 3 by 2) has three equal vertical stripes, of blue, gold and blue; superimposed on the centre of the gold band is the head of a black trident. The capital is Bridgetown.

Recent History

Barbados was formerly a British colony. The Barbados Labour Party (BLP) won a general election in 1951, when universal adult suffrage was introduced, and held office until 1961. Ministerial government was established in 1954, when the BLP's leader, Sir Grantley Adams, became the island's first Premier. He was subsequently Prime Minister of the West Indies Federation from January 1958 until its dissolution in May 1962.

Barbados achieved full internal self-government in October 1961. An election in December 1961 was won by the Democratic Labour Party (DLP), formed in 1955 by dissident members of the BLP. The DLP's leader, Errol Barrow, became Premier, succeeding Dr Hugh Cummins of the BLP. When Barbados achieved independence on 30 November 1966, Barrow became the island's first Prime Minister, having won another election earlier in the month.

The DLP retained power in 1971 but in the general election of September 1976 the BLP, led by J. M. G. M. ('Tom') Adams (Sir Grantley's son), ended Barrow's 15-year rule. The BLP successfully campaigned against alleged government corruption, winning a large majority over the DLP. Both parties were committed to retaining a system of free enterprise and alignment with the USA. At a general election in June 1981 the BLP was returned to office, owing mainly to its economic achievements in government, with 17 of the 27 seats in the newly enlarged House of Assembly. The remainder of the seats were won by the DLP. A Cabinet reshuffle took place in early 1983, and in September the Minister of Health, Dr Donald Blackman, left the Cabinet following allegations that he had publicly criticized a fellow Minister. There was also disagreement between the Government and the opposition concerning the amount spent on defence. Adams died suddenly in March 1985 and was succeeded as Prime Minister by his deputy, Bernard St John, a former leader of the BLP.

At a general election in May 1986 the DLP won a decisive victory, receiving 59.4% of the total votes and winning 24 of the 27 seats in the House of Assembly. Bernard St John and all but one of his Cabinet Ministers lost their seats, and Errol Barrow returned as Prime Minister after 10 years in opposition. The DLP promised to introduce a programme of tax reforms and to reduce spending and borrowing by the public sector. Emphasizing the Government's policy of job creation, a new Ministry of Employment was established. In June 1986 it was announced that Barrow was to review Barbados' participation in the US-supported Regional Security System (RSS), the defence force that had been established soon after the US invasion of Grenada in October 1983. Barbados, under Adams, was one of the countries whose troops supported the invasion.

Relations with Trinidad and Tobago were strained between 1982 and 1985 by publicly-stated differences over the intervention in Grenada, and by Trinidad's imposition of import restrictions, which affected Barbadian export industries. A meeting between the Trade Ministers of the two countries in August 1986 achieved a significant breakthrough, as a number of Barbadian goods were freed from the restrictions. Barbados is a member of CARICOM (see p. 108).

Government

Executive power is vested in the British monarch, represented by a Governor-General, who acts on the advice of the Cabinet. The Governor-General appoints the Prime Minister and, on the latter's recommendation, other members of the Cabinet. Legislative power is vested in the bicameral Parliament, comprising a Senate of 21 members, appointed by the Governor-General, and a House of Assembly with 27 members, elected by universal adult suffrage for five years (subject to dissolution) from single-member constituencies. The Cabinet is responsible to Parliament. Elected local government bodies were abolished in 1969 in favour of a division into 11 parishes, all of which are administered by the central government.

Defence

The Barbados Defence Force, established in April 1978, consists of 154 regular personnel. It is divided into regular defence units and a coastguard service with armed patrol boats; there is also a volunteer force and a reserve. Government spending on defence in the 1985/86 financial year was Bds $26.2m., representing 3.4% of total budget expenditure.

Economic Affairs

Traditionally, the economy of Barbados was based mainly on the cultivation of sugar cane and related activities, including the production of raw sugar, rum and molasses. In recent times, the island's economy has become diversified, so reducing the importance of sugar. Services, particularly tourism, are now the leading source of employment in Barbados, while exports of manufactured goods have overtaken agricultural exports in value. In 1984, according to estimates by the World Bank, the island's gross national product (GNP) per head, measured at average 1982–84 prices, was US $4,370. Between 1965 and 1984, it was estimated, GNP per head increased, in real terms, at an average rate of 2.5% per year.

After independence, the island's output of cane sugar fell steadily. In the late 1970s depressed world prices and increasing costs contributed to the industry's decline, and by 1978 production of raw sugar was down to 99,000 metric tons, and sugar accounted for only 6.7% of gross domestic product (GDP). There followed some recovery in raw sugar output, with the total reaching 130,000 tons in 1980, but production in 1983 was down to 81,000 tons, the lowest annual level for 35 years. The decline was partly due to smut disease which, in some cases, eradicated farmers' whole cane crops. However, production of raw sugar rose to 100,393 tons in 1984, and sales of sugar earned Bds $59m. in export earnings. By 1984 the contribution of the sugar industry to GDP was only 2.8%. The 1985 output of 100,247 tons was subsidized by a government grant of Bds $10m., and was aided further by a guarantee on a Bds $10m. bond issue by the Barbados Sugar Industry Limited. The 1986 harvest produced 111,148 tons of raw sugar. Exports of rum totalled Bds $8m. in 1985, Bds $2m. more than in 1984, helped by a bulk shipment to the United Kingdom.

Owing to volatile fluctuations in the international price of sugar on the free market, the Barbados Government has encouraged a policy of agricultural diversification. A rural development project, announced in 1980, was to invest Bds $5m. in agro-industries. Supplementary crops have been planted, most of them in rotation with sugar. Sea-island cotton, the island's original export crop, has been revived, with 754 acres (305 ha) under cultivation in 1985 and between 1,500 and 2,000 acres (600 to 800 ha) planted for the 1986 crop. Production of maize and groundnuts has also increased, although heavy rains at the beginning of 1986 were reported both to have devastated the 1986 groundnut crop and to have delayed the harvest of the 1986 cotton crop. In 1986 the Government announced a three-year pilot scheme, designed to increase production of fruits such as mango, grapefruit, avocado and papaya. By the end of 1985 the island was virtually self-sufficient in tomatoes, carrots and onions. A fishing complex, costing Bds $5m., was opened at Oistins in June 1983, as part of an overall plan to modernize the industry and to make Barbados self-sufficient in fish. As a consequence, landings of fish increased from 3,411 metric tons in 1981 to 6,522 tons in 1983. However, adverse weather conditions led to a 30% fall in fish landings in 1985.

Tourism has been greatly affected by the world recession. The steady expansion which has been maintained since the 1960s slowed in the mid-1970s. After an increase in the number of visitors between 1977 and 1979, the rate of growth dropped again between 1980 and 1982. Increased charter business and cheaper flights from the USA helped the industry in 1983, when tourist arrivals rose by 8%, boosted by short-stay visitors from the USA. Although tourism continued to grow in 1984 and between January and April 1985, Barbados experienced one of its worst summer seasons for several years between May and December 1985, with tourist arrivals declining by 13%. Real earnings in the sector were estimated to have fallen by 3% in 1985.

Government policy is to reduce dependence on tourism and to diversify industry and agriculture, thus forming a more stable, broad-based economy. It has succeeded in attracting light manufacturing industry through tax incentives, and this sector generated more than 11% of GDP in 1979. However, these industries also suffered the effects of recession in the USA, the main market for their products. The revival of the US economy in 1983 and 1984 helped to boost manufacturing exports, but local sales of clothing and furniture have been depressed by the imposition, since 1982, of import restrictions by Trinidad and Tobago (the island's main trading partner in the CARICOM region), which reduced its imports by about one-half in 1985, and by the decline of the Jamaican economy. During 1984 production of electronic components increased by 26%, but in 1985 exports fell by 20%, as a result of a slump in the US computer market. By the end of 1985, four large component assembly plants had been closed, and 1,200 jobs lost. In August 1986 the largest manufacturing enterprise in Barbados, Intel, announced that it was to close, with a loss of 900 jobs.

Infrastructure is well-developed in Barbados, and development projects planned in 1983 included a new highway linking seven industrial estates, from Bridgetown in the west to the Grantley Adams airport in the south, at a cost of Bds $52m. Work was to be completed in 1987. A new cement plant, capable of producing 1,000 tons of clinker per day, which was financed jointly by the governments of Barbados and Trinidad and Tobago, was completed in 1984.

Reserves of petroleum and natural gas have been discovered. In 1983 petroleum was being exploited at the rate of approximately 1,500 barrels per day (b/d). In 1982 the Government purchased facilities for onshore petroleum drilling and production at a cost of US $12m. Output from the Woodbourne field was increased substantially in 1983 and 1984, and in 1985, although the increase in output was more moderate, total production satisfied about 50% of the country's oil requirements. Barbados uses about 1.2m. barrels per year; the Government's aim is to be self-sufficient in petroleum (requiring production of about 4,000 b/d). Sales of natural gas reached 13.7m. cu ft (nearly 390,000 cu m) in 1985, and explorations for offshore reserves are also taking place.

After a five-year period of economic growth, real GDP declined by 2.5% in 1981, and by a further 4.4% in 1982, despite stringent economic measures, introduced in 1981, to halt the fall in government revenue and to improve the balance of payments. However, the fall in GDP had been stopped by 1983, and there was a rise of 2.9%, in real terms, in 1984. In 1985 GDP was estimated to have risen by no more than 0.3%. In October 1982 the IMF agreed to provide Bds $70m. under a stand-by arrangement in support of a 20-month economic adjustment programme; compensatory financing of Bds $28m. was also approved to offset a reduction in earnings from tourism and sugar exports. After three years of growth averaging 25.5%, the value of total domestic exports declined by about 13% in 1985. Retained imports fell by 9%, to Bds $1,016m., the lowest level in three years. In February 1984 the Government disclosed details of a five-year development plan, with emphasis on expansion by the private sector. Unemployment averaged 13.9% of the labour force in 1982, but by December 1985 had risen to 18.2%. The average rate of inflation fell from 10.3% in 1982 to 5.3% in 1983, 4.6% in 1984, 3.9% in 1985, and to only 1.3% in the year ending May 1986.

In 1985 the US Congress approved a Barbados-US Double Taxation Agreement, which has led to strong interest in Barbados' 'offshore' financial facilities. By the end of 1985 there were 520 companies registered in the offshore sector, and during 1986 several large insurance firms opened offices in Bridgetown.

Social Welfare

A social security scheme was established in 1967, and a National Drug Plan, introduced in 1980, is the first stage in a national health service, due to be completed by 1986. Old-age pensions and unemployment insurance are available. The Government has also created a building scheme of group housing for lower-income families. In 1980 Barbados had 10 hospital establishments, with a total of 2,126 beds, and in 1979 there were 201 physicians working on the island. Government expenditure on health in the 1985/86 financial year represented 13.0% of total budget spending, while social security and welfare received a further 7.1% of the total.

Education

Education is compulsory for 11 years, between five and 16 years of age. Primary education begins at the age of five and lasts for six years. Secondary education, beginning at 11 years of age, also lasts for six years, divided into two equal cycles. Enrolment of children in the primary age-group is 100%. The ratio for secondary schoolchildren was 89% (boys 86%; girls 91%) in 1983. Tuition at all government schools is free, and the state provides for approximately 86% of those eligible for primary and secondary education. The adult literacy rate was believed to be 98% in 1985. In 1984 there were 138 primary schools, 21 government-run secondary schools, 15 private secondary schools, a community college, a teacher training college, a theological college, a technical institute and a polytechnic. Degree courses in arts, law, education, natural sciences and social sciences are offered at the Barbados branch of the University of the West Indies. The faculty of medicine administers the East Caribbean Medical Scheme, while an in-service training programme for graduate teachers in secondary schools is provided by the School of Education. Government expenditure on education represented 20.6% of total budget spending in the 1985/86 financial year. In 1986 plans were announced for improvements to the primary and secondary education system, and for expansion of the technical training programme. The project is to be funded by the Inter-American Development Bank, the World Bank and the Government.

Tourism

The natural attractions of the island consist chiefly of the healthy climate and varied scenery. In addition, there are many facilities for outdoor sports of all kinds. Bathsheba, on the east coast, is a well-known health resort. Revenue from tourism increased from Bds $13m. in 1960 to an estimated Bds $568m. in 1984. The number of tourist arrivals rose from 303,778 in 1980 to 359,135 in 1985.

Public Holidays

1987: 1 January (New Year's Day), 17 April (Good Friday), 20 April (Easter Monday), 4 May (May Day), 8 June (Whit Monday), 7 July (Kadooment Day), 4 August (Caricom Day), 5 October (United Nations Day), 30 November (Independence Day), 25–26 December (Christmas).

1988: 1 January (New Year's Day), 1 April (Good Friday), 4 April (Easter Monday), 2 May (May Day), 23 May (Whit

BARBADOS

Monday), 7 July (Kadooment Day), 4 August (Caricom Day), 3 October (United Nations Day), 30 November (Independence Day), 25–26 December (Christmas).

Weights and Measures

The metric system is used.

Currency and Exchange Rates

100 cents = 1 Barbados dollar (Bds $).

Exchange rates (30 September 1986):
 £1 sterling = Bds $2.910;
 US $1 = Bds $2.011.

Statistical Survey

Sources (unless otherwise stated): Barbados Statistical Service, National Insurance Bldg, Fairchild St, Bridgetown; tel. 427-7841; Central Bank of Barbados, POB 1016, Bridgetown; tel. 436-6870.

AREA AND POPULATION

Area: 430 sq km (166 sq miles).
Population: 237,701 at census of 7 April 1970; 248,983 (males 118,565, females 130,418) at census of 12 May 1980; 253,000 (estimate, mid-1985).
Density (1985): 588 per sq km.
Principal Town: Bridgetown (capital), population 7,517 at 1980 census.
Births and Deaths (registrations, 1984): Live births 4,218 (birth rate 16.7 per 1,000); Deaths 1,954 (death rate 7.8 per 1,000).
Economically Active Population (labour force sample survey, annual average, '000 persons, excluding institutional households, 1984): Agriculture, forestry and fishing 8.5; Manufacturing 12.4; Electricity, gas and water 1.9; Construction and quarrying 6.9; Trade, restaurants and hotels 19.9; Transport, storage and communications 5.1; Financing, insurance, real estate and business services 3.3; Community, social and personal services 35.1; Total employed 93.1 (males 53.2, females 39.9); Unemployed 19.2 (males 7.9, females 11.3); Total labour force 112.3 (males 61.1, females 51.2).

AGRICULTURE, ETC.

Principal Crops (metric tons, 1984): Roots and tubers 11,000 (FAO estimate); Vegetables 12,000 (FAO estimate); (1985) Sugar cane 793,493.
Livestock (FAO estimates, '000 head, year ending September 1984): Cattle 18; Pigs 50; Sheep 54; Goats 32 (Source: FAO, *Production Yearbook*).
Livestock Products (FAO estimates, '000 metric tons, 1984): Pig meat 6; Poultry meat 6; Cows' milk 6; Hen eggs 1.0 (Source: FAO, *Production Yearbook*).
Fishing (catch in metric tons): 3,477 in 1982; 6,522 in 1983; 5,824 in 1984.

MINING

Production: (1984) Natural gas 25.3 million cu m.; Crude petroleum 635,000 barrels.

INDUSTRY

Production: (1985) Raw sugar 100,247 metric tons; (1983) Rum 1,289,000 proof gallons; Beer 1,962,000 gallons; Cigarettes 531,000 lb; Batteries 16,756; Electric energy 354m. kWh.

FINANCE

Currency and Exchange Rates: 100 cents = 1 Barbados dollar (Bds $). *Coins:* 1, 5, 10 and 25 cents; 1 dollar. *Notes:* 1, 2, 5, 10, 20 and 100 dollars. *Sterling and US Dollar equivalents* (30 September 1986): £1 sterling = Bds $2.910; US $1 = Bds $2.011; Bds $100 = £34.36 = US $49.72. *Exchange Rate:* Fixed at US $1 = Bds $2.0113 since August 1977.
Budget (Bds $ '000, year ending 31 March 1986): *Revenue:* Tax revenue 576,915 (Taxes on income and profit 204,157; Taxes on property 34,709; Taxes on goods and services 165,789; Import duties 96,870); Non-tax revenue 66,700; (Government departments 38,195); Total 643,615. *Expenditure:* General public services 135,224; Defence 26,150; Education 158,597; Health 100,149; Social security and welfare 54,911; Housing and community amenities 32,154; other community and social services 40,157; Economic services 155,213 (Agriculture 46,727; Roads and other transport 90,191); Debt charges 69,834; Total 772,389 (excluding net lending −3,226).
International Reserves (US $ million at 31 December 1985): Gold 3.39; IMF special drawing rights 0.01; Reserve position in IMF 2.37; Foreign exchange 137.39; Total 143.66 (Source: IMF, *International Financial Statistics*).
Money Supply (Bds $ million at 31 December 1985): Currency outside banks 123.47; Demand deposits at commercial banks 198.86. Source: IMF, *International Financial Statistics*.
Cost of Living (retail price index; base: March 1980 = 100): 137.7 in 1983; 144.1 in 1984; 149.7 in 1985.

Gross Domestic Product (Bds $ million in current purchasers' values): 1,990.0 in 1982; 2,112.7 in 1983; 2,303.2 in 1984.
Balance of Payments (US $ million, 1984): Merchandise exports f.o.b. 339.7; Merchandise imports f.o.b. −606.2; *Trade balance* −266.5; Exports of services 487.5; Imports of services −216.6; *Balance on goods and services* 4.4; Unrequited transfers (net) 14.7; *Current balance* 19.1; Direct capital investment (net) −1.5; Other long-term capital (net) −23.1; Short-term capital (net) 27.6; Net errors and omissions −35.8; *Total (net monetary movements)* −13.6; Valuation changes (net) 17.4; *Changes in reserves* 3.8 (Source: IMF, *International Financial Statistics*).

EXTERNAL TRADE

Principal Commodities (Bds $ '000, 1984): *Imports:* Food and live animals 159,710; Beverages and tobacco 17,931; Crude materials (inedible) except fuels 29,464; Mineral fuels, lubricants, etc. 214,126; Animal and vegetable oils and fats 13,424; Chemicals 93,194; Basic manufactures 181,055; Machinery and transport equipment 475,271; Miscellaneous manufactured articles 118,681; Other commodities and transactions 21,766; Total 1,324,623. *Exports:* Sugar 57,269; Molasses and syrup 8,365; Rum 6,531; Semi-processed and other food products 19,426; Basic manufactures 124,577; Machinery and transport equipment 369,682; Chemicals 37,958; Mineral fuels, lubricants, etc. 147,891; Other items 15,672; Total 787,371.
Principal Trading Partners (Bds $ '000, 1984): *Imports:* Aruba 79,592; Canada 74,905; CARICOM countries 148,300 (Trinidad and Tobago 113,172); Guyana 6,412; Japan 50,324; United Kingdom 100,034; USA 632,716; Total (incl. others) 1,324,623. *Exports:* Canada 12,558; CARICOM countries 123,087 (Trinidad and Tobago 74,693); Guyana 52,781; Puerto Rico 199,297; United Kingdom 54,380; USA 217,161; Total (incl. others) 787,371.

TRANSPORT

Road Traffic (motor vehicles in use, 1984): Passenger cars (incl. taxis) 30,984; Pick-ups, vans and station wagons 2,893; Lorries, buses and tractors 2,561; Motor cycles 2,991.
Shipping (international sea-borne freight traffic, '000 metric tons, 1983): Goods loaded 242; Goods unloaded 613 (Source: UN, *Monthly Bulletin of Statistics*).
Civil Aviation (1983): Aircraft movements 530,600; Freight loaded 4,309 metric tons; Freight unloaded 6,533 metric tons.

TOURISM

Tourist Arrivals: 328,375 in 1983; 367,652 in 1984; 359,135 in 1985.

COMMUNICATIONS MEDIA

Radio Receivers (1983): 191,000 in use.
Television Receivers (1983): 55,000 in use.
Telephones (1 January 1983): 72,000 in use.
Book Production (1983): 87 titles (18 books, 69 pamphlets).
Daily Newspapers (1982): 2 (circulation 39,000); Source: UNESCO, *Statistical Yearbook*).

EDUCATION

Institutions and Enrolment (1984/85):
Primary: 138 schools, 33,906 students.
Secondary: 21 schools, 21,474 students.
Technical: 1 institution, 1,600 students.
Teacher Training: 1 institution, 186 students.
Theological: 1 institution, 20 students.
Community College: 1 institution, 1,806 students.
University of the West Indies: 1 institution, 1,617 students.
There are also 15 government-aided independent schools, with 4,227 students in 1984/85.

Directory

The Constitution

The Constitution came into force on 30 November 1966, when Barbados became independent. Under its terms, protection is afforded to individuals from slavery and forced labour, from inhuman treatment, deprivation of property, arbitrary search and entry, and racial discrimination; freedom of conscience, of expression, assembly, and movement are guaranteed.

Executive power is nominally vested in the British monarch, as Head of State, represented in Barbados by a Governor-General, who appoints the Prime Minister and, on the advice of the Prime Minister, appoints other Ministers and some Senators.

The Cabinet consists of the Prime Minister, appointed by the Governor-General as being the person best able to command a majority in the House of Assembly, and not fewer than five other Ministers. Provision is also made for a Privy Council, presided over by the Governor-General.

Parliament consists of two houses, the Senate and the House of Assembly. The Senate has 21 members, 12 appointed by the Governor-General on the advice of the Prime Minister, two on the advice of the Leader of the Opposition, and seven as representatives of such interests as the Governor-General considers appropriate. The House of Assembly has (since 1981) 27 members, elected by universal adult suffrage for a term of five years (subject to dissolution). The minimum voting age is 18.

The Constitution also provides for the establishment of Service Commissions for the Judicial and Legal Service, the Public Service, the Police Service and the Statutory Boards Service. These Commissions are exempt from legal investigation; they have executive powers to deal with appointments, dismissals and disciplinary control of the services for which they are responsible.

The Government

Head of State: HM Queen ELIZABETH II.

Governor-General: Sir HUGH SPRINGER (took office 24 February 1984).

THE CABINET
(October 1986)

Prime Minister and Minister of Economic Affairs: ERROL W. BARROW.

Deputy Prime Minister, Minister of Education and Culture and Leader of the House of Assembly: L. ERSKINE SANDIFORD.

Attorney-General and Minister of Legal Affairs: MAURICE A. KING.

Minister of Agriculture, Food and Fisheries: WARWICK O. FRANKLYN.

Minister of Employment, Labour Relations and Community Development: WESLEY W. HALL.

Minister of Finance: RICHARD C. HAYNES.

Minister of Foreign Affairs and Leader of the Senate: Sir CAMERON TUDOR.

Minister of Health: N. KEITH SIMMONS.

Minister of Housing and Lands: HAROLD A. BLACKMAN.

Minister of State, Public Service: L. V. HARCOURT LEWIS.

Minister of Tourism and Industry: BRANDFORD M. TAITT.

Minister of Trade and Commerce: E. EVELYN GREAVES.

Minister of Transport, Works and Telecommunications: PHILIP M. GREAVES.

MINISTRIES

Office of the Prime Minister: Government Headquarters, Bay St, St Michael; tel. 436-6435.

Ministry of Agriculture, Food and Fisheries: Graeme Hall, Christ Church; tel. 428-4150.

Ministry of Education and Culture: Jemmot's Lane, St Michael; tel. 427-3272.

Minister of Employment, Labour Relations and Community Development: Marine House, Hastings, Christ Church; tel. 427-5420.

Ministry of Finance: Government Headquarters, Bay St, St Michael; tel. 436-6435.

Ministry of Foreign Affairs: 1, Culloden Rd, St Michael; tel. 436-2990; telex 2222.

Ministry of Health: Jemmott's Lane, St Michael; tel. 426-5080.

Ministry of Housing and Lands: Marine House, Hastings, Christ Church; tel. 427-5420.

Ministry of Legal Affairs: Marine House, Hastings, Christ Church; tel. 427-5420.

Ministry of State, Public Service: Government Headquarters, Bay St, St Michael; tel. 436-6435.

Ministry of Tourism and Industry: PO Building, Cheapside, Bridgetown; tel. 436-4830.

Ministry of Trade and Commerce: Reef Rd, Fontabelle, St Michael; tel. 427-5270.

Ministry of Transport, Works and Telecommunications: The Pine, St Michael; tel. 429-2191; telex 2203.

Legislature

PARLIAMENT

Senate

President: FRANK WALCOTT.
There are 20 other members.

House of Assembly

Speaker: LAWSON WEEKES.
Clerk of Parliament: GEORGE BRANCKER.

General Election, 28 May 1986

Party	Votes	%	Seats
Barbados Labour Party	80,028	59.45	24
Democratic Labour Party	54,367	40.38	3
Others	227	0.17	—
Total	134,622	100.00	27

Political Organizations

Barbados Labour Party: Grantley Adams House, 111 Roebuck St, Bridgetown; tel. 426-2973; f. 1938; moderate social democrat; Leader and Chair. HENRY FORDE; Sec. AARON TRUSS.

Democratic Labour Party: George St, Belleville, St Michael; tel. 429-3104; f. 1955; Leader ERROL BARROW; Pres. BRANDFORD TAITT; Gen. Sec. CORA CUMBERBATCH.

People's Pressures Movement: Bridgetown; f. 1979; Leader ERIC SEALY.

Workers' Party of Barbados: Bridgetown; tel. 425-1620; f. 1985; small left-wing organization; Gen. Sec. Dr GEORGE BELLE.

Diplomatic Representation

EMBASSIES AND HIGH COMMISSIONS IN BARBADOS

Brazil: Sunjet House, Independence Square, Bridgetown; tel. 427-1735; telex 2434; Ambassador: AMAURY BIER.

Canada: Bishops Court Hill, St Michael; tel. 429-3550; telex 2247; High Commissioner: NOBLE POWER.

China, People's Republic: 17 Golf View Terrace, Rockley, Christ Church; tel. 426-1793; telex 2363; Ambassador: (vacant).

BARBADOS

Directory

Colombia: 'Carrusel', 39 South Ridge, Kent, Christ Church; tel. 427-8804; telex 2499; Ambassador: Dr CARLOS AYERBE.
Korea, Republic: 2nd Floor, Barbados Mutual Life Building, Collymore Rock, St Michael; tel. 429-9650; telex 2532; Ambassador: CHONG CHONG-KYU.
Trinidad and Tobago: Cockspur House, Nile St, Bridgetown; tel. 429-9600/1; telex 2326; High Commissioner: REGINALD DUMAS.
United Kingdom: 147/9 Roebuck St, POB 676, Bridgetown; tel. 436-6694; telex 2219; High Commissioner: KEVIN BURNS.
USA: Canadian Imperial Bank of Commerce Bldg, Broad St, POB 302, Bridgetown; tel. 436-4950; telex 2259; Ambassador: (vacant).
Venezuela: Old Civic Bldg, corner of High and Swan Sts, Bridgetown; tel. 426-5466; telex 2339; Ambassador: ORESTES DI GIACOMO.

Judicial System

Justice is administered by the Supreme Court of Judicature, which consists of a High Court and a Court of Appeal. Final appeal lies with the Judicial Committee of the Privy Council, in London. There are Magistrates' Courts for lesser offences.
Chief Justice: Sir WILLIAM R. DOUGLAS.
Puisne Judges: D. A. WILLIAMS, C. S. HUSBANDS, L. I. WORRELL, C. A. ROCHEFORD.
Registrar: (vacant).
Magistrates' Courts: Appeals lie to a Divisional Court of the High Court.

Religion

More than 90 religious denominations and sects are represented in Barbados. According to the 1970 census, there were about 150,000 Anglicans, while the Methodist, Moravian and Pentecostal groups are next in importance. There are about 23,000 Roman Catholics, and other Christian groups have a combined membership of 50,000. There are also small groups of Hindus, Muslims and Jews.

CHRISTIANITY
The Anglican Communion
Barbados is part of the Province of the West Indies.
Bishop of Barbados: Rt Rev. DREXEL GOMEZ, Diocesan Office, Mandeville House, Bridgetown; tel. 426-2761.

The Roman Catholic Church
The diocese of Bridgetown-Kingstown, comprising Barbados and Saint Vincent and the Grenadines, is suffragan to the archdiocese of Port of Spain (Trinidad and Tobago). The Bishop participates in the Antilles Episcopal Conference (based in Kingston, Jamaica).
Bishop of Bridgetown-Kingstown: Rt Rev. ANTHONY H. DICKSON, St Patrick's Cathedral, Jemmott's Lane, Bridgetown; tel. 426-2325.

Protestant Churches
Methodist Church: Bethel Church Office, Bay St, Bridgetown; tel. 426-2223; Chair. Rev. PHILLIP SAUNDERS.
Moravian Church: Roebuck St, Bridgetown; tel. 426-2337; Superintendent Rev. RUDOLPH HOLDER.

The Press

The Bajan and South Caribbean: Carlisle House, Hincks St, POB 718C, Bridgetown; f. 1953; monthly; illustrated magazine; Man. Editor TREVOR A. D. GALE; circ. over 8,000.
Barbados Advocate (News): POB 230, Fontabelle, Bridgetown; tel. 426-1210; f. 1895; daily; Man. Dir and Publr N. S. GROSVENOR; Man. Editor ROBERT BEST; circ. 17,137.
Barbados Observer: Baxters Rd, Bridgetown; weekly.
The Beacon: 111 Roebuck St, Bridgetown; organ of the Barbados Labour Party; weekly; circ. 15,000.
The Nation: Fontabelle, St Michael; tel. 436-6240; telex 2310; f. 1973; daily; Editor-in-Chief HAROLD HOYTE; circ. 21,186 (weekday), 33,435 (weekend).
Official Gazette: Government Printing Office, Bay St, Bridgetown; tel. 426-4568; Mons. and Thurs.

Sunday Advocate (News): POB 230, Fontabelle, Bridgetown; tel. 426-1210; Man. Dir and Publr N. S. GROSVENOR; Editor ULRIC RICE; circ. 24,400.
The Sunday Sun: Fontabelle, St Michael; tel. 436-6240; telex 2310; f. 1977; Editor-in-Chief HAROLD HOYTE; circ. 34,912.

NEWS AGENCIES
Caribbean News Agency (CANA): Culloden View, Beckles Road, St Michael; tel. 429-2903; telex 2228; f. 1976; public and private shareholders from English-speaking Caribbean; Gen. Man. HARRY MAYERS.

Foreign Bureau
Agencia EFE (Spain): 48 Gladioli Drive, Husbanos, St James; tel. 425-1542; telex 2599; Rep. YUSSUFF HANIFF.
Inter Press Service (IPS) (Italy): Silver Hill, Christ Church; tel. 86646; Correspondent ALBERT BRANDFORD.
Xinhua (New China) News Agency (People's Republic of China): 29 Newton Tce, POB 22A, Christ Church, Bridgetown; telex 2458; Chief Correspondent DING BAOZHONG.

Publishers

The Cedar Press: POB 616, Bridgetown; tel. 427-2681; telex 2335; religion, sociology, education, music, agriculture, communication, politics, Caribbean history, identity and culture; Asst Publr MURIEL FORDE.
PPC Ltd: Eldino, Gills Rd, St Michael; tel. 427-5505.

Radio and Television

In 1983 there were an estimated 191,000 radio receivers and 55,000 television receivers in use.
Caribbean Broadcasting Corporation: POB 900, Bridgetown; f. 1963; Chair. Prof. MICKEY WALROND.

RADIO
Barbados Broadcasting Service: Bridgetown; f. 1981.
Barbados Rediffusion Service Ltd: River Rd, Bridgetown; tel. 426-0820; f. 1934; commercial wired service with island-wide coverage; Gen. Man. F. DUESBURY; Programme Dir A. PRAGNELL.
CBC Radio: POB 900, Bridgetown; tel. 429-2041; telex 2560; f. 1963; administered by the Caribbean Broadcasting Corporation; broadcasts 19½ hours per day; Gen. Man. DUNCAN TURNEY.
Voice of Barbados: River Rd, Bridgetown; tel. 434-1790; f. 1981; commercial station covering Barbados and Eastern Caribbean; Gen. Man. F. G. DUESBURY; Programme Dir J. E. ROGERS.

TELEVISION
CBC TV: POB 900, Bridgetown; tel. 429-2041; telex 2560; f. 1964; operated by Caribbean Broadcasting Corporation; 11 hours colour transmission Monday to Friday, 16½ hours Saturday, 15 hours Sunday; Gen. Man. DUNCAN TURNEY.

Finance

(cap. = capital; auth. = authorized; dep. = deposits; res = reserves; brs = branches; m. = million)

BANKING
Central Bank
Central Bank of Barbados: POB 1016, Treasury Bldg, Bridgetown; tel. 436-6870; telex 2251; f. 1972; bank of issue; cap. Bds $2m., res Bds $18.5m., dep. Bds $185.1m. (Dec. 1985); Gov. Dr COURTNEY N. BLACKMAN; Gen. Man. E. H. C. GRIFFITH.

Regional Development Bank
Caribbean Development Bank: Wildey, POB 408, St Michael; tel. 426-1152; associate institution of CARICOM (see p. 108); equity subscribed by former British Caribbean Territories, Canada, the United Kingdom, Colombia and Venezuela; auth. cap. US $233m. (1969 values); minimum loan US $100,000; priority given to projects in agriculture, livestock, fisheries, manufacturing, mining, tourism, housing, technical education and energy; Pres. WILLIAM DEMAS.

BARBADOS

National Development Bank
Barbados Development Bank: POB 50, Wildey, St Michael; tel. 426-0512; telex 2295; f. 1969; auth. cap. Bds $30m.; Gen. Man. RICHARD LESLIE.

National Bank
Barbados National Bank: 11 James St, Bridgetown; tel. 427-5920; telex 2271; f. 1978 by the merger of the Barbados Savings Bank, Sugar Industry Agricultural Bank, Agricultural Credit Bank and The Public Officers Housing Loan Fund; cap. Bds $13.5m., dep. Bds $74.4m. (Dec. 1978); Pres. L. V. H. LEWIS; Gen. Man. MOHAMMED YASIN; 4 brs.

Foreign Banks
Bank of Nova Scotia (Canada): POB 202, Broad St, Bridgetown; tel. 426-0230; telex 2223; Man. D. J. MACDIARMID; 7 brs.

Barclays Bank (UK): POB 301, Broad St, Bridgetown; tel. 429-5151; telex 2348; f. 1837; Man. K. L. LEWIS; 12 brs.

Canadian Imperial Bank of Commerce: POB 405, Broad St, Bridgetown; tel. 426-0571; telex 2230; Man. T. MULLOY; 10 brs and 2 sub-brs.

Caribbean Commercial Bank (Trinidad and Tobago): Lower Broad St, Bridgetown; tel. 436-6900; f. 1984; Pres. MICHAEL WRIGHT.

Royal Bank of Canada: POB 1011, Trident House, Broad St, Bridgetown; tel. 429-5249; telex 2242; f. 1911; Man. R. I. COX; 7 brs.

Trust Companies
Bank of Commerce Trust Company Barbados Ltd: POB 503, Bridgetown; tel. 426-2740.

Bank of Nova Scotia Trust Co (Caribbean) Ltd: Bank of Nova Scotia Bldg, Broad St, POB 1003B, Bridgetown; tel. 426-5285; telex 5285.

Royal Bank Trust Co (Barbados) Ltd: POB 626C, 2nd Floor, Trident House, Bridgetown; tel. 436-6596; Man. N. L. SMITH.

STOCK EXCHANGE
Barbados Stock Exchange: Bridgetown; f. 1978.

INSURANCE
The leading British and a number of US and Canadian companies have agents in the territory. Local insurance companies include the following:

Barbados Fire & General Insurance Co: POB 150, Beckwith Place, Broad St, Bridgetown; tel. 426-4291; telex 2393; f. 1880.

Barbados Mutual Life Assurance Society: Collymore Rock, St Michael; tel. 436-6750; telex 2423; f. 1840; Chair. P. McG. PATTERSON; Man. D. W. ALLAN.

Caribbean Commercial Insurance Co Ltd: 1 Broad St, POB 304, Bridgetown; tel. 436-6560.

C. F. Harrison & Co (Barbados) Ltd: 1 & 2 Broad St, POB 304, Bridgetown; tel. 426-0720; telex 2267.

Insurance Corporation of Barbados: 5 James St, Bridgetown; tel. 427-5593; telex 2317; f. 1978; cap. Bds $3m.; Gen. Man. DAVID DEANE.

Life of Barbados Ltd: Plantations Bldg, Lower Broad St, Bridgetown; tel. 426-1060; telex 2393; f. 1971; Pres. CECIL F. DE CAIRES.

United Insurance Co Ltd: POB 1215, Cowell St, Bridgetown; tel. 436-1991; telex 2343; f. 1976; Dir G. M. CHALLENOR.

Trade and Industry

CHAMBERS OF COMMERCE
Barbados Chamber of Commerce and Industry: 1st Floor, Nemwil House, Collymore Rock, POB 189, Bridgetown; tel. 426-2056; f. 1825; 153 mem. firms, 248 reps; Pres. HARTLEY RICHARDS; Exec. Dir STANLEY L. TAYLOR.

Barbados Junior Chamber of Commerce: Bridgetown; Pres. AVRIL BREWSTER; Sec. VINCENT HAYNES.

DEVELOPMENT
Barbados Agricultural Development Corporation: Fairy Valley, Christ Church; tel. 428-0250; f. 1965; programme of diversification and land reforms; Chair. GEOFFREY GARVEY; Gen. Man. E. COLERIDGE PILGRIM; Sec. FRANK B. TAYLOR (acting).

Barbados Export Production Corporation: Harbour Rd, St Michael; tel. 427-5758; telex 2486; co-ordinates activities of Barbadian manufactures; Chief Exec. PHILIP WILLIAMS.

Barbados Industrial Development Corporation: Pelican Park, Princess Alice Highway, POB 250, Bridgetown; tel. 427-5350; telex 2295; f. 1969; operates industrial estates; encourages foreign investment; advises potential customers; promotes domestic manufacturing; Chair. CECIL WILLIAMS; Gen. Man. RAWLE G. B. CHASE.

Barbados Marketing Corporation: POB 703C, Bridgetown; tel. 427-5250; telex 2253; Chair. ROBERT MORRIS; Gen. Man. CLYDE KING.

British Development Division in the Caribbean: POB 167, Carlisle House, Hincks St, Bridgetown; tel. 426-2190; telex 2236; Head MICHAEL G. BAWDEN.

STATE-OWNED COMPANIES
Barbados National Oil Company (BNOC): Woodbourne, St Philip; tel. 423-0918; telex 2334; f. 1982; exploration for petroleum and natural gas.

National Petroleum Corporation (NPC): Wildey, St Michael; tel. 426-5012; f. 1951; gas distribution.

ASSOCIATIONS
Barbados Agricultural Society: The Grotto, Culloden and Beckles Rd, St Michael; tel. 426-3434; Pres. PATRICK BETHELL; Exec. Sec. ISLA GILKES.

Barbados Hotel Association: POB 711, Bridgetown; tel. 426-5041; telex 2314; Pres. BERNARD WEATHERHEAD; Dir ROSALIND CRANE.

Barbados Manufacturers' Association: Prescod Blvd, Harbour Rd, St Michael; tel. 426-4474; f. 1964; Pres. ALLAN FIELDS; Exec. Sec. RITA ALKINS; 119 mem. firms.

Barbados Sugar Industry Ltd: POB 719C, Bridgetown; tel. 425-0010; telex 2418; Man. Dir E. A. B. DEANE; Sec. D. H. A. JOHNSON.

West Indian Sea Island Cotton Association (Inc): c/o Barbados Agricultural Development Corporation, Fairy Valley, Christ Church; Pres. E. LEROY WARD; 8 mem. associations.

EMPLOYERS' ORGANIZATION
Barbados Employers' Confederation: 1st Floor, Nemwil House, Lower Collymore Rock, St Michael; tel. 426-1574; f. 1956; Pres. CHRIS ST JOHN; Exec. Dir JAMES A. WILLIAMS; Sec.-Treas. COLLEEN BARROW; 269 mems.

TRADE UNIONS
Principal unions include:

Barbados Industrial and General Workers' Union: Bridgetown; f. 1981; Leader ROBERT CLARKE; Gen. Sec. LADEPOO SALANKEY; c. 2,000 mems.

Barbados Secondary Teachers' Union: Ryeburn House, 8th Ave, Belleville, St Michael; tel. 429-7676; f. 1948; Pres. Mrs MARGUERITE CUMMINS-WILLIAMS; Sec. PATRICK FROST; 330 mems.

Barbados Union of Teachers: POB 127, Bridgetown; f. 1974; Pres. M. MARSHALL; Gen. Sec. CARLISLE BASCOMBE; 2,000 mems.

Barbados Workers' Union: Nelson and Fairchild Sts, Bridgetown; tel. 426-3495; f. 1941; Sec.-Gen. FRANK WALCOTT; 30,000 mems.

The National Union of Public Workers: POB 174, Dalkeith Rd, Bridgetown; tel. 426-1764; f. 1944; Pres. NIGEL O. HARPER; Gen. Sec. JOSEPH GODDARD; 6,000 mems.

Transport

ROADS
Ministry of Transport and Works: POB 25, Bridgetown; tel. 429-2191; telex 2203; maintains a network of about 1,642 km (1,020 miles) of roads, of which 1,400 km (870 miles) have an asphalt surface; Chief Technical Officer C. H. ARCHER.

SHIPPING
Inter-island traffic is catered for by a fortnightly service of one vessel of the West Indies Shipping Corporation operating from Trinidad as far north as Jamaica. The CAROL container service consortium connects Bridgetown with West European ports and

several foreign shipping lines call at the port. Bridgetown harbour has berths for eight ships and simultaneous bunkering facilities for five.

DaCostas Ltd: Carlisle House, Hincks St, Bridgetown; tel. 426-0850; telex 2328.

CIVIL AVIATION

The principal airport is Grantley Adams International Airport, 18 km (11 miles) from Bridgetown.

Caribbean Air Cargo Ltd (CARICARGO): Grantley Adams International Airport, Christ Church; tel. 428-4180; telex 2417; f. 1979 by the governments of Barbados and Trinidad and Tobago (joint share-holders); services between Miami, New York, Houston and the Eastern Caribbean; Chair. PETER LOOK HONG; Man. Dir KINGSLEY CLARKE; fleet of 2 Boeing 707.

Caribbean Airways: Lower Bay St, Bridgetown; tel. 426-9900; telex 2265; f. 1970; national airline; government-owned; low-cost jet services to Brussels, Frankfurt and London; Chair. IAN DE V. ARCHER; Gen. Man. SAM WAITHE.

Tourism

Barbados Board of Tourism: Harbour Rd, POB 242, Bridgetown; tel. 427-2623; telex 2420; f. 1958; offices in London, New York, Montreal, Toronto, California and the Federal Republic of Germany; Chair. CLEVEDON MAYERS; Dir of Tourism PATRICK HINDS.

BELGIUM

Introductory Survey

Location, Climate, Language, Religion, Flag, Capital

The Kingdom of Belgium lies in north-western Europe, bounded to the north by the Netherlands, to the east by Luxembourg and the Federal Republic of Germany, to the south by France, and to the west by the North Sea. The climate is temperate. It is mild and humid on the coast, with hotter summers and colder winters inland. Temperatures in Brussels are generally between 0°C (32°F) and 23°C (73°F). Dutch, spoken in the north (Flanders), and French, spoken in the south (Wallonia), are the two main official languages. A 1963 law established four linguistic regions, the French, Dutch and German-speaking areas and Brussels, which is situated in the Flemish part but has bilingual status. Approximately 57% of the population are Dutch-speaking, 42% are French-speaking and 0.6% speak German. Almost all of the inhabitants profess Christianity, and the great majority are Roman Catholics. The national flag (proportions 15 by 13) consists of three equal vertical stripes, of black, yellow and red. The capital is Brussels.

Recent History

Since the Second World War, Belgium has become recognized as a leader of international co-operation in Europe. It is a founder member of many important international organizations, including the Council of Europe, the European Communities and the Benelux Economic Union. King Leopold III, who had reigned since 1934, abdicated in July 1951 in favour of his son, Baudouin.

In the post-war period the language dispute between French and Dutch speakers has been the country's main political problem, exacerbated by political polarization between Flanders, in the north (supporting mainly the conservative Christian Social Party and the nationalist Volksunie party), and francophone Wallonia, in the south (predominantly Socialist). All the major parties have both French and Flemish sections, although linguistic conflicts frequently override political considerations, as a result of the trend away from centralized administration towards greater regional control. Moderate constitutional reforms, produced in July 1971, were the first steps towards regional autonomy; in 1972 further concessions were made, with the German-speaking community being represented in the Cabinet for the first time, and in 1973 linguistic parity was assured in central government. Provisional legislation, passed in 1974, established separate Regional Councils and Ministerial Committees. One of the main disputes concerns the status of Brussels, as 85% of its inhabitants are francophone but the Flemish parties refuse to grant it equal status with the other two regional bodies.

In June 1977 Leo Tindemans formed a coalition between the Christian Social parties, the Socialists and two 'linguistic' parties, the Front Démocratique des Francophones (FDF) and the Volksunie. The Cabinet, in what became known as the Egmont Pact, proposed the abolition of the virtually defunct nine-province administration, and devolution of power from the central government to create a federal Belgium, comprising three political and economic regions (Flanders, Wallonia and Brussels), and two linguistic communities. These proposals, however, were not implemented. Tindemans resigned in October 1978 and the Minister of Defence, Paul Vanden Boeynants, took over as Prime Minister in a transitional government. Elections were held in December but the results showed little change in the distribution of seats in the Chamber of Representatives. Four successive Prime Ministers-designate failed to form a new government, the main obstacle again being the future status of Brussels. The six-month crisis was finally resolved when a new coalition government was formed in April 1979 under Dr Wilfried Martens, president of the Flemish Christian Social Party (CVP).

In 1980 the linguistic conflict worsened, sometimes involving violent incidents. The Government, which was also under pressure over the proposed installation of NATO nuclear missiles in Belgium and over its plans to reduce public spending at a time of high unemployment, decided that Flanders and Wallonia would be administered by regional assemblies, with control of cultural matters, public health, roads, urban projects and 10% of the national budget, while Brussels was to retain its three-member executive.

Internal disagreement over Martens' proposals for economic recovery resulted in the formation of four coalition governments between April 1979 and October 1980. The announcement of austerity measures including a 'freeze' on wages, resulted in demonstrations and lost him the support of the Socialist parties. In April 1981 a new government was formed, led by Mark Eyskens (CVP), hitherto Minister of Finance. It was a coalition of the Christian Social parties and the Socialist parties: the Cabinet remained virtually unchanged, and expressed its intention to promote investment and industrial development while cutting public spending. Lack of parliamentary support for his policies led to Eyskens' resignation in September. In December Martens formed a new centre-right government, comprising the two Christian Social parties and the two Liberal parties. In 1982 Parliament granted special powers for the implementation of austerity measures (see Economic Affairs); these were still effective in late 1986. Opposition to reductions in public spending has been vigorous, with public-sector unions undertaking damaging strike action in November 1982, September 1983 and May 1986, when two one-day general strikes took place.

The issue of the installation of 48 US 'cruise' nuclear missiles on Belgian territory led to a two-day debate in the Chamber of Representatives in November 1983 and a deferral of the final decision until 1985. A series of bombings, directed against NATO-connected targets, was carried out by left-wing terrorists during 1984, and included six explosions along an oil pipeline in December. In March 1985 the Chamber finally carried a majority vote in favour of the cruise sitings, and 16 missiles were installed at Florennes.

Following a riot in May 1985 at a football match between English and Italian clubs (in the final of the European Cup competition) at the Heysel Stadium in Brussels, which resulted in 39 deaths, calls were made for the resignation of the Interior Minister, Charles-Ferdinand Nothomb, over accusations of inefficient policing. The Deputy Prime Minister, Jean Gol, resigned over the issue in July, taking five other Liberal Cabinet members with him, and causing the collapse of the coalition. Martens offered the resignation of his Government, but this was 'suspended' by King Baudouin, and a general election was called for 13 October 1985, with the Government handling only a minimal programme until that time. A further row over education, which developed into a dispute between the two linguistic groups, led to the final dissolution of Parliament in September 1985. The general election returned the Christian Social-Liberal alliance to power, and Martens formed his sixth Cabinet in November 1985.

The incidence of terrorist attacks gathered momentum in the weeks following the election. The new Cabinet held an extraordinary session following the violent deaths of 16 people in two armed attacks on supermarkets in the Brabant region and the bombing of four banks within a week. Responsibility for the bank attacks was claimed by an extreme left-wing organization, the Cellules combattantes communistes (CCC), who were suspected of having close links with the French terrorist group Action Directe. Further attacks, mainly centred on NATO targets, were carried out before a number of arrests were made. In January 1986 the Government announced new, more stringent security legislation, which placed tighter restrictions on the sale of weapons and ammunition.

In 1983 the election of a francophone mayor in the Flemish commune of Fourons (which had been transferred from the French-speaking Liège province to Dutch-speaking Limburg in 1963) had caused a linguistic conflict which had split the

BELGIUM

Cabinet. A compromise solution failed to prevent the problem from flaring up again in October 1986, when the mayor in question, José Happart, was dismissed from his post for refusing to take a fluency test in Dutch. The incident sparked off another bitter conflict between the two linguistic groups in the coalition, leading Nothomb, the Interior Minister, to resign from the Government, and causing Martens to tender his resignation as Prime Minister. This, however, was refused by King Baudouin, and in the Chamber of Representatives a vote of confidence in the Government was avoided by 106 votes to 74.

Government

Belgium is a constitutional and hereditary monarchy, comprising nine provinces. Legislative power is vested in the King and the bicameral Parliament (the Senate and the Chamber of Representatives). The Senate has 182 members, including 106 directly elected by universal adult suffrage, 50 elected by provincial councils, 25 co-opted by the elected members and one Senator by right, the heir to the throne. The Chamber has 212 members, all directly elected by popular vote, on the basis of proportional representation. Members of both Houses serve for up to four years. Executive power, nominally vested in the King, is exercised by the Cabinet. The King appoints the Prime Minister and, on the latter's advice, other Ministers. The Cabinet is responsible to Parliament. There are political organs representing each of the linguistic regions and the capital (see Recent History).

Defence

Belgium is a member of NATO. In July 1986 the total strength of the armed forces was 91,428 (of whom 30,300 were conscripts), comprising army 67,400, navy 4,500 and air force 19,528. The defence budget for 1986 was an estimated 109,298m. Belgian francs. Military service lasts eight months for postings to Germany and 10 months for conscripts serving in Belgium.

Economic Affairs

Belgium is among the most densely populated countries in Europe, and its economy is based on diversified industrial and commercial activity. In 1984, according to estimates by the World Bank, Belgium's gross national product (GNP) per head, measured at average 1982–84 prices, was US $8,610, having increased since 1965 at an average of 3.0% per year in real terms. Industrial activity has concentrated in recent years in the increasingly populous Flemish areas of the north, but the Government is encouraging re-investment in the southern, Walloon, region. Apart from coal and, to a lesser extent, clay, sand and stone, the country has no natural resources, and it purchases essential raw materials abroad: the vital export trade is therefore dependent largely on the state of the world market. Agriculture (with forestry and fishing) employed 2.9% of the total working population in 1984, and contributed 3% of gross domestic product (GDP).

In 1984 more than 75% of Belgium's GDP was exported, making it one of the world's principal per caput exporters. About 68% of Belgium's external trade was with other members of the EEC in 1984, when the country's three main trading partners (the Federal Republic of Germany, France and the Netherlands) together accounted for 53.1% of total trade (53.6% of imports; 52.5% of exports). The overall trade deficit eased to 0.2% of GDP in 1984, compared with 3.1% in 1980, and there was expected to be a trade surplus, equal to 1.1% of GDP, in 1985. Belgium and Luxembourg constitute the Belgo-Luxembourg Economic Union (BLEU) and form a single customs region. Belgium transferred from the European currency 'snake' to the new European Monetary System (EMS) in 1979. In February 1982 the Belgian franc was devalued by 8.5% against the other currencies participating in the EMS: in March 1983 it was revalued by 1.5% in an EMS realignment.

Unemployment, which affected an average of 6.4% of the total labour force between 1972 and 1981, rose to 14.4% in 1984: it decreased to 13.5% in 1985, and was expected to fall further during 1986. There are distinct regional differences in rates of unemployment, due to the concentration of traditional industries, such as steel and textiles, in Wallonia, where in 1984 there was a 5.4% growth in the number of those out of work, compared with 1983. Meanwhile, Flanders experienced no increase, and Brussels registered a 2.7% drop, in numbers of unemployed. Government schemes to alleviate the problem include job creation and a shorter working week, with legal restraints on pay settlements being adopted in January 1983 and reinforced in 1986.

Industrial output declined by 5% in 1980, as recession affected Belgium's heavy industries, and there were several factory closures in the steel, motor vehicle and textile sectors. The two largest steel concerns merged in 1981, but the sector continued to incur severe financial losses. In 1983 the industry was granted a loan of BF 14,000m. by the EEC, and the Belgian Government approved a scheme to finance restructuring of the steel industry at a cost of BF 24,750m. However, output was to be reduced by 27%, and 35% of jobs in the state-owned Cockerill Sambre group were to be lost. In January 1984 the Belgian and Luxembourg Governments reached a 10-year agreement on the joint restructuring of their steel industries. Cockerill Sambre and Arbed (its Luxembourg equivalent) agreed to divide steel production between them so as to avoid competing with each other's products. Following approval by the Commission of the European Communities for the Government's plans to aid the steel sector in March 1984, Cockerill Sambre received BF 51,200m., but steel production was cut from 7.1m. metric tons to 4m. tons annually. In May 1985 trade unions finally agreed a programme of early retirement and a 36-hour week, as part of the restructuring, with BF 27,000m. in state support promised. Cockerill Sambre recorded a net loss of BF 6,000m. in 1985. The coal-mining industry has also experienced serious financial difficulties. In 1985 the four mines of Kempense Steenkolenmijnen (KS) received subsidies of BF 8,000m. In 1986 KS was expected to make a loss of BF 13,000m. Overall industrial output began to recover in 1984, particularly in the Flanders region, and continued to improve in 1985.

In 1978 Belgium began a programme of borrowing to finance the public sector deficit, which had been aggravated by large payments of unemployment benefits, job creation projects, rising petroleum prices and public investment. By March 1985 the public debt had reached BF 4,639,800m. Interest payments expanded from 7.7% of GDP in 1981 to about 10% in 1984, when the total government deficit was 13.1% of GDP. Debt servicing therefore represented a heavy burden, accounting for about 20% of current expenditure in the 1985 budget, and for 22% of current expenditure planned for 1986.

Under emergency powers, the first of which were granted in February 1982 and the most recent in late 1985, the Martens Government has imposed a series of austerity measures, including tax increases, wage restraints, and cuts in expenditure on health services, social security, defence and public works. These measures have been strongly opposed by the trade unions, but they had a mitigative effect on the budget deficit, which fell from 14.9% of GDP in 1983 to 13.1% in 1984, and was estimated at 12.0% in 1985. Public expenditure, which, owing to the cuts, rose by only 4.7% during 1983, had thus decreased in real terms for the first time in 10 years. A further programme of reductions, agreed in August 1986 (despite some intense trade union protest), aimed at reducing the overall public deficit to just 8% of GNP by the end of 1987 (from 11.6% in December 1985). A total of BF 195,000m. was cut from the public spending programme, mainly in the public health, educational and social security sectors. Some 'privatization' measures were also anticipated. Owing to export growth and a fall in the volume of imports, the balance of payments improved in 1983, and the current deficit fell to 1.5% of GDP from 3.6% in 1982. In 1985 a surplus of BF 35,000m. was recorded on the current account of the balance of payments, the first surplus since 1976.

In 1983 many local authorities were facing bankruptcy: by July only 62 of the 589 communes were still solvent. Attempts by the local authorities to cut their budget deficits resulted in many job losses. In July 1984 the Government announced measures to assist local authorities in financial difficulties by creating a special fund, using revenues from death duties. The rate of inflation fell from an average of 7.7% in 1983 to 6.3% in 1984, and to 4.9% in 1985. Inflation was only 0.7% in the year to July 1986.

Social Welfare

Social welfare is mainly administered by the National Office for Social Security. Contributions are paid by employers and employees towards family allowances, health insurance, unemployment benefit and pensions. Most allowances and pensions are tied to the consumer price index. Workers and employees are entitled to four weeks' holiday for every 12-month period of work. They are insured against accidents occurring on the work premises or on the way to and from work. Medical care is free to widows, pensioners, orphans and the disabled. Ordinary and supplementary family allowances are the entitlement of all families. Social welfare is also administered at a local level by Public Assistance Commissions which have been set up in every municipality. In 1981 Belgium had 521 hospital establishments, with a total of 92,436 beds (one for every 107 inhabitants), and there were 25,629 physicians working in the country. Of total expenditure by the central government in 1982, about 36,100m. francs (1.7%) was for health, and 895,900m. francs (41.0%) was for social security and welfare.

Education

Education in Belgium is compulsory from six years of age: the minimum school-leaving age was raised to 18 years in 1983. Two separate education systems exist: the Ecole officielle is a state secular school and the Ecole libre is a private denominational (usually Roman Catholic) school receiving state subsidies. Under the 1963 Language of Instruction Act, teaching is given in the language of the region: in the Brussels district teaching is in the mother language of the pupil. In June 1986 it was announced that the study of Dutch as a second language in Wallonian schools was to be introduced, and was eventually to become compulsory.

There are state-financed nursery schools for children under five years old, attended by about 90% of infants. Elementary education is for children aged six to 12 years and consists of three courses of two years each. Secondary education lasts for six years and is also divided into three two-year cycles. The Diploma of Secondary Education may be gained after an additional two years of higher teacher training.

The requirement for university entrance is a pass in the 'examination of maturity', taken after the completion of secondary studies. Courses are divided into 2–3 years of general preparation followed by 2–3 years of specialization. There are five universities, two of which are divided into French and Dutch-speaking sections, and several university centres or faculties. There are also non-university institutions of higher education for those who have successfully completed their secondary studies. These provide arts education, technical training or higher teacher training (i.e. for secondary school).

The National Study Fund provides grants where necessary and nearly 20% of students receive scholarships. Educational expenditure in 1986 was expected to amount to almost 15% of the total budget.

Tourism

Belgium has several towns of rich historic and cultural interest, such as Bruges, Ghent and Antwerp. Ostend and other seaside towns attract many visitors. The forest-covered Ardennes region is excellent hill-walking country. There were an estimated 6,785,000 tourist arrivals in 1982, when tourist receipts totalled US $1,578m.

Public Holidays

1987: 1 January (New Year's Day), 20 April (Easter Monday), 1 May (Labour Day), 28 May (Ascension Day), 8 June (Whit Monday), 21 July (Independence Day), 15 August (Assumption), 1 November (All Saints' Day), 11 November (Armistice Day), 25 December (Christmas Day).

1988: 1 January (New Year's Day), 4 April (Easter Monday), 1 May (Labour Day), 12 May (Ascension Day), 23 May (Whit Monday), 21 July (Independence Day), 15 August (Assumption), 1 November (All Saints' Day), 11 November (Armistice Day), 25 December (Christmas Day).

Weights and Measures

The metric system is in force.

Currency and Exchange Rates

100 centimes (centiemen) = 1 Belgian franc or frank (BF).

Exchange rates (30 September 1986):
 £1 sterling = 60.85 francs;
 US $1 = 42.05 francs.

Statistical Survey

Source: mainly Institut National de Statistique, 44 rue de Louvain, Brussels 1000; tel. (02) 513-96-50.

Area and Population

AREA, POPULATION AND DENSITY

Area (sq km)	30,519*
Population (census results)†	
31 December 1970	9,650,944
1 March 1981	
Males	4,810,349
Females	5,038,298
Total	9,848,647
Population (official estimates at 31 December)†	
1983	9,853,023
1984	9,857,721
1985	9,858,895
Density (per sq km) at 31 December 1985	323.0

* 11,783 sq miles. † Population is *de jure*.

PROVINCES (population at 31 December 1985)

	Population	Capital (with population)
Antwerp	1,582,786	Antwerp (483,199*)
Brabant	2,218,349	Brussels (976,536*)
Flanders (East)	1,328,805	Ghent (234,251)
Flanders (West)	1,090,387	Bruges (117,799)
Hainaut	1,277,939	Mons (90,072)
Liège	991,535	Liège (201,749)
Limburg	731,875	Hasselt (65,348)
Luxembourg	224,988	Arlon (22,118)
Namur	412,231	Namur (102,501)

* Including suburbs.

PRINCIPAL TOWNS (population at 31 December 1985)

Bruxelles (Brussel, Brussels)	976,536*
Antwerpen (Anvers, Antwerp)	483,199†
Gent (Gand, Ghent)	234,251
Charleroi	210,324
Liège (Luik)	201,749
Brugge (Bruges)	117,799
Namur (Namen)	102,501
Mons (Bergen)	90,072
Kortrijk (Courtrai)	76,230
Mechelen (Malines)	75,932
Oostende (Ostend)	68,681
Hasselt	65,348

* Including Schaerbeek, Anderlecht and other suburbs.
† Including Deurne and other suburbs.

BIRTHS, MARRIAGES AND DEATHS

	Registered live births		Registered marriages*		Registered deaths†	
	Number	Rate (per 1,000)	Number	Rate (per 1,000)	Number	Rate (per 1,000)
1978	121,983	12.4	67,127	6.8	115,060	11.7
1979	123,658	12.6	65,413	6.6	111,364	11.4
1980	124,794	12.7	66,413	6.7	114,364	11.6
1981	124,827	12.7	65,011	6.6	113,308	11.5
1982	120,382	12.2	62,423	6.3	112,506	11.4
1983	117,395	11.9	59,652	6.1	114,814	11.6
1984	115,790	11.8	58,989	6.0	110,577	11.2
1985	114,283	11.6	57,630	6.0	112,691	11.4

* Including marriages among Belgian armed forces stationed outside the country and alien armed forces in Belgium, unless performed by local foreign authority.
† Including Belgian armed forces stationed outside the country but excluding alien armed forces stationed in Belgium.

ECONOMICALLY ACTIVE POPULATION
(ISIC Major Divisions, '000 persons at 30 June each year)

	1982	1983	1984
Agriculture, forestry and fishing	106.8	106.1	106.1
Mining and quarrying	27.4	26.7	25.5
Manufacturing	848.8	830.0	821.6
Electricity, gas and water	32.9	32.6	32.8
Construction	235.6	216.8	203.2
Trade, restaurants and hotels	691.4	688.1	696.7
Transport, storage and communications	274.7	267.3	263.4
Finance, insurance, real estate and business services	252.5	264.0	271.1
Community, social and personal services*	1,202.3	1,202.1	1,214.4
Total in home employment	3,672.3	3,633.6	3,634.7
Persons working abroad	34.9	34.6	33.9
Total in employment	3,707.3	3,668.2	3,668.6
Unemployed	490.0	545.1	545.7
Total labour force	4,197.3	4,213.4	4,214.3
Males	2,588.3	2,579.2	2,561.2
Females	1,609.0	1,634.1	1,653.2

* Including members of the armed forces ('000): 92.6 in 1982; 90.8 in 1983; 89.4 in 1984.

BELGIUM   *Statistical Survey*

Agriculture

PRINCIPAL CROPS ('000 metric tons)

	1983	1984	1985
Wheat	1,003.4	1,248.6	1,149.6
Spelt	39.9	44.9	37.6
Barley	670.2	873.5	685.4
Maize	39.4	52.7	50.4
Rye	24.5	32.2	22.5
Oats	79.7	91.8	93.6
Potatoes	977.5	1,332.2	1,521.7
Linseed	6.0	8.0	7.9
Flax fibre	9	14	14
Sugar beet	5,120.1	5,763.8	5,952.2

LIVESTOCK ('000 head at 1 December)

	1983	1984	1985
Horses	28.8	27.5	26.0
Cattle	2,957.8	2,988.7	2,943.5
Pigs	5,182.4	5,268.7	5,412.1
Sheep	96.9	109.1	123.5
Goats	6.1	7.1	7.0

Poultry ('000 head at 1 December): Chickens 30,917 in 1985; Ducks 53 in 1985; Turkeys 199 in 1985.

LIVESTOCK PRODUCTS ('000 metric tons)

	1983	1984	1985
Beef and veal	282	310	317
Pig meat	698	726	717
Milk	3,872	3,819	3,781
Butter	105	102	99
Cheese	43	44	51
Hen eggs	189	184	174

Fishing*

('000 metric tons)

	1983	1984	1985
Marine fishes	33.2	31.8	31.1
Crustaceans and molluscs	2.9	2.7	2.6
Total catch	36.1	34.5	33.7

* Figures refer to marketable quantities landed, which may be less than the live weight of the catch. The total catch (in '000 metric tons) was: 48.6 in 1983; 47.9 in 1984.

Mining

	1983	1984	1985
Hard coal ('000 metric tons)	6,097	6,298	6,212
Natural gas* (million cu metres)	23	47	52

* From coal mines.

Industry

SELECTED PRODUCTS

		1983	1984	1985
Wheat flour[1]	'000 metric tons	796.8	907.5	937.7
Raw sugar	'000 metric tons	847	910	961
Margarine	'000 metric tons	158.6	168.8	171.8
Beer	'000 hectolitres	14,224.5	14,311.3	13,930.9
Cigarettes	million	29,738	29,422.2	30,355.7
Cotton yarn (pure and mixed)	metric tons	45,708	46,657	47,796
Woven cotton fabrics (pure and mixed)[2]	metric tons	51,417	51,432	53,250
Flax yarn[3]	metric tons	9,305	10,626	9,009
Jute yarn	metric tons	15,206	14,124	13,615
Other vegetable textile yarns	metric tons	15,967	17,601	18,338
Wool yarn (pure and mixed)	metric tons	86,723	92,396	90,632
Woven woollen fabrics (pure and mixed)[2]	metric tons	35,954	38,108	35,734
Rayon continuous filaments	metric tons	4,070	4,508	5,180
Woven rayon and acetate fabrics (pure and mixed)[4]	metric tons	32,746	28,134	28,617
Mechanical wood pulp	'000 metric tons	113	116	111
Chemical and semi-chemical wood pulp	'000 metric tons	260	264	256
Newsprint	'000 metric tons	111.7	101.8	100.0
Other paper and paperboard	'000 metric tons	772.7	831.8	827.2
Benzene (Benzol)	'000 metric tons	40.8	33.9	n.a.
Ethyl alcohol (Ethanol)	'000 hectolitres	157.6	162.6	175.8
Sulphuric acid (100%)	'000 metric tons	1,897.8	2,246.6	2,106.9
Nitric acid (100%)	'000 metric tons	1,445.4	1,496.4	1,532.9
Nitrogenous fertilizers[5]	'000 metric tons	755	706	715
Phosphate fertilizers[6]	'000 metric tons	460	515	490
Liquefied petroleum gas	'000 metric tons	366	310	345
Naphtha	'000 metric tons	1,733	1,290	1,304
Motor spirit (petrol)	'000 metric tons	3,942.9	3,709	3,853
Aviation gasoline	'000 metric tons	218.3	266.7	207.9
Kerosene	'000 metric tons	38	9	22
White spirit	'000 metric tons	234.1	270.1	257.5
Jet fuel	'000 metric tons	1,369	1,192.2	1,196.1
Distillate fuel oils	'000 metric tons	7,543.1	8,028	7,336.0
Residual fuel oil	'000 metric tons	4,596.9	5,286.4	3,638.2
Lubricating oils	'000 metric tons	36	37	28
Petroleum bitumen (asphalt)	'000 metric tons	704.1	526.8	516.1
Coke-oven coke	'000 metric tons	5,106	5,926	5,964
Cement	'000 metric tons	5,719	5,708	5,537
Pig-iron	'000 metric tons	8,033.2	8,968.5	8,719.0
Crude steel	'000 metric tons	10,157.0	11,303.4	10,687.3
Refined copper (unwrought)[7]	metric tons	431,264	427,707	455,459
Refined lead (unwrought)[8]	metric tons	134,152	127,711	114,293
Tin: primary	metric tons	2,214	2,408	2,298
Zinc (unwrought)[9]	metric tons	275,845	285,719	289,562
Radio receivers[10]	'000	1,006	976	1,097
Television receivers[10]	'000	766	799	833
Merchant vessels launched[11]	'000 gross reg. tons	114	178	74
Passenger motor cars[12]	'000	974.8	889.5	997.3
Commercial motor vehicles[12]	'000	33.3	38.9	37.5
Construction: new dwellings started	number	28,513	24,818	n.a.
Electric energy	million kWh.	52,689	54,656	57,321.4
Manufactured gas	million cu metres	2,223	2,577	2,526

[1] Industrial production only. [2] Including blankets.
[3] Including yarn made from tow.
[4] Including fabrics of natural silk and blankets and carpets of cellulosic fibres.
[5] Estimated production in Belgium and Luxembourg during 12 months ending 30 June of the year stated. Figures are in terms of nitrogen. Source: FAO, *Monthly Bulletin of Statistics*.
[6] Estimated production in Belgium and Luxembourg during 12 months ending 30 April of the year stated. Figures are in terms of phosphoric acid. Source: FAO, *Monthly Bulletin of Statistics*.
[7] Including alloys and the processing of refined copper imported from Zaire.
[8] Primary and secondary production, including alloys and remelted lead.
[9] Including alloys and remelted zinc.
[10] Factory shipments.
[11] Source: *Lloyd's Register of Shipping*.
[12] Assembled wholly or mainly from imported parts.

BELGIUM · Statistical Survey

Finance

CURRENCY AND EXCHANGE RATES

Monetary Units
100 centimes (centiemen) = 1 franc belge (frank) or Belgian franc (BF).

Denominations
Coins: 50 centimes; 1, 5, 10, 20 and 250 francs.
Notes: 50, 100, 500, 1,000 and 5,000 francs.

Sterling and Dollar Equivalents (30 September 1986)
£1 sterling = 60.85 francs;
US $1 = 42.05 francs;
1,000 Belgian francs = £16.43 = $23.78.

Average Exchange Rate (francs per US $)
1983 51.132
1984 57.784
1985 59.378

Note: The information on the exchange rate refers to the official market rate, used for most current transactions. There is also a free exchange market rate, applicable to most capital transactions. The average of this latter rate (francs per US dollar) was: 52.02 in 1983; 58.65 in 1984; 59.74 in 1985.

BUDGET (million Belgian francs)

Revenue	1985*	1986†
Direct taxation	846,604	890,700
Customs and excise	100,895	102,197
VAT, stamp, registration and similar duties	366,011	373,530
Other current taxes	68,544	62,180
Capital revenues	4,148	4,493
Total	1,386,202	1,433,100

Expenditure	1985*	1986†
Government departments	821,876	822,416
Public debt	375,709	428,642
Pensions	169,776	180,895
Education and cultural services	290,070	288,584
Defence	107,521	109,298
Other expenditure	136,033	143,099
Total	1,900,985	1,972,934

* Provisional.   † Official estimates.

NATIONAL BANK RESERVES*
(US $ million at 31 December)

	1983	1984	1985
Gold	1,443	1,443	1,443
IMF special drawing rights	418	445	361
Reserve position in IMF	520	511	519
Foreign exchange	3,776	3,608	3,969
Total	6,157	6,007	6.292

* Figures for gold and foreign exchange refer to the monetary association between Belgium and Luxembourg. Gold is valued at $42.22 per troy ounce. Figures exclude deposits made with the European Monetary Co-operation Fund.

Source: IMF, *International Financial Statistics*.

MONEY SUPPLY ('000 million Belgian francs at 31 December)

	1983	1984	1985
Currency outside banks	383.3	381.9	379.9
Demand deposits at commercial banks	393.7	393.3	427.7
Monetary liabilities of other monetary institutions	157.4	163.0	160.7

COST OF LIVING (Consumer Price Index. Base: 1970 = 100)

	1983	1984	1985
Food	225.2	244.3	252.7
Fuel and light	410.5	443.6	466.2
Clothing	212.4	224.4	241.9
All items (incl. others)	256.3	272.6	285.9

NATIONAL ACCOUNTS ('000 million Belgian francs at current prices)
National Income and Product

	1983	1984	1985
Compensation of employees	2,379.1	2,509.0	2,637.9
Operating surplus	978.2	1,119.4	1,247.3
Domestic factor incomes	3,357.3	3,628.4	3,885.2
Consumption of fixed capital	401.6	420.7	440.5
Gross domestic product at factor cost	3,758.9	4,049.1	4,325.7
Indirect taxes	509.8	529.5	557.4
Less Subsidies	59.3	67.7	71.0
GDP in purchasers' values	4,209.4	4,510.9	4,812.1
Factor income from abroad	326.5	387.1	465.6
Less Factor income paid abroad	363.2	414.9	500.9
Gross national product	4,172.7	4,483.1	4,776.8
Less Consumption of fixed capital	401.6	420.7	440.5
National income in market prices	3,771.1	4,062.4	4,336.3
Other current transfers from abroad	34.7	39.2	42.1
Less Other current transfers paid abroad	78.6	77.8	71.0
National disposable income	3,727.2	4,023.9	4,307.4

BELGIUM — Statistical Survey

Expenditure on the Gross Domestic Product

	1983	1984	1985
Government final consumption expenditure	761.3	800.5	850.3
Private final consumption expenditure*	2,749.5	2,958.7	3,149.1
Increase in stocks†	−27.5	−4.3	−15.9
Gross fixed capital formation	670.0	709.6	744.5
Total domestic expenditure	4,153.3	4,464.5	4,728.0
Exports of goods and services	3,003.5	3,384.8	3,556.9
Less Imports of goods and services	2,947.4	3,338.4	3,472.8
GDP in purchasers' values	4,209.4	4,510.9	4,812.1
GDP at 1980 prices	3,521.5	3,577.7	3,630.4

* Including statistical discrepancy ('000 million francs): −26.7 in 1983; −22.2 in 1984; −35.3 in 1985.
† Including adjustment in connection with gross fixed capital ('000 million francs): −6.2 in 1983; −5.3 in 1984; −8.2 in 1985.

Gross Domestic Product by Economic Activity

	1983	1984	1985
Agriculture and livestock	103.5	105.3	106.8
Forestry and logging	5.4	6.2	6.8
Fishing	1.7	1.7	1.9
Mining and quarrying	24.8	26.6	25.9
Manufacturing[1]	999.1	1,068.7	1,103.1
Electricity, gas and water	147.8	163.0	188.7
Construction	234.6	236.1	248.1
Wholesale and retail trade[2]	653.3	670.1	751.4
Distribution of petroleum products[2]	202.5	218.0	218.0
Transport, storage and communications	318.7	359.5	384.3
Finance and insurance	213.5	249.5	278.9
Real estate[3]	234.2	257.9	277.9
Business services	117.4	126.6	133.8
Public administration and defence	351.6	372.8	396.8
Education	260.3	272.3	286.2
Health services	111.5	120.3	128.5
Other community, social and personal services[4]	313.8	334.9	355.1
Domestic service of households	45.5	47.3	49.2
Sub-total	4,339.2	4,636.8	4,941.4
Imputed bank service charge	−62.7	−72.1	−78.1
Value-added tax deductible from capital formation	−69.4	−77.6	−85.9
Statistical discrepancy[5]	2.3	23.8	34.7
Total	4,209.4	4,510.9	4,812.1

[1] Including garages. [2] Including import duties. [3] Including imputed rent of owner-occupied dwellings. [4] Including restaurants and hotels.
[5] Including a correction to compensate for the exclusion of certain own-account capital investments ('000 million francs): 5.5 in 1983; 6.1 in 1984; 6.6 in 1985.

BALANCE OF PAYMENTS (US $ million)*

	1983	1984	1985
Merchandise exports f.o.b.	45,662	46,213	47,150
Merchandise imports f.o.b.	−47,478	−47,431	−47,415
Trade balance	−1,816	−1,218	−265
Exports of services	31,039	31,153	33,169
Imports of services	−28,619	−29,159	−31,664
Balance on goods and services	604	776	1,240
Private unrequited transfers (net)	−181	−176	−129
Government unrequited transfers (net)	−918	−656	−474
Current balance	−495	−55	637
Direct capital investment (net)	935	96	755
Other long-term capital (net)	−3,388	−2,416	−5,688
Short-term capital (net)	2,521	2,902	4,664
Net errors and omissions	17	−234	−17
Total (net monetary movements)	−411	295	350
Valuation changes (net)	424	−500	505
Official financing (net)	631	−306	−426
Changes in reserves	644	−511	429

* Including Luxembourg.
Source: IMF, *International Financial Statistics*.

External Trade of Belgium and Luxembourg

Note: Figures exclude trade in monetary gold, non-commercial military goods and silver specie. Exports include stores and bunkers for foreign ships and aircraft.

PRINCIPAL COMMODITIES (distribution by SITC, million Belgian francs)

Imports c.i.f.	1983	1984	1985*
Food and live animals	259,451	301,750	293,613
Dairy products and birds' eggs	38,378	40,605	40,829
Cereals and cereal preparations	57,909	72,343	60,036
Vegetables and fruit	44,641	50,267	53,488
Coffee, tea, cocoa and spices	27,564	35,348	41,451
Animal feeding-stuff (excl. cereals)	31,929	34,731	31,515
Beverages and tobacco	33,001	36,165	37,823
Crude materials (inedible) except fuels[1]	204,178	236,095	246,176
Oil seeds and oleaginous fruit	25,258	31,348	32,482
Textile fibres and waste[2]	26,103	34,201	34,001
Metalliferous ores and metal scrap[1]	77,315	82,451	89,632
Non-ferrous base metal waste and scrap	36,094	29,222	32,119
Mineral fuels, lubricants, etc. (incl. electric current)	535,706	594,990	550,422
Coal, coke and briquettes	39,223	49,163	51,352
Coal, lignite and peat	29,345	36,173	37,851
Coal (not agglomerated)	28,868	n.a.	n.a.
Petroleum, petroleum products, etc.	414,677	449,007	395,838
Crude petroleum oils, etc.	226,729	216,239	187,327
Refined petroleum products	182,707	225,953	200,323
Motor spirit (petrol) and other light oils	39,509	n.a.	n.a.
Gas oils (distillate fuels)	61,066	65,213	64,977
Residual fuel oils	68,586	101,310	75,735
Gas (natural and manufactured)	75,887	89,911	95,087
Petroleum gases, etc., in the gaseous state	68,864	80,611	85,165
Animal and vegetable oils, fats and waxes	13,864	21,343	20,850
Chemicals and related products[2]	264,113	316,233	338,618
Organic chemicals[2]	94,406	114,752	116,224
Hydrocarbons and their derivatives[2]	52,345	62,243	56,059
Artificial resins, plastic materials, etc.[2]	56,511	70,233	78,772
Products of polymerization, etc.[2]	37,037	46,153	51,410
Basic manufactures[1,2]	565,921	662,434	675,592
Paper, paperboard and manufactures[2]	50,234	62,294	66,102
Paper and paperboard (not cut to size or shape)[2]	34,332	43,549	45,986
Textile yarn, fabrics, etc.	89,247	99,939	102,686
Textile yarn	39,858	44,949	45,866
Non-metallic mineral manufactures	175,422	212,091	205,119
Pearls, precious and semi-precious stones	144,112	177,492	167,585
Non-industrial diamonds (unset)	142,587	175,454	166,431
Sorted diamonds (rough or simply worked)	84,728	107,795	106,112
Cut diamonds (unmounted)	57,859	67,647	60,304
Iron and steel	74,817	88,535	94,336
Non-ferrous metals[1,2]	89,363	103,940	103,073
Copper and copper alloys[1]	38,558	42,311	46,528
Unwrought copper and alloys[1]	33,400	35,986	40,368
Aluminium and aluminium alloys	29,405	37,883	34,917
Other metal manufactures	53,122	58,497	65,946
Machinery and transport equipment	619,348	685,516	766,113
Power generating machinery and equipment	44,286	56,600	67,134
Internal combustion piston engines (incl. parts)	32,134	42,863	50,960
Machinery specialized for particular industries	44,838	53,975	56,223
General industrial machinery, equipment and parts	65,043	75,144	81,424
Office machines and automatic data processing equipment	40,994	55,899	64,531
Automatic data processing machines, etc.	24,259	33,854	38,233
Electrical machinery, apparatus, etc.	95,466	105,706	121,199
Road vehicles and parts[3]	290,652	295,655	334,637
Passenger motor cars (excl. buses)	88,917	99,002	104,697
Parts and accessories for cars, buses, lorries, etc.	174,986	166,835	199,121
Miscellaneous manufactured articles	223,627	246,313	266,554
Clothing and accessories (excl. footwear)[2]	69,363	74,167	78,926
Other commodities and transactions	101,656	94,930	119,708
Non-monetary gold (excl. gold ores and concentrates)	35,627	30,799	35,030
Unwrought or semi-manufactured gold (excl. rolled gold)	35,484	30,642	34,853
Confidential transactions	38,856	46,456	70,717
Total	2,820,865	3,195,769	3,315,468

* Provisional.

[1] Copper matte, usually classified with metal ores and concentrates (under 'crude materials'), is included in non-ferrous metals (under 'basic manufactures').

[2] Figures exclude the value of certain confidential transactions, included in the last item of the table.

[3] Excluding tyres, engines and electrical parts.

BELGIUM   Statistical Survey

Exports f.o.b.	1983	1984	1985*
Food and live animals[1]	233,125	277,683	272,854
Meat and meat preparations	43,043	49,406	49,593
Fresh, chilled or frozen meat	30,827	35,858	36,270
Dairy products and birds' eggs	36,582	42,616	41,563
Cereals and cereal preparations	43,713	57,258	45,642
Vegetables and fruit	29,538	34,567	38,789
Beverages and tobacco	20,483	21,874	24,472
Crude materials (inedible) except fuels[1,2]	68,250	87,358	87,341
Mineral fuels, lubricants, etc. (incl. electric current)	222,605	237,210	208,600
Petroleum, petroleum products, etc.	208,403	220,305	188,954
Refined petroleum products	198,812	209,990	178,300
Motor spirit (petrol) and other light oils	58,463	54,736	54,701
Motor spirit (incl. aviation spirit)	39,984	37,101	36,387
Gas oils (distillate fuels)	53,001	53,671	40,058
Residual fuel oils	53,880	70,448	51,434
Animal and vegetable oils, fats and waxes[1]	13,429	22,542	24,980
Chemicals and related products[1]	316,733	376,342	406,136
Organic chemicals[1]	59,257	75,652	77,428
Medicinal and pharmaceutical products[1]	32,620	36,848	39,092
Artificial resins, plastic materials, etc.	112,287	133,246	143,082
Products of polymerization, etc.[1]	81,885	97,623	101,525
Polyethylene[1]	35,301	n.a.	n.a.
Basic manufactures[1]	812,628	932,014	977,237
Paper, paperboard and manufactures	36,647	41,202	44,273
Textile yarn, fabrics, etc.[1]	145,477	167,830	178,395
Textile yarn	32,258	37,700	39,939
Floor coverings, etc.[1]	46,749	54,617	56,037
Carpets, carpeting, rugs, mats, etc.	46,455	54,249	55,115
Non-metallic mineral manufactures[1]	215,634	244,668	252,127
Pearls, precious and semi-precious stones	159,060	179,920	189,158
Non-industrial diamonds (unset)	157,940	178,292	188,027
Sorted diamonds (rough or simply worked)	73,638	83,834	91,941
Cut diamonds (unmounted)	84,295	94,415	96,082
Iron and steel[1]	211,109	253,128	265,402
Ingots and other primary forms	37,169	49,002	47,638
Coils for re-rolling	29,924	n.a.	n.a.
Bars, rods, angles, shapes, etc.	44,826	51,435	53,750
Universals, plates and sheets	85,037	102,496	111,493
Thin sheets and plates (rolled but not further worked)	36,819	42,999	47,831
Non-ferrous metals[1,2]	104,574	112,998	117,380
Copper and copper alloys[1,2]	42,755	45,138	49,100
Aluminium and aluminium alloys	25,776	33,541	33,206
Other metal manufactures	55,897	64,437	68,926
Machinery and transport equipment[1]	594,562	629,669	733,425
Power generating machinery and equipment[1]	28,583	29,611	48,317
Machinery specialized for particular industries[1]	52,971	64,623	74,218
General industrial machinery, equipment and parts[1]	42,932	49,576	54,950
Telecommunications and sound equipment	43,527	44,413	48,518
Other electrical machinery, apparatus, etc.	54,239	60,886	67,008
Road vehicles and parts[1,3]	322,945	326,873	377,292
Passenger motor cars (excl. buses)	251,753	242,773	286,216
Parts and accessories for cars, buses, lorries, etc.[3]	34,065	40,111	44,691
Miscellaneous manufactured articles[1]	191,408	216,264	229,155
Furniture and parts	28,920	31,811	33,189
Clothing and accessories (excl. footwear)	38,540	42,978	44,709
Photographic apparatus, etc., optical goods, watches and clocks[1]	41,508	46,647	47,886
Photographic and cinematographic supplies	38,494	42,944	44,582
Photographic film, plates and paper	34,963	39,355	40,826
Other commodities and transactions	178,117	191,160	198,924
Confidential transactions	154,049	168,397	175,326
Total	2,651,341	2,992,116	3,163,725

* Provisional.
[1] Figures exclude the value of certain confidential transactions, included in the last item of the table.
[2] Copper matte, usually classified with metal ores and concentrates (under 'crude materials'), is included in non-ferrous metals (under 'basic manufactures').
[3] Excluding tyres, engines and electrical parts.

BELGIUM

PRINCIPAL TRADING PARTNERS*
(million Belgian francs)

Imports c.i.f.	1983	1984	1985†
Austria	14,507	16,879	23,136
Brazil	16,997	24,197	29,590
Canada	15,727	18,619	18,748
France	396,328	467,319	498,580
Germany, Federal Republic	582,294	636,575	695,014
Iraq	21,996	22,926	10,973
Italy	103,567	114,355	118,018
Japan	59,415	67,167	70,209
Libya	27,252	17,924	3,548
Netherlands	511,840	600,550	614,133
Nigeria	30,337	37,362	39,107
Norway	21,036	13,153	26,772
Saudi Arabia	29,378	21,203	22,804
South Africa and Namibia	15,881	16,870	20,684
Spain (excl. Canary Is.)	31,042	36,611	37,654
Sweden	52,123	56,413	62,512
Switzerland	72,772	77,857	77,340
USSR	71,359	108,169	74,026
United Kingdom	243,584	279,911	295,564
USA	180,685	192,387	187,752
Zaire	20,131	29,462	32,604
All countries (incl. others)	2,818,800	3,180,114	3,302,041
Not distributed	2,065	15,655	13,427
Total	2,820,865	3,195,769	3,315,468

Exports f.o.b.	1983	1984	1985†
Algeria	14,515	18,535	19,988
Austria	21,076	25,125	26,483
Canada	11,352	17,000	21,801
Denmark	26,002	27,322	34,407
France	482,963	552,404	600,102
Germany, Federal Republic	560,475	589,672	587,912
India	29,396	38,026	41,815
Israel	22,403	28,778	34,753
Italy	123,775	153,807	172,208
Japan	18,888	24,811	25,574
Netherlands	377,544	416,594	450,557
Norway	16,681	20,434	23,433
Saudi Arabia	34,287	34,677	28,159
Spain (excl. Canary Is.)	26,797	24,977	31,181
Sweden	37,891	41,149	45,843
Switzerland	75,462	80,354	76,253
USSR	34,025	31,639	37,275
United Kingdom	261,183	296,367	309,596
USA	136,381	181,390	200,573
All countries (incl. others)	2,624,928	2,966,913	3,137,224
Not distributed	26,413	25,203	26,501
Total	2,651,341	2,992,116	3,163,725

* Imports by country of production; exports by country of last consignment.
† Provisional.

Transport

RAILWAYS (traffic)

	1983	1984	1985
Passenger-km (million)	6,631	6,444	6,572
Freight ton-km (million)	6,870	7,905	8,254

ROAD TRAFFIC (motor vehicles in use at 31 December)

	1983	1984	1985
Private cars	3,262,713	3,300,248	3,342,704
Buses and coaches	17,866	17,170	16,817
Goods vehicles	261,126	265,017	272,839
Tractors (non-agricultural)	28,284	28,498	29,243

CIVIL AVIATION ('000)

	1982	1983	1984
Kilometres flown	49,812	49,113	49,591
Passenger-km	5,277,438	5,276,396	5,478,037
Ton-km	479,063	476,677	493,063
Mail ton-km	13,128	13,821	16,455

Figures refer to Sabena—Belgian World Air Lines.

SHIPPING
Fleet (at 30 June)

	1984	1985	1986
Merchant shipping:			
Steamships:			
number	2	2	2
displacement*	113.7	113.7	113.7
Motor vessels:			
number	96	99	94
displacement*	2,048.0	2,101.8	2,104.5
Inland waterways:			
Powered craft:			
number	2,505	2,419	2,327
displacement*	1,504.9	1,461.8	1,405.8
Non-powered craft:			
number	166	179	181
displacement*	253.8	294.0	323.6

* '000 gross registered tons.

Freight Traffic ('000 metric tons)

	1983	1984	1985
Sea-borne shipping:			
Goods loaded	38,771	n.a.	n.a.
Goods unloaded	66,043	n.a.	n.a.
Inland waterways:			
Goods loaded	50,299	53,513	50,414
Goods unloaded	57,245	63,144	60,922

Tourism

	1983	1984	1985†
Number of tourist nights*	8,938,904	9,347,083	9,843,452

* Foreign visitors only.
† Provisional.

Communications Media

	1983	1984	1985
Telephones in use	4,083,883	n.a.	n.a.
Television receivers in use	2,981,497	2,983,186	2,971,596
Radio licences	4,607,257	4,557,615	4,526,291

Newspapers (1982): 26 general interest dailies (combined circulation 2,204,000).

Book titles (production, 1983): 8,065, of which 6,946 were first editions.

Source: partly UNESCO, *Statistical Yearbook*.

Education

(1982/83)

	Institutions	Students
Pre-school	4,281	389,792
Primary	4,977	812,092
Secondary	2,314	848,056
Technical	250	84,588
Teacher Training	168	25,166
Universities and Higher	19	96,795

Source: Ministère de l'Education nationale et de la Culture française and Ministerie van Onderwijs.

Directory

The Constitution

The Belgian Constitution has been considerably modified by amendments since its origin in 1831. Belgium is a constitutional monarchy. The central legislature consists of a Chamber of Representatives and a Senate. The Chamber of Representatives consists of 212 members, who are elected for four years unless the Chamber is dissolved before that time has elapsed. Belgium entered 1971 with a rewritten Constitution, differing from its predecessor mainly in its treatment of the three cultural entities: French-speaking, Dutch-speaking and German-speaking. Each community has regional powers in cultural and economic affairs. Before this there had been juridical recognition of the separate, bilingual status of Brussels, and provision made for the creation of regional political organs for Brussels, Flanders and Wallonia.

ELECTORAL SYSTEM

Members must be 25 years of age, and they are elected by secret ballot according to a system of proportional representation. Suffrage is universal for citizens of 18 years or over, and voting is compulsory.

The Senate, or Second Chamber, is chosen in the following manner. It is composed of:

(1) Half as many members as the Chamber of Representatives, elected directly by the same electors.

(2) Members chosen by the Provincial Councillors, in the proportion of one for every 200,000 population.

(3) Members co-opted by groups (1) and (2), up to half the number of group (2).

(4) One Senator by right, the heir to the throne.

There are now 182 Senators.

All Senators must be over 40, with the exception of a small number of members of the royal family, who become Senators by right at the age of 18. Members are elected for four years.

THE CROWN

The King has the right to veto legislation, but he does not exercise it. Though he is supreme head of the executive, he in fact exercises his control through the Cabinet, which is responsible for all acts of government to the Chamber of Representatives. Though the King, according to the Constitution, appoints his own ministers, in practice, since they are responsible to the Chamber of Representatives and need its confidence, they are generally the choice of the Representatives. Similarly, the royal initiative is in the hands of the ministry.

LEGISLATION

Legislation is introduced either by the Government or the members in the two Houses, and as the party complexion of both Houses is generally almost the same, measures passed by the Chamber of Representatives are usually passed by the Senate. Each House elects its own President at the beginning of the session, who acts as an impartial Speaker, although he is a party nominee. The Houses elect their own committees, through which all legislation passes. They are so well organized that through them the Legislature has considerable power of control over the Cabinet. Nevertheless, according to the Constitution (Article 68), certain treaties must be communicated to the Chamber only as soon as the 'interest and safety of the State permit'. Further, the Government possesses an important power of dissolution which it uses; a most unusual feature is that it may be applied to either House separately or to both together (Article 71).

Revision of the Constitution is to be first settled by an ordinary majority vote of both Houses, specifying the article to be amended. The Houses are then automatically dissolved. The new Chambers then determine the amendments to be made, with the provision that in each House the presence of two-thirds of the members is necessary for a quorum, and a two-third majority of those voting is required.

LOCAL ADMINISTRATION

The system of local government conforms to the general European practice of being based on a combination of central officials as the executive agent and locally elected councillors as the deliberating body. The areas are the provinces and the communes, and the latter are empowered by Article 108 of the Constitution to associate for the purposes of better government.

The Government

HEAD OF STATE

King of the Belgians: HM King BAUDOUIN (BOUDEWIJN) (took the oath 17 July 1951.)

THE CABINET
(November 1986)

(PSC) and (CVP) Christian Social Party; (PRL) Parti Réformateur Libéral; (PVV) Freedom and Progress Party.

Prime Minister: Dr WILFRIED MARTENS (CVP).
Deputy Prime Minister, Minister of Justice and Institutional Reforms (French Sector): JEAN GOL (PRL).
Deputy Prime Minister, Minister for the Budget, Scientific Policy and Planning: GUY VERHOFSTADT (PVV).
Minister of Economic Affairs: PHILIPPE MAYSTADT (PSC).
Minister of the Interior, the Civil Service and Decentralization: JOSEPH MICHEL.
Minister of Foreign Affairs: LÉO TINDEMANS (CVP).
Minister of National Defence and the Brussels Region: FRANÇOIS-XAVIER DE DONNEA (PRL).
Minister of Finance: MARK EYSKENS (CVP).
Minister of Public Works: LOUIS OLIVIER (PRL).
Minister of Communications and Foreign Trade: HERMAN DE CROO (PVV).
Minister of Employment and Labour: MICHEL HANSENNE (PSC).
Ministers of Education: (Flemish Sector) DANIEL COENS (CVP); (French Sector) ANDRÉ DAMSEAUX (PRL).
Minister of Social Affairs and Institutional Reforms (Flemish Sector): JEAN-LUC DEHAENE (CVP).
Minister of the Middle Classes: JACKY BUCHMANN (PVV).

There are 10 Secretaries of State.

MINISTRIES

Office of the Prime Minister: 16 rue de la Loi, 1000 Brussels; tel. (02) 513-80-20; telex 62400.
Ministry for the Brussels Region: 21–23 blvd du Régent, 1000 Brussels; tel. (02) 513-82-00; telex 25190.
Ministry of the Budget and Planning: 26 rue de la Loi, 1040 Brussels; tel. (02) 230-15-80.
Ministry of the Civil Service: 3 rue Ducale, 1000 Brussels; tel. (02) 513-28-90.
Ministry of Economic Affairs: 23 square de Meeûs, 1040 Brussels; tel. (02) 511-19-30; telex 21062.
Ministry of Employment and Labour: 53 rue Belliard, 1040 Brussels; tel. (02) 233-51-11.
Ministry of Finance and the Middle Classes: 12 rue de la Loi, 1000 Brussels; tel. (02) 233-81-11.
Ministry of Foreign Affairs: 2 rue des Quatre Bras, 1000 Brussels; tel. (02) 516-82-11; telex 23979.
Ministry of Foreign Trade and Institutional Reforms (French Sector): 61 rue de la Régence, 1000 Brussels; tel. (02) 511-19-48.
Ministry of the Interior: 2 rue de la Loi, 1000 Brussels; tel. (02) 511-06-60; telex 21762.
Ministry of Justice: 4 place Poelaert, 1000 Brussels; tel. (02) 511-42-00; telex 62440.
Ministry of National Defence: 8 rue Lambermont, 1000 Brussels; tel. (02) 512-16-10; telex 61104.
Ministry of National Education (Flemish Sector): Centre Arts Lux., 4th and 5th Floors, 58 ave des Arts, BP 5, 1040 Brussels; tel. (02) 513-93-85; telex 26750.
Ministry of National Education (French Sector): 68A rue du Commerce, 1040 Brussels; tel. (02) 512-66-60; telex 24619.
Ministry of Posts and Telecommunications: 65 rue de la Loi, 1040 Brussels; tel. (02) 230-10-10; telex 22681.
Ministry of Public Works: 9th Floor, 155 rue de la Loi, 1040 Brussels; tel. (02) 734-91-07; telex 63477.
Ministry of Scientific Policy: 8 rue de la Science, 1040 Brussels; tel. (02) 230-41-00.
Ministry of Social Affairs and Institutional Reforms (Flemish Sector): 5th Floor, 56 rue de la Loi, 1040 Brussels; tel. (02) 230-01-70.

Legislature

CHAMBRE DES REPRÉSENTANTS/KAMER VAN VOLKSVERTEGENWOORDIGERS
(Chamber of Representatives)

General Election, 13 October 1985

	Votes	%	Seats
CVP	1,291,595	21.30	49
PSC	482,559	7.96	20
PS	834,488	13.76	35
SP	883,065	14.56	32
PRL	619,392	10.21	24
PVV	650,604	10.73	22
VU	477,408	7.87	16
Ecolo	152,481	2.51	5
Agalev	226,998	3.74	4
FDF	72,361	1.19	3
Vlaams Blok	85,330	1.41	1
UDRT/RAD	69,770	1.15	1
PCB/KPB	71,683	1.18	0
PvdA/PTB	45,685	0.75	0
Others	100,996	1.67	0
Total	6,064,415	100.00	212

SÉNAT/SENAAT

General Election, 13 October 1985

	Votes	%	Seats
CVP	1,259,244	21.01	25
PSC	475,322	7.93	10
PS	832,743	13.90	18
SP	867,305	14.47	16
PRL	588,284	9.82	13
PVV	638,639	10.66	11
VU	485,241	8.10	8
Agalev	228,918	3.82	2
Ecolo	163,357	2.73	2
FDF	69,619	1.16	1
Vlaams Blok	90,121	1.50	0
UDRT/RAD	73,054	1.22	0
PCB/KPB	70,954	1.18	0
PvdA/PTB	45,387	0.76	0
Others	104,885	1.75	0
Total	5,993,073	100.00	106

In addition, the Senate has 50 members elected by provincial councils, a further 25 co-opted by the elected members and one Senator by right, the heir to the throne.

Political Organizations

Anders Gaan Leven (Agalev) (Ecologist Party—Dutch-speaking): 78 Twee Kerkenstraat, 1040 Brussels; tel. (02) 230-66-66; f. 1982; Pres. LÉO COX.

Ecolo (Ecologist Party—French-speaking): 38 blvd Charlemagne, 1040 Brussels.

Front Démocratique des Bruxellois Francophones (FDF) (French-speaking Democratic Front): 127 chaussée de Charleroi, 1060 Brussels; tel. (02) 538-83-20; f. 1964; aims at the preservation of the French character of Brussels; Pres. GEORGES CLERFAYT; Sec.-Gen. GEORGES VERZIN.

Partei der Deutschsprachigen Belgier (PDB) (German-speaking Party): 6 Kaperberg, 4700 Eupen; f. 1971; aims at equality of rights for the German-speaking minority (65,000 approx.) as recognized in the national constitution; Pres. ALFRED KEUTGEN (Eupen).

Parti Communiste de Belgique (PCB)/Kommunistische Partij van België (KPB) (Communist Party): 18-20 ave Stalingrad, 1000 Brussels; tel. (02) 512-90-12; f. 1921; c. 14,000 mems;

BELGIUM

Pres. LOUIS VAN GEYT; Vice-Pres. (French-speaking) CLAUDE RENARD; Secs MARCEL COUTEAU, ROEL JACOBS, M. DUPPAERT, ROBERT DUSSART, DANIEL FEDRIGO.

Parti Féministe Unifié (PFU)/Vereenigde Feministische Partij (VFP): 13 ave du Pesage, 1050 Brussels; tel. (02) 648-87-38; f. 1972; aims at the creation of a humanistic, self-governing republic where basic rights of the individual and of society are respected; non-hierarchical structure; Founders NINA ARIEL, CLAIRE BIHIN, ADÈLE HAUWEL, RENÉE WATY-FOSSEPREZ.

Parti Liberal Chrétien: 46 ave de Scheut, 1070 Brussels; tel. (02) 524-39-66; Pres. L. EYKERMAN.

Parti Réformateur Libéral (PRL) (Liberal Party—French-speaking wing): Centre International Rogier, 26e étage, BP 570, 1000 Brussels; tel. (02) 219-43-30; f. 1979; 45,000 mems; formerly the Parti des Réformes et de la Liberté en Wallonie; Pres. LOUIS MICHEL; Gen.-Sec. EDOUARD C. KLEIN.

Parti Social Chrétien (PSC)/Christelijke Volkspartij (CVP) (Christian Social Party): 41 rue des deux Eglises, 1040 Brussels; tel. (02) 230-10-73 (PSC); (02) 230-60-70 (CVP); f. 1945; 186,000 mems; Pres. (PSC) GÉRARD DEPREZ; Pres. (CVP) FRANK SWAELEN; Secs JACQUES LEFÈVRE (PSC), LUDO WILLEMS (CVP).

Parti Socialiste (PS) (Socialist Party—French-speaking wing): Maison du PS, 13 blvd de L'Empereur, 1000 Brussels; tel. (02) 513-82-70; f. in 1885 as the Parti Ouvrier Belge; split from the Flemish wing in 1979; Pres. GUY SPITAELS; Sec. ROGER GAILLIEZ.

Parti Wallon (PW) (Walloon Party): 2 rue Maurice Lange, 1381 Quenast; f. 1985 by amalgamation of the Rassemblement Wallon (f. 1968), the Rassemblement Populaire Wallon and the Front Indépendantiste Wallon; advocates an independent Walloon state; ideologically a left-wing socialist party; Pres. JEAN-CLAUDE PICCIN.

Partij van de Arbeid van België (PvdA)/Parti du Travail de Belgique (PTB) (Belgian Labour Party): f. 1979; Marxist-Leninist; Leader LUDO MARTENS.

Partij voor Vrijheid en Vooruitgang (PVV) (Liberal Party—Dutch-speaking wing): 47–48 Regentlaan, bus 2, 1000 Brussels; tel. (02) 512-78-70; telex 65865; f. 1961; succeeded the former Liberal Party; Pres. GUY VERHOFSTADT.

Socialistische Partij (SP) (Socialist Party—Flemish wing): 13 blvd de l'Empereur, 1000 Brussels; tel. (02) 513-28-78; f. 1885; Pres. KAREL VAN MIERT; Sec. CARLA GALLE.

Union Démocratique pour le Respect du Travail (UDRT)/Respect voor Arbeid en Democratie (RAD) (Employers' Party): 56 blvd Lambermont, 1030 Brussels; tel. (02) 242-76-60; f. 1978; aims at fiscal reform and the defence of private property and free enterprise; Pres. ROBERT HENDRICK; Sec. (French-speaking) PASCAL ROUBAIX; Sec. (Dutch-speaking) LYDIA VAN BEEK.

Vlaams Blok (Flemish Nationalist Party): 17 Schipperijkaai, 1210 Brussels; tel. (02) 219-60-09; f. 1979; Chair. KAREL DILLEN.

Volksunie (VU) (People's Union): 12 Barrikadenplein, 1000 Brussels; tel. (02) 219-49-30; f. 1954; mems 60,000; Flemish nationalist party aiming at federal structure for the country; Pres. J. GABRIELS; Sec. P. VAN GREMBERGEN.

Diplomatic Representation

EMBASSIES IN BELGIUM

Algeria: 209 ave Molière, 1060 Brussels; tel. (02) 343-50-78; telex 64142; Ambassador: FERHAT LOUNES.

Angola: 182 rue Franz Merjay, 1180 Brussels; tel. (02) 344-49-80; telex 63170; Ambassador: NOEMIA GABRIELLA DE ALMEIDA TAVIRA.

Argentina: 225 ave Louise, BP 3, 1050 Brussels; tel. (02) 647-78-12; Ambassador: JORGE EMILIO CASAL.

Australia: 51–52 ave des Arts, 1040 Brussels; tel. (02) 511-39-97; telex 21834; Ambassador: HAROLD D. ANDERSON.

Austria: 47 rue de l'Abbaye, 1050 Brussels; tel. (02) 649-91-70; telex 22463; Ambassador: FRANZ CESKA.

Bangladesh: 29–31 rue Jacques Jordaens, 1050 Brussels; tel. (02) 640-55-00; telex 63189; Ambassador: MOHAMMED MOHSIN.

Barbados: 14 ave Lloyd George, 1050 Brussels; tel. (02) 648-13-58; telex 63926; Ambassador: RUALL CARDINAL HARRIS.

Benin: 5 ave de l'Observatoire, 1180 Brussels; tel. (02) 374-91-92; telex 24568; Ambassador: DOUWA DAVID GBAGUIDI.

Bolivia: 5 rue de la Presse, 1000 Brussels; tel. (02) 217-35-54; telex 25327; Ambassador: AUGUSTO CUADROS SÁNCHEZ.

Botswana: 169 ave de Tervueren, 1040 Brussels; tel. (02) 735-20-7; telex 22849; Ambassador: MOTEANE JOHN MELAMU.

Brazil: 350 ave Louise, BP 5, 1050 Brussels; tel. (02) 640-20-15; telex 26758; Ambassador: DAVID S. DA MOTA, Jr.

Bulgaria: 58 ave Hamoir, 1180 Brussels; tel. (02) 374-59-63; telex 22473; Ambassador: STEPHAN STOYANOV TODOROV.

Burkina Faso: 16 place Guy d'Arezzo, 1060 Brussels; tel. (02) 345-99-12; Ambassador: (vacant).

Burundi: 46 square Marie-Louise, 1040 Brussels; tel. (02) 230-45-35; telex 23572; Ambassador: CYPRIAN MBONIMPA.

Cameroon: 131 ave Brugmann, 1060 Brussels; tel. (02) 345-18-70; telex 24117; Ambassador: ZACHEE MONGO SOO.

Canada: 6 rue de Loxum, 1000 Brussels; tel. (02) 513-79-40; telex 21613; Ambassador: MAXWELL YALDEN.

Central African Republic: 416 blvd Lambermont, 1030 Brussels; tel. (02) 242-28-80; telex 22493; Ambassador: CYRIAQUE SAMBA-PANZA.

Chad: 52 blvd Lambermont, 1030 Brussels; tel. (02) 215-19-75; Ambassador: NIAMBAYE LOSSIMIAN.

Chile: 251 ave Louise, 12e étage, BP 3, 1050 Brussels; tel. (02) 648-58-81; telex 61955; Chargé d'affaires a.i.: JOSÉ MANUEL OVALLE.

China, People's Republic: 19 blvd Général Jacques, 1050 Brussels; tel. (02) 649-67-73; Ambassador: LIU SHAN.

Colombia: rue Van Eyck, 1050 Brussels; tel. (02) 649-56-79; telex 25254; Ambassador: Dr HERNANDO GALVIS ESPINOSA.

Comoros: c/o Senegal Embassy, Brussels; Ambassador: ALI MLAHAI LI.

Congo: 16-18 ave F. D. Roosevelt, 1050 Brussels; tel. (02) 648-38-56; telex 23677; Ambassador: Lt-Col ALFRED RAOUL.

Costa Rica: 437 ave Louise, 1050 Brussels; tel. (02) 640-55-41; telex 23548; Ambassador: FABIO CARBALLO MONTERO.

Cuba: 77 rue Roberts-Jones, 1180 Brussels; tel. (02) 343-00-20; telex 21945; Ambassador: TERESITA AVERHOFF FERNÁNDEZ.

Cyprus: 83 rue de la Loi (4e étage), 1040 Brussels; tel. (02) 230-12-95; telex 25172; Ambassador: ANGELOS ANGELIDES.

Czechoslovakia: 152 ave Adolphe Buyl, 1050 Brussels; tel. (02) 647-68-09; telex 21455; Ambassador: JAROSLAV KVAČEK.

Denmark: 221 ave Louise, BP 7, 1050 Brussels; tel. (02) 648-25-25; telex 22591; Ambassador: G. F. K. HARHOFF.

Ecuador: 70 chaussée de Charleroi, 1060 Brussels; tel. (02) 537-91-30; telex 63292; Ambassador: HERNÁN GUARDERAS.

Egypt: 2 ave Victoria, 1050 Brussels; tel. (02) 648-18-01; telex 64809; Ambassador: AHMED MAHER EL SAYED.

Ethiopia: 32 blvd St Michel, 1040 Brussels; tel. (02) 733-49-29; telex 62285; Ambassador: Dr GHEBRAY BERHANE.

Fiji: 66–68 ave de Cortenberg (7e étage), BP 7, 1040 Brussels; tel. (02) 736-90-51; telex 26934; Ambassador: POSECI BUNE.

Finland: 489 ave Louise, 1050 Brussels; tel. (02) 648-84-84; telex 23099; Ambassador: PENTTI TALVITIE.

France: 65 rue Ducale, 1000 Brussels; tel. (02) 512-17-15; telex 21478; Ambassador: JACQUES LECOMPT.

Gabon: 112 ave W. Churchill, 1180 Brussels; tel. (02) 343-00-55; telex 23383; Ambassador: HANGONGO NZAMBI.

Gambia: 126 ave F. D. Roosevelt, 1050 Brussels; tel. (02) 640-10-49; telex 24344; Ambassador: BABON O. JOBE.

German Democratic Republic: 80 blvd St Michel, 1040 Brussels; tel. (02) 743-91-00; telex 21585; Ambassador: ERNST WALKOWSKI.

Germany, Federal Republic: 190 ave de Tervueren, 1040 Brussels; tel. (02) 770-58-30; telex 21382; Ambassador: CHRISTIAN FEIT.

Ghana: 44 rue Gachard, 1050 Brussels; tel. (02) 649-01-63; telex 22572; Ambassador: J. A. LARYEA.

Greece: 430 ave Louise (3e étage), 1050 Brussels; tel. (02) 648-33-02; telex 25521; Ambassador: DIMITRIS HERACLIDES.

Grenada: 24 ave des Arts, 7e étage, BP 2, 1040 Brussels; tel. (02) 230-62-65; telex 64015; Chargé d'affaires a.i.: H. M. BLAIZE.

Guatemala: 3 blvd St Michel, 1040 Brussels; tel. (02) 736-03-40; telex 25130; Ambassador: HUGO ARGUETA FIGUEROA.

Guinea: 75 ave Roger Vandendriessche, 1150 Brussels; tel. (02) 771-01-90; telex 64731; Ambassador: DAOUDA KOUROUMA.

Guinea-Bissau: 2 ave Palmerston, 1040 Brussels; tel. (02) 230-41-21; telex 63631; Ambassador: MARIO CABRAL.

Guyana: 21–22 ave des Arts, 1040 Brussels; tel. (02) 230-60-65; telex 26180; Ambassador: HAROLD SAHEDEO.

Haiti: 422 ave Louise, 1050 Brussels; tel. (02) 649-73-81; Ambassador: Jean-Antoine Dardeau.

Holy See: 5–9 ave des Franciscains, 1150 Brussels (Apostolic Nunciature); tel. (02) 762-20-05; Apostolic Nuncio: Mgr Angelo Pedroni.

Honduras: 3 ave des Gaulois (5e étage), 1040 Brussels; tel. (02) 734-00-00; telex 63175; Ambassador: Manuel López Luna.

Hungary: 41 rue Edmond Picard, 1180 Brussels; tel. (02) 343-67-90; telex 21428; Ambassador: Dr József Németh.

Iceland: 19 ave des Lauriers, 1150 Brussels; tel. (02) 215-10-35; telex 23763; Ambassador: Tómas A. Tómasson.

India: 217 chaussée de Vleurgat, 1050 Brussels; tel. (02) 640-91-40; telex 22510; Ambassador: Eric Gonsalves.

Indonesia: 294 ave de Tervueren, 1150 Brussels; tel. (02) 771-20-14; telex 21200; Ambassador: Gusti Rusli Noor.

Iran: 415 ave de Tervueren, 1150 Brussels; tel. (02) 762-37-45; telex 24083; Ambassador: Alireza Salari.

Iraq: 131 ave de la Floride, 1180 Brussels; tel. (02) 374-59-92; telex 26414; Ambassador: Dr Rashid M. S. al-Rifai.

Ireland: 19 rue du Luxembourg (3e étage), 1040 Brussels; tel. (02) 513-66-33; telex 24598; Ambassador: Mary Catherine Tinney.

Israel: 40 ave de l'Observatoire, 1180 Brussels; tel. (02) 374-90-80; telex 62718; Ambassador: Itzhak S. Minerbi.

Italy: 28 rue Emile Claus, 1050 Brussels; tel. (02) 649-97-00; telex 23950; Ambassador: Alberto Cavaglieri.

Ivory Coast: 234 ave F. D. Roosevelt, 1050 Brussels; tel. (02) 672-23-57; telex 21993; Ambassador: Charles Valy Tuho.

Jamaica: 83–85 rue de la Loi (5e étage), 1040 Brussels; tel. (02) 230-11-70; telex 26644; Ambassador: Carmen Yvonne Parris.

Japan: 58 ave des Arts (7e étage), 1040 Brussels; tel. (02) 513-92-00; telex 22174; Ambassador: Shigeru Tokuhisa.

Jordan: 104 ave F. D. Roosevelt, 1050 Brussels; tel. (02) 640-77-55; Ambassador: Hasan Abu Nimah.

Kenya: 1–5 ave de la Joyeuse Entrée, 1040 Brussels; tel. (02) 230-30-65; telex 62568; Ambassador: Joseph W. N. Nyagah.

Korea, Republic: 3 ave Hamoir, 1180 Brussels; tel. (02) 375-39-80; telex 26256; Ambassador: Shin Chung-Sup.

Lebanon: 2 rue Guillaume Stocq, 1050 Brussels; tel. (02) 649-94-60; telex 22547; Ambassador: Samir el Khouri.

Lesotho: 51 ave Van Goolen, 1200 Brussels; tel. (02) 762-83-91; telex 25852; Ambassador: Lengolo Bureng Monyake.

Liberia: 18 ave des Tourists, 1640 Rhode-Saint-Genèse; tel. (02) 648-13-49; telex 61384; Ambassador: J. Rudolph Johnson.

Libya: 28 ave Victoria, 1050 Brussels; tel. (02) 649-21-12; Sec. of People's Bureau: Muftah Zawam.

Luxembourg: 75 ave de Cortenbergh, 1040 Brussels; tel. (02) 733-99-77; Ambassador: Guy de Muyser.

Madagascar: 276 ave de Tervueren, 1150 Brussels; tel. (02) 770-17-26; telex 61197; Ambassador: Pierre Désiré Ranjeva.

Malawi: 13–17 rue de la Charité, 1040 Brussels; tel. (02) 217-43-70; telex 24128; Ambassador: Stevens Erasmus Mapunda.

Malaysia: 414 ave de Tervueren, BP A, 1150 Brussels; tel. (02) 762-67-67; telex 26396; Ambassador: Datuk Mustapha Mahmud.

Mali: 487 ave Molière, 1060 Brussels; tel. (02) 345-74-32; telex 22508; Ambassador: Yaya Diarra.

Malta: 44 rue Jules Lejeune, 1060 Brussels; tel. (02) 343-01-95; telex 26616; Ambassador: Dr Paul Farrugia.

Mauritania: 6 ave de la Colombie, 1050 Brussels; tel. (02) 660-49-38; Ambassador: Ahmed Killy Ould Cheikh Sidia.

Mauritius: 68 ave des Bollandistes, 1040 Brussels; tel. (02) 733-99-88; telex 23114; Ambassador: Raymond Chasle.

Mexico: 375 ave Louise, 1050 Brussels; tel. (02) 648-26-71; telex 22355; Ambassador: Antonio González-de-León.

Monaco: 17 place Guy d'Arezzo, Box 7, 1060 Brussels; tel. (02) 347-49-87; Ambassador: François Giraudon.

Morocco: 98–100 ave F. D. Roosevelt, 1050 Brussels; tel. (02) 647-34-52; telex 21233; Ambassador: Zine El Abidine Sebti.

Netherlands: 35 rue de la Science, 1040 Brussels; tel. (02) 230-30-20; telex 21311; Ambassador: Dr Christoph Albert van der Klaauw.

New Zealand: 47–48 blvd du Régent, 1000 Brussels; tel. (02) 512-10-40; telex 22025; Ambassador: Terence O'Brien.

Nicaragua: 255 chaussée de Vleurgat, 1050 Brussels; tel. (02) 345-19-25; telex 63553; Ambassador: Giovanni Delgado Campos.

Niger: 78 ave F. D. Roosevelt, 1040 Brussels; tel. (02) 648-61-40; telex 22857; Ambassador: Habou Saley.

Nigeria: 288 ave de Tervueren, 1150 Brussels; tel. (02) 762-98-31; telex 22435; Ambassador: Joshua O. B. Iroha.

Norway: Europe Centre, 17 rue Archimède (4e et 5e étage), 1040 Brussels; tel. (02) 230-78-65; telex 21071; Ambassador: Christian Berg-Nielsen.

Pakistan: 57 ave Delleur, 1170 Brussels; tel. (02) 673-80-07; telex 61876; Ambassador: Mahdi Masud.

Panama: 23 rue Crollé, 1328 Ohain; tel. (02) 633-23-90; Chargé d'affaires a.i.: Elena Barletta de Nottebohm.

Papua New Guinea: 327 ave Louise, BP 20/21, 1050 Brussels; tel. (02) 640-34-95; telex 62249; Ambassador: Peter Ipu Peipul.

Paraguay: 42 ave de Saturne, 1180 Brussels; tel. (02) 374-87-48; telex 26535; Ambassador: Dido Florentín-Bogado.

Peru: 179 ave de Tervueren, 1150 Brussels; tel. (02) 733-33-19; telex 24577; Ambassador: Julio Ego Aguirre.

Philippines: 299 ave Molière, 1060 Brussels; tel. (02) 343-68-32; Ambassador: Mrs Rosario G. Manalo.

Poland: 29 ave des Gaulois, 1040 Brussels; tel. (02) 733-77-48; telex 21562; Ambassador: Stanisław Matosek.

Portugal: 115 rue Defacqz (5e étage), 1050 Brussels; tel. (02) 539-37-13; telex 24570; Ambassador: Alexandre Eduardo Lencastre da Veiga.

Qatar: 37 ave F. D. Roosevelt, 1050 Brussels; tel. (02) 640-29-00; telex 63754; Ambassador: Abdulla Saleh al-Mana.

Romania: 105 rue Gabrielle, 1180 Brussels; tel. (02) 345-26-80; telex 21859; Ambassador: George Ciucu.

Rwanda: 1 ave des Fleurs, 1150 Brussels; tel. (02) 763-07-02; telex 26653; Ambassador: Ildéphonse Munyeshyaka.

São Tomé and Príncipe: 42 ave Brugman, 1060 Brussels; tel. (02) 347-53-75; telex 65313; Ambassador: Fradique de Menezes.

Saudi Arabia: 45 ave F. D. Roosevelt, 1050 Brussels; tel. (02) 649-57-25; telex 64626; Ambassador: Ibrahim Saleh Bakr.

Senegal: 196 ave F. D. Roosevelt, 1050 Brussels; tel. (02) 672-90-51; telex 63951; Ambassador: Seydina Oumar Sy.

Sierra Leone: 410 ave de Tervueren, 1150 Brussels; tel. (02) 771-00-52; telex 63624; Ambassador: Abdul G. Koroma.

Singapore: 198 ave F. D. Roosevelt, 1050 Brussels; tel. (02) 660-30-98; telex 26731; Ambassador: Dr Chiang Hai Ding.

Somalia: 66 ave F. D. Roosevelt, 1050 Brussels; tel. (02) 640-16-69; telex 24807; Ambassador: Dr Mohamed Malingur.

South Africa: 26 rue de la Loi, BP 7 & 8, 1040 Brussels; tel. (02) 230-68-45; telex 23495; Ambassador: Willem Christophel Dempsey.

Spain: 19 rue de la Science, 1040 Brussels; tel. (02) 230-03-40; telex 22092; Ambassador: Mariano Berdejo.

Sri Lanka: 21–22 ave des Arts, 1040 Brussels; tel. (02) 230-48-90; telex 26927; Ambassador: Anthony N. Wiratunga.

Sudan: 124 ave F. D. Roosevelt, 1050 Brussels; tel. (02) 647-51-59; telex 24370; Ambassador: Sayed Nuri Khalil Siddig.

Suriname: 379 ave Louise, BP 20, 1050 Brussels; tel. (02) 640-11-72; telex 62680; Ambassador: Donald Aloysius MacLeod.

Sweden: 148 ave Louise, 1050 Brussels; tel. (02) 649-21-58; telex 21148; Ambassador: Kaj Sundberg.

Switzerland: 26 rue de la Loi, BP 9, 1040 Brussels; tel. (02) 230-61-45; telex 63711; Ambassador: Jean Bourgeois.

Syria: 3 ave F. D. Roosevelt, 1050 Brussels; tel. (02) 648-01-35; telex 26669; Ambassador: Mouaffac Koudsi.

Tanzania: 363 ave Louise (7e étage), 1050 Brussels; tel. (02) 640-65-00; telex 63616; Ambassador: Ernest Abel Mulokozi.

Thailand: 2 square du Val de la Cambre, 1050 Brussels; tel. (02) 640-68-10; telex 63510; Ambassador: Vitthya Vejjajiva.

Togo: 264 ave de Tervueren, 1150 Brussels; tel. (02) 770-55-63; telex 25093; Ambassador: Affionjbon Ekoue.

Trinidad and Tobago: ave de la Faisanderie, 1150 Brussels; tel. (02) 762-94-15; telex 23539; Ambassador: Maurice O. St. John.

Tunisia: 278 ave de Tervueren, 1150 Brussels; tel. (02) 771-73-95; telex 22078; Ambassador: Mohamed Megdiche.

Turkey: 74 rue Jules Lejeune, 1060 Brussels; tel. (02) 344-22-16; telex 24677; Ambassador: Faik Melek.

Uganda: 317 ave de Tervueren, 1150 Brussels; tel. (02) 762-58-25; telex 62814; Ambassador: Mrs Anna Amailuk.

BELGIUM   Directory

USSR: 66 ave de Fré, 1180 Brussels; tel. (02) 374-34-06; telex 65272; Ambassador: SERGEI NIKITIN.
United Arab Emirates: 73 ave F. D. Roosevelt, 1050 Brussels; tel. (02) 640-60-00; telex 26559; Ambassador: ESSA KHALFAN AL-HURAIMEL.
United Kingdom: 28 rue Joseph II, 1040 Brussels; tel. (02) 217-90-00; telex 22703; Ambassador: PETER CHARLES PETRIE.
USA: 27 blvd du Régent, 1000 Brussels; tel. (02) 513-38-30; telex 21336; Ambassador: GEOFFREY SWAEBE.
Uruguay: 437 ave Louise, 1050 Brussels; tel. (02) 640-11-69; telex 24663; Ambassador: MIGUEL J. BERTHET.
Venezuela: 23 ave des Phalènes, 1050 Brussels; tel. (02) 649-44-16; telex 63787; Ambassador: ANTONIO OLAVARRIA.
Yugoslavia: 11 ave Emile de Mot, 1050 Brussels; tel. (02) 647-26-52; telex 26156; Ambassador: GAVRA POPOVIĆ.
Zaire: 30 rue Marie de Bourgogne, 1040 Brussels; tel. (02) 513-66-10; telex 21983; Ambassador: EKILA LIYONDA.
Zambia: 158 ave de Tervueren, Box 2, 1150 Brussels; tel. (02) 771-21-10; telex 63102; Ambassador: SUNDIE KAZUNGA.
Zimbabwe: 21–22 ave des Arts, btes 5–6, 1040 Brussels; tel. (02) 230-85-35; telex 24133; Ambassador: SOLOMON JOHN MAHAKA.

Judicial System

The independence of the judiciary is based on the constitutional division of power between the legislative, executive and judicial bodies, each of which acts independently. Judges are appointed by the crown for life, and cannot be removed except by judicial sentence. The law of 1967, in force since 1970, unified civil procedure in the district courts, and reorganized the courts' areas of competence. Each of Belgium's nine provinces is divided into judicial districts, and these, in turn, into judicial cantons. The judiciary is organized on four levels, from the judicial canton to the district, regional and national courts. The lowest courts are those of the Justices of the Peace, of which there are 222, and the 20 Police Tribunals; each type of district court numbers 26, one in each district, including the Tribunals of the First Instance, Tribunals of Commerce, and Labour Tribunals. There are five regional Courts of Appeal, five regional Labour Courts, and one Court of Assizes in each province. The highest courts are the five civil and criminal Courts of Appeal, the five Labour Courts and the supreme Court of Cassation. The Military Court of Appeal is in Brussels.

COUR DE CASSATION/HOF VAN CASSATIE (SUPREME COURT OF JUSTICE)

First President: M. CHATEL.
President: R. SCREVENS.
Counsellors: R. JANSSENS, R. SOETAERT, P. MAHILLON, O. STRANARD, H. BOSLY, J. SACE, E. BOON, C. CAENEPEEL, J. VERVLOET, J. RAUWS, J. MATTHIJS, J. D'HAENENS, J. POUPART, P. MARCHAL, J. DE PEUTER, D. HOLSTERS, P. GHISLAIN, Y. RAPPE, C. RESTEAU, M. HELVETIUS, M. CHARLIER, H. SWINNEN, G. DE BAETS.
General Prosecutor: J. KRINGS.
First Attorney-General: L. F. DUCHATELET.
Attorneys-General: H. LENAERTS, J. VELU, A. TILLEKAERTS, R. DECLERCQ, E. LIEKENDAEL, B. JANSSENS DE BISTHOVEN, G. D'HOORE, J. M. PIRET, J. DU JARDIN.

COURS D'APPEL/HOVEN VAN BEROEP (CIVIL AND CRIMINAL HIGH COURTS)

Antwerp: First Pres. A. ROEVENS; Gen. Prosecutor R. VERHEYDEN.
Brussels: First Pres. M. DE SMEDT; Gen. Prosecutor V. VAN HONSTÉ.
Ghent: First Pres. H. VAN BEVER; Gen. Prosecutor G. VERHEGGE.
Liège: First Pres. G. MOREAU; Gen. Prosecutor L. GIET.
Mons: First Pres. P. GUERITTE; Gen. Prosecutor G. DEMANET.

Religion

CHRISTIANITY
The Roman Catholic Church

Belgium comprises one archdiocese and seven dioceses. At 31 December 1984 there were an estimated 8,726,000 adherents (about 89% of the total population).

Bishops' Conference: Bisschoppenconferentie van België/Conférence Episcopale de Belgique, 15 Wollemarkt, 2800 Mechelen; tel. (015) 21-65-01; f. 1981; Pres. Cardinal GODFRIED DANNEELS, Archbishop of Mechelen-Brussels.
Archbishop of Mechelen-Brussels: Cardinal GODFRIED DANNEELS, Aartsbisdom, 15 Wollemarkt, 2800 Mechelen; tel. (015) 21-65-01.
Bishop of Antwerp: P. VAN DEN BERGHE, 6A Justitiestraat, 2018 Antwerp; tel. (03) 231-36-34.
Bishop of Bruges: R. VANGHELUWE, 4 H. Geeststraat, 8000 Bruges; tel. (050) 33-59-06.
Bishop of Ghent: L. VAN PETEGHEM, 1 Bisdomplein, 9000 Ghent; tel. (091) 25-16-26.
Bishop of Hasselt: J. HEUSCHEN, 14 Vrijwilligersplein, 3500 Hasselt; tel. (011) 22-79-21.
Bishop of Liège: A. HOUSSIAU, 25 rue de l'Evêché, 4000 Liège; tel. (041) 23-58-20.
Bishop of Namur: R. MATHEN, 1 rue de l'Evêché, 5000 Namur; tel. (081) 22-14-25.
Bishop of Tournai: J. HUARD, 1 place de l'Evêché, 7500 Tournai; tel. (069) 22-31-91.

Protestant Churches

Belgian Evangelical Lutheran Church: 26 rue du Major René Dubreucq, 1050 Brussels; tel. (02) 511-92-47; f. 1950; 425 mems; Pres C. J. HOBUS.
Church of England: Pro-Cathedral of the Holy Trinity, Brussels; Chancellor Ven. J. LEWIS.
Eglise Protestante Unie de Belgique: 5 rue du Champ de Mars, 1050 Brussels; tel. (02) 511-44-71; 35,000 mems; Pres. Rev. M. J. BEUKENHORST; Sec. Mme R. FRAISSE-LHEUREUX.
Mission Evangélique Belge: 7 rue du Moniteur, 1000 Brussels; tel. (02) 217-23-83; f. 1918; about 2,000 mems.
Union of Evangelical Baptist Churches: 51 rue de l'Academie, 4000 Liège; tel. (041) 22-29-26; Pres HENRY BENS; Sec. Rev. JEAN DESY.

JUDAISM

There are about 35,000 Jews in Belgium.

Consistoire Central Israélite de Belgique (Central Council of the Jewish Communities of Belgium): 2 rue Joseph Dupont, Brussels; tel. (02) 512-21-90; Chair. M. GEORGES SCHNEK.

The Press

Article 18 of the Belgian constitution states: 'The Press is free; no form of censorship may ever be instituted; no cautionary deposit may be demanded from writers, publishers or printers. When the author is known and is resident in Belgium, the publisher, printer or distributor may not be prosecuted.'

There are 39 general information dailies, 21 of which are autonomous, the remainder depending largely or totally on the former (some are only, under a different title, regional editions of a larger paper). In 1985 the combined circulation of all daily newspapers averaged 2,196,011 copies per issue.

There is a trend towards concentration. The 'Le Soir' group consists of five dailies. The only other significant group consists of three Catholic papers linked with *De Standaard.*

Although there are few official political organs, it should be mentioned that nearly all the Belgian dailies have political or union leanings. It is not, however, possible to establish a parallel between the supporters of the parties and the readership of the dailies.

Although there is no easy division of the daily papers into popular and serious press, most papers strive to give a serious news coverage. The widest circulating dailies in French in 1986 were: *Le Soir* (216,395), *La Meuse/La Lanterne* (130,210), *La Libre Belgique* (90,000) and *La Dernière Heure* (100,000); and in Dutch: *Het Laatste Nieuws* (304,253), *De Standaard/Nieuwsblad/De Gentenaar* (368,385), *Het Volk* (199,078) and *Gazet van Antwerpen* (182,591). The major weeklies include *Humo* (235,007), *Flair* (230,000), *TV Ekspres* (196,389) and *Le Soir Illustré* (119,212), the latter associated with the daily *Le Soir*; and the cultural periodicals *Pourquoi Pas?* (77,836) and *Knack* (97,000). The popular women's periodical *Femmes d'Aujourd'hui* (155,694) has considerable sales in France. Some periodicals are printed in French and in Dutch.

BELGIUM
Directory

PRINCIPAL DAILIES

Antwerp

De Financieel Economische Tijd: 5 Brouwersvliet, bus 3, 2000 Antwerp; tel. (03) 231-57-56; telex 23614; f. 1968; Dutch economic and financial paper; Gen. Man. J. LAMERS; Chief Editor EUGEEN MAGIELS; circ. 21,382.

Gazet van Antwerpen: 2 Katwilgweg, 2050 Antwerp; tel. (03) 219-38-80; telex 31385; f. 1891; Christian Democrat; also weekly edition for overseas readers (Gazet Van Antwerpen-Overzee); Dir-Gen. R. VAN TONGERLOO; Editor L. DE CLERCK; circ. 182,591 (with *Gazet van Mechelen*).

Lloyd Anversois-De Lloyd: 23 Eiermarkt, 2000 Antwerp; tel. (03) 234-05-50; telex 31446; f. 1858; shipping transport, commerce, industry, finance; Dir ROGER JAUMOTTE; circ. 10,000.

De Nieuwe Gazet: 10 Leopoldstraat, 2000 Antwerp; tel. (03) 231-96-80; telex 71382; f. 1897; Liberal; Gen. Man. F. GROOTJANS; Editor F. STRIELEMAN; circ. 28,000.

Arlon

L'Avenir du Luxembourg: 38 rue des Déportés, 6700 Arlon; tel. (063) 22-03-49; telex 41503; f. 1894; Catholic; Editor JO MOTTET; circ. 34,458.

Brussels

La Cité: 26 rue St Laurent, Brussels; tel. (02) 217-23-90; telex 22998; f. 1950; Christian Democrat; Dir and Editor JEAN HEINEN; circ. 20,000.

La Côte Libre: 131 rue de Birmingham, 1070 Brussels; tel. (02) 523-01-80; telex 22648; financial; Editor P. MELAET; circ. 23,000.

Courrier de la Bourse et de la Banque: 131 rue de Birmingham, 1070 Brussels; tel. (02) 523-01-80; telex 22648; f. 1895; financial, economic, industrial and political; Admin. Dir O. DE BEAUFORT; circ. 9,500.

La Dernière Heure/Les Sports: 127 blvd Emile Jacqmain, 1000 Brussels; tel. (02) 218-30-28; telex 21448; f. 1906; independent Liberal; Dir J. L. LAMOT; Chief Editor PAUL MASSON; circ. 100,000.

Le Drapeau Rouge: 33 rue de la Caserne, Brussels; tel. (02) 512-87-00; f. 1921; Communist; Editor PIERRE BEAUVOIS; Man. JACQUES MOINS; circ. 15,000.

L'Echo de la Bourse: 131 rue de Birmingham, 1070 Brussels; tel. (02) 520-40-80; telex 23396; f. 1881; economic and financial; Dir M. KRÜGER; Editor D. DEMAIN; circ. 30,000.

Het Laatste Nieuws: 105 Emile Jacqmainlaan, 1000 Brussels; tel. (02) 219-32-90; telex 21495; f. 1888; Dutch; independent; Dir F. VINK; Editor L. SIAENS; circ. 304,253 (with *De Nieuwe Gazet*).

La Lanterne: 134 rue Royale, 1000 Brussels; tel. (02) 218-21-08; telex 22751; f. 1944; independent; Gen. Man. C. MATRIGE; Chief Editor W. MEURENS; circ. 130,210 (with *La Meuse*).

La Libre Belgique: 127 blvd Emile Jacqmain, 1000 Brussels; tel. (02) 218-60-90; telex 21550; f. 1884; Catholic; independent; Dir J. L. LAMOT; Chief Editor J. FRANCK; circ. 90,000.

De Nieuwe Gids: 105 Koningsstraat, Brussels; tel. (02) 217-21-30; f. 1944; Dutch; Dir F. VAN ERPS; circ. 200,000.

Le Soir: 112 rue Royale, 1000 Brussels; tel. (02) 217-77-50; telex 21485; f. 1887; independent; Dir-Gen. ANDRÉ DE BETHUNE; Chief Editor M. Y. TOUSSAINT; circ. 216,395.

Krantengroep De Standaard (Group combining **De Standaard, Het Nieuwsblad, De Gentenaar**): published by Vlaamse Uitgeversmaatschappij NV, 28-30 Gossetlaan, 1720 Groot-Bijgaarden; tel. (02) 467-22-11; telex 63435; Christian Socialist; Dir G. VERDEYEN; Editorial Dirs M. RUYS, L. BOSTOEN; circ. 368,385.

Charleroi

Le Journal & Independance/Le Peuple: 9 quai de Flandre, 6000 Charleroi; tel. (071) 31-01-90; telex 51277; f. 1837; Gen. Man. C RENARD; Editor JEAN GUY; circ. 27,000.

La Nouvelle Gazette (Charleroi, La Louvière, Namur); La Province (Mons): 2 quai de Flandre, 6000 Charleroi; tel. (071) 32-00-35; telex 51218; f. 1878; Man. Dir MICHEL FROMONT; Editor J.-P. VANDERMEUSE; circ. 81,883.

Le Rappel, Le Journal de Mons, l'Echo du Centre: 40 rue de Montigny, 6000 Charleroi; tel. (071) 31-22-80; telex 51203; f. 1900; independent Christian Social; Editorial Dir POL VANDROMME; circ. 35,000.

Eupen

Grenz-Echo: 8 Marktplatz, 4700 Eupen; tel. (087) 55-47-05; f. 1927; German; independent Catholic; Dir. A. KÜCHENBERG; Editor HEINZ WARNY; circ. 13,500.

Ghent

De Gentenaar: 43 Vlaanderenstraat, 9000 Ghent; tel. (091) 25-76-86; f. 1878; Catholic; Man. G. VERDEYEN.

De Morgen/Vooruit: 84–90 Moutstraat, 9000 Ghent; tel. (091) 21-80-91; telex 11264; f. 1978; independent; Dir E. VAN HORENBEECK; Editor P. GOOSSENS; circ 46,531.

Het Volk: 22 Forelstraat, 9000 Ghent; tel. (091) 25-57-01; telex 11228; f. 1891; Catholic; Dir A. VAN MELKEBEEK; Editor P. DE BAERE; circ. 199,078.

Hasselt

Het Belang van Limburg: 10 Herckenrodesingel, 3500 Hasselt; tel. (011) 29-42-11; telex 39390; f. 1879; Christian Social; Dir JAN BAERT; Editor MARC PLATEL; circ. 97,023.

Liège

La Meuse: 8-12 blvd de la Sauvenière, 4000 Liège; tel. (041) 20-08-11; telex 41253; f. 1855; independent; Gen. Man. C. MATRIGE; Editor W. MEURENS; circ. 130,210 (with *La Lanterne*).

La Wallonie: 55 rue de la Régence, 4000 Liège; tel. (041) 22-09-00; telex 41143; f. 1919; progressive; Dir ROBERT GILLON; Editor J. COPPÉ; circ. 48,000.

Mechelen

Gazet van Mechelen: 13 Befferstraat, 2800 Mechelen; tel. (015) 20-83-83; telex 31385; f. 1896; Christian Democrat; Gen. Man. R. VAN TONGERLOO; Editor L. DE CLERCK; circ. 11,429.

Namur

Vers L'Avenir: 12 blvd Ernest Mélot, 5000 Namur; tel. (081) 71-32-71; telex 59121; f. 1918; Christian Democrat; Editor JEAN CLAUDE BAFFREY; circ. 63,551.

Tournai

L'Avenir du Tournaisis: 4 ave Leray, 7500 Tournai; tel. (069) 22-10-93; f. 1894; independent Liberal; Editor P. MASSON.

Le Courrier de L'Escaut: 24 rue du Curé Notre-Dame, 7500 Tournai; tel. (069) 22-81-43; telex 57147; f. 1829; Christian Social; Dir J. DESNERCK; Chief Editor ANDRÉ SERVAIS; circ. 24,499.

Verviers

Le Jour: 91–93 rue des Déportés, 4800 Verviers; tel. (087) 22-11-71; telex 49470; f. 1893; independent; Dir J. HERMAN; Chief Editor R. MONAMI; circ. 18,000.

WEEKLIES

Antwerpse Post: 2 Katwilgweg, 2000 Antwerp; news magazine; circ. 318,886.

BS (Bonne Soirée): 13 ave des Arts, 1040 Brussels; tel. (02) 218-07-07; telex 23291; f. 1922; women's magazine in French; Chief Editor MARIE-HÉLÈNE ADLER; circ. 300,000.

Brugsch Handelsblad: 4 Eekhoutstraat, 8000 Bruges; tel. (050) 33-06-61; telex 81222; f. 1906; local, national and international news; Dirs J. HERREBOUDT and P. OP DE BEECK; Editor J. HERREBOUDT; circ. 40,000.

Chez Nous: 9 ave Frans Van Kalken, 1070 Brussels; tel. (02) 523-20-60; telex 25104; f. 1952; women's weekly; Chief Editor J. MOREAU; circ. 44,000.

Dimanche-Presse: 2 ave Nouvelle, 1040 Brussels; tel. (02) 640-04-28; Chief Editor J. L. WAUTERS.

EOS: 102 Lousbergskaai, 9000 Ghent; tel. (091) 25-57-01; telex 11228; f. 1984; scientific; Chief Editor JEF ANTHIERENS; circ. 31,000.

Femmes d'Aujourd'hui: 9 ave Frans Van Kalken, 1070 Brussels; tel. (02) 523-20-60; telex 25104; f. 1933; women's magazine; Dir L. HIERGENS; Chief Editor J. MOREAU; circ. 155,694 (French), 207,275 (Dutch).

Flair: 7 Jan Blockxstraat, 2018 Antwerp; tel. (03) 237-01-20; telex 32979.

Humo: 46 De Jonckerstraat, 1060 Brussels; tel. (02) 537-08-00; telex 23291; general weekly and TV and radio guide in Dutch; Chief Editor G. MORTIER; circ. 235,007.

Knack: 153 Tervurenlaan, 1000 Brussels; tel. (02) 736-60-40; telex 25425; independent news magazine; Dir FRANS VERLEYEN; Chief Editors HUBERT VAN HUMBEECK, FRANK DEMOOR; circ. 97,000.

Kwik/Zondag Nieuws: 105-107 Emile Jacqmainlaan, 1000 Brussels; tel. (02) 219-32-90; telex 21495; f. 1962; Dir FRANS VINK; Editor K. VANDER MIJNSBRUGGE; circ. 287,335.

Libelle/Rosita: 7 Jan Blockxstraat, 2018 Antwerp; tel. (03) 237-01-20; telex 32979; f. 1945; Dutch and French; women's magazine; Dir N. MOOLENAAR; circ. 325,100.

BELGIUM

Pallieterke: 2 Mechelsesteenweg, 2000 Antwerp; f. 1945; satirical; founder B. DE WINTER.

Panorama/Ons Land: 5–7 Jan Blockxstraat, 2018 Antwerp; tel. (03) 237-01-20; telex 32979; f. 1956; Dutch; general interest magazine; Dir K. HUYSMANS; Chief Editor K. ANTHIERENS; circ. 91,000.

De Post: 105 Emile Jacqmainlaan, 1000 Brussels; f. 1949; general illustrated; Dir K. VANDER MIJNSBRUGGE; circ. 85,000.

Pourquoi Pas?: 95 blvd Emile Jacqmain, 1000 Brussels; tel. (02) 218-13-40; telex 21180; f. 1910; news weekly; Editor JEAN WELLE; circ. 77,836.

Het Rijk der Vrouw/Ons Volk: 9 Frans Van Kalkenlaan, 1070 Brussels; tel. (02) 523-20-60; telex 25104; f. 1932; Editor L. LUCAS; circ. 200,000.

De Rode Vaan: 108 M. Lemonnielaan, 1000 Brussels; tel. (02) 512-64-15; f. 1921; Communist; Dir JEF TURF; circ. 12,000.

Le Soir Illustré: 21 place de Louvain, 1000 Brussels; tel. (02) 217-77-50; f. 1928; independent illustrated; Dir A. DECLERQ; circ. 119,212.

Story: 7 Jan Blockxstraat, 2018 Antwerp; tel. (03) 237-01-20; telex 32979; f. 1975; Dutch; women's magazine; Dir N. MOOLENAAR; circ. 262,500.

Syndicats/De Werker: 42 rue Haute, Brussels; tel. (02) 511-64-66; telex 24620; f. 1945; French and Dutch editions; organ of the Fédération Générale du Travail de Belgique.

TeVe-Blad: 86B Frankrijklei, 2000 Antwerp; tel. (03) 231-47-90; f. 1981; illustrated; Chief Editor ROB JANS; circ. 230,000.

Télémoustique: 13 ave des Arts, 1040 Brussels; tel. (02) 218-07-07; telex 23291; f. 1924; radio and TV; Dir CHARLES DUPUIS; circ. 190,000.

TV Ekspres en TV Strip: 86B Frankrijklei, 2000 Antwerp; tel. (03) 231-47-90; telex 33134; Chief Editor ROB JANS; circ. 196,389.

Le Vif: 97 Louis Schmidtlaan, 1040 Brussels; telex 25425; Dir GERALD JACOBY.

Vlaams Weekblad: 96 Steenstraat, 8000 Bruges; tel. (050) 33-45-58; f. 1911; Dir J. ROOSE; Chief Editor FRANK VAN ACKER; circ. 36,000.

Het Wekelijks Nieuws: 5 Nijverheidslaan, 8970 Poperinge; tel. (057) 33-67-21; Christian news magazine; Dirs H. and L. SANSEN; Editor H. SANSEN; circ. 56,000.

De Zeewacht: 1A Alfons Pieters, 8400 Ostend; tel. (059) 70-28-28; f. 1894; Editor HUGUES DE WAELE; circ. 30,000.

ZIE-Magazine: 86B Frankrijklei, 2000 Antwerp; tel. (03) 231-47-90; f. 1930; illustrated; Chief Editor JAN BRUSSELEERS; circ. 80,000.

Zondagsblad: 22 Forelstraat, 9000 Ghent; tel. (091) 25-57-01; f. 1949; Catholic; Dir R. VAN TONGERLOO; Editor H. CLÉMENT; circ. 92,300.

OTHER PERIODICALS

International Business Equipment: 65 rue Veydt, 1050 Brussels; tel. (02) 537-12-62; f. 1964; trilingual (French, German, English); published by Office Publications Inc.; Editor WILLIAM R. SCHULHOF; circ. 56,000.

Revue Générale: 65 ave V. Jacobs, BP 2, Brussels; f. 1865; amalg. with *Revue Belge* 1945; modern humanist; Catholic; Dirs GEORGES SION, JOSEPH BERTRAND, N. DE KERCHOVA; circ. 5,000.

La Revue Nouvelle: 26 rue Potagène, 1030 Brussels; tel. (02) 218-78-18; f. 1945; monthly; Dir MICHEL MOLITOR; circ. 4,000.

De Vlaamse Gids: 105 Emile Jacqmainlaan, 1000 Brussels; Editorial office: 28 Korte Nieuwstraat, Antwerp; tel. (03) 231-96-80; f. 1906; circ. 10,000.

NEWS AGENCIES

Agence Belga (Agence Télégraphique Belge de Presse SA)—Agentschap Belga (Belgisch Pers-telegraafagentschap NV): 1 blvd Charlemagne, BP 51, 1041 Brussels; tel. (02) 230-50-55; telex 21408; f. 1920; largely owned by daily papers; Chair. J. HUYBRECHTS; Gen. Man. R. DE CEUSTER.

Agence Europe: 10 blvd St Lazare, 1030 Brussels.

Centre d'Information de Presse (CIP): 1 blvd Charlemagne, BP 67, 1041 Brussels; f. 1946; Dir NICO DE JAGER; Chief Editor CHRIS DE SCHRYVER.

Foreign Bureaux

Agence France-Presse (AFP): 1 blvd Charlemagne, BP 3, 1041 Brussels; tel. (02) 230-83-94; telex 24889; Dir BONI DE TORHOUT.

Agencia EFE (Spain): 1 blvd Charlemagne, BP 20, 1041 Brussels; tel. 230-45-68; telex 23185; Dir ERNESTO GARCÍA HERRERA.

Directory

Agentstvo Pechati Novosti (APN) (USSR): 22 rue Général Lotz, 1180 Brussels; telex 23798; Dir IGOR ROUJENSTEV.

Agenzia Nazionale Stampa Associata (ANSA) (Italy): 1 blvd Charlemagne, BP 7, 1041 Brussels; tel. (02) 230-81-92; telex 63717; Dir GIAMPIERO GRAMAGLIA.

Algemeen Nederlands Persbureau (ANP) (Netherlands): 1 blvd Charlemagne, 1041 Brussels; tel. (02) 230-85-27; Correspondents MARTINUS VAN DIJK, RIK WINKEL.

Allgemeiner Deutscher Nachrichtendienst (ADN) (German Democratic Republic): 8 rue J. E. Raymond, BP 3, 1160 Brussels; Dir RALF KLINGSIECK.

Associated Press (AP) (USA): 1 blvd Charlemagne, BP 49, 1041 Brussels; tel. (02) 230-52-49; telex 21741; Dir ROBERT WIELAARD.

Československá tisková kancelář (ČTK) (Czechoslovakia): rue des Egyptiens 2, BP 6, 1050 Brussels; tel. 648-0133; telex 23092; Correspondent V. SUCHY.

Deutsche Presse-Agentur (dpa) (Federal Republic of Germany): 1 blvd Charlemagne, BP 17, 1041 Brussels; tel. (02) 230-36-91; telex 22356; Dir DIETER EBELING.

Inter Press Service (IPS) (Italy): 35 rue du Framboisier, 1180 Brussels; tel. (02) 374-77-18; Correspondent JACQUES ELIAS.

Jiji Press (Japan): 1 blvd Charlemagne, BP 26, 1041 Brussels; tel. (02) 736-80-15; telex 25029; Dir MAHITO TUCHIYAMA.

Kyodo Tsushin (Japan): 1 blvd Charlemagne, BP 37, 1041 Brussels; tel. (02) 230-53-34; Dir AKIHIRO ONODA.

Magyar Távirati Iroda (MTI) (Hungary): 41 rue Jean Chapelie, 1060 Brussels; Dir FERENC FÁBIÁN.

Reuters (UK): 1 blvd Charlemagne, BP 40, 1041 Brussels; tel. (02) 230-92-15; telex 21633; Chief Correspondent Y. AZMEH.

Tunis Afrique Presse (TAP): 32 rue Wéry, 1050 Brussels; Dir FATHI B'CHIR.

United Press International (UPI) (USA): 17 rue Philippe le Bon, 1040 Brussels; tel. (02) 230-43-30; telex 26997; Correspondents STEPHAN KETELE, HERMAN SAEN.

Xinhua News Agency (People's Republic of China): 32 square Ambiorix, Residence le Pavois, BP 4, 1040 Brussels; tel. (02) 230-32-54; telex 26555; Chief Correspondent SHAO TONG.

Novinska Agencija Tanjug (Yugoslavia) and TASS (USSR) also have bureaux in Brussels.

PRESS ASSOCIATIONS

Association générale des Journalistes professionnels de Belgique/Algemene Vereniging van de Beroeps-journalisten in België: 1 blvd Charlemagne, BP 54, 1041 Brussels; tel. (02) 230-62-15; f. 1979 on merger of Association Générale de la Presse Belge (f. 1885) and Union Professionnelle de la Presse Belge (f. 1914); 1,375 mems (1981); affiliated to IFJ (International Federation of Journalists); Pres. MIA DOORNAERT; Sec.-Gen. J. VANDEN HOECK.

Association belge des Editeurs de Journaux/Belgische Vereniging van de Dagbladuitgevers: 20 rue Belliard, 1040 Brussels; tel. (02) 512-17-32; telex 26854; f. 1964; 38 mems; Pres CONRAD MATRIGE; Sec.-Gen. JEAN HOET.

Fédération de la Presse Périodique de Belgique: 92 blvd Charlemagne, BP 9, 1040 Brussels; tel. (02) 230-09-99; f. 1897; Pres. (vacant).

Publishers

Acco, SV: 134-136 Tiensestraat, 3000 Louvain; tel. (016) 23-35-20; telex 62547; f. 1960; Dir HUBERT VAN SLAMBROUCK.

Altiora NV (Publishing Dept.): 1 Abdijstraat, BP 54, 3281 Averbode; tel. (013) 77-17-51; telex 39104; f. 1934; general, fiction, juvenile and religious (Roman Catholic); weekly children's periodicals; Dir T. G. SECUIANU.

Barbiaux, Drukk. G.-Uitgeverij De Garve, PVBA: 27 Groene-Poortdreef, 8200 Bruges; tel. (050) 38-07-07; f. 1909; Dir G. BARBIAUX.

De Boeck-Wesmael, SA: 203 ave Louise, BP 1, 1050 Brussels; tel. (02) 640-72-72; telex 65701; f. 1795; primary and secondary school books; Dirs CHR. DE BOECK, G. HOYOS.

Cabay, NV: 11 Agora, 1348 Louvain-la-Neuve; tel. (010) 41-91-30; telex 59324; f. 1978; academic publications; Dir R. CABAY.

Casterman, SA: 28 rue des Soeurs Noires, 7500 Tournai; tel. (069) 22-41-41; telex 57328; f. 1780; fiction, encyclopaedias, education, periodicals and children's books; Dirs L. R. and J. P. CASTERMAN.

CED-Samsom: 485 ave Louise, 1050 Brussels; tel. (02) 723-11-11; telex 64130; f. 1964; law, social, fiscal, administrative sciences, accountancy, insurance, customs, transport, occupational health and safety; Man. Dir O. CHRISPEELS.

De Clauwaert, VZW: 17 Koning Albertlaan, 3040 Korbeek-Lo; tel. (016) 46-22-29; f. 1948; general fiction, secondary school books; Dir W. VANDEN EYNDE.

Contact, NV: 33 Elsbos, 2520 Edegem; tel. (03) 157-20-24; f. 1946; Dir A. J. H. BINNEWEG.

Culture et Civilisation, SPRL: 115 ave Gabriel Lebon, 1160 Brussels; tel. (02) 734-50-05; f. 1965; Dir J. ADAM.

Davidsfonds, VZW: 79–81 Blijde-Inkomststraat, 3000 Louvain; tel. (016) 22-18-01; f. 1875; Dir N. D'HULST.

Desclée & Cie Editeurs, SA: 13 rue Barthélemy Frison, 7500 Tournai; tel. (069) 22-61-01; telex 57251; f. 1872; liturgical, philosophical, theological, Holy Scripture, Gregorian Chant; publishers to the Holy See and the Sacred Congregation of Rites; Dir A. PAUL.

Desoer NV: 31 En Hors Château, 4000 Liège; tel. (041) 23-11-05; f. 1750; science, medicine, educational materials, arts, mathematics; Dir M. LEMAÎTRE.

H. Dessain, SPRL: 7 rue Trappé, 4000 Liège; tel. (041) 23-78-83; f. 1719; school books; Dir A. MOLS.

Didier Hatier, SA: 18 rue Antoine Labarre, 1050 Brussels; tel. (02) 649-99-45; f. 1979; Dir M. TRÉVINAL.

Die Keure, NV: 108 Oude Gentweg, 8000 Bruges; tel. (050) 33-12-35; f. 1948; Dir J. P. STEEVENS.

Editions Jean Dupuis, SA: 39 rue Destrée, 6001 Marcinelle; tel. (071) 36-40-80; f. 1898; children's books, fiction and periodicals; Dir A. VERHAEGHE.

Editions Labor-Nathan: 156-158 chaussée de Haecht, 1030 Brussels; tel. (02) 216-81-50; telex 25532; f. 1925; general; *L'Ecole 2000* (periodical); Gen. Man. J. FAUCONNIER.

Editions Nauwelaerts/Publications Universitaires de Louvain: 148 Mechelsestraat, 3000 Louvain; tel. (02) 762-98-04; f. 1938; philosophical, theological, historical, legal, scientific, etc.; Dir STÉPHANE ROUGET.

Editions de l'Université de Bruxelles: 26 ave Paul Héger, BP 163, 1050 Brussels; tel. (02) 642-37-99; telex 23069; f. 1972; general scientific works; Dir Mrs MICHÈLE MAT.

Epo, VZW: 25–27 Lange Pastoorstraat, 2600 Berchem; tel. (03) 239-68-74; f. 1974; Dir M. P. DOUMEN.

Etablissements Emile Bruylant: 67 rue de la Régence, 1000 Brussels; tel. (02) 512-98-45; f. 1838; law; Dirs Mme A. VAN SPRENGEL, J. VANDEVELD.

Heideland, NV: 1 Grote Markt, 3500 Hasselt; tel. (011) 22-45-05; telex 39831; f. 1945; Dir L. NAGELS.

Heideland-Orbis: 21–23 Santvoortbeeklaan, 2100 Deurne; tel. (03) 325-68-80; telex 33649; f. 1969; encyclopaedias, dictionaries and general reference books; Dir C. VAN BAELEN.

J. Van In, IUM, NV: 39 Grote Markt, 2500 Lier; tel. (03) 480-55-11; telex 72343; f. 1833; educational and school books; Dir LAURENT WOESTENBURG.

Kluwer Algemene Uitgeverijen België (KAUB): 21-23 Santvoortbeeklaan, 2100 Deurne; tel. (03) 325-68-80; telex 33649; f. 1986; fiction and popular non-fiction, general reference books; Dir C. VAN BAELEN.

Kluwer, NVM & I: 21–23 Santvoortbeeklaan, 2100 Deurne; tel. (03) 324-78-90; telex 33649; f. 1954; Dirs J. WIJNEN, P. STOFFELS, A. MYS, I. BOVEND'AERDE.

Kritak, PVBA: 1 Andreas Vesaliusstraat, 3000 Louvain; tel. (016) 23-12-64; f. 1976; Dir ANDRÉ VAN HALEWYCK.

Lannoo, BVBA: 97 Kasteelstraat, 8880 Tielt; tel. (051) 40-25-51; telex 81555; f. 1909; Board of Mans: 6 mems.

Maison Ferdinand Larcier, SA: 39 rue des Minimes, 1000 Brussels; tel. (02) 512-47-12; f. 1839; legal publications; Dir. J. M. RYCKMANS.

Lloyd Anversois Editions, SA: 23 Eiermarkt, 2000 Antwerp; tel. (03) 234-05-50; telex 31446; f. 1858; transport, economics, insurance, trade annuals, languages; Dir M. R. JAUMOTTE.

Maklu (Maarten Kluwers' Internationale Uitgeversonderneming, NV): 13–15 Somersstraat, 2018 Antwerp; tel. (03) 231-29-00; f. 1972; Dir MAARTEN KLUWER.

Manteau, NV: 12 Beeldhouwersstraat, 2000 Antwerp; tel. (03) 237-17-92; f. 1932; Dir LIONEL DEFLO.

Mercatorfonds: 85 Meir, 2000 Antwerp; tel. (03) 231-38-40; telex 71876; f. 1965; art, ethnography, literature, music, geography and history; Dirs JAN MARTENS, R. DE VOCHT.

De Nederlandsche Boekhandel, NV: 222 Kapelsestraat, 2080 Kapellen; tel. (03) 664-53-20; telex 32242; f. 1893; Dirs J. and R. PELCKMANS.

Patmos Uitgeverij: 222 Kapelsestraat, 2080 Kapellen; tel. (03) 664-53-20; f. 1962; religion, education; Dirs J. and R. PELCKMANS.

Presses de Belgique, SA: 25 rue du Sceptre, 1040 Brussels; tel. (02) 648-80-26; f. 1942; general, philosophy, religion, history, sociology, literature, cinema, science; Man. Dir D. RENAULT.

Reinaert Uitgaven: 22 Forelstraat, 9000 Ghent; tel. (091) 25-57-01; telex 11228; f. 1946; Dir J. VAN HAVERBEKE.

La Renaissance du Livre, SA: 12 place du Petit Sablon, 1000 Brussels; tel. (02) 511-99-14; f. 1923; fiction, history, travel and educational; Admin. Dir ROLAND BOUSSON.

Sciences et Lettres: 11–19 rue de la Commune, 4020 Liège; tel. (041) 42-61-54; f. 1946; general literature; Man. Dir I. SEVERYNS.

De Sikkel: 8 Nijverheidsstraat, 2150 Malle; tel. (03) 312-47-61; telex 34641; f. 1919; education, literature, art, history of art, technical, sciences, sports, school magazines, trade papers and journals; Dir K. DE BOCK.

Soledi (Société Liégeoise d'Editions et d'Imprimerie, SA): 11 rue Saint-Vincent, 4020 Liège; tel. (041) 43-35-37; f. 1935; general and technical; Dir P. MARDAGA.

Het Spectrum, IUM, NV: 12 Bijkhoevelaan, 2110 Wijnegem; tel. (03) 353-98-00; telex 33545; f. 1953; Dir M. CORNU.

Standaard Uitgeverij: 147A Belgiëlei, 2018 Antwerp; tel. (03) 239-59-00; f. 1924; general; Dir A. G. H. A. BAART.

Story-Scientia, NVM & I: 34-35 Jamblinne de Meuxplein, 1040 Brussels; tel. (02) 736-79-10; f. 1960; Dir B. HOUDMONT.

De Tempel Uitgeverij, BVBA: 41 Tempelhof, 8000 Bruges; tel. (050) 31-55-05; f. 1985; educational and scientific; Dir M. J. VERBEKE.

Universitaire Pers Leuven/Leuven University Press: 3 Krakenstraat, 3000 Louvain; tel. (016) 22-04-31; f. 1971.

Vaillant-Carmanne, SA: BP 22, 4000 Liège; tel. (041) 22-33-61; f. 1838; scientific, technical, literary reviews and periodicals; Man. Dir G. DENGIS.

Vander: 321 Vrijwilligerslaan, bus 28, 1150 Brussels; tel. (02) 762-98-04; f. 1880; popular books and literature; Dir WILLY VANDERMEULEN.

C. de Vries-Brouwers, PVBA: 80 Haantjeslei, 2018 Antwerp; tel. (03) 237-41-80; f. 1946; Dir I. DE VRIES.

J. B. Wolters-Leuven, NV: 50 Blijde-Inkomststraat, 3000 Louvain; tel. (016) 23-34-88; telex 24525; f. 1959; education; Dir JACQUES GERMONPREZ.

Zuidnederlandse Uitgeverij, NV: 8 Cleydaellaan, 2630 Aartselaar; tel. (03) 887-83-00; telex 31739; f. 1956; Dir J. VANDE VELDEN.

PUBLISHERS' ASSOCIATIONS

Association des Editeurs Belges (ADEB): 111 ave du Parc, 1060 Brussels; tel. (02) 538-21-67; f. 1922; asscn of French-language book publishers; Pres. CHRISTIAN DE BOECK.

Cercle Belge de la Librairie: 35 rue de la Chasse Royale, 1160 Brussels; tel. (02) 640-52-41; f. 1883; asscn of Belgian booksellers and publishers; 205 mems; Pres. M. DESTREBECQ.

Vereniging van Uitgevers van Nederlandstalige Boeken: 93 Frankrijklei, 2000 Antwerp; tel. (03) 232-46-84; asscn of Dutch-language book publishers; Sec. A. WOUTERS.

Radio and Television

In 1985 there were an estimated 2,971,596 television sets in use and 4,526,291 radio licences.

FRENCH

Radio-Télévision Belge de la Communauté Culturelle Française: 52 blvd Auguste Reyers, 1040 Brussels; tel. (02) 737-21-11; Chair. JEAN HALLET; Admin-Gen. ROBERT STEPHANE; Dir of Radio Programmes PHILIPPE DANSLY; Dir of Television Programmes GEORGES KONEN; Dir of Information Service (Radio and Television) PIERRE DEVOS.

BELGIUM

DUTCH

Belgische Radio en Televisie: Instituut der Nederlandse Uitzendingen, 52 August Reyerslaan, 1040 Brussels; tel. (02) 737-31-11; telex 22486; Chair. ADRIAAN VERHULST; Admin.-Gen. CASIMIR GOOSSENS; Dir of Radio Programmes PIET VAN ROE; Dir of Television Programmes BERT HERMANS; Dir of News Department KAREL HEMMERECHTS; Dir Educational Broadcasting LEA MARTEL; Dir Technical Department MICHEL GEWILLIG.

Finance

(cap. = capital; m. = million; res = reserves;
dep. = deposits; brs = branches; frs = Belgian francs)

BANKING

Commission Bancaire: 99 ave Louise, 1050 Brussels; telex 62107; f. 1935 to supervise the application of the law relating to the legal status of banks and bankers and to the public issue of securities; also the application of the legal status of common trust funds (1957), of certain non-banking financial enterprises (1964), of holding companies (1967) and of the private savings banks (1976); Pres. W. VAN GERVEN; Man. Dirs H. BIRON, P. DUBOIS, G. GELDERS, J. VERTENEUIL.

Central Bank

Banque Nationale de Belgique: 5 blvd de Berlaimont, 1000 Brussels; tel. (02) 219-46-00; telex 21355; f. 1850; bank of issue; cap. 400m. frs; Gov. J. GODEAUX; Exec. Dirs R. BEAUVOIS, G. JANSON, W. FRAEYS, F. JUNIUS, J.-P. PAUWELS; 23 brs.

Development Banks

Gewestelijke Investeringsmaatschappij voor Vlaanderen: 1–3 Anneessensstraat, bus 1, 2000 Antwerp; tel. (03) 233-83-83; telex 34167; f. 1980; promotes creation, restructuring and extension of private enterprises, stimulation of public initiatives, implementation of the industrial policy of state and regions; cap. 2,093m. frs; Pres. R. VAN OUTRYVE D'YDEWALLE; CEO G. VAN ACKER.

Institut de Réescompte et de Garantie (IRG)/Herdiscontering-en Waarborginstituut (HWI): 78 rue du Commerce, 1040 Brussels; tel. (02) 511-73-30; f. 1935; deals with banks, public credit institutions and private savings banks (market-maker in a private discount market; refinancing of medium-term credits; export financing; bail-out operations); cap. and res 2,160.2m. frs; Chair. MARCEL D'HAEZE; Gen. Man. PIERRE NOLS.

Nationale Investeringsmaatschappij (NIM)/Société Nationale d'Investissement (SNI): 63–67 rue Montoyer, 1040 Brussels; tel. (02) 237-06-11; telex 25744; f. 1962; reconstituted in 1976 as a 100% state-owned holding company; cap. 14,000m. Belgian francs; wide cash-raising powers to muster equity capital; private sector representation on governing body and investment committee; Pres. P. WILMES.

Société Régional d'Investissement de Wallonie: 19 place Joséphine-Charlotte, 5100 Jambes; tel. (081) 30-64-11; telex 59415; f. 1979; shareholding company; promotion of creation, restructuring and extension of private enterprises; stimulation of the industrial policy of state and provinces; cap. 3,920m. frs; Pres. BERNARD MARCHAND.

Major State-owned Banks.

Caisse Générale d'Epargne et de Retraite (CGER)/Algemene Spaar-en Lijfrentekas (ASLK): BP 1436, 1000 Brussels; tel. (02) 213-61-11; telex 26860; f. 1865; cap. 34,618m. frs, dep 954.420m. frs; Pres. LUC AERTS; 1,102 brs.

Caisse Nationale de Crédit Professionnel/Nationale Kas voor Beroepskrediet: 16 blvd de Waterloo, 1000 Brussels; tel. (02) 513-64-80; telex 22026; f. 1929; res 1,411m. frs; Gen. Man. D. PONLOT.

Crédit Communal de Belgique/Gemeentekrediet van België: 44 blvd Pachéco, 1000 Brussels; tel. (02) 214-41-11; telex 26354; f. 1860; cap. and res 20,942m. frs; dep. 1,183,779m. frs; Pres. and Man. Dir FRANÇOIS NARMON; 1,412 brs.

Institut National de Crédit Agricole/Nationaal Instituut voor Landbouwkrediet: 56 rue Joseph II, 1040 Brussels; tel. (02) 234-12-11; telex 26863; f. 1937; agricultural credits; credits granted to agricultural associations; financing of agricultural products and foodstuffs; Pres. J. DETRY.

Directory

Société Nationale de Crédit à l'Industrie (SNCI)/Nationale Maatschappij voor Krediet aan de Nijverheid (NMKN): 14 ave de l'Astronomie, 1030 Brussels; tel. (02) 214-12-11; telex 25996; f. 1919; semi-public credit institution; extends long, medium and short term credits to industrial and commercial enterprises; cap. and res 8,065m. frs (Dec. 1985); Gen. Man. K. DIERCKX; 16 brs.

Major Commercial Banks

Algemene Bank Nederland (België) NV: 70/76 Pelikaanstraat, 2018 Antwerp; tel. (03) 222-02-11; telex 31628; f. 1960, name changed 1984; cap. 900m. frs, res 766m. frs, dep. 74,120m. frs (Dec. 1984); Chair. H. J. HIELKEMA; Man. Dirs W. J. KOLFF, M. EENHOORN, H. GOOSSENS.

BACOB SC: 135 Wetstraat, 1040 Brussels; tel. (02) 230-70-90; telex 62199; f. 1924; savings bank; cap. 3,205m. frs, res 4,661m. frs, dep. 233,851m. frs (Dec. 1984); Chair. H. DETREMMERIE; 488 brs.

Banco di Roma (Belgio) SA: 24 rue Joseph II, 1040 Brussels; tel. (02) 219-36-60; telex 21573; f. 1947, name changed 1976; cap. 300m. frs, res 232m. frs, dep. 37,700m. frs (June 1985); Chair. of Exec. Cttee ADHÉMAR D'ALCANTARA; Gen. Man. MANLIO DI MASE; 3 brs.

Bank van Roeselare en West-Vlaanderen NV: 38 Noordstraat, 8800 Roeselare; tel. (051) 23-52-11; telex 81734; f. 1924, name changed 1935 and 1955; cap. and res 1,988m. frs, dep. 33,936m. frs (Dec. 1985); Chair. J. SERCU; 74 brs.

Banque Belge pour l'Etranger SA: 3 rue Montagne du Parc, 1000 Brussels; tel. (02) 511-26-31; f. 1935, name changed 1972; cap. 1,100m. frs, res 119m. frs, dep. 29,653m. frs (Dec. 1984); Chair. HENRI FAYT.

Banque Belgo-Zaïroise SA (Belgolaise): 1 Cantersteen, 1000 Brussels; tel. (02) 518-72-11; telex 21375; f. 1960, name changed 1972; cap. 1,000m. frs, res 1,702m. frs, dep. 27,839 (Dec. 1985); Pres. JACQUES VERDICKT; Man. Dirs MICHEL ISRALSON, CHEVALIER BAUCHAU.

Banque du Benelux SA: 9 Grote Markt, 2000 Antwerp; tel. (03) 232-99-80; telex 31730; f. 1954, name changed 1966; cap. 700m. frs, res 410m. frs, dep. 50,284m. frs (March 1985); Chair. of Exec. Cttee JO HOLVOET; 5 brs.

Banque Bruxelles Lambert SA: 24 ave Marnix, 1050 Brussels; tel. (02) 517-21-11; telex 21421; f. 1975 by merger; cap. and res 23,787m. frs, dep. 1,334,100m. frs (Sept. 1985); Pres. JACQUES THIERRY; 985 brs.

Banque Européenne pour l'Amérique Latine SA: 59 rue de l'Association, 1000 Brussels; tel. (02) 219-00-15; telex 22431; f. 1974; cap. 1,575m. frs, res 927m. frs, dep. 41,494m. frs (Dec. 1985); Chair. XAVIER MALOU; Man. Dir NESTOR RIGA.

Banque Ippa SA: 74 rue de Namur, 1000 Brussels; tel. (03) 234-72-11; telex 33070; f. 1969; cap. 1,250m. frs, res 106m. frs, dep. 34,996m. frs (Dec. 1984); Pres. R. WYCKMANS; Gen. Man. D. DE VEUSSER; 30 brs.

Banque Nagelmackers SA: 18 place de la Cathédrale, 4000 Liège; tel. (041) 20-02-11; telex 41271; f. 1747; cap. 541m. frs, res 336m. frs, dep. 23,363m. frs (Sept. 1985); Exec. Cttee HERVÉ NAGELMACKERS, BAUDOUIN NAGELMACKERS, L.-J. BORSU, ANDRÉ PAQUOT; 60 brs.

Banque Paribas Belgique SA/Paribas Bank België NV: 162 blvd E. Jacqmain, BP 2, 1000 Brussels; tel. (02) 219-30-10; telex 21349; f. 1968; cap. 2,500m. frs, res 2,154m. frs, dep. 177,120m. frs (Dec. 1984); Chair. F. ROBERT VANES; 9 brs.

Centrale Raiffeisenkas CV (CERA)/Centrale des Caisses Rurales: 52 Parijsstraat, 3000 Leuven; tel. (016) 24-49-99; telex 24166; f. 1935; central; organization of co-operative banks; cap. 7,361m. frs, res 9,962m. frs, dep. 301,547m. frs (Dec. 1985); Chair. R. EECKLOO.

Chase Banque de Commerce SA/Chase Handelsbank NV: 9 Lange Gasthuisstraat, 2000 Antwerp; tel. (03) 223-71-11; telex 31232; f. 1893, name changed 1985; cap. 330m. frs, res 739m. frs, dep. 58,444m. frs (Dec. 1984); Chair. ROBERT D. HUNTER; Gen. Man. JOSEPH ROBINET; 13 brs.

Continental Bank SA: 227 rue de la Loi, 1040 Brussels; tel. (02) 230-61-06; telex 21219; f. 1914; total assets 58,913m. frs (Dec. 1985); Man. Dir MICHAEL ALLEN.

Crédit du Nord Belge SA: 32 rue du Fossé-aux-Loups, 1000 Brussels; tel. (02) 217-22-80; telex 21670; f. 1896; cap. 450m. frs, dep. 19,754m. frs (Dec. 1984); Man. Dir, Chair. Exec. Cttee JACQUES BAILET; 24 brs.

Crédit Général SA de Banque: 5 Grand'Place, 1000 Brussels; tel. (02) 516-12-11; telex 64540; f. 1958; cap. 1,400m. frs, res 534m.

487

frs, dep. 70,303m. frs (Dec. 1985); Chair. RICHARD EVERS; Chair. Exec. Cttee MARCEL THIENPONT.

Generale Bank/Générale de Banque: 3 rue Montagne du Parc, 1000 Brussels; tel. (02) 518-21-11; telex 21283; f. 1965 as Société Générale de Banque/Generale Bankmaatschappij, name changed 1985; cap. and res 35,092m. frs, dep. 1,105,497m. frs (Dec. 1985); Chair. JACQUES GROOTHAERT; Chair. Exec. Cttee Comte ERIC DE VILLEGAS DE CLERCAMP; 1,180 brs.

Kredietbank NV: 19 Grote Markt, 1000 Brussels; tel. (02) 517-41-11; telex 21909; f. 1935; cap. and res 21,666m. frs (March 1986); Pres. JAN HUYGHEBAERT; Chair. A. VLERICK.

Lloyds Bank (Belgium) SA: 2 ave de Tervueren, 1040 Brussels; tel. (02) 736-01-00; telex 21244; f. 1953; cap. 153m. frs, res 141m. frs, dep. 20,705m. frs (Dec. 1984); Man. Dir R. L. C. DEMOULIN.

Manufacturers Hanover Bank Belgium SA: 13 rue de Ligne, 1000 Brussels; tel. (02) 217-00-15; telex 22341; f. 1892 as Banque d'Escompte et de Travaux SA, name changed 1972; cap. 340m. frs, dep. 38,522m. frs (Dec. 1984); Pres. JOHN J. SIMONE; Man. Dir BERNARD G. GUERRA.

Mitsui Trust Bank (Europe) SA: 287 ave Louise, BP 5, 1050 Brussels; tel. (02) 640-88-50; telex 64720; f. 1980; cap. 300m. frs, res 318m. frs, dep. 94,724m. frs (Mar. 1985); Chair. MICHIO NOJI; Man. Dir YOSHIO TAKEBAYASHI.

Nippon European Bank SA: 40 blvd du Régent, BP 4, 1000 Brussels; tel. (02) 513-90-20; telex 61393; f. 1976; cap. 400m. frs, res 239m. frs (Mar. 1985); Man. Dir HIROMI YOKOYAMA.

Royal Bank of Canada (Belgium) SA: 1 rue de Ligne, 1000 Brussels; tel. (02) 217-40-40; telex 21780; f. 1934, name changed 1983; cap. 540m. frs, res 499m. frs, dep. 33,145m. frs (Sep. 1985); Chair. A. DE TAKACSY; Man. Dir D. LEPAGE.

Saitama Bank (Europe) SA: 27 ave des Arts, BP 4, 1040 Brussels; tel. (02) 230-81-00; telex 24368; f. 1980; cap. 420m. frs, res 259m. frs, dep. 38,357m. frs (Dec. 1985); Chair. SHIGETAKE IJICHI; Gen. Man. SHIGENOBU GOTO.

Takugin International Bank (Europe) SA: 17 ave Marnix, 1050 Brussels; tel. (02) 512-67-53; telex 23568; f. 1981; cap. 300m. frs, res 231m. frs, dep. 40,982m. frs (Mar. 1985); Chair. KAICHI KAWAGUCHI; Man. Dir KAZUO SANO.

Banking Associations

Association Belge des Banques/Belgische Vereniging der Banken: 36 rue Ravenstein, BP 5, 1000 Brussels; tel. (02) 512-58-68; telex 25575; f. 1936; represents only privately-owned banks; 83 mems; Pres. LÉO GOLDSCHMIDT; Dir-Gen. MICHEL DE SMET.

Association des Caisses d'Epargne Privées (Private Savings Banks): 13/14 ave des Arts, BP 1, 1040 Brussels; tel. (02) 219-43-14; telex 63186; f. 1961; Pres. H. VAN THILLO; Sec.-Gen. C. DE NOOSE.

STOCK EXCHANGE

Commission de la Bourse de Bruxelles (Stock Exchange): Palais de la Bourse, Place de la Bourse, Brussels; tel. (02) 512-51-10; telex 21374; Pres. JEAN REYERS; Sec. JACQUES LELEUX.

INSURANCE COMPANIES

Abeille-Paix, Société Anonyme Belge d'Assurances: 80 rue de la Loi, 1000 Brussels; fire, accident, general; Chair. M. M. MARCHAL; Gen. Man. M. P. MEYERSON.

Abeille-Paix Vie, Société Anonyme Belge d'Assurances: 80 rue de la Loi, 1000 Brussels; life; Chair. M. PH. DE MONPLANET; Gen. Man. M. P. MEYERSON.

Antwerpse Verzekeringsmaatschappij 'Securitas' NV: 214 Grote Steenweg, 2600 Berchem; tel. (03) 218-31-11; telex 33849; f. 1819; fire, accident, life; Chair. J. DE BROUX; Man. Dir M. LIPPENS; Gen. Man. V. CROES.

Aviabel, Compagnie Belge d'Assurances Aviation, SA: 10 ave Brugmann, 1060 Brussels; tel. (02) 345-38-40; telex 21928; f. 1935; aviation, insurance, reinsurance; Chair. G. CAMBRON; Man. J. VERWILGHEN.

AG de 1824—Compagnie Belge d'Assurances Générales 'Vie': 53 blvd Emile Jacqmain, 1000 Brussels; f. 1969; life, pensions, loans; Chair. J. DE BROUX; Gen. Man. V. CROES.

AG de 1830—Compagnie Belge d'Assurances Générales 'Incendie, Accidents et Risques Divers': 53 blvd Emile Jacqmain, 1000 Brussels; tel. (02) 214-81-11; telex 22766; f. 1830; fire insurance and consequential loss, accident, general, burglary; Chair. J. DE BROUX; Gen. Man. V. CROES.

Belgamar, Compagnie Belge d'Assurances Maritimes SA: 54 St-Katelijnevest, Bus 39/40, 2000 Antwerp; tel. (03) 231-56-62; telex 33411; f. 1945; marine reinsurance; Chair. P. VAN DER MEERSCH; Dir-Man. A. THIÈRY.

La Belgique, Compagnie d'Assurances SA: 61 rue de la Régence, 1000 Brussels; tel. (02) 511-38-40; telex 63869; f. 1855; cap. 400m. frs; Chair. HERVÉ NAGELMACKERS; Gen. Man. P. ROUSSELLE.

Compagnie d'Assurance de l'Escaut: 10 rue de la Bourse, Antwerp; f. 1821; fire, accident, life, burglary, reinsurance; Man E. DIERCXSENS.

Compagnie Belge d'Assurance-Crédit SA (COBAC): 15 rue Montoyer, 1040 Brussels; tel. (02) 513-89-30; telex 22337; f. 1929; Chair. R. LAMY; Man. Dir A. STAS DE RICHELLE.

Compagnie Financière et de Réassurances du Groupe AG: 53 blvd Emile Jacqmain, 1000 Brussels; f. 1824; all forms of reinsurance world-wide; Chair. J. DE BROUX; Gen. Man. V. CROES.

Generali Belgium SA: 149 ave Louise, 1050 Brussels; tel. (02) 536-72-11; telex 21772; fire, accident, marine, life, reinsurance; Pres. Baron LAMBERT; Dir-Gen. C. DENDAL.

Groupe Eagle-Star-Compagnie de Bruxelles 1821 SA d'Assurances: 62 rue de la Loi, 1040 Brussels; tel. (02) 237-12-11; telex 24443; f. 1821; fire, life, general; Pres. A. R. N. RATCLIFF; Gen. Man. JEAN BUISSERET.

Groupe Josi Compagnie Centrale d'Assurances 1909 SA: 11 rue des Colonies, 1000 Brussels; tel. (02) 515-12-11; telex 21463; f. 1909; accident, fire, marine, general; Pres. and Dir-Gen. J. P. LAURENT JOSI.

Lloyd Belge: 94 rue Royale, 1000 Brussels; f. 1854; fire, accident, life, reinsurance.

Les Patrons Réunis SA: 60 Chaussée de Charleroi, 1060 Brussels; tel. (02) 537-30-50; telex 64654; f. 1887; fire, life, accident; Chair. F. CASSE; Gen. Man. R. NICOLAS.

Royale Belge: 25 blvd Souverain, 1170 Brussels; tel. (02) 661-61-11; telex 23000; f. 1853; life, accident, fire, theft, reinsurance, and all other risks; Dirs P. VAN DER MEERSCH, Baron H. CAPPUYNS, M. GOBLET, Baron F. VAN DEN BERGH, Y. BOËL, J. DELORI, G. ESKÉNAZI, P. GARNY.

Société Mutuelle des Administrations Publiques: 24 rue des Croisiers, 4000 Liège; institutions, civil service employees, public administration and enterprises.

Urbaine UAP Compagnie Belge d'Assurances et de Réassurances SA: 32 rue Belliard, 1040 Brussels; tel. (02) 230-10-01; telex 62060; f. 1900; all risks; Chair. Baron R. TERLINDEN; Man. Dir R. CORNEMILLOT.

Utrecht Risques Divers: 13 rue de la Loi, 1000 Brussels; tel. (02) 512-00-58; telex 61069; f. 1948; Dirs R. WEBER, M. LACROIX.

Insurance Associations

Association des Caisses Communes d'Assurance: 5 rue de Loxum, BP 2, 1000 Brussels; Pres. R. CHARLES; Admin Dir Y. WILLEMART.

Fédération des Producteurs d'Assurances de Belgique: 40 ave Albert Elisabeth, 1200 Brussels; tel (02) 733-35-22; f. 1934; 900 mems; Pres. HENRY VAN DUYNEN; Dir JEAN SCHOUTERDEN.

Union Professionnelle des Entreprises d'Assurances Belges et Etrangères Opérant en Belgique—Beroepsvereniging der Belgische en Buitenlandse Verzekeringsondernemingen: 29 square de Meeûs, 1040 Brussels; telex 63652; f. 1921; 181 mems; affiliated to Fédération des Entreprises de Belgique; Pres. JOHN VAN WATERSCHOOT; Dir JULES DOHET.

Trade and Industry

PRINCIPAL CHAMBERS OF COMMERCE

There are chambers of commerce and industry in all major towns and industrial areas.

Kamer van Koophandel en Nijverheid van Antwerpen: 12 Markgravestraat, 2000 Antwerp; tel. (03) 232-22-19; telex 71536; f. 1969; Gen. Man. M. VERBOVEN.

Chambre de Commerce de Bruxelles: 500 ave Louise, 1050 Brussels; tel. (02) 648-50-02; telex 22082; f. 1875.

TRADE AND INDUSTRIAL ASSOCIATIONS

Fédération des Entreprises de Belgique (Belgian Business Federation): 4 rue Ravenstein, 1000 Brussels; tel. (02) 511-58-80; telex 26576; f. 1895; federates all the main industrial and non-

BELGIUM
Directory

industrial associations; Pres. ANDRÉ LEYSEN; Man. Dir RAYMOND PULINCKX.

Association Belge des Entreprises d'Alimentation à Succursales (ABEAS) (Food Chain Stores): 60 rue St Bernard, 1060 Brussels; tel. (02) 537-30-60; f. 1941; Pres. GUY BECKERS; Dir-Gen. ALPHONSE DE VADDER.

Association des Centrales Electriques Industrielles de Belgique (Industrial Electricity): 36 rue Joseph II, 1040 Brussels; f. 1922; Pres. PAUL RENDERS; Admin MARCEL DE LEENER; Man. MAURICE DE BECKER.

Association des Exploitants de Carrières de Porphyre (Porphyry): 64 rue de Belle-Vue, 1050 Brussels; f. 1967; Pres. LÉON JACQUES; Dir GEORGES HANSEN.

Association des Fabricants de Pâtes, Papiers et Cartons de Belgique (COBELPA) (Paper): 14 rue de Crayer, 1050 Brussels; tel. (02) 649-61-60; telex 22713; f. 1940; co-operative asscn; Pres. BERNARD ANCION; Dir ALFRED ROSE.

Association des Grandes Entreprises de Distribution de Belgique (AGED) (Large Distributing Concerns): 3 rue de la Science, 1040 Brussels; f. 1946; 55 mems; Pres. Baron FRANÇOIS VAXELAIRE; Dir-Gen. FRANCIS BUCHET.

Association des Industries des Carrières (AIC) (Federations of Quarrying Industries): 64 rue de Belle-Vue, 1050 Brussels; f. 1975; Pres. PHILIPPE NOTTE; Sec.-Gen. G. HANSEN.

Confédération des Brasseries de Belgique (Breweries): Maison des Brasseurs, 10 Grand' Place, 1000 Brussels; tel. (02) 512-26-96; f. 1971; Pres. ROGER VAN DER SCHUEREN; Dir MICHEL BRICHET.

Confédération Nationale de la Construction (CNC) (Civil Engineering, Road and Building Contractors and Auxiliary Trades): 34–42 rue du Lombard, 1000 Brussels; tel. (02) 513-65-32; telex 64956; f. 1946; 15,000 mems; Pres. ROBERT MATAGNE; Admin. Dir FREDDY FEYS, Man. Dir EDWIN JACOBS.

Confédération Professionnelle du Sucre et de ses dérivés (Sugar): 182 ave de Tervueren, 1150 Brussels; f. 1938; mems 10 groups, 66 firms; Pres. ARMAND MAISIN; Dir-Gen. ALAIN JOLLY.

Fédération Belge de l'Industrie de la Chaussure (FEBIC) (Footwear): 53 rue Fr. Bossaerts, 1030 Brussels; tel. (02) 735-27-01; telex 65625; f. 1968; Pres. R. SMETS.

Fédération Belge des Dragueurs de Gravier et de Sable (BELBAG-DRAGBEL) (Dredging): 1 quai des Péniches, 1020 Brussels; f. 1967; Pres. A. DEGRAIDE.

Fédération Belge des Entreprises de Distribution (FEDIS): 60 rue St-Bernard, 1060 Brussels; tel. (02) 537-30-60; telex 63201; Pres. J. BATTARD; Dir-Gens. J. DEGRAVE, H. DE VADDER.

Fédération Belge des Entreprises de la Transformation du Bois (FEBELBOIS) (Wood): Maison du Bois, 109–111 rue Royale, 1000 Brussels; tel. (02) 217-63-65; telex 64143; Man. Dir WILLY DE VYNCK.

Fédération Belge des Industries Graphiques (FEBELGRA) (Graphic Industries): 20 rue Belliard, BP 16, 1040 Brussels; tel. (02) 512-36-38; telex 26854; f. 1978; 1,400 mems; Pres. POL VERWAEST; Sec.-Gen. JOS ROSSIE.

Fédération Belge des Industries de l'Habillement (Clothing and Outfitting): 24 rue Montoyer, BP 11, 1040 Brussels; tel. (02) 230-88-90; telex 61055; f. 1946; Pres. A. DELFOSSE; Dir J. DÉCAT.

Fédération Belge du Commerce Alimentaire (FEBECA) (Foodstuffs Trade): 60 rue St-Bernard, 1060 Brussels; tel. (02) 537-30-60; telex 63201; f. 1941; Pres. GEORGES DE MEYERE; Dir-Gen. J. DEGRAVE.

Fédération Belgo-Luxembourgeoise des Industries du Tabac (FEDETAB) (Tobacco): 270–272 ave de Tervueren, BP 20, 1150 Brussels; tel. (02) 762-57-20; telex 64888; f. 1947; Pres. P. CATTELAIN; Sec.-Gen. R. DEJONGHE.

Fédération Charbonnière de Belgique (Coal): 21–22 ave des Arts, 1040 Brussels; f. 1909; Pres. PIERRE URBAIN; Dir GUY VAN BRUYSTEGEM.

Fédération de l'Industrie Cimentière (Cement): 46 rue César Franck, 1050 Brussels; tel. (02) 649-98-50; telex 21431; f. 1949; Pres. JULIEN VAN HOVE; Dir-Gen. J. P. LATTEUR.

Fédération de l'Industrie du Béton (FeBe) (Precast Concrete): 207–209 blvd August Reyers, 1040 Brussels; tel. (02) 735-80-15; f. 1936; Pres. J. SCHMIDT; Dir W. SIMONS.

Fédération de l'Industrie du Gaz (FIGAZ) (Gas): 4 ave Palmerston, 1040 Brussels; tel. (02) 230-43-85; Pres. R. G. HAVAUX; Sec.-Gen. L. BLOM.

Fédération de l'Industrie du Verre (Glass): 47 rue Montoyer, 1040 Brussels; tel. (02) 513-38-20; telex 21287; f. 1947; Pres. BERNARD NOVEL; Dir P. VAN DE PUTTE.

Fédération de l'Industrie Textile Belge (FEBELTEX) (Textiles): 24 rue Montoyer, 1040 Brussels; tel. (02) 230-93-30; telex 20183; f. 1945; 1,800 mems; Pres. ETIENNE VAN DEN BOOGAERDE; Dir-Gen. PIERRE JANSSENS.

Fédération des Carrières de Grès (Sandstone): 73 rue Franz Merjay, 1060 Brussels; f. 1947; Pres. PIERRE-ETIENNE DAPSENS; Sec. ELAINE MEERT.

Fédération des Carrières de Petit Granit (Granite): BP 3, 7400 Soignies; tel. (067) 33-41-21; telex 57444; f. 1948; Pres. JEAN-FRANZ ABRAHAM.

Fédération des Entreprises de l'Industrie des Fabrications Métalliques, Mécaniques, Electriques et de la Transformation des Matières Plastiques (FABRIMETAL) (Metalwork, Engineering, Electrics and Plastic Processing): 21 rue des Drapiers, 1050 Brussels; tel. (02) 511-23-70; telex 21078; f. 1946; Pres. EUGÈNE A. VAN DYCK; Dirs Gen. JACQUES DE STAERCKE, CLAUDE CARBONELLE, LODEWIJK COOSEMANS.

Fédération des Entreprises de Métaux non Ferreux (Nonferrous Metals): 47 rue Montoyer, 1040 Brussels; tel. (02) 513-86-34; telex 22077; f. 1918; 40 mems; Pres. JEAN ANDRÉ; Dirs STEFAN DOUKHOPELNIKOFF; CH. PIRLOT DE CORBION.

Fédération des Industries Agricoles et Alimentaires-Verbond der Landbouw en Voedingsnijverheid (Food and Agricultural Industries): 172 Kortenberglaan, bus 7, 1040 Brussels; f. 1937; Pres. P. CALLEBAUT; Dir-Gen. P. VERHAEGHE.

Fédération des Industries Céramiques de Belgique et du Luxembourg (FEDICER) (Ceramics): 4 ave Gouverneur Cornez, 7000 Mons; tel. (065) 34-80-00; telex 57865; f. 1919; Pres. C. BIENVENU; Dir P. DE BRUYCKER.

Fédération des Industries Chimiques de Belgique (Chemical Industries): 49 square Marie-Louise, 1040 Brussels; tel. (02) 230-40-90; telex 23167; f. 1919; Pres. PAUL WASHER; Man. Dir PAUL F. SMETS.

Fédération des Industries Transformatrices de Papier et Carton (FETRA) (Paper and Cardboard): 715 chaussée de Waterloo, BP 25, 1180 Brussels; telex 23442; f. 1947; 300 mems; Pres. PH. DE SONER; Dir PH. DELLA FAILLE DE LEVERGHEM.

Fédération Nationale Belge de la Fourrure et de la Peau en Poil (Furs and Skins): 4 rue de l'Autonomie, BP 4, 1070 Brussels; tel. (02) 521-79-35; f. 1947; Pres. J. ASCAREZ; Dir R. MICHIELS.

Fédération Patronale des Ports Belges (Port Employers): 33 Brouwersvliet, bus 7, 2000 Antwerp; tel. (03) 232-19-27; f. 1937; Pres. KAREL NOENINCKX; Secs WALTER BAGUE, FRANS GIELEN.

Fédération Pétrolière Belge (Petroleum): 4 rue de la Science, 1040 Brussels; tel. (02) 512-30-03; telex 26930; f. 1926; Pres. GEORGES DE GRAEVE; Man. Dir A. VERSCHUEREN.

Groupement National de l'Industrie de la Terre Cuite (Heavy Clay): 13 rue des Poissonniers, BP 22, 1000 Brussels; f. 1947; Pres. LUC JANSEN; Dir GIOVANNI PEIRS.

Groupement Patronal des Bureaux Commerciaux et Maritimes (Employers' Association of Trade and Shipping Offices): 33 Brouwersvliet, bus 7, 2000 Antwerp; tel. (03) 232-19-27; f. 1937; Pres. KAREL NOENINCKX; Sec. FRANS GIELEN.

Groupement de la Sidérurgie, ASBL (Iron and Steel): 47 rue Montoyer, 1040 Brussels; tel. (02) 513-38-20; telex 21287; f. 1982; Pres. and Dir-Gen. CHRISTIAN OURY.

Groupement des Sablières (Sand and Gravel): 49 Quellinstraat, 2018 Antwerp; tel. (03) 223-66-83; f. 1937; Pres. A. EVERARTS DE VELP; Vice-Pres ALFRED PAULUS; Sec. PAUL DE NIE.

Industrie des Huiles Minérales de Belgique (IHMB) (Mineral Oils): 49 square Marie-Louise, 1040 Brussels; tel. (02) 230-40-90; telex 23167; f. 1921; 90 mems; Pres. R. VANSLATTE; Sec. M. DONCKERWOLCKE.

Union de la Tannerie et de la Mégisserie Belges (UNITAN) (Tanning and Tawing): 11 rue d'Angleterre, 1060 Brussels; f. 1962; 13 mems; Pres. W. COLLE; Sec. Mlle D. JANUS.

Union des Armateurs Belges (Shipowners): 9 Lijnwaadmarkt, 2000 Antwerp; Chair. J. SAVERYS; Man. A. VAN MIEGHEM.

Union des Carrières et Scieries de Marbres de Belgique (UCSMB) (Marble): 40 rue Bosquet, 1060 Brussels; tel. (02) 538-46-61; telex 24235; Pres. J. VAN DEN WILDENBERG; Vice-Pres. P. STONE.

BELGIUM

Union des Exploitations Electriques en Belgique (UEEB) (Electricity): 4 galerie Ravenstein, BP 6, 1000 Brussels; tel. (02) 511-19-70; telex 62409; f. 1911; Gen. Dir E. R. MARICQ.

Union des Producteurs Belges de Chaux, Calcaires, Dolomies, et produits connexes (UCCD) (Lime, limestone, dolomite and related products): 61 rue du Trône, 1050 Brussels; f. 1942; co-operative society; Co-Pres. GUY CUVELIER, CHARLES MOREAU DE MELEN; Dir EMILE WOUTERS.

Union Professionnelle des Producteurs de Fibres-Ciment (Asbestos-Cement): World Trade Centre, 162 blvd Emile Jacqmain, BP 37, 1210 Brussels; tel. (02) 219-29-80; telex 21696; f. 1941; Pres. ETIENNE VAN DER REST; Sec. PAUL VAN REETH.

TRADE UNIONS AND PROFESSIONAL ORGANIZATIONS

Fédération Générale du Travail de Belgique (FGTB)/Algemeen Belgisch Vakverbond: 42 rue Haute, 1000 Brussels; tel. (02) 511-64-66; telex 24620; f. 1899; affiliated to ICFTU; Pres. ANDRÉ VANDEN BROUCKE; has 15 affiliated unions with a total effective membership of 1,124,072 (Dec. 1982). Affiliated unions include:

De Algemene Centrale/La Centrale Générale (Central Union): 26–28 rue Haute, 1000 Brussels; tel. (02) 513-06-25; telex 62559; Pres. JUAN FERNANDEZ; Sec.-Gen. HENRI LORENT; Nat. Secs EDDY SCHELSTRAETE, MICHEL NOLLET, ALFONS VAN NOOTEN; 260,000 mems.

Algemene Diamantbewerkersbond van België (Diamond Workers): 57 Lange Kievitstraat, bus 1, 2018 Antwerp; tel. (03) 232-48-60; f. 1896; Pres. C. DENISSE; 4,031 mems (1981).

Belgische Transportarbeidersbond (Belgian Transport Workers): 66 Paardenmarkt, 2000 Antwerp: tel. (03) 231-18-40; telex 73080; f. 1913; Pres. EGIED BAUDET; 23,000 mems (1983).

Centrale de l'Industrie du Livre et du Papier (Graphical and Paper Workers): galerie du Centre, Bloc 2, 17 rue des Fripiers, 1000 Brussels; tel. (02) 511-09-66; f. 1945; Secs ROGER DEMEYER, ROBERT LELOUP, ROGER SAGON; 12,127 mems (1985).

Centrale der Kleding en aanverwante vakken van België (Clothing Workers): 32 Ommeganckstraat, 2018 Antwerp; tel. (03) 233-56-72; f. 1898; Gen. Sec. FIRMIN VAN DE CALSEYDE; 31,081 mems (1980).

Centrale des Métallurgistes de Belgique (Metal Workers): 17 rue Jacques Jordaens, 1050 Brussels; tel. (02) 647-83-14; f. 1887; Sec.-Gen. GERMAIN DUHIN; 211,289 mems (1980).

Centrale des Travailleurs de l'Alimentation et de l'Hôtellerie (Catering and Hotel Workers): 18 rue des Alexiens, 1000 Brussels; tel. (02) 512-97-00; f. 1912; Pres. ARTHUR LADRILLE; Nat. Sec. EDOUARD PEPERMANS; 53,226 mems (1983).

Centrale Générale des Services Publics (Public Service Workers): Maison des Huit Heures, 9–11 Place Fontainas, 1000 Brussels; tel. (02) 539-39-60; telex 22563; f. 1945; Pres. R. PITON; 308,235 mems (1983).

Nationale Centrale der Mijnwerkers van België (Miners): 8 J. Stevensstraat, bus 4, 1000 Brussels; tel. (02) 511-96-45; f. 1889; Pres. J. OLYSLAEGERS; 19,560 mems (1985).

Syndicat des Employés, Techniciens et Cadres de Belgique (Employees, Technicians and Administrative Workers): 42 rue Haute, 1000 Brussels; tel. (02) 513-18-91; f. 1891; Pres. FRANÇOIS JANSSENS; 180,000 mems (1983).

Textielarbeiderscentrale van België (Textile Workers): 143 Opvoedingsstraat, 9000 Ghent; tel. (091) 21-75-11; f. 1898; Nat. Pres. JAN MONSEREZ; Nat. Sec. XAVIER VERBOVEN; 41,294 mems (1982).

Confédération des Syndicats Chrétiens (CSC): 121 rue de la Loi, 1040 Brussels; tel. (02) 233-34-11; telex 61770; Leader JEF HOUTHUYS. Affiliated unions:

Centrale Chrétienne de l'Alimentation et des Services (Food and Service Industries): 27 rue de l'Association, 1000 Brussels; f. 1919; Pres. W. VIJVERMAN; Sec.-Gen. F. BOCKLANDT; 111,049 mems (1982).

Centrale Chrétienne des Industries Graphiques et du Papier (Paper Workers): 26 ave d'Auderghem, 1040 Brussels; Pres. M. VAN ONSEM; 21,712 mems (1976).

Centrale Chrétienne des Métallurgistes de Belgique (Metal Workers): 127 rue de Heembeek, 1120 Brussels; tel. (02) 215-88-40; Pres. J. PHILIPSEN; 242,000 mems.

Centrale Chrétienne des Travailleurs de la Pierre, du Ciment, de la Céramique et du Verre (Stone, Cement, Ceramic and Glass Workers): 26–32 ave d'Auderghem, 1040 Brussels; tel. (02) 231-00-90; Pres. A. DE DECKER; 26,000 mems (1981).

Centrale Chrétienne des Ouvriers des Industries de l'Energie, de la Chimie, du Cuir et Diverses (Power, Chemical, Leather, etc., Workers); 26-32 ave d'Auderghem, 1040 Brussels; tel. 021-231-00-90; f. 1912; Pres. A. VAN GENECHTEN; Nat. Sec. J. VAN HOOF; Gen. Sec. M. SOMMEREYNS; 52,219 mems. (1979).

Centrale Chrétienne des Ouvriers du Textile et du Vêtement de Belgique (Textile and Clothing Workers): 27 Koning Albertlaan, 9000 Ghent; Pres. L. FRURU; 130,497 mems (1976).

Centrale Chrétienne des Services Publics—Christelijke Centrale van de Openbare Diensten (Public Service Workers): 26 ave d'Auderghem, 1040 Brussels; tel. (02) 231-00-90; f. 1921; Pres. F. WIEERS; Sec.-Gen. G. RASNEUR; 93,000 mems (1976).

Centrale Chrétienne des Travailleurs du Bois et du Bâtiment (Wood and Building Workers): 31 rue de Trèves, 1040 Brussels; Pres. R. MARIS; 100,000 mems (1984).

Centrale Chrétienne du Personnel de l'Enseignement Moyen et Normal Libre (Lay Teachers in Secondary and Teacher-Training Institutions): 26–32 ave d'Auderghem, 1040 Brussels; tel. (02) 231-00-90; f. 1950; Pres. ROGER DENIS; 16,000 mems (1984).

Centrale Chrétienne du Personnel de l'Enseignement Technique (Teachers in Technical Education): 26 ave d'Auderghem, 1040 Brussels; Pres. J. P. VAN DEN BERGHE; Sec.-Gen. W. KIEKENS; 33,000 mems (1982).

Centrale des Francs Mineurs (Miners' Union): 26 ave d'Auderghem, 1040 Brussels; Pres. A. DAEMEN; 31,725 mems (1976).

Centrale Nationale des Employés/Landelijke Bedienden Centrale (Employees): 107 rue de Brabant, 1030 Brussels; f. 1912; Sec.-Gen. JOSÉ ROISIN; 240,000 mems (1979).

Fédération des Instituteurs Chrétiens de Belgique/Christen Onderwijzersverbond van België (School Teachers): 203 Koningsstraat, 1210 Brussels; tel. (02) 217-40-50; f. 1893; Pres. G. BOURDEAUD'HUI; Sec.-Gen. L. VAN BENEDEN; 50,194 mems (1985).

Syndicat Chrétien des Communications et de la Culture (Christian Trade Unions of Railway, Post and Telecommunications, Shipping, Civil Aviation, Radio, TV and Cultural Workers): 26 ave d'Auderghem, 1040 Brussels; tel. (02) 231-00-90; f. 1919; Pres. H. VANTRAPPEN; Secs F. DE GRAVE, E. JANS, R. FRIPPIAT, W. THYS, P. VAN DEN DOOREN, E. VAN ELSACKER; 60,000 mems (1985).

Cartel des Syndicats Indépendants de Belgique: 36 blvd Bischoffsheim, Brussels; Pres. (public sector) EDMOND SMESMAN; Gen. Secs M. VANHAMME, JOS BOLLAERTS.

Centrale Générale des Syndicats Libéraux de Belgique (CGSLB) (General Federation of Liberal Trade Unions of Belgium): 95 blvd Albert, 9000 Ghent; tel. (091) 22-57-51; telex 12582; f. 1889; National Pres. ARMAND COLLE.

Syndicat Libre de la Fonction Publique (Public Services' Union): 25 rue de Spa, 1000 Brussels; Pres. FRANS MIEVIS; Gen. Sec. GUY DE WITTE.

Fédération Nationale des Unions Professionnelles Agricoles de Belgique: 94–96 rue Antoine Dansaert, 1000 Brussels; f. 1919; Pres. L. ERNOUX; Sec.-Gen. EMILE SCOUMANNE.

TRADE FAIRS

Foire Internationale de Bruxelles (Brussels International Trade Fair): Parc des Expositions, 1020 Brussels; tel. (02) 478-48-60; telex 23643; f. 1919; holds more than 25 fairs and trade shows each year, as well as 60 congresses and technical exhibitions; Gen. Man. J. ISAAC CASTIAU.

International Fair of Flanders: ICC Floraliapaleis, 9000 Ghent; tel. (091) 22-40-22; telex 12666; f. 1946; holds several fairs annually.

Transport

RAILWAYS

The Belgian railway network is one of the densest in the world. The main lines are operated by the SNCB under lease from the State Railways Administration and the system is complemented by the SNCV light railway network for local traffic. Five regional companies run trams, rapid transit systems and metros.

BELGIUM

Société Nationale des Chemins de Fer Belges (SNCB)/ Nationale Maatschappij der Belgische Spoorwegen (NMBS): 85 rue de France, 1070 Brussels; tel. (02) 523-62-40; f. 1926; 149.9m. passengers were carried in 1984; directed by a board of 21 members; 3,741 km of lines, of which 1,907 km are electrified; Gen. Man. M. E. Flachet.

ROADS

At 31 December 1985 there were 1,456 km of motorways, 12,587 km of other main or national roads and 13,850 km of secondary or regional roads. In addition, there are about 100,000 km of minor roads.

Société Nationale des Chemins de Fer Vicinaux (SNCV) (Light railways, buses and trams): 14 rue de la Science, 1040 Brussels; f. 1884; operates all public bus and tram services; Pres. R. Denison; Dir-Gen. Constant Henrard.

INLAND WATERWAYS

There are over 1,500 km of inland waterways in Belgium, of which 657 km are navigable rivers and 860 km are canals. In 1982 an estimated 91,222,000 metric tons of cargo were carried on the inland waterways. Under the Investment Plan started in 1957 canals and rivers have been modified to accommodate more traffic.

Ministerie van Openbare Werken: Bestuur der Waterwegen, Residence Palace, Wetstraat 155, 1040 Brussels; tel. (02) 733-96-70; telex 63477; Dir-Gen. Ir. J. Demoen.

SHIPPING

The modernized port of Antwerp is the second biggest in Europe and handles 80% of Belgian foreign trade by sea and inland waterways. It is also the largest railway port and has one of the largest petroleum refining complexes in Europe. It has 98 km of quayside and 17 dry docks, and is currently accessible to vessels of up to 75,000 tons; extensions are being carried out which will increase this limit to 125,000 tons. The port receives some 19,000 vessels and handles more than 70 million tons of cargo a year. Other ports include Zeebrugge, Ostend, Ghent, Liège and Brussels.

Régie Belge des Transports Maritimes (Belgian Maritime Transport Authority): 30 rue Belliard, 1040 Brussels; tel. (02) 230-01-80; telex 23851; Gen. Man. P. Muyldermans; Ostend–Dover lines; 1 passenger vessel, 2 jetfoils and 6 multi-purpose vessels.

De Keyser Thornton: 38 Huidevettersstraat, 2000 Antwerp; tel. (03) 233-01-05; telex 72511; liner and ship agents, forwarders and warehousemen; f. 1853; Man. Dir M. P. Ingham.

Ahlers Lines NV: 139 Noorderlaan, 2030 Antwerp; tel. (03) 543-72-11; telex 72154; services to Finland, Sweden, USSR, Norway; Dirs H. Coppieters, J. Gelens, H. Knoche.

Belfranline NV: 24–29 Meir, 2000 Antwerp; tel. (03) 234-84-11; telex 34115; f. 1957; liner services to Venezuela, Dominican Republic, Haiti, Curaçao and Jamaica; also to Central America (East Coast); Pres. J. E. Sasse; Man. Dir E. J. Sasse.

CMB SA/NV: 61 St Katelijnevest, 2000 Antwerp; tel. (03) 223-21-11; telex 72304; f. 1895, formerly known as Compagnie Maritime Belge (Lloyd Royal) SA, merged with Methania SA/NV in 1985; European service and lines to North and South America, Africa, Middle East, Indian sub-continent and Far East; Chair. and Man. Dir P. Pluys; 30 vessels for freight (conventional, container, bulk) and passengers.

ESSO Belgium SA/NV: 101 Frankrijklei, 2000 Antwerp; tel. (03) 231-96-00; telex 31144; tanker service, refining/marketing; Pres. R. Dahan; Vice-Pres. D. A. Schram.

North Sea Ferries (Belgium) NV: Leopold II Dam (Havendam), 8380 Zeebrugge; tel. (050) 54-34-11; telex 81469; operated in conjunction with North Sea Ferries Ltd, UK; roll-on/roll-off ferry services between Hull and Zeebrugge; Dirs M. Storme, G. D. S. Dunlop, M. Van Leeuwen.

Northern Shipping Service NV: Eiermarkt Building, 54 St Katelijnevest, 2000 Antwerp; tel. (03) 233-99-85; telex 32315; ship brokers and agents, regular lines, stevedoring and warehousing; Pres. L. M. Heintz.

Petrofina SA: 52 rue de l'Industrie, 1040 Brussels; tel. (02) 233-91-11; telex 21556; oil company with tanker service for exploration, production, transport, refining and marketing/distribution of oil, gas and petrochemicals; Chair. and Chief Exec. Jean-Pierre Amory.

Société Belge de Navigation Maritime/Navibel SA: Eiermarkt Building, 54 St Katelijnevest, 2000 Antwerp; tel. (03) 233-99-85; telex 32315; tramp, European, Mediterranean and North West African cargo services; Pres. R. de Vlaminck.

Ubem NV/SA: 150 Mechelse Steenweg, 2018 Antwerp; tel. (03) 237-29-50; telex 32515; bulk carriers and car ferry services; Man. Dir E. de Laet.

CIVIL AVIATION

The main international airport is at Brussels, with a direct train service from the air terminal. There are also international airports at Antwerp, Liège, Charleroi and Ostend.

SABENA (Société anonyme belge d'exploitation de la navigation aérienne) (Belgian World Air Lines): Air Terminal, 35 rue Cardinal Mercier, 1000 Brussels; tel. (02) 511-90-60; telex 21322; f. 1923; 54% state-owned; Chair. Carlos Van Rafelghem; Vice-Chair. André Pahaut; fleet of 3 Boeing 747, 15 Boeing 737, 2 Airbus A310, 5 DC-10-30 CF, 6 Cessna, 9 SF-260, 5 EMB 121 Xingu; services to most parts of the world.

BIAS Overseas NV: Antwerp Airport, B 14, 2100 Deurne; tel. (03) 230-29-65; telex 31557; f. 1968; wet or dry leasing services; Chair. R. J. M. Lucas; Man. Dir P. W. Bakker; 2 Fokker F 27.

Delta Air Transport NV: Antwerp Airport, 2100 Deurne; tel. (03) 239-58-35; telex 32602; f. 1966; Antwerp and Brussels to Amsterdam–Frankfurt–Paris (CD6)–Stuttgart, and charter service in Europe; Pres. C. van Rafelghem; Gen. Man. Tony Vangrieken; 5 FH227B.

Sobelair (Société Belge de Transports par Air) NV: 131 ave Frans Courtens, 1030 Brussels; tel. (02) 216-21-75; telex 22095; f. 1946; subsidiary of Sabena, operating charter and inclusive-tour flights; Man. Dir P. Jonnart; Dir R. Minet; Man. J. Edom; 3 Boeing 737-200, 1 Boeing 737-300, 2 Boeing 707-320C.

Trans European Airways (TEA): Bldg 117, Melsbroek Airport, 1910 Melsbroek; telex 21886; f. 1970; charter and inclusive-tour flights; Man. Dir G. P. Gutelman; 1 Airbus A300B2, 5 Boeing 737-200, 3 Boeing 737-300.

Tourism

Office de Promotion du Tourisme de la Communauté Française: 7 rue Joseph Stevens, 1000 Brussels; tel. (02) 518-12-11; telex 26816; f. 1981; promotion of tourism in French-speaking Belgium; Dir José Clossen.

Tourist Information Brussels (TIB): Hôtel de Ville, Grand-Place, 1000 Brussels; tel. (02) 513-89-40; telex 62506; Pres. Viviane Baro (acting); Sec.-Gen. Georges Renders.

Tourist Office for Flanders: 61 Grasmarkt, 1000 Brussels; tel. (02) 513-90-90; telex 63245; f. 1985; official promotion and policy body for tourism in Flemish part of Belgium; Gen. Commissioner L. R. A. Verheyden.

Atomic Energy

In 1985 an estimated 60% of Belgium's electricity was produced by nuclear power.

Commissariat à l'Energie Atomique (Atomic Energy Commission): Administration de l'Energie, Ministère des Affaires Economiques, 30 rue de Mot, 1040 Brussels; f. 1950; deals with nuclear matters falling within the competence of the Ministry of Economic Affairs.

Centre d'Etude de l'Energie Nucléaire/Studiecentrum voor Kernenergie CEN/SCK: 144 ave Eugène Plasky, 1040 Brussels; telex 22718; laboratories: 2400 Mol; f. 1952 for the training of personnel, the conduct of research and the provision of experimental facilities for industry; there are three reactors and two critical assemblies at the Centre's laboratories at Mol-Donk, Antwerp; the governing board represents industry, scientific establishments and the government; Pres. F. van den Bergh.

Institut Interuniversitaire des Sciences Nucléaires/ Interuniversitair Instituut voor Kernwetenschappen: 5 rue d'Egmont, 1050 Brussels; f. 1947 to promote research in nuclear science and solid state physics in advanced teaching and research establishments, including departments in the universities and centres at the State University (formerly Polytechnic Institute) of Mons and the Royal Military School at Brussels; 200 scientific researchers; Pres. H. Hasquin; Sec.-Gen. P. Levaux, dr.sc.

Organisme National de Déchets Radioactifs et des Matières fissiles (ONDRAF/NIRAS): 54 blvd du Régent, BP 5, Brussels; tel. (02) 513-74-60; telex 65784; f. 1981; management of radioactive waste; Gen. Man. E. Detilleux.

BELIZE

Introductory Survey

Location, Climate, Language, Religion, Flag, Capital

Belize lies on the Caribbean coast of Central America, with Mexico to the north-west and Guatemala to the south-west. The climate is sub-tropical, tempered by trade winds. The temperature averages 24°C (75°F) from November to January, and 27°C (81°F) from May to September. Annual rainfall ranges from 51 inches (1,290 mm) in the north to 175 inches (4,450 mm) in the south. The average annual rainfall in Belize City is 65 inches (1,650 mm). English is the official language but Spanish is the mother tongue of about one-half of the population, and there are small communities of Garifuna (Carib) and Maya speakers in the south. An English 'creole' is almost universally understood. Most of the population profess Christianity, dividing approximately into 60% Roman Catholics and 40% Protestants. The national flag is dark blue, with narrow horizontal red stripes at the upper and lower edges; at the centre is a white disc containing the state coat of arms, bordered by an olive wreath. The capital is Belmopan.

Recent History

Belize, known as British Honduras until June 1973, was first colonized by British settlers in the 17th century, but was not recognized as a British colony until 1862. In 1954 a new constitution granted universal adult suffrage and provided for the creation of a Legislative Assembly. The territory's first general election, in April 1954, was won by the only party then organized, the People's United Party (PUP), led by George Price. The PUP won all subsequent elections until 1984. In 1961 Price was appointed First Minister under a new ministerial system of government. The colony was granted internal self-government in 1964, with the United Kingdom retaining responsibility for defence, external affairs and internal security. Following an election in 1965, Price became Premier and a bicameral legislature was introduced. In August 1970 the capital of the territory was moved from Belize City to the newly built town of Belmopan.

The frontier with Guatemala was agreed by a convention in 1859 but this was declared invalid by Guatemala in 1940. Guatemalan claims to sovereignty of Belize date back to the middle of the 19th century and were written into Guatemala's constitution in 1945. In November 1975 and July 1977 British troops and aircraft were sent to protect Belize from the threat of Guatemalan invasion, and a battalion of troops and a detachment of fighter aircraft remained in the territory. Negotiations between the United Kingdom and Guatemala began in 1977. At a tripartite conference in May 1980 Britain suggested that it would consider unilaterally granting independence to Belize if no settlement with Guatemala was forthcoming. A series of negotiations followed, and in October the United Kingdom finally ruled out the possibility of any cession of land to Guatemala but offered economic and financial concessions. In November the UN called overwhelmingly for Belize to be granted independence, and the United Kingdom decided to proceed with a schedule for independence. A tripartite conference in March 1981 appeared to produce a sound basis for a final settlement, with Guatemala accepting Belizean independence in exchange for access to the Caribbean Sea through Belize and the use of certain offshore cays and their surrounding waters. A state of emergency was declared for three weeks in April, following strikes and serious rioting, apparently organized by the opposition in protest at the preliminary agreement which had been reached in the previous month. A constitutional conference nevertheless went ahead in April. However, further tripartite talks in May and July collapsed as a result of renewed claims by Guatemala to Belizean land. With Belizean independence imminent, Guatemala made an unsuccessful appeal to the UN Security Council to intervene, breaking off diplomatic relations with the United Kingdom and sealing its border with Belize on 7 September. However, on 21 September, as scheduled, Belize achieved independence, within the Commonwealth, with George Price becoming Prime Minister. Guatemala refused to recognize Belize's new status, and during 1982 requested the reopening of negotiations with the United Kingdom, alleging that Belize was not legally independent. Tripartite talks in January 1983 broke down after Belize rejected Guatemala's proposal that Belize should cede the southern part of the country. This claim was subsequently suspended. Tripartite talks resumed in May 1984.

At independence the United Kingdom agreed to leave troops as protection and for training of Belizean defence forces 'for an appropriate time'. Despite rumours that British troops were to be withdrawn in 1984, the British Government said in October 1983 that its policy had remained unchanged since Belize became independent. Belize is a member of CARICOM (see p. 108), whose summit conferences in 1982 and 1983 expressed support for Belize's territorial integrity against claims by Guatemala.

Internal disputes within the ruling PUP between left-wing and right-wing factions intensified during 1983, although Price succeeded in keeping the factions together. However, at the general election, held in December 1984, the PUP's 30 years of rule ended when the United Democratic Party (UDP) received 53% of the total votes and won 21 of the 28 seats in the enlarged House of Representatives. The remaining seven seats were won by the PUP, with 44% of the votes, but Price and several of his ministers lost their seats. The UDP's leader, Manuel Esquivel, became Prime Minister. The new Government pledged itself to reviving Belize's economy through increased foreign investment. In January 1985 Louis Sylvestre, the leading right-wing member of the PUP, resigned from the party and subsequently formed his own party, the Belize Popular Party (BPP).

Esquivel, although favouring closer ties with the USA, sought assurances from the British Government over its commitment to keep British troops in Belize until the resolution of the territorial dispute with Guatemala. In response, the British Government promised to honour the agreement that it had made with the former PUP Government. Talks with Guatemala resumed in February 1985, with greater optimism shown by all three parties. In July the new draft Guatemalan constitution omitted the previous unconditional claim to Belize, while Esquivel had previously acknowledged Guatemala's right of access to the Caribbean Sea. However, no settlement was forthcoming. In January 1986 Dr Marco Vinicio Cerezo was inaugurated as the elected President of Guatemala, marking a change from a military to a civilian government. In August the United Kingdom and Guatemala renewed diplomatic relations at a consular level, and in December the restoration of full diplomatic relations was announced. Meanwhile, a six-member select committee of the Belize House of Representatives was established in June 1986, to examine information on Guatemala's claim to Belize, and it was expected that further negotiations would take place between the two countries, since both Belize and Guatemala were known to be disposed towards a resolution of the border dispute.

Government

Belize is a constitutional monarchy, with the British sovereign as Head of State. Executive authority is vested in the sovereign and is exercisable by the Governor-General, who is appointed on the advice of the Prime Minister, must be of Belizean nationality, and acts in almost all matters on the advice of the Cabinet. Legislative power is vested in the bicameral National Assembly, comprising a Senate (eight members appointed by the Governor-General) and a House of Representatives (28 members elected by universal adult suffrage for five years, subject to dissolution). The Governor-General appoints the Prime Minister and, on the latter's recommendation, other Ministers. The Cabinet is responsible to the House.

Defence

The Belize Defence Force was formed in 1978 and was based on a combination of the existing Police Special Force and the Belize Volunteer Guard. The Force is of battalion size, made up of regular, volunteer and reserve elements, and includes small maritime and air wings. Provision has been made for the establishment of National Service if necessary to supplement normal recruitment. The Belize Government assumed the recurrent charges of about BZ $4m. per annum from 1981. Military service is voluntary. In July 1986 the regular armed forces totalled 600, and there were approximately 1,500 British troops in Belize. The defence budget in 1984 totalled BZ $7.2m.

Economic Affairs

The economy of Belize is primarily agricultural, based mainly on the production of sugar, bananas and citrus fruits. In 1984, according to estimates by the World Bank, the country's gross national product (GNP) per head, measured at average 1982–84 prices, was US $1,110. Between 1965 and 1984, it was estimated, the average annual growth rate of GNP per head was 2.5% in real terms.

Although 40% of the country is considered suitable for agriculture, only 15% of this area was under cultivation in 1985. Nevertheless, agriculture, forestry and fisheries were estimated to contribute more than 50% of gross domestic product (GDP) in 1984, and to employ 42% of the work-force. Belize's crops are susceptible to adverse weather conditions, and hurricanes in 1974 and 1978 caused extensive damage to citrus and banana plantations. Production of raw sugar was 97,700 metric tons in 1981, but the introduction of smut-resistant varieties increased output to 114,300 long tons in 1983. Production fell to 101,500 long tons in 1984, but sugar exports still accounted for about 46% of the total value of domestic exports, earning BZ $65.1m. Production rose slightly in 1985, to 102,000 long tons, but export earnings fell to BZ $45.9m. Belize has been protected from the most severe effects of the decline in free-market international sugar prices by quota agreements, at preferential prices, with the USA and the European Economic Community, which accept over two-thirds of Belize's sugar exports. However, in February 1986 it was announced that the US sugar quota for the year 1985/86 was to be reduced from 24,500 long tons to 16,000 long tons. In June 1985 one of the country's two sugar mills was closed after the Government refused to honour an agreement, made by the previous PUP administration, to acquire a majority shareholding in Belize Sugar Industries, the country's major sugar producer. However, in order to ensure the company's continued operations in Belize, the Government finally reached an agreement whereby the shares would be gradually transferred on behalf of the employees. In March 1986 the Government announced that the sugar mill was to reopen during 1986 for the production of ethyl alcohol (ethanol) from sugar cane juice. Production of bananas reached 10,298 metric tons in 1985, compared with 10,545 tons in 1984. The citrus crop reached 59,586 metric tons in 1985, providing export earnings of BZ $24.2m. Major expansion of the citrus industry is planned by US investors in order to supply the US market with orange juice concentrate, taking advantage of the country's geographical position and the absence of tariffs. In October 1985 it was announced that a consortium, headed by the US company Coca-Cola Foods, had bought 50,000 acres of virgin forest land on the Belize and Produce Company estate, 64 km north-west of Belize City. The company planned to clear and plant 25,000 acres (10,000 ha) of citrus initially and to build a concentrate plant. The investment of US $120m. represented the largest single investment in Belize since independence, and it was hoped that by 1995 orange concentrate would be Belize's main export. Rice, red kidney beans and maize are the principal domestic food crops, and the development of other crops, such as cocoa, coconuts and soya beans, is being encouraged. Dairy-farming, livestock and bee-keeping are also being developed. A dairy plant in the Cayo district, with a capacity of processing 400 gallons of milk per day, began operations in July 1986. Fishing provided export earnings of BZ $15m. in 1985, of which nearly 90% were accounted for by lobster sales. Belize has considerable timber reserves, particularly of tropical hardwoods.

A Five-Year Plan for 1985–89 aims to promote private investment, through tax incentives, to increase and diversify production, and to reduce dependence on imported goods. An improvement of infrastructure and a development of the international telecommunications network are also planned. Manufacturing, especially of clothing, accounted for 13.6% of GDP in 1984. In June 1984 the unemployment rate was 13.6% of a total labour force of 46,500. Immigration from neighbouring Central American countries, especially El Salvador, is matched by emigration to the USA, and remittances from Belizean workers abroad provide an important source of income.

The trade deficit, which had totalled BZ $85.9m. in 1981, fell to $69.8m. in 1984, as the total value of imports was reduced. However, owing to low international prices, the value of Belize's exports also fell, while the devaluation of the Mexican peso in 1982 seriously affected the country's re-export trade with its neighbour. In 1985 the trade deficit rose to BZ $77.4m. GDP, in real terms, increased by only 1.5% in 1981 and remained stagnant in 1982. Small increases, of 0.7% and 1.3%, were registered in 1983 and 1984 respectively, followed by a rise of 1.5% in 1985. In November 1984 the Government was forced to seek assistance from the IMF for balance-of-payments support and help in reducing the growing budget deficit. In a further effort to finance the budget deficit, the Government announced plans, in March 1986, to grant Belizean citizenship in exchange for interest-free loans of US $25,000 with a 10-year maturity. Reserves of foreign exchange fell from US $17.1m. at mid-1983 to less than US $3m. at mid-1984. However, by the end of September 1985 all debt arrears had either been paid off or rescheduled, helping to strengthen foreign reserves for 1986. The rate of inflation remained comparatively low, averaging 6% during 1984. Development assistance from the United Kingdom, Canada and various international organizations is used to improve infrastructure and public utilities.

A consortium of oil companies has undertaken exploratory drilling for petroleum in the southern region, but no commercially viable discoveries had been made by the end of 1985. Further explorations are being made off shore, and in the north-west of the country. Tourism is being promoted, but has suffered from unfavourable publicity over the Guatemalan dispute and the problems caused by drug trafficking in various parts of the country. The cultivation of hemp (marijuana), and the trafficking in illicit drugs, has proved an increasing problem for the Government, and in September 1986 the Ministry of Home Affairs announced the formation of a drug squad, intended to curb drug-related crimes. Although Mexico, with financial assistance from the USA, has helped in spraying the drug plantations with herbicides, enough of the crop survives to provide an estimated annual income of US $55m., equal to one-third of Belize's GDP.

Social Welfare

There were 10 urban and 20 rural health centres in 1980; pre-natal and child welfare clinics are sponsored by the Ministry of Health. In 1985 there were 583 hospital beds and 78 registered physicians. The infant mortality rate declined from 51 per 1,000 live births in 1970 to 19 per 1,000 in 1985.

Education

Education is compulsory for all children between the ages of six and 14 years. Primary education, beginning at six years of age and lasting for eight years, is provided free of charge, principally through subsidized denominational schools under government control. Secondary education, beginning at the age of 14, lasts for four or five years. In 1985 there were also four technical colleges, four vocational schools and a teacher-training college. The Government contributed up to 60% of the operational costs for 17 of the 22 secondary schools in 1982, while the remaining five were government-run. The Belize College of Arts, Science and Technology (BELCAST), founded in 1980, was planned as the first stage in a new University of Belize. In March 1986, however, the Government announced that it planned to divide BELCAST, with the result that it would continue as a vocational training school, with a greatly reduced budget. The Belize Teachers' College and the Bliss School of Nursing were to be re-established as independent institutions. There is an extra-mural branch of the University of the West Indies in Belize. Recurrent expenditure on education was estimated at BZ $22.2m. in 1982. The estimated adult literacy rate is over 93%.

BELIZE

Tourism

The main tourist attractions are the beaches and the barrier reef, hunting and fishing, and remains of the Mayan civilization. The Government also plans to establish three large wildlife reserves. There were 146 hotels in Belize in 1985. In 1985 there were 93,440 tourist arrivals, and income from tourism was estimated at between BZ $9m. and BZ $13m.

Public Holidays

1987: 1 January (New Year's Day), 9 March (Baron Bliss Day and Commonwealth Day), 17–20 April (Easter), 1 May (Labour Day), 8 June (Queen's Official Birthday), 10 September (St George's Cay Day), 21 September (Independence Day), 12 October (Columbus Day), 19 November (Garifuna Settlement Day), 25–26 December (Christmas).

1988: 1 January (New Year's Day), 7 March (Baron Bliss Day and Commonwealth Day), 1–4 April (Easter), 2 May (for Labour Day), 13 June (Queen's Official Birthday), 10 September (St George's Cay Day), 21 September (Independence Day), 12 October (Columbus Day), 19 November (Garifuna Settlement Day), 25–26 December (Christmas).

Weights and Measures

Imperial weights and measures are used, but petrol and paraffin are measured in terms of the US gallon (3.785 litres).

Currency and Exchange Rates

100 cents = 1 Belizean dollar (BZ $).

Exchange rates (30 September 1986):
  £1 sterling = BZ $2.894;
  US $1 = BZ $2.000.

Statistical Survey

Source (unless otherwise stated): Statistical Office of the Ministry of Economic Development, Belmopan; tel. 08-2207.

AREA AND POPULATION

Area: 22,965 sq km (8,867 sq miles).

Population: 120,936 at census of 7 April 1970; 144,857 (males 73,213; females 71,644) at census of 12 May 1980; 166,200 (official estimate, mid-1985).

Density (1985): 7.3 per sq km.

Principal Towns (estimated population at mid-1985): Belmopan (capital) 4,500; Belize City (former capital) 47,000; Corozal 10,000; Orange Walk 9,600; Dangriga (formerly Stann Creek) 7,700.

Births and Deaths (1985): Registered live births 6,659 (birth rate 40.1 per 1,000); Registered deaths 660 (death rate 4.0 per 1,000). Source: UN, *Population and Vital Statistics Report*.

Economically Active Population (1980 census): Agriculture, hunting, forestry and fishing 14,745; Mining and quarrying 32; Manufacturing 4,142; Electricity, gas and water 604; Construction 1,772; Trade, restaurants and hotels 5,646; Transport, storage and communications 1,725; Financing, insurance, real estate and business services 360; Community, social and personal services 8,956; Activities not adequately defined 1,791; Total employed 39,773 (males 31,749, females 8,024); Unemployed 7,554 (males 4,836, females 2,718); Total labour force 47,327 (males 36,585, females 10,742). Source: ILO, *Year Book of Labour Statistics*.

AGRICULTURE, ETC.

Principal Crops (1985): Sugar cane 962,000 long tons; Bananas 542,000 boxes (each of 42 lb or 19 kg); Oranges 1,043,000 boxes (each of 90 lb or 40.7 kg); Grapefruit 476,000 boxes (each of 80 lb or 36 kg); Rice (paddy) 12.1 million lb; Maize 29.0 million lb; Red kidney beans 2.3 million lb.

Livestock (FAO estimates, '000 head, year ending September 1984): Horses 5; Mules 4; Cattle 51; Pigs 20; Sheep 3; Goats 1 (Source: FAO, *Production Yearbook*).

Livestock Products (FAO estimates, '000 metric tons, 1984): Meat 4; Cows' milk 4 (Source: FAO, *Production Yearbook*); (official estimates, 1985): Beef 2.3 million lb; Honey 694,000 lb.

Forestry ('000 cu m, 1984): Roundwood removals: Industrial wood 38; Fuel wood 126; Total 164 (Source: FAO, *Yearbook of Forest Products*).

Fishing (FAO estimates, catch in metric tons): 1,400 in 1982; 1,500 in 1983; 1,600 in 1984 (Source: FAO, *Yearbook of Fishery Statistics*).

INDUSTRY

Production (1985): Raw sugar 102,000 long tons; Molasses 28,100 long tons; Cigarettes 74 million; Beer 600,000 gallons; Batteries 5,800; Fertilizers 3,670 long tons; Garments 2,734,000; Rum 4,500 gallons; Citrus concentrate 1,030,000 gallons.

FINANCE

Currency and Exchange Rates: 100 cents = 1 Belizean dollar (BZ$). *Coins:* 1, 5, 10, 25 and 50 cents. *Notes:* 1, 5, 10, 20 and 100 dollars. *Sterling and US Dollar equivalents:* (30 September 1986): £1 sterling = BZ $2.894; US $1 = BZ $2.000. BZ $100 = £34.55 = US $50.00. *Exchange rate:* Fixed at US $1 = BZ $2.000 since May 1976.

Budget (BZ $ million, proposals for year ending March 1984): Total Revenue 194.6 (Local sources 101.6; Transfer of resources 25.4; Loans 67.6); Total expenditure 194.6 (Education and legal affairs 21.6; Natural resources 33.9; Defence and home affairs 18.1; Energy and communications 35.6; Works 26.5; Health, housing and cooperatives 22.7).

International Reserves (US $ million at 31 December 1985): Reserve position in the IMF 2.09; Foreign exchange 12.73; Total 14.81 (Source: IMF, *International Financial Statistics*).

Money Supply (BZ $ million at 31 December 1985): Currency outside banks 22.64; Demand deposits at commercial banks 24.44 (Source: IMF, *International Financial Statistics*).

Gross Domestic Product (BZ $ million at current purchasers' values): 351.7 in 1983; 367.5 in 1984; 385.0 in 1985 (Source: IMF, *International Financial Statistics*).

Balance of Payments (US $ million, 1985): Merchandise exports f.o.b. 86.6; Merchandise imports f.o.b. −113.8; *Trade balance* −27.2; Exports of services 41.0; Imports of services −41.3; *Balance on goods and services* −27.5; Private unrequited transfers (net) 19.6; Government unrequited transfers (net) 12.8; *Current balance* 5.0; Direct capital investment (net) 3.7; Other long-term capital (net) 6.7; Short-term capital (net) −1.0; Net errors and omissions −12.0; *Total* (net monetary movements) 2.3; Valuation changes (net) 0.6; *Changes in reserves* 3.0. Source: IMF, *International Financial Statistics*.

EXTERNAL TRADE

Principal Commodities (BZ $ million, 1985): *Imports:* Total 256.3. *Exports:* Sugar 45.9; Molasses 1.7; Bananas 6.6; Citrus products 24.2; Fish products 15.0; Timber 1.2; Garments 31.1; Total 128.8 (excl. re-exports 51.4).

Principal Trading Partners (US $ million, 1980): *Imports:* Japan 8.0; Mexico 7.3; Netherlands Antilles 19.8; United Kingdom 23.4; USA 51.4; Total (incl. others) 148.2. *Exports:* Trinidad and Tobago 4.7; United Kingdom 24.0; USA 50.3; Total (incl. others) 82.5. (Source: UN, *Yearbook of International Trade Statistics*).

TRANSPORT

Road Traffic (motor vehicles licensed, 1985): 10,613.

Shipping (international sea-borne freight traffic, estimates, '000 metric tons, 1983): Goods loaded 160; Goods unloaded 84 (Source: UN, *Monthly Bulletin of Statistics*).

Civil Aviation (1985): Passenger movements 294,800.

TOURISM

Tourist arrivals (1985): 93,440.

COMMUNICATIONS MEDIA

Radio Receivers (1983): 79,000 in use.

Telephones (1983): 8,600 in use.

Newspapers (1985): There are no daily newspapers but six non-dailies are published.

EDUCATION

Primary (1985): 225 schools, 1,582 teachers, 38,512 students.

Secondary (1985): 24 schools, 504 teachers, 6,676 students.

Higher (1985): 5 institutions, 62 teachers, 765 students.

Directory

The Constitution

The Constitution came into effect at the independence of Belize on 21 September 1981. Its main provisions are summarized below:

FUNDAMENTAL RIGHTS AND FREEDOMS

Regardless of race, place of origin, political opinions, colour, creed or sex, but subject to respect for the rights and freedoms of others and for the public interest, every person in Belize is entitled to the rights of life, liberty, security of the person, and the protection of the law. Freedom of movement, of conscience, of expression, of assembly and association and the right to work are guaranteed and the inviolability of family life, personal privacy, home and other property and of human dignity is upheld. Protection is afforded from discrimination on the grounds of race, sex, etc, and from slavery, forced labour and inhuman treatment.

CITIZENSHIP

All persons born in Belize before independence who, immediately prior to independence, were citizens of the United Kingdom and Colonies automatically become citizens of Belize. All persons born outside the country having a husband, parent or grandparent in possession of Belizean citizenship automatically acquire citizenship, as do those born in the country after independence. Provision is made which permits persons who do not automatically become citizens of Belize to be registered as such. (Belizean citizenship is also offered, under the Belize Loans Act 1986, in exchange for interest-free loans of US $25,000 with a 10-year maturity.)

THE GOVERNOR-GENERAL

The British monarch, as Head of State, is represented in Belize by a Governor-General, a Belizean national.

THE EXECUTIVE

Executive authority is vested in the British monarch and exercised by the Governor-General. The Governor-General appoints as Prime Minister that member of the House of Representatives who, in the Governor-General's view, is best able to command the support of the majority of the members of the House, and appoints a Deputy Prime Minister and other Ministers on the advice of the Prime Minister. The Governor-General may remove the Prime Minister from office if a resolution of 'no confidence' is passed by the House and the Prime Minister does not, within seven days, either resign or advise the Governor-General to dissolve the National Assembly. The Cabinet consists of the Prime Minister and other Ministers.

The Leader of the Opposition is appointed by the Governor-General as that member of the House who, in the Governor-General's view, is best able to command the support of a majority of the members of the House who do not support the Government.

THE LEGISLATURE

The Legislature consists of a National Assembly comprising two chambers: the Senate, with eight nominated members, and the House of Representatives, with (since 1984) 28 elected members. The Assembly's normal term is five years. Senators are appointed by the Governor-General: five on the advice of the Prime Minister, two on the advice of the Leader of the Opposition or on the advice of persons selected by the Governor-General, and one after consultation with the Belize Advisory Council. If any person who is not a Senator is elected to be President of the Senate, he or she shall be an *ex-officio* Senator in addition to the eight nominees.

Each constituency returns one Representative to the House, who is directly elected in accordance with the Constitution.

If a person who is not a member of the House is elected to be Speaker of the House, he or she shall be an *ex-officio* member in addition to the 18 members provided for. Every citizen over the age of 18 is eligible to vote. The National Assembly may alter any of the provisions of the Constitution.

The Government

Head of State: HM Queen ELIZABETH II.

Governor-General: Dame ELMIRA MINITA GORDON (assumed office 21 September 1981).

THE CABINET
(October 1986)

Prime Minister, Minister of Finance and of Defence: MANUEL ESQUIVEL.
Deputy Prime Minister and Minister of Home Affairs and of Local Government: CURL THOMPSON.
Attorney-General and Minister of Foreign Affairs and of Economic Development: DEAN BARROW.
Minister of Commerce, Industry and Tourism: EDWARDO JUAN.
Minister of Natural Resources: CHARLES WAGNER.
Minister of Agriculture: DEAN LINDO.
Minister of Labour and Social Services: PHILIP GOLDSON.
Minister of Education, Youth and Sport: ELODIO ARAGÓN.
Minister of Health: ISRAEL ALPUCHE.
Minister of Housing and Public Works: HUBERT ELRINGTON.
Minister of Transport, Energy and Communications: DEREK AIKMAN.

MINISTRIES

Office of the Prime Minister: Belmopan; tel. 08-2346.
Ministry of Foreign Affairs: Belmopan; telex 102.
All other Ministries are also situated in Belmopan.

Legislature

NATIONAL ASSEMBLY
The Senate

President: DORIS GARCIA.
There are eight nominated members.

House of Representatives

Speaker: CARLOS CASTILLO.
Clerk: A. F. MONSANTO.

General Election, 14 December 1984

	Seats
United Democratic Party	21
People's United Party	7*
Christian Democratic Party	—
Independents	—

* Reduced to 6 seats in January 1985, prior to the formation of the Belize Popular Party.

Political Organizations

Belize Popular Party (BPP): Belize City; f. 1985; Leader LOUIS SYLVESTRE; Chair. MARK CUELLAR.
Christian Democratic Party: Belize City; f. 1983 after breaking away from the UDP (see below); Leader THEODORE ARANDA.
People's United Party (PUP): Belize City; f. 1950; based on organized labour; Leader GEORGE PRICE; Chair. SAID MUSA; Leader in the House of Representatives FLORENCIO MARIN.
United Democratic Party (UDP): 21 King St, Belize City; f. 1974 by merger of People's Development Movement, Liberal Party and National Independence Party; conservative; Leader MANUEL ESQUIVEL; Chair. DEAN LINDO.

Diplomatic Representation

EMBASSIES AND HIGH COMMISSIONS IN BELIZE

Colombia: Orchid Gardens, Belmopan; tel. 08-2547; Chargé d'affaires: Dr EDILBERTO RAMÍREZ DE LA PAVA.

BELIZE
Directory

France: 5574 Princess Margaret Drive, POB 230, Belize City; tel. 02-44556; telex 291; Ambassador: JEAN-PIERRE CHAUVET.
Honduras: 91 North Front St, POB 285, Belize City; tel. 02-45889; telex 103; Chargé d'affaires: MARCO A. CABALLERO.
Mexico: 20 North Park St, Belize City; tel. 02-44301; telex 277; Ambassador: MANUEL MARTÍNEZ DEL SOBRAL.
Panama: 3 Orchid Gardens, Belmopan; tel. 08-2504; Chargé d'affaires: ORLANDO BETHANCOURT.
United Kingdom: Embassy Sq., POB 91, Belmopan; tel. 08-2146; telex 284; High Commissioner: J. M. CROSBY.
USA: 29 Gabourel Lane, Belize City; tel. 02-7161; telex 213; Chargé d'affaires: D. KEITH GUTHRIE.

Judicial System

Summary Jurisdiction Courts (criminal jurisdiction) and District Courts (civil jurisdiction), presided over by magistrates, are established in each of the six judicial districts. Summary Jurisdiction Courts have a wide jurisdiction in summary offences and a limited jurisdiction in indictable matters. The maximum civil claim in which District Courts may exercise jurisdiction was increased in 1985 from BZ $500 to BZ $5,000. Appeals lie to the Supreme Court, which has jurisdiction corresponding to the English High Court of Justice and where a jury system is in operation. From the Supreme Court further appeals lie to a Court of Appeal, established in 1968, which holds an average of four sessions per year. Final appeals are made to the Judicial Committee of the Privy Council in the United Kingdom.

Court of Appeal: JAMES SMITH (President), ALBERT STAINE, Justice K. SAINT L. HENRY.
Chief Justice: T. S. COTRAN.
Puisne Judges: GEORGE BROWN, S. PONNAMBALAM.
Registrar of the Supreme Court: H. B. KNIGHT.
Magistrates: A. E. JOHNSON (Chief Magistrate), H. LORD, G. L. MITCHELL, F. BRUCE-LYLE, P. VASQUES, RAMON RAMIREZ, M. MOODY.

Religion

At mid-1985 an estimated 102,650 of the population were adherents of the Roman Catholic Church, while 63,668 were Anglican, Methodist or members of various Protestant sects, including a community of Mennonites.

CHRISTIANITY
The Roman Catholic Church

Belize comprises the single diocese of Belize City—Belmopan, suffragan to the archdiocese of Kingston in Jamaica. The Bishop participates in the Antilles Episcopal Conference (based in Jamaica).

Bishop of Belize City—Belmopan: OSMOND PETER MARTIN, Bishop's House, 144 North Front St, POB 616, Belize City; tel. 02-2122.

The Anglican Communion

Belize is part of the Province of the West Indies.
Bishop of Belize: Rt. Rev. KEITH ALFONSO MCMILLAN, Bishopthorpe, Southern Foreshore, POB 535, Belize City; tel. 3380.

The Methodist Church

Chairman and General Superintendent, Belize/Honduras District: Rev. HAROLD A. GILL, POB 212, Belize City; 2,017 mems.

OTHER RELIGIONS

There are also small communities of Hindus, Muslims and Bahá'ís.

The Press

Amandala: Amandala Press, 3304 Partridge St, POB 15, Belize City; tel. 02-7276; f. 1969; weekly; independent; Editor EVAN X. HYDE; circ. 7,000.
The Beacon: 7 Church St, Belize City; weekly; supports UDP; Editor MICHAEL FINNIGAN; circ. 4,200.

The Belize Times: 3 Queen St, POB 506, Belize City; tel. 02-45757; f. 1956; weekly; party political paper of People's United Party; Man. KATHARINE PRICE; Editor AMALIA MAI; circ. 4,200.
Government Gazette: Government Printery, Belmopan; official; weekly.
The New Belize: Government Information Service, Belmopan; tel. 08-2159; telex 138; monthly; official; circ. 12,000.
The Reporter: 147 West and Allenby St, POB 707, Belize City; tel. 02-2503; f. 1968; Editor HARRY LAWRENCE; circ. 6,000.

NEWS AGENCY

Agencia EFE (Spain): Belmopan; tel. 08-2159; Correspondent M. A. ROMERO.

PRESS ASSOCIATION

Belize Newspaper Association: POB 707, Belize City.

Radio and Television

In 1983 there were about 79,000 radio receivers in use. In August 1986 the Belize Broadcasting Authority issued licences to eight television operators for 14 channels, which mainly retransmit US satellite programmes, thus placing television in Belize on a fully legal basis for the first time.

RADIO

Radio Belize: Albert Cattouse Bldg, POB 89, Belize City; tel. 02-7246; f. 1937; government-operated semi-commercial service; transmissions for some 126 hours per week on AM and 35 hours per week on FM; broadcasts in English (80%) and Spanish; Dir RENÉ R. VILLANUEVA.

TELEVISION

Tropical Vision Channel 7: Belize City; tel. 02-2825; Man. NET VASQUEZ.
CTV-Channel 9: Belize City; tel. 02-44400; Man. MARIE HOARE.

Finance

(cap. = capital; brs = branches)

BANKING
Central Bank

Central Bank of Belize: Treasury Lane, POB 852, Belize City; tel. 02-3571; telex 225; f. 1982.

Development Bank

Development Finance Corporation: Bliss Parade, Belmopan; tel. 08-2350; issued cap. BZ $4.0m.; Chair. MICHAEL C. E. YOUNG; Man. CIRILO A. MAHUNG.

Other Banks

Atlantic Bank Ltd: 6 Albert St, POB 481, Belize City; tel. 02-7301; telex 216; f. 1971; Gen. Man. ROBERTO C. STANLEY; 1 br.
Bank of Nova Scotia: Albert St, POB 708, Belize City; tel. 02-7028; telex 218; Man. JOSÉ R. ROSADO; 4 brs.
Barclays Bank International Ltd: POB 363, 21 Albert St, Belize City; tel. 02-7211; telex 217; Man. JORGE M. AUIL; 2 brs and 4 sub-brs.
Royal Bank of Canada: 60 Market Sq., POB 364, Belize City; tel. 02-7132; telex 229; Man. KENNETH FISHER; 6 brs and 1 sub-br.

There is also a Government Savings Bank.

INSURANCE

General insurance is carried on by local companies and British, American and Jamaican companies are also represented.

Trade and Industry

Belize Export and Investment Promotion Unit: joint government and private-sector institution to encourage export and investment; Dir SYLVIA PATTOUSE.

BELIZE

Office of Economic Development: Belmopan; administration of public and private sector investment; advisory unit to Government on general economic policy and statistics agency; Head SHARMAN YVONNE HYDE.

STATUTORY BODIES

Banana Control Board: management of banana industry.
Belize Beef Corporation: f. 1978; semi-governmental organization to aid development of cattle-rearing industry.
Citrus Control Board: f. 1966; determines basic quota for each producer, fixes annual price of citrus; Chair. E. GRINAGE.
Marketing Board: POB 479, Belize City; tel. 02-7402; f. 1948 to encourage the growing of staple food crops; purchases crops at guaranteed prices, supervises processing, storing and marketing; Chair. SANTIAGO PERDOMO.
Belize Sugar Board: 2nd St South, Corozal Town; tel. 04-2005; f. 1960 to control the sugar industry and cane production; includes representatives of the Government, sugar manufacturers, cane farmers and the public sector; Exec. Sec. I. E. CRUZ.

CHAMBER OF COMMERCE

Belize Chamber of Commerce: POB 291, 9 Regent St, Belize City; tel. 02-3148; f. 1918; Pres. KENT MIFIELD; Exec. Sec. KARL VILLANUEVA; 540 mems.

DEVELOPMENT ORGANIZATION

Belize Reconstruction and Development Corporation: POB 92, Belize; tel. 02-7424; Chair. MANUEL ESQUIVEL; Gen. Man. A. BRYAN CARD.

EMPLOYERS' ASSOCIATIONS

Cane Farmers' Association: San Antonio Rd, Orange Walk; tel. 03-2005 f. 1959 to assist cane farmers and negotiate with the Sugar Board and manufacturers on their behalf; 14 district brs; Chair. BONIFACIO MOH.
Citrus Growers' Association: POB 7, Dangriga; f. 1966; citrus crop farmers' association; Chair. WILLIAM BOWMAN.
Livestock Producers' Association: 24 Craig St, POB 1052, Belize City; tel. 02-44748.

TRADE UNIONS

National Trades Union Congress of Belize (NTUCB): Pres. CYRIL DAVIS.

Principal Unions

United General Workers' Union: 1, corner West and Water Lane, Belize City; tel. 02-3916; f. 1979 by amalgamation of the Belize General Workers' Union and the Southern Christian Union; two branch unions affiliated to the central body; affiliated to ICFTU; Pres. ANTONIO GONZÁLEZ; Gen. Sec. DOMINGO PÉREZ.
Belize National Teachers' Union: POB 382, Belize City; tel. 02-2857; Pres. JOHN PINNELO; Sec. MIGUEL WONG; 600 mems.

Christian Workers' Union: 23 George St, Belize City; tel. 02-2150; f. 1962; general; Pres. DESMOND VAUGHN; 2,000 mems.
Democratic Independent Union: POB 695, Belize City; Pres. CYRIL DAVIS; 1,250 mems.
Public Service Union of Belize: POB 45, 155 West Canal St, Belize City; tel. 02-2318; f. 1922; public workers; Pres. PETER AUGUST; Sec.-Gen. CARL SMITH; 1,500 mems.

CO-OPERATIVES

In 1981 there were 38 Credit Unions, 52 Agricultural, Producer and Marketing co-operatives, nine Fishing Co-operatives, seven Bee-Keepers' Co-operatives, two Housing Co-operatives, six Transport Co-operatives and one Supplies Co-operative.

There were also three co-operative groups: Belize Credit Union League (22 mems), Fishing Co-operative Association (five mems), Honey Producers Federation (five mems).

Transport

There are no railways.

ROADS

There are about 1,600 km (1,000 miles) of all-weather main and feeder roads and about 400 km of cart roads and bush trails. A number of logging and forest tracks are usable by heavy-duty vehicles in the dry season.

SHIPPING

A new deep-water port at Belize City was opened to traffic in 1980. There is a second port at Dangriga (formerly Stann Creek), to the south of Belize City. Seven major shipping lines call at Belize City, including the Carol Line (consisting of Harrison, Hapag-Lloyd, Nedlloyd and CGM).

CIVIL AVIATION

Belize International Airport, 14 km from Belize City, can accommodate medium-sized jet aircraft and there are plans for the construction of a new terminal. There are airstrips for light aircraft on internal flights near the major towns and offshore islands.

Maya Airways Ltd: POB 458, 6 Fort St, Belize City; tel. 02-7215; telex 280; f. 1961; internal services; Dir GORDON A. ROE; fleet of 4 BN-2A Islander, 2 Cessna U206.

Tourism

Belize Tourist Bureau: 53 Regent St, POB 325, Belize City; tel. 02-7213; f. 1964; 13 mems; Chair. A. PAUL HUNT; Sec. A. B. PALACIO.

BENIN

Introductory Survey

Location, Climate, Language, Religion, Flag, Capital

The People's Republic of Benin is a narrow stretch of territory in West Africa. The country has an Atlantic coastline of about 100 km (60 miles), flanked by Nigeria to the east and Togo to the west; its northern borders are with Burkina Faso and Niger. The climate is tropical in the north, with one rainy season and a maximum temperature of 46°C (115°F), and equatorial in the south, with average temperatures of 20°–34°C (68°–93°F) and two rainy seasons. French is the official language but each of the indigenous ethnic groups has its own language. Bariba and Fulani are the major languages in the north, while Fon and Yoruba are widely spoken in the south. The majority of the people follow traditional beliefs and customs. About 15% of the inhabitants are Christians, mainly Roman Catholics, and about 13% are Muslims. The national flag (proportions 3 by 2) is green, with a five-pointed red star in the upper hoist. The capital is Porto-Novo, but most government offices and other state bodies are in Cotonou.

Recent History

Benin, called Dahomey until 1975, was formerly part of French West Africa. It became a self-governing republic within the French Community in December 1958, and an independent state on 1 August 1960. The country's history from independence until 1972 was marked by chronic political instability, with five successful coups involving the army.

Elections in December 1960 were won by the Parti Dahoméen de l'Unité, whose leader, Hubert Maga, a northerner, became the country's first President. In October 1963, following riots by workers and students, President Maga was deposed by a military coup, led by Col (later Gen.) Christophe Soglo, Chief of Staff of the Army. Soglo served as interim Head of State until the election in January 1964 of a government headed by Sourou-Migan Apithy, a southerner who had been Vice-President under Maga. Another southerner, Justin Ahomadegbé, became Prime Minister. This regime was resented in the north, where rioting occurred. In November 1965, following a series of political crises, Gen. Soglo forced Apithy and Ahomadegbé to resign. A provisional government was formed but the army intervened again in December, when Gen. Soglo assumed power at the head of a military regime. In December 1967 industrial unrest, following a ban on trade union activity, led to another coup, this time by younger officers, led by Maj. (later Lt-Col) Maurice Kouandété. An interim regime was established, with Lt-Col Alphonse Alley, formerly Chief of Staff, as Head of State and Kouandété as Prime Minister.

A return to civilian rule was attempted in 1968. A referendum in March approved a new constitution, based on a strong presidency, and a presidential election was held in May. However, leading politicians, including all former Presidents, were banned from participation in the presidential poll and called on their supporters to boycott the election. As a result, only about 26% of the electorate voted, with the abstention rate reaching 99% in the north. The election was declared void, and in June the military regime nominated Dr Emile-Derlin Zinsou, formerly Minister for Foreign Affairs, as President. In July 1968 President Zinsou was sworn in, and confirmed in office by a referendum, but in December 1969 he was deposed by Lt-Col Kouandété, then Commander-in-Chief of the Army. A Military Directorate, led by Lt-Col Paul-Emile de Souza, assumed power.

In March 1970 a presidential election was held amid violent incidents and widespread claims of irregularities. The poll was abandoned when counting revealed roughly equal support for the three main candidates, Ahomadegbé, Apithy and Maga. In May, however, the Directorate handed over power to a Presidential Council comprising these three veteran politicians. It was agreed that each member of the triumvirate would act as Head of State, in rotation, for a two-year period. As a concession to the north, Maga became the first to hold this office, being succeeded in May 1972 by Ahomadegbé.

On 26 October 1972, however, the collective civilian leadership was deposed by Maj. (later Brig.-Gen.) Mathieu Kerekou, Deputy Chief of Staff of the armed forces, who established a military regime. Kerekou promised that the new regime would be based on equal representation between northern, central and southern regions. He proclaimed a resolutely progressive policy, and in September 1973 the National Council of the Revolution (CNR) was established to carry it out.

In November 1974 Kerekou announced that the country would follow the path of 'scientific socialism', based on Marxist-Leninist principles. The vital sectors of the economy, including the banks and the distribution of petroleum products, were taken over by the state. In February 1975 Benin's co-operation agreements with France were renegotiated. Between 1974 and 1978 a decentralized local administration was set up, the education system taken over and the legal system put under review. The army and the gendarmerie were merged to form a National Defence Force. In November 1975 the Parti de la Révolution Populaire du Bénin (PRPB) was established as the 'highest expression of the political will of the people of Benin', and in December the country's name was changed from Dahomey to the People's Republic of Benin.

In August 1977 the CNR adopted a Loi Fondamentale which decreed new structures in government. Under its terms, a National Revolutionary Assembly was instituted as the supreme authority of the state, following an election, held in November 1979, for the 336 members of the Assembly: a single list of candidates was presented and approved by 97.5% of the voters. The CNR was disbanded and Kerekou's Government thus converted itself into a civilian body. At the first Ordinary Congress of the PRPB, held in December, it was decided that Lt-Col Kerekou would be the sole candidate for President of the Republic; the Assembly unanimously elected him as President in February 1980. In April 1981 it was announced that the three members of the former Presidential Council, who had been imprisoned following their overthrow in the coup of 1972, had been released from house arrest. A gradual moderation in Benin's domestic policies followed, and ministerial reshuffles in April and December 1982 reflected the Government's campaign against corruption and inefficiency, and indicated the importance of rural development in its economic policies. The changes also removed members of an extreme left-wing faction ('Les Ligueurs') from power, and resulted, for the first time, in a minority of army officers in the Government.

At a general election in June 1984, 97.9% of voters approved the single list of candidates for the National Revolutionary Assembly. The number of Assembly members was reduced from 336 to 196 in an effort to increase political efficiency, and candidates were drawn from a wider range of socio-professional groups. In July the Assembly re-elected Kerekou, the sole candidate, as President, and in the subsequent government reshuffle the National Executive Council was reduced from 23 ministers to 15. Upon his re-election, Kerekou announced an amnesty for several political prisoners, including Alphonse Alley, a former Head of State.

In an attempt to reduce smuggling, Nigeria closed its border with Benin between May 1984 and March 1986. This action adversely affected legitimate trade, including the export by Benin of sugar and cement from recently-established factories which had been co-funded by Nigeria. The closure of the border caused further problems in May 1985, when several thousand of the 700,000 illegal immigrants who had been expelled from Nigeria sought to cross Benin's frontiers in transit to Ghana.

Following a boycott of classes by students in April 1985, riots broke out in May at the University of Benin and in schools, which led to the closure by the Government of all educational establishments until the beginning of June 1985. Several students were detained following the riots, and, in an ensuing government reshuffle, both the Minister of Secondary and Higher Education and the Minister of Culture, Youth and Sports were replaced.

In November 1985 some 100 people, including teachers, engineers and high-ranking officials, were arrested on suspicion of belonging to the banned Parti communiste dahoméen (PCD). It was later alleged that the detainees were undergoing torture, while no specific charges were brought against them.

On several occasions Benin has accused foreign powers of conspiring with internal opposition to destabilize the regime. Its international standing has improved, however, with the relaxation of Kerekou's regime during the 1980s. Relations with France, Benin's main trading partner and supplier of aid, have improved since 1977, when an airborne mercenary attack, in which French involvement was alleged, was made in Cotonou. In January 1983 President Mitterrand visited Benin and participated in a ceremony to commemorate the victims of the invasion. This was the first visit by a French president since Benin's independence.

Government

In accordance with the Loi Fondamentale, adopted in August 1977 and amended in June 1984, a National Revolutionary Assembly, a body of 196 People's Commissioners representing socio-professional classes, is elected by universal suffrage every five years. The Assembly, in turn, elects the President of the Republic. Government is in the hands of the National Executive Council (NEC), under the President of the Republic, which includes heads of departments and heads of provinces, meeting monthly, and, more important, the Permanent Committee of the NEC, which comprises only ministers, meeting weekly. The Central Committee of the Parti de la Révolution Populaire du Bénin, the only permitted political party, plays a leading role in government.

Local administration is based on six provinces, divided into 84 districts. Each province is governed by a Prefect and a Secretary-General, assisted by a Provincial Revolutionary Council, a Regional Planning and Development Committee and a Conference of Heads of Regional Departments. There is a considerable degree of decentralization and financial autonomy.

Defence

Citizens of both sexes are liable for military service between the ages of 18 and 51. The army strength in July 1986 was 3,200, the air force 160, and, in addition, there were paramilitary forces numbering at least 3,500 men. The navy comprises 150 men and five patrol boats. France provides technical assistance and equipment. In 1977 a central organization, the Headquarters People's Armed Forces of Benin, was established to unify the police, customs service, armed forces and gendarmerie. It comprises three units: national defence, public security and people's militia. In 1983 the estimated defence budget was 9,500m. francs CFA.

Economic Affairs

Benin's economy is based mainly on agriculture. The agricultural sector (including forestry and fishing) engaged an estimated 70% of the labour force in 1980, compared with 81% in 1970, and provided about 43% of gross domestic product (GDP) in 1984. Despite the official policy of Marxism-Leninism, several sectors of the economy have reverted to private control. However, Benin is one of the world's less developed countries, with a low level of industrialization and literacy. In 1984, according to estimates by the World Bank, gross national product (GNP) per head, measured at average 1982–84 prices, was US $270, having increased at an average rate of only 1.0% per year, in real terms, since 1965. The average annual growth of overall GDP, measured in constant prices, was 2.2% in 1965–73, rising to 4.6% in 1973–84. The 1983–87 Development Plan stressed agriculture, transport and the expansion of small and medium-sized enterprises.

In 1975 the agricultural sector was reformed, with the introduction of a co-operative system. The land is under-utilized, however: in 1982 there were 1,200,000 ha under cultivation, representing only about 10% of potential farming area. In 1985 it was announced that the OAU was to provide $750,000 for research into agricultural production in semi-arid zones. Regional production efforts are the responsibility of the Centres d'Action Régionale pour le Développement Rural (CARDERs), through which operate regional development projects. The Arab Bank for Economic Development in Africa (BADEA) announced that in 1985 it was to lend $8m. for the support of rural development projects.

Benin's principal food crops are cassava (manioc), yams, maize and sorghum. The major cash crops are the oil palm and cotton. As a result of extensive damage to oil palm trees in the drought of 1976–77, about 29,000 ha of plantations were functioning at only 50% capacity until 1982, and it was expected that five or six years of good rainfall would be necessary to overcome the effects of this drought. Production of palm oil reached 36,000 metric tons in 1982, but only three of the six oil-processing mills are operational. Production of seed (unginned) cotton fell from more than 50,000 metric tons in 1972/73 to only 15,438 tons in 1980/81. The decline was mainly due to lack of insecticides and to adverse weather and low prices. Production rose to 31,083 tons in 1982/83, after efforts to increase the area under cultivation, and output in 1983/84 was estimated at 45,400 tons. In 1985 the French Central Fund for Economic Co-operation (CCCE) granted 75m. French francs for the construction of two cotton-ginning mills, each with an annual capacity of 20,000 tons. There are large unrecorded exports of food to Nigeria, where prices are higher and where farmers do not have to contend with the bureaucratic problems of state marketing agencies. Benin normally covers its demand for staple foods but, as a result of food shortages, all food exports were banned in December 1981. Livestock and fisheries are both small but significant sectors. The major livestock project under way is a 37,000-ha ranch at Okpara. The national fishing company is jointly owned by Benin and Libya.

The industrial sector, based on small-scale processing of primary production, contributed 14% of GDP in 1984, compared with 11.2% in 1980: the 1980–90 development plan envisaged an increase to 15.3% of GDP by 1985. Although some sectors of industry and commerce have been nationalized since December 1974, this has mainly affected Benin's external trade, and in 1978 about 60% of internal trade was conducted privately. Reserves of gold, phosphates (5m. tons) and marble have been discovered, although by 1985 the only mineral to be exploited, apart from petroleum (see below), was limestone, supplying the cement factory at Onigbolo. This factory, commissioned in mid-1982 with a capacity of 500,000 metric tons per year, was jointly financed by Nigeria, which provided 43% of the total cost (32,000m. francs CFA) of the complex. A similar arrangement was organized for the sugar factory at Savé, costing 69,000m. francs CFA, but both schemes foundered as Nigeria failed to take up its 60% of output and closed its border with Benin. In 1985 the cement works was producing only 85,000 tons per year. In December 1985 Benin secured a loan of 1,000m. francs CFA from the Banque ouest-africaine de développement (BOAD) for the rehabilitation of the textile factory at Parakou.

Petroleum has been discovered off shore, and there are estimated recoverable reserves of about 22m. barrels. Production at the Sémé field began in 1982, and in 1984 output averaged 6,900 barrels per day (b/d), almost double Benin's petroleum needs. The Norwegian Government provided 90% of the $100m. needed to finance the project. A second phase of exploitation began in 1984, and in August 1985 oil exploration rights were unexpectedly sold to a Swiss-based company, Panoco, in a US $2,000m. joint-venture agreement. In February 1986 output was estimated at only 7,200 b/d, falling far short of the 25,000 b/d projected upon Panoco's take-over of the Sémé field. Some reserves of natural gas have been discovered in the oil fields.

Other projects include the extension of Cotonou port and the construction of a dam at Nangbeto, on the Mono river, jointly with Togo. The dam will help to irrigate 42,000 ha of land in Benin, and, with a planned hydroelectric generating capacity of 62 MW, is scheduled for completion in 1987/88. Its construction is to be co-financed by the OPEC Fund for International Development and the Islamic Development Bank (IDB). In 1983 many of Benin's manufacturing units were operating at less than 50% of capacity. Nigerian petroleum revenues, which had helped to stimulate commercial activity in Benin, declined after 1981, and this contributed to the fall in demand.

Budget spending rose from 16,100m. francs CFA in 1976 to reach 60,600m. francs CFA in 1983, falling again to an estimated

57,028m. francs CFA in 1986. Benin's chronic balance-of-payments deficit decreased from an estimated US $76.3m. in 1983 to $54.7m. in 1984, largely owing to reduced imports. The trade deficit, which fell from an estimated US $270.8m. in 1982 to $52.7m. in 1984, is partly offset by unrecorded exports to Nigeria, by remittances from workers abroad, and by foreign aid. The principal donor of foreign aid is France, which in January 1983 agreed to cancel Benin's debts, amounting to 1,366m. francs CFA. In 1983–85 France provided assistance worth 32,250m. francs CFA, and the aid given in 1985 included a budget subsidy of 2,000m. francs CFA.

In August 1986 it was announced that preliminary talks had been held with the IMF regarding the implementation of a structural adjustment programme, devised in an effort to reverse the steady deterioration of the country's economy. In December 1984 the total external debt was estimated at US $582m., with debt service having risen from $8.8m. in 1980 to $38.3m. in 1984. The Government attributed the escalation of the external debt to the contracting of loans for the industrial projects at Onigbolo, Savé and Sémé (see above).

Benin is a member of the Economic Community of West African States (ECOWAS, see p. 133), of the West African Monetary Union (UMOA, p. 155), which shares a common currency (linked to the French franc), and of the West African Economic Community (CEAO, p. 121).

Social Welfare

In 1980 Benin had 204 physicians. In 1982 there were six hospitals, 31 health centres, 186 dispensaries and 65 maternity clinics. Two further hospitals were opened at Abomey and Natitingou in 1985 and 1986 respectively. There is a minimum hourly wage for workers.

Education

Following legislation in 1975, the State took control of all education, which is free, public and secular. Education is officially compulsory for five years, to be completed by children between the ages of five and 11 years. Primary education begins at five years of age and lasts for up to six years. Secondary education, beginning at the age of 11, lasts for up to seven years. Secondary school pupils and students must undertake nine months' teaching and three months' military and ideological training. In 1982 enrolment at primary schools was equivalent to 67% of children in the relevant age-group (92% of boys; 43% of girls), but the equivalent ratio for secondary enrolment was only 22% (boys 32%; girls 12%). The University of Benin was founded at Cotonou in 1970 and has more than 4,000 students. It was announced in May 1982 that three teacher-training colleges were to be built with finance from the IDA. In 1985 it was announced that the OPEC Fund for International Development was to lend US $1.5m. for the improvement of educational facilities in rural areas: in early 1986 plans were announced for the construction of 67 new primary schools in the northern provinces of Atacora, Borgou and Mono, with the help of $1.8m. in aid from UNESCO.

In 1985, according to UNESCO estimates, adult illiteracy was 74.1% (males 63.3%; females 84.3%).

Tourism

The number of foreign tourist arrivals increased from 23,000 in 1977 to 48,000 in 1982. Safaris can be arranged to two National Parks and the numerous hunting reserves.

Public Holidays

1987: 1 January (New Year's Day), 16 January (Anniversary of Mercenary Attack on Cotonou), 1 May (Labour Day), 26 October (Armed Forces Day), 30 November (National Day), 31 December (Harvest Day).

1988: 1 January (New Year's Day), 16 January (Anniversary of Mercenary Attack on Cotonou), 1 May (Labour Day), 26 October (Armed Forces Day), 30 November (National Day), 31 December (Harvest Day).

All religious holidays have been abolished and replaced by secular public holidays.

Weights and Measures

The metric system is in force.

Currency and Exchange Rates

100 centimes = 1 franc de la Communauté financière africaine (CFA).

Exchange rates (30 September 1986):
  1 franc CFA = 2 French centimes;
  £1 sterling = 480.625 francs CFA;
  US $1 = 332.125 francs CFA.

Statistical Survey

Source (unless otherwise stated): Institut National de la Statistique et de l'Analyse Economique, BP 323, Cotonou; tel. 31-40-81.

Area and Population

AREA, POPULATION AND DENSITY

Area (sq km)	112,622*
Population (census of 20–30 March 1979)	
Males	1,596,939
Females	1,734,271
Total	3,331,210
Population (official estimates at mid-year)	
1982	3,618,000
1983	3,720,000
1984	3,825,000
Density (per sq km) at mid-1984	34.0

* 43,484 sq miles.

ETHNIC GROUPS

1959 estimates: Fon 47.0%; Adja 12.2%; Bariba 9.7%; Yoruba and Mali 8.8%; Aizo 5.1%; Somba 5.0%; Fulani 3.8%; Coto-Coli 2.5%; Dendi 1.7%; others 4.4%.

BIRTHS AND DEATHS

Average annual birth rate 49.8 per 1,000 in 1970–75, 51.1 per 1,000 in 1975–80; death rate 26.6 per 1,000 in 1970–75, 24.6 per 1,000 in 1975–80 (UN estimates).

POPULATION BY PROVINCE (1979 census)

Atacora	479,604
Atlantique	686,258
Borgou	490,669
Mono	477,378
Ouémé	626,868
Zou	570,433
Total	**3,331,210**

PRINCIPAL TOWNS
(estimated population at 1 August 1981)
Cotonou 383,250; Porto-Novo (capital) 144,000.

ECONOMICALLY ACTIVE POPULATION
(ILO estimates, '000 persons at mid-1980)

	Males	Females	Total
Agriculture, etc.	598	648	1,246
Industry	91	28	118
Services	218	193	410
Total	**906**	**869**	**1,775**

Source: ILO, *Economically Active Population Estimates and Projections, 1950–2025*.

Agriculture

PRINCIPAL CROPS ('000 metric tons)

	1982	1983	1984
Rice (paddy)	9	5	8
Maize	273	282	379
Millet	8	6	9
Sorghum	60	57	82
Sweet potatoes	27	29	48
Cassava (Manioc)	610	594	639
Yams	672	671	698
Taro (Coco yam)*	12	12	13
Dry beans	29	29	37
Groundnuts (in shell)	35	34	58
Cottonseed*	20	28	34
Cotton (lint)*	10	13	16
Coconuts*	20	20	20
Palm kernels*	75	75	75
Oranges*	12	12	13
Mangoes*	12	12	13
Bananas*	13	13	13
Pineapples*	3	3	3
Coffee (green)	3*	3†	3†

* FAO estimates. † Unofficial estimate.
Source: FAO, *Production Yearbook*.

LIVESTOCK ('000 head, year ending September)

	1982	1983	1984*
Horses	6*	6*	6
Asses	1*	1*	1
Cattle	825	849	875
Pigs	490*	500*	520
Sheep	993	1,032	1,050
Goats	950*	988*	1,000

* FAO estimates.
Poultry (FAO estimates, million): 4 in 1982; 5 in 1983; 5 in 1984.
Source: FAO, *Production Yearbook*.

LIVESTOCK PRODUCTS (FAO estimates, '000 metric tons)

	1982	1983	1984
Beef and veal	12	12	13
Mutton and lamb	3	3	3
Goats' meat	3	3	3
Pig meat	5	6	6
Poultry meat	5	6	6
Other meat	7	6	6
Cows' milk	12	13	14
Goats' milk	5	5	5
Hen eggs	3.2	3.4	3.6

Source: FAO, *Production Yearbook*.

Forestry

ROUNDWOOD REMOVALS
(FAO estimates, '000 cubic metres, excluding bark)

	1982	1983	1984
Sawlogs, veneer logs and logs for sleepers*	24	24	24
Other industrial wood	184	189	195
Fuel wood	3,790	3,900	4,015
Total	3,998	4,113	4,234

* Assumed to be unchanged since 1975.
Source: FAO, *Yearbook of Forest Products*.

Fishing

('000 metric tons, live weight)

	1982	1983	1984*
Inland waters	20.0	17.0	16.4
Atlantic Ocean	3.5	3.5	3.6
Total catch	23.5	20.5	20.0

*FAO estimates.
Source: FAO, *Yearbook of Fishery Statistics*.

Mining

	1984
Crude petroleum (million barrels)	2.5

Industry

SELECTED PRODUCTS

		1981	1982	1983
Palm oil and palm kernel oil	'000 metric tons	27	36*	36*
Salted, dried or smoked fish*	'000 metric tons	2.3	2.3	2.0
Electric energy*	million kWh	5	5	5

* Provisional or estimated figures.
Source: UN, *Industrial Statistics Yearbook*.

Finance

CURRENCY AND EXCHANGE RATES

Monetary Units
100 centimes = 1 franc de la Communauté financière africaine (CFA).

Denominations
Coins: 1, 2, 5, 10, 25, 50 and 100 francs CFA.
Notes: 50, 100, 500, 1,000 and 5,000 francs CFA.

French Franc, Sterling and Dollar Equivalents
(30 September 1986)
1 French franc = 50 francs CFA;
£1 sterling = 480.625 francs CFA;
US $1 = 332.125 francs CFA;
1,000 francs CFA = £2.081 = $3.011.

Average Exchange Rate (francs CFA per US $)
1983   381.06
1984   436.96
1985   449.26

DEVELOPMENT PLAN, 1981–90
(planned public investment, '000 million francs CFA)

Agriculture	55.6
Industry/Mining	44.5
Infrastructure	297.2
Railways	188.3
Ports	30.1
Water/Dams	42.7
Roads	14.2
Total (identified)	397.3
Total (planned)	958.8

Source: *Bulletin de l'Afrique Noire*, December 1981.

BUDGET (million francs CFA)

Revenue	1981	1982
Fiscal receipts	31,737	40,602
Direct taxes	9,965	10,765
Indirect taxes (incl. import tax)	21,233	29,378
Registration and stamp duty	459	459
Non-fiscal receipts	10,807	10,335
Property income	2,102	2,108
Operations and services	1,115	418
Income from collectives and public companies	200	325
Special accounts	7,390	7,484
Total	42,564	50,937

Expenditure*	1982
Current budget	33,032
Defence	7,821
Primary education	4,063
Secondary and technical education and health	2,118
Investment budget	14,831
Grants and subsidies	3,759
Contributions, etc.	2,239
Total	47,863

* Figures for 1981 not available.
Source: Ministère des Finances, Cotonou.

1983 (million francs CFA): Current budget 60,600, investment budget 69,900.
1984 (million francs CFA): Current budget 55,914, investment budget 48,109.
1985 (draft budget, million francs CFA): Current budget 50,768, investment budget 40,588.
1986 (draft budget, million francs CFA): Current budget 57,028, investment budget 49,849.

CENTRAL BANK RESERVES (US $ million at 31 December)

	1983	1984	1985
Gold*	4.3	3.7	3.6
IMF special drawing rights	1.2	0.1	—
Reserve position in IMF	2.1	2.0	2.2
Foreign exchange	0.4	0.3	1.9
Total	8.0	6.2	7.7

* Valued at market-related prices.
Source: IMF, *International Financial Statistics*.

MONEY SUPPLY (million francs CFA at 31 December)

	1983	1984	1985
Currency outside banks	22.51	26.95	20.26
Demand deposit at deposit money banks	56.60	59.56	63.63
Checking deposits at post office	2.89	2.98	2.90
Total money	82.00	89.49	87.09

Source: IMF, *International Financial Statistics*.

NATIONAL ACCOUNTS (million francs CFA at current prices)
National Income and Product

	1976	1977	1978
Compensation of employees	30,148	35,733	38,932
Operating surplus	82,295	90,656	102,802
Domestic factor incomes	112,443	126,389	141,734
Consumption of fixed capital	8,529	8,923	10,936
Gross domestic product at factor cost	120,972	135,312	152,669
Indirect taxes	13,371	15,908	15,913
Less Subsidies	30	18	22
GDP in purchasers' values	134,313	151,202	168,560
Factor income from abroad	1,027	1,165	1,197
Less Factor income paid abroad	848	1,026	1,083
Gross national product	134,492	151,341	168,674
Less Consumption of fixed capital	8,529	8,923	10,936
National income in market prices	125,963	142,418	157,738
Other current transfers from abroad	12,171	21,432	18,600
Less Other current transfers paid abroad	1,499	1,636	1,780
National disposable income	136,635	162,214	174,558

GDP in purchasers' values ('000 million francs CFA at current prices): 193.5 in 1979; 235.9 in 1980; 287.6 in 1981; 342.9 in 1982; 385.3 in 1983.

Expenditure on the Gross Domestic Product

	1976	1977	1978
Government final consumption expenditure	12,781	14,711	14,414
Private final consumption expenditure	119,504	147,839	166,553
Increase in stocks	3,300	4,800	5,500
Gross fixed capital formation	21,962	22,887	23,203
Total domestic expenditure	157,547	190,237	209,670
Exports of goods and services	31,613	34,782	39,611
Less Imports of goods and services	54,847	73,817	80,721
GDP in purchasers' values	134,313	151,202	168,560
GDP at constant 1970 prices	86,619	76,987	75,933

Gross Domestic Product by Economic Activity (at factor cost)

	1976	1977	1978
Agriculture, hunting, forestry and fishing	53,802	59,823	73,294
Mining and quarrying	264	292	304
Manufacturing	7,992	8,671	8,854
Electricity, gas and water	852	987	1,482
Construction	5,061	5,250	5,434
Trade, restaurants and hotels	29,206	32,025	34,709
Transport, storage and communications	9,031	10,611	12,391
Public administration and defence	11,073	12,872	12,671
Other services	3,691	4,781	3,530
Total	120,972	135,312	152,669

Source: Direction des Etudes et de la Planification, Ministère des Finances, Cotonou.

BALANCE OF PAYMENTS (US $ million)

	1976	1977	1978
Merchandise exports f.o.b.	85.9	129.1	125.6
Merchandise imports f.o.b.	−208.6	−255.5	−284.8
Trade balance	−122.7	−126.4	−159.2
Exports of services	34.0	36.0	42.6
Imports of services	−64.1	−74.9	−89.2
Balance on goods and services	−152.8	−165.3	−205.8
Private unrequited transfers (net)	26.7	38.0	54.7
Government unrequited transfers (net)	53.3	66.7	54.6
Current balance	−72.8	−60.7	−96.4
Direct capital investment (net)	2.5	3.1	0.8
Other long-term capital (net)	15.4	14.1	19.1
Short-term capital (net)	27.2	19.4	37.0
Net errors and omissions	24.9	20.1	20.3
Total (net monetary movements)	−2.8	−3.9	−19.3
Valuation changes (net)	−1.0	1.0	1.6
Exceptional financing (net)	8.0	4.0	12.8
Changes in reserves	4.2	1.1	−4.8

Source: IMF, *International Financial Statistics*.

External Trade

PRINCIPAL COMMODITIES (million francs CFA)

Imports c.i.f.	1975	1976	1977
Cereals	532	1,318	2,702
Sugar and sugar products	532	454	135
Beverages	2,922	3,447	4,748
Tobacco	3,337	4,982	5,728
Construction materials	891	979	811
Petroleum products	2,579	2,954	2,990
Pharmaceutical products	1,083	1,009	817
Paper and paper products	1,013	792	831
Textiles	5,744	6,774	10,172
Clothing	2,877	4,989	7,365
Iron and steel	2,071	2,819	2,584
Non-electrical machinery	2,990	2,848	3,003
Electrical machinery	2,425	3,105	3,040
Road transport supplies	3,852	5,176	5,430
Total (incl. others)	42,080	52,207	60,354

Total imports c.i.f. (million francs CFA): 70,197 in 1978; 68,100 in 1979; 69,970 in 1980; n.a. in 1981; 156,427 in 1982.

Exports f.o.b.	1979	1980	1982*
Cocoa beans	2,950	2,940	280
Cotton	1,180	2,460	1,460
Palm products	2,990	3,690	1,890
Total (incl. others)	9,770	13,270	14,020

* Figures for 1981 are not available.
Source: IMF, *International Financial Statistics*.

PRINCIPAL TRADING PARTNERS (million francs CFA)

Imports	1975	1976	1977*
China, People's Republic	1,895	1,724	986
France	12,026	15,637	14,088
Germany, Federal Republic	3,159	3,734	4,955
Ivory Coast	1,129	1,149	1,305
Netherlands	2,634	3,007	3,580
United Kingdom	6,255	5,605	7,672
USA	2,826	3,072	3,333
Total (incl. others)	42,080	52,207	60,354

Exports	1975	1976	1977*
China, People's Republic	375	19	0
France	1,849	1,719	1,883
Germany, Federal Republic	521	193	638
Japan	348	1,008	1,534
Netherlands	472	333	1,019
Niger	591	374	242
Nigeria	1,078	542	629
Total (incl. others)	6,791	5,538	7,642

* Provisional.
Source: Direction des Etudes et de la Planification, Ministère des Finances, Cotonou.

Transport

RAILWAYS (traffic)

	1979	1981*
Passengers carried ('000)	1,665	1,934
Passenger-km (million)	143	187.6
Freight carried ('000 tons)	352	419
Freight ton-km (million)	140.4	176.5

* Figures for 1980 not available.

ROAD TRAFFIC (motor vehicles in use at 31 December)

	1977	1978	1979
Private cars	9,536	9,549	9,592
Buses and coaches / Goods vehicles	7,439	7,271	6,927

Source: *World Road Statistics* (International Road Federation, Geneva); UN, *Statistical Yearbook*.

INTERNATIONAL SEA-BORNE SHIPPING
(freight traffic at Cotonou, '000 metric tons)

	1983	1984	1985
Goods loaded	64.4	79.1	107.5
Goods unloaded	736.1	807.1	1,059.1

Source: Port Autonome de Cotonou.

CIVIL AVIATION (traffic on scheduled services)*

	1980	1981	1982
Kilometres flown (million)	1.8	1.9	1.8
Passengers carried ('000)	61	75	81
Passenger-km (million)	178	197	212
Freight ton-km (million)	18.0	21.0	21.2

* Including an apportionment of the traffic of Air Afrique.
Source: UN, *Statistical Yearbook*.

Tourism

	1980	1981	1982
Tourist arrivals ('000)	39	46	48

Source: UN, *Statistical Yearbook*.

Communications Media

	1981	1982	1983
Radio receivers ('000 in use)	250	270	290
Television receivers ('000 in use)	7	10	13

Television receivers (1984): estimated 17,250 in use.
Telephones (1978): 16,000 in use.
Books (1978): 13 titles (18,000 copies) produced.
Daily newspapers (1982): 1 (average circulation 1,000).
Source: mainly UNESCO, *Statistical Yearbook*.

Education

(1982)

	Schools	Teachers	Pupils Males	Pupils Females	Pupils Total
Pre-primary	140	267	3,129	2,538	5,667
Primary	2,723	11,339	288,779	139,406	428,185
Secondary:					
general	133	1,816	85,036	32,688	117,724
vocational	30	755	4,428	2,115	6,543
Higher	13	801	5,267	1,035	6,302

Source: mainly UNESCO, *Statistical Yearbook*.

Directory

The Constitution

On 23 May 1977 legislation (a Loi Fondamentale) was announced by the Parti de la révolution populaire du Bénin (PRPB) as preparation for the 'people's democratic revolution'. In August the Loi Fondamentale was approved by the National Revolutionary Council. In its place, a National Revolutionary Assembly was established in November 1979, comprising directly elected People's Commissioners. They, in turn, elect the President, who is Head of State. The People's Commissioners represent socio-professional classes, not geographical constituencies. At local levels, state powers are exercised by elected provincial district town and village councils. The judiciary is responsible to the National Revolutionary Assembly and the Armed Forces are under the control of the PRPB.

The Government

HEAD OF STATE

President: Brig.-Gen. MATHIEU KEREKOU (assumed office 27 October 1972; elected President 5 February 1980; re-elected 31 July 1984).

NATIONAL EXECUTIVE COUNCIL
(October 1986)

Head of Military Revolutionary Government and Minister of Defence: Brig.-Gen. MATHIEU KEREKOU.
Minister Delegate to the Presidency in charge of Interior, Security and Territorial Administration: Maj. EDOUARD ZODEHOUGAN.
Minister Delegate to the Presidency in charge of Planning and Statistics: ZUL KIFL SALAMI.
Minister of Rural Development and Co-operative Action: Maj. ADOLPHE BIAOU.
Minister of Equipment and Transport: GADO GIRIGISSOU.
Minister of Finance and Economy: HOSPICE ANTONIO.
Minister of Trade, Crafts and Tourism: SOULE DANKORO.
Minister of Primary Education: Capt. PHILIPPE AKPO.
Minister of Secondary and Higher Education: VINCENT GUEDZODJE.
Minister of Culture, Youth and Sports: OUSMANE DANKOTO.
Minister of Labour and Social Affairs: Lt-Col. NATHANAEL MENSAH.
Minister of Public Health: ANDRÉ ATCHADE.
Minister of Information and Communications: HOUDOU ALI.
Minister of Foreign Affairs and Co-operation: FRÉDÉRIC AFFO.
Minister of Justice and Inspection of Parastatal Enterprises: DIDIER DASSI.

The Prefects of the six provinces also have ministerial status.

MINISTRIES

Office of the President and Ministry of Defence: BP 2028, Cotonou; tel. 30-00-90; telex 5222.
Ministry of Culture, Youth and Sports: BP 65, Porto-Novo; tel. 21-24-30.
Ministry of Equipment and Transport: Cotonou; tel. 31-46-64.
Ministry of Finance and Economy: BP 302, Cotonou; tel. 31-40-53; telex 5009.
Ministry of Foreign Affairs and Co-operation: BP 318, Cotonou; tel. 30-04-00; telex 5200.
Ministry of Information and Communications: Cotonou; tel. 31-42-56; telex 5208.
Ministry of Inspection of Parastatal Enterprises: Cotonou; tel. 31-33-49.
Ministry of Interior, Security and Territorial Administration: Cotonou; tel. 30-11-06.
Ministry of Justice: BP 967, Cotonou; tel. 31-31-46.
Ministry of Labour and Social Affairs: BP 907, Cotonou; tel. 31-31-12.

BENIN   Directory

Ministry of Planning and Statistics: BP 342, Cotonou; tel. 30-05-41; telex 5252.
Ministry of Primary Education: Porto-Novo; tel. 21-26-51.
Ministry of Public Health: BP 882, Cotonou; tel. 31-26-70.
Ministry of Rural Development and Co-operative Action: BP 34, Porto-Novo; tel. 21-30-53.
Ministry of Secondary and Higher Education: Cotonou; tel. 30-06-81.
Ministry of Trade, Crafts and Tourism: BP 2037, Cotonou; tel. 31-52-58.

Legislature

ASSEMBLÉE NATIONALE RÉVOLUTIONNAIRE

In August 1977 the Loi Fondamentale provided for the disbanding of the National Revolutionary Council, which was to be replaced by a National Revolutionary Assembly. The Assembly was elected by direct universal suffrage in November 1979, then consisting of 336 People's Commissioners (reduced to 196 at elections in June 1984) who, in turn, elect the President. The People's Commissioners represent socio-professional classes, not geographical constituencies. In June 1984 the mandate of the National Assembly and the President of the Republic was extended from three years to five.
President of Permanent Committee: ROMAIN VILON GUEZO.

Political Organization

Parti de la révolution populaire du Bénin (PRPB): Cotonou; f. 1975; Marxist-Leninist ruling party; at the second ordinary congress of the party, held in November 1985, a cen. cttee of 45 mems was elected; this body, in turn, elected from its mems the 11-mem. Politburo. Chair. Cen. Cttee Brig.-Gen. MATHIEU KEREKOU.

Diplomatic Representation

EMBASSIES IN BENIN

Algeria: BP 1809, Cotonou; telex 5030; Ambassador: ABDELAZIZ YADI.
Bulgaria: Cotonou; Chargé d'affaires a.i.: DIMITER PERLIDANSKI.
China, People's Republic: BP 196, Cotonou; Ambassador: ZHU XIANSONG.
Cuba: BP 948, Cotonou; telex 5277; Ambassador: CARLOS CALANAS.
Egypt: BP 1215, Cotonou; telex 5274; Ambassador: ABDEL AZIZ KHALIL.
France: route de l'Aviation, BP 966, Cotonou; tel. 31-22-24; telex 5209; Ambassador: FRANÇOIS GENDREAU.
German Democratic Republic: Cotonou; Ambassador: GERHARD HAIDA.
Germany, Federal Republic: 7 route Inter-Etats, BP 504, Cotonou; tel. 31-29-67; telex 5224; Ambassador: HORST UHRIG.
Ghana: BP 488, Cotonou; tel. 30-07-46; Ambassador: C. T. K. QUARSHIE.
Korea, Democratic People's Republic: BP 317, Cotonou; Ambassador: KIM SEUNG HWAN.
Libya: 'Les Cocotiers', Cotonou; telex 5254; People's Bureau Representative: MUSTAFA AL-BUSSETTA.
Niger: BP 352, Cotonou; telex 5271; Ambassador: ABDOU ZAROUMEYE.
Nigeria: Lot 21, Patte d'Oie, Cotonou; telex 5247; Ambassador: Brother OLADUGBEWO ADEFEMIWA.
USSR: BP 2013, Cotonou; Ambassador: VITALY AGAPOV.
USA: BP 2012, Cotonou; tel. 30-17-92; Ambassador: WALTER E. STADLER.
Zaire: BP 130, Cotonou; tel. 30-19-83; Ambassador: BINDO N'KETA KIBIBI.

Judicial System

The Central People's Court controls the judicial operations of all the People's Courts at various levels. It is responsible to the National Revolutionary Assembly and to the National Executive Council.

At the lowest level, each commune, village and city ward has its own court, which does not, however, have executive powers. There is a court in each district, which has the power to try cases. There is also a court in each province which acts as an appeals court and an assizes court. The Central Court is composed of a chairman, three divisional chairmen who are professional judges, six judges and 12 lay people's judges who have the same powers as the professional judges and magistrates in judicial decision-making. The professional judges are appointed by the National Executive Council. The lay people's judges are elected for three years by the National Revolutionary Assembly on the advice of the Central Committee of the PRPB.
Cour populaire centrale (Central People's Court): Cotonou; Chair. LÉANORE AMLON.

Religion

According to the 1961 census, 65% of the population held animist beliefs, 15% were Christians (Roman Catholic 12%, Protestant 3%) and 13% Muslims. Since 1975, religious and spiritual cults have been discouraged.

CHRISTIANITY

There are 257 Protestant mission centres with a personnel of about 120. At 31 December 1984 there were an estimated 611,000 Roman Catholics (about one-sixth of the population), mainly in the south of the country.

The Roman Catholic Church

Benin comprises one archdiocese and five dioceses.
Bishops' Conference: Conférence Episcopale du Bénin, Archevêché, BP 491, Cotonou; tel. 31-31-45; Pres. Mgr CHRISTOPHE ADIMOU, Archbishop of Cotonou.
Archbishop of Cotonou: Mgr CHRISTOPHE ADIMOU, Archevêché, BP 491, Cotonou; tel. 30-01-45.

BAHÁ'Í FAITH

National Spiritual Assembly: BP 1252, Cotonou; mems resident in 285 localities.

The Press

L'Aube Nouvelle: Cotonou; daily.
Bénin-Presse Information: BP 120, Cotonou; tel. 31-26-55; publ. by the Agence Bénin-Presse; weekly.
La Croix du Bénin: BP 105, Cotonou; tel. 32-11-19; f. 1946; Roman Catholic; fortnightly; Dir BARTHÉLEMY CAKPO ASSOGBA.
Ehuzu: BP 1210, Cotonou; tel. 30-08-75; govt daily; Dir MAURICE CHABI; circ. 10,000.
Journal Officiel de la République Populaire du Bénin: Porto-Novo; publ. by the Government Information Service; monthly.

NEWS AGENCIES

Agence Bénin-Presse: BP 120, Cotonou; tel. 31-26-55; f. 1961; national news agency; section of the Ministry of Information and Communications; Dir EVARISTE DEGLA.

Foreign Bureaux

Agentstvo Pechati Novosti (APN) (USSR): 'Les Cocotiers', Lot F-12, BP 968, Cotonou; tel. 30-10-23; Dir ANDREI DOUBROVSKY.
Telegrafnoye Agentstvo Sovetskovo Soyuza (TASS) (USSR): Lot 186, Patte d'Oie, BP 928, Cotonou 6; tel. 30-01-33; telex 5204; Correspondent ALEKSANDR PROSVETOV.

Publisher

Government Publishing House

Office National d'Edition, de Presse et d'Imprimerie (ONEPI): BP 1210, Cotonou; tel. 30-08-75; f. 1975; Dir-Gen. BONI ZIMÉ MAKO.

Radio and Television

According to UNESCO, there were an estimated 290,000 radio receivers and 13,000 television receivers in use in 1983.

BENIN
Directory

Office de Radiodiffusion et de Télévision du Bénin: BP 366, Cotonou; tel. 31-20-41; telex 5132; state-owned; radio broadcasts in French, English and 18 local languages; TV transmissions 12 hours weekly; Dir-Gen. R. O. SANNI; Dir of Radio N. J. SOHOUENOU; Dir of TV SEBASTIEN AGBOTA.

Finance

(cap. = capital; dep. = deposits; res = reserves; m. = million; brs = branches; amounts in francs CFA)

BANKING

Central Bank

Banque Centrale des Etats de l'Afrique de l'Ouest (BCEAO): BP 325, Cotonou; tel. 31-24-66; telex 5211; br. in Parakou; headquarters in Dakar, Senegal; f. 1955; bank of issue for the seven states of the Union monétaire ouest-africaine (UMOA), comprising Benin, Burkina Faso, the Ivory Coast, Mali, Niger, Senegal and Togo; cap. and res 32,564m. (Sept. 1985); Gov. ABDOULAYE FADIGA; Dir in Benin GILBERT MEDJE.

State Banks

Banque Béninoise pour le Développement (BBD): 2 rue des Cheminots, BP 300, Cotonou; tel. 31-34-76; telex 5238; f. 1962; cap. 1,500m.; Pres. RICHARD ADJAHO; Man. Dir BENOÎT ZANNOU; 3 brs.

Banque Commerciale du Bénin (BCB): rue du Révérend Père Colineau, BP 85, Cotonou; tel. 31-37-13; telex 5216; f. 1962; cap. 1,500m., res 6,029m., dep. 101,484m. (Sept. 1983); conducts all govt business; Dir-Gen. FRANCIS PADONOU; 22 brs.

Caisse Nationale de Crédit Agricole (CNCA): BP 999, Cotonou; tel. 31-53-86; telex 5018; f. 1975; 51% state-owned; cap. 300m., dep. 7,089m.; Pres. ISIDORE AMOUSSOU; Dir-Gen. ASSOUMA YAKOUBOU.

INSURANCE

Société Béninoise d'Assurance: angle ave Steinmetz et rue du roi Dokodonou, Cotonou; f. 1974; cap. 40m.; Pres. V. HODONOU.

Société Nationale d'Assurances et de Réassurances (SONAR): BP 2030, Cotonou; tel. 31-16-49; telex 5231; f. 1974; cap. 300m.; state-owned; Pres. Minister of Finance and Economy; Man. Dir JEAN-BONIFACE AKANNI.

Trade and Industry

DEVELOPMENT ORGANIZATIONS

Caisse Centrale de Coopération Economique (CCCE): blvd de France, BP 38, Cotonou; tel. 31-35-80; telex 5082; Dir PAUL DERAM.

Mission Française d'Aide et de Coopération: BP 476, Cotonou; centre for administering bilateral aid from France according to the co-operation agreement signed in February 1975; Dir MICHEL MONTFORT.

Office Béninois d'Aménagement Rural (OBAR): BP 312, Porto-Novo; f. 1983; state-owned rural development organization; rural planning and promotion of hydro-agricultural development and irrigation; cap. 500m. francs CFA; Dir LÉON K. LOKOSSOU.

MARKETING BOARDS

Office National du Bois (ONAB): BP 1238, Cotonou; tel. 33-19-56; telex 5160; f. 1983; forest development and marketing of wood products; cap. 300m. francs CFA; Man. Dir D. GABRIEL LOKOUN.

Société Béninoise des Matériaux de Construction (SOBEMAC): BP 1209, Cotonou; tel. 31-25-93; telex 5262; f. 1975; monopoly of cement marketing; cap. 100m. francs CFA; Pres. MAMOUD MOUSTAPHA SOULE; Man. Dir RENÉ DOSSA MEGNIHO.

Société Nationale de Commercialisation et d'Exportation du Bénin (SONACEB): BP 933, Cotonou; tel. 31-28-22; telex 5248; f. 1972; monopoly of internal marketing of all agricultural produce except palm products, cotton and tobacco; monopoly of cement exports; Pres. ARMAND ALAPINI; Man. Dir POLYCARPE AGOSSA.

Société Nationale de Commercialisation des Produits Pétroliers (SONACOP): ave d'Ornano, BP 245, Cotonou; tel. 31-22-90; telex 5245; f. 1974; cap. 872m. francs CFA; distribution of petroleum products; Pres. DGM MCAT; Man. Dir EDMOND-PIERRE AMOUSSOU.

Société Nationale pour le Développement des Fruits et Légumes (SONAFEL): BP 2040, Cotonou; tel. 31-52-34; telex 5031; headquarters at Bohicon; f. 1975; cap. 50m. francs CFA; development of fruit and vegetable production; monopoly of export of fruit and vegetable produce; Man. Dir JOACHIM PHILIPPE D'ALMEIDA.

Société Nationale pour la Promotion Agricole (SONAPRA): BP 933, Cotonou; tel. 33-08-20; telex 5248; f. 1983; state-owned; marketing of agricultural products; Dir-Gen. H. GNONHOUE.

Société Nationale d'Equipement (SONAE): BP 2042, Cotonou; tel. 31-31-26; telex 5201; f. 1975; cap. 300m. francs CFA; import and distribution of capital goods; Man. Dir NICOLAS ADAGBE.

CHAMBER OF COMMERCE

Chambre de Commerce et d'Industrie de la République Populaire du Bénin (CCIB): ave du Général de Gaulle, BP 31, Cotonou; tel. 31-32-99; Pres. ABOU BAKAR BABA-MOUSSA; Vice-Pres. J.-V. ADJOVI, M. T. LALEYE; Sec.-Gen. N. A. VIADENOU.

EMPLOYERS' ORGANIZATIONS

Association des Syndicats du Bénin (ASYNBA): Cotonou; Pres. PIERRE FOURN.

Groupement Interprofessionnel des Entreprises du Bénin (GIBA): BP 6, Cotonou; Pres. A. JEUKENS.

Syndicat des Commerçants Importateurs et Exportateurs du Bénin: BP 6, Cotonou; Pres. M. BENCHIMOL.

Syndicat Interprofessionnel des Entreprises Industrielles du Bénin: Cotonou; Pres. M. DOUCET.

Syndicat National des Commerçants et Industriels Africains du Bénin (SYNACIB): BP 367, Cotonou; Pres. URBAIN DA SILVA.

Syndicat des Transporteurs Routiers du Bénin: Cotonou; Pres. PASCAL ZENON.

STATE ENTERPRISES

Office National de Pharmacie du Bénin (ONPB): 5 route de Porto-Novo, BP 1255, Cotonou; telex 5243; f. 1978; cap. 311m. francs CFA; manufacture of pharmaceutical products; Man. Dir EXPÉDIT VINHO.

Société Agro-Animale Bénino-Libyenne (SABLI): BP 03-1200, Cotonou; tel. 31-49-15; telex 5096; f. 1979; cap. 430m. francs CFA; 51% state-owned, 49% Libya; Man. Dir PATRICE GBEGBELEGBE.

Société d'Alimentation Générale du Bénin (AGB): BP 53, Cotonou; tel. 33-07-28; telex 5062; f. 1978; 100% state-owned; monopoly importer and distributor of basic foodstuffs, drink and tobacco; chain of 23 supermarkets and 3 wholesale stores; Man. Dir JEAN-CLAUDE SANT'ANNA.

Société Bénino-Arabe-Libyenne de Pêche Maritime (BELIPECHE): BP 1516, Cotonou; tel. 31-51-36; f. 1977; cap. US $5m.; 51% state-owned, 49% Libya; fish and fish products; Pres. LAURENT FAGBOHOUN; Dir SALEH AREIBI.

Société Bénino-Arabe-Libyenne des Mines (BELIMINES): BP 1913, Cotonou; tel. 31-59-24; telex 5128; f. 1979; cap. US $2m.; 51% state-owned, 49% Libya; mining and commercialization of marble; Pres. ANDRÉ YORO; Man. Dir HASSAN A. RAGHI.

Société Béninoise d'Electricité et d'Eau (SBEE): BP 123, Cotonou; tel. 31-22-47; f. 1973; production and distribution of electricity and water; Man. Dir EMILE-LOUIS PARAISO.

Société Béninoise de Palmier à Huile (SOBEPALH): BP 12, Porto-Novo; tel. 21-29-03; f. 1961, nationalized 1975; cap. 425m. francs CFA; 100% state-owned; production of palm oil and cotton seed oil; refineries at Monò, Hinvy and Agonvy; Pres. PHILIPPE AKPO; Man. Dir MARIUS KOKOU QUENUM.

Société des Ciments d'Onigbolo (SCO): Onigbolo; cap. 6,000m. francs CFA; 51% state-owned, 43% Nigeria; production and marketing of cement; Pres. JUSTIN GNIDEHOU; Man. Dir R. J. K. FRYMANN.

Société de Développement des Ressources Animales (SODERA): BP 2041, Cotonou; f. 1976; monopoly of import and export of meat; Man. Dir Dr PIERRE TOMAGNIMENA.

Société Nationale de Boissons (La Béninoise): route de Porto-Novo, BP 135, Cotonou; tel. 33-10-61; telex 5275; f. 1957, nationalized 1975; cap. 3,200m. francs CFA; production of beer, soft drinks and ice; Pres. BARNABÉ MIDOUZO; Dir-Gen. RICHARD MENSAH.

Société Nationale d'Irrigation et d'Aménagement Hydro-Agricole (SONIAH): BP 312, Porto-Novo; tel. 21-34-20;

BENIN

f. 1972; cap. 350m. francs CFA; development of irrigation and rice-growing projects; Dir-Gen. YENAKPONDJI CAPOCHICHI; Sec.-Gen. TOSSA JÉRÔME TONI.

Société Nationale de Raffinage (SONARAF): Cotonou; cap. 424m. francs CFA; 51% state-owned; construction of and production from petroleum refinery.

Société Nationale pour l'Industrie des Corps Gras (SONICOG): BP 312, Cotonou; tel. 31-33-71; telex 5205; f. 1962; cap. 600m. francs CFA; production of palm oil, palm kernel and groundnut oils and cakes, sheanut butter and soaps; factories at Porto-Novo, Bohicon and Cotonou; Dir-Gen. BARNABÉ BIDOUZO.

TRADE UNION

Union Nationale des Syndicats des Travailleurs du Bénin: BP 69, Cotonou; formed by integration of all previous trade union organizations; Sec.-Gen. ROMAIN VILON GUEZO.

Transport

RAILWAYS

Construction of a 650-km extension north from Parakou to Gaya, and on through Niger to Niamey, is under way and due for completion in 1988.

In 1982 the network handled almost 378,000 metric tons of goods, of which over 280,000 metric tons were in transit for Niger.

Organisation Commune Bénin-Niger des Chemins de Fer et des Transports (OCBN): BP 16, Cotonou; tel. 31-33-80; telex 5210; f. 1959; Benin has a 63% share, Niger 37%. The main line runs for 438 km from Cotonou to Parakou in the interior; a branch runs westward via Ouidah to Segboroué (34 km). There is also a line of 107 km from Cotonou via Porto-Novo to Pobé near the Nigerian border. Total length of railways: 579 km; Gen. Man. R. M. DE SOUZA.

ROADS

The system is well developed. In 1985 there were 7,445 km of classified roads (including 3,359 km of main roads) and a further 1,200 km of tracks that are suitable for motor traffic in the dry season. The roads along the coast and those from Cotonou to Bohicon and from Parakou to Malanville, a total of 700 km, are bitumen-surfaced. Five projects, costing a total of 14,191m. francs CFA, are planned, including the construction of three road bridges over the rivers Mono, Sazué and Okpara, and the improvement of sections of the Lagos–Accra and Cotonou–Malanville highways.

Société de Transit et de Consignation du Bénin (SOTRACOB): BP 253, Cotonou; tel. 31-25-65; telex 5219; f. 1975; cap. 100m. francs CFA; 65% state-owned; Man. Dir LÉONARD GBAGUIDI.

Directory

Société des Transports Routiers du Bénin (TRANSBENIN): BP 703, Cotonou; tel. 31-32-28; f. 1977; cap. 300m. francs CFA; 49% state-owned; transport of goods and passengers; Man. Dir PROSPER DJIDJOHO.

SHIPPING

The main port is at Cotonou. In 1985 the port handled 1,116,600 metric tons of goods, of which 411,600 tons were from Niger, 11,700 tons from Mali and 9,500 tons from Burkina Faso.

Capacity was 2m. metric tons in 1986, and further improvements are being carried out, with finance from Abu Dhabi, Canada, France, Norway and multilateral agencies.

Cie Béninoise de Navigation Maritime (COBENAM): BP 2032, Cotonou; tel. 31-47-87; telex 5225; f. 1974; 51% state-owned, 49% Algerian; cap. 500m. francs CFA; agents for shipping companies from France, Japan, UK, China; Man. Dir NOUHOUM ASSOUMAN.

Office Béninois des Manutentions Portuaires (OBEMAP): BP 35, Cotonou; tel. 31-39-83; has monopoly of handling merchandise at Cotonou; Man. Dir PAUL AWANOU.

Port Autonome de Cotonou: BP 927, Cotonou; tel. 31-28-90; telex 5004; Pres. Minister of Equipment and Transport; Man. Dir ODON BRICE HOUNCANRIN.

Régie de Ravitaillement des Navires: BP 863, Cotonou; telex 5292; f. 1976; state-owned; loading and unloading of ships at Cotonou; cap. 10m. francs CFA.

Société des Transports de la Province de l'Atlantique: BP 118, Cotonou; tel. 33-10-89; public transportation of passengers and freight; Dir GOUNOU DANKORO (acting).

CIVIL AVIATION

The international airport at Cotonou has a 2.4-km runway, and there are secondary airports at Parakou, Natitingou, Kandi and Abomey. There were 81,000 passengers at Cotonou in 1982. In 1981 9,763 metric tons of freight were handled.

Air Afrique: ave du Gouverneur Ballot, BP 200, Cotonou; Benin has a 7% share in Air Afrique (see under Ivory Coast); Dirs (Benin) DEMBA CISSÉ, THÉOPHILE EGAH.

Transports Aériens du Bénin (TAB): BP 824, Cotonou; tel. 30-07-97; telex 5297; f. 1978; state-owned; domestic passenger and cargo services to Savé, Parakou, Natitingou, Djougou and Kandi; regional services to Lagos, Lomé, Ouagadougou and Niamey; Man. Dir MANASSE AYAYI; fleet of 1 Fokker 28, 2 Twin Otter 300.

Tourism

Office National du Tourisme et de l'Hôtellerie (ONATHO): BP 89, Cotonou; tel. 31-26-87; telex 5032; f. 1974; Dir-Gen. CLÉMENT LOKOSSOU.

BHUTAN

Introductory Survey

Location, Climate, Language, Religion, Flag, Capital

The Kingdom of Bhutan lies in the Himalaya range of mountains, with the People's Republic of China to the north and India to the south. Average monthly temperature ranges from 4.4°C (40°F) in January to 17°C (62°F) in July. Rainfall is heavy, ranging from 150 cm (60 inches) to 300 cm (120 inches) per year. The official language is Dzongkha, spoken mainly in western Bhutan. Written Dzongkha is based on the Tibetan script. The state religion is Mahayana Buddhism, mainly the Drukpa school of the Kagyupa sect. The national flag (proportions 5 by 4) is divided diagonally from the lower hoist to the upper fly, so forming two triangles, one orange and the other maroon, with a white dragon superimposed in the centre. The capital is Thimphu.

Recent History

The first hereditary King of Bhutan was installed on 17 December 1907. An Anglo-Bhutanese Treaty, signed in 1910, placed Bhutan's foreign relations under the supervision of the Government of British India. After India became independent, that treaty was replaced in August 1949 by the Indo-Bhutan Treaty of Friendship, whereby Bhutan agrees to seek the advice of the Government of India with regard to its foreign relations, but remains free to decide whether or not to accept such advice.

King Jigme Dorji Wangchuk, installed in 1952, established the National Assembly (Tsogdu) in 1953 and a Royal Advisory Council in 1965. He formed the country's first Cabinet in May 1968. He died in July 1972 and was succeeded by the Western-educated 16-year-old Crown Prince, Jigme Singye Wangchuk. The new King stated his wish to maintain the Indo-Bhutan Treaty and further to strengthen friendship with India. In 1979, however, during the Non-Aligned Conference and later at the UN General Assembly, Bhutan voted in opposition to India, in favour of Chinese policy. In December 1983 India and Bhutan made a new trade agreement concerning overland trade with Bangladesh and Nepal. India raised no objection to Bhutan's decision to negotiate directly with the People's Republic of China over the Bhutan-China border, and discussions were begun in April 1984. The talks had made some progress by July 1986, and a fourth round of discussions was scheduled to take place in 1987.

When Chinese authority was established in Tibet in 1959, Bhutan granted asylum to about 4,000 Tibetan refugees. Because it had been discovered that many refugees were engaged in spying and subversive activities, the Bhutan Government decided in 1976 to disperse them in small groups, introducing a number of Bhutanese families into each settlement. In early 1978 discussions with the Dalai Lama of Tibet broke down after four years. In June 1979 the National Assembly approved a directive which set the end of the year as a deadline for the refugees to decide whether to take out Bhutanese citizenship or accept repatriation to Tibet. In October India announced that it would not be able to accept refugees who refused Bhutanese nationality as there were still 10,000 Tibetans in India who were awaiting rehabilitation. By July 1980, however, most of the Tibetans had chosen Bhutanese citizenship, and the remainder were to be accepted by India.

Bhutan has asserted itself as a fully sovereign, independent state, becoming a member of the UN in 1971 and of the Non-Aligned Movement in 1973. Bhutan has gradually increased the number of its diplomatic missions abroad, and in 1986 had ambassadors at the UN in New York, in New Delhi, Dhaka and Kathmandu. In March 1986 Bhutan and Japan announced their intention to establish diplomatic relations.

In 1983 Bhutan was an enthusiastic founder-member of the South Asian Regional Co-operation (SARC) organization, with Bangladesh, India, Maldives, Nepal, Pakistan and Sri Lanka. In May 1985 Bhutan was host to the first meeting of ministers of foreign affairs from SARC member countries, which agreed to give their grouping the formal title of South Asian Association for Regional Co-operation (SAARC, see p. 218). Bhutan was represented at the second SAARC summit, held in India in November 1986, when it was decided that a permanent secretariat should be established in Kathmandu.

Government

Bhutan is an absolute monarchy, without a written constitution. The system of government is unusual in that power is shared between the monarchy (assisted by the Royal Advisory Council), the Council of Ministers, the National Assembly (Tsogdu) and the monastic head (Je Khempo) of Bhutan's 6,000 lamas (Buddhist priests). The National Assembly, which serves a three-year term, has 151 members, including 105 directly elected by adult suffrage. Twelve seats in the Assembly are reserved for religious bodies, while the remainder are occupied by officials, ministers and members of the Royal Advisory Council.

Defence

The strength of the Royal Bhutanese Army, which is under the direct command of the King, is classified information. As well as the regular standing army, there is a large militia. Army training facilities are provided by an Indian military training team. Although India is not directly responsible for the country's defence, the Indian Government has indicated that any act of aggression against Bhutan would be regarded as an act of aggression against India.

Economic Affairs

In terms of average income, Bhutan is one of the poorest countries in the world. According to estimates by the World Bank, the kingdom's gross national product (GNP) per head, measured at average 1979–81 prices, was only US $80 in both 1980 and 1981. Another estimate assessed Bhutan's GNP per head at $140 in 1984.

The economy is predominantly agrarian. An estimated 95% of the economically active population were employed in agriculture, forestry and fishing in 1985, although only about 9% of the land was under cultivation. In 1983 lack of rain caused a serious decline in the production of food-grains, and, as a result, food prices increased sharply. The total annual production of cereals was expected to rise from 166,000 metric tons in 1982 to more than 200,000 tons in 1986/87. Forests cover about 70% of the country's area, and further afforestation is envisaged. Roundwood removals (mainly for fuel) totalled an estimated 3.2m. cu m in 1984. The first phase of a forest-based industrial complex at Gedu has begun, and a plant for the production of particle board was being constructed in 1983. Timber and fruit, including apples, are exported.

Bhutan has some small-scale industry, producing, for example, textiles, soap, matches, candles and carpets. Centres for the production of traditional handicrafts, such as bamboo-work, lacquer woodwork and woven carpets, have been established. Several minerals of economic importance have been discovered, and small mineral-based units have been set up, such as a graphite beneficiation plant at Paro. The Government is encouraging private entrepreneurs to set up small units, and a number of small industrial estates have been established, producing a variety of consumer goods and industrial raw materials. A cement plant was set up at Pugli in 1981, and in 1983 cement exports were worth US $3.5m. A second cement plant, at Nanglam, is scheduled for completion by 1990. There are also plans to establish a calcium carbide plant, a gypsum mining plant, at Kothakpa, and a polythene pipe manufacturing unit. A survey of reserves of tungsten ore was being carried out in 1983, and new industrial estates were being planned at Gedu, Singhigang and Gaylegphug. As an under-populated country, Bhutan is dependent on foreign labour, particularly from Nepal; to reduce this dependence, many construction activities are to be mechanized.

A series of Economic Plans began in 1961, the first two being financed entirely by India. India provided Nu 410m. of the Nu 500m. development expenditure in 1978/79, while several United Nations agencies also provided assistance for the fourth (1976–81) Plan. Of expenditure amounting to Nu 778m. under this Plan, one-half was allocated to agriculture, particularly irrigation projects. The fifth Plan, covering 1981–87, envisaged expenditure of Nu 4,338m., of which about 32% was to be allocated to agriculture and forestry and 16% to power development. Bhutan was to provide Nu 446m., with the rest being supplied by India and UN organizations. Grants from the Government of India in the 1985/86 Annual Plan provided nearly 45% of total expenditure, compared with nearly 55% in 1978/79, and assistance from international agencies contributed 11%, compared with 10% in 1978/79. Since 1982 each Plan has been administered through local government institutions, in order to encourage investment at local levels. Considerable improvements have been achieved in roads, animal husbandry, irrigation, forestry and electricity generation. Six hydroelectricity stations have been established, and exports of electric energy to India were expected to begin in 1987, with the opening of the Chukka hydroelectric project. The Indian Government is financing the establishment of an east–west link and the Indo-Bhutanese microwave link to provide Bhutan with instant communication internally and abroad. The Hashimara–Thimphu section was due to be commissioned in 1986. The 30.5m. rupees project to provide a direct link between Takhti peak and Phuntsholing was under way in 1986. Bhutan joined the Asian Development Bank (ADB, see p. 100) in 1982, and received its first US $5m. multi-project loan in September 1983, to finance agricultural equipment, construction of roads and bridges, development of solar power, and improvement of water supplies and sewerage. A second multi-project loan of $7.4m. was approved in 1984, and in 1985 the ADB provided a loan of $3.48m. for the Chirang Hill Irrigation Project (scheduled for completion in 1991), in addition to approving support for five technical assistance projects, totalling $1.5m. In September 1986 the ADB approved a loan of $4.5m. towards a $8.2m. roadworks mechanization project.

Since the 1960 ban on trade with Tibet, Bhutan's main trading partner has been India, although timber, liquor and cardamom are also exported to the Middle East and Western Europe. After the inauguration of the postal system in 1972, Bhutan's postage stamps became the main source of foreign exchange, but in 1976 this category was overtaken by tourism, which brought in an estimated US $2.3m. in 1983/84. In the year ending March 1983 there was a deficit of US $42m. on merchandise trade.

Economic growth was estimated at an annual average of 6% in the three years to March 1982, but the rate fell slightly in the year to March 1983, owing to a reduction in revenues from forestry products; low rainfall during 1983 led to poor harvests and was expected to depress overall economic growth further. Fiscal reforms, introduced in 1982/83, led to an increase in government revenue, and were expected to bring about a reduction in the budget deficit, until then equivalent to about 20% of gross domestic product annually. The projected 1985/86 budget was balanced at Nu 863.4m.

Social Welfare

In 1984 the country had 25 hospitals, and a mobile hospital unit was operating in the remote central areas. Because of a shortage of medical personnel and a lack of funds, local dispensaries are being converted into basic health units, providing basic medical services. Malaria and tuberculosis are still widespread. The budget for the financial year 1985/86 allocated Nu 53.7m. (6.2% of total expenditure) to health.

Education

Education is not compulsory. Primary education begins at seven years of age and lasts for five years. Secondary education, beginning at the age of 12, lasts for a further five years, comprising a first cycle of three years and a second cycle of two years. Free education is available, but there are insufficient facilities to accommodate all school-age children. In 1984 the total enrolment at primary schools was equivalent to an estimated 25% of children in the relevant age-group (32% of boys, 17% of girls), while the comparable ratio for secondary schools was only 4% (boys 6%, girls 1%). All schools are co-educational and follow a British syllabus. English is the language of instruction. Bhutan has no mission or private schools, and all schools are subsidized by the Government. Many Indian teachers are employed. In 1985 there were more than 200 schools, including eight high schools, one junior college, one degree college, six technical schools, 22 schools for Buddhist studies and monastic schools, two teacher training schools and four schools for Tibetan refugees. A number of Bhutanese students were receiving higher education abroad. The 1985/86 budget allocated Nu 92.5m. (10.7% of total expenditure) to education.

Tourism

Bhutan was opened to tourism in 1974, and hotels, transport and other facilities were created in the west of the country. Wildlife sanctuaries have been established. Foreign tourists may visit Bhutan in package or trekking tours, or individually, accompanied by guide/interpreters. The Government's policy is to limit the number of tourists: in 1984 and 1985 there were about 2,000 visitors per year, mainly from Europe, Japan and the USA. The Bhutan Tourism Corporation operates four hotels.

Public Holidays

1987 and 1988: The usual Buddhist holidays are observed, as well as the Birthday of HM Jigme Singye Wangchuk (11 November) and the National Day of Bhutan (17 December).

Weights and Measures

The metric system is in operation.

Currency and Exchange Rates

100 chetrum = 1 ngultrum (Nu).

Exchange rates (30 September 1986):
  £1 sterling = 18.400 ngultrum;
  US $1 = 12.716 ngultrum.

The ngultrum is fixed at par with the Indian rupee, and Indian currency is also legal tender.

Statistical Survey

Source (unless otherwise stated): Royal Government of Bhutan, Thimphu.

Area and Population

AREA, POPULATION AND DENSITY

Area (sq km)	46,500*
Population (census of December 1969)	931,514
Population (official estimates at mid-year)	
1977	1,101,053
1985	1,286,275
Density (per sq km) at mid-1985	27.7

* 17,954 sq miles.
Capital: Thimphu (estimated population 20,000 at 1 July 1985).

POPULATION OF DISTRICTS (mid-1985 estimates)

Bumthang	23,842
Chirang	108,807
Dagana	28,352
Gasa	16,907
Gaylegphug	111,283
Haa	16,715
Lhuntshi	39,635
Mongar	73,239
Paro	46,615
Pema Gatshel	37,141
Punakha	16,700
Samchi	172,109
Samdrup Jongkhar	73,044
Shemgang	44,516
Tashigang	177,718
Thimphu	58,660
Tongsa	26,017
Wangdiphodrang	47,152
Total rural population	1,119,452
Total urban population	167,823
Total	1,286,275

BIRTHS AND DEATHS

Average annual birth rate 41.0 per 1,000 in 1975–80, 39.0 per 1,000 in 1980–85; death rate 20.6 per 1,000 in 1975–80, 19.0 per 1,000 in 1980–85 (estimates).

LIFE EXPECTANCY

45.6 years (1985 estimate).

ECONOMICALLY ACTIVE POPULATION
(estimates, '000 persons, 1981/82)

Agriculture, etc.	613
Industry	6
Trade	9
Public services	22
Total	650

Agriculture

PRINCIPAL CROPS (estimates, '000 metric tons)

	1982	1983	1984
Rice (paddy)	59	60	61
Wheat	10	10	10
Barley	5	5	5
Maize	81	83	85
Millet	7	7	7
Other cereals	4	6	7
Potatoes	25	26	27
Other roots and tubers	17	17	17
Pulses	2	3	3
Tobacco	1	1	1
Jute	4	4	4
Vegetables	10	10	10
Citrus fruit	26	26	26
Other fruits	20	21	22

Source: FAO, *Production Yearbook*.

LIVESTOCK
(FAO estimates, '000 head, year ending September)

	1982	1983	1984
Cattle	305	312	315
Pigs	72	74	74
Sheep	42	43	43
Goats	44	45	45
Buffaloes	28	28	28
Horses	16	16	16
Asses	18	18	18
Mules	8	8	8

Source: FAO, *Production Yearbook*.
Cows' Milk: 11,000 metric tons in 1984 (FAO estimate).

BHUTAN

Forestry

ROUNDWOOD REMOVALS ('000 cubic metres, excl. bark)

	1979	1980*	1981*
Sawlogs, veneer logs and logs for sleepers	240	240	240
Other industrial wood*	38	38	38
Fuel wood*	2,814	2,884	2,946
Total	3,092	3,162	3,224

* FAO estimates.
1982–84: Annual output as in 1981 (FAO estimates).
Sawnwood production: 5,000 cubic metres per year (1978–84).
Source: FAO, *Yearbook of Forest Products*.

Fishing

Total catch 1,000 metric tons of freshwater fishes per year (FAO estimate).

Mining

	1983	1984	1985
Gypsum (metric tons)	4,697	13,532	12,000
Coal ('000 metric tons)	n.a.	8.6	30
Limestone ('000 metric tons)	108	126	144
Slate ('000 sq ft)	395.3	503.3	540.8
Dolomite (metric tons)	159,173	111,535	162,014

Industry

SELECTED PRODUCTS (year ending 31 March)

	1981/82	1982/83	1983/84
Cement (metric tons)	99,188	88,688	169,624
Electric energy (million kWh)	22	24	26

Finance

CURRENCY AND EXCHANGE RATES

Monetary Units
100 chetrum (Ch) = 1 ngultrum (Nu).

Denominations
Coins: 5, 10, 25 and 50 chetrum; 1 ngultrum.
Notes: 1, 2, 5, 10, 20, 50 and 100 ngultrum.

Sterling and Dollar Equivalents (30 September 1986)
£1 sterling = 18.400 ngultrum;
US $1 = 12.716 ngultrum;
1,000 ngultrum = £54.35 = $78.64.

Average Exchange Rate (ngultrum per US $)
1983   10.099
1984   11.363
1985   12.369

Note: The ngultrum is at par with the Indian rupee.

NATIONAL ACCOUNTS (million ngultrum at current prices)
Gross Domestic Product by Economic Activity

	1982	1983	1984
Agriculture	647.5	769.6	884.3
Forestry	116.8	127.9	131.9
Mining	6.2	4.7	6.7
Manufacturing	52.2	69.2	79.1
Electricity	3.0	3.1	3.2
Construction	229.3	261.4	268.5
Trade, restaurants and hotels	174.7	200.7	230.7
Transport	36.8	44.1	50.3
Financing, insurance and real estate	145.3	156.7	175.5
Public administration	177.4	196.9	221.1
Sub-total	1,589.2	1,834.3	2,051.3
Less Imputed bank service charges	29.9	30.2	38.5
Total	1,559.3	1,804.1	2,012.8

BUDGET ('000 ngultrum, year ending 31 March)

Revenue	1985/86
Internal revenue	264,253
Grants from Government of India	390,822
Grants from UN and other international agencies	96,990
Borrowing	111,325
Total	**863,390**

Expenditure	1985/86
Public works department (incl. urban development)	166,872
Power (excl. Chukka hydroelectric project)	134,759
Agriculture and irrigation (incl. Food Corpn of Bhutan)	109,637
Education	92,461
Ministry of Finance	56,288
Health	53,651
Industries and mines (incl. trade and commerce)	48,720
Forests	32,458
District administration	32,062
Post and telecommunications	20,347
Animal husbandry	19,940
Foreign Affairs	19,926
Police	15,972
Planning commission (incl. statistics)	7,101
Law courts	5,456
Department of Culture	3,478
Civil aviation	3,420
Information and broadcasting	3,330
Secretariat	10,625
Other departments	26,887
Total	**863,390**

FIFTH DEVELOPMENT PLAN (1981–87)
Estimated expenditure (million ngultrum)

Agriculture (incl. Food Corpn of Bhutan)	494.8
Animal husbandry	122.1
Education (incl. technical education)	35.3
Power	715.0
Health	340.0
Development headquarters	15.0
Information and publicity	185.3
Public works department	536.9
Forests	756.8
Industries and mines	282.1
Broadcasting, wireless, telephone and post and telegraphs	125.0
Tourism	66.6
Civil aviation	136.9
Miscellaneous	526.3
Total	**4,338.1**

SIXTH DEVELOPMENT PLAN (1987–93)
(sectoral allocation of proposed expenditure, million ngultrum)

	Total	% of total
Agriculture and irrigation	653.2	7.4
Food Corporation of Bhutan	135.0	1.5
Animal husbandry	260.2	3.0
Forestry	349.6	4.0
Industry, trade and commerce	1,787.0	20.2
Public Works Department	910.5	10.3
Power	1,118.6	12.7
Bhutan Government Transport Service	10.0	0.1
Tourism	30.0	0.3
Civil aviation	180.5	2.1
Telephone	301.6	3.4
Post, telegraph and wireless	58.0	0.7
Information and broadcasting	66.5	0.8
Education	888.3	10.1
Health	333.2	3.8
Urban development	221.8	2.5
General development	1,507.2	17.1
Total	**8,811.2***	**100.0**

* The carry-over on uncompleted projects from the Fifth Plan is expected to be 1,000m.–1,200m. ngultrum. A carry-over into the Seventh Plan of 400m.–600m. ngultrum is expected; accordingly, the estimated total outlay under the Sixth Plan is assessed at 8,200m. ngultrum.

Cost of Living (Retail Price Index; base: 1979 = 100): 129.77 in 1981; 135.14 in 1982.

BALANCE OF PAYMENTS
(US $ million, year ending 31 March)

	1980/81	1981/82	1982/83
Merchandise exports f.o.b.	16.7	20.9	16.7
Merchandise imports c.i.f.	−49.0	−52.9	−58.5
Services and private transfers (net)	−18.0	−25.7	−29.5
Official transfers and capital	56.1	61.7	74.5
Total (net monetary movements)	5.8	4.0	3.2

Source: *IMF Survey*.

External Trade

SELECTED COMMODITIES (US $'000)

Imports c.i.f.	1982	1983
Aircraft	—	4,219
Diesel fuel	4,041	4,039
Rice	1,743	1,344
Motor cars	1,151	1,100
Metal containers	n.a.	959
Soya-fortified bulgar	n.a.	792

Exports f.o.b.	1982	1983
Cement	3,809	3,516
Talc powder	459	1,428
Fruit products	980	1,095
Rosin	808	870
Cardamom	1,274	798
Sawn timber, coniferous	703	575
Potatoes	943	508

PRINCIPAL TRADING PARTNERS (US $'000)

Imports c.i.f.	1982	1983
India	48,318	32,049
Other countries	4,719	9,012

Exports f.o.b.	1982	1983
India	17,342	13,692
Other countries	263	345

Transport

ROAD TRAFFIC
In 1984 there were 3,671 vehicles, of which 827 were private cars, 1,112 were jeeps, and 664 were heavy vehicles.

CIVIL AVIATION (traffic, year ending 31 March)
Passengers flown: 4,745 in 1984/85; 5,223 in 1985/86.

Tourism

Arrivals: 2,009 in 1983; 2,000 in 1984; 2,000 in 1985.

Education

(1985)

Primary schools	143
Junior high schools	22
High schools	8
Teachers' training institutes	2
Schools for Buddhist studies and monastic schools	22
Junior college	1
Degree college	1
Technical schools	6
Schools for Tibetan refugees	4
Total pupils	53,420
Total teachers	1,875

Directory

The Constitution

The Kingdom of Bhutan has no formal constitution. However, the state system is a modified form of constitutional monarchy. Written rules, which are changed periodically, govern procedures for the election of members of the Royal Advisory Council and the Legislature, and define the duties and powers of those bodies.

The Government

Head of State: HM Druk Gyalpo ('Dragon King') JIGME SINGYE WANGCHUCK (succeeded to the throne in July 1972).

LODOI TSOKDE
(Royal Advisory Council)
(December 1986)

The Royal Advisory Council (Lodoi Tsokde), established in 1965, comprises 10 members: one nominee of the King, two monks representing the state religion, six people's representatives and a Chairman (Kalyon), also nominated by the King. The people's representatives have their names endorsed at village assemblies, forwarded by district Dzongdas (local administrative officials) and voted on by all members of the Tsogdu (National Assembly). The Council's principal task is to advise the King, as head of government, and to supervise all aspects of administration. The Council is in permanent session, virtually as a government department, and acts as the *de facto* Standing Committee of the Tsogdu. Members serve for five years and may be re-elected.

Chairman: Dasho SANGAY PENJOR.
Councillors: Dasho KIPCHU DORJI (HM Government), LOPEN YONTEN GYALTSHEN (Central Body of Monks), GELONG SAMDRUP (District Monk Bodies), TEKNATH RIZAL (South Bhutan-West), B. B. BHANDARI (South Bhutan-East), Dasho RINZIN DORJI (West Bhutan), Dasho KESANG (East Bhutan), JAMJANG GAYLEG (Central Bhutan), JAZIG (Thimphu/Paro/Ha).

LHENGYE SHUNGTSOG
(Council of Ministers)
(December 1986)

Chairman: HM Druk Gyalpo JIGME SINGYE WANGCHUCK.
Representative of His Majesty in the Ministry of Finance: HRH Ashi (Princess) SONAM CHHODEN WANGCHUCK.
Representative of His Majesty in the Ministry of Agriculture and the Ministry of Communications and Tourism: HRH Ashi DECHEN WANGMO WANGCHUCK.
Minister of Trade and Industries: (vacant).
Minister of Home Affairs: HRH NAMGYEL WANGCHUCK.
Minister of Foreign Affairs: Lyonpo DAWA TSERING.
Minister of Social Services: Lyonpo SANGYE PENJOR.

MINISTRIES
All Ministries are in Thimphu.

Legislature

TSOGDU

A National Assembly (Tsogdu) was established in 1953. The Assembly has a three-year term and meets twice yearly, in spring and autumn. The size of the membership is based, in part, on the population of the districts, and is subject to periodic revision. In 1986 the Assembly had 151 members, of whom 106 were directly elected by the public. Ten seats are reserved for religious bodies, and the remainder are occupied by officials, the ministers and members of the Royal Advisory Council. The Assembly enacts laws, advises on constitutional and political matters and debates all important issues. Both the Royal Advisory Council and the Council of Ministers are responsible to it.

LOCAL ADMINISTRATION

There are 18 districts (Dzongkhags), each headed by a Dzongda (in charge of administration and law and order) and a Thrimpon (in charge of judicial matters). Dzongdas were previously appointed by the King, but are now appointed by the Royal Civil Service Commission, established in 1982. The principal officers under the Dzongda are the Dzongda Wongma and the Dzongrab, responsible for locally administered development projects and fiscal matters respectively. Under provisions of the 1981–87 Plan, with the introduction of decentralization, Punakha and Thimphu were merged as one district. However, this did not prove successful, and by 1985 they were once more administered separately. Seven of the districts are further sub-divided into sub-districts (dungkhags) and the lowest administrative unit in all districts is the bloc (gewog) of several villages.

Political Organizations

There are no political parties in Bhutan.

Diplomatic Representation

EMBASSIES IN BHUTAN

Bangladesh: POB 178, Thorilam, Thimphu; tel. 2539; Ambassador: MAHMOOD ATIS.
India: Lungtenzampa, Thimphu; tel. 2100; Ambassador: NARESHWAR DAYAL.

BHUTAN

Judicial System

Bhutan has a Civil and a Criminal Code.

Appeal Court: The Supreme Court of Appeal is the King.

High Court (Thrimkhang Gongma): Established 1968 to review appeals from Lower Courts, although some cases are heard at the first instance; eight Judges (six nominated by the King and two elected by the Tsogdu, who serve for a five-year period), headed by the Chief Justice. Three judges form a quorum. The judges are assisted by seven senior Ramjams.

Chief Justice: Dasho Paljore J. Dorji.

Magistrates' Courts (Dzongkhag Thrimkhang): Each district has a court, headed by the Thrimpon (magistrate) and aided by a junior Ramjam, which tries most cases. Appeals are made to the High Court, and less serious civil disputes may be settled by a Gup or Mandal (Village Headman) through written undertakings.

All citizens have the right to make informal appeal for redress of grievances directly to the King, through the office of his chamberlain (Gyalpoi Zimpon).

Religion

The state religion is Mahayana Buddhism, but the southern Bhutanese are predominantly followers of Hinduism. Buddhism was introduced into Bhutan in the eighth century AD by the Indian saint Padmasambhava, known in Bhutan as Guru Rimpoche. In the 13th century Phajo Drugom Shigpo made the Drukpa school of Kagyupa Buddhism dominant in Bhutan, and this sect is still supported by the dominant race in Bhutan, the Drukpas. The main monastic group, the Central Body of Monks (comprising 1,160 monks), is led by an elected Head Abbot (Je Khempo), is directly supported by the state and spends six months of the year at Tashichhodzong and at Punakha respectively. A further 2,120 monks are sustained by the lay population. The Central Board for Monastic Affairs, established in 1984, oversees all religious bodies. Monasteries (Gompas) and shrines (Lhakhangs) are numerous. The chief monastery is situated at Tashichhodzong and contains about 2,000 lamas (Buddhist priests). There are 5,000 state-supported lamas in the kingdom, with the Je Khempo as their elected head.

The Press

Kuenphen Digest: Kuenphen Enterprise Pvt Ltd, POB 175, Phuntsholing; tel. 495; f. 1982; monthly; English; Editor Karma Tenzin Dorji.

Kuenphen Tribune: Kuenphen Enterprise Pvt Ltd, POB 175, Phuntsholing; monthly; English; Editor Karma Tenzin Dorji.

Kuensel: Dept of Information and Broadcasting, Thimphu; f. 1965; weekly govt bulletin; in English, Dzongkha and Nepali; Editor-in-Chief Rinzin Dorji; Asst Editors G. S. Upadhya (Nepali), Kinley Dorji (English), Goempo Dorji (Dzongkha); circ. 5,000.

Radio

There are 66 radio stations, of which 23 are for hydrological and meteorological purposes. In 1985 there were an estimated 15,000 radio receivers in use.

Bhutan Broadcasting Service (BBS): POB 1, Dept of Information and Broadcasting, Thimphu; tel. 2533; f. 1973 as Radio National Youth Association of Bhutan (NYAB); present name adopted 1986; short-wave radio station broadcasting three hours daily in Dzongkha, Sharchopkha, Nepali and English; Dep. Dir Louise Dorji; Programme Officer Tashi Dorji.

Finance

(cap. = capital; auth. = authorized; p.u. = paid up; res = reserves; dep. = deposits; m. = million; brs = branches; amounts in ngultrum)

BANKING

Bank of Bhutan: POB 75, Phuntsholing; tel. 225; f. 1968; 25% of shares held by State Bank of India; auth. cap. 5m., cap. p.u. 2.5m., res 130m., dep. 530m. (Dec. 1985); Dirs nominated by the Bhutan govt: Chair. Dasho Dorji Tshering; Dirs Dasho Lam Penjore, Dasho Pema Wangchuck, Dasho Chenkyab Dorji, Yeshey Zimba, Bap Kesang; Dirs nominated by the State Bank of India: K. R. Maheshwari, T. K. Basu; Man. Dir P. K. Jayaswal; 21 brs.

Royal Monetary Authority (RMA): POB 154, Thimphu; tel. 2540; f. 1982; has become the central bank, dealing with foreign exchange, currency and co-ordination of financial institutions and the framing and implementation of a unified monetary policy; began operations by taking over govt foreign-exchange deposits held by the Bank of Bhutan, which will act as an agent of the RMA; cap. p.u. 1.5m.; Man. Dir and CEO Yeshey Zimba.

Plans to establish an Industrial Development Bank were under discussion in 1986.

INSURANCE

Royal Insurance Corporation of Bhutan: POB 77, Phuntsholing; tel. 309; f. 1975; cap. 12m. (1983); Chair. HRH Ashi Sonam Chhoden Wangchuck; Man. Dir Dasho U. Dorji.

Trade and Industry

CHAMBER OF COMMERCE

Bhutan Chamber of Commerce and Industries: POB 147, Thimphu; tel. 2506; f. 1980; Pres. Karma Gayleg; Sec.-Gen. Lhab Tshering.

GOVERNMENT ORGANIZATIONS

Export Development Corporation of Bhutan (EDCB): Norzing Lam, Thimphu; tel. 2403; manages exports on behalf of the govt; brs in Phuntsholing, Gomtu and in Calcutta, India.

Food Corporation of Bhutan (FCB): Phuntsholing; tel. 241; f. 1974; activities include retailing, marketing, storage, import and export of agricultural products and establishment of regulated market yards and horticultural processing units in the country; operates a rural finance scheme, receiving loans from the Bank of Bhutan and the Royal Insurance Corpn, to assist farmers; Man. Dir Hadi Ali.

National Commission for Trade and Industry: Thimphu; tel. 403; fmrly the Industrial Development Corpn; regulates the type, quality and quantity of proposed industrial projects; Chair. HM Druk Gyalpo Jigme Singye Wangchuck.

State Trading Corpn of Bhutan (STCB): POB 76, Phuntsholing; tel. 286; manages imports on behalf of the govt; br. in Calcutta, India.

TRADE UNIONS

Trade union activity is illegal in Bhutan.

Transport

ROADS AND TRACKS

In 1984 there were 2,000 km of roads (most of which are surfaced). In addition, surfaced roads link the important border towns of Phuntsholing, Gaylegphug, Sarbhang and Samdrup Jongkhar in southern Bhutan to towns in West Bengal and Assam in India. Under the sixth development plan, the Government proposes to construct and upgrade about 1,000 km of roads to provide vital links to the national road network. In 1986 the Asian Development Bank approved a loan of US $4.5m. towards a $8.2m. roadworks mechanization project. In 1984 there were 4,439 licensed drivers in Bhutan. There is a shortage of road transport. Yaks, ponies and mules are still the chief means of transport on the rough mountain tracks.

Bhutan Government Transport Service (BGTS): Phuntsholing; Thimphu 2345; f. 1962; operates a fleet of 113 buses (1983); Man. Dir Lhendup Dorji.

Transport Corpn of Bhutan: POB 7, Phuntsholing; tel. 476; f. 1982; subsidiary of the Royal Insurance Corpn; operates coach services.

Lorries for transporting goods are operated by the private sector.

CIVIL AVIATION

There is an international airport at Paro, and a domestic airport at Yangphulla which serves the east of the country. There are numerous helicopter landing pads.

BHUTAN

Druk Air: POB 209, Tashidekhang, Main Market, Thimphu; tel. 2987; telex 3162155; national airline; became fully operational in February 1983; thrice-weekly service between Paro and Calcutta; Chair. HRH Ashi SONAM CHHODEN WANGCHUCK; Man. Dir UGYEN NAMGYEL; fleet of 2 18-seat Dornier-228 aircraft.

Tourism

The Kingdom was opened to tourism in the autumn of 1974 and the tourist seasons are from March to June and September to December. From 1974 to 1982 all tourists arrived by road via India. In 1986 Druk Air began daily flights (except on Sundays) between Calcutta and Paro. Tourists travel in organized package or trekking tours, or individually, accompanied by guides. Hotels have been constructed by the Department of Tourism at Phuntsholing, Paro and Thimphu, with lodges at Tongsa, Bumthang and Manas. There are also many small privately-run hotels and guesthouses. The first mountaineering expedition was launched in 1983, to Mt Jichudrake. Central Bhutan was also opened for trekkers and coach tours in 1982, but eastern Bhutan remains closed to foreigners. The Government intends to exercise close control over the development of tourism.

Bhutan Tourism Corporation (BTC): POB 159, Thimphu; tel. 2647; telex 3162155; state organization; operates four hotels for tourists; Gen. Man. JIGME TSHULTIM; Sales Man. DAGO BEDA.

BOLIVIA

Introductory Survey

Location, Climate, Language, Religion, Flag, Capital

The Republic of Bolivia is a land-locked state in South America, bordered by Chile and Peru to the west, by Brazil to the north and east, and by Paraguay and Argentina to the south. The climate varies, according to altitude, from humid tropical conditions in the northern and eastern lowlands, which are less than 500 m (1,640 ft) above sea-level, to the cool and cold zones at altitudes of more than 3,500 m (about 11,500 ft) in the Andes mountains. The official languages are Spanish, Quechua and Aymará. Almost all of the inhabitants profess Christianity, and the great majority are adherents of the Roman Catholic Church. The national flag (proportions 3 by 2) has three equal horizontal stripes, of red, yellow and green. The state flag has, in addition, the national emblem (an oval cartouche enclosing a mountain, an alpaca, a breadfruit tree and a sheaf of grain, all surmounted by a condor and superimposed on crossed cannons, rifles and national banners) in the centre of the yellow stripe. The legal capital is Sucre. The administrative capital and seat of government is La Paz.

Recent History

The Incas of Bolivia were conquered by Spain in 1538 and, although there were many revolts against Spanish rule, independence was not achieved until 1825. Bolivian history has been characterized by recurrent internal strife, resulting in a succession of presidents, and frequent territorial disputes with its neighbours, including the 1879–83 War of the Pacific between Bolivia, Peru and Chile, and the Chaco Wars of 1928–30 and 1933–35 against Paraguay.

At a presidential election in May 1951 the largest share of the vote was won by Dr Víctor Paz Estenssoro, the candidate of the Movimiento Nacionalista Revolucionario (MNR), who had been living in Argentina since 1946. He was denied permission to return to Bolivia and contested the election *in absentia*. However, he failed to gain an absolute majority, and the incumbent President transferred power to a junta of army officers. This regime was itself overthrown in April 1952, when a popular uprising, supported by the MNR and a section of the armed forces, enabled Dr Paz Estenssoro to return from exile and assume the presidency. His government, a coalition of the MNR and the Labour Party, committed itself to profound social revolution. It nationalized the tin mines and introduced universal suffrage (the franchise had previously been limited to literate adults) and land reform. Dr Hernán Siles Zuazo, a leading figure in the 1952 revolution, was elected President for the 1956–60 term, and Dr Paz Estenssoro was again elected President in 1960. However, the powerful trade unions came into conflict with the Government, and in November 1964, following widespread strikes and disorder, President Paz Estenssoro was overthrown by the Vice-President, Gen. René Barrientos Ortuño, supported by the army. After serving with Gen. Alfredo Ovando Candía as Co-President under a military junta, Gen. Barrientos resigned in January 1966 to campaign for the presidency. He was elected in July 1966.

President Barrientos met strong opposition from left-wing groups, including mineworkers' unions. During his term of office there was also a guerrilla uprising in south-eastern Bolivia, led by Dr Ernesto ('Che') Guevara, the Argentine-born revolutionary who had played a leading role in the Castro regime in Cuba. Guevara had travelled secretly to Bolivia in November 1966, when he began to organize a campaign to overthrow the Bolivian Government. His small guerrilla group became active in March 1967, and later received some support from miners' and students' groups. However, the insurgency was suppressed by government troops, with the help of US advisers, and guerrilla warfare ended in October 1967, when Guevara was captured and killed.

In April 1969 President Barrientos was killed in an air crash and Dr Luis Adolfo Siles Salinas, the Vice-President, succeeded to the presidency. In September 1969, however, President Siles Salinas was deposed by the armed forces, who installed Gen. Ovando in power again. He was forced to resign in October 1970, when, after a power struggle between right-wing and left-wing army officers, Gen. Juan José Torres González, who had support from leftists, emerged as President, pledging support for agrarian reform and worker participation in management. A 'People's Assembly', formed by Marxist politicians, radical students and leaders of trade unions, was allowed to meet and called for extreme socialist measures, causing disquiet in right-wing circles. President Torres was deposed in August 1971 by Col (later Gen.) Hugo Bánzer Suárez, who drew support from the right-wing Falange Socialista Boliviana and a section of the MNR, as well as from the army. In June 1973 President Bánzer announced an imminent return to constitutional government but elections were later postponed to June 1974. The MNR withdrew its support and entered into active opposition.

Following an attempted military coup in June 1974, the Cabinet was replaced by an all-military one. After an attempt to overthrow him in November 1974, President Bánzer declared that elections had been postponed indefinitely and that his military regime would retain power until at least 1980. All political and union activity was banned. Political and industrial unrest in 1976 led President Bánzer to announce that elections would be held in July 1978. Allegations of fraud rendered the elections void but Gen. Juan Pereda Asbún, the armed forces candidate in the elections, staged a successful military coup. In November 1978 his right-wing government was overthrown in another coup, led by Gen. David Padilla Aranciba, Commander-in-Chief of the Army, with the support of national left-wing elements.

Elections were held in July 1979 for a President and a bicameral Congress. The presidential poll resulted in almost equal support for two ex-Presidents, Dr Siles Zuazo (with 36.0% of the vote) and Dr Paz Estenssoro (with 35.9%), who were now leading rival factions of the MNR. Congress, convened in August to resolve the issue, failed to give a majority to any candidate. An interim government was formed under Walter Guevara Arce, President of the Senate, but this administration was overthrown on 1 November by a right-wing army officer, Col Alberto Natusch Busch. He withdrew 15 days later after failing to gain the support of Congress, which elected Dra Lidia Gueiler Tejada, President of the Chamber of Deputies, as interim Head of State pending presidential and legislative elections scheduled for June 1980.

The 1980 presidential election also yielded no clear winner and in July, before Congress could meet to decide between the two main contenders (again Dr Siles Zuazo and Dr Paz Estenssoro), a military junta led by the army commander, Gen. Luis García Meza, staged a coup—the 189th in Bolivia's 154 years of independence.

There was evidence that the new regime depended upon the proceeds of drug trafficking for much of its revenue, and this, combined with the violence of the armed forces during and after the coup, prevented its recognition by the USA and the EEC countries, which halted financial aid to Bolivia. In August 1981 a military uprising forced Gen. García to resign. In September the junta transferred power to the army commander, Gen. Celso Torrelio Villa, who declared his intention to fight official corruption and to return the country to democracy within three years. Labour unrest, provoked by Bolivia's severe economic crisis, was appeased by restitution of trade union and political rights, and a mainly civilian Cabinet was appointed in April 1982. Elections were scheduled for April 1983. The political liberalization disturbed the armed forces, who attempted to create a climate of violence, and President Torrelio resigned in July 1982, amid rumours of an impending coup. The junta installed the less moderate Gen. Guido Vildoso Calderón, the Army Chief of Staff, as President.

Unable to resolve the worsening economic crisis or to control a general strike which threatened to continue until democracy was restored, the military regime announced in September 1982 that power would be handed over in October to the Congress which had originally been elected in 1980. Dr Siles Zuazo, who had obtained most votes in both 1979 and 1980, was duly elected President by Congress, and was sworn in for a four-year term in October 1982.

President Siles Zuazo appointed a coalition Cabinet consisting of members of his own party, the Movimiento Nacionalista Revolucionario de Izquierda (MNRI), the Movimiento de la Izquierda Revolucionaria (MIR) and the Partido Comunista de Bolivia (PCB). Economic aid from the USA and Europe was resumed but the Government found itself unable to fulfil the expectations that had been created by the return to democratic rule, owing mainly to the dire economic situation, compounded by severe drought and floods. The entire Cabinet resigned in August 1983, and the President appointed a Cabinet in which the number of portfolios that were held by the right-wing of the MNRI, the Partido Demócrata Cristiano and independents was increased. The MIR joined forces with the MNR and business interests in rejecting the Government's policy of complying with IMF conditions for assistance, which involved harsh economic measures (including price increases and devaluation of the currency). The Government lost its majority in Congress and faced strikes and mass labour demonstrations. In November the opposition-dominated Senate approved an increase of 100% in the minimum wage, in defiance of the Government's austerity measures. Following a 48-hour general strike, the whole Cabinet resigned once again on 14 December, in anticipation of an opposition motion of censure; the ministers accused the Senate of planning a 'constitutional coup' and called for the formation of a government of national unity. In January 1984 President Siles Zuazo appointed a new coalition Cabinet, including 13 members of the previous Government.

The new Cabinet's main priority was to tackle Bolivia's grave economic decline. However, constant industrial agitation by the trade union confederation, the Central Obrera Boliviana (COB), coupled with rumours of an imminent coup, seriously undermined public confidence in the President. The subsequent introduction of austerity measures resulted in widespread protests, including a three-day general strike. In a move to end the prolonged industrial unrest, the Government agreed to a series of economic concessions, including a moratorium on Bolivia's foreign debt to commercial banks. In June, however, the country was again thrown into turmoil by the temporary abduction of President Siles Zuazo. Two former Cabinet ministers and some 100 right-wing army officers were arrested in connection with the kidnapping, which was believed to have been supported by leading drug dealers.

In September the Government faced another crisis, following the discovery of a plot by extreme right-wing groups to overthrow the President. Following the disclosure that Congress had ordered an enquiry into suspected links between the Government and cocaine dealers, President Siles Zuazo undertook a five-day hunger strike in a bid to secure national unity and stability. In November another general strike was held, and the President announced that he would leave office a year early, in August 1985, after a general election, to be held in June. In January 1985 a new Cabinet was formed, comprising only members of the MNRI and independents. In the same month it was announced that an attempted coup by former military officers had been thwarted.

Following the Government's decision to introduce a new series of austerity measures in February 1985, relations between the Government and the COB deteriorated even further. In March the COB called a general strike, which lasted for 16 days, causing chaos throughout the country. The Government's offer to form a 'co-administrative' joint government with the trade unions was rejected by the COB, whose leaders advocated a revolution as the only solution to the crisis. The strike was eventually halted when a majority of union leaders accepted the Government's offer of a pay increase of more than 300%.

The principal consequence of the general strike was the Government's decision to postpone the general election until July 1985. In the weeks preceding the election, there were frequent reports of electoral malpractice and poor organization. At the election, the right-wing Acción Democrática Nacionalista (ADN), whose presidential candidate was Gen. Hugo Bánzer Suárez (the former dictator), received 28.6% of the votes cast, and the MNR obtained 26.4%, while the MIR was the leading left-wing party. At a further round of voting in Congress in August, an alliance between the MNR and the leading left-wing groups, including the MIR, enabled Dr Víctor Paz Estenssoro of the MNR to secure the presidency (which he had previously held in 1952–56 and 1960–64). The military pledged their support for the new Government.

On taking office in August, the new Government immediately introduced a very strict economic programme, designed to reduce inflation, which was estimated to have reached 14,173% in the year to August. The COB rejected the programme and called an indefinite general strike in September. The Government responded by declaring the strike illegal and by ordering a 90-day state of siege throughout Bolivia. Leading trade unionists were detained or banished, and thousands of strikers were arrested. The strike was called off in October, when union leaders agreed to hold talks with the Government. The conclusion of the strike was regarded as a considerable success for the new administration which, in spite of having achieved office with the assistance of left-wing parties, had subsequently found a greater ally in the right-wing ADN. The alliance between the two parties was consolidated by the signing of a 'pacto por la democracia' in October. The state of siege ended in December.

The collapse of the world tin market in late 1985 had a catastrophic impact on the Bolivian economy, which had shown signs of improving under the Government's austerity programme. In January 1986 the Cabinet resigned to enable the President to modify government policies, but Paz Estenssoro remained fully committed to the economic programme.

In July the Government was strongly criticized by opposition groups and trade unions when 160 US soldiers arrived in Bolivia to participate in a joint campaign with the Bolivian armed forces to eradicate illegal coca plantations. The Government was accused of having contravened the Constitution by failing to consult Congress about the presence on Bolivian territory of US troops, a development which was regarded as compromising national sovereignty. However, as the allocation of US aid was to be conditional upon the elimination of Bolivia's illegal cocaine trade, the Government claimed that its actions were justified. In October the US administration agreed to provide more than US $100m. in aid to continue the drug eradication campaign.

Throughout 1986 demonstrations and strikes were held by the COB in protest at the Government's austerity measures. Following a 48-hour general strike in August, the Government imposed a state of siege for 90 days, on the grounds that left-wing extremists had conspired to overthrow the administration. Tanks and soldiers were dispatched by the Government to prevent some 5,000 miners, who were marching from Oruro to La Paz to protest against the crisis in the mining sector, from entering the capital city. More than 160 opposition politicians and trade unionists were detained under the state of siege. In September the Roman Catholic Church mediated in talks between the Government and mineworkers' leaders on the future of the industry. Although the Government continued to defend successfully its controversial economic policies against mounting public opposition, deteriorating social and economic conditions within Bolivia were expected to pose severe problems for the Government in the coming months.

The long-standing matter of possible Bolivian access to the Pacific Ocean through Chilean territory, tension over which caused a break in diplomatic relations between the two countries in 1978, has yet to be resolved. The Government of Paz Estenssoro has affirmed its intention to reopen negotiations on the issue. In September 1986 the Bolivian and Chilean Governments signed an agreement to promote improved political, social and economic ties between both countries.

Government

Legislative power is held by the bicameral Congress, comprising a Senate (27 members) and a Chamber of Deputies (130 members). Both houses are elected for a four-year term by universal adult suffrage. Executive power is vested in the President and the Cabinet, which the President appoints. The President is also directly elected for four years. If no candidate gains a majority of votes, the President is chosen by Congress. The country is divided, for administrative purposes, into nine

BOLIVIA

departments, each of which is governed by a prefect, appointed by the President.

Defence

Military service, for one year, is selective. In July 1986 the armed forces numbered 27,600 men, of whom the army had 20,000, the air force 4,000, and the navy 3,600. Defence expenditure for 1984 was 500,000m. pesos.

Economic Affairs

Although well endowed with natural resources, Bolivia is a relatively poor country in terms of average income. The main sector of the economy is agriculture, which accounts for 20% of gross domestic product (GDP) and is largely traditional and labour-intensive, with low levels of productivity. According to estimates by the World Bank, Bolivia's gross national product (GNP) per head fell from US $480 in 1983 to $410 in 1984. GNP per head was estimated at less than $300 in 1985. It was estimated that GNP per head increased at an average rate of only 0.6% per year, in real terms, between 1965 and 1983. The average annual growth of GDP, measured in constant prices, was 4.4% in 1965–73, slowing to 0.8% in 1973–84. GDP per head fell by 10% in 1983, by 6% in 1984, and was expected to fall by 7% in 1985.

Bolivia possesses large reserves of petroleum, natural gas and metalliferous ores, as well as potential for large-scale agricultural development, but lack of investment has left these resources untapped. Agriculture employs almost one-half of the working population. Although subsistence farming predominates in the central highlands, agricultural production is more effective in the tropical lowlands. Potatoes, maize, rice and wheat are the principal agricultural products for domestic consumption, while cane sugar, cotton, coffee and, increasingly, timber are the principal agricultural exports. Between 1978 and 1982 Bolivia's maize crop increased by 31.5%, and output of potatoes by 20.4%. Production of sugar fell by 14.7% in the same period, and cotton declined by 78%. In 1983 severe drought, affecting about 1.6m. people over 35% of the national territory, resulted in a 60% decline in agricultural production, and caused severe hardship. Heavy rains in February and March 1984 caused further damage to crops. The annual output of paddy rice increased from 61,729 metric tons in 1983 to an estimated 193,980 metric tons in 1984. In 1986 the Government announced that a proportion of a US $55m. loan from the World Bank would be allocated to the agricultural sector.

Between 1976 and 1980 there was rapid expansion in the cultivation of coca, a shrub whose leaves are the source of the stimulant drug cocaine, which is traded illicitly. By 1984 it was calculated that 75% of all cultivated land was used for coca production. It was reported that Bolivia's annual exports of semi-pure cocaine base were in excess of 12,000 metric tons, with a value of between $1,000m. and $2,000m. The principal coca-growing area is El Chaparé. In 1985 it was reported that the US Government intended to withhold aid for 1985/86 unless the Bolivian Government reduced coca production by 10%. Although a joint Bolivian-US campaign to eradicate illegal coca plantations, launched in mid-1986, was moderately successful, one negative consequence of the campaign was expected to be a substantial increase in the rate of unemployment, caused by the elimination of the only source of income for many of the rural population.

For many years, Bolivia has been a leading producer of tin, antimony and tungsten (wolfram), but, as a high-cost producer, Bolivia has been vulnerable to changes in market demand. By 1984 Bolivia's mining sector was operating at only 50% of total capacity. Low world prices (below the costs of production and transport) since 1980 have led to a serious decline in tin production. In 1984 output fell to an estimated 17,875 metric tons, a fall of 25% from 1983. COMIBOL, the state mining corporation, recorded losses of almost US $200m. in 1984 and $240m. in 1985. The suspension of tin trading on the London Metal Exchange in October 1985 proved to be disastrous for the Bolivian mining industry. In 1984 tin exports had generated US $247.9m., equal to 32% of total exports, hence the decline in world prices for tin was expected to result in a dramatic fall in Bolivia's earnings of foreign exchange. In August 1986 the Government announced plans to rationalize COMIBOL's operations, whereby control of 24 mines passed to the Government,

Introductory Survey

leaving COMIBOL to manage 13 mines as subsidiaries. A further two mines were to be closed, and nine mines were to be made available for leasing. Of the 27,500 workers employed in the sector, more than 30% were expected to be made redundant as a result of the crisis in the tin industry.

Lead, gold, silver and zinc are also mined. Mineral production fell by 12% in 1982, making a total drop of 30% from 1978. Production continued to decline in 1983, although copper output increased from 1,295 metric tons in 1982 to 1,982 metric tons in 1983. Copper output declined to 1,665 tons in 1985. In spite of the sector's difficulties, COMIBOL planned to construct the Bolívar and Kenko multi-metal projects and a second tin volcanization plant in Machacamarca-Oruro. In March 1984 COMIBOL won the right to control the export of all minerals and to exploit Bolivia's gold deposits. In August 1985 Bolivia's new government announced plans to exploit the reserves of lithium and potassium at Uyuni, which are estimated to be the largest of their kind in the world.

Crude petroleum has gained in importance since 1972, but production has fallen steadily since 1973, dropping by 8.5% in 1979 and by 14% in 1980, owing to the use of obsolete machinery, the lack of exploration investment and the failure to bring new oil wells into production to replace depleted wells. By August 1984 production had fallen to 22,000 barrels per day (b/d), while domestic consumption had reached 21,000 b/d. In 1984 the Government announced emergency measures to boost production, which included the use of a loan of $134m. from the Inter-American Development Bank for further exploration and the development of oilfields in Santa Cruz and Camiri. By January 1986 production had fallen to 21,000 b/d. Petroleum reserves were estimated at 151m. barrels in mid-1986. In spite of a significant discovery north of La Paz in 1985, Bolivia was expected to begin importing petroleum to meet domestic demand. The Government has expressed its eagerness to attract foreign investors to the sector, and in 1985 two US companies, Occidental Petroleum and Tesoro, were renegotiating their contracts with the Government in order to expand operations in Bolivia. Natural gas has become Bolivia's main legal export, accounting for 65% of total export earnings in 1985. Bolivia is under contract to supply 21m. cu m per day to Argentina until 1992. In 1981 Brazil agreed to buy 12m. cu m per day for 20 years. The gas was to flow 1,941 km from Santa Cruz de la Sierra to Corumba along a pipeline, expected to cost US $200m. In 1984 reserves of gas were estimated at 142,000m. cu m. The Bolivia Power Company was nationalized in 1982.

Bolivia's chief trading partners in 1983 were the USA, which supplied about 47% of imports and took 21% of exports, and Argentina, which supplied 14% of imports and took 48% of exports. Bolivia participates in the trade agreements negotiated by the Latin American Integration Association (see p. 170).

The embryonic industrial sector has received some impetus from Andean Group agreements (see p. 92). Between 1976 and 1979 industrial production increased steadily. In August 1979 the Instituto Nacional de Inversiones approved 18 new industrial projects, including schemes involving the processing of mineral and agricultural products and the establishment of textile and engineering plants. Industrial production has, however, suffered from social unrest and political instability; it declined by 26% in 1981 and by 15% in 1982. The construction industry contracted by 35% in 1981 and by 40% in 1982.

After achieving an economic growth rate averaging 6.3% annually between 1973 and 1977, Bolivia's GDP increased by only 0.8% in 1980 and fell by 2% in 1981, by 7.4% in 1982, by 7.6% in 1983 and by 3% in 1984, largely as a result of declining production of petroleum, gas and metallic minerals, and falling agricultural output. The level of investment decreased by 27% in 1981 and by 37% in 1982, when the economy was nearing a state of collapse. Corruption, linked with the cocaine trade, was rampant. Inability to pay for imports, needed as a result of natural disasters, led to food shortages. Unemployment, combined with underemployment, was estimated to affect 50% of the labour force. The public sector deficit, as a proportion of GDP, reached 25%, one of the highest levels in Latin America. Gross reserves stood at only US $200m. in April 1983, while net reserves were in deficit. The value of the peso fell from 24.5 per US dollar in February 1982 to 500 per dollar in November 1983. The failure of expensive projects resulted in a foreign debt of US $3,800m. by the end of 1982, of which $1,000m. was in the private sector, and debt servicing represented 85% of the value of legal exports. In November 1983 the peso was devalued by 60.8% against the US dollar; fuel subsidies were suspended, and food prices raised, to comply with demands by the IMF for austerity measures.

In April 1984 President Siles Zuazo imposed a series of austerity measures in an attempt to reach agreement with the IMF on a loan of $300m. and to reschedule debts to commercial banks. The peso was devalued by 75% against the US dollar; subsidies were removed from a wide range of commodities and the prices of basic foodstuffs rose by up to 460%. Such a significant reversal in the Government's economic policy led to strong protests by the trade unions. In response, the Government announced a wage increase of 130% in May, and declared a moratorium on Bolivia's debt of $1,050m. to commercial banks: Bolivia would maintain payments to foreign governments and international agencies, but these would be limited to 25% of export earnings.

In February 1985 the Government announced the devaluation of the currency to 50,000 pesos per US dollar, and ordered increases in the cost of basic goods and transport by as much as 400%. The ensuing general strike, in March, resulted in losses to the economy of US $140m. In settlement of the strike, the Government awarded pay increases of more than 300%. However, it was estimated that income per head had declined by more than 30%, in real terms, over the period 1981–85. In May the peso was devalued to 75,000 per US dollar. By July Bolivia was $147m. in arrears on payments of debt principal and interest to commercial banks. Bolivia's efforts to repay other debts were hindered by the continuing decline in foreign earnings, which fell by 11.4% in 1983 and by 7.3% in 1984. In 1984 the public sector deficit was 21.5% of GDP.

On taking office in August 1985, President Víctor Paz Estenssoro affirmed his commitment to renegotiating Bolivia's foreign debt, estimated at $4,900m., and to encouraging foreign investment in the petroleum and metal-mining sectors. However, the Government's main priority was to reduce inflation, estimated at 14,173% in the year to August. The Government's economic programme, announced in August, was based on a series of drastic anti-inflation measures, including: a 95% devaluation of the peso, a 10-fold increase in petroleum prices, the elimination of all price subsidies, a four-month 'freeze' on wages in the public sector and the lifting of currency controls. A new unit of currency, the boliviano (equivalent to 1m. pesos), was to be introduced. Although the programme resulted in the holding of a general strike in September, the disastrous condition of the Bolivian economy appeared to warrant extreme measures, and the Government's policies won the immediate support of the business community and international agencies.

Protests and strikes against the Government's economic policy continued in 1986. The Government, however, remained committed to its original programme of austerity measures. Although Bolivia failed to meet all the economic targets that had been established as conditions for financial aid from the IMF and international lending agencies, inflation was successfully reduced, from 16,259% in the year to July 1985 to 92% in the year to July 1986.

Following the onset of the international tin crisis in 1985, the United Nations organized emergency funding of US $100m. for Bolivia. In June 1986 Bolivia secured a credit of SDR50m. from the IMF. Agreement with the IMF enabled the Government to resume talks with its international creditors on the rescheduling of $680m. in outstanding debts. In September the Government announced plans to invest $2,100m., over the following three years, in a series of schemes to promote Bolivia's economic recovery. The schemes were intended to create an export-based economy capable of generating earnings of $3,000m. per year.

Social Welfare

There are benefits for unemployment, accident, sickness, old age and death. In 1978 the Government established a social security and health scheme covering 1.66m. rural workers. In 1978 there were 1,158 hospitals, clinics and medical posts, with 3,410 physicians.

Education

Primary education, beginning at six years of age and lasting for eight years, is officially compulsory and is available free of charge. Secondary education, which is not compulsory, begins at 14 years of age and lasts for up to four years. In 1983 the total enrolment at primary and secondary schools was equivalent to 72% of the school-age population (78% of boys; 67% of girls). In 1980 an estimated 77% of children in the relevant age-group (82% of boys; 72% of girls) attended primary schools, while the comparable ratio for secondary enrolment was only 16% (18% of boys; 14% of girls). There are eight state universities and two private universities. In 1976 the average rate of adult illiteracy was 36.8% (males 24.2%; females 48.6%), but by 1985, according to UNESCO estimates, the rate had declined to 25.8% (males 16.2%; females 34.9%).

Tourism

Lake Titicaca, at 3,810 m (12,500 ft) above sea-level, offers excellent fishing and the 'reed' island of Suriqui, while on its shore stands the famous Roman Catholic sanctuary of Copacabana. There are pre-Incan ruins at Tiwanaku. The Andes peaks include Chacaltaya, which has the highest ski-run in the world. In 1984 about 163,000 foreign visitors arrived at Bolivian hotels and similar establishments. Tourists come mainly from the USA, Europe and South American countries.

Public Holidays

1987: 1 January (New Year), 22 February (Oruro only), 15 April (Tarija only), 17 April (Good Friday), 1 May (Labour Day), 25 May (Sucre only), 18 June (Corpus Christi), 16 July (La Paz only), 6 August (Independence), 14 September (Cochabamba only), 24 September (Santa Cruz and Cobija only), 1 November (All Saints' Day), 10 November (Potosí only), 18 November (Beni only), 25 December (Christmas).

1988: 1 January (New Year), 22 February (Oruro only), 1 April (Good Friday), 15 April (Tarija only), 1 May (Labour Day), 25 May (Sucre only), 2 June (Corpus Christi), 16 July (La Paz only), 6 August (Independence), 14 September (Cochabamba only), 24 September (Santa Cruz and Cobija only), 1 November (All Saints' Day), 10 November (Potosí only), 18 November (Beni only), 25 December (Christmas).

Weights and Measures

The metric system is officially in force, but various old Spanish measures are also used.

Currency and Exchange Rates

100 centavos = 1 peso boliviano ($b).
Exchange Rates (30 September 1986):
 £1 sterling = 2,773,899 pesos;
 US $1 = 1,917,000 pesos.

BOLIVIA

Statistical Survey

Sources (unless otherwise indicated): Instituto Nacional de Estadística, Plaza Mario Guzmán Aspiazu No. 1, Casilla 6129, La Paz; tel. (02) 367443; Banco Central de Bolivia, Ayacucho esq. Mercado, Casilla 3118, La Paz; tel. (02) 350726; telex 2286.

Area and Population

AREA, POPULATION AND DENSITY

Area (sq km)	
Land	1,084,391
Inland water	14,190
Total	1,098,581*
Population (census results)†	
5 September 1950	2,704,165
29 September 1976	
Males	2,276,029
Females	2,337,457
Total	4,613,486
Population (official estimates at mid-year)	
1983	6,081,722
1984	6,252,721
1985	6,429,000
Density (per sq km) at mid-1985	5.9

* 424,164 sq miles.
† Figures exclude adjustment for underenumeration. This was estimated at 8.4% in 1950 and 6.99% in 1976. The adjusted total for 1950 is 3,019,031, including an estimate of 87,000 for the tribal Indian population.

DEPARTMENTS (estimated population at mid-1982)

	Population	Capital
Beni	217,700	Trinidad
Chuquisaca	435,406	Sucre
Cochabamba	908,674	Cochabamba
La Paz	1,913,184	La Paz
Oruro	385,121	Oruro
Pando	42,594	Cobija
Potosí	823,485	Potosí
Santa Cruz	942,986	Santa Cruz de la Sierra
Tarija	246,691	Tarija

PRINCIPAL TOWNS (estimated population at mid-1982)

La Paz (administrative capital)	881,404
Santa Cruz de la Sierra	376,912
Cochabamba	281,962
Oruro	132,213
Potosí	103,183
Sucre (legal capital)	79,941
Tarija	54,001

BIRTHS AND DEATHS

Average annual birth rate 45.4 per 1,000 in 1970–75, 44.8 per 1,000 in 1975–80; death rate 19.0 per 1,000 in 1970–75, 17.5 per 1,000 in 1975–80 (United Nations estimates).

ECONOMICALLY ACTIVE POPULATION (1976 census)*

	Males	Females	Total
Agriculture, hunting, forestry and fishing	604,078	88,971	693,049
Mining and quarrying	57,194	3,405	60,599
Manufacturing	88,978	56,426	145,404
Electricity, gas and water	1,987	156	2,143
Construction	81,918	529	82,447
Trade, restaurants and hotels	49,650	57,212	106,862
Transport, storage and communications	54,250	1,722	55,972
Financing, insurance, real estate and business services	10,627	2,314	12,941
Community, social and personal services	165,688	116,223	281,911
Activities not adequately described	44,963	8,637	53,600
Total labour force	1,159,333	335,595	1,494,928

* Excluding persons seeking work for the first time, numbering 6,463 (males 5,286; females 1,177).

Mid-1982 (official estimates): Total labour force 1,871,600 (males 1,437,570; females 434,030).

Agriculture

PRINCIPAL CROPS ('000 metric tons)

	1982	1983	1984
Wheat	66	40	69*
Rice (paddy)	87	62	194*
Barley	61	28	40†
Maize	450	338	489*
Sorghum	13	4	10†
Potatoes	900	316	650*
Cassava (Manioc)	271	179	200†
Other roots and tubers	74	42	45†
Soya beans	78	52	75*
Groundnuts (in shell)	19	5	15†
Cottonseed*	8	6	6
Cotton (lint)	4	3	3*
Sugar cane	3,103	2,649	2,195†
Oranges	96	96	95†
Bananas	152	154	160†
Plantains*	125*	125*	125†
Coffee (green)	21	21	18†
Natural rubber†	5	5	5

* Unofficial estimates.
† FAO estimates.
Source: FAO, *Production Yearbook*.

LIVESTOCK
(FAO estimates, '000 head, year ending September)

	1982	1983	1984
Horses	410	420	420
Mules	105	106	106
Asses	790	800	800
Cattle	4,100	4,200	4,300
Pigs	1,650	1,700	1,700
Sheep	9,200	9,200	9,200
Goats	3,100	3,200	3,200

Poultry (FAO estimates, million): 9 in 1982; 10 in 1983; 10 in 1984.
Source: FAO, *Production Yearbook*.

LIVESTOCK PRODUCTS (FAO estimates, '000 metric tons)

	1982	1983	1984
Beef and veal	90	91	93
Mutton and lamb	20	21	22
Goat's meat	6	6	6
Pig meat	33	34	35
Poultry meat	11	11	12
Cows' milk	78	78	80
Sheep's milk	28	29	29
Goats' milk	15	15	15
Cheese	7.4	7.5	7.6
Hens eggs	25.0	25.5	26.0
Wool:			
greasy	9.2	9.2	9.2
scoured	5.0	5.0	5.0
Cattle hides (fresh)	11.5	11.7	11.9
Sheep skins (fresh)	5.6	5.7	5.9

Source: FAO, *Production Yearbook*.

Forestry

ROUNDWOOD REMOVALS
('000 cubic metres, excluding bark)

	1982	1983	1984
Sawlogs, veneer logs and logs for sleepers	213	136	136
Other industrial wood	13	13*	13*
Fuel wood	1,072*	1,105*	1,133*
Total	1,298	1,254	1,282

* FAO estimates.
Source: FAO, *Yearbook of Forest Products*.

SAWNWOOD PRODUCTION ('000 cubic metres)

	1981	1982	1983
Broadleaved sawnwood	168	113	93
Railway sleepers*	4	4	4
Total	172	117	97

* FAO estimates.
1984: Production as in 1983 (FAO estimates).
Source: FAO, *Yearbook of Forest Products*.

Fishing

('000 metric tons, live weight)

	1979	1980	1981
Total catch	3.7	4.4	5.6

1982-84: Annual catch as in 1981 (FAO estimates).
Source: FAO, *Yearbook of Fishery Statistics*.

BOLIVIA
Statistical Survey

Mining

(metric tons)

	1983	1984	1985
Tin	25,278	17,875	16,136
Lead	13,138	8,400	6,242
Zinc	47,132	40,500	38,110
Copper ('000 metric tons)	1,982	1,800	1,665
Tungsten (Wolfram)	3,073	2,590*	n.a.
Antimony	12,460	9,400	8,925
Silver	170.6	139.3	101.4
Gold	1.4	1.2	0.5
Petroleum (million barrels)	8.1	7.6	n.a.
Natural gas ('000 million cu ft)	178.0	173.2	n.a.

* Estimate.
Source: Asociación Nacional de Mineros Medianos.

Industry

SELECTED PRODUCTS

	1981	1982*	1983
Flour (metric tons)	151,102	234,490	200,000†
Cement (metric tons)	369,517	324,084	314,793
Refined sugar (metric tons)	239,721	210,649	182,104
Coffee (metric tons)	21,337	17,200	21,652
Edible oil ('000 litres)	17,342	17,051	17,217
Alcohol ('000 litres)	24,689	24,373	23,281

* Provisional.
† Estimate (Source: UN, *Industrial Statistics Yearbook*).
Electric Energy (million kWh): 1,677 in 1981; 1,677 in 1982; 1,698 in 1983 (Source: UN, *Industrial Statistics Yearbook*).

Finance

CURRENCY AND EXCHANGE RATES
Monetary Units
100 centavos = 1 peso boliviano ($b).

Denominations
Coins: 20, 25 and 50 centavos; 1 and 5 pesos.
Notes: 5, 10, 20, 50, 100, 500, 1,000, 50,000, 100,000 and 500,000 pesos.

Sterling and Dollar Equivalents (30 September 1986)
£1 sterling = 2,773,899 pesos;
US $1 = 1,917,000 pesos;
10,000,000 pesos bolivianos = £3.605 = $5.216.

Average Exchange Rate (pesos per US $)
1982   64
1983   230
1984   2,314

Note: In September 1985 it was announced that the Bolivian Government intended to introduce a new currency, the boliviano, with a value equivalent to 1m. pesos.

COST OF LIVING
(Consumer Price Index for La Paz; Base: 1966 = 100)

	1981	1982	1983
Food	1,097.44	2,457.38	9,920.85
Housing	719.91	1,442.90	4,033.16
Clothes	753.00	1,724.54	6,043.10
Various	665.63	1,610.95	5,430.78
All items	923.12	2,063.52	7,750.27

BUDGET (million pesos bolivianos)*

Revenue†	1980	1981	1982
Taxation	9,070	12,299	17,118
Taxes on income, profits and capital gains	1,494	2,165	3,320
Taxes on property	171	261	389
Sales taxes	509	608	1,030
Excises	2,723	4,570	6,485
Other domestic taxes on goods and services	174	227	337
Import duties	2,748	3,557	4,352
Export duties	127	10	65
Exchange taxes and profits	623	569	311
Taxes on international transport	56	62	129
Stamp taxes	323	383	557
Interest on taxes	24	43	43
Adjustment to tax revenue	98	−156	100
Property income	1,793	1,501	1,781
Administrative fees, charges, etc.	38	41	46
Fines and forfeits	31	39	49
Other current revenue	194	403	230
Total revenue	11,126	14,283	19,224

* Figures refer to the transactions of central government units covered by the General Budget. The data exclude the activities of units (government agencies and social security institutions) with their own budgets.
† Excluding grants received (8 million pesos in 1981).

Expenditure‡	1980	1981	1982
General public services	2,914	3,924	10,352
Defence	3,192	4,814	6,436
Education	4,710	5,179	11,784
Health	2,137	1,527	1,701
Social security and welfare	173	195	345
Housing and community amenities	231	370	543
Other community and social services	91	136	182
Economic services	2,494	3,635	5,405
Agriculture, forestry and fishing	579	436	661
Mining, manufacturing and construction	167	157	186
Roads	946	988	1,382
Other transport	382	1,329	2,535
Communications	13	2	233
Other purposes	1,779	1,409	50,004
Total expenditure	17,721	21,189	86,752
Current§	16,707	19,669	85,401
Capital	1,014	1,520	1,351

‡ Excluding net lending (million pesos): 24 in 1980; 33 in 181; 76 in 1982.
§ Including interest payments (million pesos): 1,919 in 1980; 1,383 in 1981; 50,943 in 1982.
1983 (million pesos): Revenue 38,662; Expenditure 118,989.
Source: IMF, *Government Finance Statistics Yearbook*.

BOLIVIA

Statistical Survey

INTERNATIONAL RESERVES
(US $ million at 31 December)

	1983	1984	1985
Gold*	37.0	37.9	37.8
IMF special drawing rights	0.1	—	—
Foreign exchange	160.0	251.6	200.0
Total	197.1	289.5	237.8

* National valuation.

Source: IMF, *International Financial Statistics*.

MONEY SUPPLY
(million pesos bolivianos at 31 December)

	1983	1984	1985
Currency outside banks	124,755	2,887,700	176,000,000
Private sector deposits at Central Bank	2,489	50,900	—
Demand deposits at commercial banks	50,270	431,500	31,000,000
Total money	177,514	3,370,100	207,000,000

Source: IMF, *International Financial Statistics*.

NATIONAL ACCOUNTS (million pesos at 1970 prices)
Gross Domestic Product by Economic Activity

	1981*	1982*	1983
Agriculture	3,352	3,419	2,667
Mining (incl. petroleum exploration)	1,299	1,264	1,257
Industry	3,302	2,553	2,362
Construction	711	278	278
Transport and fuel	2,302	2,474	1,996
Commerce and finance	3,452	2,610	2,068
Services and rent	2,721	1,371	1,367
Public administration	1,969	3,302	1,906
Total	19,108	17,271	16,049

* Estimates.

Source: Dirección General de Presupuesto.

BALANCE OF PAYMENTS (US $ million)

	1983	1984	1985
Merchandise exports f.o.b.	755.1	724.5	623.4
Merchandise imports f.o.b.	−496.0	−412.3	−462.8
Trade balance	259.1	312.2	160.6
Exports of services	143.9	123.5	114.0
Imports of services	−647.3	−698.4	−636.5
Balance on goods and services	−244.3	−262.7	−361.9
Private unrequited transfers (net)	40.2	21.8	19.7
Government unrequited transfers (net)	65.2	66.0	59.8
Current balance	−138.9	−174.9	−282.4
Direct capital investment (net)	6.9	7.0	10.0
Other long-term capital (net)	−223.0	−154.4	−244.8
Short-term capital (net)	−113.5	204.9	−2.2
Net errors and omissions	71.5	−12.0	186.0
Total (net monetary movements)	−397.0	−129.4	−333.4
Monetization of gold	0.9	0.9	−0.1
Valuation changes (net)	5.1	4.8	3.8
Exceptional financing (net)	668.4	282.9	352.6
Official financing (net)	−230.4	−37.7	−62.7
Changes in reserves	47.0	121.5	−39.8

Source: IMF, *International Financial Statistics*.

BOLIVIA *Statistical Survey*

External Trade

PRINCIPAL COMMODITIES (US $ million)

Imports	1981	1982	1983
Consumer goods	233.6	80.4	52.3
Non-durable	115.9	47.8	35.7
Durable	117.7	32.6	16.6
Raw materials	292.6	195.9	222.6
Materials for agriculture	28.6	14.9	7.5
Materials for industry	264.0	181.0	215.1
Capital goods	384.1	209.8	257.4
Construction	49.3	4.6	38.4
Agriculture	20.4	36.0	7.1
Industry	195.3	118.2	152.4
Transport equipment	119.1	51.0	52.2
Total	**900.3**	**486.1**	**532.3**

Exports	1981	1982	1983
Minerals	556.0	419.3	347.3
Natural gas	326.2	381.6	378.2
Coffee	15.7	15.5	12.9
Sugar	5.7	8.0	12.3
Wood	12.4	11.6	7.8
Rubber	3.4	4.1	2.7
Chestnuts	2.5	2.2	n.a.
Hides	3.0	3.2	0.8
Cattle	0.9	0.6	n.a.
Total (incl. others)	**980.7**	**898.2**	**817.5**

EXPORTS OF MINING PRODUCTS (US $ '000)

	1981	1982	1983
Tin	343,095	278,343	207,906
Tungsten	42,955	n.a.	n.a.
Antimony	34,306	17,769	16,317
Lead	11,459	6,540	4,007
Zinc	40,423	38,395	33,372
Copper	4,402	3,126	2,978
Silver	71,694	37,067	58,264

PRINCIPAL TRADING PARTNERS (US $ '000)

Imports	1981*	1982*	1983
Argentina	101,344	72,357	75,562
Belgium	—	3,740	2,766
Brazil	70,654	50,519	73,860
Canada	4,677	5,795	3,994
Chile	20,187	14,799	16,215
Colombia	7,467	1,794	1,573
France	8,698	6,353	21,138
Germany, Federal Republic	77,875	36,310	29,197
Italy	7,139	8,539	3,897
Japan	121,285	54,396	38,971
Netherlands	10,750	6,288	5,670
Peru	21,172	13,599	13,473
Sweden	7,468	5,882	7,189
Switzerland	8,698	5,930	4,544
United Kingdom	25,767	19,780	20,816
USA	263,084	143,755	249,466
Total (incl. others)	**820,600**	**496,084**	**532,342**

Exports	1981†	1982†	1983
Argentina	243,124	465,119	388,770
Belgium	26,739	18,799	25,434
Brazil	36,057	19,473	12,721
Canada	8,019	74	31
Chile	36,028	10,822	8,333
Colombia	5,490	5,868	3,805
France	44,894	14,981	15,326
Germany, Federal Republic	40,775	33,314	23,548
Italy	1,326	922	602
Japan	9,443	16,224	15,358
Netherlands	45,414	35,655	49,077
Peru	26,428	23,007	14,577
Sweden	63	392	150
Switzerland	47,738	18,548	16,540
United Kingdom	73,027	30,976	19,121
USA	301,388	234,796	169,851
Total (incl. others)	**980,729**	**898,176**	**817,460**

* Estimates. † Preliminary.

Transport

RAILWAYS (traffic)

	1984
Passengers carried	2,114,848
Passenger-kilometres	684,241
Freight carried (metric tons)	1,141,923
Freight ton-kilometres	547,862

Source: Empresa Nacional de Ferrocarriles.

ROAD TRAFFIC (motor vehicles in use)

	1983
Cars	43,677
Buses	29,073
Trucks	14,627
Lorries	25,894
Jeeps	14,817
Motor cycles	40,514

CIVIL AVIATION (traffic on scheduled services)

	1980	1981	1982
Kilometres flown (million)	13.5	12.6	10.5
Passengers carried ('000)	1,342	1,220	1,160
Passenger-km (million)	944	963	780
Freight ton-km (million)	37.6	43.7	27.6

Source: United Nations, *Statistical Yearbook*.

Tourism

	1982	1983	1984
Arrivals at hotels	150,142	175,903	163,183

Education

(1981)

	Institutions	Teachers	Students
Primary and elementary	10,662	51,852	1,115,259
Pre-basic	1,920	1,192	93,985
Basic	5,970	40,686	810,889
Intermediate	2,772	9,974	210,385
Higher	548	6,179	178,217
Specialized	39	2,409	16,206
Total	11,249	60,440	1,309,682

Directory

The Constitution

Bolivia became an independent republic in 1825 and received its first constitution in November 1826. Since that date a number of new constitutions have been promulgated. Following the *coup d'état* of November 1964, the Constitution of 1947 was revived. Under its provisions, executive power is vested in the President. According to the revised Constitution, the President is elected by direct suffrage for a four-year term and is not eligible for immediate re-election. In the event of the President's death or failure to assume office, the Vice-President or, failing the Vice-President, the President of the Senate becomes interim Head of State.

The President has power to appoint members of the Cabinet, diplomatic representatives, and archbishops and bishops from a panel proposed by the Senate. The President is responsible for the conduct of foreign affairs and is also empowered to issue decrees, and initiate legislation by special messages to Congress.

Congress consists of a Senate (27 members) and a Chamber of Deputies (130 members). Congress meets annually and its ordinary sessions last only 90 working days, which may be extended to 120. Each of the nine departments (La Paz, Chuquisaca, Oruro, Beni, Santa Cruz, Potosí, Tarija, Cochabamba and Pando), into which the country is divided for administrative purposes, elects three senators. Members of both houses are elected for four years.

The supreme administrative, political and military authority in each department is vested in a prefect appointed by the President. The sub-divisions of each department, known as provinces, are administered by sub-prefects. The provinces are further divided into cantons. There are 94 provinces and some 1,000 cantons. The capital of each department has its autonomous municipal council and controls its own revenue and expenditure.

Public order, education and roads are under national control.

A decree issued in July 1952 conferred the franchise on all persons who had reached the age of 21, whether literate or illiterate. Previously the franchise had been restricted to literate persons.

The death penalty was restored in October 1971 for terrorism, kidnapping and crimes against government and security personnel. In 1981 its scope was extended to drug trafficking.

The Government

HEAD OF STATE

President: Dr Víctor Paz Estenssoro (took office 6 August 1985).
Vice-President: Julio Garret Ayllón.

THE CABINET
(October 1986)

Minister of Foreign Affairs and Religion: Guillermo Bedregal Gutiérrez.
Minister of Finance: Juan Cariaga Osorio.
Minister of Economic Planning: Gonzalo Sánchez de Lozada.
Minister of Education and Culture: Prof. Enrique Ipiña Melgar.
Minister of Labour: Walter Ríos Gamboa.
Minister of Urban Development and Housing: Franklin Anaya.
Minister of the Interior and Justice: Fernando Barthelemey.
Minister of National Defence: Dr Luis Fernando Valle.
Minister of Industry, Commerce and Tourism: Lic. Roberto Gisbert.
Minister of Transport and Communications: Andrés Petrovic.
Minister of Public Health and Social Security: Carlos Pérez.
Minister of Mining and Metallurgy: Jaime Villalobos.
Minister of Rural Affairs: Edil Sandoval Morón.
Minister of Energy and Hydrocarbons: Carlos Morales.
Minister of Aviation: Gen. Antonio Tovar Pierola.
Minister of Information: Hernán Antelo.
Secretary-General of Economic Integration: Ing. Fernando Cáceres.
Secretary-General of the Presidency: Juan Carlos Durán.

MINISTRIES

Office of the President: Palacio de Gobierno, Plaza Murillo, La Paz; tel. (02) 374030; telex 5242.
Ministry of Aviation: Avda Arce 2579, Casilla 6176, La Paz; tel. (02) 374142; telex 3413.
Ministry of Economic Planning: Avda Arce 2147, La Paz; tel. (02) 372060; telex 5321.
Ministry of Education and Culture: Avda Arce, La Paz; tel. (02) 373260; telex 5242.
Ministry of Energy and Hydrocarbons: Avda Mariscal Santa Cruz 1322, La Paz; tel. (02) 374050; telex 5366.
Ministry of Finance: Calle Bolívar, La Paz; tel. (02) 373130; telex 2617.
Ministry of Foreign Affairs and Religion: Cancellería de la República de Bolivia, Plaza Murillo esq. Ingarí, La Paz; tel. (02) 371152; telex 5242.
Ministry of Industry, Commerce and Tourism: Avda Camacho esq. Bueno, Casilla 1372, La Paz; tel. (02) 372044; telex 3259.
Ministry of the Interior and Justice: Avda Arce, La Paz; tel. (02) 370460; telex 5437.
Ministry of Labour: Calle Yanacocha, La Paz; tel. (02) 374350; telex 5242.
Ministry of Mining and Metallurgy: Avda 16 de Julio 1769, La Paz; tel. (02) 379310; telex 5564.
Ministry of National Defence: Plaza Abaroa esq. 20 de Octubre, La Paz; tel. (02) 377130; telex 5242.
Ministry of Public Health and Social Security: Plaza del Estudiante, La Paz; tel. (02) 375460; telex 5242.
Ministry of Rural Affairs: Avda Camacho 1407, La Paz; tel. (02) 374260; telex 5242.

BOLIVIA

Ministry of Transport and Communications: Edif. La Urbana, Avda Camacho, La Paz; tel. (02) 377220; telex 2648.

Ministry of Urban Development and Housing: Avda 20 de Octubre esq. F. Guachalla, Casilla 5926, La Paz; tel. (02) 372240; telex 5242.

General Secretariat of Integration: Calle Pedro Salazar 348, La Paz; tel. (02) 322753; telex 5534.

Legislature
NATIONAL CONGRESS

Election, 14 July 1985
(names of the presidential candidates are given in parentheses)

Party	Seats
Movimiento Nacionalista Revolucionario (Histórico) (Dr Víctor Paz Estenssoro)	59
Acción Democrática Nacionalista (Gen. Hugo Bánzer Suárez)	51
Movimiento de la Izquierda Revolucionaria (Jaime Paz Zamora)	16
Movimiento Nacionalista Revolucionario de Izquierda (Roberto Jordán Pando)	8
Movimiento Nacionalista Revolucionario—Vanguardia Revolucionaria 9 de Abril (Carlos Serrate Reiche)	6
Partido Socialista-Uno—Marcelo Quiroga (José María Palacios)	5
Frente del Pueblo Unido (Antonio Araníbar Quiroga)	4
Falange Socialista Boliviana (David Añez)	3
Partido Demócrata Cristiano (Dr Luis Ossio Sanjines)	3
Movimiento Revolucionario Tupac Katarí (Genaro Flores Santos)	2
Total	**157***

* Comprising 27 Senators and 130 members of the Chamber of Deputies.

President of the Senate: Ciro Humbolt Barrero (MNR).

President of the Chamber of Deputies: Willy Vargas Vacaflor (ADN).

Note: As no candidate in the presidential election obtained a clear majority of direct votes, a choice between the three leading contenders was made by the new National Congress on 4–5 August 1985. After two ballots, Dr Víctor Paz Estenssoro (MNR) was declared to have won with 94 votes. Gen. Hugo Bánzer Suárez (ADN) obtained 51 votes.

Political Organizations

Acción Democrática Nacionalista (ADN): La Paz; f. 1979; extreme right-wing; Leader Gen. Hugo Bánzer Suárez; Sec. Guillermo Fortún.

Centro Nacionalista (CEN): Héroes del Arce 1746, Of. La Voz del Pueblo, La Paz; right-wing; Leader Dr Roberto Zapata de la Barra.

Falange Socialista Boliviano (FSB): La Paz; f. 1937; right-wing; Leaders David Añez, Remy Solares; divided into two factions:

Gutiérrez: Sánchez Lima 2278, La Paz; f. 1937; Leader Dr Mario Gutiérrez.

Moreira: Canoniga Ayllón esq. Boquerón 597, Casilla 4937, La Paz; Leader Gastón Moreira Ostría; Sec.-Gen. Dr Augusto Mendizábal; 100,000 mems.

Falange Socialista Boliviana de la Izquierda (FSBI): Casilla 1649, La Paz; f. 1970; Leader Dr Enrique Riveros Aliaga; 150,000 mems.

Frente del Pueblo Unido (FPU): communist; comprising dissident members of the Movimiento de la Izquierda Revolucionaria and the Partido Comunista de Bolivia (see below).

Frente Revolucionario de Izquierda (FRI): Mercado 996, 2°, Of. 2, La Paz; left-wing; Leader Dr Manuel Morales Dávila.

Directory

Mandato de Acción y Unidad Nacional (MAN): Comercio 1057, 3°, Casilla 2169, La Paz; f. 1972; Leader Dr Gonzalo Romero Alvarez García; Sec. Dr Fernando Oblitas Mendoza; 2,000 mems.

Movimiento Agrario Revolucionario del Campesinado Boliviano (MARC): Yanacocha 448, Of. 17, La Paz; f. 1978; nationalist movement; Pres. Gen. (retd) René Bernal Escalante; Exec. Sec. Dr José Zegarra Cerruto.

Movimiento de la Izquierda Nacional (MIN): La Paz; left-wing; Leader Dr Luis Sandoval Morón.

Movimiento de la Izquierda Revolucionaria (MIR): Avda América 119, 2°, La Paz; telex 3210; f. 1971; left-wing; Leader Jaime Paz Zamora; factions include:

MIR—Araníbar: f. 1985; allied to FPU (see above); Leader Antonio Araníbar Quiroga.

MIR—Masas: f. 1985; Leader Walter Delgadillo.

Movimiento Nacionalista Revolucionario (Histórico)—MNR: Genaro Sanjines 541, Pasaje Kuljis, La Paz; formerly part of the Movimiento Nacionalista Revolucionario (MNR, f. 1942); centre-right; Leader Dr Víctor Paz Estenssoro; Exec. Sec. Javier Campero Paz; 700,000 mems.

Movimiento Nacionalista Revolucionario de Izquierda (MNRI): La Paz; f. 1979; formerly part of the Movimiento Nacionalista Revolucionario (MNR, f. 1942); left of centre; Leader Dr Hernán Siles Zuazo; Sec.-Gen. Federico Alvarez Plata.

Movimiento Nacionalista Revolucionario (MNR)—Julio: Claudio Pinilla 1648, La Paz; formerly part of the Movimiento Nacionalista Revolucionario (MNR, f. 1942); Leader Rubén Julio Castro.

Movimiento Nacionalista Revolucionario del Pueblo (MNRP): Casilla 3030, La Paz; f. 1965; nationalist movement; Leader Jaime Arellano Casteñada; 50,000 mems.

Movimiento Nacionalista Revolucionario—Vanguardia Revolucionaria 9 de Abril (MNRV): centre-right; Leader Carlos Serrate Reich.

Movimiento Revolucionario Tupac Katarí (MRTK): Linares esq. Sagáruaga 901, Casilla 3636, La Paz; f. 1978; peasant party; Pres. Juan Condori Uruchi; Leader Genaro Flores Santos; 80,000 mems.

Ofensiva de la Izquierda Democrática (OID): Edif. Herrmann 11°, Plaza Venezuela 1440, La Paz; f. 1979; Leader Luis Adolfo Siles Salinas.

Organización de Unidad Revolucionaria (OUR): Comercio 979, 1°, Of. 14, La Paz; f. 1977; Sec.-Gen. Dr Mario Lanza Suárez; 5,000 mems.

Partido Comunista de Bolivia (PCB): La Paz; f. 1950; follows Moscow line; First Sec. Simón Reyes Rivera.

Partido Comunista Marxista Leninista de Bolivia: c/o Palacio Legislativo, Palacio Murillo, La Paz; f. 1965; formerly part of the PCB; First Sec. Oscar Zamora Medinacelli.

Partido Demócrata Cristiano: Casilla 4345, La Paz; f. 1954; Pres. Dr Luis Ossio Sanjines; Sec. Miguel Rochas; Leader José Luis Roca; 50,000 mems.

Partido Indio: La Paz.

Partido Obrero Revolucionario (POR): La Paz; communist; Leader Guillermo Lora.

Partido de la Revolución Nacional (PRN): Saavedra 1026, Casilla 8466, La Paz; f. 1966; left-wing; Leader Rubén Arias Alvis; Sec.-Gen. Luis Jiménez Espinoza; 50,000 mems.

Partido Revolucionario Auténtico (PRA): Yanacocha 448, Of. 2, La Paz; f. 1960; formerly part of the Movimiento Nacionalista Revolucionario (MNR, f. 1942); Leader Dr Walter Guevara Arce.

Partido Revolucionario de la Izquierda Nacional Gueiler (PRING): Mercado 996, 2°, La Paz; Leader Dra Lidia Gueiler Tejada.

Partido Revolucionario de la Izquierda Nacionalista (PRIN): Colón 693, La Paz; f. 1964; left-wing; Leader Juan Lechín Oquendo.

Partido Social Demócrata (PSD): Edif. Barrosquira 6°, La Paz; f. 1945; Leader Dr Antonio Chiqie Dipp.

Partido Socialista-Uno (PS-1): La Paz; Leader Walter Vázquez.

Partido Socialista-Uno—Marcelo Quiroga: La Paz; Leader José María Palacios.

Partido Unión Boliviana (PUB): Pichincha 729 esq. Indaburo, La Paz; Leader Walter Gonzales Valda.

BOLIVIA

Partido de la Unión Socialista Republicana (PURS): Casilla 3724, La Paz; f. 1945; left-wing; Leader Dr CONSTANTINO CARRIÓN V.; Sec.-Gen. PEDRO MONTAÑO; 30,000 mems.

Partido de Vanguardia Obrera: Plaza Venezuela 1452, La Paz; Leader FILEMÓN ESCOBAR.

Diplomatic Representation

EMBASSIES IN BOLIVIA

Argentina: Calle Aspiazu 497, La Paz; tel. (02) 322172; telex 3300; Ambassador: GASTÓN TABOADA.

Belgium: Sánchez Lima 2400, Casilla 2433, La Paz; tel. (02) 328942; telex 3274; Ambassador: RAYMOND VAN ROY.

Brazil: Fernando Guachalla 494, Casilla 429, La Paz; tel. (02) 350718; telex 2494; Ambassador: JOÃO TABAJARA DE OLIVEIRA.

China, People's Republic: La Paz; telex 5558; Ambassador: YUAN TAO.

Colombia: Avda 6 de Agosto 2528, Casilla 1418, La Paz; tel. (02) 351199; telex 5239; Ambassador: ALFREDO URDINOLA.

Costa Rica: Avda Vera 6870, Casilla 2780, La Paz; Ambassador: GUILLERMO GAGO PÉREZ.

Cuba: Avda Arequipa 8037, Calacoto, La Paz; tel. (02) 792616; telex 2447; Ambassador: (vacant).

Czechoslovakia: Urb. Las Colinas, Calle 24, No 6, Calacoto, Casilla 2780, La Paz; tel. (02) 792530; Ambassador: STANISLAV NOVOTNÝ.

Ecuador: Edif. Herrman 14°, Plaza Venezuela, Casilla 406, La Paz; tel. (02) 321208; telex 3388; Ambassador: OLMEDO MONTEVERDE PAZ.

Egypt: Avda Ballivián 599, Casilla 2956, La Paz; tel. (02) 794616; telex 2612; Ambassador: EZZ EL-DIN EL-SAYED IZZA.

France: Edif. Bisa 7°–8°, Avda 16 de Julio 1628, Casilla 824, La Paz; tel. (02) 360431; telex 2267; Ambassador: PIERRE MUTTER.

Germany, Federal Republic: Avda Arce 2395, Casilla 5265, La Paz; tel. (02) 351980; telex 3303; Ambassador: Dr HERMAN SAÜMWEBER.

Holy See: Avda Arce 2990, Casilla 136, La Paz; tel. (02) 375007; telex 2393; Apostolic Nuncio: Mgr SANTOS ABRIL Y CASTELLO.

Hungary: Avda Los Sauces 740, entre Calles 13 y 14, Calacoto, Casilla 1822, La Paz; tel. (02) 794411; telex 3270; Ambassador: ADOLF SZELES.

Israel: Edif. Esperanza 10°, Avda Mariscal Santa Cruz, Casilla 1309, La Paz; tel. (02) 325463; telex 3297; Ambassador: BERL ZERUBAVEL.

Italy: Avda 6 de Agosto 2575, Casilla 626, La Paz; tel. (02) 327329; telex 2654; Ambassador: Dr LUCHINO CORTESE.

Japan: Calle Rosendo Gutiérrez 497, Casilla 2725, La Paz; tel. (02) 373152; telex 2548; Ambassador: (vacant).

Korea, Democratic People's Republic: La Paz; Ambassador: KIM CHAN SIK.

Korea, Republic: Avda 6 de Agosto 2592, Casilla 1559, La Paz; tel. (02) 364485; telex 3262; Ambassador: CHO KAB-DONG.

Mexico: Avda 6 de Agosto 2652, POB 430, La Paz; tel. (02) 329505; telex 3316; Ambassador: RICARDO GALÁN.

Nicaragua: Calle Rosendo Gutiérrez 666, Casilla 20362, La Paz; tel. (02) 358383; telex 3228; Ambassador: RAMÓN LEETS CASTILLO.

Panama: Calle Potosí 1270, Casilla 678, La Paz; tel. (02) 371277; telex 2314; Ambassador: Lic. JAIME RODRÍGUEZ MORALES.

Paraguay: Edif. Venus, Avda Arce esq. Montevideo, Casilla 882, La Paz; tel. (02) 322018; Ambassador: Gen. RAMÓN DUARTE VERA.

Peru: Calle Rosendo Gutiérrez 113 esq. Capitán Ravelo, Casilla 668, La Paz; tel. (02) 353550; telex 2475; Ambassador: JAIME CACHO SOUSA.

Romania: Calle Capitán Ravelo (Pasaje Isaac G. Eduardo) 2173, Casilla 20879, La Paz; tel. (02) 378632; telex 3260; Ambassador: ION FLORES.

South Africa: Calle 22, Calacoto No. 7810, Casilla 6018, La Paz; tel. (02) 792101; telex 2339; Ambassador: (vacant).

Spain: Avda 6 de Agosto 2860, Casilla 382, La Paz; tel. (02) 323245; telex 3304; Ambassador: FAUSTO NAVARRO.

Switzerland: Edif. Petrolero, Avda 16 de Julio 1616, Casilla 657, La Paz; tel. (02) 353091; telex 2325; Ambassador: (vacant).

USSR: Avda Arequipa 8128, Casilla 5494, La Paz; tel. (02) 792048; telex 2480; Ambassador: ARKADIY VLUYOV.

United Kingdom: Avda Arce 2732–2754, Casilla 694, La Paz; tel. (02) 329401; telex 2341; Ambassador: ALAN WHITE.

USA: Edif. Banco Popular del Perú, Calle Colón 290, Casilla 425, La Paz; tel. (02) 350120; telex 3268; Ambassador: EDWARD MORGAN ROWELL.

Uruguay: Avda Arce 2985, Casilla 441, La Paz; tel. (02) 353857; telex 2378; Ambassador: JOSÉ M. ALVAREZ.

Venezuela: Calle Méndez Arcos 117, Casilla 960, La Paz; tel. (02) 320872; telex 2383; Ambassador: EDUARDO MORREO BUSTAMANTE.

Yugoslavia: Benito Juárez 315, La Florida, Casilla 1717, La Paz; tel. (02) 792148; Ambassador: MIODRAG RADOVIĆ.

Judicial System

SUPREME COURT

Corte Suprema: Calle Yanacocha 417, La Paz; tel. (02) 377032; telex 2320.

Judicial power is vested in the Supreme Court. There are 12 members, appointed by Congress for a term of 10 years. The court is divided into four chambers of three justices each. Two chambers deal with civil cases, the third deals with criminal cases and the fourth deals with administrative, social and mining cases. The President of the Supreme Court presides over joint sessions of the courts and attends the joint sessions for cassation cases.

President of the Supreme Court: GUILLERMO CABALLERO SAUCEDO.

DISTRICT COURTS

There is a District Court sitting in each Department, and additional provincial and local courts to try minor cases.

ATTORNEY-GENERAL

In addition to the Attorney-General at Sucre (appointed by the President on the proposal of the Senate), there is a District Attorney in each Department as well as circuit judges.

Attorney-General: Dr JOSÉ HUGO VILAR TUFINO.

Religion

The majority of the population are Roman Catholics; there were an estimated 5,121,019 adherents in 1982. Religious freedom is guaranteed. There is a small Jewish community, as well as various Protestant denominations, in Bolivia.

CHRISTIANITY

The Roman Catholic Church

Bolivia comprises four archdioceses, four dioceses, two Territorial Prelatures and six Apostolic Vicariates.

Bishops' Conference: Conferencia Episcopal de Bolivia, Casilla 2309, La Paz; tel. 321254; f. 1972; Pres. Mgr JULIO TERRAZAS SANDOVAL, Bishop of Oruro.

Archbishop of Cochabamba: GENNARO MARÍA PRATA VUOLO, Calle Baptista 6036, Casilla 129, Cochabamba; tel. 22084.

Archbishop of La Paz: JORGE MANRIQUE HURTADO, Calle Ballivián 1277, Casilla 259, La Paz; tel. (02) 341920.

Archbishop of Santa Cruz de la Sierra: LUIS RODRÍGUEZ PARDO, Casilla 25, Ingavi 49, Santa Cruz de la Sierra; tel. 24286.

Archbishop of Sucre: Cardinal RENÉ FERNÁNDEZ APAZA, Calle Bolívar 313, Casilla 205, Sucre; tel. (064) 21703.

Protestant Churches

Baptist Convention of Bolivia: Casilla 3147, Santa Cruz; tel. 36063; Pres. Rev. HERNÁN ARTEAGA RONCALES.

Baptist Union of Bolivia: Casilla 1408, La Paz; Pres. Rev. AUGUSTO CHUIJO.

BAHÁ'Í FAITH

National Spiritual Assembly: Casilla 1613, La Paz; tel. (02) 785058; mems resident in 5,540 localities.

BOLIVIA   *Directory*

The Press

DAILY NEWSPAPERS

Cochabamba

Los Tiempos: Santiváñez 4110, Casilla 525, Cochabamba; tel. 28586; f. 1943; morning; independent; right-wing; Dir CARLOS CANELAS; circ. 18,000.

La Paz

El Diario: Loayza 118, Casilla 5, La Paz; tel. (02) 356835; telex 5530; f. 1904; morning; conservative; Dir JORGE CARRASCO VILLALOBOS; circ. 45,000.

Hoy: Avda 6 de Agosto 2170, Casilla 477, La Paz; tel. (02) 326683; telex 2613; f. 1968; morning and midday editions; independent; Dir CARLOS SERRATE REICH; circ. 25,000.

Jornada: Junín 608, Casilla 1628, La Paz; tel. (02) 353844; f. 1964; evening; independent; Dir JAIME RÍOS CHACÓN; circ. 11,500.

Meridiano: Avda 6 de Agosto 2170, Casilla 477, La Paz; f. 1981; midday; independent; Dir GUILLERMO MONJE L.; circ. 6,500.

Presencia: Avda Mariscal Santa Cruz, Casilla 1451, La Paz; tel. (02) 372340; telex 2659; f. 1952; morning; Catholic; Dir HUÁSCAR CAJÍAS K.; Man. Lic. GUSTAVO PABÓN; circ. 75,000.

Ultima Hora: Avda Camacho 309, Casilla 5920, La Paz; tel. (02) 370416; f. 1939; evening; independent; Dir JORGE SILES SALINAS; Editor JORGE CANELAS; circ. 35,000.

Oruro

El Expreso: Potosí 319 esq. Oblitas, Oruro; f. 1977; morning; independent; right-wing; Dir GENARO FRONTANILLA VISTAS; circ. 1,000.

La Patria: Avda Camacho 1892, Casilla 48, Oruro; f. 1919; morning; independent; Dir ENRIQUE MILLARES; circ. 3,500.

Potosí

El Siglo: Calle Linares 99, Casilla 389, Potosí; morning; Dir WILSON MENDIETA; circ. 1,500.

Santa Cruz

El Deber: Suárez Arana 264, Casilla 2144, Santa Cruz; tel. 23588; morning; independent; Dir PEDRO RIVERO MERCADO; circ. 8,000.

El Mundo: Florida 593, Santa Cruz; tel. 34770; f. 1979; morning; owned by Santa Cruz Industrialists' Association; Dir SIXTO NELSON FLEIG; circ. 20,000.

Tarija

La Verdad: Tarija; Dir JOSÉ LANZA; circ. 3,000.

Trinidad

La Razón: Trinidad; Dir CARLOS VÉLEZ.

PERIODICALS

Actualidad Boliviana Confidencial: Fernando Guachalla 969, Casilla 648, La Paz; weekly; Dir HUGO GONZÁLEZ RIOJA.

Aquí: Casilla 20441, La Paz; tel. (02) 365796; f. 1979; weekly; circ. 10,000.

Bolivia Libre: Edif. Esperanza 5°, Avda Mariscal Santa Cruz 2150, Casilla 6500, La Paz; fortnightly; published by the Ministry of Information.

Carta Cruceña de Integración: Casilla 2735, Santa Cruz de la Sierra; weekly; Dirs HERNÁN LLANOVARCED A., JOHNNY LAZARTE J.

Comentarios Económicos de Actualidad (CEA): Casilla 12097, La Paz; tel. (02) 377506; fortnightly; articles and economic analyses.

Extra: Oruro; weekly; Dir JORGE LAZO.

Información Política y Económica (IPE): Calle Comercio, Casilla 2484, La Paz; weekly; Dir GONZALO LÓPEZ MUÑOZ.

El Noticiero: Sucre; weekly; Dir DAVID CABEZAS; circ. 1,500.

Servicio de Información Confidencial (SIC): Elías Sagárnaga 274, Casilla 5035, La Paz; weekly; publ. by Asociación Nacional de Prensa; Dir JOSÉ CARRANZA.

Unión: Sucre; weekly; Dir JAIME MERILES.

PRESS ASSOCIATIONS

Asociación Nacional de Periodistas: Avda 6 de Agosto 2170, Casilla 477, La Paz; Pres. ALBERTO ZUAZO NATHES.

Asociación Nacional de Prensa: Comercio 1048, Casilla 3089, La Paz; Pres. CARLOS SERRATE REICH.

Asociación de Periodistas de La Paz: Comercio 1048, La Paz; tel. 369916.

NEWS AGENCIES

Agencia de Noticias Fides (ANF): Edif. Mariscal de Ayacucho, 6°, Of. 601, Calle Loayza, Casilla 5782, La Paz; tel. (02) 365152; telex 3236; owned by Catholic Church; Dir JOSÉ GRAMUNT DE MORAGAS.

Foreign Bureaux

Agencia EFE (Spain): Edif. Esperanza, Avda Mariscal Santa Cruz 2150, Casilla 7403, La Paz; tel. (02) 367205; telex 2535; Bureau Chief JUAN MARÍA CALVO.

Agentstvo Pechati Novosti (APN) (USSR): Edif. Mariscal Ballivián, Of. 401, Calle Mercado, La Paz; tel. (02) 373857; telex 3285; Correspondent VLADIMIR RAMÍREZ.

Agenzia Nazionale Stampa Associata (ANSA) (Italy): Edif. Credinform 4°, Of. 404, Calle Ayacucho esq. Calle Potosí, Casilla 7768, La Paz; tel. (02) 365530; telex 3410; Bureau Chief MABEL AZCUI.

Associated Press (AP) (USA): Edif. Mariscal de Ayacucho, Of. 1209, Calle Loayza, Casilla 4364, La Paz; tel. (02) 370128; telex 3283; Correspondent PETER J. MCFARREN.

Deutsche Presse-Agentur (dpa) (Fed. Republic of Germany): Plaza Venezuela 1456, 1°, Of. F, Casilla 135, La Paz; tel. (02) 352684; telex 2601; Correspondent ANA MARÍA CAMPERO.

Inter Press Service (IPS) (Italy): Edif. Esperanza 6°, Of. 6, Avda Mariscal Santa Cruz, Casilla 11130, La Paz; tel. (02) 365322; Correspondent OSCAR PEÑA FRANCO.

Prensa Latina (Cuba): Edif. Aries, Apto 15, Calle 10 de Obrajes esq. Hernando Siles, La Paz; tel. (02) 785357; telex 2525; Correspondent JORGE LUNA MENDOZA.

Reuters (UK): Calle Loayza, 11°, Of. 1112-3, Casilla 4057, La Paz; tel. (02) 351106; telex 2573; Correspondent JUAN JAVIER ZEBALLOS.

Telegrafnoye Agentstvo Sovetskovo Soyuza (TASS) (USSR): Casilla 6839, San Miguel, Bloque O–33, Casa 958, La Paz; tel. (02) 792108; Correspondent ELDAR ABDULLAEV.

United Press International (UPI) (USA): Plaza Venezuela 1456, 1°, Of. B, Casilla 1219, La Paz; tel. (02) 371278; telex 2453; Correspondent ALBERTO ZUAZO NATHES.

Agence France-Presse and Telam (Argentina) are also represented.

Publishers

Editorial los Amigos del Libro: Avda Heroínas E-0311, Casilla 450, Cochabamba; tel. 2920; f. 1945; general; Man. Dir WERNER GUTTENTAG.

Editorial Bruño: Casilla 4809, Calles Loayza esq. Juan de la Riva, La Paz; tel. (02) 320198; f. 1964; Dir IGNACIO LOMAS.

Editorial Difusión: Avda 16 de Julio 1601, Casilla 1510, La Paz; tel. (02) 328126; f. 1960; literature, history, politics, social studies; Man. Dir JORGE F. CATALANO.

Librería Dismo Ltda: Comercio 806, Casilla 988, La Paz; tel. (02) 353119; Dir TERESA GONZÁLEZ DE ALVAREZ.

Editorial Don Bosco: Avda 16 de Julio 1899, Casilla 4458, La Paz; tel. (02) 371149; social sciences, literature and the cinema; Dir Padre AUGUSTO BINDELLI.

Gisbert y Cía, SA: Comercio 1270, Casilla 195, La Paz; tel. (02) 356806; f. 1907; textbooks, history, law and general; Pres. JOSÉ GISBERT; Dirs JAVIER GISBERT, ARMANDO PAGANO.

Icthus Editorial: Avda 16 de Julio 1800, Casilla 8353, La Paz; tel. (02) 354007; f. 1967; general and textbooks; Man. Dir SALVADOR DE LA SERNA.

Ivar American: Calle Potosí 1375, Casilla 6016, La Paz; tel. (02) 361519; Man. Dir HÉCTOR IBÁÑEZ.

Editorial y Librería Juventud: Plaza Murillo 519, Casilla 1489, La Paz; tel. (02) 341694; f. 1946; textbooks and general; Man. Dir RAFAEL URQUIZO.

Editora Khana Cruz SRL: Avda Camacho 1372, Casilla 5920, La Paz; tel. (02) 370263; Dir JORGE SILES.

Librería La Paz: Colón 618, La Paz; tel. (02) 353323; Dir CARLOS BURGOS.

Librería La Universal: Calle Genaro Sanjines 538, Casilla 2888, La Paz; tel. (02) 342961; f. 1945; Man. Dir ROLANDO CONDORI.

BOLIVIA

Editora Lux: Edif. Esperanza, Avda Mariscal Santa Cruz, Casilla 1566, La Paz; tel. (02) 329102; Dir Mons. JESÚS LÓPEZ DE LAMA.

Editorial Popular: Plaza Pérez Velasco 787, Casilla 4171, La Paz; tel. (02) 324258; textbooks and general; Man. Dir GERMÁN VILLAMOR.

Editorial Puerta del Sol: Calle Juan de la Riva 1448, La Paz; tel. (02) 360746; f. 1965; Man. Dir OSCAR CRESPO.

Librería San Pablo: Calle Colón 627, Casilla 3152, La Paz; tel. (02) 326084; f. 1967; Man. Dirs The Daughters of San Pablo.

PUBLISHERS' ASSOCIATION

Cámara Boliviana del Libro: Edif. Las Palmas, Avda 20 de Octubre 2005, Casilla 682, La Paz; tel. (02) 327039; Pres. JAVIER GISBERT C.

Radio and Television

In 1983 there were an estimated 3.5m. radio receivers and 386,000 television receivers in use.

Dirección General de Telecomunicaciones: Edif. Guerrero, Mercado 1115, Casilla 4475, La Paz; tel. (02) 368788; telex 2595; government-controlled broadcasting authority; Dir-Gen. Ing. JORGE ESTRELLA AYALA.

RADIO

There were 158 radio stations in 1985, the majority of which were commercial. Broadcasts are in Spanish, Aymará and Quechua.

Asociación Boliviana de Radiodifusoras (ASBORA): Potosí 920, Casilla 7958, La Paz; tel. (02) 328513; broadcasting authority; Pres. MIGUEL A. DUERI; Vice-Pres. ENRIQUE COSTAS.

TELEVISION

Empresa Nacional de Televisión: Ayacucho 467, Casilla 900, La Paz; tel. (02) 323292; telex 2312; f. 1969; government network operating stations in La Paz, Oruro, Cochabamba, Potosí, Beni, Tarija and Santa Cruz; Dir-Gen. J. BARRAGÁN; Gen. Man. JUAN RECACOCHEA.

Televisión Universitaria (University Service): División de Infraestructura, Universidad Boliviana, Casilla 2255, La Paz; tel. (02) 359297; telex 3252; educational programmes; stations in Oruro, Cochabamba, Potosí, Sucre, Tarija, Beni and Santa Cruz; Dir ALFONSO VILLEGAS.

Finance

(cap. = capital; p.u. = paid up; res = reserves;
dep. = deposits; m. = million; brs = branches; amounts are in Bolivian pesos unless otherwise stated)

BANKING

Supervisory Authority

Departamento de Fiscalización del Banco Central de Bolivia: Edif. Banco Central de Bolivia, Ayacucho esq. Mercado 200, Casilla 3118, La Paz; Man. Lic. RUBÉN PANTOJA (acting).

State Banks

Banco Central de Bolivia: Ayacucho esq. Mercado, Casilla 3118, La Paz; tel. (02) 350726; telex 2286; f. 1928; bank of issue; cap. and res 671.7m. (Dec. 1981); Pres. JAVIER NOGALES; Gen. Man. RAÚL TOVAR.

Banco del Estado: Calle Colón esq. Mercado, Casilla 1401, La Paz; tel. (02) 352868; telex 3267; f. 1970; state bank incorporating banking department of Banco Central de Bolivia; cap. and res 236.9m., dep. 9.1m. (Dec. 1982); Pres. Lic. ALFREDO BUCHÓN; Gen. Man. ALFREDO OMISTE; 55 brs.

Banco Agrícola de Bolivia: Avda Mariscal Santa Cruz esq. Almirante Grau, Casilla 1179, La Paz; tel. (02) 365876; telex 3278; f. 1942; cap. 179m. (Dec. 1976); Pres. Ing. ARTURO SORNCO V.; Gen. Man. Ing. VÍCTOR G. RIVERA.

Banco Minero de Bolivia: Calle Comercio 1290, Casilla 1410, La Paz; tel. (02) 352168; telex 2568; f. 1936; finances private mining industry; cap. p.u. and res 770m. (1981); Gen. Man. RIGOBERTO PÉREZ.

Banco de la Vivienda: Avda Camacho 1336, Casilla 8155, La Paz; tel. (02) 343510; telex 2295; f. 1964; to encourage and finance housing developments; 51% state participation; initial cap. 100m.; Pres. (vacant); Gen. Man. Lic. JOSÉ RAMÍREZ MONTALVA.

Commercial Banks

Banco Boliviano Americano: Calle Loayza esq. Camacho, Casilla 478, La Paz; tel. (02) 350861; telex 2279; f. 1957; cap. and res 7,625.8m., dep. 136,507.5m. (Dec. 1984); Pres. LUIS EDUARDO SILES; Exec. Vice-Pres. JOSÉ A. ARIAS; 13 brs.

Banco de Cochabamba: Avda Camacho esq. Colón, Casilla 4314, La Paz; tel. (02) 358123; telex 2274; cap. p.u. 159.2m., res 545m., dep. 1,326m. (Aug. 1983); Pres. GUIDO QUIROGA Q.; Vice-Pres. FERNANDO SÁNCHEZ DE LOZADA; 5 brs.

Banco de Crédito Oruro: Avda Camacho No. 1472, Casilla 8156, La Paz; tel. (02) 358507; telex 2308; cap. p.u. 60.5m., res 31.5m. (Aug. 1983); Exec. Pres. ELIZABETH SALINAS; Gen. Man. BERNARDO LÓPEZ SOUX; 9 brs.

Banco de Financiamiento Industrial, SA: Washington 1402, Casilla 51, Oruro; tel. 356876; telex 2234; f. 1974 to encourage and finance industrial development; cap. p.u. 105m., res 76m. (Aug. 1983); Pres. Lic. HUGO CAMPOS; Man. FRANCISCO BERMÚDEZ.

Banco Hipotecario Nacional: Avda 16 de Julio 1630, Casilla 647, La Paz; tel. (02) 359351; telex 2290; cap. 47m. (Aug. 1983); Pres. FERNANDO ROCHERO; Gen. Man. DAVID BLANCO ZABALA.

Banco Industrial, SA: Avda 16 de Julio 1628, La Paz; tel. (02) 359471; telex 2584; f. 1963; industrial credit bank; cap. p.u. US $500m. (June 1985); Chair. of Board of Dirs JULIO LEÓN PRADO; Gen. Man. ALFREDO MOSCOSO VELARDE; 1 br.

Banco Industrial y Ganadero del Beni: Calle Mercado esq. Socabaya, Edif. Guerrero, Casilla 8717, La Paz; tel. (02) 369342; telex 2381; cap. p.u. 322m., res 64.6m., dep. 3,498m. (Dec. 1982); Pres. JAIME MUSTAFI; Gen. Man. JORGE JORDAN FERRUFINO; 10 brs.

Banco de Inversión Boliviano, SA: Edif. Herrmann 15°, Plaza Venezuela, Casilla 8639, La Paz; tel. (02) 354233; telex 2465; f. 1977; cap. 1.1m., res 32m., dep. 1.8m. (Aug. 1986); Pres. JAIME GUTIÉRREZ MOSCOSO; Vice-Pres. MAURICIO URQUIDI U.

Banco de La Paz: Avda 16 de Julio 1473, Casilla 6826, La Paz; tel. (02) 358344; telex 2423; cap. 504.5m.; dep. 2,510.4m. (Aug. 1983); Pres. Lic. GUIDO E. HINOJOSA; Man. TEDDY MERCADO COVARRUBIAS; 10 brs.

Banco Mercantil SA: Ayacucho esq. Mercado, Casilla 423, La Paz; tel. (02) 356902; telex 2270; f. 1905; cap. and res 1,825m., dep. 4,724m. (Dec. 1982); Pres. JAVIER ZUAZO; Gen. Man. EMILIO UNZUETA; 6 brs.

Banco Nacional de Bolivia: Avda Camacho esq. Colón, Casilla 360, La Paz; tel. (02) 354616; telex 2310; f. 1872; cap. and res 780.9m., dep. 27,353.2m. (Dec. 1983); Pres. Dr FERNANDO BEDOYA BALLIVIÁN; Gen. Man. Lic. MIGUEL FABRI; 10 brs.

Banco Potosí, SA: Plaza 10 de Noviembre, Casilla 85, Potosí; tel. 377174; telex 2451; Pres. Ing. JAIME BUITRAGO; Gen. Man. Lic. WALTER BELLIDO FLORES; 6 brs.

Banco del Progreso Nacional: Avda Camacho 1336, Casilla 20175, La Paz; tel. (02) 374401; telex 2460; Pres. Brig.-Gen. HERNÁN ALFARO CORTÉZ; Gen. Man. Lic. JORGE FERNÁNDEZ ARROYO.

Banco de Santa Cruz de la Sierra: Junín 154, Casilla 865, Santa Cruz; tel. 3991; telex 4230; f. 1966; cap. and res 90.3m., dep. 866.1m. (Dec. 1979); Pres. Ing. LYDERS PAREJA EGUEZ; Gen. Man. Ing. LUIS F. SAAVEDRA; 7 brs.

Banco de la Unión SA: Calle René Moreno esq. Republiquetas, Casilla 4057, La Paz; tel. (02) 46869; telex 4285; f. 1985; cap. and res US $1.8m., dep. $11m. (July 1986); Pres. Arq. CRISTÓBAL RODA DAZA; Gen. Man. JORGE CÓRDOVA; 3 brs.

Caja Central de Ahorro y Préstamo para la Vivienda: Avda Mariscal Santa Cruz 1364, 20°, Casilla 4808, La Paz; telex 5611; f. 1967; assets US $28m. (1983); Pres. ERNESTO WENDE.

Foreign Banks

Banco do Brasil SA: Avda Camacho 1448, Casilla 1650, La Paz; tel. (02) 320793; telex 5232; f. 1960; Man. JULIO LIMA DEIZAGA; 3 brs.

Banco de la Nación Argentina: Avda 16 de Julio 1486, Casilla 2745, La Paz; tel. (02) 359211; telex 5452; Man. ROBERTO VAGLIODORO MEDICI; 3 brs.

Banco Popular del Perú: Mercado esq. Colón, Casilla 907, La Paz; tel. (02) 360025; telex 2344; f. 1942; Gen. Man. Lic. EDUARDO JONES; 12 brs.

Citibank N.A. (USA): Colón 288, Casilla 260, La Paz; tel. (02) 321742; telex 2546; Vice-Pres. RICARDO LINALE.

Deutsch-Südamerikanische Bank AG (Banco Germánico de la América del Sud) and Dresdner Bank AG (Fed. Repub. of Germany): Joint representation: Avda Mariscal Santa Cruz 1285,

BOLIVIA

5°, Of. 503, Casilla 1077, La Paz; tel. (02) 374450; telex 2311; Rep. Carlos A. Martins.

Banking Association

Asociación de Bancos e Instituciones Financieras de Bolivia: Edif. Cámara Nacional de Comercio, 15°, Avda Mariscal Santa Cruz esq. Colombia, Casilla 5822, La Paz; tel. (02) 321379; telex 2439; f. 1957; Pres. Dr Fernando Bedoya Ballivián; Exec. Sec. Dr Fernando Rollano Morales; 22 mems.

INSURANCE
Supervisory Authority

Superintendencia Nacional de Seguros y Reaseguros: Calle Batallón Colorados 162, Casilla 6118, La Paz; tel. (02) 374137; f. 1975; Superintendent Dr Carlos Castañón Barrientos; Intendant Lic. Wálter Sánchez Sandoval.

National Companies
(p.i. = premium income; amounts in Bolivian pesos, $bs)

Argos, Cía de Seguros, SA: Calle Potosí 1320, Casilla 277, La Paz; tel. (02) 340029; telex 2297; f. 1962; all classes except life; p.i. $bs38,317,794 (1982); Pres. José T. Kawai; Gen. Man. Jorge Luis Gumucio.

Bolívar SA de Seguros: Avda Mariscal Santa Cruz 1287, Casilla 1459, La Paz; tel. (02) 351441; telex 2392; f. 1952; all classes; p.i. $bs1,800m. (1982); Pres. Lic. Alfredo Oporto Crespo; Gen. Man. Freddy Oporto M.

Cía Americana de Seguros y Reaseguros, SA: Edif. Sáenz 3°, Avda Camacho 1377, Casilla 6180, La Paz; tel. (02) 329374; telex 2589; f. 1970; all classes; p.i. $bs27,134,698.8 (1982); Pres. Mario Patiño Milán; Gen. Man. Julio Butrón Mendoza.

Cía Andina de Seguros y Reaseguros, SA: Edif. Alborada 2°, Mercado esq. Loayza, Casilla 4723, La Paz; tel. (02) 374371; telex 4723; f. 1974; all classes; p.i. $bs396.7m. (1982); Pres. Lic. Luis Adolfo de Ugarte; Dir Ramón Escóbar Aguilar.

Cía Boliviana de Seguros, SA: Colón 282, 1°, Casilla 628, La Paz; tel. (02) 351643; telex 2562; f. 1946; all classes; p.i. US $6,550,000 (1985); Pres. Gonzalo Bedoya H.; Gen. Man. Alfonso Ibáñez.

Cía de Seguros Primero de Mayo, SA: Edif. Naira, Of. 5, Potosí esq. Loayza, Casilla 4409, La Paz; tel. (02) 370271; f. 1978; all classes; $bs40m. (1982); Pres. Lic. Walter Sánchez; Gen. Man. Lionel Taboada.

Cía de Seguros Unión, SA: Landaeta 221, POB 2922, La Paz; tel. (02) 350879; telex 2347; f. 1961; all classes; p.i. $bs9,000m. (1984); Pres. Luis Sáenz Pacheco; Gen. Man. Germán Gaymer M.

Cía de Seguros y Reaseguros Santa Cruz, SA: Edif. Mariscal de Ayacucho 8°, Of. 808/9, Calle Loayza, Casilla 1708, La Paz; tel. (02) 365931; telex 2545; f. 1980; all classes; p.i. US $620m. (1981); Pres. Armando Pinell; Gen. Man. Antonio Olea.

La Continental de Seguros y Reaseguros, SA: Edif. Herrmann 1°, Avda 16 de Julio, Casilla 5959, La Paz; tel. (02) 356926; telex 2336; f. 1975; all classes; p.i. $bs2,198.8m. (1983); Pres. Gonzalo Bedoya; Man. Lic. Samuel Castellón.

Credinform International SA de Seguros: Edif. Credinform, Potosí esq. Ayacucho, Casilla 1724, La Paz; tel. (02) 356931; telex 2304; f. 1954; all classes; p.i. $bs4,709m.; Pres. Dr Robín Barragán Pelaez; Gen. Man. Miguel Angel Barragán Ibarguen.

Delta Insurance Co, SA: 25 de Mayo, Casilla 920, Cochabamba; tel. 26006; f. 1965; all classes except life; Pres. Juan José Galindo B.; Gen. Man. Carlos Christie J.

La Mercantil de Seguros y Reaseguros, SA: Mercado 1121, Casilla 2727, La Paz; tel. (02) 355893; telex 3313; f. 1957; all classes; p.i. $bs50m. (1982); Pres. Dr Hugo Echeverría; Gen. Man. Luis Saucedo Paz.

Real Bolivia de Seguros, SA: Edif. Litoral, Colón 150, Casilla 1847, La Paz; tel. (02) 328823; telex 2431; f. 1980; all classes; p.i. $bs30.7m.; Pres. Sebastiao Bernardes Rengel; Gen. Man. Francisco Freitas.

Reaseguradora Boliviana, SA: Edif. El Condor 15° y 16°, Calle Batallón Colorados, Casilla 6227, La Paz; tel. (02) 322991; telex 2315; f. 1977; p.i. $bs834m. (1983); Pres. Luis Sáenz Pacheco; Gen. Man. David Alcoreza Marchetti.

Seguros Illimani, SA: Edif. Mariscal de Ayacucho 10°, Calle Loayza, Casilla 133, La Paz; tel. (02) 371090; telex 3261; f. 1979; all classes; p.i. $bs66.8m.; Pres. Gastón Ibáñez; Gen. Man. Fernando Arce G.

There are also three foreign-owned insurance companies operating in Bolivia: American Life Insurance Co, American Home Assurance Co and United States Fire Insurance Co, and one company with mixed capital: Cooperativa de Seguros Cruceña Ltda.

Insurance Association

Asociación Boliviana de Aseguradores: Edif. Castilla 5°, Of. 506, Loayza 250, Casilla 4804, La Paz; tel. (02) 328804; f. 1962; Pres. David Alcoreza Marchetti; Exec. Sec. Blanca M. de Otermín.

Trade and Industry
CHAMBERS OF COMMERCE

Cámara Nacional de Comercio: Edif. Cámara Nacional de Comercio, Avda Mariscal Santa Cruz 1392, Casilla 7, La Paz; tel. (02) 379941; telex 2305; f. 1890; 30 brs and special brs; Pres. Oswaldo Irusta Méndez; Gen. Man. René Candía Navarro.

Cámara Departamental de Industria y Comercio: Avda Suárez de Figueroa 127, 3° y 4°, Casilla 180, Santa Cruz; tel. 34578; telex 4298; f. 1915; Pres. Ivo Kuljis; Dir-Gen. Justo Yépez Kakuda.

Cámara Departamental de Comercio: Calle Sucre E-0336, Casilla 493, Cochabamba; tel. 22905; f. 1922; Pres. Dr Víctor Hugo Escobar Herbas; Man. Dr Franz E. Rivero V.

Cámara Departamental de Comercio: Pasaje Guachalla, Casilla 148, Oruro; tel. 50606; f. 1895; Pres. Mario Vásquez; Man. Julio Bahoz R.

Cámara Nacional de Exportadores: Avda Villazón 1960, 1°, Casilla 20744, La Paz; tel. (02) 341220; Pres. Guillermo Crooker; Exec. Dir Dr Franz Ondarza Linares.

STATE INSTITUTES AND DEVELOPMENT ORGANIZATIONS

Agencia Promotora de Inversiones: Calle Francisco de Miranda 2045, Casilla 2355, La Paz; tel. (02) 364504; f. 1967 to promote agricultural and industrial investment in Bolivia; Man. A. Castedo Leygue.

Cámara Agropecuaria del Oriente: Bolívar 559, Casilla 116, Santa Cruz; tel. 23164; telex 4438; f. 1964; agriculture and livestock association for eastern Bolivia; Pres. Ing. Edgar Talavera Soliz; Man. Alfonso Kreidler.

Cámara Nacional Forestal: Edif. Santa Cruz 6°, Casilla 346, Santa Cruz; tel. 23996; telex 4330; f. 1971; represents the interests of the Bolivian timber industry; Pres. Ramiro Rebueta; Man. Humberto Castedo L.

Cámara Nacional de Industria: Avda Camacho 1485, Casilla 1931, La Paz; tel. (02) 374478; telex 5744; f. 1931; Pres. Javier Lupo Gamarra; Man. Dr Alfredo Arana Ruck.

Cámara Nacional de Minería: Bernardo Trigo 429, Casilla 2022, La Paz; tel. (02) 350623; f. 1953; mining institute; Pres. Antonio Mariscal Paredes; Sec.-Gen. Ing. Víctor Hugo Méndez Ugarte.

Comité Boliviano del Café (COBOLCA): Edif. Macdonald 6°, Calle Ballivián esq. Loayza, La Paz; tel. (02) 341553; controls the export, marketing and growing policies of the coffee industry; Gen. Man. Lic. Gonzalo Martínez.

Consejo Nacional de Planificación (CONEPLAN): Avda Arce, La Paz; tel. (02) 372060; f. 1985; national planning council; directly subordinate to Presidency.

Corporación Boliviana de Fomento (CBF): Edif. La Urbana, Avda Camacho 1485, Casilla 1124, La Paz; tel. (02) 357618; telex 5263; f. 1942; all aspects of national development including the production of agricultural and industrial goods, development of irrigation projects, etc.; Man. Ing. Jaime Aponte.

Corporación de las Fuerzas Armadas para el Desarrollo Nacional (Cofadena): Avda 6 de Agosto 2649, Casilla 1015, La Paz; tel. (02) 377305; telex 2284; f. 1972; industrial, agricultural and mining holding company and development organization owned by the Bolivian armed forces; Gen. Man. Carlos Morales Núñez del Prado.

Corporación Minera de Bolivia (COMIBOL): Avda Mariscal Santa Cruz 1092, Casilla 349, La Paz; tel. (02) 354044; telex 2420; f. 1952; state mining corporation; owns both mines and processing plants; Gen. Man. Ing. Gonzalo Barrientos Carreaga.

Corporación Regional de Desarrollo de La Paz (Cordepaz): Edif. Santa Isabel, 2°, Bloque A, Avda Arce esq. Pinilla, Casilla 1952, La Paz; tel. (02) 342325; telex 3256; f. 1967; decentralized government institution to foster the development of the La Paz area; Pres. Lic. OSCAR CORNEJO CLAVIJO; Gen. Man. Dr LUIS RENATO VÁLDICH.

Empresa Nacional de Electricidad, SA (Ende): Colombia No 0-0655, Casilla 565, Cochabamba; tel. 46322; telex 6251; f. 1962; state electricity company; Gen. Man. CLAUDE DE ASE.

Empresa Nacional de Fundiciones (ENAF): Avda Villazón 1966, Casilla 4301, Oruro; tel. 371251; telex 2255; f. 1966; state company for the smelting of non-ferrous minerals and special alloys; Gen. Man. Ing. SIMÓN CUENTAS CARRILLO.

Empresa Nacional de Telecomunicaciones (ENTEL): Edif. ENTEL, Calle Ayacucho, La Paz; tel. (02) 367474; telex 2220; Gen. Man. Lic. GERMÁN QUIROGA GÓMEZ.

Empresa Siderúrgica Boliviana, SA (SIDERSA): Avda 16 de Julio 1769, Casilla 7082, La Paz; tel. (02) 376488; telex 2291; f. 1973; state company for iron and steel; Man. Ing. JULIO FUENTES R.

Instituto Nacional de Inversiones (INI): Edif. Cristal 10°, Yanacocha esq. Potosí, Casilla 4393, La Paz; tel. (02) 367294; f. 1971; state institution for the promotion of new investments and the application of the Investment Law; Exec. Dir Lic. ENRIQUE RIVERA REAL.

Instituto Nacional de Preinversión (INALPRE): Calle Rosendo Gutiérrez 550, Casilla 8358, La Paz; tel. (02) 372233; f. 1974; research into and financial and technical assistance for national projects; Dir Ing. GERMÁN SANDOVAL; Exec. Vice-Dir VÍCTOR J. LOAYZA.

Yacimientos Petrolíferos Fiscales Bolivianos (YPFB): Calle Bueno, Casilla 401, La Paz; tel. (02) 356540; telex 2369; f. 1936; state petroleum enterprise; Pres. Minister of Energy and Hydrocarbons; Pres. Ing. ALFONSO ROMERO LOZA; Gen. Man. Ing. JORGE FLORES LÓPEZ.

EMPLOYERS' ASSOCIATIONS

Asociación Nacional de Mineros Medianos: Edif. Petrolero 5°, Avda 16 de Julio 1616, Of. 4, Casilla 6094, La Paz; tel. (02) 352223; telex 5589; f. 1939; association of the 27 private medium-sized mining companies; Pres. RAÚL ESPAÑA-SMITH.

Confederación de Empresarios Privados de Bolivia (CEPB): Edif. Cámara Nacional de Comercio, 7°, Avda Mariscal Santa Cruz 1392, Casilla 20439, La Paz; tel. (02) 356831; largest national employers' organization; Pres. Lic. CARLOS ITURRALDE BALLIVÍAN; Exec. Sec. Dr JAVIER MURILLO DE LA ROCHA.

There are also employers' federations in Santa Cruz, Cochabamba, Oruro, Potosí, Beni and Tarija.

TRADE UNIONS

Central Obrera Boliviana (COB): Edif. Federación de Mineros, La Paz; tel. (02) 352426; f. 1952; main union confederation; 500,000 mems; Exec. Sec. VÍCTOR LÓPEZ ARIAS; Sec.-Gen. WALTER DELGADILLO.

Affiliated unions:

Central Obrera Departamental de La Paz: Estación Central 284, La Paz; tel. (02) 352898; Sec.-Gen. EDUARDO SILES.

Confederación Sindical Unica de los Trabajadores Campesinos de Bolivia (CSUTCB): f. 1979; peasant farmers' union; Leaders GENARO FLORES SANTOS, VÍCTOR MORALES; Sec. HUGO CAYO.

Federación de Empleados de Industria Fabril: Calle Torrelio 313, La Paz; tel. (02) 371238.

Federación Sindical de Trabajadores Mineros Bolivianos (FSTMB): Plaza Venezuela 1470, La Paz; tel. (02) 340574; mineworkers' union; Pres. JUAN LECHÍN OQUENDO; Sec.-Gen. CRISTÓBAL ARANÍBAR (acting); 27,000 mems.

Federación Sindical de Trabajadores Petroleros de Bolivia: Calle México 1504, La Paz; tel. (02) 351748.

Confederación General de Trabajadores de Bolivia (CGTB): f. 1985; Leader FRANCISCO CHAMBI MANGULA.

Transport

RAILWAYS

Empresa Nacional de Ferrocarriles (ENFE): Estación Central de Ferrocarriles, Plaza Zalles, Casilla 428, La Paz; tel. (02) 26916; Avda Manco Kapac, La Paz; tel. (02) 355694; telex 2405; f. 1964; administers most of the railways in Bolivia. Total networks: 3,628 km (1984); Western Network: Total 2,202 km; Eastern Network: Total 1,426 km; Gen. Man. Ing. ARMANDO MURILLO.

There is also one private railway: Machacamarca–Uncia, owned by Corporación Minera de Bolivia (105 km). There are plans to construct a railway line with Brazilian assistance, to link Cochabamba and Santa Cruz.

ROADS

In 1984 Bolivia had 40,987 km of roads, of which 1,538 km were paved and 9,268 km were all-weather roads. Almost the entire road network is concentrated in the *altiplano* region and the Andes valleys. A 560-km highway runs from Santa Cruz to Cochabamba, serving a colonization scheme on virgin lands around Santa Cruz. The Pan-American highway, linking Argentina and Peru, crosses Bolivia from south to north-west.

INLAND WATERWAYS

By agreement with Paraguay in 1938 (confirmed in 1939) Bolivia has an outlet on the River Paraguay. This arrangement, together with navigation rights on the Paraná, gives Bolivia access to the River Plate and the sea. The River Paraguay is navigable for vessels of 12-ft draught for 288 km beyond Asunción in Paraguay and for smaller boats another 960 km to Corumbá in Brazil.

In 1974 Bolivia was granted free duty access to the Brazilian coastal ports of Belém and Santos and the inland ports of Corumbá and Port Velho. In 1976 Argentina granted Bolivia free port facilities at Rosario on the River Paraná. Most of Bolivia's foreign trade is handled through the ports of Matarani (Peru), Antofagasta and Arica (Chile), Rosario and Buenos Aires (Argentina) and Santos (Brazil).

Bolivia has over 14,000 km of navigable rivers which connect most of Bolivia with the Amazon basin.

Bolivian River Navigation Company: f. 1958; services from Puerto Suárez to Buenos Aires (Argentina).

OCEAN SHIPPING

Empresa Naviera Boliviana (ENABOL): Edif. Grover 2°, Calle Juan Joso Pérez, La Paz; tel. (02) 360730; telex 5475; Pres. A. S. KIINSKI.

CIVIL AVIATION

Bolivia has 30 airports including the two international airports at La Paz (El Alto) and Santa Cruz (Viru-Viru). In 1979 air transport accounted for 4% of cargo carried compared with 25% by rail.

Lloyd Aéreo Boliviano, SAM (LAB): Casilla 132, Aeropuerto 'Jorge Wilstermann', Cochabamba; tel. (02) 25900; telex 6290; f. 1925; partly state-owned since 1941; operates internal services linking the main localities in Bolivia, and joint services with other national lines to Argentina, Brazil, Chile, Peru, Panama, the USA and Venezuela; Pres. AUTENOR SANTA CRUZ; Gen. Man. Lic. LUIS GUERECA PADILLA; fleet: 3 Boeing 727-100, 3 Boeing 727-200, 1 Fairchild F-27M, 2 Boeing 707-323C (cargo), 1 Boeing 707-323C (passenger).

Transportes Aéreos Militares: Avda Panamericana Alto, La Paz; tel. (02) 389433; internal passenger and cargo services; Dir-Gen. Col J. M. COQUIS; fleet: 1 DC-54, 4 CV-440, 20 C-47, 1 C-46, 6 IAI Arava.

Tourism

Instituto Boliviano de Turismo: Edif. Herrmann 4°, Plaza Venezuela, Casilla 1868, La Paz; tel. (02) 367463; telex 2534; f. 1973; Exec. Dir TERESA DE VIDOVIC.

Asociación Boliviana de Agencias de Viajes y Turismo: Edif. Litoral, Mariscal Santa Cruz 1351, POB 3967, La Paz; f. 1984; Pres. EUGENIO MONROY VÉLEZ.

Atomic Energy

Instituto Boliviano de Ciencia y Tecnología Nuclear (IBTEN): Avda 6 de Agosto 2905, Casilla 4821, La Paz; tel. (02) 356877; telex 2220; f. 1983; main activities include: nuclear engineering, agricultural and industrial application of radio-isotopes, radiochemical analysis, neutron generating, nuclear physics and dosimetry; Exec. Dir Ing. JUAN CARLOS MÉNDEZ FERRY (acting).

BOTSWANA

Introductory Survey

Location, Climate, Language, Religion, Flag, Capital

The Republic of Botswana is a land-locked country in southern Africa, with South Africa to the south and east, Zimbabwe to the north-east and Namibia (South West Africa) to the west and north. A short section of the northern frontier adjoins Zambia. The climate is generally sub-tropical, with hot summers. Annual rainfall averages about 457 mm (18 in), varying from 635 mm (25 in) in the north to 228 mm (9 in) or less in the western Kalahari desert. The country is largely near-desert, and most of its inhabitants live along the eastern border, close to the main railway line. English is the official·language, and Setswana the national language. Most of the population follow African religions, but several Christian churches are also represented. The national flag (proportions 3 by 2) consists of a central horizontal stripe of black, edged with white, between two blue stripes. The capital is Gaborone.

Recent History

Botswana was formerly the Bechuanaland Protectorate, under British rule. Bechuanaland became a British protectorate, at the request of the local rulers, in 1885. It was administered as one of the High Commission Territories in southern Africa, the others being the colony of Basutoland (now Lesotho) and the protectorate of Swaziland. The headquarters of the British administration was a High Commission at Mafeking (now Mafikeng), in South Africa. The British Act of Parliament which established the Union of South Africa in 1910 also allowed for the inclusion in South Africa of the three High Commission Territories, on condition that the local inhabitants were consulted. Until 1960, successive South African governments asked for the transfer of the three territories, but the native chiefs always objected to such a scheme.

Within Bechuanaland, gradual progress was made towards self-government, mainly through nominated advisory bodies. A new constitution was introduced in December 1960, and a Legislative Council (partly elected, partly appointed) first met in June 1961. Bechuanaland was made independent of High Commission rule in September 1963, and the office of High Commissioner was abolished in August 1964. The seat of government was transferred from Mafeking to Gaberones (now Gaborone) in February 1965. On 1 March 1965 internal self-government was achieved, and the territory's first direct election, for a Legislative Assembly, was held on the basis of universal adult suffrage. Of the Assembly's 31 seats, 28 were won by the Bechuanaland Democratic Party (BDP or Domkrag), founded in 1962. The BDP was led by Seretse Khama, who had been deposed as Chief of the Bamangwato tribe in 1950 and had been exiled from Bechuanaland until 1956, when he renounced his claim to the chieftainship. Two days after the election, Khama was sworn in as the territory's first Prime Minister. Bechuanaland became the independent Republic of Botswana, within the Commonwealth, on 30 September 1966, with Sir Seretse Khama (as he had become) taking office as the country's first President.

The BDP, restyled the Botswana Democratic Party at independence, continued to dominate political life, winning elections to the National Assembly, with little opposition, in October 1969, October 1974 and October 1979. Sir Seretse, a liberal conservative, consolidated his leadership of the country while pursuing a national programme of democracy, development, self-reliance and unity, and Botswana won increasing international respect for its stability of government, non-racialism and democratic practice.

Sir Seretse Khama died in July 1980. His successor to the presidency was Dr Quett Masire, previously Vice-President and Minister of Finance. Dr Masire's presidency was renewed in September 1984, when, in a general election to the National Assembly, the ruling BDP again achieved a decisive victory, winning 28 of the 34 elective seats, with the main opposition party, the Botswana National Front (BNF), obtaining five seats. Although the BDP's success in the general election consolidated its position, some discontent among the population at the country's high level of unemployment was reflected in the outcome of the local government elections (held on the same day as the election to the National Assembly), in which the BDP lost control of all the town councils except that of Selebi-Phikwe. The BNF continued to gain strength from popular dissatisfaction with the Government in 1986. The elections to the leadership of the BDP, held in July 1985, resulted in a number of changes in the membership of the party's Central Committee, although the principal officers of the party retained their posts. A general election was expected to be held in 1989.

In southern African politics, Botswana occupies a delicate position which is reflected in a foreign policy of moderation and non-alignment. Although Botswana does not have diplomatic links with South Africa, and is openly critical of apartheid, it depends heavily on its neighbour for trade and communications. In April 1980 Sir Seretse chaired the Lusaka summit meeting which established the Southern African Development Co-ordination Conference (SADCC), an economic union of nine southern African states committed to reducing their dependence on South Africa. In July 1981 the SADCC decided to establish a permanent secretariat in Gaborone (see p. 204).

In recent years there has been increasing tension between Botswana and South Africa. In May 1984 President Masire accused South Africa of exerting pressure on Botswana to sign a non-aggression pact similar to the Nkomati accord, agreed between South Africa and Mozambique earlier that year. Relations were further strained in February 1985, when South Africa reportedly threatened to invade Botswana's territory, under the pretext of pursuing guerrilla forces of the African National Congress (ANC), a black nationalist movement that is officially outlawed in South Africa. Further tension was caused by two bomb explosions in Gaborone in February and May. At the end of February there appeared to be a slight amelioration in relations with South Africa, following talks in which South Africa reportedly abandoned its insistence that Botswana sign a formal joint security pact. However, relations deteriorated sharply again in June, when South African forces launched a raid, in which 12 people were killed, on alleged ANC bases in Gaborone. Representatives from the two countries met in September 1985 to discuss a demand by Botswana, endorsed by the UN, for compensation for the damage that had been caused by the South African raid, but they failed to reach an agreement. In November a car-bomb, planted outside a hospital in Mochudi, killed four people, but no clear connection with South Africa was established.

South Africa renewed its threats to invade Botswana in early 1986, following a land-mine explosion near the Botswana border in January. Relations improved in February, when Botswana reiterated its pledge to prohibit the use of its territory as a base for terrorist attacks. In March the Botswana Government expelled ANC representatives. However, relations deteriorated in May, when, in conjunction with attacks on Zambia and Zimbabwe, South African forces launched ground and air attacks on a complex of buildings at Mogaditsane, causing one death. South Africa again claimed that the action had been directed against ANC bases, but the attacks were internationally condemned, and were widely regarded as an attempt to disrupt the visit of the Commonwealth 'Eminent Persons Group', then taking place in South Africa. In July President Masire accused South Africa of applying selective sanctions against Botswana. At a meeting of the SADCC in August, when sanctions against South Africa were 'commended' (but not agreed upon), Botswana did not commit itself to applying sanctions.

As one of the five 'front-line' states, Botswana played a leading role in the attempts to encourage a peaceful solution

BOTSWANA

Introductory Survey

to the constitutional problems of Zimbabwe, and continues to do so for Namibia. The Botswana Defence Force (BDF) was formed in 1977, mainly to control security problems spilling over from Botswana's neighbours, and is a growing burden on development funds. Relations with Zimbabwe became strained in early 1983, when it was alleged that armed Zimbabwean dissidents were being sheltered among the 3,000 Zimbabwean refugees encamped in Botswana. The Botswana Government agreed to impose stricter controls on the refugees, and expelled about 200 from the country in May. Diplomatic relations with Zimbabwe were established in the same month, and in August it was announced that a joint trade agreement was being drafted. However, the recurrence of incidents on the Botswana-Zimbabwe border between members of the BDF and armed men wearing Zimbabwean military uniforms led to security talks between the two countries in November and December 1983. In July 1984, however, Zimbabwe claimed that Botswana had repatriated more than 1,200 Zimbabwean refugees, including more than 300 alleged guerrillas, and the first meeting of the Botswana-Zimbabwe joint commission for co-operation was held in October 1984. A new influx of refugees, following the Zimbabwe general election in July 1985, threatened to disrupt relations, but in February 1986, at a meeting of the joint commission of defence and security, the two countries agreed that they had been successful in combating South African-sponsored attacks in the border region.

Government

Legislative power is vested in the National Assembly, with 38 members holding office for five years, including 34 elected by universal adult suffrage. Executive power is vested in the President, elected by the Assembly for its duration. He appoints and leads a Cabinet, which is responsible to the Assembly. The President has powers to delay implementation of legislation for six months, and certain matters also have to be referred to the 15-member House of Chiefs for approval, although this body has no power of veto. Local government is effected through nine district councils and four town councils.

Defence

Botswana established a permanent Defence Force in 1977. In July 1986 its total strength was 3,000, including 150 in an air arm. In addition there was a paramilitary police force of 1,000. In 1984/85 defence expenditure totalled an estimated US $20.3m.

Economic Affairs

With a semi-arid climate, and periodically subject to drought, Botswana is not well suited to agriculture. Nevertheless, the country's economy was traditionally based on the nomadic herding of livestock and on the cultivation of subsistence crops. Since the 1970s, however, the exploitation of mineral deposits has become a major activity in terms of Botswana's exports and gross national product (GNP), although the mining sector provides employment for only about 4% of the labour force. The recent development of mining has made an important contribution to the country's rapid economic growth. In 1984, according to estimates by the World Bank, Botswana's GNP per head (at average 1982–84 prices) was US $960. Between 1965 and 1984, it was estimated, GNP per head increased, in real terms, at an average rate of 8.4% per year. Among all the countries of the world for which data are available over this period, Botswana ranked equal first (with Malta) in terms of the growth of GNP per head. Botswana's gross domestic product (GDP), measured at constant 1979/80 prices, increased at an average rate of 13.7% per year between 1976/77 and 1982/83.

Nearly 90% of the country's working population are engaged in agriculture. Until the early 1970s, this sector was the source of almost all of Botswana's exports. Since the early 1980s, however, agriculture has been adversely affected by successive years of drought, and the value of GDP in the agricultural sector (including forestry and fishing) declined from P87.8m. in 1981/82 to P76.1m. in 1983/84. In normal years the cattle industry is the second largest contributor to foreign exchange earnings (17% in 1982, and about 11% in 1983), and livestock accounts for about 80% of the total agricultural output. Under the provisions of the Lomé Convention (see p. 149), Botswana exports beef to the countries of the European Economic Community on favourable terms. The national herd is very unevenly distributed among the rural population, of whom almost 50% have no direct access to cattle, and it is estimated that one-half of the total number is owned by 5% of households. The effectiveness of the Government's Tribal Land Grazing Programme, initiated in 1975 to protect small-scale cattle owners and to prevent erosion of rangeland, has been limited by the severe drought. The Botswana Meat Commission (BMC) slaughtered 234,000 head of cattle in 1983, and this total rose to a record 239,000 head in 1984, when beef sales earned some P119.9m. However, the BMC's throughput declined to 220,000 head in 1985, and beef sales fell to P111.7m. Despite a decline in the carcass weight of beef exports, their value rose from about P95m. in 1984 to about P102m. in 1985, owing to fluctuations in the exchange rate. The drought reduced the national herd to some 2.6m. head by early 1985, about 500,000 fewer than pre-drought levels. Arable farming is largely undeveloped and extremely vulnerable to adverse weather conditions, and the Government's Arable Lands Development Programme and the Accelerated Rainfed Agriculture Programme have only recently had some effect. The total production of the four major crops (maize, sorghum, millet and beans) reached a record 54,300 metric tons in 1981, but, owing to drought, output declined to some 7,300 tons in 1984. Output rose to some 19,000 tons in 1985, and was forecast to reach 30,000 tons in 1986. Crop production meets only about 10% of national requirements. Food imports cost Botswana some P30.6m. in 1983, and in 1984 it was estimated that 60% of the population were receiving supplementary food aid. In that year a National Food Strategy was introduced, whereby new measures to co-ordinate food distribution were to be undertaken. In 1985 the Government introduced a Labour-based Relief Programme, whereby local inhabitants are paid to develop the rural infrastructure. There are also projects to bring extensive new areas of land under irrigation in the Chobe and Okavango regions.

The fastest growing economic sector is mining, which is now the major source of exports and government revenues, accounting for 31.7% of Botswana's total GDP in 1983/84. In addition to the established extraction of diamonds, copper-nickel and coal, there are also deposits of asbestos, chromite, copper, fluorspar, iron, manganese, silver, talc and uranium. There have been large finds of salt and natural sodium carbonate (soda ash) in the north-east, and indications of the presence of platinum, petroleum and natural gas in south-western Botswana.

Diamond production began in 1971, and in 1985 diamonds accounted for more than 75% of total export earnings. The value of diamond exports has risen significantly in recent years, reaching P622m. in 1984, and a record P1,066m. in 1985. Output rose from 2.4m. carats in 1976 to 10.9m. carats in 1983 and 12.9m. carats in 1984, making Botswana the third largest diamond producer in the world. Output fell slightly, to 12.6m. carats, in 1985. However, in 1984 it was estimated that production at the two chief mines would continue for at least 25–30 years. Much of the diamond production of 1981–83 was stockpiled in readiness for a recovery in the world market, then in recession, but, under the Sixth National Development Plan (1985–91), the Government hopes to terminate stockpiling after 1988. All current diamond production is by the De Beers Botswana Mining Company (Debswana), which is owned equally by the Botswana Government and the South African company De Beers, although Botswana takes about 70% of the profits.

The Selebi-Phikwe copper and nickel operation, in which the Government has a 15% share, began production in 1974. More than 40m. metric tons of ore were located, and production of copper-nickel matte reached about 51,850 tons in 1984, when sales of copper-nickel realized some P77.5m. Production was estimated at about 58,000 tons for 1985. However, the decline in world metal prices and markets since 1981 has reduced earnings and caused considerable financial problems for the mining company, whose total losses were estimated to have reached P750m. by mid-1985. There are further high-grade copper deposits in the Ghanzi area, but development of these will be partly subject to an improvement in world copper prices. Coal mining started in 1972, and 437,000 metric tons were produced in 1985. It is believed that there may be reserves of 17,000m. tons in the east of the country. Development of Botswana's coal resources would require the development of rail links, either through South Africa or by a trans-Kalahari railway passing through Namibia to the port of Walvis Bay, and their profitability would depend on a recovery in world coal prices. The completion of a new power station at the Morupule coalfield (scheduled for 1986) was expected to reduce dependence on South African electricity supplies. The sole major minerals project to be scheduled under the Sixth National Development Plan is the exploitation of the soda ash deposits at Sua-Pan, where there are estimated reserves of 1,000m. tons of salt and 200m. tons of soda ash.

Since independence, the Government has concentrated on improving Botswana's infrastructure, so industrial development has been limited. Progress has also been hampered by frequent drought (particularly severe in 1979 and 1982), inadequate internal and external communications, the limited domestic market and a shortage of trained manpower.

Botswana, with Lesotho and Swaziland, is linked to South Africa in a customs union. However, it left the Rand Monetary Area and established its own currency and central bank in August 1976. Real GDP fell by 0.9% in 1981/82, after an average annual growth rate of about 13% in the late 1970s. Botswana's economic difficulties required a 10% currency devaluation in May 1982, and the imposition of a 10% surcharge on goods from outside the customs union area. However, the dramatic rise in diamond output and earnings caused a revival in the economy from 1982/83, when GDP grew by 20.7% in real terms, until 1984/85, when the growth rate of real GDP was estimated at some 12%. In 1985/86 GDP was expected to grow by only about 4% in real terms. The improvement in the diamond industry also transformed the current deficit on the balance of payments, which reached $217.8m. in 1981 and $65.5m. in 1982, into a surplus of about $5m. in 1983, rising to $12m. in 1984, and to $139m. in 1985. There was also a considerable rise in foreign exchange reserves, which stood at a record P1,645m. in 1985, sufficient to cover imports for about 17 months. This increase was due not only to the recovery of the diamond industry, but also to the depressed state of the domestic economy as a result of the prolonged drought. The rise in foreign exchange reserves, together with a decline in the inflation rate from 8.3% in 1983 to 6.5% in 1984, caused a sharp increase in the value of the pula against the currencies of Botswana's principal trading partners. This was partly corrected by a 5.07% devaluation of the pula in July 1984, but the continued fall in the value of the South African rand adversely affected the competitiveness of Botswana's local industries, and in January 1985 a further devaluation of the pula, by 15%, was effected. In that year the depreciation of the pula, combined with a South African inflation rate of 17%, resulted in a rise in Botswana's rate of inflation to 10.4%.

The Sixth National Development Plan (1985–91) involves total projected investment of P1,220m. The main themes of the Plan are employment creation, rural and infrastructural development, and education. Overall economic activity was expected to slow down considerably during the period covered by the Plan, with GDP forecast to grow by only about 4.8% per year. The Botswana Development Corporation (BDC), established in 1970, aims to promote investment and assists various companies, particularly in the fields of industry and agriculture. The BDC has planned a five-year programme of investment, covering 1985/86–1989/90, roughly parallel with the Sixth National Development Plan.

Botswana's trade deficit, which was a persistent feature for more than 20 years until 1983, is usually considerable, as the rapid growth of mineral exports has been accompanied by an increased demand for imported manufactured goods and machinery. However, the trade deficit has been reduced in recent years, partly as a result of a decline in the demand for imports, due to the drought, and was converted into surpluses of $94m. and $219m. in 1984 and 1985 respectively, owing largely to the rise in diamond exports. Any deficit is also partly offset by remittances that are sent home by migrant workers. However, the recent improvement is not expected to be sustained, and a trade deficit of P70.5m. is projected for the final year of the Sixth National Development Plan. None the less, in the long term, the economic outlook is promising, despite the uncertain political situation in southern Africa, in view of Botswana's highly developed beef industry and its vast mineral resources, which offer excellent prospects for the growth of ancillary industries, employment opportunities and economic diversification.

Social Welfare

Health services are being developed, and in 1980 there were 13 general hospitals, one mental hospital, 103 clinics (32 with maternity wards), 215 health posts and 341 mobile health stops. There were 111 registered physicians, 10 dentists and 1,071 nurses. The construction at Francistown of a new hospital, the largest in the country, is due to be completed in July 1987. Medical treatment for children under 11 years of age is provided free of charge. Of total expenditure by the central government in the financial year 1983/84, about P22.6m. (5.6%) was for health, and a further P11.0m. (2.7%) was for social security and welfare.

Education

Adult illiteracy averaged 59% (males 63%; females 56%) in 1971, but, according to estimates by UNESCO, the rate had declined to 29.2% (males 27.4%; females 30.5%) by 1985. A National Literacy Programme was initiated in 1980, and over 100,000 people have been enrolled under the programme. Free primary education from the age of six years was also introduced in 1980. The government aimed to provide universal primary education by 1990, and at least two years of intermediate schooling for all soon after that date. Under the Sixth National Development Plan, P198m. is to be spent on education, including the construction of primary and secondary schools, and the expansion of technical education and of the training of teachers.

Education is not compulsory. Primary education begins at six years of age and lasts for up to seven years. Secondary education, beginning at the age of 13, lasts for a further five years, comprising a first cycle of three years and a second of two years. As a proportion of the school-age population, the total enrolment at primary and secondary schools increased from 52% (boys 48%; girls 56%) in 1975 to 65% (boys 59%; girls 71%) in 1980, and to 68% (boys 63%; girls 73%) in 1983. Enrolment at primary schools in 1980 included 75% of children in the relevant age-group (69% of boys; 82% of girls), while the comparable ratio for secondary enrolment was only 15% (boys 12%; girls 17%). In 1985 there were 223,608 pupils in primary schools, mostly financed by district councils, assisted by government grants in aid. In addition, there were 32,172 secondary students and 1,006 vocational students, and 1,434 students at the University of Botswana. There were also 1,353 students enrolled at teacher-training colleges. A teacher-training college for the secondary level opened in 1985.

Tourism

There are six game reserves, including Chobe, only a short drive from Victoria Falls (on the Zambia-Zimbabwe border) by first-class roads. Most of the main centres of population have hotels, and photographic and big-game safaris can be organized. Despite lack of infrastructure and the security problems associated with southern Africa, Botswana attracted 97,260 visitors (both holiday and day visitors) in 1981, and over 82,000 visitors in 1983, when earnings from tourism were about P40m. Efforts to expand the tourist industry include plans for the construction of new hotels and the rehabilitation of existing ones.

Public Holidays

1987: 1–2 January (New Year), 17–20 April (Easter), 28 May (Ascension Day), 15–16 July (for President's Day), 30 September–1 October (for Botswana Day), 25–26 December (Christmas).

1988: 1–2 January (New Year), 1–4 April (Easter), 12 May (Ascension Day), 15–16 July (for President's Day), 30 September–1 October (for Botswana Day), 25–26 December (Christmas).

Weights and Measures

The metric system is in use.

Currency and Exchange Rates

100 thebe = 1 pula (P).

Exchange rates (30 September 1986):
 £1 sterling = 2.674 pula;
 US $1 = 1.848 pula.

Statistical Survey

Source (unless otherwise stated): Central Statistics Office, Private Bag 0024, Gaborone; tel. 52521.

Area and Population

AREA, POPULATION AND DENSITY

Area (sq km)	582,000*
Population (census results)	
31 August 1971	574,094†
12–26 August 1981‡	
Males	443,104
Females	497,923
Total	941,027
Population (official estimates at mid-year)	
1984	1,047,000
1985	1,091,000
1986	1,131,000
Density (per sq km) at mid-1986	1.9

* 224,711 sq miles.
† Excluding 10,550 nomads and 10,861 non-citizens.
‡ Excluding 42,069 citizens absent from the country during enumeration.

POPULATION BY CENSUS DISTRICT
(1981 census results)

Barolong	15,471	Kweneng		117,127
Central	323,328	Lobatse		19,034
Chobe	7,934	Ngamiland		68,063
Francistown	31,065	Ngwaketse		104,182
Gaborone	59,657	North-East		36,636
Ghanzi	19,096	Orapa		5,229
Jwaneng	5,567	Selebi-Phikwe		29,469
Kgalagadi	24,059	South-East		30,649
Kgatleng	44,461			

PRINCIPAL TOWNS (population at 1981 census)

Gaborone (capital)	59,657			
Francistown	31,065	Kanye		20,215
Selebi-Phikwe	29,469	Lobatse		19,034
Serowe	23,661	Mochudi		18,386
Mahalapye	20,712	Maun		14,925
Molepolole	20,565	Ramotswa		13,009

BIRTHS AND DEATHS
1981: Birth rate 47.2 per 1,000; death rate 12.9 per 1,000 (census estimates).

ECONOMICALLY ACTIVE POPULATION
(persons aged 12 years and over, 1981 census)

	Males	Females	Total
Agriculture, hunting, forestry and fishing	86,436	67,135	153,571
Mining and quarrying	10,550	654	11,204
Manufacturing	3,473	1,007	4,480
Electricity, gas and water	2,238	166	2,404
Construction	16,298	787	17,085
Trade, restaurants and hotels	5,837	6,292	12,129
Transport, storage and communications	2,832	290	3,122
Financing, insurance, real estate and business services	816	661	1,477
Community, social and personal services	40,551	30,607	71,158
Activities not adequately defined	5,273	2,359	7,632
Total employed	174,304	109,958	284,262
Unemployed	14,766	17,460	32,226
Total labour force	189,070	127,418	316,488

1984/85 (survey results): Total labour force 367,949 (males 172,763; females 195,186).

EMPLOYMENT (formal sector only; August each year)

	1983	1984	1985*
Agriculture	4,500	5,400	4,000
Mining and quarrying	7,200	7,500	7,300
Manufacturing	9,800	9,500	10,100
Electricity and water	1,900	2,000	1,900
Construction	9,600	11,100	11,600
Trade, restaurants and hotels	15,300	18,100	18,300
Transport and communications	3,900	5,500	5,700
Finance and business services	6,000	6,200	6,800
Community, social and personal services	42,400	44,700	51,400
Total	100,600	110,000	117,100

* September 1985.

The number of Batswana employed in South African mines was 18,849 in 1983, 18,894 in 1984, and 16,397 in 1985.

Agriculture

PRINCIPAL CROPS ('000 metric tons)

	1982	1983	1984
Maize	12	8	2
Millet	0	0	1*
Sorghum	4	5	6
Roots and tubers*	7	7	7
Pulses*	18	15	15
Groundnuts (in shell)	0	1	1*
Sunflower seed	1	0	0
Cottonseed*	2	2	2
Cotton (lint)*	1	1	1
Vegetables*	16	16	16
Fruit*	11	11	11

* FAO estimates.
Source: FAO, *Production Yearbook*.

LIVESTOCK ('000 head, year ending September)

	1982	1983	1984
Cattle	2,979	2,818	2,685
Horses	24	23	23
Donkeys	138	142	138
Sheep	140	165	167
Goats	636	783	889
Pigs	5	5	7
Poultry	1,146	961	708

LIVESTOCK PRODUCTS (FAO estimates, '000 metric tons)

	1982	1983	1984
Beef and veal	47	41	42
Goats' meat	3	3	3
Other meat	8	8	8
Cows' milk	95	98	101
Goats' milk	5	5	5
Cheese	0.9	1.0	1.0
Butter and ghee	1.3	1.4	1.5
Hen eggs	0.7	0.7	0.7
Cattle hides	5.9	5.4	5.5

Source: FAO, *Production Yearbook*.

Forestry

ROUNDWOOD REMOVALS
(FAO estimates, '000 cubic metres)

	1982	1983	1984
Industrial wood	65	67	69
Fuel wood*	729	729	729
Total	794	796	798

* Assumed to be unchanged since 1977.
Source: FAO, *Yearbook of Forest Products*.

Fishing

	1982	1983	1984
Total catch (metric tons)	1,400	1,250	1,500

Source: FAO, *Yearbook of Fishery Statistics*.

Mining

	1983	1984	1985
Coal (metric tons)	395,087	392,854	437,088
Copper ore (metric tons)*	20,266	21,517	21,703
Nickel ore (metric tons)*	18,214	18,562	19,560
Cobalt ore (metric tons)*	223	n.a.	n.a.
Diamonds ('000 carats)	10,897	12,904	12,608

* Figures refer to the metal content of ores.

Industry

SELECTED PRODUCTS

	1982	1983	1984
Beer ('000 hectolitres)	163	162	155
Electric energy (million kWh)	604	622	660

1985: Electric energy 695 million kWh.

Finance

CURRENCY AND EXCHANGE RATES

Monetary Units
100 thebe = 1 pula (P).

Denominations
Coins: 1, 2, 5, 10, 25 and 50 thebe; 1 pula.
Notes: 1, 2, 5, 10 and 20 pula.

Sterling and Dollar Equivalents (30 September 1986)
£1 sterling = 2.674 pula;
US $1 = 1.848 pula;
100 pula = £37.39 = $54.11.

Average Exchange Rate (US $ per pula)
1983 0.9122
1984 0.7789
1985 0.5296

BUDGET ('000 pula, year ending 31 March)

Recurrent revenue	1983/84	1984/85	1985/86*
Customs and excise	156,840	155,790	149,230
Income tax	140,380	255,540	324,800
Other taxes	11,700	9,310	11,120
Interest	6,420	8,040	12,060
Other property income	171,030	289,290	548,960
Loan repayments	2,710	2,940	6,910
Other receipts	22,290	35,030	31,500
Total	511,370	755,940	1,084,580

Expenditure	1983/84	1984/85	1985/86*
Office of the President	35,616	40,960	49,460
Finance and development planning	22,655	24,610	19,290
Home affairs	7,598	9,180	10,800
Agriculture	23,661	28,810	31,920
Education	54,844	67,260	80,850
Commerce and industry	4,607	5,500	6,330
Local government and lands	37,255	50,790	60,390
Works and communications	39,164	52,550	65,220
Mineral resources and water affairs	11,158	13,440	16,200
Health	18,286	22,340	25,060
External affairs	2,352	3,100	4,660
Appropriations from revenue	156,000	244,390	282,330
Public debt interest	13,058	19,200	27,430
Other	27,692	40,250	71,640
Total	453,946	622,380	751,580

* Preliminary figures.
Source: Ministry of Finance and Development Planning, Gaborone.

NATIONAL DEVELOPMENT PLAN, 1985–91
(projected expenditure in million pula)

Office of the President	72.5
Finance and development planning	19.8
Home affairs	15.3
Agriculture	52.8
Education	198.0
Commerce and industry	19.3
Local government and lands	133.4
Works and communications	322.9
Mineral resources and water affairs	93.8
Health	69.8
Non-allocated expenditures	240.0
Total	1,222.3

Source: Ministry of Finance and Development Planning, Gaborone.

INTERNATIONAL RESERVES
(US $ million at 31 December)

	1983	1984	1985
IMF special drawing rights	7.60	8.36	10.65
Reserve position in IMF	11.84	12.10	14.20
Foreign exchange	376.23	453.83	758.35
Total	395.67	474.29	783.21

Source: IMF, *International Financial Statistics*.

MONEY SUPPLY (million pula at 31 December)

	1983	1984	1985
Currency outside banks	30.2	35.2	43.4
Demand deposits at commercial banks	107.2	115.4	144.9
Total money	137.3	150.6	188.2

Source: IMF, *International Financial Statistics*.

COST OF LIVING
(Consumer Price Index; base: 1981 = 100)

	1982	1983	1984
Food	113.2	127.8	138.8
Clothing	107.2	115.1	127.1
All items (incl. others)	111.2	122.9	133.3

Source: ILO, *Year Book of Labour Statistics*.

NATIONAL ACCOUNTS
(million pula at current prices, year ending 30 June)

Expenditure on the Gross Domestic Product

	1981/82	1982/83	1983/84
Government final consumption expenditure	230.4	281.8	340.2
Private final consumption expenditure	487.5	569.6	627.5
Increase in stocks	45.2	−12.8	−20.4
Gross fixed capital formation	304.6	320.3	337.6
Total domestic expenditure	1,067.7	1,158.9	1,284.9
Exports*	349.9	618.3	772.3
Less Imports†	638.4	749.8	780.1
GDP in purchasers' values	779.2	1,027.4	1,277.1

* Exports of goods only.
† Imports of goods plus net imports of services.

Cost-Structure of the Gross Domestic Product

	1981/82	1982/83	1983/84
Compensation of employees	347.1	409.8	476.4
Operating surplus	206.2	356.6	484.1
Domestic factor incomes	553.3	766.4	960.5
Consumption of fixed capital	107.1	129.1	151.2
GDP at factor cost	660.4	895.5	1,111.7
Indirect taxes, *less* subsidies	118.8	131.9	165.4
GDP in purchasers' values	779.2	1,027.4	1,277.1

Source: Bank of Botswana, Gaborone.

Gross Domestic Product by Economic Activity

	1981/82	1982/83	1983/84
Agriculture, hunting, forestry and fishing	87.8	77.2	76.1
Mining and quarrying	129.5	286.4	405.3
Manufacturing	71.2	78.7	82.0
Electricity, gas and water	21.8	29.7	32.3
Construction	47.6	45.0	70.5
Trade, restaurants and hotels	182.4	225.3	276.9
Transport, storage and communication	19.8	30.6	32.7
Finance, insurance, real estate and business services	87.6	98.0	127.0
Government services	144.1	171.4	202.0
Other services	32.7	37.5	43.5
Sub-total	824.5	1,079.8	1,348.3
Less Imputed bank service charge	45.3	52.4	71.2
Total	779.2	1,027.4	1,277.1

BALANCE OF PAYMENTS (US $ million)

	1983	1984	1985
Merchandise exports f.o.b.	640.3	677.7	720.4
Merchandise imports f.o.b.	−615.3	−583.4	−501.4
Trade balance	25.1	94.3	219.0
Exports of services	191.0	195.0	172.3
Imports of services	−339.3	−380.9	−335.5
Balance on goods and services	−123.2	−91.6	55.8
Private unrequited transfers (net)	−0.4	−7.3	−1.6
Government unrequited transfers (net)	128.5	110.9	85.1
Current balance	4.9	12.0	139.4
Direct capital investment (net)	25.1	62.4	58.9
Other long-term capital (net)	41.5	52.9	49.4
Short-term capital (net)	23.2	−4.5	1.9
Net errors and omissions	28.9	1.5	4.7
Total (net monetary movements)	123.6	124.3	254.3
Valuation changes (net)	−20.9	−45.7	54.7
Changes in reserves	102.7	78.6	308.9

Source: IMF, *International Financial Statistics*.

External Trade

PRINCIPAL COMMODITIES ('000 UA*)

Imports	1983	1984	1985
Food, beverages and tobacco	156,233	186,459	231,743
Fuel	103,641	104,201	130,049
Chemicals and rubber	68,225	85,795	100,852
Wood and paper	28,473	33,752	37,402
Textiles and footwear	76,269	92,357	104,649
Metal and metal products	80,425	92,360	102,389
Machinery and electrical goods	104,771	166,657	221,730
Vehicles and transport equipment	94,640	130,096	175,633
Other commodities	105,598	124,735	169,958
Total	818,275	1,016,412	1,274,405

Exports	1983	1984	1985
Meat and meat products	80,270	70,224	113,696
Diamonds	471,022	697,095	1,237,227
Copper-nickel matte	66,812	77,041	140,604
Textiles	33,494	45,551	37,730
Hides and skins	5,739	12,718	21,852
Other commodities	50,058	66,498	80,091
Total	707,395	969,127	1,631,200

* Figures are in terms of the Unit of Account (UA) used by the Customs Union of Southern Africa. This is equivalent to the South African rand. Its average value was: 1.0151 pula in 1983; 1.455 pula in 1984.

BOTSWANA   *Statistical Survey*

PRINCIPAL TRADING PARTNERS ('000 UA)

Imports	1983	1984	1985
CUSA*	680,125	793,357	966,229
Other Africa	60,212	89,156	100,962
United Kingdom	10,284	31,656	58,955
Other Europe	42,681	67,468	96,095
USA	8,678	24,324	35,146
Others	16,295	10,451	17,018
Total	818,275	1,016,412	1,274,405

Exports	1983	1984	1985
CUSA*	58,586	65,277	95,021
Other Africa	65,029	37,913	59,746
United Kingdom	30,995	20,032	83,550
Other Europe	497,057	734,384	1,269,153
USA	52,667	79,061	115,856
Others	3,061	32,460	7,854
Total	707,395	969,127	1,631,180

* Customs Union of Southern Africa, of which Botswana is a member; also including Lesotho, Namibia, South Africa and Swaziland.

Transport

RAILWAYS (year ending 30 June)

	1982/83	1983/84	1984/85
Passenger journeys*	529,984	487,298	542,692
Freight (net ton-km)	1,378,732	1,336,650	1,296,735

* Internal traffic only.

CIVIL AVIATION (traffic)

	1983	1984*	1985
Passenger journeys ('000)	127	112	136
Freight (metric tons)	278	338	n.a.
Mail (metric tons)	93	104	n.a.

* Preliminary figures.

ROAD TRAFFIC

	1983	1984	1985
Vehicles registered*	38,108	41,197	45,748

* Excluding government vehicles 4,371 in 1983).

Tourism

	1980	1981	1982
Tourist arrivals ('000)	206	227	250

Communications Media

	1981	1982	1983
Radio receivers ('000 in use)	80	100	120

Book production (first editions only, 1980): 97 titles (books 70; pamphlets 27).
Daily newspapers (1983): 1 title (estimated circulation 24,000 copies).
Sources: UNESCO, *Statistical Yearbook*; Central Statistics Office, Gaborone.
Telephones in use: 17,409 in 1983; 17,912 in 1984; 19,109 in 1985.

Education

(1985)

	Institutions	Teachers	Students
Primary	528	6,980	223,608
Secondary	65	1,283	32,172
Vocational training	17	126	1,006
Teacher training	5	86	1,353
Technical education	2	71	740
University	1	142	1,434

1984: There were 218 Batswana studying abroad.
Source: Ministry of Education, Gaborone.

Directory

The Constitution

The Constitution of the Republic of Botswana came into operation at independence on 30 September 1966.

EXECUTIVE

President

Executive power lies with the President of Botswana, who is also Commander-in-Chief of the armed forces. Election for the office of President is linked with the election of members of the National Assembly. Presidential candidates must be over 30 years of age and receive at least 1,000 nominations. If there is more than one candidate for the Presidency, each candidate for office in the Assembly must declare support for a presidential candidate. The candidate for President who commands the votes of more than half the elected members of the Assembly will be declared President. If the Presidency falls vacant the members of the National Assembly will themselves elect a new President. The President will hold office for the duration of Parliament. After the 1974 elections the President became an ex officio member of the Assembly.

Cabinet

There is also a Vice-President, whose office is Ministerial. The Vice-President is appointed by the President and deputizes in the absence of the President. The Cabinet consists of the President, the Vice-President and 10 other Ministers appointed by the President. The Cabinet is responsible to the National Assembly.

LEGISLATURE

The legislative power is vested in Parliament, consisting of the President and the National Assembly, acting after consultation in certain cases with the House of Chiefs. The President may withhold assent to a Bill passed by the National Assembly. If the same Bill is again presented after six months, the President is required to assent to it or to dissolve Parliament within 21 days.

House of Chiefs

The House of Chiefs has the Chiefs of the eight principal tribes of Botswana as ex officio members, four members elected by sub-chiefs from their own number, and three members elected by the other 12 members of the House. Bills and motions relating to chieftaincy matters and alterations of the Constitution must be referred to the House, which may also deliberate and make representations on any matter.

National Assembly

The National Assembly consists of the Speaker, the Attorney-General, who does not have a vote, 34 elected members and four specially elected members chosen by all members of the Assembly. There is universal adult suffrage. The life of the Assembly is five years.

The Constitution contains a code of human rights, enforceable by the High Court.

The Government

HEAD OF STATE

President: Dr QUETT KETUMILE JONI MASIRE (took office 18 July 1980; re-elected for a five-year term 10 September 1984).

CABINET
(October 1986)

President: Dr QUETT KETUMILE JONI MASIRE.
Vice-President and Minister of Finance and Development Planning: PETER MMUSI.
Minister of External Affairs: Dr GAOSITWE K. T. CHIEPE.
Minister of Mineral Resources and Water Affairs: ARCHIE M. MOGWE.
Minister of Presidential Affairs and Public Administration: PONATSHENGO H. K. KEDIKILWE.
Minister of Agriculture: DANIEL KWELAGOBE.
Minister of Works and Communications: COLIN BLACKBEARD.
Minister of Commerce and Industry: MOATLAGOLA P. K. NWAKO.
Minister of Health: JAMESON LESEDI T. MOTHIBAMELE.
Minister of Education: KEBATHLAMANG PITSEYOSI MORAKE.
Minister of Home Affairs: ENGLISHMAN M. K. KGABO.
Minister of Local Government and Lands: PATRICK BALOPI.
Assistant Minister of Agriculture: GEOFFREY OTENG.
Assistant Minister of Finance and Development Planning: OBED CHILUME.
Assistant Ministers of Local Government and Lands: MICHAEL R. TSHIPINARE, CHAPSON BUTALE.

MINISTRIES

Office of the President: Private Bag 001, Gaborone; tel. 55434.
Ministry of Agriculture: Private Bag 003, Gaborone; tel. 51171.
Ministry of Commerce and Industry: Private Bag 004, Gaborone; tel. 53881; telex 2674.
Ministry of Education: Private Bag 005, Gaborone; tel. 55292.
Ministry of Finance and Development Planning: Private Bag 008, Gaborone; tel. 55272; telex 2401.
Ministry of Health: Private Bag 0038, Gaborone; tel. 55557.
Ministry of Home Affairs: Private Bag 002, Gaborone; tel. 55212.
Ministry of Local Government and Lands: Private Bag 006, Gaborone; tel. 52091.
Ministry of Mineral Resources and Water Affairs: Private Bag 0018, Gaborone; tel. 52454; telex 2503.
Ministry of Works and Communications: Private Bag 007, Gaborone; tel. 55303.

Legislature

NATIONAL ASSEMBLY

Speaker: JAMES G. HASKINS.

General Election, 8 September 1984

Party	Votes	%	Seats
Botswana Democratic Party	154,863	68.0	29*
Botswana National Front	46,550	20.4	4*
Botswana People's Party	14,961	6.6	1
Botswana Independence Party	7,288	3.2	—
Botswana Progressive Union	3,036	1.3	—
Independent	1,058	0.5	—
Total	227,756	100.0	34

* A by-election was held in the Gaborone South constituency in December 1984, after the High Court ruled the September result there to be null and void. The by-election was won by the BNF, increasing the total number of seats held by the BNF to 5, and reducing the BDP total to 28.

There are six additional members of the Assembly: the Speaker, the Attorney-General and four specially elected members chosen by all members of the Assembly. The President is an ex-officio member.

House of Chiefs

The House has a total of 15 members.
Chairman: Chief SEEPAPITSO.

Political Organizations

Botswana Democratic Party (BDP): POB 28, Gaborone; f. 1962; Pres. Dr QUETT MASIRE; Chair. P. S. MMUSI; Sec.-Gen. DANIEL KWELAGOBE.

BOTSWANA

Botswana Independence Party (BIP): POB 3, Maun; f. 1962; Pres. MOTSAMAI K. MPHO; Sec.-Gen. EMMANUEL R. MOKOBI; Vice-Pres. J. G. GUGUSHE.

Botswana Liberal Party (BLP): POB 258, Francistown; f. 1983; Pres. MARTIN CHAKALISA.

Botswana National Front (BNF): POB 42, Mahalapye; f. 1967; Pres. Dr KENNETH KOMA; Parl. Leader ex-Chief BATHOEN II GASEITSIWE; Sec.-Gen. MARELEDI GIDDIE.

Botswana People's Party (BPP): POB 159, Francistown; f. 1960; Pres. Dr KNIGHT MARIPE; Chair. KENNETH MKHWA; Sec.-Gen. JOHN MOSOJANE.

Botswana Progressive Union (BPU): POB 10229, Francistown; f. 1982; Pres. D. K. KWELE; Chair. G. G. BAGWASI; Sec.-Gen. R. K. MONYATSIWA.

United Front for the Unemployed: PO Gaborone; f. 1984; Pres. M. T. MOOKETSANE.

Diplomatic Representation

EMBASSIES AND HIGH COMMISSIONS IN BOTSWANA

China, People's Republic: POB 1031, Gaborone; telex 2428; Ambassador: LU DEFENG.

Germany, Federal Republic: POB 315, Gaborone; tel. 53143; telex 2225; Ambassador: Dr KARL MAES.

Libya: POB 180, Gaborone; telex 2501; Secretary of People's Bureau: S. A. EL FALLAH.

Mozambique: Gaborone; Ambassador: RAFAEL MAGUNI.

Nigeria: POB 274, Gaborone; High Commissioner: R. O. OMOTOYE.

Romania: Gaborone; Ambassador: GHEORGHE BADRUS.

Sweden: Private Bag 0017, Gaborone; telex 2421; Ambassador: KARL-GÖRAN ENGSTRÖM.

USSR: POB 81, Gaborone; Ambassador: MIKHAIL NIKOLAYEVICH PETROV.

United Kingdom: Private Bag 0023, Gaborone; tel. 52841; telex 2370; High Commissioner: PETER A. RAFTERY.

USA: POB 90, Gaborone; tel. 53982; telex 2540; Ambassador: NATALE BELLOCCHI.

Zambia: POB 362, Gaborone; High Commissioner: N. N. K. KALALA.

Zimbabwe: POB 1232, Gaborone; tel. 4495; High Commissioner: A. M. CHIDODA.

Judicial System

There is a High Court at Lobatse and a branch at Francistown, and Magistrates' Courts in each district. Appeals lie to the Court of Appeal of Botswana.

Chief Justice: J. A. O'BRIEN-QUINN.

Puisne Judges: N. O. G. MURRAY, J. C. BARRINGTON-JONES.

President of the Court of Appeal: I. A. MAISELS.

Justices of Appeal: L. BARON, T. A. AGUDA, S. KENTRIDGE, A. N. E. AMISSAH, L. VAN WINSEN.

Registrar and Master of the High Court: FAQIR MUHAMMAD.

Chief Magistrates: R. F. HUNT, A. D. AMSTELL, G. M. OKELLO.

Senior Magistrates: K. OBENG, G. RWELENGERA, Y. D. PETKAR, S. HOOPER, M. WANNIAPPA, F. B. SWANNIKER.

Attorney-General: M. D. MOKAMA.

Religion

The majority of the population are animists; an estimated 30% are thought to be Christians. There are Islamic mosques in Gaborone and Lobatse.

CHRISTIANITY

Christian Council of Botswana: POB 355, Gaborone; Gen. Sec. (vacant).

The Anglican Communion

Archbishop of the Province of Central Africa and Bishop of Botswana: Most Rev. WALTER PAUL KHOTSO MAKHULU, POB 769, Gaborone.

Protestant Churches

African Methodist Episcopal Church: POB 141, Lobatse; Rev. L. M. MBULAWA.

Evangelical Lutheran Church in Botswana: POB 1976, Gaborone; tel. 52227; telex 2882; Bishop PHILIP ROBINSON; 13,000 mems.

Evangelical Lutheran Church in Southern Africa (ELCSA): POB 5394, Johannesburg 2000, South Africa; tel. 3377113; telex 86519; Gen. Sec. Rev. MERVYN D. ASSUR; six dioceses (one in Botswana).

  Botswana Diocese: Bishop M. NTUPING, POB 400, Gaborone; tel. 53976.

Methodist Church in Botswana: POB 260, Gaborone; Dist. Supt Rev. Z. S. M. MOSAI.

United Congregational Church of Southern Africa: POB 1263, Gaborone; tel. 52491; autonomous since 1980; Chair. Rev. K. F. MOKOBI; Sec. Rev. J. I. B. SEKGWA; 12,643 mems.

The United Methodist Church is also active in Botswana.

The Roman Catholic Church

Botswana comprises a single diocese. The metropolitan see is Bloemfontein, South Africa. The church was established in Botswana in 1928, and had an estimated 41,800 adherents in the country at 31 December 1984. The Bishop participates in the Southern Africa Catholic Bishops' Conference, based in Pretoria, South Africa.

Bishop of Gaborone: Rt Rev. BONIFACE TSHOSA SETLALEKGOSI, Bishop's House, POB 218, Gaborone; tel. 52928.

THE BAHÁ'Í FAITH

National Spiritual Assembly: POB 466, Gaborone; tel. 52532; telex 2777; mems resident in 220 localities.

The Press

DAILY NEWSPAPER

Dikgang Tsa Gompieno (Botswana Daily News): Private Bag 0060, Gaborone; tel. 52261; telex 2409; f. 1964; publ. by Dept of Information and Broadcasting; Setswana and English; Mon.–Fri.; circ. 30,000.

PERIODICALS

Agrinews: Private Bag 003, Gaborone; f. 1971; monthly; technical journal on agriculture and rural development; publ. by the Agricultural Information Service; circ. 6,000.

Botswana Advertiser: POB 130, Gaborone; weekly; publ. by Printing and Publishing Co (Botswana) (Pty) Ltd.

Botswana Guardian: POB 1641, Gaborone; tel. 52085; telex 2692; weekly; publ. by Pula Printing and Publishing (Pty) Ltd; Editor C. M. MOGALE; circ. 17,000.

Business Gazette: POB 1605, Gaborone; weekly; publ. by Proprietors' News Co Botswana (Pty) Ltd; circ. 8000.

Government Gazette: Private Bag 0081, Gaborone; tel. 53202; telex 2414.

Kutlwano: Private Bag 0060, Gaborone; telex 2409; monthly; Setswana and English; publ. by Dept of Information and Broadcasting; circ. 7,000.

Mmegi Wa Dikgang: POB 20906, Gaborone; tel. 4311; weekly; Setswana and English; publ. by the Foundation for Education with Production.

Northern Advertiser: POB 343, Francistown; weekly; publ. by Premier Investments (Pty) Ltd.

The Zebra's Voice: POB 114, Gaborone; f. 1982; quarterly; cultural magazine; publ. by the National Museum and Art Gallery; circ. 4,000.

NEWS AGENCIES

Botswana Press Agency (BOPA): Gaborone; tel. 3601; telex 2409; f. 1981.

Foreign Bureaux

Inter Press Service (IPS) (Italy): POB 1605, Gaborone.

Xinhua (New China) News Agency (People's Republic of China): Plot 5379, President's Drive, POB 1031, Gaborone; tel. 53434; telex 2428; Correspondent CHEN GUOWEI.

BOTSWANA

Publishers

A.C. Braby (Botswana) (Pty) Ltd: POB 1549, Gaborone; telex 2371; telephone directory publishers.

Department of Information and Broadcasting: Private Bag 0060, Gaborone; telex 2409; publs *Dikgang Tsa Gompieno, Kutlwano, Botswana Magazine* (annual), material on Botswana.

Longman Botswana (Pty) Ltd: POB 1083, Gaborone.

Printing and Publishing Co (Botswana) (Pty) Ltd: 5647 Nakedi Rd, POB 130, Broadhurst, Gaborone; tel. 2844; telex 2351; commercial printers; publs *Botswana Advertiser*.

Government Publishing House

Government Printer: Private Bag 0081, Gaborone; tel. 53202; telex 2414.

Radio and Television

RADIO

There were an estimated 120,000 radio receivers in use in 1983. The government is considering the introduction of a commercial radio network.

Radio Botswana: Private Bag 0060, Gaborone; tel. 52541; telex 2409; broadcasts in Setswana and English; f. 1965; Dir Mrs M. NASHA.

TELEVISION

TV Association of Botswana: Gaborone; two transmitters relaying SABC-TV programmes from South Africa, and BOP-TV programmes from Bophuthatswana; plans for a national TV service are under consideration.

Finance

(cap. = capital; p.u. = paid-up; dep. = deposits; res = reserves; m. = million; brs = branches; amounts in pula)

BANKING

Bank of Botswana: POB 712, Gaborone; tel. 51911; telex 2405; f. 1975; bank of issue; cap. p.u. 3.6m., dep. 903.4m., res 2,101.1m. (Dec. 1985); Gov. CHARLES N. KIKONYOGO; Dir of Admin. B. MATHE.

Bank of Credit and Commerce (Botswana) Ltd: Lobatse House, Industrial Sites, POB 871, Gaborone; tel. 52867; telex 2556; f. 1982; cap. and res 2.5m., dep. 37.1m.; Chair. E. A. GARDA; Gen. Man. B. N. CHOUDHURI; 4 brs.

Barclays Bank of Botswana Ltd: Commerce House, The Mall, POB 478, Gaborone; tel. (031) 52041; telex 2417; f. 1975; cap. and res 18m., dep. 189m. (Dec. 1985); Chair. LOUIS G. NCHINDO; Man. Dir ROBERT A. BIRD; 18 brs.

Botswana Co-operative Bank Ltd: Broadhurst Mall, Co-operative Bank House, POB 40106, Gaborone; tel. 71398; telex 2298; f. 1974; cap. and res 2.2m., loans 5.9m. (1985); central source of credit for registered co-operative societies; Pres. M. L. SETLHARE; Man. L. LINDKVIST.

National Development Bank: Development House, The Mall, POB 225, Gaborone; tel. 52801; telex 2553; f. 1964; cap. and res 7.7m., loans 60.3m. (March 1986); priority given to agricultural credit for Botswana farmers, and co-operative credit and loans for local business ventures; Chair. C. G. MOGAMI; Gen. Man. B. I. GASENNELWE; 6 brs.

Standard Chartered Bank Botswana Ltd: Standard House, The Mall, POB 496, Gaborone; tel. 53161; telex 2258; f. 1975; cap. and res 13.3m., dep. 136.1m. (1985); Chair. J. G. HASKINS; Man. Dir A. O'DWYER; 13 brs.

INSURANCE

Associated Insurance Brokers of Botswana (Pty) Ltd: Standard House, POB 624, Gaborone; tel. (031) 51481; telex 2539; f. 1982 by merger of Insurance Brokers Botswana (Pty) Ltd and Minet Botswana (Pty) Ltd; Man. Dir M. COWPER.

Botswana Eagle Insurance Co Ltd: 501 Botsalano House, POB 1221, Gaborone; telex 2259.

Botswana Insurance Co (Pty) Ltd: BIC House, POB 336, Gaborone; tel. 51791; telex 2359; Gen. Man. P. B. SUMMER.

Directory

ECB Insurance Brokers (Botswana) (Pty) Ltd: Botsalano House, POB 1195, Gaborone.

IGI Botswana (Pty) Ltd: IGI House, POB 715, Gaborone; tel. 51521; telex 2430; Gen. Man. J. M. WALKIN.

Trade and Industry

PUBLIC CORPORATIONS

Botswana Housing Corporation: POB 412, Gaborone; tel. 53341; telex 2729; cap. P1.3m. (March 1983); provides housing for government and local authorities, assists with housing schemes and provision of housing for other persons; Chair. P. O. MOLOSI, the Perm. Sec., Ministry of Local Govt and Lands; Gen. Man. J. D. RICHARDSON; 557 employees.

Botswana Meat Commission (BMC): Private Bag 4, Lobatse; tel. 212; telex 2420; f. 1966; cap. and res P19m. (Sept. 1985); slaughter of livestock, exports of hides and skins, carcasses, frozen and chilled boneless beef, offal tannery and cannery producing wet blue leather, canned tongue, pet foods and corned beef; Exec. Chair. D. W. FINLAY; Gen. Man. F. BOAKGOMO; 1,600 employees.

Botswana Power Corporation: Motlakase House, POB 48, Gaborone; tel. 52211; telex 2431; irredeemable cap. P13.5m.; Chair. the Dep. Perm. Sec., Ministry of Mineral Resources and Water Affairs; CEO E. D. BELL.

Botswana Telecommunications Corporation: POB 700, Gaborone; tel. 53611; telex 2252; f. 1980; cap. 17.3m. (March 1985); CEO M. T. CURRY.

Water Utilities Corporation: POB 127, Gaborone; tel. 52521; telex 2545; f. 1970; public water supply undertaking for principal townships; assets P110m.; revenue P18m. (1985); Chair. the Dep. Perm. Sec., Ministry of Mineral Resources and Water Affairs; CEO T. WATERS.

CHAMBER OF COMMERCE

The Botswana National Chamber of Commerce and Industry is being reorganized.

MARKETING BOARD

Botswana Agricultural Marketing Board: Private Bag 0053, Gaborone; tel. 51341; telex 2530; cap. P4.2m.; Chair. the Perm. Sec., Ministry of Agriculture; Gen. Man. P. R. J. MULLIGAN.

DEVELOPMENT ORGANIZATIONS

Botswana Development Corporation Ltd: Madirelo House, Mmanaka Rd, POB 438, Gaborone; tel. 51811; telex 2251; f. 1985/86; cap. P70.2m.; Chair. the Perm. Sec., Ministry of Finance and Development Planning; Gen. Man. M. O. MOLEFANE.

Botswana Enterprise Development Unit (BEDU): Plot No. 1269, Lobatse Rd, PB 0014, Gaborone; f. 1974 to promote industrialization and rural development; Dir J. LINDFORS.

Botswana Livestock Development Corporation (Pty) Ltd: POB 455, Gaborone; tel. 51949; telex 2543; cap. P3.4m. (1986); Chair. M. L. MOKONE; Gen. Man. S. M. R. BURNETT.

Financial Services Company of Botswana (Pty) Ltd: POB 1129, Gaborone; tel. 51363; telex 2207; f. 1974; cap. and res P1.9m.; provides hire purchase, mortgage and industrial leasing facilities; Chair. J. E. ANDERSON; Gen. Man. G. H. WILSON.

Trade and Investment Promotion Agency (TIPA), Ministry of Commerce and Industry: Private Bag 004, Gaborone; tel. 53881/4; telex 2674; promotes diversification of the industrial sector by encouraging investment, provides consultancy services and monitors projects, participates in trade missions and international trade fairs; Dir J. R. MONAMETSI.

EMPLOYERS' ASSOCIATION

Botswana Employers' Federation: Botsalano House, POB 432, Gaborone; f. 1971; Chair. R. MANNATHOKO; Sec.-Gen. MODIRE J. MBAAKANYI; 600 affiliated mems.

TRADE UNIONS

Botswana Federation of Trade Unions: POB 440, Gaborone; Sec.-Gen. INA KENAIRI.

Affiliated Unions

Botswana Bank Employees' Union: POB 111, Gaborone; Sec.-Gen. S. D. SHABANI.

Botswana Commercial and General Workers' Union: POB 62, Gaborone; Sec.-Gen. ALFRED J. KEBAWETSE.

BOTSWANA

Botswana Commercial Banks Supervisory and Managerial Staff Union: c/o Standard Chartered, Gaborone; Sec.-Gen. Mr PABALINGWA.

Botswana Construction Workers' Union: POB 1508, Gaborone; Sec.-Gen. BAAITSE RADITSEBE.

Botswana Co-operative Managers' Union: POB 70, Gaborone; Sec.-Gen. A. P. RAMOSAKO.

Botswana Diamond Sorters-Valuators' Union: POB 1186, Gaborone; Sec.-Gen. RONALD BAIPIDI.

Botswana Local Government Workers' Union: POB 14, Francistown; Sec.-Gen. ALLISON MANGENA.

Botswana Meat Industry Workers' Union: POB 181, Lobatse; Sec.-Gen. RUSSIA SESINYI.

Botswana Mining Workers' Union: POB 14, Selebi-Phikwe; Sec.-Gen. BALEKAMANG GABASIANE.

Botswana Railway Staff and Artisan Employees' Union: POB 1486, Gaborone; Sec.-Gen. P. MAGOWE.

Botswana Railway Workers' Union: POB 181, Gaborone; Sec.-Gen. ISAREL LESO.

Botswana Telecommunication Employees' Union: POB 2032, Gaborone; Sec.-Gen. LOFTUS S. MOTLOKWA.

Central Bank Union: POB 72, Gaborone; Sec.-Gen. C. M. TLHOMELANG.

Insurance Employees' Union of Botswana: POB 1863, Gaborone; Sec.-Gen. G. T. MMATLI.

National Union of Government Manual Workers: POB 374, Gaborone; Sec.-Gen. BAME BAFETANYE.

Non-Academic Staff Union: Private Bag 0022, Gaborone; Sec.-Gen. A. M. SEELETSO.

Orapa and Letlhakane Mines Staff Union: POB 220, Orapa; Sec.-Gen. C. M. TANGANE.

CO-OPERATIVES

Department of Co-operative Development: POB 86, Gaborone; f. 1964; by 1976 there were 116 co-operatives, of which 57 were marketing and supply co-operatives, 20 consumers' co-operatives, 29 thrift and loan societies, four credit societies, two dairy co-operatives, a horticultural co-operative, a fisheries co-operative, a co-operative union and a co-operative bank.

Transport

RAILWAYS

The main railway line from Mafikeng, South Africa, to Bulawayo, Zimbabwe, a distance of 960 km, passes through the country. There are 714 km of 1,067mm-gauge track within Botswana, including two spurs serving the Selebi-Phikwe mining complex (59 km) and the Morupule colliery (14 km). The entire main railway line in Botswana is to be rehabilitated under an SADCC project, estimated to cost US $114m. Feasibility studies were undertaken in 1984 for the construction of a trans-Kalahari rail link, about 875 km in length, which would provide Botswana with an outlet to the Atlantic Ocean on the coast of Namibia, but this project is unlikely to be implemented in the near future.

Botswana Railways: Private Bag 00125, Gaborone; the railway has been owned and operated by National Railways of Zimbabwe, but Botswana Railways has been effecting a gradual take-over. The section of railway from Ramatlabama to Mahalapye came under the control of Botswana Railways in April 1984, and it was planned that the entire length of track within Botswana should be completely controlled by Botswana Railways by January 1987.

ROADS

In 1983 there were about 15,000 km of roads. Of the 8,026 km officially maintained by the Government in 1985, 2,559 km were main roads and 2,207 km were secondary roads. There is a tarred road from Gaborone, via Francistown, to Kazungula, where the borders of Botswana, Namibia, Zambia and Zimbabwe meet. The Government plans the construction of a road between Orapa and Serowe, and the Palapye to Serowe road was completed in 1983. Under the Sixth National Development Plan, there are plans to construct several main roads and to extend the networks of both feeder and rural roads serving the remoter areas. It is possible to cross the Zambezi river into Zambia by ferry. Plans to build a bridge at the crossing are being considered.

CIVIL AVIATION

The centre of Botswana's air network is Seretse Khama Airport, the international airport at Gaborone, which opened in 1984. There are three regional airports, and airfields at all population centres and tourist areas. Air Botswana is investigating the possibility of operating a scheduled service to the village of Kasane in the Chobe area of northern Botswana. The service is projected to begin after the completion of the new Kasane Airport, which is scheduled for 1988/89. The present scheduled services of Air Botswana are supplemented by an active charter and business sector which carries 40% of the total passengers. In October 1986 British Caledonian Airways secured a licence to operate a route between London and Gaborone, to counter the effect of a possible ban on flights to South Africa.

Air Botswana (Pty) Ltd: POB 92, Gaborone; tel. 52812; telex 2413; f. 1972; owned by the Botswana Development Corporation; regular scheduled domestic services between Gaborone, Maun, Francistown and Selebi-Phikwe, connecting with regional services to South Africa, Zambia and Zimbabwe; worldwide cargo charter trading as Air Botswana Cargo; Chair. K. KUIPER; Gen. Man. C. B. POLLOCK; fleet of 1 Fokker F-27-200, 1 Dornier 228, 2 Lockheed L-100-30.

Tourism

Department of Wildlife and National Parks: POB 131, Gaborone; tel. 51461; Dir. K. T. NGWAMOTSOKO.

Tourism Development Unit, Ministry of Commerce and Industry: Private Bag 0047, Gaborone; tel. 53024; telex 2674; f. 1973; promotion of tourism in Botswana; Dir CHAWA BOGOSI.

BRAZIL

Introductory Survey

Location, Climate, Language, Religion, Flag, Capital

The Federative Republic of Brazil, the fifth largest country in the world, lies in central and north-eastern South America. To the north are Venezuela, Colombia, Guyana, Suriname and French Guiana, to the west Peru and Bolivia, and to the south Paraguay, Argentina and Uruguay. Brazil has a very long coastline on the Atlantic Ocean. Climatic conditions vary from hot and wet in the tropical rain forest of the Amazon basin to temperate in the savannah grasslands of the central and southern uplands, which have warm summers and mild winters. In Rio de Janeiro temperatures are generally between 17°C (63°F) and 29°C (85°F). The language is Portuguese. Almost all of the inhabitants profess Christianity, and about 90% are adherents of the Roman Catholic Church. The national flag (proportions 10 by 7) is green, bearing, at the centre, a yellow diamond containing a blue celestial globe with 23 white five-pointed stars (one for each state), arranged in the pattern of the southern firmament, and an equatorial scroll with the motto 'Ordem e Progresso' ('Order and Progress'). The capital is Brasília, although some administrative offices still remain in Rio de Janeiro, which was the capital of Brazil until 1960.

Recent History

Brazil was formally proclaimed a Portuguese possession in 1500. During the period of Portuguese colonial rule, many Africans were transported to Brazil to work as slaves. Following a French invasion of Portugal, the regent (later king) moved his capital from Lisbon to Rio de Janeiro in 1808. The Portuguese king returned to Europe in 1821 but his son, Crown Prince Pedro, remained as regent. In 1822 Pedro proclaimed Brazil an independent monarchy, and he took the title of Emperor Pedro I. During the liberal reign of his son, Pedro II, immigration from Europe increased and the interior of Brazil was colonized. The abolition of slavery in 1888 caused discontent among plantation owners, and Pedro II was deposed in 1889 by an army rebellion, leading to the establishment of a republic. A federal constitution for the United States of Brazil was adopted in 1891. Military leaders, in and out of office, have retained decisive influence in Brazilian politics.

Following social unrest in the 1920s, the economic crisis of 1930 resulted in a major revolt, led by Dr Getúlio Vargas, who was installed as President. He governed the country as a benevolent dictator until forced to resign by the armed forces in December 1945. During Vargas's populist rule, Brazil enjoyed internal stability and steady economic progress. He established a strongly authoritarian corporate state, similar to fascist regimes in Europe, but in 1942 Brazil entered the Second World War on the side of the Allies. Brazil was the first South American country to dispatch fighting troops to Europe, sending an expeditionary force to Italy in 1944.

In 1946 Gen. Eurico Dutra was elected President and a new constitution was adopted. Vargas was re-elected President in 1950, but failed to create the necessary stability and committed suicide in August 1954. The next President was Dr Juscelino Kubitschek, who took office in 1956. Brazil's capital was moved in 1960 from Rio de Janeiro to the newly-constructed city of Brasília, sited on a previously uninhabited jungle plateau about 1,000 km (600 miles) inland. President Kubitschek was succeeded by Dr Jânio Quadros, who was elected in October 1960 and took office in January 1961. President Quadros resigned after only seven months in office, and in September 1961 the Vice-President, João Goulart, was sworn in as President.

Military leaders suspected Goulart, the leader of the Partido Trabalhista Brasileiro (PTB), of communist sympathies, and they were reluctant to let him succeed to the presidency. As a compromise, the Constitution was amended to restrict the powers of the President and to provide for a Prime Minister. Upon taking office, President Goulart appointed Dr Tancredo de Almeida Neves, a member of the Partido Social Democrático (PSD) and a former Minister of Justice, to be Prime Minister. However, Dr Neves and most of his Cabinet resigned in June 1962. He was succeeded by Dr Francisco Brochada da Rocha, also of the PSD, who was Prime Minister from July to September 1962. His successor was Dr Hermes Lima of the PTB, hitherto Minister of Labour, but a referendum in January 1963 approved a return to the presidential system of government, whereupon President Goulart formed his own Cabinet.

Following a period of rapid inflation and allegations of official corruption, the left-wing regime of President Goulart was overthrown by a bloodless army revolution on 31 March–1 April 1964. The leader of this right-wing military coup was Gen. (later Marshal) Humberto Castelo Branco, the Army Chief of Staff, who was elected President by Congress. In October 1965 President Castelo Branco assumed dictatorial powers, and all of Brazil's 13 existing political parties were banned. In December, however, two artificially-created parties, the pro-Government Aliança Renovadora Nacional (ARENA) and the opposition Movimento Democrático Brasileiro (MDB), were granted official recognition. President Castelo Branco nominated as his successor the Minister of War, Marshal Artur da Costa e Silva, who was elected President in October 1966 and took office in March 1967. At the same time, a new constitution, changing the country's name to the Federative Republic of Brazil, was introduced. The ailing President da Costa e Silva was forced to resign in September 1969, being replaced by a triumvirate of military leaders.

During its early years the military regime promulgated a series of Institutional Acts which granted the President wide-ranging powers to rule by decree. On 20 October 1969 the ruling junta introduced a revised constitution, vesting executive authority in an indirectly-elected President. Congress, suspended since December 1968, was recalled and elected Gen. Emílio Garrastazú Médici, who took office as President on 30 October 1969. Urban guerrilla activity was widespread during 1970 but was largely eliminated by stern security measures. The next President was Gen. Ernesto Geisel, chosen by an electoral college, who took office in March 1974. Despite President Geisel's more liberal outlook, the MDB made sweeping gains in the congressional elections of November 1974, and calls were made for an end to military government. Although Gen. Geisel reaffirmed his intention to re-establish democratic institutions and to reduce press censorship, arrests and torture of political dissidents continued.

In January 1978 President Geisel's choice of Gen. João Baptista de Figueiredo as his successor was endorsed by the national convention of the ARENA. General Figueiredo was duly elected President by an electoral college in October 1978 and took office in March 1979, promising to continue the *abertura*, or opening to democratization, begun by President Geisel. In the face of growing political agitation, Congress approved various reforms that had been proposed by President Geisel. In November 1979 Congress approved legislation to end the controlled two-party system. The new parties that were subsequently formed included the first independent labour party, the Partido dos Trabalhadores (PT).

President Figueiredo suffered a heart attack in September 1981 and was replaced, until he resumed office in November, by Vice-President Antônio Aureliano Chaves de Mendonça, the first civilian to hold presidential office since 1964. Congressional, state and municipal elections were held in November 1982. The government-sponsored Partido Democrático Social (PDS) gained a majority of seats in the Senate, but failed to win an absolute majority in the Chamber of Deputies, and was also defeated in elections for the governorships of 10 states and in municipal elections in more than 75% of the main towns. The pre-election legislative measures ensured, however, that the PDS would have a majority in the presidential electoral college, due to choose a successor to Gen. Figueiredo in 1985.

In February 1983, to limit the strength of the opposition, the President issued a decree which reduced the authority of the state governors before they had even taken office, and the regime introduced other measures which concentrated political power in Brasília. Lacking a working majority in the Chamber of Deputies, the President ruled by decree laws until May 1983, when he was able to form an alliance of the PDS with the small Partido Trabalhista Brasileiro (PTB, unrelated to the former PTB, banned in 1965), thereby obtaining 248 out of 479 seats. In August 1983 the PTB withdrew from its pact with the PDS, and in October a 60-day state of emergency was declared in Brasília. In December 1983, responding to opposition demands for direct voting in the presidential election, President Figueiredo confirmed that the system of indirect election, through an electoral college, would be retained.

Throughout 1984 Brazil's political life was dominated by the issue of succession. In February the four opposition parties announced the formation of the Free Elections Movement and proposed a constitutional amendment to provide for an immediate return to direct presidential elections. The opposition's campaign was bolstered by the return to civilian rule in neighbouring Argentina in 1983. Mass rallies in Rio de Janeiro and São Paulo in April 1984, each attended by more than 1m. people, indicated the extent of public support for the opposition's campaign. In an attempt to regain the political initiative, President Figueiredo presented his own draft amendment, which proposed the return of Brazil to full democracy (including the holding of direct presidential elections) by 1988, a reduction in the presidential term of office from six to four years and the curtailment of the President's exceptional powers. In April a 60-day state of emergency was imposed in Brasília, to coincide with voting in Congress on the opposition's amendment. In spite of considerable backing from members of the PDS, the opposition narrowly failed to obtain the two-thirds majority that was required.

Following this set-back, the opposition's campaign appeared to lose momentum. In June 1984, however, a resurgence in popular protests, coupled with the Government's inability to secure a majority in support of the presidential amendment, resulted in the withdrawal of the amendment from Congress. In July Vice-President Chaves de Mendonça and the influential Marco de Oliveira Maciel, a former Governor of Pernambuco state, announced the formation of an alliance of liberal PDS members with members of the Partido do Movimento Democrático Brasileiro (PMDB). This offered the opposition a genuine opportunity to defeat the PDS in the electoral college. In August Senator Tancredo Neves, the Governor of Minas Gerais State (who had been Prime Minister in 1961–62), was named presidential candidate for the liberal alliance, while the former president of the PDS, José Sarney, was declared vice-presidential candidate. The unpopular Paolo Salim Maluf secured the nomination of the PDS but he did not enjoy the full backing of the party or the armed forces. In December the liberal alliance formed an official political party, the Partido Frente Liberal (PFL). At the presidential election, held in January 1985, Neves was elected as Brazil's first civilian President for 21 years, winning 480 of the 686 votes in the electoral college. Prior to the inauguration ceremony in March 1985, however, Neves was taken ill, and in April, following a series of operations, he died. José Sarney, who had assumed the role of acting president in Neves' absence, took office as President in April. President Sarney made no alterations to the Cabinet selected by Neves, and he affirmed his commitment to fulfilling the objectives of the late President-designate.

In May 1985 Congress approved a constitutional amendment which restored direct elections by universal suffrage. The right to vote was also extended to illiterate adults. President Sarney expressed his willingness to step down in 1989, two years before the expiry of his term of office. The first direct elections took place in November 1985, when municipal elections were held in 31 cities. At the elections the PMDB, the leading partner in the government alliance, won the mayoral contest in more than half of the municipalities, but failed to secure control of the important cities of São Paulo, Rio de Janeiro and Porto Alegre.

In February 1986 President Sarney announced a Cabinet reshuffle. The 12 new appointments to the Cabinet caused a division within the ruling alliance because the PFL (in spite of a lack of electoral support) gained control of five key ministeries, while the PMDB's position was considerably weakened.

In accordance with the plans of the late President-elect, Tancredo Neves, President Sarney authorized the formation, in September 1985, of a 50-member committee, the Comissão Provisória de Estudos Constitucionais, to prepare a draft constitution which was to have no legal significance but was to form the basis of the work of the forthcoming Constitutional Assembly. The draft constitution, composed of 468 articles, was presented to the Government in September 1986. It envisaged a radical reorganization of Brazil's governing structures to create a parliamentary system of government, including the office of Prime Minister. The current Government, however, showed only a cursory interest in the proposals, and it was suggested that the draft constitution would be submitted to the Constitutional Assembly only at the specific request of a member of the Assembly.

The introduction in February 1986 of an anti-inflation programme, the Cruzado Plan, proved to be a considerable success for the Government and boosted the personal popularity of President Sarney. The Government hoped to capitalize on its popularity at elections for the National Congress, to act as the Constitutional Assembly, in November 1986, when an electorate of some 69m. Brazilians was eligible to vote for 49 senators and 487 federal deputies. Gubernatorial elections were held concurrently with the congressional elections. At the elections the PMDB emerged as the leading party within the ruling coalition: its representatives secured a majority in the Constitutional Assembly and more than 20 state governorships. The Constitutional Assembly was to draft a new constitution and determine the length of the presidential term of office.

In addition to the problems posed by the constitutional issue, President Sarney's first months in office were further complicated by a deep division within the Cabinet between the Ministers of Planning and of the Economy. Furthermore, the Government's controversial proposals for agrarian reform, announced in May, exacerbated the already tense relations between landowners and peasants. The National Agrarian Reform Programme was launched in October 1985. Under the programme, the Government planned to distribute 40.2m. ha of land to 1.4m. landless families by 1989. However, following a protracted dispute within the Cabinet over the implementation and financing of the programme, the Minister of Land Reform and Development resigned in May 1986. Violent clashes between landowners and peasants, especially in the east Amazonian region, continued throughout 1986, resulting in the deaths of 125 people between January and June, including that of a Roman Catholic priest. The Roman Catholic Church strongly condemned the Government's apparent lack of commitment to agrarian reform, and supported the illegal occupation of land by peasant groups. By late 1986 the conflict showed no sign of abating and was, therefore, expected to be an important issue in the congressional elections.

Following the tensions created by the war in 1982 between Argentina and the United Kingdom, after the invasion of the Falkland Islands by Argentine forces, Brazil's relations with the USA improved in 1983, and Brazil gave support to US foreign policy in return for economic aid. Brazilian troops were mobilized on the frontiers with Venezuela, Guyana and Suriname. Close relations were established with Suriname, and military and economic assistance was provided, in order to undermine Suriname's links with Cuba.

Government

Brazil had a military-backed government from 1964 to 1985. Under the 1969 constitution, amended by presidential decree in 1977 and 1978, the country is a federal republic comprising 23 States, three Territories and a Federal District (Brasília). Legislative power is exercised by the bicameral National Congress, comprising the Chamber of Deputies (members elected for four years) and the Federal Senate (members elected in rotation for eight years). The number of deputies is based on the size of the population. Election is by universal adult suffrage (the franchise was extended to illiterate adults in 1985) and voting is compulsory. One-third of the Senators are elected indirectly. Executive power is exercised by the President,

BRAZIL

elected for six years. At the most recent presidential election, in January 1985, the President was chosen by an electoral college. A subsequent constitutional amendment provides that future Presidents will be elected by direct balloting. The President appoints and leads the Cabinet. Each State has a directly elected Governor and an elected legislature. A Constitutional Assembly, which was to be installed in February 1987, was to draw up a new constitution.

Defence

Military service, lasting 12 months, is compulsory for men between 18 and 45 years of age. In July 1986 the armed forces comprised 283,400 men: army 182,900, navy 49,800 and air force 50,700. Public security forces number about 240,000 men. Defence expenditure in 1984 was 1,950m. cruzados.

Economic Affairs

Brazil occupies about 48% of the South American continent. It is the world's fifth largest country, in terms of area, and the sixth most populous. Much of Brazil's interior is covered by tropical forests, on land drained by the world's largest river system, the Amazon and its many tributaries. In terms of aggregate gross national product (GNP), Brazil is among the world's 10 leading countries. Since the Second World War, the country has experienced rapid industrialization and a generally high rate of economic growth, notably in the period 1967–74, when GNP expanded at an average rate of 11% per year in real terms. In terms of employment, the major sector of the economy is still agriculture, which engaged about 30% of the labour force in 1980. Manufacturing employed about one-sixth of the working population in 1980, when its contribution to gross domestic product (GDP) was 26.6%, almost double that of the agricultural sector. In 1984, according to estimates by the World Bank, Brazil's GNP per head (at average 1982–84 prices) was US $1,720. Although annual population growth is more than 2%, it was estimated that GNP per head increased at an average rate of 4.6% per year, measured in constant prices, between 1965 and 1984. The average annual increase in overall GDP, in real terms, was 9.8% in 1965–73, slowing to 4.4% in 1973–84.

Agricultural production accounted for 11% of Brazil's GDP and provided about 40% of the country's export earnings in 1983. In 1977 Brazil became the world's second largest exporter of agricultural products. The principal agricultural exports are coffee, sugar, soya beans (soybeans), orange juice, beef, poultry and cocoa, and other crops include sisal, tobacco, maize and cotton. Agricultural production declined by 3.5% in 1982, but expanded by 2.2% in 1983, and further growth of 5% and 4.1% per year was expected in 1984 and 1985 respectively. Export earnings from soya beans reached US $1,400m. in 1984. The area planted with soya beans increased by 9% in 1984, to 9.52m. ha. The soya bean crop increased from 16m. metric tons in 1984 to 18m. tons in 1985. Brazil is normally the world's leading producer of coffee, which accounted for about 8% of export revenue in 1985. In 1981 the largest coffee harvest for 16 years produced 32m. bags (each of 60 kg); subsequent frosts reduced the crop to 17.6m. bags in 1982, recovering to an estimated 29.4m. bags in 1983. The 1984 crop was estimated to be 22m. bags and generated export earnings of $2,855m.

Between May and October 1985 Brazil experienced its most severe drought for 40 years. As a consequence, agricultural output was expected to decline by 70% in 1986, with a decline of 11.4% in the crops sector. The coffee crop was expected to fall from 30m. bags in 1985 to 11.2m. bags in 1986, of which only 7m. bags would be suitable for export. In order to satisfy the domestic demand for coffee, Brazil imported 1.5m. bags in 1986, and Colombia displaced Brazil as the world's leading exporter of coffee. The 1987 crop was expected to recover to 20m.–22m. bags, and the 1988 crop was expected to reach 26m.–28m. bags. As a result of high international prices, Brazil's export earnings from coffee were expected to increase from US $2,200m. in 1985 to more than $4,000m. in 1986. Other crops affected by the drought included cotton and soya beans, which were expected to decline by 18.7% and 27.3% respectively in 1986.

Brazil is also the world's leading producer of sugar cane, and its 1985 crop was 247m. metric tons. Output of raw sugar (in which Brazil also leads the world) rose from 8.4m. metric tons in 1981/82 to 9.3m. tons in 1982/83, but sugar's share of export revenue fell from 5% to 3% during the same period. About 1m. ha were to be irrigated for wheat production, beginning in 1982, in order to reduce imports: the harvest was estimated at 4.3m. metric tons in 1985. Brazilian orange growers benefited from three years of frosts in the USA until 1982/83, when a surplus of 100,000 tons had to be put into storage. Another frost in the USA in late 1983 led to a significant increase in Brazil's overseas sales in 1984, making orange juice Brazil's fourth most important source of foreign exchange and resulting in export earnings of $1,470m. Following the recovery of the US orange juice industry, export earnings fell to $725m. in 1985. As a consequence, Brazil was expected to seek new markets in Europe. Production of cocoa has suffered from lack of investment but exports of cocoa beans and products earned $586m. in 1984. In 1983 floods destroyed 1.5m. metric tons of rice, and imports were needed. Shortages of maize, beans and cotton were also predicted, and the suspension of imported fertilizer deliveries was expected to reduce the size of the harvests. Total production of poultry meat in 1983 was estimated at 1.7m. tons, of which about 20% was exported: 90% of exports went to the Middle East. The 1986–89 Development Plan, announced in August 1985 by the new administration, stressed the importance of developing the agricultural sector to meet the domestic demand for food. The Government intended to increase the output of food crops by 4.5% annually from 1986. In 1986 the Government announced a three-year agricultural programme which envisaged investment of CZ $71,000m. in the sector. The plan's objectives included a 10% increase in annual grain production and the establishment of a National Agricultural Fund. In June 1986 the World Bank approved a loan of US $149m. to Brazil for irrigation projects in the north-east region.

Industrial production, which accounted for 38% of GDP in 1984, is concentrated on machinery, electrical goods, construction materials, rubber, sugar and wood processing, chemicals and vehicle production. Traditional industries (textiles, clothing, food and beverages) still account for 50% of total industrial production. Manufactured goods accounted for 54% of Brazil's total exports in 1983. In 1981 the economy was hit by a severe recession: industrial production fell by 10% in 1981 and 1982, and by 6.1% in 1983. Employment fell by 20% in São Paulo, the main industrial centre, between 1980 and 1983. Manufacturing, as a whole, was working at 50% of full capacity in 1983, and factories were accumulating large stocks. However, production increased by 6.1% in 1984 and by 8.3% in 1985. In 1983 Brazil's total production of crude steel was 14.7m. metric tons and exports totalled 1.2m. tons. Production increased to 18.4m. tons in 1984 and to 20.5m. tons in 1985. The Tuberão steel mill, with an annual capacity of 3.2m. tons, was inaugurated in November 1983, but future expansion of the industry has been hindered by resistance from overseas markets, and in particular from the USA, which in 1984 imposed surcharges of up to 100% on all imports of Brazilian sheet steel. Brazil was nevertheless expected to export 1.35m. metric tons of steel to the USA in 1984, compared with 1.24m. tons in 1983. The Açominas integrated steel works, inaugurated in February 1985, were expected to come into operation by the end of 1987. The steel works were to produce 2m. tons of steel annually. The Albras aluminium refinery, with an annual capacity of 320,000 tons, was inaugurated in 1986. The construction of its associated alumina smelter, Alunorte, with an annual capacity of 1.3m. tons, has been delayed, and was not expected to resume before 1987. A new processing plant at São Luís de Maranhão, opened in 1984, will be able to produce annually 100,000 tons of aluminium and 500,000 tons of alumina. Brazil is the world's sixth largest producer of motor vehicles; exports represented 20% of total production and 12.5% of Brazil's total exports in 1985. It is also the world's fifth largest exporter of armaments. In 1984 exports of military materials earned an estimated $2,400m. The country is also a major producer of naval vessels and has a diversified and successful aerospace industry, which was expected to record a turnover of $240m. in 1984.

Brazil possesses vast mineral reserves, particularly in Minas Gerais and the Amazon area, and in 1981 the Grand Carajás project (in Amazonia) was opened. Reserves of iron ore at Carajás are estimated to be 18,000m. tons. Production began in January 1986, and planned output is 35m. tons of iron ore per year by mid-1988. Investment in the project was expected to be about US $125,000m., and the value of the Carajás minerals was assessed at $543,000m. The leading mineral export is iron ore, and Brazil is the world's second largest exporter, after Australia. In 1984 Brazil exported 87.4m. tons of iron ore. New mineral discoveries, including phosphates, uranium, manganese, titanium, copper, tin and coal, are constantly being made. Brazil is the fourth largest producer of bauxite, and extensive reserves have been located in Minas Gerais and the Amazon region, where known reserves amount to 4,600m. tons. Lack of demand, however, has 'frozen' future investment. Gold deposits at Serra Pelada, found in 1980, raised Brazil's annual gold production from 14 tons in 1980 to 53.7 tons in 1983 and to an estimated 55 tons in 1984. Production declined to 37 tons in 1985. Reserves were estimated at 341 tons in 1984. The sector was expected to expand, following foreign investment of $600m. in 1986–88. Coal reserves are estimated at 15,000m. tons. Tin production increased from 13,100 tons in 1983 to 18,877 tons in 1984 and to an estimated 23,000 tons in 1985. Brazil is the world's fastest expanding producer of tin. In addition, Brazil is the world's sixth largest tin consumer and has a smelting capacity of 13,000 tons. The world's largest tin mine, Pitinga, is located in the Amazon region and has reserves of 575,000 tons. Recent discoveries of platinum could contain one-half of the world's known reserves of the mineral. Reserves of crude petroleum were estimated at 2,200m. barrels in 1986, and were expected to increase by 300%, following the discovery of the enormous 'Marlim' field in the Baia de Campos, which was thought to contain recoverable reserves of more than 2,000m. barrels. Dependence on imported petroleum was reduced from 82.5% in 1979 to 58% in 1983, when domestic output averaged 340,000 barrels per day (b/d). Production averaged 474,000 b/d in 1984, and 564,000 b/d in 1985, and was expected to average 625,000 b/d in 1986. To reduce the cost of oil imports, an alternative energy plan, Proalcool, was devised, aiming to replace 40% of petrol consumption by combustible alcohol, derived from sugar and cassava, by 1985. In 1984 about 20% of road motor vehicles were alcohol-powered, as were 91% of all new cars produced. In view of the decline in world petroleum prices and the subsequent fall in Brazil's petroleum import bill, the Government banned the construction of new plants for the programme until 1989, in an attempt to reduce costs. It was believed that Brazil would achieve self-sufficiency in fuel by 1993. Intensive offshore exploration has revealed proven natural gas reserves of 81,600m. cu m. A new field, 'Albacora', may contain reserves of 150,000m. cu m. Production reached 15m. cu. m per day in 1985.

In 1986 some 95% of Brazil's total electricity consumption was hydro-generated. The Itaipú hydroelectric power station, on the Paraná river, has a generating capacity of 12,600 MW and is the largest in the world. This project, undertaken with Paraguay and inaugurated in 1984, will increase Brazil's installed capacity to 77,500 MW by 1990. The Tucuruí plant, on the Tocantins river, came into operation in November 1984. The estimated total hydroelectric generating potential is 213,000 MW. Brazil plans to construct two dams, at Santa Isabel and São Félix, to supply 4,000 MW to the northern region, beginning in 1992. However, the new Government's austerity programme resulted in the cancellation in July 1985 of 10 planned hydroelectric projects and development of the Tucuruí plant. It is estimated that the nuclear programme will be producing 2.5% of the nation's requirements by the late 1980s. In 1977, following the discovery of two large uranium deposits, Brazil signed an agreement with the Federal Republic of Germany to build eight nuclear power stations by the year 2000. The programme has been delayed: in 1983 one of the stations, Angra I, commenced operation; work on Angra II was expected to be completed in 1995, but work on Angra III has been suspended until 1995. Plans for two other stations were also suspended. Further delays in the development of the sector were expected to result from the Government's austerity programme. By 1983 Brazil was able to produce plutonium.

Between 1967 and 1974 Brazil's GDP grew, in real terms, by an average of 11.3% per year. The 'economic miracle' ended in 1974 at a time of worldwide recession, but real growth averaged 6.5% annually in 1975–80. GDP grew by 7.2% in 1980, but fell by 1.6% in 1981. It rose by 0.9% in 1982 but fell by 3.2% in 1983. GDP expanded by 4.4% in 1984. Unemployment has continued to increase and, including underemployment, may affect 60% of the labour force. It was estimated that 1.5m. jobs were lost between 1980 and 1983. Inflation has also continued to rise, reaching 211% in 1983. Inflation rose to 224% in 1984 and, in spite of a decline in the monthly rate to 8.9% in July 1985, a further increase to 234% was recorded in 1985. Following a devaluation of the cruzeiro by 23% in 1983, the Government has continued its policy of regular 'mini-devaluations'.

Large-scale foreign borrowing for huge, unproductive 'prestige' projects, combined with the world recession and resultant low prices for primary exports, led Brazil to incur a massive foreign debt, the largest of any country in the world. In 1982 debt servicing was consuming 85% of total export revenue, and more borrowing was needed to prevent a moratorium. Brazil was granted a loan of $4,400m. from foreign commercial banks in February 1983, and a further loan of $5,400m. was agreed with the IMF in March. In January 1984 Brazil secured a loan of $6,500m. from commercial banks. Arrears in service payments on its foreign debt were cleared in February, when Brazil received the first tranche of the loan, which amounted to $3,000m.

In spite of Brazil's failure to meet the IMF's targets for 1983, the economy appeared to make an encouraging recovery in 1984, when GDP grew by 4.4%. The improvement was principally due to a 25% increase in exports, mostly from the agricultural sector, and a lower domestic demand for imports. As a consequence, Brazil recorded a trade surplus of $13,086m. in 1984. A trade surplus of $12,466m. was achieved in 1985. Brazil was able to meet the IMF's requirements for the first half of 1984, but increases in the US prime interest rate, which reached 13% in June, posed severe problems for debt servicing. Reserves of foreign exchange increased from $4,355m. at the end of 1983 to $11,507m. at the end of 1984, which meant that Brazil did not require further funds from international banks. Reserves were $10,604m. at the end of 1985, and stood at $9,263m. in May 1986. Brazil's chronic deficit in the current account of the balance of payments ended in 1984, when a small surplus, the first since 1965, was achieved. A small deficit was recorded in 1985. Brazil's foreign debt reached $99,000m. in 1984 and was forecast to rise to $102,000m. in 1985, when its repayment obligations were expected to reach $9,718m.

In January 1985 Brazil reached a preliminary agreement with its commercial bank creditors on the rescheduling of $45,300m. in debts falling due between 1985 and 1991. In February, however, negotiations were halted, following the IMF's decision to suspend its economic agreement with Brazil. The IMF's move was thought to have been prompted by the substantial increase in the money supply (by 203% in the year to March 1985). Attempts to reach a new agreement on economic targets with the IMF were hampered by a dispute within the Cabinet between the Minister of Finance, who favoured the IMF's policy, and the Minister of Planning. In July the Government introduced an austerity programme which was expected to result in reductions of $3,600m. in government expenditure, and an increase of $2,900m. in tax revenues. Some 200,000 jobs were expected to be lost as a result of the programme. Contrary to the IMF's proposals for lower inflation and austerity, President Sarney rejected economic recession as a means of enabling Brazil to meet its debt commitments. Instead, the Government's 1986–89 Development Plan emphasized the need for economic growth and social spending. In addition, the Government planned to allocate $2,500m. to combat unemployment and poverty.

Throughout 1986 the Government maintained its opposition to the IMF's involvement in the formulation of economic policy. However, Brazil's commercial bank creditors were reluctant to agree to any rescheduling plan in the absence of an IMF-approved economic programme. In addition, relations between the Government and the banks were adversely affected by the Government's initial refusal to reimburse any of the US $455m. in losses incurred by foreign banks when three Brazilian banks collapsed in late 1985.

In February 1986 the Government, prompted by an increase of 16.2% in the monthly rate of inflation for January, announced an economic stabilization programme, the Cruzado Plan, under which a new currency, the cruzado, was introduced; prices were to be 'frozen' for one year; and salaries were to be readjusted in accordance with the rate of inflation.

Following the introduction of the Cruzado Plan, Brazil was able to reach a preliminary agreement with its commercial bank creditors on the rescheduling of $31,000m. in debts falling due in 1985/86. The agreement was signed in July. The Cruzado Plan was well received, both in Brazil and internationally, and recorded an initial success when the consumer price index declined by 1.5% in March.

One unforeseen consequence of the anti-inflation programme was a dramatic rise in consumer spending, which the Government intended to curb by introducing a further programme of economic adjustment. Under this programme, the Government was to honour its commitment to the redistribution of wealth in favour of the poor by allocating increased funds to health, education, housing and food. The budget for social programmes was to increase by 51% in 1987. In addition, the Government intended to restrict debt-servicing payments to between 2% and 2.5% of GDP, and to seek a multi-year rescheduling of Brazil's $104,000m. foreign debt without the IMF's assistance. In October the cruzado was devalued by 1.8% in relation to the US dollar. Following the Government's success at the congressional elections in November, it was able to implement the proposed new series of austerity measures, Cruzado Plan II, which included increases of up to 100% on taxes on luxury goods and an extensive revision of the consumer price index. After real GDP growth of 7.4% was achieved in 1985, growth of 8% was expected in 1986. The trade surplus of $6,100m. for the period January–June 1986 offered considerable encouragement for Brazil's immediate economic prospects.

In August 1985 Brazil and Argentina signed a trade accord (see chapter on Argentina p. 352).

Social Welfare

The social security system, in existence since 1923, was rationalized in 1960, and the National Institute for Social Security (INPS) was formed in 1966. All social welfare programmes were brought together in 1977 under the National System of Social Insurance and Assistance (SINPAS).

The INPS is in charge of benefits to urban and rural employees and their dependants. Employers and employees contribute 53.19%, the Federal Union 8.23% and other sources 36.37%. SINPAS revenue for 1983 was estimated at CR$6,636,898m. equal to 5.48% of GNP. Benefits include sickness benefit, invalidity, old age, length of service and widows' pensions, maternity and family allowances and grants. There are three government agencies: IAPAS collects contributions and revenue and supplies funds, INAMPS is in charge of medical care and CEME (Central Medicines) supplies medicines at a low price.

In 1982 there were 171,585 physicians in Brazil's hospitals, and the country had 11,590 hospital establishments, with a total of 530,501 beds. The private medical sector controls 90% of Brazil's hospitals. In response to a highly critical report on the health services, made in 1981, the Government introduced a health and welfare programme, Prevsaúde. This has been replaced by the Plan for the Reorientation of Health Aid, which proposes to adapt available resources to the requirements of the public. The plan has been co-ordinated by the Ministries of Social Welfare, Education and Health and by the State and Municipal Secretaries for Health. Under the 1986–89 Development Plan, announced in August 1985, US $4,000m. will be invested in social development schemes.

The welfare of the dwindling population of indigenous American Indians is the responsibility of the National Indian Foundation (FUNAI), which was formed to assign homelands to the Indians, most of whom are landless and threatened by the exploitation of the Amazon forest, and lack political rights.

Education

Education is free in official pre-primary schools and is compulsory between the ages of seven and 14 years. Primary education begins at seven years of age and lasts for eight years. Secondary education, beginning at 15 years of age, lasts for four years and is also free in official schools. In 1984 an estimated 79.5% of children aged seven to 14 attended primary schools, while only 14.4% of those aged 15 to 17 were enrolled at secondary schools. The Federal Government is responsible for higher education, and in 1984 there were 67 universities, of which 47 were state-run. There are a large number of private institutions in all levels of education.

Despite an anti-illiteracy drive, launched in 1971, the adult illiteracy rate stood at 21.8% in 1983, with regional variations from 15.7% in the south of the country to 55% in the northeast.

Tourism

In 1980 there were about 1.6m. visitors, but arrivals fell to 1.4m. in 1981 and to 1.1m. in 1982. In 1983 about 1.4m. tourists visited Brazil. Rio de Janeiro, with its famous beaches, is the centre of the tourist trade. Like Salvador, Recife and other towns, it has excellent examples of Portuguese colonial and modern architecture. The modern capital, Brasília, incorporates a new concept of city planning and is the nation's show-piece. Other attractions are the Iguaçu Falls, the seventh largest (by volume) in the world, and the tropical forests of the Amazon basin.

Public Holidays

1987: 1 January (New Year's Day), 21 April (Tiradentes Day), 1 May (Labour Day), 28 May (Ascension Day), 18 June (Corpus Christi), 7 September (Independence Day), 12 October (Our Lady Aparecida, patroness of Brazil), 2 November (All Souls' Day), 15 November (Proclamation of the Republic), 25 December (Christmas Day).

1988: 1 January (New Year's Day), 21 April (Tiradentes Day), 1 May (Labour Day), 12 May (Ascension Day), 2 June (Corpus Christi), 7 September (Independence Day), 12 October (Our Lady Aparecida, patroness of Brazil), 2 November (All Souls' Day), 15 November (Proclamation of the Republic), 25 December (Christmas Day).

Other local holidays include 20 January (Foundation of Rio de Janeiro) and 25 January (Foundation of São Paulo).

Weights and Measures

The metric system is in force.

Currency and Exchange Rates

100 centavos = 1 cruzado (CZ $).

Exchange rates (30 September 1986):
  £1 sterling = 20.026 cruzados;
  US $1 = 13.840 cruzados.

BRAZIL

Statistical Survey

Sources (unless otherwise stated): Banco Central do Brasil, Brasília, DF; tel. (061) 224-1453; telex (061) 1702; Fundação Instituto Brasileiro de Geografia e Estatística (FIBGE), Av. Franklin Roosevelt 166, 20.021 Rio de Janeiro, RJ; tel. (021) 252-3501.

Area and Population

AREA, POPULATION AND DENSITY

Area (sq km)	8,511,965*
Population (census results)†	
1 September 1970	93,139,037
1 September 1980	
Males	59,123,361
Females	59,879,345
Total	119,002,706
Population (official estimates at mid-year)†	
1983	129,662,000
1984	132,580,000
1985	135,564,000
Density (per sq km) at mid-1985	15.9

* 3,286,488 sq miles.
† Excluding Indian jungle population, numbering 45,429 in 1950. Census results also exclude an adjustment for underenumeration.

ADMINISTRATIVE DIVISIONS
(mid-1985, official estimates)

State	Population ('000)	Capital
Acre (AC)	358	Rio Branco
Alagoas (AL)	2,245	Maceió
Amazonas (AM)	1,728	Manaus
Bahia (BA)	10,731	Salvador
Ceará (CE)	5,893	Fortaleza
Espírito Santo (ES)	2,287	Vitória
Goiás (GO)	4,453	Goiânia
Maranhão (MA)	4,641	São Luís
Mato Grosso (MT)	1,480	Cuiabá
Mato Grosso do Sul (MS)	1,604	Campo Grande
Minas Gerais (MG)	14,600	Belo Horizonte
Pará (PA)	4,201	Belém
Paraíba (PB)	3,016	João Pessoa
Paraná (PR)	8,074	Curitiba
Pernambuco (PE)	6,776	Recife
Piauí (PI)	2,430	Teresina
Rio de Janeiro (RJ)	12,767	Rio de Janeiro
Rio Grande do Norte (RN)	2,126	Natal
Rio Grande do Sul (RS)	8,486	Porto Alegre
Rondônia (RO)	731	Porto Velho
Santa Catarina (SC)	4,096	Florianópolis
São Paulo (SP)	29,657	São Paulo
Sergipe (SE)	1,287	Aracajú
Distrito Federal (DF)	1,579	Brasília
Federal Territory:		
Amapá (AP)	214	Macapá
Roraima (RR)	104	Boa Vista

PRINCIPAL TOWNS (estimated population at mid-1985)

Brasília (capital)	1,576,657		Natal	512,241
São Paulo	10,099,086		Maceió	484,094
Rio de Janeiro	5,615,149		Teresina	476,102
Belo Horizonte	2,122,073		Santos	461,096
Salvador	1,811,367		São João de	
Fortaleza	1,588,709		Meriti	459,103
Nova Iguaçu	1,324,639		Niterói	442,706
Recife	1,289,627		Jaboatão	411,341
Curitiba	1,285,027		João Pessoa	397,715
Porto Alegre	1,275,483		Campo Grande	386,520
Belém	1,120,777		Contagem	386,272
Goiânia	928,046		Ribeirão Preto	384,604
Campinas	845,057		São José dos	
Manaus	834,541		Campos	374,526
São Gonçalo	731,061		Campos	367,134
Guarulhos	717,723		Aracaju	361,544
Duque de Caxias	666,128		Feira de Santana	356,660
Santo André	637,010		Juíz de Fora	350,687
Osasco	594,249		Londrina	347,707
São Bernardo do			Olinda	335,889
Campo	565,620		Sorocaba	328,787
São Luís	564,434			

BIRTHS AND DEATHS:
Average annual birth rate 33 per 1,000 in 1970–80; death rate 8.2 per 1,000 in 1970–80.

ECONOMICALLY ACTIVE POPULATION
(persons aged 10 years and over, 1983 estimates)

	Males	Females	Total
Agriculture, hunting, forestry and fishing	10,028,173	3,086,974	13,115,147
Manufacturing	4,991,342	1,783,444	6,774,786
Construction	4,320,158	307,574	4,627,732
Other industrial activities	801,499	88,337	889,836
Wholesale and retail trade	3,550,179	1,561,988	5,112,167
Transport and communications	1,643,552	134,101	1,777,653
Services (incl. restaurants and hotels)	2,734,850	5,158,000	7,892,850
Social services	991,316	2,616,279	3,607,595
Public administration	1,518,747	491,799	2,010,546
Other activities (not adequately described)	1,880,560	777,621	2,658,181
Persons seeking employment	1,668,144	806,063	2,474,207
Total economically active	34,128,520	16,812,180	50,940,700

1984: Total economically active population 52,443,112 (males 35,084,825, females 17,358,287).

Agriculture

PRINCIPAL CROPS ('000 metric tons)

	1983	1984	1985
Coffee*	3,343	2,841	3,753
Cotton (lint)	552	618	n.a.
Maize	18,731	21,164	22,020
Dry beans	1,581	2,626	2,548
Rice (paddy)	7,742	9,027	9,019
Cassava (Manioc)	21,848	21,466	23,111
Wheat	2,237	1,983	4,323
Potatoes	1,827	2,171	1,989
Soybeans	14,582	15,541	18,278
Sugar cane	216,037	222,318	246,542
Cocoa beans	380	330	420
Oranges	9,476	13,372	n.a.
Tobacco (leaves)	393	414	411
Bananas	6,607	6,968	n.a.
Groundnuts (in shell)	284	249	339
Natural rubber	35	33	n.a.

* Figures are in terms of dry cherries. The proportion of coffee beans is estimated at 50%.

LIVESTOCK PRODUCTS ('000 metric tons)

	1982	1983	1984
Beef and veal	2,397	2,360	2,293*
Mutton and lamb†	29	29	29
Goats' meat†	23	23	23
Pig meat*	970	950	860
Horse meat	25	20†	20†
Poultry meat	1,619	1,680	1,616†
Cows' milk	11,817	11,818	10,500*
Goats' milk†	90	90	90
Butter*	70	70	70
Cheese†	59	59	59
Dried milk*	170	180	200
Hen eggs	829*	785*	835†
Wool:			
greasy	30	31	30†
scoured	19*	19*	19†
Cattle hides (fresh)*	308	322	310

* Unofficial estimates.   † FAO estimates.
Source: FAO, *Production Yearbook*.

LIVESTOCK ('000 head)

	1982	1983	1984
Cattle	123,488	124,186	127,655
Horses	5,260	5,289	5,442
Asses	1,316	1,237	1,246
Mules	1,829	1,836	1,946
Pigs	33,176	31,678	32,327
Sheep	18,588	18,121	18,447
Goats	9,037	8,936	9,675

* Chickens (million): 470 in 1982; 451 in 1983; 450† in 1984.
* Ducks (million): 6 in 1982; 6 in 1983; 5† in 1984.
* Turkeys (million): 3 in 1982; 3 in 1983; 2† in 1984.
* Source: FAO, *Production Yearbook*.   †FAO estimate.

Forestry

ROUNDWOOD REMOVALS
(FAO estimates, '000 cubic metres, excluding bark)

	1982	1983	1984
Sawlogs, veneer logs and logs for sleepers*	31,744	31,744	31,744
Pulpwood*	20,900	20,900	20,900
Other industrial wood	4,809	4,917	5,026
Fuel wood	157,370	160,921	164,507
Total	214,823	218,482	222,177

* Assumed to be unchanged since 1980.
Source: FAO, *Yearbook of Forest Products*.

SAWNWOOD PRODUCTION ('000 cubic metres)

	1979	1980	1981
Coniferous (softwood)	7,334	7,143	7,475
Broadleaved (hardwood)	6,736	7,738	8,377
Total	14,070	14,881	15,852

1982–84: Annual production as in 1981 (FAO estimates).
Source: FAO, *Yearbook of Forest Products*.

Fishing

(metric tons)

	1982	1983	1984
Total catch	833,933	880,696	958,908

Mining

	1982	1983	1984
Bauxite ('000 metric tons)	6,290	7,199	10,355
Coal ('000 metric tons)	19,206	21,367	22,776
Iron ore ('000 metric tons)*	119,939	114,190	143,842
Manganese ore ('000 metric tons)*	2,883	2,594	3,494
Lead ('000 metric tons)*	306	372	366
Dolomite ('000 metric tons)	1,954	1,714	1,917
Sea salt ('000 metric tons)	2,888	3,259	3,578
Gold (kilograms)	25,517	53,684	37,218
Silver (kilograms)	23,250	15,112	25,792
Crude petroleum ('000 cu metres)	15,080	19,141	26,838
Natural gas (million cu metres)	3,028	4,013	4,902

* Figures refer to the gross weight of ores. The metal content (in '000 metric tons) was: Iron 88,695 in 1983, 112,133 in 1984; Manganese 1,898 in 1983, 2,457 in 1984; Lead 19.4 in 1982, 18.8 in 1983, 16.7 in 1984.

1985: Crude petroleum 31,709,000 cu metres; Natural gas 5,466 million cu metres.

Source: *Anuário Mineral Brasileiro*, Ministério das Minas e Energia.

Other ores (metal content, metric tons): Copper 24,500 in 1982, 40,000 in 1983, 44,376 in 1984; Nickel 14,451 in 1982, 15,561 in 1983, 23,532 in 1984; Zinc 71,000* in 1982, 73,000* in 1983; Tin 22,769 in 1983, 33,920 in 1984; Chromium 111,000 in 1983, 129,000 in 1984; Tungsten 1,842 in 1983, 1,892 in 1984; Uranium 290 in 1982, 300† in 1983.

* Estimate (Source: US Bureau of Mines).
† Estimate (Source UN, *Industrial Statistics Yearbook*).

Industry

SELECTED PRODUCTS

		1983	1984	1985
Asphalt	'000 metric tons	674	782	n.a.
Electric power	million kWh	161,715	176,763	188,595
Coke	'000 metric tons	4,642	n.a.	n.a.
Pig iron	'000 metric tons	12,945	17,220	18,960
Crude steel	'000 metric tons	14,671	18,385	20,450
Cement*	'000 metric tons	20,870	19,497	20,635
Tyres	'000 units	19,835	22,718	24,928
Synthetic rubber	metric tons	220,916	258,383	265,015
Passenger cars	units	748,371	679,396	759,047
Commercial vehicles	units	148,091	185,267	207,578
Tractors	units	26,627	49,785	48,976
Fertilizers	'000 metric tons	1,465	2,110	n.a.
Sugar	'000 metric tons	9,027	8,777	7,995
Newsprint	'000 metric tons	120	131	n.a.
Other paper and board	'000 metric tons	3,297	3,611	n.a.

* Portland cement only.

Finance

CURRENCY AND EXCHANGE RATES

Monetary Units
100 centavos = 1 cruzado (CZ $).

Sterling and Dollar Equivalents (30 September 1986)
£1 sterling = 20.026 cruzados;
US $1 = 13.840 cruzados;
1,000 cruzados = £49.93 = $72.25.

Average Exchange Rates (cruzados per US $)
1983   0.577
1984   1.848
1985   6.200

Note: In 1986 the cruzeiro (CR $) was replaced by a new currency unit, the cruzado, equivalent to 1,000 cruzeiros. Notes and coins issued in cruzeiros were to circulate concurrently with the cruzado, and were to remain as legal tender until March 1987. Some figures in this Survey continue to be in terms of cruzeiros.

BUDGET (CR $ million)

Revenue	1983	1984	1985
Taxes	6,536,581	14,987,695	59,389,261
Patrimonial revenue	152,000	329,408	440,410
Industrial revenue	1,213	3,023	8,046
Currency transfers	72	4,948	28,801
Miscellaneous	2,095,924	5,966,850	21,784,692
Other revenue	176,210	294,676	665,090
National Treasury total	8,989,000	21,586,600	82,316,300
Other resources	1,058,300	2,085,400	6,555,815
General total	10,047,300	23,672,000	88,872,115

Source: Secretaria de Planejamento da Presidência da República and Secretaria de Orçamento e Finanças.

MONEY SUPPLY (CR $'000 million at 31 December)

	1983	1984	1985
Currency outside banks	1,881	6,247	23,829
Demand deposits at commercial banks	4,830	13,550	57,883

Source: IMF, *International Financial Statistics*.

COST OF LIVING
(Consumer Price Index, Rio de Janeiro. Base: March 1980 = 100)

	1983	1984	1985
Foodstuffs	3,852	12,239	41,290
Clothing	3,785	11,194	42,836
Housing	5,746	14,665	42,245
Household articles	4,773	14,228	45,133
Medicines and hygiene products	4,484	12,804	43,828
Personal services	4,132	11,746	38,627
Utilities and urban transport	5,539	15,619	47,939
All items	4,312	12,796	41,838

Source: Fundação Getúlio Vargas.

Expenditure	1983	1984	1985
Legislative and auxiliary	53,828	116,271	433,024
Judiciary	58,325	112,643	349,924
Executive	4,551,684	10,171,733	37,323,428
Presidency (including Planning Secretariat)	143,177	284,931	914,560
Air	263,351	843,400	3,177,450
Agriculture	307,564	761,954	2,212,258
Communications	100,012	81,818	585,665
Education and culture	617,244	1,440,140	5,452,042
Army	297,194	615,040	2,123,301
Finance	104,862	191,680	597,273
Industry and commerce	212,687	269,270	763,433
Interior	126,813	419,121	942,357
Justice	26,033	54,260	192,920
Marine	219,338	536,654	1,899,633
Mines and power	151,440	152,865	629,548
Foreign affairs	70,681	218,250	687,370
Health	106,869	336,213	1,777,909
Work and social welfare	208,623	508,402	3,222,288
Transport	1,595,796	3,457,735	12,145,421
Unspecified items	5,383,463	13,271,353	50,765,739
Total	10,047,300	23,672,000	88,872,115

CENTRAL BANK RESERVES
(US $ million at 31 December)

	1983	1984	1985
Gold	207	488	1,004
IMF special drawing rights	—	1	1
Foreign exchange	4,355	11,507	10,604
Total	4,562	11,996	11,609

Source: IMF, *International Financial Statistics*.

NATIONAL ACCOUNTS (CZ $ '000 million)

	1981	1982	1983
Gross domestic product (GDP) at factor cost	23,120.1	45,713.7	107,982.9
Income paid abroad	1,015.4	2,590.4	6,839.9
Gross national product (GNP) at factor cost	22,104.7	43,123.3	101,143.0
Indrect tax *less* subsidies	2,511.7	5,101.6	12,284.6
GNP at market prices	24,616.4	48,224.9	113,427.6
Private	22,061.8	42,997.3	103,002.7
Governmental	2,554.6	5,227.6	10,424.9
Total domestic expenditure	25,724.8	51,150.7	117,437.3
Private consumption expenditure (incl. increase in stocks)	17,998.2	35,296.4	85,696.0
Government consumption expenditure	2,285.2	5,056.7	11,327.6
Gross fixed capital formation	5,441.4	10,797.6	20,413.7
Balance of exports and imports of goods and services	−93.0	−335.4	2,830.2
GDP at market prices	25,631.8	50,815.3	120,267.5

Source: Fundação Getúlio Vargas.

BALANCE OF PAYMENTS (US $ million)

	1983	1984	1985
Merchandise exports f.o.b.	21,898	27,002	25,634
Merchandise imports f.o.b.	−15,429	−13,916	−13,168
Trade balance	6,469	13,086	12,466
Exports of services	2,443	3,203	3,675
Imports of services	−15,857	−16,418	−16,569
Balance on goods and services	−6,945	−129	−428
Private unrequited transfers (net)	106	161	139
Government unrequited transfers (net)	2	10	16
Current balance	−6,837	42	−273
Direct capital investment (net)	1,373	1,556	1,267
Other long-term capital (net)	−2,739	−4,358	−7,944
Short-term capital (net)	−1,157	−3,195	−1,614
Net errors and omissions	−585	398	−530
Total (net monetary movements)	−9,945	−5,557	−9,094
Monetization of gold	557	336	257
Valuation changes (net)	56	229	−672
Exceptional financing (net)	9,360	10,434	8,968
Official financing (net)	−1,305	491	−385
Changes in reserves	−1,277	5,933	−926

Source: IMF, *International Financial Statistics*.

OVERSEAS INVESTMENT IN BRAZIL, 1985 (US $ '000)

Countries of origin	Investments	Reinvestments	Total
Belgium	186,482	119,849	306,331
Canada	834,478	417,524	1,252,002
France	470,776	455,052	925,828
Germany, Federal Republic	2,471,644	1,074,994	3,546,638
Japan	2,068,347	316,829	2,385,176
Luxembourg	360,035	72,457	432,492
Netherlands	369,028	149,114	518,142
Netherlands Antilles	209,195	20,704	229,899
Panama	792,518	378,932	1,171,450
Sweden	294,881	112,699	407,580
Switzerland	1,214,368	858,463	2,072,831
United Kingdom	773,378	656,418	1,429,796
USA	5,287,756	2,767,254	8,055,010
Others	2,592,446	338,863	2,931,309
Total	17,925,332	7,739,152	25,664,484

BRAZIL
Statistical Survey

External Trade

PRINCIPAL COMMODITIES (US $ '000)

Imports f.o.b.	1983	1984	1985
Vegetable products	1,136,828	1,073,543	958,117
Mineral products	8,791,801	7,556,886	6,454,820
Products of the chemical and allied industries	1,322,272	1,453,016	1,478,920
Plastic materials, resins and rubber	303,251	306,642	331,128
Paper-making materials, paper	167,917	135,853	119,206
Base metals and articles of base metal	375,712	411,188	417,918
Machinery and mechanical appliances, electrical equipment	1,894,447	1,648,162	1,971,451
Transport equipment	610,955	502,987	508,455
Optical, photographic and measuring instruments, clocks and watches	322,852	252,121	371,498
Total (incl. others)	15,428,925	13,915,821	13,153,491

Exports f.o.b.	1983	1984	1985
Live animals and animal products	658,871	729,146	751,584
Vegetable products	2,730,985	3,369,984	3,489,341
Coffee	2,347,396	2,855,975	2,632,471
Animal and vegetable oils and fats	605,579	865,149	848,116
Food, beverages, vinegar and tobacco	4,947,382	5,738,176	4,479,293
Cocoa beans	283,773	248,876	360,614
Sugar	526,802	586,293	368,682
Tobacco leaf	457,924	448,821	437,427
Mineral products	2,917,232	3,722,458	3,548,774
Haematite	1,513,010	1,605,353	1,658,143
Products of chemical and allied industries	906,034	1,137,643	1,123,947
Hides and skins	261,891	286,009	262,385
Wood, charcoal and cork	319,233	330,784	303,306
Textiles and textile articles	1,064,350	1,220,816	1,000,608
Cotton (raw)	188,510	41,556	76,754
Machinery and mechanical appliances, electrical equipment	1,553,956	1,986,729	2,166,397
Transport equipment	1,452,491	1,353,550	1,694,157
Total (incl. others)	21,899,314	27,005,336	25,639,011

PRINCIPAL TRADING PARTNERS (US $ '000 f.o.b.)

Imports	1983	1984	1985
Argentina	358,074	511,066	468,865
Belgium-Luxembourg	74,009	78,290	75,174
Canada	493,365	509,585	397,942
Chile	163,952	224,800	216,282
France	456,154	371,482	301,955
Germany, Federal Republic	704,661	628,993	863,551
Italy	213,416	202,866	187,583
Japan	560,728	553,327	549,879
Netherlands	159,675	141,532	163,716
Poland	194,125	138,553	137,179
Saudi Arabia	2,219,997	1,364,592	945,394
Sweden	144,326	65,385	92,112
Switzerland	224,323	182,328	224,867
USSR	164,152	144,744	63,718
United Kingdom	228,941	278,267	251,131
USA	2,381,547	2,256,091	2,575,321
Venezuela	663,363	541,663	257,777
Total (incl. others)	15,428,925	13,915,821	13,153,491

Imports (US $ million): Iraq 2,071 in 1983, 2,018 in 1984, 1,800 in 1985; Kuwait 272 in 1983, 227 in 1984.

Exports	1983	1984	1985
Argentina	654,627	853,110	547,793
Belgium-Luxembourg	503,088	638,368	569,761
Canada	311,781	407,558	414,332
Chile	192,838	280,854	238,756
Denmark	103,357	123,475	112,321
France	890,670	836,347	779,674
Germany, Federal Republic	1,130,716	1,255,555	1,274,415
Italy	977,237	1,115,397	1,124,878
Japan	1,432,694	1,515,323	1,394,103
Mexico	173,175	285,147	220,157
Netherlands	1,254,186	1,360,523	1,551,944
Nigeria	195,434	653,708	841,710
Norway	88,001	104,048	84,498
Peru	74,776	124,269	92,058
Poland	125,464	211,451	161,604
Saudi Arabia	386,658	261,412	168,029
Spain	526,573	495,427	523,128
Sweden	176,359	232,525	181,016
Switzerland	108,317	160,829	165,397
USSR	669,157	402,360	450,199
United Kingdom	718,564	708,169	663,339
USA	4,989,724	7,603,905	6,689,294
Venezuela	268,895	364,955	302,810
Total (incl. others)	21,899,314	27,005,336	25,639,011

Transport

RAILWAYS

	1982	1983	1984
Passengers ('000)	461,009	499,484	577,699
Passenger-km (million)	13,265	13,796	15,415
Passenger revenue (million cruzeiros)	19,528	37,893	97,207
Freight ('000 metric tons)	175,191	172,266	205,662
Freight ton-km (million)	78,022	74,966	92,421
Freight revenue (million cruzeiros)	180,555	428,322	1,517,923

Source: Empresa Brasileira de Planejamento de Transportes (GEIPOT).

ROAD TRAFFIC (motor vehicles in use at 31 December)

	1982	1983	1984
Passenger cars	8,207,437	8,761,457	9,198,447
Lorries	901,753	929,712	959,714
Buses	120,237	126,501	129,947
Commercial vehicles	759,690	812,861	861,372

Source: GEIPOT.

SHIPPING

	1982	1983	1984
Brazilian fleet (vessels)	1,788	1,890	2,135
Capacity ('000 dwt)	9,385	9,355	10,001
Freight (million metric tons):			
Total shipping	163.5	155.0	n.a.
Brazilian share (percentage)	48.4	44.5	n.a.

Source: Sunamam.

CIVIL AVIATION (embarked passengers, mail and cargo)

	1982	1983	1984
Number of passengers ('000)	14,205	13,538	12,995
Freight (metric tons)	223,208	254,840	363,529
Mail (metric tons)	3,931	16,057	16,819

Source: GEIPOT and Departamento de Aviação Civil (DAC).

Tourism

	1981	1982	1983*
Arrivals	1,357,879	1,146,881	1,400,000

* Provisional estimate.

Education

(1984)

	Institutions	Teachers	Students
Pre-primary	37,337	109,514	2,481,848
First grade	191,004	1,016,175	24,789,318
Second grade	9,107	214,225	2,951,624
Higher	847	120,632	1,399,539

Source: Serviço de Estatística da Educação e Cultura.

Directory

The Constitution

A revised constitution was introduced on 20 October 1969; the following is a summary of the main provisions (major subsequent amendments are listed below on p. 559):

Brazil is a Federative Republic consisting of 23 states, one Federal District and three Territories indissolubly united under a representative form of government to constitute the Union. The Federal District is the capital of the Union.

The Union's competence includes maintaining relations with foreign states and making treaties with them, and taking part in international organizations; declaring war and making peace; decreeing a state of siege; organizing the armed forces, planning and guaranteeing national security, issuing currency; supervising credits, etc.; establishing national services, including communications, development and education services; legislating on the execution of the Constitution and federal services and on civil, commercial, penal, procedural, electoral, agrarian, maritime and labour law. The Union, States, Federal District and Municipalities are forbidden to make any distinction between Brazilians, establish any religious cults or churches against the public interest, and to deny public documents.

The Union may intervene in state affairs only in matters of extreme urgency, such as national security, and then only by Presidential decree. The States are responsible for electing their Governors by universal suffrage by direct secret ballot. The state law will decree the establishment of Municipalities, after due consultation with the local population; it will also decree the division of the States into districts; municipal organization may vary from state to state.

LEGISLATIVE POWER

The legislative power is exercised by the National Congress, which is composed of the Chamber of Deputies and the Federal Senate. Elections for deputies and senators take place simultaneously throughout the country; candidates for Congress must be Brazilian by birth and have full exercise of their political rights. They must be at least 21 years of age in the case of deputies and at least 35 years of age in the case of senators. Congress meets twice a year in ordinary sessions, and extraordinary sessions may be convened on demand of a third of the members of either House or the President. Each Chamber arranges its own internal procedure.

The Chamber of Deputies is made up of representatives of the people, elected by direct secret ballot by men and women over 18 years of age, for a period of four years. The number of inhabitants determines the number of deputies per state. Each Territory will have one deputy.

The Federal Senate is composed of representatives of the States, elected by direct secret ballot. Each State will elect three senators with a mandate for eight years, with elections after four years of one-third of the members and after another four years of the remaining two-thirds. Each Senator is elected with his substitute.

The Senate approves, by secret ballot, the choice of Magistrates, when required by the Constitution; of the Attorney-General of the Republic, of the Ministers of the Accounts Tribunal, of the Governor of the Federal District, of the Territorial Governors and of the permanent heads of diplomatic missions.

The National Congress is responsible for legislating on all matters within the competence of the Union; national and regional plans and programmes, the strength of the armed forces in times of peace and territorial limits. Both houses vote on the budget in joint session. It is also responsible for making definitive resolutions on Presidential treaties, authorizing the President to leave the country, declaring war and approving boundary changes in the States or Territories. The Executive power must send any bills proposed by the President to the National Congress within 15 days of signing. Constitutional amendments must be proposed by at least one-third of the total number of members of both houses or by the President. Amendments are ratified by a simple majority. No changes may be made to the Constitution during a state of siege. Any Presidential bill must be considered by Congress within 45 days if so requested by the President. The President is exclusively responsible for legislation concerning finance, creating new public offices, etc., and matters concerning the administration of the Federal District and the Territories.

EXECUTIVE POWER

Executive power is exercised by the President of the Republic, aided by the Ministers of State. Candidates for the Presidency and Vice-Presidency must be Brazilian-born, be in full exercise of their political rights and be over 35 years of age. The President and Vice-President will be elected by a simple majority in open session of an electoral college composed of all members of the National Congress and delegates appointed by the State Legislatures on the basis of three for each state and one more for each 500,000 voters registered in the state. The President holds office for a term of five years and is not eligible for re-election. If the President violates any of his responsibilities he may be impeached by a two-thirds majority of the Deputies and judged by the Supreme Tribunal or the Senate according to the nature of his crime.

The Ministers of State are chosen by the President and their duties include carrying out the President's decrees, expediting instructions for the enactment of laws, decrees and regulations, and presentation to the President of an annual report of their activities.

National security is the responsibility of every citizen. There is a National Security Council, composed of the President and the Vice-President of the Republic, all the Ministers of State and the Chiefs of Staff of the armed services.

JUDICIAL POWER

Judicial power in the Union is exercised by the Supreme Federal Tribunal; the Federal Appeal Tribunals and federal judges; Military Tribunals and judges; Electoral Tribunals and judges; Labour Tribunals and judges; and State Tribunals and judges. Judges are appointed for life; they may not undertake any other employment, receive any benefits from cases tried by them or engage in any party political activity. The Tribunals elect their own presidents and organize their own internal structure.

The Supreme Federal Tribunal, situated in the Union capital, has jurisdiction over the whole national territory and is composed of 11 Ministers. The Ministers are nominated by the President after approval by the Senate, from Brazilian-born citizens, over the age of 35, of proved judicial knowledge and experience.

POLITICAL AND PERSONAL RIGHTS

Registration and voting are compulsory for all Brazilian citizens who are more than 18 years of age, except those who are illiterate or unable to express themselves in the national language or are temporarily or definitively deprived of political rights.* The organization of political parties is regulated by federal law, with the guarantee of the fundamental human rights. Congressional representation is achieved when 5% of the total electorate votes for one party, with a minimum of 7% in each of seven states.

All citizens are equal in the eyes of the law, regardless of sex, race, employment, religion or political convictions; any racialism will be prosecuted; there is no death penalty (except under military legislation in case of external war), no life imprisonment, banishment or confiscation of property. Rights concerning citizens' life, liberty, security and property are inviolable.

---

* By virtue of this clause, American Indians are classed as minors and do not, therefore, have any political rights.

The President may declare a state of siege in cases of serious breaches of order or the likelihood of their occurring; or war. Except in cases of war, the state of siege may not last longer than 60 days, with the possibility of extension with the approval of Congress. During a state of siege Congress may suspend constitutional guarantees, and also the immunity of federal deputies and senators.

The Constitution also lays down principles of economic and social order, concerning freedom of enterprise, dignity of human labour, social function of ownership, harmony and solidarity in production, economic development and repression of abuse of economic power. Strikes are not permitted in public services and essential activities, as defined by law. The Constitution lays down certain rights for workers, including limited hours of work, paid holidays and social welfare benefits; voting in trade union elections is compulsory.

The law protects family life; education is the right of all, with equal opportunity. Education will be organized by the States and the Federal District and the Union will give technical and financial assistance to develop education.

AMENDMENTS

In April 1977 the following constitutional amendments were promulgated by presidential decree:

1. The presidential term of office was increased from five to six years as from the expiry of the then incumbent's term, 15 March 1979, and the date for the presidential elections was brought forward from January 1979 to October 1978.

2. Henceforth, constitutional amendments must be approved by Congress by a simple majority, not the two-thirds majority as at present.

3. From 1978 state governors and one-third of the seats in the Senate were to be elected indirectly by electoral colleges comprising members of the state assemblies and municipal councils. Those elected (including mayors) in November 1976 were to hold office until 1982 instead of 1980. The Government restored direct elections in 1980.

4. Federal deputies to be allocated on the basis of population and not on the number of registered voters as before. Each state elects not fewer than six and not more than 55 representatives.

5. Non-budgetary tax measures will no longer require congressional approval.

6. No election candidates to be allowed to appear on radio or television to discuss campaign issues.

In December 1977 the Senate approved rules for allowing marriages to be dissolved. Brazilian citizens will be able to apply for one divorce only during their lifetime. In the case of a marriage partner becoming mentally ill, divorce proceedings cannot begin until five years after the illness has been proved.

In September further amendments were promulgated which came into force in January 1979:

1. The repeal of Institutional Act 5 which gave the President the power to close Congress, suspend a citizen's political rights for 10 years and remove members of the federal, state or municipal legislatures.

2. The repeal of Article 185 of the Constitution which imposed political ineligibility for life on those citizens penalized under Institutional Act 5.

3. The promulgation of a new National Security Law under which the death penalty, perpetual imprisonment and banishment were abrogated and under which the right of *habeas corpus* was restored for political detainees.

4. The creation of a constitutional council with the President as Chairman and comprising the Vice-President, the President of the Senate and representatives of the armed forces, to approve Presidential decrees with regard to measures designed to safeguard national security:

(a) emergency measures where public order is gravely disturbed in specific regions;

(b) state of emergency for 90 days, renewable, where public security is threatened;

(c) state of siege for 180 days, includes powers of detention, censorship, etc.

5. The creation of a new law on the formation of political parties under which a new party must have 10% of the votes in Congress or the support of 5% of the electorate.

In May 1985 the National Congress approved the following constitutional amendments:

1. The President is to be elected by direct balloting with universal suffrage.

BRAZIL

2. Illiterate citizens are permitted to vote.

Note: Following congressional elections in November 1986, a Constitutional Assembly was to be installed in February 1987 and was to draft a new constitution and determine the length of the current presidency.

The Government

HEAD OF STATE

President: José Sarney (took office as acting President on 15 March 1985, and as President on 22 April 1985, following the death of President-elect Tancredo Neves).

CABINET
(November 1986)

The Cabinet is composed of members of an alliance, the Aliança Democrática, formed by the Partido Frente Liberal (PFL) and the Partido do Movimento Democrático Brasileiro (PMDB).

Minister, Head of the Secretariat for Planning: João Sayad (PMDB).
Minister of Justice: Paulo Brossard de Souza Pinto (PMDB).
Minister of the Navy: Adm. Henrique Saboia.
Minister of the Army: Gen. Leonidas Pires Gonçalves.
Minister of the Air Force: Brig. Otávio Moreira Lima.
Minister of Foreign Affairs: Roberto Costa de Abreu Sodré (PFL).
Minister of Finance: Dilson Domingos Funaro (PMDB).
Minister of Transport: José Reinaldo Carneiro Tavares (PFL).
Minister of Agriculture: Iris Rezende Machado (PMDB).
Minister of Education: José Konder Bornhausen (PFL).
Minister of Labour: Almir Pazzianotto Pinto Urban (PMDB).
Minister of Health: Roberto Figueira Santos (PMDB).
Minister of Industry and Commerce: José Hugo Castelo Branco (PMDB).
Minister of Mines and Energy: Dr Antônio Aureliano Chaves de Mendonça (PFL).
Minister of the Interior: Ronaldo Costa Couto (PMDB).
Minister of Communications: Antônio Carlos Peixoto de Magalhães (PFL).
Minister of Social Welfare: Rafael de Almeida Magalhães (PMDB).
Head of the President's Military Household: Gen. Rubens Bayma Denys.
Minister of the Presidency and Head of the President's Civilian Household: Marco Antônio de Oliveira Maciel (PFL).
Head of the National Information Service (SNI): Gen. Ivan de Souza Mendes.
Head of the General Staff of the Armed Forces (EMFA): Col Paulo Campos Paiva.
Minister of Land Reform and Development: Dante Martins de Oliveira.
Minister of Culture: Celso Monteiro Furtado (PMDB).
Minister of Administration: Aluízio Alves (PMDB).
Minister of Science and Technology: Renato Archer da Silva (PMDB).
Minister of Housing and Urban Development: Deni Lineu Schwartz (PMDB).
Minister of Irrigation: Vicente Fialho (PMDB).

MINISTRIES

Office of the President: Palácio do Planalto, Praça dos Três Poderes, 70.150 Brasília, DF; tel. (061) 223-2714; telex (061) 1451.
Ministry of the Air Force: Esplanada dos Ministérios, Bloco M, 8°, 70.043 Brasília, DF; tel. (061) 224-5098; telex (061) 1152.
Ministry of Agriculture: Esplanada dos Ministérios, Bloco D, 8°, 70.043 Brasília, DF; tel. (061) 224-5098; telex (061) 1162.
Ministry of the Army: Esplanada dos Ministérios, Bloco A, 4°, 70.630 Brasília, DF; tel. (061) 224-6797; telex (061) 1094.
Ministry of Communications: Esplanada dos Ministérios, Bloco R, 70.044 Brasília, DF; tel. (061) 224-5614; telex (061) 1456.
Ministry of Education and Culture: Esplanada dos Ministérios, Bloco L, 70.047 Brasília, DF; tel. (061) 223-7306; telex (061) 9105.
Ministry of Finance: Esplanada dos Ministérios, Bloco P, 5°, 70.048 Brasília, DF: tel. (061) 223-2729; telex (061) 1142.
Ministry of Foreign Affairs: Itamaraty, Esplanada dos Ministérios, 70.170 Brasília, DF; tel. (061) 211-6161; telex (061) 1319.
Ministry of Health: Esplanada dos Ministérios, Bloco 11, 70.058 Brasília, DF; tel. (061) 223-8158; telex (061) 1752.
Ministry of Industry and Commerce: Esplanada dos Ministérios, Bloco 6, 70.053 Brasília, DF; tel. (061) 225-7110; telex (061) 1066.
Ministry of the Interior: Esplanada dos Ministérios, Bloco 23, 70.054 Brasília, DF; tel. (061) 224-6809; telex (061) 1015.
Ministry of Justice: Palácio da Justiça, Esplanada dos Ministérios, 70.064 Brasília, DF; tel. (061) 224-2964; telex (061) 1088.
Ministry of Labour: Esplanada dos Ministérios, Bloco F, 10°, 70.059 Brasília, DF; tel. (061) 224-2964; telex (061) 1158.
Ministry of Mines and Energy: Esplanada dos Ministérios, Bloco 3, 70.055 Brasília, DF; tel. (061) 223-2009; telex (061) 1140.
Ministry of the Navy: Esplanada dos Ministérios, Bloco 3, 70.055 Brasília, DF; tel. (061) 223-6459; telex (061) 1392.
Ministry of Social Security and Welfare: SAS, Quadra 4, Bloco N, 70.065 Brasília, DF; tel. (061) 224-9959; telex (061) 1695.
Ministry of Transport and Public Works: Esplanada dos Ministérios, Bloco 9, 70.062 Brasília, DF; tel. (061) 224-2339; telex (061) 1096.

Legislature

CONGRESSO NACIONAL
(National Congress)

President of the Federal Senate: Senator José Fragelli.
President of the Chamber of Deputies: (vacant).

General Election, 15 November 1982

	Seats	
Party	Federal Senate*	Chamber of Deputies
Partido Democrático Social (PDS)	46	235
Partido do Movimento Democrático Brasileiro (PMDB)	21	200
Partido Democrático Trabalhista (PDT)	1	24
Partido Trabalhista Brasileiro (PTB)	1	14
Partido dos Trabalhadores (PT)	—	6
Total	69	479

* Elections for one-third of Senate seats were held on 15 November 1982.

Note: Elections for a new National Congress, to act as the Constitutional Assembly, were held on 15 November 1986. The Assembly was to be installed in February 1987. See Late Information section for further details.

Governors*

STATES

Acre: Yolanda Lima Fleming (PMDB).
Alagoas: José de Medeiros Tavares (PDS).
Amazonas: Gilberto Mestrinho de Medeiros Raposo (PMDB).
Bahia: João Durval Carneiro (PDS).
Ceará: Luiz Gonzaga da Fonseca Mota (PDS).
Espírito Santo: José Morães (PMDB).
Goias: Onofre Quinan (PMDB).
Maranhão: Luiz Alves Coelho Rocha (PDS).
Mato Grosso: Wilmar Peres de Farias (PDS).
Mato Grosso do Sul: Ramez Tebet (PMDB).
Minas Gerais: Hélio Garcia (PMDB).
Pará: Jáder Fontenelle Barbalho (PMDB).

BRAZIL

Paraíba: RIVANDO BEZERRA CAVALCANTI (PDS).
Paraná: JOÃO ELÍSIO FERRAZ DE CAMPOS (PMDB).
Pernambuco: GUSTAVO KRAUSE GONÇALVES SOBRINHO (PDS).
Piauí: JOSÉ RAIMUNDO PONA MEDEIROS (PDS).
Rio de Janeiro: LEONEL DE MOURA BRIZOLA (PDT).
Rio Grande do Norte: JOSÉ AGRIPINO MAIA (PDS).
Rio Grande do Sul: JAIR DE OLIVEIRA SOARES (PDS).
Rondônia: ÂNGELO ANGELIN (PDS).
Santa Catarina: ESPIRIDIÃO AMIN HELOU (PDS).
São Paulo: ANDRÉ FRANCO MONTORO (PMDB).
Sergipe: JOÃO ALVES (PDS).

FEDERAL TERRITORIES
Amapá: JORGE NOVA DA COSTA.
Roraima: GETÚLIO ALBERTO DE SOUZA CRUZ.

FEDERAL DISTRICT
Brasília: JOSÉ APARECIDO DE OLIVEIRA.

* State Governors in office at September 1986. The Governors of the Federal Territories and Brasília are Federal Government nominees. Gubernatorial elections were held in November 1986. The new Governors were to take office in March 1987.

Political Organizations

In November 1979 Congress passed a bill disbanding the two parties in existence since 1965, the pro-Government Aliança Renovadora Nacional (ARENA) and the opposition Movimento Democrático Brasileiro (MDB), in favour of the formation of new parties. These parties were to receive legal recognition if they gained the support of 10% of the votes in Congress and of six senators. In December 1981 Congress passed a bill to cover the local and general elections due in 1982 which permitted voters to vote only for complete lists and disqualified any party which did not have branches in at least one-fifth of the *municipios* in at least nine states and which failed to contest every position in each one. In May 1985 the National Congress approved a constitutional amendment providing for the free formation of political parties.

Aliança Democrática (AD): f. 1984; electoral alliance formed to support the candidacy of the late Tancredo Neves in the presidential election of January 1985; comprises:

Partido Frente Liberal (PFL): f. 1984 by moderate members of the PDS and PMDB; Chair. MAURICIO CAMPOS; Gen. Sec. SAULO QUEIROZ.

Partido do Movimento Democrático Brasileiro (PMDB): f. 1980; moderate elements of former MDB; merged with Partido Popular February 1982; Pres. ULYSSES GUIMARÃES; Gen. Sec. MILTON REIS.

Partido Comunista Brasileiro (PCB): f. 1922; pro-Moscow; Sec.-Gen. GIACONDA DIAS.

Partido Comunista do Brasil (PC do B): f. 1962; pro-Albanian; Sec.-Gen. JOÃO AMAZONAS; 5,000 mems.

Partido Democrático Social (PDS): Senado Federal Anexo II, Presidência do PDS, 70.000 Brasília, DF; telex 2402; f. 1980 as pro-Government party in succession to ARENA (see above); (in 1984 some liberal members of the PDS united with members of the PMDB (see above) to contest the presidential election of January 1985); Pres. AMARAL PEIXATO; Leaders MURILO BADARÓ, AMARAL NETO; Sec.-Gen. VIRGILIO TÁVORA.

Partido Democrático Trabalhista (PDT): Rua 7 de Setembro 141, 4°, 20.050 Rio de Janeiro, RJ; f. 1980; formerly the PTB (Partido Trabalhista Brasileiro) renamed 1980 when the name was awarded to a dissident group after controversial judicial proceedings; Pres. DOUTEL DE ANDRADE; Gen. Sec. Dra CARMEN CYNIRA.

Partido Republicano Brasileiro (PRB): f. 1985.

Partido Revolucionário Comunista (PRC): f. 1984; Communist; Leader GENUÍNO NETO.

Partido dos Trabalhadores (PT): Brasília, DF; tel. (061) 224-1699; f. 1980; first independent labour party; associated with the *autêntico* branch of the trade union movement; 300,000 mems; Pres. LUÍS IGNÁCIO (LULA) DA SILVA; Vice-Pres. JOÃO BITTAR.

Partido Trabalhista Brasileiro (PTB): f. 1980; Pres. LUIZ GONZAGA DE PAIVA MUNIZ.

Directory

Diplomatic Representation

EMBASSIES IN BRAZIL

Algeria: Brasília, DF; tel. (061) 248-4039; telex (061) 1278; Ambassador: BACHIR OULD ROUIS.

Angola: Brasília, DF; Ambassador: FRANCISCO ROMÃO DE OLIVEIRA E SILVA.

Argentina: SEPN, Av. W-3 Quadra 513, Bloco D, Edif. Imperador, 4° andar, 70.442 Brasília, DF; tel. (061) 273-3737; telex (061) 1013; Ambassador: RAFAEL VÁSQUEZ.

Australia: SHIS, QI 09 Conj. 16, Casa 01, Lago Sul, 71.600 Brasília, DF; tel. (061) 248-5569; telex (061) 1025; Ambassador: WARWICK EDUARD WEEMAES.

Austria: SES, Av. das Nações, Lote 40, CP 07-1215, Brasília, DF; tel. (061) 243-3111; telex (061) 1202; Ambassador: Dr NIKOLAUS HORN.

Bangladesh: SHIG-Sul, Av. W-3 Sul, Quadra 705, Bloco A, Casa 19, Brasília, DF; tel. (061) 244-3521; Ambassador: Cdre MUJIBUR RAHMAN.

Belgium: Av. das Nações, Lote 32, 70.422 Brasília, DF; tel. (061) 248-0884; telex (061) 1261; Ambassador: PIERRE VAN COOPENOLLE.

Bolivia: SCS, Edif. Embaixador, 4°, 70.470 Brasília, DF; tel. (061) 223-2688; telex (061) 1946; Ambassador: Dr EDUARDO ARZE QUIROGA.

Bulgaria: SEN, Av. das Nações, Lote 8, 70.432 Brasília, DF; tel. (061) 223-5193; telex (061) 1305; Ambassador: GEORGI JEKOV GEUROV.

Cameroon: QI 3, Conj. 5, Casa 2, Lago Sul, 71.600 Brasília, DF; tel. (061) 248-4433; Ambassador: PIERRE MVONDO SHE.

Canada: SES, Av. das Nações, Lote 16, CP 07-0961, 70.410 Brasília, DF; tel. (061) 223-7615; telex 611296; Ambassador: ANTHONY T. EYTON.

Chile: SES, Av. das Nações, Lote 11, Brasília, DF; tel. (061) 225-0001; telex (061) 1075; Ambassador: ALVARO ZÚNIGA BENAVIDES.

China, People's Republic: SES, Av. das Nações, Lote 51, 70.443 Brasília, DF; tel. (061) 244-8695; telex (061) 1300; Ambassador: TAO DAZHAO.

Colombia: SES, Av. das Nações, Lote 10, 70.444 Brasília, DF; tel. (061) 226-8902; telex 1458; Ambassador: ALVARO COSTA FRANCO.

Costa Rica: SCS, Edif. Ceará 501/502, 70.303 Brasília, DF; tel. (061) 226-7212; Ambassador: ROSA LUIS GIBERSTEIN.

Cuba: Brasília, DF; Ambassador: JORGE BOLAÑOS.

Czechoslovakia: SES, Av. das Nações, Lote 21, Brasília, DF; tel. (061) 243-1263; telex (061) 1073; Ambassador VÁCLAV MALOSIK.

Denmark: SES, Av. das Nações, Lote 26, CP 07-0484, 70.416 Brasília, DF; tel. (061) 242-8188; telex (061) 1494; Ambassador: JENS OSTENFELD.

Dominican Republic: SHIS, QI 3, Conj. 2, Casa 19, Lago Sul, Brasília, DF; tel. (061) 248-1405; Ambassador: COTUBANAMA DIPP.

Ecuador: SHIS, QL 10, Conj. 1, Casa 17, 71.600 Brasília, DF; tel. (061) 248-5560; telex (061) 1290; Ambassador: LUIS PONCE ENRÍQUEZ.

Egypt: SEN, Av. das Nações, Lote 12, 70.435 Brasília, DF; tel. (061) 225-8517; telex (061) 1387; Ambassador: MOKHLESS MOHAMED GOBBA.

El Salvador: SHI-Sul, QI 9, Conj. 14, Casa 18, 71.600 Brasília, DF; tel. (061) 248-6409; Ambassador: GREGORIO CONTRERAS MORALES.

Finland: SES, Av. das Nações, Lote 27, 70.417 Brasília, DF; tel. (061) 242-8555; telex (061) 1155; Ambassador: PEKKA J. KORVENHEIMO.

France: Av. das Nações, Lote 4, 70.404 Brasília, DF; tel. (061) 223-0990; telex (061) 1491; Ambassador: BERNARD DORIN.

Gabon: SHIS, QI 9, Conj. 16, Casa 23, 70.474, Brasília, DF; tel. (061) 248-3536; telex (061) 1710; Ambassador: VICTOR MAGNAGNA.

German Democratic Republic: CP 13-1971, SHI-Sul, QL 6, Conj. 8, Casa 17, 71.600 Brasília, DF; tel. (061) 248-1008; telex (061) 1417; Ambassador: Dr WERNER HÄNOLD.

Germany, Federal Republic: CP 07-0752, SES, Av. das Nações, Lote 25, 70.415 Brasília, DF; tel. (061) 243-7466; telex (061) 1198; Ambassador: WALTER GORENFLOS.

Ghana: SQS 111, Bloco B, Apt. 603, 70.466 Brasília, DF; tel. (061) 244-2045; Ambassador: KOFI AWOONOR.

Greece: SHIS, QI 11/1, Casa 11, 70.461 Brasília, DF; tel. (061) 248-1127; telex (061) 1843; Ambassador: ALEXIS D. ZAKYTHINOS.
Guatemala: SHIS, QL 08, Conj. 05, Casa 11, Brasília, DF; tel. (061) 248-3318; Ambassador: MANUEL S. ROLDÁN.
Guyana: Edif. Venâncio III, salas 410–414, 70.460 Brasília, DF; tel. (061) 224-4397; Ambassador: HUBERT O. JACK.
Haiti: SHIS, QI 7, Conj. 16, Casa 13, Lago Sul, Brasília, DF; tel. (061) 248-6860; Ambassador: RAYMOND MATHIEU.
Holy See: SES, Av. das Nações, Lote 1, 70.401 Brasília, DF; tel. (061) 223-0794; telex (061) 2125; Apostolic Nuncio: Mgr CARLO FURNO.
Honduras: SBN, Edif. Eng. Paulo Mauricio Sampaio, 12°, sala 1209, CEP 70.040, Brasília, DF; tel. (061) 223-2773; telex (061) 3736; Ambassador: Dr JOSÉ RIGOBERTO ARRIOGA CHINCHILLA.
Hungary: SES, Av. das Nações, Lote 19, 70.413 Brasília, DF; tel. (061) 243-0822; telex (061) 1285; Ambassador: GABOR SUTO.
India: SDS, Edif. Venâncio VI, 5°, CP 11-1097, Brasília, DF; tel. (061) 226-1585; telex (061) 1245; Ambassador: DILBAGH SINGH.
Indonesia: SES, Av. das Nações, Lote 20, 70.379 Brasília, DF; tel. (061) 243-0102; Ambassador: M. SOETADI.
Iran: SES, Av. das Nações, Lote 31, 70.421 Brasília, DF; tel. (061) 242-5733; telex (061) 1347; Ambassador: SHAHMARD KANANI MOGHADDAM.
Iraq: SES, Av. das Nações, Lote 64, Brasília, DF; tel. (061) 243-1804; telex (061) 1331; Ambassador: OAIS TAWFIG ALMUKHFAR.
Israel: SES, Av. das Nações, Lote 38, 70.424 Brasília, DF; tel. (061) 244-7675; telex (061) 1093; Ambassador: RAHAMIN TIMOR.
Italy: SES, Av. das Nações, Lote 30, 70.420 Brasília, DF; tel. (061) 244-0044; telex (061) 1488; Ambassador: VIERI TRAXLER.
Ivory Coast: SEN, Av. das Nações, Lote 09, 70.473 Brasília, DF; tel. (061) 226-5810; telex (061) 1095; Ambassador: CHARLES PROVIDENCE GOMIS.
Japan: SES, Av. das Nações, Lote 39, 70.425, Brasília, DF; tel. (061) 242-6866; telex (061) 1376; Ambassador: KUNIYOSHI DATE.
Korea, Republic: SHIS, QI 11, Conj. 3, Casa 16/18, Lago Sul, 71.600 Brasília, DF; tel. (061) 225-2806; telex (061) 1085; Ambassador: GONG RO-MYUNG.
Kuwait: SHI-Sul, QI 5, Ch. 30, 70.467 Brasília, DF; tel. (061) 248-1701; telex (061) 1367; Ambassador: ALI ZAKARI ALLANSARI.
Lebanon: SES, Av. das Nações, Q.805, Lote 17, 70.411 Brasília, DF; tel. (061) 242-4801; telex (061) 1295; Ambassador: SAMIR HOBEICA.
Libya: SHIS, QI 1S, Chácara 26, CP 3505, Brasília, DF; tel. (061) 248-4830; telex (061) 1099; Ambassador: FARAG AL-SEITI.
Malaysia: SHIS, QI 05, Chácara 62, Lago Sul, 70.477 Brasília, DF; tel. (061) 248-5008; telex (061) 3666; Ambassador: (vacant).
Mexico: SES, Av. das Nações, Lote 18, 70.412 Brasília, DF; tel. (061) 244-1011; telex (061) 1101; Ambassador: ANTONIO DE ICAZA GONZÁLEZ.
Morocco: SHIS, QI 11, Conj. 05, Casa 13, Lago Sul, 71.600 Brasília, DF; Ambassador: MOHAMED LARBI MESSARI.
Netherlands: Via L-3 Sul, Quadra 801, Lote 05, 70.405 Brasília, DF; POB 07-0098, 70.000; tel. (061) 223-20-25; telex (061) 1492; Ambassador: FRITS KUPERS.
Nicaragua: SCS, Edif. Venâncio da Silva 1301/1310, 70.454 Brasília, DF; tel. (061) 225-0283; telex (061) 2495; Ambassador: JORGE JAVIER JENKINS MOLIERI.
Nigeria: SDS, Edif. Venâncio II, 4° andar, 70.000 Brasília, DF; tel. (061) 223-7839; telex (061) 1315; Ambassador: O. M. A. ABIOLA.
Norway: SES, Av. das Nações, Lote 28, 70.418, CP 07-0670, 70.359 Brasília, DF; tel. (061) 243-8720; telex (061) 1265; Ambassador: PER CONRADI PRØITZ.
Pakistan: SCS, Edif. Central, 5°, 70.304 Brasília, DF; tel. (061) 224-2922; telex (061) 2252; Ambassador: SYED MURAD AHMAD KHAIRI.
Panama: SCS, Edif. JK, 13° andar, 132/133, 70.306 Brasília, DF; tel. (061) 225-0859; Ambassador: GUSTAVO GARCÍA DE PAREDES.
Paraguay: SES, Av. das Nações, Lote 42, CP 14-2314, Brasília, DF; tel. (061) 242-3723; telex (061) 1845; Ambassador: ADOLFO M. SAMANIEGO.
Peru: SES, Av. das Nações, Lote 43, 70.428 Brasília, DF; tel. (061) 242-9933; telex (061) 1108; Ambassador: HUGO PALMA VALDERRAMA.
Philippines: SEN, Av. das Nações, Lote 1, 70.431 Brasília, DF; tel. (061) 223-5143; telex (061) 2733; Ambassador: SERGIO A. BARRERA.
Poland: SES, Av. das Nações, Lote 33, 70.423 Brasília, DF; tel. (061) 243-3438; telex (061) 1165; Ambassador: STANISŁAW PAWLISZEWSKI.
Portugal: SES, Av. das Nações, Lote 2, Brasília, DF; tel. (061) 223-1090; Ambassador: ADRIANO DE CARVALHO.
Romania: SEN, Av. das Nações, Lote 6, 70.456 Brasília, DF; tel. (061) 226-0746; Ambassador: GEORGHE APOSTOL.
Saudi Arabia: SHI-Sul, QL 10, Conj. 9, Casa 20, 70.471 Brasília, DF; tel. (061) 248-3523; telex (061) 1656; Ambassador: ABDULLAH SALEH HABABI.
Senegal: SEN, Av. das Nações, Lote 18, 70.437 Brasília, DF; tel. (061) 225-4062; telex (061) 1377; Ambassador: SAMBA NOIAYE.
South Africa: Av. das Nações, Lote 6, CP 11-1170, 70.406 Brasília, DF; tel. (061) 223-4873; telex (061) 1683; Ambassador: ALEXANDRE VAN ZYL.
Spain: SES, Av. das Nações, Lote 44, Brasília, DF; tel. (061) 242-1074; telex (061) 1313; Ambassador: MIGUEL DE ALDASORO.
Suriname: SHIS, Q7, Conj. 06, Casa 14, 71.600 Brasília, DF; telex (061) 1414; Ambassador: LIAKAT ALI ERROL ALIBUX.
Sweden: SES, Av. das Nações, Lote 29, 70.419 Brasília, DF; tel. (061) 243-1444; telex (061) 1225; Ambassador: LENNART RYDFORS.
Switzerland: SES, Av. das Nações, Lote 41, 70.448, Brasília, DF; tel. (061) 244-5500; telex (061) 1135; Ambassador: ROGER BAER.
Syria: SEN, Av. das Nações, Lote 11, 70.434 Brasília, DF; tel. (061) 226-0502; telex (061) 1721; Ambassador: ZOUHEIR MOURABET.
Thailand: SEN, Av. das Nações Norte, Lote 10, 70.433 Brasília, DF; tel. (061) 223-5105; telex (061) 3763; Ambassador: PRANON KONGSAMUT.
Togo: Brasília, DF; Ambassador: LAMBANA TCHAOU.
Trinidad and Tobago: SHIS, QL 8, Conj. 4, Casa 5, 71.600 Brasília, DF; tel. (061) 248-1268; telex (061) 1844; Ambassador: WILFRED SHEIK NAIMOOL.
Turkey: SQS 114, Bloco F, Apt. 206, 70.452 Brasília, DF; tel. (061) 242-1850; telex (061) 2252; Ambassador: YILDIRIM KESKIM.
USSR: SES, Av. das Nações, Lote A, 70.476 Brasília, DF; tel. (061) 223-6320; telex (061) 360; Ambassador: VIKTOR FEDOROVICH ISAKOV.
United Kingdom: SES, Quadra 801, Conj. K, CP 07-0586, 70.408 Brasília, DF; tel. (061) 225-2710; telex (061) 1360; Ambassador: Sir JOHN URE.
USA: SES, Av. das Nações, Lote 3, 70.403 Brasília, DF; tel. (061) 223-0120; telex (061) 41167; Ambassador: HARRY W. SCHLAUDEMAN.
Uruguay: SES, Av. das Nações, Lote 14, 70.450 Brasília, DF; tel. (061) 224-2415; telex (061) 1173; Ambassador: Dr ROBERTO VIVO BONOMI.
Venezuela: SES, Av. das Nações, Lote 13, Q-803, 70.451 Brasília, DF; tel. (061) 223-9325; telex (061) 26586; Ambassador: EDUARDO R. CALDERÓN GODOY.
Yemen Arab Republic: Brasília, DF; Ambassador: (vacant).
Yugoslavia: SES, Quadra 803, Lote 15, 70.409 Brasília, DF; tel. (061) 223-7272; Ambassador: BRANKO TRPENOVSKI.
Zaire: SHIS, QI 9, Conj. 8, Casa 20, Lago Sul, CP 07-0041, 70.439 Brasília, DF; tel. (061) 248-3348; telex (061) 1435; Ambassador: LUALABA EMELEME ALEKIA.

Judicial System

The judiciary powers of the State are held by the following tribunals: the Supreme Federal Tribunal, the Federal Tribunal of Appeal, the State Tribunals of Justice, the Superior Military, the Electoral, and the Labour Tribunals; and by judges of other courts.

The Supreme Federal Court comprises 11 ministers, nominated by the President and approved by the Senate. It judges offences committed by persons exempt from appearing before the normal courts, such as the President, Ministers of State, its own members, judges of other courts, and chiefs of permanent diplomatic missions. It also litigates in disputes between the Union and the states, between the states, or between foreign nations and the Union or the states; disputes as to jurisdiction between justices and/or tribunals of the different states, including those of the federal district and of the territories; in cases involving the extradition of criminals, in certain special cases involving the principle of *habeas corpus*, and in other cases.

The Federal Tribunal of Appeal judges the cases in which the Federal Union has interest.

The State Tribunals of Justice, apart from their normal function as a court of appeal, can sit in judgment on their own members.

BRAZIL

The number of judges varies according to the judiciary organization of each state.

The organs of the Electoral Tribunal (the Superior Tribunal, the Regional Tribunals, and the electoral judges) register the names of political parties, fix the date of elections, supervise the listing of voters, and deal with all infractions of the electoral laws. The seven judges of the Superior Electoral Tribunal are chosen: three from the Supreme Federal Tribunal, two from the Federal Tribunal of Appeal and two by the President of the Republic.

The functions of the Military Court are no more than the name implies. The Labour Tribunal deals with labour disputes.

Civil offenders usually come before the courts of the separate states and of the Federal District. Each state organizes its own judiciary system on the principles established in the Constitution, and appoints its own judges from those who have passed the State examination in law.

THE SUPREME FEDERAL TRIBUNAL

Supreme Federal Tribunal: Praça dos Três Poderes, 70.175 Brasília, DF; tel. (061) 224-8179; telex (061) 1473.

President: José Carlos Moreira Alves.

Vice-President: Luiz Rafael Mayer.

Justices: José Francisco Rezek, Djaci Alves Falcão, Célio de Oliveira Borja, Luiz O. Pires e Albuquerque Gallotti, Carlos Alberto Madeira, José Neri da Silveira, Sydney Sanches, Oscar Dias Corrêa, Aldir Guimarães Passarinho.

Procurator-General: José Paulo Sepúlveda Pertence.

Director-General (Secretariat): Ronaldo de Barros Monteiro.

Religion

CHRISTIANITY

The Roman Catholic Church

Brazil comprises 36 archdioceses, 188 dioceses (including one each for Catholics of the Maronite, Melkite and Ukrainian Rites), 16 territorial prelatures and two territorial abbacies. The Archbishop of São Sebastião do Rio de Janeiro is also the Ordinary for Catholics of other Oriental Rites in Brazil (estimated at 8,500 in 1978). The great majority of Brazil's population are adherents of the Roman Catholic Church.

Bishops' Conference: Conferência Nacional dos Bispos do Brasil, SES, Q801, Conj. B, CP 13-2067, 70.401 Brasília, DF; tel. (061) 225-2955; telex (061) 1104; f. 1980; Pres. Mgr José Ivo Lorscheiter, Bishop of Santa Maria, RS.

Latin Rite

Archbishop of São Salvador da Bahia, BA: (vacant), Primate of Brazil, Palácio da Sé, Praça da Sé 1, 40.000 Salvador; tel. (071) 243-7573.

Archbishop of Aparecida do Norte, SP: Geraldo Maria de Morais Penido.

Archbishop of Aracajú, SE: Luciano José Cabral Duarte.

Archbishop of Belém do Pará, PA: Alberto Gaudêncio Ramos.

Archbishop of Belo Horizonte, MG: João Rezende Costa.

Archbishop of Botucatú, SP: Vicente Marchetti Zioni.

Archbishop of Brasília, DF: José Freire Falcão.

Archbishop of Campinas, SP: Gilberto Pereira Lopes.

Archbishop of Campo Grande: Antônio Barbosa.

Archbishop of Cascavel, PR: Armando Cirio.

Archbishop of Cuiabá, MT: Bonifacio Piccinini.

Archbishop of Curitiba, PR: Pedro Antônio Marchetti Fedalto.

Archbishop of Diamantina, MG: Geraldo Majela Reis.

Archbishop of Florianópolis, SC: Afonso Niehues.

Archbishop of Fortaleza, CE: Cardinal Aloisio Lorscheider.

Archbishop of Goiânia, GO: Antônio Ribeiro de Oliveira.

Archbishop of Juiz de Fora, MG: Juvenal Roriz.

Archbishop of Londrina, PR: Geraldo Majela Agnelo.

Archbishop of Maceió, AL: Edvaldo Gonçalves Amaral.

Archbishop of Manaus, AM: Clóvis Frainer.

Archbishop of Mariana, MG: Oscar de Oliveira.

Archbishop of Maringá, PR: Jaime Luís Coelho.

Archbishop of Natal, RN: Nivaldo Monte.

Archbishop of Niterói, RJ: José Gonçalves da Costa.

Archbishop of Olinda e Recife, PM: José Cardoso Sobrinho.

Archbishop of Paraíba, PB: José M. Pires.

Archbishop of Porto Alegre, RS: João Cláudio Colling.

Archbishop of Porto Velho, RO: José Martins da Silva.

Archbishop of Pouso Alegre, MG: José d'Angelo Neto.

Archbishop of Ribeirão Prêto, SP: Romeu Alberti.

Archbishop of São Luís do Maranhão, MA: Paulo Eduardo Andrade Ponte.

Archbishop of São Paulo, SP: Cardinal Paulo Evaristo Arns.

Archbishop of São Sebastião do Rio de Janeiro, RJ: Cardinal Eugênio de Araújo Sales.

Archbishop of Teresina, PI: Miguel Fenelon Câmara.

Archbishop of Uberaba, MG: Benedito de Ulhôa Vieira.

Archbishop of Vitória, ES: Silvestre Luís Scandián.

Maronite Rite

Bishop of Nossa Senhora do Libano em São Paulo, SP: Jean Chedid.

Melkite Rite

Bishop of Nossa Senhora do Paraíso em São Paulo, SP: Spiridon Mattar.

Ukrainian Rite

Bishop of São João Batista em Curitiba, PR: Efrem Basilio Krevey.

The Anglican Communion

Anglicans form the Episcopal Church of Brazil (Igreja Episcopal do Brasil), comprising six dioceses.

Igreja Episcopal do Brasil: POB 965, 90.000 Porto Alegre, RS; tel. (0512) 360651; f. 1890; 65,000 mems (1986); Primate: Rt Rev. Olavo Ventura Luiz, Bishop of Southwestern Brazil.

Protestant Churches

Federação Nacional de Igrejas Presbiterianas: Rua 7 de Setembro 421, Vitória, Espirito Santo.

Igreja Cristã Reformada do Brasil: CP 2808, 01.000 São Paulo, SP; Pres. Rev. Janos Apostol.

Igreja Evangélica de Confissão Luterana no Brasil (IECLB): Rua Senhor dos Passos 202, 2° andar, CP 2876, 90.000 Pôrto Alegre, RS; tel. (0512) 213433; telex (051) 2332; f. 1949; 870,000 mems; Pres. Pastor Dr Gottfried Brakemeier.

Igreja Evangélica Congregacional do Brasil: CP 414, 98.700 Ijuí, RS; tel. (055) 332-4656; f. 1942; 40,000 mems, 270 congregations; Pres. Rev. H. Hartmut W. Hachtmann.

Igreja Evangélica Luterana do Brasil: Rua Cel. Lucas de Oliveira 895, CP 1076, 90.001 Porto Alegre, RS; tel. (0512) 32-2111; 185,000 mems; Pres. Johannes H. Gedrat.

Igreja Metodista do Brasil: General Communication Secretariat, Rua Artur Azevedo 1192, Apdo 81, Pinheiros, 05.404 São Paulo, SP; Exec. Sec. Dr Onésimo de Oliveira Cardoso.

BAHÁ'Í FAITH

National Spiritual Assembly: Rua Eng. Gama Lobo 267, Vila Isabel, 20.551 Rio de Janeiro, RJ; tel. (021) 288-9846; mems resident in 1,250 localities.

BUDDHISM

Federação das Seitas Budistas do Brasil: Av. Paulo Ferreira 1133, Piqueri, São Paulo, SP.

Sociedade Budista do Brasil: Av. Treze de Maio, 47 S/Loja 208, 20.031 Rio de Janeiro, RJ; tel. (021) 220-7486; f. 1967; Pres. João Reis Marques.

The Press

The most striking feature of the Brazilian press is the relatively small circulation of newspapers in comparison with the size of the population. The newspapers with the largest circulations are *O Día* (207,000), *Fôlha de São Paulo* (230,000), and *Jornal da Tarde* (250,000). The low circulation is mainly due to high costs resulting from distribution difficulties. In consequence there are no national newspapers. From 1978 press censorship was gradually reduced by

BRAZIL

the military Government. On taking office in March 1985, the civilian Government announced that political censorship would be abolished. The last remaining censorship on books and newspapers was abolished in July 1985.

DAILY NEWSPAPERS

Belém, PA

O Liberal: Rua Gaspar Viana 253, 66.000 Belém, PA; tel. (091) 222-3000; telex (091) 1825; Dir ROMULO MAIORANA; circ. 20,000.

Belo Horizonte, MG

Diário da Tarde: Rua Goitacases 71, 30.000 Belo Horizonte, MG; tel. (031) 226-2322; telex (031) 1166; f. 1930; evening; Dir PEDRO AGNALDO FULGÊNCIO; circ. 22,000.

Diário de Minas: Praça Raul Soares 339, 30.000 Belo Horizonte, MG; tel. (031) 224-2122; telex (031) 1255; f. 1949; Pres. PAULO NACIF; circ. 50,000.

Estado de Minas: Rua Goiás 36, 30.000 Belo Horizonte, MG; tel. (031) 226-2322; telex (031) 1166; f. 1928; morning; independent; Dir PEDRO AGNALDO FULGÊNCIO; circ. 65,000.

Blumenau, SC

Jornal de Santa Catarina: Rua São Paulo 1120, 89.100 Blumenau, SC; tel. (0473) 22-6400; telex (0473) 120; f. 1971; Dir-Gen. FLÁVIO J. A. COELHO; circ. 25,000.

Brasília, DF

Correio Braziliense: SIG, QL 2, Lotes 300/500, 70.610 Brasília, DF; tel. (061) 226-1755; telex (061) 2777; f. 1960; Pres. EDILSON CID VARELA; circ. 30,000.

Jornal de Brasília: SIG Trecho 1, Lotes 585/645, 70.610 Brasília, DF; tel. (061) 225-2515; telex (061) 1208; f. 1972; Pres. FERNANDO CÂMARA; Editor OLIVEIRA BASTOS; circ. 25,000.

Ultima Hora de Brasília: SIA Trecho 3, Lotes 1645/55, 71.200 Brasília, DF; tel. (061) 233-1210; telex (061) 1595; f. 1983; evening; Dir ANTÔNIO M. M. BRAGANÇA.

Campinas, SP

Correio Popular: Rua Conceição 124, 13.100 Campinas, SP; tel (019) 31-1055; telex (019) 1021; f. 1927; Man. HERMES SANTOS; circ. 15,000.

Curitiba, PR

O Estado do Paraná: Rua João Tachannerl 800, 80.000 Curitiba, PR; tel. (041) 233-8811; telex (041) 5388; f. 1951; Dirs LUIZ G. GOMES MUSSI, ELIAS C. ANTUN; circ. 15,000.

Gazeta do Povo: Praça Carlos Gomes 4, 80.000 Curitiba, PR; tel. (041) 224-0522; f. 1919; Pres. FRANCISCO CUNHA PEREIRA; circ. 40,000.

A Tribuna do Paraná: Cidade da Comunicações, 80.000 Curitiba PR; tel. (041) 233-8811; telex (041) 5388; f. 1956; Dir LUIZ G. GOMES MUSSI, ELIAS C. ANTUN; circ. 15,000.

Florianópolis, SC

O Estado: Rodovia SC-401, Km 3, 88.000 Florianópolis, SC; tel. (0482) 33-1866; telex (0482) 177; f. 1915; Dir JOSÉ MATUSALÉM COMELLI; circ. 20,000.

Fortaleza, CE

O Povo: Av. Aguananbi 282, 60.000 Fortaleza, CE; tel. (085) 211-9666; telex (085) 1394; f. 1928; evening; Pres. DEMÓCRITO ROCHA DUMMAR; circ. 20,000.

Tribuna do Ceará: Av. Desemb. Moreira 2470, 60.000 Fortaleza, CE; tel. (085) 224-3519; telex (085) 1207; Pres. JOSÉ A. SANCHO; circ. 12,000.

Goiânia, GO

Diário da Manhã: Av. 24 de Outubro 1240, 74.000 Goiânia, GO; tel. (062) 233-3387; telex (062) 2394; f. 1980; Pres. JULIO NASSER; circ. 16,000.

O Popular: Thomaz Edson 207, 74.000 Goiânia, GO; tel. (062) 241-5533; telex (062) 2110; f. 1938; Pres. JAIME CÂMARA, Jr; circ. 20,000.

Londrina, PR

Fôlha de Londrina: Rua Piauí 241, 86.100 Londrina PR; tel. (0432) 22-3636; telex (0432) 123; f. 1948; Pres. JOÃO MILANEZ; circ. 35,000.

Manaus, AM

A Critica: Rua Lobo D' Álmada 278, 69.000 Manaus; tel. (092) 232-1400; telex (092) 2103; f. 1949; Dir UMBERTO CALDERARO, Jr; circ. 19,000.

Niterói, RJ

O Fluminense: Rua Visconde de Iraboraí 184, 24.035 Niterói, RJ; tel. (021) 719-3311; telex (021) 32054; f. 1878; Dir ALBERTO FRANCISCO TORRES; circ. 80,000.

A Tribuna: Rua Barão do Amazonas 31, 24.030 Niterói, RJ; tel. (021) 719-1886; f. 1936; Dir JOURDAN AMORA; Dir-Gen. MARIA MADALENA A. TANURE; circ. 18,000.

Porto Alegre, RS

Zero Hora: Av. Ipiranga 1075, 90.000 Porto Alegre, RS; tel. (051) 23-4266; telex (051) 1100; f. 1964; Pres. MAURÍCIO SIROTSKY SOBRINHO; circ. 110,000 (Mon.), 115,000 (Thurs.), 220,000 (Sun.), 100,000 (other days).

Recife, PE

Diário de Pernambuco: Praça da Independência 12, 2° andar, 50.000 Recife, PE; tel. (081) 231-0129; telex (081) 1057; f. 1825; morning; independent; Dir GLADSTONE VIERA BELO; circ. 31,000.

Ribeirão Preto, SP

Diário da Manhã: Rua Duque de Caxias 179, 14.100 Ribeirão Preto, SP; tel. 634-0909; f. 1898; Dirs JOFFRE PETEAN, PAULO M. SANT'ANNA; circ. 17,000.

Rio de Janeiro, RJ

Brazil Herald: Rua do Rezende 65, 20.231 Rio de Janeiro, RJ; tel. (021) 221-2772; f. 1946; daily, except Mondays; morning; only English language daily in Brazil; Dir MAURO SALLES; circ. 18,000.

O Dia: Rua Riachuelo 359, 20.230 Rio de Janeiro, RJ; tel. (021) 292-2020; telex (021) 22385; f. 1951; morning; popular labour; Pres. ARY DE CARVALHO; circ. 207,000 weekdays, 400,000 Sundays.

O Globo: POB 1090, Rua Irineu Marinho 35, 20.233 Rio de Janeiro, RJ; tel. (021) 272-2000; telex (021) 22595; f. 1925; morning; Dir ROBERTO MARINHO; circ. 220,000 weekdays, 440,000 Sundays.

Jornal do Brasil: Av. Brasil 500, São Cristovão, 20.949 Rio de Janeiro, RJ; tel. (021) 264-4422; telex (021) 23690; f. 1891; morning; Catholic, conservative; Pres. M. F. DO NASCIMENTO BRITO; Editor FERNANDO PEDREIRA; circ. 146,943 weekdays, 250,741 Sundays.

Jornal do Comércio: Rua do Livramento 189, 20.225 Rio de Janeiro, RJ; tel. (021) 253-4069; telex (021) 22165; f. 1827; morning; Pres. AUSTREGÉSILO DE ATHAYDE; circ. 31,000 weekdays.

Jornal dos Sports: Rua Tenente Possolo 15/25, Cruz Vermelha, 20.230 Rio de Janeiro, RJ; tel. (021) 232-8010; telex (021) 23093; f. 1931; morning; sporting daily; Pres. CLIMÉRIO PEREIRA VELLOSO; circ. 38,000.

Ultima Hora: Riachuelo 359, 20.235 Rio de Janeiro, RJ; tel. (021) 223-2444; telex (021) 22385; f. 1951; evening; Pres. ARY DE CARVALHO; circ. 56,000.

Salvador, BA

A Tarde: Av. Magalhães Neto s/n, 40.000 Salvador, BA; tel. (071) 231-0077; telex (171) 1299; f. 1912; evening; Pres. REGINA SIMÕES DE MELLO LEITÃO; circ. 54,000.

Correio da Bahia: Av. Luiz Viana, Jr s/n, Gleba A, 40.000 Salvador, BA; tel. (071) 231-2811; telex (071) 1594; f. 1978; Pres. ARMANDO GONÇALVES.

Jornal da Bahia: Rua Djalma Dutra 121, 40.000 Salvador, BA; tel. (071) 233-7428; f. 1969; Dir JOÃO DA FALCÃO; circ. 20,000.

Santo André, SP

Diário do Grande ABC: Rua Catequese 562, 09.000 Santo André SP; tel. (011) 449-5533; telex (011) 44034; f. 1958; Pres. EDSON DANILLO DOTTO; circ. 85,000.

Santos, SP

Cidade de Santos: Rua do Comércio 32, 11.010 Santos, SP; tel. (013) 232-7141; telex (013) 1139; f. 1967; Pres. RENATO CASTANHARI; circ. 60,000.

A Tribuna: Rua General Câmara 90194, 11.000 Santos, SP; tel. (013) 32-7711; telex (013) 1058; f. 1894; Dir GIUSFREDO SANTINI; circ. 35,000.

BRAZIL   *Directory*

São Paulo, SP

Diário do Comércio e Indústria: Rua Alvaro de Carvalho 354, 01.050 São Paulo, SP; tel. (011) 256-5011; telex (011) 21436; f. 1933; morning; Pres. WALDEMAR DOS SANTOS; circ. 50,000.

Diário Popular: Rua Major Quedinho 28, 01.050 São Paulo, SP; tel. (011) 258-2133; telex (011) 21213; f. 1884; evening; independent; Dir WALTER L. S. HOELZ, Jr; circ. 90,000.

O Estado de São Paulo: Av. Eng. Caetano Álvares 55, 02.550 São Paulo, SP; tel. (011) 266-7099; telex (011) 23511; f. 1875; morning; independent; Dirs JÚLIO DE MESQUITA NETO, RUY MESQUITA, JOSÉ VIEIRA DE CARVALHO MESQUITA, LUIZ V. CARVALHO MESQUITA; circ. 220,000 weekdays, 460,000 Sundays.

Fôlha de São Paulo: CP 8079, Alameda Barão de Limeira 425, Campos Elísios, 01.202 São Paulo, SP; tel. (011) 220-0011; telex (011) 22930; f. 1921; morning; Dir RENATO CASTANHARI; Editor HORACIO NEVES; circ. 211,900 weekdays, 314,830 Sundays.

A Gazeta Mercantil: Rua Major Quedinho 90, 01.050 São Paulo, SP; tel. (011) 256-3133; telex (011) 37802; f. 1920; business paper; pro-government; Pres. LUIZ FERREIRA LEVY; circ. 50,000.

Jornal da Tarde: Av. Eng. Caetano Álvares 55, 02.550 São Paulo, SP; tel. (011) 266-7099; telex (011) 23511; f. 1966; evening; independent; Dirs see *O Estado de São Paulo* above; circ. 120,000, 180,000 Mondays.

Notícias Populares: Alameda Barão de Limeira 425, 01.202 São Paulo, SP; tel. 220-0011; telex (011) 22930; f. 1963; Dir LUÍS F. OLIVEIRA; circ. 150,000.

Vitória, ES

A Gazeta: Rua Chafic Murad 902, 29.000 Vitória, ES; tel. (027) 223-6333; telex (027) 2273; f. 1928; Pres. EUGÊNIO PACHECO QUEIROZ; circ. 19,000.

PERIODICALS
Rio de Janeiro, RJ

Amiga: Rua do Russell 804, 20.210 Rio de Janeiro, RJ; tel. (021) 265-2012; telex (021) 21525; weekly; women's interest; Pres. ADOLPHO BLOCH; circ. 180,000.

Antenna-Eletrônica Popular: Av. Marechal Floriano 143, CP 1131, 20.001 Rio de Janeiro, RJ; tel. (021) 223-2442; f. 1926; every 2 months; telecommunications and electronics, radio, TV, hi-fi, amateur and CB radio; Dir G. A. PENNA; circ. 25,000.

Carinho: Rua do Russell 804, 20.210 Rio de Janeiro, RJ; tel. (021) 265-2012; telex (021) 21525; monthly; women's interest; Pres. ADOLPHO BLOCH; circ. 148,000.

Casa e Jardim: Rua Felizbelo Freire 671, 20.071 Rio de Janeiro, RJ; tel. (021) 270-6262; f. 1953; monthly; homes and gardens, illustrated; Editor MILTON MADEIRA; circ. 80,000.

Conjuntura Econômica: Praia de Botafogo 188, 22.253 Rio de Janeiro, RJ; tel. (021) 551-0246; f. 1947; monthly; economics and finance; published by Fundação Getúlio Vargas; Dir JULIAN M. CHACEL.

Criativa: Rua Itapiri 1209, 21.251 Rio de Janeiro, RJ; tel. (021) 273-5522; telex (021) 23365; monthly; women's interest; Pres. OSCAR D. NEVES; circ. 121,000.

Desfile: Rua do Russell 804, 20.210 Rio de Janeiro, RJ; tel. (021) 285-0033; telex (021) 21525; f. 1969; monthly; women's interest; Dir ADOLPHO BLOCH; circ. 138,000.

Ele Ela: Rua do Russell 804, 22.210 Rio de Janeiro RJ; tel. (021) 265-2012; telex (021) 21525; f. 1969; monthly; men's interest; Dir ADOLPHO BLOCH; circ. 230,000.

Fatos e Fotos: Rua do Russell 804, 20.210 Rio de Janeiro, RJ; tel. (021) 285-0033; telex (021) 21525; illustrated weekly; general interest; Pres. ADOLPHO BLOCH; circ. 110,000.

Manchete: Rua do Russell 804, Gloria, 20.210 Rio de Janeiro, RJ; tel. (021) 285-0033; telex (021) 21525; f. 1952; weekly; general; Dir ADOLPHO BLOCH; circ. 223,000.

São Paulo, SP

Capricho: Rua Geraldo F. Gomes 61, 04.575 São Paulo, SP; tel. (011) 545-8122; telex (011) 24134; monthly; women's interest; Pres. VICTOR CIVITA; circ. 167,000.

Claudia: Rua Geraldo F. Gomes 61, 04.575 São Paulo, SP, CP 2372; tel. (011) 545-8122; telex (011) 24134; f. 1962; monthly; women's magazine; Dir VICTOR CIVITA; circ. 254,000.

Digesto Econômico: Associação Comercial de São Paulo, Rua Boa Vista 51, 01.014 São Paulo, SP; tel. (011) 239-1333; telex (011) 23355; monthly; Pres. GUILHERME ÁFIF DOMINGOS.

Dirigente Rural: Rua Afonso Celso 243, 04.119 São Paulo, SP; tel. (011) 549-4344; telex (011) 23552; monthly; agriculture; Dir HENRY MAKSOUD; Editor ISAAC JORDANOVSKI; circ. 24,000.

Exame: Rua Geraldo F. Gomes 61, 04.574 São Paulo, SP; tel. (011) 545-8122; telex (011) 24134; fortnightly; business; Dir-Gen. RICARDO FICHER; circ. 54,000.

Iris: Rua Jacucaim 67, Brooklin, 04.563 São Paulo, SP; tel. (011) 531-1299; f. 1947; monthly; photography, video and computer science; Dirs BEATRIZ DE A. MARQUES, SUSANNE A. MARQUES; circ. 62,000.

Manequim: Rua Geraldo F. Gomes 61, 04.575 São Paulo, SP; tel. (011) 545-8122; telex (011) 24134; monthly; fashion; Pres. VICTOR CIVITA; circ. 300,000.

Máquinas e Metais: Rua Dona Elisa 167, 01.155 São Paulo, SP; tel. (011) 826-4511; f. 1964; monthly; machine and metal industries; Editor JOSÉ ALVES DE SOUZA; circ. 23,000.

Mickey: Rua Bela Cintra 299, 01.415 São Paulo, SP; tel. (011) 257-0999; monthly; children's magazine; Pres. VICTOR CIVITA; circ. 141,000.

Micromundo-Computerworld do Brasil: Rua Caçapava 79, 01.408 São Paulo, SP; tel. (011) 881-6844; telex (011) 32017; monthly; computers; Gen. Dir ERIC HIPPEAU; circ. 38,000.

Mundo Elétrico: Rua Consórcio 59, 04.535 São Paulo, SP; tel. (011) 853-7185; telex (011) 30410; f. 1959; monthly; electricity; Pres. MANFREDO GRUENWALD.

Nova: Rua Geraldo F. Gomes 61, 04.575 São Paulo, SP; tel. (011) 545-8122; telex (011) 24134; f. 1973; monthly; women's interest; Pres. VICTOR CIVITA; circ. 156,000.

Pato Donald: Rua Bela Cintra 299, 01.415 São Paulo, SP; tel. (011) 257-0999; every 2 weeks; children's magazine; Pres. VICTOR CIVITA; circ. 186,600.

Placar: Rua Geraldo F. Gomes 61, 04.575 São Paulo, SP; tel. (011) 545-8122; telex (011) 24134; f. 1970; weekly; sports magazine; Pres. VICTOR CIVITA; circ. 119,000.

Quatro Rodas: Rua Geraldo F. Gomes 61, Brooklin, 04.575 São Paulo, SP; tel. (011) 545-8122; telex (011) 24134; f. 1960; monthly; motoring; Pres. VICTOR CIVITA; circ. 167,000.

Revista O Carreteiro: Rua Palacete das Aguias 284, 04.635 São Paulo, SP; tel. (011) 533-5237; monthly; transport; Dir JOSÉ A. DE CASTRO; circ. 160,000.

Saúde: Rua Geraldo F. Gomes 61, 04.575 São Paulo, SP; tel. (011) 545-8122; telex (011) 24134; monthly; health; Pres. VICTOR CIVITA; circ. 70,000.

Veja: Av. Otaviano Alves de Lima 4400, 01.390 São Paulo, SP; tel. (011) 266-0011; telex (011) 22115; f. 1968; news weekly; Pres. VICTOR CIVITA; circ. 523,000.

Visão: Rua Afonso Celso 243, 2° andar, 04.119 São Paulo, SP; tel. (011) 549-4344; telex (011) 23552; f. 1952; weekly; news magazine; Editor HENRY MAKSOUD; circ. 154,465.

NEWS AGENCIES

Abril Press: Av. Otaviano Alves de Lima 4400, CP 2372, 01.000 São Paulo, SP; tel. (011) 266-0011; telex (011) 22094; Man. EDGARD S. FARIA.

Agência ANDA: Edif. Correio Braziliense, Setor das Indústrias Gráficas 300/350, Brasília, DF; Dir EDILSON VARELA.

Agência o Estado de São Paulo: Av. Eng. Caetano Álvares 55, 02.550 São Paulo, SP; tel. (011) 222-9995; telex (011) 22700; Rep. GUILHERME DUNCAN.

Agência Fôlha de São Paulo: Alameda Barão de Limeira 425, Campos Elísios, 01.290 São Paulo; tel. (011) 243-6428; Dir TARSIO NITRINI.

Agência Globo: Rua Irineu Marinho 35, 2° andar, Centro, 20.030 Rio de Janeiro, RJ; tel. (021) 292-2000; Dir LUCIANO DE MORAIS.

Agência Jornal do Brasil: Av. Brasil 500, 6° andar, São Cristovão, 20.940 Rio de Janeiro, RJ; tel. (021) 264-4422; Rep. JAIR SOARES.

Empresa Brasileira de Notícias (EBN): SCS, Edif. Toufic 6°, 70.300 Brasília, DF; tel. (061) 223-7155; telex (061) 2227; f. 1979; Pres. RUY LOPES; Superintendent LUIZ RECENA GRASSI.

Foreign Bureaux

Agence France-Presse (AFP) (France): CP 2575-ZC-00, Rua México 21, 7° andar, 20.031 Rio de Janeiro, RJ; tel. (021) 240-6634; telex (021) 22494; Bureau Chief JACQUES THOMET; Rua Sete de Abril 230, 11° andar, Bloco B, 01.044 São Paulo, SP; tel. (011)

BRAZIL   Directory

255-2566; telex (011) 21454; Bureau Chief RICARDO UZTARROZ; SDS, Edif. Venâncio IV, sala 307, Brasília, DF; tel. (061) 224-3576; telex (061) 1291; Bureau Chief ALBERTO CARBONE.

Agencia EFE (Spain): Av. Rio Branco 25, 13° andar, 20.090 Rio de Janeiro, RJ; tel. (021) 253-4465; telex (021) 30073; Bureau Chief ZOILO G. MARTÍNEZ DE LA VEGA; SHIS, QI 3, Conj. 8, Casa 13, 71.600 Brasília, DF; tel. (061) 248-1375; Bureau Chief FRANCISCO RUBIO FIGUEROA.

Agenzia Nazionale Stampa Associata (ANSA) (Italy): Av. Pres. Antônio Carlos 40, Cobertura, CP 16095, Rio de Janeiro, RJ; tel. (021) 220-5528; telex (021) 22296; Bureau Chief MANUEL HORACIO PALLAVIDINI; Av. São Luís 258, 13° andar, Of. 1302, São Paulo, SP; tel. (011) 256-5835; telex (011) 21421; Bureau Chief RICARDO CARUCCI; c/o Correio Brasiliense, 70.610 Brasília, DF; tel. (061) 226-1755; telex (061) 2211; Bureau Chief HUMBERTO ANTONIO GIANNINI; Rua Barão do Rio Branco 556, Curitiba, PA; tel. (041) 24-5000; Bureau Chief ELOIR DANTÉ ALBERTI.

Allgemeiner Deutscher Nachrichtendienst (ADN) (German Democratic Republic): SHI-SUL, QL 14, Conj. 10, Casa 13, CP 7079, 71.600 Brasília, DF; tel. (061) 248-6499; telex (061) 3856; Correspondent WOLFGANG GERTH.

Associated Press (AP) (USA): Av. Brasil 500, sala 609, CP 72-ZC-00, 20.001 Rio de Janeiro, RJ; tel. (021) 264-4422; telex (021) 21888; Bureau Chief BRUCE HANDLER; Rua Major Quedinho 28, 6° andar, CP 3815, 01.050 São Paulo, SP; tel. (011) 256-0520; telex (011) 21595; Correspondent STAN LEHMAN; CP 14-2260, 70.343 Brasília, DF; tel. (061) 223-9492; telex (061) 1454; Correspondent SUSANA HAYWARD.

Deutsche Presse-Agentur (dpa) (Federal Republic of Germany): Av. Brasil 500, 6° andar, CP 14, Rio de Janeiro, RJ; tel. (021) 248-9156; telex (021) 22550; Bureau Chief SIEGFRIED NIEBUHR.

Inter Press Service (IPS) (Italy): Rua Evaristo de Veiga 16/1007, 20.031 Rio de Janeiro; tel. (021) 262-9429; telex (021) 34845; Correspondent MARIO CHIZUO OSAVA.

Jiji Tsushin-Sha (Japan): Rua Tenente Otavio Gomes 37, Aclimação, 01.526 São Paulo, SP; tel. (011) 278-5790; telex (011) 24594; Chief Correspondent SHOICHI OGAWA.

Kyodo Tsushin (Japan): Praia do Flamengo 168-701, Flamengo, 22.210 Rio de Janeiro, RJ; tel. (021) 285-2412; telex (021) 33653; Bureau Chief HIROAKI IDAKA.

Prensa Latina (Cuba): Marechal Mascarenha 121, Apto 203, Copacabana, 22.011 Rio de Janeiro, RJ; tel. (021) 256-7259; Correspondent SERGIO PINEDA.

Reuters (UK): SCS, Edif. Gilberto Salamão, salas 1114-6, 70.300 Brasília, DF; tel. (061) 223-5918; telex (061) 1982; Rua Líbero Badaró 377, 20°, 01.009 São Paulo, SP; tel. (011) 35-1046; telex (011) 21160; Av. Rio Branco 25, 12°, Conj. C/D, CP 266, 20.090 Rio de Janeiro, RJ; tel. (021) 233-5430; telex (021) 23222; Chief Correspondent RICHARD JARVIE.

Telegrafnoye Agentstvo Sovetskovo Soyuza (TASS) (USSR): Rua General Barbosa 34, Apto 802, Rio de Janeiro, RJ; Correspondent ALEKSANDR MAKSIMOV; Av. das Naçoes, Lote A, 70.000 Brasília, DF; Correspondent YURIY BESPALCO.

United Press International (UPI) (USA): Av. Brasil 500, 6°, CP 791, 20.940 Rio de Janeiro, RJ; tel. (021) 254-2034; Gen. Man. LUIZ CARLOS SEGALA DE MENEZES; CP 2280, São Paulo, SP; Correspondent TOMAZ MURPHY; Edif. Gilberto Salomão, Sala 813, Brasília, DF; Correspondent WALTER SOTTOMAYOR.

Xinhua (New China) News Agency (People's Republic of China): SHI/S QI 15, Conj. 16, Casa 14, CP 7089; 71.600 Brasília, DF; tel. (061) 248-5489; telex (061) 2788; Chief Correspondent WANG ZHIGEN.

Central News Agency (Taiwan) and Novosti (USSR) are also represented in Brazil.

PRESS ASSOCIATIONS

Associação Brasileira de Imprensa: Rua Araújo Pôrto Alegre 71, Castelo, 20.030 Rio de Janeiro, RJ; f. 1908; 4,000 mems; Pres. BARBOSA LIMA SOBRINHO; Sec. JOSUÉ ALMEIDA.

Federação Nacional dos Jornalistas Profissionais—FENAJ: Edif. Serra Dourada 715, SCS, 70.315 Brasília, DF; tel. (061) 223-7002; telex (061) 1792; Sec. Gen. ARMANDO ROLLEMBERG.

Publishers

There are nearly 500 publishers in Brazil. The following is a list of the most important by virtue of volume of production.

Rio de Janeiro, RJ

Bloch Editores, SA: Rua do Russell 766/804, Glória, 22.210 Rio de Janeiro, RJ; tel. (021) 265-2012; telex (021) 21525; f. 1953; general; Pres. ADOLPHO BLOCH.

Cedibra Editora Brasileira Ltda: Rua Leonídia 2, Olaria, CP 20095, 21.021 Rio de Janeiro, RJ; tel. (021) 280-7272; f. 1952; literature and children's books; Man. Dir JAN RAIS.

Distribuidora Record de Serviços de Imprensa, SA: Rua Argentina 171, São Cristóvão, CP 884, 20.921 Rio de Janeiro, RJ; tel. (021) 580-3668; telex (021) 30501; f. 1941; general fiction and non-fiction, education, textbooks, fine arts; Pres. ALFREDO C. MACHADO.

Editora Artenova, SA: Rua Pref. Olímpio de Mello 1774, Benfica, 20.030 Rio de Janeiro, RJ; tel. (021) 264-9198; f. 1971; sociology, psychology, occultism, cinema, literature, politics and history; Man. Dir ALVARO PACHECO.

Editora Brasil-América (EBAL) SA: Rua Gen. Almério de Moura 302/20, São Cristóvão, 20.921 Rio de Janeiro, RJ; tel. (021) 580-0303; telex (021) 21293; f. 1945; children's books; Dir ADOLFO AIZEN.

Editora Delta SA: Av. Almirante Barroso 63, 26° andar, CP 2226, 20.031 Rio de Janeiro, RJ; tel. (021) 240-0072; f. 1958; reference books.

Editora Globo SA: Rua Sargento Sílvio Hollenbach 350; Distrito Industrial da Fazenda Botafogo, Km 20 da Av. Brasil, Barros Filho, 21.530 Rio de Janeiro, RJ; tel. (021) 372-5959; telex (021) 32844; f. 1957; general.

Editora e Gráfica Miguel Couto SA: Rua da Passagem 78, Loja A, Botafogo, 22.290 Rio de Janeiro, RJ; tel. (021) 541-5145; f. 1969; engineering; Dir PAULO KOBLER PINTO LOPES SAMPAIO.

Editora de Guias LTB SA: Av. Pres. Wilson 165, 3° andar, 20.030 Rio de Janeiro, RJ, CP 15084; f. 1947; communications.

Editora Monterrey Ltda: Rio de Janeiro, RJ; f.1963; fiction; Dir J. GUEIROS.

Editora Nova Fronteira, SA: Rua Maria Angélica 168, Lagoa, 22.461 Rio de Janeiro, RJ; tel. (021) 286-7822; telex (021) 34695; f. 1965; fiction, psychology, history, politics, science fiction, poetry, leisure, reference; Pres. SÉRGIO C. A. LACERDA.

Editora Tecnoprint, SA: Rua da Proclamação 109, 21.040 Rio de Janeiro, RJ; tel. (021) 260-6122; f. 1939; general.

Editora Vecchi, SA: Rua do Rezende 144, Esplanada do Senado, 20.234 Rio de Janeiro, RJ; tel. (021) 221-0822; telex (021) 32756; f. 1913; general literature, juvenile, reference, cookery, magazines; Dir DELMAN BONATTO.

Editora Vozes, Ltda: Rua Frei Luís 100, 25.600 Petrópolis, RJ; tel. (021) 43-5112; f. 1901; Catholic publishers; management, theology, anthropology, fine arts, history, linguistics, science, fiction, education, data processing, etc.; Dir Dr MIGUEL GOMES MOURÃO DE CASTRO.

Exped—Espansão Editorial Ltda: Estrada dos Bandeirantes 1700, Bloco H, Jacarapeguá, 22.700 Rio de Janeiro, RJ; tel. (021) 342-0669; telex (021) 33280; f. 1967; textbooks, literature, reference; Gen. Man. FERDINANDO BASTOS DE SOUZA.

Fundação Nacional de Material Escolar (FENAME): Rua Miguel Angelo 96, Maria da Graça, 20.781 Rio de Janeiro, RJ; tel. (021) 261-7750; f. 1967; education; Dir MILTON DURÇO PEREIRA.

Gráfica Editora Primor, Ltda: Rodv. Pres. Dutra 2611, 21.530 Rio de Janeiro, RJ; tel. (021) 371-6622; telex (021) 22150; f. 1968.

Livraria Francisco Alves Editora, SA: Rua 7 de Setembro 177, 20.050 Rio de Janeiro, RJ; tel. (021) 221-3198; f. 1854; textbooks, fiction, non-fiction; Dir Supt LEO MAGARINOS DE SOUZA LEÃO.

Livraria José Olympio Editora, SA: Rua Marquês de Olinda 12, Botafogo, 22.252 Rio de Janeiro, RJ; tel. (021) 551-0642; telex (051) 21327; f. 1931; juvenile, science, history, philosophy, psychology, sociology, fiction; Dir LUIZ OCTAVIO DO ESPÍRITO SANTO.

Ao Livro Técnico SA Indústria e Comércio: Rua Sá Freire 40, São Cristóvão, 20.930 Rio de Janeiro, RJ; tel. (021) 580-4868; telex (021) 30472; f. 1946; technical, scientific, children's, languages, textbooks; Man. Dir REYNALDO MAX PAUL BLUHM.

Otto Pierre Editores Ltda: Rua Dr Nunes 1225, Olaria, 21.021 Rio de Janeiro, RJ.

Tesla Publicações Ltda: Rua da Quitanda 49, 1° andar, salas 110/12, 20.011 Rio de Janeiro, RJ; tel. (021) 242-0135; f. 1960; children's books.

São Paulo, SP

Abril SA Cultural: Av. Brig. Faria Lima 2000, Torre Norte, 3°/5° andares, 01.327 São Paulo, SP; tel. (011) 815-8055; telex (011)

BRAZIL

22765; f. 1950; science, general encyclopaedias; Man. FLAVIO BARROS PINTO.

Atual Editora Ltda: Rua José Antônio Coelho 785, Vila Mariana, 04.011 São Paulo, SP; tel. (011) 71-7795; f. 1973; design and mathematics; Dirs GELSON IEZZI, OSVALDO DOLCE.

Cia Editora Nacional: Rua Joli 294, Brás, 03.016 São Paulo, SP; tel. (011) 291-2355; f. 1925; textbooks, history, science, social sciences, philosophy, fiction, juvenile; Dirs JORGE YUNES, PAULO C. MARTI.

Cia Melhoramentos de São Paulo, Indústrias de Papel: Rua Tito 479, 05.051 São Paulo, SP; tel. (011) 262-6866; telex (011) 23151; f. 1890; history, science, juvenile education, history; Gen. Man. RAINER OELLERS.

Editora Abril SA: Av. Octaviano Alves de Lima 4400, São Paulo, SP; tel. (011) 266-0011; telex (011) 22115; f. 1950; Dir VICTOR CIVITA.

Editora Atica, SA: Rua Barão de Iguape 110, 01.507 São Paulo, SP; tel. (011) 278-9322; telex (011) 32969; f. 1965; education, economics, literature, accountancy; Pres. ANDERSON FERNANDES DIAS.

Editora Atlas SA: Rua Conselheiro Nébias 1384, Campos Elíseos, CP 7186, 01.203 São Paulo, SP; tel. (011) 221-9144; f. 1944; business administration, data-processing, economics, accounting, law, education, social sciences; Pres. LUIZ HERRMANN.

Editora Brasiliense, SA: Rua Gal. Jardim 160, 01.223 São Paulo, SP; tel. (011) 231-1422; f. 1943; education, sociology, history, administration, psychology, literature, children's books; Mans CAIO GRACO DA SILVA PRADO, THEOPHILO ISIDORE DE ALMEIDA, Jr.

Editora do Brasil SA: Rua Conselheiro Nébias 887, Campos Elíseos, 01.203 São Paulo, SP; tel. (011) 222-0211; f. 1943; commerce, education, history, psychology and sociology.

Editora Caminho Suave Ltda: Rua Fagundes 157, Liberdade, 01.508 São Paulo, SP; tel. (011) 278-5840; f. 1965; textbooks.

Editora e Encadernadora Formar Ltda: Rua dos Trilhos 1126, Mooca, CP 13250, 03.168 São Paulo, SP; tel. (011) 93-5133; f. 1962; general.

Editora F.T.D. SA: Rua Pereira Nunes 323, 20.511 Rio de Janeiro, RJ; tel. (021) 288-5846; f. 1965; textbooks; Pres. JOÃO TISSI.

Editora Moderna Ltda: Rua Afonso Brás 431, Ibirapuera, 04.511 São Paulo, SP; tel. (011) 531-5099; f. 1969; education and children's books.

Editora Revista dos Tribunais Ltda: Rua Conde do Pinhal 78, 01.501 São Paulo, SP; tel. (011) 37-2433; f. 1955; law and jurisprudence, administration, economics and social sciences; Dir ALVARO MALHEIROS.

Editora Rideel Ltda: Alameda Afonso Schmidt 877, Santa Terezinha, 02.450 São Paulo, SP; tel. (011) 267-8344; f. 1971; general; Dir ITALO AMADIO.

Encyclopaedia Britannica do Brasil Publicações Ltda: Rua Rego Freitas 192, Vila Buarque, CP 31027, 01.220 São Paulo, SP; tel. (011) 221-7122; telex (011) 21460; f. 1951; reference books.

Ênio Matheus Guazzelli & Cia Ltda (Livraria Pioneira Editora): Praça Dirceu de Lima 313, Casa Verde, 02.515 São Paulo, SP; tel. (011) 858-3199; f. 1964; architecture, political and social sciences, business studies, languages, children's books; Dir ÊNIO MATHEUS GUAZZELLI.

Gráfica Editora Michalany SA: Rua Paracatu 482, Saúde, CP 12933, 04.302 São Paulo, SP; tel. (011) 275-9716; f. 1965; biographies, economics, textbooks, geography and history.

Instituto Brasileiro de Edições Pedagógicas Ltda: Rua Joli 294, Brás, CP 5321, 03.016 São Paulo, SP; tel. (011) 291-2355; f. 1972; textbooks, foreign languages, reference books and chemistry.

Lex Editora SA: Rua Machado de Assis 47/57, Vila Mariana, CP 12888, 04.106 São Paulo, SP; tel. (011) 549-0122; f. 1937; legislation and jurisprudence; Dir AFFONSO VITALE SOBRINHO.

Luzeiro Editora Ltda: Rua Almirante Barroso 730, Brás, 03.025 São Paulo, SP; tel. (011) 292-3188; f. 1973; folklore and literature.

Rio Gráfica Educação e Cultura Ltda: Rua Lopes de Oliveira 530, Barra Funda, CP 54151, 01.152 São Paulo, SP; tel. (011) 67-4077; f. 1977; education.

Saraiva SA Livreiros Editores: Av. Marquês de São Vicente 1697, CP 2362, 01.139 São Paulo, SP; tel. (011) 826-8422; f. 1914; education, textbooks, law, economics; Pres. PAULINO SARAIVA.

Scipione Autores Editores Ltda: Rua Princesa Leopoldina 431, Alto de Lapa, 05.081 São Paulo, SP; tel. (011) 260-5878; f. 1974; textbooks, mathematics; Dir Prof. Dr SCIPIONE DI PIERRO NETTO.

Belo Horizonte, MG

Editora Lê SA: Av. D. Pedro II, 4550 Jardin Montanhês, CP 2585, 30.730 Belo Horizonte, MG; tel. (031) 462-6262; telex (031) 3340; f. 1967; textbooks.

Editora Lemi SA: Av. Nossa Senhora de Fátima 1945, CP 1890, 30.000 Belo Horizonte, MG; tel. (031) 201-8044; f. 1967; administration, accounting, law, ecology, economics, textbooks, children's books and reference books.

Editora Vigília Ltda: Rua Felipe dos Santos 508, Bairro de Lourdes, CP 2468, 30.000 Belo Horizonte, MG; tel. (031) 337-2744; f. 1960; general.

Curitiba, PR

Editora Educacional Brasileira SA: Rua XV de Novembro 178, salas 101/04, CP 7498, 80.000 Curitiba, PR; tel. (041) 223-5012; f. 1963; biology, textbooks and reference books.

PUBLISHERS' ASSOCIATIONS

Associação Brasileira do Livro: Av. 13 de Maio 23, 16°, 20.031 Rio de Janeiro, RJ; tel. (021) 232-7173; Dir ALBERJANO TORRES.

Câmara Brasileira do Livro: Av. Ipiranga 1267, 10°, 01.039 São Paulo, SP; tel. (011) 229-7855; Superintendent JOSÉ GORAYEB.

Sindicato Nacional dos Editores de Livros: Av. Rio Branco 37, 15°, 20.097 Rio de Janeiro, RJ; tel. (021) 233-5484; 170 mems; Pres. SÉRGIO C. A. LACERDA; Sec. BERTA ROSA RIBEIRO.

There are also regional publishers' associations.

Radio and Television

In 1986 there were an estimated 67m. radio receivers and 26m. television receivers in use.

Departamento Nacional de Telecomunicações (Dentel) (National Telecommunications Council): Via N2, Anexo do Ministério das Comunicações, Esplanada dos Ministérios, Bloco R, 70.066 Brasília, DF; tel. (061) 223-3229; telex (061) 1175; Dir-Gen. RUBENS BUSSACOS, Jr.

Empresa Brasileira de Radiodifusão (Radiobrás) (Brazilian Broadcasting Company): SCRN 702/3, Bloco B, no. 18, 70.323 Brasília, DF; tel. 224-3949; telex (061) 1682; f. 1976; Pres. ANTÔNIO FROTA NETO.

RADIO

In 1986 there were 2,073 radio stations in Brazil, including 15 in Brasília, 39 in Rio de Janeiro, 33 in São Paulo, 22 in Curitiba, 21 in Porto Alegre and 22 in Belo Horizonte.

The main broadcasting stations in Rio de Janeiro are: Rádio Nacional, Rádio Globo, Rádio Eldorado, Rádio Jornal do Brasil, Rádio Tupi and Rádio Mundial. In São Paulo the main stations are Rádio Bandeirantes, Rádio Mulher, Rádio Eldorado, Rádio Cultura, Rádio Pan-Americana, Rádio Record, Rádio Gazeta and Rádio Excelsior; and in Brasília: Rádio Nacional, Rádio Alvorada, Rádio Planalto and Rádio Capital.

TELEVISION

In 1986 there were 177 television stations in Brazil, of which 95 were in the state capitals and six in Brasília. PAL-M colour television was adopted in 1972 and the Brazilian system is connected with the rest of the world by satellite.

The main television networks are:

Rádio/TV Bandeirantes: Rua Radiantes 13, Morumbí, CP 372, 05.699 São Paulo, SP; tel. (011) 211-3011; telex (011) 37878; 23 television networks throughout Brazil; Pres. JOÃO JORGE SAAD.

TV Gaúcha: Rua TV Gaúcha 189, 90.000 Porto Alegre, RS; tel. (051) 33-6211; telex (051) 4118; Dir JAIME SIROTSKY.

TV Globo: Rua Lopes Quintas 303, 22.463 Rio de Janeiro, RJ; tel. (021) 294-7732; telex (021) 22795; f. 1965; 12 stations; national network; Pres. ROBERTO MARINHO.

TV Manchete: Rua do Russell 804, 22.210 Rio de Janeiro, RJ; tel. (021) 265-2012; telex (021) 33598; Pres. ADOLPHO BLOCH.

TV Record—Canal 7: Av. Miruna 713, Aeroporto, 04.085 São Paulo, SP; tel. (011) 542-9000; telex (011) 22245; Dir-Pres. PAULO MACHADO DE CARVALHO.

TVSBT—Canal 4 de São Paulo, SA: Rua Dona Santa Veloso 575, Vila Guilherme, 02.050 São Paulo, SP; tel. (011) 264-9199; telex (011) 22126; Dir JOSÉ LUIZ ANTIÓRIO.

BROADCASTING ASSOCIATIONS

Associação Brasileira de Emissoras de Rádio e Televisão (ABERT): Mezanino do Hotel Nacional, salas 5 a 8, 70.322 Brasília, DF; tel. (061) 224-4600; telex (061) 2001; f. 1962; mems: 32 shortwave, 643 FM, 1,294 medium-wave and 84 tropical-wave radio stations and 177 television stations (mid-1986); Pres. JOAQUIM MENDONÇA; Exec. Dir ANTÔNIO ABELIN.

There are regional associations for Bahia, Ceará, Goiás, Minas Gerais, Paraná, Pernambuco, Rio de Janeiro and Espírito Santo (combined), Rio Grande do Sul, Santa Catarina, São Paulo, Amazonas, Distrito Federal, Mato Grosso and Mato Grosso do Sul (combined) and Sergipe.

Finance

BANKING

(cap. = capital; p.u. = paid up; dep. = deposits; res = reserves; m. = million; brs = branches; amounts in cruzados, unless otherwise stated)

Conselho Monetário Nacional: SBS, Edif. Banco do Brasil, 6° andar, Brasília, DF; f. 1964 to formulate monetary policy and to supervise the banking system; Pres. Minister of Finance.

Central Bank

Banco Central do Brasil: Edif. Sede, SBS, Av. Pres. Vargas 84, 70.000 Brasília, DF; tel. (061) 224-1453; telex (061) 1702; f. 1965 to execute the decisions of the Conselho Monetário Nacional; bank of issue; total assets 639,423.8m. (July 1985); Pres. FERNÃO BRACHER.

State Commercial Banks

Banco do Brasil, SA: Eixo Rodoviário Sul, Sector Bancário Sul, Lote 23, CP 562, Brasília, DF; tel. (061) 212-2211; telex (061) 8121; f. 1808; cap. p.u. 8,748.5m., res 36,771.6m., dep. 230,314.2m. (Dec. 1985); Pres. CAMILLO CALAZANS DE MAGALHÃES; 3,314 brs.

Banco do Estado de Minas Gerais, SA: Rua Rio de Janeiro 471, 80, 30.000 Belo Horizonte, MG; tel. (031) 224-5882; telex (031) 1181; f. 1967; cap. and res 113.6m., dep. 1,460.5m. (May 1985); Pres. SANDOVAL SOARES DE AZEVEDO, Jr; 260 brs.

Banco do Estado do Paraná, SA: Rua Máximo João Kopp 274, CP 3331, 80.000 Curitiba, PR; tel. (041) 253-8311; telex (041) 6002; f. 1928; cap. and res 438m., dep. 918.1m. (July 1985); Pres. JOSÉ CARLOS CAMPOS HIDALGO; 309 brs.

Banco do Estado do Rio Grande do Sul, SA: Rua Capitão Montanha 177, CP 505, 90.000 Porto Alegre, RS; tel. (051) 24-1177; telex (051) 518170; f. 1928; cap. and res 230.7m., dep. 1,237.2m. (Dec. 1984); Pres. ASSIS ANHAIA DE SOUZA; 296 brs.

Banco do Estado do Rio de Janeiro, SA (BANERJ): Av. Nilo Peçanha 175, CP 21090, 20.020 Rio de Janeiro, RJ; tel. (021) 242-7679; telex (021) 23290; f. 1945; cap. and res 730.2m., dep. 8,072.9m. (Dec. 1985); Pres. CARLOS AUGUSTO RODRIGUES DE CARVALHO; 2 brs.

Banco do Estado de São Paulo, SA: Praça Antônio Prado 6, CP 30-565, 01.010 São Paulo, SP; tel. (011) 259-6622; telex (011) 21737; f. 1926; cap. and res 1,616.1m., dep. 10,435.8m. (June 1985); Pres. FERNANDO MILLIET DE OLIVEIRA; 837 brs.

Banco do Nordeste do Brasil, SA: Praça Murillo Borges 1, 60.000 Fortaleza, CE; tel. (085) 231-0688; telex (085) 1132; f. 1954; cap. and res 1,361.1m., dep. 1,100.4m. (July 1985); Pres. CARLOS MAURO CABRAL BENEVIDES; 163 brs.

Private Banks

Banco América do Sul, SA: Av. Brig. Luís Antônio 2020, CP 8075, 01.318 São Paulo, SP; tel. (011) 288-4933; telex (011) 21354; f. 1940; cap. and res 342.8m., dep. 984.4m. (July 1985); Pres. YOSUKE YOSHIDA; 102 brs.

Banco Auxiliar, SA: Rua Boa Vista 192, POB 8110, 01.014 São Paulo, SP; tel. (011) 235-7122; telex (011) 24161; f. 1928; cap. and res 569.5m., dep. 808.9m. (1985); Pres. RODOLFO MARCO BONFIGLIOLI; 127 brs; taken over by Govt, Nov. 1985.

Banco Bamerindus do Brasil, SA: Av. Pres. Kennedy 3080, 80.000 Curitiba, PR; tel. (041) 242-7411; telex (041) 5303; f. 1952; cap. and res 1,561m., dep. 2,812m. (July 1985); Pres. JOSÉ EDUARDO DE ANDRADE VIEIRA; Dir WERTHER TEIXEIRA DE AZEVEDO; 990 brs.

Banco Bandeirantes, SA: Rua Boa Vista 150, 7°, CP 8260, 01.014 São Paulo, SP; tel. (011) 239-5622; (011) 24633; f. 1944; cap. and res 259.1m., dep. 534.4m. (July 1985); Pres. Dr GILBERTO DE ANDRADE FARIA; 165 brs.

Banco Boavista, SA: Praça Pio X 118, CP 1560-ZC-00, 20.012 Rio de Janeiro, RJ; tel. (021) 291-6633; telex (021) 300053; f. 1924; cap. p.u. and res 156.5m., dep. 1,678.9m. (June 1985); Pres. LINNEO DE PAULA MACHADO; 64 brs.

Banco Bozano Simonsen SA: Av. Rio Branco 138, 20.057 Rio de Janeiro, RJ; tel. (021) 271-8000; telex (021) 22963; f. 1972; cap. and res 71.1m., dep. 207.6m. (July 1985); Pres. JÚLIO RAFAEL DE ARAGÃO BOZANO; 17 brs.

Banco Brasileiro de Descontos, SA (BRADESCO): Cidade de Deus CX, CP 8250, 06.000 Osasco, SP; tel. (011) 804-3311; telex (011) 74001; f. 1943; cap. and res 6,743.3m., dep. 28,241m. (July 1985); Pres. AMADOR AGUIAR; 1,735 brs.

Banco Cidade de São Paulo: Praça Dom José Gaspar 106, CP 30735, 01.047 São Paulo, SP; tel. (011) 258-8233; telex (011) 22198; f. 1965; cap. and res 104.4m., dep. 371.7m. (July 1985); Pres. EDMUNDO SAFDIE; 25 brs.

Banco do Comércio e Indústria de São Paulo, SA: Rua XV de Novembro 289, 01.013 São Paulo, SP; tel. (011) 239-0033; telex (011) 37680; f. 1889; cap. and res 790.6m., dep. 1,989.8m. (July 1985); Pres. CARLOS EDUARDO QUARTIM BARBOSA; 271 brs; taken over by Govt, Nov. 1985.

Banco de Crédito Nacional, SA (BCN): Rua Boa Vista 228, CP 30-243, 01.014 São Paulo, SP; tel. (011) 229-4011; telex (011) 21284; f. 1924; cap. and res 819m., dep. 831.8m. (July 1985); Pres. ANTÔNIO GRISI; 181 brs.

Banco de Crédito Real de Minas Gerais, SA: Rua Espírito Santo 495, POB 90, 30.000 Belo Horizonte, MG; tel. (031) 222-2058; telex (031) 3356; f. 1889; cap. and res 29.6m., dep. 1,311m. (May 1985); Pres. Dr DERMEVAL JOSÉ PIMENTA; 205 brs.

Banco Econômico, SA: Rua Miguel Calmon 285, 40.000 Salvador, BA; tel. (071) 254-1834; telex (071) 1647; f. 1834; cap. and res 1,125.9m., dep. 2,143.8m. (July 1985); Pres. ÂNGELO CALMON DE SÁ; 541 brs.

Banco Europeu para a América Latina (BEAL), SA: Rua Bela Cintra 952, 01.415 São Paulo, SP; tel. (011) 257-0422; telex (011) 23985; f. 1911; formerly Banco Italo-Belga; cap. and res 62.3m., dep. 287.4m. (July 1985); Gen. Man. M. BARDINI; 6 brs.

Banco Francês e Brasileiro, SA: Av. Paulista 1318, 01.310 São Paulo, SP; tel. (011) 251-4522; telex (011) 23340; f. 1948; affiliated with Crédit Lyonnais; cap. and res 834.7m., dep. 1,820.3m. (July 1985); Dir PIERRE JEAN DOSSA; 56 brs.

Banco Hispano Americano: Alameda Santos 960, 01.418 São Paulo, SP; tel. (011) 284-9355; telex (011) 35596; f. 1981; cap. and res 35.4m., dep. 161.1m. (July 1985); Dir CARLOS GUANTER PUIG.

Banco Holandês Unido SA: Rua do Ouvidor 101, 20.040 Rio de Janeiro, RJ; tel. (021) 297-2055; telex (021) 23663; f. 1917; cap. and res 64.8m., dep. 102.2m. (July 1985); Gen. Man. DURK VISSERMAN (acting); 5 brs.

Banco Itaú, SA: Rua XV de Novembro 306, 7° andar, 01.013 São Paulo, SP; tel. (011) 239-8178; telex (011) 3044; f. 1944; cap. and res 3,850.2m., dep. 7,833.3m. (July 1985); Pres. JOSÉ CARLOS DE MORÃES ABREU; 130 brs.

Banco Lar Brasileiro: Rua do Ouvidor 98, 20.040 Rio de Janeiro, RJ; tel. (021) 216-6112; telex (021) 21837; associated with the Chase Manhattan Bank, N.A.; cap. p.u. 220.9m. (June 1985); Pres. ALFREDO SALAZAR, Jr; Exec. Vice-Pres. MILTON TESSEROLLI; 44 brs.

Banco Mercantil de São Paulo, SA: Av. Paulista 1450, CP 4077, 01.310 São Paulo, SP; tel. (011) 252-2121; telex (011) 37701; f. 1938; cap. and res 200.1m., dep. 1,067.4m. (Dec. 1985); Pres. GASTÃO AUGUSTO DE BUENO VIDIGAL; 333 brs.

Banco Mercantil do Brasil, SA: Rua Rio de Janeiro 654, CP 836, 30.000 Belo Horizonte, MG; tel. (031) 201-6122; telex (031) 1762; f. 1941; cap. and res 465.2m., dep. 423.1m. (July 1985); Pres. OSWALDO DE ARAÚJO; 224 brs.

Banco Mitsubishi Brasileiro: Rua Líbero Badaró 641, CP 30179, 01.000 São Paulo, SP; tel. (011) 239-5244; telex (011) 21854; f. 1933; cap. and res 153.5m., dep. 318.9m. (July 1985); Pres. MOTOCHIKA KOBORI; 19 brs.

Banco Nacional, SA: Av. Rio Branco 123, 2° andar, 20.040 Rio de Janeiro, RJ; tel. (021) 296-7722; telex (021) 21265; f. 1944; cap. and res 880.5m., dep. 4,675.2m. (July 1985); Pres. MARCOS DE MAGALHÃES PINTO; 473 brs.

Banco Noroeste SA: Rua Alvares Penteado 216, CP 8119, 01.012 São Paulo, SP; tel. (011) 239-0844; telex (011) 23393; f. 1923; cap. and res 407.3m., dep. 1,437.8m. (July 1985); Pres. JORGE WALLACE SIMONSEN; 151 brs.

Banco Real, SA: Av. Paulista 1374, POB 5766, 01.310 São Paulo, SP; tel. (011) 286-4988; telex (011) 23520; f. 1925; cap. and res

1,334.4m., dep. 2,900.9m. (July 1985); Pres. Dr ALOYSIO DE ANDRADE FARIA; 610 brs.

Banco Royal do Canadá, SA: Rua XV de Novembro 240, 01.013 São Paulo, SP; tel. (011) 239-4533; telex (011) 23351; f. 1984; fmrly Banco Internacional SA; cap. and res 194.2m., dep. 348.2m. (June 1986); Pres. M. A. BRENNAN; 4 brs.

Banco Safra, SA: Rua XV de Novembro 212, São Paulo, SP; tel. (011) 234 6211; telex (011) 21396; cap. and res 932.9m., dep. 2,870.5m. (July 1985); Pres. CARLOS ALBERTO VIEIRA; 64 brs.

Banco Sudameris do Brasil, SA: Rua Bela Vista 739, Santo Amaro, CP 3481, 04.709 São Paulo, SP; tel. (011) 246-8066; telex (011) 21597; f. 1910; cap. and res 422.1m., dep. 1,445.9m. (July 1985); Dir GIOVANNI LENTI; 74 brs.

Banco Sul Brasileiro, SA: Rua 7 de Setembro 1028, CP 26, Porto Alegre, RS; tel. (051) 25-655; telex (051) 1357; f. 1973; cap. 14.7m., res 54.8m., dep. 333.7m. (Dec. 1983); Pres. HÉLIO PRATES DE SILVEIRA; 379 brs; (taken over by the Government in Feb. 1985).

Banco Sumitomo Brasileiro: Av. Paulista 949, CP 7961, São Paulo, SP; cap. and res 123.8m., dep. 153.8m. (July 1985); Pres. ATSUSHI SAKAI; 5 brs.

Banco de Tokyo SA: Av. Paulista 1274, 01.310 São Paulo, SP; tel. (011) 285-6011; telex (011) 21192; f. 1972; cap. and res 187.5m., dep. 481.4m. (July 1985); Pres. TOSHIRO KOBAYASHI; 6 brs.

Unibanco—União de Bancos Brasileiros, SA: Praça do Patriarca 30, POB 8185, 01.000 São Paulo, SP; tel. (011) 235-5000; telex (011) 34074; f. 1924; cap. 500m., dep. 18,782.2m. (1985); Pres. WALTHER MOREIRA SALLES; 896 brs.

Development Banks

Banco de Desenvolvimento de Minas Gerais—BDMG: Rua da Bahia 1600, Belo Horizonte, MG; tel. (031) 212-3822; telex (031) 1343; cap. and res 510.7m., dep. 2,875.5m. (May 1985); Pres. ROBERTO LÚCIO ROCHA BRANT.

Banco de Desenvolvimento do Espírito Santo, SA: Av. Princesa Isabel 64, CP 1168, 29.000 Vitoria, ES; tel. 223-8333; telex 0272-131; cap. 2.3m. (1984); Pres. ANTÔNIO DE CALDAS BRITO.

Banco do Desenvolvimento do Estado da Bahia, SA: Av. Magalhães Neto, S/N°, 40.000 Salvador, BA; tel. (071) 231-2322; telex (071) 1665; f. 1937; cap. and res 348.3m., dep. 3,076.4m. (July 1985); Pres. RAIMUNDO ALMEIDA MOREIRA.

Banco de Desenvolvimento do Estado de São Paulo, SA (BADESP): Av. Paulista 1776, 01.310 São Paulo, SP; tel. (011) 289-2233; cap. 19.7m. (1984), res 1m. (June 1978); Pres. GUSTAVO DE SÁ E SILVA.

Banco de Desenvolvimento do Estado do Rio Grande do Sul, SA (BADESUL): Rua 7 de Setembro 666, 90.000 Porto Alegre, RS; tel. (051) 21-6655; telex (051) 1159; f. 1975; cap. and res 82.9m., dep. 329.4m. (July 1985); Pres. JOSÉ MARQUES DA ROCHA.

Banco de Desenvolvimento do Paraná, SA: Av. Vicente Machado 445, CP 6042, 80.000 Curitiba, PR; tel. (041) 224-9711; telex (041) 5083; f. 1962; cap. 36.6m. (1984); Pres. MARTINHO FAUST.

Banco Nacional de Crédito Cooperativo, SA: SBN, Q.01-B1.C-4°. Par. s/n Edif. Palácio do Desenvolvimento-Asa Norte 70.057 Brasília, DF; tel. 225-2156; telex (061) 2292; established in association with the Ministry of Agriculture and guaranteed by the Federal Government to provide co-operative credit; cap. and res 534.7m., dep. 2,710.6m. (May 1985); Pres. DEJANDIR DALPASQUALE.

Banco Nacional da Habitação: Av. W-3 Norte, Quadra 507, Bloco A, 70.740 Brasília, DF; tel. (061) 272-4255; telex (061) 1340; f. 1964; development bank; cap. 718.m., res 1,638.4m., dep. 2,440.8m. (Dec. 1984); Pres. JOSÉ MARIA ARAGÃO; 23 brs.

Banco Nacional do Desenvolvimento Econômico e Social (BNDES): Av. República do Chile 100, 20.139 Rio de Janeiro, RJ; tel. (021) 277-7447; telex (021) 30447; f. 1952 to act as main instrument for financing of development schemes sponsored by the Government and to support programmes for the development of the national economy; cap. and res 10,364.1m., dep. 42,082.8m. (Dec. 1984); disbursements 6,445.1m. (1984); Pres. ANDRÉ MONTORO, Jr.

Banco Regional de Desenvolvimento do Extremo Sul (BRDE): Rua Uruguai 155, POB 139, 90.000 Porto Alegre, RS; tel. (051) 21-9200; telex (051) 1229; f. 1961; cap. and res 259.6m., dep. 386.6m. (1984); development bank for the states of Paraná, Rio Grande do Sul and Santa Catarina; acts as agent for numerous federal financing agencies and co-operates with IBRD and Eximbank; finances small- and medium-sized enterprises; Pres. CARLOS ANTÔNIO DE ALMEIDA FERREIRA; 3 brs.

Investment Banks

Banco Bozano, Simonsen de Investimento, SA: Av. Rio Branco 138, 20.057 Rio de Janeiro, RJ; tel. (021) 271-8000; telex (021) 22963; f. 1967; investment bank catering for medium- and long-term capital requirements, mergers, acquisitions; cap. 96.6m., dep. 704.7m. (Dec. 1985); Pres. JÚLIO RAFAEL DE ARAGÃO BOZANO; 6 brs.

Banco Finasa de Investimento, SA: Av. Paulista 1450, 01.310 São Paulo, SP; tel. (011) 252-2121; telex (011) 37701; f. 1965; medium- and long-term financing for industrial and commercial activities; underwriting shares and debentures; investment advisers; cap. and res 58.3m., dep. 59.1m. (Dec. 1985); Pres. GASTÃO AUGUSTO DE BUENO VIDIGAL; 6 brs.

Banco de Montreal Investimento SA (Montrealbank): Travessa Ouvidor 4, 20.040 Rio de Janeiro, RJ; tel. (021) 233-1122; cap. and res 242.8m., dep. 438.4m. (July 1985); Pres. PEDRO LEITÃO DA CUNHA; 6 brs.

Comind, Banco de Investimento, SA: Rua Libero Badaró 425, 23° andar, 01.009 São Paulo, SP; tel. (011) 239-3122; telex (011) 37226; f. 1966; cap. and res 448.3m., dep. 625.7m. (July 1985); Pres. CARLOS EDUARDO QUARTIM BARBOSA; 6 brs.

Foreign Banks

Banca Commerciale Italiana: Av. Paulista 407, 01.311 São Paulo, SP; tel. (011) 289-4666; telex (011) 23679; cap. and res 93.9m., dep. 174.6m. (July 1985); Man. MARIO CENTOSA; 2 brs.

Banco de la Nación Argentina: Av. Rio Branco 134-A, 20.040 Rio de Janeiro, RJ; tel. (021) 252-2029; telex (021) 23673; f. 1892; cap. and res 30.5m., dep. 104m. (July 1985); Man. FERNANDO LUIZ ALVES; 2 brs.

Banco Unión (Venezuela): Av. Paulista 1708, 01.310 São Paulo, SP; tel. (011) 283-3722; telex (011) 30476; cap. and res 11.7m., dep. 9.2m. (June 1986); Dir-Gen. FRANCISCO UBEDA HERMIDA.

Citibank NA (USA): Av. Rio Branco 85, 20.040 Rio de Janeiro, RJ; tel. (021) 296-1222; telex (021) 22907; f. 1812; cap. and res 389.2m., dep. 3,125.3m. (July 1985); Dir ARNOLDO SOUZA DE OLIVEIRA; 13 brs.

Deutsche Bank AG (Federal Republic of Germany): Rua 15 de Novembro 137, CP 30427, 01.013 São Paulo, SP; tel. (011) 229-0422; telex (011) 22692; f. 1969; cap. and res 77.1m., dep. 766.3m. (July 1985); Man. MANFRED HAMBURGER.

The First National Bank of Boston (USA): Rua Líbero Badaró 487, 01.009 São Paulo, SP; tel. (011) 234-5622; telex (011) 22285; cap. and res 382.1m., dep. 2,390.1m. (Mar. 1986); Senior Vice Pres. HENRIQUE DE CAMPOS MEIRELLES; 6 brs.

Lloyds Bank International Ltd (UK): Av. Brig. Faria Lima 2020, 01.452 São Paulo, SP; tel. (011) 814-1488; telex (011) 24061; cap. and res 293m., dep. 735.4m. (July 1985); Gen. Man. KEITH BURROUGHS STANGER; 14 brs.

Unión de Bancos del Uruguay: Rua 7 de Setembro 64, 20.050 Rio de Janeiro, RJ; tel. (021) 252-8070; telex (021) 31571; cap. and res 730,000, dep. 284,000 (Dec. 1982); Man. NELSON VAZ MOREIRA.

Banking Associations

Federação Nacional dos Bancos: Rua Líbero Badaró 425, 17° andar, 01.009 São Paulo, SP; tel. (011) 239-3000; telex (011) 24710; f. 1966; Pres. ANTÔNIO DE PÁDUA ROCHA DINIZ; Vice-Pres PEDRO CONDE, THEÓPHILO AZEREDO SANTOS.

Sindicato dos Bancos dos Estados do Rio de Janeiro e Espírito Santo: Av. Rio Branco 81, 19°, Rio de Janeiro, RJ; Pres. THEÓPHILO DE AZEREDO SANTOS; Vice-Pres. Dr MUFAREJ.

Sindicato dos Bancos dos Estados de São Paulo, Paraná, Mato Grosso e Mato Grosso do Sul: Rua Líbero Badaró 293, 13° andar, 01.905 São Paulo, SP; f. 1924; Pres. PAULO DE QUEIROZ.

There are eight other banking associations in Maceió, Salvador, Fortaleza, Belo Horizonte, João Pessoa, Recife, Rio de Janeiro and Porto Alegre.

STOCK EXCHANGES

Comissão de Valores Mobiliáros CVM: Rua 7 de Setembro 111, 20.050 Rio de Janeiro, RJ; tel. (021) 292-5177; telex (021) 21549; f. 1977 to supervise the operations of the stock exchanges and develop the Brazilian securities market; Pres. VITORIO CABRAL.

Bolsa de Valores do Rio de Janeiro: Praça 15 de Novembro 20, 20.010 Rio de Janeiro, RJ; tel. (021) 291-5354; telex (021) 30289; f. 1845; 639 stocks quoted; Pres. Dr ENIO CARVALHO RODRIGUES; Vice-Pres. CESAR MANOEL DE SOUZA.

BRAZIL

Bolsa de Valores de São Paulo: Rua Líbero Badaró 471, 3°, São Paulo, SP; tel. (011) 258-7222; 500 stocks quoted; Pres. Dr Eduardo Rocha de Azevedo.

There are commodity exchanges at Porto Alegre, Vitória, Recife, Santos and São Paulo.

INSURANCE

Supervisory Authorities

Superintendência de Seguros Privados (SUSEP): Rio de Janeiro, RJ; tel. (021) 231-3092; f. 1966; within Ministry of Finance; Superintendent João Régis Ricardo dos Santos.

Conselho Nacional de Seguros Privados (CNSP): Rio de Janeiro, RJ; tel. (021) 222-1423; f. 1966; Pres. Minister of Finance; Sec. Vanice da Silveira Araújo Lima.

Instituto de Resseguros do Brasil (IRB): Av. Marechal Câmara 171, CP 1440, 20.023 Rio de Janeiro, RJ; tel. (021) 297-1212; telex (021) 21237; f. 1939; reinsurance; Pres. Jorge Hilário Gouvêa Vieira.

Principal National Companies

(p.i. = premium income; cap. = capital; m. = million; amounts in cruzados, unless otherwise stated)

The following is a list of the 21 principal national insurance companies, selected on the basis of premium income.

Rio de Janeiro, RJ

Boavista, Cia de Seguros de Vida e Acidentes: Rua Barão de Itapagipe 225, 20.261 Rio de Janeiro, RJ; tel. (021) 264-0101; telex (021) 22055; f. 1950; p.i. 12.6m., cap. 4m. (1983); life and risk; Pres. Antônio Carlos de Almeida Braga.

Bradesco Seguros, SA: Rua Barão de Itapagipe 225, 20.261 Rio de Janeiro, RJ; tel. (021) 264-0101; telex (021) 22055; f. 1935; p.i. 22.4m., cap. 9.4m. (1983); general; Pres. Antônio Carlos de Almeida Braga.

Cia Internacional de Seguros: Rua Ibituruna 81, Maracanã, CP 1137, 20.271 Rio de Janeiro, RJ; tel. (021) 284-1222; f. 1920; p.i. US $40m., net assets $40m. (1985); property, life and risk; Pres. Dr Maurice Albert Bercoff.

Generali do Brasil, Cia Nacional de Seguros: Av. Rio Branco 128, 6° andar, Rio de Janeiro, RJ; tel. (021) 292-0144; telex (021) 22846; f. 1945; p.i. 7.5m., cap. 2m. (1983); general; Pres. Cláudio Bietolini.

Nacional, Cia de Seguros: Av. Pres. Vargas 850, 20.271 Rio de Janeiro, RJ; tel. (021) 296-2112; telex (021) 30881; f. 1946; p.i. 11.2m., cap. 6.3m. (1984); life and risk; Pres. Victor Arthur Renault.

Sasse, Cia Nacional de Seguros Gerais: Av. Almirante Barroso 81, 5°, 6° e 8°, Rio de Janeiro, RJ; tel. (021) 220-51967; f. 1967; p.i. 8.1m., cap. 350,000 (1984); general; Pres. Oyama Pereira.

Sul América, Cia Nacional de Seguros: Rua da Quitanda 86, Rio de Janeiro, RJ; tel. (021) 291-2020; telex (021) 30677; f. 1895; p.i. 17.2m., cap. 4.5m. (1983); life and risk; Pres. Leonídio Ribeiro, Jr; offices in São Paulo, Porto Alegre, Belo Horizonte and Recife.

Sul América Terrestres, Marítimos e Acidentes Cia de Seguros: Rua da Quitanda 86, Rio de Janeiro, RJ; tel. (021) 291-2020; telex (021) 30407; f. 1913; general; p.i. 23.3m., cap. 4.6m.; Pres. Leonídio Ribeiro.

Yorkshire-Corcovado Cia de Seguros: Av. Almirante Barroso 52, 24° andar, 20.031 Rio de Janeiro, RJ; tel. (021) 292-1125; telex (021) 22343; f. 1943; cap. 50m. (1985); life and risk; Pres. Manoel Pio Corrêa.

São Paulo, SP

Brasil, Cia de Seguros Gerais: Rua Luiz Coelho 26, 01.309 São Paulo, SP; tel. (011) 285-1533; telex (011) 21401; f. 1904; p.i. 9.9m., cap. 5m. (1983); general; Vice-Pres. Pierre Serrigny.

Cia Paulista de Seguros: Rua Líbero Badaró 158, CP 709, 01.008 São Paulo, SP; tel. (011) 229-0811; telex (011) 37787; f. 1906; p.i. 9m., cap. 1.5m. (1983); general; Pres. Roberto Pereira de Almeida.

Cia Real Brasileira de Seguros: Av. Paulista 1374, 6° andar, 01.310 São Paulo, SP; tel. (011) 285-0255; telex (011) 24744; f. 1965; p.i. 4.8m., cap. 2.1m. (1983); Pres. Aloysio de Andrade Faria.

Cia de Seguros do Estado de São Paulo: Rua Pamplona 227, 01.405 São Paulo, SP; tel. (011) 239-2911; telex (011) 21999; f. 1967; p.i. 7.8m., cap. 4m. (1983); life and risk; Pres. Herbert Júlio Nogueira.

Comind Cia de Seguros: Rua Dr Miguel Couto 58, 01.008 São Paulo, SP; tel. (011) 239-1822; telex (011) 37776; f. 1964; p.i. 8.4m., cap. 2m. (1983); life and risk; Pres. Carlos Eduardo Quartim Barbosa; Gen. Man. Paulo Pompéia Gavião Gonzaga.

Itaú Seguros SA: POB 1798, Praça Alfredo Egydio de S. Aranha 100, Bloco A, 04.390 São Paulo, SP; tel. (011) 582-3322; telex (011) 32125; f. 1921; p.i. US $169.9m., cap. $30.7m. (1985); all classes; Pres. Eudoro Libanio Villela.

Porto Seguro Cia de Seguros Gerais: Av. Rio Branco 1489, 03.242 São Paulo, SP; tel. (011) 223-0022; telex (011) 32613; f. 1945; p.i. 9.5m., cap. 1.3m. (1983); life and risk; Pres. Rosa Garfinkel.

São Paulo, Cia Nacional de Seguros: Rua Quirino de Andrade 215, 01.049 São Paulo, SP; tel. (011) 228-9322; telex (011) 24483; f. 1920; p.i. 6.6m., cap. 2m. (1983); life and risk; Pres. Décio Ferraz Novães.

Skandia-Boavista Cia Brasileira de Seguros: Av. Paulista 1415, 01.311 São Paulo, SP; tel. (011) 284-5422; f. 1914; p.i. 5m., cap. 3m. (1983); Pres. Antônio Carlos de Almeida Braga.

Sul America Bandeirante Seguros, SA: Rua Anchieta 35, 01.016 São Paulo, SP; tel. (011) 259-3555; telex (011) 24021; f. 1944; p.i. 12.6m., cap. 2.5m. (1983); life and risk; Pres. Rony Castro de Oliveira Lyrio.

Sul America Unibanco Seguradora SA: Rua Líbero Badaró 293, 32° andar, 01.009 São Paulo, SP; tel. (011) 235-5000; telex (011) 34826; f. 1866; p.i. 8.8m., cap. 7.1m. (1983); Pres. Leonídio Ribeiro.

Vera Cruz Seguradora SA: Av. Maria Coelho Aguiar 215, Bloco D, 2° andar, 05.804 São Paulo, SP; tel. (011) 545-4944; f. 1955; p.i. 6.9m., cap. 4.4m. (1983); general; Pres. Horácio Ives Freyre.

Provincial Companies

The following is a list of the principal provincial insurance companies, selected on the basis of premium income.

Bamerindus Cia de Seguros: Rua Marechal Floriano Peixoto 5500, Curitiba, PR; tel. (041) 221-2121; telex (041) 5672; f. 1938; cap. 129.1m. (1985); all classes; Pres. Hamilcar Pizzatto.

Cia de Seguros Aliança da Bahia: Rua Pinto Martins 11, 9° andar, 40.000 Salvador, BA; tel. 242-1065; f. 1870; p.i. 11.3m., cap. 3.5m. (1983); general; Pres. Pamphilo Pedreira Freire de Carvalho.

Cia de Seguros Minas-Brasil: Rua dos Caetés 745, 30.120 Belo Horizonte, MG; tel. (031) 201-5799; telex (031) 1506; f. 1938; p.i. 15.5m., cap. 130,000 (March 1986); life and risk; Pres. José Carneiro de Araújo.

Cia União de Seguros Gerais: Av. Borges de Medeiros 261, 90.020 Porto Alegre, RS; tel. (051) 26-7933; telex (051) 2530; f. 1891; cap. 100.4m. (1986); Pres. Celito de Grande.

Trade and Industry

GOVERNMENT ADVISORY BODIES

Comissão de Fusão e Incorporação de Empresa (COFIE): Ministério da Fazenda, Esplanada dos Ministérios, Edif. Sede, Ala B, 1° andar, Brasília, DF; tel. (061) 225-3405; telex (061) 1539; mergers commission; Pres. Sebastião Marcos Vital; Exec. Sec. Edgar Bezerra Leite, Jr.

Conselho de Desenvolvimento Comercial (CDC): Ministério da Indústria e do Comércio, SCS, Q.02, Edif. Pres. Dutra, 1° e 2° andares, Bloco C, No 227, Esplanada dos Ministérios, 70.300 Brasília, DF; tel. (061) 224-0685; telex (061) 2537; commercial development council; Exec. Sec. Ruy Coutinho do Nascimento.

Conselho de Desenvolvimento Econômico (CDE): Esplanada dos Ministérios, Bloco K, 8° andar, 820, 70.063 Brasília, DF; tel. (061) 215-4151; f. 1974; economic development council; Pres. João Sayad.

Conselho de Desenvolvimento Industrial (CDI): Ministério da Indústria e do Comércio, SAS Quadra 05, Lote 05, Bloco H, 70.070 Brasília, DF; tel. (061) 226-3847; telex (061) 2225; f. 1969; industrial development council; offers fiscal incentives for selected industries and for producers of manufactured goods under the Special Export Programme; Exec. Sec. José Afonso Alves Castanheira.

Conselho de Desenvolvimento Social (CDS): Esplanada dos Ministérios, Bloco K, 3° andar, 382, 70.063 Brasília, DF; tel. (061) 215-4477; social development council.

Conselho Interministerial de Preços (CIP): Av. Pres. Antônio Carlos 375, 10° andar, Rio de Janeiro, RJ; tel. (021) 240-2281; telex (021) 33314; prices commission; Exec. Sec. Aloisio Teixeira.

BRAZIL   *Directory*

Conselho Nacional do Comércio Exterior (CONCEX): Fazenda, 5° andar, Gabinete do Ministro, Esplanada dos Ministérios, Bloco 6, 70.053 Brasília, DF; tel. (061) 223-6959; telex (061) 1142; f. 1966; responsible for foreign exchange and trade policies and for the control of export activities; Sec. ROBERTO FENDT, Jr.

Conselho Nacional de Desenvolvimento Científico e Tecnológico (CNPq): Av. W-3 Norte, Quadra 507, Bloco B, 70.740 Brasília, DF; tel. (061) 274-1155; telex (061) 1089; f. 1951; scientific and technological development council; Pres. Dr CRODOVALDO PAVAN.

Conselho Nacional de Desenvolvimento Pecuário (CONDEPE): to promote livestock development.

Conselho de Não-Ferrosos e de Siderurgia (CONSIDER): Ministério da Indústria e Comércio, Esplanada dos Ministérios, Bloco 6, 5° andar, 70.053 Brasília, DF; tel. (061) 224-8039; telex (061) 1012; f. 1973; exercises a supervisory role over development policy in the non-ferrous and iron and steel industries; Exec. Sec. WILLIAM ROCHA CANTAL.

Conselho Nacional do Petróleo (CNP): SGA Norte, Quadra 603, Módulos H, I, J, 70.830 Brasília, DF; tel. (061) 226-9403; telex (061) 1673; f. 1938; directs national policy on petroleum; Pres. Gen. ROBERTO FRANCO DOMINGUES.

Fundação Instituto Brasileiro de Geografia e Estatística (IBGE): Av. Franklin Roosevelt 166, Castelo, 20.021 Rio de Janeiro, RJ; tel. (021) 220-6671; telex (021) 30939; f. 1936; produces and analyses statistical, geographical, cartographical, geodetic, demographic and socio-economic information; Dir-Gen. REGIS BONELLI.

Instituto Nacional de Metrologia, Normalização e Qualidade Industrial (INMETRO): SAS, Quadra 5, Lote 5, 70.070 Brasília, DF; tel. (061) 225-8032; telex (061) 1834; in 1981 INMETRO absorbed the Instituto Nacional de Pesos e Medidas (INPM), the weights and measures institute; Pres. JOAREZ TAVORA VEADO.

Instituto de Planejamento Econômico e Social (IPEA): SBS, Edif. BNDE, 6° andar, 70.076 Brasília, DF; tel. (061) 225-4350; telex (061) 1979; planning institute; Pres. HENRI PHILIPPE REICHSTUL.

Superintendência do Desenvolvimento da Pesca (SUDEPE): Edif. da Pesca, Av. W-3 Norte, Quadra 506, Bloco C, 70.040 Brasília, DF; tel. (061) 273-2437; telex (061) 2018; attached to the Ministry of Agriculture; assists development of fishing industry; Superintendent Dr DJACI MAGALHÃES.

REGIONAL DEVELOPMENT ORGANIZATIONS

Companhia de Desenvolvimento do Vale do São Francisco (CODEVASF): SGAN, Q 601, Lote 1, Edif. Sede, 70.830 Brasília, DF; tel. (061) 224-1709; telex (061) 1057; f. 1974; Pres. ELISEU ROBERTO DE ANDRADE ALVAS.

Superintendência do Desenvolvimento da Amazônia (SUDAM): Av. Almirante Barroso 426, Bairro do Marco, 66.000 Belém, PA; tel. (091) 226-0044; f. 1966 to develop the Amazon regions of Brazil; attached to the Ministry of the Interior; supervises industrial, cattle breeding and basic services projects; Superintendent Eng. HENRY CHECRALLA XAYATH.

Superintendência do Desenvolvimento do Nordeste (SUDENE): Praça Supt João Gonçalves de Souza, Cidade Universitária, 50.000 Recife, PE; tel. (081) 271-1044; telex (081) 1245; f. 1959; attached to the Ministry of the Interior; assists development of north-east Brazil; Superintendent JOSÉ REINAL DO CARNEIRO TAVARES.

Superintendência do Desenvolvimento da Região Centro Oeste (SUDECO): SAS, Quadra 1, Bloco A, lotes 9/10, 70.070 Brasília, DF; tel. (061) 225-6943; telex (061) 1616; f. 1967 to co-ordinate development projects in the States of Goiás, Mato Grosso, Mato Grosso do Sul, Rondônia and Distrito Federal; Superintendent ANTÔNIO MENDES CANALE.

Superintendência do Desenvolvimento da Região Sul (SUDESUL): Rua Caldas Junior 120, 20°, 90.000 Porto Alegre, RS; tel. (0512) 221-2833; telex (051) 1005; f. 1967 to co-ordinate development in the states of Rio Grande do Sul, Santa Catarina and Paraná; attached to the Ministry of the Interior; Superintendent FRANCISCO JOSÉ PEREIRA.

Superintendência da Zona Franca de Manaus (SUFRAMA): Rua Ministro João Gonçalves de Souza, Cidade Universitária, Distrito Industrial, 69.000 Manaus, AM; tel. (092) 237-3288; telex (092) 2146; to assist in the development of the Manaus Free Zone; Superintendent ROBERTO COHEN.

Other regional development organizations include Poloamazônia (agricultural and agro-mineral nuclei in the Amazon Region), Polocentro (woodland savannah in Central Brazil), Poloeste (agricultural and agro-mineral nuclei in the Centre-West), Polonordeste (integrated areas in the North-East), Procacau (expansion of cocoa industry), Prodoeste (development of the Centre-South), Proterra (land distribution and promotion of agricultural industries in the North and North-East), Provale (development of the São Francisco basin).

COMMERCIAL, AGRICULTURAL AND INDUSTRIAL ORGANIZATIONS

Associação do Comércio Exterior do Brasil: Av. General Justo 335, Rio de Janeiro, RJ; tel. (021) 240-5048; exporters' association; Pres. NORBERTO INGO ZABROZNY.

Companhia Vale do Rio Doce, SA (CVRD): Av. Graça Aranha 26, Bairro Castelo, 20.005 Rio de Janeiro, RJ; tel. (021) 272-4477; telex (021) 23162; f. 1942; state-owned mining company; owns and operates the Vitória–Minas railway, the port of Tubarão and the Carajás iron ore project; also involved in forestry and pulp production; Pres. RAYMUNDO PEREIRA MASCARENHAS.

Confederação das Associações Comerciais do Brasil: Brasília, DF; confederation of chambers of commerce in each state; Pres. AMAURY TENPORAL.

Confederação Nacional da Agricultura (CNA): Brasília, DF; tel. (061) 225-3150; national agricultural confederation; Pres. CORREA LEITE.

Confederação Nacional do Comércio (CNC): SCS, Edif. Presidente Dutra, 4° andar, Quadra 11, 70.327 Brasília, DF; tel. (061) 223-0578; national confederation comprising 35 affiliated federations of commerce; Pres. ANTÔNIO JOSÉ DOMINGUES DE OLIVEIRA SANTOS.

Confederação Nacional da Indústria (CNI): SBN, Edif. Roberto Simonsen, 16° andar, 70.040 Brasília, DF; tel. (061) 224-1328; f. 1938; national confederation of industry comprising the 21 state industrial federations; Pres. Dr ALBANO DO PRADO FRANCO; Vice-Pres. EDGAR ARP.

Confederação Nacional dos Transportes Terrestres (CNTT): Brasília, DF; tel. (061) 223-2300; confederation of land transport federations; Pres. FORTUNATO PERES, Jr.

Departamento Nacional da Produção Mineral (DNPM): SAN, Quadra 1, Bloco B, 3° andar, 70.040 Brasília, DF; tel. (061) 224-2670; telex (061) 1116; f. 1934; attached to the Ministry of Mines and Energy; responsible for geological studies and control of exploration of mineral resources; Dir-Gen. JOSÉ BELFORT DOS SANTOS BASTOS.

Federação das Indústrias do Estado de São Paulo (FIESP): Av. Paulista 1313, 01.311 São Paulo, SP; tel. (011) 251-3522; telex (011) 22130; businessmen's association; Pres. LUÍS EULÁLIO DE BUENO VIDIGAL; Vice-Pres. PAULO FRANCINI.

Instituto do Açúcar e do Álcool (IAA): Praça 15 de Novembro 42, 8°, 20.010 Rio de Janeiro, RJ; tel. (021) 231-2741; telex (021) 21391; f. 1933; government agency for the promotion and development of the sugar industry; sole exporter of raw sugar; Pres. JOSÉ RIBEIRO TOLEDO (acting).

Instituto Brasileiro do Café (IBC): Av. Rodrigues Alves 129, 10°, Cais do Porto, 20.081 Rio de Janeiro, RJ; tel. (021) 223-1592; telex (021) 23119; f. 1952; controls and promotes production of and commerce in coffee and gives technical advice to producers; government agency; Pres. PAULO GRACIANO.

Instituto Brasileiro do Desenvolvimento Florestal (IBDF): Setor de Areas Isoladas, L4 Norte, 70.080 Brasília, DF; tel. (061) 226-7101; telex (061) 1711; f. 1967; independent organization affiliated to the Ministry of Agriculture; responsible for the annual formulation of national and regional forest plans; Pres. MARCELO PALMÉRIO.

Instituto Nacional de Colonização e Reforma Agrária (INCRA): Brasília, DF; tel. (061) 223-8852; f. 1970; affiliated to the Ministry of Agriculture; Pres. Col PEDRO DANTAS.

Instituto Nacional da Propriedade Industrial (INPI): Praça Mauá 7, 11° andar, 20.081 Rio de Janeiro, RJ; tel. (021) 223-4182; telex (021) 22992; f. 1970; Pres. MAURO FERNANDO MARIA ARRUDA.

Instituto Nacional de Tecnologia (INT): Av. Venezuela 82, 8°, 20.081 Rio de Janeiro, RJ; tel. (021) 253-9422; telex (021) 30056; f. 1921; co-operates in national industrial development; Dir PAULO ROBERTO KRAHE.

BRAZIL *Directory*

PRINCIPAL STATE ENTERPRISES

In November 1986 the Government announced the closure or merger of 15 state enterprises. A further 32 organizations were to be closed or merged over the coming months.

Centrais Elétricas Brasileiras, SA (ELETROBRÁS): Av. Pres. Vargas 642, 20.071 Rio de Janeiro, RJ; tel. (021) 253-0046; telex (021) 22395; f. 1962; government holding company (7 subsidiary and 28 associated electricity companies) responsible for planning, financing and managing Brazil's electrical energy programme; Pres. MARIO PENNA BHERING.

Companhia Siderúrgica Nacional, SA (CSN): Av. 13 de Maio 13, 8° andar, Centro 20.031 Rio de Janeiro, RJ; tel. (021) 297-7177; telex (021) 23025; f. 1941; iron and steel; Pres. JUVENAL OSÓRIO GOMES.

Empresa Brasileira de Aeronáutica, SA (EMBRAER): Av. Brigadeiro Faria Lima 2.710, CP 343, 12.200 São José dos Campos, SP; tel. (123) 21-5400; telex (11) 33589; f. 1969; aeronautics industry; Chair. and Chief Executive Officer (vacant).

Empresa Brasileira de Assistência Técnica e Extensão Rural (EMBRATER): Av. W-3 Norte Q 515, LE 03, Bloco C, Brasília, DF; tel. (061) 272-3556; telex (061) 1916; Pres. ROMEU PADILHA DE FIGUEIREDO.

Empresa Brasileira de Correios e Telégrafos (ECT): Ed. Sede, 19° andar, SBN, Conj. 3, Bloco A, 70.002 Brasília, DF; tel. (061) 224-9262; telex (061) 1119; posts and telegraph; Pres. LAUMAR MELO VASCONCELOS.

Empresa Brasileira de Pesquisa Agropecuária (EMBRAPA): SCS, Supercenter Venâncio 2000, Q.08, Bloco B, No 50, 9° andar, 70.333 Brasília, DF; tel. (061) 216-5110; telex (061) 1620; f. 1973; attached to the Ministry of Agriculture; agricultural research; Pres. ORMUZ FREITAS RIVALDO.

Empresa Brasileira de Telecomunicações, SA (EMBRATEL): Av. Pres. Vargas 1012, CP 2586, 20.071 Rio de Janeiro, RJ; tel. (021) 552-1216; telex (021) 22185; f. 1965; operates national and international telecommunications system; Pres. PEDRO JORGE CASTELO BRANCO SAMPAIO.

Petróleo Brasileiro, SA (PETROBRÁS): Av. República do Chile 65, 20.035 Rio de Janeiro, RJ; tel. (021) 212-4477, ext. 3442/3; telex (021) 23335; f. 1953; has monopoly on development and production of petroleum and petroleum products; 1985 budget US $1,743m.; 50,304 employees; Pres. OZIRES SILVA.

Petrobrás Comércio Internacional, SA (INTERBRÁS): Rua do Rosário 90, Rio de Janeiro, RJ; tel. (021) 296-2033; telex (021) 21709; Pres. ARMANDO GUEDES COELHO; Vice-Pres. JOSEMAR FERREIRA NASCIMENTO.

Petrobrás Distribuidora, SA: Praça 22 de Abril 36, 8° andar, Castelo, 20.021 Rio de Janeiro, RF; tel. (021) 240-4748; telex (021) 21222; f. 1971; marketing of all petroleum by-products; Pres. CARLOS SANT'ANNA; Vice-Pres. MARCUS TÚLIO ROBERTO SAMPAIO DE MELO.

Petrobrás Fertilizantes, SA (PETROFÉRTIL): Praça Mahatma Gandhi 14, 9°/13° andares, 20.031 Rio de Janeiro, RJ; tel. (021) 220-0870; telex (021) 23880; f. 1976; Pres. MAXIMIANO DA SILVA FONSECA; Vice-Pres. AURÍLIO FERNANDES LIMA.

Petrobrás Internacional, SA (BRASPETRO): Praça Pio X 119, 20.040 Rio de Janeiro, RJ; tel. (021) 297-0102; telex (021) 21889; f. 1972; international division with operations in Algeria, Angola, People's Republic of China, the Congo, Guatemala, India, Libya and South Yemen; Pres. WAGNER FREIRE; Vice-Pres. ANTÔNIO SEABRA.

Petrobrás Mineraçao, SA (Petromisa): Av. Pres. Vargas 583, 20.071 Rio de Janeiro, RJ; tel. (021) 224-7805; telex (021) 32509; potassium exploration and non-petroleum mining; Pres. JOSÉ EDILSON DE MELO TÁVORA; Vice-Pres. RUBEN LAHYR SCHNEIDER.

Petrobrás Química, SA (PETROQUISA): Rua Buenos Aires 40, 20.070 Rio de Janeiro, RJ; tel. (021) 297-6677; telex (021) 21496; f. 1968; petrochemicals industry; controls 27 affiliated companies and 4 subsidiaries; Pres. PAULO VIEIRA BELOTTI; Vice-Pres. TARCISIO DE VASCONCELOS MAIA.

Siderurgia Brasileira, SA (SIDERBRÁS): SAS, Quadra 2, Bloco E, Edif. Siderbrás, 9° andar, 70.070 Brasília, DF; tel. (061) 223-9104; telex (061) 1542; f. 1974; steel industry; Pres. AMARO LANARI, Jr.

Other state enterprises include Aços Finos Piratini, SA, Companhia Coque e Álcool de Madeira (COALBRA), Companhia Ferro e Aço de Vitória, Companhia Nacional de Alcalis, SA, Companhia Siderúrgica de Mogi das Cruzes, Companhia Siderúrgica Paulista, SA, Usinas Siderúrgicas da Bahia and Usinas Siderúrgicas de Minas Gerais.

TRADE UNIONS

Following the return to civilian government in March 1985, the ban on trade union associations, which had been in force under military rule, was repealed.

Central Unica dos Trabalhadores (CUT): São Paulo, SP; f. 1982; central union confederation; left-wing; Pres. JAIR MENEGUELLI; Leader LUÍS IGNÁCIO (LULA) DA SILVA.

Confederação General dos Trabalhadores (CGT): São Paulo, SP; f. 1986; fmrly Coordenação Nacional das Classes Trabalhadoras; represents 1,258 labour organizations linked to PMDB; Pres. JOAQUIM DOS SANTOS ANDRADE.

Confederação Nacional dos Metalúrgicos (Metal Workers): f. 1985; Pres. JOAQUIM DOS SANTOS ANDRADE.

Confederação Nacional das Profissões Liberais (CNPL) (Liberal Professions): SCS, Edif. Gilberto Salomão, Gr. 807/810, 70.305 Brasília, DF; tel. (061) 223-2683; f. 1953; confederation of liberal professions; Pres. Dr CARLOS FALKENBERG.

Confederação Nacional dos Trabalhadores na Indústria (CNTI) (Industrial Workers): Av. W 3 Norte, Quadra 505, Lote 01, 70.730 Brasília, DF; tel. (061) 274-4150; f. 1946; Pres. ARY CAMPISTA.

Confederação Nacional dos Trabalhadores no Comércio (CNTC) (Commercial Workers): Av. W/5 Sul, Quadra 902, Bloco C, 70.390 Brasília, DF; tel. (061) 224-3511; f. 1946; Pres. ANTÔNIO DE OLIVEIRA SANTOS.

Confederação Nacional dos Trabalhadores em Transportes Marítimos, Fluvais e Aéreos (CNTTMFA) (Maritime, River and Air Transport Workers): Edif. Seguradoras, Sala 609, SBS, 70.072 Brasília, DF; tel. (061) 224-0047; f. 1960; Pres. RÔMULO AUGUSTUS PEREIRA DE SOUZA.

Confederação Nacional dos Trabalhadores em Transportes Terrestres (CNTTT) (Land Transport Workers): SBS Edif. Seguradoras, 11° andar, 70.072 Brasília, DF; tel. (061) 224-5011; telex (061) 1593; f. 1952; 300,000 mems; Pres. ORLANDO COUTINHO.

Confederação Nacional dos Trabalhadores em Comunicações e Publicidade (CONTCOP) (Communications and Advertising Workers): Edif. Serra Dourada, 7° andar, Gr. 705/708, Quadra 11, SCS, 70.365 Brasília, DF; tel. (061) 224-7926; f. 1964; Pres. JOSÉ ALCEU PORTOCARRERO.

Confederação Nacional dos Trabalhadores nas Empresas de Crédito (CONTEC) (Workers in Credit Institutions): Av. W4, SEP-SUL EQ 707/907 Lote E, 70.351 Brasília, DF; tel. (061) 224-9428; f. 1958; 693,216 mems (1982); Pres. WILSON GOMEZ DE MOURA.

Confederação Nacional dos Trabalhadores em Estabelecimentos de Educação e Cultura (CNTEEC) (Workers in Education and Culture): SAS, Quadra 4, Bloco B, 70.302 Brasília, DF; tel. (061) 226-2988; f. 1967; Pres. MIGUEL ABRAHÃO.

Confederação Nacional dos Trabalhadores na Agricultura (CONTAG) (Agricultural Workers): MSPW, Conjunto 502, Lote 2, Núcleo Bandeirante, 70.750 Brasília, DF; tel. (061) 552-0259; f. 1964; Pres. JOSÉ FRANCISCO DA SILVA.

Transport

Conselho Nacional de Transportes: Ministério dos Transportes, Esplanada dos Ministérios, Bloco 9, 7°, 70.062 Brasília, DF; tel. (061) 224-5622; telex (061) 1096; f. 1961 to study, co-ordinate and execute government transport policy and reorganize railway, road and ports and waterways councils; Pres. Minister of Transport; Exec. Sec. LAURY PEREIRA BARCELLOS.

Empresa Brasileira de Planejamento de Transportes (GEIPOT): SAN, Quadra 3, Blocos N/O, Edif. Núcleo dos Transportes, 70.040 Brasília, DF; tel. (061) 226-7335; telex (061) 1316; f. 1973; agency for the promotion of an integrated modern transport system; advises the Minister of Transport on transport policy; Pres. STANLEY FORTES BAPTISTA.

Empresa Brasileira de Transportes Urbanos (EBTU): SAN, Quadra 3, Lote A, 3°, 70.040 Brasília, DF; f. 1975 to administer resources for national urban transportation programmes costing 88,438.7m. cruzeiros between 1976 and 1982; Pres. TELMO BORBA MAGADAN.

RAILWAYS

In 1985 the Government announced plans to invest US $422m. in a project to modernize and expand the railway network. Out of a total network of 29,901 km, 2,094 km of track has been electrified.

Rêde Ferroviária Federal, SA (RFFSA) (Federal Railway Corporation): Praça Procópio Ferreira 86, 20.224 Rio de Janeiro, RJ; tel. (021) 291-2185; telex (021) 21372; f. 1957 as a holding company for 18 railways grouped into 7 regional networks, with a total of 23,837 km in 1984; a mixed company in which the government holds the majority of the shares; Pres. Ing. OSIRIS STENGHEL GUIMARÃES; Vice-Pres. FERNANDO J. F. NETO.

There are also railways owned by State Governments and several privately-owned railways:

Carajás Railway: Retorno Itaqui–Pedrinhas, Km 7, BR 135, 65.000 São Luís, MA; tel. (0982) 222-8844; telex (0982) 164/205; state-owned; transportation of iron ore, wood and rice; 890 km inaugurated in February 1985; Dir ROMILDO COELHO VELLO.

Companhia Vale de Rio Doce (Vitória–Minas Railway): Av. Graça Aranha 26, Castelo, 20.005 Rio de Janeiro, RJ; tel. (021) 272-4477; telex (021) 23162; state-owned; transportation of iron ore, general cargo, passengers; 895 km; Pres. RAYMUNDO PEREIRA MASCARENHAS.

Estrada de Ferro do Amapá: Praia de Botafogo 300, 11-A, 22.259 Rio de Janeiro, RJ; tel. (021) 552-4422; telex (021) 23774; opened 1957; 194 km open in 1983; operated by Indústria e Comércio de Minérios, SA; Pres. OSWALDO LUIZ SENRA PESSOA.

FEPASA—Ferrovia Paulista, SA: Praça Julio Prestes 148, 01.218 São Paulo, SP; tel. (011) 223-7211; telex (011) 22724; formed by merger of five railways operated by São Paulo State; 5,100 km open in 1984; Pres. SEBASTIÃO H. LEITE CINTRA.

Other privately-owned mineral lines are: Estrada de Ferro Campos do Jordão (47 km open in 1984), Estrada de Ferro Perus–Pirapora (33 km open in 1984), Estrada de Ferro Votorantim (21 km open in 1984) and Estrada de Ferro Mineração Rio do Norte (f. 1984; 35 km open in 1983).

ROADS

In 1985 there were 1,583,172 km of roads in Brazil, of which 7.3% were paved. Brasília has been a focal point for inter-regional development, and paved roads link the capital with every region of Brazil. The building of completely new roads has taken place predominantly in the north. Roads are the principal mode of transport, accounting for 70% of freight and 97% of passenger traffic, including long-distance bus services, in 1979. Major projects include the 5,000-km Trans-Amazonian Highway, running from Recife and Cabedelo to the Peruvian border, the 4,138-km Cuibá–Santarém highway, which will run in a north–south direction, and the 3,555-km Trans-Brasiliana project which will link Marabá, on the Trans-Amazonian highway, with Aceguá on the Uruguayan frontier.

Departamento Nacional de Estradas de Rodagem (DNER) (National Roads Development): Av. Pres. Vargas 522/534, 20.071 Rio de Janeiro, RJ; tel. (021) 233-2545; telex (021) 21605; f. 1945 to plan and execute federal road policy and to supervise state and municipal roads with the aim of integrating them into the national network; Dir JOÃO MARTINS RIBEIRO.

INLAND WATERWAYS

River transport plays only a minor part in the movement of goods, although total freight carried increased from 4.4m. tons in 1979 to 5.8m. tons in 1983. There are three major river systems, the Amazon, Paraná and the São Francisco. The Amazon is navigable for 3,680 km, as far as Iquitos in Peru, and ocean-going ships can reach Manaus, 1,600 km upstream. Plans have been drawn up to improve the inland waterway system and one plan is to link the Amazon and Upper Paraná to provide a navigable waterway across the centre of the country.

Companhia das Docas do Pará: Av. Pres. Vargas 41, 2°, 66.000 Belém, PA; tel. (091) 223-2055; telex (091) 1153; f. 1967; administers the port of Belém; Pres. Col RAÚL DA SILVA MOREIRA.

Empresa de Navegação da Amazônia, SA (ENASA): Av. Pres. Vargas 41, 69.000 Belém, PA; tel. (091) 223-3011; telex (091) 1311; f. 1967; cargo and passenger services on the Amazon river and its principal tributaries, connecting the port of Belém with Santarém, Manaus and other river ports; Pres. ELIAS SALAME; fleet of 10 vessels amounting to 8,564 grt.

SHIPPING

There are 36 deep-water ports in Brazil, five of which, including the port of Santos which handles 30% of all cargo, are privately owned. The largest ports are Santos, Rio de Janeiro, Paranaguá, Recife and Vitória. Tubarão, an iron ore port, and Santana (Amapá) on the Amazon, from where manganese is exported, are among the ports already equipped with automated facilities. Both ports are being expanded, as are Recife and Maceió, the sugar ports, and Ilheus, the cocoa port, on the eastern seaboard. The two main oil terminals, at São Sebastião (São Paulo) and Madre de Jesus (Bahia), are being expanded. Port expansion plans also include the building of terminals at Areia Branca, Paranaguá and Rio Grande. A new iron ore terminal is under construction at Sepetiba, and a sugar terminal is to be built in São Paulo State. All ports will be deepened to accommodate vessels of over 40,000 tons. Brazil's merchant fleet is the largest in Latin America. In 1984 it comprised 1,636 vessels (10m. tons), of which 150 were oil tankers and 1,486 were cargo vessels. In 1984 Brazil reached agreement with Bolivia on the construction of a port on the Caceres lagoon and the dredging of the Tamengo channel.

Superintendência Nacional da Marinha Mercante (SUNAMAM): Av. Rio Branco 115, 14°, 20.040 Rio de Janeiro, RJ; tel. (021) 232-1656; telex (021) 21652; f. 1941; supervisory board of the merchant marine; Superintendent MURILO R. H. DE MAZA.

Empresa dos Portos do Brasil (Portobrás): SAS, Quadra 1, Blocos 1, E/F, Brasília, DF; tel. (061) 224-1700; telex (061) 1112; f. 1975 to supervise, control and develop policies for the ports and navigable waterways; Pres. CARLOS THEOFILO DE S. MELLO.

Companhia Brasileira de Transporte de Granéis: Rua São Bento 8, 18°, 20.090 Rio de Janeiro, RJ; tel. (021) 223-4001; telex (021) 30603; f. 1976 for the carriage of liquid and solid bulk cargoes; Pres. HÉLIO PAULO FERRAZ; Exec. Dir MARCIO SALLES; 8 vessels amounting to 255,863 grt.

Companhia de Navegação Lloyd Brasileiro: Rua do Rosario 1, CP 1501, 20.041 Rio de Janeiro, RJ; tel. (021) 283-0717; telex (021) 23364; f. 1890; partly government-owned; operates between Brazil, the USA and Canada, Northern Europe, Scandinavia, the Mediterranean, East and West Africa, the Far East, the Arabian Gulf, Japan, Australia and New Zealand, and around the South American coast through the associated company **Lloyd-Libra**. Operates with pelletized, containerized and frozen cargoes, as well as with general and bulk cargoes; Pres. EDUARDO PORTELA NETO; 43 vessels amounting to 635,442 dwt; has 4 vessels under construction (2 bulk carrier, 2 full container); operates an average of 18 chartered vessels.

Companhia de Navegação Marítima (NETUMAR): Rua Monsenhor Coutinho 340, Centro Manaus, AM; Av. Presidente Vargas 482, 22°, 20.000 Rio de Janeiro, RJ; tel. (021) 2231660; telex (021) 23069; f. 1959; coastal traffic including Amazon region, foreign trade to USA and Canada, east coast and Great Lakes ports, Argentina and Uruguay; Dir JOSÉ CARLOS LEAL; 14 vessels, 229,309 dwt.

Companhia de Navegação do Norte (CONAN): Av. Rio Branco 45, 23° e 25° andares, Rio de Janeiro, RJ; tel. (021) 223-4155; telex (021) 22713; f. 1965; services to Brazil, Argentina, Uruguay and inland waterways; Pres. J. R. RIBEIRO SALOMÃO; Vice-Pres. M. J. RIBEIRO SALOMÃO; 10 vessels amounting to 121,900 grt.

Empresa de Navegação Aliança, SA: Av. Pasteur, 110 Botafogo, 22.290 Rio de Janeiro, RJ; tel. (021) 546-1122; telex (021) 23778; f. 1950; cargo services to Argentina, Europe, Baltic, Atlantic and North Sea ports; Pres. CARLOS G. E. FISCHER; 14 vessels.

Frota Amazônica, SA: Av. Presidente Vargas 112, CP 1367, Belém, PA; tel. (091) 224-0477; telex (091) 1041; cargo services between the Amazon region and the US Gulf ports, the east coast of the USA and Canada and Northern Europe; Pres. JOSÉ CARLOS FRAGOSO; 6 vessels of 35,150 grt.

Frota Oceânica Brasileira, SA: Av. Venezuela 110, CP 21-020, 20.081 Rio de Janeiro, RJ; tel. (021) 291-5153; telex (021) 22224; f. 1947; Pres. J. CARLOS FRAGOSO PIRES; Vice-Pres. LUÍS JOAQUIM CAMPOS ALHANATI; 14 vessels amounting to 365,731 grt.

Linhas Brasileiras de Navegação SA (LIBRA): Av. Rio Branco 25, 20.090 Rio de Janeiro, RJ; tel. (021) 223-2017; telex (021) 21382; Exec. Dir SYLVIO SILVA GONÇALVES; 13 cargo vessels amounting to 176,573 grt.

Petróleo Brasileiro SA (Petrobrás) (Frota Nacional de Petroleiros—Fronape): Rua Carlos Seidl, 188 Caju, CP 51015, 20.931 Rio de Janeiro, RJ; tel. (021) 580-4581; telex (021) 22286; Pres. TELMO B. SCHNEIDER; tanker fleet of 4,980,805 dwt.

Vale do Rio Doce Navegação, SA (DOCENAVE): Rua Voluntários da Pátria 143, Botafogo, 22.270 Rio de Janeiro, RJ; tel. (021) 286-8002; telex (021) 22142; bulk carrier to Japan, Persian Gulf, Europe, North America and Argentina; Dir CARLOS AUTO DE

ANDRADE; 20 bulk and 3 ore/oil carriers amounting to 1,153,826 grt (bulk) and 538,823 grt (ore/oil).

CIVIL AVIATION

There are about 1,500 airports and airstrips. Of the 48 principal airports 21 are international, although most international traffic is handled by the two airports at Rio de Janeiro and two at São Paulo. A new international airport was opened at Guarulhos, near São Paulo, in January 1985.

Serviços Aéreos Cruzeiro do Sul, SA: Av. Sílvio Noronha 365, 20.000 Rio de Janeiro, RJ; telex (021) 21765; f. 1927; in 1975 VARIG purchased an 86% participation in the company; network routes: Brazil, Argentina, Bolivia, French Guiana, Peru, Suriname, Uruguay; Pres. Dr Aguinaldo de Melo Junqueira; 1984 fleet: 6 Boeing 727-100, 6 Boeing 737-200, 2 Airbus A-300 B-4.

Transbrasil SA Linhas Aéreas: Rua Santa Luzia 651, 18°, Rio de Janeiro, RJ; tel. (021) 220-6066; telex (021) 22744; f. 1955 as Sadia, renamed 1972; scheduled passenger and cargo services to major Brazilian cities and Orlando; cargo charter flights to the USA, Caribbean and South America; Pres. Omar Fontana; 1984 fleet: 15 Boeing 727-100, 3 Boeing 767-200, 5 Boeing 707.

VARIG, SA (Viação Aérea Rio Grandense): Edif. Varig., Av. Almte Silvio Noronha 365, 20.021 Rio de Janeiro, RJ; tel. (021) 297-5141; telex (021) 22363; f. 1927; international services; Argentina, Bolivia, Chile, Colombia, Costa Rica, Ecuador, Panama, Paraguay, Peru, Uruguay, Venezuela, Mexico, Canada, the USA, Angola, the Ivory Coast, Japan, Nigeria, Mozambique, South Africa and Western Europe; domestic services to major cities of the country; cargo services; Pres. Hélio Smidt; Vice-Pres. Rubel Thomas; 1986 fleet: 10 Boeing 707-320-C, 10 Boeing 727-100, 12 Boeing 737-200, 3 Boeing 747-200B, 2 Boeing 747-300, 1 Boeing 767-200, 14 Lockheed 188, 2 Airbus A-300, 12 Douglas DC-10-30, 2 Lockheed 188-A.

Viação Aérea São Paulo, SA (VASP): 04695 Edif. VASP, Aéroporto Congonhas, São Paulo, SP; tel. (011) 533-7011; telex (011) 37913; f. 1933; controlled by São Paulo State Government; domestic services covering all Brazil; Pres. Prof. Antônio Ignacio Angarita Ferreira da Silva; 1985 fleet: 2 Boeing 727-200, 20 Boeing 737 Super Advanced, 3 Boeing 737-300, 3 Airbus A-300 B2K.

In addition to the airlines listed above, there are a number of others operating regional services.

Tourism

Centro Brasileiro de Informação Turística (CEBITUR): Rua Mariz e Barros 13, 4° andar, Praça da Bandeira, 20.270 Rio de Janeiro, RJ; tel. (021) 293-1313; telex (021) 21066.

Conselho Nacional de Turismo (CNTUR) (National Tourism Office): Ministério da Indústria e do Comércio, Rua Mariz e Barros 13, 5°, 20.270 Rio de Janeiro, RJ; tel. (021) 273-0691; f. 1966; Exec. Sec. Ricardo de Godoy Jaguaribe.

Divisão de Exposições e Feiras/Conselho de Desenvolvimento Comercial: SCS; Q-02, Bloco 1, Ministério da Indústria e do Comércio, Esplanada dos Ministérios, Brasília, DF; tel. (061) 223-0129; telex (061) 2537; f. 1967; organizes fairs and exhibitions; Dir Nelson Campos; Sec.-Gen. Roberto Nogueira Ferreira.

Divisão de Feiras e Turismo/Departamento de Promoção Comercial: Ministério das Relações Exteriores, Esplanada dos Ministérios, 2°, 70.170 Brasília, DF; tel. (061) 211-6644; f. 1977; organizes Brazil's participation in trade fairs and commercial exhibitions abroad; Dir Sergio Barcellos Telles.

Empresa Brasileira de Turismo—EMBRATUR: Rua Mariz e Barros 13, 7° andar, 20.270 Rio de Janeiro, RJ; tel. (021) 273-2212; telex (021) 21066; f. 1966; studies tourist development projects; Pres. João Dória, Jr.

Atomic Energy

Brazil's first nuclear power station, at Angra dos Reis, RJ, commenced commercial operation (power of 657 MW) in early 1985, after design faults had caused delays. Following an agreement between Brazil and the Federal Republic of Germany, two other plants, of 1,300 MW (Angra II and III), were to be constructed at the same site, with Brazilian participation, and were originally expected to become operational in 1989 and 1990 respectively. Work on two further planned plants was postponed in 1983 owing to lack of available finance. In September 1985 construction of the Angra III plant and of two further plants, Iguape I and II, was postponed indefinitely. The construction of the Angra II plant was to be completed by 1995. It is planned to install a total of 11,000 MW of nuclear power by the year 2000. Development within the sector has been severely hampered by government spending cuts in recent years.

Research reactors: The following research reactors are in operation:

(CDTN-RI) CDTN-NUCLEBRÁS, Belo Horizonte, MG; thermal power 250 kW.

(IPEN-RI) IPEN, São Paulo, SP; thermal power 10 MW.

(IEN-RI) IEN-CNEN, Rio de Janeiro, RJ; thermal power 10 kW.

(URANIE) CDTN-NUCLEBRÁS, Belo Horizonte, MG (subcritical).

(RESUCO) DEN-UFPe, Recife, Pe (subcritical).

(NC-9000) CTA, São José dos Campos, SP (subcritical).

(CAPITU) CDTN-NUCLEBRÁS, Belo Horizonte, MG (subcritical).

(SUBLIME) IME, Rio de Janeiro, RJ (planned).

Comissão Nacional de Energia Nuclear (CNEN): Rua General Severiano 90, Botafogo, 22.294 Rio de Janeiro, RJ; tel. (021) 295-7696; telex (021) 21280; f. 1956; controlling organization for: Instituto de Engenharia Nuclear—IEN (nuclear engineering); Instituto de Radioproteção e Dosimetria—IRD (radiation protection and dosimetry); Instituto de Pesquisas Energéticas e Nucleares—IPEN (energetics and nuclear research) and Centro de Energia Nuclear na Agricultura—CENA) (agricultural research); 1984 budget estimate: CR $1,431,000m.; Pres. Rex Nazaré Alves.

Empresa Nucleares Brasileiras, SA (NUCLEBRÁS): Av. Pres. Wilson 231, Castelo, 20.030 Rio de Janeiro, RJ; tel. (021) 262-8838; telex 22136; f. 1974; its main objectives are to establish fuel-cycle and NSS industries, to construct (through its subsidiary NUCON) and finance nuclear power plants and to promote the transfer of nuclear and development programmes; Pres. Licínio Marcelo Seabra.

As a result of the Brazil-Federal Republic of Germany nuclear agreement signed in July 1975, four joint-ventures between Nuclebrás and Federal German firms were established: NUCLAM (mining), NUCLEI (enrichment by the nozzle method), NUCLEN (engineering) and NUCLEP (heavy equipment) and NUSTEP (in the Federal Republic of Germany).

BRUNEI

Introductory Survey

Location, Climate, Language, Religion, Flag, Capital

The Sultanate of Brunei (Negara Brunei Darussalam) lies in South-East Asia, on the north-west coast of the island of Kalimantan (Borneo). It is surrounded and bisected on the landward side by Sarawak, one of the two eastern states of Malaysia. The country has a tropical climate, characterized by consistent temperature and humidity. Average annual rainfall ranges from about 2,400 mm (95 in) in lowland areas to about 4,000 mm (158 in) in the interior. Temperatures are high, with the annual extreme range being 23°C (73°F) to 35.8°C (96.4°F). The principal language is Malay, although Chinese is also spoken and English is widely used. The Malay population (nearly 65% of the total) are mainly Sunni Muslims. Most of the Chinese in Brunei are Buddhists, Confucians or Daoists. Europeans and Eurasians are predominantly Christians. The flag (proportions 2 by 1) is yellow, with two diagonal stripes, of white and black, running from the upper hoist to the lower fly; superimposed in the centre is the state emblem (in red, with yellow Arabic inscriptions). The capital is Bandar Seri Begawan (formerly called Brunei Town).

Recent History

Brunei, a traditional Islamic monarchy, formerly included most of the coastal regions of North Borneo (now Sabah) and Sarawak, which later became states of Malaysia. During the 19th century the rulers of Brunei ceded large parts of their territory to the United Kingdom, reducing the sultanate to its present size. In 1888, when North Borneo became a British protectorate, Brunei became a British Protected State. In accordance with an agreement made in 1906, a British Resident was appointed to the court of the ruling Sultan as an adviser on administration. Under this arrangement, a form of government that included an advisory State Council emerged.

Brunei was invaded by Japanese forces in December 1941, but reverted to its former status in 1945, when the Second World War ended. The British-appointed Governor of Sarawak was High Commissioner for Brunei from 1948 until the territory's first written constitution was promulgated in September 1959, when a further agreement was made between the Sultan and the British Government. The United Kingdom continued to be responsible for Brunei's defence and external affairs until the attainment of independence in 1984.

In December 1962 a large-scale revolt broke out in Brunei and in parts of Sarawak and North Borneo. The rebellion was carried out by the 'North Borneo Liberation Army', an organization linked with the Parti Ra'ayat Brunei (Brunei People's Party), led by A. M. Azahari, which was strongly opposed to the planned entry of Brunei into the Federation of Malaysia. The rebels proclaimed the 'revolutionary State of North Kalimantan', but the revolt was suppressed, after 10 days' fighting, with the aid of British forces from Singapore. A state of emergency was declared, the People's Party was banned, and Azahari was given asylum in Malaya. In the event, the Sultan decided in 1963 against joining the Federation. From 1962 he ruled by decree, and the state of emergency remained in force. Sir Omar Ali Saifuddin, who had been Sultan since 1950, abdicated in October 1967 in favour of his son, Hassanal Bolkiah, who was then 21 years of age. Under an agreement signed in November 1971, Brunei was granted full internal self-government.

In December 1975 the UN General Assembly passed a resolution which called for British withdrawal from Brunei, for the return of political exiles and for the holding of a general election. However, the Brunei Government remained reluctant to re-negotiate the terms of its agreement with the United Kingdom. Negotiations in 1978, following assurances by Malaysia and Indonesia that they would respect Brunei's sovereignty, resulted in an agreement (signed in January 1979) that Brunei would become fully independent within five years. Independence was duly proclaimed on 1 January 1984, and the Sultan took office as Prime Minister and Minister of Finance and of Home Affairs, presiding over a Cabinet of six other ministers (including two of the Sultan's brothers and his father, the former Sultan).

The future of the Chinese population, who control much of Brunei's private commercial sector but who, since independence, have become stateless, became uncertain in 1985, when the Sultan indicated that Brunei would become an Islamic state in which the indigenous, mainly Malay, inhabitants, known as *bumiputras* ('sons of the soil'), would receive preferential treatment. In May 1985 a number of Hong Kong and Taiwan Chinese, who were not permanent Brunei residents, were repatriated.

In May 1985 a new political party, the Brunei National Democratic Party (BNDP), was formed. The new party, which comprised businessmen loyal to the Sultan, based its policies on Islam and a form of liberal nationalism. However, the Sultan forbade employees of the Government (about 40% of the country's working population) to join the party. Members of the Chinese community were also excluded from membership. Divisions within the new party led to the formation of a second group, the Brunei National United Party, in February 1986. This party, which also received the Sultan's official approval, placed greater emphasis on co-operation with the Government, and was open to both Muslim and non-Muslim ethnic groups. In November 1986 the BNDP stated its desire for the Sultan to resign as Head of Government, in favour of an elected Prime Minister, but to remain as Head of State.

Although the Sultan was not expected to allow any relaxation of restrictions on radical political activities, it thus became clear during 1985 and 1986 that a more progressive style of government was being adopted. The death of Sir Muda Omar Ali Saifuddin, the Sultan's father, in September 1986 was expected to hasten modernization. The Sultan carried out a government reshuffle in October.

Relations with the United Kingdom had become strained during 1983, following the Brunei Government's decision in August to transfer the management of its investment portfolio from the British Crown Agents to the newly-created Brunei Investment Agency. However, normal relations were restored in September, when the British Government agreed that a battalion of Gurkha troops, stationed in Brunei since 1971, should remain in Brunei after independence, specifically to guard the oil and gas fields.

Brunei has developed close relations with the members of ASEAN (see p. 103), in particular Singapore, and became a full member of the organization immediately after independence. Royal visits were made to Thailand and Indonesia in 1984, in order to strengthen ties, and diplomatic relations with Japan were established in the same year. Brunei also joined the UN, the Commonwealth and the Organization of the Islamic Conference in 1984.

Government

The 1959 constitution confers supreme executive authority on the Sultan. He is assisted and advised by four Constitutional Councils: the Religious Council, the Privy Council, the Council of Cabinet Ministers and the Council of Succession. Since the rebellion of 1962, certain provisions of the constitution have been suspended, and the Sultan has ruled by decree.

Defence

The Royal Brunei Malay Regiment numbered 4,050 (including 150 women) in July 1986, all services forming part of the army. Military service is voluntary. Paramilitary forces comprised 1,750 Royal Brunei Police. The defence budget for 1986 was estimated at B $384m. A Gurkha battalion of the British army is stationed in Brunei.

Economic Affairs

Brunei's economy depends almost entirely on its petroleum and natural gas resources. By world standards, Brunei is not a major producer of oil and gas, but the country has a relatively small population and the development of the hydrocarbons sector has provided the inhabitants with a very high level of material prosperity. Brunei's gross domestic product (GDP), measured in current prices, reached a peak of US $4,848m. ($25,500 per head) in 1980, but falls in petroleum production and prices led to reduced GDP in subsequent years. Between 1975 and 1984, GDP expanded, in real terms, at an average rate of 3.9% annually, compared with a target growth rate of 6%: after expanding by an average of 12.2% per year during 1975–79, GDP contracted by 4.4% annually between 1980 and 1984. In terms of average income, however, Brunei remains one of the world's richest countries. In 1983, according to estimates by the World Bank, Brunei's gross national product (GNP) per head, measured at average 1981–83 prices, was US $21,140, the third highest level in the world.

Crude petroleum is produced on shore and off shore: total production in 1985 was 54.4m. barrels. In 1979 output of crude petroleum reached a peak of more than 250,000 barrels per day (b/d), but in subsequent years production steadily decreased. During 1985 average output declined to 130,000 b/d, in response to lower world demand and a need to ration reserves. Export earnings from crude petroleum, which were B $762m. in 1973, rose to B $4,778m. in 1981 but had fallen to B $3,552.3m. by 1985, reflecting reductions in both production and prices. Average output of natural gas has remained roughly constant, at about 900m. cu ft per day since 1983. Earnings from natural gas, B $46.5m. in 1973, increased to B $3,397m. in 1981, but declined to B $2,782.7m. in 1985. Sales of oil and natural gas, which in 1985 accounted for 99% of total exports, are almost entirely responsible for Brunei's favourable trade balance. Brunei's principal customer is Japan, which takes 46% of petroleum and about 97% of the total gas output; the USA and ASEAN countries are the next largest importers of Bruneian petroleum. In 1981 there was a trade surplus of B $7,327m. This fell to B $6,582m. in 1982, to B $5,629m. in 1983 and to B $4,985m. in 1985, owing to a decline in international petroleum prices, which caused a reduction in export earnings, and to an increase in imports of manufactured goods. However, Brunei's official international reserves continue to rise, and in early 1986 they were estimated at B $37,500m. These reserves are managed largely by the Brunei Investment Agency, established in August 1983, and mainly invested abroad.

Development projects to diversify the economy and to improve the infrastructure, financed by petroleum revenues, are hampered to some extent by lack of skilled labour and by the small size of the population (only 221,900 at mid-1985); foreign workers, principally from the Philippines and Malaysia, have helped to ease the labour shortage and comprised about one-third of the total labour force of 85,300 in 1985. Among the major projects which have already been completed are an international airport, a deep-water port at Muara, a petroleum refinery, with a capacity of 10,000 b/d, and a natural gas liquefaction plant, the largest in the world, at Lumut. Brunei's GDP more than doubled in the five years before 1979, when it reached an estimated B $5,795m. In 1984 GDP in current purchasers' values rose to B $8,051.5m., but in 1985 it fell to B $7,529.3m. Manufacturing and mining accounted for 76% of GDP in 1983, and for 69.3% in 1984.

In 1975 highly favourable tax concessions were introduced, with the aim of encouraging investment in new industries. The areas most suitable for industrial development are timber, paper, fertilizers, petro-chemicals and glass. Government policy is to encourage local (especially indigenous or *bumiputra*) enterprises with greater participation by Bruneians. In the 1984 budget B $950m. was allocated to the Development Fund. The 1980–84 Development Plan was designed to achieve a high level of employment, to diversify the economy through the development of agriculture, forestry and fisheries, and aimed at a minimum annual growth rate of 6%. The plan involved total expenditure of B $2,000m. The average annual rate of inflation was 6.4% in 1982 and only 1.2% in 1983, kept down by state-controlled prices for some basic commodities, including rice. The rate increased to 3.1% in 1984, but declined to 1.4% in the year to March 1986. Government revenue, largely financed by taxes from the petroleum companies, has increased significantly since 1979, and in 1985 there was an estimated surplus of B $4,985m. Expenditure in the 1985 budget totalled B $2,071m., or B $580m. less than the total allocation in 1984, although defence expenditure was increased.

In 1986, after a year of readjustment, the Government introduced a fifth Development Plan (1986–90), the first since independence. The main objectives of the Plan were to reduce dependence on income from petroleum and natural gas, to achieve self-sufficiency in food production, and to promote import substitution. The largest projects under the 1986–90 Plan were new port developments and improvements to water supplies, sewerage and telecommunications. The plan also included a review of the 1975–84 period, drawing attention to the failure of the two preceding plans to diversify the economy and to achieve significant expansion in agriculture, forestry and fishing.

A total of B $3,730m. was allocated to the 1986–90 Plan, a budget allowing for expected inflation. Of the total, industry and commerce were to receive 10% of projected expenditure, while social services were to continue to receive the largest allocation (29%). Manufacturing, timber production and agriculture were also emphasized under the 1986–90 Plan; in 1985 Brunei still imported 80% of its total food requirements, in spite of the objectives of previous plans to achieve self-sufficiency in home-grown crops and to develop potential areas of agricultural land.

In 1986 it was announced that a 20-year master plan for Brunei was under consideration, of which the 1986–90 Plan was to form a part. Long-term objectives of the master plan were the conversion of Brunei into a centre for banking and finance, and for trade and maintenance services; the establishment of a development bank, which would replace the Economic Development Board; and national pension and training schemes.

Social Welfare

Free medical services are provided by the Government. In 1981 Brunei had eight hospitals, with a total of 630 beds, and there were 97 physicians working in the country. There is a flying doctor service, as well as various clinics, travelling dispensaries and dental clinics. A non-contributory state pensions scheme for the old and disabled came into operation in 1955. The state also provides financial assistance to the poor, the destitute and widows. In the 1985 budget B $100m. was allocated to health services.

Education

Education is free, and Islamic studies form an integral part of the school curriculum. Pupils who are Brunei citizens and live more than 8 km (5 miles) from their schools are entitled to free accommodation in hostels, free transport or a subsistence allowance. Schools are classified according to the language of instruction, i.e. Malay, English or Chinese (Mandarin). In 1984 the total enrolment in the 177 primary schools was 34,373, while in the 28 general secondary schools and sixth-form centres the enrolment was 18,565. There are two teacher training colleges and four colleges for vocational and technical education. The Universiti Brunei Darussalam was formally established in 1985, but many students were also sent to universities abroad, at government expense. Adult illiteracy fell from 36% in 1971 to an estimated 29% in 1981. In the 1985 budget B $231m. was allocated to education.

Tourism

Tourism is relatively underdeveloped. In 1985 only 6,418 tourists visited Brunei.

Public Holidays

1987: 1 January (New Year's Day), February* (Chinese New Year), 23 February (National Day), 28 March† (Meraj, Ascension of the Prophet), 30 April† (First Day of Ramadan), 16 May† (Anniversary of the Revelation of the Koran), 30 May† (End of Ramadan), 2 June (for Anniversary of the Royal Brunei Malay Regiment), 15 July (Sultan's Birthday), 6 August† (Hari Raya Haji), 26 August† (Islamic New Year), 4 November† (Mouloud, Birth of the Prophet), 25 December (Christmas).

1988: 1 January (New Year's Day), February* (Chinese New Year), 23 February (National Day), 16 March† (Meraj, Ascen-

BRUNEI

sion of the Prophet), 18 April† (First Day of Ramadan), 4 May† (Anniversary of the Revelation of the Koran), 18 May† (End of Ramadan), 31 May (Anniversary of the Royal Brunei Malay Regiment), 15 July (Sultan's Birthday), 25 July† (Hari Raya Haji), 14 August† (Islamic New Year), 23 October† (Mouloud, Birth of the Prophet), 25 December (Christmas).

* From the first to the third day of the first moon of the lunar calendar.
† These holidays are dependent on the Islamic lunar calendar and may vary by one or two days from the dates given.

Weights and Measures

The imperial system is in operation but local measures of weight and capacity are used. These include the gantang (1 gallon), the tahil (1⅓ oz) and kati (1⅓ lb).

Currency and Exchange Rate

100 cents = 1 Brunei dollar (B $).

Exchange rates (30 September 1986):
  £1 sterling = B $3.141;
  US $1 = B $2.171.

Statistical Survey

Source (unless otherwise stated): Economic Planning Unit, Ministry of Finance, Bandar Seri Begawan; tel. (02) 41991; telex 2676.

AREA, POPULATION AND DENSITY

Area: 5,765 sq km (2,226 sq miles); Brunei/Muara 570 sq km (220 sq miles), Seria/Belait 2,725 sq km (1,052 sq miles), Tutong 1,165 sq km (450 sq miles), Temburong 1,305 sq km (504 sq miles).

Population (excluding transients afloat): 192,832 (males 102,942, females 89,890) at census of 25 August 1981; 221,900 (males 118,580, females 103,320), official estimates for mid-1985. *Capital:* Bandar Seri Begawan, population 55,070 (1985 estimate).

Density (per sq km): 38.5 (1985).

Ethnic Groups (1985): Malay 143,180, Chinese 44,350, Other indigenous 18,440, Others 15,930, Total 221,900.

Births and Deaths (1985): Live births 6,682 (birth rate 30.1 per 1,000); Deaths 794 (death rate 3.6 per 1,000).

Labour Force: Males 53,859, Females 16,831, Total 70,690 (incl. 2,562 unemployed). *Of which:* Community, social and personal services 29,282, Construction 12,644, Trade, restaurants and hotels 7,363, Transport, storage and communications 4,529 (census of 25 August 1981); Total 81,535 (incl. 2,800 unemployed) (1984 estimate).

AGRICULTURE, ETC.
(Source: FAO)

Principal Crops ('000 metric tons, 1984): Rice (paddy) 6, Sweet potatoes 1, Cassava (Manioc) 4, Bananas 4, Pineapples 4, Vegetables (incl. melons) 4 (FAO estimates).

Livestock ('000 head, year ending September 1984): Cattle 4, Buffaloes 15, Pigs 15, Goats 2 (FAO estimates).

Livestock Products (metric tons, 1984): Poultry meat 4,000; Hen eggs 2,320; Cattle and buffalo hides (fresh) 162 (FAO estimates).

Forestry ('000 cu m, 1984): *Roundwood removals:* Sawlogs, veneer logs and logs for sleepers 206; Other industrial wood 10*; Fuel wood 79*; Total 295. *Sawnwood production:* Total (incl. boxboards) 90.

* FAO estimates.

Fishing (metric tons, 1984): Inland waters 134 (Fishes 90, River prawn 44); Pacific Ocean 2,620 (Fishes 2,010, Shrimps and prawns 610); Total catch 2,754.

MINING

Production (1985): Crude petroleum 54,373,117 barrels; Natural gasoline 414,301 barrels; Natural gas 317,048m. cu ft.

INDUSTRY

Production ('000 metric tons, 1985): Motor spirit (petrol) 104.6; Naphthas 6.8; Distillate fuel oils 83.3; Kerosene 29.5.

FINANCE

Currency and Exchange Rates: 100 sen (cents) = 1 Brunei dollar (B $). *Coins:* 1, 5, 10, and 50 cents. *Notes:* 1, 5, 10, 50, 100, 500 and 1,000 dollars. *Sterling and US Dollar Equivalents* (30 September 1986): £1 sterling = B $3.141; US $1 = B $2.171; B $100 = £31.83 = US $46.06. *Average Exchange Rate* (Brunei dollars per US $): 2.1131 in 1983; 2.1331 in 1984; 2.2002 in 1985. Note: The Brunei dollar is at par with the Singapore dollar.

Budget (estimates, B $ million, 1984): *Revenue:* Total 6,500; *Expenditure:* Royal Brunei Malay Regiment 340.2, Public works 231.3, Education 216.2, Transfer to Development Fund 950, Total (incl. others) 2,651.

Cost of Living (Consumer Price Index; base: 1977 = 100): 138.8 in 1983; 143.1 in 1984; 146.4 in 1985.

Gross Domestic Product (B $ million in current purchasers' values): 8,015.3 in 1983; 8,051.5 in 1984; 7,529.3 in 1985.

EXTERNAL TRADE

Principal Commodities (B $ million, 1985): *Imports:* Food and live animals 196.1, Beverages and tobacco 70.5, Crude materials (inedible) except fuels 16.6, Mineral fuels, lubricants, etc. 23.9, Animal and vegetable oils and fats 7.9, Chemicals 95.1, Basic manufactures 289.9, Machinery and transport equipment 456.3, Miscellaneous manufactured articles 145.3, Total (incl. others) 1,348.4. *Exports:* Crude petroleum 3,552.3, Petroleum products 99.3, Natural gas 2,782.7, Total (incl. others) 6,532.9.

Principal Trading Partners (B $ million, 1985): *Imports:* Australia 36.9, China, People's Republic 26.9, Germany, Federal Republic 51.9, Japan 267.0, Malaysia (Peninsular) 61.1, Netherlands 23.7, Singapore 328.5, Thailand 41.7, United Kingdom 124.3, USA 300.0. *Exports:* France 0.1, Japan 4,000.0, Korea, Republic 459.0, Malaysia (Sarawak) 61.1, Philippines 34.5, Singapore 568.9, Thailand 692.9, USA 479.0.

TRANSPORT

Road Traffic (registered vehicles, 1985): Private cars 79,428, Taxis 117, Motor-cycles and scooters 3,451, Goods vehicles 10,275, Buses 388, Other vehicles 1,766, Total 95,425.

International Sea-borne Shipping (1985): *Vessels* ('000 net registered tons): Entered 24,542.3, Cleared 10,524.5. *Goods* ('000 metric tons): Loaded 49,455.0, Unloaded 680.4.

Civil Aviation (1985): Aircraft landings 4,266, aircraft take-offs 4,185; passenger arrivals 184,404, passenger departures 178,498; freight loaded 5,557,535 kg, freight unloaded 432,357 kg.

TOURISM

Tourist Arrivals (1985): 6,418.

COMMUNICATIONS MEDIA

Telephones (1985): 32,865 in use.
Radio receivers (1985): 70,000 in use.
Television receivers (1985): 45,000 in use.

EDUCATION

Pre-primary (1984): 145 schools; 363 teachers; 7,665 pupils.
Primary (1984): 177 schools; 2,131 teachers; 34,373 pupils.
General Secondary (1984, incl. Sixth-Form Centres): 28 schools; 1,526 teachers; 18,565 pupils.
Teacher Training (1984): 2 colleges; 87 teachers; 591 pupils.
Vocational (1984): 4 colleges; 188 teachers; 748 pupils.

Directory

The Constitution

Note: Certain sections of the Constitution have been in abeyance since 1962.

A new constitution was promulgated on 29 September 1959. Under its provisions, sovereign authority is vested in the Sultan and Yang Di-Pertuan, who is assisted and advised by four Councils:

THE RELIGIOUS COUNCIL

In his capacity as head of the Islamic faith in Brunei, the Sultan and Yang Di-Pertuan is advised in all Islamic matters by the Religious Council, whose members are appointed by the Sultan and Yang Di-Pertuan.

THE PRIVY COUNCIL

This Council, presided over by the Sultan and Yang Di-Pertuan, is to advise the Sultan on matters concerning the Royal prerogative of mercy, the amendment of the constitution and the conferment of ranks, titles and honours.

THE COUNCIL OF CABINET MINISTERS

Presided over by the Sultan and Yang Di-Pertuan, the Council of Cabinet Ministers considers all executive matters.

THE COUNCIL OF SUCCESSION

Subject to the Constitution, this Council is to determine the succession to the throne, should the need arise.

The State is divided into four administrative districts, in each of which is a District Officer (Malay) responsible to the Prime Minister and Minister of Home Affairs.

The Government

HEAD OF STATE

Sultan and Yang Di-Pertuan: HM Sir MUDA HASSANAL BOLKIAH MU'IZZADDIN WADDAULAH (succeeded 5 October 1967; crowned 1 August 1968).

COUNCIL OF CABINET MINISTERS
(November 1986)

Prime Minister and Minister of Defence: The Sultan and Yang Di-Pertuan, HM Sir MUDA HASSANAL BOLKIAH MU'IZZADDIN WADDAULAH.
Minister of Home Affairs and Special Adviser to the Prime Minister: Pehin Dato Haji ISA.
Minister of Foreign Affairs: Pengiran Perdana Wazir Pengiran MUDA MOHAMAD BOLKIAH.
Minister of Finance: Pengiran Di-Gadong Pengiran MUDA JEFRI BOLKIAH.
Minister of Law: Pengiran BAHRIN BIN Pengiran Haji ABAS.
Minister of Education: Pehin Dato ABDUL RAHMAN TAIB.
Minister of Development: Pengiran Dr ISMAIL.
Minister of Communications: Pehin Dato Haji ABDUL AZIZ.
Minister of Religious Affairs: Pehin Dato Haji MOHD ZAIN.
Minister of Culture, Youth and Sports: Pehin Dato Haji HUSSEIN.
Minister of Health: Dato Dr Haji JOHAR.

MINISTRIES

Office of the Prime Minister: Istana Nurul Iman, Bandar Seri Begawan; tel. (02) 29988; telex 2727.
Ministry of Communications: Batu 2½, Jalan Gadong, Bandar Seri Begawan; tel. (02) 23845.
Ministry of Culture, Youth and Sports: Jalan McArthur, Bandar Seri Begawan; tel. (02) 40585.
Ministry of Defence: Istana Nurul Iman, Bandar Seri Begawan; tel. (02) 25607.
Ministry of Development: Lapangan Terbang Lama Berakas; tel. (02) 41911.
Ministry of Education and Health: Lapangan Terbang Lama Berakas; tel. (02) 44233; telex 2577.
Ministry of Finance: Bandar Seri Begawan; tel. (02) 42405.
Ministry of Foreign Affairs: Jalan Subok, Bandar Seri Begawan; tel. (02) 41177; telex 2292.
Ministry of Home Affairs: Bandar Seri Begawan; tel. (02) 23225.
Ministry of Law: Bandar Seri Begawan; tel. (02) 44872.

Political Organizations

Partai Kebang-Saan Demokratik Brunei—PKDB (Brunei National Democratic Party—BNDP): Bandar Seri Begawan; f. 1985; pursues Islamic principles and liberal nationalism; aims to establish parliamentary democracy under a constitutional monarchy; c. 1,500 mems; Sec.-Gen. Haji ABDUL LATIF CHUCHU.

Partai Perpaduan Kebang-Saan Brunei—PPKB (Brunei National United Party—BNUP): Bandar Seri Begawan; f. 1986 after split in BNDP; pro-Government party; Sec.-Gen. AWANG HATTA Haji ZAINAL ABIDDIN.

There were formerly three other political organizations: **Parti Ra'ayat Brunei** (PRB, Brunei People's Party), which is banned and whose members are all in exile; **Barisan Kemerdeka'an Rakyat** (BAKER, People's Independence Front), founded in 1966 but no longer active; and **Parti Perdapuan Kebangsaan Ra'ayat Brunei** (PERKARA, Brunei People's National United Party), founded in 1968 but no longer active.

Diplomatic Representation

EMBASSIES AND HIGH COMMISSIONS IN BRUNEI

Australia: 4th Floor, Teck Guan Plaza, cnr Jalan Sultan and Jalan McArthur, Bandar Seri Begawan; tel. (02) 29435; telex 2582; High Commissioner: JOHN MACARTNEY STAREY.
Germany, Federal Republic: 49–50 Jalan Sultan, 6th Floor, UNF Bldg, POB 3050, Bandar Seri Begawan; tel. (02) 25547; telex 2742; Ambassador: Dr ECKARD CUNTZ.
Indonesia: LB 711, Jalan Kumbang Pasang, Bandar Seri Begawan; tel. (02) 21852; Ambassador: ZUWIR DJAMAL.
Japan: LB 16464 Kampong Mabohai, Jalan Kebangsaan, POB 3001; tel. (02) 29265; telex 2564; Chargé d'affaires: YUTAKA SHIMOMOTO.
Korea, Republic: Kampong Sungai Tilong, Batu 7, Jalan Muara; tel. (02) 30383; telex 2615; Ambassador: KANG SUNG-KU.
Malaysia: 6th Floor, Darussalam Bldg, Jalan Sultan, Bandar Seri Begawan; tel. (02) 28410; telex 2401; High Commissioner: SYED HUSSEIN BIN SYED ABU BAKAR.
Pakistan: LB 277, Kampong Telanai, Mile 3, Jalan Tutong; tel. (02) 51623; Ambassador: MIR ABAD HUSSAIN.
Philippines: 35 Kampung Pelambayan, Jalan Kota Batu, Bandar Seri Begawan; tel. (02) 28241; telex 2673; Ambassador: (vacant).
Singapore: 5th Floor, RBA Plaza, Jalan Sultan, Bandar Seri Begawan; tel. (02) 27583; telex 2385; High Commissioner: EDWARD LEE KWONG FOO.
Thailand: LB 241, Jalan Elia Fatimah, Kampong Kiarong, POB 2989, Bandar Seri Begawan; tel. (02) 29653; telex 2607; Ambassador: PONG BUA-IAM.
United Kingdom: 3rd Floor, Hongkong and Shanghai Bank Chambers, Jalan Pemancha, POB 2197, Bandar Seri Begawan; tel. (02) 22231; telex 2211; High Commissioner: ROGER WESTBROOK.
USA: 3rd Floor, Teck Guan Plaza, cnr Jalan Sultan and Jalan McArthur, Bandar Seri Begawan; tel. (02) 29670; telex 2609; Ambassador: BARRINGTON KING.

Judicial System

SUPREME COURT

The Supreme Court consists of the Court of Appeal and the High Court.

Chief Registrar, Supreme Court: Dato MOHAMMED SAIED.

BRUNEI

The Court of Appeal: composed of the President and two Commissioners appointed by the Sultan. Hears criminal and civil appeals against the decisions of the High Court.
President, Court of Appeal: Dato Sir GEOFFREY BRIGGS.

The High Court: composed of the Chief Justice and such Commissioners as the Sultan may appoint. In its appellate jurisdiction it hears appeals in criminal and civil matters against the decisions of the Subordinate Courts. Has unlimited original jurisdiction in criminal and civil matters.
Chief Justice: Sir DENYS ROBERTS.

OTHER COURTS

The Subordinate Courts: presided over by the Chief Magistrate and magistrates. Have limited original jurisdiction in civil and criminal matters.
The Courts of Kathis: deal solely with questions concerning Islamic religion, marriage and divorce. Appeals lie from these courts to the Sultan in the Religious Council.
Chief Kathi: Pehin Haji ABDUL HAMID BIN BAKAL.

Religion

The official religion of Brunei is Islam, and the Sultan is head of the Islamic population. The majority of the Malay population (about 130,000) are Muslims of the Sunni sect. The Chinese population is either Buddhist, Confucianist, Daoist or Christian. Large numbers of the indigenous races are animists of various types. The remainder of the population are mostly Christians, generally Roman Catholics, Anglicans or members of the American Methodist Church of Southern Asia.

CHRISTIANITY

The Anglican Communion
Brunei is within the Anglican diocese of Kuching, Sarawak, Malaysia.

The Roman Catholic Church
Brunei is within the Roman Catholic diocese of Kuching, Sarawak, Malaysia.

The Press

NEWSPAPERS

Borneo Bulletin: 74 Jalan Sungei, POB 69, Kuala Belait; tel. (02) 34344; telex 3336; f. 1953; weekly; Saturday; English; independent; Gen. Man. I. M. MACGREGOR; Editor K. A. MACDONALD; circ. 35,000.
Brunei Darussalam Newsletter: Information Section, Broadcasting and Information Dept, Ministry of Culture, Youth and Sports, Jalan McArthur, Bandar Seri Begawan; monthly; English; circ. 10,000.
Pelita Brunei: Information Section, Broadcasting and Information Dept, Ministry of Culture, Youth and Sports, Jalan McArthur, Bandar Seri Begawan; f. 1956; weekly; Wednesday; Malay; govt newspaper; distributed free; circ. 45,000.
Petroleum di Brunei: c/o Brunei Shell Petroleum Co Sdn Bhd, Seria; tel. (03) 72107; quarterly; English and Malay; magazine publ. by Brunei Shell Petroleum Co Sdn Bhd; circ. 7,500.
Salam: c/o Brunei Shell Petroleum Co Sdn Bhd, Seria; tel. (037) 2106; f. 1953; fortnightly; Tuesday; Malay and English in one edition; free employee newspaper publ. by the Brunei Shell Petroleum Co Sdn Bhd; circ. 9,000.

Publishers

Borneo Printers & Trading (Pte) Ltd: POB 2211; tel. (02) 24856.
The Brunei Press: POB 69, Kuala Belait; tel. (03) 34344; telex 3336; f. 1959; Gen. Man. I. M. MACGREGOR.
Capital Trading & Printing Pte Ltd: POB 1089; tel. (02) 44541.
Eastern Printers & Trading Co Ltd: POB 2304; tel. (02) 20434.

Leong Bros: 52 Jalan Bunga Kuning, POB 164, Seria; tel. (03) 22381.
Offset Printing House: POB 1111; tel. (02) 24477.

Government Publishing House
Government Printer: The Government Printing Office, Lapangan Terbang Lama, Berakas; tel. (02) 44541.

Radio and Television

In 1986 there were an estimated 74,000 radio receivers and 48,000 television receivers in use.

Radio Televisyen Brunei: Bandar Seri Begawan; tel. (02) 43111; telex 2600 (news)/2312; f. 1957; two radio networks, one broadcasting in Malay and local dialects, the other in English, Chinese (Mandarin) and Gurkha; a colour television service was opened in 1975, broadcasting in Malay and English; Dir Pg BADARUDIN Pg GHANI.

Finance

(cap. = capital; dep. = deposits; m. = million; br.(s) = branch(es); amounts in Brunei dollars)

BANKING

There is no central bank. The Treasury Department carries out most of these functions. In October 1984 there were nine banks with a total of 41 branches.

The Island Development Bank Bhd: 2nd Floor, Maya Puri Bldg, 36–37 Jalan Sultan, POB 2725, Bandar Seri Begawan; tel. (02) 20686; telex 2320; f. 1981; Man. Dir F. M. TUAZON; 2 brs.
National Bank of Brunei Bhd: 102–103 Jalan Kianggeh, POB 321, Bandar Seri Begawan; tel. (02) 26183; telex 2233; f. 1965; cap. 90m., dep. 1,417m. (Dec. 1985); Pres. HRH Prince Haji SUFRI BOLKIAH; Chair. Pehin Dato KHOO BAN HOCK; Sr Man. ROBERT TEO; 12 brs; closed down Dec. 1986; funds transferred to Hongkong and Shanghai Banking Corpn.

Foreign Banks
Bank of America NT and SA (USA): Ground Floor, Suri Bldg, Jalan Tutong, POB 2280, Bandar Seri Begawan; tel. (02) 24911; telex 2235; f. 1972; Vice-Pres. and Country Man. BRUNO CORNELIO; 2 brs.
Citibank NA (USA): 147 Jalan Pemancha, POB 2209, Bandar Seri Begawan; tel. (02) 23983; telex 2224; Country Corporate Officer DAVID CONNER; 2 brs.
The Hongkong and Shanghai Banking Corpn (Hong Kong): POB 59, cnr Jalan Sultan and Jalan Pemancha, Bandar Seri Begawan; tel. (02) 42305; telex 2273; f. 1947; Man. COLIN DUNCAN; 9 brs.
Malayan Banking Bhd (Malaysia): 148 Jalan Pemancha, POB 167, Bandar Seri Begawan; tel. (02) 42494; telex 2316; f. 1960; Man. WAN MOHD DEN WAN MOHD ZIN; 3 brs.
Overseas Union Bank Ltd: 72 Jalan Roberts, Bandar Seri Begawan; tel. (02) 25477; telex 2256; f. 1973; Man. KOH TEOW YEONG; 2 brs.
Standard Chartered Bank (UK): 145 Jalan Pemancha, POB 186, Bandar Seri Begawan; tel. (02) 42386; telex 22236; f. 1958; Man. T. A. MCCARTNEY; 4 brs.
United Malayan Banking Corpn Bhd (Malaysia): 141 Jalan Pemancha, POB 435, Bandar Seri Begawan; tel. (02) 22516; telex 2207; f. 1963; Man. LIOW CHEE HWA; 1 br.

INSURANCE

There are several locally incorporated insurance companies and a number of international insurance companies.

Trade and Industry

Trade in Brunei is largely conducted by the agency houses, European and Chinese, and by Chinese merchants.

CHAMBERS OF COMMERCE

Brunei State Chamber of Commerce: POB 2246, Bandar Seri Begawan; tel. (02) 28533; telex 2224; Chair. TIMOTHY ONG; Sec. JOHNNY P. ESCOTO; 119 mems.

Chinese Chamber of Commerce: POB 281, 9 Jalan Pretty, Bandar Seri Begawan; tel. (02) 34374; Chair. LIM ENG MING.

Indian Chamber of Commerce: POB 974, Bandar Seri Begawan; tel. (02) 23886; Pres. BIKRAMJIT BAHLLA.

Malay Chamber of Commerce: POB 156, Room 411, Malay Teachers' Bldg, Jalan Kianggeh, Bandar Seri Begawan; Chair. A. A. HAPIZ LAKSAMANA.

TRADE UNIONS

Total membership of the four trade unions was c. 4,000 in 1983.

Brunei Government Junior Officers' Union: POB 2290, Bandar Seri Begawan; Pres. Haji ALI BIN Haji NASAR; Gen. Sec. Haji OMARALI BIN Haji MOHIDDIN.

Brunei Government Medical and Health Workers' Union: POB 459, Bandar Seri Begawan; Pres. Pengiran Haji MOHIDDIN BIN Pengiran TAJUDDIN; Gen. Sec. HANAFI BIN ANAI.

Brunei Oilfield Workers' Union: POB 175, Seria; f. 1961; 505 mems; Pres. SEMITH BIN SABLI; Vice-Pres. MOHD ALI Haji YUSOF; Sec.-Gen. ABDUL WAHAB JUNAIDI.

Royal Brunei Custom Department Staff Union: Custom Dept, Kuala Belait; f. 1972; Pres. HASSAN BIN BAKAR; Gen. Sec. ABDUL ADIS BIN TARIP.

Transport

RAILWAYS

There are no public railways in Brunei. The Brunei Shell Petroleum Co Bhd maintains a 19.3-km section of light railway between Seria and Badas.

ROADS

In 1986 there were 1,025 km (637 miles) of roads in Brunei. There were also 486 km (303 miles) of district roads. The main highway connects Bandar Seri Begawan, Tutong and Kuala Belait. A new 59-km coastal road between Muara and Tutong was due for completion in 1985. Bus services operate between Brunei/Muara, Tutong and Belait districts.

Land Transport Department: Ministry of Communications, Batu 2½, Jalan Gadong, Bandar Seri Begawan; tel. (02) 23161; Controller Haji MOHD KASSIM BIN Haji JOHAN.

SHIPPING

Most sea traffic is handled by a deep-water port at Muara, 27 km from the capital. Renovation work on the port was due to be completed in 1985, including an extension of the wharf and dredging of the harbour to accommodate larger vessels. The original, smaller port at Bandar Seri Begawan itself is mainly used for local river-going vessels. There is a port at Kuala Belait which takes shallow-draught vessels and serves mainly the Shell oil field and Seria. At Seria, owing to Brunei's shallow waters, tankers are unable to come up to the shore to load and crude oil from the oil terminal is pumped through an underwater loading line to a single buoy mooring, to which the tankers are moored. At Lumut there is a 4.5-km jetty for liquefied natural gas (LNG) carriers. Rivers are the principal means of communication in the interior and boats or water taxis the main form of transport for most residents of the water villages. Larger water taxis operate daily to Temburong district.

Bee Seng Shipping Co: 1½ Miles Jalan Tutong, POB 92, Bandar Seri Begawan; telex 2219.

CIVIL AVIATION

There is an international airport at Bandar Seri Begawan which is currently undergoing a substantial upgrading. The work is due to be completed by 1987/88. The Brunei Shell Petroleum Co Sdn Bhd operates a private airfield at Anduki for helicopter services.

Directorate of Civil Aviation: Brunei International Airport; tel. (02) 30142; telex 2267; Dir JOB LIM.

Royal Brunei Airlines Ltd: Technical Centre, Mile 5, Jalan Berakas, off Jalan Costain, POB 737, Bandar Seri Begawan; tel. (02) 30737; telex 2737; f. 1974; operates services to Bangkok, Darwin, Hong Kong, Jakarta, Kota Kinabalu, Kuala Lumpur, Kuching, Manila and Singapore; Chair. Prince JEFRI BOLKIAH; Gen. Man. Pengiran TENGAH BIN Pg. Dato Paduka Haji METASSIM; fleet of 3 Boeing 737-200.

Tourism

Information Bureau: Information Dept, Ministry of Culture, Youth and Sports, 8th Floor, Arts and Handicrafts Centre, Jalan Residency, Bandar Seri Begawan; tel. (02) 28585.

BULGARIA

Introductory Survey

Location, Climate, Language, Religion, Flag, Capital

The People's Republic of Bulgaria lies in the eastern Balkans, in south-eastern Europe. It is bounded by Romania to the north, by Turkey and Greece to the south and by Yugoslavia to the west. The country has an eastern coastline on the Black Sea. The climate is one of fairly sharp contrasts between winter and summer. Temperatures in Sofia are generally between −5°C (23°F) and 28°C (82°F). The official language is Bulgarian, a member of the Slavonic group, written in the Cyrillic alphabet. Minority languages include Turkish and Macedonian. Most Christians adhere to the Bulgarian Orthodox Church, while there is a substantial minority of Muslims. The national flag (proportions 3 by 2) has three equal horizontal stripes, of white, green and red, with the state emblem (a lion, flanked by sheaves of grain and surmounted by a five-pointed red star) in the upper hoist. The capital is Sofia.

Recent History

Formerly a monarchy, Bulgaria allied with Nazi Germany in the Second World War and joined in the occupation of Yugoslavia in 1941. King Boris died in 1943 and was succeeded by his young son, Simeon II. In September 1944 the Fatherland Front, a left-wing alliance formed in 1942, seized power with help from the Soviet Union and set up a government under Kimon Georgiyev. In September 1946 the monarchy was abolished by popular referendum, and a republic was proclaimed. The first post-war election was held in October, when the Fatherland Front received 70.8% of the votes and won 364 seats (including 277 for Communists) in the 465-member National Assembly. In November Georgi Dimitrov, the First Secretary of the Communist Party and a veteran international revolutionary, became Prime Minister in a government formed from members of the Fatherland Front. All opposition parties were abolished, and a new constitution, based on the Soviet model, was adopted in December 1947. Dimitrov was replaced as Prime Minister by Vasil Kolarov in March 1949, but remained leader of the Communist Party until his death in July. His successor as Party leader, Vulko Chervenkov, also became Prime Minister in February 1950. Political trials and executions became less frequent after the death in 1953 of the Soviet leader, Stalin, and rehabilitation of those who had been disgraced began in 1956.

Todor Zhivkov succeeded Chervenkov as leader of the Communist Party in March 1954, although the latter remained Prime Minister until April 1956, when he was replaced by Anton Yugov. Following an ideological struggle within the Party, Zhivkov also became Prime Minister in November 1962. In April 1965 an attempted coup against the Government was discovered. In May 1971 a new constitution was adopted, and in July Zhivkov relinquished his position as Prime Minister to become the first President of the newly formed State Council. He was re-elected in 1976, in 1981 and in 1986. In September 1978 a purge of Communist Party membership commenced. At the twelfth Party Congress, held in March and April 1981, the Party leader was restyled General Secretary. In June, following elections to the National Assembly, a new Council of Ministers was formed, headed by Grisha Filipov, a member of the Political Bureau, in succession to Stanko Todorov, who had been Prime Minister since 1971. A broad reshuffle, affecting the top posts in the Communist Party and the Government, was announced in January 1984; it included the merging of four ministries into two in the sphere of trade and industry, and was widely believed to have economic, rather than political, ends. In 1985 the Communist Party leadership mounted a campaign against corruption and inefficiency, resulting in the dismissal and replacement of a number of ministers and senior officials, notably the Chairman of the State Planning Committee (subsequently restyled the State Planning Commission).

In January 1986 the National Assembly approved structural reforms and personnel changes in the Council of Ministers, involving the establishment of three new councils (a Council for Economic Affairs, a Council for Social Affairs and a Council for Intellectual Development), together with the abolition or reorganization of several ministries and state committees. A new Ministry of Trade was formed, incorporating the former Ministry of Foreign Trade, Ministry of Supplies and Ministry of Production and Trade in Consumer Goods. In March Grisha Filipov was replaced as Prime Minister by Georgi Atanasov, and a number of other ministerial changes took place. Six industrial and economic ministries, including the Ministry of Energy, were abolished, and a new Ministry of Agriculture and Forestry was created.

At the thirteenth Party Congress, held in April 1986, Zhivkov advocated the elimination of excessive bureaucracy, an improvement in the integration of self-governing organizations with centralized state management and an increase in the scope for initiative among such organizations. He also placed great emphasis on the importance to the national economy of an acceleration of scientific and technological progress. Following elections to the National Assembly in June, Zhivkov was unanimously re-elected President of the State Council.

In general, relations with Western states have steadily improved, and co-operation in economic and technical fields is increasing. However, relations between Bulgaria and Italy became strained in November 1982 after Mehmet Ağca, a Turkish citizen, had claimed Bulgarian involvement in his attempt to assassinate Pope John Paul II in 1981. In spite of the related arrest and detention of Sergei Antonov, a Bulgarian airline official in Rome, Ağca's claim remained unsubstantiated, and in April 1986 Antonov returned to Bulgaria, having been acquitted in the previous month, on the grounds that there was insufficient evidence to convict him.

In January 1985 reports were received in the West that Bulgaria had begun a campaign to force the country's Turkish minority to adopt Slavic names in advance of the next census, planned for the end of that year, and loss of life was claimed to have occurred where the campaign had met resistance. It was suggested that such action might have been taken in order to disguise the fact that the ethnic Turkish population, which constitutes nearly 10% of Bulgaria's total population, has a much higher rate of natural increase than the Slav population. The Bulgarian Government denied that coercion was being used in a programme in which it said the ethnic Turks were participating voluntarily. Attempts have been made in the West, without proof, to link this issue with a series of bomb attacks by unidentified terrorists in Bulgaria in 1984, in which several people were killed. Following the population census (held in December 1985), Bulgaria was condemned by the Turkish Government for 'seeking to eliminate all statistical evidence of its ethnic Turks'. The census questionnaires were criticized for allowing no scope for members of national minorities to register themselves as anything other than Bulgarian. In 1986 the Bulgarian Government continued to refute allegations, made by Amnesty International, that more than 250 ethnic Turks had been arrested or imprisoned for refusing to accept new identity cards, and that many more had been forced to resettle away from their homes, in other regions of the country.

Government

Under the 1971 constitution, the supreme organ of state power is the unicameral National Assembly, with 400 members elected for five years by universal adult suffrage in single-member constituencies. The Assembly elects the State Council (27 members were elected in June 1986) to be its permanent organ. There is no constitutional provision for a Head of State, but some of the equivalent functions are exercised by the President of the State Council. The Council of Ministers, the highest

BULGARIA

organ of state administration, is elected by (and responsible to) the Assembly.

Political power is held by the Bulgarian Communist Party (BCP), which dominates the Fatherland Front. The Front presents an approved list of candidates for elections to all representative bodies (members of the National Assembly were elected unopposed in June 1986). The BCP's highest authority is the Party Congress, convened every five years. The Congress elects a Central Committee (195 members were elected in April 1986) to supervise Party work. To direct its policy, the Committee elects a Political Bureau (Politburo), with 11 full members and six candidate members in 1986.

For local administration, Bulgaria comprises 27 provinces and three cities, each with a People's Council elected for two and a half years.

Defence

Bulgaria is a member of the Warsaw Pact. Military service is for two years in the army and air force, and for three years in the navy. According to Western estimates, the total strength of the armed forces in July 1986 was 148,500 (including 94,000 conscripts), comprising an army of 105,000, an air force of 35,000 and a navy of 8,500. Paramilitary forces include 15,000 border troops and 7,500 security police. There is a voluntary People's Militia of 150,000. Defence expenditure in 1985 was estimated at 1,010m. leva.

Economic Affairs

Bulgaria is a very fertile country. After 1945, agriculture was organized on a large-scale co-operative and mechanized basis. There are about 300 huge agro-industrial complexes. Between 1965 and 1975 the labour force in agriculture and forestry declined from 1,891,000 (44.4% of the total working population) to 1,049,000 (23.6%). The principal crops are wheat, maize, barley, sugar beet, grapes and tobacco, and in 1983 agriculture (excluding forestry) accounted for 16.5% of net material product (NMP). Tobacco is an increasingly important crop: although it occupies scarcely 2.5% of land under cultivation, it accounts for 20% of all agricultural production and 40% of the revenue of the National Agro-Industrial Union. In 1985 about 27% of Bulgaria's total agricultural output came from private plots, which occupied nearly 14% of the total area under cultivation, and accounted for almost 40% of total meat production. There is a large exportable surplus of processed agricultural products.

Between 1965 and 1975 the labour force in manufacturing increased from 991,000 (23.3% of the total) to 1,438,000 (32.3%). Food, beverages and tobacco form the largest manufacturing sector, accounting for about 27% of total output in 1983. The engineering and electronics sectors, in particular, have been greatly developed, as have the chemical fertilizer and metallurgical industries.

The 1976–80 Five-Year Plan achieved a 35% increase in industrial production, and a 20% increase in agricultural output, with three-quarters of the Plan's budget spent on further modernization and reconstruction of industry. Foreign trade increased by 80%. However, since 1977 there have been indications of a decline in the growth rate, due mainly to increases in the prices of raw materials. Industry (mining, manufacturing and utilities) provided 57.0% of NMP in 1984, when industrial production increased by 4.5%, agricultural output by 6.8% and NMP by 4.6%. In 1985 Bulgaria's NMP increased by 1.8%, and the profit realized by non-agricultural enterprises rose by 3.9%. However, a particularly cold winter, followed by a drought, seriously affected crops, and agricultural production declined by 9%. The record grain harvest of 9.3m. metric tons in 1984 was followed by a harvest of only about 5m. tons in 1985, and Bulgaria was compelled to import grain from the West. Foreign trade increased by 7.4% in 1985 (compared with a rise of 8.3% in 1984), with imports totalling 14,002m. leva and exports 13,736m. leva, 55% of exports being accounted for by products of the mechanical engineering and electronic industries. In 1985 Bulgaria imported 13.4m. metric tons of petroleum, and, in common with other CMEA countries, was unfavourably affected by the fall in the international price of oil, paying more than the average world market price for its imports from the USSR and earning little convertible currency from its re-exports.

Introductory Survey

Bulgaria has the lowest debt to the West (estimated at US $1,200m.) of all CMEA countries, but in 1985 the Government borrowed a total of $470m. in three major loans from Western banks, both to help to develop its electronic and high-technology industries and to offset some of the economic consequences of the adverse weather conditions. The drought affected not only crop production and water supplies but also electric power generation, and caused the Government to introduce wide-ranging price increases and to enforce the rationing of electricity.

The draft Five-Year Plan for 1981–85 projected a continuation of the slowdown in economic growth, with NMP rising by about 20%. Priority was to be given to the development of heavy industry. Encouragement was also to be given to the fusion of state and co-operative ownership. In 1982 a 'new economic mechanism' was introduced to increase efficiency and to ensure the elimination of the weakest enterprises: subsidies to individual companies were to be reduced, while wages were to be linked to output, although no unemployment was expected to result.

The draft Five-Year Plan for 1986–90 envisaged an acceleration of the development of science and technology and, accordingly, an increase in the production of machine tools and technical equipment. It also provided for a restructuring of foreign-trade activities and for reforms in the structure and policies of domestic economic management, with a limited amount of decentralization of decision-making and a higher degree of independence for self-governing enterprises, more than 1,500 of which were to be established during the five-year period. Tax reductions and other financial incentives for increased agricultural production in the private sector were also to be introduced.

Bulgaria produces less than one-third of its energy needs, and priority is being given to the full development of indigenous energy resources. Bulgaria's first nuclear power station, constructed by Soviet engineers, opened in 1974, and nuclear power, which was providing 29% of electric energy in 1985, was expected to provide 40% by 1990 and 60% by 2000. Construction of a fifth reactor at the nuclear power station at Kozlodui was under way in 1986, while a number of other nuclear power stations were being modernized or rebuilt. Bulgaria's first wind power station, at the Frangen plateau, north of Varna, was due to begin operating in March 1986. Coal, iron ore, copper, lead and zinc are mined, while petroleum is extracted on the Black Sea coast. Bulgaria became self-sufficient in pig-iron in 1980. Foreign trade is a state monopoly, and in 1985 75.6% was with the other members of the CMEA (see p. 126), and 56.3% with the USSR alone. Since 1980, in an attempt to increase trade and co-operation with the West, foreign companies have been encouraged to establish joint enterprises in Bulgaria. Long-term reciprocal trade agreements with Czechoslovakia and the People's Republic of China were signed in December 1985, and in January 1986 a 10-year agreement on economic, scientific and technical co-operation was signed with France. Considerable tourist development has played an important part in alleviating Bulgaria's shortage of foreign exchange.

In June 1986 the construction of a 1,635-km gas pipeline, linking Bulgaria to the USSR, was completed. In the mid-1980s the USSR supplied Bulgaria with 5,500m. cu m of gas per year, and the gas being conveyed through the new pipeline is expected to meet one-fifth of Bulgaria's demand for hydrocarbon products.

Social Welfare

State social insurance is directed by the Department of Public Insurance and the Pensions Directorate. In 1986 3,494.6m. leva (17.9% of the state budget) were allotted to social security. Workers are paid compensation during sick leave. Women are entitled to full paid leave before and after childbirth. All pensions are non-contributory. Retirement pensions consist of a basic sum plus up to 12% allowance for additional service, over the minimum requirement. The basic pension is related to the average monthly pay in three of the last 15 years of service. Retirement age varies from 45 to 60 years, depending on the job. Women retire five years earlier than men.

Since 1951 all medical services and treatment have been provided free for the whole population. In 1983 there were 80,400 hospital beds and 24,000 physicians. All medical treatment establishments and medical schools, training colleges and research institutes are controlled by the Ministry of Public Health. Departments of Public Health in the regional People's Councils supervise medical work, together with the Bulgarian Red Cross.

Education

Education in Bulgaria is free and compulsory between the ages of six and 16 years. It is administered by the Bulgarian Ministry of National Education, although direct organization of kindergartens and schools is exercised by specialized organs of local People's Councils.

In 1983 kindergartens were attended by 76% of all children between the ages of three and six. The unified secondary polytechnical school was introduced in the 1983/84 school year to provide primary and secondary education in three stages, in accordance with plans to restructure the Bulgarian system of education. The first stage covers schooling from the first to the 10th grade, while in the second stage, which lasts seven months, students obtain general vocational qualifications, and at the third stage, which lasts three months, they acquire vocational qualifications in a narrow speciality. In addition, vocational-technical schools provide primary education and workers' professional qualifications, secondary vocational-technical schools provide secondary education and workers' professional qualifications, and technical colleges (tekhnikums) offer secondary training for specialists in industry, construction, agriculture, transport, trade and public health.

After completing secondary education, students are entitled to continue their training in semi-higher institutes or in higher educational institutions.

In the 1983/84 school year 391,902 pupils attended kindergartens, 1,427,250 attended primary and secondary schools, and 93,594 students took courses at semi-higher and higher educational institutions.

Tourism

Resorts on the Black Sea coast are very popular. Most foreign visitors come from the USSR and Eastern Europe. A campaign to attract visitors from the West has resulted in a considerable increase in the number of tourists. The annual total of visitor arrivals rose from 5,771,000 (including 3,146,000 visitors in transit) in 1983 to 7,295,000 in 1985.

Public Holidays

1987: 1 January (New Year), 1–2 May (Labour Days), 24 May (Education Day), 9–10 September (National Days), 7 November (Anniversary of Russia's October Revolution).

1988: 1 January (New Year), 1–2 May (Labour Days), 24 May (Education Day), 9–10 September (National Days), 7 November (Anniversary of Russia's October Revolution).

Weights and Measures

The metric system is in force.

Currency and Exchange Rates

100 stotinki = 1 lev.

Exchange rates (30 September 1986):
 £1 sterling = 1.340 leva;
 US $1 = 92.6 stotinki.

Statistical Survey

Source (unless otherwise stated): Central Statistical Office at the Council of Ministers, Sofia, Panayot Volov St 2; tel. 46-01; telex 22001.

Area and Population

AREA, POPULATION AND DENSITY

Area (sq km)*	110,912†
Population (census results)	
2 December 1975	8,727,771
4–12 December 1985‡	
Males	4,427,040
Females	4,515,936
Total	8,942,976
Population (official estimates at 31 December)§	
1982	8,929,332
1983	8,950,144
1984	8,971,200
Density (per sq km) at December 1985	80.6

* Including territorial waters of frontier rivers (267.8 sq km).
† 42,823 sq miles.
‡ Provisional.
§ Not revised to take account of the 1985 census result.

PRINCIPAL TOWNS (estimated population at 31 December 1983)

Sofia (capital)	1,093,752	Pleven	140,440	
Plovdiv	373,235	Shumen	104,089	
Varna	295,218	Tolbukhin	102,292	
Burgas (Bourgas)	183,477	Sliven	102,037	
Ruse (Roussé)	181,185	Pernik	96,431	
Stara Zagora	144,904			

BIRTHS, MARRIAGES AND DEATHS

	Registered live births Number	Rate (per 1,000)	Registered marriages* Number	Rate (per 1,000)	Registered deaths Number	Rate (per 1,000)
1978	136,442	15.5	71,316	8.1	92,445	10.5
1979	135,358	15.3	69,693	7.9	94,403	10.7
1980	128,190	14.5	69,726	7.9	97,950	11.1
1981	124,372	14.0	66,539	7.5	95,441	10.7
1982	124,166	13.9	67,154	7.5	100,293	11.2
1983	122,993	13.7	67,032	7.5	102,182	11.4
1984†	122,641	13.7	67,256	7.5	100,888	11.3
1985†	117,893	13.2	n.a.	n.a.	107,445	12.0

* Including marriages of Bulgarian nationals outside the country but excluding those of aliens in Bulgaria.
† Provisional.

Life Expectation (1974–76): Males 68.68 years, Females 73.91 years.

ECONOMICALLY ACTIVE POPULATION (1975 census)

	Males	Females	Total
Agriculture, hunting, forestry and fishing	498,545	550,594	1,049,139
Mining and quarrying	62,534	22,310	84,844
Manufacturing	761,321	676,921	1,438,242
Electricity, gas and water	21,368	6,615	28,253
Construction	288,429	61,927	350,356
Trade, restaurants and hotels	127,031	228,721	355,752
Transport, storage and communication	231,007	67,575	298,582
Financing, insurance, real estate and business services	8,273	23,528	31,801
Community, social and personal services	366,604	443,325	809,929
Activities not adequately described	326	560	886
Total	2,365,708	2,082,076	4,447,784

EMPLOYEES IN THE 'SOCIALIZED' SECTOR*
(annual averages, '000)

	1983	1984	1985
Agriculture*	924.6	899.4	881.3
Forestry	16.8	16.7	16.0
Industry†	1,412.2	1,409.6	1,406.7
Construction	353.8	355.3	359.2
Commerce	357.2	355.9	360.5
Transport and storage	260.6	259.0	257.5
Communications	41.2	41.9	42.5
Finance and insurance services	21.5	21.9	22.0
Education and culture	303.4	308.4	311.1
Public health, welfare and sports	196.3	198.1	197.3
Administration	54.6	54.1	53.4
Science and scientific institutes	75.2	79.2	81.7
Housing and community services‡	51.3	52.7	56.1
Total (incl. others)	4,113.5	4,098.0	4,092.8

* Excluding agricultural co-operatives (employing more than 280,000 people in 1975) but including state farms and machine-tractor stations.
† Mining, manufacturing and electricity.
‡ Including water supply.

Agriculture

PRINCIPAL CROPS ('000 metric tons)

	1983	1984	1985
Wheat	3,608	4,836	3,051
Rice (paddy)	74	74*	n.a.
Barley	1,047	1,279	802
Maize	3,115	2,994	1,386
Rye	31	33*	n.a.
Oats	30	55*	n.a.
Potatoes	427	418	435
Dry beans	57	46	42
Dry peas	6	15*	n.a.
Soybeans	82	72	39
Sunflower seed	454	462	354
Seed cotton	17	15	14
Cabbages	146	160*	n.a.
Tomatoes	651	905	772
Cauliflowers	7	8*	n.a.
Pumpkins, squash and gourds	52	52*	n.a.
Cucumbers and gherkins	158	120*	n.a.
Green chillies and peppers	242	280*	n.a.
Dry onions	78	90*	n.a.
Green beans	24	20*	n.a.
Green peas	7	20*	n.a.
Water-melons	220	320*	n.a.
Grapes	1,000	1,120	n.a.
Apples	468	526	316
Pears	93	95*	n.a.
Plums	149	200*	n.a.
Peaches and nectarines	104	120*	n.a.
Apricots	32	35*	n.a.
Strawberries	14	20	11
Sugar beets	746	1,133	786
Tobacco leaves	112	141	n.a.
Flax fibre and tow	1	2*	n.a.
Hemp fibre and tow	4	4*	n.a.

* FAO estimate (Source: FAO, *Production Yearbook*).

LIVESTOCK ('000 head at 1 January each year)

	1984	1985	1986
Horses	119	118	120
Asses	351	n.a.	n.a.
Cattle	1,778	1,751	1,706
Pigs	3,769	3,734	3,912
Sheep	10,978	10,501	9,724
Goats	506	474	n.a.
Buffaloes	36	33	29
Poultry	43,078	42,277	39,227

LIVESTOCK PRODUCTS (metric tons)

	1982	1983	1984*
Beef and veal	124,000	127,000†	135,000
Buffalo meat	3,000†	3,000	2,000
Mutton and lamb	75,000†	77,000†	76,000
Goats' meat	4,000†	4,000†	5,000
Pigmeat	324,000	333,000	332,000
Poultry meat	154,000	160,000	170,000
Edible offals	49,000*	50,000*	50,000
Cow milk	2,001,000	2,092,000	2,150,000
Buffalo milk	27,000	26,000	23,000
Sheep milk	326,000	338,000	345,000
Goat milk	69,000	74,000	72,000
Butter	23,036	23,960	24,700
Cheese (all kinds)	172,753	185,631	187,300
Hen eggs	137,372	146,448	148,600
Other poultry eggs	2,503	2,543	2,500
Honey	9,796	9,074	8,600
Raw silk	172	150†	200
Wool:			
greasy	34,886	35,935	36,600
scoured	17,900	18,400	18,700
Cattle and buffalo hides	20,200*	21,400*	20,600
Sheep skins	29,400*	31,000*	31,400

* FAO estimates.   † Unofficial figure.
Source: FAO, mainly *Production Yearbook*.

Forestry

ROUNDWOOD REMOVALS
('000 cubic metres, State forests only)

	1982	1983	1984
Sawlogs, veneer logs and logs for sleepers	1,316	1,262	1,306
Pulpwood	1,150	1,118	1,175
Other industrial wood	660	637	633*
Fuel wood	1,736	1,733	1,727
Total	4,862	4,750	4,841

* Estimate.
Source: FAO, *Yearbook of Forest Products*.

SAWNWOOD PRODUCTION ('000 cubic metres)

	1982	1983	1984
Total (incl. sleepers)	1,511	1,504	1,353

Source: FAO, *Yearbook of Forest Products*.

Fishing

('000 metric tons, live weight)

	1981	1982	1983
Common carp	12.4	14.3	11.5
Hakes	6.8	8.7	4.9
Chilean jack mackerel	12.6	13.6	24.3
Cape horse mackerel	37.3	48.4	51.2
Other jack and horse mackerels	0.6	3.5	7.5
European sardine (pilchard)	8.5	—	0.5
Sprat	18.9	16.5	12.0
Other fishes (incl. unspecified)	9.3	10.2	9.0
Crustaceans and molluscs	0.3	0.4	0.3
Total catch	106.7	115.6	121.1
of which:			
Inland waters	13.2	15.6	13.7
Mediterranean and Black Seas	19.8	17.3	13.5
Atlantic Ocean	53.2	61.7	68.7
Pacific Ocean	20.5	21.0	25.1

Source: FAO, *Yearbook of Fishery Statistics*.

Mining

('000 metric tons)

	1981	1982	1983
Anthracite	89	80	83
Other hard coal	157	161	160
Lignite	23,338	26,437	26,805
Other brown coal	5,657	5,537	5,342
Iron ore*	537	474	554
Copper ore*†	62	70	80
Lead ore*†	90	95	95
Zinc ore*†	65	66	68
Manganese ore*	13.2	13.2	13.1
Salt (refined)	84	88	87
Crude petroleum‡	300	300	300
Natural gas ('000 terajoules)	5	3	4

* Figures relate to the metal content of ores.
† Source: Metallgesellschaft Aktiengesellschaft (Frankfurt am Main).
‡ UN estimates.
Sources: UN, *Industrial Statistics Yearbook;* Committee for Social Information at the Council of Ministers, Sofia.

Industry

SELECTED PRODUCTS

		1983	1984	1985*
Refined sugar	'000 metric tons	438	n.a.	n.a.
Wine	'000 hectolitres	4,549	n.a.	n.a.
Beer	'000 hectolitres	5,504.6	5,766	n.a.
Cigarettes and cigars	metric tons	91,296	92,100	94,000
Cotton yarn[1]	metric tons	85,210	83,500	82,200
Woven cotton fabrics[2]	'000 metres	367,365	367,800	349,300
Flax and hemp yarn	metric tons	9,760	9,800	9,400
Wool yarn[1]	metric tons	37,781	36,500	33,100
Woven woollen fabrics[2]	'000 metres	48,679	41,500	40,400
Woven fabrics of man-made fibres[3]	'000 metres	37,114	37,200	36,000
Leather footwear	'000 pairs	19,599	21,600	22,800
Rubber footwear	'000 pairs	9,514	7,900	n.a.
Chemical wood pulp	'000 metric tons	202.5	194.6	174.3
Paper	'000 metric tons	359.2	362.3	370.4
Paperboard	'000 metric tons	66.2	n.a.	n.a.
Rubber tyres[4]	'000	1,612.8	1,666	1,604.2
Sulphuric acid (100%)	'000 metric tons	860.7	908.3	810.0
Caustic soda (96%)	'000 metric tons	153.3	170.2	157.2
Soda ash (98%)	'000 metric tons	1,270.9	1,212.3	1,036.6
Nitrogenous fertilizers (a)[5]	metric tons	831,330	836,106	837,800
Phosphate fertilizers (b)[5]	metric tons	204,051	211,149	171,700
Soap	metric tons	29,219	n.a.	n.a.
Coke (gas and coke-oven)	'000 metric tons	1,270	1,186	1,087
Unworked glass (rectangles)	'000 sq metres	23,012	20,600	23,500
Clay building bricks	million	1,464	n.a.	n.a.
Cement	'000 metric tons	5,644	5,700	5,200
Pig-iron and ferro-alloys	'000 metric tons	1,674	1,621	1,754
Crude steel	'000 metric tons	2,831	2,878	2,926
Tractors (10 h.p. and over)	number	5,880	5,784	5,340
Metal-working lathes	number	6,310	5,564	5,476
Cranes	number	1,272	n.a.	n.a.
Fork-lift trucks	number	71,712	80,400	85,500
Refrigerators (household)	number	133,162	135,000	n.a.
Washing machines (household)	number	130,060	141,200	155,900
Radio receivers	number	42,160	40,100	41,500
Television receivers	number	126,803	112,600	110,600
Construction: dwellings completed[6]	number	69,745	68,762	n.a.
Electric energy	million kWh	42,642	44,669	41,621

* Provisional.

[1] Pure and mixed yarn. Figures for wool include yarn of man-made staple.
[2] Pure and mixed fabrics, after undergoing finishing processes.
[3] Finished fabrics, including fabrics of natural silk.
[4] Tyres for road motor vehicles (passenger cars and commercial vehicles).
[5] Figures in terms of (a) nitrogen or (b) phosphoric acid. Data for nitrogenous fertilizers include urea.
[6] Including restorations and conversions.

BULGARIA
Statistical Survey

Finance

CURRENCY AND EXCHANGE RATES

Monetary Units
100 stotinki (singular: stotinka) = 1 lev (plural: leva).

Denominations
Coins: 1, 2, 5, 10, 20 and 50 stotinki; 1, 2 and 5 leva.
Notes: 1, 2, 5, 10 and 20 leva.

Sterling and Dollar Equivalents (30 September 1986)
£1 sterling = 1.340 leva;
US $1 = 92.6 stotinki;
100 leva = £74.63 = $107.99.

Exchange Rate
Between February 1980 and February 1983 the rate was set at US $1 = 85 stotinki.

STATE BUDGET (million leva)

Revenue	1981	1982	1983
National economy	10,105.3	10,396.5	10,789.8
Other receipts	5,383.9	6,291.2	6,021.9
Total	15,489.2	16,687.7	16,811.7

Expenditure	1981	1982	1983
National economy	8,067.8	8,655.3	8,630.0
Education, health, science, art and culture	2,754.4	2,854.0	2,944.9
Social security*	2,524.4	2,714.3	2,846.3
Administration	314.2	305.2	292.7
Other expenditure	1,766.1	1,997.6	1,948.9
Total	15,426.9	16,526.4	16,662.8

* Including the pension fund for agricultural co-operatives.

1984 (draft budget, million leva): Revenue 17,754.2, Expenditure 17,739.2.

1985 (draft budget, million leva): Revenue 18,097.2, Expenditure 18,087.4.

1986 (draft budget, million leva): Revenue 19,505.8, Expenditure 19,490.8.

NATIONAL ACCOUNTS

Net Material Product* (million leva at current market prices)

Activities of the Material Sphere	1982	1983	1984
Agriculture and livestock	4,519.8	3,864.3	4,599
Forestry	81.2	80.9	
Industry†	12,237.6	13,265.4	14,091
Construction	2,207.7	2,270.4	2,367
Trade, restaurants, etc.‡	1,383.6	1,528.5	1,328
Transport and storage	1,574.6	1,601.5	1,912
Communications	221.1	243.6	
Others	623.9	624.4	611
Total	22,849.5	23,479.0	24,907

* Defined as the total net value of goods and 'productive' services, including turnover taxes, produced by the economy. This excludes economic activities not contributing directly to material production, such as public administration, defence and personal and professional services.
† Principally manufacturing, mining, electricity, gas and water supply. The figures also include the value of hunting, fishing and logging when these activities are organized.
‡ Includes material and technical supply.

External Trade

PRINCIPAL COMMODITIES (million leva)

Imports f.o.b.	1982	1983	1984
Machinery and equipment	3,717.5	4,097.3	4,373.5
Power and electro-technical machinery	286.4	346.2	568.7
Mining, metallurgical and oil-drilling equipment	254.3	221.5	253.9
Tractors and agricultural machinery	261.6	288.1	287.7
Transport rolling stock	1,488.7	1,733.1	1,801.6
Fuels, mineral raw materials and metals	5,077.4	5,538.5	6,026.4
Solid fuels	452.1	483.2	495.8
Ferrous metals	864.6	938.2	946.3
Chemicals, fertilizers and rubber	605.4	620.6	682.5
Chemicals	245.2	259.2	312.3
Agricultural crop and livestock crude materials (except foods)	501.3	588.3	640.7
Timber, cellulose and paper products	216.7	229.1	236.3
Textile raw materials and semi-manufactures	129.9	180.0	172.4
Raw materials for food production	280.3	310.8	321.5
Other industrial goods for consumption	529.2	514.9	526.2
Commodities for cultural purposes	246.0	220.8	209.3
Total (incl. others)	10,975.9	11,966.0	12,842.3

Exports f.o.b.*	1982	1983	1984
Machinery and equipment	5,097.9	5,725.1	6,197.2
Power and electro-technical machinery	367.6	408.8	392.5
Hoisting and hauling equipment	972.5	1,122.2	1,252.6
Agricultural machinery	236.7	259.5	247.6
Transport rolling stock	1,254.1	1,414.0	1,055.1
Fuels, mineral raw materials and metals	1,383.1	1,347.4	1,399.9
Ferrous metals	322.1	370.3	422.1
Chemicals, fertilizers and rubber	465.2	494.3	588.7
Chemicals	299.2	321.2	387.4
Building materials and components	187.6	223.4	255.1
Agricultural crop and livestock crude materials (except foods)	142.1	184.9	216.1
Raw materials for food production (incl. tobacco)	522.3	453.2	407.2
Foodstuffs, beverages and tobacco products	1,823.8	1,934.8	2,268.3
Meat and dairy products, animal fats and eggs	247.1	245.1	272.2
Fruit and vegetables	514.2	496.0	501.0
Wine, brandy and spirits	413.0	452.1	459.4
Cigarettes	587.5	679.5	679.6
Other industrial goods for consumption	1,028.9	1,174.5	1,315.3
Clothing and underwear	243.9	277.6	304.3
Medical, sanitary and cosmetic products	465.9	545.5	611.1
Total (incl. others)	10,880.0	11,817.5	12,987.3

* Figures include foreign aid and loans, and exports of ships' stores and bunkers for foreign vessels.

PRINCIPAL TRADING PARTNERS* (million leva)

Imports f.o.b.	1983	1984	1985
Austria	197.5	182.4	n.a.
Brazil	42.4	132.0	n.a.
Cuba	188.9	231.0	232.6
Czechoslovakia	491.8	505.7	580.0
France	96.3	140.5	n.a.
German Democratic Republic	680.9	713.5	735.4
Germany, Federal Republic	464.2	472.2	544.2
Hungary	275.5	250.2	n.a.
Iran	174.0	115.5	n.a.
Italy	106.9	125.2	160.0
Japan	106.8	74.2	88.9
Libya	252.4	306.6	400.9
Netherlands	109.5	72.2	n.a.
Poland	517.6	542.5	628.2
Romania	245.0	223.6	n.a.
Switzerland	177.9	258.7	n.a.
USSR	6,951.0	7,579.7	7,849.3
United Kingdom	105.6	106.9	n.a.
USA	63.5	61.4	152.4
Yugoslavia	122.5	136.8	n.a.
Total (incl. others)	11,966.0	12,842.3	14,002.3

Exports f.o.b.	1983	1984	1985
Brazil	33.1	102.1	n.a.
Cuba	217.2	218.2	218.1
Czechoslovakia	470.6	525.9	630.8
France	142.2	107.1	n.a.
German Democratic Republic	645.6	676.7	714.3
Germany, Federal Republic	197.5	226.2	199.2
Greece	216.1	130.1	n.a.
Hungary	270.9	249.4	264.2
India	14.7	108.6	n.a.
Iran	183.8	108.6	122.1
Iraq	302.0	357.4	421.3
Italy	98.7	66.8	67.5
Libya	473.7	601.6	619.7
Poland	378.0	460.4	475.2
Romania	255.1	243.5	291.6
Switzerland	247.8	194.4	141.3
Turkey	126.3	217.6	151.4
USSR	6,618.5	7,230.3	7,754.3
United Kingdom	108.4	202.2	n.a.
Yugoslavia	83.5	108.8	n.a.
Total (incl. others)	11,817.5	12,987.3	13,736.0

* Imports by country of purchase; exports by country of sale.

Transport

RAILWAY TRAFFIC (million)

	1983	1984	1985
Passenger-kilometres	7,255	7,538	7,785
Freight ton-kilometres	18,060	18,134	18,172

INTERNATIONAL SEA-BORNE SHIPPING

	1981	1982	1983
Vessels entered ('000 net reg. tons)	12,141	10,347	8,752.8
Goods loaded ('000 metric tons)	3,530	4,488	4,416.6
Goods unloaded ('000 metric tons)	28,862	24,751	24,704.5

INLAND WATERWAYS (million)

	1983	1984	1985
Passenger-kilometres	16	17	18
Freight ton-kilometres	2,327	2,639	2,039

CIVIL AVIATION (million)

	1983	1984	1985
Passenger-kilometres	2,870	3,057	3,231
Freight ton-kilometres	52	53	44

Tourism

	1983	1984	1985
Foreign tourist arrivals*	5,771,163	6,138,340	7,295,244

* Including visitors in transit: 3,145,997 in 1983.

VISITORS TO BULGARIA BY COUNTRY OF ORIGIN

	1983	1984	1985
Austria	45,892	39,090	46,239
Belgium	9,604	8,968	12,226
Czechoslovakia	412,873	410,024	444,638
France	37,717	32,812	39,546
German Democratic Republic	250,430	249,133	268,214
Germany, Federal Republic	149,817	127,334	188,593
Greece	125,366	107,062	98,657
Hungary	247,831	255,265	252,107
Iran*	12,340	25,958	32,687
Iraq*	6,674	3,819	3,268
Italy	13,747	12,775	17,655
Jordan*	8,722	6,379	5,854
Netherlands	16,367	13,692	16,516
Poland	352,613	384,630	477,653
Romania	246,225	243,847	207,653
Sweden	20,787	15,768	15,472
Switzerland	9,942	7,566	9,430
Turkey*	2,713,668	2,743,254	2,674,546
USSR	333,091	337,584	363,516
United Kingdom	49,854	55,038	73,350
USA	10,784	9,082	17,626
Yugoslavia	526,122	845,032	1,435,112
Unspecified	170,697	204,228	594,686
Total	5,771,163	6,138,340	7,295,244

* Mainly visitors in transit.

Communications Media

	1981	1982	1983
Telephone subscribers	1,382,100	1,513,400	1,655,000
Radio licences	2,115,100	2,085,400	2,055,139
Television licences	1,658,700	1,682,700	1,691,115
Daily newspapers (titles)	14	14	14
Book production:			
Titles*	5,036	5,070	4,924
Copies ('000)*	60,808	59,662	59,840

* Figures include pamphlets (868 titles and 6,897,000 copies in 1981; 887 titles and 6,840,000 copies in 1982; 816 titles and 9,312,000 copies in 1983).

1984: Telephone subscribers 1,810,500; Radio licences 2,043,500; Television licences 1,697,200.

1985: Telephone subscribers 1,946,300; Radio licences 2,017,400; Television licences 1,696,500.

Education

(1983/84)

	Institutions	Teachers	Students
Kindergarten	5,551	29,317	391,902
Unified secondary polytechnical	3,521	70,472	1,202,558
Special	130	2,356	17,101
Vocational technical	3	58	1,451
Secondary vocational technical	274	7,524	115,038
Technical colleges and schools of arts	229	9,336	91,102
Semi-higher institutes (teacher training)	16	629	7,305
Higher educational	30	13,205	86,275

Directory

The Constitution

Bulgaria was formerly a monarchy but on 15 September 1946 King Simeon was deposed and Bulgaria was declared a Republic. The Constitution of 1947 was replaced by a new Constitution, which was adopted by a referendum held on 16 May 1971, and proclaimed by the Fifth National Assembly on 18 May. The following are its main provisions:

The People's Republic of Bulgaria is a socialist state of the working people of towns and villages, headed by the working class. The Bulgarian Communist Party is the leading force in society and in the State. It guides the construction of a developed socialist society in the country in close fraternal co-operation with the Bulgarian Agrarian Union.

The State serves the people. It defends their interests and socialist acquisitions; directs the country's socio-economic development according to a plan; creates conditions for the constant improvement of the welfare, education and health services of the people, as well as for the all-round development of science and culture; ensures the free development of man, guarantees his rights and protects his dignity; organizes the defence of national independence, state sovereignty and the country's territorial integrity; develops and consolidates the friendship, co-operation and mutual assistance with the Union of Soviet Socialist Republics and the other socialist countries; conducts a policy of peace and understanding with all countries and peoples.

In the People's Republic of Bulgaria all power comes from the people and belongs to the people. It is realized by the people through the freely elected representative organs—the National Assembly and the People's Councils—or directly. The representative organs are elected on the basis of a general, equal and direct right to vote by secret ballot.

All the citizens of the People's Republic of Bulgaria who are 18 years of age, irrespective of sex, nationality, race, religion, education, profession, official, public or property status, excluding those under restraint, are eligible to vote and to be elected.

The People's Republic of Bulgaria is governed strictly in accordance with the Constitution and the country's laws. It belongs to the world socialist community, which is one of the main conditions for its independence and all-round development.

SOCIAL-ECONOMIC ORGANIZATION

The economic system of the People's Republic of Bulgaria is socialist. It is based on public ownership of the means of production.

The forms of ownership are: state (all people's) ownership, co-operative ownership, ownership of public organizations, and personal ownership.

Plants and factories, banks, underground resources, the natural sources of power, nuclear energy, forests, pasture land, roads, railway, water and air transport, posts, telegraphs, telephones, the radio and television are state (all people's) property.

Co-operative property belongs to collective bodies of working people who have united of their own free will for the joint carrying out of economic activity, to co-operative unions and inter-co-operative organizations. The State fosters and aids the activity of co-operatives and of co-operative farms.

The property of public organizations serves for achieving their goals, including the realization of the activities entrusted to them by state organs, and for meeting public interests.

The citizens of the People's Republic of Bulgaria have the right of personal ownership on real and movable property to meet personal needs and those of the family. The State protects the personal property, including savings, acquired by work or in some other lawful manner. Citizens cannot exercise their rights of personal ownership and their other property rights to the detriment of the public interest. The right to inherit is recognized and guaranteed.

The State directs the national economy and the other spheres of public life on the basis of unified plans for social-economic development.

Foreign trade is the exclusive right of the State.

Labour is a fundamental social-economic factor. The socialist principle 'From everyone according to his abilities, to everyone according to his work' is applied in the People's Republic of Bulgaria. The protection of labour is dealt with by the law.

THE NATIONAL ASSEMBLY

The National Assembly is the supreme representative organ which expresses the will of the people and their sovereignty. As a supreme organ of state power it combines the legislative and executive activities of the State and exercises supreme control. The term of its mandate is five years. It is composed of 400 people's representatives who are elected in constituencies with an equal number of inhabitants. The people's representatives are responsible and account to their electorate. They may be recalled before the expiry of the term for which they have been elected. Their recall is effected by decision of the electorate in a manner laid down by law. The Assembly is convened to sessions by the State Council at least three times a year.

The National Assembly is the only legislative organ of the People's Republic of Bulgaria and the supreme organizer of the planned management of social development. It realizes the supreme leadership of the home and foreign policy of the State; approves and amends the Constitution; determines which questions should be decided by referendum, and in what manner; passes, amends and revokes laws; passes the unified plans for the social-economic development of the country and the reports on their fulfilment and the State budget and the report of the Government on its realization the preceding year; establishes taxes and fixes their rate; grants amnesty; decides the questions of declaring war and concluding peace; appoints and relieves of his duties the Commander-in-Chief of the Armed Forces; may set up state-public organs with the status of ministries; elects and relieves of their duties the State Council, the Council of Ministers, the Supreme Court and the Chief Prosecutor of the People's Republic; passes laws, decisions, declarations and appeals.

Legislative initiative belongs to the State Council, the Council of Ministers, the permanent commissions of the National Assembly, the people's representatives, the Supreme Court and the Chief Prosecutor. The right of legislative initiative belongs also to public organizations in the person of the National Council of the Fatherland Front, the Central Council of Bulgarian Trade Unions, the Central Committee of the Dimitrov Young Communist League and the Executive Council of the Central Co-operative Council on questions referring to their activity.

THE STATE COUNCIL

The State Council of the People's Republic of Bulgaria is a supreme permanent organ of state power which unites the taking of decisions with their realization. Being a supreme organ of the National Assembly, the State Council ensures the blending of legislative with executive activities. It is responsible for all its activities and reports on them to the National Assembly. At its first session the National Assembly elects a State Council from among the people's representatives by a majority of more than one-half of the total number of deputies.

The powers of the State Council are in force until the newly elected National Assembly elects a State Council.

The State Council realizes the general leadership of the home and foreign policy of the State. It represents the People's Republic of Bulgaria in her international relations. The President of the State Council receives the credentials and letters of recall of foreign diplomatic representatives in the country.

The State Council appoints elections for a National Assembly and for people's councils; determines the date for holding a referendum when a decision has been passed by the National Assembly that a referendum should take place on a certain question and in a certain manner; convenes the National Assembly at sessions; issues decrees and other juridical acts on the basic questions arising from the laws and the decisions of the National Assembly; issues decrees also on questions of principle; in urgent cases by decree amends or amplifies individual provisions of the laws; carries out the general guidance of the country's defence and security; appoints and relieves of their duties the members of the State Defence Committee and of the supreme commanding staff of the Armed Forces; controls the activities of the Council of Ministers and of the heads of the Ministries and of the other Departments; at the proposal of the Chairman of the Council of Ministers relieves of their duties and appoints individual members of the Council of Ministers—it is the duty of the State Council to submit this decision to be approved at the next session of the National Assembly; issues decrees and passes decisions, appeals and declarations.

BULGARIA

THE COUNCIL OF MINISTERS

The Council of Ministers (the Government) is a supreme executive and administrative organ of the State Power. The Council effects its activities under the leadership and control of the National Assembly, and—when the latter is not in session—under the leadership and control of the State Council.

The Council of Ministers is responsible for the conducting of the internal and external policy of the State. It exercises the right of legislative initiative and secures conditions for carrying through the rights and freedoms of citizens. It also ensures public order and the country's security. It is responsible for the general leadership of the Armed Forces and concludes international agreements. It directly guides, co-ordinates and controls the activities of the ministries and other departments. The Council organizes both the implementation of the acts of the National Assembly, and of the State Council. It guides and controls the activities of the executive committees of the people's councils. It adopts decrees, instructions and decisions.

LOCAL GOVERNMENT

The territory of the Republic is divided for administrative purposes into Municipalities and Counties, which are governed by Municipal and County People's Councils, elected by the local population for a period of two and a half years. Their function is to implement all economic, social and cultural undertakings of local significance in conformity with the laws of the country. They prepare the economic plan and budget of the Municipality and the County within the framework of the State Economic Plan and the State Budget, and direct its execution. They are responsible for the correct administration of State property and economic enterprises in their areas, and for the maintenance of law and order. These councils report at least once a year to their electors on their activities.

JUSTICE

The judicial authorities apply the law. Justice is independent and subject only to the law. Lay judges (Assessors) also take part in the dispensation of justice. Judges of all ranks and assessors are elected except in special cases fixed by law. Supreme judicial control over every kind of court is exercised by the Supreme Court of the People's Republic, which is elected by the National Assembly for a term of five years.

Citizens whose rights have been violated by government organs may appeal against such violations before higher-ranking organs and courts, in accordance with the Law of Administrative Procedure, 1970.

The Chief Prosecutor, who is also elected by the National Assembly for five years, and is answerable to it alone, has supreme supervision over the correct observance of the law by Government organs, officials, and all citizens. It is his particular duty to attend to the prosecution and punishment of crimes that are detrimental to the national and economic interests of the Republic or affect its independence.

THE RIGHTS AND DUTIES OF CITIZENS

All citizens are equal before the law. No privileges or restrictions in rights based on nationality, origin, religion, sex, race, education or property are recognized. All preaching of racial, national or religious hatred is punishable by law.

Women have equal rights with men in all spheres, including equal pay for equal work. The State pays special attention to the needs of mothers and children. Marriage and the family are under State protection, although only civil marriage is legally valid. Children born out of wedlock have equal rights with legitimate offspring.

All citizens have the right to free medical treatment in hospitals.

Labour is recognized as the basic factor of public and economic life. All citizens have the right to work, and it is their duty to engage in socially useful labour, according to their abilities. Holidays, limited working hours, pensions and medical treatment are guaranteed.

All citizens have the right to free education, which is secular and democratic. Elementary education is compulsory. National minorities have the right to be educated in their own tongue, and to develop their national culture, although the study of Bulgarian is compulsory.

The Church is separate from the State. Citizens have freedom of religion and conscience. However, misuse of the Church and religion for political ends and the formation of religious organizations with a political basis is prohibited.

Citizens are guaranteed freedom of speech and of the Press, secrecy of correspondence, inviolability of persons and dwellings, and the right of meetings and rallies.

Military service is compulsory for all male citizens.

Directory

The Government

(December 1986)

HEAD OF STATE

President of the State Council: TODOR ZHIVKOV (elected 7 July 1971; re-elected 17 June 1981 and 17 June 1986).

STATE COUNCIL

President: TODOR ZHIVKOV.
First Vice-President: PETUR TANCHEV.
Vice-Presidents: GEORGI DZHAGAROV, MITKO GRIGOROV, YAROSLAV RADEV.
Secretary: NIKOLA MANOLOV.
Members: CHUDOMIR ALEKSANDROV, Mrs ASYA ANGELOVA EMILOVA, MILKO BALEV, Acad. ANGEL BALEVSKY, VLADIMIR BONEV, ANDREI BUNDZHULOV, ANGEL DIMITROV, PETUR DYULGEROV, KOSTADIN DZHATEV, GRISHA FILIPOV, GINYO GANEV, PENCHO KUBADINSKY, Mrs ELENA LAGADINOVA, YANKO MARKOV, Mrs EMILYA MIRCHEVA KOSTOVA, BORIL ORLINOV KOSEV, IVAN PANEV, DIMITUR YORDANOV DIMITROV, YORDAN YOTOV, Acad. PANTELEI ZAREV, NIKOLAI ZHISHEV, ZHIVKO ZHIVKOV.

COUNCIL OF MINISTERS

Chairman: GEORGI ATANASOV.
First Deputy Chairmen: ANDREI LUKANOV, STOYAN MARKOV.
Deputy Chairmen: OGNYAN DOINOV, Prof. IVAN ILIYEV, ALEKSI IVANOV, GEORGI KARAMANEV, GRIGOR STOICHKOV, GEORGI YORDANOV, KIRIL ZAREV.
Minister of Finance: BELCHO BELCHEV.
Minister of the Interior: Lt-Gen. DIMITUR STOYANOV.
Minister of National Defence: Gen. DOBRI DZHUROV.
Minister of Foreign Affairs: PETUR MLADENOV.
Minister of National Education: ILCHO DIMITROV.
Minister of Transport: VASIL TSANOV.
Minister of Trade: KHRISTO KHRISTOV.
Minister of Public Health: Prof. RADOI POPIVANOV.
Minister of Justice: Mrs SVETLA DASKALOVA.
Minister, the Ambassador Extraordinary and Plenipotentiary to the USSR: DIMITUR ZHULEV.
President of the Bulgarian National Bank: VASIL KOLAROV.
Chairman of the State Committee for Research and Technology: STOYAN MARKOV.
Chairman of the State Planning Commission: Prof. IVAN ILIYEV.
Chairman of the Council for Agriculture and Forestry: ALEKSI IVANOV.
Chairman of the Council for Intellectual Development: GEORGI YORDANOV.
Chairman of the Council for Economic Affairs: OGNYAN DOINOV.
Chairman of the Council for Social Affairs: GEORGI KARAMANEV.
Chairman of the Committee for State and People's Control: GEORGI GEORGIYEV.
Minister without Portfolio: GEORGI PANKOV.

MINISTRIES AND STATE COMMITTEES

Council of Ministers: 1000 Sofia, Blvd Dondukov 1; tel. 86-91.
Ministry of Finance: 1000 Sofia, Rakovsky St 102; tel. 84-91; telex 22727.
Ministry of Foreign Affairs: 1000 Sofia, Slavyanska St 1; tel. 87-48-11; telex 22530.
Ministry of the Interior: Sofia.
Ministry of Justice: Sofia; telex 22933.
Ministry of National Defence: Sofia.
Ministry of National Education: 1000 Sofia, Blvd A. Stamboliisky 18; tel. 84-81; telex 22384.
Ministry of Public Health: 1000 Sofia, pl. Lenina 5; tel. 86-31; telex 22430.
Ministry of Trade: 1000 Sofia, Sofiiska Komuna St 12; tel. 88-20-11; telex 22024.
Ministry of Transport: 1000 Sofia, Levsky St 9-11; tel. 87-10-81.

BULGARIA

Council for Agriculture and Forestry: Sofia.
Council for Economic Affairs: Sofia.
Council for Intellectual Development: 1000 Sofia, Blvd A. Stamboliisky 17; tel. 8-61-11.
Council for Social Affairs: Sofia.
State Planning Commission: 1000 Sofia, Blvd Dondukov 21; tel. 86-01.
State Committee for Research and Technology: 1574 Sofia, Chapayev St 55; tel. 73-51; telex 22341.

POLITICAL BUREAU OF THE CENTRAL COMMITTEE OF THE COMMUNIST PARTY

Members: Chudomir Aleksandrov, Georgi Atanasov, Milko Balev, Ognyan Doinov, Gen. Dobri Dzhurov, Grisha Filipov, Pencho Kubadinsky, Petur Mladenov, Stanko Todorov, Yordan Yotov, Todor Zhivkov (General Secretary).

Candidate Members: Petur Dyulgerov, Andrei Lukanov, Stoyan Markov, Grigor Stoichkov, Dimitur Stoyanov, Georgi Yordanov.

Legislature

NARODNO SOBRANIYE
(National Assembly)

The Ninth National Assembly, elected for a five-year term on 8 June 1986, has 400 members (276 are members of the Bulgarian Communist Party, 99 of the Bulgarian Agrarian Union and 25 are non-party members), who were all elected unopposed.

Chairman: Stanko Todorov.

Deputy Chairmen: Atanas Dimitrov, Milena Stamboliiska, Drazha Vulcheva.

Political Organizations

Fatherland Front: Sofia, Blvd Vitosha 18; a mass organization unifying both political parties and social organizations; it has elected local and central committees throughout the country controlled by the National Council in Sofia; the supreme body is the Congress, which is elected every five years; 4,388,000 mems.; Chair. Pencho Kubadinsky.

Bulgarian Agrarian People's Union (Bulgarsky Zemedelsky Naroden Soyuz—BZNS): Sofia, Yanko Zabunov St 1; tel. 88-19-51; telex 23302; f. 1899; peasant political organization participating in the Fatherland Front Government; 120,000 mems; Sec. Nikolai Georgiyev.

Bulgarian Communist Party (Bulgarska Komunisticheska Partiya—BKP): Sofia; f. 1891; the dominant party in the Fatherland Front; 932,055 mems (1986); Gen. Sec. of Central Committee Todor Zhivkov; Secs Chudomir Aleksandrov, Milko Balev, Grisha Filipov, Emil Khristov, Stoyan Mikhailov, Dimitur Stanishev, Vasil Tsanov, Yordan Yotov; Chair. of Central Auditing Commission Nancho Papazov.

Committee of the Movement of Bulgarian Women: Sofia, Blvd Patriyarkh Evtimii 82; f. 1948; 171 mems; Pres. Mrs Elena Lagadinova; First Vice-Pres. Yordanka Tropolova.

Dimitrov Pioneer-Children's Organization Septemvriiche: Sofia, Blvd A. Stamboliisky 11; tel. 86-81; telex 22552; f. 1944; a mass social and political organization of children; Pres. of Central Council Magdalena Yankova.

Dimitrov Young Communist League: Sofia, Blvd A. Stamboliisky 11; f. 1947; a mass social and political organization of youth, controlled by a Central Committee; First Sec. Andrei Bundzhulov.

Diplomatic Representation

EMBASSIES IN BULGARIA

Afghanistan: 1000 Sofia, Lyuben Karavelov St 34; tel. 87-23-98; Ambassador: Meraboddin Paktiawal.
Albania: Sofia, Khan Asparuh St 8; tel. 52-14-67; Ambassador: Bashkim Rama.
Algeria: Sofia, Slavyanska St 16; tel. 87-56-83; Ambassador: Ahmad Nadjib Boulbina.
Argentina: Sofia, Dunav St 1; tel. 87-95-88; Ambassador: Omar Muhammad Vaquir.
Austria: Sofia, Blvd Rusky 13; tel. 80-35-73; telex 22566; Ambassador: Dr August Tarter.
Belgium: Sofia, ul. Frédéric Joliot-Curie 19; tel. 72-35-27; telex 22455; Ambassador: Alfred Ameel.
Brazil: Sofia, Blvd Rusky 27; tel. 44-17-01; telex 22099; Ambassador: Antônio Fantinato Neto.
China, People's Republic: Sofia, Blvd Rusky 18; tel. 87-87-24; telex 22545; Ambassador: Teng Shaozhi.
Colombia: Sofia, Vasil Aprilov 17; Ambassador: Evelio Ramírez Martínez.
Cuba: Sofia, Mladezhka St 1; tel. 72-09-96; telex 22428; Ambassador: Manuel Pérez Hernández.
Czechoslovakia: Sofia, Blvd Vladimir Zaimov 9; tel. 44-62-81; Ambassador: Václav Janoušek.
Denmark: 1000 Sofia, Blvd Rusky 10, POB 1393; tel. 88-04-55; telex 22099; Chargé d'affaires a.i.: Nanna Dahlerup.
Egypt: Sofia; Tsar Ivan Assen St 91; tel. 44-19-57; telex 22270; Ambassador: (vacant).
Ethiopia: Sofia, V. Kolarov St 28; tel. 88-39-84; Ambassador: Hussein Ismael Hussein.
Finland: Sofia, Charles Darwin St 4; tel. 72-03-89; telex 22776; Ambassador: Klaus Kristian Snellman.
France: Sofia, Oborishte St 29; tel. 44-11-71; telex 22336; Ambassador: Bertrand Guilhem de Lataillade.
German Democratic Republic: Sofia, Kapitan Andreyev St 1; tel. 66-14-37; telex 22449; Ambassador: Egon Rommel.
Germany, Federal Republic: Sofia, Henri Barbusse St 7; tel. 72-21-27; Ambassador: Dr Hans Alfred Steger.
Ghana: 1113 Sofia, Tierre Degeyter St 9, Apt 37-38; Chargé d'affaires a.i.: Tetteh Tawiah.
Greece: Sofia, Blvd Klement Gottwald 68; tel. 44-37-70; telex 22458; Ambassador: Joanis Burlojanis-Tzagaridis.
Hungary: Sofia, ul. Shesti Septemvri 57; tel. 66-20-21; telex 22459; Ambassador: Gyula Gyovai.
India: Sofia, Blvd Patriyarkh Evtimii 31; tel. 87-39-44; telex 22954; Ambassador: Shiyam Sunder Nath.
Indonesia: Sofia, G. Gheorghiu-Dej St 32; tel. 44-23-49; telex 22358; Ambassador: Sajid Basoeki Sastrohardojo.
Iran: Sofia, Blvd Klement Gottwald 70; tel. 44-10-13; telex 22303; Chargé d'affaires: Sayed Reza Zargabashi.
Iraq: Sofia, Anton Chekhov St 21; tel. 87-00-13; telex 22307; Ambassador: Fausi Dakir al-Ani.
Italy: Sofia, Shipka St 2; tel. 88-17-05; telex 22173; Ambassador: Dr Giovanni Battistini.
Japan: Sofia, Lyulyakova Gradina St 14; tel. 72-39-84; telex 22397; Ambassador: Tanida Masami.
Korea, Democratic People's Republic: Sofia, Lazar Stanev St 1; tel. 72-23-60; Ambassador: Ha Don Yun.
Kuwait: Sofia, Blvd Klement Gottwald 47; tel. 44-19-92; telex 23586; Ambassador: Talib Jalal ad-Din al-Naqib.
Lebanon: Sofia; Ambassador: Hussein Mussauy.
Libya: Sofia, Oborishte St 10; tel. 44-19-21; telex 22180; Secretary of People's Bureau: Umar Muftah al-Dallah.
Mexico: Sofia, Todor Strashimirov St 1; tel. 44-32-82; telex 22087; Ambassador: Jaime Fernández-MacGregor.
Mongolia: Sofia, ul. Frédéric Joliot-Curie 52; tel. 87-41-85; telex 22274; Ambassador: Mangaljavin Dash.
Morocco: Sofia; Ambassador: Abdelhamid Dimani.
Netherlands: Sofia, Denkoglu St 19a; tel. 87-41-86; telex 22686; Ambassador: V. H. Meertins.
Nicaragua: Sofia, Mladost 1, Blvd Aliende, Res. 1; tel. 75-41-57; Ambassador: Roger Vásquez Barrios.
Pakistan: Sofia, ul. Frédéric Joliot-Curie 19; Ambassador: Ghulam Rabani.
Peru: Sofia, ul. Frédéric Joliot-Curie 19, Apt. 20; tel. 87-18-27; telex 23182; Ambassador: José Coz Botteri.
Poland: Sofia, Khan Krum St 46; tel. 88-51-66; telex 22595; Ambassador: Czesław Beck.
Portugal: Sofia, Ivats Voivoda St 6; tel. 44-35-48; telex 22082; Ambassador: R. Pereira de Sosa.
Romania: Sofia, Dimitur Polyanov St 10; tel. 44-33-81; telex 22321; Ambassador: Vasile Pungan.
Spain: Sofia, Oborishte St 47; tel. 43-00-17; telex 22308; Ambassador: Vicente Fernández Trelles.

BULGARIA
Directory

Sweden: Sofia, pl. Velchova Zavera 1; tel. 65-10-02; telex 22373; Ambassador: OKE THEODOR BERG.

Switzerland: Sofia, Shipka St 33; tel. 44-31-98; telex 22792; Ambassador: MICHAEL VON SCHENCK.

Syria: Sofia, Kliment Okhridsky St 10; tel. 44-15-85; telex 23464; Ambassador: TAHA HAIRAT.

Turkey: Sofia, Blvd Tolbukhin 23; tel. 87-23-06; telex 22199; Ambassador: ÖMER LÜTEM.

USSR: Sofia, Blvd Bulgaro-suvetska druzhba 28; tel. 66-88-19; Ambassador: LEONID IVANOVICH GREKOV.

United Kingdom: Sofia, Blvd Tolbukhin 65–67; tel. 88-53-61; telex 22363; Ambassador: JOHN HAROLD FAWCETT.

USA: Sofia, Blvd A. Stamboliisky 1; tel. 88-48-01; telex 22690; Ambassador: MELVYN LEVITSKY.

Venezuela: Sofia, ul. Frédéric Joliot-Curie 17; tel. 72-39-77; telex 23495; Ambassador: ANTONIO AVELEDO-LEAL.

Viet-Nam: Sofia, Ilya Petrov St 1; tel. 72-08-79; telex 22717; Ambassador: (vacant).

Yemen, People's Democratic Republic: Sofia, Volkolamsko St 57; tel. 65-60-05; Ambassador: MUHAMMAD HAIDARAH MASDOUS.

Yugoslavia: Sofia, G. Gheorghiu-Dej St 3; tel. 44-32-37; telex 23537; Ambassador: ILIJA DJUKIĆ.

Judicial System

Justice in the People's Republic of Bulgaria is administered by the district, regional and military courts and by the Supreme Court. All labour disputes are considered by the conciliation committees of the enterprises and by the regional courts. Civil law disputes among state enterprises, offices and co-operative and public organizations are heard by the State Court of Arbitration, and disputes connected with international trade by the Foreign Trade Court of Arbitration at the Bulgarian Chamber of Commerce and Industry.

The district court judges and assessors are elected by the district people's councils for a term of five years. Judges and assessors of the Supreme Court are elected for a term of five years by the National Assembly. Judicial control over the activities of all courts is exercised by the Supreme Court. Control for the correct observance of the law by Governmental local government authorities and officials, and by the citizens, is exercised by the Attorney-General of the Republic, who is elected by the National Assembly for a term of five years. All other prosecutors of courts are appointed and discharged by the Attorney-General. All courts and prisons are under the Ministry of Justice. All lawyers are organized in consultation offices and citizens have the right to choose their own legal representatives from among the members of any such group. State enterprises may employ their own legal adviser.

Minister of Justice: SVETLA DASKALOVA.
President of the Supreme Court: IVAN VELINOV.
Attorney-General: KOSTADIN LYUTOV.

Religion

Committee for Affairs of the Bulgarian Orthodox Church and the Religious Denominations: Sofia, Al. Zhendov St 2; deals with relations between religious organizations and the Government; Chair. LYUBOMIR POPOV.

CHRISTIANITY
The Orthodox Churches

Armenian-Apostolic-Orthodox Church: Sofia, Naicho Tzanov St 31; tel. 88-02-08; administered by Bishop DIRAYR MARDIKIYAN (resident in Bucharest); Chair. of the Diocesan Council in Bulgaria GARO DERMESROBIYAN.

Bulgarian Orthodox Church: Sofia, Synod Palace, 4 Oborishte St; f. 865; administered by the Bulgarian Patriarchy; there are 11 dioceses and one foreign diocese, each under a Metropolitan; adherents comprise 80% of the church-going population; Patriarch MAXIM.

The Roman Catholic Church

Bulgarian Catholics may be adherents of either the Latin or the Bulgarian (Byzantine-Slav) Rite. The country comprises two dioceses, both directly responsible to the Holy See.

Latin Rite
Bishop of Nikopo: SAMUIL SERAFIMOV DZHUNDRIN, 7000 Ruse, Rost. Blaskov St 14; 20,000 adherents (1968).

Bishop of Sofia and Plovdiv: (vacant), 4000 Plovdiv, Lilyana Dimitrova St 3; tel. 28430; 45,000 adherents (1980).

Bulgarian Rite
Apostolic Exarch of Sofia: METODI DIMITROV STRATIYEV (Titular Bishop of Diocletianopolis in Thrace), Sofia, ul. Pashovi 10/B.

The Protestant Churches

Supreme Episcopal Council of the Bulgarian Evangelical Methodist Church: Sofia, Rakovsky St 86; Head Pastor IVAN NOZHAROV.

Union of the Churches of the Seventh-day Adventists: Sofia, Vasil Kolarov St 10; Head Pastor NIKOLA TANEV.

Union of the Evangelical Baptist Churches: Varna, Georgi Dimitrov St 100; Head Pastor GEORGI TODOROV.

Union of the Evangelical Cathedral Churches: Sofia, Vasil Kolarov St 49; Head Pastor ASSEN M. SIMEONOV.

Union of the Evangelical Pentecostal Churches: 1557 Sofia, Bacho Kiro St 21; tel. 83-22-33; f. 1928; Head Pastor DINKO JELEV.

ISLAM

The Muslim Community: Sofia, Bratya Miladinovi St 27; adherents estimated at 14% of the actively religious population; Chief Mufti of the Turkish Muslims in Bulgaria MEHMED TOPCHIYEV; Mufti of the Bulgarian Muslims CHAVDAR ILIYEV, Smolyan.

JUDAISM

Central Jewish Theological Council: 1000 Sofia, Eksarkh Yosif St 16; tel. 83-12-73; 6,000 adherents; Head YOSIF LEVI.

The Press

As in most Communist countries, the press in Bulgaria is considered a powerful instrument of the Party and part of the educational system, and for that reason it is subject to strict control by the Government. It is largely dominated by the Communist Party and by organizations attached to the Fatherland Front, and much of its news originates from TASS, the Soviet news agency. Censorship is not usually necessary, since editors are Party members and aware of their responsibility to the Government.

There are 14 daily papers in Bulgaria, eight of which are published in Sofia, and their total daily circulation was about 2m. copies in 1980. The most important is *Rabotnichesko Delo*, the organ of the Communist Party. Other important newspapers are *Otechestven Front*, the Fatherland Front daily, and *Narodna Mladezh*, the youth newspaper.

PRINCIPAL DAILIES

Chernomorsky Front (Black Sea Front): Burgas, Milin Kamak 9; f. 1950; organ of the district committees of the Communist Party, the Fatherland Front and the District People's Council; Editor-in-Chief STOICHO STAIKOV; circ. 35,000.

Dunavska Pravda (Danubian Truth): Russe; f.1944; organ of the district committees of the Communist Party, the Fatherland Front and the District People's Council; Editor-in-Chief TSVYATKO TSVETKOV; circ. 27,500.

Kooperativno Selo (For Co-operative Farming): Sofia, 11 August St 18; tel. 83-50-33; telex 23174; f. 1951; organ of the Ministry of Agriculture; Editor-in-Chief GEORGI AVRAMOV; circ. 193,000.

Narodna Armiya (People's Army): Sofia, Ivan Vasov St 12; f. 1944; organ of the Ministry of National Defence; Editor-in-Chief Col ALEKSANDUR NIKOLOV; circ. 55,000.

Narodna Mladezh (People's Youth): Sofia, Blvd Lenin 47; f. 1944; organ of the Central Committee of the Dimitrov Communist Youth Union; Editor-in-Chief GEORGI TULIISKY; circ. 250,000.

Narodno Delo (People's Cause): Varna, Khristo Botev St 3; organ of the district committees of the Communist Party and the Fatherland Front and of the district People's Council; f. 1950; midday; Editor-in-Chief YORDAN DONCHEV; circ. 49,500.

Otechestven Front (Fatherland Front): Sofia, Blvd Lenin 47; f. 1942; organ of the National Council of the Fatherland Front; morning and evening editions; Editor-in-Chief GENCHO BUCHVAROV; total circ. 280,000.

Otechestven Glas (The Voice of the Fatherland): Plovdiv, Krakra St 9; telex 44506; f. 1943; organ of the district committees

595

of the Communist Party, the Fatherland Front and the District People's Council; Editor-in-Chief MIKHAIL MILCHEV; circ. 65,000.

Pirinsko Delo (Pirin's Cause): Blagoevrad, Assen Khristov St 19; organ of the district people's council, the district committees of the Communist Party and the Fatherland Front; Editor-in-Chief ILYA SARIN; circ. 33,000.

Rabotnichesko Delo (Workers' Cause): Sofia, Blvd Lenin 47; f. 1927; organ of the Communist Party; Editor-in-Chief Prof. YORDAN YOTOV; circ. 850,000.

Trud (Labour): Sofia, Blvd Dondukov 82; tel. 87-25-01; telex 22427; f. 1946; organ of the Central Council of Trade Unions; Editor-in-Chief DAMIYAN OBRESHKOV; circ. 300,000.

Vecherny Novini (Evening News): Sofia, Blvd Lenin 47; f. 1951; a popular advertising paper; Editor-in-Chief DELCHO KRUSTEV; circ. 125,000.

Zemedelsko Zname (Agrarian Banner): Sofia, Yanko Zabunov St 23; organ of the Agrarian People's Party; Editor-in-Chief Prof. DIMITUR DIMITROV; circ. 165,000.

PRINCIPAL PERIODICALS

Anteni (Antennae): Sofia, Khan Krum St 12; weekly on politics and culture; Editor-in-Chief VESELIN YOSIFOV; circ. 150,000.

Bulgaria: Sofia, Levsky St 1; monthly; Russian, German and Spanish; illustrated magazine; Editor-in-Chief (vacant); circ. 157,000.

Bulgaria Today: Sofia, Levsky St 1; monthly; French, English and Italian; Editor-in-Chief NIKOLA ZAKHARIYEV; total circ. 25,000.

Bulgarian Films: 1000 Sofia, Rakovsky St 96; tel. 87-66-11; telex 22447; f. 1960; 8 a year; magazine in English, French and Russian; cinema; Editor-in-Chief IVAN STOYANOVICH; circ. 21,000.

Bulgarian Foreign Trade: Sofia, Parchvich 42; tel. 8-51-51; telex 23318; f. 1952; fortnightly; French, German, English and Russian; organ of the Bulgarian Chamber of Commerce and Industry; Editor-in-Chief VENTSESLAV DIMITROV; circ. 13,000.

Bulgaro-Suvetska Druzhba: Sofia, Klement Gottwald St; organ of the All-National Committee for Bulgarian-Soviet Friendship; Editor-in-Chief ANGEL TODOROV; circ. 68,000.

Bulgarsky Voin (Bulgarian Soldier): Sofia, Sofiiska Komuna 1; monthly organ of the Chief Political Department of the People's Army; literature and arts; Editor-in-Chief VASIL CHANKOV; circ. 23,000.

Chitalishte (Reading Room): Sofia, ul. Iskar 4; monthly; organ of the Committee for Art and Culture; Editor-in-Chief BOYAN BALABANOV; circ. 5,000.

Computer for You: 1000 Sofia, Blvd Tolbukhin 51A; tel. 87-78-04; f. 1985; monthly; hardware and software; circ. 20,000.

Darzhaven Vestnik (State Newspaper): 1123 Sofia; 2 a week; publishes the laws, decrees, etc., of the National Assembly; Editor-in-Chief EMIL MITEV; circ. 63,587.

Discover Bulgaria: 1000 Sofia, Rakovsky St 127; tel. 88-37-39; f. 1958; every 2 months; French, English, German and Russian; Editor-in-Chief LILIYA GERASIMOVA; circ. 47,000.

Do It Yourself: 1000 Sofia, Blvd Tolbukhin 51A; tel. 87-50-45; f. 1981; monthly; circ. 180,000.

Economic News of Bulgaria: Sofia, Blvd A. Stamboliisky 11A; monthly; English, French, German, Spanish and Russian; published by the Bulgarian Chamber of Commerce and Industry; Editor-in-Chief LYUBEN MIKHAILOV; circ. 15,000.

Fakel (The Torch): 1000 Sofia, Angel Kanchev St 5; tel. 88-00-31; f. 1981; every 2 months; translations of Soviet literature; published by the Committee for Culture, the Bulgarian Writers' Union and the Union of Translators; Editor-in-Chief BOZHIDAR BOZHILOV; circ. 5,000.

Ikonomicheska Misal (Thoughts on Economics): Sofia, Aksakov 3; 10 a year; organ of the Institute of Economics of the Bulgarian Academy of Sciences; Editor-in-Chief KLEMANSO GROZDANOV; circ. 7,000.

Ikonomika (Economics): Sofia, Blvd Dondukov 21; f. 1946 as *Planovo Stopanstvo* (Planning of the Economy); present name adopted in 1985; monthly; organ of the State Planning Commission, Ministry of Finance, Bulgarian National Bank and Central Statistical Office; Editor-in-Chief ZVETAN MARINOV; circ. 5,000.

Izkustvo (Art): 1504 Sofia, ul. Shipka 6; 1404 Sofia, POB 139; f. 1951; 10 a year; organ of the Committee for Art and Culture, and of the Union of Bulgarian Artists; Editor-in-Chief ALEKSANDER OBRETENOV; circ. 5,000.

Kinoizkustvo (Cinematic Art): Sofia, pl. Slaveikov 11; f. 1946; monthly; cinema; Editor-in-Chief EMIL PETROV; circ. 9,000.

LIK: Sofia, Blvd Lenin 49; weekly publication of the Bulgarian Telegraph Agency; literature art and culture; Editor-in-Chief SIRMA VELEVA; circ. 17,600.

Literaturen Front: (Literary Front): Sofia, Angel Kanchev St 5; f. 1944; organ of the Bulgarian Writers' Union; Editor-in-Chief EVTIM EVTIMOV; circ. 40,000.

Lov i Ribolov (Hunting and Fishing): 1000 Sofia, Blvd Vitosha 31–33; tel. 88-42-20; f. 1895; monthly organ of the Hunting and Angling Union; Editor-in-Charge KHRISTO RUSKOV; circ. 60,000.

Mladezh (Youth): Sofia, Blvd Khristo Botev 48; f. 1945; monthly organ of the Central Committee of the Dimitrov Communist Youth Union; Editor-in-Chief BOIKO BOGDANOV; circ. 70,000.

Naroden Sport (People's Sport): Sofia, ul. Rakitin 2; tel. 44-44-29; telex 22504; f. 1944; 3 a week; organ of the Bulgarian Union for Physical Culture and Sports; Editor-in-Chief CHAVDAR KALEV; circ. 270,000.

Narodna Kultura (National Culture): 1040 Sofia, Sofiiska Komuna St 4; tel. 88-33-22; organ of the Committee for Culture; Editor-in-Chief STEFAN PRODEV; circ. 50,000.

Narodna Prosveta (National Education): Sofia, Blvd Lenin 125; monthly organ of Ministry of Education and the Union of Bulgarian Teachers; Editor DIMITUR TSVETKOV; circ. 12,125.

Nasha Rodina (Our Country): Sofia, Blvd Lenin 47; monthly; socio-political and literary; illustrated; Editor-in-Chief DIMITUR METODIYEV; circ. 35,500.

Novo Vreme (New Time): Sofia, Blvd Lenin 47; f. 1897; monthly theoretical organ of the Central Committee of the Communist Party of Bulgaria; Editor-in-Charge NIKOLAI IRIBADZHAKOV; circ. 32,000.

Orbita: 1000 Sofia, Tsar Kaloyan St; tel. 88-51-68; f. 1969; weekly publication of the Central Committee of the Dimitrov Young Communist League; science and technology; Editor-in-Chief Dr DIMITUR PEYEV; circ. 108,000.

Otechestvo (Fatherland): Sofia, Varbitsa 9; fortnightly illustrated publication of the National Council of the Fatherland Front; Editor-in-Chief SERAFIM SEVERNYAK; circ. 100,000.

Paralleli: Sofia, Blvd Lenin 49; weekly illustrated publication of the Bulgarian Telegraph Agency; Editor-in-Chief GEORGI TODOROV; circ. 135,000.

Plamak (Flame): Sofia, Angel Kanchev 5; f. 1924; every 2 weeks; literature, art and publishing; organ of the Union of Bulgarian Writers; Editor-in-Chief PETER KARANGOV; circ. 11,000.

Pogled: Sofia; organ of the Union of Bulgarian Journalists; Editor-in-Chief LYUBEN GENOV; circ. 310,000.

Science and Technology: Sofia, Blvd Lenin 49; tel. 84-61; f. 1964; weekly of the Bulgarian Telegraph Agency; Editor-in-Chief VESELIN SEIKOV; circ. 18,000.

Septemvri (September): Sofia, pl. Slaveikov 2a; monthly; organ of the Union of Bulgarian Writers; literary; Editor-in-Chief VLADIMIR GOLEV; circ. 15,000.

Septemvriiche (Septembrist): Sofia, Blvd Lenin 47; 2 a week; organ of the Central Committee of the Dimitrov Union of People's Youth; Editor-in-Chief NIKOLAI ZIDAROV; circ. 300,000.

Slavyani (Slavs): Sofia, Tsar Kaloyan St 1; monthly organ of the Slav committee in Bulgaria; Editor-in-Chief KATYA GEORGIYEVA; circ. 20,000.

Sofiiska Pravda (Sofia Truth): Sofia, Tsar Kaloyan St 3; f. 1955; 3 a week; organ of the District People's Council and the district committees of the Communist Party and the Fatherland Front; Editor-in-Chief VASIL MILUSHEV; circ. 13,000.

Sturshel (Hornet): Sofia, Blvd Lenin 47; f. 1946; weekly; humour and satire; Editor-in-Chief KHRISTO PELITEV; circ. 280,000.

Teater (Theatre): Sofia, Blvd Dondukov 82; monthly organ of the Committee of Culture and Art, Bulgarian Writers' Union and Union of Actors; Editor-in-Chief Prof. YULIYAN VUCHKOV; circ. 4,500.

Televiziya i Radio: Sofia, ul. Shishman 30; organ of the Committee for Television and Radio; Editor-in-Chief KHRISTO CHAVDAROV; circ. 100,000.

Turist: Sofia, Blvd D. Blagoev 24; tel. 51-16-41; f. 1902; monthly organ of the Bulgarian Tourist Union; Editor-in-Chief KHRISTO GEORGIYEV; circ. 25,000.

Vanshna Targoviya (Foreign Trade): Sofia, Tsar Kaloyan 8; monthly publication of the Ministry for Foreign Trade; Editor-in-Chief ALEXANDUR CHICHOVSKY; circ. 3,000.

The World Over: Sofia, Blvd Lenin 49; weekly publication of the Bulgarian Telegraph Agency; international politics; Editor-in-Chief DIMITUR KOSTOV.

Zdrave (Health): Sofia, Blvd Totleben 21; published by Bulgarian Red Cross; Editor-in-Chief MARIYA NIKOLOVA; circ. 200,000.

Zhenata Dnes: Sofia, Blvd Patriyarkh Evtimii 82; monthly organ of the Committee of the Movement of Bulgarian Women; also in Russian; Editor-in-Chief Mrs ELEONORA TURLAKOVA; circ. 580,000.

NEWS AGENCIES

Bulgarian Telegraph Agency (BTA): Sofia, Blvd Lenin 49; tel. 84-61; telex 22821; f. 1898; the official news agency, having agreements with the leading foreign agencies and correspondents in all major capitals; publishes weekly surveys of science and technology, international affairs, literature and art; Dir-Gen. BOYAN TRAIKOV.

Sofia-Press Agency: Sofia 2, Levsky St 1; f. 1967 by the Union of Bulgarian Writers, the Union of Bulgarian Journalists, the Union of Bulgarian Artists and the Union of Bulgarian Composers; publishes socio-political and scientific literature, fiction, children's and tourist literature, publications on the arts, a newspaper, magazines and bulletins in foreign languages; Dir-Gen. PETUR PETROV.

Foreign Bureaux

Agence France-Presse (AFP): Sofia, Blvd Tolbukhin 80; Correspondent NIKOLAI BOTSEV.

Agentstvo Pechati Novosti (APN) (USSR): Sofia, Dunav St 1, Apt 3; Bureau Man. PAVEL SHINKORENKO.

Allgemeiner Deutscher Nachrichtendienst (ADN) (German Democratic Republic): 1000 Sofia, Moskovska 27A; Correspondent HEIDEMARIE DREISNER.

Československá tisková kancelář (ČTK) (Czechoslovakia): 1113 Sofia, ul. Gagarin, blok 154, Apt 19; tel. 87-21-69; telex 22537; Correspondent MIROSLAV SUKUP.

Magyar Távirati Iroda (MTI) (Hungary): Sofia, ul. Frédéric Joliot-Curie 15, blok 156/3, Apt 28; Correspondent TIVADAR KELLER.

Prensa Latina (Cuba): Sofia, ul. Yuri Gagarin 22, blok 154B, Apt 2; tel. 71-91-90; Correspondent ANA MARÍA RUÍZ.

Telegrafnoye Agentstvo Sovetskovo Soyuza (TASS) (USSR): 1000 Sofia, ul. A. Gendov 1, Apt 29; Correspondent VLADIMIR BABKIN.

Xinhua (New China) News Agency (People's Republic of China): Sofia, pl. Narodno Sobraniye 3; tel. 88-49-41; telex 22539; Correspondent SUN WEIXI.

The following agencies are also represented: PAP (Poland) and Reuters (UK).

PRESS ASSOCIATION

Union of Bulgarian Journalists: Sofia, Graf Ignatiyev St 4; tel. 87-27-73; telex 22635; f. 1955; Pres. BOYAN TRAIKOV; First Vice-Pres. STOINE KRASTEV; 4,500 mems.

Publishers

Darzhavno Izdatelstvo 'Georgi Bakalov' Varna: Varna, Blvd Khristo Botev 3; popular science, fiction, economics; Dir PETUR STANEV.

Darzhavno Izdatelstvo 'Khristo G. Danov': Plovdiv, ul. Petko Karavelov 17; tel. 22-52-32; f. 1855; fiction, poetry, literary criticism; Dir PETUR ANASTASSOV.

Darzhavno Izdatelstvo Meditsina i Fizkultura: Sofia, pl. Slaveikov 11; medicine, physical culture and tourism; Dir PETUR GOGOV.

Darzhavno Izdatelstvo 'Narodna Kultura': Sofia, ul. Gavril Genov 4; tel. 87-80-63; f. 1944; foreign fiction and poetry in translation; Dir VERA GANCHEVA.

Darzhavno Izdatelstvo 'Narodna Prosveta': Sofia, ul. Vasil Drumev 37; educational publishing house; Dir SVYATKO GAGOV.

Darzhavno Izdatelstvo 'Nauka i Izkustvo': Sofia, Blvd Rusky 6; tel. 87-57-01; f. 1948; general publishers; Dir GANKA SLAVCHEVA.

Darzhavno Izdatelstvo 'Tekhnika': Sofia, Blvd Rusky 6; textbooks for technical and higher education and technical literature; Dir (vacant).

Darzhavno Izdatelstvo 'Zemizdat': 1504 Sofia, Blvd Lenin 47; tel. 46-31; f. 1949; specializes in works on agriculture, shooting, fishing, forestry, livestock-breeding, veterinary medicine and popular scientific literature and textbooks; Dir PETUR ANGELOV.

Darzhavno Voyenno Izdatelstvo: Sofia, ul. Ivan Vazov 12; military publishing house; Head Col GEORGI GEORGIYEV.

Izdatelstvo na Bulgarskata Akademiya na Naukite (Publishing House of the Bulgarian Academy of Sciences): 1113 Sofia, Acad. Georgi Bonchev St, blok 6; tel. 72-09-22; telex 23132; f. 1869; scientific works and periodicals of the Academy of Sciences; Dir Prof. Dr IVAN GARBUCHEV.

Izdatelstvo 'Bulgarsky Khudozhnik': 1000 Sofia, Moskovska 37; tel. 87-66-57; art books, children's books; Dir STEFAN KURTEV.

Izdatelstvo 'Bulgarsky Pisatel': Sofia, ul. Shesti Septemvri 35; publishing house of the Union of Bulgarian Writers; Bulgarian fiction and poetry, criticism; Dir SIMEON SULTANOV.

Izdatelstvo na CC na DKMS 'Narodna Mladezh' (People's Youth Publishing House): Sofia, ul. Kaloyan 10; politics, history, original and translated fiction, and original and translated poetry for children; Dir ROSEN BOSEV.

Izdatelstvo na Natsionalniya Savet na Otechestveniya Front (Publishing House of the National Council of the Fatherland Front): Sofia, Blvd Dondukov 32; Dir SLAV KHRISTOV KARASLAVOV.

Izdatelstvo 'Profizdat' (Publishing House of the Central Council of Bulgarian Trade Unions): Sofia, Blvd Dondukov 82; specialized literature and fiction; Dir STOYAN POPOV.

Partizdat—Izdatelstvo na Bulgarskata Komunisticheska Partiya (Publishing House of the Bulgarian Communist Party): Sofia, Blvd Lenin 47; tel. 46-31; f. 1944; Dir PENCHO ASTARDSHIYEV.

Sinodalno Izdatelstvo: Sofia; religious publishing house; Dir KIRIL BOINOV.

STATE ORGANIZATION

Jusautor: 1000 Sofia, Levsky St 7; tel. 80-30-00; telex 23042; Bulgarian copyright agency; represents Bulgarian authors of literary, scientific, dramatic and musical works, and deals with all formalities connected with the grant of options, authorization for translations, drawing up of contracts for the use of their works by foreign publishers and producers; negotiates for the use of foreign works in Bulgaria; controls the application of copyright legislation; Dir-Gen. YANA MARKOVA.

WRITERS' UNION

Union of Bulgarian Writers: Sofia, Angel Kanchev 5; f. 1913; 370 mems; Pres. LYUBOMIR LEVCHEV.

Radio and Television

Radio and television are supervised by the Committee for Television and Radio of the Committee for Culture of the Council of Ministers.

There were an estimated 2,100,000 radio receivers in use in 1985. There were about 2,002,000 television receivers in 1985. Colour television was introduced in 1977.

Bulgarian Committee for Television and Radio: 1504 Sofia, San Stefano St 29; tel. 46-81; telex 22581; Chair. LALYU DIMITROV.

RADIO

Bulgarian Radio: 1040 Sofia, Blvd Dragan Tsankov 4; tel. 85-41; telex 22558; there are four Home Service programmes and local stations at Blagoevgrad, Plovdiv, Shumen, Stara Zagora and Varna. The Foreign Service broadcasts in Bulgarian, Turkish, Greek, Serbo-Croat, French, Italian, German, English, Portuguese, Spanish, Albanian and Arabic; Dir-Gen. (vacant).

TELEVISION

Bulgarian Television: 1504 Sofia, ul. Todor Strashimirov 4; tel. 46-81; programmes are transmitted daily; Dir-Gen. (vacant).

Finance

(cap. = capital; dep. = deposits; res = reserves;
m. = million; amounts in leva)

BANKING

Bulgarska Narodna Banka (National Bank of Bulgaria): 1040 Sofia, Sofiiska Komuna St 2; tel. 85-51; telex 22031; f. c. 1879; in 1947 the National Bank of Bulgaria took over all the commercial banks of the country; in 1968 it took over the business of the Bulgarian Investment Bank; Pres. VASIL KOLAROV.

Bulgarian Foreign Trade Bank: 1040 Sofia, Sofiiska Komuna St 2; tel. 85-51; telex 22031; f. 1964; shares held by National Bank of Bulgaria and other state institutions; incorporating the Maritime

BULGARIA   Directory

Commercial Bank Ltd; cap. 120m.; res 340.4m. (Dec. 1985); Pres. IVAN DRAGNEVSKY.

Mineralbank: 1000 Sofia, Legué St 17; tel. 80-17-37; telex 23390; f. 1980; bank for new economic projects; cap. 120m.; Pres. RUMEN GEORGIYEV.

State Savings Bank: Sofia, Moskovska 19; f. 1951; provides general individual banking services; dep. 10,900m. (1982).

INSURANCE

State Insurance Institute: Sofia, Rakovsky St 102; all insurance firms were nationalized during 1947, and were re-organized into one single State insurance company; Chair. TOMA TOMOV.

Bulstrad (Bulgarian Foreign Insurance and Reinsurance Co): 1000 Sofia, Dunav St 5; POB 627; tel. 8-51-91; telex 22564; f. 1961; deals with all foreign insurance and reinsurance; Pres. G. ABADZHIYEV.

Trade and Industry

CHAMBER OF COMMERCE

Bulgarian Chamber of Commerce and Industry: 1040 Sofia, Blvd A. Stamboliisky 11A; tel. 87-26-31; telex 22374; promotes economic relations and business contacts between Bulgarian and foreign companies and organizations; organizes official participation in international fairs and exhibitions and manages the international fairs in Plovdiv; publishes economic publications in Bulgarian and foreign languages; patents inventions and registers trade marks and industrial designs; organizes foreign trade advertising and publicity; provides legal consultations etc.; Pres. PETUR RUSEV.

FOREIGN TRADE ORGANIZATIONS

Foreign trade is a state monopoly, and is conducted through foreign trade organizations and various state enterprises and corporations.

Agrocommerce: 1000 Sofia, Blvd Dondukov 86; tel. 88-23-68; telex 23223; exports the produce of the member organizations of the National Agro-Industrial Union; import and maintenance of industrial equipment; Dir-Gen. VLADIMIR DAMIYANOV.

Agromachinaimpex: Sofia, Stoyan Lepoyev St 1; tel. 20-03-91; telex 22563; export and import of agricultural machines; Dir-Gen. TODOR PASHALIYEV.

Balkancar: Sofia, Blvd Shesti Septemvri 126; tel. 56-51-21; telex 22061; production, export, import and service of electric and motor trucks, cars, buses and lorries; Dir-Gen. STEFAN DAMIYANOV.

Bulgarcoop: Sofia, Rakovsky St 99; tel. 84-41; telex 23429; export of live snails, tortoises, snakes; live game and game meat; honey and bee products; nuts, pulses, medicinal plants, rose hips and rose-hip shells, aniseed, coriander, fennel, etc.; onions and mushrooms; natural mineral water; consumer goods; Gen. Man. NENKO LECHEV.

Bulgarplodexport: Sofia, Blvd A. Stamboliisky 7; tel. 88-59-51; telex 23297; f. 1947; production, import and export of fresh and preserved fruit and vegetables; Dir-Gen. TSVETAN KARAMOCHEV.

Chimimport: Sofia, Stefan Karadja St 2; tel. 88-38-11; telex 22521; import and export of chemicals, fertilizer, plant protection preparations, tyres, synthetic rubber and rubber wares, photographic paper, aniline dyes, plastic and plastic products, fuels, etc.; Dir-Gen. BELO BELOV.

Electroimpex: Sofia, George Washington St 17; tel. 8-61-81; telex 22075; covers the export and import of electrical and power equipment; Gen. Man. KIRIL TSOCHEV.

Hemus: 1000 Sofia, Levsky St 7; tel. 80-30-00; telex 22267; import and export of books, periodicals, numismatic items, antique objects, philatelic items, art products and souvenirs; Gen. Man. IVAN ABADZHIYEV.

Hranexport: Sofia, Alabin St 56; tel. 88-22-51; telex 22525; import and export of grain, oils, feed, mixtures, etc.; Gen. Man. YOVCHO RUSEV.

Industrialimport: Sofia, Pozitano St 3; tel. 87-30-21; telex 22091; import and export of cotton, woollen and silk ready-made garments, knitwear, cotton, woollen and silk textiles, leather goods, china and glassware, sports equipment; Gen. Man. ANGEL ANGELOV.

Isotimpex: Sofia, Chapayev St 51; tel. 70-72-41; telex 22731; import and export of computing and organizational equipment, semi-conductors, radio parts, materials for computing equipment; Dir-Gen. LYUBOMIR VITANOV.

Lessoimpex: Sofia, Vladimir Poptomov St 67; tel. 87-91-75; telex 23407; import and export of timber, furniture and wooden products; Dir-Gen. BRATAN TODOROV.

Machinoexport: 1000 Sofia, Aksakov St 5; tel. 88-53-21; telex 23425; export of metal-cutting and wood-working machines, equipment, tools and spare parts; Gen. Man. NENO MITEV.

Mineralimpex: Sofia, Kliment Okhridsky St 44, Bl. 1A; tel. 66-19-66; telex 22973; export of mineral raw materials and products; import of machinery; Dir-Gen. STOIKO NIKOLOV.

Rodopaimpex: Sofia, Gavril Genov St 2; tel. 88-26-01; telex 22541; export of cattle, sheep, breeding animals, meat, meat products; dairy products, poultry, eggs; import of meat, breeding animals, tallow, artificial casing; Dir-Gen. SVETOSLAV ALEKSIYEV.

Rudmetal: Sofia, Dobrudzha St 1A; tel. 88-12-71; telex 22027; f. 1952; export and import of metal and metal products, lead, zinc, copper, pure lead, ores, etc.; Dir-Gen. YOSIF YOSIFOV.

Stroyimpex: Sofia, Eksarkh Yosif St 18; tel. 80-30-47; telex 22385; export of cement, lime, etc.; import of building materials; Dir-Gen. ATANAS VLAKHOV.

Vinimpex: Sofia, Lavele St 19; tel. 88-39-21; telex 22467; import and export of wine and spirits; Dir-Gen. GEORGI TOROMANOV.

OTHER ENTERPRISES

Bulgariafilm: 1000 Sofia, Rakovsky St 96; tel. 87-66-11; telex 22447; export and import of films; participation in international film events; Dir ALEKSANDER ILIYEV.

Bulgartabac: Sofia, Blvd A. Stamboliisky 14; POB 96; tel. 87-52-11; telex 23288; covers manufacture, import and export of raw and manufactured tobacco; Dir-Gen. DIMITER YADKOV.

Inflot: Sofia, Blvd Vl. Zaimov 88; 1000 Sofia, POB 634; tel. 87-25-34; telex 22376; agency for foreign and Bulgarian shipping, inland and maritime; Dir-Gen. DIMITUR BOTSEV.

Information Systems and System-Engineering Services: 1000 Sofia, P. Volov St 2; tel. 65-28-84; telex 22001; import and export of information systems, software and system-engineering services; Dir-Gen. OGNYAN BOZAROV.

Intercommerce: 1080 Sofia, pl. Lenina 16; tel. 87-93-64; telex 22067; all kinds of multilateral and barter deals, import and export, participation in foreign firms; Dir-Gen. KONSTANTIN GLAVANAKOV.

Interpred: 1040 Sofia, Blvd A. Stamboliisky 2; tel. 87-45-21; telex 23284; agency for the representation of foreign firms in Bulgaria; Chair. GEORGI KUMBILIYEV.

Kintex: Sofia, Blvd Anton Ivanov 66; tel. 66-23-11; telex 22471; import and export of sports and hunting goods and explosives; Dir-Gen. IVAN DAMIYANOV.

Koraboimpex: Varna, D. Blagoev St 128; tel. 88-18-25; telex 77550; imports and exports ships, marine and port equipment; Dir-Gen. KIRIL KOSTOV.

Maimex: 1431 Sofia, D. Nestorov St 15; tel. 5-81-01; telex 22712; import and export of medical equipment and pharmaceutical products; Dir TSONCHO TSONCHEV.

Pharmachim: Sofia, Iliyensko chaussée 16; tel. 38-55-31; telex 22097; import and export of drugs, pharmaceutical and veterinary products, essential oils, cosmetics and dental materials; Dir-Gen. IVAN ANDONOV.

Pirin: Sofia, Levsky St 19; tel. 88-14-43; telex 22761; f. 1965; production, export and import of leather goods; Dir-Gen. T. MANOLOV.

Raznoiznos: Sofia, Tsar Assen St 1; tel. 88-02-11; telex 23244; export and import of industrial and craftsmen's products, timber products, paper products, glassware, furniture, carpets, toys, sports equipment, musical instruments, etc.; Dir-Gen. BOTZHO BOTEV.

Ribno Stopanstvo: Sofia, Parchevich St 42; tel. 80-23-03; telex 22796; import and export of fish and fish products; Dir KHRISTO YANEV.

Technoexport: 1113 Sofia, ul. Frédéric Joliot-Curie 20, POB 541; tel. 73-81; telex 22193; import and export of machines and complete plants; renders technical assistance abroad to the construction, light and printing industries; Dir-Gen. VELIMIR DIMITROV.

Technoexportstroy: 1303 Sofia, Antim I St 11; tel. 87-85-11; telex 22128; design and construction abroad of all types of public, utility, industrial and infrastructural projects; supply of machines and technical assistance; Gen. Man. MARIN DZHERMANOV.

Technoimpex: 1080 Sofia, Graf Ignatiyev St 10, POB 932; tel. 88-15-71; telex 23783; scientific and technological assistance abroad; Dir-Gen. TSOKO KRIVIRADEV.

BULGARIA

Technoimport: Sofia, ul. Frédéric Joliot-Curie 20; tel. 73-81; telex 23421; import and export of complete plants and equipment for the metallurgical, mining and power industries; Dir-Gen. MANUIL KLEITMAN.

Technoprogress: 1000 Sofia, ul. Vela Blagoyeva 18; tel. 51-26-73; has foreign trading rights within the chemical, machine-building, transport, food, biotechnological and pharmaceutical industries.

Telecom: 1309 Sofia, Kiril Pchelinsky St 1; tel. 87-61-97; telex 22077; export and import of communications equipment and technology; Dir-Gen. NIKOLA MONOV.

TRADE UNIONS AND CO-OPERATIVES

Central Council of Bulgarian Trade Unions: Sofia, pl. D. Blagoev 1; tel. 86-61; telex 22446; f. 1904; the central Trade Union organization, to which are affiliated 16 individual trade unions; Chair. PETUR DYULGEROV; total mems 4,000,000.

Trade Unions

Trade Union of Workers in Administration and Social Organization: Sofia, ul. Alabin 52; Chair. STOYAN CHOBANOV; 147,000 mems.

Trade Union of Agricultural and Food Industry Workers: Sofia, ul. Dimo Hadzhidimov 29; Pres. MILADIN SHATEROV; 1,068,793 mems.

Trade Union of Workers in the Chemical Industry: Sofia, ul. Alabin 3; Pres. IVAN SIMOV; 101,855 mems.

Trade Union of Workers in Communications: Sofia, ul. Shesti Septemvri 4; Chair. VIOLETA STOYANOVA; 45,000 mems.

Trade Union of Construction and Building Industry Workers: Sofia, pl. Lenina 4; Chair. IVAN TODOROV; 274,500 mems.

Trade Union of Engineering Workers: Sofia, pl. Lenina 4; Chair. Ing. DOICHO DINEV; 450,000 mems.

Trade Union of Forestry and Timber Industry Workers: Sofia, ul. Dimo Hadzhidimov 29; Chair. KHRISTO VUCHOVSKY; 180,800 mems.

Trade Union of Health Service Workers: Sofia, pl. Lenina 4; Chair. Dr IVAN SECHANOV; 157,000 mems.

Trade Union of Light Industry Workers: Sofia, ul. Shesti Septemvri 4; Chair. PETUR PETROV; 215,000 mems.

Trade Union of Miners, Metallurgic and Power Industry Workers: Sofia, pl. Lenina 4; Chair. GANYU NIKOLOV; 178,000 mems.

Trade Union of Workers in the Polygraphic Industry and Cultural Institutions: Sofia, Zdanov St 7; Pres. BOICHO PAVLOV; 49,300 mems.

Trade Union of Trade Workers: Sofia, ul. Shesti Septemvri 4; Chair. PETUR TSEKOV; 520,000 mems.

Trade Union of Transport Workers: Sofia, Blvd Georgi Dimitrov 106; f. 1911; Chair. Dr Ing. KOLYO KUNCHEV; 330,000 mems.

Union of Bulgarian Actors: 1000 Sofia, ul. Papa Andrei 1; tel. 87-71-96; f. 1919; Chair. (vacant); 4,000 mems.

Union of Bulgarian Teachers: Sofia, pl. Lenina 4; tel. 88-10-07; f. 1905; Chair. ANNI SPANCHEVA; 238,000 mems.

Union of Musicians in Bulgaria: Sofia, ul. Alabin 52; Chair. Prof. GEORGI ROBEV; 6,000 mems.

Co-operatives

Central Co-operative Union: 1000 Sofia, Rakovsky 99, POB 55; tel. 84-41; telex 23229; f. 1947; the central body of all the co-operative organizations in the country. There are 384 consumers' co-operatives, 326 agrarian industrial complexes and 167 producers' co-operatives; more than 2,202,000 mems are affiliated to the Central Union; Pres. RUMEN SERBEZOV.

TRADE FAIR

Plovdiv International Fair: Plovdiv, Blvd G. Dimitrov 37; tel. 55-31-91; telex 44432; f. 1933; in 1987: International Fair of consumer goods and foodstuffs (4–10 May), International Technical Fair (28 September–5 October); organized by Bulgarian Chamber of Commerce and Industry; Dir-Gen. KIRIL ASPARUKHOV.

Transport

Ministry of Transport: 1080 Sofia, ul. Levsky 9; tel. 31-71-21; directs the state rail, road, water and air transport organizations.

Despred: 1000 Sofia, Slavyanska St 2; tel. 87-60-16; telex 23306; state forwarding enterprise; Dir-Gen. TRAIKO VURGOV.

RAILWAYS

There were 6,430 km of track in Bulgaria in 1984, of which more than 2,050 km were electrified. In June 1986 the new Sofia–Gorna Oryakhovitsa–Varna main-line railway was opened. Construction of an underground railway in Sofia began in 1979. The system was to have a total length of 100 km.

Bulgarian State Railways (BDZ): 1080 Sofia, Ivan Vazov St 3; tel. 87-30-45; telex 22423; owns and controls all railway transport; Dir-Gen. STOIL FERDOV.

ROADS

There were 37,594 km of roads in Bulgaria in 1985, including 221 km of motorways, 2,933 km of main roads and 3,828 km of secondary roads. A major motorway runs from Sofia to the coast.

Autotransport: Sofia, Gurko St 5; tel. 87-62-32; telex 22332; f. 1965; Dir-Gen. T. PEYUVSKY.

SHIPPING AND INLAND WATERWAYS

The Danube river is the main waterway. External services link Black sea ports to the USSR, the Mediterranean and Western Europe.

Bulgarian River Lines: Ruse, pl. Otets Paisi 2; Dir YORDAN RADOYEV.

Navigation Maritime Bulgare: 9000 Varna, Blvd Chervenoarmeiska 1; tel. 22-24-74; telex 77351; f. 1892; sole enterprise in Bulgaria employed in sea transport; owns tankers, bulk carriers and container, ferry and passenger vessels with a displacement of more than 1,800,000 dwt; Dir-Gen. Capt. ATANAS YONKOV.

Shipping Corporation: Varna, Panagyurishte St 17; tel. 2-63-16; telex 077524; organization of sea and river transport; carriage of goods and passengers on waterways; controls all aspects of shipping and shipbuilding, also engages in research, design and personnel training; Dir-Gen. NIKOLAI YOVCHEV.

CIVIL AVIATION

Bulgarian Airlines—Balkan: 1540 Sofia, Sofia Airport; pl. Narodno Sobraniye 12 (Head Office); tel. 7-12-01; telex 22342; f. 1947; state economic internal passenger and cargo services to Varna, Burgas, Ruse, Plovdiv, Kurdzhali, Targovishte, Silistra, Vidin and Gorna Oriakhovitsa; external services to Abu Dhabi, Algiers, Amsterdam, Ankara, Athens, Baghdad, Barcelona, Beirut, Belgrade, Berlin, Bratislava, Brussels, Bucharest, Budapest, Cairo, Casablanca, Copenhagen, Damascus, Dresden, Frankfurt am Main, Geneva, Harare, Helsinki, Istanbul, Khartoum, Kiev, Kuwait, Lagos, Leipzig, Leningrad, London, Luanda, Luxembourg, Madrid, Milan, Moscow, Nicosia, Paris, Prague, Rome, Stockholm, Tripoli, Tunis, Valletta, Vienna, Warsaw, Zürich; also agricultural aviation services; fleet of 17 TU-134, 17 TU-154, 8 AN-24, 7 Il-18, 12 Yak-40, 9 Mil Mi-8 and 3 AN-12; Dir-Gen. V. VELICHKOV.

Tourism

Balkantourist: 1040 Sofia, Blvd Vitosha 1; tel. 4-33-31; telex 22583; f. 1948; the state tourist enterprise; Dir-Gen. IVAN MILKOV.

Atomic Energy

A heterogeneous swimming-pool reactor, with a thermal capacity of 2,000 kW, came into operation near Sofia in 1961. The reactor, supplied under a bilateral agreement by the USSR, is used for the production of radioactive isotopes as well as for experimental work.

Bulgaria's first nuclear power station at Kozlodui, which opened in 1974 with an initial capacity of 440 MW, was to be expanded to have a capacity of 3,760 MW by 1988. A second nuclear power station, rated at 6,000 MW, was due to begin production in 1990. In 1985 the Kozlodui station was producing 29% of the country's electricity.

Institute for Nuclear Research and Nuclear Energy of the Bulgarian Academy of Sciences: 1784 Sofia, Blvd Lenin 72; tel. 75-80-32; telex 23561; f. 1973; Dir Acad. KHR. KHRISTOV.

BURKINA FASO

Introductory Survey

Location, Climate, Language, Religion, Flag, Capital

Burkina Faso (formerly the Republic of Upper Volta) is a land-locked state in West Africa, bordered by Mali to the west and north, by Niger to the east, and by Benin, Togo, Ghana and the Ivory Coast to the south. The climate is hot and mainly dry, with an average annual temperature of 28°C (82°F). Humidity reaches 80% in the south during the rainy season, which occurs between June and October but is often very short. The official language is French, and there are numerous indigenous languages (principally Mossi), with many dialects. The majority of the population follow animist beliefs, about 30% are Muslims and fewer than 10% Christians, mainly Roman Catholics. The national flag (proportions 3 by 2) has two equal horizontal stripes, of red and green, with a five-pointed gold star in the centre. The capital is Ouagadougou.

Recent History

Burkina Faso (known as Upper Volta until August 1984) was formerly a province of French West Africa. It became a self-governing republic within the French Community in December 1958 and achieved full independence on 5 August 1960, with Maurice Yameogo as President. In January 1966 President Yameogo was deposed in a military coup, led by Lt-Col (later Gen.) Sangoulé Lamizana, the Army Chief of Staff, who took office as President and Prime Minister. The military regime dissolved the National Assembly, suspended the Constitution and established a Supreme Council of the Armed Forces. Political activities were suspended in September 1966 but the restriction was lifted in November 1969. A new constitution, approved by popular referendum in June 1970, provided for a return to civilian rule after a four-year transitional regime of joint military and civilian administration. Elections for a National Assembly were held in December, and the Union démocratique voltaïque (UDV) won 37 of the 57 seats. In January 1971 the President appointed the UDV leader, Gérard Ouedraogo, as Prime Minister. He took office in February at the head of a mixed civilian and military Council of Ministers.

In late 1973 conflicts between the Government and the National Assembly led to deadlock, and in February 1974 the President, Gen. Lamizana, announced that the army had assumed power again. He dismissed the Prime Minister and dissolved the National Assembly. The Constitution and political activity were suspended, and the President assumed the functions of the premiership. In May the new military regime banned political parties. The Assembly was replaced by a National Consultative Council for Renewal, formed in July 1974, with 65 members nominated by the President.

Political parties were allowed to resume their activities from October 1977. A referendum in November approved a draft constitution which provided for a return to civilian democratic rule. Seven parties registered to contest elections for a new National Assembly, held in April 1978. The UDV won 28 of the 57 seats, while the newly-formed Union nationale pour la défense de la démocratie (UNDD) won 13. Gen. Lamizana was elected President in May, and the seven parties grouped themselves into three alliances in the Assembly, as required by the Constitution. The main opposition front was formed by the UNDD and the Union progressiste voltaïque (UPV). In July the Assembly elected the President's nominee, Dr Joseph Conombo (a leading member of the UDV), to be Prime Minister. The new Government's attempts to accommodate the various groups and to improve the economy were made difficult by the tacit hostility of the army and trade unions, and by the divisions in the National Assembly.

Largely as a result of the deteriorating economic situation, the country suffered a series of strikes during 1979 and 1980. After prolonged industrial unrest, President Lamizana was overthrown in November 1980 in a bloodless coup, led by Col Saye Zerbo, the military commander of the capital region, who had been Minister of Foreign Affairs during the previous period of military rule. A Comité militaire de redressement pour le progrès national (CMRPN), with 31 members (all soldiers), was established, and in December the new regime formed a Government of National Recovery, comprising both army officers and civilians. The Constitution was suspended, and the National Assembly was dissolved. Political parties and activities were banned, and a curfew was imposed. During 1981 Col Zerbo faced increasing opposition from the trade unions, a conflict which culminated in the suspension of one of the union associations and the revocation of the right to strike between November 1981 and February 1982. In November 1982, however, Col Zerbo was ousted in another military coup, led by non-commissioned army officers, in which five people were killed. Major Jean-Baptiste Ouedraogo, who had not previously been involved in politics, emerged as leader of the new military regime, setting up the Conseil de salut du peuple (CSP). The CMRPN was dissolved, and a predominantly civilian government was formed. In February 1983 several soldiers and opposition figures were arrested, following the discovery of an alleged plot to reinstate the Zerbo regime. A power struggle within the CSP became apparent with the arrest in May 1983 of radical left-wing elements within the Government, including the recently-appointed Prime Minister, Capt. Thomas Sankara. Maj. Ouedraogo announced the withdrawal of the armed forces from political life and disbanded the CSP. Sankara and his supporters were released after two weeks' detention, following a rebellion by pro-Sankara commandos at Pô, near the Ghana border.

In August 1983 Capt. Sankara seized power in a coup, in which an estimated 15 people were killed. Opposition politicians were placed under house arrest, a strict curfew was imposed and a Conseil national révolutionnaire (CNR) set up. Citizens were called to join local committees, Comités pour la défense de la révolution (CDRs), in an attempt to mobilize popular support for the regime. In September ex-President Zerbo was formally arrested, after his supporters attempted to overthrow the new Government. Administrative, judicial and military reforms were announced, and Revolutionary People's Tribunals were inaugurated to try former politicians, several of whom (including Zerbo) were imprisoned.

The Sankara regime attracted some internal criticism in March 1984, when a prominent teachers' union staged a 48-hour strike in protest at the arrest of three of its leaders. In June 1984 seven people were executed, convicted of plotting to overthrow the Government. Sankara accused an outlawed political group, the Front Progressiste Voltaïque (which comprised members of the former UPV and other left-wing groups), of complicity in the plot, alleging that it had been supported by France and other foreign powers: the French Government vigorously denied any involvement, and relations between the two countries became strained. In August 1984, on the first anniversary of the coup which had brought him to power, Sankara announced that Upper Volta would henceforth be known as Burkina Faso ('Land of the Incorruptible Men'), and a new national flag and anthem were introduced. Later that month, and following signs of growing factionalism within the CNR, Sankara dissolved the Government. The new Council of Ministers, announced in September, showed a significant reduction in the influence of the Ligue patriotique pour le développement (LIPAD), a Marxist faction which had become increasingly at odds with Sankara's populist rhetoric. Sankara proceeded to dissolve and re-form the Government in the same manner on the following two anniversaries of the coup, in August 1985 and August 1986, describing the process as a response to the 'revolutionary tradition' that was, he claimed, now established in the country.

A brief 'leaflet war', organized by trade unions in January 1985, did little to affect the relative stability of the internal political situation. It began to appear that the extended role of the CDRs in imposing government policy and organizing local affairs had consolidated both the revolution and Sankara's position as leader. In December 1985 Sankara announced the creation of the Libyan-inspired *jamahiri* system in the country: 7,300 co-ordination bureaux were to be established in order to collect and collate the views of the 'revolutionary popular masses'.

Later that month, a long-standing border dispute with Mali erupted into a six-day war which left more than 50 people dead. The conflict centred on an area known as the Agacher strip, reputed to contain significant deposits of minerals. Political tension between the two governments had been rising since mid-1985, when the Malian secretary-general of the Communauté économique de l'Afrique de l'Ouest (CEAO) was expelled from Burkina for criticizing austerity measures that had been imposed on the CEAO by Sankara. Following the cease-fire, which was arranged by the CEAO's defence grouping ANAD (Accord de non-agression et d'assistance en matière de défense), and as a result of the interim decision on the dispute that the International Court of Justice delivered in January 1986, troops were withdrawn from the Agacher area. However, tension between the two countries continued throughout 1986.

The Sankara Government has established close links with neighbouring Ghana: a series of co-operation and security agreements were consolidated in 1984, and preliminary proposals for the eventual political and economic integration of the two countries were announced in September 1986. Summit meetings of leaders from Burkina Faso and Ghana, together with Benin and Libya, have been held regularly to demonstrate 'revolutionary solidarity'.

Government

The National Assembly was dissolved in November 1980. All legislative and executive power rests with the Conseil national révolutionnaire, whose Chairman is Head of State. For administrative purposes, the country is divided into 25 provinces, which, in turn, are divided into departments, districts and villages.

Defence

National service is voluntary, and lasts for two years on a part-time basis. In July 1986 the armed forces numbered 4,000, including a small air force, and there were 2,100 men in paramilitary forces. Defence expenditure was budgeted at US $34.1m. in 1985.

Economic Affairs

The economy is predominantly agricultural. More than 80% of the working population are farmers or livestock-raising nomads. The agricultural sector contributed about 43% of gross domestic product (GDP) in 1984. The principal crops are sorghum, sugar cane, millet, beans and maize, most of which are consumed within the country. The major export crop is cotton, followed by karité nuts: since 1976 Burkina Faso has been the third largest cotton producer in West Africa. Production of seed (unginned) cotton was 79,500 tons in 1983/84, and was expected to reach about the same level in the following season. Livestock and livestock products provided about 16% of the country's export earnings in 1982.

After the devastating droughts that affected the whole Sahel region from 1968 to 1974, normal rainfall during 1975/76 brought about a considerable recovery in the levels of livestock numbers and crop production. Erratic rainfall patterns have continued to disrupt production, however: in 1981/82 output of groundnuts fell to only 483 metric tons (compared with 1,165 tons in 1980/81), while the harvest of karité nuts declined to 26,000 tons (down from 50,700 tons in 1980/81) and production of sesame seed fell to 3,700 tons (compared with annual crops of around 7,000 tons in the late 1970s). Late rains in 1983 led to an estimated shortfall in cereal production of 120,000 tons in that year, and output of raw sugar declined from 27,700 tons in 1982/83 to 26,000 tons in 1983/84.

The overall cereal deficit increased to 170,000 tons in 1984, when northern Burkina was severely affected by renewed drought. In May 1985 it was estimated that nearly 1.5m. Burkinabê were suffering from the effects of famine. Rains returned, however, in August 1985, and a 'normal' cereal harvest was forecast. During 1985 the Banque ouest-africaine de développement, in which Burkina Faso is a shareholder, granted a loan of 1,160m. francs CFA for the development of groundnut cultivation on the Mossi plateau.

The People's Development Plan, introduced in May 1984 by the Sankara regime, aimed to achieve self-sufficiency in basic foods and essential capital goods, through economic decentralization and small-scale agricultural projects. The 1986–91 Economic Plan, involving estimated total investment of 630,000m. francs CFA (of which approximately 21% was to be met from domestic resources), was to allocate a large proportion of resources to the manufacturing sector. It was hoped to achieve an average annual growth rate of 3.1% over the five-year period. In August 1984 the traditional land ownership system was abolished, and all land and mineral rights were nationalized. In June 1985 construction of a 15-MW hydroelectric dam began at Kompienga, near the Togo border. The scheme has a projected cost of 37,000m. francs CFA: it was scheduled for completion in 1988, and was expected to provide irrigation for over 7,000 ha of land. In 1986 it was announced that further dams were to be built at Bagre, on the Nankabe (White Volta) river, and at Noumbiel, on the Mouhoun (Black Volta).

There is some mining potential, but poor communications and uncertain world markets have hindered development. The Tambao manganese deposits are estimated to contain 12m. tons of high-grade ore, but plans to extend the existing railway from Ouagadougou, to facilitate the exploitation of the deposits, were finally abandoned in 1986. The Poura gold mine, which closed in 1966, was reopened in 1984, and is expected to produce an average of two tons of gold annually until 1994. In 1985 the European Investment Bank (EIB) provided a loan of 2,400m. francs CFA to assist exploitation, and in 1986 the Islamic Development Bank (IDB) financed a feasibility study on a further gold mine project at Taperko. Initial exploration of zinc and silver deposits at Perkoa began in 1984, financed by the World Bank: potential reserves are estimated at 10m. tons. Manufacturing currently contributes only about 14% of GDP: the major concerns are food processing, tobacco and textiles. Construction of a cement factory at Ouagadougou, with an annual capacity of 150,000 tons, began in 1981.

The country remains exceptionally poor, even by Third World standards. According to estimates by the World Bank, its gross national product (GNP) per head, measured at average 1982–84 prices, was US $160 in 1984, showing an annual increase of only 1.2% since 1965. The estimated average increase in overall GDP, in real terms, was 2.4% per year in 1965–73, rising to 2.9% per year in 1973–84. The country's critical financial situation has been aggravated by a chronic trade deficit, which in 1982 totalled 95,599m. francs CFA (more than five times the total value of exports), and in 1984 totalled 64,660m. francs CFA. Burkina's foreign debt totalled US $407.4m. at the end of 1984, according to the World Bank, and is estimated to have risen even higher in 1985. A strict austerity budget was adopted for 1984, balanced at 57,600m. francs CFA, a decrease of 300m. francs CFA compared with the previous year. Budget expenditure in 1985 was estimated at 72,000m. francs CFA. The Government depends on foreign sources for up to three-quarters of its national budget, and in 1982 international aid totalled US $198m. Population density is high for a country with such poor resources. Traditionally, there has been substantial emigration to the coastal countries of the region, in particular to the Ivory Coast. Remittances that are sent home by emigrant workers contribute significantly to Burkina's balance of payments.

Social Welfare

The Government provides hospitals and rural medical services. A special medical service for schools is in operation. In 1980 there were five main hospitals, with a total of 2,042 beds. There were also 254 dispensaries, 11 medical centres and 65 regional clinics. Medical services are also supplied to remote areas by 167 mobile units. In 1981 the country had 127 physicians, one per 55,858 inhabitants. By 1981 658 villages were equipped with primary health centres. An old-age and veterans' pension system was introduced in 1960, and extended workers' insurance schemes have been in operation since 1967. Of total expenditure by the central government in 1983, 6.9% was for health, and a further 7.9% was for social security and welfare.

Education

Education is available free of charge, and is officially compulsory for children between the ages of seven and 13 years. Primary education begins at seven years of age and lasts for up to six years. Secondary education, beginning at the age of 13, lasts for up to seven years. It was estimated that in 1983 about 22% of children in the relevant age-group attended primary schools (28% of boys; 16% of girls), while only about 4% of those aged 13 to 20 were enrolled at secondary schools (boys 5%; girls 3%). There is a university in Ouagadougou, and government grants are available for higher education in European and African universities. A rural radio service has been established to further general and technical education in rural areas. In August 1983 President Sankara announced plans to introduce adult 'functional literacy' programmes in national languages: in 1985, according to UNESCO estimates, adult illiteracy averaged 86.8% (males 79.3%; females 93.9%).

Tourism

The principal tourist attraction is big game hunting in the east and south-west, and along the banks of the Mouhoun (Black Volta) river. There is a wide variety of wild animals in the game reserves. Tourist arrivals at hotels rose from 14,564 in 1975 to 43,724 in 1979. Political instability affected the tourist trade in the early 1980s, with only 5% of hotel rooms being occupied in August 1983. Tourist arrivals reached only 31,000 in 1981, but rose to total 44,000 by 1985.

Public Holidays

1987: 1 January (New Year), 3 January (Anniversary of the 1966 Revolution), 20 April (Easter Monday), 1 May (May Day), 28 May (Ascension), 30 May* (Id al-Fitr, end of Ramadan), 8 June (Whit Monday), 4 August (National Day), 6 August* (Id al-Adha, Feast of the Sacrifice), 15 August (Assumption), 1 November (All Saints' Day), 4 November* (Mouloud, Birth of the Prophet), 25 December (Christmas).

1988: 1 January (New Year), 3 January (Anniversary of the 1966 Revolution), 4 April (Easter Monday), 1 May (May Day), 12 May (Ascension), 18 May* (Id al-Fitr, end of Ramadan), 23 May (Whit Monday), 25 July* (Id al-Adha, Feast of the Sacrifice), 4 August (National Day), 15 August (Assumption), 23 October* (Mouloud, Birth of the Prophet), 1 November (All Saints' Day), 25 December (Christmas).

* These holidays are dependent on the Islamic lunar calendar and may vary by one or two days from the dates given.

Weights and Measures

The metric system is in force.

Currency and Exchange Rates

100 centimes = 1 franc de la Communauté financière africaine (CFA).

Exchange rates (30 September 1986):
  1 franc CFA = 2 French centimes;
  £1 sterling = 480.625 francs CFA;
  US $1 = 332.125 francs CFA.

BURKINA FASO

Statistical Survey

Source (except where otherwise stated): Institut National de la Statistique et de la Démographie, BP 374, Ouagadougou; tel. 33-55-37.

Area and Population

AREA, POPULATION AND DENSITY

Area (sq km)	274,200*
Population (census results)	
1–7 December 1975	5,638,203
December 1985	
Males	3,846,518
Females	4,129,591
Total	7,976,019
Density (per sq km) at December 1985	29.1

* 105,870 sq miles.

PRINCIPAL TOWNS (population at 1985 census)

Ouagadougou (capital)	442,223	Ouahigouya	38,604
Bobo-Dioulasso	231,162	Banfora	35,204
Koudougou	51,670	Kaya	25,779

BIRTHS AND DEATHS

Average annual birth rate 49.3 per 1,000 in 1970–75, 48.1 per 1,000 in 1975–80; death rate 26.1 per 1,000 in 1970–75, 24.0 per 1,000 in 1975–80 (UN estimates).

ECONOMICALLY ACTIVE POPULATION
(ILO estimates, '000 persons at mid-1980)

	Males	Females	Total
Agriculture, etc.	1,550	1,414	2,964
Industry	89	57	146
Services	145	165	310
Total	1,784	1,637	3,421

Source: ILO, *Economically Active Population Estimates and Projections, 1950–2025*.

Agriculture

PRINCIPAL CROPS ('000 metric tons)

	1982	1983	1984*
Maize	111	78	60
Millet	441	398	280
Sorghum	609	611	600
Rice (paddy)	38	12	40
Sweet potatoes*	43	43	42
Cassava (Manioc)*	43	42	40
Yams*	30	29	28
Vegetables*	76	82	76
Fruit	60	65*	63
Pulses	178	176	155
Groundnuts (in shell)	73	82	77
Cottonseed	35†	46†	50
Cotton (lint)	22	29	30†
Sesame seed	8	6	5
Tobacco (leaves)*	1	1	1
Sugar cane*	350	330	320

* FAO estimates.   † Unofficial figures.

Source: FAO, *Production Yearbook*.

LIVESTOCK ('000 head, year ending September)

	1982	1983	1984
Cattle	2,871	2,850*	2,800*
Sheep	1,970	2,000	2,000*
Goats	2,459	2,600*	2,600*
Pigs	206	195*	200*
Horses	70	70*	70*
Asses	200	200*	200*
Camels*	6	6	6

* FAO estimates.

Poultry (FAO estimates, million): 13 in 1982; 14 in 1983; 15 in 1984.
Source: FAO, *Production Yearbook*.

LIVESTOCK PRODUCTS (FAO estimates, '000 metric tons)

	1982	1983	1984
Beef and veal	25	24	24
Mutton and lamb	4	4	4
Goats' meat	5	6	5
Pigs' meat	4	4	4
Horse meat	1	1	1
Poultry meat	14	14	15
Cows' milk	115	114	112
Goats' milk	10	10	10
Butter	1.2	1.3	1.3
Hen eggs	9.1	9.8	10.0
Cattle hides	4.8	4.5	4.6
Sheep skins	0.9	0.9	1.0
Goat skins	1.5	1.5	1.5

Source: FAO, *Production Yearbook*.

BURKINA FASO   Statistical Survey

Forestry

ROUNDWOOD REMOVALS
(FAO estimates, '000 cubic metres, excluding bark)

	1982	1983	1984
Sawlogs, veneer logs and logs for sleepers	5	5	5
Other industrial wood	283	290	297
Fuel wood	5,994	6,132	6,284
Total	6,282	6,427	6,586

Source: FAO, *Yearbook of Forest Products*.

Fishing

('000 metric tons, live weight)

	1980	1981	1982
Total catch	6.5	7.5	7.0

1983: Catch as in 1982 (FAO estimate).
Source: FAO, *Yearbook of Fishery Statistics*.

Industry

SELECTED PRODUCTS

		1981	1982	1983
Flour	metric tons	19,439	17,716	21,009
Soap	metric tons	9,695	11,248	10,606
Cottonseed oil (refined)	metric tons	4,176	6,272	4,376
Beer	hectolitres	747,673	709,054	701,447
Soft drinks	hectolitres	145,688	142,880	139,558
Cigarettes	'000 packets	24,876	31,177	25,570
Footwear	'000 pairs	1,478	1,628	1,313
Cotton yarn	metric tons	343	547	373*
Bicycles, motor cycles and scooters	'000	73.3	74.0	4.7†
Bicycle and motor cycle tyres	'000	1,180.6	937.9	745.4
Electric power	'000 kWh	114,595	122,825	n.a.

* Estimate.   † Motor cycles and scooters only.

Raw sugar (estimates, '000 metric tons): 26 in 1981; 28 in 1982; 28 in 1983.

Finance

CURRENCY AND EXCHANGE RATES

Monetary Units
100 centimes = 1 franc de la Communauté financière africaine (CFA).

Denominations
Coins: 1, 2, 5, 10, 25, 50 and 100 francs CFA.
Notes: 100, 500, 1,000, 5,000 and 10,000 francs CFA.

French Franc, Sterling and Dollar Equivalents (30 September 1986).
1 French franc = 50 francs CFA;
£1 sterling = 480.625 francs CFA;
US $1 = 332.125 francs CFA;
1,000 francs CFA = £2.081 = $3.011.

Average Exchange Rate (francs CFA per US $)
1983   381.06
1984   436.96
1985   449.26

COST OF LIVING (Consumer Price Index for Africans in Ouagadougou; base: 1980 = 100)

	1983	1984	1985
All items	130.6	136.9	146.3

Source: IMF, *International Financial Statistics*.

CENTRAL BANK RESERVES
(US $ million at 31 December)

	1983	1984	1985
Gold*	4.3	3.7	3.6
IMF special drawing rights	7.9	5.5	6.2
Reserve position in IMF	5.9	7.4	8.3
Foreign exchange	71.2	93.4	125.1
Total	89.3	110.0	143.1

* Valued at market-related prices.
Source: IMF, *International Financial Statistics*.

MONEY SUPPLY ('000 million francs CFA at 31 December)

	1983	1984	1985
Currency outside banks	31.74	31.24	30.97
Demand deposits at deposit money banks*	27.29	33.41	36.36
Checking deposits at post office	1.31	1.84	1.98

* Excluding the deposits of public establishments of an administrative or social nature.
Source: IMF, *International Financial Statistics*.

BURKINA FASO

BUDGET (million francs CFA)*

Revenue†	1981	1982	1983
Taxation	43,327	46,977	47,117
Taxes on income, profits, etc.	8,257	8,600	9,283
Individual taxes	4,559	5,494	5,995
Social security contributions	4,094	3,528	5,089
Domestic taxes on goods and services	7,688	9,258	9,075
Turnover tax	3,492	4,887	3,610
Excises	2,751	2,832	3,761
Taxes on international trade	20,135	22,945	20,474
Import duties	17,788	20,581	18,217
Other current revenue	5,730	6,121	4,438
Property income	3,073	3,207	3,195
Sub-total	49,057	53,098	51,555
Adjustment to cash basis	−3,294	1,039	6,191
Total current revenue	45,763	54,137	57,746
Capital revenue	46	33	17
Total revenue	45,809	54,170	57,763

Expenditure‡	1981	1982	1983
General public services	9,889	7,762	7,806
Defence	9,216	10,800	11,172
Education	7,899	9,883	10,584
Health	2,916	4,161	3,649
Social security and welfare	3,356	3,631	4,157
Housing and community amenities	98	103	172
Other community and social services	601	370	989
Economic services	10,233	10,351	8,817
General administration, regulation and research	2,463	4,477	1,717
Agriculture, forestry and fishing	2,604	2,858	2,714
Mining, manufacturing and construction	181	206	222
Transport and communications	732	56	575
Other economic services	4,253	2,754	3,589
Other purposes	5,308	10,036	5,545
Sub-total	49,516	57,047	52,891
Adjustment to cash basis	547	5,940	1,076
Total expenditure	50,063	63,037	53,967
Current§	41,140	55,354	48,343
Capital	8,923	7,683	5,624

* Figures represent a consolidation of the operations of the General Budget, covering the major units of the central government, and the National Social Security Fund.
† Excluding grants received (million francs CFA): 2,911 in 1981; 390 in 1982; 1,016 in 1983.
‡ Excluding net lending (million francs CFA): 3,331 in 1981; −2,292 in 1982; 1,270 in 1983.
§ Including interest payments (million francs CFA): 1,437 in 1981; 1,650 in 1982; 1,139 in 1983.
Source: IMF, *Government Finance Statistics Yearbook*.

1984 (estimates): Budget to balance at 57,600 million francs CFA.
1985 (budget proposals, million francs CFA): Revenue 61,000; Expenditure 72,000.

NATIONAL ACCOUNTS ('000 million francs CFA at current prices)
Expenditure on the Gross Domestic Product

	1981	1982	1983
Government final consumption expenditure	44.0	52.4	52.4
Private final consumption expenditure	302.8	322.6	348.2
Increase in stocks	4.1	5.4	1.6
Gross fixed capital formation	27.7	32.3	27.8
Total domestic expenditure	378.6	312.7	430.1
Exports of goods and services	53.6	55.2	60.7
Less imports of goods and services	125.5	132.1	144.4
GDP in purchasers' values	306.7	335.8	346.5

Source: UN, *Monthly Bulletin of Statistics*.

Gross Domestic Product by Economic Activity*

	1977	1978	1979
Agriculture, hunting, forestry and fishing	72,333	74,501	95,589
Mining and quarrying	196	250	290
Manufacturing	22,312	24,682	29,073
Electricity, gas and water	1,745	2,098	2,105
Construction	6,352	8,680	8,057
Trade, restaurants and hotels	25,738	32,107	39,824
Transport, storage and communications	12,685	12,820	16,090
Finance, insurance, real estate and business services	8,770	10,206	13,329
Community, social and personal services	1,258	1,337	1,422
Sub-total	151,389	166,681	205,780
Less Imputed bank service charges	1,758	3,443	4,592
Domestic product of industries	149,631	163,238	201,188
Government services	21,283	25,154	29,696
Private non-profit services to households	462	530	590
Domestic services of households	1,135	1,223	1,360
GDP at factor cost	172,511	190,145	232,834
Indirect taxes, *less* subsidies	20,510	22,547	19,506
GDP in purchasers' values	193,021	212,692	252,340

* Figures are provisional. Revised totals of GDP (in '000 million francs CFA) are: 184.9 in 1977; 222.5 in 1978; 259.1 in 1979.

BALANCE OF PAYMENTS (US $ million)

	1980	1981	1982
Merchandise exports f.o.b.	160.6	159.4	126.4
Merchandise imports f.o.b.	−368.3	−348.4	−359.9
Trade balance	−207.7	−189.1	−233.4
Exports of services	64.7	49.7	57.3
Imports of services	−228.0	−203.8	−193.3
Balance on goods and services	−371.1	−343.1	−369.4
Private unrequited transfers (net)	111.8	120.2	88.7
Government unrequited transfers (net)	210.6	180.8	188.6
Current balance	−48.7	−42.1	−92.1
Direct capital investment (net)	—	2.4	1.9
Other long-term capital (net)	53.4	34.8	56.1
Short-term capital (net)	9.8	27.2	18.4
Net errors and omissions	−7.9	−8.1	15.4
Total (net monetary movements)	6.6	14.2	−0.2
Allocation of IMF special drawing rights	2.2	2.1	—
Valuation changes (net)	−6.5	−13.7	−8.9
Exceptional financing (net)	4.3	0.1	—
Changes in reserves	6.6	2.7	−9.1

Source: IMF, *International Financial Statistics*.

External Trade

PRINCIPAL COMMODITIES (million francs CFA)

Imports c.i.f.	1980	1981	1982
Dairy produce	2,929	4,895	5,018
Cereals	6,860	8,288	11,758
Sugar and sugar products	113	839	1,102
Construction materials	3,538	3,803	5,323
Petroleum products	9,942	14,157	18,743
Pharmaceutical products	2,206	3,252	3,572
Textiles	2,220	2,478	3,424
Iron and steel	3,325	2,615	4,040
Non-electrical machinery	7,247	7,871	1,633
Electrical machinery	2,736	2,755	6,556
Transport equipment	10,823	10,559	36,196
Total (incl. others)	75,614	91,442	113,708

1983 (million francs CFA): Total imports 109,572.
1984 (million francs CFA): Total imports 92,100.

Exports f.o.b.	1980	1981	1982
Live animals	4,512	3,509	2,294
Vegetables	223	370	614
Groundnuts (shelled)	90	18	80
Sesame seeds	438	292	443
Karité nuts	1,535	2,984	2,312
Karité oil	103	9	738
Hides and skins	671	894	598
Raw cotton	8,369	8,174	7,592
Total (incl. others)	19,071	20,066	18,109

1983 (million francs CFA): Cotton 11,890; Total (incl. others) 21,712.
1984 (million francs CFA): Cotton 15,750; Total (incl. others) 27,440.

PRINCIPAL TRADING PARTNERS (million francs CFA)

Imports	1981	1982	1983
Belgium/Luxembourg	22,539	3,898	n.a.
China, People's Republic	1,502	2,179	2,449
France	30,408	36,703	30,626
Germany, Federal Republic	3,842	4,244	3,703
Ghana	1,015	477	529
Italy	1,840	1,567	n.a.
Ivory Coast	20,098	25,636	25,811
Japan	3,440	4,169	4,684
Netherlands	2,995	4,893	5,595
Senegal	796	1,382	1,532
Togo	1,232	1,925	1,414
United Kingdom	1,734	2,606	2,984
USA	9,831	7,544	10,284

Exports	1981	1982	1983
Belgium/Luxembourg	661	117	n.a.
China, People's Republic	1,103	n.a.	2,477
France	2,446	2,632	2,579
Germany, Federal Republic	1,138	1,346	279
Ghana	108	124	416
Italy	562	880	n.a.
Ivory Coast	6,228	3,807	1,945
Japan	1,034	943	943
Mali	310	209	1,126
Netherlands	53	366	61
Niger	484	791	512
Togo	191	261	555
United Kingdom	826	1,199	1,632

Transport

RAILWAYS (traffic)

	1980	1981	1982
Passenger journeys ('000)	3,646	3,277	2,867
Passenger-km (million)	1,250	988	856
Freight ton-km (million)	600	634	668

ROAD TRAFFIC (motor vehicles in use at 31 December)

	1982	1983
Cars	19,196	21,182
Buses	543	583
Lorries	4,658	5,146
Tractors	845	918
Motor cycles and scooters	7,159	13,411
Mopeds	21,931	n.a.

Source: International Road Federation, *World Road Statistics*.

CIVIL AVIATION (traffic on scheduled services)*

	1980	1981	1982
Kilometres flown (million)	2.1	2.3	2.1
Passengers carried ('000)	65	76	81
Passenger-km (million)	180	199	215
Freight ton-km (million)	18.0	21.0	21.2
Mail ton-km (million)	0.7	0.8	0.8
Total ton-km (million)	35	40	41

* Including an apportionment of the traffic of Air Afrique.
Source: UN, *Statistical Yearbook*.

Communications Media

	1981	1982	1983
Radio receivers ('000 in use)	118	120	122
Television receivers ('000 in use)	11	19	35

Telephones (1978): 9,000 in use.
Book production (1980): 4 titles.
Daily newspapers (1982): 1 (average circulation 1,500 copies).
Source: mainly UNESCO, *Statistical Yearbook*.

Tourism

	1983	1984	1985
Number of tourist arrivals	47,000	40,249	44,375

Receipts from tourism (million francs CFA): 1,081 in 1983; 1,788 in 1984; 2,193 in 1985.
Source: Division du Tourisme et de l'Hôtellerie, Ouagadougou.

Education

(1985)

	Institutions	Teachers	Male	Female	Total
Primary	1,537	5,415	198,180	115,340	313,520
Secondary:					
General	92	1,366	26,363	13,006	39,369
Vocational	21	274	1,936	2,277	4,213
Teacher training	2	n.a.	137	62	199
Higher	19	230	3,134	966	4,100

Source: Ministère de l'Education nationale, Ouagadougou.

Directory

The Constitution

The 1977 Constitution was suspended following the military coup of 25 November 1980. A new regime seized power in November 1982 but was, in turn, overthrown in August 1983, when power was assumed by a Conseil national de la révolution.

The Government

HEAD OF STATE

President: Capt. THOMAS SANKARA (assumed power 5 August 1983).

COUNCIL OF MINISTERS
(October 1986)

Chairman of the National Revolutionary Council: Capt. THOMAS SANKARA.
Minister of State to the Presidency in charge of Justice: Capt. BLAISE COMPAORÉ.
Minister for External Affairs and Co-operation: LEANDRE BASSOLE.
Minister of Popular Defence: Maj. BOUKARI JEAN-BAPTISTE LINGANI.
Minister of the Interior and Security: NONGMA ERNEST OUEDRAOGO.
Minister of Information: BASILE LAIETA GUISSOU.
Minister of Culture: BERNADETTE SANOU.
Minister of Economic Development: Capt. HENRI ZONGO.
Minister of Financial Resources: TALATA EUGÈNE DONDASSE.
Minister of the Budget: ADÈLE OUEDRAOGO.
Minister of Planning and Popular Development: YOUSSOUF OUEDRAOGO.
Minister of Trade and Supplies: MAMADOU TOURÉ.
Minister of Agriculture and Livestock: JEAN-MARIE SOMDA.
Minister of Peasants' Affairs: LÉONARD COMPAORÉ.
Minister of Water Resources: MICHEL KOUDA.
Minister of Equipment: MOUSSA MICHEL TAPSOBA.
Minister of Transport and Communications: ALAIN KOEFFE.
Minister of Labour and Civil Service: FIDÈLE TOE.
Minister of Environment and Tourism: BÉATRICE DAMIBA.
Minister of Family Development and National Solidarity: JOSEPHINE OUEDRAOGO.
Minister of Health: AZARA BAMBA.
Minister of Sport and Leisure: Maj. ABDUL SALAM KABORÉ.
Minister of National Education: SANSAH DAH.
Minister of Higher Education and Scientific Research: VALÈRE DIEUDONNÉ SOME.
Secretary of State for Justice: ANTOINE SAMBO KOMI.
Secretary-General of the Government and of the Council of Ministers: NAYABTIGOUNGOU EMMANUEL CONGO KABORÉ.

MINISTRIES

Presidential Office: BP 7030, Ouagadougou; telex 5221.
Ministry of Agriculture and Livestock: BP 7005, Ouagadougou.
Ministry of Culture: Ouagadougou.
Ministry of Economic Development: Ouagadougou.
Ministry of Environment and Tourism: BP 7044, Ouagadougou; tel. 33-41-65; telex 5555.
Ministry of Equipment: BP 7011, Ouagadougou.
Ministry of External Affairs and Co-operation: BP 7038, Ouagadougou; telex 5222.
Ministry of Family Development and National Solidarity: BP 515, Ouagadougou.
Ministry of Financial Resources: BP 7008, Ouagadougou; telex 5256.

Ministry of Health: BP 7009, Ouagadougou.
Ministry of Higher Education and Scientific Research: BP 7130, Ouagadougou.
Ministry of Information: BP 7045, Ouagadougou; telex 5285.
Ministry of the Interior and Security: BP 7034, Ouagadougou.
Ministry of Justice: BP 526, Ouagadougou.
Ministry of Labour and Civil Service: BP 7006, Ouagadougou.
Ministry of National Education: BP 7032, Ouagadougou; telex 5293.
Ministry of Peasants' Affairs: Ouagadougou.
Ministry of Planning and Popular Development: BP 7050, Ouagadougou; telex 5319.
Ministry of Popular Defence: BP 496, Ouagadougou; telex 5297.
Ministry of Sport and Leisure: BP 7035, Ouagadougou.
Ministry of Trade and Supplies: BP 365, Ouagadougou.
Ministry of Transport and Communications: BP 7701, Ouagadougou.
Ministry of Water Resources: Ouagadougou.
Office of the Secretary-General: BP 7030, Ouagadougou.

Legislature

ASSEMBLÉE NATIONALE

Following the coup of November 1980, the National Assembly was dissolved.

Political Organizations

The National Revolutionary Council comprises three left-wing factions:

Ligue patriotique pour le développement (LIPAD): Ouagadougou; f. 1973; Marxist and pro-Soviet; Pres. HAMIDOU COULIBALY.
Regroupement des Officiers communistes (ROC): Ouagadougou; f. 1983; Leader Capt. THOMAS SANKARA.
Union de la Lutte communiste (ULC): Ouagadougou; f. 1978.

The following parties have been banned:

Front progressiste voltaïque (FPV): fusion of the fmr Union progressiste voltaïque and other left-wing parties; Sec.-Gen. Prof. JOSEPH KI-ZERBO (in exile).
Union démocratique voltaïque (UDV): Burkina Faso section of the fmr Rassemblement démocratique africain; Leader MALO TRAORÉ.

Diplomatic Representation

EMBASSIES IN BURKINA FASO

Algeria: BP 3893, Ouagadougou.
China, People's Republic: quartier Rotonde, BP 538, Ouagadougou; Ambassador: JIANG XIANG.
Cuba: BP 3422, Ouagadougou.
Egypt: BP 668, Ouagadougou; telex 5289; Ambassador: Dr MOHAMAD ALEY EL-KORDY.
France: ave de l'Indépendance, BP 504; Ouagadougou; tel. 33-38-92; telex 5211; Ambassador: JACQUES LE BLANC.
Germany, Federal Republic: BP 600, Ouagadougou; tel. 33-60-94; telex 5217; Ambassador: MICHEL GEIER.
Ghana: BP 212, Ouagadougou; tel. 33-28-75; Ambassador: Dr KELI NORDOR.
Korea, Democratic People's Republic: BP 370, Ouagadougou; Ambassador: YI TAE-KYUN.
Korea, Republic: BP 618, Ouagadougou; telex 5307; Ambassador: CHOI KEUN-BAE.
Libya: BP 1601, Ouagadougou; telex 5311; Secretary of People's Bureau: (vacant).
Netherlands: BP 1302, Ouagadougou; telex 5303; Ambassador: P. R. BROUWER.
Nigeria: BP 132, Ouagadougou; tel. 33-42-41; telex 5236; Chargé d'affaires: R. O. OLUWOLE.
USSR: BP 7041, Ouagadougou; Ambassador: YEVGENIY MELNIKOV.
USA: BP 35, Ouagadougou; tel. 33-54-42; telex 5290; Ambassador: LEONARDO NEHER.

Judicial System

Following the August 1983 coup, Tribunaux populaires de la révolution (TPR) were established, to operate under the jurisdiction of the Appeal Courts at Ouagadougou and Bobo-Dioulasso. Tribunals consist of three magistrates from the judiciary, three military personnel and 12 representatives of local Comités pour la défense de la révolution.

Religion

Most of the population follow animist beliefs.

ISLAM

There are about 2m. Muslims in Burkina Faso.

CHRISTIANITY
The Roman Catholic Church

Burkina Faso comprises one archdiocese and eight dioceses. At 31 December 1984 there were an estimated 593,000 adherents.

Bishops' Conference: Conférence des Evêques du Burkina Faso et du Niger, BP 1195, Ouagadougou; tel. 33-62-89; f. 1978; Pres. Mgr ANSELME TITIANMA SANON, Bishop of Bobo-Dioulasso.
Archbishop of Ouagadougou: Cardinal PAUL ZOUNGRANA, BP 1472, Ouagadougou; tel. 33-51-80.

The Press

Direction de la presse écrite: Ouagadougou; official govt body responsible for media direction.

DAILIES

Bulletin Quotidien d'Information: BP 507, Ouagadougou; f. 1959; publ. by the Direction de la presse écrite; simultaneous edn publ. in Bobo-Dioulasso; Dir-Gen. HUBERT BAZIÉ; Editor PIERRE-CLAVIER TASSEMBEDO; circ. 1,500.
Dunia: BP 3013, Ouagadougou; daily news.
L'Intrus: Ouagadougou; f. 1986.
Lolowulein (Red Star): Ouagadougou; f. 1985; govt-owned.
Notre Combat: BP 507, Ouagadougou; daily.
L'Observateur: BP 810, Ouagadougou; f. 1973; independent; Dir EDOUARD OUEDRAOGO; Editor-in-Chief EDOUARD NANA; publ. suspended June 1984.
Sidwaya: Ouagadougou; f. 1984; govt-owned daily; Dir BABOU PAULIN BAMOUNI; circ. 5,000.

PERIODICALS

Armée du Peuple: Ouagadougou; f. 1982; monthly; armed forces and defence information; Editor-in-Chief Lt SEYDOU NIANG.
Bulletin Economique et Fiscal: BP 502, Ouagadougou; tel. 33-61-48; telex 5268; f. 1971; 6 a year; legislative and statutory material; distributed by the Chambre de Commerce, d'Industrie et d'Artisanat du Burkina; circ. 350.
Bulletin Mensuel de Statistique: BP 374, Ouagadougou; tel. 33-55-37; monthly; economic and demographic statistics; publ. by National Statistics Office.
Carrefour Africain: BP 507, Ouagadougou; f. 1960; monthly; govt-owned; Dir-Gen. BABOU PAULIN BAMOUNI; circ. 6,000.
Courrier Consulaire du Burkina: BP 502, Ouagadougou; tel. 33-61-48; telex 5268; f. 1960; monthly; legislative and statutory material; publ. by the Chambre de Commerce, d'Industrie et d'Artisanat du Burkina; circ. 350.
Journal Officiel du Burkina: BP 568, Ouagadougou; weekly.

NEWS AGENCIES

Agence Burkinabê de Presse: Ouagadougou; f. 1963; telex 5327; state-owned.

BURKINA FASO   *Directory*

Foreign Bureaux

Agence France-Presse (AFP): BP 391, Ouagadougou; tel. 33-56-56; telex 5204; Bureau Chief KIDA TAPSOBA.

TASS (USSR) also has a bureau in Ouagadougou.

Publishers

Presses Africaines SA: BP 1471, Ouagadougou; telex 5344; general fiction, religion, primary and secondary textbooks; Man. Dir A. WININGA.

Société Nationale d'Edition et de Presse (SONEPRESS): BP 810, Ouagadougou; f. 1972; general, periodicals; Pres. MARTIAL OUEDRAOGO.

Government Publishing House

Imprimerie Nationale du Burkina Faso (INBF): route de l'Hôpital Yalgado, BP 7040, Ouagadougou; tel. 33-52-92; f. 1963; Dir LATY SOULEYMANE TRAORÉ.

Radio and Television

There were an estimated 122,000 radio receivers and 35,000 television receivers in use in 1983.

RADIO

La Voix du Renouveau: BP 7029, Ouagadougou; f. 1959; services in French and 13 vernacular languages; Dir of Programmes KI SATURNIAN. There is a second station at Bobo-Dioulasso.

TELEVISION

Télévision Nationale du Burkina: BP 7029, Ouagadougou; tel. 33-68-01; telex 5231; f. 1963; transmissions six days per week; currently received only in Ouagadougou and Bobo-Dioulasso; public viewing centres are being set up; Dir of Programmes (vacant).

Finance

(cap.=capital; res=reserves; dep.=deposits; m.=million; brs=branches; amounts in francs CFA)

BANKING
Central Bank

Banque Centrale des Etats de l'Afrique de l'Ouest (BCEAO): BP 356, Ouagadougou; tel. 33-67-15; telex 5205; br. in Bobo-Dioulasso; headquarters in Dakar, Senegal; f. 1955; bank of issue for the seven states of the Union monétaire ouest africaine (UMOA), comprising Benin, Burkina Faso, Ivory Coast, Mali, Niger, Senegal and Togo; cap. and res 32,564m. (Sept. 1985); Gov. ABDOULAYE FADIGA; Man. in Burkina Faso MOUSSA KONE.

State Banks

Banque Internationale du Burkina SA (BIB): rue André Brunnel, BP 362, Ouagadougou; tel. 33-33-75; telex 5210; f. 1974; cap. 600m., res 219.9m., dep. 32,046m. (1983); Pres. PASCAL SANON; Gen. Man. PIERRE TAHITA; 13 brs.

Banque Internationale pour le Commerce, l'Industrie et l'Agriculture du Burkina SA (BICIA-BF): ave Georges Pompidou, BP 8, Ouagadougou; tel. 33-21-63; telex 5203; f. 1973; 51% state-owned; cap. 1,250m., res 505m., dep. 45,802m. (Sept. 1984); Pres. Minister of Finance; Man. Dir D. AUGUSTIN SOMDA; 11 brs.

Banque Nationale de Développement du Burkina Faso (BND): BP 148, Ouagadougou; tel. 33-29-96; telex 5225; f. 1962; 80% state-owned; cap. 1,100m.; Man. Dir BOUKARY OUEDRAOGO; 6 brs.

Caisse Nationale de Crédit Agricole du Burkina Faso (CNCA-BF): BP 1644, Ouagadougou; tel. 33-23-60; telex 5249; f. 1979; 54% state-owned; cap. 1,300m.; Pres. AMBROISE BATIENON; Dir-Gen. NOËL KABORÉ.

Caisse Nationale des Dépôts et des Investissements (CNDI): 4 rue du Marché, BP 585, Ouagadougou; tel. 33-41-72; telex 5269; f. 1973; state-owned; cap. 3,400m.; Pres. N. CHRISTOPHE KONE; Man. Dir DÉSIRÉ BAMSAMBDA.

INSURANCE

Société Nationale d'Assurance et de Réassurance (SONAR): BP 406, Ouagadougou; tel. 33-63-43; telex 5294; f. 1973; 51% state-owned; cap. 120m.; Man. Dir BABLO FÉLIX HEMA.

Trade and Industry

GOVERNMENT REGULATORY BODIES

Autorité des Aménagements des Vallées des Voltas (AVV): BP 524, Ouagadougou; tel. 33-65-47; telex 5401; f. 1974, integrated rural development, including economic and social planning; Man. Dir JEAN-PAUL SAWADOGO.

Bureau des Mines de la Géologie du Burkina (BUMIGEB): BP 601, Ouagadougou; tel. 33-46-79; telex 5340; f. 1978; cap. 818m. francs CFA; research into geological and mineral resources; Man. Dir KOUDOUBI FRÉDÉRIC KOALA.

Caisse de Stabilisation des Prix des Produits Agricoles (CSPPA): BP 1453, Ouagadougou; tel. 33-68-44; telex 5202; responsible for stabilization of agricultural prices; supervises trade and export; Pres. BENOÎT OUATTARA.

Office Général des Projets de Tambao: BP 12, Ouagadougou; tel. 33-42-00; telex 5261; f. 1975; cap. 100m. francs CFA; responsible for development of manganese and limestone deposits around town of Tambao; supervises construction projects; Man. Dir FRANÇOIS OUEDRAOGO.

Office National des Céréales (OFNACER): BP 53, Ouagadougou; tel. 33-67-38; telex 5317; responsible for stabilization of the supply and price of cereals.

Office National du Commerce Exterieur (ONAC): BP 389, Ouagadougou; tel. 33-62-25; telex 5258; supervises external trade; Man. Dir SYLVIE KABORÉ.

Office National de l'Eau et de l'Assainissement: BP 170, Ouagadougou; tel. 33-47-23; telex 5226; f. 1977; cap. 3,086m. francs CFA; storage, purification and distribution of water; Pres. Minister of Water Resources; Dir-Gen. OUANDÉ VICTOR OUEDRAOGO.

Office National de l'Exploitation des Ressources Animales: BP 7058, Ouagadougou; tel. 33-68-41; Dir-Gen. ROGER MOUSSA TALL.

CHAMBER OF COMMERCE

Chambre de Commerce, d'Industrie et d'Artisanat du Burkina: BP 502, Ouagadougou; tel. 33-61-48; telex 5268; br. in Bobo-Dioulasso; Pres. PAUL BALKOUMA; Sec.-Gen. DOMINIQUE I. KONATE.

DEVELOPMENT AGENCIES

Caisse Centrale de Coopération Economique (CCCE): ave Binger, BP 529, Ouagadougou; tel. 33-60-76; telex 5271; Dir FRANÇOIS PEYREDIEU DU CHARLAT.

Mission Française de Coopération: BP 510, Ouagadougou; tel. 33-43-77; telex 5211; centre for administering bilateral aid from France under co-operation agreements signed in 1961; Dir FRANÇOIS MIMIN.

EMPLOYERS' ORGANIZATIONS

Association Professionnelle des Banques et Établissements Financiers (APBEF): Ouagadougou; Pres. NOËL KABORÉ.

Groupement Professionnel des Industriels: BP 810, Ouagadougou; tel. 33-28-81; f. 1974; Pres. MARTIAL OUEDRAOGO.

Syndicat des Commerçants Importateurs et Exportateurs (SCIMPEX): BP 552, Ouagadougou; Pres. PIERRE LINAS.

Syndicat des Entrepreneurs et Industriels: BP 446, Ouagadougou.

CO-OPERATIVES

Groupement Coopératif de Ventes Internationales des Produits du Burkina (Cooproduits): BP 91, Ouagadougou; telex 5224; agricultural co-operative; exports seeds, nuts and gum arabic; Chair. and Man. Dir KÉOULÉ NACOULIMA.

Groupement des Petits Commerçants: BP 952, Ouagadougou; Pres. GABRIEL KABORÉ.

BURKINA FASO

Société de Commercialisation du Burkina 'Faso Yaar': BP 531, Ouagadougou; tel. 33-30-07; telex 5274; BP 375, Bobo-Dioulasso; tel. 99-04-23; f. 1967; 97% state-owned marketing organization with 30 retail outlets; Pres. Minister of Trade and Supplies; Man. Dir MAMADOU KARAMBIRI.

Union des Coopératives Agricoles et Maraîchères du Burkina (UCOBAM): BP 277, Ouagadougou; tel. 33-44-22; telex 5287; f. 1968; agricultural marketing organization.

TRADE UNIONS

There are over 20 autonomous trade unions and they constitute a considerable political force. The four trade union syndicates are:

Confédération Nationale des Travailleurs (CNT): BP 381, Ouagadougou; Pres. EMANUEL OUEDRAOGO.

Confédération Syndicale Burkinabê (CSB): BP 299, Ouagadougou; affiliated to Ligue patriotique pour le développement (LIPAD); mainly public service unions; Sec.-Gen. SOUMANE TOURÉ.

Organisation des Syndicats Libres: BP 99, Ouagadougou; f. 1960; 2,500 mems in seven affiliated unions; affiliated to International Confederation of Free Trade Unions (ICFTU); Sec.-Gen. BONIFACE KABORÉ.

Union Syndicale des Travailleurs: BP 301, Ouagadougou; f. 1958; 4,300 mems in 14 affiliated unions; Sec.-Gen. BONIFACE SOMDA.

Transport

RAILWAY

There is no independent railway administration in Burkina Faso.

La Régie du Chemin de Fer Abidjan-Niger (RAN): BP 192, Ouagadougou; telex 5273; Head Office: BP 1394, Abidjan, Ivory Coast; 1,173 km of track linking Ouagadougou via Bobo-Dioulasso with the coast at Abidjan (Ivory Coast); 517 km of this railway are in Burkina Faso.

ROADS

In 1983 there was a road network of 8,684 km, of which 4,576 km were main roads, and 4,108 km were regional or other roads.

The Ghana-Burkina Faso Road Transport Commission, based in Accra, was set up to implement the 1968 agreement on improving communications between the two countries.

An internationally aided programme of rehabilitation aiming to improve more than 6,000 km of roads, particularly in the northeast, and providing for the maintenance of 1,640 km, at a cost of US $73m., was begun in 1981. In 1986 plans were announced for a 133-km tarred road, to connect Bobo-Dioulasso to the Mali border via Orodara.

Régie X9: Ouagadougou; tel. 33-54-18; telex 5313; Dir NEBAMA KERE.

CIVIL AVIATION

There are international airports at Ouagadougou and Bobo-Dioulasso, 47 small airfields and 13 private airstrips. Major improvements to Bobo-Dioulasso airport were scheduled for completion by January 1987.

Air Afrique: Burkina Faso has a 7% share; see under Ivory Coast.

Air Burkina: ave Loudon, BP 1459, Ouagadougou; tel. 33-60-41; telex 203; f. 1967; state-owned airline with a monopoly of domestic services; also operates flights to and from Bamako (Mali), Lomé (Togo), Cotonou (Benin), Bouaké and Abidjan (Ivory Coast); Man. Dir BINTOU SANOGO; fleet of 1 Piper Navajo, 1 Cherokee 6, 1 DHG6 Twin Otter, 1 EMB 110 P2 Bandeirante, 1 Fokker F28.

Tourism

In 1985 there were 44,375 tourist arrivals at hotels, and receipts from tourism totalled 2,193m. francs CFA.

Division du Tourisme et de l'Hôtellerie: BP 624, Ouagadougou; tel. 33-67-64; telex 5555; Dir ABDOULAYE SANKARA.

BURMA

Introductory Survey

Location, Climate, Language, Religion, Flag, Capital

The Socialist Republic of the Union of Burma lies in the north-west region of South-East Asia, between the Tibetan plateau and the Malay peninsula. The country is bordered by Bangladesh and India to the north-west, by the People's Republic of China and Laos to the north-east and by Thailand to the south-east. The climate is tropical, with an average temperature of 27°C (80°F) and monsoon rains from May to October. Temperatures in Rangoon are generally between 18°C (65°F) and 36°C (97°F). The official language is Burmese, and there are also a number of tribal languages. About 85% of the population are Buddhists. There are animist, Muslim, Hindu and Christian minorities, and there is a Chinese community of some 350,000. The national flag is red, with a blue canton, in the upper hoist, bearing two ears of rice within a cogwheel and a ring of 14 five-pointed stars (one for each state), all in white. The capital is Rangoon.

Recent History

Burma was annexed to British India during the 19th century. It was detached from India and became a separate British dependency, with a limited measure of self-government, in 1937. Japanese forces invaded and occupied the country in February 1942, and Japan granted nominal independence under a government of anti-British nationalists. The Burmese nationalists later turned against Japan and aided Allied forces to reoccupy the country in May 1945. They formed a resistance movement, the Anti-Fascist People's Freedom League (AFPFL), led by Gen. Aung San, which became the main political force after the defeat of Japan. Aung San was assassinated in July 1947 and was succeeded by U Nu. On 4 January 1948 the Union of Burma became independent, outside the Commonwealth, with U Nu as the first Prime Minister.

During the first decade of independence Burma was a parliamentary democracy, and the Government successfully resisted revolts by communists and other insurgent groups. In 1958 the ruling AFPFL split, precipitating a political crisis. U Nu invited the Army Chief of Staff, Gen. Ne Win, to head a caretaker government and restore order. Elections in February 1960 gave an overwhelming majority to U Nu, leading the Union Party, and he resumed office in April. Despite its popularity, however, the U Nu administration proved ineffective, and on 2 March 1962 Gen. Ne Win intervened again, this time by staging a coup to depose U Nu. The new Revolutionary Council suspended the Constitution and instituted authoritarian control through the government-sponsored Burma Socialist Programme Party (BSPP). All other political parties were outlawed in March 1964.

The next decade saw the creation of a more centralized system of government, attempting to win popular support and nationalizing important sectors of the economy. A new constitution, aiming to transform Burma into a democratic socialist state, was approved in a national referendum in December 1973: new governmental organizations were created, the BSPP became the sole authorized political party and the country's name was changed to the Socialist Republic of the Union of Burma. In March 1974 the Revolutionary Council was dissolved and Ne Win (who, together with other senior army officers, became a civilian in 1972) was elected President by the State Council. Burma's economic problems increased, however, and in 1974 there were riots over food shortages and social injustices, and student demonstrations followed in 1976 as social problems increased. Following an attempted coup by members of the armed forces in July 1976, the BSPP reviewed its economic policies, and in 1977 a new plan was adopted to calm unrest.

An election in January 1978 gave Ne Win a mandate to rule for a further four years, and in March he was re-elected Chairman of the State Council. In May 1980 a general amnesty was declared for political prisoners and political exiles and rebels, including the former Prime Minister, U Nu, who returned from exile in July. More than 2,000 exiles surrendered but few senior members of the rebel forces did so.

General San Yu, formerly the Army Chief of Staff, was elected Chairman of the State Council in November 1981, following Ne Win's retirement from the office. Ne Win remained Chairman of the BSPP. The Citizenship Law of 1982 provided for three categories of citizen, and precluded members of non-indigenous races from holding important positions.

In November 1983 sentences of life imprisonment were passed on Brig. Tin Oo, formerly a member of the State Council and Joint General Secretary of the BSPP, and Col Bo Ni, formerly Minister of Home and Religious Affairs, for corruption and misuse of state funds. Brigadier Tin Oo had been regarded as Ne Win's likely successor as Chairman of the BSPP. In December two North Korean army officers were sentenced to death for their part in a bomb explosion in October, during an official visit to Rangoon by a governmental delegation from the Republic of Korea. Four South Korean cabinet ministers were among 21 people killed. Diplomatic relations with the Democratic People's Republic of Korea were severed in November 1983, and one of the assassins was executed in April 1985.

At the fifth congress of the BSPP, in August 1985, Ne Win was re-elected for a further four-year term as Chairman. U San Yu, the Chairman of the State Council, was elected to the new post of Vice-Chairman of the party. He thus moved up to second position in the party hierarchy, ahead of his closest rival U Aye Ko (who remained General Secretary of the BSPP), and established himself as Ne Win's likely successor. The congress also approved the enlargement of the party's Central Executive Committee, from 15 to 17 members, and of the Central Committee, from 260 to 280 members. Elections for a new People's Assembly were held in November. U Aye Ko was elected by the Assembly to the new position of Vice-President.

The largest of the various insurgent groups which have been fighting government forces since independence in 1948 is the Burmese Communist Party (BCP), which has gained control of areas in northern Burma and is well organized militarily. Secret peace talks with the Government in 1981 failed to reach any agreement, and government forces have continued to resist the guerrillas. The BCP formerly received support and aid from the Chinese Communist Party, but this funding gradually diminished, as the People's Republic of China began to encourage closer ties with the Burmese Government; this was illustrated by a state visit to China by U San Yu in October 1984, a reciprocal visit by the Chinese President to Rangoon in March 1985, and a visit to China later in the year by Ne Win, in his capacity as Chairman of the BSPP.

In early 1984 the Government launched one of its heaviest offensives in 35 years against the Karen National Liberation Army (KNLA), which has an estimated 4,000 armed members and is the military wing of the Karen National Union (KNU), founded in 1948. The KNU led a protracted campaign for the establishment of an independent state for the Karen ethnic group. There was serious fighting near the Thai border, with reportedly heavy casualties on both sides, and by 1986 more than 17,000 civilian refugees had been forced to flee into Thailand. The KNU is a member of the anti-communist National Democratic Front (NDF), an organization of nine ethnic minority groups, formed in 1975 (by five groups, originally) with the aim of making Burma a federal union and opposing both the Government and, initially, the BCP. In September 1983 the NDF was joined by the Kachin Independence Army (KIA), an insurgent group which, by 1985, numbered about 5,000 armed members. As well as Karen and Kachin, the NDF also comprises Karenni, Mon, Shan, Pa-O, Palaung, Wa and Arakanese parties. By May 1986 the various minority groups in the NDF had agreed to relinquish their individual demands for autonomy, in favour of a unified demand for a federal system of government. At the same time, the BCP withdrew its demand for a 'one-party' government in Burma, and entered into an alliance with the NDF: a development that was opposed by the KNU. An NDF congress was to be held in January 1987.

Part of the Government's campaign against the insurgent groups has been an attempt to intercept the smuggling routes on the border with Thailand, from which the insurgents have earned large levies from the sale of 'black market' goods. The consequent decline in financial revenue to support the guerrillas' attacks has caused them to turn instead to dealing in illicit drugs.

Defence spending, mainly for internal security, continues to account for a sizeable proportion of the budget; in 1985 it was estimated at 40% of total expenditure. About 1,500 government troops were killed during that year, but the Government also claimed to have captured 3,000 rebels, and to have killed another 9,000, between 1981 and 1985.

Government

Under the Constitution which came into force in January 1974, the highest organ of state is the 489-member People's Assembly (Pyithu Hluttaw), a legislative body elected by the people. From among its members the Assembly elects a State Council of 29 members. The Council is the chief decision-making organ of government and co-ordinates the work of central and local governmental organs. The Assembly also elects the Council of Ministers (which is responsible for the public administration of the State), the Council of People's Justices, the Council of People's Attorneys and the Council of People's Inspectors. Burma, formerly a federation, is now unitary, and is divided into States or Divisions. These, in turn, are divided into townships, and townships into wards or village-tracts. People's Councils exist for every sub-division at each of these levels.

Defence

Burma maintains a policy of neutrality and has no external defence treaties. The armed forces are largely engaged in internal security duties. In July 1986 the armed services totalled 186,000 men, of whom 170,000 were in the army, 7,000 in the navy and 9,000 in the air force. Paramilitary forces comprise a People's Police Force of 38,000 men and a People's Militia of 35,000 men. Defence expenditure allocated for 1986/87 was an estimated 1,800m. kyats.

Economic Affairs

Burma is potentially rich in agricultural, fishery, timber, mineral and water resources, of which large parts remain unexploited. In terms of average income, Burma is one of the poorest countries in Asia; in 1984, according to estimates by the World Bank, Burma's gross national product (GNP) per head, measured at average 1982–84 prices, was US $180. Between 1965 and 1984, it was estimated, GNP per head increased, in real terms, at an average rate of 2.3% per year. The average annual increase in overall gross domestic product (GDP) was 2.9% in 1965–73, rising to 6.0% in 1973–83.

The agricultural sector continues to use mainly traditional methods, and remains mostly in private ownership. In 1984/85 agriculture, including livestock and fishing, produced 46.5% of GDP and employed 64.8% of the working population. The output of the agricultural sector expanded, in real terms, by 4% in 1984/85. Rice, timber and other agricultural products have traditionally been the principal export items. Burma exported 803,000 tons of rice in 1984/85. Rice contributed 37% of total exports in 1984, but only 25% in 1985. Rice exports for 1985/86 were expected to total only 600,000 tons. In 1986 Burma exported an estimated 190,000 tons of rice to the USSR. The introduction of high-yield agricultural programmes, concentrating initially on rice, allowed the output of paddy rice to rise by more than 50% between 1975/76 and 1984/85, when the rice harvest reached a record 14.4m. metric tons. Estimates for 1985/86 showed that paddy production had risen only slightly to 15m. tons, although Burma has the potential to increase its rice output significantly by introducing double cropping. In 1984/85 52.2% of rice-growing land was sown with high-yielding varieties. The Government has also encouraged diversification into other crops, including jute, maize, tobacco and pulses.

Agricultural exports accounted for nearly 53% of total export earnings in 1983/84. Burma has the world's largest stands of broadleaved (hardwood) trees. In 1984/85 the total output of broadleaved roundwood was 1.47m. cu tons (each of 50 cu ft or 1.416 cu m), including 400,000 cu tons of teak. Export earnings from timber reached 1,003m. kyats in 1984/85, compared with 281m. kyats in 1975/76. More than 57% of forestry production was in the private sector in 1982/83.

Burma has significant deposits of petroleum, tin, copper and coal. However, insurgent activity and an inefficient and expensive system of internal transport have prevented Burma from attaining many previous production levels. Since 1980 Burma has not been self-sufficient in crude petroleum, and production declined from a peak of 11m. barrels in 1979/80 to an estimated 9.7m. barrels in 1982/83, but recovered to 10.2m. barrels in 1983/84 and to 11.8m. barrels in 1984/85, according to official figures; in 1985/86 output declined to about 8.5m. barrels. Output in 1983/84 averaged 24,500 barrels per day (b/d), compared with the 30,000 b/d necessary for self-sufficiency. Three commercially viable oilfields were discovered in 1981, with estimated total recoverable reserves of 1,717m. barrels of crude petroleum, but more recent explorations have not been successful. Burma's output of natural gas has increased significantly, however, from 8.8m. cu ft in 1977/78 to 32.6m. cu ft in 1985/86. In 1982 offshore natural gas deposits were discovered in the Gulf of Martaban, but in 1986 the Government decided to abandon a development project for the area, owing mainly to lack of funds. Proven onshore reserves of natural gas totalled 2,000,000m. cu ft (57,000m. cu m), and there were also large undeveloped deposits in the region of the Irrawaddy delta. Since the 1970s, Burma has made increasing use of hydroelectric power as the main source of domestic energy, accounting for 55% of all electricity generated in 1985/86, while natural gas power stations accounted for 38%. Other minerals known to exist in Burma include tungsten, zinc and lead.

The manufacturing sector in Burma is small, accounting for 9.4% of the country's GDP in 1984/85, and for 8.3% of the labour force; it fell short of its target growth rate during the third Four-Year Plan (1978–82), increasing by 6.6% annually instead of the projected 12%. The sector grew by 10.5% (according to official estimates) in 1984/85, but by only 6% in 1985/86. The principal industrial activities are related to agriculture: food processing and the manufacture of tobacco products. In 1984/85 1,001.1m. kyats of public sector investment was for agro-based industries. Petroleum refining and textiles are also important. In 1983/84 state-owned factories were operating at 73% of their full capacity. Of the 41,357 factories and enterprises in operation in 1984/85, 38,910 were in private hands.

Industry, transport, internal and external trade, communications and finance have been nationalized since the 1962 revolution. In 1973 the Government relaxed its opposition to foreign investment and aid, and joined the Asian Development Bank (ADB, see p. 100), which, together with the World Bank (see p. 60), provides most of Burma's multilateral support. In February 1986 the ADB granted a US $35m. loan towards an edible oil project, and in May the IDA approved a $30m. credit for a grain storage and processing project. Foreign aid was expected to total 2,600m. kyats in 1986/87. Japan is the principal unilateral aid donor, and for 1984/85 promised loans of about $190m. and other credits amounting to $45m. In November 1985 the Japanese Government agreed to provide 49,050m. yen for eight projects including the construction of an integrated liquefied petroleum gas plant and the expansion of Rangoon international airport. In November 1984 the Government announced the formation of a joint-venture company with a West German firm, to develop and produce heavy industrial equipment, using technology which is unavailable in Burma. A total of 8,058.0m. kyats was invested in the state sector in 1984/85. Burma's external debt increased from $300m. in 1975 to approximately $3,300m. at 31 March 1984, of which slightly less than one-half was undisbursed, while foreign exchange reserves were only 816m. kyats at September 1984. By 1986 the external debt was estimated at $2,600m.–3,000m., with debt-service payments equivalent to nearly 60% of the country's earnings of foreign exchange. Burma's official reserves of foreign exchange declined from $253.7m. at the end of 1980 to only $33.9m. at the end of 1985. The annual trade deficit, which increased sharply in 1982/83 to 3,277.3m. kyats (owing to a rise of 12.5% in the value of imports and a fall of 12% in exports) improved considerably in 1983/84, narrowing to 1,777.8m. kyats. The 1986/87 trade deficit was projected at 1,400m. kyats. The continuing trade deficits have led to large balance-of-payments deficits (of 209.8m. kyats in 1985/86).

The third Four-Year Plan (1978–82) achieved an average annual GDP growth rate of 6.6% (with record growth of 8.3% in 1980/81), while inflation remained below 3% per year. The 1982–86 Four-Year Plan continued to emphasize the development of agriculture, rather than an increase in industrial capacity, and envisaged average annual growth of 6.2%. In 1986 the Government announced that an average annual GDP growth of 5.5% had been achieved during the Plan period. The annual rate of inflation was officially 4.4% in 1984/85 and 5% in 1985/86.

The Four-Year Plan for 1986–90 aimed to improve economic self-sufficiency, to encourage new investment projects, to diversify exports and to reduce the public-sector deficit and reliance on foreign aid and loans. In March 1986 the Plan's target for average GDP growth was revised from 6.1% to 4.5%. During the first year of the 1986–90 Plan, GDP was expected to grow by only 3.6%

The 1986/87 budget envisaged expenditure of 42,200m. kyats and revenue of 39,000m. kyats. A total of 32,900m. kyats was allocated to recurrent spending by the state economic sector, compared with 29,900m. kyats in the previous budget. Capital expenditure by the state economic organizations, however, was cut by 8%, to 4,900m. kyats. Defence, agriculture and education were also to receive substantial allocations. A total of 7,300m. kyats was to be provided for public-sector investment, of which 2,500m. kyats would be funded by foreign aid and loans.

The economy continues to suffer from extensive trading of goods in the 'black market'; in 1985 about two-thirds of such goods were smuggled in from Thailand, and total illegal trade was thought to have a turnover of up to 50% of official trading. In November 1985, in an effort to counter this, the Government withdrew certain large-denomination bank notes from circulation; this measure had only limited success.

Burma's principal trading partner is Japan, which supplied 33.7% of the value of imports and took 6.7% of exports in 1983/84, while the European Community provided 25.8% of imports and took 12.3% of exports. India was the largest market for Burma's exports, accounting for 12.8% of total export earnings.

Social Welfare
Burma has fairly well-developed health facilities but they are not comprehensive. In 1984/85 the country had 9,481 physicians and 4,326 nurses. There were 621 hospitals, with a total of 25,599 beds. In addition, there were 1,267 rural health centres. Health treatment is free. In 1984/85 state public health expenditure was 594.6m. kyats. About 500,000 workers are covered by social security insurance, and all workers are entitled to state pensions.

Education
Education is free, where available, but is not compulsory. In 1980, according to UNESCO estimates, adult illiteracy averaged 34% (males 24%, females 44%), a relatively small proportion for a low-income country. In 1977 an estimated 65% of children aged five to nine years (66% of boys; 64% of girls) attended primary schools, while 16% of those aged 10 to 15 were enrolled at secondary schools. The third Four-Year Plan (1978–82) aimed to make basic education accessible to all. In 1984/85 the total enrolment of students was 6.3m., of whom 4.9m. were at primary school level, 993,585 in secondary education, 257,897 in high schools, 14,570 in technical, vocational and teacher training colleges, and 174,279 in universities and colleges. There were 152,982 teachers in the 29,844 schools and colleges and the two universities in 1984/85. Emphasis is placed on vocational and technical training. In 1986/87 expenditure on education was estimated at 1,200m. kyats.

Tourism
Tourism is undeveloped. Rangoon, Mandalay and Pagan possess outstanding palaces, Buddhist temples and shrines. In 1985 an estimated 30,779 tourists visited Burma.

Public Holidays
1987: 4 January (Independence Day), 12 February (Union Day), 2 March (Peasants' Day, anniversary of the 1962 coup), March* (Full Moon of Tabaung), 27 March (Armed Forces Day), April* (Maha Thingyan—Water Festival), 17 April (Burmese New Year), 1 May (Workers' Day), May* (Full Moon of Kason), 19 July (Martyrs' Day), August* (Full Moon of Waso), 6 August† (Id al-Adha—Feast of the Sacrifice), October* (Full Moon of Thadingyut), October* (Devali), November* (Tazaungdaing Festival), 25 November (National Day), 25 December (Christmas Day).

1988: 4 January (Independence Day), 12 February (Union Day), 2 March (Peasants' Day, anniversary of the 1962 coup), March* (Full Moon of Tabaung), 27 March (Armed Forces Day), April* (Maha Thingyan—Water Festival), 17 April (Burmese New Year), 1 May (Workers' Day), May* (Full Moon of Kason), 19 July (Martyrs' Day), 25 July† (Id al-Adha—Feast of the Sacrifice), August* (Full Moon of Waso), October* (Full Moon of Thadingyut), October* (Devali), November* (Tazaungdaing Festival), 23 November (National Day), 25 December (Christmas Day).

* A number of Burmese holidays depend on lunar sightings.

† These holidays are regulated by the Islamic calendar and may vary by one or two days from the dates given.

Weights and Measures
The imperial system is in force.

Currency and Exchange Rates
100 pyas = 1 kyat.
Exchange rates (30 September 1986):
 £1 sterling = 10.146 kyats;
 US $1 = 7.012 kyats.

Statistical Survey

Sources (unless otherwise stated): *Report to the Pyithu Hluttaw on the Financial, Economic and Social Conditions of the Socialist Republic of the Union of Burma* (annual), Ministry of Planning and Finance, Ministers' Office, Rangoon; tel. (01) 76066.

Area and Population

AREA, POPULATION AND DENSITY

Area (sq km)	676,552*
Population (census results)	
31 March 1973	28,885,867
1–5 April 1983†	
Males	17,507,837
Females	17,798,352
Total	35,306,189
Population (official estimates at 30 September)	
1982	34,976,000
1983	35,680,000
1984	36,392,000
Density (per sq km) at 30 September 1984	53.8

* 261,218 sq miles.
† Figures exclude 7,716 Burmese citizens (5,704 males; 2,012 females) abroad.

PRINCIPAL TOWNS (population estimates, 1983)

Rangoon	2,458,712	Moulmein	219,991
Mandalay	532,895	Akyab	143,000
Bassein	335,000	Taunggyi	80,678*

* Population at 1973 census.

BIRTHS AND DEATHS

Crude birth rate 28.4 per 1,000 in 1984; crude death rate 8.7 per 1,000 in 1984 (estimates).

EMPLOYMENT
(official estimates, '000 persons, year ending 31 March 1985)

	State sector	Co-operative and private sector	Total
Agriculture	80	9,312	9,392
Livestock and fishing	16	182	198
Forestry	93	89	182
Mining and quarrying	72	13	85
Manufacturing	178	1,056	1,234
Electricity, gas and water	16	—	16
Construction	162	78	240
Transport and communications	114	374	488
Social services	231	84	315
Administration	541	29	570
Trade	68	1,376	1,444
Activities not adequately defined	—	628	628
Total	**1,571**	**13,221**	**14,792**

Agriculture

PRINCIPAL CROPS ('000 metric tons)

	1982	1983	1984
Wheat	124	130	191
Rice (paddy)	14,373	14,392	14,500*
Maize	206	239	360
Millet	85	87	88*
Potatoes	124	140	155
Sugar cane	2,736	3,718	3,842
Pulses	498	469	573
Groundnuts (in shell)	573	550	601
Cottonseed	64	65	72
Cotton (lint)	32	33	36
Sesame seed	180	198	216
Tobacco (leaves)	51	57	62
Jute and substitutes	33	64	55
Natural rubber	16	17	16
Vegetables (incl. melons)	1,949	1,967	2,022
Fruit (excl. melons)*	1,043	1,068	1,083

* FAO estimate.
Source: FAO, *Production Yearbook*.

LIVESTOCK ('000 head, year ending September)

	1982	1983	1984*
Cattle	9,147	9,338	9,550
Buffaloes	2,018	2,049	2,100
Pigs	2,883	2,734	2,750
Sheep	300†	370†	400
Goats	873†	951†	1,000

Chickens (million): 29 in 1982; 31 in 1983; 32* in 1984.
Ducks (million): 5 in 1982; 6 in 1983; 6* in 1984.

* FAO estimates. † Unofficial estimate.
Source: FAO, *Production Yearbook*.

LIVESTOCK PRODUCTS ('000 metric tons)

	1982	1983	1984
Beef and veal*	77	78	79
Buffalo meat*	19	19	20
Mutton and lamb*	1	1	2
Goats' meat*	5	5	5
Pig meat*	81	82	83
Poultry meat	91	97	99*
Cows' milk	360†	440†	440*
Buffaloes' milk*	59	61	61
Goats' milk*	6	6	6
Butter and ghee*	7.9	9.7	9.7
Cheese*	22.6	27.6	27.6
Hen eggs	39.1	43.4	43.7*
Other poultry eggs	8.7	9.7	9.9*
Cattle and buffalo hides*	24.6	24.8	25.0

* FAO estimates. † Unofficial estimates.
Source: FAO, *Production Yearbook*.

Forestry

ROUNDWOOD REMOVALS
(FAO estimates, '000 cu m, excl. bark)

	1982	1983	1984
Sawlogs, veneer logs and logs for sleepers*	1,909	1,909	1,909
Other industrial wood	1,098	1,126	1,155
Fuel wood	15,623	16,023	16,433
Total	18,630	19,058	19,497

* Assumed to be unchanged from 1980 official estimate.
Source: FAO, *Yearbook of Forest Products*.

SAWNWOOD PRODUCTION ('000 cu m)

	1975	1976	1977
Sawnwood (incl. boxboards)	396	324	404
Railway sleepers*	11	11	11
Total	407	335	415

* FAO estimates.
1978–84: Annual production as in 1977 (FAO estimates).
Source: FAO, *Yearbook of Forest Products*.

Fishing

('000 metric tons, live weight)

	1982	1983	1984
Inland waters	133.8	142.9	144.0
Indian Ocean	450.6	442.9	468.9
Total catch	584.4	585.8	612.8

Source: FAO, *Yearbook of Fishery Statistics*.

Mining

(year ending 31 March)

	1982/83	1983/84*	1984/85*
Coal (long tons)	28,660	35,401	42,500
Crude petroleum ('000 barrels)	9,789	10,168	11,761
Natural gas (million cu ft)	17,400	18,190	24,796
Refined lead (long tons)	8,001	7,505	7,500
Antimonal lead (long tons)	273	308	250
Zinc concentrates (long tons)	7,650	7,775	9,000
Tin concentrates (long tons)	1,354	1,349	1,644
Tungsten concentrates (long tons)	592	875	997
Copper concentrates (long tons)	—	—	36,000
Iron ore (metric tons)	9,045	7,764	—
Refined silver ('000 troy oz)	576	576	576

* Provisional.
Note: Figures for metallic minerals refer to the metal content of ores mined.

Industry

SELECTED PRODUCTS (year ending 31 March)

		1982/83	1983/84*	1984/85*
Salt	('000 tons)	265	276	296
Sugar	('000 tons)	39	56	62
Cigarettes	(million)	3,189	2,882	2,760
Cotton yarn	('000 tons)	18.0	15.1	14.1
Soap	('000 metric tons)	49.9	34.6	48.2
Cement	('000 metric tons)	335	324	328
Motor spirit (petrol)	('000 gallons)	720	704	907
Kerosene	('000 gallons)	60	52	100
Diesel oil	('000 gallons)	992	939	1,178

* Provisional.

Finance

CURRENCY AND EXCHANGE RATES

Monetary Units
100 pyas = 1 kyat.

Denominations
Coins: 1, 5, 10, 25 and 50 pyas; 1 kyat.
Notes: 1, 5, 10, 15, 25, 35 and 75 kyats.

Sterling and Dollar Equivalents (30 September 1986)
£1 sterling = 10.146 kyats;
US $1 = 7.012 kyats;
1,000 kyats = £98.56 = $142.61.

Average Exchange Rate (kyats per US $)
1983   8.0355
1984   8.3855
1985   8.4749

Note: Since January 1975 the value of the kyat has been linked to the IMF's special drawing right (SDR). Since May 1977 the exchange rate has been fixed at a mid-point of SDR 1 = 8.5085 kyats.

CENTRAL GOVERNMENT BUDGET
(million kyats, year ending 31 March)

Revenue*	1980/81	1981/82	1982/83
Taxes on income and profits	182	195	239
Taxes on goods and services	2,611	2,844	2,937
Import duties	918	1,218	1,426
Property income	1,712	2,217	1,954
Fees, charges and sales	748	826	887
Sale of fixed assets	5	3	2
Total	6,176	7,303	7,445

* Excluding grants from abroad (million kyats): 415 in 1980/81; 269 in 1981/82; 658 in 1982/83.

Expenditure*	1980/81	1981/82	1982/83
General public services	928	1,004	1,151
Defence	1,342	1,529	1,499
Education	646	712	888
Health	323	429	550
Social security and welfare	415	411	467
Housing and community amenities	235	239	264
Economic services	2,062	2,504	2,780
Agriculture, forestry and fishing	1,442	1,841	2,033
Roads	288	305	371
Total (incl. others)	6,119	7,046	7,898
Current	4,653	5,497	5,637
Capital	1,466	1,549	2,261

* Excluding net lending (million kyats): −1 in 1980/81; −183 in 1981/82; −133 in 1982/83.

INTERNATIONAL RESERVES
(US $ million at 31 December)

	1983	1984	1985
Gold*	9.2	8.6	9.7
IMF special drawing rights	0.2	0.1	—
Reserve position in IMF	7.2	6.7	—
Foreign exchange	82.0	55.3	33.9
Total	98.6	70.7	43.6

* Valued at SDR 35 per troy ounce.
Source: IMF, *International Financial Statistics*.

MONEY SUPPLY
(million kyats at 31 December)

	1983	1984	1985
Currency outside banks	10,165	11,768	10,504

Source: IMF, *International Financial Statistics*.

COST OF LIVING
(Consumer Price Index for Rangoon. Base: 1978 = 100)

	1981/82	1982/83	1983/84
Food and beverages	105.4	111.5	120.7
Tobacco	103.4	105.6	109.1
Fuel and light	136.4	136.2	139.0
Clothing	99.6	111.2	113.0
Rent and repairs	103.6	114.8	111.8
Miscellaneous goods and services	110.1	112.1	113.4
All items	107.8	113.4	119.8

Source: Central Statistical Organization.

BURMA   Statistical Survey

NATIONAL ACCOUNTS
(million kyats at current prices, year ending 31 March)

National Income and Product

	1982/83	1983/84	1984/85
Compensation of employees	17,812	18,971	20,596
Operating surplus	20,470	21,949	24,225
Domestic factor incomes	38,282	40,920	44,821
Consumption of fixed capital	4,166	4,528	4,930
Gross domestic product (GDP) at factor cost	42,448	45,448	49,751
Indirect taxes, less subsidies	4,363	4,336	4,291
GDP in purchasers' values	46,811	49,784	54,042
Net factor income from abroad	−347	−510	−549
Gross national product	46,464	49,274	53,493
Less Consumption of fixed capital	4,166	4,528	4,930
National income in market prices	42,298	44,746	48,563

Source: UN, *Monthly Bulletin of Statistics*.

Expenditure on the Gross Domestic Product

	1982/83	1983/84	1984/85
Final consumption expenditure	39,747	42,831	46,028
Increase in stocks	331	−277	−42
Gross fixed capital formation	10,044	9,054	10,052
Total domestic expenditure	50,122	51,608	56,038
Exports of goods and services	3,003	3,373	3,654
Less Imports of goods and services	6,314	5,197	5,650
GDP in purchasers' values	46,811	49,784	54,042

Source: UN, *Monthly Bulletin of Statistics*.

Gross Domestic Product by Economic Activity

	1982/83	1983/84	1984/85
Agriculture	18,440	19,642	21,016
Livestock and fishing	3,204	3,562	4,132
Forestry	675	715	780
Mining and quarrying	501	490	607
Manufacturing	4,350	4,563	5,096
Electricity	210	227	267
Construction	834	872	951
Wholesale and retail trade	11,512	12,203	13,249
Transport	1,679	1,790	1,863
Communications	155	177	180
Financial institutions	1,095	1,172	1,229
Government services	2,215	2,335	2,555
Other services	1,941	2,038	2,118
GDP in purchasers' values	46,811	49,784	54,042

BALANCE OF PAYMENTS (US $ million)

	1982	1983	1984
Merchandise exports f.o.b.	422.8	375.2	364.1
Merchandise imports f.o.b.	−913.0	−728.2	−595.9
Trade balance	−490.2	−353.0	−231.7
Exports of services	95.3	68.1	66.4
Imports of services	−170.0	−141.3	−149.6
Balance on goods and services	−564.9	−426.2	−314.9
Unrequited transfers (net)	66.2	82.2	80.7
Current balance	−498.7	−344.1	−234.2
Long-term capital (net)	328.9	213.4	195.9
Short-term capital (net)	11.3	32.2	0.2
Net errors and omissions	25.5	72.4	23.4
Total (net monetary movements)	−133.0	−26.1	−14.7
Valuation changes (net)	−13.8	1.6	−1.0
Changes in reserves	−146.7	−24.5	−15.7

Source: IMF, *International Financial Statistics*.

BURMA
Statistical Survey

External Trade

PRINCIPAL COMMODITIES
(million kyats, year ending 31 March)

Imports c.i.f.	1981/82	1982/83*	1983/84*
Milk and milk products	84.4	67.5	44.8
Animal and vegetable oils, fats and waxes	88.5	43.3	6.8
Pharmaceuticals	130.7	129.1	53.4
Chemicals	133.0	144.9	118.7
Fertilizers	368.6	164.1	107.6
Cotton yarn	60.4	75.7	50.1
Refined petroleum products	68.2	70.1	7.6
Scientific instruments	180.1	84.3	38.2
Base metals and base metal manufactures	699.1	593.6	454.8
Machinery (non-electric)	2,063.7	2,978.2	720.8
Transport equipment	852.3	588.6	376.0
Electric machinery	228.9	425.4	204.9
Paper and paper products	115.2	102.4	77.0
Rubber manufactures	77.2	50.1	69.6
Total (incl. others)	5,611.3	6,313.6	5,197.3

Exports f.o.b.	1981/82	1982/83*	1983/84*
Rice and rice products	1,509.4	1,143.5	1,395.6
Matpe	134.7	111.3	138.9
Prawns	77.6	87.8	44.9
Teak	707.3	730.8	839.7
Hardwood	65.1	73.1	44.1
Base metals and ores	264.7	208.2	301.4
Silver	38.2	42.9	53.5
Oilcakes	41.0	51.6	55.9
Raw jute	28.3	4.7	—
Raw rubber	81.3	60.3	62.6
Cement	37.8	21.6	33.9
Total (incl. others)	3,452.8	3,036.3	3,419.5

* Provisional.
Source: Central Statistical Organization.

PRINCIPAL TRADING PARTNERS
(million kyats, year ending 31 March)

Imports	1981/82	1982/83	1983/84*
African countries	96.0	3.6	99.8
Australia, New Zealand and Pacific	80.5	86.0	99.9
Bangladesh	45.0	48.6	31.0
China, People's Repub.	180.4	250.5	237.1
Eastern Europe	490.4	322.6	843.8
EEC	1,415.8	1,809.9	1,340.1
India	35.1	46.7	15.6
Japan	2,107.7	2,366.7	1,752.4
North America	284.7	514.3	207.8
South-East Asian countries	381.5	426.7	251.4
Total (incl. others)	5,611.3	6,313.6	5,197.3

Exports	1981/82	1982/83	1983/84*
African countries	844.3	211.1	271.3
Bangladesh	92.9	129.1	67.9
China, People's Repub.	29.2	8.4	30.5
Eastern Europe	153.4	29.4	1.0
EEC	302.4	528.1	419.3
India	57.8	121.3	437.8
Japan	329.4	246.1	227.5
Middle East	82.2	97.3	181.9
North America	13.6	6.7	13.5
Pakistan	43.1	30.2	21.7
Sri Lanka	183.3	349.4	167.2
Total (incl. others)	3,452.8	3,036.3	3,419.5

* Provisional.
1984/85: Total imports 5,650.0m. kyats; Total exports 3,653.8m. kyats (provisional).

Transport

RAILWAYS (BURMA RAILWAYS CORPN) ('000)

	1982/83	1983/84*	1984/85*
Passengers	62,111	61,198	63,428
Passenger-miles	2,341,642	2,283,283	2,403,936
Freight tons	2,257	2,208	2,208
Freight-ton-miles	353,235	350,308	333,320

* Provisional.

ROAD TRAFFIC (ROAD TRANSPORT CORPN) ('000)

	1982/83	1983/84*	1984/85*
Passengers	154,943	111,420	118,529
Passenger-miles	789,060	648,402	754,984
Freight tons	1,248	1,217	1,238
Freight-ton-miles	157,062	147,602	150,072

* Provisional.

INLAND WATER TRANSPORT CORPN ('000)

	1982/83	1983/84*	1984/85*
Passengers	19,134	18,618	19,715
Passenger-miles	352,828	377,026	415,647
Freight tons	1,870	2,128	2,028
Freight-ton-miles	236,553	263,026	279,841

* Provisional.

INTERNATIONAL SEA-BORNE SHIPPING
('000 metric tons, year ending 31 March)

	1981/82	1982/83	1983/84
Freight loaded	1,229	1,078	1,124
Freight unloaded	692	759	475

CIVIL AVIATION (BURMA AIRWAYS CORPN)
('000, internal and external flights)

	1982/83	1983/84*	1984/85*
Passengers	552	501	422
Passenger-miles	138,795	134,462	118,402
Freight tons	5.0	5.1	3.5
Freight-ton-miles	1,528	1,411	1,604

* Provisional.

Communications Media

	1982/83	1983/84*	1984/85*
Telephones in use	50,312	51,304	52,604

* Provisional.

Tourism

	1982	1983	1984*
Number of visitors	29,910	29,668	28,575
Tourist revenue (million kyats)	75.4	82.9	80.1

* Provisional.

Education

(1984/85, provisional)

	Institutions	Teachers	Students
Primary schools	27,499	104,754	4,855,963
Middle schools	1,562	28,024	993,585
High schools	676	13,644	257,897
Teacher training colleges	18	438	3,834
Agricultural, technical and vocational schools and institutes	56	598	10,736
Universities and colleges	35	5,524	174,279

Directory

The Constitution

The Constitution came into force on 3 January 1974, following a national referendum held in December 1973. It is the basic law of the State. A summary of the main provisions follows:

GENERAL PRINCIPLES

The Socialist Republic of the Union of Burma is a sovereign, independent, socialist state. There shall be only one political party, the Burma Socialist Programme Party. Sovereign power rests with the people as represented by the People's Assembly. The State is the ultimate owner of all natural resources and shall exploit them in the interests of the people. The means of production shall be nationalized. National groups shall have the right to practise their religion and culture freely within the law and the national interest. The State shall follow an independent and peaceful foreign policy.

STATE ORGANS

The structure of the State is based on a system of local autonomy under central leadership. Government operates at four levels of administration: wards or village tracts, townships, states or divisions and at national level.

People's Assembly (Pyithu Hluttaw)

A unicameral legislature, the highest organ of State power, it exercises sovereign power on behalf of the people. It is elected directly by secret ballot for a term of four years. Regular sessions take place twice a year, the intervening period being no more than eight months. The People's Assembly may be dissolved if three-quarters of its members agree to it. It may delegate executive and judicial power to central and local state organs. It has the power to enact economic legislation, declare war and peace and the right to call referenda. It may constitute committees and commissions and invest them with powers and duties. Under certain circumstances the People's Assembly may dissolve the People's Councils.

State Council

The State Council is composed of 29 members including one representative from each of the 14 states and divisions, and the Prime Minister, elected by the People's Assembly from its members. The State Council elects a Chairman from its members who becomes President of the Union and represents the State. The term of office of the Council and the President is the same as that of the People's Assembly. The State Council is vested with executive power to carry out the provisions of the Constitution. It has the power to convene the People's Assembly in consultation with the panel of Chairmen of the Assembly. It interprets and promulgates legislation, makes decisions concerning diplomatic relations, international treaties and agreements. It is responsible for the appointment of the heads of the public services. The State Council has the power to grant pardons and amnesties. It may make orders with the force of law between sessions of the People's Assembly, and may order military action in defence of the State, declare a state of emergency and martial law subject to the subsequent approval of the People's Assembly.

Council of Ministers

The highest organ of public administration, elected by the People's Assembly from a list of candidates submitted by the State Council.

BURMA

Directory

Its term of office is the same as that of the People's Assembly. The Prime Minister is elected by the Council of Ministers from among its members. It is responsible for the management of public administration and drafting economic measures and submitting them to the People's Assembly for enactment.

Council of People's Justices
The highest judicial organ. Elected by the People's Assembly from a list of its members submitted by the State Council. Its term of office is the same as that of the People's Assembly. The People's Councils form judges' committees at local levels.

Council of People's Attorneys
Elected by the People's Assembly from a list of members submitted by the State Council. Its term of office is the same as that of the People's Assembly. It is responsible to the People's Assembly for directing state, divisional and township law officers, protecting the rights of the people and supervising the central and local organs of state power.

Council of People's Inspectors
Elected by the People's Assembly from a list of candidates submitted by the State Council. Its term of office is the same as that of the People's Assembly. It is responsible to the People's Assembly for the inspection of the activities of the local organs of state power, ministries and public bodies. There are also local inspectorates at each administrative level, responsible to the People's Council concerned.

People's Councils
The term of office of the People's Councils is the same as that of the People's Assembly. They are elected at different levels according to law. They are responsible for local economic and social affairs and public administration, the administration of local justice, local security, defence and the maintenance of law and order. Each of the People's Councils elects an executive committee to implement its decisions. The Executive Committees each elect a Chairman and a Secretary from among themselves who are also the Chairman and Secretary of the People's Council concerned.

FUNDAMENTAL RIGHTS AND DUTIES OF CITIZENS
All citizens are equal before the law irrespective of race, religion, sex or other distinction. Every citizen has the right to enjoy the benefits derived from labour, to inherit, to settle anywhere in the State according to law, to medical treatment, education and rest and recreation. Freedom of thought, conscience and expression are upheld subject to the law and the interests of state security. All citizens are bound to abstain from undermining the sovereignty and security of the State and the socialist system.

ELECTORAL SYSTEM
All citizens over 18 years are entitled to vote. Those whose parents are both citizens may stand for election to office having attained the age of 20 years (Village and Township Councils), 24 years (State and Divisional Councils), 28 years (People's Assembly). Members of religious orders and others disqualified by law are prohibited from voting or standing for election.

The Government

HEAD OF STATE
President, Chairman of the State Council: U SAN YU (elected by the People's Assembly, 9 November 1981; re-elected 4 November 1985).
Vice-President: U AYE KO.

STATE COUNCIL
(November 1986)

Chairman: U SAN YU.
Vice-Chairman: U AYE KO.
Secretary: U SEIN LWIN.
Members: U KHIN AYE, U CHIT HLAING, U JAP TU, U SOE, U SAI AUNG TUN, U SAN MAUNG, U ZAW WIN, U TIN AUNG, U TUN TIN, U TUN YI, U TUN YIN LAW, U VAN KULH, U BA HLA, U BA THAW, U BU RAL, Dr MAUNG MAUNG, U MAHN SAN MYAT SHWE, U HLA TUN, U VAMTHU HASHIM, U THA KYAW, U THAUNG TIN, U THAN SEIN, U AUNG SINT, Thura U AUNG PE, U OHN KYI, U MAUNG MAUNG KHA.

COUNCIL OF MINISTERS
(November 1986)

Prime Minister: U MAUNG MAUNG KHA.
Deputy Prime Minister and Minister for Planning and Finance: Thura U TUN TIN.
Deputy Prime Minister and Minister for Defence: Gen. Thura KYAW HTIN.
Minister for Foreign Affairs: U YE GAUNG.
Minister for Energy: U SEIN TUN.
Minister for Transport and Communications: Thura U SAW PRU.
Minister for Industry I: U TINT SWE.
Minister for Mines: U THAN TIN.
Minister for Home and Religious Affairs: U MIN GAUNG.
Minister for Industry II: U MAUNG CHO.
Minister for Trade: U KHIN MAUNG GYI.
Minister for Education: U KYAW NYEIN.
Minister for Information and Culture: U AUNG KYAW MYINT.
Minister for Labour and Social Affairs: U OHN KYAW.
Minister for Health: U TUN WAI.
Minister for Co-operatives: U THAN HLAING.
Minister for Livestock Breeding and Fisheries: Rear-Adm. MAUNG MAUNG WIN.
Minister for Construction: Maj.-Gen. MYINT LWIN.
Minister for Agriculture and Forests: Brig.-Gen. THAN NYUNT.

MINISTRIES
President's Office: Ady Rd, Rangoon; tel. (01) 60776.
Prime Minister's Office: Ministers' Office, Rangoon; tel. (01) 83742.
Office of the State Council: 15–16 Windermere Park, Rangoon; tel. (01) 32318.
Ministry of Agriculture and Forests: Ministers' Office, Rangoon; tel. (01) 75080.
Ministry of Construction: Ministers' Office, Rangoon; tel. (01) 76773.
Ministry of Co-operatives: 259/263 Bogyoke Aung San St, Rangoon; tel. (01) 77096.
Ministry of Culture: 26/42 Pansodan St, Rangoon; tel. (01) 81321.
Ministry of Defence: Signal Pagoda Rd, Rangoon; tel. (01) 71611; telex 21316.
Ministry of Education: Ministers' Office, Rangoon; tel. (01) 78597.
Ministry of Energy: Rangoon.
Ministry of Foreign Affairs: Prome Court, Prome Rd, Rangoon; tel. (01) 83333; telex 21313.
Ministry of Health: Ministers' Office, Rangoon; tel. (01) 72075.
Ministry of Home and Religious Affairs: Ministers' Office, Rangoon; tel. (01) 71952.
Ministry of Industry (No. I): 192 Kaba Aye Pagoda Rd, Rangoon; tel. (01) 50701; telex 21513.
Ministry of Industry (No. II): Ministers' Office, Rangoon; tel. (01) 78142; telex 21500.
Ministry of Information: Ministers' Office, Rangoon; tel. (01) 71409.
Ministry of Labour and Social Welfare: Ministers' Office, Rangoon; tel. (01) 78350.
Ministry of Livestock Breeding and Fisheries: Ministers' Office, Rangoon; tel. (01) 80398.
Ministry of Mines: Ministers' Office, Rangoon; tel. (01) 73996.
Ministry of Planning and Finance: Ministers' Office, Rangoon; tel. (01) 76066.
Ministry of Trade: 228/240 Strand Rd, Rangoon; tel. (01) 73613; telex 21338.
Ministry of Transport and Communications: Ministers' Office, Rangoon; tel. (01) 78438.

Legislature

PYITHU HLUTTAW
(People's Assembly)

Following national elections early in 1974, the inaugural session of the Pyithu Hluttaw was convened on 2 March 1974. New elections were held in November 1985. All the candidates were members of the BSPP. There are 489 seats and sessions are presided over by the members of a panel of chairmen in rotation.

Political Organizations

Burma Socialist Programme Party (BSPP) (Lanzin Party): 35/37 Signal Pagoda Rd, Rangoon; tel. 78180; f. 1962 by the Revolutionary Council to implement its policies; the only recognized political party; 17-mem. Cen. Exec. Cttee and 280-mem. Cen. Cttee; 2.3m. full mems (1985); Chair. U Ne Win; Vice-Chair. U San Yu; Gen. Sec. U Aye Ko; Jt Gen. Sec. U Sein Lwin.

Central Executive Committee:

U Ne Win
U San Yu
U Aye Ko
U Sein Lwin
Gen. Thura Kyaw Htin
U Chit Hlaing
Thura U Saw Pru
Lt-Gen. Saw Maung
U Sein Tun
U Tint Swe
Thura U Tun Tin
U Tun Yi
U Min Gaung
U Maung Maung Kha
U Ye Gaung
U Hla Tun
U Than Tin

Various insurgent groups are in conflict with the BSPP Government, including the following:

Burma Communist Party (BCP)—White Flag Party: f. 1946 when Communist Party (f. 1939) split into White and Red Flag factions; advocates Stalinist policies; reportedly the strongest insurgent group with up to 20,000 mems; fmrly supported by the Chinese Communist Party; Chair. of Central Cttee Thakin Ba Thein Tin.

National Democratic Front (NDF): f. 1975; aims to overthrow Burma's one-party military dictatorship and to establish a federal union based on national self-determination; comprised nine organizations (each representing an ethnic minority group) in 1986: the Karen National Union (KNU; f. 1948; Pres. Gen. Bo Mya; Military wing: Karen National Liberation Army—KNLA), Karenni National Progressive Party, New Mon State Party, Shan State Progress Party (Military wing: Shan State Army—SSA), Kachin Independence Army (KIA; Political wing: Kachin Independence Organization—KIO), Arakan Liberation Party (ALP; Military wing: Arakan Liberation Army, f. 1974), Pa-O National Organization, Palaung State Liberation Organization (Military wing: Palaung State Liberation Army) and the Wa group; Pres. Gen. Bo Mya.

In May 1986 the BCP and the NDF agreed to form a united opposition front.

Diplomatic Representation

EMBASSIES IN BURMA

Australia: 88 Strand Rd, Rangoon; tel. (01) 80711; telex 21301; Ambassador: Francis W. S. Milne.

Bangladesh: 340 Prome Rd, Rangoon; tel. (01) 32900; telex 21320; Ambassador: Mustafizur Rahman.

China, People's Republic: 1 Pyidaungsu Yeiktha Rd, Rangoon; tel. (01) 72087; telex 21346; Ambassador: Zhou Mingji.

Czechoslovakia: 326 Prome Rd, Rangoon; tel. (01) 30515; telex 21337; Ambassador: Josef Bozek.

Egypt: 81 Pyidaungsu Yeiktha Rd, Rangoon; tel. (01) 81011; Ambassador: Mahmud Ismail Sayid Issa.

France: 102 Pyidaungsu Yeiktha Rd, POB 858, Rangoon; tel. (01) 82122; telex 21314; Ambassador: Yves Rodrigue.

German Democratic Republic: 18e Inya Rd, Rangoon; tel. (01) 30933; telex 21501; Chargé d'affaires: Hans Laabs.

Germany, Federal Republic: 32 Natmauk Rd, POB 12, Rangoon; tel. (01) 50477; telex 21401; Ambassador: Dr Freiherr Marschall von Bieberstein.

India: 545–547 Merchant St, Rangoon; tel. (01) 82933; Ambassador: Dr I. P. Singh.

Indonesia: 100 Pyidaungsu Rd, Rangoon; tel. (01) 81714; Ambassador: Soeharto Pontoatnadjo.

Israel: 49 Prome Rd, Rangoon; tel. (01) 84188; telex 21319; Ambassador: Itiel Pann.

Italy: 3 Lewis Rd, Golden Valley, Rangoon; tel. (01) 30966; telex 21317; Ambassador: (vacant).

Japan: 100 Natmauk Rd, Rangoon; tel. (01) 52288; telex 21400; Ambassador: Masao Tsukamoto.

Korea, Republic: 97 University Ave, Rangoon; tel. (01) 30655; telex 21324; Ambassador: Sang Yul Lee.

Laos: 17 University Ave, Rangoon; tel. (01) 33371; telex 21519; Ambassador: Saly Khamsy.

Malaysia: 65 Windsor Rd, Rangoon; tel. (01) 31677; telex 21321; Ambassador: Mohd Amir bin Jaafar.

Nepal: 16 Natmauk Yeiktha Rd, Rangoon; tel. (01) 50633; telex 21402; Ambassador: Dr Dibya Deo Bhatt.

Pakistan: 18 Windsor Rd, Rangoon; tel. (01) 84788; Ambassador: Afzal Mahmood.

Philippines: 56 Prome Rd, 6½ Mile, Rangoon; tel. (01) 32080; Ambassador: Alfredo L. Almendrala.

Romania: 71 Mission Rd, Rangoon; tel. (01) 75891; telex 21323; Chargé d'affaires: Alexandra Voinea.

Singapore: 287 Prome Rd, Rangoon; tel. (01) 33129; Chargé d'affaires: David H. L. Low.

Sri Lanka: 34 Fraser Rd, Rangoon; tel. (01) 82066; Ambassador: W. K. M. de Silva.

Thailand: 91 Prome Rd, Rangoon; tel. (01) 82471; telex 21341; Ambassador: Thongchan Chotikasathien.

USSR: 38 Newlyn Rd, Rangoon; tel. (01) 72427; telex 21331; Ambassador: Sergei Pavlovich Pavlov.

United Kingdom: 80 Strand Rd, POB 638, Rangoon; tel. (01) 81700; telex 21216; Ambassador: Martin R. Morland.

USA: 581 Merchant St, Rangoon; tel. (01) 82055; Ambassador: Daniel A. O'Donohue.

Viet-Nam: 40 Komin Kochin Rd, Rangoon; tel. (01) 50361; Ambassador: Pham Manh Diem.

Yugoslavia: 39 Windsor Rd, Rangoon; tel. (01) 30399; telex 21325; Ambassador: Branko Vuletić.

Judicial System

A new judicial structure was established in March 1974. Its highest organ, composed of members of the People's Assembly, is the Council of People's Justices. This Council, with three members of it selected for each occasion, serves as the central Court of Justice. Below this Council are the state, divisional, township, ward and village tract courts formed with members of local People's Councils.

Chairman of the Council of People's Justices: U Tin Aung Hein.

Religion

Freedom of religious belief and practice is guaranteed. About 85% of the population are Buddhists; the remainder are animists (5%), Muslims (4%), Hindus (4%) and Christians (2%).

CHRISTIANITY

The Anglican Communion

Anglicans are adherents of the Church of the Province of Burma, comprising four dioceses.

Archbishop of Burma and Bishop of Rangoon: Most Rev. Gregory Hla Gyaw, Bishopscourt, 140 Pyidaungsu Yeiktha Rd, Dagon PO, Rangoon; tel. (01) 72668.

Protestant Churches

Burma Baptist Convention: 143 St John's Rd, Rangoon; tel. (01) 72419; Pres. Rev. U Chit Nyi; Gen. Sec. Rev. Zau Yaw.

Burma Methodist Church: Methodist Headquarters, 22 Signal Pagoda Rd, Rangoon; Bishop C. F. Chu.

Lutheran Bethlehem Church: 181–183 Theinbyu St, Kandawgalay PO 11221, POB 773, Rangoon; tel. (01) 78148; Rev. J. J. Andrews.

Presbyterian Church of Burma: Synod Office, Falam, Chin State; 22,000 mems; Rev. Sun Kanglo.

BURMA

The Roman Catholic Church

Burma comprises two archdioceses, six dioceses and one Apostolic Prefecture. At 31 December 1984 there were an estimated 407,000 adherents in the country, representing 1.1% of the total population.

Burma Catholic Bishops' Conference: 292 Prome Rd, Sanchaung PO, Rangoon; f. 1982; Pres. Mgr PAUL ZINGHTUNG GRAWNG, Bishop of Myitkyina.

Archbishop of Mandalay: Mgr ALPHONSE U THAN AUNG, Archbishop's House, 82nd and 25th St, Mandalay; tel. (02) 21997.

Archbishop of Rangoon: Mgr GABRIEL THOHEY MAHN GABY, Archbishop's House, 289 Theinbyu St, Rangoon; tel. (01) 72752.

BAHÁ'Í FAITH

National Spiritual Assembly: 355 Bowlane, Tamwe PO 11211, Rangoon; tel. (01) 51271; mems resident in 487 localities.

The Press

DAILIES

Botahtaung Daily (Vanguard Daily): 22/30 Strand Rd, Botahtaung PO, POB 539, Rangoon; tel. (01) 74310; f. 1958; state-owned; morning; Burmese; Chief Editor U THEIN; circ. 140,000.

Guardian: 392/396 Merchant St, Botahtaung PO, POB 1522, Rangoon; tel. (01) 70150; f. 1956; state-owned; morning; English; Chief Editor U SOE MYINT; circ. 19,000.

Kyemon Daily (Mirror Daily): 77 52nd St, Dazundaung PO, POB 819, Rangoon; tel. (01) 82777; f. 1951; state-owned; morning; Burmese; Chief Editor U TIN SOE; circ. 140,000.

Loktha Phyithu Nezin (Working People's Daily): 212 Theinbyu Rd, Botahtaung PO, POB 48, Rangoon; tel. (01) 73182; f. 1963; morning; Burmese and English; official; Chief Editor SAO KAI HPA; circ. 140,000.

Myanma Alin (New Light of Burma): 58 Komin Kochin Rd, Bahan PO, POB 21, Rangoon; tel. (01) 50777; f. 1914; nationalized 1969; morning; Burmese; Chief Editor (vacant); circ. 50,000.

Working People's Daily: 212 Theinbyu Rd, Rangoon; tel. (01) 73206; f. 1963; morning; English; Chief Editor U KO KO LAY; circ. 20,000.

PERIODICALS

Aurora (Moethaukpan): Myawaddy Press, 184 32nd St, Rangoon; monthly; Burmese and English; circ. 50,000.

Do Kyaung Tha: Myawaddy Press, 184 32nd St, Rangoon; monthly; circ. 100,000.

Gita Padetha: Rangoon; journal of Burma Music Council; circ. 10,000.

Guardian Magazine: 392/396 Merchant St, Botahtaung PO, POB 1522, Rangoon; tel. (01) 70150; f. 1953; nationalized 1964; monthly; English; literary magazine; circ. 50,000.

Myawaddy Magazine: 184 32nd St, Rangoon; tel. (01) 74655; f. 1952; monthly; Burmese; literary magazine; circ. 20,000.

Pyinnya Lawka Journal: 529 Merchant St, Rangoon; Publr Sarpay Beikman Management Board; quarterly; circ. 18,000.

Shetho (Forward): 22/24 Pansodan St, Rangoon; monthly; Burmese and English; publ. by the Information and Broadcasting Dept; circ. 36,000.

Shu Ma Wa Magazine: 146 Western Wing, Bogyoke Market, Rangoon; monthly; Burmese; literary.

Shwe Thwe: 529 Merchant St, Rangoon; weekly; bilingual children's journal; Publr Sarpay Beikman Management Board; circ. 100,000.

Teza: Myawaddy Press, 184 32nd St, Rangoon; monthly; English and Burmese; circ. 60,100.

Thwe/Thauk Magazine: 185 48th St, Rangoon; f. 1946; monthly; Burmese; literary.

NEWS AGENCIES

News Agency of Burma (NAB): 212 Theinbyu Rd, Rangoon; tel. (01) 70893; f. 1963; govt-sponsored; Chief Editors U YE TINT (domestic section), U KYAW MIN (external section).

Foreign Bureaux

Agence France-Presse (AFP) (France): 58A Golden Valley, Rangoon; tel. (01) 32360; Correspondent U KHIN MAUNG THWIN.

Agenzia Nazionale Stampa Associata (ANSA) (Italy): 113 Khunni St, Ward 29, Thuwunna, Rangoon; Representative U PAW HTIN.

Associated Press (AP) (USA): 283 U Wisara Rd, Sanchaung PO, Rangoon; tel. (01) 30176; telex 21327; Representative U SEIN WIN.

Deutsche Presse-Agentur (dpa) (Federal Republic of Germany): 55 Kalagar St, Kemmendine PO, Rangoon; Correspondent U CHIT TUN.

Reuters: 162 Phayre St, Rangoon; tel. (01) 11419; telex 21202; Correspondent U HLA KYI.

Telegrafnoye Agentstvo Sovetskovo Soyuza (TASS) (USSR): 41-3 Lowis Rd, Golden Valley, Rangoon; tel. (01) 31513; Correspondent YEVGENIY SHEVELEV.

Xinhua (New China) News Agency (People's Republic of China): 67A Prome Rd, Rangoon; tel. (01) 75714; telex 21351; Representative LUI JIMIN.

Publishers

Hanthawaddy Press: 157 Bo Aung Gyaw St, Rangoon; f. 1889; books and journals; Man. Editor U ZAW WIN.

Knowledge Publishing House: 130 Bo Gyoke Aung San St, Yegyaw, Rangoon; travel, fiction, religious and political books and directories.

Kyipwaye Press: 84th St, Letsaigan, Mandalay; arts, travel, religion, fiction and children's.

Myawaddy Press: 184 32nd St, Rangoon; tel. (01) 74655; journals and magazines; Chief Editor U MYA THEIN.

Sarpay Beikman Management Board: 529 Merchant St, Rangoon; tel. (01) 83611; f. 1947; Burmese encyclopaedia, literature, fine arts and general; also magazines and translations; Chair. U TAIK SOE (Dep. Information Minister); Vice-Chair. U MAUNG MAUNG KHIN.

Shumawa Press: 146 West Wing, Bogyoke Market, Rangoon; non-fiction.

Thu Dhama Wadi Press: 55-56 Maung Khine St, POB 419, Rangoon; f. 1903; religious; Propr U TIN HTOO; Man. U PAN MAUNG.

Government Publishing House

Printing and Publishing Corpn: 228 Theinbyu St, Rangoon; tel. (01) 81033; Man. Dir Col MAUNG MAUNG KHIN.

PUBLISHERS' ASSOCIATION

Burmese Publishers' Union: 146 Bogyoke Market, Rangoon.

Radio and Television

There were an estimated 800,000 radio receivers and 32,000 television receivers in use in 1984.

Burma Broadcasting Service (BBS): Prome Rd, Kamayut PO, Rangoon; tel. (01) 31355; f. 1946; broadcasts in Burmese, Arakanese, Mon, Shan, Karen, Chin, Kachin, Kayah and English; a colour television service began transmission in 1980, broadcasting two hours daily from Rangoon; Dir-Gen. U KYAW MINN; Dir of Broadcasting U AUNG KYI; Dir of Television (vacant).

Finance

(cap. = capital; p.u. = paid up; dep. = deposits; m. = million; amounts in kyats)

BANKING

All banks in Burma were nationalized in 1963 and amalgamated to form the People's Bank of the Union of Burma from November 1969. In April 1972 this was renamed the Union of Burma Bank and was reconstituted as the central bank in April 1976.

Under a law of November 1975 there are four separate state-owned banks: the Union of Burma Bank, the Myanma Economic Bank, the Myanma Foreign Trade Bank and the Myanma Agricultural Bank, each with its own management board.

Central Bank

Union of Burma Bank: 24/26 Sule Pagoda Rd, Rangoon; tel. (01) 85300; telex 21213; f. 1976; bank of issue; cap. p.u. 200m.; dep. 948m.; Chair. U MAUNG MAUNG HLA; Tech. Adviser U AYE KO.

State Banks

Myanma Agricultural Bank: 1/7 Latha St, Rangoon; tel. (01) 73018; provides agricultural credit for farmers; cap. 40m.; Man. Dir U NYUNT HLAING.

Myanma Economic Bank: 564 Merchant St, Rangoon; tel. (01) 81819; telex 21213; profits 229m. (1981); provides savings and credit facilities, extends loans and advances to state economic organizations and municipal bodies and co-operatives; Man. Dir U MAUNG MAUNG HAN.

Myanma Foreign Trade Bank: POB 203, Theingyizay C Block, Shwedagon Pagoda Rd, Rangoon; tel. (01) 84911; telex 21300; f. 1976; cap. and res. 60m., dep. 149.06m. (March 1985); handles all foreign exchange and all international banking transactions; Man. Dir U MAUNG MAUNG THAN; Gen. Man. U THAUNG TIN.

INSURANCE

Myanma Insurance Corpn: 163/167 Pansodan St, Rangoon; tel. (01) 84466; telex 21203; f. 1975; Man. Dir U NYUNT WAI.

Trade and Industry

Socialist Economic Planning Committee: Rangoon; f. 1967; 10 mems; Chair. U NE WIN; Vice-Chair. U SAN YU.

GOVERNMENT CORPORATIONS

Agricultural and Farm Produce Trade Corpn: 70 Pansodan Rd, Rangoon; tel. (01) 84044; telex 21305; Man. Dir U OHN KIN SEIN.

Agriculture Corpn: 72–74 Shwedagon Pagoda Rd, Rangoon; tel. (01) 83480; telex 21311; Man. Dir U KHIN WIN.

Construction Corpn: 60 Shwedagon Pagoda Rd, Rangoon; tel. (01) 80955; telex 21336; Man. Dir U KHIN MAUNG YIN.

Electric Power Corpn: 197–199 Lower Kemmendine Rd, Rangoon; tel. (01) 85366; telex 21306; Man. Dir U KHIN MAUNG THEIN.

Foodstuff Industries Corpn: 523 Merchant St, Rangoon; tel. (01) 84494; telex 21500; Man. Dir Col SOE LWIN.

General Industries Corpn: 128/132 Crisp St, Rangoon; tel. (01) 84031; telex 21500; Man. Dir U KO KO GYI.

Heavy Industries Corpn: 23A Kaba Aye Pagoda Rd, Rangoon; tel. (01) 52195; telex 21503; Man. Dir Lt-Col THAN SHWE.

Hotel and Tourist Corpn (Tourist Burma): 77–91 Sule Pagoda Rd, POB 1398, Rangoon; tel. (01) 77571; telex 21330; controlled by Ministry of Trade; manages all hotels, tourist offices, diplomatic stores and duty-free shops; Man. Dir U MAUNG MAUNG AYE; Gen. Man. Col TANKA DHOJ; Dep. Gen. Man. (Hotels) U TIN YEE; Dep. Gen. Man. (Tourism and Diplomatic Stores) U MYO LWIN.

Industrial Planning Department: 192 Kaba Aye Pagoda Rd, Bahan PO, POB 11201, Rangoon; tel. (01) 50744; f. 1952; Dir-Gen. Lt-Col AYE KYIN.

Inspection and Agency Corpn: Rangoon; works on behalf of Burma's state-owned enterprises to promote business with foreign companies.

Livestock Breeding Corpn: Veterinary Institute Estate, Insein, POB 1457, Rangoon; tel. (01) 40726; telex 21310; Man. Dir U KHIN LATT.

Metal Industries Corpn: 354 Prome Rd, Rangoon; tel. (01) 31518; telex 21500; Man. Dir U MYA THANT.

Myanma Export-Import Corpn: 577 Merchant St, Rangoon; tel. (01) 80260; telex 21305; Man. Dir U AUNG KYI.

Myanma Gems Corpn: 66 Kaba Aye Pagoda Rd, POB 1397, Rangoon; tel. (01) 61901; telex 21506; controlled by Ministry of Mines; Man. Dir U HLA THEIN.

Myanma Oil Corpn: 604 Merchant St, POB 1049, Rangoon; tel. (01) 82266; telex 21307; controlled by Ministry of Industry (No. II); fmrly Burma Oil Co; nationalized 1963; Man. Dir TINT LWIN.

No. 1 Mining Corpn: 226 Maha Bandoola St, Rangoon; tel. (01) 74711; telex 21307; controlled by Ministry of Mines; fmrly Myanma Bawdwin Corpn; development and mining of non-ferrous metals; Man. Dir U YOE SEIN.

No. 2 Mining Corpn: Kanbe, Yankin, Rangoon; tel. (01) 50166; telex 21511; controlled by Ministry of Mines; fmrly Myanma Tin Tungsten Development Corpn; development and mining of tin, tungsten and antimony; Man. Dir U NYAN LIN.

No. 3 Mining Corpn: Kanabe, Yankin PO, Rangoon; tel. (01) 57444; telex 21511; controlled by Ministry of Mines; production of pig iron, carbon steel, steel grinding balls, coal, barytes, gypsum, limestone and various clays, etc.; Man. Dir U MYINT THEIN.

People's Pearl and Fishery Corpn (PPFC): 654 Merchant St, Rangoon; tel. (01) 78022; telex 21310; f. 1972; Man. Dir U KAN NYUNT.

Petrochemicals Industries Corpn: 23 Prome Rd, Rangoon; tel. (01) 81943; telex 21329; controlled by Ministry of Industry (No. II); Man. Dir U TIN MAUNG AYE.

Petroleum Products Supply Corpn: 622 Merchant St, Rangoon; tel. (01) 82011; telex 21307; controlled by Ministry of Industry (No. II); Man. Dir Col MYINT SOE.

Pharmaceuticals Industries Corpn: 192 Kaba Aye Pagoda Rd, Rangoon; tel. (01) 56740; telex 21500; Man. Dir U BA NYUNT.

Posts and Telecommunications Corpn: 43 Bo Aung Gyaw St, Rangoon; tel. (01) 85499; telex 21222; Man. Dir U TIN.

Textiles Industries Corpn: 192 Kaba Aye Pagoda Rd, Rangoon; tel. (01) 52180; telex 21500; Man. Dir MYA SOE NYEIN.

Timber Corpn: POB 206, Ahlone, Rangoon; tel. (01) 83933; telex 21312; f. 1948; extraction, processing, and main exporter of Burma teak and other timber, veneers, plywood and other forest products; Man. Dir U KHIN MAUNG GYI.

CO-OPERATIVES

In 1984/85 there was a total of 21,250 co-operative societies.

Central Co-operative Society (CCS) Council: 334/336 Strand Rd, Rangoon; tel. (01) 74550; Chair. U THAN HLANG; Sec. U TIN LATT.

WORKERS' AND PEASANTS' COUNCILS

Conditions of work are stipulated in the Workers' Rights and Responsibilities Law, enacted in 1964. Regional BSPP workers' councils ensure that government directives are complied with, and that targets are met on a regional basis. In January 1985 there were 293 workers' councils in towns, with more than 1.8m. members. They are co-ordinated by a central workers' asiayone in Rangoon, formed in 1968 to replace trades union organizations which had been abolished in 1964.

Peasants' Asiayone (Organization): Rangoon; tel. (01) 82819; f. 1977; organization for the self-government of peasants; Chair. U YE GOUNG; Sec. U SAN TUN.

Workers' Asiayone: Central Committee Headquarters, Strand Rd, Rangoon; f. 1968; organization for self-government of workers; Chair. U OHN KYAW; Sec. U NYUNT THEIN.

Transport

All railways, domestic air services, passenger and freight road transport services and inland water facilities are owned and operated by state-controlled enterprises.

RAILWAYS

The railway network had 3,156 km (1,961 miles) of track in 1984/85.

Burma Railways Corpn: Bogyoke Aung San St, POB 118, Rangoon; tel. (01) 84455; telex 21361; f. 1972; govt-operated; 3,156 track km (1,961 miles) in 1984/85; Man. Dir (vacant); Gen. Man. U SAW CLYDE.

ROADS

In 1984/85 the total length of roads in Burma was 23,067 km (14,333 miles), of which 3,946 km (2,452 miles) were highways and 19,121 km (11,881 miles) were main roads.

Road Transport Corpn: 375 Bogyoke Aung San St, Rangoon; tel. (01) 82252; f. 1963 to nationalize gradually all passenger and freight road transport; in 1984/85 operated 2,695 haulage trucks and 1,335 passenger buses; Man. Dir LIN THEIN MAUNG.

INLAND WATERWAYS

The principal artery of traffic is the River Irrawaddy, which is navigable as far as Bhamo, about 1,450 km (900 miles) inland, while parts of the Salween and Chindwin rivers are also navigable.

Inland Water Transport Corpn: 50 Pansodan St, Rangoon; tel. (01) 83244; state-owned; operates cargo and passenger services throughout Burma; 19.7m. passengers and 2m. tons of freight were carried in 1984/85; Man. Dir U KHIN MAUNG THEIN.

BURMA

SHIPPING

Rangoon is the chief port. Vessels with a displacement of up to 15,000 tons can be accommodated. In 1985 a modernization plan for Rangoon port was announced in anticipation of increased foreign trade by 1990. There are also plans for the construction of a new international port at Thilawa, 13 km from Rangoon, which would also deal with the increased trade.

Burma Ports Corpn: 10 Pansodan St, POB 1, Rangoon; tel. (01) 83122; telex 21208; f. 1880; general port and harbour duties; Man. Dir U TIN MAUNG; Gen. Man. U TIN OO; fleet of 7 vessels totalling 5,766 tons gross and 36 smaller craft.

Burma Five Star Shipping Corpn: 132–136 Theinbyu Rd, POB 1221, Rangoon; tel. (01) 80022; telex 21210; f. 1959; cargo services to the Far East, South-East Asia and Europe; Man. Dir U SHWE THAN; Gen. Man. U THAN TUT; fleet of 22 coastal and ocean-going vessels.

CIVIL AVIATION

Mingaladon Airport, near Rangoon, is equipped to international standards.

Burma Airways Corpn (BAC): 104 Strand Rd, Rangoon; tel. (01) 84566; telex 21204; f. 1948; govt-controlled; internal network operates services to 25 airports; external services to Bangkok, Calcutta, Dhaka, Kathmandu and Singapore; Man. Dir THA TUN AYE THEIN; Flight Operations Man. U KYAWT MYAING; fleet of 3 F-28, 5 F-27, 3 SA330J Puma.

Tourism

Tourist Burma: 77/91 Sule Pagoda Rd, Rangoon; tel. (01) 78376; telex 21330; sole tour operator and travel agent; handles all package tours for both groups and individuals.

Atomic Energy

Atomic Energy Committee: f. 1978; Chair. U WIN MAUNG.

Union of Burma Atomic Energy Centre: Atomic Energy Dept, Central Research Organization, 6 Kaba Aye Pagoda Road, Rangoon; f. 1955; depts of nuclear mineralogical research; nuclear research; environmental radiation monitoring; Chair. Dr MAUNG MAUNG GALAY.

BURUNDI

Introductory Survey

Location, Climate, Language, Religion, Flag, Capital

The Republic of Burundi is a land-locked country lying on the eastern shore of Lake Tanganyika, in central Africa, a little south of the Equator. It is bordered by Rwanda to the north, by Tanzania to the south and east, and by Zaire to the west. The climate is tropical (hot and humid) in the lowlands, and cool in the highlands, with an irregular rainfall. The official languages are French and Kirundi, while Swahili is used, in addition to French, in commercial circles. More than 60% of the inhabitants profess Christianity, with the great majority of the Christians being Roman Catholics. A large minority still adhere to traditional animist beliefs. The national flag (proportions 3 by 2) consists of a white diagonal cross on a background of red (above and below) and green (left and right), with a white circle, containing three green-edged red stars, in the centre. The capital is Bujumbura.

Recent History

Burundi (formerly Urundi) became part of German East Africa in 1899. In 1916, during the First World War, the territory was occupied by Belgian forces from the Congo (now Zaire). Subsequently, as part of Ruanda-Urundi, it was administered by Belgium under a League of Nations mandate and later as a UN Trust Territory. Elections in September 1961, held under UN supervision, were won by the Union for National Progress party (UPRONA), which had been formed in 1958 by Ganwa (Prince) Louis Rwagasore, son of the reigning Mwami (King), Mwambutsa IV. Prince Rwagasore became Prime Minister, but was assassinated after only two weeks in office. He was succeeded by his brother-in-law, André Muhirwa. Internal self-government was granted in January 1962 and full independence on 1 July 1962, when the two parts of the Trust Territory became separate states. Burundi continued to be linked to Rwanda in a customs and monetary union, until the agreements were terminated in January 1964. In July 1966 the Mwami was deposed, after a reign of over 50 years, by his son Charles, with the help of a group of army officers, and the constitution was suspended. In November 1966 Charles, now Mwami Ntare V, was himself deposed by his Prime Minister, Capt. (later Lt-Gen.) Michel Micombero, who declared Burundi a republic.

Micombero's rule confirmed the long-established dominance of the Tutsi tribe over the Hutu tribe, who form the majority of the population. Several alleged plots against the Government in 1969 and 1971 were followed in 1972 by an abortive coup during which Ntare V was killed. The Hutus were held responsible for the attempted coup and this served as a pretext for the Tutsis to conduct a series of large-scale massacres of the rival tribe. Many Hutus fled to neighbouring countries, and repression of the tribe continued.

In 1972 Micombero began a prolonged restructuring of the executive, which resulted in 1973 in an appointed seven-man Presidential Bureau, with Micombero holding the dual office of President and Prime Minister. In July 1974 the Government introduced a new republican constitution which vested sovereignty in UPRONA, the sole legal political party in Burundi. The President was elected Secretary-General of the party and re-elected for a seven-year presidential term.

On 1 November 1976 an army coup deposed Micombero, who died in exile in July 1983. The leader of the coup, Lt-Col (later Col) Jean-Baptiste Bagaza, was appointed President by the Supreme Revolutionary Council (composed of army officers), and a new Council of Ministers was formed. The Prime Minister, Lt-Col Edouard (Ndugu) Nzambimana, announced in mid-1977 the military regime's intention to hand over power to a civilian government in 1981.

The 1978–82 five-year plan elaborated on the Government's general policy as defined in the Declaration of Fundamental Aims of 20 November 1976, with the main objectives being social justice and unity throughout the country, based on the elimination of corruption in the administration.

In October 1978 President Bagaza announced a ministerial reshuffle in which he abolished the post of Prime Minister. The first national congress of UPRONA was held in December 1979, and a party Central Committee, headed by President Bagaza, was elected to take over the functions of the Supreme Revolutionary Council in January 1980. A new constitution, adopted by national referendum in November 1981, provided for the establishment of a National Assembly, to be elected by universal adult suffrage. The first elections were held in October 1982. After the failure of five members of the Council of Ministers to be elected to the new legislative body, President Bagaza announced a number of ministerial changes in November. Having been re-elected president of UPRONA at the party's second national congress in July 1984, Bagaza was elected President of Burundi by direct suffrage for the first time in August, winning 99.63% of the votes cast; he was the only candidate for either election.

In 1985 relations between the Government and religious authorities in Burundi were affected by the arrest of several priests and the Roman Catholic Archbishop of Gitega, and by the expulsion of many foreign missionaries, all of whom were accused of holding religious services on weekdays, in defiance of government restrictions. The dispute was investigated by Amnesty International, which alleged that 20 priests were being detained without trial. An official government statement acknowledged that arrests had been made, but declared that those priests who had 'admitted their mistakes' had subsequently been released. In September 1986 the Government announced its decision to assume responsibility for the organization and administration of all lower- and intermediate-level Roman Catholic seminaries, a measure that was regarded as one of retaliation against the Roman Catholic Church, which was alleged by the Government to have been 'disseminating tendentious information abroad'.

Government

On 18 November 1981 a draft constitution was approved in a national referendum. Its provisions included the election by universal adult suffrage of a President for a five-year term, and of 52 representatives to a National Assembly, with legislative powers, for a similar period, a further 13 representatives being appointed by the President. The executive body is the Council of Ministers. Policy issues are often directed by the Central Committee of UPRONA, the only authorized political party. There are 15 provinces, administered by civilian governors, each of which is divided into districts and further subdivided into communes.

Defence

The army was merged with the police force in 1967. The total strength of the armed forces in July 1986 was 7,200, comprising an army of 5,500, a navy of 50, an air force of 150, and a paramilitary force of 1,500 gendarmes. Defence expenditure in 1985 totalled an estimated 4,200m. Burundi francs.

Economic Affairs

In terms of average income, Burundi is one of the 20 poorest countries in the world. In 1984, according to World Bank estimates, gross national product (GNP) per head was US $220 (at average 1982–84 prices), having increased at an average rate of 1.9% annually, in real terms, since 1965. The average annual rate of inflation was 12.0% in 1981, 5.8% in 1982, 8.4% in 1983 and 14.4% in 1984. According to official figures, consumer prices increased by 3.6% in 1985, and declined by 3.4% in the year to May 1986.

The economy is based almost entirely on agriculture, which employed about 94% of the labour force in 1983. The main subsistence crops are cassava and sweet potatoes, while the main cash crops are coffee and cotton. Tea is being developed, and Burundi's annual output of made tea increased from 867 metric tons in 1975 to 4,145 tons in 1985. Coffee is Burundi's principal export, and in 1983, when there was a crop of 33,999 metric tons, it accounted for 87% of export earnings, with the USA being the main customer. In 1984 coffee output fell slightly, to an estimated 32,000 tons, but the value of coffee exports rose by 52%, with coffee sales providing 84% of total export earnings. The value of coffee exports increased by a further 12.5% in 1985, when coffee sales again accounted for 84% of total export earnings, and provided 25% of government revenue and 10% of gross domestic product (GDP). Such heavy dependence on a single commodity has caused Burundi's balance of trade to react sharply to fluctuations in the world price of coffee and has prevented reliable economic planning. With proposed expenditure set at 107,000m. Burundi francs, the 1983-87 five-year plan, like its predecessor, sought to expand and diversify the country's agricultural activities in order to provide both food and work for a rapidly-increasing population, and stability for the economy. The EEC countries, in particular Belgium, France and the Federal Republic of Germany, are among Burundi's main trading partners, accounting for 45% of import costs and 60% of exports in 1983. Revenue from coffee exports rose by more than 63% in 1979 but the trade deficit continued to increase. In subsequent years the value of imports increased, while coffee earnings remained below their 1979 level. Revenue from coffee exports rose from 6,542m. Burundi francs in 1983 to 9,930m. francs in 1984 and to a record 11,172m. francs in 1985, when the visible trade deficit was 10,070m. francs (with export earnings totalling 13,280m. francs and the value of imports 23,350m. francs), compared with 10,552m. francs in 1984 (when export earnings totalled 11,831m. francs and the value of imports 22,383m. francs). Burundi's GDP expanded, in real terms, by 10.5% in 1981, but declined by 1.9% in 1982; after rising by 1.5% in 1983 and falling by 2.2% in 1984, real GDP increased by 7.1% in 1985.

The mining industry is based on the exploitation of small amounts of gold, bastnaesite, cassiterite, tungsten and tantalum, although no significant production of bastnaesite has been noted since 1978, nor of cassiterite since 1979. Burundi has the world's richest deposits of vanadium, and important deposits of nickel, estimated at 5% of world reserves, and uranium are being surveyed. Petroleum has been detected beneath Lake Tanganyika and in the Ruzizi valley, and test drilling was due to begin in 1985-86. Manufacturing, however, is still on a very small scale, accounting for less than 5% of GDP in 1983. It consists largely of the processing of agricultural products, a sector that the 1983-87 plan was to develop, with a view not only to preparing produce for export but also to establishing various import substitution industries. A native textile industry has been developed, and plantations of sugar cane have been established on the Moso plain, near Bujumbura, in association with a refinery which was due to be completed in 1987, and which was projected to meet 90% of the country's demand for sugar by 1990. Two factories at Bujumbura and Gitega, completed in 1983, are to process Burundi's entire coffee crop. In 1974 trade agreements were made with the EEC, and in 1976 Burundi established, with Zaire and Rwanda, the Economic Community of the Great Lakes Countries (CEPGL, see p. 224). In 1985 Burundi became a full member of the Preferential Trade Area for Eastern and Southern African States (see p. 218).

Most of the foreign aid to Burundi comes from Belgium, France and the Federal Republic of Germany and through the EEC's European Development Fund and the World Bank. Foreign aid to Burundi totalled US $126.7m. in 1981. In February 1984 the total amount of foreign aid required for the 1983-87 five-year plan was stated to be US $1,556m., which was to represent about 60% of the total planned investment. In August 1986 Burundi became the first member of the IMF to benefit from the Fund's Structural Adjustment Facility (SAF), established in the previous March. Under the new facility, the IMF approved a loan of SDR 20.1m., to be made over a period of three years, in support of the Burundi Government's programme of economic recovery, which aimed to reduce the country's dependence on coffee exports for foreign exchange earnings, to restore real annual GDP growth to about 4%, to restrict the deficit on the current account of the balance of payments to no more than 6.5% of GDP in 1987, and to reverse the trend of escalating debt-servicing costs. (The current-account deficit increased from 3% of GDP at the beginning of the 1980s to 8.5% of GDP in 1984, while debt-servicing costs increased from 6% of export earnings in 1981 to about 20% in 1984.) The loan was approved in addition to an 18-month stand-by credit facility of SDR 21m. that had been agreed earlier in the month, and to a US $50m. structural adjustment credit, negotiated in the previous May. Other measures taken in 1986, as part of the Government's programme of economic reform, included the raising of official prices payable to coffee producers by 28%, and, in July, the devaluation of the Burundi franc by 13% in relation to the IMF's SDR.

Unemployment has always been an enormous problem but, as 90% of the population live in rural areas, it is virtually impossible for unemployment in the countryside to decrease in absolute terms. The National Recovery Programme, initiated in 1978, aimed to mitigate this problem by continuing efforts to alleviate the food scarcity. In 1977 a stocking and trading centre was established to co-ordinate the buying and selling of foodstuffs over the whole country. The Recovery Programme also aimed to promote intensive livestock farming and new crops, such as soya beans, oil palms and sugar cane, and to create a farmers' co-operative.

Two dams are being built, and a large hydroelectric scheme on the Rwanda-Zaire border (the Ruzizi-II project) is being developed jointly with those two countries, for completion in 1987, Burundi's electricity supply hitherto having been obtained almost entirely from the hydroelectric station at Bukavu in Zaire. The exploitation of Burundi's peat bogs provided 10,000 metric tons of peat, for use as an additional source of energy, in 1982.

In 1986 the OPEC Fund for International Development agreed to provide a loan of US $3m. for the completion of the Makamba-Butembera road, which was to receive additional funding from the Saudi Fund for Development and the Burundi Government. The construction of the new road was planned with the aim of both facilitating transport in an area with good potential for agricultural development and improving road links with Tanzania.

Social Welfare

Wage-earners are protected by insurance against accidents and occupational diseases and can draw on a pension fund. Medical facilities are, however, limited. In 1978 there were 22 hospitals, nine maternity units and 100 dispensaries. In 1981 Burundi had one hospital bed for every 286 inhabitants. In 1986 Burundi and the People's Republic of China signed a protocol whereby the latter undertook to provide Burundi with medical aid in the form of drugs and equipment, and by sending a team of 12 specialists to Burundi for two years.

Education

Education is provided free of charge. Kirundi is the language of instruction in primary schools, while French is used in secondary schools. Primary education, which is officially compulsory, begins at seven years of age and lasts for six years. Secondary education, which is not compulsory, begins at the age of 13 and lasts for up to seven years, comprising a first cycle of four years and a second of three years. In 1983 the total enrolment at primary and secondary schools was equivalent to 25% of the school-age population (males 31%; females 20%), whereas in 1980 the proportion had been only 16%. Enrolment at primary schools increased from 175,856 in 1980 to 301,278 in 1983. The latter total included an estimated 35% of children in the relevant age-group (42% of boys; 29% of girls). Enrolment at secondary schools, including pupils receiving vocational instruction and teacher training, rose from 19,013 in 1980 to 26,415 in 1983. However, the latter total was equivalent to only 4% of the population in the secondary age-group. There is one university, in Bujumbura, with 1,900 students in 1981. According to official estimates, the average rate of illiteracy among the population aged 10 years and over was 66.2% (males 57.2%; females 74.3%) in 1982.

BURUNDI

Tourism
Tourism is relatively underdeveloped, but the Government plans to encourage tourists to visit Burundi. In 1977 a 150-bed hotel complex was built on the shores of Lake Tanganyika. There were about 38,000 tourist arrivals in 1982, when tourist receipts totalled US $23m.

Public Holidays
1987: 1 January (New Year's Day), 20 April (Easter Monday), 1 May (Labour Day), 28 May (Ascension), 1 July (Independence Day), 15 August (Assumption), 18 September (Victory of UPRONA Party), 1 November (All Saints' Day), 25 December (Christmas).

1988: 1 January (New Year's Day), 4 April (Easter Monday), 1 May (Labour Day), 12 May (Ascension), 1 July (Independence Day), 15 August (Assumption), 18 September (Victory of UPRONA Party), 1 November (All Saints' Day), 25 December (Christmas).

Weights and Measures
The metric system is in force.

Currency and Exchange Rates
100 centimes = 1 Burundi franc.

Exchange rates (30 September 1986):
 £1 sterling = 174.64 francs;
 US $1 = 120.69 francs.

Statistical Survey

Area and Population

AREA, POPULATION AND DENSITY

Area (sq km)	27,834*
Population (census of 16–30 August 1979)	3,992,130
Population (official estimates at mid-year)	
1983	4,421,000
1984	4,537,000
1985	4,718,000
Density (per sq km) at mid-1985	169.5

* 10,747 sq miles.

PRINCIPAL TOWNS

Bujumbura (capital), population 172,201 (census of August 1979); Gitega 15,943 (1978).

Source: Banque de la République du Burundi.

BIRTHS AND DEATHS

Average annual birth rate 46.2 per 1,000 in 1970–75, 48.3 per 1,000 in 1975–80, 47.6 per 1,000 in 1980–85; death rate 23.7 per 1,000 in 1970–75, 23.0 per 1,000 in 1975–80, 20.9 per 1,000 in 1980–85 (UN estimates).

Source: UN, *World Population Prospects: Estimates and Projections as Assessed in 1982.*

ECONOMICALLY ACTIVE POPULATION
(1983 estimates)

Traditional agriculture	2,319,595
Fishing	5,481
Traditional trades	22,820
Private sector (modern)	37,884
Public sector	95,061
Total labour force	**2,480,841**

1979 census: Total labour force 2,413,169 (Males 1,133,477; females 1,279,692).

Sources: *Revue des statistiques du travail* and Centre de recherche et de formation en population.

Agriculture

PRINCIPAL CROPS ('000 metric tons)

	1982	1983	1984
Wheat	6*	6*	4*
Maize	144	148*	103
Finger millet	40*	42*	35*
Sorghum	200*	200*	150*
Rice	9	9*	9*
Potatoes	35	36	36*
Sweet potatoes	490*	502	450*
Cassava (Manioc)	410	500	430*
Yams	6	6	7*
Taro (Coco yam)	98	100	100*
Dry beans	290	297	260*
Dry peas	29	30	32*
Palm kernels	2.1*	2.3*	2.3*
Groundnuts (in shell)	11	12	12*
Cottonseed	4*	4*	4*
Cotton (lint)	2	2*	2*
Coffee (green)	20	35*	32*
Tea (made)	2	2	2*
Tobacco (leaves)	2*	2*	2*
Bananas and plantains	960*	970*	980*

* FAO estimate.

Source: FAO, *Production Yearbook.*

LIVESTOCK ('000 head, year ending September)

	1982	1983*	1984*
Cattle	548	560	565
Sheep	320*	310	315
Goats	750*	760	770
Pigs	35*	36	37

* FAO estimates.

Poultry (FAO estimates, million): 3 in 1982; 3 in 1983; 3 in 1984.

Source: FAO, *Production Yearbook.*

LIVESTOCK PRODUCTS (FAO estimates, '000 metric tons)

	1982	1983	1984
Beef and veal	10	11	11
Mutton and lamb	1	1	1
Goats' meat	3	3	3
Pig meat	2	2	2
Cows' milk	58	58	60
Goats' milk	10	10	10
Hen eggs	2.5	2.6	2.7

Source: FAO, *Production Yearbook.*

Forestry

ROUNDWOOD REMOVALS ('000 cubic metres)

	1982	1983	1984
Sawlogs, veneer logs and logs for sleepers	2	2	2
Other industrial wood*	35	36	37
Fuel wood*	3,237	3,327	3,427
Total	3,274	3,365	3,466

* FAO estimates.
Source: FAO, *Yearbook of Forest Products*.

Fishing

(FAO estimates, '000 metric tons, live weight)

	1981	1982	1983
Dagaas	7.8	7.5	7.5
Freshwater perches	4.6	4.4	4.5
Total catch	12.4	11.9	12.0

Source: FAO, *Yearbook of Fishery Statistics*.

Mining

(metric tons)

	1977	1978	1979
Tin	36	49	16.5
Bastnaesite	28	30.5	—

Note: Bastnaesite ceased to be mined in 1979, and tin in 1980.
Source: Département de Géologie et Mines.

Industry

SELECTED PRODUCTS

	1981	1982	1983
Beer ('000 hectolitres)	687	684	644
Soft drinks ('000 hectolitres)	115	122	140
Cigarettes (million)	259	235	294
Blankets ('000)	381	345	359
Footwear ('000 pairs)	460	390	301

Source: UN, *Industrial Statistics Yearbook*.

Finance

CURRENCY AND EXCHANGE RATES

Monetary Units
100 centimes = 1 Burundi franc.

Denominations
Coins: 1, 5 and 10 francs.
Notes: 10, 20, 50, 100, 500, 1,000 and 5,000 francs.

Sterling and Dollar Equivalents (30 September 1986)
£1 sterling = 174.64 francs;
US $1 = 120.69 francs;
1,000 Burundi francs = £5.726 = $8.286.

Average Exchange Rate (Burundi francs per US dollar)
1983   92.95
1984   119.71
1985   120.69

Note: Between May 1976 and November 1983 the rate was fixed at US $1 = 90.0 Burundi francs. Since November 1983 the Burundi franc has been linked to the IMF's special drawing right (SDR), with the mid-point exchange rate initially fixed at SDR 1 = 122.7 francs. This remained in force until July 1986, when a new rate of SDR 1 = 141.0 francs was introduced.

CENTRAL BANK RESERVES
(US $ million at 31 December)

	1983	1984	1985
Gold	6.60	5.33	5.62
IMF special drawing rights	1.04	0.11	0.12
Reserve position in IMF	9.86	9.23	10.06
Foreign exchange	16.04	10.39	19.29
Total	33.54	25.06	35.09

Source: IMF, *International Financial Statistics*.

BUDGET (million Burundi francs)

Revenue	1982	1983	1984
Income tax	3,605.3	3,524.0	3,897.4
Property tax	55.8	113.4	87.8
Customs duties	3,307.2	2,620.0	4,773.0
Excise duties	2,650.9	2,150.3	2,250.9
Other indirect taxes	1,386.5	2,073.9	3,406.0
Administrative receipts	553.0	686.3	649.3
Total revenue	11,558.7	11,167.9	15,064.4

Expenditure	1982	1983	1984
Goods and services	8,764.9	8,309.7	9,085.4
Subsidies and transfers	1,571.5	2,114.3	2,792.8
Net loans	182.4	24.0	78.7
Other	1,177.0	3,258.5	3,871.1
Total expenditure	11,695.8	13,706.5	15,828.0

Sources: Ministry of Finance; Banque de la République du Burundi.

MONEY SUPPLY (million Burundi francs at 31 December)

	1983	1984	1985
Currency outside banks	7,262	7,498	7,254
Official entities' deposits at Central Bank	532	1,222	1,965
Demand deposits at commercial banks	4,985	5,090	7,902
Demand deposits at other monetary institutions	869	718	1,049
Total money	13,647	14,527	18,170

Source: IMF, *International Financial Statistics*.

COST OF LIVING
(Consumer Price Index for Bujumbura; base: 1980 = 100)

	1982	1983	1984
Food	118.2	127.8	146.0
Clothing	111.0	115.0	123.0
Rent, fuel and light	130.7	130.0	144.6
All items (incl. others)	118.5	128.3	146.7

Source: ILO, *Year Book of Labour Statistics*.

1985: All items 152.1 (Source: IMF, *International Financial Statistics*).

NATIONAL ACCOUNTS (million Burundi francs at current prices)
Expenditure on the Gross Domestic Product

	1983	1984	1985
Government final consumption expenditure	13,446	15,366	15,434
Private final consumption expenditure	78,866	90,653	100,883
Increase in stocks / Gross fixed capital formation	22,977	21,232	21,119
Total domestic expenditure	115,289	127,251	137,436
Exports of goods and services	8,990	13,439	15,475
Less Imports of goods and services	23,903	29,822	30,403
GDP in purchasers' values	100,375	110,867	122,509
GDP at constant 1980 prices	95,175	93,074	99,718

Source: IMF, *International Financial Statistics*.

Gross Domestic Product by Economic Activity*

	1982	1983	1984
Agriculture, hunting, forestry and fishing	48,081	55,202	55,084
Mining and quarrying / Electricity, gas and water	508	593	911
Manufacturing	3,809	4,806	5,650
Construction	4,953	5,742	6,417
Trade, restaurants and hotels	6,981	7,991	8,982
Transport, storage and communications	2,029	2,835	2,747
Other commercial services	1,482	1,591	1,653
Government services	7,409	7,112	8,736
Non-profit services to households	4,508	5,254	5,262
GDP at factor cost	79,760	91,126	95,442
Indirect taxes, *less* subsidies	8,747	8,114	10,061
GDP in purchasers' values	88,507	99,240	105,503

* Excluding GDP of the artisan branch (3,404 million francs in 1982).
Source: Ministère à la Présidence chargé du Plan.

External Trade

PRINCIPAL COMMODITIES (million Burundi francs)

Imports c.i.f.	1982	1983	1984
Intermediate goods	7,525.1	7,073.2	9,579.0
Capital goods	4,602.6	5,205.8	5,687.3
Consumer goods	7,152.3	4,795.9	7,116.7
Total	19,280.0	17,074.9	22,383.0

Exports f.o.b.	1982	1983	1984
Coffee	7,061.4	6,542.1	9,930.1
Cotton	223.2	249.4	82.1
Hides and skins	8.6	68.8	81.6
Tea	255.3	227.7	864.0
Minerals	4.7	5.8	0.1
Other products	345.4	401.9	870.2
Total	7,898.6	7,495.7	11,828.1

Sources: Département des Etudes et Statistiques; Banque de la République du Burundi.

PRINCIPAL TRADING PARTNERS
(million Burundi francs)

Imports	1982	1983	1984
Belgium-Luxembourg	3,057.4	2,634.6	3,284.9
France	2,269.4	1,759.3	3,123.7
Germany, Federal Republic	1,596.4	1,493.2	1,977.0
Italy	587.5	663.6	904.9
Japan	1,515.7	1,093.7	1,195.8
Kenya	792.9	638.4	757.6
Netherlands	609.0	652.8	588.7
Tanzania	597.8	464.9	504.0
United Kingdom	554.6	463.8	458.8
USA	1,020.7	561.9	1,231.2
Zaire	176.1	148.2	296.4
Others	6,502.5	6,500.5	8,060.0
Total	19,280.0	17,074.9	22,383.0

Sources: Département des Etudes et Statistiques; Banque de la République du Burundi.

Exports	1982	1983	1984
Belgium-Luxembourg	112.8	343.0	334.7
France	90.7	19.1	30.5
Germany, Federal Republic	1,865.4	3,719.0	3,965.9
Italy	173.4	254.1	341.5
Netherlands	107.3	27.7	51.6
United Kingdom	233.0	134.3	270.1
USA	2,527.7	155.0	189.4
Others	2,788.3	2,843.5	6,644.4
Total	7,898.6	7,495.7	11,828.1

Transport

ROAD TRAFFIC (motor vehicles in use)

	1982	1983	1984
Passenger cars	6,462	7,016	7,533
Vans	2,588	2,820	3,040
Lorries	1,102	1,253	1,324
All other vehicles	1,345	1,627	1,824
Total	11,497	12,716	13,721

Sources: Département des Impôts; Banque de la République du Burundi.

CIVIL AVIATION (Bujumbura Airport)

	1982	1983	1984
Passengers:			
Arrivals	23,957	21,754	19,050
Departures	24,856	21,834	19,091
Freight (metric tons):			
Arrivals	4,649	4,545	5,231
Departures	3,532	2,974	3,201

Sources: Ministry of Transport and Aviation; Banque de la République du Burundi.

LAKE TRAFFIC (Bujumbura—'000 metric tons)

	1982	1983	1984
Goods:			
Arrivals	114.0	114.5	130.0
Departures	29.2	30.4	33.9

Source: Banque de la République du Burundi.

Tourism

	1980	1981	1982
Tourist arrivals ('000)	34	37	38

Source: UN, *Statistical Yearbook*.

Communications Media

	1981	1982	1983
Radio receivers ('000 in use)	152	165	178

Source: UNESCO, *Statistical Yearbook*.

Education

(1984)

	Teachers	Pupils
Pre-primary	25	1,446
Primary	6,192	337,329
Secondary:		
General	595	9,765
Teacher training	465	7,782
Vocational	507	4,514

Source: Ministère de l'Education Nationale, *Statistiques scolaires*.

Directory

The Constitution

A new constitution for the Republic of Burundi was approved by a national referendum on 18 November 1981. Its main provisions are summarized below:

UPRONA (Union pour le progrès national) is the sole legal political party. It determines national political orientation and state policy, and supervises the action of the Government. The Head of State and the National Assembly, which holds legislative power and meets twice a year, are elected for a term of five years by direct universal adult suffrage. The sole candidate for Head of State is the President of UPRONA.

The Government

HEAD OF STATE

President: Col JEAN-BAPTISTE BAGAZA (proclaimed 9 November 1976; elected by direct suffrage 31 August 1984).

COUNCIL OF MINISTERS
(October 1986)

President and Minister of Defence: Col JEAN-BAPTISTE BAGAZA.
Minister of Parliamentary Relations: Lt-Col STANISLAS MANDI.
Minister of Economic Planning: MATHIAS SINAMENYE.
Minister of Justice: ALOYS NDENZAKO.
Minister of Internal Affairs: Lt-Col CHARLES KAZATSA.
Minister of Foreign Affairs and Co-operation: EGIDE NKURIYINGOMA.
Minister of Finance: PIERRE NGENZI.
Minister of Rural Development: JEAN KABURA.
Minister of Agriculture and Animal Husbandry: MATHIAS NTIBARIKURE.
Minister of Industry and Trade: ALBERT MUGANGA.
Minister of Transport, Posts and Telecommunications: RÉMY NKENGURUTSE.
Minister of Public Works, Energy and Mines: ISIDORE NYABOYA.
Minister of Public Health: Maj. Dr FIDÈLE NSABIMANA.
Minister of National Education: ISIDORE HAKIZIMANA.
Minister for Women's Affairs: EUPHRASIE KANDEKE.
Minister for Social Affairs: CARITAS MATEGEKO.
Minister of Labour and Professional Training: CYRILLE BARANCIRA.
Minister of Youth, Sport and Culture: BALTAZAR HABONIMANA.
Minister of Information: BENOÎT MUYEBE.
Minister of the Civil Service: DAMIEN BARAKAMFITIYE.

MINISTRIES

Office of the President and Minister of Defence: Bujumbura; tel. 6063; telex 38.
Ministry of Agriculture and Animal Husbandry: Bujumbura; tel. 4021.
Ministry of the Civil Service: Bujumbura; tel. 3514.
Ministry of Economic Planning: Bujumbura; tel. 6063.
Ministry of Finance: BP 1830, Bujumbura; tel. 23988; telex 5135.
Ministry of Foreign Affairs and Co-operation: Bujumbura; tel. 2150; telex 5065.
Ministry of Industry and Trade: Bujumbura; tel. 3820.
Ministry of Information: Bujumbura; tel. 4666.
Ministry of Internal Affairs: Bujumbura; tel. 4242.
Ministry of Justice: Bujumbura; tel. 2148.
Ministry of Labour and Professional Training: BP 2830, Bujumbura; tel. 25058.
Ministry of National Education: Bujumbura; tel. 5112.
Ministry of Parliamentary Relations: Bujumbura.
Ministry of Public Health: Bujumbura; tel. 6020.
Ministry of Public Works, Energy and Mines: Bujumbura; tel. 5268; telex 48.
Ministry of Rural Development: Bujumbura; tel. 5267.
Ministry of Social Affairs: Bujumbura; tel. 5039.
Ministry of Transport, Posts and Telecommunications: Bujumbura; tel. 2923; telex 52.
Ministry of Women's Affairs: Bujumbura; tel. 5561.
Ministry of Youth, Sport and Culture: Bujumbura; tel. 6822.

Legislature

ASSEMBLÉE NATIONALE

The first National Assembly, sanctioned by the 1981 constitution as Burundi's legislative body, was constituted following elections on 22 October 1982. Of the 65 seats in the Assembly, 52 are contested on the basis of universal adult suffrage and the remaining 13 are filled by appointees of the President of the Republic. At the 1982 elections, all 104 candidates (two for each elective seat) were members of UPRONA, the country's only legal political party, and had been chosen by local party selection committees.

President: EMILE MWOROHA.

Political Organization

Union pour le progrès national (UPRONA): BP 1810, Bujumbura; tel. 25028; telex 5057; f. 1958; following the 1961 elections, the many small parties which had been defeated subsequently merged with UPRONA, which became the sole legal political party in November 1966; in 1979 the first Party Congress adopted the party statutes and charter, and elected the Party President and the UPRONA Cen. Cttee; in 1980 there were about 1m. enrolled mems, organized into local cttees, the higher cttees being those of the zone or quarter, commune, province and finally the UPRONA Cen. Cttee, with 70 mems, and its Political Bureau of 8 mems; the supreme organ of UPRONA is the Party Congress, which is a meeting of party mems who are in the party cttees at different levels; the party guides the nation's political orientation and state policy in all fields; three movements, the Union de la Jeunesse révolutionnaire burundaise (UJRB), the Union des Femmes burundaises (UFB) and the Union des Travailleurs du Burundi (UTB), are closely allied with UPRONA and work under its control; Pres. Col JEAN-BAPTISTE BAGAZA; Sec.-Gen. EMILE MWOROHA; mems of Political Bureau Col JEAN-BAPTISTE BAGAZA, EMILE MWOROHA, Lt-Col STANISLAS MANDI, RÉMY NKENGURUTSE, EUPHRASIE KANDEKE, JEAN KABURA, KARENZO HERMENEJILDE, Lt-Col CHARLES KAZATSA.

Diplomatic Representation

EMBASSIES IN BURUNDI

Belgium: 9 ave de l'Industrie, BP 1920, Bujumbura; tel. 3676; telex 5033; Ambassador: MARCEL VAGEHNDE.
China, People's Republic: BP 2550, Bujumbura; Ambassador: SHEN LIANRUI.
Cuba: 14 ave Ngozi, BP 2288, Bujumbura; tel. 26476; telex 5140; Ambassador: DIOSDADO FERNÁNDEZ GONZÁLEZ.
Egypt: 31 ave de la Liberté, BP 1520, Bujumbura; tel. 3161; telex 5040; Ambassador: AHMED FOUAD MORSI.
France: 60 ave de l'UPRONA, BP 1740, Bujumbura; tel. 3176; telex 5044; Ambassador: ROBERT RIGOUZZO.
Germany, Federal Republic: 22 rue 18 septembre, BP 480, Bujumbura; tel. 3211; telex 5068; Ambassador: Dr IRENE GRUNDER.
Holy See: 46 chaussée Prince Louis-Rwagasore, BP 1068, Bujumbura; tel. 2326; Apostolic Pro-Nuncio: Mgr PIETRO SAMBI.
Korea, Democratic People's Republic: BP 1620, Bujumbura; Ambassador: CHOE CHONG-SOP.
Libya: ave de l'UPRONA, BP 4619, Bujumbura; telex 5088.
Romania: rue Pierre Ngendandumwe, BP 2770, Bujumbura; Chargé d'affaires a.i.: MIRCEA LAZARESCU.
Rwanda: 24 avenue du Zaïre, BP 400, Bujumbura; tel. 3140; telex 5032; Ambassador: SYMPHORIEN NTEZIRIZAZA.

BURUNDI

Tanzania: BP 1653, Bujumbura; Ambassador: H. MAKWAIA.
USSR: 9 ave de l'UPRONA, BP 1034, Bujumbura; tel. 2698; Ambassador: VALERI VASILEVICH TSYBUKOV.
USA: chaussée Prince Rwagasore, BP 1720, Bujumbura; tel. 3454; Ambassador: JAMES D. PHILLIPS.
Zaire: 5 ave Olsen, BP 872, Bujumbura; tel. 3492; Ambassador: IKOLO MBOLOKO.

Judicial System

The Constitution prescribes a judicial system wherein the judges are subject to the decisions of UPRONA made in the light of the revolutionary concept of the law. No appeal is provided for in the case of decisions of the Supreme Court.

Supreme Court: Bujumbura; tel. 5442. Four chambers: ordinary, cassation, constitutional and administrative.
Courts of Appeal: Bujumbura and Gitega.
Tribunals of First Instance: There are four national tribunals, in Bujumbura, 16 provincial tribunals and 122 smaller resident tribunals in other areas.

Religion

More than 60% of the population are Christians, mostly Roman Catholics. Anglicans number about 60,000. There are about 200,000 Protestants, of whom some 160,000 are Pentecostalists. Fewer than 40% of the population are followers of traditional belief, which is mainly in a God 'Imana'. About 1% of the population are Muslims. The Bahá'í Faith is also active in Burundi.

CHRISTIANITY

The Anglican Communion

Anglicans in Burundi form part of the Church of the Province of Burundi, Rwanda and Zaire. Since 1982 the Archbishop of the Province has been the Bishop of Butare (in Rwanda).

Bishop of Bujumbura: Rt Rev. SAMUEL SINDAMUKA, BP 1300, Bujumbura; tel. 22641.
Bishop of Buye: Rt Rev. SAMUEL NDAYISENGA, BP 94, Ngozi.
Bishop of Gitega: J. NDUWAYO.

The Roman Catholic Church

Burundi comprises one archdiocese and six dioceses. At 31 December 1984 there were an estimated 2,588,000 adherents in the country.
Bishops' Conference: Conférence des Evêques catholiques du Burundi, BP 1390, Bujumbura; f. 1980; Pres. Most Rev. JOACHIM RUHUNA, Archbishop of Gitega.
Archbishop of Gitega: Most Rev. JOACHIM RUHUNA, Archevêché, BP 118, Gitega; tel. 2149.

Other Christian Churches

Union of Baptist Churches of Burundi: Rubura, DS 117, Bujumbura 1; Pres. PAUL BARUHENAMWO; Exec. Sec. OSIAS HABINGABWA.

BAHÁ'Í FAITH

National Spiritual Assembly: BP 1578, Bujumbura.

The Press

All publications are strictly controlled by the government.

NEWSPAPERS

Burundi chrétien: BP 232, Bujumbura; weekly; French; publ. by the Roman Catholic Archdiocese of Gitega.
Le Renouveau du Burundi: Ministry of Information, BP 2870, Bujumbura; f. 1978; daily; French; circ. 20,000.
Ubumwe: BP 1400, Bujumbura; tel. 3929; f. 1971; weekly; Kirundi; circ. 20,000.

PERIODICALS

Bulletin économique et financier: BP 482, Bujumbura; bi-monthly.
Bulletin officiel du Burundi: Bujumbura; monthly.

Directory

Le Burundi en Images: BP 1400, Bujumbura; f. 1979; monthly.
Culture et Sociétés: BP 1400, Bujumbura; f. 1978; quarterly.

NEWS AGENCY

Agence burundaise de Presse (ABP): 6 ave de la Poste, BP 2870, Bujumbura; telex 5056; publ. daily bulletin.

Publishers

Imprimerie du Parti: BP 1810, Bujumbura.
Les Presses Lavigerie: 5 blvd de l'UPRONA, BP 1640, Bujumbura.

Government Publishing House

Imprimerie nationale du Burundi (INABU): BP 991, Bujumbura; tel. 4046; telex 80.

Radio and Television

In 1985 there were an estimated 180,000 radio receivers and 250 television receivers in use. The installation of a colour television network was completed in 1985.

Voix de la Révolution/Radio-Télévision Nationale du Burundi (RTNB): BP 1900, Bujumbura; tel. 23742; telex 5041; f. 1960; govt-controlled; daily radio programmes in Kirundi, Swahili, French and English; Dir-Gen. ALEXIS NTAVYO; Dir 1st Programme CHRISTINE NTAHE; Dir 2nd Programme ANTOINE NTAMIKEVYO.

Finance

(cap. = capital; p.u. = paid up; res = reserves; dep. = deposits; m. = million; amounts in Burundi francs)

BANKING

Central Bank

Banque de la République du Burundi (BRB): BP 705, Bujumbura; tel. 5142; telex 5071; f. 1964; cap. 1,494m., res 1,389m. (Dec. 1982); Gov. ALOYS NTAHONKIRIYE; Vice-Gov. PASTEUR BUDEYI; Dir MICHEL MBABAREMPORE.

Commercial Banks

Banque Belgo-Africaine du Burundi (BBAB): 16 blvd de la Liberté, BP 585, Bujumbura; tel. 2601; telex 5037; f. 1960; wholly owned by Banque Bruxelles Lambert, Belgium; cap. 72m., total assets 1,647.2m. (Dec. 1983); Chair. ROBERT DESAUVAGE.
Banque Commerciale du Burundi (BANCOBU): chaussée Prince Louis-Rwagasore, BP 990, Bujumbura; tel. 2317; telex 5051; f. 1960; 23.6% state-owned; cap. 150m., res 98m., dep. 2,800m. (Dec. 1982); Chair. DISMAS NDORERE; Man. Dir BENJAMIN MALFROID.
Banque de Crédit de Bujumbura (BCB): ave Patrice Emmery Lumumba, BP 300, Bujumbura; tel. 22091; telex 5063; f. 1964; cap. 400m., res 54m., dep. 5,697m. (Dec. 1985); Chair. A. NDORERE; Man. Dir R. THIBAUT DE MAISIÈRES.
Caisse d'Epargne du Burundi (CADEBU): BP 615, Bujumbura; tel. 2348; telex 71; f. 1964; 100% state-owned; cap. 90m.; Chair. PASTEUR BUDEYI; Man. Dir ADELIN KAREGEYA.

Development Bank

Banque Nationale pour le Développement Economique du Burundi (BNDE): BP 1620, Bujumbura; tel. 2887; telex 5091; f. 1967; cap. 500.9m. (Dec. 1983); Chair. BONUS KAMWENUBUSA; Man. Dir FRANÇOIS BARWENDERE.

INSURANCE

Société d'Assurances du Burundi (SOCABU): BP 2440, 14–18 rue de l'Amitié, Bujumbura; tel. 26803; telex 5113; f. 1977; partly state-owned; cap. p.u. 120m.; Man. ATHANASE GAHUNGU.

Trade and Industry

STATE TRADE ORGANIZATION

Office National du Commerce (ONC): Bujumbura; f. 1973; supervises international commercial operations between the govt of Burundi and other states or private organizations; also ensures the import of essential materials; brs in each province.

BURUNDI
Directory

DEVELOPMENT ORGANIZATIONS

Caisse Centrale de Mobilisation et de Financement (CAMOFI): 4 avenue de l'UJRB, BP 8, Bujumbura; tel. 5642; telex 83; f. 1977 to finance public-sector development projects and businesses; cap. 100m. (Dec. 1983); Chair. Minister of Finance; Man. Dir LÉONARD NTIBAGIRIRWA.

Comité de Gérance de la Reserve Cotonnière (COGERCO): Bujumbura; develops the cotton industry.

Fonds de Promotion Economique: PB 270, Bujumbura; tel. 5562; telex 80; f. 1981 to finance and promote industrial, agricultural and commercial activities; Man. Dir BONAVENTURE KIDWINGIRA.

Holding Arabe Libyen Burundais: Bujumbura; tel. 6635; telex 90; f. 1977 to finance development projects and businesses.

Institut des Sciences Agronomiques du Burundi (ISABU): BP 795, Bujumbura; tel. 3384; f. 1962 for the scientific development of agriculture and livestock.

Office de la Tourbe du Burundi (ONATOUR): BP 2360, Bujumbura; tel. 6480; telex 48; f. 1977 to promote the exploitation of peat bogs.

Office des Cultures Industrielles du Burundi (OCIBU): BP 450, Bujumbura; tel. 2631; supervises coffee plantations and coffee exports.

Office du Thé du Burundi (OTB): Bujumbura; telex 5069; f. 1979; develops the tea industry.

Office National du Bois (ONB): BP 1492, Bujumbura; tel. 4416; f. 1980; exploits local timber resources and imports foreign timber; Dir LAZARE RUNESA.

Office National du Logement (ONL): BP 2480, Bujumbura; tel. 6074; telex 48; f. 1974; deals with housing construction.

Société d'Economie Mixte pour l'Exploitation du Quinquina au Burundi (SOKINAB): BP 1783, Bujumbura; tel. 23469; telex 81; f. 1975 to develop and exploit cinchona trees, the source of quinine; Man. RAPHËL REMEZO.

Société de Stockage et de Commercialisation des Produits Vivriers (SOBECOV): Bujumbura; f. 1977 to stock and sell agricultural products in Burundi.

Société Mixte, Minière et Industrielle Roumano-Burundaise (SOMIBUROM): Bujumbura; f. 1977; exploitation and marketing of mineral and industrial products.

Société Sucrière du Moso (SOSUMO): BP 835, Bujumbura; tel. 6576; telex 35; f. 1982; establishes and manages sugar cane plantations.

CHAMBER OF COMMERCE

Chambre de Commerce et de l'Industrie du Rwanda et du Burundi: BP 313, Bujumbura; f. 1923; Pres. M. R. LECLERE; Hon. Sec. M. T. POJER; 130 mems.

TRADE UNION

Union des Travailleurs du Burundi (UTB): BP 1350, Bujumbura; tel. 3850; f. 1967 by amalgamation of all previous unions; closely allied with UPRONA; sole authorized union for Burundi workers; Sec.-Gen. MARIUS RURAHENYE.

Transport

RAILWAYS

There are no railways in Burundi, but in 1985 plans were being considered for the construction of a line passing through Uganda, Rwanda and Burundi, to connect with the Kigoma–Dar es Salaam line in Tanzania, which would improve Burundi's isolated trade position.

ROADS

The road network is very dense and in 1981 there was a total of 5,144 km of roads, of which 1,710 km were national highways and 1,274 km secondary roads. In 1985 a contract was awarded to construct a 133-km road linking Rugombo and Kayanza, a town on the Rwandan border.

INLAND WATERWAYS

Bujumbura is the principal port for both passenger and freight traffic on Lake Tanganyika, and the greater part of Burundi's external trade is dependent on the shipping services between Bujumbura and Tanzania, Zambia and Zaire.

CIVIL AVIATION

There is an international airport at Bujumbura, equipped to take large jet-engined aircraft.

Air Burundi: BP 2460, 40 ave du Commerce, Bujumbura; telex 80; f. 1971 as Société des Transports Aériens du Burundi; operates services to Kigali (Rwanda), Kigoma (Tanzania), Kalémié (Zaire), and internally from Bujumbura to Gitega; Man. Dir GÉRARD MUGABO; fleet of 1 Caravelle, 2 Twin Otter, 2 Piper Super Cub.

Tourism

Office National du Tourisme: BP 902, Bujumbura; tel. 22202; telex 5030; f. 1972; Dir JÉRÔME NZOJIBWAMI.

CAMEROON

Introductory Survey

Location, Climate, Language, Religion, Flag, Capital

The Republic of Cameroon lies on the west coast of Africa, with Nigeria to the west, Chad and the Central African Republic to the east, and the Congo, Equatorial Guinea and Gabon to the south. The climate is hot and humid in the south and west, with average temperatures of 26°C (80°F). The north is drier, with more extreme temperatures. The official languages are French and English, and many local languages are also spoken. Approximately 39% of Cameroonians follow traditional religious beliefs. About 40% are Christians, and about 21%, mostly in the north, are Muslims. The national flag (proportions 3 by 2) has three equal vertical stripes, of green, red and yellow, with a five-pointed gold star in the centre of the red stripe. The capital is Yaoundé.

Recent History

In 1884 a German protectorate was established in Cameroon (Kamerun). In 1916, during the First World War, the German administration was overthrown by invading British and French forces. Under an agreement made between the occupying powers in 1919, Cameroon was divided into two zones: a French-ruled area, in the east and south, and a smaller British area in the west. In 1922 both zones became subject to mandates of the League of Nations, with France and the United Kingdom as the administering powers. In 1946 the zones were transformed into UN Trust Territories, with British and French rule continuing in their respective areas.

French Cameroons became an autonomous state, within the French Community, in 1957. Under the leadership of Ahmadou Ahidjo, a northerner who became Prime Minister in 1958, the territory became independent, as the Republic of Cameroon, on 1 January 1960. The first election for the country's National Assembly, held in April 1960, was won by Ahidjo's party, the Union camerounaise. In May the new Assembly elected Ahidjo to be the country's first President.

British Cameroons, comprising a northern and a southern region, was attached to neighbouring Nigeria, for administrative purposes, prior to Nigeria's independence in October 1960. Plebiscites were held, under UN auspices, in the two regions of British Cameroons in February 1961. The northern area voted to merge with Nigeria (becoming the province of Sardauna), while the south voted for union with the Republic of Cameroon, which took place on 1 October 1961.

The enlarged country was named the Federal Republic of Cameroon, with French and English as joint official languages. It comprised two states: the former French zone became East Cameroon, while the ex-British portion became West Cameroon. John Foncha, Prime Minister of West Cameroon and leader of the Kamerun National Democratic Party, became Vice-President of the Federal Republic. Under the continuing leadership of Ahidjo, who was re-elected President in May 1965, the two states became increasingly integrated, despite Cameroon's ethnic and cultural diversity. In September 1966 a one-party regime was established when the two governing parties and several opposition groups combined to form a single party, the Union nationale camerounaise (UNC). The party expanded to embrace almost all the country's political, cultural, professional and social organizations. The only significant opposition party, the extreme left-wing Union des populations camerounaises (UPC), was finally crushed in 1971, although the leaders continued activities in exile in Paris. Meanwhile, President Ahidjo was re-elected in March 1970, when Solomon Muna (who had replaced Foncha as Prime Minister of West Cameroon in 1968) became Vice-President.

In June 1972, after approval by referendum of a new constitution, the federal system was ended and the country became the United Republic of Cameroon. The office of Vice-President was abolished. A fully centralized political and administrative system was quickly introduced, and in May 1973 a new National Assembly was elected for a five-year term. After the re-election of Ahidjo as President in April 1975, the Constitution was revised, and a Prime Minister, Paul Biya, was appointed in June. Despite opposition from anglophone intellectuals who desired a return to the federal system of government, Ahidjo was unanimously re-elected for a fifth five-year term of office in April 1980.

President Ahidjo announced his resignation in November 1982 and named Paul Biya, the Prime Minister, as his successor. No official reasons for the resignation were given. The new President, a bilingual southerner, was expected to continue the policies of national unity and non-alignment which had characterized Ahidjo's rule. Bello Bouba Maigari, a northerner, was appointed Prime Minister. Ahidjo retained the presidency of the UNC and his political influence continued. In January 1983 three members of the National Assembly, including its Vice-President, were expelled from the party.

In Cabinet reshuffles in April and June 1983, Biya introduced more technocrats into the Government and gradually removed supporters of the former President. On 22 August 1983 Biya announced the discovery of a plot to overthrow his Government, and simultaneously dismissed both the Prime Minister and the Minister of the Armed Forces. On 27 August former President Ahidjo resigned as President of the UNC and strongly criticized the regime of President Biya, accusing him of leading a police state. In September Biya was elected President of the ruling party. An amendment to the Constitution, approved in December 1983, permitted candidates who were independent of the UNC to stand for the office of President. Presidential elections took place in January 1984, and Biya was re-elected with 99.98% of the vote. In a subsequent Cabinet reshuffle, the post of Prime Minister was abolished, and it was announced that the country's name was to revert from the United Republic of Cameroon to the Republic of Cameroon.

In February 1984 Ahidjo (who was now in exile in France) and two of his close military advisers were tried for their alleged part in the coup plot of August 1983; death sentences were passed on all three men but commuted to life imprisonment two weeks later. On 6 April 1984 rebel elements in the presidential guard, led by Col Saleh Ibrahim, a northerner, attempted to seize power and overthrow the Biya government. After three days of heavy fighting, in which hundreds were reported to have been killed, the rebellion was crushed by forces loyal to the President. Trials of those implicated in the coup were held in May and November 1984, resulting in 46 executions. Following extensive changes within the military hierarchy, the UNC central committee and the leadership of state-controlled companies, in which supporters of the former President were dismissed, Biya reshuffled his government in July and introduced more stringent press censorship.

At the party conference in March 1985, the UNC changed its name to the Rassemblement démocratique du peuple camerounais (RDPC). Another Cabinet reshuffle in August further strengthened Biya's position, bringing the Ministry of Defence, the Ministry in charge of Missions and the Ministry of Computer Services and Public Contracts into the Presidency. Sweeping changes in the internal structure of the RDPC occurred as a result of elections held between January and March 1986, with more than half of the party's 49 section presidents being replaced. Many of the posts were contested by more than one candidate. In November 1986, following a reorganization of the President's office (see Government, below), Biya again reshuffled the Cabinet, appointing a total of four new ministers.

In January 1986 allegations of repression were made against the Biya regime by members of the exiled UPC movement, who claimed (at a press conference held in Paris) that between 200 and 300 people, mainly anglophones or members of clandestine opposition movements, had been arrested in the preceding months, and that some of the detainees were being subjected to torture. The Government subsequently released a number of detainees.

In July 1973 President Ahidjo announced his country's impending withdrawal from the Organisation commune africaine, malgache et mauricienne (OCAM), a grouping of mainly French-speaking African states, then based in Yaoundé. Cameroon also negotiated a revision of its co-operation agreements with France in 1974. The independent foreign policy that was pursued under President Ahidjo has been continued by his successor. Relations with France have generally remained close, although Cameroon has sought to resist overdependence: France currently accounts for around 40% of the country's foreign trade transactions. Biya paid state visits to both France and the UK during 1985.

In August 1986 Cameroon was forced to appeal for international emergency aid when an explosion of underwater volcanic gases at Lake Nyos, in the north-west of the country, led to an estimated 1,700 deaths and caused widespread suffering. The disaster coincided with a much-publicized visit to Cameroon by Shimon Peres, the Prime Minister of Israel, during which the two countries renewed diplomatic links, following a 13-year suspension of relations as a result of the Arab–Israeli war in 1973.

Government

Under the 1972 Constitution, executive power is vested in the President, as Head of State, while legislative power is held by the unicameral National Assembly, with 120 members. Both the President and the Assembly are elected for five years by universal adult suffrage. The number of deputies to the National Assembly is to increase to 150 to take account of the increase in population. The Cabinet is appointed by the President. In November 1986 the former Secretariat-General of the Presidency was replaced by two new bodies: the Secretariat-General of the Government, and the Cabinet of the President. The former Civil Cabinet became the President's Private Cabinet. Local administration is based on 10 provinces, each with a Governor who is appointed by the President.

Defence

In July 1986 Cameroon had an army of 6,600 and there were 4,000 men in paramilitary forces. The navy numbered 350 and the air force also had 350 men. France has a bilateral defence agreement with Cameroon. The defence budget for 1986/87 was 51,615m. francs CFA.

Economic Affairs

In 1984 Cameroon had one of the highest levels of income per head in tropical Africa, owing to the increased role of petroleum in the economy, which is essentially based on agriculture. In 1984, according to World Bank estimates, Cameroon's GNP per head was US $800 (at average 1982–84 prices), having increased by 2.9% annually, in real terms, since 1965. The further development of the agricultural sector and the achievement of self-sufficiency in food were stated to be the main priorities of the sixth Five-Year Plan, launched in 1986. Agriculture is well-diversified, and the main commercial products are cocoa (of which Cameroon is the world's fifth largest producer), coffee, bananas, cotton, palm oil and cane sugar. Agricultural production expanded at an average rate of almost 4% annually in 1961–80, and during that period accounted for between 70% and 75% of total export trade. The agricultural sector contributes about 22% of GDP and employs approximately 70% of the working population. In addition, Cameroon possesses considerable livestock and forestry resources. Forests cover about 40% of the total land area, and in 1983 the exploitable areas totalled 17,400,000 ha.

Output in virtually all agricultural sectors declined in 1981/82 and 1982/83, owing to persistent drought. The grain-growing northern regions were particularly affected, and the cereal shortfall in 1982/83 was estimated at 75,000 tons. Production of cocoa beans rose to 120,081 metric tons in 1984/85 (just below the 1981/82 level, from a low of 108,000 tons in 1983/84), but fell to an estimated 115,000 tons in 1985/86. Cameroon's production of coffee totalled only 64,000 tons in 1983/84, but recovered to 114,519 tons in 1984/85. In 1985/86, however, production fell to 83,131 tons, with output of the robusta variety falling to 66,356 tons from 103,958 tons in the previous season. Output of cotton increased during the early 1980s, owing to expansion of the area under cultivation: production of seed cotton (40,000 tons in 1974/75) totalled 102,000 tons in 1983, but fell back to 67,000 tons in 1984, recovering to 97,500 tons in 1985. Production of sawlogs fell to 1,298,000 cu m in 1983 from 1,700,000 cu m in 1982, as a result of the drought. Further development of Cameroon's forests depends on the creation of an adequate transport infrastructure.

The diversity of agricultural products has given rise to agro-industries, including a maize complex, sugar processing plants, tobacco factories, and cotton spinning and weaving mills. The fifth Five-Year Plan (1981–86) projected total investment of 377,200m. francs CFA for the development of the industrial sector, including mining and energy. Hydroelectricity provides around 95% of the country's power generation: the capacity of the Song-Loulou plant is currently being extended from 288 MW to 384 MW, and there are also plants at Edéa and Lagdo.

Petroleum was discovered off Rio del Rey in 1973, and Cameroon's first oil exports were shipped in 1978. Output of crude petroleum increased steadily, from 800,000 metric tons in 1978 to a record 6.7m. tons in 1985. Further offshore oilfields were discovered near the Nigerian border, in the Wouri estuary and off Kribi in 1979/80. Offshore prospecting ceased in October 1985. The capacity of the petroleum refinery, opened at Limbe (formerly Victoria) in 1980, was to be doubled to 3m. tons per year. Plans for a liquefied natural gas plant at Kribi, however, were abandoned in 1984, following revised estimates indicating that natural gas resources in these areas were less than had previously been assessed. Export earnings from petroleum were, until recently, excluded from official trade accounts, but rose from 116,677m. francs CFA in 1981 to 163,537m. francs CFA in 1983. The decrease in international oil prices reduced earnings to 95,279m. francs CFA in 1984. Oil revenues continued to decline in 1986. In 1982 the state oil corporation, Société Nationale des Hydrocarbures, obtained a 20% interest in all the petroleum-producing companies operating in Cameroon.

Bauxite deposits, estimated at 1,000m. tons, have been discovered at Minim-Martap, and are to be exploited by ALUCAM, the aluminium concern which at present uses imported bauxite from Guinea. Iron ore deposits near Kribi could also be developed in the near future. As a result of expansion in petroleum output, the mining sector's contribution to GDP rose from 12.8% in 1981/82 to 17.0% in 1983/84.

Despite the growth of exports, Cameroon continues to experience a deficit on its current balance of payments: in 1983 this totalled US $413.9m., but in 1984 it declined to $165.2m. Inflation has been a severe problem in recent years: prices in Yaoundé increased by 16.6%, on average, in 1983, but the inflation rate eased to 13.2% in the year to June 1985. The high inflation of 1983 was attributable to the Government's expansionary monetary policy, increased food prices (due to drought) and imported inflation. External debt was US $1,780m. at the end of 1985, with new loans totalling 926,900m. francs CFA in the year ending February 1986. The debt service ratio, which was equivalent to around 14% of declared export revenue in that year, and was expected to average 10% of annual export earnings in 1981–86, is one of the lowest among black African countries. The sixth Five-Year Plan, announced in 1986, involved total projected expenditure of 7,830,000m. francs CFA, of which 25% was to be devoted to rural development. Public expenditure in 1985/86 totalled 920,000m. francs CFA, with the budget figure of 740,000m. francs CFA being supplemented, in February 1986, by a special allocation of 180,000m. francs CFA from extrabudgetary oil revenue. In 1986/87 expenditure was to amount to 800,000m. francs CFA (of which 460,000m. francs CFA was to be allocated to recurrent expenditure and 340,000m. francs CFA to investment), representing a considerably reduced budget in real terms, compared with the previous year. In May 1986 plans were announced for the progressive reduction of long-term public investment in the economy: the state investment company, SNI, was to sell its existing holdings in 62 companies to local investors, and to relinquish its share capital in new industrial projects within seven years of the projects' initiation.

CAMEROON

Social Welfare
The Government and Christian missions maintain hospitals and medical centres, but there are, as yet, no welfare services covering the whole population. In 1979 Cameroon had 22,800 hospital beds in 126 hospitals and health centres and 900 dispensaries. There were 603 physicians working in the country. The 1986/87 budget allocated 27,755m. francs CFA to health expenditure. A campaign aiming at 'Health for all by the year 2000' is being carried out, with the emphasis on the development of preventive medicine. The 1986–91 Plan envisaged the development of a system of social security suitable to the country's needs.

Education
Education is provided by the Government, missionary societies and private concerns. Education in state schools is free, and the Government provides financial assistance for other schools; there is a bilingual primary school in each province, and most secondary schools are also bilingual. In 1978 a programme of standardization of curricula was introduced. Primary education begins at six years of age. It lasts for six years in Eastern Cameroon (where it is officially compulsory), and for seven years in Western Cameroon. Secondary education, beginning at the age of 12 or 13, lasts for a further seven years. In 1983 the total enrolment at primary and secondary schools was equivalent to 66% of the school-age population (74% of boys; 59% of girls): attendance at schools in the northern region, which had been as low as 32% in 1981, was estimated at 55% in 1986. In 1976 the average rate of adult illiteracy was 59.5%: by 1985, according to estimates by UNESCO, the rate had declined to 43.8% (males 31.6%; females 55.3%). The State University at Yaoundé, founded in 1962, has been decentralized, and consists of five regional campuses. Budgets in recent years have given high priority to education, with an allocation of 70,800m. francs CFA in 1986/87.

Tourism
Tourists are attracted by the cultural diversity of local customs, and by the national parks, game reserves and sandy beaches. The tourist trade is being expanded, and in 1984 there were 108,109 foreign visitors. In the course of the 1981–86 development plan, several new hotels were built, and more money was made available for the protection of animals in national parks. The 1985/86 budget allotted 1,401m. francs CFA to tourism.

Public Holidays
1987: 1 January (New Year), 11 February (Youth Day), 17 April (Good Friday), 20 April (Easter Monday), 1 May (Labour Day), 20 May (National Day), 28 May (Ascension Day), 30 May† (Djoulde Soumae, end of Ramadan), 6 August† (Festival of Sheep), 1 September (Union Nationale Camerounaise Day*), 25 December (Christmas).

1988: 1 January (New Year), 11 February (Youth Day), 1 April (Good Friday), 4 April (Easter Monday), 1 May (Labour Day), 12 May (Ascension Day), 18 May† (Djoulde Soumae, end of Ramadan), 20 May (National Day), 25 July† (Festival of Sheep), 1 September (Union Nationale Camerounaise Day*), 25 December (Christmas).

* Name of holiday to be revised.
† These holidays are dependent on the Islamic lunar calendar and may vary by one or two days from the dates given.

Weights and Measures
The metric system is in force.

Currency and Exchange Rates
100 centimes = 1 franc de la Coopération financière en Afrique centrale (CFA).

Exchange rates (30 September 1986):
  1 franc CFA = 2 French centimes;
  £1 sterling = 480.625 francs CFA;
  US $1 = 332.125 francs CFA.

CAMEROON

Statistical Survey

Source (unless otherwise stated): Direction de la Statistique et de la Comptabilité Nationale, BP 25, Yaoundé; tel. 22-07-88; telex 8203.

Area and Population

AREA, POPULATION AND DENSITY

Area (sq km)	475,442*
Population (census of 9 April 1976)†	
Male	3,754,991
Female	3,908,255
Total	7,663,246
Population (official estimates at mid-year)	
1982	8,938,000
1983	9,165,000
1984	9,542,000
Density (per sq km) at mid-1984	19.9

* 183,569 sq miles.
† Including an adjustment for underenumeration, estimated at 7.4%. The enumerated total was 7,090,115 (males 3,472,786; females 3,617,329).

PROVINCES (population at 1976 census)

	Urban	Rural	Total
Centre-South	498,290	993,655	1,491,945
Littoral	702,578	232,588	935,166
West	232,315	803,282	1,035,597
South-West	200,322	420,193	620,515
North-West	146,327	834,204	980,531
North	328,925	1,904,332	2,233,257
East	75,458	290,750	366,235
Total	2,184,242	5,479,004	7,663,246

Note: In August 1983 the number of provinces was increased to 10. Centre-South province became two separate provinces, Centre and South. The northern province was split into three: Far North, North and Adamoua.

PRINCIPAL TOWNS

1976 (population at census): Douala 458,426, Yaoundé (capital) 313,706, Nkongsamba 71,298, Maroua 67,187, Garoua 63,900, Bafoussam 62,239, Bamenda 48,111, Kumba 44,175, Limbe (formerly Victoria) 27,016.
1984 (estimated population): Douala 850,000, Yaoundé 650,000.

BIRTHS AND DEATHS

Average annual birth rate 42.9 per 1,000 in 1970–75, 43.2 per 1,000 in 1975–80; death rate 20.5 per 1,000 in 1970–75, 19.2 per 1,000 in 1975–80 (UN estimates).

ECONOMICALLY ACTIVE POPULATION
(1976 census, resident population)*

	Males	Females	Total
Agriculture, hunting, forestry and fishing	1,073,264	961,710	2,034,974
Mining and quarrying	1,188	70	1,258
Manufacturing	96,577	25,834	122,411
Electricity, gas and water	2,366	105	2,471
Construction	46,065	714	46,779
Trade, restaurants and hotels	80,862	27,180	108,042
Transport, storage and communication	35,541	718	36,259
Financing, insurance, real estate and business services	5,224	815	6,039
Community, social and personal services	178,937	26,550	205,487
Activities not adequately described	48,093	23,041	71,134
Total	1,568,117	1,066,737	2,634,854

* Excluding persons seeking work for the first time, totalling 123,045 (males 88,050, females 34,995).

1982 (official estimates): Total labour force 3,543,000 (males 2,214,000; females 1,329,000).

Agriculture

PRINCIPAL CROPS ('000 metric tons)

	1982	1983	1984*
Rice (paddy)	73	71†	40
Maize	450†	400†	400
Millet and sorghum	423	361	400
Potatoes*	33	30	32
Sweet potatoes*	140	110	130
Cassava (Manioc)†	640	600	620
Yams	400†	375†	400
Other roots and tubers	825	775	800
Dry beans*	103	105	107
Groundnuts (in shell)	90†	80*	80
Sesame seed*	10	10	10
Cottonseed*	45	65	42

	1982	1983	1984
Cotton lint†	27	37	33
Palm kernels	110†	85†	81*
Sugar cane*	1,000	1,000	1,100
Vegetables*	407	409	418
Avocados*	26	27	28
Pineapples*	31	30	32
Bananas	57†	63*	65*
Plantains*	1,000	950	970
Coffee (green)	127	64†	127†
Cocoa beans	105	108†	115†
Tobacco (leaves)	2	2†	2*
Natural rubber	18	16	16*

* FAO estimates.   † Unofficial estimates.

CAMEROON   Statistical Survey

LIVESTOCK
(FAO estimates, '000 head, year ending September)

	1982	1983	1984
Cattle	3,700	3,710	3,730
Sheep	2,180	2,190	2,180
Goats	2,200	2,100	2,000
Pigs	1,200	1,100	1,000
Horses	23	25	26
Asses	35	37	37

Poultry (FAO estimates, million): 10 in 1982; 11 in 1983; 11 in 1984.
Source: FAO, *Production Yearbook*.

LIVESTOCK PRODUCTS (FAO estimates, '000 metric tons)

	1982	1983	1984
Beef and veal	50	50	50
Mutton and lamb	8	8	8
Goats' meat	7	7	7
Pigmeat	29	27	26
Poultry meat	11	11	11
Other meat	4	3	3
Cows' milk	44	45	46
Hen eggs	9.2	9.4	9.6
Cattle hides	10.0	10.0	10.0
Sheepskins	1.6	1.6	1.6
Goatskins	1.5	1.4	1.3

Forestry

ROUNDWOOD REMOVALS ('000 cubic metres)

	1982	1983	1984
Sawlogs, veneer logs and logs for sleepers	1,707	1,776	1,776*
Other industrial wood*	606	621	638
Fuel wood*	7,994	7,994	7,994
Total	10,307	10,391	10,408

* FAO estimates.
Source: FAO, *Yearbook of Forest Products*.

SAWNWOOD PRODUCTION ('000 cubic metres)

	1982	1983	1984
Total (incl. boxboards)	383*	341†	341*

Railway sleepers (FAO estimates, '000 cubic metres): 85 in 1982; 85 in 1983; 85 in 1984.
* FAO estimate. † Unofficial estimate.
Source: FAO, *Yearbook of Forest Products*.

Fishing
(FAO estimates, '000 metric tons, live weight)

	1982	1983	1984
Inland waters	20.0	20.0	20.0
Atlantic Ocean	40.2	34.3	32.5
Total catch	60.2	54.3	52.5

Source: FAO, *Yearbook of Fishery Statistics*.

Mining
('000 metric tons)

	1983	1984	1985
Crude petroleum	5,600	6,470	6,700

Source: UN, *Monthly Bulletin of Statistics*.

Industry

SELECTED PRODUCTS

		1981	1982	1983
Palm oil	'000 metric tons	70	71*	39
Raw sugar	'000 metric tons	66	70*	58
Cocoa butter	'000 metric tons	3.5	3.6	3.0
Beer	'000 hectolitres	n.a.	2,859	3,354
Soft drinks	'000 hectolitres	n.a.	n.a.	1,033
Cigarettes	million	1,500*	1,550*	1,954
Soap	'000 metric tons	n.a.	n.a.	25.1
Cement	'000 metric tons	516*	530	598
Aluminium (unwrought)†	'000 metric tons	65.4*	64.1	53.6
Radio receivers	'000	n.a.	n.a.	12
Footwear	'000 pairs	n.a.	n.a.	6,108
Electric energy	million kWh	1,908	1,908	1,804

* Estimated production. † Using alumina imported from Guinea.
Source: UN, *Industrial Statistics Yearbook*.

CAMEROON   *Statistical Survey*

Finance

CURRENCY AND EXCHANGE RATES
Monetary Units
100 centimes = 1 franc de la Coopération financière en Afrique central (CFA).

Denominations
Coins: 1, 2, 5, 10, 25, 50, 100 and 500 francs CFA.
Notes: 100, 500, 1,000, 5,000 and 10,000 francs CFA.

French Franc, Sterling and Dollar Equivalents
(30 September 1986)
1 French franc = 50 francs CFA;
£1 sterling = 480.625 francs CFA;
US $1 = 332.125 francs CFA;
1,000 francs CFA = £2.081 = $3.011.

Average Exchange Rate (francs CFA per US $)
1983   381.06
1984   436.96
1985   449.26

BUDGET ESTIMATES
(million francs CFA, year ending 30 June)

Revenue	1983/84	1984/85
Fiscal receipts	470,264	566,000
Non-fiscal revenue	46,108	50,000
Various receipts	3,627.4	4,000
Total revenue	520,000	620,000

Expenditure	1983/84	1984/85
Current budget	326,000	400,000
Presidency	9,658.3	11,409.8
Services attached to the presidency	18,493.4	21,622.4
Armed forces	34,911.4	45,839.8
Finance	12,604.5	15,679.8
National education	50,540.6	61,476.5
Health	17,456.7	23,018.6
Equipment	19,477.6	21,163.0
Agriculture	9,531.7	11,746.1
Territorial administration	9,193.9	12,991.6
Town planning and housing	9,709.1	12,052.5
Public investment budget	198,520	220,000
Public debt servicing	46,000	60,000
Infrastructure	30.805.8	37,750
Social services	26,412	36,150
Agriculture and forestry	15,623	18,000
Transport	9,072	10,000
Defence	8,300	10,500
Total expenditure	524,520	620,000

1985/86: Budget balanced at 740,000m. francs CFA (current expenditure 430,000m.; investment expenditure 310,000m.).
1986/87: Budget balanced at 800,000m. francs CFA (current expenditure 460,000m.; investment expenditure 340,000m.).

FIFTH FIVE-YEAR PLAN (1981–86)
Proposed Expenditure (million francs CFA)

Rural economy	434,700
Industry and crafts	184,000
Mining and energy	193,200
Trade and transport	126,000
Tourism	50,600
Infrastructure	486,400
Education and training	202,400
Youth and sports	32,200
Health and social services	92,000
Housing and town planning	266,800
Administrative equipment	55,200
Information and culture	36,800
Research	29,900
Total (incl. others)	2,300,000

CENTRAL BANK RESERVES
(US $ million at 31 December)

	1982	1983	1984
Gold*	13.45	11.33	9.27
IMF special drawing rights	1.81	0.65	6.11
Reserve position in IMF	15.33	7.54	0.20
Foreign exchange	50.08	150.90	47.55
Total	80.68	170.42	63.12

* Valued at market-related prices.
Source: IMF, *International Financial Statistics*.

MONEY SUPPLY ('000 million francs CFA at 31 December)

	1982	1983	1984
Currency outside banks	107.59	127.63	134.41
Demand deposits at deposit money banks	189.39	247.94	274.85
Checking deposits at post office	1.50	1.50	1.50
Total money	298.48	377.07	410.76

COST OF LIVING (Consumer Price Index for Africans in Yaoundé. Base: 1980 = 100)

	1981	1982	1983
Food	113.0	134.5	154.4
Clothing	111.3	120.3	143.1
All items (incl. others)	110.2	125.1	145.8

1984: All items 162.4.
Source: ILO, *Year Book of Labour Statistics*.

NATIONAL ACCOUNTS ('000 million francs CFA at current prices, year ending 30 June)
Expenditure on the Gross Domestic Product

	1981/82	1982/83	1983/84
Government final consumption expenditure	192.0	248.7	306.4
Private final consumption expenditure	1,538.4	1,745.7	2,008.0
Increase in stocks	31.5	25.6	19.4
Gross fixed capital formation	507.2	654.5	809.5
Total domestic expenditure	2,269.1	2,674.5	3,143.3
Exports of goods and services	434.8	504.1	646.5
Less Imports of goods and services	531.2	560.5	594.7
GDP in purchasers' values	2,172.7	2,618.1	3,195.1

Gross Domestic Product by Economic Activity

	1981/82	1982/83	1983/84
Agriculture, hunting, forestry and fishing	586.7	607.1	702.0
Mining and quarrying	263.1	400.5	520.5
Manufacturing	247.0	290.9	358.5
Electricity, gas and water	22.2	30.1	35.2
Construction	125.0	145.8	192.6
Trade, restaurants and hotels	249.3	310.7	414.9
Transports, storage and communications	119.3	128.8	147.3
Finance, insurance, real estate and business services	285.0	355.2	396.8
Other community, social and personal services	28.0	34.5	39.2
Less imputed bank service charges	42.2	37.5	38.0
Domestic product of industries	1,883.4	2,266.1	2,769.0
Public administrations	135.3	171.8	212.8
Private non-profit services	9.2	11.0	13.6
Domestic services	18.4	22.3	26.6
Sub-total	2,046.3	2,471.2	3,022.0
Import duties	126.4	146.8	173.0
GDP in purchasers' values	2,172.7	2,618.0	3,195.0

BALANCE OF PAYMENTS (US $ million)

	1982	1983	1984
Merchandise exports f.o.b.	1,347.8	1,363.6	1,589.0
Merchandise imports f.o.b.	−1,220.1	−1,222.6	−1,064.7
Trade balance	127.7	141.0	524.2
Exports of services	442.8	467.3	450.3
Imports of services	−960.0	−1,028.1	−1,118.9
Balance on goods and services	−389.5	−419.8	−144.4
Private unrequited transfers (net)	−64.2	−73.2	−77.3
Government unrequited transfers (net)	56.7	79.1	56.5
Current balance	−396.9	−413.9	−165.2
Direct capital investment (net)	102.7	205.4	7.6
Other long-term capital (net)	121.5	336.5	371.0
Short-term capital (net)	149.5	−4.2	−174.5
Net errors and omissions	15.6	−1.4	−133.5
Total (net monetary movements)	−7.8	122.4	−94.5
Valuation changes (net)	−7.6	−29.4	−11.9
Exceptional financing (net)	0.3	0.1	—
Official financing (net)	3.6	0.1	0.5
Changes in reserves	−11.5	93.2	−106.0

Source: IMF, *International Financial Statistics*.

External Trade

PRINCIPAL COMMODITIES (million francs CFA)

Imports c.i.f.	1982	1983	1984
Tyres	4,450	4,558	6,373
Cotton fabrics	14,181	5,218	4,492
Malt	8,895	9,441	5,044
Cement	5,305	13,239	6,630
Alumina	5,414	13,649	15,373
Lubricants	4,042	4,588	3,614
Medicine	11,933	15,495	13,738
Books and newspapers	4,029	4,105	3,768
Iron and steel pipes	6,470	17,408	7,781
Paper and allied products	6,547	7,071	1,809
Drilling equipment	10,585	13,158	29,632
Footwear	3,294	2,610	3,547
Iron and steel	9,675	17,431	18,317
Cutting machinery	5,665	5,148	5,205
Generating machinery	5,004	5,469	5,282
Road transport equipment	31,888	33,512	42,342
Air transport equipment	1,089	79	810
Total (incl. others)	394,581	466,977	484,646

Exports f.o.b.	1982	1983	1984
Cocoa	37,760	50,102	100,397
Coffee (arabica)	16,506	24,781	32,706
Coffee (robusta)	34,905	49,646	61,049
Bananas	8,771	6,740	6,663
Rubber	2,420	3,740	6,843
Tobacco	3,295	3,032	3,702
Cotton fibre	11,874	13,985	10,275
Cotton fabrics	5,205	5,139	9,403
Palm nuts and kernels	128	469	1,184
Palm oil	1,804	561	591
Cocoa pulp	2,707	2,739	6,437
Cocoa butter	4,247	5,990	7,757
Logs	14,285	12,974	14,324
Sawnwood and sleepers	5,023	3,707	4,016
Aluminium	21,339	22,840	29,794
Aluminium products	5,188	5,824	5,491
Crude petroleum	154,766	163,537	95,279
Total (incl. others)	358,777	413,801	440,470

PRINCIPAL TRADING PARTNERS (million francs CFA)

Imports c.i.f.	1982	1983	1984
Belgium/Luxembourg	10,583	12,533	14,342
France	174,873	218,506	207,536
Germany, Federal Republic	27,544	30,386	32,245
Italy	16,253	17,124	22,086
Japan	24,274	30,658	34,449
Netherlands	9,807	9,057	8,470
UDEAC*	3,388	11,214	7,511
UMOA†	3,116	4,392	8,495
United Kingdom	14,121	14,164	16,828
USA	29,890	37,614	49,619
Total (incl. others)	394,581	466,977	484,646

Exports f.o.b.	1982	1983	1984
Belgium/Luxembourg	2,407	2,363	3,249
France	71,040	121,054	146,692
Germany, Federal Republic	16,522	22,742	26,996
Italy	14,022	17,259	27,670
Japan	11,193	9,850	3,882
Netherlands	64,281	75,971	109,581
UDEAC*	15,624	17,667	20,407
UMOA†	1,734	2,304	2,715
United Kingdom	2,065	2,577	3,498
USA	135,166	94,557	54,699
Total (incl. others)	358,777	405,961	440,470

* Union douanière et économique de l'Afrique centrale (Customs and Economic Union of Central Africa), comprising Cameroon, the Central African Republic, the Congo and Gabon.

† Union monétaire ouest-africaine (West African Monetary Union), comprising Benin, Burkina Faso, the Ivory Coast, Niger, Senegal and Togo.

Transport

RAILWAYS (traffic, year ending 30 June)

	1981/82	1982/83	1983/84
Passengers carried ('000)	1,578	1,867	2,218
Passenger-km (million)	324	389	444
Freight carried ('000 tons)	1,754	1,792	1,849
Freight ton-km (million)	782	327	838

1984/85 (estimate): Passengers carried: 2,480,000.

ROAD TRAFFIC (motor vehicles in use at 31 December)

	1982	1983	1984
Passenger cars	60,392	66,868	72,449
Commercial vehicles	37,068	40,094	41,301
Tractors and trailers	1,573	1,772	2,045
Motorcycles and scooters	32,027	38,931	41,579

INTERNATIONAL SEA-BORNE SHIPPING (Douala)

	1983	1984	1985
Vessels entered	1,176	1,176	1,242
Freight loaded ('000 metric tons)	887	999	1,005
Freight unloaded ('000 metric tons)	2,845	2,999	3,418

Source: Office National des Ports, Douala.

CIVIL AVIATION (traffic on scheduled services)

	1980	1981	1982
Kilometres flown (million)	7.4	7.5	6.2
Passengers carried ('000)	480	486	634
Passenger-km (million)	477	485	581
Freight ton-km (million)	27.7	31.4	45.7

Source: UN, *Statistical Yearbook*.

Tourism

FOREIGN VISITORS
Foreigners staying at least two nights: 116,386 in 1983; 108,109 in 1984.

HOTELS
In July 1986 there were 81 classified hotels, with a total of 4,073 rooms and 5,922 beds.

Source: Secrétariat d'Etat au Tourisme, Yaoundé.

Communications Media

	1981	1982	1983
Radio receivers ('000 in use)	780	800	820

Book production (first editions only, 1979): 22 titles (94,000 copies), excluding pamphlets.
Daily newspapers (1982): 2 (average circulation 35,000 copies).
Source: UNESCO, *Statistical Yearbook*.

Education

(1984/85)

	Institutions	Pupils	Teachers
Kindergarten	567	67,688	2,357
Primary	5,742	1,638,629	32,082
Post-primary	121	8,913	705
Secondary	376	238,075	8,381
Technical	164	77,555	3,239
Teacher training	28	3,880	482
Higher	5*	17,113*	839*

* 1985/86 figure.
Source: Ministère de l'Education Nationale, Yaoundé.

Directory

The Constitution

The Constitution of the United Republic of Cameroon was promulgated on 2 June 1972, after approval by a referendum on 21 May 1972. It was revised on 9 May 1975.

In January 1984 the National Assembly approved a constitutional amendment, restoring the country's original name, the Republic of Cameroon. At the same time, the Assembly adopted further constitutional reforms, abolishing the post of Prime Minister and providing that the President of the Republic would be succeeded, in the event of death or incapacity, by the President of the National Assembly.

The main provisions of the 1972 Constitution are summarized below:

The Constitution declares that the human being, without distinction as to race, religion, sex or belief, possesses inalienable and sacred rights. It affirms its attachment to the fundamental freedoms embodied in the Universal Declaration of Human Rights and the UN Charter. The State guarantees to all citizens of either sex the rights and freedoms set out in the preamble of the Constitution.

SOVEREIGNTY

1. The Federal Republic of Cameroon, constituted from the State of East Cameroon and the State of West Cameroon, shall become a unitary State to be styled the United Republic of Cameroon with effect from the date of entry into force of this Constitution. The Republic shall be one and indivisible, democratic, secular and dedicated to social service. It shall ensure the equality before the law of all its citizens. Provisions that the official languages be French and English, for the motto, flag, national anthem and seal, that the capital be Yaoundé.

2–3. Sovereignty shall be vested in the people who shall exercise it either through the President of the Republic and the members returned by it to the National Assembly or by means of referendum. Elections are by universal suffrage, direct or indirect, by every citizen aged 21 or over in a secret ballot. Political parties or groups may take part in elections subject to the law and the principles of democracy and of national sovereignty and unity.

4. State authority shall be exercised by the President of the Republic and the National Assembly.

THE PRESIDENT OF THE REPUBLIC

5. The President of the Republic, as Head of State and Head of the Government, shall be responsible for the conduct of the affairs of the Republic. He shall define national policy and may charge the Prime Minister with the implementation of this policy in certain spheres. The President may delegate to the Prime Minister his powers to direct, co-ordinate and control governmental activity in such spheres. Certain powers may also be delegated to other members of government.

6–7. Candidates for the office of President must hold civic and political rights and be at least 35 years old, and may not hold any other elective office or professional activity. Election is by a majority of votes cast by the people. The President is elected for five years and may be re-elected. Provisions are made for the continuity of office in the case of the President's resignation and for the Prime Minister to act as interim President should the President die or be permanently incapacitated.

8–9. The Prime Minister, Ministers and Vice-Ministers are appointed by the President to whom they are responsible, and they may hold no other appointment. The President is also head of the armed forces, he negotiates and ratifies treaties, may exercise clemency after consultation with the Higher Judicial Council, promulgates and is responsible for the enforcement of laws, is responsible for internal and external security, makes civil and military appointments, provides for necessary administrative services.

10. The President, by reference to the Supreme Court, ensures that all laws passed are constitutional.

11. Provisions whereby the President may declare a State of Emergency or State of Siege.

THE NATIONAL ASSEMBLY

12. The National Assembly shall be renewed every five years, though it may at the instance of the President of the Republic legislate to extend or shorten its term of office. It shall be composed of 120 members elected by universal suffrage.

13–14. Laws shall normally be passed by a simple majority of those present, but if a bill is read a second time at the request of the President of the Republic a majority of the National Assembly as a whole is required.

15–16. The National Assembly shall meet twice a year, each session to last not more than 30 days; in one session it shall approve the budget. It may be recalled to an extraordinary session of not more than 15 days.

17–18. Elections and suitability of candidates and sitting members shall be governed by law.

CAMEROON

RELATIONS BETWEEN THE EXECUTIVE AND THE LEGISLATURE

19. Bills may be introduced either by the President of the Republic or by any member of the National Assembly.

20. Reserved to the legislature are: the fundamental rights and duties of the citizen; the law of persons and property; the political, administrative and judicial system in respect of elections to the National Assembly, general regulation of national defence, authorization of penalties and criminal and civil procedure etc., and the organization of the local authorities; currency, the budget, dues and taxes, legislation on public property; economic and social policy; the education system.

21. The National Assembly may empower the President of the Republic to legislate by way of Ordinance for a limited period and for given purposes.

22–26. Other matters of procedure, including the right of the President of the Republic to address the Assembly and of the Prime Minister, Ministers and Vice-Ministers to take part in debates.

27–29. The composition and conduct of the Assembly's programme of business. Provisions whereby the Assembly may inquire into governmental activity. The obligation of the President of the Republic to promulgate laws, which shall be published in both languages of the Republic.

30. Provisions whereby the President of the Republic, after consultation with the National Assembly, may submit to referendum certain reform bills liable to have profound repercussions on the future of the Nation and National Institutions.

THE JUDICIARY

31. Justice is administered in the name of the people. The President of the Republic shall ensure the independence of the judiciary and shall make appointments with the assistance of the Higher Judicial Council.

THE SUPREME COURT

32–33. The Supreme Court has powers to uphold the Constitution in such cases as the death or incapacity of the President and the admissibility of laws, to give final judgments on appeals on the Judgment of the Court of Appeal and to decide complaints against administrative acts. It may be assisted by experts appointed by the President of the Republic.

IMPEACHMENT

34. There shall be a Court of Impeachment with jurisdiction to try the President of the Republic for high treason and the Prime Minister, Ministers and Vice-Ministers for conspiracy against the security of the State.

THE ECONOMIC AND SOCIAL COUNCIL

35. There shall be an Economic and Social Council, regulated by the law.

AMENDMENT OF THE CONSTITUTION

36–37. Bills to amend the Constitution may be introduced either by the President of the Republic or the National Assembly. The President may decide to submit any amendment to the people by way of a referendum. No procedure to amend the Constitution may be accepted if it tends to impair the republican character, unity or territorial integrity of the State, or the democratic principles by which the Republic is governed.

The Government

HEAD OF STATE

President: PAUL BIYA (took office 6 November 1982, following the resignation of Ahmadou Ahidjo; elected 14 January 1984 for a five-year term).

CABINET
(December 1986)

Secretary-General of the Government: JEAN NKUETE.

Minister Delegate at the Presidency in charge of Defence: MICHAEL MEVA-A M-EBOUTOU.

Minister Delegate at the Presidency in charge of Relations with the National Assembly: JOSEPH CHONGWAIN AWUNTI.

Minister Delegate at the Presidency in charge of the General Staff Inspectorate and Administrative Reforms: MOHAMADOU LABARANG.

Minister Delegate at the Presidency in charge of Computer Service and Public Contracts: NJIKE KAMGA.

Ministers at the Presidency in charge of Missions: TITUS EDZOA, JOSEPH CHARLES DOUMBA.

Minister of Justice and Keeper of the Seals: BENJAMIN ITOE.

Minister of Foreign Affairs: WILLIAM ETEKI MBOUMOUA.

Deputy Foreign Minister: MAHAMAT PABA SALE.

Minister of Youth and Sports: JOSEPH FOFE.

Minister of Territorial Administration: JÉRÔME-EMILIEN ABONDO.

Minister of Finance: BOTOO A'NGON.

Minister of National Education: GEORGES NGANGO.

Minister of Labour and Welfare: PHILIPPE MATAGA.

Minister of Health: VICTOR ANOMAH NGU.

Minister of Agriculture: JEAN-BAPTISTE YONKEU.

Minister of Planning and Land Management: SADOU HAYATOU.

Minister of Trade and Industry: EDOUARD NOMO ONGOLO.

Minister of Social Affairs: ROSE ZANG NGUELE.

Minister of Posts and Telecommunications: CLAUDE LEONARD MPOUMA.

Minister of Mines and Energy: MICHAEL TABONG KIMA.

Minister of Housing and Town Planning: FERDINAND-LÉOPOLD OYONO.

Minister of Transport: ANDRÉ-BOSCO CHEUWA.

Minister of Information and Culture: IBRAHIM MBOMBO NJOYA.

Minister of Equipment: HERMAN MAIMO.

Minister of the Civil Service: RENÉ ZE NGUELE.

Minister of Higher Education and Scientific Research: ABDOULAYE BABALE.

Minister of Women's Affairs: YAOU AISSATOU.

Minister of Livestock, Fishing and Animal Resources: HAMADJODA ADJOUDJI.

Junior Ministers:

Agriculture: SOLOMON MFOR GWEI.

Planning and Land Management: ELISABETH TANKEU.

Trade and Industry: MICHAEL NAMAYA.

Public Health: ISABELLE BASSONG.

Finance: TIKELA KEMONNE.

Education: NGO MBA EKO.

Information and Culture: RAPHAEL ONAMBELE.

Territorial Administration: JEAN-BAPTISTE BASCODA.

Tourism: Dr SOUAIBOU ABDOULAYE.

Defence: ALI AMADOU.

Internal Security: DENIS EKANI.

MINISTRIES

Ministries do not usually have Post Office Box numbers. Correspondence should generally be addressed to ministries c/o the Central Post Office, Yaoundé.

Office of the President: Yaoundé; tel. 23-40-25; telex 8207.

Ministry of Agriculture: Yaoundé; tel. 23-40-85; telex 8325.

Ministry of Defence: Yaoundé; tel. 23-40-55; telex 8261.

Ministry of Equipment: Yaoundé; tel. 22-16-22.

Ministry of Foreign Affairs: Yaoundé; tel. 22-01-33; telex 8252.

Ministry of Finance: BP 18, Yaoundé; tel. 23-40-00; telex 8260.

Ministry of General Inspection and Administrative Reforms: Yaoundé; tel. 22-11-17.

Ministry of Health: Yaoundé; tel. 22-29-01.

Ministry of Higher Education and Scientific Research: Yaoundé.

Ministry of Housing and Town Planning: Yaoundé; tel. 23-22-82; telex 8560.

Ministry of Information and Culture: Yaoundé; tel. 22-40-75; telex 8215.

Ministry of Justice: Yaoundé; tel. 22-01-97.

CAMEROON

Directory

Ministry of Labour and Welfare: Yaoundé; tel. 22-01-86.
Ministry of Livestock, Fishing and Animal Resources: Yaoundé; tel. 22-33-11.
Ministry of Mines and Energy: Yaoundé; tel. 23-34-04; telex 8504.
Ministry of National Education: Yaoundé; tel. 23-40-50; telex 8551.
Ministry of Planning and Land Management: Yaoundé; telex 8268.
Ministry of Posts and Telecommunications: Yaoundé; tel. 23-40-16; telex 8582.
Ministry of Social Affairs: Yaoundé; tel. 22-41-48.
Ministry of Territorial Administration: Yaoundé; tel. 23-40-90; telex 8503.
Ministry of Transport: Yaoundé; tel. 22-34-72; telex 8214.
Ministry of Youth and Sports: Yaoundé; tel. 23-32-57; telex 8568.

Legislature

ASSEMBLÉE NATIONALE

At the election held on 29 May 1983, all 120 seats were won by the Union nationale camerounaise, which was renamed the Rassemblement démocratique du peuple camerounaise in 1985.

President: SOLOMON TANDENG MUNA.
Secretary-General: El-Hadj AHMADOU HAYATOU.

Political Organizations

Rassemblement démocratique du peuple camerounais (RDPC): BP 867, Yaoundé; f. 1966 as Union nationale camerounaise (UNC) by merger of the governing party of each state of the Federation (Union camerounaise and the Kamerun National Democratic Party) and four opposition parties; renamed in March 1985; party organization comprises a Congress which meets every five years, a 12-mem. Political Bureau and a Cen. Cttee of 65 mems and 20 alt. mems; there are two ancillary organs: Organisation des femmes du RDPC and Jeunesse du RDPC; Pres. PAUL BIYA.

Union des populations camerounaises (UPC): Paris; illegal opposition movement in exile.

Diplomatic Representation

EMBASSIES IN CAMEROON

Algeria: BP 1619, Yaoundé; tel. 23-06-65; telex 8517; Ambassador: ABDELMADJID GAOUAR.
Belgium: BP 816, Yaoundé; tel. 22-27-88; telex 8314; Ambassador: PAUL JANSSENS.
Brazil: BP 348, Yaoundé; tel. 23-19-57; telex 8587; Ambassador: P. G. VILSA-BÔAS CASTRO.
Canada: Immeuble Stamatiades, BP 572, Yaoundé; tel. 23-02-03; telex 8209; Ambassador: MARC FAGUY.
Central African Republic: BP 396, Yaoundé; tel. 22-51-55; Ambassador: HUBERT ABENDON.
Chad: BP 506, Yaoundé; tel. 22-06-24; telex 8352; Chargé d'affaires: MIAAZAL ADOUM TIDJANI.
China, People's Republic: BP 1307, Yaoundé; Ambassador: SHI NAILAING.
Congo: BP 1422, Yaoundé; tel. 23-24-58; telex 8379; Ambassador: JÉRÔME OLLANDET.
Egypt: BP 809, Yaoundé; tel. 22-39-22; telex 8360; Ambassador: HASSAN GAD ELHAK.
Equatorial Guinea: BP 277, Yaoundé; tel. 22-41-49; Ambassador: ANGEL SERAFIN SERICH DOUGAN MALABO.
France: BP 1631, Yaoundé; tel. 23-40-13; telex 8233; Ambassador: YVON OMNÈS.
Gabon: BP 4130, Yaoundé; tel. 22-29-66; telex 8265; Ambassador: AUGUSTIN CHANGO.
German Democratic Republic: BP 1139, Yaoundé; tel. 22-38-41; telex 8412; Ambassador: MANFRED VOSS.
Germany, Federal Republic: BP 1160, Yaoundé; tel. 23-00-56; telex 8238; Ambassador: Dr FRIEDERICH REICHE.
Greece: BP 82, Yaoundé; tel. 22-39-36; telex 8364; Ambassador: CHRISTO KAMBAS.
Holy See: BP 210, Yaoundé; tel. 22-04-75; telex 8382; Apostolic Pro-Nuncio: Mgr DONATO SQUICCIARINI.
Israel: Yaoundé; Ambassador: (vacant).
Italy: Quartier Bastos, BP 827, Yaoundé; tel. 22-33-76; telex 8305; Ambassador: FRANCESCO LABBRUZZO.
Ivory Coast: Immeuble Ndende, quartier Bastos, BP 203, Yaoundé; tel. 22-09-69; telex 8388; Ambassador: ANTOINE KONAN KOFFI.
Korea, Republic: BP 301, Yaoundé; tel. 23-32-23; telex 8241; Ambassador: KIM DONG-HO.
Liberia: BP 1185, Yaoundé; tel. 23-26-31; telex 8227; Ambassador: AARON J. GEORGE.
Libya: BP 1980, Yaoundé; telex 8272; Head of People's Bureau: FANNOUSH HAMDI.
Morocco: BP 1629, Yaoundé; telex 8347; Ambassador: ABDERRAMMANE BOUCHAARA.
Netherlands: BP 310, Yaoundé; tel. 22-05-44; telex 8237; Ambassador: HENDRIK PHILIPSE.
Nigeria: BP 448, Yaoundé; tel. 32-24-55; telex 8267; Ambassador: AHMED SHEHU YUSUFARI.
Romania: BP 6212, Yaoundé; telex 8540; Ambassador: (vacant).
Saudi Arabia: BP 1602, Yaoundé; tel. 23-26-75; telex 8336; Ambassador: ABDOL RAHMAN AL-AKIL.
Senegal: Plateau 'Bastos', BP 1716, Yaoundé; tel. 23-26-75; telex 8303; Ambassador: PAPA LOUIS FALL.
Spain: BP 877, Yaoundé; tel. 22-35-43; telex 8287; Ambassador: MANUEL PIÑEIRO-SOUTO.
Switzerland: BP 1169, Yaoundé; tel. 23-28-96; telex 8316; Ambassador: JACQUES RIAL.
Tunisia: rue de Rotary, BP 6074, Yaoundé; tel. 22-33-68; telex 8370; Ambassador: (vacant).
USSR: BP 488, Yaoundé; tel. 22-17-14; Ambassador: SPARTAK ZYKOV.
United Kingdom: ave Winston Churchill, BP 547, Yaoundé; tel. 22-05-45; telex 8200; Ambassador: JAMES GLAZE.
USA: BP 817, Yaoundé; tel. 23-40-14; telex 8223; Ambassador: MYLES R. R. FRECHETTE.
Zaire: BP 632, Yaoundé; tel. 22-51-03; telex 8317; Ambassador: KUDIWU KENGILA-DIO.

Judicial System

Supreme Court: Yaoundé; consists of a President, titular and substitute judges (9 at present), a Procureur Général, an Avocat Général, deputies to the Procureur Général, a Registrar and clerks.

President of the Supreme Court: MARCEL NGUINI.

High Court of Justice: Yaoundé; consists of 9 titular judges and 6 substitute judges, all elected by the National Assembly.

Religion

It is estimated that 39% of the population follow traditional animist beliefs, 21% are Muslims and 40% Christians, mainly Roman Catholics.

CHRISTIANITY

The Roman Catholic Church

Cameroon comprises four archdioceses and 12 dioceses. At 31 December 1984 there were an estimated 2,508,000 adherents in the country (about 27% of the total population). There are several active missionary orders, and four major seminaries for African priests.

Bishops' Conference: Conférence Episcopale Nationale du Cameroun, BP 272, Garoua; tel. 27-13-53; f. 1981; Pres. Mgr CHRISTIAN WIYGHAN TUMI, Archbishop of Garoua.
Archbishop of Bamenda: Mgr PAUL VERDZEKOV, Archbishop's House, BP 82, Bamenda; tel. 36-12-41.
Archbishop of Douala: Mgr SIMON TONYÉ, Archevêché, BP 179, Douala; tel. 42-37-14.
Archbishop of Garoua: Mgr CHRISTIAN WIYGHAN TUMI, Archevêché, BP 272, Garoua; tel. 27-13-53.

CAMEROON

Archbishop of Yaoundé: Mgr JEAN ZOA, Archevêché, BP 207, Yaoundé; tel. 23-04-83; telex 8681.

Other Christian Churches

There are about 600,000 Protestants with about 3,000 church and mission workers, and four theological schools.

Fédération Evangélique du Cameroun et de l'Afrique Equatoriale: BP 491, Yaoundé; Admin. Sec. Pastor MOUBITANG À MEPOUI.

Presbyterian Church: BP 19, Buéa; tel. 32-23-36; telex 5613; 181,200 mems; 211 ministers; Chief Minister Rev. HENRY ANYE AWASOM.

BAHÁ'Í FAITH

National Spiritual Assembly: BP 145, Limbe; tel. 33-21-46; mems in 1,305 localities.

The Press

The Press in Cameroon has suffered from the problems of low circulations, small advertising income, high printing costs and expensive paper. Censorship has added to its difficulties. The Cameroon Press Law of December 1966 was modified in June 1981 to stipulate conditions of authorization or prohibition of newspapers, periodicals and magazines.

DAILY

Cameroon Tribune: BP 23, Yaoundé; tel. 22-27-00; telex 8311; f. 1974; govt-controlled; French; also weekly edn in English; Dir JOSEPH ZAMBOU ZOLÉCO; circ. 66,000 (daily), 30,000 (weekly).

PERIODICALS

Le Bamiléké: BP 329, Nkongsamba; monthly.
Bulletin de la Chambre de Commerce, d'Industrie et des Mines du Cameroun: BP 4011, Douala; monthly.
Bulletin Mensuel de la Statistique: BP 660, Yaoundé; monthly.
Cameroon Information: Ministry of Information and Culture, Yaoundé; every two weeks; French and English; circ. 5,000.
Cameroon Outlook: BP 124, Limbe; f. 1969; 3 a week; English; Editor CHARLES AYEAH NDI-CHIA; circ. 7,500.
Cameroon Panorama: BP 46, Buéa; f. 1962; monthly; English; Roman Catholic; Editor Sister MERCY HORGAN; circ. 3,000.
Cameroon Times: BP 200, Limbe; f. 1960; 3 a week; English; Editor-in-Chief JEROME F. GWELLEM; circ. 12,000.
Courrier Sportif du Bénin: BP 17, Douala; weekly; Dir HENRI JONG.
Essor des Jeunes: BP 363, Nkongsamba; monthly; Roman Catholic; monthly; Editor Abbé JEAN-BOCO TCHAPE; circ. 3,000.
La Gazette: BP 5485, Douala; 2 a week; Editor ABODEL KARIMOU; circ. 35,000.
The Gazette: BP 408, Limbe; tel. 33-25-67; weekly; English edn of La Gazette; Editor JEROME F. GWELLEM; circ. 70,000.
Journal Officiel de la République du Cameroun: BP 1603, Yaoundé; every two weeks; official govt gazette; circ. 1,500.
Nleb Bekristen: Imprimerie Saint-Paul, BP 763, Yaoundé; f. 1935; every two weeks; Ewondo; Dir PASCAL BAYLON MVOE; circ. 6,000.
Les Nouvelles du Mungo: BP 1, Nkongsamba; monthly; circ. 3,000.
Pistes Camerounaises: Secrétariat d'Etat au Tourisme, BP 266, Yaoundé; tel. 22-44-11; telex 8318; quarterly; tourism; Dir JOSEPH ONGUENE OWONA; publ. suspended 1984.
Recherches et Études Camerounaises: BP 660, Yaoundé; monthly; publ. by Office National de Recherches Scientifiques du Cameroun.
Revue d'Informations et d'Etudes Economiques et Financières: BP 1630, Yaoundé; quarterly.
Le Serviteur: BP 1405, Yaoundé; Protestant; monthly; Dir Pastor DANIEL AKO'O; circ. 3,000.
Le Travailleur/The Worker: BP 1610, Yaoundé; f. 1972; monthly; journal of Organisation des Sociétés de Travailleurs Camerounais; circ. 15,000.

Directory

L'Unité: BP 867, Yaoundé; monthly; trade union journal.

NEWS AGENCIES

Société de Presse et d'Edition du Cameroun (SOPECAM—Cameroon Press and Publishing Co): BP 1218, Yaoundé; tel. 23-40-12; telex 8311; f. 1978; govt body incorporating the fmr Agence Camerounaise de Press (ACAP); under the supervision of the Ministry of Information; newspaper dept produces the Cameroon Tribune; agency and publishing dept incorporates fmr ACAP functions; Dir JOSEPH ZAMBOU ZOLECO.

Foreign Bureaux

Agence France-Presse (AFP): Villa Kamdem-Kamga, BP 229, Elig-Essono, Yaoundé; telex 8218; Correspondent M. SIPA.
Xinhua (New China) News Agency (People's Republic of China): ave Joseph Omgba, BP 1583, Yaoundé; tel. 22-25-72; telex 8294; Chief Correspondent LIANG GUIHE.

Reuters (UK) and TASS (USSR) are also represented in Cameroon.

Publishers

Centre d'Edition et de Production pour l'Enseignement et la Recherche (CEPER): BP 808, Yaoundé; tel. 22-13-23; telex 8338; f. 1967; general non-fiction, history, Africana, paperbacks, science and technology, social science, university and secondary textbooks; Man. Dir WILFRED W. BANMBUH.
Editions Buma Kor: BP 727, Yaoundé; tel. 23-29-03; telex 8438; f. 1977; general, children's, educational and Christian; English and French; Man. Dir B. D. BUMA KOR.
Editions Clé: BP 1501, Yaoundé; tel. 22-35-54; f. 1963; African literature and studies; university and secondary textbooks, theology and religion; Gen. Man. JEAN DIHANG.
Editions Le Flambeau: BP 113, Yaoundé; tel. 22-36-72; f. 1977; general; Man. Dir JOSEPH NDZIE.
Editions Semences Africaines: BP 5329, Yaoundé-Nlongkak; f. 1974; fiction, history, religion, textbooks; Man. Dir PHILIPPE-LOUIS OMBEDE.
Gwellem Publications: Presbook Compound (Down Beach), BP 408, Limbe; tel. 33-25-67; f. 1983; periodicals, books and pamphlets; Dir and Editor-in-Chief JEROME F. GWELLEM.
Imprimerie Saint Paul: ave Monseigneur Vogt, BP 763, Yaoundé; education, medicine, philosophy, politics, religion and fiction.
Société Camerounaise de Publications: BP 23, Yaoundé; tel. 22-27-00; f. 1974; Man. Dir E. NGOH-HOB.
Société Kenkoson d'Etudes Africaines: BP 4064, Yaoundé; f. 1975; law, academic; CEO M. SALOMÉ.

Government Publishing House

Government Printer: BP 1091, Yaoundé; Man. Dir AMADOU VAMOULKE.

Radio and Television

In 1983 there were an estimated 820,000 radio receivers in use. A national television network, Cameroon Television (CTV), was inaugurated in March 1985, and was scheduled to become fully operational by the end of 1987.

Radiodiffusion Nationale du Cameroun: BP 281, Yaoundé; tel. 22-14-00; telex 8215; govt service; national broadcasting in French, English and vernacular languages, international broadcasting in French and English; Dir KOME EPULE; Head of Programmes HENRY BURNLEY.

Radio Buéa: BP 86, Buéa; tel. 32-25-25; programmes in English, French and 28 other local languages; Man. PETERSON CHIA YUH.
Radio Douala: BP 986, Douala; tel. 42-60-60; programmes in French, English, Douala, Bassa, Ewondo, Bakoko and Bamiléké; Dir BRUNO DJEM.
Radio Garoua: BP 103, Garoua; tel. 27-11-67; programmes in French, Hausa, English, Foulfouldé, Arabic and Choa; Dir BELLO MALGANA.

There are also provincial stations at Bertoua, Bafoussam, and Bamenda, and there is a local radio station serving Yaoundé.

Finance

(cap. = capital; res = reserves; dep. = deposits; m. = million; brs = branches; amounts in francs CFA)

BANKING

Central Bank

Banque des Etats de l'Afrique Centrale (BEAC): rue du docteur Jamot, BP 1917, Yaoundé; tel. 22-25-05; telex 8343; f. 1973 as the central bank of issue for mem. states of the Customs and Economic Union of Central Africa (UDEAC), comprising Cameroon, the Central African Republic, Chad, the Congo, Equatorial Guinea and Gabon; 5 brs in Cameroon; cap. and res 92,485m. (June 1983); Gov. CASIMIR OYÉ MBA.

Commercial Banks

Bank of America Cameroon SA: blvd de la Liberté, BP 3300, Douala; tel. 42-84-22; telex 5734; f. 1982; cap. 1,250m.; 35% state-owned, 65% by Bankamerica Holding Co SA; Pres. THOMAS EBONGALAME; Gen. Man. PAUL ROELS.

Bank of Credit and Commerce Cameroon SA (BCCC): ave John F. Kennedy, BP 1188, Yaoundé; tel. 22-29-86; telex 8558; f. 1981; 35% state-owned, 65% by BCCI Holdings (Luxembourg) SA; cap. 1,250m., dep. 75,494m. (1986); Pres. JEAN KANGA ZAMB; Man. Dir ENOW TANJONG; 3 brs.

Banque Internationale pour l'Afrique Occidentale-Cameroun (BIAO): BP 4001, Douala; tel. 42-80-11; telex 5218; f. 1974; cap. 3,500m. (1983); 35% state-owned, 65% by BIAO Paris; Pres. ETIENNE NTSAMA; Gen. Man. FRANÇOIS MPONDO MBONGUE; 42 brs.

Banque Internationale pour le Commerce et l'Industrie du Cameroun (BICIC—Cameroon): ave Ahmadou Ahidjo, BP 5, Yaoundé; tel. 23-40-07; telex 8202; f. 1962; 39% state-owned, 13% by Barclays Bank, 11.5% by Banque Nationale de Paris; cap. 4,000m., res 3,044m., dep. 334,654m. (June 1985); Chair. RAYMOND MALOUMA; Gen. Man. SADOU HAYATOU; 34 brs.

Banque Paribas Cameroun: 88 blvd de la Liberté, BP 1589, Douala; tel. 42-23-42; telex 5286; f. 1980; cap. 2,300m.; subsidiary of Banque Paribas; br. in Yaoundé; Pres. MICHAEL MEVA-A M-EBOUTOU; Dir-Gen CHARLES TCHOMTCHONA DJADJO.

Boston Bank Cameroon SA: 64 ave de la Liberté, BP 1784, Douala; tel. 42-36-12; telex 5858; f. 1981; br. in Yaoundé; cap. 1,000m. (June 1984); 66% owned by First National Bank of Boston; Chair. HERMAN MISSE; Gen. Man. KEITH TENNY.

Cameroon Bank SA: BP 1613, Yaoundé; tel. 22-25-84; telex 8342; f. 1974; 11 brs; cap. 705m. (Dec. 1984); 42.55% owned by Caisse Nationale des Hydrocarbures, 28.12% by Société Nationale d'Investissement; Chair. THÉODORE EYEFFA; Gen. Man. FRÉDÉRIC NGOMBA EKO.

Chase Bank Cameroon SA: BP 1132, 83 blvd de la Liberté, Douala; tel. 42-98-05; telex 5580; f. 1979; br. in Yaoundé; cap. 1,000m., dep. 11,911m. (June 1981); 35% state-owned, 65% owned by Chase Manhattan Overseas Banking Corpn; Pres. DAVID T. ATOGHO; Gen. Man. EMMANUEL EDING.

Société Camerounaise de Banque (SCB): rue Monseigneur Vogt, BP 145, Yaoundé; tel. 23-40-05; telex 8213; f. 1961; 49.4% state-owned, 16% Banque Camerounaise de Développement (BCD); cap. 5,000m., res 408m., dep. 205,192m. (June 1984); Chair. AHMADOU HAYATOU; Gen. Man. ROBERT MESSI MESSI; 43 brs.

Société Générale de Banques au Cameroun (SGBC): rue Joss, BP 4042, Douala; tel. 42-64-08; telex 5579; f. 1963; cap. 3,000m., res 5,414m., dep. 164,942m. (June 1984); 30% state-owned, 15% by BCD, 37.8% by Société Générale (France); Pres. AMADOU MOULIOM NJIFENJOU; Gen. Man. GASTON NGUENTI; 29 brs.

Development Agencies

Banque Camerounaise de Développement: rue du Mfoundi, BP 55, Yaoundé; tel. 22-09-11; telex 8225; f. 1960; 82% state-owned, 10% by Caisse Centrale de Coopération Economique (see below), 8% by BEAC; provides financial and technical assistance to development projects; cap. 6,000m. (June 1983); Chair. OUSMANE MEY; Man. Dir VALÈRE ABANDA METOGO.

Caisse Centrale de Coopération Economique (CCCE) (France): BP 46, Yaoundé; tel. 22-23-24; telex 8301; Dir JACQUES CHARPENTIER.

Crédit Foncier du Cameroun (CFC): ave du Président Ahidjo, BP 1531, Yaoundé; tel. 22-03-73; telex 8368; f. 1977; cap. 1,500m. (June 1983); 70% state-owned; provides financial assistance for social welfare and environment; Chair. EDOUARD AKAM MFOUMOU; Man. Dir JEAN-LOUIS ROL.

Fonds d'Aide et de Garantie des Crédits aux Petites et Moyennes Entreprises (FOGAPE): BP 1591, Yaoundé; tel. 22-37-26; reorganized 1984; provides financial and technical assistance to small and medium-sized businesses; Dir BENJAMIN MVONDO NTONGO.

Fonds National de Développement Rural (FONADER): BP 1548, Yaoundé; tel. 22-10-25; telex 8365; f. 1973; state-owned; gives financial and technical aid to agricultural and rural development projects; Chair. GILBERT ANDZE TSOUNGUI; Gen. Man. NGOME KOME ALBERT.

Société Nationale d'Investissement du Cameroun (SNI): place du Président Ahmadou Ahidjo, BP 423, Yaoundé; tel. 22-44-22; telex 8205; f. 1964; state-owned; turnover of 45,425m. (1982/83); cap. 7,000m. (June 1983); Chair. VICTOR AYISSI MVODO; Man. Dir LOUIS-CLAUDE NYASSA.

INSURANCE

Assurances Mutuelles Agricoles du Cameroun (AMACAM): BP 962, Yaoundé; tel. 22-49-66; telex 8300; f. 1965; cap. 100m.; Pres. ABEL MOUEN MALOUA; Man. Dir TIMOTHÉE MBOUMI.

Caisse Nationale de Réassurances SA (CNR): ave Foch, BP 4180, Yaoundé; tel. 22-37-99; telex 8262; f. 1965; cap. 400m.; Man. Dir DANIEL POTOUONJOU-TAPONZIE.

Compagnie Camerounaise d'Assurances et de Réassurances (CCAR): rue Franqueville, BP 4068, Douala; tel. 42-62-71; telex 5341; f. 1974; cap. 405m.; Pres. YVETTE CHASSAGNE; Dir FABIEN ATANGANA.

Guardian Royal Exchange Assurance (Cameroun) Ltd: 56 blvd de la Liberté, BP 426, Douala; tel. 43-53-65; telex 5690; cap. 300m.; Pres. V. CADDIC; Man. Dir M. E. FARRAR-HOCKLEY.

Société Camerounaise d'Assurances (SOCAR): 86 blvd de la Liberté, BP 280, Douala; tel. 42-08-38; telex 5504; f. 1973; cap. 800m.; Chair. JEAN NKUETE; Man. Dir PAUL ISALA.

Société Nouvelle d'Assurances du Cameroun (SNAC): BP 105, Douala; tél. 42-92-03; telex 5745; f. 1974; all forms of insurance; cap. 560m.; Man. Dir JEAN-CHARLES SUZEAU.

Trade and Industry

ADVISORY BODY

Economic and Social Council: BP 1058, Yaoundé; tel. 22-25-97; telex 8275; state body which advises the govt on economic and social problems; comprises 85 mems, who meet several times a year, a permanent secretariat and a president appointed by presidential decree; mems are nominated for a five-year term, while the secretariat is elected annually. Pres. LUC AYANG; Sec.-Gen. Dr JOSEPH SIMON EPALE.

CHAMBERS OF COMMERCE

Chambre d'Agriculture, de l'Elevage et des Forêts du Cameroun: Parc Repiquet, BP 287, Yaoundé; tel. 22-38-85; telex 8243; 44 mems; Pres. HUBERT OTABELA; Sec.-Gen. ABEL MOUEN MAKOUA.

Chambre de Commerce, d'Industrie et des Mines du Cameroun: BP 4011, Douala; tel. 42-28-88; telex 5616; f. 1963; branches: BP 36, Yaoundé; BP 211, Limbe; BP 59, Garoua; BP 944, Bafoussam; 138 mems; Pres. TCHOKWAGO NOUCTI; Sec.-Gen. SAMUEL BATEKI.

EMPLOYERS' ASSOCIATIONS

Groupement Interprofessionnel pour l'Etude et la Co-ordination des Intérêts Economiques au Cameroun (GICAM): ave Konrad Adenauer, BP 1134, Yaoundé; tel. 22-27-22; f. 1957; 101 mem. asscns; Pres. M. ILLE; Sec.-Gen. JACQUES FAURE.

Syndicat des Commerçants Entrepreneurs de Travaux Publics, du Bâtiment et Activités annexes au Cameroun: BP 1134, Yaoundé; br. at BP 829, Douala.

Syndicat des Commerçants Importateurs-Exportateurs du Cameroun (SCIEC): 16 rue Quillien, BP 562, Douala; tel. 42-60-04; Sec.-Gen. P. GIRMA.

Syndicat des Industriels du Cameroun (SYNINDUSTRICAM): BP 673, Douala; tel. 42-30-58; telex 5342; f. 1953; Pres. SAMUEL KONDO; Sec.-Gen. Mme DE PIERREBOURG.

Syndicat des Producteurs et Exportateurs de Bois: BP 570, Yaoundé; tel. 22-27-22; telex 8286; Pres. M. CORON; Sec.-Gen. J. FAURE.

Syndicat des Transporteurs Routiers du Cameroun: BP 834, Douala; tel. 42-55-21.

Syndicats Professionnels Forestiers et Activités connexes du Cameroun: BP 100, Douala.

Union des Syndicats Professionnels du Cameroun: BP 829, Douala; Pres. MOUKOKO KINGUE.

DEVELOPMENT ORGANIZATIONS

Cameroon Development Corporation (CAMDEV): Bota, Limbe; tel. 33-22-51; telex 5242; f. 1947, reorganized 1982; 77.9% state-owned; a statutory agricultural enterprise established to acquire and develop plantations of tropical crops, fmrly in German ownership; operates in four of 10 provinces, including francophone sector, and is the second largest employer of labour; planted area 40,000 ha out of 90,000 ha on lease from govt; operates two oil mills, three banana packing stations, three tea and four rubber factories; a smallholders' programme is under execution; cap. 4,624m. francs CFA; Chair. SAMUEL MOKA LIFAFA ENDELEY; Gen. Man. JOHN N. NGU.

Centre National d'Assistance aux Petites et Moyennes Entreprises (CAPME): BP 1377, Douala; tel. 42-58-58; telex 5590; f. 1970 by Cameroon govt and UNDP; development centre for small and medium-sized businesses; advises on industrial techniques and training and undertakes market research; Dir M. BOUBA ARDO.

Centre National du Commerce Extérieur (CNCE): 1er étage, Immeuble ONCPB, BP 2461, Douala; tel. 42-16-79; telex 5585; research into new and existing markets, commercial and economic information, and training programmes for the export market; Dir LOUIS WANSEK.

Mission de Développement des Cultures Vivrières (MIDEVIV): BP 1682, Yaoundé; tel. 22-38-29; f. 1973; development and improvement of seeds and planting materials; production and distribution of foodstuffs for urban centres; Pres. MAXIALE MAHI; Dir JEAN-BERNARD ABONG.

Mission Française de Coopération: BP 1616, Yaoundé; tel. 22-33-96; telex 8392; administers bilateral aid from France; Dir GEORGES MARTRES.

Organisation Camerounaise de la Banane (OCB): BP 221, Douala; tel. 42-31-21; telex 5694; f. 1968; development of banana plantations, marketing; Man. Dir SALOMON ELOGO METOMO.

Société Camerounaise des Tabacs (SCT): rue Joseph-Clerc, BP 29, Yaoundé; tel. 22-80-30; telex 8567; f. 1964; cap. 1,500m. francs CFA; supervises tobacco plantations and curing of tobacco; Pres. MARCEL MARIGOH MBOUA; Man. Dir LUCIEN KINGUE EBONGUE.

Société de Développement de la Culture et la Transformation du Blé (SODEBLE): BP 41, Ngaoundéré; tel. 25-10-05; telex 7642; f. 1975; development of wheat-growing and flour-milling in the Adamaoua region; cap. 4,500m. francs CFA; Man. Dir MARTIN KOUEBO.

Société de Développement du Cacao (SODECAO): BP 1651, Yaoundé; tel. 22-09-91; telex 8276; f. 1974, reorganized 1980; cap. 425m. francs CFA; development of cocoa, coffee and food crop production in the Centre-Sud province; Dir.-Gen. PAUL JOUVE.

Société de Développement du Coton (SODECOTON): BP 302, Garoua; tel. 27-10-80; telex 7617; f. 1974; cap. 4,529m. francs CFA; development of cotton and other agricultural production in the north; marketing and processing of cotton; Man. Dir MOHAMED IYA.

Société de Développement et d'Exploitation des Productions Animales (SODEPA): BP 1410, Yaoundé; tel. 22-24-28; f. 1974; cap. 375m. francs CFA; development of livestock raising and livestock products; Man. Dir Dr ADJOUDJI HAMADJODA.

Société de Développement du Périmètre de Mise en Valeur Agricole Yambassi-Bafang (SODENKAM): BP 02, Nkondjock, Yambassi-Bafang; f. 1970; cap. 136m. francs CFA; development of northern area by improving infrastructure and increasing production; Pres. Governor of the Littoral Province; Man. Dir ROBERT NKA MBOCK.

Société de Développement de la Riziculture dans la plaine des Mbo (SODERIM): BP 146, Melong; cap. 1,535m. francs CFA; expansion of rice-growing and processing; Pres. CONRAD EYOUM ESSOMBE; Man. Dir JOSEPH NGA.

Société d'Etudes des Bauxites du Cameroun (SEBACAM): BP 1090, Douala; telex 5267; f. 1970; cap. 210m. francs CFA; 40% state-owned; feasibility studies for the exploitation of bauxite reserves at Minim-Martap; Dir CLAUDE MILLET.

Société d'Expansion et de Modernisation de la Riziculture de Yagoua (SEMRY): BP 46, Yagoua; tel. 29-62-13; telex 7655; f. 1971; cap. 4,580m. francs CFA; expansion of rice-growing in areas where irrigation is possible and commercialization of rice products; Pres. AKONO NNA; Dir E. K. BUCHMANN.

PRINCIPAL CO-OPERATIVE ORGANIZATIONS

Office National de Commercialisation des Produits de Base (ONCPB): BP 378, Douala; tel. 42-67-76; telex 5260; f. 1978 to replace the Caisse de stabilisation des prix and the Cocoa Marketing Board; has monopoly of marketing cocoa, coffee, cotton, groundnuts and palm kernels; is responsible for the internal prices for the planters, the quality of the produce and development of production; holds 22% share in CAMDEV; Pres. LUC AYANG; Man. Dir ROGER MELINGUI.

Bakweri Co-operative Union of Farmers Ltd: Dibanda, Tiko; produce marketing co-operative for bananas, cocoa and coffee; 14 societies, 2,000 mems; Pres. Dr E. M. L. ENDELEY.

Cameroon Co-operative Exporters Ltd: BP 19, Kumba; f. 1953; mems: 8 socs; central agency for marketing of mems' coffee, cocoa and palm kernels; Man. A. B. ENYONG; Sec. M. M. EYOH (acting).

Centre National de Développement des Entreprises Coopératives (CENADEC): BP 120, Yaoundé; f. 1970; promotes and organizes the co-operative movement; bureaux at BP 43, Kumba and BP 26, Bamenda; Dir XAVIER ONAMBELE ETOUNDI.

Coopérative Agricole des Planteurs de la Menoua (CAPLAME): BP 130, Dschang; tel. 45-11-25; Dir PIERRE NZEFA.

Union Centrale des Coopératives Agricoles de l'Ouest (UCCAO): BP 1002, ave Samuel Wonko, Bafoussam; tel. 44-14-39; telex 7005; f. 1959; 85,000 mems; Pres. VICTOR NGNIMPEBA; Man. Dir HENRI FANKAM.

West Cameroon Co-operative Association Ltd: BP 135, Kumba; founded as central financing body of the co-operative movement; provides short-term credits and agricultural services to mem. socs; policy-making body for the co-operative movement in West Cameroon; 142 mem. unions and socs with total membership of c. 45,000; Pres. Chief T. E. NJEA; Sec. M. M. QUAN.

There are 83 co-operatives for the harvesting and sale of bananas and coffee and for providing mutual credit.

TRADE UNIONS

National Union of Private Journalists (NUPJ): Yaoundé; f. 1984; Pres. DOMINIQUE SIMI FOUDA; Vice-Pres. PADDY TAMBE JOHN, DAVID ACHIDI NDIFANG.

Organisation Syndicale des Travailleurs du Cameroun (OSTC): Yaoundé; tel. 23-00-47; f. 1985; formerly the Union National des Travailleurs du Cameroun (UNTC); Pres. DOMINIQUE FOUDA SIMA.

Transport

RAILWAYS

There are 1,115 km of track, the West Line running from Douala to Nkongsamba (172 km) with a branch line leading south-west from Mbanga to Kumba (29 km), and the Transcameroon railway which runs from Douala to Ngaoundéré (930 km), with a branch line from Ngoumou to Mbalmayo (30 km). The section from Yaoundé to Ngaoundéré (622 km) was opened in 1974. An extension of its western branch is projected from Mbalmayo to Bangui, in the Central African Republic. Improvements to the line between Douala and Yaoundé were begun in 1974; those on the section between Yaoundé and Maloumé were completed in April 1978, and those between Douala and Edéa in 1981. Improvements to the section between Edéa and Eseka, which cut the 90 km line to 82 km, were completed in 1982. Construction of the final section, between Eseka and Maloumé, began in early 1983 and was scheduled for completion in late 1987.

Régie Nationale des Chemins de Fer du Cameroun (RNCFC): BP 304, Douala; tel. 42-60-45; telex 5607; f. 1947; Chair. ANDRÉ NGONGANG OUANJI; Man. Dir YOUSSOUFA DAOUDA.

Office du Chemin de Fer Transcamerounais: BP 625, Yaoundé; tel. 22-44-33; telex 8293; supervises the laying of new

CAMEROON

railway lines and improvements to existing lines, and undertakes relevant research; Man. Dir Luc Towa Fotso (acting).

ROADS

At 30 June 1986 there were 64,065 km of roads, including 7,241 km of main roads and 13,916 km of secondary roads. Of the main and secondary roads, more than 2,600 km were bitumen-surfaced. Under the 1981/82–1985/86 Plan, 281,000m. francs CFA were allocated to the development of the road network, including the construction and strengthening of 10,564 km of roads, road transport and route studies. A fast metalled road between Douala and Yaoundé was opened in August 1985. Projects planned for 1986/87 included improvements to the roads from Edéa to Kribi and from Mbalmayo to Ebolowa, as well as to the Bamenda 'ring road'.

SHIPPING

There are two sea ports at Kribi and Limbe/Tiko, a river port at Garoua, and an estuary port at Douala, the largest port and main outlet. It has 2,510 m of quays and a minimum depth of 5.8 m in the channels, 8.5 m at the quays. In 1985 the port of Douala handled 4,601,453 metric tons, over 95% of total sea-borne traffic. Extensions and modernizations to the port were completed in January 1980, and a storage zone for the use of land-locked central African countries has been constructed. Handling capacity increased to 7m. metric tons per year. Plans are under way to increase the annual capacity of the container terminal from 1.5m. tons to 2m. tons. Facilities for ship-repair have also been provided, and there is a logistic area for oil research facilities.

Office National des Ports/National Ports Authority: 5 blvd Leclerc, BP 4020, Douala; tel. 42-01-33; telex 5270; Chair. André-Bosco Cheuoua; Gen. Man. Siegfried Dibong.

CAMATRANS (Delmas-Vieljeux Cameroun): rue Kitchener, BP 263, Douala and BP 18, Kribi; tel. 42-10-36; telex 5222; f. 1977; Dir François Perroy.

Cameroon Shipping Lines SA (CAMSHIPLINES): 18 rue Joffre, BP 4054, Douala; tel. 42-00-38; telex 5615; f. 1975; cap. 4,365m.; 67% state-owned; 6 vessels trading with western Europe, USA, Far East and Africa; Man. Dir René Mbayen.

Société Africaine de Transit et d'Affrètement (SATA): Vallée Tokoto, BP 546, Douala; tel. 42-82-09; telex 5239; f. 1950; cap. 625m.; Man. Dir Yves Lerays; Dir in Douala M. Valenza.

Société Agence Maritime de l'Ouest Africain Cameroun (SAMOA): place du Gouvernement, BP 1127, Douala; tel. 42-16-80; telex 5256; f. 1953; agents for Lloyd Triestino, Armada Shipping, Black Star Line, Gold Star Line, Nigerian Star Line, OT Africa Line, Spliethoff, Jeco Shipping, Van Uden; Dir Paul Stefani.

Société Camerounaise de Manutention et d'Acconage (SOCAMAC): BP 284, Douala; tel. 42-40-51; telex 5537; f. 1976; freight handling; Dir M. Ghoos.

Société Camerounaise de Transport et d'Affrètement (SCTA): BP 974, Douala; tel. 42-17-24; f. 1951; cap. 100m.; Pres. François Perroy; Dir-Gen. Gontran Frauciel.

Société Ouest-Africaine d'Enterprises Maritimes (Cameroun)—SOAEM: rue Alfred Saker, BP 4057, Douala; tel. 42-02-88; telex 5220; f. 1959; Man. Dir Jean-Louis Greciet.

SOCOPAO (Cameroun): BP 215, Douala; tel. 42-64-64; telex 5252; f. 1951; cap. 1,059m.; agents for Palm/Elder/Hoegh Lines, Bank Line, CNAN, CNN, Comanav, Comasersa, Dafra Line, Grand Pale, Marasia SA, Maritima del Norte, Navcoma, Nigerian Shipping Line, Niven Line, Splosna Plovba, Rossis Maritime, SSSIM, Veb Deutsche Seereederei, Polish Ocean Lines, Westwind Africa Line, Nautilus Keller Line, Estonian Shipping Co, AGTI Paris, K-Line Tokyo; Man. Dir Marc Lancrey.

Transcap Cameroun: BP 4059, Douala; tel. 42-72-14; telex 5247; Dir Michel Bardou.

CIVIL AVIATION

There are international airports at Douala and Yaoundé, and a second international airport is planned for Yaoundé. Existing facilities at Garoua are being extended to take international air traffic at an estimated cost of US $40m. There are 39 smaller airports and aerodromes.

Cameroon Airlines (Cam-Air): 3 ave du Général de Gaulle, BP 4092, Douala; tel. 42-25-25; telex 5345; f. 1971; 75% govt-owned and 25% by Air France; services to Benin, Burundi, Congo, Equatorial Guinea, France, Gabon, Italy, the Ivory Coast, Kenya, Nigeria, Switzerland, the United Kingdom and Zaire and domestic flights; fleet of 3 Boeing 737, 1 Boeing 707-Combi, 1 Boeing 747-200-B and 2 Hawker Siddeley 748; Chair. Samuel Eboua; Gen. Man. Louis-Claude Nyassa.

Tourism

Secrétariat d'Etat au Tourisme: Yaoundé; tel. 22-44-11; telex 8318; f. 1960; provincial offices in Douala, Buéa, Bamenda, Ngaoundéré, Maroua, Garoua, Bafoussam, Kribi; Sec. of State Dr Abdoulaye Souaibou.

SOCATOUR (National Tourism Company): BP 7138, Yaoundé; f. 1984.

CANADA

Introductory Survey

Location, Climate, Language, Religion, Flag, Capital

Canada occupies the northern part of North America (excluding Alaska and Greenland) and is the second largest country in the world. It extends from the Atlantic Ocean to the Pacific. Except for the boundary with Alaska in the north-west, Canada's frontier with the USA follows the upper St Lawrence Seaway and the Great Lakes, continuing west along latitude 49°N. The climate is an extreme one, particularly inland. Winter temperatures drop well below freezing but summers are generally warm. Rainfall varies from moderate to light and there are heavy falls of snow. The two official languages are English and French, the mother tongues of 61.3% and 25.7%, respectively, at the general census in 1981. More than 98% of Canadians can speak English or French. About 46% of the population are Roman Catholics. The main Protestant churches are the United Church of Canada and the Anglican Church of Canada, but most Christian denominations are represented. The national flag (proportions 2 by 1) consists of a red maple leaf on a white field, flanked by red panels. The capital is Ottawa.

Recent History

The Liberals, led by Pierre Trudeau, were returned to office at general elections in 1968, 1972, 1974, and again in 1980 after a short-lived minority Progressive Conservative administration. Foreign relations altered significantly under the Liberals, with less emphasis on traditional links with Western Europe and the USA, and a fostering of relations with the Far East, Africa and Latin America.

In 1975 Canada began to experience the effects of international economic recession. This led to a steady erosion of the Government's popularity, which finally resulted in the Liberals' defeat at general elections held in May 1979, although the Progressive Conservative administration, led by Joe Clark, lacked an overall majority. In November, Trudeau announced that he was resigning as Liberal leader, but in the following month the Government was defeated on its budget proposals. Trudeau postponed his retirement, and at general elections in February 1980 the Liberals were returned with a strong majority. Popular support for the new Government, however, fell rapidly with the persistence of adverse economic conditions, while the Progressive Conservatives gained substantially in popularity under the leadership of Brian Mulroney, a Québec labour lawyer and businessman with no previous political experience, who replaced Clark in June 1983.

With the Liberals' popular standing at a post-war low, Trudeau, who had earlier indicated that he would vacate the party leadership before the general elections due in 1985, resigned in June 1984 and was succeeded as Liberal leader and Prime Minister by John Turner, a former Minister of Finance who had left active politics in 1975 following a disagreement with Trudeau. Nine days after taking office, Turner called general elections for September. The Liberals entered the pre-election period with revived popular support, but criticism of Turner's exercise of political patronage and of his general conduct of the election campaign saw the Liberals' following recede. Mulroney, an able bilingual public speaker, led the Progressive Conservatives to the largest electoral majority in Canadian history. During 1986, however, the resignations in discordant circumstances of five cabinet ministers, together with the persistence of high rates of unemployment, particularly in Québec and the Atlantic Maritime Provinces, led to a diminution in the Government's popular support.

Since taking office, Prime Minister Mulroney has taken steps to re-establish Canada's traditional 'special relationship' with the USA, which had operated until the Trudeau period. During 1985 Canadian foreign policy moved broadly into line with that of President Reagan's administration in the USA, with the Mulroney government reinforcing its commitment to NATO defence and agreeing to the modernization of the US military radar network in northern Canada. However, Mulroney declined an invitation to participate in the US programme of space-based defence research, the Strategic Defense Initiative (SDI).

Little progress has been made in realizing Canada's wish to secure effective US government control of the emission of gases from industrial plants, which move northwards into Canada to produce environmentally destructive 'acid rain'. In April 1985 President Reagan agreed to the formation of a joint governmental commission to 'study' this problem. In 1986 the commission recommended the implementation of a US $5,000m. anti-pollution programme, to be financed jointly by the US Government and the relevant industries, although no specific arrangements were set out for funding. The Canadian Government, meanwhile, has committed itself to the reduction by 50% of acid-pollution emissions from domestic sources by 1990.

Relations between the USA and Canada came under strain in August and September 1985, when a US coastguard icebreaker traversed the Northwest Passage without seeking prior permission from Canada, asserting long-standing US claims that the channels within this 1.6m. sq km tract of ice-bound islands are international waters. The Canadian Government formally declared sovereignty of this area as from 1 January 1986.

In Québec, where four-fifths of the population speak French as a first language and which maintains its own cultural identity, the question of provincial autonomy has long been a sensitive issue. At provincial elections in 1976 the separatist Parti Québécois (PQ), led by René Lévesque, came to power, and in 1977 made French the official language of education, business and government in Québec. Certain sections of this legislation have been declared 'inoperable' and unconstitutional by the Supreme Court of Canada.

During 1977 Lévesque's Government reiterated its aim of sovereignty for Québec; however in 1978 Lévesque denied that unilateral separation was contemplated and stated that a 'sovereignty-association', with a monetary and customs union, would be sought. At a Québec provincial referendum held in May 1980, Lévesque's proposals were rejected by an electoral margin of 59.5% to 40.5%. The PQ was re-elected at provincial general elections held in April 1981, but lost seats in all subsequent by-elections. Lévesque precipitated a party split and cabinet resignations in November 1984, when he declared that Québec's economic problems were of greater urgency than the sovereignty issue. Following further by-election defeats in 1985, Lévesque resigned and was succeeded as Premier and PQ leader in October by Pierre-Marc Johnson, the province's Minister of Justice and Federal-Provincial Relations. Johnson, a member of Lévesque's faction of the PQ, called provincial elections for December. These resulted in a heavy defeat for the PQ, and the return to office of the Liberals, led by Robert Bourassa.

Constitutional reform has been an important issue in recent years. Between 1978 and 1980, a series of proposals was made by federal and provincial governments and various advisory bodies for the patriation of the Constitution, whereby the UK Parliament would transfer to Canada authority over all matters contained in British statutes relating to Canada, opening the way for the reform of central institutions and the redistribution of legislative powers between Parliament and the Provincial Legislatures.

Trudeau and the Provincial Premiers were unable to agree on reform proposals, mainly because of the wish of several of the provinces to retain full control of their natural resources. In October 1980 the Federal Government announced that it would proceed unilaterally with a constitutional reform plan incorporating patriation and a charter of rights which would be binding on all provinces. Eight of the 10 provinces challenged the plan in the Supreme Court of Canada, which ruled in September 1981 that, while the Federal Government was acting within its powers, further efforts should be made to obtain the provinces' agreement. Renewed talks between Trudeau and the provincial leaders finally resulted in all the provinces except Québec accepting compromise proposals which included a revised charter of rights and a new formula for constitutional amendments made after patriation, whereby such amendments would require the support of at least seven provinces representing more than 50% of the population. In December the plan was overwhelmingly approved by the Federal Parliament. It was adopted by the UK Parliament in March 1982 and formally took effect in April as the Constitution Act 1982. Québec, however, has maintained its opposition to the reform and its legislature has claimed the right to veto constitutional provisions, although this has been disallowed by the Supreme Court of Canada. Since the return to power in 1985 of the Liberals in Québec, the federal Progressive Conservative Government has taken new initiatives to bring Québec into the constitutional accord, a goal which Premier Bourassa has stated that he hopes will be achieved before the next federal elections, due in 1989.

The Northwest Territories (NWT), which form one-third of Canada's land mass but contain a population of only 49,000 (including 16,000 Inuit and 9,000 Indians), may eventually secure a new constitutional status. In November 1982 the Federal Government agreed in principle to implement the decision of a territorial referendum held in April, in which 56% of the voters approved a division of the NWT into two parts. In April 1985 the Federal Government stated that, subject to the eventual agreement of the Provincial Premiers and of Indian and Inuit organizations, it would incorporate into the Constitution the right to self-government of Canada's 500,000 indigenous peoples. The arrangements would include a separate legislature for Nunavut, the eastern part of the NWT. However, little progress has subsequently been reported in these negotiations.

Government

Canada is a federal parliamentary state. Under the Constitution Act 1982, executive power is vested in the British monarch, as Head of State, and exercisable by her representative, the Governor-General, whom she appoints on the advice of the Canadian Prime Minister. The Federal Parliament comprises the Head of State, a nominated Senate (104 members, appointed on a regional basis) and a House of Commons (282 members elected by universal adult suffrage for single-member constituencies). A Parliament may last no longer than five years. The Governor-General appoints the Prime Minister and, on the latter's recommendation, other ministers to form the Cabinet. The Prime Minister should have the confidence of the House of Commons, to which the Cabinet is responsible. Canada comprises 10 provinces (each with a Lieutenant-Governor and a Legislature, which may last no longer than five years, from which a Premier is chosen), and two territories constituted by Act of Parliament.

Defence

Canada co-operates with the USA in the defence of North America and is a member of NATO. Military service is voluntary. In July 1986 the armed forces numbered 83,000: army 21,000, navy 5,500, air force 15,300 and 41,200 not identified by service. Defence expenditure for 1986/87 was estimated at C $9,860m.

Economic Affairs

Canada is one of the world's leading trading nations. In 1985 it was the seventh largest exporter, with export trade valued at US $87,500m. and accounting for 4.6% of the US dollar value of world exports. It was the world's eighth largest importer, accounting for 3.8% of global imports. The Canadian economy is closely linked with that of the USA, which accounted for over 78% of total exports in 1985. Under existing agreements between the two countries, about 70% of Canadian exports entering the USA are duty-free, as are approximately 72% of US exports to Canada. Bilateral talks on a new trade agreement, aimed at an almost complete phasing-out of tariffs over a 10-year period from January 1988, with protection for the affected sectors, were opened in September 1985. By December 1986, however, these negotiations had made little effective progress. Since the Trudeau period, successful efforts have been made to develop alternative markets, notably in Japan, the People's Republic of China and the EEC, and in 1986 about 30% of Canada's gross national product (GNP) was linked with foreign trade.

Many sectors of Canadian industry rely heavily on foreign investment. Foreign control of Canadian corporations reached its peak in the early 1970s; since then, mainly as a result of government and private-sector acquisitions, such control has declined. The share of assets held by foreign-controlled corporations in the non-financial (mainly petroleum) industries declined by 0.2% to 24.3% in 1983. Corporations classified as US-controlled hold a dominant position, accounting for 71.5% of these assets in 1983. In October 1980 the Government declared its aim of reducing the foreign-owned proportion to 50% by 1990. By early 1982 the reversal of foreign investment funds caused by this policy was exerting serious pressure on the balance of payments and on the Canadian dollar exchange rate, and in June the Government eased certain restrictions on foreign investors. Since taking office in September 1984, the Progressive Conservative Government has dismantled many of the Liberals' controls on foreign ownership of Canadian corporations and energy enterprises.

Canada, one of the world's leading industrial countries, is also a major world exporter of agricultural products and, in terms of value, the world's leading fish and seafood exporter. The main exports in 1985 were motor vehicles and parts, crude petroleum, newsprint paper, softwood lumber, natural gas, wheat, wood pulp and other pulp. Canada is the world's largest producer of zinc and the second largest of nickel, asbestos, potash, uranium, gypsum, elemental sulphur, and titanium concentrates. The country is also rich in many other minerals, including gold, silver, iron, copper, cobalt and lead. There are considerable petroleum and natural gas resources in Alberta, off the Atlantic coast and in the Canadian Arctic islands. Although the development and profitability of this industry dwindled after the slump in world oil prices in 1981/82, development incentives, introduced by the Federal Government in 1985, have led to a revival in investment and production. In July 1980 construction was authorized of the initial section of the Alaska Highway Gas Pipeline, which will transport US gas from Alaska to join existing pipelines in British Columbia and Alberta for distribution in the USA and, at a later date, in Canada. The project, costing an estimated C $23,000m., is due for completion in 1987.

In 1975 Canada began to be affected by the international slump, and inflationary pressures have contributed to its economic problems. The Canadian dollar has depreciated sharply since 1976; high interest rates and tight monetary controls have been slow to take effect. Inflation reached 12.5% in 1981 before easing to 10.8% in 1982 and responding finally to anti-inflation measures, including high interest rates, by falling to 5.8% in 1983, to 4.4% in 1984 and to 4% in 1985. A further fall to 3.8% was forecast for 1986. Unemployment, however, has remained a serious problem, rising from 7.5% of the labour force in 1981 to 11% in 1982 and to 11.9% in 1983, before falling to 11.3% in 1984, 10.5% in 1985 and 9.1% in June 1986. The overall budget deficit for 1985/86 was C $34,526m. In February 1986 the Government projected a 1986/87 deficit of almost C $29,465m., although this was expected to decline to C $25,940m. for 1987/88. Growth in gross domestic product (GDP), which totalled 4.7% in 1984, retreated to 4.3% in 1985. A further decline, to 3.9%, was forecast for 1986.

Social Welfare

Almost 47% of the 1986/87 federal budget was allocated to health and social welfare. The Federal Government administers family allowances, unemployment insurance and pensions. Other services are provided by the provinces. A federal medical care insurance programme covers all Canadians against medical expenses, and a federal-provincial hospital insurance programme covers over 99% of the insurable population.

Education

Education policy is a provincial responsibility, and the period of compulsory school attendance varies. French-speaking students are entitled by law, in some provinces, to instruction in French. Primary education is from the age of five or six years to 13–14, followed by three to five years at secondary or high school. In 1981 an estimated 96% of children aged six to 11 attended primary schools, while 85% of those aged 12 to 17 were enrolled at secondary schools. There are 66 universities and 197 other institutions of higher education.

Tourism
Canada offers a wide range of outdoor tourist attractions. Its scenic, cultural and ethnic diversity add to its travel appeal, as do the developing attractions of its metropolitan centres. Most visitors are from the USA (34.1m. in 1985). Tourist spending in 1985 amounted to C $5,006m.

Public Holidays
1987: 1 January (New Year), 17 April (Good Friday), 20 April (Easter Monday), 18 May (Victoria Day), 1 July (Canada Day), 7 September (Labour Day), 12 October (Thanksgiving), 11 November (Remembrance Day), 25 December (Christmas Day), 26 December (Boxing Day).

1988: 1 January (New Year), 1 April (Good Friday), 4 April (Easter Monday), 23 May (Victoria Day), 1 July (Canada Day), 5 September (Labour Day), 10 October (Thanksgiving), 11 November (Remembrance Day), 25 December (Christmas Day), 26 December (Boxing Day).

Weights and Measures
The imperial system is in general use with the exception of the 2,000 lb American ton. A government agency, Metric Commission Canada, is responsible for the implementation of a metrication programme.

Currency and Exchange Rates
100 cents = 1 Canadian dollar (C $).

Exchange rates (30 September 1986):
 £1 sterling = C $2.010;
 US $1 = C $1.3885.

Statistical Survey

Source (unless otherwise stated): Statistics Canada, Ottawa K1A 0T6; tel. (613) 990-8116; telex 053-3585.

Area and Population

AREA, POPULATION AND DENSITY

Area (sq km)	
Land	9,215,430
Inland water	755,180
Total	9,970,610*
Population (census results)	
1 June 1976	22,992,604
3 June 1981	
Males	12,068,290
Females	12,274,890
Total	24,343,180
Population (official estimates at 1 June)	
1983	24,884,500
1984	25,124,100
1985	25,359,800
Density (per sq km) at 1 June 1985	2.5

* 3,849,674 sq miles.

PROVINCES AND TERRITORIES
(estimates at 1 June 1985)

	Area (sq km)	Population	Capital
Provinces:			
Alberta	661,190	2,358,000	Edmonton
British Columbia	947,800	2,884,700	Victoria
Manitoba	649,950	1,070,600	Winnipeg
New Brunswick	73,440	719,600	Fredericton
Newfoundland	405,720	580,700	St John's
Nova Scotia	55,490	879,800	Halifax
Ontario	1,068,580	9,064,200	Toronto
Prince Edward Island	5,660	127,400	Charlottetown
Quebec	1,540,680	6,582,700	Quebec
Saskatchewan	652,330	1,017,800	Regina
Territories:			
Northwest Territories	3,426,320	51,000	Yellowknife
Yukon Territory	483,450	23,200	Whitehorse
Total	9,970,610	25,359,800	—

PRINCIPAL TOWNS
(estimated population of metropolitan areas at 1 June 1985)

Ottawa (capital)	769,900*	Hamilton	559,700
Toronto	3,202,400	St Catharine's-Niagara	309,400
Montreal	2,878,200		
Vancouver	1,348,600	Kitchener	303,400
Edmonton	683,600	London	292,700
Calgary	625,600†	Halifax	290,600
Winnipeg	612,100	Windsor	249,800
Quebec	539,500	Victoria	245,100

* Including Hull.
† Estimate based on annual municipal census.

BIRTHS, MARRIAGES AND DEATHS

	Registered live births*		Registered marriages		Registered deaths*	
	Number	Rate (per 1,000)	Number	Rate (per 1,000)	Number	Rate (per 1,000)
1978	357,920	15.5	185,523	7.9	170,670	7.3
1979	365,475	15.2	187,711	7.9	168,183	7.1
1980	369,709	15.5	191,069	8.0	171,473	7.2
1981	371,346	15.3	190,082	7.8	171,029	7.0
1982	373,082	15.1	188,360	7.6	174,413	7.1
1983	373,689	15.0	184,675	7.4	174,484	7.0
1984	377,031	15.0	185,597	7.4	175,727	7.1
1985†	379,140	14.9	184,096	7.3	178,330	7.0

* Including Canadian residents temporarily in the USA but excluding US residents temporarily in Canada.
† Estimates.

IMMIGRATION

Country of Origin	1983	1984	1985*
United Kingdom	5,737	5,104	4,464
USA	7,381	6,922	6,763
Other	76,039	76,213	73,075
Total	89,157	88,239	84,302

* Estimates.

ECONOMICALLY ACTIVE POPULATION*
('000 persons aged 15 years and over)

	1983	1984	1985
Agriculture	476	476	488
Forestry, fishing and trapping	111	110	112
Mines, quarries and oil wells	170	182	191
Manufacturing	1,886	1,968	1,981
Construction	566	572	587
Electricity, gas and water	120	123	124
Transport and communications	750	735	760
Trade	1,850	1,929	2,001
Finance, insurance and real estate	602	631	629
Public administration	782	791	802
Other services	3,421	3,483	3,648
Total employed	10,734†	11,000‡	11,311
Unemployed	1,448	1,399	1,328
Total labour force	12,183	12,399	12,639

* Figures exclude military personnel, inmates of institutions, the Yukon and Northwest Territories, and Indian reserves.
† Comprising (in '000): Males 6,240; Females 4,495.
‡ Comprising (in '000): Males 6,367; Females 4,633.

CANADA   Statistical Survey

Agriculture

PRINCIPAL CROPS ('000 harvest units)

	1983	1984	1985
Wheat (bushels*)	976,915	778,920	891,124
Oats (bushels*)	179,817	173,197	194,316
Barley (bushels*)	472,873	470,891	571,461
Rye (bushels*)	32,595	26,131	23,568
Maize (Corn) (bushels*)	233,580	276,500	294,167
Buckwheat (bushels*)	1,651	1,205	1,133
Soybeans (bushels*)	27,000	34,302	38,500
Flax (bushels*)	17,600	26,600	35,500
Rapeseed (Canola) (bushels*)	116,020	143,120	154,700
Potatoes (cwt)	56,352	60,147	67,001
Beans (cwt)	850	1,009	1,290
Tame hay (tons)	27,407	28,284	26,221

* One bushel is 60 lb (27.2 kg) for wheat and soybeans; 34 lb (15.4 kg) for oats; 48 lb (21.8 kg) for barley; 56 lb (25.4 kg) for maize, rye and flax.

LIVESTOCK ('000 head at 1 July)

	1984	1985	1986
Milch cows	1,728	1,696	1,664
Other cattle	10,556	10,038	9,801
Sheep	791	748	722
Pigs	10,794	10,716	10,708

DAIRY PRODUCE

	1983	1984	1985
Milk (kilolitres)*	7,194,142	7,411,381	7,219,944
Creamery butter (metric tons)	103,585	107,788	94,885
Cheddar cheese (metric tons)	99,448	101,356	109,572
Ice-cream mix (kilolitres)	159,381	159,090	159,901
Eggs ('000 dozen)	504,804	489,575	487,908

* Farm sales of milk and cream.

Forestry

LUMBER PRODUCTION, 1984 (cubic metres)

	Softwoods	Hardwoods	Total
Newfoundland	87,714	1,498	89,212
Prince Edward Island	37,756	—	37,756
Nova Scotia	445,287	15,027	460,314
New Brunswick	1,011,662	54,661	1,066,323
Quebec	8,383,206	468,922	8,852,128
Ontario	3,972,358	586,229	4,558,587
Manitoba	104,985	32,607	137,592
Saskatchewan	519,921	—	519,921
Alberta	2,286,696	118,761	2,405,457
British Columbia	30,858,516	2,832	30,861,348
Total	47,708,101	1,280,537	48,988,638

Fur Industry

NUMBER OF PELTS PRODUCED

	1982/83	1983/84	1984/85
Newfoundland	29,136	30,223	34,551
Prince Edward Island	26,820	35,259	36,517
Nova Scotia	296,508	300,886	306,154
New Brunswick	84,085	82,085	79,859
Quebec	655,219	673,335	636,771
Ontario	1,572,110	1,348,028	1,431,658
Manitoba	353,190	382,464	298,537
Saskatchewan	265,770	284,146	307,062
Alberta	412,418	603,997	389,327
British Columbia	394,672	401,420	328,244
Northwest Territories	190,293	207,988	168,595
Yukon	34,890	42,280	27,018
Total	4,303,704*	4,388,585*	4,102,533

* Including Alaska fur seal.

Sea Fisheries*

LANDINGS

	1983	1984	1985†
Atlantic total	1,108,439	1,071,521	1,168,920
Cod	509,052	475,942	478,000
Crab	42,204	43,572	45,300
Small flatfishes	76,963	80,116	87,700
Haddock	39,777	32,654	36,900
Halibut	2,499	3,142	3,800
Pollock	33,843	35,216	45,000
Redfish	58,253	67,302	72,000
Herring	142,454	132,592	188,800
Salmon	1,219	858	960
Lobsters	27,655	28,694	32,500
Scallops	51,289	36,479	46,400
Tuna	417	254	120
Pacific total	190,671	169,168	212,855
Halibut	3,189	5,364	6,150
Herring	39,760	33,703	25,500
Salmon	73,851	50,431	107,600
Canada total‡	1,299,110	1,284,119	1,425,775

* Metric tons, round weight.   † Preliminary.   ‡ All sea fish.

Mining

('000)

		1983	1984	1985*
Metallic				
Bismuth	kilograms	253	166	222
Cadmium	kilograms	1,193	1,605	1,683
Cobalt	kilograms	1,410	2,123	2,676
Columbium (Cb_2O_5)	kilograms	1,745	2,767	3,300
Copper	kilograms	653,040	721,826	730,347
Gold	grams	73,512	83,446	86,044
Iron ore	metric tons	32,959	39,930	40,348
Lead	kilograms	271,961	264,301	263,890
Molybdenum	kilograms	10,194	11,557	7,569
Nickel	kilograms	125,022	173,725	175,570
Platinum group	grams	6,965	10,369	10,425
Selenium	kilograms	266	463	305
Silver	kilograms	1,197	1,327	1,209
Uranium (U_3O_8)	kilograms	6,823	10,272	10,029
Zinc	kilograms	987,713	1,062,701	1,038,504
Non-metallic				
Asbestos	metric tons	858	837	744
Gypsum	metric tons	7,507	7,775	8,384
Nepheline syenite	metric tons	523	521	488
Potash (K_2O)	metric tons	6,294	7,527	6,923
Salt	metric tons	8,602	10,235	10,043
Sulphur, in smelter gas	metric tons	678	844	773
Sulphur, elemental	metric tons	6,631	8,353	8,250
Fuels				
Coal	metric tons	44,787	57,402	60,480
Natural gas	m. cu metres	72,229	78,266	80,181
Natural gas by-products	cu metres	18,013	19,640	19,674
Petroleum, crude	cu metres	78,751	83,680	84,311
Structural materials				
Cement	metric tons	7,871	9,240	9,772
Sand and gravel	metric tons	233,408	233,759	223,724
Stone	metric tons	67,555	81,754	77,930

* Preliminary.

Industry

VALUE OF SHIPMENTS (C $ million)

	1982	1983	1984*
Food industries	28,736.4	29,591.4	31,624.2
Beverage industries	4,012.3	4,290.7	4,550.7
Tobacco products industries	1,493.8	1,516.5	1,590.2
Rubber products industries	1,936.9	2,141.2	2,507.2
Plastic products industries	2,680.2	3,042.9	3,510.4
Leather and allied products industries	1,141.4	1,166.4	1,270.5
Primary textile industries	2,318.5	2,716.6	2,729.3
Textiles products industries	1,996.2	2,394.8	2,523.0
Clothing industries	4,624.2	4,891.1	5,174.9
Wood industries	7,167.9	9,405.9	9,972.5
Furniture and fixture industries	2,403.7	2,668.2	3,021.5
Paper and allied products industries	14,261.2	15,010.8	17,471.9
Printing, publishing and allied industries	6,801.1	7,579.4	8,659.4
Primary metal industries	12,429.3	13,571.6	16,431.5
Fabricated metal products industries	11,549.4	11,098.8	12,193.1
Machinery industries	6,452.6	5,784.8	6,863.2
Transportation equipment industries	23,495.9	28,455.6	37,916.3
Electrical and electronic products industries	9,832.2	9,903.1	11,632.1
Non-metallic mineral products industries	4,420.7	4,779.1	5,246.4
Refined petroleum and coal products industries	21,760.1	23,324.4	23,336.8
Chemical and chemical products industries	14,216.7	15,750.3	17,174.9
Other manufacturing industries	3,979.8	4,172.5	4,669.8

Electric Energy (net production, million kWh): 387,460 in 1982; 394,200 in 1983.

* Preliminary.

Finance

CURRENCY AND EXCHANGE RATES

Monetary Units
100 cents = 1 Canadian dollar (C $).

Denominations
Coins: 1, 5, 10, 25 and 50 cents; 1 dollar.
Notes: 1, 2, 5, 10, 20, 50, 100 and 1,000 dollars.

Sterling and US Dollar Equivalents (30 September 1986)
£1 sterling = C $2.010;
US $1 = C $1.3885;
C $100 = £49.75 = US $72.02.

Average Exchange Rate (C $ per US $)
1983   1.2324
1984   1.2951
1985   1.3655

COST OF LIVING (Consumer Price Index. Base: 1981 = 100)

	1983	1984	1985
Food	111.2	117.4	120.8
Housing	120.2	124.7	129.0
Clothing	109.8	112.5	115.6
Transport	119.8	124.8	130.8
Health and personal care	118.2	122.8	127.2
Recreation, education and reading	115.8	119.7	124.5
Tobacco and alcohol	130.0	140.6	154.0
All items	117.2	122.3	127.2

GOLD RESERVES AND CURRENCY IN CIRCULATION
(C $ million at 31 December)

	1983	1984	1985
Gold holdings*	739.1	690.8	773.0
US dollar holdings*	2,373.8	1,692.1	1,523.9
Notes in circulation	14,163.1	15,236.0	16,672.0

* US $ million.

FEDERAL BUDGET (C $ million, year ending 31 March)

Revenue	1985/86*	1986/87†
Personal income tax	33,008	37,705
Corporate income tax	9,210	11,675
Unemployment insurance contributions	8,712	9,437
Non-resident tax	1,053	1,100
Sales tax	9,345	11,700
Customs import duties	3,971	4,205
Other excise taxes and duties	2,827	2,975
Gasoline excise tax	770	1,455
Other energy taxes	2,578	1,130
Other tax revenue	126	178
Non-tax revenue: return on investments	3,753	4,310
Other non-tax revenue	1,475	1,405
Total budgetary revenue	76,828	87,275

Expenditure	1985/86*	1986/87†
Economic and regional development	12,057	11,080
Social development	51,753	54,865
Services to government	4,385	3,380
Parliament	284	207
Defence	9,082	9,860
External affairs and aid	2,462	3,100
Fiscal arrangements	5,941	6,060
Reserves net of estimated lapse	—	813
Programme expenditures	85,964	89,365
Public debt charges	25,390	27,375
Total expenditure	111,354	116,740

1987/88: Estimated Revenue C $94,025 million; Estimated Expenditure C $119,965 million.

* Based on preliminary financial statements for the fiscal year ending 31 March 1986.
† Figures relate to Federal Budget announced in February 1986.

NATIONAL ACCOUNTS (C $ million at current prices)
National Income and Product

	1983	1984	1985
Compensation of employees	221,766	238,496	255,569
Operating surplus	93,756	110,483	118,131
Domestic factor incomes	315,522	348,979	373,700
Consumption of fixed capital	46,706	50,391	53,725
Gross domestic product at factor cost	362,228	399,370	427,425
Indirect taxes, *less* subsidies	40,189	42,851	41,171
Statistical discrepancy	3,008	1,106	1,765
GDP at market prices	405,425	443,327	476,361
Factor income from abroad*	5,540	6,177	7,439
Less Factor income paid abroad*	17,253	19,969	22,036
Gross national product	393,712	429,535	461,764
Less Consumption of fixed capital	46,706	50,391	53,725
Statistical discrepancy	−3,008	−1,106	−1,765
National income at market prices	342,998	378,038	406,274
Other current transfers from abroad†	1,653	1,729	1,754
Less Other current transfers paid abroad†	1,801	2,204	2,331
National disposable income	343,850	377,563	405,697

* Remitted profits, dividends and interest only.
† Transfers to and from persons and governments.

Expenditure on the Gross Domestic Product

	1983	1984	1985
Government final consumption expenditure	83,094	89,302	94,971
Private final consumption expenditure	232,501	251,353	274,658
Increase in stocks	−2,122	3,177	2,681
Gross fixed capital formation	81,357	84,259	92,637
Exports of goods and services	103,330	126,406	135,961
Less Imports of goods and services	89,728	110,064	122,783
Statistical discrepancy	−3,007	−1,106	−1,764
GDP at market prices	405,425	443,327	476,361
GDP at constant 1981 prices	354,780	374,462	389,324

BALANCE OF PAYMENTS (US $ million)

	1983	1984	1985
Merchandise exports f.o.b.	75,706	88,954	90,061
Merchandise imports f.o.b.	−60,829	−72,369	−77,444
Trade balance	14,877	16,585	12,617
Exports of services	12,044	12,375	13,512
Imports of services	−26,191	−27,789	−28,833
Balance on goods and services	730	1,171	−2,704
Private unrequited transfers (net)	437	753	874
Government unrequited transfers (net)	198	−32	−111
Current balance	1,365	1,893	−1,941
Direct capital investment (net)	−3,513	−1,312	−5,308
Other long-term capital (net)	3,233	2,520	5,932
Short-term capital (net)	2,778	−13	416
Net errors and omissions	−3,912	−4,910	−2,379
Total (net monetary movements)	−49	−1,822	−3,280
Valuation changes (net)	−24	−120	75
Exceptional financing (net)	497	956	3,207
Changes in reserves	425	−986	1

Source: IMF, *International Financial Statistics*.

CANADA   *Statistical Survey*

External Trade

PRINCIPAL COMMODITIES (C $ million)

Imports	1984	1985
Live animals	94.3	109.3
Food, feed, beverages and tobacco	5,812.0	5,800.2
Meat, fresh, chilled or frozen	399.4	386.7
Fish and marine animals	487.5	493.5
Fruit and vegetables	2,168.6	2,208.2
Raw sugar	189.5	154.3
Coffee	474.2	447.8
Distilled alcoholic beverages	164.7	153.2
Other beverages	265.3	287.3
Crude materials (inedible)	7,994.1	7,858.1
Fur skins (undressed)	157.1	198.3
Rubber and allied gums	140.5	118.1
Iron ores and concentrates	292.7	349.1
Aluminium ores, concentrates and scrap	500.0	477.0
Other metal ores, concentrates and scrap	955.2	753.4
Coal	1,093.5	887.4
Crude petroleum	3,375.6	3,700.4
Fabricated materials (inedible)	17,214.7	18,732.9
Wood and paper	1,422.4	1,482.9
Textiles	1,734.5	1,885.6
Chemicals	5,212.4	5,445.4
Iron and steel	1,641.3	2,008.4
Non-ferrous metals	2,258.3	2,602.2
End products (inedible)	62,811.4	70,783.0
General purpose machinery	2,600.7	2,952.4
Special industrial machinery	4,003.6	4,973.0
Agricultural machinery and tractors	1,769.3	1,738.6
Passenger automobiles and chassis	7,890.0	11,292.2
Trucks, truck tractors and chassis	2,035.9	2,624.2
Motor vehicle parts (excl. engines)	12,747.8	14,475.2
Televisions, radios and phonographs	834.0	830.3
Other telecommunication and related equipment	2,140.0	2,149.9
Miscellaneous electrical lighting distribution equipment	381.8	414.6
Miscellaneous measuring and laboratory equipment	761.6	828.5
Furniture and fixtures	382.4	433.7
Hand tools and cutlery	424.3	433.4
Electronic computers	4,149.3	3,937.8
Miscellaneous office machines and equipment	259.7	256.3
Miscellaneous equipment and tools	1,245.0	1,373.0
Special transactions, trade	1,533.5	1,630.8
Total	**95,460.0**	**104,914.2**

Exports	1984	1985
Live animals	519.0	466.8
Food, feed, beverages and tobacco	10,313.7	9,168.0
Meat, fresh, chilled or frozen	723.2	787.4
Fish, fresh or frozen	515.0	560.0
Fish, fresh or frozen, whole	314.7	380.8
Barley	636.1	319.2
Wheat	4,724.7	3,778.6
Vegetables	311.5	324.4
Whisky	363.1	352.0
Crude materials (inedible)	17,410.6	19,180.0
Rapeseed	648.5	543.6
Iron ores and concentrates	1,112.1	1,172.9
Copper ores, concentrates and scrap	499.6	518.3
Nickel ores, concentrates and scrap	580.8	560.8
Crude petroleum	4,404.2	5,916.5
Natural gas	3,923.0	3,912.3
Coal and other bituminous substances	1,846.6	2,010.3
Asbestos (unmanufactured)	498.9	446.4
Fabricated materials (inedible)	36,026.8	36,780.5
Lumber, softwood	4,182.1	4,523.6
Pulp	3,906.5	3,393.8
Newsprint	4,783.5	5,407.4
Organic chemicals	1,295.2	1,356.6
Fertilizers	1,557.1	1,294.6
Petroleum and coal products	3,196.6	3,344.0
Aluminium and alloys	1,900.7	1,906.9
Copper and alloys	799.1	661.0
Nickel and alloys	563.2	594.0
Precious metals and alloys	2,273.8	1,971.3
Electricity	1,377.8	1,408.1
End products (inedible)	44,770.8	49,952.5
Industrial machinery	2,844.9	3,058.4
Agricultural machinery and tractors	655.2	522.1
Passenger automobiles and chassis	13,771.8	16,045.7
Trucks, truck tractors and chassis	5,386.9	5,811.7
Motor vehicle engines and parts	2,119.0	2,017.3
Motor vehicle parts (excl. engines)	7,637.1	8,907.8
Office machines and equipment	1,377.4	1,363.6
Special transactions, trade	395.6	363.8
Total	**109,436.6**	**115,911.6**

CANADA   *Statistical Survey*

PRINCIPAL TRADING PARTNERS (C $ million)

Imports	1983	1984	1985
Algeria	150.1	307.0	321.9
Australia	358.4	382.1	385.6
Belgium/Luxembnourg	296.2	446.7	530.1
Brazil	500.0	668.7	808.2
China, People's Republic	245.8	333.5	403.5
Cuba	56.3	62.7	43.7
Denmark	136.9	200.8	229.7
Finland	75.8	148.2	200.1
France	841.0	1,220.3	1,373.2
Germany, Federal Republic	1,574.8	2,174.8	2,176.3
Hong Kong	820.5	966.2	886.8
India	101.1	147.1	168.2
Indonesia	40.0	71.9	81.8
Ireland	107.3	186.9	217.6
Italy	798.5	1,116.2	1,331.0
Japan	4,412.9	5,711.5	6,113.4
Korea, Republic	791.4	1,152.3	1,607.0
Malaysia	115.6	168.0	146.1
Mexico	1,089.4	1,437.8	1,330.7
Netherlands	349.8	545.3	622.6
New Zealand	156.6	122.4	160.0
Norway	313.6	133.9	187.9
Puerto Rico	146.7	177.2	199.2
Singapore	168.5	214.6	210.5
South Africa	194.1	221.8	227.7
Spain	181.9	316.4	366.5
Sweden	415.8	581.6	682.3
Switzerland	408.0	378.7	488.7
Taiwan	925.5	1,223.8	1,286.1
USSR	33.3	28.7	27.7
United Kingdom	1,809.8	2,305.1	3,281.7
USA	53,989.0	68,165.8	74,377.0
Venezuela	1,004.5	1,207.2	1,092.1
Total (incl. others)	75,520.0	95,460.0	104,914.2

Exports	1983	1984	1985
Algeria	448.5	452.3	330.8
Australia	438.0	616.2	624.6
Belgium/Luxembourg	700.1	683.0	703.2
Brazil	596.2	776.4	663.9
China, People's Republic	1,606.7	1,236.5	1,259.3
Cuba	360.6	337.6	328.5
Denmark	66.6	94.4	82.1
Finland	87.0	119.2	131.6
France	626.0	704.6	714.3
Germany, Federal Republic	1,149.9	1,190.9	1,188.6
Hong Kong	221.2	218.8	322.8
India	261.7	470.6	488.7
Indonesia	209.6	290.5	257.6
Ireland	89.2	95.7	81.6
Italy	549.3	580.5	525.3
Japan	4,721.7	5,640.8	5,745.3
Korea, Republic	555.4	720.0	775.6
Malaysia	114.0	179.7	204.4
Mexico	369.9	349.9	391.4
Netherlands	957.1	1,064.2	928.8
New Zealand	122.4	189.4	186.7
Norway	230.5	338.8	347.6
Puerto Rico	121.7	167.7	210.8
Singapore	126.7	143.0	106.4
South Africa	165.8	201.9	150.9
Spain	137.1	97.3	107.7
Sweden	146.6	165.6	179.0
Switzerland	197.8	189.4	290.1
Taiwan	341.0	423.2	429.6
USSR	1,760.8	2,119.0	1,607.9
United Kingdom	2,445.4	2,439.2	2,313.1
USA	64,206.3	82,667.9	90,344.5
Venezuela	231.0	247.9	307.1
Total (incl. others)	88,154.6	109,436.6	115,911.6

Transport

RAILWAYS* (millions)

	1983	1984	1985
Passenger-km, revenue	2,073	2,092	2,228
Ton-km, revenue freight	219,874	244,670	231,977

* Seven major rail carriers only.

ROAD TRAFFIC ('000 vehicle registrations)

	1983	1984	1985*
Passenger cars (incl. taxis and for car hire)	10,732	10,781	11,118
Truck and truck tractors (commercial and non-commercial)	3,308	3,047	3,095
Buses (school and other)	57	52	54
Motorcycles	466	470	453
Other (ambulances, fire trucks, etc.)	57	20	64

* Preliminary.

INTERNATIONAL SEA-BORNE SHIPPING

	1983	1984	1985
Goods ('000 metric tons)			
Loaded	129,490	145,322	143,421
Unloaded	48,915	60,073	60,669
Vessels (number)			
Arrived	26,100	22,515	26,555
Departed	24,439	22,636	26,438

CIVIL AVIATION (Canadian Carriers—Revenue Traffic, '000)

	1982	1983	1984
Passengers	24,447	19,658	23,561
Km flown	379,433	360,027	383,158
Passenger-km	32,527,863	31,709,869	34,641,763
Goods ton-km*	918,860	975,862	1,120,786

* Includes freight, express, mail and excess baggage.

INLAND WATER TRAFFIC
(St Lawrence Seaway, '000 metric tons)

	1982	1983	1984
Montreal—Lake Ontario	42,815	45,061	47,505
Welland Canal	49,024	50,145	53,917

Source: St Lawrence Seaway Authority.

Tourism

	1982	1983	1984
Travellers from the United States:			
Number ('000)	32,432	32,480	32,978
Expenditure (C $ million)	2,402	2,664	3,064
Travellers from other countries:			
Number ('000)	1,975	1,776	1,887
Expenditure (C $ million)	1,322	1,177	1,274

Communications Media

('000)

	1982	1983	1984
Total households	8,254	8,460	8,857
Homes with radio	8,152	8,355	8,756
Homes with television	8,101	8,286	8,681
Homes with telephone	8,084	8,267	8,727

Daily newspapers in French and English only (1984): 111; total circulation 4,551,000.

Education

(1984/85)*

	Institutions	Teachers†	Pupils†
Primary and secondary	15,624	268,515	4,956,280
Post secondary non-university	197	24,560	329,800
Universities and colleges‡	66	35,210	471,370

* Estimates.
† Full-time only.
‡ Degree-granting institutions, full-time teachers and full-time students.

Directory

The Constitution

Constitutional development has been based mainly upon five important acts of the British Parliament: the Quebec Act of 1774, the Constitutional Act of 1791, the Act of Union of 1840, the British North America Act of 1867, and the Canada Act of 1982. The British North America Act 1867 provided that the Constitution of the Dominion should be 'similar in principle to that of the United Kingdom'; that the executive authority be vested in the Sovereign, and carried on in her name by a Governor-General and Privy Council; and that legislative power be exercised by a Parliament of two Houses, the Senate and the House of Commons. The enactment of the Canada Act of 1982 was the final act of the United Kingdom Parliament in Canadian constitutional development. The Act gave to Canada the power to amend the Constitution according to procedures determined by the Constitution Act 1982, which was proclaimed in force by the Queen on 17 April 1982. The Constitution Act 1982 added to the Canadian Constitution a Charter of Rights and Freedoms, and provisions which recognize the nation's multicultural heritage, affirm the existing rights of native peoples, confirm the principle of equalization of benefits among the provinces and strengthen provincial ownership of natural resources.

THE GOVERNMENT

The national government works itself out through three main agencies. There is Parliament (consisting of the Sovereign as represented by the Governor-General, the Senate and the House of Commons) which makes the laws; the Executive (the Cabinet or Ministry) which applies the laws; and the Judiciary which interprets the laws.

Particular features similar to the British system of government are the close relation which exists between the Executive and Legislative branches, and the doctrine of cabinet responsibility which has become crystallized in the course of time. The Prime Minister is appointed by the Governor-General and is habitually the leader of the political party commanding the confidence of the House of Commons. He chooses the members of his Cabinet from members of his party in Parliament, principally from those in the House of Commons. Each Minister or member of the Cabinet is usually responsible for the administration of a department, although there may be Ministers without portfolio whose experience and counsel are drawn upon to strengthen the Cabinet, but who are not at the head of departments. Each Minister of a department is responsible to Parliament for that department, and the Cabinet as a whole is responsible before Parliament for government policy and administration generally.

Meetings of the Cabinet are presided over by the Prime Minister. From the Cabinet signed orders and recommendations go to the Governor-General for his approval, and the Crown acts only on the advice of its responsible Ministers. The Cabinet takes the responsibility for its advice being in accordance with the support of Parliament and is held strictly accountable.

THE FEDERAL PARLIAMENT

Parliament must meet at least once a year, so that twelve months do not elapse between the last meeting in one session and the first meeting in the next. The duration of Parliament may not be longer than five years from the date of election of a House of Commons. Senators (a maximum of 104 in number) are appointed until age 75 by the Governor-General in Council. They must be at least 30 years of age, residents of the province they represent and in possession of C $4,000 of real property over and above their liabilities. Members of the House of Commons are elected by universal adult suffrage for the duration of a Parliament.

Under the Constitution, the Federal Parliament has exclusive legislative authority in all matters relating to public debt and property; regulation of trade and commerce; raising of money by any mode of taxation; borrowing of money on the public credit; postal service, census and statistics; militia, military and naval service and defence; fixing and providing for salaries and allowances of the officers of the government; beacons, buoys and lighthouses; navigation and shipping; quarantine and the establishment and maintenance of marine hospitals; sea-coast and inland fisheries; ferries on an international or interprovincial frontier; currency and coinage; banking, incorporation of banks, and issue of paper money; savings banks; weights and measures; bills of exchange and promissory notes; interest; legal tender; bankruptcy and insolvency;

patents of invention and discovery; copyrights; Indians and lands reserved for Indians; naturalization and aliens; marriage and divorce; the criminal law, except the constitution of courts of criminal jurisdiction but including the procedure in criminal matters; the establishment, maintenance and management of penitentiaries; such classes of subjects as are expressly excepted in the enumeration of the classes of subjects exclusively assigned to the Legislatures of the provinces by the Act. Judicial interpretation and later amendment have, in certain cases, modified or clearly defined the respective powers of the Federal and Provincial Governments.

Both the Parliament of Canada and the legislatures of the provinces may legislate with respect to agriculture and immigration, but provincial legislation shall have effect in and for the provinces as long and as far only as it is not repugnant to any Act of Parliament. Both Parliament and the provincial legislatures may legislate with respect to old age pensions and supplementary benefits, but no federal law shall affect the operation of any present or future law of a province in relation to these matters.

PROVINCIAL AND MUNICIPAL GOVERNMENT

In each of the ten provinces the Sovereign is represented by a Lieutenant-Governor, appointed by the Governor-General in Council, and acting on the advice of the Ministry or Executive Council, which is responsible to the Legislature and resigns office when it ceases to enjoy the confidence of that body. The Legislatures are unicameral, consisting of an elected Legislative Assembly and the Lieutenant-Governor. The duration of a Legislature may not exceed five years from the date of the election of its members.

The Legislature in each province may exclusively make laws in relation to: amendment of the constitution of the province, except as regards the Lieutenant-Governor; direct taxation within the province; borrowing of money on the credit of the province; establishment and tenure of provincial offices and appointment and payment of provincial officers; the management and sale of public lands belonging to the province and of the timber and wood thereon; the establishment, maintenance and management of public and reformatory prisons in and for the province; the establishment, maintenance and management of hospitals, asylums, charities and charitable institutions in and for the province other than marine hospitals; municipal institutions in the province; shop, saloon, tavern, auctioneer and other licences issued for the raising of provincial or municipal revenue; local works and undertakings other than interprovincial or international lines of ships, railways, canals, telegraphs, etc., or works which, though wholly situtated within the province are declared by the Federal Parliament to be for the general advantage either of Canada or two or more provinces; the incorporation of companies with provincial objects; the solemnization of marriage in the province; property and civil rights in the province; the administration of justice in the province, including the constitution, maintenance and organization of provincial courts both in civil and criminal jurisdiction, and including procedure in civil matters in these courts; the imposition of punishment by fine, penalty or imprisonment for enforcing any law of the province relating to any of the aforesaid subjects; generally all matters of a merely local or private nature in the province. Further, provincial Legislatures may exclusively make laws in relation to education, subject to the protection of religious minorities; and to non-renewable natural resources, forestry resources and electrical energy, including their export from one province to another, and to the right to impose any mode or system of taxation thereon, subject in both cases to such laws not being discriminatory.

Under the Constitution Act, the municipalities are the creations of the provincial governments. Their bases of organization and the extent of their authority vary in different provinces, but almost everywhere they have very considerable powers of local self-government.

The Government

Head of State: HM Queen ELIZABETH II.
Governor-General: JEANNE SAUVÉ (took office 14 May 1984).

FEDERAL MINISTRY
(January 1987)

Prime Minister: (MARTIN) BRIAN MULRONEY.
Minister of Veterans' Affairs: GEORGE HARRIS HEES.
Leader of the Government in the Senate and Minister of State (Federal-Provincial Relations): LOWELL MURRAY.
Secretary of State for External Affairs: CHARLES JOSEPH CLARK.
Deputy Prime Minister, President of the Queen's Privy Council for Canada and Government House Leader: DONALD FRANK MAZANKOWSKI.
Minister of Justice and Attorney-General: RAYMON JOHN HNATYSHYN.
Minister of Communications: FLORA ISABEL MACDONALD.
Minister of Transport: JOHN CARNELL CROSBIE.
Minister of State: ROCH LA SALLE.
Minister of National Revenue: ELMER MACINTOSH MACKAY.
Minister of National Health and Welfare: JAKE EPP.
Minister of Agriculture: JOHN WISE.
Secretary of State and Minister responsible for Multiculturalism: DAVID EDWARD CROMBIE.
President of The Treasury Board: ROBERT R. DE COTRET.
Minister of National Defence: HENRY PERRIN BEATTY.
Minister of Finance: MICHAEL HOLCOMBE WILSON.
Minister of Consumer and Corporate Affairs: HARVIE ANDRE.
Minister of State (Fitness and Amateur Sport): OTTO JOHN JELINEK.
Minister of Fisheries and Oceans: THOMAS EDWARD SIDDON.
Minister of State (Canadian Wheat Board): CHARLES JAMES MAYER.
Minister of Indian Affairs and Northern Development: WILLIAM HUNTER MCKNIGHT.
Minister of the Environment: THOMAS MICHAEL MCMILLAN.
Minister of International Trade: PATRICIA CARNEY.
Minister of State (Transport): ANDRÉ BISSONNETTE.
Minister of Employment and Immigration: BENOÎT BOUCHARD.
Minister of Regional Industrial Expansion with responsibility for Canada Post: MICHEL CÔTÉ.
Solicitor-General: JAMES FRANCIS KELLEHER.
Minister of Energy, Mines and Resources: MARCEL MASSE.
Minister of State (Privatization) and Minister responsible for the Status of Women: BARBARA JEAN MCDOUGALL.
Minister of State (Forestry and Mines): GERALD S. MERRITHEW.
Minister of Supply and Services: MONIQUE VÉZINA.
Minister of Public Works with responsibility for Central Mortgage and Housing Corporation (CMHC): STEWART MCINNES.
Minister of State for Science and Technology: FRANK OBERLE.
Associate Minister of National Defence: PAUL WYATT DICK.
Minister of Labour: PIERRE CADIEUX.
Minister of State (Youth): JEAN CHAREST.
Minister of State (Finance): THOMAS HOCKIN.
Minister for External Relations: MONIQUE LANDRY.
Minister of State (Small Businesses and Tourism): BERNARD VALCOURT.
Minister of State (Immigration): GERRY WEINER.

MINISTRIES

Office of the Prime Minister: Ottawa K1A OA2; tel. (613) 992-4211; telex 053-3208.
Department of Agriculture: Sir John Carling Bldg, 930 Carling Ave, Ottawa K1A OC5; tel. (613) 995-5222; telex 053-3283.
Department of Communications: Journal North Tower, 300 Slater St, Ottawa K1A OC8; tel. (613) 995-8185; telex 053-4409.
Department of Consumer and Corporate Affairs: Ottawa K1A OC9; tel. (613) 997-2938; telex 053-3694.
Department of Employment and Immigration: Ottawa K1A OJ9; tel. (613) 992-4883; telex 053-3511.
Department of Energy, Mines and Resources: 580 Booth St, Ottawa K1A OE4; tel. (613) 995-3065; telex 053-3117.

CANADA

Environment Canada: Terrasses de la Chaudière, Ottawa K1A OH3; tel. (819) 997-2800; telex 053-3608.
Department of External Affairs: Lester B. Pearson Bldg, 125 Sussex Drive, Ottawa K1A OG2; tel. (613) 995-1851; telex 053-3745.
Department of Finance: Place Bell Canada, 160 Elgin St, Ottawa K1A OG5; tel. (613) 992-1573; telex 053-3336.
Department of Fisheries and Oceans: 200 Kent St, Ottawa K1A OE6; tel. (613) 992-3474; telex 053-4228.
Department of Indian and Northern Affairs: Terrasses de la Chaudière, 10 Wellington St, Ottawa K1A OH4; tel. (613) 995-5586; telex 053-3711.
Department of Justice: Justice Bldg, Kent and Wellington Sts, Ottawa K1A OH8; tel. (613) 995-2569; telex 053-3603.
Department of Labour: Labour Canada, Ottawa K1A OJ2; tel. (613) 997-2617; telex 053-3640.
Department of National Defence: 101 Colonel By Drive, Ottawa K1A OK2; tel. (613) 996-4450; telex 053-4218.
Department of National Health and Welfare: Brooke Claxton Bldg, Tunney's Pasture, Ottawa K1A OK9; tel. (613) 996-5461; telex 053-3270.
Department of Public Works: Sir Charles Tupper Bldg, Confederation Heights, Riverside Drive, Ottawa K1A OM2; tel. (613) 998-7724; telex 053-4235.
Department of Regional Industrial Expansion: 235 Queen St, Ottawa K1A OH5; tel. (613) 995-9001; telex 053-4124.
Revenue Canada (Customs and Excise): Connaught Bldg, Mackenzie Ave, Ottawa K1A OL5; tel. (613) 995-0007; telex 053-3330.
Revenue Canada (Taxation): Headquarters Bldg, 875 Heron Rd, Ottawa K1A OL8; tel. (613) 995-2960; telex 053-4974.
Department of Science and Technology: C. D. Howe Bldg, 235 Queen St, Ottawa K1A 1A1; tel. (613) 996-0326; telex 053-4396.
Secretary of State of Canada: Ottawa K1A OM5; tel. (613) 997-0055.
Solicitor-General: Sir Wilfrid Laurier Bldg, 340 Laurier Ave West, Ottawa K1A OP8; tel. (613) 996-0220; telex 053-3768.
Department of Supply and Services: Canadian Government Publishing Centre, Ottawa K1A OS9; tel. (613) 996-5861; telex 053-3580.
Department of Transport: Place de Ville, Transport Canada Bldg, 330 Sparks St, Ottawa K1A ON5; tel. (613) 996-7501; telex 053-3580.
Treasury Board: Ottawa K1A OR5; tel. (613) 996-2690; telex 053-3336.
Department of Veterans' Affairs: East Memorial Bldg, Lyon and Wellington Sts, Ottawa K1A OP4; tel. (902) 995-7774; telex 053-3377.

Federal Legislature

THE SENATE

Speaker: GUY CHARBONNEAU.

Seats at November 1986

Liberal	72
Progressive Conservative	26
Independent	3
Independent Liberal	1
Vacant	2
Total	104
Ontario	24
Quebec	24
New Brunswick	10
Nova Scotia	10
Alberta	6
British Columbia	6
Manitoba	6
Newfoundland	6
Saskatchewan	6
Prince Edward Is.	4
Northwest Territories	1
Yukon Territory	1
Total	104

HOUSE OF COMMONS

Speaker: JOHN A. FRASER.

General Election, 4 September 1984

	Seats at election	Seats at Oct. 1986
Progressive Conservative	211	209
Liberal	40	40
New Democratic Party	30	29
Independent	1	2
Vacant	—	2
Total	282	282

Provincial Legislatures

ALBERTA

Lieutenant-Governor: HELEN HUNLEY.
Premier: DON GETTY.

Election, May 1986

	Seats at election	Seats at Oct. 1986
Progressive Conservative	61	61
New Democratic Party	16	16
Liberal	4	4
Independent	2	2
Total	83	83

BRITISH COLUMBIA

Lieutenant-Governor: ROBERT G. ROGERS.
Premier: WILLIAM VANDER ZALM.

Election, October 1986

	Seats at election
Social Credit	47
New Democratic Party	22
Total	69

MANITOBA

Lieutenant-Governor: Dr GEORGE JOHNSON.
Premier: HOWARD R. PAWLEY.

Election, March 1986

	Seats at election	Seats at Oct. 1986
New Democratic Party	30	30
Progressive Conservative	26	26
Independent	1	1
Total	57	57

NEW BRUNSWICK

Lieutenant-Governor: GEORGE STANLEY.
Premier: RICHARD B. HATFIELD.

Election, October 1982

	Seats at election	Seats at Oct. 1986
Progressive Conservative	39	37
Liberal	18	20
New Democratic Party	1	1
Total	58	58

CANADA

NEWFOUNDLAND AND LABRADOR
Lieutenant-Governor: JAMES MCGRATH.
Premier: A. BRIAN PECKFORD.

Election, April 1985

	Seats at election	Seats at Oct. 1986
Progressive Conservative	36	36
Liberal	15	15
New Democratic Party	1	1
Total	52	52

NOVA SCOTIA
Lieutenant-Governor: ALAN R. ABRAHAM.
Premier: JOHN M. BUCHANAN.

Election, November 1984

	Seats at election	Seats at Oct. 1986
Progressive Conservative	42	41
Liberal	6	6
New Democratic Party	3	3
Cape Breton Labour Party	1	1
Vacant	—	1
Total	52	52

ONTARIO
Lieutenant-Governor: LINCOLN M. ALEXANDER.
Premier: DAVID R. PETERSON.

Election, May 1985

	Seats at election	Seats at Oct. 1986
Progressive Conservative	52	51
Liberal*	48	49
New Democratic Party	25	25
Total	125	125

* Formed a minority government following the May 1985 election.

PRINCE EDWARD ISLAND
Lieutenant-Governor: LLOYD G. MACPHAIL.
Premier: JOSEPH A. GHIZ.

Election, April 1986

	Seats at election	Seats at Oct. 1986
Liberal	21	21
Progressive Conservative	11	10
Vacant	—	1
Total	32	32

QUÉBEC
Lieutenant-Governor: GILLES DE LAMONTAGNE.
Premier: ROBERT BOURASSA.

Election, December 1985

	Seats at election	Seats at Oct. 1986
Liberal	99	99
Parti Québécois	23	23
Total	122	122

SASKATCHEWAN
Lieutenant-Governor: FREDERICK W. JOHNSON.
Premier: GRANT DEVINE.

Election, October 1986

	Seats at election
Progressive Conservative	38
New Democratic Party	25
Liberal	1
Total	64

Territorial Legislatures

NORTHWEST TERRITORIES
Commissioner: JOHN HAVELOCK PARKER.
Leader of the Legislative Assembly: RICHARD NERYSOO.
The Legislative Assembly, elected in November 1983, consists of 24 independent members without formal party affiliation.

YUKON TERRITORY
Commissioner: DOUGLAS LESLIE DEWEY BELL.
Leader of the Territorial Council: TONY PENIKETT.

Election, May 1985

	Seats at election	Seats at Oct. 1986
New Democratic Party	8	8
Progressive Conservative	6	6
Liberal	2	2
Total	16	16

Political Organizations

British Columbia Social Credit Party: 10691 Shellbridge Way, Suite 110, Richmond, BC V6X 2W8; tel. (604) 270-4040; conservative; governing party of British Columbia 1952–72 and since 1975; Leader WILLIAM VANDER ZALM.

Communist Party of Canada: 24 Cecil St, Toronto, Ont M5T 1N2; f. 1921; Gen. Sec. W. KASHTAN.

Green Party of Canada: 24 Ryerson Ave, Suite 302, Toronto, Ont M5T 2P3; f. 1983; environmentalist; Nat. Spokesman TREVOR G. HANCOCK.

Liberal Party of Canada: 102 Bank St, Ottawa K1P 5N4; tel. (613) 237-0740; supports Canadian autonomy, comprehensive social security, freer trade within the North Atlantic Community; Leader JOHN NAPIER TURNER; Pres. IONA CAMPAGNOLO; Nat. Dir DANIELLE DANSEREAU.

Libertarian Party of Canada: POB 190, Adelaide St Postal Station, Toronto, Ont M5C 2J1; tel. (416) 489-6057; f. 1973; Pres. DENNIS CORRIGAN; Leader VICTOR LEVIS.

New Democratic Party: 301 Metcalfe St, Ottawa K2P 1R9; tel. (613) 236-3613; f. 1961; social democratic; mem. of the Socialist International; Leader J. EDWARD BROADBENT; Pres. MARION DEWAR; Sec. DENNIS YOUNG; 120,000 individual mems, 265,000 affiliated mems.

Parti Indépendantiste: 3830 Parc Lafontaine, Montreal, Qué; tel. (514) 523-5628; f. 1984 by breakaway faction of Parti Québécois; seeks full independence for Québec; Pres. PIERRE DE BELLEFEUILLE; Leader GILLES RHEAUME.

Parti Québécois: 7370 rue St-Hubert, Montreal, Qué H2R 2N3; tel. (514) 270-5400; f. 1968; social democratic; seeks political sovereignty for Québec in an economic association with Canada; governing party of Québec from 1976–85; Pres. PIERRE-MARC JOHNSON; Chair. Nat. Exec. NADIA ASSIMOPOULOS; 160,000 mems.

Progressive Conservative Party: 161 Laurier Ave West, Suite 200, Ottawa K1P 5J2; tel. (613) 238-6111; f. 1854; advocates individualism and free enterprise and continued Canadian participation in NATO; Leader (MARTIN) BRIAN MULRONEY; Pres. BILL JARVIS; Nat. Dir JEAN-CAROL PELLETIER.

Rassemblement Démocratique pour l'Indépendance: f. 1985 by breakaway faction of Parti Québécois; seeks full independence for Québec; Leader Dr CAMILLE LAURIN.

Western Canada Concept: 10830-107th Ave, Suite 4, Edmonton, Alta T5H 0X3; tel. (403) 425-6378.

Diplomatic Representation

EMBASSIES AND HIGH COMMISSIONS IN CANADA

Algeria: 435 Daly St, Ottawa K1N 6H3; tel. (613) 232-9453; telex 053-3625; Ambassador: ABDELOUAHAD ABADA.

Antigua and Barbuda, Dominica, Saint Christopher and Nevis, Saint Lucia and Saint Vincent and the Grenadines: 112 Kent St, Suite 1701, Place de Ville, Tower B, Ottawa K1P 5P2; tel. (613) 236-8952; High Commissioner: Dr ASYLL M. WARNER.

Argentina: 90 Sparks St, Suite 620, Ottawa K1P 5B4; tel. (613) 236-2351; telex 053-4293; Ambassador: FRANCISCO JOSÉ PULIT.

Australia: 130 Slater St, 13th Floor, Ottawa K1P 5H6; tel. (613) 236-0841; telex 053-3391; High Commissioner: ROBERT STEPHEN LAURIE.

Austria: 445 Wilbrod St, Ottawa K1N 6M7; tel. (613) 563-1444; telex 053-3290; Ambassador: Dr HEDWIG WOLFRAM.

Bahamas: 150 Kent St, Suite 301, Ottawa K1P 5P4; tel. (613) 232-4724; telex 053-3793; High Commissioner: Dr PATRICIA E. J. ROGERS (acting).

Bangladesh: 85 Range Rd, Suite 402, Ottawa K1N 8J6; tel. (613) 236-0138; telex 053-4283; High Commissioner: Maj.-Gen. K. M. SAFIULLAH.

Barbados: 151 Slater St, Suite 700, Ottawa K1P 5H3; tel. (613) 236-9517; telex 053-3375; High Commissioner: PETER G. MORGAN.

Belgium: 85 Range Rd, Suites 601–604, Ottawa K1N 8J6; tel. (613) 236-7267; telex 053-3568; Ambassador: ROGER P. DENORME.

Benin: 58 Glebe Ave, Ottawa K1S 2C3; tel. (613) 237-7366; telex 053-3630; Ambassador: JOSEPH LOUIS HOUNTON.

Bolivia: 77 Metcalfe St, Suite 608, Ottawa K1P 5L6; tel. (613) 236-8237; Chargé d'affaires: MARÍIA RENÉE A. DE APARICIO.

Brazil: 255 Albert St, Suite 900, Ottawa K1P 6A9; tel. (613) 237-1090; telex 053-4222; Ambassador: RONALDO COSTA.

Bulgaria: 325 Stewart St, Ottawa KIN 6KS; tel. (613) 232-3215; telex 053-4386; Ambassador: VLADIMIR VELCHEV.

Burkina Faso: 48 Range Rd, Ottawa K1N 8J4; tel. (613) 238-4796; telex 053-4413; Chargé d'affaires a.i.: NORAOGO VINCENT OUÉDRAOGO.

Burundi: 151 Slater St, Suite 800, Ottawa K1P 5H3; tel. (613) 236-8483; Chargé d'affaires a.i.: DIDACE SUNZU.

Cameroon: 170 Clemow Ave, Ottawa K1S 2B4; tel. (613) 236-1522; telex 053-3736; Ambassador: PHILEMON YANG YUNJI.

Chile: 56 Sparks St, Suite 801, Ottawa K1P 5A9; tel. (613) 235-4402; telex 053-3774; Ambassador: ALBERTO BESA ALLAN.

China, People's Republic: 511–515 Patrick St, Ottawa K1N 5H3; tel. (613) 234-2706; telex 053-3770; Ambassador: ZHANG WENPU.

Colombia: 150 Kent St, Suite 404, Ottawa K1P 5P4; tel. (613) 230-3760; telex 053-3786; Ambassador: Dr JAIME PINZÓN LÓPEZ.

Costa Rica: 150 Argyle St, Suite 114, Ottawa K2P 1B7; tel. (613) 234-5762; telex 053-4398; Ambassador: MARIO PACHECO.

Cuba: 388 Main St, Ottawa K1S 1E3; tel. (613) 563-0141; telex 053-3135; Ambassador: RAFAEL HERNÁNDEZ MARTÍNEZ.

Czechoslovakia: 50 Rideau Terrace, Ottawa K1M 2A1; tel. (613) 749-4442; telex 053-4224; Ambassador: JÁN JANOVIČ.

Denmark: 85 Range Rd, Suite 702, Ottawa K1N 8J6; tel. (613) 234-0704; telex 053-3114; Ambassador: PER FERGO.

Dominican Republic: 260 Metcalfe St, Suite 5D, Ottawa K2P 1R6; tel. (613) 234-0363; Chargé d'affaires: ARTURO CALVENTI.

Ecuador: 150 Kent St, Suite 407, Ottawa K1P 5P4; tel. (613) 238-5032; telex 053-4846; Ambassador: Dr JUAN CARLOS FAIDUTTI ESTRADA.

Egypt: 454 Laurier Ave, Ottawa K1N 6R3; tel. (613) 234-4931; telex 053-3340; Ambassador: MAHMOUD KASSEM.

El Salvador: Copeland Bldg, 294 Albert St, Suite 302, Ottawa K1P 6E6; tel. (613) 238-2939; Chargé d'affaires a.i.: CÉSAR PENA VELASCO.

Finland: 222 Somerset St West, Suite 401, Ottawa K2P 2G3; tel. (613) 236-2389; telex 053-4462; Ambassador: JAAKKO BLOMBERG.

France: 42 Sussex Drive, Ottawa K1M 2C9; tel. (613) 232-1795; Ambassador: JEAN-PIERRE CABOUAT.

Gabon: 4 Range Rd, POB 368, Ottawa K1N 8J5; tel. (613) 232-5301; telex 053-4295; Ambassador: SIMON OMBEGUE.

Germany, Federal Republic: 1 Waverley St, Ottawa K2P 0T8; tel. (613) 232-1101; telex 053-4226; Ambassador: WOLFGANG BEHRENDS.

Ghana: 85 Range Rd, Suite 810, Ottawa K1N 8J6; tel. (613) 236-0871; telex 053-4276; High Commissioner: DANIEL O. AGYEKUM.

Greece: 76–80 MacLaren St, Ottawa K2P 0K6; tel. (613) 238-6271; telex 053-3140; Ambassador: EMMANUEL MEGALOKONOMOS.

Guatemala: 294 Albert St, Suite 500, Ottawa K1P 6E6; tel. (613) 237-3941; telex 053-3065; Ambassador: FEDERICO URRUELA-PRADO.

Guinea: 112 Kent St, Suite 208, Place de Ville, Tower B, Ottawa K1P 5P2; tel. (613) 232-1133; telex 053-4361; Ambassador: ABDOULAYE SYLLA.

Guyana: Burnside Bldg, 151 Slater St, Suite 309, Ottawa K1P 5H3; tel. (613) 235-7249; telex 053-3684; Chargé d'affaires: F. A. LAWRENCE.

Haiti: 112 Kent St, Suite 1308, Place de Ville, Tower B, Ottawa K1P 5P2; tel. (613) 238-1628; telex 053-3688; Ambassador: LAFONTAINE SAINT-LOUIS.

Holy See: Apostolic Nunciature, 724 Manor Ave, Rockcliffe Park, Ottawa K1M 0E3; tel. (613) 746-4914; telex 053-3056; Pro-Nuncio: Most Rev. ANGELO PALMAS.

Honduras: 151 Slater St, Suite 300A, Ottawa K1P 5H3; tel. (613) 233-8900; telex 053-4528; Ambassador: ALEJANDRO FLORES MENDOZA.

Hungary: 7 Delaware Ave, Ottawa K2P 0Z2; tel. (613) 232-1711; telex 053-3251; Ambassador: LAJOS NAGY.

India: 10 Springfield Rd, Ottawa K1M 1C9; tel. (613) 744-3751; telex 053-4172; High Commissioner: SUBIR JIT SINGH CHHATWAL.

Indonesia: 287 MacLaren St, Ottawa K2P 0L9; tel. (613) 236-7403; telex 053-3119; Ambassador: Dr HASJIM DJALAL.

Iran: 411 Roosevelt Ave, 4th Floor, Ottawa K2A 7X9; tel. (613) 729-0902; telex 053-4229; Chargé d'affaires a.i.: SEYED ABBAS KHADEM HAGHIGHAT.

Iraq: 215 McLeod St, Ottawa K2P 0Z8; tel. (613) 236-9177; telex 053-4310; Ambassador: ABDO ALI HAMDAN AL-DAIRI.

Ireland: 170 Metcalfe St, Ottawa K2P 1P3; tel. (613) 233-6281; telex 053-4240; Ambassador: SEAN GAYNOR.

Israel: 410 Laurier Ave West, Suite 601, Ottawa K1R 7T3; tel. (613) 237-6450; telex 053-4858; Ambassador: ELIASHIV BEN-HORIN.

Italy: 275 Slater St, 11th Floor, Ottawa K1P 5H9; tel. (613) 232-2401; telex 053-3278; Ambassador: VALERIO BRIGANTE COLONNA ANGELINI.

Ivory Coast: 9 Marlborough Ave, Ottawa K1N 8C6; tel. (613) 236-9919; Ambassador: Gen. EDMOND ISSOUF KONE.

Jamaica: 275 Slater St, Suite 402, Ottawa K1P 5H9; tel. (613) 233-9311; telex 053-3287; High Commissioner: LESLIE ARMON WILSON.

Japan: 255 Sussex Drive, Ottawa K1N 9E6; tel. (613) 236-8541; telex 053-4220; Ambassador: YOSHIO OKAWA.

Jordan: 100 Bronson Ave, Suite 701, Ottawa K1R 6G8; tel. (613) 238-8090; telex 053-4538; Ambassador: HANI KHALIFEH.

Kenya: 415 Laurier Ave East, Suite 600, K1N 6R4; tel. (613) 563-1773; High Commissioner: SOSPETER ONUKO MAGETO.

Korea, Republic: 85 Albert St, 10th Floor, Ottawa K1P 6A4; tel. (613) 232-1715; Ambassador: ROH JAE-WON.

Lebanon: 640 Lyon St South, Ottawa K1S 3Z5; tel. (613) 236-5825; telex 053-3571; Ambassador: MAKRAM ABDEL HALIM OUAIDAT.

Lesotho: 350 Sparks St, Suite 910, Ottawa K1R 7S8; tel. (613) 236-9449; telex 053-4563; High Commissioner: TSELISO THAMAE.

Malawi: 112 Kent St, Suite 905, Place de Ville, Tower B, Ottawa K1P 5P2; tel. (613) 236-8931; telex 053-3363; High Commissioner: BERNARD B. MTAWALI.

Malaysia: 60 Boteler St, Ottawa K1N 8Y7; tel. (613) 237-5182; telex 053-3064; High Commissioner: Tan Sri Datuk THOMAS JAYASURIA.

Mali: 50 Goulburn Ave, Ottawa K1N 8C8; tel. (613) 232-1501; telex 053-3361; Ambassador: SADIBOU KONÉ.

Mexico: 130 Albert St, Suite 206, Ottawa K1P 5G4; tel. (613) 233-8988; Ambassador: JOSÉ ANDRÉS DE OTEYZA.

Morocco: 38 Range Rd, Ottawa K1N 8J4; tel. (613) 236-7391; telex 053-3683; Ambassador: AHMED HAMMOUD.

Netherlands: 275 Slater St, 3rd Floor, Ottawa K1P 5H9; tel. (613) 237-5030; telex 053-3109; Ambassador: J. F. E. BREMAN.

New Zealand: Metropolitan House, 99 Bank St, Suite 801, Ottawa K1P 6G3; tel. (613) 238-5991; telex 053-4282; High Commissioner: JOHN WYBROW.

Nicaragua: 170 Laurier Ave West, Suite 908, Ottawa, K1P 5V5; tel. (613) 234-9361; telex 053-4338; Ambassador: CASIMIRO ALFONSO SOTELO.

Niger: 38 Blackburn Ave, Ottawa K1N 8A3; tel. (613) 232-4291; telex 053-3757; Ambassador: LAMBERT MESSAN.

Nigeria: 295 Metcalfe St, Ottawa K2P 1R9; tel. (613) 236-0521; telex 053-3285; High Commissioner: A. I. ATTA.

Norway: Royal Bank Centre, 90 Sparks St, Suite 932, Ottawa K1P 5B4; tel. (613) 238-6571; telex 053-4239; Ambassador: PER MARTIN ØLBERG.

Pakistan: 151 Slater St, Suite 608, Ottawa K1P 5H3; tel. (613) 238-7881; telex 053-4428; Chargé d'affaires a.i.: ANWAR KEMAL.

Peru: 170 Laurier Ave West, Suite 1007, Ottawa K1P 5V5; tel. (613) 238-1777; telex 053-3754; Ambassador: Dr OSCAR HAURTUA.

Philippines: 130 Albert St, Suite 606, Ottawa K1P 5G4; tel. (613) 233-1121; telex 053-4537; Chargé d'affaires a.i.: ELOY R. BELLO, III.

Poland: 443 Daly Ave, Ottawa K1N 6H3; tel. (613) 236-0468; telex 053-3133; Ambassador: ANDRZEJ KACALA.

Portugal: 645 Island Park Drive, Ottawa K1Y 0B8; tel. (613) 729-0883; telex 053-3756; Ambassador: LUIZ HENRIQUE CUTILEIRO NAVEGA.

Romania: 655 Rideau St, Ottawa K1N 6A3; tel. (613) 232-5345; telex 053-3101; Ambassador: EMILIAN RODEAN.

Rwanda: 121 Sherwood Drive, Ottawa K1Y 3V1; tel. (613) 722-5835; telex 053-4522; Ambassador: JOSEPH NSENGIYUMVA.

Saudi Arabia: 99 Bank St, Suite 901, Ottawa K1P 6B9; tel. (613) 237-4100; telex 053-4285; Ambassador: ZIAD SHAWWAF.

Senegal: 57 Marlborough Ave, Ottawa K1N 8E8; tel. (613) 238-6392; telex 053-4531; Ambassador: SALIOU DIODJ FAYE.

Somalia: 130 Slater St, Suite 1000, Ottawa K1P 5P2; tel. (613) 563-4541; telex 053-4739; Ambassador: MOHAMED SHEIKH HASSAN.

South Africa: 15 Sussex Drive, Ottawa K1M 1M8; tel. (613) 744-0330; telex 053-4185; Ambassador: GLENN R. W. BABB.

Spain: 350 Sparks St, Suite 802, Ottawa K1R 7S8; tel. (613) 237-2193; telex 053-4510; Ambassador: (vacant).

Sri Lanka: 85 Range Rd, Suites 102–104, Ottawa K1N 8J6; tel. (613) 233-8449; telex 053-3668; High Commissioner: Brig.-Gen. TISSA WEERATUNGA.

Sweden: 441 MacLaren St, 4th Floor, Ottawa K2P 2H3; tel. (613) 236-8553; telex 053-3331; Ambassador: OLA ULLSTEN.

Switzerland: 5 Marlborough Ave, Ottawa K1N 8E6; tel. (613) 235-1837; telex 053-3648; Ambassador: ERIK LANG.

Tanzania: 50 Range Rd, Ottawa K1N 8J4; tel. (613) 232-1509; telex 053-3569; High Commissioner: FERDINAND RUHINDA.

Thailand: 85 Range Rd, Suite 704, Ottawa K1N 8J6; tel. (613) 237-1517; telex 053-3975; Ambassador: MANASPAS XUTO.

Togo: 12 Range Rd, Ottawa K1N 8J3; tel. (613) 238-5916; telex 053-4564; telex 053-4564; Ambassador: KOSSIVI OSSEYI.

Trinidad and Tobago: 75 Albert St, Suite 508, Ottawa K1P 5E7; tel. (613) 232-2418; telex 053-4343; High Commissioner: B. L. B. PITT.

Tunisia: 515 O'Connor St, Ottawa K1S 3P8; tel. (613) 237-0330; telex 053-4161; Ambassador: ANOUAR BERRALES.

Turkey: 197 Wurtemburg St, Ottawa K1N 8L9; tel. (613) 232-1577; telex 053-4716; Ambassador: (vacant).

Uganda: 170 Laurier Ave West, Suite 601, Ottawa K1P 5V5; tel. (613) 233-7797; telex 053-4469; High Commissioner: Mrs ANNA APOKO AMAILUK.

USSR: 285 Charlotte St, Ottawa K1N 8L5; tel. (613) 235-4341; telex 053-3332; Ambassador: ALEKSEI RODIONOV.

United Kingdom: 80 Elgin St, Ottawa K1P 5K7; tel. (613) 237-1530; telex 053-3318; High Commissioner: Sir DEREK MALCOLM DAY.

USA: 100 Wellington St, Ottawa K1P 5T1; tel. (613) 238-5335; telex 053-3582; Ambassador: THOMAS M. T. NILES

Venezuela: 294 Albert St, Suite 602, Ottawa K1P 6E6; tel. (613) 235-5151; telex 053-4729; Ambassador: JOSÉ MACHIN.

Yugoslavia: 17 Blackburn Ave, Ottawa K1N 8A2; tel. (613) 233-6289; telex 053-4203; Ambassador: VLADIMIR PAVICEVIĆ.

Zaire: 18 Range Rd, Ottawa K1N 8J3; tel. (613) 236-7103; telex 053-4314; Ambassador: IKOLO BOLELAMA W'OKONDOLA.

Zambia: 130 Albert St, Suite 1610, Ottawa K1P 5G4; tel. (613) 563-0712; telex 053-4418; High Commissioner: Lt-Gen. BENJAMIN N. MIBENGE.

Zimbabwe: 112 Kent St, Suite 1315, Ottawa K1P 5P2; tel. (613) 237-4388; telex 053-4221; High Commissioner: STANISLAUS G. CHIGWEDERE.

Judicial System

FEDERAL COURTS

The Supreme Court of Canada: Supreme Court of Canada Bldg, Wellington St, Ottawa K1A 0J1; tel. (613) 995-4330; ultimate court of appeal in both civil and criminal cases throughout Canada. The judgment of the Court is final and conclusive. The Supreme Court is also required to advise on questions referred to it by the Governor in Council. Important questions concerning the interpretation of the Constitution Act, the constitutionality or interpretation of any federal or provincial law, the powers of Parliament or of the provincial legislatures or of both levels of government, among other matters, may be referred by the government to the Supreme Court for consideration.

In civil cases, appeals may be brought from any final judgment of the highest court of last resort in a province. The Supreme Court will grant permission to appeal if it is of the opinion that a question of public importance is involved, one that transcends the immediate concerns of the parties to the litigation. In criminal cases, the Court will hear appeals as of right concerning indictable offences where an acquittal has been set aside or where there has been a dissenting judgment on a point of law in a provincial court of appeal. The Supreme Court may, in addition, hear appeals on questions of law concerning both summary conviction and all other indictable offences if permission to appeal is first granted by the Court.

Chief Justice of Canada: R. G. BRIAN DICKSON.

Puisne Judges: JEAN BEETZ, WILLARD Z. ESTEY, W. R. MCINTYRE, JULIEN CHOUINARD, ANTONIO LAMER, BERTHA WILSON, GERALD LE DAIN, GÉRARD LA FOREST.

The Federal Court of Canada: Supreme Court of Canada Bldg, Wellington St, Ottawa K1A 0H9; tel. (613) 992-4238; the Trial Division of the Federal Court has jurisdiction in claims against the Crown, claims by the Crown, miscellaneous cases involving the Crown, claims against or concerning crown officers and servants, relief against Federal Boards, Commissions, and other tribunals, interprovincial and federal-provincial disputes, industrial or industrial property matters, admiralty, income tax and estate tax appeals, citizenship appeals, aeronautics-interprovincial works and undertakings, residuary jurisdiction for relief if there is no other Canadian court that has such jurisdiction, jurisdiction in specific matters conferred by federal statutes.

The Federal Court of Appeal: Supreme Court of Canada Bldg, Wellington St, Ottawa K1A 0H9; tel. (613) 996-6795; has jurisdiction on appeals from the Trial Division, appeals from Federal Tribunals, review of decisions of Federal Boards and Commissions, appeals from Tribunals and Reviews under Section 28 of the Federal Court Act, and references by Federal Boards and Commissions. The Court has one central registry and consists of the principal office in Ottawa and local offices in principal centres throughout Canada.

Chief Justice: ARTHUR L. THURLOW.

Associate Chief Justice: JAMES A. JEROME.

Court of Appeal Judges: LOUIS PRATTE, DARREL V. HEALD, JOHN J. URIE, PATRICK M. MAHONEY, LOUIS MARCEAU, JAMES K. HUGESSEN, ARTHUR J. STONE, MARK R. MACGUIGAN, BERTRAND LACOMBE.

Trial Division Judges: FRANK U. COLLIER, GEORGE A. ADDY, J. E. DUBÉ, PAUL U. C. ROULEAU, FRANCIS C. MULDOON, BARRY L. STRAYER, JOHN C. MCNAIR, BARBARA J. REED, PIERRE DENAULT, YVON PINARD, L. MARCEL JOYAL, BUD CULLEN, LEONARD A. MARTIN, MAX M. TEITELBAUM.

PROVINCIAL COURTS

Alberta

Court of Appeal

Chief Justice of Alberta: J. H. LAYCRAFT.

Court of Queen's Bench

Chief Justice: W. K. MOORE.

Associate Chief Justice: T. H. MILLER.

CANADA

British Columbia
Court of Appeal
Chief Justice of British Columbia: N. T. NEMETZ.

Supreme Court
Chief Justice: A. MCEACHERN.

Manitoba
Court of Appeal
Chief Justice of Manitoba: A. M. MONNIN.

Court of Queen's Bench
Chief Justice: B. HEWAK.
Associate Chief Justices: R. J. SCOTT, A. C. HAMILTON.

New Brunswick
Court of Appeal
Chief Justice of New Brunswick: S. G. STRATTON.

Court of Queen's Bench
Chief Justice: G. A. RICHARD.

Newfoundland
Supreme Court—Court of Appeal
Chief Justice: (vacant).

Trial Division
Chief Justice: T. A. HICKMAN.

Nova Scotia
Supreme Court—Appeal Division
Chief Justice of Nova Scotia: L. O. CLARKE.

Trial Division
Chief Justice: C. R. GLUBE.

Ontario
Supreme Court—Court of Appeal
Chief Justice of Ontario: W. G. C. HOWLAND.
Associate Chief Justice of Ontario: B. J. MACKINNON.

High Court of Justice
Chief Justice: W. D. PARKER.
Associate Chief Justice: F. W. CALLAGHAN.

Prince Edward Island
Supreme Court
Chief Justice: N. H. CARRUTHERS.

Québec
Court of Appeal
Chief Justice of Québec: J. A. MARCEL CRÊTE.

Superior Court
Chief Justice: ALAN GOLD.
Senior Associate Chief Justice: PIERRE CÔTÉ.
Associate Chief Justice: L. A. POITRAS.

Saskatchewan
Court of Appeal
Chief Justice of Saskatchewan: E. D. BAYDA.

Court of Queen's Bench
Chief Justice: MARY BATTEN.

Northwest Territories
Supreme Court
Judge of the Supreme Court: M. M. DE WEERDT.

Court of Appeal
Chief Justice: J. H. LAYCRAFT (Alberta).

Yukon Territory
Supreme Court
Judge of the Supreme Court: H. C. B. MADDISON.

Court of Appeal
Chief Justice: N. T. NEMETZ (British Columbia).

Religion

CHRISTIANITY

About 75% of the population belong to the three main Christian churches: Roman Catholic, United and Anglican. Numerous other religious denominations are represented.

The Anglican Communion

Membership of the Anglican Church of Canada totalled 912,518 in 1982.

General Synod of the Anglican Church of Canada: Church House, 600 Jarvis St, Toronto, Ont M4Y 2J6; tel. (416) 924-9192; telex 065-24128; Gen. Sec. Archdeacon H. ST C. HILCHEY.

Primate of the Anglican Church of Canada: MICHAEL GEOFFREY PEERS.

Archbishop of British Columbia: DOUGLAS WALTER HAMBIDGE, Bishop of New Westminster.

Archbishop of Canada: HAROLD LEE NUTTER, Bishop of Fredericton.

Archbishop of Ontario: JOHN CHARLES BOTHWELL, Bishop of Niagara.

Archbishop of Rupert's Land: (vacant).

The Orthodox Churches

Greek Orthodox Church: 27 Teddington Park Ave, Toronto, Ont M4N 2C4; tel. (416) 481-2223; 316,610 mems (1971 census); Bishop of Toronto His Grace SOTIRIOS.

Ukrainian Greek Orthodox Church: 9 St John's Ave, Winnipeg, Man R2W 1G8; tel. (204) 586-3093; f. 1918; 280 parishes; 150,000 mems; Metropolitan of Winnipeg and of all Canada Most Rev. WASYLY (FEDAK).

The Romanian, Syrian and Byelorussian Churches are also represented in Canada.

The Roman Catholic Church

Membership of the Roman Catholic Church totalled 10,999,964 in 1985.

Canadian Conference of Catholic Bishops: 90 Parent Ave, Ottawa K1N 7B1; tel. (613) 236-9461; telex 053-3311; Pres. Mgr BERNARD HUBERT, Bishop of Saint-Jean–Longueuil, Qué; Vice-Pres. Most Rev. JAMES HAYES, Archbishop of Halifax.

Latin Rite

Archbishop of Edmonton: JOSEPH N. MACNEIL.
Archbishop of Grouard-McLennan: HENRI LÉGARÉ.
Archbishop of Halifax: JAMES M. HAYES.
Archbishop of Keewatin-Le Pas: PAUL DUMOUCHEL.
Archbishop of Kingston: FRANCIS SPENCE.
Archbishop of Moncton: DONAT CHIASSON.
Archbishop of Montreal: PAUL GRÉGOIRE.
Archbishop of Ottawa: JOSEPH-AURÈLE PLOURDE.
Archbishop of Québec: Cardinal LOUIS-ALBERT VACHON.
Archbishop of Regina: CHARLES A. HAPLIN.
Archbishop of Rimouski: GILLES OUELLET.
Archbishop of St Boniface: MAURICE ANTOINE HACAULT.
Archbishop of St John's, Newfoundland: ALPHONSUS L. PENNY.
Archbishop of Sherbrooke: JEAN MARIE FORTIER.
Archbishop of Toronto: Cardinal G. EMMETT CARTER.
Archbishop of Vancouver: JAMES FRANCIS CARNEY.
Archbishop of Winnipeg: ADAM EXNER.

Ukrainian Rite

Ukrainian Catholic Church in Canada: 235 Scotia St. Winnipeg, Man R2V 1V7; tel. (204) 334-6368; 190,500 mems (1981 census); Archbishop-Metropolitan of Winnipeg Most Rev. MAXIM HERMANIUK.

The United Church of Canada

The United Church of Canada was founded in 1925 with the union of Methodist, Congregational and Presbyterian churches in Canada. Other free churches have since joined. In 1985 there were 2,416 pastoral charges, 3,900 ministers and 891,384 mems.

Moderator: Rt Rev. ROBERT F. SMITH.

Secretary: Rev. PHILIP A CLINE, The United Church House, 85 St Clair Ave East, Toronto, Ont M4T 1M8; tel. (416) 925-5931; telex 065-28224.

CANADA

Other Christian Churches

Canadian Baptist Federation: 219 St George St, Toronto, Ont M5R 2M2; tel. (416) 922-4775; 1,200 churches; 131,472 mems (1983); Pres. SHIRLEY BENTALL; Gen. Sec. Dr RICHARD C. COFFIN.

Christian Church (Disciples of Christ): 39 Arkell Rd, RR2, Guelph, Ont N1H 6H8; 30 churches, 2,467 mems; Exec. Minister Rev. W. RAY MILES.

Christian Reformed Church in North America: 3475 Mainway, POB 5070, Burlington, Ont L7R 3Y8; tel. (416) 336-2920; f. 1857.

Church of Jesus Christ of Latter-day Saints (Mormon): 910 70th Ave SW, Calgary, Alta; tel. (403) 252-1141; missions and institutes in nine major cities; 74,900 mems; Pres R. H. WALKER.

Lutheran Council in Canada: 25 Old York Mills Rd, Willowdale, Toronto, Ont M2P 1B5; f. 1967; tel. (416) 488-9430; 1,123 ministers; 1,003 congregations; 302,142 mems (1985); Exec. Dir LAWRENCE R. LIKNESS.

Mennonite Central Committee Canada: 134 Plaza Drive, Winnipeg, Man R3T 5K9; tel. (204) 261-6381; telex 075-5757; f. 1963; 95,000 mems in 560 congregations; Exec. Dir DANIEL ZEHR.

Pentecostal Assemblies of Canada: 10 Overlea Blvd, Toronto, Ont M4H 1A5; tel. (416) 425-1010; 185,257 mems; Gen. Supt Rev. J. M. MACKNIGHT; Gen. Sec. Rev. CHARLES YATES.

Presbyterian Church in Canada: 50 Wynford Drive, Don Mills, Ont M3C 1J7; tel. (416) 441-1111; f. 1875; 1,069 ministers, 1,053 congregations; 163,170 mems (1985); Moderator Dr J. C. HAY; Prin. Clerk Dr E. F. ROBERTS.

Religious Society of Friends: 60 Lowther Ave, Toronto, Ont M5R 1C7; tel. (416) 922-2632; Clerk of Canadian Yearly Meeting DONALD LAITIN.

Seventh-day Adventists: 1148 King St East, Oshawa, Ont L1H 1H8; tel. (416) 433-0011; org. 1901; Pres. J. W. WILSON; Sec. G. E. MAXSON.

BAHÁ'Í FAITH

Bahá'í Community in Canada: 7200 Leslie St, Thornhill, Ont L3T 6L8; tel. (416) 889-8168; f. 1902; 21,000 mems; Sec. Dr H. B. DANESH.

BUDDHISM

Buddhist Churches of Canada: 918 Bathurst St, Toronto, Ont M5R 3G5; tel. (416) 534-4302; Jodo Shinshu of Mahayana Buddhism; Bishop Rev. TOSHIO MURAKAMI.

JUDAISM

The Jews of Canada number 305,000.

Canadian Jewish Congress: 1590 ave Dr Penfield, Montreal, Qué H3G 1C5; tel. (514) 931-7531; f. 1919; Exec. Vice-Pres. ALAN ROSE.

Jewish Community Council: 151 Chapel St, Ottawa K1N 7Y2; tel. (613) 232-7306; Pres. GERALD BERGER; Exec. Dir Mrs GITTEL TATZ.

The Press

The vastness of the country hampers distribution and the establishment of a strong national press, so the daily press in Canada is essentially local in coverage, influence and distribution. Through the use of satellite transmission, a national edition of the Toronto *Globe and Mail,* established in 1981, is now available coast to coast.

The number of independently-owned daily newspapers remains limited in a country where chain ownership is predominant: over 47% of daily newspaper circulation is represented by two major groups: Thomson Newspapers Ltd (20% of daily newspaper circulation) and Southam Inc (27.3%). In 1986 the Peladeu Group accounted for 8.6% of the total circulation, while the Sun Publishing Group had 8.3%, and the Sterling Group had 1.0%. There are several smaller groups, but the number of independently-owned dailies remains limited, representing 18% of total daily newspaper circulation.

In September 1980 the Liberal government appointed a royal commission to investigate the effects of concentration of ownership in the newspaper industry. In August 1981 the commission reported that the existing concentration constituted a threat to press freedom, and recommended that some groups should be compelled to sell some of their newspaper interests in areas where there was extreme ownership concentration. While government action on the report has still to be finalized, it is expected that the Progressive Conservative government will continue to restrict cross-media ownership of newspapers, radio and television, and to prohibit non-media companies from owning daily newspapers.

In late 1986 there were 112 daily newspapers with a combined circulation of over 5.6m., representing 62% of the country's households.

In 1986 about 1,100 weekly and twice-weekly community newspapers reached an estimated 5.2m. people, mainly in the more remote areas of the country. A significant feature of the Canadian press is the number of newspapers catering for ethnic groups: there are over 80 of these daily and weekly publications appearing in over 20 languages.

There are numerous periodicals for business, trade, professional, recreational and special interest readership, although periodical publishing, particularly, suffers from substantial competition from publications originating in the USA. Among periodicals, the only one which can claim to be national in its readership and coverage is *Maclean's Canada's Weekly Newsmagazine.*

The following are among the principal newspaper publishing groups:

Southam Inc: 150 Bloor St West, Suite 900, Toronto, Ont M5S 2Y8; tel. (416) 927-1877; telex 062-3486; Pres. JOHN P. FISHER.

Sterling Newspapers Ltd: POB 10079, Pacific Centre, Vancouver, BC V7Y 1B6; tel. (604) 682-7755; Pres. F. DAVID RADLER; Vice-Pres. and Gen. Man. A. E. WEEKS.

Thomson Newspapers Ltd: 65 Queen St West, Toronto, Ont M5H 2M8; tel. (416) 864-1710; Chair. and Pres. KENNETH R. THOMSON.

Unimédia Inc: 5701 rue Christophe-Colomb, Montreal, Qué H2S 2E9; tel. (514) 274-2501; Pres. JACQUES G. FRANCOEUR.

DAILY NEWSPAPERS

(D = all day; E = evening; M = morning; S = Sunday; Publr = Publisher)

Alberta

Calgary Herald: 215 16th St SE, POB 2400, Station M, Calgary T2P 0W8; tel. (403) 235-7100; telex 038-22793; f. 1883; Publr J. PATRICK O'CALLAGAN; Man. Editor KEVIN PETERSON; circ. 141,000 (M).

Calgary Sun: 2615 12th St NE, Calgary T2E 7W9; tel. (403) 250-4200; telex 038-22734; f. 1980; Publr JIM TIGHE; Editor-in-Chief ROBERT POOLE; circ. 71,000 (M), 86,000 (S).

Edmonton Journal: 10006 101st St, Edmonton T5J 2S6; tel. (403) 429-5100; telex 037-3492; f. 1903; Publr WILLIAM NEWBIGGING; Editor STEPHEN HUME; circ. 178,000 (D).

Edmonton Sun: 9405 50th St, Edmonton T6B 2T4; tel. (403) 468-5111; telex 037-42665; f. 1978; Publr PATRICK A. HARDEN; Editor-in-Chief DAVID BAILEY; circ. 79,000 (M), 101,000 (S).

Lethbridge Herald: POB 670, Lethbridge T1J 3Z7; tel. (403) 328-4411; telex 038-49220; f. 1907; Publr and Gen. Man. DONALD R. DORAM; Man. Editor JOHN A. FARRINGTON; circ. 28,000 (E).

Medicine Hat News: POB 10, Medicine Hat T1A 7E6; tel. (403) 527-1101; telex 038-48191; f. 1910; Publr ANDREW SNADDON; Editor PETER MOSSEY; circ. 14,000 (E).

Red Deer Advocate: POB 5200, Red Deer T4N 5G3; tel. (403) 343-2400; f. 1901; Publr PAUL WILLCOCKS; Editor JOE MCLAUGHLIN; circ. 23,000 (E).

British Columbia

Daily Courier: POB 40, Kelowna V1Y 7N4; tel. (604) 762-4445; f. 1904; Publr D. F. DOUCETTE; Man. Editor DAVE HENSHAW; circ. 15,000 (E).

Daily News: POB 580, Prince Rupert V8J 3R9; tel. (604) 624-6781; Publr IRIS CHRISTISON; circ. 4,000 (E).

Kamloops News: 63 West Victoria St, Kamloops V2C 1A3; tel. (604) 372-2331; f. 1982; Publr ROLF TIMMERMANNS; Editor MEL ROTHENBURGER; circ. 22,000 (E).

Nanaimo Free Press: 223 Commercial St, POB 69, Nanaimo V9R 5K5; tel. (604) 753-3451; f. 1874; Publr S. R. BUTLER; Man. Editor FRANK PHILLIPS; circ. 9,000 (E).

Nelson Daily News: 266 Baker St, Nelson V1L 4H3; tel. (604) 352-3552; f. 1902; Publr STEEN O. JORGENSEN; Man. Editor RYON GUEDES; circ. 7,000 (M).

Penticton Herald: 186 Nanaimo Ave West, Penticton V2A 1N4; tel. (604) 492-4002; Publr JOHN J. KOBYLNIK; circ. 8,000 (E).

Prince George Citizen: POB 5700, Prince George V2L 5K9; tel. (604) 562-2441; f. 1957; Publr BRYSON W. STONE; Editor ROY K. NAGEL; circ. 24,000 (E).

CANADA

The Province: 2250 Granville St, Vancover V6H 3G2; tel. (604) 732-2222; telex 045-5695; f. 1898; Publr G. Haslam; Editor Robert D. McMurray; circ. 170,000 (m), 220,000 (s).

The Sun: 2250 Granville St, Vancover V6H 3G2; tel. (604) 732-2111; telex 045-5695; f. 1886; Publr G. Haslam; Editor Bruce Larsen; circ. 237,000 (e).

Times-Colonist: POB 300, Victoria V8W 2N4; tel. (604) 382-7211; telex 049-7288; f. 1858; Publr Colin McCullough; Man. Editor Gordon R. Bell; circ. 75,000 (d), 52,000 (s).

Manitoba

Brandon Sun: POB 460, Brandon R7A 5Z6; tel. (204) 727-2451; f. 1882; Publr and Editor Lewis D. Whitehead; Man. Editor Paul Drohan; circ. 18,000 (e).

Daily Graphic: POB 130, Portage La Prarie R1N 3B4; tel. (204) 857-3427; Publr Ian A. MacKenzie; circ. 5,000 (e).

Flin Flon Reminder: 38 Main St, POB 727, Flin Flon R8A 1N5; tel. (204) 857-3427; f. 1946; Publr and Editor T. W. Dobson; circ. 4,000 (e).

Winnipeg Free Press: 300 Carlton St, Winnipeg R3C 3C1; tel. (204) 943-9331; f. 1874; Publr Donald Nicol; Man. Editor Murray Burt; circ. 179,000 (e).

Winnipeg Sun: 1700 Church Ave, Winnipeg R2X 2W9; tel. (204) 957-0710; f. 1980; Publr Al Davies; circ. 42,000 (m).

New Brunswick

L'Acadie Nouvelle: 217 blvd St-Pierre O., Caraquet E0B 1KO; tel. (506) 727-4444; f. 1984; Gen. Man. Donat Léger.

Daily Gleaner: POB 3370, Fredericton E3B 5A2; tel. (506) 452-6671; f. 1880; Publr Tom Crowther; Editor-in-Chief Hal P. Wood; circ. 28,000 (e).

Telegraph-Journal and **Evening Times-Globe:** POB 2350, Saint John E2L 3V8; tel. (506) 632-8888; Pres. and Publr Ralph Costello; Editor-in-Chief Fred Hazel; circ. 34,000 (m), 33,000 (e).

The Times-Transcript: POB 1001, Moncton E1C 1G8; tel. (506) 853-9321; Pres. and Publr James D. Nichol; Man. Editor Mike Bembridge; circ. 45,000 (e).

Newfoundland

Evening Telegram: POB 5970, St John's A1C 5X7; tel. (709) 364-6300; f. 1879; Publr S. R. Herder; Editor Sean Finlay; circ. 38,000 (e), 54,000 (Saturday).

Western Star: POB 460, West St, Corner Brook A2H 6E7; tel. (709) 634-4348; f. 1900; Publr H. John Adderley; Editor-in-Chief C. Halloway; circ. 11,000 (e).

Nova Scotia

Amherst Daily News: POB 280, Amherst B4H 3Z2; tel. (902) 667-5102; Publr Earl J. Gouchie; circ. 4,000 (m).

Cape Breton Post: 255 George St, Sydney B1P 6K6; tel. (902) 564-5451; f. 1900; Publr James P. Milne; Exec. Editor Ian MacNeil; circ. 31,000 (e).

Chronicle-Herald and **Mail-Star:** 1650 Argyle St, POB 610, Halifax B3J 2T2; tel. (902) 426-3061; telex 019-21874; Pres. Fred G. Mounce; Man. Editor Ken Foran; circ. 80,000 (m), 59,000 (e).

Evening News: 352 East River Rd, New Glasgow B2H 5E2; tel. (902) 752-3000; f. 1910; Publr and Gen. Man. Ken Sims; Man. Editor Doug MacNeill; circ. 11,000 (e).

Truro Daily News: POB 220, Truro B2N 5C3; tel. (902) 893-9405; f. 1891; Publr Terrence W. Honey; Man. Editor Robert Paxton; circ. 9,000 (e).

Ontario

Barrie Examiner: 16 Bayfield St, Barrie L4M 4T6; tel. (416) 726-6537; f. 1864; Publr Bruce Rowland; Man. Editor Jim Haskett; circ. 13,000 (e).

Beacon Herald: POB 430, Stratford N5A 6T6; tel. (519) 271-2220; f. 1887; Co-Publr Charles W. Dingman; Co-Publr and Editor Stanford H. Dingman; circ. 13,000 (e).

Cambridge Daily Reporter: 26 Ainslie St South, Cambridge N1R 3K1; tel. (519) 621-3810; f. 1846; Publr. A. E. Wood; Man. Editor John B. Wells; circ. 13,000 (e).

Chatham Daily News: 45 Fourth St, POB 2007, Chatham N7M 2G4; tel. (519) 354-2000; f. 1862; Publr R. B. Renaud; Man. Editor Steve Zak; circ. 16,000 (e).

Citizen: POB 5020, Ottawa K2C 3M4; tel. (613) 829-9100; telex 053-4779; f. 1843; Publr Paddy Sherman; Editor Keith Spicer; circ. 189,000 (d), 241,000 (Saturday).

Directory

Cobourg Daily Star: POB 400, Cobourg K9A 4L1; tel. (416) 372-0131; Publr Bill Poirier; Man. Editor Judy Herod; circ. 5,000.

Daily Mercury: 8–14 Macdonnell St, Guelph N1H 6P7; tel. (519) 822-4310; f. 1854; Publr. J. Peter Kohl; Editor-in-Chief Gary Manning; circ. 18,000 (e).

Daily Packet and Times: 31 Colborne St East, Orillia L3V 1T4; tel. (416) 325-1355; f. 1953; Gen. Man. J. C. Marshall; Man. Editor S. Gower; circ. 10,000 (e).

Daily Press: 125 Cedar St South, Timmins P4N 2G9; tel. (705) 264-2215; f. 1933; Publr M. H. Switzer; Editor Gregory Reynolds; circ. 14,000 (e).

Daily Sentinel-Review: POB 1000, Woodstock N4S 8A5; tel. (519) 537-2341; f. 1886; Publr Paul J. Taylor; Man. Editor Bob Spence; circ. 9,000 (e).

Daily Times: 33 Queen St West, Brampton L6Y 1M1; tel. (416) 451-2020; f. 1885; Publr Victor Mlodecki; Man. Editor John L. McLeod; circ. 6,000 (e).

Le Droit: 375 Rideau St, Ottawa K1N 5Y7; tel. (613) 560-2500; f. 1913; French; Publr Jean-Robert Bélanger; Editor-in-Chief Pierre Tremblay; circ. 44,000 (e).

Evening Guide: POB 296, Port Hope L1A 3W4; tel. (416) 885-2471; Gen. Man. Ron E. David; circ. 3,000 (e).

Expositor: POB 965, Brantford N3T 5S8; tel. (519) 756-2020; f. 1852; Publr J. Howard Gaul; Editor K. J. Strachan; circ. 32,000 (e).

The Globe and Mail: 444 Front St West, Toronto M5V 2S9; tel. (416) 585-5000; telex 062-19721; f. 1844; Publr A. Roy Megarry; Editor-in-Chief Norman Webster; Man. Editor Geoffrey Stevens; circ. 320,000 (m).

Hamilton Spectator: POB 300, Hamilton L8N 3G3; tel. (416) 526-3333; telex 061-8390; f. 1846; Publr Gordon Bullock; Editor Alex M. Beer; circ. 147,000 (e).

Intelligencer: POB 5600, 45 Bridge St East, Belleville K8N 5C7; tel. (613) 962-9171; f. 1870; Publr and Gen. Man. H. Myles Morton; Man. Editor Lee Ballantyne; circ. 17,000 (e).

Kitchener-Waterloo Record: 225 Fairway Rd, Kitchener N2G 4E5; tel. (519) 894-2231; f. 1878; Publr K. A. Baird; Man. Editor William Dunfield; circ. 75,000 (e).

Lindsay Daily Post: 15 William St North, Lindsay K9V 3Z8; tel. (705) 324-2114; Pres. and Gen. Man. Thomas F. McConomy; circ. 5,000 (e).

London Free Press: POB 2280, London N6A 4G1; tel. (519) 679-1111; telex 064-5837; f. 1849; Pres. C. R. Turnbull; Editor-in-Chief William I. Morley; circ. 128,000 (m).

Niagara Falls Review: POB 270, Niagara Falls L2E 6T6; tel. (416) 358-5711; f. 1879; Publr Gordon A. Murray; Man. Editor Donald W. Mullan; circ. 20,000 (e).

Northern Daily News: 8 Duncan Ave, Kirkland Lake P2N 3L4; tel. (705) 567-5321; f. 1922; Publr William Mackie; Editor Joe Hornyak; circ. 6,000 (e).

The Nugget: POB 570, North Bay P1B 8J6; tel. (705) 472-3200; f. 1909; Publr Clifford C. Sharp; Editor Colin P. Vezina; circ. 23,000 (e).

Observer: 186 Alexander St, Pembroke K8A 4L9; tel. (613) 732-3691; f. 1855; Publr and Man. Editor W. H. Higginson; circ. 7,000 (e).

Peterborough Examiner: POB 389, Peterborough K9J 6Z4; tel. (705) 745-4641; f. 1884; Publr and Gen. Man. Bruce L. Rudd; Man. Editor Gerald F. Toner; circ. 24,000 (e).

Recorder and Times: 23 King St West, Brockville K6V 5T8; tel. (613) 342-4441; f. 1821; Co-Publrs H. S. Grant, Mrs Perry S. Beverley; circ. 14,000 (e).

St Thomas Times-Journal: 16 Hincks St, St Thomas N5P 3W6; tel. (519) 631-2790; f. 1882; Publr and Gen. Man. L. J. Beavis; Man. Editor E. Mooney; circ. 10,000 (e).

Sarnia Observer: 140 Front St South, Sarnia N7T 7M5; tel. (519) 344-3641; f. 1917; Publr and Gen. Man. T. J. Hogan; Man. Editor Jim Carnaghan; circ. 24,000 (e).

Sault Star: POB 460, Sault Ste Marie P6A 5M5; tel. (705) 253-1111; f. 1912; Publr W. R. Dane; Editor Doug Millroy; circ. 26,000 (e).

Simcoe Reformer: POB 370, Simcoe N3Y 4L2; tel. (519) 426-5710; f. 1858; Pres. John Cowlard; Man. Editor Wayne Campbell; circ. 10,000 (e).

Standard: 17 Queen St, St Catharine's L2R 5G5; tel. (416) 684-7251; f. 1891; Pres. and Publr H. B. Burgoyne; Man. Editor Murray G. Thomson; circ. 42,000 (e).

CANADA

Standard-Freeholder: 44 Pitt St, Cornwall K6J 3P3; tel. (613) 933-3160; Publr DON TOMCHICK; Man. Editor COLIN BRUCE; circ. 17,000 (E).

Sudbury Daily Star: 33 Mackenzie St, Sudbury P3C 4Y1; tel. (705) 674-5271; f. 1909; Publr DON R. HERRON; Man. Editor BRIAN GANNON; circ. 29,000 (E).

Sun Times: POB 200, Owen Sound N4K 5P2; tel. (519) 376-2250; f. 1853; Publr JOHN G. DOHERTY; Editor ROBERT HULL; circ. 21,000 (E).

The Times: 44 Richmond St West, Oshawa L1G 1C8; tel. (416) 723-3474; f. 1871; Publr A. S. TOPP; Man. Editor D. JAMES PALMATEER; circ. 22,000 (E).

Times-News and **Chronicle-Journal:** 75 Cumberland St South, Thunder Bay P7B 1A3; tel. (807) 344-3535; Publr F. M. DUNDAS; Man. Editor MICHAEL GRIEVE; circ. 9,000 (M), 28,000 (E).

Toronto Star: One Yonge St, Toronto M5E 1E6; tel. (416) 367-2000; telex 065-24387; f. 1892; Publr BELAND H. HONDERICH; Man. Editor RAY TIMSON; circ. 498,000 (D), 489,000 (S).

Toronto Sun: 333 King St East, Toronto M5A 3X5; tel. (416) 947-2222; telex 062-17688; f. 1971; Publr PAUL V. GODFREY; Editor JOHN DOWNING; Man. Editor PETER BREWSTER; circ. 284,000 (M), 450,000 (S).

Welland-Port Colborne Evening Tribune: 228 East Main St, Welland L3B 3W9; tel. (416) 732-2411; f. 1863; Publr JOHN W. VANKOOTEN; Editor JAMES R. MIDDLETON; circ. 16,000 (E).

Whig-Standard: 306 King St, Kingston K7L 4Z7; tel. (613) 544-5000; f. 1834; Publr MICHAEL L. DAVIES; Editor N. REYNOLDS; circ. 36,000 (E).

Windsor Star: 167 Ferry St, Windsor N9A 4M5; tel. (519) 255-5711; telex 064-77709; f. 1918; Publr J. S. THOMSON; Editor CARL MORGAN; circ. 87,000 (E).

Prince Edward Island

Charlottetown Guardian and Patriot: POB 760, Charlottetown C1A 4R7; tel. (902) 894-8506; f. 1887; Publr STEWART VICKERSON; Man. Editor WALTER MACINTYRE; circ. 23,000 (D).

Summerside Journal-Pioneer: POB 2480, Summerside C1N 4K5; tel. (902) 436-2121; f. 1957; Publr RALPH HECKBERT; Editor RON ENGLAND; circ. 11,000 (E).

Québec
F.—Published in French.

Le Devoir: 211 rue St-Sacrement, Montreal H2Y 1X1; tel. (514) 844-3361; f. 1910; F.; Dir BENOÎT LAUZIÈRE; Editor-in-Chief PAUL-ANDRÉ COMEAU; circ. 37,000 (M).

The Gazette: 250 ouest, St-Antoine, Montreal H2Y 3R7; tel. (514) 282-2222; telex 055-61767; f. 1778; Publr CLARK DAVEY; Man. Editor MEL MORRIS; circ. 198,000 (M), 268,000 (Saturday).

Le Journal de Montréal: 155 ouest, Port-Royal, Montreal H3L 2B3; tel. (514) 382-8800; telex 05-827591; f. 1964; F.; Pres. and Gen. Man. M. T. CUSTEAU; Editor NORMAND GIRARD; circ. 308,500 (M), 327,000 (Saturday), 314,000 (S).

Le Journal de Québec: 450 ave Béchard, Ville de Vanier G1M 2E9; tel. (613) 683-1573; f. 1967; F.; Gen. Man. JEAN-CLAUDE L'ABBÉE; Chief Editor SERGE CÔTÉ; circ. 107,000 (M).

Le Nouvelliste: 500 rue St-Georges, Trois Rivières G9A 2K8; tel. (819) 376-2501; f. 1920; F.; Publr and Editor CLAUDE MASSON; Man. Editor RENÉ FERRON; circ. 51,000 (M).

La Presse: 7 rue St-Jacques, Montreal H2Y 1K9; tel. (514) 285-7306; telex 052-4110; f. 1884; F.; Publr ROGER D. LANDRY; circ. 202,000 (M), 160,000 (S).

Le Quotidien du Saguenay, Lac St Jean: 1051 blvd Talbot, Chicoutimi G7H 5C1; tel. (418) 545-4474; f. 1973; F.; Pres. and Gen. Man. GASTON VACHON; Newsroom Dir BERTRAND GENEST; circ. 32,000 (M).

The Record: POB 1200, Sherbrooke J1H 5L6; tel. (819) 569-9511; f. 1897; Publr GEORGE R. MACLAREN; Editor CHARLES BURY; circ. 6,000 (M).

Le Soleil: 390 est, rue St Vallier, Québec G1K 7J6; tel. (418) 647-3233; telex 051-3755; f. 1896; F.; Pres. and Gen. Man. PAUL A. AUDET; Editor-in-Chief ALAIN GUILBERT; circ. 119,000 (M), 96,000 (S).

La Tribune: 1950 rue Roy, Sherbrooke J1K 2X8; tel. (819) 569-9201; f. 1910; F.; Publr YVON DUBÉ; Editor JEAN VIGNEAULT; circ. 40,000 (M).

La Voix de L'Est: 136 Principale, Granby J2G 2V4; tel. (514) 372-5433; f. 1945; F.; Publr and Gen. Man. GUY CREVIER; Newsroom Dir GINETTE LAURIN; circ. 13,000 (M).

Saskatchewan

Leader-Post: POB 2020, Regina S4P 3G4; tel. (306) 565-8211; telex 071-3131; f. 1883; Pres. MICHAEL C. SIFTON; Editor W. I. WILLIAMS; circ. 70,000 (E).

Moose Jaw Times-Herald: 44 Fairford St West, Moose Jaw S6H 1V1; tel. (306) 692-6441; f. 1889; Publr ROBERT CALVERT; Editor CLAY STACY; circ. 10,000 (E).

Prince Albert Daily Herald: 30 10th St East, Prince Albert S6V 5R9; tel. (306) 764-4276; f. 1917; Publr and Gen. Man. R. W. GIBB; Man. Editor W. ROZNOWSKY; circ. 10,000 (E).

Star-Phoenix: 204 5th Ave North, Saskatoon S7K 2P1; tel. (306) 652-9200; telex 074-2428; f. 1902; Pres. MICHAEL C. SIFTON; Editor JIM PETRO; circ. 56,000 (E).

SELECTED PERIODICALS
(W = weekly; F = fortnightly; M = monthly; Q = quarterly)

Alberta

Alberta Business: 1167 Kensington Crescent, NW, Suite 310, Calgary T2N 1X7; tel. (403) 270-7555; f. 1984; Editor ROBERTA WALKER; circ. 18,000.

Alberta Farm Life: 7708-104 St, Suite 200, Edmonton T6E 4C5; tel. (403) 433-2512; f. 1971; agriculture; Editor C. MALCOLM; circ. 20,000 (W).

Alberta Report: 17327-106th Ave, Edmonton T5S 1M7; tel. (403) 484-8884; f. 1979; news magazine; Editor STEPHEN HOPKINS; circ. 60,000 (W).

Ukrainski Visti (Ukrainian News): 10967-97th St, Edmonton T5H 2M8; tel. (403) 429-2363; f. 1929; Ukrainian and English; Editor M. CHOMIAK; circ. 17,000 (W).

Western Catholic Reporter: 10562-109th St, Edmonton T5H 3B2; tel. (403) 420-1330; Editor SHIRLEY PFISTER; circ. 36,000 (W).

British Columbia

BC Business: 200-550 Burrard St, Vancouver, V6C 2J6; tel. (604) 669-1721; telex 045-1399; f. 1973; Editor PETER MORGAN; circ. 20,000 (M).

BC Outdoors: 1132 Hamilton St, Suite 202, Vancouver V6B 2S2; tel. (604) 687-1581; telex 045-3454; f. 1945; Editor HENRY FREW; circ. 35,000; 10 a year.

Chinese Canadian Bulletin: 3289 Main St, Vancouver, V5V 3M6; tel. (604) 872-2810; f. 1961; Chinese and English; Editor MOR CHEOLIN; circ. 11,000 (M).

Pacific Yachting: 1132 Hamilton St, Suite 202, Vancouver V6B 2S2; tel. (604) 687-1581; telex 045-3454; f. 1968; Editor PAUL BURKHART; circ. 18,000 (M).

Vancouver Magazine: 1205 Richards St, Vancouver V6B 3G3; tel. (604) 685-5374; f. 1957; Editor MALCOLM F. PARRY; circ. 92,000 (M).

Western Living: 504 Davie St, Vancouver V6B 2G4; tel. (604) 669-7525; telex 045-1484; f. 1971; Editor ANDREW SCOTT; circ. 265,000 (M).

WestWorld Magazine: 320-9940 Lougheed Hwy, Burnaby, V3J 1N3; tel. (604) 421-3059; Publr PETER LEGGE; Editor LINDA AIKMAN; circ. 279,000; 10 a year.

Manitoba

The Beaver: Hudson's Bay House, 77 Main St, Winnipeg R3C 2R1; tel. (204) 934-1485; f. 1920; travel, exploration, development, ethnology and history of the Canadian West and North; Editor CHRISTOPHER DAFOE; circ. 28,000; 6 a year.

Cattlemen: 1760 Ellice Ave, Winnipeg R3H 0B6; tel. (204) 774-1861; f. 1938; animal husbandry; Editor GREN WINSLOW; circ. 41,000 (M).

Country Guide: 1760 Ellice Ave, Winnipeg R3H 0B6; tel. (204) 774-1861; f. 1882; agriculture; Editor DAVID WREFORD; circ. 231,000 (M).

Kanada Kurier: 955 Alexander Ave, Winnipeg R3C 2X8; tel. (204) 774-1883; f. 1980; German; Editor E. PRIEBE; circ. 26,000 (W).

The Manitoba Co-operator: 220 Portage Ave, 4th Floor, Winnipeg R3C 3K7; tel. (204) 943-0796; f. 1925; agricultural; Editor and Publr R. W. HAINSTOCK; circ. 48,000 (W).

Motor in Canada: POB 6900, 1077 St James St, Winnipeg R3C 3B1; tel. (204) 775-0201; f. 1915; Editor JAMES BUCHOK; circ. 12,500 (M).

CANADA

Trade and Commerce: POB 6900, 1077 St James St, Winnipeg R3C 3B1; tel. (204) 775-0201; f. 1906; Editor GEORGE MITCHELL; circ. 13,000 (M).
Ukrainian Voice/Canadian Farmer: 842 Main St, POB 3629, Station B, Winnipeg R2W 3R4; tel. (204) 589-5101; f. 1903; Ukrainian; circ. 8,000 (W).
Wildlife Crusader: 1770 Notre Dame Ave, Winnipeg R3E 3K2; tel. (204) 633-5967; f. 1944; Editor DENIS CORNEAU; circ. 8,000; 6 a year.

New Brunswick

Atlantic Advocate: POB 3370, Fredericton E3B 5A2; tel. (506) 452-6671; f. 1956; Editor H. P. WOOD; circ. 26,000 (M).

Newfoundland

Newfoundland Herald: POB 2015, St John's A1C 5R7; tel. (709) 726-7060; f. 1945; Editor COLEEN SHEA; circ. 48,000 (W).
Newfoundland Lifestyle: 197 Water St, POB 2356, St John's A1C 6E7; Editor A. D. SMITH; circ. 30,000; 6 a year.

Northwest Territories

The Drum: POB 2660, Inuvik X0E 0T0; tel. (403) 979-2623; telex 034-44527; f. 1966; English; Editor DAN HOLMAN; (W).
The Hub: POB 1250, Hay River X0E 0R0; tel. (403) 874-6577; circ. 2,000 (W).
News/North: POB 2820, Yellowknife X0E 1H0; tel. (403) 873-2661; f. 1945; circ. 11,000 (W).
Nunatsiaq News: POB 8, Frobisher Bay X0A 0H0; tel. (403) 979-5357; circ. 3,000 (W).
Yellowknife: POB 2820, Yellowknife X1A 2R1; tel. (403) 873-4,031; circ. 6,000 (W).

Nova Scotia

Atlantic Insight: 1668 Barrington St, Halifax B3J 2A2; tel. (902) 421-1214; Editor RALPH SURETTE; circ. 40,000 (M).
The Dalhousie Review: Dalhousie University Press, Sir James Dunn Science Bldg, Halifax B3H 3J5; tel. (902) 424-2541; f. 1921; literary and general; Editor Dr ALAN E. KENNEDY; (Q).

Ontario

Canada Gazette: Canadian Government Publishing Centre, Supply and Services Canada, Ottawa K1A 0S9; tel. (613) 997-1988; f. 1867; official bulletin of the Govt of Canada; Editor C. M. WHALEN; (W).
Canada Reports: External Information Services Division, Dept of External Affairs, Ottawa K1A 0G2; telex 053-3745; English and French edns; Editor CAROLE STELMACK; (F).
Canadian Aeronautics and Space Journal: 222 Somerset St West, Suite 601, Ottawa K2P 0J1; tel. (613) 234-0191; f. 1954; Chair of Editorial Board Dr G. LINDBERG; circ. 2,000 (M).
Canadian Architect: 1450 Don Mills Rd, Don Mills M3B 2X7; tel. (416) 445-6641; telex 069-66612; f. 1955; Publr and Man. Editor ROBERT GRETTON; circ. 9,000 (M).
Canadian Author & Bookman: 70 Champlain Ave, Welland L3C 2L7; f. 1921; publ. by the Canadian Authors Asscn; Editor ANNE OSBORNE; circ. 4,000 (Q).
Canadian Bar Review: Canadian Bar Asscn, 130 Albert St, Ottawa K1P 5G4; tel. (613) 237-2925; telex 053-3063; f. 1923; Editor Dr A. J. MCCLEAN; circ. 32,000 (Q).
Canadian Boating: 5200 Dixie Rd, Suite 204, Mississauga L4W 1E4; tel. (416) 625-5277; f. 1923; Editor GARY ARTHURS; circ. 17,000; 8 a year.
Canadian Chemical News: 151 Slater St, Suite 906, Ottawa K1P 5H3; tel. (613) 233-5623; telex 053-4306; f. 1949; Editor A. E. ALPER; circ. 8,000 (M).
Canadian Construction Record: 1450 Don Mills Road, Don Mills M3B 2X7; tel. (416) 445-6641; telex 069-66612; f. 1888; Editor TIM TOLTON; circ. 27,000 (M).
Canadian Dental Association Journal: 1815 Alta Vista Drive, Ottawa K1G 3Y6; tel. (613) 523-1770; f. 1935; Editor CAROLYN M. HACKLAND; Scientific Editors Dr ROBERT TURNBULL, Dr PIERRE DESAUTELS; (M).
Canadian Doctor: 1450 Don Mills Rd, Don Mills M3B 2X7; tel. (416) 445-6641; telex 069-66612; f. 1935; Editor KIM COFFMAN; circ. 33,000 (M).
Canadian Forest Industries: 1450 Don Mills Rd, Don Mills M3B 2X7; tel. (416) 445-6641; telex 069-66612; f. 1880; Editor RICHARD HOLMES; circ. 17,000 (M).

Canadian Geographic: 488 Wilbrod St, Ottawa K1N 6M8; tel. (613) 236-7493; f. 1930; publ. by the Royal Canadian Geographical Soc.; Editor R. W. SMITH; circ. 122,000; 6 a year.
Canadian Labour: 2841 Riverside Drive, Ottawa K1V 8X7; tel. (613) 521-3400; telex 053-4750; f. 1956; trade union; Asst Editor MARY KEHOE; 10 a year.
Canadian Medical Association Journal: 1867 Alta Vista Drive, Ottawa K1G 3Y6; tel. (613) 731-9331; f. 1911; Scientific Editors Dr PETER P. MORGAN, Dr BRUCE P. SQUIRES; circ. 42,000 (F).
Canadian Nurse—L' infirmière canadienne: 50 The Driveway, Ottawa K2P 1E2; tel. (613) 237-2133; f. 1908; official publ. of the Canadian Nurses' Asscn; Editor JUDITH A. BANNING; circ. 135,000.
Canadian Pharmaceutical Journal: 1785 Alta Vista Drive, Ottawa K1G 3Y6; tel. (613) 523-7877; f. 1869; Editor J.-G. CYR; circ. 12,000 (M).
Canadian Sportsman: POB 603, 25 Townline Rd, Tillsonburg N4G 4J1; tel. (519) 842-4824; f. 1870; Editor GARY FOERSTER; W (May–October), F (October–May).
Canadian Workshop: 130 Spy Court, Markham L3R 5H6; tel. (416) 475-8440; f. 1977; do-it-yourself; Editor BOB PENNYCOOK; circ. 84,000 (M).
Electronics and Communications: 1450 Don Mills Rd, Don Mills M3B 2X7; tel. (416) 445-6641; telex 069-66612; f. 1953; Assoc. Editor DENIS OLORENSHAW; circ. 17,000; 6 a year.
The Engineering Times: 1450 Don Mills Rd, Don Mills M3B 2X7; tel. (416) 445-6641; telex 069-66612; f. 1967; Man. Editor EDWARD S. CORNER; circ. 86,000 (M).
Executive: 2973 Weston Rd, Weston M9M 2T2; tel. (416) 741-1112; telex 065-27372; f. 1958; Publr DONALD COOTE; Editor PATRICIA ANDERSON; circ. 51,000; 9 a year.
Holstein Journal: 335 Lesmill Rd, Don Mills M3B 2V1; tel. (416) 441-3030; f. 1938; Editor BONNIE E. COOPER; circ. 17,000 (M).
Legion Magazine: 359 Kent St, Suite 504, Ottawa K2P 0R6; tel. (613) 235-8741; f. 1926; circ. 556,000 (M)(except July and Dec.
Modern Medicine of Canada—Médecine Moderne du Canada: 1450 Don Mills Rd, Don Mills M3B 2X7; tel. (416) 445-6641; telex 069-66612; f. 1946; Editor Dr J. A. KELLEN; English and French; circ. 42,000 (M).
Ontario Milk Producer: 6780 Campobello Rd, Mississauga L5N 2L8; tel. (416) 821-8970; f. 1925; Publr JOHN KARN; circ. 16,000.
Oral Health: 1450 Don Mills Rd, Don Mills M3B 2X7; tel. (416) 445-6641; telex 069-66612; f. 1911; Editor JANET BONELLIE; circ. 15,000 (M).
Teviskes Ziburiai (Lights of Homeland): 2185 Stavebank Rd, Mississauga L5C 1T3; tel. (416) 275-4672; Lithuanian; Editor Rev. Dr PR. GAIDA; circ. 6,000 (W).

Toronto

Akhbar El-Arab Toronto (Arab News of Toronto): 370 Queen St East, Toronto M5A 1T1; tel. (416) 362-0304; telex 065-2629; f. 1978; Arabic and English; Publr and Editor SALAH ALLAM; circ. 6,000 (F).
Books in Canada: 366 Adelaide St East, Toronto M5A 3X9; tel. (416) 363-5426; f. 1971; Editor MICHAEL SMITH; circ. 20,000; 9 a year.
Business Journal: POB 60, 3 First Canadian Place, Toronto M5X 1C1; tel. (416) 366-6811; telex 065-24036; f. 1910; Editor ALAN MORANTZ; circ. 43,000; 10 a year.
CA magazine: The Canadian Institute of Chartered Accountants, 150 Bloor St West, Toronto M5S 2Y2; tel. (416) 962-1242; telex 062-22835; f. 1911; Editor NELSON LUSCOMBE; circ. 57,000 (M).
The Campus Network: Youthstream Canada Ltd, 1541 Avenue Rd, Suite 303, Toronto M5M 3X4; tel. (416) 787-4911; 21 campus edns; Pres. CAMERON KILLORAN; circ. 196,000.
Canadian Business: 70 The Esplanade, 2nd Floor, Toronto M5E 1R2; tel. (416) 364-4266; f. 1927; Publr ROY MACLAREN; Editor CHARLES DAVIS; circ. 94,000 (M).
Canadian Churchman: 600 Jarvis St, Toronto M4Y 2J6; tel. (416) 924-9192; telex 065-24128; f. 1871; official publ. of the Anglican Church of Canada; Editor JERROLD HAMES; circ. 272,000 (M).
Canadian Defence Quarterly: 310 Dupont St, Toronto M5R 1V9; tel. (416) 968-7252; telex 065-28085; Editor JOHN GELLNER; circ. 10,000 (Q).

CANADA

Canadian Forum: 70 The Esplanade, 3rd Floor, Toronto M5E 1R2; tel. (416) 364-2431; f. 1920; political, literary and economic; Editor JOHN HUTCHESON; circ. 10,000 (M).

Canadian Journal of Economics: c/o University of Toronto Press, Front Campus, Toronto M5S 1A6; tel. (416) 978-6739; f. 1968; Editor MICHAEL PARKIN; circ. 4,000 (Q).

Canadian Living: 50 Holly St, Toronto M4S 3B3; tel. (416) 482-8600; f. 1975; Editor-in-Chief JUDY BRANDOW; circ. 510,000 (M).

Canadian Musician: 832 Mount Pleasant Rd, Toronto M4P 2L3; tel. (416) 485-8284; f. 1979; Editor TED BURLEY; circ. 26,000; 6 a year.

Canadian Travel Press: 310 Dupont St, Toronto M5R 1V9; tel. (416) 968-7252; telex 065-28085; Publr DAVID MCCLUNG; circ. 19,000 (F).

Cinema Canada: 67A Portland St, Toronto M5V 2M9; POB 398, Outremont, Que H2V 3S6; tel. (514) 272-5354; Editors JEAN-PIERRE TADROS, CONNIE TADROS; circ. 5,000.

El Popular: 2413 Dundas St West, Toronto M6P 1X3; tel. (416) 531-2495; f. 1970; Spanish; Editor MIGUEL RAKIEWICZ; circ. 14,000 (F).

Engineering Digest: 111 Peter St, Suite 411, Toronto M5V 2W2; tel. (416) 596-1624; telex 062-18852; f. 1954; Editor H. W. MEYFARTH; circ. 71,000; 10 a year.

Farm and Country: 950 Yonge St, 7th Floor, Toronto M4W 2J4; tel. (416) 924-6209; f. 1936; Publr and Editor-in-Chief JOHN PHILLIPS; circ. 72,000; 18 a year.

Financial Times of Canada: 920 Yonge St, Suite 500, Toronto M4W 3L5; tel. (416) 922-1133; f. 1912; Publr DAVID TAFLER; circ. 105,000 (W).

Hockey News: 85 Scarsdale Rd, Toronto M3B 2R2; tel. (416) 445-5702; f. 1947; Editor-in-Chief BOB MCKENZIE; circ. 112,000 (W).

Magyar Élet (Hungarian Life): 6 Alcina Ave, Toronto M6G 2E8; tel. (416) 654-2551; f. 1948; Hungarian; Publr ANDREW LASZLO; circ. 8,000 (W).

New Equipment News: 111 Peter St, Suite 411, Toronto M5V 2W2; tel. (416) 596-1624; telex 062-18852; f. 1940; Editor D. B. LEHMAN; circ. 32,200 (M).

Northern Miner: 7 Labatt Ave, Toronto M5A 3P2; tel. (416) 368-3483; telex 065-24190; f. 1915; Editor ALLAN A. JONES; circ. 26,000.

Ontario Medical Review: 250 Bloor St East, Suite 600, Toronto M4W 3P8; tel. (416) 963-9383; f. 1922; Editor RONALD E. BROWNRIDGE; circ. 18,000 (M).

Quill and Quire: 56 The Esplanade, Suite 213, Toronto M5E 1A7; tel. (416) 364-3333; f. 1935; book industry; Editor ANN VANDERHOOF; circ. 10,000 (M).

Saturday Night: 70 Bond St, Suite 500, Toronto M5B 2J3; tel. (416) 365-9510; f. 1887; Editor ROBERT FULFORD; circ. 135,000 (M).

Time (Canada edition): 620 University Ave, 11th Floor, Toronto M5G 2C5; tel. (416) 595-1229; telex 062-3245; f. 1943; Pres. MICHAEL J. MCGRATH; circ. 335,000 (W).

Toronto Life Magazine: 59 Front St East, Toronto M5E 1B3; tel. (416) 364-3333; f. 1966; Editor MARQ DE VILLIERS; circ. 93,000 (M).

TV Guide: 50 Holly St, Toronto M4S 3B3; tel. (416) 482-8600; f. 1976; Pres. JOHN VAN DE KAMER; circ. 845,000 (W).

Die Zeit: 9 Belmont St, Toronto M5R 1P9; tel. (416) 922-5258; German; Editor HAUG VON KUENHEIM; circ. 9,000 (W).

The following are all published by Maclean Hunter Ltd, 777 Bay St, Toronto M5W 1A7; tel. (416) 596-5000; telex 062-19547.

Canada & the World: tel. (416) 596-5836; telex 062-19547; f. 1937; Editor RUPERT TAYLOR; circ. 28,000; 9 a year.

Canadian Aviation: tel. (416) 596-5789; telex 062-19547; f. 1928; Editor HUGH WHITTINGTON; circ. 28,000 (M).

Canadian Building: tel. (416) 596-5760; telex 062-19547; f. 1951; Editor JOHN FENNELL; circ. 19,000 (M).

Canadian Driver/Owner: tel. (416) 596-5928; f. 1972; Editor JOHN BATES; circ. 21,000 (M).

Canadian Electronics Engineering: tel. (416) 596-5731; telex 062-19547; f. 1957; Editor PETER J. THORNE; circ. 17,000 (M).

Canadian Grocer: tel. (416) 596-5772; telex 062-19547; f. 1886; Editor GEORGE H. CONDON; circ. 17,000 (M).

Canadian Hotel & Restaurant: tel. (416) 596-5813; telex 062-19547; f. 1923; Editor ANDREW DOUGLAS; circ. 34,000 (M).

CAR (Canadian Auto Review): tel. (416) 596-5784; f. 1984; Editor RICHARD JACOBS; circ. 9,000 (M).

Chatelaine: tel. (416) 596-5422; telex 062-19547; f. 1928; women's journal; Editor MILDRED ISTONA; circ. 1,100,000 (M).

Civic Public Works: tel. (416) 596-5953; telex 062-9547; f. 1949; Editor CLIFF ALLUM; circ. 14,000 (M).

Design Engineering: tel. (416) 596-5833; telex 062-19547; f. 1955; Editor JAMES BARNES; circ. 15,000 (M).

The Financial Post: tel. (416) 596-5632; telex 062-19547; f. 1907; Editor-in-Chief NEVILLE J. NANKIVELL; circ. 188,000 (W).

Flare: tel. (416) 596-5462; telex 062-19547; f. 1984; Editor BONNIE HUROWITZ; circ. 153,000 (M).

Floor Covering News: tel. (416) 596-5940; telex 062-19547; f. 1976; Editor HELEN BAHEN; circ. 6,000; 10 a year.

Heavy Construction News: tel. (416) 596-5837; telex 062-19547; f. 1956; Editor ALEX JENKINS; circ. 25,000 (F).

Maclean's Canada's Weekly Newsmazagine: tel. (416) 596-5311; telex 062-19547; f. 1905; Editor KEVIN DOYLE; circ. 645,000 (W).

Marketing: tel. (416) 596-5835; telex 062-19547; f. 1906; Editor COLIN MUNCIE; circ. 10,000 (W).

Medical Post: tel. (416) 596-5770; telex 062-19547; f. 1965; Editor DEREK CASSELS; circ. 37,000 (F).

Office Equipment and Methods: tel. (416) 596-5920; telex 062-19547; f. 1955; Editor TOM KELLY;; circ. 60,000 (M).

Plant Management and Engineering: tel. (416) 596-5801; telex 062-19547; f. 1907; Editor RON RICHARDSON; circ. 26,000 (M).

Style: tel. (416) 596-5750; telex 062-19547; f. 1888; Editor ELIZABETH WATSON; circ. 10,000; 16 a year.

Truck Fleet Magazine: tel. (416) 596.5928; telex 062-19547; f. 1925; Editor JOHN BATES; circ. 38,000 (M).

Québec

L'Actualité: 1001 ouest, blvd De Maisonneuve, Montreal, H3A 3E1; tel. (514) 845-5141; f. 1976; general interest; French; Publr and Editor JEAN PARÉ; circ. 261,000 (M).

Le magazine Affaires: 465 rue St-Jean, 9e étage, Montreal H2Y 3S4; tel. (514) 842-6491; telex 055-61971; f. 1978; Publr CLAUDE BEAUCHAMP; circ. 64,000; 10 a year.

Allo Police: 1800 rue Parthenais, Montreal H2K 3S4; tel. (514) 527-5730; f. 1953; Editor ANDRÉ PARENT; circ. 78,000 (W).

Le Bulletin des Agriculteurs: 110 ouest, blvd Crémazie, Bureau 422, Montreal H2P 1B9; tel. (514) 382-4350; f. 1918; Publr LUCILLE FONTAINE; circ. 106,000 (M).

Canadian Arab World Review: 10935 rue Jeanne Mance, Montreal H3L 3C7; tel. (514) 331-5550; f. 1969; monthly in Arabic, English and French; Editor R. R. KNEIDER.

Châtelaine: 1001 ouest, blvd de Maisonneuve, Montreal H3A 3E1; tel. (514) 845-5141; f. 1960; French; Editor MARTINE THORNTON; circ. 304,000 (M).

CIM Bulletin: 1130 Sherbrooke St West, Suite 400, Montreal H3A 2M8; tel. (514) 842-3461; telex 055-62344; publ. by the Canadian Institute of Mining and Metallurgy; Editor PIERRE MICHAUD; circ. 11,000 (M).

Il Cittadino Canadese: 6896 blvd St Lawrence, Montreal H2S 3C7; tel. (514) 277-3181; f. 1941; Italian; Editor GIUSEPPE MANCINI; circ. 48,000 (W).

Clin d'Oeil: 100 ave Dresden, Montreal, H3P 2B6; tel. (514) 735-6361; Editor-in-Chief DANIELLE PAQUIN; circ. 125,000 (M).

Dimanche-Matin: 5701 rue Christophe-Colomb, Montreal H2S 2E9; tel. (514) 274-2501; telex 056-0688; f. 1954; French; Editor JACQUES FRANCOEUR; circ. 153,000 (W).

Echos Vedettes: 225 est, rue Roy, Montreal H2W 1M5; tel. (514) 282-9600; f. 1963; circ. 151,000 (W).

Engineering Journal: 700–2050 rue Mansfield, Montreal; tel. (514) 842-8121; f. 1918; publ. by Engineering Inst. of Canada; Editor MARTA MEANA; circ. 16,000 (Q).

L'Ingénieur: CP 6980, succursale A, Montreal H3C 3L4; tel. (514) 340-4765; f. 1915; Editor-in-Chief JOSEPH KÉLADA; circ. 10,000; 6 a year.

Jewish Eagle: 4180 De Courtrai, Bureau 218, Montreal H3S 1C3; tel. (514) 735-6577; f. 1907; Yiddish; independent; Editor B. HIRSHTAL; circ. 18,000 (W).

Le Lundi: 10000 Lajeunesse, Bureau 210, Montreal H3L 5S3; tel. (514) 382-8443; f. 1976; Editor DENIS MONETTE; circ. 121,000 (W).

CANADA   Directory

Mon Jardin: 110 ouest, blvd Crémazie, Montreal H2P 1B9; tel. (514) 382-4350; f. 1984; Dir LUCIE DUMOULIN; (Q).

Nouvelles Illustrées: 225 est, rue Roy, Montreal H2W 1M5; tel. (514) 282-9600; f. 1954; Editor M. HUGUET; circ. 27,000 (w).

Perspectives: 231 ouest, rue St-Jacques, Montreal; tel. (514) 282-2224; f. 1959; French; Publr ALBERT TREMBLAY; Editor JEAN BOUTHILLETTE; circ. 598,000 (w).

Photo Sélection: 2026 rue Persico, CP 383, Sillery G1T 2R5; tel. (418) 687-3550; f. 1980; Chief Editor YOLANDE RACINE; circ. 18,000; 8 a year.

Le Producteur de Lait Québécois: 555 blvd Roland-Thérrien, Longueuil J4H 3Y9; tel. (514) 679-0530; f. 1980; dairy farming; Dir MARIO DUMAIS; circ. 21,000 (M).

Progrès-Dimanche: 1051 blvd Talbot, Chicoutimi G7H 5C1; tel. (418) 545-4474; Pres. GASTON VACHON; circ. 52,000 (w).

Québec Construction: 465 rue St-Jean, Suite 903, Montreal H2Y 3S4; tel. (514) 842-6491; telex 055-61971; f. 1962; Pres. CLAUDE BEAUCHAMP; circ. 2,000 (w).

Le Québec Industriel: 1001 ouest, De Maisonneuve, Bureau 1000, Montreal H3A 3E1; tel. (514) 845-5141; f. 1946; Editor ANTOINE DI LILLO; circ. 16,000 (M).

Québec Science: 2875 blvd Laurier, Ste Foy G1V 2M3; tel. (418) 657-3551; telex 051-31623; f. 1969; Editor FERNAND GRENIER; circ. 22,000 (M).

Reader's Digest: 215 ave Redfern, Westmount H3Z 2V9; tel. (514) 934-0751; f. 1943; Editor ALEXANDER FARRELL; circ. 1,327,000 (M).

Relations: 8100 blvd St Laurence, Montreal H2P 2L9; tel. (514) 387-2541; f. 1941; French; Roman Catholic review; Editor-in-Chief Fr ALBERT BEAUDRY; circ. 5,000 (M).

Rénovation Bricolage: 100 rue Dresden, Montreal, H3P 2B6; tel. (514) 735-6361; f. 1976; Editor-in-Chief BORIS BRUMAT; circ. 40,000 (M).

Revue Commerce: 465 rue St-Jean, Suite 908, Montreal H2Y 2R6; tel. (514) 844-1511; f. 1898; Publr MICHEL LORD; circ. 35,000 (M).

Sélection du Reader's Digest: 215 ave Redfern, Montreal H3Z 2V9; tel. (514) 934-0751; telex 052-5800; f. 1922; Editor DENISE SURPRENANT; circ. 383,000 (M).

La Semaine: 230 est, Henri-Bourassa, Bureau 310, Montreal H3L 1B8; tel. (514) 384-6410; f. 1983; Editor BERNARD LAVOIE; circ. 69,000 (w).

Télé-Radiomonde: 225 est, rue Roy, Montreal H2W 2N6; tel. (514) 282-9600; f. 1939; Editor PIERRE NADEAU; circ. 48,000 (w).

La Terre de Chez Nous: 555 blvd Roland-Thérrien, Longueuil J4H 3Y9; tel. (514) 679-0530; f. 1929; agriculture and forestry; French; Editor MARIO DUMAIS; circ. 50,000 (w).

TV Hebdo/TV Plus: 1001 est, blvd De Maisonneuve, Bureau 1100, Montreal H2L 4P9; tel. (514) 527-9601; f. 1960; Gen. Man. JACQUES LINA; circ. 280,000 (w).

Saskatchewan

The Commonwealth: 1122 Saskatchewan Drive, Regina S4P 0C4; tel. (306) 525-8321; f. 1938; Editor RON THOMPSON; circ. 11,000; 24 a year.

Farm Light & Power: 2352 Smith St, Regina S4P 2P6; tel. (306) 525-3305; f. 1959; Publr L. T. BRADLEY; circ. 192,000; 10 a year.

Western Producer: POB 2500, Saskatoon S7K 2C4; tel. (306) 665-3500; telex 074-2690; f. 1923; world and agricultural news; Editor R. H. D. PHILLIPS; circ. 139,000 (w).

Western Sportsman: POB 737, Regina S4P 3A8; tel. (306) 352-8384; f. 1968; Editor RICK BATES; circ. 30,000; 6 a year.

Yukon Territory

Dan Sha News: 22 Nisutlin Drive, Whitehorse Y1A 3S5; tel. (403) 667-7636; telex 036-8346; circ. 3,000 (M).

The Yukon News: 211 Wood St, Whitehorse Y1A 2E4; tel. (403) 667-6285; f. 1960; circ. 6,000; 3 a week.

NEWS AGENCIES

The Canadian Press: 36 King St East, Toronto, Ont M5C 2L9; tel. (416) 364-0321; f. 1917; 104 daily newspaper mems; national news co-operative; absorbed United Press Canada in 1985; Chair. A. E. WOOD; Pres. KEITH KINCAID.

Foreign Bureaux

Agence France-Presse (AFP): 1390 ouest, rue Sherbrooke, Bureau 46, Montreal, Qué H3G 1J4; tel. (514) 844-6992; telex 052-5265 Bureau Chief HUBERT LAVERNE; also office in Ottawa.

Agencia EFE (Spain): 165 Sparks St, Suite 502, Ottawa K1P 5B9; tel. (613) 230-2282.

Agenzia Nazionale Stampa Associata (ANSA) (Italy): 150 Wellington St, Room 703, Press Gallery, Ottawa K1P 5A4; tel. (613) 235-4248; telex 053-4392; Representative CARLO GIACOBBE.

Deutsche Presse-Agentur (dpa) (Federal Republic of Germany): 702 National Press Bldg, 150 Wellington, Ottawa K1P 5A4; tel. (613) 234-6024; Representative BARBARA HALSIG.

Jiji Tsushin-Sha (Japan): 366 Adelaide St East, Toronto, Ont M5A 3X9; tel.(416) 368-8037; Chief MASATO HIRAYAMA.

Prensa Latina (Cuba): 221 rue du St-Sacrement, Montreal, Qué; tel. (514) 844-2975; Correspondent ALBERTO RABILOTTA.

Reuters (UK): POB 403, Commerce Court Postal Station, Toronto, Ont M5L 1J1; tel. (416) 869-3600; telex 062-3637; Man. WILLIAM O'SHEA; also offices in Ottawa and Montreal.

Telegrafnoye Agentstvo Sovetskovo Soyuza (TASS) (USSR): 200 Rideau Terrace, Suite 1305, Ottawa; tel. (613) 745-4310; telex 053-4504; Correspondent ARTEM MELIKIAN.

Xinhua (New China) News Agency: (People's Republic of China: 406 Daly Ave, Ottawa KIN 6H2; tel. (613) 234-8424; telex 053-4362; Chief Corresp. CAI SHUQI.

Associated Press (USA) and Central News Agency (Taiwan) are also represented.

PRESS ASSOCIATIONS

Canadian Business Press: 100 University Ave, Suite 508, Toronto, Ont M5J 1V6; tel. (416) 593-5497; Chair. GWEN PAGE; Admin. Man. E. SELLWOOD; constituent associations:

  Agricultural Press Association of Canada: Admin. Man. E. SELLWOOD.

  Magazine Publishers' Association of Canada: Pres. L. M. HODGKINSON.

  Periodical Press Association: Programme Co-ordinator M. C. GOWDY.

Canadian Community Newspapers' Association: 705-88 University Ave, Toronto, Ont M5J 1T6; tel. (416) 598-4277; f. 1919; Pres. JEAN BAKER-PEARCE; Exec. Dir JIM DILLS; 644 mems.

Canadian Daily Newspaper Publishers Association: 890 Yonge St, Suite 1100, Toronto, Ont M4W 3P4; tel. (416) 923-3567; f. 1919; Chair. TOM CROWTHER; Pres. JOHN FOY; 80 mems.

Canadian Periodical Publishers' Association: 2 Stewart St, Toronto, Ont M5V 1H6; tel. (416) 362-2546; f. 1973; Exec. Dir DINAH HOYLE.

Canadian Section, Commonwealth Press Union: 150 Bloor St West, Suite 910, Toronto, Ont M5S 2Y9; tel. (416) 927-1877; f. 1909; Hon. Sec.-Treas. R. S. MAY.

Magazines Canada (The Magazine Asscn of Canada): 250 Bloor St East, Suite 320, Toronto, Ont M4W 1E6; tel. (416) 920-6548; Chair. RALPH HANCOX; Pres. SUSAN CORRIE.

Publishers

Addison-Wesley Publishers Ltd: 26 Prince Andrew Place, POB 580, Don Mills, Ont M3C 2T8; tel. (416) 447-5101; f. 1966; mathematics, science, language, business and social sciences textbooks, trade, juvenile; CEO GEORGE MACD. BRYSON.

Thomas Allen and Son Ltd: 390 Steelcase Rd East, Markham, Ont L3R 1G2; tel. (416) 475-9126; telex 069-66716; f. 1916; Pres. JOHN D. ALLEN.

Annick Press Ltd: 5519 Yonge St, Willowdale, Ont M2N 5S3; tel. (416) 221-4802; telex 069-86766; f. 1976; children's; Co-Dirs RICK WILKS, ANNE W. MILLYARD.

Arsenal Pulp Press: POB 3868 MPO, Vancouver, BC V6B 3Z3; tel. (604) 687-4233; f. 1972; literary, native, educational.

Avon Books of Canada: 2061 McCowan Rd, Suite 201, Scarborough, Ont M1S 3Y6; tel. (416) 293-9404; Pres. PETER AUSTIN.

Black Rose Books Ltd: 3981 blvd St-Laurent, 4e étage, Montreal, Qué H2W 1Y5; tel. (514) 844-4076; f. 1970; social studies; Pres. JACQUES ROUX.

CANADA

Le Boréal Express Ltée: 5450 chemin de la Côte-des-Neiges, Bureau 212, Montreal, Que H3T 1Y6; tel. (514) 735-6267; f. 1963; history, biography, fiction, politics, economics, educational; Pres. ANTOINE DEL BUSSO.

Borealis Press Ltd: 9 Ashburn Drive, Ottawa K2E 6N4; tel. (613) 224-6837; f. 1972; general fiction and non-fiction, drama, juveniles.

Breakwater Books Ltd: POB 2188, 277 Duckworth St, St John's, Nfld A1C 6E6; tel. (709) 722-6680; f. 1973; fiction, general, children's.

Butterworths: 2265 Midland Ave, Scarborough, Ont M1P 4S1; tel. (416) 292-1421; f. 1912; a division of Reed Inc; legal, professional, academic; Pres. GEOFFREY BURN.

Canada Law Book Inc: 240 Edward St, Aurora, Ont L4G 3S9; tel. (416) 773-6300; f. 1855; law reports, law journals, legal textbooks, etc.; Pres. W. L. COWING.

Centre Educatif et Culturel: 8101 blvd Métropolitain, Anjou, Montreal, Qué H1J 1J9; tel. (514) 351-6010; telex 055-62172; f. 1956; textbooks; Pres. and Dir-Gen. DENIS VAUGEOIS.

The Coach House Press: 401 (rear) Huron St, Toronto, Ont M5S 2G5; tel. (416) 979-2217; telex 069-59372; f. 1965; fiction, poetry.

Collier Macmillan Canada Inc: 1200 Eglinton Ave East, Suite 200, Don Mills, Ont M3C 3N1; tel. (416) 449-6030; telex 069-59372; f. 1958; trade, textbooks, reference; Pres. RAY LEE.

Wm Collins, Sons and Co (Canada) Ltd: 100 Lesmill Rd, Don Mills, Ont M3B 2T5; tel. (416) 445-8221; f. 1932; trade, reference, bibles, dictionaries, juvenile, paperbacks; Pres. N. G. HARRIS.

Copp Clark Pitman: 495 Wellington St West, Toronto, Ont M5V 1E9; tel. (416) 593-9911; f. 1841; textbooks and reference material; Pres. STEPHEN MILLS.

Direction générale des publications gouvernementales: Ministère de Communications, 1283 ouest, blvd Charest, Québec, Qué G1N 2C9; f. 1867; Québec Govt publs; Dir JACQUES PIGEON.

Dominie Press Ltd: 1361 Huntingwood Drive, Unit 7, Agincourt, Ont M1S 3J1; tel. (416) 291-5857; Pres. RAYMOND YUEN.

Doubleday Canada Ltd: 105 Bond St, Toronto, Ont M5B 1Y3; tel. (416) 977-7891; f. 1944; general, trade, textbooks, mass market; Pres. PETER MAIK.

Douglas and McIntyre Ltd: 1615 Venables St, Vancouver, BC V5L 2H1; tel. (604) 254-7191; telex 062-2174; f. 1964; general non-fiction, juvenile; Pres. SCOTT MCINTYRE.

Eden Press Inc: 4626 ouest, rue Ste-Catherine, Montreal, Qué H3Z 1S3; tel. (514) 931-3910; f. 1977; scholarly, medical, scientific, general non-fiction; Pres. SHERRI CLARKSON.

Editions Bellarmin: 8100 blvd St-Laurent, Montreal, Qué H2P 2L9; tel. (514) 387-2541; f. 1891; religious, educational, politics, sociology, ethnography, history, sport, leisure; Pres. and Dir-Gen. MAURICE RUEST; Man. Rev. MAURICE RUEST, SJ.

Editions L'Etincelle (SCE): 4920 ouest, blvd de Housonneuve, Bureau 206, Westmount, Qué H3Z 1W1; tel. (514) 488-9531; telex 055-67131; f. 1972; art, social and political sciences, geography, history, juvenile; Pres. ROBERT DAVIES.

Les Editions Fides: 5710 ave Decelles, Montreal, Qué H3S 2C5; tel. (514) 735-6406; f. 1937; juvenile, history, theology, textbooks and literature; Dir-Gen. MICHELINE TREMBLAY.

Les Editions Françaises Inc: 1411 rue Ampère, CP'395, Boucherville, Qué J4B 5W2; tel. (514) 641-0514; telex 052-5107; f. 1951; textbooks; Pres. PIERRE LESPÉRANCE.

Editions France-Québec Inc: 955 rue Amherst, Montreal, Qué H2L 3K4; tel. (514) 323-1182; telex 052-4667; f. 1965; Editor BERNARD PRÉVOST.

Editions Héritage: 300 ave Arran, St-Lambert, Qué J4R 1K5; tel. (514) 672-6710; telex 052-5134; f. 1968; history, biography, sport, juveniles; Pres. JACQUES PAYETTE.

Editions de l'Hexagone: 900 est, rue Ontario, Montreal, Qué H2L 1P4; tel (514) 525-2811; f. 1953; literature; Dir-Gen. ALAIN HORIC.

Editions Hurtubise HMH: 7360 blvd Newman, Ville LaSalle, Qué H8N 1X2; tel. (514) 364-0323; telex 055-67167; f. 1960; general academic; Pres. and Dir-Gen. HERVÉ FOULON.

Editions Leméac Inc: 5111 ave Durocher, Outremont, Qué H2V 3X7; tel. (514) 273-1150; telex 052-68511; f. 1957; literary, academic, general; Pres. ROLAND ROCHT; Dir-Gen. YVES DUBÉ.

Editions Libre Expression: 244 ouest, rue St-Jacques, Montreal, Qué H2Y 1L9; tel. (514) 849-5259; f. 1976; religion, social and political sciences, general fiction and non-fiction, juvenile; Pres. ANDRÉ BASTIEN.

Editions du Pélican: CP 1182, Québec, Qué G1K 7C3; tel. (418) 688-8468; f. 1956; art, history, sport; Man. RÉAL D'ANJOU.

Les Editions la Presse: 44 ouest, rue St-Antoine, Montreal, Qué H2Y 1J5; tel. (514) 285-6981; telex 052-4110; f. 1971; general literature; Pres. NORMAND MARTIN.

Editions du Renouveau Pédagogique Inc: 8925 blvd St-Laurent, Montreal, Qué H2N 1M5; tel. (514) 384-2690; telex 058-26756; f. 1965; textbooks; Pres. ANDRÉ DUSSAULT.

Editions du Richelieu: CP 142, Saint-Jean, Qué G3B 5W3; f. 1935; general fiction and non-fiction, Roman Catholic school religious texts; Pres. FELICIEN MESSIER.

Editions de l'Université d'Ottawa: 603 ave Cumberland, Ottawa K1N 6N5; tel. (613) 564-2270; f. 1936; university texts, scholarly, general; Dir-Gen. RALPH HODGSON.

Encyclopaedia Britannica Publications Ltd: 175 Holiday Drive, POB 2249, Cambridge, Ont N3C 3N4; tel. (519) 658-4621; telex 069-59499; f. 1937; Pres. DAVID DURNAN.

Fitzhenry & Whiteside Ltd: 195 Allstate Pkwy, Markham, Ont L3R 4T8; tel. (416) 477-0030; f. 1966; textbooks, trade, educational; Pres. ROBERT I. FITZHENRY.

Gage Educational Publishing Co: 164 Commander Blvd, Agincourt, Ont M1S 3C7; tel. (416) 293-8141; f. 1844; Pres. and CEO ROBERT M. MCELMAN.

General Publishing Co Ltd: 30 Lesmill Rd, Don Mills, Ont M3B 2T6; tel. (416) 445-3333; telex 069-86664; f. 1934; fiction, history, biography, children's, general, textbooks; Pres. JACK E. STODDART.

Ginn and Company: 3771 Victoria Park Ave, Scarborough, Ont M1W 2P9; tel. (416) 497-4600; f. 1929; textbooks; Pres. RICHARD H. LEE.

GLC Publishers Ltd: 115 Nugget Ave, Agincourt, Ont M1S 3B1; tel. (416) 291-2926; Pres. DOUG PANASIS.

Grolier Ltd: 16 Overlea Blvd, Toronto, Ont M4H 1A6; tel. (416) 425-1924; f. 1912; reference; Pres. KEN PIERSON.

Harbour Publishing Co Ltd: POB 219, Madeira Park, BC V0N 2H0; tel. (604) 883-2730; f. 1972; British Columbia regional history and culture, literary, children's.

Harcourt Brace Jovanovich Canada Inc: 55 Barber Greene Rd, Don Mills, Ont M3C 2A1; tel. (416) 444-7331; f. 1922; general, medical, educational, scholarly; Pres. ANTHONY W. CRAVEN.

Harlequin Enterprises Ltd; 225 Duncan Mill Rd, Don Mills, Ont M3B 3J5; tel. (416) 445-5860; f. 1949; fiction, paperbacks; Pres. D. A. GALLOWAY.

The Frederick Harris Music Co Ltd: 529 Speers Rd, Oakville, Ont L6K 2G4; tel. (416) 845-3487; f. 1904; music.

Harvest House Ltd: 1200 Atwater Ave, Suite 1, Montreal, Qué H3Z 1X4; tel. (514) 932-0666; f. 1960; history, biography, environment and social sciences; Dir MAYNARD GERTLER.

D. C. Heath Canada Ltd: 100 Adelaide St West, Suite 1600, Toronto, Ont M5H 1S9; tel. (416) 362-6483; Pres. ROBERT H. ROSS.

Holt, Rinehart and Winston of Canada Ltd: 55 Horner Ave, Toronto, Ont M8Z 4X6; tel. (416) 255-4491; f. 1904; general trade, educational, college, reference and children's; Pres. MARK STEWART.

Hosford Publishing Ltd: 17203-103 Ave, Edmonton, Alta T5S 1J4; tel. (403) 483-2683; Pres. RICK CHECKLAND.

Houghton Mifflin Canada Ltd: 150 Steelcase Rd West, Markham, Ont L3R 1B2; tel. (416) 475-1755; educational; Pres. JOHN E. CHAMP.

House of Anansi Press Ltd: 35 Britain St, Toronto, Ont M5A 1R7; tel. (416) 363-5444; f. 1967; non-fiction, contemporary social issues, belles-lettres, fiction, Canadian poetry; Publr ANN WALL.

Hurtig Publishers: 10560 105th St, Edmonton, Alta T5H 2W7; tel. (403) 426-2359; f. 1961; non-fiction, politics, Canadiana; Pres. MEL HURTIG.

Institut de Recherches Psychologiques, Inc/Institute of Psychological Research Inc: 34, ouest, rue Fleury, Montreal, Qué H3L 1S9; tel. (514) 382-3000; f. 1968; educational and psychological texts; Pres. Dr JEAN-MARC CHEVRIER.

IPI Publishing Ltd: 44 Charles St West, Suite 2704, Toronto, Ont M4Y 1R7; tel. (416) 964-6662; Pres. Dr DANIEL BAUM.

Irwin Publishing Inc: 180 West Beaver Creek Rd, Richmond Hill, Ont L4B 1B4; tel. (416) 731-3838; telex 069-64577; f. 1945; trade and educational; Pres. JOHN W. IRWIN.

Key Porter Books: 70 The Esplanade, Toronto, Ont M5E 1R2; tel. (416) 862-7777; telex 062-18092; f. 1980; general trade.

Lancelot Press Ltd: POB 425, Hantsport, NS B0P 1P0; tel. (902) 684-9129; f. 1966; non-fiction, regional.

Lester & Orpen Dennys Ltd: 78 Sullivan St, Toronto, Ont M5T 1C1; tel. (416) 593-9602; f. 1973; fiction, non-fiction, history, art, young adult, politics, social issues; Pres. MALCOLM LESTER.

Libraire Beauchemin Ltée: 381 rue St-Jacques, Bureau 400, Montreal, Qué H2Y 3S2; tel. (514) 842-1427; f. 1842; textbooks and general; Pres. GUY FRENETTE.

Lidec Inc: 825 ave Querbes, Outremont, Qué H2V 3X1; tel. (514) 274-6521; f. 1965; educational, textbooks; Pres. and Dir-Gen. MARC-AIMÉ GUÉRIN.

James Lorimer & Co Ltd: 35 Britain St, Toronto, Ont M5A 1R7; tel. (416) 362-4762; f. 1971; urban and labour studies, children's, general non-fiction.

McClelland and Stewart, Ltd: 481 University Ave, Suite 900, Toronto, Ont M5G 2E9; tel. (416) 598-1114; telex 062-18603; f. 1906; trade, illustrated and educational; Pres. A. BENETT.

McGill-Queen's University Press: 849 ouest, rue Sherbrooke, Montreal, Qué H3A 2T5; tel. (514) 392-4421; f. 1969; scholarly; Dirs PHILIP J. CERCONE, DONALD AKENSON, PETER GOHEEN.

McGraw-Hill Ryerson Ltd: 330 Progress Ave, Scarborough, Ont M1P 2Z5; tel. (416) 293-1911; telex 065-25169; f. 1944; general; Pres. M. G. RICHARDSON.

Charles E. Merrill Publishing: 230 Basmac Drive, Weston, Ont M9L 2X5; tel. (416) 746-2200; Pres LINDA TAILNE.

Methuen Publications: 150 Laird Drive, Toronto, Ont M4G 3V7; tel. (416) 425-9200; f. 1965; trade, textbooks, professional; Gen. Man. FRED D. WARDLE.

Mosaic Press: 1252 Speers Rd, Suite 10, POB 1032, Oakville, Ont L6J 5E9; tel. (416) 825-2130; f. 1974; literary and scholarly; Dir of Operations HOWARD ASTER.

Nelson Canada: 1120 Birchmount Rd, Scarborough, Ont M1K 5G4; tel. (416) 752-9100; f. 1914; textbooks; Pres. A. G. COBHAM.

Oberon Press: 401A Delta Ottawa, 350 Sparks St, Ottawa K1R 7S8; tel. (613) 238-3275; f. 1966; poetry, children's, fiction and general non-fiction.

OISE Press: Ontario Institute for Studies in Education, 252 Bloor St West, Toronto, Ont M5S 1V6; tel. (416) 923-6641, ext. 2403; telex 062-17720; f. 1965; educational texts and scholarly.

Oxford University Press: 70 Wynford Drive, Don Mills, Ont M3C 1J9; tel. (416) 441-2941; telex 069-66518; f. 1904; general, education, religious, juvenile, Canadiana; Man. Dir MICHAEL A. MORROW.

PaperJacks Ltd: 330 Steelcase Rd East, Markham, Ont L3R 2M1; tel. (416) 475-1261; f. 1971; general paperbacks; Pres. SUSAN STODDART.

Penguin Books Canada Ltd: 2801 John St, Markham, Ont L3R 1B4; tel. (416) 475-1571; telex 069-86803; f. 1974; Pres. MORTON MINT.

Pergamon Press Canada Ltd: 150 Consumers Rd, Suite 104, Willowdale, Ont M2J 1P9; tel. (416) 497-8337; f. 1965; scientific and technical journals and books; Exec. Vice-Pres. W. D. CRAWLEY.

Pontifical Institute of Mediaeval Studies: 59 Queen's Park Crescent East, Toronto, Ont M5S 2C4; tel. (416) 926-7144; f. 1939; scholarly pubs concerning the middle ages; Dir of Publs RON B. THOMSON.

Prentice Hall Canada Inc: 1870 Birchmount Rd, Scarborough, Ont M1P 2J7; tel. (416) 293-3621; telex 065-25184; f. 1960; trade, textbooks; Pres. WALLACE A. MATHESON.

Les Presses de l'Université Laval: CP 2447, Québec, Qué G1K 7R4; tel. (418) 656-3001; f. 1950; scholarly books and periodicals; Dir CLAUDE FRÉMONT.

Les Presses de l'Université de Montréal: CP 6128, succursale A, Montreal, Qué H3C 3J7; tel. (514) 343-6929; f. 1962; scholarly and general; Dir P. STEWART (acting).

Les Presses de l'Université du Québec: CP 250, Sillery, Qué G1T 2R1; tel. (418) 657-3551; telex 051-31623; f. 1969; scholarly and general; Dir-Gen. JACKI DALLAIRE.

Random House of Canada Ltd: 1265 Aerowood Drive, Mississauga, Ont L4W 1B9; tel. (416) 624-0672; f. 1944; Pres. GORDON BAIN.

Reader's Digest Association (Canada) Ltd: 215 ave Redfern, Montreal, Qué H3Z 2V9; tel. (514) 934-0751; telex 052-5800; Pres. and CEO RONALD L. COLE.

Renouf Publishing Co Ltd: 2182 ouest, rue Ste-Catherine, Montreal, Qué H3H 1M7; tel. (514) 937-3519; telex 052-68852; f. 1888; educational, maps, atlases; Pres. INGEBORG HENNINGS.

W. B. Saunders Co Canada Ltd: 1 Goldthorne Ave, Toronto, Ont M87 5T9; tel. (416) 251-3787; telex 069-67890; Vice-Pres. TREVOR JONES.

Scholastic—TAB Publications: 123 Newkirk Rd, Richmond Hill, Ont L4C 3G5; tel. (416) 883-5300; Pres. F. LARRY MULLER.

Simon & Pierre Publishing Co Ltd: POB 280, Adelaide St Postal Station, Toronto, Ont M5C 2J4; tel. (416) 363-6767; f. 1972; drama and performing arts, fiction and non-fiction; Pres. and Editor-in-Chief MARIAN M. WILSON.

Stoddart Publishing Co Ltd: 34 Lesmill Rd, Don Mills, Ont M3B 2T6; tel. (416) 445-3333; telex 069-86664; f. 1894; a division of General Publishing Co Ltd; general; Pres. and CEO JACK E. STODDART.

Talon Books Ltd: 201–1019 East Cordova St, Vancouver, BC V6A 1M8; tel. (604) 253-5261; f. 1967; fiction and non-fiction, poetry, drama.

Turnstone Press Ltd: 603-99 King St, Suite 603, Winnipeg, Man R3B 1H7; tel. (204) 947-1555; f. 1976; literary, regional; Man. Editor PATRICIA SANDERS.

University of Alberta Press: 141 Athabasca Hall, Edmonton, Alta T6G 2E8; tel. (403) 432-3662; telex 037-2979; f. 1969; scholarly, general non-fiction.

University of British Columbia Press: 303-6344 Memorial Rd, Vancouver, BC V6T 1W5; tel. (604) 228-3259; f. 1971; humanities, science, social science and scholarly journals; Exec. Dir JAMES J. ANDERSON.

University of Ottawa Press: 603 Cumberland St, Ottawa K1N 6N5; tel. (613) 564-2270; f. 1936; scholarly works in English and French; Dir RALPH HODGSON.

University of Toronto Press: Front Campus, University of Toronto, Toronto, Ont M5S 1A6; tel. (416) 667-7791; f. 1901; academic and general university texts and journals; Dir HARALD BOHNE.

Western Producer Prairie Books: POB 2500, Saskatoon, Sask S7K 2C4; tel. (306) 665-3548; f. 1954; history, biography, photography, natural history, young adult, regional interest; Man. ROB SANDERS.

John Wiley and Sons Canada Ltd: 22 Worcester Rd, Rexdale, Ont M9W 1L1; tel. (416) 675-3580; telex 069-89189; Pres. JOHN DILL.

Government Publishing House

Canadian Government Publishing Centre: Ottawa K1A 0S9; tel. (819) 997-2560; telex 053-4296; f. 1876; books and periodicals on numerous subjects, incl. agriculture, economics, environment, geology, history and sociology; Dir G. A. GOSSELIN.

ORGANIZATIONS AND ASSOCIATIONS

Association of Canadian Publishers: 70 The Esplanade, 3rd Floor, Toronto, Ont M5E 1R2; tel. (416) 361-1408; f. 1976; 136 mems; Pres. HARALD BOHNE; Exec. Dir MARCIA GEORGE.

Canadian Book Publishers' Council: 45 Charles St East, 7th Floor, Toronto, Ont M4Y 1S2; tel. (416) 964-7231; f. 1910; 50 mems; trade asscn of firms which publish and/or represent publrs in the UK and the USA; Pres. RAY LEE; Exec. Dir JACQUELINE HUSHION.

La Société de Développement du Livre et du Périodique: 1151 Alexandre-De Seve, Montreal, Qué H2L 2T7; tel. (514) 524-7528; f. 1961; Pres. GUY SAINT-JEAN; Dir-Gen. LOUISE ROCHON; constituent asscns:

  Association des Editeurs Canadiens: f. 1943; 49 mems; Pres. CAROLE LEVERT; Sec.-Gen. JOHANE GUAY-SIMARD.

  Association des Editeurs de Périodiques Culturels Québécois: tel. (514) 523-7724; f. 1978; 39 mems; Pres. RENÉ PAYANT; Sec.-Gen. FRANCINE BERGERON.

  Association des Libraires du Québec: f. 1969; 125 mems; Pres. GISÈLE CÔTÉ; Dir-Gen. LOUISE ROCHON.

  Association Nationale des Libraires Universitaires: 8 mems; Pres. GERALD G. CAZA.

  Association Québécoise des Presses Universitaires: f. 1972; 5 mems; Pres. MARC BOUCHER; Vice-Pres. (vacant).

  Société des Editeurs de Manuels Scolaires: f. 1960; 20 mems; Pres. HERVÉ FOULON; Sec.-Gen. JOHANE MÉNARD.

Radio and Television

The 1968 Broadcasting Act set out the broadcasting policy of Canada, established the Canadian Broadcasting Corporation (CBC) as the national, publicly owned, broadcasting service and created the Canadian Radio-Television and Telecommunications Commission (CRTC) as the agency regulating radio, television and cable television. The CBC is financed mainly by public funds supplemented by revenue from television advertising. Programming policy is to use predominantly Canadian creative and other resources. Services are operated in both English and French.

Radio and television service is available to over 98% of the population: 61.4% of Canadian homes subscribe to cable television and existing wiring makes this service, which is provided by 470 cable television systems, immediately available to 80% of Canadian homes. Most television programming is in colour and 84% of homes have colour TV sets.

Many privately-owned television and radio stations have affiliation agreements with the CBC and help to distribute the national services. The major private networks are CTV, TVA (which serves the province of Québec) and Global (serving the province of Ontario), as well as the educational networks.

Canadian Broadcasting Corporation (CBC): 1500 Bronson Ave, POB 8478, Ottawa K1G 3J5; tel. (613) 724-1200; telex 053-4260; f. 1936; financed mainly by public funds, with supplementary revenue from commercial advertising on CBC television; Pres. PIERRE JUNEAU; Exec. Vice-Pres. W. T. ARMSTRONG.

Canadian Radio-Television and Telecommunications Commission (CRTC): Ottawa K1A 0N2; tel. (819) 997-0313 (Information); telex 053-4253; f. 1968; regional offices in Montreal, Halifax, Winnipeg and Vancouver; Chair. ANDRÉ BUREAU; Vice-Chair. JOHN E. LAWRENCE (Telecommunications), RÉAL THERRIEN (Broadcasting).

RADIO

The CBC operates two AM and two FM networks, one each in English and French. In the north, the CBC's northern radio service provides both national network programming in English and French, and special local and short-wave programmes, some of which are broadcast in the languages of the Indian and Inuit peoples. In March 1985 there were 839 outlets for CBC radio (79 CBC-owned stations, 629 CBC-owned relay transmitters, 131 private affiliates and rebroadcasters). CBC radio service, which is virtually free of commercial advertising, is within reach of 99.5% of the population. Radio Canada International, the CBC's overseas short-wave service, broadcasts daily in 11 languages and distributes recorded programmes free for use world-wide.

TELEVISION

The CBC operates two television networks, one in English and one in French. Northern television does not yet have the capacity for local production but it supplements the national programmes it carries with English and French programmes from other regions of Canada and with broadcasting and film documentaries in the Inuktitut language. As of March 1985, CBC television was carried on 892 outlets (28 CBC-owned stations, 610 CBC-owned rebroadcasters, 254 private affiliates and rebroadcasters). CBC television is available to over 98% of the population.

Canada was the first country to establish a domestic communications satellite system with the launching of Anik A-1 in November 1972, of Anik A-2 in April 1973, of Anik A-3 in May 1975 and, finally, of Anik-B in December 1978. In August 1982 Anik D-1 was put in orbit, followed by Anik C-3 in November 1982, and Anik C-2 in June 1983. These were joined by Anik D-2 in November 1984 and Anik C-1 in April 1985. Canada's commercial communications satellites are owned and operated by Telesat Canada.

Canadian Satellite Communication Inc (CANCOM) of Toronto, Ontario, was licensed in April 1981 by the CRTC to carry on a multi-channel television and radio broadcasting operation via Anik satellite for the distribution of CTV, TVA and independent television and radio programmes (one AM and seven FM radio stations) to serve northern and remote communities. At the same time, the CRTC approved applications to broadcast television and radio programmes to native audiences in English and several Indian languages via Anik C satellites.

In April 1983 the CRTC approved an application by CANCOM to amend its network licence by adding the distribution of the signals of the three commercial (ABC, NBC, CBS) and one non-commercial (PBS) US networks for delivery to northern and remote communities. By March 1985, 387 communities had availed themselves of this service.

There are five educational services; TV-Ontario in Ontario and Radio-Québec in Québec operate their own television stations and networks; the Access network in Alberta purchases time for educational cultural programming on the private TV stations of the province; Knowledge Network is involved in the distribution, development and co-ordination of educational television programming to British Columbia communities via Anik C satellites and cable; and Saskmedia is involved in the production, acquisition and distribution of educationally-oriented media programming.

Canadian pay television has been in operation since early 1983. All of the services initially licensed have now been reorganized in one form or another. By August 1985, Canadians had access to three general interest pay television services (one French service in eastern Canada, Premier Choix/TVEC, and two regional English services: First Choice serving eastern Canada, and Allarcom serving western Canada). New speciality discretionary services, such as MuchMusic, The Sports Network, Latinovision and Chinavision became available in 1984. In March 1985, the CRTC licensed a new health channel called Life Channel. Consideration will be given to a religious channel and a youth channel. The total number of subscribers to a Canadian discretionary service represents 12.1% of potential households.

Canadian Satellite Communication Inc: 275 Slater St, Suite 1502, Ottawa K1P 5H9; tel. (613) 232-4814.

CTV Television Network: 42 Charles St East, Toronto, Ont M4Y 1T5; tel. (416) 928-6000; telex 062-2080; 21 privately-owned affiliated stations from coast to coast, with 245 rebroadcasters; covers 97% of Canadian TV households; Pres. and Man. Dir M. CHERCOVER; Exec. Vice-Pres. J. RUTTLE.

Global Television Network: 81 Barber Green Rd, Don Mills, Ont M3C 2A2; tel. (416) 446-5311; telex 069-66767; one station and five rebroadcasters serving southern Ontario; Pres. DAVID MINTZ.

Telesat Canada: 333 River Rd, Ottawa, Ont K1L 8B9; tel. (613) 746-5920; telex 053-4184; f. 1969; Chair. D. A. GOLDEN; Pres. and CEO JOHN ALMOND.

TVA: 1600 est, blvd de Maisonneuve, CP 368, succursale C, Montreal, Qué H2L 4P2; tel. (514) 526-0476; telex 055-60626; f. 1971; French-language network, with 6 stations in Québec and 23 rebroadcasters serving 98% of the province and francophone communities in Ontario and New Brunswick; Pres. and Gen. Man. CLAUDE BLAIN.

ASSOCIATION

Canadian Association of Broadcasters: 165 Sparks St, POB 627, Station B, Ottawa K1P 5S2; tel. (613) 233-4035; telex 053-3127; Pres. DAVID BOND; Exec. Vice-Pres. WAYNE A. STACEY.

Finance

(cap. = capital; p.u. = paid up; dep. = deposits; m. = million; res = reserves; brs = branches; amounts in Canadian dollars)

BANKING

The first Canadian commercial bank was founded in 1817. A further 34 banks were established over the next 50 years, and following Confederation in 1867 the Bank Act of 1871 gave the Federal Government regulatory powers over banking operations throughout Canada.

The Bank Act of 1980 reorganized the banking structure by creating two categories of banking institution: 'Schedule A' banks, comprising the existing chartered banks; and 'Schedule B' banks, which are either subsidiaries of foreign banks (whose total Canadian assets cannot exceed 16% of those of the banking system in total), or Canadian-owned banks under private or semi-private ownership. The Act, which is subject to review at 10-year intervals to allow for changes in government policy and economic conditions, strictly limits the range of permitted operations outside the banking sphere, in order to curtail competition beteween banks and commercial enterprises. In July 1986 there were 10 'Schedule A' banks (of which no individual shareholder may control more than 10%) and 55 'Schedule B' banks.

The Bank of Canada, established as the central bank in 1934 and controlled by the Federal Government, implements government monetary and credit policies through the commercial banks. It operates the banks' clearing system and also holds the banks' primary and secondary reserves. Direct regulatory inspections of the commercial banks are carried out by the Ministry of Finance, and a federal agency insures individual deposits up to a limit of C $60,000.

At the end of 1985, there were 7,014 commercial bank branches holding deposits totalling C $188,427m. The banks' combined assets

CANADA

Directory

totalled C $441,208m., of which 45.5% were represented by foreign currency assets, reflecting the importance of international business in Canadian banking.

Trust and loan companies, which were originally formed to deal with mortgage finance and private customer loans, now play an important role in the banking system, offering current account facilities and providing access to money transfer services.

Central Bank

Bank of Canada: 234 Wellington St, Ottawa K1A 0G9; tel. (613) 563-8111; telex 053-4241; f. 1934; cap. and res 30m., dep. 2,888.3m. (Dec. 1985); Gov. JOHN W. CROW; Sr Dep. Gov. (vacant).

Principal Commercial Banks

Bank of Alberta: 10040–140th St, Edmonton, Alta T5J 3X6; tel. (403) 423-5555; f. 1984; total assets 106.4m. (Oct. 1985); Chair. and CEO FRED SPARROW; Pres. and Chief Operating Officer ROBERT A. SPLAINE.

Bank of British Columbia: 1725 Two Bentall Centre, 555 Burrard St, Vancouver, BC V7X 1K1; tel. (604) 668-4499; telex 045-08877; f. 1968; total assets 2,880m. (July 1986); Chair. and CEO EDGAR F. KAISER, Jr; 41 brs.

Bank of Montreal: 129 rue St-Jacques, CP 6002, Montreal, Qué H3C 3B1; tel. (514) 877-7110; telex 052-67661; f. 1817; cap. and res 2,945.5m., dep. 66,671.4m (Oct. 1985); Chair. and CEO WILLIAM D. MULHOLLAND.

The Bank of Nova Scotia (Scotiabank): 44 King St West, Toronto, Ont M5H 1H1; tel. (416) 866-6161; telex 062-2106; f. 1832; cap. and res 2,598m., dep. 52,704m. (Oct. 1985); Chair. and CEO C. E. RITCHIE; Dep. Chair., Pres. and Chief Operating Officer J. A. G. BELL.

Canadian Imperial Bank of Commerce: Commerce Court, Toronto, Ont M5L 1A2; tel. (416) 980-2211; telex 065-24116; f. 1961; cap. and res 3,351.5m., dep. 65,087.6m. (Oct. 1985); Chair. RUSSELL E. HARRISON; Pres. and CEO R. DONALD FULLERTON.

Continental Bank of Canada: Continental Bank Bldg, 130 Adelaide St West, Toronto, Ont M5H 3R2; tel. (416) 868-8000; telex 065-24098; f. 1979; cap. and res 271.2m., dep. 4,639.9m. (Oct. 1984); Chair. S. F. MELLOY; Pres. and CEO DAVID A. LEWIS.

National Bank of Canada: 600 ouest, rue de la Gauchetière, Montreal, Qué H3B 4L2; tel. (514) 394-4000; telex 052-5181; f. 1979; cap. and res 547.9m., dep. 16,549.7m. (Oct. 1984); Chair. and CEO MICHEL BÉLANGER; Pres. and Chief Operating Officer ANDRÉ BERARD.

The Royal Bank of Canada: 1 place Ville Marie, CP 6001, Montreal, Qué H3C 3A9; tel. (514) 874-2110; telex 055-61086; f. 1869; cap. and res 1,749.5m., dep. 77,588.3m. (Oct. 1984); Chair. ALLAN TAYLOR.

The Toronto-Dominion Bank: POB 1, Toronto Dominion Centre, 55 King St West and Bay St, Toronto, Ont M5K 1A2; tel. (416) 982-8222; telex 065-24267; f. 1856; cap. and res 852.9m., dep. 40,670m. (Oct. 1984); Chair. and CEO RICHARD M. THOMSON; Pres. R. W. KORTHALS.

Savings Banks with Federal Charters

Montreal City & District Savings Bank: 262 ouest, rue St-Jacques, Montreal, Qué H2Y 1N2; tel. (514) 284-3970; telex 052-4217; f. 1846; cap. p.u. 3m.; Chair. and CEO RAYMOND GARNEAU; Gen. Man. PIERRE GOYETTE; 117 brs.

Province of Alberta Treasury Branches: POB 1440, 9925-109 St, Edmonton, Alta T5J 2N6; tel. (403) 427-6068; telex 037-43122; f. 1938; assets 4,520m., dep. 4,527m. (March 1986); Supt A. O. BRAY; 130 brs.

Province of Ontario Savings Office: 33 King St West, 6th Floor, Oshawa, Ont L1H 8H5; tel. (416) 433-5785; f. 1921; Dir J. L. ALLEN; 21 brs.

Development Bank

Federal Business Development Bank: 800 Victoria Sq., BP 335, Tour de la Bourse, Montreal, Qué H4Z 1L4; tel. (514) 283-5904; f. 1975; auth. cap. 475m. (1984); Pres. G. A. LAVIGUEUR.

Principal Trust and Loan Companies

Canada Permanent Mortgage Corporation and Canada Permanent Trust Company: 320 Bay St, Toronto, Ont M5H 2P6; tel. (416) 361-8000; telex 062-17799; f. 1855; combined assets 6,938m. (1982); Chair., Pres. and CEO J. A. C. HILLIKER.

Canada Trustco Mortgage Co (The Canada Trust Co): POB 5703, Terminal A, London, Ont N6A 4S4; tel. (519) 663-1400; telex 064-7575; total assets 12,800m. (June 1985); Pres. and CEO M. L. LAHN; Chair. ARTHUR H. MINGAY.

Central Trust Co: 1801 Hollis St, POB 2343, Halifax, NS B3J 3C8; tel. (902) 425-7390; telex 019-22578; f. 1980; total assets 2,800m. (1984); Pres. and CEO STRUAN ROBERTSON.

Crédit Foncier: 612 rue St-Jacques, Montreal, Qué H3C 1E1; tel. (514) 392-1880; telex 052-68622; f. 1880; total assets 2,700m. (July 1985); Chair. CLAUDE CASTONGUAY; Pres. and CEO MICHEL M. LESSARD.

Guaranty Trust Company of Canada: 366 Bay St, Toronto, Ont M5H 2W5; tel. (416) 975-4500; telex 065-24107; f. 1925; total assets 3,603.2m. (1985); Pres. and CEO ALAN R. MARCHMENT.

Montreal Trust: 1 place Ville Marie, Montreal, Qué H3B 3L6; tel. (514) 397-7000; telex 055-61286; f. 1889; total assets 1,861.1m. (1983); Chair. and Pres. ROBERT GRATTON.

National Trust Co Ltd: 18 King St East, Toronto, Ont M5C 1C4; tel. (416) 364-9141; telex 062-2028; f. 1898; total assets 2,787m. (1982); Chair. and CEO J. L. A. COLHOUN.

The National Victoria and Grey Trust Co: 1 Ontario St, Stratford, Ont N5A 6S9; f. 1844; total assets 7,800m. (1984); Pres. J. C. C. WANSBROUGH; Chair. and CEO WILLIAM H. SOMERVILLE.

Royal Trustco Ltd: Royal Trust Tower, Toronto-Dominion Centre, Toronto, Ont M5H 1A2; tel. (416) 867-2000; telex 065-24306; f. 1892; total assets 7,065.9m. (1979); Chair. HARTLAND M. MACDOUGALL; Pres. and CEO MICHAEL A. CORNELISSEN.

Trust Général du Canada: 1100 rue Université, Montreal, Qué H3B 2G7; tel. (514) 871-7180; telex 055-61407; f. 1928; cap. and res 94m., total assets 3,038m. (1985); Pres. and CEO MAURICE JODOIN.

Bankers' Organizations

The Canadian Bankers' Association: 2 First Canadian Place, POB 348, Toronto, Ont M5X 1E1; tel. (416) 362-6092; telex 062-3402; f. 1891; Chair. A. BÉRARD; Pres. ROBERT M. MACINTOSH; 65 mems.

Trust Companies Association of Canada Inc: Herbert House, 335 Bay St, 7th Floor, Toronto, Ont M5H 2R3; Pres. W. W. POTTER; Dir of Admin. and Sec. J. SAYERS.

STOCK EXCHANGES

Alberta Stock Exchange: 300 Fifth Ave SW, Calgary, Alta T2P 3C4; tel. (403) 262-7791; telex 038-21793; f. 1914; 41 mems; Pres. R. J. MILLIKEN.

The Montreal Exchange: CP 61, 800 place Victoria, Montreal, Qué H4Z 1A9; tel. (514) 871-2424; telex 055-60586; f. 1874; 76 mems; Pres. and CEO (vacant).

Toronto Stock Exchange: The Exchange Tower, 2 First Canadian Place, Toronto, Ont M5X 1J2; tel. (416) 947-4700; telex 062-17759; f. 1852; 73 mems; Pres. J. P. BUNTING.

Vancouver Stock Exchange: Stock Exchange Tower, POB 10333, 609 Granville St, Vancouver, BC V7Y 1H1; tel. (604) 689-3334; telex 045-5480; f. 1907; 48 mems; Chair. G. G. FABBRO; Pres. D. J. HUDSON.

Winnipeg Stock Exchange: 955-167 Lombard Ave, Winnipeg, Man R3B 0V3; tel. (204) 942-8431; 19 mems; Pres. S. D. COHEN.

INSURANCE

Principal Companies

Abbey Life Insurance Co of Canada: 3027 Harvester Rd, Burlington, Ont L7N 3G9; Pres. W. D. MILLAR.

Antigonish Farmers' Mutual Fire Insurance Co: POB 1535, Antigonish, NS B2G 2L8; f. 1910; Man. D. J. CHISHOLM.

Blue Cross Life Insurance Co: POB 220, Moncton, NB E1C 8L3; tel. (506) 853-1811; telex 014-2233; Sec. D. R. LENNOX.

Canada Life Assurance Co: 330 University Ave, Toronto, Ont M5G 1R8; f. 1847; Pres. E. H. CRAWFORD.

Canada Security Assurance Co: 60 Yonge St, Toronto, Ont M5E 1H5; tel. (416) 362-2961; telex 062-19667; f. 1913; Pres. R. H. STEVENS.

Canadian General Insurance Co: POB 4030, Terminal A, Toronto, Ont M5W 1K4; f. 1907; Pres. R. E. BETHELL.

Canadian Home Assurance Co: 465 ouest, blvd Dorchester, Montreal, Qué H2Z 1A8; tel. (514) 866-6531; telex 052-5169; f. 1928; Pres. J. P. LUSSIER.

Canadian Indemnity Co: 165 University Ave, Toronto, Ont M5H 3B9; tel. (416) 865-0182; telex 062-19747; f. 1912; Pres. H. B. VANNAN.

CANADA

The Canadian Surety Co: Canada Sq., 2180 Yonge St, Toronto, Ont M4S 2C2; tel. (416) 486-2800; telex 065-24212; Pres. and Gen. Man. J. ROBERTSON.

Century Insurance Co of Canada: 1155 West Pender St, Vancouver, BC V6E 2P4; tel. (604) 683-0255; f. 1890; Pres. J. B. MURCH.

Confederation Life Insurance Co: 321 Bloor St East, Toronto, Ont M4W 1H1; f. 1871; Pres. P. D. BURNS.

Les Coopérants, société mutuelle d'assurance-vie, et les coopérants, compagne d'assurance générale: 333 est, rue St-Antoine, Montreal, Qué H2X 1R9; tel. (514) 287-6500; telex 052-67402; f. 1876; Pres. PIERRE SHOONER.

Crown Life Insurance Co: 120 Bloor St East, Toronto, Ont M4W 1B8; tel. (416) 928-4500; telex 062-22651; f. 1900; Chair. H. M. BURNS; Pres. A. E. MORSON.

Dominion Insurance Corpn: POB 4024, Terminal A, Toronto, Ont M5W 1K1; f. 1904; Pres. and Gen. Man. W. W. WARD.

Dominion of Canada General Insurance Co: 165 University Ave, Toronto, Ont M5H 3B9; f. 1887; Pres. D. A. WAUGH.

Eaton Life Assurance Co: 595 Bay St, Toronto, Ont M5G 2C6; f. 1920; Chair. R. BRETON; Pres. R. E. BROWN.

Economical Mutual Insurance Co: POB 700, Kitchener, Ont N2G 4C1; Pres. and Gen. Man. J. T. HILL.

Excelsior Life Insurance Co: 145 King St West, Toronto, Ont M5H 3T7; f. 1889; Chair. and CEO G. N. FARQUHAR.

Federation Insurance Co of Canada: 1080 Beaver Hall Hill, 20th Floor, Montreal, Qué H2Z 1S8; tel. (514) 875-5790; telex 055-61701; f. 1947; Pres. W. J. GREEN.

General Accident Assurance Co of Canada: The Exchange Tower, Suite 2600, 2 First Canadian Place, POB 410, Toronto, Ont M5X 1J1; tel. (416) 368-4733; telex 065-24272; f. 1906; Pres. LEONARD G. LATHAM.

Gerling Global General Insurance Co: 480 University Ave, Toronto, Ont M5G 1V6; tel. (416) 598-4651; telex 065-24108; f. 1955; Pres. Dr R. R. KERN.

Gore Mutual Insurance Co: 252 Dundas St, Cambridge, Ont N1R 5T3; tel. (519) 623-1910; telex 069-59304; f. 1839; Sec. J. M. GRAY.

Grain Insurance and Guarantee Co: 167 Lombard Ave, Suite 906, Winnipeg, Man R3B 0V9; f. 1919; Pres. and Gen. Man. A. C. AFFLECK.

The Great-West Life Assurance Co: 100 Osborne St North, Winnipeg, Man R3C 3A5; tel. (204) 946-1190; telex 075-7519; f. 1891; Pres. and CEO K. P. KAVANAGH.

Le Groupe Commerce, compagnie d'assurances: 2450 ouest, blvd Girouard, St-Hyacinthe, Qué J2S 3B3; f. 1907; Pres. and CEO GUY ST-GERMAIN.

Guardian Insurance Co of Canada: POB 4096, Station A, Toronto, Ont M5N 1N1; f. 1911; Chair. GEORGE ALEXANDER; Pres. N. CURTIS.

Halifax Insurance Co: 75 Eglinton Ave East, Toronto, Ont M4P 3A3; tel. (416) 440-1000; f. 1809; Pres. and CEO J. N. MCCARTHY.

Halifax Life Insurance Co: 75 Eglinton Ave East, Toronto, Ont M4P 3A3; tel. (416) 440-1000; f. 1911; Pres. H. J. HAFEMAN.

Imperial Life Assurance Co of Canada: 95 St Clair Ave West, Toronto, Ont M4V 1N7; tel. (416) 926-2600; f. 1896; Chair., Pres. and CEO CLAUDE BRUNEAU.

Kings Mutual Insurance Co: Berwick, NS B0P 1E0; f. 1904; Pres. C. ELLIOTT; Man. D. C. COOK.

Le Groupe La Laurentienne: 500 est, Grande-Allée, Québec, Qué G1R 2J7; Chair. and CEO CLAUDE CASTONGUAY.

Comprises the following companies in Canada:
La Laurentienne, mutuelle d'Assurance;
La Corporation du Groupe La Laurentienne;
Laurentienne Générale, Compagnie d'Assurances;
Le Bouclier Laurentien, Compagnie d'Assurances;
Le Fonds Laurentien Inc;
Imperial Life Insurance Co of Canada;
Laurentienne Agricole, Compagnie d'Assurance Inc;
La Laurentienne du Pacifique Compagnie d'Assurances;
Banque d'Epasgne de la Cité et du District du Montréal;
The Personal Insurance Co of Canada;
Les Fiduciaires de la Cité et du District de Montréal;
Yorkshire Trust Co;
La Compagnie d'Assurance—Vie Laurier;
Les Immeubles Imbrook Ltd;
Gestion Geoffrion Leclerc Inc;
Fonds F-I-C Inc;
Canagex Placements Ltd;
Les Services de santé Impco Ltd.

London Life Insurance Co: 255 Dufferin Ave, London, Ont N6A 4K1; tel. (519) 432-5281; f. 1874; Pres. and CEO EARL H. ORSER; Chair. A. T. LAMBERT.

Manufacturers Life Insurance Co: 200 Bloor St East, Toronto, Ont M4W 1E5; tel. (416) 926-0100; telex 062-17896; f. 1887; Pres. T. A. D. GIACOMO; Chair. and CEO E. S. JACKSON.

Mercantile and General Reinsurance Co of Canada: University Place, 123 Front St West, Toronto, Ont M5J 2M7; f. 1951; Pres. D. M. BATTEN.

Missisquoi and Rouville Insurance Co: 30 Principale, Frelighsburg, Qué J0J 1C0; tel. (514) 298-5251; f. 1835; Pres. and Gen. Man. J. P. COURTEMANCHE.

Montreal Life Insurance Co: 630 ouest, rue Sherbrooke, Montreal, Qué H3A 1E4; f. 1908; Pres. N. BAUER.

The Mutual Life Assurance Co of Canada: 227 King St South, Waterloo, Ont N2J 4C5, f. 1870; Chair. J. H. PANABAKER; Pres. and CEO JACK V. MASTERMAN.

The National Life Assurance Co of Canada: 522 University Ave, Toronto, Ont M5G 1Y7; tel. (416) 598-2122; telex 062-17894; f. 1897; Pres. and CEO C. T. P. GALLOWAY.

North American Life Assurance Co: 333 Broadway Ave, Winnipeg, Man R3C 0S9; tel. (204) 949-1660; f. 1881; Chair. D. G. PAYNE; Pres. HAROLD THOMPSON.

Northern Life Assurance Co of Canada: POB 2457, 380 Wellington St, Suite 1700, London, Ont; f. 1894; Pres. and CEO G. L. BOWIE; Chair. R. C. BROWN.

Portage La Prairie Mutual Insurance Co: Portage La Prairie, Man; tel. (204) 857-3415; f. 1884; Pres. E. M. BROWN; Gen. Man. H. G. OWENS.

The Laurentian General Insurance Co Ltd: 1100 ouest, Dorchester, Montreal, Qué H3B 4P4; tel. (514) 392-6174; telex 055-60752; Pres. JEAN BOUCHARD.

Québec Assurance Co: 10 Wellington St East, Toronto, Ont M5E 1L5; f. 1818; Pres. J. ROBITAILLE.

Saskatchewan Government Insurance: 2260 11th Ave, Regina, Sask S4P 0J9; tel. (306) 565-1200; telex 071-2417; f. 1945; Pres. ALEX G. WILDE.

La Sauvegarde Compagnie d'assurance sur la vie: 1 complexe Desjardins, Montreal, Qué H5B 1E2; f. 1901; Pres. HENRI LEBLOND; Dir-Gen. SERGE BEAUDOIN.

Seaboard Life Assurance Co: 2165 West Broadway, Vancouver, BC V6K 4N5; tel. (604) 734-1667; telex 045-5319; f. 1912; Pres. J. S. M. CUNNINGHAM.

Société Nationale d'Assurances: 425 ouest, De Maisonneuve, Bureau 1500, Montreal, Qué H3A 3G5; tel. (514) 288-8711; telex 055-61190; f. 1940; Pres. and Dir-Gen. HENRI JOLI-COEUR.

The Sovereign Life Assurance Co of Canada: POB 210, Main Depot, Calgary, Alta T2P 2H6; tel. (403) 292-1500; telex 038-25817; f. 1902; Pres. J. H. WALSH.

The Stanstead and Sherbrooke Insurance Co: Toronto Dominion Centre, POB 441, Toronto, Ont M5K 1L9; f. 1835; Pres. HAROLD B. GREER.

Sun Life Assurance Co of Canada: POB 4150, Station A, Toronto, Ont M5W 2C9; tel. (416) 979-9966; telex 065-24389; f. 1865; Chair. and CEO T. M. GALT; Pres. JOHN GARDNER.

Toronto Mutual Life Insurance Co: 112 St Clair Ave West, Toronto, Ont M4V 2Y3; Pres. JOHN T. ENGLISH; Chair. WALTER B. THOMPSON.

Travelers Canada: Travelers Tower, 400 University Ave, Toronto, Ont M5G 1S7; Pres. and CEO DANIEL DAMOV.

United Canadian Shares Ltd: 1661 Portage Ave, Winnipeg, Man R3J 3V8; f. 1951; Chair. R. H. JONES; Pres. C. S. RILEY, Jr.

Victoria Insurance Co of Canada: 150 Eglinton Ave East, Toronto, Ont M4P 2C3; tel. (416) 488-5999; telex 062-2237; Chair. and CEO R. W. BROUGHTON.

Waterloo Insurance Co: 14 Erb St West, POB 1604, Waterloo, Ont N2J 4C8; f. 1863; Gen. Man. K. I. TYERS.

Wawanesa Mutual Insurance Co: 191 Broadway, Winnipeg,

CANADA

Man R3C 3P1; tel. (204) 985-3811; telex 075-7564; f. 1896; Pres. I. M. MONTGOMERY.

Western Assurance Co: 10 Wellington St East, Toronto, Ont M5E 1L5; tel. (416) 366-7511; f. 1851; Pres. J. ROBITAILLE.

Western Life Assurance Co: POB 67, Hamilton, Ont L8N 3B3; f. 1910; Chair. ROBERT SHAW; Pres. and CEO C. RONALD PEARSALL.

York Fire and Casualty Insurance Co: 7501 Keele St, Suite 300, Concord, Ont L4K 1Y2; tel. (416) 738-1707; telex 069-64754; Pres. ALEXANDER A. THAIN.

Zurich Life Insurance Co of Canada: 188 University Ave, Toronto, Ont M5H 3C4; tel. (416) 593-4444; Pres. and CEO P. D. MCGARRY.

Insurance Organizations

Canadian Federation of Insurance Agents and Brokers Association: 69 Yonge St, Suite 1306, Toronto, Ont M5E 1K3; tel. (416) 367-1831; f. 1920; Pres. MARSHALL J. STEWART.

Canadian Life and Health Insurance Association: 20 Queen St West, Suite 2500, Toronto, Ont M5H 3S2; tel. (416) 977-2221; f. 1894; Pres. G. M. DEVLIN; 109 mem. cos.

Insurance Bureau of Canada: 181 University Ave, 13th Floor, Toronto, Ont M5H 3M7; tel. (416) 362-2031; Pres. J. L. LYNDON; Gen. Man. C. L. WILCKEN; 180 corporate mems.

Insurance Institute of Canada: 481 University Ave, 6th Floor, Toronto, Ont M5G 2E9; tel. (416) 591-1572; f. 1952; Chair. L. BERGERON; Pres. J. C. RHIND; 25,000 mems.

Insurers' Advisory Organization Inc: 180 Dundas St West, Toronto, Ont M5G 1Z9; tel. (416) 597-1200; f. 1855; Pres. and CEO E. F. BELTON; Sr Vice-Pres. and Chief Actuary H. J. PHILLIPS; 60 mems.

Life Insurance Institute of Canada: 20 Queen St, Suite 2500, Toronto, Ont M5H 3S2; tel. (416) 977-2221; Sec.-Treas. DEBBIE COLE-GAUER.

Life Underwriters' Association of Canada: 41 Lesmill Rd, Don Mills, Ont M3B 2T3; tel. (416) 444-5251; f. 1906; Exec. Vice-Pres. and Chief Operating Officer A. W. LINGARD; 21,000 mems.

Trade and Industry

CHAMBER OF COMMERCE

The Canadian Chamber of Commerce: 200 Elgin St, Suite 301, Ottawa K2P 2J7; tel. (613) 238-4000; telex 053-3051; f. 1925; mems: 500 community chambers of commerce and boards of trade, 80 nat. trade asscns and 4,000 business corpns; affiliated with all provincial chambers of commerce and with International Chamber and other bilateral orgs; Chair. L. R. MCGINNIS; Pres. R. B. HAMEL.

INDUSTRIAL ASSOCIATIONS

There are about 2,000 trades associations in Canada.

The Canadian Manufacturers' Association: One Yonge St, Toronto, Ont M5E 1J9; tel. (416) 363-7261; telex 065-24693; f. 1871; the nat. organization of mfrs of Canada; 8,000 mems; Pres and Exec. Dir J. L. THIBAULT.

Agriculture and Horticulture

Agricultural Institute of Canada: 151 Slater St, Suite 907, Ottawa K1P 5H4; tel. (613) 232-9459; f. 1920; 36 brs; 9 provincial sections; 9 affiliated societies; Gen. Man. A. O. TERAUDS.

Alberta Wheat Pool: POB 2700, 505-2nd St SW, Calgary, Alta T2P 2P5; tel. (403) 290-4910; telex 038-21643; Pres. A. J. MACPHERSON.

Canada Grains Council: 760-360 Main St, Winnipeg, Man R3C 3Z3; tel. (204) 942-2254; f. 1969; Pres. Dr DONALD A. DEVER.

Canadian Federation of Agriculture: 111 Sparks St, Ottawa, K1P 5B5; tel. (613) 236-9997; f. 1935; 14 mems (9 provincial feds); Pres. D. A. KNOERR; Exec. Sec. DAVID KIRK.

Canadian Horticultural Council: 3 Amberwood Crescent, Nepean, Ont K2E 7L1; tel. (613) 226-4187; telex 053-3690; f. 1922; Exec. Vice-Pres. D. DEMPSTER.

Canadian Nursery Trades Association: 1293 Matheson Blvd, Mississauga, Ont L4W 1R1; tel. (416) 629-1367; Exec. Dir ROBERT W. CHEESMAN.

Canadian Seed Growers' Association: POB 8455, Ottawa K1G 3T1; tel. (613) 236-0497; f. 1904; Exec. Dir W. K. ROBERTSON; 6,000 mems.

Directory

Canadian Society of Agricultural Engineering: 151 Slater St, Suite 907, Ottawa K1P 5H4; tel. (613) 232-9459.

Dairy Farmers of Canada: 111 Sparks St, Ottawa K1P 5B5; tel. (613) 236-9997; f. 1934; Exec. Sec. RICHARD DOYLE; 22 mem. asscns.

National Dairy Council of Canada: 704-141 Laurier Ave West, Ottawa K1P 5J3; tel. (613) 238-4116; Pres. KEMPTON L. MATTE; 250 mems.

National Farmers Union: 250c 2nd Ave South, Saskatoon, Sask S7K 2M1; tel. (306) 652-9465; 6 regional offices; Exec. Sec. STUART THIESSON.

L'Union des Producteurs agricoles: 555 blvd Roland-Therrien, Longueuil, Qué J4H 3Y9; tel. (514) 679-0530; f. 1924; Sec.-Gen. JEAN-CLAUDE BLANCHETTE; 50,000 mems.

Building and Construction

Canadian Construction Association: 85 Albert St, Ottawa K1P 6A4; tel. (613) 236-9455; telex 053-4436; f. 1918; Chair. HENRY J. F. VANDERNOOT; Pres. ROBERT E. NUTH; over 25,000 mems.

Canadian Institute of Steel Construction: 201 Consumers Rd, Suite 300, Willowdale, Ont M2J 4G8; tel. (416) 491-4552; telex 069-86547; Pres. H. A. KRENTZ; 50 mems.

Canadian Paint and Coatings Association/L'Association canadienne de l'industrie de la peinture et du revêtement: 515 St Catherine St West, Suite 825, Montreal, Qué H3B 1B4; tel. (514) 285-6381; f. 1913; Pres. R. W. MURRY; 90 mems.

Construction Specifications Canada: 1 St Clair Ave West, Suite 1206, Toronto, Ont M4V 1K6; tel. (416) 922-3159; f. 1954; Exec. Vice-Pres. RENÉ GAULIN; 1,450 mems.

National Concrete Producers' Association: 1013 Wilson Ave, Suite 101, Downsview, Ont M3K 1G1; tel. (416) 635-7179; Pres. J. ROCHELEAU; Exec. Dir MARK PATAMIA.

Ontario Painting Contractors Association: 150 Consumers Rd, Suite 508, Willowdale, Ont M2J 1P9; tel. (416) 498-1897; Exec. Dir K. EDGAR.

Clothing and Textiles

Apparel Manufacturers' Association of Ontario: 1179 King St West, Suite 117, Toronto, Ont M6K 3C5; tel. (416) 531-5707; f. 1970; Exec. Dir F. J. BRYAN; 79 mems.

Canadian Allied Textile Trades Association: 49 Front St East, Toronto, Ont M5E 1B3; tel. (416) 363-4266; telex 062-3441.

Canadian Carpet Institute: 130 Slater St, Suite 325, Ottawa K1P 6E2; tel. (613) 232-7183; telex 053-4741; f. 1961; Pres. D. S. EDWARDS.

Canadian Textiles Institute: 280 Albert St, Suite 502, Ottawa K1P 5G8; tel. (613) 232-7195; telex 053-4290; Pres. E. L. BARRY; 4 affiliated asscns.

The Shoe Manufacturers' Association of Canada: 1010 St Catherine St West, Suite 710, Montreal, Qué H3B 3R4; telex 052-68671; f. 1918; Pres. JEAN-GUY MAHEU; Exec. Sec. PIERRE ROBILLARD; 137 mems.

Tanners Association of Canada: 50 River St, Toronto, Ont M5A 3N9; tel. (416) 364-2134; Exec. Vice-Pres. IAN C. KENNEDY.

Electrical and Electronics

Canadian Electrical Association: 1 Westmount Sq., Suite 500, Montreal, Qué H3Z 2P9; tel. (514) 937-6181; telex 052-67401; f. 1891; Pres. WALLACE S. READ.

Electrical and Electronic Manufacturers Association of Canada: 10 Carlson Court, Suite 500, Rexdale, Ont M9W 6L2; tel. (416) 674-7410; Pres. D. E. P. ARMOUR; Chair. of Board E. B. PRIESTNER; 230 mems.

Electrical Bureau of Canada: 10 Carlson Court, Suite 500, Rexdale, Ont M9W 6L2; tel. (416) 674-7410.

Fisheries

Canadian Association of Fish Exporters: 77 Metcalfe St, Suite 509, Ottawa K1P 5L6; tel. (613) 232-6325; telex 053-4556.

Fisheries Association of British Columbia: 100 West Pender St, Room 400, Vancouver, BC V6B 1R8; tel. (604) 684-6454; telex 045-08441; Chair. J. B. BUCHANAN; Pres. M. HUNTER.

Fisheries Council of Canada: 77 Metcalfe St, Suite 505, Ottawa K1P 5L6; tel. (613) 238-775; telex 053-4556; Pres. R. W. BULMER; 6 mem. asscns, 173 mem. cos, 97 assoc. mem. cos.

Food and Beverages

Bakery Council of Canada: 415 Yonge St, 10th Floor, Toronto, Ont M5B 2E7; tel. (416) 598-8190; Man. Dir CHARLES W. TISDALL.

CANADA

Brewers Association of Canada: 155 Queen St, Suite 1200, Ottawa K1P 6L1; tel. (613) 232-9601; telex 053-61056; f. 1943; Pres. R. A. MORRISON; Sec. Mrs F. T. BAMFORD.

Canadian Food Brokers Association: 50 River St, Toronto, Ont M5A 3N9; tel. (416) 368-5921; Pres. IAN C. KENNEDY.

Canadian Frozen Food Association: 1306 Wellington St, Suite 303, Ottawa K1Y 3B2; tel. (613) 728-6306; telex 053-3644; Exec. Dir C. J. KYTE.

Canadian Grocery Distributors' Institute: 750 blvd Laurentien, Bureau 475, Montreal, Qué H4M 2M4; tel. (514) 747-6566; f. 1919; Pres. RAYMOND C. BERTRAND; Exec. Vice-Pres. CLAUDE PIGEON; 433 mems.

Canadian Meat Council: 5233 Dundas St West, Islington, Ont M9B 1A6; tel. (416) 239-8411; f. 1919; Gen. Man. D. M. ADAMS; 83 mems.

Canadian National Millers' Association: 155 Queen St, Suite 1101, Ottawa K1P 6L1; tel. (613) 238-2293; telex 053-3964; f. 1920; Chair. ALLAN H. JAMES; Sec. STEPHEN P. MARKEY; 19 mems.

Canadian Pork Council: 111 Sparks St, Ottawa K1P 5B5; tel. (613) 236-3633; Pres. H. MALCOLM; Exec. Sec. WILLIAM HAMILTON; 10 mem. asscns.

Confectionery Manufacturers Association of Canada: 1185 Eglinton Ave East, Don Mills, Ont M3C 3C6; tel. (416) 429-1046; f. 1919; Pres. IRENE A. GIBB; mems: 26 active, 50 associate, 2 affiliates.

Grocery Products Manufacturers of Canada: 56 Sparks St, Suite 800, Ottawa K1P 5A9; tel. (613) 236-0583; Pres. GEORGE FLEISCHMANN.

Forestry, Lumber and Allied Industries

Canadian Forestry Association: 185 Somerset St West, Ottawa K2P 0J2; tel. (613) 232-1815; f. 1900; Pres. W. K. FULLERTON; Exec. Dir A. D. HALL.

Canadian Lumbermen's Association: 27 Goulburn Ave, Ottawa K1N 8C7; tel. (613) 233-6205; telex 053-4519; f. 1908; Exec. Dir J. F. MCCRACKEN; 400 mems.

Canadian Lumber Standards: 1475-1055 West Hastings St, Vancouver, BC V6E 2E9; tel. (604) 687-2171.

Canadian Pulp and Paper Association: Sun Life Bldg, 23rd Floor, 1155 Metcalfe St, Montreal, Qué H3B 2X9; tel. (514) 866-6621; telex 055-60690; f. 1913; Pres. HOWARD HART; Exec. Vice-Pres. and Treas. GORDON MINNES; 64 mems.

Ontario Forest Industries Association: 130 Adelaide St West, Suite 1700, Toronto, Ont M5H 3P5; tel. (416) 368-6188; telex 065-24407; f. 1943; Pres. I. D. BIRD; Man. R. B. LOUGHLAN; 24 mems.

Québec Forest Industries Association Ltd: 1155 Claire-Fontaine, Bureau 1300, Québec, Qué G1R 3B2; tel. (418) 522-4027; f. 1924; Pres. and Dir-Gen. ANDRÉ DUCHESNE; 27 mems.

Hotels and Catering

Canadian Restaurant and Foodservices Association: Nu-West Center, 80 Bloor St West, Suite 1201, Toronto, Ont M5S 2V1; tel. (416) 923-8416; f. 1944; Exec. Vice-Pres. D. NEEDHAM.

Hotel Association of Canada Inc: 34 Ross St, Toronto, Ont M5T 1Z9; tel. (416) 596-7676; Pres. ADAM BOROVICH.

Mining

Canadian Gas Association: 55 Scarsdale Rd, Don Mills, Ont M3B 2R3; tel. (416) 447-6465; telex 069-66824; Pres. IAN C. MC NABB.

Canadian Petroleum Association: 633 Sixth Ave SW, Suite 1500, Calgary, Alta T2P 2Y5; tel. (403) 269-6721; Exec. Dir IAN R. SMYTH.

Mining Association of Canada: 350 Sparks St, Suite 809, Ottawa K1R 7S8; tel. (613) 233-9391; Man. Dir C. GEORGE MILLER.

Northwest Territories Chamber of Mines: POB 2818, Yellowknife, NWT X1A 2R1; tel. (403) 873-5281; f. 1967.

Ontario Mining Association: 111 Richmond St West, Suite 1114, Toronto, Ont M5H 2G4; tel. (416) 364-9301; f. 1920; Pres. C. H. BREHAUT; Exec. Dir T. P. REID; 35 mems.

Yukon Chamber of Mines: POB 4427, Whitehorse, Yukon Y1A 3T5; tel. (403) 667-2090.

Pharmaceutical

Canadian Cosmetic, Toiletry and Fragrance Association: 24 Merton St, Toronto, Ont M4S 1A1; tel. (416) 487-8111; f. 1928; Pres. KENNETH W. BAKER; Vice-Pres. SHARRON WISSLER; 290 corporate mems.

Canadian Drug Manufacturers Association: 60 St Clair Ave East, Suite 306, Toronto, Ont M4T 1N5; tel. (416) 960-3349; Chair. LUCIANO CALENTI; Exec. Dir DEBRA EKLOVE.

Pharmaceutical Manufacturers Association of Canada: 1111 Prince of Wales Drive, Ottawa, K2C 3T2; tel. (613) 236-9993; f. 1914; Pres. GUY BEAUCHEMIN; 65 mems.

Retailing

Retail Council of Canada: 210 Dundas St West, Suite 600, Toronto, Ont M5G 2E8; tel. (416) 598-4684; f. 1963; Chair. M. H. AYRE; Pres. A. J. MCKICHAN; mems represent 65% of total retail store volume.

Retail Merchants' Association of Canada Inc: 1780 Birchmount Rd, Scarborough, Ont M1P 2H8; tel. (416) 291-7903; f. 1896; Pres. and CEO JOHN GILLESPIE; nat. asscn of provincial groups, locally inc and autonomous.

Transport

Air Transport Association of Canada: 747-99 Bank St, Ottawa K1P 6B9; tel. (613) 233-7727; f. 1934; Pres. G. M. SINCLAIR; Vice-Pres. and Sec. S. T. GRANT; 165 mems.

Canadian Institute of Traffic and Transportation: 573 King St East, Toronto, Ont M5A 1M5; tel. 363-5696.

The Canadian Shippers' Council: c/o Canadian Export Association, 99 Bank St, Suite 250, Ottawa K1P 6B9; tel. (613) 238-8888; telex 053-4888; Sec. J. D. MOORE.

Canadian Trucking Association: Varette Bldg, 130 Albert St, Suite 300, Ottawa K1P 5G4; tel. (613) 239-6426; f. 1937; Exec. Dir A. KENNETH MACLAREN.

Motor Vehicle Manufacturers' Association: 25 Adelaide St East, Suite 1602, Toronto, Ont M5C 1Y7; tel. (416) 364-9333; Pres. N. A. CLARK; 9 mems.

The Railway Association of Canada: 1117 ouest, rue Ste Catherine, Bureau 721, Montreal, Qué H3B 1H9; tel. (514) 849-4274; f. 1917; Pres. J. M. BEAUPRÉ; 13 full mems and 7 associates.

The Shipping Federation of Canada: 300 St-Sacrement, Bureau 326, Montreal, Qué H2Y 1X4; tel. (514) 849-2325; f. 1903; Pres. J. A. CRICHTON; 67 mems.

Wholesale Trade

Canadian Importers' Association, Inc: World Trade Centre, 60 Harbour St, Toronto, Ont M5J 1B7; tel. (416) 862-0002; telex 065-24115; f. 1932; Pres. KEITH G. DIXON; over 850 mems.

Canadian Warehousing Association: 517 Wellington St West, Suite 209, Toronto, Ont M5V 2X5; tel. (416) 596-7489; f. 1917; Pres. DAVID I. KENTISH; 55 mems.

Miscellaneous

Canadian Shipbuilding and Ship Repairing Association: 801-100 Sparks St, Ottawa K1P 5B7; tel. (613) 232-7127; telex 053-4848; f. 1944; Pres. H. M. WALSH; 24 shipyards and ship repairing firms, 75 allied industries.

Canadian Tobacco Manufacturers Council: 1808 Sherbrooke St West, Montreal, Qué H3H 1E5; tel. (514) 937-7428; telex 052-68827; Pres. NORMAN J. MACDONALD.

Council of Printing Industries of Canada: 620 University Ave, 11th Floor, Toronto, Ont M5G 2C1; tel. (416) 591-1509; Gen. Man. FRANKLYN R. SMITH.

Industrial Developers' Association of Canada: 350 Sparks St, Suite 602, Ottawa K1R 7S8; tel. (613) 238-1490.

TRADE UNIONS

At the beginning of 1986 there were 3,730,000 union members in Canada, representing 29.7% of the civilian labour force. Of these, 39.4% belonged to unions with headquarters in the USA.

In 1986 unions affiliated to the Canadian Labour Congress represented 58% of total union membership.

Canadian Labour Congress: 2841 Riverside Drive, Ottawa K1V 8X7; tel. (613) 521-3400; telex 053-4750; f. 1956 by merger of the Canadian Congress of Labour and the Trades and Labour Congress of Canada; 2,164,345 mems (1986); Pres. SHIRLEY G. E. CARR; Sec.-Treas. RICHARD MERCIER.

Affiliated unions with over 15,000 members:

Amalgamated Clothing and Textile Workers Union: 601-15 Gervais Drive, Don Mills, Ont M3C 1Y8; tel. (416) 441-1806; Canadian Dir CHARLES (BUD) CLARK; 30,000 mems (1986).

Amalgamated Transit Union: 606-15 Gervais Drive, Don Mills, Ont M3C 1Y8; tel. (416) 445-6204; Int. Vice-Pres. JAMES H. DALEY; Exec. Dir KEN FOSTER; 20,010 mems (1986).

CANADA

American Federation of Musicians of the United States and Canada: 25 Overlea Blvd, Suite 313, Bldg 3, Toronto, Ont M4H 1B1; tel. (416) 425-1831; Vice-Pres. in Canada J. ALAN WOOD; 30,000 mems (1986).

Bakery, Confectionery and Tobacco Workers International Union: 3329 est, rue Ontario, Montreal, Qué H1W 1P8; tel. (514) 527-9371; Int. Vice-Pres. ALPHONSE DE CÉSARÉ; 16,000 mems (1986).

British Columbia Hospital Employees Union, Local 180: 2286 West 12th Ave, Vancouver, BC V6K 2N5; Prov. Pres. BILL MACDONALD; 25,000 mems (1986).

Brotherhood of Maintenance of Way Employees: 1708 Bank St, Suite 1, Ottawa K1V 7Y6; Vice-Pres in Canada A. PASSARETTI, R. Y. GAUDREAU; 18,714 mems (1986).

Brotherhood of Railway and Airline Clerks, Freight Handlers, Express and Station Employees: 99 Bank St, Suite 705, Ottawa K1P 6B9; tel. (613) 234-5811; Nat. Pres. R. C. SMITH; 18,000 mems (1986).

Canadian Brotherhood of Railway, Transport and General Workers: 2300 Carling Ave, Ottawa K2B 7G1; tel. (613) 829-8764; f. 1908; Pres. J. D. HUNTER; 39,900 mems (1986).

Canadian Paperworkers Union: 1155 ouest, rue Sherbrooke, Bureau 1501, Montreal, Qué H3A 2N3; Pres. tel. (514) 842-8931; JAMES M. BUCHANAN; 57,000 mems (1986).

Canadian Union of Postal Workers: 280 Metcalfe St, Ottawa K2P 1R7; tel. (613) 236-7238; Pres. JEAN-CLAUDE PARROT; 24,000 mems (1986).

Canadian Union of Public Employees: 21 Florence St, Ottawa K2P 0W6; tel. (613) 237-1590; telex 053-4878; Nat. Pres. JEFF ROSE; 304,269 mems (1986).

Communications and Electrical Workers of Canada: 141 Laurier Ave West, Suite 906, Ottawa K1P 5J3; tel. (613) 236-6083; Pres. FRED W. POMEROY; 40,000 mems (1986).

Energy and Chemical Workers' Union: 9940-106 St, Suite 202, Edmonton, Alta T5K 2N2; tel. (403) 422-7932; Nat. Dir CORNELIUS REIMER; 35,000 mems (1986).

Fraternité nationale des charpentiers-menuisiers, forestiers et travailleurs d'usine: 3750 est, blvd Crémazie, Montreal, Qué H2A 1B6; tel. (514) 374-5871; Pres. LOUIS-MARIE CLOUTIER; 15,000 mems (1986).

Graphic Communications International Union: 1110 Finch Ave West, Suite 600, Downsview, Ont M3J 2T2; tel. (416) 661-9761; Int. Vice-Pres. LEONARD R. PAQUETTE; 21,692 mems (1986).

Hotel Employees and Restaurant Employees International Union: 1410 rue Stanley, Bureau 500, Montreal, Qué H3A 1P8; tel. (514) 849-7511; Int. Vice-Pres JAMES STAMOS (Montreal), ALLAN E. MORGAN (Vancouver); 32,000 mems (1986).

International Association of Machinists and Aerospace Workers: 331 Cooper St, Suite 600, Ottawa K2P 0G5; tel. (613) 236-9761; Gen. Vice-Pres. VALÉRIE E. BOURGEOIS; 58,562 mems (1986).

International Woodworkers of America: 2088 Weston Rd, Weston, Ont M9N 1X4; tel. (416) 247-8628; f. 1937; Pres. J. J. MUNRO; Dir W. J. POINTON; 48,000 mems (1986).

Letter Carriers' Union of Canada: 887 Richmond Rd, Ottawa K2A 0G8; tel. (613) 728-2641; Nat. Pres. BOB MCGARRY; 23,000 mems (1986).

National Automobile, Aerospace and Agricultural Implement Workers Union of Canada (CAW-Canada): 205 Placer Court, North York, Willowdale, Ont M2H 3H9; tel. (416) 497-4110; telex 069-86509; Pres. ROBERT WHITE; 140,000 mems (1986).

National Union of Provincial Government Employees: 2841 Riverside Drive, Suite 204, Ottawa K1V 8N4; Pres. JOHN L. FRYER; 260,000 mems (1986).

Office and Professional Employees' International Union: 4740 Imperial St, Burnaby, BC V5J 1C2; tel. (604) 430-0378; Canadian Dir FRED TROTTER; 23,700 mems (1986).

Public Service Alliance of Canada: 233 Gilmour St, Ottawa K2P 0P1; tel. (613) 560-4200; telex 053-3724; f. 1966; Pres. DARYL T. BEAN; 180,238 mems (1986).

Retail, Wholesale and Department Store Union: 15 Gervais Drive, Suite 310, Don Mills, Ont M3C 1Y8; tel. (416) 441-1414; Vice-Pres. and Dir in Canada DONALD G. COLLINS; 25,000 mems (1986).

Service Employees International Union: 1 Credit Union Drive, Toronto, Ont M4A 2S6; tel. (416) 752-4073; Vice-Pres. S. E. (TED) ROSCOE, AIMÉ GOHIER; 70,000 mems (1986).

United Food and Commercial Workers International Union: 61 International Blvd, Rexdale, Ont M9W 6K4; tel. (416) 675-1104; f. 1979; Vice-Pres and Canadian Dirs CLIFFORD EVANS, F. P. BENN; 158,000 mems (1986).

United Steelworkers of America: 234 Eglinton Ave East, 7th Floor, Toronto, Ont M4P 1K7; tel. (416) 487-1571; Nat. Dir in Canada GÉRARD DOCQUIER; 160,000 mems (1986).

United Transportation Union: 99 Bank St, Suite 709, Ottawa K1P 6B9; tel. (613) 238-3717; Vice-Pres in Canada RÉAL J. PROULX, PHILIP P. BURKE; 20,724 mems (1986).

Other Central Congresses

Canadian Federation of Labour: 107 Sparks St, Suite 300, Ottawa K1P 5B5; f. 1982; Pres. JAMES A. MCCAMBLY; 13 affiliated unions representing 208,822 mems (1986).

Affiliated unions with over 15,000 members:

International Brotherhood of Electrical Workers: 45 Sheppard Ave East, Suite 401, Willowdale, Ont M2N 5Y1; tel. (416) 226-5155; Int.Vice-Pres. KEN ROSE; 68,589 mems (1986).

International Union of Operating Engineers: 17704 – 103 Ave, Edmonton, Alta T5S 1J9; tel. (403) 483-0421; Canadian Dir N. BUDD COUTTS; 36,000 mems (1986).

Sheet Metal Workers' International Association: Terrace Tower, 4445 Calgary Trail South, Suite 870, Edmonton, Alta T6H 5R7; tel. (403) 438-5475; Dir of Canadian Affairs RAYMOND A. GALL; 16,800 mems (1986).

United Association of Journeymen and Apprentices of the Plumbing and Pipe Fitting Industry of the United States and Canada: 310 Broadway Ave, Suite 702, Winnipeg, Man R3C 0S6; Vice-Pres. and Canadian Dir J. RUSS ST ELOI; 40,000 mems (1986).

Centrale des syndicats démocratiques: 1259 rue Berri, Bureau 600, Montreal, Qué H2L 4C7; tel. (514) 842-3801; f. 1972; Pres. JEAN-PAUL HÉTU; 491 affiliated unions representing 35,967 mems (1986).

Affiliated federation with over 15,000 members:

Commission des enseignantes et enseignants des commissions scolaires: 2336 Ste-Foy, CP 5800, Ste-Foy, Qué G1V 4E5; tel. (418) 658-5711; Pres. HERVÉ BERGERON; 75,000 mems (1986).

Confederation of Canadian Unions: 1331½A St Clair Ave West, Toronto, Ont M6E 1C3; f. 1969; Pres. JESS SUCCAMORE; 21 affiliated unions representing 35,683 mems (1986).

Confédération des syndicats nationaux: 1601 ave de Lorimier, Montreal, Qué H2K 4M5; f. 1921; Pres. GÉRALD LAROSE; 1,896 affiliated unions representing 222,800 mems (1986).

Affiliated federations with over 15,000 members:

Fédération des employées et employés de services publics inc: 1601 ave de Lorimier, Montreal, Qué H2K 4M5; tel. (514) 598-2231; Pres. LOUIS BOUFFARD; 27,500 mems (1986).

Fédération des affaires sociales inc: 1601 ave de Lorimier, Montreal, Qué H2K 4M5; Pres. YVES LESSARD; 93,000 mems (1986).

Fédération du commerce inc: 1601 ave de Lorimier, Bureau 122, Montreal, Qué H2K 4M5; Pres. LOUISE PARENT; 22,000 mems (1986).

Fédération de la métallurgie: 1601 ave de Lorimier, Montreal, Qué H2K 4M5; Pres. PIERRE DUPONT; 20,000 mems (1986).

Fédération nationale des syndicats du bâtiment et du bois, inc: 1601 ave de Lorimier, Montreal, Qué H2K 4M5; Pres. (vacant); 21,200 mems (1986).

The American Federation of Labor and Congress of Industrial Organizations (AFL-CIO), with headquarters in Washington, DC, USA, represented 134,915 members, or 3.6% of the total union membership in Canada, at the beginning of 1986. Affiliated unions with over 15,000 members:

International Association of Bridge, Structural and Ornamental Iron Workers: 284 King St West, Suite 501, Toronto, Ont M5V 1J1; Exec. Dir NORMAN A. WILSON; 19,940 mems (1986).

Laborers' International Union of North America: 151 Slater St, Suite 301, Ottawa K1P 5H3; tel. (613) 232-7141; Dir DOUGLAS FORGIE; 46,715 mems (1986).

United Brotherhood of Carpenters and Joiners of America: 5799 Yonge St, Suite 807, Willowdale, Ont M2M 3V3; tel. (416)

CANADA

225-8885; Officials in Canada JOHN CARRUTHERS, RONALD J. DANCER; 68,000 mems (1986).

Principal Unaffiliated Unions

Alberta Teachers' Association: 11010-142 St, Edmonton, Alta T5N 2R1; tel. (403) 453-2411; Exec. Sec. B. T. KEELER; 38,669 mems (1986).

British Columbia Nurses' Union: 1200 Burrard St, Suite 700, Vancouver, BC V6Z 2C7; Pres. COLLEEN BONNER; 18,226 mems (1986).

British Columbia Teachers' Federation: 2235 Burrard St, Vancouver, BC V6J 3H9; tel. (604) 731-8121; Pres. ELSIE MCMURPHY; 27,842 mems (1986).

Canadian Telephone Employees' Association: place du Canada, Bureau 1465; Montreal, Qué H3B 2N2; Pres. ELISABETH H. ROUSSEAU; 19,100 mems (1986).

Centrale de l'enseignement du Québec: 1415ouest, rue Jarry, Montreal, Qué H2E 1A7; tel. (514) 374-6660; telex 051-31547; Pres. YVON CHARBONNEAU; Dir-Gen. MICHEL AGNAÏEFF; 100,000 mems (1986).

Fédération des syndicats professionnels d'infirmières et d'infirmiers du Québec: 175 rue St-Jean, 4e étage, Québec, Qué G1R 1N4; tel. (418) 647-1102; Pres. HÉLÈNE PELLETIER; 17,500 mems (1986).

Federation of Women Teachers' Associations of Ontario: 1260 Bay St, Toronto, Ont M5R 2B8; Pres. CAROL DEWEY; 31,913 mems (1986).

International Brotherhood of Teamsters, Chauffeurs, Warehousemen and Helpers of America: 8th Ave West, Suite 899, Vancouver, BC V5Z 1E3; Pres. EDWARD M. LAWSON; 91,500 mems (1986).

Ontario English Catholic Teachers' Association: 65 St Clair Ave East, Toronto, Ont M4T 2Y8; Pres. JIM COONEY; 22,000 mems (1986).

Ontario Nurses' Association: 415 Yonge St, Suite 1401, Toronto, Ont M5B 2E7; tel. (416) 977-1975; Pres. DONNA ALEXANDER; 42,000 mems (1986).

Ontario Public School Teachers' Federation: 1260 Bay St, Toronto, Ont M5R 2B7; tel. (416) 928-1128; Pres. MARY C. HILL; 15,700 mems (1986).

Ontario Secondary School Teachers Federation: 60 Mobile Drive, Toronto, Ont M4A 2P3; tel. (416) 751-8300; Pres. ROD ALBERT; 35,722 mems (1986).

Professional Institute of the Public Service of Canada: 786 Bronson Ave, Ottawa K1S 4G4; tel. (613) 237-6310; Pres. IRIS CRAIG; 19,882 mems (1986).

Syndicat des fonctionnaires provinciaux du Québec: 214 ave St-Sacrement, Bureau 200, Québec, Qué G1N 4N9; tel. (418) 687-3347; Pres. JEAN-LOUIS HARGUINDEGUY; 44,000 mems (1986).

Transport

Owing to the size of the country, Canada's economy is particularly dependent upon an efficient system of transport. The St Lawrence Seaway allows ocean-going ships to reach the Great Lakes. There are almost 194,000 km (120,000 miles) of railway track, and the country's rail and canal system is being increasingly augmented by roads, air services and petroleum pipelines. The Trans-Canada Highway is one of the main features of a network of 392,000 km (243,600 miles) of roads and highways. In 1977 the Canadian Government extended its coastal jurisdiction to 370 km (200 nautical miles).

RAILWAYS

The Canadian Pacific and Canadian National Railways provide 88% of all rail transportation in Canada.

Algoma Central Railway: POB 7000, Sault Ste Marie, Ont P6A 5P6; tel. (705) 949-2113; telex 067-77146; f. 1899; diversified transportation co moving cargo by rail, water and road; also has interests in commercial property development; Chair. HENRY N. R. JACKMAN; Pres. L. N. SAVOIE.

BC Rail: POB 8770, Vancouver, BC V6B 4X6; tel. (604) 986-2012; telex 043-52752; f. 1912; 2,855 km; Pres. and CEO M. C. NORRIS.

Canadian National Railways: 935 ouest, rue LaGauchetière, CP 8100, Montreal, Qué H3C 3N4; tel. (514) 399-5430: telex 055-60519; f. 1923; 50,000 km; Chair. and CEO J. M. LECLAIR; Pres. R. E. LAWLESS.

Canadian Pacific Ltd: POB 6042, Windsor Station, Montreal, Qué H3C 3E4; tel. (514) 395-6589; telex 052-5857; f. 1881; 24,649 km of main line track; also operates Canada's largest road haulage service; interests in air and sea transport, hotels, natural resources, telecommunications, hotels and manufacturing; Chair. F. S. BURBRIDGE; Pres. and CEO W. W. STINSON.

Ontario Northland Transportation Commission: 195 Regina St, North Bay, Ont P1B 8L3; tel. (705) 472-4500; telex 067-76103; an agency of the Govt of Ontario; operates rail services over 919.1 km of track; Chair. J. W. SPOONER; Gen. Man. P. A. DYMENT.

VIA Rail Canada Inc: 2 place Ville-Marie, 4e étage, Montreal, Qué H3B 2G6; tel. (514) 871-6000; telex 052-68530; f. 1977; operates passenger services over existing rail routes throughout Canada; Chair. L. HANIGAN; Pres. and CEO P. A. H. FRANCHE.

ROADS

Provincial governments are responsible for roads within their boundaries. The federal government is responsible for major roads in the Yukon and Northwest Territories and in National Parks. In 1982 there were 391,792 km of roads (excluding municipal roads), of which 41.9% were paved.

The Trans-Canada Highway extends from St John's, Newfoundland, to Victoria, British Columbia.

INLAND WATERWAYS

The St Lawrence River and the Great Lakes provide Canada and the USA with a system of inland waterways extending from the Atlantic Ocean to the western end of Lake Superior, a distance of 3,769 km (2,342 miles). There is a 10.7-m (35-foot) navigation channel from Montreal to the sea and an 8.25-m (27-foot) channel from Montreal to Lake Erie. The St Lawrence Seaway, which was opened in 1959, was initiated partly to provide a deep waterway and partly to satisfy the demand for more electric power. Power development has been undertaken by the Provinces of Québec and Ontario, and by New York State. The navigation facilities and conditions are within the jurisdiction of the federal governments of the USA and Canada.

St Lawrence River and Great Lakes Shipping

St Lawrence Seaway Authority: Place de Ville, Ottawa K1R 5A3; tel. (613) 598-4600; telex 053-3322; opened 1959 to allow ocean-going vessels to enter the Great Lakes of North America; operated jointly with the USA; Pres. W. A. O'NEIL.

Canada Steamship Lines Inc: 759 Victoria Sq., Montreal, Qué H2Y 2K3; Chair. PAUL E. MARTIN; Pres. RAYMOND LEMAY; 34 vessels; 750,000 grt.

Halco Inc: 1303 Greene Ave, Westmount, Qué H3Z 2A7; tel. (514) 932-2147; telex 052-67630; Sr Vice-Pres. RICHARD CARSON; 6 tankers, 7 bulk cargo vessels, 1 self-unloader; 279,933 dwt.

Paterson, N. M., and Sons Ltd: POB 664, Thunder Bay, Ont P7C 4W6; tel. (807) 577-8421; telex 073-4566; bulk carriers; Vice-Pres. and Dir ROBERT J. PATERSON; 12 vessels; 95,536 grt.

Misener Shipping Ltd: 63 Church St, St Catharine's, Ont L2R 6S1; tel. (416) 688-3500; telex 061-5155; bulk cargo; Pres. DAVID K. GARDINER; 10 vessels; 184,109 grt.

Upper Lakes Shipping Ltd: 49 Jackes Ave, Toronto, Ont M4T 1E2; tel. (416) 920-7610; Pres. and Dir J. D. LEITCH; bulk carriers; 23 vessels; 475,074 grt.

SHIPPING

British Columbia Ferry Corporation: 1112 Fort St, Victoria, BC V8W 4V2; tel. (604) 381-1401; telex 045-5106; passenger and car ferries; Gen. Man. G. BALDWIN; 39 ferries.

Esso Petroleum Canada: External Supply and Transportation Division, 55 St Clair Ave West, Toronto, Ont M5W 2J8; tel. (416) 968-5309; telex 065-28049; coastal, Great Lakes and St Lawrence River, South American, Caribbean and Gulf ports to Canadian east and US Atlantic ports; Pres. G. H. THOMSON; Man. Marine Div. H. M. WESTLAKE; 11 vessels; 41,836 grt.

Fednav Ltd: 600 ouest, rue de la Gauchetière, Bureau 2600, Montreal, Qué H3B 4M3; tel. (514) 878-6500; telex 055-60637; f. 1944; shipowners, operators, contractors, terminal operators; Pres. L. G. PATHY; owned and chartered fleet of c. 50 vessels.

Marine Atlantic Inc: 100 Cameron St, Moncton, NB E1C 5Y6; tel. (506) 858-3600; telex 014-2833; Pres. and CEO R. J. TINGLEY; serves Atlantic coast of Canada; 16 vessels, incl. passenger, roll-on/roll-off and freight ferries.

CANADA

Papachristidis (Canada) Inc: 1350 Sherbrooke St West, Penthouse, Montreal, Qué H3G 1J1; tel. (514) 844-8404; telex 052-68780; Pres. Niky Papachristidis; world-wide services; 4 vessels owned and managed; 52,309 grt.

Saguenay Shipping Ltd: 85 Richmond St West, Toronto, Ont M5H 1T1; tel. (416) 364-0256.

Seaboard Shipping Co Ltd: Oceanic Plaza, 1066 West Hastings St, POB 12501, Vancouver, BC V6E 3W9; UK-Continent, Australia, New Zealand, South Africa, Mediterranean, West Indies, US Atlantic Coast; Pres. C. D. G. Roberts.

Shell Canadian Tankers Ltd: POB 400, Terminal A, Toronto, Ont; tel. (416) 597-7111; petroleum products in bulk; Pres. and CEO R. G. Naden; Vice-Pres. and Man. D. R. Maconachie; 5 Lake tankers, 20,850 grt.

Société Sofati/Soconav: 2020 rue Université, Bureau 2201, Montreal, Qué H3A 2A5; tel. (514) 284-9535; telex 052-67671; Great Lakes, St Lawrence River and Gulf, Atlantic Coast, Arctic and NWT; Chair. Michel Gaucher; Pres. Louis Rochette; Vice-Pres. (Operations) Guy Bazinet; 6 tankers, 34,811 grt.

CIVIL AVIATION

Air Canada: place Air Canada, Montreal, Qué H2Z 1X5; tel. (514) 879-7000; telex 062-17537; f. 1937; operates under jurisdiction of Ministry of Transport; Chair. Claude I. Taylor; Pres. and CEO Pierre J. Jeanniot; operates services throughout Canada and to the USA; also to the UK, Paris, Zürich, Geneva, Frankfurt, Düsseldorf, Munich, Bombay, Singapore, Antigua, Bermuda, Barbados, Bahamas, Trinidad, Guadeloupe, Martinique, Cuba, Jamaica and Saint Lucia; fleet of 33 Boeing 727, 5 Boeing 747, 14 Boeing 767, 35 DC-9, 1 DC-8-63F, 6 DC-8-73F, 14 L-1011.

CP Air: One Grant McConachie Way, Vancouver International Airport, Vancouver, BC V7B 1V1; tel. (604) 270-5211; telex 043-55587; f. 1942; acquisition by Pacific Western Airlines Ltd pending in 1987; Pres. and CEO Donald J. Carty; domestic and international scheduled services and charters; fleet of 4 Boeing 747-200B, 5 DC-10-30, 3 DC-10-10, 19 Boeing 737-200.

Eastern Provincial Airways (EPA): POB 5001, Gander, Nfld A1V 1W9; tel. (709) 256-3941; telex 016-43514; Pres. and CEO H. R. Steele; fleet of 6 Boeing 737-200, 5 HS-748.

Nordair: 1320 blvd Graham, Ville Mont-Royal, Qué H3P 3C8; tel. (514) 340-8100; telex 058-26806; f. 1947; privately-owned regional carrier; scheduled passenger and cargo services serving Québec, Ontario, Manitoba, the Eastern Arctic and the USA; Pres. Jean E. Douville; Chair. Ronald G. Lefrançois; fleet of 4 Boeing 737-200, 6 Boeing 737-200C, 5 Fairchild FH-227, 2 Lockheed Electra L-188.

Northwest Territorial Airways (NWT Air): Yellowknife International Airport, Postal Service 9000, Yellowknife, NWT X1A 2R3; tel. (403) 920-4567; telex 034-45527; f. 1961; Pres. Robert P. Engle; scheduled passenger and cargo services within the NWT, international cargo charters and scheduled cargo services to Toronto, Edmonton, Winnipeg and Vancouver; fleet of 3 Electra, 1 L-100-30 Hercules, 5 DC-3.

Pacific Western Airlines Ltd: 700 Second St SW, Calgary, Alta T2P 2W2; tel. (403) 294-2000; telex 043-55610; f. 1946; Chair. R. R. McDaniel; Pres. Murray Sigler; passenger and cargo charters and scheduled services to 50 towns in western Canada and Toronto; fleet of 2 Boeing 767, 19 Boeing 737-200.

Québecair: Montreal International Airport, CP 490, Dorval, Qué H4Y 1B5; tel. (514) 631-9802; telex 058-22584; f. 1946; regional carrier and charter services; Chair. Marc Racicot; Pres. and CEO Michel Leblanc; fleet of 4 Convair, 2 Boeing 737.

Tourism

Canadian Government Office of Tourism: Federal Dept of Regional Industrial Expansion, 235 Queen St, Ottawa K1A 0H5; tel. (613) 996-5651.

Tourism Industry Association of Canada: 130 Albert St, Suite 1016, Ottawa K1P 5G4; tel. (613) 238-3883; f. 1931; national, private sector, non-profit organization which encourages travel to and within Canada; promotes growth and development of travel services and facilities; Exec. Dir John Lawson.

Atomic Energy

Atomic Energy of Canada Ltd: 275 Slater St, Ottawa K1A 0S4; tel. (613) 237-3270; telex 053-3126; f. 1952; federal govt agency for nuclear research and development, production of radioactive isotopes and design, development and marketing of power reactors; three operational research reactors at Chalk River, Ont, and one under construction at Whiteshell Nuclear Research Establishment, Pinawa, Man; demonstration or prototype reactors located at Gentilly-1 in conjunction with Hydro-Québec; nuclear designer for CANDU (Canadian deuterium uranium) reactors; 16 commercial units now in service at five stations, providing 12.8% of Canada's total electricity generation; five others under construction in Canada; two units each in service in India, Pakistan, the Republic of Korea and Argentina, and three units under construction in Romania; Pres. and CEO James Donnelly.

Atomic Energy Control Board: POB 1046, Ottawa K1P 5S9; tel. (613) 992-9206; telex 053-3771; f. 1946; responsible for all nuclear regulatory matters; Pres. J. H. Jennekens; Sec. P. E. Hamel.

CAPE VERDE

Introductory Survey

Location, Climate, Language, Religion, Flag, Capital

The Republic of Cape Verde is an archipelago of 10 islands and five islets in the North Atlantic Ocean, about 500 km (300 miles) west of Dakar, Senegal. The country lies in a semi-arid belt, with little rain and an average annual temperature of 24°C (76°F). The official language is Portuguese, of which the locally spoken form is Creole (Crioulo). Virtually all of the inhabitants profess Christianity, and 98% are Roman Catholics. The national flag (proportions 3 by 2) comprises a vertical red stripe, at the hoist, and two equal horizontal stripes, of yellow and green. The red stripe bears, in the upper hoist, a five-pointed black star and a clamshell enclosed by a wreath of palms. The capital is Cidade de Praia.

Recent History

The Cape Verde Islands were colonized by the Portuguese in the 15th century. From the 1950s, liberation movements in Portugal's African colonies were campaigning for independence, and, in this context, the archipelago was linked with the mainland territory of Portuguese Guinea (now Guinea-Bissau). At first, however, the Partido Africano da Independência do Guiné e Cabo Verde (PAIGC) made little progress in the islands, although regarding them as an integral part of its territory. The independence of Guinea-Bissau was recognized by Portugal in September 1974, but the PAIGC leadership in the Cape Verde Islands decided to pursue separate independence rather than enter into an immediate federation with Guinea-Bissau. In December 1974 a transitional government, comprising representatives of the Portuguese Government and the PAIGC, was formed; members of other political parties were excluded. A National People's Assembly was chosen on 30 June 1975 in the islands' first general election. Only the PAIGC contested the poll, and there was 92% support for the party's platform of ultimate union with Guinea-Bissau. Independence was granted on 5 July 1975, and Aristides Pereira, Secretary-General of the PAIGC, became Cape Verde's first President. The country's first constitution was approved in September 1980.

Although Cape Verde and Guinea-Bissau remained constitutionally separate, the PAIGC supervised the activities of both states, but progress towards the ultimate goal of unification was slow. Moreover, the Cape Verde Government disapproved of the November 1980 coup in Guinea-Bissau, and in January 1981 the Cape Verde wing of the PAIGC was renamed the Partido Africano da Independência de Cabo Verde (PAICV). In February President Pereira was re-elected unanimously by the National Assembly, and all articles concerning ultimate union with Guinea-Bissau were removed from the Constitution. Reconciliation talks were held in June 1982, however, after the release of Luis Cabral, formerly the Head of State in Guinea-Bissau, and relations continued to improve during the summit meeting of lusophone African states which was held in Praia in September. Diplomatic relations between the two countries were normalized in 1982.

Sixteen people were imprisoned in June 1982 for inciting riots (in August 1981) in protest against proposed legislation on land reform, designed to expropriate absentee landlords and to transfer ownership of land to those who cultivate it.

A new National Assembly was elected in December 1985. The 83 candidates on the PAICV-approved list, of whom some were not members of the PAICV, obtained 94.5% of the votes cast. In January 1986 President Pereira was re-elected for a further five-year term by the National Assembly. Gen. Pedro Pires continued as Prime Minister, and a new government was formed. Many ministers retained their posts, but several functions were redistributed.

Cape Verde professes a non-aligned stance in foreign affairs and maintains relations with virtually all the power blocs. Cape Verde's reputation for political independence led to its being chosen as the venue for several important international conferences: for example, in 1982–83 the talks between Angola and South Africa over Namibia, and a conference of the Permanent Inter-State Committee on Drought Control in the Sahel (see p. 216), were held in Cape Verde. The country also takes an active part in co-operation between the lusophone African states. In 1985 Cape Verde agreed to accommodate up to eight members of the Basque separatist movement, ETA, who were being deported from Spain for terrorist activities. Following negotiations in June 1986 with the Spanish Minister of the Interior, José Barrionuevo, Cape Verde agreed to accept more members of ETA. In August 1986 Cape Verde established diplomatic relations with the Palestine Liberation Organization (PLO) during a visit to the islands by Yasser Arafat, the Chairman of the PLO.

Government

Under the 1980 constitution, legislative power is vested in the National People's Assembly, with 83 (formerly 56) deputies, elected by universal adult suffrage for five years. Executive power is held by the President, elected for five years by the Assembly. The President is the Head of State and governs with the assistance of an appointed Council of Ministers, led by the Prime Minister. The PAICV is the only political party permitted to operate.

Defence

The Popular Revolutionary Armed Forces have been formed from ex-combatants in the liberation wars, and numbered 1,185 (army 1,000, navy 160, air force 25) in July 1986. There is also a police force and paramilitary People's Militia. National service is by selective conscription. Estimated defence expenditure in 1981 was US $3.5m. In 1980 the USSR supplied two torpedo boats as the nucleus of a navy.

Economic Affairs

Little was done under Portuguese rule to develop the natural resources of the islands, such as the fishing grounds and the large reserves of underground water, or to alleviate the effects of the recurrent droughts and severe soil erosion. However, the World Bank has estimated that Cape Verde's gross national product (GNP) per head increased, in real terms, at an average rate of 5.3% per year between 1973 and 1983: one of the highest growth rates in Africa. In 1984, according to World Bank estimates, GNP per head was US $320 (at average 1982–84 prices), a little above the average for low-income countries.

The agricultural subsistence economy of the islands, which normally employs about three-quarters of the working population (mainly on smallholdings), has been severely affected by an almost continuous drought which was in its 18th year in 1986. Torrential rain in September 1984 was so heavy that it destroyed about half of the country's small dams, but by 1986 these had been rebuilt, along with thousands of additional dams. The staple crops are maize (production of which was estimated at 3,000 metric tons in 1984), beans and sweet potatoes, and other crops normally grown include sugar cane, cassava, castor beans, bananas, coffee and groundnuts. However, about 90% of the country's total food requirements has to be imported. Since independence, most of Cape Verde's food deficit has been met by foreign aid. In 1983 some 48,000 metric tons of cereals were imported, of which 39,000 tons were donated under food aid programmes. The 1985 grain crop reached only 2,100 tons, less than 5% of Cape Verde's total requirements. Food imports of 70,000 tons were envisaged for 1986. There is extensive rural unemployment, partly remedied by government employment schemes in soil and water conservation and reafforestation projects. The country suffers from a persistent trade deficit, which stood at US $67.3m. in 1983 and $78.8m. in 1984, while the outstanding foreign debt at the end of 1984 was an estimated $83m., equivalent to almost 100% of annual GDP.

CAPE VERDE

Between 1980 and 1984, Cape Verde's currency depreciated, in nominal terms, by 54% in relation to the US dollar.

Cape Verde's first four-year development plan was announced in 1982. It envisaged investment of US $405m., all from external sources, the main aims being to move towards self-sufficiency in food and to continue to combat desertification. In 1983 Cape Verde received aid worth $387,500 from the UN Development Programme to help to develop co-operatives and, thereby, to increase food production. In 1986 the Government prepared a new development plan, which was to be presented to potential donors by the end of the year. The 1984 budget envisaged revenue of 1,630m. escudos and expenditure of 2,134.5m. escudos. Public expenditure was to rise by 16% to cover the public debt, inflation and increases in salaries for workers in the public sector. The budget stressed the education and health sectors, whose departmental budgets were to be increased by 27% and 29% respectively. Emphasis was also to be laid on job-creation schemes: the budget set a target of 3,000 jobs to be created in 1984.

There are almost 1m. Cape Verdeans living outside the country, principally in the USA, the Netherlands, Portugal and Italy. In 1983 remittances from emigrants resident in the USA reached 2,800m. escudos, and the Government has attempted to attract emigrants' capital into the light industry and fishing sectors in Cape Verde by offering favourable tax conditions to investors. In 1985 an agreement was signed between Cape Verde and the USA, intended as the impetus to this new policy. Nevertheless, foreign aid has been indispensable, and in recent years European and Arab countries, Japan, the USA, the UN and the African Development Fund have all assisted Cape Verde. Development aid and bilateral co-operation agreements are being directed partly to the expansion of Cape Verde's network of transport and communications. Further road-building projects have been partly financed by a loan allocated by the People's Republic of China in 1986. The expansion of facilities at Amílcar Cabral international airport (on the island of Sal), with Italian and EEC aid, was scheduled for completion in 1987. In 1986 the Government discussed a Brazilian proposal to construct a new cargo terminal. The main seaport is at Mindelo, on the island of São Vicente, where a ship-building and repairing yard was opened in 1983. The ports of Praia and Porto Grande were being enlarged, and in 1982 work started on a port at Palmeira, on Sal. In 1985 Cape Verde and Angola agreed on arrangements for the sharing of port facilities, and shipping repair and refrigeration services, while co-operation in telecommunications installation and training was also agreed. Work started in 1983 on a new telecommunications network, consisting of three automatic exchanges which would provide international telephone and telex links. In 1985 France provided 1.5m. francs for a telecommunications station.

Fishing forms a large part of the islands' development potential and accounted for 70% of export revenue in 1979. The most important fish exports are usually lobster and tuna. The total annual fish catch reached 13,205 metric tons in 1983, but declined to 9,131 tons in 1984. A cold-storage plant was opened at Mindelo in 1981, and the Government was to invest a total of US $45m. to develop a modern fishing industry. In late 1985 BADEA (see p. 95) approved a loan of $300,000 for the development of Cape Verde's fisheries sector, and in January 1986 the FAO agreed to provide assistance to increase production of fish and also potatoes.

There is little manufacturing activity except for a few small fish-processing and canning plants and clothing factories, which together employ about 1,700 people and contribute only 5% of the country's GDP. However, the Government is encouraging investment in this sector, and several major projects have been undertaken: a cement plant is being constructed on the island of Maio, and a Danish company is to build a brewery. About 95% of all goods consumed in Cape Verde are imported, with Portugal remaining the principal supplier. The Government hopes to exploit the islands' resources of pozzolana, cement and salt, and to develop construction and packaging materials, soft drinks, pasta and tobacco industries.

Social Welfare

Medical facilities are limited and there is a severe shortage of staff and buildings, although plans for a national health service are being implemented. In 1980 Cape Verde had 21 hospital establishments, with a total of 632 beds, and there were 51 physicians working in government service. Development plans include the construction of more than 300 small local health units.

Education

Compulsory education is divided into Instrução Primária (for children aged seven to 12 years, of whom 95% were reportedly at school in 1980) and Escola Preparatória (for children aged 12 to 14). From the age of 14, children may attend one of the three liceus, which provide a three-year general course or a two-year pre-university course. In 1982/83 there was also one industrial and commercial school and three teacher training units. In the same year about 50,000 pupils attended 436 primary schools.

Priority is being given to the construction of schools, teacher training and the reduction of the illiteracy rate. According to official estimates, the average rate of adult illiteracy in 1985 was 52.6% (males 38.6%; females 61.4%).

Tourism

The Government launched a tourist development scheme in 1980. A large hotel already exists at Santa Maria beach, on Sal Island, and another was being built in Praia. In 1986 a third international hotel was opened on Sal. The islands of Santo Antão, São Tiago, Fogo and Brava offer a combination of mountain scenery and vast beaches.

Public Holidays

1987: 1 January (New Year), 20 January (National Heroes' Day), 8 March (Women's Day), 1 May (Labour Day), 1 June (Children's Day), 5 July (Independence Day), 12 September (Day of the Nation), 25 December (Christmas Day).

1988: 1 January (New Year), 20 January (National Heroes' Day), 8 March (Women's Day), 1 May (Labour Day), 1 June (Children's Day), 5 July (Independence Day), 12 September (Day of the Nation), 25 December (Christmas Day).

Weights and Measures

The metric system is in force.

Currency and Exchange Rates

100 centavos = 1 Cape Verde escudo.

Exchange rates (30 September 1986):
 £1 sterling = 112.43 escudos;
 US $1 = 77.70 escudos.

Statistical Survey

Source (unless otherwise stated): Statistical Service, Banco de Cabo Verde, Av. Amílcar Cabral, São Tiago; tel. 341; telex 99350.

AREA AND POPULATION

Area: 4,033 sq km (1,557 sq miles).

Population: 272,571 (census of 15 December 1970); 296,093 (census of 2 June 1980). *By island:* Boa Vista 3,397, Brava 6,984, Fogo 31,115, Maio 4,103, Sal 6,006, Santo Antão 43,198, São Nicolau 13,575, São Tiago 145,923, São Vicente 41,792 (census of 2 June 1980).

Births and Deaths (1981): Live births 9,992; deaths 2,244.

Labour force: 84,869 (census of 15 December 1970). Source: Direcção de Recenseamento e Inquéritos, Praia.

AGRICULTURE, ETC.

Principal Crops (FAO estimates, '000 metric tons, 1984): Maize 3, Potatoes 3, Cassava 2, Sweet potatoes 2, Sugar cane 9, Bananas 3.

Livestock (FAO estimates, '000 head, year ending September 1984): Cattle 13, Pigs 23, Sheep 1, Goats 77, Asses 6.

Fishing ('000 metric tons, live weight): Total catch 10.4 in 1982; 13.2 in 1983; 9.1 in 1984.

MINING

Production (metric tons, 1981): Salt (unrefined) 6,445; Pozzolana 16,300 (estimate by US Bureau of Mines).

INDUSTRY

Production (metric tons, 1981): Biscuits 432, Flour 7,942, Bread 2,340, Canned tuna 315, Frozen fish 1,300, Cigars 13, Alcoholic beverages 208,000 litres, Soft drinks 79,700 litres. Source: Direcção Geral de Estatística, Praia.

FINANCE

Currency and Exchange Rates: 100 centavos = 1 Cape Verde escudo; 1,000 escudos are known as a conto. *Coins:* 20 and 50 centavos; 1, 2½, 10, 20 and 50 escudos. *Notes:* 100, 500 and 1,000 escudos. *Sterling and Dollar Equivalents* (30 September 1986): £1 sterling = 112.43 escudos; US $1 = 77.70 escudos; 1,000 Cape Verde escudos = £8.894 = $12.870. *Average Exchange Rate* (escudos per US dollar): 58.29 in 1982; 71.69 in 1983; 84.88 in 1984.

Budget (estimates, million escudos, 1984): Revenue 1,630; Expenditure 2,134.5.

Source: *Marchés Tropicaux et Méditerranéens*.

Currency in Circulation ('000 escudos, 1976): Notes 465,609, Coins 8,415.

Cost of Living (Consumer Price Index for Praia, excluding clothing and rent; 1974 = 100): 169.4 (1977), 192.0 (1978), 205.2 (1979). Source: US Agency for International Development.

Gross Domestic Product by Economic Activity (million escudos at current prices, 1980): Agriculture and forestry 570; Fishing 180; Industry, electricity and water 120; Construction and public works 590; Trade, transport and telecommunications 1,360; Public administration 450; Other services 80; Total 3,350. Source: Centro de Estudos Economia e Sociedade, Lisbon.

Balance of Payments (million escudos, 1981): Merchandise trade (net) −3,880; Net services 15, *Balance on Goods and Services* −3,865; Private transfers 1,760; Other income 25; *Current Balance* −2,080; Public transfers 1,940; Net errors and omissions 170; Total (net monetary movements) 30. Source: Centro de Estudos Economia e Sociedade, Lisbon.

EXTERNAL TRADE

Principal Commodities ('000 escudos, 1981): *Imports:* Animals and animal products 120,498, Vegetable products 475,231, Fats and oils 141,136, Foodstuffs and beverages 475,369, Mineral products 635,240, Chemical products 201,475, Textiles and textile products 157,187, Base metals 199,678, Machinery and electrical equipment 365,056, Transport equipment 230,763; Total (incl. others) 3,451,649. *Exports:* Animals and animal products 16,728, Vegetable products 86,592, Foodstuffs and beverages 13,900, Mineral products 12,017, Skins and hides 1,135, Machinery and electrical equipment 628, Transport equipment 128, Total (incl. others) 146,996. Source: Direcção Geral de Estatística, Praia.

Principal Trading Partners ('000 escudos, 1981): *Imports:* Angola 19,971, Netherlands 342,588, Portugal 1,378,718, United Kingdom 169,878, USA 168,162; Total (incl. others) 3,451,649. *Exports:* Angola, 14,239, Central African Republic 6,502, Guinea-Bissau 1,217, Portugal 91,819, São Tomé and Principe 4, United Kingdom 599, Zaire 2,980; Total (incl. others) 146,996.

TRANSPORT

Road Traffic (motor vehicles in use, 1981): Passenger cars 4,000, Motor cycles 2,270, Lorries and buses 1,343.

Shipping (1981): Vessels entered 2,544; freight loaded 146,822 metric tons; freight unloaded 371,812 metric tons; passengers embarked 97,746; passengers disembarked 97,746. Source: Direcção Geral de Estatística, Praia, São Tiago.

Civil Aviation (Amílcar Cabral airport, 1982): Freight loaded 104.7 metric tons; freight unloaded 615.3 metric tons; passengers embarked 23,106; passengers disembarked 21,200. Source: Direcção Geral de Estatística, Praia, São Tiago.

COMMUNICATIONS MEDIA

Radio receivers (1983): 47,000 in use.

Television receivers (1985): 500 in use.

Telephones (1981): 2,000 in use.

EDUCATION

Primary (1982/83): 436 schools, 50,000 pupils, 1,459 teachers.

Preparatory (1982/83): 13 schools, 7,262 pupils, 500 teachers.

Secondary (1982/83): 3 schools, 3,192 pupils, 103 teachers.

Teacher training (1982/83): 3 units, 199 pupils, 32 teachers.

Industrial school: 1 school, 724 pupils, 40 teachers.

Source: Ministério da Educação e Cultura, CP 111, Praia, São Tiago.

Directory

The Constitution

The Constitution of the Republic of Cape Verde, the first since the country's independence in 1975, was approved on 7 September 1980. It defines Cape Verde as 'a sovereign, democratic, unitary, anti-colonialist and anti-imperialist republic'. The Head of State is the President of the Republic, who is elected by the National Assembly and has a mandate of five years, as do the Assembly deputies, elected by universal adult suffrage. The Prime Minister is nominated by the same Assembly, to which he is responsible. The President of the National Assembly may act as interim Head of State if necessary. He is not a member of the government.

The Constitution abolishes both the death sentence and life imprisonment. Citizens have equality of rights and duties, without sexual, social, intellectual, religious or philosophical distinction. This extends to all Cape Verde emigrants throughout the world. Citizens also have freedom of thought, expression, association, demonstration, religion, rights and duties and the right to health care, culture and education.

On 12 February 1981 all articles concerning plans for eventual union with Guinea-Bissau were revoked, and an amendment was inserted to provide for the creation of the Partido Africano da Independência de Cabo Verde (PAICV) to replace the Cape Verde section of the PAIGC (defined in the Constitution as 'the leading force of society').

The Government

HEAD OF STATE

President: Aristides Maria Pereira (took office 5 July 1975; re-elected February 1981 and January 1986).

COUNCIL OF MINISTERS
(October 1986)

Prime Minister: Gen. Pedro Verona Rodrigues Pires.
Minister of the Armed Forces and Security: Col Júlio de Carvalho.
Minister of Transport, Trade and Tourism: Commdt Osvaldo Lopes da Silva.
Minister of Education: André Corsino Tolentino.
Minister of Health, Labour and Social Affairs: Dr Ireneu Gomes.
Minister of Agriculture and Fishing: Commdt João Pereira Silva.
Minister of Local Administration and Town Planning: Tito Livio Santos de Oliveira Ramos.
Minister of Justice: José Eduardo Araújo.
Minister of Foreign Affairs: Silvino Manuel da Luz.
Minister of Industry and Energy: Adão Silva Rocha.
Minister of Public Works: Adriano Lima.
Minister of Information, Culture and Sport: David Hopffer Almada.
Deputy Minister to the Prime Minister: Herculano Vieira.
Deputy Minister of Planning and Co-operation: José Brito.
Deputy Minister of Finance: Dr Arnaldo Vasconcellos Franca.
Secretary of State to the Prime Minister: João de Deus Maximiano.
Secretary of State for Foreign Affairs: Aguinaldo Lisboa Ramos.
Secretary of State for Trade, Tourism and Crafts: Virgilio Burgo Fernandes.
Secretary of State for Fishing: Miguel Lima.
Secretary of State for Public Administration: Renato Cardoso.

MINISTRIES

Office of the President: Presidência da República, Praia, São Tiago; tel. 260; telex 6051.
Office of the Prime Minister: Praça 12 de Setembro, CP 16, Praia, São Tiago; tel. 248; telex 6052.
Ministry of Economy and Finance: 107 Avda Amílcar Cabral, Praia, São Tiago; tel. 329; telex 6058.
Ministry of Education and Culture: Avda Amílcar Cabral, CP 111, Praia, São Tiago; tel. 345; telex 6057.
Ministry of Foreign Affairs: Praça 10 de Mayo, CP 60, Praia, São Tiago; tel. 310; telex 6070.
Ministry of Health and Social Affairs: Praça 12 de Setembro, CP 47, Praia, São Tiago; tel. 422; telex 6059.
Ministry of the Interior: Rua Guerra Mendes, Praia, São Tiago; tel. 255; telex 6062.
Ministry of Justice: Praça 12 de Setembro, Praia, São Tiago; tel. 336; telex 6025.
Ministry of National Defence: Avda Unidade Guiné, Praia, São Tiago; tel. 448; telex 6077.
Ministry of Rural Development: Rua António Pussich, Praia, São Tiago; tel. 335; telex 6072.
Ministry of Transport and Telecommunications: Rua Guerra Mendes, CP 15, Praia, São Tiago; tel. 601; telex 6060.

Legislature

ASSEMBLÉIA NACIONAL POPULAR

The National People's Assembly consists of 83 deputies, elected for a term of five years by universal adult suffrage. The most recent general election was held on 7 December 1985, when 94.5% of the votes endorsed the single list of candidates presented by the PAICV.
President: Abílio Augusto Monteiro Duarte.

Political Organizations

Partido Africano da Independência de Cabo Verde (PAICV): (African Party for the Independence of Cape Verde): CP 22, São Tiago; telex 6022; f. 1956 as the Partido Africano da Independência do Guiné e Cabo Verde (PAIGC); name changed in 1981, following the November 1980 coup in Guinea-Bissau, which the Cape Verde govt had opposed, having previously favoured eventual unification with Guinea-Bissau; sole legal political party; Sec.-Gen. Aristides Maria Pereira; Dep. Sec.-Gen. Pedro Verona Rodrigues Pires.

The **Independent Democratic Union of Cape Verde (UCID)** is an opposition movement based in Lisbon, Portugal, formed by emigrants opposed to the PAICV regime.

Diplomatic Representation

EMBASSIES IN CAPE VERDE

Brazil: Rua Guerra Menoes, CP 93, Praia, São Tiago; tel. 385; telex 6075; Ambassador: Fernando Buarque Franco Nette.
China, People's Republic: Praia, São Tiago; Ambassador: Liang Taosheng.
Cuba: Publico CV, Praia, São Tiago; tel. 465; telex 6087; Ambassador: Gilberto García Alonso.
France: CP 192, Praia, São Tiago; tel. 290; telex 6064; Ambassador: Jacques Millot.
Portugal: Achada de Santo António, CP 160, Praia, São Tiago; tel. 408; telex 6055; Ambassador: Dr António Baptista Martins.
USSR: Praia, São Tiago; Ambassador: Nicolai Serioguine.
USA: Rua Hoji Ya Yenna 81, CP 201, Praia, São Tiago; tel. 61-43-63; telex 6068; Ambassador: Vernon Dubois Penner, Jr.

Judicial System

Supremo Tribunal de Justiça: Praia, São Tiago; the highest court.

There is a network of tribunais populares at the local level.

CAPE VERDE

Religion

CHRISTIANITY

At 31 December 1984 there were an estimated 301,475 adherents of the Roman Catholic Church, representing 97.8% of the total population. Protestant churches, among which the Nazarenes are prominent, represent about 2% of the population.

The Roman Catholic Church

Cape Verde comprises the single diocese of Santiago de Cabo Verde, directly responsible to the Holy See.

Bishop of Santiago de Cabo Verde: Mgr PAULINO DO LIVRAMENTO EVORA, CP 46, Praia, São Tiago; tel. 203.

The Press

Boletim Informativo: CP 126, Praia, São Tiago; f. 1976; weekly; publ. by the Ministry of Foreign Affairs; circ. 1,500.

Boletim Oficial da República de Cabo Verde: Imprensa Nacional, CP 113, Praia, São Tiago; weekly; official.

Raízes: CP 98, Praia, São Tiago; tel. 319; f. 1977; quarterly; cultural review; Editor ARNALDO FRANÇA; circ. 1,500.

Terra Nova: Ilha do Fogo; weekly.

Unidade e Luta: Praia, São Tiago; organ of the PAICV.

Voz do Povo: CP 118, Praia, São Tiago; weekly; publ. by Direcção Geral da Informação.

NEWS AGENCIES

Agence France-Presse (AFP): CP 26/118 Praia, São Tiago; tel. 434; Rep. Mme FATIMA AZEVADO.

Inter Press Service (IPS) (Italy): CP 14, Mindelo, São Vicente; tel. 31-10-06; Rep. JUAN A. COLOMA.

Publisher

Government Publishing House

Imprensa Nacional: CP 113, Praia, São Tiago.

Radio and Television

There were an estimated 47,000 radio receivers in use in 1983. There are two radio transmitters, both broadcasting in Portuguese and Creole. There is no Cape Verdean television service, but an estimated 500 TV receivers were in use in 1985.

Rádio Nacional de Cabo Verde

Emissora Oficial da República de Cabo Verde: CP 26, Praia, São Tiago; tel. 344; govt-controlled.

Voz de São Vicente: CP 29, Mindelo, São Vicente; f. 1974; govt-controlled; Dir FRANCISCO TOMAR.

Finance

(cap. = capital; dep. = deposits; res = reserves; m. = million; amounts in Cape Verde escudos)

BANKING

Banco de Cabo Verde: CP 101, 117 Avda Amílcar Cabral, Praia, São Tiago; tel. 374; telex 6050; f. 1975; central bank; cap. 400m., res 475m., dep. 1,997m. (1981); Gov. CORENTINO VIRGILIO SANTOS; brs on São Vicente and Sal.

The **Fundo de Solidariedade Nacional** is the main savings institution, the **Fundo de Desenvolvimento Nacional** channels public investment resources, and the **Instituto Caboverdiano** administers international aid.

Trade and Industry

Empresa Agro-industrial, EP: CP 135, Praia, São Tiago; telex 6072; f. 1986; state enterprise for fruit, vegetables and pigs; Dir JUSTINO LOPES.

Empresa Caboverdeana das Infraestruturas de Pescas (INTERBASE): CP 59, Mindelo, São Vicente; tel. 2434; telex 3084; co-ordinates and equips the fishing industry; manages the harbour, incl. cold-storage facilities (capacity 9,000 metric tons); operates ice supply and shipping agency.

Empresa Nacional de Avicultura (ENAVI): CP 135, Praia, São Tiago; tel. 61-18-59; telex 6072; f. 1979; state enterprise for poultry farming.

Empresa Nacional de Combustíveis, EP: CP 1, Mindelo, São Vicente; f. 1979; state enterprise supervising import and distribution of petroleum; Dir RUI S. LOPES DOS SANTOS.

Empresa Nacional de Produtos Farmacêuticos: CP 59, Praia, São Tiago; tel. 00-09-60; telex 6024; f. 1979; state pharmaceuticals enterprise holding monopoly of local production and medical imports.

Empresa Pública de Abastecimentos (EMPA): CP 107, Praia, São Tiago; tel. 249; telex 6054; f. 1976; state provisioning enterprise, supervising imports, exports and domestic distribution.

Instituto Nacional de Cooperativas: Praia, São Tiago; central co-operative organization.

Secretaria de Estado das Pescas (SEP): oversees the development of the fishing industry.

Sociedade de Comercialização e Apoio à Pesca Artesanal (SCAPA): Praia, São Tiago; state-run; co-ordinates small-scale fishing enterprises and promotes modern techniques.

TRADE UNION

União Nacional dos Trabalhadores de Cabo Verde—Central Sindical (UNTC—CS): Praia, São Tiago; f. 1978; Chair. ADOLINO MANUEL SILVA.

Transport

RAILWAYS

There are no railways in Cape Verde.

ROADS

In 1981 there were about 2,250 km of roads, of which 660 km were paved. In 1986 a loan of US $7.5m. from the People's Republic of China was used partly to finance new road-building projects.

SHIPPING

Cargo-passenger ships call regularly at Mindelo, on São Vicente, and Praia, on São Tiago. Praia and Porto Grande ports are being considerably enlarged, with the help of a US $7.2m. grant from the International Development Association, and a shipyard has been built at Mindelo. Work started in 1982 on a port at Palmeira on Sal.

Comissão de Gestão dos Transportes Marítimos de Cabo Verde: CP 153, São Vincente; tel. 2652; telex 3031; 3,199 grt.

Companhia Nacional de Navegação Arca Verde: CP 41, 153 Rua 5 de Julho, Praia, São Tiago; tel. 61-14-21; telex 6067; f. 1975; 5,471 grt.

Companhia de Navegação Estrella Negra: 48 Avda Kwame Nkrumah, São Vincente; telex 3030; 2,098 grt.

Companhia Nacional de Navegação Portuguesa: Agent in São Tiago: João Benoliel de Carvalho, Lda, CP 56, Praia, São Tiago.

Companhia Portuguesa de Transportes Marítimos: Agent in São Tiago: João Benoliel de Carvalho, Lda, CP 56, Praia, São Tiago.

Transportes Marítimos de Cabo Verde: Avda Kwame Nkrumah, CP 153, Mindelo, São Vicente; serves Portugal, Cádiz, Antwerp, Rotterdam, Hamburg, Ipswich, Felixstowe, Udvalla, Abidjan and Tema.

CIVIL AVIATION

The Amílcar Cabral international airport is at Espargos, on Sal Island, with capacity for aircraft of up to 50 tons. It can handle 1m. passengers per year. In 1986 work on the expansion of the airport's facilities was underway, with Italian and EEC aid. A Brazilian proposal to construct a new cargo terminal was discussed in 1986. There is also a small airport on each of the other main islands, except Brava.

CAPE VERDE

Transportes Aéreos de Cabo Verde (TACV): CP 1, Rua Guerra Mendes 11–13, Praia, São Tiago; telex 6065; f. 1955; connects São Vicente, Praia, Ilha do Sal, São Nicolau, Boavista, Fogo, São Filipe, Mosteiros and Maio; also operates weekly services to Senegal and Guinea-Bissau; Gen. Man. Valdemar Fortes de Sousa Lobo; fleet: 2 HS-748 Avro and 2 DH Twin Otter.

Tourism

Secretaria de Estado de Comércio e Turismo: CP 105, Praia, São Tiago; tel. 573; telex 6058.

THE CENTRAL AFRICAN REPUBLIC

Introductory Survey

Location, Climate, Language, Religion, Flag, Capital

The Central African Republic is a land-locked country in the heart of equatorial Africa. It is bounded by Chad to the north, by Sudan to the east, by the Congo and Zaire to the south and by Cameroon to the west. The climate is tropical, with an average annual temperature of 26°C (79°F) and heavy rains in the south-western forest areas. The national language is Sango, but French is the official language. Many of the population hold animist beliefs, but about one-third are Christians. The national flag (proportions 5 by 3) has four horizontal stripes, of blue, white, green and yellow, divided vertically by a central red stripe, with a five-pointed yellow star and crescent in the upper hoist. The capital is Bangui.

Recent History

The former territory of Ubangi-Shari (Oubangui-Chari), within French Equatorial Africa, became the Central African Republic (CAR) on achieving self-government in December 1958. Full independence was attained on 13 August 1960. The leading figure in the campaign for self-government was Barthélemy Boganda, founder of the Mouvement d'évolution sociale de l'Afrique noire (MESAN). Boganda became the country's first Prime Minister, but he was killed in an air crash in March 1959. He was succeeded by his nephew, David Dacko, who led the country to independence and in 1962 established a one-party state, with MESAN as the sole authorized party. President Dacko was overthrown on 31 December 1965 by a military coup which brought to power his cousin, Col (later Marshal) Jean-Bédel Bokassa, Commander-in-Chief of the armed forces.

In January 1966 Col Bokassa formed a new government, rescinded the Constitution and dissolved the National Assembly. Bokassa, who became Life President in March 1972 and Marshal of the Republic in May 1974, forestalled several alleged coup attempts and used stern measures to suppress opposition. A government reorganization in January 1975 included the appointment of Elisabeth Domitien, the vice-president of MESAN, to the newly-created post of Prime Minister. She thus became the first woman to hold this position in any African country, but she was dismissed in April 1976, when President Bokassa assumed the premiership.

In September 1976 the Council of Ministers was replaced by the Council for the Central African Revolution, and ex-President Dacko was named personal adviser to the President. In December the Republic was renamed the Central African Empire (CAE), and a new constitution was instituted. Bokassa was proclaimed the first Emperor, and Dacko became his Personal Counsellor. The Imperial Constitution provided for the establishment of a National Assembly but no elections were held.

The elaborate preparations for Bokassa's coronation in December 1977 were estimated to have consumed about one-quarter of the country's income. In May 1978 Bokassa reshuffled the army leadership and strengthened its powers. In July he dismissed the Council of Ministers and appointed a new Council, headed by Henri Maidou, previously a Deputy Prime Minister. In January 1979 violent protests, led by students, were suppressed, reportedly with the help of Zairian troops. Following a protest by schoolchildren against compulsory school uniforms (made by a company that was owned by the Bokassa family), many children were arrested in April. About 100 of them were killed in prison, and Bokassa himself allegedly participated in the massacre. In May the Emperor's ambassador in Paris, Gen. Sylvestre Bangui, resigned in protest, and in September he became the leader of a newly-formed government-in-exile, comprising four opposition groups. On 20 September 1979, while Bokassa was in Libya, David Dacko deposed him in a bloodless coup, strongly backed by France, and resumed power as President. The country thus became a republic again, and Henri Maidou was appointed Vice-President.

The prime concern of President Dacko was to establish order and economic stability in the CAR, but his Government was not accepted without some opposition, particularly from students who objected to the continuation in office of CAE Ministers. In August 1980 Dacko accepted demands for the dismissal of both Henri Maidou and the unpopular Prime Minister, Bernard Christian Ayandho. The new Council of Ministers was led by Jean-Pierre Lebouder, formerly Minister of Planning. Bokassa, at that time in exile in the Ivory Coast (and subsequently in Paris), was condemned to death *in absentia* in December 1980.

In February 1981 a new constitution, providing for a multi-party system, was approved by referendum and promulgated by President Dacko. He won a presidential election in March and was sworn in for a six-year term in April. Following accusations by his opponents of electoral malpractice, rioting broke out and a state of siege was declared in Bangui. Political tension increased after a bomb attack on a Bangui cinema in July, in which three people died. The Mouvement centrafricain de libération nationale claimed responsibility and was subsequently banned. A state of siege was again declared, and the Government summoned assistance from army units to maintain order. The Chief of Staff of the armed forces, Gen. André Kolingba, deposed President Dacko in a bloodless coup on 1 September, citing 'gross violations of democracy' as reasons for the military take-over, and suspending all political activity. Power was assumed by a 23-member Military Committee for National Recovery, and an all-military government was formed.

In March 1982 the exiled leader of the banned Mouvement pour la libération du peuple centrafricain (MLPC), Ange Patasse, returned to Bangui and was implicated in an unsuccessful coup attempt. Patasse, who had been the Prime Minister under Bokassa in 1976–78 and was runner-up in the presidential election of March 1981, sought asylum in the French embassy in Bangui, from where he was transported to exile in Togo. French support for Patasse strained the military regime's relations with France, but a visit by President Mitterrand to the CAR in October 1982 normalized relations. Some former government ministers were also implicated in the coup attempt, and in August 1984 two of the accused ex-ministers, Gaston Ouédane and Jérôme Allan, were sentenced to 10 years' imprisonment.

Opposition to Gen. Kolingba's regime continued, despite the suspension of all political activity in September 1981. In August 1983 a clandestine opposition movement was formed, uniting the three main opposition parties. In September 1984 Gen. Kolingba announced an amnesty for the leaders of banned political parties, who had been under house arrest since January, and reduced the sentences of the ex-ministers who had been imprisoned for involvement in the 1982 coup attempt. Shortly afterwards, in December 1984, President Mitterrand of France paid a state visit to the country. A total of 89 political prisoners were released in December 1985. Several students were arrested during anti-French demonstrations in Bangui in March 1986, following the death of 35 civilians, including many schoolchildren, as a result of the crash of a French military aircraft. Shortly afterwards, a bomb exploded on the road leading to Bangui-Mpoko airport. Two Libyan diplomats were expelled from the CAR, suspected of complicity in the bomb attack. The students were released in September, along with a further, unspecified number of political prisoners (including Gaston Ouédane and Jérôme Allan).

The appointment of several civilians as high commissioners (attached to the Council of Ministers, with responsibilities for various departments) in a government reshuffle in January 1984 was followed in September 1985 by the introduction of civilians into the Council of Ministers itself, for the first time since Gen.

CENTRAL AFRICAN REPUBLIC

Kolingba's assumption of power. In May 1986 Kolingba announced the creation of a sole legal political party, the Rassemblement démocratique centrafricain (RDC), and reiterated proposals for elections to a National Assembly, first announced in 1982. In January 1986 a constitutional commission was formed to draft a new constitution, which gave President Kolingba a further six years in office and provided for the creation of a one-party state. The new constitution was approved by an estimated 91% of the electorate in a referendum held in November 1986, and a subsequent government reshuffle in December resulted in a majority of civilians in the Council of Ministers.

In October 1986 Bokassa unexpectedly returned to the CAR, and was immediately arrested. His new trial, on charges of murder, cannibalism and embezzlement, opened in November, and was expected to continue until March 1987.

Government

Following the coup of September 1981, all legislative and executive powers rested with the Military Committee for National Recovery (Comité militaire pour le redressement national—CMRN), which had 24 members in 1984. The Government consisted entirely of army officers. In September 1985 the CMRN was dissolved and, in the ensuing reshuffle, civilians were introduced into the new Council of Ministers. The Rassemblement démocratique centrafricain (RDC), formed in 1986, is the ruling, and sole legal, political party. Legislative elections for a new National Assembly were to be held, following the electorate's approval of the new Constitution in November 1986. For administrative purposes, the country is divided into 14 prefectures and 47 sub-prefectures. At community level there are eight communes de plein exercice, four communes de moyen exercice and 164 communes rurales.

Defence

In July 1986 the armed forces numbered about 2,300 men (army 2,000; air force 300), with a further 10,000 men in paramilitary forces. Military service is selective and lasts for two years. France maintains a force of 1,600 troops in the CAR. Estimated defence expenditure in 1983 was 6,500m. francs CFA.

Economic Affairs

Since independence, the CAR's economic growth has failed to keep pace with the increase in the country's population. In 1984, according to estimates by the World Bank, the gross national product (GNP) per head (at average 1982–84 prices) was US $260, having decreased at an average rate of 0.1% per year, in real terms, since 1965. The average annual growth of overall gross domestic product (GDP), measured in constant prices, was 2.7% between 1965 and 1973, slowing to 0.7% in 1973–84. According to estimates by the UN Economic Commission for Africa, GDP declined, in real terms, in each of the four years 1979–82, with a cumulative fall of 10% over the period. During the early 1980s, however, the Kolingba regime achieved a degree of economic stability through the implementation of a series of recovery programmes, with the result that real GDP expanded by an estimated 2.5% in 1985.

About 72% of the working population are engaged in agriculture, which accounted for 39% of GDP in 1984. The most important cash crops are cotton and coffee, but subsistence farming predominates. The main subsistence crops are millet, sorghum and cassava. Since independence, both the production and export of food crops have declined. In 1986 a major livestock development programme was launched, at a total cost of US $37.3m., of which $11.9m. was provided by a loan from the International Development Association (IDA). Manufacturing is mainly small-scale and accounted for 8% of GDP in 1984, the main activities being in timber, tanning, textiles and brewing. In August 1984 the Government announced measures to encourage the development of small and medium-sized enterprises.

Production of cotton declined, following a record harvest of 60,000 tons (unginned) in 1971, to only 17,242 tons in 1981. Output increased to 33,500 tons in 1983/84 and reached 46,000 tons in 1984/85, owing mainly to an increase in the area planted and the restructuring of the national agricultural development corporation (SOCADA) as part of the Government's cotton development programme, launched in 1983. Coffee production was 18,000 tons in 1982/83, but was affected by widespread drought in 1983/84, when output fell to 10,000 tons. In 1984/85 the crop increased to 15,000 tons.

Forests, containing more than 60 species of valuable trees, cover 5.5% of land area, and total exploitable potential is estimated to be 87.3m. cu m per year. Timber exports in 1984 were 337,000 cu m. Problems of transport and organization have hampered removals, but efficiency should be increased by improvements to river navigation and by the construction of a proposed railway linking Bangui to Yaoundé, the capital of neighbouring Cameroon, and thence to the Atlantic coast.

Diamonds are found in alluvial deposits, mainly in the west of the country, and were the CAR's principal source of export earnings from the mid-1960s until 1973. The contribution of diamonds to total export earnings declined from 53% in 1968 to 17% in 1976, after which the Government adopted measures to promote investment in the industry. Revenue then steadily increased, and reached 50% of exports in 1979, before falling to only 24% in 1982. The proportion increased to 33.4% in 1983, but fell to 30.9% in 1984. Declared production in 1985 was 352,000 carats, compared with a peak of 609,000 carats in 1968. However, there is widespread evasion of export duties, with possibly 60% of total diamond production being smuggled out of the country. There is some gold mining, and a feasibility study for a state uranium-mining company, with French and Swiss participation, was begun in 1977; reserves are estimated at approximately 15,000 tons of metal at Bakouma, with a potential capacity to yield 1,000 tons per year. Exploratory drilling for petroleum deposits on the border with Chad has begun.

Annual inflation averaged 12.4% in 1984. However, salaries have not increased in line with prices, and the cost of living, measured in real terms, was estimated to have risen by 17% in the same year. The budget deficit was 9,500m. francs CFA in 1984, and was due to rise to 11,100m. francs CFA in 1985. The budget proposals for 1986 envisaged expenditure of 54,580m. francs CFA and a deficit of 7,150m. francs CFA. The trade deficit declined from 8,175m. francs CFA in 1981 to only 689m. francs CFA in 1984. The CAR relies heavily on foreign aid, especially from France, which provided 58% of aid from 1960 to 1984. French aid in 1984 amounted to 15,000m. francs CFA, of which 5,000m. francs contributed to reducing the budget deficit. The current deficit on the balance of payments was US $43.2m. in 1980. It fell to $4.3m. in 1981 but reached $54.2m. in 1982, owing to the country's severe drought and stagnant economy. The deficit declined to $34.8m. in 1983, and to $31.5m. in 1984. Accumulated arrears of debt service led to the rescheduling of payments in 1982, 1983 and 1985 on the part of Western governments. Outstanding foreign debt in March 1985 amounted to 110,000m. francs CFA, equivalent to three times the 1984 budget revenue.

The 1980/81 emergency social and economic rehabilitation plan involved expenditure of 98,000m. francs CFA, drawn largely from French and international aid: the 1983–85 recovery programme focused on the implementation of development projects totalling 31,300m. francs CFA, and succeeded in achieving a positive GDP growth rate. Both programmes concentrated on the development of agriculture and of transport infrastructure. In October 1985 the IMF approved an 18-month stand-by arrangement, authorizing purchases up to the equivalent of 15m. SDRs in support of the Government's medium-term economic recovery programme. The programme aimed to achieve cuts in the budget deficit, to 0.8% of GDP in 1985 and 0.2% in 1986, and a reduction of the current deficit on the balance of payments to 14% of GDP in 1985 and 12.1% in 1986. In July 1986 a 16-month economic restructuring programme was adopted, supported by a US $30m. structural adjustment loan from the World Bank. It was hoped that, by continuing to give priority to the potentially rich agricultural sector and by encouraging greater participation by the private sector in the economy, a real GDP growth rate of 4% per year could be achieved and maintained.

Social Welfare

An Employment Code guarantees a minimum wage for 60,000 employees and provides for the payment of benefits to compensate for accidents at work. There are 36 prefectorial hospitals, 36 maternity hospitals, 108 welfare centres and 200

CENTRAL AFRICAN REPUBLIC

first-aid centres. In 1980 the CAR had 3,605 hospital beds, but only 99 physicians were working in the country.

Education

Education is officially compulsory for eight years between six and 14 years of age. Primary education begins at the age of six and lasts for six years. Secondary education begins at the age of 12 and lasts for up to seven years, comprising a first cycle of four years and a second of three years. In 1982 an estimated 61% of children in the relevant age-group (80% of boys; 42% of girls) attended primary schools, while secondary enrolment was equivalent to only 16% (boys 24%; girls 8%). According to estimates by UNESCO, the adult illiteracy rate in 1985 averaged 59.8% (males 46.7%; females 71.4%). In January 1986 a three-year project, aimed at improving educational facilities in rural areas, was launched, with the African Development Fund providing US $7.6m. in finance. There is a university at Bangui.

Tourism

The main tourist attractions are the waterfalls, the forests and many varieties of wild animals. There are excellent hunting and fishing opportunities. There were an estimated 7,000 tourist arrivals in 1982, when tourist receipts totalled US $3m.

Public Holidays

1987: 1 January (New Year), 29 March (Anniversary of death of Barthélemy Boganda), 20 April (Easter Monday), 1 May (May Day), 28 May (Ascension), 8 June (Whit Monday), 30 June (National Day of Prayer), 13 August (Independence Day), 15 August (Assumption), 1 November (All Saints' Day), 25 December (Christmas).

1988: 1 January (New Year), 29 March (Anniversary of death of Barthélemy Boganda), 4 April (Easter Monday), 1 May (May Day), 12 May (Ascension), 23 May (Whit Monday), 30 June (National Day of Prayer), 13 August (Independence Day), 15 August (Assumption), 1 November (All Saints' Day), 25 December (Christmas).

Weights and Measures

The metric system is officially in force.

Currency and Exchange Rates

100 centimes = 1 franc de la Coopération financière en Afrique centrale (CFA).

Exchange rates (30 September 1986):
 £1 sterling = 480.625 francs CFA;
 US $1 = 332.125 francs CFA.

CENTRAL AFRICAN REPUBLIC

Statistical Survey

Source (unless otherwise stated): Direction de la Statistique Générale et des Etudes Economiques, BP 732, Bangui; tel. 61-38-00; telex 5208.

Area and Population

AREA, POPULATION AND DENSITY

Area (sq km)	622,984*
Population (census of 8–22 December 1975)	
Males	985,224
Females	1,069,386
Total	2,054,610
Population (official estimates)	
1980 (31 December)	2,362,400
1982 (31 December)	2,442,000
1985 (mid-year)	2,608,000
Density (per sq km) at mid-1985	4.2

* 240,535 sq miles.

PRINCIPAL TOWNS

Bangui (capital), population 350,000; Berbérati 100,000; Bouar 55,000 (1982 estimates).

BIRTHS AND DEATHS

Average annual birth rate 43.6 per 1,000 in 1970–75, 44.9 per 1,000 in 1975–80; death rate 25.0 per 1,000 in 1970–75, 23.5 per 1,000 in 1975–80 (UN estimates).

ECONOMICALLY ACTIVE POPULATION
(ILO estimates, '000 persons at mid-1980)

	Males	Females	Total
Agriculture, etc.	436	432	868
Industry	56	20	76
Services	131	124	255
Total	623	576	1,200

Source: ILO, *Economically Active Population Estimates and Projections, 1950–2025*.

Agriculture

PRINCIPAL CROPS ('000 metric tons)

	1982	1983	1984*
Rice (paddy)	12	13	13
Maize	48	45	43
Millet and sorghum	57	58	59
Cassava (Manioc)	940*	860	900
Yams	193*	195	197
Taro (Coco yam)	53*	55	57
Groundnuts (in shell)	127	130	130
Sesame seed	11	10	10
Cottonseed	25†	20	20
Oranges, lemons and limes	14*	14	14
Bananas	78*	80	82
Plantains	64*	64	65
Coffee (green)	17	10†	15†
Tobacco (leaves)	1	1	1
Cotton (lint)	13†	10	10

* FAO estimates.   † Unofficial figure.

Source: FAO, *Production Yearbook*.

LIVESTOCK
(FAO estimates, '000 head, year ending September)

	1982	1983	1984
Cattle	1,400	1,500*	1,500
Goats	950	960*	960
Sheep	81	80*	82
Pigs	135	137	140

* Unofficial estimates.

Chickens (estimates, million): 2 in 1982; 2 in 1983; 2 in 1984.

Source: FAO, *Production Yearbook*.

LIVESTOCK PRODUCTS (FAO estimates, metric tons)

	1982	1983	1984
Beef and veal	24,000	25,000	25,000
Mutton and lamb	1,000	1,000	1,000
Goats' meat	3,000	3,000	3,000
Pig meat	5,000	5,000	5,000
Poultry meat	2,000	2,000	2,000
Other meat	6,000	5,000	6,000
Cows' milk	4,000	4,000	4,000
Cattle hides (fresh)	3,740	3,850	3,894
Hen eggs	1,044	1,062	1,080
Honey	6,600	6,700	6,800

Source: FAO, *Production Yearbook*.

Forestry

ROUNDWOOD REMOVALS
('000 cubic metres, excluding bark)

	1982	1983	1984
Sawlogs, veneer logs and logs for sleepers	291	254	260
Other industrial wood*	208	213	218
Fuel wood*	2,613	2,680	2,680
Total	3,112	3,147	3,158

*FAO estimates.
Source: FAO, *Yearbook of Forest Products*.

SAWNWOOD PRODUCTION
('000 cubic metres)

	1982	1983	1984
Total (incl. boxboards)	63	61	58

Source: FAO, *Yearbook of Forest Products*.

Fishing

('000 metric tons, live weight)

	1975	1976	1977
Total catch (freshwater fish)	8.0	10.5	13.0

1978–84: Annual catch as in 1977.
Source: FAO, *Yearbook of Fishery Statistics*.

Mining

	1981	1982	1983
Gold (kg)	43	44	78
Gem diamonds ('000 carats)	209	186	230
Industrial diamonds ('000 carats)	103*	91*	65*

* Estimate by the US Bureau of Mines.
Source: UN, *Industrial Statistics Yearbook*.

Industry

SELECTED PRODUCTS

		1979	1980	1981
Beer	hectolitres	216,000	283,000	208,000
Soft drinks	hectolitres	33,000	32,000	34,000*
Cigarettes and cigars	million	291	316	n.a.
Woven cotton fabrics*	'000 sq metres	4,000	4,000	4,000
Footwear	'000 pairs	409	473	380
Motor cycles	number	5,000	7,000	n.a.
Bicycles	number	4,000	4,000	5,000
Electric energy	million kWh	62	64	67

1982: Woven cotton fabrics 4,000,000 sq metres*; Electric energy 68 million kWh.
1983: Woven cotton fabrics 4,000,000 sq metres*; Electric energy 68 million kWh.
* Estimated or provisional figure.
Source: UN, *Industrial Statistics Yearbook*.

Finance

CURRENCY AND EXCHANGE RATES
Monetary Units
100 centimes = 1 franc de la Coopération financière en Afrique centrale (CFA).

Denominations
Coins: 1, 2, 5, 10, 25, 50 and 100 francs CFA.
Notes: 100, 500, 1,000, 5,000 and 10,000 francs CFA.

French Franc, Sterling and Dollar Equivalents
(30 September 1986)
1 French franc = 50 francs CFA;
£1 sterling = 480.625 francs CFA;
US $1 = 332.125 francs CFA;
1,000 francs CFA = £2.081 = $3.011.

Average Exchange Rate (francs CFA per US $)
1983   381.06
1984   436.96
1985   449.26

CENTRAL BANK RESERVES
(US $ million at 31 December)

	1982	1983	1984
Gold*	5.00	4.21	3.44
IMF special drawing rights	0.19	0.74	2.54
Reserve position in IMF	1.33	1.69	0.11
Foreign exchange	44.85	44.36	50.03
Total	51.37	51.00	56.12

* Valued at market-related prices.
Source: IMF, *International Financial Statistics*.

CENTRAL AFRICAN REPUBLIC

BUDGET (million francs CFA, provisional figures)

Revenue	1981	1982
Taxation	22,778	23,650
Direct taxes	5,950	6,090
Income tax	4,260	4,080
Licences and patents	810	670
Indirect taxes	14,931	15,715
Customs duty	10,956	11,402
Domestic consumption tax	1,710	1,702
Stamp duty and registration	505	450
Accessory tax	1,392	1,395
Non-tax revenue	11,307	6,345
Special investment acounts	2,925	2,725
Goods and services	722	1,030
Property income	250	190
Subsidies	4,150	700
Loans for economic recovery	3,260	1,700
Total	**34,085**	**29,995**

Expenditure	1981	1982
Administrative budget	29,948	32,825
Interest on public debt	8	8
Services	22,758	24,937
Transfers, interventions and subsidies	n.a.	3,729
Common services	3,391	4,152
Capital budget	4,137	5,378
Communications	n.a.	1,055
Community services	n.a.	696
Participations	n.a.	617
Production	n.a.	188
Research and statistics	n.a.	22
Repayments of public debt	1,900	2,800
Total	**34,085**	**38,203**

1983 (million francs CFA): Revenue 36,200; Expenditure 43,200.

1984 (forecasts, million francs CFA): Revenue 38,500; Expenditure 48,000.

1985 (forecasts, million francs CFA): Revenue 41,420; Expenditure 52,510 (capital investment 18,000).

1986 (forecasts, million francs CFA): Revenue 47,430; Expenditure 54,580 (administrative budget 36,440, extraordinary budget 18,140).

MONEY SUPPLY ('000 million francs CFA at 31 December)

	1982	1983	1984
Currency outside banks	31.22	34.31	37.24
Demand deposits at commercial and development banks	9.01	10.09	10.69
Checking deposits at post office	0.33	0.37	0.32
Total money	**40.56**	**44.78**	**48.24**

Source: IMF, *International Financial Statistics*.

NATIONAL ACCOUNTS (estimates, million francs CFA at current prices)
Gross Domestic Product by Economic Activity

	1980	1981	1982
Agriculture, forestry and fishing	57,450	60,350	65,200
Mining and quarrying	6,110	5,360	5,370
Manufacturing	10,040	11,620	13,560
Electricity, gas and water	1,740	2,190	2,880
Construction	5,560	6,380	7,660
Trade, restaurants and hotels	22,580	25,060	28,920
Transport, storage and communications	4,980	6,050	7,470
Finance, insurance, real estate and business services	1,190	1,320	1,500
Public adminstration and defence	25,400	30,900	33,900
Other services	7,110	7,890	8,990
GDP at factor cost	**142,160**	**157,120**	**175,450**
Indirect taxes, *less* subsidies	26,240	31,680	37,050
GDP in purchasers' values	**168,400**	**188,800**	**212,500**

Source: UN Economic Commission for Africa, *African Statistical Yearbook*.

CENTRAL AFRICAN REPUBLIC

BALANCE OF PAYMENTS (US $ million)

	1982	1983	1984
Merchandise exports f.o.b.	111.5	114.6	114.7
Merchandise imports f.o.b.	−149.7	−137.5	−140.1
Trade balance	−38.2	−22.9	−25.4
Exports of services	46.4	38.6	37.5
Imports of services	−117.2	−114.8	−98.0
Balance on goods and services	−109.0	−99.1	−85.9
Private unrequited transfers (net)	−17.0	−14.8	−11.2
Government unrequited transfers (net)	71.7	79.0	65.6
Current balance	−54.2	−34.8	−31.5
Direct capital investment (net)	8.8	4.0	4.9
Other long-term capital (net)	−8.7	15.1	24.1
Short-term capital (net)	8.2	−10.6	−1.7
Net errors and omissions	18.6	4.4	3.6
Total (net monetary movements)	−27.4	−21.8	−0.6
Valuation changes (net)	−8.6	−1.4	2.5
Exceptional financing (net)	20.1	19.8	7.9
Official financing (net)	−7.8	0.7	−1.0
Changes in reserves	−23.7	−2.7	8.9

Source: IMF, *International Financial Statistics*.

External Trade

Note: The data exclude trade with other countries in the Customs and Economic Union of Central Africa (UDEAC): Cameroon, the Congo and Gabon.

PRINCIPAL COMMODITIES (distribution by SITC, US $'000)

Imports c.i.f.	1978	1979	1980
Food and live animals	5,346	8,148	11,244
Cereals and cereal preparations	1,755	4,166	5,400
Wheat flour	803	2,653	3,603
Beverages and tobacco	3,734	2,591	5,135
Beverages	3,213	2,192	4,396
Alcoholic beverages	3,056	2,039	4,109
Chemicals and related products	5,070	9,393	9,490
Medicinal and pharmaceutical products	1,884	3,200	4,588
Medicaments	1,710	3,040	4,364
Pesticides, disinfectants, etc.	405	3,331	1,497
Basic manufactures	11,802	11,448	15,393
Non-metallic mineral manufactures	2,233	2,375	3,418
Machinery and transport equipment	21,609	27,407	27,243
Power generating machinery and equipment	1,326	4,954	1,873
Internal combustion piston engines and parts	911	4,184	1,245
Machinery specialized for particular industries	1,604	3,167	2,957
General industrial machinery, equipment and parts	3,483	5,341	3,970
Electrical machinery, apparatus, etc.	3,187	2,974	4,707
Road vehicles and parts (excl. tyres, engines and electrical parts)	11,182	9,745	13,120
Motor vehicles for goods transport and special purposes	5,022	4,417	4,409
Goods vehicles (lorries and trucks)	4,983	4,128	3,989
Miscellaneous manufactured articles	6,601	4,938	8,008
Total (incl. others)	56,662	66,530	80,461

Source: UN, *International Trade Statistics Yearbook*.
Total imports (million francs CFA): 28,510 in 1981; 41,306 in 1982; 32,456 in 1983; 38,170 in 1984 (Source: IMF, *International Financial Statistics*).

CENTRAL AFRICAN REPUBLIC   Statistical Survey

Exports f.o.b.	1978	1979	1980
Food and live animals	20,957	20,447	31,766
Coffee, tea, cocoa and spices	20,956	20,358	31,759
Coffee (green and roasted)	20,830	20,265	31,611
Crude materials (inedible) except fuels	21,441	20,893	47,678
Cork and wood	11,687	9,787	33,212
Sawlogs and veneer logs	6,547	6,777	27,407
Sawn lumber	5,140	3,010	5,805
Textile fibres and waste	4,426	5,364	8,645
Cotton	4,426	5,364	8,644
Bones, ivory, horns, etc.	3,856	4,594	4,277
Basic manufactures	26,924	35,296	28,945
Non-metallic mineral manufactures	26,860	35,019	28,908
Diamonds (non-industrial)	26,860	35,019	28,898
Gold (non-monetary)	—	—	4,163
Total (incl. others)	71,717	79,547	115,400

Source: UN, *International Trade Statistics Yearbook*.

1981 (million francs CFA): Coffee 5,118; Wood 8,493; Cotton 4,991; Diamonds 7,526; Total (incl. others) 20,335.
1982 (million francs CFA): Coffee 11,759; Wood 7,141; Cotton 2,254; Diamonds 8,647; Total (incl. others) 35,461.
1983 (million francs CFA): Coffee 10,361; Wood 7,918; Cotton 3,802; Diamonds 9,475; Total (incl. others) 28,402.
1984 (million francs CFA): Coffee 10,900; Wood 9,631; Cotton 4,367; Diamonds 11,591; Total (incl. others) 37,481.

Source: IMF, *International Financial Statistics*.

PRINCIPAL TRADING PARTNERS (US $'000)

Imports c.i.f.	1978	1979	1980
Belgium/Luxembourg	627	1,100	1,298
France	32,692	42,209	48,851
Germany, Federal Republic	3,247	2,261	2,441
Guinea-Bissau	530	402	1,015
Italy	876	720	1,314
Ivory Coast	243	1,359	541
Japan	3,367	2,897	5,815
Netherlands	1,583	1,659	2,895
Nigeria	573	236	1,157
Spain	1,070	1,819	1,831
Switzerland	2,033	646	403
United Kingdom	1,516	2,176	2,221
USA	2,123	3,070	2,779
Zaire	1,190	952	2,145
Total (incl. others)	56,579	66,523	80,461

Exports f.o.b.	1978	1979	1980
Belgium/Luxembourg	17,548	16,993	16,550
Chad	1,538	527	466
Denmark	780	876	1,741
France	35,570	36,285	59,434
Israel	2,764	9,113	8,990
Italy	1,144	1,359	2,827
Netherlands	1,455	1,530	1,051
Romania	1,334	1,221	738
Spain	706	678	3,046
Switzerland	353	596	1,103
United Kingdom	1,575	1,669	2,873
USA	5,113	6,512	4,745
Yugoslavia	98	263	4,728
Total (incl. others)	71,771	79,547	111,237

Source: UN, *International Trade Statistics Yearbook*.

Transport

ROAD TRAFFIC (motor vehicles in use at 31 December)

	1981	1982	1983
Passenger cars	23,750	38,930	41,321
Buses and coaches	79	103	118
Goods vehicles	3,060	3,190	3,720
Motorcycles and scooters	170	278	397
Mopeds	62,518	71,421	79,952

Source: IRF, *World Road Statistics*.

INLAND WATERWAYS TRAFFIC—INTERNATIONAL SHIPPING (metric tons)

	1977	1978	1979
Freight unloaded at Bangui	100,034	101,989	83,632
Freight loaded at Bangui	48,022	34,475	31,000
Total	148,056	136,414	114,632

1980: Total freight traffic 263,400 metric tons.

CIVIL AVIATION (traffic on scheduled services)*

	1980	1981	1982
Kilometres flown (million)	2.5	2.4	2.3
Passengers carried ('000)	136	129	115
Passenger-km (million)	190	203	220
Freight ton-km (million)	18.1	21.1	21.3

*Including an apportionment of the traffic of Air Afrique.
Source: UN, *Statistical Yearbook*.

Tourism

	1980	1981	1982
Foreign tourist arrivals	7,000	7,000	7,000

Communications Media

	1981	1982	1983
Radio receivers	130,000	135,000	140,000
Television receivers	1,000	1,200	1,400

Source: UNESCO, *Statistical Yearbook*.

Education

(1985)

	Institutions	Teachers	Students
Pre-primary	159	369	10,445
Primary	986	4,502	294,312
Secondary:			
General	41	914	45,166
Technical	4	127	2,233
Higher*	n.a.	105	2,133

* 1983/84 figures.
Source: Ministère de l'Education Nationale, Bangui.

Directory

The Constitution

The Constitution that had been promulgated on 6 February 1981 was suspended following the coup of 1 September 1981. All legislative and executive powers were assumed by the Military Committee for National Recovery (Comité militaire pour le redressement national—CMRN). The CMRN was dissolved on 21 September 1985, and a 22-member Council of Ministers was appointed. In January 1986 a constitutional commission met to draft a new constitution, providing for a one-party state, which was approved by the electorate in a referendum held on 21 November 1986.

The Government

HEAD OF STATE

President: Gen. ANDRÉ KOLINGBA (assumed power 1 September 1981; re-elected 1986).

COUNCIL OF MINISTERS
(January 1987)

Prime Minister and Minister of Defence and War Veterans: Gen. ANDRÉ KOLINGBA.
Minister of Foreign Affairs and International Co-operation: JEAN-LOUIS PSIMHIS.
Minister of the Interior and Territorial Administration: Lt-Col CHRISTOPHE GRELOMBE.
Minister of Justice and Keeper of the Seals: Lt-Col JEAN-LOUIS GERVIL YAMBALA.
Minister of National Education: JEAN-PAUL NGOUPANDE.
Minister of Posts and Telecommunications: Commdt STANISLAS-JOSEPH POLLAGBA.
Minister of Economic and Financial Co-operation, Planning and Statistics: DIEUDONNÉ WAZOUA.
Minister of Transport and Civil Aviation: PIERRE GONIFEI-NGAIBONANOU.
Minister of the Civil Service, Labour and Professional Training: DANIEL SEHOULIA.
Minister of Higher Education and Scientific Research: JEAN-CLAUDE KAZAGUI.
Minister of Information, Arts, Culture and National Organizations: JOACHIM DA SILVA-NZENGUE.
Minister of Tourism, Water Resources, Forestry, Hunting and Fisheries: RAYMOND MBITIKON.
Minister in charge of Meetings of the Council of Ministers: JEAN WILLYBIRO-SACKO.
Minister of Mining and Energy: Lt MICHEL SALLE.
Minister of Public Health and Social Affairs: BERNARD BELLOUM.
Minister of Public Works and Territorial Development: JACQUES KITTE.
Minister of Rural Development: BASILE EREPE.
Minister of Trade and Industry: JUSTIN NDJAPOU.
Secretary of State for Economy and Finance in charge of Budget and Debt Management: TIMOTHÉE MARBOUA.
Secretary of State for Economic and Financial Co-operation, Planning and Statistics: LOUIS PAPENIA.
Secretary of State for Hydraulics: Capt. RÉMY ADELAYE.
Secretary of State for Tourism: BOUNANDELE-KOUMBA.

MINISTRIES

Office of the President: Palais de la Renaissance, Bangui; tel. 61-03-23; telex 5253.
Ministry of Agriculture and Livestock: Bangui; tel. 61-28-00.
Ministry of the Civil Service, Labour and Professional Training: Bangui; tel. 61-01-44.
Ministry of Defence and War Veterans: Bangui; tel. 61-46-11; telex 5298.
Ministry of Economy and Finance: Bangui; tel. 61-08-11; telex 5280.
Ministry of Energy and Hydraulics: Bangui; telex 5243.
Ministry of Foreign Affairs and International Co-operation: Bangui; tel. 61-15-74; telex 5213.
Ministry of Information, Arts, Culture and National Organizations: Bangui; telex 5301.
Ministry of the Interior: tel. 61-44-77.
Ministry of Justice: Bangui; tel. 61-16-44.
Ministry of National Education: BP 791, Bangui; telex 5333.
Ministry of Planning: Bangui; telex 5208.
Ministry of Posts and Telecommunications: Bangui; tel. 61-29-46; telex 5304.
Ministry of Public Health and Social Affairs: Bangui; tel. 61-29-01.
Ministry of Public Works and Urban Affairs: Bangui; tel. 61-28-00.
Ministry of Trade and Industry: Bangui; tel. 61-44-88; telex 5215.
Ministry of Transport and Civil Aviation: Bangui; tel. 61-06-36; telex 5335.

CENTRAL AFRICAN REPUBLIC   Directory

Legislature

ASSEMBLÉE NATIONALE

The February 1981 Constitution provided for the establishment of a National Assembly, whose members would serve for five years. Prior to the establishment of the proposed Assembly, the Constitution was suspended following the coup of September 1981, when legislative powers were assumed by the Military Committee for National Recovery. A new constitution was prepared in 1986. Following its approval by the electorate in November 1986, it was envisaged that legislative elections for a new National Assembly would be held in the near future.

Political Organizations

All political activity was banned between September 1981 and May 1986.

Rassemblement démocratique centrafricain: Bangui; f. May 1986 as sole legal political party.

In 1983, the main opposition groups still extant formed the **Parti révolutionnaire centrafricain (PRC)**, comprising:

Front patriotique oubanguien-Parti du Travail (FPO-PT): f. 1979 as FPO; Leader ABEL GOUMBA.

Mouvement centrafricain pour la libération nationale (MCLN): Leader Dr IDDI LALA.

Mouvement pour la libération du peuple centrafricain (MLPC): f. 1979; Leader ANGE PATASSE.

In December 1984 several opposition leaders formed a Provisional Government for National Salvation (in exile), under the aegis of the provisional executive council of the MLPC. The President of the Provisional Government is (former Brig.-Gen.) ALPHONSE MBAIKOUA. In July 1986 the MLPC and the FPO-PT announced the formation of the Front Uni, which was to campaign for a democratic system of government.

Diplomatic Representation

EMBASSIES IN THE CENTRAL AFRICAN REPUBLIC

Cameroon: BP 935, Bangui; telex 5249; Ambassador: FIDÈLE MOÏSE BONNY EBOUMBOU.
Chad: BP 461, Bangui; telex 5220; Ambassador: El Hadj MOULI SEID.
China, People's Republic: BP 1430, Bangui; Ambassador: ZHOU XIANJUE.
Congo: BP 1414, Bangui; telex 5292; Chargé d'affaires: ANTOINE DELICA.
Egypt: BP 1422, Bangui; telex 5284; Ambassador: SAMEH SAMY DARWICHE.
France: blvd du Général de Gaulle, BP 884, Bangui; tel. 61-30-00; telex 5218; Ambassador: JEAN MANO.
Gabon: BP 1570, Bangui; tel. 61-29-97; telex 5234; Ambassador: FRANÇOIS DE PAULE MOULENGUI.
Germany, Federal Republic: ave G. A. Nasser, BP 901, Bangui; tel. 61-07-46; telex 5219; Ambassador: HARRO ADT.
Holy See: ave Boganda, BP 1447, Bangui; tel. 61-26-54; Pro-Nuncio: Mgr JOHN BULAITIS.
Iraq: BP 369, Bangui; telex 5287; Chargé d'affaires: ABDUL KARIM ASWAD.
Ivory Coast: BP 930, Bangui; telex 5279; Ambassador: JEAN-MARIE AGNINI BILE MALAN.
Japan: BP 1367, Bangui; tel. 61-06-68; telex 5204; Chargé d'affaires: KIYOJI YAMAKAWA.
Korea, Democratic People's Republic: BP 1816, Bangui; Ambassador: O KYONG-HWAN.
Korea, Republic: BP 841, Bangui; tel. 61-28-88; telex 5259; Ambassador: JOUNG-SOO LEE.
Libya: BP 1732, Bangui; telex 5317; Head of Mission: EL-SENUSE ABDALLAH.
Nigeria: BP 1010, Bangui; tel. 61-39-00; telex 5269; Chargé d'affaires: T. A. O. ODEGBILE.
Romania: BP 1435, Bangui; Chargé d'affaires a.i.: MIHAI GAFTONIUC.
Sudan: BP 1351, Bangui; telex 5296; Ambassador: FAROUK ABDEL-RAHMAN.
USA: blvd David Dacko, BP 924, Bangui; tel. 61-02-00; Ambassador: DAVID C. FIELDS.
Yugoslavia: BP 1049, Bangui; Chargé d'affaires: SPIRIDON PETROVIĆ.
Zaire: BP 989, Bangui; telex 5232; Ambassador: EMBE ISEA MBAMBE.

Judicial System

Supreme Court: BP 926, Bangui; highest judicial organ; acts as a Court of Cassation in civil and penal cases and as Court of Appeal in administrative cases; operates in three sections: judicial, administrative and accounts.

President of the Supreme Court: ANTOINE GROTHE.

There is also a Court of Appeal, a Criminal Court, an administrative tribunal, 16 tribunaux de grande instance and several labour tribunals.

Religion

An estimated 60% of the population follow animist beliefs, 5% are Muslims and 35% Christians; Roman Catholics comprise about 20% of the total population.

CHRISTIANITY

The Roman Catholic Church

The Central African Republic comprises one archdiocese and five dioceses. There were an estimated 425,000 adherents at 31 December 1984.

Bishops' Conference: Conférence Episcopale Centrafricaine, BP 798, Bangui; f. 1982; Pres. Mgr JOACHIM N'DAYEN, Archbishop of Bangui.

Archbishop of Bangui: Mgr JOACHIM N'DAYEN, Archevêché, BP 1518, Bangui; tel. 61-31-48.

Protestant Church

Eglise Protestante de Bangui: Bangui.

The Press

DAILY

E Le Songo: Bangui; Sango; circ. 200.

PERIODICALS

Bangui Match: Bangui; monthly.
Le Courrier Rural: BP 850, Bangui; publ. by Chambre d'Agriculture.
Journal Officiel de la République Centrafricaine: BP 739, Bangui; f. 1974; fortnightly; economic information; Dir-Gen. GABRIEL AGBA.
Ta Tene (The Truth): BP 1290, Bangui; monthly.
Terre Africaine: Bangui; weekly.

NEWS AGENCIES

Agence Centrafricaine de Presse (ACAP): Bangui; f. 1974 following nationalization of the Bangui branch of Agence France-Presse; Gen. Man. VICTOR DETO TETEYA.

TASS (USSR) is the only foreign press agency represented in the CAR.

Publisher

Government Publishing House

Imprimerie Centrafricain: BP 329, Bangui; tel. 61-00-33; f. 1974; Dir-Gen. PIERRE SALAMATE-KOILET.

Radio and Television

There were an estimated 140,000 radio receivers in use in 1983. Television broadcasting began in 1974 with a 100 kW transmitter at Bimbo. There were an estimated 1,400 television receivers in use in 1983.

Radiodiffusion-Télévision Centrafrique: BP 940, Bangui; telex 2355; f. 1958 as Radiodiffusion Nationale Centrafricaine; govt-controlled; radio programmes in French and Sango; Dir F. P. ZEMONIAKO.

Finance

(cap. = capital; res = reserves; dep. = deposits; m. = million; amounts in francs CFA)

BANKING

Central Bank

Banque des Etats de l'Afrique Centrale (BEAC): BP 851, Bangui; tel. 61-24-00; telex 5236; headquarters in Yaoundé, Cameroon; f. 1973 as the central bank of issue for mem. states of the Customs and Economic Union of Central Africa (UDEAC), comprising Cameroon, the Central African Republic, Chad, the Congo, Equatorial Guinea and Gabon; cap. and res 92,485m. (June 1983); Gov. CASIMIR OYE-MBA; Dir in CAR ALPHONSE KOYAMBA.

Commercial Banks

Banque de Crédit Agricole et de Développement (BCAD): BP 1719, Bangui; tel. 61-32-00; telex 5207; f. 1984; cap. 600m.; 50% owned by Banque de participation et de placement (Switzerland); Pres. M. CHAUTARD; Dir-Gen. PHILIPPE NADAUD.

Banque Internationale pour l'Afrique Occidentale SA (BIAO-Centrafrique): place de la République, BP 910, Bangui; tel. 61-46-33; telex 5133; f. 1980; cap. 700m. (Dec. 1983); 20% state-owned, 75% by BIAO; Pres. RICHARD MORIN; Dir-Gen. in Bangui FRANÇOIS EPAYE.

Union Bancaire en Afrique Centrale: rue de Brazza, BP 59, Bangui; tel. 61-29-90; telex 5225; f. 1962; cap. 550m., res 155m., dep. 23,151m. (Dec. 1984); 60% state-owned; Pres. Mrs M. J. KOSSI-MAYTENGOL; Gen. Man. JOSEPH KOYAGBELE.

Investment Bank

Banque Centrafricaine d'Investissement (BCI): BP 933, Bangui; tel. 61-00-64; telex 5317; f. 1976; cap. 1,000m.; 34.8% state-owned; Pres. ALPHONSE KONGOLO; Man. Dir GÉRARD SAMBO.

Development Agency

Caisse Centrale de Coopération Economique: BP 817, Bangui; tel. 61-36-34; telex 5291; Dir NILS ROBIN.

INSURANCE

Agence Centrafricaine d'Assurances (ACA): BP 512, Bangui; tel. 61-06-23; f. 1956; cap. 3.8m.; Dir Mme R. CERBELLAUD.

Assureurs Conseils Centrafricains Faugère et Jutheau: rue de la Kouanga, BP 743, Bangui; tel. 61-19-33; f. 1968; cap. 1m.; Dir J.-Y. DEBOUDÉ.

Entreprise d'Etat d'Assurances et de Réassurances (SIRIRI): ave du Président Mobutu, BP 852, Bangui; tel. 61-36-55; telex 5248; f. 1972; general; cap. 100m.; Pres. EMMANUEL DOKOUNA; Dir-Gen. GASTON BEYINA-GBANDI.

Legendre, A. & Cie: rue de la Victoire, BP 896, Bangui; cap. 1m.; Pres. and Dir-Gen. ANDRÉ LEGENDRE.

Trade and Industry

Chambre d'Agriculture, d'Elevage, des Eaux et Forêts, Chasses et Tourisme: BP 850, Bangui; Pres. MAURICE OSCAR GAUDEVILLE.

Chambre de Commerce, d'Industrie, des Mines et de l'Artisanat: BP 813, Bangui; tel. 61-42-55; telex 5261; Pres. GABRIEL VERBIC; Sec.-Gen. YVES LAURENT KOUDOUSSINGA.

Mission Française de Coopération: BP 934, Bangui; telex 5218; administers bilateral aid from France; Dir MICHEL LANDRY.

PRINCIPAL DEVELOPMENT ORGANIZATIONS

Agence de Développement Caféière (ADECAF): Bangui; national coffee development agency; offers financial aid and training in improved farming methods.

Caisse de Stabilisation et de Péréquation des Produits Agricoles: Bangui; tel. 61-08-00; telex 5278; development of agriculture and agricultural exports; regulates consumer and producer price; Pres. JACOB GBETI.

Société Centrafricaine de Développement Agricole (SOCADA): ave David Dacko, BP 997, Bangui; tel. 61-30-33; telex 5212; f. 1964; restructured 1980; cap. 1,000m. francs CFA; 75% state-owned, 25% Compagnie française pour le développement des fibres textiles (France); cotton ginning at 20 plants, production of cotton oil (at two refineries) and groundnut oil; Pres. MAURICE METHUT; Man. Dir JEAN MAGRONDJI.

Société Centrafricaine de Palmiers à Huile (CENTRAPALM): BP 1355, Bangui; tel. 61-49-40; telex 5271; f. 1975; cap. 1,265m. francs CFA; development of palm products; operates the Bossongo agro-industrial complex (inaugurated 1986); Pres. ALBERT MANDJEKA; Gen. Man. O. COPIN.

PRINCIPAL CO-OPERATIVE ORGANIZATIONS

Office National du Diamant (OND): Bangui; f. 1966; Dir-Gen. MATHIEU GBAKPOMA.

Office National des Forêts (ONF): BP 915, Bangui; f. 1969; Dir SIMON ANZITE.

TRADE UNION

All trade union activities were suspended in May 1981.

Transport

RAILWAYS

There are no railways at present but there is a long-term project to connect Bangui to the Transcameroon railway. A railway is also due to be constructed from Sudan's Darfur region into the CAR's Vakaga province.

ROADS

In 1984 there were about 20,278 km of roads, including 5,044 km of main roads and 3,934 km of secondary roads. Both the total road length and the condition of the roads is inadequate for the traffic that uses the road system. Eight main routes leave Bangui, and those that are surfaced have been toll roads since 1971. The CAR section of the Transafrican Lagos–Mombasa highway was completed in 1984, providing a link with Cameroon.

Compagnie Nationale des Transports Routiers (CNTR): BP 330, Bangui; tel. 61-46-44; cap. 35.5m. francs CFA; Dir-Gen. GEORGES YABADA.

INLAND WATERWAYS

There are two navigable waterways. The first is open all the year, except in the dry season, and is formed by the Congo and Oubangui rivers; convoys of barges (of up to 800 tons load) ply between Bangui, Brazzaville and Pointe-Noire. The second is the river Sangha, a tributary of the Oubangui, on which traffic is seasonal. There are two ports, at Bangui and Salo, on the rivers Oubangui and Sangha respectively. Efforts are being made to develop the stretch of river upstream from Salo to increase the transportation of timber from this area, and to develop Nola as a timber port.

Agence Centrafricaine des Communications Fluviales: BP 822, Bangui; tel. 61-02-11; telex 5256; f. 1969; state-owned; development of inland waterways transport system; Man. Dir JUSTIN NDJAPOU.

Société Centrafricaine de Transports Fluviaux (SOCATRAF): BP 1445, Bangui; telex 5256; f. 1980; cap. 400m. francs CFA; 51% state-owned; Man. Dir FRANÇOIS TOUSSAINT.

CIVIL AVIATION

There is an international airport at Bangui-Mpoko, which is currently being rehabilitated at a total cost of around US $13.6m. There are also 37 small airports for internal services.

Air Afrique: BP 875, Bangui; tel. 61-46-60; telex 5281; the CAR govt has a 7% share; see under Ivory Coast; Dir in Bangui SÉVERIN TOLA.

Inter-RCA: BP 1413, Bangui; telex 5239; f. 1980 to replace Air Centrafrique; 52% state-owned, 24% by Air Afrique; extensive internal services; Man. Dir JULES BERNARD OUANDE; fleet of 1 Caravelle and 1 DC-4.

Tourism

Office National Centrafricain du Tourisme: BP 655, Bangui; tel. 61-45-66.

CHAD

Introductory Survey

Location, Climate, Language, Religion, Flag, Capital

The Republic of Chad is a land-locked country in north central Africa, bordered to the north by Libya, to the south by the Central African Republic, to the west by Niger and Cameroon and to the east by Sudan. The climate is hot and arid in the northern desert regions of the Sahara but very wet (annual rainfall 500 cm) in the south. The official languages are French and Arabic, and various African languages are also widely spoken. Almost one-half of the population are Muslims, living in the north, while most of the remainder follow animistic beliefs. About 5% are Christians. The national flag (proportions 3 by 2) has three equal vertical stripes, of blue, yellow and red. The capital is N'Djamena (formerly called Fort-Lamy).

Recent History

Formerly a province of French Equatorial Africa, Chad became an autonomous state within the French Community in November 1958. François (later N'Garta) Tombalbaye, a southerner and leader of the Parti progressiste tchadien (PPT), became Prime Minister in March 1959. Chad achieved independence on 11 August 1960, with Tombalbaye as President. In 1962 President Tombalbaye banned all opposition parties and Chad became a single-party state. Civil disturbances began in 1963, with riots in the capital, and a full-scale rebellion broke out in 1965, concentrated mainly in the north, which had until that year remained under French military control. The Muslims of northern Chad have traditionally been in conflict with their black southern compatriots, who are generally animists or Christians. The banned Front de libération nationale du Tchad (FROLINAT, founded in Sudan in 1966) assumed leadership of the revolt, which was quelled in 1968 with French military help. In 1973 several leading figures of the regime, including the Army Chief of Staff, Gen. Félix Malloum, were imprisoned on conspiracy charges. The PPT was replaced by a new political party, the Mouvement national pour la révolution culturelle et sociale (MNRCS).

In April 1975 Tombalbaye was killed in an army coup, led by the acting Chief of Staff. General Malloum was released and became President at the head of a Supreme Military Council. The provisional Government dissolved the MNRCS and launched appeals for national reconciliation. Some rebel leaders rallied to the regime, but FROLINAT maintained its opposition, receiving clandestine support from Libya, which since 1973 had held the Aozou strip of northern Chad, covering about 70,000 sq km (27,000 sq miles) and believed to contain significant deposits of uranium.

In early 1978 FROLINAT refused to negotiate, unified its command under a Revolutionary Council, led by Gen. Goukouni Oueddei, and gained large areas of territory from government forces. The advance of FROLINAT was halted with the help of French reinforcements. In August Gen. Malloum sought a new solution to the conflict in a reshuffle of his government, and a former leader of FROLINAT, Hissène (Hissein) Habré, was appointed Prime Minister. Disagreements between Habré and Malloum soon arose, and by December central authority had completely broken down. Fighting between the Government and FROLINAT flared up again in January 1979. Habré's troops took control of most of the capital, forcing Malloum to resign in March and to flee the country, leaving responsibility with the commmander of the gendarmerie, Lt-Col (later Col) Wadal Abdelkader Kamougue. French troops were sent to Chad, and a cease-fire was agreed.

In April 1979, following the failure of conferences held in Nigeria, the four main factions, notably FROLINAT and FAN (Habré's Forces armées du nord), formed a transitional government, led by Lol Mahamat Choua (Shawwa), the newly-appointed leader of the Mouvement populaire pour la libération du Tchad, also known as the 'Third Army', which was supported by Nigeria. Goukouni Oueddei became Minister of the Interior, with Habré as Minister of Defence. This government pledged not to monopolize power, but it excluded the extreme factions of the south, now under Lt-Col Kamougue and supported by Libya. Several neighbouring countries, as well as dissatisfied internal factions, denounced the regime.

Sporadic fighting continued, and there was dissension within the Government between Goukouni and Habré. In August 1979 an agreement was reached between Chad's 11 factions for the formation of an interim Gouvernement d'union nationale de transition (GUNT) under the Presidency of Goukouni, with Lt-Col Kamougue of the southern extremists as Vice-President. A Council of Ministers, representing the various factions, was appointed in November 1979.

Goukouni's authority was undermined by continual disagreements with Habré's forces, and in March 1980 the fragile truce was broken and fighting began once again in the capital. Despite numerous attempts at mediation and cease-fire agreements, the conflict remained unresolved; in May all French troops withdrew from Chad, and in June a treaty of friendship was signed between Col Gaddafi of Libya and a representative of President Goukouni, without the prior consent of the GUNT. During October 1980 Libyan forces intervened directly in the hostilities, resulting in the defeat of Habré and the retreat of the FAN from N'Djamena. A Libyan force of 15,000 men was established in the country.

In January 1981 proposals were made for a gradual merger of Chad and Libya, but the Libyan presence in Chad was unpopular, and guerrilla warfare continued. Plans were drawn up in Lomé to provide for the formation of an OAU peace-keeping force, and envisaging the holding of elections during 1981. Habré and other FAN leaders were sentenced to death *in absentia* in June. By September President Goukouni had finally renounced the proposed merger, and in November Libyan troops were withdrawn at Goukouni's request. A neutral inter-African force was installed under the auspices of the OAU.

The OAU proposed a cease-fire date of 30 March 1982, and the holding of elections by July, but neither of these suggestions was implemented, and it became clear in early 1982 that a peaceful settlement was unlikely, as President Goukouni refused to negotiate with Habré. In an attempt to strengthen the GUNT, weakened by internal conflicts, the President formed a Conseil d'Etat, appointed a Prime Minister and reshuffled the Council of Ministers in May. Fighting had intensified, however, and by April Habré was in control of one-third of the territory. N'Djamena fell to his forces on 7 June. Goukouni fled to Cameroon and thence to Algeria, where he continued to contest the leadership. In October he formed a 15-member 'government-in-exile'. The OAU force had fully withdrawn by 30 June, and in October Habré took the oath as President and formed a new government. A majority of OAU members finally agreed to recognize Habré's regime in June 1983.

Habré did not succeed in establishing national reconciliation, although some members of Kamougue's Forces armées tchadiennes (FAT) joined the ranks of the FAN to form a new national army in January 1983. By June 1983, however, Goukouni's rebel forces, with Libyan support, were in a position to capture the northern city of Faya-Largeau. Following appeals for international assistance, Habré obtained US $10m. of military aid from the USA, as well as help from Egypt, Sudan, France and Zaire. Government troops counter-attacked and repossessed Faya-Largeau at the end of July, but, after prolonged bombing by Libyan aircraft, the town again fell to the rebel forces in August. In response to Habré's renewed appeals, France sent 3,000 troops to Chad, ostensibly acting as military instructors, but with orders to retaliate should they come under attack.

In August a proposal from President Mitterrand of France for a Chad federation, as a solution to the dispute, was rejected by a spokesman for Goukouni Oueddei. At the Franco-African summit in October it was decided that the OAU should attempt to resolve the dispute by means of a reconciliation between the Government and the rebels. A defensive line separating the warring factions was set up along latitude 15°N, and in mid-September it was announced that fighting had ceased.

Following indications from both sides of a willingness to negotiate a peace settlement, a meeting of representatives from all factions was arranged for January 1984 in Addis Ababa. The talks collapsed, however, after a disagreement over protocol and representation. Renewed fighting in January led to the shooting down of a French aircraft and the death of its pilot, and prompted the French decision to extend the defensive zone 100 km northwards, to latitude 16°N. The French Minister for External Relations, Claude Cheysson, visited Chad in February. His proposal to employ a Pan-African 'observer force', however, was rejected as impracticable by the OAU.

In an attempt to consolidate his political power, Habré dissolved his former military arm, FROLINAT-FAN, in June 1984 and created a new political party, the Union Nationale pour l'Indépendance et la Révolution (UNIR). A government reshuffle followed in July. Major dissension among anti-Habré forces became evident with the formation in August of a new opposition movement, the Rassemblement des Forces Patriotiques, by GUNT factions opposed to Goukouni Oueddei's leadership.

Following a proposal in May 1984 by the Libyan leader, Col Gaddafi, for a simultaneous withdrawal of Libyan 'support elements' and French troops, a Franco-Libyan agreement was reached in September over joint evacuation of both countries' military forces. Chad was not consulted over the deal, and relations with France became strained. Following talks with President Mitterrand of France, however, Habré agreed to a joint Franco-Libyan commission monitoring the withdrawal. In mid-November it was announced that both countries' troops had been evacuated. US and Chad intelligence reports, however, maintained that 3,000 Libyan troops were still in the country, although Col Gaddafi repeatedly denied that any Libyan soldiers had remained, in contravention of the September agreement. At the Franco-African summit in December 1984, President Mitterrand declared that France would not use force to drive Libyans from northern Chad, and would intervene only if Libyan forces moved south of the 16th parallel.

The civil war in southern Chad between Habré's forces and various guerrilla commandos ('codos') escalated in October and November 1984, with the Government reportedly carrying out summary executions in an attempt to reassert its authority in the area. To escape the increasing violence, more than 50,000 Chadians were estimated to have fled to Sudan, the Central African Republic and Cameroon. In an attempt to ease unrest in the south, Habré made several tours of the area in early 1985: calm finally returned at the end of the year, when 1,200 'codos' responded to financial inducements that Habré offered (and France provided) by rallying to the government side.

At a summit meeting in August 1985, factions loyal to the GUNT formed a Conseil suprême de la révolution (CSR), which comprised most of the anti-Government groupings. Subsequent to the realignment of the 'codos', a number of former opposition factions also declared support for the Habré regime, including the Front démocratique du Tchad (FDT), led by Gen. Djibril Négué Djogo, a grouping of four factions hostile to both Habré and Goukouni (established in March 1985), and the Comité d'action et de concertation (CAC-CDR), which had split from the pro-Goukouni Conseil Démocratique Révolutionnaire (CDR) early in 1985. In response, Habré announced the release of 122 political prisoners in January 1986.

Further progress towards *rapprochement* was halted by the sudden renewal of hostilities in February, when Libyan-backed GUNT forces attacked government outposts at Kouba Olanga, Oum Chalouba and Ziguey, towns lying south of the defensive line along the 16°N latitude. Habré appealed to France for increased military aid, and a few days later French aircraft bombed the newly-completed airstrip at the Libyan-held military base of Ouadi Doum, north-east of Faya-Largeau. A retaliatory strike on N'Djamena airport caused little damage, and France undertook only a moderate build-up of its military support. Rebel attacks in the Oum Chalouba region in March were contained by government forces alone. However, the USA provided US $10m. in supplementary military aid to the Habré regime during the period of hostilities, which ceased following the destruction of a rebel base at Chicha, north of the 16°N latitude, by government forces in mid-March. The OAU arranged for reconciliation talks to take place between Habré and Goukouni in Loubomo (Congo) at the end of March, but Goukouni unexpectedly failed to attend, alleging that the OAU leadership was biased towards Habré. In the same month Habré reshuffled his Government, bringing such former opponents as Gen. Djibril Négué Djogo (FDT) and Mahamat Senoussi (CAC-CDR) into the Council of Ministers.

Goukouni's failure to attend the Loubomo talks led to a leadership crisis within the GUNT coalition and subsequently to its near-disintegration. In June Col Wadal Abdelkader Kamougue, leader of the Mouvement révolutionnaire du peuple (MRP), resigned from his position as vice-president of the GUNT, and in August Acheikh Ibn Oumar's CDR withdrew its support. In October, following a series of armed clashes between the CDR and Goukouni's Forces armées populaires (FAP) around the north-eastern town of Fada, Goukouni, who was by then virtually isolated and claiming to be under house arrest in Tripoli, declared himself willing to seek a reconciliation with Habré. He was allegedly wounded shortly afterwards, during a clash with Libyan troops in the city.

Following renewed fighting at Fada, during which Libyan forces were alleged to have launched bombing raids and ground attacks, Goukouni was replaced in November 1986 as president of the GUNT. The latter was reconstituted at a meeting of seven former pro-Goukouni factions in Cotonou (Benin), under the leadership of the CDR's president, Acheikh Ibn Oumar. Meanwhile, the FAP transferred their allegiance to Habré. In December the latter's Forces armées nationales tchadiennes (FANT) were involved, together with the FAP, in clashes with Libyan troops at Fada and at Zouar, both towns lying north of the 16th parallel. For the first time, Col Gaddafi acknowledged a Libyan military presence in Chad. In January 1987 Libyan aircraft bombed the civilian district of Arada, in the south of the country, and France, which had previously resisted any further involvement in the conflict, launched a second retaliatory bombing raid on the airbase at Ouadi Doum.

Government

The Government, which came to power through civil war, comprises a President and a Council of Ministers, appointed and led by the President. Executive and legislative power is exercised by the Council, and for administrative purposes the country is divided into 14 Prefectures. In October 1982 a Conseil national consultatif was formed, consisting of two representatives of each Prefecture and two representatives of the city of N'Djamena.

Defence

In January 1983 the various armed groups in Chad which rallied to Hissène Habré's Forces armées du nord (FAN) were merged to form a new national army, the Forces armées nationales tchadiennes (FANT). The total strength of the armed forces in July 1986 was estimated to be 14,200 (army 14,000, air force 200). In addition, there are paramilitary forces of approximately 5,700 men. Under defence agreements with France, the army receives technical and other aid. The gendarmerie, once part of the army, has been dissolved and replaced by a military police unit. Military service of three years is compulsory for men and women. Defence expenditure (excluding French subventions) in 1985 was an estimated 17,000m. francs CFA.

Economic Affairs

Chad is a severely underdeveloped country, owing partly to unfavourable climatic conditions, inadequate infrastructure and a paucity of known natural resources. During recent years, continual civil strife has aggravated economic difficulties. In 1982, according to World Bank estimates, Chad's gross national product (GNP) per head was only US $80 (at average 1980–82 prices), the lowest level among African countries and one of the lowest in the world. It was estimated that GNP per head declined at an average rate of 2.8% annually, in real terms, between 1960 and 1982.

Chad's economy is essentially one of subsistence, based on agriculture, stock-breeding and fishing, which together occupied 83% of the working population in 1980. The only significant

CHAD

cash crop is cotton, which has traditionally provided the basis for Chad's major industry and around 80% of all export earnings. The country's output of seed (unginned) cotton reached a peak of 174,062 metric tons in 1975/76 but declined in subsequent years, falling to 71,000 tons in 1981/82, when fighting in the southern cotton-growing area severely affected production. In 1983/84 output reached 158,000 tons, largely as a result of a 31% increase in the area under cultivation; it collapsed, however, to 97,000 tons in the drought year 1984/85. Production forecasts for 1985/86 envisaged a recovery to around 130,000 tons, but the sudden fall in world cotton prices which occurred during that season (exacerbated by the fall in the value of the US dollar in early 1986) led the Habré Government, in June 1986, to introduce an emergency programme in an attempt to avert the possible collapse of Chad's most important industry. The first phase of the programme, the total cost of which was put at US $47.4m., was to be part-financed by a $15m. credit from the International Development Association (IDA) and was to concentrate on the restructuring of the state-owned Société Cotonnière du Tchad (COTONTCHAD).

Sugar cane is cultivated at a 6,000-ha agro-industrial complex at Banda, and is processed at a refinery operated by the Société nationale sucrière du Tchad. Annual domestic capacity is 30,000 tons of raw sugar. Production totalled 25,000 tons in 1983/84, falling to 22,000 tons in 1984/85: it recovered slightly, to reach 23,000 tons, in 1985/86.

Lake Chad and the Logone-Chari basin are well stocked with fish, usually producing more than 100,000 tons annually. Despite government efforts to protect agriculture by irrigation and reafforestation, crops have been frequently threatened by recurring drought. N'Djamena registered only 260mm of rain in 1984, compared with an annual average of 500–600mm, and the level of the Chari river fell, causing difficulties in transporting emergency food supplies across the border from Cameroon. Lake Chad shrank in 1984 to one-third of its normal size. Heavy rainfall in July 1985 relieved the drought, but increased the problem of distributing food to the thousands of people who were affected by famine. Livestock normally accounts for about one-fifth of Chad's gross domestic product (GDP), and is the most important export after cotton. An estimated 80% of meat exports, however, are smuggled out of the country, depriving the Government of substantial tax revenue. The drought in 1984 severely depleted cattle stocks, with an estimated 200,000 head being lost.

Industry is almost entirely based on agriculture, with manufacturing accounting for only 7% of GDP. Textile production is the most important sector, followed by food and tobacco. There are proven reserves of petroleum near Lake Chad, but development has been hindered by political troubles. There are also known to be substantial deposits of uranium in the disputed northern territory.

After many years of civil war, Chad is now particularly dependent on foreign aid, with its economy in chaos, and many regions suffering critical food shortages. Drought has become increasingly severe and widespread since 1980, and the production deficit for cereals in 1984 was forecast at 300,000 tons. An estimated 2,000 people died of starvation during August–October 1984, as famine spread to the normally fertile southern areas. Emergency food aid has been supplied in recent years by the UN's World Food Programme and international donors. In 1986 the African Development Fund (ADF) granted a US $12.4m. loan towards an irrigation project in the Mamdi region, where it is hoped to cultivate maize and wheat. The total cost of the project, due to be completed in 1991, has been estimated at $25.3m.

The Habré Government's draft budget for 1986 forecast total expenditure of 22,700m. francs CFA, with revenue at 18,700m. francs CFA, of which tax revenue was to provide 17,000m. francs CFA. In 1984 the allocation for defence spending was 17,000m. francs CFA, out of a total budget expenditure of 37,635m. francs CFA. France is the main trading partner and the principal supplier of foreign aid; non-military aid from France totalled 12,000m. francs CFA in 1983, and budgetary aid of US $7.9m. was to be provided in 1986. The USA, however, contributed US $30.3m. in aid in 1984, compared with US $28m. from France. International agencies and Arab countries have provided help for agricultural and communications projects: at an aid-pledging conference, held in Geneva in December 1985, a total of US $450m. was raised in support of the interim 1986–90 Development Programme. Chad consequently has a large public debt. At the end of 1984 this debt totalled 31,900m. francs CFA externally and 32,000m. francs CFA internally.

Social Welfare

An Employment Code guarantees a minimum wage and other rights for employees. There are four hospitals, 28 medical centres and several hundred dispensaries. In 1978 there were 3,373 beds in government-administered hospital establishments, while only 90 physicians were employed in official medical services. A development programme was launched in 1986 by UNICEF, at an estimated cost of US $30m.

Education

Education is officially compulsory for six years between eight and 14 years of age. Primary education begins at the age of six and lasts for six years. Secondary education, from the age of 12, lasts for seven years, comprising a first cycle of four years and a second of three years. In 1984 only 38% of children in the primary age-group (55% of boys; 21% of girls) were enrolled at primary schools, while attendance at secondary schools was equivalent to only 6% of the relevant age-group. The Université du Tchad was opened at N'Djamena in 1971, and there are several technical colleges. In 1985, according to estimates by UNESCO, the average rate of adult illiteracy was 74.7% (males 59.5%; females 89.1%).

Tourism

Chad's potential attractions for tourists include a variety of scenery from the dense forests of the south to the deserts of the north. Wild animals abound, especially in the two national parks and five game reserves. In 1981 income from tourism was estimated at US $2m.

Public Holidays

1987: 1 January (New Year), 20 April (Easter Monday), 1 May (Labour Day), 25 May ('Liberation of Africa', anniversary of the OAU's foundation), 30 May* (Id al-Fitr, end of Ramadan), 8 June (Whit Monday), 6 August* (Id al-Adha, Feast of the Sacrifice), 11 August (Independence Day), 15 August (Assumption), 1 November (All Saints' Day), 4 November* (Maloud, Birth of the Prophet), 28 November (Proclamation of the Republic), 25 December (Christmas).

1988: 1 January (New Year), 4 April (Easter Monday), 1 May (Labour Day), 18 May* (Id al-Fitr, end of Ramadan), 23 May (Whit Monday), 25 May ('Liberation of Africa', anniversary of the OAU's foundation), 25 July* (Id al-Adha, Feast of the Sacrifice), 11 August (Independence Day), 15 August (Assumption), 23 October* (Maloud, Birth of the Prophet), 1 November (All Saints' Day), 28 November (Proclamation of the Republic), 25 December (Christmas).

* These holidays are dependent on the Islamic lunar calendar and may vary by one or two days from the dates given.

Weights and Measures

The metric system is officially in force.

Currency and Exchange Rates

100 centimes = 1 franc de la Coopération financière en Afrique centrale (CFA).

Exchange rates (30 September 1986):
 £1 sterling = 480.625 francs CFA;
 US $1 = 332.125 francs CFA.

Statistical Survey

Source (unless otherwise stated): Direction de la Statistique, des Etudes Economiques et Démographiques, BP 453, N'Djamena.

Area and Population

AREA, POPULATION AND DENSITY

Area (sq km)	
Land	1,259,200
Inland waters	24,800
Total	1,284,000*
Population (sample survey)	
December 1963–August 1964	3,254,000†
Population (official estimates at mid-year)	
1983	4,830,000
1984	4,944,000
1985	5,061,000
Density (per sq km) at mid-1985	3.9

* 495,800 sq miles.
† Including areas not covered by the survey.

PRINCIPAL TOWNS (estimated population in 1979)

N'Djamena (capital)*	402,000		Bongor	69,000
Sarh*	124,000		Doba	64,000
Moundou	87,000		Laï	58,000
			Abêché	47,000

* Fort-Lamy was renamed N'Djamena in November 1973, and Fort-Archambault was renamed Sarh in July 1972.

BIRTHS AND DEATHS

Average annual birth rate 44.6 per 1,000 in 1970–75, 44.1 per 1,000 in 1975–80; death rate 24.9 per 1,000 in 1970–75, 23.1 per 1,000 in 1975–80 (UN estimates).

PREFECTURES

	Area (sq km)	Population (1984)	Density (per sq km)
Batha	88,800	410,000	4.6
Biltine	46,850	200,000	4.3
Borkou-Ennedi-Tibesti (BET)	600,350	103,000	0.2
Chari-Baguirmi	82,910	719,000	8.7
Guéra	58,950	234,000	4.0
Kanem	114,520	234,000	2.0
Lac	22,320	158,000	7.1
Logone Occidental	8,695	324,000	37.3
Logone Oriental	28,035	350,000	12.5
Mayo-Kebbi	30,105	757,000	25.1
Moyen-Chari	45,180	582,000	12.9
Ouadaï	76,240	411,000	5.4
Salamat	63,000	121,000	1.9
Tandjilé	18,045	341,000	18.9
Total	1,284,000	4,944,000	3.9

ECONOMICALLY ACTIVE POPULATION
(ILO estimates, '000 persons at mid-1980)

	Males	Females	Total
Agriculture, etc.	1,043	318	1,361
Industry	72	4	76
Services	154	44	197
Total	1,269	366	1,635

Source: ILO, *Economically Active Population Estimates and Projections, 1950–2025.*

Agriculture

PRINCIPAL CROPS (FAO estimates, '000 metric tons)

	1982	1983	1984
Wheat	5	10	10
Rice (paddy)	23	29	29
Maize	30	26	30
Millet and sorghum	340	367	320
Other cereals	55	68	55
Potatoes	13	13	13
Sweet potatoes	35	35	35
Cassava (Manioc)	240	250	210
Yams	190	195	170
Taro (Coco yam)	8	8	8
Dry beans	40	42	35
Other pulses	18	14	13
Groundnuts (in shell)	100	80	80
Sesame seed	10	11	11
Cottonseed	64*	88*	72
Cotton (lint)	38*	51*	40
Dry onions	13	14	13
Other vegetables	57	60	55
Dates	31	32	30
Mangoes	30	32	30
Other fruit	45	50	45
Sugar cane	215	250	250

*Unofficial figures.
Source: FAO, *Production Yearbook.*

LIVESTOCK
(FAO estimates, '000 head, year ending September)

	1982	1983	1984
Cattle	3,700	3,600	3,400
Goats	2,100	2,100	2,000
Sheep	2,200	2,300	2,200
Pigs	6	6	6
Horses	150	150	150
Asses	255	255	255
Camels	420	421	421

Poultry (FAO estimates, million): 3 in 1982; 3 in 1983; 3 in 1984.
Source: FAO, *Production Yearbook.*

LIVESTOCK PRODUCTS (FAO estimates, '000 metric tons)

	1982	1983	1984
Total meat	50	50	46
Beef and veal	28	26	24
Mutton and lamb	9	9	8
Goats' meat	7	7	7
Poultry meat	3	3	3
Cows' milk	100	97	92
Sheep's milk	7	7	7
Goats' milk	14	14	12
Butter	2.2	2.1	2.1
Hen eggs	2.9	3.0	3.0
Cattle hides	4.8	4.8	4.6
Sheep skins	1.8	1.8	1.8
Goat skins	1.3	1.3	1.3

Source: FAO, *Production Yearbook*.

Forestry

ROUNDWOOD REMOVALS
(FAO estimates, '000 cubic metres, excluding bark)

	1982	1983	1984
Sawlogs, etc.	2	2	2
Other industrial wood	469	480	491
Fuel wood	2,858	2,923	2,989
Total	3,329	3,405	3,482

Source: FAO, *Yearbook of Forest Products*.

Fishing

(FAO estimates, '000 metric tons, live weight)

	1981	1982	1983
Total catch (freshwater fishes)	115	115	110

1984: Catch as in 1983 (FAO estimate).

Source: FAO, *Yearbook of Fishery Statistics*.

Industry

SELECTED PRODUCTS

		1981	1982	1983
Salted, dried or smoked fish*	'000 metric tons	20	20	20
Wheat flour‡	'000 metric tons	1†	1†	1†
Refined sugar	'000 metric tons	n.a.	18	22
Beer	'000 hectolitres	n.a.	133	130
Cigarettes	million	n.a.	212	259
Woven cotton fabrics	'000 metres	n.a.	17,124	13,075
Electric energy‡	million kWh	65	65	65

* FAO estimates.   † Provisional or estimated figure.
‡ Source: UN, *Industrial Statistics Yearbook*.

Finance

CURRENCY AND EXCHANGE RATES

Monetary Units
100 centimes = 1 franc de la Coopération financière en Afrique centrale (CFA).

Denominations
Coins: 1, 5, 10, 25, 50, 100 and 500 francs CFA.
Notes: 500, 1,000, 5,000 and 10,000 francs CFA.

French Franc, Sterling and Dollar Equivalents
(30 September 1986)
1 French franc = 50 francs CFA;
£1 sterling = 480.625 francs CFA;
US $1 = 332.125 francs CFA;
1,000 francs CFA = £2.081 = $3.011.

Average Exchange Rate (francs CFA per US $)
1983   381.06
1984   436.96
1985   449.26

GENERAL BUDGETS (million francs CFA)

Revenue	1983
Direct taxation	1,808
Poll tax	1,160
Company taxation	415
Indirect taxation	6,098
Customs receipts	5,003
Production and consumption taxes	880
Other revenue	383
Administration	260
Land	92
Extraordinary revenue	41
Total	8,330

Expenditure	1983	1984
Public debt interest	10	10
Services	31,946	32,844
Defence	15,000	17,496
Education	5,327	4,106
Interior	2,629	2,205
Public health	1,734	1,431
Community projects	3,440	3,427
State intervention	1,354	1,354
Total	36,750	37,635

1984 Budget: Revenue 11,200 million francs CFA.

1985 Budget: Proposed revenue 15,034 million francs CFA; proposed expenditure 39,847 million francs CFA.

1986 Budget: Proposed revenue 18,700 million francs CFA; proposed expenditure 22,700 million francs CFA.

CENTRAL BANK RESERVES
(US $ million at 31 December)

	1982	1983	1984
Gold*	5.00	4.21	3.44
IMF special drawing rights	0.29	1.54	0.36
Reserve position in IMF	5.58	3.62	0.25
Foreign exchange	6.54	22.84	43.54
Total	17.41	32.21	47.60

* Valued at market-related prices.
Source: IMF, *International Financial Statistics*.

MONEY SUPPLY ('000 million francs CFA at 31 December)

	1982	1983	1984
Currency outside banks	23.61	29.20	44.93
Demand deposits at commercial and development banks	9.35	11.36	20.00
Checking deposits at post office	0.20	0.20	0.20
Total money	33.16	40.75	65.13

BALANCE OF PAYMENTS (US $ million)

	1982	1983	1984
Merchandise exports f.o.b.	57.7	78.2	109.7
Merchandise imports f.o.b.	−81.7	−99.1	−128.3
Trade balance	−24.0	−20.9	−18.7
Exports of services	4.2	28.5	36.0
Imports of services	−23.0	−80.9	−96.4
Balance on goods and services	−42.8	−73.3	−79.0
Private unrequited transfers (net)	−0.7	−2.8	−1.7
Government unrequited transfers (net)	61.9	114.1	87.6
Current balance	18.5	37.9	6.9
Direct capital investment (net)	−0.1	−0.1	9.2
Other long-term capital (net)	−1.0	−18.0	−4.8
Short-term capital (net)	1.2	−3.8	−9.5
Net errors and omissions	−14.0	−8.6	8.6
Total (net monetary movements)	4.6	7.4	10.4
Valuation changes (net)	3.1	−1.7	−0.2
Exceptional financing (net)	−2.0	10.0	8.8
Official financing (net)	−0.1	0.3	0.3
Changes in reserves	5.5	16.0	19.2

Source: IMF, *International Financial Statistics*.

NATIONAL ACCOUNTS
(estimates, million francs CFA at current prices)
Gross Domestic Product by Economic Activity

	1980	1981	1982
Agriculture, hunting, forestry and fishing	81,520	92,940	110,610
Mining and quarrying	1,570	1,300	1,230
Manufacturing	18,380	16,450	16,440
Electricity, gas and water	1,350	1,070	1,070
Construction	4,990	3,390	3,080
Trade, restaurants and hotels	57,050	56,570	51,770
Transport, storage and communications	4,880	4,820	4,410
Finance, insurance, real estate and business services	1,700	1,580	1,440
Public administration and defence	26,940	28,360	27,580
Other services	2,820	2,780	2,550
GDP at factor cost	201,200	209,260	220,180
Indirect taxes, *less* subsidies	11,170	6,080	6,020
GDP in purchasers' values	212,370	215,340	226,200

Source: UN Economic Commission for Africa, *African Statistical Yearbook*.

External Trade

PRINCIPAL COMMODITIES (million francs CFA)

Imports	1983
Beverages	71.7
Cereal products	2,272.1
Sugar, confectionery, chocolate	292.7
Petroleum products	2,280.5
Textiles, clothing, etc.	392.1
Pharmaceuticals, chemicals	1,561.9
Minerals and metals	311.2
Machinery	843.2
Transport equipment	987.6
Electrical equipment	773.3
Total (incl. others)	13,539.6

Total imports (million francs CFA): 29,349 in 1981; 35,701 in 1982 (Source: IMF, *International Financial Statistics*).

Exports	1983
Live cattle	49.5
Meat	23.5
Fish	2.0
Oil-cake	8.1
Natron	8.1
Gums and resins	0.4
Hides and skins	16.6
Raw cotton	3,753.7
Total (incl. others)	4,120.0

Total exports (million francs CFA): 22,665 in 1981; 18,968 in 1982 (Source: IMF, *International Financial Statistics*).

PRINCIPAL TRADING PARTNERS (million francs CFA)

Imports	1973	1974	1975
Belgium/Luxembourg	592.9	762.6	208.8
Cameroon	725.7	932.8	1,364.2
Central African Republic	232.6	285.1	245.4
China, People's Republic	254.8	218.7	289.1
Congo	774.5	474.9	392.4
France	7,728.8	7,642.6	10,597.2
Gabon	489.4	229.4	392.4
Germany, Fed. Republic	410.9	651.0	714.9
Italy	224.7	386.0	1,107.8
Netherlands	232.9	827.9	2,116.3
Nigeria	2,194.3	2,562.4	2,805.1
Senegal	616.0	669.0	594.0
Taiwan	418.7	281.6	412.8
United Kingdom	255.4	373.4	1,542.0
USA	720.8	2,025.1	1,786.7
Total (incl. others)	18,213.5	20,858.3	28,325.2

Source: *Bulletin de Statistique*, Sous-Direction de la Statistique, N'Djamena.

Exports	1973	1974	1975
Cameroon	197.1	128.2	251.7
Central African Republic	208.4	180.4	174.1
Congo	397.9	316.9	492.1
Denmark	44.2	10.9	n.a.
France	215.0	297.6	683.8
Gabon	75.3	64.8	54.6
Germany, Fed. Republic	92.1	10.9	6.2
Libya	129.3	70.5	11.7
Nigeria	538.9	387.8	1,976.1
Spain	54.6	68.2	37.6
United Kingdom	15.3	18.0	3.9
Zaire	121.9	496.5	152.9
Total (incl. others)	8,483.2	9,052.7	10,103.3

1983 exports (million francs CFA): Cameroon 106.3; Central African Republic 35.8; Congo 9.9; France 3,806.9; Nigeria 104.6; Total (incl. others) 4,120.0.

Transport

ROAD TRAFFIC (motor vehicles in use)

	1977
Private cars	7,636
Buses, lorries and coaches	9,668
Tractors	258
Scooters and motorcycles	1,224
Trailers	1,012
Total	19,798

Source: *Annuaire Statistique du Tchad 1977*.

CIVIL AVIATION (traffic on scheduled services*)

	1980	1981	1982
Kilometres flown ('000)	3,300	2,600	2,400
Passenger-km ('000)	210,000	211,000	229,000
Freight ton-km ('000)	19,200	21,400	21,600
Mail ton-km ('000)	900	900	900

* Including an apportionment of the traffic of Air Afrique.
Source: UN, *Statistical Yearbook*.

Education

(1984)

	Institutions	Teachers	Pupils
Primary	1,231	4,494	288,478
Secondary:			
General	n.a.	n.a.	43,053
Teacher training	n.a.	59	200
Vocational	n.a.	n.a.	2,359
Higher	n.a.	n.a.	n.a.

Source: UNESCO, *Statistical Yearbook*.

Directory

The Constitution

A provisional constitution was promulgated on 29 September 1982.

The Government

HEAD OF STATE

President: HISSÈNE HABRÉ (took office 21 October 1982).

COUNCIL OF MINISTERS
(December 1986)

Minister of National Defence, Veterans and War Victims: HISSÈNE HABRÉ.
Minister of State without Portfolio: DJIDINGAR DONO NGARDOUM.
Minister of Agriculture and Rural Development: BANIARA YOYANA.
Minister of Culture, Youth and Sports: DJIBRINE GRINKY.
Minister of Finance and Data Processing: MBAILEM BANA NGARNAYAL.
Minister of Food Security and Natural Disasters: TAHER ABELDJELIL.
Minister of Foreign Affairs and Co-operation: GOUARA LASSOU.
Minister of Internal Affairs and Administrative Reform: IBRAHIM MAHAMAT ITNO.
Minister of Justice and Keeper of the Seals: Gen. DJIBRIL NÉGUÉ DJOGO.
Minister of Labour, Employment and Vocational Training: YOMITE ROMBA.
Minister for Livestock and Water Resources: TAHER GUINASSOU.
Minister of Mines and Energy: ADOUM MOUSSA SEIF.
Minister of National Education: MAHAMAT SENOUSSI.
Minister of Posts and Telecommunications: ASSILECK HALATA.
Minister of Public Health: MAHAMAT NOUR MALAYE.
Minister of Public Works, Housing and Town Planning: MOUSSA KADDAM.
Minister of Social Affairs and Women's Promotion: Mrs YONATOU RONGAR.
Minister of Tourism and Environment: MBAILAO NAIMBAYE LOZIMIAN.
Minister of Trade and Industry: HAROUNA ABDOULAY.
Minister of Transport and Civil Aviation: ABDERRAMANE ALI ABDOUL.
Minister for the Civil Service: ROUTOUANG YOMA.
Minister-adviser to the President: HOMSALA OUANGMOTCHING.
Minister-delegate to the President in charge of Planning: SOUMAILA MAHAMAT.
There are 10 Secretaries of State.

MINISTRIES

Office of the President: N'Djamena; tel. 32-15; telex 5201.
Ministry of Agriculture, Rural Development, Food Security and Natural Disasters: N'Djamena.
Ministry of Finance: N'Djamena; tel. 21-61; telex 5257.
Ministry of Foreign Affairs and Co-operation: N'Djamena; tel. 23-13; telex 5238.
Ministry of Internal Affairs and Administrative Reform: N'Djamena; tel. 20-29.
Ministry of Justice: N'Djamena; tel. 27-14.
Ministry of Labour, Employment and Vocational Training: N'Djamena; tel. 31-37.
Ministry of National Defence, Veterans and War Victims: N'Djamena; tel. 32-51.
Ministry of National Education: BP 731, N'Djamena; tel. 21-21.

CHAD

Ministry of Posts and Telecommunications: N'Djamena; tel. 25-25; telex 5256.
Ministry of Public Health: N'Djamena; tel. 37-81.
Ministry of Public Works, Housing and Town Planning: N'Djamena; tel. 26-24.
Ministry of Trade and Industry: BP 453, N'Djamena; tel. 21-61.

Legislature

ASSEMBLÉE NATIONALE

The National Assembly and the Economic and Social Council were both dissolved after the coup of 13 April 1975, and had not been reconstituted by late 1986.

Political Organizations

Union Nationale pour l'Indépendance et la Révolution (UNIR): N'Djamena; f. 1984 to succeed the cen. cttee of the Forces armées du nord (FAN), a faction of the Front de libération nationale du Tchad (FROLINAT); in control of govt since 1982; Chair. HISSÈNE HABRÉ; Exec. Sec. GOUARA LASSOU.

Various factions have professed allegiance to UNIR, including:

  Forces Armées Populaires (FAP): co-signatory to formation of CSR in 1985; approx. 3,000 mems; declared support for Habré October 1986; Leader GOUKOUNI OUEADEI.
  Rassemblement pour l'Unité et la Démocratie Tchadienne (RUDT): declared support for Habré January 1986; Leader DJIDINGAR DONO NGARDOUM.
  Rassemblement National Démocratique et Populaire (RNDP): declared support for Habré January 1986; Leader KASSIRE KOUMAKOY.
  Comité d'Action et de Concertation du Conseil Démocratique Révolutionnaire (CAC-CDR): f. 1984; fmr intellectual wing of opposition CDR, declared support for Habré November 1985; Pres. MAHAMAT SENOUSSI KHATIR.
  Front Démocratique du Tchad (FDT): f. 1985 in Paris from four anti-Goukouni opposition groups; declared support for Habré December 1985; Leader Gen. DJIBRIL NÉGUÉ DJOGO.
  Commandos Rouges (Codos): military groups representing southern interests, most of which declared support for Habré in November 1985; Leaders Col ALPHONSE KOTIGA, Sgt TOKINON.

Gouvernement d'Union Nationale de Transition (GUNT): coalition of opposition movements, initially led by GOUKOUNI OUEDDEI; in control of national government between 1979 and 1982.

In November 1986, following its near-disintegration, the movement was reconstituted under the leadership of ACHEIKH IBN OUMAR, and thereafter comprised the following factions, most of which had been signatories to the establishment of a joint council, the Conseil Suprême de la Révolution (CSR), in Bardai in 1985:

  Conseil Démocratique Révolutionnaire (CDR): f. 1979, split 1985; Pres. ACHEIKH IBN OUMAR; Leader of military wing RAKHIS MANAN.
  Forces Armées Occidentales (FAO): splinter group from MPLT; mem. of CSR; Leader MOUSSA MEDELA.
  FROLINAT 'fondamental': opposition faction of the fmr Front de Libération Nationale du Tchad; mem. of CSR; Leader HADJERO SENOUSSI.
  FROLINAT 'originel': mem. of CSR; Leader ABDELKADER YACINE.
  Mouvement Révolutionnaire du Peuple (MRP): mem. of CSR; Leader Col WADAL ABDELKADER KAMOUGUE (reported to have been expelled from movement, June 1986); Sec.-Gen. BIRE TITIMAN.
  Première Armée: f. 1984; mem. of CSR; Leader MAHAMAT ABBA SAID.
  Rassemblement des Forces Patriotiques (RFP): f. 1984; mem. of CSR; Leader FACHO BALAAM.

The following main opposition groups were also in existence:
Mouvement Populaire pour la Libération du Tchad (Troisième Armée) (MPLT): splinter group from FAP; left CSR in January 1986; Leader ABOUBAKAR ABEL RAHMANE.
Union Socialiste Tchadienne (UST): f. 1986; party aiming to negotiate with Habré regime; Leader ABDERAMAN KOULAMALLAH.

Diplomatic Representation

EMBASSIES IN CHAD

Central African Republic: BP 461, N'Djamena; tel. 32-06; Chargé d'affaires: JEAN-CLAUDE KOHO.
China, People's Republic: N'Djamena; Ambassador: YANG YONGRUI.
Congo: N'Djamena; Ambassador: ALBERT OKOUA.
Egypt: BP 1094, N'Djamena; tel. 36-60; telex 5216; Ambassador: MOHSEN AZMI.
France: rue du Lieutenant Franjoux, BP 431, N'Djamena; tel. 25-76; telex 5202; Ambassador: CHRISTIAN DUTHEIL DE LA ROCHÈRE.
Germany, Federal Republic: ave Félix Eboué, BP 893, N'Djamena; tel. 30-90; Ambassador: HANS-JOACHIM HELDT.
Nigeria: 35 ave Charles de Gaulle, BP 752, N'Djamena; tel. 24-98; telex 5242; Ambassador: SAMUEL A. OLAJIDE.
Sudan: rue de Havre, BP 45, N'Djamena; tel. 34-29; Ambassador: ELTAYEB AHMED HUMMEIDA.
USA: ave du Félix Eboué, BP 413, N'Djamena; tel. 32-69; telex 5203; Ambassador: JOHN BLANE.
Zaire: ave du 20 août, BP 910, N'Djamena; tel. 21-47; Ambassador: Gen. MALU-MALU DIANDA.

Judicial System

The Supreme Court was abolished after the coup of April 1975. There is a Court of Appeal at N'Djamena. Criminal courts sit at N'Djamena, Sarh, Moundou and Abéché, and elsewhere as necessary, and each of these four major towns has a magistrates' court. There are 43 justices of the peace. In October 1976 a permanent Court of State Security was established, comprising eight civilian or military members.

Religion

It is estimated that 45% of the population are Muslims and 6% Christians, mainly Roman Catholics. Most of the remainder follow animistic beliefs.

ISLAM

Head of the Islamic Community: Imam MOUSSA IBRAHIM.

CHRISTIANITY

The Roman Catholic Church

Chad comprises one archdiocese and three dioceses. There were an estimated 280,000 adherents at 31 December 1984.

Bishops' Conference: Conférence Episcopale du Tchad, BP 456, N'Djamena; tel. 27-11; Pres. Mgr CHARLES VANDAME, Archbishop of N'Djamena.
Archbishop of N'Djamena: Mgr CHARLES VANDAME, Archevêché, BP 456, N'Djamena; tel. 27-11.

Protestant Church

L'Entente évangélique: BP 127, N'Djamena; a fellowship of churches and missions working in Chad: includes Eglise évangélique au Tchad, Assemblées Chrétiennes, Eglise fraternelle Luthérienne and Eglise évangélique des frères.

BAHÁ'Í FAITH

National Spiritual Assembly: BP 181, N'Djamena; mems in 990 localities.

The Press

Bulletin Mensuel de Statistiques du Tchad: BP 453, N'Djamena; monthly.
Comnat: BP 731, N'Djamena; tel. 29-68; publ. by UNESCO National Commission.
Info-Tchad: BP 670, N'Djamena; daily news bulletin issued by Chad Press Agency (ATP); French; circ. 1,500.
Informations Economiques: BP 548, N'Djamena; publ. by the Chambre de Commerce, d'Agriculture et d'Industrie; weekly.
Journal Officiel de la République du Tchad: N'Djamena.

Tchad et Culture: BP 456, N'Djamena; Christian; publ. by Imprimerie du Tchad; 8 a year; circ. 5,000; publication suspended 1979.

Le Tchad en Marche: N'Djamena; publ. by Ministry of Information; monthly.

NEWS AGENCIES

Agence Tchadienne de Presse (ATP): BP 670, N'Djamena; telex 5240.

Foreign Bureaux

Agence France-Presse (AFP): BP 83, N'Djamena; Correspondent ALDOM NADJI TITO.

Reuters (UK) is also represented in Chad.

Publisher

Government Publishing House: BP 453, N'Djamena.

Radio

There were an estimated 120,000 radio receivers in use in 1982.

Radiodiffusion Nationale Tchadienne: BP 892, N'Djamena; govt station; programmes in French, Arabic and eight vernacular languages; there are four transmitters; Dir DJEDE KHOURTOU GAMMAR.

An anti-Government radio station, Radio Bardai, is operated by GUNT supporters at Bardai, northern Chad.

Finance

(cap. = capital; res = reserves; br. = branch; m. = million; amounts in francs CFA)

BANKING
Central Bank

Banque des Etats de l'Afrique Centrale: BP 50, N'Djamena; Headquarters in Yaoundé, Cameroon; tel. 24-58; telex 5220; f. 1972; central bank of issue for mem. states of the Customs and Economic Union of Central Africa (UDEAC), comprising Cameroon, the Central African Republic, Chad, the Congo, Equatorial Guinea and Gabon; cap. and res 92,485m. (June 1983); Gov. CASIMIR OYE-MBA; Dir in Chad MADJI ADAM.

National Banks

Banque de Développement du Tchad (BDT): rue Capitaine Ohrel, BP 19, N'Djamena; tel. 28-70; f. 1962; cap. 520m.; 58.4% state-owned; Man. Dir MOUTA ALI ZEZERTI.

Banque Internationale pour le Commerce et l'Industrie du Tchad (BICIT): 15 ave Charles de Gaulle, BP 38, N'Djamena; telex 5233; 40% state-owned, 30.6% by Société Financière pour les Pays d'Outre-Mer, 29.4% by Banque Nationale de Paris; Man. Dir HISSEINE LAMINE; activities temporarily suspended.

Banque Tchadienne de Crédit et de Dépôts (BTCD): 6 rue Robert-Lévy, BP 461, N'Djamena; tel. 24-77; telex 5212; f. 1963; cap. 440m.; 51% state-owned, 34% owned by Crédit Lyonnais; Pres. ABDOULAYE DOUTOU; Man. Dir MAHAMAT FARRIS; br. at Moundou.

Foreign Banks

Banque Internationale pour l'Afrique au Tchad (BIAT): BP 87, N'Djamena; tel. 26-13; telex 5228; f. 1980; cap. 450m. (Dec. 1983); 35% state-owned, 65% by Banque Internationale pour l'Afrique Occidentale; Pres. PIERRE O'QUIN; Dir in N'Djamena EMILE EMERY.

Banque Tchado-Arabe Libyenne pour le Commerce Extérieur et le Développement (BATAL): BP 104, N'Djamena; tel. 36-52; telex 5239; f. 1973; cap. 250m.; 60% owned by Libyan Arab Foreign Bank, 40% state-owned; Man. Dir ALI SAKKAH; activities suspended 1985.

Bankers' Organizations

Association Professionnelle des Banques au Tchad: N'Djamena.

Conseil National de Crédit: N'Djamena; f. 1965 to create a national credit policy and to organize the banking profession.

INSURANCE

Assureurs Conseils Tchadiens Faugère et Jutheau et Cie: N'Djamena; Dir PIERRE HUBERT.

Société de Représentation d'Assurances et de Réassurances Africaines (SORARAF): N'Djamena; Dir Mme FOURNIER.

Société Tchadienne d'Assurances et de Réassurances (STAR): N'Djamena; telex 5268; Dir PHILIPPE SABIT.

Trade and Industry

CHAMBER OF COMMERCE

Chambre de Commerce, d'Agriculture et d'Industrie de la République du Tchad: BP 458, N'Djamena; f. 1938; Pres. MADJADOUM KOLINGAR; Sec.-Gen. MAHAMAT RAHMA SALEH; brs at Sarh, Moundou and Abéché.

DEVELOPMENT ORGANIZATIONS

Caisse Centrale de Coopération Économique: BP 478, N'Djamena; Dir ALBERT LOUGNON.

Mission Française de Coopération: BP 898, N'Djamena; telex 5340; administers bilateral aid from France; Dir P. RICARD.

Office National de Développement Rural (ONDR): BP 896, N'Djamena; f. 1968; Pres. and Man. Dir HIDINI WARDOUGOU.

Société pour le Développement de la Région du Lac (SODELAC): BP 782, N'Djamena; f. 1967; cap. 180m. francs CFA; Man. Dir KAMOUGUÉ GUIDINGAR.

TRADE

Société Nationale de Commercialisation du Tchad (SONACOT): N'Djamena; telex 5227; f. 1965; cap. 150m. francs CFA; 76% state-owned; national marketing, distribution and import-export company; Man. Dir MARBROUCK NATROUD.

TRADE UNIONS

Confédération Syndicale du Tchad (CST): BP 387, N'Djamena.

Union Nationale des Travailleurs du Tchad (UNATRAT): BP 553, ave Charles de Gaulle, N'Djamena.

Transport

RAILWAYS

In 1962 Chad signed an agreement with Cameroon to extend the Transcameroon railway from N'Gaoundéré to Sarh, a distance of 500 km. Although the Transcameroon reached N'Gaoundéré in 1974, the proposed extension into Chad has been indefinitely postponed. Other possibilities of extending Sudanese and Nigerian lines into Chad are being explored.

ROADS

In 1976 there were 30,725 km of roads, of which 4,628 km were national roads and 3,512 km were secondary roads. There are also some 20,000 km of tracks suitable for motor traffic during the October–July dry season. In July 1986 the International Development Association (IDA) provided a loan of US $19.2m. towards a major road network rehabilitation programme, aimed at improving the movement of goods within the country. The EEC is helping to fund the construction of a highway leading from N'Djamena to Sarh and Lere, on the Cameroon border; meanwhile, a footbridge over the Logone river was opened in February 1985, thus providing the first all-weather road link with Cameroon.

Coopérative des Transportateurs Tchadiens (COPORTCHAD): BP 336, N'Djamena; tel. 20-49; telex 5225; road haulage; Pres. SALEH KHALIFA.

INLAND WATERWAYS

There is a certain amount of traffic on the Chari and Logone rivers which meet just south of N'Djamena. Both routes, from Sarh to N'Djamena on the Chari and from Bongor and Moundou to

CHAD

N'Djamena on the Logone, are open only during the wet season, August–December, and provide a convenient alternative when roads become impassable.

CIVIL AVIATION

The international airport at N'Djamena has been in use since 1967: proposals were announced in May 1986 for a US $3.8m. improvement programme. There are over 40 smaller airfields.

Air Afrique: BP 466, N'Djamena; tel. 30-00; Chad holds a 7% share; see Ivory Coast.

Air Tchad: 27 ave du Président Tombalbaye, BP 168, N'Djamena; f. 1966; govt majority holding with 34% UTA interest; regular passenger, freight and charter services within Chad and international charters; Pres. GEORGES N'DIGUIMBAYE; fleet of 1 Fokker F. 27-500.

Tourism

Direction du Tourisme, des Parcs Nationaux et Réserves de Faune: BP 86, N'Djamena; also at BP 88, Sarh; f. 1962; Dir DABOULAYE.

Société Hôtelière et Touristique: BP 478, N'Djamena; Dir ANTOINE ABTOUR.

CHILE

Introductory Survey

Location, Climate, Language, Religion, Flag, Capital

The Republic of Chile is a long, narrow country lying along the Pacific coast of South America, extending from Peru and Bolivia in the north to Cape Horn in the far south. Isla de Pascua (Easter Island), about 3,780 km (2,350 miles) off shore, and several other small islands form part of Chile. To the east, Chile is separated from Argentina by the high Andes mountains. Both the mountains and the cold Humboldt Current influence the climate; between Arica in the north and Punta Arenas in the extreme south, a distance of about 4,000 km (2,500 miles), the average maximum temperature varies by no more than 13°C. Rainfall varies widely between the arid desert in the north and the rainy south. The language is Spanish. There is no state religion but the great majority of the inhabitants profess Christianity, and more than 85% are adherents of the Roman Catholic Church. The national flag (proportions 3 by 2) is divided horizontally: the lower half is red, while the upper half has a five-pointed white star on a blue square, at the hoist, with the remainder white. The capital is Santiago.

Recent History

Chile was ruled by Spain from the 16th century until its independence in 1818. For most of the 19th century it was governed by a small oligarchy of land-owners. Chile won the War of the Pacific (1879–83) against Peru and Bolivia. Most of the present century has been marked by the struggle for power between right- and left-wing forces.

In September 1970 Dr Salvador Allende Gossens, the Marxist candidate of Unidad Popular (a coalition of five left-wing parties, including the Communist Party), was elected to succeed Eduardo Frei Montalva, a Christian Democrat who was President between 1964 and 1970. Allende promised to transform Chilean society by constitutional means, and imposed an extensive nationalization programme. The Government failed to obtain a congressional majority in the elections of March 1973 and was confronted with a deteriorating economic situation as well as an intensification of violent opposition to its policies. Accelerated inflation led to food shortages and there were repeated clashes between pro- and anti-Government activists. The armed forces finally intervened in September 1973, claiming that a military take-over was necessary because of the increasingly anarchic situation and economic breakdown. President Allende died during the coup.

Congress was dissolved, all political activity banned and strict censorship introduced. The military junta dedicated itself to the eradication of Marxism and the reconstruction of Chile, and its leader, Gen. Augusto Pinochet Ugarte, became Supreme Chief of State in June and President in December 1974. The junta has been widely criticized abroad for its repressive policies and violations of human rights. Critics of the regime were tortured and imprisoned, and several thousand disappeared. Some of those who had been imprisoned were released, as a result of international pressure, and sent into exile.

In September 1976 three constitutional acts were promulgated with the aim of creating an 'authoritarian democracy'. All political parties were banned in March 1977, when the state of siege was extended. Following a UN General Assembly resolution in December 1977, condemning the Government for violating human rights, Gen. Pinochet called a referendum in January 1978 to endorse the regime's policies. As more than 75% of the voters supported the President in his defence of Chile 'in the face of international aggression', the state of siege (in force since 1973) was lifted and was replaced by a state of emergency.

A plebiscite in September 1980 showed a 67% vote in favour of a new constitution which had been drawn up by the Government, although dubious electoral practices were allegedly employed. The new constitution was described as providing a 'transition to democracy' but, although Gen. Pinochet ceased to be head of the armed forces, additional clauses allowed him to maintain his firm hold on power until 1989.

Opposition to the Government from all sectors of the population, including church leaders, increased, however, and industrial and agricultural interests demanded changes in economic policies. Political demonstrations were violently broken up. In May 1983 a five-member union confederation was formed to demand the restoration of democracy. Monthly demonstrations took place in the capital and the major cities, and the population of Santiago joined in the periodic 'caceroleos', when the banging of kitchen utensils and the sounding of car horns created a deafening form of protest. By October 1983 hundreds of people had been injured in such confrontations, and a total of 68 deaths had been recorded. The regime of Gen. Pinochet received world-wide condemnation.

Political parties, which were still officially outlawed, began to re-emerge, and in July 1983 five moderate parties formed a coalition, the 'Alianza Democrática', demanding a return to democratic rule within 18 months. A left-wing coalition was also created. A 'state of internal disturbance' was declared in September, and a law banning unauthorized demonstrations was decreed in October, although, at the same time, Gen. Pinochet attempted to placate workers and debtors with populist measures and the announcement of public works projects. More than 1,000 exiles were allowed to return.

An anti-Government campaign of bombings, begun in late 1983 and directed principally against electricity installations, continued throughout 1984. In response, in January 1984 the Government announced new anti-terrorist legislation and extensive security measures. In March a 90-day state of emergency was declared, and various opposition publications were censored. Six people were killed during a national day of protest. The first May Day rally in Santiago since 1973 was attended by 150,000 people, and public protests were held throughout the country. Relations between the Roman Catholic Church and the State began to deteriorate after anti-Government demonstrations at Punta Arenas in February, for which the Government blamed the Church. Two days of violent clashes between police and demonstrators in September resulted in nine deaths, including that of a French priest. Following the demonstrations, the opposition announced its intention to call a general strike in October. During the two days of protests accompanying the strike, a further nine people were killed, and police raids on the suburbs of Santiago resulted in a large number of detentions. In November a state of siege was declared for 90 days. Two more days of anti-Government protests met with a muted response from the public.

In March 1985 three members of the Partido Comunista were abducted and murdered in Santiago. In July a judicial investigation found that officers of the Carabineros (Police) had been involved in the murders. As a consequence of this revelation, the Chief Commander of the Carabineros resigned, and 29 senior officers were dismissed. In June the state of siege was lifted and replaced by a state of emergency. However, the Government's strenuous attempts to eradicate internal opposition failed to deter the campaign of bombings and public protests, which continued throughout 1985. In September 10 people were killed and several hundred wounded during two days of anti-Government demonstrations. Opposition leaders and trade unionists were also detained and sent into internal exile. During an anti-Government protest in November, four people were killed and hundreds were arrested by the security forces. In the same month Gen. Pinochet appointed a new army representative to the junta, in what was widely regarded as a move to consolidate support for his presidency within the junta.

Throughout 1986 Gen. Pinochet's regime came under increasing attack from opposition groups, the Roman Catholic Church, guerrilla organizations (principally the Frente Patriótico Manuel Rodríguez—FPMR) and international critics including the

US administration, which had previously refrained from condemning the regime's notorious record of violations of human rights. The criticism by the US administration was especially damaging to Chile because it implied that the USA might withdraw its support for future loans to Chile by international financial agencies.

A bombing campaign by the FPMR continued intermittently: 267 acts of terrorism were recorded in the first half of 1986. Anti-Government protests were held by opposition groups and university students, and demonstrations at the beginning of May were followed by the detention of some 15,000 people from Santiago's poor districts. In April leading trade union, professional and community groups, many of whom had previously been passive critics of the Government, formed the Asamblea de la Civilidad, an organization whose aim was to seek a peaceful transition to democracy. However, during a two-day general strike called by the Asamblea in July, eight people were killed and several hundred were detained. The death of an American resident, who was reported to have been deliberately set alight by a group of soldiers, provoked international condemnation and brought renewed criticism from the USA.

In September the FPMR made an unsuccessful attempt to assassinate Gen. Pinochet. The regime's immediate response was to impose a state of siege throughout Chile, under which leading members of the opposition were detained and strict censorship was introduced. One consequence of the state of siege was the reappearance of right-wing death squads, who were implicated in a series of murders, including that of a prominent journalist, which followed the assassination attempt.

In February 1984 the Council of State, a government-appointed consultative body, began drafting a law to legalize political parties and to prepare for elections in 1989. In March Gen. Pinochet confirmed that a plebiscite would be held at an unspecified time to decide on a timetable for the elections. In September, however, Gen. Pinochet firmly rejected any possibility of a return to civilian rule before 1989. In February 1985 the Minister of the Interior, who was considered to have been the most moderate member of the Government, and the Minister of Finance resigned. Further Cabinet changes occurred in July. In August the Roman Catholic Church sponsored talks between 11 opposition groups, which resulted in the drafting of an Acuerdo Nacional para la Transición a la Plena Democracia (National Accord for the Transition to Full Democracy). President Pinochet rejected the opposition's proposals. Nevertheless, the accord was supported by a former member of the junta, Gen. Gustavo Leigh Guzmán, and by his successor, Gen. Fernando Matthei Aubel.

In 1986 reports that Gen. Pinochet intended to extend his term of office until the late 1990s caused considerable dismay among opposition groups. Although such reports were later denied by the President, the junta and the Government were thought to be divided over the issue of a return to full democracy after 1989. In October Gen. Pinochet appointed a new army representative to the junta and ordered the retirement of several army generals, including that of Gen. Luis Danús, who had publicly opposed the prolongation of Gen. Pinochet's presidency. By late 1986 the issue of the transition to democracy was still completely unresolved, and the campaign of both violent and peaceful protest against Gen. Pinochet's regime seemed certain to continue over the forthcoming months.

In 1985 the Chilean Government was strongly criticized by opposition groups and the inhabitants of Isla de Pascua (Easter Island) for its decision to extend and improve the island's Mataveri airstrip for use by the US National Aeronautic and Space Administration (NASA).

Chile has had border disputes: to the north with Bolivia and to the south with Argentina. In 1978 Bolivia broke off diplomatic relations with Chile on the grounds that it had not shown sufficient flexibility over the question of Bolivia's access to the Pacific Ocean. Chile's dispute with Argentina concerned three small islands in the Beagle Channel, south of Tierra del Fuego. The issue of sovereignty over these islands has, on occasions, brought the two countries to the verge of war. In December 1978 the case was referred to papal mediation and the resultant proposals were presented to the two Governments in December 1980. In October 1984 it was announced that total agreement had been reached. Under the terms of the settlement, Chile was awarded 12 islands and islets to the south of the Beagle Channel, including Lennox, Picton and Nueva. The agreement was formally approved by the ruling junta in April 1985, and was ratified in May by representatives of the Argentine and Chilean Governments.

Government

Chile is a republic, divided into 12 regions and a metropolitan area. Since the coup in September 1973 the country has been ruled by a military junta. In 1975 a Council of State was established to draft a new constitution, which was promulgated in March 1981 and will take full effect from 1989 (see Constitution). Meanwhile, executive and legislative power is vested in the President and the junta, assisted by a Cabinet. The clause stating that all Chilean nationals must obey the national authorities was effective from October 1980.

Defence

Military service in the army or the navy lasts two years and is compulsory for men at 19 years of age. In July 1986 the army had a strength of 57,000, the air force 15,000 and the navy 29,000. Paramilitary security forces number about 27,000 carabineros. Defence expenditure for 1985 was estimated at 200,000m. pesos.

Economic Affairs

In 1973 the junta inherited an economy with inflation between 500 and 1,000%, low monetary reserves and a declining gross domestic product (GDP). The Allende Government had introduced wide-ranging state control but the Pinochet Government attempted to establish a market-oriented economy by encouraging foreign investment, by denationalizing most of the enterprises which the Allende Government had nationalized, and by drastically reducing import tariffs. After slow growth in earlier years, production expanded considerably in 1977, when Chile's GDP rose by 9.7%, compared with a decline of 14.3% in 1975.

After the coup in 1973, the military regime reversed the agricultural reforms which had been introduced by President Allende: about 30% of the agricultural land that had been redistributed was returned to its original owners, while a further 20% was auctioned. State assistance to small farmers ended.

In 1981 about 15% of the working population were engaged in agriculture, but the sector contributes between 6.5% and 7.5% of the GDP. Although the country has great agricultural potential, land use is inefficient. The Government's refusal to protect domestic production against cheaper imports resulted in sharp falls in the production of wheat (down 29%), barley, oats, rye, oil-seeds and fruit in 1981, although production of rice, potatoes, maize and sugar beet increased. Agricultural production continued to decline in 1982. The area sown with rice fell by 17.9%. By 1983 the area sown to wheat, oats, barley, maize and rye was 35% less than in 1975. Dependence on imports increased. Wheat production fell from 650,000 metric tons in 1982 to 586,000 tons in 1983, the decline being aggravated by severe drought. In 1982 imports of wheat accounted for 60% of the total consumed. In the same period imports of oil-seeds rose from 50% to 90% of the total consumed. In 1984 production of major crops improved. Wheat production rose to 988,300 tons and maize output increased from 512,000 tons in 1983 to 721,000 tons in 1984. Wheat production was expected to be 1.2m. tons in 1985. The annual harvest of sugar beet rose from 1,643,000 tons in 1983 to 2,194,000 tons in 1984. The output of the agricultural sector expanded by 6.7% in 1984 and by 7.9% in 1985. In 1984 the Government announced plans to invest 2,400m. pesos in the sector over the following three years.

Wood and wood products account for an increasing proportion of export earnings: in 1985 foreign revenue from the sector was US $334.6m. Fishing also has great development potential, with the total catch reaching 4,499,300 metric tons in 1984. In spite of a decline in large-scale fishing, the sector was estimated to have grown by 12.6% in 1984. In 1985 exports accounted for 12% of foreign exchange earnings.

Chile became the world's leading producer of copper in 1982, when it accounted for 15% of global mine production of the metal. Chile's reserves of copper ore are estimated to represent 23% of the world's proven resources and are concentrated in the Chuquicamata and El Teniente mines. Exports of copper, in a processed or unprocessed form, provide more than 50% of

Chile's total earnings of foreign exchange, and the industry accounts for 8%–10% of GDP. Chile's production of copper rose to a record 1.3m. metric tons in 1984, compared with 1.1m. tons in 1981. Copper production was 1.4m. tons in 1985, and there are plans to increase annual output to 1.7m. tons by 1990. However, copper's share of total exports by value declined from 83% in 1973 to 44% in 1981, partly as a result of fluctuations in world demand. By 1982 the world price of copper, in real terms, had fallen to its lowest level for 50 years. Prices continued to decline, and a loss in earnings of US $244m. was recorded in 1984. However, earnings increased by $141m. in 1985. In spite of the decline in copper earnings, the Government maintained its intention to expand the sector through investment amounting to $1,400m. Expansion of the sector would be facilitated by the quality of Chile's high-grade ores and by the low cost of production. The output of gold increased by 29% in 1982, principally as a result of the opening of the El Indio mine in 1980. Production reached 17.2 tons in 1985. Gold metal and concentrates account for 5% of export revenues. Silver production was 517 tons in 1985. Chile has the largest known reserves of lithium.

Other minerals of economic importance are iron ore (for domestic consumption and export, mainly to Japan), molybdenum, manganese, lead, zinc, mercury, limestone, marble, coal, nitrates and iodine. Petroleum and natural gas are found in the south. Chile imports 60,000 barrels per day (b/d) of petroleum from Ecuador and Venezuela to meet domestic requirements but, with the discovery of large new deposits in the Magellan Straits, it is hoped to satisfy domestic oil consumption by 2003. Production averaged 34,000 b/d in 1985. In addition, Chile is eager to attract foreign investment to the sector, and it is planned to invest US $74.5m. in onshore and offshore exploration projects. In 1986 work began on the construction of a methanol plant at Cabo Negro at a cost of more than $300m. The plant was to come 'on stream' in 1988 with an annual output of 750,000 metric tons. Other domestic resources of energy, such as coal and hydroelectricity, are also being developed rapidly. Chile's potential hydroelectric generating capacity is estimated to be 18.7m. kW. The Antuco plant has a capacity of 300,000 kW and the Colbún-Machicura project, which came 'on stream' in September 1985, has an installed capacity of 490,000 kW. In 1985 the IDB allocated two loans amounting to US $230m. for the construction of a 160,000-kW plant at Alfalfal and a 130,000-kW plant at Canutillar.

Manufacturing, which accounted for about 21% of the GDP in 1983, faced very strong foreign competition after the Government's drastic reduction of import duties. Industrial production rose by 5% in 1980, and by 1.2% in 1981. Following the onset of the economic recession in mid-1981, demand slumped and high interest rates forced many businesses into liquidation. Industrial production fell by 21% in 1982. By January 1983, 61,000 small businesses had been declared insolvent, including 12 subsidiaries of the two leading industrial groups, Vial and Cruzat/Larraín. Despite claims of improved industrial output towards the end of 1983, retail traders reported a 27% drop in sales for the year, while activity in the construction sector was at its lowest level for two years. Industrial production increased by 10.3% in 1984. A slight recovery was reported in 1985, with industry expanding by 1.2% and construction by more than 8%. The Government's three-year plan, announced in 1984, contained plans to reactivate the industrial sector by investing 4,373m. pesos and creating 400,000 new jobs.

The economic decline which began in 1981 was the most spectacular in Latin America. Between 1977 and 1980 gross fixed investment represented 15.2% of GNP, one of the lowest ratios in the region. Foreign loans, which had been used for importing consumer goods and for speculation on the lucrative financial market, were no longer forthcoming by mid-1981. The collapse of the domestic economy and the numerous bankruptcies of private companies led to pressure on the private banks, which were unable to service their foreign debts, amounting to US $7,000m. by January 1983. The liquidation of several private banks panicked depositors into withdrawing a total of about $1,000m. in January 1983 alone. Chile's reserves of foreign exchange declined from $4,099m. in September 1981 to $1,218m. in April 1983. GDP contracted by 14.1%, in real terms, in 1982. A decline in world prices for copper, molybdenum and timber led to a merchandise trade deficit of $2,677m. in 1981 and only a modest surplus of $63m. in 1982.

In January 1983 Chile's foreign debt, which was US $3,500m. in 1973, reached $17,454m. (representing the highest level of debt per inhabitant in the world), of which 64% was of the private sector. An agreement on a loan of $900m. from the IMF was signed in January 1983, on the condition that strict monetarist policies would be imposed. GDP declined by 0.7% in 1983. The current deficit on the balance of payments declined from $4,733m. in 1981 to $1,165m. in 1983. By December 1983 Chile's foreign exchange reserves had risen to $2,031m.

In 1984 the economy showed signs of a modest recovery, and real GDP grew by 6.3%. Debt servicing was rendered more difficult by the continuing decline in world copper prices. However, by the end of 1984 Chile's foreign exchange reserves had risen to US $2,291m. The merchandise trade surplus declined from $1,082m. in 1983 to $447m. in 1984, when the current deficit on the balance of payments was $2,060m. Meanwhile, in February 1984 the Government revealed its plans for economic recovery, which were approved by the IMF in May. Concurrently, a loan of $780m. was secured from foreign banks. In July, however, Chile announced that it would be unable to repay any of the principal due on its foreign debt (then standing at $18,600m.) for the next five years. Interest payments would be maintained. In September the peso was devalued from 93 to 115 per US dollar. Import duties were increased to 35% to compensate for rising dollar interest rates and falling copper prices.

In May 1985 Chile reached agreement with its creditor banks on a new loan of US $1,085m. (including a loan of $300m. from the World Bank) and on the rescheduling of debts amounting to $4,450m. In addition, Chile secured further funds of $850m. from the IMF in September. In May the Government implemented a new programme of budgetary control, approved by the IMF, with the aim of restricting the budget deficit to 3.5% of GDP in 1985. The currency was devalued to 168.9 pesos per US dollar, and some import tariffs were reduced to 20%. The principal obstacle to a genuine improvement in Chile's economic performance continued to be depressed market prices for leading mineral exports. Nevertheless, real GDP grew by an estimated 2% in 1985, and a trade surplus of $759m. was recorded. GDP growth of more than 3% was expected in 1986.

In April 1986 Chile signed an agreement with its creditor banks on the rescheduling of US $2,600m. in principal falling due in 1985–87. In an attempt to reduce the foreign debt of more than $20,000m., the Government implemented a debt conversion programme, under which Chile's foreign creditors were able to exchange government-guaranteed loans for peso-denominated bonds. By mid-1986 $450m. had been deducted from the foreign debt as a result of the programme. Plans to secure a loan of $250m. from the World Bank by the end of 1986 were placed in jeopardy by the deterioration of Chile's internal situation and the subsequent reluctance of the US administration to support Chile's request for funding from international financial agencies. The loan was eventually approved by the World Bank in November. Also in November Chile reached agreement with the IMF on an economic programme for 1987–88, under which it was hoped to achieve economic growth of between 3% and 5% over the following two years.

The annual rate of inflation averaged 27.3% in 1983, but declined to 19.9% in 1984. An increase to 26.4% was recorded in 1985, but, according to official estimates, inflation averaged 17.2% in the year to July 1986. Workers' salaries in the private sector lost 50% in purchasing power between August 1981 and October 1983. In October 1984 the Government announced substantial increases, of up to 100%, in salaries, to compensate for price rises in 1984. Unemployment was officially estimated at 13.1% in July 1985, but the real level was thought to exceed 30%. In addition, 13% of the labour force were engaged in a system of minimum employment.

Social Welfare

Employees, including agricultural workers, may receive benefits for sickness, unemployment, accidents at work, maternity and retirement, and there are dependants' allowances, including family allowances. In May 1981 social security was transferred to the private sector, and run by the Administradoras de Fondo de Pensiones. All but one of the funds and 40% of the worker investors made losses, totalling US $95m., in 1981. A National Health Service was established in 1952. There were 5,671 physicians working in official medical services in 1979. Chile had 300 hospital establishments, with a total of 37,971 beds, in 1980.

Education

Pre-primary education is widely available for all children up to the age of six years. Primary education is free and compulsory for eight years, beginning at six or seven years of age. Secondary education, beginning at the age of 14, is divided into the humanities-science programme (lasting for four years), with the emphasis on general education and possible entrance to university, and the technical-professional programme (lasting for up to six years), designed to meet the requirements of specialist training. An intensive national literacy campaign, launched in 1980, reduced the rate of adult illiteracy from 11% in 1970 to an estimated 5.6% in 1983. The university law of January 1981 banned all political activity in universities, reduced the number of degree courses from 33 to 12, halved future government funding and encouraged the establishment of private specialized universities.

Tourism

Chile has a wide variety of attractions for the tourist, including fine beaches, ski resorts in the Andes, lakes and rivers. There are many opportunities for hunting and fishing in the southern archipelago, where there are plans to make an integrated tourist area with Argentina, requiring investment of US $120m. Isla de Pascua (Easter Island) may also be visited by tourists. Chile received 458,704 visitors in 1985.

Public Holidays

1987: 1 January (New Year's Day), 17–18 April (Good Friday and Easter Saturday), 1 May (Labour Day), 21 May (Battle of Iquique), 15 August (Assumption), 18 September (Independence Day), 12 October (Day of the Race), 1 November (All Saints' Day), 8 December (Immaculate Conception), 25 December (Christmas Day), 31 December (New Year's Eve).

1988: 1 January (New Year's Day), 1–2 April (Good Friday and Easter Saturday), 1 May (Labour Day), 21 May (Battle of Iquique), 15 August (Assumption), 18 September (Independence Day), 12 October (Day of the Race), 1 November (All Saints' Day), 8 December (Immaculate Conception), 25 December (Christmas Day), 31 December (New Year's Day).

Weights and Measures

The metric system is officially in force.

Currency and Exchange Rates

100 centavos = 1 Chilean peso.

Exchange rates (30 September 1986):
 £1 sterling = 282.22 pesos;
 US $1 = 195.04 pesos.

Statistical Survey

Source (unless otherwise stated): Instituto Nacional de Estadísticas, Avda Bulnes 418, Casilla 7597, Correo 3, Santiago; tel. 6991441.

Area and Population

AREA, POPULATION AND DENSITY*

Area (sq km)	756,626†
Population (census of 22 April 1970)‡	
Males	4,343,512
Females	4,541,256
Total	8,884,768
Population (official estimates at mid-year)	
1984	11,878,419
1985	12,074,477
1986	12,271,173
Density (per sq km) at mid-1986	16.2

* Excluding Chilean Antarctic Territory. † 292,132 sq miles.
‡ Excluding adjustment for underenumeration, estimated at 5.12%.

REGIONS*

		Area (sq km)	Population (30 June 1986)	Capital
I	De Tarapacá	58,786	319,171	Iquique
II	De Antofagasta	125,253	375,812	Antofagasta
III	De Atacama	74,705	192,824	Copiapó
IV	De Coquimbo	40,656	447,430	La Serena
V	De Valparaíso	16,396	1,284,646	Valparaíso
VI	Del Libertador Gen. Bernardo O'Higgins	16,456	619,483	Rancagua
VII	Del Maule	30,662	765,031	Talca
VIII	Del Bío-Bío	36,939	1,600,509	Concepción
IX	De la Araucanía	31,946	718,664	Temuco
X	De Los Lagos	68,247	869,738	Puerto Montt
XI	Aisén del Gen. Carlos Ibáñez del Campo	108,997†	72,473	Coihaique
XII	De Magallanes y Antártida Chilena	132,034‡	149,317	Punta Arenas
	Metropolitan Region (Santiago)	15,549	4,856,075	—

* Before 1975 the country was divided into 25 provinces. With the new administrative system, the 13 regions are sub-divided into 50 new provinces and the metropolitan area of Santiago.
† Area obtained as a residual.
‡ Excluding Antarctic territory.

PRINCIPAL TOWNS (population at 30 June 1985)

Gran Santiago (capital)	4,318,305*	Temuco	171,831
		Rancagua	152,132
Viña del Mar	315,947	Talca	144,656
Valparaíso	267,025	Chillán	128,920
Talcahuano	220,910	Arica	127,925
Concepción	217,756	Iquique	120,732
Antofagasta	175,486	Valdivia	119,977

* Including suburbs.

BIRTHS, MARRIAGES AND DEATHS

	Registered live births*		Registered marriages		Registered deaths	
	Number	Rate (per 1,000)	Number	Rate (per 1,000)	Number	Rate (per 1,000)
1979	234,840	21.5	80,072	7.3	74,528	6.8
1980	247,013	22.2	86,001	7.7	74,109	6.7
1981	264,809	23.4	90,564	8.0	69,971	6.2
1982	274,335	23.9	80,115	7.0	69,887	6.1
1983	260,655	22.3	82,483	7.1	74,296	6.4
1984	265,016	22.3	87,261	7.3	74,669	6.3
1985	261,978	21.7	91,099	7.5	73,534	6.1

* Figures include adjustment for underenumeration, estimated at 5% for 1978–81, 6.5% for 1982–83 and 5% for 1984–85.

ECONOMICALLY ACTIVE POPULATION*
(Sample surveys†—'000)

	1981	1982	1983
Agriculture, forestry, hunting and fishing	508.2	477.5	509.4
Mining and quarrying	63.3	54.0	59.4
Manufacturing	516.2	373.9	405.9
Construction	169.6	84.1	93.5
Electricity, gas, water and sanitary services	26.7	24.6	23.7
Commerce	620.6	509.5	550.4
Transport, storage and communication	218.1	185.1	195.8
Financial services	116.9	109.8	110.1
Others	1,031.3	1,123.8	1,267.9
Total	3,271.0	2,942.3	3,216.1

* Excluding unemployed persons seeking work for the first time.
† Covering 27,500 households.

Agriculture

PRINCIPAL CROPS ('000 metric tons)

	1982	1983	1984
Wheat	650	586	988
Rice (paddy)	131	116	165
Barley	118	73	74
Oats	118	146	163
Rye	6	4	4
Maize	425	512	721
Dry beans	162	84	94
Lentils	16	14	16
Potatoes	842	684	1,036
Sunflower seed	5	5	7
Sugar beet	963	1,643	2,194
Rapeseed	13	3	4
Tomatoes*	158	160	162
Pumpkins, etc.*	130	132	132
Onions (dry)*	127	128	130
Water melons*	168	170	172
Melons*	146	148	152
Grapes*	1,100	950	1,050
Apples	345	365	410†
Peaches	108	116	122†
Dry peas	7	6	6
Chick-peas	4	3	7

* FAO estimates. † Unofficial estimate.
Source: FAO, *Production Yearbook*.

LIVESTOCK ('000 head)

	1982	1983	1984
Horses*	430	450	460
Cattle	3,800	3,865	3,870*
Pigs	1,150	1,100	1,150*
Sheep	6,000	6,200	6,300*
Goats	600†	600	600*

* FAO estimates. † Unofficial figures.
Source: FAO, *Production Yearbook*.

LIVESTOCK PRODUCTS ('000 metric tons)

	1982	1983	1984
Beef and veal	195	208	200*
Mutton and lamb	15	13	12*
Pig meat	58	59	58*
Horse meat	6	11	11†
Poultry meat	95	86	75*
Cows' milk	1,056	900	950*
Butter	3.3	3.5	3*
Cheese	21.5	19.0	17.7
Hen eggs	71.6	65.8	66.3*
Wool:			
greasy	21.6	21.4	21.0*
clean	11.0	10.7	11.0*

* Unofficial figures. † FAO estimate.
Source: FAO, *Production Yearbook*.

Forestry

ROUNDWOOD REMOVALS
('000 cubic metres, excluding bark)

	1982	1983	1984
Sawlogs, veneer logs and logs for sleepers	3,298*	3,639	4,537
Pulpwood	3,100	3,752	3,889
Other industrial wood*	553	553	553
Fuel wood*	5,798	5,898	5,992
Total	12,749	13,842	14,971

* FAO estimates.
Source: FAO, *Yearbook of Forest Products*.

SAWNWOOD PRODUCTION ('000 cubic metres)

	1982	1983	1984
Total (incl. boxboards)	1,176	1,610	2,001

Source: FAO, *Yearbook of Forest Products*.

Fishing*

('000 metric tons, live weight)

	1982†	1983†	1984
Chilean hake	26.4	25.3	33.2
Patagonian hake	44.6	30.9	31.5
Chilean jack mackerel	1,494.7	865.3	1,426.3
Chilean sprat	46.0	18.6	38.2
Chilean pilchard (sardine)	1,779.8	2,823.4	2,571.8
Anchoveta (Peruvian anchovy)	106.0	8.0	70.7
Chub mackerel	21.0	9.3	111.9
Other marine fishes (incl. unspecified)	58.5	71.6	79.5
Total fish	3,577.0	3,852.3	4,363.1
Crustaceans	14.8	40.1	28.6
Clams	24.7	30.6	37.6
Other molluscs	41.4	40.9	50.9
Other aquatic animals‡	15.2	14.2	19.1
Total catch‡	3,673.0	3,978.1	4,499.3

* Including quantities landed by foreign fishing craft in Chilean ports.
† Source: FAO, *Yearbook of Fishery Statistics*.
‡ Excluding aquatic mammals, recorded by number rather than by weight. The number of whales caught by Chilean vessels in the Antarctic summer season was: nil in 1981/82; 1 in 1982/83.

Mining

		1983	1984	1985
Copper (metal content)	'000 metric tons	1,255.4	1,307.5	1,359.8
Coal	'000 metric tons	1,095	1,323	1,384
Iron ore*	'000 metric tons	5,974	7,116	6,510
Nitrates	'000 metric tons	623	—	—
Calcium carbonate	'000 metric tons	2,141.7	2,325.9	2,470.1
Iodine	metric tons	2,793	—	—
Sodium sulphate (hydrous)	metric tons	643	926	815
Molybdenum (metal content)	metric tons	15,264	16,861	18,389
Manganese†	metric tons	26,050	26,172	35,635
Gold	kilograms	17,759	16,829	17,240
Silver	kilograms	468,276	490,365	517,333
Petroleum	cubic metres	2,283,782	2,236,719	2,074,350
Natural gas	'000 cubic metres	4,802,775	4,897,744	4,638,176

* Gross weight. The estimated iron content is 61%.
† Gross weight. The metal content (in '000 metric tons) was: 8.5 in 1983.

Industry

SELECTED PRODUCTS

		1983	1984	1985
Sugar	'000 metric tons	193	308	285
Cement	'000 metric tons	1,255	1,390	1,429
Beer	million litres	176	178	189
Gasoline*	'000 metric tons	957	962	n.a.
Kerosene and jet fuels*	'000 metric tons	317	275	n.a.
Distillate fuel oils*	'000 metric tons	1,048	1,107	n.a.
Residual fuel oil*	'000 metric tons	1,065	1,005	n.a.
Tyres	'000	595	913	858
Cigarettes	million	7,680	—	—
Glass sheets	'000 sq metres	2,956	2,104	2,977

* Source: UN, *Monthly Bulletin of Statistics*.

Finance

CURRENCY AND EXCHANGE RATES

Monetary Units
100 centavos = 1 Chilean peso.

Denominations
Coins: 1, 5, 10 and 50 pesos.
Notes: 100, 500, 1,000 and 5,000 pesos.

Sterling and Dollar Equivalents (30 September 1986)
£1 sterling = 282.22 pesos;
US $1 = 195.04 pesos;
1,000 Chilean pesos = £3.543 = $5.127.

Average Exchange Rate (pesos per US $)
1983   78.84
1984   98.66
1985   161.08

CENTRAL BANK RESERVES
(US $ million at 31 December)

	1983	1984	1985
Gold*	566.7	540.1	540.1
IMF special drawing rights	5.4	11.5	0.3
Foreign exchange	2,030.9	2,291.4	2,449.6
Total	2,603.0	2,843.0	2,990.0

* Valued at market-related prices.
Source: IMF, *International Financial Statistics*.

BUDGET (million pesos)

Revenue	1983	1984	1985
Income from taxes	302,645	392,506	540,745
Non-tax revenue	639,234	269,595	426,666
Total current revenue	941,879	662,101	967,411

Expenditure	1983	1984	1985
Current expenditure	645,585	630,987	915,791
Operational expenditure	188,768	243,700	391,865
Remunerations	120,098	139,217	168,820
Purchase of goods and services	50,319	62,477	77,977
Interest on the public debt	18,351	42,006	145,068
Transfers	396,625	311,950	405,094
Capital expenditure	60,192	75,337	117,832
Real investment	36,288	49,868	79,112
Transfers	7,791	6,794	4,195
Amortizations	16,113	18,675	34,525
Total	705,777	706,324	1,033,623

MONEY SUPPLY (million pesos at 31 December)

	1982	1983	1984
Currency outside banks	42,960	51,880	64,180
Demand deposits at commercial banks	38,160	50,840	52,020
Total money	81,118	102,720	116,200

Source: IMF, *International Financial Statistics*.

COST OF LIVING (Consumer Price Index, annual averages. Base: December 1978 = 100)

	1981	1982	1983
Food	186.28	193.01	242.72
Housing	208.40	234.97	296.05
Clothing	178.16	183.22	225.66
Miscellaneous	195.40	230.72	301.81
All items	193.01	212.19	270.03

NATIONAL ACCOUNTS (million pesos at current prices)
National Income and Product

	1981	1982*	1983*
Compensation of employees	515,513	514,262	n.a.
Operating surplus	456,097	423,878	n.a.
Domestic factor incomes	971,610	938,140	n.a.
Consumption of fixed capital	120,054	132,812	174,692
Gross domestic product (GDP) at factor cost	1,091,664	1,070,952	n.a.
Indirect taxes, less subsidies	181,459	168,170	n.a.
GDP in purchasers' values	1,273,123	1,239,122	1,557,709
Net factor income from abroad	−57,077	−95,541	−134,180
Gross national product (GNP)	1,216,047	1,143,581	1,423,529
Less Consumption of fixed capital	120,054	132,812	174,692
National income in market prices	1,095,993	1,010,768	1,248,837

* Provisional.

Expenditure on the Gross Domestic Product

	1983*	1984*	1985*
Government final consumption expenditure	220,670	273,824	367,095
Private final consumption expenditure	1,141,863	1,381,675	1,785,245
Increase in stocks	−33,699	24,224	−13,213
Gross fixed capital formation	186,501	233,758	366,428
Total domestic expenditure	1,515,335	1,913,481	2,505,555
Exports of goods and services	374,465	459,488	71,083
Less Imports of goods and services	332,092	479,575	
GDP in purchasers' values	1,557,709	1,893,394	2,576,638
GDP at constant 1977 prices	327,180	347,926	356,447

* Provisional.

Gross Domestic Product by Economic Activity

	1981	1982*	1983*
Agriculture, forestry and fishing	80,710	69,371	88,800
Mining and quarrying	71,403	95,212	157,672
Manufacturing	284,241	233,969	320,807
Electricity, gas and water	28,948	40,137	52,163
Construction	81,836	69,670	73,571
Wholesale and retail trade	191,045	193,093	233,793
Transport, storage and communications	61,865	57,502	70,609
Other services	473,075	480,668	560,294
GDP in purchasers' values	1,273,123	1,239,122	1,557,709

* Provisional.

BALANCE OF PAYMENTS (US $ million)

	1983	1984	1985
Merchandise exports f.o.b.	3,831	3,650	3,743
Merchandise imports f.o.b.	−2,845	−3,357	−2,954
Trade balance	986	293	789
Exports of services	1,000	1,164	954
Imports of services	−3,200	−3,616	−3,111
Balance on goods and services	−1,214	−2,159	−1,368
Government unrequited transfers (net)	54	41	47
Private unrequited transfers (net)	43	58	14
Current balance	−1,117	−2,060	−1,307
Direct capital investment (net)	132	67	112
Other long-term capital (net)	−1,401	−657	−1,764
Short-term capital (net)	−1,967	589	365
Net errors and omissions	68	101	−16
Total (net monetary movements)	−4,285	−1,960	−2,610
Monetization of gold	24	62	2
Valuation changes (net)	6	41	−73
Exceptional financing (net)	3,744	1,979	2,512
Official financing (net)	12	74	−4
Changes in reserves	−499	196	−173

Source: IMF, *International Financial Statistics*.

External Trade

PRINCIPAL COMMODITIES (US $'000)

Imports c.i.f.	1983	1984	1985
Livestock and animal products	34,472	36,805	15,518
Vegetable products	292,491	231,969	120,860
Animal and vegetable fats	72,678	82,895	61,708
Manufactured foodstuffs, beverages and tobacco	105,747	91,413	31,135
Mineral products	607,421	619,079	553,975
Chemicals	325,144	241,405	356,064
Synthetic plastic rubber	152,795	179,304	151,366
Skins and leather goods	6,320	10,830	8,101
Paper and paper-making materials	69,847	73,767	63,235
Textiles	167,747	221,282	162,050
Plaster, cement, ceramics and glass	30,235	35,503	31,467
Metals and metal goods	132,656	204,631	165,248
Technical and electrical equipment	445,018	664,579	652,389
Transport equipment	137,644	165,376	187,005
Optical and precision instruments	71,460	80,608	70,550
Total (incl. others)	2,753,976	3,190,600	2,742,516

Exports f.o.b.	1983	1984	1985
Fruit and vegetables	249,732	332,781	n.a.
Meat and fish meal fodder	307,067	275,471	275,276
Chemical wood pulp	156,426	195,942	129,672
Natural sodium nitrate	28,095	28,236	32,890
Iron ore and concentrates	112,007	109,730	90,829
Copper ores, refined and unrefined copper metal	1,864,316	1,620,051	1,760,907
Chemicals	48,417	47,635	63,972
Total (incl. others)	3,835,528	3,657,248	n.a.

CHILE   *Statistical Survey*

PRINCIPAL TRADING PARTNERS (US $ million)

Imports	1983*	1984	1985
Argentina	200.6	160.9	105.9
Brazil	190.2	296.4	248.9
Canada	60.9	66.5	59.2
Ecuador	40.4	46.0	48.1
France	82.9	97.6	78.6
Germany, Federal Republic	185.2	215.7	209.0
Italy	51.3	66.1	50.3
Japan	161.2	312.7	188.5
Korea, Republic	23.3	40.7	24.2
Peru	37.2	49.2	41.1
Spain	64.3	81.1	105.5
United Kingdom	60.7	79.6	84.3
USA	703.5	747.8	654.6
Venezuela	224.8	251.8	267.7

Exports	1983*	1984	1985
Argentina	119.4	116.7	84.5
Belgium	85.3	67.1	91.0
Brazil	164.3	227.5	209.7
Canada	60.4	31.1	75.8
China, People's Republic	93.7	125.3	124.9
Colombia	42.3	43.0	44.8
France	176.7	163.4	144.6
Germany, Federal Republic	484.7	364.8	370.6
Italy	169.8	160.9	197.2
Japan	348.1	407.7	392.5
Korea, Republic	56.6	64.9	89.3
Netherlands	106.2	92.2	142.4
Peru	39.4	44.9	45.7
Spain	72.2	75.8	74.4
United Kingdom	209.2	196.1	256.2
USA	1,083.3	951.2	870.7
Venezuela	29.7	40.2	33.7

* Source: Banco Central de Chile.

Transport

PRINCIPAL RAILWAYS* ('000)

	1983	1984	1985†
Passengers (number)	9,242	8,672	8,914
Passenger/km	1,574,684	1,424,076	1,561,588
Freight (tons)	14,182	15,148	20,907

* Includes all international cargo of Ferrocarril Transandino.
† Provisional.

ROAD TRAFFIC (motor vehicles in use)

	1983	1984	1985*
Cars	618,731	630,418	624,738
Buses	20,037	20,520	21,487
Lorries	228,776	214,831	235,811
Motor cycles	31,830	31,732	33,868

* Provisional.

INTERNATIONAL SEA-BORNE SHIPPING
(freight traffic in '000 metric tons)

	1983	1984	1985*
Goods loaded	10,698	11,826	12,632
Goods unloaded	5,258	5,265	4,480

* Provisional.

CIVIL AVIATION

	1983	1984	1985*
Kilometres flown ('000)†	22,970	23,761	24,436
Passengers (number)	679,921	777,343	826,891
Freight ('000 ton-km)	267,782	270,256	274,270

* Provisional.
† Includes airline taxis.

Tourism

	1983	1984	1985*
Arrivals	335,287	417,358	458,704

* Provisional.

Communications Media

	1980	1981	1982
Radio receivers ('000 in use)	3,250	3,350	3,450
Television receivers ('000 in use)	1,225	1,250	1,300
Telephones ('000 in use)	551	595	n.a.
Book production: titles*	1,109	918	n.a.
Daily newspapers	n.a.	n.a.	37

* Figures include pamphlets (278 titles in 1981).
Source: mainly UNESCO, *Statistical Yearbook*.

Education

(Number of pupils)

	1983	1984*	1985*
Kindergarten	146,369	221,812	202,252
Basic	2,139,155	2,073,277	2,062,344
Middle	685,428	637,092	667,797
Higher (incl. universities)	126,175	184,462	196,460

* Source: Departamento de Comunicación Social, Ministerio de Educación.

Directory

The Constitution

Note: Since 1973 Government has been based on the three Constitutional Acts (see below). In accordance with the new Constitution approved by a plebiscite in 1980, the previous 1925 Constitution was abolished and the new Fundamental Law came into effect in March 1981. Provisions concerning the National Congress will be fully effective from 1989.

The three constitutional acts of 1976 provide for a 'new democratic structure' for Chilean society based on the family and rejecting class struggle. The following rights are guaranteed: the right to life and personal integrity, to a defence, to personal liberty and individual security; the right to reside in, cross or leave the country; the right of assembly, petition, association and free expression and the right to work. Men and women are accorded equal rights; no-one shall be obliged to join any association; any group considered to be contrary to morality, public order or state security shall be prohibited; the courts shall be able to prohibit any publication or broadcast considered to be contrary to public morality, order, national security or individual privacy.

The 1981 Constitution, described as a 'transition to democracy', separates the presidency from the junta and provides for presidential elections every eight years, with no re-election. The President may dissolve the legislature once during his term of office and may declare a state of emergency for up to 20 days. The bicameral legislature will consist of an upper chamber of 26 elected and nine appointed senators, who are to serve an eight-year term, and a lower chamber of 120 deputies elected for a four-year term. All former presidents are to be senators for life. There is a National Security Council consisting of the President, the Junta (comprising the heads of the armed forces and the police) and the presidents of the Supreme Court and the Senate.

All Marxist and 'totalitarian' groups are banned, limited political activity will be permitted only at the end of the 'transitional period', and there is no amnesty for terrorists. There is limited freedom of assembly and of expression: workers in public or vital sectors may not strike and other employees may strike for no more than 60 days; it is illegal to disseminate doctrines of a 'totalitarian' concept or ones which undermine public morals. The economy is based on the free market system. Abortion is prohibited.

Appended are 29 Transitory Clauses which had immediate effect in March 1981. The holding of elections is postponed until 1989, when the Junta will nominate the president and the 'no re-election' clause will be suspended. The nomination will be submitted to a referendum.

The Government

HEAD OF STATE

President: Gen. AUGUSTO PINOCHET UGARTE (assumed power as President of the Military Junta 11 September 1973; sworn in as Supreme Chief of State 27 June 1974; proclaimed President of the Republic 17 December 1974; inaugurated as President 11 March 1981).

JUNTA MILITAR DE GOBIERNO

Adm. JOSÉ TORIBIO MERINO (Navy).
Gen. RODOLFO STANGE OELCKERS (Police).
Gen. FERNANDO MATTHEI AUBEL (Air Force).
Lt-Gen. HUMBERTO GORDÓN RUBIO (Army).

THE CABINET
(November 1986)

Minister of the Interior: RICARDO GARCÍA RODRÍGUEZ.
Minister of Foreign Affairs: JAIME DEL VALLE ALLIENDE.
Minister of Labour and Social Security: ALFONSO MÁRQUEZ DE LA PLATA IRRARÁZABAL.
Minister of Finance: HERNÁN BÜCHI BUC.
Minister of Economy, Development and Reconstruction: JUAN CARLOS DÉLANO ORTÚZAR.
Minister of Public Education: SERGIO GAETE ROJAS.
Minister of Justice: HUGO ROSENDE.
Minister of National Defence: Vice-Adm. PATRICIO CARVAJAL PRADO.
Minister of Public Works: Brig.-Gen. BRUNO SIEBERT HELD.
Minister of Transport and Telecommunications: Brig. ENRIQUE ESCOBAR RODRÍGUEZ.
Minister of Agriculture: JORGE PRADO ARÁNGUIZ.
Minister of National Property: Gen. RENÉ PERI FAGERSTROM.
Minister of Planning: Brig.-Gen. FRANCISCO RAMÍREZ MIGLIASSI.
Minister of Mines: SAMUEL LIRA OVALLE.
Minister of Energy: Gen. HERMÁN BRADY ROCHE.
Minister of Public Health: Dr JUAN GIACONI GANDOLFI.
Minister of Housing and Urban Development: MIGUEL ANGEL PODUJE SAPIAIN.
Minister of Production Development (Vice-President of CORFO): Brig.-Gen. FERNANDO HORMAZÁBAL GAJARDO.
Minister Secretary-General of Government: FRANCISCO JAVIER CUADRA LINAZA.
Head of President's Consultative Committee: Brig.-Gen. SANTIAGO SINCLAIR OYANEDER.

MINISTRIES

Ministry of Agriculture: Teatinos 40, Santiago; tel. 717436; telex 240745.
Ministry of Economy, Development and Reconstruction: Teatinos 120, Santiago; tel. 725522; telex 240558.
Ministry of Energy: Teatinos 120, 7°, Santiago; tel. 6981757.
Ministry of Finance: Teatinos 120, Santiago; tel. 6982051; telex 241334.
Ministry of Foreign Affairs: Palacio de la Moneda, Santiago; tel. 6982501; telex 40595.
Ministry of Housing and Town Planning: Serrano 45, 6°, Santiago; tel. 31624; telex 40079.
Ministry of the Interior: Palacio de la Moneda, Santiago; tel. 222068; telex 241379.
Ministry of Justice: Compañia 1111, Santiago; tel. 6968151; telex 241316.
Ministry of Labour and Social Security: Huérfanos 1273, 6°, Santiago; tel. 7151333; telex 40559.
Ministry of Mines: Teatinos 120, 9°, Santiago; tel. 711593; telex 240948.
Ministry of National Defence: Plaza Bulnes s/n, 4°, Santiago; tel. 6965271; telex 40537.
Ministry of National Planning: Ahumada 48, Santiago; tel. 722033; telex 40767.
Ministry of National Property: Avda Libertador B. O'Higgins 280, Santiago; tel. 2224669.
Ministry of Production Development (CORFO): Moneda 921, Casilla 3886, Santiago; tel. 380521; telex 240421.
Ministry of Public Education: Avda Libertador B. O'Higgins 1371, Santiago; tel. 6983351; telex 240716.
Ministry of Public Health: Enrique McIver 541, 1°, Santiago; tel. 394001; telex 240136.
Ministry of Public Works: Dirección de Vialidad, Morandé 59, 2°, Santiago; tel. 724506; telex 240777.
Ministry of Transport and Telecommunications: Amunátegui 139, Santiago; tel. 726503; telex 240200.
Office of the Comptroller of the Republic: Teatinos 56, 9°, Santiago; tel. 724212; telex 40281.
Office of the Minister Secretary-General of Government: Palacio de la Moneda, Santiago; tel. 711680; telex 40073.

Legislature

CONGRESO NACIONAL

The bicameral National Congress (a Senate and a Chamber of Deputies) was dissolved by the armed forces on 13 September 1973. Until 1989 legislative functions will be exercised by the Junta, assisted by four legislative commissions.

Political Organizations

All 'Marxist' political parties were declared unlawful on 14 September 1973, and the activities of all political parties were suspended on 27 September 1973. All political parties and political activity were banned on 12 March 1977.

The most prominent political parties (some working from abroad) are:

Bloque Socialista: José Miguel de la Barra 430, Of. 72, Santiago; tel. 395747; f. 1983; socialist alliance; members include Partido Socialista de Chile and Movimiento de Acción Popular Unitaria (see below); Coordinator RICARDO NÚÑEZ MUÑOZ.

Intransigencia Democrática: Moneda 1778, Santiago; tel. 724164; f. 1985; centre-left alliance; Pres. MANUEL SANHUEZA CRUZ.

Izquierda Cristiana: Christian left; Leader LUIS MAIRA.

Movimiento de Acción Nacional (MAN): Catedral 1009, Of. 6, Santiago; tel. 724635; right-wing nationalist party; Pres. GASTÓN ACUÑA MACLEAN.

Movimiento de Acción Popular Unitaria—MAPU: Marxist; Leader OSCAR GARRETÓN (in exile); Sec.-Gen. VÍCTOR BARRUETO.

Movimiento de Izquierda Revolucionaria—MIR: revolutionary left; Leader ANDRÉS PASCAL ALLENDE (in exile).

Movimiento Social Cristiano: Santiago; tel. 6961961; f. 1984; right-wing party; Pres. JUAN DE DIOS CARMONA; Sec.-Gen. MANUEL RODRÍGUEZ.

Partido Comunista de Chile: Santiago; tel. 724164; Leader JAIME INSUNZA; Sec.-Gen. LUIS CORVALÁN LEPE (in exile).

Partido Demócrata Cristiano (PDC): Huérfanos 1022, Of. 1208, Santiago; tel. 723038; f. 1957; Pres. GABRIEL VALDÉS SUBERCASEAUX; Sec.-Gen. EUGENIO ORTEGA.

Partido Humanista: Las Urbinas 145, Depto 20, Santiago; tel. 2319089; humanist party; Pres. JOSÉ TOMÁS SÁENZ.

Partido Liberal: Tenderini 85, Of. 101, Santiago; tel. 480738; liberal party; Pres. GASTÓN URETA G.

Partido Nacional: Compañía 1357, 1°, Santiago; tel. 6992793; traditional centre-right party; Leader CARMEN SÁENZ DE PHILLIPS; Vice-Pres. FERNANDO OCHAGAVIA.

Partido Radical: Avda Santa María 281, Santiago; tel. 779903; f. 1863; social democratic; mem. of Socialist International; Pres. ENRIQUE SILVA CIMMA; Sec.-Gen. RICARDO NAVARRETE.

Partido Republicano: Sótero del Río 492, 3°, Santiago; tel. 6984167; f. 1983; centre-right party; Pres. ARMANDO JARAMILLO LYÓN; Sec.-Gen. RENÉ LEÓN ECHAIZ.

Partido Social Demócrata: París 815, Santiago; tel. 384680; Pres. RENÉ ABELIUK MANASEVICH; Sec.-Gen. LEVÍAN MUÑOZ.

Partido del Socialismo Democrático: San Antonio 220, Of. 604, Santiago; tel. 394244; democratic socialist party; Pres. LUIS ANGEL SANTIBÁÑEZ; Sec.-Gen. JAIME CARMONA DONOSO.

Partido Socialista: Santiago; left-wing; split into factions:

Partido Socialista Moderado: Santiago; moderate faction; Leader CARLOS BRIONES.

Marxist-Leninist faction: Santiago; tel. 6986109; Sec.-Gen. Dr CLODOMIRO ALMEYDA MEDINA (in exile); Leader GERMÁN CORREA.

Non-Leninist faction: San Antonio 220, Of. 609, Santiago; tel. 330445; Sec.-Gen. RICARDO NÚÑEZ MUÑOZ.

Unión Demócrata Independiente (UDI): Suecia 286, Santiago; tel. 2322686; right-wing; Leader JAIME GUZMÁN ERRÁZURIZ.

Unión Nacional: Ricardo Matte Pérez 0140, Santiago; tel. 7449915; centre-right party; Leader ANDRÉS ALLAMAND ZAVALA.

In mid-1984 a group of right-wing and centre-right parties formed a coalition, Acuerdo Democrático Nacional (ADENA), which was independent from both the Government and other opposition groupings. These groupings included: Alianza Democrática (AD, an alliance of centre and right-wing parties, incl. the Partido Demócrata Cristiano), Movimiento Democrático Popular (MDP, a coalition of left-wing parties, led by GERMÁN CORREA, declared unconstitutional in early 1985) and Proyecto para el Desarrollo Nacional (Proden, led by JORGE LAVANDEROS). The dissolution of ADENA was announced on 21 June 1985. In August 1985 a group of left- and right-wing parties signed the Acuerdo Nacional para la Transición a la Plena Democracia (National Accord for the Transition to Full Democracy). In April 1986 Chile's principal trade union, professional and community organizations formed the Asamblea de la Civilidad (Civil Assembly), with the aim of campaigning for a return to democracy. The Assembly was led by Dr JUAN LUIS GONZÁLEZ REYES. In November 1986 the Acuerdo Nacional Democrático (ANDE) was formed by 13 political organizations as a multi-party alliance whose aim was to campaign for free and open elections in 1989.

Guerrilla groups:

Acción Chilena Anticomunista (ACHA): right-wing; Pres. JUAN SERRANO.

Frente Patriótico Manuel Rodríguez (FPMR): f. 1983; supports the Partido Comunista de Chile; Leader Commdr DANIEL HUERTA.

Frente Revolucionario Nacionalista—FREN: left-wing.

Diplomatic Representation

EMBASSIES IN CHILE

Argentina: Miraflores 285, Santiago; tel. 331076; telex 240280; Ambassador: JOSÉ MARÍA ALVAREZ DE TOLEDO.

Australia: Gertrudis Echeñique 420, Casilla 33, Correo 10, Las Condes, Santiago; telex 40855; Ambassador: WILLIAM K. FLANAGAN.

Austria: Barrios Errázuriz 1968, 3°, Casilla 16196, Santiago; tel. 2234774; telex 240528; Ambassador: HARALD KREID.

Belgium: Avda Providencia 2653, 11°, Of. 1104, Santiago; tel. 2321070; telex 440088; Chargé d'affaires: MICHEL GODFRIND.

Brazil: Alonso Ovalle 1665, Santiago; tel. 6982486; telex 340350; Ambassador: JORGE CARLOS RIBEIRO.

Canada: Ahumada 11, 10°, Casilla 427, Santiago; tel. 6962256; Ambassador: MICHAEL DE GAUMOIS.

China, People's Republic: Pedro de Valdivia 550, Santiago; tel. 250755; telex 240863; Ambassador: HUANG SHIKANG.

Colombia: Darío Urzúa 2080, Santiago; tel. 747570; telex 340401; Ambassador: JORGE E. RODRÍGUEZ.

Costa Rica: Barcelona 2070, Santiago; tel. 2318915; Ambassador: FABIO CRUZ BRICEÑO.

Denmark: Avda Santa María 0182, Casilla 13430, Santiago; tel. 376056; telex 440032; Chargé d'affaires a.i.: JØRGEN ILFELDT.

Dominican Republic: Mariscal Petain 125, Santiago; tel. 2288083; Ambassador: RAFAEL VALDEZ HICARIO.

Ecuador: Avda Providencia 1979, 5°, Santiago; tel. 235742; telex 240717; Ambassador: CÉSAR VALDIVIESO CHIRIBOGA.

Egypt: Roberto del Río 1871, Santiago; tel. 748881; telex 440156; Ambassador: ABDEL-AZIZ FAHMY OMAR.

El Salvador: Calle Noruega 6595, Las Condes, Santiago; tel. 251096; Ambassador: Dr JOSÉ HORACIO TRUJILLO.

France: Avda Condell 65, Casilla 38-D, Santiago; tel. 2251030; telex 240535; Ambassador: FRANÇOIS MOUTON.

Germany, Federal Republic: Agustinas 785, 7° y 8°, Santiago; tel. 335031; telex 240583; Ambassador: HORST KULLAK-UBLICK.

Guatemala: Avda Américo Vespucio Norte 958, Casilla 36, Santiago; Ambassador: JULIO GÁNDARA VALENZUELA.

Haiti: Avda 11 de Septiembre 2155, Of. 801, Torre B, Santiago; tel. 2318233; Ambassador: MAX JADOTTE.

Holy See: Calle Nuncio Sotero Sanz 200, Casilla 507, Santiago (Apostolic Nunciature); tel. 2312020; telex 241035; Nuncio: Excmo Rev. Mgr ANGELO SODANO.

Honduras: Avda 11 de Septiembre 2155, Of. 1005, Santiago; tel. 2314161; telex 44056; Ambassador: FRANCISCO LÓPEZ REYES.

India: Triana 871, Casilla 10433, Santiago; tel. 2231548; telex 340046; Ambassador: SARV KUMAR KATHPALIA.

Israel: San Sebastián 2812, 5°, Casilla 1224, Santiago; tel. 2461570; telex 240627; Ambassador: DAVID EPHRATI.

Italy: Triana 843, Casilla 3114, Santiago; tel. 2259439; telex 44031; Chargé d'affaires a.i.: FRANCESCO CARUSO.

Japan: Avda Providencia 2653, 19°, Casilla 2877, Santiago; tel. 2321807; telex 440132; Ambassador: SHUICHI NOMIYAMA.

Jordan: Avda Providencia 545, Apto 55, Casilla 10431, Santiago; tel. 2231177; Ambassador: SAMIH EL-FARAJ.

Korea, Republic: Alcántara 74, Casilla 1301, Santiago; tel. 2284214; telex 340380; Ambassador: SUH KYUNG-SUK.

Lebanon: Isidoro Goyenechea 3607, Casilla 3667, Santiago; tel. 2325027; telex 440118; Ambassador: IBRAHIM KRAIDY.

Malta: Merced 286, 8°, Santiago; Ambassador: CORRADO ZAMPETTI.

Netherlands: Las Violetas 2368, Casilla 56-D, Santiago; tel. 2236825; telex 340381; Ambassador: PATRICK S. J. RUTGERS.

New Zealand: Avda Isidora Goyenechea 3516, Las Condes, Casilla 112, Santiago; tel. 2314204; telex 3440066; Ambassador: BARRY H. BROOKS.

Norway: Américo Vespucio Norte 548, Casilla 2431, Santiago; tel. 2281024; telex 440150; Ambassador: HELGE VINDENES.

Panama: Bustos 2199, Correo 9892, Santiago; tel. 2250147; Ambassador: RICARDO MORENO VILLALAZ.

Paraguay: Huérfanos 886, 5°, Ofs 514-515, Santiago; tel. 394640; telex 645357; Ambassador: Dr FABIO RIVAS ARAUJO.

Peru: Avda Andrés Bello 1751, Providencia, Santiago 9, Casilla 16277, Santiago; tel. 2238883; telex 440095; Ambassador: LUIS MARCHAND STENS.

Philippines: San Crecente 551, Santiago; tel. 2286135; Ambassador: RODOLFO A. ARIZALA.

Romania: Benjamín 2955, Casilla 290, Santiago; tel. 2311893; telex 440378; Chargé d'affaires a.i.: GHEORGHE PETRE.

South Africa: Carlos Antunez 1959, Casilla 16189, Santiago; tel. 2250415; telex 340484; Ambassador: Lt-Gen. ANTONIE MICHAL MULLER.

Spain: Avda Andrés Bello 1895, Casilla 16456, Santiago; tel. 742021; telex 340253; Ambassador: MIGUEL SOLANO AZA.

Sweden: Darío Urzúa 2165, Santiago; tel. 495052; telex 440153; Chargé d'affaires a.i.: HÅKAN WILKENS.

Switzerland: Avda Providencia 2653, Of. 1602, Casilla 3875, Santiago; telex 340870; Ambassador: SVEN MEILI.

Syria: Carmencita 111, Casilla 12, Correo 10, Santiago; tel. 2327471; telex 240095; Ambassador: HISHAM HALLAJ.

Turkey: N. Sótero Sanz 136, Casilla 16182, Santiago; tel. 2318952; telex 340278; Ambassador: EKREM GÖKŞIN.

United Kingdom: La Concepción 177, Casilla 72 D, Santiago; tel. 2239166; telex 340483; Ambassador: JOHN K. HICKMAN.

USA: Agustinas 1343, 5°, Santiago; tel. 710133; telex 240062; Ambassador: HARRY G. BARNES.

Uruguay: Avda Pedro de Valdivia 711, Casilla 2636, Santiago; tel. 743569; telex 340371; Ambassador: ALFREDO BIANCHI PALAZZO.

Venezuela: Mar del Plata 2055, Casilla 16577, Santiago; tel. 2250021; telex 440170; Ambassador: HÉCTOR VARGAS ACOSTA.

Judicial System

The following are the main tribunals:

The Supreme Court, consisting of 13 members, appointed for life by the President of the Republic from a list of five names submitted by the Supreme Court when vacancies arise.

There are 16 Courts of Appeal (in the cities or departments of Arica, Iquique, Antofagasta, Copiapó, La Serena, Valparaíso, Santiago, Presidente Aguirre Cerda, Rancagua, Talca, Chillán, Concepción, Temuco, Valdivia, Puerto Montt and Punta Arenas) whose members are appointed for life from a list submitted to the President by the Supreme Court. The number of members of each court varies. Judges of the lower courts are appointed in a similar manner from lists submitted by the Court of Appeal of the district in which the vacancy arises.

Corte Suprema: Plaza Montt Varas, Santiago; tel. 6980561.

President of the Supreme Court: RAFAEL RETAMAL LÓPEZ.

Ministers of the Supreme Court:

JOSÉ M. EYZAGUIRRE ECHEVERRÍA
ISRAEL BÓRQUEZ MONTERO
LUIS MALDONADO BOGGIANO
OCTAVIO RAMÍREZ MIRANDA
VÍCTOR MANUEL RIVAS DEL CANTO
ENRIQUE CORREA LABRA
OSVALDO ERBETTA VACCARO
EMILIO ULLOA MUÑOZ
MARCOS ABURTO OCHOA
ESTANISLAO ZÚÑIGA COLLAO
ABRAHAM MEERSOHN SCHIJMAN
CARLOS LETELIER BOBADILLA
SERVANDO JORDÁN LÓPEZ
HERNÁN CERECEDA BRAVO

Attorney-General: GUSTAVO CHAMORRO GARRIDO.

Secretary: RENÉ PICA URRUTIA.

Religion

CHRISTIANITY
The Roman Catholic Church

Chile comprises five archdioceses, 14 dioceses, three territorial prelatures and two Apostolic Prefectures.

Bishops' Conference: Conferencia Episcopal de Chile, Cienfuegos 47, Casilla 13191, Correo 21, Santiago; tel. 81416; f. 1982; Pres. BERNARDINO PIÑERA CARVALLO, Archbishop of La Serena.

Archbishop of Antofagasta: CARLOS OVIEDO CAVADA, Casilla E, San Martín 2628, Antofagasta; tel. 221164.

Archbishop of Concepción: JOSÉ MANUEL SANTOS ASCARZA, Calle Barros Araña 544, Casilla 65-C, Concepción; tel. 25258.

Archbishop of La Serena: BERNARDINO PIÑERA CARVALLO, Casilla 613, La Serena; tel. 211324.

Archbishop of Puerto Montt: ELADIO VICUÑA ARÁNGUIZ, Calle Benavente 285, Casilla 17, Puerto Montt; tel. 2215.

Archbishop of Santiago de Chile: Cardinal JUAN FRANCISCO FRESNO LARRAÍN, Erasmo Escala 1822, Casilla 30-D, Santiago; tel. 6963275.

The Anglican Communion

Anglicans in Chile are adherents of the Anglican Church of the Southern Cone of America, covering Argentina, Bolivia, Chile, Paraguay and Peru.

Bishop of Chile: Right Rev. COLIN FREDERICK BAZLEY, Iglesia Anglicana, Casilla 675, Santiago; tel. 2292158.

The Baptist Church

Baptist Evangelical Convention of Chile: Casilla 1055-22, Santiago; tel. 2224085; Gen. Sec. FAUSTINO AGUILERA CH.; Pres. ESTEBAN JOFRE C.

The Press

Most newspapers of nationwide circulation in Chile are published in Santiago. Since the assumption of power by the military government there has been some form of censorship in force. A decree introduced in 1981 makes it illegal for the press to 'emphasize or highlight news related to terrorist or extremist acts which have occurred within the country'. In 1984 more stringent regulations concerning censorship were imposed. In September 1986, following the imposition of a state of siege, several opposition publications were banned by the Government. According to official sources, there are 128 newspapers which appear more than twice a week, with a combined circulation of more than 900,000 copies per issue.

DAILIES
Santiago

Circulation figures listed below are supplied by the Asociación Nacional de la Prensa. Other sources give much lower figures.

Diario Oficial de la República de Chile: Agustinas 1269, Santiago; tel. 6983969; Dir ENRIQUE MENCHACA SALGADO; circ. 15,000.

Fortín Mapocho: Agustinas 1185, Of. 57, Santiago; tel. 6984973; f. 1984; independent; Dir FELIPE POZO RUIZ; (banned September 1986).

El Mercurio: Avda Santa María 5542, Casilla 13-D, Santiago; tel. 2288147; f. 1827; morning; conservative; independent; Man. Dir AGUSTÍN EDWARDS; circ. 120,000 (weekdays), 250,000 (Sundays).

La Nación: Agustinas 1269, Santiago; tel. 6982222; f. 1980 to replace government-subsidized *El Cronista*; morning; financial; Propr Sociedad Periodística La Nación; Dir ORLANDO POBLETE ITURRATE; circ. 20,000.

La Segunda: Avda Santa María 5542, Santiago; tel. 2287048; f. 1931; evening; Dir CRISTIÁN ZEGERS ARIZTÍA.; circ. 30,000.

La Tercera de la Hora: Vicuña Mackenna 1870, Santiago; tel. 517067; f. 1950; morning; independent; Dir ARTURO ROMÁN HERRERA; circ. 300,000.

Las Ultimas Noticias: Avda Santa María 5542, Santiago; tel. 2287048; f. 1902; morning; independent; Man. Dir HÉCTOR OLAVE VALLEJOS; owned by the Proprs of *El Mercurio*; circ. 150,000 (except Saturdays and Sundays).

Antofagasta

La Estrella del Norte: Calle Matta 2112, Antofagasta; tel. 222847; f. 1966; evening; Dir Roberto Retamal Pacheco; circ. 10,000.

El Mercurio: Calle Matta 2112, Antofagasta; tel. 223406; f. 1906; morning; conservative independent; Proprs Soc. Chilena de Publicaciones; Dir Darío Canut de Bon Urrutia; circ. 20,000.

Arica

Estrella de Arica: San Marcos 580, Arica; tel. 31834; telex 221051; f. 1976; Dir Enrique Jorquera Márquez; circ. 11,600.

Calama

La Estrella del Loa: Félix Hoyos 2065, Calama; tel. 212535; f. 1969; Propr Soc. Chilena de Publicaciones; Dir Roberto Retamal Pacheco; circ. 4,000 (weekdays), 7,000 (Sundays).

El Mercurio: Félix Hoyos 2071, Calama; tel. 212535; f. 1968; Propr Soc. Chilena de Publicaciones; Dir Darío Canut de Bon; circ. 4,500 (weekdays), 7,000 (Sundays).

Chillán

La Discusión de Chillán: Casilla 14-D, Calle 18 de Septiembre 721, Chillán; tel. 22651; f. 1870; morning; independent; Propr Universidad de Concepción; Dir Carlos Godoy; circ. 8,500.

Concepción

El Sur: Casilla 8-C, Calle Freire 799, Concepción; tel. 25825; f. 1882; morning; independent; Editor Hernán Alvez; circ. 35,000.

Copiapó

Atacama: Manuel Rodríguez 740, Copiapó; tel. 2255; morning; independent; Dir Samuel Salgado; circ. 6,500.

Curicó

La Prensa: Casilla 6-D, Merced 373, Curicó; tel. 132-453; f. 1898; morning; right-wing; Man. Dir Oscar Ramírez Merino; circ. 4,000.

Iquique

La Estrella de Iquique: Luis Uribe 452, Iquique; tel. 22401; telex 223134; f. 1966; evening; Dir Arcadio Castillo Ortiz; circ. 8,500.

La Serena

El Día: Casilla 13-D, Brasil 395, La Serena; tel. 211853; f. 1944; morning; Dir Antonio Puga Rodríguez; circ. 10,800.

Los Angeles

La Tribuna: Casilla 15-D, Calle Colo Colo 464, Los Angeles; tel. 23196; independent; Dir Lothar Hemmelmann Troncoso; circ. 10,000.

Osorno

Diario Austral: Plazuela Yungay 581, Osorno; tel. 5191; Dir Germán Carmona.

Diario 24 Horas: Osorno; tel. 2300; Dir Roberto Silva Bajit.

Puerto Montt

El Llanquihue: Antonio Varas 167, Puerto Montt; f. 1885; morning; independent; Dir Miguel Esteban Veyl Betanzo; circ. 6,000.

Punta Arenas

La Prensa Austral: Waldo Seguel 636, Casilla 9-D, Punta Arenas; tel. 21976; telex 380029; f. 1941; morning; independent; Dir Pablo Cruz Noceti; circ. 10,000, Sunday (*El Magallanes*; f. 1894) 12,000.

Rancagua

El Rancagüino: Campos 527, Rancagua; tel. 21483; f. 1915; independent; Dir Miguel González; circ. 10,000.

Talca

La Mañana de Talca: 1 Norte 911, Talca; tel. 33005; Dir Juan C. Bravo; circ. 5,000.

Temuco

El Diario Austral: Bulnes 699, Casilla 1-D, Temuco; tel. 232233; f. 1916; morning; commercial, industrial and agricultural interests; Dir Marco Antonio Pinto Zepeda; Propr Soc. Periodística Araucanía, SA; circ. 26,000.

Tocopilla

La Prensa: Matta 2112, Antofagasta, Casilla 2099, Tocopilla; f. 1924; morning; independent; Dir Roberto Retamal; circ. 8,000.

Valdivia

El Correo de Valdivia: Valdivia; f. 1895; morning; non-party; Dir Patricio Gómez Couchot; circ. 12,000.

El Diario Austral: Independencia 499, Valdivia; tel. 3353; telex 371011; Editor Gustavo Serrano Cotapos; circ. 4,000.

Valparaíso

La Estrella: Esmeralda 1002, Casilla 57-V, Valparaíso; tel. 258011; telex 230531; f. 1921; evening; independent; Dir Julio Hurtado Ebel; owned by the Proprs of *El Mercurio*; circ. 25,000, 30,000 (Saturdays).

El Mercurio: Esmeralda 1002, Casilla 57-V, Valparaíso; tel. 52797; f. 1827; morning; Dir Leopoldo Tassara Cavada; owned by the Proprs of *El Mercurio* in Santiago; circ. 50,000.

Victoria

Las Noticias: Casilla 92, Avda Suiza 895, Victoria; f. 1910; morning; independent; Dir Tránsito Bustamente Molina; circ. 8,000.

El Pehuén de Curacautín: Casilla 92, Avda Central 895, Victoria; morning; independent; Dir Gino Bustamente Barría; circ. 3,000.

PERIODICALS
Santiago

Análisis: Manuel Montt 425, Santiago; tel. 2234386; weekly; political, economic and social affairs; published by Emisión Ltda; Dir Juan Pablo Cárdenas; circ. 30,000; (banned September 1986).

Apsi: Alberto Reyes 032, Providencia, Casilla 9896, Santiago; tel. 775643; f. 1976; fortnightly; Dir Marcelo Contreras; circ. 30,000.

La Bicicleta: José Fagnano 614, Santiago; tel. 2223969; satirical; Dir Antonio de la Fuente; (banned September 1986).

CA Revista Oficial del Colegio de Arquitectos de Chile AG: Triana 857, Santiago; tel. 2513511; f. 1964; 4 a year; architects' magazine; Editor Arq. Jaime Márquez Rojas; circ. 5,000.

El Campesino: Tenderini 187, Casilla 40-D, Santiago; tel. 396710; telex 240760; f. 1838; monthly; farming; Dir Patricio Montt; circ. 5,000.

Carola: San Francisco 116, Casilla 1858, Santiago; tel. 336433; telex 240656; fortnightly; women's magazine; published by Editorial Antártica, SA; Dir Isabel Margarita Aguirre.

Cauce: Monjitas 454, Of. 607, Santiago; tel. 392159; weekly; political, economic and social affairs; Dir Gonzalo Figueroa Yáñez; circ. 20,000; (banned September 1986).

Chileagrícola: Casilla 2, Correo 13, Teresa Vial 1170; tel. 516039; f. 1976; monthly; farming; Dir Ing. Agr. Raúl González Valenzuela; circ. 10,000.

Chile Filatélico: Casilla 13245, Santiago; f. 1929; quarterly; Editor Ricardo Boizard G.

Chile Forestal: Bulnes 197, 2°, Santiago; tel. 6966724; f. 1974; monthly; technical information and features on forestry sector; Dir Ing. María Teresa Arames; circ. 5,600.

Cosas: Almirante Pastene 329, Providencia, Santiago; tel. 2258630; telex 340905; f. 1976; fortnightly; international affairs; Editor Mónica Comandari Kaiser; circ. 25,000.

Creces: Manuel Montt 1922, Santiago; tel. 2234337; monthly; science and technology; Dir Sergio Prenafeta; circ. 12,000.

Economía y Sociedad: Teatinos 220, Of. 91, Santiago; tel. 712445; telex 340656; Dir José Piñera; circ. 10,000.

Economic and Financial Survey: Santiago; tel. 2227553; weekly; Dir Rubén Corvalan.

Ercilla: Las Hortensias 2340, Casilla 63-D, Santiago; tel. 2255055; f. 1936; weekly; general interest; Dir Manfredo Mayol Durán; circ. 146,000.

Estanquero 11: Obispo Donoso 6, Of. A, Providencia, Santiago; tel. 2233065; f. 1985; monthly; politics; published by Sociedad Periodística Estanquero Once Ltda; Dir Gastón Acuña MacLean; circ. 6,000.

Estrategia: Rafael Cañas 114, Casilla 16845, Correo 9, Santiago; tel. 749518; telex 440001; f. 1978; weekly; financial affairs; Dir Víctor Ojeda Méndez; circ. 15,000.

Gestión: Rafael Cañas 114, Santiago; tel. 745494; monthly; management; Dir Germán Mujica Riveros; circ. 2,500.

Guía Turística: Ferrocarriles del Estado, Casilla 134-D, Santiago; tel. 394271; telex 240662; yearly tourist guides with maps, hotel, and general information; railway services; Dir Alfredo Barahona Zuleta.

CHILE

Hoy: Mons. Miller 74, Santiago; tel. 2236102; f. 1977; weekly; general interest; Dir EMILIO FILIPPI; circ. 30,000.

Jurídica del Trabajo: Avda Bulnes 180, Of. 80, Casilla 9447, Santiago; tel. 67474; Editor MARIO SOTO VENEGAS.

Mensaje: Almirante Barroso 24, Casilla 10445, Santiago; tel. 6960653; f. 1951; monthly; national and international affairs; Dir RENATO HEVIA; circ. 8,000.

Microbyte-Todo Computación: Huelén 164-B, Santiago; tel. 2231530; monthly; computer science; Dir JOSÉ KAFFMAN; circ. 9,000.

Paula: Triana 851, Santiago; tel. 2253447; fortnightly; women's magazine; Dir ANDREA ELUCHANS; circ. 20,000.

¿Qué Pasa?: Darío Urzua 2109, Casilla 13279, Santiago; tel. 2514151; telex 34129; f. 1971; weekly; general interest; Dir ROBERTO PULIDO ESPINOSA; circ. 30,000.

Revista Médica de Chile: Esmeralda 678 Interior, Casilla 23-D, Santiago; tel. 392944; f. 1872; monthly; official organ of the Sociedad Médica de Santiago; Editor ALEJANDRO GOIĆ; circ. 2,000.

Vea: Luis Thayer Ojeda 1626, Providencia, Santiago; tel. 749421; telex 240161; f. 1939; weekly; general interest, illustrated; Dir DARÍO ROJAS MORALES; circ. 40,000.

PRESS ASSOCIATION

Asociación Nacional de la Prensa: Bandera 84, Of. 411, Santiago; tel. 6966431; Pres. CARLOS PAÚL LAMAS; Sec. JAIME MARTÍNEZ WILLIAMS.

NEWS AGENCIES

Orbe Servicios Informativos, SA: Phillips 56, 6°, Of. 66, Santiago; tel. 394774; Dir EMILIO BENAVIDES.

Foreign Bureaux

Agence France-Presse (France): Avda O'Higgins 1316, 9°, Apt. 92, Santiago; tel. 60559; telex 440074; Corespondent HUMBERTO ZUMARÁN.

Agencia EFE (Spain): Coronel Santiago Bueras 188, Santiago; tel. 380179; Bureau Chief RAMIRO GAVILANES.

Agenzia Nazionale Stampa Associata (ANSA) (Italy): Moneda 1040, Of. 702, Santiago; tel. 6985811; f. 1945; Bureau Chief GIORGIO BAGONI BETTOLLINI.

Associated Press (AP) (USA): Tenderini 85, 10°, Of. 100, Casilla 2653, Santiago; tel. 335015; telex 440234; Bureau Chief RICHARD BOUDREAUX.

Deutsche Presse-Agentur (dpa) (Federal Republic of Germany): San Antonio 427, Of. 306, Santiago; tel. 393633; Correspondent CARLOS DORAT.

Inter Press Service (IPS) (Italy): Phillips 40, Of. 68, Santiago; tel. 397091; Dir OSCAR KNUST ROSALES.

Reuters (UK): Huérfanos 1117, Of. 414, Casilla 4248, Santiago; tel. 722539; telex 40584; Correspondent SIMON ALTERMAN.

United Press International (UPI) (USA): Nataniel 47, 9°, Santiago; tel. 6960162; Bureau Chief ANTHONY BOADLE.

Xinhua (New China) News Agency (People's Republic of China): Biarritz 1981, Providencia, Santiago; tel. 255033; telex 94293; Correspondent SUN KUOGUOWEIN.

Publishers

Ediciones Paulinas: Vicuña MacKenna 10777, Casilla 3746, Santiago; tel. 6989145; Catholic texts.

Ediciones Universitarias de Valparaíso: Universidad Católica de Valparaíso, Montt Saavedra 44, Casilla 1415, Valparaíso; tel. 252900; also Moneda 673, 8°, Santiago; tel. 332230; telex 230389; f. 1970; general literature, social sciences, engineering, education, music, arts, textbooks; Gen. Man. KARLHEINZ LAAGE H.

Editora Nacional Gabriel Mistral Ltda: Avda Santa María 076, Santiago; tel. 779522; literature, history, philosophy, religion, art, education; government-owned; Man. Dir JOSÉ HARRISON DE LA BARRA.

Editorial Andrés Bello/Jurídica de Chile: Avda Ricardo Lyon 946, Casilla 4256, Santiago; tel. 2253600; f. 1947; medicine, history, arts, literature, philosophy, politics, economics, military strategy, agriculture, textbooks, law and social science; Gen. Man. WILLIAM THAYER.

Directory

Editorial El Sembrador: Sargento Aldea 1041, Casilla 2037, Santiago; tel. 5569454; Dir ISAÍAS GUTIÉRREZ.

Editorial Nascimento, SA: Chiloé 1433, Casilla 2298, Santiago; tel. 5569405; f. 1898; general; Man. Dir CARLOS GEORGE NASCIMENTO MÁRQUEZ.

Editorial Universitaria, SA: María Luisa Santander 0447, Casilla 10220, Santiago; tel. 2234555; f. 1947; general literature, social science, technical, textbooks; Man. Dir GABRIELA MATTE ALESSANDRI.

Empresa Editora Zig-Zag SA: Amapolas 2075, Casilla 84-D, Santiago; tel. 2235766; telex 340455; general publishers of literary works, reference books and magazines; Pres. SERGIO MÚJICA L.; Gen. Man. RODRIGO CASTRO C.

ASSOCIATION

Cámara Chilena del Libro: Ahumada 312, Of. 806, Santiago; tel. 6989519; Pres. MANUEL MELERO ABAROA; Sec. JUAN BAGÁ BALLÚS.

Radio and Television

In 1986 there were an estimated 14,000,000 radio receivers and 2,500,000 television receivers in use. There were 5 short-wave, 149 medium-wave and 167 FM stations.

RADIO

Asociación de Radiodifusores de Chile (ARCHI): Pasaje Matte 957, Of. 801, Casilla 10476, Santiago; tel. 398755; f. 1936; 316 broadcasting stations; Pres. RICARDO BEZANILLA RENOVALES; Vice-Pres. SANTIAGO CHIESA HOWARD; Sec.-Gen. CARLOS WILSON MARÍN.

Radio Nacional de Chile: San Antonio 220, 2°, Casilla 244, Santiago; tel. 339071; government station; domestic service; Dir JOSÉ LUIS CORDOVA BALLESTEROS.

TELEVISION

Televisión Nacional de Chile: Bellavista 0990, Casilla 16104, Santiago; tel. 774552; telex 440181; government network; 113 stations; Dir-Gen. Gen. OSCAR VARGAS.

Corporación de Televisión de la Universidad Católica de Chile—Canal 13: Inés M. Urrejola 0848, Casilla 14600, Santiago; tel. 2514000; telex 440182; f. 1959; non-commercial; Exec. Dir ELEODORO RODRÍGUEZ MATTE; Production Dir RUBY ANNE GUMPERTZ; Sec.-Gen. JORGE FERNÁNDEZ PARRA.

Universidad Católica de Valparaíso—Canal 4: Variante Agua Santa s/n, Viña del Mar; Casilla 4059, Valparaíso; tel. 251024; f. 1959; Dir VÍCTOR BIELEFELD VIVAS.

Universidad de Chile—Canal 11: Inés M. Urrejola 0825, Casilla 16457, Santiago; tel. 776273; telex 340492; f. 1960; educational; Vice-Pres. JUAN PABLO O'RYAN GUERRERO.

Universidad del Norte—Red de Radiotelevisión: Carrera 1625, Casilla 1045, Antofagasta; tel. 226725; telex 40665; f. 1981; operates Canal 11-Arica, Canal 12-Iquique and Canal 3-Antofagasta; Dir HORACIO HERNÁNDEZ RIGOU.

Empresa Nacional de Telecomunicaciones, SA—ENTEL CHILE, SA: Santa Lucía 360, Casilla 4254, Santiago; tel. 712121; telex 240683; f. 1964; operates the Chilean land satellite stations of Longovilo, Punta Arenas and Coihaique, linked to INTELSAT system; Gen. Man. Lt-Col IVÁN VAN DE WYNGARD MELLADO.

Finance

(cap. = capital; p.u. = paid up; dep. = deposits; res = reserves; m. = million; amounts in pesos unless otherwise specified)

BANKING

In 1980 the law referring to banks was amended to eliminate the categories of commercial and provincial banks. New banking legislation, designed to limit new loans by banks to 5% of their capital, was introduced in November 1986.

Supervisory Authority

Superintendencia de Bancos e Instituciones Financieras: Moneda 1123, 6°, Santiago; tel. 6990072; f. 1925; run by Ministry of Finance; Superintendent GUILLERMO RAMÍREZ VILARDELL.

CHILE   *Directory*

Central Bank

Banco Central de Chile: Agustinas 1180, Santiago; tel. 6962281; telex 240658; f. 1926; under Ministry of Finance; bank of issue; cap. and res 202,174.9m., dep. 450,891.5m. (Dec. 1985); Pres. Col ENRIQUE SEGUEL; Vice-Pres. ALFONSO SERRANO; Gen. Man. JORGE COURT MOOCK; 7 brs.

State Bank

Banco del Estado de Chile: Avda B. O'Higgins 1111, Casilla 24, Santiago; tel. 716001; telex 240536; f. 1953; state bank; cap. and res 40,961.7m., dep. 663,939.5m. (Dec. 1984); Pres. HERNÁN ARZE DE SOUZA FERREIRA; Gen. Man. JORGE CASENAVE BESOAÍN; 181 brs.

National Banks

Santiago

Banco de A. Edwards: Agustinas 733, Santiago; tel. 382525; telex 441160; f. 1851; cap. and res 2,638.0m. (Dec. 1983); Pres. AGUSTÍN EDWARDS EASTMAN; Gen. Man. JULIO JARAQUEMADA LEDOUX; 21 brs.

Banco de Chile: Ahumada 251, Casilla 151-D, Santiago; tel. 383044; telex 240750; f. 1894; cap. and res 19,815m. (Dec. 1984); placed under state control Jan. 1983; Provisional Administrator ADOLFO ROJAS GANDULFO; 97 brs.

Banco Concepción: Huérfanos 1072, Casilla 80-D, Santiago; tel. 6982741; telex 340268; f. 1871; cap. and res 7,550.6m. (May 1986); Pres. MANUEL FELIÚ J.; Gen. Man. JORGE DÍAZ V.; 35 brs.

Banco Continental: Huérfanos 1219, Casilla 10492, Santiago; tel. 6968201; telex 440244; f. 1958; cap. and res 1,304.6m. (June 1986); Pres. NICOLÁS YARUR LOLAS; Gen. Man. PEDRO HERNÁN AGUILA; 2 brs.

Banco de Crédito e Inversiones: Huérfanos 1134, Casilla 136-D, Santiago; tel. 6966633; telex 340773; f. 1937; cap. and res 6,058.1m., dep. 219,431.2m. (Dec. 1984); Pres. JORGE YARUR BANNA; Gen. Man. LUIS ENRIQUE YARUR REY; 83 brs.

Banco del Desarrollo: Avda B. O'Higgins 949, 3°, Santiago; tel. 6982901; telex 340654; cap. and res 769.3m. (July 1983); Pres. DOMINGO SANTA MARÍA SANTA CRUZ; Gen. Man. VICENTE CARUZ MIDDLETON.

Banco Español-Chile: Agustinas 920, Casilla 76-D, Santiago; tel. 381501; telex 440441; f. 1926; cap. and res 4,637m. (July 1985); subsidiary of Banco de Santander, Spain; Pres. EMILIO BOTÍN SANZ DE SAUTUOLA Y GARCÍA DE LOS RÍOS; Gen. Man. MIGUEL ESTRUGO S.; 42 brs.

Banco Exterior: MacIver 225, Santiago; tel. 6962182; telex 340462; cap. and res 528.0m. (July 1983); Pres. CALIXTO RÍOS PÉREZ; Gen. Man. FRANCISCO JAVIER PERAL.

Banco Hipotecario de Fomento Nacional: Huérfanos 1234, Santiago; tel. 6981842; telex 340269; f. 1883; cap. and res 1,885.4m. (July 1983); Pres. IGNACIO COUSIÑO ARAGÓN; Gen. Man. JORGE PRIETO SÁNCHEZ; 13 brs.

Banco Industrial y de Comercio Exterior: Teatinos 220, Santiago; tel. 6982931; telex 340270; f. 1979; cap. and res 2,062m. (Dec. 1985); Pres. ELIODORO MATTE LARRAÍN; Gen. Man. GONZALO VALDÉS BUDGE; 2 brs.

Banco Internacional: San Antonio 76, Casilla 135-D, Santiago; tel. 723623; telex 341066; f. 1944; cap. 3,507.1m., dep. 73,192.8m. (Dec. 1983); placed under state control Jan. 1983; Pres BORIS SUBELMAN BORTNIC; Gen. Man. LEANDRO OMEGNA O.; 10 brs.

Banco Morgan Finansa: Moneda 843, Santiago; tel. 383536; telex 240720; cap. and res 1,420m., dep. 8,796m.; Pres. FERNANDO LÉNIZ CERDA; Gen. Man. VICTOR M. ARBULU CROUSILLAT; 15 brs.

Banco Nacional: Bandera 287, Casilla 131-D, Santiago; tel. 6982091; telex 340830; f. 1906; cap. and res 20,780m. (Dec. 1985); Pres. FRANCISCO ERRÁZURIZ TALAVERA; Gen. Man. ALFREDO NEUT BLANCO; 31 brs.

Banco O'Higgins: Bandera 201, Casilla 51-D, Santiago; tel. 723600; telex 240438; f. 1956; cap. and res 4,866.8m. (June 1985); Pres. VLADIMIR RADIC PIRAINO; Gen. Man. GONZALO MENÉNDEZ DUQUE; 21 brs.

Banco Osorno y La Unión: Eleuterio Ramírez 902, Osorno, Santiago; tel. 718164; telex 240755; f. 1908; cap. and res 2,976.7m. (Dec. 1983); placed under state control in 1986; Pres. CARLOS OLIVOS MARCHANT; Gen. Man. EDUARDO POOLEY CARVAJAL; 32 brs.

Banco del Pacífico: Moneda 888, Santiago; tel. 6981873; telex 645295; cap. and res 483m. (July 1983); Pres. FRANCISCO JAVIER COMANDARI GARCÍA; Gen. Man. FRANCISCO JAVIER AGUIRRE VALENZUELA; 6 brs.

Banco de Santiago: Bandera 172, Santiago; tel. 728072; telex 441096; f. 1977; cap. and res 12,421m., dep. 20,754m. (July 1983); placed under state control Jan. 1983; merged with Banco Colocadora Nacional de Valores in 1986; Provisional Administrator JULIO BARRIGA SILVA; 25 brs.

Banco Sudamericano: Morandé 226, Casilla 90-D, Santiago; tel. 6982391; telex 40436; f. 1944; cap. and res 4,944.1m., dep. 118,022.3m. (Dec. 1984); Pres. JOSÉ BORDA AREXTABALA; Gen. Man. GONZALO RUIZ UNDURRAGA; 23 brs.

Banco del Trabajo: Bandera 102, Casilla 9595, Santiago; tel. 714133; telex 340370; f. 1955; cap. and res 3,650.4m., dep. 127,394.5m. (Dec. 1984); Pres. ROBERTO KELLY; Gen. Man. RICARDO BACARREZA R.; 38 brs.

Banco Urquijo de Chile: Agustinas 621, Santiago; tel. 381620; telex 440430; cap. and res 1,085.5m. (July 1985); Pres. ANTONIO ZOIDO MARTÍNEZ; Gen. Man. JOSÉ LUCINIO FERNÁNDEZ LÓPEZ.

Foreign Banks

Foreign banks that have opened branches in Chile include the following:

American Express International Banking Corporation (USA), Banco do Brasil, Banco de Colombia, Banco do Estado de São Paulo (Brazil), Banco de la Nación Argentina, Banco Real (Brazil), Banco Sudameris (France), Bank of America NT & SA (USA), Bank of Tokyo (Japan), Centrobanco, Chase Manhattan Bank (USA), Chicago Continental Bank (USA), Citibank NA (USA), Hongkong and Shanghai Banking Corporation (Hong Kong), First National Bank of Boston (USA), Republic National Bank of New York (USA).

Association

Asociación de Bancos e Instituciones Financieras de Chile: Agustinas 1476, 10°; Santiago; tel. 717149; telex 340958; Pres. SERGIO MARKMANN; Gen. Man. MARÍA ELENA OVALLE M.

STOCK EXCHANGES

Bolsa de Comercio y Valores de Santiago: La Bólsa 64, Casilla 123-D, Santiago; tel. 6982001; telex 340531; f. 1893; 32 mems; Pres. EUGENIO BLANCO RUIZ; Man. JUAN GASMAN CASTRO.

Bolsa de Valores de Valparaíso: Prat 798, Casilla 218-V, Valparaíso; tel. 250677; f. 1905; Pres. CARLOS F. MARRÍN ORREGO; Man. CARLOS CASTRO SANDOVAL.

INSURANCE

In September 1986 there were 23 general insurance, 16 life insurance and three reinsurance companies operating in Chile.

Supervisory Authority

Superintendencia de Valores y Seguros: Teatinos 120, 6°, Casilla 2167, Santiago; tel. 6962194; under Ministry of Finance; Supt FERNANDO ALVARADO ELISSETCHE.

Principal Companies

(Selected by virtue of premium income)

(p.i. = premium income; m. = million; amounts in pesos)

Cía de Seguros La Chilena Consolidada: Bandera 131, Santiago; tel. 721525; telex 240474; f. 1853; general; p.i. 2,625m., total assets 2,879m. (Dec. 1985); Pres. AGUSTÍN EDWARDS EASTMAN.

Instituto de Seguros del Estado (ISE): Moneda 1025, 7°, Santiago; tel. 6964271; telex 0387; f. 1953; general; p.i. 4,171m., total assets 4,234m. (Dec. 1985); Pres. HERNÁN BÜCHI BUC.

Cía de Seguros Generales Consorcio Nacional de Seguros, SA: Bandera 236, 6°, Santiago; tel. 718232; telex 240466; f. 1916; general; p.i. 2,620m., total assets 2,231m. (Dec. 1985); Pres. CARLOS EUGENIO LAVÍN GARCÍA-HUIDOBRO.

Cía de Seguros Generales Cruz del Sur, SA: Ahumada 370, 4°, Santiago; tel. 718181; f. 1974; general; p.i. 3,131m., total assets 4,435m. (Dec. 1985); Pres. JOSÉ TOMÁS GUZMÁN DUMAS.

Cía de Seguros Interamericana: Miraflores 178, 9°, Santiago; tel. 382508; telex 440295; f. 1980; life; p.i. 3,630m., total assets 5,851m. (Dec. 1985); Pres. RICARDO PERALTA VALENZUELA.

Cía de Seguros Sudamérica, SA: Moneda 1160, Santiago; tel. 6987516; f. 1962; life; p.i. 2,368m., total assets 4,479m. (Dec. 1985); Pres. BENJAMIN DAVIS CLARKE.

Cía de Seguros de Vida Aetna Chile, SA: Coyancura 2270, 10°, Santiago; tel. 2314566; telex 242304; f. 1981; life; p.i. 2,811m., total assets 16,461m. (Dec. 1985); Pres. SERGIO BAEZA VALDÉS.

Cía de Seguros de Vida Consorcio Nacional, SA: Bandera 236, 9°, Santiago; tel. 718232; telex 240466; f. 1916; life; p.i. 8,670m., total assets 24,674m. (Dec. 1985); Pres. CARLOS EUGENIO LAVÍN GARCÍA-HUIDOBRO.

Reinsurance

Caja Reaseguradora de Chile, SA: Bandera 84, 6°, Santiago; tel. 6982941; telex 34076; f. 1927; general; total assets 13,460m. (Dec. 1985); Pres. Gen. Man. SERGIO UNDURRAEA SAAVEDRA.

Cía Reaseguradora Bernardo O'Higgins: Bandera 206, 7°, Santiago; tel. 6967929; telex 242155; f. 1982; general; total assets 1,339m. (Dec. 1985); Pres. JAIME ENCINAS PEÑARANDA.

Insurance Association

Asociación de Aseguradores de Chile: Agustinas 785, 10°, Casilla 2630, Santiago; tel. 330059; telex 340260; f. 1931; Pres. ANDRÉS CHAPARRO KAUFMAN; Gen. Man. JORGE CAÑAS SUÁREZ.

Trade and Industry

CHAMBER OF COMMERCE

Cámara de Comercio de Santiago de Chile, AG: Santa Lucía 302, 3°, Casilla 1297, Santiago; tel. 330962; telex 240868; f. 1919; 1,000 mems; Pres. LUIS CORREA PRIETO; Exec. Sec. GONZALO SERRANO.

There are Chambers of Commerce in all major towns.

STATE ECONOMIC AND DEVELOPMENT ORGANIZATIONS

In 1980 the Government began a policy of denationalization and by early 1981 over 500 state companies had been sold. Only those concerns considered to be of strategic importance continue in the state sector and each must show an annual profit of 10% of its capital.

Comisión Nacional de Energía: Teatinos 120, 7°, Casilla 14, Correo 21, Santiago; tel. 6981757; telex 240948; f. 1978 to determine Chile's energy policy and approve investments in energy-related projects; Pres. Min. of Energy; Exec. Sec. SEBASTIÁN BERNSTEIN LETELIER.

Corporación de Fomento de la Producción—CORFO: Moneda 921, Casilla 3886, Santiago; tel. 380521; telex 240421; f. 1939; holding group of principal state enterprises; under Ministry of Economic Affairs; responsible for sale of non-strategic enterprises; Vice-Pres. Brig.-Gen. FERNANDO HORMAZÁBAL GAJARDO; Gen. Man. Col GUILLERMO LETELIER S.; controls:

Cía Chilena de Electricidad—CHILECTRA: Santo Domingo 789, 2°, Casilla 1557, Santiago; tel. 391096; telex 40645; f. 1921; generation, transmission and distribution of electric energy; Exec. Vice-Pres. RUBÉN DÍAZ NIERA.

Cía de Acero del Pacífico SA: Agustinas 1161, 3°, Santiago; tel. 395666; telex 41230; f. 1946; iron and steel production; Gen. Man. ROBERTO DE ANDRACA BARBAS.

Cía de Teléfonos de Chile—CTC: San Martín 50, Santiago; tel. 86616; telex 240955; f. 1930; Man. Col GERSON ECHAVARRÍA MENDOZA.

Complejo Forestal y Maderero Panguipulli Ltda: Agustinas 785, Of. 560, Santiago; tel. 397054; Gen. Man. MANUEL F. IZQUIERDO FERNÁNDEZ.

Empresa Minera de Aysén: Arturo Prat s/n, Coyhaique; zinc and lead mining; Gen. Man. MARCOS FARDELLA.

Empresa Nacional del Carbón—ENACAR: Moneda 1025, 6°, Casilla 2056, Santiago; tel. 717201; telex 40522; in charge of coal production; Gen. Man. Col EUDORO QUIÑONES SILVA.

Empresa Nacional de Computación e Informática SA—ECOM: José Pedro Alessandri 1495, Casilla 14796, Santiago; tel. 740076; Pres. JOAQUÍN PRIETO POMAREDA.

Empresa Nacional de Electricidad—ENDESA: Santa Rosa 76, Casilla 1392, Santiago; tel. 2228646; telex 240491; f. 1944; cap. p.u. 131,961m. pesos; installed capacity 2m. kW; Dir IGNACIO CAÑAS M.; Gen. Man. HIRAM PEÑA HERNÁNDEZ.

Empresa Nacional de Explosivos—ENAEX: Agustinas 1350, 3°, Santiago; tel. 82326; Gen. Man. Col (retd) HERNÁN OPITZ DE LA BARRA.

Industria Azucarera Nacional—IANSA: Avda Bustamante 26, Casilla 6099, Correo 22, Santiago; tel. 2258077; telex 240527; f. 1953; cap. US $72.8m.; 1986 production 430,000 metric tons sugar; factories in Curicó, Linares, Rapaco, Los Angeles and Nuble; Gen. Man. M. VERÓNICA GONZÁLEZ GIL.

Sociedad Química y Minera de Chile—SOQUIMICH: Olivares 1229, Santiago; tel. 711121; telex 240762; nitrate mining and exploration; Exec. Gen. Man. EDUARDO BOBENRIETH GIGLIO.

Corporación Nacional del Cobre de Chile (CODELCO—CHILE): Huérfanos 1189; POB 150-D, Santiago; tel. 6988801; telex 240672; f. 1976 as a state-owned enterprise with four copper-producing operational divisions at Chuquicamata, Salvador, Andina and El Teniente; attached to Ministry of Mines; Exec. Pres. Brig.-Gen. (retd) ROLANDO RAMOS MUÑOZ.

Corporación Nacional Forestal—CONAF: Avda Bulnes 285, Of. 501, Santiago; telex 440138; f. 1972 to centralize forestry activities, to enforce forestry law, to promote afforestation, to administer subsidies for afforestation projects and to increase and preserve forest resources; manages 13.3m. ha designated as National Parks, Natural Monuments and National Reserves; under Ministry of Agriculture; Exec. Dir IVÁN CASTRO POBLETE.

Empresa Nacional de Minería—ENAMI: MacIver 459, 2°, Casilla 100-D, Santiago; tel. 382122; telex 240574; promotes the development of the small- and medium-sized mines; attached to Ministry of Mines; Exec. Vice-Pres. Brig.-Gen. SERGIO PÉREZ HORMAZÁBAL.

Empresa Nacional de Petróleo—ENAP: Ahumada 341, Santiago; tel. 381845; telex 240447; f. 1950; controls the petroleum industry; attached to Ministry of Mines; Pres. SAMUEL LIRA OVALLE; Gen. Man. ALEJANDRO MARTY.

Oficina de Planificación Nacional—ODEPLAN: Ahumada 48, 7°, Casilla 9140, Santiago; tel. 722033; telex 40767; f. 1967 to assist the President of the Republic in all matters relating to social and economic planning; 1982–89 projected expenditure of $10,100m. on c. 15,000 projects; Dir Minister of Planning.

PRO-CHILE: Dirección General de Relaciones Económicas Internacionales, POB 16587, Correo 9, Santiago; tel. 2317108; telex 240836; f. 1974; official export promotion agency; Dir GUILLERMO LUNECKE BRAUNING.

Servicio Agrícola y Ganadero—SAG: Avda Bulnes 140, 8°, Santiago; tel. 6982244; under Ministry of Agriculture; Exec. Dir ALEJANDRO MARCHANT BAEZA.

Sociedad Agrícola y Servicios Isla de Pascua: Miraflores 590, 1°, Of. 2, Santiago; tel. 332977; administers agriculture and public services on Easter Island; Gen. Man. FERNANDO MAIRA PALMA.

Subsecretaría de Pesca: Teatinos 120, 11°, Santiago; tel. 716620; controls fishing industry; part of the Ministry of Economic Affairs; Dir ROBERTO VERDUGO GORMAZ.

EMPLOYERS' ORGANIZATIONS

Confederación de la Producción y del Comercio: Estado 337, Of. 507, Casilla 9984, Santiago; tel. 333690; f. 1936; Pres. MANUEL FELIU J.; Man. JUAN FRANCISCO GUTIÉRREZ Y.

Affiliated organizations:

Asociación de Bancos e Instituciones Financieras de Chile (q.v.).

Cámara Chilena de la Construcción: Huérfanos 1052, 9°, Casilla Clasificador 679, Santiago; tel. 6960450; f. 1951; Pres. JORGE BRONFMAN HOROVITZ; Gen. Man. JAIME REYES GUTIÉRREZ; 1,300 mems.

Cámara Nacional de Comercio de Chile: Santa Lucía 302, 4°, Casilla 1015, Santiago; tel. 397694; telex 340110; f. 1858; Pres. DARÍO VIAL HERRERA; Man. HUMBERTO PRIETO CONCHA; 120 mems.

Sociedad de Fomento Fabril—SOFOFA: Agustinas 1357, 11°-12°, Casilla 44-D, Santiago; tel. 6982646; f. 1883; largest employers' organization; Pres. ERNESTO AYALA OLIVA; 2,000 mems.

Sociedad Nacional de Agricultura—SNA: Tenderini 187, 2°, Casilla 40-D, Santiago; tel. 396710; telex 240760; f. 1838; landowners' association; controls Radio Stations CB 57 and XQB8 (FM) in Santiago, CB-97 in Valparaíso, CD-120 in Los Angeles; Pres. MANUEL VALDÉS VALDÉS; Gen. Sec. RAÚL GARCÍA ASTABURUAGA.

Sociedad Nacional de Minería—SONAMI: Teatinos 20, 3°, Of. 33, Casilla 1807, Santiago; tel. 81696; f. 1883; Pres. MANUEL FELIÚ J.; Man. ALFREDO ARAYA MUÑOZ.

Confederación de Asociaciones Gremiales y Federaciones de Agricultores de Chile: Lautaro 218, Los Angeles; registered with Ministry of Economic Affairs 1981; Pres. DOMINGO DURÁN NEUMANN.

Confederación Gremial del Comercio Detallista de Chile: Merced 380, 8°, Santiago; retail trade; registered with Ministry of Economic Affairs 1980; Pres. ELÍAS BRUGERE.

Confederación Gremial Nacional Unida de la Mediana y Pequeña Industria, Servicios y Artesanado—CONUPIA: Estado 115, entrepiso, Santiago; registered with Ministry of Economic Affairs 1980; small- and medium-sized industries and crafts; Pres. ROBERTO PARRAQUE BONET.

There are many federations of private industrialists, organized by industry and region.

TRADE UNIONS

In September 1973 the Central Única de Trabajadores de Chile was outlawed as it was deemed to be a political organ of the Communist Party. Trade union activities have been severely curtailed under the present regime and in 1978 seven trade union federations, representing 529 trade unions and some 400,000 workers were banned, as they were deemed to be Marxist, and their property was confiscated.

New labour legislation introduced in 1979 and embodied in the 1981 constitution included: the right of association; that unions are to be organized only on a company basis; that the Government's right to control union budgets is to be abolished; that union representatives must not engage in any political activity; that strikes involving stoppages to essential public services or which endanger national security are to be prohibited and that strikes may last no longer than 60 days.

There are over 20 national labour federations and unions. The confederations include:

Confederación de Empleados Particulares de Chile—CEPCH: Teatinos 727, 3°, Santiago; tel. 722093; trade union for workers in private sector; Pres. EDMUNDO LILLO.

Confederación Marítima de Chile—COMACH: Eleuterio Ramírez 476, 8°, Valparaíso; tel. 257656; f. 1985; Leader EDUARDO RÍOS; 5,000 mems.

Confederación de Trabajadores del Cobre—CTC: MacIver 283, 5°, Santiago; tel. 380835; Pres. CARLOS OGALDE; Sec.-Gen. ROBERTO CARVAJAL.

Confederación de la Construcción: Serrano 444, Santiago; tel. 397472; trade union for workers in construction industry; Pres. SERGIO TRONCOSO; Leaders JOSÉ FIGUEROA, MANUEL BUSTAMANTE.

Coordinadora Nacional Sindical—CNS: Abdón Cifuentes 67, Santiago; tel. 6985586; national co-ordinating body; Pres. MANUEL BUSTOS HUERTA; *c.* 700,000 mems.

Federación de Trabajadores Demócrata Cristiana—FTDC: Huérfanos 1022, Of. 1306, Santiago; Christian Democratic trade union organization; Pres. ERNESTO FOGEL; Sec.-Gen. LUIS SEPÚLVEDA GUTIÉRREZ.

Grupo de los Diez: Christian Democratic trade union organization.

Unión Democrática de Trabajadores—UDT: f. 1981; 49 affiliated organizations; set up under auspices of Grupo de los Diez; Leader HERNOL FLORES; *c.* 780,000 mems.

The trade unions include:

Central Democrática de Trabajadores—CDT: Erasmo Escala 2170, Santiago; tel. 715338; eight affiliated organizations; Pres. EDUARDO RÍOS ARIAS.

Comando Nacional de Trabajadores—CNT: Santa Mónica 2015; Santiago; tel. 6989770; f. 1983; 16 affiliated organizations; Pres. RODOLFO SEGUEL MOLINA; Sec.-Gen. ARTURO MARTÍNEZ M.

Frente Nacional de Organizaciones Autónomas—FRENAO: Santa Lucía 162, Santiago; tel. 382354; Pres. MANUEL CONTRERAS LOYOLA.

Frente Unitario de Trabajadores—FUT: San Diego 379 H, Santiago; tel. 6985188; five affiliated organizations; Pres. CARLOS ROJAS; Sec.-Gen. HUMBERTO SOTO.

Transport

In April 1981 the Minister of Transport and Telecommunications announced the Government's intention to denationalize its transport and telecommunications organizations.

Ministerio de Transportes y Telecomunicaciones: Amunátegui 139, Santiago; tel. 726503; telex 240200.

RAILWAYS

The total length of the railway system in 1984 was 8,570 km, of which about 95% is state-owned. The privately-owned lines are in the north. There are also five international railways, two to Bolivia, two to Argentina and one to Peru.

In 1983 management of the State Railways system was decentralized and divided into three autonomous operating regions, consisting of Northern, Southern and the Arica–La Paz railways. Future expansion of the Santiago underground transport system is to be carried out by private enterprise.

State Railways

Empresa de los Ferrocarriles del Estado: Avda Bernardo O'Higgins 924, 4°, Casilla 134-D, Santiago; tel. 382577; telex 240662; f. 1851; 8,100 km of track (1984). The State Railways are divided between the Ferrocarriles Norte y Sur (Northern and Southern Systems) and the Ferrocarril Arica–La Paz; Gen. Man. Dir Brig.-Gen. JAIME ESTRADA LEIGH.

Private Railways

Antofagasta (Chili) & Bolivia Railway Co Ltd: Bolívar 255, Casillas S-T, Antofagasta; telex 25226; British-owned; Pres. ANDRÓNICO LUKSIC ABAROA; Gen. Man. G. M. DUQUE. The Chilean part of the system consists of the international railway from Antofagasta to Ollague on the Bolivian border, and branches; total track length 728 km.

Ferrocarril Codelco-Chile: Huérfanos 1189, 5°, Santiago; Gen. Man. M. ACEVEDO V.

  Diego de Almagro a Potrerillos: 99 km; transport of forest products, minerals and manufactures.

  Ferrocarril Rancagua–Teniente: 68 km; transport of forest products, livestock, minerals and manufactures.

Ferrocarril Tocopilla–Toco: Calle Olivares 1229, Santiago; telex 240762; owned by Sociedad Química y Minera de Chile, SA; 116 km; Gen. Man. E. BOBENRIETH.

In 1975 an underground railway in Santiago was begun:

Metro de Santiago: Red de Transporte Colectivo Independiente, Dirección General del Metro, Avda Libertador B. O'Higgins 1426, Santiago; tel. 88218; telex 40777; started operations Sept. 1975; 25 km open in Sept. 1980; 2 lines; service to be expanded by 4 km in 1985; Dir-Gen. Ing. LUDOLF LAUSEN KUHLMANN.

ROADS

Ministerio de Obras Públicas: Dirección de Vialidad, Morandé 59, 2°, Santiago; tel. 724506; telex 240777; the authority responsible for roads; the total length of roads in Chile in 1985 was 79,148 km, of which 9,500 km were paved. The road system comprises the Pan American Highway extending 3,521 km from north to south, almost completely paved, and about 57,106 km of transversal roads. Important projects include the resurfacing of sections of the Pan American Highway, the construction of the Southern Longitudinal Highway and a conservation programme to resurface the most important national routes; a two-year rehabilitation, maintenance and upgrading programme was launched in 1986, at a cost of US $280m.; investment of US $160m. annually; Dir Ing. REMBERTO URREA MUSTER.

SHIPPING

As a consequence of Chile's difficult topography, maritime transport is of particular importance. The principal ports are Valparaíso, Talcahuano, Antofagasta, San Antonio and Punta Arenas.

Chile's merchant fleet had a total capacity of 1,166,465 dwt in 1983.

Supervisory Authorities

Asociación Nacional de Armadores: Blanco 869, Valparaíso; tel. 21257; also Teatinos 20, Of. 91, 9°, Santiago; tel. 710126; shipowners' association; Pres. BELTRÁN URENDA ZEGERS; Man. SERGIO NÚÑEZ RAMÍREZ.

Cámara Marítima de Chile: Blanco 869, Valparaíso; tel. 250313; telex 230491; Pres. GABRIEL FONSO; Man. RODOLFO GARCÍA.

Dirección General de Territorio Marítimo y Marina Mercante: Errázuriz 537, 4°, Valparaíso; telex 230662; Dir Rear Adm. ERNESTO HUBER VON APPEN.

Empresa Portuaria de Chile—EMPORCHI: Blanco 839, Valparaíso; tel. 55749; telex 230313; also Huérfanos 1055, Of. 804, Santiago; tel. 6982232; telex 240624; Dir Vice-Adm. (retd) JORGE BAEZA CONCHA.

Santiago

Cía Marítima Isla de Pascua, SA (COMAIPA): MacIver 225, Of. 2001, 20°, Santiago; tel. 383036; telex 240646; Pres. FEDERICO BARRAZA.

Valparaíso

A. J. Broom y Cía, SAC: Blanco 951, POB 910, Valparaíso and Agustinas 853, 6°, POB 448, Santiago; f. 1920; Pres. Capt. JENS SORENSEN; Gen. Man. MARCELO VARGAS MUÑOZ.

Cía Chilena de Navegación Interoceánica SA: Plaza de la Justicia 59, Casilla 1410, Valparaíso; tel. 259001; telex 230386; also Avda Libertador B. O'Higgins 949, Santiago; tel. 6968147; telex 240486; f. 1930; regular sailings to Brazil, River Plate, South Africa, Japan, Republic of Korea, Taiwan, Hong Kong, USA and Europe; bulk and dry cargo services; Pres. Vice-Adm. (retd) ARTURO TRONCOSO DAROCH; Gen. Man. ANTONIO JABAT ALONSO.

Cía Sud-Americana de Vapores: Blanco 895, Casilla 49-V, Valparaíso; tel. 259061; telex 230001; also Moneda 970, 10°, 11°, Santiago; tel. 6964181; telex 240480; f. 1872; 13 cargo vessels; regular service between Chile and US/Canadian East Coast ports, US Gulf ports, North European, Mediterranean, Scandinavian and Far East ports; bulk carriers, tramp and reefer services; Pres. JOSÉ LUIS CERDA URRUTIA; Man. PATRICIO FALCONE SCHIAVETTI.

Empresa Marítima del Estado (Empremar): Almirante Gómez Carreño 49, POB 105-V, Valparaíso; tel. 258061; telex 230382; f. 1938; state-owned; 15 vessels; international and coastal services; Dir RODOLFO CALDERÓN ALDUNATE; Vice-Pres. ALVARO LARENAS L.

Naviera Chilena del Pacífico, SA: Errázuriz 556, Casilla 370, Valparaíso; tel. 250551; telex 230357; also Serrano 14, Of. 502, Santiago; tel. 333063; telex 240457; cargo; 3 vessels; Pres. ARTURO FERNÁNDEZ; Gen. Man. PABLO SIMIAN.

Naviera Interoceangas, SA: Agustinas 1357, 3°, POB 2829, Santiago; tel. 6963211; telex 240223; Man. PEDRO LECAROS MENÉNDEZ.

Pacific Steam Navigation Co: Blanco 625, 6°, Valparaíso; tel. 213191; telex 230384; also Agustinas 1070, 6°, Casilla 4087, Santiago; brs in Antofagasta and San Antonio; Man. DAVID KIMBER SMITH.

Sociedad Anónima de Navegación Petrolera (SONAP): Errázuriz 471, 3°, Casilla 1870, Valparaíso; tel. 259476; telex 230392; f. 1953; tanker services; 4 vessels; Deputy Man. EDUARDO RUIZ C.

Transmares Naviera Chilena Ltda: Blanco 853, Valparaíso; tel. 259051; telex 40483; also Moneda 970, 18°, Casilla 193-D, Santiago; tel. 722686; telex 240483; f. 1969; dry cargo service Chile–Uruguay–Brazil; Gen. Man. WOLF VON APPEN.

Several foreign shipping companies operate services to Valparaíso.

Ancúd

Sociedad Transporte Marítimo Chiloé-Aysén Ltda: Casilla 387, Ancúd; tel. 317; Deputy Man. PEDRO HERNÁNDEZ LEHMAN.

Puerto Montt

Naviera Magallanes SA (NAVIMAG): Agustinas 1357, 3°, POB 2829, Santiago; tel. 6963211; telex 240735; Man. FRANCISCO SAHLI CRUZ.

Punta Arenas

Cía Marítima de Punta Arenas, SA: Casilla 337, Punta Arenas; telex 280009; also Casilla 2829, Santiago; tel. 6963211; f. 1949; shipping agents and owners operating in the Magellan Straits; Dir ROBERTO IZQUIERDO MENÉNDEZ.

San Antonio

Naviera Aysén Ltda: Centenario 9, San Antonio; tel. 32578; telex 238603; also Huérfanos 1147, Of. 542, Santiago; tel. 6988680; telex 240982; Man. RAÚL QUINTANA A.

Naviera Paschold Ltda: Centenario 9, San Antonio; tel. 31654; telex 238603; also Huérfanos 1147, Santiago; tel. 6988680; telex 240982; Gen. Man. FERNANDO MARTÍNEZ M.

Talcahuano

Naviera Pulmalal Ltda: Anibal Pinto 85, Of. 502, Talcahuano; Dirs FELICIANO PALMA, JULIO ALEGRÍA.

CIVIL AVIATION

There are 325 airfields in the country, of which eight have long runways. Arturo Merino Benítez, 20 km north-east of Santiago, and Chacalluta, 14 km north-east of Arica, are the principal international airports.

Línea Aérea Nacional de Chile (LAN-Chile): Camino Melpilla 5300, Santiago; tel. 577505; telex 441061; government airline; f. 1929; operates scheduled internal passenger and cargo services, also Santiago–Easter Island; international services to Argentina, Bolivia, Brazil, French Polynesia, Peru, the USA, Uruguay and Venezuela; Gen. Man. JORGE PATRICIO SEPÚLVEDA CERÓN; fleet: 2 Boeing 737, 5 Boeing 707, 2 DC 10-30.

Línea Aérea del Cobre SA (LADECO): POB 13740, Avda Bulnes 147, Santiago; tel. 727226; telex 240116; f. 1958; internal services; international passenger services to Argentina, Brazil, Colombia, Ecuador, Paraguay and the USA; Pres. EUGENIO MANDIOLA; Exec. Vice-Pres. ALFREDO MORENO; fleet: 2 Boeing 737, 4 Boeing 727-100.

Tourism

Servicio Nacional de Turismo—SERNATUR: Calle Catedral 1165, 3° y 4°, Casilla 14082, Santiago; tel. 6967141; telex 240137; f. 1975; Dir MARGARITA DUCCI BUDGE.

Asociación Chilena de Empresas de Turismo—ACHET: Agustinas 1291, 2°, Of. A, Casilla 3402, Santiago; tel. 6985385; f. 1946; 150 mems; Pres. JOSÉ MARTÍNEZ URTUBIA.

Atomic Energy

Comisión Chilena de Energía Nuclear: Amunátegui 95, Casilla 188-D, Santiago; tel. 748138; telex 340468; f. 1965; government body to develop peaceful uses of atomic energy; autonomous organization that concentrates, regulates and controls all matters related to nuclear energy; Pres. Lt-Gen. HERMAN BRADY ROCHE; Exec. Dir Brig. JUAN MIR DUPOUY.

In 1980 the Government decided to postpone the building of a nuclear power station until the end of the century on grounds of commercial viability.

THE PEOPLE'S REPUBLIC OF CHINA

Note: The Pinyin system of transliteration has replaced the Wade-Giles system.

Introductory Survey

Location, Climate, Language, Religion, Flag, Capital

The People's Republic of China covers a vast area of eastern Asia, with Mongolia to the north, the USSR to the north and west, Afghanistan and Pakistan to the west, and India, Nepal, Bhutan, Burma, Laos and Viet-Nam to the south. The country borders the Democratic People's Republic of Korea in the north-east, and has a long coastline on the Pacific Ocean. The climate ranges from sub-tropical in the far south to an annual average temperature of below 10°C (50°F) in the north, and from the monsoon climate of eastern China to the aridity of the north-west. The principal language is Northern Chinese (Mandarin); in the south and south-east local dialects are spoken. The Xizangzu (Tibetans), Wei Wuer (Uighurs), Menggus (Mongols) and other groups have their own languages. The traditional religions and philosophies of life are Confucianism, Buddhism and Daoism. There are also small Muslim and Christian minorities. The national flag (proportions 3 by 2) is plain red, with one large five-pointed gold star and four similar but smaller stars, arranged in an arc, in the upper hoist. The capital is Beijing (Peking).

Recent History

The People's Republic of China was proclaimed on 1 October 1949, following the victory of Communist forces over the Kuomintang government, which fled to the island province of Taiwan. The new Communist regime received widespread international recognition, but it was not until 1971 that the People's Republic was admitted to the United Nations, in place of the Kuomintang regime, as the representative of China. Most other countries now recognize the People's Republic.

With the establishment of the People's Republic, the leading figure in China's political affairs was Mao Zedong, who was Chairman of the Chinese Communist Party (CCP) from 1935 until his death in 1976. Chairman Mao, as he was known, also became Head of State in October 1949, but he relinquished this post in December 1958. His successor was Liu Shaoqi, First Vice-Chairman of the CCP, who was elected Head of State in April 1959. Liu was dismissed in October 1968, during the Cultural Revolution (see below), and died in prison in 1969. The post of Head of State was left vacant, and was formally abolished in January 1975, when a new constitution was adopted.

The first Premier (Head of Government) of the People's Republic was Zhou Enlai, who held this office from October 1949 until his death in 1976. Zhou was also Minister of Foreign Affairs from 1949 to 1958, and subsequently remained largely responsible for China's international relations.

In the early years of the People's Republic, China was dependent on the USSR for economic and military aid, and Chinese planning was based on the Soviet model, with highly centralized control. From 1955 onwards, however, Mao Zedong set out to develop a distinctively Chinese form of socialism. As a result of increasingly strained relations between Chinese and Soviet leaders, caused partly by ideological differences, the USSR withdrew all technical aid to China in August 1960. Chinese hostility to the USSR increased, and was aggravated by territorial disputes between the two countries.

Tibet, a semi-independent region of western China, was occupied in 1950 by Chinese Communist forces. In March 1959 there was an unsuccessful armed uprising by Tibetans opposed to Chinese rule. As a result, the Dalai Lama, the head of Tibet's Buddhist clergy and thus the region's spiritual leader, fled to India, and has since remained in exile. The Chinese ended the former dominance of the lamas (Buddhist monks) and destroyed many monasteries. Tibet became an 'Autonomous Region' of China in September 1965.

Sino-Soviet friction was accompanied by an improvement in China's relations with Japan and the West during the 1970s. Almost all Western countries had recognized the Government of the People's Republic as the sole legitimate government of China, and had consequently withdrawn recognition from the 'Republic of China', which had been confined to Taiwan since 1949. The People's Republic claimed Taiwan as an integral part of its territory, although the island remained to be 'liberated'. For many years, however, the USA refused to recognize the People's Republic but, instead, regarded the Taiwan regime as the legitimate Chinese government. In February 1972 President Richard Nixon of the USA visited the People's Republic and acknowledged that 'Taiwan is a part of China'. In January 1979 the USA recognized the People's Republic and severed diplomatic relations with Taiwan.

The economic progress which was achieved during the early years of Communist rule enabled China to withstand the effects of the industrialization programmes of the late 1950s (called the 'Great Leap Forward'), the drought of 1960-62 and the withdrawal of Soviet aid in 1960. To prevent the establishment of a ruling class, Chairman Mao launched the Great Proletarian Cultural Revolution in 1966. The ensuing excesses of the Red Guards caused the army to intervene; Liu Shaoqi, Head of State, and Deng Xiaoping, General Secretary of the CCP, were disgraced. In 1971 an attempted coup by the Defence Minister, Marshal Lin Biao, was unsuccessful, and by 1973 it was apparent that Chairman Mao and Premier Zhou Enlai had retained power. In 1975 Deng Xiaoping re-emerged as first Vice-Premier and Chief of the General Staff. Zhou Enlai died in January 1976. Hua Guofeng, hitherto Minister of Public Security, was appointed Premier, and Deng was dismissed. Mao died in September 1976. His widow, Jiang Qing, tried unsuccessfully to seize power, with the help of three radical members of the CCP's Politburo. The 'gang of four' and six associates of Lin Biao were tried in November 1980. All were found guilty. The tenth anniversary of Mao's death was marked in September 1986 by an official reassessment of his life; while his accomplishments were praised, it was now acknowledged that he had made mistakes, although most of the criticism was directed at the 'gang of four'.

In October 1976 Hua Guofeng succeeded Mao as Chairman of the CCP and Commander-in-Chief of the People's Liberation Army. The 11th Congress of the CCP, held in August 1977, restored Deng Xiaoping to his former posts. In September 1980 Hua Guofeng resigned as Premier but retained his chairmanship of the CCP. The appointment of Zhao Ziyang, a Deputy Premier since April 1980, to succeed Hua as Premier, confirmed the dominance of the moderate faction of Deng Xiaoping. In June 1981 Hua Guofeng was replaced as Chairman of the CCP by Hu Yaobang, former Secretary-General of the Politburo, and as Chairman of the Military Affairs Commission by Deng Xiaoping. A sustained campaign by Deng to purge the Politburo of leftist elements led to Hua's demotion to a Vice-Chairman of the CCP and, in September 1982, to his exclusion from the Politburo.

In September 1982 the CCP was reorganized and the post of Party Chairman abolished. Hu Yaobang became, instead, General Secretary of the CCP. A year later a 'rectification' (purge) of the CCP was launched, aimed at expelling 'Maoists', who had risen to power during the Cultural Revolution, and those opposed to the pragmatic policies of Deng. China's new Constitution, adopted in December 1982, restored the office of Head of State, and in June 1983 Li Xiannian, a former Minister of Finance, became President of China.

In 1983-84 several moves were made to consolidate the authority of the Government: following the announcement of a major anti-crime drive in late 1983, thousands of people were reported to have been executed, while at the same time a campaign was launched against 'spiritual pollution'; stricter censorship was introduced to limit the effects of Western cultural influences. The reorganization of the CCP continued, and several senior cadres were dismissed or discredited. During 1984–85 a programme of modernization for the armed forces was undertaken, during which several senior officers were replaced, in accordance with the policy of rejuvenation in all areas of China's leadership. In July and October 1984 five members of the State Council (Cabinet) were replaced by considerably younger politicians, and during 1985 several more ministers were replaced. In September 1985 a special CCP conference was held (for only the second time since 1949), to approve a major reshuffle of senior CCP leaders. In a move intended to give 'new vigour' to the leadership, 10 veteran Politburo members (including, most notably, Marshal Ye Jianying, one of China's most influential military leaders) resigned to make way for six new, younger members, while five new appointments were also made to the CCP secretariat. The rejuvenated Politburo was regarded as strongly pro-Deng, while the influence of the military was perceptibly reduced, and the changes were seen as an attempt to ensure the continuation of Deng's reforms until the end of the century. In September 1986 the sixth plenary session of the CCP Central Committee adopted a detailed resolution on the 'guiding principles for building a socialist society', which redefined the general ideology of the CCP, to provide a theoretical basis for the programme of modernization and the 'open door' policy.

In January 1986 a high-level 'anti-corruption' campaign was launched, to investigate reports that many officials had exploited the programme of economic reform for their own gain. In the field of culture and the arts, however, there was a significant liberalization in 1986, with a revival of the 'Hundred Flowers' movement of 1956–57, which had encouraged the development of intellectual debate. However, a wave of student demonstrations in major cities in late 1986 was regarded by China's leaders as an indication of excessive 'bourgeois liberalization', and in the ensuing government clamp-down, in January 1987, Hu Yaobang unexpectedly resigned as CCP General Secretary, being accused of 'mistakes on major issues of political principles'. Zhao Ziyang became acting General Secretary.

China condemned Viet-Nam's invasion of Kampuchea in December 1978, and launched a punitive attack into northern Viet-Nam in February 1979. Armed clashes across the border have continued, and talks between the two countries have failed. Taiwan has repeatedly rejected China's proposals for reunification, under which Taiwan would become a 'special administrative region'. China has, however, confirmed its intention to re-establish sovereignty over Hong Kong when the existing lease on most of the territory expires in 1997; in September 1984, following protracted negotiations, China reached agreement with the British Government over the terms of Chinese administration of the territory after that date.

High-level talks with Soviet officials in 1982–85 marked a thaw in Sino-Soviet relations, and it was hoped that the signing of a five-year trade agreement between the two countries, in September 1985, would also benefit future political progress. Sino-Soviet relations improved further in 1986, after an offer by the Soviet leader, Mikhail Gorbachev, to withdraw some of the USSR's troops from Afghanistan and Mongolia, and to make some concessions over a disputed border with China at the Amur river—two issues which had long hindered any normalization of relations.

China's relations with the USA have also improved: Premier Zhao Ziyang visited Washington in January 1984, and President Ronald Reagan visited Beijing in April, when a bilateral agreement on industrial and technological co-operation was signed. The main obstacle to Sino-US relations remains the question of Taiwan, and, in particular, the continued sale of US armaments to Taiwan.

Government

China is a unitary state. Directly under the Central Government there are 21 provinces, five autonomous regions, including Xizang (Tibet), and three municipalities (Beijing, Shanghai and Tianjin). The highest organ of state power is the National People's Congress (NPC). In 1986 the NPC had 2,978 deputies, indirectly elected for five years by the provinces, autonomous regions, municipalities directly under the Central Government, and the People's Liberation Army. The NPC elects a Standing Committee to be its permanent organ. The current Constitution, adopted by the NPC in December 1982, was China's fourth since 1949. It restored the office of Head of State (President of the Republic).

Executive power is exercised by the State Council (Cabinet), comprising the Premier, Vice-Premiers and other Ministers heading ministries and commissions. The State Council is appointed by, and accountable to, the NPC.

Local people's congresses are the local organs of state power. Local revolutionary committees, created during the Cultural Revolution, were abolished in January 1980 and replaced by local people's governments.

Defence

China is divided into seven major military units. All armed services are grouped in the People's Liberation Army (PLA). In July 1986, according to Western estimates, the regular forces totalled 2,950,000: the army numbered 2,110,000, the navy 350,000 (including a naval infantry force of 56,500), and the air force 490,000. There is also a public security force and a civilian militia. Military service is by selective conscription, and lasts for three years in the army and naval infantry, and for four years in the air force and navy. Defence expenditure for 1986 was budgeted at 20,020m. yuan.

Economic Affairs

In 1984 the agricultural sector employed 68% of China's labour force and contributed 44% of net material product (NMP). China, with 21% of the world's population in 1985, accounted for 20% of the world's production of cereals and 39% of the world's pig numbers in 1984. China is the world's largest producer of rice, accounting for 38% of the world harvest in 1984. The gross value of China's farm output increased by about 50% in the decade up to 1978. In 1985 agricultural output grew by 13%, compared with an increase of 14.5% in 1984. The 1983 harvest of grain (cereals, pulses, soybeans and tubers in 'grain equivalent') exceeded all expectations, reaching 387.3m. tons, following the successful implementation of a system of 'rural responsibility' which provided more incentives for agricultural workers. In 1985 production of grain totalled 378.9m. tons, slightly lower than the 1984 harvest of 407.3m. tons. The responsibility system was taken a step further in January 1985, with the abolition of the mandatory purchase of staple crops by the State, thus permitting private grain sales by producers for the first time.

China has large mineral deposits, such as coal and iron ore, which serve the iron and steel works at Anshan, Shanghai, Baotou, Wuhan and smaller plants elsewhere. In September 1985 the first stage of the Baoshan iron and steel complex began operations. Baoshan is China's largest steel plant, with an annual production capacity of 6.5m. tons. Other important minerals include tungsten, molybdenum, antimony, tin, lead, mercury, bauxite, phosphate rock and manganese. The gross value of China's industrial output doubled in the decade to 1978. In 1979 emphasis shifted from heavy to light industry, but in 1982 this policy was reversed, and measures were adopted to accelerate the growth of heavy industry. In 1985 heavy industry contributed 53.3% of total industrial output by value, compared with 46.7% from light industry. The development of China's chemical industry is being promoted, while the electronics sector is of growing importance and has moved into areas of high technology, such as microelectronics, satellite communications and computer technology. The energy sector is being given priority in development, and the petroleum industry is expanding steadily, although around 75% of the country's fuel and power needs are still met by coal. Petroleum contributed around 18% in 1984, while hydroelectricity accounted for around 5%. In terms of consumption by economic sector, industry accounted for 64.8% in 1984, followed by domestic usage (18.3%) and agriculture (6.9%). Since 1973 China has been self-sufficient in petroleum and its derivatives, and in 1985 the country produced 125m. tons of crude petroleum. By the end of 1984, Chinese and foreign oil companies had spent US $1,600m. on the exploration of China's offshore petroleum reserves, one of the principal areas for joint-venture contracts, and it was reported in 1985 that foreign oil companies would henceforth be permitted to explore for petroleum reserves in parts of mainland China as well. China is developing its own petrochemical industries, including fibres and plastics, and is a major producer and consumer of nitrogenous fertilizers. Petrochemical products accounted for 25% of China's total export volume in 1985.

The development of the economy since 1953 has been within the framework of five-year plans, but recessions occurred in the wake of the Great Leap Forward (1958–60) and during the Cultural Revolution (1966–76). In 1980 it was decided to replace the unrealistic 1976–85 Plan by a Ten-Year Plan (1981–90) and a Five-Year Plan (1981–85), and to slow down the 'four modernizations' (agriculture, industry, defence, and science and technology). During the Sixth Five-Year Plan (1981–85) gross national product (GNP) increased at an average annual rate of 10%; industrial output increased by 12% and agricultural output by 8.1% per year. The Seventh Five-Year Plan (1986–90) aimed to continue the modernization of the economy, with priority given to reform and the expansion of the 'open door' policy. The state management of enterprises was to change gradually from direct control to indirect control, to establish 'a new socialist macro-economic management system'. Major reforms were envisaged in the sectors of banking, pricing policy, labour law and agriculture. Target growth rates were lower than during the previous Plan: GNP was planned to increase by an annual average of 7.5%, while industrial and agricultural output was targeted to increase by 6.7%. It was acknowledged that the reforms of 1984 produced excessive growth in some areas: industrial output, for example, rose by 23.1% in the first half of 1985 (compared with the same period in 1984), well above the planned increase of 8% for the whole year, and requiring a series of measures to slow the growth rate.

China's banking sector is being restructured to meet the needs of the country's rapid economic modernization, and in June 1985 the first foreign joint-venture bank was established. The services sector, in general, is of growing importance: in 1984 the output value of China's tertiary industry reached 150,200m. yuan, up 14.6% over 1983 and accounting for 22.1% of total output. In 1985 NMP reached 676,500m. yuan, an increase of 12.3% over the 1984 total. An ambitious development programme is under way, calling for output from agriculture and industry to quadruple between 1980 and 2000.

In 1984 the value of imports increased by 47.1% over the 1983 total, while exports grew by 32.5%, leaving a trade deficit of 4,000m. yuan. In 1985, however, China's exports rose by only 4.7%, while imports rose by 54.2%, resulting in a greatly increased deficit of more than 44,800m. yuan. In an attempt to restrict the deficit, strict controls were introduced on government purchases of foreign goods, and certain import duties were increased. Despite this, in the first half of 1986 imports rose by 8.6% (compared with the same period in 1985), and the trade deficit for the period totalled US $6,370m. The deficit was attributed mainly to falling export prices, especially for food products and petroleum.

As part of the drive for modernization, China has pursued a much more liberal economic policy. Joint ventures and the acceptance of foreign loans are now permitted, and commercial links have been diversified. Measures to encourage the establishment of joint ventures include the adoption, in October 1986, of a new foreign investment code, which improved credit facilities for foreign investors, and the creation of four 'Special Economic Zones', with increased autonomy and flexibility; 14 coastal cities have also been opened for investment. Around 80% of foreign investment allocated by 1986 was from Hong Kong, mainly in the fields of light industry, textiles and hotels. Outside the special zones, the commune system is being downgraded, and a degree of free enterprise is now encouraged as a means of raising living standards (the per caput annual income of peasants rose by 14.7% between 1982 and 1983). Further liberal reforms include measures to introduce capitalist-style market forces and to reduce central government control, with increased incentives for workers and a new system of taxes. It is hoped that the successes of the reforms in China's agriculture can thus be transferred to industry. The private sector of the economy has been allowed to develop, particularly in the fields of private transport and construction companies, and the sector's output increased by 88% in 1985. In 1983 official figures for China's foreign debt were published for the first time; total debts at the end of September stood at US $3,000m., mainly to the IMF, the World Bank and Japan. The external debt totalled $14,900m. at the end of 1985, and was expected to reach $49,000m. by 1990.

Social Welfare

Western and traditional Chinese medical attention is available in the cities and, to a lesser degree, in rural areas. A fee is charged. In 1984 there were 1.4m. doctors and 198,000 health establishments (including 67,000 hospitals). About 1.3m. 'barefoot doctors', semi-professional peasant physicians, assist with simple cures, treatment and the distribution of contraceptives. There were 2,165,519 hospital beds in 1984. Large factories and other enterprises provide social services for their employees. Industrial wage-earners qualify for pensions. It was announced in 1986 that China was to introduce a social security system to meet the needs of retired people and unemployed contract workers, as part of the planned reform in the labour system.

Education

The education system expanded rapidly after 1949. Fees are charged at all levels. Much importance is attached to kindergartens. Primary education begins for most children at seven years of age and lasts for five years. Secondary education usually begins at 12 years of age and lasts for a further five years, comprising a first cycle of three years and a second cycle of two years. Free higher education was abolished in 1985; instead, college students have to compete for scholarships, which are awarded according to academic ability. Since 1979 education has been included as one of the main priorities for modernization. The whole educational system is to be reformed, with the aim of introducing nine-year compulsory education in 75% of the country by 1995. As a proportion of the total school-age population, enrolment at primary and secondary schools declined from 95% in 1978 to 79% (boys 89%; girls 69%) in 1982. In 1983 China still had 235m. adult illiterates or semi-literates, representing just over 23% of the population. In 1984 some 136m. pupils attended primary schools, while 49m. were at secondary schools and 1,443,000 received higher education.

Tourism

China has enormous potential for tourism, and the sector is developing rapidly. Attractions include dramatic scenery and places of historical interest such as the Great Wall, the Ming Tombs, the Temple of Heaven and the Forbidden City in Beijing, and the terracotta warriors at Xian. Xizang (Tibet), with its monasteries and temples, has also been opened to tourists. Tours of China are organized for groups of visitors, and Western-style hotels have been built in many areas: by the end of 1985 there were more than 700 tourist hotels, with 242,000 beds. In 1985 17.8m. foreigners and overseas Chinese tourists visited China, raising US $1,250m. in foreign exchange (an increase of 10.5% over 1984).

Public Holidays

1987: January/February* (Lunar New Year), 8 March (International Women's Day), 1 May (Labour Day), 1 August (Army Day), 1–2 October (National Days).

1988: January/February* (Lunar New Year), 8 March (International Women's Day), 1 May (Labour Day), 1 August (Army Day), 1–2 October (National Days).

* From the first to the third day of the first moon of the lunar calendar.

Weights and Measures

The metric system is officially in force, but some traditional Chinese units are still used.

Currency and Exchange Rates

100 fen = 10 jiao = 1 yuan.

Exchange rates (30 September 1986):
 £1 sterling = 5.375 yuan;
 US $1 = 3.715 yuan.

Statistical Survey

Source (unless otherwise stated): State Statistical Bureau, San Li He, Beijing; tel. 868521.

Note: Wherever possible, figures in this Survey exclude Taiwan province. In the case of unofficial estimates for China, it is not always clear if Taiwan is included or excluded. Where a Taiwan component is known, either it has been deducted from the all-China figure or its inclusion is noted.

Area and Population

AREA, POPULATION AND DENSITY

Area (sq km)	9,571,300*
Population (census results)	
1 July 1964	694,580,000
1 July 1982	
Males	519,433,369
Females	488,741,919
Total	1,008,175,288
Population (official estimates at 31 December)	
1983	1,024,950,000
1984	1,034,750,000
1985	1,046,390,000
Density (per sq km) at 31 December 1985	109.3

* 3,695,500 sq miles.

BIRTHS AND DEATHS (sample survey, 1985)
Birth rate 17.8 per 1,000; Death rate 6.6 per 1,000.

LIFE EXPECTANCY (years at birth)
Males 61.8 in 1970–75, 66.0 in 1975–80; Females 64.6 in 1970–75, 68.6 in 1975–80 (UN estimates, including Taiwan).
1981 (official estimates): 67.88 (Males 66.43; Females 69.35).

ADMINISTRATIVE DIVISIONS (Previous spelling given in brackets)

	Area ('000 sq km)	Population (official estimates at 31 Dec. 1984)* Total ('000)	Density (per sq km)	Capital of province or region	Estimated population ('000), at 31 Dec. 1984†
Provinces					
Sichuan (Szechwan)	567	101,120	179	Chengdu (Chengtu)	2,540
Shandong (Shantung)	153	76,370	499	Jinan (Tsinan)	1,390
Henan (Honan)	167	76,460	458	Zhengzhou (Chengchow)	1,550
Jiangsu (Kiangsu)	103	61,710	602	Nanjing (Nanking)	2,210
Hebei (Hopei)	188	54,870	293	Shijiazhuang (Shihkiachwang)	1,130
Guangdong (Kwangtung)	212	61,660	291	Guangzhou (Canton)	3,220
Hunan (Hunan)	210	55,610	264	Changsha (Changsha)	1,120
Anhui (Anhwei)	139	51,030	366	Hefei (Hofei)	850
Hubei (Hupeh)	186	48,760	260	Wuhan (Wuhan)	3,340
Zhejiang (Chekiang)	102	39,930	392	Hangzhou (Hangchow)	1,220
Liaoning (Liaoning)	146	36,550	251	Shenyang (Shenyang)	4,130
Yunnan (Yunnan)	394	33,620	85	Kunming (Kunming)	1,480
Jiangxi (Kiangsi)	169	34,210	205	Nanchang (Nanchang)	1,090
Shaanxi (Shensi)	206	29,660	145	Xian (Sian)	2,280
Heilongjiang (Heilungkiang)	469	32,950	70	Harbin (Harbin)	2,590
Shanxi (Shansi)	156	26,000	167	Taiyuan (Taiyuan)	1,840
Guizhou (Kweichow)	176	29,320	167	Guiyang (Kweiyang)	1,350
Fujian (Fukien)	121	26,770	221	Fuzhou (Foochow)	1,160
Jilin (Kirin)	187	22,840	122	Changchun (Changchun)	1,810
Gansu (Kansu)	454	20,160	45	Lanzhou (Lanchow)	1,460
Qinghai (Tsinghai)	721	4,020	6	Xining (Hsining)	364§
Autonomous regions					
Guangxi Zhuang (Kwangsi Chuang)	236	38,060	165	Nanning (Nanning)	780
Nei Monggol (Inner Mongolia)	1,183	19,850	17	Hohhot (Huhehot)	800
Xinjiang Uygur (Sinkiang Uighur)	1,600	13,440	8	Urumqi (Urumchi)	980
Ningxia Hui (Ninghsia Hui)	66	4,060	61	Yinchuan (Yinchuen)	576§
Xizang (Tibet)	1,228	1,970	2	Lhasa (Lhasa)	105§
Municipalities					
Beijing (Peking)	17	9,470	564	—	5,760
Shanghai (Shanghai)	6	12,050	1,944	—	6,880
Tianjin (Tientsin)	11	7,990	707	—	5,300
Total	9,571	1,030,510	108		

* Excluding armed forces, totalling 4,240,000.
† Excluding population in counties under cities' administration.
‡ Excluding islands administered by Taiwan, mainly Jinmen (Quemoy) and Mazu (Matsu), with 57,847 inhabitants at 31 May 1982.
§ 1982 figures.

THE PEOPLE'S REPUBLIC OF CHINA

Statistical Survey

PRINCIPAL TOWNS
(Wade-Giles or other spellings in brackets)
Population at 31 December 1985 (official estimates in '000)

Shanghai (Shang-hai)	6,980
Beijing (Pei-ching or Peking, the capital)	5,860
Tianjin (T'ien-chin or Tientsin)	5,380
Shenyang (Shen-yang or Mukden)	4,200
Wuhan (Wu-han or Hankow)	3,400
Guangzhou (Kuang-chou or Canton)	3,290
Chongqing (Ch'ung-ch'ing or Chungking)	2,780
Harbin (Ha-erh-pin)	2,630
Chengdu (Ch'eng-tu)	2,580
Xian (Hsi-an or Sian)	2,330
Zibo (Tzu-po or Tzepo)	2,300
Nanjing (Nan-ching or Nanking)	2,250
Liupanshui	2,220
Taiyuan (T'ai-yüan)	1,880
Changchun (Ch'ang-ch'un)	1,860
Dalian (Ta-lien or Dairen)	1,630
Zaozhuang	1,590
Zhengzhou (Cheng-chou or Chengchow)	1,590
Kunming (K'un-ming)	1,490
Jinan (Chi-nan or Tsinan)	1,430
Tangshan (T'ang-shan)	1,390
Guiyang (Kuei-yang or Kweiyang)	1,380
Linyi	1,370
Lanzhou (Lan-chou or Lanchow)	1,350
Taian	1,330
Pinxiang	1,290
Suzhou (Su-chou or Soochow)	1,280
Anshan (An-shan)	1,280
Qiqihar (Chi'-ch'i-ha-erh or Tsitsihar)	1,260
Yancheng	1,250
Qingdao (Ch'ing-tao or Tsingtao)	1,250
Hangzhou (Hang-chou or Hangchow)	1,250
Fushun (F'u-shun)	1,240
Yulin	1,230
Chaozhou	1,210
Dongguan	1,210
Xiaogan	1,200
Fuzhou (Fu-chou or Foochow)	1,190
Suining	1,170
Xintai	1,160
Changsha (Chang-sha)	1,160
Shijiazhuang (Shih-chia-chuang or Shihkiachwang)	1,160
Jilin (Chi-lin or Kirin)	1,140
Nanchang (Nan-ch'ang)	1,120
Baotau (Pao-t'ou or Paotow)	1,100
Puyang	1,090
Huainan (Huai-nan or Hwainan)	1,070
Zhongshan	1,060
Luoyang (Lo-yang)	1,050
Weifang	1,040
Laiwu	1,040
Leshan	1,030
Jingmen	1,020
Ningbo	1,020
Urumqi (Urumchi)	1,000
Heze	1,000
Datong (Ta-t'ung or Tatung)	1,000

ECONOMICALLY ACTIVE POPULATION
(official estimates, '000 persons at 31 December)

	1982	1983	1984
Industry*	59,300	60,230	63,380
Construction and resources prospecting	13,400	14,810	18,580
Agriculture, forestry, water conservancy and meteorology	320,130	325,100	325,380
Transport, posts and telecommunications	8,500	9,060	10,800
Commerce, catering trade, service trade and supply and marketing of materials	18,200	20,120	23,540
Scientific research, culture, education, public health and social welfare	16,460	17,000	17,790
Government agencies and people's organizations	6,110	6,460	7,430
Others	4,960	7,260	9,070
Total labour force	447,060	460,040	475,970

* Mining, manufacturing, electricity, gas and water.

THE PEOPLE'S REPUBLIC OF CHINA

Statistical Survey

Agriculture

PRINCIPAL CROPS
(FAO estimates, unless otherwise indicated, '000 metric tons)

	1982	1983	1984
Wheat†	68,470	81,390	87,815
Rice (paddy)†	161,595	168,870	178,260
Barley	3,200	3,000	3,300
Maize†	60,560	68,210	73,410
Rye	1,200	1,300	1,400
Oats	590	560	490
Millet	6,580	7,540	7,025
Sorghum	6,985	8,355	7,715
Other cereals	2,900	3,050	3,400
Potatoes	47,000	50,000	48,000
Sweet potatoes	86,400	96,250	97,550
Cassava (Manioc)	3,600	3,800	4,000
Taro (Coco yam)*	1,308	1,365	1,469
Dry beans	1,600	1,700	1,800
Dry broad beans	2,600	2,300	2,425
Dry peas	2,000	2,000	2,100
Soybeans (Soyabeans)†	9,030	9,760	9,700
Groundnuts (in shell)†	3,916	3,951	4,815

	1982	1983	1984
Castor beans	160	180	180
Sunflower seed	1,286	1,340	1,700
Rapeseed†	5,656	4,287	4,205
Sesame seed†	342	349	476
Linseed	95	93	95
Flax fibre	62	135	68
Cottonseed	7,204	9,274	12,156
Cotton (lint)†	3,598	4,637	6,077
Vegetables and melons*	83,021	85,839	89,318
Fruit (excl. melons)*	9,483	11,192	11,913
Tree nuts*	430	469	496
Sugar cane†	36,882	31,141	39,519
Sugar beet†	6,712	9,182	8,284
Tea (made)†	397	401	414
Tobacco (leaves)	2,180	1,380	1,790
Jute and jute substitutes†	1,060	1,019	1,492
Natural rubber†	153	172	189

* Including Taiwan. † Official estimates.

Source: mainly FAO, *Production Yearbook*.

1985 (official estimates, '000 metric tons): Cotton (lint) 4,150; Sugar cane 51,470; Sugar beet 8,910; Tea (made) 440; Tobacco (leaves) 2,080; Jute and jute substitutes 3,400.

LIVESTOCK ('000 head at 31 December)

	1982	1983	1984
Horses	10,981	10,806	10,978
Mules	4,464	4,593	4,790
Asses	8,999	9,449	9,962
Cattle and buffaloes	76,073	78,084	82,128
Camels	610	564	531
Pigs	300,780	298,536	306,792
Sheep	106,568	98,916	95,193
Goats	75,222	68,035	63,207

Poultry (FAO estimates, million, year ending September): 1,000 in 1982; 1,100 in 1983; 1,200 in 1984.

1985 ('000 head at 31 December): Pigs 331,480; Sheep and goats 156,160.

LIVESTOCK PRODUCTS (FAO estimates, '000 metric tons)

	1982	1983	1984
Beef and veal*	188	218	260
Buffalo meat*	84	101	112
Mutton and lamb*	275	287	322
Goats' meat*	251	259	306
Pig meat*	13,478	13,962	15,103
Horse meat*	39	40	41
Poultry meat*	1,398	1,543	1,718
Other meat*	413	452	473
Edible offals*	682	713	763
Lard*	581	598	632
Tallow*	23	26	28
Cows' milk	1,613	1,839	2,205
Buffaloes' milk	1,450	1,500	1,560
Sheep's milk	504	510	525
Goats' milk	130	135	150
Butter*	39.8	40.5	47.9
Cheese*	112.0	115.3	123.4
Hen eggs	3,240	3,500	3,800
Other poultry eggs*	27.7	29.0	28.0
Honey*	136.6	143.6	160.6
Raw silk (incl. waste)	37.1†	36.9†	35.0
Wool:			
greasy†	202.0	194.0	187.0
clean	121.2	116.4	114.0
Cattle and buffalo hides*	83.0	94.3	106.5
Sheep skins*	72.5	76.6	78.4
Goat skins*	49.6	51.7	58.9

* Including Taiwan. † Official estimates.

Source: FAO, mainly *Production Yearbook*.

Other official estimates ('000 metric tons): Beef, buffalo meat, mutton, goats' meat and pig meat 13,508 (beef and buffalo meat 266, mutton and goats' meat 524, pig meat 12,718) in 1982, 14,021 (beef and buffalo meat 315, mutton and goats' meat 545, pig meat 13,161) in 1983, 15,406 (beef and buffalo meat 373, mutton and goats' meat 586, pig meat 14,447) in 1984, 17,550 in 1985; Cows' milk 1,618 in 1982, 1,845 in 1983, 2,186 in 1984, 2,500 in 1985.

Forestry

ROUNDWOOD REMOVALS
(FAO estimates, '000 cubic metres, including Taiwan)

	1981	1982	1983
Industrial wood	69,672	72,951	77,014
Fuel wood	154,633	154,636	154,636
Total	224,305	227,587	231,650

1984: Production as in 1983 (FAO estimate).
Source: FAO, *Yearbook of Forest Products*.
Timber production (official estimates, '000 cubic metres): 49,420 in 1981; 50,410 in 1982; 52,320 in 1983; 55,000 in 1984; 63,100 in 1985.

SAWNWOOD PRODUCTION
(FAO estimates, '000 cubic metres, including Taiwan)

	1981	1982	1983
Coniferous sawnwood	13,938	14,617	15,330
Broadleaved sawnwood	8,190	8,592	9,014
Total	22,128	23,209	24,344

1984: Production as in 1983 (FAO estimate).
Source: FAO, *Yearbook of Forest Products*.

Fishing

('000 metric tons, live weight)

	1982	1983	1984
Fishes	3,904.4	4,107.4	4,736.2
Crustaceans	525.5	549.7	580.0
Molluscs	478.8	537.2	590.7
Jellyfishes	18.0	19.0*	19.8*
Total catch	4,926.7	5,213.3	5,926.8
of which:			
Inland waters	1,562.0	1,840.8	2,249.7
Pacific Ocean	3,364.7	3,372.5	3,677.1

* FAO estimate.

Aquatic plants ('000 metric tons): 1,381.9 in 1982; 1,487.6 in 1983; 1,627.7 in 1984.

Source: FAO, *Yearbook of Fishery Statistics*.

Aquatic products (official estimates, '000 metric tons): 5,160 in 1982; 5,460 in 1983; 6,060 in 1984; 6,970 in 1985.

Mining

(Unofficial estimates, unless otherwise indicated)

		1981	1982	1983
Hard coal*	'000 metric tons	598,000	641,000	688,000
Brown coal (incl. lignite)*	'000 metric tons	23,000	25,000	27,000
Crude petroleum*	'000 metric tons	101,221	102,123	106,068
Iron ore*†	'000 metric tons	52,295	53,660	56,834
Bauxite	'000 metric tons	1,500	1,500	1,500
Copper ore†	'000 metric tons	200	200	200
Lead ore†	'000 metric tons	160	160	160
Magnesite	'000 metric tons	2,000	2,000	2,000
Manganese ore†	'000 metric tons	479	479	479
Zinc ore†	'000 metric tons	160	160	160
Salt (unrefined)*	'000 metric tons	18,320	16,380	15,876
Phosphate rock	'000 metric tons	11,500	12,500	12,500
Potash‡	'000 metric tons	20	26	25
Sulphur (native)	'000 metric tons	200	200	200
Iron pyrites (unroasted)	'000 metric tons	5,900	4,100	n.a.
Natural graphite	'000 metric tons	184	185	n.a.
Antimony ore†	metric tons	10,000	10,000	10,000
Mercury	metric tons	700	700	700
Molybdenum ore†	metric tons	2,000	2,000	2,000
Silver†	metric tons	78	78	78
Tin concentrates†	metric tons	16,000	16,000	17,000
Tungsten concentrates†	metric tons	13,480	12,530	12,530
Gold†	kg	52,876	55,986	59,097
Natural gas*	million cu m	12,740	11,930	12,210

* Official estimates.
† Figures refer to the metal content of ores and concentrates.
‡ Potassium oxide (K_2O) content of potash salts mined.

Sources for unofficial estimates: For tin, Metallgesellschaft Aktiengesellschaft (Frankfurt am Main, Federal Republic of Germany); for all other minerals, US Bureau of Mines.

Official estimates ('000 metric tons): Coal (incl. brown coal) 772,000 in 1984, 850,000 in 1985; Crude petroleum 114,530 in 1984, 125,000 in 1985; Iron ore 63,350 in 1984; Salt 16,420 in 1984; Natural gas (million cubic metres) 12,400 in 1984.

Industry

SELECTED PRODUCTS
Unofficial Estimates

		1981	1982	1983
Soyabean oil (crude)[1]	'000 metric tons	480	430	450
Palm oil (crude)[2]	'000 metric tons	190	200	200
Tung oil[2]	'000 metric tons	58	62	62
Beer[3]	'000 hectolitres	9,100	11,730	n.a.
Rayon continuous filaments[4]	'000 metric tons	80.0	80.0	85
Rayon discontinuous fibres[4]	'000 metric tons	105.0	105.0	112.0
Non-cellulosic continuous filaments[4]	'000 metric tons	55.0	67.0	75.1
Non-cellulosic discontinuous fibres[4]	'000 metric tons	292.0	302.0	325.1
Plywood[2,5]	'000 cu m	1,634	1,634	1,634
Mechanical wood pulp[2,5]	'000 metric tons	345	345	355
Chemical wood pulp[2,5]	'000 metric tons	998	998	1,000
Other fibre pulp[2,5]	'000 metric tons	3,466	3,466	3,616
Newsprint[2,5]	'000 metric tons	1,105	1,125	1,143
Other paper and paperboard[2,5]	'000 metric tons	5,583	5,663	5,745
Synthetic rubber[3]	'000 metric tons	124.9	136.0	166.0
Sulphur[6,7] (a)	'000 metric tons	300	300	300
(b)	'000 metric tons	1,800	1,800	2,100
Motor spirit (petrol)[6]	'000 metric tons	10,938	10,944	12,277
Kerosene[3]	'000 metric tons	3,670	3,840	4,102
Distillate fuel oils[6]	'000 metric tons	17,780	17,460	19,035
Residual fuel oil[6]	'000 metric tons	28,175	26,096	28,967
Aluminium (unwrought)[6]	'000 metric tons	360	370	380
Refined copper (unwrought)[6]	'000 metric tons	280	280	280
Lead (unwrought)[6]	'000 metric tons	175	175	175
Tin (unwrought)[8]	'000 metric tons	16.5	16.5	16.5
Zinc (unwrought)[6]	'000 metric tons	160	160	160

[1] Source: US Department of Agriculture. [2] Source: FAO.
[3] Source: UN, *Industrial Statistics Yearbook*.
[4] Source: Textile Economics Bureau Inc., New York, USA. [5] Including Taiwan.
[6] Source: US Bureau of Mines.
[7] Figures refer to (a) sulphur recovered as a by-product in the purification of coal-gas, in petroleum refineries, gas plants and from copper, lead and zinc sulphide ores; and (b) the sulphur content of iron and copper pyrites, including pyrite concentrates obtained from copper, lead and zinc ores.
[8] Source: Metallgesellschaft Aktiengesellschaft, Frankfurt am Main, Federal Republic of Germany.

1984 (FAO estimates, '000 metric tons): Palm oil 210; Tung oil 62.

THE PEOPLE'S REPUBLIC OF CHINA — Statistical Survey

Official Estimates

		1983	1984	1985
Raw sugar	'000 metric tons	3,771	3,800	4,450
Cotton yarn	'000 metric tons	3,270	3,219	3,510
Woven cotton fabrics	million metres	14,880	13,700	14,300
Woollen fabrics	'000 metres	142,910	180,490	210,000
Silk fabrics	'000 metres	999,000	117,800	n.a.
Chemical fibres	'000 metric tons	540.7	734.9	n.a.
Paper and paperboard	'000 metric tons	6,610	7,560	8,260
Rubber tyres	'000	12,710	15,690	n.a.
Ethylene (Ethene)	'000 metric tons	653.7	648.0	n.a.
Sulphuric acid	'000 metric tons	8,696	8,172	6,690
Caustic soda (Sodium hydroxide)	'000 metric tons	2,122.8	2,222.3	n.a.
Soda ash (Sodium carbonate)	'000 metric tons	1,793.2	1,880.3	2,000
Insecticides	'000 metric tons	331.3	298.5	205
Nitrogenous fertilizers (a)*	'000 metric tons	11,094	12,210	
Phosphate fertilizers (b)*	'000 metric tons	2,666	2,360	13,350
Potash fertilizers (c)*	'000 metric tons	29	n.a.	
Plastics	'000 metric tons	1,121	1,179	n.a.
Coke-oven coke	'000 metric tons	34,510	n.a.	n.a.
Cement	'000 metric tons	108,250	123,020	142,460
Pig-iron	'000 metric tons	37,380	40,010	n.a.
Crude steel	'000 metric tons	40,020	43,470	46,660
Internal combustion engines†	'000 horse-power	28,990	40,720	n.a.
Tractors (over 20 horse-power)	'000	37.0	39.7	44.6
Sewing machines	'000	10,872	9,348	9,860
Railway locomotives (diesel)	number	589	658	746
Railway freight wagons	number	15,785	18,100	n.a.
Road motor vehicles	'000	239.8	316.4	439
Bicycles	'000	27,582	28,611	32,350
Wrist watches	'000	34,690	37,982	41,730
Radio receivers‡	'000	19,989	22,203	n.a.
Television receivers	'000	6,840	10,038	16,220
Cameras	'000	925.6	1,261	1,800
Electric energy	million kWh	351,400	377,000	407,300

* Production in terms of (a) nitrogen; (b) phosphoric acid; or (c) potassium oxide.
† Sales.   ‡ Portable battery sets only.

Finance

CURRENCY AND EXCHANGE RATES

Monetary Units
100 fen (cents) = 1 jiao (chiao) = 1 Renminbiao (People's Bank Dollar), usually called a yuan.

Denominations
Coins: 1, 2 and 5 fen.
Notes: 10, 20 and 50 fen; 1, 2, 5 and 10 yuan.

Sterling and Dollar Equivalents (30 September 1986)
£1 sterling = 5.375 yuan;
US $1 = 3.715 yuan;
100 yuan = £18.60 = $26.92.

Average Exchange Rate (yuan per US $)
1983   1.9757
1984   2.3200
1985   2.9367

STATE BUDGET (million yuan)

Revenue	1985	1986*
Tax receipts	204,079	205,651
Funds for projects	14,679	15,000
State treasury bonds	6,061	6,000
Receipts from enterprises	4,375	9,617
Other domestic receipts	5,224	
Sub-total	234,418	236,268
Less Subsidies	50,702	27,621
Total domestic receipts	183,716	208,647
Foreign loans	2,924	5,500
Total	186,640	214,147

Expenditure	1985	1986*
Capital construction	58,380	56,780
Subsidies to enterprises	10,342	6,240
Agriculture and rural communes	10,104	11,790
Education, science and health services	31,670	35,700
National defence	19,153	20,020
Administrative expenses	13,058	14,375
Total (incl. others)	184,478	214,147

* Planned figures.

THE PEOPLE'S REPUBLIC OF CHINA

SEVENTH FIVE-YEAR PLAN, 1986-90
(proposed investment in fixed assets, '000m. yuan)

State enterprises and institutions	896
Capital construction	500
by central departments	375
by local authorities	112.5
Special Economic Zones	12.5
Technological transformation and equipment renewal	276
Other projects	120
Collective enterprises	160
Private enterprises in towns and counties	240
Total	**1,296**

INTERNATIONAL RESERVES
(US $ million at 31 December)

	1983	1984	1985
Gold*	464	435	486
IMF special drawing rights	335	406	483
Reserve position in IMF	176	255	332
Foreign exchange	14,476	16,705	11,913
Total	**15,451**	**17,801**	**13,214**

* Valued at 35 SDR per troy ounce.
Source: IMF, *International Financial Statistics*.

MONEY SUPPLY (million yuan at 31 December)

	1983	1984	1985
Total money	137,050	212,590	248,320
of which:			
Currency in circulation	52,980	79,210	98,780

Source: IMF, *International Financial Statistics*.

COST OF LIVING
(General Retail Price Index. Base: 1950 = 100)

	1982	1983	1984
All items	153.3	155.6	160.0

NATIONAL ACCOUNTS
Net Material Product* (million yuan at current prices)

	1982	1983	1984
Agriculture	186,800	209,700	249,900
Industry	180,300	196,000	228,600
Construction	20,900	25,900	29,300
Transport	15,000	16,000	18,900
Commerce	23,100	25,400	37,600
Total	**426,100**	**473,000**	**564,300**

1985: Total 676,500m. yuan.

* Defined as the total net value of goods and 'productive' services, including turnover taxes, produced by the economy. This excludes economic activities not contributing directly to material production, such as public administration, defence and personal and professional services.

BALANCE OF PAYMENTS (US $ million)

	1983	1984	1985
Merchandise exports f.o.b.	20,707	23,905	25,108
Merchandise imports f.o.b.	−18,717	−23,891	−38,231
Trade balance	**1,990**	**14**	**−13,123**
Exports of services	4,275	4,819	4,533
Imports of services	−2,289	−2,766	−3,070
Balance on goods and services	**3,976**	**2,067**	**−11,660**
Private unrequited transfers	436	305	171
Government unrequited transfers	75	137	72
Current balance	**4,487**	**2,509**	**−11,417**
Long-term capital (net)	1,172	1,608	4,439
Short-term capital (net)	−28	−411	2,270
Net errors and omissions	−848	−1,847	34
Total (net monetary movements)	**4,783**	**1,859**	**−4,674**
Valuation changes (net)	2	−42	36
Changes in reserves	**4,785**	**1,816**	**−4,638**

Source: IMF, *International Financial Statistics*.

External Trade

COMMODITY GROUPS (million yuan)

Imports f.o.b.	1982	1983	1984
Food and live animals	7,788	6,156	5,140
Beverages and tobacco	241	92	275
Crude materials (inedible) except fuels	5,585	4,848	5,696
Mineral fuels, lubricants, etc.	340	219	313
Animal and vegetable oils, fats and waxes	199	138	180
Chemicals and related products	5,444	6,277	9,492
Basic manufactures	7,241	12,402	16,457
Machinery and transport equipment	5,940	7,865	16,805
Miscellaneous manufactured articles	902	1,542	2,705
Other commodities and transactions	2,090	2,643	4,984
Total	35,769	42,182	62,047

1985 (million yuan): Total imports 125,780; total exports 80,930.

Exports f.o.b.	1982	1983	1984
Food and live animals	5,393	5,627	7,207
Beverages and tobacco	180	205	245
Crude materials (inedible) except fuels	3,064	3,732	5,328
Mineral fuels, lubricants, etc.	9,852	9,202	13,365
Animal and vegetable oils, fats and waxes	144	207	319
Chemicals and related products	2,218	2,467	3,037
Basic manufactures	7,976	8,609	11,206
Machinery and transport equipment	2,341	2,406	3,333
Miscellaneous manufactured articles	6,864	7,503	10,450
Other commodities and transactions	3,401	3,875	3,566
Total	41,433	43,833	58,056

PRINCIPAL TRADING PARTNERS (million yuan)

Imports	1982	1983	1984
Argentina	282.9	1,287.6	203.8
Australia	1,726.2	1,216.2	2,122.9
Belgium	315.4	444.6	494.2
Brazil	249.2	537.9	1,001.9
Canada	2,355.5	3,149.2	2,490.3
France	440.7	1,262.8	1,839.3
German Democratic Republic	256.8	370.8	335.3
Germany, Federal Republic	1,826.3	2,397.5	2,970.4
Hong Kong	2,482.3	3,393.2	6,765.4
Italy	599.3	601.5	1,052.4
Japan	7,386.2	10,904.8	19,417.9
Korea, Democratic People's Repub.	577.7	504.6	642.4
Romania	804.2	789.5	1,011.4
Switzerland	318.7	452.6	401.7
USSR	462.4	874.4	1,596.7
United Kingdom	489.8	1,110.3	1,189.8
USA	8,109.2	5,462.8	9,173.5
Total (including others)	35,769.2	42,182.5	62,046.8

Exports	1982	1983	1984
Brazil	715.8	716.1	896.7
Canada	323.3	413.1	591.2
France	529.6	457.7	538.8
Germany, Federal Republic	1,463.1	1,704.5	1,793.9
Hong Kong	9,801.4	11,502.5	15,389.4
Italy	444.6	461.0	706.1
Japan	9,103.2	8,962.0	11,946.0
Jordan	2,486.5	3,009.6	2,928.3
Korea, Democratic People's Repub.	534.9	542.5	533.6
Macau	492.1	531.8	710.7
Netherlands	554.2	647.3	741.5
Pakistan	381.5	444.1	598.3
Romania	526.2	578.6	706.9
Singapore	1,194.9	1,124.6	2,901.9
USSR	273.1	633.0	1,379.0
United Kingdom	581.4	1,193.1	772.7
USA	3,334.9	3,397.3	5,375.4
Total (including others)	41,433.1	43,832.7	58,055.7

Transport

	1983	1984	1985
Freight (million ton-km):			
Railways	664,600	724,700	812,500
Roads	108,400	35,900	35,500
Inland waterways	578,800	632,900	757,200
Air	230	310	415
Passenger-km (million):			
Railways	177,600	204,600	241,600
Roads	110,600	129,400	154,300
Inland waterways	15,400	15,200	17,200
Air	5,900	8,400	11,700

SEA-BORNE SHIPPING (freight traffic in '000 metric tons)

	1983	1984	1985
Goods loaded and unloaded	249,520	275,500	311,000

Communications Media

(million copies)

	1983	1984	1985
Newspapers	15,510	18,060	18,690
Magazines	1,770	2,180	2,500
Books	5,800	6,270	6,650

Radio receivers: 15m. in use in 1984.
Television receivers: 9.9m. in use in 1984.

Education

(1984)

	Institutions	Full-time Teachers ('000)	Students ('000)
Kindergartens	166,526	491	12,571
Primary schools	853,740	5,369	135,571
Secondary schools			
Lower secondary schools	75,867	2,097	38,643
Upper secondary schools	17,847	459	6,898
Secondary technical schools	2,293	118	811
Teacher training schools	1,008	42	511
Agricultural schools	4,622	55	907
Vocational schools	2,380	48	837
Special schools	330	6	39
Higher education	902	315	1,443

Directory

The Constitution

A new constitution was adopted on 4 December 1982 by the Fifth Session of the Fifth National People's Congress. Its principal provisions are set out below. The Preamble, which is not included here, states that 'Taiwan is part of the sacred territory of the People's Republic of China'.

GENERAL PRINCIPLES

Article 1: The People's Republic of China is a socialist state under the people's democratic dictatorship led by the working class and based on the alliance of workers and peasants.

The socialist system is the basic system of the People's Republic of China. Sabotage of the socialist system by any organization or individual is prohibited.

Article 2: All power in the People's Republic of China belongs to the people.

The organs through which the people exercise state power are the National People's Congress and the local people's congresses at different levels.

The people administer state affairs and manage economic, cultural and social affairs through various channels and in various ways in accordance with the law.

Article 3: The state organs of the People's Republic of China apply the principle of democratic centralism.

The National People's Congress and the local people's congresses at different levels are instituted through democratic election. They are responsible to the people and subject to their supervision.

All administrative, judicial and procuratorial organs of the state are created by the people's congresses to which they are responsible and under whose supervision they operate.

The division of functions and powers between the central and local state organs is guided by the principle of giving full play to the initiative and enthusiasm of the local authorities under the unified leadership of the central authorities.

Article 4: All nationalities in the People's Republic of China are equal. The state protects the lawful rights and interests of the minority nationalities and upholds and develops the relationship of equality, unity and mutual assistance among all of China's nationalities. Discrimination against and oppression of any nationality are prohibited; any acts that undermine the unity of the nationalities or instigate their secession are prohibited.

The state helps the areas inhabited by minority nationalities speed up their economic and cultural development in accordance with the peculiarities and needs of the different minority nationalities.

Regional autonomy is practised in areas where people of minority nationalities live in compact communities; in these areas organs of self-government are established for the exercise of the right of autonomy. All the national autonomous areas are inalienable parts of the People's Republic of China.

The people of all nationalities have the freedom to use and develop their own spoken and written languages, and to preserve or reform their own ways and customs.

Article 5: The state upholds the uniformity and dignity of the socialist legal system.

No law or administrative or local rules and regulations shall contravene the Constitution.

All state organs, the armed forces, all political parties and public organizations and all enterprises and undertakings must abide by the Constitution and the law. All acts in violation of the Constitution and the law must be looked into.

No organization or individual may enjoy the privilege of being above the Constitution and the law.

Article 6: The basis of the socialist economic system of the People's Republic of China is socialist public ownership of the means of production, namely, ownership by the whole people and collective ownership by the working people.

The system of socialist public ownership supersedes the system of exploitation of man by man; it applies the principle of 'from each according to his ability, to each according to his work.'

Article 7: The state economy is the sector of socialist economy under ownership by the whole people; it is the leading force in the national economy. The state ensures the consolidation and growth of the state economy.

Article 8: Rural people's communes, agricultural producers' co-operatives, and other forms of co-operative economy such as producers', supply and marketing, credit and consumers' co-operatives, belong to the sector of socialist economy under collective ownership by the working people. Working people who are members of rural economic collectives have the right, within the limits prescribed by law, to farm private plots of cropland and hilly land, engage in household sideline production and raise privately-owned livestock.

The various forms of co-operative economy in the cities and towns, such as those in the handicraft, industrial, building, transport, commercial and service trades, all belong to the sector of socialist economy under collective ownership by the working people.

The state protects the lawful rights and interests of the urban and rural economic collectives and encourages, guides and helps the growth of the collective economy.

Article 9: Mineral resources, waters, forests, mountains, grassland, unreclaimed land, beaches and other natural resources are owned by the state, that is, by the whole people, with the exception of the forests, mountains, grassland, unreclaimed land and beaches that are owned by collectives in accordance with the law.

The state ensures the rational use of natural resources and protects rare animals and plants. The appropriation or damage of natural resources by any organization or individual by whatever means is prohibited.

Article 10: Land in the cities is owned by the state.

Land in the rural and suburban areas is owned by collectives except for those portions which belong to the state in accordance with the law; house sites and private plots of cropland and hilly land are also owned by collectives.

The state may in the public interest take over land for its use in accordance with the law.

No organization or individual may appropriate, buy, sell or lease land, or unlawfully transfer land in other ways.

All organizations and individuals who use land must make rational use of the land.

Article 11: The individual economy of urban and rural working people, operated within the limits prescribed by law, is a complement to the socialist public economy. The state protects the lawful rights and interests of the individual economy.

The state guides, helps and supervises the individual economy by exercising administrative control.

Article 12: Socialist public property is sacred and inviolable.

The state protects socialist public property. Appropriation or damage of state or collective property by any organization or individual by whatever means is prohibited.

Article 13: The state protects the right of citizens to own lawfully earned income, savings, houses and other lawful property.

The state protects by law the right of citizens to inherit private property.

Article 14: The state continuously raises labour productivity, improves economic results and develops the productive forces by enhancing the enthusiasm of the working people, raising the level of their technical skill, disseminating advanced science and technology, improving the systems of economic administration and enterprise operation and management, instituting the socialist system of responsibility in various forms and improving organization of work.

The state practises strict economy and combats waste.

The state properly apportions accumulation and consumption, pays attention to the interests of the collective and the individual as well as of the state and, on the basis of expanded production, gradually improves the material and cultural life of the people.

Article 15: The state practises economic planning on the basis of socialist public ownership. It ensures the proportionate and co-ordinated growth of the national economy through overall balancing by economic planning and the supplementary role of regulation by the market.

Disturbance of the orderly functioning of the social economy or disruption of the state economic plan by any organization or individual is prohibited.

Article 16: State enterprises have decision-making power in operation and management within the limits prescribed by law, on condition that they submit to unified leadership by the state and fulfil all their obligations under the state plan.

State enterprises practise democratic management through congresses of workers and staff and in other ways in accordance with the law.

Article 17: Collective economic organizations have decision-making power in conducting independent economic activities, on condition that they accept the guidance of the state plan and abide by the relevant laws.

Collective economic organizations practise democratic management in accordance with the law, with the entire body of their workers electing or removing their managerial personnel and deciding on major issues concerning operation and management.

Article 18: The People's Republic of China permits foreign enterprises, other foreign economic organizations and individual foreigners to invest in China and to enter into various forms of economic co-operation with Chinese enterprises and other economic organizations in accordance with the law of the People's Republic of China.

All foreign enterprises and other foreign economic organizations in China, as well as joint ventures with Chinese and foreign investment located in China, shall abide by the law of the People's Republic of China. Their lawful rights and interests are protected by the law of the People's Republic of China.

Article 19: The state develops socialist educational undertakings and works to raise the scientific and cultural level of the whole nation.

The state runs schools of various types, makes primary education compulsory and universal, develops secondary, vocational and higher education and promotes pre-school education.

The state develops educational facilities of various types in order to wipe out illiteracy and provide political, cultural, scientific, technical and professional education for workers, peasants, state functionaries and other working people. It encourages people to become educated through self-study.

The state encourages the collective economic organizations, state enterprises and undertakings and other social forces to set up educational institutions of various types in accordance with the law.

The state promotes the nationwide use of Putonghua (common speech based on Beijing pronunciation).

Article 20: The state promotes the development of the natural and social sciences, disseminates scientific and technical knowledge, and commends and rewards achievements in scientific research as well as technological discoveries and inventions.

Article 21: The state develops medical and health services, promotes modern medicine and traditional Chinese medicine, encourages and supports the setting up of various medical and health facilities by the rural economic collectives, state enterprises and undertakings and neighbourhood organizations, and promotes sanitation activities of a mass character, all to protect the people's health.

The state develops physical culture and promotes mass sports activities to build up the people's physique.

Article 22: The state promotes the development of literature and art, the press, broadcasting and television undertakings, publishing and distribution services, libraries, museums, cultural centres and other cultural undertakings, that serve the people and socialism, and sponsors mass cultural activities.

The state protects places of scenic and historical interest, valuable cultural monuments and relics and other important items of China's historical and cultural heritage.

Article 23: The state trains specialized personnel in all fields who serve socialism, increases the number of intellectuals and creates conditions to give full scope to their role in socialist modernization.

Article 24: The state strengthens the building of socialist spiritual civilization through spreading education in high ideals and morality, general education and education in discipline and the legal system, and through promoting the formulation and observance of rules of conduct and common pledges by different sections of the people in urban and rural areas.

The state advocates the civic virtues of love for the motherland, for the people, for labour, for science and for socialism; it educates the people in patriotism, collectivism, internationalism and communism and in dialectical and historical materialism; it combats capitalist, feudalist and other decadent ideas.

Article 25: The state promotes family planning so that population growth may fit the plans for economic and social development.

Article 26: The state protects and improves the living environment and the ecological environment, and prevents and remedies pollution and other public hazards.

The state organizes and encourages afforestation and the protection of forests.

Article 27: All state organs carry out the principle of simple and efficient administration, the system of responsibility for work and the system of training functionaries and appraising their work in order constantly to improve quality of work and efficiency and combat bureaucratism.

All state organs and functionaries must rely on the support of the people, keep in close touch with them, heed their opinions and suggestions, accept their supervision and work hard to serve them.

Article 28: The state maintains public order and suppresses treasonable and other counter-revolutionary activities; it penalizes actions that endanger public security and disrupt the socialist economy and other criminal activities, and punishes and reforms criminals.

Article 29: The armed forces of the People's Republic of China belong to the people. Their tasks are to strengthen national defence, resist aggression, defend the motherland, safeguard the people's peaceful labour, participate in national reconstruction, and work hard to serve the people.

The state strengthens the revolutionization, modernization and regularization of the armed forces in order to increase the national defence capability.

Article 30: The administrative division of the People's Republic of China is as follows:

(1) The country is divided into provinces, autonomous regions and municipalities directly under the central government;

(2) Provinces and autonomous regions are divided into autonomous prefectures, counties, autonomous counties and cities;

(3) Counties and autonomous counties are divided into townships, nationality townships and towns.

Municipalities directly under the central government and other large cities are divided into districts and counties. Autonomous prefectures are divided into counties, autonomous counties, and cities.

All autonomous regions, autonomous prefectures and autonomous counties are national autonomous areas.

Article 31: The state may establish special administrative regions when necessary. The systems to be instituted in special administrative regions shall be prescribed by law enacted by the National People's Congress in the light of the specific conditions.

Article 32: The People's Republic of China protects the lawful rights and interests of foreigners within Chinese territory, and while on Chinese territory foreigners must abide by the law of the People's Republic of China.

The People's Republic of China may grant asylum to foreigners who request it for political reasons.

FUNDAMENTAL RIGHTS AND DUTIES OF CITIZENS

Article 33: All persons holding the nationality of the People's Republic of China are citizens of the People's Republic of China.

All citizens of the People's Republic of China are equal before the law.

Every citizen enjoys the rights and at the same time must perform the duties prescribed by the Constitution and the law.

Article 34: All citizens of the People's Republic of China who have reached the age of 18 have the right to vote and stand for election, regardless of nationality, race, sex, occupation, family background, religious belief, education, property status, or length of residence, except persons deprived of political rights according to law.

Article 35: Citizens of the People's Republic of China enjoy freedom of speech, of the press, of assembly, of association, of procession and of demonstration.

Article 36: Citizens of the People's Republic of China enjoy freedom of religious belief.

No state organ, public organization or individual may compel citizens to believe in, or not to believe in, any religion; nor may they discriminate against citizens who believe in, or do not believe in, any religion.

The state protects normal religious activities. No one may make use of religion to engage in activities that disrupt public order, impair the health of citizens or interfere with the educational system of the state.

Religious bodies and religious affairs are not subject to any foreign domination.

Article 37: The freedom of person of citizens of the People's Republic of China is inviolable.

No citizen may be arrested except with the approval or by decision of a people's procuratorate or by decision of a people's court, and arrests must be made by a public security organ.

Unlawful deprivation or restriction of citizens' freedom of person by detention or other means is prohibited; and unlawful search of the person of citizens is prohibited.

Article 38: The personal dignity of citizens of the People's Republic of China is inviolable. Insult, libel, false charge or frame-up directed against citizens by any means is prohibited.

Article 39: The home of citizens of the People's Republic of China is inviolable. Unlawful search of, or intrusion into, a citizen's home is prohibited.

Article 40: The freedom and privacy of correspondence of citizens of the People's Republic of China are protected by law. No organization or individual may, on any ground, infringe upon the freedom and privacy of citizens' correspondence except in cases where, to meet the needs of state security or of investigation into criminal offences, public security or procuratorial organs are permitted to censor correspondence in accordance with procedures prescribed by law.

Article 41: Citizens of the People's Republic of China have the right to criticize and make suggestions to any state organ or functionary. Citizens have the right to make to relevant state organs complaints and charges against, or exposures of, violation of the law or dereliction of duty by any state organ or functionary; but fabrication or distortion of facts with the intention of libel or frame-up is prohibited.

In case of complaints, charges or exposures made by citizens, the state organ concerned must deal with them in a responsible manner after ascertaining the facts. No one may suppress such complaints, charges and exposures, or retaliate against the citizen making them.

Citizens who have suffered losses through infringement of their civic rights by any state organ or functionary have the right to compensation in accordance with the law.

Article 42: Citizens of the People's Republic of China have the right as well as the duty to work.

Using various channels, the state creates conditions for employment, strengthens labour protection, improves working conditions and, on the basis of expanded production, increases remuneration for work and social benefits.

Work is the glorious duty of every able-bodied citizen. All working people in state enterprises and in urban and rural economic collectives should perform their tasks with an attitude consonant with their status as masters of the country. The state promotes socialist labour emulation, and commends and rewards model and advanced workers. The state encourages citizens to take part in voluntary labour.

The state provides necessary vocational training to citizens before they are employed.

Article 43: Working people in the People's Republic of China have the right to rest.

The state expands facilities for rest and recuperation of working people, and prescribes working hours and vacations for workers and staff.

Article 44: The state prescribes by law the system of retirement for workers and staff in enterprises and undertakings and for functionaries of organs of state. The livelihood of retired personnel is ensured by the state and society.

Article 45: Citizens of the People's Republic of China have the right to material assistance from the state and society when they are old, ill or disabled. The state develops the social insurance, social relief and medical and health services that are required to enable citizens to enjoy this right.

The state and society ensure the livelihood of disabled members of the armed forces, provide pensions to the families of martyrs and give preferential treatment to the families of military personnel.

The state and society help make arrangements for the work, livelihood and education of the blind, deaf-mute and other handicapped citizens.

Article 46: Citizens of the People's Republic of China have the duty as well as the right to receive education.

The state promotes the all-round moral, intellectual and physical development of children and young people.

Article 47: Citizens of the People's Republic of China have the freedom to engage in scientific research, literary and artistic creation and other cultural pursuits. The state encourages and assists creative endeavours conducive to the interests of the people that are made by citizens engaged in education, science, technology, literature, art and other cultural work.

Article 48: Women in the People's Republic of China enjoy equal rights with men in all spheres of life, political, economic, cultural and social, including family life.

The state protects the rights and interests of women, applies the principle of equal pay for equal work for men and women alike and trains and selects cadres from among women.

Article 49: Marriage, the family and mother and child are protected by the state.

Both husband and wife have the duty to practise family planning.

Parents have the duty to rear and educate their minor children, and children who have come of age have the duty to support and assist their parents.

Violation of the freedom of marriage is prohibited. Maltreatment of old people, women and children is prohibited.

Article 50: The People's Republic of China protects the legitimate rights and interests of Chinese nationals residing abroad and protects the lawful rights and interests of returned overseas Chinese and of the family members of Chinese nationals residing abroad.

Article 51: The exercise by citizens of the People's Republic of China of their freedoms and rights may not infringe upon the interests of the state, of society and of the collective, or upon the lawful freedoms and rights of other citizens.

Article 52: It is the duty of citizens of the People's Republic of China to safeguard the unity of the country and the unity of all its nationalities.

Article 53: Citizens of the People's Republic of China must abide by the Constitution and the law, keep state secrets, protect public property and observe labour discipline and public order and respect social ethics.

Article 54: It is the duty of citizens of the People's Republic of China to safeguard the security, honour and interests of the motherland; they must not commit acts detrimental to the security, honour and interests of the motherland.

Article 55: It is the sacred obligation of every citizen of the People's Republic of China to defend the motherland and resist aggression.

It is the honourable duty of citizens of the People's Republic of China to perform military service and join the militia in accordance with the law.

Article 56: It is the duty of citizens of the People's Republic of China to pay taxes in accordance with the law.

STRUCTURE OF THE STATE

The National People's Congress

Article 57: The National People's Congress of the People's Republic of China is the highest organ of state power. Its permanent body is the Standing Committee of the National People's Congress.

Article 58: The National People's Congress and its Standing Committee exercise the legislative power of the state.

Article 59: The National People's Congress is composed of deputies elected by the provinces, autonomous regions and municipalities directly under the Central Government, and by the armed forces. All the minority nationalities are entitled to appropriate representation.

Election of deputies to the National People's Congress is conducted by the Standing Committee of the National People's Congress.

The number of deputies to the National People's Congress and the manner of their election are prescribed by law.

Article 60: The National People's Congress is elected for a term of five years.

Two months before the expiration of the term of office of a National People's Congress, its Standing Committee must ensure that the election of deputies to the succeeding National People's Congress is completed. Should exceptional circumstances prevent such an election, it may be postponed by decision of a majority vote of more than two-thirds of all those on the Standing Committee of the incumbent National People's Congress, and the term of office of the incumbent National People's Congress may be extended. The election of deputies to the succeeding National People's Congress must be completed within one year after the termination of such exceptional circumstances.

Article 61: The National People's Congress meets in session once a year and is convened by its Standing Committee. A session of the National People's Congress may be convened at any time the Standing Committee deems this necessary, or when more than one-fifth of the deputies to the National People's Congress so propose.

When the National People's Congress meets, it elects a presidium to conduct its session.

Article 62: The National People's Congress exercises the following functions and powers:

(1) to amend the Constitution;

(2) to supervise the enforcement of the Constitution;

(3) to enact and amend basic statutes concerning criminal offences, civil affairs, the state organs and other matters;

(4) to elect the President and the Vice-President of the People's Republic of China;

(5) to decide on the choice of the Premier of the State Council upon nomination by the President of the People's Republic of China, and to decide on the choice of the Vice-Premiers, State Councillors, Ministers in charge of Ministries or Commissions and the Auditor-General and the Secretary-General of the State Council upon nomination by the Premier;

(6) to elect the Chairman of the Central Military Commission and, upon his nomination, to decide on the choice of all the others on the Central Military Commission;

(7) to elect the President of the Supreme People's Court;

(8) to elect the Procurator-General of the Supreme People's Procuratorate;

(9) to examine and approve the plan for national economic and social development and the reports on its implementation;

(10) to examine and approve the state budget and the report on its implementation;

(11) to alter or annul inappropriate decisions of the Standing Committee of the National People's Congress;

(12) to approve the establishment of provinces, autonomous regions, and municipalities directly under the Central Government;

(13) to decide on the establishment of special administrative regions and the systems to be instituted there;

(14) to decide on questions of war and peace; and

(15) to exercise such other functions and powers as the highest organ of state power should exercise.

Article 63: The National People's Congress has the power to recall or remove from office the following persons:

(1) the President and the Vice-President of the People's Republic of China;

(2) the Premier, Vice-Premiers, State Councillors, Ministers in charge of Ministries or Commissions and the Auditor-General and the Secretary-General of the State Council;

(3) the Chairman of the Central Military Commission and others on the Commission;

(4) the President of the Supreme People's Court; and

(5) the Procurator-General of the Supreme People's Procuratorate.

Article 64: Amendments to the Constitution are to be proposed by the Standing Committee of the National People's Congress or by more than one-fifth of the deputies to the National People's Congress and adopted by a majority vote of more than two-thirds of all the deputies to the Congress.

Statutes and resolutions are adopted by a majority vote of more than one half of all the deputies to the National People's Congress.

Article 65: The Standing Committee of the National People's Congress is composed of the following:

the Chairman;

the Vice-Chairmen;

the Secretary-General; and

members.

Minority nationalities are entitled to appropriate representation on the Standing Committee of the National People's Congress.

The National People's Congress elects, and has the power to recall, all those on its Standing Committee.

No one on the Standing Committee of the National People's Congress shall hold any post in any of the administrative, judicial or procuratorial organs of the state.

Article 66: The Standing Committee of the National People's Congress is elected for the same term as the National People's Congress; it exercises its functions and powers until a new Standing Committee is elected by the succeeding National People's Congress.

The Chairman and Vice-Chairmen of the Standing Committee shall serve no more than two consecutive terms.

Article 67: The Standing Committee of the National People's Congress exercises the following functions and powers:

(1) to interpret the Constitution and supervise its enforcement;

(2) to enact and amend statutes with the exception of those which should be enacted by the National People's Congress;

(3) to enact, when the National People's Congress is not in session, partial supplements and amendments to statutes enacted by the National People's Congress provided that they do not contravene the basic principles of these statutes;

(4) to interpret statutes;

(5) to examine and approve, when the National People's Congress is not in session, partial adjustments to the plan for national economic and social development and to the state budget that prove necessary in the course of their implementation;

(6) to supervise the work of the State Council, the Central Military Commission, the Supreme People's Court and the Supreme People's Procuratorate;

(7) to annul those administrative rules and regulations, decisions or orders of the State Council that contravene the Constitution or the statutes;

(8) to annul those local regulations or decisions of the organs of state power of provinces, autonomous regions and municipalities directly under the Central Government that contravene the Constitution, the statutes or the administrative rules and regulations;

(9) to decide, when the National People's Congress is not in session, on the choice of Ministers in charge of Ministries or Commissions or the Auditor-General and the Secretary-General of the State Council upon nomination by the Premier of the State Council;

(10) to decide, upon nomination by the Chairman of the Central Military Commission, on the choice of others on the Commission, when the National People's Congress is not in session.

(11) to appoint and remove the Vice-Presidents and judges of the Supreme People's Court, members of its Judicial Committee and the President of the Military Court at the suggestion of the President of the Supreme People's Court;

(12) to appoint and remove the Deputy Procurators-General and Procurators of the Supreme People's Procuratorate, members of its Procuratorial Committee and the Chief Procurator of the Military Procuratorate at the request of the Procurator-General of the Supreme People's Procuratorate, and to approve the appointment and removal of the Chief Procurators of the People's Procuratorates of provinces, autonomous regions and municipalities directly under the Central Government;

(13) to decide on the appointment and recall of plenipotentiary representatives abroad;

(14) to decide on the ratification and abrogation of treaties and important agreements concluded with foreign states;

(15) to institute systems of titles and ranks for military and diplomatic personnel and of other specific titles and ranks;

(16) to institute state medals and titles of honour and decide on their conferment;

(17) to decide on the granting of special pardons;

(18) to decide, when the National People's Congress is not in session, on the proclamation of a state of war in the event of an armed attack on the country or in fulfilment of international treaty obligations concerning common defence against aggression;

(19) to decide on general mobilization or partial mobilization;

(20) to decide on the enforcement of martial law throughout the country or in particular provinces, autonomous regions or municipalities directly under the Central Government; and

(21) to exercise such other functions and powers as the National People's Congress may assign to it.

Article 68: The Chairman of the Standing Committee of the National People's Congress presides over the work of the Standing Committee and convenes its meetings. The Vice-Chairmen and the Secretary-General assist the Chairman in his work.

Chairmanship meetings with the participation of the Chairman, Vice-Chairmen and Secretary-General handle the important day-to-day work of the Standing Committee of the National People's Congress.

Article 69: The Standing Committee of the National People's Congress is responsible to the National People's Congress and reports on its work to the Congress.

Article 70: The National People's Congress establishes a Nationalities Committee, a Law Committee, a Finance and Economic Committee, an Education, Science, Culture and Public Health Committee, a Foreign Affairs Committee, an Overseas Chinese Committee and such other special committees as are necessary. These special committees work under the direction of the Standing Committee of the National People's Congress when the Congress is not in session.

The special committees examine, discuss and draw up relevant bills and draft resolutions under the direction of the National People's Congress and its Standing Committee.

Article 71: The National People's Congress and its Standing Committee may, when they deem it necessary, appoint committees of inquiry into specific questions and adopt relevant resolutions in the light of their reports.

All organs of state, public organizations and citizens concerned are obliged to supply the necessary information to those committees of inquiry when they conduct investigations.

Article 72: Deputies to the National People's Congress and all those on its Standing Committee have the right, in accordance with procedures prescribed by law, to submit bills and proposals within the scope of the respective functions and powers of the National People's Congress and its Standing Committee.

Article 73: Deputies to the National People's Congress during its sessions, and all those on its Standing Committee during its meetings, have the right, in accordance with procedures prescribed by law, to the State Council or the Ministries and Commissions under the State Council, which must answer the questions in a responsible manner.

Article 74: No deputy to the National People's Congress may be arrested or placed on criminal trial without the consent of the presidium of the current session of the National People's Congress or, when the National People's Congress is not in session, without the consent of its Standing Committee.

Article 75: Deputies to the National People's Congress may not be called to legal account for their speeches or votes at its meetings.

Article 76: Deputies to the National People's Congress must play an exemplary role in abiding by the Constitution and the law and keeping state secrets and, in production and other work and their public activities, assist in the enforcement of the Constitution and the law.

Deputies to the National People's Congress should maintain close contact with the units which elected them and with the people, listen to and convey the opinions and demands of the people and work hard to serve them.

Article 77: Deputies to the National People's Congress are subject to the supervision of the units which elected them. The electoral units have the power, through procedures prescribed by law, to recall the deputies whom they elected.

Article 78: The organization and working procedures of the National People's Congress and its Standing Committee are prescribed by law.

The President of the People's Republic of China

Article 79: The President and Vice-President of the People's Republic of China are elected by the National People's Congress.

Citizens of the People's Republic of China who have the right to vote and to stand for election and who have reached the age of 45 are eligible for election as President or Vice-President of the People's Republic of China.

The term of office of the President and Vice-President of the People's Republic of China is the same as that of the National People's Congress, and they shall serve no more than two consecutive terms.

Article 80: The President of the People's Republic of China, in pursuance of decisions of the National People's Congress and its Standing Committee, promulgates statutes; appoints and removes the Premier, Vice-Premiers, State Councillors, Ministers in charge of Ministries or Commissions, and the Auditor-General and the Secretary-General of the State Council; confers state medals and titles of honour; issues orders of special pardons; proclaims martial law; proclaims a state of war; and issues mobilization orders.

Article 81: The President of the People's Republic of China receives foreign diplomatic representatives on behalf of the People's Republic of China and, in pursuance of decisions of the Standing Committee of the National People's Congress, appoints and recalls plenipotentiary representatives abroad, and ratifies and abrogates treaties and important agreements concluded with foreign states.

Article 82: The Vice-President of the People's Republic of China assists the President in his work.

THE PEOPLE'S REPUBLIC OF CHINA

The Vice-President of the People's Republic of China may exercise such parts of the functions and powers of the President as the President may entrust to him.

Article 83: The President and Vice-President of the People's Republic of China exercise their functions and powers until the new President and Vice-President elected by the succeeding National People's Congress assume office.

Article 84: In case the office of the President of the People's Republic of China falls vacant, the Vice-President succeeds to the office of President.

In case the office of the Vice-President of the People's Republic of China falls vacant, the National People's Congress shall elect a new Vice-President to fill the vacancy.

In the event that the offices of both the President and the Vice-President of the People's Republic of China fall vacant, the National People's Congress shall elect a new President and a new Vice-President. Prior to such election, the Chairman of the Standing Committee of the National People's Congress shall temporarily act as the President of the People's Republic of China.

The State Council

Article 85: The State Council, that is, the Central People's Government, of the People's Republic of China is the executive body of the highest organ of state power; it is the highest organ of state administration.

Article 86: The State Council is composed of the following: the Premier; the Vice-Premiers; the State Councillors; the Ministers in charge of ministries; the Ministers in charge of commissions; the Auditor-General; and the Secretary-General.

The Premier has overall responsibility for the State Council. The Ministers have overall responsibility for the respective ministries or commissions under their charge.

The organization of the State Council is prescribed by law.

Article 87: The term of office of the State Council is the same as that of the National People's Congress.

The Premier, Vice-Premiers and State Councillors shall serve no more than two consecutive terms.

Article 88: The Premier directs the work of the State Council. The Vice-Premiers and State Councillors assist the Premier in his work.

Executive meetings of the State Council are composed of the Premier, the Vice-Premiers, the State Councillors and the Secretary-General of the State Council.

The Premier convenes and presides over the executive meetings and plenary meetings of the State Council.

Article 89: The State Council exercises the following functions and powers:

(1) to adopt administrative measures, enact administrative rules and regulations and issue decisions and orders in accordance with the Constitution and the statutes;

(2) to submit proposals to the National People's Congress or its Standing Committee;

(3) to lay down the tasks and responsibilities of the ministries and commissions of the State Council, to exercise unified leadership over the work of the ministries and commissions and to direct all other administrative work of a national character that does not fall within the jurisdiction of the ministries and commissions;

(4) to exercise unified leadership over the work of local organs of state administration at different levels throughout the country, and to lay down the detailed division of functions and powers between the Central Government and the organs of state administration of provinces, autonomous regions and municipalities directly under the Central Government;

(5) to draw up and implement the plan for national economic and social development and the state budget;

(6) to direct and administer economic work and urban and rural development;

(7) to direct and administer the work concerning education, science, culture, public health, physical culture and family planning;

(8) to direct and administer the work concerning civil affairs, public security, judicial administration, supervision and other related matters;

(9) to conduct foreign affairs and conclude treaties and agreements with foreign states;

(10) to direct and administer the building of national defence;

(11) to direct and administer affairs concerning the nationalities, and to safeguard the equal rights of minority nationalities and the right of autonomy of the national autonomous areas;

(12) to protect the legitimate rights and interests of Chinese nationals residing abroad and protect the lawful rights and interests of returned overseas Chinese and of the family members of Chinese nationals residing abroad;

(13) to alter or annul inappropriate orders, directives and regulations issued by the ministries or commissions;

(14) to alter or annul inappropriate decisions and orders issued by local organs of state administration at different levels;

(15) to approve the geographic division of provinces, autonomous regions and municipalities directly under the Central Government, and to approve the establishment and geographic division of autonomous prefectures, counties, autonomous counties and cities;

(16) to decide on the enforcement of martial law in parts of provinces, autonomous regions and municipalities directly under the Central Government;

(17) to examine and decide on the size of administrative organs and, in accordance with the law, to appoint, remove and train administrative officers, appraise their work and reward or punish them; and

(18) to exercise such other functions and powers as the National People's Congress or its Standing Committee may assign it.

Article 90: The Ministers in charge of ministries or commissions of the State Council are responsible for the work of their respective departments and convene and preside over their ministerial meetings or commission meetings that discuss and decide on major issues in the work of their respective departments.

The ministries and commissions issue orders, directives and regulations within the jurisdiction of their respective departments and in accordance with the statutes and the administrative rules and regulations, decisions and orders issued by the State Council.

Article 91: The State Council establishes an auditing body to supervise through auditing the revenue and expenditure of all departments under the State Council and of the local government at different levels, and those of the state financial and monetary organizations and of enterprises and undertakings.

Under the direction of the Premier of the State Council, the auditing body independently exercises its power to supervise through auditing in accordance with the law, subject to no interference by any other administrative organ or any public organization or individual.

Article 92: The State Council is responsible, and reports on its work, to the National People's Congress or, when the National People's Congress is not in session, to its Standing Committee.

The Central Military Commission

Article 93: The Central Military Commission of the People's Republic of China directs the armed forces of the country.

The Central Military Commission is composed of the following: the Chairman; the Vice-Chairmen; and members.

The Chairman of the Central Military Commission has overall responsibility for the Commission.

The term of office of the Central Military Commission is the same as that of the National People's Congress.

Article 94: The Chairman of the Central Military Commission is responsible to the National People's Congress and its Standing Committee.

(Two further sections, not included here, deal with the Local People's Congresses and Government and with the Organs of Self-Government of National Autonomous Areas respectively.)

The People's Courts and the People's Procuratorates

Article 123: The people's courts in the People's Republic of China are the judicial organs of the state.

Article 124: The People's Republic of China establishes the Supreme People's Court and the local people's courts at different levels, military courts and other special people's courts.

The term of office of the President of the Supreme People's Court is the same as that of the National People's Congress; he shall serve no more than two consecutive terms.

The organization of people's courts is prescribed by law.

Article 125: All cases handled by the people's courts, except for those involving special circumstances as specified by law, shall be heard in public. The accused has the right of defence.

Article 126: The people's courts shall, in accordance with the law, exercise judicial power independently and are not subject to interference by administrative organs, public organizations or individuals.

Article 127: The Supreme People's Court is the highest judicial organ.

THE PEOPLE'S REPUBLIC OF CHINA

The Supreme People's Court supervises the administration of justice by the local people's courts at different levels and by the special people's courts; people's courts at higher levels supervise the administration of justice by those at lower levels.

Article 128: The Supreme People's Court is responsible to the National People's Congress and its Standing Committee. Local people's courts at different levels are responsible to the organs of state power which created them.

Article 129: The people's procuratorates of the People's Republic of China are state organs for legal supervision.

Article 130: The People's Republic of China establishes the Supreme People's Procuratorate and the local people's procuratorates at different levels, military procuratorates and other special people's procuratorates.

The term of office of the Procurator-General of the Supreme People's Procuratorate is the same as that of the National People's Congress; he shall serve no more than two consecutive terms.

The organization of people's procuratorates is prescribed by law.

Article 131: People's procuratorates shall, in accordance with the law, exercise procuratorial power independently and are not subject to interference by administrative organs, public organizations or individuals.

Article 132: The Supreme People's Procuratorate is the highest procuratorial organ.

The Supreme People's Procuratorate directs the work of the local people's procuratorates at different levels and of the special people's procuratorates; people's procuratorates at higher levels direct the work of those at lower levels.

Article 133: The Supreme People's Procuratorate is responsible to the National People's Congress and its Standing Committee. Local people's procuratorates at different levels are responsible to the organs of state power at the corresponding levels which created them and to the people's procuratorates at the higher level.

Article 134: Citizens of all nationalities have the right to use the spoken and written languages of their own nationalities in court proceedings. The people's courts and people's procuratorates should provide translation for any party to the court proceedings who is not familiar with the spoken or written languages in common use in the locality.

In an area where people of a minority nationality live in a compact community or where a number of nationalities live together, hearings should be conducted in the language or languages in common use in the locality; indictments, judgements, notices and other documents should be written, according to actual needs, in the language or languages in common use in the locality.

Article 135: The people's courts, people's procuratorates and public security organs shall, in handling criminal cases, divide their functions, each taking responsibility for its own work, and they shall co-ordinate their efforts and check each other to ensure correct and effective enforcement of law.

THE NATIONAL FLAG, THE NATIONAL EMBLEM AND THE CAPITAL

Article 136: The national flag of the People's Republic of China is a red flag with five stars.

Article 137: The national emblem of the People's Republic of China is Tian'Anmen in the centre illuminated by five stars and encircled by ears of grain and a cogwheel.

Article 138: The capital of the People's Republic of China is Beijing.

The Government

HEAD OF STATE

President: LI XIANNIAN (appointed at the First Session of the Sixth National People's Congress in June 1983).
Vice-President: Gen. ULANHU.

STATE COUNCIL
(January 1987)

Premier: ZHAO ZIYANG.
Vice-Premiers: WAN LI, YAO YILIN, LI PENG, TIAN JIYUN, QIAO SHI.
State Councillors:

FANG YI	JI PENGFEI	Gen. ZHANG AIPING
GU MU	ZHANG JINGFU	SONG PING
KANG SHIEN	WANG BINGQIAN	SONG JIAN
Miss CHEN MUHUA	WU XUEQIAN	

Secretary-General: CHEN JUNSHENG.
Minister of Foreign Affairs: WU XUEQIAN.
Minister of National Defence: Gen. ZHANG AIPING.
Minister in Charge of the State Planning Commission: SONG PING.
Minister in Charge of the State Economic Commission: LU DONG.
Minister in Charge of the State Commission for Restructuring the Economic System: ZHAO ZIYANG.
Minister in Charge of the State Scientific and Technological Commission: SONG JIAN.
Minister in Charge of the Commission of Science, Technology and Industry for National Defence: DING HENGGAO.
Minister in Charge of the State Nationalities Affairs Commission: ISMAIL AMAT.
Minister of Public Security: RUAN CHONGWU.
Minister of State Security: JIA CHUNWANG.
Minister of Civil Affairs: CUI NAIFU.
Minister of Justice: ZOU YU.
Minister of Finance: WANG BINGQIAN.
Auditor-General: LU PEIJIAN.
President of the People's Bank of China: Miss CHEN MUHUA.
Minister of Commerce: LIU YI.
Minister of Foreign Economic Relations and Trade: ZHENG TUOBIN.
Minister of Agriculture, Animal Husbandry and Fishery: HE KANG.
Minister of Forestry: YANG ZHONG.
Minister of Water Conservancy and Electric Power: Miss QIAN ZHENGYING.
Minister of Urban and Rural Construction and Environmental Protection: YE RUTANG.
Minister of Geology and Minerals: ZHU XUN.
Minister of Metallurgical Industry: QI YUANJING.
Minister in Charge of the State Machine-Building Industry Commission: ZHOU JIAHUA.
Minister of Nuclear Industry: JIANG XINXIONG.
Minister of Aviation Industry: MO WENXIANG.
Minister of Electronics Industry: LI TIEYING.
Minister of Astronautics Industry: LI XUE.
Minister of Coal Industry: YU HONGEN.
Minister of Petroleum Industry: WANG TAO.
Minister of Chemical Industry: QIN ZHONGDA.
Minister of Textile Industry: Miss WU WENYING.
Minister of Light Industry: YANG BO.
Minister of Railways: DING GUANGENG.
Minister of Communications: QIAN YONGCHANG.
Minister of Posts and Telecommunications: YANG TAIFANG.
Minister of Labour and Personnel: ZHAO DONGWAN.
Minister of Culture: WANG MENG.
Minister of Radio, Film and Television: AI ZHISHENG.
Minister of Public Health: CUI YUELI.
Minister in Charge of the State Education Commission: LI PENG.
Minister in Charge of the State Physical Culture and Sports Commission: LI MENGHUA.
Minister in Charge of the State Family Planning Commission: WANG WEI.

MINISTRIES

Ministry of Agriculture, Animal Husbandry and Fishery: Hepingli, Dongcheng District, Beijing; tel. 463061.
Ministry of Astronautics Industry: c/o China Astronautics Society, 31 Baishiqiao Lu, Beijing; tel. 892632.
Ministry of Aviation Industry: Beijing; tel. 444855.
Ministry of Chemical Industry: Liupukang, Deshengmenwai, Beijing; tel. 446561.
Ministry of Civil Affairs: 147 Donganmen, Beijing; tel. 551731.
Ministry of Coal Industry: Hepingli North St, Beijing; tel. 446671.

THE PEOPLE'S REPUBLIC OF CHINA

Ministry of Commerce: 45 Fuxingmenwai St, Beijing; tel. 668581.
Ministry of Communications: 10 Fuxing Rd, Beijing; tel. 8642371; telex 22462.
Ministry of Culture: Donganmen North St, Beijing; tel. 442131.
Ministry of Electronics Industry: Wanshou Rd, Beijing; tel. 810561; telex 22383.
Ministry of Finance: South Sanlihe St, Fuxingmenwai, Beijing; tel. 868451; telex 22486.
Ministry of Foreign Affairs: 225 Chaonei St, Dongsi, Beijing; tel. 553831.
Ministry of Foreign Economic Relations and Trade: 2 Changan East St, Beijing; tel. 553031; telex 22168.
Ministry of Forestry: Hepingli, Dongchang District, Beijing; tel. 463061; telex 22237.
Ministry of Geology and Minerals: Xisi Yangshi St, Beijing; tel. 668741; telex 22531.
Ministry of Justice: 2 Nan Shun Cheng Jie, Xi Zhi Men, Beijing; tel. 668971.
Ministry of Labour and Personnel: Beijing.
Ministry of Light Industry: Fuchengmenwai St, Beijing; tel. 890751.
Ministry of Metallurgical Industry: 46 West Dongsi St, Beijing; tel. 557431.
Ministry of National Defence: Beijing; tel. 667343.
Ministry of Nuclear Industry: Beijing; tel. 868381.
Ministry of Petroleum Industry: Liupukang, Deshengmenwai, Beijing; tel. 446531.
Ministry of Posts and Telecommunications: 13 West Chang-an St, Beijing; tel. 660540.
Ministry of Public Health: 44 Houhaibeiyan, Beijing; tel. 440531; telex 22193.
Ministry of Public Security: East Changan St, Beijing; tel. 553871.
Ministry of Radio, Film and Television: Outside Fu Xing Men St 2, POB 4501, Beijing; tel. 862753; telex 22236.
Ministry of Railways: 10 Fuxing Rd, Beijing; tel. 864061.
Ministry of State Security: Dongchangan St, Beijing; tel. 553871.
Ministry of Textile Industry: 12 East Changan St, Beijing; tel. 551609; telex 22661.
Ministry of Urban and Rural Construction and Environmental Protection: Baiwanzhuang, Beijing; tel. 8992211.
Ministry of Water Conservancy and Electric Power: 2 Ertiao, Baiguang St, Guanganmen, Beijing; tel. 367931; telex 22466.

COMMISSIONS

State Economic Commission: Sanlihe, Fuxingmenwai, Beijing; tel. 868521; telex 22552.
State Education Commission: 37 Damucang Hutong, Xicheng District, Beijing; tel. 658731.
State Family Planning Commission: Xizhimen South Shuncheng St, Beijing; tel. 668971.
State Machine-Building Industry Commission: Sanlihe, Beijing; tel. 868561.
State Nationalities Commission: 252 Taipingqiao St, Beijing; tel. 666931.
State Physical Culture and Sports Commission: Chongwai Stadium Rd, Beijing; tel. 757231.
State Planning Commission: Yuetan South St, Beijing; tel. 868521.
State Scientific and Technological Commission: 52 Sanlihe, Fuxingmenwai, Beijing; tel. 868361; telex 22349.

Legislature

QUANGUO RENMIN DIABIAO DAHUI
(National People's Congress)

The National People's Congress (NPC) is the highest organ of state power, and had 2,978 members in March 1985. The Fourth Session of the Sixth NPC was convened in Beijing in March 1986. The Fourth Session of the Sixth National Committee of the Chinese People's Political Consultative Conference (CPPCC), a revolutionary united front organization led by the Communist Party, took place simultaneously. The CPPCC holds democratic discussions and consultations on the important affairs in the nation's political life. Members of the CPPCC National Committee or of its Standing Committee may be invited to attend the NPC or its Standing Committee as observers.

Standing Committee

In June 1983, 133 members were elected to the Standing Committee.
Chairman: PENG ZHEN.
Vice-Chairmen:

CHEN PIXIAN	YE FEI
Gen. WEI GUOQING	BAINQEN ERDINI QOIGYI GYAINCAIN (Panchen Lama)
PENG CHONG	
Gen. SEYPIDIN	ZHU XUEFAN
GENG BIAO	WANG RENZHONG
NGAPOI NGAWANG JIGME	ZHOU GUCHENG
XU DEHENG	YAN JICI
HU JUEWEN	Lt-Gen. LIAO HANSHENG
RONG YIREN	HUANG HUA

Secretary-General: WANG HANBIN.

Local People's Congresses

Province	Chairman of People's Congress
Anhui	WANG GUANGYU
Fujian	CHENG XU
Gansu	LIU BING
Guangdong	LUO TIAN
Guizhou	ZHANG YUHUAN
Hebei	SUN GUOZHI
Heilongjiang	LI JIANBAI
Henan	ZHANG SHUDE
Hubei	HUANG ZHIZHEN
Hunan	JIAO LINYI
Jiangsu	CHU JIANG
Jiangxi	WANG SHUFENG
Jilin	ZHAO XIU
Liaoning	ZHANG ZHENGDE
Qinghai	SONG LIN
Shaanxi	YAN KELUN
Shandong	LI ZHEN
Shanxi	RUAN BOSHENG
Sichuan	HE HAOJU
Yunnan	Miss LI GUIYING
Zhejiang	LI FENGPING
Special Municipalities	
Beijing	ZHAO PENGFEI
Shanghai	HU LIJIAO
Tianjin	ZHANG ZAIWANG
Autonomous Regions	
Guangxi Zhuang	GAN KU
Nei Monggol	BATU BAGEN
Ningxia Hui	MA QINGNIAN
Xinjiang Uygur	AMUDONG NIYAZI
Xizang	NGAPOI NGAWANG JIGME

People's Governments

In July 1979 the Second Session of the Fifth NPC resolved to abolish the Revolutionary Committees, set up during the Cultural Revolution to administer each of the 29 provinces, special municipalities and autonomous regions and replace them by People's Governments with effect from January 1980.

Province	Governor
Anhui	WANG YUZHAO
Fujian	HU PING
Gansu	JIA ZHIJIE
Guangdong	YE XUANPING
Guizhou	WANG CHAOWEN
Hebei	XIE FENG
Heilongjiang	HOU JIE
Henan	HE ZHUKANG

Hubei	Guo Zhenqian
Hunan	Xiong Qingquan
Jiangsu	Miss Gu Xiulian
Jiangxi	Wu Guanzheng
Jilin	Gao Dezhan
Liaoning	Li Changchun
Qinghai	Song Ruixiang
Shaanxi	Zhang Boxing (acting)
Shandong	Li Changan
Shanxi	Wang Senhao
Sichuan	Jiang Minkuan
Yunnan	He Zhiqiang
Zhejiang	Xue Ju
Special Municipalities	Mayor
Beijing	Chen Xitong
Shanghai	Jiang Zemin
Tianjin	Li Ruihuan
Autonomous Regions	Chairman
Guangxi Zhuang	Wei Chunshu
Nei Monggol	Bu He
Ningxia Hui	Hei Boli
Xinjiang Uygur	Tomur Dawamat
Xizang	Doje Cering

Political Organizations

COMMUNIST PARTY

Zhongguo Gongchan Dang (Chinese Communist Party): Beijing; f. 1921; publ. *Renmin Ribao* (People's Daily).

The Chinese Communist Party had more than 40m. members at mid-1985. At the first plenary session of the Twelfth Central Committee, in September 1982, the post of Chairman was abolished, giving the most senior Party position to the General Secretary. At the fifth plenary session, held in September 1985, six new members were elected to the Politburo, and a further 29 full members and 35 alternate members were appointed to the Central Committee, which then consisted of 210 full members and 133 alternate members. The sixth plenary session was held in September 1986.

Twelfth Central Committee

General Secretary: Zhao Ziyang (acting).

Politburo

Members of the Standing Committee:

Hu Yaobang	Li Xiannian
Deng Xiaoping	Chen Yun
Zhao Ziyang	

Other Full Members:

Fang Yi	Gen. Yang Dezhi
Ni Zhifu	Tian Jiyun
Yu Qiuli	Qiao Shi
Peng Zhen	Li Peng
Wan Li	Wu Xueqian
Yang Shangkun	Hu Qili
Xi Zhongxun	Yao Yilin
Hu Qiaomu	

Alternate Members: Qin Jiwei, Miss Chen Muhua.

Secretariat:

Wan Li	Qiao Shi
Yu Qiuli	Miss Hao Jianxiu
Deng Liqun	Tian Jiyun
Chen Pixian	Li Peng
Hu Qili	Wang Zhaoguo

Chairman of Central Advisory Committee: Deng Xiaoping.
Vice-Chairmen: Bo Yibo, Wang Zhen, Song Renqiong.

OTHER POLITICAL ORGANIZATIONS

China Association for Promoting Democracy: tel. 447128; f. Shanghai 1945; Cen. Cttee at Beijing; mems mainly drawn from cultural and educational circles, especially teachers, editors and publrs; Chair. Ye Shengtao.

China Democratic League: Beijing; f. 1941; formed from reorganization of League of Democratic Parties and Organizations of China; mems mainly intellectuals working in education, science and culture; Chair. Fei Xiaotong.

China Democratic National Construction Association: 93 Beiheyan Dajie, Beijing; tel. 554231; f. 1945; mems mainly industrialists and businessmen; Chair. Hu Juewen; Sec. Gen. Jiang Daning.

China Zhi Gong Dang: Beijing; f. 1925; reorganized 1947; mems mainly drawn from returned overseas Chinese; Chair. Huang Dingchen.

Chinese Peasants' and Workers' Democratic Party: f. 1947; fmrly known as Provisional Action Cttee of the Kuomintang; mems mainly drawn from field of public health and medicine; Chair. Zhou Gucheng.

Communist Youth League: f. 1922; 48.5m. mems; First Sec. of Cen. Cttee Song Defu.

Guomindang (Kuomintang) Revolutionary Committee: f. 1948; mainly fmr Kuomintang mems, and those in cultural, educational, health and financial fields; Chair. Qu Wu (acting).

Jiu San (3 September) Society: f. 1945; fmrly Democratic and Science Soc.; mems mainly scientists and technologists; Chair. Xu Deheng.

Taiwan Democratic Self-Government League: f. 1947; recruits Taiwanese living on the Mainland; Chair. Su Ziheng.

The People's Liberation Army

Apart from its strategic role as a defensive force, the People's Liberation Army (PLA) is closely tied to the political leadership of the country. The People's Republic of China is divided into seven Military Units.

Chairman of Central Military Commission: Deng Xiaoping.
Vice-Chairmen: Marshal Xu Xiangqian, Marshal Nie Rongzhen, Yang Shangkun.
Chief of General Staff: Gen. Yang Dezhi.
Chief of the General Political Department (Chief Political Commissar): Yu Qiuli.
Commander, PLA Navy: Rear-Adm. Liu Huaqing.
Commander, PLA Air Force: Gen. Wang Hai.
Head, General Logistics Department: Col-Gen. Hong Xuezhi.

Military Units	Commander
Beijing	Gen. Qin Jiwei
Chengdu	Fu Quanyou
Guangzhou	Gen. You Taizhong
Jinan	Li Jiulong
Lanzhou	Zhao Xianshun
Nanjing	Gen. Xiang Shouzhi
Shenyang	Liu Jingsong

Diplomatic Representation

EMBASSIES IN THE PEOPLE'S REPUBLIC OF CHINA

Afghanistan: 8 Dong Zhi Men Wai, Da Jie Chao Yang Qu, Beijing; Ambassador: (vacant).

Albania: 28 Guang Hua Lu, Beijing; tel. 521120; Ambassador: Justin Niko Papajorgji.

Algeria: Dong Zhi Men Wai Da Jie, 7 San Li Tun, Beijing; tel. 521231; telex 22437; Ambassador: Abdelghani Akbi.

Argentina: 11 Dong Wu Jie, San Li Tun, Beijing; telex 22269; Ambassador: (vacant).

Australia: 15 Dong Zhi Men Wai Da Jie, Beijing; tel. 522331; telex 22263; Ambassador: Ross Garnaut.

Austria: 5 Xiu Shui Nan Jie, Jian Guo Men Wai, Beijing; tel. 522061; telex 22258; Ambassador: Wolfgang Wolte.

Bangladesh: 42 Guang Hua Lu, Beijing; tel. 521819; telex 22143; Ambassador: Enayetullah Khan.

Belgium: 6 San Li Tun Lu, Beijing; tel. 521736; telex 22260; Ambassador: Jan Hollants Van Loocke.

Benin: 38 Guang Hua Lu, Beijing; tel. 522741; telex 22599; Ambassador: Cosme Deguenon.

Brazil: 27 Guang Hua Lu, Beijing; tel. 522698; telex 22117; Ambassador: Italo Zappa.

Bulgaria: 4 Xiu Shui Bei Jie, Jian Guo Men Wai, Beijing; tel. 522231; Ambassador: Dontcho Georgiev Dontchev.

THE PEOPLE'S REPUBLIC OF CHINA

Burkina Faso: 52 Dong Liu Jie, San Li Tun, Beijing; telex 22666; Ambassador: MONVEL MICHEL DAH.
Burma: 6 Dong Zhi Men Wai Da Jie Chao Yang Qu, Beijing; tel. 521344; Ambassador: U TIN MAUNG MYINT.
Burundi: 25 Guang Hua Lu, Beijing; tel. 522328; telex 22271; Ambassador: NIYUNGEKO JONAPHAS.
Cameroon: 7 San Li Tun, Dong Wu Jie, Beijing; telex 22256; Ambassador: (vacant).
Canada: 10 San Li Tun Lu, Chao Yang District, Beijing; tel. 523536; telex 22717; Ambassador: RICHARD V. GORHAM.
Central African Republic: 1 Dong San Jie, San Li Tun, Beijing; tel. 522867; telex 22142; Ambassador: FERDINAND PIERRE POUNZI.
Chad: 21 Guang Hua Lu, Jianguo Men Wai, Beijing; telex 22287; Ambassador: ISSA ABBAS ALI.
Chile: 1 San Li Tun, Dong Si Jie, Beijing; tel. 521641; telex 22252; Ambassador: BENJAMIN OPAZO BRULL.
Colombia: 34 Guang Hua Lu, Beijing; tel. 523166; telex 22460; Ambassador: LUIS EDUARDO VILLAR BORDA.
Congo: 7 San Li Tun, Dong Si Jie, Beijing; tel. 521644; telex 20428; Ambassador: (vacant).
Cuba: 1 Xiu Shui Nan Jie, Jian Guo Men Wai, Beijing; tel. 521714; telex 22249; Ambassador: ROLANDO LÓPEZ DEL AMO.
Czechoslovakia: Ri Tan Lu, Jian Guo Men, Wai, Beijing; tel. 521531; Ambassador: ZDENKO CHEBEN.
Denmark: 1 Dong Wu Jie, San Li Tun, Beijing; tel. 522431; telex 22255; Ambassador: ARNE BELLING.
Ecuador: 2–41 San Li Tun, Beijing; telex 22710; Ambassador: JUAN MANUEL AGUIRRE.
Egypt: 2 Ri Tan Dong Lu, Beijing; tel. 522541; telex 22134; Ambassador: AHMED A. SELIM.
Equatorial Guinea: 2 Dong Si Jie, San Li Tun, Beijing; Ambassador: (vacant).
Ethiopia: 3 Xiu Shui Nan Jie, Jian Guo Men Wai, Beijing; telex 22306; Ambassador: PHILIPPOS WOLDE-MARIAM.
Finland: 30 Guang Hua Lu, Beijing; tel. 521753; telex 22294; Ambassador: RISTO HYVÄRINEN.
France: 3 Dong San Jie, San Li Tun, Beijing; tel. 521331; telex 22183; Ambassador: MICHEL COMBAL.
Gabon: 36 Guang Hua Lu, Beijing; tel. 522810; telex 22110; Ambassador: (vacant).
German Democratic Republic: 3 Dong Si Jie, San Li Tun, Beijing; tel. 521631; telex 22384; Ambassador: ROLF BERTHOLD.
Germany, Federal Republic: 5 Dong Zhi Men Wai Da Jie, Beijing; tel. 522161; telex 22259; Ambassador: PER FISCHER.
Ghana: 8 San Li Tun, Lu, Beijing; tel. 522288; Ambassador: OSEI BONSU AMANKWA.
Greece: 19 Guang Hua Lu, Beijing; tel. 521993; telex 22267; Ambassador: EMMANUEL E. MEGALOKONOMOS.
Guinea: 7 Dong San Jie, San Li Tun, Beijing; tel. 523649; telex 22706; Ambassador: FODE DJIBRIL CAMARA.
Guyana: 1 Xiu Shui Dong Jie, Jian Guo Men Wai, Beijing; tel. 522066; telex 22295; Ambassador: ASHIK ALTAF MOHAMMED.
Hungary: 10 Dong Zhi Men Wai Da Jie, Beijing; tel. 521683; telex 22679; Ambassador: IVAN LÁSZLÓ.
India: 1 Ri Tan Dong Lu, Beijing; tel. 521908; telex 22126; Ambassador: KIZHAKE PALAT SANKARA MENON.
Iran: Dong Liu Ji, San Li Tun, Beijing; tel. 522040; telex 22253; Ambassador: ALA ED-DIN BORUJERDI.
Iraq: 3 Ri Tan Dong Lu, Chae Yang District, Beijing; tel. 521950; telex 22288; Ambassador: Dr RASHID MOHAMED SAIED AL-RIFAI.
Ireland: 3 Ri Tan Dong Lu, Beijing; tel. 522506; telex 22425; Ambassador: DERMOT WALDRON.
Italy: 2 Dong Er Jie, San Li Tun, Beijing; tel. 522131; telex 22414; Ambassador: RAFFAELE MARRAS.
Ivory Coast: Beijing; tel. 521482; telex 22723; Ambassador: AMOAKON EJAMPAN THIEMELE.
Japan: 7 Ri Tan Lu, Jian Guo Men Wai, Beijing; tel. 522361; telex 22275; Ambassador: YOSUKE NAKAE.
Jordan: 54 Dong Liu Jie, San Li Tun, Beijing; tel. 523906; telex 22651; Ambassador: KEMAL AL HAMOUD.
Kenya: 4 Xi Liu Jie, San Li Tun, Beijing; tel. 523381; telex 22311; Ambassador: JELANI HABIB.
Korea, Democratic People's Republic: Ri Tan Bei Lu, Jian Guo Men Wai, Beijing; telex 20448; Ambassador: SIN IN HA.

Kuwait: 23 Guang Hua Lu, Beijing; tel. 522216; telex 22127; Ambassador: ABDULHADI HADJI AL-MAHMEED.
Laos: 11 East San Li Tun, Chao Yang District, Beijing; tel. 521244; telex 22144; Ambassador: THAVONE SICHALEUN.
Lebanon: 51 Dong Liu Jie, San Li Tun, Beijing; tel. 522770; telex 22113; Ambassador: FARID SAMAHA.
Lesotho: Beijing; Ambassador: CHAKA NTSANE.
Liberia: 2-62 San Li Tun, Beijing; tel. 523549; telex 22165; Ambassador: JOHN CHRISTOPHER RICKS.
Libya: 55 Dong Liu Jie, San Li Tun, Beijing; telex 22310; Secretary of the People's Bureau: ABD AL-HAMID AL-ZINTANI.
Luxembourg: 21 Nei Wu Bu Jie, Beijing; tel. 556175; telex 22638; Ambassador: PAUL SCHULLER.
Madagascar: 3 Dong Jie, San Li Tun, Beijing; tel. 521353; telex 22140; Ambassador: JEAN-JACQUES MAURICE.
Malaysia: 13 Dong Zhi Men Wai Da Jie, San Li Tun, Beijing; tel. 522531; telex 22122; Ambassador: ISMAIL MOHAMED.
Mali: 8 Dong Si Jie, San Li Tun, Beijing; telex 22257; Ambassador: BOUBACAR TOURÉ.
Malta: 2-2-71 Jian Guo Men Wai, Beijing; tel. 523114; telex 22670; Ambassador: ALFRED J. FALZON.
Mauritania: 9 Dong San Jie, San Li Tun, Beijing; tel. 521346; telex 22514; Ambassador: DIAGANA YOUSSOUF.
Mexico: 5 Dong Wu Jie, San Li Tun, Beijing; tel. 522122; telex 22262; Ambassador: EUGENIO ANGUIANO ROCH.
Mongolia: 2 Xiu Shui Bei Jie, Jian Guo Men Wai, Beijing; tel. 521203; Ambassador: N. LUVSANCHULTEM.
Morocco: 16 San Li Tun Lu, Beijing; tel. 521489; telex 22268; Ambassador: ABDERRAHIM HARKETT.
Nepal: 12 San Li Tun Lu, Beijing; tel. 521795; Ambassador: GUNA SHUMSHER JUNG BAHADUR RANA.
Netherlands: 10 San Li Tun, Dong Si Jie, Beijing; tel. 521731; telex 22277; Ambassador: (vacant).
New Zealand: 1 Ri Tan, Dong Er Jie, Chaoyang District, Beijing; tel. 522731; telex 22124; Ambassador: LINDSAY WATT.
Nicaragua: Beijing; Ambassador: ALFREDO ALANIZ.
Niger: 50 Dong Liu Jie, San Li Tun, Beijing; tel. 521616; telex 22133; Ambassador: PIERRE AUSSEIL.
Nigeria: 2 Dong Wu Jie, San Li Tun, Beijing; tel. 522274; Ambassador: ADEUGA ADEKOYE.
Norway: 1 San Li Tun, Dong Yi Jie, Beijing; tel. 522261; telex 22266; Ambassador: ARNE ARNESEN.
Oman: 6 Liang Ma He Nan Lu, San Li Tun, Beijing; tel. 523956; telex 22192; Ambassador: FARID BIN MBARAK BIN ALI AL-HINAI.
Pakistan: 1 Dong Zhi Men Wai Da Jie, Beijing; tel. 522504; Ambassador: Dr MAQBOOL AHMAD BHATTY.
Peru: 2–82 San Li Tun, Beijing; tel. 522005; telex 22278; Ambassador: ROBERTO VILLARAN KOECHLIN.
Philippines: 23 Xiu Shui Bei Jie, Jian Guo Men Wai, Beijing; tel. 523420; telex 22132; Ambassador: ALFONSO T. YUCHENGCO.
Poland: 1 Ri Tan Lu, Jian Guo Men Wai, Beijing; tel. 521235; Ambassador: ZBIGNIEW DĘMBOWSKI.
Portugal: 2-72 San Li Tun, Beijing; tel. 523220; telex 22326; Ambassador: OCTAVIO NETO VALERIO.
Romania: Jian Guo Men Wai, Xiushui, Beijing; tel. 523255; telex 22250; Ambassador: ANGELO MICULESCU.
Rwanda: 30 Xiu Shui Bei Jie, Beijing; tel. 522193; telex 22104; Ambassador: DENIS MAGIRA BIGIRIMANA.
Senegal: 1 Ri Tan Dong Yi Jie, Jian Guo Men Wai, Beijing; tel. 522576; telex 22100; Ambassador: AHMED TIDIANE KANE.
Sierra Leone: 7 Dong Zhi Men Wai Da Jie, Beijing; tel. 521222; telex 22166; Ambassador: CALEB BABATUNDA AUBEE.
Somalia: 2 San Li Tun Lu, Beijing; tel. 521752; telex 22121; Ambassador: YUSSUF HASSAN IBRAHIM.
Spain: 9 San Li Tun Lu, Beijing; tel. 523742; telex 22108; Ambassador: EUGENIO BREGOLAT Y OBIOLS.
Sri Lanka: 3 Jian Hua Lu, Jian Guo Men Wai, Beijing; tel. 52861; telex 22136; Ambassador: KANDAGE NEWTON SAMARASINGHE.
Sudan: 1 Dong Er Jie, San Li Tun, Beijing; telex 22116; Ambassador: MUHAMMAD HAMAD MUHAMMAD MATTAR.
Sweden: 3 Dong Zhi Men Wai Da Jie, Beijing; tel. 523331; telex 22261; Ambassador: LARS BERGQUIST.
Switzerland: 3 Dong Wu Jie, San Li Tun, Beijing; tel. 522736; telex 22251; Ambassador: FRITZ BOHNERT.

THE PEOPLE'S REPUBLIC OF CHINA

Syria: 6 Dong Si Jie, San Li Tun, Beijing; telex 22138; Ambassador: ZAKARIA SHURAIKI.
Tanzania: 53 Dong Liu Jie, San Li Tun, Beijing; tel. 521408; telex 22749; Ambassador: CLEMENT GEORGE KAHAMA.
Thailand: 40 Guang Hua Lu, Beijing; tel. 521903; Ambassador: TET BUNNAK.
Togo: 11 Dong Zhi Men Wai Da Jie, Beijing; tel. 522202; telex 22130; Ambassador: (vacant).
Tunisia: 1 Dong Jie, San Li Tun, Beijing; tel. 522435; telex 22103; Ambassador: RIDHA BACH BAOUAB.
Turkey: 9 Dong Wu Jie, San Li Tun, Beijing; tel. 522650; telex 210168; Ambassador: BEHIÇ HAZAR.
Uganda: 5 Dong Jie, San Li Tun, Beijing; tel. 521708; telex 22272; Ambassador: WILLIAM WYCLIFFE RWETSIBA.
USSR: 4 Dong Zhi Men Wai Zhong Jie, Beijing; telex 22247; Ambassador: OLEG TROYANOVSKI.
United Kingdom: 11 Guang Hua Lu, Jian Guo Men Wai, Beijing; tel. 521961; telex 22191; Ambassador: Sir RICHARD EVANS.
USA: 3 Xiu Shui Bei Jie, Beijing; tel. 523831; telex 22701; Ambassador: WINSTON LORD.
Venezuela: 14 San Li Tun Lu, Beijing; tel. 521295; telex 22137; Ambassador: LEONARDO DÍAZ GONZALES.
Viet-Nam: 32 Guang Hua Lu, Jian Guo Men Wai, Beijing; Ambassador: NGUYEN TRONG VINH.
Yemen Arab Republic: 4 Dongzhi Men Wai Dajie, Beijing; tel. 523346; Ambassador: HUSSEIN ABDULKHALEK AL-GALAL.
Yemen, People's Democratic Republic: 5 Dong San Jie, San Li Tun, Beijing; telex 22279; Ambassador: IBRAHIM ABDULLA SAIDI.
Yugoslavia: 56 Dong Liu Jie, San Li Tun, Beijing; tel. 421562; telex 22403; Ambassador: ZVONE DRAGAN.
Zaire: 6 Dong Wu Jie, San Li Tun, Beijing; tel. 421966; telex 22273; Ambassador: LOMBO LO MANGAMANGA.
Zambia: 5 Dong Si Jie, San Li Tun, Beijing; tel. 521554; telex 22388; Ambassador: MATHIAS MAINZA CHONA.
Zimbabwe: 62 San Li Tun, Beijing; tel. 521652; telex 22671; Ambassador: (vacant).

Judicial System

The general principles of the Chinese judicial system are laid down in Articles 123–135 of the December 1982 constitution (q.v.).

PEOPLE'S COURTS

Supreme People's Court: Dongjiaomin Xiang, Beijing; tel. 550131; f. 1949; the highest judicial organ of the state; directs and supervises work of lower courts; Pres. ZHENG TIANXIANG (term of office four years).
Special People's Courts.
Local People's Courts.

PEOPLE'S PROCURATORATES

Supreme People's Procuratorate: Donganmen Beiheyan, Beijing; tel. 550831; acts for the National People's Congress in examining govt depts, civil servants and citizens, to ensure observance of the law; prosecutes in criminal cases. Procurator-Gen. YANG YICHEN (elected by the National People's Congress for four years).
Local People's Procuratorates: undertake the same duties at the local level. Ensure that the judicial activities of the people's courts, the execution of sentences in criminal cases, and the activities of departments in charge of reform through labour, conform to the law; institute, or intervene in, important civil cases which affect the interest of the state and the people.

Religion

During the Cultural Revolution places of worship were closed. After 1977 the government adopted a policy of religious tolerance, and the 1982 Constitution states that citizens enjoy freedom of religious belief, and that legitimate religious activities are protected. Many temples, churches and mosques are reopening.

ANCESTOR WORSHIP

Ancestor worship is believed to have originated with the deification and worship of all important natural phenomena. The divine and human were not clearly defined; all the dead became gods and were worshipped by their descendants. The practice has no code or dogma and the ritual is limited to sacrifices made during festivals and on birth and death anniversaries.

BUDDHISM

Buddhism was introduced into China from India in AD 67, and flourished during the Sui and Tang dynasties (6th–8th century) when eight sects were established. The Chan and Pure Land sects are the most popular.
Buddhist Association of China: f. 1953; Pres. ZHAO PUCHU; Vice-Pres. LI RONGXI.

CHRISTIANITY

During the 19th century and the first half of the 20th century, large numbers of foreign Christian missionaries worked in China. There were an estimated 3m. Christians in China in 1984.
Chinese Catholic Patriotic Association: Chair. Mgr ZONG HUAIDE; Vice-Chair. FU TIESHAN; 3,000 mems.
Protestant Church: Chair. of Council Bishop DING GUANGXUN; 1m. adherents.
The Roman Catholic Church: Catholic Mission, Si-She-Ku, Beijing; Bishop of Beijing (vacant).

CONFUCIANISM

Confucianism is a philosophy and a system of ethics, without ritual or priesthood. The respects accorded Confucius are not paid to a prophet or god, but to a great sage whose teachings promote peace and good order in society and whose philosophy encourages moral living.

DAOISM

Daoism originated as a philosophy expounded by Lao Zi, born 604 BC. The establishment of a religion was contrary to his doctrines, but seven centuries after his death his teachings were embodied into a ritual.
China Daoist Association: Beijing; Chair. LI YUHANG.

ISLAM

According to Muslim history, Islam was introduced into China in AD 651. It had 14.6m. adherents in China in 1985, chiefly among the Wei Wuer and Hui people.
Beijing Islamic Association: Dongsi Mosque, Beijing; f. 1979; Chair. Imam Al-Hadji SALAH AN SHIWEI.
China Islamic Association: Beijing; f. 1953; Hon. Chair. BURHAN SHAHIDI; Chair. Al-Hadji MOHAMMED ALI ZHANG JIE.

The Press

In 1986 China had 2,191 newspapers. Each province publishes its own daily. Only the major newspapers and periodicals are listed below, and only a restricted number are allowed abroad.

NEWSPAPERS

Beijing Ribao (Beijing Daily): 34 Xi Biaobei Hutong, Dongdan, Beijing; tel. 553431; f. 1952; organ of the Beijing municipal cttee of the CCP; Editor-in-Chief HUANG SEN; circ. 1m.
Beijing Wanbao (Beijing Evening News): 34 Xi Biaobei Hutong, Dongdan, Beijing; tel. 553431; telex 283642; f. 1958; Editor GU XING; circ. 500,000.
Can Kao Xiao Xi (Reference News): Beijing; reprints from foreign newspapers; publ. by Xinhua (New China) News Agency; circ. 3.6m.
China Daily: 2 Jintai Xilu, Beijing; tel. 581958; telex 22022; f. 1981; English; coverage: China's political, economic and cultural developments; world, financial and sports news; Editor-in-Chief FENG XILIANG; circ. 82,000.
Dazhong Ribao (Masses Daily): 41 Lishan Rd, Jinan, Shandong Province; tel. 43821; telex 9993; f. 1939; circ. 530,000.
Fujian Ribao (Fujian Daily): Hualin Lu, Fuzhou, Fujian; tel. 57756; daily.
Gongren Ribao (Workers' Daily): Liupukeng, Andingmen Wai, Beijing; tel. 461561; f. 1949; trade union activities and workers' lives; also major home and overseas news; Editor-in-Chief XING FANGQUN; circ. 1.8m.
Guangming Ribao (Guangming Daily): 106 Yongan Lu, Beijing; tel. 338561; telex 20021; f. 1949; literature, art, science, education,

history, economics, philosophy; Editor-in-Chief Du Daozheng; circ. 1.5m. (mainly among intellectuals).

Guangzhou Ribao (Canton Daily): 10 Dongle Lu, Renmin Zhonglu, Guangzhou, Guangdong; tel. 85812; f. 1952; daily; economic and current affairs.

Guizhou Ribao (Guizhou Daily): Guiying, Guizhou Province; circ. 300,000.

Hebei Ribao (Hebei Daily): Yuhua Lu, Shijiazhuang, Hebei Province; tel. 48901; f. 1949.

Hubei Ribao (Hubei Daily): Wuluo Lu, Wuchang, Hubei; tel. 73305; f. 1949; daily.

Jiangxi Ribao (Jiangxi Daily): Nanchang, Jiangxi Province; f. 1949.

Jiefang Ribao (Liberation Daily): 274 Han Kou Rd, Shanghai; tel. 221300; telex 6078; f. 1949; Chief Editor Chen Nianyun; circ. 1m.

Jiefangjun Bao (Liberation Army Daily): Beijing; f. 1955; official organ of the PLA; circ. 100m.

Jingji Ribao (Economic Daily): 9 Xi Huangchengen Nanjie, Beijing; tel. 652018; f. 1983; financial affairs, domestic and foreign trade; Editor-in-Chief An Gang; circ. 1.59m.

Nanfang Ribao (Nanfang Daily): Dongfeng Donglu, Guangzhou, Guangdong Province; tel. 77022; f. 1949; circ. 1m.

Nongmin Ribao (Peasants' Daily): Shilipu Beili, Chao Yang Men Wai, Beijing; tel. 583431; telex 6592; f. 1980; 6 a week; for peasants in rural areas throughout China; Prin. Officer Li Qianfang; circ. 1m.

Qingdao Ribao (Qingdao Daily): 33 Taiping Lu, Qingdao, Shandong; tel. 86237; f. 1949; daily; circ. 2.6m.

Renmin Ribao (People's Daily): 2 Jin Tai Xi Lu, Beijing; tel. 596231; telex 22320; f. 1948; organ of the Chinese Communist Party; also publishes overseas edn; Dir Qian Liren; Editor-in-Chief Tan Wenrui; circ. 5m.

Shanxi Ribao (Shanxi Daily): Shuangtasi, Taiyuan, Shanxi Province; tel. 24835.

Shenzhen Tequ Bao (Shenzhen Special Zone Daily): 1 Shennan Zhonglu, Shenzhen; tel. 22840; f. 1982; reports on special economic zones open to foreigners, as well as Hong Kong and Macau.

Sichuan Ribao (Sichuan Daily): 70 Hongxing Zhonglu, Chengdu, Sichuan; tel. 22911; f. 1952; circ. 1.35m.

Tianjin Ribao (Tianjin Daily): 66 An Shan Rd, Heping District, Tianjin; tel. 25803; f. 1949; Editor-in-Chief Lu Si; circ. 600,000.

Wenhui Bao: 149 Yuanmingyuan Lu, Shanghai; tel. 211410; f. 1938; Editor-in-Chief Ma Da; circ. 1.7m.

World Economic Herald: Shanghai; f. 1980; economics and current affairs; Editor-in-Chief Qin Benli; circ. 300,000.

Xin Hua Ribao (New China Daily): 55 Zhongshan Lu, Nanjing, Jiangsu; tel. 42638; circ. 900,000.

Xin Min Wan Bao (Xin Min Evening News): Jiujianlu 41, Shanghai; tel. 217307; f. 1946; circ. 1,365,768.

Yangcheng Wanbao (Yangcheng Evening Post): 733 Dongfeng Donglu, Guangzhou, Guangdong; tel. 776211; f. 1957; daily; large-format comprehensive evening paper; circ. 1.66m.

Zhongguo Qingnian Bao (China Youth News): 2 Haiyuncang, Dongzhimen Nei, Beijing; tel. 446581; f. 1951; 4 a week; aimed at 14–25 age-group; Dir and Chief Editor She Shiguang; circ. 3m.

PERIODICALS

Ban Yue Tan (Fortnightly Conversations): Beijing; tel. 668521; f. 1980; in Chinese and Wei Wuer (Uygur); Editor-in-Chief Ming Fanlu; circ. 5m.

Beijing Review: 24 Baiwanzhuang Rd, Beijing 37; weekly; in English, French, Spanish, Japanese and German.

Chinese Literature: 24 Baiwanzhuang Rd, Beijing 37; f. 1951; quarterly; in English and French; literary; includes art reproductions; Exec. Editor Yin Shuxun.

Chinese Science Abstracts: Science Press, 137 Chaoyang Men Wai St, Beijing; tel. 44036; telex 22313; f. 1982; monthly in English; science and technology; Chief Editor Wang Mingyang.

Dianying Xinzuo (New Films): 796 Huaihai Zhonglu, Shanghai; tel. 379710; f. 1979; fortnightly; introduces new films.

Dianzi yu Diannao (Electronics and Computers): Beijing; f. 1985; scientific magazine aiming to popularize knowledge about computers and microcomputers.

Faxue Jikan (Law Quarterly): Chongqing, Sichuan; tel. 661671; f. 1979; quarterly; theoretical law journal, with summaries in English; Dirs Li Guozhi, Xu Jingcun.

Feitian (Fly Skywards): 50 Donggan Xilu, Lanzhou, Gansu; tel. 25803; f. 1961; monthly.

Guoji Xin Jishu (New International Technology): Zhanwang Publishing House, Beijing; f. 1984; also published in Hong Kong; introduces world technology, and international scientific and technical information.

Guowai Keji Dongtai (Scientific and Technical Trends Abroad): China Institute of Scientific and Technical Information, Hepingli, Beijing; tel. 462993; f. 1969; scientific journal.

Hai Xia (The Strait): 27 De Gui Lane, Fuzhou, Fujian Province; tel. 33656; f. 1981; quarterly; literary journal; Prin. Officers Yang Yu, Jwo Jong Lin.

Hong Qi (Red Flag): Shatan, Beijing; f. 1958; 2 a month; official organ of the Chinese Communist Party; Chief Editor Xiong Fu.

Huasheng Bao (Voice of Overseas Chinese): 271 Fucheng Men Wai Dajie, Beijing; tel. 891962; f. 1983; 2 a week; intended mainly for overseas Chinese and Chinese nationals resident abroad; Editor-in-Chief Zhou Ti.

Jianzhu (Construction): Baiwanzhuang, Beijing; tel. 8992849; f. 1956; monthly; Editor Fang Yueguang; circ. 500,000.

Liaowang (Outlook): Beijing; f. 1981; weekly; current affairs.

Luxingjia (Traveller): 23A Dong Jiaomin Xiang, Beijing; tel. 552631; f. 1955; monthly; Chinese beauty spots, customs, cultural relics.

Meishu Zhi You (Friends of Art): 32 Beizongbu Hutong, East City Region, Beijing; tel. 55099752; telex 5019; f. 1982; every 2 months; art review journal, providing professional and amateur artists with information on fine arts pubis in China and abroad; Editors Peng Shen, Baolun Wu.

Nianqingren (Young People): 169 Mayuanlin, Changsha, Hunan; tel. 23610; f. 1981; monthly; general interest for young people.

Nongye Zhishi (Agricultural Knowledge): 7 Shimuyuan Dongjie, Jinan, Shandong; tel. 42238; f. 1950; fortnightly; popular agricultural science; Dir Yiang Xianfen; circ. 400,000.

Renmin Huabao (People's Pictorial): Chegonzhuang, Fuchengmen Wai, Beijing 28; f. 1950; monthly; edns in 3 minority languages.

Renmin Wujing Bao (People's Armed Police Newspaper): Beijing; f. 1983; journal of the Party Cttee of the Armed Police HQ.

Shichang Zhoubao (Market Weekly): 2 Duan, Sanhao Jie, Heping District, Shenyang, Liaoning; tel. 482983; f. 1979; weekly in Chinese; trade, commodities and financial and economic affairs; circ. 1m.

Shufa (Calligraphy): 83 Kangping Lu, Shanghai; tel. 377711; f. 1978; journal on ancient and modern calligraphy.

Tiyu Kexue (Sports Science): 8 Tiyuguan Rd, Beijing; tel. 757161; f. 1981; sponsored by the China Sports Science Soc.; quarterly; in Chinese; circ. 1.2m.

Wenxue Qingnian (Youth Literature Journal): Mu Tse Fang 27, Wenzhou, Zhejiang Province; tel. 3578; f. 1981; monthly; Editor-in-Chief Chen Yushen; circ. 80,000.

Yinyue Aihaozhe (Music Lovers): 74 Shaoxing Lu, Shanghai; tel. 372608; f. 1979; quarterly; popular music knowledge.

Zhongguo Duiwai Maoyi (China's Foreign Trade): Fu Xing Men Wai St, Beijing; tel. 863790; f. 1956; monthly; in Chinese, English, French and Spanish; carries information about Chinese imports and exports and explains foreign trade and economic policies; Editor-in-Chief Ye Jixiu.

Zhongguo Ertong (Chinese Children): 23A Dongjiaomin Xiang, Beijing; tel. 552631; f. 1980; monthly; illustrated journal for elementary school pupils.

Zhongguo Funu (Women of China): 24A Shijia Hutong, Beijing; tel. 551765; f. 1956; monthly; women's rights and status, marriage and family, education, family planning, arts, cookery, etc.

Zhongguo Guanggao Bao (China's Advertising): Editorial Dept, Beijing Exhibition Hall, Xizhimen Wai, Beijing; tel. 890661; f. 1984; weekly; all aspects of advertising and marketing; offers advertising services for domestic and foreign commodities.

Zhongguo Guangbo Dianshi (China Radio and Television): 12 Fucheng Lu, Beijing; tel. 896217; f. 1982; monthly; sponsored by Ministry of Radio, Film and Television; reports and comments on radio and television.

Zhongguo Jianshe (China Reconstructs): Baiwanzhuang Lu, Beijing; tel. 892007; f. 1952; monthly; edns in English, Spanish, French, Arabic, Portuguese, Chinese and German; economic, social and cultural affairs; illustrated; Editor-in-Chief Israel Epstein.

Zhongguo Sheying (Chinese Photography): 61 Hongxing Hutong, Dongdan, Beijing; tel. 552277; f. 1957; every 2 months; reviews and comments about photography; Editor YUAN YIPING.

Zhongguo Xinwen (China News): 1 Beixinqiao Santiao, Beijing; tel. 447424; f. 1952; weekly; current affairs.

Zhongguo Zhenjiu (Chinese Acupuncture and Moxibustion): Dongzhimen, Beijing; tel. 446661; f. 1981; 2 a month; publ. by Chinese Soc. of Acupuncture and Inst. of Acupuncture under Acad. of Traditional Chinese Medicine; partly in English; available abroad.

NEWS AGENCIES

Xinhua (New China) News Agency: 57 Xuanwumen Xidajie, Beijing; tel. 668521; telex 22316; f. 1931; offices in all Chinese provincial capitals, and about 90 overseas bureaux; news service in Chinese, English, French, Spanish, Arabic and Russian, feature and photographic services; Dir-Gen. MU QING.

Zhongguo Xinwen She (China News Agency): POB 1114, Beijing; f. 1952; office in Hong Kong; supplies news features, special articles and photographs for newspapers and magazines in Chinese printed overseas; services in Chinese; Dir LIN XIUDE.

Foreign Bureaux

Agence France-Presse (AFP) (France): 10–83 Qi Jia Yuan, Beijing; tel. 521992; Bureau Chief BERNARD DEGDANNI.

Agencia EFE (Spain): 2-2-132 Jian Guo Men Wai, Beijing; tel. 523449; telex 22167; Rep. JOSEP BOSCH GRAU.

Agenzia Nazionale Stampa Associata (ANSA) (Italy): 2–81 Ban Gong Lou, 2-81 San Li Tun, Beijing; tel. 523651; telex 22290; Agent GIULIO PECORA.

Allgemeiner Deutscher Nachrichtendienst (ADN) (German Democratic Republic): Jian Guo Men Wai, Qi Jia Yuan Gong Yu 7-2-61, Beijing; telex 22109; Correspondent OTTO MANN.

Associated Press (AP) (USA): 7-2-52 Qi Jia Yuan, Diplomatic Quarters, Beijing; tel. 523419; telex 22196; Bureau Chief JAMES ABRAMS.

Bulgarian Telegraph Agency (BTA): 1–4-13 Jian Guo Men Wai, Beijing; Bureau Chief DIMITRE IVANOV MASLAROV.

Československá tisková kancelář (ČTK) (Czechoslovakia): 7-43 Qi Jia Yuan, Beijing.

Deutsche Presse-Agentur (dpa) (Federal Republic of Germany): Ban Gong Lou, San Li Tun, Apt 1–31, Beijing; tel. 521473; telex 22297; Bureau Chief HANS-JÜRGEN KAHL.

Jiji Tsushin-Sha (Japan): 9–1-13 Jian Guo Men Wai, Beijing; tel. 522924; telex 22381; Correspondent YOSHIKAZU SAITO.

Kyodo Tsushin (Japan): 3-91 Jian Guo Men Wai, Beijing; tel. 522680; telex 8522324; Bureau Chief SHIGEYOSHI FUSE.

Magyar Távirati Iroda (MTI) (Hungary): 1–42 Ban Gong Lou, San Li Tun, Beijing; Correspondent FERENC KOVÁCS.

Prensa Latina (Cuba): 6 Wai Jiao Da Lou, Beijing; tel. 521831; telex 22284; Correspondent JOSÉ LUIS ROBAINA.

Reuters (UK): 1–11 Ban Gong Lou, San Li Tun, Beijing; tel. 521921; telex 22702; Chief Correspondent G. EARNSHAW.

Telegrafnoye Agentstvo Sovetskovo Soyuza (TASS) (USSR): Jian Guo Men Wai, Qi Jia Yuan Gong Yu, Beijing; telex 22115; Correspondent GRIGORIY ARSLANOV.

United Press International (UPI) (USA): 7–1-11 Qi Jia Yuan, Beijing; tel. 523456; telex 22197; Correspondents RON REDMOND, ANN SCOTT.

The following are also represented: Agerpres (Romania), Korean Central News Agency (Democratic People's Republic of Korea), Tanjug (Yugoslavia) and VNA (Viet-Nam).

PRESS ASSOCIATION

All China Journalists' Association: Xijiaomin Xiang, Beijing; tel. 657170; Chair. WU LENGXI.

Publishers

In 1984 there were nearly 300 publishing houses in China, including a regional 'People's Publishing House' for each province.

National Publishing Administration of China (NPA): Beijing; administers publishing, printing and distribution under the Ministry of Culture; Dir BIAN CHUNGUANG.

Beijing Chubanshe (Beijing Publishing House): 51 Dong Xinglong Jie, Chongwenmen Wai, Beijing; tel. 754394; f. 1956; political theory, history, philosophy, economics, geography, etc.

Beijing Daxue Chubanshe (Beijing University Press): Beijing University, Haidian District, Beijing; tel. 283827; f. 1980; academic.

Ditu Chubanshe (Cartographic Publishing House): 3 Baizhifang Xijie, Beijing; tel. 334931; f. 1954; cartographic publr; Dir ZHANG XUELIANG.

Dolphin Books: 24 Baiwanzhuang Rd, Beijing; tel. 890951; telex 22496; f. 1986; children's books in foreign languages.

Falü Chubanshe (Law Press): 1 Baiguang Lu, Beijing; tel. 365360; f. 1980; current laws and decrees, legal textbooks, translations of important foreign legal works.

Gaodeng Jiaoyu Chubanshe (Higher Education Press): 55 Shatan Houjie, Beijing; tel. 442931; f. 1954; academic.

Gongren Chubanshe (Workers' Press): Liupukeng, Andingmen Wai, Beijing; tel. 465551; f. 1949; labour movement, trade unions, science and technology related to industrial production.

Guangdong Keji Chubanshe (Guangdong Scientific and Technical Press): 25 Xinji Lu, POB 49, Guangzhou, Guangdong; tel. 882930; f. 1978; natural sciences, technology, medicine; Dir DU YANGLIAN.

Guoji Shudian (China International Book Trading Corporation): POB 399, Chegongzhuang Xilu 21, Beijing; tel. 891203; telex 22496; f. 1949; foreign trade org. specializing in publs, including books, periodicals, art and crafts, microfilms, etc.; import and export distributors; Gen. Man. CAO JIANFEI.

Heilongjiang Kexue Jishu Chubanshe (Heilongjiang Scientific and Technical Publishing House): 28 Fenbu Jie, Nangang District, Harbin, Heilongjiang; tel. 35613; f. 1979; industrial and agricultural technology, natural sciences.

Huashan Wenyi Chubanshe (Huashan Literature and Art Publishing House): 45 Bei Malu, Shijiazhuang, Hebei; tel. 27380; f. 1982; novels, poetry, drama, etc.

Kexue Chubanshe (Science Press): 137 Chaoyangmen Nei Dajie, Beijing; tel. 444036; f. 1954; science and technology.

Lingnan Meishu Chubanshe (Lingnan Art Publishing House): 25 Xinji Lu, Xiti, Guangzhou, Guangdong Province; tel. 861251; f. 1981; works on classical and modern painting, picture albums, photographic, painting techniques; Editor-in-Chief LIN KANGSHENG.

Minzu Chubanshe (Nationalities Publishing House): Hepingli Dong Lu, Beijing; tel. 461261; f. 1953; books and periodicals in minority languages, e.g. Mongolian, Tibetan, Kazakh, Uigur, etc.

Qunzhong Chubanshe (Masses Publishing House): 14 Dongchangan St, Beijing; tel. 5121672; telex 2831; f. 1956; politics, law, judicial affairs, crime detection, public security, etc.

Renmin Jiaoyu Chubanshe (People's Educational Publishing House): 55 Shatan Houjie, Beijing; tel. 442931; f. 1950; educational, scientific.

Renmin Meishu Chubanshe (People's Fine Arts Publishing House): 32 Beizongbu Hutong, Beijing; tel. 550290; f. 1951; works by Chinese and foreign painters, picture albums, photographic, painting techniques; Dir TIAN YUWEN.

Renmin Weisheng Chubanshe (People's Medical Publishing House): 10 Tiantan Xi Li, Beijing; tel. 755431; f. 1953; medicine, pharmacology, public health; Pres. DONG MIANGUO.

Renmin Wenxue Chubanshe (People's Literature Publishing House): 166 Chaoyangmen Nei Dajie, Beijing; tel. 553177; f. 1951; largest state publr of literary works and translations into Chinese; Dir MENG WEIZAI.

Shanghai Guji Chubanshe (Shanghai Classics Publishing House): 272 Ruijin Erlu, Shanghai; tel. 370013; f. 1978; classical Chinese literature.

Shanghai Jiaoyu Chubanshe (Shanghai Educational Publishing House): 123 Yongfu Lu, Shanghai; tel. 377165; telex 3413; f. 1958; academic.

Shanghai Yiwen Chubanshe (Shanghai Translation Publishing House): 14 Lane 955, Yanan Zhonglu, Shanghai; tel. 311890; f. 1978; translations of foreign literature, especially classics.

Shangwu Yinshuguan (Commercial Press): 36 Wangfujing Dajie, Beijing; tel. 552026; f. 1897; dictionaries and reference books in Chinese and foreign languages, translations of foreign works on social sciences; Editor-in-Chief CHEN YUAN.

Shaonian Ertong Chubanshe (Juvenile and Children's Publishing House): 1538 Yanan Xi Lu, Shanghai; tel. 522519; telex 5801; f. 1952; Editor-in-Chief CHEN XIANGMING; children's educational and literary works, teaching aids and periodicals.

Waiwen Chubanshe (Foreign Languages Press): 24 Baiwanzhuang Rd, Beijing 37; tel. 892902; telex 22496; f. 1952; state publr;

books in foreign languages reflecting political, economic and cultural progress in People's Republic of China; Chief Editor LUO LIANG.

Wenwu Chubanshe (Cultural Relics Publishing House): 29 Wusi Dajie, Beijing; tel. 441761; f. 1956; books and catalogues of Chinese relics in museums and those recently discovered; Dir WANG DAIWEN.

Wuhan Daxue Chubanshe (Wuhan University Press): Wuhan University, Wuchang, Hubei; tel. 75941; f. 1952; academic.

Xiandai Chubanshe (Modern Press): 504 Anhua Li, Andingmenwai, Beijing; tel. 466251; telex 22497; f. 1982; directories, reference books, etc.

Xuelin Chubanshe (Scholar Books Publishers): 5 Shaoxing Lu, Shanghai; tel. 370176; f. 1981; academic, including personal academic works at authors' own expense.

Zhongguo Caizheng Jingji Chubanshe (China Financial and Economic Publishing House): 8 Dafosi Dongjie, Dongcheng District, Beijing; tel. 441982; f. 1961; finance, economics, commerce and accounting.

Zhongguo Dabaike Quanshu Chubanshe (Encyclopaedia of China Publishing House): A-1 Wai Guan Dong Jie, An Ding Men Wai, Beijing; tel. 464389; f. 1978; specializes in encyclopaedias; Chief Editor MEI YI; Dir CHANG PING.

Zhongguo Funü Chubanshe (Chinese Women's Publishing House): 24A Shijia Hutong, Beijing; tel. 557002; f. 1981; women's movement, marriage and family, child-care, etc.

Zhongguo Qingnian Chubanshe (China Youth Publishing House): 21 Dongsi Shiertiao Hutong, Beijing; tel. 444761; f. 1950; literature, ethics, social and natural sciences, youth work, autobiography; also periodicals; Dir CAI YUN.

Zhongguo Shehui Kexue Chubanshe (China Social Sciences Publishing House): 158A Gulou Xidajie, Beijing; tel. 441531; f. 1978; Dir ZHANG DING.

Zhonghua Shuju (Chung Hwa Book Co): 36 Wangfujing, Dajie, Beijing; tel. 554504; f. 1912; general; Gen. Man. WANG CHUNG.

Zhongguo Xiju Chubanshe (Chinese Theatrical Publishing House): 52 Dongsi Batiao Hutong, Beijing; tel. 442318; f. 1957; plays, operas, ballads, etc.

PUBLISHERS' ASSOCIATION

Publishers' Association of China: Beijing; f. 1979; arranges academic exchanges with foreign publrs; Chair. CHEN HANBO; Sec.-Gen. SONG MUWEN.

Radio and Television

At the end of 1984 there were 215 radio broadcasting stations and 575 transmitting and relay stations. In 1978, 63% of households in the countryside had loudspeakers connected to the radio rediffusion system. There were an estimated 15m. radio receivers in use in 1984.

There were 204 television stations and 507 transmitting and relay stations equipped with transmitters of 1,000 Watts or more. In 1984 there were an estimated 9.9m. television receivers in use.

Ministry of Radio, Film and Television: Outside Fu Xing Men St 2, Beijing; tel. 862753; telex 22236; controls the Central People's Broadcasting Station, the Central TV Station, Radio Beijing, China Record Company, Beijing Broadcasting Institute, Broadcasting Research Institute, the China Broadcasting Art Troupe, etc.; Minister of Radio, Film and Television AI ZHISHENG.

RADIO

Central People's Broadcasting Station: Outside Fu Xing Men St 2, Beijing; domestic service in Chinese, Guanghua (Cantonese), Zang Wen (Tibetan), Chaozhou, Min Nan Hua (Amoy), Ke Jia (Hakka), Fuzhou Hua (Foochow dialect), Hasaka (Kazakh), Wei Wuer (Uygur), Menggu Hua (Mongolian) and Chaoxian (Korean); Dir YANG ZHAOLIN.

Radio Beijing: Outside Fu Xing Men St 2, Beijing; tel. 862691; telex 22236; f. 1947; foreign service in 38 languages incl. Arabic, Burmese, Czech, English, Esperanto, French, German, Indonesian, Italian, Japanese, Lao, Polish, Portuguese, Russian, Spanish, Turkish and Vietnamese; Dir CUI YULIN.

TELEVISION

Central People's Television Broadcasting Section: Bureau of Broadcasting Affairs of the State Council, Beijing; f. 1958.

Finance

BANKING

(cap. = capital; p.u. = paid up; res = reserves; m. = million; amounts in yuan)

Central Bank

People's Bank of China: San Li He, West City, Beijing; tel. 868451; telex 22612; f. 1948; state bank and bank of issue; Pres. Miss CHEN MUHUA; Vice-Pres. LIU HONGRU.

Other Banks

Agricultural Bank of China: Fuxing Rd, Beijing; tel. 810709; telex 22017; f. 1963; functions directly under the State Council and handles state agricultural investments; total deposits 6,200m. (Aug. 1979); Pres. MA YONGWEI.

Bank of China: 17 Xi Jiao Min Xiang, Beijing; tel. 653431; telex 22254; f. 1912; handles foreign exchange and international settlements; cap. p.u. 3,000m., dep. 116,238m. (1985); Chair. and Pres. WANG DEYAN; 344 brs, 25 abroad.

Bank of Communications: 17 Xi Jiao Min Xiang, Beijing; telex 61466; f. 1908; functions under the People's Bank of China; handles state investments in the joint state-private enterprises; cap. p.u. 400m., res 245m. (1984); Gen. Man. CHANG YANQING.

China and South Sea Bank Ltd: 17 Xi Jiao Min Xiang, Beijing; f. 1920; cap. p.u. 250m., res 169m. (1984); Gen. Man. CUI PING.

China International Trust and Investment Corporation: 2 Qianmen Dongdajie, Beijing; tel. 753600; telex 22305; f. 1979; responsible to the State Council; raises funds abroad for investment in China and engages in joint investment ventures in China and abroad; auth. cap. 600m.; Pres. XU ZHAOLONG; Chair. RONG YIREN.

China Investment Bank: Sanlihe, Fu Xing Men Wai, Beijing; tel. 868451; telex 22537; f. 1981; specializes in raising foreign funds for domestic investment and credit; Chair. WU BOSHAN.

China State Bank Ltd: 17 Xi Jiao Min Xiang, Beijing; cap. p.u. 250m., res 97.5m. (1984); Gen. Man. LI PINZHOU.

Guangdong Provincial Bank: 17 Xi Jiao Min Xiang, Beijing; cap. p.u. 300m., res 166m. (1983); Gen. Man. CHENG KEDONG.

Industrial and Commercial Bank of China: Yuetan South St, Beijing; tel. 868901; f. 1984; handles industrial and commercial credits; Pres. ZHANG XIAO.

Kincheng Banking Corporation: 17 Xi Jiao Min Xiang, Beijing; telex 73405; f. 1917; cap. p.u. 300m., res 238m. (1984); Gen. Man. XIANG KEFANG.

National Commercial Bank Ltd: 17 Xi Jiao Min Xiang, Beijing; f. 1907; cap. p.u. 250m., res 174m. (1984); Gen. Man. WANG WEICAI.

People's Construction Bank of China: Sanlihe, Beijing; tel. 868451; f. 1954 to make payments for capital construction according to plan and budget approval by the state; issues long- and medium-term loans to enterprises and short-term loans to contractors; Pres. ZHOU DAOJIONG.

Sin Hua Trust, Savings and Commercial Bank Ltd: 17 Xi Jiao Min Xiang, Beijing; cap. p.u. 300m., res 193m. (1983); Gen. Man. CUI YANXU.

Yien Yieh Commercial Bank Ltd: 17 Xi Jiao Min Xiang, Beijing; cap. p.u. 250m., res 204m. (1984); Gen. Man. JIANG WENGUI.

Foreign Banks

Barclays Bank (UK): West 2, 23 Qianmen Ave East, Beijing; tel. 552417; telex 22589; Rep. W. H. SPEIRS.

First National Bank of Chicago (USA): 1604, CITIC Bldg, Jian Guo Men Wai, Beijing; tel. 5003281; telex 22433; Chief Rep. L. C. FRANKLIN.

Hongkong and Shanghai Banking Corporation (Hong Kong): POB 151, 185 Yuan Ming Yuan Lu, Shanghai; tel. 216030; telex 33058; f. 1865; Man. C. R. PAGE.

Midland Bank PLC (UK): Room 1103, CITIC Bldg, Jian Guo Men Wai, Beijing; tel. 5004410; telex 22594; Group Rep. LANCE BROWNE.

Oversea-Chinese Banking Corporation Ltd (Singapore): f. 1932; brs in Xiamen (Amoy) and Shanghai; Chair. Tan Sri TAN CHIN TUAN.

Standard Chartered Bank (UK): 9th Floor, Union Bldg, 100 Yanan Dong Lu, Shanghai; tel. 218253; telex 33067; f. 1853; Rep. TIM HOOPER.

The following foreign banks also have branches in Beijing: Banca Commerciale Italiana, Bank of Brazil, Bank of Nova Scotia, Bank of Tokyo, Banque Nationale de Paris, Banque de l'Union Européenne, Banque Indosuez, Banque Paribas, Chase Manhattan, Commerzbank, Crédit Lyonnais, Deutsche Bank, Dresdner Bank, National Bank of Pakistan, National Commercial Banking Corporation of Australia, Royal Bank of Canada, Société Generale de Banque.

INSURANCE

China Insurance Co Ltd: POB 20, 22 Xi Jiao Min Xiang, Beijing; tel. 654231; telex 22102; f. 1931; cargo, hull, freight, fire, life, personal accident, industrial injury, motor insurance, reinsurance, etc.; Man. SONG GUO HUA.

The People's Insurance Co of China (PICC): POB 2149, 22 Xi Jiao Min Xiang, Beijing; tel. 654231; telex 22102; f. 1949; hull, marine cargo, aviation, motor, life, fire, accident, liability and reinsurance, etc.; Chair. QIN DAOFU; Vice-Chair. LI PINZHOU.

Tai Ping Insurance Co Ltd: 22 Xi Jiao Min Xiang, Beijing; tel. 654231; telex 42001; marine freight, hull, cargo, fire, life, personal accident, industrial injury, motor insurance, reinsurance, etc.; Man. LIN ZHEN FENG.

Trade and Industry

EXTERNAL TRADE

All-China Federation of Industry and Commerce: 93 Beiheyan Dajie, Beijing; tel. 554231; telex 22044; f. 1953; promotes overseas trade relations; Chair. HU ZIANG.

China Council for the Promotion of International Trade: Fu Xing Men Wai St, Beijing; tel. 867504; telex 22315; f. 1952; encourages foreign trade and economic co-operation; sponsors and arranges Chinese exhbns abroad and foreign exhbns in China; helps foreigners to apply for patent rights and trade-mark registration in China; promotes foreign investment and organizes tech. exchanges with other countries; provides legal services; publishes trade periodicals; Chair. JIA SHI.

China Industry-Commerce-Economic Development Corporation (INCOMIC): 93 Bei He Yan Dajie, Beijing; tel. 554231; telex 22044; f. 1985; provides consultancy and promotion of exports and imports, both in China and internationally; Chair. HU ZIANG; Pres. ZOU SIYU.

Ministry of Foreign Economic Relations and Trade: (see under Ministries).

Export and Import Corporations

Beijing Foreign Trade Corporation: Bldg 12, Yong An Dong Li, Jian Guo Men Wai, Beijing; tel. 595182; telex 22470; controls import-export trade, foreign trade transportation, export commodity packaging and advertising for Beijing; Chair. GAO SEN; Vice-Chair. HUANG CHENGXIANG.

China International Book Trading Corporation: see under Guoji Shudian in Publishers Section.

China International Water and Electric Corporation: Liupukang, Beijing; tel. 442784; telex 22485; f. 1956, as China Water and Electric International Corpn, name changed 1983; exports equipment for projects in the field of water and electrical engineering, and undertakes such projects; Pres. ZHU JINGDE.

China Metallurgical Import and Export Corporation (CMIEC): 46 Dongsi Xidajie, Beijing; tel. 555714; telex 22461; f. 1980; imports ores, spare parts, automation and control systems, etc.; exports metallurgical products, technology and equipment; establishes joint ventures and trade with foreign companies; Gen. Man. BAI BAOHUA.

China National Aerotechnology Import-Export Corporation: 5 Liangguochang Rd, East City District, POB 1671, Beijing; tel. 445831; telex 22318; exports signal flares, electric detonators, tachometers, parachutes, general purpose aircraft, etc.; Gen. Man. SUN ZHAOQING.

China National Animal Breeding Stock Import and Export Corporation: Dongdan, Beijing; tel. 542155; telex 210101; sole agency for import and export of stud animals including cattle, sheep, goats, swine, horses, donkeys, camels, rabbits, poultry, etc., as well as pasture seeds and feed additives.

China National Arts and Crafts Import and Export Corporation: 82 Donganmen, Beijing; tel. 552187; telex 22155; deals in jewellery, ceramics, handicrafts, pottery, wicker, bamboo, etc.; Pres. YU ZHITING.

China National Cereals, Oils and Foodstuffs Import and Export Corporation: 82 Donganmen, Beijing; tel. 555180; telex 22281; imports and exports cereals, sugar, vegetable oils, meat, eggs, fruit, dairy produce, vegetables, wines and spirits, canned foods and aquatic products, etc.; Gen. Man. CAO WANTONG.

China National Chartering Corporation (SINOCHART): Import Bldg, Erlikou, Xijiao, Beijing; tel. 890931; telex 22488; f. 1950; functions under Ministry of Foreign Economic Relations and Trade; agents for SINOTRANS (see below); arranges chartering of ships, booking space, managing and operating chartered vessels; Pres. PING JIAN.

China National Chemicals Import and Export Corporation: Erlikou, Xijiao, Beijing; tel. 891289; telex 22243; deals in rubber, petroleum, paints, fertilizers, inks, dyestuffs, chemicals and drugs; Pres. SUN SUOCHANG.

China National Coal Import and Export Corporation (CNCIEC): 3A Dong Huang Si Da Jie, An Ding Men Wai, Beijing; tel. 466061; telex 22494; imports and exports coal and technology equipment for coal industry, joint coal development and compensation trade; Chair. HONG SHANGQING.

China National Electronic Technology Import and Export Corporation: 49 Fuxing Rd, Beijing; tel. 810910; telex 22475; Pres. LI DEGUANG.

China National Foreign Trade Transportation Corporation (SINOTRANS): Import Bldg, Erlikou, Xijiao, Beijing; tel. 890931; telex 22867; f. 1950; functions under Ministry of Foreign Economic Relations and Trade; agents for Ministry's import and export corpns; arranges customs clearance, deliveries, forwarding and insurance for sea, land and air transportation; Pres. PING JIAN.

China National Import and Export Commodities Inspection Corporation: 2 Dongchangan St, Beijing; tel. 55876; telex 22168; inspects, tests and surveys import and export commodities for overseas trade, transport, insurance and manufacturing firms; Gen. Man. ZHANG HUADONG.

China National Instruments Import and Export Corporation: Erlikou, Xijiao, Beijing; tel. 890931; telex 22304; imports and exports computers and technology in fields of telecommunications, electronics, navigation, chemicals, optics, nuclear physics, etc.; Pres. WANG ZHONGYUAN.

China National Light Industrial Products Import and Export Corporation: 82 Donganmen, Beijing; tel. 558831; telex 22282; imports household electrical appliances, radio and TV sets, photographic equipment, films, paper goods, building materials, etc.; exports bicycles, sewing machines, enamelware, glassware, stainless steel goods, footwear, leather goods, watches and clocks, cosmetics, stationery, electrical appliances, etc.; Pres. LI WENQUN (acting).

China National Machine Tool Corporation: San Li He, Beijing; single and multi-purpose machines, indexing-table and indexing-drum machines, vertical drilling and boring machines and transfer lines, etc.

China National Machinery and Equipment Import and Export Corporation: 12 Fuxing Menwai, Beijing; tel. 362561; telex 22186; f. 1978; imports and exports machine tools, all kinds of machinery, automobiles, hoisting and transport equipment, electric motors, photographic equipment, etc.; Gen. Dir JIA QINGLIN.

China National Machinery Import and Export Corporation: Erlikou, Xijiao, Beijing; tel. 890931; telex 22876; imports and exports machine tools, diesel engines and boilers and all kinds of machinery; Gen. Man. GU YONGJIANG.

China National Medicines and Health Products Import and Export Corporation: Bldg 12, Jian Wai Da Jie, Beijing; tel. 5003344; telex 210103; Pres. YAN RUDAI.

China National Metals and Minerals Import and Export Corporation: Erlikou, Xijiao, Beijing; tel. 892376; telex 22241; f. 1950; principal imports and exports include steel, antimony, tungsten concentrates and ferrotungsten, zinc ingots, tin, mercury, pig iron, cement, etc.; Gen. Man. WANG YAN.

China National Native Produce and Animal By-Products Import and Export Corporation (TUHSU): 82 Donganmen, Beijing; tel. 554124; telex 22283; imports and exports tea, coffee, cocoa, fibres, etc.; 5 subsidiary enterprises; 63 domestic brs; Gen. Man. QI GUANGCAI.

China National Offshore Oil Corporation (CNOOC): 31 Dongchangan St, Beijing; tel. 555225; telex 22611; Pres. QIN WENCAI.

China National Packaging Import and Export Corporation: 2 Dong Hou Xiang, An Ding Men Wai, Beijing; tel. 462124;

telex 22490; handles import and export of packaging materials, containers, machines and tools; contracts for the processing and converting of packaging machines and materials using raw materials supplied by foreign clients; Vice-Pres. XU JIANGUO.

China National Petroleum Corporation: Liupukang, Beijing; tel. 444313; telex 22312; Gen. Man. QIN WENCAI.

China National Publications Import and Export Corporation: POB 88, Beijing; tel. 440731; telex 22313; imports principally foreign books, newspapers and periodicals, records, etc., exports principally Chinese scientific and technical journals published in foreign languages; Gen. Man. CHEN WEIJIANG.

China National Publishing Industry Trading Corporation: POB 782, 504 An Hua Li, Outside An Ding Men, Beijing; tel. 466251; telex 210215; imports and exports books, journals, paintings, woodcuts, watercolour prints and rubbings; holds book fairs abroad; undertakes joint publication.

China National Seed Corporation: 16 Donghuan Bei Lu, Beijing; tel. 593619; telex 22233; imports and exports crop seeds, including cereals, cotton, oil-bearing crops and vegetables; seed production for foreign seed companies etc.; Man. HU QINGLING.

China National Technical Import Corporation: Erlikou, Xijiao, Beijing; tel. 890931; telex 22244; f. 1952; imports all kinds of complete plant and equipment, acquires modern technology and know-how from abroad, undertakes co-production and joint-venture, and technical consultation and updating of existing enterprises; Gen. Man. XU DEEN.

China National Textiles Import and Export Corporation: 82 Donganmen, Beijing; tel. 553793; telex 22280; imports synthetic fibres, raw cotton, wool, etc.; exports cotton yarn, cotton fabric, knitwear, woven garments, etc.; Pres. ZHOU YUNZHONG.

China North Industries Corporation (NORINCO): 7A Yuetan Nan Jie, Beijing; tel. 866898; telex 22339; exports measuring tools, bearings, calipers, optical instruments, hydraulic presses, dynamite, chemical products, etc.; Pres. ZHOU PEIDE.

China Nuclear Energy Industry Corporation (CNEIC): 21 Nan Lishi Rd, Beijing; tel. 867717; telex 22240; exports air filters, vacuum valves, dosimeters, radioactive detection elements and optical instruments; Gen. Man. ZHANG XINDUO.

China Petro-Chemical Corporation (SINOPEC): 24 Xiao-Guan St, An Wai, Beijing; tel. 466731; f. 1983; ministerial-level economic body directly under control of the State Council; petroleum refining, petrochemicals, synthetic fibres, etc.; 60 subordinate enterprises; approx. 500,000 employees; Chair. LI RENJUN; Pres. CHEN JINHUA.

China Road and Bridge Engineering Co: 3 Waiguan Jie, An Ding Men Wai, Beijing; tel. 463378; telex 22336; overseas building of highways, urban roads, bridges, tunnels, industrial and residential buildings, airport runways and parking areas; contracts to do all surveying, designing, pipe-laying, building, etc., and/or to provide technical or labour services; Gen. Man. MA JIANGDA.

Shanghai Foreign Trade Corporation: 27 Zhongshan Dong Yi Lu, Shanghai; tel. 217350; telex 33034; handles import-export trade, foreign trade transportation, chartering, export commodity packaging, storage and advertising for Shanghai municipality.

Shanghai International Trust and Service Corporation: 521 Henan Rd, POB 3066, Shanghai; tel. 226650; telex 33627; f. 1979; handles mail order and foreign trade, drafts contracts, arranges export, customs and deliveries for overseas Chinese, etc.

INTERNAL TRADE

State Administration for Industry and Commerce: 8 San Li He Dong Lu, Xichengqu, Beijing; tel. 863031; functions under the direct supervision of the State Council; Dir REN ZHONGLIN.

TRADE UNIONS

All-China Federation of Trade Unions: 10 Fuxingmenwai St, Beijing; tel. 367631; f. 1925; organized on an industrial basis; 15 affiliated national industrial unions, 29 affiliated local trade union councils; membership is voluntary; trade unionists enjoy extensive benefits; in 1985 there were 85m. members; Pres. NI ZHIFU.

TRADE FAIR

Chinese Export Commodities Fair (CECF): Guangzhou Foreign Trade Centre, 117 Lui Hua Rd, Guangzhou; tel. 677000; telex 44465; f. 1957; organized by the Ministry of Foreign Economic Relations and Trade; 2 trade fairs a year: 15 April–5 May; 15 October–5 November.

Transport

RAILWAYS

Ministry of Railways: 10 Fuxing Rd, Beijing; tel. 363875; controls all railways through regional divisions. The railway network has been extended to all provinces and regions except Xizang, where construction is in progress. Total length measured 51,700 km in 1984, of which at least around 3,000 km was electrified. In addition, special railways serve factories and mines. There is an extensive development programme to improve the rail network. Some of the major routes are Beijing–Guangzhou, Tianjin–Shanghai, Manzhouli–Vladivostok, Jiaozuo–Zhicheng and Lanzhou–Badou.

There is an underground system serving Beijing. Its total length was 23 km in 1984, and further lines are under construction. In 1984 Tianjin city opened its first underground line.

ROADS

In 1985 China had 940,000 km of highways. Four major highways link Lhasa with Sichuan, Xinjiang, Qinghai Hu and Kathmandu (Nepal). There are plans to build 11 motorways by 1990, with a total length of 2,000 km.

WATER TRANSPORT

Bureau of Water Transportation: Controls rivers and coast traffic. In 1984 there were 109,300 km of navigable inland waterways in China. The main rivers are the Huanghe, Changjiang and Zhu. The Changjiang is navigable by vessels of 10,000 tons as far as Wuhan, over 1,000 km from the coast. Vessels of 1,000 tons can continue to Chongqing upstream. Over one-third of internal freight traffic is carried by water.

SHIPPING

The greater part of China's shipping is handled in nine major ports: Dalian, Qinhuangdao, Xingang, Qingdao, Lianyungang, Shanghai, Huangpu (Whampoa), Guangzhou and Zhanjiang. Three-quarters of the handling facilities are mechanical, and harbour improvement schemes are constantly in progress. In 1985 China's merchant fleet ranked ninth in the world in terms of tonnage: including chartered ships, the merchant navy had a total capacity of 14.4m. dwt.

China Ocean Shipping Co (COSCO): 6 Dongchangan St, Beijing; tel. 5121188; telex 22264; br. offices: Shanghai, Guangzhou, Tianjin, Qingdao, Dalian; merchant fleet of 614 vessels of various types with a dwt of 13m. tons; serves China/Japan, China/SE Asia, China/Australia, China/Gulf, China/Europe and China/N. America; Man. Dir LIN ZUYI.

China Ocean Shipping Agency: 6 Dongchangan St, Beijing; telex 22264; f. 1953; br. offices at Chinese foreign trade ports; the sole agency which undertakes business for ocean-going vessels calling at Chinese ports; arranges sea passage, booking space, transhipment of cargoes; attends to chartering, purchase or sale of ships etc; Man. Dir LIN ZUYI.

Minsheng Shipping Co: 91 Dongzhengjie, Chongging; tel. 46109; telex 62174; f. 1984; 41 barges, 9 tugs, totalling 29,800 dwt; Dir LU GUOJI.

CIVIL AVIATION

New international airports were opened at Beijing in 1980 and Xiamen in 1983. The construction of international airports at other major centres is planned, while other airports (e.g. at Shanghai and Chengdu) are being expanded.

General Administration of Civil Aviation of China (CAAC): 115 Dong-si (West) Street, Beijing; telex 22101; established in 1949, superseded the Civil Aviation Administration of China. CAAC at present controls all civil aviation activities in China, including the current domestic network of more than 171 routes, with a total length of over 210,000 km and with services to all 29 provinces and autonomous regions except Taiwan; however, CAAC is in the process of being restructured, and its operations are to be divided between five new airlines (Air China, China Eastern Airways, China Southern Airways, China Southwestern Airways and China Capital Helicopter Service), which, despite some confusion, should be operational by 1987. External services operate from Beijing to Addis Ababa, Baghdad, Bangkok, Belgrade, Bucharest, Frankfurt, Karachi, Kuwait, London, Los Angeles, Manila, Moscow, Nagasaki, New York, Osaka, Paris, Pyongyang, Rangoon, Rome, San Francisco, Sharjah, Sydney, Teheran, Tokyo and Zürich; there is a weekly charter service between Chengdu and Hong Kong; Dir-Gen. HU YIZHOU; fleet of 5 Boeing 747, 4 707-320B, 6 707-320C,

THE PEOPLE'S REPUBLIC OF CHINA

10 737-200, 5 Ilyushin Il-62, Il-18, Trident, Antonov An-24, Il-14/Li-2 and a number of smaller aircraft; on order: 2 737-300.

Tourism

A total of 17.8m. tourists visited China in 1985, including many from Hong Kong and Macau. China's expanding tourist industry brought in US $1,250m. in foreign exchange in 1985, a rise of 10.5% over 1984.

China International Travel Service (Lüxingshe): 6 Dongchangan, Beijing; tel. 554192; telex 20052; makes travel arrangements for foreign parties; Gen. Dir and Man. ZHANG LIAN HUA; general agency in Hong Kong, business offices in London, Paris, New York and Tokyo.

Chinese People's Association for Friendship with Foreign Countries: Beijing; Pres. ZHANG WENJIN.

National Tourism Administration: 6 East Chang An Ave, Beijing; tel. 5121122; telex 22350; Chair. HAN KEHUA.

Atomic Energy

By the end of 1983 China had built 317 nuclear reactors, with a total capacity of 190m. kW. China's first 300,000 kW nuclear power station at Qinshan in Zhejiang Province, and a second plant at Daya Bay in Shenzhen Special Economic Zone, Guangdong Province (1,800,000 kW), were under construction in 1986. A third station is proposed for Sunan, in Jiangsu Province. China expects to have nuclear power plants with a combined generating power of 10,000 MW by the end of the century. In October 1983 China was admitted to the International Atomic Energy Agency (IAEA).

Atomic Energy Institute: POB 275, Beijing; f. 1958; research in the field of nuclear physics, nuclear chemistry and nuclear chemical engineering, reactor engineering, preparation of isotopes, environmental and radiation protection, radiometrology, etc.; Dir SUN ZUXUN.

Atomic Research Centre: Tarim Pendi, Xingjiang; f. 1953; Dir WANG GANZHANG.

Military Scientific Council: Beijing; Dir Dr JIAN XUESAN.

CHINA (TAIWAN)

Introductory Survey

Location, Climate, Language, Religion, Flag, Capital

The Republic of China has, since 1949, been confined mainly to the province of Taiwan (comprising one large island and several much smaller ones), which lies off the south-east coast of the Chinese mainland. The territory under the Republic's effective jurisdiction consists of the island of Taiwan (also known as Formosa) and nearby islands, including the P'enghu (Pescadores) group, together with a few other islands which lie just off the mainland and form part of the province of Fujian (Fukien), west of Taiwan. The largest of these is Chinmen (Jinmen), also known as Quemoy, which (with three smaller islands) is about 10 km from the port of Xiamen (Amoy), while five other islands under Taiwan's control, mainly Matsu (Mazu), lie further north, near Fuzhou. Taiwan itself is separated from the mainland by the Taiwan (Formosa) Strait, which is about 145 km (90 miles) wide at its narrowest point. The island's climate is one of rainy summers and mild winters. Average temperatures are about 15°C (59°F) in the winter and 26°C (79°F) in the summer. The average annual rainfall is 2,565 mm (101 in). The official language is Northern Chinese (Mandarin). The predominant religion is Buddhism but there are also Muslims, Daoists and Christians (Roman Catholics and Protestants). The philosophy of Confucianism has a large following. The national flag (proportions 3 by 2) is red, with a dark blue rectangular canton, containing a white sun, in the upper hoist. The capital of Taiwan is Taipei.

Recent History

China ceded Taiwan to Japan in 1895. The island remained under Japanese rule until 1945, when the Second World War ended. As a result of Japan's defeat in the war, Taiwan was returned to Chinese control, becoming a province of the Republic of China, then ruled by the Kuomintang (KMT, Nationalist Party). The leader of the KMT was Gen. Chiang Kai-shek, President of the Republic since 1928.

The KMT Government's forces were defeated in 1949 by the Communist revolution in China. President Chiang and many of his supporters withdrew from the Chinese mainland and established themselves on Taiwan, where they set up a KMT regime in succession to their previous all-China administration. This regime continued to assert that it was the rightful Chinese Government, in opposition to the People's Republic of China, which had been proclaimed by the victorious Communists in 1949. Since establishing their base in Taiwan, the Nationalists have successfully resisted attacks by their Communist rivals and have, in turn, declared that they intend to recover control of mainland China from the Communists.

Although its effective control was limited to Taiwan, the KMT regime continued to be dominated by politicians who had formerly been in power on the mainland. In support of the regime's claim to be the legitimate government of all China, Taiwan's legislative bodies are filled mainly by surviving mainland members, and the representatives of the island's native Taiwanese majority occupy only a minority of seats. Unable to replenish their mainland representation, the National Assembly (last elected fully in 1947) and other organs extended their terms of office indefinitely, although fewer than half of the original members were alive on Taiwan in the 1980s. While it has promised eventually to reconquer the mainland, the KMT regime has been largely preoccupied with ensuring its own survival, and promoting economic development, on Taiwan. The political domination of the island by immigrants from the mainland has caused some resentment among Taiwanese, and has led to demands for increased democratization and for the recognition of Taiwan as a state independent of China.

In 1954 the USA, which had refused to recognize the People's Republic of China, signed a mutual security treaty with the KMT Government, pledging to protect Taiwan and the Pescadores. In 1955 the islands of Quemoy and Matsu, lying just offshore from the mainland, were included in the protected area.

In spite of being confined to Taiwan, the KMT regime continued to represent China at the United Nations (and as a permanent member of the UN Security Council) until 1971, when it was replaced by the People's Republic. Nationalist China was subsequently expelled from several other international organizations. In 1986 the Taiwan regime was recognized by only 22 countries.

Legislative elections were held in December 1972, for the first time in 24 years, to fill 53 seats in the National Assembly. The new members, elected for a fixed term of six years, joined 1,376 surviving 'life-term' members of Assembly. In 1973 the Government rejected an offer from the People's Republic to hold secret talks on the reunification of China, and this policy has since been strongly reaffirmed. In October 1981 Taiwan rejected China's suggested terms for reunification, under which Taiwan would become a 'special administrative region' and would have a high degree of autonomy, including the retention of its own armed forces and its relatively high standard of living. In 1983 China renewed its offer of autonomy for Taiwan, including a guarantee to maintain the status quo in Taiwan for 100 years if the province agreed to reunification. In 1984, following the agreement between the People's Republic of China and the United Kingdom that China would regain sovereignty over the British colony of Hong Kong after 1997, Chinese leaders urged Taiwan to accept similar proposals for reunification on the basis of 'one country—two systems'. The Taipei Government insisted that Taiwan would never negotiate with Beijing until the mainland regime renounced communism. In May 1986, however, the Government was forced to make direct contact with the Beijing Government for the first time, over the issue of a Taiwanese pilot who had defected to the mainland with his aircraft, and whose fellow crew-members wished to return.

President Chiang Kai-shek remained in office until his death in April 1975. He was succeeded as leader of the ruling KMT by his son, Gen. Chiang Ching-kuo, who had been Prime Minister since May 1972. The new President was Dr Yen Chia-kan, Vice-President since 1966. In May 1978 President Yen retired and was succeeded by Gen. Chiang, who appointed Sun Yun-suan, hitherto Minister of Economic Affairs, to be Prime Minister. Economic and political stability continued to be the regime's main priority. At elections for 71 seats in the Legislative Yuan in December 1983, the KMT won an overwhelming victory, confirming its dominance over the independent 'Tangwai' (non-party) candidates. In March 1984 President Chiang was re-elected for a second six-year term, and Lee Teng-hui, a former Mayor of Taipei and a native Taiwanese, became Vice-President. In May a major government reshuffle took place, and Yu Kuo-hwa, formerly the Governor of the Central Bank, replaced Sun Yun-suan as Prime Minister.

In September 1986 135 leading opposition politicians formed the Democratic Progress Party (DPP), in defiance of the KMT's ban on the formation of new political parties. In response, the KMT announced that it would henceforth allow the establishment of new parties (although subject to approval of their policies), and that martial law (in force since 1949) would be replaced by a new national security law. Under the new law, all civilians would be tried by civilian courts, and constitutional rights of assembly and demonstration would be restored. Legislation to this effect was expected to be approved in early 1987. Elections for 84 seats in the National Assembly and 73 seats in the Legislative Yuan were held in December. The KMT achieved a decisive victory, winning 68 seats in the National Assembly and 59 in the Legislative Yuan, but the DPP received about one-quarter of the total votes, and won 11 seats in the

Assembly and 12 in the Legislative Yuan, thus more than doubling the non-KMT representation.

In January 1979 Taiwan suffered a serious setback when the USA established full diplomatic relations with the People's Republic and severed relations with Taiwan. The USA also terminated the mutual security treaty with Taiwan. Commercial links are still maintained, however, under the terms of the USA's Taiwan Relations Act of March 1979. Taiwan's purchase of armaments from the USA has remained a controversial issue and has caused increased tension with mainland China. In August 1982 Taiwan's morale was further damaged when a joint Sino-US communiqué was published, in which the USA pledged to reduce gradually its sale of armaments to Taiwan. Despite this, substantial sales of weapons have continued. In April 1984 the US President, Ronald Reagan, gave an assurance that he would continue to support Taiwan, despite the improved relations between the USA and the People's Republic, which had provoked uncertainty in Taiwan.

Government

Under the provisions of the 1947 Constitution, the Head of State is the President, who is elected for a term of six years by the National Assembly. There are five Yuans (governing bodies), the highest legislative organ being the Legislative Yuan, to which the Executive Yuan (the Council of Ministers) is responsible. In March 1986 the Legislative Yuan comprised 339 (mainly life) members. Elections for supplementary seats are held every three years. There are also Control, Judicial and Examination Yuans. Their respective functions are: to investigate the work of the executive; to interpret the Constitution and national laws; and to supervise examinations for entry into public offices. The Legislative Yuan submits proposals to the National Assembly. Elections to the Assembly are by universal adult suffrage every six years, but the great majority of Assembly seats are held by life members who formerly represented mainland constituencies. In March 1986 the Assembly had 991 members. Martial law was declared in 1949, and remained in force in 1986.

Defence

In July 1986 the armed forces totalled 424,000: army 270,000, air force 77,000, navy 38,000, with a marine corps of 39,000. Military service lasts for two years. Defence expenditure for 1986/87 was projected at NT $160,300m.

Economic Affairs

Despite the strain of maintaining large armed forces, Taiwan's economy has developed rapidly since 1950, owing mainly to the considerable expansion of foreign trade. By the 1980s, Taiwan was among the world's 20 leading exporting countries (ranking 17th in terms of total foreign trade turnover in 1985). Agriculture's role in the economy has declined significantly since the 1950s; in 1952 it provided more than 90% of total exports and contributed 56.1% of Taiwan's gross domestic product (GDP), while employing 56% of the labour force. The principal crops were rice, sugar cane and sweet potatoes. By 1983, however, agricultural products and processed food provided less than 7% of total exports; in 1985 the sector contributed only 5.8% of GDP, and employed 17.0% of the labour force.

Between 1970 and 1980, Taiwan's GDP expanded, in real terms, at an average rate of 9.5% per year, with the economy progressing towards self-sufficiency as the island's industrial infrastructure developed. Textiles were the main source of income, providing 32% of export earnings in 1970, but this proportion declined in the 1980s, as rising labour costs encouraged the development of more capital- and technology-intensive industries, such as the manufacture of electronic equipment and plastic products. In 1984 textiles accounted for one-fifth of Taiwan's total exports, and were the third largest earner of foreign exchange (after exports of machinery and electronics). Other major exports include metals, plywood and furniture, and petrochemicals. Taiwan has a 65% share of the world market in shipbreaking, centred on the port of Kaohsiung. Despite Taiwan's diplomatic isolation, trade and economic links with the rest of the world have thrived. Exports are still dominated by the US market, which accounts for more than one-third of Taiwan's foreign trade, followed by Japan and Hong Kong. However, Taiwan has come under increasing pressure from Washington to reduce its trade surplus with the USA, which reached around US $10,000m. in 1985. In July 1986 Taiwan signed an agreement to allow its textile exports to the USA to grow by just 0.5% per year from 1986 to 1988, and a similar agreement with the EEC restricted the increase in Taiwanese textile exports to 2.3% per year for the period 1987–91. In response to such protectionist measures in its traditional markets, efforts are being made to expand and diversify export markets in Europe, Africa and South-East Asia. Taiwan has also agreed to open up its domestic market to US goods, and has begun by cutting tariffs on a range of products. As a result of continued trade surpluses, Taiwan's reserves of foreign exchange increased from US $2,205m. at the end of 1980 to US $35,934m. by August 1986, leading to pressure from abroad to revalue the New Taiwan dollar (NT$). In 1985 the People's Republic of China assured Taiwan that the latter's lucrative trade links with Hong Kong would not be jeopardized by China's resumption of sovereignty over Hong Kong after 1997.

Mineral resources include coal, marble, gold, petroleum and natural gas. Taiwan's petrochemical industry is the third largest in Asia. Energy supplies have always been a problem, and Taiwan is heavily dependent on imported petroleum. There are three nuclear power plants in operation, providing around 52% of Taiwan's total power generation in 1985.

Following the recession in world markets, Taiwan's GDP grew by only 2.8% in 1982, compared with rises of 6.1% in 1981 and 7.3% in 1980. In 1983, however, following an export-led recovery, GDP grew by 7.7%, and this economic expansion continued in 1984, with GDP rising by 9.5% in real terms. In 1985 GDP grew by 4.1% in real terms, following a virtual stagnation in exports, while the value of imports decreased by around 8%. During 1986, however, the economy was revitalized by the favourable terms of foreign trade, as a fall in petroleum prices caused the cost of Taiwan's petroleum imports in the first nine months of the year to fall by 36%, while exports increased significantly, helped by a favourable exchange rate against the Japanese yen: exports in the first 10 months of 1986 were 23% higher than in the comparable period of 1985. The economy grew by 8.12% in the first half of the year, and the forecast of growth for the year as a whole was revised upwards, from 5.5% to 8.8%.

The unemployment rate was around 2.7% in 1983, falling to 2.45% in 1984. In 1985 the rate rose to 2.9%, but by June 1986 it had fallen to 2.7%. Taiwan's gross national product (GNP) per head was more than US $3,000 in 1985. The 1982–85 Four-Year Plan, which envisaged an average annual growth rate of 8%, aimed to increase investment, to stimulate trade and to develop industry. There are plans to develop Taiwan's role as an offshore banking centre, with increased financial services, while three special export-processing zones have been established to attract further foreign investment. A science-based industrial park has been established at Hsinchu, offering special incentives for foreign investors. In 1984 foreign investment in Taiwan reached US $558m., representing a growth of 50% over the 1983 figure. In 1985 new foreign investment (including investment by overseas Chinese) totalled US $720m.; the highest proportion of investments went to the chemical industry, with 30.5% of the total, while the electronics and electrical appliances sector accounted for 19.8%. Enterprises which were funded by foreign investment provided 23% of total exports in 1984. The first offshore banking licences were granted in May 1984, as the first step towards an eventual liberalization of Taiwan's foreign exchange controls.

In 1984 a major new development plan was announced: some US $20,000m. was allocated for 14 infrastructure projects, including expansion of the China Steel Corporation, construction of the Taipei underground railway system, modernization of telecommunications facilities, exploitation of petroleum and water resources and expansion of railways and highways, among many other projects. It was announced in October 1985 that US $2,500m. was to be invested in the field of chemicals over the next 10 years, and also that the majority of state enterprises were to be 'privatized'. Taiwan's hopes of maintaining a high rate of export growth rely on the continued development of high-technology products, and in July 1986 a programme of investment in technology research projects (including digital communications equipment, electronics and electro-optical technology, and research on automation schemes), totalling NT $3,200m., was announced by the Government. The services sector is also seen as a key area in Taiwan's development, with a predicted annual growth rate of 7.5% in 1986–89, and an increasing contribution to GNP.

Social Welfare

In June 1986 the Labour Security Programme covered around 4.3m. workers, providing benefits for injury, disability, birth, death and old age. At the same time, 767,000 government employees and their dependants were covered by a separate scheme. In 1978 a system of supplementary benefits for those with low incomes was introduced. In 1985 Taiwan had 12,324 hospitals and clinics, with a total of 70,806 beds, and there were 16,944 physicians (including Chinese herb doctors) working in the country.

Education

Education at primary schools and junior high schools is free and compulsory between the ages of six and 15 years. Secondary schools consist of junior and senior middle schools, normal schools for teacher-training and vocational schools. There are also a number of private schools. Higher education is provided in universities, colleges, junior colleges and graduate schools. In 1985/86 there were more than 2.3m. pupils enrolled in state primary schools, with about 1.7m. in secondary schools. There are 16 universities and 11 independent colleges.

Tourism

Festivals, ancient art treasures and the island scenery are the principal attractions. In 1985 Taiwan received 1,451,659 foreign visitors (including 256,216 overseas Chinese). Japanese visitors account for about 40% of total tourist arrivals.

Public Holidays

1987: 1 January (Founding of the Republic), 1–3 March (Chinese New Year), 29 March (Youth Day), 5 April (Ching Ming), 31 May (Dragon Boat Festival), 28 September (Teachers' Day—Birthday of Confucius), 7 October (Mid-Autumn Moon Festival), 10 October (Double Tenth Day, anniversary of 1911 revolution), 25 October (Retrocession Day, anniversary of end of Japanese occupation), 31 October (Birthday of Chiang Kai-shek), 12 November (Birthday of Sun Yat-sen), 25 December (Constitution Day).

1988: 1 January (Founding of the Republic), January/February* (Chinese New Year), 29 March (Youth Day), 5 April (Ching Ming), June† (Dragon Boat Festival), September† (Mid-Autumn Moon Festival), 28 September (Teachers' Day—Birthday of Confucius), 10 October (Double Tenth Day, anniversary of end of Japanese occupation), 31 October (Birthday of Chiang Kai-shek), 1–2 November (Birthday of Sun Yat-sen), 25 December (Constitution Day).

* From the first to the third day of the first moon of the lunar calendar.
† Exact dates vary according to the lunar calendar.

Weights and Measures

The metric system is officially in force, but some traditional Chinese units are still used.

Currency and Exchange Rates

100 cents = 1 New Taiwan dollar (NT $).

Exchange rates (30 September 1986):
 £1 sterling = NT $53.13;
 US $1 = NT $36.72.

Statistical Survey

Source (unless otherwise stated): Directorate-General of Budget, Accounting and Statistics, Executive Yuan, Taipei.

Area and Population

AREA, POPULATION AND DENSITY

Area (sq km)	36,000*
Population (census results)	
16 December 1975	16,191,609
28 December 1980	
Males	9,362,026
Females	8,587,082
Total	17,949,108
Population (official estimates at 31 December)	
1983	18,732,938
1984	19,012,512
1985	19,258,053
Density (per sq km) at 31 December 1985	534.9

* 13,900 sq miles.

PRINCIPAL TOWNS
(estimated population at 31 December 1985)

Taipei (capital)	2,507,620	Fengshan	267,022
Kaohsiung	1,302,849	Chiayi	253,573
Taichung	674,936	Chungli	237,271
Tainan	639,888	Yungho	232,519
Panchiao	479,748	Taoyuan	204,700
Shanchung	353,957	Changhwa	201,103
Keelung	351,524	Pingtun	200,441
Hsinchu	304,010	Hsintien	190,579

BIRTHS, MARRIAGES AND DEATHS

	Live births		Marriages		Deaths	
	Number	Rate (per '000)	Number	Rate (per '000)	Number	Rate (per '000)
1981	412,777	22.97	167,165	9.30	86,848	4.83
1982	404,006	22.08	161,780	8.84	87,226	4.77
1983	382,153	20.55	158,296	8.51	90,555	4.87
1984	369,725	19.59	155,052	8.22	89,576	4.75
1985	345,053	18.03	153,565	8.03	92,011	4.81

ECONOMICALLY ACTIVE POPULATION
(annual averages in '000)

	1983	1984	1985
Agriculture, forestry and fishing	1,317	1,286	1,297
Mining and quarrying	46	41	35
Manufacturing	2,305	2,494	2,488
Construction	523	521	521
Electricity, gas and water	33	34	34
Commerce	1,229	1,280	1,336
Transport, storage and communications	384	378	388
Finance and insurance	174	182	190
Other services	1,059	1,092	1,141
Total in employment	7,070	7,308	7,428
Unemployed	197	183	222
Total labour force	7,266	7,491	7,651

Agriculture

PRINCIPAL CROPS ('000 metric tons)

	1983	1984	1985
Rice*	2,485.2	2,244.2	2,173.5
Sweet potatoes	560.0	424.4	369.5
Asparagus	45.6	54.1	62.1
Soybeans	8.6	9.5	12.2
Maize	143.2	189.9	226.0
Tea	24.3	24.4	23.2
Tobacco	22.7	26.5	25.6
Groundnuts	62.5	87.0	89.1
Cassava (Manioc)	80.2	67.8	58.2
Sugar cane	7,070.1	6,545.3	6,823.4
Bananas	196.3	203.3	198.6
Pineapples	115.2	123.6	149.7
Citrus fruit	379.5	354.0	418.9
Vegetables	3,018.7	3,416.4	3,243.6
Mushrooms	56.9	59.6	59.9

* Figures are in terms of brown rice.

LIVESTOCK ('000 head at 31 December)

	1983	1984	1985
Cattle	84.7	89.5	104.8
Buffaloes	45.1	40.9	38.4
Pigs	5,888.2	6,569.3	6,674.0
Sheep and goats	197.4	217.8	231.2
Chickens	60,137.0	60,786.0	59,313.0
Ducks	11,349.0	10,576.0	10,211.0
Geese	1,746.0	1,602.0	1,546.0
Turkeys	644.0	597.0	558.0

LIVESTOCK PRODUCTS

	1983	1984	1985
Beef (metric tons)	6,619	6,482	4,351
Pig meat (metric tons)	804,805	887,816	1,008,413
Goat meat (metric tons)	662	765	678
Chickens* ('000 head)	154,815	155,000	154,686
Ducks* ('000 head)	35,901	34,456	31,896
Geese* ('000 head)	3,334	3,529	3,186
Turkeys* ('000 head)	1,281	1,274	1,163
Milk (metric tons)	58,022	66,933	87,932
Duck eggs ('000)	485,235	476,318	453,247
Hen eggs ('000)	3,070,472	3,273,463	3,344,729

* Figures refer to numbers slaughtered.

Forestry

ROUNDWOOD REMOVALS ('000 cu m)

	1983	1984	1985
Industrial wood	616.1	562.6	474.6
Fuel wood	78.7	68.5	62.4
Total	694.8	631.1	537.0

Fishing

('000 metric tons, live weight)

	1983	1984	1985
Total catch	930.6	1,002.6	1,037.7

Mining*

	1983	1984	1985
Coal	2,236,065	2,010,775	1,857,858
Gold (kg)	1,628.6	1,175.5	952.8
Silver (kg)	10,739.1	11,330.1	11,386.2
Electrolytic copper	37,960	48,436	46,734
Crude petroleum ('000 litres)	134,644	135,899	118,154
Natural gas ('000 cu m)	1,237,140	1,265,683	1,125,050
Salt	79,188	218,491	173,898
Gypsum	1,522	1,882	2,199
Sulphur	26,936	28,705	42,949
Marble	9,281,123	9,542,373	10,259,341
Talc	27,053	18,680	17,560
Asbestos	2,819	1,355	625
Dolomite	228,017	257,757	231,457

* Amounts in metric tons unless otherwise specified.

Industry

SELECTED PRODUCTS

		1983	1984	1985
Wheat flour	'000 metric tons	498.6	512.8	520.0
Refined sugar	'000 metric tons	646.4	622.4	645.6
Alcoholic beverages (excl. beer)	'000 hectolitres	1,941.4	2,143.0	2,083.7
Cigarettes	million	29,864	32,082	30,827
Cotton yarn	'000 metric tons	164.8	181.3	191.8
Paper	'000 metric tons	467.3	532.5	530.2
Sulphuric acid	'000 metric tons	677.9	761.8	733.0
Spun synthetic yarn	'000 metric tons	128.4	150.6	153.2
Motor spirit (petrol)	million litres	2,769.8	2,785.1	2,989.2
Diesel oil	million litres	3,481.4	3,493.1	3,197.4
Cement	'000 metric tons	14,809.8	14,234.4	14,417.7
Pig iron	'000 metric tons	183.6	213.5	225.7
Steel ingots	'000 metric tons	1,742.9	1,644.8	1,641.9
Transistor radios	'000 units	8,458.5	9,068.5	8,781.6
Television receivers	'000 units	5,176.8	5,165.0	3,641.3
Ships*	'000 dwt	823.7	774.4	516.7
Electric energy	million kWh	45,517	49,286	52,553
Liquefied petroleum gas	'000 metric tons	465.4	436.0	426.2

* Excluding motor yachts.

Finance

CURRENCY AND EXCHANGE RATES

Monetary Units
100 cents = 1 New Taiwan dollar (NT $).

Denominations
Coins: 50 cents; 1, 5 and 10 dollars.
Notes: 10, 50, 100, 500 and 1,000 dollars.

Sterling and US Dollar Equivalents (30 September 1986)
£1 sterling = NT $53.13;
US $1 = NT $36.72;
NT $1,000 = £18.82 = US $27.23.

Average Exchange Rate (NT $ per US $)
1983   40.065
1984   39.597
1985   39.849

INTERNATIONAL RESERVES
(US $ million at 31 December)

	1983	1984	1985
Foreign exchange	11,859	15,664	22,556

MONEY SUPPLY (NT $ million at 31 December)

	1983	1984	1985
Currency outside banks	159,616	168,160	182,808
Demand deposits at deposit money banks	453,286	501,459	568,661

BUDGET (estimates, NT $ million, year ending 30 June)

Revenue	1983/84	1984/85	1985/86
Taxes	191,456	214,056	231,633
Monopoly profits	26,086	27,129	29,136
Non-tax revenue from other sources	105,603	112,773	151,555
Total	323,145	353,958	412,324

Expenditure	1983/84	1984/85	1985/86
General administration and defence	145,927	159,961	182,098
Education, science and culture	35,415	41,163	50,982
Reconstruction and communications	26,448	29,147	33,504
Enterprise fund	29,273	29,760	35,778
Social affairs, relief and health	55,724	57,954	67,266
Obligations	13,532	17,296	12,498
Others	16,825	23,999	30,198
Total	323,145	359,280	412,324

COST OF LIVING
(Consumer Price Index for urban areas. Base: 1981 = 100)

	1983	1984	1985
Food	106.21	103.50	101.92
Clothing	103.21	104.33	102.66
Housing	106.19	107.47	108.42
Transport and communications	100.01	101.28	102.23
Medicines and medical care	102.00	107.07	110.31
Education and entertainment	108.82	112.25	117.93
All items (incl. others)	105.28	105.49	105.88

NATIONAL ACCOUNTS (NT $ million in current prices)
National Income and Product

	1983	1984	1985*
Compensation of employees	1,004,492	1,122,680	1,186,010
Operating surplus	614,664	678,545	708,795
Domestic factor incomes	1,619,156	1,801,225	1,894,805
Consumption of fixed capital	170,580	188,923	208,291
Gross domestic product (GDP) at factor cost	1,789,736	1,990,148	2,103,096
Indirect taxes	257,200	273,934	267,664
Less Subsidies	5,566	8,971	14,026
GDP in purchasers' values	2,041,370	2,255,111	2,356,734
Factor income from abroad	54,434	74,706	91,348
Less Factor income paid abroad	51,714	52,021	53,245
Gross national product (GNP)	2,044,090	2,277,796	2,394,837
Less Consumption of fixed capital	170,580	188,923	208,291
National income in market prices	1,873,510	2,088,873	2,186,546
Other current transfers from abroad	5,620	5,277	5,262
Less Other current transfers paid abroad	7,313	11,965	17,992
National disposable income	1,871,817	2,082,185	2,173,816

* Preliminary estimates. Revised totals (in NT $ million) are: GDP in purchasers' values 2,357,106; GNP 2,398,369; National income 2,187,533.

Expenditure on the Gross Domestic Product

	1983	1984	1985*
Government final consumption expenditure	335,743	365,435	398,216
Private final consumption expenditure	1,052,627	1,144,756	1,227,547
Increase in stocks	−2,910	−25	−25,761
Gross fixed capital formation	472,305	484,386	454,662
Total domestic expenditure	1,857,765	1,994,552	2,054,664
Exports of goods and services	1,102,207	1,298,953	1,306,116
Less Imports of goods and services	918,602	1,038,394	1,004,046
GDP in purchasers' values	2,041,370	2,255,111	2,356,734
GDP at constant 1981 prices	1,936,281	2,121,377	2,208,138

* Preliminary estimates. Revised totals of GDP (in NT $ million) are: 2,357,106 in current prices; 2,212,650 at 1981 prices.

Gross Domestic Product by Economic Activity

	1983	1984	1985*
Agriculture and livestock	117,708	110,398	104,263
Forestry and logging	4,417	3,414	2,900
Fishing	30,148	31,559	33,674
Mining and quarrying	14,562	14,195	14,353
Manufacturing	817,962	937,904	960,229
Construction	97,384	99,731	99,133
Electricity, gas and water	77,765	88,644	97,727
Transport, storage and communications	122,149	135,941	144,569
Trade, restaurants and hotels	277,628	309,057	328,011
Finance, insurance and real estate	72,382	79,803	83,332
Housing services†	120,190	129,795	139,953
Government services	207,455	223,065	242,942
Other services	132,348	147,106	163,091
Sub-total	2,092,098	2,310,612	2,414,177
Less Imputed bank service charge	50,728	55,501	57,443
GDP in purchasers' values	2,041,370	2,255,111	2,356,734

* Preliminary estimates.
† Including imputed rents of owner-occupied dwellings.

BALANCE OF PAYMENTS (US $ million)

	1983	1984	1985
Merchandise exports f.o.b.	25,028	30,185	30,466
Merchandise imports f.o.b.	−18,760	−20,952	−19,249
Trade balance	6,268	9,233	11,217
Exports of services	3,804	4,550	5,035
Imports of services	−5,617	−6,637	−6,709
Balance on goods and services	4,455	7,146	9,543
Private unrequited transfers (net)	−42	−170	−244
Government unrequited transfers (net)	−1	—	−5
Current balance	4,412	6,976	9,294
Direct capital investment (net)	130	131	257
Other long-term capital (net)	947	−1,255	−1,280
Short-term capital (net)	−1,797	−1,470	−2,232
Net errors and omissions	−352	−408	487
Total (net monetary movements)	3,340	3,974	6,526
Monetization of gold (net)	156	119	156
Valuation changes (net)	−18	−154	358
Changes in reserves	3,478	3,938	7,040

CHINA (TAIWAN)   *Statistical Survey*

External Trade

PRINCIPAL COMMODITIES (NT $ million)

Imports c.i.f.	1983	1984	1985
Wheat (unmilled)	5,295.0	4,959.9	5,309.5
Maize (unmilled)	19,649.6	18,873.9	16,843.0
Soybeans	14,849.9	17,378.0	15,587.8
Logs	16,314.9	15,052.0	10,482.2
Natural rubber	3,002.8	3,307.3	2,724.1
Crude petroleum	164,233.7	149,392.1	133,149.5
Raw cotton	13,166.4	16,830.4	14,355.3
Yarn from synthetic fibres	1,363.3	1,830.2	1,613.2
Distillate fuels	5,137.2	9,973.4	4,085.4
Polyacids and derivatives	5,676.0	6,253.7	7,917.2
Thin iron and steel sheets	4,872.3	4,049.1	3,817.2
Thermoplastic resins	8,619.9	8,292.3	6,741.6
Iron and steel scrap	3,775.6	4,788.2	5,696.1
Spinning, extruding machines	3,827.6	7,886.0	6,340.9
Electrical switchgear	9,788.1	11,143.8	9,240.3
Television receivers	398.4	384.6	517.2
Internal combustion engines other than for aircraft	3,115.9	3,561.8	3,814.9
Ships for breaking	12,435.4	14,501.9	14,461.2
Total (incl. others)	813,904.1	870,861.5	801,847.4

Exports f.o.b.	1983	1984	1985
Fresh bananas	1,319.4	1,604.4	1,706.5
Canned mushrooms	2,483.6	2,748.1	2,000.7
Canned asparagus	2,476.4	2,340.8	1,414.8
Raw sugar	1,554.1	984.1	917.7
Cotton fabrics	4,928.6	4,740.0	4,363.5
Yarn from synthetic fibres	11,086.2	12,246.3	13,988.2
Synthetic fabrics	16,075.2	20,472.0	24,409.5
Plywood	14,489.9	11,091.2	9,815.8
Clothing (incl. knitted and crocheted fabrics)	60,783.1	75,041.1	69,382.2
Thermionic articles, valves, tubes, photocells, transistors etc.	25,972.4	36,440.3	34,436.9
Calculating machines	19,724.4	41,204.5	54,655.1
Television receivers	17,742.7	24,116.7	16,007.0
Radio receivers	11,565.4	17,310.8	14,459.5
Plastic articles	71,307.5	95,460.0	105,436.7
Dolls and toys	23,850.7	28,892.4	23,675.4
Total (incl. others)	1,005,422.5	1,204,696.7	1,222,904.2

PRINCIPAL TRADING PARTNERS (US $ '000)

Imports c.i.f.	1983	1984	1985
Australia	682,371	777,519	800,647
Canada	361,468	400,399	368,974
Germany, Federal Republic	691,733	768,020	846,171
Hong Kong	298,896	370,355	319,679
Indonesia	344,516	422,973	413,795
Italy	179,822	222,048	234,490
Japan	5,586,697	6,441,849	5,548,848
Korea, Republic	165,094	243,909	186,617
Kuwait	1,132,490	727,640	670,769
Malaysia	493,742	550,814	481,467
Philippines	91,245	134,318	104,203
Saudi Arabia	1,925,481	1,971,220	1,361,002
Singapore	167,226	267,989	275,884
Thailand	74,462	139,980	146,920
United Kingdom	307,568	294,365	262,434
USA	4,646,443	5,041,643	4,746,274
Total (incl. others)	20,287,078	21,959,086	20,102,049

Exports f.o.b.	1983	1984	1985
Australia	634,367	831,628	747,332
Canada	727,616	916,295	944,870
Germany, Federal Republic	850,931	868,080	805,414
Hong Kong	1,643,625	2,087,131	2,539,573
Indonesia	429,072	346,206	280,900
Italy	180,666	226,742	246,076
Japan	2,477,067	3,186,462	3,460,811
Korea, Republic	222,634	230,467	253,816
Kuwait	214,299	147,489	117,163
Malaysia	223,695	232,035	194,856
Philippines	245,791	190,701	239,155
Saudi Arabia	760,238	727,732	590,013
Singapore	710,574	878,446	885,168
Thailand	263,833	244,849	236,208
United Kingdom	617,124	690,658	650,044
USA	11,333,712	14,867,709	14,772,990
Total (incl. others)	25,122,747	30,456,390	30,722,789

Transport

RAILWAYS

	1983	1984	1985
Passengers ('000)	130,390	130,592	131,268
Passenger-km ('000)	8,533,166	8,458,130	8,309,289
Freight ('000 metric tons)	30,833	29,886	29,732
Freight ton-km ('000)	2,580,966	2,492,885	2,299,840

ROAD TRAFFIC
(motor vehicles in use at 31 December)

	1983	1984	1985
Passenger cars	687,860	807,155	915,598
Buses and coaches	20,458	20,445	20,845
Goods vehicles	352,560	388,459	408,526
Motorcycles and scooters	5,594,609	6,109,083	6,588,854

INTERNATIONAL SEA-BORNE SHIPPING
(freight traffic in '000 metric tons)

	1983	1984	1985
Goods loaded	15,231	16,251	16,090
Goods unloaded	55,319	59,828	60,496

CIVIL AVIATION (scheduled services)

	1983	1984	1985
Passengers carried ('000)	10,026.6	10,861.5	10,377.7
Passenger-km (million)	10,110.3	11,193	11,246
Freight carried ('000 metric tons)	308.0	337.5	328.0
Freight ton-km (million)	1,607.3	1,830.3	1,839.0

CHINA (TAIWAN)

Communications Media

	1983	1984	1985
Television licences	5,000,000	n.a.	n.a.
Telephones	4,854,861	5,278,673	5,653,113

Education

(1985/86)

	Schools	Full-time teachers	Pupils/Students
Pre-school	2,210	12,471	234,674
Primary	2,486	72,287	2,321,700
Secondary (incl. Vocational)	1,052	76,563	1,678,767
Higher	105	20,848	428,576
Special	10	568	2,954
Supplementary	422	3,757	275,639
Total (incl. others)	6,285	186,494	4,942,310

Directory

The Constitution

On 1 January 1947 a new constitution was promulgated for the Republic of China (confined to Taiwan since 1949). The form of government that was incorporated in the Constitution is based on a five-power system and has the major features of both cabinet and presidential government. The following are the principal organs of government:

NATIONAL ASSEMBLY

The Assembly, composed of elected delegates, meets to elect or recall the President and Vice-President, to amend the Constitution, or to vote on proposed constitutional amendments that have been submitted by the Legislative Yuan. Since the overthrow of the Republic of China on the mainland, most of the seats are held by 'life-term' members, originally elected to represent mainland constituencies.

PRESIDENT

Elected by the National Assembly for a term of six years, and may be re-elected for a second term (the two-term restriction is at present suspended). Represents country at all state functions, including foreign relations; commands land, sea and air forces, promulgates laws, issues mandates, concludes treaties, declares war, makes peace, declares martial law, grants amnesties, appoints and removes civil and military officers, and confers honours and decorations. He also convenes the National Assembly, and subject to certain limitations, may issue emergency orders to deal with national calamities and ensure national security.

EXECUTIVE YUAN

Is the highest administrative organ of the nation and is responsible to the Legislative Yuan; has three categories of subordinate organization:
Executive Yuan Council (policy-making organization)
Ministries and Commissions (executive organization)
Subordinate organization (Secretariat, Government Information Office, Directorate-General of Budget, Accounting and Statistics).

LEGISLATIVE YUAN

Is the highest legislative organ of the state, composed of elected members; holds two sessions a year; is empowered to hear administrative reports of the Executive Yuan, and to change government policy. Like the National Assembly, most of its seats are held by 'life-term' members.

JUDICIAL YUAN

Is the highest judicial organ of state and has charge of civil, criminal and administrative cases, and of cases concerning disciplinary measures against public functionaries (see Judicial System).

EXAMINATION YUAN

Supervises examinations for entry into public offices, and deals with personal questions of the civil service.

CONTROL YUAN

Is a body elected by local councils to impeach or investigate the work of the Executive Yuan and the Ministries and Executives; meets once a month, and has a subordinate body, the Ministry of Audit.

The Government

HEAD OF STATE

President: CHIANG CHING-KUO (took office 20 May 1978).
Vice-President: LEE TENG-HUI.
Secretary-General: SHEN CHANG-HUAN.

THE EXECUTIVE YUAN
(January 1987)

Premier: YU KUO-HWA.
Vice-Premier: LIN YANG-KANG.
Secretary-General: WANG CHANG-CHING.
Minister of the Interior: WU POH-HSIUNG.
Minister of Foreign Affairs: CHU FU-SUNG.
Minister of National Defence: WANG TAO-YUAN.
Minister of Finance: ROBERT CHIEN-CHUN.
Minister of Education: LEE HUAN.
Minister of Justice: SHIH CHI-YANG.
Minister of Economic Affairs: LEE TA-HAI.
Minister of Communications: LIEN CHAN.
Ministers of State: LI KWOH-TING, HENRY YU-SHU KAO, CHANG FENG-HSU, CHOW HONG-TAO, CHAO YAO-TUNG, KUO WEI-FAN, HSIAO TIEN-TSANG.
Chairman of the Overseas Chinese Affairs Commission: TSENG KWANG-SHUN.
Chairman of the Mongolian and Tibetan Affairs Commission: WU HUA-PENG.
Director-General of the Government Information Office: CHANG KING-YUH.
Director-General of Directorate-General of Budget, Accounting and Statistics: YU CHIEN-MIN.
Director-General of Central Personnel Administration: PU TA-HAI.
Director-General of Department of Health: SHIH CHUN-JEN.

MINISTRIES AND COMMISSIONS

Ministry of Communications: 2 Changsha St, Sec. 1, Taipei; tel. 3112661.
Ministry of Economic Affairs: 15 Foochow St, Taipei; tel. 3517271.
Ministry of Education: 5 Chungshan South Rd, Taipei 100; tel. 3513111; telex 10894.

CHINA (TAIWAN)

Ministry of Finance: 2 Aikuo West Rd, Taipei; tel. 3511611; telex 11840.

Ministry of Foreign Affairs: 2 Chiehshou Rd, Taipei 10016; tel. 3119292; telex 11299.

Ministry of the Interior: 107 Roosevelt Rd, Sec. 4, Taipei; tel. 3415241.

Ministry of Justice: 124 Chungking South Rd, Sec. 1, Taipei 100; tel. 3113101.

Ministry of National Defence: Chiehshou Hall, Chungking South Rd, Taipei 100; tel. 3117001.

Office of the Director-General of Budget, Accounting and Statistics: 1 Chung Hsiao East Rd, Sec. 1, Taipei; tel. 3514074.

Mongolian and Tibetan Affairs Commission: 109 Roosevelt Rd, Sec. 4, Taipei; tel. 3513131.

Overseas Chinese Affairs Commission: 30 Kungyuan Rd, Taipei; tel. 3810039.

Legislature

KUO-MIN TA-HUI
(National Assembly)

Most of the seats in the Assembly are held by members who were originally elected to represent constituencies on the Chinese mainland. Since the overthrow of the Republic on the mainland in 1949, these members hold office for life. The most recent general election was held on 6 December 1986, when 84 new members were elected. In March 1986 the National Assembly had 991 members. Delegates meet to elect or recall the President and Vice-President, to amend the Constitution or to vote on proposed Constitutional amendments submitted by the Legislative Yuan.

LI-FA YUAN
(Legislative Yuan)

The Legislative Yuan is the highest legislative organ of state. As in the National Assembly, most of the seats are held by life members, originally elected on the Chinese mainland. The chamber also includes representatives appointed by the President. Other members are elected by universal suffrage for a term of three years and are eligible for re-election. In March 1986 there were 339 members (most of them holding office for life), comprising 309 KMT members, 18 independents, seven members of the Young China Party, and five members of the China Democratic Socialist Party. Elections were held on 6 December 1986 for 73 seats, of which 59 were won by the KMT, 12 by the DPP and two by independents.

President: NIEH WEN-YAH.
Vice-President: LIU KUO-TSAI.

CONTROL YUAN

Exercises powers of investigation, impeachment and censure, and powers of consent in the appointment of the President, Vice-President and the grand justices of the Judicial Yuan, and the president, vice-president and the members of the Examination Yuan, and power of audit over central and local government finances (see the Constitution).

President: YU CHUN-HSIEN.
Vice-President: HUANG TZUEN-CHIOU.

Political Organizations

China Democratic Socialist Party: 6 Lane 357, Hoping East Rd, Sec. 2, Taipei; f. 1932 by merger of National Socialists and Democratic Constitutionalists; aims to promote democracy, to protect fundamental freedoms, and to improve public welfare and social security; 30,000 mems; Chair. YANG YU-TSE; Sec.-Gen. CHANG YUN-CHING.

Democratic Progress Party (DPP): Taipei; f. 1986; aims for the end of martial law and the introduction of direct trade, tourism and postal links with mainland China, advocates 'self-determination' for the people of Taiwan; Chair. CHIANG PENG-CHIEN.

Kuomintang (KMT) (Nationalist Party of China): 11 Chung Shan South Rd, Taipei; f. 1894; the ruling party; aims to overthrow communist rule in mainland China, to promote constitutional government and to unify China under the 'Three Principles of the People'; c. 2.2m. mems; Chair. CHIANG CHING-KUO; Sec.-Gen. MA SOO-LAY; Dep. Secs-Gen. MA YING-CHIU, KUO CHE, SHAW EN-SHIN.

Young China Party: 256 King Hwa St, Taipei; f. 1923; aims to recover and maintain territorial sovereignty, to safeguard the Constitution and democracy, and to foster understanding between Taiwan and the non-communist world; Chair. LI HUANG.

Diplomatic Representation

EMBASSIES IN THE REPUBLIC OF CHINA

Costa Rica: 10 Lane 172, Chung Shan North Rd, Sec. 6, Taipei; tel. 8320832; Ambassador: RUBÉN ACÓN LEÓN.

Dominican Republic: 7th Floor, 39 Te Shing East Rd, Tien Mou, Taipei; tel. 8327811; Ambassador: LÓPEZ BALAQUER.

El Salvador: 15 Lane 34, Ku Kung Rd, Shih Lin, Taipei; tel. 8819887; Ambassador: FRANCISCO RICARDO SANTANA BERRIOS.

Guatemala: 6 Lane 88, Chien Kuo North Rd, Sec. 1, Taipei; tel. 5617043; Ambassador: ROLANDO CHINCHILLA AGUILAR.

Haiti: 3rd Floor, 246 Chungshan North Rd, Sec. 6, Taipei; tel. 8317086; Ambassador: RAYMOND PERODIN.

Holy See: 87 Ai Kuo East Rd, Taipei 106; tel. 3216847; Chargé d'affaires: Mgr PIERO BIGGIO.

Honduras: Rm 701, 142 Chung Hsiao East Rd, Sec. 4, Taipei; Ambassador: FRANCISCO ZEPEDA ANDINO.

Korea, Republic: 345 Chung Hsiao East Rd, Sec. 4, Taipei; tel. 7619360; Ambassador: KIM SANG-TAE.

Panama: 5th Floor, 13 Te Huei St, Taipei; tel. 5968563; Ambassador: AURELIO CHU YI.

Paraguay: 2nd Floor, 20 Tien Yee St, Tien Mou, Taipei; tel. 8728932; telex 13744; Ambassador: ANGEL JUAN SOUTO HERNÁNDEZ.

Saudi Arabia: 11th Floor, 550 Chung Hsiao East Rd, Sec. 4, Taipei; tel. 7035855; Ambassador: Gen. ASAAD ABDUL AZIZ AL-ZUHAIR.

South Africa: 13th Floor, Bank Tower, 205 Tun Hua North Rd, Taipei; tel. 7153251; telex 21954; Ambassador: CHRISTOFFEL PRINS.

Uruguay: 7th Floor, 16 Min Chu East Rd, Taipei; tel. 5964947; telex 26114; Ambassador: (vacant).

Judicial System

The interpretative powers of the Judicial Yuan are exercised by the Council of Grand Justices nominated and appointed for nine years by the President of the Republic of China with the consent of the Control Yuan. The President of the Judicial Yuan also presides over the Council of Grand Justices.

The Judicial Yuan has jurisdiction over the high court and district courts. The Ministry of Justice is under the jurisdiction of the Executive Yuan.

Judicial Yuan: Pres. HUANG SHAO-KU; Vice-Pres. HUNG SHOU-NAN; Sec.-Gen. FAN KUEI-SHU; the highest judicial organ, and the interpreter of the constitution and national laws and ordinances. Other judicial powers are exercised by:

Supreme Court: Court of third and last instance for civil and criminal cases; Chief Justice CHIEN KUO-CHEN.

High Courts: Courts of second instance for appeals of civil and criminal cases.

District Courts: Courts of first instance in civil, criminal and non-contentious cases.

Administrative Court: Court of last resort in cases brought against govt agencies; Chief Justice WANG CHIA-YI.

Committee on the Discipline of Public Functionaries: Chair. KU RU-SHING; metes out disciplinary measures to persons impeached by the Control Yuan.

Religion

BUDDHISM

Buddhists belong to the Mahayana and Theravada schools. Leader PAN SHENG. The Buddhist Association of Taiwan has 1,440 group members and more than 3m. adherents.

CHRISTIANITY

The Roman Catholic Church

Taiwan comprises one archdiocese and six dioceses. In 1985 there were 291,592 adherents.

CHINA (TAIWAN)

Bishops' Conference: Regional Episcopal Conference of China, POB 36603, 34 Lane 32, Kuangfu South Rd, Taipei 105; tel. 7711295; f. 1978; Pres. Mgr STANISLAUS LOKUANG, Emeritus Archbishop of Taipei.

Archbishop of Taipei: MATTHEW KIA YEN-WEN, Archbishop's House, 94 Loli Rd, POB 7-91, Taipei 10668; tel. 7071311.

The Anglican Communion

Anglicans in Taiwan are adherents of the Protestant Episcopal Church.

Bishop of Taiwan: Rt Rev. PUI-YEUNG CHEUNG, 7 Lane 105, Hangchow South Rd, Sec. 1, Taipei; c. 2,250 adherents.

Presbyterian Church

Tai-oan Ki-tok Tiu-Lo Kau-Hoe (Presbyterian Church in Taiwan): 3 Lane 269, Roosevelt Rd, Sec. 3, Taipei; tel. 3935282; telex 20588; f. 1865; Gen. Sec. Dr C. M. KAO; 210,000 mems (1986).

DAOISM (TAOISM)

There are about 1,680,102 adherents.

ISLAM

Leader DAWUD FU HSU; 54,730 adherents.

The Press

DAILIES

Taipei

Central Daily News: 83 Chung Hsiao West Rd, Sec. 1; tel. 3813939; telex 24884; f. 1928; morning; official Kuomintang organ; Publr YAO PENG.

China Daily News (Northern Edn): 131 Sungkiang Rd; tel. 5819510; morning; Chinese; f. 1946; Publr HUANG TSAO-HENG; Pres. HUANG CHAO-HENG; Editor-in-Chief WANG HSIAO-HAN.

China News: 277 Hsinyi Rd, Sec. 2; tel. 3210882; f. 1949; afternoon; English; Publr SIMONE WEI; Dir TING WEI-TUNG; Editor L. C. CHU; circ. 25,000.

China Post: 8 Fu Shun St; tel. 5969971; f. 1952; morning; English; Publr NANCY YU-HUANG; Editor HUANG CHIH-HSIANG.

China Times: 132 Da Li St; tel. 3087111; telex 26464; f. 1950; morning; Chinese; Chair. YU CHI-CHUNG; Publr YU CHIEN-HSIN; Editor HU LI-TAI; circ. 1.2m.

Chung Cheng Pao: 70 Li-hsing Rd, Shing-den; f. 1948; morning; armed forces; Publr MA CHIA-CHEN; Editor LIU CHIH-HSIU.

Commercial Times: 132 Da Li St; tel. 3087111; f. 1978; Publr YU FAN-YING; Editor-in-Chief PENG CHUI-MING.

Economic Daily News: 555 Chung Hsiao East Rd, Sec. 4; tel. 7681234; telex 27710; f. 1967; morning; Publr WANG PI-LY; Editor LIN TUNG-SHIH.

Independent Evening Post: 15 Chinan Rd, Sec. 2; tel. 3519621; f. 1947; afternoon; Chinese; Publr WU SAN-LIEN; Editor YEN WEN-SHUAN.

Mandarin Daily News: 10 Fuchow St; tel. 3412448; f. 1948; morning; Publr HSIA CHENG-YING; Editor YANG RU DER.

Min Sheng Pao: 555 Chung Hsiao East Rd, Sec. 4; tel. 7681234; telex 27710; f. 1978; Publr WANG SHAW-LAN; Editor CHEN CHI-CHIA.

Min Tsu Evening News: 235 Kunming St; tel. 3816710; f. 1950; afternoon; Chinese; Publr WANG YUNG-TAO; Editor YANG SHANG-CHIANG.

Ta Hua (Great China) Evening News: 1 Lane 61, Chiu Chuen St; tel. 5919133; f. 1950; afternoon; Publr KENG HSIU-YEH; Editor TUAN SHOU-YU.

Taiwan Hsin Sheng Pao: 110 Yenping South Rd; tel. 3119634; f. 1945; morning; Chinese; Publr SHEN YUEH; Editor HSU CHANG.

United Daily News: 555 Chung Hsiao East Rd, Sec. 4; tel. 7681234; telex 27710; f. 1951; morning; Publr WANG PI-CHENG; Editor LIU KUO-JUI.

Youth Daily News: 3 Hsinyi Rd, Sec. 1; tel. 3212778; f. 1952; morning; Chinese; armed forces; Publr MIAO LUN; Editor NIEN CHEN-YU.

Provincial

Cheng Kung Times: 244 Chi Hsien 2 Rd, Kaohsiung; f. 1985; afternoon; Publr HUANG CHAO-HENG; Dir YEN CHUNG-TSE; Editor CHENG CHI-LIN; circ. 12,000.

Directory

Chien Kuo Daily News: 36 Min Sheng Rd, Makung, Chen, Penghu; tel. 272675; f. 1949; morning; Publr YU CHIEH-TIEN; Editor CHEN KE-HSUAN; circ. 15,000.

China Daily News (Southern Edn): 57 Hsi Hwa St, Tainan; tel. 2202697; f. 1946; morning; Publr HUANG CHAO-HENG; Editor CHENG CHI-LING; circ. 260,000.

China Evening News: 98 Chung Hwa 3rd Rd, Kaohsiung; tel. 2827181; f. 1955; afternoon; Publr LIU HEN-HSIU; Editor LIU TIEN-LUNG; circ. 65,000.

Daily Free Press: 409–12 Psitun Rd, Taichung; tel. 2348366; f. 1978; morning; Publr WU A-MING; Editor SUN TING-WO; circ. 20,000.

Keng Sheng Daily News: 36 Wuchuan St, Hualien; tel. 340131; f. 1947; morning; Publr HSIEH YING-YI; Editor CHEN HSING; circ. 5,000.

Kinmen Daily News: Wu Chiang Village, Kinmen; tel. 2374; f. 1965; morning; Publr CHOU HSIAO-YU; Editor PAI CHANG-KAO; circ. 5,000.

Matsu Daily News: Matsu; tel. 2236; f. 1957; morning; Publr HUANG WEI-SUNG; Editor FANG CHING-CHING.

Min Chung Daily News: 410 Chung Shan 2 Rd, Kaohsiung; tel. 3353131; f. 1950; morning; Publr LEE SHUI-PIAO; Editor YAO CHIH-HAI; circ. 148,000.

Shang Kung Daily News: 218 Kuo Hua St, Chiayi; tel. 2240160; f. 1953; morning; Publr KUNG SHENG-TAO; Editor LIU KUEI-NAN; circ. 20,000.

Taiwan Daily News: 24 Chung Shan Rd, Taichung; tel. 2296191; morning; f. 1964; Chair. HSU HENG; Publr CHEN MAO-PANG; Editor CHANG TSU-AN; circ. 250,000.

Taiwan Shin Wen Daily News: 249 Chung Cheng 4 Rd, Kaohsiung; tel. 2212154; f. 1949; morning; Publr YEH CHIEN-LI; Editor YEH YUN-I.

Taiwan Times: 167 Chung Cheng 4 Rd, Fengshan, Kaohsiung; tel. 2725781; f. 1971; Publr HE TIEN-CHIH; Editor KANG CHI-MING; circ. 148,000.

SELECTED PERIODICALS

Agri-week: 14 Wenchow St, Taipei; tel. 3938148; f. 1975; weekly; Editor NED LIANG; Publr WANG YOU-TSAO.

Artist Magazine: 3rd Floor, 5 Lane 118, Chung Ching South Rd, Sec. 1, Taipei; tel. 3719693; f. 1975; monthly; Publr HO CHENG KWANG; circ. 22,000.

Biographical Literature: 4th Floor, 230 Hsinyi Rd, Sec. 2, Taipei; tel. 3410213; Publr LIU TSUNG-HSIANG.

China Times Weekly: 132 Da Li St, Taipei; tel. 3087111; f. 1978; weekly; Chinese; Editor-in-Chief WANG CHIANG-CHUANG.

Continent Magazine: 11-6 Foochow St, Taipei; tel 3518310; f. 1950; fortnightly; archaeology, history and literature; Publr HSU KOU-PIAO.

Crown: 21st Floor, 620 Tun Hua South Rd, Taipei; tel. 7003422; monthly; Publr PING SIN TAO.

Free China Review: 3-1 Chung Hsiao East Rd, Sec. 1, Taipei; tel. 3319540; f. 1950; monthly; English; illustrated; Publr CHANG KING-YUH; Editor BETTY WANG.

Free China Journal: 3 Chung Hsiao East Rd, Sec. 1, Taipei; tel. 3316753; f. 1984 (fmrly Free China Weekly); English; news review; Publr CHANG KING-YUH; Editor CHANG LIANG-JEN.

The Gleaner: Kaohsiung Refinery, POB 25–12, Tsoying, Kaohsiung; tel. 3621367; Publr CHIN KAI-YIN.

Harvest Farm Magazine: 14 Wenchow St, Taipei; tel. 3938148; f. 1951; fortnightly; Editor NED LIANG; Publr CHANG HSIEN-TSUI.

Information and Computer: 9th Floor, 116 Nanking East Rd, Sec. 2, Taipei; tel. 5422540; monthly; Chinese; Publr FANG HSIEN-CHI; Editor LI CHIA-AN.

Issues and Studies: Institute of International Relations, 64 Wan Shou Rd, Mucha, Taipei 11625; tel. 9394921; f. 1964; monthly; English; international affairs; Publr YU-MING SHAW; Editor DAVID S. CHOU.

Jen Chien (People's World): Taipei; f. 1985; current affairs; Editor CHEN YING-CHEN; circ. 8,000.

The Kaleidoscope Monthly: 108 Lungkiang Rd, Taipei; tel. 5365311; Publr WANG CHENG SHENG.

Music and Audiophile: 6th Floor, 271 Hsinyi Rd, Sec. 2, Taipei; tel. 3937201; f. 1973; Publr ADAM CHANG.

National Palace Museum Bulletin: Wai Shuang Hsi, Shih Lin, Taipei; tel. 8812021; f. 1966; every 2 months; art history research in Chinese with summaries in English; Publr CHING HSIAO-YI; Editor WU PING.

CHINA (TAIWAN)

National Palace Museum Monthly: Wai Shuang Hsi, Shih Lin, Taipei; tel. 8812021; f. 1983; monthly in Chinese; Publr CHIN HSIAO-YI; Editor-in-Chief SUNG LUNG-FEI; circ. 18,000.

Ours: 4th Floor, 277 Hsinyi Rd, Sec. 2, Taipei; tel. 3921612; f. 1985; Chinese; monthly; Publr CHEN MING-HUI; Editor LISA KUAN.

Reader's Digest (Chinese Edn): 3rd Floor, 872 Min Sheng East Rd, Taipei; tel. 7637206; telex 20954; monthly; Editor-in-Chief LIN TAI-YI.

Sinorama: Room 600, Central Bldg, 2 Chungshan North Rd, Sec. 1, Taipei; tel. 3123342; f. 1976; monthly; cultural; bilingual magazine with editions in Chinese with Japanese, Spanish and English; Publr CHANG KING-YUH.

Sinwen Tienti (Newsdom): 10th Floor, 207 Fuh Hsing North Rd, Taipei; tel. 3711027; f. 1945; weekly; Chinese; Dir PU SHAO-FU; Editor LI CHI-LIU.

Taiwan Pictorial: 20 Chungking South Rd, Sec. 2, Taipei; tel. 3115586; f. 1954; monthly; Chinese; general illustrated; Publr LO SEN-TUNG; Editor LIN HUA-TAI.

Tien Sia (Commonwealth Monthly): 4th Floor, 87 Song Chiang Rd, Taipei; tel. 5518627; monthly business magazine; Pres. CHARLES H. C. KAO; Publr and Editor DIANE YING.

Times Newsweekly: 132 Da Li St, Taipei; tel. 3087111; f. 1986; weekly; Chinese; Publr ALBERT C. YU; circ. 30,000.

Unitas: 561 Chung Hsiao East Rd, Sec. 4, Taipei; tel. 7666759; monthly; Chinese; literary journal; Publr CHANG PAO-CHIN; Editor KAO DAH-PENG.

Veteran's Monthly: Hua Hsin Publications, Hua Hsin Cultural Bldg, 133 Kwangfu North Rd, Taipei; tel. 3516011; Publr CHENG WEN-YUNG.

NEWS AGENCIES

Central News Agency Inc. (CNA): 209 Sungkiang Rd, Taipei 104; tel 5051180; telex 11548; f. 1924; Pres. PAN HUAN-KUN; Editor-in-Chief DAVID Y. C. WANG.

Chiao Kwang News Agency: 6th Floor, 3 Lane 1, Ta-an St, Taipei; tel. 3214803; Dir HUANG HO.

China Youth News Agency: 131 Tun Hua North Rd, Taipei 105; tel. 5961183; f. 1955; Dir PENG CHAO-HSIUNG.

Foreign Bureaux

Agence France-Presse (AFP): 6th Floor, 209 Sungkiang Rd, Taipei; tel. 7711844; telex 11069; Correspondent YANG HSIN-HSIN.

Associated Press (AP) (USA): 6th Floor, 209 Sungkiang Rd, Taipei; tel. 5036651; telex 21835; Correspondents PAN YUEH-KAN, KATHY CHANG, YANG CHI-HSIEN.

Reuter (UK): 6th Floor, 209 Sungkiang Rd, Taipei; tel. 5033034; telex 22360; Correspondents ANDREW BROWNE, C. K. CHEN.

United Press International (UPI) (USA): 6th Floor, 209 Sungkiang Rd, Taipei; tel. 5052549; Bureau Man. SHULLEN SHAW.

PRESS ASSOCIATION

Taipei Journalists Association: 555 Chung Hsiao East Rd, Sec. 4, Taipei; tel. 5051811; c. 3,080 mems representing editorial and business executives of newspapers and broadcasting stations.

Publishers

Art Book Co: 4th Floor, 18 Lane 283, Roosevelt Rd, Sec. 3, Taipei; Publr HO KUNG SHANG.

Buffalo Publishing Co: 2nd Floor, 135 Chin Shan South Rd, Sec. 1, Taipei; Publr PENG CHUNG HANG.

Business Publications Ltd: 6th Floor, Hui Feng Bldg, 18 Lane 14, Chi Lin Rd, Taipei; tel. 5216457; telex 12393; f. 1978; international business textbooks; Man. Dir MICHELLE YANG.

Cheng Chung Book Co: 20 Hengyang Rd, Taipei; humanities, social sciences, medicine, fine arts; Publr CHIANG LIEN-JU.

Cheng Wen Publishing Co: POB 22605, Taipei; tel. 7415432; Publr HUANG CHENG CHU.

Chinese Culture University Press: Hua Kang, Yangmingshan, Taipei; tel. 8611862; Publr LEE FU-CHEN.

Chung Hwa Book Co Ltd: 94 Chungking South Rd, Sec. 1, Taipei; tel. 3117365; humanities, social sciences, medicine, fine arts, school books; Gen. Man. HSIUNG DUN SENG.

The Eastern Publishing Co Ltd: 121 Sec. 1, Chungking South Rd, Taipei; tel. 3114514; Publr CHENG LI-TSU.

Directory

Far East Book Co: 10th Floor, 66–1 Chungking South Rd, Sec. 1, Taipei; tel. 3118740; art, education, history, physics, mathematics, law, literature, dictionaries; Publr GEORGE C. L. PU.

Ho Chi Book Co: 249 Wuhsing St, Taipei; Publr WU FU CHANG.

Hua Hsin Culture and Publications Center: 2nd Floor, 133 Kuang Fu North Rd, Taipei; tel. 7658848; f. 1960; Dir Dr JAMES K. CHENG; Editor-in-Chief W. L. TENG.

International Cultural Enterprises: 6th Floor, 25 Po Ai Rd, Taipei; tel. 3318080; Publr HU TZE-DAN.

Kwang Hwa Publishing Company: 3–1 Chung Hsiao East Rd, Sec. 1, Taipei; tel. 3319551; telex 11636; Publr CHANG KING-YUH.

Li-Ming Cultural Enterprise Co: 10th Floor, 3 Hsin Yi Rd, Sec. 1, Taipei; tel. 3952500; telex 27377; Publr LIU YEN-SHENG; Gen. Man. TIEN YUAN.

San Min Book Co: 61 Chungking South Rd, Sec. 1, Taipei; f. 1953; literature, history, philosophy, social sciences; Publr LIU CHEN-CHIANG.

Taiwan Kaiming Book Co: 77 Chung Shan North Rd, Sec. 1, Taipei; tel. 5415369; Publr CHAO LIU CHING-TI; Gen. Man. CHANG CHING-HWANG.

The World Book Co: 99 Chungking South Rd, Sec. 1, Taipei; tel. 3311616; f. 1921; literature, textbooks; Chair. CHEN SHEH WOO; Publr and Gen. Man. SHAW TSUNG MOU.

Youth Cultural Enterprise Co Ltd: 3rd Floor, 66–1 Chungking South Rd, Sec. 1, Taipei; Publr HU KWEI; Gen. Man. WANG SEN-NAEY.

Yuan Liou Publishing Co Ltd: 7F, 782 Ding Chou Rd, Taipei; tel. 3923707; Publr WANG JUNG-WEN.

Radio and Television

In 1986 there were an estimated 6m. licensed radio receivers, and 5.2m. licensed television sets. Broadcasting stations are mostly privately owned, but the Ministry of Communications determines power and frequencies, and the Government Information Office supervises the operation of all stations, whether private or governmental.

RADIO

In 1986 there were 33 radio broadcasting corporations, of which the following are the most important:

Broadcasting Corpn of China: 53 Jen Ai Rd, Sec. 3, Taipei 106; tel. 7710151; telex 27498; f. 1928; domestic (6 networks) and external services in 14 languages and dialects; 44 stations, 130 transmitters; Pres. P. P. TANG; Chair. PAN CHEN-CHEW.

Cheng Sheng Broadcasting Corpn: 7–8th Floors, 66–1 Chungking South Rd, Sec. 1, Taipei; f. 1950; 9 stations; Chair. JOSEPH CHING; Gen. Man. TU HSIN-SHIH.

Fu Shing Broadcasting Corpn: POB 799, 1253 Cheng Teh Rd, Shih Lin, Taipei; 27 stations; Dir HO MUH-CHAO.

TELEVISION

Taiwan Television Enterprise Ltd: 10 Pa Te Rd, Sec. 3, Taipei; tel. 7711515; telex 25714; f. 1962; Chair. HSU CHIN-TEH; Pres. STONE K. SHIH.

China Television Co: 53 Jen Ai Rd, Sec. 3, Taipei; tel. 7511247; telex 25080; f. 1969; Chair. TSU SUNG-CHIU; Pres. H. P. CHUNG.

Chinese Television Service: 100 Kuang Fu South Rd, Taipei; tel. 751-0321; telex 24195; f. 1971; cultural and educational; Chair. YEE CHIEN-CHIU; Pres. WU PAO-HUA.

Finance

(cap. = capital; p.u. = paid up; dep. = deposits; m. = million; brs = branches; amounts in New Taiwan dollars)

BANKING
Central Bank

Central Bank of China: 2 Roosevelt Rd, Sec. 1, Taipei; tel. 3936161; telex 21532; f. 1928; bank of issue; cap. 16,000m., dep. 892,662m. (June 1986); Gov. CHANG CHI-CHENG; Dep. Gov. SHIRLEY W. Y. KUO.

CHINA (TAIWAN)

Domestic Banks

Bank of Communications: 91 Heng Yang Rd, Taipei; tel. 3613000; telex 11341; f. 1907; cap. 9,000m., dep. 142,206m. (March 1986); Chair. S. C. SHIEH; Pres. C. Y. LEE; 10 brs.

Bank of Taiwan: 120 Chungking South Rd, Sec. 1, Taipei 10036; tel. 3147377; telex 11201; f. 1946; cap. 8,000m., dep. 420,680m. (June 1986); Chair. LIU SHIH-CHENG; Pres. J. T. HSIEH; 63 brs.

Co-operative Bank of Taiwan: 77 Kuan Chien Rd, Taipei; tel. 3118811; telex 23749; f. 1946; acts as central bank for co-operatives, and as major agricultural credit institution; dep. 313,508m. (June 1986); Chair. H. S. CHANG; Pres. H. A. CHEN; 66 brs.

Farmers Bank of China: 85 Nanking East Rd, Sec. 2, Taipei; tel. 5517141; telex 21610; f. 1933; cap. 3,668m., dep. 78,880m. (March 1986); Chair. C. P. YEN; Pres. C. M. PU; 25 brs.

International Commercial Bank of China: 100 Chi Lin Rd, Taipei 10424; tel. 5633156; telex 11300; f. 1912; cap. 4,705m., dep. 46,039m. (March 1986); Chair. K. H. KING; Pres. C. D. WANG; 31 brs.

Land Bank of Taiwan: 46 Kuan Chien Rd, Taipei 10038; tel. 3613020; f. 1946; cap. 4,000m., dep. 214,686m. (March 1986); Chair. Y. D. SHEU; Pres. C. C. LEE; 58 brs.

Commercial Banks

Bank of Kaohsiung: 21 Wu Fu 3rd Rd, Kaohsiung; tel. 2413051; telex 73266; f. 1982; cap. 450m., dep. 9,871m. (March 1986); Chair. K. C. CHENG; Pres. CHUN CHUNG-HUANG.

Central Trust of China: 49 Wu Chang St, Sec. 1, Taipei 10006; tel. 3111511; telex 11377; f. 1935; govt institution; cap. 2,780m., dep. 21,067m. (June 1986); Chair. W. S. KING; Pres. T. Y. CHU.

Chang Hwa Commercial Bank Ltd: 38 Tsuyu Rd, Sec. 2, Taichung; tel. 222001; telex 51248; f. 1905; cap. 3,000m., dep. 177,593m. (March 1986); Chair. K. S. LIAN; Pres. HUBERT M. F. HSU; 104 brs.

First Commercial Bank: 30 Chungking South Rd, Sec. 1, Taipei; tel. 3111111; telex 11310; f. 1899; cap. 5,768m., dep. 193,762m. (1986); Chair. CHEN PAO-CHUAN; Pres. KENNETH B. K. TSAN; 111 brs.

Hua Nan Commercial Bank Ltd: 33 Kaifeng St, Sec. 1, Taipei; tel. 3619666; telex 11307; f. 1919; cap. 3,024m., dep. 188,971m. (March 1986); Chair. YANG CHI-CHUAN; Pres. K. H. LO; 88 brs.

Overseas Chinese Commercial Banking Corpn: 8 Hsiang Yang Rd, Taipei; tel. 3715181; telex 21571; f. 1961; general banking and foreign exchange; cap. p.u. 1,575m., dep. 14,867m. (March 1986); Chair. (vacant); Gen. Man. S. LIN; 8 brs.

Shanghai Commercial and Savings Bank: 16 Jen Ai Rd, Sec. 2, Taipei; tel. 3933111; telex 22507; f. 1915; cap. p.u. 550m., dep. 5,400m. (March 1986); Chair. J. T. CHU; Pres. RICHARD J. R. YEN; 4 brs.

Taipei City Bank: 50, Sec. 2, Chungshan North Rd, Taipei 100; tel. 5425656; f. 1969; cap. 3,000m., dep. 92,400m. (March 1986); Chair. W. K. WU; Pres. LO CHI-TANG; 24 brs.

United World Chinese Commercial Bank: 65 Kuan Chien Rd, Taipei 10038; tel. 3818160; telex 21378; f. 1974; cap. 1,380m., dep. 24,425m. (March 1986); Chair. SNIT VIRAVAN; Pres. T. M. YEE.

There are also a number of Medium Business Banks throughout the country.

Foreign Banks

American Express International Banking Corpn (USA): 4th Floor, 214 Tun Hua North Rd, Taipei; tel. 7151581; telex 11349; Vice-Pres. JAMES D. VAUGHN.

Bangkok Bank Ltd (Thailand): 1st–4th Floor, 121 Sunkiang Rd, POB 22419, Taipei; tel. 5713275; telex 11289; Vice-Pres. and Man. PRASONG UTHAISANGCHAI.

Bank of America NT and SA (USA): 205 Tun Hua North Rd, Taipei; tel. 7154111; telex 11610; Vice-Pres. and Man. MYRON LAWRENCE GREENBURG.

Chase Manhattan Bank NA (USA): 72 Nanking East Rd, Sec. 2, POB 3996, Taipei; tel. 5378100; telex 26824; Vice-Pres. and Gen. Man. RODNEY D. FREED.

Chemical Bank (USA): 7th Floor, Worldwide House, 683-5 Ming Sheng East Rd, POB 48–11, Taipei; tel. 7121181; telex 22411; Vice-Pres. and Gen. Man. CHARLES R. GOW.

Citibank NA (USA): 742 Min Sheng East Rd, POB 3343, Taipei; tel. 7155931; telex 23547; Vice-Pres. FREDERICK C. COPELAND.

Continental Bank (USA): 62 Nanking East Rd, Sec. 2, Taipei; tel. 5210240; telex 28794; Gen. Man. STEVEN R. CHAMPION.

Dai-Ichi Kangyo Bank Ltd (Japan): 137 Nanking East Rd, Sec. 2, Taipei; tel. 5614371; telex 11220; Pres. TOMOYUKI INOUE.

First Interstate Bank of California (USA): 221 Nanking East Rd, Sec. 3, Taipei; tel. 7153572; telex 11830; Vice-Pres. and Gen. Man. TOM L. DOBYNS.

Hongkong and Shanghai Banking Corpn (Hong Kong): 205 Tun Hua North Rd, Taipei; tel. 7130088; telex 10934.

International Bank of Singapore: 178 Nanking East Rd, Sec. 2, Taipei; tel. 5810531; telex 25530; Branch Man. NOX WU BENG.

Irving Trust Company (USA): 10–12 Chungking South Rd, Sec. 1, Taipei; tel. 3114682; telex 21710; Vice-Pres. EDWARD J. MORIARTY.

Metropolitan Bank and Trust Co (Philippines): 52 Nanking East Rd, Sec. 1, Taipei; tel. 5214191; telex 21688; Gen. Man. HENRY SO UY (acting).

Société Générale (France): 683 Min Sheng East Rd, Taipei 10446; tel. 7155050; telex 23904; Gen. Man. CLAUDE SCHAEFFER.

Standard Chartered Bank (UK): 337 Fu Hsing North Rd, Taipei 10483; tel. 7166261; telex 12133; Man. J. J. C. BRINSDEN.

Toronto Dominion Bank (Canada): 2nd Floor, 337 Fushing North Rd, Taipei; tel. 7162162; telex 22503; Man. BYRON JOSEPH FORDYCE.

The following foreign banks also have branches in Taipei: Amsterdam-Rotterdam Bank (Netherlands), Bankers Trust Co (USA), Banque Indosuez (France), Banque Nationale de Paris (France), Banque Paribas (France), Crédit Lyonnais SA (France), Development Bank of Singapore, Dresdner Bank (Federal Republic of Germany), European Asian Bank (Federal Republic of Germany), First National Bank of Boston (USA), Grindlays Bank (UK), Hollandsche Bank-Unie NV (Netherlands), Lloyds Bank International (UK), Manufacturers Hanover Trust Co (USA), Morgan Guaranty Trust Co of New York (USA), Rainier National Bank (USA), Royal Bank of Canada, Seattle First National Bank (USA), Westpac Banking Corpn (Australia).

DEVELOPMENT CORPORATION

China Development Corpn: 13th–16th Floor, China Development Bldg 125, Nan King East Rd, Sec. 5, Taipei; tel. 7638800; telex 23147; f. 1959 as privately-owned development finance company to assist in creation, modernization and expansion of private industrial enterprises in Taiwan, to encourage participation of private capital in such enterprises; cap. 1,000m. (1984); Chair. YUNG-LIANG LIN; Pres. W. L. KIANG.

STOCK EXCHANGE

Taiwan Stock Exchange Corpn: 9th Floor, City Bldg, 85 Yen-ping South Rd, Taipei; tel. 3969271; f. 1962; 39 mems; Chair. YAO KU-HUAI.

INSURANCE

Cathay Life Insurance Co Ltd: 1 Hsiang Yang Rd, Taipei; tel. 3113575; telex 24994; f. 1962; Chair. TSAI WAN-LIN; Vice-Chair. HONG-TU TSAI.

Central Trust of China, Life Insurance Dept: 5th–7th Floor, 76 Poai Rd, Taipei; tel. 3144327; telex 21154; f. 1941; life insurance; Pres. KING WEI-SHIN.

China Mariners' Assurance Corpn Ltd: 62 Hsinsheng South Rd, Sec. 1, Taipei; tel. 3913201; telex 21748; Chair T. F. FAN; Gen. Man. K. T. FAN.

Chung Kuo Insurance Co Ltd: 10th–12th Floor, ICBC Bldg, 100 Chilin Rd, Taipei; tel. 5513345; telex 21573; fmrly China Insurance Co Ltd; Chair. GEORGE L. T. CHIEN; Pres. C. K. LIU.

Tai Ping Insurance Co Ltd: 3rd–5th Floor, 550 Chung Hsiao East Rd, Sec. 4, Taipei; tel. 7002700; telex 21641; f. 1929; Chair. GEORGE Y. L. WU; Gen. Man. C. C. HSU.

Taiwan Life Insurance Co Ltd: 17th–19th Floor, 17 Hsu Chang St, Taipei; tel. 3116411; Chair. Y. A. WU; Pres. M. H. TSAI.

There are 16 other insurance companies operating in Taipei.

Trade and Industry

CHAMBER OF COMMERCE

General Chamber of Commerce of the Republic of China: 6th Floor, 390 Fu Hsing South Rd, Sec. 1, Taipei; tel. 7080350; telex 11396; Chair. WANG YOU-THENG; Sec.-Gen. CHIANG CHI-LIN.

CHINA (TAIWAN) *Directory*

TRADE AND INDUSTRIAL ORGANIZATIONS

China External Trade Development Council: 201 Tun Hua North Rd, Taipei; tel. 7151515; telex 28094; trade promotion body; Sec.-Gen. CHIANG PIN-KUNG.

China Productivity Centre: 2nd Floor, 340 Tun Hua North Rd, Taipei; tel. 7137731; telex 22954; f. 1955; industrial management and technical consultants; Gen. Man. CASPER T. Y. SHIH.

Chinese National Association of Industry and Commerce: 17th Floor, 30 Chungking South Rd, Sec. 1, Taipei; tel. 3148001; telex 10774; Chair. KOO CHEN-FU; Sec.-Gen. WU TSU-PING.

Chinese National Federation of Industries: 12th Floor, 390 Fu Hsing South Rd, Sec. 1, Taipei; tel. 7035510; f. 1948; 127 mem. asscns; Chair. KOO CHEN-FU; Sec.-Gen. HO CHUN-YIH.

Industrial Development and Investment Centre: 10th Floor, 7 Roosevelt Rd, Sec. 1, Taipei 10757; tel. 3947213; telex 10634; f. 1959 to assist investment and planning; Dir JOHN CHANG-I NI.

Taiwan Handicraft Promotion Centre: 1 Hsu Chow Rd, Taipei; tel. 3413731; telex 28944; f. 1956; Chair. PHILLIP P. C. LIU; Man. Dir Y. C. WANG.

Trading Department of Central Trust of China: 49 Wuchang St, Sec. 1, Taipei; tel. 3111511; telex 26254; f. 1935; export and import agent for private and govt-owned enterprises.

CO-OPERATIVES

In December 1985 there were 4,341 co-operatives, with a total membership of 3,594,431 people and total capital of NT$9,112.7m. Of the specialized co-operatives the most important was the consumers' co-operative (3,559 co-ops; 2,374,892 mems; cap. NT$172.3m.).

The centre of co-operative financing is the Co-operative Bank of Taiwan (see Finance section), owned jointly by the Taiwan government and 605 co-operative units. The Co-operative Institute (f. 1918) and the Co-operative League (f. 1940), which has 424 institutional and 4,533 individual members, exist to further the co-operative movement's national and international interests; departments of co-operative business have been set up on three university campuses.

RURAL RECONSTRUCTION

Council of Agriculture (COA): 37 Nanhai Rd, Taipei 10728; tel. 3317541; f. 1984 to replace the Council for Agricultural Planning and Development (CAPD), and the Bureau of Agriculture (BOA); govt agency directly under the Executive Yuan, with ministerial status; administration of all affairs related to food, crops, forestry, fisheries and the animal industry; promotes technology and provides external assistance; Chair. Y. T. WANG; Vice-Chair. C. C. KOH; Sec.Gen. H. Y. CHEN.

TRADE UNIONS

Chinese Federation of Labour: 11th Floor, 201–18 Tun Hua North Rd, Taipei; tel. 7135111; f. 1948; mems: c. 2,000 unions representing 1,550,000 workers; Pres. CHEN HSI-CHI; Gen. Sec. LU KUO-HUA.

National Federations

Chinese Federation of Postal Workers: 9th Floor, 45 Chungking South Rd, Sec. 2, Taipei 107; tel. 3921380; f. 1930; 22,600 mems; Pres. KO YU-CHIN.

Chinese National Federation of Railway Workers: 107 Chengchou Rd, Taipei; tel. 5813354; f. 1947; 23,430 mems; Chair. LIU CHIA-YÜ.

National Chinese Seamen's Union: 2nd Floor, 115 Hang-Chow South Rd, Sec. 1, Taipei; tel. 3941321; f. 1913; 27,910 mems; Pres. KING TI-HSIEN.

Regional Federations

Taiwan Federation of Textile and Dyeing Industry Workers' Unions (TFTDWU): 2 Lane 64, Chung Hsiao East Rd, Sec. 2, Taipei; tel. 3415627; f. 1957; 33,518 mems; Chair. LI HSIN-NAN.

Taiwan Provincial Federation of Labour: 11th Floor, 44 Roosevelt Rd, Sec. 2, Taipei; tel. 3916241; f. 1948; 51 mem. unions and 913,632 mems; Pres. PENG KUANG-CHENG; Sec.-Gen. LIU JEN-HO.

Transport

RAILWAYS

Taiwan Railway Administration (TRA): 2 Yen Ping North Rd, Sec. 1, Taipei; tel. 5511131; telex 21837; a public utility under the provincial govt of Taiwan, it operates both the west line and east line systems with a route length of 1,074.9 km; the west line is the main trunk line from Keelung in the north to Kaohsiung in the south, with several branches; electrification of the main trunk line was completed in 1979; the east line runs down the east coast linking Hualien with Taitung; the north link line, with a length of 82.3 km from New Suao to Tienpu, connecting Suao and Hualien, was opened in 1980; Man. Dir Y. L. PO.

There are also 1,672 km of private narrow-gauge railroads operated by the Taiwan Sugar Corpn, the Forestry Administration and other organizations. These railroads are mostly used for freight but they also provide public passenger and freight services which connect with those of TRA.

ROADS

There were 19,676 km of highways in 1985, most of them asphalt-paved. The North–South Freeway was completed in 1978.

Taiwan Highway Bureau: 70 Chung Hsiao West Rd, Sec. 1, Taipei; tel. 3110929; f. 1946; Dir-Gen. CHI-CHANG YEN.

Taiwan Motor Transport Co Ltd: 3rd Floor, Taiwan Pineapple Bldg No. 15, Sec. 1, Chunking South Rd, Taipei; tel. 3715364; f. 1980; operates national bus service; Chair. HSIUNG YU-SHENG; Gen. Man. HU CHIEN-HUNG.

SHIPPING

Taiwan has four international ports: Kaohsiung, Keelung, Taichung and Hualien. In 1985 the merchant fleet had a total displacement of 4,267,129 grt.

China Union Lines Ltd: 2nd Floor, 7 Tsingtao West Rd, Taipei; tel. 3317521; telex 11217; f. 1948; 1 banana carrier, tramp service; Chair. Y. S. KUNG; Pres. S. Y. CHU.

Evergreen Marine Corpn: 330 Minsheng East Rd, Taipei; tel. 5057766; telex 11476; f. 1968; 56 container vessels, 1 training ship; world-wide container liner services from the Far East to the USA, the Caribbean, the Mediterranean, Europe and South-East Asia; Chair. CHANG YUNG-FA; Pres. S. S. LIN.

Far Eastern Navigation Corpn Ltd: 7th Floor, 10 Chungking South Rd, Sec. 1, Taipei; 1 bulk carrier; Chair. W. H. E. HSU.

First Steamship Co Ltd: 7th Floor, 15 Chi Nan Rd, Sec. 1, Taipei; tel. 3949412; telex 11288; 3 cargo vessels; worldwide service; Chair. S. H. HSU; Pres. S. C. CHU.

Great Pacific Navigation Co Ltd: 2nd Floor, 79 Chung Shan North Rd, Sec. 2, Taipei; tel. 5713211; telex 21983; 1 reefer vessel; fruit and refrigeration cargo services worldwide; Chair. CHEN CHA-MOU.

Taiwan Navigation Co Ltd: 6 Chungking South Rd, Sec. 1, Taipei; tel. 3113882; telex 11233; f. 1947; 4 bulk carriers, 6 tankers, 4 barges, 3 general cargo, 2 container vessels, 4 pushers, 1 refrigerator, 1 passenger vessel; Chair. T. H. CHEN; Pres. L. S. CHEN.

Yangming Marine Transport Corpn: 4th Floor, Hwai Ning Bldg, 53 Hwai Ning St, Taipei; tel. 3812911; telex 11572; 14 container vessels, 3 general cargo vessels, 10 bulk carriers, 6 tankers; Chair. CHIH MENG-BING; Pres. KUO HUNG-WEI.

CIVIL AVIATION

There are two international airports, Chiang Kai-shek (Taoyuan) near Taipei, which opened in 1979, and Kaohsiung. The former international airport at Sungshan is now used for domestic flights.

China Air Lines Ltd (CAL): 131 Nanking East Rd, Sec. 3, Taipei; tel. 7151212; telex 11346; f 1959; domestic services and international services to Hong Kong, Indonesia, Japan, Malaysia, the Philippines, Saudi Arabia, Singapore, Thailand, the Republic of Korea, the Netherlands, UAE and the USA; Chair. YEUH WU; Pres. Gen. CHI JUNG-CHUN; fleet of 3 Boeing 737, 9 747, 6 Airbus-300.

Far Eastern Air Transport Corpn: 5, Alley 123, Lane 405, Tun Hua North Rd, Taipei; telex 11639; f. 1957; domestic services and chartered flights; Chair. K. T. SIAO; Pres. T. C. HWOO; fleet of 7 Boeing 737.

CHINA (TAIWAN)

Tourism

In 1985 there were 1,451,659 foreign visitors to Taiwan.

Tourism Bureau, Ministry of Communications: 9th Floor, 280 Chung Hsiao East Rd, Sec. 4, Taipei; tel. 7218541; telex 26408; f. 1966; Dir-Gen. Yu Wei.

Taiwan Visitors' Association: 5th Floor, 111 Minchuan East Rd, Taipei; tel. 5943261; telex 20335; f. 1956; promotes domestic and international tourism; Chair. Richard C. C. Chao.

Atomic Energy

Three nuclear power plants were operational in 1985. Nuclear power generation provided about 52% of Taiwan's total power generation in 1985.

Atomic Energy Council (AEC): 67 Lane 144, Keelung Rd, Sec. 4, Taipei; tel. 3924180; telex 26554; f. 1955; promotes the advancement of nuclear science and technology, enforces safety requirements; Chair. Chen-hsing Yen; Sec.-Gen. Yu Hao-lee.

Institute of Nuclear Energy Research (INER): POB 3, Lung Tan 32500; telex 34154; f. 1968; national nuclear research centre; Dir Liu Kuang-chi.

COLOMBIA

Introductory Survey

Location, Climate, Language, Religion, Flag, Capital

The Republic of Colombia lies in the north-west of South America, with the Caribbean Sea to the north and the Pacific Ocean to the west. Its continental neighbours are Venezuela and Brazil to the east, and Peru and Ecuador to the south, while Panama connects it with Central America. The coastal areas have a tropical rain forest climate, the plateaux are temperate, and in the Andes mountains there are areas of permanent snow. The language is Spanish. Almost all of the inhabitants profess Christianity, and about 95% are Roman Catholics. There are small Protestant and Jewish minorities. The national flag (proportions 3 by 2) has three horizontal stripes, of yellow (one-half of the depth), dark blue and red. The capital is Bogotá.

Recent History

Colombia was under Spanish rule from the 16th century until 1819, when it achieved independence as part of Gran Colombia, which included Ecuador, Panama and Venezuela. Ecuador and Venezuela seceded in 1830, when Colombia (then including Panama) became a separate republic. In 1903 the province of Panama successfully rebelled and became an independent country.

For more than a century, Colombia has been dominated by two political parties, the Conservatives (Partido Conservador) and the Liberals (Partido Liberal), whose rivalry has often led to violence. Liberal governments held power in 1860–84 and 1930–46, with Conservative governments in 1884–1930 and 1946–53. From 1922 to 1953, with one exception, every President of Colombia completed his four-year term of office. The assassination in April 1948 of Bogotá's left-wing Liberal mayor, Jorge Eliécer Gaitán, led to intense political violence, amounting to civil war, between Conservative and Liberal factions. According to official estimates, lawlessness between 1949 and 1958, known as 'La Violencia', caused the deaths of about 280,000 people.

President Laureano Gómez, who had been elected 'unopposed' in November 1949, ruled as a dictator until his overthrow by a coup in June 1953, when power was seized by Gen. Gustavo Rojas Pinilla. President Rojas established a right-wing dictatorship but, following widespread rioting, he was deposed in May 1957, when a five-man military junta took power.

In an attempt to restore peace and stability, the Conservative and Liberal Parties agreed to co-operate in a National Front. Under this arrangement, the presidency was to be held by Liberals and Conservatives in rotation, while Cabinet portfolios would be divided equally between the two parties and both would have an equal number of seats in each house of the bicameral Congress. In December 1957, in Colombia's first vote on the basis of universal adult suffrage, this agreement was overwhelmingly approved by a referendum. It was subsequently incorporated in Colombia's constitution.

In May 1958 the first presidential election under the amended constitution was won by the National Front candidate, Dr Alberto Lleras Camargo, a Liberal who had been President in 1945–46. He took office in August 1958, when the junta relinquished power. During the rule of President Lleras Camargo, who was in power until 1962, left-wing guerrilla groups were established in Colombia. As provided by the 1957 agreement, he was succeeded by a Conservative, Dr Guillermo León Valencia, who held office until 1966, when another Liberal, Dr Carlos Lleras Restrepo, was elected. Despite continuing political violence, President Lleras Restrepo was able to bring about some recovery in Colombia's economy.

At the presidential election of 19 April 1970, the National Front candidate, Dr Misael Pastrana Borrero of the Conservative Party, narrowly defeated Gen. Rojas, the former dictator, who campaigned as leader of the Alianza Nacional Popular (ANAPO), with policies that had considerable appeal for the poorer sections of the population. At elections to Congress, held simultaneously, the National Front lost its majority in each of the two houses, while ANAPO became the main opposition group in each. The result of the presidential election was challenged by supporters of ANAPO, who demonstrated against alleged electoral fraud. However, the result was officially upheld, after four recounts, and in August 1970 Dr Pastrana took office as President. In June 1971 ANAPO was officially constituted as a political party, advocating a populist programme of 'Colombian socialism'. However, some ANAPO supporters, in reaction to the disputed 1970 election results, formed an armed wing, the Movimiento 19 de Abril (M-19), which began guerrilla activity against the Government. They were joined by dissident members of a pro-Soviet guerrilla group, the Fuerzas Armadas Revolucionarias de Colombia (FARC), which had been established in 1966.

The bipartisan form of government ended formally with the presidential and legislative elections of April 1974, although the 1974–78 Cabinet remained subject to the parity agreement. The Conservative and Liberal Parties together won an overwhelming majority of seats in Congress, and the vote for ANAPO was greatly reduced. The presidential election was won by the Liberal Party candidate, Dr Alfonso López Michelsen, who received 56% of the total votes. President López took office in August 1974, promising wide-ranging reforms and a more equitable distribution of income. His failure to achieve these aims led to strikes, rioting and increased guerrilla violence, and a state of siege was announced in June 1975. Meanwhile, Gen. Rojas died in January 1975 and was succeeded as leader of ANAPO by his daughter, María Eugenia Rojas de Moreno Díaz, who had been the party's presidential candidate in the 1974 election.

At elections to Congress in February 1978, the Liberal Party won a clear majority in both houses, and in June the Liberal Party candidate, Dr Julio César Turbay Ayala, won the presidential election. President Turbay kept to the National Front agreement, and attempted to tackle the problems of urban terrorism and drug trafficking, but had little success. In October 1981 a Peace Commission was set up under ex-President Lleras Restrepo. In early 1982 the guerrillas suffered heavy losses after successful counter-insurgency operations, combined with the activities of a new anti-guerrilla group which was associated with drug-smuggling enterprises, the Muerte a Secuestradores (MAS, Death to Kidnappers), whose targets later became trade union leaders and human rights activists. In April the majority of the Peace Commission resigned when the Government opposed the granting of a total amnesty, although the state of siege was lifted in June.

At congressional elections in March 1982, the Liberal Party maintained its majority in both the House of Representatives and the Senate. In the presidential election in May, the Conservative candidate, Dr Belisario Betancur Cuartas, received the most votes, owing to a division within the Liberal Party between the unpopular ex-President López, the 'official' candidate (whose career had been chequered by corruption charges), and a young Senator, Dr Luis Carlos Galán Sarmiento, who was the leader of the party's radical faction (Nuevo Liberalismo) and a protégé of ex-President Lleras Restrepo.

President Betancur, who took office in August 1982, declared a broad amnesty for guerrillas in November, reconvened the Peace Commission and ordered an investigation into the MAS. Several hundred political prisoners were released. He embarked on a programme of radical reforms. However, the internal pacification campaign, which was begun in November 1982, met with only moderate success. An estimated 2,000 guerrillas accepted the Government's offer of amnesty. In November 1983 the FARC sought a cease-fire with effect from January 1984, and revealed plans to become a political party. The Plan

Cuatrienal de Paz (Four-Year Peace Plan), launched in 1983, provided US $800m. for revitalization of the economy, further social reform, and the consolidation of economic development, with specific reference to the regions affected by guerrilla activity.

In February 1984 President Betancur announced the resumption of talks between the Peace Commission and the principal guerrilla organizations. In late March the Peace Commission and the FARC agreed conditions for a cease-fire, which was to take effect for one year from May. Under the terms of the accord, the Government agreed to the demilitarization of rural areas. The FARC was to be allowed to assume an active political role. In July, following protracted negotiations, the M-19 group (now operating as a left-wing guerrilla movement) and the Ejército Popular de Liberación (EPL) agreed to a cease-fire but refused to relinquish their weapons. In spite of the murder of the M-19's founder, Carlos Toledo Plata, and subsequent reprisals by those guerrillas still active, the peace accord was signed in August. Factions of the FARC, EPL and the M-19 group which were opposed to the truce continued to conduct guerrilla warfare against the Government.

A major setback to the Government's campaign for internal peace occurred in May 1984, when the Minister of Justice, Rodrigo Lara Bonilla, was assassinated. His murder was regarded as a consequence of his energetic efforts to eradicate the flourishing drugs industry, and Colombia's leading drugs dealers were implicated in the killing. The Government immediately declared a nation-wide state of siege and announced its intention to adopt severe measures against the dealers, including the enforcement of its hitherto unobserved extradition treaty with the USA. The state of siege was partially lifted in October 1984.

Although members of the M-19 had begun to conduct a lawful political campaign in Colombia's main cities, reports of skirmishes between the guerrillas and the armed forces increased in early 1985. In March the EPL and the M-19 temporarily withdrew from talks with the Government, claiming that discussions had reached a deadlock. Relations between the M-19 and the armed forces deteriorated, and in June the M-19 formally withdrew from the cease-fire agreement, accusing the armed forces of attempting to sabotage the truce. In addition, it criticized the Government for failing to introduce promised social reforms whose implementation had been among the conditions for the cease-fire. In October the armed forces launched a large-scale campaign to eradicate guerrilla bases in south-western Colombia. In November a dramatic siege by the M-19 at the Palace of Justice in Bogotá, during which more than 90 people (including 41 guerrillas and 11 judges) were killed, resulted in severe public criticism of the Government and the armed forces for their handling of events. Negotiations with the M-19 were suspended indefinitely. After three years, therefore, the only successful aspects of the Government's internal pacification programme had been the FARC's adherence to the cease-fire agreement and its foundation of a political party, the Unión Patriótica, in May 1985. In response to the siege and the subsequent natural disaster caused by the eruption of the Nevado del Ruiz volcano (also in November 1985), the Government declared a state of economic and social emergency.

Following the violent conclusion to the siege at the Palace of Justice, President Betancur's administration lost public support. Although the findings of an official inquiry into the siege absolved the President and the Minister of Defence, Gen. Miguel Vega Uribe, of any responsibility, the Attorney General was strongly critical of their conduct. Furthermore, it was suggested that the armed forces were responsible for the deaths of at least six of the 17 judicial officers who died in the siege. In July 1986 the Government was spared further embarrassment, when Congress declined to censure the President and Gen. Vega Uribe.

In spite of the loss of two of its principal leaders during 1986, the M-19 remained active, and there were frequent reports of clashes between guerrillas and the armed forces, especially in the city of Cali. In June an unsuccessful attempt was made by guerrillas to assassinate the Minister of the Interior. By September it was claimed that some 1,200 people had died as a result of politically-motivated violence, mostly the victims of death-squads, the security forces or guerrillas.

At congressional elections in March 1986, the traditional wing of the Partido Liberal secured a clear victory over the Partido Conservador and obtained 49% of the votes cast. The Nuevo Liberalismo wing of the Partido Liberal received only 7% of the votes and subsequently withdrew from the forthcoming presidential election. The political wing of the FARC, the Unión Patriótica, won seats in both houses of Congress. At the presidential election in May, Dr Virgilio Barco Vargas, candidate of the Partido Liberal, was elected president with 58% of the votes cast. The large majority that the Partido Liberal secured at both elections obliged the Partido Conservador to form the first formal opposition to a government for 30 years. The Partido Liberal's dominant position was consolidated by the Conservatives' refusal to participate as the minority party in a coalition government with the Liberals.

On taking office in August 1986, President Barco Vargas affirmed that his Government's principal task was to solve the problem of political violence. The new administration was committed to the peace process that had been established by former President Betancur, and intended to create an intergovernmental peace commission. The administration's plans were expected to benefit from the FARC's decision, in March 1986, to sign an indefinite cease-fire agreement. Further priorities for the Government were to be a campaign against poverty and the maintenance of Colombia's programme to combat the cultivation and trafficking of illicit drugs.

The long-standing border dispute with Venezuela has yet to be resolved, and in 1980 Nicaragua laid claim to the Colombian-controlled islands of Providencia and San Andrés. Colombia has a territorial dispute with Honduras over cays in the San Andrés and Providencia archipelago. In October 1986 the Colombian Senate approved a delimitation treaty of marine and submarine waters in the Caribbean Sea, which had been signed by the Governments of Colombia and Honduras in August. Relations with Argentina were strained following the Falklands War, but rumours of the existence of a US military base on San Andrés were denied by the Colombian Government, which announced allegiance to the Non-Aligned Movement in late 1982. The visit to Bogotá in December 1982 by President Ronald Reagan of the USA failed to secure Colombian support for US policy in Central America. President Betancur's efforts to reverse Colombian foreign policy led to improved relations with Nicaragua and Cuba, and an attempt to revive the Andean Pact. As a member of the Contadora group, Colombia sought a new peace initiative for Central America and supported the withdrawal of US forces from El Salvador and Honduras.

Government

Executive power is exercised by the President (assisted by a Cabinet), who is elected for a four-year term by universal adult suffrage. Legislation is carried out by Congress, consisting of the Senate (112 members elected for four years) and the House of Representatives (199 members elected for four years). The country is divided into 23 Departments, four Intendencies and five Commissaries.

Defence

At 18 years of age, every male (with the exception of students) must present himself as a candidate for two years' military service. In July 1986 the strength of the army was 53,000, the navy 9,000 (including 5,000 marines) and the air force 4,200. The paramilitary police force numbers about 50,000 men. Defence expenditure for 1985 was estimated at 53,289m. pesos.

Economic Affairs

The economy depends principally on coffee, of which Colombia is the world's second largest producer, with a 16% share of the world market. Sales of coffee account for more than 40% of Colombia's total earnings. Production rose from 8m. bags (each of 60 kg) in 1974/75 to 13.3m. bags in 1980/81, but declined to 11.6m. bags in 1984. Exports declined to 9m. bags in 1981/82, as a result of falling demand, but increased to 10.2m. bags in 1984/85. In 1986 the sector benefited from a poor coffee harvest in Brazil and high international prices for coffee. Colombia exported 11m. bags of coffee in 1986, which generated more than US $2,000m. in export earnings, and became the world's leading exporter of coffee. The major problems facing the industry were over-production and the appearance of coffee rust fungus in Colombia.

Other important cash crops are cotton, bananas, sugar cane, tobacco, cocoa and cut flowers. The principal food crops are rice, sorghum, maize, wheat and barley. Agricultural output accounts for about 22% of Colombia's gross domestic product (GDP), but in the years 1977–80 the increase in agricultural production was outstripped by the rise in domestic demand. In 1980 food imports reached record levels, while production grew by only 1.3%. In 1984 the agricultural sector was estimated to have grown by 3%. In May 1986 the World Bank allocated three loans amounting to US $250m. to Colombia for the agricultural sector. Colombia's new Liberal Government has announced plans to attract more private investment to the agricultural and agro-business sectors. In recent years there has been renewed interest in the issue of land reform, as 68% of cultivable land is owned by only 4% of the population. The illegal trade in Colombian hemp (marijuana) and cocaine is increasing, and it is believed that contraband exports of these drugs could now exceed the value of legal exports.

Manufacturing accounts for over 20% of the GDP, and prominent industries are food processing, textiles, chemicals, metal products and transport equipment. By 1981, when production fell by 1% after an increase of 2.6% in 1980, the sector was suffering from loss of competitiveness abroad, and industrialists were seeking the imposition of import tariffs. In 1983 the Government introduced exchange and import controls, which required more than 80% of imports to hold prior licences, and in September a ban on the import of motor cars was imposed. Import controls were eased in September 1985 and again in September 1986. The output of the manufacturing sector grew by 6% in 1984. Under the 1983–86 development plan, US $21,400m. was to be invested in 100 projects, including the development of electric energy, mining, transport and industry. The rapidly-developing construction industry, which accounts for almost 4% of GDP, received an allocation of $2,900m. to provide 400,000 additional housing units and to generate 300,000 more jobs.

In March 1982 the World Bank made a loan of US $359m. (the largest ever in Latin America) for the Guavio hydroelectric project (capacity 1,600 MW), to be completed in the late 1980s. A further loan of $70m. from the IDB has been used to construct the San Carlos hydroelectric plant (capacity 620,000 kW), near Medellín. There are plans to construct five small hydro plants with an initial installed capacity of 16,100 kW. The country's estimated total installed capacity is 93,000 MW. Hydroelectricity provided 73% of energy needs in 1983, compared with 17% in 1960. Production of crude petroleum averaged 219,043 barrels per day (b/d) in 1970, but fell to 123,836 b/d in 1979. Output rose to 145,000 b/d in 1983, reducing imports to 50,000 b/d. Output averaged 197,404 b/d in 1985. Following significant discoveries at Caño Limón in Arauca, northern Colombia, and at Vichada, recoverable reserves were estimated to be 1,280m. barrels. Joint projects with foreign companies enabled Colombia to produce sufficient petroleum for both domestic consumption and export in 1986. By late 1986 exports had reached 150,000 b/d. Production was expected to exceed 220,000 b/d in 1986. From 1986–90 the Government planned to invest $450m. in the petroleum sector, with the aim of increasing production to 400,000 b/d. In May 1985 the Government launched a programme to produce fuel alcohol from sugar cane. Production of natural gas exceeds local needs. Known gas reserves total 4,716,000m. cu ft (133,500m. cu m). The Guajira field came 'on stream' in 1977. The gas will supply power for the proposed Palomino petro-chemical complex.

Colombia possesses the largest proven reserves of coal in Latin America. Total proven reserves are 1,267m. metric tons, while potential reserves may exceed 16,200m. tons. Colombia aims to supply 10% of the world market by 1999. The richest coalfield is at El Cerrejón (with estimated reserves of 16,000m. metric tons), for which Exxon undertook a US $3,200m. development contract in 1980. Production began in 1984 and was hoped to yield 15m. metric tons per year by 1999. Colombia began exporting coal in 1983, and exports were expected to increase from 3m. tons in 1985 to 27m. tons per year after 1990. Further developments are taking place at La Loma and La Jagua. The Cerro Matoso nickel plant, costing $400m., was inaugurated in June 1982 and was expected to produce 22,600 metric tons for export annually. Proven reserves are 25m. tons, while total reserves are estimated to be 70m. tons. Colombia produces 95% of the world's emeralds. Gold, silver, platinum, lead, zinc, copper, mercury, limestone and phosphates are also mined, and there are substantial reserves of uranium. The total output of the mining sector grew by 14% in 1984.

In the late 1960s and early 1970s, Colombia's economic development was more promising than in most Latin American countries, with the annual GDP growth rate averaging 6.2% between 1966 and 1976. By 1981 the growth rate had fallen to 2.1% (from 5.4% in 1979), and by 1983 it had fallen to 1.0%. The Government continued to borrow from abroad in order to maintain economic growth, and this contributed towards high interest rates and an inflation rate of 16.8% at the end of 1983, although Colombia continued to have a low rate of indebtedness, compared with the rest of Latin America. Colombia remained the only Latin American country that was capable of raising syndicated loans on the international markets without difficulty, and in October 1983 Colombia secured a loan of US $210m. from a 21-bank syndicate. Colombia received authorization from the World Bank to borrow a further $9,600m. between 1983 and 1986, at a rate of $2,000m. per year. Although export earnings began to fall in 1981, the long-term outlook was encouraging because of developments in the mining industry, which is expected to overtake coffee in importance by the end of the decade.

In 1984 Colombia's economy was severely affected by the decline in domestic demand and the recession among its neighbours. The sharp drop in exports in 1982–83, coupled with the considerable flight of capital, resulted in a significant decline in reserves of foreign exchange, which fell from $3,489m. in December 1982 to $774m. in September 1984. Unemployment rose from 8.9% of the labour force in 1982 to 13.4% in 1984. In addition, the banking sector was severely affected by the financial difficulties of several major private concerns and by its involvement with Colombia's 'parallel' economy, centred on the flourishing trade in illicit drugs. In response to the mounting economic problems, the Government adopted a programme of austerity measures, which included a reduction in public spending, an exchange rate programme of progressive currency devaluations, and improved tax collection. In 1984 GDP grew by 3.2%, in real terms, while inflation was estimated to be 16.1%.

In May 1985 the Government reached agreement with the IMF on a programme of economic adjustment. In addition, the IMF agreed to monitor the progress of the Colombian economy. Under the agreement, Colombia received no economic aid from the IMF but the Government was able to request new funds from other creditors. In June the Government and its commercial bank creditors agreed terms for a loan of $1,000m., to cover debt servicing commitments in 1985–86. Disbursal of the loan commenced in October 1986.

As a result of high international prices for coffee in 1985–86, Colombia was expected to record a trade surplus in 1986 for the first time in several years. Following trade deficits of US $957m. and $1,378m. in 1984 and 1985 respectively, export earnings in excess of $5,000m. were anticipated for 1986 and were expected to encourage economic growth of 4.5% for the year. On taking office in August 1986, Colombia's new Liberal Government announced that the priorities of its economic policy would be to reduce unemployment (estimated at 15.1% of the labour force in mid-1986); to carry out agrarian reform; to eliminate the budget deficit (equivalent to 3.9% of GDP in 1985) and to stimulate export trade. Inflation in the year to May 1986 was 16.4%. In June 1986 Colombia's foreign debt was $13,429m., 70% of which had been incurred by the public sector.

Colombia is a member of ALADI (see p. 170) and the Andean Pact (p. 92), and became a party to GATT (p. 59) in May 1981.

Social Welfare

There is compulsory social security, paid for by the Government, employers and employees, and administered by the Institute of Social Security. It provides benefits for disability, old age, death, sickness, maternity, industrial accidents and unemployment. Large firms must provide life insurance for their employees and there is a comprehensive system of pensions. In 1977 there were 12,720 physicians working in Colombia, and in 1980 the country had 849 hospital establishments, with a total of 44,495 beds. The benefits of the health service do not reach all inhabitants, and in 1981 a report by the Family Welfare Insti-

COLOMBIA

tute estimated the level of infant mortality at 64 per 1,000 live births, one of the highest rates in the world.

Education

Primary education is free and compulsory for five years, to be undertaken by children between six and 12 years of age. No child may be admitted to secondary school unless these five years have been successfully completed. Secondary education, beginning at the age of 11, lasts for up to six years. Following completion of a first cycle of four years, pupils may pursue a further two years of vocational study, leading to the Bachiller examination. In 1985 the total enrolment at primary and secondary schools was equivalent to 90% of children aged six to 12, and 55% of children aged 13–18. In 1986 there were an estimated 231 institutions of higher education. There are plans to construct an Open University to meet the increasing demand for higher education. Adult illiteracy declined from 19.2% in 1973 to 14.8% (males 13.6%; females 16.1%) in 1981.

Tourism

The principal tourist attractions are the Caribbean coast (including the island of San Andrés), the 16th-century walled city of Cartagena, the Amazonian town of Leticia, the Andes mountains of up to 5,700 m above sea-level, the extensive forests and jungles, pre-Columbian relics and monuments of colonial art. Since 1978 tourism has been the second biggest foreign exchange earner. Most of the 715,277 visitors in 1984 came from Venezuela, Ecuador, Europe and the USA.

Public Holidays

1987: 1 January (New Year's Day), 6 January (Epiphany), 19 March (St Joseph's Day), 17 April (Maundy Thursday), 18 April (Good Friday), 1 May (Labour Day), 28 May (Ascension Day), 9 June (Thanksgiving), 18 June (Corpus Christi), 29 June (SS. Peter and Paul), 20 July (Independence), 7 August (Battle of Boyacá), 15 August (Assumption), 12 October (Discovery of America), 1 November (All Saints' Day), 11 November (Independence of Cartagena), 8 December (Immaculate Conception), 25 December (Christmas Day).

1988: 1 January (New Year's Day), 6 January (Epiphany), 19 March (St Joseph's Day), 31 March (Maundy Thursday), 1 April (Good Friday), 1 May (Labour Day), 12 May (Ascension Day), 2 June (Corpus Christi), 9 June (Thanksgiving), 29 June (SS. Peter and Paul), 20 July (Independence), 7 August (Battle of Boyacá), 15 August (Assumption), 12 October (Discovery of America), 1 November (All Saints' Day), 11 November (Independence of Cartagena), 8 December (Immaculate Conception), 25 December (Christmas Day).

Weights and Measures

The metric system is in force.

Currency and Exchange Rates

100 centavos = 1 Colombian peso.

Exchange rates (30 September 1986):
 £1 sterling = 297.45 pesos;
 US $1 = 205.56 pesos.

COLOMBIA   *Statistical Survey*

Statistical Survey

Sources (unless otherwise stated): Departamento Administrativo Nacional de Estadística (DANE), Centro Administrativo Nacional (CAN), Avda Eldorado, Apdo Aéreo 80043, Bogotá; tel. 2691100; telex 044573.

Area and Population

AREA, POPULATION AND DENSITY

Area (sq km) Total	1,141,748*
Population (census results)	
24 October 1973	22,915,229
15 October 1985	
Males	13,777,700
Females	14,060,232
Total	27,837,932
Density (per sq km) at October 1985	24.4

* 440,831 sq miles.

DEPARTMENTS (population at 15 October 1985)

Department	Population	Capital
Antioquia	3,888,067	Medellín
Atlántico	1,428,601	Barranquilla
Bogotá, DE	3,982,941	Bogotá*
Bolívar	1,197,623	Cartagena
Boyacá	1,097,618	Tunja
Caldas	838,094	Manizales
Caquetá	214,473	Florencia
Cauca	795,838	Popayán
César	584,631	Valledupar
Chocó	242,768	Quibdo
Córdoba	913,636	Montería
Cundinamarca	1,382,360	Bogotá*
La Guajira	255,310	Riohacha
Huila	647,756	Neiva
Magdalena	769,141	Santa Marta
Meta	412,312	Villaricencio
Nariño	1,019,098	Pasto
Norte de Santander	883,884	Cúcuta
Quindío	377,860	Armenia
Risaralda	625,451	Pereira
Santander del Sur	1,438,226	Bucaramanga
Sucre	529,059	Sincelejo
Tolima	1,051,852	Ibagué
Valle del Cauca	2,847,087	Cali
Intendencies		
Arauca	70,085	Arauca
Casanare	110,253	Yopal
Putumayo	119,815	Mocoa
San Andrés y Providencia Islands	35,936	San Andrés
Commissaries		
Amazonas	30,327	Leticia
Guainía	9,214	Obando
Guaviare†	35,305	San José de Guaviare
Vaupés	18,935	Mitú
Vichada‡	13,770	Puerto Carreño
Total	27,867,326	

* The capital city, Bogotá, is the capital of two departments: Bogotá, DE, and Cundinamarca. The city's population is included only in Bogotá, DE.
† Not exact.
‡ Area not covered by the census.

PRINCIPAL TOWNS
(population at 15 October 1985)

Bogotá, DE (capital)	3,982,941	Cartagena	531,426
Medellín*	2,095,147	Cúcuta*	443,093
Cali*	1,400,828	Pereira*	389,479
Barranquilla*	1,137,150	Manizales*	327,778
Bucaramanga*	595,006	Ibagué	292,965

* Metropolitan area.

BIRTHS, MARRIAGES AND DEATHS*

	Registered live births		Registered marriages		Registered deaths	
	Number	Rate (per 1,000)	Number	Rate (per 1,000)	Number	Rate (per 1,000)
1970	n.a.	n.a.	54,596	2.6	140,990	6.8
1971	797,160	36.6	52,848	2.4	160,412	7.5
1972	578,478	26.4	50,967	2.3	160,412	7.1
1973	347,380	15.4	62,469	2.8	163,563	7.3
1974	363,036	15.7	67,199	2.9	163,096	7.1
1975	386,132	16.2	72,370	3.0	153,238	6.5
1976	655,964	26.8	80,336	3.3	153,966	6.3
1977	806,492	32.0	88,401	3.5	145,426	5.8

* Data are tabulated by year of registration rather than by year of occurrence. Figures for births in 1970–73 and (except for Bogotá) marriages are based on baptisms and marriages recorded in Roman Catholic church registers. Figures for births after 1973 refer to births registered in the same year. Figures for deaths are based on burial permits. Registration is incomplete and the UN estimates average annual rates as: births 33.3 per 1,000 in 1970–75, 32.1 per 1,000 in 1975–80; deaths 9.0 per 1,000 in 1970–75, 8.2 per 1,000 in 1975–80.

ECONOMICALLY ACTIVE POPULATION
(household survey, 1980)

Agriculture, hunting, forestry and fishing	2,412,413
Mining and quarrying	49,740
Manufacturing	1,136,735
Electricity, gas and water	44,233
Construction	242,191
Trade, restaurants and hotels	1,261,633
Transport, storage and communications	352,623
Financing, insurance, real estate and business services	278,210
Community, social and personal services	1,998,460
Activities not adequately described	690,762
Total Labour Force	8,467,000*

* Males 6,247,000; females 2,220,000.

Agriculture

PRINCIPAL CROPS ('000 metric tons)

	1984	1985	1986*
Wheat	59.3	76.1	84.0
Rice (paddy)	1,695.8	1,798.2	1,757.6
Barley	28.2	60.4	68.7
Maize	864.3	762.6	913.2
Sorghum	589.6	499.4	654.4
Potatoes	2,463.0	1,910.4	2,124.8
Cassava (Manioc)	1,386.3	1,367.4	1,513.4
Soybeans	94.2	104.2	154.1
Seed cotton	243.3	339.6	341.0
Cabbages	480	n.a.	n.a.
Tomatoes	330	n.a.	n.a.
Onions	308	n.a.	n.a.
Sugar cane	11,553	13,964	13,529
Bananas	1,103.8	998.6	1,120.0
Plantains	2,145	2,185	2,249
Oranges	242†	n.a.	n.a.
Pineapples	110‡	n.a.	n.a.
Coffee (green)	693.7	677.9	686.2
Cocoa beans	39.2	42.6	44.4
Tobacco (blond and black)	33.7	28.3	29.1

* Preliminary.   † Unofficial estimate.
‡ FAO estimate (Source: FAO, *Production Yearbook*).

LIVESTOCK ('000 head)

	1982	1983	1984
Horses	1,710	1,710	1,710
Mules	590	590	590
Asses	640	640	640
Cattle	24,251	24,251	24,251
Pigs	2,179	2,244	2,311
Sheep	2,255	2,255	2,255
Goats	879	879	879
Chickens	82,800	83,000	85,100

LIVESTOCK PRODUCTS ('000 metric tons)

	1982	1983	1984
Beef and veal	635	643	672
Pig meat	93	108	110
Cows' milk	1,718	1,788	1,877
Cheese*	46.5	47.3	48.0
Butter and ghee*	12.6	12.8	12.9
Hen eggs	216	220	227
Cattle hides*	81.3	83.8	85.1

* FAO estimates (Source: FAO, *Production Yearbook*).

Forestry

ROUNDWOOD REMOVALS ('000 cu metres)

	1982	1983*	1984*
Sawlogs, veneer logs and logs for sleepers	1,960	1,960	1,960
Pulpwood	305	305	305
Other industrial wood	408	408	408
Fuel wood*	13,646	13,940	14,243
Total	16,319	16,613	16,916

* FAO estimates.
Source: FAO, *Yearbook of Forest Products*.

SAWNWOOD PRODUCTION ('000 cu metres)

	1980	1981	1982
Coniferous sawnwood	30*	30*	1
Broadleaved sawnwood	900	936	680
Railway sleepers	40	40	40*
Total	970	1,006	721

* FAO estimates.
1983 and 1984: Production as in 1982 (FAO estimates).
Source: FAO, *Yearbook of Forest Products*.

Fishing

('000 metric tons, live weight)

	1983*	1984†	1985†
Inland waters	45.3	50.8	27.7
Atlantic Ocean	3.1	8.3	3.2
Pacific Ocean	9.1	17.8	3.6
Total catch	57.5	76.9	34.5

* Source: FAO, *Yearbook of Fishery Statistics*.
† Source: Ministerio de Agricultura, *Anuario Estadístico del Sector Agropecuario 1986*.

Mining and Industry

SELECTED PRODUCTS

	1983	1984	1985
Gold ('000 troy oz)	426.5	730.7	1,142.0
Silver ('000 troy oz)	132.4	153.4	168.8
Salt (incl. sea salt) ('000 metric tons)	423.4	663.8	494.4
Iron ore (metric tons)	436,068	443,840	438,746
Crude petroleum ('000 barrels)	55,488	61,153	64,352
Diesel oil ('000 barrels)	10,367	10,507	11,150
Fuel oil ('000 barrels)	20,257	20,027	19,825
Motor fuel ('000 barrels)	21,152	22,916	21,432
Sugar (metric tons)	1,347,445	1,177,167	1,367,352
Cement ('000 metric tons)	4,721.0	5,276.4	5,315.0
Carbonates (metric tons)	118,289	129,440	114,121
Caustic soda (metric tons)	20,686	28,113	20,230
Steel ingots (metric tons)	271,733	285,663	274,416

Sources: Banco de la República, Laboratorios de Fundición y Ensaye, Concesión Salinas and Empresa Colombiana de Petróleos.

Finance

CURRENCY AND EXCHANGE RATES

Monetary Units
100 centavos = 1 Colombian peso.

Denominations
Coins: 5, 10, 20 and 50 centavos; 1, 2, 5, 10 and 20 pesos.
Notes: 1, 2, 5, 10, 20, 50, 100, 200, 500, 1,000 and 2,000 pesos.

Sterling and Dollar Equivalents (30 September 1986)
£1 sterling = 297.45 pesos;
US $1 = 205.56 pesos;
1,000 Colombian pesos = £3.362 = $4.865.

Average Exchange Rate (pesos per US $)
1983   78.85
1984 100.82
1985 142.31

INTERNATIONAL RESERVES
(US $ million at 31 December)

	1983	1984	1985
Gold	1,025	426	597
IMF special drawing rights	198	—	—
Reserve position in IMF	274	—	—
Foreign exchange	1,429	1,364	1,595
Total	2,926	1,790	2,192

Source: IMF, *International Financial Statistics*.

COST OF LIVING (Consumer price index; base: 1980 = 100).

	1983	1984	1985
All items	190.2	220.8	273.9

Source: IMF, *International Financial Statistics*.

BUDGET (million pesos)

Revenue	1983	1984	1985
Direct taxation	79,306	98,319	128,818
Indirect taxation	194,254	185,317	293,874
Rates and fines	6,829	9,991	14,169
Revenue under contracts	16,570	7,257	13,485
Credit resources	60,892	185,189	193,128
Total	357,958	486,073	643,474

Expenditure	1983	1984	1985
Public debt	45,408	64,839	88,596
Defence	39,821	53,227	53,289
Education	86,528	118,983	113,324
Public works	34,404	38,752	37,546
Police	29,981	38,640	43,516
Development	16,779	22,997	21,060
Agriculture	10,262	13,220	45,306
Health	25,459	29,811	31,132
Other items	113,157	160,569	198,121
Total	401,799	541,038	631,890

Source: Contraloría General de la República.
1986 (estimate, million pesos): Expenditure 648,000.

MONEY SUPPLY (million pesos at 31 December)

	1983	1984	1985
Currency outside banks	167,650	211,710	186,730
Demand deposits at commercial banks	220,890	267,300	341,180

Source: IMF, *International Financial Statistics*.

NATIONAL ACCOUNTS (million pesos at current prices)
Composition of the Gross National Product

	1982	1983	1984*
Compensation of employees	1,076,969	1,339,956	1,665,621
Operating surplus } Consumption of fixed capital	1,205,800	1,460,512	1,802,099
Gross domestic product (GDP) at factor cost	2,282,769	2,800,468	3,467,720
Indirect taxes	236,779	279,363	394,293
Less Subsidies	22,250	25,694	33,431
GDP in purchasers' values	2,497,298	3,054,137	3,828,582
Net factor income from abroad	−37,550	−63,193	−104,953
Gross national product (GNP)	2,459,798	2,990,944	3,723,629

* Provisional.

Expenditure on the Gross Domestic Product

	1982	1983	1984*
Government final consumption expenditure	272,766	334,565	421,635
Private final consumption expenditure	1,819,744	2,196,935	2,710,003
Increase in stocks	75,534	82,719	76,926
Gross fixed capital formation	436,091	524,847	640,090
Total domestic expenditure	2,604,135	3,139,066	3,848,654
Exports of goods and services	272,526	319,448	456,491
Less Imports of goods and services	379,363	404,377	476,563
GDP in purchasers' values	2,497,298	3,054,137	3,828,582
GDP at constant 1975 prices	542,836	551,380	568,979

* Provisional.

COLOMBIA

Gross Domestic Product by Economic Activity

	1982	1983	1984*
Agriculture, hunting, forestry and fishing	468,621	571,584	681,353
Mining and quarrying	64,538	88,646	129,266
Manufacturing	529,922	640,794	843,181
Electricity, gas and water	48,006	62,932	81,722
Construction	128,767	169,700	206,618
Wholesale and retail trade	340,848	413,726	534,262
Transport, storage and communications	207,926	254,255	307,336
Other services†	708,670	852,536	1,044,844
Total	2,497,298	3,054,137	3,828,582

* Provisional.
† Including restaurants and hotels.

BALANCE OF PAYMENTS (US $ million)

	1983	1984	1985
Merchandise exports f.o.b.	2,970	4,273	3,713
Merchandise imports f.o.b.	−4,464	−4,027	−3,734
Trade balance	−1,494	246	−21
Exports of services	1,133	1,055	1,111
Imports of services	−2,806	−3,001	−2,944
Balance on goods and services	−3,167	−1,700	−1,854
Private unrequited transfers (net)	145	289	442
Government unrequited transfers (net)	19	10	22
Current balance	−3,003	−1,401	−1,390
Direct capital investment (net)	514	561	729
Other long-term capital (net)	1,014	1,261	1,329
Short-term capital (net)	−99	−882	−207
Net errors and omissions	−271	−76	−535
Total (net monetary movements)	−1,845	−537	−74
Monetization of gold	177	−651	170
Valuation changes (net)	−90	18	104
Official financing (net)	5	4	−1
Changes in reserves	−1,753	−1,166	199

Source: IMF, *International Financial Statistics*.

External Trade

PRINCIPAL COMMODITIES (US $ '000)

Imports	1984*	1985*
Vegetables and vegetable products	193,485	243,157
Food and drink	84,038	95,964
Mineral products	466,279	464,650
Chemical products	682,763	908,761
Plastic and rubber products	221,471	277,014
Paper and paper products	198,693	168,416
Textiles and textile products	125,934	111,972
Metals	390,986	585,159
Mechanical and electrical equipment	804,563	971,661
Transport equipment	486,649	499,153
Total (incl. others)	3,982,420	4,688,876

Exports	1984*	1985*
Meat	11,491	7,045
Bananas	201,267	193,698
Raw coffee	1,730,200	1,769,962
Raw sugar	39,207	38,215
Fuel oil†	445,161	408,802
Cotton, raw and manufactured	98,188	105,996
Precious stones	20,901	24,800
Total (incl. others)	3,025,186	3,310,985

* Registrations and licences approved by INCOMEX. Export registrations do not include petroleum derivatives.
† Information according to customs declarations.

PRINCIPAL TRADING PARTNERS (US $ '000)

	1983 Imports	1983 Exports	1984 Imports	1984 Exports	1985 Imports	1985 Exports
Total ALADI	998,379	262,689	872,114	281,841	934,747	306,452
Andean Group	620,327	181,870	508,902	191,920	489,387	240,271
Bolivia	4,089	1,585	5,874	1,569	5,497	839
Ecuador	160,054	42,728	58,375	51,790	63,744	63,906
Peru	62,602	19,633	84,421	27,442	86,304	32,743
Venezuela	393,582	117,924	360,232	111,119	333,842	142,783
Other ALADI members	378,052	80,819	363,212	89,921	445,360	66,181
Argentina	49,921	42,982	51,261	52,177	95,191	31,356
Brazil	166,647	5,372	139,538	5,412	150,476	5,126
Chile	56,702	11,126	46,518	19,255	52,166	22,805
Mexico	99,214	20,762	111,236	12,858	136,809	6,517
Paraguay	1,135	203	1,918	49	1,663	29
Uruguay	4,433	374	12,741	170	9,055	348
Central American Common Market (CACM)	3,334	25,739	3,633	43,129	10,318	37,940
Rest of Latin America	87,387	59,583	86,538	46,919	116,516	84,304
Caribbean Community and Common Market (CARICOM)	818	16,456	1,118	10,312	864	8,556
USA*	1,768,627	871,985	1,371,446	977,176	1,614,830	1,036,526
Canada	176,156	26,831	174,887	40,185	121,079	38,485
Rest of North America	176,969	69,987	125,464	15,418	51,256	18,757
Eastern Europe	122,911	110,104	39,545	80,496	81,432	85,646
European Economic Community	691,528	1,022,507	637,135	1,033,429	854,194	1,127,345
European Free Trade Association	196,746	170,440	132,106	207,030	195,028	220,474
Rest of Western Europe	139,897	71,477	105,181	84,690	178,422	82,442
China, People's Republic	1,657	—	27,060	1,075	11,049	10,000
Asia (excluding Middle East and People's Republic of China)	582,789	157,003	379,043	157,406	491,753	166,111
Middle East	5,320	4,763	23,563	3,388	15,788	19,345
Africa (excluding Middle East)	9,125	41,059	2,355	40,282	8,065	66,537
Australasia and the Pacific	1,334	3,889	1,232	2,405	3,534	2,066
Unspecified	5,103	166,580	—	—	—	—
Total	4,968,080	3,080,893	3,982,420	3,025,186	4,688,876	3,310,985

* Including Puerto Rico.

Transport

RAILWAYS

	1983	1984	1985
Passengers carried ('000)	1,295	1,445	2,369
Passenger-kilometres ('000)	157,587	189,211	228,580
Freight ('000 metric tons)	1,097	1,267	1,278
Freight ton-km ('000)	553,057	726,140	776,688

Source: Ferrocarriles Nacionales de Colombia.

ROAD TRAFFIC (motor vehicles in use)

	1983
Passenger cars	509,478
Buses	48,577
Goods vehicles	257,572
Heavy-duty vehicles	213,936
Total (incl. others)	1,091,751

Source: Ministerio de Obras Públicas—INTRA.

DOMESTIC SEA-BORNE SHIPPING
(freight traffic in '000 metric tons)

	1981	1982	1983
Goods loaded and unloaded	1,318.9	1,114.8	1,254.0

INTERNATIONAL SEA-BORNE SHIPPING
(freight traffic in '000 metric tons)

	1983	1984	1985
Goods loaded	6,672	7,124	7,410
Goods unloaded	7,623	6,634	6,908

CIVIL AVIATION

	1983	1984	1985
Domestic			
Passengers carried	5,902,191	5,572,076	5,051,319
Freight carried ('000 metric tons)	82,871	84,042	84,826
International			
Passengers:			
arrivals	572,576	529,399	519,464
departures	596,584	562,598	560,516
Freight ('000 metric tons):			
loaded	73,650	67,739	67,213
unloaded	62,776	72,930	72,314

Tourism

(visitors)

Country of Origin	1982	1983	1984
Argentina	7,196	7,588	7,444
Ecuador	136,345	99,869	207,024
France	9,517	8,621	8,144
Germany, Federal Republic	9,965	9,466	9,803
Italy	8,018	6,808	6,628
Panama	7,299	8,209	8,160
Peru	9,963	8,540	9,319
Spain	9,800	9,211	8,267
USA	67,133	73,085	73,398
Venezuela	745,108	204,085	302,405
Total (incl. others)	1,083,442	506,883	715,277

Source: DAS-Corporación Nacional de Turismo.

Education

(1986*)

	Institutions	Teachers	Pupils
Nursery	5,669	11,485	276,476
Primary	36,979	135,924	4,002,543
Secondary (general)	6,336	107,084	2,136,239
Higher (incl. universities)	231	43,447	402,438

* Estimates.

Source: Ministerio de Educación Nacional, Oficina Sectorial de Planeación Educativa, División de Estadística y Sistemas.

Directory

The Constitution

The Constitution which is now in force was promulgated in 1886 and has been amended from time to time. In 1957 it was amended to provide for the alternation of the presidency between the two major parties. All citizens over 18 years of age are eligible to vote. Civil rights and social guarantees include freedom of education, the right to strike (except in the public sector), public aid to those unable to support themselves, freedom of assembly, of the press, and the right to petition. All male citizens are required to present themselves for possible military service at the age of 18.

THE PRESIDENT

Executive power is vested in the President of the Republic, who is elected by popular suffrage for a four-year term of office. The President cannot hold office for two consecutive terms but may be re-elected at a later date.

The President appoints a Cabinet, which assists in the government of the country. A substitute (primer designado) is elected by Congress, subject to biannual reappointment, to act in the event of a Presidential vacancy. The President appoints the governors of the twenty-four departments, the three intendencies and the three commissaries.

CONGRESS

Legislative power is exercised by Congress, which is composed of the Senate and the House of Representatives. Members of both chambers are elected by direct suffrage for a period of four years. The President in each House is elected for six months.

JUDICIARY

The administration of justice is in the hands of the Supreme Court, superior district tribunals, and lower courts. The magistrates of the Supreme Court of Justice are elected by serving members of the Court. The term of office is five years and the magistrates may be re-elected indefinitely.

NATIONAL ECONOMIC COUNCIL

Direction of the nation's finances is in the hands of the Consejo Nacional de Política Económica—CONPES (National Council for Economic Policy). CONPES is composed of five ministers and also representatives of banking, industrial and agricultural interests and has functioned since 1935.

LOCAL GOVERNMENT

For administrative purposes the country is divided into 23 Departments, four Intendencies and five Commissaries. The Departments are further divided into Municipalities. Governors for the Departments are appointed by the President, but regional legislatures are elected by the local inhabitants and enjoy considerable autonomy, including the management of local finances. Mayors for the Municipalities are appointed by the Governors. From 1988 popular elections for mayors will be held in all municipalities.

AMENDMENTS

Various constitutional reforms were promulgated in December 1968, including the following amendments: to increase the membership of the Senate from 106 to 112, and the maximum membership of the House of Representatives from 204 to 214; to increase from two to four years the term of office of representatives; to eliminate the two-thirds majority required for matters of importance; to enable the Government to legislate by decree for a maximum period of 90 days in any one year in the event of an economic crisis, though such decrees must relate only to the matters which caused the crisis; from 1970, proportional representation to be allowed in departmental and municipal elections; the same principle to apply to congressional elections after 1974. An amendment was also promulgated whereby the 'minority' party must have 'adequate' representation in government positions.

Note: A state of siege has been in force intermittently since 1948.

The Government

HEAD OF STATE

President: Dr VIRGILIO BARCO VARGAS (took office 7 August 1986).
Primer Designado: Dr VÍCTOR MOSQUERA CHAUX.

CABINET
(November 1986)

Minister of the Interior: Dr FERNANDO CEPEDA ULLOA.
Minister of Foreign Affairs: Col JULIO LONDOÑO PAREDES.
Minister of Justice: Dr EDUARDO SUESCÚN MONROY.
Minister of Finance and Public Credit: Dr CÉSAR GAVIRIA TRUJILLO.
Minister of National Defence: Gen. RAFAEL SAMUDIO MOLINA.
Minister of Agriculture: LUIS GUILLERMO PARRA DURÁN.
Minister of Labour and Social Security: Dr JOSÉ NAME TERÁN.
Minister of Public Health: Dr CÉSAR ESMERAL BARROS.
Minister of Economic Development: Dr MIGUEL MERINO GORDILLO.
Minister of Mines and Energy: Dr GUILLERMO PERRY RUBIO.
Minister of Education: Dra MARINA URIBE DE EUSSE.
Minister of Communications: Dr EDMUNDO LÓPEZ GÓMEZ.
Minister of Public Works and Transportation: Dr LUIS FERNANDO JARAMILLO-CORREA.

MINISTRIES

Ministry of Agriculture: Carrera 10, No 20-39, Bogotá; tel. 2419005; telex 44470.

Ministry of Communications: Edif. Murillo Toro, Carreras 7 y 8, Calle 2 y 13, Bogotá; tel. 2825465; telex 41249.

Ministry of Economic Development: Carrera 13, No 27-00, 10°, Bogotá; tel. 2419030; telex 44508.

Ministry of Education: Centro Administrativo Nacional (CAN), Of. 501, Avda Eldorado, Bogotá; tel. 2682800.

Ministry of Finance and Public Credit: Carrera 8, No 6-40, Of. 308, Bogotá; tel. 2845400; telex 44473.

Ministry of Foreign Affairs: Palacio San Carlos, Calle 10, No 5-51, Bogotá; tel. 2421501; telex 45209.

Ministry of the Interior: Calle 13, No 8-38, Of. 315, Bogotá; tel. 2862324; telex 45406.

Ministry of Justice: Calle 12, No 4-65, 2°, Bogotá; tel. 2839493.

Ministry of Labour and Social Security: Avda 19, No 6-68, Bogotá; tel. 2823032; telex 45445.

Ministry of Mines and Energy: Centro Administrativo Nacional (CAN), Avda Eldorado, Bogotá; tel. 2444520; telex 45898.

Ministry of National Defence: Centro Administrativo Nacional (CAN), 2°, Avda Eldorado, Bogotá; tel. 2884184.

Ministry of Public Health: Calle 16, No 7-39, Of. 701, Bogotá; tel. 2820002.

Ministry of Public Works and Transportation: Centro Administrativo Nacional (CAN), Of. 420, Avda Eldorado, Bogotá; tel. 2669150; telex 45656.

President and Legislature

PRESIDENT
Election, 25 May 1986

Candidate	Votes Cast
Dr Virgilio Barco Vargas (Partido Liberal)	4,198,687
Dr Alvaro Gómez Hurtado (Partido Conservador)	2,578,667
Jaime Pardo Leal (Unión Patriótica)	327,955
Regina Betancourt de Liska (Movimiento Unitario Metapolítico)	46,772

Note: Figures exclude votes cast by Colombians resident abroad.

CONGRESO
General Election, 9 March 1986

Party	Senate	House of Representatives
Partido Liberal	58	98
Partido Conservador	43	80
Nuevo Liberalismo	6	7
Unión Patriótica	3	6
Others	4	8
Total	114	199

President of the Senate: Dr Humberto Peláez Gutiérrez.

President of the House of Representatives: Dr Román Gómez.

Political Organizations

Alianza Nacional Popular (ANAPO): Bogotá; f. 1971 by supporters of Gen. Gustavo Rojas Pinilla; populist party; Leader María Eugenia Rojas de Moreno Díaz.

Democracia Cristiana: Avda 42, 18-08, Apdo 25867, Bogotá; tel. 2856639; f. 1964; Christian Democrat party; 10,000 mems; Pres. Juan Alberto Polo; Sec.-Gen. José Albendea.

Frente por la Unidad del Pueblo (FUP): Bogotá; extreme left-wing front comprising socialists and Maoists.

Movimiento Obrero Independiente Revolucionario (MOIR): Bogotá; left-wing workers' movement; Maoist; Leader Marcelo Torres.

Movimiento Unitario Metapolítico: Bogotá; f. 1985; populist-occultist party; Leader Regina Betancourt de Liska.

Partido Conservador: Calle 36, No 16-56, Bogotá; tel. 328127; f. 1849; 2.5m. mems; Leaders Dr Belisario Betancur Cuartas, Dr Alvaro Gómez Hurtado.

Partido Liberal: Avda Jiménez 8–56, Bogotá; f. 1815; divided into two factions, the official group (led by Dr Alfonso López Michelsen and Julio César Turbay) and the independent group: Nuevo Liberalismo (New Liberalism, led by Dr Luis Carlos Galán Sarmiento).

Unidad Democrática de la Izquierda (Democratic Unity of the Left): Bogotá; f. 1982; Leader Dr Gerardo Molina; left-wing coalition incorporating the following parties:

Firmes: Bogotá; democratic party.

Partido Comunista de Colombia (PCC): Bogotá; f. 1930; Moscow-line; Leader Gilberto Vieira.

Partido Socialista de los Trabajadores (PST): Bogotá; workers' socialist party; Leader María Socorro Ramírez.

Unión Patriótica (UP): f. 1985; Marxist party formed by FARC (see below); obtained legal status in 1986; Leader Jacobo Arenas; Exec. Sec. Obidio Salinas.

The following guerrilla groups are active:

Comando Ricardo Franco-Frente Sur: f. 1984; common front formed by dissident factions from the FARC and M-19 (see below); Leader Javier Delgado.

Ejército de Liberación Nacional (ELN): Castroite guerrilla movement; f. 1965; Leader Fabio Vásquez Castaño; factions include:

Frente Simón Bolívar: (ceased hostilities in December 1985).

Frente Antonio Nariño: (ceased hostilties in December 1985).

Ejército Popular de Liberación (EPL): Maoist guerrilla movement; splinter group from Communist Party; Leader Ernesto Rojas.

Fuerzas Armadas Revolucionarias de Colombia (FARC): fmrly military wing of the pro-Soviet Communist Party; composed of 27 armed fronts; 12,000 armed supporters in 1985; Leader Manuel Marulanda Vélez (alias Tirofijo); (ceased hostilities in May 1984).

Juventudes Inconformes de Colombia (JIC): disaffected youths of Colombia; left-wing; opposed to illicit trading in drugs.

Legión Aguilas Blancas (White Eagles Legion): f. 1984; extreme right-wing.

Movimiento de Autodefensa Obrera (MAO): workers' self-defence movement; Trotskyite; Leader Adelaida Abadia Rey; (reported to have joined the Unión Patriótica, July 1985).

Movimiento Revolucionario Estudantil (MRE): f. 1985; left-wing revolutionary student movement.

Movimiento 19 de Abril (M-19): f. 1970 by followers of Gen. Gustavo Rojas Pinilla and dissident factions from the FARC; left-wing urban guerrilla group; Leader Carlos Pizarro León Gómez (alias Caballo Loco).

Muerte a Secuestradores (MAS) (Death to Kidnappers): right-wing paramilitary organization; funded by drug dealers.

Patria Libre: f. 1985; left-wing guerrilla movement.

In 1984 the Government reached agreement on a cease-fire with the M-19, the FARC and the EPL. In June 1985, however, the M-19 formally withdrew from the agreement and resumed hostilities against the armed forces. In November 1985 the EPL withdrew from the agreement. The FARC maintained their commitment to the cease-fire. In late 1985 the M-19, the Comando Ricardo Franco-Frente Sur and the Quintín Lame guerrilla group (an indigenous organization active in the department of Cauca) announced the formation of a united front, the Coordinadora Guerrillera Nacional (CGN). In 1986 the CGN participated in joint campaigns with the Movimiento Revolucionario Tupac Amarú (Peru) and the Alfaro Vive ¡Carajo! (Ecuador). The alliance operated under the name of **Batallón América**.

Diplomatic Representation

EMBASSIES IN COLOMBIA

Argentina: Avda 40A, 13-09, 16°, Bogotá; tel. 2873595; telex 44576; Ambassador: Daniel Olmos.

Austria: Carrera 11, No 75-29, Bogotá; tel. 2356628; telex 41489; Ambassador: Dr Manfred Ortner.

COLOMBIA

Belgium: Calle 26, No 4A, 45, Bogotá; tel. 2828881; telex 41203; Ambassador: WILLY J. STEVENS.

Bolivia: Calle 78, No 9-57, Bogotá; tel. 2558788; telex 45583; Ambassador: GUILLERMO RIVEROS TEJADA.

Brazil: Calle 93, No 14-20, 8°, Bogotá; Ambassador: CARLOS ALBERTO LEITE BARBOSA.

Bulgaria: Calle 81, No 7-71, Bogotá; tel. 2128028; telex 41217; Ambassador: DIMITUR PETKOV POPOV.

Canada: Calle 76, No 11-52, Apdo Aéreo 53531, Bogotá 2; tel. 2355211; telex 44568; Ambassador: J. E. G. GIBSON.

Chile: Calle 100, No 11B-44, Bogotá; tel. 2147926; telex 44404; Ambassador: CARLOS MORALES RETAMAL.

China, People's Republic: Calle 71, No 2A-41, Bogotá; telex 45387; Ambassador: LI GUOXIN.

Costa Rica: Carrera 15, No 80-87, Of. 401, Bogotá; tel. 2361098; Ambassador: JULIÁN ZAMORA DOBLES.

Czechoslovakia: Avda 13, No 104A-30, Bogotá; tel. 2142240; telex 44590; Ambassador: MARIAN MASARIK.

Denmark: Calle 37, No 7-43, 9°, Apdo 52965, Bogotá; tel. 2326753; telex 44599; Ambassador: OLE PHILIPSON.

Dominican Republic: Carrera 16, No 82-9, Bogotá 2; Ambassador: RAFAEL VALERA BENÍTEZ.

Ecuador: Calle 89, No 13-07, Bogotá; tel. 2570066; telex 45776; Ambassador: Dr RODRIGO VÁLDEZ BAQUERO.

Egypt: Carrera 18, No 88-17, Bogotá; tel. 2364803; Ambassador: MAHMOUD HAFEZ EL-KAMBASHWY.

El Salvador: Carrera 16, No 79-55, Apdo 089394, Bogotá; tel. 2361178; telex 42072; Ambassador: ANDINO SALAZAR.

Finland: Calle 72, No 8-56, Bogotá; tel. 2126111; telex 44304; Ambassador: LASSE OKA.

France: Avda 39, No 7-84, Bogotá; tel. 2854311; telex 44558; Ambassador: PIERRE DE BOISDEFFRE.

German Democratic Republic: Carrera 7, No 81-57, Bogotá; tel. 2490252; telex 44412; Ambassador: HEINZ LÖHN.

Germany, Federal Republic: Carrera 4, No 72-35, Apdo Aéreo 91808, Bogotá 8; tel. 2120511; telex 44765; Ambassador: GEORG JOACHIM SCHLAICH.

Guatemala: Carrera 15, No 83-43, apt 301, Bogotá; Ambassador: MARIO MARROQUÍN NÁJERA.

Haiti: Carrera 72, No 00-86, Apdo Aéreo 52224, Bogotá; tel. 2125942; Ambassador: ALIX BALMIR.

Holy See: Carrera 15, No 36-33, Apdo Aéreo 3740, Bogotá (Apostolic Nunciature); tel. 2454260; telex 42455; Nuncio: Mgr ANGELO ACERBI.

Honduras: Carrera 13, No 63-51, Bogotá; tel. 2353158; telex 45540; Ambassador: JORGE ELÍAS FLEFIL LARACH.

Hungary: Carrera 6A, No 77-46, Bogotá; tel. 2488489; telex 43244; Ambassador: FERENC DRAGON.

India: Carrera 27, No 40-70, Bogotá; tel. 2443607; telex 41380; Ambassador: M. K. KHISHA.

Iran: Transversal 23, No 104-75, Bogotá; tel. 2142975; telex 42252; Ambassador: MUSTAFA MOKHLESI.

Israel: Calle 35, No 7-25, 14°, Bogotá; tel. 2456603; telex 44755; Ambassador: YAACOV GOTEL.

Italy: Calle 70, No 10-25, Bogotá; tel. 2354300; telex 45588; Ambassador: EGONE RATZENBERGER.

Japan: Calle 72, No 74-21, Apdo Aéreo 7407, Bogotá; telex 43327; Ambassador: YOSHIO FUJIMOTO.

Korea, Republic: Calle 94, No 9-39, Bogotá; tel. 2361616; telex 41468; Ambassador: YONG HOON LEE.

Lebanon: Calle 74, No 12-44, Bogotá; tel. 2128360; telex 44333; Ambassador: SALIM NAFFAH.

Mexico: Calle 99, No 12-08, Bogotá; tel. 2566347; telex 41264; Ambassador: JOSÉ ANTONIO ALVAREZ LIMA.

Netherlands: Carrera 9, No 74-08, Bogotá; tel. 2119600; telex 44629; Ambassador: REIJNIER FLAES.

Nicaragua: Avda 19, No 133-47, Bogotá; tel. 2583356; telex 45388; Ambassador: FRANCISCO QUIÑÓNEZ REYES.

Norway: Bogotá; Ambassador: ANTON SMITH-MEYER.

Panama: Calle 87, No 11A-64, Bogotá; tel. 2367531; Ambassador: JORGE EDUARDO RITTER.

Paraguay: Calle 13, No 62-40, Of. 403, Bogotá; tel. 2355972; Ambassador: RUBÉN RUIZ GÓMEZ.

Peru: Calle 81, No 9-73, Bogotá; tel. 2573753; telex 44453; Ambassador: JUAN JOSÉ CALLE Y CALLE.

Poland: Calle 104A, No 23-48, Bogotá; telex 44591; Ambassador: ANDRZEJ JEDYNAK.

Portugal: Calle 92, No 15-48, 4°, Bogotá; tel. 2563028; Ambassador: AMANDIO C. R. PINTO.

Romania: Carrera 7, No 92-58, Bogotá; tel. 2566438; telex 41238; Ambassador GEORGHE DROBA.

Spain: Calle 92, No 12-68, Bogotá; tel. 2312154; telex 44779; Ambassador: SALVADOR BERMÚDEZ DE CASTRO.

Sweden: Calle 72, 5-83, Bogotá; tel. 2553777; telex 44626; Ambassador: KARL WÄRNBERG.

Switzerland: Carrera 9, No 74-08/1101, Bogotá; tel. 2553945; telex 41230; Ambassador: DANIEL DAYER.

USSR: Carrera 4, No 75-00, Bogotá; tel. 2357960; telex 44503; Ambassador: LEONID ROMANOV.

United Kingdom: Calle 98, No 9-03, 4°, Apdo 4508, Bogotá; tel. 2185111; telex 44503; Ambassador: RICHARD A. NEILSON.

USA: Calle 37, No 8-61, Bogotá; tel. 2851300; telex 44843; Ambassador: CHARLES A. GUILLESPIE.

Uruguay: Carrera 100, No 14-26, Bogotá; telex 43377; Ambassador: Col (retd) ARIOSTO A. FERNÁNDEZ.

Venezuela: Calle 33, No 6-94, Bogotá; tel. 2852286; telex 44504; Ambassador: LUIS LA CORTE.

Yugoslavia: Calle 93A, No 9A-22, Apdo 91074, Bogotá; tel. 2570290; telex 45155; Ambassador: UROŠ MARKIĆ.

Judicial System

The Supreme Court of Justice is divided into four subsidiary divisions of Civil Cassation, Criminal Cassation, Labour Cassation and Constitutional Procedure. The 24 judges of the Supreme Court hold office until the age of 65 years, although they may be removed from office if considered to be unfit by reason of conduct or age. Vacancies are filled from within the Court by election by the members. For matters of great importance and government business, the three courts of the Supreme Court sit together as a Plenary Court.

The country is divided into judicial districts, each of which has a superior court of three or more judges. There are also other Courts of Justice for each judicial district, and judges for each province and municipality.

SUPREME COURT OF JUSTICE

Carrera 7a, No 27-18, 12°-24°, Bogotá.

President: FERNANDO URIBE RESTREPO.

Vice-President: Dr LUIS ENRIQUE ALDANA ROZO.

Division of Civil Cassation: Carrera 7a, No 27-18, 12°-24°, Bogotá.

President: Dr JOSÉ ALEJANDRO BONIVENTO FERNÁNDEZ.

Division of Criminal Cassation: Carrera 7a, No 27-18, 12°-24°, Bogotá.

President: Dr EDGAR SAAVEDRA ROJAS.

Division of Labour Cassation: Carrera 7a, No 27-18, 12°-24°, Bogotá.

President: Dr NEMESIO CAMACHO RODRÍGUEZ.

Division of Constitutional Procedure: Carrera 7a, No 27-18, 12°-24°, Bogotá.

President: Dr FABIO MORÓN DÍAZ.

Attorney General: CARLOS MAURO HOYOS.

Religion

Roman Catholicism is the religion of 95% of the population.

CHRISTIANITY

The Roman Catholic Church

Colombia comprises 11 archdioceses, 32 dioceses, two territorial prelatures, eight Apostolic Vicariates and seven Apostolic Prefectures.

COLOMBIA

Bishops' Conference: Conferencia Episcopal de Colombia, Apdo 7448, Calle 26, No 27-48, 4°, Bogotá; tel. 2328540; f. 1978; Pres. HÉCTOR RUEDA HERNÁNDEZ, Archbishop of Bucaramanga.

Archbishop of Barranquilla: GERMÁN VILLA GAVIRIA, Carrera 42 F, No 75B-220, Apdo Aéreo 1160, Barranquilla 4; tel. 354108.

Archbishop of Bogotá: MARIO REVOLLO BRAVO, Carrera 7a, No 10-20, Bogotá, DE; tel. 2437700.

Archbishop of Bucaramanga: HÉCTOR RUEDA HERNÁNDEZ, Calle 33, No 21-18, Bucaramanga; tel. 25132.

Archbishop of Cali: PEDRO RUBIANO SÁENZ, Carrera 5A, No 11-42, 2°, Cali; tel. 821756.

Archbishop of Cartagena: CARLOS JOSÉ RUISECO VIEIRA, Apdo Aéreo 400, Cartagena; tel. 45903.

Archbishop of Ibagué: JOSÉ JOAQUÍN FLÓREZ HERNÁNDEZ, Calle 10, No 2-58, Ibagué, Tolima; tel. 32680.

Archbishop of Manizales: JOSÉ DE JESÚS PIMIENTO RODRÍGUEZ, Carrera 23, No 19-22, Manizales; tel. 31179.

Archbishop of Medellín: Cardinal ALFONSO LÓPEZ TRUJILLO, Calle 57, No 49-44, Medellín; tel. 2517700.

Archbishop of Nueva Pamplona: RAFAEL SARMIENTO PERALTA, Calle 5, No 4-109, Nueva Pamplona; tel. 2816.

Archbishop of Popayán: SAMUEL SILVERIO BUITRAGO TRUJILLO, Calle 5, No 6-71, Popayán; tel. 21711.

Archbishop of Tunja: AUGUSTO TRUJILLO ARANGO, Calle 17, No 9-85, Tunja, Boyacá; tel. 2095.

Other Christian Churches

The Baptist Convention: Apdo Aéreo 51988, Medellín; tel. 389623; Exec. Sec. Rev. RAMIRO PÉREZ HOYOS; Pres. RAMÓN MEDINA IBÁÑEZ.

The Episcopalian Church: Bishop of Colombia: Rt Rev. BERNARDO MERINO, Carrera 6, No 49-85, Apdo Aéreo 52964, Bogotá; tel. 2883167; there are 2,780 baptized mems, 1,320 communicant mems, 22 parishes, missions and preaching stations; 4 schools with 280 pupils; 12 clergy and 2 candidates for ordination.

Iglesia Evangélica Luterana de Colombia: Calle 75, No 20-54, Apdo Aéreo 51538, Bogotá 2; tel. 2125735; 2,000 mems; Pres. VIESTURS PAVASARS.

BAHÁ'Í FAITH

National Spiritual Assembly: Apdo 51387, Bogotá 12; tel. 2174586; adherents in 1,013 localities.

JUDAISM

There is a community of about 25,000 with 66 synagogues.

The Press

DAILIES

Bogotá, DE

El Espacio: Carrera 61, No 45-35, Bogotá, DE; tel. 2636666; telex 44501; f. 1965; evening; Dir JAIME ARDILA CASAMITJANA; circ. 92,000.

El Espectador: Carrera 68, No 22-71, Apdo Aéreo 3441, Bogotá, DE; tel. 2606044; telex 44718, 44881; f. 1887; morning; Dir (vacant); Editor LUIS GABRIEL CANO; circ. 215,000.

La República: Calle 16, No 4-96, Apdo Aéreo 6806, Bogotá, DE; tel. 2821055; f. 1953; morning; economics; Dir RODRIGO OSPINA HERNÁNDEZ; circ. 20,000.

El Siglo: Avda El Dorado No 96-50, Apdo Aéreo 5452, Bogotá, DE; tel. 2345080; telex 044458; f. 1925; Conservative; Dir GABRIEL MELO GUEVARA; circ. 65,000.

El Tiempo: Avda El Dorado No 59-70, Apdo Aéreo 3633, Bogotá, DE; tel. 2635555; telex 44812; f. 1911; morning; Liberal; Dir HERNANDO SANTOS CASTILLO; circ. 200,000 (weekdays), 350,000 (Sundays).

Barranquilla, Atlántico

Diario del Caribe: Calle 42, No 50-B-32, Barranquilla, Atlántico; tel. 314660; telex 033473; f. 1946; daily; Liberal; Dir ALFONSO FUENMAYOR; circ. 30,000.

El Heraldo: Calle 53B, No 46-25, Barranquilla, Atlántico; tel. 416066; telex 033348; f. 1933; morning; Liberal; Dir JUAN B. FERNÁNDEZ; circ. 65,000.

La Libertad: Carrera 53, No 55-166, Barranquilla, Atlántico; tel. 311517; Liberal; Dir ROBERTO ESPER REBAJE; circ. 25,000.

Bucaramanga, Santander del Sur

El Deber: Carrera 12, No 30-35, Apdo Aéreo 698, Bucaramanga, Santander del Sur; f. 1923; morning; Conservative; Dir JORGE GUTIÉRREZ REYES; circ. 1,000.

Diario del Oriente: Calle 35, No 12-62, 2°, Bucaramanga, Santander del Sur; tel. 24759; Dir JOSÉ M. JAIMES; circ. 10,000.

El Frente: Calle 35, No 12-40, Apdo Aéreo 665, Bucaramanga, Santander del Sur; tel. 24949; telex 077777; f. 1942; morning; Conservative; Dir Dr RAFAEL ORTIZ GONZÁLEZ; circ. 13,000.

Vanguardia Liberal: Calle 34, No 13-42, Bucaramanga, Santander del Sur; tel. 27134; telex 77762; f. 1919; morning; Liberal; Sunday illustrated literary supplement and women's supplement; Dir and Man. ALEJANDRO GALVIS RAMÍREZ; circ. 42,000.

Cali, Valle del Cauca

Occidente: Calle 12, No 5-22, Cali, Valle del Cauca; tel. 851110; telex 55509; f. 1961; morning; Conservative; Dir ALVARO H. CAICEDO GONZÁLEZ; circ. 50,000.

El País: Carrera 2A, No 24-46, Apdo Aéreo 1608, Cali, Valle del Cauca; tel. 893011; telex 55527; f. 1950; Conservative; Dir ALVARO JOSÉ LLOREDA C.; circ. 65,071 (weekdays), 72,938 (Saturdays), 108,304 (Sundays).

El Pueblo: Avda 3A, Norte 35-N-10, Cali, Valle del Cauca; tel. 688110; telex 055669; morning; Liberal; Dir LUIS FERNANDO LONDOÑO CAPURRO; circ. 50,000.

Cartagena, Bolívar

El Universal: Calle 31, No 3-81, Cartagena, Bolívar; tel. 40028; telex 37731; daily; Liberal; Dir GONZALO ZÚÑIGA; Man. GERARDO ARAÚJO; circ. 28,000.

Cúcuta, Santander del Norte

Diario de la Frontera: Calle 14, No 3-44, Cúcuta, Santander del Norte; tel. 28494; f. 1950; morning; Conservative; Dir TEODOSIO CABEZA QUIÑONES; circ. 10,000.

La Opinión: Avda 4, No 16-12, Cúcuta, Santander del Norte; tel. 21580; f. 1960; morning; Liberal; Dir Dr EUSTORGIO COLMENARES; circ. 18,000 (Mondays), 14,500 (Mondays–Saturdays).

Manizales, Caldas

La Patria: Carrera 20, No 21-51, Apdo Aéreo 70, Manizales, Caldas; tel. 23060; telex 042583; f. 1921; morning; Conservative; Dir Dr LUIS JOSÉ RESTREPO RESTREPO; circ. 25,000.

Medellín, Antioquia

El Colombiano: Calle 54, No 51-22, Apdo Aéreo 782, Medellín, Antioquia; tel. 510444; telex 44727; f. 1912; morning; Conservative; Dir JUAN GÓMEZ MARTÍNEZ; circ. 123,707.

El Mundo: Calle 53, No 73-146, Apdo Aéreo 53874, Medellín, Antioquia; tel. 2642800; telex 65058; f. 1979; Dir DARÍO ARIZMENDI POSADA; circ. 60,000.

Neiva

Diario del Huila: Calle 8A, No 6-30, Neiva; tel. 22619; Dir MARÍA M. RENGIFO DE D.; circ. 10,000.

Pasto, Nariño

El Derecho: Calle 20, No 26-20, Pasto, Nariño; tel. 2170; telex 53740; f. 1928; Conservative; Pres. Dr JOSÉ ELÍAS DEL HIERRO; Dir EDUARDO F. MAZUERA; circ. 12,000.

Pereira, Risaralda

Diario del Otún: Carrera 8A, No 22-69, Apdo Aéreo 2533, Pereira, Risaralda; tel. 30601; telex 8754; f. 1982; Dir Dr JAVIER RAMÍREZ G.; circ. 30,000.

El Imparcial: Apdo Aéreo 57, Pereira, Risaralda; f. 1948; morning; Editor ZAHUR ZAPATA CARDONA; circ. 15,000.

La Tarde: Carrera 9A, No 20-54, Pereira, Risaralda; tel. 43013; telex 08832; f. 1975; Dir GONZALO VALLEJO RESTREPO; circ. 15,000.

Popayán, Cauca

El Liberal: Carrera 3, No 2-60, Apdo Aéreo 538, Popayán, Cauca; tel. 22418; f. 1938; Dir EDUARDO GÓMEZ CERÓN; circ. 10,000.

Santa Marta, Magdalena

El Informador: Santa Marta, Magdalena; f. 1921; Liberal; Dir JOSÉ B. VIVES; circ. 9,000.

COLOMBIA

Tunja, Boyacá

Diario de Boyacá: Tunja, Boyacá; Dir-Gen. Dr Carlos H. Mojica; circ. 3,000.

El Oriente: Tunja, Boyacá; Dir-Gen. Luis López Rodríguez.

Villavicencio, Meta

Clarín del Llano: Villavicencio, Meta; tel. 23207; Conservative; Dir Elías Matus Torres; circ. 5,000.

PERIODICALS
Bogotá, DE

Antena: Bogotá, DE; television, cinema and show business; circ. 10,000.

Arco: Carrera 5, No 35-39, Apdo Aéreo 8624, Bogotá, DE; tel. 2851500; telex 45153; f. 1959; monthly; history and politics; Dir Alvaro Valencia Tovar; circ. 10,000.

Arte en Colombia: Apdo Aéreo 90193, Bogotá, DE; tel. 2622200; telex 044611; f. 1976; quarterly; art, architecture, films and photography; English summary; Dir Celia Sredni de Birbragher; circ. 10,000.

El Campesino: Carrera 39A, No 15-11, Bogotá, DE; f. 1958; weekly; cultural; Dir Joaquín Gutiérrez Macías; circ. 70,000.

Consigna: Diagonal 34, No 5-11, Bogotá, DE; tel. 2871157; fortnightly; Turbayista; Dir Carlos Lemos; circ. 10,000.

Costa Libre: Avda 3, No 19-60, Bogotá, DE; monthly; Dir Marco Antonio Contreras.

Coyuntura Económica: Apdo Aéreo 20513, Bogotá, DE; quarterly; economics; published by Fundación para Educación Superior y el Desarrollo.

Cromos Magazine: Calle 70A, No 7-81, Apdo Aéreo 59317, Bogotá, DE; f. 1916; weekly; illustrated; general news; Dir Fernando Garavito; circ. 65,000.

As Deportes: Calle 20, No 4-55, Bogotá, DE; f. 1978; sports; circ. 25,000.

Documentos Políticos: Bogotá, DE; monthly; organ of the pro-Moscow Communist Party.

Economía Colombiana: Edif. de los Ministerios, Of. 126A, No 6-40, Bogotá, DE; f. 1984; published by Contraloría General de la República; monthly; economics.

Escala: Calle 30, No 17-70, Bogotá, DE; f. 1962; monthly; architecture; Dir David Serna Cárdenas; circ. 16,000.

Estrategía: Bogotá, DE; monthly; economics; Dir Rodrigo Otero.

Guión: Carrera 16, No 36-89, Bogotá, DE; f. 1977; weekly; general; Conservative; Dir Juan Carlos Pastrana; circ. 35,000.

Hit: Calle 20, No 4-55, Bogotá, DE; cinema and show business; circ. 20,000.

El Informador Andino: Carrera 7, No 22-86, 2°, Bogotá, DE; economic affairs.

MD en Español: Bogotá; medicine.

Menorah: Apdo Aéreo 9081, Bogotá, DE; tel. 2433609; f. 1950; independent monthly review for the Jewish community; Dir Eliécer Celnik; circ. 10,000.

Nueva Frontera: Carrera 7A, No 17-01, 5°, Bogotá, DE; tel. 2343763; f. 1974; weekly; political; Liberal; Dir Carlos Lleras Restrepo; circ. 20,000.

Pluma: Apdo Aéreo 12190, Bogotá, DE; monthly; art and literature; Dir Jorge Valencia Jaramillo; circ. 70,000.

Que Hubo: Bogotá, DE; weekly; general; Editor Consuelo Montejo; circ. 15,000.

Revista Diners: Carrera 10, No 64-65, 3°, Bogotá, DE; tel. 2122873; telex 45304; f. 1963; Dir Consuelo Mendoza de Riaño; circ. 110,000.

Semana: Calle 85, No 10-46, Bogotá, DE; tel. 2575400; general; Dir Felipe López Caballero.

Síntesis Económica: Bogotá, DE; tel. 2325434; weekly; economics; Dir Daniel Mazuera Gómez.

Sucesos: Bogotá, DE; weekly; Dir Néstor Espinoza; circ. 15,000.

Teorema: Bogotá, DE; art and literature; Dir Alberto Rodríguez; circ. 5,000.

Tribuna Médica: Calle 8A, No 68A-41, Bogotá, DE; tel. 2628200; telex 43195; f. 1961; fortnightly; medical and scientific; Editor Salomón Lerner; circ. 55,000.

Tribuna Roja: Apdo Aéreo 19042, Bogotá, DE; tel. 2430371; f. 1971; quarterly; organ of the MOIR (pro-Maoist Communist party); Dir Carlos Naranjo; circ. 300,000.

Vea: Calle 20, No 4-55, Bogotá, DE; weekly; popular; circ. 90,000.

Voz Proletaria: Carrera 34, No 9-28, Apdo Aéreo 19857/8886, Bogotá, DE; f. 1957; weekly; Communist; Dir M. Cepeda Vargas; circ. 45,000.

NEWS AGENCIES

Ciep—El País: Carrera 16, No 36-55, Bogotá; tel. 2326816; Dir Jorge Téllez.

Colprensa: Diagonal 34, No 5-63, Apdo Aéreo 20333, Bogotá; tel. 2872200; telex 45153; f. 1980; Dir Alberto Saldarriaga.

Foreign Bureaux

Agence France-Presse (AFP): Carrera 5, No 16-14, Of. 807, Apdo Aéreo 4654, Bogotá 1; tel. 848613; telex 44726; Dir Daniel Priollet.

Agencia EFE (Spain): Carrera 16, No 39-69, Apdo 16038, Bogotá; tel. 2851576; telex 44577; Bureau Chief Carlos Lareau Urzanqui.

Agentstvo Pechati Novosti (APN) (USSR): Carrera 7, No 14-40, Of. 701, Bogotá; tel. 2437394; Rep. José Arizala.

Agenzia Nazionale Stampa Associata (ANSA) (Italy): Carrera 4, No 67-30, Apdo Aéreo 16077, Bogotá; tel. 2125409; telex 42266; Bureau Chief Alberto Rojas Morales.

Associated Press (AP) (USA): Calle 80, No 8-14, Of. 102, Bogotá; tel. 111311; telex 44641; Bureau Chief Thomas G. Wells.

Central News Agency Inc. (Taiwan): Carrera 13A, No 98-34, Bogotá; tel. 256342; Correspondent Christina Chow.

Deutsche Presse-Agentur (dpa) (Federal Republic of Germany): Carrera 7, No 17-01, Of. 915, Apdo Aéreo 044245, Bogotá; tel. 2818065; Correspondent Carlos Alberto Rueda.

Inter Press Service (IPS) (Italy): Calle 20, No 7-17, Of. 608, Apdo 7739, Bogotá; tel. 2418841; Correspondent Ramón Martínez Gorriarán.

Prensa Latina (Cuba): Calle 57, No 35A-41, Apdo Aéreo 30372, Bogotá; tel. 2115266; Correspondent Tomás Díaz Acosta.

Reuters (UK): Carrera 6A, No 14-98, Of. 13-05, Apdo Aéreo 29848, Bogotá; tel. 2438819; telex 44537; Correspondent Hernando Orozco.

Telegrafnoye Agentstvo Sovetskovo Soyuza (TASS) (USSR): Calle 20, No 7-17, Of. 901, Bogotá; tel. 2437394; Correspondent Gennady Kochuk.

United Press International (UPI) (USA): Carrera 5, No 16-14, Of. 502, Apdo Aéreo 57570, Bogotá; tel. 2119106; telex 44892; Man. Dr Luis Eduardo Azuaje.

Xinhua (New China) News Agency (People's Republic of China): Calle 74, No 4-26, Apdo 501, Bogotá; tel 2115347; telex 45620; Dir Wu Huizhong.

PRESS ASSOCIATIONS

Asociación Colombiana de Periodistas: Avda Jiménez, No 8-74, Of. 509, Bogotá.

Asociación de Diarios Colombianos (ANDIARIOS): Calle 61, No 5-20, Apdo Aéreo 13663, Bogotá; tel. 2114181; f. 1962; 30 affiliated newspapers; Pres. Dr Carlos Pinilla Barrios; Exec. Dir Luis Guillermo Angel Correa.

Círculo de Periodistas de Bogotá: Calle 26, No 13A-23, P-23, Bogotá; Pres. María Teresa Herrán.

Publishers
Bogotá

Aguirre Editor: Calle 53, No 49-123, Apdo Aéreo 1395, Medellín; tel. 2394801; fiction; Dir Alberto Aguirre.

Comunicadores Técnicos Ltda: Calle 40A, No 13-30, Apdo Aéreo 28797, Bogotá; technical; Dir Pedro P. Morcillo.

Cultural Colombiana Ltd: Calle 72, No 16-15 y 16-21, Apdo Aéreo 6307, Bogotá; tel. 2355494; f. 1951; textbooks; Dir José Porto.

Ediciones Lerner: Calle 8A, No 68A-41, Apdo Aéreo 8304, Bogotá; tel. 430567; telex 43195; f. 1959; literature, history, medicine; Man. Dir Jack Grinberg.

Ediciones Paulinas: Carrera 23, No 169-98, Apdo 100383, Bogotá; tel. 2345036; f. 1956; religion, culture; Dir Antonio J. Ortiz.

COLOMBIA   Directory

Ediciones Tercer Mundo Ltda: Carrera 30, No 42-32, Apdo Aéreo 4817, Bogotá; tel. 2695129; f. 1961; social science; Man. Dir Luis Carlos Ibáñez.

Editorial El Globo, SA: Calle 16, No 4-96, Apdo Aéreo 6806, Bogotá.

Editorial Interamericana, SA: Carrera 17, No 33-71, Apdo Aéreo 6131, Bogotá; tel. 2454786; university textbooks; Gen. Man. Víctor Cortes.

Editorial Mercurio, SA: Calle 70A, No 7-81, Apdo Aéreo 59317, Bogotá; tel. 2110800; telex 41384; f. 1977; Pres. Dr Rafael Sanabria V.

Editorial Norma y Cía SCA: Apdo Aéreo 46, Cali; tel. 614289; telex 55555; f. 1964; children's, textbooks, education; Gen. Man. Fernando Gómez.

Editorial Presencia, Ltda: Calle 23, No 24-20, Apdo Aéreo 006642, Bogotá; tel. 2681817; textbooks, general; Gen. Man. Alberto Umaña C.

Editorial Temis SA: Calle 13, No 6-45, Apdo Aéreo 5941, Bogotá; tel. 2690713; f. 1951; law, sociology, politics; Man. Dir Jorge Guerrero.

Editorial Voluntad, SA: Carrera 7, No 24-89, 24°, Apdo 29834; tel. 2858711; f. 1930; school books; Man. Gastón de Bedout.

Fundación Centro de Investigación de Educación Popular: Carrera 5, No 33A-08, Apdo Aéreo 25916, Bogotá; tel. 2324440; f. 1959; politics, economics and sociology; Man. Dir Manuel Uribe Ramón.

Instituto Caro y Cuervo: Carrera 11, No 64-37, Apdo Aéreo 51502, Bogotá; tel. 2558289; f. 1942; philology, general linguistics and reference; Man. Dir Rafael Torres Quintero; Gen. Sec. Francisco Sánchez Arévalo.

Legis Editores, SA: Avda Eldorado No 81-10, Apdo Aéreo 98888, Bogotá; tel. 2634100; f. 1952; economics, law, general; Pres. Ramiro Montoya.

Publicar SA: Calle 15, No 8-68, 6°, Apdo Aéreo 8010, Bogotá; tel. 2345600; telex 44588; f. 1954; directories; Man. Dr Fabio Cabal P.

Siglo XXI Editores de Colombia Ltda: Avda 3, No 17-73, Apdo Aéreo 19434, Bogotá; tel. 2813906; f. 1966; arts, politics, anthropology, history, fiction, etc.; Man. Dir Santiago Pombo V.

Medellín

Editorial Bedout, SA: Calle 61, No 51-04, Apdo Aéreo 760, Medellín; tel. 316900; f. 1889; social science, literature and textbooks; Man. Héctor Quintero Arredondo.

ASSOCIATION

Cámara Colombiana de la Industria Editorial: Carrera 7A, No 17-51, Of. 410, Apdo Aéreo 8998, Bogotá; tel. 2821117; f. 1951; Exec. Dir Martha Lía Correa Arango.

Radio and Television

In 1985 there were an estimated 25,000,000 radio receivers, and an estimated 4,500,000 television receivers in use.

Ministerio de Comunicaciones, División de Telecomunicaciones: Edif. Murillo Toro, Apdo Aéreo 14515, Bogotá; broadcasting authority; Dir Minister of Communications.

Instituto Nacional de Radio y Televisión—INRAVISION: Centro Administrativo Nacional (CAN), Vía del Aeropuerto Eldorado, Bogotá; tel. 2697242; telex 43311; f. 1954; government-run TV and radio broadcasting network; educational and commercial broadcasting; Dir Fernando Sánchez Torres.

RADIO

In 1985 there were 486 radio stations officially registered with the Ministry of Communications. Most radio stations belong to ASOMEDIOS. The principal radio networks are as follows:

Cadena Líder de Colombia: Carrera 5, No 14-80, 3°, Bogotá; tel. 2831323; Pres. Efraín Paez Espitía.

CARACOL (Primera Cadena Radial Colombiana, SA): Calle 19, No 8-48, Apdo Aéreo 9291, Bogotá; tel. 2822088; telex 044880; 44 stations; radio and television services; Pres. Fernando Londoño Henao.

Circuito Todelar de Colombia: Calle 57, No 18-13, Bogotá; tel. 2111690; 66 stations; Pres. Germán Tobón Martínez.

RCN (Radio Cadena Nacional, SA): Calle 13, No 37-32, Bogotá; 64 stations; official network; Gen. Man. Dr Oscar Bayter Posada.

Radiodifusora Nacional: CAN, Vía Eldorado, Bogotá; tel. 690350; Dir Hjalmar de Greiff Bernal.

Super Radio: Calle 39, No 18-12, Apdo Aéreo 23316, Bogotá; 27 stations; Man. Alvaro Pava Camelo.

TELEVISION

Television services began in 1954 and are operated by the state monopoly, INRAVISION, which controls two commercial and one educational station. Broadcasting time is distributed among competing programmers through a public tender and most of the commercial broadcast time is dominated by programmers such as RTI, Punch, CARACOL and Colvisión. The first channel broadcasts daily for about 17 hours, the second channel for about 15 hours. The educational station broadcasts for 5½ hours per day. The NTSC colour television system was adopted in 1979.

ASSOCIATIONS

Asociación Nacional de Medios de Comunicación (ASOMEDIOS): Carrera 22, No 85-72, Bogotá; f. 1978 and merged with ANRADIO (Asociación Nacional de Radio, Televisión y Cine de Colombia) in 1980; Pres. Dr Tulio Angel Arbeláez.

Federación Nacional de Radio (FEDERADIO): Calle 18, No 6-47, Of. 501, Bogotá; Dir Libardo Taborda Bolívar.

Finance

(cap. = capital; p.u. = paid up; res = reserves; dep. = deposits; m. = million; amounts are given in pesos)

Contraloría General de la República: Calle 17, No 9-82, P4, Bogotá; tel. 2823549; Controller-General Dr Rodolfo González García.

BANKING

In 1976 the Government legislated that all foreign banks operating in Colombia should be at least 51% locally owned by 30 June 1978.

Superintendencia Bancaria: Carrera 7A, No 7-56, Apdo Aéreo 3460, Bogotá; tel. 2437050; telex 41443; Banking Superintendent Germán Tabares Cardona.

Junta Monetaria (Monetary Board): Carrera 7, 14-78, Bogotá; regulates banking operations and monetary policy; Advisers Dr Carlos Caballero Argaez, Dr Manuel Ramírez.

Central Bank

Banco de la República: Carrera 7, No 14-78, Apdo Postal 402, Aéreo 3531, Bogotá; tel. 2831111; telex 0044559; f. 1923; sole bank of issue; cap. 153.9m., res 463.3m. (Dec. 1983); Gen. Man. Dr Francisco J. Ortega Acosta; 33 brs.

The Banco de la República also administers the following financial funds that channel resources to priority sectors:

Fondo de Inversiones Privadas: f. 1963; private investment fund for industrial development.

Fondo Financiero Agrario: agriculture and livestock finance fund.

Fondo Financiero Industrial: industrial finance fund.

Fondo de Ahorro y Vivienda: savings and housing finance fund.

Fondo de Desarrollo Eléctrico: electric development finance fund.

Commercial Banks

Bogotá

Banco Anglo-Colombiano (fmrly Bank of London and South America Ltd): Carrera 8, No 15-46, Apdo Aéreo 3532, Bogotá; tel. 2811788; telex 044884; f. 1976; cap. and res 963.9m., dep. 11,948.4m. (Dec. 1984); Pres. José Joaquín Casas Fajardo; Regional Man. M. P. Mulholland; 35 brs.

Banco de Bogotá: Calle 36, No 7-47, Apdo Aéreo 3436, Bogotá; tel. 2881188; telex 44730; f. 1870; cap. and res 10,796.8m., dep. 127,614.5m. (Dec. 1984); Vice-Pres. Dr Alejandro Figueroa; 251 brs.

Banco Cafetero: Calle 28, No 13-53, Apdo Aéreo 240332, Bogotá; tel. 2846800; telex 44546; f. 1953; cap. and res 4,925.4m., dep. 64,168.3m. (June 1984); government-owned; acts both as a commercial lending institution and development bank for rural coffee regions; Pres. (vacant); 288 brs.

Banco Central Hipotecario: Carrera 6a, No 15-32, Bogotá; tel. 2813840; telex 45720; f. 1932; cap. 8,688.2m., dep. 182,302.1m. (June

1985); provides urban housing development credit; Gen. Man. Dr MARIO CALDERÓN RIVERA; 123 brs.

Banco de Colombia: Calle 30A, No 6-38, Apdo Aéreo 6836, Bogotá; tel. 2850300; telex 44744; f. 1874; cap. and res 3,556.3m. (May 1984), dep. 22,948.3m. (1983); nationalized in January 1986; Pres. GUILLERMO VILLAVECES MEDINA; 270 brs.

Banco Colombo-Americano (fmrly Bank of America): Carrera 7A, No 24-89, 47°, Apdo Aéreo 12327, Bogotá; tel. 2816700; telex 44511; cap. 332.1m. (June 1984), dep. 1,175.8m. (June 1983); Gen. Man. KEITH PARKER; 12 brs.

Banco Colpatria: Carrera 7A, No 24-89, 9°, Apdo Aéreo 7762, Bogotá; tel. 2412020; telex 44637; f. 1955; cap. and res 864.7m. (June 1984), dep. 24,608.4m. (June 1983); Pres. JUAN MANUEL CÁRDENAS; 26 brs.

Banco del Comercio: Calle 13, No 8-52, Apdo Aéreo 4749, Bogotá; tel. 2826400; telex 044450; f. 1949; cap. and res 2,181.9m. (June 1984), dep. 14,411.5m. (June 1983); Pres. JAMES A. THERRIEN W.; 129 brs.

Banco de Crédito: Carrera 10A, No 16-39, 6°, Apdos Aéreos 6800, 6454, Bogotá; tel. 2827288; telex 44789; f. 1963; cap. and res 544.7m. (June 1984), dep. 1,474.5m. (June 1983); Pres. LUIS FERNANDO MESA PRIETO; 10 brs.

Banco de Crédito y Comercio (fmrly Banco Mercantil): Carrera 7A, No 14-23, Apdo Aéreo 6826, Bogotá; tel. 2848800; telex 44709; f. 1954; cap. and res 1,014.0m. (June 1984), dep. 2,600.6m. (June 1983); Exec. Pres. Dr JOSÉ EDUARDO ZÁRATE MIRANDA; 22 brs.

Banco del Estado: Carrera 10A, No 18-15, 11°, Apdo Aéreo 8311, Bogotá; tel. 2338100; telex 44719; f. 1884; cap. and res 1,230.2m., dep. 7,614.0m. (June 1983); Pres. Dr HERNÁN RINCÓN; 58 brs.

Banco Exterior de Los Andes y de España de Colombia—EXTEBANDES DE COLOMBIA: Calle 74, No 6-65, Apdo Aéreo 241247, Bogotá; tel. 2127200; telex 45374; f. 1982; cap. and res 500m., dep. 4,792m. (Dec. 1984); Gen. Man. ARMANDO GONZÁLEZ QUINTERO.

Banco Ganadero: Carrera 9, No 72-21, Apdo Aéreo 53851, Bogotá; tel. 2170100; telex 45448; f. 1956; government-owned; provides financing for cattle development; cap. and res 1,864.9m. (June 1984), dep. 18,942.1m. (June 1983); Pres. JESÚS ENRIQUE VILLAMIZAR; 115 brs.

Banco Internacional de Colombia: Avda Jiménez, No 8-89, Apdo Aéreo 4134, Bogotá; tel. 2835888; telex 44721; cap. and res 869.9m. (June 1984), dep. 2,987.8m. (June 1983); Pres. CLEVELAND A. CHRISTOPHE; 23 brs.

Banco Real de Colombia (fmrly Banco Real SA): Carrera 7A, No 33-80, Apdo Aéreo 034262, Bogotá; tel. 2879300; telex 44688; f. 1976; cap. and res 301.5m. (June 1984), dep. 876.6m. (June 1983); Pres. Dr LUSIVANDER FURLANI LEITE; 9 brs.

Banco Royal Colombiano (fmrly Royal Bank of Canada): Carrera 8A, No 14-35, 3°, Apdo Aéreo 3438, Bogotá; tel. 2820077; telex 44609; cap. and res 576.1m. (June 1984), dep. 1,956.0m. (June 1983); Gen. Man. PHILLIP BRUCE ARTHUR WILLIAMS; 11 brs.

Banco Santander: Carrera 10A, No 28-49, 10°, Bavaria Torre A, Apdo Aéreo 4740, Bogotá; tel. 2843100; telex 45417; cap. and res 1,161.8m. (June 1984), dep. 3,602.5m. (June 1983); Pres. Dr JAIME HENAO LÓPEZ; 37 brs.

Banco Sudameris Colombia (fmrly Banco Francés e Italiano): Carrera 8, No 15-42, Apdo Aéreo 3440, Bogotá; tel. 2838700; telex 044725; cap. and res 1,084.4m., dep. 11,455.5m. (Dec. 1984); Pres. LUCIANO BALA BONA; 25 brs.

Banco Tequendama: Carrera 7A, No 26-15, Bogotá; tel. 2875711; telex 33475; f. 1976; cap. and res 725.8m. (June 1984); Pres. ANDRÉS ALVARO CAMACHO MARTÍNEZ; 11 brs.

Banco de los Trabajadores: Calle 13, No 7-60, Apdo Aéreo 17645, Bogotá; tel. 2338200; telex 41430; f. 1974; cap. and res 405.4m. (June 1984), dep. 1,706.8m. (June 1983); Pres. WINSTON MEDINA LOZANO; 19 brs.

Caja de Crédito Agrario, Industrial y Minero: Carrera 8A, No 15-43, Apdo Aéreo 3534, Bogotá; tel. 2844600; telex 44457; f. 1931; cap. and res 17,519m., dep. 121,783m. (June 1986); government-owned development bank; Gen. Man. Dr MARIANO OSPINA HERNÁNDEZ; 877 brs.

Caja Social de Ahorros: Calle 59, No 10-60, 9°, Apdo Aéreo 53889, Bogotá; tel. 112930; telex 45685; Jesuit-run; cap. and res 688.5m., dep. 15,811.4m. (Dec. 1984); Gen. Man. JORGE MARMOREK ROJAS; 69 brs.

Cali

Banco de Occidente: Carrera 5A, No 12-42, Apdo Aéreo 4400, Cali; tel. 711132/39; telex 55655; cap. and res 1,874.5m. (June 1984),
dep. 9,825.3m. (June 1983); Pres. FRANCISCO CASTRO ZAWADSKY; 98 brs.

Banco Popular: Carrera 4A, No 9-60, Apdo Aéreo 1869, Cali; tel. 893124/29; telex 055656; f. 1950; government-owned; cap. and res 7,019.3m., dep. 82,621m. (Dec. 1984), dep. 28,724.9m. (June 1983); Pres. FLORÁNGELA GÓMEZ ORDÓÑEZ; 182 brs.

Manizales

Banco de Caldas: Carrera 22, No 21-03, Apdo Aéreo 617, Manizales; tel. 30438; telex 83512; f. 1965; cap. and res 480.3m. (June 1984), dep. 1,888.7m. (June 1983); Pres. ALBERTO MEJÍA JARAMILLO; 13 brs.

Medellín

Banco Comercial Antioqueño: Edif. Vicente Uribe Rendón 14°, Carrera 46, No 52-36, Medellín; tel. 515200; telex 65339; f. 1912; cap. and res 6,145.3m., dep. 231,396.3m. (Dec. 1985); Pres. FERNANDO PLAZA CASTRO; 122 brs.

Banco Industrial Colombiano: Calle 50, No 51-66, Apdo Aéreo 45635, Medellín; tel. 317900; telex 06743; f. 1945; cap. and res 1,289.6m. (June 1984), dep. 9,037.3m. (June 1983); Pres. JAVIER GÓMEZ RESTREPO; 83 brs.

Banking Association

Asociación Bancaria de Colombia: Carrera 7A, No 17-01, 3°, Apdo Aéreo 13994, Bogotá; f. 1936; 56 mem. banks; Pres. GUILLERMO NÚÑEZ VERGARA; Vice-Pres. GERARDO A. MONCADA VEGA.

STOCK EXCHANGES

Comisión Nacional de Valores: Carrera 7A, No 31-10, 4°, Apdo Aéreo 39600, Bogotá; tel. 2873300; telex 44326; f. 1979 to regulate the securities market; Pres. Dr JAIME ALBERTO GÓMEZ.

Bolsa de Bogotá: Carrera 8A, No 13-82, 8°, Apdo Aéreo 3584, Bogotá; tel. 2436501; telex 044807; f. 1928; Pres. CARLOS DEL CASTILLO; Vice-Pres. CARLOS BURAGLIA; Sec.-Gen. NORA LUCIA SANÍN DE SAFFÓN.

Bolsa de Medellín: Carrera 50, No 50-48, 2°, Apdo Aéreo 3535, Medellín; tel. 318708; telex 66788; Pres. FRANCISCO PIEDRAHITA E.

Bolsa de Occidente SA: Calle 8, No 3-14, 17°, Cali; tel. 817022.

INSURANCE

Principal National Companies
(selected on the basis of premium income)

(n.p.i. = net premiums issued; amounts in pesos)

Aseguradora Colseguros SA: Calle 17, No 9-82, Bogotá; tel. 2839100; telex 044710; f. 1874; n.p.i. 9,616m. (1985); Pres. Dr ORLANDO CABRALES MARTÍNEZ; Gen. Sec. Dr JOSÉ PABLO NAVAS PRIETO.

Aseguradora del Valle, SA: Edif. Carvajal 8°, Calle 13, No 4-25, Cali; tel. 93895061; telex 055703; n.p.i. 648.1m. (1983); Pres. Dr JORGE E. HOLGUÍN CÓRDOBA.

Aseguradora Grancolombiana SA: Calle 31, No 6-41, 4°, 12° y 15°, Apdo Aéreo 10454, Bogotá; tel. 2856520; telex 41328; n.p.i. 3,225.7m. (1983); Pres. RAFAEL PADILLA ANDRADE.

Colpatria, Compañía de Seguros Patria SA: Carrera 7A, No 24-89, Apdo 7762, Bogotá; tel. 2412020; telex 43200; n.p.i. 1,260.8m. (1983); Pres. CARLOS PACHECO DEVÍA; 40 brs.

Cía Agrícola de Seguros SA: Calle 67, No 7-94, 15°-22°, Bogotá; tel. 2121100; telex 45501; f. 1952; n.p.i. 1,843.6m. (1983); Pres. Dr ARIEL JARAMILLO ABAD.

Cía Central de Seguros: Carrera 5A, No 15-80, 21°, Apdo Aéreo 5764, Bogotá; tel. 2435519; n.p.i. 1,151.5m. (1983); f. 1957; Man. Dir J. EFRÉN OSSA GÓMEZ.

Cía Mundial de Seguros, SA: Calle 33, No 6-94, 2° y 3°, Apdo 30270, Bogotá; tel. 2855600; telex 43183; n.p.i. 556.3m.; Pres. GUILLERMO CÁCERES LINARES.

Cía de Seguros Bolívar, SA: Carrera 10A, No 16-39, Apdo Aéreo 4421, Bogotá; tel. 2830100; telex 044873; f. 1939; n.p.i. 3,496m. (1983); Pres. Dr JOSÉ ALEJANDRO CORTÉS O.

Cía de Seguros Colmena: Carrera 7, No 73-47, 5°, 6° y 7°, Bogotá; tel. 2119111; telex 45217; f. 1951; n.p.i. 607.6m.; Pres. Dr BERNARDO BOTERO MORALES.

Cía de Seguros La Andina, SA: Carrera 7, No 72-13, 8° y 10°, Bogotá; tel. 2118411; telex 45713; n.p.i. 529.7m.; Man. JOHN S. PHILLIPS.

Cía de Seguros La Fénix de Colombia SA: Carrera 7A, No 32-33, 5°, Bogotá; tel. 2811400; telex 41335; n.p.i. 732.3m. (1983); Pres. PHILIP M. TIBBLE.

COLOMBIA

Cía Suramericana de Seguros, SA: Centro Suramericana, Carrera 64B, No 49A-30, Apdos Aéreos 780 y 2030, Medellín; tel. 942302100; telex 66639; f. 1944; n.p.i. 3,813.5m. (1983); Pres. Dr NICANOR RESTREPO SANTAMARÍA.

La Continental Cía de Seguros, SA: Carrera 13, No 26-45, 9°, Bogotá; tel. 2420670; n.p.i. 774.3m. (1983); Gen. Man. ROBERT W. REINECKE.

La Interamericana Cía de Seguros Generales, SA: Calle 78, No 9-57, 5°, Bogotá; tel. 2559700; telex 44631; n.p.i. 862.4m. (1983); Pres. GLEN LAWSON.

La Nacional Cía de Seguros Generales, SA: Calle 42, No 56-01, Apdo Aéreo 5627, Bogotá; tel. 2685800; telex 44567; f. 1952; n.p.i. 2,530m. (1983); Pres. EDUARDO VERANO PRIETO.

Seguros Colina, SA: Calle 38, No 8-66, 14°-16°, Bogotá; tel. 2854600; telex 43120; n.p.i. 558.4m.; Gen. Man. LYLE SWEENEY.

Seguros del Comercio, SA: Calle 71A, No 6-30, 2°, Apdo Aéreo 57227, Bogotá; tel. 2124900; telex 044582; f. 1954; n.p.i. 2,213.4m. (1985); Pres. MARISTELLA SANÍN DE ALDANA.

Seguros del Estado, SA: Carrera 11, No 87, Bogota; telex 6810; n.p.i. 672.3m.; Pres. Dr JORGE MORA SÁNCHEZ.

Seguros Médicos Voluntarios, SA: Calle 72, No 6-44, 9°, Apdo 11777, Bogotá; tel. 2127611; telex 43354; n.p.i. 1,200.8m. (1983); Gen. Man. Dr FRANCISCO DI DOMENICO.

Seguros Tequendama, SA: Carrera 7A, No 26-20, 7°, Apdo 7988, Bogotá; tel. 2858200; telex 0441426; n.p.i. 737.3m. (1982); Pres. Dr JULIÁN EFRÉN OSSA.

Skandia Seguros de Colombia, SA: Avda 19, No 113-30, Apdo Aéreo 100327, Bogotá; tel. 2141200; telex 043398; n.p.i. 2,700m. (1984); Pres. JAN CARENDI.

Numerous foreign companies are also represented.

Insurance Association

Unión de Aseguradores Colombianos—FASECOLDA: Carrera 7a, No 26-20, 11° y 12°, Apdo Aéreo 5233, Bogotá; tel. 2876611; telex 45708; f. 1976; 64 mems; Pres. Dr WILLIAM R. FADUL.

Trade and Industry

CHAMBERS OF COMMERCE

Confederación Colombiana de Cámaras de Comercio—CONFECAMARAS: Carrera 13, No 27-47, Of. 502, Apdo Aéreo 29750, Bogotá; tel. 2881200; telex 44416; f. 1969; 40 mem. organizations; Exec.-Pres. NICOLÁS DEL CASTILLO MATHIEU; Pres. JAIRO PATIÑO GUTIÉRREZ.

Cámara de Comercio de Bogotá: Carrera 9A, No 16-21, Apdo Aéreo 29824, Bogotá; tel. 2819900; telex 45574; f. 1878; 1,500 mem. organizations; Dir Dr MARIO SUÁREZ MELO; Pres. Dr ARIEL JARAMILLO.

There are also local Chambers of Commerce in the capital towns of all the Departments and in many of the other trading centres.

STATE INDUSTRIAL AND TRADE ORGANIZATIONS

Carbones de Colombia—CARBOCOL: Carrera 7, No 31-10, 13°, Apdo Aéreo 29740, Bogotá; tel. 2873100; telex 45779; f. 1976; initial cap. 350m. pesos; state enterprise for the exploration, mining, processing and marketing of coal; Pres. ALVARO PUPO PUPO; Vice-Pres. RAIMUNDO ALDANA.

Colombiana de Minería—COLMINAS: Bogotá; state mining concern; Man. ALFONSO RODRÍGUEZ KILBER.

Corporación de la Industria Aeronáutica Colombiana SA: Aeropuerto Internacional Eldorado Entrada 1 Interior 2, Bogotá; tel. 2684642; telex 45254; Man. Gen. ALVARO MEJÍA SOTO.

Departamento Nacional de Planeación: Calle 26, No 13-19, Bogotá; tel. 2824055; telex 45634; supervises and administers development projects; approves foreign investments; Dir MARÍA MERCEDES CUELLAR.

Empresa Colombiana de Minas—ECOMINAS: Avda 34, No 19-05, Apdo Aéreo 17878, Bogotá; tel. 2875588; administers state resources of emerald, copper, gold, sulphur, gypsum, phosphate rock and other minerals except coal and uranium; Gen. Man. CECILIA GARCÍA BAUTISTA.

Empresa Colombia de Niquel—ECONIQUEL: Carrera 7, No 26-20, Bogotá; tel. 2323839; telex 43262; administers state nickel resources; Dir JAVIER RESTREPO TORO.

Directory

Empresa Colombiana de Petróleos—ECOPETROL: Carrera 13, No 36-24, Apdo Aéreo 5938, Bogotá; tel. 2856400; f. 1951; responsible for exploration, production and refining of petroleum; Pres. JOSÉ FRANCISCO CHONA.

Instituto Colombiano de Petróleo: f. 1985; research into all aspects of the hydrocarbon industry; Dir JORGE BENDECK OLIVELLA.

Empresa Colombiana de Uranio—COLURANIO: Centro Administrativo Nacional (CAN), 4°, Ministerio de Minas y Energía, Bogotá; tel. 2445440; telex 45898 f. 1977 to further the exploration, processing and marketing of radio-active minerals; initial cap. US $750,000; Dir JAIME GARCÍA.

Empresa de Comercialización de Productos Perecederos—EMCOPER: Carrera 30, No 45A-68, Bogotá; tel. 2442421; attached to Ministry of Agriculture; Dir LUIS FERNANDO LONDOÑO RUIZ.

Empresa Nacional de Telecomunicaciones—TELECOM: Calle 23, No 13-49, Bogotá; tel. 2694077; national telecommunications enterprise; Pres. EMILIO SARAVIA.

Fondo de Promoción de Exportaciones—PROEXPO: Calle 28, No 13A-15, 35°-42°, Apdo Aéreo 240092, Bogotá; tel. 2825151; telex 44452; f. 1967; aims to diversify exports, strengthen the balance of payments and augment the volume of trade, by granting financial aid for export operations and acting as consultant to export firms, also undertaking market studies; Dir ALBERTO SCHLESINGER VÉLEZ.

Fondo Nacional de Proyectos de Desarrollo—FONADE: Calle 26, No 13-19, 18°, Apdo Aéreo 24110, Bogotá; tel. 2829400; telex 45634; f. 1968; responsible for channelling loans towards economic development projects; administered by a committee under the head of the Departamento Administrativo de Planeación; FONADE works in close association with other official planning organizations; Man. RAÚL SANABRIA.

Fundación para el Desarrollo Integral del Valle del Cauca: Calle 8, No 3-14, 17°, Apdo Aéreo 7482, Cali; industrial development organization; Pres. GUNNAR LINDAHL HELLBERG; Exec. Pres. FABIO RODRÍGUEZ GONZÁLEZ.

Industria Militar—INDOMUL: Diagonal 40, No 47-75, Apdo Aéreo 7272, Bogotá; tel. 2699911; telex 45816; attached to Ministry of Defence; Man. Maj. Gen. HERNÁN HURTADO VALLEJO.

Instituto Colombiano Agropecuario—ICA: Calle 37, No 8-43, 8°, Apdo Aéreo 7984, Bogotá; tel. 2855520; telex 44586; Man. FERNANDO GÓMEZ MONCAYO.

Instituto Colombiano de Comercio Exterior—INCOMEX: Calle 28, No 13A-15, Apdo Aéreo 240193, Bogotá, DE; tel. 2833284; telex 44860; government agency; sets and executes foreign trade policy; Dir ALBERTO YOHAI.

Instituto Colombiano de Energía Eléctrica—ICEL: Carrera 13, No 27-00, Apdo Aéreo 16243, Bogotá; tel. 2420181; telex 43319; formulates policy for the development of electrical energy; Man. DIEGO OTERO.

Instituto Colombiano de Hidrología, Meteorología y Adecuación de Tierras—HIMAT: Carrera 5, No 15-18, 20°, Apdo Aéreo 20032, Bogotá; tel. 2836927; telex 44345; f. 1976; responsible for irrigation, flood control, drainage, hydrology and meteorology; Dir ENRIQUE SANDOVAL GARCÍA.

Instituto Colombiano de la Reforma Agraria—INCORA: Apdo Aéreo 151046, Bogotá; tel. 2447520; f. 1962; a public institution which, on behalf of the Government, administers public lands and those it acquires; reclaims land by irrigation and drainage facilities, roads, etc. to increase productivity in agriculture and stock-breeding; provides technical assistance and loans; supervises the redistribution of land throughout the country; Man. ANTONIO GÓMEZ MERLANO.

Instituto de Crédito Territorial—ICT: Carrera 13, No 18-51, Apdo Aéreo 40377, Bogotá; tel. 2343560; telex 44826; Man. MARÍA EUGENIA ROJAS DE MORENO DÍAZ.

Instituto de Fomento Industrial—IFI: Calle 16, No 6-66, Apdo Aéreo 4222, Bogotá; tel. 2822055; telex 044642; f. 1940; state finance corporation for the promotion of manufacturing activities; cap. 5,160.2m. pesos, res 160.2m. pesos (1984); Man. SERGIO RESTREPO LONDOÑO.

Instituto de Mercadeo Agropecuario—IDEMA: Carrera 10, No 16-82, Apdo Aéreo 4534, Bogotá; tel. 2829911; telex 43315; state enterprise for the marketing of agricultural products; Man. AUGUSTO RAMÍREZ RAMÍREZ.

Instituto Nacional de Fomento Municipal—INSFOPAL: Centro Administrativo Nacional (CAN), Apdo Aéreo 8638, Bogotá; tel. 2690177; telex 45328; Gen. Man. NELSON AMAYA.

Instituto Nacional de Investigaciones Geológico-Mineras—INGEOMINAS: Diagonal 53, No 34-53, Apdo Aéreo 4865, Bogotá; tel. 2211400; telex 32363500; f. 1968; responsible for mineral research, geological mapping and research including hydrogeology, remote sensing, geochemistry and geophysics; Dir ALFONSO LÓPEZ REINA.

Instituto de Desarrollo de Recursos Naturales Renovables y del Ambiente—INDERENA: Diagonal 34, No 5-18, 3°, Apdo Aéreo 13458, Bogotá; tel. 2854417; telex 44428; f. 1968; agency regulating the development of natural resources; Dir Dra MARGARITA MARIÑO DE BOTERO.

Superintendencia de Industria y Comercio—SUPERINDUSTRIA: Carrera 13, No 27-00, 5°, Bogotá; tel. 2342035; supervises chambers of commerce; controls standards and prices; Man. Dr DIEGO NARANJO MEZA; Supt ROBERTO NAVARRO DE LA OSSA.

Superintendencia de Sociedades—SUPERSOCIEDADES: Calle 14, No 7-19, 5° al 16°, Apdo Aéreo 4188, Bogotá; tel. 2830562; oversees activities of local and foreign corporations; Supt LUIS FERNANDO SANMIGUEL.

There are several other agricultural and regional development organizations.

TRADE FAIR

Corporación de Ferias y Exposiciones, SA: Carrera 40, No 22C-67, Apdo Aéreo 6843, Bogotá; tel. 2440141; telex 44553; f. 1954; holds the biannual Bogotá International Fair and the biannual International Agricultural Fair (AGROEXPO); Man. OSCAR PÉREZ GUTIÉRREZ.

EMPLOYERS' AND PRODUCERS' ORGANIZATIONS

Asociación Colombiana Popular de Industriales (ACOPI): Carrera 23, No 41-94, Apdo Aéreo 16451, Bogotá, DE; tel. 2442741; f. 1951; association of small industrialists; Pres. JUAN A. PINTO SAAVEDRA; Man. RAMIRO SERNA JARAMILLO.

Asociación Nacional de Cultivadores de Caña de Azúcar (ASOCAÑA): Calle 58N, No 3N-15, 4°, Apdo Aéreo 4448, Cali; tel. 689111; telex 51136; f. 1959; sugar planters' association; Pres. HERNÁN BORRERO URRUTIA.

Asociación Nacional de Exportadores (ANALDEX): Carrera 7A, No 26-20, 27°, Apdo Aéreo 4448, Bogotá; tel. 2859303; telex 43326; exporters' association; Pres. ALFONSO ROJAS LLORENTE.

Asociación Nacional de Exportadores de Café de Colombia: Carrera 7, No 32-33, Of. 25-04, Bogotá; tel. 2830669, 2830698; telex 44802; f. 1938; private association of coffee exporters; Pres. GILBERTO ARANGO LONDOÑO.

Asociación Nacional de Industriales (ANDI) (National Association of Manufacturers): Calle 52, No 47-48, Apdo 997, Medellín; tel. 420200; telex 06631; f. 1944; Pres. FABIO ECHEVERRI CORREA; 7 brs; 722 mems.

Expocafé: Bogotá; f. 1985; coffee exporting organization; comprises 53 coffee co-operatives.

Federación Colombiana de Ganaderos (FEDEGAN): Carrera 14, No 36-65, Apdo Aéreo 9709, Bogotá; tel. 2327129; f. 1975; cattle raisers' association; about 350,000 affiliates; Pres. HERNÁN VALLEJO MEJÍA.

Federación Nacional de Algodoneros: Carrera 8A, No 15-73, 5°, Apdo Aéreo 8632, Bogotá; tel. 2343221; telex 44864; f. 1953; federation of cotton growers; Gen. Man. ANTONIO AVELLO ROCA; 14,000 mems.

Federación Nacional de Cacaoteros: Carrera 17, No 30-39, Bogotá; federation of cocoa growers.

Federación Nacional de Cafeteros de Colombia (National Federation of Coffee Growers): Avda Jiménez de Quesada, No 7-65, 5°, Apdo Aéreo 3938, Bogotá; tel. 2829200; telex 44723; f. 1927; totally responsible for fostering and regulating the coffee economy; Gen. Man. JORGE CÁRDENAS GUTIÉRREZ; 203,000 mems.

Federación Nacional de Cultivadores de Cereales (FENALCE): Carrera 7, No 79-75, Of. 402, Apdo Aéreo 8694, Bogotá; tel. 2112015; f. 1960; federation of grain growers; Gen. Man. ADRIANO QUINTANA SILVA; 1,500 mems.

Sociedad de Agricultores de Colombia (SAC) (Colombian Farmers' Society): Carrera 7A, No 24-89, 44°, Apdo Aéreo 3638, Bogotá; tel. 2821989; f. 1871; Pres. (vacant).

There are several other organizations, including those for rice growers, engineers and financiers.

TRADE UNIONS

According to official figures, an estimated 900 of Colombia's 2,000 trade unions are independent.

Confederación Sindical de Trabajadores de Colombia—CSTC: Calle 16, No 13-49, Of. 202 Bogotá; tel. 2412441; Communist; Pres. Dr. GUSTAVO OSORIO; Sec.-Gen. ANGELINO GARZÓN.

Frente Sindical Democrática (FSD): f. 1984; centre-right trade union alliance; comprises:

Unión de Trabajadores de Colombia—UTC (National Union of Colombian Workers): Carrera 10, No 7-33, Bogotá; tel. 2336745; f. 1946; mainly Conservative; incorporates 22 regional federations, 5 industry federations and 18 national unions; affiliated to the ICFTU and ORIT; Pres. VÍCTOR M. ACOSTA VALDEBLÁNQUEZ; Vice-Pres. JORGE CARRILLO ROJAS; 1.2m. mems.

Confederación de Trabajadores de Colombia—CTC (Colombian Confederation of Workers): Calle 16, No 14-13, 5°, Apdo Aéreo 4780, Bogotá; tel. 2430040; f. 1934; mainly Liberal; 600 affiliates, including 6 national organizations and 20 regional federations; admitted to ICFTU; Pres. MANUEL FELIPE HURTADO; 400,000 mems.

Confederación General de Trabajadores—CGT: Calle 19, No 13A-12, 6°, Apdo Aéreo 5415, Bogotá; tel. 2835817; Christian Democrat; Pres. Dr ALVARO RAMÍREZ PINILLOS.

Transport

Land transport in Colombia is rendered difficult by high mountains, so the principal means of long-distance transport is by air. As a result of the development of the El Cerrejón coal field, Colombia's first deep-water port has been constructed at Bahia de Portete, and a 150-km rail link between El Cerrejón and the port became operational in 1986.

Instituto Nacional del Transporte (INTRA): Edif. Minobras (CAN), 6°, Apdo Aéreo 24990, Bogotá; tel. 2449100; government body; Dir Dr EUGENIO MARULANDA GÓMEZ.

RAILWAYS

Ferrocarriles Nacionales de Colombia (National Railways of Colombia): Calle 13, No 18-24, Bogotá; tel. 2775577; Pres. Dr LUIS FERNANDO JARAMILLO; Man. Dr TITO RUEDA G.

The Administrative Council for the National Railways operated 3,403 km of track in 1984. The system is divided into five divisions, each with its own management: Central, Pacific, Antioquia, Santander and Magdalena.

The Medellín urban transport project, which will provide a 29-km underground system with 24 stations, was scheduled to be operational by 1988. A similar transit project has been proposed for Bogotá.

ROADS

Fondo Vial Nacional: Bogotá; f. 1966; administered by the Ministerio de Obras Públicas; to execute development programmes in road transport.

In 1980 there were 74,735 km of roads. The country's main highways are the Caribbean Trunk Highway, the Eastern and Western Trunk Highways, the Central Trunk Highway and there are also roads into the interior. There are plans to construct a Jungle Edge highway to give access to the interior, a link road between Turbo, Bahía Solano and Medellín, a highway between Bogotá and Villavicencio and to complete the short section of the Pan-American highway between Panama and Colombia.

There are a number of national bus companies and road haulage companies.

INLAND WATERWAYS

Dirección de Navegación y Puertos: Edif. Minobras (CAN), Of. 562, Bogotá; tel. 2694827; telex 45656; responsible for river transport; the waterways system is divided into four sectors: Magdalena, Atrato, Orinoquia, and Amazonia; Dir-Gen. DANIEL LORDUY; Man. Dr ALFREDO LAVERDE LÓPEZ.

The Magdalena river is the centre of river traffic and is navigable for 1,761 km, while the Atrato is navigable for 687 km. The River Orinoco is navigable for 2,259 km (mainly through Venezuela) and the Amazon for 3,336 km (mainly through Brazil). There are plans to construct an Atrato–Truandó inter-oceanic canal.

SHIPPING

The four most important ocean terminals are Buenaventura on the Pacific coast and Santa Marta, Barranquilla and Cartagena on the Atlantic coast. The port of Tumaco on the Pacific coast is gaining in importance and there are plans for construction of a deep-water port at Bahía Solano. In 1986 the World Bank allocated a loan of US $43m. to Colombia for the rehabilitation of port facilities at Buenaventura, Cartagena and Santa Marta.

Empresa Puertos de Colombia—COLPUERTOS (Colombian Port Authority): Carrera 10A, No 15-22, 10°, Apdo Aéreo 13037, Bogotá; tel. 2343574; f. 1959; Man. Capt. (retd) JAIME SÁNCHEZ CORTÉS.

Flota Mercante Grancolombiana, SA: Carrera 13, No 27-75, Apdo Aéreo 4482, Bogotá; tel. 2836600; telex 44853; owned by the Colombian Coffee Growers' Federation (80%) and Ecuador Development Bank (20%); f. 1946; one of Latin America's leading cargo carriers serving 45 countries worldwide and transporting 70% of all government imports; Pres. Dr ENRIQUE VARGAS R.; Sec.-Gen. Dr HUMBERTO VELÁSQUEZ; 15 vessels.

Colombiana Internacional de Vapores, Ltda (Colvapores): Avda Caracas, No 35-02, Apdo 17227, Bogotá; cargo services mainly to the USA.

Líneas Agromar, Ltda: Carrera 30 y Calle 4, Apdo Aéreo 3259, Barranquilla; tel. 328896; telex 33462; Pres. M. DEL DAGO F.

Several foreign shipping lines call at Colombian ports.

CIVIL AVIATION

Colombia has more than 100 airports, including 11 international airports: Bogotá (Eldorado Airport), Medellín, Cali, Barranquilla, Bucaramanga, Cartagena, Cúcuta, Leticia, Pereira, San Andrés and Santa Marta. Aerocivil operates 520 airports and the Fondo Aeronáutico Nacional operates 74 airports.

Airports Authority

Departamento Administrativo de Aeronáutica Civil (Aerocivil): Aeropuerto Internacional Eldorado, Bogotá; tel. 2669200; telex 44620; Dir YESID CASTAÑO GONZÁLEZ.

National Airlines

AVIANCA (Aerovías Nacionales de Colombia): Avda Eldorado 93-30, 4°, Bloque 1, Bogotá; telex 44427; f. 1919; operates domestic services to all cities in Colombia and international services to Argentina, Brazil, Chile, Ecuador, Mexico, Panama, Peru, Uruguay, Venezuela, the Dominican Republic, Haiti, the Netherlands Antilles, Puerto Rico, the USA, France, the Federal Republic of Germany and Spain; Pres. Dr ORLANDO CABRALES MARTÍNEZ; fleet: 3 Boeing 747, 10 Boeing 727-100, 7 Boeing 727-200, 8 Boeing 707.

Sociedad Aeronáutica de Medellín Consolidada, SA (SAM): Edif. SAM, Calle 52, No 52-11, Apdo Aéreo 1085, Medellín; Avda Jiménez, No 5-14, Bogotá; telex 06774; f. 1945; subsidiary of Avianca; internal services; and international cargo services to Costa Rica, El Salvador, Guatemala, Nicaragua, Panama and the USA; Gen. Man. JAVIER ZAPATA; fleet: 3 Boeing 727-100, 2 Boeing 727-100C.

Servicio Aéreo a Territorios Nacionales (Satena): Aeropuerto Internacional Eldorado, Entrada No 1, Interior No 11, Carrera 10, Bogotá; tel. 2679578; telex 44561; f. 1962; commercial enterprise attached to the Ministry of National Defence; internal services; Man. Brig. ALBERTO GUZMAN MOLINA; fleet: 1 Fokker F-28, 2 HS-748, 6 Pilatus Porter PC 6, 5 Casa 212-200.

In addition the following airlines operate scheduled domestic passenger and cargo services: Aerolíneas Centrales de Colombia, SA (ACES), Aerovías de Pesca y Colonización del Suroeste Colombiano (Aeropesca) and Aerovías Colombianas (ARCA).

Tourism

Corporación Nacional de Turismo: Calle 28, No 13A-15, 16°, Apdo Aéreo 8400, Bogotá; tel. 2839466; telex 441350; f. 1968; Gen. Man. Dr ALFREDO RIASCOS NOGUERA; 8 brs throughout Colombia and brs in Europe, the USA and Venezuela.

Asociación Colombiana de Agencias de Viajes y Turismo—ANATO: Carrera 21, No 83-63/71, Apdo Aéreo 7088, Bogotá; tel. 2562290; telex 45675; f. 1949; Pres. Dr OSCAR RUEDA GARCÍA.

Atomic Energy

Instituto de Asuntos Nucleares—IAN: Avda Eldorado, Carrera 50, Apdo Aéreo 8595, Bogotá 1, DE; tel. 2440809; telex 45898; f. 1959; experimental facilities; Dir Dr ERNESTO VILLARREAL SILVA.

THE COMOROS*

Introductory Survey

Location, Climate, Language, Religion, Flag, Capital

The Federal Islamic Republic of the Comoros is an archipelago in the Mozambique Channel, between the island of Madagascar and the east coast of the African mainland. The group comprises four main islands (Njazidja, Nzwani and Mwali, formerly Grande-Comore, Anjouan and Mohéli respectively, and Mayotte) and numerous islets and coral reefs. The climate is tropical, with considerable variations in rainfall and temperature from island to island. The official languages are Arabic and French but the majority of the population speak Comoran, a blend of Swahili and Arabic. Islam is the state religion. The flag is green, with a white crescent moon and four five-pointed white stars in the centre. The capital is Moroni, on Njazidja.

Recent History

Formerly attached to Madagascar, the Comoros became a separate French Overseas Terrritory in 1947. The islands achieved internal self-government in December 1961, with a Chamber of Deputies and a Government Council to control local administration.

Elections in December 1972 produced a large majority for parties advocating independence, and Ahmed Abdallah became President of the Government Council. In June 1973 he was restyled President of the Government. A referendum in December 1974 resulted in a 96% vote in favour of independence, despite the opposition of the Mayotte Party, seeking the status of a French Department for the island of Mayotte.

On 6 July 1975, after France decided that any constitutional settlement must be ratified by all the islands voting separately, the Chamber of Deputies voted for immediate independence. The Chamber elected Abdallah to be first President of the Comoros and constituted itself as the National Assembly. France made no attempt to intervene but maintained control of Mayotte. President Abdallah was deposed in August, and the Assembly was abolished. A National Executive Council was established, with Prince Saïd Mohammed Jaffar, leader of the opposition Front National Uni, as its head, and Ali Soilih, leader of the coup, among its members. In November the Comoros was admitted to the UN, as a unified state comprising the whole archipelago, but France continued to support Mayotte, although recognizing the independence of the three remaining islands in December. In February 1976 Mayotte voted overwhelmingly to retain its links with France.

As relations with France deteriorated, all development aid and technical assistance were withdrawn. Ali Soilih was elected Head of State in January 1976, and a new constitution gave him extended powers. Many citizens reported political repression.

In May 1978 Soilih was shot dead, following a coup by a group of about 50 European mercenaries, led by a Frenchman, Bob Denard, on behalf of the exiled former President, Ahmed Abdallah. A Federal Islamic Republic was proclaimed. In July the Comoros was expelled from the Organization of African Unity (OAU) because of the continued presence of the mercenaries.

A new constitution was drawn up and approved by a referendum in October, on the three islands excluding Mayotte, by 99.31% of votes. Abdallah was elected President in the same month, and in December elections were held to form a Federal Assembly. In January 1979 the Assembly approved the formation of a one-party state. Unofficial opposition groups, however, continue to exist, and 150 people were arrested in February 1981 after officially-denied reports of an attempted coup. Ali Mroudjae, former Minister of Foreign Affairs and Co-operation, was appointed Prime Minister in February 1982, and legislative elections were held in March. Constitutional amendments, adopted in October, strengthened the President's power by reducing that of each island's Governor. In May 1983 President Abdallah announced an amnesty for all political prisoners who were serving sentences of less than 10 years. In December a plot to overthrow the Government was discovered. A group of British mercenaries was to have staged a coup on behalf of a former Comoran diplomat, Saïd Ali Kemal, but the plot was foiled by the arrest of the mercenary leaders in Australia. Abdallah was the sole candidate at a presidential election in September 1984. Despite calls by the opposition for voters to boycott the election, there was a turn-out of 98%. Abdallah's candidacy was endorsed by 99.44% of voters, and he was therefore returned to office for a further six years. In January 1985 the Constitution was amended to abolish the position of Prime Minister, and President Abdallah assumed the office of Head of Government. In March 1985 an attempt by presidential guardsmen to overthrow Abdallah, while he was absent on a private visit to France, was foiled, and in November 17 people, including Mustapha Saïd Cheikh, secretary-general of the banned opposition movement, Front démocratique (FD), were sentenced to forced labour for life, while 50 others were also imprisoned for their part in the coup attempt. However, in December 1985 President Abdallah granted an amnesty to about 30 political prisoners, many of whom were FD members, and in May 1986 a further 15 detainees, convicted after the attempted coup, were also given amnesty. In September 1985 Abdallah effected a major ministerial reshuffle—the third in 11 months. The four 'super-ministries' which had been created earlier in the year were abolished and replaced by nine ministries and three secretariats of state. This was followed by a minor government reshuffle in February 1986. In January 1987 President Abdallah announced a further amnesty for political prisoners, and the holding of legislative elections in April.

Diplomatic relations with France were resumed in July 1978, and in November the two countries signed agreements on military and economic co-operation, apparently deferring any decision on the future of Mayotte. In February 1979 the OAU readmitted the Comoros. In July 1986 the OAU reiterated its appeal to France for the return of Mayotte to the Comoros. In January 1985 the Comoros was admitted as the fourth member state of the Indian Ocean Commission (IOC), an organization founded by Madagascar, Mauritius and Seychelles to promote regional co-operation and economic development. In July 1986 Saïd Kafe, the Minister of Foreign Affairs, Foreign Trade and Co-operation, visited France for negotiations over Mayotte, and in October the French Prime Minister, Jacques Chirac, visited the Comoros and Mayotte.

Government

According to the Constitution of October 1978 (q.v.), the Comoros is ruled by a President, elected for six years by universal adult suffrage. He is assisted by an appointed Council of Ministers. Legislative power lies with the Federal Assembly, with 38 members directly elected for five years, while each island has a degree of autonomy under a Governor and Council. Constitutional amendments in October 1982 gave the President the power to appoint each Governor, while the Federal Government became responsible for each island's resources.

Defence

The national army, the Forces Armées Comoriennes, has 700–800 men, and there are about 20 French officers.

---

* Some of the information contained in this chapter refers to the whole Comoros archipelago, which the independent Comoran state claims as its national territory. However, the island of Mayotte (Mahoré) is, in fact, administered by France. Separate information on Mayotte may be found in the chapter on French Overseas Possessions.

Economic Affairs

The economy of the Comoros is severely underdeveloped. In 1984 the gross domestic product (GDP) totalled about 43,100m. Comoros francs, an increase of 3.3%, in real terms, over the previous year. Apart from a minute industrial sector, which concentrates on the distillation of essences, vanilla processing, soft drinks and woodwork, the population work in primitive agriculture. The soil, however, is over-exploited, ill-suited to arable or pasture and, in places, severely eroded. In 1980 an estimated 83% of the working population were engaged in the agricultural sector (including fishing). Cassava, sweet potatoes, bananas and rice are the main food crops, but more than one-half of the islands' food is imported. Rice imports totalled 2,279m. Comoros francs in 1983 and about 5,651m. francs in 1985, following the virtual destruction of the domestic crop by a hurricane in 1984. The dominant sector, that of the colonial plantations, is geared exclusively to the cultivation of vanilla, cloves, ylang-ylang and copra for export to a world market in recession, and earnings are quite inadequate to cover the cost of imports. In 1985 earnings from exports of vanilla, the principal export commodity, were estimated at 4,689m. Comoros francs. The cost of total imports in the same year was estimated at CF16,481m.

Over-population, high unemployment, poor harvests, landlessness, lack of natural resources, poor communications and the emigration of trained personnel to the oil-rich countries bordering the Persian Gulf all add to the country's economic problems. However, the Government is aiming for self-sufficiency in basic foodstuffs, and by 1981 major projects involving maize, coconuts and poultry had also been established. Plans were made to develop the raising of livestock, and in late 1986 breeding stock were to be introduced to improve the quality of the local cattle. Small fishing concerns are also planned, as studies have shown that the Comoros has a potential catch of 25,000–30,000 metric tons of tuna each year, which could provide the basis for a processing industry.

Economic growth has barely kept pace with the increase in the islands' population in recent years. In 1982, according to estimates by the World Bank, the gross national product (GNP) of the Comoros (excluding Mayotte), measured at average 1980–82 prices, was US $120m., equivalent to $340 per head. Between 1973 and 1982, it was estimated, the country's GNP increased, in real terms, at an average rate of 2.7% per year, while the annual population growth rate was 2.6%. Over a longer period, the average rise in real GNP per head between 1960 and 1982 was an estimated 0.9% per year. According to estimates by the UN Economic Commission for Africa, the Comoros' GDP, measured in constant prices, increased at an average rate of 5.6% per year between 1976 and 1982, but, in real terms, GDP was lower in 1982 than in 1974.

Until 1975 French aid underpinned the Comoros' economy, but no effort to develop a basis for an independent economy was made. When France cut off all aid in July 1975, it left the islands virtually bankrupt. After diplomatic relations were restored in July 1978, aid resumed, and in 1985 budgetary aid totalled 24m. French francs and direct grants totalled 13m. francs. Saudi Arabia, Kuwait, the United Arab Emirates and the EEC also contribute to development projects. The country's first international aid donors' conference, held in July 1984, was attended by 17 countries and 24 aid agencies. The conference considered projects outlined in the 1983–90 Development Plan, and raised US $114.6m. in project finance. Of this, $15.25m. was allocated for the construction of a hydroelectric power plant on Nzwani. In November 1985 the EEC agreed to allocate 7,065m. Comoros francs to finance the agricultural sector from 1986 to 1990.

In 1986 the Comoros debt was estimated at 96,000m. Comoros francs. The 1986 budget projected expenditure totalling 19,768m. francs with a planned deficit of 1,608m. francs and expenditure of 2,840m. francs on debt servicing. The Government was to introduce austerity measures, including a reduction of the number of civil servants on the payroll by 350, a campaign to curb tax evasion, a reduction in operating expenditure and a reorganization of public companies.

The balance of trade showed a deficit of CF5,680m. in 1983, rising to CF15,700m. in 1984 and decreasing to CF9,433m. in 1985. The country's balance-of-payments deficit was estimated at CF3,202m. in 1984. In mid-1986 the OPEC Fund for International Development granted US $1m. to the Comoros for balance-of-payments support.

Social Welfare

In 1978 the Government administered six hospital establishments, with a total of 698 beds, and there were 20 physicians working in the country. In 1983 the Government was granted a loan of $2.8m. by the International Development Association for a programme to curb population growth and to improve health facilities on the islands. Two new maternity clinics were planned, and existing health centres were to be renovated.

Education

Education is officially compulsory for eight years between seven and 15 years of age. Primary education begins at the age of six and lasts for six years. Secondary education, beginning at 12 years of age, lasts for seven years, comprising a first cycle of four years and a second of three years. Total enrolment at primary and secondary schools, as a proportion of all school-age children, increased from 19% in 1970 to 58% (boys 70%; girls 47%) in 1980. Secondary education ceased after the withdrawal of all French teaching staff in late 1975 but some schools were reopened in 1976 with the aid of teachers from other French-speaking countries. According to a UNICEF study, there are enough Comoran teachers to provide basic education for all children through traditional Koranic schools, which 31,600 pupils were attending in 1978/79. In 1980 there were 59,709 pupils attending primary schools and 13,798 pupils at secondary schools. There were 509 Comorans studying abroad in 1978/79. An education project was launched in 1980, financed by the African Development Fund.

Tourism

There is a developing tourist industry but fewer than 2,000 tourists per year stay in the islands' four hotels. In July 1986 South African developers initiated plans to build three new hotels and to refurbish existing hotels, thus providing an infrastructure for tourism in the Comoros. The scheme aims to attract South African and European tourists to the Comoros. The chief attractions are the beaches, underwater fishing and mountain trips.

Public Holidays

1987: 28 March* (Leilat al-Meiraj, Ascension of the Prophet), 30 April* (Ramadan begins), 30 May* (Id al-Fitr, end of Ramadan), 6 July (Independence Day), 6 August* (Id al-Adha, Feast of the Sacrifice), 26 August* (Muharram, Islamic New Year), 4 September* (Ashoura), 4 November* (Mouloud, Birth of the Prophet).

1988: 16 March* (Leilat al-Meiraj, Ascension of the Prophet), 18 April* (Ramadan begins), 18 May* (Id al-Fitr, end of Ramadan), 6 July (Independence Day), 25 July* (Id al-Adha, Feast of the Sacrifice), 14 August* (Muharram, Islamic New Year), 23 August* (Ashoura), 23 October* (Mouloud, Birth of the Prophet).

* Religious holidays, which are dependent on the Islamic lunar calendar, may differ by one or two days from the dates given.

Weights and Measures

The metric system is in force.

Currency and Exchange Rates

100 centimes = 1 Comoros franc (CF).

Exchange rates (30 September 1986):
  1 Comoros franc = 2 French centimes;
  £1 sterling = 480.625 Comoros francs;
  US $1 = 332.125 Comoros francs.

Statistical Survey

Source (unless otherwise stated): Ministère de l'Economie et des Finances, BP 324, Moroni; tel. 2767; telex 219.
Note: Unless otherwise indicated, Statistical Survey does not include figures for Mayotte.

AREA AND POPULATION

Area: 1,862 sq km (719 sq miles) *By island:* Njazidja (Grande-Comore) 1,146 sq km, Nzwani (Anjouan) 424 sq km, Mwali (Mohéli) 290 sq km.

Population: 356,000 (census of March 1980); 395,000 (official estimate for December 1985). *By island:* Njazidja 189,000, Nzwani 148,000, Mwali 19,000 (census of March 1980).

Principal Towns (population at census of March 1980): Moroni (capital) 18,000; Mutsamudu 13,000; Fomboni 5,400.

Births and Deaths (including figures for Mayotte): 8,700 registered live births (birth rate 30.7 per 1,000) in 1973; 5,284 registered deaths (death rate 19.5 per 1,000) in 1970. Average annual birth rate 46.8 per 1,000 in 1970–75, 46.5 per 1,000 in 1975–80; average annual death rate 18.3 per 1,000 in 1970–75, 17.1 per 1,000 in 1975–80 (UN estimates).

Economically Active Population (ILO estimates, '000 persons at mid-1980, including figures for Mayotte): Agriculture, forestry and fishing 150; Industry 10; Services 20; Total 181 (males 104, females 77). Source: ILO, *Economically Active Population Estimates and Projections, 1950–2025*.

AGRICULTURE, ETC.

Principal Crops ('000 metric tons, 1985): Cassava (Manioc) 20.2, Sweet potatoes and yams 8.4, Rice (paddy) 2.5, Maize 4.3, Coconuts 41.3, Bananas 39.5.

Livestock ('000 head at 31 December 1985): Cattle 40, Sheep 5, Poultry 66.

Fishing (metric tons, live weight): Total catch 4,000 per year (FAO estimates) in 1978–84; 4,400 in 1985.

INDUSTRY

Electric energy (production by public utilities): 10 million kWh in 1983.

FINANCE

Currency and Exchange Rates: 100 centimes = 1 Comoros franc. *Coins:* 1, 2, 5, 10 and 20 francs. *Notes:* 50, 100, 500, 1,000 and 5,000 francs. *Sterling and Dollar Equivalents* (30 September 1986): £1 sterling = 480.625 Comoros francs; US $1 = 332.125 Comoros francs; 1,000 Comoros francs = £2.081 = $3.011. *Average Exchange Rate* (Comoros francs per US $): 381.06 in 1983; 436.96 in 1984; 449.26 in 1985. Note: The Comoros franc has a fixed link to French currency, with an exchange rate of 1 French franc = 50 Comoros francs.

Budget (estimates, million Comoros francs, 1986): *Current revenue:* Indirect taxes 5,816. *Current expenditure:* Public debt 2,840, Federal Assembly 284, President of the Republic 575, National defence 872, Foreign affairs and co-operation 395, National education, culture, youth and sports 2,477, Home affairs, information and press 221, Finance and budget 238, Equipment, planning and environment 204, Production and agriculture 136, Health and population 652, Immigration 16, Telecommunications 8, Transport and tourism 93, Justice and civil service 143, Other expenditure 1,226; Total 10,380. *Capital budget:* Revenue 17,372, Expenditure 17,372.

Gross Domestic Product by Kind of Economic Activity (estimates, million Comoros francs at current factor cost, 1982): Agriculture, hunting, forestry and fishing 12,972; Manufacturing 1,619 Electricity, gas and water 183; Construction 3,325; Trade, restaurants and hotels 4,288; Transport, storage and communications 495; Finance, insurance, real estate and business services 789; Public administration and defence 5,010; Other services 259; GDP at factor cost 28,940; Indirect taxes (net of subsidies) 3,640; GDP in purchasers' values 32,580. Source: UN Economic Commission for Africa, *African Statistical Yearbook*.

EXTERNAL TRADE

Principal Commodities (estimates, million Comoros francs, 1985): *Imports:* Fuels 1,445, Rice 5,651; Total (incl. others) 16,481. *Exports:* Vanilla 4,689, Ylang-ylang 657, Cloves 1,376, Copra 65; Total (incl. others) 7,048. Source: Direction des Douanes des Comores.

Principal Trading Partners (million French francs): *Imports:* People's Republic of China 4.0, France 33.6, Kenya and Tanzania 7.6, Madagascar 16.1, Pakistan 6.8; Total (incl. others) 81.1. *Exports:* France 28.8, Federal Republic of Germany 1.5, Madagascar 2.2, USA 9.4; Total (incl. others) 44.0.

TRANSPORT

Road Traffic (1977): 3,600 motor vehicles in use.

Shipping (international sea-borne freight traffic, estimates in '000 metric tons, 1983): Goods loaded 11; Goods unloaded 90. Source: UN, *Monthly Bulletin of Statistics*.

Civil Aviation (1973): 15,227 passenger arrivals, 15,674 passenger departures, 909 tons of freight handled.

COMMUNICATIONS MEDIA

Radio receivers (1983): 54,000 in use.

EDUCATION

Primary (1980): 236 schools; 1,292 teachers; 59,709 pupils.

Secondary (1980): 449 teachers (general education 432; teacher training 8; vocational 9); 13,798 pupils (general education 13,528; teacher training 119; vocational 151).

Directory

The Constitution

The Constitution of the Federal Islamic Republic of the Comoros was approved by popular referendum on 1 October 1978. Several amendments were made in October 1982 and in January 1985. It is not in effect on the island of Mayotte (q.v.), which it envisages as eventually 'rejoining the Comoran community'.

GENERAL PRINCIPLES

The preamble affirms the will of the Comoran people to derive from the state religion, Islam, inspiration for the regulation of government, to adhere to the principles laid down by the Charters of the UN and the OAU, and to guarantee the rights of citizens in accordance with the UN Declaration of Human Rights. Sovereignty resides in the people, through their elected representatives. All citizens are equal before the law.

ISLAND AND FEDERAL INSTITUTIONS

The Comoros archipelago constitutes a Federal Islamic Republic. Each island has autonomy in matters not assigned by the Constitution to the federal institutions, which comprise the Presidency and Council of Government, the Federal Assembly, and the Supreme Court. There is universal secret suffrage for all citizens over 18 in full possession of their civil and political rights. The number of political parties may be regulated by federal law.

The President of the Republic is Head of State and Head of Government and is elected for six years by direct suffrage, and may not serve for more than two terms. He nominates ministers to form the Council of Government. The Governor of each island is nominated by the President of the Republic for five years, and appoints not more than four Commissioners to whom administration is delegated. Should the Presidency fall vacant, the President of the Supreme Court temporarily assumes the office until a presidential election takes place.

The Federal Assembly is directly elected for five years. Each electoral ward elects one deputy. The Assembly meets for not more than 45 days at a time, in April and October and if necessary in extraordinary sessions. Matters covered by federal legislation include defence, posts and telecommunications, external and inter-island transport, civil, penal and industrial law, external trade, federal taxation, long-term economic planning, education and health.

The Council of each island is directly elected for four years. Each electoral ward elects one councillor. Each Council meets for not more than 15 days at a time, in March and December and if necessary in extraordinary sessions. The Councils are responsible for non-federal legislation.

THE JUDICIARY

The judiciary is independent of the legislative and executive powers. The Supreme Court acts as a Constitutional Council in resolving constitutional questions and supervising presidential elections, and as High Court of Justice it arbitrates in any case where the government is accused of malpractice.

The Government

HEAD OF STATE

President and Head of Government: AHMED ABDALLAH ABDEREMANE (elected 22 October 1978; re-elected 30 September 1984).

COUNCIL OF MINISTERS
(November 1986)

Minister of Foreign Affairs, Foreign Trade and Co-operation: SAÏD KAFE.
Minister of the Interior, Information and Broadcasting: OMAR TAMOU.
Minister of Finance, Budget, Economy, Trade, Management of State Companies and Commercial and Industrial Public Organizations: SAÏD AHMED SAÏD ALI.
Minister of Planning, Construction, Environment, Urban Development and Housing: MIKIDACHE ABDEL-RAHIM.
Minister of National Education, Culture, Youth and Sports: SALIM IDAROUSSE.
Minister of Production, Rural Development, Industry and Crafts: MOHAMMED ALI.
Minister of Justice, Public Administration, Employment and Professional Training: Dr BEN ALI BACAR.
Minister of Public Health and Population: ALI HASSAN ALI.

Secretaries of State
Secretary of State for the Interior: ABDEL-AZIZ HAMADI.
Secretary of State for Transport and Tourism: ATHOUMANE ABDOU.
Secretary of State for Posts and Telecommunications: AHMED BEN DAOUD.

MINISTRIES

Office of the Head of Government: BP 421, Moroni; tel. 2413; telex 233.
Ministry of Agricultural Production and Small Manufacturing: BP 41, Moroni; tel. 2292; telex 240.
Ministry of the Civil Service, Labour and Employment: BP 109, Moroni; tel. 2098; telex 219.
Ministry of Defence: BP 246, Moroni; tel. 2646; telex 233.
Ministry of Finance and Economy: BP 324, Moroni; tel. 2767; telex 219.
Ministry of Foreign Affairs and Foreign Trade: BP 428, Moroni; tel. 2306; telex 219.
Ministry of Justice and Information: BP 520, Moroni; tel. 2411; telex 219.
Ministry of National Education, Culture, Youth and Sports: BP 446, Moroni; tel. 2420; telex 229.
Ministry of Posts and Telecommunications: Moroni; tel. 2343.
Ministry of Public Health: BP 42, Moroni; tel. 2277; telex 219.
Ministry of Transport and Tourism: Moroni; tel. 2098; telex 244.

Legislature

ASSEMBLÉE FÉDÉRALE

Elections for a Federal Assembly of 38 members were held in two stages, on 7 and 14 March 1982. All candidates stood on a non-party basis.
President: MOHAMED TAKI ABDULKARIM.

Political Organizations

During Ali Soilih's presidency, political parties ceased to play an active role, though still legally in existence. The 1978 Constitution provided for the free activity of political parties, but in January 1979 the Federal Assembly voted for the establishment of a one-party system for the following 12 years. The **Union comorienne pour le progrès (Udzima)** became the sole legal party in February 1982.

Various unofficial opposition groups continue to exist, mostly based in France. These include **FNUK-UNIKOM** (f. from the merger of the Front national uni des komores and the Union des komoriens), led by ABUBAKAR AHMED NURDIN; the **Comité national de salut public**, led by SAÏD ALI KEMAL; the **Union pour une République Démocratique des Comores (URDC)**, led by MOUZAOIR ABDALLAH; and the **Association des stagiaires et des étudiants comoriens.** An opposition group known as the **Front démocratique (FD)**, led by MUSTAPHA SAÏD CHEIKH, is active within the Comoros.

THE COMOROS

Diplomatic Representation

EMBASSIES IN THE COMOROS

China, People's Republic: Moroni; tel. 2721; Ambassador: LIU QINGYOU.

France: blvd de Strasbourg, BP 465, Moroni; tel. 73-07-53; telex 220; Ambassador: ALAIN DESCHAMPS.

USA: Moroni; Ambassador: FERNANDO E. RONDON.

Judicial System

The Supreme Court consists of two members chosen by the President of the Republic, two elected by the Federal Assembly, one by the Council of each island, and former Presidents of the Republic; Pres. HARIBOU CHEBANI.

Religion

The majority of the population are Muslims. There are an estimated 2,000 adherents of the Roman Catholic Church.

CHRISTIANITY
The Roman Catholic Church

Apostolic Administrator of the Comoros: (vacant), BP 46, Moroni; tel. 2270.

The Press

NEWS AGENCY

Agence Comores Presse (ACP): Moroni.

Foreign Bureau

Agence France-Presse (AFP): c/o Radio-Comoros, BP 250, Moroni; tel. 2261; telex 241; Rep. ALI SOILIH.

Radio and Television

In 1983 there were an estimated 54,000 radio receivers in use. In 1986 France announced that it would be funding the construction of a television station.

Radio-Comoros: BP 250, Moroni; tel. 2261; telex 241; govt-controlled since 1975; home service in Comoran and French; international services in Arabic, French, English, Malagasy and Swahili; Tech. Dir KOMBO SOULAIMANA.

Finance

BANKING

(cap. = capital; m. = million; amounts in Comoros francs)

Central Bank

Banque Centrale des Comores: BP 405, Moroni; tel. 2101; telex 215; f. 1981; bank of issue; cap. 500m.; Pres. AHMED DAHALANI; Dir-Gen. MOHAMED HALIFA.

Other Banks

Banque de Développement des Comores: BP 298, place de France, Moroni; tel. 73-08-18; telex 246; f. 1982; provides loans, guarantees and equity participation for small and medium-scale projects; Banque Centrale des Comores and Comoran govt hold two-thirds of shares, European Investment Bank and Caisse Centrale de Coopération Economique (France) each own one-sixth; cap. 300m. (Dec. 1983); Dir-Gen. CAABI ELYACHROUTU.

Banque Internationale des Comores (BIC): BP 1009, Place de France, Moroni; tel. 2543; telex 242; subsidiary of Banque Internationale pour l'Afrique Occidentale; cap. 300m. (Dec. 1983); Dir-Gen. NICOLAS SEGUIN DE BROIN.

BIC Afribank: Moroni; telex 274.

Trade and Industry

CEFADER: a rural design, co-ordination and support centre, with branches on each island.

Chambre de Commerce, d'Industrie et d'Agriculture: BP 66, Moroni.

Mission Permanente de Coopération: Moroni; centre for administering bilateral aid from France; Dir GABRIEL COURCELLE.

Office National du Commerce: Moroni, Njazidja; Chair. SAÏD MOHAMED DJOHAR.

Société de développement de la pêche artisanale des Comores (SODEPAC): state-run agency overseeing fisheries development programme.

TRADE UNION

Union des Travailleurs des Comores: BP 405, Moroni.

Transport

RAILWAYS

There are no railways in the Comoros.

ROADS

There are approximately 750 km of roads serviceable throughout the year, of which 398 km are paved. A major road-improvement scheme was launched in 1979, with foreign assistance, and in 1984 a French company won the contract to resurface 170 km of roads on Njazidja and Nzwani islands.

SHIPPING

Large vessels anchor off Moroni, Mutsamudu and Fomboni, and the port of Mutsamudu can now accommodate vessels of up to 11 m draught. The Government is planning to develop Moroni port and was seeking financial aid for the project in 1986. Goods from Europe come via Madagascar, and coasters serve the Comoros from the east coast of Africa.

Société Comorienne de Navigation: Moroni; services to Madagascar.

CIVIL AVIATION

The international airport is at Moroni-Hahaya on Njazidja and each of the three other islands has a small airfield.

Air Comores (Sociéte Nationale des Transports Aériens): BP 544 Moroni; telex 218; f. 1975; state-owned; services to Nzwani, Mwali and Dzaoudzi; Gen. Man. DJAMALEDDINE AHMED; fleet of 1 Boeing 737 and 1 Fokker F27.

Tourism

Fewer than 2,000 tourists a year stay in the islands' four hotels, owing to limited accommodation, few flights to the islands and their political and commercial isolation. In 1981 the Government was studying projects aimed at increasing hotel capacity from 87 to 166 rooms, which included the construction of a new hotel in Moroni. In July 1986 South African developers initiated plans to refurbish existing hotels and to construct three new ones, and thus provide an infrastructure for tourism in the Comoros.

Société Comorienne de Tourisme et d'Hôtellerie (COMOTEL): Itsandra Hotel Njazidja; tel. 2365; national tourist agency.

THE CONGO

Introductory Survey

Location, Climate, Language, Religion, Flag, Capital

The People's Republic of the Congo is an equatorial country on the west coast of Africa. It has a coastline of about 170 km on the Atlantic Ocean, from which the country extends northward to Cameroon and the Central African Republic. It is bordered by Gabon in the west, with Zaire to the east, while in the south there is a short frontier with the Cabinda exclave of Angola. The climate is tropical, with temperatures averaging 21°–27°C (70°–80°F) throughout the year. The average annual rainfall is about 1,200 mm (47 in). The official language is French, and many African languages are also used. More than 50% of the population follow traditional beliefs, although over 30% are Roman Catholics. There are small Protestant and Muslim minorities. The national flag is red, with the state emblem (two green palms enclosing a crossed hammer and hoe, surmounted by a gold star) in the upper hoist. The capital is Brazzaville.

Recent History

Formerly part of French Equatorial Africa, Middle Congo became the autonomous Republic of the Congo, within the French Community, in November 1958. The Congo became fully independent on 15 August 1960. The leading figure in this period was the Abbé Fulbert Youlou, a former Roman Catholic priest who, in contravention of ecclesiastical orders, became involved in politics and was suspended from priestly office. In November 1958 Youlou became Prime Minister, and in November 1959 he was elected President of the Republic by the National Assembly. After independence, the Assembly approved a new constitution for the Congo in March 1961. Under its provisions, Youlou was re-elected President (unopposed) by popular vote. Proposals to establish a one-party state were announced by President Youlou in August 1962 and overwhelmingly approved by the National Assembly in April 1963.

However, on 15 August 1963 (the third anniversary of independence and the date scheduled for the introduction of one-party rule) Youlou was forced to resign, following anti-Government demonstrations and strikes by trade unionists. On the following day, a provisional government was formed, with the support of military and trade union leaders. Alphonse Massamba-Débat, a former Minister of Planning, became Prime Minister. In December a national referendum approved a new constitution, and a general election was held for a new National Assembly. Later in the month, Massamba-Débat was elected President for a five-year term. The new regime adopted a policy of 'scientific socialism', and in July 1964 the Mouvement national de la révolution (MNR) was established as the sole political party. In June 1965 ex-President Youlou was sentenced to death *in absentia*.

Tension between the armed forces and the MNR culminated in a military coup in August 1968. The leader of the coup was Capt. (later Major) Marien Ngouabi, a paratroop officer, who became Chief of the General Staff. The National Assembly was replaced by the National Council of the Revolution, led by Ngouabi. The President was briefly restored to office, with reduced powers, but was dismissed again in September, when Capt. (later Major) Alfred Raoul, the new Prime Minister, also became Head of State, a position that he relinquished in January 1969 to Major Ngouabi, while remaining Prime Minister until the end of that year.

Ngouabi set up a regime which proclaimed itself Marxist but maintained close economic ties with France. The People's Republic of the Congo, as it became in January 1970, was governed by a single political party, the Parti congolais du travail (PCT). The regime was threatened by left-wing protests and attempted coups, and there were serious ethnic jealousies between the rival tribes. In 1973 Ngouabi introduced a new constitution and a National Assembly with delegates elected from a single party list. However, Ngouabi felt increasingly insecure, and in 1976 he dismissed the Political Bureau of the PCT, replacing it by a Special Revolutionary General Staff.

In March 1977 Ngouabi was assassinated. Ex-President Massamba-Débat was charged with organizing the attempted coup and later executed. The Government was taken over by an 11-member Military Committee of the PCT, and in April 1977 Col (later Brig.-Gen.) Joachim Yhombi-Opango, the Chief of Staff, was named as the new Head of State.

The worsening economic crisis and the inherited regional and ethnic imbalances, however, made Yhombi-Opango's regime vulnerable to both left and right. In April 1977 he abrogated the Constitution and suspended the National Assembly. In August 1978 a plot to overthrow the Government was reported. In February 1979 Yhombi-Opango and the Military Committee handed over their powers to the Central Committee of the PCT. Following an election in March, Col Denis Sassou-Nguesso became President of the Republic, having assumed power in the interim month as head of a Provisional Committee. In July a National Assembly and regional councils were also elected, and the new socialist Constitution was overwhelmingly approved in a referendum. At the Third PCT Congress in July 1984, Sassou-Nguesso was unanimously re-elected President of the PCT Central Committee and President of the Republic for a second five-year term. Under the provisions of a constitutional change, the President of the Central Committee also became Head of Government. An extensive government reshuffle followed in August, with the aim of 'strengthening the revolutionary process'. Ange-Edouard Poungui, a former Vice-President, became Prime Minister in succession to Col Louis Sylvain Goma, who had held the post since December 1975. Sassou-Nguesso assumed control of the Ministry of Defence and Security. Ex-President Yhombi-Opango, who had been detained since March 1979, was released in November 1984.

Economic decline continued, and in November 1985 the introduction of austerity measures into the system of awarding grants to students resulted in violent demonstrations in Brazzaville, during which three people were reported to have been killed. Several students were arrested. In December, following a reorganization of the secretariat of the PCT Central Committee, a further government reshuffle took place, with the number of portfolios being reduced from 27 to 22 in an attempt to improve administrative efficiency. In August 1986 10 people went on trial before the Revolutionary Court of Justice in Brazzaville, accused of complicity in bomb attacks in the capital in 1982, during which nine people died. The accused included Claude Ernest Ndalla, a former Minister of Education who was condemned to death, and Jean-Pierre Thystère-Tchicaya, a member of the PCT Central Committee's Politburo at the time of his arrest in 1984. In November 1986 the membership of the Politburo was reduced from 13 to 10, and that of the secretariat of the PCT Central Committee from 10 to eight; in December the Council of Ministers was reshuffled, and the number of portfolios further reduced, to 19.

In foreign policy, the Congo has moved away from being within the Soviet sphere of influence, as was apparent in the mid-1970s, and has fostered links with France, the USA and the People's Republic of China. There was an improvement in relations with France following the victory of the French left in the 1981 elections, and President Mitterrand paid an official visit to the Congo in October 1982. Western nations, particularly France, remain the chief source of development aid, but some Eastern bloc aid is received in the form of military and security assistance. The Congo is committed to the survival of the OAU (see p. 186), of which President Sassou-Nguesso was elected chairman in 1986, and is a member of the Customs and Economic Union of Central Africa (UDEAC) (see p. 155).

Government

There is only one political party, the Parti congolais du travail (PCT), which professes Marxist-Leninist principles. The Presi-

THE CONGO

dent of the Central Committee of the PCT is the President of the Republic, Head of State and Head of Government, elected for a five-year term by the Congress of the PCT, which also elects the 75-member Central Committee. To direct its policy, the Central Committee elects a Politburo, which comprised 10 members in December 1986. The senior executive body of the PCT is the Secretariat of the Central Committee, with eight members in December 1986. Supreme executive power rests with the Council of Ministers, under the chairmanship of the President of the Republic. The main legislative body is the People's National Assembly, which was re-established in 1979. The 153 members are elected by universal adult suffrage from a list proposed by the PCT. The Assembly is responsible to the Prime Minister, himself responsible to the PCT.

Responsibility for local administration is vested in nine Popular Regional Councils, each with an Executive Committee elected by universal franchise. They act under the direction of 10 Commissars designated by the Central Committee of the PCT.

Defence

In July 1986 the army numbered 8,700, the navy 200 and the air force 500. There were 6,100 men in paramilitary forces, and 500 Cuban troops were stationed in the country. National service is voluntary for men and women, and lasts for two years. The defence budget for 1985 was 25,000m. francs CFA.

Economic Affairs

Prior to the development of the petroleum industry, the most important economic activity was forestry, which, together with agriculture, engaged an estimated 62% of the labour force in 1980. Forests cover approximately 60% of the country's area, and more than half is exploitable. Reserves of timber are estimated to be between 90m. and 120m. cu m, with a production capacity of 850,000 cu m per year. Species include okoumé and limba. In 1978 major eucalyptus plantations were installed, and plans have been announced for a wood-pulp plant near Pointe-Noire, at a cost of 60,000m. francs CFA. Poor transport facilities have greatly hindered the development of forestry production. As a result of the decline in world demand for timber in the early 1970s, production of industrial logs, which totalled 837,000 cu m in 1971, had virtually ceased by 1975. The market began to recover in 1976, as a result of public investment, both in reafforestation and in research, but in 1983 exports amounted to only 363,000 cu m. In 1984 timber production was 586,736 cu m. The state-owned timber monopoly, Société Nationale d'Exploitation des Bois, incurred financial losses totalling 81.4m. francs CFA in 1982, largely owing to stagnation in world timber prices.

As a result of the rapid rise in earnings from petroleum, the agricultural sector's share of gross domestic product (GDP) declined during the early 1980s. Agriculture, forestry and fishing contributed 16.7% of total GDP in 1978, but the proportion had fallen to 7% by 1984. The staple crops are cassava and plantains, while maize, groundnuts and rice are also cultivated. The major cash crops are sugar cane, oil palm, cocoa and coffee. Sugar development has been taken over by a Franco-Dutch concern, and the annual output of raw sugar rose to 31,000 metric tons in 1984, from a low of 21,000 tons in 1983. Production of palm oil declined during the early 1980s, totalling only 1,093 tons in 1984 (compared with 2,460 tons in 1982), but was expected to improve as a result of the implementation of development projects in the Ouesso region, which commenced in 1986. Cocoa is cultivated on 8,000 ha in the north-west Sangha region, and production of cocoa beans in 1984 was estimated at 2,000 tons. Coffee production totalled an estimated 3,000 tons in 1984. Cultivation of tobacco, once a major cash crop, has dwindled as a result of the drift of producers into more profitable crops. The Government is undertaking extensive development and plantation projects to revive production of palm oil, coffee and cocoa, following a general decline in agricultural production since independence: in 1984 the Congo imported 75% of its food requirements, at an estimated cost of 46,000m. francs CFA.

Since 1960, when the Congo's first oilfield, at Pointe-Indienne, went into production, petroleum has been the driving force behind the country's economy, contributing between 60% and 70% of revenue to the national budget during the early 1980s

Introductory Survey

and providing more than 90% of export earnings. The sector experienced a particularly rapid growth over this period, due to a high level of investment and increasing exports. By 1983 there were seven oilfields in operation, and annual production of crude petroleum had risen to 5.4m. tons, compared with only 2.6m. tons in 1979. However, reserves in almost all the major fields were by then declining, and further exploration was being carried out on and off shore. Annual output reached a peak of 6m. tons in 1984, before slackening in 1985 to 5.8m. tons. Production at the new Tchibouela field, which has estimated reserves of 12m. tons, was due to begin in late 1986, and total annual petroleum output was expected to stabilize at around 6m. tons in 1986 and 1987. There are reserves of 600m. tons in the largest field, Emeraude: their heavy viscous nature would, however, necessitate expensive methods of extraction, which are not considered to be viable. The operative oil companies are mainly French and Italian, and interest has been shown by US oil corporations, with Conoco taking over a second offshore concession in May 1985, following Amoco's contract in 1984. The Congo is not a member of OPEC. A refinery at Pointe-Noire, with an annual distillation capacity of 1m. tons, began production in 1982, to handle 25% of national output, producing heavy fuel oil, kerosene and motor spirit. There are deposits of natural gas at Pointe-Indienne, where production was 1.4m. cu m in 1979, but remaining reserves are not large enough to warrant commercial exploitation.

Recent fluctuations in the price of petroleum, and in particular the collapse of world oil prices in early 1986 as a result of continuing high OPEC production levels, have made the Government adopt a flexible approach to planned spending. In recent years development planning has been concentrated on improving the transport infrastructure, to enable forest potential to be exploited, increasing food production, and halting the increasing rural exodus. An intensive programme of structural adjustment measures was commenced in 1985, and the 1986/87 development plan sought to concentrate on the diversification of production, both of food for the domestic market and of goods for export. The decline in export revenue from oil meant that agricultural development was to take place at the expense of some existing industrial projects. The revised 1986 budget allocated only 259,484m. francs CFA to public expenditure, compared with 449,000m. francs CFA in 1985. In order to ease the burden of debt service, which in recent years has accounted for around 40% of the Congo's foreign earnings, US $500m. of the public external debt (estimated to total $1,396m. at the end of 1984) was rescheduled at a July 1986 meeting of the 'Paris Club' of Western creditor governments, following the conclusion of a SDR 22.4m. stand-by agreement with the IMF. Since independence, economic growth has been closely linked with the performance of the petroleum sector. During the late 1960s the expansion of real GDP averaged only 2.6% annually, despite a high rate of investment. Following a period of stagnation, GDP growth in 1973–84 increased to an annual average of 8.1%, mainly as a result of increased petroleum production and higher prices.

In 1984, according to World Bank estimates, the Congo's GNP per head was US $1,140 (at average 1982–84 prices), one of the highest levels in sub-Saharan Africa. It was estimated that the average annual increase in GNP per head was 3.7%, in real terms, between 1965 and 1984.

Social Welfare

There is a state pension scheme and a system of family allowances and other welfare services. The health system consists of three general hospitals, 31 medical centres, 419 dispensaries, 98 infirmaries and seven centres for contagious diseases, giving a total of 7,048 hospital beds. Plans were announced in 1986 for the construction of a new hospital at Loubomo, in the Niari region. In 1981 there were 266 physicians and 849 qualified nurses working in the Congo.

Education

Education is officially compulsory for 10 years between six and 16 years of age. Primary education begins at the age of six and lasts for six years. Secondary education, from 12 years of age, last for seven years, comprising a first cycle of four years and a second of three years. In 1985, according to estimates by UNESCO, the average rate of adult illiteracy was 37.1% (males

28.6%, females 44.6%, one of the lowest in Africa. In 1965 all private schools were taken over by the Government. A number of students go to France for technical instruction. The Marien Ngouabi University, at Brazzaville, was founded in 1971.

Tourism

There were 558 hotel rooms in 1981 but provision was made in the 1982–86 development plan to increase this to 1,000 rooms. Brazzaville has three international hotels, but there is a shortage of accommodation in Pointe-Noire, where the oil and business sectors have increased demand. A regional hotel chain is to be set up to cater for travellers in the provinces. There are plans to turn Mbamou Island into a tourist attraction. There were 62,000 tourist arrivals in 1981, when tourist receipts totalled US $13m.

Public Holidays

1987: 1 January (New Year's Day), 18 March ('Day of Supreme Sacrifice', anniversary of President Ngouabi's assassination), 17 April (Good Friday), 20 April (Easter Monday), 1 May (Labour Day), 31 July (Revolution Day), 15 August (Independence Day), 25 December (Christmas), 31 December (Foundation of the Party).

1988: 1 January (New Year's Day), 18 March ('Day of Supreme Sacrifice', anniversary of President Ngouabi's assassination), 1 April (Good Friday), 4 April (Easter Monday), 1 May (Labour Day), 31 July (Revolution Day), 15 August (Independence Day), 25 December (Christmas), 31 December (Foundation of the Party).

Weights and Measures

The metric system is in force.

Currency and Exchange Rates

100 centimes = 1 franc de la Coopération financière en Afrique centrale (CFA).

Exchange rates (30 September 1986):
 1 franc CFA = 2 French centimes;
 £1 sterling = 480.625 francs CFA;
 US $1 = 332.125 francs CFA.

Statistical Survey

Source (unless otherwise stated): Centre National de la Statistique et des Etudes Economiques, Ministère du Plan, BP 2031, Brazzaville; tel. 81-43-24; telex 5210.

Area and Population

AREA, POPULATION AND DENSITY

Area (sq km)	342,000*
Population (census results)	
7 February 1974	1,319,790
1985	1,912,429
Density (per sq km) at census of 1985	5.6

* 132,047 sq miles.

REGIONS (estimated population at 1 January 1983)*

Brazzaville	456,383	Kouilou	78,738
Pool	219,329	Lékoumou	67,568
Pointe-Noire	214,466	Sangha	42,106
Bouenza	135,999	Nkayi	40,419
Cuvette	127,558	Likouala	34,302
Niari	114,229	Loubomo	33,591
Plateaux	110,379	**Total**	**1,675,067**

* Figures have not been revised to take account of the 1985 census results.

PRINCIPAL TOWNS (population at 1974 census)

Brazzaville (capital)	302,459	Loubomo (Dolisie)	28,577
Pointe-Noire	140,367	Ngamaba-Mfilou	18,944
Nkayi (Jacob)	28,957	Loandjili	15,738
		Mossendjo	11,913

1980 estimates: Brazzaville 422,400; Pointe-Noire 185,110; Nkayi 32,520; Loubomo 30,830.

BIRTHS AND DEATHS

Average annual birth rate 45.4 per 1,000 in 1970–75, 44.7 per 1,000 in 1975–80; death rate 21.7 per 1,000 in 1970–75, 20.1 per 1,000 in 1975–80 (UN estimates).

ECONOMICALLY ACTIVE POPULATION
(ILO estimates, '000 persons at mid-1980)

	Males	Females	Total
Agriculture, etc.	181	224	405
Industry	73	4	77
Services	136	30	166
Total	**390**	**258**	**649**

Source: ILO, *Economically Active Population Estimates and Projections, 1950–2025.*

Agriculture

PRINCIPAL CROPS (FAO estimates, '000 metric tons)

	1982	1983	1984
Maize	6*	7	7
Rice (paddy)	2	2	2
Sugar cane	320	250	250
Potatoes	2	2	2
Sweet potatoes	13	13	13
Cassava (Manioc)	650	600	600
Yams	14	14	14
Other roots and tubers	21	22	22
Dry beans	4	4	4
Dry peas	3	3	3
Tomatoes	8	9	9
Other vegetables	26	27	27
Avocados	19	20	20
Pineapples	104	105	105
Bananas	32	32	32
Plantains	60	62	62
Palm kernels	0.5	0.5	0.5
Groundnuts (in shell)	15	15	15
Coffee (green)	2*	3	3
Cocoa beans	2*	2*	2*
Natural rubber	2	2	2

* Unofficial figure.
Source: FAO, *Production Yearbook.*

LIVESTOCK
(FAO estimates, '000 head, year ending September)

	1982	1983	1984
Cattle	67	68	68
Pigs	37	40	42
Sheep	60	60	60
Goats	179	180	182

Poultry: 1,183,000 (FAO estimate) in 1982.
Source: FAO, *Production Yearbook.*

LIVESTOCK PRODUCTS
(FAO estimates, '000 metric tons)

	1982	1983	1984
Beef and veal	2	2	3
Pig meat	2	2	2
Poultry meat	5	5	5
Other meat	5	6	5
Cows' milk	3	3	3
Hen eggs	0.9	0.9	1.0

Source: FAO, *Production Yearbook.*

Forestry

ROUNDWOOD REMOVALS
('000 cubic metres, excluding bark)

	1982	1983	1984
Sawlogs, veneer logs and logs for sleepers	517	514	587
Other industrial wood*	208	213	219
Fuel wood	1,467	1,511	1,551
Total	2,192	2,238	2,357

* FAO estimates.
Source: FAO, *Yearbook of Forest Products*.

SAWNWOOD PRODUCTION
('000 cubic metres)

	1982	1983	1984
Total (incl. boxboards)	66	65	60

Fishing

('000 metric tons, live weight)

	1982	1983	1984
Inland waters	12.0	12.0	12.0
Atlantic Ocean	17.9	19.9	19.3
Total catch	29.9	31.9	31.3

Source: FAO, *Yearbook of Fishery Statistics*.

Mining

	1981	1982	1983
Crude petroleum ('000 metric tons)	4,124	4,481	5,365
Natural gas (terajoules)	100	n.a.	n.a.
Copper ore ('000 metric tons)*	6.3	3.4	3.9
Gold (kg.)	2	3	8
Lead concentrates ('000 metric tons)*	2.3	1.2	1.4
Zinc concentrates ('000 metric tons)*	4.5	2.4	2.8

Crude petroleum ('000 metric tons): 6,007 in 1984; 5,826 in 1985.
* Figures refer to the metal content of ores and concentrates.

Industry

SELECTED PRODUCTS

		1983	1984	1985
Palm oil	'000 metric tons	2	1	1
Wheat flour	'000 metric tons	8	3	n.a.
Raw sugar	'000 metric tons	21	39	46
Beer	'000 hectolitres	788	906	882
Soft drinks	'000 hectolitres	278	279	n.a.
Cigarettes	metric tons	895	903	1,027
Veneer sheets	'000 cu metres	74	65	n.a.
Soap	metric tons	5,100	5,500	1,900
Cement	'000 metric tons	29	n.a.	62
Electricity	million kWh	233	253	n.a.
Footwear	'000 pairs	928	995	1,128

THE CONGO

Statistical Survey

Finance

CURRENCY AND EXCHANGE RATES

Monetary Units
100 centimes = 1 franc de la Coopération financière en Afrique centrale (CFA).

Denominations
Coins: 1, 2, 5, 10, 25, 50 and 100 francs CFA.
Notes: 100, 500, 1,000, 5,000 and 10,000 francs CFA.

French Franc, Sterling and Dollar Equivalents
(30 September 1986)
1 French franc = 50 francs CFA;
£1 sterling = 480.625 francs CFA;
US $1 = 332.125 francs CFA;
1,000 francs CFA = £2.081 = $3.011.

Average Exchange Rate (francs CFA per US $)
1983   381.06
1984   436.96
1985   449.26

BUDGET (million francs CFA)

Revenue	1981	1982	1983
Tax receipts	121,546	159,460	219,915
Income tax and domestic taxes	19,589	32,800	55,915
Tax on oil companies	80,498	97,660	124,000
Customs duty	21,459	29,000	40,000
Income from property and services	44,238	54,040	84,085
Property income	192	471	1,684
Petroleum revenue	42,653	52,340	80,000
Services	1,393	1,229	2,401
Total	165,784	213,500	304,000

Expenditure	1981	1982	1983
Personnel	43,800	53,800	58,270
Material	17,000	20,600	24,355
Common services	10,400	13,100	13,139
Public debt	28,200	49,300	97,019
Transfers	66,500	76,700	111,216
Investment budget	45,100	50,000	n.a.
Total	165,800	213,500	304,000

Source: Centre National de la Statistique et des Etudes Economiques, Brazzaville.

1984: Revised budget balanced at 368,200m. francs CFA (recurrent budget 253,000m. francs CFA; investment budget 115,000m. francs CFA).
1985: Revised budget estimate 449,000m. francs CFA (recurrent budget 324,000m. francs CFA; investment budget 125,000m. francs CFA).
1986: Revised budget estimate 259,484m. francs CFA (recurrent budget 192,400m. francs CFA; investment budget 67,084m. francs CFA).

CENTRAL BANK RESERVES
(US $ million at 31 December)

	1982	1983	1984
Gold*	5.00	4.21	3.44
IMF special drawing rights	1.06	0.22	2.09
Reserve position in IMF	3.64	3.12	0.47
Foreign exchange	32.32	4.02	1.56
Total	42.02	11.57	7.55

* Valued at market-related prices.
Source: IMF, *International Financial Statistics*.

1982–86 DEVELOPMENT PLAN
(proposed expenditure in million francs CFA)

Primary sector	
Stockraising and agriculture	73,420
Marine fishing	7,450
Water, forestry and freshwater fishing	194,830
Mining and power	132,050
Secondary sector	
Industry	95,550
Public works and construction	195,360
Tertiary sector	
Presidency and ministries	120,310
Transport	138,780
Trade	20,330
Information, posts and telecommunications	36,530
Social services and health	28,040
Education	22,660
Tourism	11,900
Culture	5,880
Miscellaneous	25,820
Total	1,108,900

MONEY SUPPLY ('000 million francs CFA at 31 December)

	1982	1983	1984
Currency outside banks	43.20	42.92	43.68
Demand deposits at commercial and development banks	51.82	43.93	52.59
Checking deposits at post office	2.59	3.65	5.07
Total money	97.60	90.50	101.34

Source: IMF, *International Financial Statistics*.

NATIONAL ACCOUNTS
(million francs CFA at current prices)
National Income and Product*

	1978	1980	1981
Compensation of employees	83,024	119,568	158,649
Operating surplus	46,884	142,561	232,507
Domestic factor incomes	129,908	262,129	391,156
Consumption of fixed capital	36,464	41,191	60,391
Gross domestic product (GDP) at factor cost	166,372	303,320	451,547
Indirect taxes	32,223	60,164	96,916
Less Subsidies	282	3,087	6,757
GDP in purchasers' values	198,313	360,397	541,706
Factor income from abroad	770	2,201	4,511
Less Factor income paid abroad	13,422	34,877	37,690
Gross national product	185,661	327,721	508,527
Less Consumption of fixed capital	36,464	41,191	60,391
National income in market prices	149,197	286,530	448,136
Other current transfers from abroad	4,970	4,193	13,054
Less Other current transfers paid abroad	4,259	19,070	16,289
National disposable income	149,908	271,653	444,901

* Data for 1979 are not available.
GDP (million francs CFA): 711,514 in 1982; 799,386 in 1983; 920,128 in 1984.

THE CONGO

Expenditure on the Gross Domestic Product*

	1978	1980	1981
Government final consumption expenditure	45,505	63,385	72,839
Private final consumption expenditure	117,888	147,924	220,622
Increase in stocks	7,934	10,157	21,057
Gross fixed capital formation	46,360	118,744	239,734
Total domestic expenditure	217,687	340,210	554,252
Exports of goods and services	78,562	203,029	314,318
Less Imports of goods and services	97,936	182,842	326,864
GDP in purchasers' values	198,313	360,397	541,706

* Data for 1979 are not available.

Gross Domestic Product by Economic Activity*

	1978	1980	1981
Agriculture and fishing	27,834	34,429	36,074
Forestry and logging	3,959	7,699	6,613
Mining and quarrying	31,937	120,980	212,807
Manufacturing	19,363	27,079	34,344
Electricity, gas and water	3,250	2,906	3,545
Construction	6,020	17,060	25,076
Trade, restaurants and hotels	28,700	35,053	60,087
Transport, storage and communications	17,699	32,781	43,865
Other marketable services	14,584	26,042	51,762
Government services	36,064	45,352	54,860
Private non-profit services to households	500	700	1,000
Sub-total	189,910	350,081	530,033
Import duties	10,427	17,494	21,959
Less Imputed bank service charge	2,024	7,178	10,286
GDP in purchasers' values	198,313	360,397	541,706

* Data for 1979 are not available.

BALANCE OF PAYMENTS (US $ million)

	1982	1983	1984
Merchandise exports f.o.b.	1,108.5	1,066.2	1,268.4
Merchandise imports f.o.b.	−663.8	−649.5	−617.6
Trade balance	444.7	416.7	650.8
Exports of services	97.2	93.2	86.8
Imports of services	−855.4	−906.7	−524.8
Balance on goods and services	−313.5	−396.8	212.8
Private unrequited transfers (net)	−47.2	−41.1	−45.0
Government unrequited transfers (net)	29.9	37.7	44.9
Current balance	−330.8	−400.2	212.8
Direct capital investment (net)	35.3	56.1	34.9
Other long-term capital (net)	413.6	118.9	66.1
Short-term capital (net)	−246.6	121.7	−236.7
Net errors and omissions	43.4	71.2	−139.8
Total (net monetary movements)	−85.0	−32.3	−62.6
Valuation changes (net)	−4.1	2.8	4.6
Exceptional financing (net)	3.4	—	54.2
Official financing (net)	−0.6	−0.1	0.6
Changes in reserves	−86.4	−29.7	−3.2

Source: IMF, *International Financial Statistics*.

External Trade

Note: Figures exclude trade with other states of the Customs and Economic Union of Central Africa (UDEAC).

PRINCIPAL COMMODITIES (million francs CFA)

Imports c.i.f.	1983	1984	1985
Machinery	68,257.4	54,452.5	62,481.4
Transport equipment	29,783.5	32,598.5	28,225.9
Petroleum products	5,672.6	9,766.1	8,290.2
Chemicals and related products	14,501.5	21,084.2	20,545.5
Textile materials and manufactures	6,724.0	10,495.1	8,648.9
Iron and steel	29,884.5	29,911.0	36,053.3
Food, beverages and tobacco	38,005.1	49,370.0	47,318.9
Plastic and rubber goods	7,548.8	7,923.8	7,046.5
Precision instruments, watches, etc.	5,606.7	6,143.3	6,307.1
Total (incl. others)	239,969.9	259,820.0	306,198.4

Source: Direction Générale des Douanes et des Droits Indirects.

Exports f.o.b.	1983	1984	1985
Petroleum and petroleum products	213,682.9	474,146.3	455,554.0
Wood	8,888.8	19,919.5	12,363.0
Diamonds	13,697.8	6,090.8	5,010.2
Coffee	1,103.8	2,548.8	952.4
Iron and steel	1,750.6	5,221.4	6,054.6
Total (incl. others)	243,719.7	516,700.0	488,365.7

THE CONGO
Statistical Survey

PRINCIPAL TRADING PARTNERS (million francs CFA)

Imports c.i.f.	1983	1984	1985
Belgium/Luxembourg	5,133	4,782	6,214
China, People's Republic	3,063	5,505	4,279
France	143,637	136,793	118,797
Germany, Fed. Republic	10,853	15,412	12,176
Italy	9,353	7,778	21,567
Japan	8,001	9,480	8,917
Netherlands	6,186	5,827	7,010
Spain	4,456	8,639	11,495
USA	19,106	14,819	17,267
Total (incl. others)	239,970	259,820	306,198

Exports f.o.b.	1983	1984	1985
Belgium/Luxembourg	12,195	12,265	5,140
France	2,808	5,919	53,262
Germany, Fed. Republic	1,659	2,523	1,322
Italy	31,197	8,409	8,955
Netherlands	2,848	11,011	29,562
Spain	8,084	9,526	67,762
USA	176,032	400,780	293,112
Total (incl. others)	243,720	516,700	488,366

Transport

RAILWAYS (traffic)

	1981	1982	1983
Passenger-km (million)	358	390	381
Freight ton-km (million)	546*	511*	437

* Including service traffic and passengers' baggage.

ROAD TRAFFIC ('000 motor vehicles in use)

	1980	1981	1982
Passenger cars	45.4	49.0	30.5
Commercial vehicles	38.6	60.0	78.6

Source: Régie Nationale des Transports et des Travaux Publics.

INLAND WATERWAYS (freight traffic in '000 metric tons)

Port of Brazzaville	1981	1982	1983
Goods loaded	76.0	88.5	86.6
Goods unloaded	485.9	432.4	457.2

INTERNATIONAL SEA-BORNE SHIPPING

Port of Pointe-Noire	1981	1982	1983
Vessels entered ('000 net registered tons)	5,936	6,671	6,686
Goods loaded ('000 metric tons)	6,205	6,364	7,656
Goods unloaded ('000 metric tons)	826	896	547

CIVIL AVIATION (traffic on scheduled services)*

	1980	1981	1982
Kilometres flown (million)	2.9	3.1	3.0
Passengers carried ('000)	117	154	161
Passenger-km (million)	197	229	247
Freight ton-km (million)	18.5	21.4	21.7

* Including an apportionment of the traffic of Air Afrique.
Source: UN, *Statistical Yearbook*.

Communications Media

	1979	1980	1981
Radio receivers ('000 in use)	92	93	98
Television receivers ('000 in use)	3.3	3.5	3.7
Telephones ('000 in use)	14	n.a.	17
Daily newspapers	3	n.a.	n.a.

1982: Radio receivers 102,000; television receivers 4,000; daily newspapers 1; non-daily newspapers 2.
1983: Radio receivers 100,000; television receivers 4,500.
Sources: UNESCO, *Statistical Yearbook*; UN, *Statistical Yearbook*.

Education

(1982)

	Institutions	Pupils	Teachers
Pre-primary	42	4,567	482
Primary	1,428	422,874	7,329
Secondary:			
General	n.a.	189,831	3,996
Teacher-training*	n.a.	1,938	187
Vocational*	n.a.	18,806	1,261
University	n.a.	8,288*	292†

* 1981 figures. † 1980 figure.
Source: UNESCO, *Statistical Yearbook*.

Directory

The Constitution

A new constitution was approved by national referendum on 8 July 1979. The Constitution was amended in July 1984. The following is a summary of its provisions:

FUNDAMENTAL PRINCIPLES

The People's Republic of the Congo is a sovereign independent state, in which all power springs from the people and belongs to the people. Treason against the people is the greatest crime. All nationals are guaranteed freedom of conscience and religion, and religious communities are free to practise their faith, but political organizations based on religion are banned. The land is the property of the people, and as necessary the state shall regulate its use. The state directs the economic life and development of the country according to the general plan. The right to own and inherit private property is guaranteed, and expropriation is governed by law.

HEAD OF STATE

The Chairman of the Central Committee of the Parti congolais du travail (PCT) is the President of the Republic, Head of State and Head of Government. He is elected for a five-year term by the Congress of the PCT.

THE EXECUTIVE

Executive power is vested in the Council of Ministers, under the Chairmanship of the President of the Republic. It directs and orientates the action of the Government; Ministers are appointed by the Prime Minister, who is responsible to the party.

THE LEGISLATURE

Most legislative powers are vested in the People's National Assembly. It has 153 members, elected by all adults over the age of 18 from a list put out by the PCT, with representatives from the party, mass organizations (including women and students), and workers, peasants and craftsmen. It is responsible to the Prime Minister and undertakes tasks entrusted to him by the party. The President of the National Assembly is second in rank only to the President of the Republic.

THE PARTY

The sole political party is the Parti congolais du travail (PCT). Its Political Bureau of 10 members takes part in government. Its Central Committee consists of 75 members, including the Political Bureau, most of the Ministers and the Chief of Staff of the army, chaired by the President of the Republic and Head of State. The Central Committee's powers include the initiation of revisions to the constitution, which become final when approved by the National Assembly, and the appointment of judges to the Revolutionary Court of Justice.

Note: In August 1984 a Constitutional Council was established by Presidential statute, assuming powers hitherto exercised by the Constitutional Chamber of the Supreme Court.

The Government

HEAD OF STATE

President: Col DENIS SASSOU-NGUESSO (appointed President of the Provisional Committee of the PCT 8 February 1979; elected President of the Republic 31 March 1979; re-elected July 1984).

COUNCIL OF MINISTERS
(December 1986)

Prime Minister: ANGE-EDOUARD POUNGUI.
Minister of Defence and Security: Col DENIS SASSOU-NGUESSO.
Minister of Finance and Budget: JUSTIN LEKOUNDZOU ITIHI OSSETOUMBA.
Minister of Administration and Local Government: RAYMOND DAMAS-NGOLLO.
Minister of Rural Development: Col FRANÇOIS-XAVIER KATALI.
Minister of Foreign Affairs and Co-operation: ANTOINE NDINGA OBA.
Minister of Transport and Civil Aviation: HILAIRE MOUNTHAULT.
Minister of Public Works, Construction, Housing and Urban Affairs: Lt-Col BENOÎT MOUNDELE NGOLO.
Minister of Secondary and Higher Education, Culture and Arts: JEAN-BAPTISTE TATI-LOUTARD.
Minister of Economy and Planning: PIERRE MOUSSA.
Minister of Basic Education and Literacy: PIERRE-DAMIEN BASSOUKOU-BOUMBA.
Minister of Industry, Fisheries and Crafts: AMBROISE NOUMAZALAYE.
Minister of Mines and Energy: RODOLPHE ADADA.
Minister of Scientific Research and Environment: CHRISTOPHE BOURAMOUÉ.
Minister of Forestry: OSSEBI DOUNIAM.
Minister of Labour, Social Security and Justice: DIEUDONNÉ KIMBEMBE.
Minister of Tourism, Sports and Leisure: JEAN-CLAUDE GANGA.
Minister of Trade and Small and Medium Enterprises: ALPHONSE POATI.
Minister of Health and Social Affairs: BERNARD COMBO MATSIONA.
Minister of Information, Posts and Telecommunications: CHRISTIAN GILBERT BEMBERT.
Head of the President's Office: AIME EMMANUEL YOKA.

MINISTRIES

All Ministries are in Brazzaville.
Office of the President: Palais du Peuple, Brazzaville; telex 5210.
Ministry of Education: BP 169, Brazzaville; tel. 81-24-60; telex 5210.
Ministry of Finance: Centre Administratif, quartier Plateau, BP 2093, Brazzaville; tel. 81-06-20; telex 5210.
Ministry of Foreign Affairs and Co-operation: BP 2070, Brazzaville; tel. 81-06-48; telex 5210.
Ministry of Health and Social Affairs: Palais du Peuple, Brazzaville; tel. 81-27-27; telex 5210.
Ministry of Industries: Palais du Peuple, Brazzaville; tel. 81-46-85; telex 5210.
Ministry of Information, Posts and Telecommunications: Brazzaville; telex 5331.
Ministry of Planning: BP 2031, Brazzaville; tel. 81-43-24; telex 5210.
Ministry of Trade: Brazzaville; tel. 81-18-27; telex 5210.

Legislature

ASSEMBLÉE NATIONALE POPULAIRE

A new body of 153 members was elected on 8 July 1979.

Political Organization

Parti congolais du travail (PCT): Brazzaville; telex 5335; f. 1969 to replace the Mouvement national de la révolution; Marxist-Leninist party committed to 'scientific socialism'. The National Party Congress, the highest authority of the PCT, meets every five years; most recent meeting July 1984; the 75-mem. Cen. Cttee, which meets three times a year, directs party policy; the 8-mem. Secretariat of the Cen. Cttee is the PCT's senior executive body; the day-to-day direction of the party is in the hands of a 10-mem. Politburo, which exercises the powers of the Cen. Cttee between its sessions. There is a 13-mem. Military Cttee and three specialized organs: Confédération syndicale congolaise (CSC),

THE CONGO

Union révolutionnaire des femmes congolaises (URFC) and Union de la jeunesse socialiste congolaise (UJSC). Pres. of Cen. Cttee Col DENIS SASSOU-NGUESSO; Gen. Sec. CAMILLE BONGOU.

Diplomatic Representation

EMBASSIES IN THE CONGO

Algeria: BP 2100, Brazzaville; tel. 81-39-15; telex 5303; Ambassador: DJAMEL-EDINE GHERNATI.
Angola: BP 388, Brazzaville; tel. 81-14-71; telex 5321; Ambassador: JOSÉ AGOSTINHO NETO.
Belgium: BP 225, Brazzaville; tel. 81-29-63; telex 5216; Ambassador: CHRISTIAN DELEU.
Bulgaria: BP 2460, Brazzaville; tel. 81-27-33; Ambassador: GEORGI VLADIKOV.
Cameroon: BP 2136, Brazzaville; tel. 81-34-04; telex 5242; Ambassador: JEAN-HILAIRE MBEA MBEA.
Central African Republic: BP 10, Brazzaville; tel. 81-40-14; Ambassador: TIMOTHÉE KONGBA MENGUI.
Chad: BP 386, Brazzaville; tel. 81-22-22; Chargé d'affaires a.i.: NEATOBEI BIDI.
China, People's Republic: BP 213, Brazzaville; tel. 81-11-20; Ambassador: DU YI.
Cuba: BP 80, Brazzaville; tel. 81-20-91; telex 5308; Ambassador: DIEGO ERNESTO GONZÁLEZ.
Czechoslovakia: BP 292, Brazzaville; tel. 81-08-37; Ambassador: LUBOMIR HALUSKA.
Egypt: BP 917, Brazzaville; tel. 81-44-28; Ambassador: NOSRAT ALY NAIM.
France: rue Alfassa, BP 2089, Brazzaville; tel. 81-14-23; telex 5239; Ambassador: ROBERT DELOS SANTOS.
Gabon: ave Fourneau, BP 2033, Brazzaville; tel. 81-05-90; telex 5225; Ambassador: CONSTANT TSOUMOU.
German Democratic Republic: rue de la Musique Tambourinée, BP 2244, Brazzaville; tel. 81-44-54; telex 5219; Ambassador: RONALD WEIDEMANN.
Germany, Federal Republic: BP 2022, Brazzaville; tel. 81-29-90; telex 5235; Ambassador: BERNHARD KALSCHEUER.
Guinea: BP 2477, Brazzaville; tel. 81-24-66; Ambassador: BONATA DIENG.
Italy: 2-3 blvd Lyautey, BP 2484, Brazzaville; tel. 81-40-47; Ambassador: VITTORIO FUMO.
Korea, Democratic People's Republic: BP 2032, Brazzaville; tel. 81-41-98; Ambassador: PAK CHANG-SOK.
Libya: BP 920, Brazzaville; Secretary of People's Bureau: SAAD ABDESSALEM BAAIU.
Nigeria: BP 790, Brazzaville; tel. 81-13-16; telex 5263; Ambassador: EJOH ABUAH.
Romania: BP 2413, Brazzaville; tel. 81-32-79; telex 5259; Ambassador: GHEORGHE POPESCU.
United Kingdom: ave du Général de Gaulle, Plateau, BP 1038, Brazzaville; tel. 81-49-44; telex 5366; Chargé d'affaires a.i.: CLIVE ALMOND.
USSR: BP 2132, Brazzaville; tel. 81-44-39; Ambassador: VLADIMIR KONSTANTINOVICH LOBACHEV.
USA: BP 1015, Brazzaville; tel. 81-20-70; Ambassador: ALAN W. LUKENS.
Viet-Nam: BP 988, Brazzaville; tel. 81-26-21; Ambassador: TRAN XUAN MAN.
Yugoslavia: BP 2062, Brazzaville; tel. 81-42-46; telex 5316; Chargé d'affaires a.i.: DJUSO MAJKIĆ.
Zaire: 130 ave de l'Indépendance, BP 2450, Brazzaville; tel. 81-29-38; Ambassador: YENDE BUKU.

Judicial System

Supreme Court: Brazzaville; telex 5298; acts as a Cour de Cassation; Pres. CHARLES ASSEMEKANG.
Revolutionary Court of Justice: f. 1969; has jurisdiction in cases involving the security of the state; comprises nine judges selected by Cen. Cttee of PCT; Pres. POPOSSI MANZIMBA.

In August 1978, after the discovery of a plot to overthrow the Government, a state security court was established by decree to try 'current and future crimes against the Congolese revolution'. There is a court of appeal, labour courts, and tribunaux coutumiers (courts of common law), the latter to be replaced by tribunaux d'instance.

Religion

It is estimated that about one-half of the population follow traditional animist beliefs. The remainder are mostly Christians. Muslims number about 40,000. In February 1978 the Government banned all religions and sects, except the Roman Catholic Church, the Congo Evangelical Church, the Salvation Army, Islam and the followers of Simon Kimbangu Prophète, Lassy Zephirin Prophète and Terynkyo.

CHRISTIANITY
The Roman Catholic Church

The Congo comprises one archdiocese and four dioceses. There were an estimated 730,000 adherents at 31 December 1984.
Bishops' Conference: Conférence Episcopale du Congo, BP 2301, Brazzaville; Pres. Mgr GEORGES SINGHA, Bishop of Owando.
Archbishop of Brazzaville: Mgr BARTHÉLEMY BATANTU, Archevêché, BP 2301, Brazzaville; tel. 81-17-93.

Other Christian Churches
Eglise Evangélique du Congo: BP 3205, Brazzaville; 107,819 mems (1982); Pres. Rev. JEAN MBOUNGOU.
Protestant Churches: In all four equatorial states (the Congo, the CAR, Chad and Gabon) there are nearly 1,000 mission centres with a total personnel of about 2,000.

The Press

Media censorship has been in operation since 1972.

DAILIES

ACI: BP 2144, Brazzaville; tel. 81-05-91; telex 5285; daily news bulletin publ. by Agence Congolaise d'Information; circ. 1,000.
L'Eveil de Pointe-Noire: BP 66, Pointe-Noire.
Mweti: BP 991, Brazzaville; tel. 81-10-87; national news; Dir EMMANUEL KIALA-MATUMBA; Chief Editor JONATHAN NZOUSSI-SOUNDA; circ. 8,000.

PERIODICALS

Bakento Ya Congo: BP 309, Brazzaville; tel. 81-27-44; quarterly; Dir MARIE LOUISE MAGANGA; Chief Editor CHARLOTTE BOUSSE; circ. 3,000.
Bulletin Mensuel de la Chambre de Commerce de Brazzaville: BP 92, Brazzaville; monthly.
Bulletin Mensuel de Statistique: Centre Nationale de la Statistique et des Etudes Economiques, BP 2031, Brazzaville; monthly.
Combattant Rouge: Brazzaville; tel. 81-02-53; Dir SYLVIO GEORGES ONKA; Chief Editor GILLES OMER BOUSSI.
Congo-Magazine: BP 114, Brazzaville; tel. 81-43-81; monthly; Dir GASPARD MPAN; Chief Editor THEODORE KIAMOSSI; circ. 3,000.
Effort: BP 64, Brazzaville; monthly.
Jeunesse et Révolution: BP 885, Brazzaville; tel. 81-44-13; weekly; Dir JEAN-ENOCH GOMA-KENGUE; Chief Editor PIERRE MAKITA.
La Semaine Africaine: BP 2080, Brazzaville; tel. 81-03-28; f. 1952; weekly; publ. by Archdiocese of Brazzaville; circulates in the Congo, Gabon, Chad and the CAR; Dir Fr FRANÇOIS DE PAUL MOUNDANGA; Chief Editor BERNARD MACKIZA; circ. 8,000.
Le Stade: BP 114, Brazzaville; tel. 81-11-85; telex 5285; weekly; sports; Dir STEPH MALONGA; Chief Editor ALBERT OBOUA; circ. 10,000.
Voix de la Classe Ouvrière (Voco): BP 2311, Brazzaville; tel. 81-36-66; every 2 months; Dir MICHEL JOSEPH MAYOUNGOU; Chief Editor MARIE-JOSEPH TSENGOU; circ. 4,500.

NEWS AGENCIES

Agence Congolaise d'Information (ACI): BP 2144, Brazzaville; tel. 81-05-91; telex 5285; f. 1961; Dir AUGUSTIN MATONGO-AVELEY.

THE CONGO

Foreign Bureaux

Agence France-Presse (AFP): BP 4174, Brazzaville; telex 5285; Correspondent BOY BUTA LOUMBWELE.

Agentstvo Pechati Novosti (APN) (USSR): BP 170, Brazzaville; tel. 81-43-44; telex 5227; Bureau Chief OLEG KHLASTOUNOV.

Inter Press Service (Italy): Poto-Poto, BP 4174, Brazzaville; tel. 81-05-65; telex 5285; Correspondent BOY BUTA LOUMBWELE.

Telegrafnoye Agentstvo Sovetskovo Soyuza (TASS) (USSR): BP 379, Brazzaville; tel. 81-44-33; telex 5203; Correspondent BORIS PHILIPOV.

Xinhua (New China) News Agency (People's Republic of China): 40 ave Maréchal Lyauté, BP 373, Brazzaville; tel. 81-44-01; telex 5230; Chief Correspondent XU ZHENQIANG.

Reuters (UK) is also represented in the Congo.

Publishers

Imprimerie Centrale d'Afrique (ICA): BP 162, Pointe-Noire; f. 1949; Man. Dir M. SCHNEIDER.

Société Congolaise Hachette: BP 919, Brazzaville; telex 5291; general fiction, literature, education, juvenile, textbooks.

Government Publishing House

Imprimerie Nationale: BP 58, Brazzaville.

Radio and Television

A television service began in 1963 and now operates for 46 hours per week, with most programmes in French but some in Lingala and Kikongo. Colour transmissions began in 1983. In 1983 there were an estimated 100,000 radio receivers and 4,500 television receivers in use.

Radiodiffusion-Télévision Nationale Congolaise: BP 2241, Brazzaville; tel. 81-24-73; telex 5299; Dir GUY-NOËL PANKIMA.

La Voix de la Révolution Congolaise: BP 2241, Brazzaville; tel. 81-24-73; national broadcasting station; radio programmes in French, Lingala, Kikongo, Subia, English and Portuguese; transmitters at Brazzaville and Pointe-Noire; foreign service to Namibia in English and vernacular languages; Dir JEAN-PASCAL MONGO-SLYM.

Finance

(cap. = capital; res = reserves; dep. = deposits; br. = branch; m. = million; amounts in francs CFA unless otherwise stated)

BANKING

Central Bank

Banque des Etats de l'Afrique Centrale (BEAC): BP 126, Brazzaville; tel. 81-28-14; telex 5200; Headquarters in Yaoundé, Cameroon; f. 1973 as the central bank of issue for mem. states of the Customs and Economic Union of Central Africa (UDEAC), comprising Cameroon, the Central African Republic, Chad, the Congo, Equatorial Guinea and Gabon; cap. and res 92,485m. (June 1983); br. in Pointe-Noire; Gov. CASIMIR OYE-MBA; Man. in the Congo GABRIEL BOKILO.

Commercial Banks

Banque Commerciale Congolaise (BCC): ave Amílcar Cabral, BP 79, Brazzaville; tel. 81-08-80; telex 5237; f. 1962; cap. 3,500m., res 3,787m., dep. 89,169m. (Dec. 1984); 57.8% state-owned, 25% by Credit Lyonnais (France); Chair. AMBROISE NOUMAZALAY; Gen. Mans CLÉMENT MOUAMBA, MICHEL TRICAUD; 12 brs.

Banque Internationale du Congo (BIDC): ave Patrice Lumumba, BP 645, Brazzaville; tel. 81-14-11; telex 5339; f. 1983; cap. 600m.; 51% state-owned, 19% by Banque Internationale pour l'Afrique Occidentale (France); Chair. Minister of Finance; Gen. Man. CLÉMENT MOUAMBA.

Banque Nationale de Développement du Congo (BNDC): ave Foch, BP 2085, Brazzaville; tel. 81-30-13; telex 5312; f. 1961; cap. 1,087m.; 79% state-owned; provides financial and technical help for development projects; Chair. Minister of Finance; Man. Dir ANDRÉ BATANGA.

Union Congolaise de Banques SA (UCB): ave Amílcar Cabral, BP 147, Brazzaville; tel. 81-10-68; telex 5206; f. 1974 by the merger of Société Générale de Banques au Congo and Banque Internationale pour le Commerce et l'Industrie; cap. 3,000m., res 1,248m., dep. 75,247m. (Dec. 1983); 51% state-owned; Chair. PIERRE MOUSSA; Man. Dir PAUL ANDELY; 8 brs.

Development Bank

Banque de Développement des Etats de l'Afrique Centrale (BDEAC): BP 1177, Brazzaville; tel. 81-02-12; telex 5306; f. 1975; cap. 41,880m. (Nov. 1983); shareholders: Cameroon, CAR, Chad, Congo, Equatorial Guinea and Gabon (13.09% each), BEAC (10.1%), France (4.76%), Federal Republic of Germany (2.39%), Kuwait (2.39%), Banque Africaine de Développement (1.91%); Man. Dir CÉLESTIN GAOMBALET.

Financial Institution

Caisse Congolaise d'Amortissement: 410 allée du Chaillu, BP 2090, Brazzaville; tel. 81-28-79; telex 5294; Man. Dir ETIENNE NOTÉ.

INSURANCE

Assurances et Réassurances du Congo (ARC): ave Amílcar Cabral, BP 977, Brazzaville; tel. 81-01-71; telex 5236; f. 1973 to acquire the businesses of all insurance companies operating in the Congo; cap. 350m.; 50% govt-owned; Dir-Gen. RAYMOND IBATA; brs at Pointe-Noire and Loubomo.

Trade and Industry

DEVELOPMENT AGENCIES

Bureau pour le Développement de la Production Agricole (BDPA): BP 2222, Brazzaville; tel. 81-29-77; Dir M. GARREAU.

Caisse Centrale de Coopération Economique (CCCE): BP 96, Brazzaville; tel. 81-15-95; telex 5202; cap. 500m. French francs; Dir PHILIPPE PROUST.

Mission Française de Coopération: BP 2175, Brazzaville; tel. 81-15-03; f. 1959; administers bilateral aid from France according to the January 1974 co-operation agreement; Dir GÉRARD LA COGNATA.

Société de Développement Régional de la Vallée de Niari et de Kayes: Kayes; f. 1966; controlled by the BNDC; Dir JEAN-MICHEL MOUMBOUNOU.

MARKETING BOARDS

Office Congolais des Bois (OCB): BP 1229, Pointe-Noire; tel. 94-22-38; telex 8248; f. 1974; cap. 1,500m. francs CFA; monopoly of purchase and marketing of all log products; Man. Dir ALEXANDRE DENGUET-ATTIKI.

Office Congolais des Forêts: BP 839, Pointe-Noire; tel. 94-02-79; Dir MARC PROSPER BAYONNE.

Office Congolais des Matériaux de Construction (OCMC): BP 2913, Brazzaville; tel. 81-22-80; f. 1964; cap. 130m. francs CFA; building projects agency; Man. Dir ALBERT AHOUE OWANGO.

Office du Café et du Cacao (OCC): BP 2488, Brazzaville; tel. 81-19-03; telex 5273; f. 1978; cap. 1,500m. francs CFA; state-owned; marketing and export of coffee and cocoa; Man. Dir PAUL YORA.

Office National de Commercialisation des Produits Agricoles (ONCPA): BP 144, Brazzaville; tel. 81-24-01; telex 5273; f. 1964; marketing of all agricultural products except sugar; promotion of rural co-operatives; Dir JEAN-PAUL BOCKONDAS.

Office National du Commerce (OFNACOM): BP 2305, Brazzaville; tel. 81-43-99; telex 5309; f. 1964; importer and distributor of general merchandise; monopoly importer of salted and dried fish, cooking salt, rice, tomato purée, buckets, enamelled goods and blankets; Dir-Gen. VALENTIN EHOUSSA MBONGO.

Office National d'Importation et de Vente de Viande en Gros (ONIVEG): BP 2130, Brazzaville; tel. 81-30-33; telex 5240; f. 1975; cap. 177m. francs CFA; monopoly importer and distributor of wholesale meats; Man. Dir ROBERT PAUL MANGOUTA.

CHAMBERS OF COMMERCE

Chambre de Commerce, d'Agriculture et d'Industrie de Brazzaville: BP 92, Brazzaville; tel. 81-10-89; Pres. M. NOTÉ; Sec.-Gen. GERMAIN TCHIKAYA.

Chambre de Commerce, d'Agriculture et d'Industrie du Kouilou: 3 ave Charles de Gaulle, BP 665, Pointe-Noire; tel. 94-12-80; f. 1948; Chair. FRANÇOIS LUC MACOSSO; Sec.-Gen. GEORGES MBOMA.

PROFESSIONAL ORGANIZATION

Union Patronale et Interprofessionnelle du Congo (UNICONGO): BP 42, Brazzaville; tel. 81-05-51; telex 5289; employers' union; Pres. Jacques-Guy Huguet.

NATIONALIZED INDUSTRIES

Cimenterie Domaniale de Loutété (CIDOLOU): BP 72, Loutété; tel. 92-61-08; telex 5244; f. 1968; cap. 900m. francs CFA; production of cement; Man. Dir M. Missongo-mi-Makusso.

Minoterie, Aliments de Bétail, Boulangerie (MAB): BP 789, Pointe-Noire; tel. 94-19-09; telex 8283; f. 1978; cap. 2,650m. francs CFA; monopoly importer of cereals; production of flour and animal feed; Man. Dir Denis Tempere.

Régie Nationale des Palmeraies du Congo (RNPC): BP 8, Brazzaville; tel. 81-08-25; f. 1966; cap. 908m. francs CFA; production of palm oil; Man. Dir Rene Macosso.

Société Congolaise de Pêches Maritimes (COPEMAR): BP 784, Pointe-Noire; tel. 94-20-32; telex 8322; f. 1981; cap. 860m. francs CFA; processing of fish products; Man. Dir Pascal Issanga.

Société Congolaise Industrielle des Bois d'Ouesso: Ouesso; cap. 2,500m. francs CFA; 51% state-owned.

Société Mixte Bulgaro-Congolaise de Recherche et d'Exploitation de Phosphates (SOPHOSCO): Brazzaville; f. 1976; cap. 250m. francs CFA; 51% state-owned, 49% Bulgarian-owned; mining of phosphate.

Société Nationale de Construction (SONACO): BP 1126, Brazzaville; tel. 81-06-54; f. 1979; cap. 479m. francs CFA; building works; Man. Dir Denis M'Bomo.

Société Nationale de Distribution d'Eau (SNDE): BP 229 and 365, ave Sergent Malamine, Brazzaville; tel. 81-41-69; telex 5272; water supply and sewerage; holds monopoly over wells and import of mineral water; Chair. and Man. Dir F. S. Sita.

Société Nationale d'Elevage (SONEL): BP 81, Loutété, Massangui; f. 1964; cap. 80m. francs CFA; development of semi-intensive stock-rearing; exploitation of by-products in co-operation with SIA-CONGO; Man. Dir Théophile Bikawa.

Société Nationale d'Exploitation des Bois (SNEB): BP 1198, Pointe-Noire; tel. 94-02-09; f. 1970; cap. 1,779m. francs CFA; production of timber; merged with wood-processing firm SONATRAB 1983; Pres. Rigobert Ngoulou; Man. Dir Robert Zinga Kanza.

Société Nationale de Recherche et d'Exploitation Pétrolières (HYDRO-CONGO): ave Amílcar Cabral, BP 2008, Brazzaville; tel. 81-34-59; telex 5215; f. 1973; cap. 710m. francs CFA; research into and production of petroleum resources; has monopoly of distribution of petroleum products in the Congo; refinery at Pointe-Noire; Chair. Rodolphe Adada; Man. Dir Auxence Ickonga.

Société des Potasses du Congo (SPC): Brazzaville; f. 1986; cap. 100m. francs CFA; 51% state-owned, 49% Entreprise Minière Chimique (France); prospecting, researching and study of potassium deposits in the Congo.

Société des Textiles du Congo (SOTEXCO): BP 3222, Brazzaville; tel. 81-33-83; f. 1966; cap. 1,700 francs CFA; operates cotton spinning mills, dyeing plants and weaving plants in Kinsoundi; Man. Dir M. Kombo-Kitombo.

Société des Verreries du Congo (SOVERCO): BP 1241, Pointe-Noire; tel. 94-05-84; telex 9288; f. 1977; cap. 500m. francs CFA; manufacture of glassware; Chair. Jean Itadi; Man. Dir M. Babetana.

Sucrerie du Congo (SUCO): BP 71, Nkayi; tel. 92-11-00; f. 1978; cap. 500m. francs CFA; sugar production; Dir Jean de Dieu Nitoud.

TRADE UNION

Confédération Syndicale Congolaise (CSC): BP 2311, Brazzaville; telex 5304; f. 1964; Sec.-Gen. Jean-Michel Boukamba Yangouma.

Transport

Agence Transcongolaise des Communications (ATC): BP 711, Pointe-Noire; tel. 94-15-32; telex 5302; f. 1969 to control nationalization of transport; is the largest state enterprise with a capital of 23,888m. francs CFA; has three sections: Congo-Océan Railway, inland waterways and general transport facilities, and the port of Pointe-Noire; Man. Dir François Bita.

RAILWAYS

There are 510 km of track from Brazzaville to Pointe-Noire. A 286-km section of privately-owned line links the manganese mines at Moanda (in Gabon), via a cableway to the Congo border at M'Binda, with the main line to Pointe-Noire; a realignment of 91 km of track was completed in July 1985.

Chemin de Fer Congo-Océan (CFCO): BP 651, Pointe-Noire; tel. 94-25-63; telex 8231; Dir Noël Bouanga.

INLAND WATERWAYS

The Congo and Oubangui rivers form two axes of a highly developed inland waterway system. The Congo river and seven tributaries in the Congo basin provide 2,300 km of navigable river and the Oubangui river, developed in co-operation with the Central African Republic, 2,085 km.

ATC—Direction des Voies Navigables, Ports et Transports Fluviaux: BP 2048, Brazzaville; tel. 81-06-27; waterways authority; Dir J.-P. Bockondas.

Société Congolaise de Transports (SOCOTRANS): BP 617, Pointe-Noire; tel. 94-23-31; f. 1977; cap. 17m. francs CFA; Mans Yves Criquet, Henri Benatouil.

Transcap-Congo: BP 1154, Pointe-Noire; tel. 94-01-46; telex 8218; f. 1962; Chair. Marc Bonnet.

SHIPPING

A major expansion programme for Brazzaville port is expected to be completed by the end of 1987. The project, which was to cost an estimated 1,900m. francs CFA, was part-financed by the European Investment Bank (EIB) and aimed at making the port into a container traffic centre for several central African countries, such as Chad, the CAR and the western part of Cameroon.

ATC—Direction du Port de Brazzaville: BP 2048, Brazzaville; tel. 81-00-42; port authority; Brazzaville, on the river Congo, is an inland port; nationalized in 1977; Dir Jean-Paul Bockondas.

ATC—Direction du Port de Pointe-Noire: BP 711, Pointe-Noire; tel. 94-00-52; telex 8318; nationalized in 1977; port authority; Pointe-Noire is the main port of the Congo; Dir Alphonse M'Bama.

La Congolaise de Transport Maritime (COTRAM): f. 1984; national shipping company; state-owned; scheduled to become fully operational by 1986 and handle 40% of the Congo's traffic.

ROADS

In 1980 there were 8,246 km of roads usable throughout the year, of which 849 km were bituminized. The network consists of 4,519 km of main roads and 3,727 km of secondary roads, with the principal routes linking Brazzaville to Pointe-Noire, in the south, and to Ouesso, in the north.

Régie Nationale des Transports et des Travaux Publics: BP 2073, Brazzaville; tel. 81-35-58; f. 1965; civil engineering, upkeep of roads and public works; Man. Dir Hector Bienvenu Ouamba.

CIVIL AVIATION

There are international airports at Brazzaville (Maya-Maya) and Pointe-Noire. There are also 37 smaller airfields. An aeronautical development programme covering 1982–86 included the construction of airports at six regional capitals.

Agence Nationale de l'Aviation Civile (ANAC): BP 128, Brazzaville; Gen. Man. A. Bouiti.

Air Afrique: BP 1126, Pointe-Noire; tel. 81-01-73; telex 8342; the Congo govt holds a 7% share; see under Ivory Coast; Dir in the Congo Benjamin Dedegbe.

Lina Congo (Lignes Nationales Aériennes Congolaises): ave Amílcar Cabral, BP 2203, Brazzaville; tel. 81-30-66; telex 5243; f. 1965; state-owned; operates an extensive internal network, plus services to Gabon; Man. Dir M. Carombo-Oukouno; fleet of 1 Boeing 737-200QC, 1 Fokker F.28-1000, 1 F.27-600, 2 Twin Otter 300.

Tourism

Direction Générale du Tourisme: BP 456, Brazzaville; tel. 81-09-53; telex 5325; Dir-Gen. Félix Taba-Goma.

COSTA RICA

Introductory Survey

Location, Climate, Language, Religion, Flag, Capital

The Republic of Costa Rica lies in the Central American isthmus, with Nicaragua to the north, Panama to the south, the Caribbean Sea to the east and the Pacific Ocean to the west. The climate is warm and damp in the lowlands (average temperature 27°C (81°F)) and cooler on the Central Plateau (average temperature 22°C (72°F)), where two-thirds of the population live. The language is Spanish. Almost all of the inhabitants profess Christianity, and the overwhelming majority adhere to the Roman Catholic Church, the state religion. The national flag (proportions 3 by 2) has five horizontal stripes, of blue, white, red, white and blue, the red stripe being twice the width of the others. The state flag, in addition, has on the red stripe (to the left of centre) a white oval enclosing the national coat of arms, showing three volcanic peaks between the Caribbean and the Pacific. The capital is San José.

Recent History

Costa Rica was ruled by Spain from the 16th century until 1821, when independence was declared. The only significant interruption in the country's constitutional government since 1920 occurred in February 1948, when the result of the presidential election was disputed. The legislature annulled the election in March but a civil war ensued. The anti-Government forces, led by José Figueres Ferrer, were successful, and a revolutionary junta took power in April. Costa Rica's army was abolished in December 1948. After the preparation of a new constitution, the victorious candidate of the 1948 election took office in January 1949.

Figueres, who founded the socialist Partido de Liberación Nacional (PLN), dominated national politics for decades, holding presidential office in 1953–58 and 1970–74. Under his leadership, Costa Rica became one of the most democratic countries in Latin America. Since the 1948 revolution, there have been frequent changes of power, all achieved by constitutional means. Figueres' first government nationalized the banks and instituted a comprehensive social security system. The presidential election of 1958 was won by a conservative, Mario Echandi Jiménez, who reversed many PLN policies. His successor, Francisco Orlich Bolmarich (President from 1962 to 1966), was supported by the PLN but continued the encouragement of private enterprise. Another conservative, José Joaquín Trejos Fernández, held power in 1966–70. In 1974 the PLN candidate, Daniel Oduber Quirós, was elected President. He continued the policies of extending the welfare state and of establishing friendly relations with communist states. Communist and other left-wing parties were legalized in 1975. In 1978 Rodrigo Carazo Odio of the conservative Partido Unidad Opositora (PUO) coalition (subsequently the Coalición Unidad) was elected President. During Carazo's term of office the worsening instability in Central America led to diplomatic tension, and in 1981 the President was criticized for his alleged involvement in illegal arms trafficking between Cuba and El Salvador.

At presidential and legislative elections in February 1982, Luis Alberto Monge Alvarez of the PLN gained a comfortable majority and his party won 33 of the 57 seats in the Legislative Assembly. Monge was inaugurated as President in May. He announced a 100-day emergency economic programme and a policy of fiscal conservatism in an attempt to rescue the country from the near-bankruptcy inherited from President Carazo. Unlike other members of the Socialist International, Monge did not denounce the elections in El Salvador in March 1982, although he continued a policy of neutrality regarding Nicaragua. Incursions from across the border increased, and in May a national alert was declared. The rebel Nicaraguan, Edén Pastora Gómez, was expelled from Costa Rica to prevent the country from becoming a base for military activity against the Sandinista regime in Nicaragua. Relations with Nicaragua continued to worsen, as guerrilla activity spread to San José and included a spate of kidnappings.

Throughout 1983, President Monge came under increasing pressure, from liberal members of the Cabinet and PLN supporters, to adopt a more neutral stance in foreign policy. Three leading members of the anti-Sandinista (Contra) movement were expelled from Costa Rica in May, and 80 of Pastora's supporters were arrested in September. In addition, some 82 guerrilla camps were dismantled by the Civil Guard. In November 1983 President Monge declared Costa Rica's neutrality in an attempt to elicit foreign support for his country. This declaration was opposed by the USA and led to the resignation of the Minister of Foreign Affairs.

In January 1984 the cancellation of a US-financed plan, involving the use of American soldiers in construction work along Costa Rica's border with Nicaragua, was regarded as an indication of the Government's desire to seek improved relations with Nicaragua. In May, however, relations deteriorated, following reports of an air raid by the Nicaraguan Air Force on a border village in Costa Rica and of an increasing number of incursions by the Sandinista forces. Public opposition to any renunciation of neutrality was emphasized by a demonstration in support of peace and neutrality, held in San José and attended by over 20,000 people. In an attempt to defuse the tense situation at the border, the Costa Rican and Nicaraguan Governments, assisted by representatives of the Contadora group (Colombia, Mexico, Panama and Venezuela), which seeks to mediate in disputes involving Central America, agreed to form a commission of supervision and prevention, to monitor events in the border area. In late May, however, the attempt to assassinate Edén Pastora Gómez near the Costa Rican border exacerbated the rift within the Cabinet concerning government policy towards Nicaragua.

Relations between Costa Rica and Nicaragua deteriorated rapidly in December 1984, when the Government accused Nicaragua of violating international law, following an incident involving a Nicaraguan refugee at the Costa Rican embassy in Managua. As a result of the dispute, diplomatic relations were reduced to a minimal level, and Costa Rica boycotted a meeting of the Contadora group in February 1985. Reports of clashes between the Sandinista forces and Costa Rican Civil Guardsmen along the joint border became increasingly frequent. In 1985 the Government's decision to create an anti-guerrilla battalion, to be trained by US military advisers, increased public scepticism about the Government's commitment to maintaining Costa Rica's neutrality.

During 1983 there were signs of increasing urban unrest in response to the Government's austerity measures and to the agrarian crisis, which had produced high unemployment, principally among workers on banana plantations. By August 1984 the Government's position was regarded as unstable. The division within the Cabinet over policy towards Nicaragua, coupled with the effects of the unpopular austerity programme and a protracted strike by banana plantation workers, which had resulted in two deaths, led to fears of a coup. At President Monge's request, the Cabinet resigned, and in the subsequent reshuffle four Ministers were replaced.

At presidential and legislative elections in February 1986, Oscar Arias Sánchez, the candidate of the PLN, was elected President, with 52% of the votes cast. The PLN also obtained a clear majority in the Legislative Assembly. The new Government was committed to the development of a 'welfare state', whereby 25,000 new jobs and 20,000 new dwellings were to be created each year. In addition, the Government planned to renegotiate the country's external debt and to reach agreement on a social pact with the trade unions. Furthermore, President Arias Sánchez was resolved to maintain and reinforce Costa Rica's policy of neutrality, a decision which was expected to antagonize relations with the US administration.

COSTA RICA

In February 1986 diplomatic relations with Nicaragua were fully restored, and it was decided to establish a permanent inspection and vigilance commission at the common border. In accordance with the Government's pledge to protect neutrality, Costa Rica objected to the allocation of US $100m. in US aid to the Contra forces in mid-1986. In addition, the Government embarked on a series of arrests and expulsions of Contras resident in Costa Rica, and closed down illegal hospitals and an airstrip (which had been built during ex-President Monge's administration with the assistance of the Costa Rican Civil Guard). In October, however, an aeroplane crash in Nicaraguan territory, involving four US citizens, caused considerable embarrassment to the Costa Rican Government and encouraged scepticism about Costa Rica's participation in the anti-Sandinista campaign. Relations with the USA were expected to be impaired further by the Government's claim that the US administration's decision to reduce financial aid to Costa Rica would undermine national stability and was an attempt to coerce Costa Rica to support the Contras.

Government

Under the Constitution of 1949, executive power is vested in the President, assisted by two Vice-Presidents (or, in exceptional circumstances, one Vice-President) and an appointed Cabinet. The President is elected for a four-year term by compulsory adult suffrage, and a successful candidate must receive at least 40% of the votes. The legislative organ is the unicameral Legislative Assembly, with 57 members who are similarly elected for four years.

Defence

There have been no armed forces since 1948. In July 1986, rural and Civil Guards totalled 9,500 men. In 1985 an anti-terrorist battalion was formed, composed of 750 Civil Guards. Spending on the security forces was estimated to be US $20.2m. in 1984. Military aid from the USA amounted to an estimated $3.7m. in 1986.

Economic Affairs

Costa Rica's economy is based mainly on the export of coffee, bananas, meat, sugar and cocoa. Staples such as maize, beans and potatoes are also grown. In 1983 the agricultural sector (including forestry and fishing) employed 28% of the labour force and provided 20.8% of the country's gross domestic product (GDP). The sector usually contributes about 60% of Costa Rica's exports. In 1984 coffee and bananas accounted for 27% and 25% of export earnings respectively. The fall in the banana price was offset by a rise in production, but the fall in the world coffee price, which did not recover until 1982, considerably worsened the balance of trade. Following the collapse of the banana industry on the Pacific coast, when sales to Japan, the industry's principal market, were taken over by the Philippines, the industry was to be concentrated on the Caribbean coast. In 1984 a 72-day strike by banana plantation workers resulted in losses in banana taxes of an estimated US $500m. As a result of the strike and rising costs, the United Brands' subsidiary, Compañía Bananera de Costa Rica, closed down its operations in the country. In March 1985 the Government reached agreement with United Brands on the purchase of 1,700 ha of the abandoned plantations (which totalled 2,300 ha) and 500 buildings. The plantations were to be converted to the cultivation of cocoa. Exports declined by some 25% in 1985, resulting in losses in revenue amounting to more than $50m. and precipitating a crisis in the industry. However, there were plans to invest 500m. colones in development projects in 1986/87. In 1983 a record coffee harvest of 2.3m. bags (each of 60 kg) was produced, and export earnings reached $237m., thereby encouraging government hopes that the coffee industry would play an important part in the country's economic recovery. In 1984 production was in excess of 3m. bags, in spite of coffee rust disease and a shortage of credit. The increase in the world coffee price in 1985/86 was expected to result in additional export earnings of $150m. in 1986. In 1984 a record output of 245,000 metric tons of raw sugar was expected. However, a 33% reduction in Costa Rica's quota for exports of sugar to the USA was expected to result in the loss of $7m. in foreign exchange earnings in 1986 and a reduction in output. In 1984 the total output of the agricultural sector grew by 8%.

The Government is to develop the estimated 150m. tons of bauxite which has been discovered in the Boruca region. Construction of an aluminium smelter (annual production 280,000 metric tons) and an associated hydroelectric scheme was due to be completed by the late 1980s.

The principal branches of the manufacturing sector are food processing, textiles, chemicals and plastics. During 1984 industrial output increased by 10%. Investment is concentrated on the energy sector. Hydroelectric capacity totalled 460 MW in 1983 and is scheduled to rise to about 1,000 MW by 1988, with the opening of four new stations. Costa Rica's entire electricity requirements are expected to be fulfilled when the Arenal hydro project (opened in 1979) reaches its full capacity of 1,974 MW. In 1986 the Government announced plans to construct a 55-MW geothermal power station at Miravalle. In 1983 trade agreements were signed with Romania and Mexico to provide technical assistance for the design and building of tourist projects, and financial aid of US $28m. for petroleum exploration in Valle Talamanca. Petroleum production began on a small scale in June 1984. The petroleum refinery at Puerto Limón has a capacity of 15,000 barrels per day.

From a comparatively healthy position in the late 1970s, Costa Rica's economy began to deteriorate in 1981, when GDP declined, in real terms, by 2.3%. A further decline, of 7.3%, occurred in 1982, but GDP grew by 2.9% in 1983. The trade deficit rose to US $522m. in 1980, as a result of the rising cost of petroleum, the fall in coffee prices and increased imports of consumer goods. However, it improved to $22m. in 1982. Between 1980 and 1983 industrial investment in Costa Rica fell by 38%, with manufacturers working at only 30%–45% of their total capacity. The public sector debt rose from $1,800m. in December 1980 to $2,400m. in September 1981. All $40m. of gold reserves were sold off in May 1981. Although Costa Rica had broken three IMF agreements in two years, in December 1982 the IMF agreed to a loan of $100.7m., conditional upon the implementation of an austerity programme. IMF demands included devaluation of the colón, which fell on the free market to 62 per US dollar, representing an 86% depreciation since December 1980. The average annual rate of inflation increased from 18.1% in 1980 to 37.1% in 1981 and to 90.1% in 1982. However, inflation declined to 32.6% in 1983 and to only 12% in 1984. It rose to 15.1% in 1985, but stood at 11.6% in the year to June 1986. Unemployment rose from 4.5% of the labour force in 1978 to 9.4% in 1982, easing to 9.0% in 1983. Wages declined in real terms by 40% from 1982 to 1983. In 1983 the USA gave $145m. in economic aid under the Caribbean Basin Initiative. In September 1983, after two years of negotiations with 200 of its creditor banks, Costa Rica finally agreed terms for rescheduling debts of $1,200m.

In September 1984 the IMF allocated SDR 18.6m. to Costa Rica, after Costa Rica agreed to a programme of austerity measures. In 1984 GDP grew by an estimated 7.3%. The colón was devalued by a total of 10% in 1984. In 1984 the public sector deficit was 2.5% of GDP. The USA was expected to allocate $180m. in economic aid to Costa Rica in 1984, and $198m. in 1985.

In January 1985 the Government reduced state subsidies on various basic goods. In March the IMF approved a short-term credit of SDR 54m. for Costa Rica. As a result of obtaining this loan, the Government was able to reach agreement with creditor banks in April on the rescheduling of US $150m. in debts falling due in 1985 and on a further loan of $75m. In addition, a structural adjustment loan, amounting to $80m., was secured from the World Bank. The principal problem for the Government was servicing the foreign debt of $4,500m. In recent years debt servicing has absorbed more than 50% of foreign exchange earnings.

Following the elections in February 1986, Costa Rica's new Government inherited a relatively stable economy. However, it was evident that the new administration would need to stimulate the growth of GDP, which fell to 1.2% in 1985, in order to finance its ambitious welfare schemes. In May the Government announced the gradual elimination of tariffs on imports of finished goods, in an attempt to encourage non-traditional exports and to reduce the trade deficit, which increased from US $87m. in 1984 to more than $100m. in 1985.

As a result of Costa Rica's failure to meet economic targets for 1985–86, the IMF did not disburse the final tranche of the

SDR 54m. credit that had been agreed in 1985. Furthermore, the World Bank and the US Agency for International Development delayed the disbursement of loans amounting to US $80m. Consequently, Costa Rica experienced an acute shortage of foreign exchange, and in May 1986 the Government announced the temporary suspension of interest payments on the foreign debt. Arrears on debt servicing were estimated at $110m. In October Costa Rica requested the rescheduling, over a period of 25 years, of $1,400m. in debt owing to foreign commercial banks. The Government sought to limit debt servicing costs to 1.5% of GDP and to obtain concessionary rates of interest for repayments. Although the creditor banks were not expected to agree to such terms, a settlement was anticipated, especially in view of the IMF's willingness to allocate a further credit of SDR 60m. to Costa Rica. Doubts remained, however, concerning the Government's ability to implement the controversial programme of austerity measures which formed the IMF's principal condition for financial assistance.

Social Welfare

Costa Rica possesses one of the world's most advanced social welfare systems, which provides a complete programme of care and assistance for all wage earners and their dependants.

All social services are co-ordinated by the National Development Plan, run by the Ministry of Planning, and are organized by state institution. Approximately 7% of the GDP and 12% of public spending are allocated to the social services. The Social Security Fund provides health services and general social insurance, the National Insurance Institute provides professional insurance and the Ministry of Health operates a preventive health programme through a chain of health units throughout the country. Benefits include disability and retirement pensions, workers' compensation and family assistance. In 1979 there were 1,506 registered physicians, not all resident and working in Costa Rica. In 1982 there were 28 hospitals and 76 health centres, with a total of 7,706 beds.

Education

All education is free, and elementary education is compulsory between six and 13 years of age. Official secondary education is free and consists of a three-year basic course, followed by a more highly specialized course of two years. Attendance figures are very high: in 1982 an estimated 91% of children aged six to 16 received secondary education. There are four universities, one of which is an 'open' university. At 94%, Costa Rica has the highest adult literacy rate in Central America. The education system received 8,086.2m. colones of budget expenditure in 1985.

Tourism

The main tourist features are the Irazú and Poás volcanoes, the Orosí valley, the ruins of the colonial church at Orosí and the jungle train to Limón. Tourists also visit San José, the capital, and the Pacific beaches of Guanacaste and Puntarenas. Tourism is a major growth sector. In 1984 Costa Rica received 273,901 tourists.

Public Holidays

1987: 1 January (New Year's Day), 19 March (Feast of St Joseph), 11 April (Anniversary of the Battle of Rivas), 16 April (Maundy Thursday), 17 April (Good Friday), 1 May (Labour Day), 18 June (Corpus Christi), 29 June (SS. Peter and Paul), 25 July (Anniversary of the Annexation of Guanacaste Province), 2 August (Our Lady of the Angels), 15 August (Assumption), 15 September (Independence Day), 12 October (Columbus Day), 8 December (Immaculate Conception), 25 December (Christmas Day), 28–31 December (San José only).

1988: 1 January (New Year's Day), 19 March (Feast of St Joseph), 31 March (Maundy Thursday), 1 April (Good Friday), 11 April (Anniversary of the Battle of Rivas), 1 May (Labour Day), 2 June (Corpus Christi), 29 June (SS. Peter and Paul), 25 July (Anniversary of the Annexation of Guanacaste Province), 2 August (Our Lady of the Angels), 15 August (Assumption), 15 September (Independence Day), 12 October (Columbus Day), 8 December (Immaculate Conception), 25 December (Christmas Day), 28–31 December (San José only).

Weights and Measures

The metric system is in force.

Currency and Exchange Rates

100 céntimos = 1 Costa Rican colón.

Exchange rates (30 September 1986):
 £1 sterling = 82.877 colones;
 US $1 = 57.275 colones.

COSTA RICA

Statistical Survey

Source (unless otherwise stated): Dirección General de Estadística y Censos, Ministerio de Economía y Comercio, Apdo 10163, San José; tel. 210883.

Area and Population

AREA, POPULATION AND DENSITY

Area (sq km)	
Land	51,060
Inland water	40
Total	51,100*
Population (census results)	
14 May 1973	1,871,780
11 June 1984†	
Males	1,231,024
Females	1,229,202
Total	2,460,226
Population (official estimates at mid-year)‡	
1981	2,271,000
1982	2,324,257
1983	2,378,598
Density (per sq km) at June 1984	47.3§

* 19,730 sq miles.
† Figures are provisional. The revised total is 2,416,809.
‡ Not adjusted to take account of the 1984 census result.
§ Based on revised total.

PROVINCES (population at 1984 census)

	Population	Capital (with population)
Alajuela	427,962	Alajuela (33,929)
Cartago	271,671	Cartago (23,884)
Guanacaste	195,208	Liberia (14,093)
Heredia	197,575	Heredia (20,867)
Limón	168,076	Limón (43,158)
Puntarenas	265,883	Puntarenas (47,851)
San José	890,434	San José (245,370)
Total	2,416,809	—

BIRTHS, MARRIAGES AND DEATHS (rates per 1,000)

Births 31.0 in 1981, 30.7 in 1982, 29.6 in 1983, 32.3 in 1984; Marriages 7.3 in 1981, 7.7 in 1982, 7.5 in 1983, 8.5 in 1984; Deaths 3.9 in 1981, 3.9 in 1982, 3.8 in 1983, 4.1 in 1984.

ECONOMICALLY ACTIVE POPULATION
(census, June 1984)

	Males	Females	Total
Agriculture, hunting, forestry and fishing	241,851	7,549	249,400
Mining, quarrying and manufacturing	76,666	30,929	107,595
Construction	41,412	348	41,760
Electricity, gas, water, transport, storage and communications	26,731	2,779	29,510
Commerce	76,680	31,142	107,822
Community, social and personal services	91,921	84,172	176,093
Activities not adequately described	63,605	18,641	82,246
Total	618,866	175,560	794,426

Agriculture

PRINCIPAL CROPS ('000 metric tons)

	1982	1983	1984
Rice (paddy)	146	241	127*
Maize	85	95	104*
Beans (dry)	16	14	20*
Palm kernels†	7	7	7
Palm oil†	24	24	24
Sugar cane	2,466	2,544	2,850†
Bananas	1,136	1,021	950*
Coffee (green)	115	123	124*
Cocoa beans	5	2	3*

* Unofficial figure. † FAO estimates.
Source: FAO, *Production Yearbook*.

LIVESTOCK ('000 head, year ending September)

	1982	1983	1984
Horses*	113	113	113
Cattle	2,276	2,585*	2,550†
Pigs†	243	236	223

Poultry (million): 5* in 1982; 6* in 1983; 6* in 1984.
* FAO estimate. † Unofficial figures.
Source: FAO, *Production Yearbook*.

COSTA RICA *Statistical Survey*

LIVESTOCK PRODUCTS ('000 metric tons)

	1982	1983	1984
Beef and veal	68*	56	62*
Pig meat	9	9	8†
Poultry meat†	5	5	5
Cows' milk	302	325	340†
Cheese†	6	6	6
Butter and ghee†	4	4	4
Hen eggs	17*	18*	18†
Cattle hides (fresh)*	9	8	8

* Unofficial figures. † FAO estimates.
Source: FAO, *Production Yearbook*.

Forestry

ROUNDWOOD REMOVALS
('000 cubic metres, excluding bark)

	1982	1983	1984
Sawlogs, veneer logs and logs for sleepers	723	595	720
Pulpwood*	10	10	10
Other industrial wood*	167	171	176
Fuel wood*	2,362	2,428	2,489
Total	3,262	3,204	3,395

* FAO estimates.
Source: FAO, *Yearbook of Forest Products*.

SAWNWOOD PRODUCTION ('000 cubic metres)

	1982*	1983	1984
Total	378	306	412

* FAO estimate.
Source: FAO, *Yearbook of Forest Products*.

Fishing

('000 metric tons, live weight)

	1982	1983	1984
Inland waters	0.5	0.5	0.2
Atlantic Ocean	0.2	0.2	0.5
Pacific Ocean	10.2	8.5	11.2
Total catch	10.9	9.2	11.9

Source: FAO, *Yearbook of Fishery Statistics*.

Industry

SELECTED PRODUCTS

	1981	1982	1983
Cement ('000 metric tons)*	694	750	750
Salt (unrefined)* ('000 metric tons)	39	41	n.a.
Fish (tinned) ('000 metric tons)	1.9	1.2*	1.3*
Palm oil* ('000 metric tons)	23	24	24
Raw sugar ('000 metric tons)	190	194*	206*
Cocoa powder (metric tons)	468	n.a.	n.a.
Cocoa butter (metric tons)	1,208	n.a.	n.a.
Cigarettes (million units)	2,320	1,976	2,200
Nitrogenous fertilizers*†‡ ('000 metric tons)	40	42	46
Motor spirit (petrol) ('000 metric tons)	85	80	85
Kerosene ('000 metric tons)	18	18	20
Distillate fuel oils ('000 metric tons)	150	140	150
Residual fuel oils ('000 metric tons)	150	170	175
Bitumen ('000 metric tons)	15	12	15
Electric energy (million kWh)	2,362	2,500	2,700

* Estimates.
† Twelve months ending 30 June of the year stated.
‡ Production in terms of nitrogen.
Source: UN, *Industrial Statistics Yearbook*.

COSTA RICA

Statistical Survey

Finance

CURRENCY AND EXCHANGE RATES

Monetary Units
100 céntimos = 1 Costa Rican colón.

Denominations:
Coins: 5, 10, 25 and 50 céntimos; 1, 2, 5, 10 and 20 colones.
Notes: 5, 10, 20, 50, 100, 500 and 1,000 colones.

Sterling and Dollar Equivalents (30 September 1986)
£1 sterling = 82.877 colones;
US $1 = 57.275 colones;
1,000 Costa Rican colones = £12.07 = $17.46.

Average Exchange Rate (colones per US $)
1983 41.09
1984 44.53
1985 50.45

CENTRAL BANK RESERVES
(US $ million at 31 December)

	1983	1984	1985
Gold	34.98	n.a.	n.a.
IMF special drawing rights	2.98	0.11	0.02
Foreign exchange	308.29	404.89	506.35
Total	346.25	n.a.	n.a.

Source: IMF, *International Financial Statistics*.

MONEY SUPPLY (million colones at 31 December)

	1983	1984	1985
Currency outside banks	6,941	8,588	9,938
Demand deposits at commercial banks	18,401	21,399	22,367

Source: IMF, *International Financial Statistics*.

COST OF LIVING (Consumer price index for San José metropolitan area; base: 1975 = 100)

	1983	1984	1985
Food	611.4	665.2	746.7
Rent	383.2	410.3	485.7
Clothing	301.1	316.7	343.7
Miscellaneous	571.2	707.1	840.8
All items (incl. others)	509.4	570.3	656.1

BUDGET (million colones)

Revenue*	1983	1984	1985
Tax revenue	26,768.5	32,640.0	37,130.0
Taxes on income, profits and capital gains	4,713.6	4,737.7	5,062.1
Social security contributions	7,072.2	8,668.2	10,855.5
Taxes on property	146.9	157.0	128.5
Domestic taxes on goods and services	8,750.7	11,304.3	12,388.7
Sales tax	4,664.1	5,732.7	5,530.2
Excises	3,944.7	6,475.1	6,695.1
Import duties	1,712.9	4,252.9	5,359.6
Export duties	3,350.4	3,148.6	2,970.4
Banana tax	1,745.6	1,586.0	1,320.6
Exchange profits	—	16.6	0.1
Stamp taxes	180.5	510.9	583.9
Non-tax current revenue	1,312.4	3,731.3	3,880.6
Property income	607.0	2,689.6	2,768.7
Social security funds	350.3	659.0	1,196.5
Administrative fees and charges and non-industrial sales	212.3	450.6	365.3
Contributions to government employee pension funds within government	305.3	378.8	475.7
Capital revenue	0.2	4.7	—
Total	28,081.1	36,382.0	41,010.6

* Excluding grants (million colones): 10.4 in 1981; 28.9 in 1982; 34.0 in 1983.

Source: IMF, *Government Finance Statistics Yearbook*.

Expenditure†	1983	1984	1985
General public services	2,677.0	3,495.7	4,149.9
Defence	927.5	1,139.7	1,202.4
Education	5,906.9	6,841.1	8,086.2
Health, social security and welfare	11,261.2	13,286.5	16,162.0
Housing and community amenities	813.0	2,158.6	804.1
Housing	450.8	998.6	250.8
Sanitary services	290.5	353.2	339.1
Other community and social services	1,559.3	971.4	1,012.9
Economic services	6,145.3	7,036.9	7,471.0
General administration, regulation and research	109.1	132.3	149.8
Agriculture, forestry and fishing	1,614.6	1,472.8	1,586.8
Roads	3,836.4	4,942.0	5,382.5
Other transport and communications	124.2	159.4	175.3
Other purposes	3,134.8	4,073.9	4,935.7
Sub-total	32,425.0	39,003.8	43,824.2
Adjustment	−1,935.0	−1,805.5	−688.7
Total	30,490.0	37,198.3	43,135.5

† Excluding lending minus repayments (million colones): 215.8 in 1983; 378.3 in 1984; 342.0 in 1985.

BALANCE OF PAYMENTS (US $ million)

	1983	1984	1985
Merchandise exports f.o.b.	852.5	997.5	930.3
Merchandise imports f.o.b.	−897.8	−996.7	−1,005.2
Trade balance	−45.3	0.8	−74.9
Exports of services	319.9	315.9	336.9
Imports of services	−627.5	−613.7	−636.3
Balance on goods and services	−352.9	−297.0	−374.3
Private unrequited transfers (net)	22.9	31.9	34.3
Government unrequited transfers (net)	13.4	9.0	12.7
Current balance	−316.6	−256.1	−327.3
Direct capital investment (net)	55.3	52.0	67.0
Other long-term capital (net)	−119.2	−235.2	−206.1
Short-term capital (net)	−60.1	−99.0	−54.2
Net errors and omissions	82.3	108.4	117.5
Total (net monetary movements)	−358.3	−429.9	−403.1
Monetization of gold (net)	7.5	−13.7	11.3
Valuation changes (net)	6.4	11.5	−20.4
Exceptional financing (net)	428.6	425.1	530.2
Official financing (net)	−23.3	−51.2	−54.3
Changes in reserves	61.0	−58.2	−63.7

Source: IMF, *International Financial Statistics*.

External Trade

PRINCIPAL COMMODITIES (US $ million)

Imports	1982	1983	1984
Consumer durables	32.6	47.6	7.6
Consumer non-durables	134.4	167.7	171.2
Oil and fuel	86.5	100.0	83.3
Primary commodities	435.4	478.2	511.6
Building material	29.2	37.3	36.1
Machinery and equipment	167.2	151.9	50.3
Others	7.9	5.1	233.6
Total	893.2	987.8	1,093.7

Exports	1982	1983	1984
Coffee	236.9	230.1	267.3
Bananas	239.0	240.5	251.0
Sugar	13.2	17.4	35.5
Cattle and meat	54.7	32.7	43.7
Total (incl. others)	871.6	866.1	1,006.4

PRINCIPAL TRADING PARTNERS (US $ million)

Imports	1982	1983	1984
El Salvador	22.6	29.7	30.8
Germany, Federal Republic	35.1	46,7	56.2
Guatemala	56.2	59.4	59.4
Japan	37.1	52.8	82.4
Netherlands	40.6	6.1	10.5
United Kingdom	23.8	12.6	14.2
USA	316.8	372.9	394.5
Total (incl. others)	893.1	987.8	1,093.7

Exports	1982	1983	1984
El Salvador	33.1	41.6	44.5
Germany, Federal Republic	122.2	110.6	131.5
Guatemala	64.3	88.5	75.9
Japan	6.1	4.8	4.5
Netherlands	24.9	21.0	22:1
United Kingdom	26.1	12.2	16.8
USA	261.2	274.5	711.1
Total (incl. others)	870.4	872.6	1,006.4

Transport

RAILWAYS

	1982	1983	1984
Passenger journeys	2,397,147	2,508,959	2,000,933

ROAD TRAFFIC (motor vehicles in use at 31 December)

	1982	1983	1984
Cars and jeeps	91,350	101,251	106,233
Lorries	62,309	62,363	63,350
Buses	3,640	3,310	3,315
Industrial vehicles	10,322	10,812	11,109
Motor cycles	33,979	32,308	33,317
Total	201,600	210,044	217,324

1985: Cars and jeeps 109,802; Lorries 65,974; Buses 3,573.

INTERNATIONAL SEA-BORNE SHIPPING
(freight traffic in '000 metric tons)

	1981	1982	1983
Goods loaded	6,685.8	1,603.7	1,063.7
Goods unloaded	1,871.1	1,583.1	1,031.2

CIVIL AVIATION

	1981	1982	1983
Passengers:			
Domestic	119,249	123,892	70,943
International	464,061	517,658	529,947
Freight (metric tons):			
Domestic	454,400	383,700	175,900
International	19,107,400	17,746,600	19,602,500

Source (all transport statistics): Ministry of Public Works and Transport, San José.

Tourism

	1982	1983	1984
Visitors	371,582	326,242	273,901
Revenue (US $)	131,142,737	130,613,348	117,338,570

Source: Instituto Costarricense de Turismo.

Education

(1984)

	Institutions	Teachers	Pupils
Primary	3,068	12,223	353,958
Secondary	241	9,152	148,032

Directory

The Constitution

The present Constitution of Costa Rica was promulgated in November 1949. Its main provisions are summarized below:

GOVERNMENT

The government is unitary: provincial and local bodies derive their authority from the national Government. The country is divided into seven Provinces, each administered by a Governor who is appointed by the President. The Provinces are divided into Cantons, and each Canton into Districts. There is an elected Municipal Council in the chief city of each Canton, the number of its members being related to the population of the Canton. The Municipal Council supervises the affairs of the Canton. Municipal government is closely regulated by national law, particularly in matters of finance.

LEGISLATURE

The government consists of three branches: legislative, executive and judicial. Legislative power is vested in a single chamber, the Legislative Assembly, which meets in regular session twice a year—from 1 May to 31 July, and from 1 September to 30 November. Special sessions may be convoked by the President to consider specified business. The Assembly is composed of 57 deputies elected for four years. The chief powers of the Assembly are to enact laws, levy taxes, authorize declarations of war and, by a two-thirds vote, suspend, in cases of civil disorder, certain civil liberties guaranteed in the Constitution.

Bills may be initiated by the Assembly or by the Executive and must have three readings, in at least two different legislative periods, before they become law. The Assembly may override the presidential vote by a two-thirds vote.

EXECUTIVE

The executive branch is headed by the President, who is assisted by the Cabinet. If the President should resign or be incapacitated, the executive power is entrusted to the First Vice-President; next in line to succeed to executive power are the Second Vice-President and the President of the Legislative Assembly.

The President sees that the laws and the provisions of the Constitution are carried out, and maintains order; has power to appoint and remove Cabinet ministers and diplomatic representatives, and to negotiate treaties with foreign nations (which are, however, subject to ratification by the Legislative Assembly). The President is assisted in these duties by a Cabinet, each member of which is head of an executive department.

ELECTORATE

Suffrage is universal, compulsory and secret for persons over the age of 18 years.

DEFENCE

A novel feature of the Costa Rican Constitution is the clause outlawing a national army. Only by a continental convention or for the purpose of national defence may a military force be organized.

COSTA RICA

The Government

HEAD OF STATE

President: Lic. Oscar Arias Sánchez (took office 8 May 1986).
Vice-Presidents: Victoria Garrón de Doryan, Jorge Manuel Dengo.

THE CABINET
(December 1986)

Minister of the Presidency: Lic. Rodrigo Arias Sánchez.
Minister of Foreign Affairs: Rodrigo Madrigal Nieto.
Minister of the Interior: Lic. Guido Fernández Saborío.
Minister of Finance: Lic. Fernando Naranjo Villalobos.
Minister of Labour and Social Welfare: Lic. Edwin León Villalobos.
Minister of Health: Dr Edgar Mohs Villalta.
Minister of Public Works and Transport: Ing. Guillermo Constenla Umaña.
Minister of Public Security: Hernán Garrón Salazar.
Minister of Agriculture and Livestock: Ing. Alberto Esquivel Volio.
Minister of Public Education: Dr. Francisco Antonio Pacheco.
Minister of Economy and Trade: Lic. Luis Diego Escalante Vargas.
Minister of Energy and Mines: Alvaro Umaña Quesada.
Minister of Culture, Youth and Sport: Lic. Carlos Francisco Echeverría Salgado.
Minister of National Planning and Economic Policy: Lic. Otón Solís Fallas.
Minister of Justice and Grace: Dr Luis Paulino Mora.
Minister of Housing and Human Settlement: Dr Fernando Zumbado Jiménez.
Minister of Foreign Trade: Licda. Muni Figueres de Jiménez.
Minister of Science and Technology: Dr Rodrigo Zeledón Araya.

MINISTRIES

Ministry of Agriculture and Livestock: Apdo 10.094, San José; tel. 312341.
Ministry of Culture, Youth and Sport: Apdo 10.227, San José; tel. 227581.
Ministry of Economy and Trade: Apdo 10.216, San José; tel. 238036; telex 2414.
Ministry of Finance: Apdo 10.104, San José; tel. 229122; telex 2277.
Ministry of Foreign Affairs: Apdo 10.027, San José; tel. 237555; telex 2107.
Ministry of Health: Apdo 10.123, San José; tel. 230333.
Ministry of Housing and Human Settlement: Paseo Estudiantes 222, San José; tel. 332579.
Ministry of Energy and Mines: Avda 8–10, Calle 25, Apdo 4752, San José; tel. 334533; telex 3363.
Ministry of the Interior: Apdo 10.006, San José; tel. 232395.
Ministry of Justice and Grace: Apdo 5685, San José; tel. 237344.
Ministry of Labour and Social Welfare: Apdo 10.133, San José; tel. 237166.
Ministry of National Planning and Economic Policy: Apdo 10.127, San José; tel. 232322; telex 2962.
Ministry of the Presidency: Casa Presidencial, Apdo 10.089, San José; tel. 246155.
Ministry of Public Education: Apdo 10.087, San José; tel. 231666.
Ministry of Public Security: Apdo 1006, San José; tel. 232395; telex 3308.
Ministry of Public Works and Transport: Apdo 10.176, San José; tel. 260033; telex 2493.

Directory

President and Legislature

PRESIDENT

Presidential Election, 2 February 1986

Candidates	Percentage of Votes Cast
Oscar Rafael Arias Sánchez (PLN)	52.3
Rafael Angel Calderón Fournier (PUSC)	45.8
Alvaro Montero (PU)	
Alejandro Madrigal (ANC)	
Eugenio Jiménez Sancho (PI)	1.9
Rodrigo Gutiérrez Sáenz (AP)	

ASAMBLEA LEGISLATIVA

President: Dra Rosemary Kasspinsky de Murillo.

General Election, 2 February 1986

Party	Seats
Partido Liberación Nacional (PLN)	29
Partido Unidad Social Cristiana (PUSC)	25
Coalición Pueblo Unido (PU)	1
Alianza Popular (AP)*	1
Acción Agrícola Cartaginesa	1
Total	57

* A left-wing coalition, formed to contest the elections by the Partido del Pueblo Costarricense and several other parties.

Political Organizations

NATIONAL PARTIES

Acción del Pueblo (AP): San José; Pres. Angel Ruiz Zúñiga; Sec. Henry Mora Jiménez.
Alianza Nacional Cristiana (ANC): Pres. Victor Hugo González Montero; Sec. Juan Rodríguez Venegas.
Coalición Pueblo Unido (PU): Calle 4, Avda 7 y 9, San José; tel. 230032; Sec. Alberto Salom Echeverría; left-wing coalition comprising:
    Partido del Pueblo Costarricense: Apdo 6613, 100 San José; tel. 225517; f. 1931; Communist; Sec.-Gen. Manuel Mora Valverde.
    Partido Socialista Costarricense: San José; socialist; Pres. Alvaro Montero Mejía; Sec. Alberto Salom Echeverría.
    Partido de los Trabajadores: San José; Maoist; Pres. Johnny Francisco Araya Monge; Sec. Ilse Acosta Polonio.
Movimiento Nacional (MN): San José; Pres. Mario Echandi Jiménez; Sec. Rodrigo Sancho Robles.
Partido Concordia Costarricense: Calle 2 y 4, Avda 10, San José; tel. 232497; Pres. Emilio Piedra Jiménez; Sec. Roberto Francisco Salazar Madriz.
Partido Independiente (PI): San José; Pres. Eugenio Jiménez Sancho; Sec. Gonzalo Jiménez Chaves.
Partido de Liberación Nacional (PLN): Calle 28, Avda Central y 2, Apdo 2.244, San José; tel. 227489; f. 1948; social democratic party; affiliated to the Socialist International; 367,000 mems; Pres. Lic. Daniel Oduber Quirós; Sec.-Gen. Rolando Araya Monge.
Partido Nacional Democrático: San José; Pres. Rodolfo Cerdas Cruz; Sec. Eladio Jara Jiménez.
Partido Radical Demócrata: San José; Pres. Juan José Echeverría Brealey; Sec. Rodrigo Esquivel Rodríguez.
Partido Republicano Nacional: San José; Pres. Rolando Rodríguez Varela; Sec. Fernando Peña Herrera.
Partido Unidad Social Cristiana (PUSC): San José; Pres. Cristián Tattembach Yglesias; Sec. Roberto Tovar Faja.

COSTA RICA
Directory

Partido Unión Generaleña: Pérez Zeledón, Apdo 440-8000, San José; tel. 710524; f. 1981; Pres. Dr CARLOS A. FERNÁNDEZ VEGA; Sec. HUGO SÁENZ MARÍN.

Partido Unión Nacional: San José; Pres. OLGA MARTA ULATE ROJAS; Sec. RODRIGO GONZÁLEZ SABORÍO.

The following party is in suspension:

Acción Socialista: San José; Pres. MARCIAL AGUILUZ ORELLANA; Sec. ARNOLDO FERRETO SEGURA.

PROVINCIAL PARTIES

Acción Agrícola Cartaginesa: Cartago; Pres. JUAN BRENES CASTILLO; Sec. RODRIGO FALLAS BONILLA.

Acción Democrática Alajuelense: Alajuela; Pres. FRANCISCO ALFARO FERNÁNDEZ; Sec. JUAN BAUTISTA CHACÓN SOTO.

Partido Auténtico Limonense: Limón; Pres. MARVIN WRIGTH LINDO; Sec. GUILLERMO JOSEPH WIGNALL.

LOCAL PARTIES

Partido Alajuelita Nueva: Alajuela; Pres. ANNIE BADILLA CALDERÓN; Sec. CARLOS ALBERTO RETANA R.

Partido Laborista: La Unión; Pres. MIGUEL ANGEL MENDOZA HERNÁNDEZ; Sec. JORGE PACHECO ALVARADO.

The following guerrilla groups are active:

Ejército del Pueblo Costarricense (EPC): f. 1984; right-wing.

Patria y Libertad: f. 1985.

Diplomatic Representation

EMBASSIES IN COSTA RICA

Argentina: Calle 27, Avda Central, Apdo 1963, San José; tel. 213438; telex 2117; Ambassador: RUBÉN ANTONIO VELA.

Belgium: 4A, entrada de Los Yoses, Apdo 3.725, 100 San José; tel. 256255; telex 2909; Ambassador: Baron PANGAERT D' OPDORP.

Brazil: Edif. Plaza de la Artillería 7°, Calle 4, Avda Central y 1, Apdo 10.132, San José; tel. 234325; telex 2270; Ambassador: R. B. DENYS.

Bulgaria: Edif. Delcoré 3°, 100 m Sur Hotel Balmoral, Apdo 4.752, San José; Ambassador: KIRIL ZLATKOV NIKOLOV.

Canada: Edif. Cronos 6°, Avda Central, Calle 3, Apdo 10.303, San José; tel. 230446; telex 2179; Ambassador: STANLEY E. GOOCH.

Chile: De la Pulpería La Luz 125 metros Norte, Casa 116, Apdo 10.102, San José; tel. 244243; telex 2207; Ambassador: PEDRO PALACIOS CAMERÓN.

China (Taiwan): Edif. Mendiola 3°, Avda Central 917, Apdo 907, San José; tel. 213752; telex 2174; Ambassador: H. K. SHAO.

Colombia: Calle 5A, Avda 5A, San José; tel. 210725; telex 2198; Ambassador: CARLOS BORDA MENDOZA.

Czechoslovakia: Residencial El Prado, Carretera a Curridabat 75 metros oeste de la POPS, Apdo 3.910, San José; telex 2323; Chargé d'affaires: MIROSLAV GREPL.

Dominican Republic: Frente costado al norte de la Nunciatura Apostólica, Barrio Rohrmoser, Apdo 4.746, San José; telex 3210; Ambassador: JOSÉ MARCOS IGLESIAS IÑIGO.

Ecuador: Edif. Jiménez 3°, Avda 5 y Calle 1, Apdo 1.374, San José; tel. 236281; telex 2601; Ambassador: RAÚL SORROZO ENCALDA.

El Salvador: Edif. Trianón 3°, Avda Central y Calle 5A, Apdo 1.378, San José; tel. 225536; telex 2641; Ambassador: CARLOS MATAMOROS GUIROLA.

France: Carretera a Curridabat Del Indoor Club, 200 al Sur y 25 al Oeste, Apdo 10.177, San José; tel. 250733; telex 2191; Ambassador: JEAN-LOUIS MARFAING.

Germany, Federal Republic: Calle 36, Avda 3A, San José; tel. 215811; telex 2183; Ambassador: FRANZ ELLES.

Guatemala: Avda Primera detrás Más y Menos del Paseo Colón, Avda 2, San José; tel. 228991; Ambassador: Dr CARLOS URRUTIA-APARICIO.

Holy See: Urbanización Rohrmoser, Sabana Oeste, Apdo 992, Centro Colón, San José; tel. 322128; Apostolic Nuncio: Mgr PIER GIACOMO DE NICOLÒ.

Honduras: Edif. Jiménez de la Guardia 2°, Calle 1, Avda 5, Apdo 2.239, San José; tel. 222145; telex 2784; Ambassador: (vacant).

Israel: Calle 2, Avdas 2 y 4, Apdo 5.147, San José; tel. 216444; telex 2258; Ambassador: DAVID TOURGEMAN.

Italy: Calles 35 y 37, Avda 10, Los Yoses, Apdo 1.729, San José; tel. 246574; telex 2769; Ambassador: Dr ROSARIO GUIDO NICOSIA.

Japan: De la 1a entrada del Barrio Rohrmoser (Sabana Oeste) 500 metros y 100 Norte, Apdos 501 y 10.145, San José; tel. 321255; telex 2205; Ambassador: HIROYUKI KIMOTO.

Korea, Republic: Calle 28, Avda 2, Barrio San Bosco, Apdo 3.150, San José; tel. 212398; telex 2512; Ambassador: JAE HOON KIM.

Mexico: Avda 7, No 1371, Apdo 10.107, San José; tel. 225496; telex 2218; Ambassador: JESÚS CABRERA MUÑOZ LEDO.

Netherlands: 2a entrada de Los Yoses, 100m al sur, Avda 8, Calle 37, Apdo 10.285, San José; tel. 253516; telex 2187; Ambassador: JAN-WILLEM BERTENS.

Nicaragua: Edif. Trianón, Calle 25 y 27, Avda Central, San José; tel. 224749; telex 2316; Ambassador: CLAUDIA CHAMORRO BARRIOS.

Panama: 200m al sur, 25m al este de Higueron, La Granja, San Pedro de Montes de Oco, San José; tel. 253401; Ambassador: JOAQUÍN MEZA I.

Peru: Edif. Plaza Artillería 7°, Calle 4 y Avda Central, Apdo 4.248, San José; tel. 225644; Ambassador: ALFONSO ESPINOSA PALACIOS.

Poland: San José; Ambassador: (vacant).

Romania: Avda 1A, Calles 29–33, Barrio Escalante 2981, San José; tel. 225479; telex 2337; Ambassador: (vacant).

Spain: Paseo Colón No 3072, Apdos 10.150 y 2.058, San José; tel. 211933; telex 2438; Ambassador: MERCEDES RICO CARABIAS.

Switzerland: Calle 5, Avda 3 y 5, San José; tel. 214829; telex 2512; Ambassador: (vacant).

USSR: Apdo 6.340, San José; tel. 255780; telex 2299; Ambassador: YURI PAVLOV.

United Kingdom: Edif. Centro Colón 11°, Apdo 815, 1007 San José; tel. 215566; telex 2169; Ambassador: M. F. DALY.

USA: Calle 1, Avda 3, Apdo 10.054, San José; tel. 331155; Ambassador: (vacant).

Uruguay: Calle 2, Avda 1, San José; tel. 232512; Ambassador: (vacant).

Venezuela: Avda Central 5A entrada Los Yoses, Apdo 10.230, San José; tel. 255813; telex 2413; Ambassador: FRANCISCO QUIJADA G.

Yugoslavia: Calles 30 y 32, Paseo Colón, San José; tel. 220619; Ambassador: (vacant).

Judicial System

Ultimate judicial power is vested in the Supreme Court, the 17 justices of which are elected by the Assembly for a term of eight years, and are automatically re-elected for an equal period, unless the Assembly decides to the contrary by a two-thirds vote. Judges of the lower courts are appointed by the Supreme Court in plenary session.

The Supreme Court may also meet as the Corte Plena, with power to declare laws and decrees unconstitutional. There are also four appellate courts, criminal courts, civil courts and special courts. The jury system is not used.

La Corte Suprema: Apdo 01, San José 1000; tel. 230666; telex 1548.

President of the Supreme Court: ULISES ODIO SANTOS.

Religion

Under the Constitution, all forms of worship are tolerated. Roman Catholicism is the official religion of the country. Various Protestant Churches are represented. There are an estimated 7,000 members of the Methodist Church.

CHRISTIANITY
The Roman Catholic Church

Costa Rica comprises one archdiocese, three dioceses and one Apostolic Vicariate. At 31 December 1984 there were an estimated 2,295,000 adherents in the country, representing about 90% of the total population.

Bishops' Conference: Conferencia Episcopal de Costa Rica, Arzobispado, Apdo 3187, San José; tel. 210947; f. 1977; Pres. ROMÁN ARRIETA VILLALOBOS, Archbishop of San José de Costa Rica.

Archbishop of San José de Costa Rica: ROMÁN ARRIETA VILLALOBOS, Arzobispado, Apdo 497, 1000 San José; tel. 336029.

COSTA RICA

The Baptist Church
Baptist Convention of Costa Rica: Apdo 454, 2400 Desamparados, San José; tel. 301823; Pres. JORGE CORDERO.

BAHÁ'Í FAITH
National Spiritual Assembly: Apdo 3751, San José; tel. 225335; resident in 238 localities.

The Press

General Directorate of Information and the Press: Presidential House, Apdo 520, Zapote, San José; tel. 256205; telex 2376; Dir Lic. LIDIETTE BRENES DE CHARPENTIER.

DAILIES
Boletín Judicial: La Uruca, Apdo 5.024, San José; tel. 315222; f. 1878; journal of the judiciary; Dir ISAÍAS CASTRO VARGAS; circ. 2,500.
Diario Extra: Calle 4, Avda 4, Apdo 177-1009, San José; tel. 239505; f. 1978; morning; independent; Dir WILLIAM GÓMEZ.
La Gaceta: La Uruca, Apdo 5.024, San José; tel. 315222; f. 1878; official gazette; Dir ISAÍAS CASTRO VARGAS; circ. 5,000.
La Nación: Llorente de Tibás, Apdo 10.138, San José; tel. 351211; telex 2358; f. 1946; morning; independent; Dir EDUARDO ULIBARRI; circ. 85,000.
La Prensa Libre: Calle 4, Avda 4, Apdo 10.121, San José; tel. 236666; f. 1889; evening; independent; Dir ANDRÉS BORRASÉ SANOU; circ. 50,000.
La República: Barrio Tournón, Goicoechea, Apdo 2.130, San José; tel. 230266; f. 1950, reorganized 1967; morning; independent; Dir JOAQUÍN VARGAS GENE; circ. 58,000.

PERIODICALS
Abanico: Calle 4, esq. Avda 4, Apdo 10.121, San José; tel. 236666; weekly supplement of La Prensa Libre; women's interests; Editor ANGELA OROZCO SÁNCHEZ; circ. 50,000.
Acta Médica: Sabana Sur, Apdo 548, San José; tel. 323433; f. 1954; organ of the Colegio de Médicos; every 3 months; Editor Dr CLAUDIO CORDERO CABEZAS; circ. 1,000.
Contrapunto: La Uruca, Apdo 7-1980, San José; tel. 313333; f. 1978; fortnightly; publication of Sistema Nacional de Radio y Televisión; Dir FABIO MUÑOZ CAMPOS; circ. 10,000.
Eco Católico: Avda 10, Calles 5 y 7, Apdo 1.064, San José; tel. 225903; f. 1931; Catholic weekly; Dir ARMANDO ALFARO; circ. 15,000.
Libertad: Calle 0, Avdas 16 y 18, San José; tel. 239394; f. 1962; weekly; organ of the Partido Vanguardia Popular; Dir CÉSAR OLIVARES; circ. 25,000.
Mujer y Hogar: Avda 15, Casa 1916, Apdo 89, Barrio Aránjuez, San José; tel. 223525; f. 1943; weekly; women's journal; Editor and Gen. Man. CARMEN CORNEJO MÉNDEZ; circ. 15,000.
Noticiero del Café: Calle 1, Avdas 18 y 20, Apdo 37, San José; tel. 226411; telex 2279; f. 1964; monthly; coffee journal; owned by the Instituto del Café; Dir ROCÍO BOGANTES MADRIGAL; circ. 5,000.
Perfil: Llorente de Tibás, Apdo 10138, San José; tel. 351211; telex 2358; fortnightly; women's interest; Dir GRETTEL ALFARO.
Polémica: Icadis, Apdo 1.006, Paseo de los Estudiantes, San José; tel. 333964; f. 1981; every 4 months; left-wing; Dir GABRIEL AGUILERA PERALTA.
Rumbo Centroamericano: Llorente de Tibás, Apdo 10.138, San José; tel. 351211; telex 2358; f. 1984; general; Dir MARCELA ANGULO GRILLO; circ. 15,000.
San José News: Apdo 7-2.730, San José; 2 a week; Dir CHRISTIAN RODRÍGUEZ.
Semanario Universidad: Ciudad Universitaria Rodrigo Facio, San Pedro Montes de Oca, San José; tel. 255857; telex 2544; f. 1970; weekly; general; Dir Lic. CARLOS MORALES CASTRO; circ. 15,000.
The Tico Times: Calle 6, diagonal a la Corte Suprema de Justicia, Apdo 4.632, San José; tel. 220040; weekly; in English; Dir RICHARD DYER; circ. 12,000.

PRESS ASSOCIATIONS
Colegio de Periodistas de Costa Rica: Sabana Este, Calle 42, Avda 4, Apdo 5.416, San José; tel. 335850; f. 1969; 450 mems; Admin. Dir WILLIAM MONGE.
Sindicato Nacional de Periodistas: Sabana Este, Calle 42, Avda 4, Apdo 5416, San José; tel. 227589; f. 1970; 105 mems; Sec.-Gen. BERNI QUIRÓS HERRERA.

FOREIGN NEWS BUREAUX
ACAN-EFE (Central America): Costado Sur, Casa Matute Gómez, Casa 1912, Apdo 84930, San José; tel. 226785; telex 3197; Correspondent WILFREDO CHACÓN SERRANO.
Agence France-Presse (France): Calle 13, entre Avdas 9 y 11, Apdo 5276, San José; tel. 330757; telex 2403; Correspondent JEAN-PIERRE BOUSQUET.
Agencia EFE (Spain): Avda 10, Calles 19 y 21, No 1912, Apdo 84930, San José; tel. 226785; telex 3197.
Agentstvo Pechati Novosti (APN) (USSR): De la Casa Italiana 100 Este, 50 Norte, Apdo 1011, San José; tel. 241560; telex 2711.
Agenzia Nazionale Stampa Associata (ANSA) (Italy): c/o Diario la República, Barrio Tournón, Guadalupe, Apdo 2.130, San José; tel. 230840; telex 2538; Correspondent YEHUDI MONESTEL ARCE.
Associated Press (AP) (USA): Calles 11 y 13, Avda 7, Apdo 2218, San José; tel. 216146; Correspondent OLDEMAR RAMÍREZ.
Deutsche Presse-Agentur (dpa) (Federal Republic of Germany): Edif. Trifami, Of. 606, Calle 2, Avda 1, Apdo 7156, San José; tel. 330604; Correspondent DANILO ARIAS MADRIGAL.
Inter Press Service (IPS) (Italy): Calle 11 entre Avda 1 y 3, No 152, Apdo 70.1002, San José; tel. 236952; telex 3239; Dir LUIS PÁSARA.
Prensa Latina (Cuba): 150 Sur Edif. Ana Lorena (IDA), Barrio Betania, San José; tel. 342606; telex 3223; Correspondent LUIS BÁEZ.
Telegrafnoye Agentstvo Sovetskovo Soyuza (TASS) (USSR): De la Casa Italia 1000 Este, 50 Norte, Casa 675, Apdo 1011, San José; tel. 241560; telex 2711; Correspondent ENRIQUE MORA.
United Press International (UPI) (USA): Calle 15, Avda 2, Radio Reloj, Apdo 4.334, San José; tel. 222644; Correspondent WILLIAM CESPEDES CHAVARRÍA.
Xinhua (New China) News Agency (People's Republic of China): Apdo 4774, San José; tel. 313497; telex 3066; Correspondent XU BIHUA.

Publishers

Alfalit Internacional: Diagonal a los Tribunales de Justicia, Apdo 292, Alajuela; f. 1961; educational; Dir GILBERTO BERNAL.
Antonio Lehmann Librería, Imprenta y Litografía, Ltda: Calles 1 y 3, Avda Central, Apdo 2.014, San José; tel. 231212; telex 2540; f. 1896; general fiction, educational, textbooks; Man. Dir ANTONIO LEHMANN STRUVE.
Editorial Caribe: Apdo 1.307, San José; tel. 227244; f. 1949; religious textbooks; Dir JOHN STROWEL.
Editorial Costa Rica: Calle 1A, Avda 18, Apdo 10.010, San José; tel. 234875; f. 1959; government-owned; Gen. Admin. MARY NASSAR DE OLASO.
Editorial Fernández Arce: Apdo 6.523, 1000 San José; tel. 216321; f. 1967; textbooks for primary, secondary and university education; Dir Dr MARIO FERNÁNDEZ LOBO.
Editorial Texto Ltda: Calle 26, Avdas 5 y 7, Apdo 2.988-1.000, San José; tel. 227661; Dir FRANK THOMAS GALLARDO.
Editorial de la Universidad Autónoma de Centroamérica (UACA): Apdo 7637-1.000, San José; tel. 235822; telex 2907; f. 1981; Dir RODOLFO PIZA.
Editorial de la Universidad Estatal a Distancia (EUNED): Plaza González Víquez, Apdo 2, San José; tel. 235430; telex 3003; f. 1979; Dir CARLOS ALBERTO ARCE.
Editorial Universitaria Centroamericana (EDUCA): Apdo 64, Ciudad Universitaria Rodrigo Facio, 2060 San José; tel. 258740; telex 3011; f. 1969; organ of the CSUCA; science, art, philosophy; Editorial Dir CARMEN NARANJO.
Mesen Editores: Apdo 146-2.400, Desamparados, San José; tel. 592455; f. 1978; general; Dir DENIS MESÉN SEGURA.
Trejos Hermanos Sucs, SA: Curridabat, Apdo 10.096, San José; tel. 242411; telex 2875; f. 1912; general and reference; Man. ALVARO TREJOS.

ASSOCIATION
Cámara Costarricense del Libro: San José; Pres. LUIS FERNANDO CALVO FALLAS.

COSTA RICA   *Directory*

Radio and Television

In 1984 there were an estimated 420,000 radio receivers and 426,000 television receivers in use.

Control Nacional de Radio: Dirección Nacional de Comunicaciones, Ministerio de Gobernación y Policia, Apdo 10.006, 1000 San José; tel. 257421; f. 1954; governmental supervisory department; Dir WARREN MURILLO MARTÍNEZ.

Cámara Nacional de Medios de Comunicación Colectiva (CANAMECC): Calle 3 Bis, Avda 7 y 9, Apdo 6.574, San José; tel. 224820; f. 1954; Pres. CLAUDIO REYES ACOSTA.

Cámara Nacional de Radio (CANARA): Calle 3 Bis, Avda 7 y 9, Edif. Teresa, Apdo 6.574, San José; tel. 224820; Pres. GERARDO LEE ROJAS.

Asociación Costarricense para Información y Cultura (ACIC): San José; f. 1983; independent body; controls private radio stations; Pres. EUGENIO PIGNATARO PACHECO.

RADIO
Non-Commercial

Faro del Caribe: Apdo 2.710, 1000 San José; tel. 262618; f. 1948; call letters TIFC; religious and cultural programmes in Spanish and English; Man. JUAN JACINTO OCHOA F.

Radio Costa Rica: Apdo 365, 1009 San José; tel. 336628; f. 1985; broadcasts Voice of America news bulletins (in Spanish) and locally-produced educational and entertainment programmes; Pres. EUGENIO PIGNATARO PACHECO.

Radio Fides: Avda 4, Curia Metropolitana, Apdo 5.079, 1000 San José; tel. 221252; f. 1952; Catholic station; Dir P. JORGE LUIS CAMPOS.

Radio Santa Clara: Santa Clara, San Carlos, Ciudad Quesada, Alajuela; tel. 471264; f. 1986; Roman Catholic station; Dir P. MARCO A. SOLÍS V.

Radio Universidad de Costa Rica: Ciudad Universitaria Rodrigo Facio, San José; tel. 253936; f. 1949; classical music; Dir JOSÉ TASIES SOLÍS.

Commercial

There are about 40 commercial radio stations including:

Cadena de Emisoras Columbia: Apdo 708, San José; tel. 340354; operates Radio Columbia, Radio Uno, Radio Sabrosa, Radio Puntarenas; Dir ARNOLDO ALFARO CHAVARRÍA.

Cadena Musical: 13 Moravia, Apdo 854, San José; tel. 362026; f. 1954; operates Radio Musical, Radio Cucu and Radio Sonora; Dir RIGOBERTO URBINA PINTO.

Circuito Radial Titania: Apdo 10.279, San José; tel. 226033; operates Radio Titania and Radio Sensación; Dir RODOLFO BAZO ODOR.

Grupo Centro: Apdo 6.133, San José; tel. 223041; operates Radio Centro, Radio Centro Turrialba, Radio W Liberia, Radio W San Isidro, MI Radio (Alajuela), Stereo Azul; Dir ROBERTO HERNÁNDEZ RAMÍREZ.

Radio Chorotega: Santa Cruz de Guanacaste, Apdo 92; tel. 680447; f. 1983; Catholic station; Dir P. ROHANY VALLEJO.

Radio Emasus: San Visto de Coto Brus; tel. 773101; f. 1962; Roman Catholic station; Dir P. ALVARO COTO.

Radio Fundación: Apdo 301, 2400 San José; tel. 591213; operated by the Fundación 'Ciudadelas de Libertad' to promote educational and cultural development; Man. VÍCTOR BERMÚDEZ MORA.

Radio Monumental/Radio Linda: Apdo 800, San José; tel. 220000; f. 1929; all news station; Dir NORA RUIZ DE ANGULO.

Radio Sinai/Radio Eraus: Apdo 262, San Isidro del General, Pérez Zeledón; tel. 710367; f. 1957; Dir P. ALVARO COTO OROZCO.

Sistema Radiofónico: Apdo 341, San José; tel. 224344; operates Radio Reloj and Radio Sonido 1120; Dir RÓGER BARAHONA GÓMEZ.

TELEVISION
Government-Owned

Red Nacional de TV: Apdo 7-1.980, San José; tel. 329627; cultural; Dir Lic. ARMANDO VARGAS ARAYA.

Commercial

Corporación Costarricense de Televisión: Apdo 1.860, San José; tel. 210255; telex 2443; Gen. Man. MARIO SOTELA BLEN.

Multivisión de Costa Rica: Apdo 4.666, San José; tel. 334444; telex 3043; operates Radio Sistema Universal A.M. (f. 1956), Channel 9 (f. 1962) and Channel 4 (f. 1964) and FM (f. 1980); Gen. Man. ARNOLD VARGAS V.

Telenac—Canal 2: Apdo 2.860, San José; tel. 312222; Pres. MARIO SOTELA BLEN.

Televisora de Costa Rica, SA (Teletica): Apdo 3.876, San José; tel. 322222; telex 2220; f. 1960; operates Channel 7; Pres. OLGA DE PICADO; Gen. Man. RENÉ PICADO COZZA.

Canal 6: Apdo 2.860, San José; tel. 329255; f. 1965; Pres. MARIO SOTELA BLEN.

Canal 11: Apdo 5.542, San José; tel. 331011; Pres. FRANZ ULRICH.

Finance

(cap. = capital; p.u. = paid up; res = reserves; dep. = deposits; m. = million; brs = branches; amounts in colones)

BANKING

Banco Central de Costa Rica: Apdo 10.058, San José; tel. 334233; telex 2163; f. 1950; cap. 5m., dep. 32,445.5m. (Dec. 1985); Exec. Pres. Dr EDUARDO LIZANO; Gen. Man. RODRIGO BOLAÑOS.

State-Owned Banks

Banco Anglo-Costarricense: Apdo 10.038, San José; tel. 223322; telex 2132; f. 1863; responsible for servicing commerce; cap. and res 893.6m., dep. 9,293.3m. (Dec. 1984); Pres. JORGE ARAYA WESTOVER; Gen. Man. JOSÉ MANUEL PERAZA.

Banco de Costa Rica: Avda Fernández Güell y Calle 4, Apdo 10.035, 1000 San José; tel. 331100; telex 2103; f. 1877; responsible for industry; cap. and res 1,547.4m., dep. 22,169.6m. (Dec. 1985); Pres. Lic. ROLANDO FERNÁNDEZ S.; Gen. Man. Lic. RODOLFO ULLOA A.; 20 brs.

Banco Crédito Agrícola de Cartago: Calle 5 a 2, Apdo 297, Cartago; tel. 513011; telex 8006; f. 1918; responsible for housing; cap. 377,049m., dep. 3,341m. (Aug. 1984); Pres. JORGE EDUARDO COTO BARBOZA; Gen. Man. FRANCISCO MARÍN ALVARADO; 5 brs.

Banco Nacional de Costa Rica: Calles 2 y 4, Avda 1A, Apdo 10.015, San José; tel. 232221; telex 02120; f. 1914; responsible for the agricultural sector; cap. and res 2,201.8m., dep. 31,865.4m. (Dec. 1984); Pres. OSCAR AUILAS; Gen. Man. Lic. PORFIRIO MORERA BATRES; 13 brs.

Banco Popular y de Desarrollo Comunal: Calle 1, Avda 2 y 4, Apdo 10.190, San José; tel. 228122; telex 2844; f. 1969; cap. 260m., res 6m., dep. 940m. (June 1981); Pres. MARIO MONTENEGRO MORA; Gen. Man. ALVARO UREÑA ALVAREZ.

Private Banks

Banco de la Construcción, SA: Edif. Colón, Apdo 5.099, San José; tel. 215811; telex 2473; f. 1974; cap. p.u. 10m. (Dec. 1978); Pres. Dr ANTONIO PEÑA CHARANÍA; Man. HERNÁN VOLIO CALLEJA.

Banco Latinoamericano (Costa Rica), SA: San José; f. 1974; cap. 5m.; Pres. FERNANDO BERROCAL S.; Man. FRED O'NEILL G.

Banco Lyon, SA: Calle 2, No 32 Norte, Apdo 10.184, San José; tel. 212611; telex 2577; f. 1871; res 11.8m. (June 1984); Pres. JORGE LYON CHAVARRÍA; Gen. Man. JORGE ARTURO GRANADOS M.

Banco de Santander (Costa Rica), SA: Avda 2, Calle Central, Apdo 6.714, San José; tel. 228066; telex 2666; f. 1977; cap. 35m. (1985); Pres. EMILIO BOTÍN SANZ DE S.; Gen. Man. JOSÉ LUIS ALBERO VERANO.

Bank of America, SA: Calle Central, Avdas 3 y 5, Apdo 5.445, San José; tel. 219911; f. 1968; cap. p.u. 5m., res 2.6m. (June 1978); Pres. DONN R. DAVIS; Man. VÍCTOR PEDROSO.

Credit Co-operatives

Federación Nacional de Cooperativas de Ahorro y Crédito y de Servicios Múltiples (Fedecrédito): Calle 1, 471, Apdo 4.748, San José; tel. 230301; f. 1963; 125 co-operatives, with 147,500 mems; combined cap. US $50m.; Gen. Man. Lic. MANUEL A. ARAYA BARBOZA.

STOCK EXCHANGE

Bolsa Nacional de Valores, SA: Edif. Cartagena 7°, Calle Central, Avda 1, Apdo 1.736, San José; tel. 228011; telex 2863; f. 1972; Exec. Pres. Ing. HUMBERTO PÉREZ BONILLA.

COSTA RICA
Directory

INSURANCE

Instituto Nacional de Seguros: Calles 9 y 9B, Avda 7, Apdo 10.061, 1000 San José; tel. 235800; telex 2290; f. 1924; administers the state monopoly of insurance; services of foreign insurance companies may be used only by authorization of the Ministry of Economy and after the Instituto has certified it will not accept the risk; cap. and res 3,389m. colones (Dec. 1983); Exec. Pres. Dr JORGE ELÍAS RAMÍREZ; Gen. Man. VÍCTOR JULIO BRENES ZÚÑIGA.

Trade and Industry

STATE AGENCIES

Cámara Nacional de Artesanía y Pequeña Industria de Costa Rica: Calle 11, Avda 1, Apdo 8–6.540, San José; tel. 232763; f. 1963; development, marketing and export of small-scale industries and handicrafts; Man. MIREYA GUEVARA DE PADILLA.

Centro de Promoción de Exportaciones e Inversiones: Apdo 5.418, San José; tel. 217166; telex 2385; f. 1968 to encourage increased investment in export oriented activities and greater exports of non-traditional products; Exec. Dir EDUARDO ALONSO.

CINDE: Apdo 7.170, 1000 San José; tel. 231711; coalition for development initiatives to attract foreign investment for production and export of new products; Dir FEDERICO VARGAS PERALTA.

CODESA: Apdo 10.254, San José; tel. 224423; f. 1972; state development corporation; Pres. LUIS GARITA BONILLA.

Consejo Nacional de Producción: Calle 36 a 12, Apdo 2.205, San José; tel. 236033; telex 2273; f. 1948 to encourage agricultural and fish production and to regulate production and distribution of basic commodities; Pres. ANTONIO ALVAREZ DESANTI.

Instituto Costarricense de Acueductos y Alcantarillados: Avda Central, Calle 5, Apdo 5.120, San José; tel. 332155; telex 2724; water and sewerage; Exec. Pres. Ing. ELADIO PRADO.

Instituto Costarricense de Electricidad: Apdo 10.032, 1000 San José; tel. 327732; telex 2140; state power and telecommunications agency; Pres. Ing. TEÓFILO DE LA TORRE A.; Gen. Man. Ing. RODRIGO SUÁREZ MEJIDO.

Instituto de Fomento y Asesoría Municipal: Apdo 10.187, San José; tel. 233714; f. 1970; municipal development institute; Pres. JORGE URBINA ORTEGA; Exec. Dir HARRY JAGER CONTRERAS.

Instituto de Desarrollo Agrícola (IDA): Apdo 5.054, 1000 San José; tel. 246066; Exec. Pres. Lic. Ing. SERGIO QUIRÓS MAROTO.

Instituto Mixto de Ayuda Social (IMAS): Calle 29, entre Avdas 2 y 4, Apdo 2.613, San José; tel. 252555; telex 1559; Pres. Lic. DENIS GARCÍA URBINA.

Instituto Nacional de Fomento Cooperativo: Apdo 10.103, San José; tel. 234355; f. 1973; to encourage the establishment of co-operatives and to provide technical assistance and credit facilities; cap. 11m. (May 1986); Pres. JOSÉ WALTER OROZCO FONSECA; Exec. Dir Lic. RAFAEL A. ROJAS JIMÉNEZ.

Instituto Nacional de Vivienda y Urbanismo: Apdo 2.534, San José; tel. 215266; telex 2908; housing and town planning institute; Exec. Pres. Minister of Housing and Human Settlement; Man. Dr HERMÁN VOLIO.

Ministerio de Planificación Nacional y Política Económica: Apdo 10.127, 1000 San José; tel. 237833; telex 2962; f. 1963; formulates and supervises execution of the National Development Plan; main aims: to increase national productivity; to improve distribution of income and social services; to increase citizen participation in solution of socio-economic problems; Dir Minister of National Planning and Economic Policy.

Oficina del Café: Calle 1, Avdas 18 y 20, Apdo 37, San José; tel. 226411; telex 2279; f. 1948 to develop the coffee industry, to control production and to regulate marketing; Pres. ODALIER VILLALOBOS; Exec. Dir. Lic. MARIO FERNÁNDEZ URPÍ.

Refinadora Costarricense de Petróleo (Recope): Apdo 4351, San José; tel. 239611; telex 2215; f. 1961; state petroleum organization; Gen. Man. ROBERTO DOBLES.

CHAMBERS OF COMMERCE AND INDUSTRY

Cámara de Comercio de Costa Rica: Urbanización Tournón, Apdo 1.114, 1000 San José; tel. 210005; telex 2646; f. 1915; 1,000 mems; Pres. SAMUEL HIDALGO SOLANO; Exec. Dir JULIO UGARTE.

Cámara de Industrias de Costa Rica: Calles 13–15, Avda 6, Apdo 10.003, San José; tel. 232411; telex 2474; f. 1943; Pres. JORGE WOODBRIDGE; Exec. Dir GUSTAVO GUTIÉRREZ CASTRO.

Unión de Cámaras: Apdo 539-1002, Paseo de Estudiantes, San José; tel. 210778; f. 1974; business federation; Pres. VÍCTOR E. HERRERA ALFARO.

AGRICULTURAL ORGANIZATIONS

Cámara de Azucareros: Calle 3, Avda Fernández Güell, Apdo 1.577, 1000 San José; tel. 212103; f. 1949; sugar growers; Pres. RODOLFO JIMÉNEZ BORBÓN.

Cámara Nacional de Agricultura: Avda 1, Calles 24 y 28, Apdo 1671, 1000 San José; tel. 216864; telex 3489; f. 1947; Pres. ALFREDO ROBERT POLINI.

Cámara Nacional de Bananeros: Calle 3, Avda Central y Primera, Edif. Jiménez, Apdo 10.273, San José; tel. 227891; f. 1967; banana growers; Pres. Ing. ASDRÚBAL CARBALLO CHAVES.

Cámara Nacional de Cafetaleros: Calle 3, Avdas 6 y 8, Apdo 1.310, San José; tel. 218207; telex 2525; f. 1948; 300 mems; coffee growers; Pres. TOBÍAS UMAÑA.

Cámara Nacional de Ganaderos: Edif. Ilifilán 4°, Calles 2 y 4, Avda Central Apdo 4.564, San José; tel. 221652; cattle farmers; Pres. VÍCTOR WOLF FOURNIER.

TRADE UNIONS

Central Auténtica de Trabajadores Democráticos (Democratic Workers' Union): Calle 13 a 10 y 12, Solera; tel. 532971; Sec.-Gen. Prof. CARLOS VARGAS.

Central de Trabajadores Costarricenses (Costa Rican Workers' Union): Calle 20 a 3 y 5, San José; tel. 217701; Sec.-Gen. ALSIMIRO HERRERA TORRES.

Confederación Costarricense de Trabajadores Democráticos (Costa Rican Confederation of Democratic Workers): Calles 3–5, Avda 12, Apdo 2.167, San José; tel. 221981; telex 2167; f. 1966; mem. ICFTU and ORIT; Sec.-Gen. MIGUEL CALDERÓN SANDÍ; 50,000 mems.

Confederación Unitaria de Trabajadores (CUT): Calles 1 y 3, Avda 12, Casa No 142, San José; tel. 335805; f. 1980 from a merger of the Federación Nacional de Trabajadores Públicos and the Confederación General de Trabajadores; linked to Coalición Pueblo Unido; 53 affiliated unions; Pres. MARIO DEVANDAS; Sec.-Gen. Lic. RODRIGO UREÑA QUIRÓS; c. 55,000 mems.

Federación Sindical Agraria Nacional (FESIAN) (National Agrarian Confederation): 20,000 member families.

Transport

Ministerio de Obras Públicas y Transportes: Apdo 10.176, San José; tel. 260033; telex 2493; the ministry is responsible for setting tariffs, allocating funds, maintaining existing systems and constructing new ones.

Cámara Nacional de Transportes: Calle 20, Avda 7, San José; tel. 225394; national chamber of transport.

RAILWAYS

Instituto Costarricense de Ferrocarriles (INCOFER): Apdo No 1, 1009 FE al P Estación, Zona 3, San José; tel. 260011; telex 2393; government-owned; 700 km, of which 320 km are electrified; Exec. Pres. Ing. JOSÉ F. NICOLÁS ALVARADO.

INCOFER comprises:

División I: San José to Limón; Río Frío to Limón; f. 1986; 130 km of track are electrified.

División II: Alajuela to San José; San José to Puntarenas.

Other railways in Costa Rica include 48 km of track belonging to the United Fruit Company of Boston (USA).

ROADS

In 1984 there were 28,410 km of roads, of which 2,834 km were paved, excluding 683 km of the Pan-American Highway.

SHIPPING

Local services operate between the Costa Rican ports of Puntarenas and Limón and those of Colón and Cristóbal in Panama and other Central American ports. The multi-million dollar project at Caldera on the Gulf of Nicoya is now in operation as the main Pacific port; Puntarenas is being used as the second port. The Caribbean coast is served by the port complex of Limón/Moír. International services are operated by various foreign shipping lines.

COSTA RICA

Cooperativa de Pescadores del Pacífico: Apdo 336, Puntarenas; 2 vessels.

Junta de Administración Portuaria y de Desarrollo Económico de la Vertiente Atlántica (JAPDEVA): Calle 17, Avda 7, Apdo 8–5.330, 1000 San José; tel. 335301; telex 2435; state agency for the development of Atlantic ports; Exec. Pres. Lic. RAFAEL BARRIENTOS GERMÉ.

Instituto Costarricense de Puertos del Pacífico (INCOP): Calle 36 a 3, San José; tel. 237111; state agency for the development of Pacific ports; Exec. Pres. RODRIGO ARAÚZ BONILLA.

Naviera Multinacional del Caribe, SA (NAMUCAR): Avda No 2 Calle 7 y 9, 746, Apdo 10.095, San José; tel. 213666; telex 2463; 2 vessels.

CIVIL AVIATION

Costa Rica's main international airport is the Juan Santamaría Airport, 16 km from San José at El Coco and there are regional airports at Liberia, Limón and Pavas (Tobías Bolaños Airport).

Líneas Aéreas Costarricenses, SA—LACSA (Costa Rican Airlines): Apdo 1.531, San José; tel. 323555; telex 2188; f. 1946; operates international services to Colombia, El Salvador, Guatemala, Mexico, Panama, Puerto Rico, Venezuela and the USA; Chair. and Chief Exec. Capt. OTTO ESCALANTE W.; fleet: 3 Boeing 727-200, 1 DC-8-62F (cargo).

Servicios Aéreos Nacionales, SA (SANSA): Paseo Colón, Apdo 999-1000, Centro Colón, San José; tel. 332714; telex 2914; internal services; Gen. Man. Lic. CARLOS MANUEL DELGADO AGUILAR; fleet: 2 Aviocar C-212.

Tourism

A total of 273,901 tourists visited Costa Rica in 1984. The political instability elsewhere in Central America has discouraged foreign visitors.

Cámara Nacional de Turismo: Centro Comercial, 2°, Apdo 828, 2000 San José; tel. 311558.

Instituto Costarricense de Turismo: Apdo 777, San José; tel. 231733; telex 2281; f. 1964; Exec. Pres. ROBERTO LOBO ANAYA.

Atomic Energy

Comisión de Energía Atómica de Costa Rica: Calle 5, No 555, Apdo Postal 6681, San José; tel. 231997; f. 1967; Pres. Dr MANUEL CONSTENLA UMAÑA; Dir Dr NILO VICARIOLI CORRADI.

CUBA

Introductory Survey

Location, Climate, Language, Religion, Flag, Capital

The Republic of Cuba is an archipelago of two main islands, Cuba and the Isle of Youth (formerly the Isle of Pines), and about 1,600 keys and islets. It lies in the Caribbean Sea, 145 km (90 miles) south of Florida, USA. Other nearby countries are the Bahamas, Mexico, Jamaica and Haiti. The climate is tropical, with the annual rainy season from May to October. The average annual temperature is 25°C (77°F) and hurricanes are frequent. The language is Spanish. Most of the inhabitants are Christians, of whom the great majority are Roman Catholics. The national flag (proportions 2 by 1) has five equal horizontal stripes, of blue, white, blue, white and blue, with a red triangle, enclosing a five-pointed white star, at the hoist. The capital is Havana (La Habana).

Recent History

Cuba was ruled by Spain from the 16th century until 1898, when the island was ceded to the USA after Spain's defeat in the Spanish–American War. Cuba became an independent republic on 20 May 1902, but the USA retained its naval bases on the island and, until 1934, reserved the right to intervene in Cuba's internal affairs. In 1933 an army sergeant, Fulgencio Batista Zaldivar, came to power at the head of a military revolt. Batista ruled the country, directly or indirectly, until 1944, when he retired after serving a four-year term as elected President.

In March 1952, however, Gen. Batista (as he had become) seized power again, deposing President Carlos Prío Socarrás in a bloodless coup. Batista's new regime soon proved to be unpopular and became harshly repressive. In July 1953 a radical opposition group, led by Dr Fidel Castro Ruz, attacked the Moncada army barracks in Santiago de Cuba. Castro was captured, with many of his supporters, but later released. He went into exile and formed a revolutionary movement which was committed to Batista's overthrow. In December 1956 Castro landed in Cuba with a small group of followers, most of whom were captured or killed. However, 12 survivors, including Castro and the Argentine-born Dr Ernesto ('Che') Guevara, escaped into the hills of the Sierra Maestra, where they formed the nucleus of the guerrilla forces which, after a prolonged struggle, forced Batista to flee from Cuba on 1 January 1959. The Batista regime collapsed, and Castro's forces occupied Havana.

The assumption of power by the victorious rebels was initially met with great popular acclaim. The 1940 constitution was suspended in January 1959, being replaced by a new 'Fundamental Law'. Executive and legislative power was vested in the Council of Ministers, with Fidel Castro as Prime Minister and his brother Raúl as his deputy. Guevara reportedly ranked third in importance. The new regime ruled by decree but promised to hold elections within 18 months. When it was firmly established, the Castro Government adopted a radical economic programme, including agrarian reform and the nationalization of industrial and commercial enterprises. These drastic reforms, combined with the regime's authoritarian nature, provoked opposition from some sectors of the population, including former supporters of Castro, and many Cubans went into exile.

All US business interests in Cuba were expropriated, without compensation, in October 1960, and the USA severed diplomatic relations in January 1961. A US-sponsored force of anti-Castro Cuban émigrés landed in April 1961 at the Bahía de Cochinos (Bay of Pigs), in southern Cuba, but the invasion was thwarted by Castro's troops. Later in the year, all pro-Government groups were merged to form the Organizaciones Revolucionarias Integradas (ORI). In December 1961 Fidel Castro publicly announced that Cuba had become a Communist state, and he proclaimed a 'Marxist-Leninist' programme for the country's future development. In January 1962 Cuba was excluded from active participation in the Organization of American States (OAS). The USA instituted a full economic and political blockade of Cuba. Hostility to the USA was accompanied by increasingly close relations between Cuba and the USSR. In October 1962 the USA revealed the presence of Soviet missiles in Cuba but, after the imposition of a US naval blockade, the weapons were withdrawn. The missile bases, capable of launching nuclear weapons against the USA, were dismantled, so resolving one of the most serious international crises since the Second World War. In 1964 the OAS imposed diplomatic and commercial sanctions against Cuba.

The ORI was replaced in 1962 by a new Partido Unido de la Revolución Socialista Cubana (PURSC), which was established, under Fidel Castro's leadership, as the country's sole legal party. Guevara resigned his military and government posts in April 1965, subsequently leaving Cuba to pursue revolutionary activities abroad. In October 1965 the PURSC was renamed the Partido Comunista Cubano (PCC). Although it is ostracized by most other Latin American countries, the PCC Government has maintained and consolidated its internal authority, with little effective opposition. Supported by considerable aid from the USSR, the regime has made significant progress in social and economic development, including improvements in education and public health. At the same time, Cuba has continued to give active support to left-wing revolutionary movements in Latin America and in many other parts of the world. Guevara was killed in Bolivia, following an unsuccessful guerrilla uprising under his leadership, in October 1967.

In July 1972 Cuba's links with the Eastern bloc were strengthened when the country became a full member of the Council for Mutual Economic Assistance (CMEA, see p. 126), a Moscow-based organization linking the USSR and other communist states. As a result of its admission to the CMEA, Cuba received preferential trade terms and more technical advisers from the USSR and East European countries.

In June 1974 the country's first elections since the revolution were held for municipal offices in Matanzas province. Cuba's first 'socialist' constitution was submitted to the first Congress of the PCC, held in December 1975, and came into force in February 1976, after being approved by popular referendum. The PCC Congress also elected a new Central Committee and an enlarged Politburo. In addition, the existing six provinces were reorganized to form 14. As envisaged by the new constitution, elections for municipal assemblies were held in October 1976. These assemblies later elected delegates to provincial assemblies and deputies to the National Assembly of People's Power, inaugurated in December 1976 as 'the supreme organ of state'. The National Assembly chose the members of a new Council of State, with Fidel Castro as President. The second Congress of the PCC was held in December 1980, when Fidel and Raúl Castro were re-elected First and Second Secretaries respectively. The Politburo and the Central Committee were enlarged, and details of the 1981–85 Plan were announced. Election of candidates to the 169 municipal assemblies took place in October 1981. The National Assembly was inaugurated for a second five-year term in December. Fidel Castro was re-elected by the Assembly as President of the Council of State, and Raúl Castro re-elected as First Vice-President.

Although the OAS voted in favour of allowing member countries to normalize their relations with the Cuban Government in 1975, Cuba remained excluded from participation in OAS activities. Relations with the USA deteriorated because of Cuban involvement in the Angolan war in 1976 and in the Ethiopian–Somali war in 1977, and withdrawal of Cuban troops from Africa was made the condition for lifting the US trade embargo. The raising of emigration restrictions in April 1980 resulted in an attempt by more than 125,000 Cubans to enter the USA by landing in Florida. In 1981 the hostility between the two countries was exacerbated by US allegations concerning the extent of Cuban political and military activity abroad, and by the Cuban accusation that the USA had been instrumental in introducing the five agricultural diseases and epidemics that had decimated Cuban crops and livestock, resulting in the deaths of more than 150 people.

In 1981 Cuba expressed interest in discussing foreign policy with the USA, and declared that the shipment of arms to guerrilla groups in Central America had ceased. High-level talks between the two countries took place in November 1981 but US hostility increased. Economic sanctions were tightened, the major air link was closed, and tourism and investment by US nationals was prohibited in April 1982. A naval blockade was considered. Cuba's support of Argentina during the 1982 crisis concerning the Falkland Islands improved relations with the rest of Latin America, and the country's legitimacy was finally acknowledged when it was elected to the chair of the UN General Assembly Committee on Decolonization in September 1982, while continuing to play a leading role in the Non-Aligned Movement despite its firm alliance with the Soviet bloc.

In July 1983 President Castro announced his support for the peace initiative of the Contadora group (Colombia, Mexico, Panama and Venezuela), which called for a negotiated settlement to the problems in Central America. In addition, President Castro proposed a reciprocal arrangement between Cuba and the USA to allow for a reduction in the number of military personnel in Central America and for a halt to the supply of armaments to the region. However, an increase in US military activity in Honduras and the Caribbean region led President Castro to declare a 'state of national alert' in August. The US invasion of Grenada in October, and the ensuing short-lived confrontation between US forces and Cuban personnel on the island, severely damaged hopes that the two countries might reach an agreement over Central America, and left Cuba isolated in the Caribbean, following the weakening of its diplomatic and military ties with Suriname in November.

Cuba's concern that the re-election of the US President, Ronald Reagan, in November 1984 would increase the possibility of an invasion by the USA, aimed at the overthrow of the Castro regime, prompted moves to expand and strengthen the civil defence system. In public speeches throughout 1984, however, President Castro appeared to adopt a more conciliatory approach towards relations with the USA. In June Cuba granted the release of 48 Cuban and US prisoners who had been detained for political and criminal offences. In July official negotiations were begun with the USA on the issues of immigration and repatriation. In December agreement was reached on the resumption of Cuban immigration to the USA and the repatriation of 2,746 Cuban 'undesirables', who had accompanied other Cuban refugees to the USA in 1980. The repatriation of Cuban 'undesirables' began in February 1985, but relations between Cuba and the USA deteriorated rapidly in May, following the inauguration of Radio Martí, a radio station sponsored by the 'Voice of America' radio network, which began to broadcast Western-style news and other programmes to Cuba from Florida, USA. The establishment of Radio Martí was regarded by the Cuban Government as an act of provocation by the USA. The Government retaliated by suspending its immigration accord with the USA and by banning all visits to Cuba by US residents of Cuban origin. In October the US Government imposed restrictions on visits to the USA by PCC members and Cuban government officials. Attempts to revive negotiations concerning immigration in July 1986 failed. However, in September, more than 100 Cuban political prisoners and members of their families were permitted to leave for the USA, as a result of the mediation of US Roman Catholic bishops. Relations between the Cuban Government and the Roman Catholic Church showed further improvement, following the visit of Mother Teresa, the Nobel Peace Prize winner, to the island in July 1986.

In May–June 1985 a series of ministerial changes was rumoured to have caused friction within the Government, which resulted in the postponement of a planned PCC Congress from December 1985 to February 1986. The Third Congress of the PCC duly opened in February 1986, and drastic changes were made within the Central Committee. Almost one-third of the 146 full members were replaced. Nine of the 24 members of the new Politburo were elected for the first time, with several senior members, veterans of the 1959 revolution, being replaced by younger persons. A new Council of State was elected in December.

Throughout 1984 the number of Cuban personnel in Ethiopia was reduced, from 10,000 to 5,000 men. However, the Cuban Government stated in 1986 that it would not withdraw its troops (estimated at 27,000 in mid-1986) from Angola until apartheid was dismantled in South Africa.

Since 1985 Cuba has succeeded in establishing stronger ties with other Latin American countries, notably Argentina, Brazil, Peru and Uruguay. Relations with Spain, however, became more strained in 1986 after the attempted kidnapping in December 1985, by four employees of the Cuban embassy in Madrid, of a Cuban citizen, Manuel Sánchez Pérez, who had allegedly been involved in espionage activities and who had sought political asylum in Spain. The four diplomats were expelled from Spain. In September 1986 Cuba expelled the bureau chiefs of a British and a French news agency for publishing an interview with a human rights activist.

Government

Under the 1976 constitution, the first since the 1959 revolution, the supreme organ of state, and the sole legislative authority, is the National Assembly of People's Power, with 499 deputies elected for five years by municipal assemblies. The National Assembly elects 31 of its members to form the Council of State, the Assembly's permanent organ. The Council of State is the highest representative of the State, and its President is both Head of State and Head of Government. Executive and administrative authority is vested in the Council of Ministers, appointed by the National Assembly on the proposal of the Head of State. Municipal, regional and provincial assemblies have also been established. The Partido Comunista Cubano (PCC), the only authorized political party, is 'the leading force of society and the state'. The PCC's highest authority is the Party Congress, which elects a Central Committee (225 members in February 1986) to supervise the Party's work. To direct its policy, the Central Committee elects a Politburo (24 members in 1986).

Defence

Conscription for military service is for a three-year period from 17 years of age, and conscripts also work on the land. In July 1986, according to Western estimates, the army numbered 130,000, the navy 13,500 and the air force 18,500. Army reserves were estimated to be 120,000. Paramilitary forces include 15,000 State Security troops, 3,500 border guards and a Youth Labour Army of about 100,000. A local militia organization (Milicias de Tropas Territoriales—MTT), comprising 1.2m. men and women, was formed in 1980. Estimated expenditure on defence and internal security for 1985 was 1,471m. pesos. Considerable aid is received from communist countries, notably the USSR. Despite Cuban hostility, the USA maintains a base at Guantánamo Bay, with about 2,100 military (mostly naval) personnel in 1986.

Economic Affairs

The state-controlled Cuban economy is basically agricultural, and is heavily dependent upon the annual output of cane sugar, which provided the country with 70% of its export revenue in 1985. Production of raw sugar reached a record 8.2m. metric tons in the 1981/82 season, and seven new sugar mills were under construction. Most of Cuba's sugar exports are sold at fixed prices under long-term agreements, mainly to the USSR and other countries in the Eastern bloc. Any surplus production for export is sold on the free market. However, the world sugar price of 8 US cents per lb. in 1982, down from 28 cents per lb. in 1980, did not even cover production costs. A further setback for the industry was the devastating rainfall during the first four months of 1983, which reduced the annual output of raw sugar to 7.2m. metric tons. Because of the fall in production, Cuba was unable to fulfil its quota (2.4m. metric tons) of free-market exports under the International Sugar Agreement. Production increased to 8.2m. metric tons in 1984 and remained at about the same level in 1985, in spite of being affected by drought. Nevertheless, in 1985 Cuba was obliged to purchase 500,000 tons of sugar on the open market in order to meet its export commitments. Hurricane Kate, which struck Cuba in November 1985, damaged about 1m. ha of cane plantations (25% of the country's cultivated land), and in March 1986 harvesting of this crop was severely hampered by more heavy rains, especially in Camagüey Province. Further losses resulted from the use of inefficient manual cane-cutting methods. Additional resources were to be devoted to increasing production, and it was hoped that the annual output of raw sugar would reach 12m. metric tons by 1990.

The annual harvest of Cuba's second most important export crop, tobacco, was also severely damaged by the rains in 1983, following a record output of 54,600 tons in 1981/82, and amounted to only 45,000 tons in 1982/83. It declined to 30,200 tons in 1983/84, but increased to an estimated 45,000 tons in 1984/85. The financial loss which was caused by the destruction of other crops in 1983 amounted to US $60m. Cuban exports of citrus fruits are of increasing significance. With heavy investment by other CMEA countries, Cuba planned to increase overall production of citrus fruits to 1.4m. tons in 1985, and to 2.6m. tons in 1990, in an attempt to reduce dependence on sugar. Dairy cattle are being introduced on a large scale, and the livestock sector expanded by 6.2% in 1983. As a result of extensive government investment in the fishing industry, Cuba's total catch rose from 27,100 tons in 1959 to a record 213,000 tons in 1978. In 1985 Cuba joined the International Coffee Agreement (see p. 222) as an exporting member.

Cuba possesses about one-tenth of the world's known nickel reserves, and nickel is Cuba's second most important export commodity. In the 10 years to 1986 the Government invested more than 1,200m. pesos in the development of the industry. Production of nickel and cobalt fell from 39,257 metric tons in 1983 to 33,227 tons in 1984. The opening of the Punta Gorda plant, scheduled for 1985, was expected to increase nickel output to 100,000 tons per year by 1992. However, the first of the three new refineries did not start operating until February 1986, and the third was not expected to begin operations until 1990. Cuba supplies 35% of the CMEA's nickel requirements. There are also deposits of copper, chromite, manganese and iron ore. Projects brought into operation in August 1986 included a chrome-ore dressing plant near Moa, built with Czechoslovak aid, and the Maj.-Gen. Carlos Roloff iron foundry in Guantánamo, built in co-operation with Poland. Cuba is dependent on the USSR for 98% of its petroleum requirements of 206,000 barrels per day. Cuba was guaranteed 61m. tons of petroleum in 1981–85. In 1985 42% of Cuba's total convertible currency earnings of US $1,350m. derived from the re-export of Soviet petroleum. Heavy losses were envisaged in 1986, following the sharp decline in international petroleum prices. Exploration for petroleum in Cuba is being undertaken with Soviet and Mexican assistance, and considerable finds on the northern coast, near Varadero, have been announced. Domestic production of crude petroleum rose from 253,000 metric tons in 1981 to 770,000 tons in 1984 and was scheduled to reach 2m. tons in 1989. A new petroleum refinery, under construction at Cienfuegos, was due to come into operation in 1987, and a new oil terminal is planned for the port of Matanzas to be built jointly by the INA oil enterprise of Yugoslavia, and a French company. Cuba's refining capacity is 6.5m. tons per year. A nuclear energy plant is also under construction at Juraguá, Cienfuegos, and will have a generating capacity of 1,668 MW. It is estimated that nuclear power will provide 15% of Cuba's energy requirements by 1990. Under the 1986–90 Energy Plan, some 250 small hydro plants were to be built, principally for irrigation purposes. An eight-unit thermoelectric plant was to be constructed at Habana del Este, with a planned capacity of 1m. kW.

The bulk of installed industrial capacity is made up of plants for processing agricultural produce and for the production of cement, fertilizers, textiles, domestic consumer goods and agricultural machinery. Industrial development is accorded high priority and the 1983 budget allocated 3,500m. pesos to industrial concerns. Cuba's output of crude steel rose from 301,200 metric tons in 1982 to 338,200 tons in 1984. Plans for Cuban-Soviet co-operation, announced in 1981, included an integrated steelmill with an annual capacity of 1.3m. tons. In 1981 the Karl Marx cement factory, with a capacity of 1.65m. metric tons per year, was completed at a cost of US $208m. (equivalent). A plant for the assembly of motor vehicles from imported parts is planned. Industrial production is hampered by Cuba's dependence on Western technology and by a shortage of spare parts for US-made industrial machinery. The industrial sector recorded growth of 4.7% in 1983 and 6.4% in 1984.

In November 1980 an economic exchange agreement was signed, pledging Soviet aid up to the year 2000 at a total value of at least US $35,000m. US trade sanctions have restricted potential trade with Western countries and increased dependence on the USSR, with which Cuba conducts two-thirds of its trade. In the mid-1980s it was estimated that the USSR was supplying Cuba with petroleum, subsidized trade and financial aid amounting to $4,100m. annually. Cuba's total debt to the USSR was estimated to be between $8,500m. and $23,000m. Following the signing of four trade and economic co-operation agreements in April 1986, the USSR was to provide the island with new credits totalling 2,500m. roubles between 1986 and 1990, an increase of 50% over the previous five-year period. In 1984 Cuba's trade turnover (imports plus exports) with Eastern bloc countries amounted to 10,900m. pesos, representing about 85% of total foreign trade.

In January 1983 Cuba announced that there would be no repayments on its foreign debt principal falling due between January 1983 and December 1985. Interest payments would be maintained. Cuba's total debt to the West was US $3,200m. in 1984. In December 1984 agreement was reached on the rescheduling of $100m. of debt. In spite of President Castro's calls for the repudiation of the foreign debts of all Latin American countries, Cuba continued to reschedule its own debt to Western creditors in 1985. In July 10 Western creditor countries agreed to reschedule some $145m. in debt due for repayment in 1985. In August Cuba's Western creditor banks agreed to reschedule $85m. in debt, also due in 1985.

In 1986 the decline in world oil prices and the damage that Hurricane Kate caused to sugar and banana crops resulted in severe economic problems. Instead of the planned US $260m. trade surplus, Cuba recorded a deficit estimated at $200m. To compensate for hurricane damage, the UN World Food Programme and the FAO granted aid to the country. Owing to the increasingly serious shortage of foreign exchange, Cuba and its Western creditors continued to negotiate the rescheduling of the country's $3,500m. debt repayment in 1986. The Government was seeking $300m. in new loans to support the refinancing arrangements. In July 1986 Cuba suspended payment of its medium- and long-term foreign debt and also of its short-term commercial debt.

The first Five-Year Development Plan (1981–85), based on high projected world prices for sugar, proved to be too ambitious and costly. Although the economy had achieved an overall average growth rate of 7.3% during 1981–85, with industrial output rising by an average of 8.8%, shortcomings were reported in several sectors, particularly in the sugar industry. State subsidies were reduced by about two-thirds, with a loss of more than 170m. pesos to state enterprises, while public spending and imports both declined in 1982. Consumer prices rose by 10%, and unemployment was estimated to be 3.4% of the labour force. After 1970, financial incentives were introduced to boost productivity, and in 1980 a free market for surplus agricultural produce was introduced to undermine the 'black market' which had developed as a result of shortages and rationing. However, the free market was suspended after corrupt practices were discovered. In spite of severe economic measures, a consumer boom was reported, revealing an increase in the level of personal income of 218.6% between 1970 and 1982. In February 1982 Cuba's need for convertible currency prompted an invitation to foreign companies to engage in joint projects to build factories and tourist facilities, with the prospect of obtaining a 49% interest and generous fiscal incentives. Several companies expressed interest but were deterred by fear of US sanctions.

Under the 1986–90 Development Plan an annual economic growth rate of 5% was envisaged. Among the measures were a strict austerity programme for state organizations and enterprises, increased investment in the agricultural and industrial sectors, the diversification of export production and a policy of import substitution. Total exports were to increase by an average rate of 5% annually, while the growth in imports was to be restricted to 1.5%. The contribution of the industrial sector to the GNP was planned to rise to 50%.

Social Welfare

Through the State Social Security System, employees receive benefits for sickness, accidents, maternity, disability, retirement and unemployment. Health services are free. In 1984 there were 63,016 hospital beds and 20,490 physicians. The 1984 budget allocation for health and education was 2,556.9m. pesos.

Education

Education is universal and free at all levels. Education is based on Marxist-Leninist principles and combines study with manual work. The 1981–85 Development Plan emphasized improvement of professional and technological education, especially in medicine, economics, accountancy and teaching.

Pre-school national schools are run by the State for children of five years of age, and day nurseries are available for all children after their 45th day. Primary education, from six to 12 years of age, is compulsory, and secondary education lasts from 13 to 16 (to be extended to 18) years of age. In 1982 an estimated 97.3% of children in the primary school age-group attended primary schools, while 84.4% of those in the secondary school age-group were enrolled at secondary schools. In 1985 there were 212,155 students in higher education. Workers undergoing university courses receive a state subsidy to provide for their dependants. Courses at intermediate and higher levels have an emphasis on technology, agriculture and teacher training. In 1979 the estimated illiteracy rate among persons aged 15 to 49 was only 4.6% (males 4.3%; females 4.9%). Adult education centres gave basic education to 292,067 people in 1984/85.

Tourism

Cuba has much to attract the tourist, including a colonial cultural heritage, forests, mountains and a coastline with many bays and inlets, providing excellent bathing, diving and fishing. Tourism began to develop after 1977, with the lifting of travel restrictions by the USA, and the country subsequently attracted European tourists. The majority of visitors come from Canada, Spain and Mexico. US travel restrictions were reimposed in 1982. However, an estimated 240,000 tourists visited Cuba in 1985, compared with only 4,000 in 1973. Twenty-nine new hotels were opened between 1976 and 1981, and 30 new hotels are planned, with a projected total capacity of 20,200 rooms. Under the 1986–90 Development Plan, some 500m. pesos were to be invested in the sector, which was expected to become Cuba's principal source of foreign exchange by 1990.

Public Holidays

1987: 1 January (Liberation Day), 1 May (Labour Day), 25–27 July (Anniversary of the 1953 Revolution), 10 October (Wars of Independence Day).

1988: 1 January (Liberation Day), 1 May (Labour Day), 25–27 July (Anniversary of the 1953 Revolution), 10 October (Wars of Independence Day).

Weights and Measures

The metric system is in force.

Currency and Exchange Rates

100 centavos = 1 Cuban peso.

Exchange rates (31 August 1986):
 £1 sterling = 1.123 pesos;
 US $1 = 76.0 centavos.

Statistical Survey

Source (unless otherwise stated): Cámara de Comercio de Cuba, Calle 21, No 661, Apdo 4237, Vedado, Havana; tel. 30-3356; telex 51-1752; Comité Estatal de Estadísticas, Havana, Cuba; tel. 31-5171.

Area and Population

AREA, POPULATION AND DENSITY

Area (sq km)	110,860*
Population (census results)	
6 September 1970	8,569,121
11 September 1981	
Males	4,914,873
Females	4,808,732
Total	9,723,605
Population (official estimates at 31 December)	
1982	9,841,989
1983	9,945,700
1984	10,042,800
Density (per sq km) at 31 December 1984	90.6

* 42,803 sq miles.

Population: 10,099,000 (official estimate) at mid-1985.

EMPLOYMENT IN THE STATE SECTOR
(annual averages, '000 persons)

	1982	1983	1984
Industry*	599.9	630.5	665.7
Construction	260.7	283.7	308.5
Agriculture	615.6	595.3	581.7
Forestry	20.7	26.0	26.9
Transport	179.5	184.7	187.2
Communications	23.5	24.6	25.5
Trade	324.1	347.7	367.2
Social services	85.7	96.9	108.0
Science and technology	21.3	22.5	25.5
Education	357.0	370.6	380.1
Arts and culture	35.0	37.2	38.0
Public health	153.7	169.8	184.9
Total (incl. others)	2,881.7	2,999.7	3,114.8

* Mining, manufacturing, electricity, gas and water.

Total labour force (persons aged 15 years and over, 1981 census): 3,617,620 (males 2,479,733; females 1,137,887).

PRINCIPAL TOWNS
(estimated population at 31 December 1984)

La Habana (Havana, the capital)	1,992,620	Cienfuegos	107,850
		Matanzas	104,583
		Bayamo	104,363
Santiago de Cuba	356,033	Pinar del Río	99,649
Camagüey	287,392	Las Tunas	89,006
Holguín	194,113	Ciego de Ávila	79,510
Santa Clara	176,917	Sancti Spíritus	74,922
Guantánamo	172,491		

BIRTHS, MARRIAGES AND DEATHS*

	Registered live births†		Registered marriages‡		Registered deaths	
	Number	Rate (per 1,000)	Number	Rate (per 1,000)	Number	Rate (per 1,000)
1977	168,960	17.7	62,113	6.5	56,084	5.9
1978	148,249	15.4	58,361	6.1	55,100	5.7
1979	143,551	14.8	62,834	6.5	54,838	5.6
1980	136,900	14.1	68,941	7.1	55,707	5.7
1981	136,211	14.0	72,824	7.5	57,814	5.9
1982	159,759	16.3	80,295	8.2	56,485	5.8
1983	165,284	16.7	76,365	7.7	58,346	5.9
1984	166,281	16.6	75,254	7.5	59,798	6.0

* Data are tabulated by year of registration rather than by year of occurrence.
† Births registered in the National Consumers Register, established on 31 December 1964.
‡ Including consensual unions formalized in response to special legislation.

Agriculture

PRINCIPAL CROPS ('000 metric tons)

	1982	1983	1984
Sugar cane	74,137.6	74,375.3	73,810.6
Maize*†	96	96	97
Cassava (Manioc)*	330‡	335†	340†
Potatoes	258.3	206.7	223.4
Sweet potatoes	177.4	201.0	335†
Plantains	79.8	113.7	172*
Rice (paddy)	519.8	517.6	504.8
Tobacco (leaves)	44.9	30.2	45*
Tomatoes	226.5	153.3	79.3
Citrus fruits	530.0	631.5	502.8
Bananas	191.9	199.6	265.8
Mangoes	52.3	39.1	39*
Coffee (green)*	29	18	21†

* Source: FAO, *Production Yearbook*.
† FAO estimates.   ‡ Unofficial figure.

LIVESTOCK ('000 head; state enterprises only)

	1982	1983	1984
Horses	819.9	812.2	792.0
Pigs	853.1	910.6	1,008.9
Sheep	317.1	352.0	430.9
Poultry	23,052.4	25,744.1	26,734.5

LIVESTOCK PRODUCTS ('000 metric tons)

	1982	1983	1984
Beef and veal	300.0	303.2	n.a.
Pig meat	70.6	72.7	81.9
Poultry meat	75.9	89.9	106.6
Cows' milk	928.7	948.2	942.9
Hen eggs (million)	2,012.9	2,231.1	2,557.6

Forestry

ROUNDWOOD REMOVALS
('000 cubic metres, excluding bark)

	1981	1982	1983
Sawlogs, veneer logs and logs for sleepers*	35	35	35
Other industrial wood*	350	350	350
Fuel wood	2,802	2,850	2,747
Total	3,187	3,235	3,132

* FAO estimates (output is assumed to be unchanged since 1971).
1984: Output as in 1983 (FAO estimates).
Source: FAO, *Yearbook of Forest Products*.

SAWNWOOD PRODUCTION ('000 cubic metres)

	1981	1982	1983
Total	85	74	84

1984: Production as in 1983 (FAO estimates).
Source: FAO, *Yearbook of Forest Products*.

Fishing

('000 metric tons, live weight)

	1982	1983	1984
Inland waters	13.6	14.1	16.2
Atlantic Ocean	94.8	128.7	149.3
Pacific Ocean	86.8	55.6	34.1
Total catch	195.2	198.5	199.6

Source: FAO, *Yearbook of Fishery Statistics*.

Mining

		1982	1983	1984
Crude petroleum	'000 metric tons	541	742	770
Natural gas	'000 cu metres	10,700	8,300	3,400
Copper concentrates	metric tons	2,645	2,667	2,701
Nickel and cobalt	metric tons	37,603	39,257	33,227
Refractory chromium	metric tons	27,300	33,600	37,900
Salt	metric tons	198,000	179,800	183,600
Silica and sand	'000 cu metres	4,652	5,118	5,461
Crushed stone	'000 cu metres	8,887	9,849	10,681

Industry

SELECTED PRODUCTS

		1982	1983	1984
Crude steel	'000 metric tons	301.2	363.7	338.2
Corrugated steel bars	'000 metric tons	203.6	241	270.4
Grey cement	'000 metric tons	3,163.3	3,231.1	3,346.9
Mosaics	'000 sq metres	2,305.2	2,584.4	2,918.4
Motor spirit (Gasoline)	metric tons	846,700	889,800	983,900
Kerosene	metric tons	456,700	493,800	505,600
Sulphuric acid (98%)	'000 metric tons	332.9	356.3	336.2
Fertilizers	metric tons	1,026,400	1,082,000	1,036,200
Tyres	'000	218.3	353.7	450.3
Woven textile fabrics	'000 sq metres	153,336.7	170,300	172,100
Cigarettes	million	17,043.6	16,801.9	18,697.4
Cigars	million	358.4	332.8	301.6
Raw sugar*	'000 metric tons	7,777.6	7,231.9	7,513.5
Leather footwear	'000 pairs	13,500	13,200	12,500
Electric energy	million kWh	11,069.7	11,551.4	12,291.3

* Corresponding to calendar year.

Finance

CURRENCY AND EXCHANGE RATES

Monetary Units:
100 centavos = 1 Cuban peso.

Denominations:
Coins: 1, 5, 20 and 40 centavos; 1 peso.
Notes: 1, 3, 5, 10, 20 and 50 pesos.

Sterling and Dollar Equivalents (31 August 1986)
£1 sterling = 1.123 pesos;
US $1 = 76.0 centavos;
100 Cuban pesos = £89.01 = $131.58.

NATIONAL ACCOUNTS

Net Material Product (NMP) by Economic Activity*
(million pesos at current prices)

	1982	1983	1984
Agriculture, forestry and fishing	1,396.6	1,342.1	1,380.5
Industry†	3,920.6	4,134.9	4,755.7
Construction	942.1	1,078.5	1,291.3
Trade, restaurants, etc.	4,943.9	5,336.4	5,142.1
Transport and communications	909.2	958.6	1,055.8
Other activities of the material sphere	63.1	76.1	94.3
Total	12,175.5	12,926.6	13,719.7

* NMP is defined as the total net value of goods and 'productive' services, including turnover taxes, produced by the economy. This excludes economic activities not contributing directly to material production, such as public administration, defence and personal and professional services.
† Principally manufacturing, mining, electricity, gas and water.
Source: UN, *Monthly Bulletin of Statistics*.

STATE BUDGET (million pesos)

	1984	1985
Total revenue	11,471.3	11,311.2
Total expenditure	10,793.0	11,060.9
Productive sector	3,535.1	3,329.7
Housing and community services	731.2	723.8
Education and public health	2,405.0	2,556.9
Other social, cultural and scientific activities	1,766.9	1,885.8
Government administration and judicial bodies	659.3	647.6
Defence and public order	1,168.6	1,470.9
Other	526.9	446.2

INTERNATIONAL RESERVES
(million pesos at 31 December)

	1983	1984
Gold and other precious metals	13.5	13.5
Cash and deposits in foreign banks (convertible currency)	271.4	165.8
Sub-total	284.9	179.3
Deposits in foreign banks (in transferable roubles)	47.3	83.5
Total	332.2	262.8

External Trade

PRINCIPAL COMMODITIES (million pesos)

Imports	1982	1983	1984
Food and live animals	810.6	786.7	808.2
Beverages and tobacco	10.0	9.5	7.7
Animal and vegetable fats and oils	47.6	64.7	79.2
Crude materials (inedible) except fuels	185.1	197.2	252.5
Mineral fuels, lubricants, etc.	1,497.9	1,857.5	2,217.6
Chemicals and related products	357.6	415.7	425.8
Basic manufactures	717.0	762.5	959.8
Machinery and transport equipment	1,712.3	1,903.0	2,195.9
Miscellaneous manufactured articles	192.5	225.3	260.6
Total	5,530.6	6,222.1	7,207.3

Exports	1982	1983	1984
Sugar and sugar products	3,808.1	4,096.0	4,126.2
Minerals and concentrates	299.8	299.0	300.6
Tobacco and tobacco products	103.8	102.9	56.1
Fish and fish preparations	98.6	106.6	91.8
Other agricultural products	151.9	185.1	156.2
Total (incl. others)	4,933.2	5,534.9	5,462.1

PRINCIPAL TRADING PARTNERS ('000 pesos)

Imports c.i.f.	1982	1983	1984
Argentina	12,900	82,000	146,300
Bulgaria	170,261	193,289	190,200
Canada	47,290	37,312	56,400
China, People's Republic	218,900	152,900	242,800
Czechoslovakia	182,222	179,266	176,400
France	33,734	100,148	98,000
German Democratic Republic	205,698	247,586	266,900
Germany, Federal Republic	54,032	64,614	91,200
Hungary	97,316	128,881	132,100
Italy	24,283	18,785	58,600
Japan	135,899	85,236	218,400
Mexico	16,000	22,900	72,800
Netherlands	33,000	37,000	34,600
Poland	68,383	89,557	65,300
Romania	182,800	121,600	149,100
Spain	95,184	106,128	104,800
Sweden	31,852	16,705	31,500
Switzerland	17,300	32,000	21,400
USSR	3,744,391	4,245,949	4,775,800
United Kingdom	49,670	92,629	92,200
Viet Nam	21,100	17,200	32,100
Total (incl. others)	5,530,604	6,217,672	7,207,200

Exports f.o.b.	1982	1983	1984
Algeria	68,300	44,200	11,900
Bulgaria	160,258	183,650	188,200
Canada	46,188	39,111	43,700
China, People's Republic	306,100	212,900	203,100
Czechoslovakia	113,282	127,416	163,600
Egypt	50,700	51,000	23,500
France	45,259	61,059	33,800
German Democratic Republic	163,891	199,589	217,900
Germany, Federal Republic	44,348	68,266	14,200
Hungary	62,293	15,710	23,800
Iraq	31,500	25,600	15,600
Italy	26,167	23,339	18,900
Japan	71,236	68,058	49,700
Libya	17,300	20,200	10,300
Mexico	43,700	17,200	10,600
Poland	12,764	14,810	15,000
Spain	87,985	94,137	64,400
Switzerland	55,300	34,600	39,200
Syria	23,200	18,500	16,600
USSR	3,289,610	3,874,189	3,938,000
United Kingdom	24,318	30,332	15,300
Total (incl. others)	4,933,200	5,522,700	5,462,100

Transport

RAILWAYS

	1982	1983	1984
Passengers ('000)	23,139.1	23,500.0	24,600.0
Passenger-kilometres (million)	2,073.3	2,143.6	2,359.8
Freight carried ('000 metric tons)	18,248.3	17,696.9	18,407.2
Freight ton-kilometres (million)	2,668.9	2,723.8	2,723.8

ROAD TRAFFIC ('000 motor vehicles in use)

	1980	1981	1982
Passenger cars	154.4	171.4	182.2
Commercial vehicles	132.6	142.8	152.4

Source: UN, *Statistical Yearbook*.

INTERNATIONAL SEA-BORNE SHIPPING
(freight traffic, '000 metric tons)

	1982	1983	1984
Goods loaded	8,838.6	8,169.6	8,307.0
Goods unloaded	16,897.8	16,968.1	17,817.8

CIVIL AVIATION

	1982	1983	1984
Passengers carried ('000)	894.5	1,000.0	1,000.0
Passenger-kilometres (million)	1,939.0	2,150.5	2,514.2
Freight ton-kilometres (million)	24.8	33.4	37.6

Education

(1984/85)

	Schools*	Teachers	Pupils
Pre-primary	n.a.	4,931	109,061
Primary	10,866	79,610	1,174,453
Secondary: general	1,291	64,495	793,516
Technical and professional	605	25,304	305,556
Higher	33	17,717	212,155

* Figures for 1984.

Directory

The Constitution

Following the assumption of power by the Castro regime on 1 January 1959, the Constitution was suspended and a Fundamental Law of the Republic was instituted with effect from 7 February 1959. In February 1976 Cuba's first socialist Constitution came into force after being submitted to the first Congress of the Communist Party of Cuba in December 1975 and to popular referendum in February 1976.

POLITICAL, SOCIAL AND ECONOMIC PRINCIPLES

The Republic of Cuba is a socialist state in which all power belongs to the working people. The Communist Party of Cuba is the leading force of society and the state. The socialist state carries out the will of the working people and guarantees work, medical care, education, food, clothing and housing. The Republic of Cuba is part of the world socialist community. It bases its relations with the Union of Soviet Socialist Republics and with other socialist countries on socialist internationalism, friendship, co-operation and mutual assistance. It hopes to establish one large community of nations within Latin America and the Caribbean.

The State organizes and directs the economic life of the nation in accordance with a central social and economic development plan. Foreign trade is the exclusive function of the State. The State recognizes the right of small farmers to own their lands and other means of production and to sell that land. The State guarantees the right of citizens to ownership of personal property in the form of earnings, savings, place of residence and other possessions and objects which serve to satisfy their material and cultural needs. The State also guarantees the right of inheritance.

Cuban citizenship is acquired by birth or through naturalization.

The State protects the family, motherhood and matrimony.

The State directs and encourages all aspects of education, culture and science.

All citizens have equal rights and are subject to equal duties.

The State guarantees the right to medical care, education, freedom of speech and press, assembly, demonstration, association and privacy. In the socialist society work is the right and duty, and a source of pride for every citizen.

GOVERNMENT

National Assembly of People's Power

The National Assembly of People's Power is the supreme organ of the State and is the only organ with constituent and legislative authority. It is composed of deputies over the age of 18 elected by the Municipal Assemblies of People's Power, for a period of five years. All Cuban citizens over the age of 16, except those who are mentally incapacitated or who have committed a crime, are eligible to vote. The National Assembly of People's Power holds two ordinary sessions a year and a special session when requested by one-third of the deputies or by the Council of State. More than half the total number of deputies must be present for a session to be held.

All decisions made by the Assembly, except those relating to constitutional reforms, are adopted by a simple majority of votes. The deputies may be recalled by their electors at any time.

The National Assembly of People's Power has the following functions:

to reform the Constitution;

to approve, modify and annul laws;

to supervise all organs of the State and government;

to decide on the constitutionality of laws and decrees;

to revoke decree-laws issued by the Council of State;

to discuss and approve economic and social development plans, the state budget, monetary and credit systems;

to approve the general outlines of foreign and domestic policy, to ratify and annul international treaties, to declare war and approve peace treaties;

to approve the administrative division of the country;

to elect the President, First Vice-President, the Vice-Presidents and other members of the Council of State;

to elect the President, Vice-President and Secretary of the National Assembly;

to appoint the members of the Council of Ministers on the proposal of the President of the Council of State;

to elect the President, Vice-President and other judges of the People's Supreme Court;

to elect the attorney-general and the deputy attorney-generals;

to grant amnesty;

to call referendums.

The President of the National Assembly presides over sessions of the Assembly, calls ordinary sessions, proposes the draft agenda, signs the Official Gazette, organizes the work of the commissions appointed by the Assembly and attends the meetings of the Council of State.

Council of State

The Council of State is elected from the members of the National Assembly and represents that Assembly in the period between sessions. It comprises a President, one First Vice-President, five Vice-Presidents, one Secretary and 23 other members. Its mandate ends when a new Assembly meets. All decisions are adopted by a simple majority of votes. It is accountable for its actions to the National Assembly.

The Council of State has the following functions:

to call special sessions of the National Assembly;

to set the date for the election of a new Assembly;

to issue decree-laws in the period between the sessions of the National Assembly;

to decree mobilization in the event of war and to approve peace treaties when the Assembly is in recess;

to issue instructions to the courts and the Office of the Attorney General of the Republic;

to appoint and remove ambassadors of Cuba abroad on the proposal of its President, to grant or refuse recognition to diplomatic representatives of other countries to Cuba;

to suspend those provisions of the Council of Ministers that are not in accordance with the Constitution;

to revoke the resolutions of the Executive Committee of the local organs of People's Power which are contrary to the Constitution or laws and decrees formulated by other higher organs.

The President of the Council of State is Head of State and Head of Government and for all purposes the Council of State is the highest representative of the Cuban state.

Head of State

The President of the Council of State is the Head of State and the Head of Government and has the following powers:

to represent the State and Government and conduct general policy;

to call and preside over the sessions of the Council of State and the Council of Ministers;

to supervise the ministries and other administrative bodies;

to propose the members of the Council of Ministers to the National Assembly of People's Power;

to receive the credentials of the heads of foreign diplomatic missions;

to sign the decree-laws and other resolutions of the Council of State;

to assume command of the Revolutionary Armed Forces.

In the case of absence, illness or death of the President of the Council of State, the First Vice-President assumes the President's duties.

The Council of Ministers

The Council of Ministers is the highest-ranking executive and administrative organ. It is composed of the Head of State and Government, as its President, the First Vice-President, the Vice-Presidents, the Ministers and the President of the Central Planning Board. Its Executive Committee is composed of the President, the First Vice-President and the Vice-Presidents of the Council of Ministers.

The Council of Ministers has the following powers:

to conduct political, economic, cultural, scientific, social and defence policy as outlined by the National Assembly;

to approve international treaties;

CUBA

to propose projects for the general development plan and, if they are approved by the National Assembly, to supervise their implementation;

to conduct foreign policy and trade;

to draw up bills and submit them to the National Assembly;

to draw up the draft state budget;

to conduct general administration, implement laws, issue decrees and supervise defence and national security.

The Council of Ministers is accountable to the National Assembly of People's Power.

LOCAL GOVERNMENT

The country is divided into 14 provinces and 169 municipalities. The provinces are: Pinar del Río, Habana, Ciudad de la Habana, Matanzas, Villa Clara, Cienfuegos, Sancti Spíritus, Ciego de Avila, Camagüey, Las Tunas, Holguín, Granma, Santiago de Cuba and Guantánamo.

Voting for delegates to the municipal assemblies is direct, secret and voluntary. All citizens over 16 years of age are eligible to vote. The number of delegates to each assembly is proportionate to the number of people living in that area. A delegate must obtain more than half the number of votes cast in the constituency in order to be elected. The Municipal Assemblies are elected for a period of two-and-a-half years and are headed by Executive Committees elected from the members of the Municipal Assemblies. The members of the Executive Committees form five Regional Assemblies and the members of the Regional Assemblies in turn form Provincial Assemblies also headed by Executive Committees. Membership of regional and provincial executive committees is proposed by a commission of Communist Party members and youth and trade union representatives. The President and Secretary of each of the regional and the provincial assemblies are the only full-time members, the other delegates carrying out their functions in addition to their normal employment.

The regular and extraordinary sessions of the local Assemblies of People's Power are public. More than half the total number of members must be present in order for agreements made to be valid. Agreements are adopted by simple majority.

JUDICIARY

Judicial power is exercised by the People's Supreme Court and all other competent tribunals and courts. The People's Supreme Court is the supreme judicial authority and is accountable only to the National Assembly of People's Power. It can propose laws and issue regulations through its Council of Government. Judges are independent but the courts must inform the electorate of their activities at least once a year. Every accused person has the right to a defence and can be tried only by a tribunal.

The Office of the Attorney-General is subordinate only to the National Assembly and the Council of State and is responsible for ensuring that the law is properly obeyed.

The Constitution may be modified only by a two-thirds majority vote in the National Assembly of People's Power.

The Government
(January 1987)

Head of State: Dr FIDEL CASTRO RUZ (took office 2 December 1976; re-elected December 1981 and December 1986).

COUNCIL OF STATE

President: Dr FIDEL CASTRO RUZ.
First Vice-President: Gen. RAÚL CASTRO RUZ.
Vice-Presidents:
JUAN ALMEIDA BOSQUE.
OSMANY CIENFUEGOS GORRIARÁN.
JOSÉ RAMÓN MACHADO VENTURA.
PEDRO MIRET PRIETO.
Dr CARLOS RAFAEL RODRÍGUEZ RODRÍGUEZ.
Secretary: Dr JOSÉ M. MIYAR BARRUECO.
Members:
JOSÉ RAMÓN BALAGUER CABRERA.
Dr ARMANDO HART DÁVALOS.
PEDRO CHÁVEZ GONZÁLEZ.
MERCEDES DIAZA HERRERA.
LÁZARO TRENCILLO FIS.
RAMIRO VALDÉS MENÉNDEZ.
FELIX VILLAR BENCOMO.
FLAVIO BRAVO PARDO.
GUILLERMO GARCÍA FRIAS.
CARLOS LAGE DAVILA.
ROBERTO VEIGA MENÉNDEZ.
VILMA ESPÍN GUILLOIS DE CASTRO.
JOSÉ RAMÍREZ CRUZ.
ARMANDO ACOSTA CORDERO.
SEVERO AGUIRRE DEL CRISTO.
ORLANDO LUGO FONTE.
ROBERTO ROBALNA GONZÁLEZ.
JOSÉ RAMÓN FERNÁNDEZ ALVAREZ.
PEDRO CANISIO SAEZ JOVE.
ZEIDA SUÁREZ PREMIER.
Gen. SENÉN CASAS REGUEIRO.
Gen. ABELARDO COLOMÉ IBARRA.
LIDIA TABLADA ROMERO.

COUNCIL OF MINISTERS

President: Dr FIDEL CASTRO RUZ.
First Vice-President: Gen. RAÚL CASTRO RUZ.
Vice-Presidents:
Dr CARLOS RAFAEL RODRÍGUEZ RODRÍGUEZ.
RAMIRO VALDÉS MENÉNDEZ.
JOEL DOMENECH BENÍTEZ.
ANTONIO ESQUIVEL YEDRA.
DIOCLES TORRALBA GONZÁLEZ.
JOSÉ RAMÓN FERNÁNDEZ ALVAREZ.
JOSÉ A. LÓPEZ MORENO.
OSMANY CIENFUEGOS GORRIARÁN.
PEDRO MIRET PRIETO.
Secretary: OSMANY CIENFUEGOS GORRIARÁN.
Minister of Agriculture: ADOLFO DÍAZ SUÁREZ.
Minister of Foreign Trade: RICARDO CABRISAS RUIZ.
Minister of Internal Trade: MANUEL VILA SOSA.
Minister of Communications: MANUEL CASTILLO RABASA.
Minister of Construction: RAÚL CABRERA NÚÑEZ.
Minister of Culture: Dr ARMANDO HART DÁVALOS.
Minister of Education: JOSÉ RAMÓN FERNÁNDEZ ÁLVAREZ.
Minister of Higher Education: FERNANDO VECINO ALEGRET.
Minister of the Revolutionary Armed Forces: Gen. RAÚL CASTRO RUZ.
Minister of the Food Industry: ALEJANDRO ROCA IGLESIAS.
Minister of the Sugar Industry: JUAN HERRERA MACHADO.
Minister of Light Industry: ANTONIO ESQUIVEL YEDRA.
Minister of the Fishing Industry: JORGE A. FERNÁNDEZ-CUERVO VINENT.
Minister of the Iron and Steel and Metallurgical Industries: Ing. MARCOS LAGE COELLO.
Minister of Heavy Industry: MARCOS PORTAL LEÓN.
Minister of the Interior: JOSÉ ABRAHANTES FERNÁNDEZ.
Minister of Justice: Dr JUAN ESCALONA REGUERA.
Minister of Foreign Affairs: ISIDORO MALMIERCA PEOLI.
Minister of Public Health: JULIO TEJAS PÉREZ.
Minister of Transport: DIOCLES TORRALBA GONZÁLEZ.
Minister, President Central Planning Board: JOSÉ LÓPEZ MORENO.
Minister, State Committee for Technical and Material Supplies: SONIA RODRÍGUEZ.
Minister, State Committee for Economic Co-operation: ERNESTO MELÉNDEZ BACH.
Minister, State Committee for Statistics: FIDEL VASCOS GONZÁLEZ.
Minister, State Committee for Finance: RODRIGO GARCÍA LEÓN.
Minister, State Committee for Standardization: RAMÓN DARIAS RODÉS.
Minister, State Committee for Prices: ARTURO GUZMÁN PASCUAL.
Minister, State Committee for Labour and Social Security: FRANCISCO LINARES CALVO.

CUBA   Directory

Minister, President of the Banco Nacional de Cuba: HÉCTOR RODRÍGUEZ LLOMPART.
Minister, President of the Academy of Sciences of Cuba: ROSA ELENA SIMEÓN.
Ministers without Portfolio: JOSÉ A. NARANJO MORALES, LEVY FARAH BALMASEDA, ANTONIO RODRÍGUEZ MAURELL.

MINISTRIES

Ministry of Agriculture: Avda Independencia, entre Conill y Sta Ana, Havana; tel. 70-8091; telex 511966.
Ministry of Communications: Plaza de la Revolución 'José Martí', Havana; tel. 70-5581; telex 51945.
Ministry of Construction: Avda Carlos M. de Céspedes y Calle 35, Havana; tel. 70-9411; telex 511275.
Ministry of Culture: Calle 2, entre 11 y 13, Vedado, Havana; tel. 30-3124; telex 511400.
Ministry of Education: Obispo No 160, Havana; tel. 62-4011; telex 511188.
Ministry of the Fishing Industry: Ensenda de Pote y Atarés, Havana; tel. 99-1561; telex 511206.
Ministry of the Food Industry: Calle 41, No 4455, Playa, Havana; tel. 2-6801; telex 511163.
Ministry of Foreign Affairs: Calzada No 360, Vedado, Havana; tel. 32-3279; telex 511122.
Ministry of Foreign Trade: Infanta No 16, Vedado, Havana; tel. 70-9341; telex 511174.
Ministry of Heavy Industry: Avda Salvador Allende, No 666, Havana; tel. 70-7711; telex 511183.
Ministry of Higher Education: Calle 23, No 565 esq. a F, Vedado, Havana; tel. 3-6655; telex 511253.
Ministry of the Interior: Plaza de la Revolución, Havana.
Ministry of Internal Trade: Calle Habana, No 258, Havana; tel. 6-6984; telex 511171.
Ministry of the Iron and Steel and Metallurgical Industries: Avda Rancho Boyeros y Calle 100, Havana; tel. 44-2211; telex 511179.
Ministry of Justice: Calle 0, No 216, Vedado, Havana; tel. 32-4526; telex 511331.
Ministry of Light Industry: Empedrado No 302, Havana; tel. 61-7971; telex 511141.
Ministry of Public Health: Calle 23, No 201, Vedado, Havana; tel. 32-2561; telex 511149.
Ministry of the Revolutionary Armed Forces: Plaza de la Revolución, Havana.
Ministry of the Sugar Industry: Calle 23, No 171, Vedado, Havana; tel. 30-5061; telex 511664.
Ministry of Transport: Rancho Boyeros y Tulipán, Havana; tel. 70-7751; telex 511181.
Central Planning Board: 20 de Mayo y Ayestarán, Plaza de la Revolución, Havana; tel. 79-7501; telex 511158.
State Committee for Economic Co-operation: Calle 1a, No 201, Vedado, Havana; tel. 3-6661; telex 511297.
State Committee for Finance: Obispo esq. Cuba, Havana; tel. 61-1691; telex 511101.
State Committee for Labour and Social Security: Calle 23, esq. Calle P, Vedado, Havana; tel. 70-4571; telex 511225.
State Committee for Prices: Amistad No 552, Havana; tel. 6-7050.
State Committee for Standardization: Egido No 610 entre Gloria y Apodaca, Havana; tel. 6-7901; telex 511422.
State Committee for Statistics: Almendares No 156, Havana; tel. 79-6506; telex 511257.
State Committee for Technical and Material Supplies: Monserrate No 261, Havana; tel. 6-8881; telex 511757.

Legislature

ASAMBLEA NACIONAL DEL PODER POPULAR

The National Assembly of People's Power was constituted on 2 December 1976. The Assembly's third five-year term began in December 1986. It consists of 499 deputies.
President: FLAVIO BRAVO PARDO.
Vice-President: SEVERO AGUIRRE DEL CRISTO.
Secretary: JOSÉ ARAÑABURO GARCÍA.

Political Organization

Partido Comunista Cubano (PCC) (Communist Party of Cuba): Havana; f. 1961 as the Organizaciones Revolucionarias Integradas (ORI) from a fusion of the Partido Socialista Popular (Communist), Fidel Castro's Movimiento 26 de Julio and the Directorio Revolucionario 13 de Marzo; became the Partido Unido de la Revolución Socialista Cubana (PURSC) in 1962; renamed as the Partido Comunista Cubano in 1965; 225-member Central Committee (146 full mems and 79 candidate mems were elected in February 1986), Political Bureau (14 full mems and 10 candidate mems in 1986), Secretariat and 5 Commissions; 500,000 mems (1985).
Political Bureau: Full mems Dr FIDEL CASTRO RUZ, Gen. RAÚL CASTRO RUZ, JUAN ALMEIDA BOSQUE, Dr ARMANDO HART DÁVALOS, JOSÉ RAMÓN MACHADO VENTURA, CARLOS RAFAEL RODRÍGUEZ RODRÍGUEZ, PEDRO MIRET PRIETO, JORGE RISQUET VALDÉS-SALDAÑA, JULIO CAMACHO AGUILERA, OSMANY CIENFUEGOS GORRIARÁN, VILMA ESPÍN GUILLOIS DE CASTRO, ESTEBAN LAZO HERNÁNDEZ, Gen. ABELARDO COLOMÉ IBARRA, ROBERTO VEIGA MENÉNDEZ.
Secretariat: Dr FIDEL CASTRO RUZ (First Sec.), Gen. RAÚL CASTRO RUZ (Second Sec.), JORGE RISQUET VALDÉS-SALDAÑA, JOSÉ RAMÓN MACHADO VENTURA, LIONEL SOTO PRIETO, JESÚS MONTANE OROPESA, JULIÁN RIZO ALVAREZ, JAIME CROMBET HERNÁNDEZ-BAQUERO, JOSÉ RAMÓN BALAGUER CABRERA, SIXTO BATISTA SANTANA.

Diplomatic Representation

EMBASSIES IN CUBA

Afghanistan: Calle 24, No 4314, Miramar, Havana; tel. 29-3555; Ambassador: ABDOL MAJID SARBOLAND.
Albania: Calle 13, No 851, Vedado, Havana; tel. 30-2788; Ambassador: GEZIM ARAPI.
Algeria: Calle 13, No 760, Vedado, Havana; tel. 3-9947; Ambassador: HOCINE ZATOUT.
Angola: Avda 5, No 1012, entre 10 y 12, Miramar, Havana; tel. 29-2205; Ambassador: MANUEL PEDRO PACAVIRA.
Argentina: Calle 36, No 511, entre 5a y 7a, Miramar, Havana; tel. 29-4992; telex 511138; Ambassador: LUIS RAÚL CLARASO DE LA VEGA.
Austria: Calle 4, No 101 entre 1 y 3, Miramar, Havana; tel. 22-4394; telex 511415; Ambassador: (vacant).
Belgium: Avda 5a, No 7408, Miramar-Playa, Havana; tel. 29-6440; telex 511482; Ambassador: WILLY VERRIEST.
Benin: Calle 20, No 119, Miramar, Havana; tel. 2-3595; Ambassador: FRÉDÉRIC ASSOGBA AFFO.
Bulgaria: Calle B, No 252, Vedado, Havana; tel. 30-0256; Ambassador: PETAR IVANOV MARINKOV.
Burkina Faso: Avda 5a, No 11003, entre 110 y 112, Miramar; tel. 2-8935; Ambassador: NARAOGO V. OUÉDRAOGO.
Canada: Calle 30, No 518, esq. a 7a, Miramar, Havana; tel. 2-6421; telex 511586; Ambassador: K. B. WILLIAMSON.
China, People's Republic: Calle 13, No 551, Vedado, Havana; tel. 32-5205; Ambassador: (vacant).
Congo: Avda 5, No 1003, Miramar, Havana; tel. 2-6513; Ambassador: ROGER ISSOMBO.
Czechoslovakia: Avda Kohly, No 259, Nuevo Vedado, Havana; tel. 30-0024; Ambassador: STANISLAV SVOBODA.
Denmark: Paseo de Martí No 20, Apdo 4-C, Havana; tel. 61-6610; telex 511100; Chargé d'affaires a.i.: NIELS NEUSTRUP.
Ecuador: Avda 5a-A, No 4407, Miramar, Havana; tel. 29-2004; telex 511770; Ambassador: MANUEL ARAUJO HIDALGO.
Egypt: Avda 5, No 1801, Miramar, Havana; tel. 22-2541; telex 511551; Ambassador: HASSAN A. EL ABBADÍ.
Ethiopia: Calle 6, No 318, Miramar, Havana; tel. 22-1260; Ambassador: NADEW ZEKARIAS.
Finland: Avda 5a, No 9202, Miramar, Apdo. 3304, Havana; tel. 22-4098; telex 511485; Ambassador: TERO LEHTOVAARA.
France: Calle 14, No 312, Miramar, Havana; tel. 295980; telex 511195; Ambassador: JEAN-LOUIS MARFAING.

CUBA

German Democratic Republic: Calle 13, No 652, entre A y B, Vedado, Havana; tel. 3-6626; telex 511127; Ambassador: KARLHEINZ MÖBUS.

Germany, Federal Republic: Calle 28, No 313, entre 3a y 5a, Miramar, Havana; tel. 22-2560; telex 511433; Ambassador: JOACHIM KAMPMANN.

Ghana: Avda 5a, No 1808, esq. Calle 20, Miramar, Havana; tel. 29-3513; Ambassador: KOJO AMOV-GATTFRIED.

Greece: Havana; Ambassador: ELISABETH PAPAZOI.

Guinea: Calle 20, No 504, Miramar, Havana; tel. 2-6428; Ambassador: LAMINE SOUGOULÉ.

Guinea-Bissau: Calle 14, No 113, Miramar, Havana; tel. 2-8794; Ambassador: PASCOAL CORREIA ALVES.

Guyana: Calle 18, No 506, Miramar, Havana; tel. 22-1249; telex 511498; Ambassador: CECIL STANLEY PILGRIM.

Holy See: Calle 12, No 514, Miramar, Havana (Apostolic Nunciature); tel. 29-5700; Apostolic Pro-Nuncio: Mgr GIULIO EINAUDI.

Hungary: Calle 19, No 407, Vedado, Havana; tel. 32-6526; telex 511368; Ambassador: ISTVÁN BOGNÁR.

India: Calle 21, No 202, Vedado, Havana; tel. 32-5777; telex 511414; Ambassador: V. C. KHANNA.

Iran: Avda 5a, No 3002, esq. a 30, Miramar, Havana; tel. 29-4575; telex 512186; Ambassador: MUHAMMAD H. FADAIE FARD.

Iraq: Avda 5a, No 8201, Miramar, Havana; tel. 2-6461; telex 511413; Ambassador: SAHEB HUSSEIN TAHER.

Italy: Paseo No 606 (altos), Vedado, Havana; tel. 30-0378; telex 511352; Ambassador: VINCENZO MANNO.

Japan: Calle 17, No 552, esq. a D, Vedado, Havana; tel. 32-5554; telex 511260; Ambassador: HARUYUKI MABUCHI.

Kampuchea: Avda 5a, No 7001, Miramar, Havana; tel. 29-6779; Ambassador: LONG VISALO.

Korea, Democratic People's Republic: Calle 17, No 752, Vedado, Havana; tel. 30-5132; telex 511553; Ambassador: PAK YONG SE.

Laos: Avda 5a, No 2808, esq. 30, Miramar, Havana; tel. 2-6198; Ambassador: SOUKTHAVON KEOLA.

Lebanon: Calle 174, No 1707, Siboney, Havana; tel. 21-9030; Ambassador: GILBERTO GAZZI.

Libya: Calle 8, No 309, Miramar, Havana; tel. 2-4892; telex 511570; Ambassador: MUHAMMAD AL-EJILI.

Malta: Calle 20, No 712, 1°, entre 7a y 9a, Miramar, Havana; Ambassador: FERNANDO ESPÁ Y CUENCA BENET.

Mexico: Calle 12, No 518, Miramar, Havana; tel. 2-8634; telex 511298; Ambassador: ENRIQUE OLIVARES SANTANA.

Mongolia: Calle 66, No 505, Miramar, Havana; tel. 2-5080; Ambassador: BAYARJUUGUIN NANZAD.

Mozambique: Calle 36a, No 704, Miramar, Havana; tel. 22-8332; Ambassador: DANIEL ANTÓNIO.

Netherlands: Calle 8, No 307, Miramar, Havana; tel. 2-6511; telex 511279; Ambassador: COENRAAD FREDRICK STORK.

Nicaragua: Avda 7a, No 1402, Miramar, Havana; tel. 2-6810; Ambassador: LUIS ENRIQUE FIGUEROA AGUILAR.

Nigeria: Avda 5a, No 1401, Apdo 6232, Miramar, Havana; tel. 29-1091; telex 1589; Ambassador: PETER OCHALA OSUMAN.

Panama: Calle 26, No 109, Miramar, Havana; tel. 22-4096; Ambassador: MANUEL ORESTES NIETO DE ICAZA.

Peru: Calle 36a, No 704, Miramar, Havana; tel. 29-4477; telex 511289; Chargé d'affaires: JORGE VELÁZQUEZ DE LA TORRE.

Poland: Avda 5, No 4405, Miramar, Havana; tel. 29-1015; Ambassador: CZESŁAW DĘGA.

Portugal: Avda 5a, No 6604, Miramar, Havana; tel. 2-6871; telex 511411; Ambassador: CONSTANTINO RIBEIRO VAZ.

Romania: Calle 21, No 307, Vedado, Havana; tel. 32-4303; Ambassador: VICTOR BOLOJAN.

Sierra Leone: Calle 36, No 716, Miramar, Havana; tel. 29-1897; Ambassador: ALIMAMY YAMBA KOMEH.

Spain: Cárcel No 51, esq. Zulueta, Havana; tel. 6-4741; telex 511367; Ambassador: ANTONIO SERRANO DE HARO MEDIALDES.

Sweden: Avda 31, No 1411, Miramar, Havana; tel. 29-2871; telex 511208; Ambassador: JAN STÅHL.

Switzerland: Avda 5, No 2005, Miramar, Havana; tel. 2-6452; telex 511194; Ambassador: PETER HOLLENWEGER.

Syria: Avda 5, No 7402, Miramar, Havana; tel. 22-5266; telex 511394; Ambassador: MUHAMMAD NAJDY AL-JAZZAR.

Turkey: Avda 1a A, No 4215, entre 42 y 44, Miramar, Havana; tel. 22-3933; Ambassador: GUNDOGDU CAN.

USSR: Calle 13, No 651, Vedado, Havana; tel. 3-3667; Ambassador: ALEKSANDR KAPTO.

United Kingdom: Edif. Bolívar, Cárcel No 101–103, e Morro y Prado, Apdo 1069, Havana; tel. 61-5681; telex 511656; Ambassador: ANDREW PALMER.

USA: (Relations broken off in 1961); Calzada entre L y M, Vedado, Havana; tel. 32-0551; Counsellor: CURTIN KAMMAN.

Venezuela: Avda 5a, No 7802, Miramar, Havana; tel. 22-5497; telex 511384; Ambassador: (vacant).

Viet-Nam: Avda 5a, No 1802, Miramar, Havana; tel. 2-3367; Ambassador: HOANG LUONG.

Yemen, People's Democratic Republic: Avda 7a, No 1086, Miramar, Havana; tel. 22-2594; telex 511488; Ambassador: OMAR HUSSEIN AL-HURUBI.

Yugoslavia: Calle 42, No 115, Miramar, Havana; tel. 2-4982; Ambassador: MIHAJLO POPOVIĆ.

Judicial System

The judicial system comprises the People's Supreme Court, the People's Provincial Courts and the People's Municipal Courts. The People's Supreme Court exercises the highest judicial authority.

PEOPLE'S SUPREME COURT

The People's Supreme Court comprises the Plenum, the five Courts of Justice in joint session and the Council of Government. When the Courts of Justice are in joint session they comprise all the professional and lay judges, the Attorney-General and the Minister of Justice. The Council of Government comprises the President and Vice-President of the People's Supreme Court, the Presidents of each Court of Justice and the Attorney-General of the Republic. The Minister of Justice may participate in its meetings.

President: Dr JOSÉ RAÚL AMARO SALUP.

Vice-President: (vacant).

Criminal Court:
President: Dr JOSÉ GARCÍA ALVAREZ.
Eight professional judges and 12 lay judges.

Civil and Administrative Court:
President: Dr LUIS M. BUCH RODRÍGUEZ.
Two professional judges and 12 lay judges.

Labour Court:
President: Dr WILFREDO PÉREZ MARCHANTE.
Three professional judges and 12 lay judges.

Court for State Security:
President: Dr EVERILDO DOMÍNGUEZ DOMÍNGUEZ.
Three professional judges and 12 lay judges.

Military Court:
President: JUAN F. GARCÍA GARCÍA.
Three professional judges and 12 lay judges.

Attorney-General: Dr RAMÓN DE LA CRUZ OCHOA.

Religion

There is no established Church, and all religions are permitted, though Roman Catholicism predominates.

CHRISTIANITY

The Roman Catholic Church

Cuba comprises two archdioceses and five dioceses. At 31 December 1984, according to diocesan estimates, there were 4.1m. adherents in the country, representing about 40% of the total population. The number of practising Roman Catholics was estimated at only 100,000 in 1986.

Bishops' Conference: Conferencia Episcopal de Cuba, Calle Habana 152, Apdo 594, Havana; tel. 80-3005; f. 1983; Pres. ADOLFO RODRÍGUEZ HERRERA, Bishop of Camagüey.

Archbishop of San Cristóbal de la Habana: JAIME LUCAS ORTEGA Y ALAMINO, Calle Habana 152, Apdo 594, Havana; tel. 6-8463.

CUBA
Directory

Archbishop of Santiago de Cuba: PEDRO MEURICE ESTIU, Sánchez Hechevarría 607, Apdo 26, Santiago de Cuba; tel. 5-4801.

The Protestant Church

Convención Bautista de Cuba Oriental: Apdo 581, Calle 1, No 101, Rpto Fomento, Santiago; tel. 6643; f. 1905; Pres. Rev. VÍCTOR RUIZ VICTORES; Sec. Rev. FÉLIX SANTOS PERRAND.

The Press

DAILIES

Havana

Granma: Avda General Suárez y Calle Territorial, Plaza de la Revolución José Martí, Apdo 6260, Havana; tel. 70-3521; f. 1965 to replace *Hoy* and *Revolución;* official Communist Party organ; morning and weekly editions; also weekly editions in Spanish, English, French and Portuguese; Editor JORGE ENRIQUE MENDOZA; circ. 700,000.

Juventud Rebelde: Prado, 533, Havana 2; tel. 61-6274; f. 1965; organ of the Young Communist Union; evening; Dir JORGE LÓPEZ PIMENTEL; circ. 300,000.

Trabajadores: Virtudes 257, esq. a Aguila, Havana; tel. 6-7593; f. 1970; organ of the trade-union movement; daily; Dir JORGE LUIS CANELA CIURANA; circ. 150,000.

Tribuna de la Habana: Virtudes 257 entre Aguila y Galiano, Havana; tel. 70-6164; f. 1980; Dir ROBERTO PAVÓN TAMAYO; circ. 60,000.

Provinces

Adelante: Goyo Benítez 19, Camagüey; f. 1959; morning; Dir ARMANDO BOUDET; circ. 32,000.

Ahora: Frexes y Rastro, Holguín; f. 1962; Dir EZEQUIEL HERNÁNDEZ; circ. 20,000.

Cinco de Septiembre: Calle 35, No 5609, entre 56 y 58, Cienfuegos; f. 1980; Dir ENRIQUE ROMÁN HERNÁNDEZ; circ. 6,000.

La Demajagua: Calle Martí 68, Bayamo; f. 1978; Dir JOSÉ FERNÁNDEZ VEGA; circ. 14,000.

Escambray: Adolfo del Castillo 10, Sancti Spíritus; f. 1979; Dir RAFAEL GARCÍA RUIZ; circ. 9,300.

Girón: San Juan de Díos 3, Matanzas; f. 1960; Dir OTHONIEL GONZÁLEZ QUEVEDO; circ. 25,000.

Guerrillero: Colón esq. Delicias y Adela Azcuy, Pinar del Río; f. 1969; Dir RONALD SUÁREZ; circ. 21,000.

Invasor: Marcial Gómez 401 esq. Estrada Palma, Ciego de Avila; Dir DIGNO ROLANDO CEDEÑO; circ. 6,000.

Sierra Maestra: Santa Lucía 356, Santiago de Cuba; f. 1959; Dir ORLANDO GUEVARA NÚÑEZ; circ. 25,000.

Vanguardia: Matanzas; f. 1962; Dir PEDRO HERNÁNDEZ SOTO; circ. 24,000.

Venceremos: Cuartel 715 entre Narcisco López y J. del Sol, Guantánamo; f. 1962; Dir ROBERTO TORRES; circ. 3,000.

Ventiseis: Calle Colón 157 entre Francisco Vega y Julián Santana, Las Tunas; Dir JOSÉ INFANTES REYES; circ. 4,500.

Victoria: Calle 41 entre 24 y 26, Nueva Gerona, Isla de la Juventud; f. 1967; Dir NIEVE VARONA PUENTE; circ. 9,400.

PERIODICALS

ANAP: Línea 351, Vedado, Havana; f. 1961; monthly; information for small farmers; Dir RICARDO MACHADO; circ. 90,000.

Bohemia: Avda de Rancho Boyeros y San Pedro, Havana; tel. 7-4820; f. 1908; weekly; politics; Dir MAGALI GARCÍA MORÉ; circ. 257,000.

El Caimán Barbudo: Paseo 613, Vedado, Havana; f. 1966; monthly; cultural; Dir ROBERTO ROMAY REQUEIRO; circ. 30,000.

Casa de las Américas: Calle 3a y Avda G, Vedado, Havana; tel. 32-3587; telex 511019; f. 1960; every 2 months; literary; Dir ROBERTO FERNÁNDEZ RETAMAR; circ. 15,000.

Con la Guardia en Alto: Avda Salvador Allende 601, Havana; f. 1961; monthly; for mems of the Committees for the Defence of the Revolution; Dir AURELIO ALVAREZ; circ. 60,000.

Cuba Internacional: Avda Simón Bolívar 352, Apdo 3603, Havana; tel. 6-5323; f. 1959; monthly; political; in Spanish and Russian; Dir AURELIO MARTÍNEZ; circ. 30,000.

Cubatabaco: Amargura 103, Havana; tel. 61-8453; telex 511123; f. 1972; quarterly; tobacco industry; Dir ZOILA COUCEYRO; circ. 10,000.

Cubatabaco International: Amargura 103, Havana; tel. 61-8453; telex 511123; f. 1979; 2 a year; tobacco industry; Dir ZOILA COUCEYRO; circ. 3,000 (in English).

El Deporte Derecho del Pueblo: Vía Blanca y Boyeros, Havana; f. 1964; monthly; sport; Dir MARIO TORRES; circ. 15,000.

Granma Campesino: Gen. Suárez y Territorial, Havana; f. 1966; Dir ROBERTO MENDOZA; circ. 100,000.

Industria Alimenticia: Amargura 103, Havana; tel. 61-8453; telex 511123; f. 1977; quarterly; food industry; Dir ZOILA COUCEYRO; circ. 10,000.

Juventud Técnica: O'Reilly 251, Havana; f. 1965; monthly; scientific-technical; Dir HOMERÓ ALFONSO; circ. 50,000.

L.P.V.: Vía Blanca y Boyeros, Havana; f, 1961; weekly; sport; Dir IRENES FORBES; circ. 15,000.

Magacín: Havana; f. 1975; monthly; commerce; Dir MIRTA MUÑIZ; circ. 40,000.

Mar y Pesca: San Ignacio 303, Havana; f. 1965; monthly; fishing; Dir FABIÁN DELGADO PÉREZ; circ. 44,000.

El Militante Comunista: Calle 11, No 160, Vedado, Havana; tel. 32-7581; f. 1967; monthly; Communist Party publication; Dir MANUEL MENÉNDEZ; circ. 200,000.

Moncada: Belascoaín esq. Zanja, Havana; f. 1966; monthly; Dir JESÚS HERNÁNDEZ; circ. 40,000.

Muchachas: Galiano 264 esq. Neptuno, Havana; f. 1980; young women's magazine; Dir CAROLINA AGUILAR; circ. 84,000.

Mujeres: Galiano 264 esq. Neptuno, Havana; f. 1961; monthly; women's magazine; Dir CAROLINA AGUILAR; circ. 270,000.

Opina: Calle Línea 157 entre K y L, Vedado, Havana; f. 1979; monthly; consumer-orientated; published by Institute of Internal Demand; Dir EUGENIO RODRÍGUEZ BALARI; circ. 500,000.

Palante: Calle 21, No 954, entre 8 y 10, Vedado, Havana; f. 1961; weekly; humorous; Dir ROSENDO GUTIÉRREZ ROMÁN; circ. 150,000.

Pionero: Calle 17, No 354, Havana 4; tel. 32-4571; f. 1961; weekly; children's magazine; Dir PEDRO GONZÁLEZ (PÉGLEZ); circ. 225,000.

Prisma: Reina 352, Havana; f. 1979; Man. Dir LUIS SUARDÍAZ; circ. 30,000 (Spanish), 20,000 (English), 15,000 (Portuguese).

Revolución y Cultura: Ministerio de Cultura, Avda 47, No 2822 esq. 28 y 34, Reparto Kohly, Municipio Playa, Havana; f. 1972; monthly; cultural; Dir GILDA BETANCOURT ROA; circ. 15,000.

RIL: O'Reilly 358, Havana; tel. 62-0777; telex 511592; f. 1972; bi-monthly; technical; Dir Exec. Council of Publicity Dept, Ministry of Light Industry; Chief Officer MIREYA CRESPO; circ. 8,000.

Sol de Cuba: Calle 19, No 60 entre M y N, Vedado, Havana 4; tel. 32-9881; telex 511955; f. 1983; every 3 months; Spanish, English and French editions; Gen. Dir GARY GONZÁLEZ; Editorial Dir RAÚL PALAZUELOS; circ. 50,000.

Somos Jóvenes: Calle 17, No 354, esq. H, Vedado, Havana; f. 1977; monthly; Dir GUILLERMO CABRERA; circ. 200,000.

Verde Olivo: Avda de Rancho Boyeros y San Pedro, Havana; tel. 79-8373; f. 1959; weekly; organ of the Revolutionary Armed Forces; Dir Maj. EDUARDO YASELLS; circ. 100,000.

PRESS ASSOCIATIONS

Unión de Periodistas de Cuba: Calle 23, No 452, Vedado, Apdo 6646, Havana; f. 1963; Sec.-Gen. ERNESTO VERA MÉNDEZ.

Unión de Escritores y Artistas de Cuba (Union of Writers and Artists): Calle 17, No 351, Vedado, Havana; tel. 32-4551; Pres. NICOLÁS GUILLÉN; Exec. Vice-Pres. LISANDRO OTERO.

NEWS AGENCIES

Agencia de Información Nacional (AIN): Calle 23, No 358 esq. a J, Vedado, Havana; tel. 32-1269; national news agency; Dir FAUSTO SUÁREZ.

Prensa Latina (Agencia Informativa Latinoamericana, SA): Calle 23, No 201 esq. a N, Vedado, Havana; tel. 32-5561; telex 511132; f. 1959; Dir PEDRO MARGOLLES VILLANUEVA.

Foreign Bureaux

Agence France-Presse (AFP): Calle O, No 202, esq. 23, 5°, Depto 18, Vedado, Havana; tel. 32-0949; telex 511191; Bureau Chief (vacant).

CUBA

Agencia EFE (Spain): Calle 36, No 110, entre 1a y 3a, Apdo 5, Miramar, Havana; tel. 22-4958; telex 511395; Bureau Chief JUAN J. AZNARES MOZAS.

Agentstvo Pechati Novosti (APN) (USSR): Calle 28, No 510, entre 5a y 7a, Miramar, Havana; tel. 22-4129; Bureau Chief IOSIF BATIEV.

Agenzia Nazionale Stampa Associata (ANSA) (Italy): Calle Paseo 158, Apdo 403, Vedado, Havana; tel. 3-7474; telex 511903; Correspondent GIANNINA BERTARELLI.

Allgemeiner Deutscher Nachrichtendienst (ADN) (German Democratic Republic): Edif. M. Fajardo, Calle 17, Apdo 27A, Vedado, Havana; tel. 32-9247; Bureau Chief ROLF HEMPEL.

Bulgarian Telegraph Agency (BTA): Edif. Focsa, Calle 17 esq. M, Apdo 22-E, Vedado, Havana; tel. 32-4779; Bureau Chief RUMEN POPOV.

Československá tisková kancelář (ČTK) (Czechoslovakia): Edif. Fajardo, Calle 17, Apto 3-A, Vedado, Havana; tel. 32-6101; telex 511397; Bureau Chief ILONA KOVARIKOVA.

Inter Press Service (IPS) (Italy): Calle 84 No 313, Bajos entre 3a y 5a Avda, Miramar, Havana; tel. 2-6040; telex 512247; Correspondent JESÚS GARCÍA CANOURA.

Korean Central News Agency (Democratic People's Republic of Korea): Calle 10, No 613 esq. 25, Apto 6, Vedado, Havana; tel. 31-4201; Bureau Chief CHE GUAN SON.

Magyar Távirati Iroda (MTI) (Hungary): Calle 21, No 4 entre N y O, Apto 52, Vedado, Havana; tel. 32-8353; Correspondent TAMÁS SIMÁRDI.

Novinska Agencija Tanjug (Yugoslavia): Calle 5a F, No 9801 esq. 98, Miramar, Havana; tel. 22-7671; Bureau Chief ANTON HOCEVAR.

Polska Agencja Prasowa (PAP) (Poland): Calle E, entre Línea y Calzada, No 158, Apdo 11-A, Vedado, Havana; tel. 32-5930; Bureau Chief RYSZARD RYMASZEWSKI.

Reuters (UK): Edif. Altamira, Apto 116, Calle O, No 58, Vedado, Havana 4; tel. 32-4345; telex 511584.

Telegrafnoye Agentstvo Sovetskovo Soyuza (TASS) (USSR): Calle 96, No 317, entre 3a y 5a, Miramar, Havana 4; tel. 29-2528; Bureau Chief ALEXANDER VOROPAEV.

Viet-Nam Agency (VNA): Calle 16, No 514, 1°, entre 5a y 7a, Miramar, Havana; tel. 2-4455; Bureau Chief NGUYEN DUY CUONNG.

Xinhua (New China) News Agency (People's Republic of China): Calle G, No 259, esq. 13, Vedado, Havana; tel. 32-4616; telex 511692; Bureau Chief YAN WEIMIN.

Publishers

Casa de las Américas: Calle 3a y Avda G, Vedado, Havana; tel. 32-3587; telex 511019; f. 1960; Latin American literature and philosophy; Dir ROBERTO FERNÁNDEZ RETAMAR.

Ciencias Sociales: Calle 14, No 4104, entre 41 y 43, Miramar, Playa, Havana; tel. 2-3959; f. 1967; owned by the Ministry of Culture; social and political literature, history, philosophy, juridical sciences and economics; Dir RICARDO GARCÍA PAMPÍN.

Científico-Técnica: Calle 2, No 58, entre 3a y 5a, Vedado, Havana; tel. 3-9417; owned by the Ministry of Culture; technical and scientific literature; Dir JORGE LUIS VICTORERO.

Ediciones Unión: Calle 17, No 351, Vedado, Havana; tel. 32-8114; publishing arm of the Unión de Escritores y Artistas de Cuba; Cuban literature, art; Dir EMILIO COMAS PARET.

Editorial Arte y Literatura: Calle O'Reilly, No 4, esq. Tacón, Habana Vieja, Patrimonio de la Humanidad, Havana; tel. 62-3708; owned by the Ministry of Culture; world literature and art; Dir MIGUEL A. BOTALÍN.

Editorial José Martí: Havana; f. 1985; owned by the Ministry of Culture; foreign language publishing.

Editorial Política: Havana; publishing institution of the Partido Comunista Cubano.

Empresa Editorial Pueblo y Educación: Calle 3a A, No 4605, entre 46 y 60, Playa, Havana; tel. 22-1490; textbooks; Dir CATALINA LAJUD HERRERO.

Letras Cubanas: Calle O'Reilly, No 4, Habana Vieja, Havana; owned by the Ministry of Culture; general, particularly contemporary Cuban literature and philosophy; Dir ABEL E. PRIETO.

Orbe: Havana; tel. 3-5138; Dir HUMBERTO GONZÁLEZ.

Oriente: Havana; owned by Ministry of Culture; general.

Government Publishing House

Instituto Cubano del Libro: Palacio del Segundo Cabo, Calle O'Reilly, No 4, esq. a Tacón, Havana; tel. 6-8341; state printing and publishing organization attached to the Ministry of Culture which combines three publishing houses and an international book trade network; Pres. PABLO PACHECO LÓPEZ.

Radio and Television

In 1984 there were an estimated 2,130,000 radio receivers and an estimated 725,000 television receivers in use.

Ministerio de Comunicaciones: Plaza de la Revolución José Martí, Havana; tel. 70-0911; Dir of Radiocommunications JOSÉ HIDALGO.

Empresa Cubana de Radio y Televisión: Calle K, No 352, esq. 19, Vedado, Havana; tel. 32-1746; telex 511600; Man. Dir CARLOS MAZORRA.

Instituto Cubano de Radio y Televisión: Televisión Nacional, Calle 23, No 258, Vedado, Havana 4; tel. 32-5501; telex 511613; f. 1962; Pres. ISMAEL GONZÁLEZ; Vice-Pres. SERGIO CORRIERI HERNÁNDEZ.

RADIO

In 1985 there were 5 national networks and 1 international network; 18 provincial radio stations and 29 municipal radio stations.

Radio Enciclopedia: Calle N, No 266, Vedado, Havana; tel. 32-1180; instrumental music programmes; 24 hours daily; Dir DANIEL MARTÍN.

Radio Habana Cuba: Avda Menocal, No 105, Apdo 7026, Havana; tel. 7-4954; f. 1961; shortwave station; broadcasts in Spanish, English, French, Arabic, Portuguese, Quechua, Guaraní and Creole; Dir PEDRO ROJAS.

CMBF—Radio Musical Nacional: Infanta No 105, Centro Habana, Havana; tel. 79-8479; telex 1766; f. 1948; national network; classical music programmes; 17 hours daily; Dir JUAN ANTONIO POLA.

Radio Progreso: Avda Menocal, No 105, Havana; tel. 70-4561; national network; mainly entertainment and music; 24 hours daily; Dir JUAN RIVERO.

Radio Rebelde: Calle 23, No 258, Vedado, Havana; Apdo 6277, Havana; tel. 32-0435; telex 511777; f. 1984 (after merger of former Radio Rebelde and Radio Liberación); national network; 24-hour news programmes, music and sports; Dir-Gen. JUAN B. HERNÁNDEZ.

Radio Reloj: Edif. Radiocentro, Calle 23 entre L y M, Vedado, Havana; tel. 32-9689; f. 1947; national network; 24-hour news service; Dir LÁZARA RODRÍGUEZ ALEMÁN.

TELEVISION

In 1985 there were two national networks with 73 transmitters.

Canal 6: Calle M, No 312, Vedado, Havana; tel. 32-5000; broadcasts in colour; Dir OMAR GONZÁLEZ.

Canal Tele Rebelde: Calle M, No 312, Vedado, Havana; tel. 32-6940; telex 511661; broadcasts in colour; Dir OVIDIO CABRERA.

Finance

Comité Estatal de Finanzas: Obispo esq. a Cuba, Havana; tel. 61-1691; f. 1976; charged with the direction and control of the State's financial policy, including preparation of the budget.

BANKING

All banks were nationalized in October 1960. Legislation establishing the national banking system was approved by the Council of State in October 1984.

Central Bank

Banco Nacional de Cuba (National Bank of Cuba): Cuba 402, esq. a Lamparilla, Apdo 736, Havana 1; tel. 62-5361; telex 511146; f. 1950, reorganized 1975; total assets 11,115.0m. pesos (31 Dec. 1985); sole bank of issue; arranges short- and long-term credits, finances investments and operations with other countries, and acts as the clearing and payments centre; 162 throughout the country; Pres. HÉCTOR RODRÍGUEZ LLOMPART; First Vice-Pres OSVALDO FUENTES TORRES (Domestic), LUIS GUTIÉRREZ (International).

CUBA
Directory

Finance Bank
Banco Financiero Internacional, SA: Calle Línea, No 1, Vedado, Havana; tel. 32-5972; telex 512405; f. 1984; autonomous; capital 10m. pesos (1985); promotes Cuban exports and banking relations; Chair. EMILIO ARAGONÉS; Gen. Man. ARNALDO ALAYÓN.

Savings Bank
Banco Popular del Ahorro: Havana; f. 1983; savings bank.

INSURANCE
State Organizations
Empresa del Seguro Estatal Nacional (ESEN): Obispo esq. a Cuba, Apdo 109, Havana; tel. 62-2963; f. 1981; Man. Dir CÉSAR GARCÍA AMPUDIA.

Empresa de Seguros Internacionales de Cuba—Esicuba: Obispo No 257, 3°, Apdo 79, Havana; tel. 61-8906; telex 511616; f. 1963; Man. Dir ANDRÉS GONZÁLEZ HERRERA.

Trade and Industry

IMPORT-EXPORT BOARDS

Alimport (Empresa Cubana Importadora de Alimentos): Infanta 16, 3°, Apdo 7006, Havana; tel. 7-4971; telex 511454; controls import of foodstuffs and liquors; Man. Dir BADITH SAKER.

Autoimport (Empresa Central de Abastecimiento y Venta de Equipos de Transporte Ligero): Galiano 213, entre Concordia y Virtudes, Havana; tel. 62-5926; telex 511417; imports cars, light vehicles, motor cycles and spare parts; Man. Dir RAFAEL LÓPEZ MARTÍNEZ.

Aviaimport (Empresa Cubana Importadora y Exportadora de Aviación): Calle 182, No 126 entre la y 5a, Reparto Flores, Havana; tel. 70-3096; telex 511174; import of aircraft and components; Man. Dir MANUEL GONZÁLEZ FERNÁNDEZ.

Caribex (Empresa Exportadora del Caribe): Ensenada de Pote y Atarés, Habana Vieja, Apdo 138, Havana; tel. 9-5349; telex 511189; import and export of seafood and marine products; Man. Dir CLAUDIO BETANCOURT.

Construimport (Empresa Central de Abastecimiento y Venta de Equipos de Construcción y sus Piezas): Carretera de Varona, Km. 1½, Capdevila, Havana; tel. 44-2111; telex 511213; controls the import and export of construction machinery and equipment; Man. Dir JESÚS SERRANO.

Consumimport (Empresa Cubana Importadora de Artículos de Consumo General): Calle 23, No 55, Apdo 6427, Vedado, Havana; tel. 70-3571; telex 511174; imports and exports general consumer goods; Dir EVELIO LASTRA.

Copextel (Corporación Productora y Exportadora de Tecnología Electrónica): Calle 194 y 7a, Siboney, Havana; tel. 20-5818; telex 512459; exports LTEL personal computers and micro-computer software; Man. Dir LUIS J. CARRASCO.

Coprefil (Empresa Comercial y de Producciones Filatélicas): Calle Infanta No 58 esq. P, Vedado, Apdo 1000, Havana 1; tel. 7-8812; telex 512479; imports and exports postage stamps, postcards, calendars, handicrafts, communications equipment, electronics, watches, etc.; Man. Dir ONELIO ALFONSO PÉREZ.

Cubaelectrónica (Empresa Importadora y Exportadora de Productos de la Electrónica): Calle 23, No 55, Vedado, Havana; imports and exports electronic equipment and devices; Man. Dir LUIS BLANCA.

Cubaequipos (Empresa Cubana Importadora de Productos Mecánicos y Equipos Varios): Calle 23, No 55, Vedado, Havana; tel. 70-2546; telex 511371; imports of mechanical goods and equipment; Man. Dir JORGE DOMÍNGUEZ.

Cubaexport (Empresa Cubana Exportadora de Alimentos y Productos Varios): Calle 23, No 55, Vedado, Apdo 6719, Havana; tel. 70-4521; telex 511178; export of foodstuffs; Man. Dir JOSÉ M. BARROS.

Cubafrutas (Empresa Cubana Exportadora de Frutas Tropicales): Calle 23, No 55, Vedado 4, Apdo 6683, Havana; tel. 70-4521; telex 511849; f. 1979; controls export of fruits, vegetables and canned foodstuffs; Man. Dir JORGE AMARO.

Cubaindustria (Empresa Cubana Exportadora de Productos Industriales): Calle 15, No 410, entre F y G, Vedado, Havana; tel. 32-5522; telex 511677; controls export of industrial products; Man. Dir JORGE REYES.

Cubametales (Empresa Cubana Importadora de Metales, Combustibles y Lubricantes): Infanta 16, 4°, Apdo 6917, Vedado, Havana; tel. 70-2561; telex 511452; controls import of metals (ferrous and non-ferrous), crude oil and oil products; also engaged in the export of oil products and ferrous and non-ferrous scrap; Pres. PEDRO PÉREZ.

Cubaniquel (Empresa Cubana Exportadora de Minerales y Metales): Calle 23, No 55, Apdo 6128, Havana; tel. 7-8460; telex 511178; sole exporter of minerals and metals; Man. Dir WALTER S. LEO.

Cubatabaco (Empresa Cubana del Tabaco): O'Reilly No 104, Apdo 6557, Havana; tel. 62-1857; telex 511174; f. 1962; controls export of leaf tobacco, cigars and cigarettes; Man. Dir FRANCISCO PADRÓN.

Cubatécnica (Empresa de Contratación de Asistencia Técnica): Avda 1a, No 4, entre 0 y 2, Hotel Sierra Maestra, Miramar, Havana; tel. 22-2574; telex 511360; controls export and import of technical assistance; Man. Dir JUAN NUIRY SÁNCHEZ.

Cubatex (Empresa Cubana Importadora de Fibras, Tejidos, Cueros y sus Productos): Calle 23, No 55, Vedado, Apdo 7115, Havana; tel. 70-2531; telex 511175; controls import of fibres, textiles, hides and by-products and export of fabric and clothing; Dir SILVIA ORTA.

Cubazucar (Empresa Cubana Exportadora de Azúcar y sus Derivados): Calle 23, No 55, 7°, Apdo 6647, Havana; tel. 70-3526; telex 511147; f. 1962; controls export of sugar, molasses and alcohol; Man. Dir EMILIANO LEZCANO VIQUEIRA.

Decuba (Empresa de Intercambio de Mercancías y Exportación de Artesanías): Vedado, Havana; tel. 32-4740; telex 512347; controls import and export of various surplus produce and export of Cuban handicrafts; Man. Dir JESÚS O. PIREZ GARCÍA.

Ecimact (Empresa Comercial de Industrias de Materiales, Construcción y Turismo): Avda Independencia y 19 de Mayo, Plaza de la Revolución, Apdo 6039, Havana; tel. 79-5282; telex 511926; controls import and export of engineering services and plant for industrial construction and tourist complexes; Man. Dir JOSÉ SALERO JURE.

Ecimetal (Empresa Comercial para la Industria Metalúrgica y Metal mecánica): Avda Independencia y 19 de Mayo, Havana; tel. 7-5648; telex 511555; controls import of plant for shaping and milling metals; Man. Dir ARMANDO SÁNCHEZ CARNOT.

Ediciones Cubanas (Empresa de Comercio Exterior de Publicaciones): Obispo 461, Apdo 605, Havana; tel. 6-9174; telex 511424; controls import and export of books and periodicals; Man. Dir JOSÉ MANUEL CASTRO RODRÍGUEZ.

Egrem (Empresa de Grabaciones y Ediciones Musicales): Campanario No 315, entre San Miguel y Neptuno, Apdo 2217, Havana; tel. 62-2998; telex 512171; controls the import and export of records, tapes, printed music and musical instruments; Man. Dir MIGUEL COMAS.

Emexcon (Empresa Exportadora de la Construcción): Calle 25, No 2606, Miramar, Havana; tel. 2-4093; telex 511693; f. 1978; consulting engineer services, contracting, import and export of building materials and equipment; Pres. Lic. ELIODORO PÉREZ.

Emidict (Empresa Especializada Importadora, Exportadora y Distribuidora para la Ciencia y la Técnica): Calle 16, No 102, Miramar, Havana 13; tel. 2-5316; telex 512233; controls import and export of scientific and technical products and equipment; Man. Dir ABELARDO IGLESIAS.

Empoft (Empresa Operadora de Fuerza de Trabajo—UNECA): Calle 9a, No 614, entre 6 y 10, Miramar, Havana; tel. 29-4576; telex 511678; manages specialized personnel for building projects; Man. Dir ALEJANDRO GAUBECA.

Empresa Cubana de Acuñaciones: Aguiar No 402, Havana; tel. 62-5181; telex 511146; f. 1976; controls export of coins, jewels and precious metals; Man. Dir GUILLERMO TRIANA.

Energoimport (Empresa Importadora de Objetivos Electroenergéticos): Calle 7a No 2602, esq. a 26, Miramar, Havana; tel. 2-8156; telex 511812; f. 1977; controls import of equipment for electricity generation; Dir LÁZARO HERNÁNDEZ.

Eprob (Empresa de Proyectos para las Industrias de la Básica): Avda Independencia y 19 de Mayo, Havana; tel. 70-7074; telex 512413; exports consulting services and processing of engineering construction projects, consulting services and supplies of complete industrial plants and turn-key projects; Man. Dir EDUARDO BARADA.

Eproyiv (Empresa de Proyectos para Industrias Varias): Avda Independencia y 19 de Mayo, Plaza de la Revolución, Havana; tel. 7-7092; telex 515004; exports consulting services to third-world

CUBA

countries for plant acquisition, tender analysis and tender application; industrial design; Man. Dir RIGOBERTO RAMÍREZ.

Fecuimport (Empresa Cubana Importadora y Exportadora de Ferrocarriles): Avda 7a, No 6209, entre 62 y 66, Miramar, Havana; tel. 2-3764; telex 511174; imports and exports railway equipment; Man. Dir RICARDO ESPINO MARTÍNEZ.

Ferrimport (Empresa Cubana Importadora de Artículos de Ferretería): Calle 23, No 55, 2°, Apdo 6258, Vedado, Havana; tel. 70-2531; telex 511144; import of ironware; Man. Dir MIGUEL SOSA.

Fondo Cubano de Bienes Culturales: Muralla No 107, esq. S. Ignacio, Havana; tel. 62-0085; telex 511400; controls export of fine handicraft and works of art; Man. Dir NISIA AGÜERO.

ICAIC (Empresa Distribuidora Internacional de Películas): Calle 23, No 1155, Vedado, Havana 4; tel. 3-4400; telex 511419; f. 1960; imports and export films and newsreel; Man. Dir ANTONIO RODRÍGUEZ.

Imexin (Empresa Importadora y Exportadora de Infraestructura): Avda 5a, No 1007, esq. a 12, Miramar, Havana; tel. 29-2700; telex 511404; controls import and export of infrastructure; Man. Dir RAÚL BENCE.

Imexpal (Empresa Importadora y Exportadora de Plantas Alimentarias, sus Completamientos y Derivados): Calle 22, No 313, entre 3a y 5a, Miramar, Havana; tel. 29-1671; telex 511404; controls import and export of food processing plants and related items; Man. Dir Ing. MARIO A. TRAVIESO.

Maprinter (Empresa Cubana Importadora y Exportadora de Materias Primas y Productos Intermedios): Infanta 16, Apdo 2110, Havana; tel. 70-0975; telex 511453; controls import and export of raw materials and intermediate products; Man. Dir CARLOS DANTÍN ACOSTA.

Maquimport (Empresa Cubana Importadora de Maquinarias y Equipos): Calle 23, No 55, Vedado, Apdo 6052, Havana; tel. 70-2546; telex 511371; controls import of machinery and equipment; Man. Dir ARMANDO VERA GIL.

Marpesca (Empresa Cubana Importadora y Exportadora de Buques Mercantes y de Pesca): Conill No 580, esq. Avda 26, Nuevo Vedado, Havana; tel. 30-1971; telex 511687; imports and exports ships and port and fishing equipment; Man. Dir REYNALDO LUIS CABRERA.

Medicuba (Empresa Cubana Importadora y Exportadora de Productos Médicos): Máximo Gómez 1, esq. a Egido, Havana; tel. 6-7936; telex 511658; enterprise for the export and import of medical and pharmaceutical products; Man. Dir ORLANDO ROMERO.

Quimimport (Empresa Cubana Importadora de Productos Químicos): Calle 23, No 55, Vedado, Apdo 6088, Havana; tel. 70-8066; telex 511283; controls import of chemical products; Man. Dir NANCY BLANCO MIR.

Tecnoimport (Empresa Cubana Importadora y Exportadora de Productos Técnicos): Infanta 16, Apdo 7024, Havana; tel. 22-3861; telex 511572; imports technical products; Man. Dir CARMEN GARCÍA ROSQUETE.

Tractoimport (Empresa Central de Abastecimiento y Venta de Maquinaria Agrícola y sus Piezas): Avda Rancho Boyeros y Calle 100, Apdo 6301, Havana; tel. 44-2411; telex 511162; f. 1960 for the import of tractors and agricultural equipment; also exports pumps and agricultural implements; Man. Dir MANUEL CASTRO AGUILA.

Transimport (Empresa Central de Abastecimiento y Venta de Equipos de Transporte Pesados y sus Piezas): Calle 102 y Avda 63, Marianao, Apdo 6665, Havana; tel. 20-0325; telex 511150; controls import of land vehicles and transportation equipment; Man. Dir LORENZO ORTEGA.

UNECA (Unión de Empresas Constructoras Caribe): Avda 9a, No 614, entre 6 y 10, Miramar, Havana; tel. 29-4576; telex 511678; undertakes construction work abroad; Man. Dir ANGEL GÓMEZ TRUEBA.

CHAMBER OF COMMERCE

Cámara de Comercio de la República de Cuba: Calle 21, No 661, Apdo 4237, Vedado, Havana; tel. 30-3356; telex 511752; f. 1963; mems include all Cuban foreign trade enterprises and the most important agricultural and industrial enterprises; Pres. JOSÉ ANTONIO GARCÍA LARA (acting).

AGRICULTURAL ORGANIZATION

Asociación Nacional de Agricultores Pequeños—ANAP (National Association of Small Farmers): Calle 1, No 206, Vedado, Havana; tel. 32-4541; telex 511294; f. 1961; 201,000 mems (July 1984); Pres. JOSÉ RAMÍREZ CRUZ; Vice-Pres. PEDRO MANUEL ROCHE.

TRADE UNIONS

All workers have the right to become members of a national trade union according to their industry and economic branch.

The following industries and labour branches have their own unions: Agriculture, Chemistry and Energetics, Civil Workers of the Revolutionary Armed Forces, Commerce and Gastronomy, Communications, Construction, Culture, Education and Science, Food, Forestry, Health, Light Industry, Merchant Marine, Mining and Metallurgy, Ports and Fishing, Public Administration, Sugar, Tobacco and Transport.

Central de Tradajadores de Cuba—CTC (Confederation of Cuban Workers): Palacio de los Trabajadores, San Carlos y Peñalver, Havana; tel. 7-4901; telex 511403; f. 1939; affiliated to WFTU and CPUSTAL; 17 national trade unions affiliated; Gen. Sec. ROBERTO VEIGA MENÉNDEZ; 2,666,000 mems (1982).

Transport

The Ministry of Transport controls all public transport.

RAILWAYS

The total length of railways in 1986 was 14,547 km, of which 9,638 km were used by the sugar industry. The remaining 4,909 km (of which 151 km are electrified) are public service railways operated by Ferrocarriles de Cuba. All railways were nationalized in 1960.

Ferrocarriles de Cuba: Ministerio del Transporte, Avda Independencia y Tulipán, Havana; tel. 70-7751; f. 1960; operates public services; Dir-Gen. LEONARDO CRUZ GONZÁLEZ; divided as follows:

División Occidente: serves Pinar del Río, Ciudad de la Habana, Havana Province and Matanzas.

División Centro: serves Villa Clara, Cienfuegos and Sancti Spíritus.

División Centro-Este: serves Camagüey, Ciego de Avila and Tunas.

División Oriente: serves Santiago de Cuba, Granma, Guantánamo and Holguín.

División Camilo Cienfuegos: serves part of Havana Province and Matanzas.

ROADS

The total length of roads in 1984 was 34,000 km, of which 10,127 km were paved. The Central Highway runs from Pinar del Río in the west to Santiago, for a length of 1,144 km. In addition to this paved highway, there are a number of secondary and 'farm-to-market' roads. A small proportion of these secondary roads is paved, but the majority are unsurfaced earth roads. There are in addition many hundred kilometres of tracks and paths, some of which can be used by motor vehicles during the dry season.

SHIPPING

Cuba's principal ports are Havana (which handles 60% of all cargo), Santiago de Cuba, Cienfuegos, Nuevitas, Matanzas, Antilla, Guayabal and Mariel. Maritime transport has developed rapidly since 1959, and in 1984 there was a merchant fleet of 107 ships. In 1983 there was a coastal trading and deep-sea fleet of 65 ships. Cuba's merchant fleet had a total capacity of 1,071,500 dwt in 1984. During 1986–90 the merchant fleet was to be expanded by 35 ships. A supertanker port is under construction at Matanzas, with co-operation from Soviet and French enterprises, and is scheduled for completion in 1987. A major development of the port of Nuevitas has been planned.

Empresa Consignataria Mambisa: Lamparilla No 2, 2°, Apdo 1785, Havana; tel. 6-8311; telex 511197; shipping agent, ship-chandlers; Man. Dir JULIO AIRA PRADO.

Empresa Cubana de Fletes (Cuflet): Calle Oficios No 170, entre Teniente Rey y Amargura, Apdo 6755, Havana; tel. 6-7355; telex 512181; freight agents for Cuban cargo; Man. Dir ORLANDO BORREGO DÍAZ.

Empresa de Navegación Caribe (Navecaribe): Lamparilla 2, 4°, Apdo 1784, Havana; tel. 62-3605; telex 511262; operates Cuban coastal fleet; Gen. Man. Capt. HUGO VIVAR CASTILLO.

Empresa de Navegación Mambisa: San Ignacio No 104, Apdo 543, Havana; tel. 61-7901; telex 511131; operates dry cargo, reefer and bulk carrier vessels; Gen. Man. JORGE FERNÁNDEZ.

Flota Cubana de Pesca: Apdo 14, Zona Postal No 1, Havana; tel. 61-9223; telex 51189; fishing fleet.

There are regular passenger and cargo services by Cuban vessels between Cuba and northern Europe, the Baltic, the Mediterranean, the Black Sea and Japan and by Soviet, Bulgarian and Czechoslovak vessels between Cuba and the Baltic and the Black Sea. A regular Caribbean service is maintained by Empresa Multinacional del Caribe (Namucar). The Cuban fleet also runs regular container services to northern Europe, the Mediterranean and the Black Sea.

CIVIL AVIATION

There are international airports at Havana, Holguín, Santiago de Cuba and Varadero. Improvements to Havana and Santiago de Cuba airports are scheduled for completion in 1990.

Empresa Cubana de Aviación (Cubana): Calle 23 y P, No 64, Apdo 6215, La Rampa, Vedado, Havana; tel. 7-4911; telex 511737; f. 1929; international services to Angola, Argentina, Barbados, Belgium, Canada, Czechoslovakia, France, German Democratic Republic, Guinea, Guyana, Jamaica, Iraq, Libya, Mexico, Nicaragua, Panama, Peru, Spain and Trinidad; internal services from Havana to 7 other cities; Gen. Man. PEDRO RODRÍGUEZ HEREDIA; fleet: 12 Ilyushin 62, 2 Ilyushin 18, 4 Ilyushin 14, 5 Tupolev, 1 Britannia 300, 7 Antonov 24 and 6 YAK 40.

Tourism

Empresa de Turismo Internacional (Cubatur): Calle 23, No 156, Apdo 6560, Vedado, Havana; tel. 32-4521; telex 511366; Gen. Dir BERNARDO BARRERA HERNÁNDEZ.

Empresa de Turismo Nacional (Viajes Cuba): Calle 20, No 352, entre 21 y 23, Vedado, Havana; tel. 30-0587; telex 511366; f. 1981; Dir ELEUTERIO GUERRA GÓMEZ.

Instituto Nacional de Turismo (INTUR): Avda de Malecón y G, Vedado, Havana 4; tel. 32-0571; telex 511238; f. 1959; Pres. RAFAEL SED PÉREZ; Vice-Pres ENRIQUE RODRÍGUEZ, OROSMÁN QUINTERO.

Atomic Energy

In 1980 construction of Cuba's first nuclear power station was approved. It is to be built in Cienfuegos with help from the USSR and will have a capacity of 1,668 MW. The first 417-MW reactor is due to begin operations in 1990. In 1983 plans were announced to modernize the national research institute. The institute will also receive a 10 MW reactor.

Comisión de Energía Atómica Cuba (CEAC): Apdo 6795, Havana 6; f. 1980; concerned with the peaceful uses of atomic energy; Pres. JOSÉ R. FERNÁNDEZ; Exec. Sec. FIDEL CASTRO DÍAZ-BALART.

Instituto de Investigaciones Nucleares: Managua, Havana; Dir Ing. RAIMUNDO FRANCO PARELLADA.

CYPRUS

Introductory Survey

Location, Climate, Language, Religion, Flag, Capital

The Republic of Cyprus is an island in the eastern Mediterranean Sea, about 100 km south of Turkey. The climate is mild, although snow falls in the mountainous south-west between December and March. Temperatures in Nicosia are generally between 5°C (41°F) and 36°C (97°F). About 75% of the population speak Greek and almost all of the remainder speak Turkish. The Greek-speaking community is overwhelmingly Christian, and almost all Greek Cypriots adhere to the Orthodox Church of Cyprus, while most of the Turks are Muslims. The national flag (proportions 3 by 2) is white, with a gold map of Cyprus, garlanded by olive leaves, in the centre. The capital is Nicosia.

Recent History

A guerrilla war against British rule in Cyprus was begun in 1955 by Greek Cypriots seeking unification (*Enosis*) with Greece. Their movement, the National Organization of Cypriot Combatants (EOKA), was led politically by Archbishop Makarios III, head of the Greek Orthodox Church in Cyprus, and militarily by Gen. George Grivas. Archbishop Makarios was suspected by the British authorities of being involved in EOKA's campaign of violence, and in March 1956 he and three other leaders of the *Enosis* movement were deported. They were released in 1957 but not allowed to return to Cyprus. After a compromise agreement between the Greek and Turkish communities, a constitution for an independent Cyprus was finalized in 1959. Following his return from exile, Makarios was elected the country's first President in December 1959. Cyprus became independent on 16 August 1960, although the United Kingdom retained sovereignty over two military base areas.

Following a constitutional dispute, the Turks withdrew from the central government in December 1963 and serious intercommunal fighting occurred. In 1964 a UN peace-keeping force was established to keep Greeks and Turks apart. The effective exclusion of the Turks from political power led to the creation of separate administrative, judicial and legislative organs for the Turkish community. Relations between the two communities gradually improved, and in 1968 talks on the establishment of a more equitable constitutional arrangement began. These talks continued sporadically for six years, never producing an agreement, with the Turks favouring some form of federation, while the Greeks advocated a unitary state. Each community received military aid from its mother country, and the Greek Cypriot National Guard was controlled by officers of the Greek Army.

In 1971 Gen. Grivas returned to Cyprus, revived EOKA, and began a terrorist campaign for *Enosis*, directed against the Makarios government and apparently supported by the military regime in Greece. Grivas died in January 1974, and in June Makarios ordered a purge of EOKA sympathizers from the police, National Guard and civil service, accusing the Greek regime of subversion. On 15 July President Makarios was deposed by a military coup, led by Greek officers of the National Guard, who appointed Nicos Sampson, an extremist Greek Cypriot politician and former EOKA terrorist, to be President. Makarios escaped from the island on the following day and travelled to Britain. At the invitation of Rauf Denktaş, the Turkish Cypriot leader, the Turkish army intervened to protect the Turkish community and to prevent Greece from using its control of the National Guard to take over Cyprus. Turkish troops landed on 20 July and rapidly occupied the northern third of Cyprus, dividing the island along what became the Attila Line, which runs from Morphou through Nicosia to Famagusta. President Sampson resigned on 23 July, and Glavcos Clerides, the President of the House of Representatives, became acting Head of State. The military regime in Greece collapsed on the same day. In December Makarios returned to Cyprus and resumed the presidency. However, the Turkish Cypriots' effective control of northern Cyprus enabled them to establish a *de facto* government, and in February 1975 to declare the establishment of the 'Turkish Federated State of Cyprus' ('TFSC'), with Denktaş as President.

President Makarios died in August 1977. He was succeeded by Spyros Kyprianou, a former Minister of Foreign Affairs, who had been President of the House of Representatives since 1976. In September 1980 a ministerial reshuffle by President Kyprianou caused the powerful communist party, AKEL, to withdraw its support from the ruling Democratic Party. Kyprianou therefore lost his overall majority in the House of Representatives. At the next general election, held in May 1981, AKEL and the Democratic Rally each won 12 seats in the House. The Democratic Party, however, won only eight seats, so the President still depended on the support of AKEL.

In the 'TFSC' a new Cabinet was formed in December 1978 under Mustafa Çağatay of the National Unity Party (NUP), a former minister. In the elections held in June 1981, President Rauf Denktaş was returned to office, but his party, the NUP, lost its previous majority, and the government that was subsequently formed by Çağatay was defeated in December. In March 1982 a coalition government, comprising the NUP, the Democratic People's Party and the Turkish Unity Party, was formed by Çağatay.

In September 1980 the intermittent UN-sponsored intercommunal peace talks were resumed. In August 1981 the Turkish Cypriots offered to hand back 3%–4% of the 35% of the area of Cyprus which they controlled, and also to resettle 40,000 of the 200,000 refugees who fled from northern Cyprus in 1974. The constitutional issue remained the main problem: the Turkish Cypriots want equal status for the two communities, with equal representation in government and strong links with the mother country, while the Greeks, although they agree to the principle of an alternating presidency, favour a strong central government, and object to any disproportionate representation for the Turkish community, who form less than 20% of the population.

In November 1981 a UN plan (involving a federal council, an alternating presidency and the allocation of 70% of the island to the Greek community) was presented, but talks faltered in February 1982, when the Greek Prime Minister, Andreas Papandreou, called for the withdrawal of all Greek and Turkish troops and an international conference, rather than the continuation of intercommunal talks.

In February 1983 Kyprianou was re-elected President, with the support of AKEL, gaining 56.5% of the votes. In May the UN General Assembly voted in favour of the withdrawal of Turkish troops from Cyprus, whereupon President Denktaş of the 'TFSC' threatened to boycott any further intercommunal talks and to seek recognition for the 'TFSC' as a sovereign state; simultaneously it was announced that the Turkish lira was to replace the Cyprus pound as legal tender in the 'TFSC'. UN proposals for a summit meeting between Denktaş and Kyprianou in late 1983 were unsuccessful.

On 15 November 1983 the 'TFSC' made a unilateral declaration of independence as the 'Turkish Republic of Northern Cyprus' ('TRNC'), with Denktaş continuing as President. An interim government was formed in December, led by Nejat Konuk (Prime Minister of the 'TFSC' from 1976 to 1978 and President of the Legislative Assembly from 1981), pending elections in 1984. Like the 'TFSC', the 'TRNC' was recognized only by Turkey, and the declaration of independence was condemned by the UN Security Council. Conciliatory proposals by the 'TRNC', including the resettlement of 40,000 Greek Cypriot refugees in. Famagusta, under UN administration, were rejected by the Cyprus Government in January 1984, while the 'TRNC', in turn, refused to accept Kyprianou's proposal that the Turkish Cypriots should be allowed to administer 25% of the island, on condition that the declaration of independence be withdrawn. The establishment of diplomatic links between the 'TRNC' and Turkey in April 1984 was followed by a formal rejection by the 'TRNC' of UN proposals for a suspension of its declaration of independence prior to further talks. In August and September the Greek and Turkish Cypriots conferred (separately) with the UN Secretary-General, whose aim was to bring the two sides together for direct negotiations. The Turkish Cypriots reiterated that they would accept the proposed creation of a two-zone federation only if power were to be shared equally between the north and the south. In December 1984, after a third round of negotiations, the leaders of the two communities, Spyros Kyprianou and Rauf Denktaş, agreed to hold a summit meeting in January 1985. No agreement was reached, despite some concessions by the Turkish Cypriots. Kyprianou came under severe criticism from some members of the House of Representatives over the failure of the talks, and immediately reshuffled his Council of Ministers.

In July 1985 the UN Secretary-General presented further proposals, which the Greek Cypriots accepted. The proposals envisaged a bi-zonal federal Cyprus (in which the Turkish Cypriots would occupy 29% of the land), with a Greek Cypriot president and a Turkish Cypriot vice-president, both having limited power of veto over federal legislation. Ministers would be appointed in a ratio of seven Greek Cypriots to three Turkish Cypriots, and one important ministry would always be held by a Turkish Cypriot. There would be two assemblies: an upper house, with a 50:50 community representation, and a lower house, weighted 70:30 in favour of the Greek Cypriots. A tripartite body, including one non-Cypriot voting member, would have the final decision in constitutional disagreements. However, serious problems remained over the crucial questions of a timetable for the withdrawal of Turkey's troops and of the nature of international guarantees for a newly-united Republic of Cyprus. This plan was given the guaranteed support of foreign governments (in effect the USA), which were to provide financial help. The Turkish Cypriots rejected these proposals, principally because they wanted Turkish troops to remain on the island indefinitely, in order to protect their interests, and they felt that any peace settlement should include Turkey as a guarantor.

In November 1985, following a debate on President Kyprianou's leadership, the House of Representatives was dissolved. A general election for an enlarged House was held in December. The Democratic Rally won 19 seats, President Kyprianou's Democratic Party won 16 seats and AKEL won 15 seats. AKEL and the Democratic Rally therefore failed to secure the two-thirds majority required to amend the Constitution and thus challenge the President's tenure of power. The election result was seen as a vindication of President Kyprianou's policies and as a setback to the UN peace proposals.

During 1984 a 'TRNC' constituent assembly, comprising the members of the Legislative Assembly and 30 nominated members, drew up a new constitution, which was approved by a referendum in May 1985. At the presidential election on 9 June, Rauf Denktaş was returned to office with over 70% of the vote. A general election followed on 23 June, with the NUP winning more seats than any other party but failing to secure an overall majority in the Legislative Assembly. In July 1986 Turgut Özal, the Prime Minister of Turkey, made his first visit to the 'TRNC', thus increasing Greek Cypriot fears that there might be further international recognition of the Turkish Cypriot state.

In August terrorists carried out a rocket and mortar attack on the British sovereign air-base at Akrotiri, wounding several people. A hitherto unknown Arab group, the Unified Nasserite Organization, claimed responsibility, stating that the attack was a reprisal for the British Government's decision to allow US bombers to use British bases from which to attack Libya in April.

Further meetings to discuss the draft peace plan were held in March 1986. On this occasion the Turkish Cypriots accepted the plan, while the Greek Cypriots did not. Their principal objections were that the plan failed to envisage: the withdrawal of the 17,000 Turkish troops in Cyprus prior to implementation of the plan; the removal from Cyprus of settlers from the Turkish mainland; the provision of suitable international guarantors for the settlement, with the exclusion of Turkey; and the assurance of the 'three basic freedoms', namely the right to live, move and work anywhere in Cyprus. The Greek Cypriot leaders, as well as Prime Minister Papandreou of Greece, still favoured a 'summit' meeting between Kyprianou and Denktaş, or an international conference. The latter suggestion was first proposed by the USSR, which also suggested a complete withdrawal of all foreign troops from the island, including the UN Peace-keeping Force (UNFICYP). The UN Secretary-General had presented three sets of peace proposals in less than two years, to no avail, and in late 1986 the problems appeared to be intractable.

Government

The 1960 Constitution provided for a system of government in which power would be shared by the Greek and Turkish communities in proportion to their numbers. This constitution remains in force officially but since the ending of Turkish participation in the government in 1963, and particularly since the creation of a separate Turkish area in northern Cyprus in 1974, each community has administered its own affairs, refusing to recognize the authority of the other's government. The Greek Cypriot administration claims to be the government of all Cyprus, and is generally recognized as such, although it has no Turkish participation. The northern area is under the *de facto* control of the 'Turkish Republic of Northern Cyprus' (for which a new constitution was drawn up in 1984 by a constituent assembly, and approved by a referendum in May 1985). Each community has its own president, council of ministers, legislature and judicial system.

Defence

The National Guard was set up by the House of Representatives in 1964, after the withdrawal of the Turkish members. Men between the ages of 18 and 50 are liable to 26 months' conscription. In July 1986 it comprised an army of 13,000, mainly composed of Cypriot conscripts, but with some seconded Greek Army officers and NCOs. There is also a Greek Cypriot paramilitary force of 3,000 armed police. The Turkish community has a security force of about 4,500 men and total armed forces of 36,500, of whom 25,000 are conscripts. Cyprus also contains the UN Peace-keeping Force (UNFICYP, see p. 49) of 2,301 (July 1985) and the British military bases at Akrotiri and Dhekelia.

Economic Affairs

The Cypriot economy was gravely affected by the events of 1974. However, despite the loss of 80% of the island's citrus fruit groves, 30% of its factories, 60% of the tourist installations and the main port of Famagusta, the economy of the southern (Greek Cypriot) part of the island made a remarkable recovery until 1980, when it was clear that the boom was over. The northern third of the island, under Turkish Cypriot control, is closely linked to the economy of Turkey (the source of about 45% of the area's imports), and has almost no economic contacts with the south of the island. The unilateral declaration of independence by the Turkish Cypriots in November 1983 reinforced the international economic embargo which has caused serious problems for the northern sector. The northern economy has not recovered as quickly as that in the south, and continues to rely heavily on aid from Turkey: annual budget expenditure was set at TL 103,079.6m. in 1986, of which TL 26,000m. (about 25%) was to come from Turkey. Grants from the Greek Government to the Greek Cypriot sector amounted to C£10.6m., or 3.7% of budget revenue, in 1985.

The southern economy is basically agricultural, with potatoes and citrus fruit as the principal crops. Before the economic disaster of 1974, agriculture employed 35% of the working population (1972) and provided 49% of exports (1973). Industry was growing rapidly, but mining, mainly for copper, had been in decline for some years. A large trade deficit was covered by income from tourism, foreign military expenditure and remittances sent home by Cypriot expatriates.

Although citrus and cereal production in the southern part of the island has remained low because of reduced areas of cultivation, production of other fruits and vegetables, particularly potatoes, has expanded. Vegetables and fruit accounted for 26.6% of domestic exports (mainly to the United Kingdom) in 1982, declining to 22.4% in 1983 but recovering to 24.6% in 1984. In 1985 vegetables and fruit accounted for only 20.6% of

CYPRUS

domestic exports, owing to adverse weather conditions. Export earnings from citrus fruit were £18.3m. in 1985, compared with £14.3m. in 1984, while exports of potatoes, the single most important crop, fell sharply, from £30.2m. in 1984 to £10.4m. in 1985.

The construction sector developed rapidly in the Greek Cypriot area after the 1974 Turkish invasion, with the need to rehouse refugees and to re-establish the tourist industry. It registered an average annual growth of 40% in 1975–79, and a record 9,449 units of housing were constructed in 1979, although the total declined to 6,327 units in 1984. The contribution of the construction sector to GDP declined from C£101m. in 1980 to C£87.1m. in 1985. Manufacturing also recovered strongly after 1974. Clothing and footwear accounted for 24.2% of domestic exports in 1982, rising to 33.9% in 1984 and reaching 33.3% in 1985. Although manufacturing has gradually declined as a proportion of GDP, the sector continues to expand in real terms. The value of the output of manufactured goods increased from C£132.2m. in 1980 to C£161.5m. in 1985. The main areas of growth were in the production of leather articles, canned goods, paper products and pumps. The main areas of decline were cement, bricks, wine and petroleum products. The restructuring of industry created a large demand for imports, and this, combined with a parallel decline in exports, brought the trade deficit, which was C£60m. in 1976, to C£460m. in 1984. The trade deficit continued to widen, despite a reduction in visible imports, and totalled a record £471.7m. in 1985. The increase in real GDP declined from 4.8% in 1982 to 2.7% in 1983, but recovered to 5.1% in 1984. However, it declined to 3.5% in 1985. Unemployment has increased, but from only 1.8% of the labour force in 1979 to 3.3% in 1983–85. There were 8,094 people out of work in November 1985, compared with 9,169 in August 1983 (when unemployment reached 4%, the highest rate since March 1977). Inflation rose from an annual average of 4% in 1976–77 to 13.4% in 1980, falling to 10.8% in 1981 and to 5.1% in 1983, but rose to 6% in 1984. Inflation declined to 5% in 1985, and the Government expected a further fall, to between 2% and 3%, in 1986.

In the Turkish-controlled north, emphasis has been laid on restoring the production and export of citrus fruit from damaged groves, relying on seasonal labour from the Turkish mainland, and on improving the communications network. Exports from the Turkish Cypriot area totalled an estimated $50.7m. in 1983, compared with $45.3m. in 1982. Imports were worth an estimated $139.7m. in 1982 and $170.1m. in 1983. Inflation exceeded 100% in 1984, compared with 33.8% in 1983, but by November 1986 it had declined to 42%. A Five-Year Plan, based on aid from Turkey, was introduced in 1978 and envisaged annual growth in GDP of 7.5%, but this was not achieved: in 1980 and 1981 GDP fell slightly, and in 1982 growth was only 0.9%. In 1985 GNP per head was estimated at US $1,620 (compared with $1,350 in 1977), but this was still less than one-third of the level in the south of the island. A second Five-Year Plan, covering 1984–88, envisages an average annual growth rate of 6.5% in GDP.

Since 1975, the Middle East (chiefly Lebanon, Syria, the Arabian peninsula and Libya) has become a major market for Greek Cypriot exports. Arab countries together took 48% of total exports, worth C£140m., in 1985, including the greater part of the manufactured goods. EEC countries are Cyprus's main suppliers, providing 57% of total imports in 1985, and the majority of agricultural exports also go to the EEC (25% of total exports in 1984). The United Kingdom is the single main trading partner of both the government-controlled and the Turkish-occupied areas, although in recent years this trade has been threatened by EEC regulations. Since 1972, Cyprus has been linked with the European Community by an association agreement (see p. 148), although the initial lifting of Community restrictions on most Cypriot industrial products was not followed, as planned, by the removal of barriers to agricultural produce. In November 1985 the EEC Council of Ministers approved the admission of Cyprus to a customs union with the Community, but by late 1986 the two sides had failed to reach agreement on the terms of such a union. The EEC proposals envisaged the gradual elimination of many tariffs and the reduction of many duties over 10 years. The proposals also provided for Cyprus to adopt the EEC's common customs tariff after the 10-year period had elapsed. There has been strong disagreement with the EEC over the recognition of the Turkish north in trade agreements.

Social Welfare

A comprehensive social insurance scheme, covering every working male and female and their dependants, is in operation. It includes provisions for protection against arbitrary and unjustified dismissal, for industrial welfare and for tripartite co-operation in the formulation and implementation of labour policies and objectives. Benefits and pensions from the social insurance scheme cover unemployment, sickness, maternity, widows, orphans, injury at work, old age and death. An improved scheme, involving income-related contributions and benefits, was introduced in October 1980. The provision of health services to Greek Cypriots in 1981 included 134 hospital establishments, with a total of 3,535 beds, and 601 physicians.

Education

Greek Cypriot education, under the control of the Greek communal chamber until 31 March 1965, is now organized by the Ministry of Education. Elementary education, which is free and compulsory, is provided in six grades for children between five and 11 years of age. In the towns and certain large villages there are separate junior schools consisting of the first three grades. Secondary education lasts for six years and is provided by trade schools, technical schools, the Gymnasion-Lykeion (classics, science and economics), the Agricultural Gymnasion and the Upper School of Options (Lykeion Epilogis Mathemation), which was introduced in 1977. The first three years are spent at the Gymnasion, and the second three at technical school or the Lykeion. Secondary education is free for all years of study at technical school and for the first four years in all other schools. There are no universities in southern Cyprus. Higher education for teachers, engineers, foresters, nurses and health inspectors is provided by technical and vocational colleges.

Education in the Turkish Cypriot zone is controlled by the 'TRNC'. It is divided into two sections, formal (nursery, primary, secondary and higher) and adult education. A university, the Eastern Mediterranean University, was opened in November 1986 near Famagusta. It has two main faculties: engineering and business and economics.

Tourism

Before the coup and Turkish intervention in July 1974, tourism was developing at a rapid rate. In 1973 nearly 265,000 tourists visited Cyprus. The tourist industry was severely disrupted by the invasion, and in 1975, with 90% of the hotels in Turkish Cypriot hands, the number of tourists fell to 47,000. Revenue from tourism fell from C£24m. in 1973 to C£14m. in 1974, and to C£5.4m. in 1976. However, the Government has made great efforts to restore the tourist industry: tourist earnings were C£102.4m. in 1981, rising to C£212m. in 1984, when there were 736,972 foreign visitors to the Greek Cypriot area. In 1985 there were 813,607 foreign visitors to the Greek Cypriot area, and revenue from tourism rose to C£365.7m., compared with 76,631m. Turkish liras from 125,075 visitors to the Turkish Cypriot area.

Public Holidays

1987: 1 January (New Year's Day), 6 January (Epiphany)*, 19 January (Name Day)*, 2 March (Green Monday)*, 25 March (Greek Independence Day)*, 17–20 April (Easter)*, 23 April (National Sovereignty and Children's Day)†, 1 May (Workers' Day and Spring Day), 19 May (Youth and Sports Day)†, 30 May (Ramazam Bayram—end of Ramadan)†, 20 July (Peace and Freedom Day, anniversary of the Turkish invasion in 1974)†, 6 August (Kurban Bayram)†, 30 August (Victory Day)†, 1 October (Independence Day)*, 28 October (Greek National Day)*, 29 October (Turkish Republic Day)†, 4 November (Birth of the Prophet)†, 15 November (TRNC Day)†, 25–26 December (Christmas)*.

1988: 1 January (New Year's Day), 6 January (Epiphany)*, 19 January (Name Day), 22 February (Green Monday)*, 25 March (Greek Independence Day)*, 8–11 April (Easter)*, 23 April (National Sovereignty and Children's Day)†, 1 May (Workers' and Spring Day)†, 18 May (Ramazam Bayram—end of Ramadan)†, 20 July (Peace and Freedom Day, anniversary of the Turkish invasion in 1974)†, 25 July (Kurban Bayram)†, 30

CYPRUS

August (Victory Day)†, 1 October (Independence Day)*, 23 October (Birth of the Prophet)†, 28 October (Greek National Day)*, 29 October (Turkish Republic Day)†, 15 November (TRNC Day)†, 25–26 December (Christmas)*.

* Greek and Greek Orthodox.
† Turkish and Turkish Muslim.

Weights and Measures

Although the imperial and the metric systems are understood, Cyprus has a special internal system:

Weights: 400 drams = 1 oke = 2.8 lb (1.27 kg.).
44 okes = 1 Cyprus kantar.
180 okes = 1 Aleppo kantar.

Capacity: 1 liquid oke = 2.25 pints (1.28 litres).
1 Cyprus litre = 5.6 pints (3.18 litres).

Length and Area: 1 pic = 2 feet (61 cm).

Area: 1 donum = 14,400 sq ft (1,338 sq m).

Currency and Exchange Rates

100 cents = 1 Cyprus pound (C£).

Exchange rates (30 September 1986):
£1 sterling = 74.84 Cyprus cents;
US $1 = 51.72 Cyprus cents.

In the 'Turkish Republic of Northern Cyprus' the Turkish lira (TL) has replaced the Cyprus pound.

Statistical Survey

Source: Statistics and Research Department, Ministry of Finance, Nicosia; tel. (02) 403286.

Note: Since July 1974 the northern part of Cyprus has been under Turkish occupation, so some of the statistics relating to subsequent periods may not cover the whole island. Some separate figures for the 'TRNC' are given on p. 847.

AREA AND POPULATION

Area: 9,251 sq km (3,572 sq miles), incl. Turkish-occupied region.

Population: 631,778 (males 312,566; females 319,212) at census of 1 April 1973; 612,851 (males 306,144; females 306,707), incl. estimate for Turkish-occupied region, at census of 30 September 1976; 665,200 (provisional estimate for mid-1985).

Ethnic Groups (estimates for mid-1985): Greeks 532,600, Turks 124,100, others 8,500; Total 665,200.

Principal Towns (estimated population at October 1982): Nicosia (capital) 149,100 (excl. Turkish-occupied portion), Limassol 107,200, Larnaca 48,300, Famagusta (Gazi Magosa) 39,500 (mid-1974).

Births and Deaths (estimates, 1985): Live births 13,000 (birth rate 19.5 per 1,000); Deaths 5,700 (death rate 8.5 per 1,000).

Employment (government-controlled area, 1984): Agriculture, hunting, forestry and fishing 43,100; Manufacturing 44,000; Construction 20,500; Trade, restaurants and hotels 43,600; Other services 62,600; Total (incl. others) 216,300.

AGRICULTURE, ETC.

Principal Crops (government-controlled area, '000 metric tons, 1984): Wheat 9, Barley 83, Potatoes 185, Carobs 10, Olives 12, Grapes 199, Oranges 51, Grapefruit 65, Lemons 27.

Livestock (government-controlled area, '000 head, December 1984): Cattle 38, Sheep 334, Goats 235, Pigs 235, Chickens 2,400.

Fishing (government-controlled area, metric tons, live weight, 1984): Inland waters 56; Mediterranean Sea 2,205; Total catch 2,261.

MINING

Exports (government-controlled area, metric tons, 1985): Asbestos 16,948, Iron pyrites 65,423, Gypsum (calcined) 4,449, Terra umbra 6,704.

INDUSTRY

Selected Products (government-controlled area, 1985): Cement 659,000 metric tons, Bricks 46.9 million, Mosaic tiles 1,540,000 sq metres, Cigarettes 2,365.9 million, Footwear (excluding plastic and semi-finished shoes) 7,311,000 pairs, Beer 24.7 million litres, Wines 38.7 million litres, Intoxicating liquors 3.4 million litres.

FINANCE

Currency and Exchange Rates: 100 cents = 1 Cyprus pound (Cyprus £). *Coins:* ½, 1, 2, 5, 10, 20, 50 cents; 1 pound. *Notes:* 25 and 50 cents; 1, 5 and 10 pounds. *Sterling and US Dollar Equivalents* (30 September 1986): £1 sterling = 74.84 Cyprus cents; US $1 = 51.72 Cyprus cents; Cyprus £100 = £133.62 sterling = $193.35. *Average exchange rate* (US $ per Cyprus £): 1.9015 in 1983; 1.7039 in 1984; 1.6407 in 1985.

Budget (estimates, Cyprus £, government-controlled area, year ending 31 December 1985): *Revenue:* Direct taxes 78,715,000, Indirect taxes 129,375,150, Sale of goods and services 18,794,695, Interest, dividends, rents and royalties 18,779,900, Transfers 12,902,550, Greek government grants 10,600,000, Loan proceeds 18,002,000, Other 1,531,980, Total 288,701,275; *Expenditure:* Agriculture and forests 4,513,977, Water development 3,991,032, Public works 3,854,149, Cyprus army and tripartite agreement 4,588,873, Customs and excise 11,791,736, Public debt charges 86,124,433, Pensions and grants 11,727,880, Medical 23,784,237, Police 24,398,037, Subsidies, subventions and contributions 64,702,600, Education grants 45,776,796, Other 71,308,628, Total 356,563,428. **1986** (estimates, Cyprus £ million, government-controlled area): Revenue 359; Expenditure 504.8. **1987** (estimates, Cyprus £ million): Revenue 404.1; Expenditure 540.3.

Development Budget (Cyprus £'000, government-controlled area, 1985): Water development 22,005.4, Road network 8,053.0, Harbours 6, Agriculture 7,992.5, Commerce and industry 1,833.2, Airports 1,030.0. **1986** (Cyprus £'000): Total estimated expenditure 64,389.9. **1987** (Cyprus £ million): Total estimated expenditure 67.9.

International Reserves (US $ million at 31 December 1985): Gold 13.3, IMF special drawing rights 0.1, Reserve position in IMF 5.1, Foreign exchange 590.0; Total 608.5.

Money Supply (government-controlled area, Cyprus £ million at 31 December 1985): Currency outside banks 127.9, Demand deposits at deposit money banks 157.7; Total money 285.6.

Cost of Living (Retail Price Index, government-controlled area; base: 1981 = 100): 111.81 in 1983; 118.51 in 1984; 124.47 in 1985.

Gross Domestic Product in Purchasers' Values (government-controlled area, Cyprus £ million at current prices): 1,015.5 in 1982; 1,124.1 in 1983; 1,315.7 in 1984.

Balance of Payments (Cyprus £ million, government-controlled area, 1984): Merchandise exports f.o.b. 307.5, Merchandise imports f.o.b. −720.7, *Trade balance* −413.2; Receipts from services and transfers 534.6, Payments for services and transfers −238.1, *Current balance* −116.7; Long-term loans (net) 94.1, Other long-term capital (net) 40.0, Short-term capital (net) 12.8, Net errors and omissions 13.9. *Total* (net monetary movements) 44.1.

EXTERNAL TRADE

Principal Commodities (Cyprus £ '000, government-controlled area only, distribution by SITC, 1985): *Imports c.i.f.:* Food and live animals 82,525 (Cereals and cereal preparations 35,021); Petroleum, petroleum products, etc. 129,106 (Crude petroleum oils, etc. 60,282, Refined petroleum products 68,533); Chemicals and related products 57,004; Basic manufactures 176,993 (Textile yarn, fabrics, etc. 56,896); Machinery and transport equipment 199,401 (Road vehicles and parts, excl. tyres, engines and electrical parts, 58,668); Miscellaneous manufactured articles 56,628; Total (incl. others) 762,312. *Exports f.o.b.:* Fresh or simply preserved vegetables 15,459 (Fresh or chilled potatoes 10,375); Fresh or dried fruit and nuts 25,692 (citrus fruit 18,284); Beverages and tobacco 14,138 (Beverages 9,154); Basic manufactures 14,428; Machinery and transport equipment 12,995; Clothing and accessories (excl. footwear) 49,686 (Men's and boys' outer garments of non-knitted textile fabrics, excl. headgear, gloves, stockings, etc., 12,709, Women's, girls' and infants' outer garments of non-knitted textile fabrics, excl. headgear, gloves, stockings, etc., 20,633); Footwear 16,680; Total (incl. others) 199,305. Figures for exports exclude (Cyprus £ '000): Re-exports 55,837; Stores for ships and aircraft 35,468.

Principal Trading Partners (Cyprus £'000, government-controlled area, 1985): *Imports c.i.f.:* France 71,592; Federal Republic of Germany 62,737; Greece 58,724; Iraq 44,803; Italy 95,480; Japan 67,844; Spain 22,124; Syria 13,343; USSR 19,348; United Kingdom 103,476; USA 33,973; Total (incl. others) 762,309. *Exports f.o.b.:* Egypt 15,104; Federal Republic of Germany 5,320; Greece 11,372; Kuwait 6,258; Lebanon 25,427; Libya 23,206; Saudi Arabia 21,651; USSR 9,591; United Arab Emirates 8,057; United Kingdom 47,004; USA 6,383; Total (incl. others) 254,660. Figures for exports exclude (Cyprus £'000): Stores for ships and aircraft 35,468; Unspecified items sent by parcel post 482.

TRANSPORT

Road Traffic (licensed motor vehicles, government-controlled area, 1985): Private cars 121,498, Taxis and self-drive cars 4,154, Lorries and buses 47,305, Motor cycles 40,002, Tractors, etc. 7,424, Total 220,383.

Shipping (government-controlled area, 1985): *Freight traffic* ('000 metric tons, excluding goods loaded and unloaded at Larnaca and Paphos airports): Goods loaded 1,310, Goods unloaded 2,765; *Vessels* (steam or motor vessels and sailing vessels entered, '000 net reg. tons): 11,436.

Civil Aviation (Cyprus Airways, 1985): Kilometres flown 10,254,000, Passenger arrivals 867,741, Passenger departures 864,110, Freight landed (metric tons) 6,836, Freight cleared (metric tons) 20,196.

CYPRUS
Statistical Survey, Directory

TOURISM

Foreign Visitors by Country of Origin (excluding one-day visitors and visitors to the Turkish-occupied zone, 1985): Greece 42,892, Israel 6,564, Lebanon 89,310, United Kingdom 238,295, USA 16,823; Total (incl. others) 813,607.

EDUCATION

1985/86 (government-controlled area): Kindergarten: 423 institutions, 16,810 pupils; Primary schools: 380 institutions, 50,990 pupils; Secondary schools: 92 institutions, 4,621 teachers, 41,399 pupils; Technical and vocational: 11 institutions, 458 teachers, 4,760 pupils; Teacher-training (1984/85): 1 institution, 37 teachers, 415 pupils; Other post-secondary (1984/85): 15 institutions, 252 teachers, 2,719 pupils.

'Turkish Republic of Northern Cyprus'*

Source: Office of the London Representative of the 'Turkish Republic of Northern Cyprus', 28 Cockspur St, London SW1; tel. (01) 839-4577; telex 8955363.

AREA AND POPULATION

Area: 3,355 sq km (1,295 sq miles).
Population: (official estimate): 162,676 (mid-1986).
Capital: Lefkoşa (Nicosia), population 68,286 (Turkish-occupied sector, 1978).

FINANCE

Currency and Exchange Rates: Turkish currency: 100 kuruş = 1 Turkish lira (TL) or pound. *Coins:* 1, 5, 10, 25 and 50 kuruş; 1, 2½, 5 and 10 liras. *Notes:* 5, 10, 20, 50, 100, 500, 1,000 and 5,000 liras. *Sterling and Dollar Equivalents* (30 September 1986): £1 sterling = 1,011.0 liras; US $1 = 698.7 liras; 10,000 Turkish liras = £9.89 = $14.31. *Average Exchange Rate* (liras per US dollar): 225.46 in 1983; 366.68 in 1984; 521.98 in 1985.

Budget (estimates, million Turkish liras, year ending 31 December 1986): *Revenue:* Local taxes 45,500.0, Foreign aid and loans 57,267.8, Total 102,767.8; *Expenditure:* Current expenditure 76,762.9, Defence 6,365.0; Development 19,639.9; Total 102,767.8.

EXTERNAL TRADE

Principal exports (first and second grade, metric tons, 1982): Citrus fruits 115,163, Potatoes 8,449, Carobs 5,309, Tobacco 358.
1983 (US $ million): Imports 145.3; Exports 41.
Principal Trading Partners (US $ million, 1985): *Imports:* Turkey 65.9, EEC 53.9, Total (incl. others) 143.2; *Exports:* Turkey 5.4, EEC 34.8, Total (incl. others) 45.4.

TOURISM

Visitors (1985): 125,075 (incl. 103,791 from Turkey).

EDUCATION

1985/86: Secondary schools and lycées 31 institutions, 661 teachers, 11,139 pupils; Technical lycées and technical secondary schools 10 institutions, 260 teachers, 1,826 pupils; Girls' technical training schools and women's technical training centres 47 institutions, 57 teachers, 1,700 pupils; one university (opened November 1986), with 50 teachers, 1,200 students.

* Note: Following a unilateral declaration of independence in November 1983, the 'Turkish Federated State of Cyprus' became known as the 'Turkish Republic of Northern Cyprus'.

Directory

The Constitution

The Constitution, summarized below, entered into force on 16 August 1960, when Cyprus became an independent republic.

THE STATE OF CYPRUS

The State of Cyprus is an independent and sovereign Republic with a presidential regime.

The Greek Community comprises all citizens of the Republic who are of Greek origin and whose mother tongue is Greek or who share the Greek cultural traditions or who are members of the Greek Orthodox Church.

The Turkish Community comprises all citizens of the Republic who are of Turkish origin and whose mother tongue is Turkish or who share the Turkish cultural traditions or who are Muslims.

The official languages of the Republic are Greek and Turkish.

The Republic shall have its own flag of neutral design and colour, chosen jointly by the President and the Vice-President of the Republic.

The Greek and the Turkish Communities shall have the right to celebrate respectively the Greek and the Turkish national holidays.

THE PRESIDENT AND VICE-PRESIDENT

Executive power is vested in the President and the Vice-President, who are members of the Greek and Turkish Communities respectively, and are elected by their respective communities to hold office for five years.

The President of the Republic as Head of the State represents the Republic in all its official functions; signs the credentials of diplomatic envoys and receives the credentials of foreign diplomatic envoys; signs the credentials of delegates for the negotiation of international treaties, conventions or other agreements; signs the letter relating to the transmission of the instruments of ratification of any international treaties, conventions or agreements; confers the honours of the Republic.

The Vice-President of the Republic, as Vice-Head of the State, has the right to be present at all official functions; at the presentation of the credentials of foreign diplomatic envoys; to recommend to the President the conferment of honours on members of the Turkish Community, which recommendation the President shall accept unless there are grave reasons to the contrary.

The election of the President and the Vice-President of the Republic shall be direct, by universal suffrage and secret ballot, and shall, except in the case of a by-election, take place on the same day but separately.

The office of the President and of the Vice-President shall be incompatible with that of a Minister or of a Representative or of a member of a Communal Chamber or of a member of any municipal council including a Mayor or of a member of the armed or security forces of the Republic or with a public or municipal office.

The President and Vice-President of the Republic are invested by the House of Representatives.

The President and the Vice-President of the Republic in order to ensure the executive power shall have a Council of Ministers composed of seven Greek Ministers and three Turkish Ministers. The Ministers shall be designated respectively by the President and the Vice-President of the Republic who shall appoint them by an instrument signed by them both. The President convenes and presides over the meetings of the Council of Ministers, while the Vice-President may ask the President to convene the Council and may take part in the discussions.

CYPRUS

The decisions of the Council of Ministers shall be taken by an absolute majority and shall, unless the right of final veto or return is exercised by the President or the Vice-President of the Republic or both, be promulgated immediately by them.

The executive power exercised by the President and the Vice-President of the Republic conjointly consists of:

Determining the design and colour of the flag.

Creation or establishment of honours.

Appointment of the members of the Council of Ministers.

Promulgation by publication of the decisions of the Council of Ministers.

Promulgation by publication of any law or decision passed by the House of Representatives.

Appointments and termination of appointments as in Articles provided.

Institution of compulsory military service.

Reduction or increase of the security forces.

Exercise of the prerogative of mercy in capital cases.

Remission, suspension and commutation of sentences.

Right of references to the Supreme Constitutional Court and publication of Court decisions.

Address of messages to the House of Representatives.

The executive powers which may be exercised separately by the President and Vice-President include: designation and termination of appointment of Greek and Turkish Ministers respectively; the right of final veto on Council decisions and on laws concerning foreign affairs, defence or security; the publication of the communal laws and decisions of the Greek and Turkish Communal Chambers respectively; the right of recourse to the Supreme Constitutional Court; the prerogative of mercy in capital cases; and addressing messages to the House of Representatives.

THE COUNCIL OF MINISTERS

The Council of Ministers shall exercise executive power in all matters, other than those which are within the competence of a Communal Chamber, including the following:

General direction and control of the government of the Republic and the direction of general policy.

Foreign affairs, defence and security.

Co-ordination and supervision of all public services.

Supervision and disposition of property belonging to the Republic.

Consideration of Bills to be introduced to the House of Representatives by a Minister.

Making of any order or regulation for the carrying into effect of any law as provided by such law.

Consideration of the Budget of the Republic to be introduced to the House of Representatives.

THE HOUSE OF REPRESENTATIVES

The legislative power of the Republic shall be exercised by the House of Representatives in all matters except those expressly reserved to the Communal Chambers.

The number of Representatives shall be 50, subject to alteration by a resolution of the House of Representatives carried by a majority comprising two-thirds of the Representatives elected by the Greek Community and two-thirds of the Representatives elected by the Turkish Community.

Out of the number of Representatives 70% shall be elected by the Greek Community and 30% by the Turkish Community separately from amongst their members respectively, and, in the case of a contested election, by universal suffrage and by direct and secret ballot held on the same day.

The term of office of the House of Representatives shall be for a period of five years.

The President of the House of Representatives shall be a Greek, and shall be elected by the Representatives elected by the Greek Community, and the Vice-President shall be a Turk and shall be elected by the Representatives elected by the Turkish Community.

THE COMMUNAL CHAMBERS

The Greek and the Turkish Communities respectively shall elect from amongst their own members a Communal Chamber.

The Communal Chambers shall, in relation to their respective Community, have competence to exercise legislative power solely with regard to the following:

All religious, educational, cultural and teaching matters.

Personal status; composition and instances of courts dealing with civil disputes relating to personal status or to religious matters.

Imposition of personal taxes and fees on members of their respective Community in order to provide for their respective needs.

THE PUBLIC SERVICE AND THE ARMED FORCES

The public service shall be composed as to 70% of Greeks and as to 30% of Turks.

The Republic shall have an army of 2,000 men, of whom 60% shall be Greeks and 40% shall be Turks.

The security forces of the Republic shall consist of the police and gendarmerie and shall have a contingent of 2,000 men. The forces shall be composed as to 70% of Greeks and as to 30% of Turks.

OTHER PROVISIONS

The following measures have been passed by the House of Representatives since January 1964, when the Turkish members withdrew:

The amalgamation of the High Court and the Supreme Constitutional Court (see Judicial System section).

The abolition of the Greek Communal Chamber and the creation of a Ministry of Education.

The unification of the Municipalities.

The unification of the Police and the Gendarmerie.

The creation of a military force by providing that persons between the ages of 18 and 50 years can be called upon to serve in the National Guard.

The extension of the term of office of the President and the House of Representatives by one year intervals from July 1965 until elections in February 1968 and July 1970 respectively.

New electoral provisions; abolition of separate Greek and Turkish rolls; abolition of post of Vice-President, which was re-established in 1973.

The Government*

HEAD OF STATE

President: SPYROS KYPRIANOU (took office 3 August 1977, re-elected 28 February 1978 and 13 February 1983).

COUNCIL OF MINISTERS
(December 1986)

Minister of Foreign Affairs: GEORGIOS IACOVOU.

Minister of Finance: CHRISTOS MAVRELLIS.

Minister of the Interior: CONSTANTINOS MICHAELIDES.

Minister of Defence: ELIAS ELIADHIS.

Minister of Agriculture and Natural Resources: ANDREAS A. PAPASOLOMONTOS.

Minister of Health: CHRISTOS PELEKANOS.

Minister of Education: ANDREAS N. CHRISTOFIDES.

Minister of Commerce and Industry: MICHALAKIS P. MICHAELIDES.

Minister of Communication and Works: ROIS G. NICOLAIDES.

Minister of Labour and Social Insurance: ANDREAS M. MOUSIOUTTAS.

Minister of Justice: DEMETRIOS P. LIVERAS.

* Under the Constitution of 1960, the vice-presidency and three posts in the Council of Ministers are reserved for Turkish Cypriots. However, there has been no Turkish participation in the government since December 1963. In 1968 President Makarios announced that he considered the office of vice-president in abeyance until Turkish participation in the government is resumed, but the Turkish community elected Rauf Denktaş vice-president in February 1973.

MINISTRIES

All ministries are in Nicosia.

Ministry of Agriculture and Natural Resources: tel. (02) 402171; telex 4660.

Ministry of Commerce and Industry: tel. (02) 403441; telex 2283.

CYPRUS Directory

Ministry of Communications and Works: tel. (02) 402161; telex 3678.
Ministry of Defence: telex 3553.
Ministry of Education: tel. (02) 403331.
Ministry of Finance: tel. (02) 403201; telex 3399.
Ministry of Foreign Affairs: tel. (02) 402307; telex 2366.
Ministry of Health: tel. (02) 403243.
Ministry of the Interior: tel. (02) 402423.
Ministry of Justice: tel. (02) 402355.
Ministry of Labour and Social Insurance: tel. (02) 403481.

House of Representatives

The House of Representatives originally consisted of 50 members, 35 from the Greek community and 15 from the Turkish community, elected for a term of five years. In January 1964 the Turkish members withdrew and set up the 'Turkish Legislative Assembly of the Turkish Cypriot Administration' (see p. 850). The Greek membership of the House was expanded from 35 to 56 members at the 1985 elections.

Elections for the Greek Representatives, 8 December 1985

Party	Votes	% of Votes	Seats
Democratic Rally	107,223	33.56	19
Democratic Party	88,322	27.65	16
AKEL (Communist Party)	87,643	27.43	15
EDEK (Socialist Party)	35,371	11.07	6
Independents	923	0.29	—
Total	319,467	100.00	56

Political Organizations

Anorthotiko Komma Ergazomenou Laou (AKEL) (Progressive Party of the Working People): 8 Akamas St, POB 1827, Nicosia; tel. (02) 441121; f. 1941; successor to the Communist Party of Cyprus (f. 1926); over 14,000 mems; Gen. Sec. EZEKIAS PAPAIOANNOU.

Demokratiko Komma (DIKO) (Democratic Party): Stasikratous 16, Balmona Bldg, Nicosia; tel. (02) 472002; f. 1976; supports settlement of the Cyprus problem based on UN resolutions; Pres. SPYROS KYPRIANOU.

Demokratikos Synagermos (DISY) (Democratic Rally): 4 C. Palamas St, Nicosia; tel. (02) 449791; f. 1976; opposition party; absorbed Democratic National Party (DEK) in 1977; advocates greater active involvement by the West in the settlement of the Cyprus problem; 10,000 mems; Chair. GLAVKOS CLERIDES; Gen. Sec. ALEKOS MARKIDIS.

Enosi Kentrou (EK) (Centre Union): c/o Tassos Papadopoulos, Chanteclair Bldg, Apt 205, Nicosia; tel. (02) 461962; f. 1981; Pres. TASSOS PAPADOPOULOS.

Ethniki Demokratiki Enosi Kyprou (EDEK)—Sosialistiko Komma (Cyprus National Democratic Union): 23A Const. Paleologos Ave, Nicosia; tel. (02) 463961; telex 3182; f. 1969; the Socialist Party of Cyprus; supports independent, non-aligned, unitary, demilitarized Cyprus; advocates the establishment of a socialist structure; Pres. Dr VASSOS LYSSARIDES.

Komma Phileleftheron (Liberal Party): Nicosia; f. 1986; Pres. NIKOS ROLANDIS.

Nea Demokratiki Parataxi (NEDIPA) (New Democratic Camp): Nicosia; tel. (02) 461400; f. 1981 by deputies from Democratic Party; Pres. ALECOS MICHAELIDES.

Pankyprio Ananeotiko Metopo (PAME) (Pancyprian Renewal Front): Achilleos 27, Strovolos, Nicosia; tel. (02) 425678; f. 1981; Pres. CHRYSOSTOMOS SOFIANOS.

Diplomatic Representation

EMBASSIES AND HIGH COMMISSIONS IN CYPRUS

Australia: 4 Annis Komninis St, 2nd Floor, Nicosia; tel. (02) 473001; telex 2097; High Commissioner: MARY MCPHERSON.

Bulgaria: 15 St Paul St, Nicosia; tel. (02) 472486; telex 2188; Ambassador: BOCHO V. BOCHEV.

China, People's Republic: 27 Clementos St, POB 4531, Nicosia; tel. (02) 473041; Ambassador: LUO YISU.

Cuba: 39 Regas Feros St, Acropolis, Nicosia; tel. (02) 427211; telex 2306; Ambassador: GUILLERMO GÓMEZ.

Czechoslovakia: 7 Kastoryas St, Nicosia; tel. (02) 311683; telex 2490; Ambassador: LADISLAV ŠKEŘÍK.

Egypt: 3 Egypt Ave, POB 1752, Nicosia; tel. (02) 465144; Ambassador: YEHIA HOSNI KABEL.

France: 6 Ploutarchou St, Engomi, POB 1671, Nicosia; tel. (02) 465258; telex 2389; Ambassador: JEAN-DOMINIQUE PAOLINI.

German Democratic Republic: 115 Prodromos St, Nicosia; tel. (02) 444193; telex 2291; Ambassador: KURT MEIER.

Germany, Federal Republic: 10 Nikitaras St, POB 1795, Nicosia; tel. (02) 444362; telex 2460; Ambassador: Dr THILO RÖTGER.

Greece: 8/10 Byron Ave, POB 1799, Nicosia; tel. (02) 441880; telex 2286; Ambassador: C. STOFOROPOULOS.

Holy See: POB 1964, Paphos Gate, Paphos St, Nicosia; tel. (02) 462132; Apostolic Pro-Nuncio: Archbishop CARLO CURIS.

India: Anemomylos Bldgs, POB 5544, Nicosia; tel. (02) 461741; telex 4146; High Commissioner: G. M. JAMBHOLKAR.

Israel: 44 Archbishop Makarios III Ave, POB 1049, Nicosia; tel. (02) 445195; telex 2238; Ambassador: AMOS SHETIBEL.

Italy: 15 Themistocli Dezvi St, POB 1452, Nicosia; tel. (02) 473183; telex 3847; Ambassador: UGO TOSCANO.

Lebanon: 1 Vasilissis Olga St, POB 1924, Nicosia; tel. (02) 442216; telex 3056; Chargé d'affaires a.i.: ALEXANDER AMMOUN.

Libya: 9A Kypranoros St, POB 3669, Nicosia; tel. (02) 49363; Secretary of People's Bureau: SALEM SHWEIHDI.

Romania: 37 Tombazis St, Nicosia; tel. (02) 445845; telex 2431; Chargé d'affaires a.i.: ION AGAFICIOAIA.

Syria: Corner Androcleous and Thoukidides Sts, POB 1891, Nicosia; tel. (02) 474481; telex 2030; Chargé d'affaires a.i.: ANVAR SHEIKHOUNI.

USSR: 4 Gladstone St, POB 1845, Nicosia; tel. (02) 472141; Ambassador: YURI FOKIN.

United Kingdom: Alexander Pallis St, POB 1978, Nicosia; tel. (02) 473131; telex 2208; High Commissioner: W. J. A. WILBERFORCE.

USA: Dositheon St, and Therissos St, Lycavitos, Nicosia; tel. (02) 465151; telex 4160; Ambassador: RICHARD WOOD BOEHM.

Yemen, People's Democratic Republic: Nicosia; Ambassador: ABDO ALI ABDUL-RAHMAN.

Yugoslavia: 2 Vasilissis Olgas St, Nicosia; tel. (02) 445511; Ambassador: VESELIN POPOVAĆ.

Judicial System

Supreme Council of Judicature: Nicosia. The Supreme Council of Judicature is composed of the Attorney-General, the President and Judges of the Supreme Court. It is responsible for the appointment, promotion, transfer, etc., of the judges exercising civil and criminal jurisdiction in the District Courts and the Assize Courts.

SUPREME COURT

Supreme Court: Char. Mouskos St, Nicosia; tel. (02) 402398. The Constitution of 1960 provided for a separate Supreme Constitutional Court and High Court but in 1964, in view of the resignation of their neutral presidents, these were amalgamated to form a single Supreme Court.

The Supreme Court is the final appellate court in the Republic and the final adjudicator in matters of constitutional and administrative law, including recourses on conflict of competence between state organs on questions of the constitutionality of laws, etc. It deals with appeals from Assize Courts and District Courts as well as from the decisions of its own judges when exercising original jurisdiction in certain matters such as prerogative orders of *habeas corpus, mandamus, certiorari*, etc., and in admiralty and certain matrimonial causes.

President: M. A. TRIANTAFYLLIDES.

Judges: ANTONIS KOURRIS, A. N. LOIZOU, Y. CH. MALACHTOS, D. GR. DEMETRIADES, L. G. SAVVIDES, A. LORIS, D. STYLIANIDES, G. PIKIS.

OTHER COURTS

Assize Courts and District Courts: As required by the Constitution a law was passed in 1960 providing for the establishment, jurisdiction and powers of courts of civil and criminal jurisdiction, i.e. of six District Courts and six Assize Courts.

Ecclesiastical Courts: There are seven Orthodox Church tribunals having exclusive jurisdiction in matrimonial causes between members of the Greek Orthodox Church. Appeals go from these tribunals to the appellate tribunal of the Church.

'Turkish Republic of Northern Cyprus'

The Turkish intervention in Cyprus in July 1974 resulted in the establishment of a separate area in northern Cyprus under the control of the Autonomous Turkish Cypriot Administration with a Council of Ministers, and separate judicial, financial, military and educational machinery serving the Turkish community.

On 13 February 1975 the Turkish-occupied zone of Cyprus was declared the 'Turkish Federated State of Cyprus', and Rauf Denktaş declared president. At the second joint meeting held by the Executive Council and Legislative Assembly of the Autonomous Turkish Cypriot Administration, it was decided to set up a Constituent Assembly which would prepare a constitution for the 'Turkish Federated State of Cyprus' within 45 days. This Constitution, which was approved by the Turkish Cypriot population in a referendum held on 8 June 1975, was regarded by the Turkish Cypriots as a first step towards a federal republic of Cyprus. The main provisions of the Constitution are summarized below:

The 'Turkish Federated State of Cyprus' is a democratic, secular republic based on the principles of social justice and the rule of law. It shall exercise only those functions which fall outside the powers and functions expressly given to the (proposed) Federal Republic of Cyprus. Necessary amendments shall be made to the Constitution of the 'Turkish Federated State of Cyprus' when the Constitution of the Federal Republic comes into force. The official language is Turkish.

Legislative power is vested in a Legislative Assembly, composed of 40 deputies, elected by universal suffrage for a period of five years. The President is Head of State and is elected by universal suffrage for a period of five years. No person may be elected president for more than two consecutive terms. The Council of Ministers shall be composed of a prime minister and 10 ministers. Judicial power is exercised through independent courts.

Other provisions cover such matters as the rehabilitation of refugees, property rights outside the 'Turkish Federated State', protection of coasts, social insurance, the rights and duties of citizens, etc.

On 15 November 1983 a unilateral declaration of independence brought into being the 'Turkish Republic of Northern Cyprus', which, like the 'Turkish Federated State of Cyprus', was not granted international recognition.

The Constituent Assembly, established after the declaration of independence, prepared a new Constitution, which was approved by the Turkish Cypriot electorate on 5 May 1985. The new constitution is very similar to the old one, but the number of deputies in the Legislative Assembly has been increased to 50.

Rauf Denktaş was re-elected president on 9 June 1985, and elections to the Legislative Assembly were held on 23 June 1985.

President of the 'Turkish Republic of Northern Cyprus': RAUF R. DENKTAŞ (assumed office as President of the 'Turkish Federated State of Cyprus' 13 February 1975; became President of the 'TRNC' 15 November 1983; re-elected for a five-year term 9 June 1985).

CABINET
(December 1986)

Prime Minister: Dr DERVIŞ EROĞLU.
Minister of Foreign Affairs and Defence: Dr KENAN ATAKOL.
Minister of Finance and Customs: MEHMET BAYRAM.
Minister of Public Works, Communications and Tourism: NAZIF BORMAN.
Minister of Economics, Commerce and Industry: ERDAL ONURHAN.
Minister of the Interior, Rural Affairs and Natural Resources: TAŞKENT ATASAYAN.
Minister of Health and Social Welfare: Dr MUSTAFA ERBILEN.
Minister of Labour, Youth and Sport: GÜNAY CAYMAZ.
Minister of Rehabilitation: ONAY DEMIRCILER.
Minister of Agriculture and Forestry: AYTAÇ BEŞEŞLER.
Minister of Education and Culture: SALIH COŞAR.

MINISTRIES

All ministries are in Nicosia (Lefkoşa).
Prime Minister's Office: tel. (905) 20-72141; telex 57178.
Ministry of Agriculture and Forestry: tel. (02) 4073594.
Ministry of Economics, Commerce and Industry: tel. (02) 4071751; telex 57174.
Ministry of Education and Culture: tel. (02) 4073116.
Ministry of Finance and Customs: tel. (02) 4073626; telex 57268.
Ministry of Foreign Affairs and Defence: tel. (02) 4072241; telex 57178.
Ministry of Health and Social Welfare: tel. (02) 4073611.
Ministry of the Interior, Rural Affairs and Natural Resources: tel. (02) 4071176.
Ministry of Labour, Youth and Sport: tel. (02) 4071444; telex 57178.
Ministry of Public Works, Communications and Tourism: tel. (02) 4072331; telex 57165.
Ministry of Rehabilitation: tel. (02) 4073457.
Ministry of Tourism and Social Assistance: tel. (02) 4071341; telex 57174.

PRESIDENT

Election, 9 June 1985

Candidates	Votes	%
RAUF R. DENKTAŞ (Independent)	55,352	70.47
ÖSKER ÖZGÜR (Republican Turkish Party)	14,413	18.35
ALPAY DURDURAN (Communal Liberation Party)	7,221	9.19
ARIF T. DESEM (Independent)	693	0.88
SERVET S. DEDECAY	528	0.67
AYHAN KAYMAK	335	0.43
Total	78,542	100.00

LEGISLATIVE ASSEMBLY

Election, 23 June 1985

Party	Seats
National Unity Party	24
Republican Turkish Party	12
Communal Liberation Party	10
New Dawn Party	4
Total	50

Speaker: HAKKI ATUN.

POLITICAL ORGANIZATIONS

Atilimci Halk Partisi (Democratic People's Party): 15A Şerif Arzik St, Nicosia; tel. (02) 73222; telex 57244; f. 1979; based on social democratic principles; nationalist and secular; aims at a bizonal, bi-communal and non-aligned federal republic of Cyprus; Leaders İSMET KOTAK and İRSEN KÜCÜK.

Calişan Halkin Partisi (Working People's Party): 2F Müftü Ziyai Efendi St, Nicosia; tel. (02) 76179; f. 1983; extreme left-wing; Leader BEKIR AZGIN.

Cumhuriyetçi Türk Partisi (Republican Turkish Party): 99A Şehit Salahi, Şevket St, Nicosia; tel. (02) 73300; f. 1970 by members of the Turkish community in Cyprus; socialist principles with anti-imperialist stand; district organizations at Famagusta, Kyrenia, Morphou and Nicosia; Leader ÖSKER ÖZGÜR; Gen. Sec. NACI TALAT USAR.

Kibris Demokrasi Partisi (Cyprus Democratic Party): 22 Şerif Arzik St, Nicosia; tel. (02) 79053; f. 1984 by fmr mems of the Toplumcu Kurtuluş Partisi; left of centre; believes in social justice and a mixed economy; Leader ERKEM URAL.

CYPRUS

Directory

Kuzey Kibris Sosyalist Partisi (Northern Cyprus Socialist Party): 44 Alay Bey St, Nicosia; tel. (02) 79245; f. 1985; favours absolute independence; Gen. Sec. DOĞAN HARMAN.

Sosyal Demokrat Partisi (Social Democratic Party): 10 Mahmut Paşa St, Nicosia; tel. (02) 75250; f. 1982; aims at a bi-zonal, bi-communal federal republic of Cyprus; Gen. Sec. HASAN NIDAI MESUTOĞLU.

Toplumcu Kurtuluş Partisi (Communal Liberation Party): 13 Mahmut Paşa St, Nicosia; tel. (02) 72555; f. 1976; left of centre; social democratic principles, social justice; believes in the leading role of organized labour; wants a solution of Cyprus problem as an independent, non-aligned, bi-zonal and bi-communal Federal state; Leader ISMAIL BOZKURT; Gen. Sec. MUSTAFA AKINCI.

Ulusal Birlik Partisi (National Unity Party): 9 Atatürk Meydani, Nicosia; tel. (02) 73972; f. 1975; right of centre; based on Atatürk's reforms, social justice and peaceful co-existence in an independent, bi-zonal, federal state of Cyprus; Leader DERVIŞ EROĞLU; Gen. Sec. OLGUN PAŞALAR.

Yeni Doğuş Partisi (New Dawn Party): 1 Cengiz Han St, Nicosia; tel. (02) 72558; f. 1984; right of centre; supports a mixed economy; Leader AYTAÇ BEŞESLER; Gen. Sec. VURAL ÇETIN.

Yeni Türk Birliği Partisi (New Turkish Unity Party): Han Apt 12/D2, Cengiz Han St, Nicosia; tel. (02) 75891; f. 1985; extreme right-wing party; Leader ISMAIL TEZER.

DIPLOMATIC REPRESENTATION

Turkey: Nicosia; Ambassador: BEDRETTIN TUNABAŞ.

Turkey is the only country to have recognized the 'Turkish Republic of Northern Cyprus'.

JUDICIAL SYSTEM

Supreme Council of Judicature: The Supreme Council of Judicature, composed of the President and Judges of the Supreme Court, a retired member of the Supreme Court, the Attorney-General of the 'Turkish Republic of Northern Cyprus' and the elected President of the Cyprus Turkish Bar, is responsible for the appointment, promotion, transfer, leave and discipline of all judges in accordance with the powers vested by the Constitution of the 'Turkish Federated State of Cyprus'. The appointment of the President and judges of the Supreme Court must be approved by the President of the 'Turkish Republic of Northern Cyprus'.

Supreme Court: The Supreme Court functions as the Constitutional Court, the Court of Appeal and the Supreme Administrative Court.

President: ŞAKIR SIDKI İLKAY.

Judges: SALIH SAMI DAYIOĞLU, NAZIM ERGIN SALÂHI, NIYAZI FAZIL KORKUT, AZIZ ALTAY, HAMDI ATALAY, CELAL KARABACAK, TANER ERGINEL.

Subordinate Courts: Judicial power other than that exercised by the Supreme Court is exercised by the Assize, District and Family Courts.

Religion

Greeks form 77% of the population and most of them belong to the Orthodox Church. Most Turks (about 18% of the population) are Muslims. At the 1960 census, religious adherence was:

Greek Orthodox	441,656
Muslims	104,942
Armenian Apostolic	3,378
Maronite	2,752
Anglican	
Roman Catholic	18,836
Other	

CHRISTIANITY

The Orthodox Church of Cyprus

The Autocephalous Orthodox Church of Cyprus, founded in AD 45, is part of the Eastern Orthodox Church; the Church is independent, and the Archbishop, who is also the Ethnarch (national leader of the Greek community), is elected by universal suffrage; 500,000 members.

Archbishop of Nova Justiniana and all Cyprus: Archbishop CHRYSOSTOMOS, POB 1130, Nicosia; tel. (02) 474411.

Metropolitan of Paphos: Bishop CHRYSOSTOMOS.

Metropolitan of Kitium: Bishop CHRYSOSTOMOS.

Metropolitan of Kyrenia: Bishop GREGORIOS.

Metropolitan of Limassol: Bishop CHRYSANTHOS.

Metropolitan of Morphou: Bishop CHRYSANTHOS.

Metropolitan of Salamis: Bishop BARNABAS.

The Roman Catholic Church

Most of the Roman Catholics in Cyprus are adherents of the Maronite rite. The Archbishop of Cyprus resides in Lebanon. At 31 December 1984 the archdiocese contained an estimated 193,880 Maronite Catholics.

Maronite Church of Cyprus: 8 Favieros St, Nicosia; tel. (02) 463212; Archbishop of Cyprus: Mgr ELIE FARAH, Maronite Archbishopric, POB 70400, Antelias, Lebanon (winter); tel. 961-410020; Cornet-Chahouane, Lebanon (summer); tel. 925005; Vicar General for Cyprus: Mgr JEAN FORADARIS.

The Anglican Communion

Anglicans in Cyprus are adherents of the Episcopal Church in Jerusalem and the Middle East.

Bishop in Cyprus and The Gulf: Right Rev. JOHN E. BROWN, Diocesan Office, Grigoris Afxentiou St, POB 2075, Nicosia; tel. (02) 451220.

ISLAM

Most of the adherents in Cyprus are Sunnis of the Hanafi Sect. The religious head of the Muslim community is the Mufti.

Mufti of Cyprus: AHMET CEMAL İLKTAÇ (acting), POB 142, Nicosia, Mersin 10, Turkey.

The Press

GREEK CYPRIOT DAILIES

Agon (Struggle): Tryfon Bldg, Eleftheria Sq, POB 1417, Nicosia; tel. (02) 477181; f. 1964; morning; Greek; independent, right-wing; Owner and Dir N. KOSHIS; Chief Editor GEORGE A. LEONIDAS; circ. 7,500.

Alithia (Truth): 5 Gr. Xenopoulos St, Nicosia; tel. (02) 463040; Dir FRIXOS KOULEPMOS; Chief Editor ALECOS CONSTANTINIDES.

Apogevmatini (Afternoon): Flat 303, 12 Dem. Dervis St, Nicosia; tel. (02) 443858; f. 1972; afternoon; Greek; independent; moderate; Co-owner and Chief Editor ANTHOS LYKAVGHIS; circ. 11,000.

Cyprus Mail: POB 1144, 75 Vasilou Voulgaroktonos St, Nicosia; tel. (02) 462074; f. 1945; English; independent, conservative; Dir. IACOVOS IACOVIDES; Chief Editor MIKE WARD; circ. 2,340.

Eleftherotypia (Free Press): 6 Themistoklis Dervis St, Nicosia; tel. (02) 454400; f. 1981; Greek; right of centre; organ of DIKO party; Chief Editor YIANNIS SPANOS.

Havavgi (Dawn): POB 1556, Etak Bldg, 8 Akamas St, Nicosia; tel. (02) 476356; f. 1956; Greek; organ of AKEL (Communist Party); Dir GEORGE SAVVIDES; Chief Editor ANDREAS KANNAOUROS; circ. 14,384.

Phileleftheros (Liberal): Themistocles Dervis 12, Nicosia; tel. (02) 463922; telex 4999; f. 1955; morning; Greek; independent, moderate; Chief Editor CHR. KATSAMBAS; circ. 19,500.

Simerini (Today): POB 1836, 4 Annis Komnenis St, Nicosia; tel. (02) 448708; telex 3826; f. 1976; morning; Greek; right-wing; Dir COSTAS HADJICOSTIS; Chief Editor SAVVAS JACOVIDES.

Ta Nea (The News): 23B Constantine Palaelogos Ave, POB 1064, Nicosia; tel. (02) 449766; f. 1970; morning; Greek; organ of EDEK party; Editor TAKIS KOUNNAFIS; circ. 6,250.

TURKISH CYPRIOT DAILIES

Birlik (Unity): 43 Yediler St, Nicosia, Mersin 10, Turkey; tel. (02) 472959; f. 1980; Turkish; organ of National Unity Party; Chief Editor OLGUN PAŞALAR; circ. 2,500.

Bozkurt (Grey Wolf): 142 Kyrenia St, Nicosia, Mersin 10, Turkey; tel. (02) 471565; f. 1951; morning; Turkish; independent; Editor SADI TOGAN; circ. 3,000.

Halkin Sesi (Voice of the People): 172 Kyrenia St, Nicosia, Mersin 10, Turkey; tel. (02) 473141; f. 1942; morning; Turkish; independent Turkish Nationalist; Chief Editor AKAY CEMAL; circ. 5,500.

Kibris Postasi (Cyprus Post): 5 Hükümet Yolu, Famagusta; tel. (036) 6611; telex 57244; f. 1982; Turkish; organ of the Atilimci Halk Partisi (Democratic People's Party); Chief Editor ŞENER LEVENT; circ. 4,000.

CYPRUS

Ortam (Conditions): 158A Girne St, Nicosia, Mersin 10, Turkey; tel. (02) 474872; Turkish; organ of the Toplumcu Kurtuluş Partisi (Communal Liberation Party); Editor KEMAL AKTUNÇ; circ. 1,250.

Yeni Duzen (New System): Yeni Sanayi St, Nicosia, Mersin 10, Turkey; tel. (02) 474906; Turkish; organ of the Cumhuriyetçi Türk Partisi (Republican Turkish Party); Chief Editor ERGÜN VEHBI; circ. 1,000.

GREEK CYPRIOT WEEKLIES

Agrotiki Phoni (Farmers' Voice): A. Karyos St, Engomi Industrial Estate, Nicosia; tel. (02) 449766; Greek; organ of the Farmers' Union; affiliated to EDEK party; Chief Editor M. IERIDES.

Ammochostos: 57 Ledra St, POB 3561, Nicosia; tel. (02) 448022; Greek; right-wing; reflects views of Famagusta refugees; Dir and Chief Editor NICOS FALAS; circ. 3,152.

Anexartitos (Independent): Tryfon Bldg, Eleftheria Sq, Nicosia; tel. (02) 451086; f. 1974; Greek; independent socialist; Dir and Chief Editor RENOS PRENTZAS; circ. 7,000.

Cyprus Weekly: POB 1992, 216 Mitsis 3 Bldg, Archbishop Makarios Ave, Nicosia; tel. (02) 441433; telex 2260; f. 1979; English; independent; Dirs and Editors GEORGES DER PARTHOGH, ALEX EFTHYVOULOS, ANDREAS HADJIPAPAS; circ. 7,500.

Demokratiki (Democratic): POB 1074, Tryfon Bldg, Eleftheria Sq, Nicosia; tel. (02) 444603; Greek; independent, left of centre; Dir and Co-owner EFTHYMIOS HADJIEFTHYMIOU; Co-owner and Chief Editor ANTHOS LYKAVGHIS; circ. 18,000.

Eleftherotypia Tis Defteras (Monday's Free Press): POB 3821, Hadjisavvas Bldg, Eleftheria Sq, Nicosia; tel. (02) 454400; f. 1980; Greek; right of centre; organ of DIKO party.

Ergatiki Phoni (Workers' Voice): POB 5018, Nicosia; tel. (02) 441142; f. 1946; Greek; organ of Cyprus Workers' Confederation; Editor CHRISTODOULOS MICHAELIDES; circ. 8,440.

Ergatiko Vima (Workers' Tribune): POB 1885, Archermos St 31–35, Nicosia; tel. (02) 473192; f. 1956; Greek; organ of the Pancyprian Federation of Labour; Editor-in-Chief PANTELIS VARNAVAS; circ. 13,000.

Kirykas (Herald): 12 Diagorou St, Nicosia; tel. (02) 461961; f. 1981; Greek; right of centre; organ of Centre Union party; Dir and Chief Editor GEORGE ELIADES.

Official Gazette: Printing Office of the Republic of Cyprus, Nicosia; tel. (02) 462202; f. 1960; Greek; published by the Government of the Republic of Cyprus.

Phakos Tis Epikerotitos (Mirror of Current Events): Hadjisavas Bldg, Evagoras Ave, Nicosia; tel. (02) 41657; Greek; independent; Editor PHAEDON KOTSONIS.

Synghroni Politiki (Current Politics): 306 Omirou 2B, Nicosia; f. 1981; Greek; independent; political and economic review.

TURKISH CYPRIOT WEEKLIES

Demokratik Halk Gazetesi (Democratic People's Gazette): Serif Arzif Sok., Nicosia; tel. (02) 473222; f. 1977; Turkish; Editor AHMET GAZIOGLU; circ. 4,000.

Ekonomi (The Economy): Bedrettin Demirel Ave, POB 718, Nicosia, Mersin 10, Turkey; tel. (020) 78760; telex 57137; f. 1958; Turkish; published by the Turkish Cypriot Chamber of Commerce; Editor-in-Chief SAMI TAŞARKAN; circ. 3,000.

Günaydin Kibris (Good Morning, Cyprus): 26 Müftü Ziyai St, Nicosia; tel. (02) 471472; telex 57240; f. 1982; Turkish; Editor REŞAT AKAR; circ. 1,900.

Kuzey Kibris (North Cyprus): Mehmet Akif Cad., Nicosia; tel. (02) 73498; telex 57177; f. 1963 as *News Bulletin*, under present name 1981; English; published by Public Information Office of the 'TRNC'; Chief Editor SAMI TAŞARKAN; circ. 4,000.

Olay: 5 Hükümet St, Famagusta; tel. (036) 66111; telex 57244; Turkish.

Yön (Direction): Selen Otopark, Nicosia; tel. (02) 475250; f. 1983; Editor AYDIN ARIF AKKURT; circ. 1,000.

OTHER WEEKLIES

Lion: British Forces Post Office 53; tel. (052) 21021; British Sovereign Base Areas weekly with British Forces Broadcasting Service and Services Sound and Vision Corporation programme guide; Editor Capt. RAEC; circ. 2,600.

Middle East Economic Survey: Middle East Petroleum and Economic Publications (Cyprus), POB 4940, Nicosia; tel. (02) 445431; telex 2198; f. 1957 (in Beirut); weekly review of petroleum, economic and political news; Publisher BASIM W. ITAYIM; Editor IAN SEYMOUR.

GREEK CYPRIOT PERIODICALS

Apostolos Varnavas: Archbishopric of Cyprus, POB 1130, Nicosia; monthly; Greek; organ of the Orthodox Church of Cyprus; Dir Dr ANDREAS N. MITSIDES; circ. 1,200.

Countryman: Nicosia; f. 1943; quarterly; Greek; published by the Cyprus Public Information Office; circ. 6,000.

Cyprus Bulletin: Nicosia; tel. (02) 446281; f. 1964; fortnightly; Arabic, French, German, Greek, Russian, Spanish, Turkish; weekly English edition; published by the Cyprus Press and Information Office; circ. 28,000.

Cyprus Medical Journal: POB 1393, Nicosia; f. 1947; quarterly; English and Greek; Editor Dr G. N. MARANGOS.

Cyprus Today: c/o Ministry of Education, Nicosia; f. 1963; quarterly; English; cultural and informative review of the Ministry of Education; published and distributed by Press and Information Office; free of charge; Chair. Editorial Board P. SERGHIS; circ. 16,000.

Deltio Omilou Pedagogigon Erevnon (Bulletin of Educational Research): 18 Archbishop Makarios III Ave, 2nd Floor, Nicosia; 2 a year; for teachers and researchers; publ. by the Cyprus Educational Research Asscn; Editor A. D. CHRISTODOULIDES; circ. 1,000.

Dimosios Ypallilos (Civil Servant): 2 Andreas Demetriou St, Nicosia; tel. (02) 442278; fortnightly; published by the Cyprus Civil Servants' Trade Union; circ. 10,800.

Eso-Etimos (Ever Ready): POB 4544, Nicosia; tel. (02) 443587; f. 1913; quarterly; Greek; published by Boy Scouts of Cyprus; circ. 2,500; Editor C. CHRISTOU.

International Crude Oil and Product Prices: Middle East Petroleum and Economic Publications (Cyprus), POB 4940, Nicosia; tel. (02) 445431; telex 2198; f. 1971 (in Beirut); 2 a year; review and analysis of oil price trends in world markets; Publisher BASIM W. ITAYIM.

Kypriakos Logos (Cypriot Speech): 10 Kimonos St, Engomi, Nicosia; f. 1969; Greek; every 2 months; philological, literary, historical and philosophical; Editor P. STYLIANOU; circ. 4,000.

Mathitiki Estia (Student Hearth): Pancyprian Gymnasium, Nicosia; f. 1950; annually; Greek; organ of the Pancyprian Gymnasium students; Editor GEORGE HADJINICOLAOU.

Nea Epochi (New Epoch): POB 1581, Stasandrou 15, Nicosia; tel. (02) 444605; f. 1959; every two months; Greek; literary; Editor ACHILLEAS PYLIOTIS; circ. 2,000.

O Kosmos Tou Kypriakou Vivliou (The World of Cypriot Books): POB 1722, Nicosia; tel. (02) 472744; Greek; journal of the book trade; publ. by MAM (see Publishers).

Oikogeneia Kai Scholeio (Family and School): 18 Archbishop Makarios III Ave, 2nd Floor, Nicosia; tel. (02) 454466; every 2 months; Greek; for parents and teachers; publ. by the Pancyprian School for Parents; Editor A. D. CHRISTODOULIDES; circ. 7,000.

Paediki Hara (Children's Joy): 18 Archbishop Makarios III Ave, Nicosia; tel. (02) 442638; monthly; for pupils; published by the Pancyprian Union of Greek Teachers; Editor GEORGHIOS LOUCA; circ. 13,000.

Pnevmatiki Kypros (Cultural Cyprus): Nicosia; tel. (02) 659001; f. 1960; monthly; Greek; literary; Owner Dr KYPROS CHRYSANTHIS.

Radio Programme: Cyprus Broadcasting Corp., Broadcasting House, POB 4824, Nicosia; tel. (02) 422231; telex 2333; fortnightly; Greek and English; published by the CBC; radio and TV programme news; circ. 25,000.

Synergatistis (The Co-operator): POB 4537, Nicosia; f. 1961; monthly magazine; Greek; official organ of the Pancyprian Confederation of Co-operatives; Editor G. I. PHOTIOU; circ. 4,300.

Trapezikos (Bank Employee): POB 1235, Nicosia; tel. (02) 449900; f. 1960; bank employees' magazine; Greek; monthly; Editor G. S. MICHAELIDES; circ. 17,500.

TURKISH CYPRIOT PERIODICALS

Egitim Bülteni (Education Bulletin): Ministry of Education, Nicosia, Mersin 10, Turkey; tel. (02) 472136; f. 1972; monthly; Turkish; published by Ministry of Education of the 'Turkish Republic of Northern Cyprus'; circ. 3,000.

Kooperatif (Co-operative): Dept. of Co-operative Devt, Nicosia, Mersin 10, Turkey; tel. (02) 471207; f. 1970; monthly; Turkish; published by Department of Co-operative Development of the 'Turkish Republic of Northern Cyprus', circ. 2,000.

Ögretmen (Teacher): Nicosia, Mersin 10, Turkey; tel. (02) 472802; f. 1972; monthly; Turkish; organ of Cyprus Turkish Secondary Schools' Teachers' Asscn; circ. 1,200.

CYPRUS
Directory

Söz (Word): Sabri Orient Otel Alti, Nicosia, Mersin 10, Turkey; tel. (02) 476179; f. 1985; Turkish; Chief Editor ARIF TAHSIN.

OTHER PERIODICAL

The Blue Beret: HQ UNFICYP, POB 1642, Nicosia; tel. (02) 464000; monthly; English; circ. 2,200.

NEWS AGENCIES

Cyprus News Agency: POB 3947, Nicosia; tel. (02) 458413; telex 4787; f. 1976; English; Dir IOANNIS SOLOMOU.

Kuzey Kıbrıs Haber Ajansi (Northern Cyprus News Agency): 30 Osman Paşa Ave, Nicosia, Mersin 10, Turkey; tel. (02) 473892; f. 1977.

Pan Basin-Yayin Ajansi (Pan Press and Publications Agency): 49 Müftü Raci Efendi St, Nicosia, Mersin 10, Turkey; tel. (02) 472633; f. 1980; Dir ARMAN RATIP.

Türk Ajansi Kıbrıs (TAK) (Turkish News Agency of Cyprus): 35A Müftü Raci Efendi St, Nicosia, Mersin 10, Turkey; tel. (02) 471818; telex 57219; f. 1973; Dir KEMAL AŞIK.

Foreign Bureaux

Agence France-Presse (AFP) (France): 4 Democritos Bldg, Flat 84, Stasikratous and Mnasiadoir, Nicosia; tel. (02) 475738; telex 2824; Rep. DIMITRIS ANDREOU.

Agentstvo Pechati Novosti (APN) (USSR): 6 Kreontos St, POB 4051, Nicosia; Rep. V. M. SAFRONOV.

Agenzia Nazionale Stampa Associata (ANSA) (Italy): c/o The Cyprus Weekly, POB 1992, Nicosia; tel. (02) 41433; telex 2260; Rep. GEORGES DER PARTHOGH.

Associated Press (AP) (USA): POB 4853, 4 Andreas Zakos St, Engomi, Nicosia; tel. (02) 447086; telex 2459; Rep. ALEX EFFY.

Athinaikon Praktorion Eidision (Greece): 4 Andreas Patsalides St, Engomi, Nicosia; tel. (02) 441110; Rep. GEORGE LEONIDAS.

Československá tisková kancelář (ČTK) (Czechoslovakia): 30 Evagoros Pallikarides St, Strovolos, Nicosia; Rep. STAVROS ANGELIDES.

Deutsche Presse Agentur (dpa) (Federal Republic of Germany): 9 Diadalou St, Nicosia; Rep. ANTHOS LYKAVGIS.

Iraqi News Agency: POB 1098, Nicosia; tel. (02) 477031; telex 2197; Rep. CHRISTAKIS KATSAMBAS.

Jamahiriya News Agency (JANA) (Libya): 93 Kennedy Ave, Nicosia; Rep. MUHAMMAD ALI SHEWEIHDI.

Novinska Agencija Tanjug (Yugoslavia): 3A Vassilis Michaelides St, Engomi, Nicosia; tel. (02) 450212; telex 3087; Rep. NADA DUGONJIĆ.

Polska Agencja Prasowa (PAP) (Poland): Prodromos St 24, POB 2373, Nicosia; Rep. MICHALAKIS PANTELIDES.

Prensa Latina (Cuba): 12 Demophon St, 5th Floor, Apt 501, Nicosia; tel. (02) 464131; telex 4505; Rep. LEONEL NODAL.

Reuters (UK): POB 5725, Karandokis Bldg, Zena de Tyras St, Nicosia; tel. (02) 475030; telex 4922; f. 1984; Bureau Chief THOMAS O'DWYER.

Telegrafnoye Agentstvo Sovetskovo Soyuza (TASS) (USSR): 3 Philellinon St, Nicosia; tel. (02) 475375; telex 2368; Rep. VSEVOLOD POLONSKI.

United Press International (UPI) (USA): POB 1992, 24A Heroes Ave, Nicosia 109; tel. (02) 449809; telex 2260; Rep. GEORGES DER PARTHOGH.

Xinhua (New China) News Agency (People's Republic of China): POB 7024, Flat 32, 6 Nafpactos St, Nicosia; tel. (02) 456703; telex 5265; Rep. JING BIHUA.

Publishers

Bozkurt Basimevi: 142 Kyrenia Ave, Nicosia, Mersin 10, Turkey; tel. (02) 471565; Turkish Cypriot.

Devlet Basimevi (Turkish Cypriot Government Printing House): Şerif Arzik St, Nicosia, Mersin 10, Turkey; tel. (02) 472010; Dir ŞABRI ERTÜRK.

MAM (The House of Cyprus Publications): POB 1722, Nicosia; tel. (02) 472744; f. 1965; specializes in publications on Cyprus and international organizations and by Cypriot authors.

Radio and Television

In December 1985, in the government-controlled areas, it was estimated that there were 171,000 radio receivers and 88,500 television receivers (including about 50,000 colour receivers) in use.

Cyprus Broadcasting Corporation: POB 4824, Broadcasting House, Nicosia; tel. (02) 22231; telex 2333; Chair. GABRIEL SCOTTIS; Dir-Gen. D. KYPRIANOU; Chief Engineer C. G. ANASTASSIADES; Dir of Programmes CH. PAPADOPOULOS.

Radio: f. 1952; Programme I in Greek, Programme II in Greek, Turkish, English, Arabic and Armenian; two medium wave transmitters of 20 kW in Nicosia with relay stations at Paphos and Limassol; two 30 kW ERP VHF FM stereo transmitters on Mount Olympus; international service in English and Arabic.

Television: f. 1957; one Band III 200/10 kW transmitter on Mount Olympus with 35 transposer stations.

Bayrak Radio and TV Corpn (BRT): Atatürk Square, Nicosia, Mersin 10, Turkey; tel. (02) 471281; in July 1983 it became an independent Turkish Cypriot Corpn partly financed by the govt; Dir. Gen. D. ÖZER BERKEM.

Radio Bayrak: f. 1963; home service in Turkish, overseas services in Turkish, Greek, English, Arabic and German; broadcasts 29 hours a day; Dir of Broadcasting H. NESHET ERKMAN; Tech. Dir YUSUF GAZI; Admin. Dir S. TÜREM.

Bayrak TV: f. 1976; transmits programmes in Turkish, Greek, English and Arabic on six channels.

Services Sound and Vision Corpn, Cyprus: Dhekelia, British Forces Post Office 58, Cyprus; tel. (357) 41-53000; telex 2853; incorporates the British Forces Broadcasting Service, Cyprus; broadcasts a 24-hour radio service in English VHF and medium wave and a four-hour TV service; Gen. Man. JOHN M. CAMPBELL; Engineering Man. ROGER DUNN.

Türkiye Radyo Televizyon (TRT): Turkish television programmes are transmitted to the Turkish sector of Cyprus.

Finance

(brs = branches; cap. = capital; p.u. = paid up; auth. = authorized; dep. = deposits; res = reserves; m. = million; amounts in Cyprus pounds)

BANKING
Central Bank

Central Bank of Cyprus: POB 5529, 36 Metochiou St, Nicosia; tel. (02) 445281; telex 2424; f. 1963; became the Bank of Issue in 1963; cap. p.u. 100,000, res 328m., dep. 330.4m. (July 1986); Gov. A. C. AFXENTIOU.

Greek Cypriot Banks

Bank of Cyprus Ltd: POB 1472, 86–90 Phaneromenis St, Nicosia; tel. (02) 464064; telex 2451; f. 1899, reconstituted 1943 by the amalgamation of Bank of Cyprus, Larnaca Bank Ltd and Famagusta Bank Ltd; cap. p.u. 9m., res 7.1m., dep. 470m. (Dec. 1985); Chair. GEORGE C. CHRISTOFIDES; Gov. ANDREAS PATSALIDES; 136 brs throughout Cyprus.

Co-operative Central Bank Ltd: POB 4537, Gregoris Afxentiou St, Nicosia; tel. (02) 442921; telex 2313; f. 1937 under the Co-operative Societies Law; banking and credit facilities to member societies; dep. 110m. (Dec. 1984); Chair B. BALTAYIAN; Gen. Man. D. PITSILLIDES; 5 brs.

Cyprus Popular Bank Ltd: Popular Bank Bldg, POB 2032, 39 Archbishop Makarios III Avenue, Nicosia; tel. (02) 450000; telex 2494; f. 1901; cap. p.u. 8.2m., dep. 328m., res 21.1m. (Dec. 1985); Chair. EVAGORAS C. LANITIS; Group Chief Exec. KIKIS N. LAZARIDES; 95 brs.

Hellenic Bank Ltd: POB 4747, 92 Dhigenis Akritas Ave, Nicosia; tel. (02) 447000; telex 3311; f. 1974; cap. p.u. 2.5m., res 0.8m., dep. 87m. (Dec. 1985); Chair. PASCHALIS L. PASCHALIDES; Gen. Man. PANOS C. GHALANOS; 36 brs.

Mortgage Bank of Cyprus Ltd: POB 1472, 86–90 Phaneromenis St, Nicosia; tel. (02) 464064; telex 2451; f. 1944; wholly owned subsidiary of Bank of Cyprus Ltd; cap. p.u. 1m., dep. 61.9m. (Dec. 1985); Chair. GEORGE C. CHRISTOFIDES; Gov. ANDREAS PATSALIDES; 136 brs.

CYPRUS

Turkish Cypriot Banks
(amounts in Turkish liras)

Cyprus Turkish Co-operative Central Bank, Ltd: POB 1861, Mahmout Pasha St, Nicosia, Mersin 10, Turkey; tel. (02) 464257; telex 57143; banking and credit facilities to member societies, bodies and individuals; Gen. Man. MEHMET ESHREF.

Kibris Endüstri Bankasi (Cyprus Industrial Bank): 3 Memduh Asaf Sok., Nicosia, Mersin 10, Turkey; tel. (02) 471830; telex 57257.

Kibris Kredi Bankasi (Cyprus Credit Bank): İplik Pazari St, Nicosia, Mersin 10, Turkey; tel. (020) 71666; telex 57246; f. 1978; cap. p.u. 288.3m., dep. 11,162.3m. (Dec. 1985); Chair. SALIH BOYACI; Gen. Man. MUSTAFA YILDIRIM; 9 brs.

Kibris Ticaret Bankasi Ltd (Cyprus Commercial Bank Ltd): 7 Atatürk Sq., Nicosia, Mersin 10, Turkey; tel. (02) 475180; telex 57197; f. 1982; auth. cap. 1,000m., res 9m., dep. 2,650m. (Dec. 1985); Chair. YÜKSEL AHMET RAŞIT; 6 brs.

Turkish Bank Ltd: POB 242, 92 Kyrenia St, Nicosia, Mersin 10, Turkey; tel. (02) 471313; telex 2585; f. 1901; cap. p.u. and res TL 3,233m., dep. TL 42,344m. (Dec. 1985); Chair. and Gen. Man. M. TANJU OZYOL; 15 brs.

Investment Organization

Cyprus Investment and Securities Corporation: Nicosia; tel. (02) 451535; telex 4449; f. 1982 to encourage industrial investment: shareholders: Bank of Cyprus, Cyprus Development Bank and the International Finance Corporation; auth. cap. 1m.; cap. p.u. 500,000; Gen. Man. ANDREAS ALONEFTIS.

Development Bank

Cyprus Development Bank Ltd: 50 Makarios III Avenue, Alpha House, POB 1415, Nicosia; tel. (02) 457575; telex 2797; f. 1963; cap. p.u. 2m.; reserves 594,000 (Dec. 1984); provides medium- and long-term loans for productive projects, particularly in manufacturing and processing industries, tourism and agriculture, and technical, managerial and administrative assistance and advice; performs related economic and technical research; Chair. MIKIS N. TSIAKKAS; Gen. Man. JOHN G. JOANNIDES; Asst Gen. Man. L. D. SPARSIS; 1 br.

INSURANCE
Greek Cypriot Insurance Companies

Office of the Superintendent of Insurance: Treasury Department, Ministry of Finance, Nicosia; tel. (02) 402224; telex 2366; f. 1969 to control insurance companies, insurance agents, brokers and agents for brokers in Cyprus.

Apac Ltd: Apt 1, 5 Mourouzi St, POB 5403, Nicosia 133; tel. (02) 455186; telex 2766; f. 1983; captive offshore company operating outside Cyprus; Chair. KYPROS CHRYSOSTOMIDES; Principal Officer GEORGHIOS POYATZIS.

Allied Assurance & Reinsurance Co Ltd: 12 Themistoclis Dervis Ave, Ivory Tower, POB 5509, Nicosia 136; tel. (02) 457311; telex 4265; f. 1982; offshore company operating outside Cyprus; Chair. HENRI J. CHALHOUB; Gen. Man. CONSTANTINOS AXIOTIS.

Atlantic Insurance Co Ltd: 34 Theophanis Theodotou St, POB 4579, Nicosia 136; tel. (02) 444052; telex 2535; f. 1983; Chair. P. FRYER; Gen. Man. N. MARATHOVOUNIOTIS.

Commercial Union Assurance (Cyprus) Ltd: 4th Floor, Lavinia Bldg, Corner of Santa Rosa Ave and Mykinon St, POB 1312, Nicosia; tel. (02) 445045; telex 2547; f. 1974; Chair. J. CHRISTOPHIDES.

Compass Insurance Co Ltd: 3rd Floor, Themis Tower, Corner Gladstone and Olympion Sts, POB 1183, Limassol; tel. (051) 53155; telex 4938; f. 1981; Chair. P. LOUCAIDES; Gen. Man. PHAEDON MAKRIS.

Cosmos (Cyprus) Insurance Co Ltd: 1st Floor, Flat 12, 6 Áyia Eleni St, POB 1770, Nicosia 135; tel. (02) 441235; telex 3433; Chair. ELIZABETH PLAKIDOU; Gen. Man. KYRIACOS TYLLIS.

General Insurance Company of Cyprus Ltd: 20 Katsonis St, POB 1668, Nicosia 150; tel. (02) 450883; telex 2311; f. 1951; Chair. G. CH. CHRISTOFIDES; Gen. Man. S. SOPHOCLEOUS.

Hermes Insurance Co Ltd: 1st Floor, Office 101–103, 8 Michalakis Karaolis St, POB 4828, Nicosia; tel. (02) 448130; telex 3466; f. 1980; Chair. and Man. Dir P. VOGAZIANOS.

Laiki Insurance Co Ltd: Laiki Tower, 11 Archbishop Makarios III Ave, POB 2069, Nicosia 136; tel. (021) 49900; telex 2474; f. 1981; Chair. E. K. LANITIS; Man. Y. E. SOLOMONIDES.

Minerva Insurance Co Ltd: 8 Epaminondas St, POB 3554, Nicosia 137; tel. (02) 445134; telex 2608; f. 1970; Chair. and Gen. Man. K. KOUTSOKOUMNIS.

Directory

Paneuropean Insurance Co Ltd: First Floor, Avenue Court, Corner Severis Ave and Katsonis St, POB 3506, Nicosia; tel. (02) 444399; telex 3419; f. 1980; Chair. ZENON SEVERIS; Man. Dir ALECOS PULCHERIOS.

Philiki Insurance Co Ltd: 1st Floor, 2 Demokritos Bldg, Corner Archbishop Makarios III Ave and J. Clerides St, POB 2274, Nicosia; tel. (02) 444433; telex 2353; Chair. LOUKIS PETRIDES; Gen. Man. DOROS ORPHANIDES.

Saudi Stars Insurance Co Ltd: No. 2 Corner Archbishop Makarios III Ave and Methonis St, POB 1493, Nicosia; tel. (02) 445874; telex 3156; f. 1979; offshore company operating outside Cyprus; Chair. M. F. AL-HAJRI; Man. PAN. MEGALEMOS.

Seven Stars Insurance Co Ltd: 256 Archbishop Makarios III Ave, Eftapaton, Limassol 225; tel. (051) 445045; telex 2547; f. 1983; offshore company operating outside Cyprus; Chair. KYPROS CHRYSOSTOMIDES.

Universal Life Insurance Company Ltd: Universal Tower, 85 Dighenis Akritas Ave, POB 1270, Nicosia 135; tel. (02) 461222; telex 3116; f. 1970; Chair. J. CHRISTOPHIDES; Gen. Man. ANDREAS GEORGHIOU.

Turkish Cypriot Insurance Companies

Can Holding Ltd: 42–46 Girne St, Nicosia, Mersin 10, Turkey; tel. (02) 71132.

Şark Ltd: 41 Yediler St, Nicosia, Mersin 10, Turkey; tel. (02) 73150.

Şeker Sigorta: K.T. Kooperatif Merkez Bankasi, Nicosia, Mersin 10, Turkey; tel. (02) 71207; telex 57216.

There were 34 foreign insurance companies operating in Cyprus in 1986.

Trade and Industry

GREEK CYPRIOT CHAMBERS OF COMMERCE AND INDUSTRY

Cyprus Chamber of Commerce and Industry: 38 Grivas Dhigenis Ave, POB 1455, Nicosia; tel. (02) 449500; telex 2077; Pres. ANDREAS AVRAAMIDES; Vice-Pres. PHANOS EPIPHANIOU, GEORGE ROLOGIS; Sec.-Gen. PANAYIOTIS LOIZIDES; 4,000 mems, 48 affiliated trade asscns.

Famagusta Chamber of Commerce and Industry: POB 777, Famagusta; temporary address: Stylianides Bldg, 3rd Floor, 1 Koumandarias St, POB 3124, Limassol; tel. (051) 70165; telex 4519; f. 1952; Pres. DEMETRIOS P. IOANNOU; Vice-Pres. TAKIS KYRIAKIDES; Sec.-Gen. IACOVOS HADJIVARNAVAS; 300 mems.

Larnaca Chamber of Commerce and Industry: 12 Gregoris Afxentiou Ave, Apt 43, POB 287, Larnaca; tel. (04) 55051; telex 3187; Pres. Dr A. FRANCIS; Vice-Pres. ANDREAS MOUSCOS; Sec. OTHON THEODOULOU; 350 mems.

Limassol Chamber of Commerce and Industry: 25 Spyros Araouzos St, POB 347, Limassol; tel. (05) 62556; telex 2890; Pres. KYRIACOS HAMBOULLAS; Vice-Pres. CHRISTAKIS GEORGIADES.

Nicosia Chamber of Commerce and Industry: 38 Grivas Dhigenis Ave, POB 1455, Nicosia; tel. (02) 449500; telex 2077; Pres. LEANDROS ZACHARIADES; Vice-Pres. COSTAS CONSTANTINIDES.

Paphos Chamber of Commerce and Industry: POB 82, Paphos; tel. (06) 35115; telex 2888; Pres. MICHALAKIS E. CONIOTIS; Vice-Pres. THEODOROS ARISTODEMOU.

TURKISH CYPRIOT CHAMBERS OF COMMERCE AND INDUSTRY

Turkish Chamber of Industry: Müftü Racı St, Ontaş İşhanı B24, Nicosia, Mersin 10, Turkey; tel. (02) 471870.

Turkish Cypriot Chamber of Commerce: Bedrettin Demirel Cad. POB 718, Nicosia, Mersin 10, Turkey; tel. (02) 78760; telex 57137; f. 1958; Pres. MUSTAFA YILDIRIM; Sec.-Gen. ÖMER ALGANER.

EMPLOYERS' ORGANIZATIONS
Greek Cypriot Employers' Organizations

At 31 December 1980 there were 28 employers' associations, including 14 independent associations, with a total membership of 4,115.

Cyprus Employers' & Industrialists' Federation: 30 Grivas-Dhigenis Ave, POB 1657, Nicosia; tel. (02) 445102; f. 1960; 22 member Trade Associations, 360 direct and 1,100 indirect members; Dir-Gen. ANT. PIERIDES; Chair. MICHAEL COLOCASSIDES. The largest of the Trade Association members are: Cyprus Building

CYPRUS

Contractors' Association; Cyprus Hotel Keepers' Association; Clothing Manufacturers' Association; Cyprus Shipping Association; Shoe Makers' Association; Cyprus Metal Industries Association; Cyprus Bankers Employers' Association; Motor Cars, Tractors & Agricultural Machinery Importers' Association.

Turkish Cypriot Employers' Organizations

Kibris Türk İşverenler Sendikasi (Cyprus Turkish Employers Association): P.K. 674, Nicosia, Mersin 10, Turkey; tel. (02) 76173; Chair. ALPAY ALI RIZA GÖRGÜNER.

TRADE UNIONS

At 31 December 1980 there were 97 trade unions with 240 branches, six union federations and five confederations.

Greek Cypriot Trade Unions

Pankypria Ergatiki Omospondia—PEO (Pancyprian Federation of Labour): POB 1885, 31–35 Archermos St, Nicosia; tel. (02) 473192; f. 1946, registered 1947; previously the Pancyprian Trade Union Committee f. 1941, dissolved 1946; 11 unions and 122 brs with a total membership of 71,000; affiliated to the World Federation of Trade Unions; Gen. Sec. A. ZIARTIDES.

Synomospondia Ergaton Kyprou (Cyprus Workers' Confederation): 23 Alkaiou St, POB 5018, Engomi, Nicosia; tel. (02) 441142; f. 1944, registered 1950; 7 Federations, 5 Labour Centres, 47 unions, 12 brs with a total membership of 50,770; affiliated to the Greek Confederation of Labour and the ICFTU; Gen. Sec. MICHAEL IOANNOU.

Pankyprios Omospondia Anexartition Syntechnion (Pancyprian Federation of Independent Trade Unions): 1 Menadrou St, Nicosia; tel. (02) 442233; f. 1956, registered 1957; has no political orientations; 8 unions with a total membership of 798; Pres. COSTAS ANTONIADES; Gen. Sec. KYRIACOS NATHANAEL.

Demokratiki Ergatiki Omospondia Kyprou (Democratic Labour Federation of Cyprus): POB 1625, 25 Constantinou Paleologou Ave, Nicosia; tel. (02) 456506; f. 1962; 4 unions with a total membership of 4,250; Hon. Pres. PETROS STYLIANOU; Gen. Sec. RENOS PRENTZAS.

Cyprus Civil Servants' Trade Union: 2 Andreas Demetriou St, Nicosia; tel. (02) 442278; f. 1949, registered 1966; restricted to persons in the civil employment of the government and public authorities; 6 brs with a total membership of 13,030; Pres. A. PAPANASTASSIOU; Gen. Sec. G. IACOVOU.

Union of Cyprus Journalists: c/o A. Kannaouros, Haravghi, Nicosia.

Turkish Cypriot Trade Unions

Kıbrıs Türk İşçi Sendikaları Federasyonu (TÜRK-SEN) (Turkish-Cypriot Trade Union Federation): Sehit Mehmet R. Hüseyin Sok., POB 829, Nicosia, Mersin 10, Turkey; tel. (02) 472444; f. 1954, registered 1955; 15 unions with a total membership of 12,000; affiliated to ICFTU, ETUC, CTUC and the Confederation of Trade Unions of Turkey; Pres. HÜSEYIN CURCIOĞLU; Gen. Sec. (vacant).

Devrimci İşçi Sendikalari Federasyonu (Dev-İş) (Revolutionary Trade Unions Federation): 30 Beliğ Paşa Sok., Nicosia, Mersin 10, Turkey; tel. (02) 472640; f. 1976; two unions with a total membership of 4,500; affiliated to WFTU; Pres. HASAN SARICA; Gen.-Sec. BAYRAM ÇELIK.

TRADE FAIRS

Cyprus International (State) Fair: POB 3551, Nicosia; tel. (02) 448918; telex 3344; 12th Fair scheduled for 23 May–7 June 1987.

Transport

There are no railways in Cyprus.

ROADS

In 1985 there were 11,657 km of roads, of which 5,608 km were paved and 6,049 km were earth or gravel roads. The construction of the Nicosia–Limassol four-lane dual carriageway was completed in 1985. A project is under way to link the Nicosia–Limassol highway with another four-lane highway to Larnaca. Bus and taxi services between Nicosia and the principal towns and villages, which were severely disrupted by the Turkish invasion, have since been restored, but the north and south are now served by separate transport systems, and there are no services linking the two sectors.

SHIPPING

Until 1974 Famagusta was the island's most important harbour, handling about 83% of the country's cargo. Famagusta is a natural port capable of receiving ships of a maximum draught of 9.2 m. Since its capture by the Turkish army in August 1974 the port has been officially declared closed to international traffic. However, it continues to serve the Turkish-occupied region.

The main ports which serve the island's maritime trade at present are Larnaca and Limassol, which were constructed in 1973 and 1974 respectively. Both ports have been expanded: the quay of the new Limassol port is 1,280 m long and 11 m deep, while the port of Larnaca has a quay length of 866 m and a depth of 10 m. There is also an industrial port at Vassiliko, with a quay 555 m long and 9 m deep, and there are three specialized petroleum terminals, at Larnaca, Dhekelia and Moni.

In 1985, 4,786 vessels with a total registered tonnage of 13,480,000 visited Cyprus. Limassol handled approximately two thirds of ships entered and cleared.

Both Kyrenia and Karavostassi are under Turkish occupation and have been declared closed to international traffic. Karavostassi used to be the country's major mineral port dealing with 76% of the total mineral exports. However, since the war minerals have been passed through Vassiliko and Limni which are open roadsteads. In 1977 a hydrofoil service was started between Kyrenia and Mersin on the Turkish mainland.

The number of merchant vessels registered in Cyprus rose from 314 (with a total displacement of 1,575,702 grt) in 1970 to 1,510 (10,406,649 grt) in March 1986.

Greek Cypriot Shipping Companies

Brasal Offshore Services Ltd: POB 1518, Limassol; tel. (051) 21022; telex 2105; salvage craft, survey launch, suction dredger; Man. Dir E. BRANCO.

A. Elias (Overseas) Co Ltd: POB 1165, 104 Archbishop Makarios III Ave, Limassol; tel. (05) 67025; telex 2108; four cargo ships; Chair. A. ELIAS; Man. Dir I. ELIAS.

Eurointerlink Ltd: 48–48A Omonia Ave, Limassol; tel. (05) 65806; telex 2587; four cargo ships; Gen. Man. TASSOS THOMAIDES.

Hanseatic Shipping Co Ltd: POB 127, 111 Sp. Araouzou, Limassol; tel. (05) 65262; telex 2290; 63 ships; Man. Dir Capt. J. MEYER.

Lefkaritis Bros Marine Ltd: POB 162, 1 Kilkis St, Larnaca; tel. (04) 52142; telex 2224; f. 1974; three tankers; Chair. and Man. Dir TAKIS C. LEFKARITIS.

Josef Roth (Cyprus) Shipping Co Ltd: POB 1536, 28 Archbishop Makarios III Ave, 6th Floor, Limassol; telex 2848; six cargo ships.

Sol Maritime Services Ltd: POB 1682, 140B Franklin Roosevelt St, Limassol; tel. (05) 69000; telex 2882; f. 1977; three car ferries, one roll-on/roll-off ferry; Man. Dir TAKIS SOLOMONIDES.

Turkish Cypriot Shipping Companies

Savarona Maritime Ltd: 8 Bekiroğlu İshani, Müftü Ziya Efendi Sok., Nicosia, Mersin 10, Turkey; tel. (02) 475179; telex 57246.

Traverway Maritime Ltd: Onar Ishani, Mahkemeler Onu, Nicosia, Mersin 10, Turkey; tel. (02) 472323; telex 57249.

Orion Navigation Ltd: Seagate Court, Famagusta, Mersin 10, Turkey; tel. (03) 62006; telex 57228; f. 1976; shipping agents; Dir O. LAMA; Shipping Man. L. LAMA.

CIVIL AVIATION

There is an international airport at Nicosia, which can accommodate all types of aircraft, including jets. It has been closed since July 1974 following the Turkish invasion. A new international airport was constructed at Larnaca, from which flights operate to Europe, the Middle East and the Gulf. Another international airport at Paphos began operations in November 1983.

In 1975 the Turkish authorities opened Ercan (formerly Tymbou) airport, and a second airport was opened at Geçitkale in 1986.

Cyprus Airways: POB 1903, 21 Alkeou St, Nicosia; tel. (02) 43054; telex 2225; f. 1947; jointly owned by Cyprus government and local interests; charter subsidiary Cyprair Tours; Exec. Pres. STAVROS GALATARIOTIS; Man. Dir S. NATHANAEL; services to Abu Dhabi, Alexandria, Athens, Bahrain, Beirut, Birmingham, Cairo, Cologne, Dhahran, Damascus, Doha, Dubai, Frankfurt, Geneva, Jeddah, Kuwait, London, Manchester, Munich, Muscat, Paris, Rhodes,

Tel-Aviv and Zürich from Larnaca Airport; fleet of 3 Airbus 310, 4 Boeing 707-120B and 3 BAC 1-11-500.

Cyprus Turkish Airlines Ltd: Bedreddin Demirel Ave, Nicosia, Mersin 10, Turkey; tel. (02) 471901; telex 57133; f. 1974; jointly owned by the 'Turkish Republic of Northern Cyprus' and Turkish Airlines; Gen. Man. O. URAL; routes from Ercan Airport, Nicosia, to Ankara, Adana, Istanbul and İzmir; fleet of 1 Boeing 727-200, 1 DC9-30 and 1 A310.

Tourism

Cyprus Tourism Organization: Zena Bldg, 18 Th. Theodotou St, POB 4535, Nicosia; tel. (02) 443374; telex 2165; Chair. CHRISTAKIS GEORGIADES; Dir-Gen. ANTONIOS ANDRONICOU.

Cyprus Turkish Tourism Enterprises: Kordon Boyu, Kyrenia, Mersin 10, Turkey; tel. (90–581) 52165; telex 57128.

CZECHOSLOVAKIA

Introductory Survey

Location, Climate, Language, Religion, Flag, Capital

The Czechoslovak Socialist Republic lies in central Europe. Its neighbours are Poland to the north, the German Democratic Republic to the north-west, the Federal Republic of Germany to the west, Austria to the south-west, Hungary to the south-east and the USSR to the extreme east. The state is composed of two main population groups, the Czechs (63.5% of the total population in 1983) and the Slovaks (31.2%). The climate is continental, with warm summers and cold winters. The average mean temperature is 9°C (49°F). The official languages, which are mutually understandable, are Czech and Slovak, members of the west Slavonic group. There is a Hungarian-speaking minority in Slovakia. Most of the country's inhabitants profess Christianity: about 70% are Roman Catholics, and 15% Protestants. The national flag (proportions 3 by 2) has two equal horizontal stripes, of white and red, on which is superimposed a blue triangle (half the length) at the hoist. The capital is Prague (Praha).

Recent History

At the end of the First World War, in 1918, the Austro-Hungarian Empire was dissolved, and its former western Slavonic provinces became Czechoslovakia. The boundaries of the new republic, fixed by treaty in 1919, included the Sudetenland, an area in northern Bohemia that was inhabited by about 3m. German-speaking people. After the Nazis, led by Adolf Hitler, came to power in Germany in 1933, there was increased agitation in the Sudetenland for autonomy within, and later secession from, Czechoslovakia. In 1938, to appease German demands, the British, French and Italian Prime Ministers made an agreement with Hitler, by which the Sudetenland was ceded to Germany, while other parts of Czechoslovakia were transferred to Hungary and Poland. The remainder of Czechoslovakia was invaded and occupied by Nazi Germany in March 1939.

After Germany's defeat in the Second World War (1939–45), the pre-1938 frontiers of Czechoslovakia were restored, although a small area in the east was ceded to the USSR in June 1945. Almost all of the German-speaking inhabitants of Czechoslovakia were expelled, and the Sudetenland was settled by Czechs from other parts of Bohemia. At elections in 1946 the Communists emerged as the leading party, gaining 38% of the votes. The Communist Party's leader, Klement Gottwald, became Prime Minister in a coalition government. After Ministers of other parties resigned, Communist control became complete on 25 February 1948. A People's Republic was established on 9 June 1948. Gottwald replaced Edvard Beneš as President, a position that he held until his death in 1953. The country aligned itself with the Soviet-led East European bloc, joining the Council for Mutual Economic Assistance (CMEA) and the Warsaw Pact (see pp. 126 and 206 respectively).

Under Gottwald, government followed a rigid Stalinist pattern, and in the early 1950s there were many political trials. Although these ended under Gottwald's successors, Antonín Zápotocký and, from 1956, Antonín Novotný, 'de-Stalinization' was late in coming to Czechoslovakia, and no relaxation was felt until 1963, when a new government, with Jozef Lenárt (hitherto President of the Slovak National Council) as Prime Minister, was formed. Meanwhile, the country was renamed the Czechoslovak Socialist Republic, under a new constitution, proclaimed in July 1960.

In January 1968 Alexander Dubček succeeded Novotný as Party Secretary, and in March Gen. Ludvík Svoboda succeeded him as President. Oldřich Černík became Prime Minister in April 1968. The policies of the new government were more independent and liberal, and envisaged widespread reforms. These were seen by other members of the East European bloc as endangering their unity, and in August 1968 Warsaw Pact forces occupied Prague and other major cities. The Soviet Government exerted heavy pressure on Czechoslovak leaders to suppress their reformist policies, and in April 1969 Dubček was replaced by Dr Gustáv Husák as First (subsequently General) Secretary of the Communist Party. Although Dr Husák resisted some pressure for stricter control and political trials, there was a severe purge of Communist Party membership, and most of Dubček's supporters were removed from the Government. The first elections since 1964 were held in November 1971 and showed a 99.81% vote in favour of National Front candidates.

In May 1975 Dr Husák was appointed President of the Republic while still holding the positions of Chairman of the National Front and General Secretary of the Communist Party. Dr Husák was re-elected Party leader in April 1976 and again in April 1981 and in March 1986, and was re-elected President in May 1980 and May 1985.

In January 1977 a manifesto known as Charter 77, protesting against the lack of civil rights in Czechoslovakia, was published in the West. Many of the hundreds of Czechoslovak intellectuals and former politicians who signed the Charter were arrested, tried on various charges and imprisoned, but, despite attempts by the Government to suppress the activists, the civil rights campaign continued. A purge of Party members began in 1979 and, although almost all of those protesters who were originally detained had been released by 1983, sporadic arrests and harassment continued. By 1985 the movement's field of comment had broadened, and in that year spokesmen for the signatories issued appeals for the dissolution of NATO and the Warsaw Pact alliance, for the withdrawal of Soviet troops and nuclear weapons from Czechoslovakia, and for the Czechoslovak Government to adopt an attitude in favour of economic reforms, such as was developing in other East European countries.

Relations between the Czechoslovak Government and the Roman Catholic Church, which had long been strained, did not improve in spite of a series of discussions with representatives of the Vatican in late 1983 and 1984. The discussions mainly concerned the Government's desire to fill vacant bishoprics with politically acceptable incumbents, and its objection to a Vatican decree of 1982, forbidding priests to join, among other 'political' bodies, the peace organization Pacem in Terris, which was backed by the Czechoslovak Government. Several foreign Roman Catholic dignitaries, including Pope John Paul II, were refused visas to attend celebrations, which took place in Czechoslovakia in July 1985, to mark the 1,100th anniversary of the death of St Methodius.

The 17th Communist Party Congress was held in March 1986. Dr Husák was re-elected General Secretary of the Party's 195-member Central Committee. Three additional alternate members were elected to the Presidium of the Central Committee, while the Party Secretariat remained unchanged. Legislative elections were held in May 1986. Changes in the Federal Government, appointed in June, included the creation of the new post of First Deputy Prime Minister.

Government

Czechoslovakia is a federal state of two nations of equal rights, the Czechs and the Slovaks, and composed of two republics, each having its own government. The supreme organ of state power is the Federal Assembly, elected for a five-year term by all citizens over the age of 18 years, and having two chambers, the House of the People and the House of Nations. Membership of the former is proportional to the population of the country. In May 1986, 134 deputies were elected from the Czech Socialist Republic and 66 from the Slovak Socialist Republic. The House of Nations has 150 members: 75 from each of the republics. The Federal Assembly elects the President for a five-year term of office. The President, in turn, appoints the Federal Government, led by the Prime Minister, to hold executive authority. Ministers are responsible to the Assembly.

Each of the two constituent republics has its own government (responsible for all matters except external relations, defence, overseas trade, transport and communications) and its own elected National Council or parliament.

Political power is held by the Communist Party of Czechoslovakia, which dominates the National Front (including four other minor parties). All candidates for representative bodies are sponsored by the Front. The Communist Party's highest authority is the Party Congress, which elects the Central Committee (133 full members and 62 candidate members were elected in March 1986) to supervise Party work. The Committee elects a Presidium (11 full and six alternate members in March 1986) to direct policy.

Defence

Czechoslovakia is a member of the Warsaw Pact. Military service is compulsory and lasts for two years in the army and three years in the air force. Service with the reserve lasts until the age of 50. In July 1986, according to Western estimates, the army numbered 145,000 (100,000 conscripts) and the air force 56,000 (18,000 conscripts); border troops numbered 11,000. The People's Militia comprises 120,000 part-time personnel. The defence budget for 1986 was 27,000m. korunas. Since the invasion of 1968, Soviet forces have occupied permanent positions on the frontier with the Federal Republic of Germany.

Economic Affairs

Although Czechoslovakia depends on the USSR for many raw materials, it is a highly industrialized country. In 1984 industrial activity contributed 59.6% of net material product (NMP), and construction 11.1%. Industry is state-owned. Output of motor cars and cycles is important, and other manufactures are glass, beer, ceramics, footwear and textiles. Mining of coal and lignite is an important activity, output totalling 126.6m. tons in 1985. Other minerals, such as copper and zinc, are also extracted. In 1985 large gold deposits were confirmed to exist near Prague.

In the mid-1980s a long-term programme to develop the generation of electricity by means of nuclear and hydroelectric power was being implemented. In 1985 nuclear power stations generated 14.6% of the total output of electricity; this proportion was expected to rise to more than 25% in 1987 (with a projected output of 21.5m. MWh), and to reach 60% by the year 2000. In 1984 hydroelectric power stations generated 3.7m. MWh, and the country's hydroelectric power potential was to be increased from 36% in 1986 to 63% by the year 2000. As a consequence of the rapid development of nuclear power plants, the extraction of coal and lignite was projected to decline from 122.7m. metric tons in 1986 (accounting for the generation of 69% of the total output of electricity) to 119m. tons in 1990 (63.4%).

Agriculture has been collectivized and about 95% of the land is under agricultural co-operatives, state farms or communal enterprises. Agriculture accounted for 8.5% of NMP in 1984. Important crops are wheat, barley, potatoes, hops and sugar beet. Forestry is also significant; in 1985 there were 4.58m. ha of forests, covering about 26% of the territory.

The targets of the fifth Five-Year Plan (1971–75) were exceeded. NMP rose by 31.7%, 3.7% above the target, and investment went up by 44.1%. Gross output of goods and material services increased by 38%, and industrial output grew by 37.5%. During the period of the sixth Five-Year Plan (1976–80) gross output rose by 20%. Industrial output grew by 25% (the engineering sector by 38%), and agricultural production by 9%. After 1977, however, Czechoslovakia experienced an economic slowdown, owing to adverse weather conditions, poor harvests (necessitating large imports of grain), labour shortages, energy problems and less favourable terms of trade, although in 1984 a record grain harvest of 12m. metric tons helped to boost agricultural production. Grain production fell slightly, to 11.7m. tons, in 1985, and to an estimated 10.8m. tons in 1986, while storm damage to hop fields, which cover some 11,800 ha, in 1986 led to a shortfall in the production of beer, which is exported to more than 60 countries and is an important source of foreign exchange earnings.

The seventh Five-Year Plan (1981–85) envisaged a 10–14% increase in NMP; the increase was 3.2% in 1984 and 3.3% in 1985, bringing the overall increase for 1981–85 to 11.3%. The development of industry (particularly the engineering sector, which increased production by 28.7% in 1981–85) was given priority, resulting in a steady rise in exports. In 1985 industrial growth was 3.4%, while agricultural production increased by 4.8%, compared with the annual average for 1981–84. Industrial production during the seventh Five-Year Plan rose by 14.8%, and agriculture by 9.7%, compared with 1976–80.

The Government has sought to resolve the current economic problems through internal measures rather than by external borrowing, and has urged stringent economies, particularly with regard to imported fuels, and increased efficiency and quality in production. Wide-ranging adjustments in the retail prices of food products were made in January 1982, and increases in the wholesale price of energy and raw materials, which averaged 6.4% and were not to be passed on to consumers, took effect in January 1984. A proposed new planning system for enterprises was to create scope for material incentives with the aim of raising production. Investment, which amounted to 150,000m. korunas in 1980, was reduced in subsequent years to stand at 147,900m. korunas in 1984. The 1987 draft budget envisaged total expenditure of 381,900m. korunas, 4.8% more than in 1986.

The eighth Five-Year Plan (1986–90) envisaged a 19% increase in NMP. Increased labour productivity was projected to account for 92% of this increase, and the growth of employment was to contribute only 8%. Industrial production was to increase by 15.8%, and agricultural production by 6.8%, while total investment was to amount to almost 900,000m. korunas (compared with 811,000m. korunas in 1981–85). The proportion of the applied NMP intended for the internal use of the population, society and the economy was to increase from 3.1% to 15.9%, while a further 3.9% was to be allocated to scientific and technological development.

Czechoslovakia is a member of the Council for Mutual Economic Assistance (CMEA) (see p. 126), and member countries, together with Yugoslavia and the People's Republic of China, accounted for 78.8% of total trade turnover (of which 44.8% was with the USSR) in 1985. During 1981–85 exports increased by 50% and imports by 48%. Principal exports include machinery and equipment, chemicals and fuels, and glass and other manufactured goods. There is considerable trade with Western European countries, notably the Federal Republic of Germany, Austria and the United Kingdom. However, Czechoslovakia's share in world trade fell from 1.5% in 1965 to 0.9% in 1980. A determined attempt is now being made to increase this share, particularly through the export of industrial products and especially those of the engineering sector, which were planned to rise by 47% in 1986–90. In 1985 the country's trade deficit was US $88m., with the value of imports totalling $17,642m. and that of exports $17,554m. Czechoslovakia's external debt was estimated at US $3,000m. in 1983, compared with $3,400m. in 1982. The gross debt in 1984 was estimated at $3,300m.

Social Welfare

A single and universal system of social security was established in Czechoslovakia after the Second World War. All workers and employees benefit equally from the insurance scheme. Protection of health is provided for by law, with particular emphasis on the prevention of illness rather than treatment and cure. Medical care, treatment, medicines, etc. are free for the entire Czechoslovak population, and in 1985 28,400m. korunas were spent on the health service. In 1985 there were almost 55,000 physicians and 195,500 hospital beds. The National Health Insurance Scheme is administered by the Revolutionary Trade Union Movement, which also supervises other aspects of social welfare. Sickness benefit is paid for a maximum period of two years, after which time disablement pension applies. Social security is guaranteed for all through different schemes: for wage-earners, members of co-operative societies, members of agricultural co-operatives, pensioners and members of the armed forces. Benefits and rights are the same for all these groups. Great importance is attached to maternity benefits and family allowances.

Education

Education at all levels is provided free. Many children between the ages of three and six years attend kindergarten (mateřská škola). Education is compulsory between the ages of six and 16 years, when children attend the basic school (základní škola). A general curriculum is followed by more specialized subjects.

CZECHOSLOVAKIA

Most Czechoslovak children continue their education after the basic school. Secondary grammar schools provide four years of general education, and prepare students for university. Education of the same level is provided by working people's secondary schools, which had 30,970 students in 1983/84. Four-year secondary vocational schools train young people as specialists in the fields of economics, administration and culture, or prepare them for studies at institutes of higher learning. Courses at the specialized apprentice training centres last from two to four years, and prepare young people for workers' professions.

Tourism

Czechoslovakia has magnificent scenery, with winter sports facilities. Prague is the best known of the historic cities, and there are famous castles and cathedrals, numerous resorts and 57 spas with natural mineral springs, notably Mariánské Lázně (Marienbad) and Karlovy Vary (Carlsbad). In 1984 foreign tourist arrivals totalled 17.5m., including excursionists and visitors in transit.

Public Holidays

1987: 1 January (New Year's Day), 20 April (Easter Monday), 1 May (Labour Day), 9 May (National Day), 25–26 December (Christmas).

1988: 1 January (New Year's Day), 4 April (Easter Monday), 1 May (Labour Day), 9 May (National Day), 25–26 December (Christmas).

Weights and Measures

The metric system is in force.

Currency and Exchange Rates

100 haléřů (hellers) = 1 koruna (Czechoslovak crown or Kčs.).

Exchange rates (31 August 1986):
  £1 sterling = 15.31 Kčs.;
  US $1 = 10.36 Kčs.

Statistical Survey

Source: mainly Federal Statistical Office, Sokolovská 142, 180 00 Prague 8; tel. (2) 814; telex 121197.

Area and Population

AREA, POPULATION AND DENSITY

Area (sq km)	127,903*
Population (census results)	
1 December 1970	14,344,987
1 November 1980	
Males	7,441,160
Females	7,841,935
Total	15,283,095
Population (official estimates at mid-year)	
1982	15,369,091
1983	15,414,360
1984	15,459,303
Density (per sq km) at mid-1984	120.9

* 49,384 sq miles.

PRINCIPAL TOWNS
(estimated population at 1 January 1985)

Praha (Prague, capital)	1,189,828	Hradec Králové	98,476
Bratislava	409,100	Pardubice	93,822
Brno	383,443	České Budějovice	93,520
Ostrava	325,431	Havířov	91,013
Košice	218,238	Ústí nad Labem	90,520
Plzeň (Pilsen)	174,555	Žilina	89,847
Olomouc	105,516	Gottwaldov (Zlín)	85,383
Liberec	100,048	Nitra	83,338

REGIONS

	Area (sq km)	Population (1 Jan. 1984)	Density (per sq km)
Czech Socialist Republic:			
Central Bohemia	11,003	1,141,163	104
Southern Bohemia	11,345	694,642	61
Western Bohemia	10,876	875,036	80
Northern Bohemia	7,810	1,180,269	151
Eastern Bohemia	11,240	1,245,964	111
Southern Moravia	15,028	2,055,908	137
Northern Moravia	11,067	1,953,649	177
Prague (city)	495	1,189,828	2,404
Total	78,864	10,336,459	131
Slovak Socialist Republic:			
Western Slovakia	14,491	1,711,911	118
Central Slovakia	17,986	1,570,456	87
Eastern Slovakia	16,195	1,451,716	90
Bratislava (city)	367	409,100	1,115
Total	49,039	5,143,183	105
Grand total	127,903	15,479,642	121

POPULATION BY NATIONALITY (estimates, 31 December 1983)

	Czech Socialist Republic '000	%	Slovak Socialist Republic '000	%	Total '000	%
Czech	9,746	94.4	58	1.1	9,804	63.5
Slovak	383	3.7	4,426	86.6	4,810	31.2
Magyar (Hungarian)	21	0.2	567	11.1	587	3.8
German	55	0.5	3	0.1	57	0.4
Polish	68	0.7	3	0.1	71	0.5
Ukrainian and Russian	15	0.1	40	0.8	55	0.4
Others and unspecified	38	0.4	13	0.3	52	0.3
Total	10,326	100.0	5,110	100.0	15,436	100.0

CZECHOSLOVAKIA

Statistical Survey

BIRTHS, MARRIAGES AND DEATHS

	Registered live births Number	Rate (per 1,000)	Registered marriages Number	Rate (per 1,000)	Registered deaths Number	Rate (per 1,000)
1978	279,094	18.4	134,579	8.9	174,914	11.6
1979	272,352	17.9	127,134	8.3	175,786	11.5
1980	248,901	16.3	117,921	7.7	186,116	12.2
1981	237,728	15.5	116,805	7.6	180,039	11.8
1982	234,356	15.2	117,376	7.6	181,158	11.8
1983	229,484	14.9	120,547	7.8	186,907	12.1
1984	226,595	14.7	121,376	7.9	182,351	11.8
1985	225,193	14.5	n.a.	7.7	182,581	11.8

CIVILIAN LABOUR FORCE EMPLOYED
('000 persons, excluding apprentices)

	1982	1983	1984
Agriculture	946	933	941
Forestry	93	92	93
Mining, manufacturing, gas and electricity	2,806	2,821	2,831
Construction	714	716	723
Trade, restaurants, etc.	655	665	673
Other commerce	182	184	185
Transport	385	383	385
Communications	109	110	112
Services	266	271	278
Education and culture	530	537	550
Science and research	167	168	171
Health and social services	352	359	365
Civil service, jurisdiction	121	120	119
Others	109	107	108
Total in employment	**7,435**	**7,466**	**7,534**
Women on maternity leave	347	342	339
Total labour force	**7,782**	**7,808**	**7,873**

Agriculture

PRINCIPAL CROPS ('000 metric tons)

	1982	1983	1984
Wheat and spelt	4,606	5,820	6,170
Rye*	583	751	710
Barley	3,654	3,276	3,677
Oats†	488	473	479
Maize	941	722	940
Sugar beet	8,210	6,041	7,513
Potatoes	3,608	3,177	3,978
Dry peas	97	151	181
Dry broad beans	41	31	30
Grapes	275	317	234
Linseed	15	15	12
Rapeseed	178	314	300
Poppy seed	4	n.a.	n.a.
Hops	13	12	11
Tobacco	6	6	5
Carrots	138	125	180
Onions	139	131	168

	1982	1983	1984
Garlic	9	12	12
Tomatoes	122	112	79
Cabbages	290	246	377
Cauliflowers	77	74	86
Lettuce	21	n.a.	n.a.
Cucumbers and gherkins	159	114	78
Apples	504	427	378
Pears	42	53	46
Plums	63	47	47
Sweet cherries	37	36	25
Sour cherries	9	10	10
Peaches	19	19	16
Apricots	19	22	24
Strawberries	21	24	21
Currants	27	32	37
Walnuts	14	19	14
Flax fibre	20	24	27

* Including mixed crops of rye and wheat.
† Including mixed crops of oats and barley.
Source: mainly FAO, *Production Yearbook*.

CZECHOSLOVAKIA

Statistical Survey

LIVESTOCK ('000 head at end of year)

	1981	1982	1983
Cattle	5,103	5,131	5,190
Pigs	7,302	7,126	7,070
Sheep	959	990	1,041
Goats	52	52	55
Horses	44	44	45

Chickens (million): 45 in 1981; 47 in 1982; 49 in 1983.
Source: FAO, *Production Yearbook*.

LIVESTOCK PRODUCTS ('000 metric tons)

	1982	1983	1984
Beef and veal	373	384	406
Pig meat	743	796	815
Poultry meat	182	178	181
Cows' milk	5,931	6,496	6,763
Butter	138.4	149.2	151.7
Cheese	187.0	188.2	192.6
Condensed and evaporated milk	120.4	146.7	155.0
Hen eggs	251.5	261.6	275.2
Honey	10.4	14.9	15.3*
Wool: greasy	4.7	5.0	5.3
clean	2.8	3.0	3.2
Cattle hides	54.3	56.0	58.4

* FAO estimate.
Source: FAO, *Production Yearbook*.

Forestry

ROUNDWOOD REMOVALS ('000 cubic metres, excluding bark)

	1982	1983	1984
Planned	18,539	18,739	19,229
Unplanned	421	177	122
Production	18,960	18,916	19,451
Deliveries	18,775	18,833	18,913
of which:			
Industrial	17,421	17,505	17,607
Fuel wood	1,354	1,328	1,306

SAWNWOOD PRODUCTION ('000 cubic metres)

	1982	1983	1984
Coniferous	4,140	4,206	4,300
Broadleaved	819	809	800
Total	4,959	5,015	5,100

Fishing*

(metric tons)

	1982	1983	1984
Carp	14,351	15,618	15,693
Others	3,690	3,907	3,965
Total catch	18,041	19,525	19,658

* Figures refer only to fish caught by the State Fisheries and members of the Czech and Slovak fishing unions.

Mining

	1982	1983	1984
Hard coal ('000 metric tons)	27,463	26,915	26,421
Brown coal ('000 metric tons)	95,504	98,878	101,084
Lignite ('000 metric tons)	3,440	3,538	3,659
Kaolin ('000 metric tons)	648	662	668
Iron ore:			
gross weight ('000 metric tons)	1,861	1,903	1,869
metal content ('000 metric tons)	499	507	n.a.
Crude petroleum ('000 metric tons)	89	93	91
Salt (refined) ('000 metric tons)	327	241	243
Magnesite ('000 metric tons)	672	662	660
Antimony ore (metric tons)*	731	753	n.a.
Copper concentrates (metric tons)*	26,980	28,382	29,608
Lead concentrates (metric tons)*	5,220	5,270	5,129
Mercury (metric tons)	151	144	152
Tin concentrates (metric tons)*	295	307	425
Zinc concentrates (metric tons)*	13,857	14,199	14,370

* Figures refer to the metal content of ores and concentrates.

Industry

SELECTED PRODUCTS

		1982	1983	1984
Wheat flour	'000 metric tons	1,339	1,296	1,305
Refined sugar	'000 metric tons	894	836	936
Margarine	metric tons	38,936	36,601	34,898
Wine	'000 hectolitres	1,303	1,378	1,563
Beer	'000 hectolitres	24,912	24,957	23,768
Cigarettes	million	24,006	25,016	24,603
Cotton yarn (pure and mixed)	metric tons	138,762	140,110	140,003
Woven cotton fabrics*	'000 metres	582,942	585,321	597,932
Wool yarn (pure and mixed)	metric tons	57,979	58,364	57,467
Woven woollen fabrics*	'000 metres	61,025	61,732	61,786
Chemical fibres	'000 metric tons	179.9	185.6	188.8
Chemical wood pulp	'000 metric tons	679.2	692.4	789.4
Newsprint	'000 metric tons	79.4	68.0	72.2
Other paper	'000 metric tons	848.4	866.2	866.8
Leather footwear	'000 pairs	57,617	57,374	58,285
Rubber footwear	'000 pairs	6,786	6,461	6,140
Other footwear	'000 pairs	64,071	63,803	66,159
Synthetic rubber	metric tons	65,200	67,200	n.a.
Rubber tyres	'000 units	4,954	4,931	5,095
Sulphuric acid	'000 metric tons	1,252	1,244	1,246
Hydrochloric acid	'000 metric tons	223.5	224.5	228.0
Caustic soda	'000 metric tons	325.1	331.6	328.6
Soda ash	'000 metric tons	106.4	95.0	101.3
Nitrogenous fertilizers(a)†	'000 metric tons	568.3	590.8	575.8
Phosphate fertilizers(b)†	'000 metric tons	335.4	326.2	343.7
Plastics and synthetic resins	'000 metric tons	956.3	1,002	1,039
Liquefied petroleum gas	'000 metric tons	145	141	n.a.
Motor spirit (petrol)	'000 metric tons	1,365	1,500	n.a.
Kerosene and jet fuel	'000 metric tons	309	390	404
Distillate fuel oils	'000 metric tons	3,798	3,753	3,688
Residual fuel oils	'000 metric tons	7,565	7,450	7,357
Petroleum bitumen (asphalt)	'000 metric tons	1,023	1,042	n.a.
Coke-oven coke	'000 metric tons	10,566	10,340	10,302
Cement	'000 metric tons	10,325	10,498	10,530
Pig iron‡	'000 metric tons	9,525	9,466	9,561
Crude steel	'000 metric tons	14,992	15,024	14,831
Rolled steel products	'000 metric tons	10,657	10,733	10,910
Aluminium (unwrought)	metric tons	33,830	36,156	31,635
Refined copper (unwrought)	metric tons	25,636	25,746	26,068
Lead (unwrought)	metric tons	21,071	21,030	21,134
Radio receivers§	number	278,675	278,381	259,137
Television receivers	number	391,385	415,494	383,636
Passenger cars	number	173,517	177,505	180,150
Goods vehicles	number	47,270	43,194	46,872
Motor cycles‖	number	133,728	136,160	123,628
Electric locomotives	number	137	148	131
Diesel locomotives	number	482	505	517
Trams	number	972	950	901
Tractors	number	33,523	34,176	34,160
Electric energy	million kWh	74,749	76,275	78,388
Manufactured gas	million cu metres	7,808	7,604	7,694
Construction:				
New dwellings completed	number	101,829	95,701	91,863

* After undergoing finishing processes.
† Production of fertilizers is measured in terms of (a) nitrogen or (b) phosphoric acid. The figures for phosphate fertilizers include ground rock phosphate.
‡ Including blast furnace ferro-alloys.   § Excluding radiograms.
‖ Engine capacity of 100 cc and over.

Finance

CURRENCY AND EXCHANGE RATES

Monetary Units
100 haléřů (singular haléř—heller) = 1 koruna (Czechoslovak crown or Kčs.).

Denominations
Coins: 5, 10, 20 and 50 haléřů; 1, 2 and 5 Kčs.
Notes: 10, 20, 50, 100, 500 and 1,000 Kčs.

Sterling and Dollar Equivalents (31 August 1986)
£1 sterling = 15.31 Kčs.;
US $1 = 10.36 Kčs. (non-commercial rates);
1,000 Kčs. = £65.30 = $96.53.

Note: The rates quoted above are applicable to tourism. Foreign trade transactions are valued according to the commercial exchange rate. On this basis, the average value of the koruna was: 15.86 US cents in 1983; 15.02 US cents in 1984; 14.58 US cents in 1985.

BUDGET (million Kčs.)

Revenue	1983	1984
State budget	213,691	222,446
From socialist economy	231,433	246,384
Taxes and rates	44,335	45,891
Other receipts	1,467	1,702
Minus grants and subsidies to local administrative organs	63,544	71,531
Budgets of local administrative organs	110,436	121,359
Total	324,127	343,805

Expenditure	1983	1984
State budget	213,598	222,373
National economy	82,301	87,090
Science and technology	7,856	8,306
Money-order and technical services	5,724	5,972
Culture and social welfare	88,659	90,819
Defence	25,261	26,276
Administration	3,797	3,910
Budgets of local administrative organs	110,292	119,819
Total	323,890	342,192

1985: Total revenue Kčs. 359,700m.; Total expenditure Kčs. 358,000m.

COST OF LIVING
(Consumer Price Index. Base: 1 January 1967 = 100)

	1982	1983	1984
Food	117.5	118.2	119.0
Industrial goods	132.5	134.0	135.5
Public catering	132.9	133.7	135.7
Services	131.2	132.5	134.2
All items	127.1	128.2	129.4

NATIONAL ACCOUNTS

Net Material Product*
('000 million Kčs. at current market prices)

Activities of the material sphere	1982	1983	1984
Agriculture, hunting and fishing	37.4	39.6	40.8
Forestry and logging	4.9	4.5	4.5
Industry†	300.5	311.1	318.0
Construction	51.6	52.6	59.5
Trade, restaurants, etc.	74.2	72.5	87.6
Transport and storage	21.2	21.1	24.4
Communications	4.4	4.6	4.7
Others	1.8	2.0	1.9
Total	496.0	507.9	541.5

* Defined as the total net value of goods and 'productive' services, including turnover taxes, produced by the economy. This excludes economic activities not contributing directly to material production, such as public administration, defence and personal and professional services.
† Principally manufacturing, mining, electricity, gas and water supply.

External Trade

PRINCIPAL COMMODITIES (distribution by SITC, million Kčs.)

Imports f.o.b.	1981	1982	1983
Food and live animals	6,481.2	6,667.4	5,846.7
Cereals and cereal preparations	1,210.9	1,389.4	916.0
Vegetables and fruit	2,022.4	1,890.7	1,643.7
Crude materials (inedible) except fuels	9,218.6	9,233.9	9,467.0
Cotton fibres and waste	1,326.7	1,336.4	1,439.3
Metalliferous ores and metal scrap	3,528.6	3,472.6	3,591.6
Mineral fuels, lubricants, etc. (incl. electric current)	20,548.3	26,601.1	31,117.5
Coal, coke and briquettes	1,408.7	1,806.5	1,959.3
Petroleum, petroleum products, etc.	13,862.6	17,817.6	20,623.8
Gas (natural and manufactured)	4,764.6	6,409.3	7,875.6
Chemicals and related products	7,032.4	6,917.9	7,352.3
Organic chemicals	1,380.9	1,202.8	1,235.6
Manufactured fertilizers	n.a.	1,094.4	1,453.2
Basic manufactures	9,091.2	8,987.3	9,588.8
Iron and steel	2,036.1	2,057.6	2,395.4
Non-ferrous metals	3,515.1	3,121.4	3,461.7
Machinery and transport equipment	27,591.2	28,985.8	32,315.9
Power generating machinery and equipment	1,738.8	2,408.8	2,383.8
Machinery specialized for particular industries	7,300.5	7,865.1	8,216.0
Agricultural machinery (excl. tractors) and parts	1,473.3	1,564.6	1,877.2
Civil engineering and contractors' plant, equipment and parts	1,452.1	1,710.2	1,476.1
Metalworking machinery	2,116.5	1,916.2	2,177.8
Machine-tools for working metal	1,393.7	1,323.4	1,446.7
General industrial machinery, equipment and parts	7,443.1	7,868.0	9,297.8
Office machines and automatic data processing equipment	1,332.8	1,732.0	2,052.2
Automatic data processing machines and units	n.a.	1,031.8	1,409.2
Road vehicles and parts*	2,990.4	2,785.9	3,254.4
Parts and accessories for cars, buses, lorries, etc.*	2,215.1	2,264.4	2,496.4
Miscellaneous manufactured articles	3,558.9	3,840.0	4,578.8
Total (incl. others)	86,275.6	94,177.0	103,012.4

* Excluding tyres, engines and electrical parts.

Total imports (million Kčs.): 113,754 in 1984; 120,323 in 1985.

Exports f.o.b.	1981	1982	1983
Food and live animals	2,878.6	2,889.3	2,437.2
Crude materials (inedible) except fuels	3,098.8	3,345.5	3,495.8
Mineral fuels, lubricants, etc. (incl. electric current)	4,165.7	4,852.7	4,987.2
Coal, coke and briquettes	2,188.0	2,424.4	2,337.8
Coal, lignite and peat	1,409.9	1,489.8	1,483.4
Petroleum, petroleum products, etc.	1,764.7	1,965.6	2,232.0
Chemicals and related products	5,403.2	5,803.5	6,278.3
Organic chemicals	1,468.5	1,668.8	1,647.5
Artificial resins, plastic materials, etc.	1,186.4	1,256.5	1,407.3
Basic manufactures	16,191.0	16,754.0	18,019.4
Textile yarn, fabrics, etc.	2,755.2	3,042.0	3,436.0
Non-metallic mineral manufactures	2,791.1	2,907.0	2,978.6
Iron and steel	6,803.8	6,741.7	7,206.4
Iron and steel	6,803.8	6,741.7	7,206.4
Bars, rods, angles, shapes, etc.	1,970.5	1,869.5	2,031.8
Universals, plates and sheets	1,538.4	1,604.5	1,616.9
Tubes, pipes and fittings	1,854.4	1,880.5	2,095.3
Machinery and transport equipment	43,425.2	47,737.4	54,008.5
Power generating machinery and equipment	3,030.5	3,822.8	3,680.8
Steam power units, steam engines and parts	1,022.5	1,588.1	1,218.5
Machinery specialized for particular industries	11,348.4	12,811.7	15,212.9
Agricultural machinery (excl. tractors) and parts	1,255.4	1,321.6	1,602.1
Civil engineering and contractors' plant, equipment and parts	1,467.8	1,589.5	1,686.1
Textile and leather machinery and parts	3,692.0	4,563.7	4,983.0
Metalworking machinery	4,405.7	4,457.4	4,274.4
Machine-tools for working metal	2,779.7	2,837.4	3,169.1
General industrial machinery, equipment and parts	9,798.3	10,787.7	12,720.3
Office machines and automatic data processing equipment	1,005.8	1,175.2	1,303.5
Telecommunications and sound equipment	1,197.5	1,368.9	1,562.4
Other electrical machinery, apparatus, etc.	2,161.0	2,317.1	2,776.0
Road vehicles and parts*	7,662.6	8,176.1	8,913.9
Motor vehicles for goods transport and special purposes	2,532.9	2,593.4	3,137.9
Parts and accessories for cars, buses, lorries, etc.*	2,858.8	3,136.7	3,480.8
Railway vehicles and associated equipment	2,348.4	2,399.4	3,082.7
Miscellaneous manufactured articles	10,322.8	11,545.4	12,429.0
Furniture and parts	1,012.9	1,324.0	1,413.3
Footwear	2,977.3	3,156.3	3,150.1
Total (incl. others)	87,689.1	95,313.8	103,837.9

* Excluding tyres, engines and electrical parts.

Total exports (million Kčs.): 114,515 in 1984; 119,818 in 1985.

CZECHOSLOVAKIA

PRINCIPAL TRADING PARTNERS
(million Kčs., country of consignment)

Imports f.o.b.	1982	1983	1984
Austria	3,062.8	2,940.0	2,251
Belgium	514.7	453.0	461
Brazil	738.2	676.3	484
Bulgaria	2,551.0	2,842.3	3,226
China, People's Republic	484.3	622.0	825
Cuba	758.5	776.1	1,061
France	730.2	790.9	882
German Democratic Republic	8,948.4	10,635.2	11,783
Germany, Federal Republic*	4,408.5	4,659.3	4,731
Hungary	5,132.8	5,145.6	6,387
Iran	741.9	604.0	904
Italy	730.3	926.4	836
Japan	576.5	443.6	455
Netherlands	761.2	695.0	740
Poland	5,932.3	6,411.4	8,193
Romania	2,476.7	2,382.5	2,320
Switzerland	2,093.7	2,158.3	2,342
USSR	40,917.1	47,573.7	53,230
United Kingdom	1,535.4	1,321.3	1,376
USA	895.3	592.8	305
Yugoslavia	4,346.9	4,365.1	3,866
Total (incl. others)	94,177.0	103,012.4	113,737

* Excluding imports from West Berlin (million Kčs.): 74.3 in 1982; 75.5 in 1983.

Exports f.o.b.	1982	1983	1984
Austria	2,862.7	2,817.1	2,917
Bulgaria	2,657.4	2,945.0	3,186
China, People's Republic	837.4	551.9	1,056
Cuba	1,297.4	1,225.8	1,438
France	929.7	899.3	942
German Democratic Republic	8,635.1	9,314.9	10,107
Germany, Federal Republic†	4,841.2	4,928.2	5,365
Hungary	5,089.5	5,522.8	5,688
Iran	334.5	720.8	302
Iraq	955.8	953.1	964
Italy	1,228.8	1,074.5	1,084
Libya	1,066.7	1,361.2	1,219
Netherlands	768.2	811.2	904
Poland	5,949.0	7,327.1	8,134
Romania	2,434.1	1,880.8	1,981
Switzerland	1,520.3	1,045.0	1,066
Syria	934.7	1,624.5	1,873
Turkey	666.8	813.0	667
USSR	38,745.4	43,420.7	49,606
United Kingdom	1,005.2	1,139.3	1,256
Yugoslavia	3,934.5	4,429.2	4,683
Total (incl. others)	95,313.8	103,837.9	114,230

† Excluding exports to West Berlin (million Kčs.): 180.7 in 1982; 186.8 in 1983.

Transport

	1982	1983	1984
Railway transport:			
Freight ('000 tons)	288,650	291,691	299,021
Passengers (million)	413	411	422
Public road transport:			
Freight ('000 tons)	368,121	358,736	349,979
Passengers (million)	2,196	2,221	2,260
Waterway transport:			
Freight ('000 tons)	11,393	11,858	13,374
Air transport:			
Freight (tons)	21,400	23,000	23,054
Passengers ('000)	1,052	1,135	1,139

ROAD TRAFFIC (vehicles in use at 30 June)

	1982	1983	1984
Passenger cars	2,441,472	2,511,269	2,639,564
Buses and coaches	32,363	33,072	34,747
Goods vehicles	357,868	362,544	378,113
Motorcycles and scooters	662,987	636,281	612,487

Tourism

	1982	1983	1984
Foreign tourist arrivals*	12,471,206	14,301,839	17,510,459

* Including excursionists and visitors in transit. Visitors spending at least one night in the country totalled 3,370,000 in 1982.

Communications Media

	1982	1983	1984
Telephones in use	3,306,155	3,401,775	3,489,022
Radio receivers in use	4,132,865	4,164,844	4,208,538
Television receivers in use	4,307,748	4,322,765	4,346,022
Book production: titles*	7,164	7,202	7,128
Newspapers (dailies)	30	30	30
Periodicals	1,070	1,071	1,072

* Figures include pamphlets (1,415 in 1982), and refer to titles produced by centrally managed publishing houses only; the total number of titles produced was 10,519 in 1982 and 9,574 in 1983.

Education
(1984/85)

	Institutions	Teachers	Students
Nursery	11,601	51,181	700,478
Primary (classes 1–8)	6,398	94,404	2,037,121
Secondary (classes 9–12)			
Universal	342	9,302	138,436
Special (technical, etc.)	565	16,748	271,234
Continuation schools	1,362	n.a.	413,217
Higher	36	5,670	174,304

Directory

The Constitution

A new Constitution was proclaimed on 11 July 1960. It was amended in October 1968, July 1971 and May 1975. A summary of the main provisions of the Constitution follows:

The Czechoslovak Socialist Republic is a Federal State of two fraternal nations possessing equal rights, the Czechs and the Slovaks.

According to the Constitution, work in the interests of the community is a primary duty and the right to work a primary right of every citizen. All citizens have equal rights and equal duties without regard to nationality and race. Remuneration for work done is based on its quantity, quality and social importance. Men and women have equal status. All citizens have the right to health protection, education and leisure after work including paid holidays. Other rights include: freedom of expression, assembly, inviolability of the person, the home, mail, etc. Everyone has the right to profess any religious faith or to be without religious conviction.

The economic foundation of the State is the Socialist economic system which excludes every form of exploitation of man by man. The means of production are socially owned and the entire national economy is directed by plan. Socialist ownership includes both national property such as mineral wealth, the means of industrial production, banks, etc., and co-operative property. The land of members of agricultural co-operatives remains the personal property of the individual members, but is jointly farmed by the co-operative. Small private enterprises based on the labour of the owner himself and excluding exploitation of another's labour power are permitted. Personal ownership of consumer goods, family houses and savings derived from labour is inviolable. Inheritance of such personal property is guaranteed.

The Czechoslovak Constitution does not restrict itself to laying down a system of state organs but also sets forth the principles by which the life of society is to be guided. It is not just a Constitution of the State but a constitution for the whole of society. In economic, political and cultural life, in questions of social security and many other spheres it emphasizes the participation of citizens in the administration of public affairs and even transfers a number of functions that have hitherto pertained to state organs to the working people and their voluntary organizations.

The guiding force in society and in the State is the Communist Party of Czechoslovakia, a voluntary militant alliance of the most active and politically conscious citizens. It is associated with the other political parties, the Trade Union Movement and other people's organizations in the National Front of Czechs and Slovaks.

FEDERAL ASSEMBLY

The supreme organ of state power in the Czechoslovak Socialist Republic is the Federal Assembly (Parliament) which is elected for a five-year term and elects the President of the Republic. The President may be relieved of his or her duties by the Assembly in the event of having been unable to fulfil them for over a year. The Federal Assembly consists of two chambers of equal rights: the House of the People and the House of Nations. The composition of the House of the People, which has 200 deputies, corresponds to the composition of the population of the Czechoslovak Socialist Republic. The House of Nations has 150 deputies on parity basis: 75 are elected in the Czech Socialist Republic and 75 in the Slovak Socialist Republic.

PRESIDENT

The President, elected by the Federal Assembly, appoints the Federal Government. The Government is the supreme executive organ of State power in Czechoslovakia; it consists of a Prime Minister, 10 Deputy Prime Ministers (including a First Deputy Prime Minister, a new post created in 1986) and 16 Ministers. The Ministries of Foreign Affairs, of National Defence, of Foreign Trade, of Transport and of Posts and Telecommunications, are within the exclusive competence of the Federation, i.e. there are no corresponding portfolios in the governments of the republics. The second group of Federal Government organs share authority with organs of the two republics, i.e. there are corresponding portfolios in the national governments.

ELECTORAL SYSTEM

All representative bodies are elected, and the right to elect is universal, equal and by secret ballot. Every citizen has the right to vote on reaching the age of 18, and is eligible for election on reaching the age of 21. Deputies must maintain constant contacts with their constituents, heed their suggestions and be accountable to them for their activity. A member of any representative body may be recalled by his or her constituents at any time.

For election purposes, the country is divided into electoral districts; there are 200 electoral districts in the Czechoslovak Socialist Republic, each represented by one deputy in the House of the People, and 75 electoral districts each in the Czech and Slovak Socialist Republics, which send one deputy each to the House of Nations.

All candidates are National Front candidates, put forward by the Communist Party of Czechoslovakia and by the other political parties and social organizations associated in the National Front. One or more candidates can be nominated for one electoral district. Appropriate National Front organs select the candidates from the list of nominees, and submit their names for registration.

The principle of simple majority obtains in the elections: the candidate is elected when he obtains more than 50% of the votes cast, provided that the majority of all voters in his electoral district exercise their right to vote. When either of the two conditions is not met, new elections are held in the electoral district concerned within two weeks. When a seat becomes vacant, the Presidium of the Federal Assembly calls a by-election in the constituency; this is not mandatory in the last year of the deputies' term of office.

NATIONAL COUNCILS

Each of the republics has its own parliament: the Czech National Council and the Slovak National Council. The members are elected for a five-year term of office. The Czech National Council has 200 deputies, the Slovak National Council 150 deputies. There are also separate Czech and Slovak Governments, each consisting of a Prime Minister, a First Deputy Prime Minister (a new post created in 1986), three Deputy Prime Ministers and up to 15 other Ministers.

NATIONAL COMMITTEES

National committees are the organs of popular self-government in the regions, districts and localities. The members are elected for a five-year term of office. They rely on the active participation of the working people of their area and co-operate with other organizations of the people. They direct local economic and cultural development, ensure the protection of socialist ownership and the maintenance of socialist order in society, see to the implementation and observance of laws, etc. They take part in drafting and carrying out the State plan for the development of the national economy and draw up their own budgets which form a part of the State budget. Commissions elected by the national committees are charged with various aspects of public work and carry out their tasks with the aid of a large number of citizens who need not be elected members of the national committees.

JUDICIAL SYSTEM

The execution of justice is vested in elected and independent courts. Benches are composed of professional judges and of judges who carry out their function in addition to their regular employment. Both categories are equal in making decisions. Judges are independent in the discharge of their office and bound solely by the legal order of the socialist State. The supervision of the observance of the laws and other legal regulations by public bodies and by individual citizens rests with the Office of the Procurator. The Procurator-General is appointed and recalled by the President of the Republic and is accountable to the Federal Assembly.

The Government

(December 1986)

HEAD OF STATE

President of the Republic: Dr Gustáv Husák (elected 29 May 1975; re-elected 22 May 1980 and 22 May 1985).

CZECHOSLOVAKIA

FEDERAL GOVERNMENT

Prime Minister: LUBOMÍR ŠTROUGAL.
First Deputy Prime Minister: RUDOLF ROHLÍČEK.
Deputy Prime Ministers: KAROL LACO, JOSEF KORČÁK, PETER COLOTKA, MATEJ LÚČAN, LADISLAV GERLE, SVATOPLUK POTÁČ, JAROMÍR OBZINA, PAVOL HRIVNÁK, MIROSLAV TOMAN.
Minister of Agriculture and Food: MIROSLAV TOMAN.
Minister of Finance: JAROMÍR ZAK.
Minister of Foreign Affairs: BOHUSLAV CHŇOUPEK.
Minister of Foreign Trade: BOHUMIL URBAN.
Minister of Fuel and Power: VLASTIMIL EHRENBERGER.
Minister of General Engineering: LADISLAV LUHOVY.
Minister of the Interior: VRATISLAV VAJNAR.
Minister of Labour and Social Affairs: MILOSLAV BODA.
Minister of Metallurgy and Heavy Engineering: EDUARD SAUL.
Minister of the Electrotechnical Industry: MILAN KUBÁT.
Minister of National Defence: Gen. MILAN VACLAVIK.
Minister of Posts and Telecommunications: JIŘÍ JIRA.
Minister of Transport: Ing. VLADIMÍR BLAŽEK.
Minister, Chairman of the Federal Prices Office: MICHAL SABOLČÍK.
Minister, Chairman of the People's Control Commission: FRANTIŠEK ONDŘICH.
Minister, Chairman of the State Commission for Research and Development and Investment Planning: JAROMÍR OBZINA.
Chairman of the State Planning Commission: SVATOPLUK POTÁČ.
Minister, Vice-Chairman of the State Planning Commission: VLADIMÍR JANZA.

MINISTRIES
All Ministries are in Prague.

STATE GOVERNMENTS
Czech Government
Prime Minister: JOSEF KORČÁK.
First Deputy Prime Minister: LADISLAV ADAMEC.
Deputy Prime Ministers: ZDENĚK KRČ, FRANTIŠEK ŠRÁMEK, JAROSLAV TLAPAK.
Minister of Agriculture and Food: ONDREJ VANEK.
Minister of Construction: KAREL POLÁK.
Minister of Culture: MILAN KLUSÁK.
Minister of Education: MILAN VONDRUŠKA.
Minister of Finance: JIŘÍ NIKODYM.
Minister of Forestry and Water Conservancy: FRANTIŠEK KALINA.
Minister of Health: JAROSLAV PROKOPEC.
Minister of Industry: PETR HOJER.
Minister of the Interior: JOSEF JUNG.
Minister of Justice: ANTONÍN KAŠPAR.
Minister of Labour and Social Affairs: NASTA BAUMRUKOVA.
Minister of Trade: JOSEF RAB.
Minister, Chairman of the People's Control Commission: JAN MOTL.
Ministers without Portfolio: VLADIMÍR SIMEK, KAREL LÖEBL.
Chairman of the Czech Planning Commission: ZDENĚK KRČ.
Chairman of the Czech Prices Office: BEDŘICH HABÁRT.
Chairman of the Czech Commission for Research and Development and Investment Planning: FRANTIŠEK ŠRÁMEK.

Slovak Government
Prime Minister: PETER COLOTKA.
First Deputy Prime Minister: JÚLIUS HANUS.
Deputy Prime Ministers: JAROSLAV KANSKÝ, PAVOL BAHYL, MILAN RUSNAK.
Minister of Agriculture and Food: JÚLIUS VARGA.
Minister of Construction: DUŠAN MIKLÁNEK.
Minister of Culture: MIROSLAV VÁLEK.
Minister of Education: LUDOVIT KILAR.
Minister of Finance: FRANTIŠEK MIŠEJE.
Minister of Forestry and Water Conservancy: VLADIMÍR MARGETIN.
Minister of Health: EVA TOKOLYOVA.
Minister of Industry: ŠTEFAN URBAN.
Minister of the Interior: ŠTEFAN LAZAR.
Minister of Justice: Maj.-Gen. JÁN PJEŠČOK.
Minister of Labour and Social Affairs: KAZIMIR NAGY.
Minister of Trade: JAROSLAV ZELKO.
Minister, Chairman of the People's Control Commission: ŠTEFAN FERENCEI.
Chairman of the Slovak Planning Commission: PAVOL BAHYL.
Chairman of the Slovak Prices Office: JÁN ZERVAN.
Chairman of the Slovak Commission for Research and Development and Investment Planning: MILAN RUSNAK.

PRESIDIUM OF THE CENTRAL COMMITTEE OF THE COMMUNIST PARTY OF CZECHOSLOVAKIA

Secretary-General: Dr GUSTÁV HUSÁK.
Full Members: VASIL BIL'AK, PETER COLOTKA, KAREL HOFFMANN, Dr GUSTÁV HUSÁK, ALOIS INDRA, MILOŠ JAKEŠ, ANTONÍN KAPEK, JOSEF KEMPNÝ, JOSEF KORČÁK, JOZEF LENÁRT, LUBOMÍR ŠTROUGAL.
Alternate Members: JÁN FOJTÍK, JOSEF HAMAN, VLADIMÍR HERMAN, MILOSLAV HRUŠKOVIČ, IGNAC JANAK, FRANTIŠEK PITRA.

Legislature

FEDERÁLNÍ SHROMÁŽDĚNÍ
(Federal Assembly)

The Federal Assembly consists of 350 deputies elected for a five-year term. The Assembly is bicameral, comprising the House of the People (200 members) and the House of Nations (150 members). General elections to both chambers were held on 23–24 May 1986. All the members, nominated by the National Front, were elected unopposed.
Chairman: ALOIS INDRA.

Sněmovna Lidů
(House of the People)

This House has 200 members. At the May 1986 elections, 134 were from the Czech Socialist Republic, and 66 from the Slovak Socialist Republic.
Chairman: VLADIMIR VEDRA.

Sněmovna Národů
(House of Nations)

This House has 150 members: 75 each from the Czech and Slovak Socialist Republics.
Chairman: DALIBOR HANES.

NATIONAL COUNCILS

Czech National Council: Prague; 200 deputies elected for a five-year term; Chair. JOSEF KEMPNÝ.
Slovak National Council: Bratislava; 150 deputies elected for a five-year term; Chair. VILIAM ŠALGOVIČ.

Political Organizations

National Front of the Czechoslovak Socialist Republic: Škrétova 6, 120 59 Prague 2; a political organization embracing all political parties and mass organizations; Chair. Dr GUSTÁV HUSÁK.
National Front of the Czech Socialist Republic: Prague; Chair. JOSEF KEMPNÝ.
National Front of the Slovak Socialist Republic: Bratislava; Chair. JOZEF LENÁRT.
Communist Party of Czechoslovakia—CPCZ (Komunistická Strana Československa—KSČ): nábř. Ludvíka Svobody 12, 125 11 Prague 1; f. 1921; incorporating the former Czechoslovak Social Democratic Party and the Slovak Labour Party; the leading political force in the National Front; 1,675,000 mems (1986); Gen. Sec. of Central Committee Dr GUSTÁV HUSÁK; Secretariat of Central Committee MIKULÁŠ BEŇO, VASIL BIL'AK, JÁN FOJTÍK, JOSEF HAMAN,

CZECHOSLOVAKIA

Josef Havlín, Zdeněk Hoření, Miloš Jakeš, Marie Kabrhelova, František Pitra, Jindřich Poledník.

Communist Party of Slovakia—CPSL (Komunistická Strana Slovenska—KSS): Hlboká 2, 883 33 Bratislava; First Sec. Josef Lenárt.

Czechoslovak People's Party: Revoluční 5, 110 15 Prague 1; f. 1919; Christian Party; Chair. Zbynek Žalman; Head of the Secretariat Josef Andrš.

Czechoslovak Socialist Party: nám. Republiky 7, 111 49 Prague 1; Chair. Dr Bohuslav Kučera; Central Sec. Jiří Fleyberk.

Revolutionary Trade Union Movement—ROH: nám. A. Zápotockého 2, 113 59 Prague 3; f. 1945; 7,194,694 mems; is a member of the National Front and is headed by the Central Council of Trade Unions (see below); federated to WFTU; Pres. Karel Hoffmann.

Slovak Freedom Party: Stefánikova 6C, 892 18 Bratislava; f. 1946 as a splinter party from the Slovak Democratic Party; Chair. Kamil Brodziansky; Sec.-Gen. Juraj Moravec.

Slovak Reconstruction Party: Sedliárska 7, 801 00 Bratislava; f. 1948 from the Slovak Democratic Party; Chair. Jozef Šimúth; Sec.-Gen. Dalibor Laborecký.

Socialist Union of Youth (Socialistický svaz mládeže): nám. M. Gorkého 24, 116 47 Prague 1; f. 1970; a united mass youth movement; 1.6m. mems; Chair. Jaroslav Jenerál; Chair. of Czech Cen. Cttee Vasil Mohorita; Chair. of Slovak Cen. Cttee Jozef Durica.

Diplomatic Representation

EMBASSIES IN CZECHOSLOVAKIA

Afghanistan: V Tišině 6, 160 00 Prague 6; tel. (2) 373537; Ambassador: Abdul Wakil.

Albania: Pod Kaštany 22, 125 20 Prague; Chargé d'affaires a.i.: Agim Kasa.

Algeria: Korejská 16, 125 21 Prague; tel. (2) 325189; Ambassador: Abdulhamid Latreche.

Argentina: Washingtonova 25, 125 22 Prague 1; Ambassador: Angel María Oliveri López.

Austria: Viktora Huga 10, 125 43 Prague 5; tel. (2) 546550; telex 121849; Ambassador: Paul Ullmann.

Belgium: Valdštejnská 6, 125 24 Prague 1; tel. (2) 534051; telex 122362; Ambassador: Hugo Walschap.

Bolivia: Ve Smečkách 25, 125 59 Prague; tel. (2) 263209; Chargé d'affaires a.i.: Teodolfo Imani Castro.

Brazil: Bolzanova 5, 125 01 Prague 1; tel. (2) 229254; telex 122292; Ambassador: Manuel Antônio de Pimentel Brandão.

Bulgaria: Krakovská 6, 125 25 Prague 1; tel. (2) 264310; telex 121381; Ambassador: Khristo Petkov.

Burma: Romaina Rollanda 3, 125 23 Prague 6; Ambassador: U Min Naung.

Canada: Mickiewiczova 6, 125 33 Prague 6; tel. (2) 326941; telex 121061; Ambassador: Terence Charles Bacon.

China, People's Republic: Majakovského 22, 125 26 Prague; Ambassador: Zhang Dake.

Colombia: Veverkova 11, 125 01 Prague 7; tel. (2) 378895; Ambassador: Jorge Arango Mejía.

Costa Rica: Konevova 192, 130 00 Prague 3; Ambassador: Arnoldo Amrhein Pinto.

Cuba: Sibiřské nám. I, 125 35 Prague 6; tel. (2) 341341; telex 93184; Ambassador: Mario Rodríguez Martínez.

Denmark: U Havlíčkových sadů I, 120 21 Prague 2; tel. (2) 254715; telex 122209; Ambassador: Hans Jespersen.

Ecuador: Opletalova 43, 125 01 Prague 1; tel. (2) 241289; telex 123286; Ambassador: Arturo Lecaro Bustamante.

Egypt: Majakovského 14, 125 46 Prague 6; tel. (2) 341051; telex 123552; Ambassador: Umar Gad Mohamed el Sayed Gad.

Finland: Dřevná 2, 125 01 Prague 2; tel. (2) 205541; telex 121060; Ambassador: Eero Yrjölä.

France: Velkopřevorské nám. 2, 118 00 Prague 1; tel. (2) 533042; Ambassador: Jacques Alexandre Humann.

German Democratic Republic: Gottwaldovo nábřeží 32, 125 39 Prague 1; tel. (2) 299551; telex 121528; Ambassador: Helmut Ziebart.

Germany, Federal Republic: Vlašska 19, 125 60 Prague 1; tel. (2) 532351; telex 122814; Ambassador: Dr Werner Schattmann.

Ghana: V Tisine 4, 160 00 Prague 6; tel. (2) 373058; telex 122263; Ambassador: A. K. Agyemang.

Greece: Španělská 24, 125 45 Prague 2; tel. (2) 247597; Ambassador: Vasileios Elevtheriadhis.

Hungary: Mičurinova I, 125 37 Prague; tel. (2) 365041; telex 123535; Ambassador: Béla Kovács.

India: Valdštejnská 6, 125 28 Prague 1; tel. (2) 536293; telex 121901; Ambassador: Uday Chand Soni.

Indonesia: Nad Buďánkami II/7, 125 29 Prague 5; tel. (2) 546041; telex 121443; Ambassador: Raffly Rasad.

Iran: Na Zátorce 18, 160 00 Prague 6; tel. (2) 371480; telex 122732; Ambassador: Mohammad Ali Sarmadi Rad.

Iraq: Na Zátorce 10, 125 01 Prague 6; Ambassador: (vacant).

Italy: Nerudova 20, 125 31 Prague 1; tel. (2) 532646; telex 122704; Ambassador: Dr Giulio Bilancioni.

Japan: Maltézské nám. 6, 125 32 Prague 1; tel. (2) 535751; telex 121199; Ambassador: Tadashi Otaka.

Kampuchea: Na Hubalcé 1, 169 00 Prague 6; Ambassador: Chim Nguon.

Korea, Democratic People's Republic: R. Rollanda 10, 125 34 Prague; Ambassador: Kim Kwang Sop.

Lebanon: Gottwaldovo nábřeží 14, 110 00 Prague 1; tel. (2) 293633; telex 123583; Ambassador: Sleiman Younes.

Libya: Bubenecka 59, 125 01 Prague; Secretary of People's Bureau: Omar Nasser Abdelgalil.

Mexico: Karlovo nám. 19, 125 49 Prague 2; tel. (2) 297514; Ambassador: Sergio Pitol.

Mongolia: Korejská 5, 160 00 Prague 6; tel. (2) 328992; telex 121921; Ambassador: Yondongiyn Ochir.

Netherlands: Maltézské nám. 1, 125 40 Prague 1; tel. (2) 531378; telex 122643; Ambassador: Count de Marchant et d'Ansembourg.

Nicaragua: Na Baště sv. Jiří 3, 125 46 Prague 6; tel. (2) 123336; Ambassador: Ramon Bayardo Altamirano López.

Nigeria: Pred Bateriemi 18, 162 00 Prague 6; tel. (2) 354294; telex 123575; Ambassador: Dr Musa Otigba.

Norway: Žitná 2, 125 41 Prague 1; tel. (2) 298856; telex 122200; Ambassador: Georg Krane.

Peru: Hradecká 18, 125 01 Prague 1; telex 123345; Ambassador: Jaime Cacho-Sousa.

Poland: Valdštejnská 8, 125 42 Prague 1; tel. (2) 536951; telex 121841; Ambassador: Andrzej Jedynak.

Portugal: Na Florenci 23, 11 000 Prague; tel. (2) 244167; telex 121354; Ambassador: Mário Júlio de Melo Freitas.

Romania: Nerudova 5, 125 44 Prague; Ambassador: Cornel Pînzaru.

Spain: Pevnostní 9, 160 00 Prague 6; tel. (2) 327124; telex 121974; Ambassador: Manuel García Miranda.

Sweden: Úvoz 13, 125 52 Prague 1; tel. (2) 533344; telex 121840; Ambassador: Karl-Wilhelm Woehler.

Switzerland: Pevnostní 7, 162 00 Prague 6; tel. (2) 320406; Ambassador: Jan Straka.

Syria: Pod Kaštany 16, 125 01 Prague; telex 121532; Chargé d'affaires a.i.: Ziad Hadad.

Tunisia: Štěpánská 18, Prague 2; tel. (2) 242251; telex 122512; Ambassador: Mongi Kooli.

Turkey: Pevnostní 3, 125 01 Prague 6; Ambassador: Orhan Aka.

USSR: Pod Kaštany I, 160 00 Prague 6; Ambassador: Viktor Pavlovich Lomakin.

United Kingdom: Thunovská 14, 118 00 Prague 1; tel. (2) 533347; telex 121011; Ambassador: Stephen Barrett.

USA: Tržiště 15, 125 48 Prague; tel. (2) 536641; telex 121196; Ambassador Julian M. Niemczyk.

Uruguay: Václavské nám. 64, 111 21 Prague 1; tel. (2) 244778; telex 121291; Ambassador: Adolfo Linardi Montero.

Venezuela: Janáčkovo nábřeží 49, 150 00 Prague 2; tel. (2) 536051; telex 122146; Ambassador: Oreste di Giacomo.

Viet-Nam: Holeckova 6, 125 55 Prague; telex 121824; Ambassador: Nguyen Phu Soai.

Yemen Arab Republic: Washingtonova 17, 125 22 Prague 1; tel. (2) 220371; telex 123300; Ambassador: Abd al-Latif Muhammad Dayfallah.

Yemen, People's Democratic Republic: Hradešínská 58, 110 00 Prague 10; telex 123541; Ambassador: Saif Mohsin Hussain.

Yugoslavia: Mostecká 15, 118 00 Prague; tel. (2) 531443; telex 123284; Ambassador: Dusan Rodić.

Judicial System

Justice is executed through elected courts which consist of three ranks of law courts: the Supreme Court of the Czechoslovak Socialist Republic (together with Supreme Courts of the Czech and Slovak Socialist Republics), Regional and District Courts. There are also Military Courts which are subject to special regulations. Judges of the Czechoslovak Supreme Court are elected by the Federal Assembly; judges of the Czech and Slovak Supreme Courts and of the Regional and District Courts are elected by the National Councils of the respective republics. Judges are of two kinds, professional and lay judges, the latter having other occupations, but both types have equal authority. Lay judges are elected by District National Committees. Supervision of the observance of laws and legal regulations rests with the Procurator-General who is appointed by the President of the Republic and accountable to the Federal Assembly.

Chairman of the Supreme Court: Dr Josef Ondřej.
Procurator-General: Dr Ján Feješ.

Religion

CHRISTIANITY

Secretariat for Ecclesiastical Affairs: f. 1949; controls church affairs; Dir Vladimír Janků.

The Roman Catholic Church

Czechoslovakia comprises three archdioceses and 10 dioceses, including one (directly responsible to the Holy See) for Catholics of the Slovak (Byzantine) rite.

Latin Rite
Bohemia

Archbishop of Prague: Hradčanské nám. 16, 119 02 Prague 1; tel. (2) 539548; HE Cardinal František Tomášek.
Bishops:
České Budějovice: (Vicarius capitularis) Josef Kavale.
Hradec Králové: (Vicarius capitularis) Dr Karel Jonáš.
Litoměřice: (Vicarius capitularis) Josef Hendrich.

Moravia

Archbishop of Olomouc: Wurmova 9, 771 01 Olomouc; tel. (68) 25726; (vacant); Apostolic Administrator Mgr Josef Vrana, Titular Bishop of Octabia.
Bishops:
Brno: (Vicarius capitularis) Canon Prof. Ludvík Horký.

Slovakia

Archbishop of Trnava: Svätoplukovo 3, 917 66 Trnava; tel. (805) 26235; (vacant); Apostolic Administrator Dr Július Gábriš, Titular Bishop of Decoriana.
Bishops:
Banská Bystrica: (Bishop) Josef Feranec.
Košice: (Vicarius capitularis) Štefan Onderko.
Nitra: (Bishop) Dr Ján Pasztor.
Rožňava: (Vicarius capitularis) Zoltán Belák.
Spišske Podhradie (Vicarius capitularis) Štefan Garaj.

Slovak Rite
Bishop of Prešov: Greckokatolicky biskupský urad, Slovenskej Republiky rád 8, Prešov; tel. 34622; (vacant); 356,648 adherents (31 December 1984).

The Orthodox Church

The (Eastern) Orthodox Church: V Jámě, 6, 111 21 Prague 1; divided into four eparchies: Prague, Olomouc, Prešov, Michalovce; Head of the Autocephalous Church Metropolitan of Prague and of all Czechoslovakia Dorotej; 150,000 mems; 150 parishes; Theological Faculty in Prešov.

Protestant Churches

Brethren Church: Soukenická 15, 110 00 Prague 1; 10,000 mems, 31 congregations, 200 preaching stations; Pres. Dr Jan Urban; Sec. J. Michal.

Czechoslovak Baptists: Na Topolce 10, 140 00 Prague 4; tel. (2) 430974; f. 1919; 4,000 mems; Pres. Rev. Dr Pavel Titéra; Sec. Rev. Stanislav Švec.
Evangelical Church of Czech Brethren (Presbyterian): Jungmannova 9, 111 21 Prague 1; united since 1918; activities extend over Bohemia, Moravia, and Silesia; 230,000 adherents and 272 parishes; Pres. Dr Miloslav Hájek; Gen. Sec. Dr Jiří Otter.
Reformed Christian Church in Slovakia: Kalininova 14/IV, 040 10 Košice; 180,000 mems and 310 parishes; Bishop Dr Imrich Varga.
Silesian Evangelical Church of the Augsburg Confession in the Czech Socialist Republic (Silesian Lutheran Church): Na Nivách 7, 737 01 Český Těšín; tel. 56656; founded in the 16th century during the Luther reformation, reorganized in 1948; 46,700 mems; Bishop Dr Vladislav Kiedroń.
Slovak Lutheran Church (Evangelical Church of the Augsburg Confession in Czechoslovakia); 326 parishes in 14 seniorates; 369,000 baptized mems; Bishop-Gen. Prof. Dr Ján Michalko, Palisády 46, 811 06 Bratislava; Eastern District Bishop Dr Július Fillo, Jesenského 1, 040 01 Košice; Bishop of the Western District Rudolf Koštial, Námestie SNP 17, 960 01 Zvolen.
Unitarians: Karlova 8, 110 00 Prague 1; f. 1923; 5,000 mems; Presiding Officer Dr D. J. Kafka.
Unity of Brethren (Jednota bratrská) (Moravian Church): Hálkova, 5, 120 00 Prague 2; f. 1457; 7,000 mems; Pres. Rev. Jindřich Halama.

Other Christian Churches

Czechoslovak Hussite Church: Kujbyševa 5, 160 00 Prague 6; f. 1920; 500,000 mems; divided into five dioceses; Bishop-Patriarch Miroslav Novák.
Old Catholic Church: Šámalova 23, 615 00 Brno; 1,500 mems, 3 parishes; Bishop Gen. Vicar Rudolf Trousil.

JUDAISM

The present community is estimated at approximately 15,000 people, and is divided under two central organizations:
Council of Jewish Communities in the Czech Socialist Republic (Rada židovských náboženských obcí v České socialistické republice): Maiselova 18, 110 01 Prague 1; 2,700 mems; Chair. Dezider Galsky; Sec.-Gen. Ing. Artur Radvanský; Chief Rabbi of Prague Daniel Meyer.
Union of the Jewish Religious Communities in the Slovak Socialist Republic (Ústredný zväz židovských náboženských obcí ve Slovenskej socialistickej republike): Šmeralova ul. 21, 801 00 Bratislava; 3,300 mems; Chair. Bedřich Grünwald; Chief Rabbi Samuel Grossmann (Košice).

The Press

Although the Czechoslovak press was considerably affected by the events of 1968, its basic purpose is still as defined in the October 1966 Press Law: 'to give as far as possible complete information... to advance the interest of socialist society... to promote the people's socialist awareness of the policy of the Communist Party as the leading force in society and state'.

This law, which codified previous legislation on the rights and duties of journalists and publishers states that 'freedom of expression and of the press is guaranteed by the fact that publishers and press organizations... have been placed at the disposal of the working people and their organizations'. Hence, only political parties and such social institutions associated with the National Front as trade unions, youth unions, cultural associations and rural co-operatives may own newspapers and periodicals. Private ownership is forbidden. Even collective ownership rests upon official approval; papers must be registered with the Czech or Slovak Office for the Press and Information, and when the editor fails to observe the conditions under which approval was given, the paper may be suspended.

During 1968 there was freedom of publication and Western books circulated in large editions. Censorship was abolished in June, but restored in September. In 1969 censorship was again abolished, but the necessity for official approval has since prevented the publication of ideologically dissenting journals. The editor of a paper or periodical bears full responsibility for its contents.

The Czechoslovak people far exceed other East European nations in their consumption per head of newspapers and magazines. There are 30 daily papers, including nine in Prague and nine (one in Hungarian and the rest in Slovak) in Bratislava. About 800 weekly

CZECHOSLOVAKIA

papers and magazines and an even greater number of less frequent periodicals are also published. In addition, farms and factories produce their own daily or weekly news-sheets, dealing mainly with local issues. All registered periodicals receive an allocation of newsprint.

Political speeches and articles on social and economic development are given special prominence. In contrast with much of the East European press, which is often characterized as dull and lacking in popular appeal, the Czechoslovak press is relatively lively and colourful and allows a qualified scope for criticism. There is no tabloid press as the policy is to play down such items as constitute the sort of sensationalism familiar to the West. Advertising is now more common than formerly, and although mainly concerned with state enterprises, it includes some material from abroad. Sales are mainly by subscription.

The most widely read and influential papers are the Prague dailies, headed by *Rudé právo*. This paper is the chief organ of the Czechoslovak Communist Party. It is eight pages long and has a nation-wide circulation of 950,000 copies. Its sister paper, the Slovak CP's *Pravda* (330,000), is the leading provincial daily. The Czech and the Slovak trade-union organs are *Práce* and *Práca* in their respective cities. Three other important metropolitan dailies are *Lidová demokracie* and *Svobodné slovo* produced respectively by the People's Party and the Socialist Party, and *Mladá Fronta*, published by the Central Committee of the Socialist Union of Youth.

There are also many small circulation periodicals—often of very high quality—dealing with specialized subjects. One should also note several very popular and colourful women's magazines, such as *Vlasta* (740,000), and the satirical *Dikobraz*, famous for its political cartoons.

The national news agency, Československá tisková kancelář (ČTK), receives a state subsidy and is controlled by the federal government through its presidium.

PRINCIPAL DAILIES
Prague

Československý sport (Czechoslovak Sport): Na Poříčí 30, 115 23 Prague 1; telex 121514; central organ of the Czech Association for Physical Training; Editor JAROMÍR TOMÁNEK; circ. 185,000.

Lidová demokracie (People's Democracy): Karlovo nám. 5, 112 08 Prague 1; telex 121403; f. 1945; morning; official organ of the Czechoslovak People's Party (Catholic); Editor Dr STANISLAV TOMS; circ. 217,000.

Mladá fronta (Youth Front): Panská 8, 112 22 Prague 1; telex 122468; f. 1945; morning; organ of the Central Committee of the Socialist Union of Youth; Editor IVAN KULHÁNEK; circ. 239,000.

Práce (Labour): Václavské nám. 15, 112 58 Prague 1; telex 121134; f. 1945; morning; published by the Central Council of Trade Unions; Editor CYRIL SMOLÍK; circ. 317,000.

Rudé právo (Red Right): Na Poříčí 30, 112 86 Prague 1; tel. (2) 249851; telex 121184; f. 1920; morning; central organ of the Czechoslovak Communist Party; Editor-in-Chief ZDENĚK HOŘENÍ; circ. 950,000.

Svoboda (Freedom): Na Florenci 3, 113 29 Prague 1; telex 121856; organ of the Central Bohemian Regional Committee of the Communist Party of Czechoslovakia; Editor VLADIMÍR PÁNEK; circ. 57,000.

Svobodné slovo (Free Word): Václavské nám. 36, 112 12 Prague 1; telex 121432; f. 1907; organ of the Czechoslovak Socialist Party; Editor MIROSLAV STRAKA; circ. 228,000.

Večerní Praha (Evening Prague): Na Poříčí 30, 112 86 Prague 1; telex 121883; f. 1955; evening; edited by the Prague City Committee of the Communist Party; Editor FRANTIŠEK NEBL; circ. 120,000.

Zemědělské noviny (Farmer's News): Václavské nám. 47, 113 78 Prague 1; telex 121435; f. 1945; organ of the Ministry of Agriculture and Food; Editor VLADISLAV KULHÁNEK; circ. 342,000.

Banská Bystrica

Smer (Course): Partizánska cesta, 975 43 Banská Bystrica; organ of the Central Committee of the Communist Party of Slovakia; Editor ANTON KAMAS.

Bratislava

Hlas ludu (Voice of the People): Žabotova 6, 897 18 Bratislava; telex 93398; f. 1949; morning; West Slovakia Regional Committee of the Communist Party of Slovakia; Editor Dr IZIDOR LEDNÁR; circ. 42,000.

L'ud (People): Gorkého 9/1, 897 16 Bratislava; telex 93254; f. 1948; organ of the Slovak Reconstruction Party; Editor Ing. VLADIMÍR PALOVIČ; circ. 17,000.

Práca (Labour): Odborárske nám. 3, 897 17 Bratislava; telex 93283; f. 1946; organ of the Slovak Trades Union Council; Editor-in-Chief JÁN VIŠVÁDER; circ. 230,000.

Pravda (Truth): Štúrova 4, 893 39 Bratislava; telex 93386; f. 1920; organ of Slovak Communist Party; Editor-in-Chief BOHUMIL TRÁVNÍČEK; circ. 330,000.

Rol'nicke noviny (Farmer's News): Fučíkova 6, 883 41 Bratislava; f. 1946; organ of the Slovak Ministry of Agriculture; Editor PAVEL HAVLÍČEK; circ. 73,000.

Smena (Shift): Dostojevského rad 21, 897 14 Bratislava; telex 93341; f. 1947; organ of Slovak Central Committee of the Socialist Union of Youth; Editor HELMUT VÁCHA; circ. 129,000.

Šport (Sport): Volgogradská 1, 893 44 Bratislava; organ of the Slovak Central Committee of the Czechoslovak Sports Association; Editor-in-Chief HELMUT VÁCHA; circ. 60,000.

Új Szó (New World): Gorkého 10, 893 38 Bratislava; telex 92308; f. 1948; midday; Hungarian-language paper of the Communist Party of Slovakia; Editor JOZEF KISS; circ. 85,000.

Večernik (Evening Paper): Októbrové nám. 7, 893 13 Bratislava; telex 92296; f. 1956; evening; organ of the City Committee of the Slovak Communist Party; Editor Dr FRANTIŠEK BARTOŠEK; circ. 50,000.

Brno

Brněnský večernik (Brno Evening News): Běhounská 18, 658 44 Brno; f. 1968; organ of the Brno City Committee of the Communist Party; Editor-in-Chief JOSEF KORGER; circ. 35,000.

Rovnost (Equality): nám. Rudé armády 13, 658 22 Brno; f. 1885; published by South Moravian Regional Committee of the Communist Party; morning; Editor JOSEF ČÍŽEK; circ. 115,000.

České Budějovice

Jihočeská Pravda (Truth of Southern Bohemia): Vrbenská 23, 370 45 České Budějovice; published by the South Bohemian Regional Committee of the Communist Party; Editor ANTONÍN BEZDĚČKA; circ. 55,000.

Hradec Králové

Pochodeň (Torch): Škroupova 695, 501 72 Hradec Králové; published by the East Bohemian Regional Committee of the Communist Party; Editor OLDŘICH ENGE; circ. 54,000.

Košice

Večer (Evening): Švermova 47, 042 97 Košice; organ of the City Committee of the Communist Party of Slovakia; Editor IVAN FECKO; circ. 21,000.

Východoslovenské noviny (East Slovak News): Švermova 47, 042 66 Košice; organ of the East Slovakia Regional Committee of the Communist Party of Slovakia; Editor ANDREJ HLAVÁČ; circ. 56,000.

Ostrava

Nová Svoboda (New Freedom): Novinářská 3, 709 07 Ostrava; f. 1945; morning; published by the Regional Committee of the Communist Party; Editor JAN HŘÍBEK; circ. 198,000.

Plzeň

Pravda (Truth): Leninova 15, 304 83 Plzeň; f. 1919; published by the West Bohemian Regional Committee of the Communist Party; Editor VÁCLAV JAKL; circ. 72,000.

Ústí nad Labem

Průboj (Forward): Švermova 83, 400 90 Ústí nad Labem; published by the North Bohemian Regional Committee of the Communist Party; Editor JIŘÍ ŠKODA; circ. 76,000.

PRINCIPAL PERIODICALS
Czech language

Ahoj na sobotu (Hallo Saturday): Václavské nám. 36, 112 12 Prague; illustrated family weekly published by the Czechoslovak Socialist Party; Editor SLAVOMIL OLŠÁK; circ. 200,000.

Architektura ČSR (Czech Architecture): Letenská 5, 118 45 Prague 1; f. 1939; 10 a year; journal of the Union of Architects of the Czech Socialist Republic; Editor Dr JAN NOVOTNÝ; circ. 6,000.

Automobil (The Automobile): Spálená 51, 113 02 Prague 1; f. 1957; technical monthly on motor car construction and production; Editor Ing. MILAN JOZIF; circ. 69,000.

CZECHOSLOVAKIA

Československá fotografie: Mrštíkova 23, 100 00 Prague 10; f. 1946; monthly; photographic; Editor Eva Horská; circ. 50,500.

Československý architekt (Czechoslovak Architect): Letenská 5, 118 45 Prague 1; f. 1955; fortnightly; Editor Dr Jan Novotný.

Československý voják (Czechoslovak Soldier): Vlastina 710, 162 00 Prague 6; fortnightly; pictorial; published by the Political Administration of the People's Army; Editor Jiří Pražák; circ. 60,000.

Československý život (Czechoslovak Life): Vinohradská 46, 120 41 Prague 2; telex 122948; f. 1946; illustrated monthly magazine; political, economic, social, cultural and sports; published by Orbis Press Agency in English, French, German, Italian and Spanish; Editor Karel Beba.

Dikobraz (The Porcupine): Na Poříčí 30, 112 86 Prague 1; telex 121184; f. 1945; satirical weekly; published by *Rudé právo*; Chief Editor Jindřich Bešta; circ. 525,000.

Film a doba (Film and Time): Václavské nám. 43, 116 48 Prague 1; monthly; Editor Vladimír Kolár; circ. 7,000.

Hospodářské noviny (Economic News): Na Poříčí 30, 112 86 Prague 1; telex 121184; weekly; published by Communist Party of Czechoslovakia; Editor Ing. Rudolf Kostka; circ. 115,000.

Hudební rozhledy (Musical Review): Valdštejnské nám. 1, 118 00 Prague 1; f. 1948; fortnightly review; published by the Association of Czech Composers and Concert Artists; Editor Dr Vilém Pospíšil; circ. 4,200.

Kino: Václavské nám. 43, 116 48 Prague 1; an illustrated film magazine published by General Management of Czechoslovak Film; fortnightly; Editor Vaclav Vondra; circ. 150,000.

Kulturni práce (Cultural Work): Václavské nám. 15, 110 00 Prague 1; telex 121134; trade union monthly; Editor Borek Sýkora; circ. 14,500.

Květy (Flowers): Na Poříčí 30, 112 86 Prague 1; telex 12184; f. 1834; illustrated weekly; published by *Rudé právo*; Editor Dr Milan Codr; circ. 360,000.

Literární měsíčník (Literary Monthly): Národní třída 11, 111 47 Prague 1; published by the Union of Czech Writers; Editor Oldřich Rafaj; circ. 15,000.

Mladý svět (Young World): Panská 8, 112 22 Prague 1; telex 121510; illustrated weekly for young people published by the Central Committee of the Socialist Union of Youth; Editor Olga Čermáková; circ. 470,000.

Motoristická současnost (Motoring Today): Jungmannova 24, 113 66 Prague 1; tel. (2) 260651; f. 1969; monthly; published by Naše vojsko; Editor Miloš Kovářík; circ. 105,000.

Naše rodina (Our Family): Karlovo nám. 5, 120 00 Prague 2; f. 1968; Christian and cultural weekly published by Czechoslovak People's Party; Editor Dr Libuše Daňková; circ. 169,000.

Novinář (Journalist): Pařížská ul. 9, 110 00 Prague 1; f. 1949; monthly; published by the Union of Czechoslovak Journalists; Editor Dagmar Petružálkova; circ. 6,000.

Nový Orient (New Orient): Lázeňská 4, 118 37 Prague 1; 10 a year; cultural and political magazine; published by the Oriental Institute of the Czechoslovak Academy of Science; Editor Dr Jaroslav Cesar; circ. 2,550.

Obrana lidu (People's Defence): Jungmannova 24, 113 66 Prague 1; weekly; published by the Political Administration of the People's Army; Editor František Chadalík; circ. 200,000.

Odborář (Trade Unionist): nám. M. Gorkého 23, 112 82 Prague 1; fortnightly; Editor Ing. Helena Mandová; circ. 160,000.

100+1ZZ: Opletalova 5, 111 44 Prague 1; fortnightly foreign press digest of the Czechoslovak News Agency (ČTK); Editor Juraj Rácz; circ. 100,000.

Prager Volkszeitung (Prague's People's Newspaper): Helénská 4, 120 00 Prague 2; weekly; general politics and culture; published by the Central Committee of the Czechoslovak National Front and the Cultural Union of the German citizens in Czechoslovakia; Editor Heribert Panster; circ. 17,000.

Právnik (The Lawyer): Národní třída 18, 116 91 Prague 1; tel. (2) 201620; f. 1861; monthly; law; published by Czechoslovak Academy of Sciences (Institute of State and Law); Editor Dr Josef Blahož; circ. 4,700.

Revue Obchod-průmysl-hospodářství (Trade-Industry-Economy Review): ul. 28 října 13, 112 79 Prague 1; telex 121142; monthly; journal of the Czechoslovak Chamber of Commerce; published in Czech; Editor František Hrouda; circ. 5,300.

Rozhlas (Radio): Vinohradská 12, 120 99 Prague 2; telex 121100; f. 1923; weekly; cultural and sound radio journal; published by the Czechoslovak Radio; Editor Ing. Ludmila Karbanová; circ. 265,000.

Socialistické Československo (Socialist Czechoslovakia): Vinohradská 46, 120 41 Prague 2; telex 122948; illustrated monthly magazine published by Orbis Press Agency; also in German and Russian; Chief Editor Petra Frankeovác.

Stadion (Stadium): Klimentská 1, 115 88 Prague; illustrated sport weekly published by the Czech Central Committee for Physical Training; Editor Zvonimír Šupich; circ. 162,500.

Svět motorů (World of Motors): Jungmannova 24, 113 66 Prague 1; f. 1947; weekly; motoring; Editor Miroslav Ebr; circ. 350,000.

Svět práce (The World of Labour): Václavské nám. 15, 112 58 Prague 1; telex 121134; f. 1946, reorganized 1968; political, economic and cultural weekly; published by Central Council of Trade Unions; Editor Ladislav Höschl; circ. 65,000.

Svět socialismu (The World of Socialism): Smetanovo nábř. 18, 115 65 Prague 1; illustrated weekly; published by the Union of Czechoslovak-Soviet Friendship; Editor Vladimír Pánek; circ. 105,000.

Svět v obrazech (World in Pictures): Pařížská 9, 110 00 Prague; illustrated weekly published by the Czech Union of Journalists; Editor Dr Zdeněk Hrabica; circ. 150,000.

Světová literatura (World Literature): Na Florenci 3, 115 86 Prague 1; f. 1956; published by Odeon, bi-monthly; contemporary foreign literature; Editor Zdeněk Volný; circ. 12,000.

Technický týdenik (Technical Weekly): nám. Gorkého 23, 112 82 Prague 1; technical weekly; published by Central Council of Trade Unions; Editor Jaroslav Kašpar; circ. 33,000.

Tribuna (Tribune): Olšanská 1, 130 00 Prague 3; f. 1956; published by Odeon; bi-monthly of the Czechoslovak Communist Party; Editor Jaroslav Kojzar; circ. 78,000.

Tvorba (Creation): Na Poříčí 30, 112 86 Prague 1; telex 121184; weekly; political and cultural; published by the Rudé Právo Publishing House; Editor Jaroslav Kořínek; circ. 81,000.

Týdeník československé televize (Czechoslovak Television Weekly): Na Poříčí 30, 112 86 Prague 1; telex 121184; f. 1965; weekly cultural and television journal; published by *Rudé právo*; Editor Jana Kolárová; circ. 500,000.

Věda a život (Science and Life): nám. Družby národů 5, 602 00 Brno; f. 1954; monthly; published by Czech Central Committee of Socialist Academy; Editor František Kala; circ. 13,500.

Vesmír (Universe): Vodičkova 40, 112 29 Prague 1; f. 1871; a monthly popular science magazine of the Czechoslovak Academy of Science; Editor prof. Dr Emil Hadač; circ. 13,500.

Vlasta: Jindřišská 5, 116 08 Prague 1; f. 1946; illustrated weekly; published by the Union of Czech Women; concerned with the status of women in society, problems of family and education; Editor Libuše Sekerová; circ. 740,000.

Zlatý Máj (Golden May): Na Perštýně 1, 110 01 Prague 1; telex 121605; magazine on literature for children; 10 a year; published by Albatros Publishing House; Editor Dr Jiří Lapáček; circ. 3,100.

Slovak language

Express: Obráncov Mieru 14, 801 00 Bratislava; f. 1969; weekly digest of the foreign press; organ of the Union of Slovak Writers; Editor Karol Hulman; circ. 60,000.

Film a divadlo (Film and Theatre): Volgogradská 8, 801 00 Bratislava; f. 1956; fortnightly organ of the Institute for Theatre; Editor Miro Procházka; circ. 43,000.

Hét (Week): Obchodná 7, 890 44 Bratislava; Hungarian; weekly pictorial; organ of the Cultural Union of Hungarians in the Czechoslovak Socialist Republic; Editor Juraj Strasser; circ. 30,000.

Horizont: Bezručova 9, 893 33 Bratislava; f. 1965; monthly; magazine of the Union of Czechoslovak-Soviet Friendship; Editor Karol Hederling; circ. 30,000.

Katolícke noviny (Catholic News): Kapitulská 9, 890 21 Bratislava; f. 1849; weekly; published by the St Vojtech League; Editor Dr Alojz Martinec; circ. 130,000.

Krásy Slovenska (Beauty of Slovakia): Vajnorská 100, 832 58 Bratislava; illustrated monthly; published by Sport, publishing house of the Slovak Physical Culture Organization; Editor Dr Tibor Sásik; circ. 18,000.

Nö (Woman): Martanovičová 20, 801 00 Bratislava; f. 1952; Hungarian; weekly pictorial; published by the Slovak Women's Union; Editor Alžbeta Harasztiová; circ. 35,000.

Nové Slovo (New Word): Leškova 5, 894 21 Bratislava; f. 1944; weekly; politics, culture, economy; organ of the Central Committee of the Communist Party of Slovakia; Editor Emil Polák; circ. 50,000.

CZECHOSLOVAKIA

Príroda a spoločnosť (Nature and Society): Štúrova 5, 890 17 Bratislava; f. 1953; fortnightly; organ of the Socialist Academy of Slovakia; Editor PAVOL BERTA; circ. 20,000.

Revue svetovej literatúry (Revue of World Literature): Obráncov mieru 14, 815 93 Bratislava; tel. (7) 47764; f. 1965; 7 a year; organ of the Slovak Literary Fund; Editor-in-Chief VLADIMÍR LUKÁN; circ. 7,000.

Rodina (Family): Volgogradská 8, 893 39 Bratislava; published by Pravda; Editor JÁN LAPŠANSKÝ; circ. 121,000.

Roháč (Stag-Beetle): Obráncov mieru 47, 893-26 Bratislava; f. 1948; humorous, satirical weekly; published by Pravda, publishing house of the Communist Party of Slovakia; Editor PETER BÁN; circ. 120,000.

Sloboda (Freedom): Obráncov mieru 8, 892 18 Bratislava; f. 1946; weekly; organ of the Freedom Party of Slovakia; Editor VLADIMÍR ŽABKAY; circ. 4,500.

Slovenka (Slovak Woman): Štúrova 12, 897 19 Bratislava; f. 1949; weekly pictorial published by the Slovak Women's Union: Editor LIBUŠA MINÁČOVÁ; circ. 220,000.

Slovenské pohl'ady (Slovak Views): Leningradská 2, 897 28 Bratislava; f. 1846; reissued 1881; monthly of the Union of Slovak Writers; works of Slovak prose writers and poets, literary criticism, translations from world literature; Editor VLADIMÍR REISEL; circ. 6,000.

Svet socializmu (World of Socialism): Bezručova 9, 893 33 Bratislava; f. 1951; weekly pictorial of the Union of Czechoslovak-Soviet Friendship; Editor KAROL HEDERLING; circ. 200,000.

Štart (Start): Vajnorská 100/A, 893 44 Bratislava; telex 93330; f. 1956; illustrated weekly; organ of the Slovak Sports Organization; Editor JOZEF MAZÁG; circ. 68,000.

Technické noviny (Technical News): Obráncov mieru 19, 897 17 Bratislava; f. 1953; weekly of the Slovak Council of Trade Unions; Editor MICHAL KIMLIK; circ. 70,000.

Tip: Vajnorská 100A, 832 58 Bratislava; telex 93330; f. 1969; weekly; football and ice-hockey; published by the Slovak Physical Training Organization; Editor FERDINAND KRÁLOVIČ; circ. 45,000.

Učitelské noviny (Teachers' Gazette): Nábř. arm. gen. L. Svobodu 15, 816 41 Bratislava; f. 1959; organ of the Slovak Ministry of Education; Editor EMIL NANDORY; circ. 35,000.

Uj ifjúság (New Youth): Praźská 11, 897 14 Bratislava; Hungarian; weekly; organ of the Slovak Central Committee of the Socialist Union of Youth; Editor Dr JURAJ ŠTRASSER; circ. 21,000.

Výber (Digest): Októbrové nám. 7, 893 46 Bratislava; f. 1968; weekly; digest of home and foreign press; in Czech and Slovak; published by the Union of Slovak Journalists; Editor VERONIKA TÖKÖLYOVÁ; circ. 21,000.

Život (Life): Gorkého 8, 882 12 Bratislava; f. 1951; illustrated weekly; political, economic, social and cultural matters; Editor Ing. LADISLAV TOMÁŠEK; circ. 180,000.

Foreign languages

Czechoslovak Foreign Trade: ul. 28 října 13, 112 79 Prague 1; tel. (2) 226651; telex 121142; f. 1961; monthly; journal of the Czechoslovak Chamber of Commerce and Industry; published in English, German, Spanish, Russian and French by Rapid, Czechoslovak Advertising Agency; Editor-in-Chief JAROSLAV BERANEK; circ. 12,000.

Czechoslovak Heavy Industry: ul. 28 října 13, 112 79 Prague 1; telex 121142; f. 1955; scientific, technical monthly for heavy industry published by Rapid in English, French, German, Spanish and Russian; Editor IVAN KUBA; circ. 10,000.

Czechoslovak Motor Review: ul. 28 října 13, 112 79 Prague 1; telex 121142; monthly; published by Rapid in English, French, German, Russian and Serbo-Croat; Editor KAREL RŮŽIČKA.

Czechoslovak Trade Unions: Václavské nám. 17, 112 58 Prague 1; tel. (2) 268879; telex 121134; review of the Central Trades Union Council; 6 a year; English, French, German, Russian, Italian, Swedish, Portuguese and Spanish; Editor-in-Chief H. SEMÍNOVÁ; circ. 35,000.

The Democratic Journalist: Pařížská 9, 110 01 Prague 1; tel. (2) 220911; telex 122631; f. 1953; 12 a year; press organ of the International Organization of Journalists; English, French, Spanish and Russian; Editor RUDOLF PŘEVRÁTIL.

For You from Czechoslovakia: ul. 28 října 13, 112 79 Prague 1; telex 121142; quarterly; published by Rapid in English, German, Russian, Spanish and French; Editor MARIE SŮVOVÁ.

Glass Review: ul. 28 října 13, 112 79 Prague 1; telex 121142; glass-making and ceramics; monthly; published by Rapid in English, French, German and Russian; Editor ZDENKA KALABISOVÁ.

Investa: ul. 28 října 13, 112 79 Prague 1; telex 121142; f. 1970; quarterly; export magazine dealing with machines for the footwear, tanning and textile industries, knitting and sewing machines; published by Rapid in English, French, German, Russian and Spanish; Editor-in-Chief LUDMILA HÁLKOVOVÁ.

Kovoexport: ul. 28 října 13, 112 79 Prague 1; telex 121142; f. 1955; 6 a year; export magazine dealing with all branches of precision engineering; published by Rapid in English, French, German, Russian and Spanish; Editor-in-chief LUDMILA HÁLKOVOVÁ.

Neue Prager Presse: Vinohradská 46, 120 41 Prague 2; telex 122948; weekly; politics, culture, economy, tourism; published by Orbis in German; Editor JOSEF KOLONIČKÝ.

News Service: 17 November St, 110 01 Prague 1; fortnightly; magazine of the International Union of Students; English, French and Spanish; Editor LAJOS DEMCSÁK; circ. 8,000.

NEWS AGENCIES

Československá tisková kancelář (ČTK) (Czechoslovak News Agency): Opletalova 5–7, 111 44 Prague 1; tel. (2) 2147; telex 122841; f. 1918; news and photo exchange service with all international and many national news agencies; maintains wide network of foreign correspondents; English, Russian, French and Spanish news service for foreign countries; publishes weekly bulletin in Russian, English, Spanish, French and German; pubs specialized economic bulletins and documentation surveys in Czech; Gen. Dir Dr OTAKAR SVĚRČINA.

Orbis Press Agency: Vinohradská 46, 120 41 Prague 2; telex 122948; f. 1977; supplies information about Czechoslovakia to the foreign press and foreign publishing houses on a commercial basis; Dir Dr VLADIMÍR VIPLER.

ČTK—Made in ... publicity: Kotorská 16, 140 04 Prague 4; telex 122501; f. 1963; organization of the Czechoslovak News Agency for advertising foreign products and services in Czechoslovakia; Gen. Dir Ing. OTAKAR DUŠEK.

Foreign Bureaux

Agence France-Presse (AFP): Zitná 10, 120 00 Prague 2; Bureau Chief BERNARD NICOLAS.

Agentstvo Pechati Novosti (APN) (USSR): Italská 36, 120 00 Prague 2; Bureau Chief ANDREY SHAMSHIN.

Agenzia Nazionale Stampa Associata (ANSA) (Italy): Smečkách 2, 110 00 Prague 1; tel. (2) 247434; telex 122734; Bureau Chief FILIPPO MARIA TULLI.

Allgemeiner Deutscher Nachrichtendienst (ADN) (German Democratic Republic): nábř. B. Engelse 78, 120 00 Prague 2; Bureau Chief STEFFI GENSICKE.

Associated Press (AP) (USA): Růžová 7, 110 00 Prague 1; tel. (2) 243592; telex 121987; Correspondent IVA DRÁPALOVÁ.

Bulgarian Telegraph Agency (BTA): Ždanova 46, 160 00 Prague 6; telex 121066; Bureau Chief VIOLETA MICEVA.

Deutsche Presse-Agentur (dpa) (Federal Republic of Germany): Želivského 11/4/13, 130 31 Prague 3; tel. (2) 276595; telex 122706; Bureau Chief LADISLAV VALEK.

Inter Press Service (IPS) (Italy): Rubešová 12, 120 00 Prague 2; tel. (2) 2147; telex 122885; Correspondent FERMIN BARNO.

Kyodo Tsushin (Japan): Brevnov Liborova 24, Prague 6; tel. (2) 356797; Bureau Chief KIYOSHI HASUMI.

Magyar Távirati Iroda (MTI) (Hungary): Smaltovný 17, Prague 7; Bureau Chief GÁBOR SZÜCS.

Prensa Latina (Cuba): Petrská nám. 1, 110 00 Prague 1; telex 121083; Bureau Chief FRANCISCO FORTEZA.

Telegrafnoye Agentstvo Sovetskovo Soyuza (TASS) (USSR): Pevnostní 5, 162 00 Prague 6; Bureau Chief LEONID LATYSEV.

Xinhua (New China) News Agency (People's Republic of China): Majakovskho 22, Prague 6; tel. (2) 326144; telex 121561; Correspondent YU JUNMIN.

The following are also represented: Agerpres (Romania), PAP (Poland) and Tanjug (Yugoslavia).

PRESS ASSOCIATIONS

Czechoslovak Union of Journalists: Pařížská 9, 110 00 Prague 1; f. 1946; 6,777 mems; Chair. JÁN RIŠKO.

CZECHOSLOVAKIA

Czech Union of Journalists: Pařížská 9, 110 01 Prague 1; f. 1877; 4,000 mems; Pres. Dr JOSEF VALENTA.

Slovak Union of Journalists: Októbrové nám. 7, 893 46 Bratislava; f. 1968; 2,206 mems; Pres. Dr ŠTEFAN BACHÁR.

Publishers

In May 1949 legislation was passed making the publication, printing, illustration, and distribution of all books and music the prerogative of the State. These activities are now restricted to the Government, political parties, trade unions, and national and communal bodies. However, churches and religious bodies are permitted to publish if the State will accept their work for printing.

CZECH PUBLISHING HOUSES

Academia: Vodičkova 40, 112 29 Prague 1; f. 1953; publishing house of the Czechoslovak Academy of Sciences; scientific books, periodicals; Dir RADOSLAV ŠVEC.

Albatros: Na Perštýně 1, 110 01 Prague 1; telex 121605; f. 1949; literature for children and young people; Dir VÁCLAV MIKEŠ.

Artia: Ve Smečkách 30, 111 27 Prague 1; telex 121065; f.1953; part of the Artia Foreign Trade Corporation; children's books, art books and encyclopaedias; Dir Dr VILÉM ŠILAR.

Avicenum: Malostranské nám. 28, 118 02 Prague 1; f. 1953; medical books and periodicals; Dir VÁCLAV CIPRA.

Blok: Rooseveltova 4, 657 00 Brno; regional literature, fiction, general; Dir IVO ODEHNAL.

Československý spisovatel (Czechoslovak Writer): Národní 19, 111 47 Prague 1; telex 122645; publishing house of the Czech Literary Fund; poetry, fiction, literary theory and criticism; Dir Dr JAN PILAŘ.

Horizont: Nekázanka 7, 111 21 Prague 1; f. 1968; publishing house of the Czech Socialist Academy; general; Dir VOJTĚCH SVAROVSKÝ.

Kartografie: Fr. Křižíka 1, 170 20 Prague 7; state map publishing house; Dir Ing DRAHOMÍRA JOŠTOVÁ.

Kruh: Dlouhá 108, 500 21 Hradec Králové; regional literature, fiction and general; Dir Dr JOSEF KUBÍČEK.

Lidové nakladatelství: Václavské nám. 36, 115 65 Prague 1; f. 1968; formerly Svět Sovětů; publishing house of the Union of Czechoslovak-Soviet Friendship; classical and contemporary fiction, general, magazines; Dir Dr JAN NOVÁK.

Melantrich: Václavské nám. 36, 112 12 Prague 1; telex 121432; f. 1919; publishing house of the Czechoslovak Socialist Party; general, fiction, newspapers and magazines; Dir Ing. JAN KRÁTKÝ.

Merkur: Gorkého nám. 11, 115 69 Prague 1; telex 121648; commerce, tourism, catering; Dir JIŘÍ LINHART.

Mladá fronta: Panská 8, 112 22 Prague 1; telex 121510; f. 1945; publishing house of the Central Committee of the Socialist Union of Youth; literature for young people, fiction and non-fiction, newspapers and magazines; Dir Dr KORNEL VAVRINČÍK.

Nakladatelství dopravy a spojů: Hybernská 5, 115 78 Prague 1; state publishing house for transport and communications; Dir Dr OLDŘICH BREJCHA.

Naše vojsko: Na Děkance 3, 128 12 Prague 1; publishing house of the Czechoslovak Army; fiction, general; Dir Dr STANISLAV MISTR.

Odeon: Národní třída 36, 115 87 Prague 1; telex 123055; f. 1953; literature, poetry, fiction (classical and modern), literary theory, art books, reproductions; Dir JOSEF KULÍČEK.

Olympia: Klimentská 1, 115 88 Prague 1; f. 1954; sports, tourism, illustrated books; Dir LUDVÍK UHLÍŘ.

Panorama: Hálkova 1, Prague 2; Dir FRANTIŠEK HANZLÍK.

Panton: Říční 12, 118 39 Prague 1; f. 1958; publishing house of the Czech Musical Fund; books on music, sheet music, records; Dir. MILOŠ KONVALINKA.

Práce: Václavské nám. 17, 112 58 Prague 1; tel. (2) 266151; telex 121134; f. 1945; publishing house of the Trade Union Movement; trade union movement, fiction, general, periodicals; Dir Dr JURAJ HIMAL.

Profil: Ciklářská 51, 702 00 Ostrava 1; regional literature, fiction and general; Dir IVAN ŠEINER.

Rapid: ul. 28 října 13, 112 79 Prague 1; telex 121142; foreign trade; Dir JOSEF MAREŠ.

Růže: Žižkovo nám. 5, 371 96 České Budějovice; regional literature, fiction and general; Dir FRANTIŠEK PODLAHA.

Severočeské nakladatelství: Velká Hradební 33, 400 21 Ústí nad Labem; regional literature, fiction and general; Dir JAN SUCHL.

Státní nakladatelství technické literatury: Spálená 51, 113 02 Prague 1; state publishing house of technical literature; technology, applied sciences, dictionaries, periodicals; Dir Ing. JINDŘICH SUCHARDA.

Státní pedagogické nakladatelství: Ostrovní 30, 113 01 Prague 1; f. 1775; state publishing house; school and university textbooks, dictionaries; Dir Ing. JOSEF PAPEŽ.

Státní zemědělské nakladatelství: Václavské nám. 47, 113 11 Prague 1; state publishing house; agriculture; periodicals; Dir Ing. KAREL KOUKAL.

Středočeské nakladatelství knihkupectví: U Prašné brány 3, 116 29 Prague 1; regional literature, fiction, general; Dir Dr VLADIMÍR PÍŠA.

Supraphon: Palackého 1, 122 99 Prague 1; telex 121218; state publishing house for gramophone records and music; Dir JAN KVÍDERA.

Svoboda: Revoluční 15, 113 03 Prague 1; publishing house of the Central Committee of the Communist Party of Czechoslovakia; politics, history, philosophy, fiction, general; Dir Dr EVŽEN PALONCY.

Ústřední církevní nakladatelství: Ječná 2, 120 00 Prague 2; f. 1952; religion; Dir KAREL KNOBLOCH.

Vyšehrad: Karlovo nám. 5, 120 78 Prague 2; publishing house of the Czechoslovak People's Party; general fiction, newspapers and magazines; Dir KAREL HRUNEK.

Západočeské nakladatelství: Moskevská 36, 301 35 Plzeň; regional literature, fiction, general; Dir MIROSLAV JIRKA.

SLOVAK PUBLISHING HOUSES

Alfa: Hurbanovo nám. 3, 815 89 Bratislava; previously the Slovak Publishing House of Technical Literature; technical and economic literature, dictionaries; Dir Ing. RUDOLF SCHALLER.

Cirkevné vydavateľstvo: Palisády 64, 801 00 Bratislava; religious literature; Dr ONDREJ LIŠČIK.

Matica Slovenská: Hostihora 2, 036 52 Martin; f. 1863; literary science, bibliography, biography and librarianship; literary archives and museums; life of the Slovaks living abroad; Dir ONDREJ KUČERA.

Mladé Letá (Young Years): nám. SNP 11, 894 26 Bratislava; telex 93421; state publishing house; f. 1950; literature for children and young people; Dir Dr RUDO MORIC.

Obzor (Horizon): ul. ČS armády 35, 893 36 Bratislava; state publishing house; educational, encyclopedias, popular scientific, fiction, textbooks, law; Dir Ing. JÁN PRINC.

Osveta (Education): Osloboditeľov 55, 036 54 Martin; f. 1953; medical, educational, photographic and regional literature; Dir JÁN KRAJČ.

Pallas: Štúrova 1A, 882 09 Bratislava; publishing house of the Slovak Fund of Fine Arts; books about art; Dir GUSTAV HUPKA.

Práca: Obráncov mieru 19, 897 17 Bratislava; f. 1946; publishing house of the Slovak Trade Unions Council; economics, labour, work safety, etc.; Dir. JÁN DUŽI.

Pravda: Gunduličova 12, 882 05 Bratislava; f. 1969; publishing house of the Central Committee of the Communist Party of Slovakia; politics, philosophy, history, economics, fiction, children's literature; Dir Ing. VILIAM KAČER.

Príroda: Križkova 7, 894 17 Bratislava; agricultural literature, gardening books; Dir Ing. VINCENT ŠUGÁR.

Slovenské pedagogické nakladateľstvo: Sasinková 5, 891 12 Bratislava; pedagogical literature, educational, school texts, dictionaries; Dir FRANTIŠEK MRÁZ.

Slovenský spisovateľ: Leningradská 2, 897 28 Bratislava; publishing house of the Union of Slovak Writers; fiction, poetry; Dir VOJTĚCH MIHALIK.

Smena: Pražská 11, 897 14 Bratislava; publishing house of the Slovak Central Committee of the Socialist Union of Youth; fiction, literature for young people; Dir RUDOLF BELAN.

Šport: Vajnorská 100, 893 44 Bratislava; telex 93330; publishing house of the Central Committee of the Slovak Physical Culture Organization; sport, physical culture, guide books, periodicals; Dir Ing. FRANTIŠEK MIKLOŠ.

Tatran: Michalská 9, 891 34 Bratislava; f. 1949; fiction, art books; Dir Dr ANTON MARKUŠ.

CZECHOSLOVAKIA

Directory

Veda (Science): Klemensova 27, 895 30 Bratislava; f. 1953; publishing house of the Slovak Academy of Science: scientific and popular scientific books and periodicals; Dir Ing. MIROSLAV MURÍN.

Východoslovenské vydavateľstvo: Alejová 3, 040 11 Košice; regional literature, fiction, general; Dir MIKULÁŠ JÁGER.

WRITERS' UNIONS

Svaz československých spisovatelů (Union of Czechoslovak Writers): Národní třída 11, 110 47 Prague 1; Chair. Dr JAN KOZÁK.

Svaz českých spisovatelů (Union of Czech Writers): Národní třída 11, 111 47 Prague 1; f. 1972; 165 mems; Chair. IVAN SKÁLA.

Zväz slovenských spisovateľov (Union of Slovak Writers): 890 08 Bratislava; f. 1949; Chair. (vacant).

Radio and Television

In 1985 there were 4,208,538 radio licences and an estimated 4,360,000 television receivers in use.

RADIO

There are five national networks in Czechoslovakia: Radios Prague and Bratislava (long and medium wave), Radio Hvězda (long, medium and VHF—popular and youth programmes), and Radios Vltava and Děvín (VHF from Prague and Bratislava respectively—programmes on Czech, Slovak, socialist and progressive western culture).

Local stations broadcast from Prague (Central Bohemian Studio), Banská Bystrica, Brno, České Budějovice, Hradec Králové, Košice, Ostrava, Plzeň, Prešov, Ústí nad Labem and other towns.

Foreign broadcasts are made in Arabic, English, French, German, Greek, Hungarian, Italian, Portuguese, Spanish, Ukrainian, and Czech and Slovak.

Československý rozhlas (Czechoslovak Radio): Vinohradská 12, 120 99 Prague 2; telex 121100; f. 1923; Dir-Gen. Dr JÁN RIŠKO.

Český rozhlas (Czech Radio): Vinohradská 12, 120 99 Prague 2; telex 121100; Dir Dr KAREL KVAPIL.

Československý rozhlas na Slovensku (Czechoslovak Radio in Slovakia): Mýtna 1, 812 90 Bratislava; tel. (7) 47697; telex 93353; f. 1926; Dir Dr ŠTEFAN BACHÁR.

Československé zahraniční vysílání (Czechoslovak Foreign Broadcasts): Vinohradská 12, 120 99 Prague 2; telex 121189; Dir Dr JOSEF HORA.

TELEVISION

There are television studios in Prague, Brno, Ostrava, Bratislava and Košice.

Československá televize (Czechoslovak Television): nám. M. Gorkého 29, 111 50 Prague 1; tel. (2) 221247; telex 121800; f. 1953; Dir-Gen. Dr JAN ZELENKA.

Československá televize na Slovensku (Czechoslovak TV in Slovakia): nám. SNP 38, 899 40 Bratislava; telex 93294; Dir Dr MILOŠ MARKO.

Finance

(cap. = capital; dep. = deposits; m. = million; res = reserves)

BANKS

Československá obchodní banka a.s. (Commercial Bank of Czechoslovakia): na Příkopě 14, 115 20 Prague 1; tel. (2) 2132; telex 122201; f. 1965; commercial and foreign exchange transactions; cap. 1,000m. Kčs., res 4,231.4m. Kčs., dep. 54,430.3m. Kčs. (Dec. 1982); Gen. Man. Ing. KVĚTOSLAV BRDIČKA.

Státní banka československá (State Bank of Czechoslovakia): Na Příkopě 28, 110 03 Prague 1; tel. (2) 2112; telex 121831; the State Monetary Agency; f. 1950; bank of issue, a bank for granting long-term and short-term credits, maintaining payments relations, financing and control of capital construction, and buying and selling securities; a deposit centre; a central bank for directing and securing banking economic relations with foreign countries; and a cash clearing centre of the ČSSR. Statutory Funds 5,000m. Kčs.; General Reserve 2,521m. Kčs. (Dec. 1982); Pres. Ing. JAN STEJSKAL.

Živnostenská banka: Na Příkopě 20, 113 80 Prague 1; tel. (2) 224346; telex 122313; f. 1868; cap. 250m. Kčs., res 113m. Kčs. (Dec. 1983); Gen. Man. Dr KAREL PROCHÁZKA.

SAVINGS BANKS

Česká státní spořitelna (Czech State Savings Bank): Václavské nám. 42, 113 98 Prague 1; telex 121010; accepts deposits and issues loans; 13,373,128 depositors (June 1983); Gen. Dir Ing. FRANTIŠEK PAZDERA.

Slovenská štátna spořitelna (Slovak State Savings Bank): Leningradská 24, 801 00 Bratislava; telex 93133; Dir Ing. JOZEF LAŠŠÁK.

INSURANCE

Česká státní pojišťovna (Czech State Insurance and Reinsurance Corporation): Spálená 16, 113 04 Prague 1; tel. (2) 294342; telex 121112; many home branches and some agencies abroad; controls all insurance; issues life, accident, fire, aviation and marine policies, all classes of reinsurance; Lloyd's agency; Gen. Man. Ing. JOSEF VEČEŘA.

Slovenská štátna poisťovňa (Slovak State Insurance Corporation): Strakova 1, 815 74 Bratislava; telex 93375; Gen. Dir RASTISLAV HAVERLIK.

Trade and Industry

CHAMBER OF COMMERCE

Československá obchodní a průmyslová komora (Czechoslovak Chamber of Commerce and Industry): Argentinská 38, 170 05 Prague 7; tel. (2) 8724111; telex 121862; f. 1949; its 859 mems are all Czechoslovak foreign trade corporations and the majority of the industrial enterprises, banks and research institutes; Pres. Ing. JAROSLAV JAKUBEC.

FOREIGN TRADE CORPORATIONS

Artia: Ve Smečkách 30, 111 27 Prague 1; imports and exports cultural commodities; Gen. Dir Ing. MIROSLAV MARUŠKA.

Centrotex: nám. Hrdinů 3/1634, 140 61 Prague 4; imports and exports textiles; Gen. Dir Ing. JIŘÍ KOUTNÍK.

Čechofracht: Na Příkopě 8, 111 83 Prague 1; f. 1949; shipping and international forwarding corporation; Gen. Dir JIŘÍ KADANÍK.

Chemapol: Kodaňská 46, 100 10 Prague 10; tel. (2) 715; telex 122021; f. 1948; imports and exports chemical and pharmaceutical products and raw materials; Gen. Dir Ing. VÁCLAV VOLF.

Czechoslovak Ceramics: V Jámě 1, 111 91 Prague 1; exports and imports ceramics; Gen. Dir Ing. MIROSLAV DOBEŠ.

Czechoslovak Filmexport: Václavské nám. 28, 111 45 Prague 1; import and export of films; Gen. Dir Ing. JIŘÍ JANOUŠEK.

Drevounia: Dr V. Clementisa 10, 826 10 Bratislava; tel. (7) 229962; telex 93291; imports and exports wood and furniture; Gen. Dir Ing. JIŘÍ JIRAVA.

Exico: Panská 9, 111 77 Prague 1; tel. (2) 246941; telex 122211; f. 1966; exports and imports leather, shoes, skins; Gen. Dir Ing. KAREL HOLEŠÍNSKÝ.

Ferromet: Opletalova 27, 111 81 Prague 1; imports and exports metallurgical products; Gen. Dir Ing. BŘETISLAV SEDLÁK.

Inspekta: Na Strži 63, 140 62 Prague 4; control of goods in foreign trade; Gen. Dir Ing. JAN SVIHEL.

Jablonex: Palackého 41, 467 37 Jablonec nad Nisou; exports of imitation jewellery and decorations; Gen. Dir Ing. VÍT RYŠÁNEK.

Koospol: Leninova 178, 160 67 Prague 6; imports and exports foodstuffs; Gen. Dir LADISLAV MALÝ.

Kovo: Jankovcova 2, 170 88 Prague 7; imports and exports precision engineering products; Gen. Dir Ing. VÁCLAV HALEŠ.

Ligna: Vodičkova 41, 112 09 Prague 1; imports and exports timber, wood products, musical instruments and paper; Gen. Dir Ing. MILOŠ ŠVACH.

Merkuria: Argentinská 38, 170 05 Prague 7; exports and imports tools and consumer goods; Gen. Dir Ing. JOSEF ANDĚL.

Metalimex: Štěpánská 34, 112 17 Prague 1; imports and exports metals, natural gas and solid fuels; Gen. Dir Ing. MIROSLAV HLAVIČKA.

Motokov: Na Strži 63, 140 62 Prague 4; imports and exports vehicles and light engineering products; Gen. Dir Ing. JÁN MACHAJ.

Omnipol: Nekázanka 11, 112 21 Prague 1; import and export of sports and civil aircraft; Gen. Dir Ing. LUDVÍK ŠKOČDOPOLE.

Pragoexport: Jungmannova 34, 112 59 Prague 1; imports and exports consumer goods; Gen. Dir Ing. FRANTIŠEK FREMUND.

CZECHOSLOVAKIA
Directory

Pragoinvest: Českomoravská 23, 180 56 Prague 9; tel. (2) 822741; telex 122379; import and export of machinery and complete plant equipment; Gen. Dir Ing. MILOSLAV KOČÁREK.

Simex: Václavské nám. 8, 110 00 Prague 1; imports and exports machines and components; Gen. Dir JOSEF ŠEBESTA.

Skloexport: tř. 1. máje 52, 461 52 Liberec; exports glass; Gen. Dir Ing. JAROSLAV KŘIVÁNEK.

Škodaexport: Václavské nám. 56, 113 32 Prague 1; tel. (2) 2131; telex 122413; exports and imports power engineering and metallurgical plants, engineering works, electrical locomotives and trolleybuses, tobacco machines; Gen. Dir Ing. MILOSLAV MIKEŠ.

Strojexport: POB 662, Václavské nám. 56, 113 26 Prague 1; tel. (2) 2131; telex 121753; f. 1953; imports and exports machines and machinery equipment; Gen. Dir Ing. JOSEF LEVORA.

Strojimport: Vinohradská 184, 130 52 Prague 3; tel. (2) 713; telex 122241; imports and exports machines and industrial plant; Gen. Dir Ing. JAN ŠTĚRBA.

Technoexport: Václavské nám. 1, 113 34 Prague 1; tel. (2) 247351; telex 121268; imports and exports chemical and foodstuff engineering plant; Gen. Dir Ing. OLDŘICH KUCHTA.

Tuzex: Rytířská 13, 113 43 Prague 1; retail goods for foreign currency; Gen. Dir Ing. ANTONÍN RAČANSKÝ.

TRADE UNIONS

Ústřední rada odborů (ÚRO) (Central Council of Trade Unions): nám. A. Zápotockého 2, 113 59 Prague 3; f. 1945; governing body of Revoluční odborové hnutí—ROH (Revolutionary Trade Union Movement); Chair. Ing. KAREL HOFFMANN.

Česká odborová rada (ČOR) (Czech Trade Union Council): nám. A. Zápotockého 2, 113 59 Prague 3; Chair. Ing. VÁCLAV BĚŽEL.

Slovenská odborová rada (SOR) (Slovak Trade Union Council): Odborárske nám. 3, 897 17 Bratislava; Chair. IVAN GOŇKO.

Odborový svaz civilních pracovníků Československé lidové armády (Civil Employees of the Czechoslovak People's Army): nám. Svobody 471, 160 00 Prague 6; Chair. VLADIMÍR CHRASTIL.

Odborový svaz pracovníků chemického, papírenského a sklářského průmyslu a tisku (Chemical, Paper, Glass and Printing Industry): nám. A. Zápotockého 2, 113 59 Prague 3; Chair. LADISLAV ŠANOVSKÝ; 336,386 mems.

Odborový svaz pracovníků dopravy a silničního hospodářství (Transport and Roads): Vinohradská 10, Prague 2; Chair. MIROSLAV VALOUŠEK; 247,667 mems.

Odborový svaz pracovníků dřevoprůmyslu, lesního a vodního hospodářství (Woodwork Industry, Forestry and Water Conservancy): nám. A. Zápotockého 2, 113 59 Prague 3; Chair. MICHAL REGULÝ; 263,000 mems.

Odborový svaz pracovníků hornictví a energetiky (Mining and Power Generating Industries): nám. A. Zápotockého 2, 113 59 Prague 3; Chair. VLADIMÍR POLEDNÍK; 398,843 mems.

Odborový svaz pracovníků kovoprůmyslu (Metal): nám. A. Zápotockého 2, 113 59 Prague, 3; Chair. JOSEF TREJBAL; 1,236,374 mems.

Odborový svaz pracovníků místního hospodářství (Communal Enterprises): nám. M. Gorkého 23, 112 82 Prague 1; Chair. RICHARD ŠTĚCH; 359,755 mems.

Odborový svaz pracovníků obchodu (Commerce): nám. M. Gorkého 23, 112 82 Prague 1; Chair. MARIE HADRABOVÁ; 690,383 mems.

Odborový svaz pracovníků potravinářského průmyslu (Food Industry): nám. A. Zápotockého 2, 113 59 Prague 3; Chair. (vacant); 231,357 mems.

Odborový svaz pracovníků školství a vědy (Education and Science): nám. M. Gorkého 23, 112 82 Prague 1; f. 1945; Chair. Dr DRAHOMÍRA HANZALOVÁ; 467,486 mems.

Odborový svaz pracovníků spojů (Post and Telecommunications): nám. A. Zápotockého 2, 113 59 Prague 3; f. 1972; Chair. DARINA PRISTACHOVÁ; 134,626 mems.

Odborový svaz pracovníků státních orgánů, peněžnictví a zahraničního obchodu (Government and Financial Institutions and Foreign Trade): nám. M. Gorkého 23, 118 82 Prague 1; Chair. BOHUMIL HANUŠ; 281,515 mems.

Odborový svaz pracovníků stavebnictví a ve výrobě stavebních hmot (Building and Building Materials Industry): nám. M. Gorkého 23, 118 82 Prague 1; Chair. VILIAM EICHENBERGER; 641,466 mems.

Odborový svaz pracovníků textilního, oděvního, a kožedělného průmyslu (Textile, Clothing and Leather Industry): nám. A. Zápotockého 2, 113 59 Prague 3; Chair. MÁRIA TRVALOVÁ; 438,518 mems.

Odborový svaz pracovníků umění, kultury a společenských organizací (Art, Cultural and Social Organizations): nám. M. Gorkého 23, 112 82 Prague 1; f. 1945; Chair. Dr JIŘÍ NEUŽIL; 167,803 mems.

Odborový svaz pracovníků zdravotnictví (Health Workers): nám. A. Zápotockého 2, 113 59 Prague 3; Chair. MARCELA OKROUHLÍKOVÁ; 389,345 mems.

Odborový svaz pracovníků železnic (Railway Workers): nám. A. Zápotockého 2, 113 59 Prague 3; Chair. FRANTIŠEK VÁLA; 296,736 mems.

Odborový svaz pracovníků zemědělství (Agricultural Workers): nám. A. Zápotockého 2, 113 59 Prague 3; Chair. VLADISLAV TŘEŠKA; 442,049 mems.

TRADE FAIR

BVV Trade Fairs and Exhibitions: Výstaviště 1, 602 00 Brno; tel. (5) 3141111; telex 62294; f. 1959; international engineering fair yearly in September; international consumer goods fair yearly in April or May; Gen. Dir Ing. KAREL SVOBODA.

Transport

RAILWAYS

In 1983 the total length of the Czechoslovak railways was 13,142 km; of this total, 3,221 km were electrified, including the connection Prague–Warsaw via Bohumín. The densest section of the network links the north with the south, and there is a direct rail link between the west and east of the country.

Československé státní dráhy (Czechoslovak State Railways): Na Příkopě 33, 110 05 Prague 1; tel. (2) 2122; telex 121096; Dir LADISLAV STROS.

Prague Metropolitan Railway: Dopravní podniky hlavního města Prahy, Bubenská 1, 170 26 Prague 7; the Prague underground railway opened in 1974, and by Nov. 1984 22.3 km were operational; Gen. Dir Ing. MIKULÁŠ LACEK; Gen. Sec. EDUARD STRAKA.

ROADS

In 1983 there were 74,064 km of roads in Czechoslovakia. Over 90% of the total road network is hard surfaced. The Prague–Brno–Bratislava motorway was opened in 1980.

Československá státní automobilová doprava—ČSAD (Czechoslovak State Road Transport): Hybernská 32, 111 21 Prague 1; f. 1949; the organization has 11 regional head offices.

Sdružení československých mezinárodních automobilových dopravců (ČESMAD) (Czechoslovak International Road Transport Enterprises Association): Perucká 5, 120 67 Prague 2; f. 1966; Chair. M. JUŘENA.

INLAND WATERWAYS

The total length of navigable waterways in Czechoslovakia is 480 km. The Elbe and its tributary the Vltava connect the country with the North Sea via the port of Hamburg. The Oder provides a connection with the Baltic Sea and the port of Szczecin. The Danube provides a link with Western Germany, Austria, Hungary, Yugoslavia, Bulgaria, Romania and the USSR. Czechoslovakia's river ports are Prague, Mělník, Ústí nad Labem and Děčín on the Vltava and Elbe, and Bratislava and Komárno on the Danube; in 1983, work began on a new port at Praha Radotin, which is to be the largest on the Vltava and Elbe.

Československá plavba dunajská národný podnik (Czechoslovak Danube River Shipping): Červenej armády 35, 890 24 Bratislava; telex 92338; Man. Dir Ing. PAVOL ČIBÁK.

Československá plavba labsko-oderská (ČSPLO) (Czechoslovak Elbe-Oder River Shipping): K. Čapka 1, 405 02 Děčín; telex 184241; carries out transport of goods on the Vltava, Elbe and Oder rivers as well as other waterways; transfer and storage of goods in Czechoslovak ports; operates the river ports of Prague, Mělník, Kolín, Ústí nad Labem and Děčín; Man. Dir Ing. KAREL ADAMOVSKÝ.

SHIPPING

Československá námořní plavba, mezinárodní akciová společnost (Czechoslovak Ocean Shipping, International Joint-Stock Company): Počernická 168, 100 99 Prague 10; telex 122137;

CZECHOSLOVAKIA

f. 1959; a shipping company operating the Czechoslovak seagoing fleet; 14 ships totalling 264,000 dwt; Man. Dir ANTONIN SOKOLÍK.

Czechoslovak Danube Navigation: Červenej armády 35, 890 24 Bratislava; telex 92338; five ships totalling 8,954 grt; Man. Dir Ing. PAVOL CIBÁK.

CIVIL AVIATION

There are civil airports at Prague (Ruzyně), Brno, Bratislava, Gottwaldov (Holešov), Karlovy Vary, Košice, Mariánské Lázně, Lucenec, Ostrava, Piešťany, Poprad-Tatry, Sliač (Banská Bystrica), Uherske Hradiste and Zilina, served by ČSA's internal flights. International flights serve Prague, Bratislava and Poprad-Tatry.

ČSA (Československé aerolinie, Czechoslovak Airlines): Head Office: Ruzyně Airport, 160 08 Prague; telex 120338; f. 1923; external services to most European capitals, the Near, Middle and Far East, North and Central America and North Africa; Gen. Dir Ing. JINDŘICH KOPŘIVA; fleet of 6 Ilyushin Il-62, 5 Ilyushin Il-62M, 13 Tupolev TU-134A, 2 Ilyushin Il-18 and 16, Yak-40.

Slov-Air: Ivanka Airport, Bratislava; telex 93568; f. 1971; domestic scheduled and charter services; Dir ONDREJ HUDOBA; fleet of small turboprop aircraft including four Let L-410 and two An-2.

Tourism

Čedok (Travel and Hotels Corporation): Na Příkopě 18, 111 35 Prague 1; telex 121064; the official Czechoslovak Travel Agency; 146 travel offices; branches throughout Europe and the USA; Dir VÁCLAV PLESKOT.

Atomic Energy

Nuclear power accounted for 14.6% of total electricity production in 1985.

Czechoslovak Atomic Energy Commission (ČSKAE): Slezská 9, 120 29 Prague 2; responsible for the peaceful utilization of atomic energy and for co-ordinating the atomic energy programme; Chair. Ing. STANISLAV HAVEL.

Ministry of Fuel and Power: Vinohradská 8, 120 70 Prague 2; responsible for nuclear power station construction plants at Jaslovské Bohunice (1,320 MW in operation, 440 MW under construction in 1985), Dukovany (440 MW in operation, 1,320 MW under construction), Mochovce (1,760 MW under construction), Temelín (4,000 MW under construction); Minister VLASTIMIL EHRENBERGER.

Ústav jaderného výzkumu (Institute of Nuclear Research): CS-250 68 Řež; telex 122626; f. 1955; Dir VASIL KRETT.

DENMARK

Introductory Survey

Location, Climate, Language, Religion, Flag, Capital

The Kingdom of Denmark is situated in northern Europe. It consists of the peninsula of Jutland, the islands of Zealand, Funen, Lolland, Falster and Bornholm, and 480 smaller islands. The country lies between the North Sea, to the west, and the Baltic Sea, to the east. Denmark's only land frontier is with the Federal Republic of Germany, to the south. Norway lies to the north of Denmark, across the Skagerrak, while Sweden, whose most southerly region is separated from Zealand by a narrow strait, lies to the north-east. Outlying territories of Denmark are Greenland and the Faeroe Islands in the North Atlantic Ocean. Denmark is low-lying and the climate is temperate, with mild summers and cold, rainy winters. The language is Danish. Almost all of the inhabitants profess Christianity: the Danish Lutheran Church, to which 94% of the population belong, is the established Church, and there are also small communities of other Protestant groups and of Roman Catholics. The national flag (proportions 37 by 28) displays a white cross on a red background, the upright of the cross being to the left of centre. The capital is Copenhagen (København).

Recent History

In 1945, following the end of German wartime occupation, Denmark recognized the independence of Iceland, which had been declared in the previous year. In 1947 King Frederik IX succeeded to the throne on the death of his father, Christian X. Home rule was granted to the Faeroe Islands in 1948 and to Greenland in 1979. Denmark was a founder member of NATO in 1949 and of the Nordic Council in 1952. Denmark's constitution was radically revised in 1953: new provisions allowed for female succession to the throne, abolished the upper house of parliament and amended the franchise. King Frederik died in January 1972, and his eldest daughter, Margrethe, became the first queen to rule Denmark for nearly 600 years. Following a referendum, Denmark entered the EEC in January 1973.

The system of proportional representation which is embodied in the 1953 constitution makes it difficult for a single party to gain a majority in the Folketing (Parliament), and the tendency of Danish parties to fragment has, in recent years, produced a series of coalition and minority governments, all of which have had to face economic problems and popular discontent with Denmark's EEC membership. The Liberal Party's minority Government, led by Poul Hartling and formed in 1973, was followed in 1975 by a minority Social Democratic Government under the leadership of Anker Jørgensen. In August 1978, facing the need for economic reform to deal with a substantial national debt, the Government (re-elected in February 1977) formed a coalition with the Liberal Party, introducing stringent financial measures which included the imposition, in March 1979, of a two-year statutory limit on wage rises. In September 1979, however, the Liberals' refusal to support a proposed profit-sharing scheme for industrial workers forced the Government to resign, although general elections in October reinstated the Social Democrats in a minority government, with Jørgensen remaining as Prime Minister.

In May 1980 the Government, with the support of the three centre parties (the Radical Liberals, the Centre Democrats and the Christian People's Party), implemented measures, including increased taxes and a cut in public spending, in an attempt to tighten control of the economy and redirect public spending emphasis from social services towards investments with the potential to ease Denmark's perennial balance-of-payments problems. There was considerable industrial unrest during 1981, with unemployment at a post-war record of 9%; a crisis arose when the three centre parties withdrew their support for a compromise economic package presented by the Social Democrats, and the Government resigned in November. General elections, held in December, were inconclusive and Jørgensen again formed a minority Social Democrat administration, with small centrist parties holding the balance in the Folketing. By September 1982 Jørgensen's economic policy, including attempts to reduce the budget deficit by imposing new taxation, had once more led to disagreements within the Cabinet, and the Government resigned.

The Conservatives, who had been absent from Danish coalitions since 1971, formed a centre-right four-party government (with the Liberals, the Centre Democrats and the Christian People's Party), led by Poul Schlüter, who became Denmark's first Conservative Prime Minister since 1894. Holding only 66 of the Folketing's 179 seats, the coalition narrowly avoided defeat in October 1982, when it introduced stringent economic measures (including a six-month 'freeze' on wages), and again in September 1983, when larger cuts in public spending were proposed. In December the anti-tax Progress Party withdrew its support for further spending cuts, and the Government was defeated. Elections to the Folketing were held in January 1984, and Schlüter's Government remained in office, with its component parties holding a total of 77 seats. With the anticipated support of 10 Radical Liberal members and three from the Faeroes and Greenland, the Government had a theoretical majority of one. In a Cabinet reshuffle in March 1986 nine portfolios changed hands, and six new ministers were appointed. The Centre Democrats lost one of their four posts, while the number of Conservative posts increased from eight to nine.

In the Folketing a government is expected to resign only if its defeated proposals have been presented as a 'vital element' of policy. This practice enabled the coalition to survive a series of defeats on foreign policy, including several attempts by the Folketing to dissociate itself from particular aspects of NATO defence strategy. In November 1984 the Government ignored a Folketing decision in favour of a ban on any first use of nuclear weapons by the Western alliance. In March 1985 the Folketing voted against any inclusion of nuclear power stations in public energy plans, and in May a majority approved a motion opposing Danish involvement in research connected with the US Government's 'Strategic Defense Initiative' (a plan, first announced by President Ronald Reagan in March 1983, to test the feasibility of creating a space-based defensive 'shield' against attack by ballistic missiles). This vote was a further defeat for Schlüter's Government. The left-wing parties have also committed the Government to work actively towards the creation of a nuclear-free zone in the Nordic region.

In January 1986 tension arose between Denmark and the other members of the EEC when the left-wing parties in the Folketing combined to defeat proposals for a programme of EEC reforms. These reforms had been designed to accelerate decision-making by the EEC's Council of Ministers, by removing the need for unanimity, and to lift internal trade barriers within the Community. The Social Democrats, who led the opposition, argued that the adoption of the reforms would lead to a diminution of Denmark's powers to protect its own environmental standards, forcing the country to alter its stringent import controls. The reform proposals were rejected in the Folketing by a narrow majority, making any amendment to the EEC's Treaty of Rome impossible, since a positive vote by the legislatures of all member states was required. Schlüter announced that a national referendum on the issue would take place in February, arguing that Danish rejection of the proposals would be the first stage towards Denmark's withdrawal from the EEC, and all parties agreed to respect the referendum result: 56.2% of the votes cast were in favour of the reforms, which were formally approved by the Folketing in May.

In July 1985 social unrest in Denmark was heightened when three bomb explosions, for which the Islamic Jihad (Holy War), a fundamentalist organization of Iranian origin, claimed responsibility, injured 27 people in Copenhagen, and the incidents were followed by a series of attacks on Middle Eastern

DENMARK

refugees in Denmark. Further explosions and attacks occurred in September and October, despite attempts to tighten security. In November the Folketing considered draft legislation to reduce the flow of Middle Eastern refugees, estimated at around 200 per week, by altering the procedures for granting asylum. In September 1986 the Folketing announced that it was seeking a solution whereby refugee arrivals would be shared between all European countries, and uniform refugee regulations would be imposed. A law aimed at reducing the flow of arrivals in Denmark by at least one-half was adopted in October 1986.

In May 1986 the Folketing approved the implementation of a total ban on trade in goods and services with South Africa, to take effect from December 1986, in protest at that country's racial policies.

Government

Denmark is a constitutional monarchy. Under the 1953 constitutional charter, legislative power is held jointly by the hereditary monarch (who has no personal political power) and the unicameral Folketing (Parliament), with 179 members, including 175 from metropolitan Denmark and two each from the Faeroe Islands and Greenland. Members are elected for four years (subject to dissolution) on the basis of proportional representation. A referendum in September 1978 reduced the age of suffrage from 20 to 18. Executive power is exercised by the monarch through a Cabinet, led by the Prime Minister, which is responsible to the Folketing. Denmark comprises 14 counties (amtskommuner), one city and one borough, all with elected councils.

Defence

In July 1986 Denmark maintained an army of 15,600 men, a navy of 6,925 men and an air force of 7,000 men. The army had about 162,700 reservists, and there was a volunteer Home Guard numbering 72,200. Military service is for nine–12 months. Denmark abandoned its neutrality after the Second World War and has been a member of NATO since 1949. The estimated defence budget for 1986 was 12,771m. kroner.

Economic Affairs

Denmark's economy is based mainly on agriculture and manufacturing, with small enterprises predominant in both sectors. The country has a high standard of living, with well-developed social services. In 1984, according to estimates by the World Bank, Denmark's gross national product (GNP) per head, measured at average 1982–84 prices, was US $11,170, one of the highest levels among industrialized countries. It was estimated that GNP per head increased at an average rate of 1.8% per year, in real terms, between 1965 and 1984.

Danish agriculture is internationally competitive and is organized on a co-operative basis. The co-operatives are united in national federations. Cheese, beef and bacon are the main agricultural exports. The proportion of the working population employed in agriculture declined from 21% in 1950 to 6% in 1985, although in the latter year over 67% of the land surface was cultivated. Intensive farming and subsidies from the EEC have stimulated production, although rising mortgage interest rates caused many farms to close in the early 1980s. During this period, pig farming experienced difficulties, owing to an outbreak of foot-and-mouth disease, but it was hoped that a five-year investment plan, begun in 1984, would increase the annual value of pig production to 18.2m. kroner by 1989. During the first seven months of 1986 agricultural exports fell by 9%, compared with the corresponding period in 1985. Exports of pig meat suffered a particularly sharp decline, and the Minister of Agriculture planned to seek additional government funding for the promotion and marketing of exports. In 1983 the value of fish products was 8,810m. kroner, with a total catch of 1,862,000 metric tons, and in 1985 the Government announced its intention to seek a higher Danish catch quota for North Sea herring in 1986.

Denmark's industry has developed considerably since 1945, and in 1983 the manufacturing sector accounted for about 62% of the country's exports. In spite of a shortage of raw materials, the iron and metal industry is now the most important producing group. The other major branches of manufacturing include food-processing and beverages, engineering and chemicals. The manufacturing of electronic goods is one of Denmark's fastest-growing industries, exporting 90% of its output. Exports were estimated at 11,000m. kroner in 1985, an increase of 1,500m. kroner on the 1984 total. In August 1986 it was announced that the Danish shipbuilding industry was to receive state help in the form of loans and more flexible investment rules. Several shipyards had been in danger of closure, owing to the lack of new orders since the end of 1984.

Denmark's economy suffers from the country's dependence on petroleum for most of its energy needs (66% in 1982); it was decided in January 1980 not to develop nuclear energy. However, exploration of hydrocarbon reserves in the Danish sector of the North Sea had revealed proven reserves of 359m. barrels of crude petroleum and 83m. cu m of natural gas by 1983. Dansk Undergrunds Consortium (DUC), formed by a Danish industrial group and foreign concessionaires, produced an average of 43,000 barrels per day (b/d) in 1983, and in 1984 seven new consortia were given exploration licences. In 1985 DUC announced an expansion plan, costing an estimated $250m., for its Dan F oilfield. Great emphasis has been placed on the development of natural gas reserves, and a $1,000m. scheme to connect 48 offshore wells with the mainland was completed in 1984, leaving only the construction of a pipeline to northern Jutland outstanding. In 1985 oil and gas flows were able to supply 50% of domestic demand. Since 1981 Danish oil and gas fields have gradually been brought under state control. In 1982 a total of 500 unexplored tracts, covering 74,000 sq km, were returned to the state by DUC, and all exploration groups are required to have a Danish interest of at least 20%.

Denmark's reliance on imported petroleum has contributed to current deficits on the balance of payments since 1963, and these have been financed by large loans contracted abroad. Since 1973 Denmark's current balance-of-payments deficits have averaged 4% of gross domestic product (GDP). Despite attempts by the Jørgensen Government to raise employment levels, and to bolster industry by the exploitation of petroleum, the number of unemployed rose to an average of 8.9% of the work-force in 1981, and the average rate of inflation reached 11.7%.

In their 'programme for the restoration of the Danish economy', aiming principally to balance the deficit on the current account by 1988, the Conservative-led coalition imposed a six-month 'freeze' on wages in October 1982, together with a longer-term ban on inflation-linked indexation, and reductions in welfare and unemployment benefits. Nevertheless, unemployment in that year reached 9.5%, as inflation rose to 10.1%. During 1983 collective wage agreements in both public and private sectors were held to an average increase of 4.5%. Inflation for the year fell to an average of 6.9%, and the current deficit on the balance of payments was reduced from 18,725m. kroner in 1982 to 10,785m. kroner, or 2.4% of GDP, in 1983.

By 1984 the current account deficit had risen to 17,200m. kroner, and external indebtedness had increased to 38% of GDP, compared with 32% in 1982. However, unemployment had been reduced to 9.8% of the labour force by November, and this success was accompanied by a rise of 4.5% in GDP in 1984, and by a reduction in the balance-of-payments deficit.

In 1985 the current account deficit rose to 28,400m. kroner, 4.6% of GDP, but unemployment fell to 9%. For the first time in 12 years, a budget surplus was achieved at the end of the financial year 1985/86. A series of austerity measures was introduced during 1985 and 1986, in an effort to reduce the balance-of-payments deficit, to improve the trade balance and to reduce domestic demand. Demonstrations and strikes followed the imposition of stringent wage settlements in March 1985, whereby pay increases were 'frozen' at 2% per year until 1987. In December 1985 central government levies were imposed on local programmes of public building and construction, and taxes on energy were increased. These were raised again in March 1986, when the Government also announced increases in the price of alcohol, tobacco and other luxury items. In October the Government introduced a further austerity programme, including taxation on domestic consumer lending, further increases in energy taxation and incentives for domestic savings. In the draft budget for 1987 the Government forecast a growth in GDP of 2.5%, following projected growth of 3.1% in 1986, and a decrease in the annual rate of inflation from 3.1% to 2.8%. Plans to eliminate the current account deficit by

DENMARK

1988 were abandoned, but the Government expressed the hope that a small reduction would be achieved in 1987.

Social Welfare

Denmark was one of the first countries to introduce state social welfare schemes. Principal services cover unemployment, sickness, old age and disability, and are financed largely by state subventions. In 1979 Denmark had 132 hospital establishments, and in 1984 there was a total of 36,405 hospital beds, with 12,800 physicians working in the country. In 1984 almost 30% of proposed budget expenditure was allocated to social services. In the same year the Government introduced a new system whereby social benefits are regulated according to the individual's means.

Education

Education is compulsory for nine years between seven and 16 years of age, though exemption may be granted after seven years. The State is obliged to offer a pre-school class and a tenth voluntary year. State-subsidized private schools are available, but about 90% of pupils attend municipal schools. The 1975 Education Act, with effect from August 1976, increased parental influence, introduced a comprehensive curriculum for the first 10 years and offered options on final tests or a leaving certificate thereafter.

Primary and lower secondary education begins at six or seven years of age and lasts for nine (optionally 10) years. At the age of 16 or 17, pupils may transfer to an upper secondary school (Gymnasium), leading to the Upper Secondary School Leaving Examination (Studentereksamen) after three years, or they may take a two-year course, leading to the Higher Preparatory Examination; both courses give admission to university studies. Students may transfer to vocational courses or apprenticeship training at this point. Enrolment at primary and secondary schools is equivalent to virtually 100% of school-age children.

There are three universities, two university centres, and several other institutions of further and higher education. The traditional folk high schools offer a wide range of further education opportunities, which do not confer any professional qualification.

Tourism

Tourists visit Denmark mainly for the peaceful charm of its countryside and old towns, or for the sophistication of Copenhagen. There were an estimated 2,113,707 tourist arrivals at accommodation establishments in 1985, when tourist receipts totalled US $1,423m. Revenue from tourism totalled 14,051m. kroner in 1985.

Public Holidays

1987: 1 January (New Year's Day), 16–20 April (Easter), 15 May (General Prayer Day), 28 May (Ascension Day), 5 June (Constitution Day), 8 June (Whit Monday), 25–26 December (Christmas).

1988: 1 January (New Year's Day), 31 March–4 April (Easter), 29 April (General Prayer Day), 12 May (Ascension Day), 23 May (Whit Monday), 5 June (Constitution Day), 25–26 December (Christmas).

Weights and Measures

The metric system is in force.

Currency and Exchange rates

100 øre = 1 Danish krone.

Exchange rates (30 September 1986):
 £1 sterling = 11.08 kroner;
 US $1 = 7.655 kroner.

Statistical Survey

Note: The figures in this survey relate only to 'metropolitan' Denmark, excluding the Faeroe Islands and Greenland, which are dealt with in separate chapters (see pp. 903 and 905 respectively).
Source (unless otherwise stated): Danmarks Statistik, Sejrøgade 11, 2100 Copenhagen Ø; tel. (01) 29-82-22.

Area and Population

AREA, POPULATION AND DENSITY

Area (sq km)	43,092*
Population (census results)	
9 November 1970	4,937,579
1 January 1981	
Males	2,528,225
Females	2,595,764
Total	5,123,989
Population (official estimates at 1 January)	
1984	5,112,130
1985	5,111,108
1986	5,116,273
Density (per sq km) at 1 January 1986	118.7

* 16,638 sq miles.

CIVILIAN LABOUR FORCE EMPLOYED (ISIC Major Divisions, '000 persons aged 15 to 74 at October each year)

	1983	1984	1985
Agriculture, forestry and fishing	182.0	178.6	175.3
Mining and quarrying	2.0	2.2	2.2
Manufacturing	468.8	491.8	524.4
Electricity, gas and water	15.8	16.0	16.3
Construction	146.1	151.3	157.8
Trade, restaurants and hotels	323.7	336.0	345.4
Transport, storage and communications	171.4	174.8	179.3
Financing, insurance, real estate and business services	201.9	211.9	228.3
Community, social and personal services	911.6	917.8	929.1
Total	2,423.3	2,480.4	2,558.1

PRINCIPAL TOWNS (population at 1 January 1985)

København (Copenhagen, the capital)	1,358,540*	Horsens	46,586
		Vejle	43,867
Århus (Aarhus)	194,348	Helsingør (Elsinore)	43,581
Odense	136,803		
Ålborg (Aalborg)	113,865	Kolding	41,770
Esbjerg	70,975	Roskilde	39,663
Randers	55,780	Næstved	38,177

* Copenhagen metropolitan area, including Frederiksberg.

BIRTHS, MARRIAGES AND DEATHS

	Registered live births		Registered marriages		Registered deaths	
	Number	Rate (per 1,000)	Number	Rate (per 1,000)	Number	Rate (per 1,000)
1978	62,036	12.2	28,763	5.6	52,864	10.4
1979	59,464	11.6	27,842	5.4	54,654	10.7
1980	57,293	11.2	26,448	5.2	55,939	10.9
1981	53,089	10.4	25,411	5.0	56,359	11.0
1982	52,658	10.3	24,330	4.8	55,368	10.8
1983	50,822	9.9	27,096	5.3	57,156	11.2
1984	51,800	10.1	28,624	5.6	57,109	11.2
1985	53,749	10.5	29,322	5.7	58,378	11.4

Expectation of life at birth: Males 71.5 years; females 77.5 years (1983–84).

Agriculture

PRINCIPAL CROPS ('000 metric tons)

	1983	1984	1985
Wheat	1,548	2,446	1,972
Barley	4,423	6,072	5,251
Rye	315	608	565
Oats	85 }	158	{ 152
Mixed grain	8 }		{ 17
Potatoes	853	1,121	1,100
Pulses	78	285	542
Rapeseed	309	474	543
Sugar beet	2,616	3,614	3,515

LIVESTOCK ('000 head at June-July)

	1983	1984	1985
Horses	33.1	33.2	31.9
Cattle	2,851.6	2,749.9	2,617.7
Pigs	9,253.1	8,717.0	9,089.0
Sheep	52.1	54.8	70.4
Chickens	14,766.2	14,418.8	14,066.9
Turkeys	414.1	339.0	392.8
Ducks	887.7	675.2	703.0
Geese	116.0	70.3	56.4

LIVESTOCK PRODUCTS ('000 metric tons)

	1983	1984	1985
Beef and veal	255.6	263.1	252.1
Pig meat	1,095.5	1,082.9	1,132.0
Poultry meat	112.0	110.8	114.7
Cows' milk	5,427	5,234	4,899
Butter	131.1	104.4	109.7
Cheese	251.4	295.1	255.5
Eggs	80.6	80.1	79.7

Fishing*

('000 metric tons, live weight)

	1982	1983	1984
Trouts	21.1	24.3	22.3
European plaice	36.3	30.5	35.2
Atlantic cod	193.1	185.6	193.4
Haddock	33.9	34.3	24.2
Norway pout	341.4	317.9	275.3
Blue whiting (Poutassou)	58.1	82.8	94.3
Whiting	46.0	32.6	32.8
Sandeels (Sandlances)	544.0	526.8	641.9
Capelin	18.0	—	7.9
Atlantic horse mackerel	7.4	4.0	24.8
Atlantic herring	83.7	173.9	117.5
Sprat (Brisling)	337.7	239.9	162.0
Atlantic mackerel	24.9	35.8	20.5
Other fishes (incl. unspecified)	97.6	92.3	101.1
Total fish	1,843.3	1,780.7	1,753.2
Blue mussel	69.5	66.5	81.5
Other aquatic animals	13.8	15.4	12.0
Total catch	1,926.6	1,862.6	1,846.6
Inland waters	21.6	24.6	22.7
Atlantic Ocean	1,905.0	1,838.0	1,823.9

* Data include quantities landed by Danish fishing craft in foreign ports and exclude quantities landed by foreign fishing craft in Danish ports.

Source: FAO, *Yearbook of Fishery Statistics*.

Mining

('000 metric tons)

	1983	1984	1985
Crude petroleum	2,149	2,219	2,853
Salt (unrefined)	452	523	574
Sulphur*	7	11	7
Limestone flux and calcareous stone	2,169	n.a.	2,058

* Sulphur of all kinds, other than sublimed sulphur, precipitated sulphur and colloidal sulphur.

Industry

SELECTED PRODUCTS

		1982	1983	1984
Pig meat:				
Fresh, chilled or frozen	'000 metric tons	n.a.	552	645
Salted, dried or smoked	'000 metric tons	184	167	167
Poultry meat and offals	'000 metric tons	n.a.	n.a.	109
Fish fillets: fresh, chilled, frozen	'000 metric tons	n.a.	n.a.	99
Salami, sausages, etc	'000 metric tons	67	n.a.	74
Meat in airtight containers:				
Hams	'000 metric tons	60	72	74
Other meat	'000 metric tons	84	86	30
Meat preparations, pâtés, etc	'000 metric tons	36	39	97
Beet and cane sugar (solid)	'000 metric tons	473	405	533
Beer	'000 hectolitres	8,787	8,671	8,286
Flours, meals and pastes of fish	'000 metric tons	336	342	437
Oil cake and meal	'000 metric tons	196	169	136
Cigarettes	million	9,846	10,583	10,966
Cement	'000 metric tons	1,657	1,667	1,983
Motor spirit (Petrol)	'000 metric tons	1,053	1,088	1,175
Motor and fuel oils	'000 metric tons	n.a.	4,721	4,405
Powder asphalt	'000 metric tons	2,581	2,451	2,307
Washing powders, etc	'000 metric tons	187	199	203
Paper and paperboard	'000 metric tons	319	n.a.	n.a.
Refrigerators for household use	'000	n.a.	n.a.	219
New dwellings completed	number	22,152	26,863	22,867
Electric energy	million kWh	20,385	20,830	26,903
Manufactured gas	'000 gigajoules	4,297	4,369	4,043

Finance

CURRENCY AND EXCHANGE RATES

Monetary Units
100 øre = 1 Danish krone (plural: kroner).

Denominations
Coins: 5, 10 and 25 øre; 1, 5 and 10 kroner.
Notes: 20, 50, 100, 500 and 1,000 kroner.

Sterling and Dollar Equivalents (30 September 1986)
£1 sterling = 11.08 kroner;
US $1 = 7.655 kroner;
1,000 Danish kroner = £90.27 = $130.63.

Average Exchange Rate (kroner per US $)
1983   9.145
1984 10.357
1985 10.596

NATIONAL BANK RESERVES (million kroner)

	1983	1984	1985
Gold	6,137	5,661	4,772
IMF special drawing rights	1,227	1,747	1,759
European currency units	4,085	3,234	4,194
Gross foreign assets	27,569	27,189	41,328
Reserve position in IMF	7,351	7,854	6,993
Total official reserves	46,369	45,685	59,046

BUDGET (million kroner)

Revenue	1986*	1987†
Income and property taxes	97,810	101,420
Customs and excise duties	105,327	119,636
Other revenue	} −29,773	} −24,818
Interest (net)		
Total	173,364	196,238

Expenditure	1984*	1985†
Social services	64,213	61,114
Education	15,067	16,527
Defence	11,971	12,938
Public works	1,905	2,706
Agriculture	1,972	2,013
Justice	4,019	4,181
Finance ministry	1,016	1,115
Greenland	2,228	2,292
Other expenditure	85,448	92,554
Total	187,839	195,440

* Approved.   † Estimates.

DENMARK   Statistical Survey

MONEY SUPPLY ('000 million kroner at 31 December)

	1983	1984	1985
Currency outside banks	21.17	26.09	28.65
Demand deposits with commercial banks and savings banks	115.77	135.58	174.96
Savings deposits with commercial banks and savings banks	80.48	97.56	102.87
Short-term government bills outside banks	18.13	18.11	14.75
Total money	235.55	277.33	321.23

COST OF LIVING
(Consumer Price Index. Base: 1980 = 100)

	1983	1984	1985
Food	130	142	148
Fuel and light	146	146	151
Clothing	118	126	134
Rent	130	140	147
All items	131.5	139.8	146.4

NATIONAL ACCOUNTS (million kroner at current prices)
National Income and Product

	1983	1984	1985
Compensation of employees	282,471	305,392	329,840
Operating surplus	108,728	120,439	132,436
Domestic factor incomes	391,200	425,831	462,276
Consumption of fixed capital	46,700	50,400	55,100
Gross domestic product at factor cost	437,900	476,231	517,376
Indirect taxes	91,413	102,358	114,070
Less Subsidies	16,977	18,715	18,577
GDP in purchasers' values	512,336	559,874	612,869
Factor income from abroad	10,415	14,310	17,729
Less Factor income paid abroad	28,842	37,089	42,439
Gross national product	493,908	537,095	588,159
Less Consumption of fixed capital	46,700	50,400	55,100
National income in market prices	447,208	486,695	533,059
Other current transfers from abroad	3,920	7,753	7,232
Less Other current transfers paid abroad	8,859	9,459	11,445
National disposable income	442,269	484,989	528,846

Expenditure on the Gross Domestic Product

	1983	1984	1985
Government final consumption expenditure	140,492	146,198	154,717
Private final consumption expenditure	279,470	305,590	334,567
Increase in stocks	1,000	6,500	6,500
Gross fixed capital formation	81,231	95,556	115,423
Total domestic expenditure	502,193	553,823	611,207
Exports of goods and services	186,282	208,725	226,348
Less Imports of goods and services	176,140	202,674	224,686
GDP in purchasers' values	512,336	559,874	612,869

DENMARK

Gross Domestic Product by Economic Activity (million kroner at current factor cost)

	1983	1984	1985
Agriculture and hunting	21,647	27,794	26,354
Forestry and logging	1,040	956	1,062
Fishing	2,359	2,435	2,515
Mining and quarrying	3,320	4,599	6,826
Manufacturing	85,728	97,697	108,552
Electricity, gas and water	7,665	6,096	6,042
Construction	25,225	26,481	30,864
Wholesale and retail trade	58,317	62,998	71,004
Restaurants and hotels	5,683	6,152	7,122
Transport, storage and communication	36,045	37,849	41,313
Finance and insurance	11,182	14,833	16,184
Owner-occupied dwellings	39,727	44,275	47,137
Business services	20,972	23,475	27,094
Market services of education and health	5,777	6,295	6,659
Recreational and cultural services	4,230	4,362	4,638
Household services (incl. vehicle repairs)	12,182	13,237	13,669
Government services	105,298	109,126	114,128
Other producers	2,749	2,986	3,236
Sub-total	449,147	491,646	534,401
Less Imputed bank service charges	11,247	15,414	17,025
Total	437,900	476,231	517,376

BALANCE OF PAYMENTS (US $ million)

	1983	1984	1985
Merchandise exports f.o.b.	16,210	16,079	17,116
Merchandise imports f.o.b.	−15,974	−16,285	−17,887
Trade balance	236	−206	−771
Exports of services	6,301	6,365	6,975
Imports of services	−7,524	−7,864	−8,798
Balance on goods and services	−988	−1,705	−2,594
Private unrequited transfers (net)	−94	−7	−55
Government unrequited transfers (net)	−94	76	−80
Current balance	−1,176	−1,637	−2,728
Direct capital investment (net)	2,562	1,988	} 4,451
Other long-term capital (net)	567	20	
Short-term capital (net)	567	−20	255
Net errors and omissions	−482	−611	−456
Total (net monetary movements)	1,375	−367	1,522
Valuation changes (net)	−2	−241	888
Official financing (net)	−18	−4	10
Changes in reserves	1,355	−612	2,420

Source: IMF, *International Financial Statistics*.

External Trade

PRINCIPAL COMMODITIES (distribution by SITC, million kroner)

Imports c.i.f.	1983	1984	1985*
Food and live animals	14,862.8	16,430.3	16,663.6
Fish, crustaceans and molluscs	2,768.7	3,281.3	3,818.0
Animal feeding-stuff (excl. cereals)	4,721.2	4,530.1	3,920.9
Oil-cake, etc.	4,105.2	3,798.5	3,258.1
Crude materials (inedible) except fuels	8,342.5	8,340.3	8,273.6
Mineral fuels, lubricants, etc.	29,267.8	31,305.9	33,053.7
Coal, coke and briquettes	3,956.3	4,237.0	5,994.5
Coal, lignite and peat	3,872.0	4,141.3	5,866.9
Coal (not agglomerated)	3,852.8	4,121.7	n.a.
Petroleum, petroleum products, etc	23,963.9	25,863.7	26,248.8
Crude petroleum oils, etc.	10,813.3	11,610.4	10,404.9
Refined petroleum products	12,445.4	13,341.4	14,903.4
Gas oils (distillate fuels)	5,153.7	5,910.5	7,190.6
Chemicals and related products	16,099.9	19,520.9	20,437.1
Artificial resins and plastic materials, etc.	4,928.3	5,931.8	6,328.3
Products of polymerization, etc.	3,461.0	4,191.9	4,425.0
Basic manufactures	29,191.8	35,636.6	36,730.1
Paper, paperboard and manufactures	4,848.4	5,814.7	6,354.6
Textile yarn, fabrics, etc.	5,265.0	6,119.5	6,721.3
Iron and steel	6,715.0	7,743.8	8,569.0
Machinery and transport equipment	33,413.8	41,086.5	50,624.2
Machinery specialized for particular industries	3,990.4	5,130.5	6,771.6
General industrial machinery, equipment and parts	5,334.0	5,938.0	7,126.3
Office machines and automatic data processing equipment	4,325.4	5,704.1	6,583.9
Automatic data processing machines, etc.	2,567.9	3,433.0	3,643.8
Telecommunications and sound equipment	2,444.0	3,219.1	3,710.1
Other electrical machinery, apparatus, etc.	4,937.0	6,205.5	7,209.4
Road vehicles and parts (excl. tyres, engines and electrical parts)	7,906.7	10,530.4	12,393.0
Passenger motor cars (excl. buses)	3,966.1	5,189.0	5,895.1
Miscellaneous manufactured articles	13,628.8	16,777.5	19,471.1
Clothing and accessories (excl. footwear)	3,548.5	4,386.7	5,320.9
Total (incl. others)	148,896.5	171,825.8	191,371.0

* Provisional figures.

DENMARK   Statistical Survey

Exports f.o.b.	1983	1984	1985*
Food and live animals	41,210.3	45,961.2	48,055.2
Meat and meat preparations	18,272.2	19,758.9	20,545.5
Fresh, chilled or frozen meat	10,092.9	10,888.2	11,615.9
Pig meat	6,000.3	6,906.6	7,831.2
Salted, dried or smoked meat	3,608.5	3,550.7	3,243.8
Other prepared or preserved meat	4,570.8	5,320.0	5,685.7
Dairy products and birds' eggs	7,257.5	7,656.9	7,359.0
Cheese and curd	3,563.5	4,080.2	3,873.6
Fish, crustaceans and molluscs	7,112.1	7,886.8	8,921.7
Fresh, chilled or frozen fish	4,063.8	4,470.3	4,848.9
Cereals and cereal preparations	2,853.3	4,181.9	4,497.1
Crude materials (inedible) except fuels	9,833.6	9,935.2	11,507.5
Hides, skins and furskins	3,792.7	3,256.3	3,630.7
Mineral fuels, lubricants, etc.	7,289.8	8,540.5	9,643.0
Petroleum, petroleum products, etc.	6,371.0	7,689.7	8,174.5
Refined petroleum products	3,954.5	5,615.2	5,580.7
Chemicals and related products	12,701.5	14,954.9	16,011.3
Medicinal and pharmaceutical products	4,024.2	4,706.8	5,276.1
Medicaments (incl. veterinary medicaments)	2,758.4	3,181.3	3,649.6
Basic manufactures	18,028.3	20,388.5	19,464.9
Textile yarn, fabrics, etc.	3,217.3	3,726.7	3,887.6
Machinery and transport equipment	34,816.1	37,774.3	43,480.1
Power generating machinery and equipment	2,429.9	3,506.8	4,257.3
Machinery specialized for particular industries	5,518.2	5,990.2	6,839.6
General industrial machinery, equipment and parts	9,796.4	11,106.0	12,203.7
Electrical machinery, apparatus, etc.	6,959.9	8,129.0	9,121.7
Transport equipment	8,371.7	7,102.0	8,432.5
Ships, boats and floating structures	5,777.4	4,070.4	5,252.2
Miscellaneous manufactured articles	19,551.9	23,980.3	26,870.5
Furniture and parts	4,597.7	5,991.3	6,668.5
Clothing and accessories (excl. footwear)	3,489.0	4,373.0	4,961.6
Professional, scientific and controlling instruments, etc.	2,953.8	3,520.1	3,845.1
Total (incl. others)	146,800.3	165,346.4	179,338.9

* Provisional figures.

PRINCIPAL TRADING PARTNERS* (million kroner)

Imports c.i.f.	1983	1984	1985
Austria	1,500.6	1,784.0	2,021.0
Belgium/Luxembourg	4,808.1	5,051.7	6,364.5
Brazil	1,702.0	2,324.6	2,435.2
Finland	6,053.6	6,013.3	6,342.7
France (incl. Monaco)	6,699.6	7,655.8	8,534.4
German Dem. Rep.	1,581.7	1,875.1	1,896.8
Germany, Fed. Rep.	29,701.2	35,002.1	40,354.7
Italy	5,187.0	6,181.3	6,836.4
Japan	5,376.3	6,705.3	7,728.6
Kuwait	2,255.7	3,364.2	3,127.7
Netherlands	8,816.8	9,208.2	10,000.3
Norway	6,135.8	7,066.9	7,720.5
Poland	1,012.0	1,864.0	1,818.3
Spain (excl. Canary Is)	1,290.6	1,703.8	1,950.8
Sweden	19,634.0	23,944.7	24,979.0
Switzerland	2,759.5	3,176.1	3,590.0
USSR	2,531.6	3,424.1	3,012.9
United Kingdom	15,829.4	15,458.6	17,898.6
USA	8,019.8	8,930.3	11,365.6
Total (incl. others)	148,896.5	171,825.8	191,371.0

Exports f.o.b.	1983	1984	1985
Belgium/Luxembourg	2,616.0	2,803.5	3,245.9
Canada	1,063.8	1,545.2	1,788.6
Finland	2,942.7	3,230.8	3,699.2
France (incl. Monaco)	8,079.0	7,317.2	7,941.9
Germany, Fed. Rep.	25,354.1	26,644.4	28,418.7
Greenland	1,791.4	2,189.2	2,233.0
Italy	6,487.5	6,450.6	7,121.4
Japan	2,705.0	4,696.6	5,527.7
Netherlands	5,947.7	5,545.3	6,512.9
Norway	9,379.8	10,515.9	12,066.8
Panama	250.2	310.7	1,733.7
Saudi Arabia	2,315.1	1,639.4	1,384.3
Sweden	15,410.6	18,874.4	21,668.8
Switzerland	2,957.4	3,067.6	3,413.0
United Kingdom	19,785.9	21,228.4	21,881.8
USA	10,694.4	15,914.5	18,147.6
Total (incl. others)	146,800.3	165,346.4	179,338.9

* Imports by country of production; exports by country of consumption.

DENMARK

Transport

RAILWAYS ('000)

	Private railways 1984	State railways 1983	State railways 1984
Number of journeys	11,181	132,972	133,974
Passenger-kilometres	197,130	4,391,000	4,420,900
Ton-kilometres	11,696	1,621,000	1,658,000

ROAD TRAFFIC (motor vehicles in use at 31 December)

	1983	1984	1985
Private cars	1,376,877	1,426,078	1,486,155
Taxis, hire cars, etc.	13,462	13,915	14,791
Buses, coaches	7,762	7,836	8,010
Vans, lorries	236,633	244,881	259,397
Tractors	144,015	143,308	143,570
Trailers	174,432	197,117	221,781
Motor cycles	38,637	40,238	41,395

CIVIL AVIATION (Scandinavian Airlines System)

	1983	1984
Kilometres flown ('000)	121,230.3	123,856.4
Passengers carried ('000)	9,367.6	10,250.7
Passenger-kilometres (million)	11,332.0	11,789.2
Cargo and mail carried ('000 metric tons)	150.2	155.0
Cargo and mail tonne-kilometres (million)	438.9	451.7

SHIPPING
Danish Merchant Marine
(vessels above 20 gross registered tons, at 31 December)

	1984 Number	1984 Gross tonnage	1985 Number	1985 Gross tonnage
Steamers	16	1,520,681	14	1,202,914
Motor vessels	2,816*	3,728,640	2,790	3,717,131
Total	2,832	5,249,321	2,804	4,913,045

* Including four sailing-ships, displacement (1984) 180 grt.

Sea-borne Freight Traffic at Danish Ports*
('000 metric tons loaded and unloaded)

	1983	1984	1985
Aalborg	4,874	4,939	5,087
Copenhagen	6,240	6,973	6,790
Fredericia	6,197	6,089	6,637
Kalundborg	6,203	5,961	6,669
Skaelskør	4,676	5,692	5,449
Others	26,825	26,181	31,584
Total	55,015	55,835	62,216

* Excluding international ferry traffic.
Source: *Danmarks skibe og skibsfart*.

International Sea-borne Shipping
(Freight traffic in '000 metric tons)

	1983	1984	1985
Goods loaded	8,947	11,074	11,007
Goods unloaded	29,846	31,056	33,324

* Excluding international ferry traffic.
Source: *Danmarks skibe og skibsfart*.

Tourism

(income from visitors, million kroner)

	1983	1984	1985
Scandinavian visitors	3,633	4,314	4,849
German visitors	3,564	3,478	3,333
All other visitors	4,755	5,592	5,869
Total	11,952	13,384	14,051

OVERNIGHT STAYS (foreign visitors)

	1983	1984	1985
In hotels	4,501,200	4,608,300	4,590,800
At camping sites	4,670,200	4,126,700	3,986,300
Total	9,171,400	8,735,000	8,577,100

Communications Media

	1983	1984	1985
Radio licences*	115,896	123,451	174,000
Television licences (black and white)	463,960	416,812	383,000
Television licences (colour)	1,425,337	1,477,417	162,200
Telephone subscribers	2,403,245	n.a.	n.a.
Number of newspapers	47	47	47
Total circulation (weekdays)	1,805,000	1,837,000	1,855,000
Books published	9,460	10,660	9,554

* Radios only, excluding combined radio and television licences.

Education

(1985/86)

	Institutions	Teachers	Students
Primary and secondary schools	2,422	74,095	782,650
Universities	5	2,984*	54,375

* January 1984, excluding part-time teachers.
Source: Economical and Statistical Division of the Danish Ministry of Education.

Directory

The Constitution

The constitutional charter (*Grundlov*), summarized below, was adopted on 5 June 1953.

GOVERNMENT

The form of government is a limited (constitutional) monarchy. The legislative authority rests jointly with the Crown and Parliament. Executive power is vested in the Crown, and the administration of justice is exercised by the courts. The Monarch can constitutionally 'do no wrong'. She exercises her authority through the Ministers appointed by her. The Ministers are responsible for the government of the country. The Constitution establishes the principle of Parliamentarism under which individual Ministers or the whole Cabinet must retire when defeated in Parliament by a vote of no confidence.

MONARCH

The Monarch acts on behalf of the State in international affairs. Except with the consent of the Parliament, she cannot, however, take any action which increases or reduces the area of the Realm or undertake any obligation, the fulfilment of which requires the co-operation of the Parliament or which is of major importance. Nor can the Monarch, without the consent of the Parliament, terminate any international agreement which has been concluded with the consent of the Parliament.

Apart from defence against armed attack on the Realm or on Danish forces, the Monarch cannot, without the consent of the Parliament, employ military force against any foreign power.

PARLIAMENT

The Parliament is an assembly consisting of not more than 179 members, two of whom are elected in the Faeroe Islands and two in Greenland. It is called the Folketing. Danish nationals, having attained 18 years of age, with permanent residence in Denmark, have the franchise and are eligible for election. The members of the Folketing are elected for four years. Election is by a system of proportional representation, with direct and secret ballot on lists in large constituencies. A bill adopted by the Folketing may be submitted to referendum, when such referendum is claimed by not less than one-third of the members of the Folketing and not later than three days after the adoption. The bill is void if rejected by a majority of the votes cast, representing not less than 30% of all electors.

The Government

HEAD OF STATE

Queen of Denmark: HM Queen Margrethe II (succeeded to the throne 14 January 1972).

THE CABINET
(December 1986)

A coalition of the Conservative People's Party (KF), the Liberal Party (V), Centre Democrats (CD) and the Christian People's Party (KRF).

Prime Minister: Poul Schlüter (KF).
Minister of Finance: Palle Simonsen (KF).
Minister of Foreign Affairs: Uffe Ellemann-Jensen (V).
Minister of Labour: Henning Dyremose (KF).
Minister of Housing and Building: Thor Pedersen (V).
Minister of Energy: Svend Erik Hovmand (V).
Minister of Fisheries: Lars Gammelgaard (KF).
Minister of Defence: Hans Engell (KF).
Minister of the Interior: Knud Enggaard (V).
Minister of Justice: Eric Ninn-Hansen (KF).
Minister of Industry: Nils Wilhjelm (KF).
Minister of Economic Affairs: Anders Andersen (V).
Minister of Inland Revenue: Isi Foighel (KF).
Minister for Ecclesiastical Affairs: Mette Madsen (V).
Minister for Cultural Affairs: Hans Peter Clausen (KF).
Minister of Agriculture: Britta Schall-Holberg (V).
Minister of the Environment and for Nordic Affairs: Christian Christiansen (KRF).
Minister for Greenland: Tom Høyem (CD).
Minister for Social Affairs: Mimi Stilling Jakobsen (CD).
Minister of Transport and Public Works: Frode Noer Christiansen (CD).
Minister of Education: Bertel Haarder (V).

MINISTRIES

Office of the Prime Minister: Christiansborg, Prins Jørgens Gaard 11, 1218 Copenhagen K; tel. (01) 11-30-38; telex 27027.
Ministry of Agriculture: Slotsholmsgade 10, 1216 Copenhagen K; tel. (01) 12-37-17; telex 27157.
Ministry of Cultural Affairs: Nybrogade 2, 1203 Copenhagen K; tel. (01) 13-93-01; telex 27385.
Ministry of Defence: Slotsholmsgade 10, 1216 Copenhagen K; tel. (01) 11-62-60.
Ministry of Ecclesiastical Affairs: Frederiksholms Kanal 21, 1220 Copenhagen K; tel. (01) 14-62-63.
Ministry of Economic Affairs: Slotsholmsgade 12, 1216 Copenhagen K; tel. (01) 11-62-11; telex 16833.
Ministry of Education: Frederiksholms Kanal 21-25, 1220 Copenhagen K; tel. (01) 92-50-00.
Ministry of Energy: Slotsholmsgade 1, 1216 Copenhagen K; tel. (01) 92-75-00; telex 15505.
Ministry of the Environment: Slotsholmsgade 12, 1216 Copenhagen K; tel. (01) 12-76-88; telex 31209.
Ministry of Finance: Christiansborg Slotsplads 1, 1218 Copenhagen K; tel. (01) 11-44-88; telex 16140.
Ministry of Fisheries: Stormgade 2, 1470 Copenhagen K; tel. (01) 92-65-00; telex 16144.
Ministry of Foreign Affairs: Asiatisk Plads 2, 1448 Copenhagen K; tel. (01) 92-00-00; telex 31292.
Ministry for Greenland: Hausergade 3, 1128 Copenhagen K; tel. (01) 13-68-25; telex 27125.
Ministry of Housing and Building: Slotsholmsgade 12, 1216 Copenhagen K; tel. (01) 92-61-00; telex 31401.
Ministry of Industry: Slotsholmsgade 12, 1216 Copenhagen K; tel. (01) 12-11-97; telex 22373.
Ministry of Inland Revenue: Slotsholmsgade 12, 1216 Copenhagen K; tel. (01) 12-53-20; telex 16939.
Ministry of the Interior: Christiansborg Slotsplads 1, 1218 Copenhagen K; tel. (01) 11-69-00; telex 16140.
Ministry of Justice: Slotsholmsgade 10, 1216 Copenhagen K; tel. (01) 12-09-06; telex 15530.
Ministry of Labour: Laksegade 19, 1063 Copenhagen K; tel. (01) 92-59-00; telex 19320.
Ministry of Social Affairs: Slotsholmsgade 6, 1216 Copenhagen K; tel. (01) 12-25-17; telex 27343.
Ministry of Transport and Public Works: Frederiksholms Kanal 25-27, 1220 Copenhagen K; tel. (01) 12-62-42; telex 22275.

Legislature

FOLKETING

President of the Folketing: Svend Jakobsen.
Secretary-General: Helge Hjortdal.
Clerk of the Folketing: L. E. Hansen-Salby.

DENMARK

General Election, 10 January 1984
(metropolitan Denmark only)

	Votes	%	Seats
Social Democrats	1,062,602	31.38	56
Conservative People's Party	788,225	23.27	42
Liberals	405,722	11.98	22
Socialist People's Party	387,115	11.43	21
Radical Liberals	184,634	5.45	10
Centre Democrats	154,557	4.56	8
Progress Party	120,631	3.56	6
Christian People's Party	91,633	2.71	5
Left Socialists	89,359	2.64	5
Others	102,255	3.02	—
Total	3,386,733	100.00	175

The Folketing also contains two members from Greenland and two from the Faeroe Islands.

Political Organizations

Centrum-Demokraterne (Centre Democrats): Folketinget, Christiansborg, 1218 Copenhagen K; tel. (01) 11-66-00; f. 1973; opposes extreme ideologies, supports EEC and NATO; Leader ERHARD JACOBSEN, Sec.-Gen. YVONNE HERLØV ANDERSEN.

Danmarks Kommunistiske Parti (Danish Communist Party): Dr Tværgade 3, 1302 Copenhagen K; f. 1919; Chair. JØRGEN JENSEN.

Danmarks Retsforbund (Justice Party): Lyngbyvej 42, 2100 Copenhagen Ø; tel. (01) 20-44-88; f. 1919; programme is closely allied to Henry George's teachings (single tax, free trade); Chair. POUL GERHARD C. KRISTIANSEN.

Europæiske Centrum-Demokrater (European Centre Democrats): Christiansborg, 1218 Copenhagen K; tel. (01) 11-66-00; f. 1974; supports co-operation within EEC and provides information about the workings of the EEC; Chair. ERHARD JACOBSEN.

Fremskridtspartiet (Progress Party): Folketinget, Christiansborg, 1218 Copenhagen K; tel. (01) 11-66-00; telex 19461; f. 1972; movement whose policies include gradual abolition of income tax, disbandment of most of the civil service, and abolition of diplomatic service and about 90% of legislation; Chair. P. S. HANSEN.

Konservative Folkeparti (Conservative People's Party): Tordenskjoldsgade 21, 1055 Copenhagen K; tel. (01) 13-41-40; f. 1916; advocates free initiative and the maintenance of private property, but recognizes the right of the State to take action to keep the economic and social balance; Chair. POUL SCHLÜTER; Sec.-Gen. TORBEN RECHENDORFF.

Kristeligt Folkeparti (Christian People's Party): Skindergade 24, 1159 Copenhagen K; tel. (01) 11-31-60; telex 19306; f. 1970; interdenominational grouping opposed to pornography and abortion; favours social-liberal economic policy, and emphasizes significance of cultural and family policy; Chair. FLEMMING KOFOD-SVENDSEN; Sec.-Gen. CARSTEN LARSEN.

Det Radikale Venstre (Danish Social-Liberal Party): Det Radikale Venstres sekretariat, Christiansborg, 1240 Copenhagen K; tel. (01) 12-72-51; telex 16485; f. 1905; supports international détente and co-operation within regional and world organizations, social reforms without socialism, incomes policy, workers' participation in industry, state intervention in industrial disputes, state control of trusts and monopolies, strengthening private enterprise; Chair. THORKILD MØLLER; Leader NIELS HELVEG PETERSEN; Gen. Sec. JENS CLAUSAGER.

Socialdemokratiet (Social-Democratic Party): Thorvaldsensvej 2, 1998 Frederiksberg C; tel. (01) 39-15-22; telex 22309; f. 1871; finds its chief adherents among workers, employees and public servants; 100,000 members; Chair. ANKER JØRGENSEN; Gen. Sec. STEEN CHRISTENSEN.

Socialistisk Folkeparti (Socialist People's Party): Folketinget, Christiansborg, 1218 Copenhagen K; tel. (01) 12-70-11; telex 1458; f. 1958, with socialist aims, by Aksel Larsen; Chair. GERT PETERSEN; Sec. LILLIAN UBBESEN.

Venstre (Liberal Party): Søllerødvej 30, 2840 Holte; tel. (02) 80-22-33; telex 37783; f. 1870; supports free trade, a minimum of state interference, and the adoption, in matters of social expenditure, of a modern general social security system; Chair. UFFE ELLEMANN-JENSEN; Sec.-Gen. CLAUS HJORT FREDERIKSEN.

Venstresocialisterne (Left Socialist Party): Rosenørns Allé 44, 1970 Copenhagen F.C.; tel. (01) 35-60-99; f. 1967 as a result of a split from the Socialist People's Party; collective leadership.

Diplomatic Representation

EMBASSIES IN DENMARK

Argentina: Store Kongensgade 45, 1264 Copenhagen K; tel. (01) 15-80-82; telex 27182; Ambassador: Mrs RUTH GUEVARA ACHÁVAL.

Australia: Kristianiagade 21, 2100 Copenhagen Ø; tel. (01) 26-22-44; telex 22308; Ambassador: ANTHONY F. DINGLE.

Austria: Grønningen 5, 1270 Copenhagen K; tel. (01) 12-46-23; telex 27023; Ambassador: Dr GERHARD GMOSER.

Belgium: Øster Allé 7, 2100 Copenhagen Ø; tel. (01) 26-03-88; telex 22624; Ambassador: GILBERT LOQUET.

Brazil: Ryvangs Allé 24, 2100 Copenhagen Ø; tel. (01) 20-64-78; telex 19322; Ambassador: WLADIMIR MURTINHO.

Bulgaria: A. N. Hansens Allé 5, 2900 Hellerup; tel. (01) 62-11-20; telex 27020; Ambassador: IVAN SPASSOV (designate).

Burkina Faso: Svanemøllevej 20, 2100 Copenhagen Ø; tel. (01) 18-40-22; telex 19375; Ambassador: NONGOMA BRUNO ZIDOUEMBA.

Canada: Kr. Bernikowsgade 1, 1105 Copenhagen K; tel. (01) 12-22-99; telex 27036; Ambassador: DOROTHY J. ARMSTRONG.

Chile: Kastelsvej 15^3, 2100 Copenhagen Ø; tel. (01) 38-58-34; telex 15099; Chargé d'affaires: JAIME LAGOS ERAZO.

China, People's Republic: Øregårds Allé 25, 2900 Hellerup; tel. (01) 62-58-06; Ambassador: CHEN LUZHI.

Colombia: Esplanaden 7, 1263 Copenhagen K; tel. (01) 11-26-03; telex 22691; Ambassador Dr PEDRO LÓPEZ MICHELSEN.

Cuba: Dag Hammarskjölds Allé 42^2, 2100 Copenhagen Ø; tel. (01) 42-05-15; telex 16852; Ambassador: Mme MARTA JIMÉNEZ MARTÍNEZ.

Czechoslovakia: Ryvangs Allé 14, 2100 Copenhagen Ø; tel. (01) 29-18-88; telex 27112; Ambassador: ALOJZ KUSALÍK.

Egypt: Nyropsgade 47, 1602 Copenhagen V; tel.(01) 12-76-41/42; telex 19892; Ambassador: MAMDOUH ZAKI ABDEL-SALAM.

Finland: Hammerensgade 5, 1267 Copenhagen K; tel. (01) 13-42-14; telex 27084; Ambassador: EVA-CHRISTINA MÄKELÄINEN.

France: Kongens Nytorv 4, 1050 Copenhagen K; tel. (01) 15-51-22; telex 27029; Ambassador: LÉON BOUVIER.

German Democratic Republic: Svanemøllevej 48, 2100 Copenhagen Ø; tel. (01) 29-22-77; telex 19677; Ambassador: NORBERT JAESCHKE.

Germany, Federal Republic: Stockholmsgade 57, 2100 Copenhagen Ø; tel. (01) 26-16-22; telex 27166; Ambassador: Dr HELMUT REDIES.

Ghana: Egebjerg Allé 13, 2900 Hellerup; tel. (01) 62-82-22; Ambassador: BENJAMIN SAM.

Greece: Borgergade 16, 1300 Copenhagen K; tel. (01) 11-45-33; telex 27279; Ambassador: DIMITRI MANOLATOS.

Holy See: Immortellevej 11, 2950 Vedbæk; tel. (02) 89-35-36; Apostolic Pro-Nuncio: Mgr HENRI LEMAÎTRE.

Hungary: Strandvejen 170, 2920 Charlottenlund; tel. (01) 63-16-88; telex 27186; Ambassador: Mme PIROSKA KIRÁLY.

Iceland: Dantes Plads 3, 1556 Copenhagen V; tel. (01) 15-96-04; telex 15954; Ambassador: HÖRDUR HELGASON.

India: Vangehusvej 15, 2100 Copenhagen Ø; tel. (01) 18-28-88; telex 15964; Ambassador: RAMESH CHANDRA SHUKLA.

Indonesia: Ørehøj Allé 1, 2900 Hellerup; tel. (01) 62-44-22; Ambassador: SUTADI SUKARYA.

Iran: Grønningen 5, 1270 Copenhagen K; tel. (01) 14-12-38; Ambassador: HEIDAR ALI ALIZADEH ELYSEIE.

Ireland: Østbanegade 21, 2100 Copenhagen Ø; tel. (01) 42-32-33; telex 22995; Ambassador: LIAM RIGNEY.

Israel: Lundevangsvej 4, 2900 Hellerup; tel. (01) 62-62-88; telex 23136; Ambassador: SHAMAY CAHANA.

Italy: Vordingborggade 18-22, 2100 Copenhagen Ø; tel. (01) 26-04-00; telex 27078; Ambassador: ALESSANDRO CORTESE DE BOSIS.

Ivory Coast: Gersonsvej 8, 2900 Hellerup; tel. (01) 62-88-22; telex 22351; Ambassador: EMILE ZOHORÉ BLÉHOUAN.

Japan: Oslo Plads 14, 2100 Copenhagen Ø; tel. (01) 26-33-11; telex 27082; Ambassador: MICHIO MIZOGUCHI.

DENMARK

Korea, Democratic People's Republic: Skelvej 2, 2900 Hellerup; tel. (01) 62-50-70; Ambassador: TAK KWAN CHOL.

Korea, Republic: Dronningens Tværgade 8, 1302 Copenhagen K; tel. (01) 14-31-23; Ambassador: MIN-GIL CHUNG.

Lesotho: Østerkildevej 14, 2820 Gentofte; tel. (01) 65-14-42; telex 16687; Ambassador: (vacant).

Libya: Rosenvængets Hovedvej 4, 2100 Copenhagen Ø (People's Bureau); tel. (01) 26-36-11; telex 22652; Chargé d'affaires: El Hadj OMAR EL-HERIK.

Mexico: Gammel Vartov Vej 18, 2900 Hellerup; tel. (01) 20-86-00; telex 27503; Ambassador: SERGIO MOTA MARÍN.

Morocco: Øregårds Allé 19, 2900 Hellerup; tel. (01) 62-45-11; telex 22913; Ambassador: OMAR BELKORA.

Netherlands: Toldbogade 95, 1253 Copenhagen K; tel. (01) 15-62-93; telex 27093; Ambassador: EDUARD BEELAERTS VAN BLOKLAND.

Norway: Trondhjems Plads 4, 2100 Copenhagen Ø; tel. (01) 38-89-85; telex 27114; Ambassador: OLE ÅLGÅRD.

Pakistan: Valeursvej 17, 2900 Hellerup; tel. (01) 62-11-88; Chargé d'affaires: QAZI HUMAYUN.

Peru: Rosenvængets Allé 20, 2100 Copenhagen Ø; tel. (01) 38-38-75; Chargé d'affaires a.i.: CLAUDIO DE LA PUENTE RIBEYRO.

Poland: Richelieus Allé 12, 2900 Hellerup; tel. (01) 62-72-44/46; telex 19264; Ambassador: LUCJAN PIATKOWSKI.

Portugal: Hovedvagtsgade 6, Mezz., 1103 Copenhagen K; tel. (01) 13-13-01; telex 16586; Ambassador: ANTÓNIO CASCAIS.

Romania: Strandagervej 27, 2900 Hellerup; tel. (01) 62-42-04; telex 27017; Ambassador: Mrs CORNELIA FILIPAȘ.

Saudi Arabia: Lille Strandvej 27, 2900 Hellerup; tel. (01) 62-12-00; telex 15931; Ambassador: Sheikh FUAD SAFWAT HUSSEINI.

Spain: Upsalagade 26, 2100 Copenhagen Ø; tel. (01) 42-47-00; telex 27145; Ambassador: MARIANO UCELAY.

Sweden: Skt. Annæ Plads 15A, 1250 Copenhagen K; tel. (01) 14-22-42; telex 22960; Ambassador: CARL DE GEER.

Switzerland: Amaliegade 14, 1256 Copenhagen K; tel. (01) 14-17-96; telex 16239; Ambassador: CHARLES BRUGGMANN.

Thailand: Norgesmindevej 18, 2900 Hellerup; tel. (01) 62-50-10; Ambassador: SATHIT SATHIRATHAYA.

Turkey: Vestagervej 16, 2100 Copenhagen Ø; tel. (01) 20-55-00; telex 27476; Ambassador: TANER BAYTOK.

Uganda: Sofievej 15, 2900 Hellerup; tel. (01) 62-05-40; telex 15689; Ambassador: Mrs EDITH GRACE SSEMPALA.

USSR: Kristianiagade 5, 2100 Copenhagen Ø; tel. (01) 42-55-85; Ambassador: BORIS NIKOLAYEVICH PASTUKHOV.

United Kingdom: Kastelsvej 40, 2100 Copenhagen Ø; tel. (01) 26-46-00; telex 27106; Ambassador: PETER W. UNWIN.

USA: Dag Hammarskjölds Allé 24, 2100 Copenhagen Ø; tel. (01) 42-31-44; telex 22216; Ambassador: TERENCE A. TODMAN.

Venezuela: Strandvejen 735, 2930 Klampenborg; tel. (01) 63-69-58; telex 15309; Ambassador: Dr EDUARDO MORREO BUSTAMANTE (designate).

Yugoslavia: Svaneænget 36, 2100 Copenhagen Ø; tel. (01) 29-71-61; Ambassador: Mrs ANA JOVANOVIĆ.

Judicial System

In Denmark the judiciary is independent of the Government. Judges are appointed by the Crown on the recommendation of the Minister of Justice and cannot be dismissed except by judicial sentence.

The ordinary courts are divided into three instances, the Lower Courts, the High Courts and the Supreme Court. There is one Lower Court for each of the 84 judicial districts in the country. These courts must have at least one judge trained in law and they hear the majority of minor cases. The two High Courts serve Jutland and the islands respectively. They serve as appeal courts for cases from the lower courts, but are also used to give first hearing to the more important cases. Each case must be heard by at least three judges. The Supreme Court, at which at least five judges must sit, is the court of appeal for cases from the Higher Courts. Usually only one appeal is allowed from either court, but in special instances the Minister of Justice may give leave for a second appeal, to the Supreme Court, from a case which started in a lower court.

There is a special Maritime and Commercial Court in Copenhagen, consisting of a President and two Vice-Presidents with legal training and a number of commercial and nautical assessors; and also a Labour Court, which deals with labour disputes.

An Ombudsman is appointed by Parliament, after each general election, and is concerned with defects in the laws or administrative provisions. He must present an annual report to Parliament.

President of the Supreme Court: P. M. CHRISTENSEN.
President of the East High Court: K. HAULRIG.
President of the West High Court: O. AGERSNAP.
President of the Maritime and Commercial Court: EMIL FRANK POULSEN.
President of the Labour Court: P. HØEG.
Ombudsman: N. EILSCHOU HOLM.

Religion

CHRISTIANITY

The Protestant Churches

Den evangelisk-lutherske Folkekirke i Danmark (Danish Lutheran Church): Nørregade 11, 1165 Copenhagen K; tel. (01) 13-35-08; telex 16217; the established Church of Denmark, supported by the State; membership is 4,750,000 people (93% of the population).

Bishop of Copenhagen: OLE BERTELSEN.
Bishop of Helsingør: JOHS JOHANSEN.
Bishop of Roskilde: B. WIBERG.
Bishop of Nykøbing: TH. GRAESHOLT.
Bishop of Odense: V. LIND.
Bishop of Ålborg: HENRIK CHRISTIANSEN.
Bishop of Viborg: GEORG S. GEIL.
Bishop of Århus: H. ERIKSEN.
Bishop of Ribe: H. SKOV.
Bishop of Haderslev: O. LINDEGAARD.

Church of Jesus Christ of Latter-day Saints (Mormons): Informationstjenesten, Annexgårdsvej 37, 2610 Rødovre; tel. (01) 70-90-43; f. (in Denmark) 1850; 4,500 mems.

Det Danske Baptistsamfund (Baptist Union of Denmark): Köbnerhus, Lärdalsgade 5.1, 2300 Copenhagen S; tel. (01) 59-07-08; f. 1839; 6,400 mems; Pres. Rev. OLE JOERGENSEN; Gen. Sec. Rev. GUNNAR KRISTENSEN.

First Church of Christ Scientist: Nyvej 7, 1851 Frederiksberg C; also in Århus.

German Lutheran Church: Sankt Petri Church, Nørregade, Copenhagen; Hauptpastorat: Larslejsstræde 11, 1451 Copenhagen K; tel. (01) 13-38-34.

Methodist Church: Centralmissionen, Stokhusgade 2, 1317 Copenhagen K; tel. (01) 15-25-96.

Moravian Brethren: The Brethren Community, 6070 Christiansfeld.

Norwegian Lutheran Church: Kong Haakons Kirke, Ved Mønten 9, 2300 Copenhagen S; tel. (01) 57-11-03.

Reformed Church: Reformed Synod of Denmark, Dronningensgade 51, 7000 Fredericia; Rev. WALTER EBLING KAISER.

Seventh-day Adventists: Adventistsamfundet, Concordiavej 16, 2850 Nærum; tel. (02) 80-56-00.

Society of Friends: Danish Quaker Centre, Vendersgade 29, 1363 Copenhagen K; tel. (01) 11-82-48.

Swedish Lutheran Church: Svenska Gustafskyrkan, Folke Bernadottes Allé, 2100 Copenhagen Ø; tel. (01) 15-54-58; also V. Strandvej 24, 9990 Skagen; tel. (08) 44-23-11.

Unitarians: Unitarernes Hus, Dag Hammarskjölds Allé 30, 2100 Copenhagen Ø; Chair. P. BOVIN; mems: 100 families.

The Roman Catholic Church

Denmark comprises a single diocese, directly responsible to the Holy See. At 31 December 1984 there were an estimated 27,387 adherents in the country. The Bishop participates in the Scandinavian Episcopal Conference (based in Norway).

Bishop of Copenhagen: HANS LUDVIG MARTENSEN, Katolsk Bispekontor, Bredgade 69A, 1260 Copenhagen K; tel. (01) 11-60-80.

Other Christian Churches

Church of England: St Alban's House, Stigårdsvej 6, 2900 Hellerup; f. 1728; Chaplain Rev. KENNETH POVEY.

Russian Orthodox Church: Alexander Nevski Church, Bredgade 53, 1260 Copenhagen K.

DENMARK

BAHÁ'Í FAITH

Bahá'í: Det Nationale Åndelige Råd, Sofievej 28, 2900 Hellerup; tel. (01) 62-35-18; National Centre for the Bahá'í faith in Denmark.

ISLAM

The Muslim Community: Nusrat Djahan Mosque (and Ahmadiyya Mission), Eriksmunde Allé 2, 2650 Hvidovre, Copenhagen; tel. (01) 75-35-02; telex 16600.

JUDAISM

Jewish Community: The Synagogue, Krystalgade 12, Copenhagen; Mosaisk Trossamfund, Ny Kongensgade 6, 1472 Copenhagen K; tel. (01) 12-88-68; 8,000 mems; Chief Rabbi BENT MELCHIOR.

The Press

Denmark's long press history dates from the first newspaper published in 1666, but it was not until press freedom was introduced by law in 1849 that newspapers began to assume their present importance. The per caput circulation of Danish newspapers is one of the highest in the world. There are over 220 separate newpapers, and over 40 main dailies.

The freedom of the press is embodied in the 1953 Constitution and all censorship laws have been abolished. The legal limits to press comment are wide, legislation on defamation being chiefly concerned to protect the reputation of the individual. The Law of 1938 included provision for a Board of Denials and Corrections to be established to guard the individual's right to require a newspaper to correct factual errors. This Press Law makes editors legally responsible for the contents of a paper with the exception of signed articles for which the author is responsible.

Most newspapers and magazines are privately owned and published by joint concerns, co-operatives or limited liability companies. The main concentration of papers is held by the Berlingske Tidende Group which owns *Berlingske Tidende, Weekendavisen, B.T.*, the provincial *Jydske Tidende* and three weekly magazines. Another company, Politiken A/S, owns several dailies, including *Politiken, Ekstra Bladet* and *Roskilde Tidende*, one weekly and a large publishing house. De Bergske Blade owns a group of six Liberal papers.

There is no truly national press. Copenhagen accounts for 16% of the national dailies and about half the total circulation. The provincial press has declined since the last war, but still tends to be more politically orientated than the majority of Copenhagen dailies. The Communist Party's *Land og Folk* is the only paper to be directly owned by a political party, although all papers show a fairly pronounced political leaning. The three Social Democrat papers, headed by Copenhagen's *Aktuelt*, are owned and subsidized by the trade unions.

The major Copenhagen dailies are *Berlingske Tidende, Ekstra Bladet, B.T., Politiken* and *Aktuelt*. The serious evening paper *Information* and the weekly *Weekendavisen* are also influential. The *Aalborg Stiftstidende* and *Fyens Stiftstidende*, published at Odense, are the largest provincial papers.

PRINCIPAL DAILIES

Ålborg

Aalborg Stiftstidende: Nytorv 7, 9100 Aalborg; tel. 12-58-00; telex 69747; f. 1767; weekday evenings; Saturday and Sunday mornings; independent Liberal; Publisher and Chief Editor ERLING BRØNDUM; approx. circ. weekdays 72,000, Sundays 103,000.

Århus

Aarhuus Stiftstidende: Kannikegade 14, Århus; tel. (06) 12-40-00; telex 64321; f. 1794; evening; independent Liberal; Editors PAGE HOLM-PEDERSEND, AAGE LUNDGAARD; circ. 71,000 weekdays, 90,000 Sundays.

Jyllands-Posten: 8260 Viby J; tel. (06) 14-66-77; telex 68747; f. 1871; morning; independent; Man. Chief Editors A. N. LARSEN, N. THOSTRUP, T. TOLSTRUP; circ. weekdays 125,000, Sundays 230,000.

Copenhagen

Aktuelt: Rådhuspladsen 45, 1595 Copenhagen V; tel. (01) 32-40-01; telex 19785; f. 1871; morning; Social Democratic; Editors MOGENS JØRGENSEN, HARRY RASMUSSEN; Dir A. STENDELL JENSEN; circ. 56,000 weekdays, 114,000 Sundays.

Berlingske Tidende: Pilestræde 34, 1147 Copenhagen K; tel. (01) 15-75-75; telex 27143; f. 1749; morning; independent Conservative; Chief Editor HANS DAM; circ. weekdays 135,000, Sundays 208,000.

Børsen: Møntergade 19, 1116 Copenhagen K; tel. (01) 15-72-50; telex 22903; f. 1896; morning; independent; business news; Chief Editor JAN CORTZEN; circ. 40,000.

B.T.: Kr. Bernikowsgade 6, 1147 Copenhagen K; tel. (01) 14-12-34; f. 1916; morning; independent; Chief Editor PETER DALL; circ. 216,000.

Ekstra Bladet: Rådhuspladsen 33, 1585 Copenhagen V; tel. (01) 11-85-11; telex 16885; f. 1904; evening; Liberal; Editor-in-Chief SU. O. GADE; Man. Dir E. BONNERUP NIELSEN; circ. 246,000.

Information: Store Kongensgade 40, 1264 Copenhagen K; tel. (01) 14-14-26; telex 22658; f. (underground during occupation) 1943, legally 1945; morning; independent; Chief Editor TORBEN KROGH; circ. 31,000.

Kristeligt Dagblad: Frederiksborggade 5, 1360 Copenhagen K; tel. (01) 12-35-35; f. 1896; morning; independent; Editors GUNNAR RYTGAARD, JENS RAVN OLESEN; Dir IB NORDLAND; circ. 18,000.

Land og Folk (Land and People): Dr Tværgade 1-3, 1302 Copenhagen K; tel. (01) 14-01-14; telex 27126; f. 1911; morning; publ. by Danish Communist Party; Editor GUNNAR KANSTRUP; circ. weekdays 8,000, Saturdays 31,000.

Politiken: Politikens Hus, Rådhuspladsen 37, 1585 Copenhagen V; tel. (01) 11-85-11; telex 16885; f. 1884; morning; Liberal; Editors HERBERT PUNDIK, AGNER AHM, JÖRGEN GRUNNET; Man. Dir E. BONNERUP NIELSEN; circ. weekdays 155,000, Sundays 222,000.

Esbjerg

Vestkysten: Banegårdspladsen, 6700 Esbjerg; tel. (01) 12-45-00; telex 54123; f. 1917; evening; Liberal; Editors THYGE MADSEN, EGON HANSEN; circ. 56,000.

Fredericia

Fredericia Dagblad: Gothersgade 37, 7000 Fredericia; tel. (05) 92-26-00; evening; Liberal; Editors STEFFEN BORCH, B. W. EILERSEN; circ. 11,000.

Frederikshavn

Frederikshavns Avis: Danmarksgade 3, 9900 Frederikshavn; tel. (08) 42-22-77; independent; circ. 7,000; Editor BENT EILERSTEN.

Herning

Herning Folkeblad: Østergade 25, 7400 Herning; tel. (07) 22-39-89; f. 1869; evening; Liberal; Chief Editor GORM ALBRECHTSEN; circ. 17,000.

Hillerød

De Begske Blad: Milnersvej 44, 3400 Hillerød; tel. (02) 26-27-00; circ. 133,644.

Frederiksborg Amts Avis: Milnersvej 44-46, 3400 Hillerød; tel. (02) 26-31-00; f. 1874; morning; Liberal; Editor SEJR CLAUSEN; circ. weekdays 37,000, Sundays 52,000.

Hjørring

Vendsyssel Tidende: Østergade, 9800 Hjørring; tel. (08) 92-17-00; f. 1872; evening; Liberal; Editor MOGENS LORENTSEN; circ. weekdays 27,000, Sundays 33,000.

Holbæk

Holbæk Amts Venstreblad: Ahlgade 1, 4300 Holbæk; tel. (03) 43-20-48; telex 44148; f. 1905; evening; Radical Liberal; Editor ALFRED HANSEN; circ. 22,000.

Holstebro

Dagbladet: Holstebro, Struer, Herning, Nygade 10-12, 7500 Holstebro; tel. (07) 42-17-22; evening; Liberal independent; Editor ERIK MOELLER; circ. 15,000.

Horsens

Horsens Folkeblad: Søndergade 47, 8700 Horsens; tel. (05) 62-45-00; telex 61626; f. 1866; evening; Liberal; Editor MOGENS AHRENKIEL; circ. 24,000.

Kalundborg

Kalundborg Folkeblad: Skibbrogade 40, 4400 Kalundborg; tel. (03) 51-24-60; telex 44351; f. 1917; evening; Liberal Democrat; Editor JØRGEN JENSEN; circ. 11,000.

Kolding

Jydske Tidende: Jernbanegade 46-50, 6000 Kolding; tel. (05) 52-33-33; telex 51340; f. 1849; morning; independent; Editor ERIK RANDEL; circ. 40,000, Sundays 55,000.

DENMARK

Kolding Folkeblad: Jernbanegade 33, 6000 Kolding; tel. (05) 52-20-00; telex 51362; f. 1871; evening; Liberal; Editor LARS GREGERS HANSEN; circ. 20,000.

Naskov

Ny Dag: Højevej 15, 4900 Naskov; tel. (03) 92-14-00; telex 47551; evening; Social Democrat; Editor JØRGEN MATHIESEN; circ. 12,000.

Næstved

Næstved Tidende: Ringstedgade 13, 4700 Næstved; tel. (03) 72-45-11; telex 46243; f. 1866; Liberal; Editor OLE C. JØRGENSEN; circ. 24,000.

Nykøbing

Folketidende: Tværgade 14, 4800 Nykøbing F; tel. (03) 85-20-66; f. 1873; evening; Liberal; Editor PALLE BRANDT; circ. 24,000.

Odense

Fyens Stiftstidende: Jernbanegade 1, 5000 Odense; tel. (09) 11-11-11; telex 59858; f. 1772; evening; independent; Editors BENT A. KOCH, EGON TØTTRUP; circ. weekdays 72,000, Sundays 108,000.

Randers

Amtsavisen: L. Voldgade 3, 8900 Randers; tel. (06) 42-75-11; telex 65173; f. 1810; evening; independent; Chief Editor POUL BØGH; circ. 34,000.

Ringkøbing

Ringkøbing Amts Dagblad: St. Blichersvej 5, 6950 Ringkøbing; tel. (07) 32-07-22; evening; Editor KRISTIAN SAND; circ. 15,000.

Ringsted

Dagbladet: Søgade 4, 4100 Ringsted; tel. (03) 61-25-00; telex 45111; evening; Liberal; Editor TORBEN DALBY LARSEN; circ. 31,000.

Roskilde

Roskilde Tidende: Algade 18, 4000 Roskilde; tel. (02) 35-66-66; evening; independent; Editor Mrs SØREN JAKOBSEN; circ. 9,000.

Silkeborg

Midtjyllands Avis: Vestergade 30, 8600 Silkeborg; tel. (06) 82-13-00; f. 1857; daily except Sundays; Chief Editor VIGGO SØRENSEN; circ. 23,000.

Skive

Skive Folkeblad: Slotsgade 3, 7800 Skive; tel. (07) 52-34-11; telex 66735; f. 1880; Social-Liberal; Editor HANS LARSEN; circ. 14,304.

Slagelse

Sjællands Tidende og Kalundborg Folkeblad: Korsgade 4, 4200 Slagelse; tel. (03) 52-37-00; telex 45372; f. 1815; evening; Liberal; for western part of Zealand; Editors HANS-KR. STENBÆK and ERIK LJUNGGREN; circ. 23,000.

Svendborg

Fyns Amts Avis: Sct. Nicolajgade 3, 5700 Svendborg; tel. (09) 21-46-21; telex 58118; f. 1863; Liberal; Editor UFFE RIIS SØRENSEN; circ. 25,000.

Thisted

Thisted Dagblad: Jernbanegade 15-17, 7700 Thisted; tel. (07) 92-33-22; Liberal independent; Editor HANS PETER KRAGH; circ. 11,800.

Vejle

Vejle Amts Folkeblad: Kirketorvet 10-16, 7100 Vejle; tel. (05) 82-80-00; f. 1865; evening; Liberal; Editor VAGN NYGAARD; circ. 27,000.

Viborg

Viborg Stifts Folkeblad: Sct Mathiasgade 7, 8800 Viborg; tel. (06) 62-68-00; f. 1877; Liberal Democrat; evening; also published: Viborg Nyt, Skive Bladet (weekly); Aktuel Jordbrug (monthly); Editor PER SUNESEN; circ. 14,000.

Viby

Jyllands-Posten, Morgenavisen: Grondalsvej, 8260 Viby J; tel. (06) 14-66-77; telex 68747; independent; circ. 125,000, Sundays 230,000.

WEEKLY NEWSPAPERS

Bilen: Pilestræde 34, 1147 Copenhagen K; tel. (01) 15-75-75; telex 27143; Thursday; Chief Editor FINN KNUDSTRUP; circ. 126,000.

Den Blå Avis: Meinungsgade 6, 2200 Copenhagen N; tel. (01) 37-37-37; Thursday/Friday; circ. 44,000.

Boligen: Pilestræde 34, 1147 Copenhagen K; tel. (01) 15-75-75; telex 27094; Thursday; circ. 130,607.

Demokraten Weekend: Jeppe Huus, Rømersgade 22, 1362 Copenhagen K; tel. (01) 11-35-22; Friday; circ. 14,800.

Weekendavisen Berlingske Aftenavis: Gammel Mønt 1, 1147 Copenhagen K; tel. (01) 15-75-75; telex 27143; f. 1749; Independent Conservative; Friday; Chief Editor JOERGEN SCHLEIMANN; circ. 45,000.

POPULAR PERIODICALS

Alt for Damerne: Vognmagergade 11, 1148 Copenhagen K; tel. (01) 15-19-25; telex 16705; f. 1946; weekly; women's magazine; Publr KJELD LUCAS; Editor EBBA EILERTZEN; circ. 145,910.

Alt om Sport: Store Kongensgade 40 H, 1264 Copenhagen K; tel. (01) 32-85-00; monthly; sports magazine; Editor ASGER STROM; circ. 25,632.

Anders And & Co: Vognmagergade 11, 1148 Copenhagen K; tel. (01) 15-19-25; telex 16705; weekly; children's magazine; Editor NANCY DEJGAARD; circ. 141,677.

Bådnyt: Nørre Farimagsgade 49, 1375 Copenhagen K; tel. (01) 12-66-12; telex 15712; monthly; sailing boats and motor boats; Editor FREDDY NIELSKOV; circ. 29,427.

Basserne: Krogshøjvej 32, 2880 Bagsværd; tel. (02) 98-52-27; telex 37416; 26 a year; children and youth; circ. 89,000.

Det Bedste fra Reader's Digest A/S: Jagtvej 169, 2100 Copenhagen Ø; tel. (01) 18-12-13; telex 27357; monthly; Danish Reader's Digest; Editor OLE KNUDSEN; circ. 132,000.

Bilen Motor og Sport: Nørre Farimagsgade 49, 1375 Copenhagen K; tel. (01) 12-66-12; telex 15712; monthly; cars, motor sport; Editor FLEMMING HASLUND; circ. 60,000.

Billed Bladet: Gl. Mønt 1, 1147 Copenhagen K; tel. (01) 15-20-55; telex 22200; f. 1938; weekly; family picture magazine; Editor JØRGEN EJBØL; circ. 282,325.

Bo Bedre: Nørre Farimagsgade 49, 1375 Copenhagen K; tel. (01) 12-66-12; telex 15712; monthly; homes and gardens; Editor-in-Chief ALLAN STRAUSS; circ. 112,654.

Camping: Gammel Kongevej 74, 1850 Copenhagen; tel. (01) 21-06-04; monthly; circ. 50,000.

Eva: Nørre Farimagsgade 49, 1375 Copenhagen K; tel. (01) 12-66-12; telex 15712; 6 a year; fashion, beauty; Editor VIBEKE HELLES; circ. 45,773.

Familie Journalen: Vigerslev Allé 18, 2500 Valby, Copenhagen; tel. (01) 30-33-33; f. 1877; weekly; Editor ANKER SVENDSEN-TUNE; circ. 366,600.

Femina: Vigerslev Allé 18, 2500 Valby, Copenhagen; tel. (01) 30-33-33; f. 1873; weekly; Editor JUTTA LARSEN; circ. 142,000.

Foto-Avisen: Ravnehusvej 35, 300 Värlöse; 4 a year; photography; Editor FINN LICHT; circ. 28,000.

Helse—Familiens Lægeblad: Østerbrogade 115A, 2100 Copenhagen Ø; tel. (01) 29-77-00; 6 a year; family health; circ. 510,000.

Hendes Verden: Vognmagergade 11, 1148 Copenhagen K; tel. (01) 15-19-25; telex 16705; f. 1937; weekly; for women; Editor EVA RAVN; circ. 142,076.

Hi Fi & elektronik: Nørre Farimagsgade 49, 1364 Copenhagen K; tel. (01) 12-66-12; monthly; electronics and hi-fi equipment; Editor THOMAS WEDEL; circ. 31,729.

Hjemmet (The Home): Vognmagergade 11, 1148 Copenhagen K; tel. (01) 15-19-25; telex 16705; weekly; Chief Editor KAJ DORPH-PETERSEN; circ. 265,000.

Hus og Hjem: Kronprinsensgade 1, 1114 Copenhagen K; tel. (01) 15-95-95; f. 1896; weekly; for women; Editor KAY HOLKENFELDT; circ. 16,660.

Ide-nyt: Gl. Klausdalsbrovej 482, 2730 Herlev; tel. (02) 94-60-40; telex 35148; 4 a year; free magazine; homes and gardens; circ. 2,300,000.

Landsbladet: Vester Farimagsgade 6, 1606 Copenhagen V; tel. (01) 11-22-22; farmer's weekly; Man. Dir NIKO WIEGMAN; circ. 90,000.

Min Hest: Semic Forlagene, Krogshøjvej 32, 2880 Bagsværd; tel. (02) 42-32-33; telex 37416; monthly; for young girls; circ. 19,000.

Motor: Blegdamsvej 124, 1200 Copenhagen Ø; tel. (01) 38-21-12; telex 15857; fortnightly; cars and motor-tourism; circ. 170,000.

Notat: Nordkystvejen 2F, 8961 Allingåbro; tel. (06) 48-16-00; weekly; family magazine; circ. 30,000.

DENMARK

Samvirke: Roskildevej 65, 2620 Albertslund; tel. (02) 64-88-11; telex 33311; f. 1928; consumer monthly; Publr and Chief Editor Aa. Büchert; circ. 750,000.

Se og Hør: Vigerslev Allé 18, 2500 Valby, Copenhagen; tel. (01) 30-33-33; telex 22390; f. 1940; news and TV; Editor Mogens E. Pedersen; circ. 315,000.

Søndags-B.T.: Østergade 5, 1147 Copenhagen K; tel. (01) 11-75-75; telex 27143; f. 1921; weekly; family magazine; Editor Alice Vestergaard; circ. 171,694.

TV Bladet: Gl. Mønt 1, 1147 Copenhagen K; tel. (01) 15-20-55; telex 27094; weekly; television and radio programmes; circ. 287,730.

Ude og Hjemme: Vigerslev Allé 18, 2500 Valby, Copenhagen; tel. (01) 30-33-33; f. 1926; family weekly; Editor Jørn Bauenmand; circ. 180,437.

Ugens Rapport: Skt. Annæ Plads 8, 1250 Copenhagen K; tel. (01) 13-60-60; f. 1971; men's weekly; Editor-in-chief Hans-Ulrik Buchwald; circ. 80,401.

Vi Unge: Hellerupvej 66, 2900 Hellerup; tel. (01) 62-32-22; f. 1958; teenagers' monthly; Editor Carl W. Baerentzen; circ. 55,000.

SPECIALIST PERIODICALS

ABF-Nyt: Istedgade 1, 1650 Copenhagen V; tel. (01) 24-75-02; monthly; Editor Jan Hansen; circ. 19,008.

Aktuel Data & EDB: Skelbækgade 4, 1717 Copenhagen V; tel. (01) 21-68-01; 6 a year; computing and information technology; circ. 45,649.

Alt om Data: St. Kongensgade 72, 1264 Copenhagen K; tel. (01) 11-32-83; 6 a year; circ. 24,000.

Amt- og Kommune Bladet: Tordenskjoldsgade 27, 1055 Copenhagen K; tel. (01) 14-00-10; monthly; community news; circ. 20,079.

Arbejdsgiveren: Vester Voldgade 113, 1503 Copenhagen V; tel. (01) 93-40-00; telex 16464; 20 a year; management; circ. 50,555.

Arbejdslederen: Vermlandsgade 67, 2300 Copenhagen S; tel. (01) 57-56-22; 15 a year; circ. 61,293.

Arte nyt: Hvidkildevej 64, 2400 Copenhagen NV; tel. (01) 10-16-22; 4 a year; circ. 39,896.

Automatik: Egebjergvej 13, 4500 Nykøbing sj; tel. (03) 41-23-10; engineering; monthly; circ. 15,760.

Beboerbladet: Studiestræde 50, 1554 Copenhagen V; tel. (01) 11-11-22; 4 a year; home-renting; circ. 394,484.

Boligen: Studiestræde 50, 1554 Copenhagen V; tel. (01) 11-11-22; 10 a year; housing and architecture; circ. 19,000.

Byggeri: Skelbækgade 4, 1717 Copenhagen V; tel. (01) 21-68-01; telex 16368; f. 1980; 23 a year; building and construction; circ. 20,000.

Civilforsvar: Datavej 18, 3460 Birkerørd; tel. (02) 82-00-66; 6 a year; defence; circ. 20,500.

Computerworld: Torvegade 52, 1400 Copenhagen K; tel. (01) 95-56-95; telex 31566; f. 1981; weekly; computing; Chief Officers Jens Michael Damm, Lars Olsen; circ. 19,800.

Cyklister: Dansk Cyklist Forbund, Kjeld Langes Gade 14, 1367 Copenhagen K; tel. (01) 14-42-12; f. 1905; 6 a year; organ of Danish Cyclists' Asscn; circ. 30,000.

Danmarks Restauranter: Vodroffsvej 46, 1900 Copenhagen V; tel. (01) 35-60-88; monthly; catering; Editor Jens G. Eilertzen; circ. 10,867.

Effektivt Landbrug: Skelbækgade 4, 1717 Copenhagen V; tel. (01) 21-68-01; 23 a year; farming; circ. 37,116.

Eleven: Vesterbrogade 20, 1620 Copenhagen V; tel. (01) 22-49-22; 4 a year; organ of students' union; circ. 90,000.

Expert Video Club: Roholmsvej 5, 2620 Albertslund; tel. (02) 62-12-55; 4 a year; circ. 20,000.

Folkeskolen: Søtoften 62, 8250 Egå; tel. (06) 22-03-89; telex 220942; weekly; teaching; Editor J. C. Jørgensen; circ. 80,250.

Forbrugsforeningsbladet: Knabrostræde 12, 1210 Copenhagen K; tel. (01) 13-88-22; monthly; circ. 28,000.

Fremtiden: Amaliegade 40A, 1256 Copenhagen K; tel. (01) 14-88-86; f. 1945; international affairs; 4 a year; publ. by Danish Foreign Policy Society; Editors Mogens Espersen, Hugo Gården; circ. 1,000.

Gør-det-Selv: Nr. Farimagsgade 49, 1375 Copenhagen K; tel. (01) 12-66-12; monthly; do-it-yourself; circ. 85,000.

Hair News: Gothersgade 103, 1123 Copenhagen K; tel. (01) 11-17-21; 6 a year; Editor S. Pjedsted; circ. 10,000.

Handicap Information: Idrættens Hus, 2605 Brøndby; tel. (02) 45-55-55; telex 33111; 10 a year; circ. 12,000.

Havebladet: Frederikssundsvej 308B, 2700 Brønshøj; tel. (01) 28-87-50; 4 a year; gardening; circ. 44,000.

Haven: Åby Bækgardsvej 6, 8230 Åbyhøj; tel. (06) 15-56-88; monthly; horticulture and gardening; circ. 89,445.

High Fidelity: St. Kongensgade 72, 1264 Copenhagen K; tel. (01) 11-25-47; 11 a year; circ. 22,500.

Hippologisk Tidsskrift: V. Farimagsgade 6, 1606 Copenhagen V; tel. (01) 11-22-22; f. 1888; monthly; equestrianism; Editor I. C. Christensen; circ. 13,740.

Hunden: Parkvej 1, Jersie Strand, 2680 Solred Strand; tel. (03) 14-15-66; 10 a year; organ of the kennel club; circ. 28,000.

Huset: Nørre Voldgade 2, 1358 Copenhagen K; tel. (01) 12-03-30; monthly; home-owning; Editor Jen Henning; circ. 10,825.

Idrætsliv: Idrætens Hus, 2600 Glostrup; tel. (02) 45-55-55; monthly; athletics; circ. 13,500.

Ingeniøren: Skelbækgade 4, 1717 Copenhagen V; tel. (01) 21-68-01; weekly engineers' magazine; circ. 55,464.

Jagt og Fiskeri: Jørgensvej 4, 5610 Assens; tel. (09) 71-40-31; monthly; hunting, fishing, sport; Editor Villy Andersen; circ. 140,000.

Kommunal-Arbejderen: Nitivej 6, 2000 Copenhagen F; tel. (01) 19-90-22; monthly; circ. 130,000.

Maleren: Tomsgardsvej 23c, 2400 Copenhagen NV; tel. (01) 34-75-22; monthly; painting; circ. 15,000.

MC-Revy: Nørre Farimagsgade 49, 1375 Copenhagen K; tel. (01) 12-66-12; 4 a year; motorcycling and mopeds; circ. 24,500; Editor Flemming Haslund.

Musik Nyt: J. A. Schwartzgade 30, 2100 Copenhagen Ø; tel. (01) 26-22-49; monthly; music; circ. 15,000.

Populær Elektronik: Greve Strandvej 42, 2670 Greve Strand; tel. (02) 90-86-00; monthly; engineering and electronics; circ. 38,290.

Post og Tele: Tietensgade 37, 1530 Copenhagen V; tel. (01) 15-66-10; 4 a year; circ. 30,000.

Sundhedsmagasinet Praxis: Gl. Bjert 22, 6091 Bjert; tel. (05) 57-27-00; 8 a year; circ. 100,000

Sygeplejersken: Vimmelskaftet 38, 1008 Copenhagen K; tel. (01) 15-15-55; 50 a year; nursing; circ. 56,703.

Thema Dänemark/Denmark Today/Danmark Idag: Scandinavian News Inf., St. Kongensgade 68, 1264 Copenhagen K; 6 a year; news for business, exports, etc.; circ. 105,000.

Tidernes Tegn: Børstenbindervej 4, 5230 Odense M; every 2 months; religion; circ. 17,000.

Transport: Skelbækgade 4, 1717 Copenhagen V; tel. (01) 21-68-01; telex 16368; 20 a year; circ. 19,112.

Ugeskrift for Læger: Trondhjemsgade 9, 2100 Copenhagen Ø; tel. (01) 38-55-00; weekly; medical; circ. 20,000.

NEWS AGENCY

Ritzaus Bureau I/S: Mikkel Bryggersgade 3, 1460 Copenhagen K; tel. (01) 12-33-44; telex 22362; f. 1866; general, financial and commercial news; works in conjuction with Reuters, Agence France-Presse, Deutsche Presse-Agentur and European national agencies; owned by all Danish newspapers; Chair. of Board of Dirs Aage Deleuran; Gen. Man. and Editor-in-Chief Per Winther.

Foreign Bureaux

Agence France-Presse (AFP): Mikkel Bryggersgade 5, 1460 Copenhagen K; tel. (01) 13-23-31; telex 19584; Bureau Chief Francis Powley.

Agencia EFE (Spain): Mikkel Bryggersgade 5, 1460 Copenhagen K; Chief Camino Sánchez.

Agentstvo Pechati Novosti (APN) (USSR): Vestagervej 7, 2100 Copenhagen Ø; tel. (01) 20-04-44; telex 15618; Chief Editor Ilja Baranikas.

Agenzia Nazionale Stampa Associata (ANSA) (Italy): Hvalsoevej 6, 2700 Broensholm; tel. (01) 80-04-13; telex 15487; telex 15487; Agent Vittorio Spadanuda.

Allgemeiner Deutscher Nachrichtendienst (ADN) (German Democratic Republic): 2660 Bröndbystrand, Kisumparken 65 st. th., Copenhagen; Bureau Chief Herbert Hansch.

Associated Press (AP) (USA): Kristen Bernikowsgade 4, 2nd floor, 1105 Copenhagen K; tel. (01) 11-36-17; telex 22381; Bureau Chief William C. Mann.

DENMARK

Deutsche Presse-Agentur (dpa) (Federal Republic of Germany): Mikkel Bryggersgade 5, 1460 Copenhagen K; tel. (01) 14-22-19; Chief Correspondent THOMAS BORCHERT.

Reuter (UK): 24 Læderstræde, 1201 Copenhagen K; tel. (01) 15-53-09; telex 16846.

Telegrafnoye Agentstvo Sovetskovo Soyuza (TASS) (USSR): Uraniavej 9B, 1, 1878 Copenhagen; tel. (01) 24-04-03; telex 19304; Correspondent YEVGENI KISELYEV.

United Press International (UPI) (USA): Store Strandstræde 8, Copenhagen; Bureau Chief BØRGE MORS.

PRESS ASSOCIATIONS

Danske Dagblades Forening (Danish Newspapers Association): The House of the Press, Skindergade 7, 1159 Copenhagen K; tel. (01) 12-21-15; telex 27183; comprises managers and editors-in-chief of all newspapers; general spokesman for the Danish press.

Illustrated Press Publishers' Association: Copenhagen; publishers of magazines.

Københavnske Dagblades Samraad (Copenhagen Newspaper Publishers' Association): c/o Det Berlingske Hus, Pilestræde 34, 1147 Copenhagen K; Chair. W. REVES.

Publishers

Forlaget ålökke A/S: 26 Tulinpanparken, 8700 Horsens; tel. (05) 65-77-84; educational, audio-visual and other study aids; Dir BERTIL TOFT HANSEN.

Akademisk Forlag AmbA: Store Kannikestræde 6–8, POB 54, 1002 Copenhagen K; tel. (01) 11-98-26; f. 1962; textbooks, scientific literature and educational materials; Man. Dir PER HOLM RASMUSSEN; Chief Editor NIELS PERSSON.

Alrune Forlaget: Snertinge Markvej 57, 4760 Vordingborg; tel. (03) 78-25-73; children's books.

Apostrof Forlaget: Berggreensgade 24, 2100 Copenhagen Ø; tel. (01) 20-84-20; Dirs MIA TIMM, OLE THESTRUP.

Arnkrone Publishers Ltd: Fuglebækvej 4, 2770 Kastrup; tel. (01) 50-70-00; f. 1941; popular medicine, art and cultural history; children's fiction and non-fiction, psychotherapy, contemporary fiction and humour; Man. Dir J. JUUL RASMUSSEN.

Aschehoug Dansk Forlag A/S: Klosterrisvej 7, 2100 Copenhagen Ø; tel. (01) 29-44-22; telex 16987; f. 1914; school and textbooks; Man. Dir ERIK IPSEN.

  J. Fr. Clausens Forlag: popular specialist literature.

  Grafisk Forlag: textbooks, handbooks, children's books.

  H. Hagerups Forlag: school and textbooks.

  H. Hirschsprungs Forlag: textbooks.

Peter Asschenfeldt's Stjernbøger A/S: Njalsgade 19.1C, 2300 Copenhagen S; tel. (01) 54-10-58; bestseller paperbacks; Dir PETER ASSCHENFELDT.

Forlaget Det Bedste fra Reader's Digest ApS: Jagtvej 169, 2100 Copenhagen Ø; popular science, medicine, cars, gardening, maps and atlases; Man. Dir JOHN MADSEN.

Bergs Forlag ApS: Peder Skramsgade 5, 1054 Copenhagen K; tel. (01) 13-54-80; f. 1965; art books; Man. H. M. BERG.

Bibelselskabets Forlag og Vajsenhusets Forlag: Frederiksborggade 50, 1360 Copenhagen K; tel. (01) 12-78-35; religious works; Man. Dir NIELS JØRGEN CAPPELÖRN.

Bibliotekscentralens Forlag: 7–11 Tempovej, 2750 Ballerup; tel. (02) 97-40-00; telex 35730; f. 1939; bibliographies, indexes and library literature; Man. Dir ASGER HANSEN.

Thomas Bloms Forlag ApS: Rudolph Berghsgade 18, 2100 Copenhagen Ø; tel. (01) 29-17-49; non-fiction, children's books; Owners CONNIE and THOMAS BLOM.

Bierman og Bierman ApS: Vestergade 120, 7200 Grindsted; tel. (05) 32-02-88; f. 1968; fiction, non-fiction, children's books, general culture, magazines; Man. Dir B. LORENTZEN.

Bogans Forlag A/S: Kastaniebakken 8, 3540 Lynge; tel. (02) 18-80-55; f. 1974; general paperbacks, popular science and occult; Owner EVAN BOGAN.

Bonniers Specialmagasiner A/S: Nørre Farimagsgade 49, 1375 Copenhagen K; tel. (01) 12-66-12; telex 15712; f. 1960 as Fogtdals Blade A/S; handbooks, part-works and magazines; Man. Dir ERIK SKIPPER LARSEN.

Directory

Borgens Forlag A/S: Valbygårdsvej 33, 2500 Valby; tel. (01) 46-21-00; f. 1948; fiction, non-fiction, handicrafts, religion, children's, computer books and textbooks; Man. Dir JARL BORGEN; Dirs ERIK CRILLESEN, NIELS BORGEN.

Börnegudstjeneste-Forlaget: 25 Korskaervej, 7000 Fredericia; tel. (05) 92-61-00; religion, children's books; Man. Dir B. HANSEN.

Børsen Forlaget A/S: Møntergade 19, 1116 Copenhagen K; tel. (01) 15-72-50; telex 22903; business information (daily news, magazines, newsletters and books), electronic publishing; Man. Dir PREBEN SCHACK.

Branner og Korchs Forlag A/S: H.C. Örstedsvej 7B, 1879 Frederiksberg C; tel. (01) 22-45-11; f. 1949; handbooks, fiction, juveniles; Dir TORBEN SCHUR.

Carit Andersens Forlag A/S: Malmögade 3, 2100 Copenhagen Ø; tel. (01) 26-06-21; telex 16121; illustrated books, fiction, science fiction; Dir ERIK ALBRECHTSEN.

Centrum, Jyllands-Posten Forlag: Gunnar Clausensvej 66, 8260 Viby J; tel. (06) 29-69-77; fiction, handbooks, children's, school books; Dir SVEN BEDSTED.

Dansk Historisk Håndbogsforlag A/S: Klintevej 25, 2800 Lyngby; tel. (02) 88-52-48; genealogy, heraldry, culture and local history, facsimile editions, microfiches produced by subsidiary co; Owners and Man. Dirs RITA JENSEN, HENNING JENSEN.

Dansklærerforeningens Forlag: Nørre Søgade 49C, 1370 Copenhagen K; tel. (01) 15-04-99; school books, Danish literature; Man. Dir ASGER UHD JEPSEN.

Delta Forlag A/S: Kroghsgade 5, 2100 Copenhagen Ø; tel. (01) 26-38-01; fiction, non-fiction, juveniles, educational, feminist; Dir JÖRGEN MARTENS.

Christian Ejlers' Forlag ApS: Brolæggerstræde 4, POB 2228, 1018 Copenhagen K; tel. (01) 12-21-14; f. 1967; general, art, social and political science; Dir CHRISTIAN EJLERS.

Chr. Erichsens Forlag A/S: Kronprinsensgade 1, 1114 Copenhagen K; tel. (01) 15-95-95; f. 1902; fiction, children's handbooks; Man. Dir KAY HOLKENFELDT.

Forlaget Europa: Nyhavn 40, 1051 Copenhagen K; tel. (01) 15-62-73; telex 19280; school and university texts, tourist and restaurant guides; Dir LARS KVISTSKOV LARSEN.

FADL Forlag A/S (Foreningen af danske Lægestuderendes Forlag): Blegdamsvej 30, 2200 Copenhagen N; tel. (01) 35-62-87; telex 16698; f. 1964; medicine, biology; Man. Dir HANS JESPERSEN.

Forlaget for Faglitteratur A/S: Vandkunsten 6, 1467 Copenhagen K; tel. (01) 13-79-00; medicine, technology.

Palle Fogtdal A/S: Nygade 7, 1164 Copenhagen K; tel. (01) 15-39-15; art books, general trade books, non-fiction; Man. Dir PALLE FOGTDAL.

Forlaget Forum A/S: Snaregade 4, 1205 Copenhagen K; tel. (01) 14-77-14; f. 1940; fiction, quality paperbacks and children's books; Dir CLAUS BRØNDSTED.

Forlaget Fremad af 1979 A/S: Rentemestervej 45-47, 2400 Copenhagen NV; tel. (01) 33-40-40; f. 1912; fiction, non-fiction, popular science, textbooks, juveniles, reissues; Man. Dir PETER JOHANSEN.

FSRS Forlag: Kronprinsessegade 8, 1306 Copenhagen K; tel. (01) 93-91-91; telex 22491; textbooks, legal, economic, financial, business; Man. Dir OLE PHILIPSEN.

J. Frimodts Forlag: Korskærvej 25, 7000 Fredericia; tel. (05) 93-44-55; religion, fiction, devotional; Man. Dir BENT HANSEN.

G.E.C. Gads Forlag: Vimmelskaftet 32, 1161 Copenhagen K; tel. (01) 15-05-58; university and school books, legal and reference; Man. AXEL KIELLAND.

Gjellerup og Gad Forlagsaktieselskab: Vimmelskaftet 32, 1161 Copenhagen K; tel. (01) 15-05-58; textbooks, school books, audio-visual aids; Mans GRETHE BRYNER, HARALD BERTELSEN.

Forlaget GMT: Meilgård, 8585 Glæsborg; tel. (06) 31-75-11; f. 1971; history, philosophy, politics, social sciences, general fiction, textbooks; Publrs HANS JØRN CHRISTENSEN, ERIK BJØRN OLSEN.

Grevas Forlag: Auningvej 33, Sdr. Kastrup 8544 Mørke; tel. (06) 16-83-87; f. 1966; novels, debate; Dir LUISE HEMMER PIHL.

Gyldendalske Boghandel-Nordisk Forlag A/S: Klareboderne 3, 1001 Copenhagen K; tel. (01) 11-07-75; telex 15887; f. 1770; fiction, non-fiction, reference books, paperbacks, children's books, textbooks; Dirs NIELS ÅGNER, KURT FROMBERG, KLAUS RIFBJERG, EGON SCHMIDT.

P. Haase & Søns Forlag A/S: Lövstræde 8, 1152 Copenhagen K; tel. (01) 11-59-99; f. 1877; Man. Dir N. J. HAASE; educational books, audio-visual aids, children's books, fiction, non-fiction.

DENMARK

Forlaget Hamlet A/S: 25 Linnésgade, 1361 Copenhagen K; tel. (01) 13-16-50; handbooks, art books.

Hekla Forlag: Store Kongensgade 61A and B, POB 9011, 1022 Copenhagen K; tel. (01) 91-19-33; f. 1979; general trade fiction and non-fiction; Owner HELGA W. LINDHARDT.

Hernovs' Forlag: Bredgade 14-16, 1260 Copenhagen K; tel. (01) 15-62-84; f. 1941; fiction, memoirs, children's; Owner JOHS. G. HERNOV; Dir PER LESLIE HOLST.

Forlag Hønsetryk: Rosenørns Allé 18, 1970 Copenhagen V; tel. (01) 54-81-51; Owner Gjellerup Forlags-Aktieselskab.

Høst & Søns Forlag: Dronningens Tværgade 5, 1302 Copenhagen K; tel. (01) 15-30-31; f. 1836; crafts and hobbies, languages, books on Denmark, children's books; Dir ERIK C. LINDGREN.

Forlaget Hovedland: POB 1953, Elsdyrvej 4, 8270 Højberg; tel. (06) 27-44-70; Owner STEEN PIPER.

Finn Jacobsens Forlag: Gothersgade 56, 1123 Copenhagen K; tel. (01) 14-36-32; non-fiction, science, cultural history; Owner FINN JACOBSEN.

Forlaget Kaleidoscope ApS: Njalsgade 19–21, 2300 Copenhagen S; tel. (01) 95-83-33; educational, audio-visual, fiction for youth; Man. Dir JENS BENDTSEN.

Forlaget Per Kafod ApS: Ved Stranden 16, 1061 Copenhagen K; tel. (01) 15-03-47.

Forlaget Komma A/S: Frederiksborggade 26, Israels Plads, POB 2163, 1016 Copenhagen K; tel. (01) 14-55-83; telex 19149; f. 1977; reference, history, maritime, cookery, instructional; Man. Dir LUDVIG E. BRAMSEN.

Morten A. Korch's Forlag: Aurehøjvej 2, 2900 Hellerup; tel. (01) 62-08-59; children's books; Owner MORTEN KORCH.

Krak: Nytorv 17, 1450 Copenhagen K; tel. (01) 12-03-08; telex 16652; f. 1770; reference works, maps and yearbooks; Dir IB LE ROY TOPHOLM.

Lademann Ltd, Publishers: Linnésgade 25, POB 2163, 1016 Copenhagen K; tel. (01) 13-16-50; telex 19149; f. 1954; novels, history, text books, reference books, encyclopedias, paperbacks; Man. Dir JØRGEN LADEMANN.

Lindhardt og Ringhof, Forlag ApS, og Jespersen og Pio's Forlag: Studiestræde 14, 1455 Copenhagen K; tel. (01) 11-19-55; f. 1971; general fiction and non-fiction, paperbacks; Owners OTTO B. LINDHARDT, GERT RINGHOF.

Lohses Forlag: Korskærvej 25, 7000 Fredericia; tel. (05) 93-44-55; f. 1868; religion, memoirs, travel; Man. Dir BENT HANSEN.

Mallings Forlag ApS: Gammel Kongevej 3-5, 1610 Copenhagen V; tel. (01) 24-35-55; telex 15817; f. 1975; Dir HANNAH MALLING.

Martins Forlag: Thorsbjerggård L1 Fjellenstrupvej 25, 3250 Gilleleje; tel. (02) 30-11-00; telex 19203; fiction, non-fiction, juveniles; Man. Dir JENS ERIK HALKIER.

Medicinsk Forlag ApS: Tranevej 2, 3650 Ölstykke; tel. (02) 17-65-92; medical and scientific books; Man. Dir ANNI LINDELÖV.

Forlaget Melgaard ApS: Østerbrogade 119, 2100 Copenhagen Ø; tel. (01) 18-45-47; travel, general fiction, non-fiction; Owner SØREN MELGAARD.

Forlaget Modtryk AMBA: Anholtsgade 4–6, 8000 Århus C; tel. (0045) 61-27-912; telex 4556785; f. 1972; politics, children's and school books, fiction, thrillers and poetry; Man. Dir PREBEN BACH.

Munksgårds Forlag: POB 2148, Nørre Søgade 35, 1016 Copenhagen K; tel. (01) 12-70-30; telex 19431; f. 1917; agents to Royal Danish Academy, and various learned societies; specializing in medical and natural science, international scientific journals, humanities, school books and computer software; Man. Dir OLUF V. MØLLER.

Forlaget Natur og Harmoni: Lövstræde 8, 1152 Copenhagen K; tel. (01) 11-59-99; alternative health books; Owner P. Haase & Søns Forlag A/S.

Nordiske Landes Bogforlag: Mariendalsvej 33, 2000 Frederiksberg; tel. (01) 34-80-76; illustrated books, travel, fiction books about Greenland; Owner JÖRGEN FISKER.

Nyt Nordisk Forlag-Arnold Busck A/S: Koebmagergade 49, 1150 Copenhagen K; tel. (01) 11-11-03; f. 1896; textbooks, school books, non-fiction; Dir OLE ARNOLD BUSCK.

Det Schønbergske Forlag A/S: Landemærket 5, 1119 Copenhagen K; tel. (01) 11-30-66; f. 1857; fiction, travel, history, biography, paperbacks, textbooks; Man. OLE STENDER.

Forlaget Optima ApS: Møllevænget 16, 7800 Skive; tel. (07) 53-55-80; education; Dir INGRID CHRISTIANSEN.

Jørgen Paludans Forlag ApS: Fiolstræde 32, 1171 Copenhagen K; tel. (01) 11-82-03, ext. 45; language teaching, natural sciences, psychology, history, sociology, politics, economics; Man. Dir JØRGEN PALUDAN.

Publishers D/Forlaget Henrik Borberg: Store Kongensgade 110A, 1264 Copenhagen K; tel. (01) 32-88-48; non-fiction, reference, software packaging; Man. Dir HENRIK BORBERG.

Politikens Forlag A/S: Vestergade 26, 1456 Copenhagen K; tel. (01) 11-21-22; f. 1947; dictionaries, reference books, handbooks, yearbooks, collected works and maps; Dir JOHANNES RAVN.

Rasmus Navers Forlag: Lövstræde 8, 1152 Copenhagen K; tel. (01) 11-59-99; humour, poetry, fiction; Owner P. Haase & Søns Forlag A/S.

Hans Reitzel Publishers Ltd: Dronningens Tværgade 5, 1302 Copenhagen K; tel. (01) 14-04-51; f. 1949; reference and textbooks, psychology, sociology; Man. Dir JOACHIM MALLING; Editors BEATE NELLEMANN, OLE GAMMELTOFT.

C.A. Reitzels Forlag A/S: Nørregade 20, 1165 Copenhagen K; tel. (01) 12-24-00; f. 1819; Owner and Man. Dir SVEND OLUFSEN.

Rhodos, International Science and Art Publishers: Niels Brocks Gård, Strandgade 36, 1401 Copenhagen K; tel. (01) 54-30-20; telex 31502; f. 1959; science, art, literature, politics, professional, criticism; Man. Dir NIELS BLAEDEL.

Rosenkilde og Baggers Forlag: POB 2184, 1017 Copenhagen K; tel. (01) 15-70-44; f. 1941; manuals, cultural history, facsimiles; Owner BENT W. DAHLSTRØM.

Forlaget Rosinante ApS: POB 5, Kirkevej 15, 2920 Charlottenlund; tel. (01) 63-32-05; f. 1984; general trade books, non-fiction, fiction; Owner and Man. Dir MERETE RIES.

Samlerens Forlag A/S: Christian den Niendes Gade 2, 1111 Copenhagen K; tel. (01) 13-10-23; social sciences, health, art, paperbacks, manuals, biographies, history, politics; Man. Dir BØRGE PRISKORN.

A/S J. H. Schultz Forlag: Møntergade 21 (1), 1116 Copenhagen K; tel. (01) 12-11-95; f. 1661; printers, publishers, booksellers; printers to the Danish Government and the Copenhagen University; subsidiary: Schultz Medical Information; Publishing Man. POUL BAY.

Semic Forlagene A/S: Krogshøjvej 32, 2880 Bagsværd; tel. (02) 44-32-33.

Forlaget Sesam A/S: Frederiksborggade 26A, 1360 Copenhagen K; history, educational, children's; Dir GEORG VEJEN.

Skarv ApS: Kongevejen 45B, 2840 Holte; tel. (01) 42-47-45; children's, educational, general; Owner and Man. Dir SÖREN KOUSTRUP.

A/S Skattekarteteket: Informationskontor, Palægade 4, 1261 Copenhagen K; tel. (01) 11-78-74; books on taxation; Man. Dir P. TAARNHØJ.

Sommer & Sörensen Forlag ApS: Mynstersvej 19, 1827 Frederiksberg C; tel. (01) 23-25-55; Dirs AAGE BÖRGLUM SÖRENSEN, ERIK SOMMER.

Forlaget Spektrum A/S: Snaregade 4, 1205 Copenhagen K; tel. (01) 14-77-14; general literature, paperbacks; Dir CLAUS BRØNSTED.

Strandbergs Forlag: Topstykket 17, 3460 Birkeröd; tel. (02) 81-63-97; cultural history, computer science; Owner HANS JÖRGEN STRANDBERG.

Strubes Forlag A/S: POB 827, 2100 Copenhagen Ø; tel. (01) 42-07-16; psychic, occult, philosophy, art, naval; Man. Dir POUL STRUBE.

Teaterforlaget Drama: Ladegårdsskov 14, 6300 Gråsten; tel. (04) 65-11-41; theatrical literature, drama; Man. Dir OVE KIRKETERP.

Teknisk Forlag A/S: Skelbækgade 4, 1717 Copenhagen V; tel. (01) 21-68-01; telex 16368; f. 1948; technical books and periodicals; Man. Dir PETER MÜLLER.

Teknologisk Institus Forlag: POB 141, 2630 Tåstrup; tel. (02) 99-66-11; technical, crafts, industries.

Tellerup Ltd: POB 109, 2900 Hellerup; tel. (01) 62-37-00; f. 1972; children's, young adults fiction, science fiction, fiction; Dir K. TELLERUP.

Thaning & Appels Forlag A/S: H.C. Ørstedsvej 7B, 1879 Frederiksberg C; tel. (01) 22-45-11; f. 1866; fiction, art, popular sciences; Dir AKSEL PEDERSEN.

Forlaget Tiderne Skifter ApS: Skt. Peder Stræde 28B, 1453 Copenhagen K; tel. (01) 13-65-03; fiction, sexual and cultural politics, psychology, criticism, arts, children's books; Man. Dir CLAUS CLAUSEN.

DENMARK   *Directory*

Forlaget Tommeliden: Odensevej 92, Herrested, 5853 Ørbøk; tel. (09) 98-23-74; fiction, school books, handbooks, juveniles; Man. Dir JES TRØST JØRGENSEN.

Unitas Forlag, De Unges Forlag: Valby Langgade 19, 2500 Valby; tel. (01) 16-60-33; religion, fiction, education; Man. Dir LORENS HEDELUND.

Vandrer mod Lysets Forlag ApS: Ellevadsvej 3, 2920 Charlottenlund; tel. (01) 63-22-26; religion, science, philosophy, ethics; Dir BØRGE BRØNNUM.

Forlaget Vindrose: Nybrogade 14, 1203 Copenhagen K; tel. (01) 13-50-00; f. 1980; general trade, fiction and non-fiction; Dir ERIK VAGN JENSEN.

Vitafakta ApS: Kohavevej 28, 2950 Vedbæk; tel. (02) 89-21-03; health books, school books; Dir INGER MARIE HAUT.

Wangels Forlag A/S: 8 Gammeltorv, POB 1061, 1008 Copenhagen K; tel. (01) 15-61-11; telex 19387; f. 1946; fiction, book club; Gen. Man. BENNY FREDERIKSEN.

Edition Wilhelm Hansen: 9-11 Gothersgade, 1123 Copenhagen K; tel. (01) 11-78-88; telex 19912; educational books, books on music; Owners HANNE WILHELM HANSEN, LONE WILHELM HANSEN, TINE BIRGER CHRISTENSEN.

Winthers Forlag ApS: Naverland 1A, 2600 Glostrup; tel. (02) 96-06-66; f. 1945; general fiction, paperbacks; Man. Dir PREBEN C. C. MØLLER.

Forlag Wøldike: Stægers Allé 13, 2000 Frederiksberg; tel. (01) 86-39-54; fiction and non-fiction; Publr OVE MØLBECK.

Government Publishing House

Statens Informationstjeneste (State Information Service): Bredgade 20, POB 1103, 1009 Copenhagen K; tel. (01) 92-92-00; acts as press, public relations and information body for the government in all media; publishes Official Gazette, etc.

PUBLISHERS' ASSOCIATION

Den danske Forlæggerforening: Købmagergade 11, 1150 Copenhagen K; tel. (01) 15-66-88; f. 1837; 78 mems; Chair. OLE A. BUSCK; Dir ERIK V. KRUSTRUP.

Radio and Television

In 1986 there were 2,061,000 current licences for radio receivers and 1,953,000 licences for television receivers.

Radio Denmark: Radio House, Rosenørns Allé 22, 1999 Copenhagen V; tel. (01) 35-06-47; telex 22695; Dir-Gen. HANS JØRGEN JENSEN; Dir of Radio Programmes SVEN FUGL; Dir of Television Programmes HENRIK ANTONSEN.

Finance

The first Danish commercial bank was founded in 1846. In January 1975 restrictions on savings banks were lifted, giving commercial and savings banks equal rights and status. Several foreign banks have representative offices in Copenhagen, and in January 1975 restrictions on the establishment of full branches of foreign banks were removed. In 1985 there were about 80 commercial banks and 150 savings banks, considerably fewer than 20 years earlier. All banks are under government supervision, and public representation is obligatory on all bank supervisory boards.

BANKING

(cap. = capital; p.u. = paid up; res = reserves; dep. = deposits; m. = million; brs = branches; amounts in kroner)

Central Bank

Danmarks Nationalbank: Havnegade 5, 1093 Copenhagen K; tel. (01) 14-14-11; telex 27051; f. 1818; self-governing; sole right of issue; administers foreign exchange rates and regulations; regulates money-traffic and the extension of credit; capital fund 50m.; gold in coin and bullion 4,772m.; notes in circ. 18,599m. (1985); brs in Århus and Odense; Govs E. HOFFMEYER, O. THOMASEN, R. MIKKELSEN.

Commercial Banks

Århus Discontobank A/S: Søndergade 9, 8100 Århus C; tel. (06) 12-01-88; telex 64518; f. 1894; cap. 25m., res 51.7m., dep. 443m. (1985); Gen. Man. PREBEN ANDERSEN; 7 brs.

Aktivbanken A/S: POB 2350, Ladegårdsvej 3, 7100 Vejle; tel. (05) 85-81-33; telex 61113; f. 1971; cap. 150m., res 679m., dep. 4,187m. (1985); Gen. Mans E. HØGSAA, E. K. LARSEN; 53 brs.

Amagerbanken A/S: Amagerbrogade 25, 2300 Copenhagen S; tel. (01) 95-60-90; telex 31262; f. 1903; cap. and res 834m., dep. 5,350m. (Dec. 1985); Chief Gen. Man. KNUD CHRISTENSEN; 27 brs.

Andelsbanken Danebank: Staunings Plads 1-3, 1643 Copenhagen V; tel. (01) 14-51-14; telex 27086; f. 1925; cap. (p.u.) 653.5m., dep. 21,393m. (1985); Chief Gen. Mans Mrs BODIL NYBOE ANDERSEN, A. C. JACOBSEN, H. LUNDAGER, K. ØBERG; 235 brs.

Arbejdernes Landsbank A/S: Vesterbrogade 5, 1502 Copenhagen V; tel. (01) 14-88-77; telex 15633/27235; f. 1919; cap. (p.u.) 300m. (1985); Man. Dirs S. NIBELIUS, J. CHRISTENSEN, J. BAGGE MØLHOLM; 53 brs.

Bikuben: Silkegade 8, 1113 Copenhagen K; tel. 12-01-33; telex 19832; f. 1877; cap. 1,071.9m., res 2,158.4m., dep. 24,801.0m. (Dec. 1985); Gen. Mans HANS ERIK BALLE, KNUD BRANDENBORG, BOERGE MUNK EBBESEN, PEDER ELKJAER; 304 brs.

Bonusbanken A/S: 7400 Herning; tel. (07) 12-11-14; telex 62314; f. 1958; total assets 371m. (1986); Gen. Man. I. ØSTERBY HANSEN; 1 br.

Bornholmerbanken A/S: St. Torv 15, 3700 Rønne, Bornholm; tel. (03) 95-00-61; telex 48117; f. 1966; cap. and res 81m., dep. 391m. (Dec. 1984); Man. SØREN ANDERSEN; 8 brs.

C og G Banken A/S: Dronningens Tuærgade 26, 1302 Copenhagen K; tel. 13-88-99; telex 16127; f. 1890; cap. 40m., res 12.0m., dep. 497.9m. (1984); Chair. VAGN BLINDKILDE; Gen. Mans FLEMMING PEDERSEN, PETER A. JERICHOW.

Copenhagen Handelsbank A/S: 2 Holmens Kanal, 1091 Copenhagen K; tel. (01) 12-86-00; telex 12186; f. 1873; cap. and res 6,795m., dep. 50,658m. (Dec 1985); Chair. B. GOMARD; Chief Exec. B. HANSEN; 350 brs.

Den Danske Bank af 1871 A/S: Holmens Kanal 12, 1092 Copenhagen K; tel. (01) 15-65-00; telex 27000; f. 1871; cap. and res 9,221m., dep. 107,483m. (Dec 1985); Chair. POUL J. SVANHOLM; Man. Dirs TAGE ANDERSEN, ERIK BAGGER, JOHN RAMMER, PETER STRAARUP, KNUD SØRENSEN, HENRIK THUFASON; 285 brs.

Den Danske Provinsbank A/S: Kannikegade 4-6, 8100 Århus C; tel. (06) 12-25-22; telex 64403; main offices in Århus, Odense, Copenhagen and Ålborg; f. 1967 by merger; cap. 920m., res 2,228m., dep. 23,599 (June 1986); Gen. Mans HANS-VERNER LARSEN, B. DALSGAARD; 224 brs.

Djurslands Bank: 5 Torvet, 8500 Grenå; tel. (06) 32-15-55; telex 63488; f. 1965; cap. and res 141m., dep. 1,053m. (1985); Gen. Mans F. JUHL KRISTENSEN, H. STEENBERG; 31 brs.

Egnsbank Nord A/S: Jernbanegade 4-6, 9900 Frederikshavn; tel. (08) 42-04-33; telex 67102; f. 1970; total assets 3,077m. (Dec. 1985); Gen. Mans JENS OLE JENSEN, B. WAMMEN, OLE KRISTENSEN; 39 brs.

Esbjerg Bank A/S: Kongesgade 70, 6700 Esbjerg; tel. (05) 12-82-00; telex 54161; f. 1916; total assets 943m. (Dec. 1985); Man. B. HAABER CHRISTIANSEN; 6 brs.

Fællesbanken for Danmarks Sparekasser A/S: Borgergade 24, 1347 Copenhagen K; tel. (01) 11-27-33; telex 22396; f. 1940; cap. 406.3m., dep. 2,190m. (1985); Dir H. LINDEGAARD; 8 brs.

Forstædernes Bank A/S: Malervangen 1, 2600 Glostrup; tel. (02) 96-17-20; telex 33261; f. 1902; total assets 3,600m. (Sept. 1986); Chair. V. B. CHRISTENSEN; Gen. Man. F. MARCUSSEN; 14 brs.

Haandværker-, Handels- og Landbrugsbanken A/S: Jernbanegade 9, 4700 Næstved; tel. (03) 72-45-55; telex 46255; f. 1901; cap. and res 71m, dep. 421m. (1985); Man. OLE MEYER; 7 brs.

A/S H & L Banken (Handels- og Landbrugsbanken i Thisted): Jernbanegade 7A, 7700 Thisted; tel. (07) 92-21-11; telex 66699; f. 1915; res 30.8m., dep. 412.9m. (1985); Gen. Mans K. E. SØRENSEN, N. JENSEN; 22 brs.

Hellerup Bank A/S: Østergade 16, 1006 Copenhagen K; tel. (01) 12-85-00; telex 16812; f. 1922; total assets 2,534m. (Dec. 1985); Chair. EJVIND BRANDT; Gen. Man. O. LORENTZEN; 18 brs.

Himmerlandsbanken A/S: Adelgade 31, 9500 Hobro; tel. (08) 52-10-00; telex 65864; f. 1892; cap. and res 139.9m., dep. 787.4m. (1985); Man. BENT HANSEN; 14 brs.

Holstebro Bank A/S: Torvet 1, 7500 Holstebro; tel. (07) 42-21-44; telex 66433; f. 1871; cap. and res 265m., dep. 1,361m. (1985); Man. K. E. ANDERSEN; 10 brs.

Jyske Bank: Vestergade 8-16, 8600 Silkeborg; tel. (06) 82-11-22; telex 63231; f. 1855, amalgamated in 1967; dep. 19,650.7m. (Dec. 1985); Chief Exec. POUL NORUP; 147 brs.

DENMARK

Landbobanken i Skive, Salling Bank A/S: Frederiksgade 6, 7800 Skive; tel. (07) 52-33-66; telex 66726; f. 1926; cap. 18m., dep. 596m. (1985); Chair. Lars E. Andersen; Man. P. E. Bastrup; 13 brs.

Langelands Bank A/S: Østtedsgade 6, 5900 Rudkøbing; tel. (09) 51-10-22; telex 50594; f. 1872; cap. and res 61.9m., dep. 275m. (1985); Man. Torben Rasmussen; 17 brs.

Lollands Bank A/S: Nybrogade 3, 4900 Nakskov, Lolland; tel. (03) 92-11-33; telex 47542; f. 1907; cap. 12m., res 51.5m., dep. 336.5m. (1985); Man. Mogens Nielsen; 7 brs.

Midtbank A/S: Østergade 2, 7400 Herning; tel. (07) 12-48-00; telex 62142; f. 1965; cap. and res 472m., dep. 3,123m. (Sept. 1986); Gen. Mans B. Jensen, H. Martinussen, M. Mouritzen; 49 brs.

Morsø Bank A/S: Algade, 7900 Nykøbing M.; tel. (07) 72-14-00; telex 60714; f. 1876; cap. 21m., res 67m., dep. 526m. (1985); Man. Dir H. J. Christensen; 11 brs.

Næstved Diskontobank A/S: Axeltorv 4, 4700 Næstved; tel. (03) 72-15-00; telex 46227; f. 1871; total assets 35,287m. (Dec. 1984); Gen. Man. A. Hove Andreasen; 10 brs.

Nordvestbank A/S: Torvet 4-5, 7620 Lemvig; tel. (07) 82-07-77; telex 66536; f. 1874; cap. and res 165m., dep. 624m. (1985); Chair. E. Thorndahl; Gen. Man. J. Holt; 8 brs.

Nørresundby Bank A/S: Torvet 4, 9400 Nørresundby; tel. (08) 17-33-33; telex 69776; f. 1898; cap. and res 275m., dep. 1,321m. (1985); Man. H. Wormslev; 14 brs.

Privatbanken A/S: Torvegade 2, POB 1000, 2400 Copenhagen NV; tel. (01) 11-11-11; telex 27196; f. 1857; cap. and res 4,413m., dep. 74,448m. (June 1986); Chair. of Board Ole Damgaard-Nielsen; Man. Dirs L. Johansen, E. Lunderskov, Bent Pedersen, S. Rasborg; 215 brs.

Ringkjøbing Bank: Torvet 2, POB 19, 6950 Rinkjøbing; tel. (07) 32-03-22; telex 62442; f. 1872; cap. and res 152m., dep. 963m. (Dec. 1985); Man. Dir Mogens Svensson; 8 brs.

Ringkjøbing Landbobank A/S: Torvet 1, 6950 Ringkjøbing; tel. (07) 32-11-66; telex 60385; f. 1886; cap. and res 240m., dep. 1,112m. (1985); Man. P. J. Madsen; 13 brs.

Roskilde Bank A/S: Algade 14, 4000 Roskilde; f. 1884; tel. (02) 35-17-00; telex 43122; cap. and res 174m., dep. 1,112m. (1985); Man. N. Valentin Hansen; 17 brs.

Skælskør Bank A/S: Algade 18, 4230 Skælskør; tel. (03) 59-60-70; telex 40139; f. 1876; total assets 688m. (Sept. 1985); Man. P. W. Olsen; 6 brs.

Sparekassen SDS: 8 Kongens Nytorv, 1050 Copenhagen K; tel. (01) 13-13-39; telex 15745; f. 1973; cap. and res 4,616m., dep. 34,849m. (1985); Chair. L. Ringaard; 365 brs.

Sydbank A/S: Kirkepladsen 2, POB 169, 6200 Åbenrå; tel. (04) 62-12-22; telex 52114; f. 1970; cap. and res 851m., dep. 5,285m. (1985); Gen. Mans M. C. Andersen, N. Jakobsen, S. Olsen; 63 brs.

Varde Bank A/S: Kongensgade 62-64, 6701 Esbjerg; tel. (05) 12-68-11; telex 54138; f. 1872; cap. 150m., res 744m., dep. 3,470m. (1985); Chair. Starup-Jensen; Man. Dirs C. K. Hansen, Alex Holm Jensen, Kaj Thomsen; 46 brs.

Vestjysk Bank (Hostelbro Landmandsbank): Vestergade 1, 7500 Holstebro; tel. (07) 42-26-11; telex 66412; f. 1887; total assets 1,649m. (Aug. 1985); Mans H. E. Sørensen, G. V. Møller; 4 brs.

BANKERS' ORGANIZATIONS

Den Danske Bankforening (Bankers' Association): Bankernes Hus, Amaliegade 7, 1256 Copenhagen K; tel. (01) 12-02-00; telex 16102; f. 1950; 80 mem. banks; Man. Dir Karsten Hillestrøm.

Danmarks Sparekasseforening (Savings Banks Association): Købmagergade 62, POB 2189, 1017 Copenhagen K: tel. (01) 15-18-11; telex 15965.

STOCK EXCHANGE

Københavns Fondsbørs (Copenhagen Stock Exchange): Nikolaj Plads 2, 1067 Copenhagen K; tel. (01) 93-33-66; telex 16496; f. 1861; Chair. Christen Sørensen; Chief Exec. Ib Paaschburg.

INSURANCE

State Insurance Company

Statsanstalten for Livsforsikring (Government Life Assurance Institution): Kampmannsgade 4, 1645 Copenhagen V; tel. (01) 15-15-15; telex 15283; f. 1842; Gen. Dir Søren Rasmussen.

Principal Private Companies

Alm. Brand af 1792 gs: Lyngby Hovedgade 4, POB 1792, 2800 Lyngby; tel. (02) 87-33-22; telex 37512; f. 1792; Chief Gen. Man. Bent Knie-Andersen.

Assurance-Companiet Baltica, Aktieselskab: Bredgade 40, 1299 Copenhagen K; tel. (01) 12-24-36; telex 16322; f. 1982 by merger; all classes except life; Chief Gen. Man. Peter Christoffersen.

Assurance-Compagniet Baltica, Livsforsikringsaktieselskab: life.

Baltica-Nordisk Reinsurance Company A/S: Groenningen 25, 1270 Copenhagen K; tel. (01) 14-13-67; telex 15367; Gen. Man. Kaj Ahlmann.

Forsikringsselskabet Codan A/S: Codanhus, Gl. Kongevej 60, Frederiksberg C; tel. (01) 21-21-21; telex 15469; f. 1915; all classes except life; Gen. Man. Peter Zobel.

Forsikringsselskabet Codan Liv A/S: f. 1943; life.

A/S Det Kjøbenhavnske Reassurance-Compagni: Amaliegade 39, POB 2093, 1013 Copenhagen K; tel. (01) 14-30-63; telex 19617; reinsurance.

Forsikringsaktieselskabet Hafnia: Holmens Kanal 22, 1097 Copenhagen K; tel. (01) 13-14-15; telex 15546; f. 1872; all classes except life; Chair. E. J. B. Christensen.

Livsforsikringsaktieselskabet Hafnia-Haand i Haand: Holmens Kanal 22, 1097 Copenhagen K; tel. (01) 13-14-15; telex 15546; f. 1980; life; Chair. E. J. B. Christensen.

Livsforsikringsaktieselskabet Hafnia Pension Invest: Holmens Kanal 22, 1097 Copenhagen K; tel. (01) 13-14-15; telex 15546; f. 1983; life; Chair. E. J. B. Christensen.

Skadeforsikringsaktieselskabet Hafnia-Haand i Haand: Holmens Kanal 22, 1097 Copenhagen K; tel. (01) 13-14-15; telex 15546; f. 1890; all classes except life; Chair. E. J. B. Christensen.

Det kongelige octroierede almindelige Brandassurance-Co. A/S (The Royal Chartered General Fire Insurance Co. Ltd): Hojbro Plads 10, 1248 Copenhagen K; tel. (01) 14-15-16; telex 16016; f. 1798; all branches; Man. Jens Vissing.

Købstædernes almindelige Brandforsikring: Grønningen 1, 1270 Copenhagen K; tel. (01) 14-37-48; f. 1761; fire; Chair. Ingvardt Pedersen; Gen. Man. Alf Torp-Pedersen.

Pensionsforsikringsanstalten A/S: Marina Park, Sundkrogsgade 4, 2100 Copenhagen Ø; tel. (01) 20-77-11; telex 16183; life; Gen. Mans Andre Lublin, A. Kühle.

Top-Danmark A/S: Borupvang 4, 2750 Ballerup; tel. (02) 65-33-11; telex 35107; f. 1985; Man. Dir Henning Birch.

Forsikringsselskabet-Topsikring A/S: Borupvang 4, 2750 Ballerup; f. 1985; non-life; Man. Dir Thorkild Kristiansen.

Topsikring A/S Livsforsikringsselskabet: Borupvang 4, 2750 Ballerup; life; Man. Dir Torben V. Holm.

Top International A/S: Borupvang 4, 2750 Ballerup; Man. Dir Eric Guy Whitton.

Top-Center A/S: Borupvang 4, 2750 Ballerup; f. 1985; Man. Dir Henning Birch.

Tryg Forsikring gs: POB 300, Forsikringshuset, Parallelvej, 2800 Lyngby; tel. (02) 87-88-11; telex 37449; f. 1973 by merger; all classes.

Insurance Association

Assurandør-Societetet: Amaliegade 10, 1256 Copenhagen K; tel. (01) 13-75-55; Chair. Bent Møller Hansen; Dir Steen Leth Jeppesen; 111 mems.

Trade and Industry

ADVISORY BODIES

Det Økonomiske Råd (Economic Council): Kampmannsgade 1, IV, 1604 Copenhagen V; tel. (01) 13-51-28; f. 1962, under the Economic Co-ordination Act, to watch national economic development and help to co-ordinate the actions of economic interest groups; 27 members representing both sides of industry, the government and independent economic experts; Co-Chair. Prof. Christen Sørensen, Prof. Peder J. Pedersen, Prof. C. Vastrup.

Industrirådets Industriregister (Federation of Danish Industries' Register of Industries): H. C. Andersens Blvd 18, 1596 Copenhagen V; tel. (01) 15-22-33; telex 22993.

DENMARK

Landsforeningen Dansk Arbejde (National Association for Enterprise): Købmagergade 45, 1150 Copenhagen K; tel. (01) 11-36-22.

CHAMBERS OF COMMERCE

Danish National Committee of International Chamber of Commerce: Børsen, 1217 Copenhagen K; Chair. KNUD OLESEN; Sec.-Gen. H. SEJER-PETERSEN.

Provinshandelskammeret (Provincial Chamber of Commerce): Børsen, 1217 Copenhagen K; tel. (01) 13-90-66; f. 1901; Pres. H. E. HEMPEL-HANSEN; Man. Dir P. NEERGAARD.

Grosserer-Societetet (Chamber of Commerce of Copenhagen): Børsen, 1217 Copenhagen K; tel. (01) 15-53-20; telex 19520; f. 1742; approx. 2,500 mems; Pres. AAGE RASK-PEDERSEN; Sec.-Gen. H. SEJER-PETERSEN.

EMPLOYERS' ORGANIZATIONS

Bryggeriforeningen (Danish Brewers' Association): Frederiksberggade 11, 1459 Copenhagen K; f. 1899; Chair. POUL J. SVANHOLM; Dir POUL ANTONSEN; 21 mems.

Danmarks Textiltekniske Forening (Textile Technical Society): Fredericiavej 99, 7100 Vejle; f. 1942; Pres. AAGE JESPERSEN; Vice-Pres. MOGENS NISSEN; 500 mems.

Dansk Arbejdsgiverforening (Employers' Confederation): Vester Voldgade 113, 1503 Copenhagen V; tel. (01) 93-40-00; telex 16464; f. 1896; Chair. BENNED HANSEN; Dir-Gen. HANS SKOV CHRISTENSEN; 22,800 mems.

Danske Husmandsforeninger (Family Farmers' Association): Landbrugsmagasinet, Vester Farimagsgade 6, 1606 Copenhagen V; tel. (01) 12-99-50; f. 1906; Chair. CHR. SØRENSEN; Sec.-Gen. KURT LÆNKHOLM; 30,000 mems.

De danske Mejeriers Fællesorganisation (Danish Dairy Board): Frederiks Allé 22, 8000 Århus; f. 1912; Chair. THOMAS JØRGENSEN; Sec. A. TIRSGAARD; 100 mems.

Fællesforeningen for Danmarks Brugsforeninger (Co-op of Denmark): Roskildevej 65, 2620 Albertslund; f. 1896; Chair. BJARNE MØGELHØJ; Chief Exec. BENT J. LE FÈVRE; 975,000 mems.

Foreningen af danske Cementfabrikker (Association of Cement Manufacturers): N. Voldgade 34, Copenhagen; f. 1898; Chair. POUL SKOVGAARD; Sec. PER LAURENTS; 4 mems.

Foreningen af Fabrikanter i Jernindustrien i København (Manufacturers' Federation of the Copenhagen Iron Industry): N. Voldgade 30, Copenhagen; f. 1885; Chair. BENNED HANSEN; Sec. E. ENGELHARDT; 172 mems.

Foreningen af Fabrikanter i Jernindustrien i Provinserne (Manufacturers' Federation of the Provincial Iron Industry): N. Voldgade 34, Copenhagen; tel. (01) 12-22-78; telex 16068; f. 1895; Chair. VAGN-AAGE JENSEN; Sec. GLENN SØGAARD; 435 mems.

Håndværksrådet (Federation of Crafts and Smaller Industries): Amaliegade 15, 1256 Copenhagen K; tel. (01) 12-36-76; telex 16600; f. 1879; comprises about 450 asscns with 57,000 mems; Chair. KLAUS BONDE LARSEN; Man. LAUE TRABERG SMIDT.

Industrirådet (Federation of Industries): H. C. Andersens Blvd 18, 1596 Copenhagen V; tel. (01) 15-22-33; telex 22993; f. 1910; Pres. OTTO CHRISTENSEN; Dir OVE MUNCH; 2,250 mems.

Det kongelige danske Landhusholdningsselskab (The Royal Agricultural Society): Rolighedsvej 26, 1958 Frederiksberg C; tel. (01) 35-02-27; f. 1769 to promote agricultural progress; Pres JENS N. HENRIKSEN, A. NEIMANN-SØRENSEN, P. SKAK OLUFSEN; Dir JENS WULFF; 3,100 mems.

De danske Landboforeninger (Farmers' Unions): Axelborg, Vesterbrogade 4A, 1620 Copenhagen V; tel. (01) 12-75-61; f. 1893; Pres. H. O. A. KJELDSEN; Chief Sec. JØRGEN SKOVBAK; 99,000 mems.

Landbrugsrådet (Agricultural Council): Axelborg, Axeltorv 3, 1609 Copenhagen V; tel. (01) 14-56-72; telex 16772; f. 1919; Pres. H. O. A. KJELDSEN; Dir KJELD EJLER; 32 mems.

Sammenslutningen af Arbejdsgivere indenfor den keramiske Industri (Federation of Employers of the Ceramic Industry): N. Voldgade 34, Copenhagen; tel. (01) 15-17-00; f. 1918; Chair. P. BREDEGAARD; Sec. I. SEHESTED HANSEN; 22 mems.

Sammenslutningen af Landbrugets Arbejdsgiverforeninger (SALA) (Agricultural Employers' Federation): Vesterbrogade 6D, 1620 Copenhagen V; tel. (01) 13-46-55.

Skibværftsforeningen (Association of Danish Shipbuilders): St Kongensgade 128, 1264 Copenhagen K; tel. (01) 13-24-16; telex 19582.

Directory

Textilindustrien (Federation of Textile Industries): Bredgade 41, POB 300, 7400 Herning; f. 1895; Pres. C. WICHMANN MADSEN; Man. Dir J. BOLLERUP JENSEN; 310 mems.

TRADE UNIONS

Landsorganisationen i Danmark (LO) (Federation of Trade Unions): Rosenørns Allé 12, 1634 Copenhagen V; tel. (01) 35-35-41; telex 16170; Pres. KNUD CHRISTENSEN; Vice-Pres. FINN THORGRIMSON; Treas. ERIK HEMMINGSEN; 1,403,826 mems (1985); 1,393 affiliated unions.

Dansk Beklædnings- og Tekstilarbejderforbund (Textile and Garment Workers); Nyropsgade 14, 1602 Copenhagen V; tel. (01) 11-67-65; f. 1978 by merger of Garment Workers' Union and Textile Workers' Union; Pres. and Gen. Sec. TOVE STENKJÆR; 32,760 mems.

Dansk Bogbinder- og Kartonnagearbejder Forbund (Bookbinders and Cardboard Box Workers): Grafisk Forbundshus, Lygten 16, 2400 Copenhagen NV; tel. (01) 81-42-22; Pres. SVEND MAABJERG; 8,819 mems.

Dansk El-Forbund (Electricians' Union): Vodroffsvej 26, 1900 Frederiksberg C; tel. (01) 21-14-00; Pres. FREDDY ANDERSEN; 24,053 mems.

Dansk Funktionærforbund (Service Trade Employees); Upsalagade 20, 2100 Copenhagen Ø; tel. (01) 38-65-95; Pres. HANS JØRGEN JENSEN; 25,133 mems.

Dansk Jernbane Forbund (Railway Workers); Bredgade 21, 1260 Copenhagen K; tel. (01) 14-33-00; f. 1899; Pres. E. NYGAARD JESPERSEN; 10,887 mems.

Dansk Kommunal Arbejderforbund (Municipal Workers); Nitivej 6, 2000 Frederiksberg; tel. (01) 19-90-22; telex 27481; Pres. POUL WINCKLER; 119,106 mems.

Dansk Metalarbejderforbund (Metalworkers): Nyropsgade 38, 1602 Copenhagen V; tel. (01) 12-82-12; telex 16526; f. 1888; Pres. GEORG POULSEN; 138,500 mems.

Dansk Postforbund (Postmen): Vodroffsvej 13A, 1900 Frederiksberg C; tel. (01) 21-41-24; f. 1908; Pres. AAGE ANDERSEN; 16,697 mems.

Dansk Typograf-Forbund (Printers): Grafisk Forbundshus, Lygten 16, 2400 Copenhagen NV; tel. (01) 81-42-22; Pres. KAJ PEDERSEN; 9,927 mems.

Handels- og Kontorfunktionærernes Forbund i Danmark (Commercial and Clerical Employees): H. C. Andersens Blvd 50, POB 268, 1501 Copenhagen V; tel. (01) 12-43-43; f. 1900; Pres. JØRGEN EIBERG; 311,220 mems.

Hotel-og Restaurationspersonalets Forbund i Danmark (Catering Workers): Uplandsgade 52A, 2300 Copenhagen S; Chair. BENT MOOS; 8,039 mems.

Husligt Arbejder Forbund (Domestic Workers): Rådhuspladsen 77, 1550 Copenhagen V; tel. (01) 13-40-00; Pres. MARGIT VOGNSEN; 71,526 mems.

Kvindeligt Arbejderforbund (Unskilled Women Workers); Ewaldsgade 3, 2200 Copenhagen N; tel. (01) 39-31-15; f. 1901; Pres. LILLIAN KNUDSEN; 105,000 mems.

Malerforbundet i Danmark (Housepainters): Tomsgårdsvej 23c, 2400 Copenhagen NV; tel. (01) 34-75-22; f. 1890; Pres. AGNER CHRISTENSEN; 13,919 mems.

Murerforbundet i Danmark (Bricklayers): Mimersgade 47, 2200 Copenhagen N; tel. (01) 81-99-00; Pres. BENDT JENSEN; 12,806 mems.

Nærings- og Nydelsesmiddelarbejder Forbundet (Food, Sugar Confectionery, Chocolate, Dairy Produce and Tobacco Workers): C.F. Richs Vej 103, 2000 Frederiksberg; tel. (01) 87-15-22; Pres. E. ANTON JOHANNSEN; 43,994 mems.

Pædagogisk Medhjælper Forbund (Teachers' assistants): St Kongensgade 79, 1264 Copenhagen K; tel. (01) 11-03-43; Pres. JAKOB SØLVHØJ; 22,829 mems.

Snedker- og Tømrerforbundet i Danmark (Joiners, Cabinet-makers and Carpenters): Mimersgade 47, 2200 Copenhagen N; tel. (01) 81-99-00; Pres. BENT LARSEN; 46,253 mems.

Specialarbejderforbundet i Danmark (Unskilled and Semi-skilled Workers): Nyropsgade 30, 1602 Copenhagen V; tel. (01) 14-21-40; telex 19596; Pres. HARDY HANSEN; 318,066 mems.

Træindustriarbejderforbundet i Danmark (Woodworkers); Mimersgade 47, 2200 Copenhagen N; tel. (01) 81-99-00; Pres. JENS PEDER JENSEN; 17,458 mems.

Akademikernes Centralorganisation (Academic employees): Nørre Voldgade 29, 1358 Copenhagen K; tel. (01) 12-85-40.

Den Almindelige Danske Lægeforening (Danish Medical Association): Trondhjemsgade 9, 2100 Copenhagen Ø; tel. (01) 38-55-00.

Dansk Journalistforbund (Journalists); Gammel Strand 46, 1202 Copenhagen K; tel. (01) 14-23-88; f. 1961; Pres. Ms TOVE HYGUM JAKOBSEN; 5,600 mems.

Funktionærernes og Tjenestemændenes Fællesråd (Federation of Civil Servants' and Salaried Employees' Organizations): Niels Hemmingsensgade 12, 1010 Copenhagen K; tel. (01) 15-30-22; f. 1952; Chair. MARTIN RØMER; 350,000 mems.

Transport

RAILWAYS

In June 1986 government plans were announced for a 20-km combined tunnel-and-bridge link for trains across the Great Belt, linking the islands of Zealand and Funen. Work was to start in 1987 and was due to be completed in 1992. A meeting between the Governments of Denmark and Sweden was held in October 1986 to discuss plans for a bridge-and-tunnel link between the two countries.

DSB (Danish State Railways): Sølvgade 40, 1349 Copenhagen K; tel. (01) 14-04-00; telex 22225; controls 2,471 km of line, of which 145 km in the Copenhagen suburban area are electrified; Dir-Gen. OLE ANDRESEN.

A total of 514 km, mostly branch lines, is run by 13 private companies.

ROADS

At 31 December 1985 Denmark had 70,147 km (43,595 miles) of paved roads, including 603 km (374 miles) of motorways and 3,996 km (2,483 miles) of other national roads.

Ministry of Public Works (Transport Department): Frederiksholms Kanal 27, 1220 Copenhagen K; tel. (01) 12-62-42; telex 22275; f. 1894; administers general traffic problems, road traffic, air traffic, harbours, roads, private railways; Perm. Sec. JØRGEN L. HALCK.

FERRIES

DSB (Danish State Railways): Sølvgade 40, 1349 Copenhagen K; tel. (01) 14-04-00; telex 22225; operates passenger train and motor car ferries between the mainland and principal islands. Train and motor car ferries are also operated between Denmark, Sweden and Germany in co-operation with German Federal Railways, and German and Swedish State Railways; Gen. Man. OLE ANDRESEN.

Other services are operated by private companies.

SHIPPING

The Port of Copenhagen is the largest port in Denmark and the only one including a Free Port Zone. The other major ports are Århus, Ålborg and Esbjerg, which provides daily services to the United Kingdom. There are oil terminals at Kalundborg, Fredericia and Skælskør.

Farvandsdirektoratet (National Administration of Shipping and Navigation): Overgaden oven Vandet 62B, 1001 Copenhagen K; tel. (01) 57-40-50; telex 31319.

Principal Shipping Companies

(Figures for the number of ships and their displacement refer only to Danish flag vessels.)

Corral Line: POB 49, 6300 Gråsten; tel. (04) 65-00-19; telex 52814; 2 livestock carriers of 4,000 grt; shipowners, managers, chartering agents; worldwide; Man. Dir B. CLAUSEN.

Rederiet Otto Danielsen: Kongevejen 40, 2840 Holte; tel. (02) 42-32-55; telex 15704; 7 vessels of 9,200 grt; general tramp trade, chartering, ship sales; Man. Dirs OTTO and KNUD DANIELSEN.

Dannebrog Rederi A/S: Rungsted Strandvej 113, 2960 Rungsted Kyst; tel. (02) 86-65-00; telex 37204; f. 1883; owners of live sheep carriers, tankers and roll-on, roll-off vessels; Liner service: Dafra Line: Europe–West Africa, Nordana Line: US Gulf–Caribbean, Mediterranean; Man. Owner E. WEDELL-WEDELLSBORG.

DFDS A/S: Skt Annæ Plads 30, 1295 Copenhagen; tel. (01) 15-63-00; telex 19435; f. 1866; 10 vessels of 98,100 grt; passenger and car ferry services Denmark–UK, Denmark–Norway, Sweden–UK, Germany–UK, liner trade to Spain, Portugal and South America; Man. Dir NIELS BACH.

The East Asiatic Co Ltd A/S: Holbergsgade 2, 1099 Copenhagen K; tel. (01) 11-83-00; telex 12100; f. 1897; 6 vessels of 189,300 grt; trading, industry, plantations, shipping; Chair. T. W. SCHMITH; Board of Management H. H. SPARSØ, J. A. HANSEN, O. F. ANDREASEN, F. HASLE.

Kosan Tankers A/S: Studiestræde 61, 1581 Copenhagen V; tel. (01) 14-34-00; telex 22214; f. 1951; 19 gas carriers of 29,754 grt; Gen. Man. GUNNER NIELSEN.

Knud I. Larsen: Århusgade 129, Frihavnen, 2100 Copenhagen Ø; tel. (01) 18-00-44; telex 22251; f. 1983; 14 vessels of 20,200 grt; general cargo and container ships; Man. Owners KNUD I. LARSEN, FINN SAKSØ LARSEN.

J. Lauritzen A/S: Skt Annæ Plads 28, 1291 Copenhagen K; tel. (01) 11-12-22; telex 15522; f. 1884; 173,800 grt; world-wide service with refrigerated vessels, product tankers and bulk carriers; drilling rigs, polar vessels, cruise traffic; Pres JENS KASTEN, TORBEN V. RASMUSSEN.

Mercandia Rederierne: Amaliegade 27, 1256 Copenhagen K; tel. (01) 12-01-55; telex 19762; f. 1964; 21 roll-on, roll-off vessels totalling 763,600 grt; tramp and liner services; Owner and Man. PER HENRIKSEN.

A. P. Møller: Esplanaden 50, 1098 Copenhagen K; f. 1904; 85 ships of 3,024,000 grt; container ships, car carriers, gas and oil tankers, bulk-carriers, supply-ships and anchor-handling vessels, drilling rigs; principal services: USA, Far East, West Africa, Persian (Arabian) Gulf, Europe; Chair. MAERSK MCKINNEY MØLLER.

Mortensen + Lange: POB 2703, Strandvejen 32D, 2100 Copenhagen Ø; tel. (01) 29-55-33; telex 15100; 18 vessels of 14,800 grt; worldwide tramping; Man. Dir HANS MORTENSEN.

Dampskibsselskabet Norden A/S: Amaliegade 49, 1256 Copenhagen K; tel. (01) 15-04-51; telex 22374; f. 1871; 7 bulk carriers and product tankers of 189,700 grt; tramp; Dir J. KRUHL.

Ove Skou Rederiaktieselskab: H. C. Andersens Blvd 44/46, 1553 Copenhagen V; tel. (01) 15-36-00; telex 19900; 3 ships totalling 45,200 grt; worldwide tramping; Man. Dir LARS OREBY HANSEN.

A/S Em. Z. Svitzer Bjergnings-Enterprise: Kvæsthusgade 1, 1251 Copenhagen K; tel. (01) 15-51-95; telex 15983; f. 1833; 25 tugs and salvage vessels of 5,500 grt; worldwide salvage, towage and offshore services; Gen. Man. JØRN HANSEN.

A/S D/S Torm: Holmens Kanal 42, 1060 Copenhagen K; tel. (01) 12-24-37; telex 22315; f. 1889; 5 bulk carriers and product tankers of 122,800 grt; liner services USA–West Africa; Man. Dir ERIK BEHN.

Association

Danmarks Rederiforening (Danish Shipowners' Asscn): Amaliegade 33, 1256 Copenhagen K; tel. (01) 11-40-88; telex 16492; f. 1884; representing 4,029,000 grt; Chair. of the Board ERIK BEHN; Man. Dir KNUD PONTOPPIDAN.

CIVIL AVIATION

The International Airport is about 10 km from the centre of Copenhagen. Domestic airports include Roskilde in Sjælland (Zealand), Tirstrup at Århus, Ålborg, Billund, Esbjerg, Karup, Skrydstrup, Stauning, Sønderborg and Thisted in Jutland, Rønne in Bornholm and Odense in Fyn (Funen).

Statens Luftfartsvæsen (Civil Aviation Administration): Luftfartshuset, POB 744, 2450 Copenhagen SV; tel. (01) 44-48-48; telex 27096.

Det Danske Luftfartselskab A/S—DDL (Danish Airlines): Industriens Hus, H. C. Andersens Blvd 18, 1553 Copenhagen V; tel. (01) 14-13-33; telex 22437; f. 1918; partner in SAS (see under Sweden) and SCANAIR; Chair. HALDOR TOPSØE; Man. Dir R. SØKILDE.

National Airlines

Conair A/S (Consolidated Aircraft Corporation): Hangar 276, Copenhagen Airport, 2791 Dragoer; tel. (01) 53-17-00; telex 31423; operates charter and inclusive-tour flights to the Mediterranean and Africa for Spies Travel Organization, which owns the airline; Chair. ROBERT KOCH-NIELSEN; fleet of 5 Boeing 720B.

Danair A/S: Kastruplundgade 13, 2770 Kastrup; f. 1971; owned by SAS (see under Sweden), Maersk Air and Cimber Air; operates domestic services between Copenhagen and Ålborg, Billund, Esbjerg, Karup, Odense, Roenne, Skrydstrup, Sønderborg, Thisted, Tirstrup and the Faeroe Islands; Chair. F. AHLGREEN ERIKSEN; Man. Dir GUNNAR TIETZ; fleet of DC-9, B-737, Dash-7, Shorts-360 and ATR-42 on lease from parent companies.

DENMARK

Cimber Air A/S: Sonderborg Airport, 6400 Sonderborg; telex 52315; operates services between Copenhagen and Sonderborg for Danair, operates charter flights and total route systems for other companies; Pres. I. L. NIELSEN; Man. Dir H. I. NIELSEN; fleet of 2 Fokker F.28-3000, 2 Nord 262, 3 ATR-42-42-3000, 2 King Air 200, 1 Falcon 20.

Maersk Air: Copenhagen Airport, 2791 Dragoer; tel. (01) 53-44-44; telex 31126; provides charter flights for Scandinavian tour operators, operates a scheduled service between Billund and Southend, England and in 1983 acquired the commuter airline Air Business, linking the oil centres of Esbjerg and Stavanger; Pres. BJARNE HANSEN; fleet of 4 Boeing 737-200, 2 737-300, 3 Dash 7, 2 Shorts 360, 1 HS.125-700B, 3 Bell 212, 2 Aérospatiale Super Puma.

Sterling Airways: Hangar 144, Copenhagen Airport, 2791 Dragoer; tel. (01)53-53-53; telex 31231; owned by Tjaereborg International Holdings A/S, operates inclusive-tour flights to Europe, North Africa, North America and Sri Lanka; Chair. STEFFEN GULMANN; Pres. PETER VANGE; fleet of 2 DC-8-65, 3 Boeing 727-200, 6 Caravelle 10B, 2 Corvette, 1 King Air C90.

Tourism

Danmarks Turistråd (Tourist Board): Vesterbrogade 6D, 1620 Copenhagen V; tel. (01) 11-14-15; Information Bureau, H. C. Andersens Blvd 22, 1553 Copenhagen V; tel. (01) 11-13-25; telex 27586; f. 1967; Dir ERIK PALSGAARD.

Atomic Energy

Danish Energy Agency: Landemærket 11, 1119 Copenhagen K; tel. (01) 92-67-00; telex 22450; f. 1976; Dir HANS VON BÜLOW.

Risø National Laboratory: Forsogsanlæg Risø, POB 49, 4000 Roskilde; tel. (02) 37-12-12; telex 43116; f. 1958; research laboratory for utilization of energy; Dir N. E. BUSCH; Asst Dirs H. BJERRUM MØLLER, K. SINGER, S. P. STRANDDORF.

DANISH EXTERNAL TERRITORIES

THE FAEROE ISLANDS

Introductory Survey

Location, Climate, Language, Religion, Flag, Capital

The Faeroe (Faroe) Islands are a group of 18 islands (of which 17 are inhabited) in the Atlantic Ocean, between Scotland and Iceland. The main island is Streymoy, where more than one-third of the population resides. The climate is mild in winter and cool in summer, with a mean temperature of 7°C (45°F). Most of the inhabitants profess Christianity: the majority of Faeroese are Lutherans, belonging to the Danish National Church. The principal language is Faeroese, but Danish is a compulsory subject in all schools. The flag (proportions 22 by 16) displays a red cross, bordered with blue, on a white background, the upright of the cross being to the left of centre. The capital is Tórshavn, which is situated on Streymoy.

History and Government

The Faeroe Islands have been under Danish administration since Queen Margrete of Denmark inherited Norway in 1380. The islands were occupied by the United Kingdom while Denmark was under German occupation during the Second World War, but they were restored to Danish control immediately after the war. The Home Rule Act of 1948 gave the Faeroese control over all their internal affairs. There is a local parliament (the Løgting), but the Danish Folketing, to which the Faeroese send two members, is responsible for defence and foreign policy, constitutional matters and the judicial and monetary systems. The Faeroe Islands did not join the EEC with Denmark in 1973.

The centre-left coalition government of Social Democrats, Republicans and the People's Party, formed in 1978, collapsed in 1980 over a plan, opposed by the conservative People's Party, to extend through the winter months a government-owned ferry service linking the islands with Denmark, Norway and Scotland. At a general election, held in November, conservative political groups slightly increased their share of the popular vote. Although there was no material change in the balance of party representation in the Løgting, the Union Party formed a centre-right coalition with the People's Party and the Home Rule Party in January 1981. A general election was held in November 1984, and in December a four-party, centre-left coalition government was formed, comprising the Social Democratic Party, the Home Rule Party, the Republican Party and the Christian People's Party combined with the Progressive and Fishing Industry Party.

Economic Affairs

Only about 6% of the land surface is cultivated. As the summers are too cool for cereal production, the main crops are potatoes and vegetables, and grass for the large number of sheep raised on the islands. Coal is mined at Suderoy, and about one-fifth of the working population is engaged in handicrafts. The most important sector of the Faeroese economy is fishing, which employed 17% of the labour force in 1977 and contributed 22% of the total GDP in 1980, accounting for more than 90% of the islands' exports. In January 1974 the Løgting decided not to join the EEC but to negotiate a special trade agreement which would protect the fishing industry. Following Faeroese pressure, an agreement was reached on limiting the annual catch of cod and haddock by foreign trawlers from January 1974. In March 1977, despite protests from the EEC, the Faeroes imposed stringent conservation measures, curbing fishing within a limit of 200 nautical miles (370 km) from the coast. In an attempt to shield the economy from changing market conditions in fishing, tourism has been developed, with a luxury hotel being built at Tórshavn in 1984. Danish subsidies account for about 15% of the Faeroese GNP.

In 1940 the Faeroese krona was introduced. It must, however, always be freely interchangeable with the Danish krone at the rate of 1: 1. For exchange rate, see under Denmark.

Education and Social Welfare

The education system is similar to that of Denmark, except that Faeroese is the language of instruction. Danish is, however, a compulsory subject in all schools. Plans for the upgrading of the Faeroese Academy to university status were under way in 1986.

In 1981 government medical services included three hospitals, with a total of 357 beds, and 64 physicians.

Statistical Survey

Source: Føroya Landsstýri (Faeroese Government),
Tinganes, 3800 Tórshavn, Faeroe Islands.

AREA AND POPULATION

Area: 1,398.9 sq km (540.1 sq miles).

Population (official estimates at mid-year): 44,479 in 1982; 44,805 in 1983; 45,464 in 1984.

Principal Town: Tórshavn (capital), estimated population 13,408 in 1984.

Births and Deaths (1985): Registered live births 740 (birth rate 16.2 per 1,000); Deaths 330 (death rate 7.2 per 1,000). Source: UN, *Population and Vital Statistics Report*.

Labour Force (census of 22 September 1977): Males 12,808; Females 4,777; Total 17,585.

AGRICULTURE, ETC.

Fishing ('000 metric tons, live weight, 1984): Atlantic cod 62.0, Haddock 13.4, Saithe (Coalfish) 56.9, Norway pout 28.0, Blue whiting (Poutassou) 62.3, Capelin 45.3, Atlantic herring 2.5, Atlantic mackerel 9.2, Other fishes 55.0, Crustaceans and molluscs 12.9; total catch 347.5. Figures include quantities landed by Faeroes fishing craft in foreign ports but exclude quantities landed by foreign fishing craft in Faeroes ports.

FINANCE

Government Accounts ('000 kroner, year ending 31 March 1984): Net revenue 1,135,105; Expenditure 1,074,050.

Cost of Living (consumer price index; base: 1980 = 100): 114.8 in 1981; 127.8 in 1982.

Gross National Product (million kroner at current prices): 3,700 in 1982; 4,450 in 1983; 4,907 in 1984.

EXTERNAL TRADE

Principal Commodities (million kroner, 1984): *Imports c.i.f.:* Food and live animals 233.9; Mineral fuels, lubricants, etc. 452.6 (Petroleum products 452.3); Chemicals and related products 97.2; Basic manufactures 347.0; Machinery 368.8 (Non-electric machinery 200.7, Electric machinery, apparatus, etc. 168.1); Transport equipment 830.6 (Road vehicles and parts 154.5, ships and boats 676.1); Miscellaneous manufactured articles 253.3; Total (incl. others) 2,707.7. *Exports f.o.b.:* Fresh, chilled or frozen fish 893.1 (Fresh or frozen fish fillets 675.1); Salted, dried or smoked fish 317.1 (Salted cod 183.2); Crustaceans and molluscs 188.9; Animal feeding-stuff (excl. cereals) 196.0; Total (incl. others) 1,640.4.

Principal Trading Partners (million kroner, 1984): *Imports c.i.f.:* Denmark 1,594.8; Fed. Repub. of Germany 389.9; Norway 406.2; Sweden 81.2; United Kingdom 43.3; Total (incl. others) 2,707.7. *Exports f.o.b.:* Denmark 342.7; France (incl. Monaco) 121.7; Fed. Repub. of Germany 224.9; Greece 29.0; Italy 112.5; Norway 26.4; Spain 26.6; Sweden 32.5; United Kingdom 229.2; USA 309.4; Total (incl. others) 1,640.4.

TRANSPORT

Shipping (1983): Merchant fleet (displacement) 68,000 gross registered tons; International sea-borne freight traffic (estimates, '000 metric tons): Goods loaded 188, Goods unloaded 313. (Source: UN, *Monthly Bulletin of Statistics*).

DANISH EXTERNAL TERRITORIES

Directory

GOVERNMENT

The legislative body is the Løgting, elected on a basis of proportional representation. All Faeroese over the age of 20 years have the right to vote. Based on the strength of the parties in the Løgting, a small Government, the Landsstýri, is formed. This is the administrative body in certain spheres, chiefly relating to Faeroese economic affairs. The Løgmadur (Chairman) has to ratify all Løgting laws. A commissioner, known as the Ríkisumboðsmaður, represents the Danish Government.

Ríkisumboðsmaður: NIELS BENTSEN.

Landsstýri
(December 1986)

Løgmadur and Minister of Fisheries: ATLI DAM (Social Democratic Party).
Deputy Chairman and Minister of Education and Agriculture: JÓGVAN DURHUUS (Republican Party).
Minister of Industry and Justice: VILHELM JOHANESEN (Social Democratic Party).
Minister of Social Services: Rev. NIELS PAULI DANIELSEN (CPP, PFIP).
Minister of Transport and Communications, and Cultural and Religious Affairs: LASSE KLEIN (Home Rule Party).
Minister of Finance: JÓNGERD PURKHÚS (Republican Party).

Government Offices

Færøernes Hjemmestyre (Faeroese Home Rule Government): Landskontoret, 3800 Tórshavn; tel. (042) 1-10-80.

Løgting

The Løgting has 32 members, elected by universal adult suffrage.
Speaker: JAKUP LINDENSKOV (Social Democratic Party).
Deputy Speaker: JÓGVAN SUNDSTEIN (People's Party).

Election, 8 November 1984

	Votes	Seats
Javnaðarflokkurin (Social Democratic Party)	5,879	8
Fólkaflokkurin (People's Party)	5,446	7
Sambandsflokkurin (Union Party)	5,330	7
Tjóveldisflokkurin (Republican Party)	4,921	6
Sjálvstýrisflokkurin (Home Rule Party)	2,135	2
CPP, PFIP (Christian People's Party, Progressive and Fishing Industry Party)	1,466	2

POLITICAL ORGANIZATIONS

The address of each of the following organizations is Løgtingid, Aarvegi, 3800 Tórshavn.

Fólkaflokkurin (People's Party): f. 1940; favours free enterprise and wider political and economic autonomy for the Faeroes within the Kingdom of Denmark; Chair. JÓGVAN SUNDSTEIN.

Framburds- og Fiskivinnuflokkurin (Progressive and Fishing Industry Party): non-socialist, social, anti-communist centre party; has strong links with the Fishermen's Association.

Javnaðarflokkurin (Social Democratic Party): f. 1928; Chair. ATLI P. DAM.

Sambandsflokkurin (Union Party): f. 1906; favours the maintenance of close relations between the Faeroes and the Kingdom of Denmark; conservative in internal affairs; Chair. PAULI ELLEFSEN.

Sjálvstýrisflokkurin (Home Rule Party): f. 1906; social-liberal party advocating political independence for the Faeroes within the Kingdom of Denmark; Leader HILMAR KASS.

Tjodveldisflokkurin (Republican Party): f. 1948; advocates the secession of the Faeroes from Denmark; Chair. ERLENDUR PATURSSON.

RELIGION

Christianity

The Faeroes Church comes under the jurisdiction of the Lutheran Bishop of Copenhagen, who exercises control through a suffragan bishop. The largest independent group is the 'Plymouth Brethren'. There is also a small Roman Catholic community.

THE PRESS

There are no daily papers in the Faeroe Islands.

Dagblaðið: POB 23, 3800 Tórshavn; tel. (042) 17600; telex 81338; 3 a week; People's Party; circ. 5,500.

Dimmalætting: POB 19, 3800 Tórshavn; tel. (042) 11212; telex 81222; 3 a week; Union Party; circ. 11,700.

Friu Føroyar: POB 2055, 3800 Argir; tel. (042) 12098; f. 1983; weekly; socialist.

Norðlýsið: POB 58, 3870 Klaksvík; tel. (042) 56285; weekly; circ. 2,000.

Oyggjatíðindi: POB 312, 3800 Tórshavn; tel. (042) 14411; 2 a week; circ. 5,000.

Tíðindablaðið Sosialurin: POB 76, 3800 Tórshavn; tel. (042) 11820; f. 1927; 3 a week; Editor JAN MÜLLER; Social Democratic Party; circ. 6,000.

Tingakrossur: R. C. Effersøesgøta 16, 3800 Tórshavn; tel. (042) 15474; weekly; Home Rule Party; circ. 1,600.

14 September: POB 62, 3800 Tórshavn; tel. (042) 14412; 2 a week; circ. 4,000.

NEWS AGENCY

Faeroe Press Agency: P/f Salvará, Tjarnardeild 12, Tórshavn; f. 1980; covers Ritzaus Bureau of Copenhagen, Danmarks Radio and Morgunblaðið of Reykjavík, Iceland; Man. JÓGVAN ARGE.

PUBLISHER

Útvarp Føroya: Norðari Ringvegur, POB 328, 3800 Tórshavn; tel. (042) 16568; telex 81226; f. 1957; fiction and periodicals; Man. NIELS JUEL ARGE.

RADIO AND TELEVISION

In 1984 there were an estimated 9,000 television receivers, and in 1985 16,800 radio receivers were estimated to be in use.

Sjónvarp Føroya (Faeroese Television): POB 21, 3800 Tórshavn; tel. (042) 17780; telex 81391; f. 1982; Man. J. A. SKAALE.

Útvarp Føroya (Faeroese Broadcasting Corporation): POB 328, 3800 Tórshavn; tel. (042) 16566; telex 81226; f. 1957; Man. N. J. ARGE.

BANKS

(cap. = capital; dep. = deposits; m. = million; amounts in kroner; brs = branches)

Føroya Banki AS: POB 14, Niels Finsengøta 15, 3800 Tórshavn; tel. (042) 11350; telex 81227; f. 1906; total assets 3,561m. (Dec. 1985); Chair. POUL JOHS. JOHANSEN; Gen. Mans HANS-JORGEN LAURSEN, JOHAN SIMONSEN, NIELS JOEL NATTESTAD; 32 brs.

Sjovinnubankin PF (Fisheries Bank): 3800 Tórshavn; tel. (042) 14900; telex 81229; f. 1932; total assets 2,470m. (Dec. 1985); Chair. BIRGIR DANIELSEN; Mans STEINGIRM NIELSEN, REGIN OLSEN; 29 brs.

TRANSPORT

The main harbour is at Tórshavn; the other ports are at Fuglafjordur, Klaksvík, Skálafjordur, Tvøroyri, Vágur and Vestmanna. Between mid-May and mid-September, a summer roll-on, roll-off ferry service links the Faeroe Islands with Iceland, Shetland, Denmark and Norway.

There is an airport on Vágar. Danair operates services to Bergen and Copenhagen, and Icelandair operates a service to Reykjavík.

TOURISM

Føroya Ferdamannafelag: 3800 Tórshavn; tel. (042) 15788; telex 81375; tourism information and travel agency.

Kunningarstovan Tórshavn: 3800 Tórshavn; tel. (042) 15788; telex 81375; tourism information and tour operator.

DANISH EXTERNAL TERRITORIES

Greenland

GREENLAND

Introductory Survey

Location, Climate, Language, Flag, Capital

Greenland is the world's largest island, with a total area of 2,175,600 sq km, and lies in the North Atlantic Ocean, east of Canada. Most of it is permanently covered by ice but 341,700 sq km of coastland are habitable. Danish and Greenlandic are the official languages. The flag displays a circular rising sun, set against a red and white background. Nuuk (Godthåb) is the capital.

History, Government, Defence

Greenland first came under Danish rule in 1380. In the revision of the Danish constitution in 1953, Greenland became part of the Kingdom. The island sends two members to the Danish Folketing, and the Danish authorities are represented in Greenland by the High Commissioner (Rigsombudsmanden).

In October 1972 the Greenlanders voted by 9,658 to 3,990 against joining the European Community but, as part of Denmark, were bound by the Danish decision to join. Resentment of Danish domination of the economy, education and the professions continued, taking expression in 1977 in the formation of a nationalist left-wing party, the Siumut. In 1975 the Minister for Greenland appointed a commission to devise terms for Greenland home rule. Its proposals for a Parliament (Landsting) and Executive (Landsstyre), with several responsibilities, including foreign policy and defence, remaining under Danish control, were approved by 73.1% to 26.9% in a referendum among the Greenland electorate in January 1979. The Siumut, led by a Lutheran pastor, Jonathan Motzfeldt, secured 13 seats in the 21-member Landsting at a general election in April, and a five-member Landsstyre, with Motzfeldt as Prime Minister, took office in May. Since 1979 the island has been gradually assuming full administration of its internal affairs.

In February 1982 a referendum was held to decide Greenland's continued membership of the European Community. This resulted in a 53% majority in favour of withdrawal. Negotiations were begun in May 1982, with the Danish Government acting on Greenland's behalf, and were concluded in March 1984 (with effect from 1 February 1985): Greenland was accorded the status of an overseas territory in association with the Community, with preferential access to EEC markets (see below).

At the April 1983 general election to the Landsting (enlarged, by measures adopted in 1982, to between 23 and 26 seats, depending on the proportion of votes cast), the Siumut and Atassut parties won 12 seats each, while the Inuit Ataqatigiit (IA) won two seats. The Siumut party once again formed a government, led by Motzfeldt, dependent on the support of the IA members in the Landsting: this support was withdrawn in March 1984, when the IA members voted against the terms of withdrawal from the European Community, and Motzfeldt resigned. In the ensuing general election, held in June, the Siumut and Atassut parties won 11 seats each while the IA won three. Motzfeldt once again formed a coalition government, comprising the Siumut party and the IA.

Economic Affairs

Seal-hunting has traditionally been the main occupation in Greenland and it is still very important in the northern districts. In the south, sheep-rearing is on the increase, while in the central coastal areas fishing is of prime importance. In June 1980 the Danish Government declared an economic zone extending 200 nautical miles (370 km) off the east coast of Greenland. Under the terms of Greenland's withdrawal from the European Community, which took effect in February 1985, Community member countries retained fishing rights in Greenland waters, in return for an annual payment of 26.5m. ECUs (US $21.2m.) for an initial period of five years: a proportion of the total catch was to be reserved for Greenland, and preferential access to EEC markets for Greenland fish products was to be maintained.

The exploitation of mineral resources and of hydroelectric power is subject to agreement between the Danish Government and the Greenland Home Rule Authorities. In 1985 the only exploitation of mineral resources was at a lead and zinc mine in Marmorilik. In 1975 exploration began of three potential petroleum-producing areas off the western shores, but no oil was found and the concessions were terminated in 1978. A concession for exploration in eastern Greenland was issued in 1984, and geological testing was started in 1985. Apart from minerals, fish and fish produce, the main exports are sealskin and foxskin.

The economy is still dependent on large subsidies of about 2,500m. kroner per year from Denmark. As an EEC member, Greenland received about 83.7m. ECUs (US $67m.) in assistance from the European Regional Development Fund between 1975 and 1983; the total in 1983 was 19.24m. ECUs for 92 investment projects, including airport improvements and energy supply projects. It was hoped that the loss of such assistance, incurred through leaving the Community, would be offset by income from the sale of fishing rights.

Until 1950 Denmark had a monopoly of trade and industry in Greenland. The abolition of this monopoly opened the market to other European countries, particularly Sweden, Norway and Finland. However, Denmark still took about 75% of exports in 1985, and provided 60% of imports, thereby maintaining a substantial control over trade. Other members of the EEC took 17% of exports in 1985, while the USA took about 2%.

Education and Social Welfare

The educational system is based on that of Denmark, except that the main language of instruction is Greenlandic. Danish is, however, quite widely used. There is a school in every settlement and a teacher training college in Nuuk. In 1985/86 there were about 100 primary and lower secondary schools, with 9,400 pupils and 1,070 teachers.

There is a free health service for all residents, administered by the Danish Government, with a total of 16 hospitals.

Statistical Survey

Source: Ministry for Greenland, *Annual Report*.

AREA, POPULATION AND DENSITY

Area: Total 2,175,600 sq km (840,000 sq miles); Ice-free portion 341,700 sq km (131,930 sq miles).

Population (official estimate for 1 January 1986): 53,406 (incl. 44,053 born in Greenland).

Density (1986): 0.025 per sq km.

Capital: Nuuk (Godthåb), population 10,972 (1986).

Births and deaths (1985): Registered live births 1,150 (birth rate 21.6 per 1,000); Deaths 444 (death rate 8.4 per 1,000). Source: UN, *Population and Vital Statistics Report*.

Labour Force (census of 26 October 1976): Males 14,234; Females 7,144; Total 21,378.

AGRICULTURE, ETC.

Livestock (1984): Sheep 20,200, Reindeer 3,000.

Hunting (1984): 1,384 Fox skins, 45 Polar bears.

Fishing ('000 metric tons, landings, 1984): Atlantic cod 16.7, other fishes 18.1, Northern prawn 25.3: Total catch 60.1. The figure excludes seals, which are recorded by number rather than by weight. In 1984 a total of 99,485 seals were caught.

MINING

Production (concentrates, '000 metric tons, 1985): Lead 26; Zinc 119.

FINANCE

Danish currency is in use.

Government Accounts (million kroner, 1984): Revenue 1,157; Expenditure 1,204.

EXTERNAL TRADE

Principal Commodities* (million kroner, 1985): *Imports c.i.f.:* Food and live animals 335.0 (Meat and meat preparations 97.9); Beverages and tobacco 229.1 (Beverages 206.3); Mineral fuels, lubricants etc. 527.5 (Petroleum products 525.5); Chemicals 110.8; Basic manufactures 462.8; Machinery and transport equipment 850.7 (Machinery 518.9, Transport equipment 331.8); Miscellaneous manufactured articles 406.3; Total (incl. others) 3,130.7. *Exports f.o.b.:* Fresh, chilled or frozen fish 186.0; Salted, dried or smoked fish 58.4; Crustaceans and molluscs 1,139.6; Other tinned and prepared fish 28.8; Crude materials (inedible) except fuels 338.8 (Lead ores and concentrates 41.9, Zinc ores and concentrates 290.3); Total (incl. others) 1,827.6.

* Preliminary figures.

Principal Trading Partners (million kroner, 1985): *Imports c.i.f.:* Denmark 1,852.3, Finland 52.5, France and Monaco 57.6, Federal Republic of Germany 120.4, Japan 114.8, Norway 284.7, Sweden 263.5, USA 114.1; Total (incl. others) 3,130.7. *Exports f.o.b.:* Belgium and Luxembourg 76.6, Denmark 1,377.1, Federal Republic of Germany 126.4, France and Monaco 79.6; Total (incl. others) 1,827.6.

Directory

GOVERNMENT

The legislative body is the Landsting, with 25 members elected on a basis of proportional representation. Greenlanders and Danes resident in Greenland over the age of 18 years have the right to vote. Based on the strength of the parties in the Landsting, a seven-member executive, the Landsstyre, is formed. During a transitional period the Landsstyre will gradually assume control of the administration of Greenland's internal affairs. Jurisdiction in constitutional matters, foreign affairs and defence remains with Denmark.

Landsstyre
(December 1986)

Prime Minister and Secretary for Administration: JONATHAN MOTZFELDT.
Secretary for Fisheries and Industry: MOSES OLSEN.
Secretary for the Economy: HANS PAVIA ROSING.
Secretary for Schools, Ecclesiastical and Cultural Affairs: STEPHEN HEILMANN.
Secretary for Social Affairs and Housing: ARQALUK LYNGE.
Secretary for the Development of Settlements, and for Labour and Youth: HENDRIK NIELSEN.
Secretary for Vocational Training and Trade: JOSEF MOTZFELDT.

Government Offices

Grønlands Hjemmestyre (Greenland Home Rule Government): POB 1015, 3900 Nuuk; tel. (009) 299-2-30-00; telex 90613; Denmark office Sjælboderne 2, 1122 Copenhagen K; tel. (01) 13-42-24.

Landsting
Election, 6 June 1984

	Votes	Seats
Siumut (Forward Party)	9,949	11
Atassut (Feeling of Community Party)	9,873	11
Inuit Ataqatigiit (Eskimo Brotherhood)	2,732	3

POLITICAL ORGANIZATIONS

Atassut (Feeling of Community Party): POB 399, 3900 Nuuk; formed as a national organization in 1978; moderate, non-socialist party; Leader OTTO STEENHOLDT.

Inuit Ataqatigiit (Eskimo Brotherhood): POB 321, 3900 Nuuk; f. 1978; Marxist-Leninist organization, calling for Greenland citizenship to be restricted to those of Eskimo parentage; advocates Greenland's eventual independence from Denmark; Chair. ARQALUK LYNGE.

Siumut (Forward Party): POB 357, 3900 Nuuk; f. 1977; aims to improve the status of hunters, fishermen and workers, to promote collective ownership and co-operation, and to develop greater reliance on Greenland's own resources; Chair. JONATHAN MOTZFELDT.

JUDICIAL SYSTEM

The island is divided into 18 court districts and these courts all use lay assessors. For most cases these lower courts are for the first instance and appeal is to the Landsret, the higher court in Nuuk, which is the only one with a professional judge. This court hears the more serious cases in the first instance and appeal in these cases is to the High Court (Østre Landsret) in Copenhagen.

RELIGION
Christianity

The Greenlandic Church comes under the jurisdiction of the Landsstyre and of the Lutheran Bishop of Copenhagen, who exercises control through a suffragan bishop.

THE PRESS

There are no daily newspapers in Greenland.

Atuagagdliutit/Grønlandsposten: POB 39, 3900 Nuuk; Advertising Dept, Bladforlagene, Dr Tværgade 30, 1302 Copenhagen K; weekly; Editor JØRGEN FLEISCHER.

Sermitsiag: POB 150, 3900 Nuuk; weekly; Editor HAGEN HØJER CHRISTENSEN.

PUBLISHER

Grønlandske Forlag: POB 1009, 3900 Nuuk; tel. (009 299) 22122; telex 90636; f. 1956; general, children's and textbooks; Man. REPSE THAÁRUP HØEGH.

RADIO AND TELEVISION

In 1984 there were an estimated 18,000 radio receivers and 12,000 television receivers in use.

Kalaallit Nunaata Radioa/Grønlands Radio: POB 1007, 3900 Nuuk; tel. (009 299) 21172; telex 90606; 8 AM stations, 28 FM stations, 1 Short Wave station; bilingual programmes in Greenlandic and Danish, 17 hours a day; TV in most parts of the west coast, distributed by cable and transmitters, fed from Nuuk by microwave link; Man. Dir PETER F. ROSING; Tech. Dir THOMAS MIKKELSEN.

American Forces Radio and Television Service (AFRTS)—Air Force Arctic Broadcasting Squadron (AFABS): Station Manager, OL-A Det 1 AFABS, APO New York, NY 09121, USA; station at Søndre Strømfjord; 2 FM radio stations broadcast 24 hours a day; television transmissions 16 hours daily.

BANKS
(cap. = capital; dep. = deposits; m. = million; amounts in kroner; br. = branch)

Grønlandsbanken A/S: POB 1033, 3900 Nuuk; tel. (009 299) 21380; telex 90611; f. 1967; cap. 179m., dep. 707m. (1984); Man. S. E. DANIELSEN; 3 brs.

Nuna Bank A/S (commercial bank): POB 1031, 3900 Nuuk; tel. (009 299) 21360; Man. JØRGEN ULRICHSEN.

TRANSPORT

Inland traffic is mainly by aircraft (fixed-wing and helicopter), boat and dog-sled. There are airports at Kangerlussuag (Søndre Strømfjord) for flights to Denmark, operated by Scandinavian Airlines System (SAS), and at Narsarsuq for flights to Denmark via Iceland, operated by Greenlandair, and for internal flights. Nuuk (Godthåb) has an airport for internal flights and for flights to Iceland and Canada, and Ilulissat (Jakobshavn) has an airport for internal flights. Another airport opened in 1985 at Constable Point, on the east coast, for flights to Iceland. The main port is at Nuuk; there are also all-year ports at Paamiut (Frederikshåb), Maniitsoq (Sukkertoppen) and Sisimiut (Holsteinsborg). In summer, two Icelandic air companies operate passenger services between Iceland and Kulusuk (on the east coast); and coastal motor vessels operate passenger services along the west coast from Upernavik to Nanortalik.

Grønlandsfly A/S (Greenlandair Inc.): POB 1012, 3900 Nuuk; tel. (009 299) 24488; telex 90602; f. 1960; air services to all towns and main settlements in Greenland, and to Copenhagen (Denmark), Reykjavík and Keflavík (Iceland) and Frobisher Bay (Northwest Territories, Canada); Pres. CLAES PIPER; Chair. LARS EMIL JOHANSEN; Exec. Vice-Pres. EGON SØRENSEN; fleet of 2 DHC-7, 3 DHC-6, 4 S-61N, 6 Bell-212, 5 Bell-206A/B, 1 Beechcraft King Air E-90, 1 Piper PA 31T and 1 Cessna 172 Spyhawk.

DJIBOUTI

Introductory Survey

Location, Climate, Language, Religion, Flag, Capital

The Republic of Djibouti is in the Horn of Africa, at the southern entrance to the Red Sea. It is bounded on the north, west and south-west by Ethiopia, and on the south-east by Somalia. The land is volcanic desert and the climate hot and arid. There are two main ethnic groups, the Issa, who are of Somali origin and comprise 50% of the population, and the Afar, who comprise 40% of the population and are of Ethiopian origin. Both groups are Muslims, and they speak related Cushitic languages. The official languages are Arabic and French. The flag has two equal horizontal stripes, of blue and green, with a white triangle, enclosing a five-pointed red star, at the hoist. The capital is Djibouti.

Recent History

French involvement in the territory began in 1859 and centred on the port of Djibouti, whose position at the entrance to the Red Sea invests the country with its strategic importance and economic potential. In 1945 the area (then known as French Somaliland) was proclaimed an overseas territory, and in 1967 was renamed the French Territory of the Afars and the Issas. The Afars and the Issas have strong connections with Ethiopia and Somalia respectively.

In the late 1950s divisions between the two communities were not marked, the Issas dominating local politics through their greater numbers in the port, but in the 1960s conflicting interests in the Horn of Africa and the French policy of favouring the minority Afar community combined to reveal tensions in the Territory. Demands for independence were growing, and the violence which had been sporadic since 1967 brought matters to a head in 1975, when Ali Aref Bourhan, Vice-President of the Council of Ministers, lost the support of 13 of his deputies. International assurances to respect the rights of a free Djibouti ushered in negotiations for its independence.

Ali Aref resigned in July 1976, and it was finally agreed that a referendum on independence and elections to a new Chamber of Deputies would be held simultaneously in May 1977, and that independence would follow in June; all parties united to form the Rassemblement Populaire pour l'Indépendance, which became the Rassemblement Populaire pour le Progrès (RPP) in 1979.

The Territory voted overwhelmingly for independence in the referendum, while in the parallel elections to the Chamber of Deputies 77% of votes cast were in support of a single list of candidates. Hassan Gouled Aptidon was elected President and on 27 June 1977 Djibouti became independent.

The most important task facing the new state was that of resolving tensions between Afar and Issa. The first administration attempted to balance all ethnic and political interests, but the Afars soon complained of discrimination and attacked the Government's pro-Somali policies; following the arrest of 600 Afars in December 1977, Ahmed Dini, the Prime Minister, and four other Afar Ministers resigned. A special Commission of Afars was created, and the President agreed to its demands for more Afar representation in the Government, the civil service and the armed forces, and the release of most Afar detainees. In February 1978 a new Council of Ministers, with a careful tribal balance, was announced, and in September Barkad Gourad Hamadou, a former Minister of Health, became Prime Minister and declared a policy of 'rapid detribalization'.

In February 1981 a law providing for the election of the President by universal suffrage was passed; President Gouled, the sole candidate, was subsequently re-elected in June. Other laws, passed in October, led to the establishment of a one-party state. Legislative elections were held in May 1982, when candidates were chosen from a single list approved by the RPP, with 91% of the electorate voting. The new Government, formed in June, differed little from its predecessor. In October 1986 President Gouled announced a ministerial reshuffle, in which three newcomers joined the Government.

Separate treaties of friendship and co-operation were signed in 1981 with Ethiopia, Somalia, Kenya and Sudan in an effort to begin the peace process in East Africa. In August 1984 the Minister of Foreign Affairs reaffirmed Djibouti's policy of maintaining a neutral stance in the conflict between its neighbours in the Horn of Africa, and expressed his Government's willingness to act as a mediator. A joint ministerial committee has been formed between Djibouti and Ethiopia, to strengthen existing relations and co-operation between the two countries, and at the first session, held in July 1985, it was agreed to improve technical and scientific co-operation in the agricultural sector. Djibouti's role in promoting regional co-operation was illustrated by the creation, in February 1985, of the six-nation Inter-Governmental Authority on Drought and Development (IGADD, see p. 217); Djibouti was chosen as the site of the new organization's permanent secretariat, and President Gouled became the first chairman. At IGADD's inaugural session, in January 1986, the heads of state of Ethiopia and Somalia met for the first time in 10 years.

Djibouti suspended air and sea links with the People's Democratic Republic of Yemen in August 1986, following an incident in which an Air Djibouti aircraft was intercepted by Yemeni fighter aircraft and forced to land at Aden. Djibouti had played a prominent part in the evacuation of foreign nationals from Aden during the fighting there in January 1986.

In April 1984 a new scheme for repatriating Ethiopian refugees (estimated to number 35,000), under the aegis of the UNHCR, was begun. By December 1984 it was estimated that around 16,000 had returned to Ethiopia. Djibouti also suffered the effects of drought in 1984–85, and was granted US $215,000 in famine relief aid from the EEC.

Government

The Government is formed from the Chamber of Deputies, consisting of 65 members elected for five years by universal adult franchise. It comprises a Council of Ministers, presided over by a Prime Minister, and an elected President, to whom it is responsible. The Republic forms a single electoral district. Djibouti became a one-party state in October 1981.

Defence

Since French withdrawal, a large portion of the annual budget has been set aside for military expenditure, and defence costs were estimated at US $32.2m. in 1985. In July 1986 there were about 4,000 French troops stationed in Djibouti. The total armed forces of Djibouti itself, in which all services form part of the army, numbered 2,870 (including 40 naval and 90 air force personnel), and there was a paramilitary force of 1,500 gendarmes.

Economic Affairs

There is little arable farming in Djibouti. The land is mainly volcanic desert, one of the least hospitable and productive terrains in Africa. More than one-half of the population are pastoral nomads, herding goats, sheep and camels. The agricultural sector contributed only 5.2% to gross domestic product (GDP) in 1983. The development of underground water supplies for irrigation is being studied, and deep-water wells have been sunk in an attempt to alleviate the effects of periodic drought. A two-phase fisheries development programme had helped to triple catches by 1985, and aims to raise the per caput income of fishers to US $400 per year, from $285.

Industry is limited to a few small-scale enterprises. A mineral-bottling factory was opened in 1981, and a dairy plant came into operation in 1985. Manufacturing accounted for 10% of GDP in 1983. There were plans for a small-scale fodder mill and slaughterhouse to be built, with finance provided by the Arab Fund for Economic and Social Development. Several industry and infrastructure contracts, worth more than US $80m., were awarded in 1983, including one for the construction of a cement works in the capital, with an expected output of 100,000 metric tons per year. A geothermal exploration scheme was announced in 1984, funded by foreign aid, which should make Djibouti self-sufficient in gas and also enable it to export gas to neighbouring countries. In June 1986 Saudi Arabia gave a grant of $21.4m. for the purchase and installation of three electricity generators, with a capacity of 15 MW.

Political uncertainty in the Horn of Africa has discouraged the creation of new industries, despite the existence of a free zone, and almost all consumer goods are imported (mainly from France). Imports totalled 39,307m. Djibouti francs in 1983 (a decrease of 2.2% from 1982), while exports fell to 1,919m. Djibouti francs, 14% lower than in 1982. However, exports excluding 'special transactions' rose by 48.8% in the same year. Despite the country's development problems, some economic diversification has taken place, and GDP rose by 3% annually in 1979–82, reversing the annual 2.7% decline in 1977–79. In 1984 GDP rose by less than 1%, after an increase of 1.03% in 1983. The 25,000 refugees from the Ogaden region of Ethiopia who are still in Djibouti represent a huge burden on the economy.

Djibouti's economic potential depends, at present, on its developing service sector, which provided 71.6% of GDP in 1983. The sector is based on the expanding seaport, the modern airport, the Djibouti–Addis Ababa railway and the growing activity in banking, which is aided by the freely convertible Djibouti franc and the absence of exchange controls. The war between Ethiopia and Somalia temporarily closed the railway, which carried about one-half of Ethiopia's foreign trade, thus threatening Djibouti's economic viability. Having suffered badly during the closure of the Suez Canal (1967–75), the port has also found it difficult to compete with the rising Arab ports nearby: total traffic decreased by 10.4% in 1984 and by 20.5% in 1985. Djibouti was established as a free port in 1981. Land-locked African countries, including Uganda and Zaire, air-freight their goods to Djibouti for export. The main hope for the future is to develop Djibouti as a major entrepôt for trade between East Africa and the Arab countries. An international container terminal, capable of handling 40,000 metric tons per year, was inaugurated in 1985. The terminal includes 'roll-on, roll-off' facilities, and a refrigerated warehouse, and further improvements are planned. An undersea telecommunications cable, linking Djibouti with Saudi Arabia, was inaugurated in September 1986. Djibouti also has two earth satellite stations, forming part of the network of the Arab Satellite Communication Organization (see p. 172).

Djibouti is dependent on foreign aid, which, owing to the country's strategic position, is readily forthcoming, particularly from France and the oil-rich states of the Persian Gulf, as well as from the USA and from other European countries. This assistance, along with a surplus in services and transfers, means that Djibouti usually achieves a positive balance of payments (US $5.3m. in 1981). In 1986, however, Djibouti's budgetary deficit was expected to reach 8.5% of GDP. The national treasury reserves were reported to have fallen from 10,000m. Djibouti francs in December 1981 to 500m. francs in July 1986. Aid from France for 1985–86 was to total 24m. French francs, while under the terms of the third Lomé convention with the EEC, of March 1986, Djibouti was allocated 58m. ECUs in aid.

The Djibouti Government's first Development Plan (1982–84) aimed to direct foreign aid into a co-ordinated development strategy. The 1984–89 Development Plan envisaged total expenditure of $570m.; a high proportion (62%) of the funds needed for this Plan was raised following a successful conference of aid donors, held in November 1983. Development plans under way include the expansion of Djibouti's airport, modernization of the communications network, and an urban rehabilitation project for Djibouti town. In 1980 Djibouti became a member of the World Bank and of the International Finance Corporation.

Social Welfare

The social insurance scheme in Djibouti is divided into three categories, according to whether the worker is employed in the private sector, the civil service or the army. Employees receive benefits in case of accidents at work, and are allocated retirement pensions after the age of 55. In 1985 there were 18 hospital establishments, with a total of 1,283 beds, and 703 medical personnel, including 68 physicians.

Education

Since independence, the Government has assumed overall responsibility for education. Primary education generally begins at seven years of age and lasts for six years. Secondary education, usually starting at the age of 13, lasts for seven years. In 1985/86 there were 25,212 primary school pupils and 6,934 pupils at secondary schools.

Tourism

The Government is attempting to encourage tourists, the main attractions being the desert scenery of the interior and the potential for underwater sports on the coast. In 1985 there were 316 hotel rooms, and in the same year 17,037 tourists stayed in hotels in Djibouti.

Public Holidays

1987: 1 January (New Year's Day), 1 May (Workers' Day), 30 May* (end of Ramadan), 27 June (Independence Day), 6 August* (Id al-Adha, Feast of the Sacrifice), 26 August* (Muharram, Islamic New Year), 4 November* (Mouloud, Birth of the Prophet), 25 December (Christmas Day).

1988: 1 January (New Year's Day), 1 May (Workers' Day), 18 May* (end of Ramadan), 27 June (Independence Day), 25 July* (Id al-Adha, Feast of the Sacrifice), 14 August* (Muharram, Islamic New Year), 23 October* (Mouloud, Birth of the Prophet), 25 December (Christmas Day).

* These holidays are dependent on the Islamic lunar calendar and may vary by one or two days from the dates given.

Weights and Measures

The metric system is in force.

Currency and Exchange Rates

100 centimes = 1 Djibouti franc.

Exchange rates (30 September 1986):
£1 sterling = 257.16 Djibouti francs;
US $1 = 177.72 Djibouti francs.

Statistical Survey

Source (unless otherwise stated): Ministère du Commerce, de l'Industrie, des Transports et du Tourisme, BP 1846, Djibouti; tel. 35331.

AREA AND POPULATION

Area: 23,200 sq km (8,958 sq miles).

Population: 220,000 (1976 estimate), including Afars 70,000, Issas and other Somalis 80,000, Arabs 12,000, Europeans 15,000, other foreigners 40,000; 430,000 (1985 estimate, including refugees and resident foreigners).

Principal Towns (1981): Djibouti (capital), population 200,000; Dikhil; Ali-Sabieh; Tadjourah; Obock.

AGRICULTURE, ETC.

Principal Crops ('000 metric tons, 1984): Vegetables 12.

Livestock (FAO estimates, '000 head, year ending September 1984): Cattle 44, Sheep 400, Goats 543, Asses 7, Camels 54.

Livestock Products: (FAO estimates, metric tons, 1984): Meat 6,000, Goatskins 475.

Fishing (metric tons, live weight): Total catch 251 in 1980; 385 in 1981; 426 in 1982.

INDUSTRY

Electric energy (million kWh): 148 in 1983; 146 in 1984; 164 in 1985.

FINANCE

Currency and Exchange Rates: 100 centimes = 1 Djibouti franc. *Coins:* 1, 2, 5, 10, 20, 50 and 100 Djibouti francs. *Notes:* 500, 1,000 and 5,000 Djibouti francs. *Sterling and Dollar Equivalents* (30 September 1986): £1 sterling = 257.16 Djibouti francs; US $1 = 177.72 Djibouti francs; 1,000 Djibouti francs = £3.889 = $5.627. *Exchange Rate* (Djibouti francs per US $): 177.72 since February 1973.

Budget (million Djibouti francs, 1984): *Revenue:* Taxation 16,900.3 (Direct taxes 5,321.5, Indirect taxes 10,742.4, Registration and stamp duty 691.3), Non-tax current revenue 2,627.5, Grants 1,486.9, Repayment of loans 57.5, Loans received 160.0, Transfers from reserve fund 4,683.2, Total 25,915.4; *Expenditure:* General administration 8,955.2, Defence 4,711.8, Education 1,360.4, Health 1,567.0, Economic services 1,221.3, Debt servicing 433.6, Other current expenditure 1,783.8, Capital expenditure 2,742.8, Total 22,775.9.

Gross Domestic Product (million Djibouti francs at current prices): 59,997 in 1983; 60,234 in 1984.

Balance of Payments (million Djibouti francs, 1982): Exports f.o.b. (incl. re-exports) 20,830, Imports c.i.f. −38,523, *Trade Balance* −17,693; Services, port 847, Unrequited transfers (net) 8,909, *Current Balance* −4,366; Capital movements 1,942, Changes in reserves −2,424.

EXTERNAL TRADE

Principal Commodities (million Djibouti francs, 1983): *Imports:* Machinery and electrical equipment 4,301, Textiles 4,713, Food 7,488, Qat 3,550, Petroleum and derivatives 3,708, Road vehicles 4,749; Total (incl. others) 39,307. *Exports:* Live animals 592, Food 356; Total (incl. others) 1,919.

Principal Trading Partners (million Djibouti francs): *Imports, 1983:* Benelux 2,900, Ethiopia 3,850, France 13,900, Italy 1,700, Japan 3,000, United Kingdom 1,500; Total (incl. others) 39,300. *Exports, 1980:* France 1,459, Italy 127, Somalia 110, Spain and Portugal 2, United Kingdom 8; Total (incl. others) 2,220.

TRANSPORT

Railways (Djibouti-Ethiopian Railway, 1984): Freight traffic ('000 metric tons): Ethiopian imports 109.7, Ethiopian exports 94.1, Internal traffic 2.7; Freight (million ton-km): Ethiopian imports 58.6, Ethiopian exports 52.9, Internal traffic 0.2.

Shipping (Djibouti port, 1985): Vessels entered 898; Goods loaded 140,000 metric tons; Goods unloaded 471,000 metric tons; Passenger arrivals 1,915; Passenger departures 1,284.

Civil Aviation (Djibouti airport, 1985): Freight loaded 1,655 metric tons; Freight unloaded 6,627 metric tons; Passenger arrivals 55,023; Passenger departures 48,256; Mail unloaded 223 metric tons.

COMMUNICATIONS MEDIA

Radio Receivers (1983): 23,000 in use.

Television Receivers (1983): 11,000 in use.

Telephones (1981): 6,000 in use.

EDUCATION

Primary (1985/86): 58 schools (51 state schools, 7 private schools); 25,212 pupils (22,720 at state schools, 2,492 at private schools); 514 teachers (state schools only).

Secondary and Technical (1985/86): 19 schools (8 state schools, 11 private schools); 6,934 pupils (5,975 at state schools, 959 at private schools); 293 teachers (state schools only).

Teacher Training (1985/86): 107 pupils; 13 teachers.

Directory

The Constitution

In February 1981 the National Assembly approved the first constitutional laws controlling the election and terms of office of the President, who is elected by universal suffrage for six years and may serve for no more than two terms. Candidates for the presidency must be presented by a regularly constituted political party and represented by at least 25 members of the Chamber of Deputies.

Deputies are elected for five years from a single list of candidates proposed by the Rassemblement populaire pour le progrès.

In October 1984 a new constitutional law was proposed, specifying that, when the office of President falls vacant, the President of the Supreme Court will assume the power of Head of State for a minimum of 20 days and a maximum of 35 days, during which period a new President shall be elected.

Laws approving the provisional establishment of a single-party system were adopted in October 1981.

The Government

HEAD OF STATE

President and Commander-in-Chief of the Armed Forces: HASSAN GOULED APTIDON (took office 27 June 1977).

COUNCIL OF MINISTERS
(November 1986)

Prime Minister and Minister of Ports: BARKAD GOURAD HAMADOU.
Minister of the Interior and of Telecommunications: YOUSEF ALI CHIRDON.
Minister of Justice and Muslim Affairs: ELAF ORBISS ALI.
Minister of Foreign Affairs and Co-operation: MOUMIN BAHDON FARAH.
Minister of Defence: (vacant).
Minister of Commerce, Transport and Tourism: MOUSSA BOURALE ROBLE.
Minister of Finance and National Economy: MUHAMMAD DJAMA ELABE.
Minister of the Civil Service: HELEM HOUMED.
Minister of Industry and Industrial Development: SALEM ABDOU.
Minister of Labour and Social Welfare: MUHAMMAD DEL WAIS.
Minister of Education, Youth and Sports: SULEIMAN FARAH LODON.
Minister of Public Works and Housing: BOURHAN ALI WARKI.
Minister of Agriculture and Rural Development: AHMAD HASSAN LIBAN.
Minister of Health and Social Affairs: MUHAMMAD ABADO KAKO.

MINISTRIES

Office of the Prime Minister: BP 2086, Djibouti; tel. 351494; telex 5871.
Ministry of Agriculture and Rural Development: BP 453, Djibouti; tel. 351297; telex 5871.
Ministry of the Civil Service: BP 155, Djibouti; tel. 351464; telex 5871.
Ministry of Commerce, Transport and Tourism: BP 121, Djibouti; tel. 352540; telex 5871.
Ministry of Defence: BP 42, Djibouti; tel. 352034; telex 5871.
Ministry of Education, Youth and Sports: BP 2102, Djibouti; tel. 351689; telex 5871.
Ministry of Finance and National Economy: BP 13, Djibouti; tel. 353331; telex 5871.
Ministry of Foreign Affairs and Co-operation: BP 1863, Djibouti; tel. 352471; telex 5871.
Ministry of Health and Social Affairs: BP 296, Djibouti; tel. 353331; telex 5871.
Ministry of Industry and Industrial Development: BP 175, Djibouti; tel. 350137; telex 5871.
Ministry of the Interior: BP 33, Djibouti; tel. 350791; telex 5871.
Ministry of Justice and Muslim Affairs: BP 12, Djibouti; tel. 351506; telex 5871.
Ministry of Labour and Social Welfare: BP 170, Djibouti; tel. 350497; telex 5871.
Ministry of Ports: BP 2086, Djibouti; tel. 351280; telex 5871.
Ministry of Public Works and Housing: BP 11, Djibouti; tel. 350006; telex 5871.
Ministry of Telecommunications: Djibouti; tel. 350971; telex 5871.

Legislature

CHAMBRE DES DÉPUTÉS

Elections for a 65-seat Chamber of Deputies were held on 21 May 1982. A single list of candidates, comprising 26 Issas, 23 Afars and 16 Arabs, was presented by the Rassemblement populaire pour le progrès. A total of 78,031 votes (from a possible 85,995) were cast; in addition, 1,349 invalid votes and 6,615 abstentions were recorded.

President of the Chamber: ABDOULKADER WABERI ASKAR.

Political Organizations

Rassemblement populaire pour le progrès (RPP): Djibouti; formed in 1979 to succeed the Ligue populaire africaine pour l'indépendance, which participated in the 1977 elections as part of the fmr Rassemblement populaire pour l'indépendance; became sole legal party in October 1981; Pres. HASSAN GOULED APTIDON; Sec.-Gen. MOUMIN BAHDON FARAH.

The following organizations are banned:

Front de Libération de la Côte des Somalis (FLCS): f. 1963; Issa-supported; headquarters in Mogadishu, Somalia; participated in 1977 elections as part of Rassemblement populaire pour l'indépendance; Chair. ABDULLA WABERI KHALIF; Vice-Chair. OMAR OSMAN RABEH.

Front démocratique pour la libération de Djibouti (FDLD): f. 1979 by a merger of the fmr Mouvement populaire de libération and Union nationale pour l'indépendance; Afar-supported; Sec. MUHAMMAD KAMIL ALI.

Mouvement pour la libération de Djibouti (MLD): f. 1964; Afar-supported; headquarters in Dire Dawa, Ethiopia; Leader SHEHEM DAOUD.

Parti populaire djiboutien: f. 1981; mainly Afar party; Leader MOUSSA AHMAD IDRIS.

Diplomatic Representation

EMBASSIES IN DJIBOUTI

China, People's Republic: Djibouti; tel. 352246; telex 5926; Ambassador: XU CHENGHUA.
Egypt: BP 1989, Djibouti; tel. 351231; telex 5880; Ambassador: (vacant).
Ethiopia: BP 230, Djibouti; tel. 350718; Ambassador: BERHANU DINKA.
France: 45 blvd du Maréchal Foch, BP 2039, Djibouti; tel. 350963; telex 5861; Ambassador: ROBERT THOMAS.
Iraq: BP 1983, Djibouti; tel. 353469; telex 5877; Ambassador: ABDEL AZIZ AL-GAILANI.
Libya: BP 2073, Djibouti; tel. 353339; telex 5874; Ambassador: JALAL MUHAMMAD AL-DAGHELY.
Oman: BP 1996, Djibouti; tel. 350852; telex 5876; Ambassador: SAOUD SALEM HASSAN AL-ANSI.

DJIBOUTI

Saudi Arabia: BP 1921, Djibouti; tel. 351645; telex 5865; Chargé d'affaires: Mowaffak al-Doligane.
Somalia: BP 549, Djibouti; tel. 353521; telex 5815; Ambassador: Muhammad Shek Muhammad Malingur.
Sudan: Djibouti; tel. 351483; Ambassador: Tag el-Sir Muhammad Abass.
USSR: BP 1913, Djibouti; tel. 352051; Ambassador: Viktor Zhuravlev.
USA: Villa Plateau du Serpent, blvd Maréchal Joffré, BP 185, Djibouti; tel. 353849; Ambassador: John P. Ferriter.
Yemen Arab Republic: BP 194, Djibouti; tel. 352975; Ambassador: Muhammad Abdoul Wassi Hamid.
Yemen, People's Democratic Republic: BP 1932, Djibouti; tel. 353704; Chargé d'affaires: Awad Salem Baabad.

Judicial System

The cour suprême was established in October 1979. There is a tribunal supérieur d'appel and a tribunal de première instance in Djibouti; each of the five administrative districts has a tribunal coutumier.

Religion

ISLAM

Almost the entire population are Muslims.

Qadi of Djibouti: Mogue Hassan Dirir, BP 2900, Djibouti; tel. 352989.

CHRISTIANITY

The Roman Catholic Church

Djibouti comprises a single diocese, directly responsible to the Holy See. There were an estimated 8,500 adherents in the country at 31 December 1984.

Bishop of Djibouti: Michel-Joseph-Gérard Gagnon, BP 94, Djibouti; tel. 350140.

Other Christian Churches

Eglise Protestante: blvd de la République, BP 416, Djibouti; tel. 351820; f. 1967; Pastor J.-Cl. Leveille.
Greek Orthodox Church: blvd de la République, Djibouti; tel. 351325; c. 350 adherents; Archimandrite Stavros Georganas.

The Press

Carrefour Africain: BP 393, Djibouti; fortnightly; publ. by the Roman Catholic mission; circ. 500.
Djibouti Aujourd'hui: Djibouti; f. 1977; monthly; Editor Ismael Omar Guelleh.
La Nation de Djibouti: place du 27 juin, BP 32, Djibouti; tel. 352201; weekly; Dir Ismael H. Tani; circ. 4,000.

FOREIGN NEWS AGENCY

Agence France-Presse (AFP): BP 97, Djibouti; tel. 352294; telex 5863; Correspondent Haidar Khalid Abdullah.

Radio and Television

There were an estimated 23,000 radio receivers and 11,000 television receivers in use in 1983. In 1980 Djibouti became a member of the Arab Satellite Communication Organization, and opened an earth station for radio, television and telecommunications; a second earth station was inaugurated in June 1985.

Radiodiffusion-Télévision de Djibouti (RTD): BP 97, Djibouti; tel. 352294; telex 5863; f. 1956; state-owned; programmes in French, Afar, Somali and Arabic; 21 hours radio and 3 hours television daily; Dir Muhammad Djama Aden.

Finance

(cap. = capital; p.u. = paid up; dep. = deposits; m. = million; res = reserves; br. = branch; amounts in Djibouti francs)

BANKING

Banque Nationale de Djibouti: BP 2118, Djibouti; tel. 352751; telex 5838; f. 1981; will eventually take over some of the functions carried out by the Trésor National; Gov. Luc A. Aden.
Trésor National de la République de Djibouti: blvd de la République, BP 2119, Djibouti; in charge of monetary issue.

Commercial Banks

Bank of Credit and Commerce International: 10 ave Pierre Pascal, BP 2105, Djibouti; tel. 351741; telex 5810; Dir Nasim Ahmad.
Banque de Djibouti et du Moyen Orient SA: 6 rue de Marseille, BP 2471, Djibouti; tel. 351133; telex 5943; f. 1983; cap. 125m.; 55% owned by Middle East Bank; Chair. Majid Muhammad al-Futtaim; Man. Dir T. M. Sheth.
Banque Indosuez (Mer Rouge) (France): 10 place Lagarde, BP 88, Djibouti; tel. 353016; telex 5829; f. 1908; cap. 1,500m. (Dec. 1983); Chair. and Man. Dir Pascal Mouradian; 5 brs.
Banque pour le Commerce et l'Industrie (Mer Rouge): place Lagarde, BP 2122, Djibouti; tel. 350857; telex 5821; f. 1977; 51% of shares owned by Banque Nationale de Paris Intercontinentale; cap. 1,500m., res 600m., dep. 19,391m. (Dec. 1984); Pres. Jean-Claude Clarac; 8 brs.
British Bank of the Middle East (Hong Kong): place Lagarde, BP 2112, Djibouti; tel. 353291; telex 5826; Man. Christopher Reddington.
Caisse de Développement de Djibouti: rue de l'Ethiopie, BP 520, Djibouti; tel. 353391; f. 1983; national development bank; cap. 250m.; 51% govt-owned; Chair. Luc Aden.
Commercial and Savings Bank of Somalia: BP 2004, Djibouti; tel. 351282; telex 5879; Man. Hassan Bulhan.
Commercial Bank of Ethiopia: BP 187, Djibouti; tel. 352101; telex 5835; f. 1980; Man. Alemayehu Adafre.

Banking Association

Association Professionnelle des Banques: c/o Banque pour le Commerce et l'Industrie (Mer Rouge), place Lagarde, BP 2122, Djibouti; tel. 350857; Pres. Muhammad Aden.

INSURANCE

Assurances Générales de France (AGF): 3 rue Marchand, Djibouti; tel. 352339.
State Insurance Co of Somalia (SICOS): BP 50, Djibouti; tel. 352707; telex 5819; all classes of insurance.

About 10 European insurance companies maintain agencies in Djibouti.

Trade and Industry

Chambre Internationale de Commerce et d'Industrie: place Lagarde, BP 84, Djibouti; tel. 350826; telex 5957; f. 1912; 24 mems; 12 assoc. mems; Pres. Said Ali Coubeche; First Vice-Pres. Muhammad Aden.
Djibouti Labour Federation: Pres. Idris Omar.

Transport

RAILWAYS

Compagnie du chemin de fer Djibouti-Ethiopien: BP 2116, Djibouti; tel. 350353; POB 1051, Addis Ababa; tel. 447250; f. 1908 as Compagnie du Chemin de Fer Franco-Ethiopien, renamed 1981; jtly-owned by govts of Djibouti and Ethiopia; plans to grant autonomous status were announced by the two govts in July 1985; 781 km of track, 100 km in Djibouti, linking Djibouti with Addis Ababa; Pres. Y. Ali Chirdon; Man. Dir Channie Tamiru.

ROADS

In 1985 there were 2,895 km of roads, of which over 300 km were bitumen-surfaced, including the 185-km road along the Ethiopian frontier. Of the remainder, 1,000 km are serviceable throughout the year, the rest only during the dry season. Half the roads are usable only by lorries. In 1981 the 40-km Grand Bara road was opened, linking the capital with the south. A 114-km road linking the capital with Tadjourah, due for completion by 1988, is under construction.

SHIPPING

Djibouti was established as a free port in 1981.

Compagnie Générale Maritime: Immeuble Plein Ciel, BP 182, Djibouti; tel. 353825; telex 5817; agents for Mitsui OSK Line.

Compagnie Maritime Auxiliaire d'Outre-Mer: ave des Messageries Maritimes, BP 89, Djibouti; tel. 352022; telex 5825; agents for Adriatic Red Sea Line, British Petroleum, Compagnie Générale Maritime, Comp. Navale des Pétroles, Deutsche Ost Afrika Line, Djakarta Lloyd, Hapaglloyd, Hungarian Shipping Line, Jadranska Line, Nedlloyd Line, Scandinavian East Africa Line, Shell International, Sovinflot; Gen. Man. L. J. Hughes.

Gellatly Hankey et Cie (Djibouti) SA: rue de Genève, BP 81, Djibouti; tel. 352012; telex 5860; f. 1942; Lloyd's agents, and shipping agents for Nippon Yusen Kaisha, Waterman Line, P & O, Cosco, Sinochart and others.

J. J. Kothari & Co Ltd: BP 171, rue de Soleillet, Djibouti; tel. 350219; agents for American President Lines, Shipping Corpn of India, Mogul Line, United Arab Maritime, Sudan Shipping Line, Finnland Steamship Co; also stevedores, freight forwarders; Dirs S. J. Kothari, N. Kothari.

Mitchell Cotts Djibouti SARL: blvd de la République, BP 85, Djibouti; tel. 351204; telex 5812; agents for Clan Line, Ellerman City Liners, Fearnley and Eger, Harrison Line, Iraqi Maritime Transport Co, Maldivian National Trading Corpn, Farell Lines, Central Gulf, Yemen Gulf Lines, Société Navale Caennaise, OCL, Beacon and other shipping and forwarding cos; Dir Fahmy Said Cassim.

Société d'Armement et de Manutention de la Mer Rouge (SAMER): BP 10, Djibouti; agents for Pacific International Line, Cunard Brocklebank, Wilhelm Wilhelmsen Co, Pakistan Shipping Lines, Aktiebolaget Svenska Östasiatiska Kompaniet, Texaco, Chevron Shipping Co, Kie Hock Shipping Co, Barber Lines, Supreme Shipping Co, Scandutch; Chair. John Collins; Man. Dir Vincent Dell'Aquilla.

Société Maritime L. Savon et Ries: ave Saint-Laurent du Var, BP 2125, Djibouti; agents for Chargeurs Réunis, NCHP, Sudcargos, Svedel Line, Lloyd Triestino, Hellenic Lines, Messina, Polish Ocean Lines; Dir M. Aarstad.

CIVIL AVIATION

There is an international airport at Ambouli, 6 km from Djibouti, and there are six internal airports.

Air Djibouti (Red Sea Airlines): BP 505, rue Marchand, Djibouti; telex 5820; f. 1971, when Air Somalie took over the fmr Air Djibouti (f. 1963); the Djibouti govt holds 62.5% of shares, and Air France 32.3%; internal flights connecting the six major centres and international services to the Yemen Arab Republic, Somalia, the United Arab Emirates, France, Italy, Egypt, Ethiopia and Saudi Arabia; Gen. Man. Paul Botbol; fleet of 2 Twin Otter and 1 Boeing 727.

Tourism

Office de Développement du Tourisme: place du 27 juin, BP 1938, Djibouti; tel. 353790; telex 5938.

DOMINICA

Introductory Survey

Location, Climate, Language, Religion, Flag, Capital

The Commonwealth of Dominica is situated in the Windward Islands group of the West Indies, lying between Guadeloupe, to the north, and Martinique, to the south. The climate is tropical, though tempered by sea winds which sometimes reach hurricane force, especially from July to September. The average temperature is about 27°C (80°F), with little seasonal variation. Rainfall is heavy, especially in the mountainous areas, where the annual average is 6,350 mm (250 inches), compared with 1,800 mm (70 inches) along the coast. English is the official language but a local French patois is widely spoken. Almost all of the inhabitants profess Christianity, and about 80% are Roman Catholics. The national flag has a green field, with equal stripes of yellow, white and black forming an upright cross, on the centre of which is superimposed a red disc containing a parrot surrounded by ten five-pointed green stars (one for each of the island's parishes). The capital is Roseau.

Recent History

A British possession since the 18th century, Dominica formed part of the Leeward Islands federation until 1939. In 1940 it was transferred to the Windward Islands and remained attached to that group until the federal arrangement was ended in December 1959. Under a new constitution, effective from January 1960, Dominica (like each other member of the group) achieved a separate status, with its own Administrator and an enlarged Legislative Council. Dominica was a member of the West Indies Federation between 1958 and its dissolution in 1962.

At the January 1961 elections to the Legislative Council, the ruling Dominica United People's Party was defeated by the Dominica Labour Party (DLP), formed from the People's National Movement and other groups. Edward LeBlanc, leader of the DLP, became Chief Minister. In March 1967 Dominica became one of the West Indies Associated States, gaining full autonomy in internal affairs, with the United Kingdom retaining responsibility for defence and foreign relations only. The Legislative Council was replaced by a House of Assembly, the Administrator became Governor and the Chief Minister was restyled Premier. At elections to the House in October 1970, the Labour Party was divided into two factions, one campaigning as the DLP and the other, led by the Premier, as the LeBlanc Labour Party. The Premier was returned to power and the DLP was subsequently reunited.

In July 1974 LeBlanc retired, being replaced as DLP leader and Premier by Patrick John, formerly Deputy Premier and Minister of Finance. Elections to an enlarged House of Assembly were held in March 1975, when the DLP was returned again, winning 16 of the 21 elective seats. Following a decision in 1975 by the Associated States to seek independence separately, Dominica became an independent republic within the Commonwealth on 3 November 1978. Frederick Degazon, formerly Speaker of the House of Assembly, became President, and Patrick John became Prime Minister.

In May 1979 two people were killed by the defence force at a demonstration against the Government's attempts to introduce legislation which would restrict the freedom of the trade unions and the press. The killings fuelled increasing popular opposition to the Government, and a Committee for National Salvation (CNS), formed to bring down the Government, demanded John's resignation. On his refusal, opponents of the Government organized a general strike which lasted 25 days, with John finally agreeing to hand over power to an interim President only after all his Cabinet ministers had resigned. Oliver Seraphin, the candidate proposed by the CNS, was elected Prime Minister, and an interim government was then formed to prepare for elections in six months.

Elections were eventually held in July 1980, when the Dominica Freedom Party (DFP) gained a convincing victory, winning 17 of the 21 elective seats in the House of Assembly. Eugenia Charles, the party's leader, became the Caribbean's first woman Prime Minister. Both Patrick John, who contested the elections as leader of the DLP, and Oliver Seraphin, who stood as leader of the newly formed Democratic Labour Party (DEMLAB), lost their seats. The DFP's victory was attributed to its continued integrity, while the DLP and DEMLAB had suffered from major political scandals.

Fears for the island's security dominated 1981. In January the Government disarmed the defence force as a result of reports that weapons were being traded for marijuana. There were shooting incidents between police and Rastafarians in February, and the Government declared a state of emergency after murders and kidnapping had risen to an unacceptable level. In March a plot to overthrow the Government, with the aid of US mercenaries, was uncovered, implicating former Prime Minister Patrick John and the two most senior officers in the defence force, who were all gaoled pending trial. The state of emergency was lifted in August, only to be reinstated in January 1982, following a second attempted coup in December 1981. This second plot involved an unsuccessful attempt to free Patrick John from prison. In June 1982 John and his fellow prisoners were tried and acquitted but, owing to the Government's continued opposition to this verdict, they were retried in October 1985, when John and the former deputy defence force commander each received a prison sentence of 12 years. In August 1986 the former commander of the defence force, Frederick Newton, was hanged for the murder of a policeman during the attempt to free John. Five other soldiers who had been involved in the escape attempt had their death sentences commuted to life imprisonment.

After his release in June 1982, John attempted to form a new left-wing coalition party, and in 1983 a new DLP was formed upon its reunification with DEMLAB. In January 1985 agreement was reached between the DLP, the United Dominica Labour Party and the Dominica Liberation Movement, to form a united left-wing grouping, known as the Labour Party of Dominica (LPD), to contest the next general election, with Michael Douglas, a former Minister of Finance, as leader. During the election campaign, Eugenia Charles stressed the economic achievements of her administration and accused members of the LPD of having 'pro-Communist' links. At the general election, held on 1 July, the DFP was returned to power, winning 15 of the 21 elective seats in the House of Assembly. The opposition LPD won five seats, with the remaining seat being won by Rosie Douglas, the brother of the LPD leader, whose candidature was not officially endorsed by the LPD. In May 1986 a by-election in the St Joseph constituency increased the DFP's strength in the House to 16 seats, with five seats still being held by the LPD.

In foreign policy, Dominica has close links with France and the USA. France helped in putting down the coup attempts against the DFP government, and Dominica was the first Commonwealth country to benefit from the French aid agency, FAC. In October 1983 Dominica, as a member of OECS (see p. 109), contributed a small contingent to the US-backed invasion of Grenada.

Government

Dominica is a republic. Legislative power is vested in the unicameral House of Assembly, containing 30 members (nine nominated and 21 elected for five years by universal adult suffrage). Executive authority is vested in the President, elected by the House, but in most matters the President is guided by the advice of the Cabinet and acts as a constitutional Head of State. He appoints the Prime Minister, who must be able to command a majority in the House, and (on the Prime Minister's recommendation) other Ministers. The Cabinet is responsible to the House.

Defence

The Dominican Defence Force was officially disbanded in April 1981. There is a police force of about 300, which includes a coastguard service. A patrol boat was received from the USA in 1983.

Economic Affairs

Agriculture is the principal economic activity, accounting for 32% of gross national product (GNP) in 1983, and bananas are the main crop. In 1978 bananas accounted for 70% of exports and 20% of GNP, but hurricane damage in 1979 virtually stopped all production. Regular shipments to the United Kingdom, the principal recipient, recommenced in April 1981, and production reached 26,800 tons in 1982, when sales of bananas represented 44.1% of exports. In 1983 26,165 tons were exported, creating revenue of EC $30.3m. Production increased by 11% in 1984, but the fluctuations in international currency rates caused a reduction in export earnings. Exports of bananas totalled 31,433 tons in 1984 and 33,294 tons in 1985, when the proportion of bananas being field-packed rose to 70% from 40% in 1984. Export revenue from bananas in 1985 totalled EC $28.3m., an increase of 16% on the 1984 figure. In August 1986 the Government announced that it had annulled a EC $4.9m. debt incurred between 1977 and 1980 by the Dominica Banana Growers' Association (DBGA) to finance its operating deficits and inherited by the Dominica Banana Marketing Corporation (DBMC), which replaced the DBGA in 1982. The Government's action was in recognition of the improved financial management and operational efficiency achieved by the DBMC.

Other important crops include coconuts (which provide copra for export as well as edible oil and soap), limes and other citrus fruits. Plans were made in 1983 to revitalize the lime industry, with TT $3.49m. from the Caribbean Food Corporation, both to improve processing and to modernize cultivation methods. In 1986 a 5,500-acre coconut rehabilitation scheme was begun, financed by Canadian aid. This followed a sharp decline in coconut oil exports in 1985. Dominica also exports bay oil and patchouli oil.

In February 1986 the Government announced plans for the establishment of an export-import agency and for a 2,000-acre land reform scheme, both intended to increase agricultural production and exports. Under the scheme, the Government purchased land in prime agricultural areas and guaranteed a minimum holding, with security of tenure, to small farmers and landless farm workers. It also promised to provide services and equipment. In June 1986 further plans for the agricultural industry were announced, including the construction of feeder roads and farm access roads, a grant of EC $4.7m. for the banana industry and EC $1.8m. support for the crop diversification plan. A loan from the International Fund for Agricultural Development was also received. The Dominica Export-Import Agency (Dexia) came into operation in July 1986, replacing the Agriculture Marketing Board and the External Trade Bureau, and is intended to assist in the development of a wide range of agricultural exports.

There is a small amount of livestock but this is reared mainly for domestic consumption. Fishing is a traditional occupation for the islanders, and a number of co-operatives have been established to provide vessels and equipment to fishermen on a hire basis. A loan was received from Taiwan in November 1985 for upgrading the fishing industry, and a further loan was offered in June 1986 for the establishment of a fishing development. Taiwan also presented the country with the gift of a fishing vessel. Quarrying of pumice was suspended in 1974 but resumed in 1977. Attempts are being made to exploit Dominica's extensive timber reserves, to provide lumber for export, prefabricated houses, and to supply furniture manufacturers.

An Industrial Development Corporation was established in 1974 to promote and encourage the growth of new industries in Dominica, and to diversify the island's economic base. There are factories for the manufacture and refining of crude and edible vegetable oils and for the production of cigarettes, canned juices and soaps. Soaps accounted for 38% of domestic products in 1982 and export earnings totalled EC $23.4m. Exports declined in 1983, however, and in 1984 had fallen to $14.9m., but an increase of around 30% was recorded in 1985. Dominica is now using its own plentiful reserves of water to export to other, drier Caribbean islands, such as Aruba, in return for money to help to improve water supply infrastructure. Dominica generates more than 75% of its electricity by means of hydro-electric power stations.

Tourism is not as developed as in many of the other Caribbean islands, but the number of visitors had grown to 33,000 in 1982, contributing EC $4m. to the economy. The number of visitors rose in 1983 and again in 1984, when arrivals totalled 40,971. Despite an increase of over 100% in cruise passenger arrivals in 1985, the number of stopover arrivals decreased by 3.4%.

The island's crops and infrastructure are still recovering from the destructive effect of a severe hurricane in August 1979, when the Government declared the whole country a disaster area. Reconstruction is taking place with aid from an international consortium of aid donors and loans from international organizations, but received a setback in 1980, when a second hurricane hit the country. Before 1980, the Government had a growing budget deficit on its current transactions. However, the funding of capital expenditure projects through foreign aid and loans, and the imposition of fiscal restraint, helped to convert the current balance from a deficit of EC $17.3m. in 1980/81 to a surplus of EC $400,000 in 1984/85. A loan of EC $37m. was secured from the IMF for balance-of-payments support for the period 1981–84, and a further SDR 1.4m. stand-by credit was approved in 1984. As a result, the current account deficit on the balance of payments was reduced from EC $38.6m. in 1980 to $6.2m. in 1983, representing a reduction from 55.5% of gross domestic product (GDP) to 9.5%. However the deficit increased in 1984, reaching EC $29m. GDP grew, in real terms, by 7.9% in 1980, by 4.5% in 1984, but by only 1.1% in 1985. The 1986/87 budget, presented in June 1986, aimed for an annual GDP growth rate of at least 4% over three years under a structural adjustment programme assisted by the IMF and the World Bank. The rate of inflation fell from 32.7% in 1980 to 4.2% in 1983 and to 2.1% in 1984. Unemployment also fell, from 23% of the labour force in 1980 to 13% by 1984. The level of imports continued to rise over the same period while, in spite of a reduction in the trade deficit to EC $47.5m. in 1983, the poor international price for Dominica's exports produced little change in export earnings. Export earnings fell in 1984, and this decline, combined with a further increase in imports, produced a trade deficit of EC $86.9m.

Social Welfare

There are main hospitals at Roseau and Portsmouth, with 242 and 50 beds respectively, and two cottage hospitals, at Marigot and Grand Bay. A loan was received from France in 1986 for the construction of a polyclinic at the Princess Margaret Hospital, Roseau. There are 44 health centres, located throughout the island. In 1985 there were approximately 25 physicians working in Dominica.

Education

Education is free and is provided by a mixture of government and denominational schools. There are also a number of schools catering for the mentally and physically handicapped. Education is compulsory for 10 years between five and 15 years of age. Primary education begins at the age of five and lasts for seven years. Secondary education, beginning at 12 years of age, also lasts for seven years, comprising a first cycle of five years and a second of two years. A teacher training college provides further education, and there is also a branch of the University of the West Indies on the island. Adult illiteracy was only 5.9% in 1970.

Tourism

Despite its many natural attractions, Dominica has never achieved the tourist success of its neighbours, and the effects of two hurricanes temporarily hampered the growth experienced in 1978. The Government has designated areas of the island as nature reserves to ensure that there will always be areas of natural beauty to attract visitors. There were 40,971 tourist arrivals in 1984.

DOMINICA

Public Holidays

1987: 1 January (New Year's Day), 17–20 April (Easter), 1 May (Labour Day), 8 June (Whit Monday), 2 July (Caricom Day), 3 August (August Monday), 2–3 November (Independence Days), 25–26 December (Christmas).

1988: 1 January (New Year's Day), 1–4 April (Easter), 2 May (for Labour Day), 23 May (Whit Monday), 2 July (Caricom Day), 1 August (August Monday), 2–3 November (Independence Days), 25–26 December (Christmas).

Weights and Measures

The imperial system is in use, although the metric system is to be introduced.

Currency and Exchange Rates

100 cents = 1 East Caribbean dollar (EC $).

Exchange rates (30 September 1986):
 £1 sterling = EC $3.907;
 US $1 = EC $2.700.

Statistical Survey

Sources (unless otherwise stated): Ministry of Finance, Roseau; OECS Economic Affairs Secretariat, *Annual Digest of Statistics*.

AREA AND POPULATION

Area: 750.6 sq km (289.8 sq miles).

Population: 70,513 at census of 7 April 1970; 73,795 (males 36,754, females 37,041) at census of 7 April 1981; 83,266 (estimate, 1984).

Principal Towns (population at 1981 census): Roseau (capital) 8,279; Portsmouth 2,200.

Births and Deaths (1984): Registered live births 1,716 (birth rate 20.8 per 1,000); Deaths 432 (death rate 5.2 per 1,000).

Economically Active Population (1981 census): Agriculture, hunting, forestry and fishing 7,843; Mining and quarrying 8; Manufacturing 1,417; Electricity, gas and water 245; Construction 2,306; Trade, restaurants and hotels 1,613; Transport, storage and communications 914; Financing, insurance, real estate and business services 257; Community, social and personal services 4,980; Activities not adequately defined 1,004; Total employed 20,587 (males 14,057; females 6,530); Unemployed 4,746 (males 2,641; females 2,105); Total labour force 25,333 (males 16,698, females 8,635). Source: ILO, *Yearbook of Labour Statistics*.

AGRICULTURE, ETC.

Principal Crops ('000 metric tons, 1984): Bananas 37, Dasheen 12, Tannias 6, Grapefruit 5, Limes 6.

Livestock (FAO estimates, year ending September 1984): Cattle 4,000, Pigs 9,000, Sheep 4,000, Goats 6,000. Source: FAO, *Production Yearbook*.

Fishing (metric tons, live weight): Total catch 1,545 in 1982; 1,000 in 1983 (FAO estimate); 400 in 1984 (FAO estimate). Source: FAO, *Yearbook of Fishery Statistics*.

MINING

Pumice ('000 metric tons, 1982): Estimated production 109. Source: UN, *Industrial Statistics Yearbook*.

INDUSTRY

Production (1984): Soap 4,068 metric tons; Electricity (1983) 18,225,000 kWh.

FINANCE

Currency and Exchange Rates: 100 cents = 1 East Caribbean dollar (EC $). *Coins:* 1, 2, 5, 10, 25 and 50 cents. *Notes:* 1, 5, 20 and 100 dollars. *Sterling and US Dollar Equivalents* (30 September 1986): £1 sterling = EC $3.907; US $1 = EC $2.700; EC $100 = £25.60 = US $37.04. *Exchange Rate:* Fixed at US $1 = EC $2.70 since July 1976.

Budget (estimates 1984/85, EC $ million): Revenue 76.2; Recurrent Expenditure 73.2.

International reserves (US $ million at 31 December 1985): Reserve position in IMF 0.01; Foreign exchange 3.26; Total 3.27. Source: IMF, *International Financial Statistics*.

Money Supply (EC $ million at 31 December 1985): Currency outside banks 9.64; Demand deposits 21.58; Total money 31.22. Source: IMF, *International Financial Statistics*.

Cost of Living (Retail Price Index, base: 1980 = 100): All items 123.2 in 1983; 125.9 in 1984; 128.5 in 1985.

National Accounts (EC $ million in current prices): Gross Domestic Product 191.7 in 1982; 207.07 in 1983; 223.84 in 1984.

Balance of Payments (US $ million, 1985): Merchandise exports f.o.b. 28.7, Merchandise imports f.o.b. −52.0; *Trade balance* −23.3; Exports of services 10.4, Imports of services −13.6; *Balance on goods and services* −26.5; Unrequited transfers (net) 21.0; *Current balance* −5.6; Long-term capital 5.7, Short-term capital −0.3; Net errors and omissions 0.1; *Total* (net monetary movements) −0.1; Valuation changes (net) −1.4; Exceptional financing (net) 0.1; *Changes in reserves* −1.4.

Source: IMF, *International Financial Statistics*.

EXTERNAL TRADE

Principal Commodities (EC $ million, 1984): *Imports c.i.f.:* Food and live animals 32.4; Beverages and tobacco 4.8; Crude materials (inedible) except fuels 2.6; Mineral fuels, lubricants, etc. 15.4; Animal and vegetable oils, fats and waxes 5.8; Chemicals and related products 13.9; Basic manufacturers 33.9; Machinery and transport equipment 38.9; Miscellaneous manufactured articles 8.4; Total (incl. others) 156.1. *Exports f.o.b.:* Bananas 30.0; Soap 14.9; Vegetable oils 5.7; Galvanized sheets 6.6; Grapefruit 1.6; Total (incl. others) 67.3.

Principal Trading Partners (EC $ million, 1984): *Imports:* Asia 18.6; Barbados 3.4; Canada 12.0; Netherlands 4.9; Saint Lucia 8.5; Saint Vincent and the Grenadines 4.5; Trinidad and Tobago 12.0; United Kingdom 20.0; USA 41.6; Total (incl. others) 156.1. *Exports:* Antigua and Barbuda 8.6; Barbados 2.1; Grenada 3.0; Jamaica 10.8; Trinidad and Tobago 9.8; United Kingdom 31.7; USA 1.1; Total (incl. others) 67.3.

TRANSPORT

Road Traffic (registered motor vehicles, 1983): 2,261 passenger vehicles; 1,616 commercial vehicles (incl. jeeps); 156 motor cycles; Total (incl. others) 6,552.

Shipping (international sea-borne freight traffic, '000 metric tons, estimates, 1983): Goods loaded 30; Goods unloaded 48 (Source: UN, *Monthly Bulletin of Statistics*).

Civil Aviation (1981): Aircraft arrivals 3,670.

EDUCATION

Primary and Secondary Schools (1983/84): 56 primary schools, 584 primary teachers, 17,456 primary pupils; 9 secondary schools, 157 teachers, 3,443 secondary pupils; 1 sixth form college, 13 teachers, 113 pupils.

Further Education (1982): 1 teacher training college; 15 teachers; 60 students; 1 technical college, 18 teachers, 120 students.

TOURISM

1984: 40,971 tourist arrivals (7,017 by sea; 33,954 by air).

Directory

The Constitution

The Constitution came into effect at the independence of Dominica on 3 November 1978. Its main provisions are summarized below:

FUNDAMENTAL RIGHTS AND FREEDOMS

The Constitution guarantees the rights of life, liberty, security of the person, the protection of the law and respect for private property. The individual is entitled to freedom of conscience, of expression and assembly and has the right to an existence free from slavery, forced labour and torture. Protection against discrimination on the grounds of sex, race, place of origin, political opinion, colour or creed is assured.

THE PRESIDENT

The President is elected by the House of Assembly for a term of five years. A presidential candidate is nominated jointly by the Prime Minister and the Leader of the Opposition and on their concurrence is declared elected without any vote being taken; in the case of disagreement the choice will be made by secret ballot in the House of Assembly. Candidates must be citizens of Dominica aged at least 40 who have been resident in Dominica for five years prior to their nomination. A President may not hold office for more than two terms.

PARLIAMENT

Parliament consists of the President and the House of Assembly, composed of 21 elected Representatives and nine Senators. According to the wishes of Parliament, the latter may be appointed by the President—five on the advice of the Prime Minister and four on the advice of the Leader of the Opposition—or elected. The life of Parliament is five years.

Parliament has the power to amend the constitution. Each constituency returns one Representative to the House who is directly elected in accordance with the Constitution. Every citizen over the age of 18 is eligible to vote.

THE EXECUTIVE

Executive authority is vested in the President. The President appoints as Prime Minister the elected member of the House who commands the support of a majority of its elected members, and other Ministers on the advice of the Prime Minister. Not more than three Ministers may be from among the appointed Senators. The President has the power to remove the Prime Minister from office if a resolution of 'no confidence' in the Government is passed by the House and the Prime Minister does not resign within three days or advise the President to dissolve Parliament.

The Cabinet consists of the Prime Minister, other Ministers and the Attorney-General in an ex officio capacity.

The Leader of the Opposition is appointed by the President as that elected member of the house who, in the President's judgement, is best able to command the support of a majority of the elected members who do not support the Government.

The Government

HEAD OF STATE

President: Sir CLARENCE SEIGNORET (assumed office 19 December 1983).

CABINET
(December 1986)

Prime Minister and Minister of Finance, Defence, Foreign and Economic Affairs: MARY EUGENIA CHARLES.
Attorney-General and Minister of Legal Affairs, Immigration and Labour: BRIAN G. K. ALLEYNE.
Minister of Housing, Community Development and Social Affairs: HESKEITH ALEXANDER.
Minister of Health, Water and Sewage: RONAN DAVID.
Minister of Agriculture, Industry, Tourism, Trade, Lands and Surveys: CHARLES MAYNARD.
Minister of Communications, Works and Roads: ALLEYNE CARBON.
Minister of Education and Sports: HENRY GEORGE.

MINISTRIES

Office of the President: Victoria St, Roseau; tel. 2054.
Office of the Prime Minister: Government Headquarters, Kennedy Ave, Roseau; tel. 2406.
All other Ministries are at Government Headquarters, Kennedy Ave, Roseau; tel. 2401.

Legislature

HOUSE OF ASSEMBLY

Speaker: MARIE DAVIES PIERRE.
Clerk: ALBERTHA JNO BAPTISTE.
Nominated Members: 9.
Elected Members: 21.

Election, 1 July 1985

Party	Seats
Dominica Freedom Party	15
Labour Party of Dominica	5
United Dominica Labour Party*	1†

* Represented by a single candidate, not officially endorsed by the Labour Party of Dominica.
† At a by-election in May 1986 the seat was won by the Dominica Freedom Party, increasing the DFP's seats to 16.

Political Organizations

Dominica Freedom Party (DFP): Cross St, Roseau; tel. 2104; Leader MARY EUGENIA CHARLES.
Dominica Progressive Force: Roseau; f. 1983 from split in DLP; left-wing; Leader LENNARD BAPTISTE.
Labour Party of Dominica (LPD): Roseau; f. 1985 as a reunification of all groups and movements of socialistic orientation; Leader MICHAEL A. DOUGLAS; Deputy Leader R. E. HENRY; Gen. Sec. JEROME BARZEY; consists of:
  Dominica Labour Party (DLP): 19 Federation Drive, Roseau; tel. 2321; f. 1961; split into two factions in 1979: the DLP, under the leadership of PATRICK JOHN, and the Democratic Labour Party (DEMLAB), under OLIVER SERAPHIN; remerged with DEMLAB in 1983 to form stronger left-wing alliance.
  Dominica Liberation Movement (DLM): 69 Queen Mary St, Roseau; tel. 4256; f. 1979 from alliance of four leftist groupings; Leader ATHERTON MARTIN; Gen. Sec. BILL RIVIERE.
  United Dominica Labour Party (UDLP): Roseau; f. 1981 as a result of split in Democratic Labour Party (DEMLAB); Leader MICHAEL A. DOUGLAS.

Diplomatic Representation

EMBASSY IN DOMINICA

Venezuela: 37 Cork St, 3rd Floor, Roseau; tel. 3348; telex 8643; Chargé d'affaires: FRANCISCO ITURBE.

Judicial System

Justice is administered by the Eastern Caribbean Supreme Court, consisting of a Court of Appeal and a High Court. One of the six puisne judges of the High Court is resident in Dominica and presides over the Court of Summary Jurisdiction. The District Courts deal with summary offences and civil offences involving sums of not more than EC $500.

DOMINICA

Religion

CHRISTIANITY
The Roman Catholic Church
Dominica comprises the single diocese of Roseau, suffragan to the archdiocese of Castries (Saint Lucia). At 31 December 1984 there were an estimated 65,000 adherents in the country, representing a large majority of the inhabitants. The Bishop participates in the Antilles Episcopal Conference (based in Kingston, Jamaica).

Bishop of Roseau: Rt Rev. ARNOLD BOGHAERT; Bishop's House, 20 Virgin Lane, Roseau; tel. 2837.

The Anglican Communion
Anglicans in Dominica are adherents of the Church in the Province of the West Indies. The country forms part of the diocese of the Windward Islands (the Bishop resides in Kingstown, Saint Vincent).

Other Christian Churches
There are churches of various denominations, including Methodist, Pentecostal, Baptist, Church of Christ, Seventh-day Adventists and Jehovah's Witnesses.

The Press

New Chronicle: 7 Queen Mary St, POB 124, Roseau; tel. 2121; f. 1909; Saturday; progressive independent; Man. J. A. WHITE; Editor J. VANTERPOOL; circ. 25,000.

Official Gazette: Government Printery, Roseau; tel. 2401; telex 8613; weekly; circ. 550.

Radio and Television

There were an estimated 39,000 radio receivers in use in 1983. There is no national television service, although there is a cable television network serving one-third of the island.

Dominica Broadcasting Corporation: Victoria St, Roseau; tel. 3283; government station; daily broadcasts in English; 2 hrs weekly in French patois; 10 kW transmitter on the medium wave band; programmes received throughout Caribbean excluding Jamaica and Guyana.

Gospel Broadcasting Corporation: POB 205, Roseau; tel. 4391; religious; 126 hrs weekly; Man. Dir WAYNE K. DEBOER.

Finance

BANKS
Agricultural, Industrial and Development (AID) Bank: POB 215, 64 Hillsborough St, Roseau; tel. 2853; telex 8620; f. 1971; state-owned; cap. EC $5m. (1982); Man. VANS T. LEBLANC.

Banque Française Commerciale: corner of Queen Mary St and Gt Marlborough St, POB 166, Roseau; tel. 4040; telex 8629; Man. P. INGLISS.

Barclays Bank plc: Old St, Roseau; tel. 82571; telex 8618; sub-branch in Portsmouth; Man. R. L. SHIPMAN.

National Commercial Bank of Dominica: POB 271, 64 Hillsborough St, Roseau; tel. 4401/5; telex 8620; public-owned; share cap. EC $10m. (1978); Chair. FRANK A. BARON; Gen. Man. LAMBERT V. LEWIS.

Royal Bank of Canada: Bay St, POB 144, Roseau; tel. 2771; telex 8367; Man. H. PINARD.

There is a Government Savings Bank with four branches.

INSURANCE
Several British and US companies have agents in Roseau. Local companies include the following:

J. B. Charles and Co. Ltd: POB 121, Roseau; tel. 2855.

Insurance Services Ltd: 8 Castle St, Roseau; tel. 3079.

Tonge Inc: POB 20, 17 Great George St, Roseau; tel. 4027; telex 8631.

Walton's Insurance Agency Ltd: POB 209, 8 Castle St, Roseau; tel. 3079.

Trade and Industry

Co-operative Citrus Growers' Association: 21 Hanover St, Roseau; tel. 2062; telex 8615; f. 1954; processing and marketing of citrus fruits; Pres. P. NORMAN ROLLE.

DOMLEC: POB 13, Castle St, Roseau; tel. 2681; telex 8655; state-owned national electricity service.

Dominica Association of Industry and Commerce (DAIC): POB 85, 14 Church St, Roseau; tel. 2874; f. 1972 by a merger of the Manufacturers' Association and the Chamber of Commerce to represent the business sector and to stimulate commerce and industry; autonomous organization liaising with the Government on questions of trade, overseas investment, fiscal and other incentives to industry; 91 mems; Pres. PATRICIA GARRAWAY-INGLIS; Exec. Sec. CHERYL P. J. ROLLE.

Dominica Banana Marketing Corporation (DBMC): Corner of Queen Mary St and Turkey Lane, Roseau; tel. 2671; telex 8648; f. 1934; state-supported; Chair. VANOULST JNO CHARLES; Exec. Sec. E. M. ANGOL; Gen. Man. E. C. JAMES.

Dominica Employers' Federation: 14 Church St, Roseau; tel. 2314; Pres. DERMOT SOUTHWELL; Sec. SHIRLEY GUYE.

Dominica Export-Import Agency (Dexia): Roseau; opened July 1986, replacing the Dominica Agricultural Marketing Board and the External Trade Bureau.

Dominica Manufacturers' Association (DMA): Roseau; f. 1984; Chair. PARRY BELLOT.

Industrial Development Corporation (IDC): POB 293, Old St, Roseau; tel. 2045; telex 8642; f. 1974; promotes local and foreign investment to increase employment, production and exports; Chair. DERMOT SOUTHWELL.

MARKETING AND CO-OPERATIVE ORGANIZATIONS
At the end of 1980 there were 26 registered credit unions, with 15,171 members and share capital of EC $3.3m. There were also 36 other registered co-operatives, of which 19 were agricultural (citrus, fisheries, craft, poultry, vegetables, bay oil, bananas and sugar cane), with 1,861 members and share capital of approximately EC $72,000.

TRADE UNIONS
Dominica Farmers' Union (DFU): 17 Church St, Roseau; tel. 4244; Gen. Sec. RICHARD CHARLES; 2,500 mems.

Dominica Trade Union: 70–1 Queen Mary St, Roseau; tel. 2903; f. 1945; Pres. R. L. KIRTON; Gen. Sec. VERONICA G. NICHOLAS; 650 mems.

Civil Service Association: Valley Rd/Windsor Lane, Roseau; tel. 2102; f. 1940 and registered as a Trade Union in 1960, representing all grades of civil servants, including firemen, prison officers, nurses, teachers and postal workers; Pres. JOHN ALEXIS; Sec. ARTHUR R. SMITH; 2,700 mems.

Dominica Amalgamated Workers' Union: 22 Hillsborough St, POB 137, Roseau; tel. 3048; f. 1960; Gen. Sec. A. FREDERICK JOSEPH; 5,000 mems.

Waterfront and Allied Workers' Union: 43 Hillsborough St, Roseau; tel. 2343; f. 1965; Pres. LOUIS BENOIT; Gen. Sec. CURTIS AUGUSTUS; 5,000 mems.

Transport

ROADS
At the end of 1976 there were 327 km (231 miles) of first-class, 262 km (163 miles) of second-class and 117 km (73 miles) of third-class motorable roads, as well as 282 miles (454 km) of tracks. Despite hurricane damage and extensive flooding in 1979 and 1980, most of the roads were operational in 1982. Extensive road development was completed in 1986 at a cost of US $39m.

SHIPPING
A deep-water harbour at Woodridge Bay serves Roseau, which is the principal port. Several foreign shipping lines call at Roseau,

and ships of the Geest Line also call at Portsmouth to collect bananas.

CIVIL AVIATION

Melville Hall Airport, 64 km (40 miles) from Roseau, and Canefield airstrip are the two airports on the island. A loan was received from France in 1986 for an improvement-scheme at Canefield airstrip and was to include the construction of a terminal building and lighting of the runway.

Tourism

Dominica Tourist Board: 37 Cork St, POB 73, Roseau; tel. 2351; telex 8649; Chair. GERRY AIRD; Dir of Tourism VALDA LAVILLE. There were 40,971 visitors in 1984.

Dominica Hotel Association: POB 5, Roseau; tel. 6244; telex 619.

THE DOMINICAN REPUBLIC

Introductory Survey

Location, Climate, Language, Religion, Flag, Capital

The Dominican Republic occupies the eastern part of the island of Hispaniola, which lies between Cuba and Puerto Rico in the Caribbean Sea. The country's only international frontier is with Haiti, to the west. The climate is sub-tropical, with an average annual temperature of 27°C (80°F). In Santo Domingo, temperatures are generally between 19°C (66°F) and 31°C (88°F). The west and south-west of the country are arid. Hispaniola lies in the path of tropical cyclones. The official language is Spanish. Almost all of the inhabitants profess Christianity, and more than 90% are Roman Catholics. There are small Protestant and Jewish communities. The national flag (proportions 23 by 15) is blue (upper hoist and lower fly) and red (lower hoist and upper fly), quartered by a white cross. The state flag has, in addition, the national coat of arms, showing a quartered shield in the colours of the flag (on which are superimposed national banners, a cross and an open Bible) between scrolls above and below, at the centre of the cross. The capital is Santo Domingo.

Recent History

The Dominican Republic became independent in 1844, although it was occupied by US military forces between 1916 and 1924. General Rafael Leonidas Trujillo Molina overthrew the elected President, Horacio Vázquez, in 1930 and dominated the country until his assassination in May 1961. The dictator ruled personally from 1930 to 1947 and indirectly thereafter. His brother, Héctor Trujillo, was President from 1947 until August 1960, when he was replaced by Dr Joaquín Balaguer, hitherto Vice-President. After Rafael Trujillo's death, President Balaguer remained in office, but in December 1961 he permitted moderate opposition groups to participate in a Council of State, with legislative and executive powers. Balaguer resigned in January 1962, when the Council of State became the Provisional Government. A presidential election in December 1962, the country's first free election for 38 years, was won by Dr Juan Bosch Gaviño, the founder and leader of the Partido Revolucionario Dominicano (PRD), who had been in exile since 1930. President Bosch, a left-of-centre democrat, took office in February 1963 but was overthrown in the following September by a military coup. The leaders of the armed forces transferred power to a civilian triumvirate, led by Emilio de los Santos. In April 1965 a revolt by supporters of ex-President Bosch overthrew the triumvirate. Civil war broke out between pro-Bosch forces and military units headed by Gen. Elías Wessin y Wessin, who had played a leading role in the 1963 coup. The violence was eventually suppressed by the intervention of some 23,000 US troops, who were formally incorporated into an Inter-American peace force by the Organization of American States after they had landed. The peace force withdrew in September 1965.

Following a period of provisional government under Héctor García Godoy, a presidential election in June 1966 was won by ex-President Balaguer, the candidate of the Partido Reformista Social Cristiano (PRSC), who won 57% of the votes cast, while ex-President Bosch won 39%. The PRSC, founded in 1964, also won a majority of seats in both houses of the National Congress. President Balaguer took office in July. A new constitution was promulgated in November 1966. Despite his association with the Trujillo dictatorship, Balaguer initially proved to be a popular leader, and in May 1970 he was re-elected for a further four years. In February 1973 a state of emergency was declared when guerrilla forces landed on the coast. Captain Francisco Caamaño Deño, the leader of the 1965 revolt, and his followers were killed. Bosch and other opposition figures went into hiding. Bosch later resigned as leader of the PRD (founding the Partido de la Liberación Dominicana—PLD), undermining hopes of a united opposition in the May 1974 elections, when President Balaguer was re-elected with a large majority. In June 1975 guerrilla forces of Dominican émigrés from Cuba landed on the island in an unsuccessful attempt to overthrow Balaguer.

In the May 1978 presidential election, Dr Balaguer was defeated by the PRD candidate, Silvestre Antonio Guzmán Fernández. This was the first occasion in the country's history when an elected President yielded power to an elected successor. An attempted military coup in favour of Dr Balaguer was prevented by pressure from the US Government. On assuming office in August, President Guzmán undertook to professionalize the armed forces by removing politically ambitious high-ranking officers. In June 1981 he declared his support for Jacobo Majluta Azar, his Vice-President, as his successor but in November the PRD rejected Majluta's candidacy in favour of Dr Salvador Jorge Blanco, a left-wing senator, who was elected President in May 1982. In the Congressional elections, held at the same time, the PRD gained a majority in both the Senate and the Chamber of Deputies. President Guzmán committed suicide in July after allegations of fraud were made against his government and members of his family. Vice-President Majluta was immediately sworn in as interim President until Dr Blanco assumed office in August. Although a member of the Socialist International, Blanco maintained good relations with the USA (on which the country is economically dependent) and declared that he would not resume relations with Cuba. In December 1982 the Government revealed that it would not nationalize foreign property, including extensive holdings owned by oil companies, in the Dominican Republic.

In 1983 popular discontent with the Government's austerity programme led to the occupation of the Ministry of Agriculture by peasants, and calls for agrarian reform. In August 1983 a two-week purge of subversives took place on the orders of President Blanco. Two visiting Cuban academics were deported, and Socialist and Communist Party sympathizers were arrested. The Government's move came in response to a report which implicated Cuban and Nicaraguan involvement in the increased left-wing activity in the country.

In April 1984 a series of public protests against substantial increases in the cost of essential items erupted into violent confrontations between government forces and demonstrators in Santo Domingo and four other cities, which lasted for three days. In the course of the protests, more than 50 people were killed, some 200 injured and over 4,000 arrested. The Government held opposition groups of the extreme right and left responsible for the unrest. In May the Government responded to the prospect of further demonstrations by ordering the arrest of more than 100 trade union and left-wing leaders. In August, in anticipation of civil unrest at the announcement of new price increases, more arrests were made among trade union and opposition leaders. Rumours of a plot against the Government by left-wing sympathizers caused serious disquiet throughout the country. In November a new Secretary of State for Finance was named for the second time in 1984, the previous change having been made in May. Further demonstrations, including one attended by 40,000 people in Santo Domingo, were held in protest at the continuing economic decline.

In February 1985 a further series of substantial price increases led to violent clashes between demonstrators and police, during which four people died and more than 50 were injured. Public unrest was exacerbated by the Government's decision, in April, to accept the IMF's terms for further financial aid. In June a 24-hour general strike was organized by trade unions, in protest at the Government's economic policy and its refusal to increase the minimum wage. In July, however, the threat of a 48-hour general strike prompted the Government to order an immediate increase in the minimum wage.

Further violence preceded the presidential and legislative elections of May 1986. Several people were killed, and many more injured, in clashes between rival political supporters. The three principal candidates in the presidential election were all former Presidents: Dr Joaquín Balaguer of the PRSC; Jacobo Majluta, who, having registered La Estructura, his right-wing faction of the PRD, as a separate political party in July 1985, nevertheless secured the candidacy of the ruling PRD; and Dr Juan Bosch of the PLD. The counting of votes was suspended twice, following allegations by Majluta of fraud by the PRSC and by the Central Electoral Board, two of the three members of which then resigned. Dr Balaguer was finally declared the winner by a narrow margin of votes over Majluta, his nearest rival. In the simultaneous legislative elections, the PRSC won 21 of the 30 seats in the Senate and 56 of the 120 seats in the Chamber of Deputies. Upon taking office as President (for the fifth time) in August 1986, Dr Balaguer pledged to combat poverty and corruption, and appealed for national reconciliation, proposing a two-year truce to the opposition parties.

Government

The Dominican Republic comprises 26 provinces, each administered by an appointed governor, and a Distrito Nacional (DN) containing the capital. Under the 1966 Constitution, legislative power is exercised by the bicameral National Congress, with a Senate of 30 members and a Chamber of Deputies (120 members). Members of both houses are elected for four years by universal adult suffrage. Executive power lies with the President, who is also elected by direct popular vote for four years. He is assisted by a Vice-President and a Cabinet containing Secretaries of State.

Defence

Military service is voluntary and lasts for four years. In July 1986 the armed forces totalled 21,300 men: army 13,000, air force 4,300 and navy 4,000. Paramilitary forces number 1,000. Defence expenditure for 1986 was estimated at RD $203.9m.

Economic Affairs

Between 1968 and 1974 the annual increase in the Dominican Republic's gross domestic product (GDP) averaged 10.6% in real terms, one of the highest growth rates in the world. Over the same period, GDP per head grew by 7.4% annually. However, the country is dependent on fuel imports to meet its energy requirements, and in the later 1970s, following sharp rises in the world price of petroleum, its economic progress was slower. Between 1975 and 1981 GDP expanded, in real terms, by 4.5% per year, with GDP per head growing at an average annual rate of 1.8%. GDP increased by 1.7% in 1982, by 3.9% in 1983, but by only 0.4% in 1984. There was an estimated fall of 2.2% in real GDP in 1985. In 1984, according to estimates by the World Bank, the Dominican Republic's gross national product per head (at average 1982-84 prices) was US $970, having increased at an average rate of 3.2% per year, in constant prices, since 1965.

Agriculture employs more than 50% of the working population, and agricultural products provided about 50% of export earnings in 1985. However, the contribution of the agricultural sector (excluding forestry and fishing) to GDP declined from 19.5% in 1980 to 16.8% in 1983. The principal commercial crop is sugar cane. In 1985 raw sugar accounted for an estimated 21.5% of the value of total exports, compared with 34.6% in 1982, when earnings from sugar amounted to US $266m. Output of raw sugar in 1982/83 totalled 1.2m. metric tons. However, the outlook was poor as the price had dropped to below the cost of production, earnings fell by 43% between 1981 and 1982, and the USA subsequently introduced tariffs on sugar imports. The USA's decision to reduce its sugar import quota by 44% in 1985 led to a crisis within the industry. Exports of sugar to the USA declined from 686,071 metric tons in 1981 to 412,840 tons in 1985. Export earnings from raw sugar fell from $272m. in 1984 to an estimated $158m. in 1985, and estimates for 1986 predicted a further decline. The USA's quota for sugar imports from the Dominican Republic in 1987, announced in December 1986, was only 145,000 tons. The sector suffered a setback in June 1984, when Gulf and Western, the major private sugar company (accounting for about one-third of national sugar output), announced its intention to cease operations and to sell its property.

The Government has encouraged the cultivation of coffee and cocoa in order to diversify exports. In 1985 exports of coffee and cocoa totalled an estimated $86m. and $58m. respectively.

Tobacco and bananas are also grown. The tobacco industry also faced a crisis in 1985, owing partly to a drop in sales. In 1980 the Sabana Yegua dam, designed to irrigate 600,000 ha of land, was opened. The Government also undertook to develop the Madrigal water supply project for Santo Domingo, and the Río Nizao irrigation project. In 1983 loans of $1,000m. were secured from the Inter-American Development Bank (IDB) to aid agricultural producers and small business concerns. In December 1985 a further $55m. loan from the IDB was agreed, to continue this industrial recovery programme. The agricultural sector is highly vulnerable, suffering from the loss of the entire pig population after an outbreak of African swine fever in 1978, from damage (valued at an estimated $1,000m.) inflicted by Hurricane David in 1979, from further weather hazards in 1981, and from declines in world prices for coffee, cocoa and tobacco in 1980 and for sugar in 1981 and 1984-85.

The mining sector accounted for 5.3% of GDP in 1980, but the proportion fell to 2.2% in 1983. The principal mineral resources are bauxite (with reserves of 18m. tons at Cabo Rojo), gold, silver and ferro-nickel. Production of bauxite, however, ceased in early 1984, when the US company Alcoa announced withdrawal from the country. The value of ferro-nickel exports rose from US $24.2m. in 1982 to an estimated $120.7m. in 1985. Earnings from the gold-silver alloy, doré, fell from $163.6m. in 1982 to an estimated $113.6m. in 1985. Foreign oil companies have been granted concessions to undertake exploratory drilling, and in 1981 a petroleum deposit was discovered at Charco Largo, Barahona. Its potential output was estimated at 20,000 barrels per day (b/d). National consumption is estimated at 28,000 b/d. In 1984 the cost of imports of petroleum and petroleum products rose to $504.8m. Substantial savings were anticipated in 1986, following the decline in international petroleum prices. In 1984 the IDB provided financing of US $11m. for petroleum exploration. Attempts were being made to find alternative energy sources, and hydroelectricity is now being developed. In 1983 a hydroelectric generator with a capacity of 40,000 kW became operational at the Tavera dam. The hydroelectric plant, Niza II, was to start operations in 1986 with an annual production capacity of 28m. kWh. Two further plants are to be built on the Yaque de Norte river. The first coal-fired plant in the Caribbean region, the 125 MW Haina station, was under construction in 1985.

Government investment has been concentrated on agriculture, energy and tourism. In 1983 tourism generated foreign exchange income equal to 43% of total export receipts, and therefore surpassed earnings from sugar. Revenue from tourism increased to US $370m. in 1984 and to US $470m. in 1985. Remittances from Dominicans resident in the USA are also significant, totalling an estimated $600m. in 1985.

Between 1969 and 1976 great economic progress was made, mainly owing to massive US aid, the high level of world sugar prices, substantial public and private investment and increased foreign participation. After the hurricane disaster in 1979, the Government attempted to achieve economic recovery through a high level of public expenditure, and added 50,000 employees to the government payroll. By preventing growth of the money supply in 1981, inflation was reduced to 10%. The budget deficit was US $183m. in 1982. Falling earnings from the narrow range of raw material and commodity exports resulted in a severe shortage of convertible currency. The trade deficit rose from $389.1m. in 1984 to an estimated $546.6m. in 1985. The 1986 budget envisaged total expenditure of 2,161m. pesos, 10% of which was expected to be granted by international organizations and bilateral financing agencies.

In 1983 a three-year loan of $466m. was agreed with the IMF. In early 1984 the disbursement of some US $70m. (including $40m. from the IMF) was halted, pending the Dominican Republic's fulfilment of the IMF's conditions, principally the introduction of a unified exchange rate for the peso. In April 1984 the Government introduced price increases of over 80% on basic items and of 300% on import tariffs. In May, however, negotiations with the IMF were broken off after the Government rejected the IMF's proposed austerity programme. The principal issue of contention had been the IMF's insistence upon an immediate transfer of all imports to the 'parallel' exchange rate of 2.97 pesos per US dollar, to allow for an increase of between 20% and 300% in the cost of petroleum products and electricity. Negotiations were resumed, and in August agree-

THE DOMINICAN REPUBLIC

ment was reached on an interim loan. In January 1985 the long-standing parity of the currency with the US dollar was ended, and a new exchange rate of about 3 pesos per dollar was established. In April 1985 the Government obtained a stand-by credit of SDR 78.5m. from the IMF. Consequently, the Government was able to reach provisional agreement on the renegotiation of US $360m. of debts with creditor governments and of $787m. of debts with creditor banks. In November 1985 the IMF approved a loan of SDR 15.5m., under its compensatory financing facility, to offset the decline in the Dominican Republics earnings from sugar exports. The Government's continuing compliance with the IMF's demands for austerity prompted a series of general strikes and protests in 1985.

In 1985 unemployment affected 29.8% of the labour force, not including 30% under-employment. Inflation increased from an annual average of 6.9% in 1983 to 24.4% in 1984. A further increase to nearly 40% was recorded during 1985. On taking office in 1982, the Government of President Blanco introduced 125 emergency economic measures as part of a fiscal reform programme, aimed at cutting the public sector deficit of $330m., and at achieving a current payments surplus by 1984/85. In July 1983 the Government announced its Public Investment Programme for 1983–85, providing $1,666.2m. in funding for 412 projects.

In 1986, after two years of austerity measures, the economy began to recover. Inflation was only 6.1% in the year to June 1986, compared with an annual average of 37.5% in 1985. In January 1986 President Blanco reduced the price of petrol by 12% to 3.96 pesos per gallon, and halved the 36% surcharge on traditional exports. The main economic problems confronting the incoming Government of President Balaguer in August 1986 were the creation of new jobs, to decrease the country's reliance on the sugar industry, and to reduce its $3,551m. foreign debt.

In July 1984 the Dominican Republic was granted observer status in CARICOM (see p. 108).

Social Welfare

A voluntary national contributory scheme, introduced in 1947, provides insurance cover for sickness, unemployment, accidental injury, maternity, old age and death. Only 42% of the population are thought to benefit from the system. In 1980 there were 571 hospitals and clinics, 2,142 physicians and 8,953 hospital beds under the auspices of the public health and welfare department and the Institute of Social Security.

Education

Education is, where possible, compulsory for children between seven and 14 years of age. Primary education begins at the age of seven and lasts for six years. Secondary education, starting at 13 years of age, also lasts for six years, comprising a first cycle of two years and a second of four years. As a proportion of the school-age population, the total enrolment at primary and secondary schools increased from 66% in 1970 to 83% in 1981, but declined to 73% in 1983. There are five universities. In 1985, according to UNESCO estimates, the average rate of adult illiteracy was 22.7%.

Tourism

Strenuous efforts are being made to develop the tourist industry. Hotels, casinos and seaside resorts are being built, and tours to the old Spanish colonial settlements have been organized. It was planned to spend RD $150m. on a tourism development programme, to be completed in the mid-1980s. Tourist complexes are under construction at Puerto Plata, Samana, La Romana, La Altagracia and Santiago de los Caballeros. In 1984 there were 680,000 tourist arrivals, including visits by nationals resident abroad, and tourist receipts totalled about US $370m., rising to $470m. in 1985.

Public Holidays

1987: 1 January (New Year's Day), 6 January (Epiphany), 21 January (Our Lady of Altagracia), 26 January (Duarte), 27 February (Independence), 14 April (Pan-American Day), 17 April (Good Friday), 1 May (Labour Day), 16 July (Foundation of Sociedad la Trinitaria), 16 August (Restoration Day), 24 September (Our Lady of Mercedes), 12 October (Columbus Day), 24 October (United Nations Day), 1 November (All Saints' Day), 25 December (Christmas Day).

1988: 1 January (New Year's Day), 6 January (Epiphany), 21 January (Our Lady of Altagracia), 26 January (Duarte), 27 February (Independence), 1 April (Good Friday), 14 April (Pan-American Day), 1 May (Labour Day), 16 July (Foundation of Sociedad la Trinitaria), 16 August (Restoration Day), 24 September (Our Lady of Mercedes), 12 October (Columbus Day), 24 October (United Nations Day), 1 November (All Saints' Day), 25 December (Christmas Day).

Weights and Measures

The metric system is officially in force but the imperial system is often used.

Currency and Exchange Rates

100 centavos = 1 Dominican Republic peso (RD $).
Exchange rates (30 September 1986):
  £1 sterling = 4.240 pesos;
  US $1 = 2.930 pesos.

Statistical Survey

Source (unless otherwise stated): Oficina Nacional de Estadísticas, Edif. de Oficinas Públicas, Avda México esq. Leopoldo Navarro, Santo Domingo; Banco Central de la República Dominicana, Santo Domingo; tel. 689-8141; telex 346-0052.

Area and Population

AREA, POPULATION AND DENSITY

Area (sq km)	
Land	48,072
Inland water	350
Total	48,422*
Population (census results)	
9 January 1970	4,009,458
12 December 1981	
Males	2,832,454
Females	2,815,523
Total	5,647,977
Population (official estimates at mid-year)	
1983	5,961,891
1984	6,101,775
1985	6,244,500
Density (per sq km) at mid-1985	129.0

* 18,696 sq miles.
1981 ('000): Births 218.1; Marriages 25.2.

PRINCIPAL TOWNS (Population at 12 December 1981)

Santo Domingo, DN (capital)	1,313,172
Santiago de los Caballeros	278,638
La Romana	91,571
San Pedro de Macorís	78,562
San Francisco de Macorís	64,906
Concepción de la Vega	52,432
San Juan	49,764
Barahona	49,334
San Felipe de Puerto Plata	45,348

ECONOMICALLY ACTIVE POPULATION (1981 census)

Total: 1,915,388 (Males 1,361,109; Females 554,279).
Source: ILO, *Year Book of Labour Statistics*.

Agriculture

PRINCIPAL CROPS ('000 metric tons)

	1982	1983	1984
Rice (paddy)	447	355	344
Maize	28	42	76
Sorghum	16	42	66
Potatoes	12	19	20
Sweet potatoes	19	35	60
Cassava (Manioc)	68	102	118
Yams	5	9	14
Other roots and tubers	40	30	43
Dry beans	58	48	54
Groundnuts (in shell)	36	38	38
Coconuts*	78	80	85
Copra†	11	13	14
Tomatoes	153	155	181
Sugar cane	11,805	11,520	11,750†
Oranges*	73	74	75
Lemons and limes*	14	14	14
Avocados	135*	136*	136
Mangoes	182*	184*	185
Pineapples	25†	25†	25*
Bananas	320†	320†	320*
Plantains	600†	605†	605*
Coffee (green)	63	68	49
Cocoa beans	43	45	44†
Tobacco (leaves)	34	34	35†

* FAO estimates.   † Unofficial figures.
Source: FAO, *Production Yearbook*.

LIVESTOCK ('000 head, year ending September)

	1982	1983	1984
Horses	204*	204*	204†
Mules†	99	99	99
Asses†	120	120	120
Cattle	1,969	1,998	1,994†
Pigs	54	375	382*
Sheep	76	76	78†
Goats	459	463	465†

* Unofficial figures.   † FAO estimates.
Chickens (FAO estimates, million): 8 in 1982; 9 in 1983; 9 in 1984.
Source: FAO, *Production Yearbook*.

LIVESTOCK PRODUCTS ('000 metric tons)

	1982	1983	1984*
Beef and veal	54	56	57
Poultry meat	61	74	74
Cows' milk	450†	460†	460
Butter	1.4	1.5	1.5
Cheese	2.5	3.0	3.0
Hen eggs	19.6†	17.3†	17.5
Cattle hides (fresh)	7.2*	7.4*	7.4

* FAO estimates.   † Unofficial figures.
Source: FAO, *Production Yearbook*.

THE DOMINICAN REPUBLIC

Fishing

('000 metric tons, live weight)

	1980	1981	1982
Inland waters	2.5	2.8	1.7
Atlantic Ocean	8.2	9.2	11.4
Total catch	10.7	12.0	13.2

1983 and 1984: Annual catch as in 1982 (FAO estimates).
Source: FAO, *Yearbook of Fishery Statistics*.

Mining

	1982	1983	1984*
Ferro-nickel (metric tons)	14,375	52,278	63,966
Bauxite (metric tons)	152,250	n.a.	n.a.†
Gold (troy oz)	386,309	354,023	338,272
Silver (troy oz)	2,197,680	1,329,138	1,207,472

* Estimates.
† Production of bauxite ceased in early 1984.

Industry

SELECTED PRODUCTS*

		1982	1983	1984
Wheat flour	'000 tons	181.2	172.5	213.6
Refined sugar	'000 tons	109.6	101.9	108.5
Molasses	'000 US gallons	77,992.4	71,992.4	65,903.8
Fertilizers	'000 tons	176.0	188.4	n.a.
Cement	'000 tons	948.5	1,064.1	1,143.0
Beer	million litres	86.3	96.3	94.5
Spirits	million litres	22.3	22.4	26.4
Cigars	million	12.0	13.3	n.a.
Cigarettes	million	4,421.0	4,288.4	3,683.5
Electricity	million kWh	2,225.4	2,825.4	2,932.4
Cardboard boxes	million units	356.7	369.1	n.a.

* Provisional.

Finance

CURRENCY AND EXCHANGE RATES

Monetary Units
100 centavos = 1 Dominican Republic peso (RD $ or peso oro)

Denominations
Coins: 1, 5, 10, 25 and 50 centavos; 1 peso.
Notes: 1, 5, 10, 20, 50, 100, 500 and 1,000 pesos.

Sterling and Dollar Equivalents (30 September 1986)
£1 sterling = 4.240 pesos;
US $1 = 2.930 pesos;
100 Dominican Republic pesos = £23.59 = US $34.13.

Note: Prior to January 1985, the Dominican Republic peso was officially at par with the US dollar. The average exchange rate for 1985 was US $1 = RD $3.113.

CENTRAL BANK RESERVES
(US $ million at 31 December)

	1983	1984	1985
Gold*	31.3	7.9	5.9
IMF special drawing rights	0.2	0.4	28.8
Reserve position in IMF	7.4	—	—
Foreign exchange	163.3	253.1	308.5
Total	202.2	261.4	343.2

* Valued at market-related prices.
Source: IMF, *International Financial Statistics*.

MONEY SUPPLY (RD $ million at 31 December)

	1983	1984	1985
Currency outside banks	414.7	592.8	677.2
Demand deposits at commercial banks	358.4	516.7	657.8

Source: IMF, *International Financial Statistics*.

BUDGET (RD $ million)

Revenue	1983	1984	1985*
Tax revenue	798.1	1,067.5	1,548.0
Non-tax revenue	107.5	81.4	80.1
Other receipts†	267.0	167.6	282.3
Total	1,172.6	1,316.5	1,910.4

* Preliminary.
† Including loans from domestic banks and from abroad (RD $ million): 265.9 in 1982.

Expenditure	1983	1984	1985
Presidency	189.9	157.7	493.6
Interior and police	83.8	122.2	132.9
Armed forces	129.3	163.9	190.8
Education	151.5	174.4	213.0
Health	96.9	119.5	141.1
Others	547.3	540.9	715.4
Total	1,198.7	1,278.6	1,886.8

COST OF LIVING (Consumer Price Index. Base: Year ending April 1977 = 100)

	1983	1984	1985
Food, beverages and tobacco	161.23	196.61	273.78
Housing	184.73	224.46	271.98
Clothing, shoes and accessories	181.66	266.84	449.71
Others	166.37	212.19	289.99
All items	168.97	210.27	289.18

THE DOMINICAN REPUBLIC — Statistical Survey

NATIONAL ACCOUNTS (RD $ million at current prices, provisional estimates)

National Income and Product

	1982	1983	1984
Domestic factor incomes*	7,014.5	7,490.4	9,279.3
Consumption of fixed capital	437.7	510.2	637.0
Gross domestic product at factor cost	7,488.2	8,000.6	9,916.3
Indirect taxes, *less* subsidies	472.8	574.2	789.3
GDP in purchasers' values	7,961.0	8,574.8	10,705.6
Net factor income from abroad	−254.1	−297.1	−241.4
Gross national product	7,706.9	8,277.7	10,464.2
Less Consumption of fixed capital	473.7	510.2	637.0
National income in market prices	7,233.2	7,767.5	9,827.2

* Compensation of employees and the operating surplus of enterprises.

Expenditure on the Gross Domestic Product

	1982	1983	1984
Government final consumption expenditure	779.4	786.3	870.8
Private final consumption expenditure*	5,978.7	6,299.4	7,813.7
Increase in stocks†	99.3	62.4	33.5
Gross fixed capital formation	1,496.4	1,762.5	2,174.6
Total domestic expenditure	8,374.1	8,910.6	10,892.6
Exports of goods and services	1,141.8	1,241.8	1,369.6
Less Imports of goods and services	1,534.6	1,577.6	1,556.6
GDP in purchasers' values	7,961.0	8,574.8	10,705.6
GDP at constant 1970 prices	3,072.5	3,193.6	3,205.5

* Obtained as a residual.
† Including only mining, manufacturing, groundnuts, raw tobacco and beans.

Gross Domestic Product by Economic Activity

	1981	1982	1983
Agriculture	951.6	952.0	976.7
Livestock	352.9	410.5	461.7
Forestry and fishing	45.0	49.4	50.0
Mining	270.6	193.5	185.3
Manufacturing	1,133.1	1,454.8	1,527.5
Construction	537.1	535.1	648.8
Wholesale and retail trade	1,197.6	1,350.3	1,449.3
Transport	345.2	359.9	371.4
Communications	63.2	69.3	77.2
Electricity	66.8	82.4	77.5
Finance	286.8	335.8	367.6
Owner-occupied dwellings	681.2	693.4	750.5
Government services	608.0	663.7	704.2
Other services	727.8	810.9	927.1
Total	7,266.9	7,961.0	8,574.8

THE DOMINICAN REPUBLIC *Statistical Survey*

BALANCE OF PAYMENTS (US $ million)

	1982	1983	1984
Merchandise exports f.o.b	767.7	785.2	868.1
Merchandise imports f.o.b.	−1,257.3	−1,279.0	−1,257.1
Trade balance	**−489.6**	**−493.8**	**−389.0**
Exports of services	378.5	463.5	507.3
Imports of services	−536.5	−602.6	−546.7
Balance of goods and services	**−647.6**	**−632.9**	**−428.4**
Private unrequited transfers (net)	190.0	195.0	205.0
Government unrequited transfers (net)	15.0	20.0	60.0
Current balance	**−442.6**	**−417.9**	**−163.4**
Direct capital investment (net)	−1.4	48.2	68.5
Other long-term capital (net)	200.7	14.4	225.6
Short-term capital (net)	−153.6	−134.4	−70.0
Net errors and omissions	−31.1	10.6	29.7
Total (net monetary movements)	**−428.0**	**−479.1**	**−90.4**
Monetization of gold (net)	−16.4	−14.6	−22.1
Valuation changes (net)	2.8	7.8	7.7
Exceptional financing (net)	179.7	361.1	−1.1
Official financing (net)	101.5	−20.9	−7.8
Changes in reserves	**−160.4**	**−145.7**	**82.7**

Source: IMF, *International Financial Statistics.*

External Trade

PRINCIPAL COMMODITIES (US $ '000)

Imports	1982	1983	1984
Cars and other vehicles (incl. spares)	55,292	44,350	65,300
Chemical and pharmaceutical products	71,875	70,339	65,944
Cotton and manufactures	7,423	10,829	9,660
Foodstuffs	120,095	103,388	112,295
Petroleum and petroleum products	451,646	461,296	504,842
Iron and steel manufactures (excl. building materials)	63,819	57,594	61,118
Machinery (incl. spares)	112,949	104,285	83,660
Total (incl. others)	1,255,817	1,279,020	1,146,827

Exports	1983	1984	1985*
Raw sugar	263,562	271,886	158,477
Molasses	11,660	14,217	9,693
Cocoa beans	55,518	70,064	58,078
Coffee (green)	76,288	95,072	86,149
Tobacco (unmanufactured)	21,816	24,228	17,612
Ferro-nickel	83,471	108,522	120,715
Alloy of gold and silver	150,758	131,810	113,611
Furfural	22,486	19,854	16,505
Total (incl. others)	785,176	868,076	738,548

* Estimates.

PRINCIPAL TRADING PARTNERS (US $ '000)

Imports	1982	1983	1984*
Belgium and Luxembourg	5,013	10,736	7,540
Brazil	14,994	20,131	21,537
Canada	32,466	29,684	19,222
France	13,916	13,741	9,351
Germany, Federal Republic	32,908	40,405	33,396
Italy	10,489	11,221	9,745
Japan	64,596	55,032	58,621
Mexico	170,659	151,816	147,660
Netherlands	3,202	10,145	14,752
Netherlands Antilles	48,306	45,611	23,159
Puerto Rico	21,363	24,640	21,869
Spain	46,540	43,886	27,942
United Kingdom	14,338	12,619	11,661
USA	469,867	438,353	407,646
Venezuela	221,045	271,547	332,726
Total (incl. others)	1,255,817	1,279,020	1,146,827

* Estimates.

Exports	1983	1984	1985*
Belgium and Luxembourg	26,388	11,737	19,971
Canada	34,397	20,542	17,686
France	1,289	417	2,008
Haiti	5,420	6,339	5,623
Italy	1,960	2,587	3,901
Japan	6,973	15,146	13,229
Morocco	6,498	8,905	758
Netherlands	31,386	60,430	53,023
Puerto Rico	32,434	43,087	52,129
Spain	16,765	12,770	10,897
Switzerland	48,318	111	200
United Kingdom	3,148	561	670
USA	503,643	625,977	508,569
Venezuela	3,689	12,950	1,810
Total (incl. others)	785,176	868,076	738,548

Transport

ROAD TRAFFIC (motor vehicles in use at 31 December)

	1982	1983	1984
Passenger cars	94,601	87,605	101,979
Trucks and lorries	50,883	52,197	54,571
Buses	4,463	4,814	6,736

INTERNATIONAL SEA-BORNE SHIPPING
(freight traffic in '000 metric tons)

	1982	1983	1984
Goods loaded*	2,017	1,750	1,777
Goods unloaded	3,163	3,560	3,649

* Not including exports to duty-free zones.

CIVIL AVIATION (traffic on scheduled services)

	1981	1982
Kilometres flown (million)	4.7	5.5
Passengers carried ('000)	440	414
Passengers-km (million)	374	481
Freight ton-km (million)	11.0	9.0

Source: UN, *Statistical Yearbook*.

Tourism

	1982	1983	1984
Total visitors	621,530	600,295	680,778

Education

1983/84

	Institutions	Teachers	Students
Primary	5,864	29,667	1,039,405
Secondary	1,664	9,610	384,091

* Estimates.
1977/78: Higher education: 59,321 students in 5 establishments.

Directory

The Constitution

The present Constitution of the Dominican Republic was promulgated on 28 November 1966. Its main provisions are summarized below:

The Dominican Republic is a sovereign, free, independent State; no organizations set up by the State can bring about any act which might cause direct or indirect intervention in the internal or foreign affairs of the State or which might threaten the integrity of the State. The Dominican Republic recognizes and applies the norms of general and American international law and is in favour of and will support any initiative towards economic integration for the countries of America. The civil, republican, democratic, representative Government is divided into three independent powers: legislative, executive and judicial.

The territory of the Dominican Republic is as laid down in the Frontier Treaty of 1929 and its Protocol of Revision of 1936.

The life and property of the individual citizen are inviolable; there can be no sentence of death, torture nor any sentence which might cause physical harm to the individual. There is freedom of thought, of conscience, of religion, freedom to publish, freedom of unarmed association, provided that there is no subversion against public order, national security or decency. There is freedom of labour and trade unions; freedom to strike, except in the case of public services, according to the dispositions of the law.

The State will set about agrarian reform, dedicating the land to useful interests and gradually eliminating the latifundios (large estates). The State will do all in its power to support all aspects of family life. Primary education is compulsory and all education is free. Social security services will be developed. Every Dominican has the duty to give what civil and military service the State may require. Every legally entitled citizen must exercise the right to vote, i.e. all persons over 18 years of age and all who are or have been married even if they are not yet 18.

GOVERNMENT

Legislative power is exercised by Congress which is made up of the Senate and Chamber of Deputies, elected by direct vote. Senators, one for each of the 26 Provinces and one for the Distrito Nacional, are elected for four years; they must be Dominicans in full exercise of their citizen's rights, and at least 25 years of age. Their duties are to elect judges, the President and other members of the Electoral and Accounts Councils, and to approve the nomination of diplomats. Deputies, one for every 50,000 inhabitants or fraction over 25,000 in each Province and the Distrito Nacional, are elected for four years and must fulfil the same conditions for election as Senators.

Decisions of Congress are taken by absolute majority of at least half the members of each house; urgent matters require a two-thirds majority. Both houses normally meet on 27 February and 16 August each year for sessions of 90 days, which can be extended for a further 60 days.

Executive power is exercised by the President of the Republic, who is elected by direct vote for a four-year term. The President must be a Dominican citizen by birth or origin, over 30 years of age and in full exercise of citizen's rights. The President must not have engaged in any active military or police service for at least a year prior to election. The President takes office on 16 August following the election. The President of the Republic is Head of the Public Administration and Supreme Chief of the armed forces and police forces. The President's duties include nominating Secretaries and Assistant Secretaries of State and other public officials, promulgating and publishing laws and resolutions of Congress and seeing to their faithful execution, watching over the collection and just investment of national income, nominating, with the approval of the Senate, members of the Diplomatic Corps, receiving foreign Heads of State, presiding at national functions, decreeing a State of Siege or Emergency or any other measures necessary during a public crisis. The President may not leave the country for more than 15 days without authorization from Congress. In the absence of the President, the Vice-President will assume power, or failing him, the President of the Supreme Court of Justice.

LOCAL GOVERNMENT

Government in the Distrito Nacional and the Municipalities is in the hands of local councils, with members elected proportionally

THE DOMINICAN REPUBLIC

to the number of inhabitants, but numbering at least five. Each Province has a civil Governor, designated by the Executive.

JUDICIARY

Judicial power is exercised by the Supreme Court of Justice and the other Tribunals; no judicial official may hold another public office or employment, other than honorary or teaching. The Supreme Court is made up of at least nine judges, who must be Dominican citizens by birth or origin, at least 35 years old, in full exercise of their citizen's rights, graduates in law and have practised professionally for at least 12 years. There are also five Courts of Appeal, a Lands Tribunal and a Court of the First Instance in each judicial district; in each Municipality and in the Distrito Nacional there are also Justices of the Peace.

Elections are directed by the Central Electoral Board. The armed forces are essentially obedient and apolitical, created for the defence of national independence and the maintenance of public order and the Constitution and Laws.

The artistic and historical riches of the country, whoever owns them, are part of the cultural heritage of the country and are under the safe-keeping of the State. Mineral deposits belong to the State. There is freedom to form political parties, provided they conform to the principles laid down in the Constitution. Justice is administered without charge throughout the Republic.

This Constitution can be reformed if the proposal for reform is supported in Congress by one-third of the members of either house or by the Executive. A special session of Congress must be called and any resolutions must have a two-thirds majority. There can be no reform of the method of government, which must always be civil, republican, democratic and representative.

The Government

HEAD OF STATE

President: Dr Joaquín Balaguer (took office 16 August 1986).
Vice President: Carlos Morales Troncoso.

CABINET
(November 1986)

Secretary of State to the Presidency: Dr Rafael Bello Andino.
Secretary of State for the Armed Forces and General Chief of Staff of the Armed Forces: Maj.-Gen. Antonio Imbert Barreras.
Secretary of State for External Relations: Dr Donald Reid Cabral.
Secretary of State for the Interior and Police: Gen. (retd) Elías Wessin y Wessin.
Secretary of State for Finance: Lic. Roberto Saladín S.
Secretary of State for Education and Culture: Dr Pedro C. Pichardo.
Secretary of State for Agriculture: Dr Norberto Quezada.
Secretary of State for Public Works and Communications: Ing. Simón Tomás Fernández.
Secretary of State for Employment: Julio César Castaños.
Secretary of State for Health and Social Welfare: Dr Ney Arias Lora.
Secretary of State for Industry and Commerce: Lic. Roberto Martínez Villanueva.
Secretary of State for Tourism: Lic. Fernando Rainieri Marranzini.
Secretary of State for Sport, Physical Education and Recreation: Lic. Andrés Vanderhorst.
Secretary of State without Portfolio: Ing. Manuel Guaroa Liranzo.
Administrative Secretary to the Presidency: Lic. Glory Consuelo Torres Mejía.
Technical Secretary to the Presidency: Dr Guillermo Caram.
Governor of the Central Bank: Dr Luis Julián Pérez.

SECRETARIATS OF STATE

Secretariat of State for Agriculture: Centro de los Héroes de Constanza, Santo Domingo, DN; tel. 533-7171; telex 346-0393.

Secretariat of State for the Armed Forces: Plaza de la Independencia, Avda 27 de Febrero, Santo Domingo, DN; tel. 533-5131; telex 346-0652.
Secretariat of State for Education and Culture: Avda Máximo Gómez, Santo Domingo, DN; tel. 689-9161.
Secretariat of State for Employment: Santo Domingo, DN.
Secretariat of State for External Relations: Avda Independencia, Santo Domingo, DN; tel. 533-4121; telex 326-4192.
Secretariat of State for Finance: Avda México, Santo Domingo, DN; telex 346-0437.
Secretariat of State for Health and Social Welfare: Santo Domingo, DN.
Secretariat of State for Industry and Commerce: Edif. de Oficinas Gubernamentales 7°, Avda México, Santo Domingo, DN; tel. 685-5171.
Secretariat of State for the Interior and Police: Edif. de Oficinas Gubernamentales 3°, Avda Leopoldo Navarro a esq. México, Santo Domingo, DN; tel. 689-1979.
Secretariat of State for the Presidency: Santo Domingo, DN.
Secretariat of State for Public Works and Communications: Ensanche La Fé, Santo Domingo, DN; tel. 567-4929.
Secretariat of State for Sport, Physical Education and Recreation: Calle Pedro Henríquez Ureña, Santo Domingo, DN; tel. 688-0126; telex 346-0471.
Secretariat of State for Tourism: Calle César Nicolás Pensón 59, Santo Domingo, DN; telex 346-0303.

President and Legislature

PRESIDENT

Election, 16 May 1986

Candidates	Votes
Dr Joaquín Balaguer (PRSC)	855,565
Lic. Jacobo Majluta Azar (PRD*)	706,588
Dr Juan Bosch Gaviño (PLD)	387,881

There were three other candidates.

* Although Majluta had registered La Estructura, his right-wing faction of the PRD, as a separate political party in July 1985, he succeeded in securing the PRD candidacy.

CONGRESO NACIONAL

President: Lic. Florencio Carvajal Suero.
Vice-President: Maximo Antonio Nova Zapata.

The National Congress comprises a Senate and a Chamber of Deputies.

General Election, 16 May 1986

	Senate	Chamber
Partido Reformista Social Cristiano (PRSC)	21	56
Partido Revolucionario Dominicano (PRD)	7	48
Partido de la Liberación Dominicana (PLD)	2	16
Total	30	120

Political Organizations

La Estructura: f. 1985; right-wing dissident faction of PRD (see below); formed by Jacobo Majluta Azar; Pres. Andrés van der Horst.

Movimiento de Conciliación Nacional (MCN): Calle Pina 207, Santo Domingo, DN; f. 1969; centre party; 659,277 mems; Pres. Dr Jaime M. Fernández; Sec. Víctor Mena.

Movimiento de Integración Democrática (MIDA): Las Mercedes 607, Santo Domingo, DN; tel. 687-8895; centre-right; Leader Dr Francisco Augusto Lora.

THE DOMINICAN REPUBLIC

Movimiento Popular Dominicano: Santo Domingo, DN; left-wing; Leader JULIO DE PEÑA VALDÉS.

Partido Comunista Dominicano: Avda Independencia 89, Santo Domingo, DN; tel. 685-3540; f. 1944; Leader JOSÉ ISRAEL CUELLO; Sec.-Gen. NARCISO ISA CONDE.

Partido Demócrata Popular: Arz. Meriño 259, Santo Domingo, DN; tel. 685-2920; opposition party; Leader LUIS HOMERO LÁJARA BURGOS.

Partido de la Liberación Dominicana (PLD): Avda Independencia 401, Santo Domingo, DN; tel. 685-3540; f. 1973 by breakaway group of PRD; left-wing; Leader Dr JUAN BOSCH GAVIÑO; Sec.-Gen. LIDIO CADET.

Partido Quisqueyano Demócrata (PQD): 27 de Febrero 206, altos, Santo Domingo, DN; tel. 567-7970; f. 1968; right-wing; 600,000 mems; Pres. Gen. (retd) ELÍAS WESSIN Y WESSIN; Sec.-Gen. Lic. JUAN MANUEL TAVERAS.

Partido Reformista Social Cristiano (PRSC): Avda San Cristóbal, Ensanche La Fe, Apdo 1332, Santo Domingo, DN; tel. 566-7089; f. 1964; centre-right party; Leader Dr JOAQUÍN BALAGUER; Sec.-Gen. JOAQUÍN RICARDO.

Partido Revolucionario Dominicano (PRD): Espaillat 118, Santo Domingo, DN; tel. 687-2193; f. 1939; democratic socialist; mem. of Socialist International; split in 1985 when right-wing faction, led by JACOBO MAJLUTA, formed La Estructura; 400,000 mems; Pres. JOSÉ FRANCISCO PEÑA GÓMEZ; Sec.-Gen. VICENTE SÁNCHEZ BARET.

Partido Revolucionario Social Cristiano (PRSC): Las Mercedes 141, Santo Domingo, DN; tel. 688-3511; f. 1961; left-wing; Pres. Dr CLAUDIO ISIDORO ACOSTA; Sec.-Gen. Dr ALFONSO LOCKWARD.

Partido de los Trabajadores Dominicanos: Avda Duarte No 69, altos, Santo Domingo, DN; tel. 685-7705; f. 1979; workers' party; Sec.-Gen. RAFAEL CHALJUB MEJÍA.

Other parties include Unión Cívica Nacional (UCN), Partido Alianza Social Demócrata (ASD—Leader Dr JOSÉ RAFAEL ABINADER), Movimiento Nacional de Salvación (MNS—Leader LUIS JULIÁN PÉREZ), Partido de Veteranos Civiles (PVC), Partido Acción Constitucional (PAC), Partido Unión Patriótica (PUP—Leader ROBERTO SANTANA), Partido de Acción Nacional (right-wing) and Movimiento de Acción Social Cristiana (ASC). The Partido Comunista Dominicano, outlawed in 1962, was authorized again in 1977.

An opposition front, the Frente Izquierda Dominicana, has been formed by 53 political organizations and trade unions.

Diplomatic Representation

EMBASSIES IN THE DOMINICAN REPUBLIC

Argentina: Avda Máximo Gómez 10, Santo Domingo, DN; tel. 682-2977; telex 346-0154; Ambassador: JORGE VÁSQUEZ.

Brazil: Avda Anacaona 5, esq. Calle Angel Liz, Mirador Sur, Santo Domingo, DN; tel. 533-9466; telex 346-0155; Ambassador: NESTOR DOS SANTOS LIMA.

Chile: Avda Anacaona 11, Santo Domingo, DN; telex 346-0395; Ambassador: GASTÓN LLANEX FERNÁNDEZ.

China (Taiwan): Avda Abraham Lincoln, Santo Domingo, DN; tel. 566-1277; telex 346-0267; Ambassador: MICHAEL T. S. TUNG.

Colombia: Avda Abraham Lincoln 502, 2°, Santo Domingo, DN; tel. 567-6836; Ambassador: Dr ERNESTO TORRES DÍAZ.

Costa Rica: Andrés Julio Aybar 15, Santo Domingo, DN; tel. 565-7294; Chargé d'affaires: ODALISCA AUED RODRÍGUEZ.

Ecuador: Gustavo M. Ricart 90, Santo Domingo, DN; tel. 565-0822; telex 326-4556; Ambassador: ADAIBERTO ORTIZ Q.

El Salvador: Avda Abraham Lincoln 167, Santo Domingo, DN; tel. 567-6084; Ambassador: Dr JOSÉ R. JOVEL PINEDA.

France: Avda Jorge Washington 353, Santo Domingo, DN; tel. 689-2161; telex 346-0392; Ambassador: CLAUDE FOUQUET.

Germany, Federal Republic: Mejía y Cotes 37, Santo Domingo, DN; tel. 565-8811; Ambassador: ULRICH SCHOENING.

Guatemala: Z No 8, Naco, Santo Domingo, DN; tel. 566-8881; Ambassador: (vacant).

Haiti: Cub Scouts 11, Naco, Santo Domingo, DN; tel. 567-2511; telex 346-0851; Ambassador: MELIÈRE DUPLAN.

Holy See: Máximo Gómez No 27, Apdo 312, Santo Domingo, DN; tel. 682-3773; Apostolic Nuncio: BLASCO COLLAÇO.

Honduras: Avda Winston Churchill, Santo Domingo, DN; tel. 566-5707; Ambassador: M. DE J. TRONCOSO.

Israel: Avda Sarasota 38, Santo Domingo, DN; tel. 533-7359; telex 346-0139; Ambassador: SHMUEL TEVET.

Italy: Rodríguez Objío 4, Santo Domingo, DN; tel. 689-3684; telex 346-0543; Ambassador: (vacant).

Japan: Avda Bolívar 202-A, Santo Domingo, DN; tel. 689-9181; Ambassador: MASAHIRO MAEDA.

Jordan: L E Vicioso 12, Santo Domingo, DN; tel. 532-9429.

Korea, Republic: Avda Sarasota 98, Santo Domingo, DN; tel. 532-4314; telex 326-4368; Ambassador: KIM SUNG-SHIK.

Mexico: Moises García 40, Santo Domingo, DN; tel. 687-2357; telex 326-4187; Ambassador: RUBÉN GONZÁLEZ SOSA.

Nicaragua: El Recodo, Santo Domingo, DN; tel. 532-8846; telex 326-4542; Ambassador: RICARDO ZAMBRANA.

Panama: E de Marchena 36, Santo Domingo, DN; tel. 685-6950; Chargé d'affaires a.i.: Lic. CRISTÓBAL SARMIENTO.

Peru: Cancillería, Winston Churchill, Santo Domingo, DN; tel. 565-5851; Ambassador: RAÚL GUTIÉRREZ.

Romania: Santo Domingo, DN; Ambassador: (vacant).

Spain: Independencia 1205, Santo Domingo, DN; tel. 533-1425; telex 346-0158; Ambassador: LUIS MARIÑAS OTERO.

USA: César Nicolás Pensón, esq. Leopoldo Navarro, Santo Domingo, DN; tel. 682-2171; telex 346-0013; Ambassador: ROBERT ANDERSON.

Uruguay: Avda México 169, Santo Domingo, DN; tel. 565-2669; Ambassador: JAIME WOLFSON KOT.

Venezuela: Cancillería, Avda Bolívar 832, Santo Domingo, DN; tel. 687-5066; telex 326-4279; Ambassador: Lic. ABEL CLAVIJO OSTOS.

Judicial System

The Judicial Power resides in the Supreme Court of Justice, the Courts of Appeal, the Tribunals of the First Instance, the municipal courts and the other judicial authorities provided by law. The Supreme Court is composed of nine judges and the Attorney-General and exercises disciplinary authority over all the members of the judiciary. The Attorney-General of the Republic is the Chief of Judicial Police and of the Public Ministry which he represents before the Supreme Court of Justice. All judges are elected by the Senate.

Corte Suprema: Centro de los Héroes de Constanza, Santo Domingo, DN; tel. 533-3522.

President: Dr MANUEL BERGÉS CHUPANI.

Attorney-General: RAMÓN GONZÁLEZ HARDY.

Religion

More than 90% of the inhabitants belong to the Roman Catholic Church, but freedom of worship exists for all denominations. The Baptist, Evangelist, Seventh-day Adventist and Jewish faiths are also represented.

CHRISTIANITY

The Roman Catholic Church

The Dominican Republic comprises one archdiocese and seven dioceses.

Bishops' Conference: Conferencia del Episcopado Dominicano, Apdo 186, Santo Domingo, DN; tel. 685-3141; f. 1985; Pres. Mgr. NICOLÁS DE JESÚS LÓPEZ RODRÍGUEZ, Archbishop of Santo Domingo.

Archbishop of Santo Domingo: NICOLÁS DE JESÚS LÓPEZ RODRÍGUEZ, Arzobispado, Apdo 186, Isabel la Católica No 55, Santo Domingo, DN; tel. 685-3141.

BAHÁ'Í FAITH

National Spiritual Assembly of the Bahá'ís of the Dominican Republic: Cambronal 152 esq. Beller, Santo Domingo, DN; f. 1961; tel. 687-1726; 415 localities.

The Press

DAILIES

Santo Domingo, DN

El Caribe: Autopista Duarte, Km 7½, Apdo 416, Santo Domingo, DN; tel. 566-8161; f. 1948; morning; Dir GERMÁN E. ORNES; circ. 28,000.

Diario Las Américas: Avda Tiradentes, Santo Domingo, DN; tel. 566-4577.

Listín Diario: Calle 19 de Marzo 59, Apdo 1455, Santo Domingo, DN; tel. 689-7171; f. 1889; morning; Dir RAFAEL HERRERA; circ. 55,000.

El Nacional: Avda San Martín 236, Santo Domingo, DN; tel. 565-5581; f. 1966; evening and Sunday; Dir MARIO ALVAREZ DUGAN; circ. 45,000.

La Noticia: Julio Verne 14, Santo Domingo, DN; tel. 687-3131; f. 1973; evening; Pres. JOSÉ A. BREA PEÑA; Dir SILVIO HERASME PEÑA.

El Sol: Carrera Sánchez, Km 6½, Santo Domingo, DN; tel. 532-9511; morning; Pres. QUITERIO CEDEÑO; Dir BOLÍVAR DÍAZ SANTANA.

Ultima Hora: Paseo de los Periodistas 52, Ensanche Miraflores, Santo Domingo, DN; tel. 688-3361; evening; Exec. Dir ANÍBAL DE CASTRO.

Puerto Plata

El Porvenir: Puerto Plata; f. 1872; Dir ALONSO RODRÍGUEZ.

Santiago de los Caballeros

La Información: Las Carreras 157, Santiago de los Caballeros; tel. 685-2225; f. 1915; morning; Editor LUIS E. FRANCO; circ. 15,000.

PERIODICALS AND REVIEWS

Santo Domingo, DN

Agricultura: Santo Domingo, DN; organ of the State Secretariat of Agriculture and Colonization; f. 1905; monthly; Dir MIGUEL RODRÍGUEZ, Jr.

Agroconocimiento: Apdo 345-2, Santo Domingo, DN; monthly; agricultural news and technical information; Dir DOMINGO MARTE; circ. 10,000.

¡Ahora!: Avda San Martín 236, Apdo 1402, Santo Domingo, DN; tel. 565-5581; telex 346-0423; f. 1962; weekly; Dir MARIO ALVAREZ DUGAN.

La Campiña: San Martín 236, Apdo 1402, Santo Domingo, DN; f. 1967; Dir Ing. JUAN ULISES GARCÍA B.

Carta Dominicana: Avda Tiradentes 56, Santo Domingo, DN; tel. 566-0119; f. 1974; monthly; economics; Dir JUAN RAMÓN QUIÑONES M.

Deportes: San Martín 236, Apdo 1402, Santo Domingo, DN; f. 1967; sports; fortnightly; Dir L. R. CORDERO; circ. 5,000.

Eva: San Martín 236, Apdo 1402, Santo Domingo, DN; f. 1967; fortnightly; Dir MAGDA FLORENCIO.

Horizontes de América: Alexander Fleming 2, Santo Domingo, DN; tel. 565-9717; f. 1967; monthly; Dir ARMANDO LEMUS CASTILLO.

Letra Grande, Arte y Literatura: Leonardo de Vinci 13, Mirador del Sur, Santo Domingo, DN; tel. 533-4522; f. 1980; monthly; art and literature; Dir JUAN RAMÓN QUIÑONES M.

Renovación: Calle José Reyes esq. El Conde, Santo Domingo, DN; fortnightly; Dir OLGA QUISQUEYA Viuda MARTÍNEZ.

FOREIGN PRESS BUREAUX

Agencia EFE (Spain): Avda 27 de Febrero, Galerías Comerciales 5°, Of. 507, Santo Domingo, DN; tel. 567-7617; telex 02024176; Bureau Chief ANTONIO CASTILLO URBERUAGA.

Agenzia Nazionale Stampa Associata (ANSA) (Italy): Calle Navarro 79, 3°, Sala 17, Apdo 1486, Correo Principal, Santo Domingo, DN; tel. 685-8765; telex 201-4537; Bureau Chief HUMBERTO ANDRÉS SUAZO.

Inter Press Service (IPS) (Italy): Edif. Palamara, El Conde 407, Apto 202, Santo Domingo, DN; tel. 689-6449; Correspondent MARCIA SCANTLEBURY.

United Press International (UPI) (USA): Carrera A. Manoguaybo 16, Manoguaybo, DN; tel. 689-7171; telex 346-0206; Chief Correspondent SANTIAGO ESTRELLA VELOZ.

Publishers

Santo Domingo, DN

Arte y Cine, C por A: Isabel la Católica 42, Santo Domingo, DN.

Editora Alfa y Omega: José Contreras 69, Santo Domingo, DN; tel. 532-5577.

Editora de las Antillas: Calle Pedro Henríquez Ureña, Santo Domingo, DN; tel. 685-2197.

Editora Colonial, C por A: Calle Moca 27-B, Apdo 2569, Santo Domingo, DN; tel. 688-2394; Pres. DANILO ASENCIO.

Editora Dominicana, SA: 23 Oeste, No 3 Lup., Santo Domingo, DN; tel. 688-0846.

Editora El Caribe, C por A: Autopista Duarte, Km 7½, Apdo 416, Santo Domingo, DN; tel. 566-8161; f. 1948; Dir Dr GERMÁN E. ORNES.

Editora El País: Carretera Sánchez, Km 6½, Santo Domingo, DN; tel. 532-9511.

Editora Hoy, C por A: Avda San Martín, 236, Santo Domingo, DN; tel. 566-1147; telex 346-0423.

Editora Listín Diario, C por A: Paseo de los Periodistas 52, Ensanche Miraflores, Santo Domingo, DN; tel. 689-7171; f. 1889; Pres. Dr ROGELIO A. PELLERANO.

Editorama, SA: Avda Tiradentes 56, Apdo 2074, Santo Domingo, DN; tel. 566-0119.

Editorial Padilla: San F. de Macorís 14, Santo Domingo, DN; tel. 682-3101.

Editorial Santo Domingo: Central 40, Santo Domingo, DN; tel. 532-9431.

Editorial Stella: 19 de Marzo, Santo Domingo, DN; tel. 682-2281.

Julio D. Postigo e Hijos: Mercedes 49, Santo Domingo, DN; f. 1949; fiction; Man. J. D. POSTIGO.

Publicaciones América: Arz. Meriño, Santo Domingo, DN; Dir PEDRO BISONÓ.

Santiago de los Caballeros

Editora el País, SA: Carrera Sánchez, Km 6½, Santiago de los Caballeros, SD; tel. 532-9511.

Radio and Television

In 1984 there were about 225,000 radio receivers and 388,000 television receivers (including 7,500 colour sets) in use.

Dirección General de Telecomunicaciones: Isabel la Católica 73, Santo Domingo, DN; tel. 682-2244; government supervisory body; Dir.-Gen. WILLIAM SOTO MEDINA.

RADIO

There were 103 commercial stations in 1980. The government-owned broadcasting network Radio Televisión Dominicana operates 10 radio stations.

TELEVISION

Radio Televisión Dominicana: Dr Tejada Florentino 8, Apdo 969, Santo Domingo, DN; tel. 689-2121; government station; two channels, two relay stations; Dir-Gen. R. A. FONT BERNARD; Gen. Man. AGUSTÍN MERCADO.

Rahintel Televisión: Centro de los Héroes de Constanza, Apdo 1220, Santo Domingo, DN; tel. 533-3151; telex 3460213; commercial station; two channels; Pres. LEONEL ALMONTE V.

Color-Visión (Corporación Dominicana de Radio y Televisión): Calle Emilio A. Morel esq. Luis E. Pérez, Ensanche La Fé, Apdo 30043, Santo Domingo, DN; tel. 566-5875; telex 326-4327; commercial station; two channels: Channel 2 (Santiago) and Channel 9 (Santo Domingo, Puerto Plata, La Romana, San Juan); Dir-Gen. M. QUIROZ.

Teleantillas: Autopista Duarte, Km 7½, Apdo 415, Santo Domingo, DN; tel. 567-7751; owned by Editora del Caribe.

Tele-Inde Canal 13: 30 de Marzo, No 80, Santo Domingo, DN; commercial station; Proprietor JOSÉ A. SEMORILE.

Telesistema Dominicana: Calle El Vergel 88, Ensanche El Vergel, Santo Domingo; tel. 567-5151; Dir OCTAVIO A. BERAS-GOICO.

THE DOMINICAN REPUBLIC

Finance

(cap. = capital; dep. = deposits; m = million; p.u. = paid up; res = reserves; amounts in pesos)

In May 1981 the Government announced a 12-month prohibition on the opening of new agencies for commercial banks and other financial institutions.

BANKING

Supervisory Body

Superintendencia de Bancos: Avda México esq. Leopoldo Navarro, Apdo 1326, Santo Domingo, DN; tel. 685-8141; telex 346-0653; f. 1947; Superintendent SOFÍA LEONOR SÁNCHEZ BARET.

Central Bank

Banco Central de la República Dominicana: Avda Pedro Henríquez Ureña esq. Leopoldo Navarro, Santo Domingo, DN; tel. 689-7121; telex 346-0052; f. 1947; cap. and res 55.9m., total assets 6,156.0m. (June 1985); Gov. Dr LUIS JULIÁN PÉREZ; Man. FÉLIX SANTANA.

Commercial Banks

Banco del Comercio Dominicano: Avda 27 de Febrero, esq. Winston Churchill, Santo Domingo, DN; tel. 567-8871; telex 346-0324; f. 1979; cap. and res. 57.7m., dep. 418.1m. (June 1986); Pres. JOSÉ UREÑA ALMONTE; 19 brs.

Banco Dominico-Hispano, SA: Avda 27 de Febrero 102, Santo Domingo, DN; tel. 567-8211; f. 1948; cap. and res 6.4m., dep. 1.5m. (June 1985); Exec. Vice-Pres. Lic. AUGUSTO PEIGNAND.

Banco Fiduciario Dominicano, SA: Avda San Martín 122, Apdo 1101, Santo Domingo, DN; tel. 565-9971; f. 1983; cap. and res 5.1m., dep. 17.8m. (June 1985); Exec. Vice-Pres. GEORGE MANUEL HAZOURY PEÑA.

Banco Metropolitano: Avda Lope de Vega esq. Gustavo Mejía Ricart, Apdo 1872, Santo Domingo, DN; tel. 562-2442; telex 346-0419; f. 1974; cap. and res 10.5m., dep. 80.9m. (June 1985); Gen. Dir ADALBERTO PÉREZ; 8 brs.

Banco Nacional de Crédito: Avda Lope de Vega 95, Apdo 1502, Santo Domingo, DN; tel. 567-9581; telex 326-4522; f. 1981; cap. and res 8.6m., dep. 32.8m. (June 1985); Dir HÉCTOR CASTRO NOBOA; 4 brs.

Banco Popular Dominicano: Isabel la Católica 251, Apdo 1441, Santo Domingo, DN; tel. 682-9141; telex 346-0105; f. 1963; cap. and res 40.9m., dep. 491.1m. (June 1986); Pres. PEDRO A. RODRÍGUEZ; 35 brs.

Banco del Progreso Dominicano, SA: Avda John F. Kennedy 3, Santo Domingo, DN; tel. 566-7171; telex 346-0181; f. 1975; cap. and res 6.1m., dep. 62.6m. (June 1985); Exec. Vice-Pres. MICHAEL A. KELLY; 6 brs.

Banco Regional Dominicano, SA: Restauración esq. San Luis, Apdo 308, Santiago; tel. 582-7173; f. 1982; cap. and res 4.9m., dep. 19.5m. (June 1985); Pres. LORENZO GARCÍA T.; 2 brs.

Banco de Reservas de la República Dominicana: Isabel la Católica 201, Apdo 1353, Santo Domingo, DN; tel. 688-2241; telex 346-0012; f. 1941; cap. and res 101.9m., dep. 685.6m. (June 1985); Gen. Administrator FRIXO MESSINA R.; 37 brs. . .

Banco de Santander Dominicano: Avda John F. Kennedy, Santo Domingo, DN; tel. 566-5811; telex 346-0321; f. 1949 as Banco de Crédito y Ahorros; cap. and res 8.9m., dep. 94.6m. (June 1985); Dir-Gen. RICARDO HERNÁNDEZ; 13 brs.

Banco de los Trabajadores de la República Dominicana: El Conde esq. Arz. Meriño, Santo Domingo, DN; tel. 688-0181; telex 346-4500; f. 1972; state-controlled; cap. and res 9.2m., dep. 16.7m. (June 1985); Pres. PEDRO SOSA GERMÁN; 4 brs.

Banco Universal, SA: El Conde 105, Apdo 2065, Santo Domingo, DN; tel. 688-6666; f. 1982; cap. and res 5.0m., dep. 13.1m. (June 1985); Pres. LEONEL ALMONTE.

Development Banks

Banco Agrícola de la República Dominicana: Avda G. Washington 601, Apdo 1057, Santo Domingo, DN; tel. 533-1171; f. 1945; government agricultural development bank; cap. and res 204.5m. (June 1985); Gen. Administrator Lic. RAFAEL ANGELES SUÁREZ; 31 brs.

Banco de Crédito Hipotecario, SA: Avda Bolívar esq. Socorro Sánchez, Apdo 497-2, Santo Domingo, DN; tel. 682-3191; telex 346-0820; f. 1983; cap. and res 3.6m., dep. 4.0m. (July 1986); Pres. Lic. ENRIQUE DALET LOZANO.

Directory

Banco Hipotecario Central de Créditos: Juan I. Jiménez 1, Santo Domingo, DN; tel. 689-8005; f. 1983; cap. and res 6.2m., dep. 4.4m. (July 1986); Exec. Vice-Pres. Lic. JOSÉ MANUEL LÓPEZ VÁLDEZ.

Banco Hipotecario de la Construcción, SA (BANHICO): Avda Tiradentes (Altos Plaza Naco), Santo Domingo, DN; tel. 562-1281; f. 1977; cap. and res 8.4m., dep. 0.4m. (June 1985); Man. Dr JAIME ALVAREZ DUGAN.

Banco Hipotecario Dominicano, SA: Avda 27 de Febrero esq. Winston Churchill, Apdo 266-2, Santo Domingo, DN; tel. 567-7281; telex 4546; f. 1972; housing development bank; cap. and res 20.3m., (June 1985); Pres. SAMUEL CONDE; 5 brs.

Banco Hipotecario Financiero, SA: Avda 27 de Febrero esq. Avda Tiradentes, Apdo 385-2, Santo Domingo, DN; tel. 566-5151; f. 1978; cap. and res 2.6m., dep. 12.9m. (June 1985); Pres. Dr LUCAS T. GUERRA C.

Banco Hipotecario Horizontes, SA: Avda Rómulo Betancourt 1410, Santo Domingo, DN; tel. 532-3122; f. 1984; cap. and res 3.5m., dep. 0.1m. (June 1985); Pres. HÉCTOR MARTÍNEZ CASTRO.

Banco Hipotecario Miramar, SA: Avda John F. Kennedy 10, Apdo 2424, Santo Domingo, DN; tel. 566-5681; telex 326-4202; f. 1976; cap. and res 12.0m., dep. 8.2m. (June 1985); Pres. Ing. GUILLERMO ARMENTEROS; 5 brs.

Banco Hipotecario Popular, SA: Avda 27 de Febrero 261, Santo Domingo, DN; tel. 567-5511; f. 1978; cap. and res 32.1m., dep. 74.1m. (July 1986); Pres. MANUEL E. JIMÉNEZ F.

Banco Hipotecario Unido, SA: Calle El Sol 42, Apdo 290, Santiago; tel. 583-6409; f. 1983; cap. and res 1.8m., dep. 0.7m. (June 1985); Exec. Pres. LUIS MARTÍNEZ VILCHEZ.

Banco Hipotecario Universal, SA: Avda Santa Rosa esq. Gregorio Luperón, Apdo 259, La Romana; tel. 556-2183; f. 1979; cap. and res 3.9m., dep. 0.1m. (June 1985); Pres. LEONEL ALMONTE; 2 brs.

Banco Inmobiliario Dominicano, SA: Calle El Sol 10, Santiago; tel. 583-4331; f. 1979; cap. and res 13.6m., dep. 0.5m. (June 1985); Dir Dr MANUEL PITTALUGA NIVAR; 3 brs.

Banco Nacional de la Construcción: Avda Alma Mater esq. Pedro Henríquez Ureña, Santo Domingo, DN; tel. 685-9776; f. 1977; cap. and res 3.7m., dep. 0.9m. (June 1985); Gen. Man. LUIS MANUEL PELLERANO.

There were 18 development finance societies and 18 savings and lending associations in 1985.

Foreign Banks

Bank of Nova Scotia (Canada): Avda John F. Kennedy esq. Lope de Vega, Santo Domingo, DN; tel. 566-5671; telex 346-0067; f. 1920; cap. and res 9.5m., dep. 101.1m. (June 1985); Gen. Man. IVAN L. LESSARD; 12 brs.

Chase Manhattan Bank (USA): Avda John F. Kennedy, Apdo 1480, Santo Domingo, DN; tel. 565-4441; telex 346-0096; f. 1962; cap. and res 11.6m., dep. 140.8m. (June 1985); Man. WILLIAM D. GAMBREL; 6 brs.

Citibank NA (USA): Avda John F. Kennedy 1, Apdo 1492, Santo Domingo, DN; tel. 566-5611; telex 346-0083; f. 1962; cap. and res 14.1m., dep. 97.2m. (June 1985); Vice-Pres. MICHAEL CONTRERAS; 5 brs.

INSURANCE

Supervisory Body

Superintendencia de Seguros: Secretaría de Estado de Finanzas, Leopoldo Navarro esq. Avda México, Santo Domingo, DN; tel. 688-1245; Superintendent Dr JUAN ESTEBAN OLIVERO FELIZ.

National Companies

La Americana, SA: Edif. La Cumbre, Avda Tiradentes, Santo Domingo, DN; tel. 567-0171; telex 346-0185; f. 1975; life; Pres. Dr LUIS AGOSTO GINEBRA H.

Centro de Seguros La Popular, C por A: Gustavo Mejía Ricart 61, Santo Domingo, DN; tel. 566-1988; general except life; Pres. Lic. FABIO A. FIALLO.

Citizens Dominicana, SA: Avda Winston Churchill esq. Paseo de los Locutores 4°, Santo Domingo, DN; tel. 562-2705; f. 1978; Pres. MIGUEL E. SAVIÑÓN TORRES.

Cía Dominicana de Seguros, C por A: Edif. Buenaventura, Avda Independencia 201, Dr Delgado esq., Apdo 176, Santo Domingo, DN; tel. 689-6127; general except life; Pres. Lic. HUGO VILLANUEVA.

THE DOMINICAN REPUBLIC
Directory

Cía Nacional de Seguros, C por A: Avda Máximo Gómez 31, Apdo 916, Santo Domingo, DN; tel. (809) 685-2121; telex 346-0117; general; Pres. Máximo A. Pellerano.

Cía de Seguros Quisqueyana, SA: Edif. Galerías Comerciales, 6a Planta, Avda 27 de Febrero, Apdo 21-443, Santo Domingo, DN; tel. 567-0133; telex 346-0637; general; Pres. Polibio Díaz.

La Colonial, SA: Edif. Haché 2°, Avda John F. Kennedy, Santo Domingo, DN; tel. 565-9926; f. 1971; general; Pres. Dr Miguel Feris Iglesias.

El Condor Seguros, SA: Avda 27 de Febrero No 12, Apdo 20077, Santo Domingo, DN; tel. 689-4146; telex 346-0210; f. 1977; general; Pres. Juan Pablo Reyes.

General de Seguros, SA: Avda Bolívar 805, 2-6, Apdo 2183, Santo Domingo, DN; tel. 685-9102; general; Man. Dr Fernando A. Ballista.

La Intercontinental de Seguros, SA: Avda Tiradentes, Centro Comercial Naco, Apdo 825, Santo Domingo, DN; tel. 562-1211; general; Gen. Man. Ramón Báez Figueroa.

Latinoamericana de Seguros, SA: Plaza Naco, Avda Tiradentes 2a, Apdo 1215, Santo Domingo, DN; tel. 562-2959; life; Pres. Rafael Castro Martínez.

La Metropolitana de Seguros, C por A: Edif. Alico, 4a, Avda Abraham Lincoln, Apdo 131, Santo Domingo, DN; tel. (809) 532-0541; telex 346-0366; managed by American International Underwriters (AIU); Gen. Man. Rafael Armando Pichardo.

La Mundial de Seguros, SA: Edif. Mella 5°, Avda George Washington, Santo Domingo, DN; tel. 688-4477; telex 346-0466; general except life and financial; Pres. John Richards.

Patria, SA: Avda 27 de Febrero 10, Santo Domingo, DN; tel. 687-3151; general except life; Pres. Dr Miguel Angel Luna Morales.

La Real de Seguros, SA: Avda 27 de Febrero 80, Santo Domingo, DN; tel. 566-5195; general; Pres. Lic. Mario Viñas Betances.

Reaseguradora Internacional, SA: Avda Pasteur 17, Santo Domingo, DN; tel. 685-3903; general; Pres. Lic. Fabio A. Fiallo.

Reaseguradora Nacional, SA: Avda Máximo Gómez 31, Apdo 916, Santo Domingo, DN; tel. 685-3177; f. 1971; general; Pres. Máximo A. Pellerano.

Reaseguradora Profesional, SA: Edif. Concordia 2°, Avda Abraham Lincoln esq. José Amado Soler, Santo Domingo, DN; tel. (809) 562-5291; telex 346-0385; f. 1985; Pres. Alejandro Grullón.

Reaseguradora Santo Domingo, SA: Centro Comercial Jardines del Embajador, 2a Planta, Avda Sarasota, Apdo 25005; Santo Domingo, DN; tel. (809) 532-2586; telex 346-0566; general; Pres. Dr Luis Agosto Ginebra H.

San Rafael, C por A: Leopoldo Navarro 61, Santo Domingo, DN; tel. 688-2231; telex 346-0169; general; Pres. Fernando Casanova.

Seguros La Alianza: Padre Fantino Falcó, Plaza Naco, Avda Tiradentes, Santo Domingo, DN; tel. 562-6361; general; Pres. Virgilio Alvarez Bonilla.

Seguros América, C por A: Edif. La Cumbre 4°, Avda Tiradentes, Santo Domingo, DN; tel. 567-0181; telex 346-0185; f. 1966; general; Pres. Dr Luis Ginebra Hernández.

Seguros La Antillana, SA: Avda Abraham Lincoln No 708, Apdo 146, Santo Domingo, DN; tel. 567-4481; telex 346-0411; general; Pres. Andrés A. Freites V.

Seguros del Caribe, SA: Edif. Galerías Comerciales 5°, Avda 27 de Febrero, Santo Domingo, DN; tel. 567-0242; general; Pres. Eduardo González.

Seguros Horizontes, SA: Avda Lope de Vega 50 (altos), Santo Domingo, DN; tel. 562-6591; telex 346-0812; f. 1974; general and life; Pres. Emilio Antonio Lama S.

Seguros Pepín, SA: Mercedes 470 esq. Palo Hincado, Santo Domingo, DN; tel. 689-8171; general; Pres. Dr Bienvenido Corominas.

Unión de Seguros, C por A: Avda 27 de Febrero 263, Santo Domingo, DN; tel. 566-2191; f. 1964; general; Pres. Belarminio Cortina.

La Universal de Seguros, C por A: Edif. Motorambar 2° y 3°, Avda Abraham Lincoln 1054, Santo Domingo, DN; tel. 562-3011; general; Pres. Ernesto Izquierdo.

Insurance Association

Cámara Dominicana de Aseguradores y Reaseguradores, Inc.: Edif. Central 1°, Avda Winston Churchill esq. Max Henríquez Ureña, Santo Domingo, DN; Pres. Marino Ginebra Hurtado.

Trade and Industry

TRADE AND DEVELOPMENT ORGANIZATIONS

Asociación Dominicana de Hacendados y Agricultores Inc.: Avda Sarasota 4, Santo Domingo, DN; farming and agricultural organization; Pres. Lic. Silvestre Alba de Moya.

Asociación de Industrias de la República Dominicana Inc.: Avda Sarasota 20, Apdo 850, Santo Domingo, DN; tel. 532-5523; f. 1962; industrial organization; Pres. Ing. José del Carmen Ariza.

Centro Dominicano de Promoción de Exportaciones (CEDOPEX): Plaza de la Independencia, Sección de Herrera, Apdo 199-2, Santo Domingo, DN; tel. 566-9131; telex 346-0351; organization for the promotion of exports; Dir Lic. Eduardo Tejera.

Consejo Estatal del Azúcar (CEA) (State Sugar Council): Calle de los Héroes, PO Box 1256/1258, Santo Domingo, DN; tel. 533-1161; telex 346-0043; f. 1966; autonomous administration for each of the 12 state sugar mills; Pres. Víctor Manuel Báez.

Consejo Promotor de Inversiones (Investment Promotion Council): Edif. Cianave, 2° Piso, Avda México 66, Santo Domingo; tel. 682-2323; Chair. Lic. José Antonio Najri.

Corporación Dominicana de Electricidad: Avda Independencia, Santo Domingo, DN; tel. 533-1131; state electricity company; Man. Ing. Marcelo Jorge Pérez.

Corporación Dominicana de Empresas Estatales (CORDE) (Dominican State Corporation): Avda General Antonio Duvergé, Apdo 1378, Santo Domingo, DN; tel. 533-5171; telex 346-0311; f. 1966 to administer, direct and develop 26 state enterprises; auth. cap. RD $25m.; Exec. Dir Lic. Partenio Ortiz O.

Corporación de Fomento Industrial (CFI): Avda 27 de Febrero, Apdo 1472, Santo Domingo, DN; tel. 533-8151; telex 346-0049; f. 1962 to promote agro-industrial development; auth. cap. RD $25m.; Dir-Gen. Lic. Roger Ogando Piña.

Dirección General de Minería e Hidrocarburos: Edif. de Oficinas Gubernamentales 10°, Avda México esq. Leopoldo Navarro, Santo Domingo, DN; tel. 685-8191; f. 1947; government mining and hydrocarbon organization; Dir-Gen. Ing. Miguel A. Peña.

Fondo de Inversión para el Desarrollo Económico—FIDE (Economic Development Investment Fund): c/o Banco Central de la República Dominicana, Avda Pedro Henríquez Ureña, Santo Domingo, DN; f. 1965; associated with AID, IDB; resources RD $10m.; encourages economic development in productive sectors of economy, excluding sugar; authorizes complementary financing to private sector for establishing new industrial and agricultural enterprises and developing existing ones.

Fundación Dominicana de Desarrollo (Dominican Development Foundation): Apdo 857, Santo Domingo, DN; f. 1962 to mobilize private resources for collaboration in financing small-scale development programmes; 384 mems; assets US $10.7m.; Exec. Dir Jaime R. Fernández Quezada.

Instituto Agrario Dominicano (IAD): Santo Domingo, DN; Dir Ing. Agron. Diomedes Castellanos.

Instituto Azucarero Dominicano (INAZUCAR): Avda Jiménez Moya, Apdo 667, Santo Domingo, DN; tel. 532-5571; sugar institute; f. 1965; Exec. Dir Lic. Miguel Guerrero.

Instituto de Desarrollo y Crédito Cooperativo (IDECOOP): Avda México, Santo Domingo, DN; tel. 689-6155; f. 1963 to encourage the development of co-operatives; cap. 100,000 pesos.

Instituto de Estabilización de Precios (INESPRE): Avda Luperón, Santo Domingo, DN; tel. 533-3111; price commission; Dir José Michelén.

Instituto Nacional de la Vivienda: Antiguo Edif. del Banco Central, Calle Pedro Henríquez Ureña esq. Leopoldo Navarro, Apdo 1506, Santo Domingo, DN; tel. 685-4181; f. 1962; low-cost housing institute; Dir-Gen. Lic. Elpidio Ramírez.

CHAMBER OF COMMERCE

Cámara Oficial de Comercio, Agricultura e Industria del Distrito Nacional: Arz. Nouel 206, Apdo Postal 815, Santo Domingo, DN; tel. 682-2688; f. 1910; 950 active mems; Pres. Juan Félix Aróstegui; Sec.-Gen. Lic. Aquiles O. Farias Monje.

There are official Chambers of Commerce in the larger towns.

EMPLOYERS' ASSOCIATIONS

Confederación Patronal de la República Dominicana: Edif. Mella, Cambronal/G. Washington, Santo Domingo, DN; Pres. Ing. Heriberto de Castro.

THE DOMINICAN REPUBLIC   *Directory*

Consejo Nacional de Hombres de Empresa Inc.: Edif. Motorambar 7°, Avda Abraham Lincoln 1056, Santo Domingo, DN; Pres. Antonio Najri.

Federación Dominicana de Comerciantes: Santo Domingo, DN; Pres. Juan Valerio Sánchez.

TRADE UNIONS

It is estimated that 13% of the total work-force belong to trade unions.

Central General de Trabajadores—CGT: Tunti Cáceres 222, Santo Domingo, DN; f. 1972; 13 sections; Sec.-Gen. Nelsida Marmolejos; 65,000 mems.

Central Unitaria de Trabajadores—CUT: Santo Domingo, DN; f. 1978; left-wing.

Confederación Autónoma de Sindicatos Clasistas—CASC (Autonomous Confederation of Trade Unions): J. Erazo 39, Santo Domingo, DN; tel. 687-8533; f. 1962; supports PRSC; Sec.-Gen. Gabriel Del Río.

Confederación de Trabajadores Dominicanos—CTD (Confederation of Dominican Workers): Santo Domingo, DN; f. 1920; 11 provincial federations totalling 150 unions are affiliated; Sec.-Gen. Julio de Peña Váldez; 188,000 mems. (est.).

Unión General de Trabajadores Dominicanos—UGTD: Santo Domingo, DN; f. 1978; supports PRD.

Transport

RAILWAYS

Oficina Nacional de Transporte Terrestre (ONATRATE): Santo Domingo, DN; Dir Virgilio Bonilla.

Ferrocarril Unidos Dominicanos: Santo Domingo; government-owned; 142 km of track from La Vega to Sánchez principally used for the transport of exports.

There are also a number of semi-autonomous and private railway companies for the transport of sugar cane, including:

Ferrocarril de Central Romana: La Romana; 375 km open; Pres. C. Morales.

Ferrocarril Central Río Haina: Apdo 1258, Haina; 113 km open.

ROADS

In 1983 there were 12,297 km of roads. There is a direct route from Santo Domingo to Port-au-Prince in Haiti. In 1980 a project to improve the main road between Santo Domingo and Santiago de los Caballeros, at a cost of US $61m., was launched.

SHIPPING

The Dominican Republic has 14 ports, of which Santo Domingo is by far the largest, handling about 80% of imports. In 1983 the country's merchant fleet had a total displacement of 11,963 grt.

A number of foreign shipping companies operate services to the island.

Armadora Naval Dominicana, SA: Calle Isabel la Católica 165, Apdo 2677, Santo Domingo, DN; tel. 689-6191; telex 346-0465; Man. Dir Capt. Einar Wettre.

Líneas Marítimas de Santo Domingo, SA: José Gabriel García 8, Apdo 1148, Santo Domingo, DN; tel. 682-1206; telex 326-4274; Pres. C. Lluberes; Vice-Pres. K. H. Windeler.

CIVIL AVIATION

There are international airports at Santo Domingo (Aeropuerto Internacional de las Américas) and Puerto Plata. The airport at La Romana is authorized for international flights, providing that three days' notice is given. Most main cities have domestic airports.

Aerolíneas Argo: Avda 27 de Febrero 409, Santo Domingo, DN; tel. 566-1844; telex 346-0531; f. 1971; cargo and mail services to USA, Puerto Rico and US Virgin Islands; fleet: 1 L-749 Constellation, 1 Curtiss C-46.

Dominicana de Aviación C por A: Calle El Donde 83, Santo Domingo, DN; telex. 346-0394; f. 1944; operates on international routes connecting Santo Domingo with the Netherlands Antilles, the USA and Venezuela; charter flights in USA, Canada and Europe; Chair. Dr Eudoro Sánchez y Sánchez; fleet: 1 Boeing 727-100, 1 727-100C, 2 727-200, 1 707-320C, 2 DC-6B.

Alas del Caribe, C por A: Avda Luperón, Aeropuerto de Herrera, Santo Domingo, DN; tel. 566-2141; f. 1968; internal routes; Pres. Jacinto B. Peynado; Dir Manuel Pérez Negrón.

Tourism

Secretaría de Estado de Turismo: Calle César Nicolás Pensón 59, Santo Domingo, DN; telex 346-0303; Sec. of State for Tourism Lic. Fernando Rainieri Marranzini.

Asociación Dominicana de Agencias de Viajes: Carrera Sánchez 201, Santo Domingo, DN; tel. 687-8984; Pres. Ramón Prieto.

Atomic Energy

Comisión Nacional de Asuntos Nucleares: Edif. de la Defensa Civil, Dr Delgado 58, Santo Domingo, DN; tel. 565-5090; telex 346-0461; Pres. Dr Abel González Massenet.

ECUADOR

Introductory Survey

Location, Climate, Language, Religion, Flag, Capital

The Republic of Ecuador lies on the west coast of South America. It is bordered by Colombia to the north, by Peru to the east and south, and by the Pacific Ocean to the west. The Galapagos Islands, about 1,000 km (600 miles) off shore, form part of Ecuador. The climate is affected by the Andes mountains, and the topography ranges from the tropical rain forest on the coast and in the eastern region to the tropical grasslands of the central valley and the permanent snowfields of the highlands. The official language is Spanish, but Quechua and other indigenous languages are very common. Almost all of the inhabitants profess Christianity, and about 90% are Roman Catholics. The national flag (proportions 2 by 1) has three horizontal stripes, of yellow (one-half of the depth), blue and red. The state flag has, in addition, the national emblem (an oval cartouche, showing Mt Chimborazo and a steamer on a lake, surmounted by a condor) in the centre. The capital is Quito.

Recent History

Ecuador was ruled by Spain from the 16th century until 1822, when it achieved independence as part of Gran Colombia. In 1830 Ecuador seceded and became a separate republic. A long-standing division between Conservatives (Partido Conservador), whose support is generally strongest in the highlands, and Liberals (Partido Liberal, subsequently Partido Liberal Radical), based in the coastal region, began in the 19th century. Until 1948 Ecuador's political life was characterized by a rapid succession of presidents, dictators and juntas. Between 1830 and 1925 the country was governed by 40 different regimes. From 1925 to 1948 there was even greater instability, with a total of 22 heads of state.

Dr Galo Plaza Lasso, who was elected in 1948 and remained in power until 1952, was the first President since 1924 to complete his term of office. He created a climate of stability and economic progress. Dr José María Velasco Ibarra, who had previously been President in 1934–35 and 1944–47, was elected again in 1952 and held office until 1956. A 61-year-old tradition of Liberal Presidents was broken in 1956, when a Conservative candidate, Dr Camilo Ponce Enríquez, was elected in June (though with only 29% of the votes cast) and took office in September. He was succeeded in September 1960 by ex-President Velasco, who campaigned as a non-party Liberal. In November 1961, however, President Velasco was deposed by a coup, and succeeded by his Vice-President, Dr Carlos Julio Arosemena Monroy. The latter was himself deposed in July 1963 by a military junta, led by Capt. (later Rear-Adm.) Ramón Castro Jijón, the Commander-in-Chief of the Navy, who assumed the office of President. In March 1966 the High Command of the Armed Forces dismissed the junta and installed Clemente Yerovi Indaburu, a wealthy businessman and a former Minister of Economics, as acting President. Yerovi was forced to resign when the Constituent Assembly, elected in October 1966, proposed a new constitution which prohibited the intervention of the armed forces in politics. In November he was replaced as provisional President by Dr Otto Arosemena Gómez, who held office until the elections of June 1968, when Dr Velasco returned from exile to win the Presidency for the fifth time. He took office in September.

In June 1970 President Velasco, with the support of the army, suspended the Constitution, dissolved the National Congress and assumed dictatorial powers to cope with a financial emergency. In February 1972 he was overthrown for the fourth time by a military coup, led by Brig.-Gen. Guillermo Rodríguez Lara, the Commander-in-Chief of the Army, who proclaimed himself Head of State. In January 1976 President Rodríguez resigned, and power was assumed by a three-man military junta, led by Vice-Adm. Alfredo Poveda Burbano, the Chief of Staff of the Navy. The new junta announced its intention to lead the country to a truly representative democracy. A national referendum approved a newly-drafted constitution in January 1978 and presidential elections took place in July. No candidate achieved an overall majority, and a second round of voting was held in April 1979, when a new Congress was also elected. Jaime Roldós Aguilera of the Concentración de Fuerzas Populares (CFP) was elected President and he took office in August, when the Congress was inaugurated and the new constitution came into force. President Roldós promised social justice and economic development, and guaranteed freedom for the press, but he met antagonism from both the conservative sections of the Congress and the trade unions. In May 1981 the President died in an air crash and was replaced by the Vice-President, Dr Osvaldo Hurtado Larrea, who faced opposition from left-wing politicians and unions for his efforts to cut government spending. He was also opposed by right-wing and commercial interests, which feared encroaching state intervention in the private economic sector.

A dispute between Hurtado and Vice-President León Roldós Aguilera in January 1982 led to the resignation of two Ministers belonging to Roldós' party, Pueblo, Cambio y Democracia (PCD), which then went into opposition. Hurtado replaced the Ministers with members of the CFP, creating a new pro-government majority with a coalition of members of Democracia Popular-Unión Demócrata Cristiana, CFP, Izquierda Democrática and seven independents. The heads of the armed forces resigned and the Defence Minister was dismissed in January 1982, when they opposed Hurtado's attempts to settle amicably the border dispute with Peru (see below). In August Hurtado lost his majority again when two CFP Ministers resigned over energy policy. A state of emergency was declared in October, after a general strike and violent demonstrations against price rises, but it was lifted in November. From October 1982 to January 1983 Ecuador suffered extremely heavy rainfall and flooding, which resulted in loss of life (landslides claimed over 100 victims), extensive damage to agriculture and devastation of property. A state of emergency was declared in Quito.

In March 1983 the Government introduced a series of austerity measures, which encountered immediate opposition from the trade unions and workers in the private sector. A 48-hour general strike was called. During the ensuing demonstrations, one person was killed and 50 injured. Three Ministers resigned in July, and a new Cabinet was appointed in August. Discontent with the Government's performance was reflected in the results of the concurrent presidential and general elections of January 1984, when the ruling party, Democracia Popular-Unión Demócrata Cristiana, lost support. Seventeen political parties contested the elections. Of the nine presidential candidates competing for votes, the two leading contenders were León Febres Cordero, leader of the Partido Social Cristiano (PSC) and candidate of the conservative Frente de Reconstrucción Nacional (FRN), and Rodrigo Borja, representing the left-wing Izquierda Democrática. As neither candidate won an absolute majority, a second round of voting was held in May 1984. After an often acrimonious campaign, Febres Cordero unexpectedly won the second round, securing 52.2% of the votes cast.

After taking office in August, President Febres Cordero reaffirmed his commitment to his campaign promise of 'bread, roofs and jobs' and announced his plans for renewed economic prosperity, which was to be achieved by the expansion of the private sector and the imposition of austerity measures. The President's policies were expected to encounter strong resistance in Congress, where a loose coalition of left-wing parties formed the majority grouping.

In September a serious constitutional dispute concerning the appointments procedure for the Supreme Court arose between the Government and Congress. Following violent confrontations in Congress and fears of a coup, both the Government and

ECUADOR

Congress made appointments to the Supreme Court. As a result of the ensuing impasse, proceedings in both Congress and the Supreme Court came to a halt. In spite of the establishment of a bipartite commission to restructure the Supreme Court, the two sides remained in conflict. The dispute was finally resolved in December 1984, when Congress agreed to allow the Government to appoint the new Supreme Court justices.

In March 1984 a state of emergency was declared for 11 days in two northern provinces, following unrest and acts of sabotage by workers in the petroleum industry. In October a 24-hour general strike was called by the Frente Unitario de Trabajadores (FUT) and opposition groups, to protest against the restrictions on press freedom and the austerity measures that had been imposed by the new Government. In January 1985 a 48-hour general strike was called by the opposition after the Government announced increases in the cost of petroleum products and public transport fares. In the course of public demonstrations, seven people were killed and more than 100 were arrested. The trade unions staged another 24-hour general strike in September 1986, aimed at doubling the minimum wage.

In March 1986 the dismissal of the Chief of Staff of the Armed Forces and Commander of the Air Force, Lt-Gen. Frank Vargas Pazos, resulted in a military crisis. Refusing to accept his dismissal, Lt-Gen. Vargas barricaded himself in at the Mantas military base, along with several hundred of his supporters. After several days, the siege ended peacefully with the resignation of the Minister of Defence, Gen. Luis Piñeiros, and that of the army commander, Gen. Manuel Albuja, who were both accused by Lt-Gen. Vargas of embezzlement. While in detention at the Mariscal Sucre air base, near Quito, Lt-Gen. Vargas secured support for his cause from the base's personnel, and staged a second act of rebellion. Troops loyal to President Febres Cordero attacked the base, capturing Lt-Gen. Vargas and arresting 400 of his supporters, including 200 civilians. Although the incident was the most serious crisis that his government had faced (necessitating the imposition of a state of emergency), the President denied that the country had been threatened by a coup attempt. In January 1987 President Febres Cordero was abducted by supporters of Lt-Gen. Vargas. He was released in exchange for Vargas.

Meanwhile, in March 1985 a dispute between the Government and Congress broke out over the Government's decision to veto a congressional ruling on an increase in the minimum wage which exceeded the Government's own proposed increase. The Government was accused by its opponents of acting in an unconstitutional and undemocratic manner. In July the Government obtained a majority in Congress, when five opposition members of Congress changed their political allegiance to support the Government. In June 1986 the mid-term legislative elections for 59 provincial seats (postponed from January 1986) took place. As a result, President Febres Cordero lost his congressional majority. Following the elections, the pro-Government parties retained only 27 of the 71 seats in Congress, the parties of the FRN (of which President Febres Cordero's PSC was the principal component) having won only 17 of the 59 renewable seats. President Febres Cordero was also defeated in a simultaneous referendum on a question of constitutional reform, that of whether independent candidates, unaffiliated to political parties, should be allowed to contest elections. Following these setbacks, the President reorganized his Cabinet.

The long-standing border dispute with Peru over the Cordillera del Cóndor erupted into war in January 1981. A cease-fire was declared a few days later under the auspices of the guarantors of the Rio Protocol of 1942 (Argentina, Brazil, Chile and the USA). The Protocol was not recognized by Ecuador as it awarded the area, which affords access to the Amazon river system, to Peru. Further clashes occurred along the border with Peru in December 1982 and January 1983. In addition, skirmishes between Ecuadorean and Colombian forces were reported to have taken place in the border zone in December 1982. Following a series of diplomatic disagreements, Ecuador broke off diplomatic relations with Nicaragua in October 1985. In addition, Ecuador withdrew from a support group of countries for the Contadora Group (see p. 230).

Government

Ecuador comprises 20 provinces, including the Galapagos Islands. Each province has a Governor, who is appointed by the President. Executive power is vested in the President, who is directly elected by universal adult suffrage for a four-year term. The President is not eligible for re-election. Legislative power is held by the 71-member unicameral Congress, which is also directly elected: 12 members are elected on a national basis and serve a four-year term, while 59 members are elected on a provincial basis and are replaced every two years, being ineligible for re-election. In April 1980 the future formation of an upper chamber was agreed.

Defence

Military service, which lasts two years, is selective for men at the age of 20. In July 1986 there were 42,000 men in the armed forces: army 35,000, navy 4,000 (including 1,500 marines) and air force 3,000. Defence expenditure for 1984 was estimated to be 14,000m. sucres.

Economic Affairs

Despite a rapid increase in population (estimated at 2.9% in each year from 1977 to 1986), Ecuador has experienced significant economic growth in recent years, owing mainly to the development of the country's petroleum resources. In 1984, according to estimates by the World Bank, Ecuador's gross national product (GNP) per head, measured at average 1982–84 prices, was US $1,150. Between 1965 and 1984, it was estimated, GNP per head increased, in real terms, at an average rate of 3.8% per year. The average annual increase in overall gross domestic product (GDP), measured in constant prices, was 7.2% in 1965–73, slowing to 4.8% in 1973–84. In terms of employment, the most important sector of the economy is agriculture. According to census results, however, the proportion of the working population engaged in agriculture, forestry and fishing declined from 54% in 1974 to 35% in 1982. Until the exploitation of petroleum in 1972, Ecuador's main source of income was agriculture. In 1984 the leading agricultural exports were bananas (of which Ecuador is the world's leading exporter), coffee and cocoa. African palm, rice and other grains are also grown. The agricultural sector expanded by 6.7% in 1984, but by only 2.4% in 1985. Banana exports declined from 1.25m. metric tons in 1982 to 864,000 tons in 1984. In 1985, however, exports rose to 1.3m. tons, worth US $138m. Bananas usually account for 45% of agricultural exports, while coffee accounts for about 25%. In 1984 Ecuador's production of coffee was estimated to be 90,000 metric tons, and in 1985 output increased to 96,000 tons. Despite a refining capacity of 130,000 metric tons, Ecuador's annual production of cocoa beans decreased from 97,000 tons in 1982 to 45,000 tons in 1983, and was estimated at 55,000 tons in 1984. However, estimated output rose to 128,000 tons in 1985.

The severe weather of late 1982 not only caused damage amounting to 3,000m. sucres but also had a devastating impact upon agriculture. The soya and cotton crops were cut by 50%, and banana production by 40%. Agricultural production in the coastal region fell by 32% as a result of rain damage, and the newly-developed activity of poultry farming in Manabí province was destroyed, at a cost of $15m. Ecuador's output of raw sugar declined from 254,000 metric tons in 1982 to 220,000 tons in 1983, but production recovered to 328,000 tons in 1984. In 1983 total agricultural production fell by 30%, but a rapid recovery in 1984 resulted in an increase in output of 22%.

Fishing has benefited considerably from official development programmes, and the total catch was a record 867,496 metric tons in 1984. However, the industry has been particularly badly affected by the adverse presence in the Pacific Ocean of the warm water current known as El Niño. The shrimp industry has continued to thrive and generated export earnings of US $185m. in 1985. The industry underwent cumulative growth of 314% between 1979 and 1983, and shrimps now constitute Ecuador's fourth most important export. However, in 1986 the industry faced a crisis, owing primarily to a lack of larvae. There was a need for new investment and technology to build new larva hatcheries and so secure the future of the industry. The fishing sector grew by 14% in 1984. Ecuador's extensive forests yield valuable hardwoods, and Ecuador is the world's principal producer of balsawood.

In 1985 proven reserves of petroleum amounted to 2,100m. barrels. With the completion in 1972 of the trans-Andean pipeline (capacity 400,000 barrels per day), linking the oilfields of Oriente Province with the tanker-loading port of Esmeraldas, Ecuador became a petroleum-exporting nation. The Corporación Estatal Petrolera Ecuatoriana (CEPE), founded in 1972 as the state petroleum corporation, bought a 25% share in Texaco-Gulf's operations in Ecuador in 1974, and bought Gulf's 37.5% holding in 1977. Ecuador's average output of crude petroleum increased from 215,000 barrels per day (b/d) in 1981 to 237,132 b/d in 1983, and to 292,000 b/d in November 1985. Domestic consumption increased by 14% annually from 1972 until 1982. By 1986 domestic requirements accounted for 110,000 b/d of Ecuador's output of crude petroleum. In 1983 the Government introduced new legislation to assist the industry. Foreign oil companies were encouraged to increase investment and exploration, and in June 1983 the Government opened 11 new blocks of territory for exploration. Between 1984 and 1988 Occidental Petroleum, a major US oil company, is scheduled to invest $50m. in petroleum exploration, and, under the terms of a 20-year contract signed in 1985, British Petroleum is to invest $28m. Between 1984 and 1989 the Government plans to invest $1,590m. to increase the industry's refining and petrochemical capacity, and $883m. will be spent on the Atahualpa refinery, on the Guayaquil coast, which is projected to have an eventual capacity of 75,000 b/d. In November 1986 a contract was signed for the construction of the Amazon refinery, which should increase the country's installed refining capacity by 10,000 b/d. In March 1986 the 503-km trans-Ecuadorean pipeline was nationalized. In January 1985 economic difficulties obliged the Government to suspend temporarily its adherence to the output quota, established by OPEC, which had been reduced by 17,000 b/d in 1984. By October petroleum production had increased to 290,000 b/d, considerably in excess of the OPEC quota of 183,000 b/d. Following OPEC's refusal to permit a 55% increase in Ecuador's output quota, the Government announced Ecuador's temporary withdrawal from OPEC in October. In early 1986 production surpassed 300,000 b/d for the first time. Petroleum accounted for about two-thirds of Ecuador's total export revenue in 1985, but substantial losses were expected in 1986, following the sharp decline in international oil prices. As a result of OPEC meetings in 1986, Ecuador's quota for the first six months of 1987 was fixed at 210,000 b/d.

In 1981 70% of energy generation was by thermoelectric plants. Between 1973 and 1983 the capacity of Ecuador's electric generating plants increased from 481,543 kW to 1,380,000 kW. An estimated 52% of the population have access to electricity. In 1982 electricity provided about one-quarter of energy generation. The Government hopes to expand the hydroelectric sector into the principal source of energy. A series of projects includes the Paute scheme, with a planned capacity of 500,000 kW, which was scheduled for completion in 1986. In February 1983 the Daniel Palacios Dam was inaugurated as part of the Paute scheme. Production of natural gas declined from a peak of 40m. cu m in 1978 to 31m. cu m in 1980, when total reserves were estimated at 58,000m. cu m. Production rose to 33m. cu m in 1981. The Amistad field contained 209m. cu m of proven reserves and up to 537m. cu m of possible reserves. There are plans to construct pipelines from Esmeraldas and Shushufindi to Quito. A plant for the production of liquefied petroleum gas at Shushufindi was opened in 1982. Ecuador's other mineral resources include gold, silver, copper, sulphur, titanium, antimony, lead and zinc, all mined in small quantities.

Manufacturing, mainly consisting of textiles, food processing, cement and pharmaceuticals, developed rapidly in the 1970s, despite shortages of electric energy. Industrial production rose by 6.6% in 1981, but declined by 5.6% in 1983, as a result of falling production throughout the sector. In 1985 manufacturing output expanded by 1.4%, compared with a decline of 2.1% in 1984. The value of industrial exports fell from US $615m. in 1980 to $211m. in 1983, and was expected to decline further. There is little heavy industry but some sectors, such as petrochemicals, steel and the assembly of motor vehicles, are being developed through the Andean Group. An $800m. petrochemical complex was completed in 1983, and a $180m. integrated steel mill was expected to be functioning by 1985.

With a real GDP growth rate of 13.6% in 1974, Ecuador had one of Latin America's fastest growing economies, owing to the development of the petroleum sector. The growth rate was 4.5% in 1981 but fell to 1.4% in 1982. The country's GDP contracted by 3.5% in 1983. The rapid deterioration in 1982 and 1983 resulted principally from a decline in petroleum prices and a contraction in the markets for Ecuador's traditional agricultural exports. The average annual rate of inflation increased from 16.3% in 1982 to 48.4% in 1983. Reserves of foreign exchange declined from $961m. at the end of 1980 to $570m. one year later, and to $205m. in March 1983. From August 1982 the flow of foreign funds into Ecuador stopped, with severe consequences for the public sector, which accounted for 74% of public borrowing. In March 1983 the Government agreed to assume responsibility for the repayment, over six years, of a large proportion of the private-sector debt on the understanding that the private sector would repay the Government in local currency.

In March 1983, to avert a national crisis, the Government introduced a stabilization programme consisting of a series of austerity measures. The sucre was devalued by 21%, from 33.15 to 42.00 per US dollar. The commercial interest rate was increased from 14% to 16%, new exchange regulations were introduced and export subsidies were eliminated. Further subsidies were removed from flour, petrol, diesel oil and other fuels. As a result of the Government's new measures, the current deficit on the balance of payments declined from $1,195m. in 1982 to $104m. in 1983. The economic programme proved highly unpopular within the country, but it did enable Ecuador to reach agreement with the IMF over further financial assistance. In July Ecuador obtained $170m. in special drawing rights (SDRs) from the IMF, and reached agreement with a consortium of international banks on the rescheduling of $269m. of debt. In November 1984 the Government and the IMF reached agreement, in general terms, on further financing. Following this accord, the Government and commercial bank creditors concluded in December the renegotiation of Ecuador's foreign debt until 1989 (amounting to $4,629m.). Under the terms of the agreement, Ecuador secured additional financing of $2,000m. In March 1985 Ecuador obtained a one-year stand-by credit, amounting to 105.5m. SDRs, from the IMF. In April Ecuador's creditor governments agreed to reschedule debt that was due to be repaid in 1985–87. In August Ecuador secured a further loan of $200m. from its creditor banks, and in December 1985 an agreement to reschedule payment of $4,600m. of Ecuador's foreign debt was signed. In January 1986 the World Bank granted two loans amounting to $106m. to aid Ecuador's economic recovery. This was followed by two further loans, totalling $145m., in April. In early 1986 Ecuador also secured loans and grants totalling $196m. from the IDB.

After taking office in August 1984, President Febres Cordero confirmed that his Government's economic priorities would be to encourage more foreign investment in Ecuador and to liberalize the economy. In September the policy of mini-devaluations was ended, and official exchange rates for the sucre were established for sales and purchases. A unified exchange rate was established in September 1985. However, the currency was further devalued in 1986, by 12.4% in January and by 23% in August.

In 1985 the economy showed signs of improvement: GDP growth was estimated at almost 4% (compared with a decline of 3.5% in 1983), and a trade surplus of $1,147m. was achieved. After rising to $248m. in 1984, the current account deficit fell to $85m. in 1985. The annual rate of inflation declined from 28% in 1984 to 23.5% in 1985. Unemployment decreased from 13% of the labour force in 1984 to 9% in 1985. In 1986, however, the fall in oil prices resulted in a serious shortfall in export earnings. By mid-1986 foreign exchange reserves had declined to $145m., and in September a surcharge of up to 30% was imposed on imported goods. To offset the losses in petroleum revenues, Ecuador obtained further assistance from the IMF, and in October 1986 secured a loan of $220m. from foreign commercial banks. By late 1986, therefore, Ecuador's total external debt was approaching $8,000m. Economic growth for the year, originally projected at 6%, was negligible.

The Government's determination to encourage foreign investment in Ecuador was demonstrated by the liberalization of foreign trade laws in May 1985. The Government's strategy for foreign trade included the establishment of two free-trade zones and the revision of the tariff system. In support of its policy, the Government threatened to withdraw from the Andean Group if the Group's rules on trading were not liberalized. The level of foreign investment in Ecuador declined unexpectedly

ECUADOR

in 1985, when it totalled 4,509m. sucres, compared with 6,459m. sucres in 1984.

Ecuador is a member of the Andean Group (see p. 92) and of OPEC (see p. 195).

Social Welfare

Social insurance is compulsory for all employees. Benefits are available for sickness, industrial accidents, disability, maternity, old age, widowhood and orphanhood. In 1980 about 125,000 peasants were integrated into social security schemes; the 1980–84 Development Plan aimed to increase the number to 335,000. Hospitals and welfare institutions are run by Central Public Assistance Boards. In 1973 Ecuador had 221 hospital establishments, with a total of 13,594 beds, and in 1977 there were 4,660 physicians working in the country.

Education

Education is compulsory for six years, to be undertaken between six and 14 years of age, and all public schools are free. Private schools continue to play a vital role in the educational system. Primary education begins at six years of age and lasts for six years. Secondary education, in general and specialized technical or humanities schools, begins at the age of 12 and lasts for up to six years, comprising two equal cycles of three years each. In 1975 the enrolment ratios for the respective age-groups were 80% in primary schools and 28% in secondary schools. By 1979 primary enrolment had risen to 87%. In 1982 the total enrolment at primary and secondary schools was equivalent to 88% of the school-age population. University courses extend for up to six years, and include programmes for teacher training. A number of adult schools and literacy centres have been built, aimed at reducing the rate of adult illiteracy, which averaged 26.1% in 1974 and 16.1% in 1982. There are 16 universities. In many rural areas, Quechua and other indigenous Indian languages are used in education.

Tourism

The main tourist attractions are the magnificent mountain and forest scenery of the highlands, the tropical jungles of the Upper Amazon, the Galapagos Islands (although tourist numbers are limited by ecological considerations) and the relics of Indian and colonial Spanish cultures. Plans have been announced to construct an important tourist attraction on the equator, to be known as 'Mitad del Mundo'. The Government has spent US $1.3m. on developing a village and facilities for tourists. There are a number of coastal resorts from which deep-sea fishing is possible. In 1982 Ecuador received a total of 217,008 foreign visitors, compared to 244,485 in 1980 and approximately 172,000 in 1975.

Public Holidays

1987: 1 January (New Year's Day), 6 January (Epiphany), 3–4 March (Carnival), 16 April (Holy Thursday), 17 April (Good Friday), 18 April (Easter Saturday), 1 May (Labour Day), 24 May (Battle of Pichincha), 24 July (Birth of Simón Bolívar), 10 August (Independence of Quito), 9 October (Independence of Guayaquil), 12 October (Discovery of America), 1 November (All Saints' Day), 2 November (All Souls' Day), 3 November (Independence of Cuenca), 6 December (Foundation of Quito), 25 December (Christmas Day).

1988: 1 January (New Year's Day), 6 January (Epiphany), 16–17 February (Carnival), 31 March (Holy Thursday), 1 April (Good Friday), 2 April (Easter Saturday), 1 May (Labour Day), 24 May (Battle of Pichincha), 24 July (Birth of Simón Bolívar), 10 August (Independence of Quito), 9 October (Independence of Guayaquil), 12 October (Discovery of America), 1 November (All Saints' Day), 2 November (All Souls' Day), 3 November (Independence of Cuenca), 6 December (Foundation of Quito), 25 December (Christmas Day).

Weights and Measures

The metric system is in force.

Currency and Exchange Rates

100 centavos = 1 sucre.
Exchange rates (30 September 1986):
 £1 sterling = 204.46 sucres;
 US $1 = 141.30 sucres.

ECUADOR

Statistical Survey

Sources (unless otherwise stated): Banco Central de Ecuador, Quito; Ministerio de Industrias, Comercio e Integración, Quito; Instituto Nacional de Estadística y Censos, 10 de Agosto 229, Quito; tel. 519-320.

Area and Population

AREA, POPULATION AND DENSITY

Area (sq km)	
Land	263,950
Inland water	6,720
Total	270,670*
Population (census results)†	
8 June 1974	6,521,710
28 November 1982	
Males	4,021,034
Females	4,039,678
Total	8,060,712
Population (official estimates at mid-year)†	
1984	9,114,866
1985	9,377,980
1986	9,647,107
Density (per sq km) at mid-1986	35.6

* 104,506 sq miles.
† Figures exclude nomadic tribes of indigenous Indians. Census results also exclude any adjustment for underenumeration.

PROVINCES (estimated population at mid-1986)*

	Population	Capital
Azuay	513,343	Cuenca
Bolívar	164,741	Guaranda
Cañar	198,322	Azogues
Carchi	143,274	Tulcán
Cotopaxi	312,671	Latacunga
Chimborazo	369,229	Riobamba
El Oro	406,822	Machala
Esmeraldas	297,376	Esmeraldas
Guayas	2,485,763	Guayaquil
Imbabura	281,032	Ibarra
Loja	404,036	Loja
Los Ríos	533,685	Babahoyo
Manabí	1,039,408	Portoviejo
Morona Santiago	85,619	Macas
Napo	151,745	Tena
Pastaza	38,531	Puyo
Pichincha	1,710,275	Quito
Tungurahua	374,322	Ambato
Zamora Chinchipe	59,113	Zamora
Archipiélago de Colón (Galápagos)	7,954	Puerto Baquerizo (Isla San Cristóbal)
Total	9,577,261	

* Figures exclude persons in unspecified areas, totalling 69,846.

PRINCIPAL TOWNS (estimated population at mid-1986)

Guayaquil	1,509,108	Portoviejo	134,393
Quito (capital)	1,093,278	Manta	129,578
Cuenca	193,012	Ambato	122,139
Machala	137,321	Esmeraldas	115,138

BIRTHS, MARRIAGES AND DEATHS*
(excluding nomadic Indian tribes)

	Registered live births		Registered marriages		Registered deaths	
	Number	Rate (per 1,000)	Number	Rate (per 1,000)	Number	Rate (per 1,000)
1976	252,456	34.9	42,895	5.9	60,669	8.4
1977	251,734	33.8	47,198	6.3	59,150	7.9
1978	262,027	34.2	46,500	6.1	56,101	7.3
1979	267,372	33.9	46,278	5.9	59,951	7.6
1980	262,778	32.4	48,306	5.9	57,020	7.0
1981	264,963	31.7	49,936	6.0	54,910	6.6
1982	262,102	30.5	49,341	5.7	53,009	6.2
1983	253,990	28.7	49,571	5.6	55,202	6.2

* Registration is incomplete. For the period 1980–85 the average annual rates are estimated to have been: births 36.8 per 1,000; deaths 8.1 per 1,000.

ECONOMICALLY ACTIVE POPULATION*
(ISIC Major Divisions, 1982 census)

	Males	Females	Total
Agriculture, hunting, forestry and fishing	727,880	59,092	786,972
Mining and quarrying	6,912	494	7,406
Manufacturing	214,063	72,467	286,530
Electricity, gas and water	11,946	1,237	13,183
Construction	154,683	3,326	158,009
Trade, restaurants and hotels	185,127	86,787	271,914
Transport, storage and communications	96,345	4,976	101,321
Financing, insurance, real estate and business services	29,865	14,251	44,116
Community, social and personal services	343,627	211,288	554,915
Activities not adequately described	28,567	10,027	38,594
Total	1,799,015	463,945	2,262,960

* Figures refer to persons aged 12 years and over, excluding those seeking work for the first time, totalling 83,103 (males 62,637; females 20,466).

Agriculture

PRINCIPAL CROPS (metric tons)

	1982	1983*	1984*
Coffee (green)	83,938	81,000	90,000†
Bananas	1,998,749	1,642,000	1,124,000†
Potatoes	416,417	314,000	363,000†
Rice (paddy)	384,356	274,000	470,000†
Barley	35,435	30,000	33,000†
Wheat	38,538	27,000	24,000†
Maize	323,978	229,000	300,000†
Cocoa beans	96,952	45,000	60,000†
Seed cotton	25,196	7,000‡	7,000‡
Sugar cane	5,421,000	5,620,000	6,000,000‡
Palm kernels	7,920*	6,208	8,000‡

* Source: FAO, *Production Yearbook*.
† Unofficial figure.   ‡ FAO estimate.

LIVESTOCK ('000 head, year ending September)

	1982	1983	1984
Cattle	3,200	3,270	3,300*
Sheep	2,341†	2,303†	2,311†
Pigs	3,520	3,735	4,278†

Poultry (million): 41 in 1982; 42* in 1983; 43* in 1984.
* FAO estimate.   † Unofficial figure.
Source: FAO, *Production Yearbook*.

LIVESTOCK PRODUCTS ('000 metric tons)

	1982	1983	1984
Beef and veal	94	92	110*
Mutton and lamb*	9	9	9
Pig meat*	57	59	61
Poultry meat*	28	29	30
Cows' milk	967	981	990*
Butter*	4.4	4.4	4.4
Cheese*	12.8	12.8	13.1
Hen eggs	49.4	50.0*	50.2*
Wool:			
greasy	3.1†	3.3*	3.4*
clean*	1.6	1.6	1.7
Cattle hides (fresh)*	11.7	12.5	14.5

* FAO estimate.   † Unofficial figure.
Source: FAO, *Production Yearbook*.

Fishing

('000 metric tons, live weight)

	1982	1983	1984
Herrings, sardines, anchovies, etc.	243.0	130.3	413.0*
Chub mackerel	248.0	96.5	306.1*
Other marine fishes	127.4	40.8	109.3*
Other sea creatures	35.8	39.7	39.1*
Total catch	654.1	307.3	867.5

* FAO estimate.
Source: FAO, *Yearbook of Fishery Statistics*.

Forestry

ROUNDWOOD REMOVALS
('000 cubic metres, excluding bark)

	1982	1983	1984
Sawlogs, veneer logs and logs for sleepers	1,961*	1,962	2,077
Pulpwood	71*	69	73
Other industrial wood	20	77	82
Fuel wood	5,580	5,800	5,996
Total	7,632	7,908	8,228

* FAO estimate.
Source: FAO, *Yearbook of Forest Products*.

SAWNWOOD PRODUCTION ('000 cubic metres)

	1982	1983	1984
Total (incl. boxboards)	978	1,140	1,210

Source: FAO, *Yearbook of Forest Products*.

Mining

	1981	1982	1983
Gold (troy oz)	1,286.0	1,601.1	607.6
Silver (troy oz)	32,146.4	10,076.0	3,137.6
Copper (kg)	825,000	25,370	7,960
Zinc (kg)	742,000	47,320	14,820
Petroleum ('000 barrels)	77,062.1	77,072.2	86,691.3

Industry

SELECTED PRODUCTS

		1980	1981	1982
Diesel oil	'000 barrels	5,014.8	5,224.4	4,373.7
Kerosene	'000 barrels	2,206.6	2,530.4	2,059.1
Gasoline	'000 barrels	7,801.6	7,563.9	6,118.8
Residual fuel oils	'000 barrels	14,322.4	14,491.2	12,485.6
Distillate fuel oils	'000 barrels	131.5	81.8	169.2
Turbo-fuels	'000 barrels	1,146.9	1,064.4	906.7
Liquefied natural gas	'000 barrels	694.3	763.1	642.7
Structural steel	metric tons	98,048	139,130	163,617
Cement	metric tons	1,238,122	1,584,796	1,491,977
Electricity	'000 kWh	3,704,022	4,265,977	n.a.

1982 ('000 metric tons): Raw sugar 246; Frozen and tinned fish (estimate) 58.6; Cocoa powder (1981, exports only) 6.6; Cocoa butter (1981, estimate, exports only) 6.3 (Source: UN, *Industrial Statistics Yearbook*).

Finance

CURRENCY AND EXCHANGE RATES

Monetary Units
100 centavos = 1 sucre.

Denominations
Coins: 10, 20 and 50 centavos; 1 sucre.
Notes: 5, 10, 20, 50, 100, 500 and 1,000 sucres.

Sterling and Dollar Equivalents (30 September 1986)
£1 sterling = 204.46 sucres;
US $1 = 141.30 sucres;
1,000 sucres = £4.891 = $7.077.

Average Exchange Rate (sucres per US dollar)
1983   44.115
1984   62.536
1985   69.556

CENTRAL BANK RESERVES (US $ million at 31 December)

	1983	1984	1985
Gold*	124.3	124.3	124.3
IMF special drawing rights	0.1	0.5	28.8
Reserve position in IMF	12.0	—	—
Foreign exchange	632.4	610.7	689.4
Total	768.8	735.5	842.5

* Valued at $42.22 per troy ounce prior to October 1982, and at $300 per ounce thereafter.
Source: IMF, *International Financial Statistics*.

MONEY SUPPLY (million sucres at 31 December)

	1982	1983	1984
Currency outside banks	20,519	25,421	35,314
Private sector deposits at central bank	6,487	11,077	11,447
Demand deposits at private banks	46,124	58,647	82,297
Total money	73,130	95,145	129,058

Source: IMF, *International Financial Statistics*.

COST OF LIVING*
(Consumer Price Index; average for urban area)

	1983	1984	1985
Food and drink	344.6	438.1	556.4
Housing	202.1	239.6	269.9
Clothing	237.0	296.0	368.2
Miscellaneous	242.7	305.3	390.7
All items	272.0	340.2	423.1

* Base: May 1978–April 1979 = 100.

ECUADOR

BUDGET (million sucres)

Revenue	1981	1982
Taxation	24,603.1	23,929.8
Export tax	381.7	18.0
Import tax	9,127.4	8,312.8
Income tax	6,744.8	5,658.9
Taxes on financial transactions	524.2	767.7
Capital taxes	250.6	250.7
Taxes on consumption and production	7,479.8	8,854.3
Transport tax	53.3	54.4
Stamps	32.4	13.0
Other taxes	8.9	—
Non-tax revenue	14,056.1	19,550.2
Interest rates	316.0	327.9
Royalties	100.7	118.3
Mining rights	13,639.4	18,279.4
Other revenue	1,179.3	824.6
Transfers	296.6	361.0
Gross current revenue and transfers	38,955.8	43,841.0
Effective current revenue and transfers	39,297.4	44,820.3
Capital revenue	23,192.8	28,607.8
Total	62,490.2	73,428.1

Expenditure	1981	1982
Justice	893.4	921.4
Presidency	629.3	429.7
Ministry of the Interior and Police	2,137.9	3,285.2
Ministry of National Defence	5,847.6	6,869.8
Ministry of Finance	1,733.1	1,553.9
Ministry of Education	15,042.6	17,054.9
Ministry of Labour and Social Welfare	670.4	661.0
Ministry of Public Health	4,367.7	4,951.6
Agriculture	2,227.2	2,644.7
Ministry of Agriculture and Livestock	1,824.8	1,547.2
Ministry of Natural Resources and Energy	582.8	648.6
Ministry of Commerce	420.6	396.6
Transport and Communications	4,540.2	5,214.6
Public debt	11,044.6	18,287.7
Total (incl. others)	62,490.2	73,428.1

NATIONAL ACCOUNTS

Expenditure on the Gross Domestic Product (million sucres in current prices)

	1981	1982*	1983*
Government final consumption expenditure	49,742	57,509	65,921
Private final consumption expenditure	214,665	260,199	365,622
Increase in stocks	3,162	4,481	3,772
Gross fixed capital formation	77,628	91,289	91,939
Total domestic expenditure	345,197	413,478	527,254
Exports of goods and services	75,906	87,779	138,895
Less Imports of goods and services	72,441	84,298	100,347
Gross domestic product in purchasers' values	348,662	416,959	565,802

* Provisional.

Gross Domestic Product by Economic Activity (million sucres in constant 1975 prices)

	1981	1982*	1983*
Agriculture, hunting, forestry and fishing	22,647	23,138	20,015
Mining and quarrying	15,992	15,471	19,261
Manufacturing	29,159	31,178	30,586
Electricity, gas and water	1,117	1,264	1,514
Construction	7,239	7,193	6,331
Trade, restaurants and hotels	25,032	25,098	21,738
Transport, storage and communications	10,517	10,841	10,881
Finance and business services	11,552	11,824	12,180
Ownership of dwellings	6,722	6,909	6,997
Other services	8,240	8,726	9,027
Sub-total	138,217	141,642	138,530
Less Imputed bank service charge	5,059	5,147	5,850
Domestic product of industries	133,158	136,495	132,680
Government services	14,000	14,234	14,405
Domestic services of households	688	695	704
Sub-total	147,846	151,424	147,789
Customs duties (net of import subsidies)	5,597	4,712	3,142
GDP in purchasers' values	153,443	156,136	150,931

* Provisional.

ECUADOR

Statistical Survey

BALANCE OF PAYMENTS (US $ million)

	1983	1984	1985
Merchandise exports f.o.b.	2,348.0	2,622.0	2,870.0
Merchandise imports f.o.b.	−1,408.0	−1,567.0	−1,723.0
Trade balance	940.0	1,055.0	1,147.0
Exports of services	340.0	350.0	390.0
Imports of services	−1,408.0	−1,673.0	−1,647.0
Balance on goods and services	−128.0	−268.0	−110.0
Private unrequited transfers (net)	} 24.0	20.0	25.0
Government unrequited transfers (net)			
Current balance	−104.0	−248.0	−85.0
Direct capital investment (net)	50.0	50.0	60.0
Other long-term capital (net)	−1,200.0	−898.0	−745.0
Short-term capital (net)	−1,098.0	−249.0	—
Net errors and omissions	−81.9	9.9	−86.1
Total (net monetary movements)	−2,433.9	−1,335.1	−856.1
Valuation changes (net)	14.1	21.9	−39.4
Exceptional financing (net)	2,473.0	1,327.0	881.0
Official financing (net)	74.0	−72.0	—
Changes in reserves	127.2	−58.3	−14.4

Source: IMF, *International Financial Statistics*.

External Trade

PRINCIPAL COMMODITIES (US $ '000)

Imports c.i.f.	1980	1981	1982
Foodstuffs	63,523	38,680	33,385
Processed foods	110,408	122,923	104,715
Inedible animal and vegetable products	94,248	98,306	106,462
Mineral products	306,445	294,699	290,634
Chemical products	253,915	253,981	295,179
Agricultural equipment	58,072	63,004	59,585
Industrial machinery	345,649	298,543	258,818
Transport equipment	408,238	494,312	265,542
Vehicles	58,301	37,457	44,884
Construction materials	119,890	89,763	60,734
Total (incl. others)	2,249,519	2,102,146	1,917,197

1983 (US $'000): Total imports 1,497,703.

Exports f.o.b.	1981	1982	1983
Bananas	207,878	213,297	152,926
Coffee	105,870	138,758	148,607
Cocoa	43,838	63,064	8,366
Seafood	83,207	129,346	179,340
Petroleum	1,560,062	1,388,284	1,636,757
Cocoa products	105,713	55,939	26,398
Seafood products	99,043	81,470	27,134
Petroleum derivatives	166,530	136,383	106,168
Total (incl. others)	2,541,361	2,343,579	2,357,629

PRINCIPAL TRADING PARTNERS (US $ million)

Imports c.i.f.	1981	1982	1983
Brazil	68.3	123.8	114.1
Chile	10.9	47.1	41.4
Colombia	44.4	43.9	46.1
Germany, Federal Republic	144.9	137.8	109.9
Italy	71.4	61.1	57.9
Japan	222.8	206.1	116.4
Mexico	53.8	19.9	26.7
Spain	29.2	43.4	35.7
Taiwan	48.2	47.8	22.0
United Kingdom	58.0	52.3	39.6
USA	656.5	713.0	574.6
Total (incl. others)	2,102.1	1,917.2	1,497.7

Exports f.o.b.	1981	1982	1983
Brazil	65.5	281.0	2.7
Chile	73.7	29.2	36.4
Colombia	82.6	91.9	133.3
Japan	311.1	16.9	39.9
Panama	17.8	70.1	219.5
Taiwan	14.2	11.6	129.6
USA	956.0	1,073.5	1,383.9
Uruguay	100.8	32.4	0.3
Venezuela	53.0	54.3	2.0
Total (incl. others)	2,541.4	2,343.6	2,357.6

Transport

RAILWAYS (million)

	1977	1978	1979
Passenger-kilometres	72	65	69
Net ton-kilometres	25	34	29

Source: UN, *Statistical Yearbook*.

ROAD TRAFFIC

('000 motor vehicles in use, 1985): Passenger cars 261.3, Goods vehicles 23.8, Buses and Coaches 12.9 (Source: IRF, *World Road Statistics*).

INTERNATIONAL SEA-BORNE SHIPPING
(estimated freight traffic, '000 metric tons)

	1981	1982	1983
Goods loaded	7,894	7,303	9,924
Goods unloaded	2,725	2,424	2,541*

* Estimate.
Source: UN, *Monthly Bulletin of Statistics*.

CIVIL AVIATION (traffic on scheduled services)

	1981	1982
Passengers carried ('000)	692	676
Passenger-km (million)	946	862
Freight ton-km (million)	38.8	36.4

Source: UN, *Statistical Yearbook*.

Tourism

	1980	1981	1982
Foreign visitors	244,485	226,297	217,008

Education

(1983/84*)

	Institutions	Teachers	Pupils
Primary	11,480	41,973	1,407,898
Middle	1,099	27,289	477,829
Basic	338	3,287	50,772
Specialized	415	15,565	279,159
Technical	346	8,437	147,898
Higher†	12	8,854	227,233

* Provisional.   † 1980 figures.

Directory

The Constitution

The 1945 Constitution was suspended in June 1970. In January 1978 a referendum was held to choose between two draft Constitutions, prepared by various special constitutional committees. In a 90% poll, 43% voted for a proposed new Constitution and 32.1% voted for a revised version of the 1945 Constitution. The new Constitution came into force on 10 August 1979. Its main provisions are summarized below:

CHAMBER OF REPRESENTATIVES

The Constitution of 1979 states that legislative power is exercised by the Chamber of Representatives which sits for a period of 60 days from 10 August. The Chamber is required to set up four full-time Legislative Commissions to consider draft laws when the House is in recess. Special sessions of the Chamber of Representatives may be called.

Representatives are elected for four years from lists of candidates drawn up by legally-recognized parties. Twelve are elected nationally; two from each Province with over 100,000 inhabitants, one from each Province with fewer than 100,000; and one for every 300,000 citizens or fractions of over 200,000. Representatives are eligible for re-election.

In addition to its law-making duties, the Chamber ratifies treaties, elects members of the Supreme and Superior Courts, and (from panels presented by the President) the Comptroller-General, the Attorney-General and the Superintendent of Banks. It is also able to overrule the President's amendment of a bill which it has submitted for Presidential approval. It may reconsider a rejected bill after a year or request a referendum, and may revoke the President's declaration of a state of emergency. The budget is considered in the first instance by the appropriate Legislative Commission and disagreements are resolved in the Chamber.

PRESIDENT

The presidential term is four years, and there is no re-election. The President appoints the Cabinet, the Governors of Provinces, diplomatic representatives and certain administrative employees, and is responsible for the direction of international relations. In the event of foreign invasion or internal disturbance, the President may declare a state of emergency and must notify the Chamber, or the Tribunal for Constitutional Guarantees if the Chamber is not in session.

As in other post-war Latin-American Constitutions, particular emphasis is laid on the functions and duties of the State, which is given wide responsibilities with regard to the protection of labour; assisting in the expansion of production; protecting the Indian and peasant communities; and organizing the distribution and development of uncultivated lands, by expropriation where necessary.

Voting is compulsory for every Ecuadorean citizen who is literate and over 18 years of age. An optional vote has been extended to illiterates (under 15% of the population by 1981). The Constitution guarantees liberty of conscience in all its manifestations, and states that the law shall not make any discrimination for religious reasons.

The Government

HEAD OF STATE

President: Ing. LEÓN FEBRES CORDERO RIVADENEIRA (took office 10 August 1984).

Vice-President: Dr BLASCO PEÑAHERRERA PADILLA.

ECUADOR

THE CABINET
(January 1987)

Minister of the Interior: Lic. LUIS ROBLES PLAZA.
Minister of Foreign Affairs: RAFAEL GARCÍA VELASCO.
Minister of Finance and Public Credit: Econ. DOMINGO CORDÓVEZ.
Minister of Industry, Trade, Integration and Fisheries: Econ. XAVIER NEIRA MENÉNDEZ.
Minister of Agriculture and Livestock: MARCOS ESPINEL.
Minister of Energy and Mines: Ing. XAVIER ESPINOZA TERÁN.
Minister of Labour and Human Resources: Dr JORGE EGAS PEÑA.
Minister of Education and Culture: Dr IVÁN GALLEGOS DOMÍNGUEZ.
Minister of Defence: Gen. MEDARDO SALAZAR NAVAS.
Minister of Public Health: Dr JORGE BRACHO OÑA.
Minister of Social Welfare: Dr ERNESTO VELÁSQUEZ BAQUERIZO.
Minister of Public Works and Communications: Ing. CÉSAR RODRÍGUEZ BAQUERIZO.
Secretary-General for Public Administration: Lic. PATRICIO QUEVEDO TERÁN.
Secretary-General for Public Information: Lic. MARCO LARA GUZMÁN.
President of the National Monetary Board: Ing. FEDERICO ARTETA RIVERA.
General Manager of the Central Bank: Dr CARLOS JULIO EMANUEL MORÁN.

MINISTRIES

Office of the President: Palacio Nacional, García Moreno 1043, Quito; tel. 216-300; telex 23751.
Office of the Vice-President: Manuel Larrea y Arenas, N 2, 21, Quito; tel. 550-033.
Ministry of Agriculture and Livestock: Avda Eloy Alfaro y Amazonas, Quito; tel. 554-122; telex 2291.
Ministry of Defence: Exposición 208, Quito; tel. 216-150; telex 2703.
Ministry of Education, Culture and Sport: Mejía 348, Quito; tel. 216-224.
Ministry of Energy and Mines: Santa Prisca 223 y Manuel Larrea, Quito; tel. 239-100; telex 2271.
Ministry of Finance and Public Credit: Avda 10 de Agosto 1661 y Jorge Washington, Quito; tel. 544-500; telex 2358.
Ministry of Foreign Affairs: Avda 10 de Agosto y Carrión, Quito; tel. 230-500; telex 2441.
Ministry of Industry, Trade, Integration and Fisheries: Juan León Mera y Roca, Quito; tel. 524-666; telex 2166.
Ministry of the Interior: Espejo y Benalcázar, Quito; tel. 216-080; telex 2354.
Ministry of Labour and Human Resources: Ponce y Luis Felipe Borja, Quito; tel. 524-666; telex 2898.
Ministry of Public Health: Juan Larrea 444, Quito; tel. 521-114.
Ministry of Public Works and Communications: Avda 6 de Diciembre y Wilson, Quito; tel. 242-666; telex 2353.
Ministry of Social Welfare: Robles 6, Quito; tel. 540-750; telex 2898.

President and Legislature

PRESIDENTIAL ELECTION

In the second round of voting, held on 6 May 1984, LEÓN FEBRES CORDERO RIVADENEIRA (PSC) polled 52.2% of the valid votes cast, and RODRIGO BORJA CEVALLOS (ID) polled 47.8%.

CONGRESO NACIONAL
Cámara Nacional de Representantes
President of Congress: ANDRÉS VALLEJO.
Vice-President of Congress: ENRIQUE AYALA.

Party	Seats after elections* 29 January 1984	1 June 1986
Izquierda Democrática (ID)	24	17
Partido Social Cristiano (PSC)†	9	15
Concentración de Fuerzas Populares (CFP)†	7	4
Frente Radical Alfarista (FRA)†	6	3
Partido Demócrata (PD)†	5	1
Democracia Popular (DP)	4	8
Partido Liberal Radical (PLR)†	4	3
Movimiento Popular Democrático (MPD)	3	4
Partido Roldosista Ecuatoriano (PRE)	3	5
Frente Amplio de la Izquierda (FADI)	2	3
Partido Conservador (PC)†	2	1
Partido Nacionalista Revolucionario (PNR)†	1	—
Partido Socialista (PSE)	1	6
Pueblo, Cambio y Democracia (PCD)	—	1
Total	**71**	**71**

* The 59 seats allocated on a provincial basis are renewable after two years. The January 1986 mid-term elections were postponed until June 1986. The remaining 12 deputies, elected on a national basis in January 1984, retain their seats until 1988.

† These parties support the Government of President Febres Cordero.

Note: In June 1985 five deputies of the FRA and two deputies of the ID left the opposition bloc within Congress in order to support the Government. Consequently, the Government obtained a majority within Congress for the first time since the general election in January 1984. Following the mid-term elections of June 1986, however, the pro-Government bloc held only 27 seats and had thus lost its majority.

Political Organizations

Concentración de Fuerzas Populares (CFP): Quito; f. 1946; Leader GALO VAYAS; Dir Dr AVERROES BUCARAM SAXIDA.
Democracia Popular-Unión Demócrata Cristiana (DP-UDC): Saá No 153 y Hnos Pazmiño, Casilla 2300, Quito; tel. 547-388; f. 1978; Christian democrat; Pres. Dr WILFRIDO LUCERO BOLAÑOS.
Frente Progresista Democrático: f. 1984 to succeed Convergencia Democrática; regrouped June 1986; also known as Bloque Progresista; left-wing coalition comprising the following parties:
  Frente Amplio de la Izquierda (FADI): Quito; f. 1977; left-wing alliance comprising the following parties: Partido Comunista Ecuatoriano, Partido Socialista Revolucionario, Movimiento para la Unidad de la Izquierda, Movimiento Revolucionario de la Izquierda Cristiana; Dir Dr RENÉ MAUGÉ M.
  Izquierda Democrática (ID): Juan León Mera 268 y Jorge Washington, Quito; f. 1977; Leader RODRIGO BORJA CEVALLOS; Dir XAVIER LEDESMA.
  Movimiento Popular Democrático (MPD): Maoist; Leader Dr JAIME HURTADO GONZÁLEZ.
  Partido Demócrata (PD): Quito; Leader Dr FRANCISCO HUERTA MONTALVO.
  Partido Socialista (PSE): Quito.
  Pueblo, Cambio y Democracia (PCD) Popular Roldosista: Quito; f. 1980; centre-left; committed to policies of fmr Pres. Jaime Roldós; Dir LEÓN ROLDÓS AGUILERA; Sec.-Gen. ERNESTO BUENANO CABRERA.
  Unión Democrática Popular (UDP): Leader JORGE CHIRIBOGA.
Frente Radical Alfarista (FRA): Quito; f. 1972; Leader IVÁN CASTRO PATIÑO.
Frente de Reconstrucción Nacional (FRN): centre-right coalition comprising the following parties:
  Alianza Popular Revolucionaria Ecuatoriana (APRE): centrist.
  Coalición Nacional Republicana (CNR): Quito; f. 1986; fmrly Coalición Institucionalista Demócrata (CID).

ECUADOR

Partido Conservador (PC): Quito; f. 1855, traditional rightist party; Dir José Terán Varea.

Partido Liberal Radical (PLR): Quito; f. 1895; held office from 1895 to 1944 as the Liberal Party which subsequently divided into various factions; carries on the traditions of the old party; Dir Carlos Julio Plaza A.

Partido Nacionalista Revolucionario (PNR): Calle Pazmiño 245, Of. 500, Quito; f. 1969; supporters of Dr Carlos Julio Arosemena Monroy; Dir Dr Mauricio Gándara.

Partido Nacional Velasquista (PNV): f. 1952; centre-right; Leader Alfonso Arroyo Robelly.

Partido Social Cristiano (PSC): Quito; f. 1951; centre-right party; Pres. Camilo Ponce; Leaders Sixto Durán Ballén, León Febres Cordero Rivadeneira.

Partido Roldosista Ecuatoriano (PRE): Quito; f. 1982; Dir Abdalá Bucaram Ortiz.

The following guerrilla groups are active:

Fuerzas Armadas Populares Eloy Alfaro—Alfaro Vive ¡Carajo! (Eloy Alfaro Popular Armed Forces—Alfaro Lives, Damn it!): f. 1982; left-wing; supports Izquierda Democrática; Leader Rosa Mireya Cárdenas; 3,000 mems (est).

Montoneros Patria Libre (MPL): f. 1986; advocates an end to authoritarianism.

Diplomatic Representation

EMBASSIES IN ECUADOR

Argentina: Avda Amazonas 477, Apdo 2937, Quito; tel. 562-292; telex 2136; Ambassador: (vacant).

Belgium: Austria 219 e Irlanda, Quito; telex 2767; Ambassador: Roger Tyberghein.

Bolivia: Quito; Ambassador: Eusebio Moreira.

Brazil: Camilo Destruge 130, Quito; telex 2218; Ambassador: José de Meira Penna.

Bulgaria: Quito; Chargé d'affaires: Marin Kostov.

Chile: Edif. Rocafuerte 4° y 5°, Avda Amazonas 325 y Washington, Quito; telex 2167; Ambassador: Gabriel van Schouwen Figueroa.

China, People's Republic: Quito; Ambassador: Pan Wenjie.

Colombia: Calle San Javier 169, Casilla 2923, Quito; telex 2156; Ambassador: Laureano Alberto Arellano.

Costa Rica: Quito; Ambassador: Félix Cortez.

Cuba: Quito; Ambassador: Carlos Zamora.

Czechoslovakia: Calle General Salazar 459 y Coruña, Quito; telex 2478; Ambassador: Julius Stang.

Dominican Republic: Avda 6 de Diciembre 4629, Quito; Ambassador: Mario Pena.

Egypt: Edif. Araucaria 9°, Baquedano 222 y Reina Victoria, Apdo 9355, Sucursal 7, Quito; tel. 235-046; telex 2154; Ambassador: Esmat Naguib.

El Salvador: Calle Antonio de Ulloa 2835, Sector Rumipamba, Quito; tel. 245-315; telex 2411; Ambassador: Manuel A. Calderón.

France: Plaza 107 y Avda Patria, Apdo 536, Quito; tel. 560-789; telex 2146; Ambassador: Michel Perrin.

German Democratic Republic: Calle Ignacio Bossano 460 y Játiva, Apdo 102, Quito; tel. 453-814; telex 2241; Ambassador: Heinz Löhn.

Germany, Federal Republic: Avda Patria y 9 de Octubre, Quito; telex 2222; Ambassador: Dr Josef Engels.

Guatemala: Avda 6 de Diciembre 2636, Quito; Ambassador: Juan Rendón M.

Holy See: (Apostolic Nunciature), Avda Orellana 692, Apdo 4543-A, Quito; tel. 528-783; Nuncio: Mgr Vincenzo Farano.

Honduras: Cordero 279 y Plaza, Quito; telex 2805; Ambassador: Antonio Molina O.

Hungary: Avda República de El Salvador 733 y Avda Portugal, Quito; tel. 459-700; telex 2255; Ambassador: Ferenc Dragon.

Israel: 12 de Octubre 532, 4°, Quito; telex 2174; Ambassador: Naphtali Gal.

Italy: Calle La Isla 111, POB 072-A, Quito; tel. 522-015; telex 2715; Ambassador: Severio Callea.

Japan: Avda Amazonas 239 y 18 de Septiembre, Quito; telex 2185; Ambassador: H. Nishamiya.

Directory

Korea, Republic: Edif. el Libertador 5° A y B, Carrión 256, Quito; telex 2868; Ambassador: Yoon Tae-Hyun.

Mexico: Avda 6 de Diciembre 4843, Casilla 6371, Quito; tel. 457-820; telex 2395; Ambassador: Carlos A. de Icaza.

Netherlands: Edif. Club de Leones Central 3°, Avda de las Naciones Unidas entre Avdas 10 de Agosto y Amazonas, Apdo 2840, Quito; telex 2576; Ambassador: Dr J. Weidema.

Panama: Calle Pazmiño 245 y Avda 6 de Diciembre, Quito; Ambassador: Roberto Samuel Fábrega Goytia.

Paraguay: Avda Gaspar de Villarroel 2013 y Avda Amazonas, Casilla 139-A, Quito; tel. 245-871; telex 2260; Ambassador: Dr Gilberto Caniza Sánchiz.

Peru: Edif. España Pent-House, Avda Colón y Amazonas, Quito; Ambassador: Felipe Valdivieso Belaúnde.

Poland: Quito; Chargé d'affaires: Czesław Bugajski.

Romania: Avda República del Salvador 482 e Irlanda, Quito; telex 2230; Ambassador: Gheorghe Dobra.

Spain: La Pinta 455 y Amazonas, Casilla 9322, Quito; tel. 232-557; telex 2816; Ambassador: José Luis de la Guardia.

Sweden: Avda 10 de Agosto 1865, Quito; telex 2396; Ambassador: Christian Bausch.

Switzerland: Catalina Herrera 120 y Avda Amazonas, 2°, Casilla 4815, Quito; tel. 241-504; telex 2592; Chargé d'affaires a.i.: François Pillonel.

USSR: Reina Victoria 462 y Roca, Quito; Ambassador: Guerman E. Chliapnikova.

United Kingdom: González Suárez 111, Casilla 314, Quito; tel. 230-070; telex 2138; Ambassador: Michael W. Atkinson.

USA: Avda 12 de Octubre y Patria 120, Quito; tel. 548-000; telex 2329; Ambassador: Fernando E. Rondon.

Uruguay: Edif. Sonelsa 2°, Calle Mariscal Foch s/n y Avda 6 de Diciembre, Quito; tel. 237-151; telex 2657; Ambassador: Dr Jorge Pérez Otermin.

Venezuela: Coruña 1733 y Belo Horizonte, Apdo 688, Quito; tel. 230-781; telex 22160; Ambassador: Luis Rodríguez Malaspina.

Yugoslavia: Gen. Francisco Salazar 958 y 12 de Octubre, Quito; tel. 526-218; telex 2633; Ambassador: Samuilo Protić.

Judicial System

Note: In August 1984 an amendment to the Constitution was passed to reduce the term of Supreme Court justices from six to four years. Following the appointment of the 16 Supreme Court justices by Congress, a dispute broke out between Congress and the Government, which opposed the appointments on the grounds that they were 'unconstitutional'. In December 1984 the dispute was resolved when Congress agreed to waive its prerogative to select the 16 Supreme Court justices and allowed the Government to make the new appointments.

Attorney-General: Jorge Maldonado.

Supreme Court of Justice: Palacio de Justicia, Avda 6 de Diciembre y Piedrahita, Quito; tel. 230-200; Pres. Fernando Cásares; 15 Judges and two Fiscals.

Higher or Divisional Courts: Ambato, Cuenca, Guayaquil, Ibarra, Loja, Portoviejo, Quito, Riobamba, El Oro-Latacunga and Esmeraldas; 44 judges.

Provincial Courts: in 15 towns; 35 Criminal, 42 Provincial, 87 Cantonal, 445 Parochial Judges.

Special Courts: for juveniles and for labour disputes.

Religion

There is no state religion but about 90% of the population are Roman Catholics. There are representatives of various Protestant Churches and of the Jewish faith in Quito and Guayaquil.

CHRISTIANITY

The Roman Catholic Church

Ecuador comprises three archdioceses, 10 dioceses, one territorial prelature, seven Apostolic Vicariates and one Apostolic Prefecture.

Bishops' Conference: Conferencia Episcopal Ecuatoriana, Apdo 1081, Avenida América 1866 y Lagasca, Quito; tel. 524-568; f. 1985; Pres. Bernardino Echeverría Ruiz, Archbishop of Guayaquil.

ECUADOR

Archbishop of Cuenca: Luis Alberto Luna Tobar, Casilla 46, Calle Bolívar 736, Cuenca; tel. 823-651.
Archbishop of Guayaquil: Bernardino Echeverría Ruiz, Arzobispado, Apdo 254, Calle Clemente Ballén 501, Guayaquil; tel. 512-778.
Archbishop of Quito: Antonio J. González Zumárraga, Arzobispado, Apdo 106, Calle Chile 1122, Quito; tel. 210-703.

The Baptist Church
The Baptist Convention of Ecuador: POB 3236, Guayaquil; tel. 384-865; Pres. Rev. David Fajarde; Sec. Jorge Moreno Chavarría.

The Methodist Church
The Methodist Church: Evangelical United Church, Rumipamba 915, Apdo 236-A, Quito; 800 mems, 2,000 adherents.

BAHÁ'Í FAITH
The National Spiritual Assembly of the Bahá'ís: Apdo 869-A, Quito; tel. 231-379; mems resident in 1,121 localities.

The Press

PRINCIPAL DAILIES
Quito
El Comercio: Chile 1347, Apdo 57, Quito; tel. 260020; telex 2246; f. 1906; morning; conservative; Proprs Compañía Anónima El Comercio; Dir Jaime Chávez Granja; circ. 130,000.

Hoy: Quito; liberal; Editor Benjamín Ortiz.

El Tiempo: Avda América y Villalengua, Apdo 3117, Quito; f. 1965; morning; independent; Proprs Editorial La Unión, CA; Pres. Antonio Granda Centeno; Editor Eduardo Granda Garces; circ. 35,000.

Ultimas Noticias: Chile 1345, Apdo 57, Quito; tel. 260020; telex 2246; f. 1938; evening; independent; commercial; Proprs Compañía Anónima El Comercio; Dir David Mantilla Cashmore; circ. 90,000.

Guayaquil
Expreso: Guayaquil; morning; independent; Dir Galo Martínez; circ. 30,000.

La Razón: Avda 9 de Octubre 427, Apdo 5832, Guayaquil; evening; independent; f. 1964; Dir Jorge Pérez Concha; circ. 28,000.

El Telégrafo: Avda 10 de Agosto 601 y Boyacá, Apdo 415, Guayaquil; tel. 323-265; telex 3473; f. 1884; morning; independent; commercial; Proprs El Telégrafo CA; Dir-Gen. Gen. Eduardo Arosemena Gómez; Man. Roberto Ycaza Vega; circ. 35,000 (weekdays), 52,000 (Sundays).

El Universo: Escobedo y 9 de Octubre, Apdo 531, Guayaquil; f. 1921; morning; independent; Dir Carlos Pérez Perasso; circ. 190,000 (weekdays), 210,000 (Sundays).

There are local daily newspapers of very low circulation in other towns.

PERIODICALS
Quito
La Calle: Casilla 2010, Quito; f. 1956; weekly; politics; Dir Carlos Enrique Carrión; circ. 20,000.

Carta Económica del Ecuador: Toledo 1448 y Coruña, Apdo 3358, Quito; f. 1969; weekly; economic, financial and business information; Pres. Dr Lincoln Larrea B.; circ. 8,000.

Comercio Ecuatoriano: Calle Guayaquil 1242, Apdo 202, Quito; monthly; commerce.

Ecuador Guía Turística: Meja 438, Oficina 43, Quito; f. 1969; tourist information in Spanish and English; Propr Prensa Informativa Turística; Dir Jorge Vaca O.; circ. 30,000.

F × 2t (Fuerza por Talento y Trabajo): Calle Carlos Ibarra No 206, Quito; tel. 519-563; f. 1985; fortnightly; political information; Dir Wilson Almeida Muñoz; Man. Fernando Cedeño; circ. 15,000.

Integración: Solano 836, Quito; quarterly; economics of the Andean countries.

Letras del Ecuador: Casa de la Cultura Ecuatoriana, Avda 6 de Diciembre, Casilla 67, Quito; f. 1944; monthly; literature and art; non-political; Dir Dr Teodoro Vanegas Andrade.

Directory

El Libertador: Olmedo 931 y García Moreno, Quito; f. 1926; Pres. Dr Benjamín Terán Varea.

Mensajero: Benalcázar 562, Apdo 4100, Quito; f. 1884; monthly; religion, culture, economics and politics; Dir José González Poyatos, s.i.; circ. 5,000.

Nueva: Apdo 3224, Quito; monthly; left-wing; Dir Magdalena Jaramillo de Adoum.

Solidaridad: Calle Oriente 725, Quito; tel. 216-541; f. 1982; monthly; publ. of Confederation of Catholic Office Staff and Students of Ecuador; Dir Wilson Almeida Muñoz; Man. Johny Merizalde; circ. 15,000.

This is Ecuador: La Ni a 555 y Avda Amazonas, Quito; f. 1968; monthly; English; tourism; Dir Gustavo Vallejo.

Guayaquil
Análasis Semanal: Guayaquil; weekly; economic and political affairs; Editor Walter Spurrier Baquerizo.

Boletín del Sindicato Médico: Guayaquil; f. 1911; monthly; scientific, literary; independent.

Ecuador Ilustrado: Guayaquil; f. 1924; monthly; literary; illustrated.

Estadio: Aguirre 724 y Boyacá, Apdo 1239, Guayaquil; fortnightly; sport; Dir Xavier Alvarado Roca; circ. 70,000.

Hogar: Aguirre 724 y Boyacá, Apdo 1239, Guayaquil; telex 3423; f. 1964; monthly; Man. Editor Rosa Amelia Alvarado; circ. 35,000.

Vistazo: Aguirre 724 y Boyacá, Apdo 1239, Guayaquil; tel. 326-683; telex 3423; f. 1957; fortnightly; general; Pres. Xavier Alvarado Roca; circ. 85,000.

NEWS AGENCIES
Foreign Bureaux
Agencia EFE (Spain): Palacio Arzobispal, Chile 1178, Apdo 4043, Quito; tel. 512-427; telex 2602; Bureau Chief Emilio Crespo.

Agenzia Nazionale Stampa Associata (ANSA) (Italy): Apdo 2748, Quito; tel. 260-020; telex 2246; Bureau Chief Santiago Jervis Simmons.

Associated Press (AP) (USA): Edif. Sudamérica, 4°, Of. 44, Calle Venezuela 1018 y Mejía, Quito; tel. 570-235; telex 2296; Correspondent Sergio Carrasco.

Deutsche Presse-Agentur (dpa) (Federal Republic of Germany): Pasaje San Luis 104, Edif. Recalde, Of. 402, Quito; tel. 571-214; Correspondent Jorge Ortiz.

Inter Press Service (IPS) (Italy): Edif. Sudamérica 1°, Of. 14, Quito; tel. 215-616; Correspondent Matilde Wolter.

Prensa Latina (Cuba): Edif. Sudamérica 2°, Of. 24, Venezuela 1081 y Mejía, Quito; tel. 519-333; telex 2625; Bureau Chief Omar Sepúlveda.

Reuters (UK): Chile 1345, 4°, Casilla 4112, Quito; tel. 518-185; telex 22620; Correspondent Jorge Aguirre.

Telegrafnoye Agentstvo Sovetskovo Soyuza (TASS) (USSR): Calle Roca 328 y 6 de Diciembre, 2°, Dep. 6, Quito; tel. 511-631; telex 3566; Correspondent Vladimir Gostev.

United Press International (UPI) (USA): Quito; Correspondent Ricardo Polit.

Xinhua (New China) News Agency (People's Republic of China): Edif. Portugal, Avda Portugal y Avda de la República del Salvador No 730, 10°, Quito; telex 2268; Bureau Chief Lin Minzhong.

Publishers

Artes Gráficas Ltda: Avda 12 de Octubre 1637, Apdo 533, Casilla 456-A, Quito; Man. Manuel de Castillo.

Cromograf, SA: Coronel 2207, Casilla 4285, Guayaquil; tel. 346-400; telex 3387; children's books, paperbacks, art productions.

Editorial Ariel: Avda 10 de Agosto No 504, Guayaquil; tel. 519-282; literature, sociology and history.

Editorial de la Casa de la Cultura Ecuatoriana 'Benjamín Carrión': Avda 6 de Diciembre 794, Apdo 67, Quito; tel. 651-753; f. 1944; general fiction and non-fiction, general science; Dir Dr Teodoro Vanegas Andrade.

Editorial Claridad: Quito; tel. 517-442; economics, history, sociology and politics.

Editorial Interamericana del Ecuador: Avda América 542, Quito; tel. 510-592; Man. Manuel de Castillo.

ECUADOR

Editorial y Librería Selecciones: Avda 9 de Octubre No 724 y Boyacá, Guayaquil; tel. 305-807; history, geography and sociology.
Pontificia Universidad Católica del Ecuador: 12 de Octubre 1076 y Carrión, Apdo 2184, Quito; tel. 529-240; literature, natural science, law, anthropology, sociology, politics, economics, theology, philosophy, history and archaeology.
Universidad Central del Ecuador: Departamento de Publicaciones, Servicio de Almacén Universitario, Ciudad Universitaria, Quito.
Universidad de Guayaquil: Departamento de Publicaciones, Biblioteca General, Apdo 3834, Guayaquil; tel. 392-430; f. 1930; general literature, history, philosophy, fiction; Man. Dir LEONOR VILLAO DE SANTANDER.

Radio and Television

There were about 1,900,000 radio receivers and 600,000 television sets in use in 1985.
Asociación Ecuatoriana de Radiodifusión: 911–915 Edif. Gran Pasaje, Guayaquil; independent association; Pres. JORGE AGUILAR V.
Instituto Ecuatoriano de Telecomunicaciones (IETEL): Casilla 3066, Quito; telex 2150; Gen. Man. Ing. VÍCTOR H. GARCÉS POZO.

RADIO

There are nearly 300 commercial stations, 10 cultural stations and 10 religious stations. The following are some of the most important commercial stations:
CRE, Cadena Radial Ecuatoriana: Edif. El Torreón 8°, Avda Boyacá 642, Apdo 4144, Guayaquil; tel. 307-896; telex 3825; Dir R. GUERRERO.
Emisoras Gran Colombia: Casilla 2246, Quito; tel. 211-670; f. 1943; Dir EDUARDO CEVALLOS C.
Radio Colón: Diguja 327, Quito; tel. 453-288; Dir ATAHUALPA RUIZ RIVA.
Radio Cristal: Luque 1407, Guayaquil; Dir ARMANDO ROMERO.
Radio Nacional del Ecuador: Chile 1267, Quito.
Radio Quito: Chile 1347, Quito; tel. 511-228; Dir ALFONSO LASSO BERMEJO.
Radio Tropicana: Edif. El Torreón 8°, Avda Boyacá 642, Apdo 4144, Guayaquil; tel. 307-900; telex 3825; Dir R. GUERRERO.
La Voz de los Andes: Casilla 691, Quito; tel. 241-550; telex 22734; f. 1931; operated by World Missionary Fellowship; programmes in 14 languages including Spanish, English and Quechua; private, non-commercial, cultural, religious; Pres. Dr RONALD A. CLINE; Dir of Broadcasting ROGER STUBBE.

TELEVISION

Corporación Ecuatoriana de Televisión: C. del Carmen, Casilla 1239, Guayaquil; tel. 300-150; telex 3409; Pres. XAVIER ALVARADO ROCA.
Cadena Ecuatoriana de Televisión: Avda de las Américas, frente al Aeropuerto, Guayaquil; tel. 391-555; telex 3530; f. 1969; commercial; Gen. Man. JORGE PÉREZ.
Canal Universitario Católica: Humbolt 3170, Cuenca; tel. 823040; telex 048567; Dir. CÉSAR CORDERO MOSCOSO.
Teleamazonas: Casilla 4844, Quito; tel. 249-600; telex 2244; commercial; Pres. A. GRANDA C.
Telecuatro Guayaquil, SA: 9 de Octubre 1200, Guayaquil; tel. 308-194; telex 3198; Dir. JOSÉ ORUZ GUERRA.
Telemanabí: Apdo 50, Portoviejo; Dir. EDUARDO IZAGUIRRE.
Televisión Esmeraldeña Compañía de Economía Mixta—TESEM: Edif. Mutual V. Torres, Casilla 108, Esmeraldas; tel. 710090; Dir HÉCTOR ENDARA E.
Televisión del Pacífico SA (Telenacional): Murgeón 732, Casilla 130-B, Quito; tel. 540-877; telex 2435; commercial; Man. MODESTO LUQUE BENÍTEZ.
Televisora Ecuatoriana: Emeraldas 865; tel. 234-421; commercial; Dir. GERARDO BABORICH.
Televisora Nacional Cía Ltda—Canal 8: Bellavista, Casilla 3888, Quito; tel. 244-888; telex 2888; commercial; Exec. Pres. CRISTINA MANTILLA DE LARA.

Directory

Finance

(cap. = capital; p.u. = paid up; res = reserves; dep. = deposits; m. = million; amounts in sucres)

Junta Monetaria Nacional (National Monetary Board): Quito; Pres. Ing. FEDERICO ARTETA RIVERA.

BANKING
Supervisory Authority

Superintendencia de Bancos y Seguros: Avda 12 de Octubre 1561, Apdo 424, Quito; tel. 541-582; telex 2148; f. 1927; Superintendent Dr ALFONSO TRUJILLO BUSTAMANTE.

State Banks

Banco Central del Ecuador: Avda 10 de Agosto, Plaza Bolívar, Casilla 339, Quito; tel. 511-649; telex 2165; f. 1927; cap. 841m., res 2,533m., dep. 51,363m. (June 1986); Pres. Ing. FEDERICO ARTETA RIVERA; Gen. Man. Dr CARLOS JULIO EMANUEL MORÁN.
Banco de Desarrollo del Ecuador, SA (BEDE): Páez 655 y Ramírez Dávalos, Casilla 373, Quito; tel. 551-870; telex 2655; f. 1976; cap. 33,343m., res 368m. (July 1984); Pres. CARLOS JULIO AROSEMENA; Gen. Man. MARCO FLORES.
Banco Ecuatoriano de la Vivienda: Avda l0 de Agosto 2270 y Cordero, Casilla 3244, Quito; tel. 521-311; telex 2399; f. 1962; cap. 4,706m., res 560m., dep. 3,955m. (June 1984); Pres. Arq. SIXTO DURÁN BALLÉN C.; Gen. Man. FRANCISCO ALBÓRNOZ CAZARES.
Banco Nacional de Fomento: Ante 107 y 10 de Agosto, Casilla 685, Quito; tel. 230-010; telex 2256; f. 1928; cap. 3,000m., res 2,837m., dep. 9,289m. (June 1984); Pres. JULIO RABASCAL MOSCOSO; Gen. Man. JUAN SALA LARRETA.
Corporación Financiera Nacional CFN: Juan León Mera 130 y Avda Patria, Casilla 163, Quito; tel. 541-600; telex 2193; f. 1964; cap. 2,000m., res 119m. (July 1984); Pres. EDUARDO VILLAQUIRÁN LEBED; Gen. Man. Dr TEODORO ARÍZAGA VEGA.

Commercial Banks
Quito

Banco Amazonas: Avda Amazonas y Santa María, Casilla 1211, Quito; tel. 545-123; telex 2393; f. 1976; affiliated to Banque Paribas; cap. 400m., res 38.1m., dep. 1,065m. (June 1985); Pres. Dr FRANCISCO PARRA GIL; Gen. Man. CARLOS MOSQUERA.
Banco de los Andes: Avda Amazonas 477, Casilla 3761, Quito; tel. 554-215; telex 2214; f. 1973; affiliated to Banco de Bogotá; cap. 247m., res 57m., dep. 1,298m. (June 1984); Pres. RAFAEL ANDRADE OCHOA; Gen. Man. Dr MAURICIO PÉREZ M.
Banco Caja de Crédito Agrícola Ganadero, SA: Avda 6 de Diciembre 225 y Piedrahita, Quito; tel. 528-521; telex 2559; f. 1949; cap 132m., res 41m., dep. 592m. (Aug. 1984); Man. HUGO GRIJALVA GARZÓN; Pres. NICOLÁS GUILLÉN.
Banco Consolidado del Ecuador: Avda Patria 724 y 9 de Octubre, Apdo 9150, Quito; tel. 552-044; telex 2634; f. 1981; cap. 150m., res 1m., dep. 401m. (June 1984); Pres. Dr MARCO TULIO GONZÁLEZ; Gen. Man. RAFAEL PAZMIÑO HOLGUÍN.
Banco Co-operativas: Avda 10 de Agosto 937, Casilla 2244, Quito; tel. 551-933; telex 2651; f. 1965; cap. 75m., res 3m., dep. 693m. (June 1983); Pres. Dr MANUEL PAREJA; Gen. Man. Dr CÉSAR MOSQUERA.
Banco Internacional: Avda Patria 660, Casilla 2114, Quito; tel. 546-222; telex 2195; f. 1973; cap. 238m., res 40m., dep. 3,434m. (June 1984); Pres. FRANCISCO URIBE LASSO; Gen. Man. MANUEL FERNÁNDEZ NEIRA.
Banco del Pichincha, SA: Avda 10 de Agosto y Bogotá, Casilla 717-A, Quito; tel. 210-020; telex 2207; f. 1906; cap. 777m., res 250m., dep. 12,137m. (June 1984); Pres. Dr GONZALO MANTILLA MATA; Gen. Man. JAIME ACOSTA VELASCO.
Banco Popular del Ecuador: Amazonas 648, Casilla 696, Quito; tel. 548-100; telex 2234; f. 1953; cap. 675m., res 302m., dep. 6,068m. (June 1985); Pres. and Gen. Man. GERMÁNICO PINTO DÁVILA (acting).
Banco de Préstamos, SA: Venezuela 659, Casilla 529, Quito; tel. 216-360; telex 2854; f. 1909; cap. 150m., res 21m., dep. 691m. (June 1984); Pres. ALFREDO ALBÓRNOZ ANDRADE; Gen. Man. MAURO INTRIAGO DUNN.
Banco de la Producción, SA: Avda Amazonas y Japón, Apdo 38-A, Quito; tel. 454-100; telex 2376; f. 1978; cap. 260m., res 91m., dep. 1,099m. (June 1984); Pres. RODRIGO PAZ DELGADO; Gen. Man. Lic. JOSÉ MORILLO BATLLE.

ECUADOR

Ambato
Banco de Tungurahua: Montalvo 630, Casilla 173, Ambato; tel. 821-122; telex 02-7186; f. 1979; cap. 50m., res 2m., dep. 329m. (June 1984); Pres. GEORG SONNENHOLZNER; Gen. Man. Dr RODRIGO VÁSCONEZ SEVILLA.

Cuenca
Banco del Austro: Bolívar 547, Casilla 167, Cuenca; tel. 830-222; telex 04-8560; f. 1977; cap. 180m., res 16m., dep. 792m. (June 1984); Pres. JUAN ELJURI ANTÓN; Gen. Man. ANTONIO CHAMOUN JORGGE.

Banco del Azuay, S.A.: Bolívar 797, Casilla 33, Cuenca; tel. 823-130; telex 04-8579; f. 1913; cap. 267m., res 33m., dep. 1,860m. (June 1984); Pres. Dr LUIS CORDERO CRESPO; Gen. Man. Dr CARLOS RENDÓN MORA.

Guayaquil
Banco Bolivariano CA: Pichincha 412, Casilla 10184, Guayaquil; tel. 321-420; telex 04-3659; f. 1980; cap. 437.4m., res 186m., dep. 2,904m. (June 1986); Pres. Abog. JOSÉ SALAZAR BARRAGÁN; Gen. Man. ANGEL TORRES N.; 8 brs.

Banco Continental: General Cordova 811 y Víctor Manuel Rendón, Casilla 9348, Guayaquil; tel. 303-300; telex 04-3418; f. 1974; cap. 501m., res 77m., dep. 2,695m. (June 1984); Pres. ALBERTO BUSTAMANTE ILLINGWORTH; Gen. Man. Dr LEÓNIDAS ORTEGA TRUJILLO.

Banco de Crédito e Hipotecario: P. Icaza 302, Casilla 60, Guayaquil; tel. 306-630; telex 04-3336; f. 1871; cap. 160m., res 11m., dep. 547m. (June 1984); Pres. LUIS NOBOA NARANJO; Gen. Man. PATRICIO FUENTES LEÓN.

FILANBANCO: 12 de Octubre y Pichincha, Apdo 149, Guayaquil; tel. 511-780; telex 04-3173; f. 1908; cap. 920m., res 189m., dep. 7,020m. (June 1984); Pres. Dr LUIS PERE CABANAS; Gen. Man. MIGUEL BADUY AHUAD.

Banco de Guayaquil: P. Ycaza 105, Casilla 1300, Guayaquil; tel. 309-300; telex 04-3671; f. 1923; cap. 297m., res 160m., dep. 3,179m. (June 1984); Pres. Dr José SANTIAGO CASTILLO; Gen. Man. DANILO CARRERA D.

Banco Industrial y Comercial: Pichincha 335 e Illingworth, Casilla 5817, Guayaquil; tel. 522-015; telex 04-3199; f. 1965; cap. 80m., res 42m., dep. 823m. (June 1984); Pres. Dr JUAN A. ILLINGWORTH BAQUERIZO; Gen. Man. GABRIEL MARTÍNEZ INTRIAGO.

Banco del Pacífico: P. Ycaza 200 y Pichincha, Casilla 988, Guayaquil; tel. 522-200; telex 04-3240; f. 1972; cap. 1,001m., res 349m., dep. 10,740m. (June 1984); Exec. Pres. VÍCTOR MASPONS Y BIGAS; Gen. Man. MAURICIO DE WIND.

Banco del Progreso: Primero de Mayo y P. Moncayo, Casilla 11100, Guayaquil; tel. 312-100; telex 04-3662; f. 1981; cap. 850m., res 15m., dep. 3,260m. (Aug. 1986); Pres. ARCADIO AROSEMENA GALLARDO; Gen. Man. FERNANDO ASPIAZU S.

Banco Sociedad General de Crédito: 9 de Octubre 1404 y Machala, Casilla 5501, Guayaquil; tel. 396-700; telex 04-3138; f. 1972; cap. 150m., res 37m., dep. 1,274m. (June 1984); Pres. JOSÉ ANTÓN DÍAZ; Gen. Man. FRANCISCO R. DE AZUERO Y MACHADO.

Banco Territorial: Panamá 814 y V.M. Rendón, Casilla 227, Guayaquil; tel. 305-210; f. 1886; cap. 125m., res 94m., dep. 147m. (Aug. 1985); Pres. FEDERICO GOLDBAUM; Gen. Man. HUGO SUÁREZ BAQUERIZO.

La Previsora Banco Nacional de Crédito: Avda 9 de Octubre 110 y Pichincha, Apdo 1324, Guayaquil; tel. 306-100; telex 04-3429; f. 1919; cap. 350m., res 13m., dep. 3,562m. (June 1984); Pres. JUAN JOSÉ MEDINA; Gen. Man. REINALDO NAVARRETE.

Loja
Banco de Loja: esq. Bolívar y Rocafuerte, Casilla 300, Loja; tel. 960-381; telex 04-4132; f. 1968; cap. 40m., res 47m., dep. 731m. (June 1984); Pres. Dr VÍCTOR EMILIO VALDIVIESO C.; Gen. Man. OSWALDO BURNEO VALDIVIEZO.

Machala
Banco de Machala: Avda 9 de Mayo y Rocafuerte, Casilla 711, Machala; tel. 920-022; telex 04-4479; f. 1962; cap. 330m., res 121.4m., dep. 2,698m. (June 1986); Pres. Dr JOSÉ UGARTE VEGA; Gen. Man. ESTEBAN QUIROLA FIGUEROLA; 6 brs.

Portoviejo
Banco Comercial de Manabí, SA: 10 de Agosto 600 y 18 Octubre, Portoviejo; tel. 653-888; telex 6180; f. 1980; cap. 117m., res 21m., dep. 720m. (June 1985); Pres. Dr RUBÉN DARÍO MORALES; Gen. Man. ARISTO ANDRADE DÍAZ.

Foreign Banks
Banco Holandés Unido, SA (Netherlands): Avda 10 de Agosto 911, Casilla 42, Quito; tel. 239-765; telex 2153; f. 1959; cap. 104m., res 68m., dep. 1,335m. (June 1984); Pres. KEES DOEFF; Gen. Man. JEROEN J. B. SANDERS; br. at Guayaquil.

Bank of America (USA): Edif. Cofiec, Avda Amazonas y Patria, Casilla 344, Quito; tel. 527-011; telex 2152; f. 1966; cap. 250m., res 162m., dep. 1,206m. (June 1986); Gen. Man. STEPHEN HOTCHKISS; br. at Guayaquil.

Bank of London and South America Ltd (UK): Avda Amazonas 580, Casilla 556-A, Quito; tel. 548-066; telex 2215; f. 1936; cap. 170m., res 46m., dep. 1,894m. (June 1984); Pres. PETER KNIGHT; Man. MICHAEL HARDING-JONES.

Citibank, NA (USA): Juan León Mera 130 y Patria, Casilla 1393, Quito; tel. 563-300; telex 2134; f. 1959; cap. 253m., res 347m., dep. 4,729m. (July 1985); Gen. Man. JAMES V. DEANE; 2 brs.

Finance Corporations
COFIEC—Compañía Financiera Ecuatoriana de Desarrollo: Avdas Patria y Amazonas, Casilla 411, Quito; f. 1965; cap. 678m., res 85m. (July 1984); Pres. Dr JOSÉ ANTONIO CORREA E.

Financiera Guayaquil, SA: Carchi 702 y 9 de Octubre, 7°, Casilla 2167, Guayaquil; f. 1976; cap. 458m., res 69m. (July 1984); Gen. Man. Dr MIGUEL BABRA LYON.

FINANSA—Financiera Nacional, SA: Avda 6 de Diciembre 2417, entre Orellana y la Niña, Casilla 6420-CCI, Quito; tel. 546200; telex 2884; f. 1976; cap. 694m., res 103.6m. (June 1986); Gen. Man. RICHARD A. PEARSE.

FINANSUR—Financiera del Sur, SA: 9 de Mayo y 9 de Octubre, Casilla 7436, Machala; f. 1979; cap. 600m., res 30m. (July 1984); Pres. Econ. DANILO CARRERA DROUET.

Associations
Asociación de Bancos Privados del Ecuador: Edif. Banco de Préstamos, Avdas 10 de Agosto y Patria, Casilla 768, Quito; f. 1965; 28 mems; Pres. LEÓNIDAS ORTEGAT.

Asociación de Compañías Financieras del Ecuador—AFIN: Robles 653 y Amazonas, 13°, Of. 1310-1311, Casilla 9156, Quito; tel. 550-623; telex 2809; Pres. Dr JOSÉ ANTONIO CORREA.

STOCK EXCHANGE
Bolsa de Valores de Quito CA: Avda Río Amazonas 540, Quito; f. 1969; volume of operations in 1978 US $196m.; Pres Dr MARCO ANTONIO GUZMÁN; Gen. Man. Dr BOLÍVAR CHIRIBOGA VALDIVIESO.

INSURANCE
Instituto Ecuatoriano de Seguridad Social: Avda 10 de Agosto y Bogotá, Apdo 2640, Quito; tel. 547-400; telex 2280; f. 1928; various forms of state insurance provided; the Institute directs the Ecuadorean social insurance system; it provides social benefits, medical service and housing programmes; Dir-Gen. Dr VICENTE BURNEO BURNEO.

National Companies
In 1981 there were 27 insurance companies operating in Ecuador. The following is a list of the eight principal companies, selected by virtue of capital.

Amazonas Cía Anónima de Seguros: V. M. Rendón y Córdova, Apdo 3285, Guayaquil; tel. 306-300; telex 3176; f. 1966; cap. 110m. sucres (1984); Exec. Pres. ANTONIO AROSEMENA.

Cía Reaseguradora del Ecuador, SA: Junín No 105 y Malecón Simón Bolívar, Casilla 6776, Guayaquil; f. 1977; tel. 304-458; telex 04-42960; cap. 20m. sucres (1983); Man. Dir Dr EDUARDO PEÑA TRIVIÑO.

Cía de Seguros Condor, SA: P. Ycaza 302, Apdo 5007, Guayaquil; tel. 305-200; f. 1966; cap. 40m. sucres; Gen. Man. JAIME GUZMÁN ITURRALDE.

Cía de Seguros Ecuatoriano-Suiza, SA: Avda 9 de Octubre 2101 y Tulcán, Apdo 397, Guayaquil; tel. 372-222; telex 3386; f. 1954; cap. 65m. sucres (1986); Gen. Man. Econ. ENRIQUE SALAS CASTILLO.

La Nacional Cía de Seguros Generales, SA: Panamá 809, Apdo 1085, Guayaquil; tel. 307-700; telex 3420; f. 1941; cap. 100m. sucres (1984); Gen. Man. LUCIANO CAGNATO CALIGO.

Panamericana del Ecuador, SA: Avda Amazonas 477 entre Roca y Robles, Edif. Banco de los Andes, 4°, Apdo 3902, Quito; tel. 235-358; telex 2352; f. 1973; cap. 38m. sucres (1984); Gen. Man. JOSÉ ANDINO C.

Seguros Rocafuerte, SA: P. Carbo 505 y 9 de Octubre, Apdo 6491, Guayaquil; f. 1967; cap. 40m. sucres; Gen. Man. Ing. DANIEL CAÑIZARES AGUILAR.

La Unión Cía Nacional de Seguros: Malecón esq. Gral Franco, Apdo 1294, Guayaquil; f. 1943; cap. 62m. sucres; Man. DAVID ALBERTO GOLDBAUM MORALES.

Trade and Industry

CHAMBERS OF COMMERCE AND INDUSTRY

Federación Nacional de Cámaras de Comercio del Ecuador: Avda Olmedo 414, Casilla Y, Guayaquil; tel. 524-928; federation of chambers of commerce; Pres. JORGE BEJARANO ORRANTIA.

Cámara de Comercio de Cuenca: Presidente Córdova 7-51, Casilla 4929, Cuenca; tel. 827116; telex 04 8630; f. 1919; 4,100 mems; Pres. MARCELO BATALLAS ESPINOZA.

Cámara de Comercio de Quito: Avdas República y Amazonas, Casilla 202, Quito; tel. 453011; telex 2638; f. 1906; 6,000 mems; Pres. Dr ALFREDO GALLEGOS.

Cámara de Comercio de Guayaquil: Avda Olmedo 414, Guayaquil; tel. 511130; f. 1889; 3,700 mems; Pres. JORGE BEJARANO ORRANTIA.

Federación Nacional de Cámaras de Industrias: Avdas República y Amazonas, Casilla 2438, Quito; f. 1974; Pres. Ing. PEDRO KOHN TOEPFER.

Cámara de Industrias de Cuenca: Edif. Las Cámaras, Avda Federico Malo 1-155, Casilla 326, Cuenca; tel. 830845; telex 8631; f. 1936; Pres. Dr RAFAEL VEGA VINTIMILLA.

Cámara de Industrias de Guayaquil: Avda 9 de Octubre 910, Casilla 4007, Guayaquil; tel. 302705; telex 3686; f. 1936; Pres. RODOLFO KRONFLE AKEL.

STATE ENTERPRISES AND DEVELOPMENT ORGANIZATIONS

Centro de Desarrollo Industrial del Ecuador—CENDES: Avda Orellana 1715 y 9 de Octubre, Casilla 2321, Quito; tel. 527-100; f. 1962; carries out industrial feasibility studies, supplies technical and administrative assistance to industry, promotes new industries, supervises investment programmes; Gen. Man. Ing. ENRIQUE MACÍAS CHÁVEZ.

Centro Nacional de Promoción de la Pequeña Industria y Artesanía (CENAPIA): Quito; agency to develop small-scale industry and handicrafts; Dir Ing. ARTURO CELY LAZO.

Centro de Reconversión Económica del Austro (CREA): Bolívar y Cueva, Cuenca; tel. 830799; telex 8610; f. 1959; development organization; Dir Lic. DANIEL TORAL V.

Consejo Nacional de Desarrollo (CONADE): Juan Larrea y Arenas, Quito; formerly Junta Nacional de Planificación y Coordinación Económica; aims to formulate a general plan of economic and social development and supervise its execution; also to integrate local plans into the national; Chair. Dr BLASCO PEÑAHERRERA PADILLA.

Corporación Estatal Petrolera Ecuatoriana (CEPE) (Ecuadorean State Petroleum Corporation): Avda Colón No 1021, 8° piso, Edif. Banco Continental, Casillas 5007/8, Quito; tel. 544-939; telex 2861; f. 1972 to promote exploration for and exploitation of petroleum and natural gas deposits by initiating joint ventures with foreign and national companies and to act as the agency controlling the concession of onshore and offshore exploration rights; began international marketing of crude petroleum in 1974 and took over the domestic marketing and distribution of petroleum products in 1976; Gen. Man. Gen. Ing. CARLOS ROMO-LEROUX.

Empresa de Comercio Exterior (ECE): Quito; f. 1980 to promote non-traditional exports; State owns 33% share in company; share capital 25m. sucres.

Empresa Pesquera Nacional: state fishing enterprise.

Fondo de Desarrollo del Sector Rural Marginal (Foderuma): f. 1978 to allot funds to rural development programmes in poor areas; initial cap. 100m. sucres.

FONADE—Fondo Nacional de Desarrollo: f. 1973; national development fund to finance projects as laid down in the five-year plan.

Fondo Nacional de Preinversión—FONAPRE: f. 1974 to undertake feasibility projects before investment is made by FONADE; Gen. Man. Econ. ALBERTO CÁRDENAS DÁVILA.

Fondo de Promoción de Exportaciones—FOPEX: Juan León Mera 130 y Avda Patria, Casilla 163, Quito; f. 1972; export promotion; Dir Dr JUAN VILLACÍS A.

Instituto de Colonización de la Región Amazónica (INCRAE): f. 1978 to encourage settlement in and economic development of the Amazon region.

Instituto Ecuatoriano de Electrificación (INECEL): f. 1961; state enterprise for the generation, transmission and distribution of electric energy; Gen. Man. Ing. HANS COLLIN MORALES.

Instituto Ecuatoriano de Recursos Hidráulicos—INEHRI: undertakes irrigation and hydroelectric projects; Man. Ing. PEDRO ALAVA GONZÁLEZ.

Instituto Ecuatoriano de Reforma Agraria y Colonización (IERAC): f. 1973 to supervise the Agrarian Reform Law under the auspices and co-ordination of the Ministry of Agriculture; Dir Ing. RAFAEL PÉREZ REINA.

Organización Comercial Ecuatoriana de Productos Artesanales—OCEPA: Páez 552 y Carrión, Casilla 2948, Quito; tel. 230-879; telex 22062; f. 1964; to develop and promote national arts and crafts; Gen. Man. NANCY VARGAS.

Programa Nacional del Banano y Frutas Tropicales: Pichincha 103, Guayaquil; to promote the development of banana and tropical fruit cultivation.

Programa Regional de Desarrollo del Sur del Ecuador (PREDESUR): Muroz 146, Quito; f. 1972 to promote the development of the southern area of the country; Dir Ing. LUIS CARRERA DE LA TORRE.

Superintendencia de Compañías del Ecuador: Roca 660 y Avda Amazonas, Casilla 1387, Quito; tel. 525-022; telex 2595; responsible for the social and economic development of commercial enterprises; Pres. TERESA MINUCHE DE MERA.

EMPLOYERS' ASSOCIATIONS

Asociación de Cafecultores del Cantón Piñas: García Moreno y Abdón Calderón, Piñas; coffee growers' association.

Asociación de Comerciantes e Industriales: Boyacá 1416, Guayaquil; traders' and industrialists' association.

Asociación de Industriales Textiles del Ecuador—AITE: Avdas República y Amazonas, Edif. Las Cámaras 8°, Casilla 2893, Quito; telex 2770; f. 1938; textile manufacturers' association; 34 mems; Pres. RICHARD C. HANDAL; Sec.-Gen. JOSÉ LUIS ALARCÓN.

Asociación de Productores Bananeros del Ecuador—APROBANA: Malecón 2002, Guayaquil; banana growers' association.

Asociación Nacional de Empresarios—ANDE: Edif. España 6°, Of. 67, Avda Colón y Amazonas, Casilla 3489, Quito; tel. 238-507; national employers' association.

Asociación Nacional de Exportadores de Cacao y Café: Casilla 4774, Manta; cocoa and coffee exporters' association.

Cámara de Agricultura: Casilla 560, Quito; tel. 230-195; Pres. Ing. NICOLÁS GUILLÉN.

Consorcio Ecuatoriano de Exportadores de Cacao y Café: Abdón Calderón y García Moreno, Piñas; cocoa and coffee exporters' consortium.

Corporación Nacional de Exportadores de Cacao y Café: Sucre 106 y Malecón, Guayaquil; cocoa and coffee exporters' corporation.

Federación Nacional de Cooperativas Cafetaleras: Guayaquil 1242, Of. 304, Quito; coffee co-operatives federation.

There are several other coffee and cocoa organizations.

TRADE UNIONS

Frente Unitario de Trabajadores (FUT): f. 1971; left-wing; 300,000 mems; Pres. FROILAN ASANZA; comprises:

Confederación Ecuatoriana de Organizaciones Clasistas—CEDOC: POB 3207, Calle Rocafuerte 1477, Quito; tel. 519-351; f. 1938; affiliated to CMT and CLAT; socialist; Pres. DAVID TENESACA; Sec.-Gen. GERMÁN BARRAGÁN; 130,000 mems (est.) organized in 19 provinces.

Confederación Ecuatoriana de Organizaciones Sindicales Libres—CEOSL: Casilla 1373, Quito; tel. 522-511; f. 1962; affiliated to ICFTU and ORIT; Pres. JOSÉ CHÁVEZ CHÁVEZ; Sec.-Gen. JULIO CHANG CRESPO.

Confederación de Trabajadores del Ecuador—CTE (Confederation of Ecuadorean Workers): Casa del Obrero, Plaza del Teatro, Manabí 267, Quito; f. 1944; admitted to WFTU and

ECUADOR

CSTAL; backed by Communist party; Leaders JUAN VÁSQUEZ, EDGAR PONCE; 55,000 mems (est.) in 200 affiliated unions.

Central Católica de Obreros: Avda 24 de Mayo 344, Quito.

A number of trade unions are not affiliated to the above groups. These include the Federación Nacional de Trabajadores Marítimos y Portuarios del Ecuador—FNTMPE (National Federation of Maritime and Port Workers of Ecuador) and both railway trade unions.

Transport

Ministerio de Obras Públicas y Comunicaciones: Avda 6 de Diciembre y Wilson, Quito; tel. 242-666; telex 2353.

RAILWAYS

All railways are government-controlled. Extensive construction work is being undertaken.

Empresa Nacional de Ferrocarriles del Estado: POB 159, Calle Bolívar 443, Quito; tel. 216-180; Gen. Man. F. M. SÁNCHEZ.

Total length 965 km (1986).

There are divisional state railway managements for the following lines: Guayaquil–Quito, Sibambe–Cuenca and Quito–San Lorenzo.

ROADS

There were 36,187 km of roads in 1985, of which 9,988 km were paved. The Pan-American Highway runs north from Ambato to Quito and to the Colombian border at Tulcán and south to Cuenca and Loja. The severe weather of 1982/83 damaged 1,120 km of roads. In January 1984 the Government announced plans to construct 18 new roads throughout the country.

SHIPPING

Some US $160m. is to be invested in the modernization of Ecuador's principal ports: Guayaquil, Esmeraldas, Manta and Puerto Bolívar.

Flota Bananera Ecuatoriana, SA: Edif. Gran Pasaje 9°, Picaza 437, Casilla 6883, Guayaquil; tel. 309-333; telex 43218; f. 1967; owned by Government of Ecuador and private stockholders; Pres. DIEGO SÁNCHEZ; Gen. Man. JORGE BARRIGA; 5 vessels.

Flota Mercante Grancolombiana, SA: Calle 2 Aguirre 104 y Malecón Simón Bolívar, Casilla 3714, Guayaquil; tel. 512-791; telex 3210; f. 1946 with Colombia and Venezuela; on Venezuela's withdrawal in 1953, Ecuador's 10% interest was increased to 20%; operates services from Colombia and Ecuador to European ports, US Gulf ports and New York, Mexican Atlantic ports and East Canada; offices in Quito, Cuenca, Bahía, Manta and Esmeraldas; Man. Naval Capt. J. ALBERTO SÁNCHEZ; fleet of 29 vessels (21 owned by it and 8 chartered).

Flota Petrolera Ecuatoriana—FLOPEC: Edif. España 4°, Avda Colón y Amazonas, Casilla 535-A, Quito; tel. 552-100; telex 22211; f. 1973; 7 vessels; Pres. S. CORAL.

Transportes Navieros Ecuatorianos—Transnave: Edif. Citibank 6°, Avda 9 de Octubre 416 y Chile, Apdo 4706, Guayaquil; tel. 308-400; telex 43249; 5 vessels; transports general cargo within the European South Pacific Magellan Conference, Japan West Coast South America Conference and Atlantic and Gulf West Coast South America Conference; Pres. MARIO JARAMILLO DEL CASTILLO; Gen. Man. Ing. BORIS TOLEDO BARBERO.

Various foreign lines operate between Ecuador and European ports.

CIVIL AVIATION

There are two international airports: Mariscal Sucre, near Quito, and Simón Bolívar, near Guayaquil.

Aerolíneas Nacionales del Ecuador, SA—ANDES: Apdo 3317, Aeropuerto Simón Bolívar, Guayaquil; telex 3228; f. 1961; headquarters in Miami, USA; regular cargo services Miami–Panamá–Quito, Guayaquil, Cuenca; Chair. Dr ARMANDO ARCE; fleet: 2 CL-44, 1 DC-8-30F, 1 DC-8-50F.

Empresa Ecuatoriana de Aviación—EEA: Edif. Rocafuerte, Avda Jorge Washington 718, Apdo 505, Quito; nationalized 1974; international scheduled passenger services to Argentina, Brazil, Chile, Colombia, Costa Rica, Mexico, Panama, Peru, USA and Venezuela; Pres. Col. LUIS A. ESTRADA; fleet: 2 DC-10-30, 3 Boeing 707-320-B, 1 707-320-C, 3 Boeing 720-B.

Transportes Aéreos Nacionales Ecuatorianos—TAME: Avda Amazonas 1354 y Colón, 6°, Casilla 2665, Quito; brs in Guayaquil and 10 other cities; f. 1962; domestic scheduled services for passengers and freight; charter services abroad; Gen. Man. Brig.-Gen. (retd.) IVÁN PUYOL; fleet: 4 Electra Jet Prop., 2 Twin Otter, 2 HS748, 1 Boeing 727-200, 1 727-100.

The following airlines also offer national and regional services:

Aerotaxis Ecuatorianos, SA—ATESA; Cía Ecuatoriana de Transportes Aéreos—CEDTA; Ecuastol Servicios Aéreos, SA; Ecuavia Cía Ltda; Sociedad Ecuatoriana de Transportes Aéreos—SAETA; Servicios Aéreos Nacionales—SAN; Aeroturismo Cía Ltda—SAVAC.

Tourism

The number of tourists visiting Ecuador rose from 172,000 in 1975 to 217,008 in 1982.

Asociación Ecuatoriana de Agencias de Viajes y Turismo—ASECUT: Amazonas 657 y Ramírez Dávalos, Casilla 1210, Quito; Apdo 510, Guayaquil; tel. 529-253; telex 2924; f. 1953; Pres. ANDRÉS PÉREZ ESPINOSA.

Dirección Nacional de Turismo: Reina Victoria 514 y Roca, Quito; f. 1964; tel. 239-044; Exec. Dir FRANCISCO AVILÉS.

Atomic Energy

Comisión Ecuatoriana de Energía Atómica: Cordero 779 y Avda 6 de Diciembre, Casilla 2517, Quito; f. 1968; research in nuclear physics radio-isotopes, radio-biology, chemistry and medicine; in 1975 it took over the production and sale of radioactive minerals; Exec. Dir. Ing. FAUSTO MUÑOZ RIBADENEIRA.

EGYPT

Introductory Survey

Location, Climate, Language, Religion, Flag, Capital

The Arab Republic of Egypt occupies the north-eastern corner of Africa, with an extension across the Gulf of Suez into the Sinai Peninsula, sometimes regarded as lying within Asia. Egypt is bounded to the north by the Mediterranean Sea, to the north-east by Israel, to the east by the Red Sea, to the south by Sudan, and to the west by Libya. The climate is arid, with a maximum annual rainfall of only 200 mm (8 in) around Alexandria. More than 90% of the country is desert, and some 99% of the population live in the valley and delta of the River Nile. Summer temperatures reach a maximum of 43°C (110°F) and winters are mild, with an average day temperature of about 18°C (65°F). Arabic is the official language. Many educated Egyptians also speak English or French. More than 80% of the population are Muslims, mainly of the Sunni sect. The remainder are mostly Christians, principally Copts, who number some 6m. The national flag (proportions 3 by 2) has three equal horizontal stripes, of red, white, and black; the white stripe has, in the centre, the national emblem (a shield superimposed on a hawk, with a scroll beneath) in gold. The capital is Cairo.

Recent History

Egypt, a province of Turkey's Ottoman Empire from the 16th century, was occupied by British forces in 1882. The administration was controlled by British officials, although Egypt remained nominally an Ottoman province until 1914, when a British protectorate was declared. The United Kingdom (UK) granted nominal independence to Egypt on 28 February 1922. Fuad I, the reigning Sultan since 1917, became King of Egypt. He was succeeded in 1936 by his son, King Faruq (Farouk). The Anglo-Egyptian Treaty of 1936 recognized full Egyptian sovereignty and provided for the gradual withdrawal of British troops, while giving the UK the right to maintain a garrison on the Suez Canal, which links the Mediterranean and Red Seas, and to use Alexandria and Port Said as naval bases. The treaty also restored the Anglo-Egyptian condominium over the Sudan (which remained in force until Sudanese independence on 1 January 1956). The Italian invasion of Egypt in 1940 and the subsequent Libyan campaign postponed the departure of British forces. After the Second World War, British forces withdrew from Egypt, except for a military presence in the Suez Canal Zone. When the British mandate in Palestine was ended in 1948, Arab armies intervened to oppose the newly-proclaimed State of Israel. A cease-fire was agreed in 1949, leaving Egyptian forces occupying the Gaza Strip.

On 23 July 1952 King Farouk's unpopular regime, widely recognized as corrupt, was overthrown by a bloodless military coup. Power was seized by a group of young army officers, the 'Free Officers', led by Lt-Col Gamal Abd an-Nasir (Nasser). Three days later, Farouk abdicated in favour of his infant son, Ahmad Fuad II, and went into exile. After the coup, Gen. Muhammad Nagib (Neguib) was appointed Commander-in-Chief of the Army and Chairman of the Revolution Command Council (RCC), a nine-member military junta. In September 1952 Gen. Neguib was appointed Prime Minister and Military Governor of Egypt, with Col Nasser as Deputy Prime Minister. In December 1952 the 1923 Constitution was abolished, and in January 1953 all political parties were dissolved. On 18 June 1953 the monarchy was abolished and Egypt was proclaimed a republic, with Gen. Neguib as President and Prime Minister. In April 1954 President Neguib was succeeded as Prime Minister by Col Nasser. In October Egypt and the United Kingdom signed an agreement concerning the Suez Canal, providing for the withdrawal of all British forces by June 1956. In November 1954, following a dispute within the military regime, President Neguib was relieved of all his remaining posts, and Col Nasser became acting Head of State.

The establishment of military rule was accompanied by wide-ranging reforms, including the redistribution of land, the promotion of industrial development and the expansion of social welfare services. In foreign affairs, the new regime was strongly committed to Arab unity, and Egypt played a prominent part in the Non-Aligned Movement. In 1955, having failed to secure Western armaments on satisfactory terms, Egypt accepted military assistance from the USSR.

In January 1956 Col Nasser proclaimed a new Egyptian constitution, providing for a strong presidency. On 23 June the Constitution was approved by a national referendum, and Nasser was elected President (unopposed). The RCC was dissolved on the next day. In July 1956, following the departure of British forces, the US and British Governments withdrew their offers of financial assistance for Egypt's most ambitious development project, the construction of the Aswan High Dam on the River Nile. In response, President Nasser announced the nationalization of the Suez Canal Company, so that revenue from Canal tolls could be used to finance the High Dam's construction. The take-over of the Canal was a cause of great concern to Israel, Britain and France, and Israel invaded the Sinai Peninsula on 29 October. Britain and France began military operations against Egypt two days later. Strong pressure from the UN and the US Government resulted in a cease-fire on 6 November, and supervision by the UN of the invaders' withdrawal.

Egypt and Syria, although geographically separate, merged in February 1958 to form a single country, the United Arab Republic (UAR), with Nasser as President. The new nation strengthened earlier ties with the USSR and other countries of the East European bloc. In September 1961 Syria seceded from the UAR, and resumed its separate independence, after the army had seized power there. However, Egypt retained the title of UAR until September 1971. Further attempts at federating Egypt, Syria and Iraq during the early 1960s proved unsuccessful. Earlier, in 1958, the UAR and Yemen formed a federation called the United Arab States, but this was dissolved at the end of 1961. Following the death in September 1962 of the Imam Ahmad of Yemen, a military coup deposed his successor, and the rebels proclaimed the Yemen Arab Republic (YAR). Civil war broke out between royalist forces, supported by Saudi Arabia, and republicans, aided by Egyptian troops. The republicans eventually gained control, and Egyptian forces withdrew from the YAR in 1967.

President Nasser continued to enjoy immense prestige throughout the Arab world and beyond. Internally, he was regarded as the founder of modern Egypt. In December 1962 Nasser established the Arab Socialist Union (ASU) as the country's only recognized political organization. In May 1967 he secured the withdrawal of the UN Emergency Force from Egyptian territory. Egypt subsequently reoccupied Sharm esh-Sheikh, near the southern tip of the Sinai Peninsula, and closed the Straits of Tiran to Israeli shipping. These actions provoked the 'Six-Day War' of June 1967, when Israel quickly defeated neighbouring Arab states, including Egypt. The war left Israel in control of the Gaza Strip and a large area of Egyptian territory, including the whole of Sinai. The Suez Canal was blocked, and remained closed until June 1975. Following the Arab defeat, President Nasser announced his resignation but, in response to massive public demonstrations of support, he agreed to remain in office.

In December 1969 the office of Vice-President was re-established when Col Anwar Sadat, who had held the post in 1964–66, was reappointed. President Nasser died suddenly in September 1970, and was succeeded by Col Sadat. In October the accession of President Sadat was confirmed by referendum. In September 1971 the UAR was renamed the Arab Republic of Egypt, and a new constitution took effect. In the early years of his rule, Sadat followed Nasser's aim of unity with other Arab states. However, plans for union with Libya came to nothing in 1973. The Federation of Arab Republics (Egypt, Libya and Syria) came into being in 1972, but proved ineffective. Relations with

Libya later deteriorated to such an extent that open warfare occurred on the border in July 1977.

Egypt's relations with the USSR also deteriorated in the 1970s. In 1972 the Egyptian Government expelled Soviet military advisers, and in March 1976 Egypt terminated its Treaty of Friendship with the USSR. Relations with the USA, on the other hand, became closer when President Sadat came to rely increasingly on US aid.

An uneasy cease-fire with Israel lasted until October 1973, when Egyptian troops crossed the Suez Canal to recover territory which had been lost in 1967. After 18 days of fighting, a cease-fire was arranged. Dr Henry Kissinger, the US Secretary of State, negotiated disengagement agreements in 1974 and September 1975, by which Israel evacuated territory in Sinai, and Israeli and Egyptian forces were separated by a buffer zone under the control of UN forces.

A dramatic peace-making initiative was made by President Sadat in November 1977, when he visited Israel and addressed the Knesset. Many Arab countries opposed the visit on the grounds that it undermined Arab unity. Syria, Libya, Algeria, Iraq and the People's Democratic Republic of Yemen, together with the Palestine Liberation Organization (PLO), condemned Egypt in December 1977, and Egypt consequently broke off diplomatic relations with them.

As a result of its isolation, Egypt experienced difficulty in attempting to produce anything tangible out of Sadat's peace initiative, but in September 1978, after talks at Camp David in the USA (under the guidance of President Carter), President Sadat and Menachem Begin, Prime Minister of Israel, signed two agreements. The first was a 'framework of peace in the Middle East' and the second was a 'framework for the conclusion of a peace treaty between Egypt and Israel'. The first agreement provided for a five-year transitional period during which the inhabitants of the Israeli-occupied West Bank of the Jordan and the Gaza Strip would obtain full autonomy and self-government, and the second agreement provided for the signing of a peace treaty between Egypt and Israel by 17 December 1978. After some difficulties, the peace treaty was signed in March 1979, and Israel subsequently made phased withdrawals from the Sinai Peninsula, the last of which took place in April 1982. Syria, Algeria, Libya and the PLO had met in Damascus in September 1978 and condemned the Camp David agreements, and in Baghdad in March 1979 the Council of the Arab League expelled Egypt from the League and introduced political and economic sanctions. Oman, Sudan and Somalia were the only Arab countries which did not sever their ties with Egypt. Egypt, however, continued to strengthen relations with Israel, and in February 1980 the two countries exchanged ambassadors for the first time.

In 1974 Sadat began to introduce a more liberal political and economic regime. Foreign investment was encouraged but was slow to arrive. Inflation, overcrowding and administrative shortcomings were the main internal problems.

Political parties (banned since 1953) were allowed in the 1976 elections for the People's Assembly. They were legalized in June 1977 but overshadowed in July 1978, when Sadat formed a new political party, the National Democratic Party, with himself as leader. The special constitutional status of the ASU was terminated in April 1979. Sadat was engaged in a massive campaign of arrests of Muslim fundamentalists, whose influence had grown after the Iranian revolution in 1979, when he was assassinated on 6 October 1981 by members of Islamic Jihad, a group of fundamentalists (belonging to the community of Islamic extremists called gamaat, or 'the (Islamic) groups'), led by Lt Khalid Islambouly, who was later executed. Sadat was succeeded by Lt-Gen. Hosni Mubarak, who had been Vice-President since April 1975 and was previously Commander-in-Chief of the Air Force. Although many detainees were released, Mubarak has continued to order the arrest of fundamentalists, and several thousand have been detained since October 1981. The state of emergency was extended for another year in October 1982 and October 1983. Sadat's ban on demonstrations was lifted in October 1983 but, at the same time, the Minister of the Interior revealed that 13 terrorist organizations had been discovered in the preceding year. Mubarak twice reshuffled the Council of Ministers in 1982, in January and August, in an effort to secure a better economic performance and instituted a campaign against corruption in government.

An electoral law, adopted in July 1983, required parties to receive a minimum of 8% of the total vote to be represented in the People's Assembly. This prompted opposition parties to boycott elections to local councils and to the Shura Council, an advisory assembly. In January 1984 the legality of the re-formed New Wafd Party, perhaps the only opposition party with any prospect of wide popular support, was upheld by the courts after the Government had refused to recognize it on its re-emergence in August 1983.

The new electoral requirements ensured a wide margin of victory for the ruling National Democratic Party (NDP) at elections to the People's Assembly on 27 May 1984. The NDP received 72.9% of the total vote, winning 389 of the 448 elective seats in the Assembly. Of the four other participating parties, only the New Wafd, with 15.1% of the vote, crossed the 8% threshold, and won the remaining 59 seats. It was suggested that the New Wafd's electoral alliance with the Muslim Brotherhood cost the party the support of many of Egypt's estimated 6m. Copts. The opposition parties protested that the elections were undemocratic, accusing the Government of fraud and the intimidation of voters. Dr Ahmad Fuad Mohi ed-Din, who had been Prime Minister since January 1982 and was also Secretary-General of the NDP, died on 5 June 1984. As a result, President Mubarak reshuffled the Council of Ministers on 16 July, appointing Gen. Kamal Hassan Ali, hitherto a Deputy Prime Minister and the Minister of Foreign Affairs, as Prime Minister.

A joint Egypt/Sudan Nile Valley Parliament, a Higher Integration Council and a Joint Fund were established by charter in October 1982. The Parliament's first session was held in May 1983. Relatively powerless in itself, the Parliament was designed as the first step towards the ultimate political and economic integration of the two states. The Higher Integration Council meets regularly to co-ordinate joint economic projects and the progress towards federation, while also acting as a forum to determine policy in foreign affairs in general and on Pan-Arab questions in particular.

In foreign affairs, signs in the mid-1980s that Egypt's period of estrangement from other Arab states was drawing to a close made increasingly plain a division in the Arab world between a 'moderate' grouping (including Jordan, Iraq and, less vocally, the Gulf states), which views the participation of Egypt as indispensable to any diplomatic initiatives for solving the problems of the region, and a 'radical' grouping, led by Syria, which has devoted itself to taking Egypt's place as the leader of the Arab community. Arab investment in Egypt is estimated to have doubled between 1982 and 1984, and in early 1984 it was contributing about 21% of all foreign investment. Libya and Syria are now the only Arab nations to continue the trade boycott of Egypt, and they, together with the People's Democratic Republic of Yemen, dissented from the decision, taken in January 1984, to readmit Egypt to membership of the Organization of the Islamic Conference (OIC, see p. 193). While Libya and Syria have supported the rebels in the revolt against Yasser Arafat's leadership of the Palestine National Liberation Movement (Fatah), the main guerrilla group within the PLO, Egypt has openly backed Arafat, the PLO chairman. In recognition of this fact, Arafat visited President Mubarak for talks in Cairo in December 1983, marking the end of a six-year period of estrangement between Egypt and the PLO. Then, in September 1984, Jordan decided to resume diplomatic relations with Egypt. Although relations between Egypt and Israel cooled, Egypt's progressive rehabilitation had occurred without its being forced to renounce the Camp David agreements or the treaty of 1979 with Israel (much to the annoyance of Syria and Libya).

Egypt's new-found confidence in international affairs in 1984 was demonstrated in its proposal of two formulas for peace in the Gulf war, though neither was taken up by Iran and Iraq. President Mubarak, accompanied by King Hussein of Jordan, made a surprise visit to Baghdad in March 1985, to demonstrate his support for the Iraqi President, Saddam Hussain, despite the fact that there have been no formal diplomatic relations between Egypt and Iraq since 1979. The division of loyalties in the Gulf war reflects the wider split in the Arab world, with Egypt, Jordan, Saudi Arabia and the remaining Gulf states supporting Iraq, while Libya and Syria have backed Iran.

In October 1984 Egypt unilaterally withdrew from the confederation agreement for a 'Union of Arab Republics' which it had signed with Libya and Syria in 1971; while alleged Libyan terrorist and espionage activities, and the continued problem of Muslim fundamentalists pursuing Islamic revolution, encouraged the Government to extend the national state of emergency for 18 months from October 1984 and for a further two years from April 1986.

In April 1985 President Nimeri of Sudan was deposed in a bloodless coup by Lt-Gen. Abd ar-Rahman Swar ad-Dahab. The uncertainty of relations between Egypt and the new regime cast into doubt the tenability of the integration agreements that had been made when President Nimeri was in power. Col Gaddafi of Libya visited Khartoum in May, to show support for the new government, and urged Arabs to overthrow 'reactionary regimes', implicitly including Egypt. Diplomatic relations between Libya and Sudan were restored in April, and a military protocol was signed in Tripoli in July. It was also feared that the presence of ex-President Nimeri in Egypt, where he had been granted political asylum, would embitter relations with the new Sudanese regime, but Lt-Gen. Swar ad-Dahab reaffirmed Sudan's commitment to the integration agreement of 1982 during a visit to Egypt in October, when he and President Mubarak announced the formation of a new joint committee to oversee the acceleration of the integration process in the fields of agriculture and industry. In July 1986, in Cairo, Sudanese lawyers representing the Government of Sudan requested Nimeri's extradition.

Relations with Libya have continued to deteriorate. In July 1985 Col Gaddafi barred Egyptian workers (of whom there were some 100,000 in the country at the time) from Libya, in retaliation against a similar Egyptian measure preventing Libyans from working in Egypt.

Consolidating the contacts that were first made between them after Yasser Arafat's expulsion from Lebanon at the end of 1983, the PLO leader, King Hussein of Jordan and President Mubarak continued their discussions in pursuit of a negotiated settlement of the Palestinian question during 1984 and 1985. Mubarak backed the agreement of February 1985, reached by Yasser Arafat and King Hussein, establishing the principle of a joint Jordanian-Palestinian delegation to take part in a proposed Middle East peace conference, to include the permanent members of the UN Security Council. Israel's rejection of any PLO representation in such a delegation, its demand for direct talks with Jordan, and the USA's refusal to accept the PLO as a negotiating partner until it recognizes Israel's right to exist, prevented the Jordanian-Palestinian initiative from making significant progress.

The credibility of the PLO as a participant in peace negotiations, and of the Jordanian-Palestinian agreement, which had already been damaged by the murder of three Israelis by Palestinian guerrillas in Larnaca, Cyprus, in September 1985, was further compromised, with direct and damaging consequences for Egypt's relations with the USA, when an Italian cruise liner, the *Achille Lauro*, was hijacked in the eastern Mediterranean by four Palestinians, belonging to the Palestine Liberation Front (PLF), on 7 October. The terrorists murdered an American passenger before surrendering to the Egyptian authorities in Port Said. Rather than hold them for trial in Egypt, President Mubarak handed the Palestinians over to Abu al-Abbas, the leader of one of two groups calling themselves the PLF and a member of the PLO's Executive Committee nominally loyal to Arafat, to be tried, as he thought, by the PLO. The USA accused Abu al-Abbas of organizing the hijack, and criticized Mubarak for allowing him to go free. On 10 October US fighter aircraft intercepted the Egyptian airliner that was taking al-Abbas and the hijackers to Tunis, forcing it to land at a US air force base in Sicily. This action aroused considerable anti-American feeling in Egypt. In November an EgyptAir airliner was hijacked to Malta by Palestinians, whom Egypt immediately linked with the renegade PLO leader, Abu Nidal, and his Libyan supporters, though the only clear claim of responsibility came from a group calling itself 'Egypt's Revolution'. Egyptian special forces were sent to Malta to release the 98 passengers who had been taken hostage, but their assault on the aircraft resulted in the deaths of 58 passengers and strong criticism of Egypt's handling of the affair.

The campaign by Muslim fundamentalists in Egypt for the legal system fully to adopt the principles of the Shari'ah (Islamic holy law) intensified in 1985. An amendment to the Constitution, approved by the People's Assembly in 1980, made Islamic law the basis of Egyptian law, and this provision was largely, though not fully, implemented. As well as taking into account the views of a potentially volatile puritan Islamic section of the community, Mubarak wishes to avoid alienating the country's Coptic Christians, who occupy important positions in commerce, industry and the professions. In May 1985 the People's Assembly rejected immediate changes in the legal system, and advocated a thorough study of the small proportion of Egyptian law which does not conform to Islamic precepts before proceeding further. Numerous Muslim fundamentalists, including militant leader Sheikh Hafez Salama, were detained in July for crimes of agitation. However, the relative freedom of the press and of political association, which distinguishes Mubarak's regime from that of Sadat, remains.

The resumption of full diplomatic relations with the Soviet Union was announced in April 1984, and ambassadors were exchanged later in the year. Relations had ceased in 1981, when President Sadat expelled the Soviet Ambassador and 1,000 Soviet experts from Egypt.

Dr Ali Lutfi, a former Minister of Finance under President Sadat, was appointed Prime Minister on 4 September 1985, following the resignation of Gen. Kamal Hassan Ali and his Council of Ministers. The new Council of Ministers contained nine new appointments, and three members, while retaining their former portfolios, were elevated to the rank of Deputy Prime Minister, a post already held by the Minister of Defence, Field Marshal Muhammad Abd al-Halim Abu Ghazalah. The appointment of Dr Lutfi reflected the priority that President Mubarak placed on improving the condition of the economy.

Relations between Egypt and Israel were strained by the latter's invasion of Lebanon in June 1982, and Israel has repeatedly accused Egypt of contraventions of the military provisions of the 1979 peace treaty. In January 1985 Israel and Egypt embarked on a series of talks, the first for two years, to determine the sovereignty of the minute coastal strip of Taba, on the Red Sea, which Israel did not vacate when it left Sinai in 1982. The solution of this problem is viewed by both sides as a precondition of improvement in bilateral relations. In January 1986 Israel agreed to submit the dispute to international arbitration, provided that this was preceded by an eight-month period of conciliation, during which the chosen arbitrators would attempt to secure a compromise solution before delivering a binding decision. After the appointment of arbitrators (three independent and one each from Egypt and Israel) and the demarcation of the Taba enclave had been agreed, the arbitration document was finally approved by both countries on 10 September 1986. The process of arbitration began in December.

On 11 September 1986 President Mubarak of Egypt and Prime Minister Peres of Israel met in Alexandria, Egypt, to discuss ways of reviving the Middle East peace process. After the 'summit' meeting (the first between Egypt and Israel since August 1981), and following the signing of the Taba arbitration agreement, President Mubarak appointed Muhammad Bassiouni, Egypt's former chargé d'affaires in Tel-Aviv, as ambassador to Israel. The previous Egyptian ambassador had been recalled from Israel in 1982, after the Israeli invasion of Lebanon.

In February 1986, reacting to a rumour that their period of service was to be extended by one year to four years, some 17,000 poorly-paid conscripts to the Central Security Force (CSF) went on the rampage in and around Cairo, destroying two luxury hotels and damaging other buildings used by tourists in the Pyramids area of the city. The disturbances lasted for three days and there were clashes between conscripts and the army, which was attempting to restore order. According to government figures, 107 people died as a result of the mutiny; more than 2,500 arrests were made, but some 8,000 conscripts were unaccounted for when the riots ended. There were reports of violence in other cities, including Asyut, Ismailia and Sohag. The Minister of the Interior, Ahmad Rushdi, who was held responsible for the failure of the intelligence services to detect signs of unrest in the CSF, was dismissed and replaced by Maj.-Gen. Zaki Badr.

In November 1986 President Mubarak accepted the resignation of the Prime Minister, Ali Lutfi, and a new Council of Ministers, containing, among 11 changes, a new Minister of

Finance and three other new ministers in positions related to the management of the economy, was appointed under a new Prime Minister, Atif Sidqi. President Mubarak was believed to be critical of Ali Lutfi for his indecisive approach to the country's economic problems, and for giving the impression that Egypt and the IMF were close to reaching an agreement on radical economic reforms which were a condition of financial aid.

Government

Legislative power is held by the unicameral Majlis ash-Sha'ab (People's Assembly). At the general election of May 1984 the number of members in the Assembly was increased from 392 to 458: 10 nominated by the President and 448 directly elected for five years from 48 constituencies. The Assembly nominates the President, who is elected by popular referendum for six years (renewable). The President has executive powers and appoints one or more Vice-Presidents, a Prime Minister and a Council of Ministers. There is also a 210-member advisory assembly, the Shura Council. The country is divided into 26 governorates.

Defence

In July 1986 Egypt had total armed forces of 445,000 (army 320,000, air defence command 80,000, navy 20,000, air force 25,000), with 380,000 reserves. There is a selective three-year period of National Service. Defence expenditure in 1985/86 was estimated at £E 3,650m.

Economic Affairs

Egypt's economy comprises a prosperous, relatively efficient, private sector and a heavily-subsidized, generally inefficient, public sector. In 1983, according to estimates by the World Bank, Egypt's gross national product per head (at average 1981–83 prices) was US $700, having increased at an average rate of 4.1% per year, in real terms, since 1965. The average annual growth of overall gross domestic product (GDP), measured in constant prices, was 3.8% in 1965–73, rising to 8.8% in 1973–83. The rate of growth had declined by the mid-1980s, owing largely, in the view of most observers, to the oil glut which has depressed the economies of the Gulf states.

The move towards a free market economy, which is advocated by many Egyptian experts, seems unlikely, as it would mean the removal of food subsidies and the state enterprises on which, however inefficient, many poor Egyptians depend. As yet, therefore, the Nasserite model prevails. Nasser nationalized private industry, closed the economy to Western investment and created a huge public sector. State enterprises provide about 70% of Egypt's industrial output. Under Sadat, the economy was liberalized and from 1974 an 'open door' policy (*infitah*) was pursued regarding foreign investment. An attempt to cut food subsidies in 1977, however, prompted riots which threatened to topple the Government. An IMF study showed that the proportion of GDP devoted to subsidies rose from 7% in 1978 to 13% in 1981, and has since risen to 25%.

Subsidies on petroleum also place a considerable strain on the nation's finances: the estimated $3,600m. spent on them in 1983 kept oil products at about 17% of their price in the rest of the world. As a result of this support, oil consumption in Egypt is increasing faster than production. According to the Egypt Energy Planning Agency, the consumption of petroleum products in 1982/83 (20m. tons, worth $4,000m.) was 15% up on 1981/82. In 1984 it was estimated that domestic petroleum consumption was rising at an annual rate of between 12% and 15%, while production was increasing by about 7% annually. Domestic use accounted for 46.5% (19.5m. tons) of output in 1983/84, compared with 42.5% in 1982/83. If, as expected, the domestic requirement continues to rise at this rate relative to production, Egypt, which has been a petroleum surplus country only since 1976, will become a net importer again by 1995. The Government is taking some small steps to reduce subsidies but the political sensitivity of the issue has prevented any drastic reform of the system of subsidization. President Mubarak had to withdraw increases in the prices of pasta and cooking fat after rioting in the town of Kafr ed-Dawar in September 1984, though increases in the prices of flour, sugar and sesame seed were retained. Subsidies cost the Government £E 2,996m. ($3,595m.) in 1983/84, about 18% of total budgeted expenditure of £E 16,209m. ($19,450m.). According to IMF estimates, Egypt spent more than $4,000m. or 7% of its GNP on food and fuel subsidies in 1985.

Petroleum production in Egypt is small by Middle East standards, averaging about 785,000 b/d in 1983/84, and between 865,000 b/d and 870,000 b/d in 1984/85, compared with capacity of 1m. b/d. Of the average daily output in 1984/85, about 50% was used locally and 200,000 b/d–250,000 b/d were taken by foreign oil companies under production contracts, which left only some 225,000 b/d available for export. Average output in 1985/86 was almost 900,000 b/d. Petroleum has been the principal earner of foreign currency (accounting for more than 50% of total export revenue in 1984/85) followed by workers' remittances from abroad, Suez Canal tolls and tourism. Revenue from petroleum, however, has been affected by the fall in prices, resulting from the world oil glut and the restriction that is placed on the amount of petroleum available for export by the growth in local consumption. Earnings from exports of petroleum were estimated at $2,142m. in 1984/85, compared with $2,567m. in 1983/84 and a peak of about $3,000m. in 1981/82. Egypt, not being a member of OPEC and having been suspended from membership of OAPEC, is able to maintain a flexible pricing policy. During 1983 the market stabilized to the extent that Egypt, having cut the price of its Suez blend by $2 to $27 per barrel in April, was able to restore the price to $28.50 by a series of four increases up to September. The price of Suez crude petroleum was reduced to $28 per barrel in 1984, and that price was maintained until February 1985. This was consistent with Egypt's policy of supporting OPEC's programme to prevent a collapse in world oil prices. Egypt voluntarily reduced its petroleum production by 30,000 b/d in November 1984, but in 1985 it dissociated itself from OPEC's policies, steadily reducing the price of Suez oil to $25.25 per barrel by July, as demand for oil remained slack. A decline in the value of the US dollar, and in Iranian oil exports, led to increases in the price of all Egyptian blends. After rises in September and October, the price of Suez rose to $26.70 per barrel in December. During 1986, however, the world oil price, already weakened by a surplus of supplies, fell sharply after OPEC decided to increase production in order to secure a 'fair' share of the reduced market. Egypt was forced to cut production and to reduce prices in order to remain competitive, so that, in July, after a series of reductions, the Suez blend was priced at only $7.35 per barrel. Egypt's average output (which was probably about 950,000 b/d in December 1985, rather than the officially acknowledged 870,000 b/d, so as to maximize earnings while prices were relatively high) was cut by some 300,000 b/d in early 1986, and in April exports were reduced to about 50,000 b/d, compared with more than 250,000 b/d at the end of 1985. After OPEC members decided in August 1986 to reintroduce production quotas, the price of petroleum on world markets began to increase again. Accordingly, for the second half of January after several increases, the Suez blend was priced at $17.60 per barrel. Production also rose after August, rising to 940,000 b/d at the end of the year. In January 1987 Egypt promised to reduce its production by 7%, to 870,000 b/d, in line with OPEC quotas. Net petroleum revenues for the first half of 1986 were $341m., compared with $2,612m. for the whole of 1985.

Suez Canal transit rates were raised by an average of 5% in January 1984 and 1985, and by an average of 3.4% in January 1986. Revenue from this source in 1985/86 totalled a record $1,030m., compared with $897m. in 1984/85 and $974m. in 1983/84. The rise in earnings was attributed to the increase in the value of the US dollar, the currency in which canal tolls are paid.

Income in the form of remittances from an estimated 2m. to 2.5m. Egyptians working abroad increased unexpectedly from $1,450m. in 1981/82 to $2,150m. in 1982/83, though they were subject to deteriorating economic conditions in the oil-producing countries where most emigrants work. Adjustments in the exchange rate and improved banking services for expatriate workers increased remittances to $3,931m. in 1983/84, making them Egypt's largest foreign currency earner in that year. There was an unexpectedly small decline of 3.7% in the value of remittances, to $3,785m., in 1984/85. None the less, Egypt is already facing the problem of finding employment for former expatriates after their return from Libya, where Egyptian workers were barred from employment in 1985, and from the Gulf states, where there are fewer jobs and lower wages than heretofore, owing to the recession in the petroleum industry. Egypt estimated that up to 500,000 Egyptians working abroad would be made redundant before the end of 1985. Revenue from tourism fell from $1,000m. in 1981/82, to $600m. in 1982/83 and to about $300m. in 1983/84, but rose to about $1,000m. in 1984/85. An increase in terrorist activity in the Middle East during the second half of 1985, the anti-American reaction in the region following the bombing of Libyan cities by US forces in April 1986, and the revolt of 17,000 conscripts of the Egyptian Central Security Force in February, combined to deter tourists, particularly Americans, from visiting Egypt. Income from tourism was expected to fall by 30% in 1985/86 to about $700m.

In 1978 the agricultural sector accounted for approximately 60% of total export earnings, but by 1979 its contribution had fallen to 50%, and it has continued to decrease, as population growth has outstripped production, and agriculture figured less in government development plans. The proportion of the total labour force involved in agriculture declined from 41.5% in 1977 to 34.6% in 1984/85. Egypt, from a position of self-sufficiency in food during the 1970s, now has to import more than one-half of its food, at an estimated cost of $4,100m. in 1984. The high birth rate puts a strain on this sector of the economy, as it does on the others, and agricultural production (which rose from $19,500m. in 1981/82 to $24,500m. in 1984/85) is failing to keep up with the growth in population. Since 1960 annual per caput wheat consumption has risen from 80 kg to 180 kg, making Egyptians the world's biggest consumers of wheat. Imports of wheat and wheat flour totalled 5.9m. tons in 1983 and an estimated 6.2m. tons in 1984. The returns from the three most lucrative agricultural exports (cotton, rice and oranges) declined after 1974, owing to inadequate investment.

Egypt's external trade deficit has persisted almost without interruption since before the Second World War. It increased from $3,980m. in 1980/81 to $4,620m. in 1981/82. The situation did not improve in 1982/83 and the trade deficit was $5,559m. in 1983/84. By 1984/85 the trade deficit had risen to $7,000m. (imports $10,800m., exports $3,800m.) but, according to IMF estimates, it fell to about $5,700m. in 1985/86 (imports $8,900m., exports $3,200m.), as imports declined, largely owing to a shortage of convertible currency and to limitations on the importation of luxury consumer items, such as cars and hi-fi. The deficit on the current account rose to $1,527m. in 1984/85 from $1,421 in 1983/84, but including imports of US military equipment which do not figure in Central Bank calculations, the deficit was $2,500m. in 1983/84 and $2,950m. in 1984/85. In September 1986 a ban was placed on the import of 210 items, including cars, a range of foodstuffs, building materials and household goods, and 10 new tariff scales were introduced.

As a result of the foreign trade deficits mentioned above, foreign debt servicing costs have increased. In September 1986 the IMF estimated that the overall foreign debt (both civil and military) had risen to US $38,600m. in 1985/86, from $32,500m. in 1984/85, largely owing to petroleum revenue losses. The servicing of foreign debt is the biggest drain on Egypt's resources of foreign currency, accounting for $3,100m. (or about 35% of current earnings) in 1984/85 and $3,400m. in 1985/86, according to IMF estimates. Egypt stands second only to Israel in the amount of aid which it receives from the USA. Egypt's military debt to the USA amounted to $4,550m. at the end of 1984/85 and the interest payment due in 1985/86 was $555m., compared with $481.6m. in the previous year. Egypt is seeking to reschedule its debt and has asked the IMF for a stand-by loan of $1,000m., but has met opposition to the request. Both the IMF and the USA have made further loans and aid to Egypt conditional on the introduction of economic reforms, in particular the reform of the system of state subsidies. Egyptian officials say that the IMF is demanding a 75% cut in the level of subsidies. In 1986 the USA delayed disbursement of $265m. in economic aid (which in 1985/86 totalled $1,300m. of overall aid of $2,300m.) to demonstrate its dissatisfaction with Egypt's progress towards economic reform. However, it released $150m. in March 1986, following the riots in Cairo in February.

In June 1986 the Majlis (People's Assembly) approved a budget for 1986/87 which included a 15% cut in government subsidies to £E 1,700m., from £E 2,000m. in 1985/86 (though the actual level of spending on subsidies is usually significantly higher than the budgeted figure: according to the Central Agency for Mobilization and Statistics, in 1983/84 actual subsidies on basic foods were £E 2,055m. ($2,466m.), compared with the budgeted allowance of £E 1,358m. ($1,630m.)). To compensate those affected by the cut in subsidies and the consequent rise in the prices of basic commodities, a system of cash welfare benefits was proposed, though the political and practical obstacles to enacting such a radical reform are considerable.

A new Five-Year Plan for 1982–87 was unveiled at the end of 1982 with the aims of increasing total investment (particularly in public-sector industrial and agricultural production) and of limiting the growth of the services sector. Particular emphasis was placed on the hydrocarbons sector, with £E 1,300m. being allocated to increase production of petroleum and natural gas from 34.6m. tons in 1981 to 63m. tons in 1987. However, these plans have had to be revised, owing to the crisis in the world petroleum market, and the target for 1986/87 was less than 50m. tons, including 44.2m. tons of oil. The Plan set an average annual real growth rate target of 7.9%. According to the World Bank, however, in a study published in 1985, Egypt has fallen well short of its targets under the Plan. The study puts the growth of GDP in the first two years at only about 6%, while real investment rose by 2.9%, compared with the target of 10.5%.

In December 1984 Egypt's four public sector banks were authorized to purchase dollars at a rate of £E 1.20 = US $1 to attract remittances from Egyptians working abroad who prefer to deal on the 'black market'. A rate of £E 1.12 to the dollar, introduced earlier in the year, failed to attract remittances. Only about 40% of the estimated $4,000m. which is generated annually in remittances reaches Egyptian banks. In January 1985, at the behest of Dr Mustafa as-Said, the Minister of the Economy, a 'floating' exchange rate was established to reflect more accurately the value of the Egyptian pound against the US dollar, to restrain rising imports, and to counter black market transactions by attracting remittances. The rate of exchange remained some 10% below the 'black market' level and failed to divert remittances to the banks. Meanwhile, measures increasing the number of import items requiring official approval, and banking regulations (including the obligation to purchase letters of credit in Egyptian pounds), proved too restrictive, causing long delays for importers, particularly in the private sector, who were competing for short supplies of currency in the banks. Dr as-Said was heavily criticized for the failure of his policies and resigned in March 1985, following a banking scandal which resulted from his 1983 decree banning banks from dealing with certain 'black market' currency operators. As-Said was replaced by Dr Sultan Abu Ali, who immediately withdrew his predecessor's currency regulations. In April 1985 importers were once again allowed to open letters of credit with foreign currency obtained from available sources, including the 'black market'. With the 'floating' exchange rate still in operation, an inevitable consequence of the lifting of import restrictions and the increase in foreign exchange liquidity was that the Egyptian pound lost 20% of its value against the US dollar on the free market. In September the pound slumped against the US dollar, losing more than 25% of its value, to stand at US $1 = £E 1.83. It subsequently strengthened slightly but fell to US $1 = £E 1.95 in December and to US $1 = £E 2.07 in April 1986. The pound stood at US $1 = £E 1.90 in September 1986.

Although it rejects the more far-reaching of the IMF's requested economic reforms (such as a 75% cut in the subsidies bill and the floating of the Egyptian pound), since the end of July 1986 Egypt has begun to implement some of the IMF's minor reforms, abolishing one of the country's four foreign currency exchange rates and reducing subsidies by small amounts on certain commodities, such as petroleum.

Social Welfare

Great progress has been made in social welfare services in recent years. There are comprehensive state schemes for sickness benefits, pensions, health insurance and training. In 1982 Egypt had around 1,480 hospital establishments, with a total of 84,000 beds. The current five-year plan (1982/83–1986/87) aims to increase the number of beds to 88,000. In 1982 there were about

EGYPT

92,000 registered physicians and other medical personnel, although not all of them were resident and working in Egypt.

Education

Primary education is officially compulsory for six years between six and 12 years of age. In 1981, however, enrolment at primary schools was equivalent to 78% of children in the relevant age-group (boys 90%; girls 65%). Secondary education, beginning at 12 years of age, lasts for a further six years, comprising two equal cycles of three years each. Enrolment at secondary schools in 1981 was equivalent to 54% of children in this age-group (boys 62%; girls 46%). About 8m. people were receiving state education in the 1980/81 school year. There are 13 universities. Education is free at all levels. In 1976 adult illiteracy averaged 61.8% (males 46.4%; females 77.6%).

Tourism

Egypt has always been a considerable tourist centre. Historical remains of ancient civilization include the Pyramids and the temples at Abu Simbel. The River Nile is popular for cruises. A total of 1,560,500 tourists visited Egypt in 1984.

Public Holidays

1987: 1 January (New Year), 28 March (Leilat al-Meiraj, Ascension of Muhammad), mid-April (Sham an-Nessim), 30 May (Id al-Fitr, end of Ramadan), 18 June (Evacuation Day, proclamation of the republic), 23 July (Revolution Day), 6 August (Id al-Adha, feast of the Sacrifice), 26 August (Islamic New Year), 6 October (Armed Forces Day), 24 October (Popular Resistance Day), 4 November (Mouloud, Birth of Muhammad), 23 December (Victory Day).

1988: 1 January (New Year), 16 March (Leilat al-Meiraj), mid-April (Sham an-Nessim), 18 May (Id al-Fitr), 18 June (Evacuation Day, proclamation of the republic), 23 July (Revolution Day), 25 July (Id al-Adha), 14 August (Islamic New Year), 6 October (Armed Forces Day), 23 October (Mouloud), 24 October (Popular Resistance Day), 23 December (Victory Day).

Coptic Christian holidays include: Christmas (7 January), Palm Sunday and Easter Sunday.

Weights and Measures

The metric system is in force, but some Egyptian measurements are still in use.

Currency and Exchange Rates

1,000 millièmes = 100 piastres = 5 tallaris = 1 Egyptian pound (£E).

Exchange rates (30 September 1986):
  £1 sterling = £E 1.013;
  US $1 = 700 millièmes.

EGYPT
Statistical Survey

Statistical Survey

Source (unless otherwise stated): Central Agency for Public Mobilization and Statistics, POB 2086, Nasr City, Cairo; tel. (02) 604632; telex 92395; Research Department, National Bank of Egypt, Cairo; International Monetary Fund.

Area and Population

AREA, POPULATION AND DENSITY

Area (sq km)	997,738.5*
Population (census results)	
30 May 1966	30,075,858
22–23 November 1976	
Males	18,647,289
Females	17,978,915
Total	36,626,204
Population (official estimates at mid-year)†	
1983	45,915,000
1984	47,191,000
1985	48,503,000
Density (per sq km) at mid-1985	48.6

* 385,229 sq miles. Inhabited and cultivated territory accounts for 35,189 sq km (13,587 sq miles).
† Including Egyptian nationals abroad (1,572,000 at the 1976 census).

ECONOMICALLY ACTIVE POPULATION
(Egyptians only, '000 persons)

	1982/83	1983/84	1984/85
Agriculture, forestry and fishing	4,296.4	4,384.9	4,464.2
Manufacturing and mining	1,514.2	1,603.2	1,722.0
Petroleum and petroleum products	25.2	26.5	27.0
Housing and construction	867.3	917.4	982.2
Electricity, gas and water	138.3	139.4	147.0
Transport and communications	446.3	463.8	492.2
Suez Canal	18.9	19.2	19.7
Trade	1,161.2	1,187.8	1,214.2
Finance and insurance	88.4	92.5	96.4
Tourism, hotels and restaurants	144.2	149.7	157.2
Social and private services	942.2	939.9	956.9
Social insurance	31.5	33.0	34.9
Government services	2,436.6	2,511.7	2,576.7
Total labour force	**12,110.7**	**12,469.0**	**12,890.6**

GOVERNORATES

Governorate	Area (sq km)	Capital
Cairo	214.2	Cairo
Alexandria	2,679.4	Alexandria
Port Said	72.1	Port Said
Ismailia	1,441.6	Ismailia
Suez	17,840.4	Suez
Damietta	589.2	Damietta
Dakahlia	3,470.9	Mansura
Sharkia	4,179.5	Zagazig
Kalyubia	1,001.1	Benha
Kafr esh-Sheikh	3,437.1	Kafr esh-Sheikh
Gharbia	1,942.2	Tanta
Menufia	1,532.1	Shibin el-Kom
Behera	10,129.5	Damanhur
Giza	85,153.2	Giza
Beni Suef	1,321.7	Beni Suef
Fayum	1,827.2	Fayum
Menia	2,261.7	Menia
Asyut	1,553.0	Asyut
Suhag	1,547.2	Suhag
Kena	1,850.7	Kena
Aswan	678.5	Aswan
Al-Bahr al-Ahmar	203,685.0	Al-Ghaurdaqah
Al-Wadi al-Jadid	376,505.0	Al-Kharijah
Matruh	212,112.0	Matruh
North Sinai*	60,714.0	El-Arish
South Sinai*		Et-Toor

* Area not occupied by Israel at time of 1976 census.

PRINCIPAL TOWNS (population at census of November 1976, excluding nationals abroad)

El-Qahira (Cairo, the capital)	5,074,016	Asyut	213,751
El-Iskandariyah (Alexandria)	2,317,705	Zagazig	202,575
		Es-Suweis (Suez)	193,965
El-Giza	1,230,446	Damanhur	170,633
Shoubra el-Kheima	394,223	El-Faiyum	166,910
El-Mahalla el-Koubra	292,114	El-Minya (Menia)	146,366
Tanta	283,240	Kafr ed-Dawar	146,248
Bur Sa'id (Port Said)	262,760	Ismailia	145,930
El-Mansoura	259,387	Aswan	144,654
		Beni Suef	117,910

Greater Cairo (November 1976): 6,808,318, (July 1979): 7,258,000, (1984): c. 10,000,000.

Agriculture

PRODUCTION OF LINT COTTON
('000 kantars*, year ending 30 June)

	1981/82	1982/83	1983/84
Giza 70	1,960	1,835	1,540
Giza 45	147	114	76
Giza 69	808	862	614
Giza 67	595	—	—
Dandara	1,337	1,232	962
Total (incl. others)	9,985	9,208	8,004

* 1 metric kantar = 50 kg.
1984/85: Total production 7,981,000 kantars.

LIVESTOCK ('000 head, year ending September)

	1982	1983	1984
Cattle	1,826	1,828*	1,825*
Buffaloes	2,393	2,397*	2,410*
Sheep	1,394	1,420*	1,450
Goats	1,498	1,499*	1,500*
Pigs	15	15	15*
Horses	9	9*	10*
Asses	1,775	1,778*	1,780*
Camels	76	80*	82*

Chickens (million): 28 in 1982; 29* in 1983; 28* in 1984.
Ducks (million): 4 in 1982; 4* in 1983; 4* in 1984.
* FAO estimate.
Source: FAO, *Production Yearbook*.

OTHER PRINCIPAL CROPS ('000 metric tons)

	1982	1983	1984
Wheat	2,017	1,996	1,815
Maize	3,347	3,509	3,170
Millet	596	621	560
Barley	121	132	145
Rice (paddy)	2,441	2,442	2,236
Broad beans*	260	295	297
Lentils	6	7	10
Onions*	651	452	400
Sugar cane	8,740	8,396	8,634

* Dry crop (the production of onions includes interplanted crop).

LIVESTOCK PRODUCTS ('000 metric tons)

	1982	1983*	1984*
Beef and veal	120*	133	136
Buffalo meat	127*	121	134
Mutton and lamb	22*	25	29
Goats' meat	23†	23	24
Pig meat	3†	3	3
Poultry meat	158*	177	192
Other meat	24*	25	25
Edible offals	58*	58	60
Cows' milk	650*	650	655
Buffaloes' milk	1,250*	1,300	1,320
Sheep's milk	21*	21	21
Goats' milk	9*	9	9
Butter	68.1*	68.1	68.9
Cow and buffalo cheese	240.1*	241.3	244.3
Hen eggs	101.0†	121.9	132.0
Honey	9.7*	7.5	7.5
Wool: greasy	1.2	2.1	2.1
Cattle and buffalo hides	38.0*	37.6	38.2
Sheep skins	2.6*	3.0	3.6
Goat skins	3.1*	3.4	3.8

* FAO estimates.   † Unofficial figure.
Source: FAO, mainly *Production Yearbook*.

Forestry

ROUNDWOOD REMOVALS
(FAO estimates, '000 cubic metres, excluding bark)

	1982	1983	1984
Industrial wood	86	89	91
Fuel wood	1,776	1,821	1,867
Total	1,862	1,910	1,958

Source: FAO, *Yearbook of Forest Products*.

Fishing

('000 metric tons, live weight)

	1981	1982	1983
Marine	33.6	24.6	26.1
Freshwater	108.1	112.6	112.3
Total catch	141.7	137.2	138.4

Source: FAO, *Yearbook of Fishery Statistics*.

Mining

('000 metric tons)

	1982/83	1983/84	1984/85
Crude petroleum	34,100	38,700	43,300
Iron ore*	2,223	2,236	n.a.
Salt (unrefined)†	918	n.a.	n.a.
Phosphate rock†	783	725	754
Natural gas	2,600	3,280	3,780

Small quantities of lead and zinc are also mined.

* Figures refer to the metal content of ores.
† Source: US Bureau of Mines.

Industry

SELECTED PRODUCTS

		1980/81	1981/82	1982/83
Wheat flour*	'000 metric tons	3,537	3,487	n.a.
Refined sugar	'000 metric tons	619	630	720
Dairy products	'000 metric tons	214	377	324
Margarine	'000 metric tons	154	166	n.a.
Rice (bleached)	'000 metric tons	650	650	650
Cottonseed oil	'000 metric tons	208	102	90
Wine	'000 hectolitres	15.9	15.2	n.a.
Beer	'000 hectolitres	460	506	314
Cigarettes	million	33,000	36,000	44,000
Manufactured tobacco	metric tons	10,690	11,732	n.a.
Cotton yarn (pure)	'000 metric tons	239	245	229
Woven cotton fabrics (pure and mixed)	million square metres	754	996	922
Flax yarn†	'000 metric tons	0.6	0.5	0.6
Jute yarn and fabrics	'000 metric tons	69	66	65
Woollen yarn and fabrics	'000 metric tons	n.a.	35	32
Woven rayon and acetate fabrics	'000 metric tons	3	5	6
Paper and paperboard	'000 metric tons	134	54	56
Rubber tyres and tubes‡	'000	2,448	1,901	2,882
Ethyl alcohol	'000 hectolitres	260	290	270
Sulphuric acid (100%)	'000 metric tons	44	45	45
Caustic soda (Sodium hydroxide)	'000 metric tons	43	45	46
Fertilizer nitrates	'000 metric tons	3,346	3,950	4,200
Fertilizer phosphates	'000 metric tons	474	620	936
Motor spirit (petrol)	'000 metric tons	1,984	1,400	1,571
Kerosene	'000 metric tons	1,475	1,750	1,862
Distillate fuel oils	'000 metric tons	2,159	2,018	n.a.
Residual fuel oil (Mazout)	'000 metric tons	6,781	7,456	8,513
Petroleum bitumen (asphalt)	'000 metric tons	291	235	275
Coke-oven coke	'000 metric tons	920	974	n.a.
Cement	'000 metric tons	3,446	4,300	4,800
Pig-iron	'000 metric tons	297	293	n.a.
Crude steel	'000 metric tons	800	900	1,000
Radio receivers	'000	198	211	n.a.
Television receivers	'000	441	593	n.a.
Passenger motor cars (assembly)	number	18,734	17,035	n.a.
Electric energy	million kWh	19,000	21,000	n.a.

* Source: International Wheat Council, *World Wheat Statistics*.
† Including waste and yarn made from tow.
‡ Tyres and inner tubes for road motor vehicles (including motorcycles) and bicycles.

Finance

CURRENCY AND EXCHANGE RATES

Monetary Units
1,000 millièmes = 100 piastres = 5 tallaris = 1 Egyptian pound (£E).

Denominations
Coins: 1, 2 and 5 millièmes; 1, 2, 5 and 10 piastres.
Notes: 5, 10, 25 and 50 piastres; 1, 5, 10 and 20 pounds.

Sterling and Dollar Equivalents (30 September 1986)
£1 sterling = £E1.013;
US $1 = 700 millièmes;
£E100 = £98.73 sterling = $142.86.

Note: The information on exchange rates refers to the official rate of the Central Bank, fixed at US $1 = 700 millièmes (£E1 = $1.4286) since January 1979. However, a system of multiple exchange rates is in operation, and the official rate is applicable only to a limited range of transactions, including payments for selected imports and exports. At 30 September 1986 the 'premium' rate, applicable to other imports and exports, was $1 = £E1.36 (£E1 = 73.53 US cents), while the 'parallel' rate, applicable to most transactions by the private sector, was $1 = £E1.90 (£E1 = 52.63 US cents).

CENTRAL BANK RESERVES
(US $ million at 31 December)

	1983	1984	1985
Gold*	757	679	578
Reserve position in IMF	32	—	—
Foreign exchange	739	736	792
Total	1,528	1,415	1,370

* From June 1981 gold is valued at market-related prices.
Source: IMF, *International Financial Statistics*.

BUDGET ESTIMATES* (£E million, year ending 30 June)

	1984/85	1985/86	1986/87
Expenditure	18,277	19,910	20,001
Current spending	13,412	14,480	12,535
Investment	4,865	5,430	7,466
Subsidies	2,058	2,000	1,700
Revenue	12,877	15,010	14,386
Gross deficit	5,400	4,900	5,615
Financing	4,200	4,000	4,835
Net deficit	1,200	900	780

Source: *Al-Ahram*, Cairo.

* The government does not provide up-to-date figures on actual spending and income. A number of observers, including the IMF, believe that the gross and net deficits for 1984/85 and 1985/86 were higher than budgeted. A major reason for the discrepancy is that the expenditure on subsidies tends to exceed its allocation. Estimates by the IMF put the actual spending on subsidies in 1984/85 at about £E2,600m.

MONEY SUPPLY (£E million at 31 December)

	1983	1984	1985
Currency outside banks	6,475	7,098	8,285
Demand deposits at deposit money banks	3,798	4,554	5,606

Source: IMF, *International Financial Statistics*.

GDP GROWTH TARGETS UNDER 1982/83–1986/87 PLAN (£E million, year ending 30 June)

	GDP 1982/83	GDP 1986/87	Overall growth 1982/83–1986/87 (%)	Average annual growth rate 1982/83–1986/87 (%)	Proportion of total GDP (%) 1982/83	Proportion of total GDP (%) 1986/87
Commodity sector	11,584.9	15,836.9	36.7	8.1	54.3	54.8
Agriculture	4,000.0	4,660.0	16.5	3.9	18.8	16.1
Mining and industry	2,905.8	4,359.4	50.0	10.7	13.6	15.1
Petroleum and products	3,547.6	5,238.9	47.7	10.2	16.6	18.1
Electricity	126.8	194.6	53.5	11.3	0.6	0.7
Building and construction	1,004.7	1,384.0	37.8	8.3	4.7	4.8
Productive services	5,703.8	7,597.6	33.2	7.4	26.8	26.2
Communications, transport and storage	916.0	1,363.3	48.9	10.5	4.3	4.7
Suez Canal	719.6	899.0	24.9	5.7	3.4	3.1
Commerce	2,680.4	3,488.0	30.1	6.8	12.6	12.1
Finance	1,097.0	1,455.0	32.6	7.3	5.2	5.0
Insurance	51.3	69.0	34.5	7.7	0.2	0.2
Hotels and restaurants	239.5	323.3	35.0	7.8	1.1	1.1
Social services	4,027.3	5,485.5	34.6	8.0	18.9	19.0
Housing	401.0	548.7	36.8	8.2	1.9	1.9
Public utilities	42.0	72.3	72.1	14.5	0.2	0.2
Social and private services	866.0	1,126.8	30.1	6.8	4.1	3.9
Social insurance	22.3	30.3	35.9	8.0	0.1	0.1
Government services	2,696.0	3,707.4	37.5	37.5	12.6	12.8
Total GDP	21,316.0	28,920.0	35.7	7.9	100.0	100.0

Source: Ministry of Planning.

BALANCE OF PAYMENTS (US $ million)

	1982	1983	1984
Merchandise exports f.o.b.	4,018	3,693	3,864
Merchandise imports f.o.b.	−7,733	−7,515	−9,250
Trade balance	−3,715	−3,822	−5,386
Exports of services	3,202	3,570	3,512
Imports of services	−3,820	−3,847	−4,188
Balance on goods and services	−4,332	−4,099	−6,062
Unrequited transfers (net)	2,481	3,688	3,981
Current balance	−1,852	−411	−2,081
Direct capital investment (net)	285	471	713
Portfolio investment (net)	—	6	1
Other long-term capital (net)	1,105	179	527
Short-term capital (net)	83	−377	459
Net errors and omissions	132	213	115
Total (net monetary movements)	−245	81	−266
Valuation changes (net)	−191	−77	24
Exceptional financing (net)	460	74	211
Changes in reserves	24	79	−32

Source: IMF, *International Financial Statistics*.

External Trade

PRINCIPAL COMMODITIES (£E million)

Imports c.i.f.	1981	1982	1983
Foodstuffs	2,051.6	1,863.6	1,811.4
Cereals and milling products	1,004.1	895.2	696.2
Animal and vegetable oils	193.0	191.1	214.2
Petroleum	55.0	64.3	103.4
Petroleum products	83.4	157.2	263.8
Paper and paper products	127.7	121.6	118.4
Tobacco	73.3	105.1	136.4
Chemical products	472.1	406.2	438.2
Wood, hides and rubber	476.0	327.8	396.1
Machinery and electrical apparatus	977.6	1,156.0	1,335.6
Transport equipment	787.9	701.7	868.9
Watches, clocks, scientific apparatus	79.7	76.9	104.3
Total (incl. others)	6,187.5	6,354.5	7,192.7

1984: Total imports £E7,536.1m.

Exports f.o.b.	1982	1983	1984
Textile fibre and products	426.4	510.8	n.a.
Raw cotton	286.0	308.8	340.0
Cotton yarn	86.6	137.1	154.4
Cotton fabrics	15.8	28.3	n.a.
Potatoes	28.8	21.4	25.6
Rice	8.1	5.0	11.4
Edible fruits	42.1	60.6	n.a.
Sugar and sugar confectionery	18.9	9.5	n.a.
Leather products and footwear	3.9	5.8	3.8
Crude petroleum	1,211.2	1,070.7	1,030.5
Petroleum products	235.5	330.5	233.1
Total (incl. others)	2,184.3	2,250.3	2,197.9

PRINCIPAL TRADING PARTNERS (£E million)

Imports c.i.f.	1982	1983	1984
Australia	149.4	130.2	n.a.
Belgium/Luxembourg	91.7	133.9	n.a.
Czechoslovakia	94.0	95.9	67.1
Finland	36.5	83.4	n.a.
France	476.9	496.6	586.0
German Dem. Rep.	57.4	59.3	65.7
Germany, Fed. Rep.	629.2	763.8	769.2
Greece	217.8	268.8	n.a.
India	42.4	57.7	n.a.
Italy	480.6	575.3	644.0
Japan	288.4	357.3	477.9
Netherlands	222.8	251.2	263.3
Romania	138.4	190.1	221.5
Saudi Arabia	36.5	166.8	136.5
Spain	149.1	244.8	n.a.
Sweden	109.8	140.6	n.a.
Switzerland	122.4	150.6	n.a.
Turkey	75.2	59.2	n.a.
USSR	123.0	140.0	150.8
United Kingdom	278.6	257.9	264.0
USA	1,208.5	1,160.2	858.6
Yugoslavia	93.5	126.6	157.4
Total (incl. others)	6,354.5	7,192.7	7,536.1

Exports f.o.b.	1982	1983	1984
China, People's Rep.	24.8	20.4	25.8
Czechoslovakia	26.2	35.2	28.9
France	151.0	213.3	144.5
German Dem. Rep.	9.4	18.9	24.0
Germany, Fed. Rep.	88.2	49.3	73.7
Greece	45.2	44.6	n.a.
Iraq	0.5	2.6	15.1
Italy	482.5	408.0	379.0
Japan	55.1	59.0	70.3
Lebanon	14.6	11.1	9.0
Netherlands	118.8	88.8	114.1
Poland	—	8.2	n.a.
Romania	129.0	84.2	183.9
Saudi Arabia	60.1	57.2	50.8
Sudan	46.8	11.3	20.7
Switzerland	25.4	28.1	n.a.
USSR	94.9	160.5	116.2
United Kingdom	53.5	34.8	38.2
USA	103.2	148.6	121.9
Yugoslavia	38.2	23.0	22.3
Total (incl. others)	2,184.1	2,250.3	2,197.9

Transport

RAILWAYS (year ending 30 June)

	1980/81	1981/82	1982/83
Total freight (million ton-km)	2,334	2,307	2,303
Total passengers (million passenger-km)	11,000	12,478	14,468
Track length (km)	4,385	4,321	5,327

ROAD TRAFFIC (motor vehicle licences at 31 December)

	1983	1984	1985
Buses	24,284	26,029	28,273
Tractors	202,940	237,889	264,573
Cars	597,869	679,425	719,199
Motor cycles	199,218	223,370	247,182

SHIPPING (Suez Canal traffic)

	1983	1984	1985
Transits (number)	22,224	21,361	19,991
Displacement ('000 net tons)	378,226	371,039	352,579
Northbound goods traffic ('000 metric tons)	141,002	154,237	151,901
Southbound goods traffic ('000 metric tons)	115,703	109,491	105,695
Net tonnage of tankers ('000)	136,472	131,285	122,794

Source: Suez Canal Authority.

CIVIL AVIATION (scheduled services)

	1980	1981	1982
Kilometres flown (million)	30.5	33.6	34.9
Passengers carried ('000)	2,028	2,233	2,433
Passenger-km (million)	2,870	3,269	3,643
Freight ton-km (million)	29.4	39.0	53.5

Source: UN, *Statistical Yearbook*.

Tourism

TOURIST ARRIVALS BY REGION

	1981	1982	1983
Arabs	578,786	618,331	598,673
Europeans	480,393	485,663	536,910
Americans	201,269	193,065	219,505
Others	115,579	126,192	142,837
Total	1,376,027	1,423,251	1,497,925

1984: Total tourist arrivals 1,560,500.

Education

(number of pupils, 1980/81)

	General Education Male	General Education Female	General Education Total	Azhar Education Male	Azhar Education Female	Azhar Education Total
Primary*	2,709,893	1,838,165	4,548,058	75,450	36,939	112,389
Preparatory	978,545	595,688	1,574,233	54,538	12,589	67,127
Secondary	307,708	178,159	485,867	89,357	35,508	124,865
Technical	379,468	239,849	619,317	—	—	—
Teacher training	25,538	25,458	50,996	—	—	—

* In 1980/81 there were 140,146 teachers in primary education; in 1981/82 there were 141,562.

Directory

The Constitution

A new constitution for the Arab Republic of Egypt was approved by referendum on 11 September 1971.

THE STATE

Egypt is an Arab Republic with a democratic, socialist system based on the alliance of the working people and derived from the country's historical heritage and the spirit of Islam.

The Egyptian people are part of the Arab nation, who work towards total Arab unity.

Islam is the religion of the State; Arabic is its official language and the Islamic code is a principal source of legislation. The State safeguards the freedom of worship and of performing rites for all religions.

Sovereignty is of the people alone which is the source of all powers.

The protection, consolidation and preservation of the socialist gains is a national duty: the sovereignty of law is the basis of the country's rule, and the independence of immunity of the judiciary are basic guarantees for the protection of rights and liberties.

THE FUNDAMENTAL ELEMENTS OF SOCIETY

Social solidarity is the basis of Egyptian society, and the family is its nucleus.

The State ensures the equality of men and women in both political and social rights in line with the provisions of Muslim legislation.

Work is a right, an honour and a duty which the State guarantees together with the services of social and health insurance, pensions for incapacity and unemployment.

The economic basis of the Republic is a socialist democratic system based on sufficiency and justice in a manner preventing exploitation.

Ownership is of three kinds, public, co-operative and private. The public sector assumes the main responsibility for the regulation and growth of the national economy under the development plan.

Property is subject to the people's control.

Private ownership is safeguarded and may not be sequestrated except in cases specified in law nor expropriated except for the general good against fair legal compensation. The right of inheritance is guaranteed in it.

Nationalization shall only be allowed for considerations of public interest in accordance with the law and against compensation.

Agricultural holding may be limited by law.

The State follows a comprehensive central planning and compulsory planning approach based on quinquennial socio-economic and cultural development plans whereby the society's resources are mobilized and put to the best use.

The public sector assumes the leading role in the development of the national economy. The State provides absolute protection of this sector as well as the property of co-operative societies and trade unions against all attempts to tamper with them.

PUBLIC LIBERTIES, RIGHTS AND DUTIES

All citizens are equal before the law. Personal liberty is a natural right and no one may be arrested, searched, imprisoned or restricted in any way without a court order.

Houses have sanctity, and shall not be placed under surveillance or searched without a court order with reasons given for such action.

The law safeguards the sanctities of the private lives of all citizens; so have all postal, telegraphic, telephonic and other means of communication which may not therefore be confiscated, or perused except by a court order giving the reasons, and only for a specified period.

Public rights and freedoms are also inviolate and all calls for atheism and anything that reflects adversely on divine religions are prohibited.

The freedom of opinion, the Press, printing and publications and all information media are safeguarded.

Press censorship is forbidden, so are warnings, suspensions or cancellations through administrative channels. Under exceptional circumstances as in cases of emergency or in war time, censorship may be imposed on information media for a definite period.

Egyptians have the right to permanent or provisional emigration and no Egyptian may be deported or prevented from returning to the country.

Citizens have the right to private meetings in peace provided they bear no arms. Egyptians also have the right to form societies which have no secret activities. Public meetings are also allowed within the limits of the law.

SOVEREIGNTY OF THE LAW

All acts of crime should be specified together with the penalties for the acts.

Recourse to justice, it says, is a right of all citizens, and those who are financially unable, will be assured of means to defend their rights.

Except in cases of *flagrante delicto,* no person may be arrested or their freedom restricted unless an order authorizing arrest has been given by the competent judge or the public prosecution in accordance with the provisions of law.

SYSTEM OF GOVERNMENT

The President, who must be of Egyptian parentage and at least 40 years old, is nominated by at least one-third of the members of the People's Assembly, approved by at least two-thirds, and elected by popular referendum. His term is for six years and he 'may be re-elected for another subsequent term'. He may take emergency measures in the interests of the State but these measures must be approved by referendum within 60 days.

The People's Assembly, elected for five years, is the legislative body and approves general policy, the budget and the development plan. It shall have 'not less than 350' elected members, at least half of whom shall be workers or farmers, and the President may appoint up to 10 additional members. In exceptional circumstances the Assembly, by a two-thirds vote, may authorize the President to rule by decree for a specified period but these decrees must be approved by the Assembly at its next meeting. The law governing the composition of the People's Assembly was amended in May 1979 (see People's Assembly, below).

The Assembly may pass a vote of no confidence in a Deputy Prime Minister, a Minister or a Deputy Minister, provided three days' notice of the vote is given, and the minister must then resign. In the case of the Prime Minister, the Assembly may 'prescribe' his

EGYPT

responsibility and submit a report to the President: if the President disagrees with the report but the Assembly persists, then the matter is put to a referendum: if the people support the President the Assembly is dissolved; if they support the Assembly the President must accept the resignation of the Government. The President may dissolve the Assembly prematurely, but his action must be approved by a referendum and elections must be held within 60 days.

Executive Authority is vested in the President, who may appoint one or more vice-presidents and appoints all ministers. He may also dismiss the vice-presidents and ministers. The President has 'the right to refer to the people in connection with important matters related to the country's higher interests.' The Government is described as 'the supreme executive and administrative organ of the state'. Its members, whether full ministers or deputy ministers, must be at least 35 years old. Further sections define the roles of Local Government, Specialized National Councils, the Judiciary, the Higher Constitutional Court, the Socialist Prosecutor General, the Armed Forces and National Defence Council and the Police.

POLITICAL PARTIES

In June 1977 the People's Assembly adopted a new law on political parties, which, subject to certain conditions, permitted the formation of political parties for the first time since 1953. The law was passed in accordance with Article Five of the Constitution which describes the political system as 'a multi-party one' with four main parties: 'the ruling National Democratic Party, the Socialist Workers (the official opposition), the Liberal Socialists and the Unionist Progressive'. (The legality of the re-formed New Wafd Party was established by the courts in January 1984.)

1980 AMENDMENTS

On 30 April 1980 the People's Assembly passed a number of amendments, which were subsequently massively approved at a referendum the following month. A summary of the amendments follows:

(i) the regime in Egypt is socialist-democratic, based on the alliance of working people's forces.

(ii) the political system depends on multiple political parties; the Arab Socialist Union is therefore abolished.

(iii) the President is elected for a six-year term and can be elected for 'other terms'.

(iv) the President shall appoint a Consultative Council to preserve the principles of the revolutions of 23 July 1952, and 15 May 1971.

(v) a Supreme Press Council shall safeguard the freedom of the press, check government censorship and look after the interests of journalists.

(vi) Egypt's adherence to Islamic jurisprudence is affirmed. Christians and Jews are subject to their own jurisdiction in personal status affairs.

(vii) there will be no distinction of race or religion.

The Government

THE PRESIDENCY

President: MUHAMMAD HOSNI MUBARAK (confirmed as President by referendum, 13 October 1981, after assassination of President Sadat).

Vice-President: (vacant).

COUNCIL OF MINISTERS
(December 1986)

Prime Minister: Dr ATIF SIDQI.

Deputy Prime Minister and Minister of Defence and Military Production: Field-Marshal MUHAMMAD ABD AL-HALIM ABU GHAZALAH.

Deputy Prime Minister and Minister of Foreign Affairs: Dr AHMAD ESMAT ABD AL-MEGUID.

Deputy Prime Minister and Minister of Planning and International Co-operation: Dr KAMAL AHMAD AL-GANZURI.

Deputy Prime Minister and Minister of Agriculture and Food Security: Dr YOUSSEF AMIN WALI.

Minister of Finance: Dr MUHAMMAD AHMAD AR-RAZZAZ.

Minister of Social Insurance and Social Affairs: Dr AMAL ABD AR-RAHIM OSMAN.

Minister of Reconstruction and for New Communities and Land Reclamation: Eng. HASABALLAH AL-KAFRAWI.

Minister of Manpower and Vocational Training: ASIM ABD AL-HAQ SALIH.

Minister of Justice: AHMAD MAMDUH ATIYAH.

Minister of Transport, Communications and Naval Transport: Eng. SULAYMAN MUTAWALLI SULAYMAN.

Minister of Electricity and Energy: Eng. MUHAMMAD MAHIR ABAZAH.

Minister of Culture: Dr AHMAD ABD AL-MAKSOUD HEIKAL.

Minister of Information: MUHAMMAD SAFWAT MUHAMMAD YOUSSEF ASH-SHARIF.

Minister of Health: Dr MUHAMMAD RAGIB DUWAYDAR.

Minister of Local Government: Dr AHMAD SALAMAH MUHAMMAD.

Minister of Tourism and Civil Aviation: Dr FOUAD SULTAN.

Minister of Economy and Foreign Trade: Dr YUSRI ALI MUSTAPHA.

Minister of Supply and Internal Trade: Dr MUHAMMAD JALAL AD-DIN ABU ADH-DHAHAB.

Minister of the Interior: Maj.-Gen. ZAKI BADR.

Minister of Irrigation: Eng. ESAM RADI ABD AL-HAMID RADI.

Minister of Industry: Eng. MUHAMMAD FARAG ABD AL-WAHHAB.

Minister of Petroleum and Mineral Resources: ABD AL-HADI MUHAMMAD KANDIL.

Minister of Cabinet Affairs and Minister of State for Administrative Development: Dr ATEF MUHAMMAD OBEID.

Minister of National Education: Dr AHMAD FATHI SURUR.

Minister of Housing, Utilities and Urban Complexes: Eng. HASABALLAH MUHAMMAD AL-KAFRAWI.

Minister of Wakfs (Islamic Endowment): Dr MUHAMMAD ALI MAHGOUB.

Minister of State for Foreign Affairs: Dr BOUTROS BOUTROS GHALI.

Minister of State for Military Production: Dr GAMAL AS-SAYED IBRAHIM.

Minister of State for Immigration and Egyptian Expatriates: ADLI ABD ASH-SHAHID BISHAY.

Minister of State for Scientific Research: Dr ADEL ABD AL-HAMID IZZ.

Ministers of State for People's Assembly and Shura (Advisory) Council Affairs: MUHAMMAD ABD AL-HAMID RADWAN, Dr AS-SAYED ALI AS-SAYED.

MINISTRIES

Ministry of Agriculture: Sharia Wizaret az-Ziraa, Dokki, Giza; tel. (02) 702677.

Ministry of Civil Aviation: Sharia Matar, Cairo (Heliopolis); tel. (02) 969555.

Ministry of Communications: 22 Sharia Ramses, Cairo.

Ministry of Culture: 110 Sharia al-Galaa, Cairo; tel. (02) 971995.

Ministry of Development and New Communities: 1 Ismail Abaza, Kasr el-Eini, Cairo; tel. (02) 92571.

Ministry of Economic Co-operation: 9 Sharia Adly, Cairo; telex 348.

Ministry of Economy: 8 Sharia Adly, Cairo; tel. (02) 920050.

Ministry of Education: Sharia el-Falaky, Cairo; tel. (02) 27363.

Ministry of Scientific Research: 4 Sharia Ibrahim Nagiv, Cairo (Garden City).

Ministry of Electricity and Energy: Cairo (Nasr City); tel. (02) 831204.

Ministry of Finance: Sharia Magles esh-Sha'ab, Lazoughli Sq., Cairo; tel. (02) 24857.

Ministry of Foreign Affairs: Tahrir Sq., Cairo; telex 92220.

Ministry of Foreign Trade: Lazoughli Sq., Cairo; tel. (02) 22957.

Ministry of Health: Sharia Magles esh-Sha'ab, Cairo; tel. (02) 981177; telex 94107.

Ministry of Housing and Reconstruction: 1 Sharia Ismail Abaza, Cairo; telex 92571.

Ministry of Industry and Mineral Resources: 2 Sharia Latin America, Cairo (Garden City); tel. (02) 31845; telex 93112.

Ministry of Information: Radio and TV Building, Cairo (Maspiro); tel. (02) 749518.

EGYPT

Ministry of Irrigation: Sharia Kasr el-Eini, Cairo; tel. (02) 24527.

Ministry of Justice: Justice Bldg, Cairo (Lazoughli); tel. (02) 31176.

Ministry of Land Reclamation: Land Reclamation Building, Dokki, Giza; tel. 703011.

Ministry of Manpower and Vocational Training: Sharia Youssef Abbas, Nasr City, Abbasia, Cairo.

Ministry of Military Production: 5 Sharia Ismail Abaza, Kasr el-Eini, Cairo; tel. (02) 27487.

Ministry of Naval Transport: 4 Sharia el-Bataisa, Alexandria; tel. 35763; telex 54147.

Ministry of Petroleum: 2 Sharia Latin America, Cairo (Garden City); tel. (02) 25022; telex 92197.

Ministry of Planning: Sharia Salah Salem, Cairo (Nasr City).

Ministry of Social Affairs: Sharia Sheikh Rihan, Cairo; telex 94105.

Ministry of Social Insurance: 3 Sharia el-Alfi, Cairo; tel. (02) 922717.

Ministry of Supply and Internal Trade: 99 Sharia Kasr el-Eini, Cairo; tel. (02) 33882; telex 93497.

Ministry of Tourism: 110 Sharia Kasr el-Eini, Tahrir Sq., Cairo; tel. (02) 31921; telex 94040.

Ministry of Transport: Sharia Kasr el-Eini, Cairo; telex 92802.

Ministry of Wakfs: Sharia Sabri Abu Alam, Ean el-Luk, Cairo; tel. (02) 746305.

Legislature

MAJLIS ASH-SHA'AB
(People's Assembly)

The law governing election to, and the composition of, the People's Assembly was amended on 20 July 1983. Parties are now required to gain a minimum of 8% of the total vote to be represented in the Assembly. There are now 48 constituencies, which each elect between three and 12 members to the Assembly. In 31 constituencies, an extra member, who must be a woman, is automatically added to the list of elected members from the majority party. Ten members are appointed by the President.

Speaker: Dr RIFA'AT EL-MAHGOUB.

Deputy Speakers: IHAB MAQLAD (workers), AHMAD MOUSSA (professions).

Leader of the Opposition: MUMTAZ NASSAR (New Wafd Party).

Elections, 27 May 1984

Party	Votes	%	Seats
National Democratic Party	3,756,359	72.9	389
New Wafd Party	778,131	15.1	59
Socialist Labour Party	364,040	7.1	—
National Progressive Unionist Party	214,587	4.2	—
Liberal Socialist Party	33,448	0.6	—
Total	5,146,565	100.0	448*

* There are, in addition, 10 members (4 Copts, 4 Socialist Labour Party, 1 National Progressive Unionist Party, 1 public personality of no party political allegiance) appointed by the President.

In September 1980 elections were held for a 210-member **Shura (Advisory) Council,** which replaced the former Central Committee of the Arab Socialist Union. Of the total number of members, 140 are elected and the remaining 70 are appointed by the President. The National Democratic Party holds all the elected seats. The opposition parties boycotted elections to the Council in October 1983, and again in October 1986, in protest against the 8% electoral threshold.

Speaker: Dr ALI LUTFI.

Deputy Speakers: THARWAT ABAZAH, AHMAD AL-IMADI.

Political Organizations

Liberal Socialist Party: Cairo; f. 1976; advocates expansion of 'open door' economic policy and greater freedom for private enterprise; Leader MUSTAFA KAMEL MURAD.

National Democratic Party: Cairo; f. July 1978; government party established by Anwar Sadat; has absorbed Arab Socialist Party; Leader MUHAMMAD HOSNI MUBARAK; Sec.-Gen. Dr YOUSSEF AMIN WALI; Political Bureau: Chair. MUHAMMAD HOSNI MUBARAK; mems: KAMAL HASSAN ALI, Dr MUSTAFA KHALIL, Dr RIFA'AT EL-MAHGOUB, Dr SUBHI ABD AL-HAKIM, Dr MUSTAFA KAMAL HILMI, FIKRI MAKRAM OBEID, Dr ISMAT ABD AL-MEGUID, Dr AMAL OSMAN, SAFWAT ASH-SHARIF, Dr YOUSSEF AMIN WALI, HASSAN ABU BASHA, KAMAL HENRY BADIR, Dr AHMAD HEIKAL.

National Progressive Unionist Party: 1 Sharia Karim ed-Dawlah, Cairo; f. 1976; left wing; Leader KHALED MOHI ED-DIN; Sec. Dr RIFA'AT ES-SAID; 160,000 mems.

New Wafd Party: Cairo; original Wafd Party f. 1919; banned 1952; re-formed as New Wafd Party February 1978; disbanded June 1978; re-formed August 1983; Leader FOUAD SERAG ED-DIN; Sec.-Gen. IBRAHIM FARAG.

Socialist Labour Party: 12 Sharia Awali el-Ahd, Cairo; f. September 1978; official opposition party; Leader IBRAHIM SHUKRI.

Ummah Party: Islamic religious party, based in Khartoum, Sudan; Leader SADIQ AL-MAHDI (Prime Minister of Sudan).

Diplomatic Representation

EMBASSIES IN EGYPT

Afghanistan: *Interests served by India.*

Albania: 29 Sharia Ismail Muhammad, Cairo (Zamalek); tel. (02) 3415651; Ambassador: ALKYZ CERGA.

Algeria: *Interests served by India.*

Angola: 12 Midan en-Nasr, Cairo (Dokki); tel. (02) 707602; Ambassador: KAMU D'ALMEIDA.

Argentina: 8 Sharia as-Saleh Ayoub, Cairo (Zamalek); tel. (02) 650862; Ambassador: (vacant).

Australia: 5th Floor, Cairo Plaza Annexe, Corniche en-Nil, Cairo; tel. (02) 717022; telex 92257; Ambassador: KENNETH ROGERS.

Austria: Riyadh Tower, Cnr 5 Sharia Wissa Wassef, Cairo (Giza); tel. (02) 651898; telex 92258; Ambassador: FRANZ BOGEN.

Bahrain: *Interests served by Pakistan.*

Bangladesh: 18 Sharia Souris, Madinet el-Mohandessin, Cairo (Dokki); tel. (02) 706294; Ambassador: HEDAYET AHMAD.

Belgium: 20 Sharia Kamel esh-Shennawi, Cairo (Garden City); tel. (02) 3547494; telex 92264; Ambassador: JACQUES GÉRARD.

Bolivia: El Misr Bldg, Midan ar-Rimaha, Cairo (Giza); Chargé d'affaires (a.i.): ENRIQUE SORIA NAU.

Brazil: 1125 Corniche en-Nil, Cairo (Maspiro); tel. (02) 756877; Ambassador: MARCUS ANTÔNIO DE SALVO COIMBRE.

Brunei: Room 401, Nile Hilton, Tahrir Sq., Cairo; tel. (02) 750666.

Bulgaria: 36 Sharia el-Missaha, Cairo (Dokki).

Burkina Faso: 40 Sharia es-Sawra, Medinat ez-Zobbat, Cairo (Dokki); tel. (02) 709754; Ambassador: HAROUNA KOUELA.

Burma: 24 Sharia Muhammad Mazhar, Cairo (Zamalek); tel. (02) 3404176; Ambassador: U AYE PE.

Burundi: 13 Sharia el-Israa, Madinet el-Mohandessin, Cairo (Dokki); tel. (02) 698991; Ambassador: GEDEON MAGETE.

Cameroon: POB 2061, 42 Sharia Babel, Cairo (Dokki); tel. (02) 704843; Ambassador: HAYATOU SOUAIBOO.

Canada: 6 Sharia Muhammad Fahmy es-Sayed, Cairo (Garden City); tel. (02) 3543110; telex 92677; Ambassador: MARC PERRON.

Central African Republic: 13 Sharia Chebab, Madinet el-Mohandessin, Cairo (Dokki); tel. (02) 713291; Ambassador: PIERRE FIDÈLE BAKRI.

Chad: POB 1869, 31 Sharia Adnan Oumar Sedki, Cairo (Dokki); tel. (02) 703232; Ambassador: NGARASANAM DINGAMHASDE REBEYE.

Chile: 5 Sharia Chagaret ed-Dorr, Cairo (Zamalek); tel. (02) 3408711; telex 92519; Ambassador: VICTOR LARENAS.

China, People's Republic: 14 Sharia Bahgat Aly, Cairo (Zamalek); tel. (02) 809459; Ambassador: WEN YEZHAN.

Colombia: Apt 141, 1 Sharia Sad el-Ali, Cairo (Dokki); tel. (02) 717278; Ambassador: VIRGINIA OBREGÓN BORRERO.

Cuba: 9 Sharia Hussein Ahmad Rashad, Cairo (Dokki); tel. (02) 381704; telex 93966; Ambassador: LUIS KARAKADZE BERRAYARZA.

Cyprus: 23A Sharia Ismail Muhammad, Cairo (Zamalek); tel. (02) 699288; telex 2059; Ambassador: SOTIRIS ELLINAS.

Czechoslovakia: 4 Sharia Dokki, Cairo (Giza); tel. (02) 981706; Ambassador: MILOS VESELY.
Denmark: 12 Sharia Hassan Sabri, Cairo (Zamalek); tel. (02) 3407411; telex 92254; Ambassador: WILLIAM THUNE ANDERSEN.
Djibouti: 157 Sharia Mohandessin, Sharia Sudan, Cairo; tel. (02) 709787; telex 93143.
Ecuador: 8 Sharia Abd ar-Rahman Fahmy, Cairo (Garden City); tel. (02) 26372; Ambassador: LUCINDO ALMEIDA.
Ethiopia: 12 Midan Bahlawi, Cairo (Dokki); tel. (02) 705133; Ambassador: Ato BETROU KIDANE MARIAM.
Finland: 10 Sharia el-Kamel Muhammad, Cairo (Zamalek); tel. (02) 699722; Ambassador: (vacant).
France: 29 Sharia Giza, Cairo; tel. (02) 728033; telex 92032; Ambassador: PIERRE HUNT; also looks after Lebanese interests at 5 Sharia Ahmad Nassim, Cairo (Giza); tel. (02) 728266; telex 92227.
Gabon: 15 Sharia Make el-Moukarama, Cairo (Dokki); tel. (02) 381395; telex 92323; Ambassador: ALAIN MAURICE MAYOMBO.
German Democratic Republic: 13 Sharia Hussein Wassef, Cairo (Dokki); tel. (02) 3484525; telex 22354; Ambassador: WOLFGANG SCHÜSSLER.
Germany, Federal Republic: 8 Sharia Hassan Sabri, Cairo (Zamalek); tel. (02) 3410015; telex 92023; Ambassador: Dr KURT MÜLLER.
Ghana: 24 Sharia el-Batal Ahmad Abd al-Aziz, Cairo (Dokki); tel. (02) 704275; Ambassador: Dr W. C. YAW ANOFF.
Greece: 18 Sharia Aicha et-Taimouria, Cairo (Garden City); tel. (02) 30443; Ambassador: ANTOINE NOMIKOS.
Guatemala: 29 Sharia Dr Muhammad Mandour Madinet Nasr, Cairo; tel. (02) 600371; telex 93242; Ambassador: Gen. FELIPE DOROTEO MONTERROSO MIRANDA.
Guinea: 46 Sharia Muhammad Mazhar, Cairo (Zamalek); tel. (02) 699088; Ambassador: AMIROU DIALLO.
Guinea-Bissau: 37 Sharia Lebanon, Madinet el-Mohandessin, Cairo.
Holy See: Apostolic Nunciature, Safarat al-Vatican, 5 Sharia Muhammad Mazhar, Cairo (Zamalek); tel. (02) 3406152; Pro-Nuncio: Mgr GIOVANNI MORETTI.
Hungary: 55 Sharia Kods esh-Sherif, Cairo (Mohandessin); tel. (02) 805091; Ambassador: Dr ERNŐ SIMONYI.
India: 5 Sharia Aziz Abaza, Cairo (Zamalek); tel. (02) 3413051; telex 92081; Ambassador: ALFRED GONZALVES; also looks after Afghanistan interests at 59 Sharia Orouba (Heliopolis), Algerian interests at 14 Sharia Brasil (Zamalek), Yemen Arab Republic interests at 28 Amin ar-Rifai (Dokki).
Indonesia: 13 Sharia Aicha et-Taimouria, Cairo (Garden City); tel. (02) 27200; Ambassador: Maj.-Gen. (retd) BARKAT TIRTADIDJAJA.
Iran: *Interests served by Switzerland.*
Iraq: *Interests served by Yugoslavia.*
Ireland: POB 2681, 3 Sharia Abu el-Feda, Cairo (Zamalek); tel. (02) 3408264; telex 92778; Ambassador: EAMONN RYAN.
Israel: 6 Ibn el-Malek, Cairo (Giza); tel. (02) 726000; telex 93363; Ambassador: MOSHE SASSON.
Italy: 15 Sharia Abd ar-Rahman Fahmi, Cairo (Garden City); tel. (02) 3543195; telex 94229; Ambassador: GIOVANNI MIGLIUOLO.
Ivory Coast: 39 Sharia el-Kods esh-Sherif, Madinet el-Mohandessin, Cairo (Dokki); tel. (02) 699009; telex 2334; Ambassador: KOUAME KOFFI.
Japan: Immeuble Cairo Centre, 3rd Floor, 2 Sharia Abd al-Kader Hamza, 106 Kasr el-Eini; tel. (02) 3553962; telex 92226; Ambassador: YOSHIYA KATO.
Jordan: 6 Sharia Juhaini, Cairo; tel. (02) 982766; Ambassador: HUSSEIN HAMAMI.
Kampuchea: 2 Sharia Tahawia, Cairo (Giza); tel. (02) 3489966; Ambassador: IN SOPHEAP.
Kenya: 20 Sharia Boulos Hanna, POB 362, Cairo (Dokki); tel. (02) 704455; telex 92021; Ambassador: OCHIENG ADALA.
Korea, Democratic People's Republic: 6 Sharia es-Saleh Ayoub, Cairo (Zamalek); tel. (02) 699532; Ambassador: O CHANG RIM.
Kuwait: 4 Sharia al-Montazeh, Cairo (Zamalek); tel. (02) 816252.
Lebanon: *Interests served by France.*
Liberia: 11 Sharia Brasil, Cairo (Zamalek); tel. (02) 819864; telex 92293; Ambassador: GABRIEL FARNGALO.

Malaysia: 7 Sharia Wadi en-Nil, Mohandessin, Cairo (Agouza); tel. (02) 699162; Ambassador: ABDULLAH ZAWAWI BIN HAJI MUHAMMAD.
Mali: 3 Sharia al-Kawsar, Cairo (Dokki); tel. (02) 701641; Ambassador: MUPHTAH AG-HAIRY.
Mauritania: 31 Sharia Syria, Cairo (Dokki); tel. (02) 707229; telex 92274.
Mauritius: 72 Sharia Abd el-Moneim Riad, Cairo (Agouza); tel. (02) 807642; telex 93631; Ambassador: Dr SABIR AHMAD KHAN CHATTAROO.
Mexico: 5 Dar es-Shifa, Cairo; tel. (02) 28622; Ambassador: JORGE PALACIOS TREVINO.
Mongolia: 3 Midan en-Nasr, Cairo (Dokki); tel. (02) 650060; Ambassador: SONOMDORJIN DAMBADARJAA.
Morocco: *Interests served by Senegal.*
Nepal: 9 Sharia Tiba, Cairo (Dokki); tel. (02) 704541; Ambassador: KRISHNA BAHADUR MONANDHAR.
Netherlands: 18 Sharia Hassan Sabri, Cairo (Zamalek); tel. (02) 3408744; telex 92028; Ambassador: Dr NICOLAAS H. BIEGMAN.
Niger: 28 Sharia Pahlaw, Cairo (Dokki); tel. (02) 987740; telex 2880; Ambassador: SORY MAMADOU DIALLO.
Nigeria: 13 Sharia Gabalaya, Cairo (Zamalek); tel. (02) 3406042; telex 92038; Ambassador: U. B. WALI.
Norway: 8 Sharia el-Gezireh, Cairo (Zamalek); tel. (02) 3403340; telex 92259; Ambassador: AAGE F. BOTHNER.
Oman: 30 Sharia Montazah, Cairo (Zamalek); tel. (02) 698073; telex 92272; Ambassador: GHALEB ABDULLAH JOUBRAN.
Pakistan: 8 Sharia es-Salouli, Cairo (Dokki); tel. (02) 988977; Ambassador: SUED ZAFARUL ISLAM; also looks after Bahrain interests at 8 Sharia Jamaiat an-Nisr, Cairo (Dokki); tel. (02) 705052; telex 2084.
Panama: Apt 9, 97 Sharia Mirghani, Cairo (Heliopolis); tel. (02) 662547; telex 92776; Ambassador: MARCO OCTAVIO AROSEMENA JAEN.
Peru: 11 Sharia Brasil, Cairo (Zamalek); tel. (02) 301971; telex 93663; Ambassador: JORGE PLASENCIA.
Philippines: 5 Sharia ibn el-Walid, Cairo (Dokki); tel. (02) 703596; Ambassador: (vacant).
Poland: 5 Sharia Aziz Osman, Cairo (Zamalek); tel. (02) 698410; Ambassador: TADEUSZ ZAREBA.
Portugal: 15A Sharia Mansour Muhammad, Cairo (Zamalek); tel. (02) 3405583; telex 20325; Ambassador: JOSÉ DE MATTOS-PARREIRA.
Qatar: 10 Sharia ath-Thamar, Midan an-Nasr, Madinet al-Mohandessin, Cairo; tel. (02) 704537; telex 92287.
Romania: 6 Sharia Kamel Muhammad, Cairo (Zamalek); tel. (02) 698107; telex 93807; Ambassador: ION COZMA.
Rwanda: 9 Sharia Ibrahim Osman, Mohandessin, Cairo, PB 485; tel. (02) 361079; telex 92552; Ambassador: JEAN NTIGURA.
Saudi Arabia: 12 Sharia al-Kamel Muhammad, Cairo (Zamalek); tel. (02) 819111.
Senegal: 46 Sharia Abd al-Moneim Riad, Mohandessin, Cairo (Dokki); tel. (02) 815647; telex 92047; Ambassador: SHAMS ED-DINE NDOYE; also looks after Tunisian interests at 26 Sharia el-Jazirah, Cairo (Zamalek); tel. (02) 698940.
Sierra Leone: 6 Sharia Hindawi, Midan Finny, Cairo (Dokki); tel. (02) 700699; Ambassador: (vacant).
Singapore: POB 356, 40 Sharia Babel, Cairo (Dokki); tel. (02) 704744; telex 21353; Ambassador: Haji YA'ACOB BIN MOHAMED.
Somalia: 38 Sharia esh-Shahid Abd el-Moneim Riad, Cairo (Dokki); tel. (02) 704038; Ambassador: HUSSEIN HASSAN FAREH.
Spain: 9 Hod el-Laban, Cairo (Garden City); tel. (02) 3547069; telex 92255; Ambassador: CARLOS FERNÁNDEZ-LONGORIA.
Sri Lanka: POB 1157, 8 Sharia Yehia Ibrahim, Cairo (Zamalek); tel. (02) 699138; telex 23575; Ambassador: A. KATHIRAMALAINATHAN.
Sudan: 4 Sharia el-Ibrahimi, Cairo (Garden City); tel. (02) 25043; Ambassador: AL-AMIN ABD AL-LATIF.
Sweden: POB 131, 13 Sharia Muhammad Mazhar, Cairo (Zamalek); tel. (02) 651132; telex 92256; Ambassador: OLOV ARTHUR TERNSTROM.
Switzerland: 10 Sharia Abd al-Khalek Saroit, POB 633, Cairo; tel. (02) 758133; telex 92267; Ambassador: Dr LUCIANO MORDASINI; also looks after Iranian interests at 12 Sharia Rifa'a, Cairo (Dokki); tel. (02) 985116.
Tanzania: 9 Sharia Abd al-Hamid Lotfi, Cairo (Dokki); tel. (02) 704155; telex 23537; Ambassador: MUHAMMAD A. FOUM.

EGYPT

Thailand: 2 Sharia al-Malek el-Afdal, Cairo (Zamalek); tel. (02) 3408356; telex 94231; Ambassador: CHAMRAS CHOMBHUBOL.

Tunisia: *Interests served by Senegal.*

Turkey: ave en-Nil, Cairo (Giza); tel. (02) 726115; Ambassador: BERDUK OLGAÇAY; also looks after United Arab Emirates interests at 4 Sharia ibn Sina, Al-Gezira, Cairo; tel. (02) 729955.

Uganda: 9 Midan el-Missaha, Cairo (Dokki); tel. (02) 3485544; telex 92087; Ambassador: (vacant).

USSR: 95 Sharia Giza, Cairo (Giza); tel. (02) 731416; Ambassador: ALEKSANDR BELONOGOV.

United Arab Emirates: *Interests served by Turkey.*

United Kingdom: Sharia Ahmad Raghab, Cairo (Garden City); tel. (02) 3540852; telex 94188; Ambassador: Sir ALAN URWICK.

USA: 5 Sharia Latin America, Cairo (Garden City); tel. (02) 28219; telex 93773; Ambassador: FRANK WISNER.

Uruguay: 6 Sharia Loutfallah, Cairo (Zamalek); tel. (02) 3415137; telex 92435; Ambassador: RAMIRO PIRIZ BALLÓN.

Venezuela: 15A Sharia Mansour Muhammad, Cairo (Zamalek); tel. (02) 813517; telex 93638; Ambassador: ABEL CLAVIJO OSTOS.

Viet-Nam: 21 Sharia el-Madina el-Mounawara, Cairo (Dokki); tel. (02) 704838; Ambassador: NGUYEN TU HUYEN.

Yemen Arab Republic: *Interests served by India.*

Yugoslavia: 33 Sharia Mansour Muhammad, Cairo (Zamalek); tel. (02) 3404061; Ambassador: MILAN ZUPAN.

Zaire: 5 Sharia Mansour Muhammad, Cairo (Zamalek); tel. (02) 699069; Ambassador: NGANDU MWALBA.

Zambia: POB 1464, 22 Sharia en-Nakhil, Cairo (Dokki); tel. (02) 709620; telex 92262; Ambassador: WINDSOR K. NKOWANI.

Judicial System

The Courts of Law in Egypt are principally divided into two juridical court systems: Courts of General Jurisdiction and Administrative Courts. Since 1969 the Supreme Constitutional Court has been at the top of the Egyptian judicial structure.

THE SUPREME CONSTITUTIONAL COURT

Is the highest court in Egypt. It has specific jurisdiction over: (i) judicial review of the constitutionality of laws and regulations; (ii) resolution of positive and negative jurisdictional conflicts and determination of the competent court between the different juridical court systems, e.g. Courts of General Jurisdiction and Administrative Courts, as well as other bodies exercising judicial competence; (iii) determination of disputes over the enforcement of two final but contradictory judgments rendered by two courts each belonging to a different juridical court system; (iv) rendering binding interpretation of laws and decree laws in the event of a dispute in the application of said laws or decree laws, always provided that such a dispute is of a gravity requiring conformity of interpretation under the Constitution.

COURTS OF GENERAL JURISDICTION

The Courts of General Jurisdiction in Egypt are basically divided into four categories, as follows: (i) The Court of Cassation (ii) The Courts of Appeal; (iii) The Tribunals of First Instance; (iv) The District Tribunals; each of the above courts is divided into Civil and Criminal Chambers.

(i) Court of Cassation: Is the highest court of general jurisdiction in Egypt. Its sessions are held in Cairo. Final judgments rendered by Courts of Appeal in criminal and civil litigation may be petitioned to the Court of Cassation by the Defendant or the Public Prosecutor in criminal litigation and by any of the parties in interest in civil litigation on grounds of defective application or interpretation of the law as stated in the challenged judgment, on grounds of irregularity of form or procedure, or violation of due process, and on grounds of defective reasoning of judgment rendered. The Court of Cassation is composed of the President, 41 Vice-Presidents and 92 Justices.

President: Hon. ABD AL-BORHAN NOOR.

(ii) The Courts of Appeal: Each has geographical jurisdiction over one or more of the governorates of Egypt. Each Court of Appeal is divided into Criminal and Civil Chambers. The Criminal Chambers try felonies, and the Civil Chambers hear appeals filed against such judgment rendered by the Tribunals of First Instance where the law so stipulates. Each Chamber is composed of three superior judges. Each Court of Appeal is composed of President, and sufficient numbers of Vice-Presidents and Superior Judges.

(iii) The Tribunals of First Instance: In each governorate there are one or more Tribunals of First Instance, each of which is divided into several Chambers for criminal and civil litigations. Each Chamber is composed of: (a) a presiding judge, and (b) two sitting judges. A Tribunal of First Instance hears, as an Appellate Court, certain litigations as provided under the law.

(iv) District Tribunals: Each is a one-judge ancillary Chamber of a Tribunal of First Instance, having jurisdiction over minor civil and criminal litigations in smaller districts within the jurisdiction of such Tribunal of First Instance.

PUBLIC PROSECUTION

Public prosecution is headed by the Attorney General, assisted by a number of Senior Deputy and Deputy Attorneys General, and a sufficient number of chief prosecutors, prosecutors and assistant prosecutors. Public prosecution is represented at all levels of the Courts of General Jurisdiction in all criminal litigations and also in certain civil litigations as required by the law. Public prosecution controls and supervises enforcement of criminal law judgments.

Attorney General: Hon. ABD AL-AZIZ IBRAHIM MUSTAFA AL-JUNDI.

ADMINISTRATIVE COURTS SYSTEM (CONSEIL D'ETAT)

The Administrative Courts have jurisdiction over litigations involving the State or any of its governmental agencies. The Administrative Courts system is divided into two courts: the Administrative Courts and the Judicial Administrative Courts, at the top of which is the High Administrative Court. The Administrative Prosecutor investigates administrative crimes committed by government officials and civil servants.

President of Conseil d'Etat: Hon. MUHAMMAD HILAL KASEM.

Administrative Prosecutor: Hon. RIFA'AT KHAFAGI.

THE STATE COUNCIL

Is an independent judicial body which has the authority to make decisions in administrative disputes and disciplinary cases within the judicial system.

THE SUPREME JUDICIAL COUNCIL

The Supreme Judicial Council was reinstituted in 1984, having been abolished in 1969. It exists to guarantee the independence of the judicial system from outside interference and is consulted with regard to draft laws organizing the affairs of the judicial bodies.

Religion

About 90% of Egyptians are Muslims, and almost all of these follow Sunni tenets. There are about 6m. Copts, forming the largest religious minority. Besides the Copts there are other Christian minorities numbering about a quarter of a million and consisting of Greek Orthodox, Roman Catholics, Armenians and Protestants. There is also a small Jewish minority.

ISLAM

Grand Sheikh of Al-Azhar: Sheikh JAD AL-HAQ ALI JAD AL-HAQ.

Grand Mufti of Egypt: Dr MUHAMMAD SAYED ATTIYAH TANTAWI.

CHRISTIANITY

Coptic Orthodox Church: Anba Ruess Building, Ramses St, Abbasiya, Cairo; f. AD 61; Leader Pope SHENOUDA III; about 8 million followers in Egypt, Sudan, other African countries, the USA, Canada, Australia, Europe and the Middle East. In September 1981 Pope Shenouda was banished to a monastery by President Sadat and a committee of five bishops was appointed to administer the Church. This decree was rescinded in April 1982 and the church's synod called upon to elect a new pope. However, Pope Shenouda was released from internal exile by President Mubarak and permitted to resume his duties in January 1985.

Coptic Catholic Church: Patriarch Cardinal STEPHANOS II, SIDAROUSS, 34 Sharia ibn Sandar, Koubbeh Bridge, Cairo; tel. (02) 821740; 4 dioceses; 200,000 mems.

Greek Catholic Patriarchate: POB 50076, Beirut, Lebanon; 16 rue Daher, Cairo; Patriarch of Antioch, of Alexandria and of Jerusalem His Beatitude MAXIMOS V HAKIM; 500,000 mems in the Middle East.

EGYPT
                                                                                           Directory

Greek Orthodox Church: Patriarch (vacant).

Armenian Apostolic Church: 179 Ave Ramses, Cairo, POB 48-Faggalah; tel. 901385; Archbishop ZAVEN CHINCHINIAN; 12,000 mems.

Armenian Catholic Patriarchate: 36 Sharia Muhammad Sabri Abou Alam, Cairo; Archbishop RAPHAEL BAYAN.

Maronite Church: 15 Sharia Hamdi, Daher, Cairo; Archbishop JOSEPH MERHI.

Syrian Catholic Church: 46 Sharia Daher, Cairo; Bishop BASILE MOUSSA DAOUD.

JUDAISM

Jewish Community: Office of the Chief Rabbi, Rabbi HAIM DOUEK, 13 Sharia Sebil el-Khazindar, Abbassia, Cairo.

The Press

Despite a fairly high illiteracy rate, the Egyptian Press is well developed. Cairo is the biggest publishing centre in the Middle East.

Legally all newspapers and magazines come under the control of the Supreme Press Council. The four big publishing houses of al-Ahram, Dar al-Hilal, Dar Akhbar al-Yawm and Dar al-Gomhouriya, operate as separate entities and compete with each other commercially. Dar al-Hilal is concerned only with magazines and publishes *Al-Mussawar*, *Hawa'a* and *Al-Kawakeb*. Dar Akhbar al-Yawm publishes the daily newspaper *Al-Akhbar*, the weekly newspaper *Akhbar al-Yawm* and the weekly magazine *Akher Saa*.

Dar al-Gomhouriya publishes the daily *Al-Gomhouriya*, the daily English language paper *Egyptian Gazette*, the daily French newspaper *Le Progrès Egyptien* and the afternoon paper *Al-Misaa'*.

The most authoritative daily newspaper is the very old-established *Al-Ahram*. Other popular large circulation magazines are *Rose al-Youssef*, *Sabah al-Kheir* and *Al-Iza'a wat-Television*.

In May 1975 President Sadat set up the Supreme Press Council, under the Chairmanship of the First Secretary of the Arab Socialist Union, to supervise the Press.

In November 1978, however, President Sadat abolished the Ministry of Culture and Information, but major papers remained under government ownership. A Press Law of July 1980 liberalized the organization of the major papers and, while continuing to provide for 49% ownership by the employees, arranged for the transfer of the remaining 51% from the defunct Arab Socialist Union to the new Shura (Advisory) Council. The editorial board of a national newspaper should consist of at least five members, headed by an editor-in-chief who is selected by the Shura Council. In June 1984 the Shura Council approved a proposal made by the Supreme Press Council that the posts of chairman of the board and editor-in-chief be held separately and not by one individual.

DAILIES
Alexandria

Barad ach-Charikat (Companies' Post): POB 813, Alexandria; f. 1952; Arabic; evening; commerce, finance, insurance and marine affairs, etc.; Editor S. BENEDUCCI; circ. 15,000.

Al-Ittihad al-Misri (Egyptian Unity): 13 Sharia Sidi Abd ar-Razzak, Alexandria; f. 1871; Arabic; evening; Propr ANWAR MAHER FARAG; Dir HASSAN MAHER FARAG.

Le Journal d'Alexandrie: 1 Sharia Rolo, Alexandria; French; evening; Editor CHARLES ARCACHE.

La Réforme: 8 passage Sherif, Alexandria; f. 1895; French; noon; Propr Comte AZIZ DE SAAB; circ. 7,000.

As-Safeer (The Ambassador): 4 Sharia as-Sahafa, Alexandria; f. 1924; Arabic; evening; Editor MUSTAFA SHARAF.

Tachydromos-Egyptos: 4 Sharia Zangarol, Alexandria; tel. 35650; f. 1879; Greek; morning; liberal; Publr PENY COUTSOUMIS; Editor DINOS COUTSOUMIS; circ. 2,000.

Cairo

Al-Ahram (The Pyramids): Sharia al-Galaa, Cairo; tel. (02) 745666; telex 2001; f. 1875; Arabic; morning, incl. Sundays (international edition published in London, England); Editor and Chair. IBRAHIM NAFEH; circ. 900,000 (weekdays), 1.1m. (Friday).

Al-Akhbar (The News): Dar Akhbar al-Yawm, Sharia as-Sahafa, Cairo; tel. (02) 758888; telex 92215; f. 1952; Arabic; Chair. (vacant); Man. Editor AHMAD ZEIN; circ. 789,268.

Arev: 3 Sharia Soliman Halaby, Cairo; f. 1915; Armenian; evening; official organ of the Armenian Liberal Democratic Party; Editor AVEDIS YAPOUDJIAN.

Egyptian Gazette: 24–26 Sharia Zakaria Ahmad, Cairo; tel. (02) 751511; telex 92475; f. 1880; English; morning; Editor-in-Chief SAMI ESH-SHAHED; circ. 35,000.

Al-Gomhouriya (The Republic): 24 Sharia Zakaria Ahmad, Cairo; tel. (02) 751511; telex 92475; f. 1953; Arabic; morning; Chair. MOHSEN MUHAMMAD; Editor MAHFOUZ AL-ANSARI; circ. 650,000.

Journal d'Egypte, Le: 1 Sharia Borsa Guédida, Cairo; f. 1936; French; morning; Gen. Man. LITA GALLAD; Editor-in-Chief MUHAMMAD RACHAD; circ. 72,000.

Mayo (May): Sharia al-Galaa, Cairo; organ of National Democratic Party; Supervisor MUHAMMAD SAFWAT ASH-SHARIF; circ. 500,000.

Al-Misaa' (The Evening): 24 Sharia Zakaria Ahmad, Cairo; telex 92475; f. 1956; Arabic; evening; Editor-in-Chief HAMDI EN-NAHAS; circ. 105,000.

Misr (Egypt): Cairo; f. 1977; organ of the Arab Socialist Party.

Phos: 14 Sharia Zakaria Ahmad, Cairo; f. 1896; Greek; morning; Editor S. PATERAS; Man. BASILE A. PATERAS; circ. 20,000.

Le Progrès Egyptien: 24 Sharia Zakaria Ahmad, Cairo; tel. (02) 741611; telex 92475; f. 1890; French; morning including Sundays; Editor-in-Chief KHALED ANWAR BAKIR; circ. 21,000.

PERIODICALS
Alexandria

Al-Ahad al-Gedid (New Sunday): 88 Sharia Said M. Koraim, Alexandria; tel. 807874; f. 1936; Editor-in-Chief and Publisher GALAL M. KORAITEM; circ. 60,000.

Alexandria Medical Journal: 4 G. Carducci, Alexandria; f. 1922; English, French and Arabic; quarterly; publ. by Alexandria Medical Asscn; Editor AMIN RIDA; circ. 1,500.

Amitié Internationale: 59 avenue Hourriya, Alexandria; tel. 23639; f. 1957; publ. by Asscn Egypt d'Amitié Internationale; Arabic and French; quarterly; Editor Dr ZAKI BADAOUI.

L'Annuaire des Sociétés Egyptiennes par Actions: 23 Midan Tahrir, Alexandria; f. 1930; annually in December; French; Propr ELIE I. POLITI; Editor OMAR ES-SAYED MOURSI.

L'Echo Sportif: 7 Sharia de l'Archevêché, Alexandria; French; weekly; Propr MICHEL BITTAR.

L'Economiste Egyptien: 11 Sharia de la Poste, Alexandria, POB 847; f. 1901; weekly; Proprs MARGUERITE and JOFFRE HOSNI.

Egypte-Sports-Cinéma: 7 avenue Hourriya, Alexandria; French; weekly; Editor EMILE ASSAAD.

Egyptian Cotton Gazette: POB 433, Alexandria; organ of the Cotton Exporters Association; English; 2 a year; Chief Editor AHMAD H. YOUSSEF.

Egyptian Cotton Statistics: Alexandria; English; weekly.

Egyptian Customs Magazine: 2 Sharia Sinan, Alexandria; deals with invoicing, receipts, etc.; Man. MUHAMMAD ALI EL-BADAWI.

La Gazette d'Orient: 5 Sharia Borsa Guédida, Alexandria; Propr MAURICE BETITO.

Guide des Industries: 2 Sharia Adib, Alexandria; French; annual; Editor SIMON A. BARANIS.

Informateur des Assurances: 1 Sharia Sinan, Alexandria; f. 1936; French; monthly; Propr ELIE I. POLITI; Editor SIMON A. BARANIS.

La Réforme Illustrée: 8 passage Sherif, Alexandria; f. 1925; French; weekly; Propr Comte AZIZ DE SAAB; circ. 20,000.

Répertoire Permanent de Législation Egyptienne: 27 ave el-Guesch, Chatby-les-Bains, Alexandria; f. 1932; French and Arabic; Editor V. SISTO.

Sina 'at en-Nassig (L'Industrie Textile): 5 rue de l'Archevêché, Alexandria; Arabic and French; monthly; Editor PHILIPPE COLAS.

Voce d'Italia: 90 Sharia Farahde, Alexandria; Italian; fortnightly; Editor R. AVELLINO.

Cairo

Al-Ahali (The People): 23 Sharia Abd al-Khalek, Tharwat, Cairo; tel. (02) 759114; weekly; Managing Editor MUHAMMAD SID AHMAD.

Al-Ahram al-Iqtisadi (The Economic *Al-Ahram*): Sharia al-Galaa, Cairo; telex 2001; Arabic; weekly; economic and political affairs; owned by Al-Ahram publrs; Chief Editor ISSAM RIFA'AT; circ. 60,000.

Al-Ahrar (The Liberals): Cairo; f. 1977; weekly; published by Liberal Socialist Party; Editor MUHAMMAD AMER.

Akhbar al-Yawm (Daily News): 6 Sharia as-Sahafa, Cairo; f. 1944; Arabic; weekly (Saturday); Editor-in-Chief IBRAHIM ABU SADAH; Man. Dir TALAAT EZ-ZOHEIRI; circ. 1,087,177.

Akher Sa'a (Last Hour): Dar Akhbar al-Yawm, Sharia as-Sahafa, Cairo; telex 92215; f. 1934; Arabic; weekly (Wednesday); independent; Editor-in-Chief MUHAMMAD WAJDI GANDIL; circ. 97,832.

Al-Azhar: Idarat al-Azhar, Sharia al-Azhar, Cairo; f. 1931; Arabic; Islamic monthly; supervised by the Egyptian Council for Islamic Research of Al-Azhar University; Dir MUHAMMAD FARID WAGDI.

Contemporary Thought: University of Cairo, Cairo; quarterly; Editor Dr Z. N. MAHMOUD.

Ad-Da'wa (The Call): Cairo; Arabic; monthly; organ of the Muslim Brotherhood.

Ad-Doctor: 8 Sharia Hoda Shaarawy, Cairo; f. 1947; Arabic; monthly; Editor Dr AHMAD M. KAMAL; circ. 30,000.

Echos: 1–5 Sharia Mahmoud Bassiouni, Cairo; f. 1947; French; weekly; Dir and Propr GEORGES QRFALI.

The Egyptian Mail: 24–26 Sharia Zakaria Ahmad; telex 92475; weekly; Saturday edition of *The Egyptian Gazette*; English; circ. 35,000.

Études Médicales: Collège de la Ste Familie Faggalah, Cairo; quarterly; Editor HUBERT DE LEUSSE.

Études Scientifiques: Cairo; scientific and technical quarterly; Editor HUBERT DE LEUSSE.

Al-Fusoul (The Seasons): 17 Sharia Sherif Pasha, Cairo; Arabic; monthly; Propr and Chief Editor MUHAMMAD ZAKI ABD AL-KADER.

Al-Garidat at-Tigariyat al-Misriya (The Egyptian Business Paper): 25 Sharia Nubar Pasha, Cairo; f. 1921; Arabic; weekly; circ. 7,000.

Hawa'a (Eve): Dar al-Hilal, 16 Sharia Muhammad Ezz el-Arab, Cairo; telex 92703; women's magazine; Arabic; weekly; Chief Editor SUAD AHMAD HILMI; circ. 160,837.

Al-Hilal Magazine: Dar al-Hilal, 16 Sharia Muhammad Ezz el-Arab, Cairo; telex 92703; f. 1895; Arabic; literary monthly; Editor Dr HUSSAIN MONES.

Industrial Egypt: POB 251, 26A Sharia Sherif Pasha, Cairo; f. 1924; quarterly bulletin and year book of the Federation of Egyptian Industries in English and Arabic; Editor DARWISH M. DARWISH.

Informateur Financier et Commercial: 24 Sharia Soliman Pasha, Cairo; f. 1929; weekly; Dir HENRI POLITI; circ. 15,000.

Al-Iza'a wat-Television (Radio and Television): 13 Sharia Muhammad Ezz el-Arab, Cairo; f. 1935; Arabic; weekly; Editor and Chair. AHMAD BAHGAT; circ. 80,000.

Al-Kawakeb (The Stars): Dar al-Hilal, 16 Sharia Muhammad Ezz el-Arab, Cairo; tel. (02) 27954; f. 1952; Arabic; weekly; film magazine; Editor KAMEL EN-NAGMI; circ. 86,381.

Kitab al-Hilal: Dar al-Hilal, 16 Sharia Muhammad Ezz el-Arab, Cairo; monthly; Founders EMILE and SHOUKRI ZEIDAN; Editor Dr HUSSAIN MONES.

Al-Liwa' al-Islami (Islamic Standard): 11 Sharia Sherif Pasha, Cairo; f. 1982; Arabic; weekly; government paper to promote official view of Islamic revivalism; Propr AHMAD HAMZA; Editor MUHAMMAD ALI SHETA; circ. 30,000.

Lotus Magazine (Afro-Asian Writings): 104 Sharia Kasr el-Eini, Cairo; f. 1968; quarterly; English, French and Arabic.

Magallat al-Mohandeseen (The Engineer's Magazine): 28 avenue Ramses, Cairo; f. 1945; published by The Engineers' Syndicate; Arabic and English; 10 a year; Editor and Sec. MAHMOUD SAMI ABD AL-KAWI.

Al-Magallat az-Zira'ia (The Agricultural Magazine): Cairo; monthly; agriculture; circ. 30,000.

Medical Journal of Cairo University: Manyal University Hospital, Sharia Kasr el-Eini, Cairo; f. 1933; Kasr el-Eini Clinical Society; English; quarterly.

The Middle East Observer: 8 Sharia Chawarby, Cairo; f. 1954; English; weekly; specializing in economics of Middle East and African markets; also publishes supplements on law, foreign trade and tenders; Man. Owner AHMAD FODA; Chief Editor AHMAD SABRI; circ. 30,000.

Al-Musawwar: Dar al-Hilal, 16 Sharia Muhammad Ezz el-Arab, Cairo; tel. (02) 27954; telex 92703; f. 1924; Arabic; weekly; Editor-in-Chief MAKRAM MUHAMMAD AKRAM; circ. 130,423.

October: 1119 Sharia Corniche en-Nil, Cairo; tel. (02) 746834; telex 847031; monthly; Chair. and Editor-in-Chief ANIS MANSUR; circ. 140,500.

Progrès Dimanche: 24 Sharia Galal, Cairo; tel. 741611; telex 92475; weekly; French; Sunday edition of *Le Progrès Egyptien*; Editor-in-Chief KHALED ANWAR BAKIR.

Riwayat al-Hilal: Dar al-Hilal, 16 Sharia Muhammad Ezz el-Arab, Cairo; Arabic; monthly; Proprs EMILE and SHOUKRI ZEIDAN; Editor Dr HUSSAIN MONES.

Rose al-Youssef: 89A Sharia Kasr el-Eini, Cairo; f. 1925; Arabic; weekly; political; circulates throughout all Arab countries, includes monthly English section; Chair. of Board ABD AL-AZIZ KHAMIS; Editor MUHAMMAD TUHAMI; Editor English section IBRAHIM EZZAT; circ. 35,000.

As-Sabah (The Morning): 4 Sharia Muhammad Said Pasha, Cairo; f. 1922; Arabic; weekly; Editor MUSTAFA EL-KACHACHI.

Sabah al-Kheir (Good Morning): 18 Sharia Muhammad Said Pasha, Cairo; Arabic; weekly; light entertainment; Chief Editor LOUIS JIRYIS; circ. 70,000.

Ash-Shaab (The People): Sharia Corniche en-Nil, Cairo; organ of Socialist Labour Party; weekly; Editor-in-Chief HAMED ZAIDAN; circ. 50,000.

At-Tahrir (Liberation): 5 Sharia Naguib, Rihani, Cairo; Arabic; weekly; Editor ABD AL-AZIZ SADEK.

At-Taqaddum (Progress): c/o 1 Sharia Jarim ed-Dawlah, Cairo; f. 1978; organ of National Progressive Unionist Party; replaced Al-Ahali.

Tchehreh Nema: 14 Sharia Hassan el-Akbar (Abdine), Cairo; f. 1904; Iranian; monthly; political, literary and general; Editor MANUCHEHR TCHEHREH NEMA MOADEB ZADEH.

Up-to-Date International Industry: 10 Sharia Galal, Cairo; Arabic and English; monthly; foreign trade journal.

Al-Wafd: Cairo; f. 1984; weekly; organ of the New Wafd Party; Editor-in-Chief MUSTAFA SHARDI; circ. 360,000.

Watani (My Country): Cairo; weekly newspaper of the Coptic Orthodox Church; Editor MEGUID ATTAIA.

Yulio (July): July Press and Publishing House, Cairo; f. 1986; weekly; Nasserist; Editor ABDULLAH IMAM; and a monthly cultural magazine, Editor MAHMOUD AL-MARAGHI.

NEWS AGENCIES

Middle East News Agency: 4 Sharia Sherifin, Cairo; tel. (02) 36160; f. 1955; regular service in Arabic, English and French; Chair. MUHAMMAD ABD AL-GAWAD MANSOUR; Editors MUHAMMAD EL-BIALI, KAMAL AMER and MUSTAFA NAGUIB.

Foreign Bureaux

Agence France-Presse (AFP): 33 Sharia Kasr el-Nil, Apt 12, Cairo; tel. (02) 767044; telex 92225; Correspondent MICHEL GARIN.

Agencia EFE (Spain): 35a Sharia Abul Feda, 4th Floor, Apt 14, Cairo (Zamalek); Correspondent JOSÉ LUIS VIDAL COY.

Agenzia Nazionale Stampa Associata (ANSA) (Italy): 19 Sharia Abd al-Khalek Sarwat, Cairo; tel. (02) 770403; telex 93365; Chief ETTORE MENCACCI.

Allgemeiner Deutscher Nachrichtendienst (ADN) (German Democratic Republic): 17 Sharia el-Brazil, Apt 59, Cairo (Zamalek); Correspondent RAINER HÖHLING.

Associated Press (AP) (USA): 33 Sharia Kasr en-Nil, POB 1077, Cairo; tel. (02) 779089; telex 92211; Chief WILLIAM C. MANN.

Bulgarian Telegraph Agency (BTA): 13 Sharia Muhammad Kamel Morsi, Aguza, Cairo; Chief DIMITER MASLAROV.

Deutsche Presse-Agentur (dpa) (Federal Republic of Germany): 33 Sharia Kasr en-Nil, Apt 13/4, Cairo; tel. (02) 767019; telex 92054; Chief WOLFGANG KOYDL.

Jiji Tsushin-Sha (Japan): Room 12, 5th Floor, 3 Gezira el-Wosta, Cairo (Zamalek); tel. (02) 3041443; Corresp. KYOSUKE NAITO.

Kyodo Tsushin (Japan): 9 Sharia el-Kamel Muhammad, Flat 2, Cairo (Zamalek); tel. (02) 3406105; telex 20435; Correspondent SHIRO ONISHI.

Magyar Távirati Iroda (MTI) (Hungary): 11 Sharia Ahmad Heshmat, Flat 15, Cairo (Zamalek); Chief KÁROLY PATAK.

Reuters (United Kingdom): Apt 43, North Block, Immobilia Bldgs, 26 Sharia Sherif Pasha, Cairo, POB 2040; tel. (02) 745667; Chief J. ROGERS.

Telegrafnoye Agentstvo Sovetskovo Soyuza (TASS) (USSR): 30 Sharia Muhammad Mazhar, Cairo (Zamalek); Correspondent YURI TYSOVSKY.

United Press International (UPI) (USA): 4 Sharia Eloui, POB 872, Cairo; Chief WADIE KIROLOS.

Xinhua (New China) News Agency (People's Republic of China): 19 Sharia Gezira el-Wosta, Cairo (Zamalek); tel. (02) 411648; telex 93812; Chief WANG GENBAO.

The Iraqi News Agency (INA) reopened its office in Cairo in October 1985.

Publishers

General Egyptian Book Organization: 117 Sharia Corniche en-Nil, Cairo; tel. (02) 775000; telex 93932; f. 1961; affil. to Min. of Culture; Chair. Dr EZZ ED-DIN ISMAIL.

Alexandria

Alexandria University Press: Shatby, Alexandria.

Artec: 10 Sharia Stamboul, Alexandria.

Dar Nashr ath-Thaqata: Alexandria.

Egyptian Book Centre: A. D. Christodoulou and Co, 5 Sharia Adib, Alexandria; f. 1950.

Egyptian Printing and Publishing House: Ahmad es-Sayed Marouf, 59 Safia Zaghoul, Alexandria; f. 1947.

Maison Egyptienne d'Editions: Ahmad es-Sayed Marouf, Sharia Adib, Alexandria; f. 1950.

Maktab al-Misri al-Hadith li-t-Tiba wan-Nashr: 7 Sharia Noubar, Alexandria; also at 2 Sharia Sherif, Cairo; Man. AHMAD YEHIA.

Cairo

Al-Ahram Establishment: Sharia al-Galaa, Cairo; tel. (02) 758333; telex 92001; f. 1875; publishes newspapers, magazines and books, incl. *Al-Ahram*; Chair. ABDALLA ABD AL-BARI.

Akhbar al-Yawm Publishing House: 6 Sharia as-Sahafa, Cairo; f. 1944; publishes *Al-Akhbar* (daily), *Akhbar al-Yawm* (weekly), and colour magazine *Akher Sa'a*; Pres. MOUSA SABRI; Dir-Gen. AMIN ADLY.

Al-Arab: 28 Sharia Faggalah, Cairo; tel. (02) 908025; f. 1900; fiction, poetry, history, biography, philosophy, religion, Arabic language and literature etc.; Man. Dir Dr SALADIN BOUSTANI.

Argus Press: 10 Sharia Zakaria Ahmad, Cairo; Owners KARNIG HAGOPIAN and ABD AL-MEGUID MUHAMMAD.

Dar al-Gomhouriya: 24 Sharia Zakaria Ahmad, Cairo; affiliate of At-Tahrir Printing and Publishing House; publications include the dailies, *Al-Gomhouriya*, *Al-Misaa'*, *Egyptian Gazette* and *Le Progrès Egyptien*; Pres. MOHSEN MUHAMMAD.

Dar al-Hilal Publishing Institution: Sharia 16 Muhammad Ezz el-Arab, Cairo; tel. (02) 20610; telex 92703; f. 1892; publishes *Al-Hilal*, *Riwayat al-Hilal*, *Kitab al-Hilal*, *Tabibak al-Khass* (monthlies); *Al-Mussawar*, *Al-Kawakeb*, *Hawaa*, *Samir*, *Mickey* (weeklies); Chair. MAKRAN MUHAMMAD AHMAD.

Dar al-Kitab al-Arabi: Misr Printing House, Sharia Noubar, Bab al Louk, Cairo; f. 1968; Man. Dir Dr SAHAIR AL-KALAMAWI.

Dar al-Kitab al-Masri: POB 156, Cairo; tel. (02) 742168; telex 22481; f. 1929; religion, history, geography, poetry, philosophy, science, etc.; Man. Dir EZ-ZEIN HASSAN.

Dar al-Maaref: 1119 Sharia Corniche en-Nil, Cairo; tel. (02) 777077-87; telex 92199; f. 1890; publishing, printing and distribution of all kinds of books in Arabic and other languages; publishers of *October* magazine; Chair. and Man. Dir SALAH MUNTASSAR.

Dar ash-Shorouk: 16 Sharia Gawad Hosni, Cairo; tel. (02) 774814; telex 93091; f. 1968; publishing, printing and distribution; publishers of books on modern Islamic politics, philosophy and art, and books for children; Chair. M. I. EL-MOALLIM.

Documentation and Research Centre for Education (Ministry of Education): 33 Sharia Falaky, Cairo; f. 1956; Dir Mrs ZEINAB M. MEHREZ; bibliographies, directories, information and education bulletins.

Editions Horus: 1 Midan Soliman Pasha, Cairo.

Editions le Progrès: 6 Sharia Sherif Pasha, Cairo; Propr WADI SHOUKRI.

Editions et Publications des Pères Jésuites: 1 Sharia Boustan al-Maksi, Faggalah, Cairo; religious publications in Arabic.

Les Editions Universitaires d'Egypte: 41 Sharia Sherif Pasha, Cairo; university textbooks.

Egyptian Co for Printing and Publishing: 40 Sharia Noubar, Cairo; tel. (02) 21310; Chair. MUHAMMAD MAHMOUD HAMED.

Higher University Council for Arts, Letters and Sciences: University of Cairo, Cairo.

Lagnat at-Taalif wat-Targama wan-Nashr (Committee for Writing, Translating and Publishing Books): 9 Sharia el-Kerdassi (Abdine), Cairo.

Librairie La Renaissance d'Egypte (Hassan Muhammad & Sons): 9 Sharia Adly, POB 2172, Cairo; f. 1930; Man HASSAN MUHAMMAD; religion, history, geography, medicine, architecture, economics, politics, law, philosophy, psychology, children's books, atlases, dictionaries.

Maktabet Misr: POB 16, 3 Sharia Kamel Sidki, Cairo; tel. (02) 908920; f. 1932; publs wide variety of fiction, biographies and textbooks for schools and universities; Man. AMIR SAID GOUDA ES-SAHHAR.

Muhammad Abbas Sid Ahmad: 55 Sharia Noubar, Cairo.

National Library Press (Dar al-Kutub): Midan Ahmad Maher, Cairo; bibliographic works.

New Publications: J. Meshaka and Co, 5 Sharia Maspiro, Cairo.

The Public Organization for Books and Scientific Appliances: Cairo University, Orman, Ghiza, Cairo; f. 1965; state organization publishing academic books for universities, higher institutes, etc.; also imports books, periodicals and scientific appliances; Chair. KAMIL SEDDIK; Vice-Chair. FATTHY LABIB.

Senouhy Publishers: 54 Sharia Abd al-Khalek Sarwat, Cairo; f. 1956; Dirs LEILA A. FADEL, OMAR RASHAD.

At-Tahrir Printing and Publishing House: 24 Sharia Zakaria Ahmad, Cairo; tel. (02) 751511; telex 92475; f. 1953; affil. to Shura (Advisory) Council; Chair. MOHSEN MUHAMMAD; Man. Dir ABD AL-HAMID HAMROUSH.

Other Cairo publishers include: Dar al-Fikr al-Arabi, Dar al-Fikr al-Hadith Li-t-Tab wan-Nashr, Dar wa Matabi, Dar an-Nahda al-Arabiya, Dar al-Misriya Li-t-Talif wat-Tardjma, Dar al-Qalam, Dar ath-Thagapa, Majlis al-Ala Li-Riyyat al-Funun, Maktaba Ain Shams, Maktaba al-Andshilu al-Misriya, Maktabat ach-Chandshi, Maktabat an-Nahira al-Hadith, Markaz Tasjil al-Athar al-Misriya, Matbaat ar-Risala, al-Qaumiya li-t-Tibaa wan-Nashr-Wizarat az-Ziraa Maslahat al-Basatin, Az-Zahraa for Arab Information.

Radio and Television

In 1985 there were an estimated 12m. radio receivers and 3.86m. television receivers in use.

RADIO

Egyptian Radio and Television Corporation (ERTV): Radio and TV Building, Sharia Maspiro, Corniche en-Nil, POB 1186, Cairo; tel. (02) 757155; telex 92152; f. 1928; 300 hours daily; Pres. HUSSEIN ENAN; Head of Eng. Section Eng. FAROUK IBRAHIM ALI; Head of Int. and Public Relations and Liaison Officer Mrs SOURAYAH HAMDAN. Home Service radio programmes in Arabic, English, French, Armenian, German, Greek, Italian, Russian and Hebrew; foreign services in Arabic, English, French, Swahili, Hausa, Bengali, Urdu, German, Spanish, Indonesian, Malay, Thai, Hindi, Pushtu, Persian, Turkish, Somali, Portuguese, Fulani, Italian, Zulu, Shona, Sindebele, Lingala, Afar, Amharic, Yoruba, Wolof, Bambara.

Middle East Radio: Société Egyptienne de Publicité, 24–26 Sharia Zakaria Ahmad, Cairo; f. 1964; commercial service with 500-kW transmitter; UK Agents: Radio and Television Services (Middle East) Ltd, 21 Hertford St, London, W1.

TELEVISION

Egyptian Television Organization: Radio and TV Bldg, Sharia Maspiro, Corniche en-Nil, Cairo; f. 1960; 22.5 hours daily (three channels); Pres. Mrs SAMIA SADEK.

Finance

(cap. = capital; auth. = authorized; p.u. = paid up; dep. = deposits; res = reserves; m. = million; brs = branches; amounts in £ Egyptian unless otherwise stated)

BANKING

The whole banking system was nationalized in 1961. Since 1974 foreign and private sector banks have been allowed to play a role in the economy, and about 50 foreign banks have been established. More than 200 financial institutions are now operating in Egypt.

EGYPT

Central Bank

Central Bank of Egypt: 31 Sharia Kasr en-Nil, Cairo; tel. (02) 751529; telex 92237; f. 1961; cap. 5.0m., dep. 10,246m., res 195m. (June 1986); 3 brs; Gov. and Chair. MUHAMMAD SALAH AD-DIN HAMID.

Commercial and Specialized Banks

Agricultural Bank: there are 17 Agricultural Banks in governorates throughout Egypt.

Alexandria Altogary and Al-Bahari Bank: 85 Sharia el-Horreya, Alexandria; f. 1981.

Alexandria Commercial and Maritime Bank: 85 avenue el-Horreya, POB 2376, Alexandria; tel. 4921556; telex 54553; f. 1981; cap. p.u. US $30m., dep. 97.5m. (Dec. 1985); Chair MUSTAFA W. HANNO; Man. Dir MUHAMMAD M. FAHMY.

Arab Land Bank: 33 Sharia Abd al-Khalek Sarwat, POB 26, Cairo; tel. (02) 748506; telex 92208; f. 1958; cap. p.u. 2m.; Chair. AHMAD AMIN.

Bank of Alexandria, SAE: 6 Sharia Salah Salem, Alexandria; and 49 Sharia Kasr en-Nil, Cairo; tel. 806212 (Alexandria), (02) 913822 (Cairo); telex 54107 (Alexandria), (02) 92069 (Cairo); f. 1957; cap. p.u. 25m. (Sept. 1984); 79 brs; Chair. MUHAMMAD ALI EL-BARBARY.

Bank of Commerce and Development (Altogariyoon): 30 Sharia Ramses, Cairo; f. 1980.

Banque du Caire, SAE: 22 Sharia Adly, POB 1495, Cairo; tel. (02) 762545; telex 92022; f. 1952; cap. and res 426.6m. (June 1985); 109 brs; Chair. MAHMOUD F. LABAN.

Banque Misr, SAE: 151 Sharia Muhammad Farid, Cairo; tel. (02) 912711; telex 92242; f. 1920; cap. 20m., res 300m., dep. 3,769m. (June 1984); 300 brs; Chair. MUHAMMAD NABIL IBRAHIM.

Crédit Foncier Egyptien: 11 Sharia el-Mashadi, POB 141, Cairo; tel. (02) 910197; telex 93863; f. 1880; cap. p.u. 25m. (June 1983); Chair. Dr ALI SABRI YASSIN.

Development Industrial Bank: 110 Sharia el-Galaa, Cairo; tel. (02) 779087; telex 92643; f. 1975; cap. p.u. 34m., dep. 30m. (June 1985); Chair. Dr Eng. MUHAMMAD ES-SAYED EL-GHAROURI.

Egyptian Export Development Bank: Evergreen Bldg, 10 Sharia Talaat Harb, Cairo; f. 1983 to replace National Import-Export Bank; tel. (02) 777033; telex 20850; auth. cap. 100m., issued cap. 50m.; Chair. HAZEM EL-BEBLAWI.

Egyptian Workers Bank: 90 Sharia el-Galaa, Cairo; f. 1983.

Hong Kong Egyptian Bank: Abu el-Feda Bldg, Sharia Abu el-Feda, Zamalek, Cairo; tel. (02) 3409186; telex 20471; f. 1982.

National Bank for Development: 5 Sharia el-Borsa el-Gedida, POB 647, Cairo; tel. (02) 763528; telex 20878; f. 1980; cap. p.u. and res 48.5m.; Chair. MUHAMMAD ALI Z. EL-ORABI; Dep. Chair. and Man. Dir MUHAMMAD I. FARID; there are affiliated National Banks for Development in 16 governorates.

National Bank of Egypt: 24 Sharia Sherif, Cairo; tel. (02) 744175; telex 92238; f. 1898; nationalized 1960; handles all commercial banking operations; total assets 7,856m., cap. 40m., dep. 4,824m. (June 1985); Chair. MUHAMMAD ABD AL-MONEIM ROUSHDI; Gen. Man. ABD AL-KARIM ABD AL-HAMID; 205 brs.

Principal Bank for Development and Agricultural Credit: 110 Sharia Kasr el-Eini, Cairo; tel. (02) 31057; telex 93045; f. 1976 to succeed former Credit organizations; cap. p.u. 18.6m. (June 1982); Chair. FATAHALLA RIFA'AT MUHAMMAD.

Social Bank

Nasser Social Bank: 35 Sharia Kasr en-Nil, POB 2552, Cairo; tel. (02) 744377; telex 92754; f. 1971; interest-free savings and investment bank for social and economic activities, participating in social insurance, specializing in financing co-operatives, craftsmen and social institutions; Chair. IBRAHIM M. LUTFI.

Multinational Banks

Arab African International Bank: 5 Midan es-Saray al-Koubra, POB 60, Garden City, Maglis esh-Shaab, 11516 Cairo; tel. (02) 3545094; telex 93531; f. 1964; auth. cap. US $500m., cap. p.u. US $284m. (June 1986); commercial investment bank; shareholders are governments of Kuwait, Egypt, Algeria, Jordan and Qatar, Bank Al-Jazira (Saudi Arabia), Rafidain Bank (Iraq), individuals and Arab institutions; Chair. and Man. Dir IBRAHIM AL-IBRAHIM; Deputy Chair. and Man. Dir ABD AL-HAMID KABODAN; Chief Gen. Man. ESSAM ED-DIN SHAFIK GABR; Gen. Man. MUHAMMAD A. AZAB; brs in Cairo, Alexandria, Heliopolis, Beirut, Dubai, Abu Dhabi, London (2), Nassau, and New York.

Arab International Bank: 35 Sharia Abd al-Khalek Sarwat, POB 1563, Cairo; tel. (02) 916120; telex 92079; f. 1971 as Egyptian International Bank, renamed 1974; cap. p.u. US $150m., res US $86m., dep. US $1,862m. (June 1985); offshore bank; aims to promote trade and investment in shareholders' countries and other Arab countries; Chair. Dr MUSTAFA KHALIL.

Commercial Foreign Venture Banks

Alexandria-Kuwait International Bank: 110 Sharia Kasr el-Eini, POB 1004, Cairo; tel. (02) 779776; telex 23535; f. 1978; cap. US $23m. (October 1985); dep. US $256m. (Dec. 1983); Egyptian/Kuwaiti businessmen have 62% interest, Bank of Alexandria 25%, Sharjah Group 3.5%, Principal Bank for Development and Agric. Credit 4.5%, Egyptian Kuwait Real Estate Devt Co 5%; 5 brs; Chair. and Man. Dir M. F. EL-ASSY.

Alwatany Bank of Egypt: 1113 Sharia Corniche en-Nil, POB 750, Cairo; tel. (02) 740705; telex 93268; f. 1980; cap. p.u. 13.8m., dep. 111m. (Dec. 1984); Chair. FAT'HALLAH RIFA'AT MUHAMMAD; Man. Dir TEWFIK GAMIL YASSIN.

Bank of Credit and Commerce (Misr), SAE: Cairo Centre Building, 106 Sharia Kasr el-Eini, POB 303, Garden City, Cairo; tel. (02) 557321; telex 93806; f. 1981; member of BCC Group; cap. p.u. 12.7m., dep. 308m. (Dec. 1984); 19 brs; Chair. MUHAMMAD ABDULLAH MERZBAN; Man. Dir QAISER RAZA.

Banque du Caire Barclays International, SAE: 12 Midan esh-Sheikh Youssef, Garden City, Cairo; tel. (02) 3549422; telex 93734; cap. 10m., dep. 205m. (Dec. 1984); Chair. M. F. LABAN; Joint Gen. Mans MUHAMMAD ABD AL-FATH ABD AL-AZIZ and A. M. JABLONOWSKI.

Banque du Caire et de Paris: 3 Sharia Latin America, Garden City, POB 2441, Cairo; tel. (02) 28322; telex 93722; f. 1977; Banque du Caire has 51% interest and Banque Nationale de Paris 49%; cap. p.u. 10.3m., dep. 108m. (Dec. 1985); Chair. ABD AL-WAHAB H. EL-ABIARI.

Cairo Far East Bank: 104 Corniche en-Nil, POB 757, El-Agoza, Cairo; tel. (02) 710280; telex 93977; f. 1978; cap. p.u. 7m., dep. 33.9m.; Chair. Dr AHMAD ABU ISMAIL.

Chase National Bank (Egypt), SAE: Nile Tower, 21-23 Sharia Giza, Giza; tel. 726132; telex 92394; f. 1975; National Bank of Egypt has 51% interest and Chase Manhattan Bank 49%; cap. 10m.; total assets US $878.5m., dep. US $680.7m. (1984); Chair. AHMAD ISMAIL; Man. Dir JAMES E. LEWIS.

Crédit International d'Egypte: Sharia Talaat Harb, POB 831, Cairo; tel. (02) 759738; telex 93680; f. 1977; Egyptian National Bank has 51% interest, Crédit Commercial de France 39% and Berliner Handels und Frankfurter Bank 10%; cap. 7m.; Chair. ABD AL-GHANI GAMEH.

Delta International Bank: Arab Socialist Union Building, 1113 Corniche en-Nil, POB 1159, Cairo; tel. (02) 753484; telex 93833; f. 1978; cap. p.u. US $17.5m. (1983); dep. US $217.2m., res US $5.6m. (Dec. 1982); Chair. MAHMOUD SEDKI MOURAD.

Egyptian Gulf Bank: Cairo Centre Bldg, 2 Sharia Abd al-Kader Hamza, POB 50 Maglis esh-Shaab, Cairo; tel. (02) 3542390; telex 93545; f. 1981; cap. p.u. 17.8m., dep. 160.4m. (1985); 4 brs; Chair. KAMAL HASSAN ALI; Gen. Man. GAMIL HUSSAM ED-DIN ABUS-SU'UD.

Egyptian-American Bank: 4 Sharia Hassan Sabri, Zamalek, POB 1825, Cairo; tel. (02) 316150; telex 92683; f. 1976; Bank of Alexandria has 51% interest and American Express Int. Banking Corpn 49%; total assets 453.5m. (1983); Chair. ES-SAYED EL-HABASHI; Man. Dir Dr FARID W. SAAD.

Faisal Islamic Bank of Egypt: 1113 Corniche en-Nil, POB 2446, Cairo; tel. (02) 753109; telex 93877; f. 1979; all banking operations conducted according to Islamic principles; cap. US $70m., dep. US $1,837m. (July 1986); Chair. Prince MUHAMMAD AL-FAISAL AS-SAOUD; Gov. Dr MAHMOUD MUHAMMAD EL-HELW; 10 brs.

Misr Exterior Bank, SAE: Cairo Plaza Bldg, Corniche en-Nil, POB 272, Cairo; tel. (02) 778552; telex 94061; f. 1981; Banco Exterior de España has a 40% interest, Banque Misr has 40%, Egyptian/Saudi Arabian businessmen have 20%; cap. p.u. US $20m., dep. 100.1m. (Aug. 1985); 4 brs; Chair. MUHAMMAD NABIL IBRAHIM; Man. Dirs ABDULLAH ABD AL-FATAH TAYEL, JUAN JOSÉ PUYOL.

Misr International Bank, SAE: 14 Sharia el-Alfy, POB 631, Cairo; tel. (02) 931002; telex 92688; f. 1975; cap. p.u. 10.9m.; dep. 1,436m.; Chair. SARWAT ABD AL-GHAFAAR.

Misr-America International Bank: 8 Sharia Ibrahim Naguib, POB 1003, Garden City, Cairo; tel. (02) 32247; telex 92830; f. 1977; Development Industrial Bank has 26% interest, Misr Insurance Co

EGYPT

has 25%; while Bank of America has 40%, Kuwait Real Estate Bank 4.5% and First Arabian Corporation 4.5%; cap. p.u. 5m., dep. 175,127m. (Dec. 1983); Chair. Dr MUHAMMAD IBRAHIM DAKROURI; Man. Dir MICHEL ROWIHAB.

Misr-Romanian Bank, SAE: POB 35, 35 Sharia Abu el-Feda, Zamalek, Cairo; tel. (02) 3419275; telex 93653; f. 1977; Banque Misr has 51% interest, while Romanian Bank for Foreign Trade (Bucharest) has 19%, Bank for Agriculture and Food Industries (Bucharest) 15%, and Investments Bank (Bucharest) 15%; cap. p.u. US $10m., dep. 107.7m. (June 1985); 3 brs; Chair. HUSSEIN AMER; Deputy Chair., Man. Dir and Gen. Man. GHEORGHE IDITOIU and BAHIR ABD AL-KERIM FAHMI.

Mohandes Bank: 30 Sharia Ramses, POB 2778, Cairo; tel. (02) 750972; telex 93950; f. 1979; cap. p.u. 12.5m., dep. 200.6m., res 12.4m. (Dec. 1984); Chair. AHMAD ALI KAMAL; Gen. Man. MUHAMMAD ABD AS-SALEM BADREDDIN.

Nile Bank, SAE: 35 Sharia Ramses, POB 2741, Cairo; tel. (02) 741417; telex 20825; f. 1978; cap. p.u. US $30m. (Dec. 1985); dep. 212.9m., res 7.3m. (Dec. 1984); 12 brs; Chair. and Man. Dir EYSSA EL-AYOUTI.

Pyramids Bank (El-Ahram Bank): 12 Sharia Itehad el-Mohameen el-Arab, Garden City, Cairo; tel. (02) 3555464; telex 20623; f. 1980; auth. cap. 50m., cap. p.u. 28m. (1985); Chair. Dr TAHER AMIN HASSAN; Gen. Man. MUHAMMAD ABDULLAH MAHMOUD.

Suez Canal Bank: 11 Sharia Muhammad Sabry Abu Alam, POB 2620, Cairo; tel. (02) 751066; telex 93852; f. 1978; total assets 1,270m. (Dec. 1985); Chair. ZAKARIA TAWFIK ABD AL-FATAH; Gen. Man. MUSTAFA FAYEZ HABLAS.

Non-Commercial Banks

Arab Investment Bank (Federal Arab Bank for Development and Investment): 1113 Corniche en-Nil, POB 1147, Cairo; tel. (02) 753301; telex 93792; f. 1978; cap. p.u. US $13m., dep. US $102m., total assets US $180m. (Dec. 1983); 6 brs; Chair. and Man. Dir Prof. FOUAD HASHEM AWAD.

Banque Nationale Société Générale, SAE: 4 Sharia Talaat Harb, 2nd Floor, POB 2664, Cairo; tel. (02) 770291; telex 93894; National Bank of Egypt has 51% interest, Société Générale, Paris has 49%; f. 1978; cap. 10m.; Gen. Man. JEAN DUBOIS.

Egypt Arab African Bank: POB 61, Magles esh-Shaab, 5 Midan es-Saray, El-Koubra, Garden City, Cairo; tel. (02) 3550948; telex 20965; f. 1982; Arab African International Bank has 49% interest, Egyptian businessmen have 16%, Arab African International Bank Pension Fund, Bank of Alexandria, Banque du Caire, Egyptian Reinsurance Co, and Development Industrial Bank each have 7%; cap. p.u. 20m., dep. 292.8m., res 13.7m. (Dec. 1984); merchant and investment bank services; Chair. and Man. Dir ALI GAMAL ED-DIN DABBOUS.

Egyptian Investment Finance Corporation: Cairo; f. 1985; cap. 17m.; merchant bank services.

Housing and Development Bank: 26 Batal Ahmad Abd al-Aziz, POB 234, Cairo (Dokki); tel. (02) 717170; telex 94075; f. 1979; cap. p.u. 18m., dep. 46.4m., res. 12.9m. (June 1986); 3 brs; Chair. MUHAMMAD AMIN AL-HIZZAWI.

Islamic International Bank for Investment and Development: 4 Sharia Addy, Mesaha Sq., Dokki, POB 180, Cairo; tel. (02) 843936; telex 94248; f. 1980; auth. cap. US $12, cap. p.u. US $10m. (June 1984); Chair. and Gen. Man. AHMAD A. FOUAD.

Misr Iran Development Bank: The Nile Tower, 21–23 Sharia Giza, POB 219, El-Orman; tel. (02) 727311; telex 22407; f. 1975; cap. p.u. US $40m., dep. US $335m. (1983); brs in Cairo and Port Said; Chair. MUHAMMAD ALI EL-BARBARY; Man. Dir AL-MOTAZ MANSOUR.

Société Arabe Internationale de Banque: 10 Sharia Abd as-Salam Aref, POB 2673, Cairo; tel. (02) 747266; telex 92693; f. 1976; cap. p.u. US $16m.; dep. US $172m. (Dec. 1984); 2 brs; Chair. Dr HASSAN ABBAS ZAKI; Gen. Man. HISHAM ESH-SHIATI.

Branches of Principal Foreign Banks

American Express International Banking Corporation, Arab Bank Ltd, Banca Commerciale Italiana, Banco do Brasil, Bank Melli Iran, Bank Saderat Iran, Bank of America, Bank of Credit and Commerce-International, Bank of Nova Scotia, Bank of Tokyo, Banque Nationale de Paris, Banque Paribas, Chemical Bank, Citibank, Commerzbank AG, Crédit Lyonnais, Crédit Suisse, Deutsche Bank AG, Dresdner Bank AG, Jammal Trust Bank, Lloyds Bank International Ltd, Middle East Bank Ltd, Midland Bank, National Bank of Abu Dhabi, National Bank of Greece, National Bank of Oman Ltd, National Bank of Pakistan, National Bank of Sudan, Rafidain Bank Iraq, Royal Bank of Canada, Sumitomo Bank Ltd, Swiss Bank Corpn.

Offshore Bank

Manufacturers Hanover Trust Co: 3 Sharia Ahmad Nessim, Giza, POB 1962, Giza, Cairo; tel. (02) 726703; telex 92297; Vice-Pres. and Man. R. DOLAN.

STOCK EXCHANGES

Capital Market Authority: 26 Sharia Gomhouriya, Cairo; tel. (02) 900392; telex 94282; f. 1979; Chair. MUHAMMAD HASSAN FAG AN-NOUR.

Cairo Stock Exchange: 4 Sharia esh-Sherifein, Cairo; f. 1883; Pres. MUHAMMAD ALI HASSAN.

Alexandria Stock Exchange: Pres. FOUAD SHAHEEN.

INSURANCE

Arab International Insurance Co: POB 2704, 28 Sharia Talaat Harb, Cairo; tel. (02) 746322; telex 92599; f. 1976; a joint-stock free zone company established by Egyptian and foreign insurance companies; Chair. GAMAL EL-BOROLLOSSI; Gen. Man. HASSAN M. HAFEZ.

Ach-Chark Insurance Co, SAE: 15 Sharia Kasr en-Nil, Cairo; tel. (02) 753333; f. 1931; Chair. AMIN EL-HIZZAWI; general and life.

The Egyptian Reinsurance Co, SAE: 7 Sharia Dar esh-Shifa, Garden City, POB 950, Cairo; tel. (02) 3543354; telex 92245; f. 1957; Chair. MUSTAFA KAMEL ESH-SHAMI.

L'Epargne, SAE: Immeuble Chemla, Sharia 26 July, POB 548, Cairo; all types of insurance.

Al-Iktisad esh-Shabee, SAE: 11 Sharia Emad ed-Din, POB 1635, Cairo; f. 1948; Man. Dir and Gen. Man. W. KHAYAT.

Misr Insurance Co: 44A Sharia Dokki, Giza; tel. 700158; telex 93320; f. 1934; all classes of insurance and reinsurance; cap. p.u. 6m.; Chair. FATHI MUHAMMAD IBRAHIM.

Mohandes Insurance Co: 36 Sharia Batal Ahmad Abd al-Aziz, Mohandeseen, Giza; tel. 701074; telex 93392.

Al-Mottahida: 9 Sharia Soliman Pasha, POB 804, Cairo; f. 1957.

National Insurance Co of Egypt, SAE: 33 Sharia Nabi Danial, POB 446, Alexandria; tel. 2333; telex 54212; f. 1900; Chair. ALI RA'AFAT NAWITO.

Provident Association of Egypt, SAE: 9 Sharia Sherif Pasha, POB 390, Alexandria; f. 1936; Man. Dir G. C. VORLOOU.

Trade and Industry

CHAMBERS OF COMMERCE

Alexandria

Egyptian Chamber of Commerce, Alexandria: Sharia el-Ghorfa Altogariya, Alexandria; tel. 808993; Pres. ABD AL-HAMID SERRI; Sec. AHMAD EL-ALFI MUHAMMAD; Gen. Dir MUHAMMAD FATHI MAHMOUD.

Cairo

Cairo Chamber of Commerce: 4 Sharia Midan el-Falaki, Cairo; tel. (02) 22897; f. 1913; Pres. MUHAMMAD EL-BELEDI; Gen. Dir SAID EL-BARRAD.

FOREIGN INVESTMENT ORGANIZATION

General Authority for Investment and Free Zones: 8 Adly St, POB 1007, Cairo; tel. (02) 906796; telex 92235; Deputy Chair. SULTAN ABOU ALI.

NATIONALIZED ORGANIZATIONS

In November 1975 a Presidential Decree ratified the establishment of Higher Councils for the various sectors of industry. During 1978, however, various government ministries took increasing control of industries. In 1980 it was estimated that the government controlled about 350 companies. The majority of the larger, more important industrial and commercial companies are now either State-owned or run under government supervision.

PETROLEUM

Egyptian General Petroleum Corporation (EGPC): POB 2130, Nasr City, Cairo; tel. (02) 837388; telex 92049; state supervisory authority generally concerned with the planning of policies relating to petroleum activities in Egypt with the object of securing the development of the oil industry and ensuring its effective administration; Chair. HAMAD AYYOUB.

EGYPT

Belayim Petroleum Co (PETROBEL): Sharia Gharb el-Istad, Nasr City, Cairo; f. 1957; capital equally shared between EGPC and International Egyptian Oil Co, which is a subsidiary of ENI of Italy; oil and gas exploration, drilling and production.

General Petroleum Co (GPC): 8 Sharia Dr Moustafa Abou Zahra, Nasr City, Cairo; f. 1957; wholly owned subsidiary of EGPC; operates mainly in Eastern Desert.

Gulf of Suez Petroleum Co (GUPCO): POB 2400, Cairo; f. 1965; partnership between EGPC and Amoco-Egypt Co, USA; developed the El-Morgan oilfield in the Gulf of Suez, also holds other exploration concessions in the Gulf of Suez and the Western Desert; output was averaging 24.5m. b/d in 1982; Chair. Dr Eng. HAMDI EL-BANBI.

Western Desert Petroleum Co (WEPCO): POB 412, Alexandria; tel. 4928710; telex 54075; f. 1967 as partnership between EGPC and Phillips Petroleum and later Hispanoil with 15% interest; developed Alamein, Yidma and Umbarka fields in the Western Desert and later Abu Qir offshore gas field in 1978; Chair. Eng. MUHAMMAD MOHI ED-DIN BAHGAT.

Arab Petroleum Pipelines Co (SUMED): 9 Sharia Amin Yehia-Zizinia, POB 2056, Alexandria; tel. (58) 64138; telex 54295; f. 1974; Suez-Mediterranean crude oil transportation pipeline (capacity: 80m. tons per year) and oil terminal operators; Chair. and Man. Dir Dr MUHAMMAD RAMZY EL-LEITHY.

Numerous foreign oil companies are prospecting for oil in Egypt under agreements with EGPC.

EMPLOYERS' ORGANIZATIONS

Federation of Egyptian Industries: POB 251, 26A Sharia Sherif Pasha, Cairo, and 65 Gamal Abdel Nasser Ave, Alexandria; tel. (02) 39488 (Cairo), 28622 (Alexandria); f. 1922; Pres. Dr ADEL GAZAREIN; represents the industrial community in Egypt.

TRADE UNIONS

Egyptian Trade Union Federation (ETUF): 90 Sharia Galaa, Cairo; f. 1957; 21 affiliated unions; 2.5m. mems; affiliated to the International Confederation of Arab Trade Unions and to the Organization of African Trade Union Unity; Pres. SAAD M. AHMED; Gen. Sec. IBRAHIM SHALABI.

General Trade Union of Agriculture: 31 Sharia Mansour, Bab el Louk, Cairo; 150,000 mems; Pres. MOKHTAR ABD AL-HAMID; Gen. Sec. MUHAMMAD ABD AL-KHALEK GOUDA.

General Trade Union of Air Transport: 5 Sharia Ahmad Sannan, St Fatima, Heliopolis; 11,000 mems; Pres. ABD AL-MONEM FARAG EISA; Gen. Sec. SHEKATA ABD AL-HAMID.

General Trade Union of Banks and Insurance: 2 Sharia el-Kady el-Fadel, Cairo; 56,000 mems; Pres. MAHMOUD MUHAMMAD DABBOUR; Gen. Sec. ABDOU HASSAN MUHAMMAD ALI.

General Trade Union of Building Workers: 9 Sharia Emad ed-Din, Cairo; 150,000 mems; Pres. HAMID HASSAN BARAKAT; Gen. Sec. SALEM ABD AR-RAZEK.

General Trade Union of Business and Management Services: 2 Sharia Muhammad Haggag, Midan et-Tahrir, Cairo; 100,000 mems; Pres. ABD AR-RAHMAN KHEDR; Gen. Sec. MAHMOUD MUHAMMAD.

General Trade Union of Commerce: 70 Sharia el-Gomhouriya, Cairo; tel. 914124; f. 1903; more than 100,000 mems; Pres. ABD AR-RAZEK ESH-SHERBEENI; Gen. Sec. KAMEL HUSSEIN A. AWAD.

General Trade Union of Food Industries: 3 Sharia Housni, Hadaek el-Koba, Cairo; 111,000 mems; Pres. SAAD M. AHMED; Gen. Sec. ADLY TANOUS IBRAHIM.

General Trade Union of Health Services: 22 Sharia esh-Sheik Kamar, Es Sakakiny, Cairo; 56,000 mems; Pres. IBRAHIM ABOU EL-MUTI IBRAHIM; Gen. Sec. AHMAD ABD AL-LATIF SALEM.

General Trade Union of Maritime Transport: 36 Sharia Sharif, Cairo; 46,000 mems; Pres. THABET MUHAMMAD ES-SEFARI; Gen. Sec. MUHAMMAD RAMADAN ABOU TOR.

General Trade Union of Military Production: 90 Sharia el-Galaa, Cairo; 55,000 mems; Pres. MOUSTAFA MUHAMMAD MOUNGI; Gen. Sec. IBRAHIM LUTFI ZANATI.

General Trade Union of Mine Workers: 5 Sharia Ali Sharawi, Hadaek el-Koba, Cairo; 14,000 mems; Pres. ABBAS MAHMOUD IBRAHIM; Gen. Sec. AMIN HASSAN AMER.

General Trade Union of Petroleum and Chemical Industries: 90 Sharia el-Galaa, Cairo; 103,000 mems; Pres. AHMAD AHMAD EL-AMAWI; Gen. Sec. ABD AL-KADER HASSAN ABD AL-KADER.

General Trade Union of Posts, Telegrams and Telephones: 90 Sharia el-Galaa, Cairo; 80,000 mems; Pres. MUHAMMAD KHAIRI HASHEM; Gen. Sec. MUHAMMAD ABD AR-RAUF DIRRAZ.

General Trade Union of Press, Printing and Information: 90 Sharia el-Galaa, Cairo; 43,100 mems; Pres. MUHAMMAD ALI EL-FIKKI; Gen. Sec. ABD AL-AZIZ MUHAMMAD BASUNI.

General Trade Union of Public Utilities: 22 Sharia Sharif, Cairo; 64,000 mems; Pres. MANSOUR ABD AL-MONEM MANSOUR; Gen. Sec. MUHAMMAD TALAAT HASSAN.

General Trade Union of Railways: 15 Sharia Emad ed-Din, Cairo; 89,000 mems; Pres. MAHMOUD ATITO; Gen. Sec. SAID MOUSTAFA ABOU EL-ELA.

General Trade Union of Road Transport: 90 Sharia el-Galaa, Cairo; 243,000 mems; Pres. MUHAMMAD MUHAMMAD AHMAD EL-OKALI; Gen. Sec. MUHAMMAD KAMAL LABIB.

General Trade Union of Textile Workers: 327 Sharia Shoubra, Cairo; 244,000 mems; Pres. ALI MUHAMMAD DOUFDAA; Gen. Sec. HASSAN TOULBA MARZOUK.

General Trade Union of Hotels and Tourism Workers: 90 Sharia el-Galaa, Cairo; 35,000 mems; Pres. MOUSTAFA IBRAHIM; Gen. Sec. AMIN ABUBAKR.

General Trade Union of Workers in Engineering, Metal and Electrical Industries: 90 Sharia el-Galaa, Cairo; tel. 742519; 130,000 mems; Pres. SAID GOMAA; Gen. Sec. GAMAL TARABISHI.

Transport

RAILWAYS

The area of the Nile Delta is well served by railways. Lines also run from Cairo southward along the Nile to Aswan, and westward along the coast to Sollum.

Egyptian Railways: Station Bldg, Midan Ramses, Cairo; tel. (02) 75100; telex 92616; f. 1851; length 5,327 km; 25 km electrified; Chair. Dr Eng. MUHAMMAD MAHER EL-MORSI.

Alexandria Passenger Transport Authority: 2 Sharia Aflatone, POB 466, Alexandria; tel. 5961810; telex 54637; f. 1863; controls City Tramways (28 km), Ramleh Electric Railway (16 km), suburban buses (450 km); Chair. Eng. MUHAMMAD ABD AR-RAHMAN AMIN; Tech. Dir Eng. MUHAMMAD AHMAD BAYOUMY.

Heliopolis Co for Housing and Inhabiting: 28 Sharia Ibrahim el-Lakkany, Heliopolis, Cairo; 50 km, 148 railcars; Gen. Man. ABD AL-MONEIM SEIF.

Work on the first underground transport system in Africa or the Middle East began in Cairo in 1982. Following delays, the system is now scheduled for completion in 1988. A 430-km line to carry iron ore from the Bahariya mines to the Helwan iron and steel works was opened in August 1973.

ROADS

There are good metalled main roads as follows: Cairo–Alexandria (desert road); Cairo–Benna–Tanta–Damanhur–Alexandria; Cairo–Suez (desert road); Cairo–Ismailia–Port Said or Suez; Cairo–Fayum (desert road); in 1984 there were over 90,000 km of roads. The Ahmad Hamdi road tunnel (1.64 km) beneath the Suez Canal was opened in October 1980. A road from Aswan to Wadi Halfa, in Sudan, was due to be completed in 1985.

Egyptian General Organization of Inland Transport for Provinces Passengers: Sharia Kasr el-Eini, Cairo; Pres. HASSAN MOURAD KOTB.

SHIPPING

Egypt's principal ports are Alexandria, Port Said and Suez. A port constructed at a cost of £E315m. and designed to handle up to 16m. tons of grain, fruit and other merchandise per year (22% of the country's projected imports by 2000) was opened at Damietta in July 1986.

Alexandria Port Authority: 66 ave Gamal Abd al-Nasser, Alexandria; Head Office: 106 Sharia el-Horreya, Alexandria; tel. 34321; telex 54147; Chair. Adm. ANWAR HEGAZY.

Major Shipping Companies

Alexandria Shipping and Navigation Co: 557 ave el-Horreya, POB 812, Alexandria; tel. 62923; telex 54029; services between Egypt, N. and W. Europe, USA, Red Sea and Mediterranean; Chair. and Man. Dir Eng. MAHMOUD ISMAIL; Gen. Man. I. ABAZZA.

Egyptian Navigation Co: 2 Sharia en-Nasr, POB 82, Alexandria; tel. 800050; telex 4131; f. 1930; owners and operators of Egypt's

EGYPT

mercantile marine; services Alexandria/Europe, USA, Black Sea, Adriatic Sea, Mediterranean Sea, Indian Ocean and Red Sea; 48 vessels; Chair. Adm. M. A. Ra'afat.

Pan-Arab Shipping Co: 13 Sharia Salah Salem, POB 39, Alexandria; tel. 4837360; telex 54123; f. 1974; Arab League Co; Dir-Gen. Capt. Hassan Said Mahmoud.

THE SUEZ CANAL

In 1984 21,361 vessels, with a net displacement of 371m. tons, used the Suez Canal, linking the Mediterranean and Red Seas.

Length of Canal 195 km; maximum permissible draught: 16.2 m (53 ft); breadth of canal at water level and breadth between buoys defining the navigable channel 365 m. and 180 m. respectively in the northern section and 305 m. and 175 m. in the southern section.

Suez Canal Authority (Hay'at Canal as-Suess): Irshad Bldg, Ismailia; tel. (064) 20000; telex 63238; Cairo Office: 6 Sharia Lazokhli, Garden City, Cairo; f. 1956; Chair. Muhammad Ezzat Adel.

CIVIL AVIATION

The main international airport is at Heliopolis, 23 km from Cairo. A second terminal was opened at Cairo International Airport in July 1986. An international airport was opened at Nuzhah in December 1983.

EgyptAir: Cairo International Airport, Heliopolis, Cairo; tel. (02) 455099; telex 22221; f. 1932 as Misr Airwork; known as United Arab Airlines 1960–1971; operates internal services in Egypt and external services throughout the Middle East, Far East, Africa, Europe and the United States; Chair. General Muhammad Fahim Rayan; fleet of one Boeing 747-100, one Boeing 747-200, 3 Boeing 767-200 ER, 6 Boeing 707-320C, 7 Boeing 737-200, 8 Airbus A300B4-203, one DC10, 3 Fokker F-27.

Egyptian Civil Aviation Authority: 31 Sharia 26 July, Cairo; tel. (02) 660632; Chair. Ali Osman Zeiko.

Tourism

Ministry of Tourism: 110 Sharia Kasr el-Eini, Cairo; f. 1965; branches at Alexandria, Port Said, Suez, Luxor and Aswan; Minister of Tourism and Civil Aviation Dr Fouad Sultan.

Egyptian General Authority for the Promotion of Tourism: Misr Travel Tower, Abbassia Sq., Cairo; tel. (02) 823570; telex 20799; Chair. Muhammad Nassim.

Egyptian General Co for Tourism and Hotels: 4 Latin America St, Garden City, Cairo; tel. (02) 32158; telex 92363; f. 1961; affiliated to the Ministry of Tourism.

Authorized foreign exchange dealers for tourists include the principal banks and the following:

American Express of Egypt Ltd: 15 Sharia Kasr en-Nil, POB 2160, Cairo; tel. (02) 750444; telex 92715; f. 1919; 7 brs.

Thomas Cook Overseas Ltd: 5 Sharia Talaat Harb, Cairo; tel. (02) 767420; telex 92413.

Atomic Energy

A 32-man Higher Nuclear Council was formed in August 1975. Work has begun on two of the eight 1,000 MW nuclear power stations to be built by the year 2000, which it is hoped will provide 40% of total energy requirements.

Atomic Energy Organization: 101 Sharia Kasr el-Eini, Cairo; f. 1955; Chair. Dr Ibrahim Hamouda; Vice-Chair. Dr Saleh Hashish; Dir of Nuclear Research Centre Dr E. Abd al-Aziz; Dir of Nat. Centre for Radiation Research and Technology Dr H. R. el-Kadi.

Nuclear Power Plants Authority: POB 8191, Masaken, Nasr City, 108 Abbassia; tel. 608291; telex 20761; f. 1976; Chair. Dr A. F. as-Saidi.

EL SALVADOR

Introductory Survey

Location, Climate, Language, Religion, Flag, Capital
The Republic of El Salvador lies on the Pacific coast of Central America. It is bounded by Guatemala to the west and by Honduras to the north and east. The climate varies from tropical on the coastal plain to temperate in the uplands. The language is Spanish. About 80% of the population are Roman Catholics, and other Christian churches are represented. The national flag (proportions 3 by 2) consists of three equal horizontal stripes, of blue, white and blue, with the national coat of arms in the centre of the white stripe. The capital is San Salvador.

Recent History
El Salvador was ruled by Spain until 1821, and became independent in 1839. Since then the country's history has been one of frequent coups and outbursts of political violence. General Maximiliano Hernández Martínez became President in 1931, and ruthlessly suppressed a peasant uprising, with an alleged 30,000 killings, in 1932. President Hernández was deposed in 1944, and the next elected President, Gen. Salvador Castañeda Castro, was overthrown in 1948. His successor as President, Lt-Col Oscar Osorio (1950–56), relinquished power to Lt-Col José María Lemus, who was deposed by a bloodless coup in 1960. He was replaced by a military junta, which was itself supplanted by another junta in January 1961. Under this junta, the conservative Partido de Conciliación Nacional (PCN) was established and won all 54 seats in the elections to the Legislative Assembly in December 1961. A member of the junta, Lt-Col Julio Adalberto Rivera, was elected unopposed to the presidency in 1962. He was succeeded by a former Minister of the Interior, Gen. Fidel Sánchez Hernández, the candidate of the ruling PCN, in 1967.

In the 1972 presidential election Col Arturo Armando Molina Barraza, candidate of the ruling PCN, was elected. His rival, José Napoleón Duarte, the leader of the left-wing coalition party Unión Nacional de Oposición, launched an abortive coup in March, and Col Molina took office in July, despite allegations of massive electoral fraud. These allegations were repeated in the 1977 presidential election, after which the PCN candidate, Gen. Carlos Humberto Romero Mena, took office.

Reports of violations of human rights by the Government were increasingly prevalent in 1979. The polarization of left and right after 1972 became evident in the rise in guerrilla activity. In October 1979 President Romero was overthrown and replaced by a junta of civilians and army officers. The junta promised to install a democratic system and to call elections, declared a political amnesty and invited participation from the guerrilla groups, but violence continued between government troops and guerrilla forces, and elections were postponed. In January 1980 an ultimatum from progressive members of the Government resulted in the formation of a new government, a coalition of military officers and the Partido Demócrata Cristiano (PDC). In March the country moved closer to full-scale civil war with the assassination of the Roman Catholic Archbishop of San Salvador, Oscar Romero y Galdames, an outspoken supporter of human rights.

In December 1980 José Napoleón Duarte, the 1972 presidential candidate and a member of the junta, was sworn in as President. In January 1981 the guerrillas launched their 'final offensive' and, after initial gains, the opposition front, Frente Democrático Revolucionario—FDR (allied with the guerrilla front, the Farabundo Martí de Liberación Nacional—FMLN), called for negotiations with the USA. The US authorities referred them to the Salvadorean Government, which refused to recognize the FDR while it was linked with the guerrillas. The USA affirmed its support for the Duarte Government and provided civilian and military aid. During 1981 the guerrilla forces unified and strengthened their hold on the north and east of the country. They continued their attacks on key economic targets, mainly bridges, electricity pylons and military installations, while the army retaliated by indiscriminately punishing the local population in guerrilla-controlled areas. By December 1981 there were an estimated 300,000 refugees, many of whom were in neighbouring countries. Large areas of Morazán, Chalatenango and Cabañas provinces were almost completely depopulated. Despite participation by Honduran and Guatemalan forces in counter-insurgency operations against the guerrillas, no victory was attained.

Elections to a Constituent Assembly, to take place in March 1982, were approved by an electoral law in December 1981 and backed by the USA, which secured support from the Organization of American States. The elections were boycotted by left-wing groups. The leader of the FDR urged the guerrillas not to disrupt the elections, but violence occurred in the preceding days and at least 40 people were killed on election day. A high turn-out of about 75% of voters was recorded. The PDC failed to win an absolute majority against the five right-wing parties which, with 60% of the vote between them, formed a Government of National Unity. Major Roberto D'Aubuisson Arrieta, leader of the extreme right-wing Alianza Republicana Nacionalista (ARENA), emerged as the most powerful figure and became President of the Constituent Assembly. In April a politically independent banker, Dr Alvaro Magaña Borja, was elected interim President of El Salvador, after pressure from the armed forces. However, the Assembly voted itself wide powers over the President. Military leaders then demanded that five ministerial posts be given to members of the PDC, fearing that, otherwise, US military aid would be withdrawn. A presidential election was scheduled for 1983, and a new constitution was to be drafted.

During 1982 about 1,600 Salvadorean troops were trained in the USA, and US military advisers were reported to be actively participating in the conflict. Agrarian reform was suspended in May by the Government, which ruled out negotiation with guerrillas. It was estimated that 4,000 civilians were killed in the first nine months of 1982, making a total of about 35,000 deaths in three years. The Government failed to curb violations of human rights by the armed forces. The guerrillas embarked on a new offensive in October 1982. In November a military coup was forestalled by Gen. José Guillermo García, the Minister of Defence, who removed several right-wingers from key military posts. In October the FDR-FMLN called for an unconditional dialogue with the Government, and in November Maj. D'Aubuisson failed to force through the Assembly a measure which would have blocked any dialogue with the left. President Magaña's position was strengthened in December, when a split within the PCN gave the moderates a majority in the Assembly.

The presidential election, originally planned for 1983, was postponed until March 1984 as a result of disagreement in the Constituent Assembly over the new constitution, which finally entered into force in December 1983. The agrarian reform programme caused a serious dispute between Maj. D'Aubuisson's ARENA party and the PDC, and led to a campaign by right-wing 'death squads' against trade unionists and peasant leaders. In October 1983 the Assembly voted to allow a maximum permissible holding of 262 ha per landowner. This result represented a victory for the ARENA party, which had been isolated in the Assembly following the collapse of its alliance with the PCN in February.

The issue of human rights abuse continued to be a serious problem for the Government throughout 1983. Following a period of intense activity by the death squads in September and October, when the weekly total of murders exceeded 200, the US Government called for the removal of several high-level officials, military officers and political figures who were linked with death squads. In January 1984, despite warnings from the US Congress that it would make substantial cuts in aid to El Salvador if the situation was allowed to deteriorate, the US

Government announced that military and economic aid in excess of US $450m. would be allocated to El Salvador in the year ending September 1985.

The failure of the US-trained 'rapid reaction' battalions and frequent reports of army atrocities (including the murder of the President of the Human Rights Commission, Marianela García Villas, in March 1983) undermined both public confidence in the Government and President Ronald Reagan's efforts to secure further US aid for El Salvador. In June 1983, in response to the guerrillas' successful offensive against the important agricultural region of Usulatán, the army launched 'Operation Well-being', a large-scale pacification programme. The campaign achieved only limited success, and by December 7,282 soldiers had been killed or wounded in the course of the year's hostilities. Following their capture of the strategically important towns of Berlín and San Miguel, the guerrillas struck a crucial blow against the Government with the attack on the garrison at El Paraíso and the destruction of the Cuscatlán bridge in January 1984. In February the FDR-FMLN proposed the formation of a broad-based provisional government, as part of a peace plan without preconditions. The plan was rejected by the Government. The guerrillas refused to participate in the presidential election, due to be held in March 1984, and threatened to prevent voting in various provinces. The election was marked by a low turn-out of voters, resulting partly from chaotic voting conditions and poor organization and partly from disruptions by the guerrillas. As no candidate emerged with a clear majority, a second round of voting was planned for May, when the contest was between José Napoleón Duarte, candidate of the PDC, and Maj. D'Aubuisson, candidate of ARENA. In an attempt to attract more votes, D'Aubuisson adopted a more moderate line towards his opponent, but his campaign was seriously damaged by reports which linked him to the right-wing death squads. At the second round of voting, Duarte secured a clear majority over D'Aubuisson, obtaining 54% of the votes cast.

Following his inauguration in June, President Duarte ordered a purge of the armed forces, which resulted in several high-ranking officers being sent abroad, and the reorganization of the police force, including the disbanding of the notorious Treasury Police. Both the FDR-FMLN and the President expressed their willingness to commence peace negotiations. Following pressure from the Roman Catholic Church and trade unions, the Government opened discussions with guerrilla leaders in Chalatenango in October. A second round of negotiations was held in November but the talks ended amid accusations of intransigence from both sides.

In August 1984 President Duarte appointed a five-member commission to investigate various crimes against human rights, including the murder of Archbishop Romero y Galdames. The Government had been prompted to act following reports of the massacre of more than 150 peasants by the armed forces in Cabañas and Chalatenango. By October it was estimated that 44,456 civilians had been killed in the course of the conflict. In January 1985, 20 politically-motivated assassinations were reported, including the murder of the Government's leading investigator into corruption. Prior to the legislative and municipal elections in March, there was a resurgence in the activities of right-wing 'death squads'. Following the elections, President Duarte guaranteed renewed investigations into such clandestine organizations.

In spite of the peace negotiations, confrontations between government forces and the guerrillas increased in late 1984. In October more than 200 soldiers and guerrillas were killed in fighting at the town of Suchitoto. During 1985 an increase in the aerial bombardment of guerrilla-occupied territory enabled the armed forces to claim a greater measure of success in their counter-insurgency campaign. However, a consequence of this strategy was an increase in the number of civilian casualties. In July the guerrillas launched a new campaign directed at urban centres.

Contrary to public predictions, the PDC won a convincing victory over the ARENA-PCN electoral alliance at the legislative and municipal elections in March 1985, thereby securing a clear majority in the new National Assembly. The PDC's victory, coupled with internal divisions within the right-wing grouping, precipitated a decline in the popularity and influence of the alliance, which culminated in the resignation of ARENA's leader, Roberto D'Aubuisson, in September.

Following its electoral success, the Government announced plans to introduce extensive social reforms in the spheres of health, education and local government services. Although President Duarte reaffirmed his intention to resume talks with the FDR-FMLN, both parties failed to agree on preconditions for renewing their dialogue. The murder of four US marines in June and an attack on the army's principal training centre at La Unión in October, in the course of which some 40 soldiers were killed, only served to worsen relations between the two sides.

In September 1985 Inés Duarte Durán, President Duarte's eldest daughter, was abducted by guerrillas. In view of the President's personal involvement in the issue, the Government was obliged to negotiate with the guerrillas. In November 118 guerrillas were released from prison in exchange for Inés Duarte. The Government was severely criticized by the opposition and the armed forces for its handling of the abduction, which had dominated internal affairs and rendered the Government virtually inactive in other spheres for almost two months.

Public discontent with President Duarte was compounded by the introduction of a series of controversial austerity measures in January 1986. The new policy was intended to revive El Salvador's economy, but it succeeded only in antagonizing the trade unions and the private sector. The trade unions demonstrated their opposition by holding strikes and protests throughout the year. A further problem for the Government was the deterioration in its relations with the Roman Catholic Church, following allegations that the Church was offering assistance to members of the rebel forces.

In October 1986 a severe earthquake caused extensive damage to the capital, San Salvador; more than 1,000 people were reported to have died and some 30,000 people were injured. More than 200,000 people were made destitute by the earthquake, which caused damage estimated to be in excess of US $1,500m. The disaster was expected to have calamitous social and economic consequences for El Salvador.

In November 1986 El Salvador was implicated in the controversy that followed the shooting-down of a US aircraft over Nicaragua. It was suggested that Ilopango Airport (located near San Salvador) was used as a supply-base by the Nicaraguan Contra rebels in their campaign against the Sandinista Government. The allegations caused embarrassment to the Salvadorean Government and were expected to pose further difficulties for President Duarte's administration in 1987.

Throughout 1985 and 1986 there was reported to be a noticeable decline in the number of politically-motivated murders and violations of human rights. In March 1986 President Duarte attempted to revive the dialogue with the guerrillas by proposing simultaneous talks between himself and the FDR-FMLN and the Nicaraguan Government and the Contra rebels. In April private talks were held in Lima, Peru, between representatives of the Salvadorean Government and the guerrillas, and in June President Duarte made a firm offer to the guerrillas to resume negotiations in September, with mediation by the Roman Catholic Church. Although the FDR-FMLN agreed to attend the talks, the negotiations failed to take place, after a dispute between the Government and the guerrillas over the agenda for the meeting and security arrangements. Although these developments enabled President Duarte to affirm his commitment to securing a negotiated settlement with the FDR-FMLN, there was increasing speculation that a military solution would be sought to end the civil war. Such speculation was supported by reports of the armed forces' growing domination of the conflict and by the success of the army's 'Unidos para reconstruir' campaign, a social and economic programme, launched in July 1986, to recover areas that had been devastated by the protracted fighting. Although the guerrillas mounted a successful attack against the army garrison at San Miguel in June, they failed to make any significant gains in 1986, and it was reported that a substantial number of guerrillas had defected to the Government's side. The state of siege, which had been in force since 1979, was lifted in January 1987.

El Salvador has a territorial dispute with Honduras over three islands in the Gulf of Fonseca and a small area of land on the joint border. In an attempt to resolve the issue, the dispute was submitted to the International Court of Justice for arbitration in December 1986.

EL SALVADOR

Government

Executive power is held by the President, assisted by the Vice-President and the Council of Ministers. The President is elected for a five-year term by universal adult suffrage. Legislative power is vested in the National Assembly (which replaced the National Constituent Assembly in March 1985), with 60 members elected by universal adult suffrage for a three-year term.

Defence

Military service is by compulsory conscription of men between 18 and 30 years of age for one year. In July 1986 the army totalled 38,650 men, the navy 1,290 and the air force 2,700. Paramilitary forces number 11,600 men, and the territorial civil defence force 7,000. Defence expenditure in 1985 was estimated at 630m. colones. The US Government granted US $125.4m. in military aid to El Salvador for the year ending September 1986.

Economic Affairs

The economy is primarily agricultural, with foodstuffs providing 71% of export earnings in 1984. The principal commercial crop is coffee, which accounted for 62% of export earnings in 1984. Coffee's contribution to GDP declined from 21.6% in 1977 to 8.8% in 1984. Prices fell by about 30% in 1981, and the crop was damaged by rust disease. Production declined from 3.4m. bags (each of 60 kg) in 1979 to 2.9m. bags in 1982. About 75% of coffee producers were making losses and were unable to harvest the crop as credit was no longer available. In 1983 production was affected by drought, followed by heavy rainfall. In addition, the guerrilla forces undertook a successful offensive against the agricultural region centred on Usulután, causing a further reduction in final production figures for coffee of up to 25%. The 1984 harvest was estimated to be 1.66m. bags. Losses in production were expected to amount to US $360m., or 10% of GNP. Between 1979 and 1985 coffee production declined by 34%. In spite of the destruction of an estimated 80,000 quintales (each of 46 kg) of coffee by the guerrilla forces, foreign exchange earnings from coffee were expected to increase substantially in 1986, as a result of high international prices.

Other major crops are cotton, sugar cane, maize, beans and rice. The annual output of maize increased from 9m. quintales in 1982/83 to 9.6m. quintales in 1983/84. Cotton production has fallen sharply since 1981, when the area planted was reduced by 50% from 1978. The annual harvest of seed (unginned) cotton fell from 2.6m. quintales in 1980/81 to 2m. quintales in 1981/82. The 1983/84 crop declined by 27%, causing a dramatic fall in export earnings, from US $55m. in 1983 to $9m. in 1984. The continued rural warfare and the displacement of population have reduced productivity. Nevertheless, agricultural production increased by 1% in 1984 and by an expected 2% in 1985. In 1986 the IDB allocated a loan of $830,000 to El Salvador to finance a programme to improve the use of resources in some 200 farming co-operatives.

The agrarian reform plan, introduced in March 1980 as part of the junta's political and economic programme, provided for land expropriation in three stages: farms of more than 500 ha; farms of between 150 and 500 ha; all rented cultivated land to be turned over to tenant farmers. Some success was achieved with the first stage: 12% of total arable land was taken over by the government agency, ISTA, and 330 estates were allocated to 30,000 workers in the form of co-operatives. Production fell by 10% in 1980/81 but average yields exceeded those of the private sector. A high proportion of funds was used to compensate landowners, and there were allegations of incompetence and excessive bureaucracy. By December 1982 only 52,000 out of a potential 150,000 tenants had benefited from the redistribution of land, and landowners had begun to reclaim their expropriated land by force. It was estimated that more than 9,000 peasants who were eligible for land had been evicted, either by landowners or the army. In March 1983 the Constituent Assembly approved a 10-month extension of the third phase of the reform programme, which enabled peasants to apply for title to 7 ha of land. Of the 48,000 peasants who had applied for land by September 1983, it was believed that only 2,600 had received their allocations. In December the Assembly voted to allow a maximum permissible holding of 245 ha, extended the third phase by a further six months and blocked the possibility of further reform, owing to the scarcity of land available for redistribution. In June 1984 the Assembly revoked Article 207 of the land reform law, which provided for a third phase of the programme.

El Salvador is the most highly industrialized country in the Central Americn Common Market (CACM). Manufacturing, concentrated in food processing, textiles, clothing, leatherwork and pharmaceuticals, accounted for 15.5% of GDP in 1984. The sector was severely affected by the armed conflict in 1981, when production of large and small businesses declined by 35% and 60% respectively. The sabotage campaign that was mounted by the left-wing guerrillas in mid-1981 caused damage estimated at US $4.8m., and all industry was operating at 52% capacity. The flight of capital has been estimated at $1,800m. since 1979. In 1985 underemployment was estimated to be 40% and unemployment was estimated to be 30%. In spite of a series of strikes which preceded the presidential election in May, industrial output increased by 2% in 1984. In November 1985 El Salvador's principal trade unions held a series of strikes in protest at the Government's economic policies. Real wages were estimated to have declined by 54% between 1980 and 1985.

GDP declined, in real terms, by 23.5% between 1978 and 1982. Export earnings fell by 33% over the same period. Private investment in fixed capital fell by 64% in 1981 to US $500m. Foreign exchange reserves declined from $114m. in 1979 to $71.8m. in 1982. Reserves recovered between 1983 and 1985, and reached $169.7m. by August 1985. The Government has become increasingly dependent on foreign aid, which amounted to $464.9m. in 1981. The USA provided $133m. in civilian aid in 1981, the World Bank $77m., the IMF $123m. and the IDB $102m. US economic aid amounted to $1,700m. between 1980 and 1985. The balance of payments had a current surplus of $30.6m. in 1980, but showed a deficit of $250m. in 1981, easing to $152m. in 1982, to $65m. in 1983 and to $53.5m. in 1984. In 1982 El Salvador received $32.2m. in special drawing rights from the IMF and was able to hold down the cost of debt servicing, owing to assistance from the US Government. In September 1983 El Salvador requested loans amounting to $20m. from commercial banks in the USA and Europe, and received $40m. from the IDB. In 1985 El Salvador's foreign debt was $1,900m. The budget deficit fell from 1,005.3m. colones in 1984 to 365m. colones in 1985. It has been estimated that 47% of government revenue is absorbed by the internal conflict. In accordance with IMF policy, the Government has introduced austerity measures. Public spending was reduced by 19% in 1983. The average annual rate of inflation was 13.1% in 1983 and fell to 11.6% in 1984. Inflation increased to 22.3% in 1985. In January 1984 a 14% value-added tax was introduced. In July 1984 the Federal Republic of Germany approved financing of $18m. for El Salvador. In 1985 the protracted civil war was estimated to have resulted in losses to the economy valued at $1,214m. In spite of continuing difficulties, real GDP growth of 1.5% and 1.6% was recorded in 1984 and 1985 respectively.

In January 1986 the Government introduced a programme of austerity measures, in an attempt to reverse the prevailing economic decline. Under the programme, the colón was devalued by 50% and a single exchange rate of 5 colones per US dollar was established; the minimum wage was increased by 15%; a price 'freeze' was imposed on basic foodstuffs; limits were imposed on imports of non-essential goods and cars; public transport fares were increased by 20%; and a temporary tax of 15% was imposed on exceptional profits derived from coffee earnings. The new programme proved to be highly controversial and prompted an increase in protests by trade unions against the Government. In spite of the austerity measures, no economic growth was expected in 1986, and the annual rate of inflation rose to an estimated 38%.

The Government's problems were exacerbated by a severe earthquake in October, which caused damage estimated at more than US $1,500m. In view of this catastrophe and the continuing failure to secure agreement on a cease-fire in the internal conflict, the prospects for any improvement in the economy in 1987 were generally regarded to be negligible.

El Salvador is a member of CACM (see p. 110), SELA (p. 218) and the IDB (p. 157).

EL SALVADOR

Social Welfare

In 1952 the Instituto Salvadoreño del Seguro Social (ISSS) was established. This institute provides hospital facilities, medicines and benefits for industrial injury, sickness, accident, disability, maternity, old age and death. Health and welfare insurance is financed by contributions from workers, employers and the State. In 1979 El Salvador had 82 hospital establishments, with a total of 7,848 beds. In 1980 there were 1,491 physicians working in the country. The Ministry of Health runs 250 medical units, including 14 hospitals. In 1985 its budget was 164.7m. colones.

Education

In 1984 there were 3,516 public and private schools. There were 1,208,488 students receiving education in 1985. There is one national university and 33 private universities. State education is free, and there are also numerous private schools. Primary education, beginning at seven years of age and lasting for nine years, is officially compulsory. However, only 69% of children in the relevant age-group were enrolled at primary schools in 1983, compared with 72% in 1978. Secondary education begins at the age of 16 and lasts for three years. Enrolment at secondary schools, as a proportion of children in this age-group, was estimated to be 25% in 1984. In 1980 the illiteracy rate among people aged 10 and over was 30.2% (males 42.6%, females 57.4%). The rate was 15.5% in urban areas but 42.2% among the rural population. The budgetary allocation for education in 1985 was 347.6m. colones.

Tourism

El Salvador was one of the centres of the ancient Mayan civilization, and the ruined temples and cities are of great interest. The volcanoes and lakes of the uplands provide magnificent scenery, while there are fine beaches along the Pacific coast. The civil war, in progress since 1979, has devastated the tourist industry. The number of tourist arrivals declined from 293,000 in 1978 to 82,000 in 1981, although the total rose to 99,000 in 1982 and to 106,000 in 1983.

Public Holidays

1987: 1 January (New Year's Day), 17–20 April (Easter), 1 May (Labour Day), 18 June (Corpus Christi), 4–6 August* (San Salvador Festival), 15 September (Independence Day), 12 October (Discovery of America), 2 November (All Souls' Day), 5 November (First Call of Independence), 24–25 December (Christmas).

1988: 1 January (New Year's Day), 1–4 April (Easter), 1 May (Labour Day), 2 June (Corpus Christi), 4–6 August* (San Salvador Festival), 15 September (Independence Day), 12 October (Discovery of America), 2 November (All Souls' Day), 5 November (First Call of Independence), 24–25 December (Christmas).

* 5–6 August in other cities.

Weights and Measures

The metric system is officially in force. Some old Spanish measures are also used, including:
 25 libras = 1 arroba;
 4 arrobas = 1 quintal (46 kg).

Currency and Exchange Rates

100 centavos = 1 Salvadorean colón.

Exchange rates (30 September 1986):
 £1 sterling = 7.235 colones;
 US $1 = 5.000 colones.

EL SALVADOR

Statistical Survey

Sources (unless otherwise stated): Banco Central de Reserva de El Salvador, 1a Calle Poniente y 7a Avda Norte, San Salvador; tel. 22-1144; Dirección General de Estadística y Censos, Calle Arce No 953, San Salvador; tel. 71-5011.

Area and Population

AREA, POPULATION AND DENSITY

Area (sq km)	
Land	21,073
Inland water	320
Total	21,393*
Population (census results)†	
2 May 1961	2,510,984
28 June 1971	
Males	1,763,190
Females	1,791,458
Total	3,554,648
Population (official estimates at mid-year)	
1983	4,724,154
1984	4,779,525
1985	4,819,000
Density (per sq km) at mid-1985	227

* 8,260 sq miles.
† Excluding adjustments for underenumeration.
Capital: San Salvador (population 452,614 at 1 July 1984).

BIRTHS AND DEATHS (per 1,000)

	1982	1983	1984
Birth rate	33.6	30.5	29.8
Death rate	7.1	6.9	6.0

ECONOMICALLY ACTIVE POPULATION*
(household survey, January–June 1980)

	Males	Females	Total
Agriculture, hunting, forestry and fishing	520,699	115,918	636,617
Mining and quarrying	4,103	291	4,394
Manufacturing	144,115	103,506	247,621
Electricity, gas and water	8,828	853	9,681
Construction	79,737	352	80,089
Trade, restaurants and hotels	78,785	177,301	256,086
Transport, storage and communication	62,994	2,599	65,593
Financing, insurance, real estate and business services	10,430	5,433	15,863
Community, social and personal services	121,145	129,013	250,158
Activities not adequately defined	112	112	224
Total labour force	1,030,948	535,378	1,566,326

* Excluding persons seeking work for the first time, totalling 27,027 (males 8,498; females 18,529).

Agriculture

PRINCIPAL CROPS (production in '000 quintals*)

	1982/83	1983/84	1984/85†
Coffee (green)	3,400	3,439	3,350
Seed cotton	2,308	1,690	1,737
Maize	9,000	9,630	11,462
Beans	830	927	1,056
Rice (paddy)	501	611	899

* Figures are in terms of the old Spanish quintal, equivalent to 46 kg (101.4 lb).
† Provisional.
Sugar cane ('000 metric tons): 2,372 in 1982; 2,984 in 1983; 3,200 (unofficial estimate) in 1984.

LIVESTOCK ('000 head, year ending September)

	1982	1983	1984
Horses*	89	90	90
Mules*	23	23	23
Cattle	1,106	954	937
Pigs	400	400	379
Sheep*	4	4	4
Goats*	14	14	14

* FAO estimates.
Chickens (million): 5 in 1982; 4 in 1983; 4 in 1984 (FAO estimate).
Source: FAO, *Production Yearbook*.

LIVESTOCK PRODUCTS ('000 metric tons)

	1982	1983	1984
Beef and veal*	30	30	30
Pigmeat†	13	13	13
Poultry meat	16	16	16†
Cows' milk†	268	249	249
Cheese†	17.6	17.7	17.7
Hen eggs	38.0*	35.3†	36.4†

* Unofficial figures.   † FAO estimates.
Source: FAO, *Production Yearbook*.

EL SALVADOR

Forestry

ROUNDWOOD REMOVALS
(FAO estimates, '000 cubic metres, excluding bark)

	1982	1983	1984
Sawlogs, veneer logs and logs for sleepers	70	60	60
Other industrial wood	50	30	30
Fuel wood	4,275	4,404	4,530
Total	4,395	4,494	4,620

Source: FAO, *Yearbook of Forest Products*.

SAWNWOOD PRODUCTION ('000 cubic metres)

	1981	1982*	1983*
Coniferous	30	30	25
Broadleaved	10	10	8
Total	40	40	33

* FAO estimates.
1984: Production as in 1983 (FAO estimates).
Source: FAO, *Yearbook of Forest Products*.

Fishing

('000 metric tons, live weight)

	1982	1983	1984
Freshwater fishes	0.6	0.8	1.7
Marine fishes	2.7	1.2	1.4
Squat lobsters	7.1	3.2	1.8
Other crustaceans	3.2	2.4	7.1
Molluscs	—	—	0.2
Total catch	13.5	7.6	12.2

Source: FAO, *Yearbook of Fishery Statistics*.

Industry

SELECTED PRODUCTS

	1981	1982	1983
Raw sugar ('000 metric tons)	182	199	259
Beer ('000 hectolitres)	427	420	n.a.
Cigarettes (million)	2,328	2,291	2,500*
Motor spirit (petrol)† ('000 metric tons)	115	107	120
Distillate fuel oils ('000 metric tons)	182	171	185
Residual fuel oils ('000 metric tons)	193	182	190
Cement ('000 metric tons)	459	276	320*
Electric energy (million kWh)	1,474	1,500	1,610

* Estimated production.
† Including aviation gasoline.
Source: UN, *Industrial Statistics Yearbook*.

Finance

CURRENCY AND EXCHANGE RATES

Monetary Units
100 centavos = 1 Salvadorean colón.

Denominations
Coins: 1, 2, 3, 5, 10, 25 and 50 centavos.
Notes: 1, 2, 5, 10, 50 and 100 colones.

Sterling and Dollar Equivalents (30 September 1986)
£1 sterling = 7.235 colones;
US $1 = 5.000 colones;
100 Salvadorean colones = £13.82 = $20.00.

Exchange Rate
Prior to January 1986, the official exchange rate was fixed at US $1 = 2.50 colones. In January 1986 a new rate of $1 = 5.00 colones was introduced.

BUDGET (million colones)

Current Revenue	1983	1984	1985
Taxes	1,079.8	1,350.6	1,659.4
Non-tax revenue	130.7	208.3	202.8
Current transfers	15.0	16.0	4.2
Other revenue	3.4	2.5	44.7
Total	1,229.0	1,577.5	1,911.0

Expenditure	1983	1984	1985
Remunerations	789.2	1,006.0	1,180.8
Purchase of goods and services	226.7	229.8	207.6
Interest on public debt	143.7	187.9	171.4
Private sector transfers	48.6	137.2	79.4
Public sector transfers	154.7	185.2	201.8
Foreign transfers	3.1	2.7	3.1
Expenditure from previous years	53.7	48.3	33.1
Capital investment	304.2	368.8	248.2
Amortization of public debt	123.2	519.2	152.6
Total	1,847.1	2,685.0	2,276.0

EL SALVADOR

CENTRAL BANK RESERVES
(US $ million at 31 December)

	1983	1984	1985
Gold*	19.8	19.8	19.8
IMF special drawing rights	0.1	—	—
Foreign exchange	160.1	165.8	179.6
Total	180.0	185.6	199.4

* Valued at US $42.22 per troy ounce.
Source: IMF, *International Financial Statistics*.

COST OF LIVING
(Consumer Price Index for Urban Areas. Base: 1980 = 100)

	1982	1983	1984
Food	130.2	147.6	168.5
Clothing	141.3	159.6	175.0
Rent, electricity and water	131.4	n.a.	165.4
All items	128.3	145.1	162.1

1985: Food 200.3; All items 198.2.
Source: ILO, mainly *Year Book of Labour Statistics*.

NATIONAL ACCOUNTS (million colones at current prices)
National Income and Product

	1982	1983	1984*
Domestic factor incomes†	7,979.7	8,923.6	9,955.5
Consumption of fixed capital	370.8	417.4	471.9
Gross domestic product at factor cost	8,350.5	9,341.0	10,427.4
Indirect taxes, *less* subsidies	615.7	750.7	982.4
GDP in purchasers' values	8,966.2	10,091.7	11,409.8
Net factor income from abroad	−228.8	−369.7	−392.1
Gross national product	8,737.4	9,722.0	11,017.7
Less Consumption of fixed capital	370.8	417.4	471.9
National income in market prices	8,366.6	9,304.6	10,545.8

* Provisional.
† Compensation of employees and the operating surplus of enterprises. The amount is obtained as a residual.

Expenditure on the Gross Domestic Product

	1982	1983	1984*
Government final consumption expenditure	1,414.7	1,504.3	1,703.0
Private final consumption expenditure†	6,876.6	7,938.6	9,248.1
Increase in stocks	55.8	43.9	58.5
Gross fixed capital formation	1,129.5	1,179.8	1,335.9
Total domestic expenditure	9,476.6	10,666.6	12,345.5
Exports of goods and services	2,042.3	2,461.4	2,407.2
Less Imports of goods and services	2,552.7	3,036.3	3,342.9
GDP in purchasers' values	8,966.2	10,091.7	11,409.8
GDP at constant 1962 prices	2,847.7	2,870.4	2,912.9

* Provisional.
† Including a statistical discrepancy.

Gross Domestic Product by Economic Activity

	1982	1983	1984*
Agriculture, hunting, forestry and fishing	2,075.4	2,160.5	2,354.9
Mining and quarrying	13.6	15.2	17.7
Manufacturing	1,381.8	1,572.1	1,767.5
Construction	300.6	343.4	365.8
Electricity, gas and water	199.7	243.9	281.9
Transport, storage and communications	346.7	411.5	482.0
Wholesale and retail trade	2,088.8	2,513.1	2,924.0
Finance, insurance, etc.	330.8	357.8	392.1
Owner-occupied dwellings	471.0	537.9	613.9
Public administration	1,049.7	1,113.2	1,261.9
Private services	708.0	823.1	947.7
Total	8,966.2	10,091.7	11,409.8

* Provisional.

EL SALVADOR

BALANCE OF PAYMENTS (US $ million)

	1982	1983	1984
Merchandise exports f.o.b.	704.1	735.4	725.9
Merchandise imports f.o.b.	−825.9	−830.9	−914.5
Trade balance	−121.8	−95.5	−188.6
Exports of services	168.3	172.9	228.3
Imports of services	−369.6	−385.8	−400.8
Balance of goods and services	−323.1	−308.4	−361.1
Private unrequited transfers (net)	51.7	52.6	118.0
Government unrequited transfers (net)	119.0	190.8	189.6
Current balance	−152.4	−65.0	−53.5
Direct capital investment (net)	−1.0	28.1	12.4
Other long-term capital (net)	150.2	300.7	12.0
Short-term capital (net)	22.7	−118.7	−14.8
Net errors and omissions	−93.9	−25.4	−42.5
Total (net monetary movements)	−74.4	119.7	−86.5
Valuation changes (net)	1.6	15.2	11.7
Exceptional financing (net)	81.8	−90.4	79.6
Official financing (net)	−36.0	−5.6	13.6
Changes in reserves	−27.0	38.9	18.4

Source: IMF, *International Financial Statistics*.

External Trade

PRINCIPAL COMMODITIES (million colones)

Imports c.i.f.	1982	1983*	1984*
Foodstuffs	366.4	353.3	336.4
Dairy products	47.4	57.4	18.9
Wheat	77.8	50.9	61.2
Fruits and fruit preparations	48.4	34.1	27.4
Vegetables	75.1	44.5	37.6
Raw materials, inedible	417.8	416.3	419.3
Crude petroleum	335.5	316.4	325.8
Animal and vegetable oils and fats	48.1	58.7	80.6
Chemical products	458.7	502.1	561.9
Chemical elements and compounds	66.7	94.2	108.0
Medicinal and pharmaceutical products	122.0	126.6	152.5
Perfume materials and other toiletries	45.8	36.8	44.1
Manufactured fertilizers	45.9	66.8	62.7
Basic manufactures and miscellaneous manufactured articles	560.4	594.3	658.5
Paper, cardboard and manufactures	70.7	82.4	94.4
Textile yarn and thread	52.6	41.2	45.9
Textile fabrics, other than cotton	27.0	22.3	30.5
Iron and steel	63.1	65.9	67.4
Clothing (excl. footwear)	19.7	18.9	18.4
Machinery and transport equipment	283.1	296.7	376.8
Mining, construction and industrial machinery	78.1	85.7	92.6
Electrical machinery and apparatus	132.9	131.3	131.4
Road motor vehicles	38.6	34.9	82.3
Total (incl. others)	2,141.9	2,228.7	2,443.6

* Provisional.
1985: Total imports 2,403.4 million colones.
Source: IMF, *International Financial Statistics*.

Exports f.o.b.	1982	1983*	1984*
Foodstuffs	1,159.2	1,206.8	1,279.7
Fresh shrimps	53.2	36.7	58.3
Coffee	1,014.2	1,019.0	1,106.9
Raw materials, inedible	129.1	167.7	49.0
Cotton	115.7	140.8	25.9
Chemical products	72.4	100.6	100.8
Miscellaneous manufactures	324.2	294.3	300.9
Clothing (excl. footwear)	52.2	24.1	19.0
Petroleum products	30.2	38.1	38.4
Total (incl. others)	1,748.6	1,838.2	1,793.4

* Provisional.
1985 (million colones): Coffee 1,131.4; Total (incl. others) 1,690.3.
Source: IMF, *International Financial Statistics*.

PRINCIPAL TRADING PARTNERS (million colones)

Imports c.i.f.	1982	1983	1984*
Canada	33.6	33.8	28.5
Costa Rica	89.9	106.6	116.7
France	48.8	22.7	9.3
Germany, Federal Republic	99.5	90.8	107.9
Guatemala	524.8	430.6	468.7
Honduras	20.5	38.0	41.7
Italy	17.4	12.0	17.3
Japan	66.9	78.1	104.8
Mexico	176.6	205.8	243.4
Netherlands	48.5	44.6	37.7
Nicaragua	17.0	8.8	8.1
Panama	59.7	59.1	78.4
Spain	16.6	21.7	23.5
Taiwan	n.a.	n.a.	20.1
USA	581.9	722.6	811.3
Venezuela	190.2	174.1	164.6
Total (incl. others)	2,207.2	2,228.7	2,443.6

Exports f.o.b.	1982	1983	1984*
Canada	27.0	32.7	28.9
Costa Rica	53.9	55.2	67.5
Germany, Federal Republic	512.1	349.6	403.0
Guatemala	329.0	307.6	293.2
Italy	19.3	7.1	1.2
Japan	58.5	91.5	99.1
Netherlands	5.8	5.7	1.6
Nicaragua	43.2	37.4	12.8
Panama	20.5	39.9	13.1
Spain	13.1	41.7	38.1
Taiwan	2.8	30.9	0.4
USA	619.3	711.8	669.9
Total (incl. others)	1,760.0	1,838.2	1,793.4

* Provisional.

Transport

RAILWAYS

	1982	1983	1984
Passengers ('000)	380.8	246.8	290.1
Freight ('000 metric tons)	301.5	364.5	315.0

Source: Comisión Ejecutiva Portuaria Autónoma.

ROAD TRAFFIC ('000 motor vehicles in use)

	1980	1981	1982*
Passenger cars	81.4	82.6	72.5
Commercial vehicles	62.5	64.0	67.8

* Source: UN, *Statistical Yearbook*.

SHIPPING

	1982	1983	1984
Vessels entered ('000 tons)	3,930	4,234	4,295
Freight ('000 metric tons)			
Loaded	281.4	402.3	267.7
Unloaded	552.1	897.4	855.1

Source: Comisión Ejecutiva Portuaria Autónoma.

CIVIL AVIATION (scheduled services)

	1982	1983	1984
Passengers arriving	123,450	129,488	144,576
Passengers leaving	120,956	139,820	164,654
Freight loaded (tons)	2,634.8	3,677.1	4,795.7
Freight unloaded (tons)	4,388.7	5,254.7	6,362.6

Source: Comisión Ejecutiva Portuaria Autónoma.

Tourism

	1980	1981	1982
Tourist arrivals ('000)	118	82	99

Source: UN, *Statistical Yearbook*.

Communications Media

	1981	1982	1983
Radio receivers ('000 in use)	n.a.	n.a.	1,900
Television receivers ('000 in use)	310	320	330
Telephones ('000 in use)	100	n.a.	n.a.
Daily newspapers	n.a.	6	n.a.

Source: mainly UNESCO, *Statistical Yearbook*.

Education

(1984)

	Institutions	Teachers	Students
Pre-Primary	550	1,144	60,902
Primary	2,631	19,978	883,214
Secondary	329	3,590	85,906
Higher	34	3,803	74,113

Directory

The Constitution

The Constitution of the Republic of El Salvador came into effect on 20 December 1983.

The Constitution provides for a republican, democratic and representative form of government, composed of three Powers—Legislative, Executive, and Judicial—which are to operate independently. Voting is a right and duty of all citizens over 18 years of age. Presidential and congressional elections may not be held simultaneously.

The Constitution binds the country, as part of the Central American Nation, to favour the total or partial reconstruction of the Republic of Central America. Integration in a unitary, federal or confederal form, provided that democratic and republican principles are respected and that basic rights of individuals are fully guaranteed, is subject to popular approval.

LEGISLATIVE ASSEMBLY

The Legislative Power is vested in a single Chamber, the Legislative Assembly, whose members are elected every three years and are eligible for re-election. The Assembly's term of office begins on 1 May. The Assembly's duties include the choosing of the President and Vice-President of the Republic from the two citizens who shall have gained the largest number of votes for each of these offices, if no candidate obtains an absolute majority in the election. It also selects the members of the Supreme and subsidiary courts; of the Elections Council; and the Accounts Court of the Republic. It fixes taxes; ratifies treaties concluded by the Executive with other States and international organizations; sanctions the Budget; regulates the monetary system of the country; determines the conditions under which foreign currencies may circulate; and suspends and reimposes constitutional guarantees. The right to initiate legislation may be exercised by the Assembly (as well as by the President, through the Council of Ministers, and by the Supreme Court). The Assembly may override, with a two-thirds majority, the President's objections to a Bill which it has sent for presidential approval.

PRESIDENT

The President is elected for five years, the term beginning and expiring on 1 June. The principle of alternation in the presidential office is established in the Constitution, which states the action to be taken should this principle be violated. The Executive is responsible for the preparation of the Budget and its presentation to the Assembly; the direction of foreign affairs; the organization of the armed and security forces; and the convening of extraordinary sessions of the Assembly. In the event of the President's death, resignation, removal or other cause, the Vice-President takes office for the rest of the presidential term; and, in case of necessity, the Vice-President may be replaced by one of the two Designates elected by the Legislative Assembly.

JUDICIARY

Judicial Power is exercised by the Supreme Court and by other competent tribunals. The Magistrates of the Supreme Court are elected by the Legislature, their number to be determined by law. The Supreme Court alone is competent to decide whether laws, decrees and regulations are constitutional or not.

The Government

HEAD OF STATE

President: Ing. JOSÉ NAPOLEÓN DUARTE (sworn in 1 June 1984).
Vice-President: Lic. RODOLFO ANTONIO CASTILLO CLARAMOUNT.

COUNCIL OF MINISTERS
(December 1986)

Minister of the Interior: EDGAR ERNESTO BELLOSO FUNES.
Minister of the Presidency: Dr JORGE EDUARDO TENORIO.
Minister of Justice: Dr JULIO ALFREDO SAMAYOA.
Minister of Health and Social Security: Dr BENJAMÍN VALDES H.
Minister of Finance: RICARDO J. LÓPEZ.
Minister of Economy: Dr RICARDO PARDOMO.
Minister of Foreign Trade: Dr RICARDO GONZÁLEZ.
Minister of Foreign Affairs: Dr RICARDO ACEVEDO PERALTA.
Minister of Defence and Public Security: Gen. CARLOS EUGENIO VIDES CASANOVA.
Minister of Education: Prof. JOSÉ ALBERTO BUENDÍA FLORES.
Minister of Agriculture and Livestock: Ing. CARLOS AQUILINO DUARTE FUNES.
Minister of Planning and Economic and Social Development: Dr FIDEL CHÁVEZ MENA.
Minister of Labour and Social Welfare: MIGUEL ALEJANDRO GALLEGOS.
Minister of Public Works: Ing. LÓPEZ CERÓN.
Minister of Culture and Communications: Lic. JULIO ADOLFO REY PRENDES.
Secretary of Information to the Presidency: Prof. LUIS ANGEL LAGOS GÓMEZ.

MINISTRIES

Ministry of the Presidency: Casa Presidencial, San Salvador; telex 20522.
Ministry of Agriculture and Livestock: Blvd de Los Héroes y 21a Calle Poniente, San Salvador; telex 20228.
Ministry of Defence and Public Security: Palacio Nacional, San Salvador; telex 30345.
Ministry of Economy: Centro de Gobierno, 4a Avda Norte 233, San Salvador.
Ministry of Education: Calle Delgado y 8a Avda Norte, San Salvador.
Ministry of Finance: 3a Avda Norte y 13 Calle Poniente, San Salvador.
Ministry of Foreign Affairs: Blvd Dr Manuel Enrique Araújo, Km 6, San Salvador; telex 20179.
Ministry of Foreign Trade: Paseo Gral Escalón 4122, Apdo 0119, San Salvador; tel. 24-3000; telex 20269.
Ministry of Health and Social Security: Calle Arce 827, San Salvador.
Ministry of the Interior: Palacio Nacional, San Salvador.
Ministry of Justice: 3a Avda Norte y 11 Calle Poniente, San Salvador.
Ministry of Labour and Social Welfare: Edif. Ministerio del Interior, Palacio Nacional, San Salvador; telex 20016.
Ministry of Planning and Economic and Social Development: 10 Avda Sur, Costado Noroeste de Casa Presidencial, San Salvador; telex 30309.
Ministry of the Presidency: Casa Presidencial, San Salvador.
Ministry of Public Works: Palacio Nacional, San Salvador.

President

In the second round of voting in the presidential election, held on 6 May 1984, JOSÉ NAPOLEÓN DUARTE, candidate of the Partido Demócrata Cristiano (PDC), received 752,625 (53.6%) of the votes cast, while Maj. ROBERTO D'AUBUISSON ARRIETA, candidate of the Alianza Republicana Nacional (ARENA), received 651,741 (46.4%) of the votes.

Legislature

ASAMBLEA NACIONAL

President: Dr GUILLERMO ANTONIO GUEVARA LACAYO (PDC).
First Vice-President: ALFONSO ARÍSTEDES ALVARENGA.

EL SALVADOR

General Election, 31 March 1985

Party	Seats
Partido Demócrata Cristiano (PDC)	33
Alianza Republicana Nacionalista (ARENA)	13
Partido de Conciliación Nacional (PCN)	12
Partido Acción Democrática (PAD)	1
Partido Auténtico Institucional Salvadoreño (PAISA)	1
Total	60

Political Organizations

OFFICIALLY RECOGNIZED PARTIES

Alianza Republicana Nacionalista (ARENA): San Salvador; f. 1981; right-wing; united with PCN to contest March 1985 elections; Leader ALFREDO CRISTIANI; Sec.-Gen. MARIO REPDAELLI.

Movimiento Estable Republicano Centrista (MERECEN): San Salvador; f. 1982; centre party; Sec.-Gen. JUAN RAMÓN ROSALES Y ROSALES.

Partido Acción Democrática (PAD): Apdo 01124, San Salvador; f. 1981; right-wing; Leader RENÉ FORTÍN MAGAÑA.

Partido Acción Renovadora (PAR): San Salvador; f. 1944; advocates a more just society; Leader ERNESTO OYARBIDE.

Partido Auténtico Institucional Salvadoreño (PAISA): San Salvador; f. 1982; formerly right-wing majority of the PCN; aligned with ARENA; Sec.-Gen. Dr ROBERTO ESCOBAR GARCÍA.

Partido de Conciliación Nacional (PCN): Calle Arce 1128, San Salvador; f. 1961; right-wing; Pres. HUGO CARRILLO; Leader FRANCISCO JOSÉ GUERRERO; Sec.-Gen. RAÚL MOLINA MARTÍNEZ.

Partido Demócrata Cristiano (PDC): 3a Calle Poniente 836, San Salvador; f. 1960; 150,000 mems; anti-imperialist, advocates self-determination and Latin American integration; Sec.-Gen. Lic. RODOLFO ANTONIO CASTILLO CLARAMOUNT.

Partido de Orientación Popular (POP): San Salvador; f. 1981; extreme right-wing.

Partido Popular Salvadoreño (PPS): POB (01) 425, San Salvador; tel. 23-2265; f. 1966; right-wing; represents business interests; Sec.-Gen. FRANCISCO QUIÑÓNEZ AVILA.

Partido Unionista Centroamericana (PUCA): San Salvador; advocates reunification of Central America; Pres. Dr GABRIEL PILOPA ARAÚJO.

Parties awaiting legal recognition are Partido Centrista Salvadoreño (f. 1985; Leader TOMÁS CHAFOYA MARTÍNEZ); Partido de Empresarios, Campesinos y Obreros (ECO, Leader Dr LUIS ROLANDO LÓPEZ) and Partido Independiente Democrático (PID, f. 1985; Leader EDUARDO GARCÍA TOBAR).

Other parties include: Partido de la Revolución Salvadoreña (Sec.-Gen. JOAQUÍN VILLALOBOS) and Patria Libre (f. 1985; right-wing; Leader HUGO BARRERA).

OPPOSITION GROUPING

Frente Democrático Revolucionario-Farabundo Martí de Liberación Nacional (FDR-FMLN): San Salvador; f. 1980 as a left-wing opposition front to the PDC-military coalition government; the FDR is the political wing and the FMLN is the guerrilla front; military operations are co-ordinated by the Dirección Revolucionaria Unida (DRU); Pres. (FDR) GUILLERMO UNGO; Vice-Pres. (FDR) EDUARDO CALLES; the front comprises c. 20 groups, of which the principal are:

Bloque Popular Revolucionario (BPR): guerrilla arm: Fuerzas Populares de Liberación (FPL, Leader 'Commander GERÓNIMO'); based in Chalatenango; First Sec. LEONEL GONZÁLEZ; Second Sec. DIMAS RODRÍGUEZ.

Frente de Acción Popular Unificado (FAPU): guerrilla arm: Fuerzas Armadas de la Resistencia Nacional (FARN); Leaders FERMÁN CIENFUEGOS, SAÚL VILLALTA.

Frente Pedro Pablo Castillo: f. 1985.

Ligas Populares del 28 de Febrero (LP-28): guerrilla arm: Ejército Revolucionario Popular (ERP); Leaders JOAQUÍN VILLALOBOS, ANA GUADALUPE MARTÍNEZ.

Movimiento Nacional Revolucionario (MNR): San Salvador.

Movimiento Obrero Revolucionario Salvado Cayetano Carpio (MOR).

Movimiento Popular Social Cristiano: formed by dissident members of PDC; Leader RUBÉN ZAMORA.

Partido Comunista Salvadoreño (PCS): guerrilla arm: Fuerzas Armadas de Liberación (FAL); Leader JORGE SCHAFIK HANDAL; Deputy Leader AMÉRICO ARAÚJO RAMÍREZ.

Partido Revolucionario de los Trabajadores Centroamericanos (PRTC): Leaders ROBERTO ROCA, MARÍA CONCEPCIÓN DE VALLADARES (alias Commdr NIDIA DÍAZ).

Unión Nacional Democrática (UND): communist.

OTHER GROUPS

Partido de Liberación Nacional (PLN): political-military organization of the extreme right; the military wing is the Ejército Secreto Anti-comunista (ESA); Sec.-Gen. and C.-in-C. AQUILES BAIRES.

The following guerrilla groups are dissident factions of the Fuerzas Populares de Liberación (FPL):

Frente Clara Elizabeth Ramírez: f. 1983; Marxist-Leninist group.

Movimiento Laborista Cayetano Carpio: f. 1983.

There are also several right-wing guerrilla groups and 'death squads' not officially linked to any of the right-wing parties.

Diplomatic Representation

EMBASSIES IN EL SALVADOR

Argentina: 71a Avda Sur 227, Colonia Escalón, San Salvador; tel. 24-2006; telex 20221; Ambassador: Dr VÍCTOR JOSÉ BIANCULLI.

Brazil: Edif. la Centroamericana, Alameda Roosevelt 3107 5°, San Salvador; tel. 23-1214; telex 20096; Ambassador: MARIO LOUREIRO DIAS COSTA.

Chile: Pasaje Belle Vista No 121, Entre 9a C.P. y 9a C.P. bis, Colonia Escalón, San Salvador; tel. 23-7132; telex 20377; Ambassador: RENÉ PÉREZ NEGRETE.

China (Taiwan): 89a Avda Norte 335, Colonia Escalón, San Salvador; tel. 23-6920; telex 20152; Ambassador: Gen. LO YU-LUM.

Colombia: Edif. Inter-Capital 2°, Paseo Gral Escalón y Calle La Ceiba, Colonia Escalón, San Salvador; tel. 23-0126; telex 20247; Ambassador: Dr LUIS GUILLERMO VÉLEZ TRUJILLO.

Costa Rica: Edif. la Centroamericana 3°, Alameda Roosevelt 3107, San Salvador; tel. 23-8282; telex 30271; Ambassador: Lic. OSCAR CASTRO VEGA.

Dominican Republic: 77a Avda Norte 422, Colonia Escalón, San Salvador; tel. 23-6636; Ambassador: ALBERTO EMILIO DESPRADEL CABRAL.

Ecuador: Blvd Hipódromo 803, Colonia San Benito, San Salvador; tel. 24-5921; telex 20445; Ambassador: JAIME SÁNCHEZ LEMOS.

France: Colonia La Mascota, Pasaje A 41-46, Casilla 474, San Salvador; tel. 23-0728; telex 20243; Ambassador: ALAIN ROUQUIÉ.

Germany, Federal Republic: 3a Calle Poniente 3831, Colonia Escalón, Apdo 693, San Salvador; tel. 23-6173; telex 20149; Ambassador: GUIDO HEYMER.

Guatemala: 15 Avda Norte 135, San Salvador; tel. 21-6097; Ambassador: Brig.-Gen. LUIS FEDERICO FUENTES CORADO.

Holy See: 87a Avda Norte y 7a Calle Poniente, Colonia Escalón, Apdo 01-95, San Salvador (Apostolic Nunciature); tel. 23-2454; Apostolic Nuncio: Mgr FRANCESCO DE NITTIS.

Honduras: 9a Calle Poniente 4612 y 89a Avda Norte, Colonia Escalón, San Salvador; tel. 24-6662; telex 20524; Ambassador: Lic. ROBERTO SUAZO TOMÉ.

Israel: 85 Avda Norte, No 619, Colonia Escalón, Apdo 1776, San Salvador; tel. 23-8770; telex 20777; Ambassador: ARYEH AMIR.

Italy: 1a Calle Poniente y 71a Avda Norte 204, San Salvador; tel. 23-7325; telex 20418; Ambassador: Dr TEODORO FUXA (also represents the interests of Somalia).

Japan: Avda La Capilla 615, Colonia San Benito, San Salvador; tel. 24-4597; Chargé d'affaires: HIROYUKI KIMOTO.

Mexico: Paseo Gral Escalón 3832, San Salvador; tel. 23-4243; telex 20070; Ambassador: FEDERICO URUCHÚA DURAND.

Nicaragua: 27a Avda Norte 1134, Colonia Layco, San Salvador; tel. 25-7281; telex 20546; Chargé d'affaires: FRANCISCO TENORIO MORA.

EL SALVADOR

Panama: Edif. Balam Quitzé 68-1, Calle Circunvalación y 89a Avda Sur, Colonia Escalón, San Salvador; tel. 23-7893; Ambassador: DAVID SAMUEL PERÉ RAMOS.
Paraguay: Avda La Capilla 414, Colonia San Benito, San Salvador; tel. 23-5951; Ambassador: JUAN ALBERTO LLÁNEZ.
Peru: Edif. La Centroamericana 2°, Alameda Roosevelt 3107, San Salvador; tel. 23-0008; Ambassador: ALBERTO MONTAGNE.
Spain: 51 Avda Norte 138, San Salvador; tel. 23-7961; telex 20372; Ambassador: FERNANDO ALVAREZ DE MIRANDA.
United Kingdom: 17a Calle Poniente 320, Centro de Gobierno, Apdo 1591, San Salvador; tel. 22-6104; telex 20174; Chargé d'affaires: DAVID RIDGWAY.
USA: 25 Avda Norte 1230, San Salvador; tel. 26-7100; telex 20648; Ambassador: EDWIN G. CORR.
Uruguay: Edif. Intercapital, Calle La Ceiba y Paseo Gral Escalón 1°, San Salvador; tel. 24-6661; telex 20391; Ambassador: ALFREDO LAFONE.
Venezuela: 93 Avda Norte 619, Colonia Escalón, San Salvador; tel. 23-5809; telex 20388; Ambassador: Dr PEDRO E. COLL.

Judicial System

Supreme Court of Justice: Centro de Gobierno José Simeón Cañas, San Salvador; tel. 71-3511; composed of 14 Magistrates, one of whom is its President. The Court is divided into four chambers: Constitutional Law, Civil Law, Penal Law and Litigation.
President: Dr FRANCISCO JOSÉ GUERRERO.
Chambers of 2nd Instance: 14 chambers composed of two Magistrates.
Courts of 1st Instance: 87 courts in all chief towns and districts.
Courts of Peace: 193 courts throughout the Republic.
Attorney-General: SANTIAGO MENDOZA AGUILAR (PDC).

Religion

Roman Catholicism is the dominant religion, but other denominations are also permitted. In 1982 there were about 200,000 Protestants. Seventh-day Adventists, Jehovah's Witnesses, the Baptist Church and the Church of Jesus Christ of Latter-day Saints (Mormons) are represented.

CHRISTIANITY
The Roman Catholic Church
El Salvador comprises one archdiocese and four dioceses. About 90% of the country's inhabitants are adherents.
Bishops' Conference: Conferencia Episcopal de El Salvador, 15 Avda Norte 1420, Colonia Layce, Apdo 1310, San Salvador; tel. 25-8997; telex 20420; f. 1974; Pres. Mgr MARCO RENÉ REVELO CONTRERAS, Bishop of Santa Ana.
Archbishop of San Salvador: Mgr ARTURO RIVERA Y DAMAS, Arzobispado, Calle San José y Avda Las Américas, Urb. Isidro Menéndez, Apdo 2253, San Salvador; tel. 26-6066..

The Baptist Church
Baptist Association of El Salvador: Apdo 347, San Salvador; tel. 25-1636; f. 1933; Pres. EUDORA MARY C. KALIL; Exec. Sec. Rev. Lic. CARLOS ISIDRO SÁNCHEZ.

BAHÁ'Í FAITH
National Spiritual Assembly: 33a Calle Oriente Bis 315, Apdo 01-151, San Salvador; tel. 25-8563; mems resident in 295 localities.

The Press

DAILY NEWSPAPERS
San Salvador
El Diario de Hoy: 11a Calle Oriente 271, Apdo 495, San Salvador; tel. 21-5340; telex 20291; f. 1936; independent; Dir ENRIQUE ALTAMIRANO MADRIZ; Man. FRANCISCO MARCHESINI; circ. 75,710 (weekdays), 75,786 (Sundays).
Diario Latino: 23a Avda Sur 225, Apdo 96, San Salvador; tel. 21-3240; f. 1890; evening; Editor MIGUEL ANGEL PINTO; circ. 20,000.

Directory

Diario Oficial: 4a Calle Poniente 829, San Salvador; tel. 21-9101; f. 1875; Dir ALONSO MIRA; circ. 2,100.
El Mundo: 2a Avda Norte 211, Apdo 368, San Salvador; tel. 21-9188; f. 1967; evening; Dir CRISTÓBAL IGLESIAS; circ. 58,032 (weekdays), 61,822 (Sundays).
La Prensa Gráfica: 3a Calle Poniente 130, San Salvador; tel. 71-3333; f. 1915; general information; conservative, independent; Editor RODOLFO DUTRIZ; circ. 97,312 (weekdays), 115,564 (Sundays).

Santa Ana
Diario de Occidente: 1a Avda Sur No. 3, Santa Ana; tel. 41-2931; f. 1910; Editor ALEX E. MONTENEGRO; circ. 6,000.

PERIODICALS
Anaqueles: 8a Avda Norte y Calle Delgado, San Salvador; review of the National Library.
Cultura: Ministerio de Educación, Pasaje Contreras 145, San Salvador; quarterly; educational; Dir Dr DAVID ESCOBAR GALINDO.
El Salvador Filatélico: Avda España 207, Altos Vidrí Panades, San Salvador; f. 1940; publ. quarterly by the Philatelic Society of El Salvador.
Orientación: Palacio Arzobispal, 1a Calle Poniente 3462, San Salvador; tel. 24-5099; Catholic weekly; Dir ROBERTO TORROELLA.
Proceso: Apdo (01) 168, San Salvador; tel. 24-0011; f. 1980; weekly newsletter, published by the Documentation and Information Centre of the Universidad Centroamericana José Simeón Cañas.
Revista del Ateneo de El Salvador: 13a Calle Poniente, Centro de Gobierno, San Salvador; tel. 22-9686; f. 1912; 3 a year; official organ of Salvadorean Athenaeum; Pres. Dr MANUEL LUIS ESCAMILLA; Sec.-Gen. Dr CARLOS RIVAS TEJADA.
Revista Judicial: Centro de Gobierno, San Salvador; tel. 22-4522; organ of the Supreme Court; Dir Dr MANUEL ARRIETA GALLEGOS.

PRESS ASSOCIATION
Asociación de Periodistas de El Salvador (Press Association of El Salvador): Edif. Casa del Periodista, Paseo Gral Escalón 4130, San Salvador; tel. 23-8943; Pres. JOSÉ LUIS URRUTIA.

FOREIGN NEWS AGENCIES
Agencia EFE (Spain): Condominio Los Héroes, Nivel 13, Blvd de Los Héroes Local 13D, San Salvador; tel. 26-0110; telex 20455, Bureau Chief CRISTINA HASBÚN DE MERINO.
Agenzia Nazionale Stampa Associata (ANSA) (Italy): Edif. Panamericano 411/25, Avda Norte y 27 Calle Poniente; tel. 26-7328; telex 20083; Bureau Chief RENÉ ALBERTO CONTRERAS.
Associated Press (AP) (USA): Hotel Camino Real, Suite 201, Blvd de Los Héroes, San Salvador; tel. 24-4885; telex 20463; Correspondent BRYNA BRENNAN.
Deutsche Presse-Agentur (dpa) (Federal Republic of Germany): Avda España 225, 2°, Of. 1, San Salvador; tel. 22-2640; Correspondent JORGE ARMANDO CONTRERAS.
Inter Press Service (IPS) (Italy): IPS Third World, Aconcagua 5 bis, Col. Miramonte, San Salvador; tel. 26-6814; telex 20523; Correspondent VIRGINIA AGUIRRE.
Reuters (UK): Hotel Camino Real, Suite 220, Blvd de Los Héroes, San Salvador; tel. 23-4736; telex 20634; Bureau Chief ADRIAN R. ALDANA.
UPI (USA) is also represented.

Publishers

Editorial Universitaria: Ciudad Universitaria, Universidad de El Salvador, Apdo 1703, San Salvador; tel. 25-6604; f. 1923; Dir ALFREDO MONTTI.
Dirección de Publicaciones: Ministerio de Educación, 17 Avda Sur 430, San Salvador; tel. 22-9152; f. 1953; educational and general; Dir JOSÉ ROBERTO HENRÍQUEZ.
UCA: Apdo 06668, San Salvador; tel. 24-0011; f. 1975; social science, religion and economy; Dir RODOLFO CARDENAL.

PUBLISHERS' ASSOCIATIONS
Asociación Salvadoreña de Agencias de Publicidad: San Salvador; f. 1962.
Cámara Salvadoreña del Libro: Calle Arce No 423, Apdo 2296, San Salvador; tel. 21-7206; f. 1974; Pres. OTTO KURT WAHN CABRALES.

EL SALVADOR

Radio and Television

In 1985 there were an estimated 2,000,000 radio receivers and 350,000 television receivers in use.

Administración Nacional de Telecomunicaciones (ANTEL): Edif. Administrativo ANTEL, Centro de Gobierno, San Salvador; tel. 21-8702; telex 20252; f. 1963; Pres. Ing. JULIO CÉSAR GÓMEZ; Gen. Sec. RAFAEL ANTONIO RODEZNO.

RADIO

Asociación Salvadoreña de Radiodifusores (ASDER): 4a Calle Oriente 528, Apdo 210, San Salvador; tel. 22-0872; Pres. MANUEL ANTONIO FLORES BARRERA.

YSS Radio El Salvador: Dirección General de Medios, Ministerio de Cultura y Comunicaciones, San Salvador; tel. 21-4376; telex 20145; non-commercial cultural station; Dir-Gen. (vacant).

There are 75 commercial radio stations. The guerrilla group, ERP, operates its own station, Radio Venceremos, and the FPL operate Radio Farabundo Martí.

TELEVISION

Canal 2, SA: Apdo 720, San Salvador; tel. 23-6744; telex 20443; commercial; Pres. B. ESERSKI; Gen. Man. EDUARDO ANAYA.

Canal 4, SA: Carretera de San Salvador a Santa Tecla, Apdo 444, San Salvador; tel. 24-4555; commercial; Pres. BORIS ESERSKI; Man. RONALD CALVO.

Canal 6, SA: Alameda Dr Manuel E. Araújo Km. 6, Apdo (06) 1801, San Salvador; tel. 23-5122; commercial; Pres. JOSÉ A. GONZÁLEZ L.; Man. Dr PEDRO LEONEL MORENO MONGE.

Canal 8 and 10: Final 13 Avda Sur, Apdo 4, Nueva San Salvador; tel. 28-0499; government station; Dir Prof. CARLOS ANTONIO BURGOS.

Canal 12: 5a Avda las Acacias 130, Col. San Benito, San Salvador; tel. 246171.

Finance

(cap. = capital; p.u. = paid up; res = reserves; dep. = deposits; m. = million; brs = branches; amounts in colones unless otherwise stated)

BANKING

The banking system was nationalized in March 1980.

Supervisory Body

Superintendencia del Sistema Financiero: Edif. Banco Central de Reserva de El Salvador, 1a Calle Poniente y 7a Avda Norte, San Salvador; tel. 21-6360; Superintendent Dr EUSEBIO MARTELL.

Central Bank

Banco Central de Reserva de El Salvador: 1a Calle Poniente y 7a Avda Norte, San Salvador; tel. 22-1144; telex 20088; f. 1934; nationalized Dec. 1961; sole right of note issue; cap. p.u. 2.5m., res 330.9m., dep. 2,426.67 (June 1986); Pres. Lic. ALBERTO BENÍTEZ BONILLA; Man. Lic. ARMANDO BARRIOS; 7 brs.

Commercial and Mortgage Banks

Banco Agrícola Comercial de El Salvador: 5a Avda Norte y Calle Arce, San Salvador; tel. 71-2666; telex 20092; f. 1955; cap. 30m., res 6.3m., dep. 1,009.2m. (June 1986); Pres. Lic. RAFAEL TOMÁS CARBONELL; 16 brs.

Banco Capitalizador: 1a Calle Poniente 531, San Salvador; tel. 71-2311; telex 20254; f. 1955; cap. 14m., res 2.7m., dep. 464.7m. (June 1986); Pres. Dr ERNESTO ARBIZÚ MATA; 17 brs.

Banco de Comercio de El Salvador: 4a Calle Oriente 224 y 4a Avda Sur, Apdo 237, San Salvador; tel. 71-4144; telex 20124; f. 1949; cap. 35m., res 1.9m., dep. 683.5m. (June 1986); Pres. AUGUSTO RAMÓN ÁVILA; Gen. Man. EUSEBIO MARTELL; 21 brs.

Banco de Crédito Popular: 4a Calle Oriente 224 y 4a Avda Sur, Apdo (06) 994, San Salvador; tel. 71-1122; telex 20208; f. 1957; cap. 23m., res 2.1m., dep. 369.2m. (June 1986); Pres. JOSÉ ALBERTO CERNA; 12 brs.

Banco Cuscatlán: 6a Avda Sur 118, San Salvador; tel. 24-6333; telex 20220; f. 1972; cap. p.u. 31.5m., res 13.5m., dep. 1,133.2m. (June 1986); Pres. Lic. RAFAEL EDMUNDO GIRÓN CARBALLO; 11 brs.

Banco de Desarrollo e Inversión, SA: 67a Avda Norte y Blvd San Antonio Abad, Plaza las Américas, San Salvador; tel. 23-7415;

Directory

telex 20261; f. 1978; cap. 17m., res 4.1m., dep. 185.6m. (June 1986); Pres. XÓCHITL TIRZA DE MERINO; 6 brs.

Banco Financiero: Edif. Torre Roble, Blvd de Los Héroes, Apdo 1562, San Salvador; tel. 23-9255; telex 20319; f. 1977; cap. 5m., res 0.204m., dep. 91.8m. (July 1986); Pres. RODOLFO SANTOS MORALES; 2 brs.

Banco Hipotecario de El Salvador: 4a Calle Oriente y 2a Avda Sur, San Salvador; tel. 22-2122; telex 20309; f. 1934; mortgage bank; cap. p.u. 0.9m., res 21.6m., dep. 810.4m. (June 1986); Pres. FILADELFO BAIRES PAZ; Man. JULIO RIVAS; 16 brs.

Banco Mercantil, SA: 1a Calle Poniente y 7a Avda Norte, frente al Banco Central de Reserva, San Salvador; tel. 23-3022; telex 20723; f. 1978; cap. 10m., res 3.2m., dep. 171m. (June 1986); Pres. RAFAEL SALVADOR VELIS; 4 brs.

Banco Salvadoreño: 2a Avda Norte 129, San Salvador; tel. 71-2122; telex 20172; f. 1885; cap. 25m., res 3.5m., dep. 502.4m. (June 1986); Pres. JOSÉ DANIEL CASTELLANOS; 14 brs.

Public Institutions

Banco de Fomento Agropecuario: 15a Avda Sur y 6a Calle Poniente, Apdo (06) 490, San Salvador; tel. 71-3011; telex 20027; f. 1973; cap. 465m., res 8.2m., dep. 34.2m. (June 1986); Pres. Ing. JOAQUÍN GUEVARA MORÁN; Man. RAFAEL ANTONIO ALVARENGA LÓPEZ; 27 brs.

Banco Nacional de Fomento Industrial (BANAFI): 1a Calle Poniente No 2310, San Salvador; tel. 24-6677; telex 20285; Pres. Lic. ERNESTO ALWODS LAGOS.

Financiera Nacional de la Vivienda (FNV): 49 Avda Sur 820, San Salvador; tel. 23-8822; national housing finance agency; f. 1963 to improve housing facilities through loan and savings associations; cap. 5.2m., res 18.9m. (June 1985); Pres. Ing. REMO BARDI; Man. ARMANDO ESTRADA VALDEZ.

Financiera Nacional de Tierras Agrícolas (FINATA): 5a Calle Poniente 149, San Salvador; tel. 71-2444; Pres. JUAN PABLO MEJÍA RODRÍGUEZ; Man. Lic. ERNESTO TORRES CHICO.

Savings and Loan Associations

Asociación de Ahorro y Préstamo, SA (ATLACATL): Blvd de Los Héroes y Calle Poniente 25, Apdo 1100, San Salvador; tel. 25-5555; f. 1964; savings and loan association; cap. 19.2m., dep. 276.8m. (June 1986); Pres. OSCAR ARGUETA; 17 brs.

Ahorro, Préstamos e Inversiones, SA (APRISA): Blvd de Los Héroes 1017, San Salvador; tel. 26-0011; f. 1977; cap. 3.1m., res 0.3m., dep. 89.5m. (June 1986); Pres. Dr NAPOLEÓN ARNOLDO MONTERROSA VALLE; 9 brs.

Ahorros Metropolitanos, SA (AHORROMET): Calle Arce y 9a Avda Norte 532, San Salvador; tel. 71-0888; f. 1972; cap. 4.5m., res 0.3m., dep. 118.2m. (June 1986); Pres. Lic. EFRAÍN FUENTES ALVARENGA; 12 brs.

La Central de Ahorros, SA: Alameda Roosevelt y 43 Avda Sur, San Salvador; tel. 24-4840; f. 1979; cap. 5m., res 0.7m., dep. 40.1m. (June 1986); Pres. ISMAEL ESCOBAR; 4 brs.

Construcción y Ahorro SA (CASA): 1a Calle Poniente y 9a Avda Norte, San Salvador; tel. 71-5533; f. 1964; saving and building finance; cap. 8m., res 6.2m., dep. 234.2m. (June 1986); Pres. Lic. JOSÉ OSCAR MEDINA; 14 brs.

CRECE, SA: Alameda Roosevelt y 59 Avda Norte, Apdo (05) 25, San Salvador; tel. 23-8299; f. 1973; cap. 5.5m., res 0.6m., dep. 119m. (June 1986); Pres. MAURICIO ERNESTO MARTÍNEZ; 8 brs.

Crédito Inmobiliario, SA (CREDISA): Edif. CREDISA, 3a y 7a Calle Poniente, San Salvador; tel. 23-4111; f. 1964; cap. 9m., res 0.2m., dep. 210.5m. (June 1986); Pres. Dr Ing. RINALDO GALDÁMEZ DE LEÓN; 14 brs.

Foreign Banks

Banco de Santander y Panamá, SA: Alameda Roosevelt 3425, Apdo (01) 231, San Salvador; tel. 24-1099; telex 20003; Pres. MAXIMINO BELLOSO; Man. MARÍA LAURA BAIRE RIVAS.

Bank of America NT and SA (USA): Edif. San José, Planta Alta, 29 Avda Norte 1223, Apdo (05) 93, San Salvador; tel. 26-7391; telex 20072; Pres. Dr ARMANDO PEÑA QUEZADA.

Bank of London and South America Ltd: 2a Calle Oriente 215, Apdo (06) 197, San Salvador; tel. 22-4244; telex 20198; Man. R. A. FAIRHURST.

Banking Associations

Federación de Asociaciones Cooperativas de Ahorro y Crédito de El Salvador de RL (FEDECACES): 23a Avda Norte y 25a Calle Poniente, No. 1301, Colonia San Jorge, Apdo 156, San Salvador; tel. 26-8925.

EL SALVADOR

Federación de Cajas de Crédito (FEDECREDITO): 25a Avda Norte y 23a Calle Poniente, San Salvador; tel. 25-5553; telex 20392; f. 1943; Pres. Lic. Rafael Pleitez Menéndez; Man. Lic. Sebastián Obdulio Varela Dueñas.

STOCK EXCHANGE

Bolsa de El Salvador: Edif. Noljer, Avda La Capilla, Colonia San Benito, San Salvador; tel. 23-8342; San Salvador; f. 1964.

INSURANCE

American Life Insurance Co.: Edif. Omnimotores, Km 4½, Carretera a Santa Tecla, Apdo 169, San Salvador; tel. 23-4925; telex 20627; f. 1963; cap. 1m.; Man. Carlos F. Pereira.

Aseguradora Agrícola Comercial, SA: Alameda Roosevelt 3104, Apdo 1855, San Salvador; tel. 23-8200; telex 20288; f. 1973; cap. 1.5m.; Pres. Luis Escalante A.; Man. Jean Paul Bolens.

Aseguradora Popular, SA: 4a Calle Oriente y 2a Avda Sur No 212, Apdo 1991, San Salvador; tel. 71-6033; telex 20531; f. 1975; cap. 2m.; Man. Lic. Roberto José Cantón.

Aseguradora Suiza Salvadoreña, SA: Alameda Dr Manuel Enrique Araújo y Calle La Reforma, Plaza Suiza, San Salvador; tel. 23-2111; telex 20581; f. 1969; cap. 2.5m.; Pres. Roberto Schildknecht.

La Auxiliadora, SA: Avda Olímpica y 63 Avda Sur, Colonia Escalón, Apdo 665, San Salvador; tel. 23-7736; telex 30153; f. 1958; cap. 1.5m., dep. 9m.; Pres. María Eugenia Brizuela de Avila.

La Centro Americana, SA, Cía Salvadoreña de Seguros: Alameda Roosevelt 3107, Apdo 527, San Salvador; tel. 23-6666; telex 20176; f. 1915; cap. 5m.; Gen. Man. Lic. Rufino Garay.

Compañía Anglo Salvadoreña de Seguros, SA: Paseo General Escalón 3848, San Savador; tel. 24-2399; telex 20466; f. 1976; cap. 2m.; Exec. Vice-Pres. Dr José Luis Urrutia Escobar.

Compañía General de Seguros, SA: Edif. General de Seguros, 2a Avda Sur 302, San Salvador; tel. 71-3111; telex 20218; f. 1955; cap. 6m.; Exec. Chair. Dr Rafael Cáceres Viale.

La Seguridad Salvadoreña: Km 4½, Carretera a Santa Tecla, Apdo 1527, San Salvador; tel. 23-4100; telex 20626; f. 1974; cap. 2m.; Pres. Carlos F. Pereira.

Seguros Desarrollo, SA: Calle Loma Linda No. 265, Colonia San Benito, Apdo 05-92, San Salvador; tel. 24-3800; telex 20773; f. 1975; cap. 2m.; Exec. Pres. Ismael Warleta Fernández.

Seguros e Inversiones, SA (SISA): Edif. SISA, Alameda Dr Manuel Enrique Araújo 3530, Apdo 1350, San Salvador; tel. 23-1200; telex 20772; f. 1962; cap. 3m.; Man. Mauricio Samayoa R.

Unión de Seguros, SA: Avda Morazán 110, San Salvador; tel. 21-9644; f. 1974; cap. 1m.; Man. Federico Denis Badgerow.

Trade and Industry

CHAMBER OF COMMERCE

Cámara de Comercio e Industria de El Salvador: 9a Avda Norte y 5a Calle Poniente, Apdo (06) 1640, San Salvador; tel. 71-2055; telex 20753; f. 1915; 850 mems; Pres. Víctor A. Steiner; Sec. Ing. Ricardo Flores Cena.

TRADE ORGANIZATIONS

Asociación Cafetalera de El Salvador—ACES: Edif. Instituto del Café 4°, San Salvador; tel. 21-3580; f. 1930; coffee growers' asscn; Pres. Dr Francisco García Rossi.

Asociación de Ganaderos de El Salvador: 1a Avda Norte 1332, San Salvador; tel. 25-7208; telex 20213; f. 1932; livestock breeders' asscn; Pres. Lic. Carlos Arturo Muyshondt.

Asociación Salvadoreña de Beneficiadores y Exportadores de Café (ABECAFE): 87a Avda Norte 720, Apdo A, Colonia Escalón, San Salvador; tel. 23-3292; telex 20231; coffee producers' and exporters' asscn; Pres. Ing. Sergio Catani.

Asociación Salvadoreña de Industriales: Calles Roma y Liverpool, Colonia Roma, Apdo Postal (06) 48, San Salvador; tel. 23-7788; telex 20235; f. 1958; 317 mems; manufacturers' asscn; Pres. Eduardo Menéndez; Exec. Dir Roberto Ortiz Avalos.

Co-operativa Algodonera Salvadoreña Ltda: 7a Avda Norte 418, Apdo (06) 616, San Salvador; tel. 22-0399; telex 20374; f. 1940; 1,057 mems; cotton growers' asscn; Pres. Luis Méndez Novoa.

Instituto Nacional del Azúcar: Paseo Gral Escalón y 87 Avda Norte, San Salvador; tel. 24-6044; telex 30024; national sugar institute; Pres. Raimundo Rodríguez.

Instituto Nacional del Café (INCAFE): 6a Avda Sur 133, San Salvador; tel. 71-3311; telex 20138; f. 1942; national coffee institute; Pres. Ing. Humberto Dalponte Mori; Gen. Man. Lic. Miguel Angel Aguilar.

STATE AND DEVELOPMENT ORGANIZATIONS

Comisión Ejecutiva Hidroeléctrica del Río Lempa (CEL): 9a Calle Poniente 950, San Salvador; tel. 71-0855; telex 20303; state energy agency dealing with electricity generation, transmission, distribution and non-conventional energy sources; Pres. Col Jaime Abdul Gutiérrez.

Comisión Nacional del Petróleo (CONAPE): 9a Calle Poniente 950, San Salvador; telex 20301; state petroleum enterprise.

Corporación de Exportadores de El Salvador (COEXPORT): Edif. ASI, Calle Roma y Liverpool, Colonia Roma, San Salvador; tel. 24-4019; telex 20355; f. 1973 to establish a policy of export incentives; Man. Lic. Silvia Cuéllar Sicilia.

Corporación Salvadoreña de Inversiones (CORSAIN): 1a Calle Poniente entre 43 y 45 Avda Norte, San Salvador; tel. 24-6677; telex 20257; Pres. Dr Jorge A. Hernández Gutiérrez.

Fondo de Financiamiento y Garantía para la Pequeña Empresa (FIGAPE): Diagonal Principal y 1a Diagonal, Apdo 1990, San Salvador; tel. 25-9466; f. 1973; government body to assist small-sized industries; Pres. Leopoldo Samayoa.

Fondo de Garantía para el Crédito Educativo (EDUCREDITO): Avda España 726, San Salvador; tel. 22-2181; f. 1973; Pres. Ing. Juan José Interiano; Dir Lic. Erasmo Sermeño.

Fondo Social para la Vivienda (FSV): Edif. Torre Roble, Blvd de Los Héroes, San Salvador; tel. 26-3011; f. 1973; Pres. Baltasar Perla.

Instituto Salvadoreño de Transformación Agraria (ISTA): Km 5, Carretera a Santa Tecla, San Salvador; tel. 24-6000; f. 1976 to promote rural development; empowered to buy inefficiently cultivated land; Pres. Samuel Maldonado.

Instituto de Vivienda Urbana (IVU): Centro Urbano Libertad, San Salvador; tel. 23-3011; government housing agency; Pres. Ricardo Moreno Calderón; Man. Cristobal A. Huezo Nativi.

EMPLOYERS' ORGANIZATIONS

There are several business associations, the most important of which is the Alianza Nacional de Empresa Privada (National Private Enterprise Alliance; Pres. Juan Maldonado), which has a political organization, the Alianza Productiva.

TRADE UNIONS

Asociación de Sindicatos Independientes—ASIES (Association of Independent Trade Unions).

Confederación General de Sindicatos—CGS (General Confederation of Unions): 3a Calle Oriente 226, San Salvador; f. 1958; admitted to ICFTU/ORIT; 27,000 mems.

Confederación General de Trabajadores Salvadoreños —CGTS (General Confederation of Salvadorean Workers): San Salvador; f. 1957; 10 affiliated unions; Sec.-Gen. José Alberto López; 3,500 mems.

Coordinadora de Solidaridad de los Trabajadores (CST): f. 1985; conglomerate of independent left-wing trade unions.

Federación Campesina Cristiana de El Salvador-Unión de Trabajadores del Campo (FECCAS-UTC): allied illegal Christian peasants' organizations; Universidad Nac., Apdo 4000, San Salvador.

Federación Revolucionaria de Sindicatos (Revolutionary Federation of Unions): Sec.-Gen. Salvador Chávez Escalante.

Federación Unitaria Sindical de El Salvador (Unitary Federation of Unions): San Salvador.

MUSYGES (United Union and Guild Movement): labour federation previously linked to FDR; 50,000 mems (est.).

UCS: pro-government peasant association; 100,000 mems; Gen. Sec. Guillermo Blanco.

Unidad Nacional de Trabajadores Salvadoreños—UNTS: San Salvador; f. 1986; largest trade union conglomerate; Leader Marco Tulio Lima; affiliated unions include:

Unidad Popular Democrática (UPD): San Salvador; f. 1980; led by a committee of 10; 500,000 mems.

EL SALVADOR

Unión Nacional Obrera-Campesina—Unoc: San Salvador; f. 1986; pro-government labour organization.

Some unions, such as those of the taxi drivers and bus owners, are affiliated to the Federación Nacional de Empresas Pequeñas Salvadoreñas—Fenapes, the association of small-scale business.

Transport

Comisión Ejecutiva Portuaria Autónoma—CEPA: Edif. Torre Roble, Blvd de Los Héroes, Apdo 2667, San Salvador; tel. 24-1133; telex 20194; f. 1952; operates and administers the ports of Acajutla and Cutuco and the El Salvador International Airport, as well as Ferrocarriles Nacionales de El Salvador; Chair. Arq. MARCELO SUÁREZ BARRIENTOS; Gen. Man. Ing. JOSÉ RICARDO HERNÁNDEZ P.

RAILWAYS

There are about 600 km of railway track in the country. The main track links San Salvador with the ports of Acajutla and Cutuco and with San Jerónimo on the border with Guatemala. The International Railways of Central America run from Anguiatú on the El Salvador–Guatemala border to the Pacific ports of Acajutla and Cutuco and connect San Salvador with Guatemala City and the Guatemalan Atlantic ports of Puerto Barrios and Santo Tomás del Castillo.

Ferrocarriles Nacionales de El Salvador—Fenadesal: Avda Peralta 903, Apdo 2292, San Salvador; tel. 21-8940; telex 20194; 600 km open; in 1975 Ferrocarril de El Salvador and the Salvadorean section of International Railways of Central America (429 km open) were merged and are administered by the Railroad Division of CEPA (see above); Man. Ing. H. REYES V.

ROADS

The country's highway system is well integrated with its railway services. There are some 12,146 km of roads, including: the Pan-American Highway: 306 km; paved highways: 1,700 km; improved roads: 2,827 km; dry-weather roads: 3,872 km. A coastal highway, with interconnecting roads, was under construction in the late 1980s.

SHIPPING

The ports of Acajutla and Cutuco are administered by CEPA (see above). Services are also provided by foreign lines.

CIVIL AVIATION

AESA Aerolíneas de El Salvador, SA de CV: Centro Comercial Beethoven, Sobre Paseo Gen. Escalón, Apdo (06) 1830; tel. 24-6166; cargo and mail service between San Salvador and Miami; Pres. E. CORNEJO LÓPEZ; Gen. Man. JORGE MARCHESSINI.

TACA International Airlines: Edif. Caribe 2°, San Salvador; tel. 23-2244; telex 30156; f. 1939; passenger and cargo services to Belize, Guatemala, Honduras, Mexico, Nicaragua, Panama and the USA; Pres. Dr ENRIQUE BORGO BUSTAMANTE; Exec. Pres. FEDERICO BLOCH; fleet: 2 BAC One Eleven 400, 3 Boeing 737-200, 1 Electra-188-C.

Tourism

Buró de Convenciones y Visitantes de San Salvador: 9a Avda Norte 406, San Salvador; tel. 22-4375.

Cámara Salvadoreña de Turismo: Hotel Sheraton, 89 Avda Norte y 11 Calle Poniente, Colonia Escalón, Apdo (01) 337, San Salvador; tel. 24-2222; Pres. ROBERTO CALDERÓN.

Instituto Salvadoreño de Turismo (ISTU) (National Tourism Institute): Calle Rubén Darío 619, San Salvador; tel. 22-8000; telex 20775; f. 1947; Pres. RAMÓN DÍAZ BACH; Asst Man. MILAGRO DE ROCHAC.

Atomic Energy

Comisión Salvadoreña de Energía Nuclear (COSEN): c/o Ministerio de Economía, 4a Avda Norte 233, San Salvador; f. 1961; atomic energy research institute.

EQUATORIAL GUINEA

Introductory Survey

Location, Climate, Language, Religion, Flag, Capital

The Republic of Equatorial Guinea consists of the islands of Bioko (formerly Fernando Póo and subsequently renamed Macías Nguema Biyogo under the regime of President Macías), Corisco, Great Elobey, Small Elobey and Pagalu (formerly known as Annobón), and the mainland territory of Río Muni (Mbini) on the west coast of Africa. Cameroon lies to the north and Gabon to the east and south of Río Muni, while Bioko lies off shore from Cameroon and Nigeria. The small island of Pagalu lies far to the south, beyond the islands of São Tomé and Príncipe. The climate is hot and humid, with average temperatures higher than 26°C (80°F). The official language is Spanish. In Río Muni the Fang language is spoken, as well as those of coastal tribes such as the Combe, Balemke and Bujeba, while in Bioko the principal local language is Bubi, although pidgin English and Ibo are also widely understood. An estimated 96% of the population are adherents of the Roman Catholic Church. The national flag (proportions 3 by 2) has three equal horizontal stripes, of green, white and red, with a light blue triangle at the hoist. The state flag has, in addition, the national coat of arms (a white shield, containing a tree, with six yellow stars above and a scroll beneath) on the white stripe. The capital is Malabo (formerly Santa Isabel).

Recent History

Portugal ceded the territory to Spain in 1778. The mainland region and the islands were periodically united for administrative purposes. In July 1959 Spanish Guinea, as the combined territory was known, was divided into two provinces: Río Muni, on the African mainland, and Fernando Póo (with other nearby islands). From 1960 the two provinces were represented in the Spanish legislature. In December 1963 they were merged again, to form Equatorial Guinea, with a limited measure of self-government.

After 190 years of Spanish rule, independence was declared on 12 October 1968, following a referendum on the proposed constitution. In presidential elections, held in September 1968, the Prime Minister of the autonomous government, Bonifacio Ondo Edu, was defeated by Francisco Macías Nguema. President Macías formed a coalition government from all the parties represented in the new National Assembly. Relations with Spain became strained in early 1969 after a series of anti-European incidents and an attempted coup in March by the Minister for Foreign Affairs, Atanasio Ndongo Miyone, who was killed.

In February 1970 the President outlawed all existing political parties and formed the Partido Unico Nacional (PUN), which later became the Partido Unico Nacional de los Trabajadores (PUNT). Macías appointed himself Life President in July 1972. A new constitution, giving absolute powers to President Macías and abolishing the provincial autonomy previously enjoyed by Fernando Póo (then renamed Macías Nguema Biyogo), was adopted in July 1973. President Macías controlled both radio and press and all citizens were forbidden to leave the country, although many fled during his rule. During 1976 and 1977 there were many arrests and executions. Nigerian workers were repatriated in 1976 after reports of maltreatment and forced labour. Foreign affairs were dominated by close relations with the Soviet bloc.

In August 1979 President Macías was overthrown in a coup led by his nephew, Lt-Col (later Col) Teodoro Obiang Nguema Mbasogo, hitherto the Deputy Minister of Defence. Macías was later captured, tried on charges of treason, genocide, embezzlement and violation of human rights, and executed by a military firing squad. The Spanish Government, which admitted prior knowledge of the coup, was the first to recognize the new regime, and remains its major supplier of financial and technical aid. Obiang Nguema appointed civilians to the Supreme Military Council for the first time in December 1981. In August 1982 he was reappointed President for a further seven years, and later that month a new constitution, which provided for an eventual return to civilian government, was approved by 95% of voters in a referendum. Obiang Nguema's regime continues to be opposed by Equatorial Guineans living in exile (estimated to number around 130,000 in 1983), many of whom have criticized both the continuing depressed economic situation and the lack of political freedom which resulted from the banning of all political parties in 1979. In April 1983 representatives of five exiled opposition groups met at Zaragoza, in north-eastern Spain, and formed a Co-ordinating Board of Opposition Forces. Equatorial Guinea held its first legislative elections in more than 19 years in August 1983, when an estimated 50,000 voters elected 41 candidates (unopposed) to a new House of Representatives; in 1986 the House received a mandate from the President to draft a law that would provide for the existence of political opposition groups within the country.

Obiang Nguema's rule has been threatened on a number of occasions. Attempted coups were reported in April 1981, May 1983 and November 1983. In January 1986, following rumours of discontent among the Río Muni armed forces, the President reshuffled the Supreme Military Council and reinforced his control by assuming the post of Minister of Defence, previously held by his uncle, Deputy Prime Minister Fructuoso Mba Oñana Nchama, who was instead made responsible for public works. In July 1986 an attempt to occupy the presidential palace in Malabo was quelled by loyalist forces, and in August a military tribunal, headed by the Deputy Defence Minister, passed sentence upon 13 senior civilian and military officials who had been arrested for complicity in the coup attempt. The alleged leader, Eugenio Abeso Mondu (a former diplomat and a member of the House of Representatives), was sentenced to death and executed by firing squad, while prison sentences were passed on 12 others, including former Defence Minister Fructuoso Mba Oñana, Planning Minister Marcos Mba Ondo and the national director of the Banque des Etats de l'Afrique Centrale (BEAC), Damian Ondo Mañe. Mba Oñana and Mba Ondo were replaced in the Supreme Military Council in a minor reshuffle in October.

Relations with Spain have been variable, but improved following a visit to Madrid by President Obiang Nguema in August 1983, during which Spain agreed to the refinancing of the US $45m. debt that was owed to it by Equatorial Guinea. Equatorial Guinea's entry into the Customs and Economic Union of Central Africa (UDEAC, see p. 155) in December 1983 marked a significant move away from the country's traditional links with Spain and towards greater integration with neighbouring francophone countries. Obiang Nguema was appointed to the presidency of UDEAC in December 1985. In January 1985 the country joined the Franc Zone (see p. 155), with financial assistance from France, which also applied pressure on the 'Paris Club' of creditor nations to achieve a rescheduling of Equatorial Guinea's debts in July.

Government

After the coup of August 1979 the Supreme Military Council ruled by decree. In August 1982 a new constitution was approved in a referendum, making provision for presidential and legislative elections by universal suffrage, a State Council of 11 members and a House of Representatives of the People (elected for a five-year term in August 1983). The Constitution also provides for a transition from rule by the Supreme Military Council to constitutional government at an unspecified date.

Defence

In July 1986 there were 2,300 men in the army, 150 in the navy and 150 in the air force. There was also a paramilitary force of 2,000. Military service is voluntary. The estimated defence expenditure for 1982 was US $6m. Spain has provided military advisers and training since October 1979, and the presidential

EQUATORIAL GUINEA

guard is staffed by Moroccans. Foreign military aid totalled $1.1m. in 1986.

Economic Affairs

The economy is based mainly on agriculture, the principal products being cocoa, coffee, palm oil, bananas, cassava and okoumé timber. About 90% of all cocoa production comes from Bioko. Coffee and timber are produced mainly in Río Muni. Between 1970 and 1975, according to World Bank estimates, Equatorial Guinea's gross national product (GNP) per head declined at an average rate of 6% annually. With the departure of the Nigerian workers in 1976, the economic situation deteriorated further. According to estimates by the UN Economic Commission for Africa, the country's gross domestic product (GDP) in 1976 was 54% lower, in real terms, than in 1974. Real GDP continued to fall, with declines in each of the four years 1977–80. Over the six-year period 1974–80, there was a cumulative fall of 66% in real GDP. Thereafter, some recovery was achieved, with estimated GDP growth of 2.2% in 1981 and 3.9% in 1982.

The cocoa crop was 38,207 metric tons in 1966/67, but the subsequent political upheavals caused it to fall to 5,000 tons in 1979. Production rose to 8,300 tons in 1983, and to an estimated 10,000 tons in 1984. A programme of replanting, recruitment and training, and the possible return of Nigerian workers, should lead to gradual recovery. Output of cocoa in 1985 was estimated to have risen by 25%, compared with 1984. Coffee production declined from 8,450 tons in 1968 to only 120 tons in 1982. Most of the coffee crop is smuggled out of the country. Production was estimated at 700 tons in 1984. Timber production grew rapidly after 1979, reaching 60,000 tons in 1981, but there was a general fall in agricultural output in 1982, and wood production fell to 20,000 tons. A new sawmill, with an annual capacity of 20,000 cu m, was built with Italian aid in 1982. Equatorial Guinea's total area of exploitable forests is estimated at 800,000 ha, and exports of timber in 1984 totalled 103,000 cu m. Output of bananas, palm oil and cassava is gradually increasing, but there are still widespread food shortages and industry is minimal. In 1986 a livestock development project was under way at Moka, with aid of US$12.6m. from the African Development Fund. In 1981, according to World Bank estimates, Equatorial Guinea's GNP per head was only US $180 (at average 1979–81 prices), the third lowest level among African countries.

At the time of the overthrow of President Macías, the economy was effectively in ruins. Under President Obiang Nguema, aid has been secured, principally from Spain, France, the EEC, the IMF and the People's Republic of China. An international aid conference, held in Geneva in April 1982, aimed to provide US $140m. for projects in agriculture, transport and communications, water resources, housing and urbanization, and industry, mining and energy, and in July 1983 the World Food Programme approved an aid programme of $3.9m. to feed the country's vulnerable groups. In July 1985 Equatorial Guinea received its first IMF stand-by credit, totalling $9.2m., for a programme of structural adjustment. In May 1986 the World Bank approved a $10.5m. loan to finance imports of goods needed to boost agricultural production. Further discussion on a new IMF stand-by facility was to take place in late 1986. The annual cost of servicing the country's public external debt, which at the end of 1984 totalled $102.6m., is equivalent to 95% of export earnings, and represents a severe burden. A rescheduling of $28m. of debt was arranged in July 1985.

In a bid to further its economic development, Equatorial Guinea joined the Communauté Economique des États de l'Afrique Centrale (CEEAC), which was set up in October 1983. In December 1983 Equatorial Guinea was admitted to the Customs and Economic Union of Central Africa (UDEAC, see p. 155), and in January 1985 the franc CFA was introduced to replace the epkwele, which had been linked to the Spanish peseta. It was hoped that Equatorial Guinea's entry into the Franc Zone would bring the country out of economic isolation by encouraging foreign trade and investment. A UDEAC technical assistance programme was agreed in September 1984, designed to help strengthen Equatorial Guinea's administrative structures.

In June 1982 there were 350 Spanish development workers in Equatorial Guinea, working mainly in education and health.

Spanish aid between 1979 and 1982 totalled 13,000m. pesetas, but in December 1983 Spain indicated that aid would be reduced in the fields of education, health and defence, following Equatorial Guinea's decision to join UDEAC and thereby gain admission to the Franc Zone. Spanish credits in 1986 totalled 1,925m. pesetas. France has increased its aid considerably, following Equatorial Guinea's entry into UDEAC, donating 21.9m. French francs in 1984.

There are prospects for the development of offshore and onshore reserves of petroleum, and exploration was under way in 1984 with the co-operation of French and Spanish companies. Preliminary surveys have indicated that oil reserves are adequate to meet Equatorial Guinea's domestic demand. Natural gas has been discovered off shore, but in 1984 the viability of the deposits was still to be determined. Indications of deposits of gold, manganese and uranium have been detected, but prospecting is difficult because of the equatorial forest and the near-total absence of a road network. A law was announced in 1981 that declared all mineral deposits to be state property. These developments and the country's considerable agricultural resources should provide the base for a return to economic viability, and possibly to future prosperity, and in 1983 financial forecasts were optimistic. Spain is by far the largest trading partner, and in 1983 it was estimated that, apart from wood, 75% of Equatorial Guinea's trade turnover was with Spain. The value of exports to France was 80m. French francs in 1984, compared with only 12m. francs in 1983.

Social Welfare

Health services are extremely limited and diseases such as malaria, infectious hepatitis, whooping cough and dysentery are endemic. In 1975 Equatorial Guinea had only five physicians, compared with 25 in 1971. There were 65 hospital establishments, with a total of 3,577 beds, in 1977.

Education

The 1982 constitution made education the state's first priority, and free and compulsory basic education was to be provided. Education is officially compulsory for eight years between six and 14 years of age. In 1986 primary education in nine grades was provided for 65,000 pupils in 550 schools. More advanced education for 3,013 pupils took place in 14 centres with 288 teachers in 1980/81. Since 1979, assistance in the development of the educational system has been provided by Spain, which had 100 teaching staff working in Equatorial Guinea in 1986. Two higher education centres, at Bata and Malabo, are administered by the Spanish Universidad Nacional de Educación a Distancia (UNED) and had 500 students in 1986. In 1980, according to estimates by UNESCO, the average rate of adult illiteracy was 63%.

Tourism

During the rule of President Macías, very few foreigners were allowed into Equatorial Guinea. Tourism remains undeveloped.

Public Holidays

1987: 1 January (New Year's Day), 5 March (Independence Anniversary), 17–20 April (Easter), 1 May (Labour Day), 25 May (OAU Day), 10 December (Human Rights Day), 25 December (Christmas).

1988: 1 January (New Year's Day), 5 March (Independence Day), 1–4 April (Easter), 1 May (Labour Day), 25 May (OAU Day), 10 December (Human Rights' Day), 25 December (Christmas).

Weights and Measures

The metric system is in force.

Currency and Exchange Rates

100 centimes = 1 franc de la Coopération financière en Afrique centrale (CFA).

Exchange rates (30 September 1986):
 1 franc CFA = 2 French centimes;
 £1 sterling = 480.625 francs CFA;
 US $1 = 332.125 francs CFA.

Statistical Survey

Source (unless otherwise stated): Dirección Técnica de Estadística, Secretaría de Estado para el Plan de Desarrollo Económico y Cooperación, Malabo.

AREA AND POPULATION

Area: 28,051 sq km (Río Muni (Mbini) 26,017 sq km, Bioko 2,017 sq km, Pagalu 17 sq km).

Population: 246,941 (Río Muni 200,106, Bioko 44,820, Pagalu 2,015) at December 1965 census; 300,000 (Río Muni 240,804, Bioko 57,190, Pagalu 2,006) at census of July 1983 (Source: Ministerio de Asuntos Exteriores, Madrid).

Provinces (population, census of July 1983): Kie-Ntem 70,202, Litoral 66,370, Centro-Sur 52,393, Wele-Nzas 51,839, Bioko Norte 46,221, Bioko Sur 10,969, Pagalu 2,006.

Principal towns (population at 1983 census): Malabo (capital) 15,253, Bata 24,100.

Births and Deaths (UN estimates): Average annual birth rate 42.3 per 1,000 in 1970-75, 42.5 per 1,000 in 1975-80; death rate 24.5 per 1,000 in 1970-75, 22.7 per 1,000 in 1975-80.

Economically Active Population (estimates, '000 at mid-1980): Agriculture, etc. 104 (males 48, females 56); Industry 18 (males 16, females 2); Services 36 (males 28, females 8); Total 159 (males 93, females 65). Source: ILO, *Economically Active Population Estimates and Projections, 1950-2025*.

AGRICULTURE, ETC.

Principal Crops (FAO estimates, metric tons, 1984): Sweet potatoes 35,000, Cassava 54,000, Coconuts 8,000, Palm kernels 3,000, Bananas 18,000, Cocoa beans 10,000, Green coffee 700 (Source: FAO, *Production Yearbook*).

Livestock (FAO estimates, year ending September 1984): Cattle 4,000, Pigs 5,000, Sheep 34,000, Goats 7,000 (Source: FAO, *Production Yearbook*).

Forestry (1984): Roundwood removals (FAO estimates, '000 cu m): Fuel wood 447, Industrial wood 140, Total 587 (Source: FAO, *Yearbook of Forest Products*).

Fishing (metric tons, live weight): Total catch 2,500 in 1980; 2,500 per year (FAO estimates) in 1981-83 (Source: FAO, *Yearbook of Fishery Statistics*).

INDUSTRY

Palm oil (FAO estimates, '000 metric tons): 4.9 in 1982; 5.0 in 1983; 5.2 in 1984 (Source: FAO, *Production Yearbook*).

Electric energy (million kWh): 15 in 1981; 14 in 1982; 15 in 1983 (Source: UN, *Industrial Statistics Yearbook*).

FINANCE

Currency and Exchange Rates: 100 centimes = 1 franc de la Coopération financière en Afrique centrale (CFA). *Coins:* 1, 2, 5, 10, 25, 50, 100 and 500 francs CFA. *Notes:* 100, 500, 1,000, 5,000 and 10,000 francs CFA. *French Franc, Sterling and Dollar Equivalents* (30 September 1986): 1 French franc = 50 francs CFA; £1 sterling = 480.625 francs CFA; US $1 = 332.125 francs CFA; 1,000 francs CFA = £2.081 = $3.011. *Average Exchange Rate* (francs CFA per US dollar): 381.06 in 1983; 436.96 in 1984; 449.26 in 1985. *Note:* In January 1985 Equatorial Guinea adopted the franc CFA in place of the epkwele (plural: bipkwele), which had been linked to the Spanish peseta at the rate of 1 peseta = 2 epkwele since June 1980. Some of the figures in this Survey are still in terms of bipkwele.

Budget (estimates, million bipkwele, 1982): Revenue 2,980 (Sales of goods and services 407, Direct and indirect taxes 2,263, Other 310); Expenditure 4,038 (Compensation of employees 2,444, Other goods and services 1,060, Interest on public debt 200, Transfers 173, Other 161).

Gross Domestic Product by Economic Activity (estimates, million bipkwele at current prices, 1982): Agriculture, forestry and fishing 2,060; Manufacturing 260; Electricity, gas and water 20; Construction 270; Trade, restaurants and hotels 480; Transport and communications 110; Finance, insurance, real estate and business services 40; Public administration and defence 1,560; Other services 200; GDP at factor cost 5,000; Indirect taxes (net of subsidies) 450; GDP in purchasers' values 5,450. Source: UN Economic Commission for Africa, *African Statistical Yearbook*.

Balance of Payments (US $'000, 1981): Merchandise exports f.o.b. 16,120.3, Merchandise imports f.o.b. −30,643.6, *Trade balance* −14,523.3; Exports of services 4,616.4, Imports of services −7,282.0, Transfers (net) −400.1, *Current balance* −17,588.9; *Capital balance* −2,120.0; Net errors and omissions −4,250.7; *Total* −23,959.6.

EXTERNAL TRADE

Principal Commodities (million bipkwele, 1981): *Imports:* Food, beverages and tobacco 1,990, Petroleum and petroleum products 1,787, Clothing 478, Iron and steel products 993, Motor vehicles and machinery 1,389; Total (incl. others) 7,982. *Exports:* Cocoa 1,788, Coffee 70, Timber 611; Total (incl. others) 2,502. **1982** (million bipkwele): Total imports 10,857; Total exports 3,837.

Principal Trading Partners (million bipkwele, 1981): *Imports:* Cameroon 574, Spain 6,375. *Exports:* Federal Republic of Germany 87, Netherlands 81, Spain 2,170.

TRANSPORT

Shipping (international sea-borne freight traffic, '000 metric tons, 1982): Goods loaded 85, Goods unloaded 52 (Source: UN, *Statistical Yearbook*).

COMMUNICATIONS MEDIA

Radio receivers 115,000 in use in 1983; Television receivers 2,000 in use in 1983; Daily newspapers 2 in 1982 (Source: UNESCO, *Statistical Yearbook*).

EDUCATION

Primary (1980/81): Schools 511; Teachers 647; Pupils 40,110.

Secondary and Further (1980/81): Schools 14; Teachers 288; Pupils 3,013. There were 175 pupils studying abroad.

Directory

The Constitution

A new constitution was approved by referendum on 15 August 1982. The transition from rule by the Supreme Military Council to constitutional government was to take place at a solemn and public ceremony.

FUNDAMENTAL PRINCIPLES

Education is the first priority of the state. Civil liberties and basic human rights are guaranteed. The state has sole control of minerals and coal mines, electricity and water supply, posts and telecommunications, and radio and television.

PRESIDENT OF THE REPUBLIC

The President, who is Head of State, leader of the Government and Supreme Commander of the Armed Forces, has the power to appoint and dismiss ministers and to determine and direct national policy. At the expiry of the presidential term of seven years, an election by universal suffrage is to be held. (President Obiang Nguema was appointed for a term of seven years immediately before the publication of this constitution.)

STATE COUNCIL

The State Council has 11 members (including the Chairman of the House of Representatives, the President of the Supreme Tribunal and the Minister of Defence), and is responsible for defending national sovereignty, unity between the territorial units of Equatorial Guinea, peace and justice, and the proper conduct of democracy. The Council acts as an electoral college to approve or reject a presidential candidature, may refuse to accept the resignation of the President of the Republic, and may declare the President physically or mentally unfit to continue in office.

HOUSE OF REPRESENTATIVES

The House of Representatives is elected for a term of five years, and its members should be between 45 and 60 years of age. It sits twice a year, in March and September, for two-month periods, unless an extraordinary session is requested by the President, or by petition of three-quarters of the members of the House.

The Government

HEAD OF STATE

President: Col TEODORO OBIANG NGUEMA MBASOGO (took office 25 August 1979).

SUPREME MILITARY COUNCIL
(December 1986)

President and Minister of Defence: Col TEODORO OBIANG NGUEMA MBASOGO.
Prime Minister and Minister of Health: CRISTINO SERICHE BIOKO MALABO.
Deputy Prime Minister and Minister of Territorial Administration: EYI MONSUY ANDEME.
Minister of Public Works: ALEJANDRO ENVORO OVONO.
Minister of Education and Sport: FORTUNATO NZAMBI MACHINDE.
Minister of Information and Tourism: LEANDRO MBOMIO NSUE.
Minister of Labour: ANACLETO EJAPA BOLEKIA.
Minister of Communications: DEMETRIO ELO.
Minister of Agriculture: ALFREDO ABESCO NVONO.
Minister of Industry and Commerce: OBAMA EYEGUE.
Minister of Economic Planning: HILARIO NSUE ALENE.
Minister of Justice and Religion: ANGEL NDONG MICHA.
Minister of the Civil Service: MECHEBA IKAKA.
Minister of Energy: JUAN OLO MBA NSENG.
Minister of Water Resources and Forestry: ALOGO NCHAMA.
Minister of Foreign Affairs: MARCELINO NGUEMA ONGUENE.
Minister of Economy and Finance: FELIPE INESTROCA IKAKA.
Deputy Minister of Defence: MELANIO EBENDENG NSOMO.
Secretary-General for the Presidency: MARTÍN MKA ESONO.

MINISTRIES

All Ministries are in Malabo.
Ministry of Finance: Malabo; tel. 20-43.
Ministry of Foreign Affairs and Co-operation: Malabo; tel. 32-20.

Legislature

CÁMARA DE REPRESENTANTES DEL PUEBLO

The 41-member House of Representatives of the People was elected for a five-year term on 28 August 1983. All candidates were nominated by President Obiang Nguema and were elected unopposed.

Political Organizations

Since the coup in August 1979 there has been no recognition of political organizations in Equatorial Guinea. However, in 1986 President Obiang Nguema gave the House of Representatives a mandate to draft a law for their legalization. Groupings that call from exile for the restoration of democracy include the following:

Convergencia Social Democrática (CSD): Paris, France; f. 1984; comprises:
  Partido Socialista de Guinea Ecuatorial (PSAGE): Oviedo, Spain.
  Reunión Democrática para la Liberación de Guinea Ecuatorial (RDLGE): Paris, France: f. 1981; formed 12-mem. provisional govt-in-exile 1983; Pres. MANUEL RUBÉN NDONGO.

Co-ordinating Board of Opposition Forces: Zaragoza, Spain; f. 1983; Sec.-Gen. SEVERO MOTO NSA; comprises:
  Alianza Nacional de Restauración Democrática de Guinea Ecuatorial (ANRDGE): BP 335, 1211 Geneva 4, Switzerland; f. 1974; Sec.-Gen. MARTÍN NSOMO OKOMO.
  Frente de Liberación de Guinea Ecuatorial (FRELIGE).
  Movimiento de Liberación y Futuro de Guinea Ecuatorial (MOLIFUGE).
  Partido del Progreso de Guinea Ecuatorial: Madrid; Leader SEVERO MOTO NSA.

Revolutionary Command Council of Socialist Guinean Patriots and Cadres: f. 1981; Leader DANIEL OYONO.

Diplomatic Representation

EMBASSIES IN EQUATORIAL GUINEA

China, People's Republic: Malabo; Ambassador: DAI SHIQI.
Cuba: Malabo; Ambassador: ALBERTO SUÁREZ.
France: 13 Calle de Argelia, Apdo 326, Malabo; tel. 29-68; Ambassador: MARCEL CAUSSE.
Gabon: Apdo 648, Douala, Malabo; tel. 420; telex 1125; Ambassador: HENRI AUGÉ.
Korea, Democratic People's Republic: Malabo; Ambassador: KANG SU-MYONG.
Nigeria: 4 Paseo de los Cocoteros, Apdo 78, Malabo; Ambassador: Navy Capt. FESTUS PORBENI.
Spain: Malabo; Ambassador: ANTONIO NÚÑEZ GARCÍA-SAUCO.
USSR: Malabo; Ambassador: BORIS KRASNIKOV.
USA: Malabo; tel. 2507; Ambassador: FRANCIS S. RUDDY.

Judicial System

The structure of judicial power was established in February 1981. The Supreme Tribunal in Malabo, consisting of a President of the Supreme Tribunal, the Presidents of the three chambers (civil, criminal and administrative), and two magistrates from each chamber, is the highest court of appeal. There are Territorial High

EQUATORIAL GUINEA

Courts in Malabo and Bata, which are also courts of appeal. Courts of the First Instance exist in Malabo and Bata, and may be convened in the other provincial capitals, and Local Courts may be convened when necessary.

Religion

An estimated 96% of the population are nominally adherents of the Roman Catholic Church. Traditional forms of worship are also followed.

CHRISTIANITY
The Roman Catholic Church

Equatorial Guinea comprises one archdiocese and two dioceses. There were an estimated 313,000 adherents in the country at 31 December 1984.

Bishops' Conference: Arzobispado, Apdo 106, Malabo; f. 1984; Pres. Mgr RAFAEL MARÍA NZE ABUY, Archbishop of Malabo.

Archbishop of Malabo: Mgr RAFAEL MARÍA NZE ABUY, Arzobispado, Apdo 106, Malabo; tel. 21-76.

The Press

Ebano: Malabo; Spanish; daily; circ. 1,000.
Hoja Parroquial: Malabo; weekly.
Potopoto: Apdo 236, Bata; Fang; daily.
Unidad de la Guinea Ecuatorial: Malabo; irregular.

NEWS AGENCY

Agencia EFE (Spain): 50 Calle del Presidente Nasser, Apdo 128, Malabo; tel. 31-65; Bureau Chief ANGEL ASENSIO CASANUEVA.

Radio and Television

There were an estimated 115,000 radio receivers and 2,000 television sets in use in 1983.

RADIO

There are two radio stations, both operated by the Government.

Radio Ecuatorial Bata: Apdo 57, Bata; tel. 182; commercial station; programmes in Spanish and vernacular languages; Dir JESÚS OBIANG NGUEMA NDONG.

Radio Santa Isabel: Apdo 195, Malabo; tel. 382; programmes in Spanish, English, Fang, Bubi, Annobonés and Combe; Dir JUAN EYENE OPKUA NGUEMA.

TELEVISION

Director of Television: SATURNINO MBA ELO.

Finance

(cap. = capital; res = reserves; m. = million; br. = branch; amounts in francs CFA)

BANKING
Central Bank

Banque des Etats de l'Afrique Centrale (BEAC): Apdo 1917, Malabo; tel. 22-25-05; telex 8343; headquarters in Yaoundé, Cameroon; f. 1973 as the central bank of issue for mem. states of the Customs and Economic Union of Central Africa (UDEAC), comprising Cameroon, the Central African Republic, Chad, the Congo, Equatorial Guinea and Gabon; cap. and res 92,485m. (June 1983); br. in Bata; Gov. CASIMIR OYE MBA; Dir in Malabo (vacant).

Commercial Banks

Banco de Crédito y Desarrollo: 1 Avda de la Libertad, Apdo 39, Malabo; tel. 35-35; cap. 8.75m.; 100% state-owned; br. in Bata; Chair. MARCELO EKONG AWONG; Man. Dir FELICIANO NTUGU NSA.

Banco Exterior de Guinea Ecuatorial y España (GUINEXTEBANC): 67 Calle del Presidente Nasser, Apdo 261, Malabo; export bank.

BIAO-Guinée Equatorial: Malabo; f. 1986; cap. 300m.; 51% owned by the Banque Internationale pour l'Afrique Occidentale, Paris, 49% state-owned.

Trade and Industry

Cámara de Comercio, Agrícola y Forestal de Malabo: Apdo 51, Malabo.

Cámaras Oficiales Agrícolas de Guinea: Bioko and Bata; buys cocoa and coffee from indigenous planters, who are partially grouped in co-operatives.

Empresa General de Industria y Comercio (EGISCA): Malabo; f. 1986 to replace the defunct Empresa Estatal de Comercio Interior y Exterior; parastatal body jtly operated with the French Société pour l'Organisation, l'Aménagement et le Développement des Industries Alimentaires et Agricoles (SOMDIA); import-export agency.

Empresa Guineano-Española de Petróleos (GEPSA): 33 Avda de la Independencia, Apdo 30, Malabo; tel. 23-00; f. 1980; owned equally by the govt and Hispanoil; legislation governing petroleum production was passed in 1981; wells drilled in early 1982 produced some positive results; also conducts natural gas exploration.

Sociedad Anonima de Desarollo del Comercio (SOADECO-Guinée): Malabo; f. 1986 to replace the defunct Empresa Estatal de Comercio Interior y Exterior; parastatal body jtly operated with the French Société pour l'Organisation, l'Aménagement et le Développement des Industries Alimentaires et Agricoles (SOMDIA); development of commerce.

Transport

RAILWAYS

There are no railways in Equatorial Guinea.

ROADS

Bioko: a semi-circular tarred road serves the northern part of the island from Malabo to Batete in the west and from Malabo to Bacake Grande in the east, with a feeder road from Luba to Moka and Bahía de la Concepción; total length of roads: about 160 km.

Río Muni: a tarred road links Bata with Mbini (Río Benito) in the west; another road, partly tarred, links Bata with the frontier post of Ebebiyin in the east and then continues into Gabon; other earth roads join Acurenam, Mongomo de Guadelupe and Nsork; total length of roads: 1,015 km.

SHIPPING

The main ports are Malabo (general cargo), Luba (bananas), Bata (general), Mbini and Kogo (timber). A regular monthly service is operated by the Spanish Compañía Transmediterránea from Barcelona, calling at Malabo and Bata.

CIVIL AVIATION

There are international airports at Bata and Malabo. In 1985 discussions took place with the French Government regarding the foundation of a new national airline to provide a regular service between the two centres.

Aerolíneas Guinea Ecuatorial (ALGESA): Malabo; f. 1982 to operate regular services to Cameroon, Gabon and Nigeria; fleet of 2 HS 748, 1 Cessna 402.

Tourism

Prior to the fall of President Macías Nguema in 1979, few foreigners visited Equatorial Guinea. Tourism remains undeveloped.

ETHIOPIA

Introductory Survey

Location, Climate, Language, Religion, Flag, Capital

Socialist Ethiopia extends inland from the Red Sea coast of eastern Africa. The country has a long frontier with Somalia near the Horn of Africa. Sudan lies to the west, Djibouti to the east and Kenya to the south. The climate is mainly temperate because of the high plateau terrain, with an average annual temperature of 13°C (55°F), abundant rainfall in most years and low humidity. The lower country and valley gorges are very hot and subject to periodic drought. The official language is Amharic, but many other local languages are also spoken. English is widely used in official and commercial circles, and Arabic is spoken in the province of Eritrea. The Ethiopian Orthodox (Tewahido) Church, an ancient Christian sect, has a wide following in the north and on the southern plateau. In much of the south and east there are Muslims and followers of animist beliefs. The national flag (proportions 3 by 2) has three horizontal stripes, of green, yellow and red. The capital is Addis Ababa.

Recent History

Ethiopia was dominated for more than 50 years by Haile Selassie, who became Regent in 1916, King in 1928 and Emperor in 1930. He ruled the country, except during the Italian occupation of 1936–41, until his deposition by the armed forces in September 1974 in the wake of serious regional famine, inflation and unemployment, and growing demands for democratic reform. The Emperor's rule was highly personal and autocratic, but he consolidated the expansion of Ethiopian territory and the gradual process of national modernization which had been begun by the Emperor Menelik (1865–1913). The former Italian colony of Eritrea was merged with Ethiopia, in a federal arrangement, in September 1952, and annexed to Ethiopia as a province in November 1962. Haile Selassie died, a captive of the present military regime, in August 1975.

The revolution of September 1974 was engineered by an Armed Forces Co-ordinating Committee, known popularly as the Dergue ('Shadow'), which controls ultimate power. The Dergue established a Provisional Military Government (PMG), headed by Lt-Gen. Aman Andom. In November, after a dispute in the military leadership, Gen. Andom was deposed and shot. The PMG was replaced by a Provisional Military Administrative Council (PMAC), led by Brig.-Gen. Teferi Benti; the monarchy was abolished in March 1975. Ethiopia was declared a socialist state in December 1974, and a national programme, called Ethiopia Tikdem (Ethiopia First), was carried out in the following year. Insurance companies, banks, financial institutions, large industrial enterprises, rural and urban land and schools were nationalized, while peasant co-operatives and industrial workers' councils were established.

Widespread unrest continued throughout 1975 and 1976, despite moves by the Dergue to ease tension by releasing some detainees and promising a return to civilian rule, at an unspecified date. Strains within the Dergue were reflected by its reorganization in December 1976. However, in February 1977 Lt-Col Mengistu Haile Mariam executed Brig.-Gen. Teferi Benti and his closest associates, and replaced him as chairman of the PMAC and Head of State.

The Government continued to meet political and armed opposition from various groups, both Marxist and anti-Marxist. During 1977 and 1978 thousands of opponents of the Government were killed or imprisoned in a programme of 'rehabilitation' or 'liquidation'. Until July 1977 the Dergue was assisted by Mei'son (the Marxist All-Ethiopia Socialist Movement) but later formed its own party, Abyot Seded (Revolutionary Flame), which sought to enlist civilian support. However, all political groupings were theoretically swept away in late 1979 when a Commission for Organizing the Party of the Working People of Ethiopia (COPWE) was established.

The Central Committee of COPWE, which was dominated by military personnel, held its first congress in June 1980. It announced in February 1981 that peasant co-operatives were to be encouraged, and that mass organizations for youth, women, peasants and workers were to be strengthened. The third congress and the formal establishment of the Workers' Party of Ethiopia (WPE), which replaced COPWE, took place in September 1984, to coincide with the 10th anniversary of the revolution. Lt-Col Mengistu was unanimously elected Secretary-General of the party, which was modelled on the Communist Party of the Soviet Union. The congress also elected an 11-member Politburo and a 136-member Central Committee. It was reported that the PMAC would be dissolved at a future date.

In June 1986, in preparation for the eventual transfer of power from the PMAC to a civilian government, a draft constitution was published. Under its provisions, a National Assembly (Shengo) would be established, while locally-elected assemblies would administer the regions (including Eritrea). Power would be vested in the WPE, as the sole legal party, operating on the basis of 'democratic centralism', and Ethiopia would become a People's Democratic Republic. However, the sensitive issue of the exact degree of self-determination for the regions was left open, and the timing of the return to civilian rule was not specified. The Constitution was approved at a national referendum in January 1987, following further discussion and amendment.

In December 1985 the Commissioner for Relief and Rehabilitation, Dawit Wolde Giorgis, defected while on a fundraising visit to the USA. He later accused the Ethiopian regime of being authoritarian and rigidly doctrinaire, and criticized aspects of the Government's famine-relief policy. These accusations were reinforced by the Minister of Foreign Affairs, Goshu Wolde, who also defected in October 1986. Berhanu Bayih, formerly Minister of Labour and Social Affairs, became the new Minister of Foreign Affairs.

Numerous secessionist movements, encouraged by the confusion created by the revolution, seek the destruction of the empire created by Menelik and Haile Selassie. These are strongest in the Ogaden region and Eritrea. Somalia lays claim to the Ogaden, which is inhabited mainly by ethnic Somalis, and regular Somali troops have supported incursions by forces of the Western Somali Liberation Front (WSLF). In 1977 the Somalis made major advances in the Ogaden, but in 1978 were forced to retreat. By the end of 1980 the Ethiopian defence forces were in control of virtually the whole of the Ogaden, but armed clashes have continued in the region. In 1980 an OAU committee declared the Ogaden to be an integral part of Ethiopia.

Secessionist movements have existed in Eritrea since its annexation in 1962, and also in Tigre, claiming to control large tracts of the provinces. In January 1982 the Government announced 'Operation Red Star', to bring the political, social and economic development of Eritrea into line with the rest of the country. However, the accompanying military campaign to allow the implementation of these projects had failed by May. The strongest movement, the Eritrean People's Liberation Front (EPLF), faced a major government offensive outside its stronghold of Nakfa in mid-1983, while a similar campaign was waged against the Tigre People's Liberation Front (TPLF) in western Tigre province. In early 1984 the EPLF launched a major new campaign, and, during heavy fighting, government troops suffered severe losses. The EPLF captured the town of Tessenei, near the Sudanese border, and defeated the army on three fronts in the Eritrean highlands. In January 1985 three of the Eritrean factions agreed to merge as the Eritrean Unified National Council (EUNC), but the EPLF refused to collaborate with this group. It was revealed that secret talks had been held sporadically between the EPLF and the Ethiopian Government since 1977, aimed at reaching agreement on autonomy for the region, but had so far been unproductive. In March the Government launched a large-scale offensive in Tigre and Eritrea, and by September had made significant gains, including the recapture of the strategic towns of Barentu and Tessenei.

The continued fighting in the north during 1984–85 compounded problems facing areas of Ethiopia already severely affected by famine. In 1984 the rains failed for the third consecutive crop season, and in May the Relief and Rehabilitation Commission estimated that 7m. people could face starvation. Following large-scale media attention, Ethiopia at last received emergency food aid from many Western nations, but distribution of the aid posed a major problem, as the ports rapidly became congested. Some famine relief was airlifted to affected areas, while Western food agencies sent food and medical supplies into Eritrea through Sudan. Some rainfall in 1985 eased the drought in the northern provinces, but Ethiopia remained dependent on foreign aid during 1986. The 1986 grain harvest was threatened by a devastating plague of locusts, and the Government estimated that 2.5m. people could face starvation in 1987. Part of the Government's solution to the famine was the controversial plan to resettle more than 1.5m. people from the northern areas to the more fertile lowlands, but critics saw this as an attempt to remove opposition from the disputed areas. By May 1986 some 600,000 people had been resettled, but then the programme was suspended, in response to international criticism.

After Lt-Col Mengistu's coup in February 1977, the USSR supplanted the USA as the principal supplier of armaments to Ethiopia. In 1978 a treaty of friendship and co-operation between Ethiopia and the USSR was signed. Relations with the USA improved slightly in December 1985, however, when Ethiopia agreed to pay compensation to US companies, on claims dating back to the 1975 nationalizations. In August 1981, in response to US military interests in Somalia, Oman and Egypt, a treaty of friendship and co-operation was also signed between Ethiopia, Libya and the People's Democratic Republic of Yemen, which are all Soviet-influenced states. Ethiopia has also developed closer diplomatic links with its neighbours, Kenya and Djibouti, which have attempted to bring about a reconciliation with Somalia. Under the mediation of the President of Djibouti, in January 1986 Mengistu met the Somali President, Mohamed Siad Barre, for the first time since 1977. Talks between the two Ministers of Foreign Affairs took place later in 1986, when the issue of the Ogaden was discussed. Following the military coup in Sudan in April 1985, which displaced President Nimeri, it was announced that full diplomatic relations would be restored between Ethiopia and Sudan.

Government

Ethiopia has been ruled since November 1974 by a Provisional Military Administrative Council (PMAC), chaired by the Head of State. A General Congress comprising all members of the PMAC, or Dergue (whose original 120 members were reduced to about 80), decides policy; a Central Committee of 32, elected by the Congress, and a Standing Committee (originally 16 members, but reduced in 1979 to eight), elected from the Central Committee of the Congress, execute the decisions of the Congress. The powers of the largely civilian Council of Ministers, appointed by the PMAC, are closely defined. The Chairman of the PMAC presides over each of its three sections, is Chairman of the Council of Ministers, Head of State and Commander-in-Chief of the armed forces. Local government is carried out by kebelles (urban dwellers' associations) and peasant associations. These have elected committees with extensive administrative and judicial powers. There are more than 1,200 kebelles and about 30,000 peasant associations, organized into the All-Ethiopia Peasants' Association in 1978.

In 1979 the regime formed a Commission for Organizing the Party of the Working People of Ethiopia (COPWE), which established, and was subsequently replaced by, the Marxist-Leninist Workers' Party of Ethiopia (WPE) in September 1984, in preparation for the eventual transfer of power from the PMAC to a civilian government.

Defence

In July 1986, according to Western estimates, the army (including the People's Militia) numbered 220,000, the air force 4,000 and the navy 3,000. Military service is compulsory, and lasts for 30 months. In addition, all men and women between 18 and 50 years of age undergo six months' reserve training. Ethiopia receives armaments and technical assistance from Warsaw Pact countries, Cuba, Libya and the People's Democratic Republic of Yemen; there are an estimated 4,000 Cubans serving in the armed forces. Defence expenditure in 1984/85 was estimated at 925m. birr.

Economic Affairs

Ethiopia is, economically, one of the least developed countries in the world. It suffers from unfavourable climatic conditions, an inadequate infrastructure, a shortage of skilled labour and, in recent years, adverse terms of trade. Economic difficulties have been aggravated by years of civil strife between the central government and numerous dissident or secessionist groups. Natural disasters, including droughts, floods and plagues of locusts, have contributed to widespread famine and have increased the already huge refugee problem arising from military hostilities. In 1984, according to World Bank estimates, Ethiopia's GNP per head was only US $110 (at average 1982–84 prices), the second lowest level among African countries and one of the six lowest in the world. It was estimated that GNP per head had increased by only 0.4% annually, in real terms, between 1965 and 1984. The average annual growth in overall GDP, in constant prices, was 4.1% in 1965–73, slowing to 2.3% in 1973–83.

The economy is mainly agricultural and pastoral, with agriculture producing almost one-half of GDP in years of normal rainfall. Agricultural products provide about 90% of Ethiopia's export earnings. Revenue from coffee usually accounts for more than 60% of all export receipts. Annual production of coffee generally averages around 200,000 tons, but in 1984/85 it fell to about 150,000 tons, as a result of the drought. In 1985/86, however, quotas were surpassed in several regions, and 61,000 tons of coffee were exported, earning more than 595m. birr. Agricultural output in general has been devastated by recent drought: the IMF estimated that in 1984/85 domestic food production was reduced by 25%, while export earnings fell by 15% as a result of the drought. Output of food crops totalled 4.6m. metric tons in 1984, compared with a pre-famine total of 7.2m. tons in 1982/83. In 1985/86, however, following improved rainfall in many areas, agricultural production increased by 21.5%, but the good harvests were threatened by a serious plague of locusts in Tigre and Gondar regions.

Apart from coffee, Ethiopia's major exports include hides and skins, pulses and oilseeds, and refined petroleum products. In recent years the USA has been the largest single export market, taking nearly 20% of total overseas sales in 1984, while the EEC accounts for around one-third of both imports and exports. The bulk of Ethiopia's imports come from the USSR (23% in 1984). Export earnings consistently fail to pay for imports, and the gap has been widening since 1975: in 1984/85 the trade deficit reached 1,400m. birr. Fishing and forestry are still small-scale activities, but international aid is to be sought to develop the fishing industry, which could provide a major long-term solution to the country's food supply problems. In 1975 a radical land reform programme, aimed at stimulating agricultural development by demolishing the feudal system of tenure which existed before the overthrow of the monarchy in 1974, was initiated after all land had been nationalized. In the 1980s the Government embarked on a policy of 'villagization', grouping farmers together in collective units in order to provide better facilities and to improve production; by June 1986 20,000 such villages had been established, mainly in Hararge region, but there were allegations that the programme was enforced and that it had disrupted agriculture and reduced harvests. By 1994/95 some 50% of farms are scheduled to be organized into co-operatives, compared with 1% in 1984/85. Only about 18% of Ethiopia's total area is cultivated, and in addition only 100,000 ha of land is irrigated, out of a potential of more than 2m. ha. Much of the production of cash crops takes place on state farms, which cover a total of about 300,000 ha. By 1994/95 this area is planned to increase to 500,000 ha. About 45% of agricultural production is at subsistence level. Soil erosion, due to poor agricultural techniques, deforestation and overgrazing, is an increasing problem, and land is becoming barren at an estimated rate of 200,000 ha per year.

Industrial activity, which contributes about 16% of Ethiopia's

GDP, is confined mainly to food processing and the manufacture of textiles and goods for local consumption. Industrial production increased by 5.1% in 1985/86. About one-half of Ethiopia's industry is in Eritrea, although the war there has forced many factories to close. Ethiopia has small reserves of gold, platinum, copper and potash, which are being exploited with the assistance of the USSR. There has also been Soviet-led exploration for petroleum, and in 1986 bidding for 25 petroleum-drilling concessions was opened to international companies. The cost of petroleum imports generally accounts for more than 50% of Ethiopia's foreign exchange earnings. The capacity of Ethiopia's only petroleum refinery, at Assab, had reached 800,000 metric tons per year by 1982. Ethiopia has massive hydroelectric power resources, which provide the bulk of electricity generation. In addition, geothermal resources are being assessed, mainly in the Lake Langano area in the Rift Valley. A five-year programme of rehabilitation for the power sector, at a cost of $106.8m., was announced in 1986. Banks, insurance companies and many large industrial concerns, including shipping and maritime services, are all nationalized.

Ethiopia suffered from its worst drought and famine for 10 years in 1982–84, when it was estimated that up to 7m. people were affected. The northern and western provinces were the most severely hit. In February 1985 the Government announced an austerity programme, which introduced compulsory contributions for all wage-earners and private companies to an emergency famine relief fund, and also outlined restrictions on petrol consumption and a ban on the import of luxury items, including motor cars and textiles. The problem of drought was exacerbated by the fighting in Eritrea, the Ogaden and Tigre, which displaced millions of people. Relief attempts were hindered by the continuing conflicts within Ethiopia, the lack of foreign exchange, owing to defence expenditure requirements, and by political differences with the West.

Economic development is hampered by a lack of adequate transport and communications. However, a port development project, financed by the IDA, is under way at Assab, and will increase the port's capacity, while a railway linking the port with Addis Ababa is also planned. Other obstacles to the country's development are the lack of trained manpower and financial investment, and the dislocations caused by political change. In 1978 the Government began a series of one-year plans under a National Revolutionary Development Campaign, which resulted in considerable economic recovery in 1978–81. The 10-year plan for 1984/85–1993/94 aims to achieve self-sufficiency in food and to develop the industrial sector. Over the period of the plan, industry's contribution to GDP is projected to increase from 16% to 26%, while agriculture's share is expected to fall to 35%. During the plan period, GDP is expected to grow by around 6% per year in real terms. The state's share of agricultural production is to be significantly expanded, while 216 industrial projects are to be carried out, with the aim of making Ethiopia less dependent on imported capital goods. The plan's success depends largely on foreign assistance (almost 45% of funding is envisaged to come from external sources), and the Government hopes to attract foreign private investment, following the publication of a joint-venture code in 1983. A three-year intermediate plan was announced in 1986, for the period 1986/87–1988/89 (forming part of the 10-year 'perspective' plan). During the plan period, GDP (at 1980/81 prices) was expected to grow by 6.3% per year (from 8,641m. birr in 1985/86 to 10,370m. birr). Agriculture was expected to grow by 6.8% per year, and industry by 8.3%.

Ethiopia's external debt totalled around $1,000m. in mid-1984 (about 20% of GDP), but the country has an excellent record of debt repayment. It was estimated that by 1987/88 the external debt would reach $2,000m., not including Ethiopia's military debt to the USSR (estimated at $2,500m.–$4,000m. in October 1985). In the 1970s the development aid that Ethiopia received was the lowest per head among the UN-designated least developed countries, but by the end of 1984 large amounts of extra emergency aid had been given, following extensive foreign news coverage of the drought, and by 1985 Ethiopia was the largest recipient of EEC aid. Under the Lomé III agreement with the EEC, Ethiopia was granted $224m., most of which was allocated to the agricultural sector, followed by development of ports and telecommunications. Other loans announced in 1986 included $44.5m. from the USSR, to expand the industrial sector, and $40m. from the IMF, to compensate for the drop in export earnings.

Social Welfare

The scope of modern health services has been greatly extended since 1960, but they still reach only a small section of the population. In 1980 Ethiopia had 86 hospital establishments, with a total of 11,147 beds, and there were 428 physicians working in the country. Relative to the size of the population, the provision of hospital beds and physicians was the lowest among African countries. There are also 1,500 clinics and health centres. With foreign assistance, health centres and clinics are steadily expanding into the rural areas. In times of famine, however, Ethiopian health services are totally inadequate. In 1977 free medical care for the needy was introduced.

Education

Education in Ethiopia is free and, after a rapid growth in numbers of schools, it is hoped to introduce compulsory primary education shortly. A major literacy campaign was launched in 1979. By 1983 more than 10m. people had been enrolled for tuition programmes, and the adult illiteracy rate was reportedly reduced from 93% to 45%.

Since September 1976 most primary and secondary schools have been controlled by local peasant associations and urban dwellers' associations. Primary education begins at seven years of age and lasts for six years. Secondary education, beginning at the age of 13, lasts for a further six years, comprising a first cycle of two years and a second of four years. As a proportion of children in the relevant age-group, enrolment at primary schools rose from 16% in 1970 to 46% (60% of boys; 33% of girls) in 1981. Secondary enrolment in 1981 was equivalent to only 12% of children in the appropriate age-group. There are two universities.

Tourism

The principal tourist attractions are hunting, the early Christian monuments and churches, and the ancient capitals of Gondar and Axum. Tourism has been adversely affected by political uncertainty since 1974, and only 3,297 tourists visited the country in 1978. However, the Tourism and Hotel Commission launched a major campaign to win back tourists in 1980, with 48,830 visitors in 1981 and almost 58,000 in 1982. Tourist arrivals in 1983/84 were about 69,000. Tourism brought in an estimated 30m. birr in foreign exchange in 1983/84, compared with 11m. birr in 1979.

Public Holidays

1987: 7 January* (Christmas), 19 January* (Epiphany), 2 March (Battle of Adowa), 6 April (Victory Day), 13 April* (Palm Sunday), 20 April* (Easter), 1 May (May Day), 30 May (Id al-Fitr, end of Ramadan), 6 August (Id al-Adha/Arafat), 11 September (New Year's Day), 12 September (Popular Revolution Commemoration Day), 27 September* (Feast of the True Cross), 4 November (Mouloud, Birth of the Prophet).

1988: 7 January* (Christmas), 19 January* (Epiphany), 2 March (Battle of Adowa), 28 March* (Palm Sunday), 4 April* (Easter), 6 April (Victory Day), 1 May (May Day), 18 May (Id al-Fitr, end of Ramadan), 25 July (Id al-Adha/Arafat), 11 September (New Year's Day), 12 September (Popular Revolution Commemoration Day), 27 September* (Feast of the True Cross), 23 October (Mouloud, Birth of the Prophet).

* Coptic holidays.

Note: Ethiopia uses its own solar calendar; the Ethiopian year 1979 began on 11 September 1986.

Weights and Measures

The metric system is officially in use. There are many local weights and measures.

Currency and Exchange Rates

100 cents = 1 birr.

Exchange rates (30 September 1986):
 £1 sterling = 2.995 birr;
 US $1 = 2.070 birr.

Statistical Survey

Source (unless otherwise stated): Central Statistical Office, POB 1143, Addis Ababa; tel. 113010.

Area and Population

AREA, POPULATION AND DENSITY

Area (sq km)	1,223,600*
Population (census of 9 May 1984†)	
Males	21,018,900
Females	21,150,303
Total	42,169,203
Density (per sq km) at May 1984	34.5

* 472,435 sq miles.
† Including an estimate for areas not covered by the census.

ADMINISTRATIVE REGIONS (July 1980 estimates)*

	Area (sq km)	Population
Arussi	24,600	1,149,400
Bale	128,300	879,200
Eritrea	117,400	2,426,200
Gemu Goffa	40,100	1,003,400
Gojam	64,500	2,037,900
Gondar	73,400	2,053,400
Hararge	254,800	3,125,200
Illubabor	50,800	810,800
Kefa (Kaffa)	53,000	1,615,400
Shoa†	85,500	6,362,200
Sidamo	116,700	2,808,300
Tigre	65,700	2,162,100
Wollega	69,800	2,019,200
Wollo	79,000	2,612,600
Total	**1,223,600**	**31,065,300**

* Figures for population have not been revised to take account of the results of the May 1984 census.
† Data include the capital, Addis Ababa, which is also a separate Administrative Region.

PRINCIPAL TOWNS (estimated population at July 1980)

Addis Ababa (capital)	1,277,159	Harar	62,921
Asmara	424,532	Bahr Dar	52,188
Dire Dawa	82,024	Debre Zeit	49,570
Gondar (incl. Azeso)	76,932	Mekele	46,846
Dessie	75,616	Debre Markos	40,686
Nazret	69,865	Keren	37,931
Jimma	63,837	Akaki	35,022
		Assela	34,874
		Massawa	32,977

BIRTHS AND DEATHS

Average annual birth rate 49.6 per 1,000 in 1970–75, 49.3 per 1,000 in 1975–80; death rate 23.2 per 1,000 in 1970–75, 23.4 per 1,000 in 1975–80 (UN estimates).

ECONOMICALLY ACTIVE POPULATION
(ILO estimates, '000 persons at mid-1970)

	Males	Females	Total
Agriculture, etc.	5,866	3,240	9,106
Industry	394	233	627
Services	782	307	1,090
Total	**7,042**	**3,781**	**10,823**

Source: ILO, *Labour Force Estimates and Projections, 1950–2000*.

1984 census: Total labour force 18,492,300 (males 11,243,065; females 7,249,235).

Agriculture

PRINCIPAL CROPS ('000 metric tons)

	1982	1983	1984*
Wheat	917	900†	675
Barley	1,168	1,130†	848
Maize	1,603	1,700†	1,275
Oats	62	63†	47
Millet (Dagusa)	240	193	145
Sorghum	1,356	1,160	870
Other cereals	1,372	1,214	910
Potatoes*	240	242	182
Yams*	280	282	212
Other roots and tubers*	1,000	1,050	788
Dry beans	37	35*	26
Dry peas	133	150*	113
Dry broad beans	601	600*	450
Chick-peas	101	118	89
Lentils	52	42	32
Other pulses	103	108	81
Sugar cane*	1,450	1,600	1,650

	1982	1983	1984
Soybeans	12	6	6*
Groundnuts (in shell)*	33	31	28
Castor beans*	12	12	12
Rapeseed*	22	22	22
Sesame seed*	37	36	36
Linseed	36	36*	30*
Safflower seed*	32	32	32
Cottonseed†	59	44	48
Cotton (lint)†	27	20	22
Vegetables and melons*	499	507	513
Bananas*	73	74	74
Other fruit (excl. melons)*	133	135	136
Coffee (green)	202	220†	240†
Tobacco (leaves)*	3	3	3
Fibre crops (excl. cotton)*	15	16	16

* FAO estimates. † Unofficial estimates.
Source: FAO, *Production Yearbook*.

ETHIOPIA   Statistical Survey

LIVESTOCK (FAO estimates, '000 head, year ending September)

	1982	1983	1984
Cattle	26,200	26,300	26,000
Sheep	23,350	23,400	23,450
Goats	17,220	17,240	17,250
Asses	3,900	3,905	3,910
Horses	1,550	1,560	1,570
Mules	1,455	1,460	1,465
Camels	1,000	1,010	1,020
Pigs	19	19	19

Poultry (FAO estimates, million): 54 in 1982; 55 in 1983; 55 in 1984.
Source: FAO, *Production Yearbook*.

LIVESTOCK PRODUCTS (FAO estimates, '000 metric tons)

	1982	1983	1984
Beef and veal	215	216	216
Mutton and lamb	85	86	86
Goats' meat	61	63	65
Pig meat	1	1	1
Poultry meat	69	70	70
Other meat	111	112	116
Edible offals	90	91	92
Cows' milk	605	610	611
Goats' milk	95	95	95
Sheep's milk	58	60	61
Butter	8.9	9.0	9.0
Hen eggs	74.5	75.2	75.9
Honey*	21.0	21.0	21.0
Wool:			
greasy	12.3	12.4	12.4
clean	6.3	6.4	6.4
Cattle hides	41.3	41.4	41.6
Sheep skins	15.3	15.5	15.5
Goat skins	13.0	13.3	13.7

* Unofficial estimates.
Source: FAO, *Production Yearbook* and *Monthly Bulletin of Statistics*.

Forestry

ROUNDWOOD REMOVALS
('000 cubic metres, excluding bark)

	1982	1983	1984*
Sawlogs, etc.	120	120	120
Other industrial wood	1,645	1,693	1,693
Fuel wood*	27,804	28,540	29,341
Total	29,569	30,353	31,154

* FAO estimates.
Source: FAO, *Yearbook of Forest Products*.

SAWNWOOD PRODUCTION ('000 cubic metres)

	1981	1982	1983
Total (including boxboards)	65*	45	45

* FAO estimate.
1984: Production as in 1983 (FAO estimate).
Source: FAO, *Yearbook of Forest Products*.

Fishing

(FAO estimates, '000 metric tons, live weight)

	1981	1982	1983
Inland waters	3.5	3.4	3.5
Indian Ocean	0.3	0.4	0.4
Total catch	3.8	3.8	3.9

1984: Catch as in 1983 (FAO estimates).
Source: FAO, *Yearbook of Fishery Statistics*.

Mining

(year ending 10 September)

	1978/79	1979/80	1980/81
Gold (kilograms)	247.9	289.0	386.0
Platinum (kilograms)	3.4	3.5	n.a.

ETHIOPIA   *Statistical Survey*

Industry

SELECTED PRODUCTS (year ending 10 September)

		1979/80	1980/81	1981/82
Wheat flour	'000 metric tons	175	160	164
Macaroni	'000 metric tons	54	24	11
Raw sugar	'000 metric tons	163	154	177
Wine	'000 hectolitres	77	74	86
Beer	'000 hectolitres	552	604	616
Soft drinks	'000 hectolitres	711	720	625
Mineral waters	'000 hectolitres	160	173	177
Cigarettes	million	1,458	1,575	1,300*
Cotton yarn	'000 metric tons	9	7	9
Woven cotton fabrics	million sq metres	86	87	92
Blankets	number	1,158	847	899
Woollen carpets	'000 sq metres	21	17	17
Nylon fabrics	million sq metres	5.9	5.9	5.9
Footwear	'000 pairs	6,936	6,936	7,511
Soap	'000 metric tons	10.3	10.6	12.2
Ethyl alcohol	'000 hectolitres	7	8	5
Liquefied petroleum gas	'000 metric tons	4	5	5
Motor gasoline†	'000 metric tons	81	94	99
Distillate fuel oils†	'000 metric tons	154	146	193
Residual fuel oils†	'000 metric tons	243	193	300
Clay building bricks	million	23	23	20
Quicklime	'000 metric tons	9	5	4
Cement	'000 metric tons	123	142	159
Electric energy	million kWh	668	696	763

1982/83: Wheat flour 160,000 metric tons*; Raw sugar 207,000 metric tons; Cigarettes 1,300m.*; Woollen carpets 17,000 sq metres; Liquefied petroleum gas 5,000 metric tons; Motor gasoline 102,000 metric tons†; Distillate fuel oils 209,000 metric tons†; Residual fuel oils 303,000 metric tons†; Cement 150,000 metric tons; Electric energy 753m. kWh.

* Estimate.

† Figures refer to calendar year, e.g. output in 1980 appears under 1979/80.

Source: UN, *Industrial Statistics Yearbook*.

Finance

CURRENCY AND EXCHANGE RATES

Monetary Units
100 cents = 1 birr.

Denominations
Coins: 1, 5, 10, 25 and 50 cents.
Notes: 1, 2, 10, 50 and 100 birr.

Sterling and Dollar Equivalents (30 September 1986)
£1 sterling = 2.995 birr;
US $1 = 2.070 birr;
100 birr = £33.39 = $48.31.

Exchange Rate
Fixed at US $1 = 2.070 birr since February 1973.

NATIONAL BANK RESERVES
(US $ million at 31 December)

	1983	1984	1985
Gold*	21.3	21.3	21.3
IMF special drawing rights	2.4	2.9	0.2
Reserve position in IMF	4.4	—	—
Foreign exchange	119.1	41.4	147.8
Total	147.2	65.6	169.3

* Valued at US $102 per troy ounce.

Source: IMF, *International Financial Statistics*.

MONEY SUPPLY (million birr at 31 December)

	1983	1984	1985
Currency outside banks	1,251	1,272	1,418
Demand deposits at commercial banks*	892	1,037	1,285
Total money*	2,141	2,309	2,702

* From August 1984, data exclude the Djibouti branch of the Commercial Bank of Ethiopia.

Source: IMF, *International Financial Statistics*.

COST OF LIVING (General Index of Retail Prices for Addis Ababa, excluding rent; base: 1980 = 100)

	1981	1982	1983
Food	104.7	111.0	111.8
Fuel, light and soap*	115.3	119.5	111.1
Clothing	102.0	101.2	99.1
All items (incl. others)	106.1	112.1	111.6

* Including certain kitchen utensils.

1984: Food 124.1; All items 120.8.

Source: ILO, *Year Book of Labour Statistics*.

ETHIOPIA

Statistical Survey

BUDGET ESTIMATES (million birr, year ending 7 July)*

Revenue	1979/80	1980/81	1983/84†
Direct taxes	361.4	381.2	638.2
Domestic indirect taxes	342.7	384.8	495.5
Taxes on foreign trade	623.3	578.5	572.1
Charges and fees	11.8	22.4	23.9
Sales of goods and services	32.1	37.7	43.0
Property and investment	137.0	224.4	439.1
Miscellaneous	21.0	6.0	7.0
Pension contributions	17.9	19.9	26.0
External assistance	151.6	216.8	219.4
Capital receipts	273.0	312.5	433.4
Total	**1,971.8**	**2,184.2**	**2,897.6**

Expenditure	1979/80	1980/81	1983/84†
Current			
National defence	750.8	736.8	869.6
Internal order and justice	143.7	150.6	174.0
Organs of state	104.3	113.4	161.7
Public works and communications	43.0	44.8	63.2
Agriculture, industry, commerce and mining	75.8	86.7	96.9
Education and culture	221.2	229.7	252.0
Public health and social welfare	114.6	130.4	136.2
Pensions	66.0	82.6	100.0
Public debt	92.0	107.8	192.6
Bank charges	1.5	2.0	2.8
Unallocated	41.6	56.3	107.6
Total current	**1,654.6**	**1,741.1**	**2,224.8**
Capital			
Economic development	594.6	795.5	1,078.2
Social development	89.1	120.6	148.2
General services	26.7	21.2	8.6
Total capital	**710.4**	**937.3**	**1,234.9**
Total	**2,365.0**	**2,678.4**	**3,459.8**

* Figures for 1981/82 and 1982/83 are not available.
† Projected.

NATIONAL ACCOUNTS (million birr at current prices, year ending 7 July)

Expenditure on the Gross Domestic Product

	1981/82	1982/83	1983/84
Government final consumption expenditure	1,487	1,733	1,868
Private final consumption expenditure*	7,349	8,013	7,913
Gross fixed capital formation	1,082	1,119	1,284
Total domestic expenditure	**9,918**	**10,865**	**11,065**
Exports of goods and services	1,076	1,142	1,267
Less Imports of goods and services	1,824	1,991	2,277
GDP in purchasers' values	**9,169**	**10,016**	**10,055**

* Including increase in stocks. The figures are obtained as a residual.

Gross Domestic Product by Economic Activity*

	1979/80	1980/81	1981/82
Agriculture and livestock	3,723.6	3,872.0	3,879.1
Forestry	143.4	147.1	151.0
Hunting	1.3	1.3	4.9
Fishing	3.6	3.6	
Mining and quarrying	8.1	8.1	9.8
Manufacturing	533.5	464.4	600.1
Handicraft and small industry	296.5	306.9	317.8
Building and construction	295.9	308.1	325.9
Electricity and water	55.4	58.0	59.5
Wholesale and retail trade	812.2	853.4	889.2
Transport and communications	355.1	376.7	434.0
Banking, insurance and real estate	244.5	291.7	304.4
Public administration and defence	535.3	584.5	617.4
Ownership of dwellings	200.2	206.3	212.0
Educational services			
Medical and health services	283.5	298.7	319.0
Domestic services			
Other services	161.7	167.4	174.1
GDP at factor cost	**7,653.8**	**8,048.2**	**8,298.2**
Indirect taxes, *less* subsidies	845.1	806.2	820.6
GDP at market prices	**8,498.9**	**8,854.4**	**9,118.8**

* Figures are provisional. Revised totals (in million birr) are: 8,500 in 1979/80; 8,907 in 1980/81; 9,169 in 1981/82.

Source: National Revolutionary Development Campaign and Central Planning Supreme Council Secretariat.

BALANCE OF PAYMENTS (US $ million)

	1982	1983	1984
Merchandise exports f.o.b.	402.8	402.6	416.8
Merchandise imports f.o.b.	−675.2	−740.0	−800.0
Trade balance	−272.4	−337.3	−383.2
Exports of services	176.5	169.6	210.3
Imports of services	−239.8	−252.9	−290.1
Balance on goods and services	−335.7	−420.6	−463.0
Private unrequited transfers (net)	38.1	92.1	144.9
Government unrequited transfers (net)	102.4	158.1	186.1
Current balance	−195.2	−170.4	−132.0
Long-term capital (net)	69.5	207.4	192.3
Short-term capital (net)	39.5	−35.9	29.6
Net errors and omissions	10.8	−54.8	−149.0
Total (net monetary movements)	−75.4	−53.6	−59.2
Valuation changes (net)	−0.6	7.8	3.9
Exceptional financing	—	0.1	1.2
Changes in reserves	−76.0	−45.8	−54.1

Source: IMF, *International Financial Statistics*.

External Trade

PRINCIPAL COMMODITIES ('000 birr)

Imports c.i.f.	1982	1983	1984
Food and live animals	124,320	207,269	170,736
Cereals and cereal preparations	90,259	170,625	122,346
Crude materials (inedible) except fuels	50,229	58,130	43,264
Mineral fuels, lubricants, etc.	399,781	350,231	319,784
Petroleum	357,792	315,344	262,480
Chemicals and related products	173,415	209,275	205,875
Inorganic chemicals	48,115	36,872	36,720
Manufactured fertilizers	13,030	42,040	37,788
Basic manufactures	262,727	263,778	290,167
Textile yarn, fabrics, etc.	45,664	37,375	37,199
Iron and steel	78,620	67,171	76,307
Machinery and transport equipment	513,601	603,434	664,861
General industrial machinery	203,568	229,250	234,439
Electrical machinery, apparatus, etc.	82,729	114,801	86,740
Road vehicles	179,843	187,971	191,535
Miscellaneous manufactured articles	64,579	68,796	59,823
Total (incl. others)	1,623,397	1,813,325	1,813,842

Exports f.o.b.	1982	1983	1984
Food and live animals	591,135	596,994	619,090
Coffee	514,388	519,956	545,707
Crude materials (inedible) except fuels	171,640	158,208	164,077
Goatskins	21,119	17,258	18,592
Sheepskins	49,134	52,512	59,746
Cotton lint	21,775	9,342	7,849
Qat	32,862	28,862	32,014
Mineral lubricants, etc.	63,921	68,917	63,851
Furnace and fuel oils	63,919	68,917	63,851
Total (incl. others)	835,983	832,491	861,759

Source: Ethiopian Chamber of Commerce.

1985 (million birr): Coffee 432.7; Hides and skins 103.6; Total (incl. others) 689.4 (Source: IMF, *International Financial Statistics*).

PRINCIPAL TRADING PARTNERS ('000 birr)

Imports	1982	1983	1984
China, People's Rep.	8,210	8,775	8,201
France	56,841	51,494	62,654
German Dem. Rep.	31,848	39,086	31,724
Germany, Fed. Rep.	157,866	179,419	201,171
India	17,429	8,098	9,560
Italy	185,505	243,045	190,418
Japan	145,431	168,147	124,015
Kenya	10,828	9,757	9,382
Korea, Rep.	42,941	46,257	10,306
Netherlands	30,424	51,879	37,571
Saudi Arabia	17,957	18,002	20,172
Sweden	38,499	36,108	25,344
Switzerland	31,382	38,798	42,401
USSR	441,821	379,063	412,318
United Kingdom	122,795	137,638	124,577
USA	63,559	83,192	190,579
Total (incl. others)	1,623,397	1,813,325	1,813,842

Source: Ethiopian Chamber of Commerce.

Exports	1982	1983	1984
Djibouti	77,516	65,333	59,830
Egypt	10,999	6	1
France	44,280	63,319	43,720
Germany, Fed. Rep.	133,565	137,789	155,321
Italy	43,913	62,177	63,695
Japan	62,171	62,805	64,510
Netherlands	10,504	16,476	17,471
Saudi Arabia	56,015	47,931	36,080
Sudan	1,008	1,525	10,337
USSR	5,042	3,684	39,074
United Kingdom	16,886	13,435	20,055
USA	216,013	169,508	167,800
Yemen, People's Dem. Rep.	48,980	54,893	49,680
Yugoslavia	15,154	2,204	2,012
Total (incl. others)	835,983	832,491	861,759

Transport

RAILWAYS (traffic)*

	1978/79	1979/80	1980/81
Addis Ababa–Djibouti:			
Passenger-km ('000)	171,000	247,000	310,000
Freight ('000 net ton-km)	148,000	148,000	131,000

* Excluding Eritrea but including traffic on the portion of the Djibouti–Addis Ababa line which runs through the Republic of Djibouti.

1983: Passenger-km 360m., Freight 122m. ton-km.

ROAD TRAFFIC (motor vehicles in use at 31 December)

	1983	1984	1985
Cars	43,387	43,558	41,250
Buses and coaches	4,681	3,908	3,622
Goods vehicles	14,077	9,161	15,537
Motorcycles and scooters	1,291	1,292	1,437
Total	63,436	57,919	61,846

Source: International Road Federation, *World Road Statistics*.

SHIPPING
(Ports of Assab and Massawa, year ending 7 July)

	1979/80	1980/81	1981/82*
Vessels entered ('000 net reg. tons)	2,265	2,604	n.a.
Goods loaded ('000 metric tons)	518	625	547
Goods unloaded ('000 metric tons)	1,695	1,595	1,753

* Provisional figures.

CIVIL AVIATION (traffic on scheduled services)

	1980	1981	1982
Kilometres flown (million)	10.5	12.0	12.6
Passengers carried ('000)	243	328	335
Passenger-km (million)	647	760	762
Freight ton-km (million)	24.8	21.0	24.5

Source: UN, *Statistical Yearbook*.

Tourism

	1980	1981	1982
Tourist arrivals ('000)	42	46	60

Source: UN, *Statistical Yearbook*.

ETHIOPIA

Communications Media

	1981	1982	1983
Radio receivers ('000 in use)	n.a.	3,000	3,300
Television receivers ('000 in use)	31	40	40
Book production: titles	150*	n.a.	457
Daily newspapers:			
Number	n.a.	3	n.a.
Average circulation ('000 copies)	n.a.	40	n.a.
Non-daily newspapers:			
Number	n.a.	4	n.a.
Average circulation ('000 copies)	n.a.	39	n.a.

* Excluding pamphlets (214 in 1983).
Source: UNESCO, *Statistical Yearbook*.
Telephones: 86,000 in use (1980).

Education

(1982)

	Teachers	Students
Primary	42,347	2,511,050
Secondary: general	12,570	535,152
Higher:		
Universities, etc.	1,001	10,512
Other	268	5,605

Source: UNESCO, *Statistical Yearbook*.

Directory

The Constitution

The 1931 Constitution was abolished by military decree in September 1974. Plans were announced in 1976 for the future promulgation of a new constitution, and in 1984 it was stated that the newly-formed Workers' Party of Ethiopia (WPE) was to draw up a new constitution. In June 1986 a draft constitution was published, providing for a unitary state comprising administrative and autonomous regions. The new constitution was to be submitted for approval to a national assembly (to be established at a later date), culminating in the proclamation of Ethiopia as a People's Democratic Republic.

The Government

HEAD OF STATE

Chairman of the Provisional Military Administrative Council (PMAC): Lt-Col MENGISTU HAILE MARIAM (assumed power 3 February 1977).

PMAC STANDING COMMITTEE
(December 1986)

Chairman: Lt-Col MENGISTU HAILE MARIAM.
Secretary-General: Lt-Col FIKRE-SELASSIE WOGDERES.
Deputy Secretary-General: FISSEHA DESTA.
Military Affairs: Lt-Gen. TESFAYE GEBRE-KIDAN.
Security: TEKA TULU.
Development and Planning: ADDIS TEDLA.
Party Organization: LEGESSE ASFAW.
Administrative and Legal Affairs: WUBSHET DESSIE.
Other Members: GESSESSE WOLDE-KIDAN, ENDALE TESSEMA, KASSAHUN TAFESSE, Lt-Col BERHANU BAYIH.

COUNCIL OF MINISTERS
(December 1986)

Chairman: Lt-Col MENGISTU HAILE MARIAM.
Deputy Chairman: Lt-Col FIKRE-SELASSIE WOGDERES.
Minister of Transport and Communications: YOUSSOUF MOHAMMED.
Minister of Culture, Sports and Youth Affairs: Maj. GIRAM YILMA.
Minister of Education: BILILIGNE MANDEFRO.
Minister of Finance: TESFAYE DINKA.
Minister of Industry: HAILU YIMENU.
Minister of Law and Justice: AMANUEL AMDE-MIKHAIL.
Minister of Foreign Affairs: Lt-Col BERHANU BAYIH.
Minister of Agriculture: GEREMEW DEBELE.
Minister of the Interior: Brig.-Gen. TAYE TILAHUN.
Minister of Mines and Energy: Eng. TEKIZE-SHOA AYITENFISU.
Minister of Labour and Social Affairs: (vacant).
Minister of Defence: Brig.-Gen. TESFAYE GEBRE-KIDAN.
Minister of Public and National Security: TESFAYE WOLDE-SELASSIE.
Minister of Health: Brig.-Gen. Dr GIZAW TSEHAY.
Minister of Housing and Urban Development: TESFAYE MARRU.
Minister of Foreign Trade: WOLLIE CHEKOL.
Minister of Construction: KASSA GEBRE.
Minister of Information and National Guidance: Dr FELEKE GDELE-GIORGIS.
Minister of Domestic Trade: MERSHA WODAJO.
Minister of Planning: MERSIE EJIGU.
Minister of State Farms: YOSEPH MULETA.
Minister of Tea and Coffee Development: TEKOLA DEJENE.
Commissioner for Hotels and Tourism: (vacant).
Commissioner for National Water Resources: KELKILEW TADESSE.
Commissioner for Relief and Rehabilitation: BERHANU JEMBERE.

MINISTRIES AND COMMISSIONS

Office of the Chairman of the Council of Ministers: POB 1013, Addis Ababa; tel. 123400.
Ministry of Agriculture: POB 1223, Addis Ababa; tel. 448040.
Ministry of Construction: Addis Ababa; tel. 155406.
Ministry of Culture, Sports and Youth Affairs: POB 1902, Addis Ababa; tel. 446338.
Ministry of Defence: POB 125, Addis Ababa; tel. 445555; telex 21261.
Ministry of Domestic Trade: POB 1769, Addis Ababa; tel. 448200.
Ministry of Education: POB 1362, Addis Ababa; tel. 112039.
Ministry of Finance: POB 1905, Addis Ababa; tel. 113400; telex 21147.
Ministry of Foreign Affairs: POB 393, Addis Ababa; tel. 447345; telex 21050.
Ministry of Foreign Trade: POB 2559, Addis Ababa; tel. 151066; telex 21320.

ETHIOPIA

Ministry of Health: POB 1234, Addis Ababa; tel. 157011.
Ministry of Housing and Urban Development: POB 3386, Addis Ababa; tel. 150000.
Ministry of Industry: POB 704, Addis Ababa; tel. 448025.
Ministry of Information and National Guidance: POB 1020, Addis Ababa; tel. 111124.
Ministry of the Interior: POB 2556, Addis Ababa; tel. 113334.
Ministry of Labour and Social Affairs: POB 2056, Addis Ababa; tel. 447080.
Ministry of Law and Justice: POB 1370, Addis Ababa; tel. 447390.
Ministry of Mines and Energy: POB 486, Addis Ababa; tel. 448250; telex 21448.
Ministry of Public and National Security: POB 125, Addis Ababa; tel. 154258.
Ministry of State Farms: POB 1223, Addis Ababa; tel. 154600.
Ministry of Tea and Coffee Development: POB 3222, Addis Ababa; tel. 448005; telex 21130.
Ministry of Transport and Communications: POB 1629, Addis Ababa; tel. 155011.
Commission for Hotels and Tourism: POB 2183, Addis Ababa; tel. 447470.
Commission for National Water Resources: POB 486, Addis Ababa; tel. 447597; telex 21219.
Commission for Relief and Rehabilitation: POB 5686, Addis Ababa; tel. 153011; telex 21281.

POLITICAL BUREAU OF THE CENTRAL COMMITTEE OF THE WORKERS' PARTY OF ETHIOPIA

General Secretary: Lt-Col MENGISTU HAILE MARIAM.
Members: FIKRE-SELASSIE WOGDERES, FISSEHA DESTA, Lt-Gen. TESFAYE GEBRE-KIDAN, BERHANU BAYIH, ADDIS TEDLA, LEGESSE ASFAW, HAILU YIMENU, AMANUEL AMDE-MIKHAIL, ALEMU ABEBE, SHIMELIS MAZENGIA.
Alternate Members: TEKA TULU, FASIKA SIDELIL, SHEWANDAGN BELETE, TESFAYE DINKA, TESFAYE WOLDE-SELASSIE, KASSA GEBRE.

Legislature

Parliament was suspended by military decree in September 1974.

Political Organizations

Workers' Party of Ethiopia (WPE): Addis Ababa; f. 1984; Marxist-Leninist; sole legal political party; Sec.-Gen. Lt-Col MENGISTU HAILE MARIAM.

The following separatist groups are in armed conflict with the Ethiopian government:

Afar Liberation Front (ALF): operates in Hararge and Wollo Administrative Regions; Leader ALI MIRAH.
Eritrean People's Liberation Front (EPLF): f. 1970 as a breakaway from the Eritrean Liberation Front; Marxist-Leninist; Christian and Muslim support; maintains Eritrean People's Liberation Army (EPLA) of 25,000–30,000 men; Sec.-Gen. RAMADAN MOHAMMED NUR.
Eritrean Unified National Council (EUNC): f. 1985 by merger of the Eritrean Liberation Front-Revolutionary Council (f. 1958), the People's Liberation Forces-Unified Organization and the People's Liberation Forces-Revolutionary Committee; Pres. YOHANNES ZERE MARIAM; Chair. OSMAN SALEH SABBE.
Oromo Liberation Front (OLF): operates among the Oromo (or Galla) people in Shoa Administrative Region with Somali military assistance.
Somali Abo Liberation Front (SALF): operates in Bale Administrative Region with Somali military assistance; Sec.-Gen. MUHAMMAD HASAN GABABA.
Tigre People's Liberation Front (TPLF): f. 1975; Marxist; operates in Tigre Administrative Region.
Western Somali Liberation Front (WSLF): POB 978, Mogadishu, Somalia; f. 1975; aims to unite the Ogaden region with Somalia; maintains guerrilla forces of c. 3,000 men supported by regular Somali forces; Sec.-Gen. ISSA SHAYKH ABDI NASIR ADAN.

Diplomatic Representation

EMBASSIES IN ETHIOPIA

Algeria: POB 5740, Addis Ababa; tel. 441334; Ambassador: HOCINE MESLOUB.
Argentina: Addis Ababa; telex 21172; Ambassador: Dr H. R. M. MOGUES.
Australia: Addis Ababa; Chargé d'affaires: LES LUCK.
Austria: POB 137, Addis Ababa; tel. 202144; telex 21060; Ambassador: Dr HERBERT TRAXL.
Belgium: Fikre Mariam St, Higher 16, Kebelo, POB 1239, Addis Ababa; tel. 181813; telex 21157; Ambassador: PAUL VERMEIRSCH.
Bulgaria: POB 987, Addis Ababa; tel. 153822; Ambassador: G. P. KASSOV.
Burundi: POB 3641, Addis Ababa; tel. 159564; telex 21069; Ambassador: A. SIMBANAIYE.
Cameroon: Bole Rd, POB 1026, Addis Ababa; telex 21121; Ambassador: S. N. ETOUNGOU.
Canada: African Solidarity Insurance Bldg, Haile Selassie I Sq., POB 1130, Addis Ababa; tel. 151100; telex 21053; Ambassador: W. AGNES.
Chad: Addis Ababa; Ambassador: J. B. LAOKOLE.
China, People's Republic: POB 5643, Addis Ababa; telex 21145; Ambassador: ZHANG RUIJIE.
Congo: POB 5571, Addis Ababa; tel. 154331; telex 21406; Ambassador: C. STANISLAS BATHEAS-MOLLOMB.
Cuba: Jimma Voad Ave, POB 5623, Addis Ababa; tel. 202010; telex 21306; Ambassador: FRANCISCO CABRERA.
Czechoslovakia: POB 3108, Addis Ababa; tel. 446382; telex 21021; Ambassador: EDUARD KUKAN.
Djibouti: POB 1022, Addis Ababa; tel. 183200; telex 21317; Chargé d'affaires: DJIBRIL DJAMA ELABE.
Egypt: POB 1611, Addis Ababa; tel. 113077; telex 21254; Ambassador: SAMIR AHMED.
Equatorial Guinea: POB 246, Addis Ababa; Ambassador: FELIX MBA ONDO NCHAMA.
Finland: Tedla Desta Bldg, Bole Rd, POB 1017, Addis Ababa; tel. 445881; telex 21259; Chargé d'affaires a.i.: ESKO JÄÄSALO.
France: Kabana, POB 1464, Addis Ababa; tel. 110681; Ambassador: JOSE PAOLI.
Gabon: POB 1256, Addis Ababa; tel. 181075; telex 21208; Ambassador: DENIS DANGUE REWAKA.
German Democratic Republic: POB 5507, Addis Ababa; tel. 181506; telex 21170; Ambassador: HANS JAGENOW.
Germany, Federal Republic: Kabana, POB 660, Addis Ababa; tel. 120433; telex 21015; Ambassador: BERND OLDENKOTT.
Ghana: POB 3173, Addis Ababa; tel. 201402; telex 21249; Ambassador: BONIFACE KWAME ATERPOR.
Greece: Africa Ave, POB 1168, Addis Ababa; tel. 110612; telex 21092; Chargé d'affaires: M. DIAMANTOPOULOS.
Guinea: POB 1190, Addis Ababa; tel. 449712; Ambassador: PIERRE BASSAMBA CAMARA.
Holy See: POB 588, Addis Ababa; tel. 202100; Apostolic Pro-Nuncio: Archbishop THOMAS A. WHITE.
Hungary: Sudan St, POB 1213, Addis Ababa; tel. 167610; telex 21176; Ambassador: GYULA BOGNAR.
India: Kabana, POB 528, Addis Ababa; tel. 128100; telex 21148; Ambassador: C. V. RANGANATHAN.
Indonesia: POB 1004, Mekanisa Rd, Addis Ababa; tel. 202104; telex 21264; Ambassador: IMAM ABIKUSNO.
Iran: 317/02 Jimma Rd, Old Airport Area, POB 1144, Addis Ababa; tel. 200369; telex 21118; Chargé d'affaires: HASSEN DABIR.
Italy: Villa Italia, POB 1105, Addis Ababa; tel. 113040; telex 21342; Ambassador: SERGIO ANGELETTI.
Ivory Coast: POB 3668, Addis Ababa; tel. 448330; telex 21081; Ambassador: (vacant).
Jamaica: National House, Africa Ave, POB 5633, Addis Ababa; tel. 183656; telex 21137; Ambassador: R. A. PIERCE.
Japan: Finfinne Bldg, Revolution Sq., POB 5650, Addis Ababa; tel. 448215; telex 21108; Ambassador: SUKETORO ENOMOTO.
Kenya: Fikre Mariam Rd, POB 3301, Addis Ababa; tel. 180033; telex 21103; Ambassador: F. K. NGANATHA.

ETHIOPIA
Directory

Korea, Democratic People's Republic: POB 2378, Addis Ababa; Ambassador: SOK TAE UK.

Korea, Republic: Jimma Rd, Old Airport Area, POB 2047, Addis Ababa; tel. 444490; telex 21140; Ambassador: DEUK PO KIM.

Liberia: POB 3226, Addis Ababa; telex 21083; Ambassador: NATHANIEL EASTMAN.

Libya: POB 5728, Addis Ababa; telex 21214; Secretary of People's Bureau: K. BAZELYA.

Malawi: POB 2316, Addis Ababa; tel. 44829536; telex 21087; Ambassador: D. P. W. KACHIKUWO.

Mexico: Tsige Mariam Bldg 292/21, 4 Piso, Churchill Rd, POB 2962, Addis Ababa; tel. 443456; Ambassador: CARLOS FERRER.

Mozambique: Addis Ababa; Ambassador: ALBERTO SITHOLE.

Netherlands: Old Airport Area, POB 1241, Addis Ababa; tel. 203300; telex 21049; Ambassador: (vacant).

Niger: POB 5791, Addis Ababa; tel. 15611; telex 21284; Ambassador: IBRAHIM MOUSSA.

Nigeria: POB 1019, Addis Ababa; tel. 120644; telex 21028; Ambassador: HALIDU HANNANNIYA.

Poland: Bole Rd, POB 1123, Addis Ababa; tel. 180196; telex 21185; Ambassador: ANDRZEJ K. KONOPACKI.

Romania: Africa Ave, POB 2478, Addis Ababa; tel. 181191; telex 21168; Ambassador: BARBU POPESCU.

Rwanda: Africa House, Higher 17 Kelele 20, POB 5618, Addis Ababa; tel. 180300; telex 21199; Ambassador: JEAN-MARIE VIANNEY NDAGIJIMANA.

Saudi Arabia: Old Airport Area, POB 1104, Addis Ababa; tel. 448010; telex 21194; Chargé d'affaires: HASSAN M. ATTAR.

Senegal: Africa Ave, POB 2581, Addis Ababa; tel. 446332; telex 21027; Ambassador: LATYR KAMARA.

Sierra Leone: POB 5619, Addis Ababa; tel. 203210; telex 21144; Ambassador: FRANCIS E. KAREMO.

Spain: Entoto St, POB 2312, Addis Ababa; tel. 114987; telex 21107; Ambassador: E. ROMEU.

Sudan: Kirkos, Kabele, POB 1110, Addis Ababa; telex 21293; Ambassador: OSMAN NAFI.

Sweden: Ras Tesemma Sefer, POB 1029, Addis Ababa; tel. 448110; telex 21039; Ambassador: NILS G. REVELIUS.

Switzerland: Jimma Rd, Old Airport Area, POB 1106, Addis Ababa; tel. 201107; telex 21123; Ambassador: FRANZ BIRRER.

Tanzania: POB 1077, Addis Ababa; tel. 441064; telex 21268; Ambassador: FATUMA TATU NURU.

Turkey: POB 1506, Addis Ababa; tel. 152321; telex 21257; Ambassador: SUPHI MERIÇ.

Uganda: POB 5644, Addis Ababa; tel. 9816945; telex 21143; Chargé d'affaires: ROBERT CANON UCUNGI.

USSR: POB 1500, Addis Ababa; Ambassador: (vacant).

United Kingdom: POB 858, Addis Ababa; tel. 182354; telex 21299; Ambassador: H. B. WALKER.

USA: Entoto St, POB 1014, Addis Ababa; tel. 110666; Chargé d'affaires: JAMES R. CHEEK.

Venezuela: Dedre Zeit Rd, POB 5584, Addis Ababa; tel. 157575; telex 21102; Chargé d'affaires: L. SOSA-VAAMONDE.

Viet-Nam: POB 1288, Addis Ababa; Ambassador: NGUYEN DUY KINH.

Yemen Arab Republic: POB 664, Addis Ababa; Ambassador: Lt-Col HUSSEIN MOHASIN AL-GHAFFARI.

Yemen, People's Democratic Republic: POB 664, Addis Ababa; Ambassador: SALIH ABU BAKR BIN HUSAYNUN.

Yugoslavia: POB 1341; Addis Ababa; tel. 447804; Ambassador: NUSRET SEFEROVIĆ.

Zaire: Makanisa Rd, POB 2723, Addis Ababa; tel. 204385; telex 21043; Ambassador: WAKU YIZILA.

Zambia: POB 1909; Addis Ababa; tel. 44815; telex 21065; Ambassador: GEORGE CHIPAMPATA.

Zimbabwe: POB 5624, Addis Ababa; tel. 183872; telex 21351; Ambassador: TICHAONA J. B. JOKONYA.

Judicial System

Special People's Courts were established in 1981 to replace the former military tribunals. Judicial tribunals are elected by members of the urban dwellers' and peasant associations. In April 1977 powers were introduced to detain suspected saboteurs for up to six months without trial. There is no appeal against the decision of the Supreme Judicial Tribunal.

The Supreme Court: Addis Ababa; comprises a president and two other judges; has jurisdiction only to hear appeals from the High Court.

The High Court: Addis Ababa; hears appeals from the Provincial and sub-Provincial Courts; has original jurisdiction.

Awraja Courts: Provincial courts composed of three judges, criminal and civil.

Warada Courts: Sub-Provincial; one judge sits alone with very limited jurisdiction, criminal only.

Religion

About 45% of the population are Muslims and about 40% belong to the Ethiopian Orthodox (Tewahido) Church. There are also significant Evangelical Protestant and Roman Catholic communities. The Pentecostal Church and the Society of International Missionaries carry out mission work in Ethiopia. There are also Hindu and Sikh religious institutions and a small Jewish population.

CHRISTIANITY
Ethiopian Orthodox (Tewahido) Church

The Ethiopian Orthodox (Tewahido) Church is one of the five oriental orthodox churches. It was founded in AD 328, and in 1986 had more than 22m. members, 20,000 parishes and 250,000 clergy. The Supreme Body is the Holy Synod and the National Council, under the chairmanship of the Patriarch. There are 24 Archbishops and Bishops. The Church administers 1,139 schools and 12 relief and rehabilitation centres throughout Ethiopia.

Patriarchate Head Office: POB 1283, Addis Ababa; tel. 116507; telex 21489; Patriarch: His Holiness ABUNA TEKLE HAIMANOT; Gen. Sec. L. M. ABEBAW YIGZAW.

Other Christian Churches

Armenian Orthodox Church: Pres. ABEDIS TERZIAN, POB 116, St George's Armenian Church, Addis Ababa; f. 1923.

Ethiopian Evangelical Church (Mekane Yesus): Pres. Ato FRANCIS STEPHANOS, POB 2087, Addis Ababa; tel. 111200; telex 21528; f. 1958; affiliated to Lutheran World Federation; 685,796 mems (1984).

Greek Orthodox Church: Metropolitan of Axum: Most Rev. PETROS GIAKOUMELOS, POB 571, Addis Ababa.

The Roman Catholic Church: At 31 December 1984 there were an estimated 112,000 adherents of the Alexandrian-Ethiopian rite and 145,000 adherents of the Latin rite.

   Alexandrian-Ethiopian Rite: There is one archdiocese (Addis Ababa) and two dioceses (Adigrat and Asmara); Archbishop of Addis Ababa: Cardinal PAULOS TZADUA, POB 2109, Addis Ababa; tel. 111667.

   Latin Rite: There are five Apostolic Vicariates (Asmara, Awasa, Harar, Nekemte and Soddo-Hosanna) and one Apostolic Prefecture (Meki); Vicar Apostolic of Asmara: (vacant), POB 224, Asmara; tel. 110631.

Seventh-day Adventist Church: Pastor GEBRE-MICHAEL TELLEMA, POB 145, Addis Ababa; 32,000 mems.

ISLAM
Leader: Haji MOHAMMED HABIB SANI.

JUDAISM

Following the secret airlifts to Israel in 1984–85 of about 13,000 Falashas (Ethiopian Jews), there were estimated to be some 8,000 Falashas still in the country, living mainly in Gondar and Tigre Administrative Regions.

TRADITIONAL BELIEFS

It is estimated that between 5% and 15% of the population follow animist rites and ceremonies.

The Press

DAILIES

The following three newspapers are published by the Ministry of Information and National Guidance:

ETHIOPIA

Addis Zemen: POB 30145, Addis Ababa; f. 1941; Amharic; Editor-in-Chief TSEHAJU DEBALKEW (acting); circ. 37,000.

Ethiopian Herald: POB 30701, Addis Ababa; tel. 119050; f. 1943; English; Editor-in-Chief KIFLOM HADGOI; circ. 6,000.

Hibret: POB 247, Asmara; Tigrinya; Editor-in-Chief GURJA TESFA SELASSIE; circ. 4,000.

PERIODICALS

Al-Alem: POB 30232, Addis Ababa; weekly; Arabic; publ. by the Ministry of Information and National Guidance; Editor-in-Chief TELSOM AHMED; circ. 2,500.

Berisa: POB 30232, Addis Ababa; f. 1976; weekly; Oromogna; publ. by the Ministry of Information and National Guidance; circ. 2,000.

Ethiopia: POB 247, Asmara; weekly; Amharic; publ. by Ministry of Information and National Guidance; Editor-in-Chief ABRAHA GEBRE HIWOT; circ. 2,000.

Ethiopian Trade Journal: POB 517, Addis Ababa; tel. 448240; telex 21213; publ. by the Chamber of Commerce; quarterly; English; Editor-in-Chief GETACHEW ZICKE.

Maedot (Passover): POB 1283, Addis Ababa; tel. 116507; telex 21489; Amharic and English; publ. by the Ethiopian Orthodox Church.

Meskerem: POB 80001, Addis Ababa; quarterly; theoretical political journal; circ. 100,000.

Negarit Gazzetta: POB 1031, Addis Ababa; fortnightly; Amharic and English; official gazette of laws, orders and notices.

Nigdina Limat: POB 2458, Addis Ababa; tel. 158039; telex 21213; monthly; Amharic; publ. by the Chamber of Commerce.

Revolutionary Police: POB 40046, Addis Ababa; fortnightly; Amharic; police journal.

Serto Ader (Worker): POB 80123, Addis Ababa; f. 1980; weekly; organ of the WPE; Editor TESFAYE TADESE; Dep. Editor GEZAHEGN GEBRE; circ. 100,000.

Tatek (Get Armed): POB 1901, Addis Ababa; fortnightly; Amharic; army journal.

Tinsae (Resurrection): POB 1283, Addis Ababa; tel. 116507; telex 21489; Amharic and English; publ. by the Ethiopian Orthodox Church.

Trade and Development Bulletin: POB 856, Asmara; tel. 110814; telex 42079; monthly; Amharic and English; publ. by the Chamber of Commerce; Editor TAAME FOTO.

Yezareitu Ethiopia (Ethiopia Today): POB 30232, Addis Ababa; weekly; Amharic; publ. by the Ministry of Information and National Guidance; Editor-in-Chief ABIYE MEIZURIA (acting); circ. 30,000.

NEWS AGENCIES

Ethiopia News Agency (ENA): POB 530, Patriots' St, Addis Ababa; tel. 120014; telex 21068.

Foreign Bureaux

Agence France-Presse (AFP): POB 3537, Addis Ababa; tel. 157386; telex 21031; Chief SEYOUM AYELE.

Agentstvo Pechati Novosti (APN) (USSR): POB 239, Addis Ababa; telex 21237; Chief VITALI POLIKARPOV.

Allgemeiner Deutscher Nachrichtendienst (ADN) (German Democratic Republic): POB 2387, Addis Ababa; telex 21025; Chief BERND HINKELMANN.

Agenzia Nazionale Stampa Associata (ANSA) (Italy): POB 1001, Addis Ababa; telex 115704; Chief BRAHAME GHEBREZGHI-ABIHER.

Novinska Agencija Tanjug (Yugoslavia): POB 5743, Addis Ababa; telex 21150; Chief JOVIĆ RADOSLAV.

Prensa Latina (Cuba): 5th Floor, Gen. Makonnen Bldg, nr Ghion Hotel, opposite National Stadium, POB 5690, Addis Ababa; tel. 449299; telex 21151; Chief ROBERTO CORREA WILSON.

Telegrafnoye Agentstvo Sovetskovo Soyuza (TASS) (USSR): POB 998, Addis Ababa; tel. 181255; telex 21091; Chief GENNADI G. GABRIELYAN.

Xinhua (New China) News Agency (People's Republic of China): POB 2497, Addis Ababa; tel. 151064; telex 21504; Correspondent TENG WENQI.

PRESS ASSOCIATION

Ethiopian Journalists' Association: Addis Ababa; Chair. IMERU WORKU (acting).

Publishers

Addis Ababa University Press: POB 1176, Addis Ababa; tel. 119148; telex 21205; f. 1968; educational and reference works in English; Editor INNES MARSHALL.

Ethiopia Book Centre: POB 1024, Addis Ababa; privately-owned.

Kuraz Publishing Agency: POB 30933, Addis Ababa; state-owned.

Government Publishing House
Government Printing Press: POB 1241, Addis Ababa.

Radio and Television

There were an estimated 3.3m. radio receivers and 40,000 television receivers in use in 1983.

Board of Telecommunications of Ethiopia: POB 1047, Addis Ababa; Gen. Man. G. ENGDAYEHU.

RADIO

Voice of Revolutionary Ethiopia: POB 1020, Addis Ababa; tel. 121011; f. 1941; Amharic, English, French, Arabic, Afar, Oromigna, Tigrinya and Somali; Gen. Man. MULUGETA LULE.

TELEVISION

Ethiopian Television: POB 5544, Addis Ababa; tel. 16701; telex 21429; f. 1964; state-controlled; commercial advertising is accepted; programmes are transmitted from Addis Ababa to 17 regional stations; broadcasts cover all of Ethiopia except two Administrative Regions; Dir-Gen. A. TEFERRA GIZAW; Head of TV WOLE GURMU.

Finance

(cap. = capital; p.u. = paid up; dep. = deposits; m. = million; res = reserves; amounts in birr)

BANKING

On 1 January 1975 all privately-owned banks and other financial institutions were nationalized.

Central Bank
National Bank of Ethiopia: POB 5550, Addis Ababa; tel. 447430; telex 21020; f. 1964; bank of issue; cap. 30m., res 146.5m. (June 1983); Gov. TADESSE GEBRE-KIDAN.

Other Banks
Agricultural and Industrial Development Bank: POB 1900, Addis Ababa; tel. 151188; telex 21173; provides development finance for industry and agriculture, technical advice and assists in project evaluation; cap. p.u. 100m.; Gen. Man. TSEGAYE ASFAW; 9 brs.

Commercial Bank of Ethiopia: POB 255, Addis Ababa; tel. 155000; telex 21037; f. 1964; state-owned; merged with Addis Bank 1980; cap. 65m., res 39m. (Dec. 1984); Gen. Man. ALEMU ABERRA; 146 brs.

Housing and Savings Bank: POB 3480, Addis Ababa; tel. 152300; f. 1975; provides credit for housing construction; cap. p.u. 6m., dep. 212.3m. (June 1984); Gen. Man. GETACHEW YIFRU; 7 brs.

INSURANCE
Ethiopian Insurance Corporation: POB 2545, Addis Ababa; tel. 156348; telex 21120; f. 1976 to carry out all insurance business; Gen. Man. AYALEW BEZABEH.

Trade and Industry

CHAMBER OF COMMERCE
Ethiopian Chamber of Commerce: POB 517, Mexico Sq., Addis Ababa; tel. 448240; telex 21213; f. 1947; city chambers in Addis Ababa, Asmara, Bahr Dar, Dire Dawa, Nazret, Jimma, Gondar and Dessie; Pres. (vacant); Sec.-Gen. MEBRATE MENGISTU.

ETHIOPIA

AGRICULTURAL ORGANIZATION

All-Ethiopia Peasants' Association (AEPA): f. April 1978 to promote improved agricultural techniques, cottage industries, education, public health and self-reliance; mems: 30,000 peasant asscns with total membership of c. 7m.; Chair. ABDELA SONESA.

TRADE AND INDUSTRIAL ORGANIZATIONS

Ethiopian Beverages Corporation: POB 1285, Addis Ababa; tel. 186185; telex 21373.

Ethiopian Cement Corporation: POB 5782, Addis Ababa; tel. 122323; telex 21308.

Ethiopian Chemical Corporation: POB 5747, Addis Ababa; tel. 184305; telex 21011.

Ethiopian Coffee Marketing Corporation: POB 2591, Addis Ababa; tel. 155330; telex 21174.

Ethiopian Food Corporation: Higher 21, Kebele 04, Mortgage Bldg, Addis Ababa; tel 158522; telex 21292; f. 1975; produces and distributes food items including edible oil, ghee substitute, pasta, bread, maize, wheat flour etc.

Ethiopian Fruit and Vegetable Marketing Enterprise: POB 2374, Addis Ababa; tel. 449192; telex 21106; f. 1980; sole wholesale domestic distributor and exporter of fruit and vegetables, spices and floricultural products; Gen. Man. HAILU BALCHA.

Ethiopian Handicrafts and Small-Scale Industries Development Agency: POB 704, Addis Ababa; tel. 157366.

Ethiopian Import and Export Corporation (ETIMEX): POB 2313, Addis Ababa; tel. 152400; telex 21009; f. 1975; state trading corpn under the supervision of the Ministry of Foreign Trade; import of building materials, foodstuffs, stationery and office equipment, textiles, clothing, chemicals, general merchandise, capital goods.

Ethiopian Livestock and Meat Corporation: POB 5579, Addis Ababa; tel. 159011; telex 21095.

Ethiopian Oil Seeds and Pulses Export Corporation: POB 5719, Addis Ababa; tel. 150532; telex 21137; Gen. Man. SHIFERAW BEKELE.

Ethiopian Petroleum Organization: POB 3375, Addis Ababa; telex 21054; f. 1976; operates Assab petroleum refinery; Gen. Man. KEBEDE AKALE WOLDE.

Ethiopian Pharmaceuticals and Medical Supplies Corporation: POB 21904, Addis Ababa; tel. 134599; telex 21248; f. 1976; manufacture, import, export and distribution of pharmaceuticals, chemicals, dressings, surgical and dental instruments, hospital and laboratory supplies; Gen. Man. BERHANU ZELEKE.

Ethiopian Sugar Corporation: POB 133, Addis Ababa; tel. 159700; telex 21038.

Hides and Skins Marketing Corporation: POB 1238, Addis Ababa; tel. 126244; telex 21256.

National Leather and Shoe Corporation: POB 2516, Addis Ababa; tel. 150832; telex 21096; f. 1975; produces and sells semi-processed hides and skins, finished leather, leather goods and footwear.

National Textiles Corporation: POB 2446, Addis Ababa; tel. 157316; telex 21129; f. 1975; production of yarn, fabrics, knitwear, blankets, bags, etc.; Gen. Man. BEKELE HAILE.

Natural Gums Processing and Marketing Enterprise: POB 62322, Addis Ababa; tel. 159931; telex 21336.

TRADE UNIONS

All trade unions must register with the Ministry of Labour and Social Affairs, and 'subordinate' unions must comply with directives issued by 'higher' unions.

All-Ethiopia Trade Union (AETU): POB 3653, Addis Ababa; f. 1975 by the govt to replace the Confederation of Ethiopian Labour Unions; comprises nine industrial unions and 16 regional unions with a total membership of c. 240,000 (1983); Chair. TADESSE TAMRAT; Sec.-Gen. ABERA AFFIN.

Transport

RAILWAYS

Ethio-Djibouti Railway Company: POB 1051, Addis Ababa; tel. 47250; telex 21414; f. 1897; 781 km of track, of which 681 km is in Ethiopia; runs from Addis Ababa to Djibouti; owned equally by Ethiopian and Djibouti govts; plans to grant autonomous status were announced by the two govts in July 1985; Dir-Gen. CHANNIE TAMIRU.

ROADS

In 1985 the total road network comprised 37,871 km of primary, secondary and feeder roads and trails, of which 12,839 km were main roads. A highway links Addis Ababa with Nairobi in Kenya, forming part of the Trans-East Africa Highway.

Ethiopian Transport Construction Authority: POB 1770, Addis Ababa; tel. 447170; telex 21180; f. 1951; constructs roads, bridges, airfields, ports and railways, and maintains roads and bridges throughout Ethiopia; Gen. Man. KELLETTA TESFA MICHAEL.

National Freight Transport Corporation: POB 2538, Addis Ababa; tel. 151841; telex 21238; f. 1974; truck and tanker operations throughout the country.

National Public Transport Authority: POB 5780, Addis Ababa; tel. 156044; telex 21371; f. 1977; urban bus services in Addis Ababa and Jimma, and services between towns.

Road Transport Authority: POB 2504, Addis Ababa; enforcement of road transport regulations, registering of vehicles and issuing of driving licences.

SHIPPING

The Ethiopian merchant shipping fleet totalled 28,409 grt in July 1983. There are irregular services by foreign vessels to Massawa and Assab (the port for Addis Ababa), which can handle over 1m. metric tons of merchandise annually. It has an oil refinery with an annual capacity of 500,000 metric tons. Much trade goes through Djibouti (in the Republic of Djibouti) to Addis Ababa, and Ethiopia has permission to use the Kenyan port of Mombasa. Transport and maritime services were nationalized in September 1979.

Ethiopian Shipping Lines Corporation: POB 2572, Addis Ababa; tel. 444204; telex 21045; f. 1964; state-owned; serves Red Sea and Europe with its own and chartered vessels; Chair. YUSUF AHMED; Gen. Man. TESEMA GEZAW; 12 vessels.

Marine Transport Authority: POB 1861, Addis Ababa; tel. 446448; telex 21280; f. 1978; administers and operates the ports of Assab and Massawa, manages inland waterways, handles cargo.

Maritime and Transit Services Corporation: POB 1186, Addis Ababa; tel. 150666; telex 21125; f. 1979; handles cargoes for import and export; operates shipping agency service.

CIVIL AVIATION

Ethiopia has four international airports and around 40 airfields.

Civil Aviation Authority: POB 978, Addis Ababa; tel. 180266; telex 21162; constructs and maintains airports; provides air navigational facilities.

Ethiopian Airlines: Bole International Airport, POB 1755, Addis Ababa; tel. 152222; telex 21012; f. 1945; operates regular domestic services and flights to 31 international destinations in Africa, Europe, Middle East, India and the People's Republic of China; Chair. YUSUF AHMAD; Gen. Man. Capt. MUHAMMAD AHMAD; fleet of 2 Boeing 767, 5 Boeing 720B, 2 707-320C, 3 727-200, 9 DC-3, 2 DHC-5A Buffalo, 6 DHC-6A, 11 Cessna 172, 2 Seneca III, 1 Piper Aztec.

Tourism

Ethiopian Tourism Commission: POB 2183, Addis Ababa; tel. 447470; telex 21067; f. 1961; Commr (vacant).

FIJI

Introductory Survey

Location, Climate, Language, Religion, Flag, Capital

Fiji comprises more than 300 islands, of which 100 are inhabited, situated about 1,930 km (1,200 miles) south of the equator in the Pacific Ocean. The four main islands are Viti Levu (on which almost 70% of the country's population lives), Vanua Levu, Tavenui and Kadavu. The climate is tropical, with temperatures ranging from 16° to 32°C (60°–90°F). Rainfall is heavy on the windward side. Fijian and Hindi are the principal languages but English is also widely spoken. In 1966 about 51% of the population were Christians (mainly Methodists), 40% Hindus and 8% Muslims. The national flag (proportions 2 by 1) is light blue, with the United Kingdom flag as a canton in the upper hoist. In the fly is the main part of Fiji's national coat of arms: a white field quartered by a red upright cross, the quarters containing sugar canes, a coconut palm, a bunch of bananas and a dove bearing an olive branch; in chief is a red panel with a yellow lion holding a coconut. The capital is Suva, on Viti Levu.

Recent History

The first documented sighting of the islands by Europeans was made by a Dutch expedition, led by Abel Tasman, in 1643. The first Europeans to settle on the islands were sandalwood traders, missionaries and shipwrecked sailors. Under their influence, local fighting and jealousies reached unprecedented heights, until by the 1850s, one chief, Thakombau, had gained a tenuous influence over the whole of the western islands. Thakombau came into conflict with US interests during the 1850s. As a result, he turned to the British for assistance, unsuccessfully at first, but the United Kingdom agreed to a second offer of cession, and on 10 October 1874 Fiji was proclaimed a British possession.

In September 1966 the British Government introduced a new constitution for Fiji. It provided for a ministerial form of government, an almost wholly elected Legislative Council and the introduction of universal adult suffrage. Rather than using a common roll of voters, however, the Constitution introduced an electoral system that combined communal (Fijian and Indian) rolls with cross-voting. In September 1967 the Executive Council became the Council of Ministers, with Ratu Kamisese Mara, leader of the multiracial (but predominantly Fijian) Alliance Party (AP), as Fiji's first Chief Minister. Following a constitutional conference in April–May 1970, Fiji achieved independence, within the Commonwealth, on 10 October 1970. The Legislative Council was renamed the House of Representatives, and a second parliamentary chamber, a nominated Senate, was established. The British-appointed Governor became Fiji's first Governor-General, while Ratu Sir Kamisese Mara (as he had become in 1969) took office as Prime Minister. Mara has remained Prime Minister since independence.

Before independence, Fiji was troubled by racial tensions. The descendants of Indian workers who were brought to Fiji in the late 19th century had grown to outnumber the native inhabitants but were discriminated against in political representation and land ownership rights. A new electoral system was adopted in 1970 to ensure a racial balance in the legislature.

At the general election held in March and April 1977 the National Federation Party (NFP), traditionally supported by the Indian population, won 26 of the 52 seats in the House of Representatives but was unable to form a government and subsequently split into two factions. The AP governed in a caretaker capacity until another election in September, when it was returned with its largest-ever majority. While these two main parties profess multiracial ideas, the Fijian Nationalist Party campaigned on a 'Fiji for the Fijians' platform in order to foster nationalist feeling.

In 1980 Ratu Sir Kamisese Mara's suggestion that a government of national unity be formed was overshadowed by renewed political disagreement between the AP and the NFP (whose two factions had drawn closer together again) over land ownership. Fijians own 83% of the land and are strongly defending their traditional rights, while the Indian population is pressing for greater security of land tenure. The July 1982 elections were also dominated by racial issues. The Alliance Party retained power after winning 28 seats, but their majority had been cut from 20 to four. The NFP won 22 seats and the Western United Front (WUF), which professes a multiracial outlook, took the remaining two seats. Allegations by the two major political parties that foreign political and business interests had been involved in each other's election campaign prompted the appointment of a Royal Commission of Inquiry which, however, failed to uncover any conclusive proof of the allegations during its investigations in 1983.

All except one of the 24 members of the opposition parties in the House of Representatives supported their leader, Jai Ram Reddy, in his boycott of Parliament, which had begun in December 1983 after Reddy was ordered to leave the House for refusing at one point to stand while addressing the Speaker. The Opposition's demand that the Speaker, Tomasi Vakatora, be removed from his post was unheeded, and the boycott ended in June 1984 after Reddy had resigned his seat in May and had been replaced as parliamentary leader of the NFP, and of the opposition coalition, by Siddiq Koya, whom he had defeated for the leadership in 1977. The subsequent by-election for Reddy's seat generated renewed division within the NFP; finally, the candidate whom Koya supported was narrowly defeated by a candidate sponsored by the party's Youth Wing. Koya immediately raised 'legal objections'; demands for Koya's resignation were suspended as the issue went before the courts.

In February 1985 the Government held its first economic 'summit conference'; the meeting was boycotted, however, by both the parliamentary opposition and the Fiji Trades Union Congress (FTUC), in protest against a government-imposed 'freeze' on wages, in force since November 1984. A meeting of union leaders in May 1985 marked the beginning of discussions which culminated in the founding of the Fiji Labour Party, officially inaugurated in Suva in July 1985. Sponsored by the FTUC, and under the presidency of Dr Timoci Bavadra, the new party was formed with the aim of presenting a more effective parliamentary opposition, and has declared free education and a national medical scheme to be among its priorities. However, since it hoped to work through farmers' organizations to win votes among rural electorates, which are traditionally supporters of the NFP, there was speculation that it would merely dilute NFP support and thus give the AP an even bigger majority.

During 1985 and 1986 disagreements between the Government and the FTUC over economic policies became increasingly acrimonious, and in February 1986, having failed to reach agreement with the labour unions on an acceptable increase in wages for 1986, the Government arbitrarily fixed the increase at 2.25%. This provoked an outbreak of labour unrest, leading to the withdrawal, in June 1986, of government recognition of the FTUC as the unions' representative organization. The FTUC responded by holding public protest rallies and by seeking an international suspension of air and sea links with Fiji. The dispute was finally settled in January 1987, when the FTUC, the Fiji Employers' Consultative Association and the Government signed an agreement whereby a guideline of 5.5% was fixed for pay increases in 1987.

In 1986 representatives from the Fijian Government and the Soviet Union met to discuss trade links, tourism and the possibility of securing a fishing agreement. A ban, imposed in response to Soviet military intervention in Afghanistan, and under which Soviet ships had been prohibited from entering Fiji's ports, was subsequently lifted, although no agreement on Soviet fishing rights was signed. In October 1986 Fiji was one of a group of South Pacific island states to conclude a five-year fishing agreement with the USA, whereby the US tuna fleet was granted a licence to operate vessels within Fiji's exclusive fishing zone.

In early 1986 an NFP working committee was formed to conduct an inquiry into the decline of the party, which had lost a number of parliamentary seats as a result of both by-election defeats and the defection of several of its sitting members (including the former deputy leader, Irene Jai Narayan), who chose to classify themselves as independent. Subsequently, in May Koya resigned from the leadership of the NFP, and was replaced by Harish Chandra Sharma. The party continued to lose internal support, and in August a further three of its parliamentary members transferred their allegiance to the Fiji Labour Party.

A general election was due to be held in April 1987, with the NFP, the WUF and the Fiji Labour Party proposing to form an electoral alliance, in an attempt to defeat the ruling AP. The alliance partners declared their support for the Labour Party president, Dr Timoci Bavadra, as prospective Prime Minister.

Government

The Head of State is the British sovereign, represented locally by an appointed Governor-General, who is required to act in accordance with the advice of the Cabinet except in certain constitutional functions. The Prime Minister, who heads the Cabinet, is chosen by the House of Representatives. Legislative power is vested in the bicameral Parliament, comprising the House and the nominated Senate.

The House of Representatives has 52 members, elected for five years by voting on national and communal rolls, divided into three categories: Fijian, Indian and General (those ineligible for the first two rolls). Twelve Fijians, 12 Indians and three General members are elected on the communal rolls. Ten Fijians, 10 Indians and five General members are elected on the national rolls.

The Senate is an appointed Upper House with 22 members: eight are appointed by the Great Council of Fijian Chiefs; seven by the Prime Minister; six by the Leader of the Opposition; and one by the Council of Rotuma (Island). Senators serve a six-year term.

Defence

The Royal Fiji Military Forces consist of men in the regular army, the Naval Squadron, the conservation corps and the territorials. The conservation corps was created in 1975 to make use of unemployed labour in construction work. In July 1986 the total armed forces numbered 2,670 men: 2,500 in the army and 170 in the navy. The defence budget for 1986 was $F 16.3m.

Economic Affairs

The economy is basically agricultural, and the principal cash crop is sugar cane. The instability of the international sugar market seriously affected the Fijian economy in the mid-1970s but, as a member of the group of African, Caribbean and Pacific (ACP) countries which has been linked to the EEC by the Lomé Convention since 1975, Fiji benefits from the Convention's Sugar Protocol, which guarantees that EEC member-states import raw cane sugar from ACP countries at a fixed price. In recent years this price has been far above the prevailing international price of raw sugar on the free market.

In 1982 Fiji produced a record 486,000 metric tons of raw sugar. However, the combined effects of a lengthy drought and a hurricane in March 1983 severely affected the yield in 1983 and, with an output of only 275,877 tons, sugar had to be imported for domestic consumption in order that Fiji might meet its export contracts. In 1984 Fiji produced 483,000 tons of raw sugar, just below the record level of 1982, but, as a result of low free-market prices for sugar and cuts in Fiji's export quota to the USA, the Fiji Sugar Corporation made the first operating loss in its history. In 1985 production of raw sugar declined to 340,000 tons, owing to cyclone damage. However, long-term trade agreements with New Zealand, the People's Republic of China and Malaysia, negotiated in 1985 and 1986, were expected to increase revenue from sugar sales. The USA increased Fiji's sugar export quota from 12,012 metric tons in 1986 to 25,190 tons in 1987, in order to compensate for previous losses of sugar exports to the USA, due to a statistical error.

Fiji's principal trading partners are Australia, Japan, New Zealand, Singapore, the United Kingdom and the USA. Since 1982 tourism has overtaken the sugar industry to become the major source of foreign exchange earnings. Tourist receipts totalled almost $F 170m. in 1985, compared with sugar exports of almost $F 111m. Other important exports are fish, gold and coconut products.

In an effort to diversify the economy, domestic industries such as cement, timber, cigarettes and tuna canning are being encouraged by income tax concessions and export incentive reliefs, and these measures succeeded in reducing the trade deficit from $F 248m. in 1983 to $F 174m. in 1984. The trade deficit was $F 240.2m. in 1985, when the value of exports totalled $F 263.9m. and that of imports $F 504.1m.

The seventh Five-Year Development Plan (1976–80) aimed to expand production and to develop the infrastructure, and gave priority to agriculture. In 1978 an Australian aid project, involving an estimated investment of $A 7.5m. over 10 years, was launched. It aimed to bring 324,000 ha of hilly and largely undeveloped land into production by establishing 103 individual farm holdings, with an emphasis on livestock and grazing. In 1977 agreement was reached on the need for a policy of wage restraint to combat inflation, which fell from 13.7% in 1975 to 4.4% in the year to December 1985, the lowest rate attained for 14 years. As a result of a wage 'freeze' and price controls, imposed by the Government—in spite of resistance from the trade unions—in November 1984 and remaining in force until February 1986, the country's balance of payments improved, and there was expected to be a current surplus of $F 11m. in 1986, compared with a deficit of $F 5m. in 1985. The four cyclones that struck Fiji in early 1985, killing 29 people and causing considerable damage to crops, had an adverse effect on the economy: GDP declined by 1.7% in 1985, with agricultural production declining by 8.8% and manufacturing by 4.7%. During 1979–85 GDP grew by an average of only 1.4% per year in real terms, compared with an average growth of 4.6% per year during 1970–78.

Under Fiji's eighth Five-Year Development Plan (1981–85), sugar production and tourism remained the dominant industries, but it was hoped that the proposed development of cocoa, ginger, citrus fruits, timber, beef, goats' meat, fish and dairy farming would help to diversify the economy. Moreover, in 1985 there were plans to spend $F 6m. on projects to bring more land under rice cultivation and, under the South Pacific Regional Trade Economic Co-operation Agreement (SPARTECA, see p. 202), which gives access to the Australian and New Zealand markets for manufactured goods, to diversify into the production of items such as washing machines, wheelbarrows and cement mixers. Reliance on imported petroleum products is to be reduced by the development of hydroelectricity (an important scheme, opened in October 1983 at Monasavu, reduced oil imports by 20% in 1984) and by exploring the possibilities of converting coconut oil into fuel. In 1986 construction began of a sawmill and chipmill at Lautoka, on Viti Levu, which was due to be in full operation by 1989. The new mill was expected to process 215,000 cu m of pine wood per year, and annual export earnings, mainly from sales of sawn timber to Australia and Japan, were projected to be $F 12.5m. Following the expansion of the joint Fijian and Australian-owned Vatukoula gold mine, ore capacity was increased, and output raised to an estimated 1,893 kg in 1985. An agreement with Japan, signed in October 1986, secured a grant of more than $A8m. for the construction of a fisheries port at Lautoka.

Fiji's ninth Five-Year Development Plan (1986–90) aimed to achieve an average growth in GDP of 5% per year in real terms. Continuing emphasis was to be placed on resource-based industries, such as sugar, coconut and gold production, and on the development of the tourist industry. A tourist resort under construction at Vunaniu Bay, at an expected cost of US $65m., was due to open in 1987, and $F 40m. of new investment was expected annually during 1986–88. A target figure of 400,000 tourist visitors was set for the year 1990. Both a continuing need for wage restraint and a planned shift towards consumption-based taxes were also envisaged.

The 1987 budget proposals envisaged total revenue of $F 400.5m. and expenditure of $F 477.6m., of which some $F 5.2m. was to be used to finance a programme of tax relief for low-paid workers, by establishing a higher income-tax threshold. Increased excise charges were to be levied on a number of items, including alcohol, tobacco products and petrol.

Social Welfare
The Fiji National Provident Fund, established in 1966, contains provision for retirement pensions, widows' pensions, an insurance scheme and housing loans. Employers and employees contribute equally. In June 1981 there were 125,441 members. Medical and dental treatment is provided for all at a nominal charge. In 1984 Fiji had 27 hospitals (with a total of 1,736 beds), 48 health centres, 90 nursing centres and 339 physicians.

Education
Education in Fiji is not compulsory, but in 1983 nearly 100% of school-age children were enrolled at the country's schools, and the Government's plan to provide free education covered the first eight years of schooling. Primary education begins at six years of age and lasts for six years. Secondary education, beginning at the age of 12, lasts for a further six years. State subsidies are available for secondary and tertiary education in cases of hardship. In 1984 there were 672 state primary schools (with a total enrolment of 127,286 pupils in 1985), 139 state secondary schools (with an enrolment of 41,505 pupils in 1985), 36 vocational and technical institutions (with 3,639 students), three teacher-training colleges (with 181 students) and a school of medicine (with 213 students). There were 876 holders of Fiji government scholarships at the University of the South Pacific in Fiji in 1981. The adult illiteracy rate in 1976 averaged 21% (males 16%; females 26%), but in 1985, according to estimates by UNESCO, the rate was only 14.5% (males 9.8%; females 19.1%).

Tourism
Scenery, climate and fishing attract visitors to Fiji, where tourism is an increasingly important industry. In 1983 there were 191,616 visitors to Fiji, compared with 203,636 in the previous year, a decrease that resulted from the devastation caused by a severe hurricane in March 1983. However, tourism recovered in 1984, when there were 235,227 visitors. A succession of cyclones in early 1985 again had a detrimental effect on the tourist industry, but, with plans for up to $F 200m. to be invested in new hotels, this was not expected to be lasting. After declining slightly, to 228,175, in 1985, the number of visitors rose to an estimated 260,000 in 1986.

Public Holidays
1987: 1 January (New Year's Day), 17–20 April (Easter), 15 June (for Queen's Official Birthday), 3 August (Bank Holiday), 12 October (for Independence Day), 22 October (Diwali), 4 November* (Birth of the Prophet Muhammad), 16 November (for Birthday of the Prince of Wales), 25–28 December (Christmas).

1988: 1 January (New Year's Day), 1–4 April (Easter), 13 June (for Queen's Official Birthday), 1 August (Bank Holiday), 10 October (Independence Day), 23 October* (Birth of the Prophet Muhammad), October/November (Diwali), 14 November (Birthday of the Prince of Wales), 25–27 December (Christmas).

* This Islamic holiday is dependent on the lunar calendar and may vary by one or two days from the dates given.

Weights and Measures
The metric system is in force.

Currency and Exchange Rates
100 cents = 1 Fiji dollar ($F).

Exchange rates (30 September 1986):
 £1 sterling = $F 1.691;
 US $1 = $F 1.169.

Statistical Survey

Source (unless otherwise stated): Bureau of Statistics, POB 2221, Government Bldgs, Suva; tel. 315144; telex 2167.

AREA AND POPULATION

Area (incl. the Rotuma group): 18,376 sq km (7,095 sq miles).
Population: 588,068 (296,950 males, 291,118 females) at census of 13 Sept. 1976; 714,548 (provisional) at census of 31 Aug. 1986.
Principal Town: Suva (capital), population 69,481 (provisional) at 1986 census.
Ethnic Groups (estimates for 31 Dec. 1984): Indians 345,148, Fijians 312,121, Part Europeans 11,486, Rotumans 8,411, Chinese 4,672, Europeans 3,181, Others 5,662, Total 690,681.
Births and Deaths (registrations, 1984): Live births 19,502 (birth rate 28.4 per 1,000); Deaths 3,162 (death rate 4.6 per 1,000).
Economically Active Population (census of 13 Sept. 1976): Agriculture, hunting, forestry and fishing 76,886, Manufacturing 13,039, Construction 11,186, Trade, restaurants and hotels 17,372, Community, social and personal services 29,134, Total (incl. others and unemployed) 175,785 (males 146,315, females 29,470).

AGRICULTURE, ETC.

Principal Crops (1985, metric tons): Sugar cane 3,000,000, Coconuts 240,000, Cassava 97,000, Copra 25,000, Rice (paddy) 22,000, Sweet potatoes 8,000, Bananas 5,000, Yams 10,000, Taro 38,000 (FAO estimates). Source: FAO, *Production Yearbook*.
Livestock ('000 head, year ending September 1985): Cattle 159, Pigs 30, Goats 56, Horses 41 (FAO estimates). Source: FAO, *Production Yearbook*.
Forestry (FAO estimates, 1984): *Roundwood removals* ('000 cu m): Sawlogs and veneer logs 181, Fuel wood and charcoal 28, Other industrial wood 4; Total 213 (Source: FAO, *Yearbook of Forest Products*).
Fishing (metric tons, live weight): Total catch 28,225 in 1982; 29,090 in 1983; 31,313 in 1984. Source: FAO, *Yearbook of Fishery Statistics*.

MINING

Production: Gold 1,509 kg (1984), Silver 473 kg (1984), Crushed metal 133,891 cu m (1984).

INDUSTRY

Production (1984, metric tons unless otherwise stated): Beef 3,383, Sugar 480,106, Copra 23,644, Coconut oil 16,289, Soap 7,252, Cement 97,888, Paint 1,822 ('000 litres), Beer 18,551 ('000 litres), Soft drinks 3,518 ('000 litres), Cigarettes 513,118,600 (number), Timber 176 ('000 cu m), Matches 105 ('000 gross boxes).

FINANCE

Currency and Exchange Rates: 100 cents = 1 Fiji dollar ($F).
Coins: 1, 2, 5, 10, 20 and 50 cents. *Notes:* 1, 2, 5, 10 and 20 dollars.
Sterling and US Dollar Equivalents (30 September 1986): £1 sterling = $F 1.691; US $1 = $F 1.169; $F 100 = £59.13 = US $85.56.
Average Exchange Rate (US $ per $F): 0.9842 in 1983; 0.9250 in 1984; 0.8676 in 1985.
Budget ($F '000, 1984): *Revenue:* Customs duties and port dues 113,115, Income tax and estate and gift duties 153,773, Interest 507, All other income 70,263, Total 337,658; *Expenditure:* Public debt charges 58,576, Pensions and gratuities 24,390, Works annually recurrent 37,554, Departmental expenditure 223,887, Total 334,407.
International Reserves US $ million at 31 Dec. 1985): Gold (valued at market-related prices) 0.42, IMF special drawing rights 5.65, Reserve position in IMF 8.60, Foreign exchange 116.59; Total 131.26 (Source: IMF, *International Financial Statistics*).
Money Supply ($F million at 31 Dec. 1985): Currency outside banks 61.8; Demand deposits at commercial banks 84.6; Total money 146.4 (Source: IMF, *International Financial Statistics*).
Cost of Living (Consumer Price Index, 1979 = 100): 145.4 (1983), 153.1 (1984), 160.0 (1985).
Gross Domestic Product by Economic Activity (1984, $F million at constant 1977 factor cost): Agriculture, forestry and fishing 180.9, Mining and quarrying 0.7, Manufacturing 91.0, Electricity, gas and water 9.1, Building and construction 43.9, Distribution (incl. tourism) 124.9, Transport and communications 86.3, Finance and insurance 97.8, Government and other services 132.7, Total (after deduction of imputed bank service charges of $F 22.4m.) 744.9.
Gross Domestic Product by Expenditure (1984, $F million, provisional estimates at current prices): Final consumption expenditure 1,051.5 (private 804.0, government 247.5), Gross fixed capital formation 232.2 (private 105.0, public 127.2), Net change in stocks 10.9, Exports of goods and services 549.2, GDP at current market prices (forementioned items *less* Imports of goods and services 561.5) 1,282.3, GDP at factor cost (GDP at current market prices *less* Net indirect taxes 124.4) 1,157.9.
Balance of Payments (US $ million, 1985): Merchandise exports f.o.b. 209.1; Merchandise imports f.o.b. −382.7; *Trade balance* −173.5; Exports of services 315.1; Imports of services −176.4; *Balance on goods and services* −34.8; Private unrequited transfers (net) −10.4; Government unrequited transfers (net) 38.4; *Current balance* −6.8; Direct capital investment (net) 33.6; Other long-term capital (net) −25.5; Short-term capital (net) 1.8; Net errors and omissions −7.8; *Total* (net monetary movements) −4.6; Valuation changes (net) 16.6; *Change in reserves* 12.0. Source: IMF, *International Financial Statistics*.

EXTERNAL TRADE

Principal Commodities (1984, $F '000, provisional): *Imports:* Machinery and electrical goods 65,435, Transport equipment 21,064, Textile yarn and fabrics 24,246, Iron and steel 16,880, Food 74,714, Petroleum products 103,657, Clothing 5,105, Tape recorders 791, Watches 3,986, Total imports (incl. others) 487,105. *Exports:* Sugar 109,955, Gold 20,520, Coconut oil 18,467, Molasses 6,678, Green ginger 2,004, Veneer sheets 2,860, Biscuits 1,161, Prepared fish 14,243, Cement 395, Lumber 4,341, Silver 93. *Re-exports:* Petroleum products 51,497, Fish 220, Textile yarns and fabrics 4,746, Clothing 1,083. Total exports (incl. others) 279,418.
Principal Trading Partners (1984, $F '000): *Imports:* Australia 168,415, Canada 2,579, Germany, Federal Republic 7,488, Hong Kong 8,713, India 4,981, Japan 78,843, Netherlands 2,008, New Zealand 78,484, Singapore 27,210, United Kingdom 24,549, USA 19,675. *Exports:* Australia 38,153, Canada 5,042, Germany, Federal Republic 444, Japan 7,229, New Zealand 10,961, Singapore 1,612, Tonga 8,835, United Kingdom 6,297, USA 28,092, Western Samoa 9,861.

TRANSPORT

Road Traffic (motor vehicles registered at 31 December 1985): Passenger cars 32,453, All other vehicles 33,834.
Shipping (international traffic, 1984): Freight loaded 661,000 metric tons; freight unloaded 807,000 metric tons; vessels entered 747 (with a total displacement of 3,554,000 net reg. tons); vessels cleared 747 (with a total displacement of 3,554,000 net reg. tons).
Civil Aviation (1984): Passengers arriving 267,233, Passengers departing 267,568, Transit passengers 176,362.

TOURISM

Foreign Tourist Arrivals: 191,616 (1983), 235,227 (1984), 228,175 (1985).

COMMUNICATIONS MEDIA

Radio receivers (1983): 400,000 in use.
Telephones (1981): 46,000 in use.
Book production (1980): 110 titles (84 books, 26 pamphlets); 273,000 copies (229,000 books, 44,000 pamphlets).
Daily newspapers (1982): 3 (combined circulation 67,000 copies per issue).
Non-daily newspapers (1982): 4 (combined circulation 74,300).

EDUCATION

Primary: 672 schools (1984), 127,286 pupils (1985).
Secondary: 139 schools (1984), 41,505 pupils (1985).
Vocational and Technical (1984): 36 institutions, 3,639 students.
Teacher Training (1984): 3 institutions, 181 students.
Medical (1984): 1 institution, 213 students.

Directory

The Constitution

The Constitution came into force on 10 October 1970, when Fiji achieved independence. It contains provisions relating to the protection of fundamental rights and freedoms, the powers and duties of the Governor-General, the Cabinet, the House of Representatives, the Senate, the Judiciary, the Public Service and finance.

It provides that every person in Fiji regardless of race, place of origin, political opinion, colour, creed or sex is entitled to the fundamental rights of life, liberty, security of the person and protection of the law, freedom of conscience, expression, assembly and association; protection of the privacy of his or her home and other property and from the deprivation of property without compensation. The enjoyment of these rights, however, is subject to the proviso that they do not prejudice the rights and freedom of others, or the public interest.

EXECUTIVE

HM the Queen appoints a Governor-General as her representative in Fiji.

The Cabinet consists of the Prime Minister, the Attorney-General and any other Minister whom the Governor-General might appoint on the advice of the Prime Minister. The Governor-General appoints as Leader of the Opposition in the House of Representatives either the leader of the largest Opposition party or, if there is no such party, the person whose appointment would be most acceptable to the leaders of the Opposition parties in the House.

PARLIAMENT

The Fiji Parliament consists of a Senate and a House of Representatives. The Senate has 22 members: 8 nominated by the Council of Chiefs, 7 nominated by the Prime Minister, 6 nominated by the Leader of the Opposition and one nominated by the Council of the Island of Rotuma. Their appointments are for a six-year term. The President and Vice-President of the Senate are elected from members who are neither Ministers nor Assistant Ministers. The House of Representatives has 52 members, elected for five years: 27 elected on the communal roll and 25 on the national roll (a cross-voting system by which all races vote together). The House elects a Speaker and a Deputy Speaker from among its non-ministerial members.

PROVINCIAL GOVERNMENT

There are 14 provinces, each headed by a provincial council.

The Government

Head of State: HM Queen ELIZABETH II.

Governor-General: Ratu Sir PENAIA GANILAU (took office 12 February 1983).

THE CABINET
(January 1987)

Prime Minister and Minister for Foreign Affairs: Ratu Sir KAMISESE KAPAIWAI TUIMACILAI MARA.
Deputy Prime Minister and Minister for Fijian Affairs: Ratu DAVID TOGANIVALU.
Second Deputy Prime Minister and Minister of Finance: MOSESE QIONIBARAVI.
Minister for Education: FILIPE BOLE.
Minister for Housing and Urban Affairs: EDWARD BEDDOES.
Minister for Employment and Industrial Relations: MOHAMMED RAMZAN.
Minister for Primary Industries and Minister of State for Co-operatives: CHARLES WALKER.
Minister for Communications, Transport and Works: APISAI TORA.
Minister for Home Affairs: AKARIVA NAMBATI.
Minister for Lands, Energy and Mineral Resources: JONE NAISARA.
Minister for Health and Social Welfare: Dr APENISA KURISAQILA.
Minister of State for Forests: Ratu Sir JOSAIA TAVAIQIA.
Minister for Economic Development, Planning and Tourism: PETER STINSON.
Minister of State for Rural Development: Ratu TIMOCI VEFIKULA.
Minister for Information: Dr AHMED ALI.
Attorney-General and Minister for Justice: QORINIASI BALE.

MINISTRIES

All Ministries are in Suva.

Legislature

PARLIAMENT
The Senate

There are 22 appointed members.
President: W. J. CLARK.
Vice-President: Ratu TEVITA VAKALALABURE.

House of Representatives

Speaker: TOMASI VAKATORA.
Deputy Speaker: VIJAYA PARMANANDAM.
Leader of the Opposition: HARISH CHANDRA SHARMA.

General Election, 10–17 July 1982

	% of votes	Seats*
Alliance Party	51.80	28
National Federation Party	41.15	22
Western United Front	3.86	2
Fijian Nationalist Party	2.82	—
Independents	0.37	—

* Following a number of by-elections and changes of political allegiance, the distribution of seats in 1986 was as follows: Alliance Party 30, National Federation Party 16, Western United Front 2, Fiji Labour Party 4. A general election was to be held in April 1987.

Political Organizations

Alliance Party (AP): 41 Gladstone Rd, POB 688, Suva; f. 1965; multiracial; ruling party; Pres. Ratu Sir KAMISESE K. T. MARA; Sec.-Gen. JONE BANUVE.

Fiji Labour Party: Suva; f. 1985; Pres. Dr TIMOCI BAVADRA; Sec.-Gen. KRISHNA DATT.

Fijian Nationalist Party: POB 1336, Suva; f. 1974; seeks more parliamentary representation for persons of Fijian ethnic origin and for general pro-Fijian reforms; Chair. WAISALE BAKALEVU; Sec. SAKIASI BUTADROKA.

National Federation Party (NFP): POB 228, Suva; f. 1960; fusion of two parties: the Federation Party, which was mainly Indian but multiracial, and the National Democratic Party, a purely Fijian party; Leader HARISH CHANDRA SHARMA; Pres. JAI RAM REDDY.

Western United Front (WUF): POB 263, Sigatoka; f. 1981; mainly Fijian, favouring co-existence and co-operation among all communities; 10,000 mems; Pres. Ratu OSEA GAVIDI; Sec. ISIKELI NADALO.

Diplomatic Representation

EMBASSIES AND HIGH COMMISSIONS IN FIJI

Australia: Dominion House, POB 214, Suva; tel. 312844; telex 2126; High Commissioner: JOHN PIPER.

China, People's Republic: 147 Queen Elizabeth Drive, Suva; telex 2136; Ambassador: JI CHAOZHU.

France: 1st Floor, Dominion House, Suva; tel. 311993; telex 2326; Ambassador: DANIEL DUPONT.

FIJI

India: POB 405, Suva; tel. 312255; telex 2110; High Commissioner: THETTALIL PARAMESWARAN PILLAI SREENIVASAN.
Japan: 2nd Floor, Dominion House, Suva; tel. 25631; telex 2253; Ambassador: KIKUO YOSHIDA.
Korea, Republic: 8th Floor, Vanua House, PMB, Suva; tel. 311977; telex 2175; Ambassador: KIM HYON-CHIN.
Malaysia: Air Pacific House, Suva; tel. 312166; telex 2295; High Commissioner: Miss TING WEN LIAN.
New Zealand: 10th Floor, Reserve Bank of Fiji Bldg, POB 1378, Suva; tel. 311422; telex 2161; High Commissioner: RODNEY GATES.
Papua New Guinea: 6th Floor, Ratu Sukuna House, POB 2447, Suva; telex 2113; High Commissioner: DENIS KEPORE.
Tuvalu: Suva; telex 2297; High Commissioner: SEMU TAAFAKI.
United Kingdom: Victoria House, 47 Gladstone Rd, POB 1355, Suva; tel. 311033; telex 2129; High Commissioner: ROGER A. R. BARLTROP.
USA: 31 Loftus St, POB 218, Suva; tel. 314466; telex 2255; Ambassador: C. EDWARD DILLERY.

Judicial System

Justice is administered by the Fiji Court of Appeal, the Supreme Court and the Magistrates' Courts. The Supreme Court of Fiji is the superior court of record presided over by the Chief Justice, who is also the President of the Fiji Court of Appeal.
Chief Justice: Sir TIMOCI TUIVAGA.
Puisne Judges: G. O. L. DYKE, R. A. KEARSLEY, F. X. ROONEY, B. P. CULLINAN, K. GOVIND, M. J. SHEEHAN.
Chief Registrar: F. JITOKO.

Religion

Most Fijians are Christians, mainly Protestant. The Indians are mostly Hindus, and there is also a Muslim and a Sikh community.

CHRISTIANITY
The Anglican Communion
Anglicans in Fiji are adherents of the Church of the Province of New Zealand.
Bishop in Polynesia: Rt Rev. JABEZ LESLIE BRYCE, Bishop's House, 7 Disraeli Rd, POB 35, Suva; tel. 24357.

The Roman Catholic Church
Fiji comprises a single archdiocese. At 31 December 1984 there were an estimated 58,000 adherents in the country.
Bishops' Conference: Episcopal Conference of the Pacific, POB 109, Suva; tel. 22851; f. 1974; Pres. Most Rev. PETERO MATACA, Archbishop of Suva.
Archbishop of Suva: Most Rev. PETERO MATACA, Archdiocesan Office, POB 109, Suva; tel. 22851.

Other Christian Church
Methodist Church: Epworth Arcade, Nina St, POB 357, Suva; f. 1835; Pres. Rev. PAULA NIUKULA; Gen. Sec. Rev. INOKE NABULIVOU; 170,000 adherents.

BAHÁ'Í FAITH
National Spiritual Assembly: POB 639, Suva; tel. 22776; mems resident in 316 localities.

The Press

NEWSPAPERS AND PERIODICALS
Coconut Telegraph: POB 249, Savusavu, Vanua Levu; f. 1975; monthly; serves widely-scattered rural communities; Editor Mrs LEMA LOW.
Fiji Beach Press: News (South Pacific) Ltd, POB 5176, Raiwaqa, Suva; tel. 311211; telex 2138; weekly in English (circ. 8,000), twice a year in English for overseas (circ. 40,000); tourist paper; Editor MERE MOMOIVALU.
Fiji Fantastic: George Rubine Ltd, POB 12511, Suva; tel. 311944; telex 2463; f. 1978; fortnightly; English; Editor-in-Chief LEIGH MARTIN; circ. 10,000.

Directory

Fiji Royal Gazette: Printing Dept, POB 99, Suva; f. 1874; weekly; English.
Fiji Sun: Newspapers of Fiji Ltd, POB 354, Suva; tel. 311944; telex 2333; f. 1974; daily; English; Editor PETER LOMAS; circ. 26,000.
Fiji Times: 20 Gordon St, POB 1167, Suva; tel. 312111; telex 2124; f. 1869; publ. by Fiji Times Ltd; daily; English; Gen. Man. REX GARDNER; circ. 27,000.
Fiji Today: Dept of Information, Suva; tel. 211700; annual; English; Editor WALTER THOMAS; circ. 25,000.
Islands Business: 24 Des Voeux Rd, POB 12718, Suva; tel. 312040; telex 2528; f. 1980; monthly; English; Man. Dir ROBERT KEITH-REID; Editor JOHN RICHARDSON; circ. 8,000.
Jagriti: POB 9, Nadi; f. 1950; 3 a week; Hindi; circ. 5,500.
Nai Lalakai: 20 Gordon St, POB 1167, Suva; tel. 314111; telex 2124; f. 1962; publ. by Fiji Times Ltd; weekly; Fijian; Editor DALE TONAWAI; circ. 18,000.
Shanti Dut: 20 Gordon St, POB 1167, Suva; f. 1935; publ. by Fiji Times Ltd; weekly; Hindi; Editor M. C. VINOD; circ. 8,000.
Siga Rarama: Newspapers of Fiji Ltd, POB 354, Suva; tel. 311944; telex 2333; f. 1974; weekly; Fijian; Editor MIKA TURAGA; circ. 10,000.
Sunday Sun: Newspapers of Fiji Ltd, POB 354, Suva; tel. 311944; telex 2333; f. 1974; weekly; English; Editor PETER LOMAS; circ. 26,000.
Sunday Times: Fiji Times Ltd, POB 1167, Suva; weekly; English; Gen. Man. REX GARDNER.

Publishers

Fiji Times Ltd: POB 1167, Suva; tel. 314111; telex 2124; f. 1869; largest newspaper publr; also publrs of books and magazines; Gen. Man. REX GARDNER.

Government Publishing House
Printing Department: POB 98, Suva.

Radio and Television

There were an estimated 400,000 radio receivers in use in 1983. In 1985 a 12-year contract to establish and operate a commercial television broadcasting service was awarded to Pacific Television Pty Ltd, a subsidiary of an Australian television network, Publishing and Broadcasting Ltd; operations were due to begin in September 1987. There were estimated to be between 30,000 and 40,000 video recorders in use in Fiji in 1985.
Fiji Broadcasting Commission (Radio Fiji): POB 334, Broadcasting House, Suva; tel. 314333; telex 2142; f. 1954; broadcasts from 10 AM and one FM station in two national networks; programmes in English, Fijian and Hindustani; Chair. Dr ISOA BAKANI; Gen. Man. Dr LASARUSA VUSONIWAILALA.
FM96: Suva; f. 1985; commercial; broadcasts 24 hrs per day; Man. Dir WILLIAM PARKINSON.

Finance

(cap.=capital; res=reserves; m.=million; brs=branches; amounts in Fiji dollars)

BANKING
Central Bank
Reserve Bank of Fiji: POB 1220, Suva; tel. 313611; telex 2165; f. 1984 to replace Central Monetary Authority of Fiji; bank of issue; cap. 2m., res 14m. (1985); Chair. and Gov. SAVENACA SIWATIBAU.

Commercial Bank
National Bank of Fiji: 107 Victoria Parade, POB 1166, Suva; tel. 311999; telex 2135; f. 1973; cap. 5.0m., dep. 65m. (1985); Chair. KANTILAL TAPPOO; Chief Man. GORDON RYAN; 11 brs.

Development Bank
Fiji Development Bank: POB 104, Suva; tel. 314866; telex 2578; f. 1967; finances the development of natural resources, agriculture, transportation and other industries and enterprises; statutory body; cap. 34m. (1986); Chair. LYLE N. CUPIT; Man. Dir LAISENIA QARASE; 9 brs.

FIJI   Directory

Merchant Bank
Merchant Bank of Fiji Ltd: Suva; f. 1986; Gen. Man. PETER ALLINGHAM.

Foreign Banks
Australia and New Zealand Banking Group Ltd: 4th Floor, Civic House, POB 179, Suva; tel. 314000; telex 2194; Chief Man. (Pacific Islands) W. G. BARNES.

Bank of Baroda (India): POB 57, Suva; telex 2120; Man. for Fiji J. K. SHAH.

Bank of New Zealand: PMB, Suva; telex 2132; Regional Man. K. W. W. TAYLOR; 8 brs.

Westpac Banking Corporation (Australia): 1 Thomson St, POB 238, Suva; tel. 311666; telex 2133; Chief Man. R. J. HUEY; 11 brs.

INSURANCE
Colonial Mutual Life Assurance Society Ltd: Private Bag, Suva; tel. 314400; telex 2254; f. 1876; Man. T. VUETILOVONI.

Panpacific Insurance Co Ltd: POB 119, Suva; tel. 22601; telex 2361; f. 1982; Office Man. SAMSON M. SINGH.

Queensland Insurance (Fiji) Ltd: Queensland Insurance Center, Victoria Parade, POB 101, Suva; tel. 315455; telex 2414; Gen. Man. R. JACKSON.

Trade and Industry

DEVELOPMENT CORPORATIONS
Commonwealth Development Corporation: Office of the Representative for Pacific Islands, Velop House, 371 Victoria Parade, POB 161, Suva; tel. 25607; telex 2412; Rep. M. C. HODGSON.

Economic Development Board: Velop House, Govt Bldgs, POB 2303, Suva; tel. 313295; telex 2355; f. 1980 to promote and stimulate foreign and local economic development investment; Chair. Sir JOHN (IAN) SUTHERLAND THOMSON; Dir NARENDRA P. SINGH.

Fijian Development Fund Board: POB 122, Suva; tel. 22231; f. 1951; funds derived from payments of $F20 a ton from the sales of copra by indigenous Fijians only; deposits bear interest at 2.5%; funds used only for Fijian development schemes; dep. $F959,500 (1980); Chair. Ratu Sir KAMISESE MARA; Sec. N. MORRIS.

Fiji Development Company Ltd: POB 161, Suva; f. 1960; subsidiary of the Commonwealth Development Corpn; Man. P. DAYAL.

Land Development Authority: c/o Ministry of Primary Industries, POB 358, Suva; tel. 311233; f. 1961 to co-ordinate development plans for land and marine resources; Chair. Ratu Sir JOSAIA TAVAIQIA.

CHAMBER OF COMMERCE
Suva Chamber of Commerce: 7th Floor, Honson Bldg, Thomson St, POB 337, Suva; f. 1902; Chair. R. P. A. PROBERT; Sec. P. B. Sloan; 94 mems.

MARKETING ORGANIZATIONS
Fiji Pine Commission: POB 521, Lautoka; tel. 61511; telex 5294; f. 1976; development of forest plantations, and marketing of forest products through subsidiary joint venture Forestry Development Service Ltd; Gen. Man. P. J. DRYSDALE; Sec. S. D. SHARMA.

Fiji Sugar Cane Growers' Council: 4th Floor, Dominion House, Thomson St, Suva; tel. 314490; telex 2271; f. 1985; aims to develop the sugar industry and protect the interests of registered growers; CEO Sir VIJAY R. SINGH; Chair. S. M. KOYA; Sec. BHAN SINGH.

Fiji Sugar Corporation Ltd: 5th Floor, Dominion House, Thomson St, POB 283, Suva; tel. 313455; telex 2119; nationalized 1974; buyer of sugar cane and raw sugar mfrs; Chair. LYLE N. CUPIT; Man. Dir RASHEED A. ALI.

Fiji Sugar Marketing Co Ltd: 5th Floor, Dominion House, Thomson St, POB 1402, Suva; tel. 311588; telex 2271; Man. Dir JOHN MAY.

National Marketing Authority: POB 5085, Raiwaqa, Suva; tel. 385888; telex 2413; f. 1971; a statutory body set up to develop markets for agricultural and marine produce locally and overseas; exporters of fresh fruit and vegetables, fish, fresh, syruped and crystallized ginger; Chair. REG WOODMAN; Gen. Man. Ratu EPELI KANAIMAWI.

Sugar Commission of Fiji: 4th Floor, Dominion House, Thomson St, Suva; tel. 315488; Chair. GERALD BARRACK.

CO-OPERATIVES
In 1986 there were 1,203 registered co-operatives.

EMPLOYERS' ORGANIZATIONS
Fiji Employers' Consultative Association: 7th Floor, Honson Bldg, Thomson St, POB 575, Suva; tel. 25688; represents 133 major employers; Pres. Col P. F. MANUELI; Dir KENNETH A. J. ROBERTS.

Fiji Manufacturers' Association: 7th Floor, Honson Bldg, Thomson St, POB 1308, Suva; f. 1902; Pres. CHANDU RANIGA; Sec. P. B. SLOAN; 108 mems.

TRADE UNIONS
Fiji Trades Union Congress (FTUC): 32 Des Voeux Rd, POB 1418, Suva; tel. 315377; f. 1951; affiliated to ICFTU and ICFTU—APRO; 36 affiliated unions; more than 40,000 mems; Pres. JALE TOKI; Nat. Sec. JAMES R. RAMAN. Principal affiliated unions:

Fiji Public Service Association: 298 Waimanu Rd, POB 1405, Suva; tel. 311922; 7,267 mems; Pres. D. P. SINGH; Gen. Sec. M. P. CHAUDHRY.

Fiji Registered Ports Workers' Union: f. 1947; Gen. Sec. TANIELA VEITATA.

Fiji Sugar and General Workers' Union: POB 330, Lautoka; 3,000 mems; Pres. Ratu INIA; Gen. Sec. ANNAND REDDY.

Fiji Teachers' Union: 211 Edinburgh Drive, POB 3582, Samabula; tel. 381585; f. 1930; 3,500 mems; Pres. KRISHNA DATT; Gen. Sec. PRATAP CHAND.

Mineworkers' Union of Fiji: Vatukoula; f. 1986.

National Union of Factory and Commercial Workers: POB 989, Suva; 3,800 mems; Pres. CAMA TUILEVUKA; Gen. Sec. JAMES R. RAMAN.

Public Employees' Union: POB 781, Suva; 5,000 mems; Pres. Ratu NABORISI CAGILABA; Gen. Sec. JOVECI GAVOKA.

Other important unions include the Building Workers' Union, the Fijian Teachers' Asscn, the National Union of Hotel and Catering Workers, the Fiji Bank Employees' Union, the National Union of Electricity Workers and the Fiji Sugar and Tradesmen's Union. There were 42 registered trade unions in October 1984.

Transport

RAILWAYS
Fiji Sugar Corporation Railway: Rarawai Mill, POB 155, Ba; tel. 74044; telex 6248; 725 km of permanent track and 225 km of temporary track, serving cane-growing areas at Ba, Lautoka and Penang on the island of Viti Levu; also Labasa on the island of Vanua Levu.

In 1985 the Asian Development Bank was financing a feasibility study of the potential for the creation of a major passenger railway system.

ROADS
At the end of 1982 there were 4,295 km of roads in Fiji, of which 1,250 km were main or national roads and 563 km secondary roads. A 500-km highway circles the main island of Viti Levu. Of the total road network, 13% is paved.

SHIPPING
There are ports of call at Suva, Lautoka and Levuka. The main port, Suva, handles more than 800 ships a year, including large passenger liners. Lautoka handles more than 300 vessels and liners and Levuka mainly handles commercial fishing vessels.

Inter-Ports Shipping Corpn Ltd: 25 Eliza St, Walu Bay; POB 152, Suva; tel. 313638; telex 2703; f. 1984; Man. Dir LEO B. SMITH.

Transcargo Express Fiji Ltd: POB 936, Suva; f. 1974; Man. Dir LEO B. SMITH.

Williams Taoniu Shipping Co Ltd: POB 1270, Suva; inter-island shipping.

The main foreign companies serving Fiji are: Karlander (Aust.) Pty Ltd, Sofrana-Unilines (Fiji Express Line), Pacific Forum Line, and Pacific Navigation of Tonga operating cargo services between Australia and Fiji; Union Steam Ship Co of New Zealand from New Zealand; Blue Star Line Ltd and Crusader Shipping Co Ltd calling at Fiji between North America and New Zealand, and P & O between the USA and Australia; Nedlloyd operates to Fiji from New Zealand, the UK and Northern Europe; Bank Line Ltd from

FIJI

the UK and the Netherlands; NYK Line and Daiwa Lines from Japan; Marshall Islands Maritime Co from Honolulu and Tonga; Kyowa Shipping Co Ltd from Hong Kong, Taiwan, the Republic of Korea and Japan; and Jebsen Line from various Asian ports.

CIVIL AVIATION

There is an international airport at Nadi (about 210 km from Suva), a domestic airport at Nausori and 13 other airfields.

Air Coral Coast: Korolevu; telex 3241; domestic airline; Man. Dir GORDON OLIVER; fleet of 1 Britten Norman Islander, 1 Cessna 206.

Air Pacific Ltd: Air Pacific Centre, Grantham Rd, Raiwaqa; tel. 386444; telex 2131; f. 1951; domestic services from Nausori Airport (serving Suva) to Nadi and Labasa, and international services to Tonga, Solomon Islands, Vanuatu, Western Samoa, Australia and New Zealand; in December 1984 management was taken over by the Australian airline Qantas, initially for three years, with an option for renewal for a further two years; Chair. Sir JOHN (IAN) SUTHERLAND THOMSON; CEO JOHN SCHAAP; fleet of 1 Boeing 737-200, 1 Fokker F-27-600, 4 ATR 42.

Fiji Air Ltd: 219 Victoria Parade, POB 1259, Suva; tel. 22666; telex 2258; domestic airline operating over 200 scheduled services a week to 17 destinations; international service to Tuvalu; charter operations, aerial photography and surveillance also conducted; partly owned by the Fijian govt; CEO M. C. D. TYLER; fleet of 3 DHC6 Twin Otters, 1 Britten Norman Islander, 1 Cessna 404, 1 Beech Baron C55, 1 Piper Navajo Chieftain.

Sunflower Airlines: Nadi; telex 5183; domestic airline; fleet of 3 Britten Norman Islander, 1 Riley Heron, 1 Aztec.

Tourism

Fiji Visitors Bureau: POB 92, Suva; tel. 22867; telex 2180; f. 1923; Chair. RADIKE QEREQERETABUA; Gen. Man. MALAKAI GUCAKE.

FINLAND

Introductory Survey

Location, Climate, Language, Religion, Flag, Capital

The Republic of Finland lies in northern Europe, bordered to the far north by Norway and to the north-west by Sweden. The USSR adjoins the whole of the eastern frontier. Finland's western and southern shores are washed by the Baltic Sea. The climate varies sharply, with warm summers and cold winters. The mean annual temperature is 5°C (41°F) in Helsinki and −0.4°C (31°F) in the far north. There are two official languages: 93.5% of the population speak Finnish and 6.3% speak Swedish. Finnish is a member of the small Finno-Ugrian group of languages, which includes Hungarian. There is a small Lapp population in the north. Almost all of the inhabitants profess Christianity, and more than 90% belong to the Evangelical Lutheran Church. The Orthodox Church has the status of a second national church, while there are small groups of Roman Catholics, Methodists, Jews and other religious sects. The national flag (proportions 18 by 11) displays an azure blue cross (the upright to the left of centre) on a white background. The state flag has, at the centre of the cross, the national coat of arms (a yellow-edged red shield containing a golden lion and nine white roses). The capital is Helsinki.

Recent History

Finland was formerly an autonomous part of the Russian Empire. During the Russian revolution of 1917 the territory proclaimed its independence. Following a brief civil war, a democratic constitution was adopted in 1919. The Soviet regime which came to power in Russia attempted to regain control of Finland but acknowledged the country's independence in 1920.

Demands by the USSR for military bases in Finland and for the cession of part of the Karelian isthmus, in south-eastern Finland, were rejected by the Finnish Government in November 1939. As a result, the USSR attacked Finland, and the two countries fought the 'Winter War', a fiercely contested conflict lasting 15 weeks, before Finnish forces were defeated. Following its surrender, Finland ceded an area of 41,880 sq km (16,170 sq miles) to the USSR in March 1940. In the hope of recovering the lost territory, Finland joined Nazi Germany in attacking the USSR in 1941. However, a separate armistice between Finland and the USSR was concluded in 1944.

In accordance with a peace treaty signed in February 1947, Finland agreed to the transfer of about 12% of its pre-war territory (including the Karelian isthmus and the Petsamo area on the Arctic coast) to the USSR, and to the payment of reparations which totalled about US $570m. when completed in 1952. Meanwhile, in April 1948, Finland and the USSR signed the Finno-Soviet Pact of Friendship, Co-operation and Mutual Assistance (the YYA treaty), which was extended for periods of 20 years in 1955, 1970 and again in 1983. A major requirement of the treaty is that Finland repel any attack made on the USSR by the Federal Republic of Germany, or its allies, through Finnish territory. Finnish policy, however, is one of neutrality in foreign affairs. Finland's trade agreement with the European Communities, signed in October 1973, was followed by the signing of a 15-year trade agreement with the USSR in May 1977. Finland joined the United Nations and the Nordic Council in 1955, became an associate member of EFTA in 1961 and a full member in 1985.

Since becoming independent in 1917, Finland has had more than 60 governments, including numerous minority coalitions. Political instability has been characterized by a succession of caretaker governments and premature elections.

Disputes over economic policy caused the dissolution of the Government of National Emergency, a five-party coalition led by Martti Miettunen (Centre Party), in September 1976, after 10 months in office. Miettunen then reluctantly agreed to lead a new three-party minority coalition, excluding the Social Democrats and Communists, to implement measures intended to overcome the country's economic crisis. At the President's request for a majority government, this coalition resigned in May 1977; a new five-party government was formed by Kalevi Sorsa, leader of the Social Democratic Party and a former Prime Minister. Sorsa embarked on a plan to stimulate domestic demand by assisting private business through tax relief, and thereby to combat Finland's growing unemployment.

In February 1978, when the Finnish markka was devalued for the third time within a year, disagreements within the Council of State over the extent of the devaluation led to the resignation of the Government. The majority coalition was re-formed under Sorsa in March, but did not include the Swedish People's Party. In the face of dissent from trade unions over the effects of the devaluation, and the possibility of a general strike, the new four-party coalition implemented a 1.5% pay rise which had been due in January 1979, and slightly relaxed the stringent financial policy. Although the Conservative opposition gained significant support at a general election in March 1979, a new centre-left coalition government was formed in May by Dr Mauno Koivisto, a Social Democratic economist, ex-Premier and former Governor of the Bank of Finland. This four-party Government, comprising the Centre Party, the Social Democratic Party, the Swedish People's Party and the Finnish People's Democratic League (SKDL), continued to pursue deflationary economic policies, although crises arose within the Council of State in 1981 because of disagreements over social welfare policy and budgetary matters.

In October 1981 the 81-year-old President, Dr Urho Kekkonen, who had held office since 1956, resigned, and in January 1982 Dr Koivisto was elected President. By the time of his resignation, Dr Kekkonen had established significant presidential influence over foreign affairs, particularly concerning the maintenance of stable relations between Finland and the USSR. He died in August 1986. The new President Koivisto was succeeded as head of the coalition by former Prime Minister Sorsa, who reshuffled the Council of State in January and again in July. In October a crisis arose when three ministers belonging to the SKDL refused to support austerity measures which had been adopted to counteract the effects on the Finnish economy of a Swedish currency devaluation. A further refusal by SKDL ministers to support an increase in defence spending led to the re-formation of the coalition on 30 December, without the SKDL, until the general election of March 1983.

At this election the Social Democrats won 57 of the 200 seats in Parliament (compared with 52 in the 1979 election), while the opposition National Coalition Party lost three seats. In May Sorsa formed another centre-left coalition, comprising the Social Democrats, the Swedish People's Party, the Centre Party (which had merged with the Liberal Party in 1982) and the Rural Party: the coalition parties had a total of 122 parliamentary seats. The aims of the new Government, which retained office throughout 1984 and 1985 without any major disruption, were to reduce inflation and unemployment, to curb the rise in gross taxation, to limit state borrowing, and to expand trade with Western countries. In May 1985 the coalition was threatened when the Government announced that it would resign if an anti-nuclear parliamentary motion, introduced by the Rural Party and the Swedish People's Party, was not withdrawn. The motion, which demanded the dismantling of Finland's four nuclear reactors, was subsequently withdrawn by both parties. The Government also survived a motion of 'no confidence', proposed by the Conservative opposition, for its alleged failure to provide accurate information following the accident in April 1986 at the Chernobyl nuclear power station in the USSR, which resulted in radio-active fall-out over Finland.

In 1985 relations between Finland and the USSR were threatened when the Communist Party of Finland (SKP) expelled several groups of pro-Soviet dissidents. Nevertheless, in April 1985 the Centre Party had announced its support for President Koivisto in his efforts to develop better relations with Moscow. In April 1986 the pro-Soviet groups that had been expelled from the SKP announced the formation of a separate electoral organization, called the Democratic Alternative, and elected a separate central committee of the Committee of SKP Organizations. Further expulsions were made in June, by both the SKP and the Finnish People's Democratic League (SKDL), of pro-Soviet groups and deputies. The Democratic Alternative was officially registered as a political party in July, when it formally severed its links with SKP.

Government

Finland has a republican constitution which combines a parliamentary system with a strong presidency. The unicameral Parliament (Eduskunta) has 200 members, elected by universal adult suffrage for four years (subject to dissolution by the President) on the basis of proportional representation. The President, entrusted with supreme executive power, is elected for six years by a college of 301 electors, chosen by popular vote in the same manner as members of Parliament. Legislative power is exercised by Parliament in conjunction with the President. For general administration, the President appoints a Council of State (Cabinet), which is headed by a Prime Minister and is responsible to Parliament. Finland has 12 provinces, each administered by an appointed Governor.

Defence

The armed forces of Finland are restricted by treaty to 41,900, and in July 1986 numbered 34,900 (of whom 25,000 were conscripts serving up to 11 months), comprising an army of 30,000, an air force of 2,900 and a navy of 2,000. There were also about 700,000 reserves and 4,400 frontier guards. Estimated defence expenditure in 1986 was 5,146m. markkaa.

Economic Affairs

Apart from extensive forests and large reserves of copper ore, Finland has few natural resources. The country also has a harsh climate (no port is ice-free throughout the year) and a rugged terrain. Nevertheless, the people of Finland enjoy a high standard of living and the benefits of a modern welfare state. In 1984, according to estimates by the World Bank, Finland's gross national product (GNP) per head, measured at average 1982–84 prices, was US $10,770, having increased at an average rate of 3.3% per year, in real terms, since 1965.

Forests cover 65% of Finland's land area, and forestry products (mainly wood, pulp and paper) provided over 36% of export earnings in 1985. Increased competition from the USA and Sweden, in particular, and a shortage of timber for industrial use reduced Finland's share of the world market in forestry products from 25% in the 1960s to only 9% in 1983. Between 1983 and 1985, the annual capacity of Finnish sawmills declined by 2m. cu m, as the result of a decrease in exports, owing to reduced international demand for some forest products. This affected both the pulp and the paper industries, where export prices fell sharply during the second half of 1985 and the volume of exports declined. At the end of the logging year 1984/85 a 20% increase in felling was recorded, but during the year 1985/86 felling of marketable timber declined by 14%, employment in the sector was reduced by around 20% and 21 large sawmills stopped production. However, export prices recovered and the volume of exports increased during the first half of 1986.

The metal and engineering sector (particularly ship-building and the manufacture of machinery for the paper industry) accounted for 35% of total exports in 1984. During 1985, however, a sharp fall in the export of ships, particularly to the USSR, caused a decline in the growth of exports in the sector. The capacity for expansion in Finland's industry is limited by a lack of skilled labour and by the need to import some raw materials and energy. Apart from hydroelectric power and peat, there are no indigenous forms of energy, and all of Finland's gas, coal and petroleum requirements must be imported. Energy accounted for around 24% of total imports in 1985. Finland annually imports about 4,000m. kWh of electricity and 85% of its crude petroleum from the USSR. A 400-km natural gas pipeline linking Finland and the USSR was extended westwards from Kouvola to Tampere and Helsinki during 1985 and 1986, and was officially put into service in November 1986. It was expected that 1,200 m. cu m of gas would be imported from the USSR by the end of 1986.

In 1985 41% of electricity was generated by nuclear power, and four nuclear power stations were in operation. In May 1986 the Government announced that the construction of a proposed fifth power station was to be postponed indefinitely, reflecting the widespread negative attitude to nuclear power, following the accident at the USSR's nuclear power station at Chernobyl in April. Plans were being discussed during 1986 for an increase in imports of coal, to be used for electricity generation. Construction work was due to begin in 1987 on a peat-fired power station at Haapavesi in Oulu Province. It was expected to be in operation by 1990. Two coal-fired power stations were also to be built.

Cereal and dairy farming are highly mechanized. State subsidies are provided to encourage exports, and by late 1985 the country had a grain surplus of 800,000 metric tons, despite a system of levies and taxes, aimed at curbing over-production. The export of grain was begun in 1986.

A trade agreement between Finland and the EEC countries came into effect in 1974, leading to the abolition of tariffs on most goods by 1977. Finland has also participated in a trade agreement with the CMEA since 1973, and in 1985 CMEA countries took about 23% of Finnish exports and provided 24% of imports. In 1985 EEC member-states together provided 37% of Finnish imports and took 36% of exports; EFTA countries accounted for 18% of imports and 20% of exports. The abolition of all trade restrictions on industrial goods between the EEC and EFTA, with effect from 1 January 1984, was expected to increase Finland's trade with western Europe. The USSR accounted for 26% of both imports and exports in 1983, and in September 1984 a new five-year trade agreement was signed, envisaging an expansion of 12% in trade between the two countries.

Despite being sheltered, to some extent, from the effects of world recessions by its bilateral trade agreement with the USSR, the Finnish economy was adversely affected by cyclic recessions which occurred following the sharp rises in world petroleum prices in 1974 and 1979. Economic policies, aimed at stimulating domestic demand when export markets weakened, enabled Finland to sustain a relatively high rate of growth between 1977 and 1982. During this period GDP increased, in real terms, by an average annual rate of 4.0%, although depressed markets and high energy costs limited growth to 1.8% in 1981. The average annual growth rate between 1982 and 1985 was 3%.

A revival in world trade in the mid-1980s led to a marked expansion in exports, particularly to Western countries. In 1984 exports to the USSR fell by 13%, while those to Western markets increased by 27%. Exports totalled 80,904m. markkaa in 1984, compared with under 70,000m. markkaa in the previous year, while the value of imports increased by 4.4%, giving an overall trade surplus of 6,200m. markkaa. Finnish exports to Western markets decreased by 2% during 1985, owing mainly to a decline in demand for forest products towards the end of the year and a fall in the US dollar in relation to the markka, which reduced the competitiveness of Finnish industries. Although the annual growth in GDP was estimated at 4% during the first half of 1985, it subsequently fell to 2%. However, exports to CMEA countries increased in value by 16%, and the volume of total exports rose by 1%. Despite an increase in imports, an overall trade surplus of 2,616m. markkaa was achieved.

A sharp fall in the price of petroleum in December 1985 caused a disruption in trade with the USSR during the first half of 1986. Negotiations took place between the two countries to adjust the terms of the bilateral trade pact for 1986–90 in order to offset the reduced value of Finnish oil imports and to reduce the widening surplus in the trade account. Contracts were concluded in June for increased imports of coal, electricity and chemical raw materials. However, the reduction in imports between January and July, from 9,786m. markkaa to 6,515m., led to a reduction in exports to the USSR, with the metal, engineering, textile, clothing and footwear industries being particularly badly affected. Tax reforms relating to energy were announced in June, in an effort to reduce costs for export industries by shifting from excise-based taxation to a value-added sales tax. Major strikes during March, April and May disrupted economic activity, and, although some recovery was expected during the second half of the year, GDP growth was not expected to be above 2%.

Despite the rapid economic growth that occurred in the late 1970s, unemployment rose considerably in 1977, and reached a peak of nearly 9% of the labour force in the first quarter of 1978. The level of unemployment was gradually reduced, and stood at 5% in the latter half of 1981. In 1983 and 1984 the Government made financial allocations to stimulate employment, and temporarily lowered employers' social security contributions. There was also a reduction in working hours. However, by 1984 the average rate of unemployment stood at 6.2%. In 1985 a works and employment programme costing an estimated 7,100m. markkaa was approved, with employment projects being focused particularly on areas of high unemployment, such as northern Finland. Total employment rose by 1% but labour supply also increased and the unemployment rate rose slightly, to 6.3%. Unemployment at the end of July 1986 stood at 6.7%.

In March 1986 a 58-hour strike was staged by 250,000 members of the Central Organization of Finnish Trade Unions (SAK), to support demands for pay increases and the introduction of a 35-hour working week. A two-year wage settlement was reached, whereby average wages would rise by 2.4% in 1986 and by 2.6% in 1987. The average working week was to be reduced from 40 to 37½ hours by 1990. A 45-day strike by state employees during April and May affected air and rail transport and communication services. The Union of State Employees had been demanding pay increases of 20% and eventually accepted a settlement providing basic increases of 20%, spread over two years.

Since 1976 the central bank has followed an unyieldingly tight credit policy, aimed at checking escalation in foreign debt. Devaluations of the markka in 1977 and 1978 led to a trade surplus of 2,800m. markkaa in 1978, and a brief revival followed, causing the markka to be revalued by 3% in 1979. By 1981, however, deteriorating terms of international trade had exacerbated rising inflation, which reached 11.8%. By late 1982 deflationary measures (including a two-year national wage agreement implemented in 1980, reductions in planned public spending, and regulated prices) had reduced inflation to 9.25%. The expiry of the wage agreement in February 1983, however, slowed the rate of decrease, and inflation stood at 8.5% by the end of the year. The markka was devalued twice in October, by 4.3% and again by 6%, in response to a 16% devaluation of the Swedish krona. The result was an increase of 5% in Finland's export competitiveness, but the markka value of Finland's international debt was also increased, reaching 53,220m. markkaa by the end of 1984 and 53,500m. markkaa by the end of 1985 (equivalent to 18% of annual GDP). The Government's policy of borrowing to sustain economic growth had also increased the state's share of the foreign debt from 15% in 1977 to about 44% in 1983. In 1984 a further national wage agreement was introduced, and government expenditure rose by only 2.5% in comparison with the 1983 figure. As a result, inflation declined from an annual average of 8.4% in 1983 to 7.1% in 1984, and continued to fall, reaching 5.9% in 1985. In the year ending September 1986 it fell even further, to 3.3%.

In May 1986 intense speculation against the markka in foreign exchange markets, as a result of industrial strikes and the devaluation of the Norwegian krone, led to a devaluation of the currency by about 2%. Finland's reserves of foreign exchange totalled 22,650m. markkaa in December 1985, but they fell during 1986 to below 11,000m. markkaa by mid-August, with the net outflow especially high during the first week of August. In an effort to stabilize the reserves, the annual rate of interest payable on 'call money' was temporarily raised to 40%. The interest rate was subsequently lowered in September, and a series of measures was announced, aimed at stimulating the development of the money market.

The budget for 1987 envisaged a rise in government spending of 8%, with total expenditure projected to reach 109,500m. markkaa. The annual rate of inflation was expected to fall to around 2.5%.

Social Welfare

Social policy covers social security (national pensions, disability insurance, sickness insurance), social assistance (maternity, child, housing, education and other allowances and accident compensation) and social welfare (care of children, the aged, disabled and maladjusted, including residential services). Sickness insurance covers a considerable part of the costs of medical care outside hospital, while the general hospitals charge moderate fees. The National Health Act of 1972 provided for the establishment of health centres in every municipality, and the abolition of doctors' fees. In 1984 Finland had 61,103 hospital beds. In the same year there were 9,979 physicians working in the country.

Education

Compulsory education, introduced in 1921, lasts for nine years between seven and 16 years of age. By the 1977/78 school year, the whole country had transferred to a new comprehensive education system. Tuition is free and instruction is the same for all students. The compulsory course comprises six years at primary school, beginning at the age of seven, followed by three years at secondary school, beginning at the age of 13. After completing compulsory education, the pupil may transfer to an upper secondary school or other vocational school or institute for a further three years. In 1982 the total enrolment at all primary and secondary schools was equivalent to 98% of the school-age population. After three years in upper secondary school, a student takes a matriculation examination. Students who pass this examination are entitled to seek admission at one of the 22 universities and colleges of further education.

Tourism

Vast forests, Europe's largest inland water system, magnificent unspoilt scenery and the possibility of holiday seclusion are the chief attractions for the visitor to Finland. The winter sports season is long. The number of tourists visiting Finland has increased substantially since the early 1970s, with most visitors coming from other Scandinavian countries, the Federal Republic of Germany and the USSR. Tourist receipts totalled 2,845m. markkaa in 1983.

Public Holidays

1987: 1 January (New Year's Day), 10 January (for Epiphany), 17 April (Good Friday), 20 April (Easter Monday), 1 May (May Day), 23 May (for Ascension Day), 6–7 June (Whitsun), 20 June (Midsummer Day, Flag Day), 31 October (for All Saints' Day), 6 December (Independence Day), 25–26 December (Christmas).

1988*: 1 January (New Year's Day), 8 January (for Epiphany), 1 April (Good Friday), 4 April (Easter Monday), 2 May (for May Day), 12 May (Ascension Day), 21–22 May (Whitsun), 19 June (Midsummer Day, Flag Day), 1 November (All Saint's Day), 6 December (Independence Day), 25–26 December (Christmas).

* Public holidays for 1988 may be subject to alteration.

Weights and Measures

The metric system is in force.

Currency and Exchange Rates

100 penniä=1 markka (Finnmark).

Exchange Rates (30 September 1986):
 £1 sterling=7.0945 markkaa;
 US $1=4.907 markkaa.

FINLAND

Statistical Survey

Sources (unless otherwise specified): Central Statistical Office of Finland, POB 504, 00101 Helsinki; *Maataloustilastollinen Kuukausikatsaus* (Monthly Review of Agricultural Statistics), Board of Agriculture Statistical Office, Mariankatu 23, 00170 Helsinki; and *Bank of Finland Monthly Bulletin*.

Area and Population

AREA, POPULATION AND DENSITY

Area (sq km)	
Land	304,623
Inland water	33,522
Total	338,145*
Population (census results)	
31 December 1970	4,598,336
1 November 1980	
Males	2,313,165
Females	2,471,545
Total	4,784,710
Population (official estimates at 31 December)	
1982	4,841,715
1983	4,869,858
1984	4,893,748
Density (per sq km) at 31 December 1984	14.5

* 130,559 sq miles.

PROVINCES (estimated population at 31 December 1984)

	Land Area (sq km)*	Population
Uudenmaan (Nylands)	9,898	1,175,373
Turun-Porin (Åbo-Björneborgs)	22,169	712,439
Ahvenanmaan (Åland)	1,527	23,595
Hämeen (Tavastehus)	17,010	675,127
Kymen (Kymmene)	10,783	341,709
Mikkelin (St Michels)	16,343	209,256
Kuopion (Kuopio)	16,511	255,740
Pohjois-Karjalan (Norra Karelens)	17,782	177,633
Vaasan (Vasa)	26,447	443,743
Keski-Suomen (Mellersta Finlands)	16,230	247,351
Oulun (Uleåborgs)	56,866	430,902
Lapin (Lapplands)	93,057	200,879
Total	304,623	4,893,748

* Excluding inland waters, totalling 33,522 sq km.

PRINCIPAL TOWNS
(estimated population at 31 December 1984)

Helsinki (Helsingfors) (capital)	484,263
Tampere (Tammerfors)	168,150
Turku (Åbo)	162,282
Espoo (Esbo)	152,929
Vantaa (Vanda)	141,991
Oulu (Uleåborg)	96,525
Lahti	94,347
Pori (Björneborg)	78,933
Kuopio	77,371
Jyväskylä	64,834
Kotka	59,474
Vaasa (Vasa)	54,497
Lappeenranta (Villmanstrand)	53,966
Joensuu	46,354
Hämeenlinna (Tavastehus)	42,461

BIRTHS, MARRIAGES AND DEATHS

	Registered live births*		Registered marriages†		Registered deaths*	
	Number	Rate (per 1,000)	Number	Rate (per 1,000)	Number	Rate (per 1,000)
1977	65,659	13.9	30,966	6.5	44,065	9.3
1978	63,983	13.5	29,760	6.3	43,692	9.2
1979	63,428	13.3	29,277	6.1	43,738	9.2
1980	63,064	13.2	29,388	6.1	44,398	9.3
1981	63,469	13.2	30,100	6.3	44,404	9.2
1982	66,103	13.7	30,459	6.3	43,408	9.0
1983	66,892	13.8	28,311	5.8	45,388	9.3
1984	65,076	13.6	28,632	5.9	45,098	9.2

* Including Finnish nationals temporarily outside the country.
† Data relate only to marriages in which the bride was domiciled in Finland.

ECONOMICALLY ACTIVE POPULATION*
('000 persons aged 15 to 74 years)

	1982	1983	1984
Agriculture, forestry and fishing	312	302	294
Mining and quarrying	10	10	10
Manufacturing	581	571	562
Electricity, gas and water	26	25	27
Construction	183	183	183
Trade, restaurants and hotels	326	337	342
Transport, storage and communications	180	177	180
Finance, insurance, real estate and business services	136	135	147
Community, social and personal services	616	646	664
Activities not adequately described	7	4	4
Total employed	2,377	2,390	2,413
Unemployed	149	156	158
Total labour force	2,526	2,546	2,572

* Excluding persons on compulsory military service (30,000 in 1982, 29,000 in 1983 and 28,000 in 1984).

Agriculture

PRINCIPAL CROPS
('000 metric tons; farms with arable land of 1 hectare or more)

	1982	1983	1984
Wheat	435.4	549.5	478.3
Barley	1,598.5	1,764.4	1,715.3
Rye	35.0	116.1	92.3
Oats	1,319.9	1,406.5	1,320.9
Mixed grain	28.7	40.1	39.8
Potatoes	601.1	804.0	745.0
Rapeseed	96.3	101.2	85.7
Sugar beet	756.1	955.0	823.4

LIVESTOCK ('000 head at 1 June; farms with arable land of 1 hectare or more)

	1984	1985	1986
Horses	19.2	18.8	18.5
Cattle	1,643.1	1,608.3	1,567.3
Sheep	109.7	111.7	116.1
Reindeer	347.0	345.0	n.a.
Pigs*	1,957.6	1,295.2	1,322.7
Chickens }	7,957.6	7,469.4	7,089.1
Other poultry }			
Beehives†	40.0	35.0	n.a.

* Including piggeries of dairies. † '000 hives.

LIVESTOCK PRODUCTS ('000 metric tons)

	1983	1984	1985
Beef	119.7	122.3	125.4
Veal	0.9	0.7	0.7
Pig meat	185.2	170.5	172.4
Poultry meat	18.3	19.7	20.5
Cows' milk*	2,943.1	3,123.7	2,987.5
Butter	84.0	79.9	72.5
Cheese	72.0	75.9	79.1
Hen eggs	82.6	88.2	85.6
Cattle hides	14.6	14.9	n.a.

* Million litres.

Forestry

ROUNDWOOD REMOVALS ('000 cu m, excl. bark)

	1982	1983	1984
Sawlogs, veneer logs and logs for sleepers	15,790	17,143	17,633
Pulpwood	17,182	16,618	18,656
Other industrial wood	1,379	1,405	1,433
Fuel wood	3,305	3,242	3,153
Total	37,656	38,408	40,875

Source: FAO, *Yearbook of Forest Products*.

SAWNWOOD PRODUCTION ('000 cu m, incl. boxboards)

	1982	1983	1984
Coniferous (softwood)	7,230	7,925	8,146
Broadleaved (hardwood)	70	70	86
Total	7,300	7,995	8,232

Railway sleepers ('000 cu m): 22 in 1982; 28 in 1983; 33 in 1984.
Source: FAO, *Yearbook of Forest Products*.

Fishing

('000 metric tons, live weight)

	1982	1983	1984
Freshwater fishes	29.0	28.6	28.8
Diadromous fishes	18.5	20.0	22.3
Atlantic herring	85.0	95.9	97.4
Other marine fishes	13.1	12.7	12.4
Total catch	145.6	157.1	160.9
Inland waters	33.0	33.7	33.9
Atlantic Ocean	112.6	123.4	127.0

Source: FAO, *Yearbook of Fishery Statistics*.

Mining

	1982	1983	1984
Copper ore* ('000 metric tons)	38.1	37.7	29.5
Lead ore* ('000 metric tons)	1.9	2.1	2.5
Zinc ore* ('000 metric tons)	54.7	56.3	60.2
Silver (metric tons)	36.9	30.5	34.9
Gold (kilograms)	1,144	784	880

* Metal content.

Industry

SELECTED PRODUCTS

		1982	1983*	1984*
Cellulose	'000 metric tons	4,043	4,387	4,771
Machine pulp (for sale)	'000 metric tons	36	31	37
Newsprint	'000 metric tons	1,355	1,285	1,499
Other paper, boards and cardboards	'000 metric tons	4,397	5,008	5,748
Plywoods and veneers	'000 cubic metres	537	519	551
Cement	'000 metric tons	1,906	1,969	1,645
Pig iron and ferro-alloys	'000 metric tons	1,944	1,900	2,034
Electricity	million kWh	36,660	40,120	43,201
Cotton yarn	metric tons	10,067	6,666	6,916
Cotton fabrics	metric tons	16,576	14,241	12,818
Sugar	metric tons	292,368	242,816	172,331
Rolled steel products	metric tons	1,847,000	1,955,000	1,987,000
Copper (cathodes)	metric tons	47,969	55,422	57,318
Cigarettes	million	8,491	8,329	8,345

* Provisional figures.

Finance

CURRENCY AND EXCHANGE RATES

Monetary Units
100 penniä (singular: penni) = 1 markka (Finnmark).

Denominations
Coins: 5, 10, 20 and 50 penniä; 1, 5 and 10 markkaa.
Notes: 5, 10, 50, 100 and 500 markkaa.

Sterling and Dollar Equivalents (30 September 1986)
£1 sterling = 7.0945 markkaa;
US $1 = 4.907 markkaa;
100 markkaa = £14.095 = $20.379.

Average Exchange Rate (markkaa per US $)
1983   5.570
1984   6.010
1985   6.198

BUDGET (million markkaa)

Revenue	1982	1983	1984
Direct taxes	17,160	19,565	21,894
Indirect taxes	35,023	36,713	43,967
Social security	1	1	0
Other	15,859	20,074	20,750
Total	68,043	76,353	86,611

Expenditure	1982	1983	1984
Education	11,266	12,824	13,756
Social security	9,325	12,627	14,535
Health	5,935	6,785	7,156
Agriculture and forestry	8,912	7,394	8,026
Transport and communications	6,439	7,131	7,405
Defence	4,154	4,543	4,866
Public debt	4,580	6,558	9,224
Other	17,397	19,329	20,780
Total	68,008	77,191	85,748

Budget Estimates (million markkaa): 1985: Revenue 93,863, Expenditure 93,860; 1986: Revenue 100,781, Expenditure 100,780.

INTERNATIONAL RESERVES
(US $ million at 31 December)

	1983	1984	1985
Gold*	238.0	211.8	384.2
IMF special drawing rights	38.7	142.8	171.8
Reserve position in IMF	128.7	131.1	143.1
Foreign exchange	1,070.3	2,480.4	3,435.0
Total	1,475.7	2,966.1	4,134.1

* Valued at market-related prices.
Source: IMF, *International Financial Statistics*.

MONEY SUPPLY (million markkaa at 31 December)

	1983	1984	1985
Currency outside banks	5,628	5,876	6,143
Demand deposits at deposit money banks	15,798	19,007	21,483
Total money*	21,427	24,945	27,694

* Including private-sector deposits at the Bank of Finland.
Souce: IMF, *International Financial Statistics*.

COST OF LIVING (Consumer Price Index. Base: 1981 = 100)

	1983	1984	1985
Food	120	129	139
Beverages and tobacco	125	132	140
Clothing and footwear	113	120	126
Rent, heating and lighting	118	124	131
Furniture, household equipment	114	123	130
All items	119	127	135

FINLAND

NATIONAL ACCOUNTS (million markkaa at current prices)*
National Income and Product

	1982	1983	1984†
Compensation of employees	133,945	148,426	165,370
Operating surplus	49,375	57,825	64,734
Domestic factor incomes	183,320	206,251	230,104
Consumption of fixed capital	36,379	40,063	43,990
Gross domestic product at factor cost	219,699	246,314	274,094
Indirect taxes	33,208	36,978	43,534
Less Subsidies	7,735	8,856	9,752
GDP in purchasers' values	245,172	274,436	307,876
Factor income received from abroad	3,598	3,738	4,926
Less Factor income paid abroad	8,891	9,458	11,988
Gross national product	239,879	268,716	300,814
Less Consumption of fixed capital	36,379	40,063	43,990
National income in market prices	203,500	228,653	256,824

* Accounts adjusted in 1984. † Provisional figures.

Expenditure on the Gross Domestic Product

	1982	1983	1984
Government final consumption expenditure	46,661	53,305	59,890
Private final consumption expenditure	134,161	149,607	164,677
Increase in stocks	2,001	1,670	1,335
Gross fixed capital formation	60,987	68,987	72,079
Statistical discrepancy	−688	−424	1,843
Total domestic expenditure	243,142	273,145	299,824
Exports of goods and services	76,397	84,061	95,875
Less Imports of goods and services	74,367	82,770	87,823
GDP in purchasers' values	245,172	274,436	307,876

Gross Domestic Product by Economic Activity

	1982	1983	1984
Agriculture, hunting, forestry and fishing	19,199	20,784	22,864
Mining and quarrying	919	1,009	1,100
Manufacturing	57,348	63,936	72,530
Electricity, gas and water	7,737	8,233	8,633
Construction	17,662	20,571	21,786
Trade, restaurants and hotels	25,336	27,803	30,337
Transport, storage and communication	17,648	19,832	22,216
Finance, insurance and business services	18,348	21,369	25,296
Owner-occupied dwellings	15,009	16,274	17,688
Public administration and defence	10,262	11,769	13,052
Other community, social and personal services	34,918	40,108	45,310
Sub-total	224,386	251,698	280,812
Less Imputed bank service charge	5,564	6,165	7,207
GDP in basic values	218,822	245,533	273,605
Commodity taxes	31,859	35,361	41,442
Less Commodity subsidies	5,509	6,458	7,171
GDP in purchasers' values	245,172	274,436	307,876

FINLAND

BALANCE OF PAYMENTS (US $ million)

	1983	1984	1985
Merchandise exports f.o.b.	12,172	13,087	13,520
Merchandise imports f.o.b.	−12,010	−11,593	−12,637
Trade balance	162	1,494	882
Exports of services	3,177	3,267	3,280
Imports of services	−4,132	−4,590	−4,654
Balance on goods and services	−793	171	−491
Private unrequited transfers (net)	−23	−20	−33
Government unrequited transfers (net)	−121	−145	−152
Current balance	−936	5	−677
Direct capital investment (net)	−241	−360	−261
Other long-term capital (net)	601	1,423	1,541
Short-term capital (net)	193	852	−54
Net errors and omissions	156	−103	36
Total (net monetary movements)	−228	1,817	586
Valuation changes (net)	−37	−253	475
Official financing (net)	1	8	−3
Changes in reserves	−264	1,572	1,058

Source: IMF, *International Financial Statistics*.

External Trade

PRINCIPAL COMMODITIES (distribution by SITC, million markkaa)

Imports c.i.f.	1982	1983	1984
Food and live animals	4,247.3	3,724.5	4,031.2
Coffee, tea, cocoa and spices	1,180.4	1,277.8	1,619.8
Crude materials (inedible) except fuels	3,899.6	4,403.1	4,972.9
Mineral fuels, lubricants, etc.	17,753.7	19,245.5	18,654.0
Coal, coke and briquettes	2,133.9	1,794.9	1,502.0
Petroleum, petroleum products, etc.	14,721.0	16,441.3	16,018.0
Crude petroleum oils, etc.	11,341.0	12,559.6	11,867.0
Refined petroleum products	3,219.3	3,759.0	4,017.6
Gas oils (distillate fuels)	1,627.6	1,587.3	1,862.9
Chemicals and related products	5,652.5	6,702.6	7,123.2
Chemical elements and compounds	1,788.8	2,006.7	2,096.4
Plastic materials, etc.	1,665.3	2,052.9	2,223.8
Basic manufactures	9,290.8	10,086.2	10,838.0
Textile yarn, fabrics, etc.	2,501.2	2,627.3	2,718.1
Woven textile fabrics (excl. narrow or special fabrics)	1,179.3	1,211.4	1,234.5
Iron and steel	2,086.8	2,034.5	2,309.2
Non-ferrous metals	969.8	1,170.0	1,190.9
Other metal manufactures	1,416.0	1,535.5	1,690.5
Machinery and transport equipment	18,236.5	20,876.9	22,169.3
Non-electric machinery	9,234.2	10,163.9	10,946.1
Electrical machinery, apparatus, etc.	3,566.7	4,283.9	5,095.8
Transport equipment	5,435.5	6,429.1	6,127.5
Road vehicles and parts*	4,056.0	4,547.0	4,919.5
Passenger motor cars (excl. buses)	1,753.9	2,040.6	2,253.9
Miscellaneous manufactured articles	4,849.5	5,671.2	6,184.3
Scientific instruments, watches, etc.	1,553.2	1,810.4	1,882.5
Total (incl. others)	64,751.4	71,527.9	74,681.6

* Excluding tyres, engines and electrical parts.
1985: Total imports 81,406 million markkaa.

Exports f.o.b.	1982	1983	1984
Food and live animals	1,877.4	2,385.9	2,642.1
Crude materials (inedible) except fuels	8,415.4	9,415.8	11,352.5
Wood, lumber and cork	3,587.0	4,321.0	4,792.2
Shaped or simply worked wood	3,152.0	3,919.3	4,308.5
Shaped coniferous lumber	3,127.2	3,891.1	4,286.4
Sawn coniferous lumber	2,886.0	3,603.1	3,598.3
Pulp and waste paper	3,064.1	3,259.9	4,148.6
Chemical wood pulp	3,027.2	3,251.9	4,063.0
Mineral fuels, lubricants, etc.	2,555.2	3,597.2	4,452.1
Petroleum, petroleum products, etc.	2,394.1	3,539.8	4,391.0
Refined petroleum products	2,366.5	3,491.4	4,340.2
Chemicals and related products	3,188.6	3,725.4	4,366.1
Basic manufactures	23,897.4	26,358.0	30,134.9
Wood and cork manufactures (excl. furniture)	2,296.7	2,218.2	2,016.3
Veneers, plywood boards, etc.	1,472.5	1,538.1	1,629.8
Paper, paperboard and manufactures	14,018.7	15,672.2	18,985.6
Paper and paperboard	12,614.9	14,065.3	17,339.5
Newsprint paper	2,776.9	3,013.1	3,518.9
Other printing and writing paper in bulk	4,875.1	5,650.8	7,745.2
Kraft paper and paperboard	1,348.1	1,432.3	1,640.7
Articles of paper pulp, paper or paperboard	1,403.8	1,606.9	1,646.1
Iron and steel	2,283.9	2,817.9	3,275.0
Non-ferrous metals	1,631.5	2,067.9	2,532.4
Other metal manufactures	1,855.6	1,663.1	1,304.7
Machinery and transport equipment	15,889.4	17,167.8	20,121.7
Non-electric machinery	6,937.2	6,537.9	7,468.1
Electrical machinery, apparatus, etc.	2,687.2	2,923.8	3,115.2
Transport equipment	6,264.6	7,706.1	9,538.5
Ships and boats	4,866.0	6,260.6	7,967.0
Miscellaneous manufactured articles	6,906.9	6,723.0	7,416.1
Clothing (excl. footwear)	3,127.8	2,798.8	3,003.8
Clothing not of fur	2,780.2	2,494.9	2,752.6
Non-knitted textile clothing (excl. accessories and headgear)	1,943.6	1,844.5	2,040.6
Total (incl. others)	63,026.1	69,692.3	80,904.1

1985: Total exports 84,022 million markkaa.

PRINCIPAL TRADING PARTNERS (million markkaa)*

Imports c.i.f.	1982	1983	1984
Austria	806.4	836.8	838.2
Belgium/Luxembourg	1,148.1	1,254.9	1,445.1
Denmark	1,501.4	1,728.0	1,821.0
France	2,023.3	2,336.1	2,362.8
Germany, Federal Republic	8,585.8	9,464.2	10,385.8
Iran	323.6	719.4	341.2
Italy	1,707.9	2,140.7	2,347.6
Japan	2,723.2	3,903.3	4,165.6
Netherlands	1,714.5	1,903.2	2,047.1
Norway	1,456.5	1,885.0	1,557.4
Poland	938.5	904.6	1,159.0
Saudi Arabia	1,362.7	772.7	959.8
Sweden	7,869.7	7,995.6	9,154.1
Switzerland	1,059.4	1,208.3	1,230.3
USSR	15,910.0	18,388.8	17,274.0
United Kingdom	4,642.0	4,765.9	5,758.3
USA	3,947.0	4,043.0	3,734.0
Total (incl. others)	64,751.4	71,527.9	74,681.6

Exports f.o.b.	1982	1983	1984
Belgium/Luxembourg	869.6	1,085.2	1,193.4
Denmark	2,282.5	2,580.8	3,297.7
France	2,486.6	2,847.9	3,188.0
Germany, Federal Republic	5,699.8	6,668.8	7,775.8
Iraq	728.4	422.4	266.9
Italy	1,134.9	1,300.2	1,715.8
Netherlands	1,928.1	2,771.3	2,865.5
Norway	3,084.5	2,376.8	3,663.3
Sweden	7,547.2	8,635.2	9,961.4
Switzerland	838.7	947.3	1,006.4
USSR	16,805.3	18,243.6	15,297.0
United Kingdom	6,827.3	7,199.7	9,737.7
USA	2,007.5	2,860.3	6,614.5
Total (incl. others)	63,026.1	69,692.3	80,904.1

* Imports by country of production; exports by country of consumption.

FINLAND

Statistical Survey

Transport

RAILWAYS (traffic)

	1982	1983	1984
Passenger-km (million)	3,326	3,339	3,276
Freight ton-km (million)	8,000	8,089	7,981

ROAD TRAFFIC (registered motor vehicles at 31 December)

	1983	1984	1985
Passenger cars	1,410,438	1,472,975	1,546,094
Lorries and vans	167,831	173,784	179,637
Buses	9,102	9,069	9,017
Special purpose vehicles	10,585	11,159	11,867

CIVIL AVIATION (scheduled services, '000)

	1982	1983	1984
Kilometres flown	36,743	36,581	36,959
Passenger-kilometres	2,589,497	2,629,768	2,696,235
Cargo ton-kilometres	66,867	77,274	79,408

SHIPPING
Merchant Fleet (1984)

	Ships	Displacement ('000 gross reg. tons)
Passenger vessels	160	230
Tankers	44	1,006
Others	268	831
Total	472	2,067

International Sea-borne Freight Traffic

	1982	1983	1984
Vessels ('000 net reg. tons):			
Entered	49,750	51,108	50,722
Cleared	49,479	51,214	50,717
Goods ('000 metric tons):			
Loaded	16,040	17,845	20,729
Unloaded	30,260	30,915	29,418

CANAL TRAFFIC

	1981	1982	1983
Vessels in transit	48,372	52,535	57,553
Timber rafts in transit	14,442	12,839	11,459
Goods carried ('000 tons)	8,292	7,940	9,512

Tourism

NUMBER OF NIGHTS AT ACCOMMODATION FACILITIES

Country of Domicile	1982	1983	1984
Denmark	49,356	51,499	55,017
France	50,753	46,481	58,842
Germany, Federal Republic	269,726	255,136	277,889
Netherlands	36,078	36,767	44,140
Norway	174,181	169,833	166,007
Sweden	628,088	563,497	540,861
Switzerland	70,020	75,024	79,824
USSR	227,770	245,001	245,766
United Kingdom	96,078	104,067	108,073
USA	114,480	150,011	157,477
Total (incl. others)	2,024,681	2,060,562	2,112,508

Communications Media

	1982	1983	1984
Telephones in use	2,643,574	2,777,073	2,899,000
Television receivers*	1,678,249	1,770,130	1,770,000
Book production: titles†	7,436	8,594	8,563
Newspapers and periodicals	4,684	4,652	n.a.

* Number of licensed sets.
† Including pamphlets (1,874 in 1982; 2,312 in 1983).

Education

(1983/84)

	Institutions	Staff	Students
First level	4,230	25,139	369,047
Secondary, general	1,082	22,356	316,740
Secondary vocational			116,906
Universities and other education at the third level	571	21,938	119,982

Directory

The Constitution

The Constitution (summarized below) was adopted on 17 July 1919. The first report of the Constitutional Committee on possible reforms of the fundamental laws was presented in April 1974. The multi-party system and the constitutional checks on revision of the fundamental laws are likely to delay any major changes until later in the 1980s, but several issues have emerged as potential areas for reform. Generally, the right-wing parties are suspicious of reform, but the left has won some support from the centre.

Three main topics have been discussed by the Committee: the respective powers of the President, the Council of State (Cabinet) and Parliament (Eduskunta); legislative procedure, particularly the strength of the protection to be given to parliamentary minorities; the basic economic, social and cultural rights of the individual and security of ownership. The Committee has also recommended the implementation of employee participation in decision-making. The most basic reform under discussion is the left's proposal that Parliament should be the supreme state organ, and that much of the President's power should be transferred to the Council of State. There are also proposals that citizens should vote directly for a presidential candidate, and that the President should be restricted to a maximum of two successive terms of office.

GOVERNMENT

For the general administration of the country, there is a Council of State, appointed by the President, and composed of the Prime Minister and the Ministers of the various Ministries. The members of the Council, who must enjoy the confidence of the Parliament, are collectively responsible to it for their conduct of affairs, and for the general policy of the administration, while each member is responsible for the administration of his own Ministry.

To this Council the President can appoint supernumerary Ministers, who serve either as assistant Ministers or as Ministers without portfolio. The President also appoints a Chancellor of Justice, who must see that the Council and its members act within the law. If, in the opinion of the Chancellor of Justice, the Council of State or an individual Minister has acted in a manner contrary to the law, the Chancellor must report the matter to the President of the Republic or, in certain cases, to the Parliament. In this way Ministers are rendered legally as well as politically responsible for their official acts.

THE PRESIDENT

The President is elected for a term of six years by 301 electors. The electors are chosen by public vote in the same manner as members of Parliament.

The President of the Republic is entrusted with supreme executive power. The President's decisions are made known in meetings of the Council of State on the basis of the recommendation of the minister responsible for the matter. The President has the right to depart even from a unanimous opinion reached by the Council of State. Legislative power is exercised by the Parliament in conjunction with the President. Both the President and the Parliament have the right of initiative in legislation. Laws passed by the Parliament are submitted to the President, who has the right of veto. If the President has not within three months assented to a law, this is tantamount to a refusal of assent. A law to which the President has not given assent will nevertheless come into force, if the Parliament elected at the next general election adopts it without alteration.

The President has also the right to issue decrees in certain events, to order new elections to the Parliament, to grant pardons and dispensations, and to grant Finnish citizenship to foreigners.

The President's approval is necessary in all matters concerning the relations of Finland with foreign countries. The President is Supreme Commander of the Defence Forces of the Republic.

Such decisions as are arrived at by the President are made in the Council of State, except in matters pertaining to military functions and appointments.

THE PARLIAMENT

The Parliament is an assembly of one chamber with 200 members elected for four years by universal suffrage on a system of proportional representation, every man and woman aged 18 years or over being entitled to vote and everyone over 20 being eligible. It assembles annually at the beginning of February. The ordinary duration of a session is 120 days but the Parliament can, at its pleasure, extend or shorten its session. The opposition of one-third of the members can cause ordinary legislative proposals to be deferred until after the next elections. Discussion of questions relating to the constitutional laws belongs also to Parliament, but for the settlement of such questions certain delaying conditions (fixed majorities) are prescribed. The Parliament, besides taking part in legislation, has the right to determine the estimates, which, though not technically a law, are published as a law.

Furthermore, the Parliament has the right, in a large measure, to supervise the administration of the Government. For this purpose it receives special reports (the Government also submitting an account of its administration every year) and a special account of the administration of national finances. The Chancellor of Justice submits a yearly report on the administration of the Council of State. The Parliament elects five auditors, who submit to it annual reports of their work, to see that the estimates have been adhered to. The Parliament also appoints every four years a Parliamentary Ombudsman (Judicial Delegate of Parliament) who submits to it a report, to supervise the observance of the laws.

The Parliament has the right to interrogate the Government. It can impeach a member of the Council of State or the Chancellor of Justice for not having conformed to the law in the discharge of his duties. Trials are conducted at a special court, known as the Court of the Realm, of 13 members, six of whom are elected by Parliament for a term of four years.

The Government

(December 1986)

HEAD OF STATE

President: Dr MAUNO KOIVISTO (assumed duties 10 September 1981; elected 26 January 1982).

COUNCIL OF STATE

(Valtioneuvosto)

A coalition of the Centre Party (KP), Social Democratic Party (SDP), Swedish People's Party (SFP) and Finnish Rural Party (SMP), formed in May 1983.

Prime Minister: KALEVI SORSA (SDP).

Deputy Prime Minister and Minister for Foreign Affairs: PAAVO VÄYRYNEN (KP).

Minister of Foreign Trade: JERMU LAINE (SDP).

Minister of Justice: CHRISTOPHER TAXELL (SFP).

Minister of the Interior: KAISA RAATIKAINEN (SDP).

Minister of the Environment: MATTI AHDE (SDP).

Minister of Defence: VEIKKO PIHLAJAMÄKI (KP).

First Minister of Finance: ESKO OLLILA (KP).

Second Minister of Finance: PEKKA VENNAMO (SMP).

First Minister of Education: Mrs PIRJO ALA-KAPEE (SDP).

Second Minister of Education: GUSTAV BJÖRKSTRAND (SFP).

Minister of Agriculture and Forestry: TOIVO YLÄJÄRVI (KP).

Minister of Transport and Communications: MATTI LUTTINEN (SDP).

Minister of Trade and Industry: SEPPO LINDBLOM (SDP).

First Minister of Social Affairs and Health: Dr EEVA KUUSKOSKI-VIKATMAA (KP).

Second Minister of Social Affairs and Health: MATTI PUHAKKA (SDP).

Minister of Labour: URPO LEPPÄNEN (SMP).

MINISTRIES

Prime Minister's Office: Aleksanterinkatu 3D, 00170 Helsinki; tel. (90) 1601; telex 124636.

Ministry of Agriculture and Forestry: Hallituskatu 3A, 00170 Helsinki; tel. (90) 1601; telex 125621.

Ministry of Defence: Et. Makasiinikatu 8A, 00130 Helsinki; tel. (90) 625801; telex 124667.

FINLAND

Ministry of Education: Kirkkokatu 3, 00170 Helsinki; tel. (90) 171636; telex 122079.
Ministry of the Environment: POB 306, 00531 Helsinki; tel. (90) 1601; telex 123717.
Ministry of Finance: Snellmaninkatu 1A, 00170 Helsinki; tel. (90) 1601; telex 123241.
Ministry of Foreign Affairs: Ritarikatu 2B, 00170 Helsinki; tel. (90) 1601; telex 124636.
Ministry of the Interior: Kirkkokatu 12, 00170 Helsinki; tel. (90) 1601; telex 123644.
Ministry of Justice: Eteläesplanadi 10, 00130 Helsinki; tel. (90) 18251.
Ministry of Labour: Eteläesplanadi 4, 00130 Helsinki; tel. (90) 18561; telex 121441.
Ministry of Social Affairs and Health: Snellmaninkatu 4-6, 00170 Helsinki; tel. (90) 1601; telex 125073.
Ministry of Trade and Industry: Aleksanterinkatu 10, 00170 Helsinki; tel. (90) 1601; telex 124645.
Ministry of Transport and Communications: Eteläesplanadi 16, 00130 Helsinki; tel. (90) 17361; telex 125472.

Legislature

EDUSKUNTA

Speaker: ERKKI PYSTYNEN (KOK).
First Deputy Speaker: MATTI LOUEKOSKI (SD).
Second Deputy Speaker: VEIKKO PIHLAJAMÄKI (KESK).
Secretary-General: ERKKI KETOLA.

General Election, 20–21 March 1983

	Votes	%	Seats
Social Democratic Party	795,953	26.71	57
National Coalition Party	659,078	22.12	44
Centre Party	525,207	17.63	38
Finnish People's Democratic League	400,930	13.46	26
Finnish Rural Party	288,711	9.69	17
Swedish People's Party	137,423	4.61	10
Finnish Christian Union	90,410	3.03	3
Greens			2
Others	81,982	2.75	3
Total	2,979,694	100.00	200

Note: A general election was scheduled for March 1987.

Political Organizations

Demokraattinen Vaihtoehto (Democratic Alternative): Helsinki; f. 1986 by a minority faction of the Communist Party of Finland; Chair. KRISTIINA HALKOLA; Gen. Sec. JOUKO KAJANOJA.
Kansallinen Kokoomus (KOK) (National Coalition Party): Kansakoulukuja 3, 00100 Helsinki; tel. (90) 6942611; telex 124591; f. 1918; moderate conservative political ideology; 80,000 mems.; Chair. ILKKA SUOMINEN; Sec.-Gen. JUSSI ISOTALO; Chair. Parliamentary Group ULLA PUOLANNE.
Keskustapuolue (KP) (Centre Party): Pursimiehenkatu 15, Helsinki; tel. (90) 170311; f. 1906; a radical centre party founded to promote the interests of the rural population, especially that of the numerous small farmers, on the lines of individual enterprise; also favours decentralization; 304,000 mems; Chair. PAAVO VÄYRYNEN; Sec. SEPPO KÄÄRIÄNEN; Chair. Parliamentary Group KAUKO JUHANTALO.
Liberaalinen Kansanpuolue (LKP) (Liberal People's Party): Fredrikinkatu 58A 6, Helsinki; tel. (90) 440227; f. 1965 as a coalition of the Finnish People's Party and the Liberal Union; 8,000 mems; Chair. KYÖSTI LALLUKKA; Sec.-Gen. JARI P. HAVIA.
Perustuslaillinen Oikeistopuolue-Konstitutionella högerpartiet r.p. (Constitutional Party of the Right): Mannerheimintie 146A, 00270 Helsinki; tel. (90) 419063; f. 1973; conservative; seeks to protect constitutional rights and parliamentary democracy; Chair. GEORG C. EHRNROOTH; Sec. PANU TOIVONEN.
Suomen Eläkelästen Poulue (Finnish Pensioners' Party): f.1986; represents the interests of pensioners; Chair. YRJOE VIRTANEN.
Suomen Kansan Demokraattinen Liitto r.p. (SKDL) (Finnish People's Democratic League): Kotkankatu 11, 00510 Helsinki; f. 1944 by social democrats, socialists and communists; co-operative organization of communists, socialists and other leftist groups; member organizations: Finnish Communist Party, Women's, Youth and Student Leagues; 120,000 mems; Chair. ESKO HELLE; Sec.-Gen. REIJO KÄKELÄ; Chair. Parliamentary Group VEIKKO SAARTO.
Suomen Kommunistinen Puolue (SKP) (Communist Party of Finland): Sturenkatu 4, Helsinki; tel. (90) 77081; f. 1918; proscribed until 1944 after the signing of the Armistice with USSR; Chair. ARVO AALTO; Deputy Chair. HELJÄ TAMMISOLA; Gen. Sec. ESKO VAINIONPÄÄ.
Suomen Kristillinen Liitto (SKL) (Finnish Christian Union): Töölönkatu 50 D, 00250 Helsinki; f. 1958; 18,000 mems; Chair. E. ALMGREN; Sec. JOUKO JÄÄSKELÄINEN; Chair. Parliamentary Group C. P. OLAVI RONKAINEN.
Suomen Maaseudun Puolue (SMP) (Finnish Rural Party): Hämeentie 157, 00560 Helsinki; tel. (90) 790299; f. 1959; non-socialist programme; represents lower-middle-class elements, small farmers, small enterprises etc.; Chair. PEKKA VENNAMO; Sec. AARO NIIRANEN; Chair. Parliamentary Group J. JUHANI KORTESALMI.
Suomen Sosialidemokraattinen Puolue (SDP) (Finnish Social Democratic Party): Saariniemenkatu 6, 00530 Helsinki; f. 1899; constitutional socialist programme; mainly supported by the working and middle classes and small farmers; approx. 97,000 mems; Chair. KALEVI SORSA; Sec. ERKKI LIIKANEN; Chair. Parliamentary Group PERTTI PAASIO.
Svenska Folkpartiet (SFP) (Swedish People's Party): Bulevarden 7A, PB 146, 00121 Helsinki; tel. (90) 640313; telex 121844; f. 1906; a liberal party representing the interests of the Swedish-speaking minority; 50,000 mems; Chair. CHRISTOFFER TAXELL; Sec. PETER STENLUND; Chair. Parliamentary Group OLE NORRBACK.

Diplomatic Representation

EMBASSIES IN FINLAND

Argentina: Bulevardi 10A 14, Helsinki; tel. (90) 607630; telex 122794; Ambassador: RAÚL A. MEDINA MUÑOZ.
Austria: Eteläesplandi 18, Helsinki; tel. (90) 634255; Ambassador: HANS GEORG RUDOFSKY.
Belgium: Kalliolinnantie 5, Helsinki; tel. (90) 170412; Ambassador: JEAN ADRIAENSSEN.
Brazil: Mariankatu 7A 3, Helsinki; tel. (90) 177922; Ambassador: JOSÉ AUGUSTO DE MACEDO SOARES.
Bulgaria: Itäinen puistotie 10, Helsinki; tel. (90) 661707; Ambassador: IVAN VRAZHILOV.
China, People's Republic: Vanha Kelkkamäki 9–11, Helsinki; tel. (90) 688371; Ambassador: LIN AILI.
Colombia: Kulosaarentie 9A, Helsinki; tel. (90) 689132; Ambassador: (vacant).
Cuba: Paasivuorenkatu 3, Helsinki; tel. (90) 766199; telex 121017; Ambassador: MAGALY T. GOZÁ LEÓN.
Czechoslovakia: Armfeltintie 14, Helsinki; tel. (90) 171169; Ambassador: JÁN HUSÁK.
Denmark: POB 178, Yrjönkatu 9, 00121 Helsinki 12; tel. (90) 641948; telex 124782; Ambassador: PETER MEYER MICHAELSEN.
Egypt: Stenbäckinkatu 22A, Helsinki; tel. (90) 413288; telex 124216; Ambassador: HAZEM M. MAHMOUD.
France: Itäinen puistotie 13, Helsinki; tel. (90) 171521; Ambassador: HENRI OURMET.
German Democratic Republic: Vähäniityntie 9, 00570 Helsinki 57; tel. (90) 688138; telex 12643; Ambassador: Dr STEFAN DOERNBERG.
Germany, Federal Republic: Fredrikinkatu 61, Helsinki; tel. (90) 6943355; telex 124568; Ambassador: Dr KLAUS TERFLOTH.
Greece: Lönnrotinkatu 15C 26, Helsinki; tel. (90) 645202; Ambassador: SPYRIDON A. ADAMOPOULOS.
Holy See: Bulevardi 5 as. 12, Helsinki; tel. (90) 644664; Apostolic Nuncio: HENRI LEMAÎTRE.
Hungary: Kuusisaarenkuja 6, Helsinki; tel. (90) 484144; Ambassador: ÁRPÁD HARGITA.
India: Satamakatu 2A 8, Helsinki; tel. (90) 608927; telex 125202; Ambassador: KALARICKAL PRANCHU FABIAN.
Indonesia: Eerikinkatu 37, 00180 Helsinki; tel. (90) 6947744; Ambassador: PONGKI SUPARDJO.

FINLAND

Iran: Bertel Jungintie 4, Helsinki; tel. (90) 687133; Ambassador: ROSTAM ALI ROSTAMI TARESI.
Iraq: Lars Sonckintie 2, Helsinki; tel. (90) 689177; Ambassador: PETER YOUSIF JEJJOUNI.
Israel: Vironkatu 5A, Helsinki; tel. (90) 175177; Ambassador: MORDECHAI LADOR.
Italy: Fabianinkatu 29c 4, 00100 Helsinki; tel. (90) 175144; telex 121753; Ambassador: EMANUELE COSTA.
Japan: Yrjönkatu 13, Helsinki; tel. (90) 644206; Ambassador: SHOTARO TAKAHASHI.
Korea, Democratic People's Republic: Kulosaaren puistotie 32, Helsinki; tel. (90) 688195; Ambassador: LI NAM-KYU.
Korea, Republic: Mannerheimintie 76 A 7, Helsinki; tel. (90) 498955; Ambassador: WOO YOUNG CHUNG.
Mexico: Pohjoisranta 14A 16, Helsinki 17; tel. (90) 631621; telex 122021; Ambassador: RODOLFO NAVARRETE TEJERO.
Netherlands: Raatimiehenkatu 2A 7, Helsinki; tel. (90) 661737; telex 121779; Ambassador: WILLEM JAN DE VOS VAN STEENWIJK.
Norway: Rehbinderintie 17, Helsinki; tel. (90) 171234; Ambassador: KJELL COLDING.
Peru: Fredrikinkatu 16A 22, Helsinki; tel. (90) 631354; Ambassador: AUGUSTO SALAMANCA REGALADO.
Poland: Armas Lindgrenintie 21, Helsinki; tel. (90) 688077; Ambassador: HENRYK BURCZYK.
Portugal: Itäinen puistotie 11B, Helsinki; tel. (90) 171717; Ambassador: ANTÓNIO CABRAL DE MONCADA.
Romania: Stenbäckinkatu 24, Helsinki; tel. (90) 413624; Ambassador: MARIA STĂNESCU.
South Africa: Rahapajankatu 1A, Helsinki; tel. (90) 658288; Ambassador: I. D. DU PLESSIS.
Spain: Bulevardi 10A 8, Helsinki; tel. (90) 647351; telex 122193; Ambassador: FERNANDO SARTORIUS Y ALVAREZ DE BOHORQUES.
Sweden: P. Esplanadi 7B, Helsinki; tel. (90) 651255; Ambassador: KNUT THYBERG.
Switzerland: Uudenmaankatu 16A, Helsinki; tel. (90) 649422; Ambassador: MARIANNE VON GRUENIGEN.
Turkey: Topeliuksenkatu 3B A 1-2, Helsinki; tel. (90) 406058; Ambassador: DOGAN TÜRKMEN.
USSR: Tehtaankatu 1B, Helsinki; tel. (90) 661876; Ambassador: V. M. SOBOLEV.
United Kingdom: Uudenmaankatu 16-20, 00120 Helsinki 12; tel. (90) 647922; telex 121122; Ambassador: H. A. JUSTIN STAPLES.
USA: Itäinen puistotie 14A, Helsinki 14; tel. (90) 171931; telex 121644; Ambassador: ROCKWELL A. SCHNABEL.
Venezuela: Mikonkatu 13A, Helsinki; tel. (90) 177433; Ambassador: GERMÁN DE PÉREZ CASTILLO.
Yugoslavia: Kulosaarentie 36, Helsinki; tel. (90) 688522; telex 122099; Ambassador: IVAN TOŠEVSKI.

Judicial System

The administration of justice is independent of the Government and judges can be removed only by judicial sentence.

SUPREME COURT
Korkein oikeus: Consists of a President and 21 Justices appointed by the President of the Republic. Final court appeal in civil and criminal cases, supervises judges and executive authorities, appoints judges.
President: CURT OLSSON.

SUPREME ADMINISTRATIVE COURT
Korkein hallinto oikeus: Consists of a President and 21 Justices appointed by the President of the Republic. Highest tribunal for appeals in administrative cases.
President: ANTTI SUVIRANTA.

COURTS OF APPEAL
There are Courts of Appeal at Turku, Vaasa, Kuopio, Helsinki, Kouvola, and Rovaniemi, consisting of a President and an appropriate number of members.

DISTRICT AND MUNICIPAL COURTS
Courts of first instance for almost all suits. Appeals lie to the Court of Appeal, and then to the Supreme Court. District Courts consist of a judge and from five to seven jurors. The decision rests with the judge, but the jurors may overrule him if they are unanimous. Municipal Courts are the municipal equivalent of District Courts, consisting of three judges of whom one or two may be lay judges, and presided over by the burgomaster.

CHANCELLOR OF JUSTICE
The Oikeuskansleri is responsible for seeing that authorities and officials comply with the law. He is the chief public prosecutor, and acts as counsel for the Government.
Chancellor of Justice: JORMA S. AALTO.

PARLIAMENTARY SOLICITOR-GENERAL
The Eduskunnan Oikeusasiamies is the Finnish Ombudsman appointed by Parliament to supervise the observance of the law.
Parliamentary Solicitor-General: (vacant).

Religion

CHRISTIANITY
Protestant Churches
Evangelical Lutheran Church of Finland (Suomen evankelisluterilainen kirkko): Office of Foreign Affairs, Satamakatu 11, POB 185, 00160 Helsinki; tel. (90) 18021; telex 122357; over 90% of the population (4,910,712 people) belong; Archbishop Dr JOHN VIKSTRÖM.
Adventists (Suomen Adventtikirkko): Uudenmaantie 50, 20720 Turku; tel. (21) 365100; f. 1894; membership 6,385; Pres. OLAVI ROUHE; Sec. JOEL NIININEN.
Baptists, Finnish-speaking (Suomen Baptistiyhdyskunta): 40800 Vaajakoski; membership 1,787; Pres. Rev. JOUKO NEULANEN.
Baptists, Swedish-speaking (Finlands Svenska Baptistmission): Rådhusgatan 44A, 65100 Vasa; tel. (967) 118559; f. 1856; membership 1,732.
Church of Sweden in Finland: Minervagatan 6, Helsinki; f. 1919; membership 1,779; Rector Dr JARL JERGMAR.
Free Church of Finland (Suomen Vapaakirkko): Sibeliuksenkatu 17, 13100 Hämeenlinna; tel. (917) 65211; f. 1923; membership 12,284; Moderator ERKKI VERKKONEN; Chair. SEPPO KOLEHMAINEN; World Mission Secs RIITTA SIIKANEN, JUHANI KIVELÄ.
Jehovah's Witnesses (Jehovan Todistajat): Kuismatie 58, 01300 Vantaa; membership 16,300.
Methodists (Suomen metodistikirkko): 17310 Vesirehmaa; membership 2,033; Moderator Rev. ANTTI MUSTONEN.

Other Christian Churches
Orthodox Church (Suomen ortodoksinen kirkko): 58,000 mems; tel. (Admin.) (971) 122611; PAAVALI Archbishop of Karelia and all Finland, Karjalankatu 1, 70300 Kuopio; TIIHON Bishop of Joensuu, Kirkkokatu 30A, 80120 Joensuu; JOHANNES Metropolitan of Helsinki, Unioninkatu 39, 00170 Helsinki; LEO Metropolitan of Oulu, Nummikatu 30, 90100 Oulu.
Catholic Church in Finland (Katolinen kirkko Suomessa): Rehbinderintie 21, 00150 Helsinki; tel. (358-0) 637907; membership 3,800; Finland comprises the single diocese of Helsinki, directly responsible to the Holy See; Bishop of Helsinki, PAUL M. VERSCHUREN.

JUDAISM
Jewish Community of Helsinki (Helsingin Juutalainen Seurakunta): Synagogue and Community Centre, Malminkatu 26, 00100 Helsinki; tel. (90) 6941302; membership 1,082; Pres. WOLF DAVIDKIN.

The Press

The 1919 Constitution provided safeguards for press freedom in Finland, and in the same year the Freedom of the Press Act developed and qualified this principle by defining the rights and responsibilities of editors and the circumstances in which the Supreme Court may confiscate or suppress a publication. In practice there are few restrictions. The most notable offences for news-

FINLAND

papermen concern libel and copyright. Two notable features of the press are the public's legal right of access to all official documents (with important exceptions), and since 1966 the right of the journalist to conceal his source of news.

Almost all daily newspapers are independent companies, most of which are owned by large numbers of shareholders. Newspaper chains are virtually unknown, but the Finnish press is a party press. The small number of papers which are generally considered left-orientated are usually owned by the political parties concerned, by trade unions, or by other workers' associations (the Social Democratic Party's chief organ is *Suomen Sosialidemokraatti* and the Finnish Communist Party publishes *Kansan Uutiset*). Most of the right-wing newspapers are owned by private shareholders, and some belong to private endowments. The leading organ of the National Coalition Party is *Aamulehti* in Tampere. The left-wing papers are subject to considerably closer influence from the parties to which they are affiliated than their right-wing counterparts. Privately owned newspapers—including some of the largest such as *Helsingin Sanomat* and *Turun Sanomat*—are usually independent of political parties.

Helsinki is the only large press centre, with a large number of daily papers. Several large dailies are produced in provincial towns, as are a number of weekly and twice-weekly papers. In 1986 there were 97 daily newspapers in Finland with a total circulation of about 3,013,004. Twelve of these dailies are printed in Swedish. A further 148 small local non-daily papers were also registered.

The most popular daily papers are *Helsingin Sanomat, Aamulehti, Turun Sanomat, Ilta-Sanomat, Uusi Suomi, Savon Sanomat* and *Hufvudstadsbladet*. Those most respected for their standard of news coverage and commentary are *Helsingin Sanomat*, an independent paper, and the smaller *Uusi Suomi*.

The total circulation of periodicals amounts to about 23m. copies per issue, of which the business and trade press contribute 11.5m. The largest publishers are Kustannusosakeyhtiö Apulehti, Yhtyneet Kuvalehdet Oy, Lehtimiehet Oy and Sanoma Osakeyhtiö. Consumer co-operatives use their periodicals as information media for both their members and their customers. *Pirkka, YV, Me* and *Yhteishyvä* are among the most important.

There are about 1,100 periodicals, of which some 200 are in the nation's second language, Swedish. Among the leading weekly periodicals are the general interest *Seura, Apu* and the illustrated news magazine *Suomen Kuvalehti*. The publications of the consumer co-operatives enjoy large circulations, as do the chief women's magazines *Anna, Me naiset* and *Kotiliesi*. The more popular serious magazines include the fortnightly *Pellervo* specializing in agricultural affairs, and *Valitut Palat*, the Finnish *Reader's Digest*.

PRINCIPAL DAILIES

Helsinki

Helsingin Sanomat: Ludviginkatu 6-8, POB 240, 00101 Helsinki; tel. (90) 1221; telex 124897; f. 1889; independent; Editors-in-Chief HEIKKI TIKKANEN, SEPPO KIEVARI, SIMOPEKKA NORTAMO, KEIJO K. KULHA; circ. 429,816 weekdays, 511,976 Sunday.

Hufvudstadsbladet: Mannerheimvägen 18, 00100 Helsinki; tel. (90) 12531; telex 124402; f. 1864; Swedish language; independent; Editor Prof. JAN-MAGNUS JANSSON; circ. 66,996 weekdays, 70,200 Sunday.

Iltalehti: POB 139, 00101 Helsinki; tel. (90) 53031; telex 124898; f. 1981; independent; Editor-in-Chief RALF FRIBERG; circ. 77,000 afternoon, 20,000 weekend.

Ilta-Sanomat: POB 375, Korkeavuorenkatu 34, 00101 Helsinki; tel. (90) 1221; telex 124897; f. 1932; afternoon; independent; Editors-in-Chief VESA-PEKKA KOLJONEN, LAURI HELVE; circ. 187,000 weekdays, 216,496 Sunday.

Kansan Uutiset: Niittaajankatu 8, 00810 Helsinki; tel. (90) 75881; telex 12663; f. 1957; organ of the Finnish Communist Party and People's Democratic League of Finland; Editor ERKKI KAUPPILA; circ. 45,731.

Kauppalehti (The Commercial Daily): POB 189, 00100 Helsinki; tel. (90) 53031; telex 125827; f. 1898; morning; Editor-in-Chief ARTO TUOMINEN; circ. 72,392.

Suomen Sosialidemokraatti: Putkitie 3, 00880 Helsinki; tel. (90) 7554211; telex 12433; f. 1918; chief organ of the Social Democratic Party; Editor SEPPO HEIKKI SALONEN; circ. 34,099.

Suomenmaa: Atomitie 5c, 00371 Helsinki; tel. (90) 5625044; f. 1908; Centre; Editor SEPPO SARLUND; circ. 32,802.

Uusi Suomi: POB 139, 00101 Helsinki; tel. (90) 53031; telex 124898; f. 1847; morning; independent; Editors JOHANNES KOROMA, JYRKI VESIKANSA; circ. 92,596 morning, 96,686 Sunday.

Hämeenlinna

Hämeen Sanomat: Vanajantie 7, 13200 Hämeenlinna; tel. 23011; f. 1879; independent; Man. AIMO VIHERVUORI; Editor-in-Chief ALLAN LIUHALA; circ. 30,382.

Hyrylä

Keski-Uusimaa: Klaavolantie 5, 04300 Hyrylä; tel. (90) 255255; independent; circ. 22,238.

Iisalmi

Iisalmen Sanomat: POB 11, 74100 Iisalmi; tel. (977) 24511; telex 4416; Centre; circ. 18,766.

Joensuu

Karjalainen: POB 99, Torikatu 33, 80101 Joensuu; tel. (973) 21321; telex 46126; f. 1874; National Coalition; Editor SEPPO VENTO; circ. 53,364.

Jyväskylä

Keskisuomalainen: POB 159, Aholaidantie 3, 40101 Jyväskylä; tel. (0941) 201211; telex 28211; f. 1871; Centre; Editor ERKKI LAATIKAINEN; circ. 76,283.

Kajaani

Kainuun Sanomat: POB 150, Viestitie 2, 87700 Kajaani; tel. (986) 1661; telex 33172; f. 1918; Centre; Editor OTSO KUKKONEN; circ. 30,000.

Kemi

Pohjolan Sanomat: Sairaalakatu 2, 94100 Kemi; tel. (80) 2911; telex 3643; f. 1915; Centre; Editors MATTI LAMMI, REIJO ALATÖRMÄNEN; circ. 39,149.

Kokkola

Keskipohjanmaa: Kosila POB 45, 67101 Kokkola; tel. (968) 14322; telex 76118; f. 1917; Centre; Editor PENTTI PULAKKA; circ. 32,746.

Kouvola

Kouvolan Sanomat: POB 40, Tommolankatu 2, 45101 Kouvola; tel. (951) 16911; telex 52210; f. 1909; Editor MARTTI JOUTSEN; circ. 32,496.

Kuopio

Savon Sanomat: POB 68, Vuorikatu 21, 70101 Kuopio; tel. 121000; telex 42111; f. 1907; Centre; Editor MAURI AUVINEN; Dir RISTO SUHONEN; circ. 84,712.

Lahti

Etelä-Suomen Sanomat: POB 80, Ilmarisentie 7, 15101 Lahti; tel. (918) 42811; telex 16132; f. 1900; independent; Dir JAAKKO UKKONEN; Editor-in-Chief KAUKO MÄENPÄÄ; circ. 64,237.

Lappeenranta

Etelä-Saimaa: POB 3, 53100 Lappeenranta; tel. 15600; telex 58217; f. 1885; Centre; Man. Dir RAIMO TUKIA; Editor LAURI SARHIMAA; circ. 32,915.

Mikkeli

Länsi-Savo: POB 6, 50101 Mikkeli; tel. (955) 10555; telex 55154; circ. 27,296.

Oulu

Kaleva: POB 70, 90101 Oulu; tel. (981) 326111; telex 32112; f. 1899; Liberal independent; Editor TEUVO MÄLLINEN; circ. 88,177.

Kansan Tahto: POB 61, 90101 Oulu; tel. (981) 221722; f. 1906; organ of the People's Democratic League; 5 a week; circ. 16,936.

Pori

Satakunnan Kansa: POB 58, 28101 Pori; tel. (939) 328111; telex 66102; f. 1873; National Coalition; Editor ERKKI TEIKARI; circ. 60,807.

Rauma

Länsi-Suomi: Kaivopuistontie 1, 26100 Rauma; tel. 3361; telex 65160; National Coalition Party; circ. 19,453.

Rovaniemi

Lapin Kansa: Veitikantie 6-8, 96100 Rovaniemi; tel. 2911; telex 37213; f. 1928; independent; Editor JUHANI NURMELA; circ. 39,942.

Salo

Salon Seudun Sanomat: POB 117, Örninkatu 14, 24101 Salo; tel. (924) 11661; circ. 20,637.

FINLAND
Savonlinna
Itä-Savo: POB 35, 57101 Savonlinna; tel. (957) 29171; telex 5611; Centre; circ. 22,242.

Seinäjoki
Ilkka: POB 60, Kouluk, 60101 Seinäjoki; tel. (964) 141100; telex 72130; f. 1906; organ of Centre Party; Editor KARI HOKKANEN; circ. 53,465.

Tammisaari
Västra Nyland: Genvägen 4, 10600 Ekenäs; tel. (911) 62800; telex 13150; f. 1881; Swedish; independent; Editor KARL OLOF SPRING; circ. 12,200.

Tampere
Aamulehti: Patamäenkatu 7, Tampere; tel. (931) 666111; telex 22111; f. 1881; National Coalition; Editors Prof. PERTTI PESONEN, EERO SYVÄNEN, RAIMO SEPPÄLÄ; circ. 140,918 weekdays, 146,687 Sunday.

Kansan Lehti: Sarvijaakonkatu 16, 33540 Tampere; tel. (931) 616440; telex 22257; f. 1899; Social Democratic; Editor PAAVO LUOKKALA; circ. 11,000.

Turku-Åbo
Åbo Underrättelser (Åbo News): Slottsgatan 10, 20101 Turku-Åbo; tel. (921) 333886; telex 962368; f. 1824; morning; Independent; Editor Bo STENSTRÖM; circ. 8,016.

Turun Päivälehti: Nuppulantie 21, 20310 Turku; tel. (921) 392111; telex 62129; f. 1898; morning; Social Democratic; Editor AIMO MASSINEN; circ. 10,325.

Turun Sanomat: Kauppiaskatu 5, 20100 Turku; tel. (921) 693311; telex 62213; f. 1904; independent; Man. Dir KEIJO KETONEN; Editor JARMO VIRMAVIRTA; circ. 131,630 weekdays, 140,312 Sunday.

Vaasa
Pohjalainen: POB 37, Pitkäkatu 37, 65101 Vaasa; tel. (961) 111411; telex 74212; f. 1903; National Coalition; Editor ERKKI MALMIVAARA; circ. 64,007.

Vasabladet: POB 52, Sandögatan 6, Vaasa 10; tel. (961) 121866; telex 74269; f. 1856; Liberal independent; Editor BIRGER THÖLIX; circ. 27,407.

POPULAR PERIODICALS

Aku Ankka (Donald Duck): POB 113, 00381 Helsinki; tel. (90) 1201; telex 125848; f. 1951; weekly; children's; Editor KIRSTI TOPPARI; circ. 281,251.

Anna: Hietalahdenranta 13, 00180 Helsinki; tel. (90) 18211; telex 121364; f. 1963; weekly; women's; Editor-in-Chief SONJA TANTTU; circ. 176,835.

Apu: Hitsaajankatu 7, 00810 Helsinki; tel. (90) 782311; telex 124698; f. 1933; weekly; family journal; Editor-in-Chief VELI-ANTTI SAVOLAINEN; circ. 300,832.

Avotakka: Hitsaajankatu 10, 00810 Helsinki; tel. (90) 782311; telex 124732; f. 1967; monthly; house and garden; Editor-in-Chief LEENA NOKELA; circ. 80,137.

Eeva: Hitsaajankatu 10, 00810 Helsinki; tel. (90) 782311; telex 124732; f. 1933; monthly; women's; Editor-in-Chief ULLA LESKINEN; circ. 115,000.

Emäntälehti: Uudenmaankatu 24A, 00120 Helsinki; tel. (90) 646211; f. 1902; monthly; women's; Editor MAIJA RIIHIJÄRVI-SAMUEL; circ. 26,721.

Et-lehti: POB 113, 00381 Helsinki; tel. (90) 1201; telex 125848; pensioners' magazine; Editor MARJUKKA LUOMALA; circ. 95,688.

Hymy: Puutarhakatu 16, 33210 Tampere; tel. (90) 6943311; telex 122730; monthly; family journal; Editor-in-Chief RAIMO VESA; circ. 130,213.

Kaks plus: Puutarhakatu 16, 33210 Tampere; telex 122730; home and children; Editor-in-Chief ANTTI NURMINEN; circ. 52,860.

Katso: Hitsaajankatu 7, 00810 Helsinki; weekly; tel. (90) 872311; telex 124732; TV, radio and video; Editor-in-Chief REIJO TELARANTA; circ. 65,608.

Kodin Kuvalehti: POB 113, 00318 Helsinki; tel. (90) 1201; telex 125848; fortnightly; family magazine; Editor EIJA AILASMAA; circ. 180,020.

Kotiliesi: Hietalahdenranta 13, 00180 Helsinki; tel. (90) 18211; telex 121364; f. 1922; fortnightly; home journal; Editor-in-Chief LEENA HÄYRINEN; circ. 212,653.

Koululainen: Hietalahdenranta 13, 00180 Helsinki; tel. (90) 18211; telex 121364; 17 a year; for pupils of comprehensive schools; circ. 64,000.

Makasiini: Hitsaajankatu 7, 00810 Helsinki; tel. (90) 782311; f. 1978; monthly; home; Editor-in-Chief KITI ANDREJEW; circ. 82,782.

Me naiset: POB 113, 00381 Helsinki; tel. (90) 1201; telex 125848; f. 1952; weekly; women's; Editor ULLA-MAIJA PAAVILAINEN; circ. 130,065.

Nykyposti: Puutarhakatu 16, 33210 Tampere; tel. (90) 6943311; telex 122730; f. 1977; monthly; family journal; Editor-in-Chief LASSE ASKOLIN; circ. 226,070.

Seura: Hietalahdenranta 13, 00180 Helsinki; tel. (90) 18211; telex 121364; f. 1934; family journal; Editors-in-Chief HANNU PARPOLA, HEIKKI PARKKONEN; circ. 323,969.

Suomen Kuvalehti: Hietalahdenranta 13, 00180 Helsinki; tel. (90) 18211; telex 121364; f. 1916; weekly; illustrated news; Editors-in-Chief MIKKO POHTOLA, PEKKA HYVÄRINEN; circ. 125,000.

Suosikki: Eerikinkatu 3B, 00100 Helsinki; tel. (90) 6943311; telex 122730; monthly; youth, music; Editor-in-Chief JYRKI HÄMÄLÄINEN; circ. 120,101.

Teknikan Maailma: Eerinkatu 3B, 00100 Helsinki; tel. (90) 6943311; telex 122730; 20 a year; popular technical review; circ. 121,777.

Urkki: Helsinki; tel. (90) 627149; monthly; men's; circ. 72,559.

Valitut Palat: Halsuantie 4, 00420 Helsinki; tel. (90) 5632011; telex 122489; monthly; Finnish Reader's Digest; Editor-in-Chief ERKKI HAGLUND; circ. 330,000.

SPECIALIST PERIODICALS

Aja: Sturenkatu 27, 00550 Helsinki; tel. (90) 73101; quarterly; motoring; Editor MATTI VAKKILAINEN; circ. 100,000.

Arkkitehti: Eteläesplanadi 22A, 00130 Helsinki; tel. (90) 640801; 8 a year; architectural; Editor-in-Chief MARJA-RIITTA NORRI; circ. 5,000.

Bank of Finland Monthly Bulletin: POB 160, 00101 Helsinki; tel. (90) 1832629; telex 121224; f. 1921; monthly; in English; economics; Editor-in-Chief ANTERO ARIMO.

Duodecim: Kalevankatu 11A, 00100 Helsinki; tel. (90) 611050; f. 1885; 2 a month; medical; Editor Dr KARI RAIVIO; circ. 15,000.

Eevaneule: Hitsaajankatu 7, 00810 Helsinki; tel. (90) 782311; telex 124698; knitting fashion; Editor-in-Chief SEIJA MÄKI; circ. 42,157.

Eläinmaailma: POB 113, 00381 Helsinki; tel. (90) 1201; telex 125848; f. 1979; monthly; animals and nature; Editor JYRKI LESKINEN; circ. 43,395.

Energia: POB 161, 00161 Helsinki; tel. (90) 626235; telex 122751; 10 a year; energy in Finland; Editor PENTTI AVOMAA; circ. 5,000.

Erä: Eerinkatu 3B, 00100 Helsinki; tel. (90) 6943311; telex 122730; monthly; outdoor life; Editor SEPPO SUURONEN; circ. 27,064.

Finnfacts: Yrjönkatu 13, 00120 Helsinki; tel. (90) 642980; telex 121640; 8 a year; economic and industrial information; in English, French, German, Japanese, Spanish, Swedish.

Finnish Trade Review: POB 908, 00101 Helsinki; tel. (90) 69591; telex 121696; f. 1930; 8 a year; in English; publ. by the Finnish Foreign Trade Asscn; Editor ELINA JOENSUU-MAMADOU; circ. 25,000.

Forum för ekonomi och teknik: Mannerheimv. 18, 00100 Helsinki; tel. (90) 643445; f. 1968; fortnightly; industry and trade; Editor-in-Chief RAGNHILD ARTIMO; circ. 12,800.

Idea: Ratavartijankatu 2, 00520 Helsinki; tel. (90) 15901; telex 123629; 32 a year; electronics; circ. 12,427.

Ilmailu: Malmin Lentoasema, 00700 Helsinki; f. 1938; monthly; aviation; Editor ARJA VARTIA; circ. 9,500–10,000.

Kameralehti: Eerikinkatu 7C 8, 00100 Helsinki; tel. (90) 6944051; f. 1950; 11 a year; photographic; Editor PEKKA PUNKARI; circ. 15,514.

Kanava: Hietalahdenranta 13, 00180 Helsinki; tel. (90) 18211; telex 121364; f. 1933; 9 a year; journal for Finnish culture and policy; Editor SEIKKO ESKOLA; circ. 6,901.

Karjatalous: POB 69, 00371 Helsinki; tel. (90) 5681; telex 123427; monthly; dairy farming; Editor-in-Chief KALEVI JÄNTTI; circ. 72,030.

Kauneus ja Terveys: Hitsaajankatu 10, 00810 Helsinki; tel. (90) 782311; telex 124698; monthly; women's; beauty and health; Editor-in-Chief KRISTIINA DRAGON; circ. 75,332.

Kauppa ja Koti: Kalevankatu 6, 00100 Helsinki; tel. (90) 6191; telex 121722; free to customers of retail stores; Editor-in-Chief TAPANI LEHMUSVAARA; circ. 387,245.

Kauppakamarilehti: POB 139, 00101 Helsinki; tel. (90) 53031; telex 124898; f. 1920; monthly; trade and industry; publ. by the

FINLAND

Central Chamber of Commerce in co-operation with Uusi Suomi Oy; Chief Editor MARKKU KOSOLA; circ. 16,043.

Kirjastolehti: Museokatu 18A 5, 00100 Helsinki; tel. (90) 441984; monthly; libraries, booksellers, publishers, teachers; f. 1908; Chief Editor HANNELE KOIVUNEN ; circ. 7,500.

Koiramme- Våra Hundar: Bulevardi 14A, 00120 Helsinki; tel. (90) 643101; monthly; dogs; circ. 47,731.

Koneviesti: Revontulentie 8B, 02100 Espoo; tel. 43731; bi-monthly; farming and forestry; Editor RISTO KNAAPI; circ. 50,321.

Kotilääkäri: Hietalahdenranta 13, 00180 Helsinki; tel. (90) 18211; telex 122772; f. 1889; monthly; home nursing; Editor-in-Chief IRMA HEYDEMANN; circ. 54,479.

Kuuloviesti: Mäkipellontie 15, 00320 Helsinki; tel. (90) 578244; monthly; magazine for the deaf and hard of hearing; Editor RAIJA ARHO; circ. 13,000.

Lakimiesuutiset-Juristnytt: Uudenmaankatu 4-6A 5, 00120 Helsinki; tel. (90) 649201; monthly; law; Editor LIISA GRÖNROOS; circ. 10,160.

Liiketaloudellinen aikakauskirja (Journal of Business Economics): Runeberginkatu 14-16, Helsinki; quarterly; summaries in English.

Look at Finland: POB 53, 00521 Helsinki; tel. (90) 144511; quarterly; tourist information, travel and general articles; publ. by Finnish Tourist Board and Ministry for Foreign Affairs; Editor-in-Chief BENGT PIHLSTRÖM; circ. 40,000.

MARK markkinoinnin ammattilehti: Fabianinkatu 4B 10, 00130 Helsinki; tel. (90) 651500; f. 1979; 10 a year; advertising and marketing; Editor-in-Chief MARJA-LIISA KINTURI; circ. 7,657.

Meidän Talo: Hitsaajankatu 7, 00810 Helsinki; tel. (90) 782311; telex 124698; f. 1978; monthly; home, garden and building; Editor-in-Chief JUHA TOLVANEN; circ. 56,845.

Merkonomi: Yrjönkatu 12-14B, 00120 Helsinki; tel. (90) 602533; 8 a year; commercial; Editor-in-Chief ILKKA PELTTARI; circ. 20,900.

Metsälehti (Forestry News): Maistraatinportii 4A, 00240 Helsinki; tel. (90) 1562333; f. 1933; fortnightly; Editor PAAVO SEPPÄNEN; circ. 91,339.

Metsästäjä: Frederinkatu 47, 00100 Helsinki; tel. (90) 640514; bi-monthly organ of the Jagarnas Centralorganisation (hunting); Editor MATTI VALTONEN; circ. 280,000.

Navigator: POB 161, 00161 Helsinki; tel. (90) 626235; 14 a year; shipping, shipbuilding, ports; Editor ANTTI KYYNÄRÄINEN; circ. 5,000.

Paperi ja Puu-Papper och Trä (Paper and Timber): POB 176, 00141 Helsinki; tel. (90) 664166; f. 1919; monthly; several languages, mainly Finnish and English; sawn goods, wood panel, pulp and paper technology; Editor-in-Chief ANNELI HATTARI; circ. 3,600.

Parnasso: Yhtyneet Kuvalehdet Oy, Hietalahdenranta 13, 00180 Helsinki; tel. (90) 18211; telex 12364; f. 1951; 8 a year; non-political, literary; Editor-in-Chief JUHANI SALOKANNEL; circ. 6,412.

Rakennuslehti: Mannerheimintie 40, Helsinki 10; tel. (90) 499455; weekly; building and construction; Editor HEIKKI RANSSI; circ. 29,854.

Science 2000 (Tiede 2000): POB 113, 00381, Helsinki; tel. (90) 1201; f. 1980; 10 a year; popular science; Editor JALI RUUSKANEN; circ. 30,000.

Sosiaalinen Aikakauskirja: POB 267, 00170 Helsinki; tel. (90) 1605411; telex 125073; 6 a year; social policy; summaries in English; Editor KARI PURO.

Sosiologia: c/o University of Helsinki, Dept of Sociology, Helsinginkatu 34C, 00530 Helsinki; tel. (90) 765911; f. 1963; quarterly journal of the Westermarck Society (Finnish Sociological Asscn) circ. 2,000.

Suomen Kunnat: Albertinkatu 34, 00180 Helsinki; tel. (90) 6948800; f. 1921; fortnightly; municipal review; Editor-in-Chief MIKKO JOKELA; circ. 20,000.

Suomen Lääkärilehti (Finnish Medical Journal): Ruoholahdenkatu 4, 00180 Helsinki; tel. (90) 6944022; telex 125336; 36 a year; medical journal published by the Finnish Medical Asscn; Editor ILKKA VARTIOVAARA; circ. 17,500.

Suomen Lehdistö (Finland's Press): Kalevankatu 4, 00100 Helsinki; tel. (90) 607786; telex 123990; 10 a year; organ of the Finnish Newspaper Publishers' Asscn; Editor OLAVI RANTALAINEN; circ. 4,120.

Suuri Käsityökerho: POB 113, 00381 Helsinki; tel. (90) 1201; telex 125848; f. 1974; monthly; needlework and clothing magazine; Editor PIA SALO; circ. 102,036.

Talouselämä: P. Roobertinkatu 13B, 00130 Helsinki; tel. (90) 643411; f. 1938; business weekly; Editor-in-Chief RAUNO LARSIO; circ. 45,900.

Tekniikan Maailma: Eerikinkatu 3B, 00100 Helsinki; tel. (90) 6943311; bi-monthly; engineering, cars; Editor-in-Chief RAUNO TOIVONEN; circ. 124,092.

Tekniset: POB 146, 00131 Helenski; tel. (90) 658611; telex 122728; 16 a year; industrial technology; Editor LAURI TUOMINEN; circ. 70,000.

Tuulilasi: Hitsaajankatu 7, 00810 Helsinki; monthly; independent; Editor-in-Chief ERKKI RAUKKO; circ. 84,826.

Unitas: Aleksanterinkatu 30, Helsinki; tel. (90) 1651; telex 124407; f. 1929; quarterly economic review in English, German, Swedish and Finnish; Editor KALEVI KOSONEN; circ. 29,000.

Vene: Eerinkatu 3B, 00100 Helsinki; tel. (90) 6943311; telex 122730; monthly; sailing; Editor-in-Chief MATTI MURTO; circ. 35,954.

Yritys Tietoisku: Pakilantie 78, 00660 Helsinki; tel. (90) 743055; monthly; politics and current affairs; circ. 56,000.

CO-OPERATIVE JOURNALS

E: POB 740, 00101 Helsinki; tel. (90) 7331; bi-monthly; management of co-operative societies; Editor HILKKA KEMPPINEN; circ. 7,631.

Elanto, Elanto-Tidningen: Hämeentie 11, 00530 Helsinki; tel. (90) 7341; monthly magazine of Elanto Co-operative Society.

Kymppi: Pohjoisesplanadi 35A, 00100 Helsinki; tel. (90) 18271; telex 125768; f. 1954; 8 a year; publ. by Finnish Savings Banks Asscn, free to customers; Editor-in-Chief V.-M. HEPOLUHTA; circ. 182,000.

Lantmän och Andelsfolk: Nylandsgatan 34A, 00120 Helsinki; tel. (90) 653009; monthly; co-operative farming; Editor RAINER MATTSSON; circ. 9,500.

Me: Hameentie 19A, 00500 Helsinki; tel. (90) 7331; telex 124454; fortnightly; organ of Finnish consumers' societies; Editor-in-Chief HILKKA KEMPPINEN; circ. 361,699.

Pellervo: Simonkatu 6, 00100 Helsinki; tel. (90) 6955203; f. 1899; fortnightly; agricultural and co-operative journal; organ of the Central Union of Agricultural Co-operative Societies; Editor-in-Chief MARTTI SEPPÄNEN; circ. 92,488.

Pirkka: Rauhankatu 15, 00170 Helsinki; tel. (90) 175566; monthly; Swedish; free to customers of retail stores; Editor-in-Chief OSMO LAMPINEN; circ. 1,477,734.

Samarbete: Vilhelmsgatan 7, 00100 Helsinki; tel. (90) 1881; telex 124456; f. 1909; monthly; circ. 40,364.

Yhteishyvä: Vilhonkatu 7, 00100 Helsinki; tel. (90) 1881; telex 124456; f. 1905; 18 a year; free to customers of co-operative shops; Editor-in-Chief PENTTI TÖRMÄLÄ; circ. 488,833.

YV: Arkadiankatu 23, 00100 Helsinki; tel. (90) 4041; free to customers of co-operative banks; Editor-in-Chief MATTI PAAVONSALO; circ. 514,585.

NEWS AGENCIES

Oy Suomen Tietotoimisto-Finska Notisbyrån Ab (STT-FNB): Yrjönkatu 22C, 00100 Helsinki; tel. (90) 646224; telex 124534; f. 1887; six provincial branches; independent national agency distributing domestic and international news in Finnish and Swedish; Pres. ERKKI TEIKARI; Gen. Man. and Editor-in-Chief PER-ERIK LÖNNFORS.

Foreign Bureaux

Agence France-Presse (AFP) (France): c/o Suomen Tietotoimisto-Finska Notisbyran (STT-FNB), Yrjönkatu 22, 00100 Helsinki.

Agencia EFE (Spain): Mariankatu 7B 8, 00170 Helsinki; Correspondent HANNU VUORI.

Agenzia Nazionale Stampa Associata (ANSA) (Italy): Iso Roobertinkatu 46 B 31, 00120 Helsinki; tel. (90) 639799; Agent MATTI BROTHERUS.

Allgemeiner Deutscher Nachrichtendienst (ADN) (German Democratic Republic): Aarholmankuja 4C 27, 00840 Helsinki; Correspondent BRUNO STORM.

Associated Press (AP) (USA): Yrjönkatu 27A, 2nd floor, 00100 Helsinki 10; tel. (90) 646883; Correspondent RISTO MÄNPÄÄ.

Inter Press Service (IPS) (Italy): c/o Ylioppilaslenti, Mannerheimintie 5c, 5th floor, 01000 Helsinki 10; tel. 176616; Editor ANTTI ANTIO.

Reuters (UK): c/o Suomen Tietotoimisto-Finska Notisbyrån (STT-FNB), POB 550 Helsinki 10.

FINLAND

Telegrafnoye Agentstvo Sovetskovo Soyuza (TASS) (USSR): Ratakatu 1A 10, Helsinki 12; Correspondent ALEXANDER GORBUNOV.

United Press International (UPI) (USA): Ludviginkatu 3-5, 00130 Helsinki; tel. (90) 605701; telex 124403; Bureau Man. SIRKA LIISA KANKURI.

Xinhua (New China) News Agency (People's Republic of China): Hopeasalmentie 14, 00570 Helsinki; tel. (90) 687587; telex 122552; Correspondent ZHENG HUANGING.

PRESS ASSOCIATIONS

Aikakauslehtien Liitto (Periodical Publishers' Association): Lönnrotinkatu 33A 1, 00180 Helsinki; tel. (90) 603311; f. 1946; protects the interests of periodical publishers and liaises with the authorities, postal services and advertisers; organizes training courses to improve the quality of periodicals; Man. Dir OLLI KINNUNEN.

Suomen Sanomalehtimiesten Liitto (Union of Journalists): Yrjönkatu 11A, 00120 Helsinki; f. 1921; Pres. ANTERO LAINE; Sec.-Gen. EILA HYPPÖNEN; 7,200 mems.

Sanomalehtien Liitto—Tidningarnas Förbund (Newspaper Publishers' Association): Kalevankatu 4, 00100 Helsinki; tel. (90) 607786; telex 123990; f. 1908; negotiates newsprint prices, postal rates; represents the press in relations with government and advertisers; undertakes technical research; Man. Dir VEIKKO LÖYTTYNIEMI; 107 mems.

Publishers

Gummerus Publishers: POB 479, 00101 Helsinki; tel. (90) 644301; telex 123727; f. 1872; fiction, non-fiction, juvenile and reference books; Pub. Dir RISTO LEHMUSOKSA.

Holger Schildts Förlagsaktiebolag: Anneg. 16, 00120 Helsinki; tel. (90) 604892; f. 1913; all subjects in Swedish only; Man. Dir J. AF HÄLLSTRÖM.

Karisto Oy: Paroistentie 2, POB 102, 13101 Hämeenlinna; tel. (917) 161551; telex 2348; f. 1900; non-fiction and fiction; Man. Dir SIMO MOISIO.

Kirjayhtymä Oy: Eerikinkatu 28, 00180 Helsinki; tel. (90) 6944522; f. 1958; fiction, non-fiction, textbooks; Man. Dir P. NURMIO; Publishing Dir K. IMMONEN.

Kustannusosakeyhtiö Kansanvalta: Putkitie 3, 00880 Helsinki; tel. (90) 7554211; telex 124433; f. 1918; Labour publishing company; publishes newspaper *Suomen Sosialidemokraatti*; Dir KIMMO JOKELA.

Kustannusosakeyhtiö Otava: Uudenmaankatu 10, 00120 Helsinki; tel. (90) 647022 (19961 from 1 May 1987); telex 124560; f. 1890; non-fiction, fiction, science, juvenile, textbooks and encyclopaedias; Chair. HEIKKI A. REENPÄÄ; Man. Dir OLLI REENPÄÄ.

Kustannusosakeyhtiö Tammi: Eerikinkatu 28, 00180 Helsinki; tel. (90) 6942700; telex 125482; f. 1943; fiction, non-fiction, juvenile; Man. Dir OLLI ARRAKOSKI.

Sanoma Corporation: POB 240, 00101 Helsinki 10; tel. (90) 1221; telex 122772; f. 1889; publishes daily newspapers *Helsingin Sanomat* and *Ilta-Sanomat*; also magazines and books, cable television and electronic publishing; Chair. AATOS ERKKO; Man. Dir JAAKKO RAURAMO.

Söderström & Co. Förlags Ab: Murbacksgatan 6, Helsinki 21; tel. (90) 6923681; f. 1891; all subjects in Swedish only; Man. Dir CARL APPELBERG.

Weilin+Göös: Ahertajantie 5, 02100 Espoo; tel. 43771; telex 122597; f. 1872; fiction, non-fiction, reference books, juvenile, textbooks, software; Man. Dir JUHA VUORI-KARVIA.

Werner Söderström Osakeyhtiö: Bulevardi 12, 00120 Helsinki; tel. (90) 61681; telex 122644; f. 1878; fiction and non-fiction, science, juvenile, textbooks, movies, graphic industry; Man. Dir H. TARMIO.

Government Printing Centre

Valtion Painatuskeskus: Hakuninmaantie 2, POB 516, 00101 Helsinki; tel. (90) 56601; telex 123458; f. 1859; non-fiction, textbooks and state publications; Man. Dir OLAVI PERILÄ.

PUBLISHERS' ASSOCIATION

Suomen Kustannusyhdistys: Merimiehenkatu 12A 6, 00150 Helsinki; tel. (90) 179185; f. 1858; Chair. HANNU TARMIO; Sec. UNTO LAPPI; 53 mems.

Radio and Television

In 1984 there were an estimated 2,515,000 radio receivers in use. In the same year, there were 1,738,432 television licences. Some 100,000 homes are linked to cable television in Finland.

Office of the Director-General of Posts and Telecommunications: POB 1001, 00101 Helsinki; tel. (90) 1954004; telex 122695; Dir-Gen. P. TARJANNE.

Oy Yleisradio Ab (YLE) (Finnish Broadcasting Company): Kesäkatu 2, 00260 Helsinki; f. 1926, state controlled since 1934, with management appointed according to the political character of Parliament; Dir-Gen. SAKARI KIURU; Dir of Radio and Deputy Dir-Gen. JOUNI MYKKÄNEN; Dir of TV Programme 1 ARNE WESSBERG; Dir of TV Programme 2 TAPIO SIIKALA; Dir of Swedish Radio and TV BENGT BERGMAN; Dir of Regional Programming OLAVI PELTOLA; Dir of Finance and Admin. AIMO HAAPANEN; Dir of Engineering ERKKI LARKKA.

RADIO

Oy Yleisradio Ab (YLE) (Finnish Broadcasting Company): POB 10, 00241 Helsinki; tel. (90) 418811; telex 124735; Finnish main programme: both light and serious programmes; Finnish second programme: mainly musical and educational; Swedish programme: Swedish language and music; also regional stations, belonging to a local radio union; Foreign Service: broadcasts to Europe, Africa, the Middle and Far East and America in Finnish, Swedish, German and English.

Experimental Finnish local radio began operations in 1984, and 23 such licences were granted in 1985.

TELEVISION

The state operates two television channels, and broadcasting time is leased from them by commercial companies. A co-operation project between Yleisradio and the Nokia electronics company for a third television channel was approved by the Government in 1986. Transmissions began in September 1986.

TV Programme 1: about 45 hours per week (commercial programmes included).

TV Programme 2: about 40 hours per week (commercial programmes included).

In 1986 the television companies of Finland, Sweden and Denmark began an exchange of teletext news pages in a new service designed to speed up news reports between Nordic countries. There were an estimated 135,000 teletext sets in Finland in 1986.

Oy Yleisradio Ab (YLE) (Finnish Broadcasting Company): Programme 1: POB 10, 00241 Helsinki; tel. (90) 418811; telex 121270; Programme 2: Tohlopinranta 12, 33270 Tampere; tel. 445445; telex 22176.

MTV Oy: Ilmalantori 2, 00240 Helsinki; tel. (90) 15001; telex 125144; f. 1957; independent commercial TV company producing programmes on both channels; about 20 hours per week; Pres. EERO PILKAMA; Exec. Vice-Pres. JAAKKO PAAVELA; Vice-Pres. of Programming TAUNO AIJÄLÄ.

Finance

The Bank of Finland is the country's central bank and the centre of Finland's monetary and banking system. It functions 'under guarantee and supervision of Parliament and the Bank supervisors delegated by Parliament'.

There are four deposit bank groups in Finland: commercial banks, savings banks, co-operative banks and the state-owned Postipankki. The total number of branches in 1985 was more than 3,500.

The commercial banks constitute the most important group of deposit banks. At the end of 1985 there were 10 commercial banks, with a total of 967 offices. Two of these banks are national, and three are foreign-owned. The Bank of Helsinki merged with the Union Bank of Finland in November 1986.

The savings banks and co-operative banks are regional, providing mainly local banking services. At 31 December 1985 there were 254 savings banks, with 1,062 branch offices, and 370 co-operative banks, with 854 branch offices. Postipankki has 47 branch offices. In addition, 3,211 post offices handle certain Postipankki operations.

There are six mortgage banks operating in Finland, and several special credit institutions. The insurance institutions, of which 56 are private companies, granted credits in 1985. Finance companies, development companies and other special institutions have also joined the money-market.

FINLAND

BANKING

(cap. = capital; dep. = deposits; m. = million; res = reserves; brs = branches; amounts in markkaa)

Central Bank

Suomen Pankki—Finlands Bank (The Bank of Finland): POB 160, Snellmaninaukio, 00170 Helsinki; tel. (90) 1831; telex 121224; f. 1811; Bank of Issue under the guarantee and supervision of Parliament; cap. and res 7,187m. (Aug. 1986); Gov. ROLF KULLBERG; 12 brs.

Commercial and Mortgage Banks

Ålandsbanken Ab (Bank of Åland Ltd): Nygatan 2, 22100 Mariehamn; tel. (928) 29011; telex 63119; f. 1919; cap. and res 127m., dep. 876m. (Aug. 1986); 20 brs; Chair. FOLKE WOIVALIN; Chief Gen. Man. FOLKE HUSELL.

Kansallisluottopankki Oy (Kansallis Mortgage Bank Ltd): Aleksanterinkatu 42, POB 10, 00101 Helsinki; tel. (90) 1631; telex 124702; f. 1985; cap. and res 100m.; Chair. JAAKKO LASSILA; Man. Dir EERO HERTTOLA.

Kansallis-Osake-Pankki: POB 10, Aleksanterinkatu 42, 00101 Helsinki; tel. (90) 1631; telex 124702; f. 1889; cap. and res 4,832m., dep. 35,509m. (Aug. 1986); Chair. AATOS ERKKO; Chief Gen. Man. JAAKKO LASSILA; 463 brs.

Mortgage Bank of Finland Ltd: Eteläesplandi 8, 00130 Helsinki; tel. (90) 650066; telex 121840; f. 1956; cap. 215m. (Dec. 1985); Chair. ROLF KULLBERG; Man. Dir ILPO NIITTI.

Okobank (Osuuspankkien Keskuspankki Oy) (Central Bank of the Co-operative Banks of Finland Ltd): Arkadiankatu 23, 00101 Helsinki; tel. (90) 4041; telex 124714; f. 1902; cap. and res 1,480m., dep. 1,751m. (Aug. 1985); Chair. of Board of Admin. ESA TIMONEN; Chair. Board of Management PAULI KOMI; 1,224 brs.

Postipankki: Unioninkatu 20, 00007 Helsinki; tel. (90) 1641; telex 121698; f. 1886; operates through its head office, 47 branches and the 3,211 local post offices; assets 39,804m., dep. 32,409m. (Dec. 1985); Chair. ROLF KULLBERG; Chief Gen. Man. HEIKKI TUOMINEN.

PSP-Kuntapankki Oy (PSP Municipality Bank Ltd): Unionkatu 20, 00007 Helsinki; tel. (90) 1641; telex 121428; cap. and res 21m.; Chair. HEIKKI TUOMINEN; Man. Dir REIJO MARJANEN.

Skopbank (Säästöpankkien Keskus-Osake-Pankki) (Central Bank of the Finnish Savings Banks): Mikonkatu 4, 00100 Helsinki; tel. (90)17251; telex 122284; f. 1908; cap. and res 1,297m., dep. 2,489m. (Aug. 1986); Chair. of Board and Chief Exec. MATTI ALI-MELKKILÄ.

Suomen Hypoteekkiyhdistys (Mortgage Society of Finland): POB 509, Yrjönkatu 9, Helsinki 12; tel. (90) 647401; telex 123646; f. 1860; cap. and res 65m. (Dec. 1985); Pres. OSMO KALLIALA.

Suomen Kiinteistöpankki Oy—Fastighetsbanken i Finland Ab (Finnish Real Estate Bank Ltd): Mikonkatu 4, POB 428, 00100 Helsinki; tel. (90) 17251; telex 122284; f. 1907; cap. 40m., res 10.1m. (June 1986); Pres. PAAVO PEKKANEN; Man. Dir TOIVO IHO.

Suomen Teollisuuspankki Oy, Industribanken i Finland Ab (Industrial Bank of Finland Ltd): Fabianinkatu 8, 00130 Helsinki; tel. (90) 177521; telex 121839; f. 1924; cap. and res 575m. (Dec. 1985); Chair. MIKA TIIVOLA; Man. Dir ARTO VALIO.

Union Bank of Finland Ltd (Suomen Yhdyspankki Oy/Föreningsbanken i Finland Ab): Aleksanterinkatu 30, POB 868, 00101 Helsinki; tel. (90) 1651; telex 124407; f. 1862; cap. and res 4,949m., dep. 28,018m. (Aug. 1986); Chair. Board of Man. and Chief Exec. MIKA TIIVOLA; 647 brs and service-points.

Banking Associations

Osuuspankkien Keskusliitto r.y. (Central Union of the Co-operative Banks): Arkadiankatu 23, 00100 Helsinki; tel. (90) 4041; f. 1928; in 1985 there were 370 co-operative banks (1,224 offices) with a membership of 494,000; Gen. Man. MATTI LATOLA.

Pankkien neuvottelukunta (Joint Delegation of the Finnish Banks): Eteläranta 10, 00130 Helsinki; tel. (90) 629712; Chair. HEIKKI TUOMINEN.

Suomen Pankkiyhdistys r.y. (Bankers Association): Fabianinkatu 8, 00130 Helsinki; tel. (90) 177521; telex 121839; f. 1914; Chair. JAAKKO LASSILA; Man. Dir RISTO PIEPPONEN; Dir EERO KOSTAMO.

Suomen Säästöpankkiliitto (Savings Bank Association): Pohjoisesplanadi 35A, 00101 Helsinki; tel. (90) 18271; telex 125768; f. 1906; 243 mems; 1,072 offices; Chair. MATTI ALI-MELKKILÄ; Man. Dir KALEVI KAUNISKANGAS.

STOCK EXCHANGE

Helsinki Stock Exchange: Fabianinkatu 14, 00100 Helsinki; tel. (90) 624161; telex 123460; f. 1912; Chair. of Supervisory Board MIKA TIIVOLA; Man. Dir MATTI MÄENPÄÄ.

INSURANCE

Alandia Group: Ålandsvägen 31, 22100 Mariehamn; tel. (928) 29000; telex 63117; f. 1961; life, non-life and marine; comprises three subsidiaries; Gen. Man. JOHAN DAHLMAN.

Ålands Ömsesidiga Försäkringsbolag (Åland Mutual Insurance Co), **Återförsäkringsaktiebolaget Hamnia** (Hamnia Reinsurance Co): Köpmansgatan 6, 22100 Mariehamn; tel. (928) 15100; telex 63191; Gen. Man. BJARNE OLOFSSON.

Keskinäinen Vakuutushtiö Autoilijat (Autoilijat Mutual Insurance Co): Hietalahdenranta 3, POB 165, 00150 Helsinki; tel. (90) 12321; telex 123625; f. 1938; Gen. Man. PETER KÜTTNER.

EFFOA-yhtymän Keskinäinen Vakuutusyhtiö (Effoa Gp Mutual Insurance Co): Eteläranta 8, POB 290, 00130 Helsinki; tel. (90) 1781; telex 121410; f. 1942; insurance for Effoa-Finland Steamship Co; marine; Chair. N.-G. PALMGREN.

Hämeen Vakuutus Keskinäinen Yhtiö (Hämeen Vakuutus Mutual Insurance Co): Raatihuoneenkatu 19, 13100 Hämeenlinna; tel. (917) 69311; telex 2304; f. 1896; Gen. Man. AIMO KORHONEN.

Eläkevakuutusosakeyhtiö Ilmarinen (Ilmarinen Pension Insurance Co Ltd): Eerikinkatu 41, 00180 Helsinki; tel. (90) 1841; telex 122932; f. 1961; Gen. Man. JUHANI SALMINEN.

Kansa Corpn Ltd: Hämeentie 33, POB 78, 00501 Helsinki; tel. (90) 73161; telex 122209; f. 1919; parent company of several domestic and overseas subsidiaries in insurance, reinsurance and finance; Pres. CEO ERKKI PESONEN.

Lähivakuutus Keskinäinen Yhtiö (Local Mutual Insurance Co): Annankatu 25, 00100 Helsinki; tel. (90) 12941; f. 1917; Gen. Man. SIMO CASTRÉN.

Meijerien Keskinäinen Vakuutusyhtiö (Dairies' Mutual Co): Meijeritie 6, POB 68, 00370 Helsinki; tel. (90) 5681; f. 1920; Gen. Man. KEIJO RAUTIO.

Suomen Merivakuutus Osakeyhtiö (Finnish Marine Insurance Co): Melkonkatu 22A, 00210 Helsinki; tel. (90) 6927166; telex 121013; f. 1898; Man. Dir CARL-HENRIK LUNDELL.

Osuuspankkien Keskinäinen Vakuutusyhtiö (Mutual Insurance Co of the Co-operative Banks): Temppelikatu 6B, 00100 Helsinki; tel. (90) 4041; f. 1964; non-life; Gen. Man. ASKO KUTVONEN.

Keskeytysvakuutusosakeyhtiö Otso (Otso Loss of Profits Insurance Co): POB 126, Bulevardi 10, 00120 Helsinki; tel. (90) 61691; telex 121061; f. 1939; non-life; Gen. Man. MAGNUS NORDLING.

Keskinäinen Vakuutusyhtiö Palonvara (Palonvara Mutual Co): Rautatienkatu 19, 15110 Lahti; tel. (918) 522611; f. 1912; non-life; Gen. Man. JUHANI SORRI.

Vakuutusosakeyhtiö Pankavara (Pankavara Insurance Co): Kanavaranta 1, POB 309, 00160 Helsinki; tel. (90) 16291; telex 121438; f. 1943; non-life; Gen. Man. VELI KORPI.

Patria Insurance Co Ltd: Vattuniemenkuja 8A, 00210 Helsinki; tel. (90) 69611; telex 124832; f. 1881; non-life and reinsurance; Man. Dir ANTTI SAVOLAINEN.

Pohjola Group: Lapinmäentie 1, 00300 Helsinki; tel. (90) 5591; telex 124556; life and non-life, reinsurance; three subsidiaries; Pres., Man. Dir PENTTI TALONEN.

Säästöpankkien Keskinäinen Vakuutusyhtiö (Savings Banks' Mutual Insurance Co): Iso Roobertinkatu 4–6, 00120 Helsinki; tel. (90) 18271; f. 1971; Gen. Man. JUHANI LAINE.

Sampo Group: Yliopistonkatu 27, 20100 Turku; tel. (921) 663311; telex 62242; life, non-life, pensions and reinsurance; Gen. Man. ANTTI KATAJA.

Svensk-Finland Ömsesidiga Försäkringsbolaget (Svensk-Finland Mutual Insurance Co): Malminkatu 20, POB 549, 00100 Helsinki; tel. (90) 6944122; telex 125093; f. 1925; non-life; Man. Dir PER-IVAR GUSTAFSSON.

Tapiola Insurance Group: Revontulentie 7, 02100 Espoo; tel. (90) 4531; telex 121073; life, non-life, livestock, pensions; Chair. PERTTI PALOHEIMO; Man. Dir JUKKA SYRJÄNEN.

Keskinäinen yhtiö Teollisuusvakuutus (Industrial Mutual Insurance Co): Vattuniemenkuja 8, 00210 Helsinki; tel. (90) 69611; telex 124832; f. 1890; Gen. Man. CARL-OLAF HOMÉN.

FINLAND
Directory

Keskinäinen Vakuutusyhtiö Tulenvara (Tulenvara Mutual Insurance Co): Porkkalankatu 3, 00180 Helsinki; tel. (90) 13211; telex 124633; f. 1948; non-life; Gen. Man. YRJÖ PESSI.

Jälleenvakuutusosakeyhtiö Turva (Turva Reinsurance Co): Annankatu 42c, POB 347, 00101 Helsinki; tel. (90) 13221; telex 124627; f. 1897; Man. Dir KARI MALMIVUO.

Työväen Keskinäinen Vakuutusyhtiö Turva (Turva Employees' Mutual Co): Hämeenkatu 25, POB 117, 33200 Tampere; tel. (931) 193111; f. 1910; Gen. Man. RAIMO VUORINEN.

Jälleenvakuutusosakeyhtiö Varma (Varma Reinsurance Co): Lönnrotinkatu 19, 00120 Helsinki; tel. (90) 6949344; f. 1919; Gen. Man. LEIF MARTINSEN.

Keskinäinen Vakuutusyhtiö Varma (Varma Mutual Co): Hämeenkatu 9, POB 48, 33100 Tampere; f. 1920; tel. (931) 31211; telex 22611; Gen. Man. HARRI PYHÄLTÖ.

Pension-Varma: Annankatu 18A, 00120 Helsinki; tel. (90) 61651; telex 125415; f. 1947; pension and general life insurance; Gen. Man. JUHANI KOLEMAIHNEN.

Henkivakuutusosakeyhtiö Verdandi (Verdandi Life Co): Olavintie 2, 20700 Turku; tel. (921) 690011; telex 62601; life, pension; Man. Dir KURT LJUNGMAN.

Wärtsilän Keskinäinen Vakuutusyhtiö (Wärtsilä Mutual Insurance Co): John Stenbergin ranta 2, 00530 Helsinki; tel. (90) 70951; f. 1943; non-life; Gen. Man. MARTTI ALOPAEUS.

Keskinäinen yhtiö Yrittäjäinvakuutus-Fennia (Enterprise-Fennia Mutual Insurance Co): Asemamiehenkatu 3, 00520 Helsinki; tel. (90) 15031; telex 121280; f. 1928; insurance in all non-life classes; Gen. Man. KARI ELO.

Insurance Associations

Federation of Accident Insurance Institutions: Bulevardi 28, 00120 Helsinki; tel. (90) 19251; telex 123511; f. 1920; Man. Dir PENTTI VIRTANEN.

Federation of Employment Pension Institutions: Lastenkodinkuja 1, 00180 Helsinki; tel. (90) 6940122; f. 1964; Man. Dir PENTTI KOSTAMO.

Federation of Finnish Insurance Companies: Bulevardi 28, 00120 Helsinki; tel. (90) 19251; telex 123511; f. 1942; Chair. JUKKA SYRJÄNEN; Man. Dir MATTI L. AHO; 48 mems.

Finnish Atomic Insurance Pool, Finnish Pool of Aviation Insurers, Finnish General Reinsurance Pool: Bulevardi 10, 00120 Helsinki; tel. (90) 61691; telex 121061; Man. Dir K.-M. STRÖMMER.

Finnish Marine Underwriters' Association: Hietaniemenkatu 19, 00100 Helsinki; tel. (90) 441248; telex 122044; f. 1956; Man. Dir LARS BECKMAN.

Finnish Motor Insurers' Bureau: Bulevardi 28, 00120 Helsinki; tel. (90) 19251; telex 123511; f. 1959; Man. Dir PENTTI AJO.

Insurance Rehabilitation Agency: Asemamiehenkatu 3, 00520 Helsinki; tel. (90) 15041; f. 1964; joint bureau of the Finnish carriers of employment accident insurance, motor insurance and pension insurance, to carry out vocational rehabilitation as part of the insurance compensation; Man. Dir RISTO SEPPÄLÄINEN.

Trade and Industry

CHAMBERS OF COMMERCE

Central Chamber of Commerce (Keskuskauppakamari): Fabianinkatu 14, POB 1000, 00100 Helsinki; tel. 650133; telex 123814; f. 1918; Pres. JAAKKO LASSILA; Gen. Man. MATTI AURA; 23 local chambers of commerce represented by 8 mems each on Board.

Finnish Foreign Trade Association: POB 908, Arkadiankatu 4-6B, 00101 Helsinki; tel. (90) 69591; telex 121696; f. 1919; Chair. MIKA TIIVOLA; Vice-Chair. HARRY B. BERNER, MATTI NUUTILA; Chair. of Board TIMO RELANDER; Man. Dir PERTTI HUITU.

Helsinki Chamber of Commerce: Kalevankatu 12, 00100 Helsinki; tel. (90) 644601; f. 1917; Pres. JUHANI PESONEN; Man. Dir HEIKKI HELIÖ; 3,000 mems.

TRADE AND INDUSTRIAL ORGANIZATIONS

E-osuuskunta Eka (Eka Co-operative Society): Hämeentie 19, Helsinki 50; tel. (90) 7331; telex 124454; f. 1983 as a merger of 40 co-operatives; Pres. EINO MALINEN.

Enigheten Centrallaget (Butter and Cheese Export): Päiväläisentie 2, Helsinki 39; tel. (90) 5624188; telex 122835; Chair. and Man. Dir B. LEMBERG; 10 mems.

Finnish Cabinet Makers' and Wood Turners' Association: P. Esplanadikatu 25A, Helsinki; f. 1944; Man. Dir JUHO SAVIO.

Finnish Joinery Association: P. Esplanadikatu 25A, Helsinki; Man. Dir JUHO SAVIO.

Hankkija Wholesale Co-operative Society: POB 80, 00101 Helsinki; f. 1905; agricultural produce; Chair. and Chief Exec. JORMA JÄRVI.

Kalatalouden Keskusliitto (Federation of Fisheries Associations): Köydenpunojankatu 7B 23, 00180 Helsinki; f. 1891; Sec. M. ARO; 398,000 mems.

Kaukomarkkinat Oy/Kauko International: Kutojantie 4, 02631 Espoo; tel. (90) 5211; telex 124469; f. 1947; exports and international trade in chemical and mechanical forest industry, chemical industry, and metal and engineering industries; Pres AHTI SIRKIÄ, JUHA WARIS.

Kesko Oy (Retailers' Wholesale Co): Satamakatu 3, 00160 Helsinki; tel. (90) 1981; telex 124748; f. 1941; retailer-owned wholesale corporation, trading in foodstuffs, textiles, shoes, consumer goods, agricultural and builders' supplies, and machinery; Pres. E. O. MANSUKOSKI.

Kotimaisen Työn Liitto (Association for Domestic Work): POB 177, Bulevardi 5A, 00121 Helsinki; tel. (90) 645733; f. 1978; public relations for Finnish products and for Finnish work; Chair. of Council SEPPO LINDBLOM; Chair. of Board of Dirs PAAVO PREPULA; Man. Dir RAUNO BISTER; about 1,000 mems.

Kulutusosuustoiminnan Keskusliitto (KK) r.y. (Central Union of Consumer Co-operation): Hämeentie 19, POB 740, 00101 Helsinki; tel. (90) 7331; telex 124454; f. 1916; Chair. VEIKKO HELLE; Dir-Gen. NIILO HÄMÄLÄINEN; 65 mem. societies, 640,000 individuals.

Maataloustuottajain Keskusliitto (Central Union of Agricultural Producers): Simonkatu 6, 00100 Helsinki; tel. (90) 69551; telex 122474; f. 1917; Chair. Board of Dirs HEIKKI HAAVISTO; Sec.-Gen. ESKO LINDSTEDT; 310,652 mems.

Munakunta (Co-operative Egg Producers' Association): POB 38, Helsinki 39, f. 1921; Chair. and Man. Dir SIMO PALOKANGAS; 12,700 mems.

Oy Labor Ab (Agricultural Machinery): Mikkolantie 1, 00640 Helsinki; tel. (90) 7291; telex 124660; f. 1898; Gen. Man. KIMMO VARJOVAARA.

Pellervo-Seura (Pellervo Society): Simonkatu 6, Helsinki 10; tel. (90) 69551; f. 1899; central organization of farmers' co-operatives; Man. Dir AARNE HAKALA; 790 mem. societies (incl. 8 central co-operative societies).

Suomen Betoniteollisuuden Keskusjärjestö r.y. (Concrete Industry Association): Iso Roobertinkatu 30, 00120 Helsinki; tel. (90) 648212; telex 121394; f. 1929; Chair. SEPPO PAATELAINEN; Man. Dir RISTO PESONEN; 100 mems.

Suomen Metsäteollisuuden Keskusliitto r.y. (Central Association of Finnish Forest Industries): Eteläesplanadi 2, 00130 Helsinki; tel. (90) 13261; telex 121823; f. 1918; Chair. CASIMIR EHRNROOTH; Man. Dir MATTI PEKKANEN; mems: 41 companies in the forestry industry and the following sales or trade associations:

Converta (Finnish Paper and Board Converters' Association): Fabianinkatu 9, POB 35, 00131 Helsinki; tel. (90) 661316; telex 124622; f. 1944; Man. Dir ANTTI RISLAKKI; 9 mems.

Finnboard (Finnish Board Mills Association): Eteläesplanadi 2, POB 36, 00131 Helsinki; tel. (90) 13251; telex 121460; f. 1943; Man. Dir JARL H. F. KÖHLER; 13 mems.

Finncell: Eteläesplanadi 2, POB 60, 00101 Helsinki; tel. (90) 18051; telex 124459; f. 1918; Man. Dir T. NYKOPP; 14 mems.

Finnpap (Paper Mills' Association): Eteläesplanadi 2, POB 380, 00101 Helsinki; tel. (90) 13241; telex 124429; f. 1918; sales organization for the Finnish paper industry; Man. Dir THOMAS NYSTÉN; 17 mems.

Suomen Kuitulevy-yhdistys (Wood Fibre Panel Association—FFA): Opastinsilta 8b B, 00520 Helsinki; tel. (90) 141122; telex 124858; f. 1953, reorganized 1960; Man. Dir A. PENTINSAARI; 4 mems.

Suomen Lastulevy-yhdistys (Particle Board Association): Opastinsilta 8b B, 00520 Helsinki; tel. (90) 141122; telex 124858; Man. Dir ERIK LINDSTRÖM; 6 mems.

Suomen Sahanomistajayhdistys (Finnish Sawmill Owners' Assoctaion): Fabianinkatu 29c, 00100 Helsinki; tel. (90) 661801; telex 121851; f. 1895; Man. Dir PEKKA SNÄLL; 32 mems.

Suomen Vaneriyhdistys (Association of Finnish Plywood Industry): Opastinsilta 8b B, 00520 Helsinki; f. 1939; Man. Dir ERIK LINDSTRÖM; 8 mems.

FINLAND   *Directory*

Suomen Osuuskauppojen Keskusliitto (SOKL) (Co-operative Union): Vilhonkatu 7, 00100 Helsinki; tel. (90) 1881; telex 121341; f. 1908; Chair. SEPPO TÖRMÄLÄ; 81 mems.

Suomen Teknillinen Kauppaliitto (Technical Traders Association): Mannerheimintie 14B, 00100 Helsinki; f. 1918; organization of the main importers dealing in iron, steel, and non-ferrous metals, machines and equipment, heavy chemicals and raw materials; Chair. K. KUOSMANEN; Man. Dir KLAUS VARTIOVAARA; 67 mems.

Suomen Tukkukauppiaiden Liitto r.y. (Wholesalers' and Importers' Association): Mannerheimintie 76, 00250 Helsinki; f. 1920; Man. OLAVI FAGERSTRÖM; 400 mem. firms include those of 17 affiliated organizations.

Svenska Lantbruksproducenternas Centralförbund (Union of Swedish Agricultural Producers): Fredriksgatan 61, 00100 Helsinki; f. 1945; Swedish-speaking producers; Chair. O. ROSENDAHL; 21,517 mems.

Teknisen Tukkukaupan Keskusliitto (TTK) (Central Federation of Technical Wholesale Traders): Mannerheimintie 14B, Helsinki 10; 10 branch associations with 250 mems.

Tuottajain Lihakeskuskunta (Farmers' Meat Marketing Association): Vanha talvitie 5, 00500 Helsinki; tel. (90) 717911; telex 124813; f. 1936; Pres. GUSTAV SANDELIN; 8 mem. co-operatives.

Valio Finnish Co-operative Dairies' Association: POB 390, 00101 Helsinki; tel. (90) 5681; telex 123-427; f. 1905; Man. Dir IIKKA HAKA; 134 mems (dairies).

EMPLOYERS' ORGANIZATIONS

Liiketyönantajain Keskusliitto (LTK) r.y. (Confederation of Service Industries): Eteläranta 10, 00130 Helsinki; tel. (90) 19281; f. 1945; divided into seven member associations and consists of about 6,500 member enterprises with about 300,000 employees; Chair. PENTTI KIVINEN; Man. Dir JARMO PELLIKKA.

Suomen Työnantajain Keskusliitto (STK) (Finnish Employers' Confederation): Eteläranta 10, 00130 Helsinki; tel. (90) 17281; f. 1907 to safeguard the interests of its member enterprises by negotiating and signing collective agreements and by influencing general decisions which affect business life; comprises 28 different branch associations with about 6,334 member enterprises employing about 618,868 employees. Chair. KRISTER AHLSTRÖM; Dir-Gen. PENTTI SOMERTO.

Ålands Arbetsgivareförening r.f. (Åland Employers' Association): Ringvägen 19, 22100 Mariehamn; tel. (928) 12469; Chair. KJELL CLEMES; Man. Dir ROLF BERGMAN; 27 mems.

Autoalan Työnantajaliitto r.y. (Federation of Motor Vehicle Trade Employers): Liisankatu 21B 11, 00170 Helsinki; tel. (90) 171410; Chair. ROLF EHRNROOTH; Man. Dir LEO GYLDÉN; 361 mems.

Autoliikenteen Työnantajaliitto r.y. (Employers' Federation of Road Transport): Nuijamiestentie 7A, 00400 Helsinki; tel. (90) 585022; Chair. LAASE VAANO; Man. Dir HANNU PARVELA; 535 mems.

Autonrengasliitto r.y. (Tyre Federation): Nordenskiöldinkatu 6A 1, 00250 Helsinki; tel. (90) 492554; Chair. HEIKKI HELENIUS; Man. Dir NILS ANDERSSON; 61 mems.

Graafisen Teollisuuden Työnantajaliitto (Employers' Association of the Graphic Arts Industries): Lönnrotinkatu 11A, 00120 Helsinki; tel. (90) 602911; Chair. JAAKKO RAURAMO; Man. Dir TURKKA LAINE; 387 mems.

Kenkäteollisuuden Työnantajaliitto r.y. (Employers' Federation of the Shoe Industry): Eteläranta 10, 00130 Helsinki; tel. (90) 19231; Chair. ESKO HEINO; Man. Dir TAPANI KAHRI; 51 mems.

Konttorikoneliikkeiden Yhdistys r.y. (Association of Office Machine Merchants): Mannerheimintie 76B, 00250 Helsinki; tel. (90) 494413; Chair. TOM HYNNINEN; Man. Dir KALLE-VEIKKO HAVAS; 83 mems.

Kultaseppien Työnantajaliitto r.y. (Employers' Association of Goldsmiths): Eteläranta 10, 00130 Helsinki; tel. (90) 19231; Chair. and Man. Dir JORMA NURMI; 29 mems.

Metsäteollisuuden Työnantajaliitto (Employers' Association of Forest Industries): Fabianinkatu 9A, POB 5, 00131 Helsinki; tel. (90) 174877; telex 122986; Chair. OLLI PAROLA; Man. Dir MAURI MOREN; 123 mems.

Nahkateollisuuden Työnantajaliitto r.y. (Leather Industry Employers' Federation): Eteläranta 10, 00130 Helsinki; tel. (90) 19231; Chair. PERTTI HELLEMAA; Man. Dir TAPANI KAHRI; 35 mems.

Osuusteurastamoiden Työnantajaliitto r.y. (Association of Co-operative Abattoir Employers): Eteläranta 10, 00130 Helsinki; tel. (90) 19231; Chair. GUSTAV SANDELIN; Man. Dir RISTO VARA; 9 mems.

Puhelinlaitosten Työnantajaliitto (Employers' Association of Telephone Companies): Yrjönkatu 13A, 00120 Helsinki; tel. (90) 642811; telex 124845; Chair. ERKKI RIPATTI; 51 mems.

Puusepänteollisuuden Liitto r.y. (Employers' Association of the Furniture and Joinery Industries): Fabianinkatu 9A, 00130 Helsinki; tel. (90) 174877; f. 1917; Chair. RAIMO VAARA; Man. Dir ARTO TÄHTINEN; 121 mems.

Rannikko—ja Sisävesiliikenteen Työnantajaliitto (RASILA) r.y. (Coastal Shipping and Inland Waterways Transportation Employers' Federation): see under Shipping.

Sähkötyönantajain Liitto r.y. (Employers' Association of Electrical Contractors): Yrjönkatu 13A, 00120 Helsinki; tel. (90) 642811; telex 124845; Chair. JUKKA RYTÖVUORI; Man. Dir MATTI HÖYSTI; 230 mems.

Suomen Kiinteistöliitto r.y. (Finnish Real-Estate Association): Annankatu 24, 00100 Helsinki; tel. (90) 641331; f. 1907; Chair. JOUKO KIVIHARJU; 164 mems.

Suomen Konsulttitoimistojen Liitto (SKOL) r.y. (Finnish Association of Consulting Firms (SKOL)): Pohjantie 12A, 02100 Espoo; tel. (90) 460122; Chair. ANTTI SÄÄSKILAHTI; 193 mems.

Suomen Lasitus- ja Hiomoliitto r.y. (Finnish Glass Dealers' and Glaziers' Association): P. Hesperiankatu 11, 00260 Helsinki; tel. (90) 441100; Chair. and Man. Dir MARTTI LINDBLOM; 141 mems.

Suomen Lastauttajain Työnantajaliitto r.y. (Finnish Employers' Association of Stevedores): Kalevankatu 12, 00100 Helsinki; tel. (90) 643131; telex 122977; f. 1920; Chair. JUHANI FORSS; Man. Dir JAN-ERIK EHRSTRÖM; 43 mems.

Suomen Metalliteollisuuden Työnantajaliitto (Finnish Metal Industries Employers' Association): Eteläranta 10, 00130 Helsinki; tel. (90) 19231; telex 124635; f. 1903; Chair. REIJO KAUKONON; Man. Dir HARRI MALMBERG; 850 mems.

Suomen Rakennusteollisuusliitto r.y. (Finnish Building Industry Federation): Unioninkatu 14, 00130 Helsinki; tel. (90) 658211; telex 125321; f. 1946; Chair. KAUKO MAIJALA; Man. Dir MATTI LOUKOLA; 1,966 mems.

Suomen Tiiliteollisuusliitto r.y. (Finnish Brick Industry Association): Laturinkuja 2, 02600 Espoo; tel. (90) 519133; telex 125103; Chair. ARVI PALOHEIMO; Man. Dir JUKKA SUONIO; 11 mems.

Suomen Varustamoyhdistys r.y. (Finnish Shipowners' Association): Satamakatu 4A, 00160 Helsinki; tel. (90) 174722; Chair. ROLF SUNDSTRÖM; Man. Dir PER FORSSKÄHL; 14 mems.

Tekstiiliteollisuuden Työnantajaliitto (Textile Industries Employers' Association): Aleksis Kiven katu 10, 33210 Tampere; tel. (931) 32277; f. 1905; Chair. J. SUOMALAINEN; Man. Dir MATTI JÄRVENTIE; 145 mems.

Työnantajain Yleinen Ryhmä (Employers' General Group): Eteläranta 10, 00130 Helsinki; Chair. HARRY MILDH; Man. Dir TAPANI KAHRI; 533 mems.

Vaatetusteollisuuden Työnantajaliitto r.y. (Clothing Industry Employers' Federation): Eteläranta 10, 00130 Helsinki; tel. (90) 19231; Chair. SEPPO HYYPPÄ; Man. Dir TAPANI KAHRI; 200 mems.

Voimalaitosten Työnantajaliitto r.y. (Employers' Association of Power Plants): Yrjönkatu 13A, 00120 Helsinki; tel. (90) 642811; telex 124845; f. 1945; Chair. KALEVI NUMMINEN; Man. Dir MATTI HÖYSTI; 100 mems.

TRADE UNIONS

Suomen Ammattiliittojen Keskusjärjestö (SAK) r.y. (Central Organization of Finnish Trade Unions): Siltasaarenkatu 3A, 00530 Helsinki; f. 1907; 27 affiliated unions; 1,055,055 mems (1985); Pres. PERTTI VIINANEN; Vice-Pres OLAVI HÄNNINEN, RAIMO KANTOLA; Secs PEKKO AHMAVAARA, LAURI IHALAINEN.

Principal affiliated unions (membership of over 5,000):

Auto- ja Kuljetusalan Työntekijäliitto (AKT) r.y. (Transport Workers): Haapaniemenkatu 7–9B, 00530 Helsinki; tel. (90) 70911; f. 1948; Pres. RISTO KUISMA; Secs KAUKO LEHIKOINEN, LEO ROPPOLA; 42,888 mems.

Hotelli- ja Ravintolahenkilökunnan Liitto (HRHL) r.y. (Hotel and Restaurant Workers): Haapaniemenkatu 7-9, 00530

FINLAND

Helsinki; f. 1933; Pres. Matti Haapakoski; Sec. Jorma Kallio; 46,000 mems.

Kemian Työntekijäin Liitto r.y. (Chemical Workers): Haapaniemenkatu 7-9, 00530 Helsinki; tel. (90) 70911; f. 1970; Pres. Heikki Pohja; Sec. Mikko Kulmala; 20,297 mems.

Kiinteistötyöntekijäin Liitto r.y. (Caretakers): Viherniemenkatu 5A, 00530 Helsinki; f. 1948; Pres Jaakko Kiviranta, Teuvo Peltola; Secs Raimo Kähärä, Eva-Kaija Laakkonen; 12,000 mems.

Kumi- ja Nahkatyöväen Liitto (KNL) r.y. (Rubber and Leather Workers): Siltasaarenkatu 4, 00530 Helsinki; tel. (90) 750044; f. 1937; Pres. Hilkka Häkkilä; Sec. Kalevi Urpelainen; 16,000 mems.

Kunnallisten työntekijäin ja viranhaltijain liitto (KTV) r.y. (Municipal Workers' and Employees' Union): Kolmas linja 4, 00530 Helsinki; tel. (90) 77031; f. 1931; Pres. Pekka Salonen; Asst Gen. Sec. Jouni Riskilä; 185,000 mems.

Lasi- ja Posliinityöväen Liitto r.y. (Glass and Porcelain Workers): Haapaniemenkatu 7-9, 00530 Helsinki; f. 1906; Pres. Risto Sainio; Sec. Toivo Partanen; 5,371 mems.

Liiketyöntekijäin Liitto r.y. (Commercial Workers): Siltasaarenkatu 6, 00530 Helsinki; f. 1917; Pres. Kauko Suhonen; Sec. Mauno Hietikko; 100,000 mems.

Maaseututyöväen Liitto r.y. (Forest and Agricultural Workers): Haapaniemenkatu 7-9, 00530 Helsinki; f. 1945; Pres. Esa Ihalainen; Vice Pres. Kalevi Väisänen; Secs Raimo Lindlöf, Lauri Ainasto; 24,000 mems.

Metallityöväen Liitto r.y. (Metalworkers): Siltasaarenkatu 3-5A, 00530 Helsinki; tel. (90) 77071; telex 122571; f. 1899; Pres. Per-Erik Lundh; Vice-Pres. Veikko Lehtonen; Secs Osmo Isoviita, Erik Lindfors; 157,000 mems.

Paperiliitto r.y. (Paperworkers): Pl.326, 00531 Helsinki; f. 1906; Pres. Antero Mäki; Gen. Sec. Artturi Pennanen; 51,800 mems.

Puutyöväen Liitto r.y. (Woodworkers): Haapaniemenkatu 7-9B, 00530 Helsinki; tel. (90) 70911; f. 1973; Pres Heikki Peltonen, Timo Rautarinta; Secs Onni Kuutsa, Kalevi Hölttä; 42,000 mems.

Rakennustyöläisten Liitto r.y. (Building Workers): Siltasaarenkatu 4, 00530 Helsinki; tel. (90) 77021; f. 1930; Pres. Aarno Aitamurto; Vice-Pres. Matti Ojala; Sec. Hannu Alanoja; 91,000 mems.

Suomen Elintarviketyöläisten Liitto r.y. (Food Workers): Siltasaarenkatu 6, PL 213, 00531 Helsinki; tel. (90) 717877; f. 1905; Pres. Jarl Sund; Sec. Arto Talasmäki; 40,000 mems.

Suomen Kirjatyöntekijäin Liitto r.y. (Bookworkers): Ratakatu 9, 00120 Helsinki; tel. (90) 649717; f. 1894; Pres. Pentti Levo; Sec. Pekka Lahtinen; 27,635 mems.

Suomen Merimies-Unioni—Finlands Sjömans-Union r.y. (Seamen): Siltasaarenkatu 6, 00530 Helsinki; tel. (90) 716177; telex 124795; f. 1916; Pres. Reijo Anttila; Vice-Pres. Risto Ahola; Sec. Per-Erik Nelin; 11,000 mems.

Suomen Sähköalantyöntekijäin Liitto r.y. (Electricity Workers): Hämeenkatu 17A, 33200 Tampere; tel. (931) 34700; f. 1955; Pres. Seppo Salisma; Vice-Pres. Alpo Holi; Secs Paavo Talala, Heikki Varjonen; 28,052 mems.

Tekstiili- ja Vaatetustyöväen Liitto r.y. (Textile and Clothing Workers): Hämeenkatu 5B, 33100 Tampere; tel. (931) 32340; f. 1970; Pres. Seppo Niemi; Vice-Pres. Aura Järvinen; Secs Tuulikki Kannisto, Orvo Pantti; 43,000 mems.

Virkamiesten ja Työntekijäin Yhteisjärjestö (VTY) r.y. (Joint Organization of Civil Servants and Workers): Haapaniemenkatu 7-9B-talo, 00530 Helsinki; tel. (90) 70911; f. 1946; Pres. Raimo Rannisto; Sec.-Gen. Pertti Ahonen; 103,513 mems.

Toimihenkilö- ja Virkamiesjärjestöjen Keskusliitto (TVK) r.y. (Confederation of Salaried Employees): Asemamiehenkatu 4, 00520 Helsinki; tel. (90) 1551; telex 122505; f. 1922; 15 affiliates; Chairs Matti Kinnunen, Riitta Prusti; approx. 370,000 mems.

Principal affiliated unions (membership of over 5,000):

Ammattioppilaitosten opettajien liitto (Vocational School and College Teachers): Asemamiehenkatu 4, 00520 Helsinki; tel. (90) 1551; f. 1930; Chair. Jarmo Nurmio; 8,000 mems.

Erityisalojen Toimihenkilöliitto (ERTO) (Federation of Special Service and Clerical Employees): Vironkatu 6A, 00170 Helsinki; tel. (90) 177350; f. 1968; Chair. Matti Hellsten; 8,000 mems.

Kunnallisvirkamiesliitto (KVL)—Kommunaltjänstemannaförbundet (KTF) r.y. (Federation of Municipal Officers): Asemamiehenkatu 4, 00520 Helsinki; tel. (90) 1551; f. 1918; Chair. Taisto Mursula; 57,000 mems.

Pankkitoimihenkilöliitto (Bank Employees): Asemapäällikönkatu 3c, 00520 Helsinki; tel. (90) 141066; f. 1931; Pres. Pauli Salmio; Sec.-Gen. Raimo Pohjaväre; 34,000 mems.

Suomen Liikeväen Liitto (Commercial Employees): Asemamiehenkatu 4, 00520 Helsinki; f. 1906; Chair. Nils Komi; Exec. Dir E. Suumäki; 23,000 mems.

Suomen Perushoitajaliitto (Nursing Assistants): Asemamiehenkatu 2, 00520 Helsinki; tel. (90) 141833; f. 1948; Chair. Salme Pihl; 26,000 mems.

Suomen Poliisien Liitto (Police Federation): Haapaniemenkatu 7-9B, 00520 Helsinki; tel. (90) 739091; f. 1923; Chair. Timo Mikkola; 7,000 mems.

Suomen Teollisuustoimihenkilöiden Liitto (Salaried Employees in Industry): Asemamiehenkatu 4, 00520 Helsinki; tel. (90) 1551; f. 1917; Chair. Tuulikki Väliniemi; Exec. Dir Tarmo Hyvärinen; 45,000 mems.

Terveydenhuoltoalan ammattijärjestö Tehy (Health Professionals): Asemamiehenkatu 4, 00520 Helsinki; tel. (90) 1551; f. 1982; Chair. Aila Jokinen; 65,000 mems.

Vakuutusväen Liitto (Insurance Employees): Asemamiehenkatu 4, 00520 Helsinki; tel. (90) 1551; telex 122505; f. 1945; Chair. Irma Teräväinen; Exec. Dir Pekka Porttila; 9,000 mems.

Valtion Laitosten ja Yhtiöiden Toimihenkilöliitto (Employees in State-owned Institutions and Companies): Topparikuja 5, 00520 Helsinki; f. 1945; Chair. Eila Salminen; Exec. Dir Risto Nuutilainen; 11,000 mems.

Virkamiesliitto (Civil Servants): Asemamiehenkatu 4, 00520 Helsinki; tel. (90) 1551; f. 1917; Chair. Keijo Rantala; 68,000 mems.

STATE-OWNED INDUSTRIES

It has never been government policy in Finland to nationalize industries. Occasionally, however, it has been found necessary for various reasons to give substantial state aid in setting up a company and the State has retained a majority of shares in these companies. All are administered as limited companies, the State being represented on the Board of Management and at the General Meeting of Shareholders by either the relevant Minister or an official of the relevant Ministry.

Alko Ltd: Salmisaarenranta 7, POB 350, Helsinki 00101; tel. (90) 60911; telex 121045; f. 1932; production, import, export and sale of alcoholic beverages and spirits; has monopoly of retail sale of all alcoholic beverages except medium beer; 99.9% state-owned; Board of Admin. Chair. Ilkka Suominen; Board of Management Chair. Heikki Koski; 2,800 employees.

Enso-Gutzeit Oy: Kanavaranta 1, 00160 Helsinki; tel. (90) 16291; telex 124438; f. 1872; wood processing, paper, engineering, chemicals, forestry, merchant shipping, acquiring and installing hydroelectric power; 52.5% state-owned; Supervisory Board Chair. E. Ollila; Board of Dirs Chair., Pres., and CEO Pentti Salmi; 13,079 employees.

Finnair Oy: see Civil Aviation.

Imatran Voima Oy: POB 138, 00101 Helsinki; tel. (90) 6944811; telex 124608; f. 1932; electric power, including nuclear energy; 95% state-owned; Chair. Supervisory Council Paavo Aitio; Chair. Board of Dirs Kalevi Numminen; 4,500 employees.

Kemijoki Oy: POB 457, 00100 Helsinki; tel. (90) 6944811; telex 124608; f. 1954; electric power; 77.08% state-owned; Chair. Supervisory Board Paavo Väyrynen; Chair. Board of Management Teuvo Hiltunen; 511 employees.

Kemira Group: POB 330, Porkkalankatu 3, 00101 Helsinki; tel. (90) 13211; telex 121191; f. 1920; 15 plants in Finland, 25 overseas; fertilizers, agricultural and industrial chemicals, biotechnical products, explosives, safety equipment, man-made fibres, paints, filters and engineering services; Chair. Supervisory Board Heimo Linna; Chair. Board of Management Yrjö Pessi; 12,000 employees.

Neste Oy: Keilaniemi, 02150 Espoo 15; tel. (90) 4501; telex 124641; f. 1948; oil refining, petrochemicals, plastics, industrial chemicals and lubricants, shipping, natural gas, batteries; 97.96% state-owned; (see also under Shipping); Chair. Supervisory Board Ulf Sundqvist; Chair. Board of Management Jaakko Ihamuotila; 5,370 employees.

Outokumpu Oy: POB 280, 00101 Helsinki; tel. (90) 4031; telex 124441; f. 1932; exploration, mining, mineral processing, metal

FINLAND

refining and processing, equipment manufacture, engineering contracting; 81% state-owned; Chair. Supervisory Board ERKKI LIIKANEN; Chair. Board of Dirs and Pres. PERTTI VOUTILAINEN; 9,000 employees.

Rautaruukki Oy: POB 217, Kiilakiventie 1, 90101 Oulu; tel. (81) 327711; telex 32109; f. 1960; steel processing; 98.96% state-owned; Chair. Supervisory Board AHTI KARJALAINEN; Chair. Board of Management, Pres. MIKKO KIVIMÄKI; 7,500 employees.

Oy Sisu-Auto Ab: POB 307, 00101 Helsinki; tel. (90) 542011; telex 121245; f. as private company in 1931; in 1975 the State bought 70% of the shares; 99.9% state-owned (1986); manufacture, sale and maintenance of lorries, buses and special vehicles; Chair. Supervisory Board REINO BREILIN; Chair. Board of Management VEIKKO JÄÄSKELÄINEN; Pres. and CEO JORMA S. JERKKU; 1,290 employees.

Valmet Corpn: POB 155, Punanotkonkatu 2, 00131 Helsinki; tel. (90) 13291; telex 124427; f. 1946; engineering, shipbuilding and automation; 99% state-owned; Chair. Admin. Council JERMU LAINE; Chair. Board of Dirs MATTI KANKAANPÄÄ; 17,143 employees.

Valvilla Oy: POB 108, 20101 Turku; telex 62156; f. 1978; wool and linen spinning, weaving and sales; 98.2% state-owned; Chair. Supervisory Board ARTO LAMPINEN; Chair. Board of Management KAUKO SALMINEN; 1,140 employees.

Veitsiluoto Oy: Kemi; f. 1932; wood processing; 88.8% state-owned; Chair. Supervisory Board JAAKO PAJULA; Chair. Board of Management PENTTI O. RAUTALAHTI; 4,700 employees.

TRADE FAIRS

Osuuskunta Suomen Messut (Finnish Fair Corporation): Helsinki Fair Centre, POB 21, 00521 Helsinki; tel. (90) 15091; telex 121119; f. 1919; principal annual events: Helsinki International Boat Show, Medicine (exhibition of medicine, nursing and health care), Caravan (caravans and towing vehicles), Skiexpo (skiing and winter tourism); bi-annually: business machines and equipment, Elkom (professional electronics), FinnConsum (Helsinki International Trade Fair), Habitare (furniture and interior decoration), FinnBuild (Helsinki International Building Fair); every 3 years: FinnTec (Helsinki International Technical Fair), FinnTexMa (textile industry machines and accessories); every 4 years: Hepac (heating), Maxpo (construction machinery), Eltek (electrical technology); Chair. of Supervisory Board RAIMO ILASKIVI; Chair. of Admin. Board KARI O. SOHLBERG; Man. Dir MATTI HURME.

Transport

RAILWAYS

There are 5,883 km of railways, providing internal services and connections with Sweden and the USSR, and 1,445 km of track are electrified. An underground railway service has been provided by Helsinki City Transport since 1982.

Jo-Fo Oy: Forssa; Man. Dir A. J. HAAPAKOSKI.

Karhula Railway: Ratakatu 8, 48600 Karhula; tel. (952) 62396; f. 1937; goods transport; Man. PERTTI HONKALA; Man. of Traffic OLLI KOKKOMÄKI.

Valtionrautatiet (State Railways): Finnish State Railways, Board of Administration, Vilhonkatu 13, POB 488, 00101 Helsinki; tel. (90) 7071; telex 301151; began operating 1862; operates 5,877 km of railways; wide gauge (1,524 mm); privately-owned total 6 km; 1,445 km of route are electrified; Dir-Gen. HERBERT RÖMER; Chief Dir and Dir of Traffic Dept PANU HAAPALA.

ROADS

At 31 December 1985 there were 76,061 km of public roads, of which 205 km were motorways, 11,210 km other main roads (I and II class), 29,666 km other highways and 35,185 km local roads (excluding urban streets). In addition, there are about 51,397 km of private roads subsidized for their maintenance.

Tie-ja vesirakennushallitus (Roads and Waterways Administration): POB 33, 00521 Helsinki; tel. (90) 1541; telex 124589; f. 1799; central office and 13 road and waterways districts; in charge of developing road and water traffic, including planning, constructing and maintaining roads, bridges and ferries, water channels, canals, ports and piers; Dir-Gen. JOUKO LOIKKANEN; Dir-in-Chief VÄINÖ SUONIO.

INLAND WATERWAYS

Lakes cover 31,500 sq km. The inland waterway system comprises 6,100 km of buoyed-out channels, 40 open canals and 25 lock canals. The total length of canals is 76 km. In 1983 the waterways carried about 1,754m. ton-km of goods and 0.5m. domestic passengers.

In 1963 the USSR agreed to lease to Finland the right to use the southern part of the Saimaa Canal. In the summer of 1968 the rebuilt Saimaa Canal was opened for vessels. In 1983 a total of 1,400,000 tons of goods were transported along the canal.

Tie- ja vesirakennushallitus (Roads and Waterways Administration): see Roads.

Suomen Uittajainyhdistys r.y. (Association of Finnish Floaters): Fabianinkatu 9A, 00130 Helsinki; 332 mems; Chair. RISTO HYTÖNEN; Sec. ILKKA PURHONEN.

SHIPPING

The chief export port is Kotka, where construction of a new deep harbour was due to start in 1987; the main import port is Helsinki, which has five specialized harbours. The West Harbour handles most of the transatlantic traffic, the East Harbour coastal and North Sea freight, and the South Harbour passenger traffic. North Harbour deals only in local launch traffic. Sörnäinen is the timber and coal harbour; Herttoniemi specializes in oil. Other important international ports are Turku (Åbo), Rauma and Hamina.

Associations

Ålands Redarförening r.f. (Åland Shipowners' Association): Alandsvägen 31, 22100 Mariehamn; tel. (928) 13430; telex 63117; f. 1934; Chair. INGMAR INGVESGÅRD; Man. Dir JUSTUS HARBERG.

Rannikko- ja Sisävesiliikenteen Työnantajaliitto (RASILA) r.y. (Employers' Federation of Coastal and Inland Waterways Transportation): Fabianinkatu 9A, 00130 Helsinki; tel. (90) 174877; branch of STK (see Trade and Industry); Chair. KARI LAHTINEN; Man. Dir ILMO RINKINEN; 20 mems.

Suomen Varustamoyhdistys—Finlands Rederiförening (Finnish Shipowners' Association): Satamakatu 4, POB 155, 00161 Helsinki; tel. (90) 174722; telex 122751; f. 1932; Chair. R. SUNDSTRÖM; Man. Dir PER FORSSKÅHL; 14 mems.

Principal Companies

Oy Bore Line Ab: Pohjoisranta 2D, Norra kajen, POB 151, 00170 Helsinki; tel. 651899; telex 123503; and Länsilaituri 169, POB 106, 20200 Turku 20; tel. 304888; telex 62230; f. 1897; routes: Baltic and North Sea cargo services; Man. Dir RALF SUNDMAN.

Effoa—Finland Steamship Co Ltd: Eteläranta 8, POB 290, 00130 Helsinki; tel. (90) 1781; telex 121410; f. 1883; liner and contract services: see Finncarriers; passenger services operated by Silja Line and Finnjet Line; Man. Dir ROBERT G. EHRNROOTH; 14 cargo vessels and 3 cruise ferries.

Etelä-Suomen Laiva Oy: Hitsaajankatu 12, 00810 Helsinki; tel. (90) 782655; telex 124453; world-wide tramp services; Man. Dir K. MERISALO; 6 cargo vessels.

Oy Finnlines Ltd: Lönnrotinkatu 21, POB 406, 00121 Helsinki; tel. (90) 16621; telex 124462; f. 1947; cargo traffic, chartering, agencies; ship management, marine consulting; member of freight pools; Pres. ROLF SUNDSTRÖM; 31 cargo vessels, (17 general cargo carriers, 7 roll-on roll-off ships, 5 bulk carriers, 1 ore carrier, 1 passenger ferry).

Oy Finncarriers Ab: Eteläranta 8, 00130 Helsinki; tel. (90) 1781; telex 122822; f. 1975; liner and contract services between Finland and other European countries, the Mediterranean, North Africa, the Middle East and South and Central America; Man. Dir BO ÅBERG.

Lundqvist Rederierna: N. Esplanadgt. 9, 22100 Mariehamn; tel. (928) 16411; telex 63113; f. 1927; liner services; Pres. STIG LUNDQVIST; 3 vessels, total tonnage 15,883 dwt.

Neste Oy: Keilaniemi, 02150 Espoo 15; tel. (90) 4501; telex 124641; f. 1948; (see also under State-owned Industries); Pres. JAAKKO IHAMUOTILA; Corporate Vice-Pres. Shipping RAIMO ROOS; 17 tankers, 3 LPG carriers, 4 tugs; 942,241 dwt.

Oy Henry Nielsen Ab: Lönnrotinkatu 18, 00120 Helsinki; tel. (90) 17291; telex 122519; f. 1923; managing owners for about 123,804 dwt tanker and dry cargo; shipbrokers, liner- and forwarding-agents; Man. BERNDT NIELSEN.

Oy R. Nordström & Co Ab: POB 67, 07901 Loviisa; tel. (15) 531801; telex 1812; f. 1928; shipowners; shipbrokers at Loviisa, Walkom; Dirs KLAUS LAGUS, M.-R. NORDSTRÖM, L. ÖRÖ, R.-R. NORDSTRÖM, H. NORDSTRÖM.

John Nurminen Oy: Pasilankatu 2, 00240 Helsinki; tel. (90) 15071; telex 124562; f. 1886; international transports, export and import forwarding, air cargo, aircraft ground handling, ocean line agencies, ships' clearance, stevedoring, forwarding for fairs and

FINLAND

exhibitions, project transports, terminal and warehouse services; branch offices at Helsinki Airport and 22 main towns; Man. Dir JUHA NURMINEN.

Rederiaktiebolaget Gustaf Erikson: POB 49, 22101 Mariehamn; tel. (928) 12070; telex 63112; f. 1913; Chair. BJÖRN ERIKSON; 14 dry cargo and refrigerated vessels.

Rederiaktiebolaget Sally: Hamngatan 8, 22100 Mariehamn; tel. (928) 16711; telex 63115; ferry services to Sweden, England, France; Caribbean cruises; Man. Dir INGMAR INGVESGÅRD; 7 ferries and 2 cruisers; total tonnage 78,627 grt.

SF Line Ab: Norra Esplanadg. 3, 22100 Mariehamn; tel. (928) 14120; telex 63151; f. 1963; 3 car/passenger vessels; Chair. STIG LUNDQVIST; Man. Dir GUNNAR EKLUND; total tonnage 59,151 grt.

CIVIL AVIATION

An international airport is situated at Helsinki-Vantaa, 19 km from Helsinki. Internal flights connect Helsinki to Ivalo, Joensuu, Jyväskylä, Kajaani, Kemi, Kokkola/Pietarsaari, Kuopio, Kuusamo, Lappeenranta, Mariehamn, Mikkeli, Oulu, Pori, Rovaniemi, Savonlinna, Tampere, Turku, Vaasa and Varkaus. Seasonal flights also to Kittilä.

In 1985 7.3m. passengers passed through Finnish airports.

Finnair Oy: Head Office: Mannerheimintie 102, 00250 Helsinki; tel. (90) 410411; telex 124404; f. 1923; 76.1% state-owned; 21 domestic services and services to 34 cities in Europe, the Middle East, South-East Asia and North America; Chair. GUNNAR KORHONEN; Pres. RISTO OJANEN; fleet of 3 Fokker F-27 200, 2 ATR 42-300, 1 DC-8, 18 DC-9, 4 DC-10, 3 MD-82, 2 MD-83.

Finnaviation Oy (FA): POB 39, 01531 Vantaa; tel. (90) 377022; telex 121931; f. 1979; 60% owned by Finnair Oy; scheduled domestic services link Helsinki, Oulu, Kuusamo, Vaasa, Kuopio, Jyväskylä, Tampere and Turku; also a service from Vaasa to Umeå and Sundsvall, Sweden; Man. Dir LARS DAHLBERG; fleet of 1 Dassault Falcon 20, 3 Embraer EMB-110-P1 Bandeirante, 1 Cessna 441, 1 Cessna 425, 1 Cessna 402.

Karair Oy: 01530 Vantaa, tel. (90) 8251; telex 124769; f. 1957; internal services and charter flights abroad; Dir TUOMAS KARHUMÄKI; fleet of 1 DC-8-62, 1 EMB-110-P1 Bandeirante, 1 DHC-6-300 Twin Otter.

Tourism

Matkailun edistämiskeskus (Tourist Board): Asemapäällikönkatu 12B, 00520 Helsinki; tel. (90) 144511; telex 122690; f. 1973; Chair. KALERVO HENTILÄ; Dir BENGT PIHLSTRÖM.

Atomic Energy

Atomic Energy Commission: Ministry of Trade and Industry, Aleksanterinkatu 10, 00170 Helsinki; tel. (90) 1605256; telex 12645; consultative body which advises the government; the Ministry of Trade and Industry is the administrative and licensing authority; Chair. Prof. PEKKA JAUHO; Sec.-Gen. L. MATTILA; Admin. Sec. M. HOVI.

Finnish Centre for Radiation and Nuclear Safety: POB 268, 00101 Helsinki; tel. (90) 61671; telex 122691; f. 1958; responsible for the supervision of radiation protection and nuclear safety.

Finnish Nuclear Society: c/o Technical Research Centre of Finland, Nuclear Engineering Laboratory, Lönnrotinkatu 37, 00180 Helsinki; tel. (90) 648931; telex 122972.

Lappeenranta University of Technology: Dept of Energy Technology, POB 20, 53851 Lappeenranta; tel. (50) 27570; telex 58290.

Technical Research Centre of Finland: Division for Energy Technology, Vuorimiehentie 5, 02150 Espoo; tel. (90) 4561; telex 122972.

Teknillinen korkeakoulu (Helsinki University of Technology): Department of Technical Physics, 02150 Espoo; tel. (90) 4512458; telex 125161; the Department provides engineering education in technical physics, laser technology, nuclear engineering, computer and information science, process physics and instrumentation and related theory; Dirs Dr E. A. BYCKLING, Lic. Tech. I. HARTIMO, Dr T. E. KATILA, Dr T. KOHONEN, Dr J. KURKIJÄRVI, Dr J. T. ROUTTI, Dr R. SALOMAA.

Imatran Voima Oy: see State-Owned Industries.

Teollisuuden Voima Oy (Industrial Power Co Ltd): Fredrikinkatu 51-53, 00100 Helsinki; tel. (90) 605022; telex 122065.

FRANCE

Introductory Survey

Location, Climate, Language, Religion, Flag, Capital

The French Republic is situated in Western Europe. It is bounded to the north by the English Channel, to the east by Belgium, Luxembourg, the Federal Republic of Germany, Switzerland and Italy, to the south by the Mediterranean Sea and Spain, and to the west by the Atlantic Ocean. The island of Corsica is part of metropolitan France, while four overseas departments, two overseas 'collectivités territoriales' and four overseas territories also form an integral part of the Republic. The climate is temperate throughout most of the country, but in the south it is of the Mediterranean type, with warm summers and mild winters. Temperatures in Paris are generally between 0°C (32°F) and 24°C (75°F). The principal language is French, which has numerous regional dialects, and small minorities speak Breton or Basque. Almost all French citizens profess Christianity, and about 90% are adherents of the Roman Catholic Church. Other Christian denominations are represented, and there are also Muslim and Jewish communities. The national flag (proportions three by two) has three equal vertical stripes, of blue, white and red. The capital is Paris.

Recent History

In September 1939, following Nazi Germany's invasion of Poland, France and the United Kingdom declared war on Germany, thus entering the Second World War. In June 1940, however, France was forced to sign an armistice, following a swift invasion and occupation of French territory by German forces. After the liberation of France from German occupation in 1944, a provisional government was set up under Gen. Charles de Gaulle, leader of the 'Free French' forces during the wartime resistance. The war in Europe ended in May 1945, when German forces surrendered at Reims. In 1946, following a referendum, the Fourth Republic was established and Gen. de Gaulle retired from public life.

France had 26 different governments from 1946 until the Fourth Republic came to an end in 1958 with an insurrection in Algeria (then an overseas department) and the threat of civil war. In May Gen. de Gaulle was invited by the President, René Coty, to form a government. In June he was invested as Prime Minister by the National Assembly, with the power to rule by decree for six months. A new constitution was approved by referendum in September 1958 and promulgated in October; thus the Fifth Republic came into being, with Gen. de Gaulle taking office as its first President in January 1959. The new system provided a strong, stable executive. Real power rested in the hands of the President, who strengthened his authority through direct appeals to the people in national referendums.

The early years of the Fifth Republic were overshadowed by the Algerian crisis. De Gaulle suppressed a revolt of French army officers and granted Algeria independence in 1962, withdrawing troops and repatriating French settlers. A period of relative tranquillity was ended in 1968, when dissatisfaction with the Government's authoritarian policies on education and information, coupled with discontent at low wage rates and lack of social reform, fused into a serious revolt of students and workers. For a month the republic was threatened, but the student movement collapsed and the general strike was settled by large wage rises. In April 1969 President de Gaulle resigned after defeat in a referendum on regional reform.

Georges Pompidou, who had been Prime Minister between April 1962 and July 1968, was elected President in June 1969. He attempted to continue Gaullism, while also responding to the desire for change which had been manifested in 1968. The Gaullist hold on power was threatened, however, by the Union of the Left, formed in 1972 by the Parti Socialiste (PS) and the Parti Communiste Français (PCF). Leaders of the PS and the PCF agreed a common programme for contesting legislative elections. At a general election for the National Assembly in March 1973, the Government coalition was returned with a reduced majority.

President Pompidou died in April 1974. Valéry Giscard d'Estaing, formerly leader of the Républicains Indépendants (RI), supported by the Gaullist Union des Démocrates pour la République (UDR) and the centre parties, was elected President in May, narrowly defeating François Mitterrand, the First Secretary of the PS and the candidate of the Union of the Left (which was abandoned in 1977). A government was formed from members of the RI, the UDR and the centre parties. In August 1976 Jacques Chirac resigned as Prime Minister and was replaced by Raymond Barre, hitherto Minister of External Trade. Chirac undertook the transformation of the UDR into a new Gaullist party, the Rassemblement pour la République (RPR). In February 1978 the non-Gaullist parties in the Government formed the Union pour la Démocratie Française (UDF), to compete with RPR candidates in the National Assembly elections held in March, when the governing coalition retained a working majority.

In the April/May 1981 presidential elections, Mitterrand, the candidate of the PS, defeated Giscard d'Estaing, receiving nearly 52% of the votes in the second ballot (with the support of Communist voters). He appointed Pierre Mauroy, the Mayor of Lille, to be Prime Minister and dissolved the National Assembly. At elections for a new Assembly, held in June, the PS and associated groups, mainly the Mouvement des Radicaux de Gauche (MRG), won 285 of the 491 seats, while the PCF won 44. Four Communists were included in the first left-wing Council of Ministers for 23 years. The new Government introduced a programme of reforms: social benefits and working conditions were substantially improved, and several major industrial enterprises and financial institutions were brought under state control. A law of March 1982 initiated the complex process of decentralization, and the transfer of administrative and financial power from government-appointed Préfets to locally-elected departmental assemblies. Cantonal elections for these bodies were held in the same month, with right-wing candidates winning 1,187 of the 2,014 contested seats.

By 1983 the effects of economic recession had led to the adoption of deflationary policies, including reductions in public expenditure, and there was evidence of decreasing support for the Government. Following a decline in support for the PS and other left-wing parties at nationwide municipal elections held in March 1983, Mauroy resigned, but was immediately requested to form a new administration by President Mitterrand. Elections for one-third of the seats in the newly-enlarged Senate in September 1983 resulted in an overall majority for the opposition right-wing and centre parties, which subsequently controlled 179 of the 317 seats, with the left-wing parties holding 133 seats. In the June 1984 elections to the European Parliament, the PS suffered a serious setback, taking only 20 of the 81 seats allocated to France, while the RPR/UDF opposition alliance, led by Simone Veil, won 41 seats. As a result of increased support for the extreme right-wing Front National (FN), already apparent in several earlier municipal by-elections, the party received 11% of the total vote and took 10 seats (as many as the PCF).

Dissension between the PCF and the PS over the Government's continued programme of economic austerity became increasingly bitter as plans for further 'industrial restructuring' were revealed. After forceful protest by opposition politicians and Roman Catholic pressure-groups, a government proposal to introduce a unified, state-run secular education system was abandoned in July 1984, and the Minister of Education, Alain Savary, resigned. President Mitterrand accepted Mauroy's subsequent resignation, and appointed Laurent Fabius, the former Minister for Industry, as Prime Minister. Following Fabius's declared intention to continue policies of economic rigour, the PCF refused to participate in the new Council of Ministers, whose immediate priorities, according to Fabius, were economic modernization and national solidarity. Relations between the Government and the mainly right-wing Senate became strained in 1984 as opposition proposals to hold a referendum on the education issue were rejected by the Government as unconstitutional, while a subsequent proposal by the Government to hold a referendum to amend the Constitution accordingly (so that referendums could be held on matters concerning civil liberties, including education, instead of being confined to the organization of public authorities) was rejected in September.

A general election for an enlarged National Assembly (increased from 491 to 577 seats) was held in March 1986. In accordance with legislation introduced in 1985, the voting, except in three small overseas possessions, was based on a system of proportional representation (with voters choosing from party lists in each department or territory), rather than under the previous system of single-member constituencies. As in the 1981 general election, the PS and the MRG formed a left-wing alliance, while the RPR and the UDF formed a centre-right alliance. The PS remained the largest single party in the Assembly but lost its overall majority: the PS/MRG alliance won 209 seats, while its share of the total votes was only 31.4% (compared with 37.5% of the first-round votes in 1981). The RPR/UDF alliance received 41.0% of the votes (compared with 40.0% in 1981) and won 277 seats. With the support of 14 deputies from minor right-wing parties, the RPR/UDF was able to control a majority of seats in the new Assembly. Meanwhile, the PCF suffered a severe decline in support, obtaining only 9.8% of the votes (compared with 16.2% in 1981) and winning 35 seats. The FN, previously unrepresented in the Assembly, also won 35 seats, with 9.7% of the votes, whereas the combined support for all extreme right-wing parties in 1981 was only 0.4%.

Following the March 1986 election, President Mitterrand invited Jacques Chirac, the leader of the RPR (the dominant party in the centre-right alliance), to become Prime Minister (Chirac, the Mayor of Paris since 1977, had previously been Prime Minister in 1974–76). A new Council of Ministers, comprising RPR/UDF politicians and a few non-party members, was formed. This resulted in an unprecedented situation in France: a right-wing Government 'cohabiting' with a Socialist President, as Mitterrand had expressed his intention to remain in office until the expiry of his presidential term in 1988.

On the same day as the election for the National Assembly, voting took place throughout France for regional councils, using direct suffrage in all areas for the first time (the councils in metropolitan France had previously been chosen by indirect election, except in Corsica—see below). The regional elections also resulted in a swing to the right: the RPR/UDF received 39.3% of the votes and won 790 of the 1,840 seats on the regional councils, while the PS, with 29.1% of the votes, won 552 seats. Of the 22 regional councils in metropolitan France, 20 elected right-wing presidents (compared with 16 hitherto). In some regions, however, the right-wing alliances lacked a clear majority, and in nine regional councils they formed coalitions with the FN in order to maintain their control.

In April 1986 Chirac introduced highly controversial enabling legislation to allow his Government to circumvent the normal parliamentary process and to legislate by decree on economic and social issues, and on the proposed reversion to the single-seat majority voting system for elections to the National Assembly. The PS attempted to delay the legislation by submitting about 600 amendments, but the Government invoked the 'guillotine' procedure (setting a time-limit for parliamentary consideration of legislative proposals) to restrict further debate. A Socialist motion expressing 'no confidence' in the Government, introduced to delay the legislation further, was defeated in the Assembly. However, President Mitterrand announced that he would accept only a limited number of decrees on specific issues, and insisted on his presidential right to refuse to sign decrees that undermined the previous Government's achievements on social reform. Chirac was therefore forced to use the 'guillotine' procedure to gain parliamentary approval for contentious legislation, which the President would be constitutionally obliged to sign within 15 days, following its approval by the Senate (with a large right-wing majority) and the Constitutional Council.

In mid-1986 the Chirac Government succeeded in implementing a major part of its programme. In July the 'guillotine' procedure was used to enact legislation quickly through the National Assembly and the Senate to approve plans for the 'privatization' of 65 state-owned companies, and in November the shares in the state-owned Compagnie de Saint-Gobain, a conglomerate producing pipes, glass and building materials, were offered for sale to private investors. The Government implemented its programme of deregulation of the French broadcasting system, which included the privatization of TF1 (the state-owned television channel), the use of private communications companies to construct cable networks, and the termination of concessions on two new commercial television channels and two satellite television stations, which the Socialist Government had allotted to companies with a centre-left bias earlier in 1986, in an attempt to prevent domination of broadcasting by right-wing groups. The Chirac Government established a new broadcasting authority, the Commission Nationale de la Communication et des Libertés (CNCL), to oversee the reform programme. The Government also repealed a 1984 law which had been introduced to reform the press and to restrict right-wing press monopolies. In October 1986, however, the Constitutional Council added amendments to the broadcasting legislation to limit a single company's ownership of newspapers and other media outlets. In July the National Assembly adopted the right-wing coalition's proposals for stringent legislation on immigration, which enabled local authorities to expel illegal immigrants, removed the right of automatic French citizenship from children of foreign parents and granted more extensive powers to frontier police officers to refuse entry to immigrants accused of breaking the law. In October about 1,700 illegal immigrants were expelled from France. Chirac had also introduced tough anti-terrorism measures in May, following a series of bombings in Paris, which were carried out by the Committee of Solidarity with Arab and Middle Eastern Political Prisoners (CSPPA), a group seeking the release of three members of the Lebanese Armed Revolutionary Faction (FARL), who had been convicted of terrorist offences. The measures gained the general support of the National Assembly, and were implemented in mid-September, following a renewal of terrorist activities in Paris by the CSPPA, which resulted in 10 deaths. In elections for one-third of the seats in the enlarged Senate in late September, the right-wing parties consolidated their majority.

By the end of 1986 the Government's popularity had slumped, owing to two consecutive crises. In late November the largest student demonstrations since 1968 took place throughout France in protest against proposed legislation on education, which aimed to introduce selection procedures for university places, to increase registration fees, and reform the degree and baccalauréat systems. The use of riot police, and the death of one student during the demonstrations, provoked much criticism. In mid-December the Government was forced to withdraw the proposed legislation, and Alain Devaquet, the Minister Delegate attached to the Minister of National Education, resigned. In late December transport unions went on strike over pay and working conditions. The Government withdrew plans to introduce merit-linked salaries in January 1987, but remained determined that increases in wages should not exceed the limit of 2%–3% per year, set by the austerity policy. President Mitterrand exploited the weakened position of the Government and vociferously supported the students and transport workers.

As a result of the decentralization legislation of 1982, Corsica was elevated from regional status to that of a 'collectivité territoriale', with its own directly-elected 61-seat Assembly, and an administration with greater executive powers in economic, social and other spheres. This measure failed to pacify the pro-independence Front de Libération Nationale de la Corse (FLNC) and the Consulte des Comités Nationalistes (CCN), which were banned in 1983, following a terrorist campaign. A new independence movement, the Mouvement Corse pour l'Autodétermination (MCA), was immediately formed by members of the banned CCN, and terrorist activities have continued sporadically since 1984. The MCA won three seats in the Corsican Assembly at elections held in August 1984.

Since 1984 the French Government has also faced growing terrorist activity in the Pacific overseas territory of New Caledonia, where Kanak (indigenous Melanesian) separatists are campaigning for independence from metropolitan France. In July 1986 the Chirac Government cancelled its predecessor's plans to allow New Caledonians to vote for independence in association with France, and proposed to hold a vote in New Caledonia within 12 months on the question of total independence or the adoption of a statute to incorporate the territory firmly as part of the French Republic. Following pressure from the South Pacific Forum and the Kanak Socialist National Liberation Front (FLNKS), the UN General Assembly voted in December to place New Caledonia under the supervision of the UN Special Committee on Decolonization to ensure genuine self-determination for the islanders. However, the French Government announced that it would continue to implement its declared policy on New Caledonia.

Terrorist attacks in the Basque region of south-western France escalated in 1983 and 1984, as violence between Spanish right-wing extremists and members of the Basque separatist movement, ETA, spread across the border from Spain. In June 1984, responding to pressure from the Spanish Government, the French Government agreed to stop granting refugee status to ETA members seeking asylum in France, and in July 1986 the two governments agreed to increase collaboration over ETA. Many ETA members have subsequently been deported, detained, or expelled to other countries.

France is a founder-member of the European Communities. In 1966 it withdrew from the integrated military structure of NATO, but remained a member of the alliance. In 1984 President Mitterrand expressed support for the controversial deployment of US nuclear missiles in Europe, and the 1984–88 defence plan envisages the strengthening of France's independent nuclear deterrent, while reducing conventional armed forces. In 1986 the French Government became more active in NATO, and expressed willingness for France to be used as a landing place for NATO reinforcements during time of war. France and the Federal Republic of Germany agreed to intensify military links and to play a more active joint role in international affairs, while Chirac advocated a Western European Union charter to reinforce European co-operation on defence. In November the French Government introduced a five-year defence budget which envisaged that spending on military equipment would increase by 6% per year.

France has been conducting tests of nuclear weapons on the South Pacific atoll of Mururoa, in French Polynesia, since 1966, despite protests from countries in the region, particularly Australia and New Zealand. In mid-1985 France's relations with these countries were further damaged by the discovery that French secret service agents had been responsible for the sinking of the trawler *Rainbow Warrior* (flagship of the international environmental protection group, Greenpeace) in the New Zealand port of Auckland. In September the head of the secret service, Adm. Pierre Lacoste, was dismissed, and the Minister of Defence, Charles Hernu, was forced to resign. In December 1985 the French Government agreed to compensate Greenpeace, but controversy remained over the fate of the secret service agents, who had been imprisoned on charges of manslaughter by the New Zealand authorities, and over the issue of compensation for the New Zealand Government. In April 1986 the new Chirac Government gave priority to the release of the agents, and used trade sanctions against New Zealand imports. By July an agreement was reached between the two governments: New Zealand returned the agents on the condition that they were confined to Hao Atoll, a French military base in the Pacific, for three years, while France issued a formal apology and paid US $7m. compensation to New Zealand, and approved New Zealand butter quotas. In November France signed a treaty with the South Pacific Forum countries to eradicate nuclear and other pollution from the area.

France granted independence to most of its former colonies after the Second World War. In Indo-China, after prolonged fighting, Laos, Cambodia (now Kampuchea) and Viet-Nam became fully independent in 1954. In Africa most of the French colonies in the West and Equatorial regions attained independence in 1960, but have retained their close economic and political ties with France. In February 1985 the first Francophone summit was held in Paris to promote cultural and diplomatic links among former French colonies. Guerrilla warfare and other forms of civil strife in ex-colonies have involved French troops as peace-keeping forces in recent years. In 1983, under the terms of a co-operation agreement, a large contingent of French troops was sent to Chad as a result of continuing hostilities between government forces and Libyan-backed rebels. In September 1984 an agreement was signed between France and Libya, and both countries began a gradual evacuation of their forces from Chad. By December 1985 Libyan troops had been reinforced in northern Chad, and in February 1986 they attacked government forces. France sent 200 more troops to N'Djamena, the Chadian capital, and bombed a Libyan-built airbase at Ouadi Doum. A retaliatory strike followed on N'Djamena airport. In order to counter further attack, the French stationed an airstrike force at N'Djamena airport. After further fighting between government forces and rebels, and an escalation of Libyan hostilities in late 1986, the French Government was prepared to consider further military action in January 1987.

In 1986 the Chirac Government changed the direction of French foreign policy in the Middle East. From 1978 France had the largest contingent of soldiers in the UN Intervention Force in Lebanon (UNIFIL), with 1,400 men in a force of 5,800. Following increasing numbers of casualties among French soldiers, Chirac requested the UN to redefine UNIFIL's role, and by November 1986 the Government had announced the withdrawal of more than one-half of the French contingent of UNIFIL from Lebanon. The Chirac Government began to normalize relations with Iran, which had been hostile to France, owing to French sales of military equipment to Iraq since the outbreak of the Iran–Iraq war in September 1980. In 1986 the French Government reached a settlement with Iran over the repayment of a US $100m. loan from the Iranian Government of the late Shah in 1974, expelled leaders of the Mujaheddin resistance (opposed to the Iranian regime of Ayatollah Khomeini) from France and closed the Mujaheddin headquarters in Paris. Improved relations between France and Iran resulted in the release of five out of nine French hostages being detained by a pro-Iranian group, Islamic Jihad, in Lebanon. The French Government also thanked Syria for its role in the release of the hostages, and continued to maintain good relations with Syria, despite French approval of the British Government's anti-Syrian measures at an EEC summit in early November.

Government

Under the 1958 constitution, legislative power is held by the bicameral Parliament, comprising a Senate and a National Assembly. The Senate has 319 members (296 for metropolitan France, 13 for the overseas departments, 'collectivités territoriales' and territories, and 10 for French nationals abroad), increased in 1986 from 317 members. Senators are elected for a nine-year term by an electoral college composed of the members of the National Assembly, delegates from the Councils of the Departments and delegates from the Municipal Councils. One-third of the Senate is renewable every three years. The National Assembly has 577 members (increased in 1986 from 491), with 555 for metropolitan France and 22 for overseas departments, 'collectivités territoriales' and territories. In the March 1986 general election, members of the Assembly were directly elected by universal adult suffrage, using a system of proportional representation. The Assembly's term is five years, subject to dissolution. The Government that took power after the election introduced legislation, in preparation for the next elections, whereby the single-member constituency system of direct election is to be reintroduced, using a second ballot if the first ballot fails to produce an absolute majority for any one candidate.

Executive power is held by the President. Since 1962 the President has been directly elected by popular vote (using two ballots if necessary) for seven years. The President appoints a Council of Ministers, headed by the Prime Minister, which administers the country and is responsible to Parliament.

Metropolitan France comprises 21 administrative regions containing 96 departments. Under the decentralization law of March 1982, administrative and financial power in metropolitan France was transferred from the Préfets, who became Commissaires de la République, to locally-elected departmental assemblies (Conseils généraux) and regional assemblies (Conseils régionaux). The special status of a 'collectivité territoriale' was granted to Corsica, which has its own directly-elected legislative Assembly.

There are four overseas departments (French Guiana, Guadeloupe, Martinique and Réunion), two overseas 'collectivités

FRANCE

'territoriales' (Mayotte and St Pierre and Miquelon) and four overseas territories (French Polynesia, the French Southern and Antarctic Territories, New Caledonia and the Wallis and Futuna Islands), all of which are integral parts of the French Republic (see p. 1088). Each overseas department is administered by an elected Conseil général and Conseil régional, each 'collectivité territoriale' by an appointed government commissioner, and each overseas territory by an appointed high commissioner.

Defence

French military policy is decided by the Supreme Defence Council. Military service is compulsory and lasts for 12–18 months. In July 1986 the total armed forces numbered 557,493 (including 253,300 conscripts), comprising an army of 296,480, a navy of 66,345, an air force of 95,978, inter-service central staffs of 4,517, a Service de Santé of 8,465 and a gendarmerie of 85,708. Total reserves stood at 391,000 (army 305,000; navy 28,000; air force 58,000). The defence budget for 1986 was 158,026m. francs. France is a member of NATO, but withdrew from its integrated military organization in 1966.

Economic Affairs

France is one of the world's leading industrial countries, with extensive and diversified industrial and commercial activity. Much of the country's industrial base has been acquired since the Second World War, while there has been an increasing role in the economy for state-controlled enterprises. Since the late 1950s France has experienced significant economic growth, and its people enjoy a high standard of living. In 1984, according to estimates by the World Bank, France's GNP per head (at average 1982–84 prices) was US $9,760, having increased since 1965 at an average annual rate of 3.0% in real terms, one of the fastest growth rates in Western Europe. The average annual increase in overall gross domestic product (GDP), measured in constant prices, was 5.5% in 1965–73, slowing to 2.3% in 1973–84.

France remains Western Europe's leading agricultural nation, with 32m. ha, nearly 60% of its area, used for farming. The number of workers engaged in agriculture, however, declined as a proportion of the total employed population from 15% in 1968 to 7.8% in 1984. Co-operatives are very common in both supply and sales of most sectors, accounting for between one-third and one-half of all business. After intensive state-assisted marketing efforts, there was a record trade surplus in the agricultural sector of 17,000m. francs in 1980 and 21,900m. in 1981, compared with a deficit of 3,300m. in 1977. The surplus fell to 18,600m. francs in 1982, but rose again to approximately 23,000m. francs in 1983, and to 28,000m. francs in 1985. Agriculture accounted for about 17% of total exports in 1981: the chief items were cereals, sugar, dairy produce, wine and livestock. Protest against the EEC's Common Agricultural Policy (particularly the import of EEC-subsidized meat from the United Kingdom and the reduction of France's annual milk production quota by 1m. metric tons) was widespread in 1984. In 1986 the Government proposed to increase aid to beef and dairy farmers, and granted 1,300m. francs of aid, following a drought in mid-1986. Average farm incomes declined by 7.1% in 1985 (according to November estimates), compared with a fall of 3.1% in 1983. By the end of 1984 farmers' debts had risen to a total of 190,000m. francs. Despite France's 14m. ha of woodland, forestry has remained a minor industry. After a trade deficit of 14,000m. francs in wood and wood products was announced in 1982, the Government introduced measures to modernize the industry and to increase its efficiency.

Since the Second World War, French industry has expanded extremely rapidly. During 1970–80 industrial production increased by 33%, in spite of a fall in 1975 (owing to the world recession). After virtual stagnation during 1980–82, industrial production increased by 1.5% between May 1983 and March 1984, by 0.8% in the year to August 1985 and by an estimated 1.5% in 1986. The major branches of the manufacturing sector are steel, motor vehicles, aircraft, mechanical and electrical engineering, textiles, chemicals and food processing.

In 1986 the incoming Government of Jacques Chirac introduced a five-year programme to 'privatize' 65 state-owned industrial, banking and financial holding companies, including companies that had been nationalized by the Socialist Government in 1982. The Chirac Government hoped to raise about 200,000m. francs from the sale of state assets, at a rate of 40,000m. francs per year. The newly-privatized companies would remain 10% government-owned, 10% of shares would be allocated to company employees and a maximum of 20% of the shares would be sold to foreign groups. It was hoped that the sale of state-owned companies would reduce the state debt, and finance a reduction of 40,000m. francs in taxation and also government spending on the loss-making state-owned steel and motor vehicle industries before their eventual privatization. Chirac appointed new heads of state-owned companies to introduce rationalization programmes, and encouraged companies to enlarge their capital and to issue non-voting shares on the stock exchange, which would be converted into ordinary voting shares after privatization. By the end of 1986, the Compagnie de Saint-Gobain, producing glass, pipes and building materials, had been privatized, while two financial groups, Paribas and Assurances Générales de France, were due to be privatized in early 1987. The losses for the nationalized sector increased from 1,900m. francs in 1980 to 36,400m. francs in 1984, but decreased to 9,000m. francs in 1985.

Government grants to nationalized industries in 1987 were to be reduced by 10%, to 24,400m. francs. Losses by the coal industry rose from 115m. francs in 1982 to 750m. francs in the following year, and in 1984 the Socialist Government announced plans for restructuring, involving the closure of several coal mines and the loss of 30,000 jobs by 1988. By 1985 losses had increased to 8,900m. francs, although a loss of only 4,000m. francs was expected in 1986. Under the 1984 plan, subsidies were to be 'frozen' until 1989. In 1986 and 1987 the coal industry was to receive an annual subsidy of 7,400m. francs, representing a reduction in real terms. Output of coal was expected to be reduced from 18.5m. tons in 1983 to around 12m. tons by 1988. The French steel industry incurred losses of 38,000m. francs over the period 1980–85, and a loss of 4,000m. francs was forecast for 1986. The Government appointed a new chairman in 1986 to head the two steel companies, to carry out a rationalization programme. The industry aimed to reduce annual steel production to 16m. tons by 1990, and proposed to decrease the work-force from 75,000 to 50,000 by 1988.

Modernization plans in the private sector led to industrial unrest in 1983 and 1984, particularly in the motor manufacturing industry, which has suffered as a result of foreign competition: France's share in the market for road vehicles, both at home and abroad, declined steadily between 1979 and 1984. The performance of Renault, the state-owned vehicle manufacturer began to improve in 1985–86: its deficit was 10,925m. francs in 1985, compared with 12,555m. francs in 1984; exports increased by 1.8% in the first half of 1986, and sales grew by 17% in 1986. A restructuring programme was envisaged, to reduce car production, and 9,000 redundancies were planned for the end of 1986. In 1986 the Government reduced aid to the five major ship-building yards, and proposed rationalization plans whereby only one of the five yards would remain operational. A feature of the Socialist Government's restructuring plans was the creation of industrial conversion zones in areas where the decline of traditional heavy industry has led to high unemployment, while financial incentives were introduced to stimulate the development of small and medium-sized enterprises in these areas. In 1986 the Government planned to establish three corporate-tax-free zones, near the three ailing Normed ship-building operations, which would attract industrial investments to France.

France was the world's fifth largest exporting country in 1980. There were, however, heavy trade deficits as France's market share of world trade in manufactured goods declined from 11.1% in 1980 to 9.3% in 1985. The deficit reached a record 93,300m. francs in 1982, but declined to 48,900m. francs in 1983 and to around 25,000m. francs in 1984, owing to increased competitiveness after devaluations of the franc in 1981, 1982 and March 1983, and reduced domestic demand, caused by government austerity measures. In 1985 the trade deficit was reduced to 24,000m. francs, and by 1986 there was an estimated surplus of 5,000m. francs. However, this was a disappointing improvement, as the fall in the value of the US dollar and in the price of petroleum had been expected to add 60,000m. francs to the trade balance. A more substantial improvement in the trade balance was inhibited by the Government's policy of dismantling exchange controls to encourage repatriation of funds. There has been a marked improvement in the balance of payments in recent years: the current deficit decreased from US $12,082m. in 1982 to $876m. in 1984, and there was a surplus of $907m. in 1985, reflecting improved earnings from services especially from tourism. Since 1980 dependence on imported energy (which accounted for about 22% of France's imports in 1979) has been reduced, and in 1983 France provided almost 38% of its own energy requirements, an increase of 4% over the previous year; about 65% of electricity was produced by nuclear power in 1985, and this proportion is expected to increase to 75% by 1990. France's principal trading partners are the other members of the EEC, especially the Federal Republic of Germany, Italy and Belgium. Exports to major industrialized countries increased in 1983, but there was concern over increasing trade deficits with Japan and the Federal Republic of Germany. Tourism is one of France's largest sources of foreign exchange earnings, contributing some 32,000m. francs to the country's current account in 1985, but the industry was expected to suffer from US cancellations in 1986, owing to fears of terrorism. France remains the world's third largest exporter of armaments, despite a drop in sales in 1983. It also plays a leading part in the European aerospace industry. In 1985, however, there was a 14% decline in aircraft exports, although it was forecast that sales would rise in 1987, on the basis of contracts already signed.

France's GDP (in 1970 prices) increased by 3.3% in 1979, but by only 1.0% in 1980 and 0.5% in 1981. The growth rate recovered to 1.8% in 1982, but fell to 0.7% in 1983, reflecting declines in consumer spending and investment. In 1984 GDP grew by 1.5%, but in 1985 the growth rate fell to 1.1%. Growth of 2.3% was estimated for 1986. For 1987 the Government's target growth rate was 3%. Industrial stagnation and the effects of restructuring nationalized industries led to increased unemployment, particularly among young people. In July 1986 there was a 2.5% increase over the 1985 mid-year figure, with an estimated 2.47m. unemployed (some 9.8% of the total workforce), of whom more than 1m. were under 25 years of age. The Government established job-creation and youth-employment schemes, but by 1985 only 200,000 places had been created on such schemes, whereas it was estimated that some 500,000 jobs had been lost in French industry in the period 1981–84. In 1986 the new Government used public spending to create jobs for young people by paying 25%–100% of employers' social security contributions if they employed young workers. The Government also introduced legislation to encourage more flexible working patterns, with short-term labour contracts and an increased number of part-time jobs. In September, however, the Government introduced a law allowing employers to issue redundancies more easily. The 1987 GDP growth rate forecast was pessimistic with regard to the reduction of the rate of unemployment, as the French labour force was expected to rise by 0.8% per year in 1986–90. The number of unemployed was forecast to rise to 3.2m. by the end of 1987.

After the Socialists' electoral victory in 1981, the nationalization measures were accompanied by a series of social measures, including higher minimum wages and higher welfare allowances, funded by new taxes on persons with high incomes. The 1982 budget was reflationary, increasing expenditure by 27% to stimulate consumption. However, the expected improvement in investment and exports did not follow, while inflation rose and the deficit on the current balance of payments trebled in 1982 to 78,000m. francs, making necessary a heavy increase in foreign borrowing (the foreign medium- and long-term debt rose from 187,000m. francs at the end of 1981 to 528,500m. francs at the end of 1984, exacerbated by the strength of the US dollar). Austerity measures were therefore introduced, including a temporary 'freeze' on wages in 1982, increased taxation and price controls, with the aim of reducing the rate of inflation and the trade deficit. The average annual rate of inflation declined from 13.4% in 1981 to 4.7% in 1985, and inflation was only 2.4% in the year to November 1986. The budget for 1984 continued 'exceptional' taxes, introduced in the previous year, and limited the increase in government spending to 6.5%; the aim of keeping the budget deficit to below 3% of annual GNP, however, was not achieved, and there was a final deficit of some 130,000m. francs, equivalent to 3.3% of GNP.

The 1985 budget reduced direct taxation (in accordance with an undertaking to reduce by 1% the ratio of taxation and compulsory levies to GDP, estimated at 45% in 1984) but increased the prices of petroleum products and charges for public services; government expenditure was to rise by only 5.9%. This budget was rejected by the Communist Party, hitherto parliamentary supporters of the Socialist Government. Another austerity budget was proposed for 1986. It aimed to restrain government spending, to maintain confidence in the franc and to continue the reduction in the rate of inflation. Public spending was to be reduced by 1%–2% in real terms, and grants to nationalized companies were to be drastically cut. The budget deficit was projected at 145,000m. francs, or 3% of GDP.

Following the general election in March 1986, the new right-wing Government introduced a series of economic measures which aimed to limit the annual rate of inflation to 2.3% and to reduce the budgetary deficit by 1,300m. francs. The Government announced a 6% devaluation of the franc, a partial lifting of controls on prices and foreign exchange transactions, a 'freeze' in the real growth of civil service salaries and a reduction of 15,000m. francs in planned government spending for the year. The Government also proposed to raise an estimated 200,000m. francs over five years by the disposal of state assets through its privatization programme (see above). The budget for 1987 reflected the Government's determination to implement its economic programme, despite slower growth of GDP than previously forecast. Taxation was to be reduced by 27,000m. francs, including cuts of 15,000m. francs in personal taxes, owing to the abolition of the Socialist-sponsored wealth tax and to an increase in the level of minimum earnings liable to taxation. These measures were offset by an increase of 15,000m. francs in social security and pension fund contributions. The effect of new reductions in corporation tax of 11,000m. francs was balanced by cuts of 10% in government aid to industry. Attempts to reduce government expenditure would also result in the loss of 19,000 jobs in the civil service, and in November the Government introduced an incomes policy, with a limit of 2%–3% on public-sector salary increases. The proposals for 1987 increased projected expenditure by 1.8%, i.e. by less than the estimated rate of inflation for 1986, which benefited job retraining schemes and defence. The projected budget deficit was reduced to 128,600m. francs equivalent to 2.5% of expected annual GDP.

Social Welfare

France has evolved a comprehensive system of social security, which is compulsory for all wage-earners and self-employed people. State insurance of wage-earners requires contributions from both employers and employees, and provides for sickness, unemployment, maternity, disability through industrial accident, and substantial allowances for large families. The self-employed must make these contributions in full. War veterans receive pensions and certain privileges, and widows the equivalent of three months' salary and pension. About 95% of all medical practitioners adhere to the state scheme. The patient pays directly for medical treatment and prescribed medicines, and then obtains reimbursement for all or part of the cost. Sickness benefits and pensions are related to the insured person's income, age and the length of time for which he or she has been insured. Of total expenditure by the central government in 1982, about 227,300m. francs (14.6%) was for health, and a further 688,200m. francs (44.6%) for social security and welfare. In 1977 France had 3,548 hospital establishments, with a total of 644,118 beds, equivalent to one for every 82 inhabitants. In 1983 there were 147,402 physicians registered in France. A national minimum hourly wage is in force, and is periodically adjusted to keep pace with inflation.

Education

France is divided into 27 educational districts, called Académies, each responsible for the administration of education, from primary to higher levels, in its area.

Education is compulsory and free for children aged six to 16 years. Primary education begins at six years of age and lasts for five years. At the age of 11 all pupils enter the first cycle of the Enseignement secondaire, with a four-year general course. At the age of 15 they may then proceed to the second cycle,

FRANCE

choosing a course leading to the baccalauréat examination after three years or a course leading to the brevet d'études professionnelles after two years, with commercial, administrative or industrial options. In 1963 junior classes in the Lycées were gradually abolished in favour of new junior comprehensives, called Collèges. Alongside the collèges and lycées, technical education is provided in the Lycées professionnels and the Lycées techniques. About 15% of children attend France's 10,000 private schools, most of which are administered by the Roman Catholic Church. The Socialist Government's plans to merge private schools into the state system were abandoned in 1984, following strong public protest; compromise measures were introduced, however, involving continued government financial assistance and greater involvement in the appointment of teachers at private schools.

Educational reforms, introduced in 1980, aimed to decentralize the state school system: the school calendar now varies according to three zones, and the previously rigid and formal syllabus has been replaced by more flexibility and choice of curricula. Further decentralization measures have included, from 1986, the transfer of financial responsibility for education to the local authorities.

The minimum qualification for entry to university faculties is the baccalauréat. There are three cycles of university education. The first level, the Diplôme d'études universitaires générales (DEUG), is reached after two years of study, and the first degree, the Licence, is obtained after three years. The master's degree (Maîtrise) is obtained after four years of study, while the doctorate requires six or seven years' study and the submission of a thesis. The prestigious Grandes Ecoles complement the universities; entry to them is by competitive examination, and they have traditionally supplied France's administrative élite. The 1968 reforms in higher education aimed to increase university autonomy and to render teaching methods less formal. Several new diploma courses were instituted in 1982 and 1984, and more directly vocational and professional qualifications are planned. However, Government plans to revise the baccalauréat, to introduce further selection procedures for entry to the universities, to restrict places on courses and to award separate degrees in each university were abandoned in December 1986, following widespread student demonstrations.

Expenditure on education by central and local government in 1982 was about 159,700m. francs, equivalent to 9.2% of total government spending. Different forms of financial aid are available to university students, but in 1983/84 only 18% of French students obtained a grant.

Primary teachers are trained in Ecoles Normales. Secondary teachers must hold either the Certificat d'Aptitude au Professorat d'Enseignement Général des Collèges (CAPEGC), the Certificat d'Aptitude au Professorat de l'Enseignement du Second Degré (CAPES) or the Agrégation.

Tourism

France draws tourists from all over the world. Paris is famous for its boulevards, historic buildings, theatres, art treasures, fashion houses and restaurants, and for its many music halls and night clubs. The Mediterranean and Atlantic coasts and the French Alps are the most popular tourist resorts. Among other attractions are the many ancient towns, the châteaux of the Loire, the fishing villages of Brittany and Normandy, and spas and places of pilgrimage, such as Vichy and Lourdes. Corsica also attracts many tourists. Gastronomy is a tourist attraction throughout France. There were 36,748,000 tourist arrivals in 1985, when tourist receipts totalled 32,000m. francs. The leading sources of visitors are the Federal Republic of Germany, Belgium, the United Kingdom, the Netherlands and Switzerland.

Public Holidays

1987: 1 January (New Year's Day), 20 April (Easter Monday), 1 May (Labour Day), 8 May (Liberation Day), 28 May (Ascension Day), 8 June (Whit Monday), 14 July (National Day, Fall of the Bastille), 15 August (Assumption), 1 November (All Saints' Day), 11 November (Armistice Day), 25 December (Christmas Day).

1988: 1 January (New Year's Day), 4 April (Easter Monday), 1 May (Labour Day), 8 May (Liberation Day), 12 May (Ascension Day), 23 May (Whit Monday), 14 July (National Day, Fall of the Bastille), 15 August (Assumption), 1 November (All Saints' Day), 11 November (Armistice Day), 25 December (Christmas Day).

Weights and Measures

The metric system is in force.

Currency and Exchange Rates

100 centimes = 1 French franc.

Exchange rates (30 September 1986):
 £1 sterling = 9.6125 francs;
 US $1 = 6.6425 francs.

FRANCE

Statistical Survey

Statistical Survey

Unless otherwise indicated, figures in this survey refer to metropolitan France, excluding Overseas Departments and Territories.

Area and Population

AREA, POPULATION AND DENSITY

Area (sq km)	543,965*
Population (census results, *de jure*)†	
20 February 1975	52,655,802
4 March 1982	54,334,871
Population (official estimates at mid-year)	
1983	54,730,000
1984	54,947,000
1985	55,170,000
Density (per sq km) at mid-1985	101.4

* 210,026 sq miles.
† Excluding professional soldiers and military personnel outside the country with no personal residence in France. These were estimated at 44,000 in 1975.

PRINCIPAL TOWNS
(population at 1982 census, provisional figures)

Paris (capital)	2,188,960	Dijon	140,900
Marseille		Limoges	139,320
(Marseilles)	867,260	Angers	137,760
Lyon (Lyons)	408,860	Tours	133,580
Toulouse	345,780	Amiens	130,880
Nice	335,240	Nîmes	126,780
Strasbourg	248,040	Aix-en-Provence	119,140
Nantes	242,340	Villeurbanne	116,660
Bordeaux	205,960	Caen	115,180
Saint-Etienne	204,120	Besançon	114,040
Le Havre	199,120	Metz	113,360
Montpellier	196,360	Saint-Nazaire	112,000
Rennes	195,260	Perpignan	110,540
Reims (Rheims)	178,380	Mulhouse	107,480
Toulon	177,920	Orléans	103,660
Lille	164,900	Rouen	101,700
Grenoble	156,440	Boulogne-	
Brest	154,020	Billancourt	101,360
Clermont-Ferrand	148,040	Roubaix	100,820
Le Mans	147,140		

NATIONALITY OF THE POPULATION (1982 census*)

Country of citizenship	Population	%
France	50,593,100	93.22
Algeria	795,920	1.47
Belgium	50,200	0.09
Germany	43,840	0.08
Italy	333,740	0.61
Morocco	431,120	0.79
Poland	64,820	0.12
Portugal	764,860	1.41
Spain	321,440	0.59
Tunisia	189,400	0.35
Turkey	123,540	0.23
Yugoslavia	64,420	0.11
Others	496,800	0.93
Total	**54,273,200**	**100.00**

* Figures based on a 5% sample of census returns.

REGIONS (1982 census*)

	Area (sq km)	Population	Density (per sq km)
Ile-de-France	12,012.3	10,064,840	837.9
Champagne-Ardennes	25,605.8	1,344,820	52.5
Picardie (Picardy)	19,399.5	1,740,460	89.7
Haute-Normandie	12,317.4	1,659,520	134.7
Centre	39,150.9	2,265,340	57.9
Basse-Normandie	17,589.3	1,350,480	76.8
Bourgogne (Burgundy)	31,581.9	1,592,300	50.4
Nord-Pas-de-Calais	12,414.1	3,919,240	315.7
Lorraine	23,547.1	2,334,740	99.2
Alsace	8,280.2	1,553,740	187.6
Franche-Comté	16,202.4	1,078,700	66.6
Pays de la Loire	32,081.8	2,937,980	91.6
Bretagne (Brittany)	27,207.9	2,703,440	99.4
Poitou-Charentes	25,809.5	1,567,600	60.3
Aquitaine	41,308.4	2,655,800	64.3
Midi-Pyrénées	45,347.9	2,308,740	50.9
Limousin	16,942.3	736,340	43.5
Rhône-Alpes	43,698.2	5,022,800	114.9
Auvergne	26,012.9	1,329,180	51.0
Languedoc-Roussillon	27,375.8	1,929,520	70.5
Provence-Alpes-Côte d'Azur	31,397.9	3,942,980	125.6
Corse (Corsica)	8,681.5	234,640	27.0
Total	**543,965.4**	**54,273,200**	**99.8**

* Figures for population are based on a 5% sample of census returns.

BIRTHS, MARRIAGES AND DEATHS*

	Registered live births		Registered marriages		Registered deaths	
	Number	Rate (per 1,000)	Number	Rate (per 1,000)	Number	Rate (per 1,000)
1978	737,062	13.8	354,628	6.7	546,916	10.3
1979	757,354	14.1	340,405	6.7	541,805	10.1
1980	800,376	14.9	334,377	6.2	547,107	10.2
1981	805,483	14.9	315,117	5.8	554,823	10.3
1982†	797,970	14.7	311,910	5.6	543,160	10.0
1983†	748,790	13.7	299,820	5.5	558,740	10.2
1984†	760,480	13.8	280,960	5.1	540,600	9.8
1985†	769,070	14.1	n.a.	4.9	552,490	10.1

* Including data for national armed forces outside the country.
† Provisional figures.

Expectation of Life at Birth (1981): Males 70.4 years; Females 78.5 years.

IMMIGRATION AND EMIGRATION

	1979	1980	1981
Algerian workers and their families:			
Arriving from Algeria in France	970,244	1,185,280	1,338,674
Returning from France to Algeria	913,373	1,098,878	1,239,550
Other immigrants:			
Permanent	48,523	51,462	n.a.
Seasonal	124,490	120,211	n.a.

ECONOMICALLY ACTIVE POPULATION*

	1975 Census† Males	1975 Census† Females	1975 Census† Total	Official estimate 1984‡
Agriculture, hunting, forestry and fishing	1,470,700	628,400	2,099,100	1,659,300
Mining and quarrying	171,400	9,900	181,300	121,800
Manufacturing	4,014,800	1,805,100	5,819,900	4,991,900
Electricity, gas and water	144,300	30,000	174,400	217,200
Construction	1,797,400	101,600	1,899,000	1,578,900
Trade, restaurants and hotels	1,759,700	1,426,900	3,186,600	3,454,400
Transport, storage and communications	978,000	277,900	1,255,800	1,369,900
Finance, insurance, real estate and business services	705,100	581,200	1,286,300	1,655,700
Community, social and personal services	2,223,600	2,813,900	5,037,500	6,205,500
Activities not adequately described	3,200	900	4,100	—
Total employed	13,268,200	7,675,800	20,944,000	21,254,600
Unemployed	374,500	456,400	830,900	2,318,700
Total labour force	13,642,700	8,132,200	21,774,900	23,573,300

* Including regular members of the armed forces, numbering 244,000 (males 235,300; females 8,700) in 1975 and 313,800 (males 303,400; females 10,400) in 1984, but excluding persons on compulsory military service.

† Based on a 5% sample of census returns. According to a 20% sample, the total labour force was 22,041,770, (males 13,909,585; females 8,132,185).

‡ Figures relate to persons 17 years of age and over. The total labour force comprised 13,708,500 males (12,636,300 employed; 1,072,200 unemployed) and 9,864,800 females (8,618,300 employed; 1,246,500 unemployed).

1982 Census (5% sample): Total labour force 23,776,500 (males 14,191,780; females 9,584,720).

Source: ILO, *Year Book of Labour Statistics*.

Agriculture

PRINCIPAL CROPS ('000 metric tons)

	1983	1984	1985
Wheat	24,745	32,977	29,030
Rye	293	349	298
Barley	8,772	11,543	11,424
Oats	1,419	1,875	1,743
Maize*	10,525	10,493	11,839
Sorghum	248	262	192
Rice (paddy)	38	36	61
Sugar beet	26,319	28,752	28,476
Potatoes	5,731	6,964	7,814
Pulses	715	881	1,058
Soybeans	29	46	58
Sunflower seed	833	980	1,510
Rapeseed	969	1,354	1,400
Tobacco (leaves)	36	37	38
Artichokes	96	95	83

	1983	1984	1985
Cabbages	254‡	266‡	270†
Carrots	508	551	580
Cauliflowers	542	372	538
Cucumbers and gherkins	100‡	109‡	105†
Melons	222	235	246
Dry onions	170	175	195
Green peas	440	480	400
Tomatoes	770	833	887
Apples	1,983	2,960	2,315‡
Apricots	102	82	98
Grapes†	10,000	9,370	10,000
Peaches and nectarines	447	482	489
Pears	430	485	450
Plums	177	225	185

* Figures refer to main, associated and catch crops.
† FAO estimate.
‡ Unofficial estimate.

Source: FAO, *Production Yearbook*.

LIVESTOCK ('000 head at 31 December)

	1982	1983	1984
Cattle	23,656	23,519†	23,099†
Pigs	11,709	11,251	10,975
Sheep†	12,251	11,231	10,824
Goats	1,208	1,042	962
Horses	306	310*	310*
Asses*	23	23	23
Mules	12*	12	12*

Chickens (million): 187 in 1982; 185* in 1983; 188* in 1984.
Ducks (million): 10* in 1982; 10* in 1983; 10* in 1984.
Turkeys (million): 16* in 1982; 16* in 1983; 17* in 1984.
* FAO estimate.
† Unofficial figure.
Source: FAO, *Production Yearbook*.

LIVESTOCK PRODUCTS ('000 metric tons)

	1983	1984	1985
Beef and veal	1,811	1,991	1,900*
Mutton and lamb	171	174	177*
Goats' meat	8	8*	8*
Pig meat	1,795	1,819	1,810
Horse meat	28	29	28
Poultry meat	1,284	1,249	1,281
Other meat	294	292	295
Edible offals*	405	423	418
Cows' milk	33,515	33,918	33,000*
Sheep's milk	1,080	1,060	1,060*
Goats' milk	445	455*	450*
Butter	622	597	570
Cheese	1,207	1,245	1,275
Hen eggs	908	917	915
Wool:			
greasy	22.5*	24.0	24.0†
clean*	11.0	11.1	11.3

* FAO estimate.
† Unofficial figure.
Source: FAO, *Production Yearbook* and *Monthly Bulletin of Statistics*.

Forestry

ROUNDWOOD REMOVALS
('000 cubic metres, excluding bark)

	1982	1983	1984
Sawlogs, veneer logs and logs for sleepers	17,755	18,611	18,611
Pulpwood	8,419	8,974	8,974
Other industrial wood	807	672	672*
Fuel wood*	10,418	10,418	10,424
Total	37,399	38,675	38,681

* FAO estimate.
Source: FAO, *Yearbook of Forest Products*.

SAWNWOOD PRODUCTION
('000 cubic metres, including boxboards)

	1982	1983	1984
Coniferous (softwood)	5,388	5,483	5,667
Broadleaved (hardwood)	3,400	3,313	3,485
Total	8,788	8,796	9,152

Railway sleepers ('000 cubic metres): 261 in 1982; 209 in 1983.
Source: FAO, *Yearbook of Forest Products*.

Fishing*

('000 metric tons, live weight)

	1982	1983	1984
Atlantic cod	46.0	46.7	56.4
Ling	14.7	16.2	15.2
Haddock	22.5	19.4	17.8
Saithe (Pollock)	68.7	63.7	68.2
Whiting	43.8	39.5	34.2
European hake	18.3	22.4	21.0
Monk (Anglerfish)	21.2	23.0	23.0
Atlantic herring	15.1	16.8	22.4
European sardine (pilchard)	28.4	26.0	24.3
Skipjack tuna	26.5	39.9	48.8
Yellowfin tuna	31.7	35.0	44.4
Atlantic mackerel	18.1	12.4	13.3
Sharks, rays, skates, etc.	20.6	23.3	21.2
Other fishes (incl. unspecified)	139.0	154.7	146.1
Total fish	514.6	538.8	556.1
Crustaceans	30.3	30.3	27.8
Oysters	87.1	106.2	79.5
Blue mussel	75.0	57.8	47.4
Other molluscs	38.4	40.7	27.6
Other marine animals	0.5	0.3	0.3
Total catch	746.0	774.1	738.8
Mediterranean and Black Sea	57.7	52.4	46.4
Atlantic Ocean	680.2	699.2	613.6
Indian Ocean	8.2	22.6	78.7

* Figures include quantities landed by French craft in foreign ports and exclude quantities landed by foreign craft in French ports. Data exclude aquatic plants ('000 metric tons): 40.7 in 1982; 47.7 in 1983; 64.2 in 1984. Catch from inland waters (28,065 metric tons in 1980) is also excluded.

Source: FAO, *Yearbook of Fishery Statistics*.

Mining

	1982	1983	1984
Hard coal ('000 metric tons)	16,896	17,022	16,594
Brown coal (incl. lignite) ('000 metric tons)	3,065	2,606	2,426
Iron ore:			
gross weight ('000 metric tons)	19,411	15,967	14,840
metal content ('000 metric tons)	6,200	5,174	4,679
Bauxite ('000 metric tons)	1,610	1,595	1,522
Crude petroleum ('000 metric tons)	1,646	1,661	2,064
Potash salts ('000 metric tons)*	1,824	1,651	1,873
Native sulphur ('000 metric tons)	1,839	1,654	1,589
Phosphate rock ('000 metric tons)	11	3.4	n.a.
Salt (unrefined) ('000 metric tons)	6,694	5,686	5,779
Lead concentrates (metric tons)†	5,860	1,511	1,607
Zinc concentrates (metric tons)†	37,020	33,970	35,112
Natural gas (million cu m)	6,586	6,662	6,344

* Figures refer to recovered quantities of K_2O.
† Figures refer to the metal content of concentrates.

Source: Ministère de l'Industrie, des Postes et Télécommunications et du Tourisme.

Industry

SELECTED PRODUCTS

		1982	1983	1984
Wheat flour	'000 metric tons	3,454	3,427	3,499
Raw sugar	'000 metric tons	4,825	3,875	4,305
Margarine	'000 metric tons	164	162	154
Wine	'000 hectolitres	79,950	68,800	64,150
Beer	'000 hectolitres	22,409	22,086	22,287
Cigarettes and cigarillos	million	62,510	62,147	60,729
Cotton yarn (pure and mixed)[1]	metric tons	141,281	148,471	146,863
Woven cotton fabrics (pure and mixed)	metric tons	134,099	127,940	126,123
Wool yarn (pure and mixed)	metric tons	113,709	108,061	106,978
Woven woollen fabrics (pure and mixed)	metric tons	49,742	47,816	47,231
Rayon and acetate continuous filaments	metric tons	8,592	8,394	7,523
Rayon and acetate discontinuous fibres[2]	metric tons	37,826	29,839	20,980
Non-cellulosic continuous filaments	metric tons	64,787	63,227	63,513
Non-cellulosic discontinuous fibres	metric tons	140,187	143,895	152,392
Woven fabrics of non-cellulosic (synthetic) fibres[3]	metric tons	73,756	66,613	n.a.
Mechanical wood pulp	'000 metric tons	406	398	460
Chemical wood pulp	'000 metric tons	1,223	1,338	1,456
Newsprint	'000 metric tons	248	219	265
Other printing and writing paper	'000 metric tons	2,072	2,128	2,154
Other paper and paperboard	'000 metric tons	2,807	2,915	3,046
Synthetic rubber	'000 metric tons	286	306	337
Rubber tyres[4]	'000	41,478	45,606	47,817
Sulphuric acid	'000 metric tons	4,166	4,325	4,531
Caustic soda (Sodium hydroxide)	'000 metric tons	1,448	1,393	1,470
Nitrogenous fertilizers (a)[5]	'000 metric tons	1,553	1,530	1,600
Phosphate fertilizers (b)[5]	'000 metric tons	1,300	1,200	1,230
Potash fertilizers (b)[5]	'000 metric tons	1,726	1,601	1,685
Plastics and synthetic resins	'000 metric tons	2,950	3,098	3,319
Liquefied petroleum gas[6]	'000 metric tons	2,467	2,359	2,291
Motor spirit (petrol)	'000 metric tons	16,709	16,173	16,009
Jet fuel	'000 metric tons	4,085	4,474	4,436
Distillate fuel oils	'000 metric tons	11,115	9,358	10,328
Residual fuel oil	'000 metric tons	36,515	33,948	32,914
Petroleum bitumen (asphalt)	'000 metric tons	2,652	2,437	2,238
Coke-oven coke	'000 metric tons	9,935	8,458	8,999
Cement	'000 metric tons	26,141	24,503	22,724
Pig-iron	'000 metric tons	15,047	13,770	15,036
Crude steel	'000 metric tons	18,402	17,582	19,000
Rolled steel products	'000 metric tons	16,462	15,342	16,543
Aluminium (unwrought): primary	'000 metric tons	390.5	360	343
secondary (incl. alloys)	'000 metric tons	154.8	162.1	159
Refined copper (unwrought)	metric tons	46,000	45,000	41,000
Lead (unwrought): primary	'000 metric tons	144	116	118
secondary	'000 metric tons	38	37	34
Zinc (unwrought)[7]	'000 metric tons	283	286	292
Radio receivers	'000	2,733	2,489	2,128
Television receivers	'000	2,155	2,033	2,001
Merchant ships launched	'000 gross reg. tons	287	307	n.a.
Passenger motor cars	'000	2,777.1	2,960.8	2,713.3
Lorries	'000	324.5	332.9	306.0
Mopeds	'000	504	409	450
Construction: dwellings completed[8]	'000	n.a.	314	n.a.
Electric energy	million kWh	265,281	281,589	307,107
Manufactured gas	million kWh	63	19	n.a.

[1] Including tyre-core yarn.   [2] Including cigarette filtration tow.
[3] Including fabrics of natural silk.
[4] Tyres for road motor vehicles other than bicycles and motor cycles.
[5] Twelve months ending (a) 30 June or (b) 30 April of year stated. Production is in terms of plant nutrients: nitrogen, phosphoric acid and K_2O.
[6] Excluding production in natural gas processing plants ('000 metric tons): 265 in 1982.
[7] Including both primary and secondary production, but excluding remelted zinc.
[8] Including restorations and conversions but excluding single rooms without kitchens.

Source: Ministère de l'Industrie, des Postes et Télécommunications et du Tourisme.

FRANCE   *Statistical Survey*

Finance

CURRENCY AND EXCHANGE RATES

Monetary Units:
100 centimes = 1 French franc.

Denominations:
Coins: 1, 5, 10, 20 and 50 centimes; 1, 2, 5, 10 and 100 francs.
Notes: 10, 50, 100, 200 and 500 francs.

Sterling and Dollar Equivalents (30 September 1986)
£1 sterling = 9.6125 francs;
US $1 = 6.6425 francs;
1,000 French francs = £104.03 = $150.55.

Average Exchange Rate (francs per US $)
1983   7.621
1984   8.739
1985   8.985

BANK OF FRANCE AND EXCHANGE FUND RESERVES* (US $ million at 31 December)

	1983	1984	1985
Gold†	30,786	26,832	27,580
IMF special drawing rights	442	572	900
Reserve position in IMF	1,352	1,265	1,370
Foreign exchange	18,057	19,102	24,319
Total	50,637	47,772	54,169

* Excluding deposits made with the European Monetary Co-operation Fund.
† Valued at market-related prices.
Source: IMF, *International Financial Statistics*.

COST OF LIVING (Consumer Price Index for Urban Households, average of monthly figures; base: 1980 = 100)

	1982	1983	1984
Food	128.4	140.3	151.4
Fuel and light	137.8	150.7	162.8
Clothing and household linen	120.0	132.3	145.7
Rent	123.9	136.0	146.5
All items (incl. others)	126.8	139.0	149.3

1985: Food 158.9; All items 158.0.
Source: ILO, mainly *Year Book of Labour Statistics*.

BUDGET (million francs)

Revenue	1984	1985	1986
Tax revenue	950,037	1,009,104	1,062,332
Income tax	203,397	204,155	210,507
Corporation tax	89,290	93,720	99,930
Value-added tax	415,800	444,624	470,895
Stamp duty, etc.*	49,980	53,167	56,024
Other customs revenue	10,455	11,256	12,031
Petroleum revenue	67,396	85,291	90,915
Other taxes	113,719	116,981	122,030
Non-tax revenue	54,002	60,475	63,746
Special accounts	10,623	11,649	11,980
Tax relief and reimbursements	−73,620	−98,570	−107,400
Other deductions, e.g. EEC	−107,912	−115,284	−129,088
Total	833,130	867,374	901,570

* Including registration duties and tax on stock exchange transactions.

Expenditure	1984	1985	1986
Public authorities, general administration	108,694	116,114	128,704
Education and culture	223,084	238,566	246,505
Social services, health and employment	199,688	200,859	199,042
Agriculture and rural areas	24,365	25,179	25,726
Housing and town planning	42,765	46,939	48,023
Transport and communications	42,795	42,920	43,052
Industry and services	46,490	50,853	51,301
Foreign affairs	27,479	26,150	26,236
Defence	150,769	159,531	167,834
Others	94,671	111,060	117,355
Total	960,800	1,018,171	1,053,778

Source: Ministère de l'Economie et des Finances.

CURRENCY IN CIRCULATION
('000 million francs at 31 December)

	1983	1984	1985
Currency outside banks	190.6	198.8	207.4

Source: Banque de France, Paris.

NATIONAL ACCOUNTS (million francs at current prices)
National Income and Product

	1983	1984	1985
Compensation of employees	2,188,954	2,343,837	2,476,196
Operating surplus	764,250	832,204	1,001,965
Domestic factor incomes	2,953,204	3,176,041	3,478,161
Consumption of fixed capital	487,800	513,335	572,785
Gross domestic product at factor cost	3,441,004	3,689,376	4,050,946
Indirect taxes	578,065	695,948	639,749
Less Subsidies	84,062	102,481	105,357
GDP in purchasers' values	3,935,007	4,282,843	4,585,338
Factor income received from abroad / Less Factor income paid abroad	2,709	15,296	15,239
Gross national product	3,932,298	4,267,547	4,570,099
Less Consumption of fixed capital	487,800	513,335	572,785
Less Net indirect taxes paid to supranational organizations	6,657	7,927	4,914
National income in market prices	3,437,841	3,746,085	3,992,400

Source: Ministère de l'Economie et des Finances.

Expenditure on the Gross Domestic Product

	1981	1982	1983
Government final consumption expenditure	491,780	578,489	644,656
Private final consumption expenditure*	2,008,720	2,302,420	2,544,860
Increase in stocks†	−6,679	31,162	−1,325
Gross fixed capital formation†	665,989	742,184	778,702
Total domestic expenditure*	3,159,810	3,654,255	3,966,890
Exports of goods and services	735,396	822,347	930,353
Less Imports of goods and services	784,598	909,622	962,236
GDP in purchasers' values*	3,110,610	3,566,980	3,935,010
GDP at constant 1970 prices*	1,123,000	1,143,210	1,151,560

* Totals are generally rounded to the nearest 10 million francs.
† Construction of non-residential buildings is included in 'Increase in stocks'.

Gross Domestic Product by Economic Activity

	1981	1982	1983
Agriculture and hunting	108,367	140,509	142,177
Forestry and logging	9,718	8,937	10,349
Fishing	3,137	3,232	3,640
Mining and quarrying	27,019	28,313	29,061
Manufacturing	787,847	898,268	992,224
Electricity, gas and water	67,701	77,150	96,970
Construction	201,750	227,553	236,219
Wholesale and retail trade	314,707	354,890	387,075
Restaurants and hotels	67,135	76,616	87,620
Transport, storage and communications	165,904	187,397	206,051
Finance, insurance, real estate and business services*	536,774	605,820	684,396
Government services	386,767	455,085	505,720
Other community, social and personal services	253,198	292,664	330,539
Private non-profit services to households / Domestic services of households	22,888	25,932	28,166
Sub-total†	2,952,910	3,382,370	3,740,210
Value-added tax and import duties	282,911	331,619	360,160
Less Imputed bank service charges	125,217	147,003	165,360
Total†	3,110,610	3,566,980	3,935,010

* Including imputed rents of owner-occupied dwellings.
† Rounded to the nearest 10 million francs.

FRANCE — *Statistical Survey*

BALANCE OF PAYMENTS (US $ million)*

	1983	1984	1985
Merchandise exports f.o.b.	89,706	92,214	96,033
Merchandise imports f.o.b.	−98,460	−96,865	−100,565
Trade balance	−8,754	−4,651	−4,532
Exports of services	55,572	55,491	58,613
Imports of services	−48,169	−48,818	−50,574
Balance on goods and services	−1,351	2,022	3,507
Private unrequited transfers (net)	−1,737	−1,013	−1,312
Government unrequited transfers (net)	−2,077	−1,884	−1,288
Current balance	−5,166	−876	907
Direct capital investment (net)	12	279	317
Other long-term capital (net)	9,301	4,937	3,518
Short-term capital (net)	−339	−2,204	−2,422
Net errors and omissions	358	650	60
Total (net monetary movements)	4,166	2,786	2,380
Valuation changes (net)	482	−2,626	2,981
Official financing (net)	−561	148	316
Changes in reserves	4,087	308	5,677

* Figures refer to transactions of metropolitan France, Monaco and the French overseas departments and territories with the rest of the world.

Source: IMF, *International Financial Statistics*.

FINANCIAL FLOWS TO DEVELOPING COUNTRIES
(US $ million)

	1982	1983	1984*
Official development assistance:			
To individual countries	3,312	3,145	3,170
To multilateral institutions	716	670	618
Other official capital flows	429	467	1,246
Private capital	9,123	5,052	3,862
Total flow of resources	13,580	9,334	8,896

* Provisional.

FINANCIAL FLOWS BY RECEIVING COUNTRIES
(US $ million)

	1982	1983	1984*
Overseas Departments and Overseas Territories (DOM-TOM)	1,560	1,497	1,422
African and Malagasy States	4,146	3,015	1,611
Algeria	−107	379	449
Morocco and Tunisia	613	351	559
Other countries	6,389	3,002	3,715
International organizations	843	906	828
Total	13,444	9,150	8,584

* Provisional.

Source: Ministère des Relations Extérieures, Paris.

FRANCE

Statistical Survey

External Trade

Note: Figures refer to the trade of metropolitan France and Monaco with the rest of the world, excluding trade in war materials, goods exported under the off-shore procurement programme, war reparations and restitutions and the export of sea products direct from the high seas. The figures include trade in second-hand ships and aircraft, and the supply of stores and bunkers for foreign ships and aircraft.

PRINCIPAL COMMODITIES
(distribution by SITC, million francs)

Imports c.i.f.	1982	1983	1984‡
Food and live animals	66,485.5	75,948.9	82,798.8
Meat and meat preparations	13,387.4	15,159.0	15,178.4
Fresh, chilled or frozen meat	12,260.6	13,889.0	13,792.0
Vegetables and fruit	16,036.4	18,090.9	20,725.2
Coffee, tea, cocoa and spices	9,146.7	10,975.3	13,549.9
Beverages and tobacco	7,067.8	7,636.5	8,975.4
Crude materials (inedible) except fuels	37,475.0	40,210.2	48,335.9
Mineral fuels, lubricants, etc. (incl. electric current)	202,966.7	196,289.6	219,869.1
Petroleum, petroleum products, etc.	165,403.3	158,056.4	176,668.6
Crude petroleum oils, etc.	129,483.2	120,669.1	138,180.2
Refined petroleum products	33,717.1	34,762.4	35,623.8
Gas (natural and manufactured)	25,396.9	27,180.3	30,780.4
Animal and vegetable oils, fats and waxes	4,418.6	4,718.8	7,197.9
Chemicals and related products	64,852.8	72,339.8	86,922.1
Organic chemicals	16,189.4	18,524.0	22,453.8
Inorganic chemicals	10,861.4	10,304.2	13,195.5
Artificial resins, plastic materials, etc.	13,937.8	16,151.6	19,286.3
Basic manufactures	117,776.5	124,630.9	144,032.3
Paper, paperboard and manufactures	13,307.4	15,262.3	18,122.3
Paper and paperboard	9,931.7	11,466.7	13,758.4
Textile yarn, fabrics, etc.	22,931.1	24,507.8	28,398.8
Non-metallic mineral manufactures	12,128.2	12,563.6	14,095.4
Iron and steel	26,883.3	26,024.3	30,573.8
Non-ferrous metals	16,865.5	19,254.6	22,544.8
Other metal manufactures	14,499.0	15,082.6	16,765.9
Machinery and transport equipment	180,429.4	193,823.5	213,480.0
Power generating machinery and equipment	16,784.3	18,044.8	19,526.7
Machinery specialized for particular industries	20,175.1	20,229.3	21,811.4
General industrial machinery, equipment and parts	23,645.8	24,472.9	26,643.6
Office machines and automatic data processing equipment	20,659.2	25,427.9	31,170.6
Automatic data processing machines and units	10,860.9	13,412.8	18,276.8
Electrical machinery, apparatus, etc.	37,342.9	39,668.8	47,461.2
Road vehicles and parts*	48,306.3	52,977.9	54,779.9
Passenger motor cars (excl. buses)	25,813.5	28,703.0	29,185.9
Parts and accessories for cars, buses, lorries, etc.*	10,514.2	12,089.4	13,132.4
Miscellaneous manufactured articles	74,452.2	82,327.4	92,113.9
Clothing and accessories (excl. footwear)	16,869.8	18,357.2	21,127.3
Other commodities and transactions†	1,670.2	1,828.0	1,695.8
Total	757,594.9	799,753.6	905,421.2

* Excluding tyres, engines and electrical parts.
† Including items not classified according to kind (million francs): 231.1 in 1982; 211.2 in 1983; 220.7 in 1984.
‡ Figures are provisional. Revised total is 904,676 million francs.

1985: Total imports 962,722 million francs.

Exports f.o.b.	1982	1983	1984‡
Food and live animals	78,336.4	90,042.1	102,676.9
Dairy products and birds' eggs	12,456.3	13,387.3	15,082.9
Cereals and cereal preparations	25,594.8	32,915.7	39,158.2
Wheat and meslin (unmilled)	11,533.1	15,594.7	18,041.5
Beverages and tobacco	17,023.7	19,894.6	23,951.7
Beverages	16,422.3	19,206.6	23,167.6
Alcoholic beverages	15,732.4	18,330.6	22,102.5
Crude materials (inedible) except fuels	21,996.1	28,319.7	32,995.2
Mineral fuels, lubricants, etc. (incl. electric current)	24,558.6	27,052.6	30,425.1
Petroleum, petroleum products, etc.	20,717.1	20,919.0	22,449.4
Refined petroleum products	18,957.3	19,190.0	20,968.2
Animal and vegetable oils, fats and waxes	2,064.0	2,384.6	3,683.5
Chemicals and related products	76,572.3	90,177.2	109,645.5
Organic chemicals	18,356.0	21,830.2	27,255.8
Hydrocarbons and their derivatives	10,726.0	13,162.2	16,406.4
Inorganic chemicals	12,183.3	12,427.2	15,559.2
Essential oils, perfume materials and cleansing preparations	9,332.3	11,363.0	14,327.5
Artificial resins, plastic materials, etc.	13,998.9	17,426.9	20,905.8
Basic manufactures	120,979.9	133,936.7	158,565.6
Paper, paperboard and manufactures	9,088.2	10,495.8	13,334.1
Textile yarn, fabrics, etc.	19,016.5	21,389.5	25,425.9
Non-metallic mineral manufactures	12,492.8	14,909.6	16,706.3
Iron and steel	36,720.2	36,928.4	46,047.8
Universals, plates and sheets	9,086.4	10,511.1	13,211.2
Non-ferrous metals	10,630.0	13,747.0	16,602.1
Other metal manufactures	19,134.2	20,538.7	22,493.4
Machinery and transport equipment	206,677.6	236,383.4	272,188.2
Power generating machinery and equipment	15,910.1	17,953.1	21,199.5
Machinery specialized for particular industries	21,390.7	22,795.0	23,197.3
General industrial machinery, equipment and parts	27,772.0	30,421.4	32,425.3
Office machines and automatic data processing equipment	11,055.5	15,178.4	19,908.7
Electrical machinery, apparatus, etc.	36,317.0	43,663.2	51,373.3
Road vehicles and parts*	64,656.7	73,293.7	82,560.8
Passenger motor cars (excl. buses)	32,402.5	35,953.2	39,943.3
Parts and accessories for cars, buses, lorries, etc.*	20,083.7	25,362.0	29,311.1
Other transport equipment	25,738.5	28,045.8	37,227.5
Aircraft, etc., and parts*	16,887.1	16,953.2	24,430.8
Miscellaneous manufactured articles	53,697.6	62,070.3	73,728.3
Clothing and accessories (excl. footwear)	11,746.8	13,108.7	15,098.1
Other commodities and transactions†	4,187.7	4,388.5	5,142.8
Total	606,093.9	694,649.6	813,002.8

* Excluding tyres, engines and electrical parts.
† Including items not classified according to kind (million francs): 1,875.4 in 1982; 2,725.4 in 1983; 2,733.3 in 1984).
‡ Figures are provisional. Revised total is 813,537 million francs.

1985: Total exports 871,641 million francs.

FRANCE

Statistical Survey

PRINCIPAL TRADING PARTNERS (million francs)*

Imports c.i.f.	1982	1983	1984†
Algeria	25,815.4	23,372.8	25,900.6
Australia	3,724.9	3,928.0	5,501.1
Austria	4,474.1	4,668.1	5,660.2
Belgium and Luxembourg	58,488.1	64,277.1	74,345.8
Brazil	7,630.5	9,101.5	9,886.1
Canada	5,264.2	5,660.5	6,760.3
Denmark	5,534.4	6,528.5	6,065.9
Egypt	2,258.8	3,960.4	5,336.0
Finland	3,609.3	4,375.1	5,223.4
Germany, Federal Republic	127,572.7	135,459.7	147,290.8
Iran	6,067.8	7,238.1	6,774.4
Iraq	2,666.4	3,777.9	6,808.8
Ireland	4,409.9	5,003.2	5,685.9
Italy	72,781.6	79,356.4	89,186.0
Ivory Coast	3,591.2	4,058.3	4,851.3
Japan	20,049.2	20,874.8	23,846.0
Libya	3,973.0	6,477.1	7,124.6
Mexico	4,877.2	5,530.5	7,087.2
Morocco	3,972.7	4,476.0	5,206.0
Netherlands	41,987.9	47,686.0	55,085.1
Nigeria	12,047.0	15,002.5	19,766.5
Norway	9,453.4	9,839.9	11,011.1
Portugal	3,734.1	5,064.9	5,793.2
Saudi Arabia	46,203.8	26,652.7	18,753.5
South Africa	4,816.1	4,422.0	5,954.9
Spain (excl. Canary Is.)	23,106.0	27,047.0	30,745.1
Sweden	11,170.6	12,028.0	13,833.0
Switzerland and Liechtenstein	15,243.8	16,061.8	18,062.2
USSR	18,668.2	21,242.3	22,286.7
United Arab Emirates	10,555.9	9,663.0	8,182.1
United Kingdom	45,974.7	56,800.6	73,350.6
USA and Puerto Rico	59,738.4	61,760.3	69,910.9
Total (incl. others)	757,594.8	799,753.5	905,421.1

Exports f.o.b.	1982	1983	1984†
Algeria	13,990.7	18,565.8	23,583.7
Austria	4,682.2	5,510.7	6,048.9
Belgium and Luxembourg	52,328.7	59,334.3	69,818.0
Brazil	3,987.4	4,881.9	4,890.6
Cameroon	4,231.5	4,501.8	5,218.5
Canada	4,625.9	5,476.2	8,657.6
Denmark	4,357.8	5,351.9	6,259.6
Egypt	6,580.8	8,428.2	8,283.1
Germany, Federal Republic	89,558.8	108,066.5	119,443.0
Greece	6,332.1	6,121.0	7,016.1
Indonesia	4,939.3	3,572.6	2,766.0
Iraq	9,228.6	6,163.3	5,984.1
Italy	68,383.4	74,114.2	88,551.4
Japan	7,061.8	8,248.6	8,972.8
Kuwait	2,048.0	3,444.3	6,259.0
Morocco	7,346.5	6,258.3	6,979.3
Netherlands	27,950.4	32,992.9	38,645.1
Nigeria	8,076.8	7,002.2	7,942.3
Norway	3,540.1	3,923.8	6,235.8
Portugal	5,240.4	5,258.5	5,718.2
Saudi Arabia	12,886.2	13,732.1	19,905.6
Spain (excl. Canary Is.)	18,823.2	22,101.0	26,207.6
Sweden	6,950.4	9,005.8	10,728.7
Switzerland and Liechtenstein	24,161.5	29,048.8	31,620.1
Tunisia	6,069.0	6,440.6	6,601.1
USSR	10,168.7	16,949.8	16,837.6
United Kingdom	43,883.0	52,677.1	64,367.1
USA and Puerto Rico	34,326.9	43,823.8	65,894.5
Total (incl. others)	606,093.8	694,649.5	813,002.7

* Imports by country of production; exports by country of last consignment.
† Figures are provisional. Revised totals (in million francs) are: Imports 904,676; Exports 813,537.

Source: Direction Générale des Douanes et Droits Indirects.

Transport

RAILWAYS (traffic)

	1983	1984	1985
Paying passengers ('000 journeys)	736,000	839,000	825,000
Freight carried ('000 metric tons)	176,000	177,000	171,000
Passenger-km (million)	58,430	60,200	61,900
Freight ton-km (million)*	59,400	60,100	58,400

* Including passengers' baggage.
Source: Société Nationale des Chemins de Fer Français, Paris.

ROAD TRAFFIC (motor vehicles in use at 31 December)

	1983	1984	1985
Passenger cars	20,600,000	20,800,000	20,940,000
Goods vehicles	3,037,000	3,111,000	3,225,000
Buses and coaches	62,000	62,000	64,000
Motor cycles and scooters	650,000	665,000	630,000
Mopeds	4,600,000	4,400,000	3,400,000

Source: International Road Federation, *World Road Statistics*.

SHIPPING
Merchant Fleet (vessels registered at 30 June)

	Displacement ('000 gross reg. tons)		
	1980	1981	1982
Oil tankers	7,777	7,400	6,557
Total (incl. others)	11,925	11,455	10,771

* Provisional figures.
Source: UN, *Statistical Yearbook*.

Sea-borne Freight Traffic ('000 metric tons)

	1983	1984	1985
Goods loaded (excl. stores)	70,109.9	70,562.8	75,175.9
International	59,420.0	60,028.6	64,997.1
Coastwise	10,689.9	10,534.3	10,178.8
Goods unloaded (excl. fish)	196,449.8	202,206.4	199,081.2
International	183,399.8	189,762.0	186,492.5
Coastwise	13,050.0	12,444.4	12,588.7

Source: Direction des Ports et de la Navigation Maritimes, Secrétariat d'Etat à la Mer.

FRANCE

INLAND WATERWAYS

	1979	1980	1981
Freight carried ('000 metric tons)	92,862	92,197	83,571
Freight ton-km (million)	11,898	12,151	11,068

CIVIL AVIATION (revenue traffic on scheduled services)

	1980	1981	1982
Kilometres flown (million)	276.3	270.5	270.7
Passengers carried ('000)	19,521	21,591	22,372
Passenger-km (million)	34,130	36,718	37,916
Freight ton-km (million)	1,985.8	2,128.4	2,185.2
Mail ton-km (million)	107.1	111.1	112.1
Total ton-km (million)	5,131	5,509	5,670

Source: UN, *Statistical Yearbook*.

Tourism

FOREIGN TOURIST ARRIVALS BY COUNTRY ('000)

	1982	1983	1985
Belgium	2,856	2,658	3,117
Canada	250	283	477
Germany, Federal Republic	8,403	8,059	8,723
Italy	2,000	2,193	2,646
Latin America	412	414	590
Netherlands	3,888	3,806	3,655
Spain	893	813	995
Switzerland	3,215	3,267	3,603
United Kingdom	5,864	5,934	5,862
USA	1,355	2,050	2,778
Total (incl. others)	33,466	34,018	36,748

Note: Figures for 1984 are not available.
Estimated Revenue from Tourism: 32,000 million francs (net) in 1985.
Source: Ministère de l'Industrie, des Postes et Télécommunications et du Tourisme.

Communications Media

	1981	1982	1983
Radio receivers ('000 in use)	n.a.	46,300	47,000
Television receivers ('000 in use)	19,500	20,000	20,500
Telephones ('000 in use)	26,940	n.a.	n.a.
Book production (titles):			
Books	25,190	27,152	25,632
Pamphlets	12,118	15,034	11,944

Source: mainly UNESCO, *Statistical Yearbook*.
Newspapers (1983): 84 dailies (circulation 11.3 million).

Education

	Schools 1983/84	Teachers 1983/84	Students 1983/84
Pre-primary	17,012	84,046	2,461,400
Primary	49,356	246,994	4,233,400
Secondary	11,181	372,605	5,453,400

Universities: 1,124,900 students enrolled in 1983/84.
Source: Ministère de l'Education Nationale.

Directory

The Constitution

The Constitution of the Fifth Republic was adopted by referendum on 28 September 1958 and promulgated on 6 October 1958.

PREAMBLE

The French people hereby solemnly proclaims its attachment to the Rights of Man and to the principles of national sovereignty as defined by the Declaration of 1789, confirmed and complemented by the Preamble of the Constitution of 1946.

By virtue of these principles and that of the free determination of peoples, the Republic hereby offers to the Overseas Territories that express the desire to adhere to them, new institutions based on the common ideal of liberty, equality and fraternity and conceived with a view to their democratic evolution.

Article 1. The Republic and the peoples of the Overseas Territories who, by an act of free determination, adopt the present Constitution thereby institute a Community.

The Community shall be based on the equality and the solidarity of the peoples composing it.

I. ON SOVEREIGNTY

Article 2. France shall be a Republic, indivisible, secular, democratic and social. It shall ensure the equality of all citizens before the law, without distinction of origin, race or religion. It shall respect all beliefs.

The national emblem shall be the tricolour flag, blue, white and red.

The national anthem shall be the 'Marseillaise'.

The motto of the Republic shall be 'Liberty, Equality, Fraternity'.

Its principle shall be government of the people, by the people, and for the people.

Article 3. National sovereignty belongs to the people, which shall exercise this sovereignty through its representatives and through the referendum.

No section of the people, nor any individual, may attribute to themselves or himself the exercise thereof.

Suffrage may be direct or indirect under the conditions stipulated by the Constitution. It shall always be universal, equal and secret.

All French citizens of both sexes who have reached their majority and who enjoy civil and political rights may vote under the conditions to be determined by law.

Article 4. Political parties and groups may compete for votes. They may form and carry on their activities freely. They must respect the principles of national sovereignty and of democracy.

II. THE PRESIDENT OF THE REPUBLIC

Article 5. The President of the Republic shall see that the Constitution is respected. He shall ensure, by his arbitration, the regular functioning of the public powers, as well as the continuity of the State.

He shall be the guarantor of national independence, of the integrity of the territory, and of respect for Community agreements and for treaties.

Article 6. The President of the Republic shall be elected for seven years by direct universal suffrage. The method of implementation of the present article shall be determined by an organic law.

Article 7. The President of the Republic shall be elected by an absolute majority of the votes cast. If such a majority is not obtained at the first ballot, a second ballot shall take place on the second following Sunday. Those who may stand for the second ballot shall be only the two candidates who, after the possible withdrawal of candidates with more votes, have gained the largest number of votes on the first ballot.

Voting shall begin at the summons of the Government. The election of the new President of the Republic shall take place not less than 20 days and not more than 35 days before the expiration of the powers of the President in office. In the event that the Presidency of the Republic has been vacated for any reason whatsoever, or impeded in its functioning as officially declared by the Constitutional Council, after the matter has been referred to it by the Government and which shall give its ruling by an absolute majority of its members, the functions of the President of the Republic, with the exception of those covered by Articles 11 and 12 hereunder, shall be temporarily exercised by the President of the Senate and, if the latter is in his turn unable to exercise his functions, by the Government.

In the case of vacancy or when the impediment is declared to be final by the Constitutional Council, the voting for the election of the new President shall take place, except in case of force majeure officially noted by the Constitutional Council, not less than 20 days and not more than 35 days after the beginning of the vacancy or of the declaration of the final nature of the impediment.

If, in the seven days preceding the latest date for the lodging of candidatures, one of the persons who, at least 30 days prior to that date, publicly announced his decision to be a candidate dies or is impeded, the Constitutional Council can decide to postpone the election.

If, before the first ballot, one of the candidates dies or is impeded, the Constitutional Council orders the postponement of the election.

In the event of the death or impediment, before any candidates have withdrawn, of one of the two candidates who received the greatest number of votes in the first ballot, the Constitutional Council shall declare that the electoral procedure must be repeated in full; the same shall apply in the event of the death or impediment of one of the two candidates standing for the second ballot.

All cases shall be referred to the Constitutional Council under the conditions laid down in paragraph 2 of article 61 below, or under those determined for the presentation of candidates by the organic law provided for in Article 6 above.

The Constitutional Council can extend the periods stipulated in paragraphs 3 and 5 above provided that polling shall not take place more than 35 days after the date of the decision of the Constitutional Council. If the implementation of the provisions of this paragraph results in the postponement of the election beyond the expiry of the powers of the President in office, the latter shall remain in office until his successor is proclaimed.

Articles 49 and 50 and Article 89 of the Constitution may not be put into application during the vacancy of the Presidency of the Republic or during the period between the declaration of the final nature of the impediment of the President of the Republic and the election of his successor.

Article 8. The President of the Republic shall appoint the Premier. He shall terminate the functions of the Premier when the latter presents the resignation of the Government.

At the suggestion of the Premier, he shall appoint the other members of the Government and shall terminate their functions.

Article 9. The President of the Republic shall preside over the Council of Ministers.

Article 10. The President of the Republic shall promulgate the laws within 15 days following the transmission to the Government of the finally adopted law.

He may, before the expiration of this time limit, ask Parliament for a reconsideration of the law or of certain of its articles. This reconsideration may not be refused.

Article 11. The President of the Republic, on the proposal of the government during [Parliamentary] sessions, or on joint motion of the two Assemblies published in the *Journal Officiel*, may submit to a referendum any bill dealing with the organization of the public powers, entailing approval of a Community agreement, or providing for authorization to ratify a treaty that, without being contrary to the Constitution, might affect the functioning of the institutions.

When the referendum decides in favour of the bill, the President of the Republic shall promulgate it within the time limit stipulated in the preceding article.

Article 12. The President of the Republic may, after consultation with the Premier and the Presidents of the Assemblies, declare the dissolution of the National Assembly.

General elections shall take place 20 days at the least and 40 days at the most after the dissolution.

The National Assembly shall convene by right on the second Thursday following its election. If this meeting takes place between the periods provided for ordinary sessions, a session shall, by right, be opened for a 15 day period.

There may be no further dissolution within a year following these elections.

Article 13. The President of the Republic shall sign the ordinances and decrees decided upon in the Council of Ministers.

He shall make appointments to the civil and military posts of the State.

Councillors of State, the Grand Chancellor of the Legion of Honour, Ambassadors and Envoys Extraordinary, Master Councillors of the Audit Office, prefects, representatives of the Government in the Overseas Territories, general officers, rectors of academies [regional divisions of the public educational system] and directors of central administrations shall be appointed in meetings of the Council of Ministers.

An organic law shall determine the other posts to be filled in meetings of the Council of Ministers, as well as the conditions under which the power of the President of the Republic to make appointments to office may be delegated by him to be exercised in his name.

Article 14. The President of the Republic shall accredit Ambassadors and Envoys Extraordinary to foreign powers; foreign Ambassadors and Envoys Extraordinary shall be accredited to him.

Article 15. The President of the Republic shall be commander of the armed forces. He shall preside over the higher councils and committees of national defence.

Article 16. When the institutions of the Republic, the independence of the nation, the integrity of its territory or the fulfilment of its international commitments are threatened in a grave and immediate manner and the regular functioning of the constitutional public powers is interrupted, the President of the Republic shall take the measures required by these circumstances, after official consultation with the Premier and the Presidents of the Assemblies, as well as with the Constitutional Council.

He shall inform the nation of these measures in a message.

These measures must be prompted by the desire to ensure to the constitutional public powers, in the shortest possible time, the means of accomplishing their mission. The Constitutional Council shall be consulted with regard to such measures.

Parliament shall meet by right.

The National Assembly may not be dissolved during the exercise of exceptional powers.

Article 17. The President of the Republic shall have the right of pardon.

Article 18. The President of the Republic shall communicate with the two Assemblies of Parliament by means of messages, which he shall cause to be read, and which shall not be the occasion for any debate.

Between sessions, the Parliament shall be convened especially to this end.

Article 19. The acts of the President of the Republic, other than those provided for under Articles 8 (first paragraph), 11, 12, 16, 18, 54, 56 and 61, shall be counter-signed by the Premier and, should circumstances so require, by the appropriate ministers.

III. THE GOVERNMENT

Article 20. The Government shall determine and conduct the policy of the nation.

It shall have at its disposal the administration and the armed forces.

It shall be responsible to the Parliament under the conditions and according to the procedures stipulated in Articles 49 and 50.

Article 21. The Premier shall direct the operation of the Government. He shall be responsible for national defence. He shall ensure the execution of the laws. Subject to the provisions of Article 13, he shall have regulatory powers and shall make appointments to civil and military posts.

He may delegate certain of his powers to the ministers.

He shall replace, should the occasion arise, the President of the Republic as the Chairman of the councils and committees provided for under Article 15.

He may, in exceptional instances, replace him as the chairman of a meeting of the Council of Ministers by virtue of an explicit delegation and for a specific agenda.

Article 22. The acts of the Premier shall be counter-signed, when circumstances so require, by the ministers responsible for their execution.

Article 23. The functions of Members of the Government shall be incompatible with the exercise of any parliamentary mandate, with the holding of any office, at the national level, in business, professional or labour organizations, and with any public employment or professional activity.

An organic law shall determine the conditions under which the holders of such mandates, functions or employments shall be replaced.

The replacement of the members of Parliament shall take place in accordance with the provisions of Article 25.

IV. THE PARLIAMENT

Article 24. The Parliament shall comprise the National Assembly and the Senate.

The deputies to the National Assembly shall be elected by direct suffrage.

The Senate shall be elected by indirect suffrage. It shall ensure the representation of the territorial units of the Republic. Frenchmen living outside France shall be represented in the Senate.

Article 25. An organic law shall determine the term for which each Assembly is elected, the number of its members, their emoluments, the conditions of eligibility, and the system of ineligibilities and incompatibilities.

It shall likewise determine the conditions under which, in the case of a vacancy in either Assembly, persons shall be elected to replace the deputy or senator whose seat has been vacated until the holding of new complete or partial elections to the Assembly concerned.

Article 26. No Member of Parliament may be prosecuted, searched for, arrested, detained or tried as a result of the opinions or votes expressed by him in the exercise of his functions.

No Member of Parliament may, during parliamentary session, be prosecuted or arrested for criminal or minor offences without the authorization of the Assembly of which he is a member except in the case of *flagrante delicto*.

When Parliament is not in session, no Member of Parliament may be arrested without the authorization of the Secretariat of the Assembly of which he is a member, except in the case of *flagrante delicto*, of authorized prosecution or of final conviction.

The detention or prosecution of a Member of Parliament shall be suspended if the assembly of which he is a member so demands.

Article 27. Any compulsory vote shall be null and void.

The right to vote of the members of Parliament shall be personal.

The organic law may, under exceptional circumstances, authorize the delegation of a vote. In this case, no member may be delegated more than one vote.

Article 28. Parliament shall convene by right in two ordinary sessions a year.

The first session shall begin on the first Tuesday of October and shall end on the third Friday of December.

The second session shall open on the last Tuesday of April; it may not last longer than three months.

Article 29. Parliament shall convene in extraordinary session at the request of the Premier or of the majority of the members comprising the National Assembly, to consider a specific agenda.

When an extraordinary session is held at the request of the members of the National Assembly, the closure decree shall take effect as soon as the Parliament has exhausted the agenda for which it was called, and at the latest 12 days from the date of its meeting.

Only the Premier may ask for a new session before the end of the month following the closure decree.

Article 30. Apart from cases in which Parliament meets by right, extraordinary sessions shall be opened and closed by decree of the President of the Republic.

Article 31. The members of the Government shall have access to the two Assemblies. They shall be heard when they so request.

They may call for the assistance of Commissioners of the Government.

Article 32. The President of the National Assembly shall be elected for the duration of the legislature. The President of the Senate shall be elected after each partial re-election [of the Senate].

Article 33. The meetings of the two Assemblies shall be public. An *in extenso* report of the debates shall be published in the *Journal Officiel*.

Each Assembly may sit in secret committee at the request of the Premier or of one-tenth of its members.

V. ON RELATIONS BETWEEN PARLIAMENT AND THE GOVERNMENT

Article 34. Laws shall be voted by Parliament.

They shall establish the regulations concerning:

Civil rights and the fundamental guarantees granted to the citizens for the exercise of their public liberties; the obligations imposed by the national defence upon the person and property of citizens;

Nationality, status and legal capacity of persons; marriage contracts, inheritance and gifts;

Determination of crimes and misdemeanours as well as the penalties imposed therefor; criminal procedure; amnesty; the creation of new juridical systems and the status of magistrates;

The basis, the rate and the methods of collecting taxes of all types; the issue of currency.

They likewise shall determine the regulations concerning:

The electoral system of the Parliamentary Assemblies and the local assemblies;

The establishment of categories of public institutions;

The fundamental guarantees granted to civil and military personnel employed by the State;

The nationalization of enterprises and the transfers of the property of enterprises from the public to the private sector.

Laws shall determine the fundamental principles of:

The general organization of national defence;

The free administration of local communities, of their competencies and their resources;

Education;

Property rights, civil and commercial obligations;

Legislation pertaining to employment unions and social security.

The financial laws shall determine the financial resources and obligations of the State under the conditions and with the reservations to be provided for by an organic law.

Laws pertaining to national planning shall determine the objectives of the economic and social action of the State.

The provisions of the present article may be detailed and supplemented by an organic law.

Article 35. Parliament shall authorize the declaration of war.

Article 36. Martial law shall be decreed in a meeting of the Council of Ministers.

Its prorogation beyond 12 days may be authorized only by Parliament.

Article 37. Matters other than those that fall within the domain of law shall be of a regulatory character.

Legislative texts concerning these matters may be modified by decrees issued after consultation with the Council of State. Those legislative texts which shall be passed after the entry into force of the present Constitution shall be modified by decree only if the Constitutional Council has stated that they have a regulatory character as defined in the preceding paragraph.

Article 38. The Government may, in order to carry out its programme, ask Parliament for authorization to take through ordinances, during a limited period, measures that are normally within the domain of law.

The ordinances shall be enacted in meetings of Ministers after consultation with the Council of State. They shall come into force upon their publication but shall become null and void if the bill for their ratification is not submitted to Parliament before the date set by the enabling act.

At the expiration of the time limit referred to in the first paragraph of the present article, the ordinances may be modified only by the law in those matters which are within the legislative domain.

Article 39. The Premier and the Members of Parliament alike shall have the right to initiate legislation.

Government bills shall be discussed in the Council of Ministers after consultation with the Council of State and shall be filed with the secretariat of one of the two Assemblies. Finance bills shall be submitted first to the National Assembly.

Article 40. The bills and amendments introduced by the Members of Parliament shall be inadmissible when their adoption would have as a consequence either a diminution of public financial resources or an increase in public expenditure.

Article 41. If it shall appear in the course of the legislative procedure that a Parliamentary bill or an amendment is not within the domain of law or is contrary to a delegation granted by virtue of Article 38, the Government may declare its inadmissibility.

In case of disagreement between the Government and the President of the Assembly concerned, the Constitutional Council, upon the request of one or the other, shall rule within a time limit of eight days.

Article 42. The discussion of bills shall pertain, in the first Assembly to which they have been referred, to the text presented by the Government.

An Assembly given a text passed by the other Assembly shall deliberate on the text that is transmitted to it.

Article 43. Government and Parliamentary bills shall, at the request of the Government or of the Assembly concerned, be sent for study to committees especially designated for this purpose.

Government and Parliamentary bills for which such a request has not been made shall be sent to one of the permanent committees, the number of which is limited to six in each Assembly.

Article 44. Members of Parliament and of the Government have the right of amendment.

After the opening of the debate, the Government may oppose the examination of any amendment which has not previously been submitted to committee.

If the Government so requests, the Assembly concerned shall decide, by a single vote, on all or part of the text under discussion, retaining only the amendments proposed or accepted by the Government.

Article 45. Every Government or Parliamentary bill shall be examined successively in the two Assemblies of Parliament with a view to the adoption of an identical text.

When, as a result of disagreement between the two Assemblies, it has been impossible to adopt a Government or Parliamentary bill after two readings by each Assembly, or, if the Government has declared the matter urgent, after a single reading by each of them, the Premier shall have the right to bring about a meeting of a joint committee composed of an equal number from both Assemblies charged with the task of proposing a text on the matters still under discussion.

The text elaborated by the joint committee may be submitted by the Government for approval of the two Assemblies. No amendment shall be admissible except by agreement with the Government.

If the joint committee does not succeed in adopting a common text, or if this text is not adopted under the conditions set forth in the preceding paragraph, the Government may, after a new reading by the National Assembly and by the Senate, ask the National Assembly to rule definitively. In this case, the National Assembly may reconsider either the text elaborated by the joint committee, or the last text voted by it, modified when circumstances so require by one or several of the amendments adopted by the Senate.

Article 46. The laws that the Constitution characterizes as organic shall be passed and amended under the following conditions:

A Government or Parliamentary bill shall be submitted to the deliberation and to the vote of the first Assembly notified only at the expiration of a period of 15 days following its introduction;

The procedure of Article 45 shall be applicable. Nevertheless, lacking an agreement between the two Assemblies, the text may be adopted by the National Assembly on final reading only by an absolute majority of its members;

The organic laws relative to the Senate must be passed in the same manner by the two Assemblies;

The organic laws may be promulgated only after a declaration by the Constitutional Council on their constitutionality.

Article 47. The Parliament shall pass finance bills under the conditions to be stipulated by an organic law.

Should the National Assembly fail to reach a decision on first reading within a time limit of 40 days after a bill has been filed, the Government shall refer it to the Senate, which must rule within a time limit of 15 days. The procedure set forth in Article 45 shall then be followed.

Should Parliament fail to reach a decision within a time limit of 70 days, the provisions of the bill may be enforced by ordinance.

Should the finance bill establishing the resources and expenditures of a fiscal year not be filed in time for it to be promulgated before the beginning of that fiscal year, the Government shall urgently request Parliament for the authorization to collect the taxes and shall make available by decree the funds needed to meet the Government commitments already voted.

The time limits stipulated in the present article shall be suspended when the Parliament is not in session.

The Audit Office shall assist Parliament and the Government in supervising the implementation of the finance laws.

Article 48. The discussion of the bills filed or agreed upon by the Government shall have priority on the agenda of the Assemblies in the order determined by the Government.

One meeting a week shall be reserved, by priority, for questions asked by Members of Parliament and for answers by the Government.

Article 49. The Premier, after deliberation by the Council of Ministers, shall make the Government responsible, before the National Assembly, for its programme or, should the occasion arise, for a declaration of general policy.

When the National Assembly adopts a motion of censure, the responsibility of the Government shall thereby be questioned. Such a motion is admissible only if it is signed by at least one-tenth of the members of the National Assembly. The vote may not take place before 48 hours after the motion has been filed. Only the votes that are favourable to a motion of censure shall be counted; the motion of censure may be adopted only by a majority of the members comprising the Assembly. Should the motion of censure be rejected, its signatories may not introduce another motion of censure during the same session, except in the case provided for in the paragraph below.

The Premier may, after deliberation by the Council of Ministers, make the Government responsible before the National Assembly for the adoption of a vote of confidence. In this case, this vote of confidence shall be considered as adopted unless a motion of censure, filed during the twenty-four hours that follow, is carried under the conditions provided for in the preceding paragraph.

The Premier shall have the right to request the Senate for approval of a declaration of general policy.

Article 50. When the National Assembly adopts a motion of censure, or when it disapproves the programme or a declaration of general policy of the Government, the Premier must hand the resignation of the Government to the President of the Republic.

Article 51. The closure of ordinary or extraordinary sessions shall by right be delayed, should the occasion arise, in order to permit the application of the provisions of Article 49.

VI. ON TREATIES AND INTERNATIONAL AGREEMENTS

Article 52. The President of the Republic shall negotiate and ratify treaties.

He shall be informed of all negotiations leading to the conclusion of an international agreement not subject to ratification.

Article 53. Peace treaties, commercial treaties, treaties or agreements relative to international organization, those that commit the finances of the State, those that modify provisions of a legislative nature, those relative to the status of persons, those that call for the cession, exchange or addition of territory may be ratified or approved only by a law.

They shall go into effect only after having been ratified or approved.

No cession, no exchange, no addition of territory shall be valid without the consent of the populations concerned.

Article 54. If the Constitutional Council, the matter having been referred to it by the President of the Republic, by the Premier, or by the President of one or the other Assembly, shall declare that an international commitment contains a clause contrary to the Constitution, the authorisation to ratify or approve this commitment may be given only after amendment of the Constitution.

Article 55. Treaties or agreements duly ratified or approved shall, upon their publication, have an authority superior to that of laws, subject, for each agreement or treaty, to its application by the other party.

VII. THE CONSTITUTIONAL COUNCIL

Article 56. The Constitutional Council shall consist of nine members, whose mandates shall last nine years and shall not be renewable. One-third of the membership of the Constitutional Council shall be renewed every three years. Three of its members shall be appointed by the President of the Republic, three by the President of the National Assembly, three by the President of the Senate.

In addition to the nine members provided for above, former Presidents of the Republic shall be members *ex officio* for life of the Constitutional Council.

The President shall be appointed by the President of the Republic. He shall have the deciding vote in case of a tie.

Article 57. The office of member of the Constitutional Council shall be incompatible with that of minister or Member of Parliament. Other incompatibilities shall be determined by an organic law.

Article 58. The Constitutional Council shall ensure the regularity of the election of the President of the Republic.

It shall examine complaints and shall announce the results of the vote.

Article 59. The Constitutional Council shall rule, in the case of disagreement, on the regularity of the election of deputies and senators.

Article 60. The Constitutional Council shall ensure the regularity of the referendum procedure and shall announce the results thereof.

Article 61. Organic laws, before their promulgation, and regulations of the parliamentary Assemblies, before they come into application, must be submitted to the Constitutional Council, which shall rule on their constitutionality.

To the same end, laws may be submitted to the Constitutional Council, before their promulgation, by the President of the Republic, the Premier, the President of the National Assembly, the President of the Senate, or any 60 deputies or 60 senators.

In the cases provided for by the two preceding paragraphs, the Constitutional Council must make its ruling within a time limit of one month. Nevertheless, at the request of the Government, in case of urgency, this period shall be reduced to eight days.

In these same cases, referral to the Constitutional Council shall suspend the time limit for promulgation.

Article 62. A provision declared unconstitutional may not be promulgated or implemented.

The decisions of the Constitutional council may not be appealed to any jurisdiction whatsoever. They must be recognised by the public powers and by all administrative and juridical authorities.

Article 63. An organic law shall determine the rules of organization and functioning of the Constitutional Council, the procedure to be followed before it, and in particular of the periods of time allowed for laying disputes before it.

VIII. ON JUDICIAL AUTHORITY

Article 64. The President of the Republic shall be the guarantor of the independence of the judicial authority.

He shall be assisted by the High Council of the Judiciary.

An organic law shall determine the status of magistrates.

Magistrates may not be removed from office.

Article 65. The High Council of the Judiciary shall be presided over by the President of the Republic. The Minister of Justice shall be its Vice-President *ex officio*. He may preside in place of the President of the Republic.

The High Council shall, in addition, include nine members appointed by the President of the Republic in conformity with the conditions to be determined by an organic law.

The High Council of the Judiciary shall present nominations for judges of the Court of Cassation [Supreme Court of Appeal] and for First Presidents of courts of appeal. It shall give its opinion under the conditions to be determined by an organic law on proposals of the Minister of Justice relative to the nominations of the other judges. It shall be consulted on questions of pardon under conditions to be determined by an organic law.

The High Council of the Judiciary shall act as a disciplinary council for judges. In such cases, it shall be presided over by the First President of the Court of Cassation.

Article 66. No one may be arbitrarily detained.

The judicial authority, guardian of individual liberty, shall ensure the respect of this principle under the conditions stipulated by law.

IX. THE HIGH COURT OF JUSTICE

Article 67. A High Court of Justice shall be instituted.

It shall be composed, in equal number, of members elected, from among their membership, by the National Assembly and by the Senate after each general or partial election to these Assemblies. It shall elect its President from among its members.

An organic law shall determine the composition of the High Court, it rules, as well as the procedure to be applied before it.

Article 68. The President of the Republic shall not be held accountable for actions performed in the exercise of his office except in the case of high treason. He may be indicted only by the two Assemblies ruling by identical vote in open balloting and by an absolute majority of the members of said Assemblies. He shall be tried by the High Court of Justice.

The members of the Government shall be criminally liable for actions performed in the exercise of their office and rated as crimes or misdemeanours at the time they were committed. The procedure defined above shall be applied to them, as well as to their accomplices, in case of a conspiracy against the security of the State. In the cases provided for by the present paragraph, the High Court shall be bound by the definition of crimes and misdemeanours, as well as by the determination of penalties, as they are established by the criminal laws in force when the acts are committed.

X. THE ECONOMIC AND SOCIAL COUNCIL

Article 69. The Economic and Social Council, at the referral of the Government, shall give its opinion on the Government bills, ordinances and decrees, as well as on the Parliamentary bills submitted to it.

A member of the Economic and Social Council may be designated by the latter to present, before the Parliamentary Assemblies, the opinion of the Council on the Government or Parliamentary bills that have been submitted to it.

Article 70. The Economic and social council may likewise be consulted by the Government on any problem of an economic or social character of interest to the Republic or to the Community. Any plan, or any bill dealing with a plan, of an economic or social character shall be submitted to it for advice.

Article 71. The composition of the Economic and Social Council and its rules of procedure shall be determined by an organic law.

XI. ON TERRITORIAL UNITS

Article 72. The territorial units of the Republic shall be the communes, the Departments, and the Overseas Territories. Any other territorial unit shall be created by law.

These units shall be free to govern themselves through elected councils and under the conditions stipulated by law.

In the Departments and the Territories, the Delegate of the Government shall be responsible for the national interests, for administrative supervision, and for seeing that the laws are respected.

Article 73. Measures of adjustment required by the particular situation of the Overseas Departments may be taken with regard to the legislative system and administrative organization of those Departments.

Article 74. The Overseas Territories of the Republic shall have a particular organization, taking account of their own interests within the general interests of the Republic. This organization shall be defined and modified by law after consultation with the Territorial Assembly concerned.

Article 75. Citizens of the Republic who do not have ordinary civil status, the only status referred to in Article 34, may keep their personal status as long as they have not renounced it.

Article 76. The Overseas Territories may retain their status within the Republic.

If they express the desire to do so by decision of their Territorial Assemblies taken within the time limit set in the first paragraph of Article 91, they shall become either Overseas Departments of the Republic or, organized into groups among themselves or singly, member States of the Community.

XII. ON THE COMMUNITY

Article 77. In the Community instituted by the present Constitution, the States shall enjoy autonomy; they shall administer themselves and, democratically and freely, manage their own affairs.

There shall be only one citizenship in the Community.

All citizens shall be equal before the law, whatever their origin, their race and their religion. They shall have the same duties.

Article 78. The Community shall have jurisdiction over foreign policy, defence, the monetary system, common economic and financial policy, as well as the policy on strategic raw materials.

In addition, except by special agreement, control of justice, higher education, the general organization of external and common transport, and telecommunications shall be within its jurisdiction.

Special agreements may establish other common jurisdictions or regulate the transfer of jurisdiction from the Community to one of its members.

Article 79. The member States shall benefit from the provisions of Article 77 as soon as they have exercised the choice provided for in Article 76.

Until the measures required for implementation of the present title go into force, matters within the common jurisdiction shall be regulated by the Republic.

Article 80. The President of the Republic shall preside over and represent the Community.

The Community shall have, as organs, an Executive Council, a Senate and a Court of Arbitration.

Article 81. The member States of the Community shall participate in the election of the President according to the conditions stipulated in Article 6.

The President of the Republic, in his capacity as President of the Community, shall be represented in each State of the Community.

Article 82. The Executive Council of the Community shall be presided over by the President of the Community. It shall consist of the Premier of the Republic, the heads of Government of each of the member States of the Community, and of the ministers responsible for the common affairs of the Community.

The Executive Council shall organize the co-operation of members of the Community at Government and administrative levels.

The organization and procedure of the Executive Council shall be determined by an organic law.

Article 83. The Senate of the Community shall be composed of delegates whom the Parliament of the Republic and the legislative assemblies of the other members of the Community shall choose from among their own membership. The number of delegates of each State shall be determined, taking into account its population and the responsibilities it assumes in the Community.

The Senate of the Community shall hold two sessions a year, which shall be opened and closed by the President of the Community and may not last more than one month each.

The Senate of the Community, upon referral by the President of the Community, shall deliberate on the common economic and financial policy, before laws in these matters are voted upon by the Parliament of the Republic, and, should circumstances so require, by the legislative assemblies of the other members of the Community.

The Senate of the Community shall examine the acts and treaties or international agreements, which are specified in Articles 35 and 53, and which commit the Community.

The Senate of the Community shall take enforceable decisions in the domains in which it has received delegation of power from the legislative assemblies of the members of the Community. These decisions shall be promulgated in the same form as the law in the territory of each of the States concerned.

An organic law shall determine the composition of the Senate and its rules of procedure.

Article 84. A Court of Arbitration of the Community shall rule on litigations occurring among members of the Community.

Its composition and its competence shall be determined by an organic law.

Article 85. By derogation from the procedure provided for in Article 89, the provisions of the present title that concern the functioning of the common institutions shall be amendable by identical laws passed by the Parliament of the Republic and by the Senate of the Community.

The provisions of the present title may also be revised by agreements concluded between all states of the Community: the new provisions are enforced in the conditions laid down by the Constitution of each state.

Article 86. A change of status of a member State of the Community may be requested, either by the Republic, or by a resolution of the legislative assembly of the State concerned confirmed by a local referendum, the organization and supervision of which shall be ensured by the institutions of the Community. The procedures governing this change shall be determined by an agreement approved by the Parliament of the Republic and the legislative assembly concerned.

Under the same conditions, a Member State of the Community may become independent. It shall thereby cease to belong to the Community.

A Member State of the Community may also, by means of agreement, become independent without thereby ceasing to belong to the Community.

An independent State which is not a member of the Community may, by means of agreements, adhere to the Community without ceasing to be independent.

The position of these States within the Community is determined by the agreements concluded for that purpose, in particular the agreements mentioned in the preceding paragraphs as well as, where applicable, the agreements provided for in the second paragraph of Article 85.

Article 87. The particular agreements made for the implementation of the present title shall be approved by the Parliament of the Republic and the legislative assembly concerned.

XIII. ON AGREEMENTS OF ASSOCIATION

Article 88. The Republic or the Community may make agreements with States that wish to associate themselves with the Community in order to develop their own civilisations.

XIV. ON AMENDMENT

Article 89. The initiative for amending the Constitution shall belong both to the President of the Republic on the proposal of the Premier and to the Members of Parliament.

The Government or Parliamentary bill for amendment must be passed by the two Assemblies in identical terms. The amendment shall become definitive after approval by a referendum.

Nevertheless, the proposed amendment shall not be submitted to a referendum when the President of the Republic decides to submit it to Parliament convened in Congress; in this case, the proposed amendment shall be approved only if it is accepted by a three-fifths majority of the votes cast. The Secretariat of the Congress shall be that of the National Assembly.

No amendment procedure may be undertaken or followed if it is prejudicial to the integrity of the territory.

The republican form of government shall not be the object of an amendment.

XV. TEMPORARY PROVISIONS

Article 90. The ordinary session of Parliament is suspended. The mandate of the members of the present National Assembly shall expire on the day that the Assembly elected under the present Constitution convenes.

FRANCE

Until this meeting, the Government alone shall have the authority to convene Parliament.

The mandate of the members of the Assembly of the French Union shall expire at the same time as the mandate of the members of the present National Assembly.

Article 91. The institutions of the Republic, provided for by the present Constitution, shall be established within four months counting from the time of its promulgation.

This period shall be extended to six months for the institutions of the Community.

The powers of the President of the Republic now in office shall expire only when the results of the election provided for in Articles 6 and 7 of the present Constitution are proclaimed.

The Member States of the Community shall participate in this first election under the conditions derived from their status at the date of the promulgation of the Constitution.

The established authorities shall continue in the exercise of their functions in these States according to the laws and regulations applicable when the Constitution goes into force, until the establishment of the authorities provided for by their new regimes.

Until its definitive constitution, the Senate shall consist of the present members of the Council of the Republic. The organic laws that shall determine the definitive constitution of the Senate must be passed before 31 July 1959.

The powers conferred on the Constitutional Council by Articles 58 and 59 of the Constitution shall be exercised, until the establishment of this Council, by a committee composed of the Vice-President of the Council of State, as Chairman, the First President of the Court of Cassation, and the First President of the Audit Office.

The peoples of the member States of the Community shall continue to be represented in Parliament until the entry into force of the measures necessary to the implementation of Chapter XII.

Article 92. The legislative measures necessary to the establishment of the institutions and, until they are established, to the functioning of the public powers, shall be taken in meetings of the Council of Ministers, after consultation with the Council of State, in the form of ordinances having the force of law.

During the time limit set in the first paragraph of Article 91, the Government shall be authorized to determine, by ordinances having the force of law and passed in the same way, the system of elections to the Assemblies provided for by the Constitution.

During the same period and under the same conditions, the Government may also adopt measures, in all domains, which it may deem necessary to the life of the nation, the protection of citizens or the safeguarding of liberties.

ELECTORAL LAW, 1985

At the elections of March 1986, the 577 Deputies of the National Assembly for Metropolitan France and for the Overseas Departments and Territories (except Mayotte, St Pierre and Miquelon and the Wallis and Futuna Islands) were elected under a system of proportional representation, the increase from 491 to 577 giving a ratio of approximately one deputy per 108,000 inhabitants. Within each department, seats were allocated to candidates in the order in which they appeared on party lists, and the votes for any party receiving less than 5% of the total vote were reapportioned among the remaining lists.

ELECTORAL LAW, OCTOBER 1986

The 577 Deputies of the National Assembly are to be directly elected under the former single-member constituency system, with two ballots where the first does not produce an absolute majority. A candidate will require a simple majority in the second ballot to be successful. Candidates polling less than 5% of the votes will lose their deposit.

The Government

HEAD OF STATE

President: FRANÇOIS MITTERRAND (took office 21 May 1981).

COUNCIL OF MINISTERS
(January 1987)

A coalition of the Rassemblement pour la République (RPR) and the Union pour la Démocratie Française (UDF), which includes the Centre des Démocrates Sociaux (CDS), the Parti Radical (Rad.), the Parti Républicain (PR) and the Parti social-démocrate (PSD).

Prime Minister: JACQUES CHIRAC (RPR).

Minister of State for the Economy, Finance and Privatization: EDOUARD BALLADUR (RPR).

Minister of Justice and Keeper of the Seals: ALBIN CHALANDON (RPR).

Minister of Defence: ANDRÉ GIRAUD (UDF-PR).

Minister for Culture and Communication: FRANÇOIS LÉOTARD (UDF-PR).

Minister of Foreign Affairs: JEAN-BERNARD RAIMOND.

Minister of the Interior: CHARLES PASQUA (RPR).

Minister of Equipment, Housing, Regional Planning and Transport: PIERRE MÉHAIGNERIE (UDF-CDS).

Minister for the Overseas Departments and Territories: BERNARD PONS (RPR).

Minister of National Education: RENÉ MONORY (UDF-CDS).

Minister of Social Affairs and Employment: PHILIPPE SÉGUIN (RPR).

Minister of Industry, Postal Services, Telecommunications and Tourism: ALAIN MADELIN (UDF-PR).

Minister of Agriculture: FRANÇOIS GUILLAUME.

Minister of Co-operation: MICHEL AURILLAC (RPR).

Minister for Relations with Parliament: ANDRÉ ROSSINOT (UDF-Rad.).

Ministers Delegate attached to the Prime Minister:
  Civil Service, Social Economy and the Plan: HERVÉ DE CHARETTE (UDF-PR).
  Administrative Reform: CAMILLE CABANA (RPR).

Ministers Delegate attached to the Minister for the Economy, Finance and Privatization:
  Budget: ALAIN JUPPÉ (RPR).
  Foreign Trade: MICHEL NOIR (RPR).
  Trade, Artisan Industries and Services: GEORGES CHAVANES (UDF-CDS).

Minister Delegate attached to the Minister of Foreign Affairs:
  European Affairs: BERNARD BOSSON (UDF-CDS).

Ministers Delegate attached to the Minister of the Interior:
  Local Government: YVES GALLAND (UDF-Rad.).
  Security: ROBERT PANDRAUD (RPR).

Ministers Delegate attached to the Minister of Equipment, Housing, Regional Planning and Transport:
  Transport: JACQUES DOUFFIAGUES (UDF-PR).
  Environment: ALAIN CARIGNON (RPR).

Minister Delegate attached to the Minister of National Education:
  Research and Higher Education: JACQUES VALADE (RPR).

Minister Delegate attached to the Minister of Social Affairs and Employment:
  Health and Family Affairs: Mme MICHÈLE BARZACH (RPR).

Minister Delegate attached to the Minister of Industry, Postal Services and Telecommunications and Tourism:
  Postal Services and Telecommunications: GÉRARD LONGUET (UDF-PR).

SECRETARIES OF STATE

Attached to the Prime Minister:
  French Language: Mme LUCETTE MICHAUX-CHEVRY (RPR).
  Human Rights: CLAUDE MALHURET (UDF-PR).
  Youth and Sport: CHRISTIAN BERGILIN (RPR).

Attached to the Minister of State for the Economy, Finance and Privatization:
  Consumer Affairs and Competition: JEAN ARTHUIS (UDF-CDS).

Attached to the Minister for Culture and Communication: PHILIPPE DE VILLIERS (UDF-PR).

Attached to the Minister of Foreign Affairs: DIDIER BARIANI (UDF-Rad.).

Attached to the Minister for the Overseas Departments and Territories:
  South Pacific Problems: GASTON FLOSSE (RPR).

Attached to the Minister of National Education:
  Teaching: Mme MICHÈLE ALLIOT-MARIE (RPR).
  Vocational Training: Mme NICOLE CATALA (RPR).

FRANCE   Directory

Attached to the Minister of Social Affairs and Employment:
  Social Security: ADRIEN ZELLER (UDF-CDS).
Attached to the Minister of Industry, Postal Services and Telecommunications and Tourism:
  Tourism: JEAN-JACQUES DESCAMPS (UDF-PR).
Attached to the Minister of Defence:
  Defence: JACQUES BOYON (RPR).
  Armed Forces Veterans: GEORGES FONTÈS (RPR).
  Repatriates: ANDRÉ SANTINI (UDF-PSD).
  The Sea: AMBROISE GUELLEC (UDF-CDS).

MINISTRIES

Office of the President: Palais de l'Elysée, 55–57 rue du Faubourg Saint Honoré, 75008 Paris; tel. (1) 42-92-81-00; telex 650127.
Office of the Prime Minister: 57 rue de Varenne, 75700 Paris; tel. (1) 42-75-80-00; telex 200724.
Ministry of Agriculture: 78 rue de Varenne, 75700 Paris; tel. (1) 45-55-95-50; telex 200814.
Ministry of Co-operation: 20 rue Monsieur, 75700 Paris; tel. (1) 47-83-10-10; telex 202363.
Ministry of Culture and Communication: 3 rue de Valois, 75042 Paris; tel. (1) 42-96-10-40; telex 210293.
Ministry of Defence: 14 rue Saint Dominique, 75700 Paris; tel. (1) 45-55-95-20; telex 201375.
Ministry of the Economy, Finance and Privatization: 246 blvd St-Germain, 75700 Paris; tel. (1) 42-60-33-00; telex 217068.
Ministry of Equipment, Housing, Regional Planning and Transport: 45 ave Georges-Mandel, 75016 Paris; tel. (1) 46-47-31-32.
Ministry of Foreign Affairs: 37 quai d'Orsay, 75700 Paris; tel. (1) 45-55-95-40; telex 202329.
Ministry of Industry, Postal Services and Telecommunications and Tourism: 101 rue de Grenelle, 75700 Paris; tel. (1) 45-56-36-36.
Ministry of the Interior: place Beauvau, 75800 Paris; tel. (1) 45-22-90-90; telex 290922.
Ministry of Justice and Overseas Legislation: 13 place Vendôme, 75042 Paris Cedex 01; tel. (1) 42-61-80-22; telex 211320.
Ministry of National Education: 110 rue de Grenelle, 75700 Paris; tel. (1) 45-50-10-10; telex 201244.
Ministry of Overseas Departments and Territories: 27 rue Oudinot, 75700 Paris; tel. (1) 47-83-01-23.
Ministry for Relations with Parliament: 72 rue de la Varenne, 75700 Paris; tel. (1) 42-75-80-00.
Ministry of Social Affairs and Employment: 127 rue de Grenelle, 75700 Paris; tel. (1) 45-67-55-44.

President and Legislature

PRESIDENT
Elections of 26 April and 10 May 1981

	First ballot	Second ballot
HUGUETTE BOUCHARDEAU (Parti Socialiste Unifié)	321,353	
JACQUES CHIRAC (Rassemblement pour la République)	5,225,848	
MICHEL CRÉPEAU (Mouvement des Radicaux de Gauche)	642,847	
MICHEL DEBRÉ (Independent Gaullist)	481,821	
MARIE-FRANCE GARAUD (Independent Gaullist)	386,623	
VALÉRY GISCARD D'ESTAING (Non-Party)	8,222,432	14,642,306
ARLETTE LAGUILLER (Lutte Ouvrière)	668,057	
BRICE LALONDE (Mouvement d'Ecologie Politique)	1,126,254	
GEORGES MARCHAIS (Parti Communiste Français)	4,456,922	
FRANÇOIS MITTERRAND (Parti Socialiste)	7,505,960	15,708,262

Figures published by Ministry of the Interior, after corrections by the Conseil Constitutionnel (see p. 1061).

PARLEMENT
(Parliament)

Assemblée Nationale
(National Assembly)

President: JACQUES CHABAN-DELMAS.

The Assembly has 577 members, elected under a system of proportional representation for up to five years.

General election, 16 March 1986

Parties and Groups	Votes cast	%	Seats
Parti Socialiste (PS)	8,702,137	31.04	206*
Union UDF-RPR	6,017,207	21.46	147
Rassemblement pour la République (RPR)	3,142,373	11.21	76†
Union pour la Démocratie Française (UDF)	2,330,072	8.31	53
Front National (FN)	2,705,838	9.65	35
Parti Communiste	2,740,972	9.78	35
Various right-wing	1,094,336	3.90	14
Various left-wing	287,177	1.02	5
Mouvement des Radicaux de Gauche (MRG)	107,754	0.38	2
Union de la Gauche	56,044	0.20	2
Other extreme left-wing	427,753	1.53	—
Ecologists	340,138	1.21	—
Other extreme right-wing	57,334	0.20	—
Regionalists	28,045	0.10	—
Total	28,037,180	100.00	575*†

* Not including the deputy for St Pierre and Miquelon, elected in a second round of voting on 23 March 1986.
† Not including the deputy for the Wallis and Futuna Islands, elected in a second round of voting on 23 March 1986.

Note: By-elections were held in Haute-Corse in August and in Haute-Garonne in September 1986, following a ruling by the Constitutional Council that the March results were invalid, owing to electoral irregularities. The distribution of seats remained unchanged.

Sénat
(Senate)

President: ALAIN POHER.

Members of the Senate are indirectly elected for a term of nine years, with one-third of the seats renewable every three years.

After the most recent election, held on 28 September 1986, the Senate had 319 seats: 296 for metropolitan France; 13 for the overseas departments and territories; and 10 for French nationals abroad. The strength of the parties was as follows:

	Seats
Groupe communiste	15
Groupe de la Gauche démocratique	35
Groupe de l'Union centriste des Démocrates de Progrès	70
Groupe de l'Union des Républicains et des Indépendants	54
Groupe du Rassemblement pour la République	77
Groupe socialiste	64
Non-attached	4
Total	319

Note: Until the September 1986 election, the Senate had 317 seats. The two additional members represent French nationals abroad.

Political Organizations

Centre National des Indépendants et Paysans (CNIP): 106 rue de l'Université, 75007 Paris; tel. (1) 47-05-49-64; f. 1949; right-wing; Pres. PHILIPPE MALAUD; Sec.-Gen. FRANÇOIS-XAVIER PARENT.

Fédération des Socialistes Démocrates (FSD): 8 rue Saint Marc, 75002 Paris; Pres. CHRISTIAN CHAUVEL; Sec.-Gen. GILBERT PÉROT.

FRANCE

Front National (FN): 8 rue du Général Clergerie, 75116 Paris; tel. (1) 47-27-56-66; f. 1972; extreme right-wing nationalist; Pres. JEAN-MARIE LE PEN; Sec.-Gen. JEAN-PIERRE STIRBOIS.

Ligue Communiste Revolutionnaire (LCR): c/o Rouge, 2 rue Richard Lenoir, 93100 Montreuil; tel. (1) 48-59-23-00; f. 1974; Trotskyist; French section of the Fourth International; Leader ALAIN KRIVINE.

Lutte Ouvrière (LO): BP 233, 75865 Paris Cedex 18; Trotskyist; Leaders ARLETTE LAGUILLER, F. DUBURG, J. MORAND.

Mouvement des Démocrates: 71 rue Ampère, 75017 Paris; tel. (1) 47-63-99-40; f. 1974; Leader MICHEL JOBERT.

Mouvement gaulliste populaire (MGP): 103 rue Quincampoix, 75003 Paris; f. 1982 by merger of Union démocratique du travail and Fédération des républicains de progrès; Gaullist party; Leaders JACQUES DUBÛ-BRIDEL, PIERRE DABEZIES.

Mouvement des Radicaux de Gauche (MRG): 3 rue la Boétie, 75008 Paris; tel. (1) 47-42-22-41; f. 1973; formed by splinter group from Parti Radical; left-wing; Pres. FRANÇOIS DOUBIN.

Parti Communiste Français (PCF): 2 place du Colonel Fabien, 75940 Paris Cedex 19; tel. (1) 42-38-66-55; telex 650818; subscribed to the common programme of the United Left (with the Parti Socialiste) until 1977 when the United Left split over nationalization issues; aims to follow the democratic path to socialism and advocates an independent foreign policy; mems 702,800 (1979); Sec.-Gen. GEORGES MARCHAIS.

Parti Socialiste (PS): 10 rue de Solférino, 75007 Paris; tel. (1) 45-50-34-35; telex 200174; f. 1971; subscribed to the common programme of the United Left (with the Parti Communiste) until 1977, when the United Left split over nationalization issues. Belief in a planned economy, full employment and the eventual attainment of socialism through the nationalization of key industries; 200,000 mems; First Sec. LIONEL JOSPIN.

Parti Socialiste Unifié (PSU): 9 rue Borromée, 75015 Paris; tel. (1) 45-66-45-37; f. 1960; left-wing party; 7,000 mems; National Secs SERGE DEPAOUIT, JACQUES SALVATOR.

Rassemblement pour la République (RPR): 123 rue de Lille, 75007 Paris; tel. (1) 45-50-32-19; telex 260820; f. 1976 from the Gaullist party Union des Démocrates pour la République (UDR) after the resignation of Jacques Chirac as Prime Minister in Giscard d'Estaing's Government; Pres. JACQUES CHIRAC; Political adviser CLAUDE LARBÉ; Sec.-Gen. JACQUES TOUBON.

Union Centriste et Radicale (UCR): f. 1984 after dissolution of Mouvement des Sociaux Libéraux; Pres. OLIVIER STIRN; Sec.-Gen. FRANÇOIS GARCIA.

Union pour la Démocratie Française (UDF): 42 bis, blvd de Latour Maubourg, 75007 Paris; tel. (1) 45-50-34-20; formed in 1978 to unite for electoral purposes non-Gaullist 'majority' candidates; Chair. JEAN LECANUET; Sec.-Gen. MICHEL PINTON.

Affiliated parties:

Centre des Démocrates Sociaux (CDS): 205 blvd Saint Germain, 75007 Paris; tel. (1) 45-44-72-50; f. 1976 by merger of Centre Démocrate and Centre Démocratie et Progrès; Pres. PIERRE MÉHAIGNERIE; Sec.-Gen. JACQUES BARROT.

Parti Radical et Radical-Socialiste: 1 place de Valois, 75001 Paris; tel. (1) 42-61-56-32; f. 1901; Pres. ANDRÉ ROSSINOT; Sec.-Gen. YVES GALLAND.

Parti Républicain (PR): 1 rue Villersexel, 75007 Paris; tel. (1) 45-44-44-20; formed May 1977 as a grouping of the Fédération Nationale des Républicains Indépendants (FNRI) and three smaller 'Giscardian' parties; Hon. Pres. MICHEL PONIATOWSKI; Sec.-Gen. FRANÇOIS LÉOTARD.

Parti social-démocrate (PSD): 110 rue de Sèvres, 75015 Paris; tel. (1) 45-66-74-73; f. 1973 as Mouvement des démocrates socialistes de France, name changed 1982; Pres. MAX LEJEUNE; Sec.-Gen. CHARLES BAUR.

Les Verts: Cité Fleurie, 90 rue Vergniaud, 75013 Paris; tel. (1) 45-89-99-11; f. 1984; ecologist party; National Secs MICHEL CARRÉ, MICHEL DELORE.

Small left-wing parties include Organisation Communiste Internationale, Communistes Démocrates et Unitaires, Révolution, Parti communiste révolutionnaire (marxiste-léniniste), and Union des communistes de France (marxiste-léniniste). Small right-wing and opposition parties include Nouvelle Action Française (f. 1971), Oeuvre Française (f. 1968), Parti Démocrate Française (f. 1982), Parti des Forces Nouvelles (f. 1974), and Restauration Nationale (f. 1947). There are also regional movements in Brittany, the Basque country, Corsica and Occitania (Provence-Languedoc).

Diplomatic Representation

EMBASSIES IN FRANCE

Afghanistan: 32 ave Raphaël, 75016 Paris; tel. (1) 45-27-66-09; Chargé d'affaires a.i.: ABDULLAH KESHTMAND.

Albania: 131 rue de la Pompe, 75116 Paris; tel. (1) 45-53-51-32; telex 611534; Ambassador: MAXHUM PEKA.

Algeria: 50 rue de Lisbonne, 75008 Paris; tel. (1) 42-25-70-70; Ambassador: ABDELHAMID MEHIRI.

Angola: 19 ave Foch, 75116 Paris; tel. (1) 45-01-58-20; Ambassador: LUIS JOSÉ DE ALMEIDA.

Argentina: 6 rue Cimarosa, 75116 Paris; tel. (1) 45-53-14-69; telex 613819; Ambassador: CARLOS ORTIZ DI ROZAS.

Australia: 4 rue Jean Rey, 75724 Paris Cedex 15; tel. (1) 45-75-62-00; telex 202313; Ambassador: PETER CAMPBELL JOHN CURTIS.

Austria: 6 rue Fabert, 75007 Paris; tel. (1) 45-55-95-66; telex 200708; Ambassador: ERIC NETTEL.

Bahrain: 15 ave Raymond Poincaré, 75116 Paris; tel. (1) 45-53-01-19; telex 620924; Ambassador: SALMAN MOHAMED AL-SAFFAR.

Bangladesh: 5 sq. Pétrarque, 75016 Paris; tel. (1) 45-53-41-20; telex 630868; Ambassador: Dr A. MAJEED KHAN.

Belgium: 9 rue de Tilsit, 75840 Paris Cedex 17; tel. (1) 43-80-61-00; telex 650484; Ambassador: RITTWEGER DE MOOR.

Benin: 87 ave Victor Hugo, 75116 Paris; tel. (1) 45-00-98-82; telex 610110; Ambassador: SOULER ISSIFOU IDRISSOU.

Bolivia: 12 ave Président Kennedy, 75016 Paris; tel. (1) 42-24-93-44; Ambassador: GASTÓN ARAOZ.

Brazil: 34 cours Albert 1er, 75008 Paris; tel. (1) 42-25-92-50; telex 650063; Ambassador: ANTÔNIO CORRÊA DO LAGO.

Bulgaria: 1 ave Rapp, 75007 Paris; tel. (1) 45-51-85-90; Ambassador: GUEORGUI YOVKOV.

Burkina Faso: 159 blvd Haussmann, 75008 Paris; tel. (1) 43-59-90-63; telex 201058; Ambassador: EMMANUEL SALEMBERE.

Burma: 60 rue de Courcelles, 75008 Paris; tel. (1) 42-25-56-95; Ambassador: KHIN MAUNG WIN.

Burundi: 3 rue Octave Feuillet, 75016 Paris; tel. (1) 45-20-60-61; telex 611463; Chargé d'affaires a.i.: SEBASTIEN NTAHUGA.

Cameroon: 73 rue d'Auteuil, 75016 Paris; tel. (1) 47-43-98-33; telex 620312; Ambassador: JACQUES-ROGER BOOH-BOOH.

Canada: 35 ave Montaigne, 75008 Paris; tel. (1) 47-23-01-01; telex 280806; Ambassador: LUCIEN BOUCHARD.

Central African Republic: 29 blvd de Montmorency, 75016 Paris; tel. (1) 42-24-42-56; telex 611908; Ambassador: GABRIEL M'BANGAS.

Chad: 65 rue des Belles Feuilles, 75116 Paris; tel. (1) 45-53-36-75; telex 610629; Ambassador: AHMED ALLAM-MI.

Chile: 2 ave de la Motte-Piquet, 75007 Paris; tel. (1) 45-51-46-68; telex 260075; Ambassador: EDUARDO CISTERNAS.

China, People's Republic: 11 ave George V, 75008 Paris; tel. (1) 47-23-34-45; telex 270114; Ambassador: ZHOU JUE.

Colombia: 22 rue de l'Elysée, 75008 Paris; tel. (1) 42-65-46-08; telex 640935; Chargé d'affaires a.i.: OCTAVIO GALLÓN.

Comoros: 13-15 rue de la Néva, 75008 Paris; tel. (1) 47-63-81-78; telex 642390.

Congo: 37 bis rue Paul Valéry, 75116 Paris; tel. (1) 45-00-60-57; telex 611954; Ambassador: JEAN-MARIE EWENGUÉ.

Costa Rica: 74 ave Paul-Doumer, 75116 Paris; tel. (1) 45-04-50-93; telex 648046; Chargé d'affaires a.i.: FRANCISCO OREAMUNO.

Cuba: 16 rue de Presles, 75015 Paris; tel. (1) 45-67-55-35; telex 200815; Ambassador: ALBERTO BOZA HIDALGO-GATO.

Cyprus: 23 rue Galilée, 75116 Paris; tel. (1) 47-20-86-28; telex 610664; Ambassador: PETROS MICHAELIDES.

Czechoslovakia: 15 ave Charles Floquet, 75007 Paris; tel. (1) 47-34-29-10; telex 611032; Ambassador: MECISLAV JABLONSKY.

Denmark: 77 ave Marceau, 75116 Paris; tel. (1) 47-23-54-20; telex 620172; Ambassador: GUNNAR RIBERHOLDT.

Djibouti: 26 rue Emile Ménier, 75116 Paris; tel. (1) 47-27-49-22; telex 614970; Ambassador: AHMED IBRAHIM ABDI.

Dominican Republic: 2 rue Georges-Ville, 75116 Paris; tel. (1) 45-00-77-71; telex 615333; Ambassador: MILTON LEONIDAS RAY GUEVARA.

Ecuador: 34 ave de Messine, 75008 Paris; tel. (1) 45-61-10-21; telex 641333; Ambassador: PATRICIO F. AVELLÁN.

FRANCE

Egypt: 56 ave d'Iéna, 75116 Paris; tel. (1) 47-20-97-70; telex 611691; Ambassador: ALI SAMIR SAFOUAT.
El Salvador: 12 rue Galilée, 75116 Paris; tel. (1) 47-20-42-02; telex 612572; Chargé d'affaires a.i.: JOAQUÍN RODEZNO.
Equatorial Guinea: 6 rue Alfred de Vigny, 75008 Paris; tel. (1) 47-66-44-33; Ambassador: JESÚS ELA ABEME.
Ethiopia: 35 ave Charles Floquet, 75007 Paris; tel. (1) 47-83-83-95; Chargé d'affaires: (vacant).
Finland: 2 rue Fabert, 75007 Paris; tel. (1) 47-05-35-45; telex 200054; Ambassador: OSSI SUNELL.
Gabon: 26 bis ave Raphaël, 75016 Paris; tel. (1) 42-24-79-60; telex 610146; Ambassador: JEAN-CLAUDE LABOURA.
German Democratic Republic: 24 rue Marbeau, 75116 Paris; tel. (1) 45-00-00-10; telex 620569; Ambassador: ALFRED MARTER.
Germany, Federal Republic: 13–15 ave Franklin D. Roosevelt, 75008 Paris; tel. (1) 43-59-33-51; telex 280136; Ambassador: FRANZ-JOACHIM SCHOELLER.
Ghana: 8 Villa Said, 75116 Paris; tel. (1) 45-00-09-50; telex 611020; Ambassador: JOSEPH QUAO CLELAND.
Greece: 17 rue Auguste Vacquerie, 75116 Paris; tel. (1) 47-23-72-28; telex 612747; Ambassador: CHRISTOS ROKOFYLLOS.
Guatemala: 73 rue de Courcelles, 75008 Paris; tel. (1) 42-27-78-63; telex 650850; Ambassador: GUILLERMO PUTZEIS-ALVAREZ.
Guinea: 24 rue Emile Ménier, 75116 Paris; tel. (1) 45-53-72-25; telex 611748; Ambassador: SEKOU DECAST CAMARA.
Haiti: 10 rue Théodule Ribot, 75017 Paris; tel. (1) 47-63-47-78; Ambassador: JEAN-CLAUDE ANDRÉ.
Holy See: 10 ave du Président Wilson, 75116 Paris; tel. (1) 47-23-58-34; Apostolic Nuncio: Mgr ANGELO FELICI.
Honduras: 6 place Vendôme, 75001 Paris; tel. (1) 42-61-34-75; telex 215535; Ambassador: RAFAEL LEIVA VIVAS.
Hungary: 5 bis sq. de l'Avenue Foch, 75116 Paris; tel. (1) 45-00-41-59; telex 610822; Ambassador: Dr REZSŐ PALOTAS.
Iceland: 124 blvd Haussmann, 75008 Paris; tel. (1) 45-22-81-54; telex 290314; Ambassador: HARALDUR KRÖYER.
India: 15 rue Alfred Dehodencq, 75016 Paris; tel. (1) 45-20-39-30; telex 610621; Ambassador: Air Chief Marshall (retd) I. H. LATIF.
Indonesia: 49 rue Cortambert, 75016 Paris; tel. (1) 45-03-07-60; telex 611005; Ambassador: BACHTIAR RIFAI.
Iran: 4 ave d'Iéna, 75116 Paris; tel. (1) 47-23-61-22; telex 610600; Chargé d'affaires: ALI REZA MOAYERI.
Iraq: 53 rue de la Faisanderie, 75116 Paris; tel. (1) 45-01-51-00; telex 613706; Ambassador: MOHAMED SADIQ EL MASCHAT.
Ireland: 12 ave Foch, 75116 Paris; tel. (1) 45-00-20-87; telex 620557; Ambassador: ANDREW O'ROURKE.
Israel: 3 rue Rabelais, 75008 Paris; tel. (1) 42-56-47-47; telex 650831; Ambassador: OVADIA SOFER.
Italy: 51 rue de Varenne, 75007 Paris; tel. (1) 45-44-38-90; telex 270827; Ambassador: WALTER GARDINI.
Ivory Coast: 102 ave Raymond Poincaré, 75116 Paris; tel. (1) 45-01-53-10; telex 611915; Ambassador: EUGÈNE AIDARA.
Japan: 7 ave Hoche, 75008 Paris; tel. (1) 47-66-02-22; telex 660493; Ambassador: MORIYUKI MOTONO.
Jordan: 80 blvd Maurice Barrès, 92200 Neuilly-sur-Seine; tel. (1) 46-24-51-38; telex 630084; Chargé d'affaires a.i.: MOHAMED AFANA.
Kenya: 3 rue Cimarosa, 75116 Paris; tel. (1) 45-53-35-00; telex 620825; Ambassador: SIMEON B. ARAP BULLUT.
Korea, Republic: 125 rue de Grenelle, 75007 Paris; tel. (1) 47-05-64-10; Ambassador: YOON UK-SUP.
Kuwait: 2 rue de Lubeck, 75116 Paris; tel. (1) 47-23-54-25; telex 620513; Ambassador: ISSA AL-HAMAD.
Laos: 74 ave Raymond Poincaré, 75116 Paris; tel. (1) 45-53-70-47; telex 610711.
Lebanon: 3 villa Copernic, 75116 Paris; tel. (1) 45-00-22-25; telex 611087; Ambassador: FAROUK ABILLAMA.
Liberia: 8 rue Jacques Bingen, 75017 Paris; tel. (1) 47-63-58-55; telex 290288; Ambassador: EDITH BOWEN CARR.
Libya (People's Bureau): 2 rue Charles Lamoureux, 75116 Paris; tel. (1) 47-04-71-60; telex 620643; Sec. of People's Bureau: HAMED EL HOUDERI.
Luxembourg: 33 ave Rapp, 75007 Paris; tel. (1) 45-55-13-37; telex 204711; Ambassador: PIERRE WURTH.
Madagascar: 4 ave Raphaël, 75016 Paris; tel. (1) 45-04-62-11; telex 610394; Ambassador: FRANÇOIS DE PAULE RABOTOSON.

Malaysia: 2 bis rue Bénouville, 75116 Paris; tel. (1) 45-53-11-85; Ambassador: Tan Sri LIM TAIK CHOON.
Mali: 89 rue du Cherche-Midi, 75006 Paris; tel. (1) 45-48-58-43; telex 260002; Ambassador: MAMADOU DIAWARA.
Malta: 92 ave des Champs Elysées, 75008 Paris; tel. (1) 45-62-53-01; telex 641023; Chargé d'affaires: MICHAËL BORG.
Mauritania: 5 rue de Montévidéo, 75116 Paris; tel. (1) 45-04-88-54; telex 620506; Ambassador: M. HAMOUD OULD ELY.
Mauritius: 68 blvd de Courcelles, 75017 Paris; tel. (1) 42-27-30-19; telex 660233; Ambassador: RAMDUTHSING JADDOO.
Mexico: 9 rue de Longchamp, 75116 Paris; tel. (1) 45-53-76-43; telex 610332; Ambassador: JORGE CASTAÑEDA Y ALVAREZ DE LA ROSA.
Monaco: 22 blvd Suchet, 75016 Paris; tel. (1) 45-04-74-54; telex 611088; Ambassador: CHRISTIAN ORSETTI.
Mongolia: 5 ave Robert Schuman, 92100 Boulogne-Billancourt; tel. (1) 46-05-23-18; telex 200656; Ambassador: (vacant).
Morocco: 3–5 rue Le Tasse, 75016 Paris; tel. (1) 45-20-69-35; telex 611025; Ambassador: Dr YOUSSEF BEN ABBES.
Mozambique: 82 rue Laugier, 75017 Paris; tel. (1) 47-64-91-32; telex 641527; Ambassador: ISAAC MURARGY.
Nepal: 7 rue Washington, 75008 Paris; tel. (1) 43-59-28-61; telex 643929; Ambassador: DILLY RAJ UPRETY.
Netherlands: 7–9 rue Eblé, 75007 Paris; tel. (1) 43-06-61-88; telex 200070; Ambassador: MAX VEGELIN VAN CLAERBERGEN.
New Zealand: 7ter rue Léonard de Vinci, 75116 Paris; tel. (1) 45-00-24-11; telex 611929; Ambassador: J. G. MCARTHUR.
Nicaragua: 11 rue de Sontay, 75116 Paris; tel. (1) 45-00-35-42; telex 612017; Ambassador: ROBERTO ARGÜELLO HURTADO.
Niger: 154 rue de Longchamp, 75116 Paris; tel. (1) 45-04-80-60; telex 611080; Ambassador: ABDOU GARBA.
Nigeria: 173 ave Victor Hugo, 75116 Paris; tel. (1) 47-04-68-65; telex 620106; Ambassador: PETER LUIS UDOH.
Norway: 28 rue Bayard, 75008 Paris; tel. (1) 47-23-72-78; telex 280947; Ambassador: ASBJØRN SKARSTEIN.
Oman: 50 ave d'Iéna, 75116 Paris; tel. (1) 47-23-01-63; telex 613765; Ambassador: MOHAMED HASSAN ALI.
Pakistan: 18 rue Lord Byron, 75008 Paris; tel. (1) 45-62-23-32; telex 660000; Ambassador: JAMSHEED MARKER.
Panama: 145 ave de Suffren, 75015 Paris; tel. (1) 47-83-23-32; telex 205970; Ambassador: GASPAR WITTGREEN.
Paraguay: 8 ave Charles Floquet, 75007 Paris; tel. (1) 47-83-54-77; Ambassador: Dr JORGE HAMUY-DACAK.
Peru: 50 ave Kléber, 75116 Paris; tel. (1) 47-04-46-63; telex 611081; Ambassador: HUGO OTERO.
Philippines: 39 ave Georges Mandel, 75116 Paris; tel. (1) 47-04-65-50; telex 218458; Ambassador: FELIPE MABILANGAN.
Poland: 1–3 rue Talleyrand, 75007 Paris; tel. (1) 45-51-60-80; telex 611029; Ambassador: JANUSZ STEFANOWICZ.
Portugal: 3 rue de Noisiel, 75116 Paris; tel. (1) 47-27-35-29; telex 620905; Ambassador: LUÍS GASPAR DA SILVA.
Qatar: 57 quai d'Orsay, 75007 Paris; tel. (1) 45-51-90-71; telex 270074; Ambassador: ABDUL RAHMAN BIN HAMAD.
Romania: 5 rue de l'Exposition, 75007 Paris; tel. (1) 47-05-49-54; Ambassador: PETRE GIGEA.
Rwanda: 70 blvd de Courcelles, 75017 Paris; tel. (1) 42-27-36-31; telex 650930; Ambassador: BONAVENTURE UBALIJORO.
San Marino: 6 ave Franklin Roosevelt, 75008 Paris; tel. (1) 43-59-22-28; telex 643445; Minister: CAMILLO DE BENEDETTI.
Saudi Arabia: 5 ave Hoche, 75008 Paris; tel. (1) 47-66-02-06 and 42-27-81-12; telex 641508; Ambassador: JAMIL AL-HEJAILAN.
Senegal: 14 ave Robert Schuman, 75007 Paris; tel. (1) 47-05-39-45; telex 611563; Ambassador: AMADOU MOKTAR CISSE.
Seychelles: 53 bis rue François 1er, 75008 Paris; tel. (1) 47-23-98-11; Ambassador: D. DE SAINT JORRE.
Singapore: 12 sq. de l'Avenue Foch, 75116 Paris; tel. (1) 45-00-33-61; Ambassador: DAVID SAUL MARSHALL.
Somalia: 26 rue Dumont d'Urville, 75116 Paris; tel. (1) 45-00-76-51; telex 611828; Ambassador: AHMED SHIRE MAHMOUD.
South Africa: 59 quai d'Orsay, 75007 Paris; tel. (1) 45-55-92-37; telex 200280; Ambassador: ABRAHAM DU PLOOY.
Spain: 13 ave Georges V, 75008 Paris; tel. (1) 47-23-61-83; telex 280689; Ambassador: JUAN DURÁN-LÓRIGA RODRIGÁÑEZ.

FRANCE

Sri Lanka: 15 rue d'Astorg, 75008 Paris; tel. (1) 42-66-35-01; telex 642337; Ambassador: D. G. B. DE SILVA.
Sudan: 56 ave Montaigne, 75008 Paris; tel. (1) 47-20-07-34; telex 660268; Ambassador: YOUSIF MOUKHTÁR YOUSIF.
Sweden: 17 rue Barbet de Jouy, 75007 Paris; tel. (1) 45-55-92-15; telex 204740; Ambassador: CARL LIDBOM.
Switzerland: 142 rue de Grenelle, 75007 Paris; tel. (1) 45-50-34-46; telex 270969; Ambassador: FRANÇOIS DE ZIEGLER.
Syria: 20 rue Vaneau, 75007 Paris; tel. (1) 45-50-24-90; Ambassador: YOUSSEF CHAKKOUR.
Tanzania: 70 blvd Péreire, 75017 Paris; tel. (1) 47-66-21-77; telex 643968; Ambassador: TATU NURU.
Thailand: 8 rue Greuze, 75116 Paris; tel. (1) 47-04-32-22; telex 270837; Ambassador: PRACHA GUNA-KASEM.
Togo: 8 rue Alfred Roll, 75017 Paris; tel. (1) 43-80-12-13; telex 290497; Ambassador: BOUMBÉRA ALASSOUNOUMA.
Tunisia: 25 rue Barbet de Jouy, 75007 Paris; tel. (1) 45-55-95-98; telex 200639; Ambassador: MUSTAPHA ZAANOUNI.
Turkey: 16 ave de Lamballe, 75016 Paris; tel. (1) 45-24-52-24; telex 610850; Ambassador: FAIK MELEK.
Uganda: 13 ave Raymond Poincaré, 75116 Paris; tel. (1) 47-27-46-80; telex 630028; Ambassador: DAVID NABETA.
USSR: 40–50 blvd Lannes, 75016 Paris; tel. (1) 45-04-05-50; telex 611761; Ambassador: YAKOV RIABOV.
United Arab Emirates: 3 rue de Lota, 75116 Paris; tel. (1) 45-53-94-04; telex 620003; Chargé d'affaires a.i.: HILAL SAEED ALZAABI.
United Kingdom: 35 rue du Faubourg Saint Honoré, 75383 Paris Cedex 08; tel. (1) 42-66-91-42; telex 650264; Ambassador: Sir JOHN FRETWELL.
USA: 2 ave Gabriel, 75008 Paris; tel. (1) 42-96-12-02; telex 650221; Ambassador: JOE RODGERS.
Uruguay: 15 rue Lesueur, 75116 Paris; tel. (1) 45-00-91-50; telex 610564; Chargé d'affaires a.i.: JORGE SILVA CENCIO.
Venezuela: 11 rue Copernic, 75016 Paris; tel. (1) 45-53-29-98; telex 610683; Ambassador: RAMÓN ESCOVAR SALÓM.
Viet-Nam: 62 rue Boileau, 75116 Paris; tel. (1) 45-24-50-63; telex 613240; Ambassador: HA VAN LAU.
Yemen Arab Republic: 21 ave Charles Floquet, 75007 Paris; tel. (1) 43-06-66-22; telex 200076; Ambassador: GHALEB ALI JAMIL.
Yemen, People's Democratic Republic: 25 rue Georges Bizet, 75116; tel. (1) 47-23-61-76; telex 610231; Ambassador: ABDALLAH ABODA HAMMAM.
Yugoslavia: 54 rue de la Faisanderie, 75116 Paris; tel. (1) 45-04-05-05; Ambassador: BORIS SNUDERL.
Zaire: 32 cours Albert 1er, 75008 Paris; tel. (1) 42-25-57-50; telex 280661; Ambassador: SAKOMBI INONGO.
Zambia: 76 ave d'Iéna, 75016 Paris; tel. (1) 47-23-43-52; telex 610483; Ambassador: HENRY KOSAM MATIPA.
Zimbabwe: 5 rue de Tilsit, 75008 Paris; tel. (1) 47-63-48-31; telex 643505; Ambassador: BEN KUFAKUNESU JAMBGA.

Judicial System

The Judiciary is independent of the Government. Judges of the Court of Cassation and the First President of the Court of Appeal are appointed by the executive from nominations of the High Council of the Judiciary.

Subordinate cases are heard by Tribunaux d'instance, of which there are 471, and more serious cases by Tribunaux de grande instance, of which there are 181. Parallel to these Tribunals are the Tribunaux de commerce, for commercial cases, composed of judges elected by tradesmen and manufacturers among themselves. These do not exist in every district. Where there is no Tribunal de commerce, commercial disputes are judged by Tribunaux de grande instance.

The Conseils de Prud'hommes (Boards of Arbitration) consist of an equal number of workers or employees and employers ruling on the differences which arise over Contracts of Work.

The Tribunaux correctionnnels (Correctional Courts) for criminal cases correspond to the Tribunaux de grande instance for civil cases. They pronounce on all graver offences (délits), including those involving imprisonment. Offences committed by juveniles of under 18 years go before specialized tribunals for children.

From all these Tribunals appeal lies to the Cours d'appel (Courts of Appeal).

The Cours d'assises (Courts of Assize) have no regular sittings, but are called when necessary to try every important case, for example, murder. They are presided over by judges who are members of the Cours d'appel and composed of elected judges (jury). Their decision is final, except where shown to be wrong in law, and then recourse is had to the Cour de Cassation (Court of Cassation). The Cour de Cassation is not a supreme court of appeal but a higher authority for the proper application of the law. Its duty is to see that judgments are not contrary either to the letter or the spirit of the law; any judgment annulled by the Court involves the trying of the case anew by a court of the same category as that which made the original decision.

COUR DE CASSATION

Palais de Justice, 75 quai de l'Horloge, 75055 Paris; tel. (1) 43-29-12-55.
First President: SIMONE ROZÈS.
Presidents of Chambers: JEAN-MICHEL AUBOUIN (2ème Chambre Civile), JACQUES BAUDOUIN (Chambre Commerciale), JEAN LEDOUX (Chambre Criminelle), MICHEL MONEGIER DE SORBIER (3ème Chambre Civile), ROGER FABRE (1ère Chambre Civile), JEAN JONQUÈRES (Chambre Sociale).
Solicitor-General: PIERRE ARPAILLANGE.
There are 84 Counsellors, one First Attorney-General and 19 Attorneys-General.
Chief Clerk of the Court: DANIEL AUTIÉ.
Council of Advocates at Court of Cassation: Pres. JACQUES ROUVIÈRE.

COUR D'APPEL DE PARIS

Palais de Justice, blvd de Palais, 75001 Paris.
First President: PIERRE DRAI.
There are also 58 Presidents of Chambers.
Solicitor-General: YVES MONNET.
There are also 125 Counsellors, 22 Attorneys-General and 38 Deputies.

TRIBUNAL DE GRANDE INSTANCE DE PARIS

Palais de Justice, blvd de Palais, 75001 Paris.
President: ROBERT DIET.
Solicitor of Republic: MICHEL RAYNAUD.

TRIBUNAL DE COMMERCE DE PARIS

1 quai de Corse, 75181 Paris Cedex 04.
President: JACQUES BON.

ADMINISTRATIVE JURISDICTION

Certain cases arising between civil servants (when on duty) and the government, or between any citizen and the government are judged by special administrative courts.

The Tribunaux Administratifs, of which there are 22, are situated in the capital of each area; the Conseil d'Etat (see below) has its seat in Paris.

TRIBUNAL DES CONFLITS

Decides whether cases shall be submitted to the ordinary or administrative courts.
President: The Minister of Justice.
Vice-President: PIERRE NICOLAI.
There are also four Counsellors of the Cour de Cassation and three Counsellors of State.

COUR DES COMPTES

13 rue Cambon, 75100 Paris; tel. (1) 42-98-95-00.
An administrative tribunal charged with judging the correctness of public accounts. It is the judge of common law of all public accounts laid before it. The judgments of the Court may be annulled by the Conseil d'Etat.
First President: ANDRÉ CHANDERNAGOR.
Presidents: JUSTIN ROHMER, RENÉ VACQUIER, CHARLES DE VILLAINES, MAURICE BERNARD, FRANCIS RAISON, FRANÇOIS MOSES.
Attorney-General: PIERRE MOINOT.
Secretary-General: FRANÇOIS LOGEROT.
Solicitors-General: MICHEL LAGRAVE, CHRISTIAN DESCHEEMAEKER, JEAN-PIERRE GASTINEL.

FRANCE   Directory

CHAMBRES RÉGIONALES DES COMPTES
In 1983 jurisdiction over the accounts of local administrations (Régions, Départements and Communes) and public institutions (hospitals, council housing, etc.) was transferred from the Cour des Comptes to local Chambres Régionales. The courts are autonomous but under the jurisdiction of the State. Appeals may be brought before the Cour des Comptes.

CONSEIL D'ETAT
Palais-Royal, 75100 Paris; tel. (1) 42-61-52-29.

A council of the central power and an administrative tribunal. As the consultative organ of the government, it gives opinions in the legislative and administrative domain (interior, finance, public works and social sections). In administrative jurisdiction it has three functions: to judge in the first and last resort such cases as appeals against excess of power laid against official decrees or individuals; to judge appeals against judgments made by administrative tribunals and resolutions of courts of litigation; and to annul decisions made by various specialized administrative authorities which adjudicate without appeal, such as the Cour des Comptes.

President: JACQUES CHIRAC.

Vice-President: PIERRE NICOLAY.

Presidents of Sections: JACQUES BOUTET, FERNAND GREVISSE, SUZANNE GREVISSE, GUY BRAIBANT, MICHEL COMBARNOUS, JEAN KAHN.

General Secretary: MICHEL FRANC.

Religion

CHRISTIANITY
The Roman Catholic Church
In 1976 there were an estimated 45,175,724 Roman Catholics in France, equivalent to about 90% of the population.

Ecclesiastically, France comprises nine Apostolic Regions, together forming 18 archdioceses (of which one, Marseille, is directly responsible to the Holy See), 75 dioceses (including two, Metz and Strasbourg, directly responsible to the Holy See) and one Territorial Prelature. The Archbishop of Paris is also the Ordinary for Catholics of Oriental Rites.

Bishops' Conference: Conférence Episcopale Française, 106 rue de Bac, 75341 Paris Cedex 07; tel. (1) 42-22-57-08; telex 260757; f. 1975; Pres. Mgr JEAN VILNET, Bishop of Lille.

Latin Rite

Archbishop of Lyon and Primate of Gaul: Cardinal ALBERT DECOURTRAY, Archevêché, 1 place de Fourvière, 69321 Lyon Cedex 05; tel. 78-25-12-27; telex 380835.

Archbishop of Aix: Mgr BERNARD PANAFIEU.

Archbishop of Albi: Mgr JOSEPH RABINE.

Archbishop of Auch: Mgr GABRIEL VANEL.

Archbishop of Avignon: Mgr RAYMOND BOUCHEX.

Archbishop of Besançon: Mgr LUCIEN DALOZ.

Archbishop of Bordeaux: Mgr MARIUS MAZIERS.

Archbishop of Bourges: Mgr PIERRE PLATEAU.

Archbishop of Cambrai: Mgr JACQUES DELAPORTE.

Archbishop of Chambéry: Mgr CLAUDE FEIDT.

Archbishop of Marseille: Mgr ROBERT COFFY.

Archbishop of Paris: Cardinal JEAN-MARIE LUSTIGER.

Archbishop of Reims: Mgr JACQUES MÉNAGER.

Archbishop of Rennes: Mgr JACQUES JULLIEN.

Archbishop of Rouen: Mgr JOSEPH DUVAL.

Archbishop of Sens: Mgr EUGÈNE ERNOULT.

Archbishop of Toulouse: Mgr ANDRÉ COLLINI.

Archbishop of Tours: Mgr JEAN HONORÉ.

Armenian Rite

Apostolic Exarch of France: KRIKOR GHABROYAN, Titular Bishop of Amida (Diyarbakir, Turkey), 10 bis rue Thouin, 75005 Paris; tel. (1) 43-26-50-43; 30,000 adherents (1984).

Ukrainian Rite

Apostolic Exarch of France: MICHEL HRYNCHYSHYN, Titular Bishop of Zygris, 186 boulevard Saint-Germain, 75006 Paris; tel. (1) 45-48-48-65; 16,000 adherents (1984).

Protestant Churches
There are some 850,000 Protestants in France.

Fédération Protestante de France: 47 rue de Clichy, 75009 Paris; tel. (1) 48-74-15-08; telex 642380; f. 1906; Pres. JACQUES STEWART; Vice-Pres. J. BAEUERLÉ, J. P. MONSARRAT, TH. KLIPFFEL, A. THOBOIS; Gen. Sec. LOUIS SCHWEITZER.

The Federation comprises the following Churches:

Alliance Nationale des Eglises Luthériennes de France: 1A quai Saint Thomas, Strasbourg; tel. 88-32-45-86; f. 1945; 220,000 mems; groups the two Lutheran churches below; Pres. Pasteur A. APPEL; Sec. Pastor PHILIPPE GUNTHER.

Eglise de la Confession d'Augsbourg d'Alsace et de Lorraine: 1A quai Saint Thomas, 67081 Strasbourg Cedex; tel. 88-32-45-86; Pres. ANDRÉ APPEL; Gen. Secs Pastor W. JURGENSEN, P. ISSLER.

Eglise Evangélique Luthérienne de France: 16 rue Chauchat, 75009 Paris; tel. (1) 47-70-80-30; 65 parishes grouped in 2 directorates: Paris and Montbéliard; Pres. Pastor MICHEL MARLIER; Sec. Pastor JACQUES FISCHER.

Eglise Méthodiste: 3 rue Paul Verlaine, 30100 Alès; the total Methodist community was estimated at 2,900 mems in 1982.

Eglise Réformée d'Alsace et de Lorraine: 2 rue du Bouclier, 67000 Strasbourg; 45,000 mems; Pres. Pastor THÉRÈSE KLIPFFEL.

Eglise Réformée de France: 47 rue de Clichy, 75009 Paris; tel. (1) 48-74-90-92; Pres. National Council Pastor JEAN-PIERRE MONSARRAT.

Fédération des Eglises Evangéliques Baptistes de France: 48 rue de Lille, 75007 Paris; tel. (1) 42-61-13-96; Pres. Pastor ANDRÉ THOBOIS.

Union Nationale des Eglises Réformées Evangéliques Indépendantes: 7 rue Godin, 30000 Nîmes; Pres. Pastor MAURICE LONGEIRET.

The Orthodox Churches
Administration of Russian Orthodox Churches in Europe (Jurisdiction of the Oecumenical Patriarchate): 12 rue Daru, 75008 Paris; presided over by His Eminence the Most Reverend GEORGES, Archbishop of Russian Orthodox Churches in Europe.

Greek Orthodox Cathedral of St Etienne: 7 rue Georges Bizet, 75116 Paris; tel. (1) 47-20-82-35; Superior The Most Rev. MELETIOS CARABINIS, Greek Archbishop of France, Spain and Portugal.

Other Christian Churches
Société Religieuse des Amis (Quakers) et Centre Quaker International: 114 rue de Vaugirard, 75006 Paris; tel. (1) 45-48-74-23.

ISLAM
Islam is the second most important religion in France; in 1985 there were about 2.5m. adherents, of whom more than 750,000 resided in the Marseille area.

Muslim Institute of the Paris Mosque: place du Puits de l'Ermite, 75005 Paris; tel. (1) 45-35-97-33; f. 1923; cultural, diplomatic, social, judicial and religious sections; research and information and commercial annexes; Dir Cheikh EL ABBAS BENCHEIKH EL HOCINE.

JUDAISM
Consistoire Central Israélite de France et d'Algérie: 17 rue Saint Georges, 75009 Paris; tel. (1) 45-26-02-56; f. 1808; 120 asscns; Chief Rabbi of France RENÉ SAMUEL SIRAT; Chief Rabbi of the Consistoire Central JACOB KAPLAN; Pres. JEAN PAUL ELKANN; Exec. Dir LÉON MASLIAH.

Consistoire Israélite de Paris (Jewish Consistorial Association of Paris): 17 rue Saint Georges, 75009 Paris; tel. (1) 42-85-71-09; Pres. EMILE TOUATI; Chief Rabbi ALAIN GOLDMANN; Sec.-Gen. SERGE GUEDJ.

BUDDHISM
World Federation of Buddhists, French Regional Centre: 98 chemin de la Calade, 06250 Mougins; Sec. Mme TEISAN PERUSAT STORK.

Association Zen Internationale: 17 rue des Cinq Diamants, 75013 Paris; tel. (1) 45-80-10-00; Sec. JANINE MANNOT.

The Press

The legislation under which the French press operates mostly dates back to an Act of 1881 which established very liberal conditions for journalism, asserting the right of individuals to produce newspapers without any prior authorization. At the same time the law defined certain offences which the press might commit, such as incitement to crime, disturbance of the peace by the publication of false information, libel and defamation, the publication of material offensive to the President and revealing official secrets. Further legislation in the 1940s somewhat extended these restrictions on the press, particularly with regard to children's literature. A law to prevent the concentration of newspaper and magazine ownership in the hands of a small number of press conglomerates was adopted in September 1984. However, the measures did not come into force until 1986 and they proved to be ineffective: in January the Hersant Group took over *Le Progrès* and gained a 95% virtual monopoly of the press in Lyon. Hersant claimed immunity as an MEP, and by June the new right-wing Government had abrogated the 1984 law and a 1944 ordinance, thus increasing the proportion of the total circulation of daily newspapers that an individual was permitted to control. The Constitutional Council added amendments which attempted to prevent the use of 'front' companies and intermediaries to increase an individual company's holdings in the French press.

An estimated 14,000 newspapers and periodicals are published in France. In 1983 there were 11 daily papers published in Paris with a national circulation and some 73 provincial dailies covering all the French regions. The circulations of the two groups in 1980 were 3.8m. for the Parisian press and 7.5m. for the provincial press. These figures showed a remarkable decline from the situation in 1946, when 28 Parisian dailies had a circulation of 5m. and 175 provincial dailies shared 9m. circulation. In recent years sharply rising costs and falling advertising revenue have increased the difficulties caused by declining circulation. National dailies have been particularly badly affected by the economic crisis and increasing competition from radio and television. Many are in serious financial difficulty. The prestigious daily, *Le Monde*, issued shares to avoid a financial crisis in late 1985. The press was given approximately 4,000m. francs of state assistance in 1983.

The provincial press, already strong under the Third Republic, achieved a leading role during the German occupation (1940–44), when Paris was cut off from the rest of France. Since the war, it has proved more adept than the national press at dealing with the fall in revenue and rising costs. The best-selling provincial dailies can now almost match the most popular Paris dailies for circulation and they have initiated various rationalization schemes. Six groups of provincial papers have been formed to pool advertising and, in some cases, copy and printing facilities. The largest of these groups are those centred on *Le Dauphiné Libéré* (Grenoble) and *Le Progrès* (Lyon) and the group in East France led by *L'Est Républicain*. In an attempt to prevent the domination of the press in Lyon by the Hersant Group (following its take-over of *Le Progrès* in January 1986), two national dailies, *Le Monde* and *Libération*, started to produce regional editions in Lyon. By late 1986 the Hersant Group had launched a regional edition of *Le Figaro*, which was also based in Lyon.

The weekly news magazines have expanded in recent years; the two best examples of this are *L'Express* and *Le Nouvel Observateur*. Radio and TV magazines have greatly increased in popularity: total weekly circulation of 3m. in 1970 rose to 7m. in 1983 for the nine titles now on the market.

The only major daily which acts as the organ of a political party is the Communist paper, *L'Humanité*. All others are owned by individual publishers or by the powerful groups which have developed round either a company or a single personality. The major groups are as follows:

Amaury Group: 25 ave Michelet, 93400 Saint-Ouen; owns *Le Parisien Libéré*, the provincial dailies *Le Courrier de l'Ouest* and *Le Maine Libre*, the sports daily *L'Equipe*, several weeklies, incl. *Points de Vue*, and monthlies, incl. *Marie-France;* Man. Dir ROGER BELIN.

Bayard Presse: 3 rue Bayard, 75008 Paris; tel. (1) 45-62-51-51; telex 641868; important Catholic press group; owns the national *La Croix-L'Evénement, Le Pèlerin, Panorama d'Aujourd'hui, Notre Temps,* important magazines for young people and several specialized religious publications; Pres. BERNARD PORTE.

Editions Mondiales: 2 rue des Italiens, 75009 Paris; telex 643932; formerly Del Duca Group; owns several popular weekly magazines, incl. *Nous Deux, Intimité, Modes de Paris, Télé-Poche* and also specialized magazines; Man. Dir JEAN MAMERT.

Expansion Group: 67 ave de Wagram, 75017 Paris; tel. (1) 47-63-12-11; owns a number of magazines, incl. *L'Expansion, L'Entreprise, Architecture d'Aujourd'hui, Harvard L'Expansion, Voyages;* Chair. and Man. Dir JEAN-LOUIS SERVAN-SCHREIBER.

Filipacchi Group: 63 ave des Champs Elysées, 75008 Paris; tel. (1) 42-56-72-72; controls a number of large-circulation magazines incl. *Paris-Match, Salut, 7 à Paris, OK!, Girls, Podium, Top 50, Newlook, Penthouse, Union, Echo des Savanes, Les Grands Ecrivains, Femme, Pariscope, Jazz Magazine, Lui* and *Photo.*

Hachette Group: 100 rue Réaumur, 75002 Paris; telex 205133; f. 1826; taken over by Matra Group in 1981; publs incl. *Le Journal du Dimanche, France-Dimanche, Elle, Le Jardin des Modes, Le Point, Télé-7-Jours, Parents*; has 36% holding in *Le Parisen Libre* and *l'Equipe;* Chair. and Man. Dir JEAN-LUC LAGARDÈRE.

Hersant Group: one of the largest of the provincial daily press groups; owns 20 dailies, numerous weeklies, fortnightlies and periodicals; dailies incl. *Le Progrès, L'Eclair, Le Dauphiné Libéré, Nord-Matin* and *Nord-Eclair;* has a majority holding in *Le Figaro, France-Soir, l'Aurore* and *Paris-Turf;* Chair. and Man. Dir ROBERT HERSANT.

Among the metropolitan dailies, the outstanding papers are *Le Monde* (circulation 357,117), which carries no photographs, and *Le Figaro* (394,517). Also popular are *France-Soir* and *Le Parisien Libéré*. The English language *International Herald Tribune* (170,234) is also important. The major provincial dailies are *Ouest-France* (Rennes), *Dépêche du Midi* (Toulouse), *Sud-Ouest* (Bordeaux), *Le Dauphiné Libéré* (Grenoble), *La Voix du Nord* (Lille), *Le Progrès* (Lyon), and *Le Provençal* (Marseille). Many provincial dailies cater for rural readership by producing local subsidiary editions.

Metropolitan weekly papers range from the popular press, such as *France-Dimanche* (693,380) and *Ici-Paris* (700,000), through to the more serious current affairs magazines like *L'Express, Le Nouvel Observateur* and the satirical *Canard Enchainé*. Among the popular periodicals must be mentioned the weekly illustrated *Paris-Match* (912,137) and the women's journals *Marie-Claire* (677,772), *Elle* (412,000) and *Marie-France* (522,248).

DAILY PAPERS (PARIS)

L'Aurore: 37 rue du Louvre, 75081 Paris; telex 220310; f. 1944; Dir ROGER ALEXANDRE; circ. 35,000 (1983).

La Croix: 3-5 rue Bayard, 75008 Paris; tel. (1) 45-62-51-51; f. 1883; Catholic; Dir BERNARD PORTE; Editors-in-Chief JEAN POTIN, ANDRÉ GÉRAUD, NOËL COPIN; circ. 113,028.

Les Echos: 37 ave des Champs Elysées, 75381 Paris Cedex 08; tel. (1) 45-62-19-68; telex 290275; f. 1908; economic and financial; Editor J. BEYTOUT; circ. 78,000.

L'Equipe: 10 rue du Faubourg Montmartre, 75438 Paris Cedex 09; tel. (1) 42-46-92-33; telex 280390; f. 1946; sport; Man. Dir JACQUES GODDET; circ. 239,632.

Le Figaro: 25 ave Matignon, 75398 Paris Cedex 08; tel. (1) 42-56-80-80; telex 211112; f. 1828; morning; news and literary; magazine on Saturdays; Chair. and Man. Dir ANDRÉ BOUSSEMART; Vice-Pres. and Dir-Gen. PHILIPPE VILLIN; circ. 394,517.

France-Soir: 100 rue Réaumur, 75002 Paris; tel. (1) 45-08-28-00; f. 1941 as *Défense de la France*, present title 1944; merged with *Paris-Presse L'Intransigeant* 1965; magazine on Saturdays, merged with *TV-France-Soir,* 1987; Chair. and Man. Dir JACQUES HERSANT; circ. 405,388.

L'Humanité: 5 rue du Faubourg Poissonière, 75440 Paris Cedex 09; tel. (1) 42-46-82-69; f. 1904 by Jean Jaurès; organ of the French Communist Party; morning; Dir ROLAND LEROY; Editor-in-Chief CLAUDE CABANES; circ. 117,005.

International Herald Tribune: 181 ave Charles de Gaulle, 92521 Neuilly Cedex; tel. (1) 46-37-93-00; telex 612718; f. 1887; English language; Co-Chairs W. S. PALEY, K. GRAHAM, A. O. SULZBERGER; Editor WALTER WELLS; circ. 170,234.

Le Journal Officiel de la République Française: 26 rue Desaix, 75015 Paris; f. 1870; official journal of the Government; publishes laws, decrees, parliamentary proceedings, and economic bulletins; Dir ROBERT BOUQUIN.

Libération: 9 rue Christiani, 75883 Paris Cedex 18; tel. (1) 42-62-34-34; telex 641917; f. 1973; non-conformist; Dir SERGE JULY; circ. 116,682.

Le Matin de Paris: 21 rue Hérold, 75001 Paris; tel. (1) 42-96-16-65; f. 1977; left-wing; weekly Nord-Pas-de-Calais supplement; magazine on Saturdays; Man. Dir MAX THÉRET; Dirs VINCENT LALU, GUY CLAISSE; circ. 100,000 (1984).

FRANCE

Le Monde: 5 rue des Italiens, 75427 Paris Cedex 09; tel. (1) 42-47-97-27; telex 650572; f. 1944; liberal; independent; week-end supplements; Dir ANDRÉ FONTAINE; Editor-in-Chief DANIEL VERNET; circ. 357,117.

Paris ce Soir: 31 rue de Tournon, 75006 Paris; tel (1) 43-26-01-45; f. 1985; evening; Dir PIERRE PLANCHER.

Paris-Turf/Sport Complet: 100 rue de Richelieu, 75002 Paris; racing, sport; Dir PIERRE JANROT; circ. 150,000.

Le Parisien Libéré: 25 ave Michelet, 93400 Saint Ouen; tel. (1) 42-52-88-00; telex 660041; f. 1944; morning; Chair. and Man. Dir PHILLIPE AMAURY; Man. Dir MARTIN DESPREZ; circ. 339,271.

Le Quotidien du Médecin: Le France, 2 rue Ancelle, 92200 Neuilly-sur-Seine; medical journal; Dir Dr MARIE CLAUDE TESSON MILLET; Editor GÉRARD BADOU; circ. 62,000.

Le Quotidien de Paris: 2 rue Ancelle, 92521 Neuilly-sur-Seine Cedex; tel. (1) 47-47-12-32; telex 610806; f. 1974, relaunched 1979; Man. Dir ROBERT TOUBON; Editor PHILIPPE TESSON; circ. 75,000 (1986).

La Tribune de l'Economie: 12 rue Béranger, 75003 Paris; tel. (1) 48-04-99-99; telex 230735; f. 1986; economic and financial; Dir HUGUES-VINCENT BARBE; Editor JACQUES LÉGER; circ. 59,000.

SUNDAY PAPERS (PARIS)

France-Dimanche: 6 rue Ancelle, 92521 Neuilly Cedex; tel. (1) 47-45-14-41; Dir DENIS JACOB; circ. 693,380.

L'Humanité-Dimanche: 5 rue du Faubourg Poissonnière, 75440 Paris Cedex 09; tel. (1) 42-46-82-69; f. 1946; weekly magazine of the French Communist Party; Dir ROLAND LEROY; Editor FRANÇOIS HILSUM; circ. 360,000.

PRINCIPAL PROVINCIAL DAILY PAPERS

Amiens
Le Courrier Picard: 14 rue Alphonse Paillat, BP 206D, 80010 Amiens Cedex; tel. 22-91-71-81; telex 145558; f. 1944; Chair. DANIEL MARCOURT; Man. Dir JACQUES BENESSE; Chief Editor FRANÇOIS PERRIER; circ. 86,000.

Angers
Courrier de l'Ouest: blvd Albert Blanchoin, BP 728, 49005 Angers Cedex; tel. 41-66-21-31; telex 720997; f. 1944; Chair. and Man. Dir J. M. DESGREES DU LOU; circ. 109,968.

Angoulême
La Charente Libre: Zone Industrielle no. 3, BP 106, 16001 Angoulême; tel. 45-69-33-33; telex 791950; Dir L. G. GAYAN; circ. 45,000.

Auxerre
L'Yonne Républicaine: 8-12 ave Jean Moulin, 89006 Auxerre; f. 1944; Gen. Man. L. CLÉMENT; circ. 41,606.

Besançon
Le Comtois: 60 rue Grande, 25000 Besançon; f. 1914; Dir. PIERRE BRANTUS; circ. 15,532.

Bordeaux
La France—Nouvelle République de Bordeaux et du Sud-Ouest: 10 rue Porte Dijeaux, 33000 Bordeaux; f. 1944; Dir J. M. BLANCHY; circ. 22,000.

Sud-Ouest: 8 rue de Cheverus, 33000 Bordeaux; tel. 56-90-92-72; telex 570670; f. 1944; independent; Man. Dir JEAN-FRANÇOIS LEMOINE; Chief Editor PIERRE VEILLETET; circ. 356,989.

Calais
Nord Littoral: 39 blvd Jacquard, 62100 Calais; tel. 21-34-41-00; f. 1944; Editor J. J. BARATTE; circ. 9,819.

Chalon-sur-Saône
Courrier de Saône-et-Loire: 9 rue des Tonneliers, 71104 Chalon-sur-Saône; f. 1826; Dir RENÉ PRÉTET; circ. 46,021.

Charleville-Mézières
L'Ardennais: 36 cours Aristide Briand, 08102 Charleville-Mézières; tel. 24-32-91-51; f. 1944; Man. Dir PIERRE DIDRY; circ. 28,186.

Chartres
L'Echo Républicain: 39 rue de Châteaudun, 28004 Chartres; f. 1929; Chair. and Man. Dir ALAIN PLOUVIER; Editor-in-Chief ALAIN GENESTAR; circ. 31,817.

Chaumont
La Haute-Marne Libérée: 14 rue du Patronage Laïque, 52003 Chaumont; f. 1944; Editor JEAN BLETNER; circ. 15,055.

Cherbourg
La Presse de la Manche: 14 rue Gambetta, 50104 Cherbourg; tel. 33-44-20-08; telex 171623; f. 1944; Chair. and Man. Dir DANIEL JUBERT; circ. 27,605.

Clermont-Ferrand
La Montagne (Centre-France): 28 rue Morel Ladeuil, 63003 Clermont-Ferrand; tel. 73-93-22-91; telex 990588; f. 1919; independent; Dir RENÉ BONJEAN; circ. 252,457.

Dijon
Le Bien Public: 7 blvd Chamoine Kir, 21015 Dijon Cedex; f. 1850; Dirs Baron THÉNARD, M. BACOT; circ. 53,383.

Les Dépêches du Centre-Est: 17 rue de Colmar, BP 570, 21015 Dijon; tel. 80-65-17-45; f. 1936; Chair. FRANCIS BOILEAU; Man. Dir MICHEL-YVES LAURENT; circ. 34,030.

Epinal
Liberté de l'Est: 40 quai des Bons Enfants, 88001 Epinal Cedex; tel. 29-82-98-00; f. 1945; Man. SERGE CLÉMENT; circ. 31,319.

Grenoble
Le Dauphiné Libéré: Les Iles Cordées, 38113 Veurey-Voroize; tel. 76-88-71-00; telex 320822; f. 1944; Chair. CHARLES DEBBASCH; circ. 360,000.

Le Havre
Havre Libre: 25 ave René Coty, 76066 Le Havre; f. 1944; Dir and Editor-in-Chief DENIS HEURTAS; circ. 28,268.

Lille
Nord-Matin: 19 rue Ed Delesalle, 59023 Lille Cedex; f. 1944; Gen. Man. R. GRUSS; circ. 78,167.

La Voix du Nord: 8 place du Général de Gaulle, 78167 Lille; f. 1944; Chair. and Man. Dir RENÉ DECOCK; circ. 376,073.

Limoges
L'Echo du Centre: 46 rue Turgot, 87000 Limoges; tel. 55-34-46-35; f. 1943; five editions; Communist; Dir DENIS TRICLOT; Chief Editor DOMINIQUE FAVIER; circ. 65,000.

Le Populaire du Centre: rue du Général Catroux, BP 54, 87011 Limoges Cedex; f. 1905; four editions; Chair and Man. Dir RENÉ BONJEAN; Editor-in-Chief ROGER QUEYROI; circ. 55,881.

Lyon
Le Progrès: 85 rue de la République, 69293 Lyon Cedex 1; f. 1859; Chair. ROBERT HERSANT; Vice-Chair. DENIS HUERTAS; Man. Dir GUY LESCOEUR; circ. Monday–Saturday 353,608, Sunday 447,289.

Marseille
La Marseillaise: 17 cours Honoré d'Estienne d'Orves, BP 1862, 13222 Marseille Cedex 1; tel. 91-54-92-13; f. 1944; Communist; Dir PAUL BIAGGINI; circ. 165,000.

Le Méridional-La France: 4 rue Cougit, 13316 Marseille Cedex 15; f. 1944; independent; 12 regional editions; Chair. RENÉ MERLE; circ. 100,000.

Le Provençal: 248 ave Roger Salengro, 13015 Marseille; tel. 90-84-45-45; f. 1944; the biggest daily paper in the south-east (evening edition **Le Soir**); Chair. and Man. Dir ANDRÉ POITEVIN; circ. 345,000.

Metz
Le Républicain Lorrain: 3 rue de St Eloy, BP 89, 57104 Metz-Woippy; tel. 87-33-22-00; f. 1919; independent; Pres. Mme MARGUERITE PUHL-DEMANGE; Dir-Gen. CLAUDE PUHL; circ. 200,011.

Montpellier
Midi-Libre: Mas de Gulle, 34063 Montpellier; tel. 67-42-00-44; f. 1944; Dir CLAUDE BUJON; circ. 200,000.

Morlaix
Le Télégramme de Brest et de l'Ouest: rue A. Le Braz, BP 243, 29205 Morlaix Cedex; tel. 98-62-11-33; telex 940652; f. 1944; Dir JEAN-PIERRE COUDURIER; circ. 201,963 (1985).

Mulhouse
L'Alsace: 25 ave du Président Kennedy, 68053 Mulhouse; tel. 89-43-99-44; telex 881818; f. 1944; Editor GILBERT KLEIN; circ. 137,035.

Nancy
L'Est Républicain: 5 bis ave Foch, 54042 Nancy; tel. 88-29-80-54; f. 1889; Dir Gérard Lignac; circ. 252,383.

Nantes
L'Eclair: 5 rue Santeuil, 44010 Nantes Cedex; f. 1945; radical; Gen. Man. Rolande Hersant; circ. 20,230.

Presse Océan: 7–8 allée Duguay Trouin, BP 1142, 44024 Nantes Cedex 01; tel. 40-47-09-33; telex 710505; f. 1944; independent; Chair. and Man. Dir Philippe Mestre; Editor-in-Chief Jean-Marie Gautier; circ. 93,180.

Nevers
Journal du Centre: 3 rue du Chemin de Fer, BP 14, 58001 Nevers; f. 1943; Editor M. Berthelot; circ. 37,834.

Nice
Nice-Matin: 214 route de Grenoble, BP 4, 06029 Nice Cedex; tel. 93-83-91-91; telex 460788; f. 1944; Chair and Man. Dir Michel Bavastro; circ. 261,980.

Orléans
La République du Centre: rue de la Halte, Saran, BP 35, 45403 Fleury les Aubrais Cedex; tel. 38-86-37-68; telex 780702; f. 1944; Chair. and Man. Dir Marc Carré; Editor Jacques Rameau; circ. 85,000.

Pau
Eclair-Pyrénées: 40 rue Emile Guichenné, 64006 Pau; f. 1944; Dir Henri Loustalan; circ. 16,500.

Perpignan
L'Indépendant: 4 rue Emmanuel Brousse, 66004 Perpignan; f. 1846; also **Indépendant-Dimanche** (Sunday); Dir Paul Chichet; circ. 73,610.

Poitiers
Centre Presse: 5 rue Victor Hugo, BP 299, 86007 Poitiers; f. 1958; Man. Dir Cyrille Duval; Editor-in-Chief Roland Barkat; circ. 20,000.

Reims
L'Union: 87–91 place Drouet d'Erlon, 51052 Reims Cedex; f. 1944; telex 830751; Dir Philippe Hersant; Editor-in-Chief Jacques Richard; circ. 152,000.

Rennes
Ouest-France: Zone Industrielle Rennes-Chantepie, 35051 Rennes Cedex; tel. 99-03-62-22; telex 730965; f. 1944; Chair. François-Régis Hutin; circ. 803,701 (1985).

Roubaix
Nord-Eclair: 21 rue du Caire, 59052 Roubaix Cedex 1; tel. 20-75-92-56; telex 160740; f. 1944; Chair. A. Diligent; Man. Dir A. Farine; circ. 102,773.

Rouen
Paris-Normandie: 19 place du Général de Gaulle, BP 563, 76004 Rouen; f. 1944; tel. 35-88-45-88; telex 771507; Publr Société Normande de Presse Républicaine; Chair. and Man. Dir Jean Allard; circ. 129,030.

Saint-Etienne
Loire-Martin-La Dépêche: 14 place Jean Jaurès, 42000 Saint-Etienne; tel. 73-32-79-97; f. 1944; Editor François Gaillard; circ. 23,743.

La Tribune: 10 place Jean Jaurès, 42000 Saint-Etienne; Editor J.-C. Lignel; circ. 91,387.

Strasbourg
Dernières Nouvelles d'Alsace: 17-19-21 rue de la Nuée Bleue, BP 406/R1, 67000 Strasbourg; tel. 88-23-31-23; telex 880445; f. 1877; non-party; Dir Jacques Puymartin; circ. 218,636.

Le Nouvel Alsacien: 6 rue Finkmatt, 67000 Strasbourg; tel. 88-32-37-14; f. 1885; Man. Bernard Deck; circ. 15,245.

Tarbes
La Nouvelle République des Pyrénées: 48 ave Bertrand Barère, 65001 Tarbes; tel. (Tarbes) 93-90-90; f. 1944; Man. Jean Gaits; circ. 17,765.

Toulon
Var/Matin: route de la Seyne à Ollioules, 83190 Toulon; f. 1946; Man. Dir Christian de Barbarin; circ. 81,000.

Toulouse
Dépêche du Midi: ave Jean Baylet, 31095 Toulouse; f. 1870; radical; Gen. Man. Mme Evelyne-Jean Baylet; circ. 247,533.

Tours
La Nouvelle République du Centre-Ouest: 4-18 rue de la Préfecture, 37048 Tours Cedex; tel. 47-61-81-46; telex 750693; f. 1944; non-party; Chair Jacques Saint-Cricq; circ. 271,790 (1985).

Troyes
L'Est-Eclair: 55 rue Urbain IV, 10000 Troyes; tel. 25-79-90-10; f. 1945; Dirs Jean Bruley and André Bruley; circ. 33,000.

Libération-Champagne: 126 rue Général de Gaulle, BP 713, 10003 Troyes Cedex; tel. 25-73-11-55; Dir Gilbert Boutsoque; circ. 21,074.

SELECTED PERIODICALS

The following is a selection from the total of about 14,000 periodicals published in France.

General, Political and Literary

Annales—Economies, sociétés, civilisations: 54 blvd Raspail, 75006 Paris; tel. (1) 45-48-25-64; f. 1929; every 2 months; Dirs F. Braudel, A. Burguière, M. Ferro, J. le Goff, B. Lepetit, E. le Roy Ladurie, C. Morazé, J. Revel, L. Valensi.

L'Arc: Editions Le Jas, 04230 Le Revest Saint Martin; tel. 92-75-17-16; f. 1957; Dir J. F. Guesnier; Editor-in-Chief Micheline Hountou; circ. 7,000.

Aspects de la France: 10 rue Croix des Petits Champs, 75001 Paris; tel. (1) 42-96-12-06; f. 1947; weekly; monarchist; organ of L'Action Française; Dir Pierre Pujo.

Autre Journal: 7 rue d'Argout, 75002 Paris; tel. (1) 42-36-33-86; f. 1984, fmrly Nouvelles Littéraires; monthly; literature, medicine, science, technology, news; Dir Michel Butel; circ. 220,000.

Le Canard Enchaîné: 173 rue Saint Honoré, Paris 75001; tel. (1) 42-60-31-36; f. 1915; weekly; political satire; Chair. and Man. Dir André Ribaud; circ. 500,000.

Carrefour: 114 ave des Champs Elysées, 75008 Paris; f. 1944; weekly; moderate; Dir Jean Dannenmuller; circ. 100,000.

Le Courrier de la République: 25 rue du Louvre, 75001 Paris; f. 1959; monthly; political; Publr Laurence Carvallo.

Le Crapouillot: 49 ave Marceau, 75016 Paris; f. 1915; satire and humorous; Man. Dir J.-C. Goudeau; Editor Patrice Boizeau.

Critique: Editions de Minuit, 7 rue Bernard Palissy, 75006 Paris; tel. (1) 45-44-23-16; f. 1946; monthly; general review of French and foreign literature; Editor Jean Piel.

Croissance des Jeunes Nations: 163 blvd Malesherbes, 75017 Paris; tel. (1) 47-66-01-86; f. 1961; monthly on the developing nations; circ. 35,000.

Diogène: Unesco House, 1 rue Miollis, 75732 Paris Cedex 15; tel. (1) 45-68-27-34; f. 1951; quarterly; international review of human sciences; three editions, in English, French and Spanish; anthologies in Arabic, Chinese, Hindi, Japanese and Portuguese; Editor Jean d'Ormesson.

Les Ecrits de Paris: 9 passage des Marais, 75010 Paris; f. 1944; monthly; current affairs; circ. 25,000.

Esprit: 212 rue St-Martin, 75003 Paris; tel. (1) 48-04-92-90; f. 1932; monthly; Dir Paul Thibaud; Editor-in-Chief Olivier Mongin; circ. 10,000.

Europe: 146 rue du Faubourg Poissonnière, 75010 Paris; tel. (1) 42-81-91-03; f. 1923; monthly; literary review; Chair. Pierre Gamarra; Editors Charles Dobzynski, Jean-Baptiste Para.

L'Evénement du Jeudi: 2 rue Christine, 75006 Paris; tel. (1) 43-54-84-80; f. 1984; weekly; current affairs; Dir Jean-François Kahn; circ. 160,000.

L'Express: 61 ave Hoche, 75380 Paris; f. 1953; weekly; Editors Yves Cuau, Yann de l'Ecotais; circ. 585,000.

Gauche: 80 rue du Bac, 75007 Paris; tel. (1) 45-49-14-80; f. 1984; monthly; left-wing political review; Editor Elisabeth Azoulay; circ. 15,000.

Le Hérisson: 2–12 rue de Bellevue, 75019 Paris; f. 1936; weekly; humorous; Dir J. P. Ventillard; Editor A. Moreuil; circ. 270,000.

Ici-Paris: 29 rue Galilée, 75116 Paris; f. 1941; weekly; Editor Louis Balayé; circ. 700,000.

Jours de France: 7 Rond Point des Champs Elysées, 75008 Paris; tel. (1) 43-59-53-19; f. 1954; weekly; news and fashion magazine; Chief Editor Marcel Dassault; circ. 673,000.

FRANCE

Lire: 61 ave Hoche, 75380 Paris Cedex 08; tel. (1) 42-67-97-98; monthly; literary review; Editor BERNARD PIVOT.

Lutte Ouvrière: BP 233, 75865 Paris Cedex 18; f. 1968; weekly; Editor MICHEL RODINSON.

Minute: 34 rue Jean Jaurès, 92800 Paris; tel. (1) 49-00-02-02; f. 1962; right-wing weekly; Pres. and Dir-Gen. M. BOIZEAU; Man. Dir PATRICK BUISSON; circ. 300,000.

Le Monde Diplomatique: 7 rue des Italiens, 75427 Paris Cedex 09; tel. (1) 42-47-97-27; telex 650572; f. 1954; monthly; political and cultural; Dir CLAUDE JULIEN; Editor MICHELINE PAUNET; circ. 128,000.

Le Nouvel Observateur: 14 rue Dussoubs, 75081 Paris; telex 680729; f. 1964; weekly; left-wing political and literary; Dir JEAN DANIEL; Editorial Dir FRANZ-OLIVIER GIESBERT; circ. 324,200.

La Nouvelle Revue Française (NRF): 5 rue Sébastien Bottin, 75007 Paris; tel. (1) 45-44-39-19; telex 204121; f. 1909; monthly; literary; Editor GEORGES LAMBRICHS.

Parents: 6 rue Ancelle, 92521 Neuilly; magazine for parents; circ. 403,130.

Paris-Match: 63 ave des Champs Elysées, 75008 Paris; f. 1949; weekly; magazine of French and world affairs; Dir ROGER THÉROND; circ. 912,137.

Le Peuple: 263 rue de Paris, Case 432, 93514 Montreuil Cedex; tel. 48-51-83-06; telex 213060; f. 1921; fortnightly; official organ of the Confédération Générale du Travail (trade union confederation); Dir JEAN-CLAUDE LAROZE.

Poétique: Editions du Seuil, 27 rue Jacob, 75261 Paris Cedex 06; tel. (1) 43-29-12-15; telex 600605; quarterly.

Le Point: 140 rue de Rennes, 75006 Paris; f. 1972; politics and current affairs; Man. Dir OLIVIER CHEVRILLON; Editor CLAUDE IMBERT; circ. approx. 328,000.

Point de Vue-Images du Monde: 116 bis ave des Champs Elysées, 75008 Paris; weekly; Dir C. GIRON; circ. 370,311.

Politique Hebdo: 14–16 rue des Petits Hotels, 75010 Paris; weekly; review of world socialist studies and practice.

Politique Internationale: 11 rue du Bois de Boulogne, 75116 Paris; 4 a year.

Quinzaine Littéraire: 43 rue du Temple, 75004 Paris; tel. (1) 48-87-48-58; f. 1966; fortnightly; Dir MAURICE NADEAU; circ. 40,000.

Révolution: 15 rue Montmartre, 75001 Paris; tel. (1) 42-33-61-26; f. 1980; weekly; political and cultural; Dir GUY HERMIER; Chief Editors JEAN-PAUL JOUARY, GÉRARD STREIFF.

Revue des Deux Mondes: 15 rue de l'Université, 75007 Paris; tel. (1) 42-61-21-49; f. 1829; monthly; current affairs; Dir JEAN JAUDEL.

Revue d'Histoire Littéraire de la France: 14 rue de l'Industrie, 75013 Paris; f. 1894; 6 a year; Editor RENÉ POMEAU.

Rivarol: 9 passage des Marais, 75010 Paris; f. 1951; weekly; political, literary and satirical; circ. 45,000.

Rouge: 2 rue Richard Lenoir, 93100 Montreuil; tel. 48-59-00-80; f. 1969; weekly; extreme left; circ. 12,000.

Sélection du Reader's Digest: 212 blvd Saint Germain, 75439 Paris Cedex 07; monthly; Chair. CLAUDE POTHIER; circ. 1,130,000.

Les Temps Modernes: 22 rue de Condé, 75006 Paris; tel. (1) 43-29-08-47; f. 1945 by J.-P. Sartre; monthly; literary review; publ. by Les Presses d'Aujourd'hui; Dir S. DE BEAUVOIR.

La Tribune des Nations: 150 ave des Champs Elysées, 75008 Paris; f. 1933, re-launched 1983; monthly; politics and foreign affairs; Dir FABRICE HULMANN.

L'Unité: 12 cité Malesherbes, 75009 Paris; f. 1972; weekly; organ of the Socialist Party; Dir NICOLE CHAILLOT; Editor CLAUDE ESTIER.

Art

L'Architecture d'Aujourd'hui: 67 ave de Wagram, 75017 Paris; tel. (1) 47-63-12-11; telex 650242; f. 1930; publ. by Groupe Expansion; Editor-in-Chief M. EMERY; circ. 25,791.

Art et Décoration: 2 rue de l'Echelle, 75001 Paris; tel. (1) 42-60-30-05; f. 1897; 6 a year; Dir ANDRÉ MASSIN; circ. 451,443.

Gazette des Beaux-Arts: 140 Faubourg Saint Honoré, 75008 Paris; tel. (1) 45-63-01-00; f. 1859; monthly; the oldest review of the history of art; Dir DANIEL WILDENSTEIN.

L'Oeil: 10 rue Guichard, 75116 Paris; tel. (1) 45-25-85-60; f. 1955; monthly; Vice-Chair. FRANÇOIS DAULTE; Gen. Sec. and Editor SOLANGE THIERRY.

Bibliography

Bulletin des Bibliothèques de France: 3–5 blvd Pasteur, 75015 Paris; tel. (1) 45-39-25-75; f. 1956; 6 a year; circ. 2,200.

Livres-Hebdo: 30 rue Dauphine, 75006 Paris; tel. (1) 43-29-73-50; f. 1979; 46 a year; Dir P. GARNIER.

Livres de France: 30 rue Dauphine, 75006 Paris; tel. (1) 43-29-73-50; f. 1979; 11 a year; Dir P. GARNIER.

Economic and Financial

Les Affaires: 61 rue de Malte, 75011 Paris; f. 1963; monthly; Dir R. MONTEUX; circ. 25,000.

L'Assurer-Conseil: 31 rue d'Amsterdam, 75008 Paris; tel. (1) 48-74-19-12; monthly; produced by Syndicat National des Courtiers d'Assurances; Editor-in-Chief ALAIN FARSHIAN.

L'Economie: 26 rue du Bouloi, 75001 Paris; f. 1945; weekly; national and international economics; Chair. and Man. Dir PHILIPPE LE PROUX DE LA RIVIÈRE; circ. 30,000.

L'Expansion: 67 ave de Wagram, 75017 Paris; tel. (1) 47-63-12-11; telex 650242; f. 1967; every 2 weeks; economics and business; Dir JEAN-LOUIS SERVAN-SCHREIBER; Editor-in-Chief JEAN BOISSONNAT; circ. 171,004.

Express Documents: 61 rue de Malte, 75011 Paris; weekly; fiscal, judicial and social; Dir ROBERT MONTEUX.

Le Nouvel Economiste: 22 rue de la Tremoille, 75008 Paris; tel. (1) 47-23-01-05; f. 1975 by merger of *l'Entreprise* and *Les Informations*; weekly; Chair. and Man. Dir FRANK TENOT; Man. Dirs JEAN-MARIE VENDROUX, MICHEL TARDIEU; circ. 117,090.

Revue Economique: 54 blvd Raspail, 75006 Paris; tel. (1) 45-44-39-79; f. 1950; every 2 months; Chair. J. M. PARLY.

Science et Vie Economique: 2 rue de la Baume, 75008 Paris; f. 1984; monthly; economics; Dir PAUL DUPUY; Editor GILLES COVILLE; circ. 300,000.

L'Usine Nouvelle: 59 rue du Rocher, 75008 Paris; f. 1945; weekly with monthly supplements; technical and industrial journal; Chair. and Man. Dir C. BREGOU; Man. Dir J. P. JIROU NAJOU; circ. 60,000.

Valeurs Actuelles: 14 rue d'Uzès, 75081 Paris Cedex 02; f. 1967; weekly; politics, economics, international affairs; Editor R. BOURGINE; circ. 150,000.

La Vie Française-l'Opinion: 2 rue du Pont Neuf, 75001 Paris; f. 1945; weekly; economics and finance; Dir and Editor-in-Chief BRUNO BERTEZ; circ. 101,002.

History and Geography

Acta geographica: 184 blvd Saint Germain, 75006 Paris; tel. (1) 45-48-54-62; f. 1821; quarterly; Chair. JACQUELINE BEAUJEU-GARNIER.

Annales de géographie: 103 blvd Saint Michel, 75005 Paris; tel. (1) 46-34-12-19; telex 201269; f. 1891; every 2 months; Dirs J. BEAUJEU-GARNIER, E. DALMASSO, F. DOUMENGE, P. GEORGE, A. GODARD, P. MONBEIG, J. TRICART.

Cahiers de civilisation médiévale: 24 rue de la Chaine, 86022 Poitiers; tel. 49-41-03-86; f. 1958; quarterly; Dirs PIERRE BEC, ROBERT FAVREAU.

XVIIe siècle: c/o Collège de France, 11 place Marcelin Berthelot, 75231 Paris Cedex 05; tel. (1) 45-48-85-24; f. 1948; quarterly; Dir M. FUMAROLI; Pres. J. TRUCHET; circ. 1,500.

Histoire, Economie et Société: 88 blvd St-Germain, 75005 Paris.

Historia: 91 rue de Rennes, 75006 Paris; f. 1946; monthly; Dirs JACQUES JOURQUIN, CHRISTIAN MELCHIOR-BONNET; circ. 170,000.

Revue d'histoire diplomatique: 13 rue Soufflot, 75005 Paris; f. 1887; quarterly; Dir GEORGES DETHAN.

Revue de l'histoire des religions: 12 rue Jean de Beauvais, 75005 Paris; tel. (1) 43-26-22-16; f. 1880; quarterly; Dirs HENRI-CHARLES PUECH, ANTOINE GUILLAUMONT; Editor CHARLES AMIEL.

Revue historique: 26 rue Geoffrey l'Asnier, 75005 Paris; tel. (1) 48-87-93-80; f. 1876; quarterly; Dirs JEAN FAVIER, RENÉ RÉMOND.

Revue de synthèse: Centre International de Synthèse, 12 rue Colbert, 75002 Paris; tel. (1) 42-97-50-68; f. 1900; quarterly; Dir JACQUES ROGER.

Law

Propriété Immobilière: 17 rue d'Uzès, 75002 Paris; f. 1945; monthly; Chair. MARC N. VIGIER; Man. Dir JEAN-MARC PILPOUL; circ. 5,846.

Revue Critique de Droit International Privé: 22 rue Soufflot, 75005 Paris; f. 1905; quarterly; publ. by Editions Sirey; Dirs Prof

H. Batiffol and Prof. Ph. Francescakis; Editor-in-Chief Prof. Paul Lagarde; Gen. Sec. Prof. Y. Lequette.

Leisure

Cahiers du Cinéma: 9 passage de la Boule Blanche, 75012 Paris; tel. (1) 43-43-92-20; telex 220064; f. 1951; monthly; film reviews; Dir and Editor Serge Toubiana; circ. 80,000.

France-Football: 10 rue du Faubourg Montmartre, 75009 Paris; tel. (1) 42-46-92-33; telex 280390; weekly; owned by Amaury Group.

Le Miroir du Cyclisme: 10 rue des Pyramides, 75001 Paris; monthly; cycling.

Photo: 63 ave des Champs-Elysées, 75008 Paris; f. 1960; monthly; specialist photography magazine; circ. 213,000.

Télé-Magazine: 5 rue de Chartres, 92522 Neuilly; f. 1955; weekly; circ. 220,000.

Télé-Poche: 2 rue des Italiens, 75009 Paris; f. 1966; weekly; television magazine; Dir Antoine de Clermont-Tonnerre; circ. 1,805,651.

Télérama: 129 blvd Malesherbes, 75017 Paris; f. 1972; weekly; radio, TV, film, literature and music; circ. 450,000.

Télé 7 Jours: 2 rue Ancelle, 92521 Neuilly-s/Seine; f. 1960; weekly; television; Dir J.-P. Ollivier; Chief Editor Philippe Gosset; circ. 3,063,412.

Military

Armées d'Aujourd'hui: 19 blvd de Latour Maubourg, BP 11307, 75326 Paris Cedex 07; 10 a year; military and technical; produced by the Service d'information et de relations publiques des armées (SIRPA).

Revue de Défense Nationale: Ecole Militaire, 1 place Joffre, 75700 Paris; tel. (1) 45-55-92-30; f. 1939; monthly; publ. by Committee for Study of National Defence; military, economic, political and scientific problems; Chair. General Jean Richard; Editor Amiral Jacques Hugon.

TAM (Terre, air, mer): 19, blvd de Latour-Maubourg, 75326 Paris Cedex 07; f. 1962; monthly; publ. by Ministry of Defence; circ. 170,000.

Music

Diapason-Harmonie: 2 rue des Italiens, 75009 Paris; tel. (1) 48-24-46-21; telex 643932; f. 1956; monthly; Pres. and Dir-Gen. Jean-Pierre Roger; Chief Editor Yves Petit de Voize; circ. 70,000.

Revue de Musicologie: 2 rue Louvois, 75002 Paris; f. 1917; 2 a year; publ. by Société française de musicologie; Editors Christian Meyer, Adelaïde de Place; circ. 1,000.

Overseas and Maritime

L'Annuaire des Entreprises et Organismes d'Outremer: 190 blvd Haussmann, 75008 Paris; annual listing firms and organizations in francophone Africa; Publr René Moreux et Cie.

Le Droit Maritime Français: 190 blvd Haussmann, 75008 Paris; tel. (1) 45-63-11-55; telex 290131; f. 1949; monthly; maritime law; Pres. Serge Marpaud; Dirs Pierre Bonnefont, Jean Gueneau.

Europe Outremer: 178 Quai Louis Blériot, 75016 Paris; tel. (1) 46-47-78-44; f. 1923; monthly; Dir R. Taton; circ. 17,800.

Industries et Développement International: 190 blvd Haussmann, 75008 Paris; tel. (1) 45-63-11-55; telex 290131; f. 1953; monthly; analysis and information on developing economies; Pres. Serge Marpaud; Dirs Pierre Bonnefont, Jean Gueneau.

Le Journal de la Marine Marchande et du Transport Multimodal: 190 blvd Haussmann, 75008 Paris; tel. (1) 45-63-11-55, telex 290131; f. 1919; weekly shipping publication; Pres. Serge Marpaud; Dir-Gen. Pierre Bonnefont.

Marchés Tropicaux et Méditerranéens: 190 blvd Haussmann, 75008 Paris; tel. (1) 45-63-11-55; telex 290131; f. 1945; weekly; African trade review; Pres. Serge Marpaud; Dirs Pierre Bonnefont, Jean Gueneau.

Navires, Ports et Chantiers: 190 blvd Haussmann, 75008 Paris; tel. (1) 45-63-11-55; telex 290131; f. 1950; monthly; international shipbuilding and harbours; Pres. Serge Marpaud; Dirs Pierre Bonnefont, Jean Gueneau.

La Pêche Maritime: 190 blvd Haussmann, 75008 Paris; tel. (1) 45-63-11-55; telex 290131; f. 1919; monthly; fishing industry; Pres. Serge Marpaud; Dirs Pierre Bonnefont, Jean Gueneau.

Philosophy, Psychology

Bibliographie de la Philosophie: Librairie J. Vrin, 6 place de la Sorbonne, 75005 Paris; f. 1937; quarterly.

Les études philosophiques: 2–8 rue François de Croisset, 75018 Paris; f. 1926, 1946 (new series); quarterly; Dirs P. Aubenque, J. Brun, L. Millet.

Psychologie française: 28 rue Serpente, 75006 Paris; f. 1956; quarterly; revue of the Société Française de Psychologie; Editor C. Bonnet.

Revue d'Esthétique: 162 rue Saint Charles, 75740 Paris Cedex 15; tel. (1) 61-23-09-26; telex 521001; f. 1948; 2 a year; Dirs Olivier Revault d'Allonnes, Mikel Dufrenne; circ. 2,500.

Revue des sciences philosophiques et théologiques: Librairie J. Vrin, 6 place de la Sorbonne, 75005 Paris; f. 1907; quarterly.

Revue philosophique de la France et de l'étranger: 108 blvd Saint Germain, 75006 Paris; f. 1876; quarterly; Dirs Pierre Maxime Schuhl, Yvon Bres; circ. 1,200.

Religion

L'Actualité Religieuse dans le Monde: 163 blvd Malesherbes, 75017 Paris; tel. (1) 47-66-01-86; f. 1983; Editor José de Broucker; circ. 30,000.

Etudes: 14 rue d'Assas, 75006 Paris; tel. (1) 45-48-52-51; f. 1856; monthly; general interest; Editor R. P. Paul Valadier.

France Catholique: 12 rue Edmond Valentin, 75007 Paris; tel. (1) 47-05-43-31; weekly; Dir A. Chabadel; circ. 20,000.

Le Pèlerin: 3 rue Bayard, 75008 Paris; f. 1873; weekly; Dir Guy Baudrillart; Editors-in-Chief Henry Caro, Guy Mauratille; circ. 523,405.

Prier: 163 blvd Malesherbes, 75017 Paris; tel. (1) 47-66-01-86; telex 649333; f. 1978; monthly; review of modern prayer and contemplation; circ. 85,000.

Témoignage Chrétien: 49 rue du Faubourg Poissonnière, 75009 Paris; tel. (1) 42-46-37-50; telex 290562; f. 1941; weekly; cultural; Dir Georges Montaron; circ. 100,000.

La Vie: 163 blvd Malesherbes, 75017 Paris; tel. (1) 47-66-01-86; telex 649333; f. 1945; weekly; Chair. and Man. Dir André Schafter; Dir José de Broucker; circ. 400,000.

Science and Mathematics

Annales de chimie: 120 blvd Saint Germain, 75280 Paris Cedex 06; tel. (1) 46-34-21-60; f. 1789; every 2 months; chemistry.

Astérisque: BP 126-05, 75226 Paris Cedex 05; tel. (1) 46-33-79-36; f. 1973; monthly; Dir M. Herman.

L'Astronomie: 3 rue Beethoven, 75016 Paris; tel. (1) 42-24-13-74; f. 1887; monthly; publ. by Société Astronomique de France; Chair. P. Simon.

Biochimie: 120 blvd Saint Germain, 75280 Paris Cedex 06; tel. (1) 46-34-21-60; telex 260946; f. 1914; monthly; bio-chemistry; Scientific Editor Mme M. Grunberg-Manago; Editor Yves Raoul.

Bulletin de la Société mathématique de France: BP 126-05, 75226 Paris Cedex 05; tel. (1) 46-33-39-42; f. 1872; quarterly; Dir P. Schapira; Sec. H. Nocton.

Bulletin des sciences mathématiques: Centrale des Revues, 11 rue Gossin, 92543 Montrouge Cedex; telex 260776; f. 1870; quarterly; circ. 800.

Science et vie: 5 rue de la Baume, 75382 Paris; f. 1913; monthly; Pres. Jacques Dupuy.

Technical and Miscellaneous

L'Argus de l'Automobile: 1 place Boieldieu, 75002 Paris; tel. (1) 42-61-83-03; telex 214633; f. 1927; motoring weekly.

Aviation Magazine International: 48 blvd des Batignolles 75017 Paris; tel. (1) 43-87-32-05; telex 290163; f. 1950; fortnightly; circ. 30,000.

Bureaux d'Études Automatismes: 33 rue la Boëtie, 75008 Paris; tel. (1) 42-56-16-54; 8 issues a year; automated systems design and CAD; publ. by CEP Information Technologie.

L'Echo de la Presse: 19 rue des Prêtres Saint-Germain l'Auxerrois, 75039 Paris Cedex 01; f. 1945; weekly; journalism, advertising; Editor Noel Jacquemart; circ. 8,100.

Ingénieurs de l'Automobile: 3 ave Président-Wilson, 75116 Paris; tel. (1) 47-20-93-23; f. 1927; monthly; formerly *Journal de la S.I.A.*; technical automobile review; Dir Paul Bardez.

Machine Moderne: 2 cité Bergère, 75009 Paris; tel. (1) 48-24-23-24; telex 650702; f. 1906; monthly; technical magazine; Dir J. P. Poncier; circ. 10,000.

Matériaux et Techniques: 76 rue de Rivoli, 75004 Paris; tel. (1) 42-78-52-20; f. 1913; monthly; review of engineering research and progress on industrial materials; Chief Editor R. DROUHIN.

Le Monde de l'Education: 5 rue des Italiens, 75427 Paris; monthly; circ. 80,955 (1984).

Le Moniteur des Travaux Publics et du Bâtiment: 17 rue d'Uzès, 75002 Paris; f. 1903; weekly; Editor JACQUES GUY; Chair. and Man. Dir MARC N. VIGIER; circ. 75,982.

La Revue Générale des Chemins de Fer: C.D.R., 11 rue Gossin, 92543 Montrouge Cedex; telex 260776; f. 1878; monthly; Chief Editor J. P. BERNARD; circ. 4,000.

La Revue Pratique du Froid et du Conditionnement de l'Air: 254 rue de Vaugirard, 75740 Paris Cedex 15; tel. (1) 45-32-27-19; telex 202639; f. 1945; fortnightly; industrial and technical review on cold storage, heat pumps and heat recovery and air-conditioning; Dir P. BENICHOU; Editor-in-Chief MICHÈLE LERY; circ. 5,079.

Technologies et Formations: 254 rue de Vaugirard, 75740 Paris Cedex 15; tel. (1) 45-32-27-19; telex 202639; f. 1945; every 2 months; review intended for vocational schools and training managers; Dir P. BENICHOU; circ. 3,900.

Traitement Thermique: 254 rue de Vaugirard, 75740 Paris Cedex 15; tel. (1) 45-32-27-19; telex 202639; f. 1963; 9 a year; technical review for engineers and technicians of heat treatment; Dir PIERRE BENICHOU; circ. 2,420.

La Vie des Métiers: Z.A. 34630 St Thibéry; tel. 67-77-80-35; monthly; Man. Editor YVES JEAN.

Women's and Fashion

Alma: 3 rue Bayard, 75008 Paris; f. 1986; monthly; publ. by Bayard-Presse; Chief Editor GENEVIÈVE JURGENSEN.

Bonne Soirée: 8 rue Bellini, 75782 Paris Cedex 16; f. 1922; weekly; French and Belgian; Chief Editor M. H. ADLER; circ. 234,637.

Echo de la Mode: 9 rue d'Alexandrie, 75002 Paris; f. 1890; weekly; publ. by Editions de Montsouris; Chair. and Man. Dir ALBERT DE SMAELE; circ. 405,000.

Elle: 6 rue Ancelle, 92521 Neuilly-s/Seine Cedex; weekly; Dir PAUL GIANNOLI; Editors D. FILIPACCHI, R. PAGNIEZ, R. THÉROND; circ. 412,000.

Femme d'Aujourd'hui: 20–22 rue de Clichy, 75009 Paris; tel. (1) 42-80-64-65; telex 643433; f. 1933; weekly; circ. 850,000.

Femme Pratique: 20–22 rue de Clichy 75009 Paris; tel. (1) 42-80-64-65; telex 643433; f. 1958; monthly; French and Belgian; circ. 380,000.

Intimité: 2 rue des Italiens, 75009 Paris; f. 1949; weekly; illustrated stories; Dir ANTOINE DE CLERMONT-TONNERRE; circ. 650,000.

Jardin des Modes: 80 ave du Maine, 75014 Paris; tel. (1) 43-20-13-11; f. 1921; monthly; Publr and Editor ALICE MORGAINE; circ. 80,000.

La Maison de Marie-Claire: 11 bis rue Boissy d'Anglas, 75008 Paris; f. 1967; Dir EVELYNE PROUVOST; circ. 203,347.

Maison et Jardin: 10 blvd du Montparnasse, 75724 Paris Cedex 15; tel. (1) 45-67-35-05; telex 204191; f. 1950; 10 a year, 2 special issues (*Maison Magazine*); associated with *House and Garden*, New York and London, *Casa Vogue*, Italy; Publr PATRICK DELCROIX; circ. 125,000.

Marie-Claire: 11 bis rue Boissy d'Anglas, 75008 Paris; monthly; Dir EVELYNE PROUVOST; circ. 677,772.

Marie-France: 114 ave des Champs Elysées 75008 Paris; f. 1944; monthly; Man. Dir MAURICE BRÉBART; Chief Editor DANIÈLE BOTT; circ. 522,284.

Modes et travaux: 10 rue de la Pépinière, 75380 Paris Cedex 08; f. 1919; monthly; Dir PHILIPPE CHOPIN; circ. 1,500,000.

Nous Deux: 2 rue des Italiens, 75009 Paris; f. 1947; illustrated stories; Dir ANTOINE DE CLERMONT-TONNERRE; circ. 1,000,000.

Vogue: 4 place de Palais Bourbon, 75007 Paris; f. 1921; 10 a year, plus 10 a year of *Vogue Hommes* and 2 a year of *Vogue Spéciale Beauté;* Dirs JEAN PONIATOWSKI (*Vogue*), GÉRALD ASARIA (*Vogue Hommes*, also Editor); Editor FRANCINE CRESCENT.

NEWS AGENCIES

Agence France-Presse: 11–15 place de la Bourse, 75002 Paris; f. 1944; tel. (1) 42-33-44-66; telex 210064; 24-hour service of world political, financial, sporting news, etc.; 110 agencies and 1,500 correspondents all over the world; Chair. and Man. Dir JEAN-LOUIS GUILLAUD; Sec.-Gen. PIERRE JEANTET.

Agence Parisienne de Presse: 18 rue Saint Fiacre, 75002 Paris; f. 1949; Man. Dir MICHEL RAVELET.

Agence Républicaine d'Information: 22 rue de Châteaudun, 75009 Paris; French domestic and foreign politics; Dir ALBERT LEBACQZ.

Presse Services: 111 ave Victor Hugo, 75116 Paris; f. 1929; Chair. and Man. Dir C. CAZENAVE DE LA ROCHE.

Science-Service—Agence Barnier: 10 rue Notre Dame de Lorette, 75009 Paris; medical, scientific, technical, recreation news; Man. Dir DENISE BARNIER.

Foreign Bureaux

Agencia EFE (Spain): 7 rue d'Aguesseau, 75008 Paris; tel. (1) 42-65-98-31; telex 660829; Delegate D. ERNESTO GARCÍA HERRERA.

Agentstvo Pechati Novosti (APN) (USSR): 8 rue Prony, 75017 Paris; Bureau Chief G. BOTCHKAREU.

Agenzia Nazionale Stampa Associata (ANSA) (Italy): 29 rue Tronchet, 75008 Paris; tel. (1) 42-65-55-16; telex 042-290120; Bureau Chief ADA PRINCIGALLI.

Allgemeiner Deutscher Nachrichtendienst (ADN) (German Democratic Republic): 23 rue Erlanger, 75016 Paris; Bureau Chief JOACHIM SONNENBERG.

Associated Press (AP) (USA): 162 rue du Faubourg Saint-Honoré, 75008 Paris; tel. (1) 43-59-86-76; telex 280770; Bureau Chief HARRY DUNPHY.

Československá tisková kancelář (ČTK) (Czechoslovakia): 6 rue du Dr Finlay, 75015 Paris; tel. (1) 45-79-00-24; telex 201735; Bureau Man. KAREL BARTAK.

Deutsche Presse-Agentur (dpa) (Federal Republic of Germany): 30 rue Saint Augustin, 75002 Paris; tel. (1) 47-42-95-02; telex 212995 (Hamburg, Fed. Republic of Germany); Bureau Chief CHRISTIAN VOLBRACHT.

Inter Press Service (Italy): 39 rue Volta, 75003 Paris; tel. 42-74-47-12; telex 217511; Dir ANNE VALIER.

Jiji Tsushin-sha (Japan): 175 blvd Malesherbes, 75017 Paris; tel. (1) 42-27-43-27; telex 660616; Bureau Chief JOJI HARANO.

Kyodo Tsushin (Japan): 19 rue Paul Lelong, 75002 Paris; tel. (1) 42-60-13-16; telex 680516; Bureau Chief HIROSHI SASAKI.

Magyar Távirati Iroda (MTI) (Hungary): 8 rue Octave Feuillet, 75116 Paris; Correspondent LÁSZLÓ BALÁZS.

Middle East News Agency (Egypt): 6 rue de la Michodière, 75002 Paris; tel. (1) 47-42-16-03; telex 230011; f. 1956; Dir ESSAM SALEH.

Prensa Latina (Cuba): 22 ave de l'Opéra, 75001 Paris; tel. (1) 42-60-22-18; telex 214682; Bureau Chief RAMÓN MARTÍNEZ CRUZ.

Reuters (UK): 101 rue Réaumur, 75080 Paris; tel. (1) 42-60-31-63; telex 210003; Chief Correspondent J. MORRISON.

Telegrafnoye Agentstvo Sovetskovo Soyuza (TASS) (USSR): 27 ave Bosquet, 75007 Paris; Correspondent YURI LOPATIN.

United Press International (UPI) (USA): 2 rue des Italiens, 75009 Paris; tel. (1) 47-70-91-70; telex 650547; Bureau Chief ALINE MOSBY.

Wikalat al-Maghreb al-Arabi/Agence Maghreb Arabe Presse (Morocco): Bur. 4, Place de la Concorde, 75008 Paris; tel. (1) 42-65-40-45; telex 214759; Corespondent CHAKIB LAAROUSSI.

Xinhua (New China) News Agency (People's Republic of China): 148 rue Petit Leroy, Chevilly-Larue, 94150 Rungis; tel. (1) 46-87-12-08; telex 204398; Correspondent WANG WEN.

The following Agencies are also represented: Jamahiriya News Agency (Libya) and Central News Agency (Taiwan).

PRESS ASSOCIATIONS

Comité de Liaison Professionnel de la Presse: 49 rue Cambon, 75011 Paris; liaison organization for press, radio and cinema; mems. Fédération Nationale de la Presse Française, Confédération de la Presse Française, Chambre Syndicale de la Presse Filmée, Fédération Française des Agences de Presse; Gen. Sec. CHRISTIAN LOYAUTÉ.

Confédération de la Presse Française: 17 place des Etats Unis, 75116 Paris; tel. (1) 47-23-36-36; Chair. PIERRE ARCHAMBAULT; Dir JEAN-CLAUDE GATINEAU.

Fédération Française des Agences de Presse: 49 rue Cambon, 75011 Paris; Chair. HENRI DERAMOND; Vice-Pres. JEAN GORINI.

Fédération Nationale de la Presse d'Information Spécialisée: 6 bis rue Gabriel Laumain, 75484 Paris Cedex 10; tel. (1) 47-70-93-86; Chair. HUBERT ZIESENISS; Dir MAURICE VIAU.

FRANCE   *Directory*

Fédération Nationale de la Presse Française: 6 bis rue Gabriel Laumain, 75010 Paris; tel. (1) 48-24-98-30; f. 1944; mems. Syndicate de la Presse Parisienne, Syndicat de la Presse Hebdomadaire Parisienne, Syndicat des Quotidiens Régionaux, Syndicat des Quotidiens Départementaux, Fédération de la Presse Hebdomadaire et Périodique, Union Nationale de la Presse Périodique d'Information, Fédération Nationale de la Presse d'Information Spécialisée; Chair. ROBERT BUJON; Dir MICHEL CABART.

Fédération Nationale des Syndicats et Associations Professionnelles de Journalistes Français: 52 rue Richer, 75009 Paris; tel. (1) 48-24-65-71; f. 1888, under present title since 1937; 7,000 mems; Chair. ARMAND MACÉ; Vice-Chair. PIERRE MITANCHEZ, GEORGES VERPRAET, ROBERT POIRIER, DENIS PERIER-DAVILLE; Sec.-Gen. BERNARD HENNEQUIN.

Union de la Presse Française à Diffusion Nationale et Internationale: 6 bis rue Gabriel Laumain, 75010 Paris; tel. (1) 48-24-98-30; mems Syndicat de la Presse Parisienne, Fédération Nationale de la Presse Hebdomadaire et Périodique, Syndicat des Publications d'Informations Générales, Syndicat des Publications d'Informations Spécialisées, Syndicat des Publications Economiques et Techniques; Chair. ANDRÉ LOUIS DUBOIS.

Union Nationale de la Presse Périodique d'Information: 6 bis rue Gabriel Laumain, 75010 Paris; tel. (1) 48-24-98-30; f. 1978; mems Syndicat National de la Presse Hebdomadaire Régionale d'Information, Syndicat National des Publications Régionales, Syndicat de la Presse Judiciaire de Province, Fédération de la Presse Agricole; Chair. ALBERT GARRIGUES; Vice-Pres P.,FLANDRE, MATAGRIN, V. BASTIDE, J. TRINET.

PRESS INSTITUTE

Institut Français de Presse et des Sciences de l'Information: 83 bis rue Notre Dame Des Champs, 75006 Paris; tel. (1) 43-20-12-24; f. 1953; studies all aspects of communication and the media; maintains research and documentation centre; higher specialized teaching of all aspects of information services; open to research workers, students, journalists; Dir PIERRE ALBERT.

Publishers

Editions Albin Michel: 22 rue Huyghens, 75014 Paris Cedex 14; tel. (1) 43-20-12-20; telex 203379; f. 1900; general, fiction, history, classics; Chair. and Man. Dir FRANCIS ESMÉNARD.

Editions Arthaud: 20 rue Monsieur le Prince, 75006 Paris; tel. (1) 43-29-12-20; telex 205641; f. 1870; literature, arts, history, travel books, reference, sports; Chair. and Man. Dir CHARLES-HENRI FLAMMARION; Dir ROSELYNE DE AYALA.

Assimil: 13 rue Gay Lussac, Z.I. 94430 Chennevières-sur-Marne; tel. (1) 45-76-87-37; telex 232775; f. 1929; self-study language methods; Man. Dir JEAN-LOUP CHEREL.

Editions Aubier-Montaigne: 13 quai de Conti, 75006 Paris; tel. (1) 43-26-55-59; telex 205641; f. 1924; literature, philosophy and religion, history and sociology; Chair and Man. Dir HENRI FLAMMARION; Dir PATRICE MENTHA.

J. B. Baillière: 10 rue Thénard, 75005 Paris; tel. (1) 46-34-21-10; telex 201326; f. 1814; science, medicine, agriculture and technical books; Dirs MICHEL ROUX-DESSARPS and HENRI MOREL D'ARLEUX.

Editions André Balland: 33 rue Saint André des Arts, 75006 Paris; tel. (1) 43-25-74-40; f. 1967; fine art, literature, history, humanities; Chair. and Man. Dir ANDRÉ BALLAND.

Bayard-Presse: 3–5 rue Bayard, 75008 Paris; tel. (1) 45-62-51-51; telex 280626; f. 1873; children's books, religion, literature; owns *La Croix, Le Pèlerin, Notre Temps, Panorama d'Aujourd'hui*, etc.; Chair. JEAN GELAMUR.

Beauchesne Editeur: 72 rue des Saints Pères, 75007 Paris; tel. (1) 45-48-80-28; f. 1900; scripture, religion and theology, philosophy, religious history, politics, encyclopaedias, periodicals; Dir MONIQUE CADIC.

Editions Belfond: 216 blvd Saint Germain, 75007 Paris; tel. (1) 45-44-38-23; telex 260717; f. 1963; fiction, poetry, documents, history, arts; Chair. PIERRE BELFOND; Dir-Gen. FRANCA BELFOND.

Berger-Levrault SA: 229 blvd Saint Germain, 75007 Paris; tel. (1) 47-05-56-14; telex 270797; f. 1676; architecture, art, social and economic sciences, juvenile, law, history; Man. Dir MARC FRIEDEL.

Editions E. de Boccard: 11 rue de Médicis, 75006 Paris; tel. (1) 43-26-00-37; f. 1866; history, archaeology, religion, orientalism; Dir DOMINIQUE CHAULET.

Bordas: 17 rue Rémy Dumoncel, BP 50, 75661 Paris Cedex 14; tel. (1) 43-20-15-50; telex 260776; f. 1946; encyclopaedic, scientific, history, geography, arts, children's and educational; Chair. and Man. Dir JEAN MANUEL BOURGOIS.

Editions Bornemann: 15 rue de Tournon, 75006 Paris; tel. (1) 43-26-05-88; f. 1829; art, educational children's books, sports, nature, easy readers; Chair. and Man. Dir PIERRE C. LAHAYE.

Buchet-Chastel: 18 rue de Condé, 75006 Paris; tel. (1) 43-26-92-00; f. 1929; dietetics, religion, sociology, history, music, literature, biographies, documents; Dir GUY BUCHET.

Calmann-Lévy: 3 rue Auber, 75009 Paris; tel. (1) 47-42-38-33; telex 270105; f. 1836; fiction, history, social sciences, economics, sport, religion; Chair. and Man. Dir JEAN-ETIENNE COHEN-SÉAT; Dir ALAIN OULMAN.

Casterman: 66 rue Bonaparte, 75006 Paris; tel. (1) 43-25-20-05; telex 200001; f. 1780; juvenile, comics, fiction, education, leisure interests; Chair. and Man. Dir ETIENNE POLLET.

Les Editions du Cerf: 29 blvd de Latour Maubourg, 75340 Paris Cedex 07; tel. (1) 45-50-34-07; telex 200684; f. 1929; juvenile, religion, social science; Pres. MICHEL HOUSSIN; Dir-Gen. PASCAL MOITY.

Champion-Slatkine: 7 quai Malaquais, 75006 Paris; tel. (1) 46-34-07-29; f. 1973; medieval literature, music, law, history, psychology, comics, ethnology, linguistics; Dir MICHEL SLATKINE.

Chiron (Editions): 40 rue de Seine, 75006 Paris; tel. (1) 43-26-47-56; telex 205434; f. 1907; technical, sport, education, leisure; Chair. and Man. Dir D. FERRANDO-DURFORT.

Armand Colin: 103 blvd Saint Michel, 75240 Paris Cedex 05; tel. (1) 46-34-12-19; telex 201269; f. 1870; philosophy, history, law, geography and science, pedagogy, music, poetry, maps and textbooks; Chair. and Man. Dir JEAN-MAX LECLERC.

Editions du CNRS (Centre National de la Recherche Scientifique): 15 quai Anatole France, 75700 Paris; tel. (1) 45-55-92-25; telex 260034; f. 1939; public institution under the Ministry of Research; science and social science; Dir GÉRARD LILAMAND.

Dalloz (Jurisprudence Générale): 11 et 14 rue Soufflot, 75240 Paris Cedex 05; tel. (1) 43-29-50-80; telex 206446; f. 1824; law, philosophy, political science, business and economics; Chair. and Man. Dir PATRICE VERGÉ.

Dargaud Editeur: 12 rue Blaise Pascal, 92201 Neuilly-sur-Seine; tel. (1) 47-47-11-33; telex 620631; f. 1943; juvenile, cartoons, music, science-fiction; Chair. and Man. Dir GEORGES DARGAUD.

Editions la Découverte: 1 place Paul Painlevé, 75005 Paris; tel. (1) 46-33-41-16; f. 1959; economic and political science, literature, history, pedagogy; Man. Dir FRANÇOIS GÈZE.

Librairie Delagrave (SARL): 15 rue Soufflot, 75240 Paris Cedex 05; tel. (1) 43-25-88-66; telex 204252; f. 1865; textbooks; Man. FABRICE DELAGRAVE.

Editions Denoël: 19 rue de l'Université, 75007 Paris; tel. (1) 42-61-50-85; f. 1930; general literature, sport, politics, economics; Dir GÉRARD BOURGADIER.

Editions Des Femmes: 6 rue de Mézières, 75006 Paris; tel. (1) 42-22-60-74; telex 202397; f. 1973; mainly women authors; fiction, essays, art, history, politics, psychoanalysis, talking books; Dirs ANTOINETTE FOUQUE, MARIE-CLAUDE GRUMBACH.

Desclée De Brouwer: 76 bis rue des Saints Pères, 75007 Paris; tel. (1) 45-44-07-36; telex 202098; f. 1875; religion, reference, textbooks, arts, psychiatry, juvenile; Chair. and Man. Dir GÉRARD LANDRIEU.

Deux Coqs d'Or: 28 rue la Boétie, 75008 Paris; tel. (1) 45-62-10-52; telex 650780; f. 1949; children's books, art, science; Chair. and Man. Dir JEAN-MICHEL AZZI; Dir FRANÇOIS MARTINEAU.

Didot-Bottin SA: 28 rue Docteur Finlay, 75738 Paris Cedex 15; tel. (1) 45-78-61-66; telex 204286; f. 1796; publs *Bottin Mondain* and other commercial registers and directories, encyclopaedias, business and administration; Chair. and Man. Dir VINCENT HOLLARD.

La Documentation Française: 29–31 quai Voltaire, 75340 Paris Cedex 07; tel. (1) 42-61-50-10; telex 204826; f. 1945; government publs; political, economical, topographical, historical, sociological documents and audio-visual material; Dir FRANÇOISE GALLOUEDEC-GENUYS.

Editions ESF/Entreprise Moderne d'Edition: 17 rue Viète, 75854 Paris Cedex 17; tel. (1) 47-63-68-76; f. 1947; business and technical books, humanities, social sciences; Chair. GÉRARD DIDIER; Man. Dir CLAUDE CHICHET.

Eyrolles: 61 blvd Saint Germain, 75240 Paris Cedex 05; tel. (1) 46-34-21-99; telex 203385; f. 1918; scientific, technical; Chair. and Man. Dir C. SCHOEDLER.

Librairie Arthème Fayard: 75 rue des Saints Pères, 75278 Paris Cedex 06; tel. (1) 45-44-38-45; telex 240918; f. 1850; general fiction, literature, biography, history, religion, essays, philosophy, geography, music, science; Chair. and Man. Dir CLAUDE DURAND.

Flammarion et Cie: 26 rue Racine, 75278 Paris Cedex 06; tel. (1) 43-29-12-20; telex 205641; f. 1875; general literature, art, human sciences, history, children's books, medicine; Chair. CHARLES-HENRI FLAMMARION; Dirs JEAN-DIDIER CONDUT and P. FORBIN.

Fleuve Noir: 6 rue Garancière, 75278 Paris Cedex 06; tel. (1) 46-34-21-61; telex 204870; f. 1949 (Presses de la Cité); crime and science fiction, paperbacks; Dir Gen. PATRICK SIRY.

Foucher: 128 rue de Rivoli, 75038 Paris Cedex 01; tel. (1) 42-36-38-90; telex 240231; f. 1935; science, economics, law, medicine; Chair. and Man. Dir BERNARD FOULON.

Editions Gallimard: 5 rue Sébastien Bottin, 75007 Paris; tel. (1) 45-44-39-19; telex 204121; f. 1911; general fiction, literature, history, poetry, philosophy; Chair. and Man. Dir CLAUDE GALLIMARD.

Garnier Frères: BP 168, 19 rue des Plantes, 75014 Paris; tel. (1) 45-40-98-15; telex 270105; f. 1833; general, classics, pocket editions, dictionaries, essays, juvenile literature, comics; Chair. and Man. Dir BERNARD GARNIER; Dir B. VEREANO.

Librairie Générale de Droit et de Jurisprudence: 20 rue Soufflot, 75005 Paris; tel. (1) 43-54-07-19; telex 210023; f. 1836; law and economy; Man. Dir J.-P. HÉBERT; Dir F. MARTY.

Librairie Générale Française: 79 blvd Saint Germain, 75006 Paris; tel. (1) 46-34-86-34; telex 204434; *Livres de Poche* paperback series, general literature, dictionaries, encyclopaedias; f. 1953; Dir FREDERIC DITIS.

Librairie Orientaliste Paul Geuthner SA: 12 rue Vavin, 75006 Paris; tel. (1) 46-34-71-30; f. 1901; philology, travel books, studies and learned perodicals concerned with the Orient; Dir MARC F. SEIDL-GEUTHNER.

Editions Grasset et Fasquelle: 61 rue des Saints Pères, 75006 Paris; tel. (1) 45-44-38-14; f. 1907; contemporary literature, criticism, general fiction and children's books; Chair. and Man. Dir JEAN CLAUDE FASQUELLE.

Librairie Gründ: 60 rue Mazarine, 75006 Paris; tel. (1) 43-29-87-40; telex 204926; f. 1880; art, natural history, children's, books, guides; Chair. MICHEL GRÜND; Man. Dir ALAIN GRÜND.

Hachette: 12 rue François 1er, 75008 Paris; tel. (1) 43-59-79-59; telex 643476; f. 1826; general; all types of book, especially textbooks; Vice-Pres. and CEO YVES SABOURET.

Librairie A. Hatier, SA: 8 rue d'Assas, 75006 Paris; tel. (1) 45-44-38-38; telex 202732; f. 1880; text books, art, audio-visual materials, dictionaries, general literature, geographical maps, books for young people, computer software; Man. Dir MICHEL FOULON.

Hermann: 293 rue Lecourbe, 75015 Paris; tel. (1) 45-57-45-40; telex 200595; f. 1870; sciences and art, humanities; Chair. and Man. Dir PIERRE BERÈS.

Import Diffusion Music: 42–44 rue du Fer à Moulin, 75005 Paris; tel. (1) 45-35-44-25; telex 201947; f. 1972; music; Dirs ALAIN PIERSON, PHILIPPE AGEON.

J'ai Lu: 27 rue Cassette, 75006 Paris; tel. (1) 45-44-38-76; telex 202765; f. 1958; fiction, paperbacks; subsidiary of Flammarion et Cie; Chair. and Man. Dir CHARLES-HENRI FLAMMARION; Literary Dir JACQUES SADOUL.

Julliard: 8 rue Garancière, 75278 Paris Cedex 06; tel. (1) 46-34-12-80; telex 204807; f. 1931; general literature, history, political science, biographies and documents; Chair. and Man. Dir CLAUDE NIELSEN; Man. Dir BERNARD de FALLOIS.

Editions Klincksieck: 11 rue de Lille, 75007 Paris; tel. (1) 42-60-38-25; f. 1842; human sciences, architecture, literature, history, fine art, philosophy, music; Chair. and Man. Dir Mme ANDRÉE LAURENT-KLINCKSIECK.

Jeanne Laffitte: 1 place Francis Chirat, BP 1903, 13225 Marseille Cedex 02; tel. 91-54-14-44; f. 1972; art, geography, culture, medicine, history; Chair. and Man. Dir JEANNE LAFFITTE.

Editions Robert Laffont: 6 place Saint Sulpice, 75279 Paris Cedex 06; tel. (1) 43-29-12-33; telex 250877; f. 1941; literature, history, art, translations; Chair. and Man. Dir ROBERT LAFFONT.

Librairie Larousse SA: 17 rue du Montparnasse, 75298 Paris Cedex 06; tel. (1) 45-44-38-17; telex 250828; f. 1852; general, specializing in dictionaries, illustrated books on scientific subjects, encyclopaedias, classics, textbooks and periodicals; Pres. and Dir-Gen. BRUNO ROHMER.

Editions Jean-Claude Lattès: 17 rue Jacob, 75006 Paris; tel. (1) 46-34-03-10; telex 205652; f. 1968; general fiction and non-fiction, biography, music; Chair. and Man. Dir NICOLE LATTÈS.

Letouzey et Ané: 87 blvd Raspail, 75006 Paris; tel. (1) 45-48-80-14; f. 1885; history and archaeology of Catholic Church; history of religions; ecclesiastical encyclopaedias and dictionaries, biography; Dirs J. LETOUZEY, FLORENCE LETOUZEY-DUMONT.

Editions Magnard: 122 blvd Saint Germain, 75264 Paris Cedex 06; tel. (1) 43-26-39-52; telex 202294; f. 1933; children's and educational books; Man. Dir LOUIS MAGNARD.

Librairie Maloine, SA: 27 rue de l'Ecole de Médecine, 75006 Paris; tel. (1) 43-25-60-45; telex 203215; f. 1881; medical textbooks, sciences and humanities; Chair. and Man. Dir ANTONIN PHILIPPART.

Editions Maritimes et d'Outre-mer: 17 rue Jacob, 75006 Paris; tel. (1) 46-34-03-10; telex 205652; f. 1839; yachting, marine, maritime history, navigation; Chair. and Man. Dir PIERRE GUTELLE.

Masson: 120 blvd Saint Germain, 75280 Paris Cedex 06; tel. (1) 46-34-21-60; telex 260946; f. 1804; medicine and science, books and periodicals; publrs for various academies and societies; Chair. and Man. Dir JÉROME TALAMON.

Mercure de France, SA: 26 rue de Condé, 75006 Paris; tel. (1) 43-29-21-13; f. 1890; general fiction, history, psychology, sociology; Chair. and Man. Dir SIMONE GALLIMARD.

Les Editions de Minuit: 7 rue Bernard Palissy, 75006 Paris; tel. (1) 42-22-37-94; f. 1945; general literature; Chair. and Man. Dir JÉRÔME LINDON.

Fernand Nathan Editeur: 9 rue Méchain, 75676 Paris Cedex 14; tel. (1) 45-89-89-49; telex 204525; f. 1881; affiliated to Librairie Larousse; school, and children's books, encyclopaedias, educational journals and games, fine arts, literature; Chair. and Man. Dir JEAN-JACQUES NATHAN.

Les Editions d'Organisation (Editions Hommes et Techniques): 5 rue Rousselet, 75007 Paris; tel. (1) 45-67-18-40; f. 1952; subsidiary of Eyrolles; management and business economy; Chair. and Man. Dir SERGE EYROLLES.

Editions Ouvrières: 12 ave Soeur Rosalie, 75621 Paris Cedex 13; tel. (1) 43-37-93-85; f. 1929; religious, educational, political and social, including labour movement; Dir A. JONDEAU.

Payot: 106 blvd Saint Germain, 75006 Paris; tel. (1) 43-29-74-10; telex 203246; f. 1912; general science, biography, philosophy, religion, education, history; Chair. and Man. Dir J.-L. PIDOUX-PAYOT.

Librairie Académique Perrin: 8 rue Garancière, 75285 Paris; tel. (1) 46-34-12-80; telex 204807; f. 1884; historical and literary biographies, fine arts, humanities, trade books; Chair. and Man. Dir CLAUDE NIELSEN.

A. et J. Picard: 82 rue Bonaparte, 75006 Paris; tel. (1) 43-26-96-73; f. 1869; archaeology, architecture, history of art, history, prehistory, auxiliary sciences, linguistics, musicological works, antiquarian books, *Catalogue Varia* (old and rare books, documentary books, quarterly); Chair. and Man. Dir CHANTAL PASINI-PICARD.

Plon: 8 rue Garancière, 75285 Paris; tel. (1) 46-34-12-80; telex 204807; f. 1844; fiction, travel, history, anthropology, science, trade books and suspense series; Chair. and Man. Dir CLAUDE NIELSEN.

Présence Africaine: 25 bis rue des Ecoles, 75005 Paris; tel. (1) 43-54-13-74; telex 200891; f. 1949; general books; Dir-Gen. YANDÉ CHRISTIANE DIOP.

Presses de la Cité: 8 rue Garancière, 75285 Paris; tel. (1) 46-34-12-80; telex 204807; f. 1947; general fiction, history, paperbacks; group comprises Plon, G.P. Rouge et Or, Solar, Librairie Académique Perrin, Julliard, Presses Pocket, Editions Fleuve Noir, Messageries Centrales du Livre, Editions Christian Bourgois, le Rocher, UGE 10/18; Chair. and Man. Dir CLAUDE NIELSEN.

Presses de la Fondation Nationale des Sciences Politiques: 27 rue Saint Guillaume, 75341 Paris Cedex 07; tel. (1) 42-22-09-85; f. 1975; history, politics, linguistics, economics, sociology; Chair. and Man. Dir LOUIS BODIN.

Presses Universitaires de France: 108 blvd Saint Germain, 75006 Paris; tel. (1) 46-34-12-01; telex 600474; f. 1921; philosophy, psychology, psychoanalysis, psychiatry, education, sociology, theology, history, geography, economics, law, linguistics, literature, science, the 'Que Sais-Je?' series, and official pubs of universities; Chair. PIERRE ANGOULVENT.

Presses Universitaires de Grenoble: Domaine Universitaire, BP 47 X, 38040 Saint Martin d'Hères, Grenoble; tel. 76-44-43-78; telex 980910; f. 1972; architecture, anthropology, law, economics, management, history, statistics, literature, medicine, science, politics; Dir CHRISTIAN AUGUSTE.

Privat: 14 rue des Arts, 31000 Toulouse; tel. 61-23-09-26; telex 521001; f. 1840; regional publs, history, medicine, philosophy, religion, tourism, education; Dir-Gen. YVES SUAUDEAU; Dir DOMINIQUE AUTIÉ.

FRANCE

Editions Quillet: 11 blvd de Sébastopol, 75001 Paris; tel. (1) 42-61-80-95; f. 1898; general; specializes in dictionaries and encyclopaedias; Chair. and Man. Dir VINCENT BRUGÈRE-TRÉLAT.

Editions Seghers, SA: 6 place Saint Sulpice, 75279 Paris; tel. (1) 43-29-12-33; telex 250877; f. 1939; poetry, novels, politics, philosophy, biographies; Chair. and Man. Dir ROBERT LAFFONT.

Editions du Seuil: 27 rue Jacob, 75261 Paris Cedex 06; tel. (1) 43-29-12-15; telex 600605; f. 1936; modern literature, fiction, illustrated books, non-fiction; Chair. and Man. Dir MICHEL CHODKIEWICZ.

Editions Stock: 103 blvd St Michel, 75005 Paris; tel. (1) 46-34-89-34; f. 1710; subsidiary of Librairie Hachette; foreign literature, novels, general literature, law, science, philosophy, sport; Chair. and Man. Dir JEAN ROSENTHAL.

Editions de la Table Ronde: 40 rue du Bac, 75007 Paris; tel. (1) 42-22-28-91; f. 1944; history, leisure, medicine, children's books; Man. Dir GWENN-AËL BOLLORÉ.

Editions Tallandier: 61 rue de la Tombe Issoire, 75677 Paris Cedex 14; tel. (1) 43-20-14-33; telex 210311; f. 1865; literature, history, magazines, popular editions, book club edition; Chair. and Man. Dir JAQUES JOURQUIN.

Editions Vigot Frères: 23 rue de l'Ecole de Médecine, 75006 Paris; tel. (1) 43-29-54-50; telex 201708; f. 1890; medicine, pharmacology, languages, tourism, veterinary science, sport; Chair. and Man. Dir CHRISTIAN VIGOT; Dir DANIEL VIGOT.

Vilo: 25 rue Ginoux, 75015 Paris; tel. (1) 45-77-08-05; telex 200305; f. 1950; non-fiction, art, history, geography, tourism, sport; Chair. and Man. Dir M. LARFILLON.

Librairie Philosophique J. Vrin: 6 place de la Sorbonne, 75005 Paris; tel. (1) 43-54-03-47; f. 1911; university textbooks, philosophy, education, science, law, religion; Chair. and Man. Dir A. PAULHAC-VRIN.

Librairie Vuibert: 63 blvd Saint Germain, 75005 Paris; tel. (1) 43-25-61-00; telex 201005; f. 1877; economics, business, mathematics, physics, science; Chair. JEAN ADAM.

CARTOGRAPHERS

Blondel La Rougery: 7 rue Saint Lazare, 75009 Paris; tel. (1) 48-78-95-54; f. 1902; maps; specialized prints of maps and charts; Chair. J. BARBOTTE.

Girard et Barrère: 2 place du Puits de l'Ermite, 75005 Paris; f. 1780; maps and globes; Mans MM BARRY, GOURIER, VUILLERET.

Institut Géographique National: 136 bis rue de Grenelle, 75700 Paris; tel. (1) 45-50-34-95; telex 204989; f. 1940; surveying and mapping of France and many other countries; Dir CLAUDE MARTINAND.

Cartes Taride: 2 bis place du Puits de l'Ermite, 75005 Paris; f. 1852; tourists' maps, guides and maps of the world, globes; Mans MM BARRY, GOURIER, VUILLERET.

PUBLISHERS' ASSOCIATIONS

Cercle de la Librairie (Syndicat des Industries et Commerces du Livre): 35 rue Grégoire de Tours, 75006 Paris Cedex; tel. (1) 43-29-21-01; f. 1847; a syndicate of the book trade, grouping the principal asscns of publishers, booksellers and printers; Chair. YVON CHOTARD; Man. Dir PIERRE FREDET; Sec.-Gen. MARC FRIEDEL.

Fédération Française des Syndicats de Libraires: 259 rue Saint Honoré, 75001 Paris; tel. (1) 42-60-93-93; f. 1892; booksellers' asscn; 2,000 mems; Chair. BERNARD BOLLENOT; Gen. Man. MICHÈLE BOURGUIGNON.

Syndicat National de l'Edition: 35 rue Grégoire de Tours, 75279 Paris Cedex 06; tel. (1) 43-29-21-01; f. 1892; c. 350 mems; publishers' asscn; Chair. ALAIN GRUND; Man. Dir P. FREDET.

Chambre Syndicale des Editeurs de Musique de France: 175 rue Saint Honoré, 75040 Paris Cedex 01; tel. (1) 42-96-89-11; telex 212740; f. 1873; music publishers' asscn; Chair. FRANÇOIS LEDUC; Sec. DIDIER DUCLOS.

Syndicat Professionnel Annuaires, Télématique, Communication (ATC): 35 rue Grégoire de Tours, 75279 Paris Cedex 06; tel. (1) 43-29-21-01; f. 1984; Pres. HUBERT MOULET.

Chambre Syndicale de l'Edition Musicale (CSDEM): 57 ave de Villiers, 75017 Paris; music publishers; Chair. PHILIPPE SEILLER.

Syndicat Général des Imprimeries de Paris et de la Région Parisienne: 46 rue de Bassano, 75008 Paris; tel. (1) 47-20-45-90; f. 1970; printers' asscn; 650 mems; Chair. RENÉ MARQUET.

Union Parisienne des Syndicats Patronaux de l'Imprimerie: 46 rue de Bassano, 75008 Paris; tel. (1) 47-20-45-90; f. 1923; Chair. JACQUES NOULET.

Directory

Union Syndicale des Libraires de France (USLF): 40 rue Grégoire de Tours, 75006 Paris; tel. (1) 46-34-74-20; Pres. RAYMOND PÉJU; Sec.-Gen. ROBERT BOISTEAU.

Radio and Television

From 1964 to 1974 broadcasting was administered by the Office de Radiodiffusion-Télévision Française (ORTF), under the tutelage of the Ministry of Information. From 1968 onwards, the ORTF was subject to repeated strikes, accusations of political bias, from both the right and the left, and scandalous revelations of economic mismanagement. In 1975 it was replaced by seven independent state-financed companies, comprising four organizations with responsibility for programmes (one for each television channel and one for radio), an audiovisual institute, a company responsible for carrying out major production work for the radio and television institutions, and an establishment with general responsibility for broadcasting. Each company has its own budget and an administrative council composed of two representatives of the state, and one representative each of parliament, the press and the staff. This structure was modified under the broadcasting law of July 1982, which aimed to establish the independence of the broadcasting system from any form of political pressure, and a nine-member committee was formed to safeguard the independence of the networks, and to appoint their heads. In 1986 the committee was replaced by a 13-member Commission Nationale de la Communication et des Libertés (CNCL), with the additional responsibilities of allocating concessions for privatized channels, and overseeing the telecommunications and cable television sectors. The CNCL also assumed responsibility for allocating airwaves from Télédiffusion de France (TDF), the state-owned broadcasting agency, which is due to be partly privatized. In December 1986 the CNCL announced a series of new appointments to the chairs of television and radio networks. The state monopoly of broadcasting was ended, now applying only to transmission. A controlled amount of advertising is accepted on all channels. The creation of several specialized companies was envisaged to complement the existing seven.

In 1983 there were an estimated 47m. radio receivers and 20.5m. television receivers in use.

Commission Nationale de la Communication et des Libertés (CNCL): 100 ave Raymond Poincaré, 75016 Paris; tel. (1) 45-01-58-88; telex 614595; f. 1986; supervises all French broadcasting, allocates concessions for privatized channels, distributes cable networks and frequencies, appoints heads of state-owned radio and television companies, oversees telecommunications sectors and other specialized services planned for deregulation, monitors programme standards; consists of 13 members appointed for nine years: two nominated by the Pres. of the Republic; two by the Pres. of the National Assembly; two by the Pres. of the Senate; one mem. of the Conseil d'Etat, elected by the Conseil d'Etat; one magistrat from the Cour de Cassation, elected by the Cour de Cassation; one magistrate from the Cour des Comptes, elected by the Cour des Comptes; one mem. of the Académie Française, elected by the Académie Française; and three specialists in television, telecommunications and journalism, co-opted by the other 10 mems; Pres. GABRIEL DE BROGLIE.

Institut National de la Communication Audiovisuelle: Tour Gamma A, 193–197 rue de Bercy, 75582 Paris Cedex 12; tel. (1) 43-47-64-00; f. 1975; research and professional training in the field of broadcasting; radio and TV archives; Chair. JANINE LANGLOIS-GLANDIER.

Radio Télévision Française d'Outre-Mer (RFO): 5 ave du Recteur Poincaré, 75016 Paris; tel. (1) 45-24-71-00; controls broadcasting in the French overseas territories; Chair. JEAN-CLAUDE MICHAUD; Dir of DOM-TOM CLAUDE LEFÈVRE; Dir of Foreign Affairs ANDRÉ BRIÈRE.

Société France Media International (FMI): 78 ave Raymond Poincare, 75116 Paris; merchandising in France and abroad for all TV programmes except news and sport, co-productions with foreign TV companies: Chair. PHILIPPE ROSSIGNOL; Man. Dir ANDRÉ HARRIS.

Télédiffusion de France (TDF): 21–27 rue Barbès, 92512 Montrouge; tel. (1) 46-57-11-15; telex 25738; f. 1975; responsible for broadcasting programmes produced by the production companies (Radio France, TF1, A2, FR3), for the organization and maintenance of the networks, for study and research into radio and television equipment; administrative council comprising 16 members, of which six are representatives of the State; Pres. XAVIER GOUYOU-BEAUCHAMPS; Man. Dir PASCAL MANCHUEL.

FRANCE

RADIO

Société Nationale de Radiodiffusion (Radio France): 116 ave Président Kennedy, 75786 Paris Cedex 16; tel. (1) 45-24-24-24; telex 200002; f. 1975; production of radio programmes; Chair. and Man. Dir ROLAND FAURE; Dir JEAN IZARD; Dir. France Inter JÉRÔME BELLAY; Information Dir MICHEL MEYER; Dir France Culture JEAN-MARIE BORZEIX; Dir of programmes and musical services ALAIN DUREL; Radio France Internationale HENRI TÉZENAS DU MONTZEL.

Radio France Home Services

France-Inter: Entertains and informs. Broadcasts transmitted for 24 hours a day; they can be received by 98% of the population and by listeners outside France. There are two main programmes, France-Inter and France-Inter Variétés. Other specialized and regional items are also produced. France-Inter is broadcast on long, medium and short waves and France-Inter Variétés is broadcast on medium wave and high fidelity (frequency modulated) transmitters.

France Culture: Serious programme on art, culture and thought; broadcasts can be received by 95% of the population.

France Musique: Transmission on frequency modulation transmitters. Nearly 95% of the programme is devoted to music; there are regular stereophonic transmissions.

Radio Bleue: medium-wave transmission for the elderly.

Radio-Sorbonne: Low-power transmission of educational programmes. Only available in the Paris region.

There are 49 regional and local radio stations, which relay Parisian programmes as well as transmitting their own broadcasts.

Radio France International

Home Service: Broadcasts in France for foreign workers in Arabic, Cambodian, Lao, Portuguese, Serbo-Croat, Spanish, Turkish, Vietnamese (on France-Culture network).

Foreign Service: Broadcasts 24 hours daily to Europe (in French, German, Portuguese, Polish, Romanian and Spanish), Eastern Europe (in French and Russian), Africa/Indian Ocean (in French, English and Portuguese), North America (in French), Latin America (in French, Portuguese and Spanish) and Asia (in French).

Private Radio

A number of radio stations based in countries on France's perimeter have very large French audiences. These include notably RTL (Luxembourg), Europe No. 1 (Saarbrücken), Radio Monte Carlo (Monaco). The French Government has a major shareholding in RTL. The state monopoly of broadcasting was ended in 1982, and in 1986 the French Government sold its controlling stake in Europe No. 1 to Hachette, the largest publishing group in France. By the end of 1983 approximately 800 private radio stations ('radios libres') had been authorized. Advertising on private radio was legalized in September 1984.

TELEVISION

In 1986 there were three state-run channels. On the first channel (now TF1) transmission is on a 819-line system and covers 98.5% of the population. The channel began a gradual conversion to colour broadcasting in 1976. In August 1986 legislation was adopted by the new right-wing Government to privatize TF1, and in October restrictions on the ownership of media outlets were announced, with the aim of preventing a single communications company from owning more than 25% of a national television station. TF1 was expected to be offered for sale by March 1987. The second channel (now A2) is on a 625-line system in colour and 96.5 per cent of the population can receive it. There are 135 transmitting stations and about 3,000 relay stations for the first two channels. The third network (now FR3), introduced in 1973, is on a 625-line system in colour and 70% of the population can receive it. A fourth channel, Canal Plus introduced in November 1984, is on a 625 line system in colour, and was expected to reach 90% of the country by 1987. The channel is to provide subscribers with 20 hours of daily broadcasts, mainly cinema and sport, and is to carry no advertising. A further channel, TV5, consisting of programmes relayed from French, Belgian and Swiss television, began broadcasting by satellite in January 1984. In 1985 two new commercial television networks, La 5 and TV6, were approved by the Government. La 5 was controlled by a group of French and Italian investors, and its transmissions consisted mainly of foreign light entertainment programmes and films. TV6 was owned by French media groups, and offered music and video programmes. Both channels started broadcasting in February 1986, but their contracts were cancelled and opened to new bids in late 1986. Government approval was granted in 1984 for the transmission of France's first breakfast television, and by early 1986 free videotex data screens had been installed in millions of homes. In May 1984 agreement was reached with Luxembourg to finance jointly a communal direct-broadcasting satellite television system (TDF-1). However, the intention of the Compagnie Luxembourgeoise de Télédiffusion (CLT) to operate a channel on TDF-1 was ignored when the French Government decided to grant concessions for two channels to a European consortium. The launch of TDF-1, scheduled for November 1986, was postponed until early 1987, owing to the loss of the Ariane satellite-carrying rocket in June 1986, and a series of technical problems. In late 1986 the new right-wing Government cancelled the European consortium's concessions and offered them to the general market on different financial terms. After two years of controversy, government approval was given in 1984 to plans to develop a cable television network, and in December 1986 Paris Câble started broadcasting to 100 homes in the Parisian suburbs for a six-month trial period. The responsibility for construction of the networks has been opened to private communications companies rather than to the state-owned postal and telecommunications service.

Télé-Luxembourg, Télé-Belge and Télé-Monte-Carlo have large regional audiences in France. German-speaking inhabitants of Alsace watch programmes from the Federal Republic.

Canal Plus: 78 rue Olivier de Serres, 75015 Paris; tel. (1) 45-33-74-74; f. 1984; independent channel, financed by audience subscription and commercial sponsoring of programmes; Pres. ANDRÉ ROUSSELET.

Société Nationale de Télévision—Télévision Française 1 (TF1): 15 rue Cognacq Jay, 75330 Paris Cedex 07; tel. (1) 45-55-35-35; telex 200006; f. 1975; production of programmes on the first TV channel; Chair. and Man. Dir HERVÉ BOURGES; Asst Man. Dirs JEAN LALLIER, MICHEL ASTORG.

Société Nationale de Télévision en Couleur—Antenne 2 (A2): 22 ave Montaigne, 75387 Paris Cedex 08; tel. (1) 42-99-42-42; telex 642313; f. 1975; production of programmes on the second TV channel; Chair. CLAUDE CONTAMINE; Dir JEAN-MARIE CAVADA; Editorial Dir ELIE VANNIER.

Société Nationale de Programmes—France Régions 3 (FR3): 5 ave Recteur Poincaré, 75782 Paris Cedex 16; tel. (1) 45-24-22-22; f. 1975; production of programmes on the third TV channel; responsible for regional and overseas TV; Chair. and Man. Dir RENÉ HAN; Dir-Gen. JACQUES GOUJAT.

La 5: f. 1986; independent channel; 60% owned by French investors, 40% owned by Fininvest, a private Italian TV co; financed by advertising sold by La 5; Dir JERÔME SEYDOUX.

TV5: 21 rue Jean Goujon, 75008 Paris; communal channel for francophone European countries, transmitted by ECS 1 satellite; Chair. PAUL PEYRE.

TV6: f. 1986; independent channel; 25% owned by Films Gaumont, 18% by NRJ private radio station, 25% by Publicus and 12% by Agence Gilbert Gros advertising agencies, and 20% by private shareholders; music; Dir MAURICE LÉVY.

Société Française de Production: 36 rue des Alouettes, 75935 Paris; tel. (1) 42-03-99-04; telex 240888; f. 1975; production of major programmes for cinema and TV; Chair. FRANÇOIS LEMOINE; Dir FRANCIS BRUN-BUISSON.

Finance

(cap. = capital; p.u. = paid up; dep. = deposits; res = reserves; m. = million; Frs = Francs)

BANKING

In 1982 the Socialist Government nationalized 36 banks, bringing 95% of all deposits under state control. These banks are marked * in the following list. Those marked † had previously been nationalized and became wholly nationalized in 1982.

The banking law of July 1984 strengthened government control of local banks. All banks, including foreign-controlled banks, became unified 'credit establishments', supervised by the Association française des établissements de crédit. In July 1986 the right-wing Government adopted a Privatization Law, and produced a plan to denationalize 65 state-owned companies including banks, in the following three years.

Central Bank

Banque de France: 1 rue de la Vrillière, 75001 Paris; tel. (1) 42-92-42-92; telex 220932; f. 1800; cap. and res 304,151.4m. Frs (Dec. 1984); nationalized from 1946; the Governor and two Deputy

FRANCE

Governors are nominated by decree of the President of the Republic; the bank has 234 offices or brs throughout France; Gov. JACQUES DE LAROSIÈRE.

Commercial Banks

Al Saudi Banque: 49/51 ave George V, 75008 Paris; tel. (1) 47-23-00-55; telex 630349; f. 1976; cap. 200m. Frs, dep. 3,852m. Frs (Dec. 1984); Chair. CHAFIC AKHRAS.

American Express Bank (Finance): 12-14 Rond Point des Champs Elysées, 75408 Paris; tel. 42-25-15-16; telex 643177; cap. 91m. Frs; Chair. FRANÇOIS GISCARD D'ESTAING; 4 brs.

Banque Arabe et Internationale d'Investissement (BAII): 12 place Vendôme, 75001 Paris; tel. (1) 42-60-34-01; telex 680330; investment bank; cap. 300m. Frs (Dec. 1985); subsidiary of Baii Holdings, Luxembourg; Chair. and CEO YVES LAMARCHE.

Banque Centrale des Coopératives et des Mutuelles: 12 place de la Bourse, 75002 Paris; tel. (1) 42-33-44-71; telex 211038; f. 1922; cap. 72m. Frs, res 3m. Frs (Dec. 1984); two-thirds of shares are held by 136 co-operative socs; Chair. and Man. Dir MICHEL BAROIN; Dir-Gen. JEAN-MICHEL REFFET; 36 brs.

Banque Commerciale pour l'Europe du Nord (Eurobank): 79-81 blvd Haussmann, 75382 Paris Cedex 08; tel. (1) 42-66-92-80; telex 280200; f. 1921; cap. 720m. Frs, dep. 559m. Frs (Dec. 1984); Chair. and Man. Dir BERNARD DUPUY; Dir-Gen. HENRI ROCHE.

Bank of Credit and Commerce International (Overseas) Ltd: 125 ave des Champs Elysées, 75008 Paris; tel. (1) 47-23-90-19; telex 611710; Dir NAZIZ CHINOY.

Banque Courtois: 33 rue de Rémusat, 31000 Toulouse; tel. 61-29-61-29; telex 531580; f. 1960; cap. 46.3m. Frs, res 26m. Frs, dep. 1,251m. Frs (Dec. 1984); Chair. and Gen. Man. GILBERT COURTOIS DE VIÇOSE.

*__Banque de Bretagne:__ 283 ave du Général Patton, 35040 Rennes Cedex; tel. 99-28-36-44; telex 730094; f. 1909; cap. 65.9m. Frs (1985); Chair. X. HENRY DE VILLENEUVE.

Banque de la Méditerranée-France: 49 ave Hoche, 95008 Paris; tel. (1) 47-66-51-56; telex 648528; cap. 70m. Frs, res 13.5m. Frs, dep. 1,733m. Frs (1984); Chair. and Man. Dir JOSEPH GHOLAM.

Banque de Neuflize, Schlumberger, Mallet: 3 ave Hoche, 75008 Paris; tel. (1) 47-66-61-11; telex 640653; f. 1966 after merger of Neuflize, Schlumberger and Mallet Frères; merged with Banque Jordaan 1980; subsidiary of Algemene Bank Nederland NV; cap. 120m. Frs, dep. 4,846m. Frs, res 291m. Frs (1984); Chair. Supervisory Bd JEAN-PIERRE MALLET; Chair. Man. Bd ANTOINE DUPONT-FAUVILLE.

*__Banque de l'Union Européenne:__ 4 rue Gaillon, 75107 Paris Cedex 02; tel. (1) 42-66-20-30; telex 210942; f. 1920; merged with CIC group April 1984; cap. 400m. Frs, dep. 6,930m. Frs (1985); res 183m. Frs (1984); Chief Exec. Officer JEAN DROMER.

Banque Européenne de Tokyo: 4-8 rue Saint Anne, 75001 Paris; tel. (1) 42-61-58-55; telex 210436; f. 1968; cap. and res 207m. Frs, dep. 3,418m. Frs (Dec. 1985); Pres. and Gen. Man. HIROO SATO.

Banque Fédérative du Crédit Mutuel SA: 34 rue du Wacken, 67002 Strasbourg; tel. 88-35-90-35; telex 890702; f. 1895; cap. 300m. Frs, res 55m. Frs (1985); Chair. Supervisory Board ETIENNE PFIMLIN; Chair. Management Board RAYMOND CROMBECQUE.

Banque Française de l'Agriculture et du Crédit Mutuel: 21 blvd Malesherbes, 75008 Paris; tel. (1) 42-66-31-40; telex 650582, 641040; f. 1933; cap. 60m. Frs, res 9m. Frs, dep. 565m. Frs (1984); Chair. ALAIN ROSTAND.

Banque Française de Crédit Coopératif: 33 rue des Trois Fontanot, 92002 Nanterre Cedex; tel. (1) 47-24-89-00; telex 620496; f. 1969; cap. 30m. Frs, dep. 3,650m. Frs; Chair. Supervisory Board JACQUES MOREAU; Gen. Man. ROBERT DURAND; 34 brs.

Banque Française du Commerce Extérieur: 21 blvd Haussmann, 75009 Paris; tel. (1) 42-47-47-47; telex 660370; f. 1947; cap. 660m. Frs, res 138m. Frs, dep. 19,936m. Frs (1984); Chair. MICHEL FREYCHE; Man. Dir PIERRE ANTONI.

*__Banque Hervet SA:__ 1 place de la Préfecture, 18004 Bourges; 127 ave Charles de Gaulle, 92201 Neuilly-sur-Seine; tel. 47-58-90-00; telex 620433; f. 1830; cap. 142.4m. Frs, res 165m. Frs, dep. 4,284m. Frs (1984); Chair. JEAN BAYARD; Man. Dir JEAN-CHARLES GAUDRION.

*__Banque Indosuez:__ 96 blvd Haussmann, 75008 Paris; tel. (1) 45-61-20-20; telex 650409; f. 1975 by merger between Banque de l'Indochine and Banque de Suez and de l'Union des Mines; cap. 2,100m. Frs, dep. 67,741m. Frs (Dec. 1986); Chair. RENAUD DE LA GÉNIÈRE; Pres. and CEC ANTOINE JEANCOURT-GALIGNANI; 41 brs.

*__Banque Industrielle et Mobilière Privée, SA:__ 22 rue Pasquier, 75383 Paris Cedex 08; tel. (1) 42-66-91-52; telex 640586; f. 1967; cap. 31m. Frs, dep. 1,264m. Frs, res 41m. Frs (1984); Chair. PASCAL GENDREAU.

Directory

Banque Intercontinentale Arabe: 67 ave Franklin Roosevelt, 75008 Paris; tel. (1) 43-59-91-49; telex 660630; f. 1975 by Banque Extérieure d'Algérie and Libyan Arab Foreign Bank; cap. 310m. Frs, res 18m. Frs, dep. 1,438m. Frs (1984); Chair. MOURAD KHELLAF; Vice-Pres. MOHAMED ABDULJAWAD.

Banque Internationale de Commerce, SA: 62 ave Marceau, 75008 Paris; tel. (1) 47-20-57-39; telex 630151; f. 1919; cap. 10m. Frs, res 7m. Frs (1984); Chair. Princess ISABELLE DE BOURBON DE PARME; Vice-Chair. and Man. Dir HUBERT PÉRIN.

Banque Libano-Française (France): 33 rue Monceau, 75008 Paris; tel. (1) 42-59-51-88; telex 640823; f. 1968; cap. 40m. Frs (1983), res 38m. Frs, dep. 3,826m. Frs (1984); Chair. GILLES DOUBRÈRE; Gen. Man. BERNARD DELAVALLÉE.

Banque Louis-Dreyfus: 6 rue Rabelais, 75008 Paris; tel. (1) 43-59-07-59; telex 290063; f. 1905; cap. 240m. Frs (Aug. 1985); dep. 2,023m. Frs (Dec. 1985); Chair. JEAN-CLAUDE SEYS.

†**Banque Nationale de Paris, SA:** 16 blvd des Italiens, 75009 Paris; tel. (1) 42-44-45-46; telex 280605; f. 1966 by merger of the Banque Nationale pour le Commerce et l'Industrie (f. 1932) with the Comptoir National d'Escompte de Paris (f. 1848); cap. 1,633m. Frs, dep. 284,115m. Frs (1984); Chair. and Man. Dir RENÉ THOMAS; Man. Dirs JACQUES MASSON, JACQUES WAHL.

> **Banque pour l'Expansion Industrielle (BANEXI):** 1 blvd Haussmann, 75009 Paris; tel. (1) 42-44-48-95; cap. 270m. Frs (1984); Chair. ALBERT COSTA DE BEAUREGARD.

> **Banque Nationale de Paris Intercontinentale:** Siège Social; 20 blvd des Italiens, 75009 Paris; Direction Générale: 28 rue Drouot, 75009 Paris; tel. (1) 42-44-22-11; telex (Head Office) 641419; f. 1940; cap. 125m. Frs, dep. 10,717m. Frs (1985); Chair. RENÉ THOMAS; Gen. Man. JEAN-CLAUDE CLARAC.

*__Banque Odier Bungener Courvoisier, SA:__ 57 ave d'Iéna, 75116 Paris; tel. (1) 45-01-50-00; telex 630889; f. 1960; subsid. of Crédit Commercial de France 1983; cap. 60m. Frs, dep. 1,269m. Frs, res 53m. Frs (Dec. 1984); Chair. and Man. Dir GABRIEL D'ALLEZ.

Banque Paribas: 3 rue d'Antin, 75002 Paris; tel. (1) 42-98-12-34; telex 210041; f. 1872; cap. 1,000m. Frs, dep. 49,723m. Frs (1984); Chair. MICHEL FRANÇOIS-PONCET; Dirs-Gen. FRANÇOIS MORIN, HUBERT DE SAINT-AMAND.

*__Banque Parisienne de Crédit:__ 56 rue de Châteaudun, 75009 Paris; tel. (1) 42-80-68-68; telex 280179; f. 1920; cap. 52.1m. Frs, res 207m. Frs (Dec. 1984); Chair. GUY CHARTIER; 73 brs.

*__Banque Régionale de l'Ain:__ 2 ave Alsace-Lorraine, 01001 Bourg-en-Bresse; tel. 74-22-82-22; telex 310435; f. 1849; mem. of Crédit Industriel et Commercial Group; cap. 60m. Frs; dep. 2,271m. Frs (1984); Pres. JEAN-NOËL RELIQUET; Dir-Gen. PAUL DEGUERRY.

*__Banque Régionale de l'Ouest:__ 7 rue Gallois, 4003 Blois Cedex; tel. 54-78-96-28; telex 750408; f. 1913; mem. of Crédit Industriel et Commercial Group; cap. 30m. Frs, res 50m. Frs, dep. 3,389m. Frs (1984); Chair. J. DE LA CHAUVINIÈRE; Gen. Man. J. C. CAMUS.

Banque Rivaud: 13 rue Notre Dame des Victoires, 75082 Paris Cedex 02; tel. (1) 42-61-52-43; telex 680231; f. 1906; cap. 90m. Frs, res 24.2m. Frs, dep. 2,140m. Frs (Dec. 1985); Chair. Comte DE RIBES; Gen. Man. B. DE BUFFEVENT.

Banque Scalbert-Dupont: 37 rue du Molinel, 59023 Lille; tel. 20-06-92-52; telex 820650; f. 1838; cap. 71m. Frs, res 182m. Frs, dep. 10,012m. Frs (Dec. 1984); Chair. and Man. Dir CLAUDE LAMOTTE.

Banque Sudameris: 4 rue Meyerbeer, 75429 Paris Cedex 09; tel. (1) 45-23-72-22; telex 641669; formerly Banque Française et Italienne pour l'Amérique du Sud-Sudameris; f. 1910; cap. 395.6m. Frs (1985); Chair. G. RAMBAUD.

Banque Transatlantique, SA: 17 blvd Haussmann, 75428 Paris Cedex 09; tel. (1) 42-47-13-00; telex 650729; f. 1881; cap. 58m. Frs, res 78.1m. Frs (1984); Pres. Dir-Gen. F. DE SIÈGES.

*__Banque Vernes et Commerciale de Paris:__ 52 ave Hoche, 75382 Paris Cedex 08; tel. (1) 47-54-40-40; telex (Foreign Dept) 290322; f. 1971 by merger of Banque Vernes (f. 1821) and Banque Commerciale de Paris (f. 1952); cap. 233m. Frs, dep. 8,076m. Frs (1985); Chair. GILBERT LASFARGUES; Man. Dir CLAUDE BARRET; 30 brs.

*__Banque Worms SA:__ 45 blvd Haussmann, 75427 Paris Cedex 09; tel. (1) 42-66-90-10; telex 210895; f. 1928; cap. 450m. Frs, dep. 14,658m. Frs, res 746m. Frs (Dec. 1984); Chair. JEAN-MICHEL BLOCH-LAINÉ; Gen. Man. J. H. GOUGENHEIM.

Barclays Bank SA: 33 rue du Quatre Septembre, BP 24X 75460 Paris Cedex 10; tel. (1) 42-65-65-65; telex 210015; cap. 400m. Frs, dep. 5,409m. Frs, res 222m. Frs (1984); Chair. PIERRE DE LALANDE; Vice-Pres HENRI LAMBERT, AMBROISE ROUX.

FRANCE   *Directory*

Caisse Centrale des Banques Populaires: 115 rue Montmartre; 75002 Paris; tel. (1) 42-96-15-15; telex 210993; f. 1921; the central banking institution of 37 co-operative regional Banques Populaires; cap. 300m. Frs, dep. 53,400m. Frs (1985); Chair. JEAN MARTINEAU; Gen. Man. PAUL LORIOT.

Caisse Nationale de Crédit Agricole (CNCA): 91–93 blvd Pasteur, 75015 Paris; tel. (1) 43-23-52-02; telex 250971; f. 1920; government-supervised central institution for 94 regional agricultural co-operative banks; densest banking network in France, with 13,700 domestic branch offices; broad range of banking services with special emphasis on agribusiness; international network includes brs in Chicago, Frankfurt, London, New York, Milan, Hong Kong, rep. offices in Madrid, Barcelona, Rio de Janeiro, San Francisco, Beijing, Cairo and Caracas; total assets 929,182m. Frs, cap. and res 38,442m. Frs (1985); Chair. MARCEL DENEUX; CEO and Man. Dir BERNARD AUBERGER.

Compagnie Parisienne de Réescompte, SA: 59–61 rue La Fayette, 75009 Paris; tel. (1) 42-80-62-28; telex 290942 (5 lines); f. 1928; discount bank; cap. 230m. Frs, dep. 70m. Frs, res 222m. Frs (Dec. 1984); Chair. and Gen. Man. RENÉ CASSOU; Joint Gen. Mans. R. GAYOUX and J.-C. MARTINI.

***Crédit Chimique SA:** 20 rue Treilhard, 75008 Paris; tel. (1) 45-61-94-00; telex 650838; f. 1889; cap. 100m. Frs, dep. 5,555m. Frs, res 69m. Frs (1984); Chair. and Man. Dir J. L. JAVAL.

***Crédit Commercial de France (CCF) SA:** 103 ave des Champs Elysées, 75008 Paris; tel. (1) 47-20-92-00; telex 630300; f. 1894; cap. 899m. Frs, res 2,065m. Frs, dep. 47,009m. Frs (1984); Chair. and Chief Exec. Officer G. PALLEZ; 246 brs in France, 13 abroad.

Crédit du Nord: 28 place Rihour, 59000 Lille (reg. office); tel. 20-30-61-61; telex 120342; 6–8 blvd Haussmann, 75009 Paris (administrative headquarters); tel. (1) 42-47-12-34; telex 641379; f. 1974 by merger; cap. 792.6m. Frs, dep. 37.1m. Frs (1985); Chair. BRUNO DE MAULDE.

Crédit Foncier de France, SA: 19 rue des Capucines, 75001 Paris; tel. (1) 42-60-35-30; telex 230079; f. 1852; cap. 304m. Frs, res 473.8m. Frs (Dec. 1981); Gov. GEORGES BONIN; Sec.-Gen. MARCEL GONTARD.

***Crédit Industriel d'Alsace et de Lorraine (CIAL):** 31 rue Jean Wenger-Valentin, 67000 Strasbourg; tel. 88-37-61-23; telex 870015; f. 1919; cap. 143.7m. Frs, dep. 11,432m. Frs, res 486m. Frs (1984); Man. Dir ALAIN WEBER.

***Crédit Industriel de l'Ouest, SA:** 4 rue Voltaire, 44000 Nantes; tel. 40-35-91-91; telex 700590; f. 1957; cap. 82m. Frs, dep. 9,826m. Frs (1984); Chair. BERNARD MADINIER; Man. Dir JEAN-LOUIS RUSTERHOLTZ.

***Crédit Industriel de Normandie:** 15 place de la Pucelle d'Orléans, 76041 Rouen; tel. 35-08-64-00; telex 770950; f. 1932; cap. 33m. Frs, res 33m. Frs, dep. 3,205m. Frs (1984); Chair. and Man. Dir ANDRÉ LECOMTE.

***Crédit Industriel et Commercial de Paris, SA:** 66 rue de la Victoire, 75009 Paris; tel. (1) 42-80-80-80; telex 290692; f. 1859; merged with Banque de l'Union Européenne Feb. 1983; cap. 1,456m. Frs, dep. 30,495m. Frs (1985); Chair. JEAN DROMER; Pres. CHRISTIAN GIACOMOTTO; 114 brs.

†Crédit Lyonnais, SA: Central Office: 19 blvd des Italiens, 75002 Paris; tel. (1) 42-95-70-00; telex 612400; Head Office: 18 rue de la République, 69002 Lyon; f. 1863; cap. 1,344m. Frs, dep. 258,272m. Frs (1984); Chair. J. M. LEVÊQUE; Man. Dir BERNARD THIOLON; 1,854 brs.

***L'Européenne de Banque:** 21 rue Lafitte, 75428 Paris Cedex 08; tel. (1) 42-47-82-47; telex 280952; f. 1817 as Rothschild Frères; became Banque Rothschild 1968; present name adopted 1982; affiliated to Crédit Commercial de France 1984; cap. 209m. Frs, res 149m. Frs, dep. 4,400m. Frs (Dec. 1984); Chair. and Man. Dir ROGER PRAIN.

Frab-Bank International (French Arab Bank for International Investment): 90 ave des Champs Elysées, 75008 Paris; tel. (1) 43-59-99-49; telex 642528; cap. 150m. Frs; Chair. NEVILLE MILLS; Gen. Man. M. T. M. GÉDEON.

Grindlays Bank SA: 96 ave Raymond Poincaré, 75016 Paris Cedex 09; tel. (1) 45-01-51-61; telex 614193; f. 1969 as Banque Ottomane (France) SA, renamed Banque Grindlay Ottomane 1971–79; cap. 60m. Frs, res 7m. Frs, dep. 15,495m. Frs (Dec. 1984); 9 brs in France, 2 in Monaco; Chair. HUBERT MARTIN; Man. Dir P. A. CARPENTER.

Midland Bank France SA: 6 rue Piccini, 75016 Paris; tel. (1) 45-02-80-80; telex 658022; f. 1978; cap. 302m. Frs, res 159m. Frs, dep. 3,206m. Frs (Dec. 1984); Chair. LEON BRESSLER.

Société Bancaire de Paris: 24 rue Murillo, 75008 Paris; tel. (1) 47-66-02-00; telex 643296; Chair. M. C. ESPIRITO SANTO SILVA; Man. Dir M. LAFFINEUR.

***Société Bordelaise de Credit Industriel et Commercial, SA:** 42 cours du Chapeau Rouge, 33001 Bordeaux; tel. 56-48-52-90; telex (Foreign Dept) 550850; f. 1880; cap. 127m. Frs, dep. 3,104m. Frs, res 3m. Frs (1984); Chair. and Man. Dir LOUIS PIERRE BLANC.

***Société Centrale de Banque:** 5 blvd de la Madeleine, 75001 Paris; tel. (1) 42-61-51-30; telex 680014; f. 1880; cap. 168.7m. Frs, res 12.7m. Frs, dep. 7,422.2m. Frs (Dec. 1985); Chair. YANN GAILLARD; Gen. Man. PIERRE PICHOT.

Société de Banque Occidentale (SDBO): 8 rue de la Rochefoucauld, 75009 Paris; tel. (1) 42-81-91-61; telex 650159; f. 1969 as Banque Occidentale pour l'Industrie et le Commerce SA; merged with Société de Banque et de Crédit (f. 1907) Nov. 1981, when present name was adopted; wholly-owned subsidiary of Crédit Lyonnais; cap. 260m. Frs (Dec. 1984), res. 129.9m. Frs, dep. 5,412.4m. Frs (Dec. 1985); Chair. MICHEL GALLOT; Gen. Man. PIERRE DESPESSAILLES; 5 brs.

†Société Générale, SA: 29 blvd Haussmann, 75009 Paris; tel. (1) 42-98-20-00; telex 290842; f. 1864; cap. 1,250m. Frs, dep. 229,892m. Frs (1984); Chair. MARC VIÉNOT; Gen. Man. J. P. DELACOUR; 2,600 brs.

***Société Générale Alsacienne de Banque:** 8 rue du Dôme, 67000 Strasbourg; tel. 88-32-99-27; telex 870720; f. 1881; cap. 216.3m. Frs, dep. 19,626m. Frs (1984); Chair. and Man. Dir RENÉ GERONIMUS.

***Société Lyonnaise de Banque SA:** 8 rue de la République, 69001 Lyon; tel. 78-92-02-12; telex 330532; f. 1865; cap. 206m. Frs, dep. 17,154m. Frs, res 232m. Frs (Dec. 1984); Chair. and Man. Dir JEAN CARRIÈRE.

***Société Marseillaise de Crédit, SA:** 75 rue Paradis, 13006 Marseille; tel. 91-54-91-12; telex 430232; f. 1865; cap. 100m. Frs, dep. 9,076m. Frs (1984); Chair. JEAN-PAUL ESCANDE.

***Société Nancéienne Varin-Bernier:** 4 place André Maginot, Nancy; tel. 83-37-65-45; telex 960205; f. 1881; cap. 115m. Frs, dep. 10,834m. Frs; Pres. BERNARD YONCOURT; Gen. Man. HENRI DESFORGES.

Standard Chartered Bank: BP 43, 4 rue Ventadour, 75001 Paris; tel. (1) 42-60-35-50; telex 670638; 2 brs.

***Union de Banques à Paris:** 22 place de la Madeleine, 75381 Paris; tel. (1) 42-68-33-33; telex 640664; f. 1935; cap. 86m. Frs, dep. 3,000m. Frs, res. 131m. Frs. (Dec. 1984); Chair. and Man. Dir ROGER PUJOL; 53 brs.

Union de Banques Arabes et Françaises (UBAF): 190 ave Charles de Gaulle, 92523 Neuilly Cedex; tel. (1) 47-38-01-01; telex 610334; f. 1970; cap. 250m. Frs, res 152m. Frs (1984); Chair. MOHAMED ABUSHADI; Vice-Chair. BERNARD THIOLON.

Union Française de Banques: 5 ave Kléber, 75791 Paris Cedex 16; tel. (1) 45-71-60-60; telex 200015; f. 1950; cap. 428m. Frs, res 253m. Frs, dep. 346m. Frs (Dec. 1984); Chair. and Gen. Man. J. M. BOSSUAT.

Supervisory Body

Association Française des Etablissements de Crédit: 36 rue Taitbout, 75009 Paris; tel. (1) 48-24-34-34; f. 1983; advises government on monetary and credit policy and supervises the banking system; Pres. JEAN DROMER; Gen. Man. ROBERT PELLETIER.

Banking Association

Association Française des Banques: 18 rue La Fayette, 75009 Paris; tel. (1) 42-46-92-59; telex 660282; f. 1941; 384 mems; Chair. DOMINIQUE CHATILLON; Delegate-Gen. JEAN-JACQUES BURGARD.

STOCK EXCHANGES

La Bourse de Paris: Palais de la Bourse, 4 place de la Bourse, 75080 Paris Cedex 02; tel. (1) 40-26-85-90; f. 1808; run by:

Compagnie des Agents de Change: Chambre Syndicale des Agents de Change, 4 place de la Bourse, 75080 Paris Cedex 02; tel. (1) 42-61-85-90; telex 230844; undertakes the organization and management of French stock exchanges; 102 mems; Chair. XAVIER DUPONT.

There are also provincial exchanges in Bordeaux, Lille, Lyon, Marseille, Nancy and Nantes.

Stock Exchange Association

Commission des Opérations de Bourse: Tour Mirabeau 39–43 quai André Citroën, 75739 Paris Cedex 15; tel. (1) 45-78-33-33; telex 205238; f. 1967; 90 mems; Chair. YVES LE PORTZ; mems JEAN

FRANCE

JONQUÈRES, XAVIER DUPONT, PIERRE BALLEY; Govt Commr PHILIPPE JAFFRE; Alternates ROBERT LÉON, JEAN-CHRISTIAN METZ; Sec.-Gen. GÉRARD DE LA MARTINIÈRE.

INSURANCE

A list is given below of some of the more important insurance companies:

L'Alsacienne: 1 chemin du Wacken, 67000 Strasbourg; f. 1820; Chair. ROBERT MATT (Leader of Groupe des Mutuelles Alsaciennes, composed of: L'Alsacienne, La Cité, Cuspide, Condor, Economic, La Cité Européenne, Le Comptoir).

Assurances Abeille-Paix (Groupe Victoire): 52 rue de la Victoire, 75009 Paris; tel. (1) 42-80-75-75; cap. 283.4m. Frs; Chair. PHILIPPE CHAREYRE; Gen. Mans YVES LESSARD, MICHEL MARCHAL.

Assurances du Groupe de Paris (La Paternelle RD, La Paternelle Vie, Prévoyance Mutuelle MACL): AGP, 21 rue de Châteaudun, 75009 Paris; tel. (1) 42-82-82-12; telex 280-638; Chair. BERNARD PAGEZY; Man. Dir ETIENNE BENEZECH.

Assurances Mutuelles de France: 7 ave Marcel Proust, 28032 Chartres; tel. 37-28-82-28; telex 760511; f. 1819; Chair. CHRISTIAN SASTRE.

Caisse Industrielle d'Assurance Mutuelle (CIAM): 7 rue de Madrid, 75383 Paris Cedex 08; Chair. MICHEL LEOHET; Gen. Man. HENRI DORON.

La Concorde: 5 rue de Londres, 75456 Paris Cedex 09; tel. (1) 42-80-66-00; telex 650734; f. 1905; Chair. ANDRÉ ROSA; Gen. Man. RENÉ PERILLIER.

France Incendie, Accidents et Risques Divers: 7–9 blvd Haussmann, 75439 Paris Cedex 09; f. 1837; Gen. Man. GEORGES SOLEILHAVOUP.

Garantie Mutuelle des Fonctionnaires: 76 rue de Prony, 75857 Paris Cedex 17; tel. (1) 47-66-52-24; telex 640377; f. 1934; Chair. and Man. Dir (vacant).

Groupe des Assurances Générales de France: 87 rue de Richelieu, 75060 Paris Cedex 02; tel. (1) 42-44-04-44; telex 210697; f. 1968 by merger of Assurances Générales and Phénix, both f. 1819; insurance and reinsurance; cap. 407m. Frs; Chair. and Man. Dir MICHEL ALBERT; Gen. Man. ROGER PAPAZ.

Groupe des Assurances Nationales (GAN): 2 rue Pillet Will, 75448 Paris Cedex 09; tel. (1) 42-47-50-00; telex 280006; f. 1820 (fire), 1830 (life), 1865 (accident), reorganized 1968; Chair. FRANÇOIS HEILBRONNER; Chief Exec. JACQUES BONNAUD.

Groupement Français d'Assurances (GFA): 38 rue de Châteaudun, 75009 Paris; Chair. and Man. Dir G. MASSOUD.

Mutuelle Centrale d'Assurances (MCA): 65 rue de Monceau, 75008 Paris; Gen. Man. A. JANNIN.

La Mutuelle du Mans: 37 rue Chanzy, 72000 Le Mans; tel. 43-84-96-25; telex 720664; f. 1828 (fire); Chair. and Man. Dir J. PERROUD.

Mutuelle Générale Française, Groupe des Sociétés: 19–21 rue Chanzy, 72030 Le Mans Cedex; tel. 43-84-96-40; telex 720764; life and general insurance; f. 1883; Chair. JEAN CLAUDE JOLLAIN; Gen. Man. MICHEL COSSON.

Mutuelles Unies: 3037x, 76029 Rouen Cedex, and 10 rue de Londres, 75440 Paris Cedex 09; tel. 35-80-40-40 (Rouen), (1) 42-80-62-19 (Paris); telex 180559 (Rouen), 640584 (Paris); f. 1817; comprises Mutuelles Unies IARD, Mutuelles Unies-Vie, La Mutualité Générale Risques Divers; Chair. and Gen. Man. C. BEBEAR.

P.F.A.: 92076 Paris la Défense Cedex 43; tel. (1) 42-91-10-10; telex 615030; Chair. GUY VERDEIL; Gen. Man. GÉRARD BOUCHER.

Présence: 30 rue Laffitte, 75439 Paris Cedex 09; tel. (1) 42-82-14-40; f. 1986 from merger between Présence-Vie, La Providence IARD and Le Secours; Chair. VICTOR ROSSET.

La Réunion Française: 7 rue de la Bourse, 75002 Paris; tel. (1) 48-24-03-04; telex 648083; f. 1899; insurance and reinsurance; Chair. ALAIN DU COUËDIC; Gen. Man. FRANÇOIS DROUAULT.

Rhin et Moselle-Assurances Françaises: 1 rue des Arquebusiers, 67002 Strasbourg Cedex; tel. 88-25-31-31; telex 890332; f. 1881; comprises Compagnie Générale d'Assurances et de Réassurances (cap. 120m. Frs), Compagnie d'Assurances sur la Vie (cap. 60m. Frs); Chair. and Man. Dir MICHEL LEONET.

Société Anonyme Française de Réassurances: 34–36 blvd de Courcelles, 75849 Paris Cedex 17; tel. (1) 42-67-50-00; telex 650493; reinsurance; Chair. and Gen. Man. J. BOURTHOUMIEUX.

Société Commerciale de Réassurance (SCOR): Immeuble SCOR, 92074 Paris la Défense Cedex 39; tel. (1) 42-91-04-32; telex 614151; f. 1969; Chair. PATRICK PEUGEOT; Gen. Man. FRANÇOIS NEGRIER.

Société de Réassurance des Assurances Mutuelles Agricoles (SOREMA): 20 rue Washington, 75008 Paris; tel. (1) 45-61-99-50; telex 640774; f. 1978; reinsurance; Chair. and Man. Dir L. BORDEAUX MONTRIEUX.

UAP Réassurances: 372 rue Saint Honoré, 75001 Paris; tel. (1) 42-61-50-77; telex 210141; f. 1919; reinsurance; Chair. and Man. Dir ROBERT POUPART-LAFARGE; Man. Dir GÉRARD FRANÇOIS.

L'Union des Assurances de Paris: Tour Assur, Cedex 14, 92083 Paris La Défense; includes L'UAP-Vie, L'UAP-Incendie-Accidents and L'UAP-Capitalisation; Chair. YVETTE CHASSAGNE.

Via Assurances IARD Nord et Monde: 52 rue Laffitte, 75439 Paris Cedex 09; Chair. EMMANUEL GAUTIER; Man. Dir JACQUES LEFÈVRE.

Insurance Associations

Fédération Française des Sociétés d'Assurances: 26 blvd Haussmann, 75009 Paris; tel. (1) 42-47-90-00; telex 640477; f. 1925; Chair. JACQUES LALLEMENT.

Fédération Nationale des Syndicats d'Agents Généraux d'Assurances de France: 104 rue Jouffroy, 75017 Paris; tel. (1) 47-66-04-25; Chair. ANDRÉ MIGEO.

Syndicat français des Assureurs-Conseils: 14 rue de la Grange Batelière, 75009 Paris; tel. (1) 45-23-25-26; Chair. GILBERT BAYOU.

Syndicat National des Courtiers d'Assurances et de Réassurances: 31 rue d'Amsterdam, 75008 Paris; tel. (1) 48-74-19-12; f. 1896; produces monthly bulletin; Chair. PATRICK LUCAS; c. 900 mems.

Trade and Industry

CHAMBERS OF COMMERCE

There are Chambers of Commerce in all the larger towns for all the more important commodities produced or manufactured.

Chambre de Commerce et d'Industrie de Paris: 27 ave de Friedland, 75382 Paris Cedex 08; tel. (1) 45-61-99-00; f. 1803; Chair. PHILIPPE CLEMENT; Man. Dir FRANÇOIS ESSIG.

DEVELOPMENT ORGANIZATION

Institut de Développement Industriel (IDI): 4 rue Ancelle, 92203 Neuilly-sur-Seine: tel. (1) 47-58-14-11; telex 630006; f. 1970 as a state agency assisting small and medium-sized businesses by taking equity shares in enterprises and offering advisory services; Chair. CLAUDE MANDIL.

TRADE COUNCIL

Conseil National du Commerce: 53 ave Montaigne, 75008 Paris; tel. (1) 42-25-01-25; Chair. J. DERMAGNE.

EMPLOYERS' ORGANIZATION

Conseil National du Patronat français (CNPF): 31 ave Pierre Ier de Serbie, 75016 Paris; f. 1946; an employers' organization grouping some 900,000 industrial, trading and banking concerns; Chair. FRANÇOIS PÉRIGOT; Vice-Pres. LOUIS-CHARLES BARY.

INDUSTRIAL AND TRADE ASSOCIATION

Syndicat Général du Commerce et de l'Industrie—Union des Chambres Syndicales de France: 163 rue Saint Honoré, 75001 Paris; tel. (1) 42-60-66-83; Chair. G. NONCLERCQ.

INDUSTRIAL ORGANIZATIONS

Assemblée Permanente des Chambres d'Agriculture (APCA): 9 ave George V, 75008 Paris; tel. (1) 47-23-55-40; telex 280720; f. 1929; Chair. LOUIS PERRIN; Gen. Sec. PIERRE CORMORECHE.

Association Nationale des Industries Agro-alimentaires (ANIA): 52 rue Faubourg Saint Honoré, 75008 Paris; tel. (1) 42-26-40-14; f. 1971; food and agricultural produce; Chair. FRANCIS LEPATRE; 47 affiliated federations.

Centre de Liaisons Intersyndicales des Industries et des Commerces de la Quincaillerie: 91 rue du Miromesnil, 75008 Paris; tel. (1) 45-61-99-44; telex 650680; f. 1913; hardware; Chair. MM. BLANC; Pres. OLIVIER BLONDET; Sec.-Gen. M. PASSEBOSC; mems 14 syndicates.

FRANCE

Centre des Jeunes Dirigeants d'Entreprise (CJD): 19 ave Georges V, 75008 Paris; tel. (1) 47-23-43-43; telex 642541; junior management; Chair. GUY JEANJEAN; Sec.-Gen. PHILIPPE GUILHAUME; 3,000 mems.

Chambre Syndicale de la Sidérurgie Française: 5 bis rue de Madrid, 75379 Paris Cedex 08; tel. (1) 45-22-83-00; telex 650392; f. 1945; steel-making; Chair. MICHEL COLLAS; Delegate-Gen. YVES PIERRE SOULÉ.

Chambre Syndicale de l'Ameublement, Négoce de Paris et de l'Ile de France: 15 rue de la Cerisaie, 75004 Paris; tel. (1) 42-72-13-79; f. 1860; furnishing; Chair. GEORGES GIDOIN; Sec.-Gen. PAUL MENANTAUD; 407 mems.

Chambre Syndicale de l'Amiante: 10 rue de la Pépinière, 75008 Paris; tel. (1) 45-22-12-34; f. 1898; asbestos; Chair. CYRIL X. LATTY; 17 mems.

Chambre Syndicale des Céramistes et Ateliers d'Art: 62 rue d'Hauteville, 75010 Paris; tel. (1) 47-70-95-83; telex 660005; f. 1937; ceramics and arts; Chair. M. BLIN; 1,200 mems.

Chambre Syndicale des Constructeurs d'Automobiles: 2 rue de Presbourg, 75008 Paris; tel. (1) 47-23-54-05; telex 610-446; f. 1909; motor manufacturing; Chair. RAYMOND RAVENEL; 10 mems.

Chambre Syndicale des Constructeurs de Navires: 47 rue de Monceau, 75008 Paris; tel. (1) 45-61-99-11; telex 280756; shipbuilding; Chair. GILBERT FOURNIER; Vice-Chair. JACQUES DOLLOIS; Gen. Man. DOMINIQUE DE MAS LATRIE.

Chambre Syndicale des Industries Minières: 30 ave de Messine, 75008 Paris; tel. (1) 45-63-02-66; f. 1974; mining industry; Chair. J. AUDIBERT; Sec.-Gen. G. JOURDAN; 40 mems.

Comité Central de la Laine et des Fibres Associées (Groupement Général de l'Industrie et du Commerce Lainiers Français): 12 rue d'Anjou, 75008 Paris; tel. (1) 42-66-11-11; telex 212591; f. 1922; manufacture of wool and associated textiles; Chair. JEAN ARPENTINIER; Vice-Chair. ROBERT SERRES; 530 mems.

Comité Central des Armateurs de France: 73 blvd Haussmann, 75008 Paris; tel. (1) 43-65-36-04; telex 660532; f. 1903; shipping; Pres. PHILIPPE POIRIER D'ANGÉ D'ORSAY; Delegate-Gen. PATRICK GAUTRAT; 120 mems.

Confédération des Commerçants-Détaillants de France et d'Outre-Mer: 21 rue du Château d'Eau, 75010 Paris; tel. (1) 42-08-17-15; retailers; Chair. M. FOUCAULT.

Confédération des Industries Céramiques de France: 44 rue Copernic, 75116 Paris; tel. (1) 45-00-18-56; telex 611913; f. 1937; ceramic industry; Chair. JACQUES ARDOUIN; Man. Dir ROBERT BOUCHET; 300 mems, 12 affiliates.

Confédération Générale des Petites et Moyennes Entreprises: 1 ave du Général de Gaulle, Terrasse Bellini, 92806 Puteaux Cedex; tel. (1) 47-78-16-38; telex 630358; f. 1945; small and medium-sized enterprises; Chair. RENÉ BERNASCONI; 3,000 affiliated asscns.

Fédération des Chambres Syndicales de l'Industrie du Verre: 3 rue de la Boétie, 75008 Paris; tel. (1) 42-65-60-02; f. 1874; glass industry; Chair. PIERRE BREITENSTEIN.

Fédération des Chambres Syndicales des Minerais et Métaux non-Ferreux: 30 ave de Messine, 75008 Paris; tel. (1) 45-63-02-66; f. 1945; minerals and non-ferrous metals; Chair. JEAN PIERRE GERIN; Delegate-Gen. G. JOURDAN; 14 affiliated syndicates.

Fédération des Exportateurs des Vins et Spiritueux de France: 13 rue d'Aguesseau, 75008 Paris; tel. (1) 42-66-37-20; telex 643941; f. 1921; exporters of wines and spirits; Pres. LOUIS LATOUR; Delegate-Gen. LOUIS RÉGIS AFFRE; 450 mems.

Fédération des Industries Electriques et Electroniques (FIEE): 11 rue Hamelin, 75783 Paris Cedex 16; tel. (1) 45-05-14-27; telex 611045; f. 1925; electrical and electronics industries; Chair. A. MERCIER; Delegate-Gen. PAUL ROGER SALLEBERT; c. 1,000 mems.

Fédération des Industries Mécaniques et Transformatrices des Métaux: BP 3515, 11 ave Hoche, 75382 Paris Cedex 08; tel. (1) 45-63-02-00; telex 280900; f. 1840; mechanical and metal-working; Chair. ROLAND KOCH; Man. Dir G. IMBERT; Secs.-Gen. M. GONDRAN, M. CLAIRE, M. BAY.

Fédération des Industries Nautiques: Port de la Bourdonnais, 75007 Paris; tel. (1) 45-55-10-49; telex 203963; Chair. MICHEL RICHARD.

Fédération Française de la Bijouterie, Joaillerie, Orfèvrerie du Cadeau, Diamants, Pierres et Perles et Activités qui s'y rattachent (BJOC): 58 rue du Louvre, 75002 Paris; tel. (1) 42-33-61-33; telex 214351; jewellery and precious stones; Chair. M. ARTHUS-BERTRAND; 1,500 mems.

Directory

Fédération Française de la Tannerie-Mégisserie: 122 rue de Provence, 75008 Paris; tel. (1) 45-22-96-45; f. 1885; leather industry; Pres. BERNARD SOL; 350 mems.

Fédération Française de l'Imprimerie et des Industries graphiques (FFIIG): 115 blvd Saint Germain, 75006 Paris; tel. (1) 46-34-21-15; printing; Co-Chairs: MM. DE CLERCK, HUAN, NOULET, PIC, PRETRE.

Fédération Française du Commerce du Bois: 8 rue du Colonel Moll, 75017 Paris; tel. (1) 42-67-64-75; telex 640438; timber trade; Chair. GÉRARD LEMAIGNEN; Man. Dir DENIS SPIRE; Delegate-Gen. L. THOMAS D'ANNEBAULT.

Fédération Nationale de la Musique: 57 ave de Villiers, 75017 Paris; tel. (1) 42-67-05-50; f. 1946; includes Chambre Syndicale de la Facture Instrumentale, Syndicat National de l'Edition Phonographique and other groups; musical instruments and recordings; Chair. LUCIEN ADES; Sec.-Gen. PIERRE CHESNAIS.

Fédération Nationale de l'Industrie Hôtelière (FNIH): 22 rue d'Anjou, 75383 Paris Cedex 08; tel. (1) 42-65-04-61; telex 640033; Chair. J. BLAT.

Fédération Nationale des Entreprises à Commerces Multiples: 11 rue Saint Florentin, 75008 Paris; tel. (1) 42-60-36-02; f. 1937; Chair. M. LANIER; Vice-Chair. JACQUES DU CLOSEL.

Fédération Nationale des Industries Électrométallurgiques, Électrochimiques et Connexes: 33 rue de Lisbonne, 75008 Paris; tel. (1) 45-61-06-63; telex 641446; Chair. ANDRÉ LEGENDRE.

Fédération Nationale du Bâtiment: 33 ave Kléber, 75784 Paris Cedex 16; tel. (1) 47-20-10-20; f. 1906; building trade; Chair. JACQUES BRUNIER; Dir-Gen. CHRISTIAN MAURETTE; 55,000 mems.

Fédération Nationale du Bois: 1 place André Malraux, 75001 Paris; tel. (1) 42-60-30-27; telex 215409; timber and wood products; Chair. J. NANTY; Dir JEAN FAHYS; 4,000 mems.

Groupement des Industries Françaises Aéronautiques et Spatiales: 4 rue Galilée, 75782 Paris Cedex 16; tel. (1) 47-23-55-56; aerospace industry; Pres. JACQUES BENICHOU; Chair. J. MITTERRAND.

Syndicat Général de l'Industrie Cotonnière Française: 3 ave Ruysdaël, 75008 Paris; tel. (1) 42-67-97-23; telex 640324; f. 1902; cotton manufacturing; Chair. JEAN-FRANÇOIS VIRLET; Vice-Chair. DENIS CHAIGNE; mems 80 (spinning), 191 (weaving).

Syndicat Général des Cuirs et Peaux Bruts: Bourse de Commerce, 2 rue de Viarmes, 75040 Paris Cedex 01; tel. (1) 45-08-08-54; f. 1977; untreated leather and hides; Chair. PIERRE DUBOIS; 60 mems.

Syndicat Général des Fabricants de Papiers, Cartons et Celluloses de France: 154 blvd Haussmann, 75008 Paris; tel. (1) 45-62-87-07; telex 290544; f. 1864; paper, cardboard and cellulose; Chair. PAUL BRETON; Gen. Man. JEAN-FRANÇOIS HEMON-LAURENS; 133 firms affiliated.

Syndicat Général des Fabricants d'Huile et de Tourteaux de France: 10 rue de la Paix, 75002 Paris; tel. (1) 42-61-57-21; f. 1928; edible oils; Pres. PIERRE RINGENBACH; Sec.-Gen. J. C. BARSACQ.

Syndicat Général des Fondeurs de France et Industries connexes: 2 rue Bassano, 75783 Paris Cedex 16; tel. (1) 47-23-55-50; telex 620617; f. 1897; metal smelting; Chair. AUDRÉ DOAT; Delegate-Gen. GÉRARD CORNET; 500 mems.

Syndicat National de l'Industrie Pharmaceutique (CSNIP): 88 rue de la Faisanderie, 75782 Paris Cedex 16; tel. (1) 45-03-21-01; telex 612828; pharmaceuticals; Chair. M. HUBERT-LOUIS.

Union des Armateurs à la Pêche de France: 59 rue des Mathurins, 75008 Paris; tel. (1) 42-66-32-60; telex 660143; f. 1945; fishing-vessels; Chair. FERNAND LEBURGNE; Delegate-Gen. A. PARRES; Sec.-Gen. P. SOISSON.

Union des Chambres Syndicales de l'Industrie du Pétrole: 16 ave Kléber, 75116 Paris; tel. (1) 45-02-11-20; telex 630545; petroleum industry; Chair. JEAN-LOUIS BREUVIL-JARRIGE.

Union des Fabricants de Porcelaine de Limoges: 7 rue du Général Cérez, Limoges; tel. 55-77-29-18; porcelain manufacturing; Chair. ANDRÉ RAYNAUD; Sec.-Gen. MARIE-THÉRÈSE PASQUET.

Union des Industries Chimiques: 64 ave Marceau, 75008 Paris; tel. (1) 47-20-56-03; telex 630611; f. 1860; chemical industry; Chair. J.-C. ACHILLE; Dir-Gen. M. C. MARTIN; 63 affiliated unions.

Union des Industries Métallurgiques et Minières: 56 ave de Wagram, 75017 Paris; tel. (1) 47-66-51-15; metallurgy and mining; Chair. JEAN CLAUDE; Vice-Pres. PIERRE GUILLEN.

FRANCE

Union des Industries Textiles (Production): 10 rue d'Anjou, 75008 Paris; tel. (1) 42-66-11-11; telex 640969; f. 1901; Chair. Louis-Charles Barry; 3,000 mems.

TRADE UNIONS

There are three major trade union organizations:

Confédération Générale du Travail (CGT): Complexe Immobilier Intersyndical CGT, 263 rue de Paris, 93516 Montreuil Cedex; tel. (1) 48-51-80-00; telex 214182; f. 1895; a founder member of the World Federation of Trade Unions since 1945; National Congress is held every three years; Sec.-Gen. Henri Krasucki; approx. 1.6m. mems.

Affiliated unions:

Agroalimentaire et Forestière (FNAF): 263 rue de Paris, 93100 Montreuil Cedex; Sec.-Gen. Freddy Huck.

Bois (Woodworkers): 171/3 ave Jean Jaurès, 75940 Paris Cedex 10; Sec.-Gen. Georges Lhericel.

Cheminots (Railway Workers): 263 rue de Paris, 93100 Montreuil Cedex; Sec.-Gen. Georges Lanoue.

Construction (Building): 263 rue de Paris, 93100 Montreuil Cedex; Sec.-Gen. Robert Brun.

Eclairage (Lighting): 16 rue de Candale, 93057 Pantin Cedex; Sec.-Gen. François Duteil.

Education, Recherche et Culture: 263 rue de Paris, 93100 Montreuil Cedex; Sec.-Gen. Joël Hedde.

Employés: 263 rue de Paris, 93100 Montreuil Cedex; Sec.-Gen. Pierre Blanchard.

Energie Atomique: Bâtiment 38, Centre d'Etudes Nucléaires de Saclay, 91191 Gif-sur-Yvette Cedex; Sec.-Gen. J. Trelin.

Enseignements Techniques et Professionnels (Technical and Professional Teachers): 12 promenée Venise Gosnat, 94200 Ivry-sur-Seine; tel. (1) 46-70-01-59; Sec.-Gen. Michèle Baracat.

Equipements (Outfitters): 263 rue de Paris, Case 543, 93515 Montreuil Cedex; tel. (1) 48-51-82-81; Sec.-Gen. Jean-Claude Boual.

Finances: 263 rue de Paris, 93100 Montreuil Cedex; Sec.-Gen. Jean-Christophe le Duigou.

Fonctionnaires (Civil Servants): Bourse Nationale du Travail, 263 rue de Paris, 93515 Montreuil Cedex; tel. (1) 48-51-82-31; telex 218912; groups National Education, Finance, Technical and Administrative, Civil Servants, Police, etc.; mems about 70 national unions covered by six federations; Sec.-Gen. Thérèse Hirszberg.

Industries Chimiques (Chemical Industries): 263 rue de Paris, 93100 Montreuil Cedex; Sec.-Gen. Jean Vincent.

Industries du Livre du Papier et de la Communication (FILPAC) (Printing and Paper Products): Case 426, 263 rue de Paris, 93514 Montreuil Cedex; tel. (1) 48-51-80-45; Sec.-Gen. Jacques Piot.

Ingénieurs, Cadres et Techniciens (Engineers, Managerial Staff and Technicians): 263 rue de Paris, 93100 Montreuil Cedex; Sec.-Gen. Alain Obadia.

Journalistes: 50 rue Edouard Pailleron, 75019 Paris; tel. (1) 42-09-23-00; Sec.-Gen. Gérard Gatinot.

Marine Marchande (Merchant Marine): Case 420, 263 rue de Paris, 93514 Montreuil Cedex; three federations.

Métaux (Metal): 263 rue de Paris, 93100 Montreuil Cedex; Sec.-Gen. André Sainjon.

Personnels du Commerce, de la Distribution et des Services: Case 425, 263 rue de Paris, 93514 Montreuil Cedex; tel. (1) 48-51-83-11; Sec.-Gen. Michelle Commergnat.

Police: 26 rue Saint Félicité, 75015 Paris; Sec.-Gen. Claude Toulouse.

Ports et Docks: 263 rue de Paris, 93100 Montreuil Cedex; Sec.-Gen. Gérard Leclercq.

Postes et Télécommunications: 263 rue de Paris, 93100 Montreuil Cedex; Sec.-Gen. Albert Leguern.

Santé (Health): 263 rue de Paris, 93100 Montreuil Cedex; Sec.-Gen. Bernard Desormière.

Services Publics (Community Services): 263 rue de Paris, 93100 Montreuil Cedex; Sec.-Gen. Alain Pouchol.

Sous-sol (Miners): Case 535, 263 rue de Paris, 93515 Montreuil Cedex; Sec.-Gen. Augustin Dufresne.

Spectacle, Audio-Visuel et Action Culturelle (Theatre, Media and Culture): 14-16 rue des Lilas, 75017 Paris; tel. (1) 46-07-62-22; Sec.-Gen. Claude Quemy.

Directory

Syndicats Maritimes (Seamen): Case 420, 263 rue de Paris, 93514 Montreuil Cedex; tel. (1) 48-51-84-21; Sec.-Gen. F. Lagain.

Tabac et Allumettes (Tobacco and Matches): 263 rue de Paris, 93100 Montreuil Cedex; Sec.-Gen. Bertrand Page.

THC (Textiles): 263 rue de Paris, 93100 Montreuil Cedex; Sec.-Gen. Christian Larose.

Transports: 263 rue de Paris, 93100 Montreuil Cedex; Sec.-Gen. Sylvie Salmon Tharreau; 50,000 mems.

Travailleurs de l'Etat (State Employees): 263 rue de Paris, 93100 Montreuil Cedex; Sec.-Gen. Henri Berry.

Verre et Céramique (Glassworkers and Ceramics): Case 417, 263 rue de Paris, 93514 Montreuil Cedex; Dir-Gen. Jacques Beauvoir.

Voyageurs-Représentants, Cadres et Techniciens de la Vente (Commercial Travellers): 263 rue de Paris, 93100 Montreuil Cedex; tel. (1) 42-72-96-99; Sec.-Gen. Alain Serre.

Force Ouvrière: 198 ave du Maine, 75680 Paris Cedex 14; tel. (1) 45-39-22-03; telex 203405; f. 1947 by breakaway from the CGT (above); Force Ouvrière is a member of ICFTU and the European Trade Union Confederation; Sec.-Gen. André Bergeron; approx. 1m. mems.

Affiliated federations:

Action Sociale: 8 rue de Hanovre, 75002 Paris; tel. (1) 42-68-08-01; Sec. Michel Pinaud.

Agriculture et Alimentation (Food and Agriculture): 198 ave du Maine, 75680 Paris Cedex 14; tel. (1) 45-39-22-03; Secs-Gen. Gérard Fosse, Alain Kerbriand.

Bâtiment, Travaux Publics, Bois, Céramiques, Papier-Carton et Matériaux de Construction (Building and Building Materials, Public Works, Wood, Ceramics and Pasteboard): 170 av Parmentier, 75010 Paris; tel. (1) 42-01-30-00; Sec.-Gen. Marcel Hupel.

Cadres et Ingénieurs (UCI) (Engineers): 2 rue de la Michodière, 75002 Paris; tel. (1) 47-42-39-69; Sec.-Gen. Hubert Bouchet.

Cheminots (Railway Workers): 60 rue Vergniaud, 75640 Paris Cedex 13; tel. (1) 45-80-22-98; f. 1948; Sec.-Gen. Jean Jacques Carmentran; 16,350 mems.

Coiffeurs, Esthétique et Parfumerie (Hairdressers, Beauticians and Perfumery): 3 ave Charles de Gaulle, 94470 Boissy Saint Léger; tel. (1) 45-99-20-22; Sec.-Gen. Michel Bourlon.

Cuirs-Textiles-Habillement (Leather and Textiles): 8 rue de Hanovre, esc. B., 75002 Paris; tel. (1) 47-42-92-70; Sec. Francis Desrousseaux.

Education et Culture: 4 blvd de Strasbourg, 75010 Paris; tel. (1) 42-06-27-87; Sec.-Gen. François Chaintron; 20,000 mems.

Employés et Cadres (Managerial Staff): 28 rue des Petits Hôtels, 75010 Paris; tel. (1) 42-46-46-64; Sec.-Gen. Yves Simon.

Energie Electrique et Gaz (Gas and Electricity): 60 rue Vergniaud, 75640 Paris Cedex 13; tel. (1) 45-88-91-51; f. 1947; Sec.-Gen. Gabriel Gaudy; 22,000 mems.

Finances: 46 rue des Petites Ecuries, 75010 Paris; tel. (1) 42-46-75-20; Sec. André Roulet.

Fonctionnaires (Civil Servants): 46 rue des Petites Ecuries, 75010 Paris; tel. (1) 42-46-48-56; Sec. André Giauque.

Industries Chimiques (Chemical Industries): 60 rue Vergniaud, 75640 Paris Cedex 13; tel. (1) 45-80-14-90; Sec.-Gen. F. Grandazzi.

Livre (Printing Trades): 198 ave du Maine, 75014 Paris Cedex 14; tel. (1) 45-40-69-44; Sec.-Gen. Roger Carpentier.

Métaux (Metals): 60 rue Vergniaud, 75640 Paris Cedex 13; tel. (1) 45-80-22-96; Sec.-Gen. Michel Huc.

Mineurs, Miniers et Similaires (Mine Workers): 169 ave de Choisy, 75624 Paris Cedex 13; tel. (1) 45-87-10-98; Sec.-Gen. René Mertz.

Personnels Civils de la Défense Nationale (National Defence, Civil Servants' Section): 46 rue des Petites Ecuries, 75010 Paris; tel. (1) 42-46-00-05; Sec.-Gen. Jacques Pe.

Personnels des Services des Départements et des Régions: 46 rue des Petites Ecuries, 75010 Paris; tel. (1) 42-46-50-52; Sec.-Gen. Michèle Simonnin.

Pharmacie (Chemists): 198 ave du Maine, 75680 Paris Cedex 14; tel. (1) 45-39-97-22; Sec.-Gen. Marguerite Adenis.

Police: 6 et 8 rue Albert Bayet, 75013 Paris; tel. (1) 45-82-28-08; f. 1948; Sec. Roger Brosse; 8,000 mems.

FRANCE

PTT (Post, Telegraphs and Telephones): 60 rue Vergniaud, 75640 Paris Cedex 13; tel. (1) 40-78-31-50; telex 200644; Sec.-Gen. Jacques Marçot.

Services d'Administration Générale de l'État: 46 rue des Petites Ecuries, 75010 Paris; tel. (1) 42-46-40-19; f. 1948; Sec.-Gen. Lucien Lepresle; 20,000 mems.

Services Publics et de Santé (Health and Public Services): 153–155 rue de Rome, 75017 Paris; tel. (1) 46-22-26-00; f. 1947; Sec.-Gen. René Champeau; 130,000 mems.

Spectacles, Presse et Audiovisuel (Theatre and Cinema Performers, Press and Broadcasting): 2 rue de la Michodière, 75002 Paris; tel. (1) 47-42-35-86; Sec.-Gen. Michel Lesage.

Tabacs et Allumettes (Tobacco and Matchworkers): 198 ave du Maine, 75680 Paris Cedex 14; tel. (1) 45-39-66-32; Sec. Daniel Dreux.

Transports: 198 ave du Maine, 75680 Paris Cedex 14; tel. (1) 45-40-68-00; Sec. Gilbert Doriat.

Travaux Publics et Portuaires de la Marine et des Transports (Transport and Public Works): 46 rue des Petites Ecuries, 75010 Paris; tel. (1) 42-46-36-63; telex 643115; f. 1932; Sec.-Gen. René Valladon; 50,000 mems.

Voyageurs-Représentants-Placiers (Commercial Travellers): 6 et 8 rue Albert Bayet, 75013 Paris Cedex 14; tel. (1) 45-82-28-28; f. 1930; Sec. Henry Dupille.

Confédération Française Démocratique du Travail (CFDT): 4 blvd de la Villette, 75955 Paris Cedex 19; tel. (1) 42-03-80-00; telex 240832; constituted in 1919 as Confédération Française des Travailleurs Chrétiens—CFTC, present title and constitution adopted in 1964; co-ordinates 2,500 trade unions, 102 departmental and overseas federations and 22 affiliated professional federations, all of which are autonomous. There are also 22 regional orgs; in 1984 its membership was estimated at 700,000; affiliated to European Trade Union Confederation; Sec.-Gen. Edmond Maire.

Principal affiliated federations:

Agroalimentaire (FGA): 26 rue de Montholon, 75439 Paris Cedex 09; tel. (1) 42-47-73-32; f. 1980; Sec.-Gen. Marc Gagnaire.

Anciens Combattants (War Veterans): 37 rue Bellechasse, 75007 Paris Cedex 09; tel. (1) 45-50-32-55; Sec.-Gen. Nicole Delvaux.

Banques (Banking): 26 rue de Montholon, 75439 Paris Cedex 09; tel. (1) 42-47-76-25; Sec.-Gen. Régis de Berranger.

Construction-Bois: 26 rue de Montholon, 75439 Paris Cedex 09; tel. (1) 42-47-73-02; f. 1934; Sec.-Gen. Jean Auboeuf.

EDF-GDF (Electricity and Gas of France): 5 rue Mayran, 75439 Paris Cedex 09; tel. (1) 42-85-39-31; f. 1946; Sec.-Gen. Alain Chupin.

Education Nationale (SGEN-CFDT) (National Education): 5 rue Mayran, 75009 Paris; tel. (1) 42-47-74-01; f. 1937; Sec.-Gen. Jean Michel Boullier.

Enseignement Privé (Non-State education): 26 rue de Montholon, 75439 Paris Cedex 09; tel. (1) 48-78-32-72; Sec.-Gen. Michel Villeminot.

Etablissements et Arsenaux de l'Etat: 26 rue de Montholon, 75439 Paris Cedex 09; tel. (1) 42-47-75-74; Sec.-Gen. Alain Petitjean.

Finances et Affaires Economiques (Finance): 26 rue de Montholon, 75439 Paris Cedex 09; tel. (1) 42-47-72-63; f. 1936; civil servants and workers within government financial departments; Sec.-Gen. Jean-Marie Pernot.

Fonctionnaires et Assimilés (UFFA-CFDT) (Civil Servants): 26 rue de Montholon, 75439 Paris Cedex 09; tel. (1) 42-47-76-50; f. 1972; Sec.-Gen. Roselyne Vieillard.

Habillement, Cuir et Textile (HACUITEX): 26 rue de Montholon, 75439 Paris Cedex 09; tel. (1) 42-47-75-60; f. 1963; Sec.-Gen. Daniel Torqueo.

Industries Chimiques (FUC) (Chemicals): 26 rue de Montholon, 75439 Paris Cedex 09; tel. (1) 42-47-73-30; Sec.-Gen. Christian Marquette.

Information, Livre, Audiovisuel et Culture (FILAC): 43 rue du Faubourg Montmartre, 75009 Paris; tel. (1) 42-46-50-64; Sec.-Gen. Michel Mortelette.

Ingénieurs et Cadres (UCC-CFDT): 26 rue de Montholon, 75439 Paris Cedex 09; tel. (1) 42-80-01-01; Sec.-Gen. Daniel Croquette.

Justice: 25 rue de la Fontaine au Roi, 75011 Paris; tel. (1) 48-05-70-56; Sec.-Gen. Jean-Marie Pillard.

Mines et Métallurgie (Miners and Metal Workers): 5 rue Mayran, 75009 Paris; tel. (1) 42-47-74-00; telex 660154; Sec.-Gen. Georges Granger.

Personnel du Ministère de l'Intérieur et des Collectivités Locales (INTERCO): 3 cité d'Hauteville, 75010 Paris; tel. (1) 48-24-23-36; telex 660154; Sec.-Gen. Jacques Nodin.

Protection Sociale, Travail-Emploi (Social Security): 26 rue de Montholon, 75439 Paris Cedex 09; tel. (1) 42-47-75-67; Sec.-Gen. Gilbert Claudel.

PTT (Post, Telegraph and Telephone Workers): 26 rue de Montholon, 75439 Paris Cedex 09; tel. (1) 42-85-13-20; telex 650346; Sec.-Gen. Denis Tonnerre.

Santé et Services Sociaux (Hospital Workers): 26 rue de Montholon, 75439 Paris Cedex 09; tel. (1) 42-47-73-31; Sec.-Gen. Jean-René Masson.

Services: 26 rue de Montholon, 75439 Paris Cedex 09; tel. (1) 42-47-76-20; Sec.-Gen. Marguerite Bertrand.

Transports et Equipement: 26 rue de Montholon, 75439 Paris Cedex 09; tel. (1) 42-47-73-33; f. 1977; Sec.-Gen. Michel Pernet.

Union Confédérale des Retraités (UCR): 26 rue de Montholon, 75439 Paris Cedex 09; tel. (1) 42-47-76-88; Sec.-Gen. Marcel Gonin.

Confédération Française de l'Encadrement (CGC): 30 rue de Gramont, 75002 Paris; tel. (1) 42-61-81-76; f. 1944; organizes managerial staff, professional staff and technicians; co-ordinates unions in every industry and sector; Pres. Paul Marchelli; Delegate-Gen. Jean de Santis; 300,000 mems.

Confédération Française des Travailleurs Chrétiens (CFTC): 13 rue des Ecluses Saint Martin, 75483 Paris Cedex 10; tel. (1) 42-05-79-66; telex 214046; f. 1919; present form in 1964 after majority CFTC became CFDT (see above); absorbed Confédération Générale des Syndicats Indépendants 1977; Chair. Jean Bornard; Gen. Sec. Guy Drilleaud; 270,000 mems.

Confédération des Syndicats Libres (CSL) (formerly Confédération française du Travail): 13 rue Péclet, 75015 Paris; tel. (1) 45-33-62-62; telex 201390; f. 1959; right-wing; Sec.-Gen. Auguste Blanc; 250,000 mems.

Fédération de l'Education Nationale (FEN): 48 rue La Bruyère, 75440 Paris Cedex 09; tel. (1) 42-85-71-01; telex 648356; f. 1948; federation of teachers' unions; Sec.-Gen. Jacques Pommatau; 500,000 mems.

Fédération Nationale des Syndicats Autonomes: 19 blvd Sébastopol, 75001 Paris; f. 1952; groups unions in the private sector; Sec.-Gen. Michel-André Tillières.

Fédération Nationale des Syndicats d'Exploitants Agricoles (FNSEA) (National Federation of Farmers' Unions): 11 rue de la Baume, 75008 Paris; tel. (1) 45-63-11-77; telex 660587; f. 1946; divided into 92 departmental federations and 30,000 local unions; Chair. Raymond Lacombe; Sec.-Gen. Luc Guyau; Man. Dir Michel Ménard; 700,000 mems.

PRINCIPAL STATE-CONTROLLED COMPANIES

Aerospatiale: 37 blvd de Montmorency, 75781 Paris Cedex 16; tel. (1) 45-24-43-21; manufacturer of aircraft, helicopters, strategic missiles, space and ballistic systems; 35,222 employees; Chair. and Gen. Man. Henri Martre.

Avions Marcel Dassault—Breguet Aviation: 33 rue du Professeur Victor Pauchet, 92420 Vaucresson; f. 1967 by merger; state took 46% of shares in 1982; design and production of civil and military aircraft; 16,200 employees; Chair. Claude Vallières.

Charbonnages de France (CdF): Tour Albert 1er, 65 ave de Colmar, 92507 Rueil Malmaison; tel. (1) 47-32-92-34; telex 631450; established under the Nationalization Act of 1946; responsible for coal mining, sales and research in metropolitan France; CdF Chimie undertakes chemical manufacturing (petrochemicals, plastics, resins, fertilizers, paints and inks); there are also engineering and informatics divisions; 60,000 employees (15,000 of whom work for CdF Chimie); Chair. Francis Grangette; Man. Dir (CdF) Bernard Pache; Man. Dir (CdF-Chimie) Serge Tchuruk.

Compagnie Générale d'Electricité (CGE): 54 rue la Boétie, 75382 Paris Cedex 08; tel. (1) 45-63-14-14; telex 280953; f. 1898; nationalized 1982; energy and transportation, nuclear energy, electrical contracting and industrial process control, telecommunications and business systems, cables, batteries; 153,800 employees (of whom 133,000 are in France); turnover 78,500m. Frs (1985); Chair. Pierre Suard.

Electricité de France: 32 rue de Monceau, 75008 Paris; tel. (1) 47-55-94-10; telex 280098; established under the Electricity and

Gas Industry Nationalization Act of 1946; responsible for generating and supplying electricity for distribution to consumers in metropolitan France; 120,000 employees; Chair. MARCEL BOITEUX; Man. Dir JEAN GUILHAMON.

Société Nationale Elf Aquitaine (SNEA): Tour Elf, 2 place de la Coupole, 92400 Paris la Défense; tel. (1) 47-44-45-46; telex 615400; 67% owned by ERAP—Entreprise de Recherches et d'Activités Pétrolières, a state enterprise; undertakes exploration for and production of petroleum and natural gas, chiefly in France, Africa (Cameroon, the Congo, Gabon and Nigeria), the North Sea and the USA; in 1985 it produced 17m. metric tons of crude petroleum and 18,100m. cu m of natural gas; has four refineries in France and a share in four others, with total capacity of 29.4m. metric tons per year. Elf Aquitaine also exploits uranium and non-energy minerals, and has subsidiaries in petrochemicals (ATOCHEM) and pharmaceuticals (SANOFI). Chair. and Chief Exec. MICHEL PECQUEUR; Vice-Chair. and Exec. Vice-Pres. GILBERT RUTMAN.

Gaz de France: 23 rue Philibert Delorme, 75840 Paris Cedex 17; tel. (1) 47-54-20-20; telex 650483; established under the Electricity and Gas Industry Nationalization Act of 1946; responsible for distribution of gas in metropolitan France; about 17.5% of gas is produced in France (Aquitaine) and the rest imported from Algeria, the Netherlands, Norway and the USSR; Chair. JACQUES FOURNIER; Gen. Man. PIERRE DELAPORTE.

Matra: 4 rue de Presbourg, 75116 Paris; tel. (1) 47-23-54-04; became 51% state-owned in 1982; military, space, telecommunications, data processing, components, automobile electronics, transport, control and automation systems, horology, automobiles; Chair. JEAN-LUC LAGARDÈRE; Man. Dir JEAN-LOUIS GERGORIN.

Péchiney: 23 rue Balzac, 75008 Paris; telex 290503; nationalized 1982; aluminium, fine metallurgy and advanced materials, ferroalloys and carbon products, copper fabrication; 49,160 employees; turnover 29,009m. Frs (1983); Chair. and CEO JEAN GANDOIS.

Régie Nationale des Usines Renault: 34 quai du Point du Jour, BP 103, 92109 Boulogne-Billancourt; tel. (1) 46-09-15-30; telex 205677; nationalized in 1945; in 1984 1.74m. passenger cars and small vans were manufactured; sales totalled 117,584m. Frs; Chair. RAYMOND LÉVY.

Rhône-Poulenc: 25 quai Paul Doumer, 92408 Courbevoie Cedex; f. 1858; nationalized 1982; chemicals, pharmaceuticals, animal foodstuffs, film, textiles, communications; 80,000 employees (of whom 48,000 in France); turnover 56,000m. Frs (1984); Chair. and CEO JEAN-RENÉ FOURTOU.

Sacilor: Cedex 34, 92072 Paris la Défense; tel. (1) 47-67-80-00; telex 612557; nationalized 1982; steel; about 75,000 employees (1985, incl. Usinor, see below); Chair. and Man. Dir FRANCIS MER; Man. Dirs CLAUDE INK, JEAN-PIERRE HUGON, JEAN JACQUET.

Société Nationale d'Etude et de Construction de Moteurs d'Avion (SNECMA): 2 blvd Victor, 75724 Paris Cedex 15; tel. (1) 45-54-92-00; telex 202834; f. 1905; nationalized 1945; manufactures engines for civil and military aircraft, electronic and meteorological equipment; Chair. and Man. Dir MICHEL VIRET.

Société Nationale d'Exploitation Industrielle des Tabacs et des Allumettes (SEITA): 53 quai d'Orsay, 75340 Paris Cedex 07; tel. (1) 45-55-91-50; telex 250604; responsible for the production and marketing of tobacco and matches in France; sales totalled 32,454m. Frs in 1984; 8,000 employees; Chair. and Man. Dir F. EYRAUD.

Thomson SA: 173 blvd Haussmann, 75379 Paris Cedex 08; tel. (1) 45-61-96-00; telex 650143; f. 1893 as Compagnie Française Thomson-Houston; nationalized 1982; holding company for Thomson group; electrical and electronics industry; 129,000 employees; turnover 46,500m. Frs (1982); Chair. ALAIN GOMEZ; Chief Exec. NOËL GOUTARD.

Usinor: Immeuble 'Ile-de-France', Cedex 33, 92070 Paris la Défense 9; tel. (1) 47-67-10-10; telex 614730; f. 1948; nationalized 1981; steel; Chair. and Man. Dir FRANCIS MER.

Transport

RAILWAYS

Most of the French railways are controlled by the Société Nationale des Chemins de fer Français (SNCF) which took over the activities of the five largest railway companies in 1937. The SNCF is divided into five Réseaux (Systems) which are further subdivided into 25 Régions (Areas), all under the direction of a general headquarters in Paris. In December 1985 the SNCF operated 34,676 km of track, of which 11,488 km were electrified. The Parisian transport system is controlled by a separate authority, the Régie Autonome des Transports Parisiens (RATP, see below). A number of small railways in the provinces are run by independent organizations. In 1986 the French and British Governments agreed to construct a rail link between the two countries, under the English Channel, which would be completed by 1991. Further plans were proposed to link the Channel tunnel to towns in the Netherlands, Belgium and the Federal Republic of Germany, by building a railway network in northern France.

Société Nationale des Chemins de fer Français (SNCF): 88 rue Saint Lazare, 75436 Paris Cedex 09; tel. (1) 42-85-60-00; telex 290936; f. 1937; formerly 51% state-owned, wholly nationalized 1982; Dir-Gen. JEAN DUPUY; Pres. PHILIPPE ESSIG.

Réseau de l'Est: 13 rue d'Alsace, 75475 Paris Cedex 10; tel. (1) 42-03-96-31; Dir MICHEL FLEURY.

Réseau du Nord: 18 rue de Dunkerque, 75475 Paris Cedex 10; tel. (1) 42-80-63-63; Dir PHILIPPE VICAIRE.

Réseau de l'Ouest: 20 rue de Rome, 75008 Paris; tel. (1) 42-85-88-00; Dir LOUIS LEMAIRE.

Réseau du Sud-Ouest: 1 place Valhubert, 75634 Paris Cedex 13; tel. (1) 45-84-14-18; Dir CHARLES VIGNIER.

Réseau du Sud-Est: place Louis Armand, 75571 Paris Cedex 12; tel. (1) 43-46-12-12; Dir CLAUDE ARNOLD.

Metropolitan Railways

Régie Autonome des Transports Parisiens (RATP): 53 ter quai des Grands Augustins, POB 75-06, 75271 Paris Cedex 06; tel. (1) 40-46-41-41; telex 200000; f. 1948; state-owned; operates the Paris underground and suburban railways, and buses; Chair. PAUL REVERDY; Gen. Man. MICHEL ROUSSELOT.

Three provincial cities also have underground railway systems: Marseille (first section opened 1977), Lyon and Lille.

ROADS

At 31 December 1985 there were 6,150 km of motorways (autoroutes). There are also about 28,500 km of national roads (routes nationales), 350,000 km of secondary roads, 420,000 km of other urban roads and 700,000 km of rural roads.

Fédération Nationale des Transports Routiers: 2 ave Velasquez, 75008 Paris; tel. (1) 45-63-16-00; road transport; Chair. MAURICE VOIRON.

INLAND WATERWAYS

In 1981 there were 8,623 km of navigable waterways, of which 1,617 km were accessible to craft of 3,000 tons.

SHIPPING

At 30 June 1982 the French merchant shipping fleet had a total displacement of 10,771,000 grt, of which oil tankers accounted for 6,557,000 grt. In 1965 control of seaports was transferred from the State to autonomous authorities. The State retains supervisory powers. In 1986 the Government announced a two-year scheme, costing 1,400m. francs, to revitalize the merchant fleet.

Principal Shipping Companies

CETRAMAR, Consortium Européen de Transports Maritimes: 32 rue Boissy d'Anglas, 75008 Paris; tel. (1) 42-68-44-44; telex 640738; tramping; Man. Dir P. RAYMOND; tonnage 339,797 gross.

Chargeurs Réunis: 3 blvd Malesherbes, BP 9808, 75360 Paris Cedex 08; tel. (1) 42-68-44-44; telex 280034; f. 1964; Europe to and from West Africa, South Africa and Far East-North America (east coast) to and from West Africa and Far East to West Africa; Chair. G. ROY; Gen. Man. M. PALANDJIAN; tonnage 246,207 gross.

Compagnie de Navigation d'Orbigny: 10 ave de Messine, 75008 Paris; tel. (1) 45-62-54-66; telex 641208; f. 1865; cargo services from French, Belgian and German ports to Brazilian, Uruguayan and Argentine ports; Chair. and Man. Dir ROBERT DE LAMBILLY; tonnage 13,208 gross.

Compagnie Générale Maritime: Tour Winterthur, 102 Quartier Boieldieu, 92085 Paris la Défense, Cedex 18; tel. (1) 47-76-70-00; telex 630387; f. 1976 from merger of Compagnie Générale Transatlantique and Compagnie des Messageries Maritimes; holding co. Compagnie Générale Maritime et Financière (CGMF); 99.9% state-owned; freight services to USA, Canada, West Indies, Central and South America, Northern Europe, USSR, the Middle East, India, Australia, New Zealand, Indonesia and other Pacific and Indian Ocean areas; Chair. CLAUDE ABRAHAM; Man. Dir JACQUES RIBIÈRE; tonnage 1,819,555 dwt.

Compagnie Nationale de Navigation: 2 square Pétrarque, 75116 Paris; tel. (1) 47-04-61-70; telex 610549; Chair. and Man. Dir G. WESSELS; tonnage 495,156 dwt; 3 tankers.

Compagnie Navale Worms: 50 blvd Haussmann, 75441 Paris Cedex 09; holding co. with subsidiaries: Société Française de Transports Maritimes (Navale et Commerciale Havraise Péninsulaire, Société Française de Transports Pétroliers, Société Nantaise des Chargeurs de l'Ouest, Cie Morbihannaise de Navigation, Truckline Ferries France), Feronia International Shipping (FISH) and other subsidiaries abroad; Chair. and Man. Dir J. BARNAUD.

Esso SAF: 92093 Paris la Défense Cedex 2; tel. (1) 43-34-60-00; telex 620031; ocean-going tankers; Chair. M. KOPFF; Marine Man. A. CALVARIN; fleet of 4 cargo carriers (1m. grt) and 2 coasters.

Gazocéan: Tour Fiat, 1 place de la Coupole, 92084 Paris la Défense Cedex 16; tel. (1) 47-96-60-60; telex 615234; f. 1957; fleet with a capacity of about 300,000 cu m of liquefied gas; world-wide gas sea transportation and trade; Chair. JACQUES PETITMENGIN; Man. Dir ALESSANDRO BRONZINI.

Nouvelle Compagnie de Paquebots: 33 rue J. F. Leca, Marseille; tel. 91-91-91-21; telex 440003; f. 1965; cap. 10,229,100 Frs; passenger cruise services; Chair. and Man. Dir BERNARD MAURIAC; tonnage 27,658 gross.

Louis-Dreyfus et Cie: 87 ave de la Grande Armée, 75782 Paris Cedex 16; tel. (1) 45-01-54-45; telex 611234; tramping; Chair. GÉRARD LOUIS-DREYFUS; Man. Dir P. D'ORSAY; tonnage 630,000 gross.

Mobil Oil Française: Tour Septentrion, 92081 Paris la Défense Cedex 09; tel. (1) 47-73-42-41; telex 610412; bulk petroleum transport; refining and marketing of petroleum products; Chair. MARC CASANOVA.

Société d'Armement Fluvial et Maritime (SOFLUMAR): 5 ave Percier, 75008 Paris; tel. (1) 45-62-50-50; telex 650252; coastal tankers and tramping; Man. Dir M. F. VALLAT; 52,754 gross.

Société Française de Transports Pétroliers: 1 rue de Mogador, 75009 Paris; tel. (1) 42-85-19-00; telex 650371; oil and chemical tankers; Chair. J. P. PAGE; 1,055,534 dwt.

Société Maritime des Pétroles BP et Cie: 10 quai Paul Doumer, 92412 Courbevoie Cedex; tel. (1) 47-68-40-00; telex 630546; oil tankers; Man. Dir YVES METGE; tonnage 1,049,105 dwt.

Société Maritime Shell: 29 rue de Berri, 75397 Paris Cedex 08; tel. (1) 45-61-82-82; telex 660487; oil tankers; Man. Dir M. JOLIVET; 1,663,764 dwt.

Société Nationale des Chemins de Fer Français (SNCF): 3 rue Ambroise Paré, 75010 Paris; tel. (1) 42-80-48-48; telex 280549; cross-Channel passenger, accompanied motorcar, freight and roll on/roll off on train-ferries and car-ferries; Chair. P. ESSIG; tonnage 45,000 gross.

Société Nationale Maritime Corse-Méditerranée: 61 blvd des Dames, 13002 Marseille; tel. 91-56-32-00; telex 440068; passenger and roll on/roll off ferry services between France and Corsica, Sardinia, North Africa; Pres. J. RIBIÈRE; Man. Dir J. P. ISOARD; 13 vessels.

Société Navale Caennaise: 58 ave Pierre Berthelot, Caen; tel. 31-82-21-76; telex 170122; f. 1901; regular lines; Chair. JEAN-MICHEL BLANCHARD; Man. Dir Y. LENEGRE; tonnage 43,501 grt.

Société Navale Chargeurs Delmas-Vieljeux: 16 ave Matignon, 75008 Paris; tel. (1) 42-56-44-33; telex 290354; f. 1867; cargo service from French, German and Dutch ports to West and East Africa, also ocean tramping and tankers, bulk liquids; Chair. TRISTAN VIELJEUX; Vice-Pres. PATRICE VIELJEUX; tonnage 440,279 dwt.

Total Compagnie Française de Navigation: 24 rue du Pont, 92521 Neuilly-sur-Seine Cedex; tel. (1) 47-45-13-35; telex 611759; f. 1931; cap. 120m. Frs; oil tankers; Chair. LOUIS BOUZOLS; tonnage 2,516,747 dwt.

Union Industrielle et Maritime: 36 rue de Naples, 75008 Paris; tel. (1) 42-93-13-03; telex 650416; cargo services, continental, North Africa, transatlantic; Chair. P. E. CANGARDEL; Man. Dirs J. M. CANGARDEL, A. GODILLON; tonnage 105,642 gross.

Union Navale: 3 blvd Malesherbes, 75008 Paris; tel. (1) 42-68-44-44; telex 650254; bulk transport; Man. Dir PIERRE RAYMOND.

Van Ommeren (France): 5 ave Percier, 75008 Paris; tel. (1) 45-62-50-50; telex 650252; coastal tankers and tramping; Man. Dir M. F. VALLAT; tonnage 55,556 gross.

CIVIL AVIATION

There are international airports at Orly, Roissy and Le Bourget (Paris), Bordeaux, Lyon, Marseille and Nice.

National Airlines

Air France: 1 sq Max Hymans, 75757 Paris Cedex 15; tel. (1) 43-23-81-81; telex 200666; f. 1933; international, European and inter-continental services; flights to Africa, Madagascar, Americas, Middle and Far East and West Indies; Chair. (vacant); Pres. HENRI SAUVAN; Sec.-Gen. MARC MAUGARS; Senior Vice-Pres. GERARD ORIZET, JEAN-DIDIER BLANCHET, CLAUDE POSTEL, ALAIN VARINI; fleet (1986) 7 Concorde, 33 Boeing 747, 14 Boeing 737, 17 Airbus A300, 29 Boeing 727, 6 Airbus A310.

Air Inter: 1 ave du Maréchal Devaux, 91550 Paray Vieille Poste; tel. (1) 46-75-12-12; telex 250932; f. 1954; operates internal services within metropolitan France; Air France and the SNCF are the part owners; in 1978 Air Inter agreed with Air France to cease charter operations and received 20% of Air France's subsidiary Air Charter International; Chair and Man. Dir PIERRE EELSEN; fleet (1984) 14 Airbus, 11 Mercure, 12 Super 12, 7 Fokker F27.

Private Airlines

Union de Transports Aériens (UTA): 3 blvd Malesherbes, 75008 Paris; tel. (1) 42-66-30-30 and 776-41-33; telex 610692; f. 1963; services to West and South Africa, Middle and Far East, Australia, New Caledonia, New Zealand, Japan, Tahiti and the west coast of the USA; Chair. RENÉ LAPAUTRE; Man. Dir GUY SENE; fleet of 6 DC-10, 5 Boeing 747.

Nineteen small private companies provide regional air services. Small private airlines flying services outside France include:

Euralair: 93350 Aéroport du Bourget, Paris; tel. (1) 48-35-95-22; telex 680096; f. 1964; Chair. ALEXANDRE COUVELAIRE.

Europe Aéro Service SA: Aérodrome de Perpignan-Rivesaltes, 66028 Perpignan; telex 500084; f. 1965; internal passenger and cargo services, freight services to Frankfurt, Zürich, Milan, Algiers, Tunis, Casablanca and Barcelona; Chair. GEORGES MASUREL.

Transport Aérien Transrégional (TAT): 4 bis rue Jules Favre, 37000 Tours; tel. 47-54-21-45; telex 750876; f. 1968; took over Air Alpes 1981; took over Air Alsace routes following its demise in 1982; Chair. and Man. Dir MICHEL MARCHAIS.

Airlines Association

Chambre Syndicale du Transport Aérien (CSTA): 43 blvd Malesherbes, 75008 Paris; tel. (1) 47-42-11-00; telex 281491; f. 1946 to represent French and foreign airlines at national level; Chair. PIERRE EELSEN; Delegate-Gen. Adj. JEAN-YVES SAVINA; 17 mems.

Tourism

Ministère de l'Industrie, de Postes et Télécommunications et du Tourisme: 101 rue de Grenelle, 75007 Paris; Minister ALAIN MADELIN.

Direction de l'Industrie Touristique: 17 rue de l'Ingénieur Robert Keller, 75041 Paris Cedex 15; tel. (1) 45-75-62-16; Dir FRANCESCO FRANGIALLI.

There are Regional Delegates of the Direction du Tourisme in the 23 regions and 4 overseas départements. There are over 5,000 Offices de Tourisme and Syndicats d'Initiative (tourist offices run by the local authorities) throughout France.

Atomic Energy

Commissariat à l'Energie Atomique (CEA) (Atomic Energy Commissariat): 31–33 rue de la Fédération, 75752 Paris Cedex 15; tel. (1) 40-56-10-00; telex 200671; f. 1945; Gen. Administrator JEAN-PIERRE CAPRON; High Commissioner JEAN TEILLAC; Sec.-Gen. JEAN MARMOT.

The CEA is an establishment of scientific, industrial and technological character. Its function is to promote the uses of nuclear energy in science, industry and national defence; the fields in which it is active, either directly or through its own subsidiaries and participation in private companies, are: production of nuclear materials; reactor development; fundamental research; innovation and transfer of technologies; military applications; bio-technologies; robotics; electronics; new materials; radiological protection and nuclear safety.

Administration is in the hands of a 15-member Comité de l'Energie Atomique (Atomic Energy Committee), presided over by the Prime Minister and consisting of government officials and representatives of sciences and industry.

FRANCE

Institutes and Administrative Bodies:

Direction des Applications Militaires (Military Applications Division): Dir ALAIN VIDART.

Institut de Protection et de Sûreté Nucléaire (Institute for Nuclear Protection and Security): CEN/Fontenay-aux-Roses, BP 6, 92260 Fontenay-aux-Roses; Dir FRANÇOIS COGNE.

Institut de Recherche Fondamentale (Fundamental Research Institute): Orme des Merisiers, 91191 Gif-sur-Yvette Cedex; Dir JULES HOROWITZ.

Institut de Recherche Technologique et de Développement Industriel (Institute of Technological Research and Industrial Development): 31 rue de la Fédération, 75752 Paris Cedex 15; tel. (1) 40-56-10-00; Dir MICHEL RAPIN.

Office des Rayonnements Ionisants: CEN Saclay, 91191 Gif-sur-Yvette Cedex; Dir YVES LE GALLIC.

Agence Nationale pour la Gestion des Déchets Radioactifs: 31–33 rue de la Fédération, 75752 Paris Cedex 15; tel. (1) 40-56-15-15; Dir JEAN CHATOUX.

Institut National des Sciences et Techniques Nucléaires (National Institute of Nuclear Science and Technology): CEN Saclay-INSTN, 91191 Gif-sur-Yvette Cedex; f. 1956; Dir. Y. CHELET.

Research Centres:

Centre d'Etudes Nucléaires de Cadarache (CEN-CA) (Cadarache Nuclear Research Centre): BP 1, 13115 Saint-Paul-les-Durance, Bouches-du-Rhône; tel. 42-25-70-00; telex 440678; f. 1960; Dir CLAUDE MORANVILLE.

Centre d'Etudes Nucléaires de Fontenay-aux-Roses (Fontenay-aux-Roses Nuclear Research Centre): BP 6, 92265 Fontenay-aux-Roses Cedex; tel. (1) 46-54-70-80; f. 1945; Dir G. VIAL.

Centre d'Etudes Nucléaires de Grenoble (CEN-G) (Grenoble Nuclear Research Centre): 85X, 38041 Grenoble Cedex; tel. 76-88-44-00; telex 320323; f. 1956; 40 laboratories; Dir MICHEL SUSCILLON.

Centre d'Etudes Nucléaires de Saclay (CENS) (Saclay Nuclear Research Centre): 91191 Gif-sur-Yvette Cedex; tel. (1) 69-08-60-00; telex 690641; f. 1949; Dir PHILIPPE SACHNINE.

Centre d'Etudes Nucléaires de la Vallée du Rhône (CEN-VALRHO): BP 171, 30205 Bagnols-sur-Cèze Cedex; tel. 66-79-60-00; telex 480816; Dir ALBERT TEBOUL.

Société des Participations du CEA: CEA-Industrie: 31–33 rue de la Fédération, 75752 Paris Cedex 15; tel. (1) 42-73-60-60; principal affiliates CISI, COGEMA, FRAMATOME, TECHNICATOME, ORIS-INDUSTRIE, etc.; Pres. JEAN-PIERRE CAPRON; Dir-Gen. DENIS MORTIER.

Centre national de la recherche scientifique (CNRS): 15 quai Anatole France, 75700 Paris; tel. (1) 45-55-92-25; telex 260-034; there are nuclear research centres attached to this institution in Strasbourg, Grenoble and Orsay.

Groupe de Laboratoires de Strasbourg-Cronenbourg: rue du Loess, BP 20 CRO, 67037 Strasbourg Cedex; f. 1957; Dirs P. DEJOURS. B. METZ, G. MONSONEGO, J. H. VIVIEN, A. GALLMANN.

FRENCH OVERSEAS POSSESSIONS

Ministry of Overseas Departments and Territories: rue Oudinot 27, 75700 Paris, France; tel. 47-83-01-23.
Minister: BERNARD PONS.

The national flag of France, proportions three by two, with three equal vertical stripes, of blue, white and red, is used in the Overseas Possessions.

French Overseas Departments

The four Overseas Departments (départements d'outre-mer) are French Guiana, Guadeloupe, Martinique and Réunion. They are integral parts of the French Republic, and the administrative structure is similar to that of the Departments of Metropolitan France. Overseas Departments, however, have their own Courts of Appeal. Until 1982 each Overseas Department was administered by a Prefect, with elected General Councils, indirectly-elected Regional Councils and with elected representatives in the French National Assembly and Senate of the Republic in Paris. Under the decentralization law of March 1982, the appointed Prefect in each Overseas Department was restyled Commissaire de la République (Government Commissioner). The former executive power of the Prefect was transferred to the General Council. A proposal to replace the General and Regional Councils by a single assembly was rejected by the French Constitutional Council in December 1982. As a compromise between autonomy and complete assimilation into France, the Regional Councils' powers were increased in 1983. In February the first direct elections for the Regional Councils were held. Their wider powers included responsibility for economic, social and cultural affairs. In March 1986 elections were held in all Overseas Departments for the French National Assembly and for the Regional Councils, and in September elections were held in Guadeloupe and Martinique for representatives to the Senate in Paris.

FRENCH GUIANA

Introductory Survey

Location, Climate, Language, Religion, Capital

French Guiana (Guyane) lies on the north coast of South America, with Suriname to the west and Brazil to the south and east. The climate is humid, with a season of heavy rains from April to July and another short rainy season in December and January. Average temperature at sea-level is 27°C (85°F), with little seasonal variation. French is the official language but a creole patois is also spoken. The majority of the population belong to the Roman Catholic Church, although other Christian churches are represented. The capital is Cayenne.

Recent History

French occupation commenced in the early 17th century. After brief periods of Dutch, English and Portuguese rule, the territory was finally confirmed as French in 1817. The colony steadily declined, after a short period of prosperity in the 1850s as a result of the discovery of gold in the basin of the Apprrouague river. French Guiana, including the notorious Devil's Island, increasingly became used as a penal colony, and as a place of exile for convicts and political prisoners, before the practice was stopped in 1937. The colony became a department of France in 1946.

French Guiana's reputation as a political and economic backwater has been dispelled by the growth of pro-independence sentiments, and the use of violence by a small minority, compounded by tensions between the Guyanais and large numbers of immigrant workers. In 1974 demonstrations against unemployment, the worsening economic situation, and French attitudes towards the department, led to the detention of leading trade unionists and pro-independence politicians. In 1975 a large-scale plan for the revitalization of French Guiana was announced by Olivier Stirn, Secretary of State for the Overseas Departments. However, much of the promised expansion and development failed to materialize, owing to the lack of interest and of investment, and also because of the problems which have been encountered in developing French Guiana's interior. As a result of growing industrial and political unrest in the late 1970s, there were increased demands for greater autonomy for the department by the Parti Socialiste Guyanais (PSG), the strongest political party. In 1980 there were several bomb attacks against 'colonialist' targets by an extremist group known as Fo nou Libéré la Guyane (FNLG). Reforms, introduced by the French Socialist Government in 1982 and 1983, succeeded in decentralizing some power over local affairs to a new Regional Council. The French Government, however, has refused to countenance any change in French Guiana's departmental status.

In the February 1983 elections to the Regional Council, the left-wing parties gained a majority of votes, but not of seats, and the balance of power was held by the separatist Union des Travailleurs Guyanais (UTG), which was restyled the Parti National Populaire Guyanais (PNPG) in November 1985. In May 1983 French Guiana was the target for bombings by the Alliance Révolutionnaire Caraïbe (ARC), an extremist independence movement based in Guadeloupe, another French Overseas Department in the West Indies. At elections to the General Council, held in March 1985, the PSG and left-wing independents succeeded in increasing their representation to 13 seats out of a total of 19.

For the general election to the French National Assembly in March 1986, French Guiana's representation was increased from one to two deputies. The incumbent member, Elie Castor of the PSG, received 48.1% of the total votes (compared with 51.2% in the 1981 general election) and was re-elected. The right-wing Rassemblement pour la République (RPR) and the centrist Union pour la Démocratie Française (UDF), which had formed an electoral alliance in 1981 and for the 1983 regional elections, presented separate candidates in 1986: Paulin Bruné of the RPR was elected, with 34.2% of the votes. On the same day as the elections to the Assembly, direct elections were held for the 31 seats on the Regional Council. The PSG, with 42.1% of the votes, increased its strength on the Council from 14 to 15 members, and Georges Othily of the PSG was re-elected president of the Council. The RPR won nine seats, and the UDF three, while four seats were secured by Action Démocratique Guyanaise.

Government

France is represented in French Guiana by an appointed Government Commissioner. There are two Councils with local powers: the General Council, with 19 members, and the Regional Council, with 31 members. Both are elected by universal adult suffrage for a period of six years. Under the system of proportional representation used for the elections of March 1986 (as applied in metropolitan France), French Guiana elected two representatives to the French National Assembly in Paris, compared with one at the 1981 elections. French Guiana sends one elected representative to the French Senate.

Defence

In 1986 France maintained a military force of about 7,900 in French Guiana and the Antilles.

FRENCH OVERSEAS DEPARTMENTS

French Guiana

Economic Affairs

The economy of French Guiana is heavily dependent on France for budgetary aid and imports of food and manufactured goods. Local production is mainly in the agricultural sector, particularly forestry and fisheries. In 1982, according to estimates by the World Bank, the gross national product (GNP), measured at average 1980–82 prices, was US $210m. ($3,230 per head).

Fishing, especially for shrimps, has grown in importance since 1965, and in 1982 fish products accounted for 64.1% of export earnings. Most of the catch is made by foreign vessels and landed in French Guiana for processing, prior to export, mainly to the USA. Forests cover 90% of the territory's area and contain valuable reserves of tropical hardwoods, such as rosewood, mahogany and satinwood. However, poor communications, lack of development and the difficulties involved in working in the tropical rain forest have prevented these vast reserves from being exploited to any significant extent. Production of sawlogs between 1973 and 1984 increased from 30,100 cu m to 69,200 cu m. Local sawmills provide finished products for export, including plywoods and veneers. Rosewood oil is also extracted. Total timber exports amounted to 20,585 metric tons in 1982, with a value equivalent to 11.8% of total export earnings. Agricultural cultivation is confined to the coastal strip, where 90% of the population is concentrated. Rice, cassava, bananas and vegetables are grown for local consumption, while sugar cane is cultivated for use in rum production. The rearing of livestock has been developed since 1975 by stock farms on the coastal plain.

Mineral resources have been shown to exist, but their exploitation at the present time does not seem to be economically viable, considering the huge investment needed. An estimated 42m. tons of bauxite exists on the Kaw plateau, and 40m. tons of kaolin near Saint-Laurent-du-Maroni. Other minerals are present in smaller quantities, but only gold is mined with any success, with production totalling 249 kg in 1983.

Tourism is growing, but improvements are needed in transport and hotel facilities. Unemployment is high, affecting about 30% of the labour force, and is a particularly serious problem among young people. In 1982 a new investment bank, SOFIDEG, was set up to encourage agricultural development. In 1968 a rocket launching base was established at Kourou, where *Ariane*, the European Space Agency's communications satellite launcher, was developed. After initial setbacks, successful launches between 1983 and 1986 confirmed the centre's future commercial prospects. A new town was created to house the resident engineers and technicians. A second launch pad was constructed at Kourou, and the first rocket was launched from the new site in March 1986. However, following the mid-air destruction of a rocket in June, the Arianespace company announced that, pending the report of an independent commission of inquiry into the causes of the failure, no further rockets would be launched. A new schedule of launchings was nevertheless announced in September 1986. The next launch was planned for February 1987.

There has been a steady flow of emigrants away from French Guiana, while the Government has tried to attract up to 30,000 immigrants to boost the labour force. These have included civil servants from France, and members of the Hmong tribe from Laos. There are also large numbers of illegal immigrants, estimated at over 20,000, from Haiti, other Caribbean islands, and from French Guiana's neighbours. Although French Guiana is underpopulated and suffering from a shortage of skilled labour, most immigrants remain in Cayenne, and impose a strain on the city's resources. In 1983 46% of births were children of immigrant parents.

French Guiana, in common with other French Overseas Departments, is heavily dependent on imports of food and energy. The cost of imports grew from 1,355m. francs in 1981 to 2,158m. francs in 1984, while the value of French Guiana's exports remained low, producing a trade deficit of 1,831m. francs in 1984.

Social Welfare

In 1984 there were two hospitals, with a total of 611 beds, a health centre and three private clinics. The Institut Pasteur undertakes research into malaria and other tropical diseases. There is a system of social security similar to the French model. In 1984 there were 154 physicians working in French Guiana.

Education

Education is modelled on the French system, and is compulsory for 10 years between the ages of six and 16 years. State education is free. There are also a number of private denominational schools. Between 1974 and 1985 the number of children attending primary schools increased from 6,465 to 10,512. Over the same period, the total enrolment at secondary (including vocational) schools rose from 5,251 to 9,757. This expansion has placed a strain on the education system. Higher education in law is provided by a branch of the Universitaire Antilles-Guyane in Cayenne.

Tourism

Tourism has expanded recently, but there is still much scope for development and improvement of tourist facilities. The main attractions are the natural beauty of the tropical scenery, and the Amerindian villages of the interior.

Public Holidays

1987: 1 January (New Year's Day), 3–4 March (Lenten Carnival), 17–20 April (Easter), 1 May (Labour Day), 28 May (Ascension Day), 8 June (Whit Monday), 14 July (National Day), 11 November (Armistice Day), 25 December (Christmas Day).

1988: 1 January (New Year's Day), 16–17 February (Lenten Carnival), 1–4 April (Easter), 2 May (for Labour Day), 12 May (Ascension Day), 14 July (National Day), 11 November (Armistice Day), 25 December (Christmas Day).

Weights and Measures

The metric system is in use.

Currency and Exchange Rates

French currency: 100 centimes = 1 franc.

Exchange rates (30 September 1986):
£1 sterling = 9.6125 francs;
US $1 = 6.6425 francs.

Statistical Survey

Source (unless otherwise stated): Institut national de la statistique et des études économiques, 81 rue Ch. Colomb, BP 755, 97306 Cayenne; tel. 311279.

AREA AND POPULATION

Area: 90,000 sq km (34,750 sq miles).

Population: 73,012 (males 38,448; females 34,564) at census of 9 March 1982; 84,177 (estimate for 1 January 1986); *Capital:* Cayenne, population 38,135 (1982).

Births, Marriages and Deaths (1984): Live births 2,297; Marriages 287; Deaths 287.

Economically Active Population (1982 census): Employed 26,423 (males 17,205, females 9,218); Unemployed 4,760; Total labour force 31,183 (excl. armed forces).

AGRICULTURE, ETC.

Principal Crops (FAO estimates, metric tons, 1985): Sugar cane 9,000, Cassava 8,000, Rice (paddy) 6,000. Source: FAO, *Production Yearbook*.

Livestock (FAO estimates, year ending September 1985): Cattle 14,000, Pigs 10,000. Source: FAO, *Production Yearbook*.

Forestry (cu m, 1984): Sawlogs 69,200, Sawnwood 34,679.

Fishing (landings in metric tons, 1984): Fish 402.9; Shrimps 1,861.5; Total 2,264.4.

MINING

Production (1983): Gold 249 kg. Source: UN, *Industrial Statistics Yearbook*.

INDUSTRY

Production (1984): Rum 2,159 hl, Electricity 116 million kWh (1983).

FINANCE

Currency and Exchange Rates: 100 centimes = 1 French franc. *Coins:* 1, 5, 10, 20 and 50 centimes; 1, 2, 5 and 10 francs. *Notes:* 10, 50, 100, 200 and 500 francs. *Sterling and Dollar Equivalents* (30 September 1986): £1 sterling = 9.6125 francs; US $1 = 6.6425 francs; 1,000 French francs = £104.03 = $150.55.

Budget (1981): 291.5 million francs.

Aid from France (1976): US $81 million.

Cost of Living (consumer price index for Cayenne; base: January 1980 = 100): 163.0 in December 1984.

EXTERNAL TRADE

Principal Commodities (million francs, 1982): *Imports:* Food 516.2; Petroleum products 322.5; Total (incl. others) 1,643.1;

FRENCH OVERSEAS DEPARTMENTS — French Guiana

Exports: Shrimps 129.5; Timber 25; Fish 6.3; Total (incl. others) 211.8.
Principal Trading Partners (million francs, 1984): *Imports:* France 1,181.0; Trinidad and Tobago 280.8; Japan 101.2; USA 62.1; Total (incl. others) 2,158.1. *Exports:* France 29.7; Japan 59.1; Martinique 22.9; USA 135.5; Total (incl. others) 326.7.

TRANSPORT

Road Traffic (vehicles in use, 1984): Passenger cars 24,000, Commercial vehicles 4,610. Source: IRF, *World Road Statistics.*
Shipping (1983): Ships entered 234, Freight unloaded 242,318 metric tons, Freight loaded 17,322 metric tons.
Civil Aviation (1984): Freight carried 3,914 metric tons, Passengers carried 181,266.

EDUCATION

Primary (1985/6): 54 schools; 10,512 pupils.
Secondary (1985/6): Secondary and technical schools 21; 9,757 pupils.

Directory

The Government

(January 1987)

Government Commissioner: JACQUES DEWATRE.
President of the General Council: ELIE CASTOR (PSG).
Deputies to the French National Assembly: ELIE CASTOR (PSG), PAULIN BRUNÉ (RPR).
Representative to the French Senate: RAYMOND TARCY (PSG).

REGIONAL COUNCIL

President: GEORGES OTHILY (PSG).

Election, 16 March 1986

	Votes	%	Seats
PSG	6,704	43.00	15
RPR	4,319	27.69	9
ADG	1,906	12.22	4
UDF	1,390	8.91	3
FN	571	3.66	—
PNPG	533	1.41	—
Others	490	3.14	—
Total	15,913	100.00	31

Political Organizations

Action Démocratique Guyanaise (ADG): ave d'Estrées, Cayenne; Leader ANDRÉ LECANTE.
Front National: place Newton, 97310 Kourou; extreme right-wing; Leader GUY MALON.
Parti National Populaire Guyanais (PNPG): ave d'Estrées, Cayenne; f. 1985; independence party; Leader CLAUDE ROBO.
Parti Socialiste Guyanais (PSG): Cité Césaire, Cayenne; f. 1956; Sec.-Gen. GÉRARD HOLDER.
Rassemblement pour la République (RPR): 84 ave Léopold Héder, Cayenne; f. 1946; right-wing; Pres. PAULIN BRUNÉ.
Union pour la Démocratie Française (UDF): 111 bis rue Christophe Colomb, BP 472, 97331 Cayenne; tel. 311710; f. 1979; Leader CLAUDE HO A CHUCK.

Judicial System

See: Judicial System, Martinique.

Religion

The majority of the population belong to the Roman Catholic Church.

CHRISTIANITY
The Roman Catholic Church

French Guiana comprises the single diocese of Cayenne, suffragan to the archdiocese of Fort-de-France, Martinique. At 31 December 1984 there were an estimated 62,000 adherents in French Giuana, representing more than 75% of the total population.
Bishop of Cayenne: FRANÇOIS MORVAN, Evêché, BP 378, 24 rue Madame-Payé, 97328 Cayenne; tel. 310118.

Other Christian Churches

The Seventh-day Adventist, Evangelist, Assembly of God, and Jehovah's Witnesses Churches are also represented.

The Press

France-Guyane: 28 rue Félix Eboué, Cayenne; telex 910552; 2 a week; Dir LUC GERMAIN; circ. 4,000.
Guyane-Matin: 42 blvd Jubelin, Cayenne; tel. 313524; daily; Dir FABIEN ROUBAUD; circ. 1,000.
La Presse de Guyane: 26 rue Lieutenant Brassé, 97300 Cayenne; daily; Dir JEAN SERGE; circ. 16,000.

Radio and Television

In 1983 there were an estimated 60,000 radio receivers and 12,000 television receivers in use.
Cayenne FM: Hôtel PLM Montabo, BP 581, 97334 Cayenne; tel. 313938; 120 hours weekly.
Radio-Télévision Française d'Outre-mer (RFO): rue du Dr Devèze, BP 336, 97305 Cayenne; tel. 311500; telex 910526; Radio-Guyane Inter: 16 hours broadcasting daily; Téléguyane: 2 channels, 32 hours weekly; Dir MARCEL BEAUDZA.
Radio Antipa: 1 place Schoëlcher, Cayenne; tel. 310037; 126 hours weekly.
Radio Tout Moune: route de Montabo, BP 74, Cayenne; tel. 318074; 24 hours a day; Dir HECTOR JEAN-LOUIS.

Finance

(cap. = capital; dep. = deposits; m. = million; frs = French francs; brs = branches)

BANKING
Central Bank

Caisse Centrale de Coopération Economique: 13 rue Louis Blanc, Cayenne; tel. 314133; telex 910570; Dir HERVÉ MAURICE.

Commercial Banks

Banque de la Guyane: 2 place Victor Schoëlcher, BP 35, Cayenne; tel. 303866; telex 910522; f. 1855; cap. 5m. frs, res 1.5m. frs (Dec. 1977); Dir M. BLONDEL; 2 brs.
Banque Française Commerciale: 8 place Palmistes, Cayenne; tel. 303577; telex 910559; Dir ANDRÉ GEROLIMATOS.
Crédit Populaire Guyanais: Caisse de Crédit Mutuel, 93 rue Lallouette, BP 818, 97338 Cayenne; tel. 301523; Dir MICHEL AUBERGE.

Development Bank

Société financière de développement de la Guyane (SOFIDEG): 25 rue F. Arago, Cayenne; tel. 300418; telex 910556; Dir PATRICE PIN.

Trade and Industry

Chambre de Commerce de la Guyane: 8 ave Général de Gaulle, Cayenne; tel. 303000; telex 910537; Pres. JEAN-PIERRE PRÉVÔT.
Jeune Chambre Economique de Cayenne: 2 bis rue Docteur Saint-Rose, BP 1094, Cayenne; Pres. MADELEINE GEORGES.

TRADE UNIONS

Confédération Française des Travailleurs: 113 rue Christophe Colomb, BP 383, Cayenne; tel. 310232; Sec.-Gen. RENÉ SYDALZA.
Fédération de l'Education Nationale: 68 rue Justin Catayee, BP 807, Cayenne; Sec.-Gen. ELIANE NIEL.

FRENCH OVERSEAS DEPARTMENTS

Force Ouvrière (FO): 107 rue Barthélemy, Cayenne; Sec.-Gen. M. Xavero.

Syndicat National des Instituteurs (SNI): Ecole Maximilien Sabas, BP 265, Cayenne; Sec.-Gen. Claude Leonardi.

Union des Travailleurs Guyanais (UTG): 7 ave de la Digue Ronjon, Cayenne; tel. 312642; Sec.-Gen. Paul Cécilien.

Transport

RAILWAYS

There are no railways in French Guiana.

ROADS

There are 372 km of Routes Nationales (66 asphalt) and 341 km of departmental roads (127 asphalt) along the coastal strip, linking the main towns with the capital, Cayenne. There were 40,651 registered vehicles in February 1986.

SHIPPING

The new port of Dégrad-des-Cannes, on the estuary of the river Mahury, has become the major port. There are other ports at Le Larivot, Saint-Laurent-du-Maroni and Kourou. Saint-Laurent is used primarily for the export of timber. There is a ferry service across the Maroni river between Saint-Laurent and Albina, Suriname. The rivers provide the best means of access to the interior, although numerous rapids prevent navigation by large vessels.

CIVIL AVIATION

Rochambeau International Airport, situated 17.5 km from Cayenne, is equipped to handle the largest jet aircraft. Air Guyane operates internal air services.

Guyane Air Transport (GAT): Rochambeau, Cayenne; tel. 317200; Dir M. Frédéric.

Tourism

There were 503 hotel rooms in 1982.

Office du Tourisme: Jardin Botanique, BP 801, 97303 Cayenne; tel. 300900; telex 910356; Dir H. Condé-Salazar.

Délégation régionale au Tourisme: Préfecture, rue Fiedmond, 97300 Cayenne; tel. 300520; telex 910532.

GUADELOUPE

Introductory Survey

Location, Climate, Language, Religion, Capital

Guadeloupe is the most northerly of the Windward Islands group in the West Indies. Dominica lies to the south, and Antigua and Montserrat to the north-west. Guadeloupe is formed by two large islands, Grande-Terre and Basse-Terre, separated by a narrow sea channel, with a smaller island, Marie-Galante, to the south-east, and another, La Désirade, to the east. There are also a number of small dependencies, mainly Saint-Barthélemy and the northern half of Saint-Martin (the remainder being part of the Netherlands Antilles), among the Leeward Islands. The climate is tropical, with an average temperature of 26°C (79°F), and a more humid and wet season between June and November. French is the official language, but a creole patois is widely spoken. The majority of the population profess Christianity, and belong to the Roman Catholic Church. The capital is the town of Basse-Terre; the other main town and principal commercial centre is Pointe-à-Pitre on Grande-Terre.

Recent History

Guadeloupe was first occupied by the French in 1635, and has remained French territory, apart from a number of brief occupations by the British in the 18th and early 19th century. It gained departmental status in 1946.

Economic and political power has been the monopoly of the white Creole population who wish to maintain the country's relationship with France, and the right-wing and centre parties have traditionally been the strongest political force on the islands. Most Guadeloupeans, however, are dissatisfied with the economic results of departmentalization and the attitudes of central government towards Guadeloupe's own identity, and they have sought greater internal autonomy for the department. The principal left-wing party, the Parti Communiste Guadeloupéen (PCG), was founded in 1958 in response to greater nationalist feeling. The PCG has rejected independence at any cost, preferring to seek internal autonomy. The deterioration of the economy and rising unemployment provoked industrial and political unrest during the 1960s and 1970s, including outbreaks of serious rioting in 1967. Pro-independence parties have rarely won more than 5% of the total vote at elections in Guadeloupe, but their activities have served to increase tension on the islands. Several have turned to violence as a means of expressing their opposition to what they see as French colonialism. In 1980 and 1981 there was a series of bomb attacks on hotels, government offices and other targets by a group called the Groupe Libération Armée (GLA), and in 1983 and 1984 there were further bombings by a group called the Alliance Révolutionnaire Caraïbe (ARC). The Government responded by outlawing the ARC and reinforcing the military and police presence on the islands. Further sporadic acts of violence continued into 1985, but in October the ARC suspended its bombing campaign, prior to the holding of legislative elections. However, in November 1986 a further series of bomb attacks began.

In 1974 Guadeloupe was granted the status of a region, and an indirectly-elected Regional Council was formed. In direct elections to a new Regional Council in February 1983, held as a result of the decentralization reforms that were introduced by the Socialist Government of President Mitterrand, the centre-right coalition succeeded in gaining a majority of the seats and control of the administration. In January 1984 Lucette Michaux-Chevry, the president of the General Council, formed a new conservative centre party, Le Parti de la Guadeloupe (LPG), to provide a more Guadeloupean approach to continued relationships with France, although the LPG remained in alliance with the right-wing Rassemblement pour la République (RPR). However, at the elections for the General Council, held in March 1985, the left-wing combination of the Parti Socialiste (PS) and the PCG gained a majority of seats on the enlarged Council, and Dominique Larifla of the PS was elected its president. In July demonstrations and a general strike, organized by pro-separatist activists in order to obtain the release of a leading member of the Mouvement populaire pour une Guadeloupe indépendante (MPGI), quickly intensified into civil disorder and rioting in the main town, Pointe-à-Pitre.

For the general election to the French National Assembly in March 1986, Guadeloupe's representation was increased from three to four deputies, with voting based on a system of proportional representation, rather than on the previous system of single-member constituencies. The local branches of the RPR and the Union pour la Démocratie Française (UDF), which had campaigned jointly at the 1981 general election and the 1983 regional elections, presented separate candidates. In February 1986 the president of the Regional Council, José Moustache, resigned from the RPR and joined the UDF. As a result of this split, the incumbent PCG and PS members of the Assembly (Ernest Moutoussamy and Frédéric Jalton respectively) were re-elected, but the other deputy seeking re-election, Marcel Esdras of the UDF, was defeated, and the two remaining seats were won by RPR candidates (Lucette Michaux-Chevry and Henri Beaujean).

In the concurrent elections for the 41 members of the Regional Council, the two left-wing parties together received 52.4% of the total votes (compared with 43.1% in 1983) and won a majority of seats, increasing their combined strength from 20 to 22 members (PS 12, PCG 10). As a result, Moustache was replaced as president of the Council by Félix Proto of the PS. The elections were boycotted by the Union Populaire pour la Libération de la Guadeloupe. In September the publication of a report (prepared at Proto's request) criticizing the management of finances by the former RPR/UDF majority on the Regional Council, led by Moustache, caused disruption within the Council and, as expected, had repercussions on the indirect elections for the two Guadeloupe members of the French Senate later in the month: there was a decline in support for centre-right candidates, and, as before, two left-wing Senators were elected (one from the PCG and one from the PS).

Government
France is represented in Guadeloupe by an appointed Government Commissioner. There are two councils with local powers: the 43-member General Council and the 41-member Regional Council. Both are elected by universal adult suffrage for a period of up to six years. Under the system of proportional representation used for the elections of March 1986, Guadeloupe elected four (hitherto three deputies) to the French National Assembly in Paris. Guadeloupe sends two indirectly elected representatives to the Senate.

Defence
In 1986 France maintained a military force of about 7,900 in French Guiana and the Antilles.

Economic Affairs
Guadeloupe's economy is based on agriculture, tourism and light industry, but is heavily dependent on French aid and imports. In 1982, according to estimates by the World Bank, the gross national product (GNP), measured at average 1980–82 prices, was US $1,370m. ($4,330 per head).

Agricultural production is dominated by the sugar industry, but this traditional sector of the economy is in decline. In 1983 less than 35% of available agricultural land was planted with sugar cane. The annual harvest of cane declined from 1.8m. metric tons in 1962 to 498,000 tons in 1984, and production of raw sugar consequently dropped from 184,812 tons in 1965 to 41,244 tons in 1984. Only four sugar factories remain in operation, and these suffer from inefficiency, lack of investment and large financial deficits. The production of rum, derived from sugar cane, has also declined: 64,883 hectolitres were distilled in 1984, compared with more than 90,000 hectolitres in 1982. Government attempts to revitalize the sugar industry by encouraging smallholders have been less successful than hoped. However, in 1982 a plan was agreed which provides a fixed price for sugar and subsidies for small-scale farmers. A three-year replantation scheme was launched in 1983, and it was intended that 10,000 ha would be replanted during that period. In 1985 the harvest of cane was 531,393 tons.

Bananas are the other major crop, and provide about 50% of Guadeloupe's export earnings. Exports of bananas totalled 133,413 metric tons in 1984, compared with 122,390 tons in 1982. Attempts have been made to diversify agricultural production by developing the cultivation of tropical fruits and vegetables, but Guadeloupe still relies heavily on imported food, which cost 587m. francs in 1983. In spite of a high level of unemployment, affecting 25% of the labour force in 1983, there is an acute shortage of agricultural labour, caused by the reluctance of young people to accept less than the minimum wage (wages are linked to those of metropolitan France). This has led to a large influx of immigrant workers from Haiti and Dominica, and to tensions in some areas of the towns.

Tourism is an important sector of the economy, but it employs only about 9% of the working population. Adverse publicity from the terrorist attacks in 1983 and 1984 led to many cancellations from tourists, and tourist arrivals at hotels declined in 1984 by more than 15%, to 163,469. The number declined still further in 1985, to 150,884.

The development of industrial activity has been promoted by the Government, and 36 companies were created between 1980 and 1982 at an investment of 120m. francs. However, the industrial sector employs only about 3,000 people, and contributes 10% of GDP. There is an industrial zone and freeport at Jarry. The 65% of the active population engaged in the administrative and service sector produce 80.5% of GDP. Civil servants from France receive a 40% bonus on their basic earnings, and other incentives, for working in the French Antilles. Local investment is concentrated in the import/export business, and in the discount stores which sell imported goods.

France provides more than 85% of Guadeloupe's imports, which totalled 5,230.7m. francs in 1984. Imports of energy, 83% of which are provided by the other French Overseas Departments, increased by around 50% between 1982 and 1984. This dependence on imported fuel, combined with the rapid rise in prices, contributed to a massive trade deficit, which rose from 2,680m. francs in 1981 to 4,480m. francs in 1984. In 1982 Guadeloupe received 2,960m. francs in aid from the French Government, but produced a deficit of 2,700m. francs. Between 1981 and 1984, the annual rate of inflation declined from 14% to 7.8%.

Social Welfare
There are two main public hospitals, a pyschiatric hospital and 10 private clinics, with a total of 2,314 beds in 1978. In 1979 there were 373 physicians and 78 dentists working in Guadeloupe.

Education
Education is free and compulsory in state schools between the ages of six and 16 years. The system is similar to that of France, with primary, junior and secondary academic and technical education. Primary education begins at six years of age and lasts for five years. Secondary education, beginning at the age of 11, lasts for up to seven years, comprising a first cycle of four years and a second of three years. Higher education is provided by a branch of the Universitaire Antilles-Guyane, containing faculties of law, economics and science.

Tourism
Guadeloupe is a popular tourist destination, especially for visitors from France and the USA. The main attractions are the beaches, the mountainous scenery and the unspoilt beauty of the island dependencies. In 1984 there were 74 hotels providing a total of 3,336 rooms. There were 227,180 tourist arrivals (including cruise-ship passengers) in 1984, compared with 259,450 in 1983.

Public Holidays
1987: 1 January (New Year's Day), 17–20 April (Easter), 1 May (Labour Day), 28 May (Ascension Day), 8 June (Whit Monday), 14 July (National Day), 21 July (Victor Schoëlcher Day), 11 November (Armistice Day), 25 December (Christmas Day).
1988: 1 January (New Year's Day), 1–4 April (Easter), 2 May (for Labour Day), 12 May (Ascension Day), 23 May (Whit Monday), 14 July (National Day), 21 July (Victor Schoëlcher Day), 11 November (Armistice Day), 25 December (Christmas Day).

Weights and Measures
The metric system is in use.

Currency and Exchange Rates
French currency is used (see French Guiana).

Statistical Survey

Source (unless otherwise stated): Institut national de la statistique et des études économiques, ave Paul Lacavé, BP 96, 97102 Basse-Terre; tel. 990250.

AREA AND POPULATION
Area: 1,780 sq km (687.3 sq miles), of which dependencies (La Désirade, Les Saintes, Marie-Galante, Saint-Barthélemy, Saint-Martin) 269 sq km.

Population: 327,002 (males 160,112; females 166,890) at census of 9 March 1982; 332,000 (estimate for 1 January 1985): *Principal Towns:* Basse-Terre (capital) 13,656, Pointe-à-Pitre 25,310 (1981 estimates).

Births, Marriages and Deaths (1984): Live births 6,676; Marriages 1,653; Deaths 2,239.

Economically Active Population (persons aged 16 years and over, 1982 census): Agriculture, forestry and fishing 12,997; Manufacturing, mining and quarrying 6,643; Electricity, gas and water 703; Construction 9,997; Wholesale and retail trade 10,062; Transport, storage and communications 4,819; Financing, insurance, real estate and business services 15,109; Community, social and personal services (incl. restaurants and hotels) 26,106; Activities not adequately defined 5,963; Total employed 92,399 (males 54,529, females 37,870); Unemployed 29,427 (males 14,629, females 14,798); Civilian labour force 121,826 (males 69,158, females 52,668); Armed forces 2,062 (all males); Total labour force 123,888.

AGRICULTURE, ETC.
Principal Crops (FAO estimates, '000 metric tons, 1985): Sugar cane 622, Bananas 153, Aubergines 6, Coconuts 3, Pineapples 2. Source: FAO, *Production Yearbook*.

Livestock (1985): Cattle 91,000, Pigs 46,000, Goats 52,000 (estimate), Sheep 4,000 (estimate). Source: FAO, *Production Yearbook*.

Fishing (estimated catch in metric tons, 1984): 8,940. Source: FAO, *Yearbook of Fishery Statistics*.

FRENCH OVERSEAS DEPARTMENTS Guadeloupe

INDUSTRY
Production (1984): Raw sugar 41,244 metric tons, Rum 64,883 hl, Electricity 446 million kWh.

FINANCE
Currency and Exchange Rates: French currency is used (see French Guiana).
Aid from France (1981): US $215 million.
Consumer Price Index (base: April 1978-March 1979 = 100): 171.5 in 1983; 185.6 in 1984.
Gross Domestic Product (million francs at current prices): 6,639 in 1981; 7,649 in 1982; 8,486 in 1983.

EXTERNAL TRADE
Principal Commodities (million francs, 1984): *Imports:* Agricultural products 278.5; Food products 917.2; Energy (petroleum) 896.9; Total (incl. others) 5,230.7. *Exports:* Agricultural products 438.8; Food products 190.3; Total (incl. others) 750.7.
Principal Trading Partners (million francs, 1984): *Imports:* France 3,072.2; Japan 137.9; Martinique 599.4; USA 153.7; Total (incl. others) 5,230.7. *Exports:* France 540.9; French Guiana 11.0; Martinique 118.0; Total (incl. others) 750.7.

TRANSPORT
Road Traffic (vehicles in use, 1981): Passenger cars 87,785, Commercial vehicles 33,350.
Shipping (1984): Ships entered 1,222; Freight loaded 338,000 metric tons; Freight unloaded 1,139,000 metric tons.
Civil Aviation (commercial traffic, 1984): Number of flights 31,687; Passengers carried 1,168,670, Freight carried 11,213 metric tons.

TOURISM
Visitors (1984): 227,180.

EDUCATION
Primary (1982): Schools 238, Teachers 2,408, Students 50,576.
Secondary (1982): Schools 59 (1981), Teachers 2,964, Students 49,062.
Higher (1981): The Universitaire Antilles-Guyane comprises, in Guadeloupe, a College of Arts, a College of Law and Economics and a College of Physical and Natural Sciences. In 1981 it was attended by 3,800 students. There is also an Ecole Normale for teacher training.

Directory

The Government
(January 1987)

Government Commissioner: YVES BONNET.
President of the General Council: DOMINIQUE LARIFLA (PS).
President of the Economic and Social Council: GUY FRÉDÉRIC.
Deputies to the French National Assembly: ERNEST MOUTOUSSAMY (PCG), FRÉDÉRIC JALTON (PS), LUCETTE MICHAUX-CHEVRY (RPR), HENRI BEAUJEAN (RPR).
Representatives to the French Senate: HENRI BANGOU (PCG), FRANÇOIS LOUISY (PS).

REGIONAL COUNCIL
President: FÉLIX PROTO (PS).

Election, 16 March 1986

	Votes	%	Seats
RPR	25,371	33.09	15
PS	21,969	28.65	12
PCG	18,229	23.77	10
UDF	8,217	10.71	4
Others	2,876	3.78	—
Total	76,662	100.00	41

Political Organizations

Alliance Révolutionnaire Caraïbe: Pointe-à-Pitre; f. 1983; illegal pro-independence alliance; left-wing; supports armed struggle.
Fédération Guadeloupéenne du Parti Socialiste (PS): Avenue de Général de Gaulle, Cité Jardin du Raizet, 97110 Abymes; Sec.-Gen. DOMINIQUE LARIFLA.
Fédération Guadeloupéenne du Rassemblement pour la République (RPR): 1 rue Baudot, Basse-Terre; tel. 811069; Pres. RAYMOND GUILLIOD.
Fédération Guadeloupéenne de l'Union pour la Démocratie Française (UDF): Pointe-à-Pitre; Pres. MARCEL ESDRAS.
Mouvement populaire pour une Guadeloupe indépendante (MPGI): Pointe-à-Pitre; f. 1982; extremist independence party; Sec-Gen. LUC REINETTE.
Mouvement Socialiste Départmentaliste Guadeloupéen: Mairie de Morne-à-l'Eau, 97111 Morne-à-l'Eau; Sec.-Gen. ABDON SAMAN.
Parti Communiste Guadeloupéen (PCG): 119 rue Vatable, 97110 Pointe-à-Pitre; f. 1944; Sec.-Gen. GUY DANINTHE.
Le Parti de la Guadeloupe (LPG): Pointe-à-Pitre; f. 1984; centre party; Leader LUCETTE MICHAUX-CHEVRY.
Union Populaire pour la Libération de la Guadeloupe (UPLG): Basse-Terre; f. 1978; semi-clandestine pro-independence movement; Pres. Dr CLAUDE MAKOUKE.

Judicial System

Cour d'Appel: Palais de Justice, 97100 Basse-Terre; First Pres. JEAN THIERRY; Procurator-Gen. ROLAND GIRARD; two Tribunaux de Grande Instance, four Tribunaux d'Instance.

Religion

The majority of the population belong to the Roman Catholic Church.

CHRISTIANITY

The Roman Catholic Church

Guadeloupe comprises the single diocese of Basse-Terre, suffragan to the archdiocese of Fort-de-France, Martinique. At 31 December 1984 there were an estimated 260,000 adherents, representing more than 75% of the total population. The Bishop participates in the Antilles Episcopal Conference, based in Kingston, Jamaica.

Bishop of Basse-Terre: Mgr ERNEST CABO, Evêché, BP 50, 97101 Basse-Terre; tel. 813669.

The Press

Combat Ouvrier: Valette, 97180 St Anne; monthly; trade union publ.
L'Etincelle: 119 rue Vatable, 97110 Pointe-à-Pitre; weekly; organ of the Communist Party; Dir ROBERT BARON; circ. 5,000.
France-Antilles: 1 rue Hincelin, BP 658, 97159 Pointe-à-Pitre; telex 919728; daily; Dir CLAUDE PROVENÇAL; circ. 25,000.
Guadeloupe 2000: Résidence Massabielle, 97110 Pointe-à-Pitre; fortnightly; right-wing extremist; Dir EDOUARD BOULOGNE; circ. 4,000.
Information Caraïbe (ICAR): BP 958, Pointe-à-Pitre; tel. 825606; f. 1973; weekly; Dir P. FERTIN.
Jakata: 18 rue Condé, 97110 Pointe-à-Pitre; f. 1977; fortnightly; Dir FRANTZ SUCCAB; circ. 6,000.
Magwa: Résidence Vatable, Bâtiment B, 97110 Pointe-à-Pitre; fortnightly; independent.
Match: 33 rue St John Perse, 97110 Pointe-à-Pitre; tel. 820187; fortnightly; Dir CAMILLE JABBOUR; circ. 6,000.
Le Progrès social: rue du Dr Cabre, 97110 Basse-Terre; tel. 811041; weekly; Dir HENRI RODES; circ. 5,000.
Télé Sept Jours: Agence Promovente, Immeuble Lagland Bergevin, 97110 Pointe-à-Pitre; weekly; TV.

FRENCH OVERSEAS DEPARTMENTS   *Guadeloupe*

NEWS AGENCIES

Agence France-Presse (AFP) and **Agence Centrale Parisienne de Presse (ACP)**: BP 1105, 97181 Pointe-à-Pitre; tel. 821476; telex 919728; Rep. RENÉ CAZIMIR-JEANON.

Foreign Bureaux

Agencia EFE (Spain): BP 1016, 97178 Pointe-à-Pitre; Correspondent DANNICK ZANDRONIS.

Associated Press (AP) (USA): BP 1105, 97181 Pointe-à-Pitre; tel. 821476; telex 919728; Rep. RENÉ CAZIMIR-JEANON.

United Press International (UPI) (USA): BP 658, 97159 Pointe-à-Pitre; Rep. STÉPHANE DELANNOY.

Radio and Television

In 1983 there were an estimated 98,000 radio receivers and 64,000 television receivers in use.

Société nationale de radio-télévision françaises d'Outre-Mer (RFO): BP 402, 97163 Pointe-à-Pitre Cedex; tel. 836320; 17 hours radio and 10 hours television broadcast daily; Dir ROGER BORDY.

Radio Antilles: 55 rue Henri IV, 97110 Pointe-à-Pitre.

Radio Caraïbes International: Tour Cecid, Blvd Legitimus, 97110 Pointe-à-Pitre; tel. 821746; telex 019083. Dir OLIVIER GARON.

Finance

(cap. = capital; dep. = deposits; m. = million; frs = French francs; brs = branches)

BANKING

Central Bank

Caisse Centrale de Coopération Economique: Faubourg Frébault, BP 160, 97154 Pointe-à-Pitre; tel. 833272; telex 919074.

Commercial Banks

Banque des Antilles Françaises: place de la Victoire, 97110 Pointe-à-Pitre; tel. 822593; telex 919726; rue de Cours Nolivos, 97100 Basse-Terre; f. 1853; cap. 32,583m. frs (1983); Dir d'Agence JEAN-FRANÇOIS JEANTES; Dir-Gen. MICHEL GENADINOS; 4 brs.

Banque Française Commerciale: 21 rue Gambetta, 97110 Pointe-à-Pitre; tel. 821201; telex 919764; f. 1977; cap. 21m. frs (Dec. 1981); Dir RENÉ MOUTTET; 4 brs.

Banque Nationale de Paris: place de la Rénovation, 97110 Pointe-à-Pitre; tel. 829696; telex 919706; Dir HENRI BETBEDER; 6 brs.

Banque Populaire de la Guadeloupe—Crédit Guadeloupéen: 10 rue Achille René-Boisneuf, 97110 Pointe-à-Pitre; f. 1926; tel. 914560; telex 919713; dep. 550m. frs (1983); Pres. CHRISTIAN RIMBAUD; Dir RICHARD NALPAS; 6 brs.

Caisse Régionale de Crédit Agricole Mutuel de la Guadeloupe: BP 134, Rue Félix Eboué Prolongée, 97154 Pointe-à-Pitre; tel. 821897; telex 919708; Dir THÉLÈME GEDEON; 5 brs.

Crédit Martiniquais: Angle des rues P. Lacavé et Cités Unies, 97100 Pointe-à-Pitre; tel. 831859; f. 1987, in succession to Chase Manhattan Bank (USA).

Société Générale de Banque aux Antilles (SGBA): 30 rue Frébault, 97110 Pointe-à-Pitre; tel. 825423; telex 919735; f. 1979; cap. 15m.; Pres. GEORGES GUITTON; Dir JEAN-CLAUDE GOETZ; 4 brs.

INSURANCE

Compagnie Antillaise d'Assurances, Société d'Assurances à forme mutuelle: 12 rue Gambetta, BP 409, 97110 Pointe-à-Pitre; tel. 832332; telex 919945; f. 1937; Dir-Gen. FÉLIX CHERDIEU D'ALEXIS; Man. A. ZOGG.

Foreign Companies

Some 30 of the principal European insurance companies are represented in Pointe-à-Pitre, and another six companies have offices in Basse-Terre.

Trade and Industry

Agence pour la promotion industrielle de la Guadeloupe (APRIGA): BP 1229, 97184 Pointe-à-Pitre; tel. 834897; telex 919780; f. 1979; development agency; Pres. GEORGES MARIANNE; Dir CHARLY BLONDEAU.

Centre Technique de la Canne et du Sucre: Morne l'Epingle, 97139 Les Abymes; tel. 829470; Pres. ANTOINE ANDREZE-LOUISON; Dir PHILIPPE DOUCHEL.

Chambre de Commerce et d'Industrie de Pointe-à-Pitre: Assainissement, BP 64, 97152 Pointe-à-Pitre; tel. 900808; telex 919780; Pres. GEORGES MARIANNE; Dir-Gen. JEAN-CLAUDE PARIS.

Chambre de Commerce et d'Industrie de Basse-Terre: 6 rue Victor Hugues, BP 17, 97100 Basse-Terre; tel. 811656; telex 919781; f. 1832; 24 mems; Pres. GÉRARD PENCHARD; Sec.-Gen. GERMAIN WILLIAM.

Chambre d'Agriculture de la Guadeloupe: 27 rue Sadi-Carnot, 97110 Pointe-à-Pitre; tel. 821130; telex 919286; Pres. CHRISTIAN FLEREAU; Dir VICTORIEN LUREL.

Société d'Intérêt Collectif Agricole (Sica-Assobag): Desmarais, 97100 Basse-Terre; tel. 810552; telex 919727; f. 1967; banana producers; Pres. FRANÇOIS LE METAYER; Dir JEAN-CLAUDE PETRELLUZZI.

Syndicat des Producteurs-Exportateurs de Sucre et de Rhum de la Guadeloupe et Dépendances: Zone Industrielle de la Pointe Jarry, 97122 Baie-Mahault, BP 2015, 97191 Pointe-à-Pitre; tel. 266212; f. 1937; 4 mems; Pres. AMÉDÉE HUYGHUES-DESPOINTES; Sec.-Gen. JACQUES GRENIER.

TRADE UNIONS

Confédération Générale du Travail de la Guadeloupe: 4 cité Artisanale de Bergevin, 97110 Pointe-à-Pitre; f. 1973; Sec.-Gen. CLAUDE MORVAN; 15,000 mems.

Union Départementale de la Confédération Française des Travailleurs Chrétiens: Pointe-à-Pitre; f. 1937; Sec.-Gen. E. DEMOCRITE; about 3,500 mems.

Union Départementale des Syndicats CGT-FO: 59 rue Lamartine, Pointe-à-Pitre; Gen. Sec. CLOTAIRE BERNOS; about 1,500 mems.

Union Générale des Travailleurs de la Guadeloupe: 5 Immeuble Diligenti, 97110 Pointe-à-Pitre; tel. 900539; confederation of pro-independence trade unions.

Union Interprofessionnelle de la Guadeloupe: Bergevin, 97110 Pointe-à-Pitre; tel. 831650; (affiliated to the Confédération Française Démocratique du Travail (CFDT) of France); Institut National de la Recherche Agronomique (INRA), Domaine de Duclos, 97170 Petit-Bourg; Secs M. GONFIE and AUBERT PARFAIT.

Transport

RAILWAYS

There are no railways in Guadeloupe.

ROADS

There are 1,975 km of roads in Guadeloupe, of which 323 km are Routes Nationales.

SHIPPING

The major port is at Pointe-à-Pitre, and a new port for the export of bananas has been built at Basse-Terre.

CIVIL AVIATION

Air Guadeloupe: Raizet Airport, 97110 Abymes; tel. 822161; telex 919008; f. 1970; regular flights to Antigua, Dominica, St Martin; connects the various dependent islands; fleet of 2 Fairchild F-27-J, 4 Twin Otters.

Tourism

Office du Tourisme: 5 square de la Banque, POB 1099, 97181 Pointe-à-Pitre; tel. 820930; telex 029715; Dir-Gen. ERICK W. ROTIN; Pres. PHILIPPE CHAULET.

Bureau Industrie et Tourisme: Préfecture de la Guadeloupe, rue de Lardenoy, 97109 Basse-Terre; tel. 817681; telex 919707; Dir FRANÇOIS VOSGIEN.

Syndicat d'Initiative de la Guadeloupe: 28 rue Sadi-Carnot, 97110 Pointe-à-Pitre; Pres. Dr EDOUARD CHARTOL.

FRENCH OVERSEAS DEPARTMENTS

MARTINIQUE

Introductory Survey

Location, Climate, Language, Religion, Capital

Martinique is one of the Windward islands in the West Indies, with Dominica to the north and Saint Lucia to the south. The island is dominated by the volcanic peak of Mont Pelée. The climate is tropical, but tempered by easterly and north-easterly breezes. The more humid and wet season runs from July to November, and the average temperature is 26°C (80°F). French is the official language, but a creole patois is widely spoken. The majority of the population profess Christianity and belong to the Roman Catholic Church. The capital is Fort-de-France.

Recent History

Martinique has been a French possession since 1635. The prosperity of the island was based on the sugar industry, which was dealt a devastating blow by the volcanic eruption of Mont Pelée in 1902. Martinique became a department of France in 1946, when the Governor was replaced by a Prefect, and an elected General Council was created.

The French Government's policy of assimilation since 1946 has created a strongly French society, bound by linguistic, cultural and economic ties to metropolitan France. The island enjoys a better infrastructure and a higher standard of living than its immediate Caribbean neighbours but, in consequence, it has also become heavily dependent on France. In 1960 the French Government granted the island's General Council the power to discuss political, as well as administrative, questions, partly in response to civil disturbances, and partly to the growth of nationalist feeling in the 1950s, as expressed by Aimé Césaire's Parti Progressiste Martiniquais (PPM), and the Parti Communiste Martiniquais (PCM). However, economic power remained concentrated in the hands of the *békés* (descendants of white colonial settlers), who own most of the agricultural land, and control the lucrative import/export market. This led to little incentive for innovation or self-sufficiency, and resentment at lingering colonial attitudes.

In 1974 Martinique, together with Guadeloupe and French Guiana, was given regional status as part of France's governmental reorganization. An indirectly-elected Regional Council was created, with some control over the local economy. In 1982 and 1983 the Socialist Government of President François Mitterrand, which had pledged itself to decentralizing power in favour of the overseas departments, made further concessions towards autonomy by giving the local councils greater control over taxation, local police and the economy. In the first direct elections to the new Regional Council, held in February 1983, left-wing parties gained a small majority of votes and seats. This success, and the election of Aimé Césaire as the Council's President, strengthened his influence against the pro-independence elements in his own party. Full independence for Martinique is supported by only a small minority of the population, while the majority seek reforms that would bring greater autonomy within French control. The Mouvement Indépendantiste Martiniquais (MIM), the most vocal of the separatist parties, fared badly in the elections, gaining less than 3% of the total vote. Late in 1983, and in 1984, Martinique became a target for the terrorist activities of the outlawed Alliance Révolutionnaire Caraïbe (ARC), which claimed responsibility for a number of bombings on the island. At elections to an enlarged General Council, held in March 1985, the left-wing parties increased their representation to 19 seats out of a total of 44, but the coalition of right-wing and centre parties maintained their control of the administration.

For the general election to the French National Assembly in March 1986, Martinique's representation was increased from three to four deputies, with voting based on a system of proportional representation, rather than the previous system of single-member constituencies. Martinique was the only French department in which the major left-wing parties presented a unified list of candidates. The left-wing alliance received 51.2% of the votes, and two of its candidates were elected: Aimé Césaire (who retained his seat) and Louis-Joseph Dogué of the Fédération Socialiste de la Martinique (FSM), the local branch of the Parti Socialiste. The joint list of the right-wing Rassemblement pour la République (RPR) and the centrist Union pour la Démocratie Française (UDF) obtained 42.4% of the votes, and each party won one seat. For the concurrent elections to the Regional Council, the Union of the Left (including the PPM, the FSM and the PCM) similarly campaigned with a joint programme, winning 21 of the 41 seats (as the three parties had together won in 1983), although with a reduced share (41.3%) of the votes. The RPR and the UDF together obtained 49.8% of the votes and won the 20 remaining seats. Aimé Césaire retained the presidency of the Council.

In September 1986 indirect elections were held for the two Martinique seats in the French Senate. As in the March elections, the left-wing parties united, and, as a consequence, Martinique acquired a left-wing Senator for the first time since 1958: Rodolphe Désiré of the PPM was elected, while the other successful candidate was an incumbent Senator, Roger Lise of the UDF.

Government

France is represented in Martinique by an appointed Government Commissioner. There are two councils with local powers: the 44-member General Council and the 41-member Regional Council. Both are elected by universal adult suffrage for a period of up to six years. Under the system of proportional representation used for the general election of March 1986, Martinique elected four (hitherto three) deputies to the French National Assembly in Paris. Martinique sends two indirectly elected representatives to the Senate.

Defence

In 1986 France maintained a military force of about 7,900 in French Guiana and the Antilles.

Economic Affairs

Martinique's economic development, in common with that of Guadeloupe, has created a society that combines a relatively high standard of living, and the benefits of a developed island, with a weak economic base in agricultural and industrial production, and a chronic trade deficit. This has contributed to problems such as high unemployment, emigration and social unrest. In 1983, according to estimates by the World Bank, Martinique's gross national product (GNP), measured at average 1981–83 prices, was US $1,320m., equivalent to $4,260 per head.

Sugar cane is the main agricultural crop, but the plantations have been allowed to decline in order to protect growers of sugar beet in France and other EEC countries. Martinique's annual output of raw sugar fell from 12,500 metric tons in 1968 to 2,000 tons in 1982, while only one sugar mill remained in production on the island. Martinique's sugar production now fails to satisfy one-quarter of local demand, and sugar is imported from Guadeloupe. Production increased in 1983 and reached 5,462 tons in 1984. Most is used in the production of rum for export. In the 1970s local investment was diverted from sugar cane towards the development of banana plantations. Bananas are the second major crop, but the plantations suffered damage from Hurricane Allen in 1980. Exports of bananas increased from 161,799 tons in 1984 to 170,873 tons in 1985. Exports to France totalled 167,209 tons, and the remainder was exported to Italy and other Mediterranean countries. The Government is trying to diversify agricultural products by developing underused areas of the country, and encouraging smallholders. Pineapples, aubergines, avocados and other tropical fruits are produced for the export market. However, agriculture provides only about 6.5% of GDP, and the island still remains dependent on imported food supplies. A large proportion of the island's meat requirements has to be imported, and virtually all the vegetables. This contributes to the massive trade deficit, which stood at 4,724m. francs in 1984.

Light industry and small businesses have been encouraged by specialist government agencies in an attempt to fill the gap left by the decline in agriculture. Two industrial zones have been established, tax incentives are in operation, and 154m. francs were invested between 1980 and 1983. However, industry provides only about 10% of GDP and employs 6,000 of the workforce. Between 1960 and 1980 the percentage of the working population employed in agricultural and industrial production declined from 62% to 29%. The majority of workers are employed in services and administration, and investment by the white landowners has been redirected into the more profitable food import and tourism sectors. There is also a large community of white civil servants, and other immigrants from France, attracted by the high standard of living and the close links with France.

Tourism is a major activity on the island, but numbers of tourists have fallen since 1981, partly owing to the recession, and partly as a result of the terrorist campaign in which bombs were planted outside hotels. However, the number of tourist arrivals at hotels rose by 4.4% in 1984, to 183,789, although the number of cruise-

FRENCH OVERSEAS DEPARTMENTS

Martinique

ship passengers calling at Martinique declined. In 1985 hotel arrivals totalled 190,255, and the number of cruise-ship passengers increased by almost 13%.

Unemployment is high, especially in the under-25 age group; in 1984 it was estimated to affect 25% of the labour force. There is extensive emigration to France and, to a lesser extent, French Guiana, at a rate of about 15,000 annually. The linking of wage levels to those of metropolitan France, despite the island's lower level of productivity, has increased labour costs and restricted development. France supports Martinique's economy by providing large amounts of government aid. In 1982 the island received 5,150m. francs in French aid.

Social Welfare

Martinique has a system of social welfare similar to that of metropolitan France. In 1981 there were 14 hospitals, with a total of 4,117 beds, and 361 physicians.

Education

There is free and compulsory education in government schools for children aged six to 16 years. Higher education in law, science and economics is provided by a branch of the Universitaire Antilles-Guyane.

Tourism

Martinique's tourist attractions are its beaches and coastal scenery, its mountainous interior, and the historic towns of Fort-de-France and St Pierre. In 1985 there were 190,255 tourist arrivals at hotels and 152,989 cruise-ship passenger arrivals.

Public Holidays

1987: 1 January (New Year's Day), 17–20 April (Easter), 1 May (Labour Day), 28 May (Ascension Day), 8 June (Whit Monday), 14 July (National Day), 11 November (Armistice Day), 25 December (Christmas Day).

1988: 1 January (New Year's Day), 1–4 April (Easter), 2 May (for Labour Day), 12 May (Ascension Day), 23 May (Whit Monday), 14 July (National Day), 11 November (Armistice Day), 25 December (Christmas Day).

Weights and Measures

The metric system is in use.

Currency and Exchange Rates

French currency is used (see French Guiana).

Statistical Survey

Source: Institut national de la statistique et des études économiques, Pointe de Jaham Schoëlcher, BP 605, 97261 Fort-de-France; tel. 717179.

AREA AND POPULATION

Area: 1,100 sq km (424.7 sq miles).

Population: 326,717 (males 158,415, females 168,302) at census of 9 March 1982; 327,073 (estimate for 1 January 1984); *Capital:* Fort-de-France, population 97,814 (1982).

Births, Marriages and Deaths (1984): Live births 5,715; Marriages 1,297; Deaths 2,072.

Economically Active Population (persons aged 16 years and over, 1982 census): Agriculture, hunting, forestry and fishing 9,844; Mining and quarrying 1,853; Manufacturing 4,001; Electricity, gas and water 1,006; Construction 7,832; Trade, restaurants and hotels 9,864; Transport, storage and communications 5,197; Financing, insurance, real estate and business services 17,878; Community, social and personal services 29,382; Activities not adequately defined 7,707; Total employed 94,564 (males 54,121, females 40,443); Unemployed 35,936 (males 18,086, females 17,850); Total labour force 130,500 (males 72,207, females 58,293).

AGRICULTURE, ETC.

Principal Crops (FAO estimates, '000 metric tons, 1985): Sugar cane 230, Bananas 205, Pineapples 26. Source: FAO, *Production Yearbook.*

Livestock (FAO estimates, year ending September 1985): Cattle 52,000, Pigs 42,000, Sheep 73,000, Goats 27,000. Source: FAO, *Production Yearbook.*

Fishing (estimated catch in metric tons): 5,174 in 1982. Source: FAO, *Yearbook of Fishery Statistics.*

INDUSTRY

Production (1984): Raw sugar 5,462 metric tons, Rum 104,003 hl, Cement 118,985 metric tons, Refined petroleum products 603,270 tons, Electricity 386 million kWh.

FINANCE

Currency and Exchange Rates: French currency is used (see French Guiana).

Budget (million francs, 1983): Revenue 1,742, Expenditure 5,868.

Aid from France (provisional estimate, 1980): 2,124 million francs.

Cost of Living (consumer price index; base: 1979 = 100): 160.9 in 1983; 173.8 in 1984.

Gross Domestic Product (million francs at current prices): 7,367 in 1981; 8,949 in 1982; 9,963 in 1983.

EXTERNAL TRADE

Principal Commodities (million francs, 1984): *Imports:* Food products 1,204.4; Energy (petroleum) 1,092.1; Total (incl. others) 5,647.8; *Exports:* Agricultural products 473.0; Food products 168; Total (incl. others) 924.2.

Principal Trading Partners (million francs, 1984): *Imports:* France 3,247; Venezuela 365; EEC (minus France) 534; *Exports:* France 633; Guadeloupe 164; French Guiana 34.

TRANSPORT

Road Traffic (motor vehicles in use at 31 December 1984): Passenger cars 140,000; Buses and coaches 700; Goods vehicles 2,000. Source: IRF, *World Road Statistics.*

Shipping (freight traffic in '000 metric tons, 1984): Goods loaded 542.7; Goods unloaded 1,241.8.

Civil Aviation (1984): Passengers carried 949,700, Freight 10,373 metric tons.

TOURISM

Tourist Arrivals (1984): Arrivals at hotels 190,255; Cruise passengers 152,989.

EDUCATION

Primary (1982): 226 schools, 1,927 teachers, 41,928 students.

Secondary (1982): 3,042 schools (1980), 3,142 teachers, 47,087 students. Source: UNESCO, *Statistical Yearbook.*

Higher (1983): 2,100 students at the Universitaire Antilles-Guyane which, in Martinique, comprises a College of Economic Science and a College of Law. There is also a teacher-training college.

Directory

The Government

(January 1987)

Government Commissioner: EDOUARD LACROIX.

President of the General Council: ÉMILE MAURICE (RPR).

Deputies to the French National Assembly: AIMÉ CÉSAIRE (PPM), LOUIS-JOSEPH DOGUÉ (FSM), MICHEL RENARD (RPR), JEAN MARAN (UDF-Parti Républicain).

Representatives to the French Senate: ROGER LISE (UDF), RODOLPHE DÉSIRÉ (PPM).

REGIONAL COUNCIL

President: AIMÉ CÉSAIRE (PPM).

Election, 16 March 1986

	Votes	%	Seats
Union de la Gauche*	50,372	41.34	21
RPR	37,573	30.83	11
UDF	23,087	18.94	9
Others	5,807	8.89	—
Total	121,839	100.00	41

* Including the PPM, the FSM and the PCM.

FRENCH OVERSEAS DEPARTMENTS	*Martinique*

Political Organizations

Fédération Socialiste de la Martinique (FSM): Cité la Meynard, 97200 Fort-de-France; tel. 503477; local branch of the Parti Socialiste; Leader MICHEL YOYO.

Groupe Révolution Socialiste (GRS): 40 rue Pierre Semar, 97200 Fort-de-France; tel. 703649; f. 1973; Trotskyist; Leader GILBERT PAGO.

Mouvement Indépendantiste Martiniquais (MIM): Fort-de-France; pro-independence party; also known as La Parole au peuple; Leader ALFRED MARIE-JEANNE.

Parti Communiste Martiniquais (PCM): Fort-de-France; f. 1957; Leader ARMAND NICOLAS.

Parti Progressiste Martiniquais (PPM): Fort-de-France; f. 1957; Pres. AIMÉ CÉSAIRE; Sec.-Gen. CAMILLE DARSIÈRES.

Rassemblement pour la République (RPR): Fort-de-France; Sec. MICHEL RENARD.

Union pour la Démocratie Française (UDF): Fort-de-France; Pres. JEAN MARAN.

Parti Républicain (PR): Fort-de-France; Leader JEAN BALLY.

Judicial System

Cour d'Appel de Fort-de-France: Fort-de-France; tel. 706262; telex 912525; highest court for Martinique and French Guiana; Pres. ROBERT BOSC; Procurator-Gen. HENRI JACQUEMIN.

Two Tribunaux de Grande Instance at Fort-de-France and Cayenne (French Guiana) and three Tribunaux d'Instance, two in Fort-de-France and one in Cayenne.

Religion

The majority of the population belong to the Roman Catholic Church.

CHRISTIANITY
The Roman Catholic Church

Martinique comprises a single archdiocese, with an estimated 290,000 adherents (nearly 90% of the total population) at 31 December 1984. The Archbishop participates in the Antilles Episcopal Conference, based in Kingston, Jamaica.

Archbishop of Fort-de-France: MAURICE MARIE-SAINTE, Archevêché, Route du Viet-Nâm héroïque, BP 586, 97207 Fort-de-France; tel. 637070.

The Press

Antilla: BP 46, Lamentin; monthly; Dir ALFRED FORTUNE.

L'Arbalète: Cité Saint-Georges, Fort-de-France; weekly.

Aujourd'hui Dimanche: presbytère de Bellevue, Fort-de-France; tel. 714897; weekly; Dir Père GAUTHIER; circ. 12,000.

Carib Hebdo: 23 rue Yves Goussard, Fort-de-France; Dir MAURICE TAÏLAMÉ.

Combat Ouvrier: BP 386, Immeuble C, Apt 34, Cité Saint-Georges, Fort-de-France; weekly; Dir M. G. BEAUJOUR.

France-Antilles: place Stalingrad, 97200 Fort-de-France; tel. 710883; telex 912677; f. 1964; daily; Dir DENIS HUERTAS; circ. 30,000 (Martinique edition).

Information Caraïbe (ICAR): 18 allée des Perruches, 97200 Fort-de-France; tel. 730429; weekly; Editor DANIEL COMPÈRE.

Justice: rue E. Zola, Fort-de-France; weekly; organ of the PPM; Dir G. THIMOTÉE; circ. 8,000.

Le Naif: voie no 7, route du Lamentin, Fort-de-France; weekly; Dir R. LAOUCHEZ.

Le Progressiste: rue de Tallis Clarière, Fort-de-France; weekly; organ of the PPM; Dir PAUL GABOURG; circ. 13,000.

Révolution Socialiste: BP 1031, 97200 Fort-de-France; tel. 703649; f. 1973; weekly; organ of the GRS; Dir PHILIPPE PIERRE CHARLES; circ. 2,500.

L'Union: weekly; organ of l'Union Departmentaliste Martiniquaise; Fort-de-France; Dir JEAN MARAN.

Radio and Television

In 1983 there were an estimated 45,000 radio sets and 41,500 television sets in use.

Radio-Télévision Française d'Outre-mer (RFO): La Clairère, BP 662, Fort-de-France; tel. 711660; Dir PIERRE GIRARD.

Radio Caraïbe Internationale (RCI): Immeuble Massal, Croix de Bellevue, 97209 Fort-de-France; tel. 731212; telex 019579; Dir-Gen. OLIVIER GARON.

Finance

(cap. = capital; dep. = deposits; m. = million;
frs = French francs; brs = branches)

BANKING
Central Bank

Caisse Centrale de Coopération Economique: 12 blvd du Général de Gaulle, BP 804, 97200 Fort-de-France; Dir JEAN BRUTOT.

Major Commercial Banks

Banque des Antilles Françaises: 34 rue Lamartine, 97200 Fort-de-France; tel. 719344; f. 1853; cap. 32.5m. frs (1983); Pres. Dir BERNARD NOGRET.

Banque Française Commerciale: 6–10 rue Ernest Deproge, 97200 Fort-de-France; telex 912526; cap. 50m. frs (1983); Dir HENRI DE MALEZIEUX.

Banque Nationale de Paris: 72 ave des Caraïbes, 97200 Fort-de-France; tel. 737111; telex 912619; Dir MICHEL MASSE.

Caisse Nationale d'Epargne et de Prévoyance: 82 rue Perrinon, 97200 Fort-de-France; telex 912435; Dir Mme M. E. ANDRE.

Caisse Régionale de Crédit Agricole Mutuel: 106 blvd Général de Gaulle, BP 583, 97207 Fort-de-France; tel. 717607; telex 912657; f. 1950; 9,500 mems; Pres. M. SAINTE-ROSE; Dir MAURICE LAOUCHEZ; 27 brs.

Crédit Maritime Mutuel: 45 rue Victor Hugo, 97200 Fort-de-France; tel. 730093; telex 912477.

Crédit Martiniquais: rue de la Liberté, Fort-de-France; tel. 711240; telex 912612; f. 1922; associated with Crédit Lyonnais (France), Banque Paribas (France) and, since 1987, with Chase Manhattan Bank (USA); cap. 30.4m. frs (1983); Pres. ROGER MARRY; Gen. Man. PIERRE MICHAUX; 11 brs.

Crédit Ouvrier: 30 rue Franklin Roosevelt, Fort-de-France; Dir ALAIN LOUTOBY.

Crédit Populaire: ave Jean Jaurès, 97200 Fort-de-France; Dir M. L. ASSELIN DE BEAUVILLE.

Crédit Social des Fonctionnaires: 63 rue Perrion, 97200 Fort-de-France; Dir FRED AUGUSTIN.

Société Générale de Banque aux Antilles: 19 rue de la Liberté, BP 408, 97200 Fort-de-France; tel. 716983; telex 912545; f. 1979; cap. 15m. frs; Dir MICHEL SAMOUR.

Société Martiniquaise de Financement (SOMAFI): route de Saint Thérèse, 97200 Fort-de-France; Dir JEAN MACHET.

INSURANCE

Cie Antillaise d'Assurances: 19 rue de la Liberté, 97205 Fort-de-France; tel. 730450.

Caraïbe Assurances: 11 rue Victor Hugo, BP 210, 97202 Fort-de-France; tel. 639229; telex 912096.

Groupement Français d'Assurances: 46–48 rue Ernest Deproge, 97205 Fort-de-France; tel. 605455; telex 912403.

La Nationale (GAN): 30 blvd Général de Gaulle, BP 185, Fort-de-France; tel. 713007; Reps MARCEL and ROGER BOULLANGER.

La Protectrice: 27 rue Blénac, 97205 Fort-de-France; tel. 702545; Rep. RENÉ MAXIMIN.

Le Secours: 74 ave Duparquet, 97200 Fort-de-France; tel. 700379; Dir Y. ANGANI.

L'Union des Assurances de Paris: 28 rue de la République, Fort-de-France; tel. 700470; Rep. R. DE REYNAL.

Trade and Industry

CHAMBER OF COMMERCE

Chambre de Commerce et d'Industrie de la Martinique: 50–56 rue Ernest Deproge, Fort-de-France; tel. 700008; telex 912633;

f. 1907; Pres. Alex Huyghues-Despointes; Dir-Gen. Henri Titina; 26 mems.

DEVELOPMENT

Agence pour le Développement Economique de la Martinique: 26 rue Lamartine; BP 803, 97207 Fort-de-France; tel. 734581; telex 912633; f. 1979; promotion of industry.

Bureau de l'Industrie de l'Artisanat: Préfecture, 97262 Fort-de-France; tel. 713627; telex 029650; f. 1960; government agency; research, documentation and technical and administrative advice on investment in industry and tourism; Dir Raphaël Firmin.

Société de Crédit pour le Développement de la Martinique (SODEMA): 12 blvd du Général de Gaulle, BP 575, 97200 Fort-de-France; tel. 605758; f. 1970; cap. 14.7m. frs; medium- and long-term finance.

Société de Développement Régional Antilles-Guyane (SODERAG): 109 rue Ernest Deproge, 97200 Fort-de-France; tel. 635978; telex 912343; Dir-Gen. J. Jack Elot; Sec.-Gen. Fernand Lerychard.

ASSOCIATIONS

Chambre Départementale d'Agriculture: 55 rue Isambert, BP 432, Fort-de-France; tel. 715146; Pres. Marcel Fabre.

Chambre de Métiers de la Martinique: Morne Tartenson, 97200 Fort-de-France; tel. 713222; f. 1970; 40 mems; Pres. P. Samot.

Groupement de Producteurs d'Ananas de la Martinique: BP 12, 97201 Fort-de-France; f. 1967; Pres. C. de Gryse.

Société d'Intérêt Collectif Agricole Bananière de la Martinique (SICABAM): Centre Commercial de Dillon, 97200 Fort-de-France; telex 912617; f. 1961; 1,000 mems; Pres. M. Garcin; Dir H. Hayot.

Syndicat des Distilleries Agricoles: Immeuble Clément, rive droite Levassor, Fort-de-France; tel. 712546.

Syndicat des Planteurs et Manipulateurs de la Canne: 33 rue Lamartine, Fort-de-France; tel. 712453; Pres. Jean de Laguarigue.

Syndicat des Producteurs de Rhum Agricole: Dillon, 97200 Fort-de-France.

Union Départementale des Coopératives Agricoles de la Martinique: Fort-de-France; Pres. M. Ursulet.

TRADE UNIONS AND PROFESSIONAL ORGANIZATIONS

Centrale Démocratique Martiniquaise des Travailleurs: BP 21, 97201 Fort-de-France; Sec.-Gen. Line Beausoleil.

Chambre Syndicale des Hôtels de Tourisme de la Martinique: Entrée Montgéralde, Route de Chateauboeuf, BP 1011, Fort-de-France; tel. 702780.

Confédération Générale du Travail: Maison des Syndicats, Jardin Desclieux, Fort-de-France; tel. 712589; f. 1936; affiliated to WFTU; Sec.-Gen. Victor Lamon; about 12,000 mems.

Ordre des Médecins de la Martinique: 35 rue Victor-Sévère, 97200 Fort-de-France; tel. 702701; Pres. Dr René Legendri.

Ordre des Pharmaciens de la Martinique: Zone Industrielle de la Lézarde, 97232 Lamentin; tel. 511356.

Syndicat National des Instituteurs: 3 rue de la Mutualité, Fort-de-France.

Union Départementale des Syndicats—FO: BP 1114, 97209 Fort-de-France; affiliated to ICFTU; Sec.-Gen. R. Fabien; about 2,000 mems.

Transport

RAILWAYS

There are no railways in Martinique.

ROADS

There are 262 km of autoroutes and first class roads, and 615 km of secondary roads.

SHIPPING

Alcoa Steamship Co, Alpine Line, Agdwa Line, Delta Line, Raymond Witcomb Co, Moore MacCormack, Eastern Steamship Co: c/o Ets René Cottrell, 48 rue Ernest Deproge, Fort-de-France.

Compagnie Générale Maritime: BP 574, ave Maurice Bishop, 97206 Fort-de-France; tel. 700040; telex 912049; also represents other passenger and freight lines; Rep. Guy Adam.

Compagnie de navigation Mixte: Immeuble Rocade, La Dillon, BP 1023, 97209 Fort-de-France; Rep. R. M. Michaux.

Compagnie Maritime des Chargeurs Réunis: 34 rue Ernest Deproge, 97200 Fort-de-France; Rep. M. G. Plissonneau.

CIVIL AVIATION

Martinique's international airport is at Lamentin, 6 km from Fort-de-France, and is served by the following airlines: Air Canada, American Airlines (USA), Air France, LIAT (Antigua), Pan Am and Eastern Airlines (USA).

Air Martinique: Aéroport du Lamentin, 97232 Le Lamentin; tel. 510990; telex 912385; f. 1981; scheduled and charter services; Chair. Michel Zeigler; Dir-Gen. Michel Gouze; fleet of 2 Twin Otters, 2 Islanders, and 1 Beech 99.

Tourism

Délégation Régionale au Tourisme: Préfecture, Fort-de-France; Dir. Gilbert Lecurieux.

Office du Tourisme: Pavillon du Tourisme, blvd Alfassa, BP 520, 97200 Fort-de-France; tel. 717960; Pres. Jean-Baptiste Edmond; Dir Jacques Guannel.

Syndicat d'Initiative: BP 299, 97203 Fort-de-France; Pres. M. R. Rose-Rosette.

RÉUNION

Introductory Survey

Location, Climate, Language, Religion, Capital

Réunion is an island in the Indian Ocean, lying about 800 km (500 miles) east of Madagascar. The climate varies greatly according to altitude: at sea-level it is tropical, with average temperatures between 20°C (68°F) and 28°C (82°F), but in the uplands it is much cooler, with average temperatures between 8°C (46°F) and 19°C (66°F). Rainfall is abundant, averaging 4,714 mm annually in the uplands, and 686 mm at sea-level. The population is of mixed origin, including people of European, African, Indian and Chinese descent. The official language is French. A large majority of the population are Christians belonging to the Roman Catholic Church. The capital is Saint-Denis.

Recent History

Réunion was first occupied by France in 1642, and was ruled as a colony until 1946, when, in common with certain Caribbean territories, it received full departmental status. In 1974 it became an Overseas Department with the status of a region.

In June 1978 the liberation committee of the OAU adopted a report recommending measures to hasten the independence of the island, and condemned its occupation by a 'colonial power'. However, this view seems to have little support among the people of Réunion themselves. Although the left-wing political parties on the island advocate increased autonomy (amounting to virtual self-government), few people are in favour of complete independence.

In 1982 the French Government proposed a decentralization scheme, envisaging the dissolution of the General and Regional Councils in the Overseas Departments and the creation in each territory of a single assembly, to be elected on the basis of proportional representation. However, this plan met with considerable opposition in Réunion and the other Overseas Departments, and the Government was eventually forced to abandon the project. Revised legislation on decentralization in the Overseas Departments was approved by the French National Assembly in December 1982. Elections for the new Regional Council were held in Réunion in February 1983, when left-wing candidates won 50.77% of the votes cast.

For the general election to the French National Assembly in March 1986, Réunion's representation was increased from three to five deputies, with voting based on a system of proportional representation, rather than on the previous system of single-member constituencies. The Parti Communiste Réunionnais (PCR) won two seats, while the Union pour la Démocratie Française (UDF), the Rassemblement pour la République (RPR) and a newly-formed right-wing party, France-Réunion-Avenir (FRA), each secured one seat. In the concurrent elections to the Regional Council, the centre-right RPR/UDF alliance and FRA together received 54.1% of the votes cast, winning respectively 18 and eight of the 45 seats, while the PCR won 13 seats. Pierre Lagourgue of FRA was elected President of the Regional Council.

In September 1986 the French Government's plan to introduce a programme of economic reforms (see Economic Affairs) provoked controversy on the island. The left-wing parties claimed that the Government's proposals should grant the Overseas Departments social equality with metropolitan France through similar levels of taxation and benefits. Before Jacques Chirac, the French Prime Minister, visited Réunion to announce the reforms in October, the PCR Secretary-General, Paul Vergès, accused France of instituting 'social apartheid' in the Overseas Departments, and presented his case to the European Parliament in Strasbourg.

In January 1986 France was admitted to the Indian Ocean Commission (IOC, see p. 217), on account of its sovereignty over Réunion. Réunion was given the right to host ministerial meetings of the IOC, but would not be allowed to occupy the presidency, owing to its status as a non-sovereign state.

Government

France is represented in Réunion by an appointed Government Commissioner. There are two councils with local powers: the 36-member General Council and the 45-member Regional Council. Both are elected for up to six years by direct universal suffrage. Under the system of proportional representation used for the general election of March 1986, Réunion elected five (hitherto three) deputies to the National Assembly in Paris. Réunion sends three indirectly elected representatives to the Senate.

Defence

Réunion is the headquarters of French military forces in the Indian Ocean. In 1986 there were 3,300 French troops stationed on Réunion and Mayotte.

Economic Affairs

The economy has traditionally been based on agriculture, which employed 14.7% of the working population in 1982. Sugar cane is the principal crop and has formed the basis of the economy for over a century. Only 25% of the land area can be cultivated because of the volcanic origin of the soil, but over 70% of the arable land is used for sugar cane. Annual production of raw sugar declined from 258,100 tons in 1982, to 223,700 tons in 1983, owing to drought. Output increased to 246,400 tons in 1984 but declined to about 233,000 tons in 1985. In 1985 sugar exports accounted for 75% of total exports by value. Other crops include vanilla, tobacco and geraniums, vetiver and ylang-ylang, which are grown for the production of tropical essences. Réunion is far from self-sufficient in food, and substantial imports are necessary. The only industry of importance is the processing of sugar and rum.

France remains the major trading partner, supplying 64.9% of imports and buying 80% of exports in 1984. However, Réunion suffers from a substantial trade deficit: in 1984 receipts from exports covered only 11.9% of the import bill. The difference is partly made up by financial support from France, which totalled 500m. francs in 1982, and by receipts from expatriate workers. Tourism is becoming more important, and it is hoped that increased investment in this sector will lead to higher receipts and will help to reduce the trade deficit, as well as providing new jobs. The rate of population growth has dropped sharply since 1973, from 3% per year to around 1.5%, but the population density remains extremely high (205.3 per sq km in 1982). Réunion has a high level of unemployment. The 1982 census recorded 54,338 people, or 31.4% of the labour force, as unemployed, and by October 1986 the number of unemployed reached about 72,000, or 37.1% of the labour force. Since 1980 the Government has invested heavily in a series of public works projects in an effort to create jobs and to alleviate the high level of seasonal unemployment following the sugar cane harvest. However, large numbers of workers still emigrate in search of employment, principally to France. In mid-1986 Réunion was expected to benefit from French legislation reducing employers' payments to young persons' social security contributions, in an attempt to encourage youth employment. The French Government also introduced a programme of reforms in October 1986 to enhance the Overseas Departments' economic status by 1991. The reforms included a removal of taxation from investments in all economic sectors of the Overseas Departments for a renewable period of 10 years. The Integrated Development Operation (OID) for the Overseas Departments, initiated in 1979 by local assemblies in conjunction with the French Government, would be continued, and 400m. francs was to be provided for Réunion (over a five-year period) from various sources, including the French Government, the EEC, and from revenue resulting from the implementation of the 1986 programme of reforms. The rate of inflation decreased from 13.9% in 1981 to 8.2% in 1983 and has since stabilized at 7.7% in 1984 and at 7.2% in 1985. In 1984, according to estimates by the World Bank, Réunion's gross national product (GNP), measured at average 1982–84 prices, was US $1,950m., equivalent to $3,690 per head. Between 1973 and 1983, it was estimated, GNP per head increased, in real terms, at an average rate of only 0.6% per year. Réunion's economic future is largely dependent on France's willingness to continue the subsidies implicit in the island's status as a department, despite the low tax yield from its generally unprosperous citizens.

Social Welfare

In 1985 Réunion had 3,849 hospital beds; there were 813 physicians, 181 nurses and 221 dentists.

Education

Education is compulsory for children aged six to 16 years, and consists of five years' primary and five years' secondary schooling.

FRENCH OVERSEAS DEPARTMENTS
Réunion

In 1985 there were 499 primary schools and 69 secondary schools, comprising 59 junior comprehensives, or collèges, and 10 lycées, on the island. There is a teacher training college and a university college, which was upgraded to full university status, with several faculties, in 1982. The illiteracy rate among the population over 15 years of age was 21.3% in 1982.

Tourism
Tourism is being extensively developed. A three-year plan, launched in 1979, invested 13.4m. francs in the sector. Several new hotels were built, and in 1983 a 'holiday village' was opened in Saint-Gilles. In 1984 about 79,000 tourists stayed in the island's hotels.

Weights and Measures
The metric system is in use.

Currency and Exchange Rates
French currency is used (see French Guiana).

COMMUNICATIONS MEDIA
Radio receivers (1983): 120,000 in use.
Television receivers (1983): 90,000 in use.
Telephones (1981): 60,000 in use.
Book production (1983): 79 titles.
Daily newspapers (1982): 3 (average circulation 59,000 copies).
Non-daily newspapers (1982): 2 (average circulation 9,000 copies).

EDUCATION
Primary (incl. pre-primary): Teachers 4,963 (1981/82), Pupils 113,330 (1984/85), Schools 499 (1985).
Secondary: Teachers 4,042 (1981/82), Pupils 69,417 (1984/85), Schools 69 (1985).
University: Teaching Staff 74 (1982/83), Students 2,995 (1984/85). There is also a teacher training college.
* Provisional figures.

Statistical Survey

Source: Institut National de la Statistique et des Etudes Economiques, Service Régional de la Réunion, Saint-Denis.

AREA AND POPULATION
Area: 2,512 sq km (970 sq miles).
Population: 515,798 (males 252,997, females 262,801) at census of 9 March 1982; 532,000 (estimate for 1 January 1984).
Principal Towns (population at 1982 census): Saint-Denis (capital) 109,068; Saint-Paul 58,410; Saint-Pierre 50,081.
Births and Deaths (1984): Births 13,129, Birth rate (per 1,000) 24.4; Deaths 3,079, Death rate (per 1,000) 5.7.
Labour Force (1982 census): Employed 118,490 (males 77,270, females 41,220); Unemployed 54,338 (males 33,548, females 20,790).

AGRICULTURE, ETC.
Principal Agricultural Products (FAO estimates, '000 metric tons, 1985): Sugar cane 2,100, Raw sugar 233, Maize 14.
Livestock (FAO estimates, '000 head, year ending September 1985): Cattle 20, Pigs 72, Goats 43, Sheep 3.
Fishing (landings, metric tons): 2,787 (1982); 2,448 (1983); 2,144 (1984).

FINANCE
Currency and Exchange Rates: French currency is used (see French Guiana).
Budget (million francs, 1984): Revenue 2,228.2; Expenditure 5,685.0.
Cost of Living (Consumer Price Index for December each year; base: 1978 = 100): 158.1 in 1982; 171.0 in 1983; 183.2 in 1984.
Gross Domestic Product (million francs at current prices): 10,128.1 in 1981; 12,008.9 in 1982; 13,410.6 in 1983.

EXTERNAL TRADE
Principal Commodities (million francs): *Imports* (1984*): Agricultural, fishing and forestry products 410, Processed agricultural products 1,310, Fuels 740, Intermediate goods 1,110, Capital goods 1,730, Consumer goods 1,590; Total 6,890. *Exports* (1984*): Sugar 612.4, Rum 34.2, Oil of geranium 20.9, Oil of vetiver root 13.0, Vanilla 10.0; Total (incl. others) 816.6.
Principal Trading Partners (million francs): *Imports* (1984): France 4,475.5, Others 2,414.5. *Exports* (1982): France 418.8, Others 270.2.

TRANSPORT
Road Traffic (motor vehicles in use, 1982): Passenger cars 108,725; Vans 24,997; Total (incl. others) 158,257.
Shipping: Vessels entered (1983) 390; Freight unloaded (1984) 1,098,500 metric tons; Freight loaded (1984) 294,400 metric tons; Passenger arrivals (1983) 407; Passenger departures (1983) 365.
Civil Aviation (1984): Passenger arrivals 205,640; Passenger departures 206,667; Freight unloaded 6,181 metric tons; Freight loaded 3,938 metric tons.

Directory

The Government
(January 1987)

Government Commissioner: JEAN ANCIAUX.
President of the General Council: AUGUSTE LEGROS (RPR).
President of the Economic and Social Council: EDMOND LAURET.
Deputies to the French National Assembly: MICHEL DEBRÉ (RPR), PAUL VERGÈS (PCR), ELIE HOARAU (PCR), JEAN-PAUL VIRAPOULLÉ (UDF-CDS), ANDRÉ THIEN AH KOON (FRA).
Representatives to the French Senate: PAUL BÉNARD (RPR), ALBERT RAMASSAMY (PS), LOUIS VIRAPOULLÉ (centre).

REGIONAL COUNCIL
Place Barachois, 97405 Saint-Denis.
President: PIERRE LAGOURGUE (FRA).

Election, 16 March 1986

Party	% of Votes	Seats
RPR/UDF	36.8	18
PCR	28.2	13
FRA and other right-wing	17.3	8
PS	14.1	6
Others	3.6	—
Total	100.0	45

Political Organizations

France-Réunion-Avenir (FRA): Saint-Denis; f. 1986; right-wing; Leader ANDRÉ THIEN AH KOON.

Front National (FN): Saint-Denis; f. 1972; extreme right-wing policies; advocates continuing relations with South Africa; Leader ALIX MOREL.

Mouvement des Radicaux de Gauche (MRG): BP 991, 97479 Saint-Denis; f. 1977; campaigns for independence and an economy separate from, but assisted by, France; Pres. JEAN-MARIE FINCK.

Mouvement pour l'Indépendance de la Réunion (MIR): f. 1981 from Mouvement pour la libération de la Réunion; groups all those favouring autonomy.

Parti Communiste Réunionnais (PCR): Saint-Denis; f. 1959; Sec.-Gen. PAUL VERGÈS.

Parti Socialiste (PS)—Fédération de la Réunion: 85 rue d'Après, 97400 Saint-Denis; tel. 21-77-95; telex 916445; Sec.-Gen. JEAN-CLAUDE FRUTEAU.

Rassemblement des Démocrates pour l'Avenir de la Réunion (RADAR): BP 866, 97477 Saint-Denis Cedex; f. 1981; centre party.

FRENCH OVERSEAS DEPARTMENTS   *Réunion*

Rassemblement des Socialistes et des Démocrates (RSD): Saint-Denis; Sec.-Gen. Daniel Cadet.

Rassemblement pour la République (RPR): 23 rue Victor MacAuliffe, 97400 Saint-Denis; tel. 20-06-09; telex 916080; Department Sec. François Mas.

Union pour la Démocratie Française (UDF): Saint-Denis; f. 1978; Sec.-Gen. Gilbert Gérard.

Centre des Démocrates Sociaux (CDS).

Judicial System

Cour d'appel: Palais de Justice, 166 rue Juliette Dodu, 97488 Saint-Denis; tel. 21-75-39; telex 916149; Pres. Henri Thiriot.

There are two **Tribunaux de grande instance**, one **Cour d'assises**, four **Tribunaux d'instance**, two **Tribunaux pour enfants** and two **Conseils de prud'hommes**.

Religion

A large majority of the population are adherents of the Roman Catholic Church.

CHRISTIANITY
The Roman Catholic Church

Réunion comprises a single diocese, directly responsible to the Holy See. At 31 December 1984 there were an estimated 465,000 adherents, representing 87% of the population.

Bishop of La Réunion: Mgr Gilbert Aubry, Evêché, 36 rue de Paris, BP 55, 97462 Saint-Denis; tel. 21-28-49.

The Press

DAILIES

Journal de l'Ile de la Réunion: 42 rue Alexis de Villeneuve, BP 98, 97463 Saint-Denis; tel. 21-32-64; telex 916453; f. 1956; Dir Philippe Baloukjy; circ. 26,500.

Quotidien de la Réunion: BP 303, 97467 Saint-Denis Cedex; tel. 28-10-10; telex 916183; f. 1976; Dir Maximin Chane Ki Chune; circ. 29,000.

Témoignages: 21 bis rue de l'Est, BP 192, 97465 Saint-Denis; f. 1944; organ of the Parti Communiste Réunionnais; Dir Elie Hoarau; circ. 6,000.

PERIODICALS

Al-Islam: BP 437, 31 rue M. A. Leblond, 97410 Saint-Pierre; tel. 25-19-65; publ. by the Centre Islamique de la Réunion; monthly; Dir Saïd Ingar.

Cahiers de la Réunion et de l'Océan Indien: 24 blvd des Cocotiers, 97434 Saint-Gilles-les-Bains; Man. Dir Claudette Saint-Marc.

Les Cahiers du Centre Universitaire de la Réunion: ave de la Victoire, 97400 Saint-Denis; Dir Anne Jacquemin.

Gazette de l'Ile de la Réunion: rues Bouvet/Monthyon, Saint-Denis; weekly.

Le Memento Industriel et Commercial Réunionnais: 80 rue Pasteur, 97400 Saint-Denis; tel. 21-94-12; Dir Catherine Louapre Pottier; circ. 10,000.

974 Ouest: Montgaillard, 97400 Saint-Denis; monthly; Dir Denise Elma.

Les Nouvelles Economiques: BP 120, 5 bis rue de Paris, 97463 Saint-Denis; tel. 21-53-66; telex 916278; monthly; Dir Jean-Pierre Fourtoy.

La Réunion Agricole: Chambre d'Agriculture, 24 rue de la Source, BP 134, 97464 Saint-Denis Cedex; tel. 21-25-88; monthly; Dir Marcel Bolon; Chief Editor René Bouisseau; circ. 17,000.

Télé 7 Jours Réunion: BP 405, 9469 Saint-Denis; weekly; Dir Michel Mekdoud; circ. 25,000.

Témoignage Chrétien de la Réunion: 21 bis rue de l'Est, 97465 Saint-Denis; weekly; Dir. René Payet; circ. 2,000.

Visu: BP 405, 9469 Saint-Denis; monthly.

Radio and Television

In 1983 there were an estimated 120,000 radio receivers and 90,000 television receivers (including 20,000 colour receivers) in use. Since 1985 there has been a growth in the number of private local radio stations.

Radio France d'Outre-Mer (RFO): place Sarda Garriga, 97405 Saint-Denis; home radio and television relay services in French; a second TV channel was opened in 1983; Dir Yves Le Garrec.

Télé Free-DOM: Saint-Denis; f. 1986; private TV channel; Dir Dr Camille Sudre.

Finance

(cap. = capital; res = reserves; brs = branches; amounts in French francs)

BANKING
Central Bank

Institut d'Emission des Départements d'Outre-mer: 1 cité du Retiro, 75008 Paris, France; Office in Réunion: 4 rue de la Compagnie, 97487 Saint-Denis Cedex; tel. 21-18-96; Dir Jacques Pierrat.

Commercial Banks

Banque Française Commerciale: 60 rue Alexis de Villeneuve, 97400 Saint-Denis; tel. 21-82-50; telex 916162; affiliated to Banque Indosuez; Dir Roger Vincenti; 9 brs.

Banque Nationale de Paris Intercontinentale: 67 rue Juliette Dodu, BP 113, 97463 Saint-Denis; telex 916133; Man. Dir Serge Nicolaoui; 13 brs.

Banque de la Réunion: 27 rue Jean-Chatel, 97400 Saint-Denis; tel. 21-32-20; telex 916134; f. 1849; affiliated to Crédit Lyonnais; cap. 36.3m.; res 54m. (1983); Pres. Tanneguy de F. de Chauvin; Man. Dir Jean-François Maulandi; 11 brs.

Caisse Régionale de Crédit Agricole Mutuel de la Réunion: cité des Lauriers 'les Camélias', BP 84, 97462 Saint-Denis; f. 1949; affiliate of Caisse Nationale de Crédit Agricole; Chair. Henry Isautier; Dir Henri Pavie.

Development Bank

Banque Populaire Fédérale de Développement: 33 rue Victor MacAuliffe, 97400 Saint-Denis; tel. 21-18-11; telex 916582; Dir Olivier Devisme; 3 brs.

INSURANCE

More than 20 major European insurance companies are represented in Saint-Denis.

Trade and Industry

Association pour le Développement industriel de la Réunion: 18 rue Milius, 97468 Saint-Denis Cedex; f. 1975; 149 mems; Pres. Abdeali Goulamaly.

Chambre de Commerce et d'Industrie de la Réunion: 25 bis rue de Paris, BP 120, 97463 Saint-Denis; telex 916278; f. 1830; Pres. Alex How-Choong; Man. Dir Jean-Pierre Fourtoy.

Direction de l'Action Economique: Secrétariat Général pour les Affairs Economiques, ave de la Victoire, 97405 Saint-Denis; tel. 21-86-10; telex 916111.

Jeune Chambre Economique de Saint-Denis de la Réunion: BP 1151, 25 rue de Paris, 97483 Saint-Denis; f. 1963; 30 mems; Chair. Olivier Moreau.

Société de Développement Economique de la Réunion (SODERE): 133 rue Maréchal Leclerc, 97469 Saint-Denis; tel. 20-01-68; telex 916471; Chair. Pierre Peyron; Man. Dir Albert Trimaille.

Syndicat des Exportateurs d'Huiles Essentielles, Plantes Aromatiques et Medicinales de Bourbon: 38 bis rue Labourdonnais, 97400 Saint-Denis; tel. 20-10-23; exports oil of geranium, vetiver and vanilla; Pres. Rico Ploenières.

Syndicat des Fabricants de Sucre de la Réunion: BP 57, 97462 Saint-Denis; tel. 21-67-00; telex 916138; Chair. Armand Barau.

Syndicat des Producteurs de Rhum de la Réunion: BP 57, 97462 Saint-Denis; tel. 21-67-00; telex 916138; Chair. ARMAND BARAU.

Syndicat Patronal du Bâtiment de la Réunion: BP108, 97463 Saint-Denis; tel. 21-03-81; telex 916393; Pres. B. LENFANT; Sec.-Gen. Mlle C. D'HANENS.

TRADE UNIONS

Confédération Générale du Travail de la Réunion (CGTR): 104 rue Maréchal Leclerc, 97400 Saint-Denis; Sec.-Gen. BRUNY PAYET.

Réunion also has its own sections of the major French trade union confederations, **Confédération Française Démocratique du Travail (CFDT), Force Ouvrière (FO), Confédération Française de l'Encadrement** and **Confédération Française des Travailleurs Chrétiens (CFTC).**

Transport

RAILWAYS

There are no railways in Réunion.

ROADS

A route nationale runs all round the island, generally following the coast and linking all the main towns. Another route nationale crosses the island from south-west to north-east linking Saint-Pierre and Saint-Benoît. In 1982 there were 345.7 km of routes nationales, 731.5 km of departmental roads and 1,602.9 km of other roads.

SHIPPING

In 1986 work started on the expansion of the Port de la Pointe des Galets.

Compagnie Générale Maritime (CGM): 2 rue de l'Est, BP 10, 97420 Le Port; tel. 42-00-88; agents for Mitsui OSK Lines, Unicorn Lines, Black Sea Shipping, Marine Chartering, Taiyo Shipping, Unigas Oceangas; Dir HENRI-PIERRE SIGNEUX.

Navale et Commerciale Havraise Péninsulaire: résidence du Barachois, BP 62, 97462 Saint-Denis; rue de St Paul, BP 29, 97420 Le Port; freight only.

Société de Manutention et de Consignation Maritime (SOMACOM): BP 7, Le Port; agents for Scandinavian East Africa Line, Bank Line, Clan Line, Union Castle Mail Steamship Co and States Marine Lines.

CIVIL AVIATION

There is an international airport at Saint-Denis Gillot.

Réunion Air Service: BP 611, 97473 Saint-Denis; tel. 28-22-51; telex 916236; f. 1975; subsidiary of Air France; scheduled service to Mayotte; Gen. Man. B. POPINEAU; fleet of 1 HS748, 1 Piper Chieftain, 1 Cherokee Six, 2 SA315B Lama, 1 Alouette II, 2 Alouette III.

Tourism

In 1984 about 79,000 tourists stayed in the island's hotels.

L'Agence Régionale du Tourisme et des Loisirs (ARTL): 2 rue de la Victorie, 97400 Saint-Denis; Pres. BERTHO AUDIFAX.

Délégation Régionale au Commerce, à l'Artisanat et au Tourisme: Préfecture/Commissariat de la République, 97405 Saint-Denis; tel. 21-86-10; telex 916068; Dir JEAN-FRANÇOIS DESROCHES.

Office du Tourisme: rue Rontaunay 97400 Saint-Denis; tel. 21-24-53; telex 916486; Chair. S. PERSONNÉ.

French Overseas Collectivités Territoriales

The two Overseas Collectivités Territoriales are Mayotte and St Pierre and Miquelon. Their status is between that of an overseas department and that of an overseas territory. They are integral parts of the French Republic and are both administered by a Government Commissioner, appointed by the French Government. The Government Commissioner is assisted by an elected General Council. The collectivités territoriales are represented in the French National Assembly and in the Senate in Paris.

MAYOTTE

Introductory Survey

Location, Climate, Language, Religion, Capital
The island of Mayotte forms part of the Comoro archipelago, which lies between the island of Madagascar and the east coast of the African mainland. The climate is tropical. The official language is French, and Islam is the main religion. The capital is Dzaoudzi.

Recent History
Since the Comoros unilaterally declared independence in July 1975, Mayotte (Mahoré) has been administered separately by France. The independent Comoran state claims Mayotte as part of its territory and officially represents it in international organizations, including the United Nations. In December 1976 France introduced the special status of collectivité territoriale for the island. Following the coup in the Comoros in May 1978, Mayotte rejected the new government's proposal that it should rejoin the other islands under a federal system, and reaffirmed its intention of remaining linked to France. In December 1979 the French National Assembly approved legislation to prolong Mayotte's special status for another five years, during which the islanders were to be consulted. However, in October 1984 the National Assembly further prolonged Mayotte's status, and the referendum on the island's future was postponed indefinitely. The UN General Assembly has adopted several resolutions reaffirming the sovereignty of the Comoros over the island, and urging France to come to an agreement with the Comoran government as soon as possible. The main political party on Mayotte, the Mouvement populaire mahorais (MPM), demands full departmental status for the island, but France has been reluctant to grant this in view of Mayotte's undeveloped condition.

Following the general election to the French National Assembly in March 1986, the RPR/UDF alliance formed a new government in mainland France. At the election, a UDF-CDS candidate was elected as deputy for Mayotte. The RPR/UDF coalition shared the MPM's aim to elevate Mayotte to the status of an overseas department. In October Jacques Chirac became the first French Prime Minister to visit Mayotte, and he assured the islanders that they would remain French citizens for as long as they wished. Meanwhile, the French Minister of Overseas Departments and Territories, Bernard Pons, prepared a five-year Development Plan (see Economic Affairs) which included the reform of laws relating to land, labour, town-planning, public markets and penal procedure, to be implemented by decree if necessary. As the OAU shares the UN's policy on Mayotte (in July 1986 reiterating its appeal to France for the return of Mayotte to the Comoros), the French Government may face an embarrassing situation in Franco-African diplomacy, and relations between Mayotte and the Comoros may deteriorate further. For further details of the recent history of the island, see the chapter on the Comoros, p. 794.)

Government
The French Government is represented in Mayotte by an appointed Government Commissioner. There is a General Council, with 17 members, elected by universal adult suffrage. Mayotte elects one deputy to the French National Assembly, and one representative to the Senate.

Defence
There were 300 French troops stationed on Mayotte in 1984.

Economic Affairs
The economy of the island is entirely agricultural. Vanilla, ylang-ylang, coffee and copra are the main products. In 1985 Mayotte produced 18 metric tons of ylang-ylang. Exports of ylang-ylang were worth about 3m. francs in 1983. In the same year 3.8 tons of vanilla and 9.2 tons of coffee were exported, and in 1983 receipts from vanilla totalled 814,000 francs. In 1985 500 ha of forest were planted. Livestock rearing and fishing are secondary agricultural activities. Mayotte is not self-sufficient, and has to import substantial quantities of foodstuff, at a cost of 43.8m. francs in 1984.

France is Mayotte's major trading partner: in 1983 France supplied imports to the value of 96.7m. francs and bought exports worth 4.4m. francs. Mayotte has a large trade deficit, owing to its reliance on imports, which cost 182.8m. francs in 1984, compared with export earnings of 34m. francs. The island is dependent on French aid, which totalled 84m. francs in 1983. In 1985 Mayotte's external assets totalled 168.5m. francs, and banking aid reached 24.1m. francs. In 1984 Mayotte's budget expenditure was an estimated 159m. francs.

In 1986 the French Minister of Overseas Departments and Territories, Bernard Pons, announced a five-year Development Plan for Mayotte, involving projected expenditure of 100m. francs. The island has invested in public works, including roads, ports and buildings: during the period 1978–85 a total of 22 administrative buildings and 600 dwellings were constructed. There is considerable potential for tourism, although any economic progress in Mayotte is largely dependent on French aid.

Statistical Survey

Source: Office of the Prefect/Government Commissioner, Dzaoudzi.

AREA AND POPULATION
Area: 376 sq km (145 sq miles).
Population: 67,138 (census of August 1985, preliminary results); *Principal towns:* Dzaoudzi (capital) 5,675, Mamoudzou 12,119.

FINANCE
Currency and Exchange Rates: French currency is used (see French Guiana).
Budget (million francs): 144.3 in 1983; 168 in 1984; 313 in 1985 (provisional).

EXTERNAL TRADE
Principal Commodities ('000 francs, 1984): *Imports:* Foodstuffs 43,787, Hydrocarbons 34,836, Wood 9,554, Cement 6,037, Total (incl. others) 182,836; *Exports:* Total 33,951.
Principal Trading Partners ('000 francs, 1984): *Imports:* France 96,656, Bahrain 20,616, Kenya 14,053, Thailand 12,735, South Africa 10,818. *Exports* (1983): France 4,405, Others 3,294.

TRANSPORT
Roads (1984): 93 km of main roads, of which 72 km are tarred, 137 km of local roads, of which 40 km are tarred, and 54 km of tracks unusable in the rainy season; 1,528 vehicles.
Civil Aviation (1984): *Arrivals:* 7,747 passengers, 120 metric tons of freight; *Departures:* 7,970 passengers, 41 metric tons of freight.

EDUCATION
Primary (1984): 441 teachers, 14,992 pupils.
Secondary (1984): 66 teachers, 1,374 pupils.

FRENCH OVERSEAS COLLECTIVITÉS TERRITORIALES   *Mayotte, St Pierre and Miquelon*

Directory

The Constitution

In a referendum in April 1976, the population of Mayotte voted to renounce the status of an overseas territory. They expressed their desire for departmental status, but this has been rejected by the French Government. The change in status of the island to a collectivité territoriale involved the election of a General Council with 17 members to assist the Prefect (now Government Commissioner) in the administration of the island. In December 1979 the French National Assembly voted to extend this status for five years. A further referendum was due to be held in 1984, but was postponed indefinitely in December of that year.

The Government

(January 1987)

Government Commissioner: AKLI KHIDER.
Secretary-General: PHILIPPE SCHAEFER.
Deputy to the French National Assembly: HENRY JEAN-BAPTISTE (UDF-CDS).
Representative to the French Senate: MARCEL HENRY (MPM).

GENERAL COUNCIL

The General Council has 17 members, of whom nine represent the Mouvement populaire mahorais (MPM). The most recent election was in March 1985.

President of the General Council: YOUNOUSSA BAMANA.

Political Organizations

Fédération de Mayotte du Rassemblement pour la République: Dzaoudzi; Mayotte branch of the French (Gaullist) RPR; holds six seats in the General Council; Sec.-Gen. MANSOUR KAMARDINE.
Mouvement populaire mahorais (MPM): Dzaoudzi; seeks departmental status for Mayotte; Leader YOUNOUSSA BAMANA.
Parti pour le rassemblement démocratique des mahorais (PRDM): Dzaoudzi; f. 1978; demands unification with the Comoros; Leader DAROUÈCHE MAOULIDA.
Union pour la Démocratie Française (UDF).
  Centre des Démocrates Sociaux (CDS).

Judicial System

Tribunal Supérieur d'Appel: Pres. CLAUDE BAURAIN.
Procureur de la République: JEAN JACQUES LECOMTE.
Tribunal d'Instance: Pres. JEAN-PASCAL MARTRES.

Religion

Muslims comprise about 98% of the population. Most of the remainder are Christians, mainly Roman Catholics.

The Press

Le Journal de Mayotte: BP 108, 97610 Dzaoudzi; daily.

Radio and Television

In 1983 there were an estimated 13,800 radio receivers in use.

Société Nationale de Radio-Télévision Française d'Outre-mer (RFO)—Mayotte: BP 103, Dzaoudzi, 97610 Mayotte; tel. 60-10-17; telex 915822; govt-owned; radio broadcasts in French and Mahorian; television transmissions began in December 1986; Station Man. YVES COPIN.

Finance

BANKS

Institut d'Emission d'Outre-mer: Dzaoudzi, 97610 Mayotte.
Banque Française Commerciale: Mamoudzou, 97600 Mayotte; branch at Dzaoudzi.

Transport

ROADS

The main road network totals approximately 93 km, of which 72 km are bituminized. There are 137 km of local roads, of which 40 km are tarred, and 54 km of minor tracks which are unusable during the rainy season.

SHIPPING

Coastal shipping is provided by locally-owned small craft. A deep-water port is under construction at Longoni.

CIVIL AVIATION

There is an airfield at Dzaoudzi, serving four-times weekly commercial flights to Réunion and twice-weekly services to Njazidja, Nzwani and Mwali.

ST PIERRE AND MIQUELON

Introductory Survey

Location, Climate, Language, Religion, Capital

The territory of St Pierre and Miquelon (Iles Saint-Pierre-et-Miquelon) consists of a number of small islands which lie about 25 km (16 miles) from the southern coast of Newfoundland, Canada, in the North Atlantic Ocean. The climate is cold and wet, with temperatures falling to −20°C (−4°F) in winter, and averaging between 10° and 20°C (50°–68°F) in summer. The islands are often shrouded in mist and fog. The language is French, and the majority of the population profess Christianity and belong to the Roman Catholic Church. The capital is Saint-Pierre, on the island of Saint-Pierre.

Recent History

The islands of Saint Pierre and Miquelon are the remnants of the once extensive French possessions in North America. They were confirmed as French territory in 1816, and gained departmental status in July 1976.

The departmentalization proved unpopular with many of the islanders, since it incorporated the territory's economy into that of the EEC, and other institutions of metropolitan France, neglecting the islands' isolation and their dependence on Canada for supplies and transport links. In 1978 and 1980 general strikes were called by local trade unionists to protest at the negative effects of departmental status. In March 1982 Socialist and other left-wing candidates, campaigning for a change in the islands' status, were elected unopposed to all 14 seats in the department's General Council. Saint Pierre and Miquelon was excluded from the Mitterrand Government's decentralization reforms.

In 1976 Canada imposed an economic interest zone extending to 200 nautical miles (370 km) around its shores. As a result of French fears over the loss of traditional fishing areas, and the threat to the livelihood of the fishermen of Saint Pierre, the Government claimed a similar zone around the islands. The possibility of discovering valuable reserves of petroleum and natural gas in the area has heightened the tension between France and Canada. In December 1984 legislation was approved to help solve both the internal and external problems by giving the islands the status of a collectivité territoriale with effect from June 1985. This would allow Saint Pierre and Miquelon to receive the investment and development that are suitable for its position, and would allay Canadian fears of EEC exploitation of its offshore waters. Local representatives, however, continued to remain apprehensive about the outcome of negotiations between the French and Canadian Governments to settle the dispute over coastal limits. In February 1985 the Government Commissioner was expelled from Saint Pierre by striking workers during the course of an industrial dispute, while in June disagreements between members of the General Council led to the temporary resignations of four council members.

A general election to the French National Assembly was held in March 1986. The islands' incumbent deputy, Albert Pen (representing the Parti Socialiste), was re-elected. Pen was also the sole candidate at the indirect election to choose the islands' representative in the French Senate in September. A fresh election for a deputy to the National Assembly was held in November, when Gérard Grigon, representing the Union pour la Démocratie Française, was elected.

Government
The French Government is represented in Saint Pierre by an appointed Government Commissioner. There is a General Council, with 14 members elected by adult universal suffrage for a period of six years. St Pierre and Miquelon elects one deputy to the French National Assembly and one representative to the Senate.

Economic Affairs
The islanders have traditionally earned their living by fishing, and by acting as a supply base for fishing fleets operating in the rich seas off Newfoundland. However, the economy has been experiencing a long decline. The number of French and foreign ships coming to fish, and calling at Saint Pierre, declined from 1,290 in 1976 to 774 in 1983. An agreement with Canada, signed in 1972, which expired in 1986, limited the amounts of fish caught by French ships in the Gulf of Saint Lawrence to 20,500 metric tons per year. The agreement also granted permanent fishing rights to fishing vessels from Saint Pierre, provided that they fished 'on an equal footing' with Canada. Disagreements arose in 1984 over Saint Pierre's right to use a modern vessel that enabled fish to be treated on board and thus exported immediately, while Canadian fishermen were obliged to return to port with their catch. Discussions between France and Canada were opened in Geneva in 1986 to decide the terms of a new fishing agreement. Interpêche, the primary company in the fishing sector on the islands (and a major employer), has been in financial difficulties, and required government subsidy. Unemployment affected 11% of the labour force in 1983.

Around 70% of imported goods, including fuel and building materials, come from Canada. Items such as clothing and consumer goods are imported from France via Nova Scotia. The proximity of Canada, and the islands' reliance on imported goods, has caused a high rate of inflation, averaging 17.7% in 1983. The failure of government employees' salaries to rise in line with inflation has led to a series of damaging general strikes on the islands, including one in 1983, and a threatened stoppage in 1984. High wage demands and rates of social security contributions are resented by employers. In June 1984 a plan for future development projects was agreed, which included improvements in the fishing industry, infrastructural developments such as the upgrading of the airport, and health projects, at a total cost to the Government of 42.5m. francs.

Social Welfare
In 1981 there was one general hospital, with 68 beds, and maternity and hospice establishments. In 1977 there were six physicians working in the islands.

Education
The education system is modelled on the French system, and education is compulsory for children between the ages of six and 16 years. There are nine primary schools (of which five are privately-run), three secondary schools (of which two are private) and six technical schools.

Tourism
The French way of life attracts many visitors from Canada and the USA to the islands, despite the unfavourable climate. There were 11,293 tourist arrivals in 1982.

Public Holidays
1987: 1 January (New Year's Day), 17–20 April (Easter), 1 May Labour Day), 28 May (Ascension Day), 8 June (Whit Monday), 14 July (National Day), 11 November (Armistice Day), 25 December (Christmas Day).
1988: 1 January (New Year's Day), 1–4 April (Easter), 2 May (for Labour Day), 12 May (Ascension Day), 23 May (Whit Monday), 14 July (National Day), 11 November (Armistice Day), 25 December (Christmas Day).

Weights and Measures
The metric system is in use.

Currency and Exchange Rates
French currency is used (see French Guiana).

Statistical Survey

Source (unless otherwise stated): Préfecture, 97500 Saint Pierre; tel. 412801.

AREA AND POPULATION
Area: 242 sq km (93.4 sq miles).
Population: 6,041 (census of 9 March 1982); Saint-Pierre 5,415, Miquelon 626.
Births and Deaths (1981): Live births 109 (birth rate 18.2 per 1,000); Deaths 50 (death rate 8.3 per 1,000).
Labour Force (1982 census): Employed 2,145 (males 1,483, females 662); Unemployed 235 (males 141, females 94).

AGRICULTURE, ETC.
Agriculture and Livestock: Vegetables are grown, and some cattle, sheep and pigs are kept for local consumption.
Fishing (metric tons, live weight): Total catch 12,511 (incl. Atlantic cod 9,988) in 1984. Source: FAO, *Yearbook of Fishery Statistics*. Fishing is the only industry of consequence, and fish products are the main exports.

FINANCE
Currency and Exchange Rates: French currency is used (see French Guiana).
Aid from France (1980): 17 million francs.

EXTERNAL TRADE
Total ('000 francs, 1982): *Imports:* 275,390 (Fuel, meat, clothing, electrical equipment and machinery); *Exports:* 41,045 (Fish, marine equipment). Most trade is with Canada, France and the franc zone, and the USA.

TRANSPORT
Road Traffic (31 December 1982): 2,406 motor vehicles in use.
Shipping (1982): Ships entered 865, Freight entered 58,656 metric tons, Freight cleared 3,688 metric tons.
Civil Aviation (1982): Passengers carried 15,644, Freight carried 97 metric tons.

TOURISM
Tourist Arrivals (1982): 11,293.

EDUCATION
Primary (1982): 9 schools, 50 teachers, 1,023 students.
Secondary (1982): 3 schools, 55 teachers, 748 students.
There are also 6 technical schools.

Directory

The Government
(January 1987)

Government Commissioner: BERNARD LEURQUIN.
Representative to the Social and Economic Council: RÉMY BRIAND.
Deputy to the French National Assembly: GÉRARD GRIGNON (UDF-CDS).
Representative to the French Senate: ALBERT PEN (PS).

FRENCH OVERSEAS COLLECTIVITÉS TERRITORIALES   *St Pierre and Miquelon*

GENERAL COUNCIL

The General Council has 14 members. All 14 seats are currently held by the Parti Socialiste (PS) and other left-wing parties, who were elected unopposed.

President of the General Council: MARC PLANTEGENEST (PS).

Political Organizations

Parti Socialiste (PS).
Union pour la Démocratie Française (UDF).
Centre des Démocrates Sociaux (CDS).

Judicial System

Tribunal Supérieur d'Appel at Saint-Pierre (Pres. FRANÇOIS DENEAUVE); Tribunal de Première Instance (Pres. LIONEL RINUY).

Religion

Almost all of the inhabitants are adherents of the Roman Catholic Church.

CHRISTIANITY
The Roman Catholic Church

The islands form the Apostolic Vicariate of the Iles Saint-Pierre et Miquelon. At 31 December 1984 there were an estimated 6,038 adherents (about 98% of the total population).

Vicar Apostolic: FRANÇOIS JOSEPH MAURER (Titular Bishop of Chimaera), Vicariat Apostolique, BP 4245, 97500 Saint-Pierre; tel. 412035.

The Press

Journal Officiel: Saint-Pierre; published by the Government Printer; f. 1886; fortnightly.

Radio and Television

In 1983 there were an estimated 4,000 radio receivers and 3,400 television receivers in use.

Radio-Télévision Française d'Outre-mer (RFO): BP 4227, 97500 Saint-Pierre; tel. 413824; telex 914428; the government station, broadcasts 16 hours of radio programmes daily, and 80 hours of television programmes weekly on two channels; Dir CLAUDE ESPERANDIEU.

Finance

MAJOR BANKS

Banque des Iles Saint-Pierre-et-Miquelon: rue Jacques-Cartier, Saint-Pierre; tel. 412217; telex 914435; f. 1889; cap. 7.5m. francs; Pres. and Gen. Man. GEORGES LANDRY; Man. GUY ROULET.

Crédit Saint Pierrais: 20 place du Général de Gaulle, BP 4218, Saint-Pierre; tel. 412249; telex 914429; Pres. MARCEL GIRARDIN; Man. G. COQUELIN.

PRINCIPAL INSURANCE COMPANIES

La Foncière-Cie: Saint-Pierre.

Comité Central des Assureurs Maritimes de France: 16 rue M. Georges Lefèvre, BP 4222, 97500 Saint-Pierre; tel. 414355; telex 914420; Reps GUY PATUREL, BERNARD HARAN.

Mutuelle Générale Française: Saint-Pierre; Rep. J. ANDRIEUX.

Trade and Industry

Chambre de Commerce, d'Industrie et de Métiers: blvd Constant Colmay, BP 4207, 97500 Saint-Pierre; tel. 414512; telex 914437; Pres. LOUIS E. HARDY.

TRADE UNION

Force Ouvrière (FO): 15 rue Dr Dunan, 97500 Saint-Pierre; tel. 412522; telex 914427; Sec.-Gen. MAX OLAÏSOLA.

Transport

SHIPPING

Packet boats run to Halifax, Sydney and Louisbourg in Canada, and there are container services between Saint-Pierre and Halifax, Nova Scotia. The seaport at Saint Pierre has three jetties and 1,200 metres of quays.

CIVIL AVIATION

There is an airport at Saint Pierre, served by airlines linking the territory with France and Canada.

Air Saint-Pierre: 18 rue Albert Briand St Pierre, POB 4225, 97500 Saint-Pierre; telex 914422; f. 1961; connects the territory with Sydney (Canada) and directly with Halifax, Nova Scotia, in association with Eastern Provincial Airways; Pres. RÉMY L. BRIAND; fleet of 1 HS. 748, 1 Navajo Chieftain, 1 Aztec, and 1 Apache. Saint-Pierre is also served by Air Canada and Air France.

Tourism

Office du Tourisme: 97500 Saint-Pierre; tel. 412222; telex 914437; f. 1959; Pres. ANDRÉ PATUREL; Man. JEAN-CHARLES GIRARDIN.

There were 11,293 tourist arrivals in 1982.

French Overseas Territories

The four Overseas Territories (territoires d'outre-mer) are French Polynesia, the French Southern and Antarctic Territories, New Caledonia, and the Wallis and Futuna Islands. They are integral parts of the French Republic. Each is administered by a High Commissioner or Chief Administrator, who is appointed by the French Government. Each Territory also has a Territorial Assembly or Congress, elected by universal adult suffrage. Certain members of the Territorial Assembly or Congress sit in the French National Assembly and the Senate of the Republic in Paris. The Territories have varying degrees of internal autonomy.

FRENCH POLYNESIA

Introductory Survey

Location, Climate, Language, Religion, Flag, Capital

French Polynesia comprises several scattered groups of islands in the south Pacific Ocean, lying about two-thirds of the way between the Panama Canal and New Zealand. Its nearest neighbours are the Cook Islands, to the east, and the Line Islands (part of Kiribati), to the north-east. French Polynesia consists of the following island groups: the Iles du Vent (including the islands of Tahiti and Moorea) and the Iles Sous le Vent (located about 160 km north-west of Tahiti) which, together, constitute the Society Archipelago; the Tuamotu Archipelago, which comprises 78 islands scattered east of the Society Archipelago in a line stretching north-west to south-east for about 1,500 km; the Gambier Islands, located 1,600 km south-east of Tahiti; the Austral Islands, lying 640 km south of Tahiti; and the Marquesas Archipelago, which lies 1,450 km north-east of Tahiti. There are 120 islands in all. The average monthly temperature throughout the year varies between 20°C (68°F) and 29°C (84°F), and most rainfall occurs between November and April, the average annual precipitation being 1,625 mm. The official language is French, and Polynesian languages are spoken by the indigenous population. The principal religion is Christianity, 55% of the population being Protestant and 24% Roman Catholic. Provision was made in a statute of 6 September 1984 for the adoption of a French Polynesian flag, to fly alongside the French tricolour. The capital is Papeete, on the island of Tahiti.

Recent History

The first Europeans to visit French Polynesia were Spanish and Portuguese explorers in the 16th century. Descriptions of Tahiti and other Society islands by Samuel Wallis, who first visited in 1767, and by Capt. James Cook and his officers, gave rise in Europe to their reputation as the 'islands of love', but contact with Europeans allowed disease to cause a rapid decline in the indigenous population, while others were killed in internal warfare.

Tahiti was made a French protectorate in 1842 and a colony in 1880. The other island groups were annexed during the last 20 years of the 19th century. The islands were governed from France under a decree of 1885 until 1957, when French Polynesia became an Overseas Territory, administered by a Governor in Papeete. A Territorial Assembly and a Council of Government were elected to advise the Governor.

Between May 1975 and May 1982 a majority in the Territorial Assembly sought independence for French Polynesia. Following pressure by Francis Sanford, leader of the largest autonomist party in the Assembly, a new constitution for the Territory was negotiated with the French Government and approved by a newly-elected Assembly in 1977. Under the provisions of the new statute, France retained responsibility for foreign affairs, defence, monetary matters and justice, but the powers of the territorial Council of Government were increased, especially in the field of commerce. The French Governor was replaced by a High Commissioner, who was to preside over the Council of Government and was head of the administration, but had no vote. The Council's elected Vice-President, responsible for domestic affairs, was granted greater powers. An Economic and Social Committee, responsible for all development matters, was also created, and French Polynesia's economic zone has been extended to 200 nautical miles (370 km) from the islands' coastline.

Following elections to the Territorial Assembly in May 1982, the Tahoeraa Huiraatira Party of Gaston Flosse, with 13 of the 30 seats, formed successive ruling coalitions, first with the Ai'a Api Party and in September with John Teariki's Pupu Here Ai'a Party. Seeking greater (but not full) independence from France, especially in economic matters, elected representatives of the Assembly held discussions with the French Government in Paris in 1983. In spite of feelings expressed by the Assembly, that the French proposals for increased internal autonomy did not go far enough, a new statute was approved by the French National Assembly in September 1984. This allowed the territorial government greater powers, mainly in the sphere of commerce and development; the Council of Government was replaced by a Council of Ministers, whose President was to be elected from among the members of the Territorial Assembly. Gaston Flosse became the first President of the Council of Ministers.

In February 1985 Flosse and his New Caledonian counterpart, Dick Ukeiwé, signed an anti-independence alliance protocol, calling for closer economic, cultural and political co-operation within the French Republic; it was immediately described as 'illegal' and 'unconstitutional' by France's High Commissioner to New Caledonia, and subsequently annulled by a French administrative tribunal in that territory.

The testing of nuclear devices by the French Government began in 1966 at Mururoa Atoll, in the Tuamotu Archipelago. In 1983, in spite of strong protests by many Pacific nations, the Government indicated that tests would continue for a number of years. In October 1983 Australia, New Zealand and Papua New Guinea accepted a French invitation jointly to send scientists to inspect the test site, but the team's subsequent report was widely criticized for being inconclusive with regard to the problem of nuclear waste disposal, and, although the French test programme appeared to present no immediate health hazards, there was definite evidence of environmental damage, resulting from the underground explosions, which had caused subsidence by weakening the rock structure of the atoll.

A series of tests in May and June 1985, involving bigger explosions than hitherto, prompted a renewed display of opposition. In July the trawler *Rainbow Warrior*, the flagship of the anti-nuclear environmentalist group, Greenpeace, which was to have led a protest flotilla to Mururoa, was sunk in Auckland Harbour, New Zealand, in an explosion that killed one crew member. Two agents of the French secret service, the Direction générale de sécurité extérieure (DGSE), were subsequently convicted of manslaughter and imprisoned in New Zealand. (In 1986 they were transferred to Hao Atoll, in the Tuamotu Archipelago, where they were to serve the remainder of their 10-year sentence.) However, in September 1985 the French President, François Mitterrand, visited the test site to reaffirm France's nuclear policy and its strategic interests in the Pacific, and declared that the tests at Mururoa would continue for as long as necessary. In October the Greenpeace yacht, *Vega*, was seized by French naval commandos, as it sailed into the prohibited zone around the atoll, in an unsuccessful attempt to disrupt further scheduled tests; although the protest as a whole ended in deadlock, it succeeded in attracting world-wide attention. Further tests were conducted in 1985 and 1986, bringing the total number of underground tests since 1975 to 86 by mid-December 1986.

At elections held in March 1986, the Tahoeraa Huiraatira Party gained the first outright majority to be achieved in the territory, winning 24 of the 41 seats in the Territorial Assembly, after a recount in one constituency, and the decision of two successful independent candidates to join the ruling party. Leaders of opposition parties subsequently expressed dissatisfaction with the election result, claiming that the Tahoeraa Huiraatira Party's victory had been secured only as a result of one of the five constituencies' having been allocated a disproportionately large number of seats in the Territorial Assembly, whereby the weight carried by its constituents' votes was effectively increased. The constituency at

FRENCH OVERSEAS TERRITORIES

French Polynesia

the centre of the dispute was that comprising the Mangareva and Tuamotu islands, where the two French army bases at Hao and Mururoa constituted a powerful body of support for Flosse and the Tahoeraa Huiraatira Party, which, in spite of winning a majority of seats, had obtained a minority of individual votes in the election (30,571, compared with the opposition parties' 43,771). At the concurrent elections for French Polynesia's two seats in the National Assembly in Paris, Flosse and Alexandre Léontieff, the candidates of the Rassemblement pour la République, were elected, Flosse subsequently ceding his seat to Edouard Fritch.

In April 1986 Flosse was re-elected President of the Council of Ministers, supported by the votes of 25 of the 41 members of the Territorial Assembly. Meanwhile, in March, the incoming French Prime Minister, Jacques Chirac, appointed Flosse to a post in the French Council of Ministers, assigning him the portfolio of Secretary of State for South Pacific Problems. Flosse resigned as President of the Territory's Council of Ministers in February 1987.

Flosse faced severe criticism from leaders of the opposition for his allegedly inefficient and extravagant use of public funds, and was accused, in particular, of corrupt electoral practice, through having distributed government-financed gifts of construction materials, food and clothing, in an attempt to influence voters during his pre-election campaign. In September 1986 a formal complaint against Flosse was made by Quito Braun-Ortega, one of the leaders of the Amuitahiraa Mo Porinesia (a coalition of opposition parties), who accused Flosse of appropriating public funds for his own personal and political purposes.

Government

The French Government is represented in French Polynesia by its High Commissioner to the territory, and controls various important spheres of government, including defence, foreign diplomacy and justice. A local Territorial Assembly, with 41 members, is elected for a five-year term by universal adult suffrage. The Assembly may elect a President of an executive body, the territorial Council of Ministers, who, in turn, submits a list of between five and 10 members of the Assembly to serve as Ministers, for approval by the Assembly.

In addition, French Polynesia elects two deputies to the French National Assembly in Paris (under a system of proportional representation in March 1986), one representative to the French Senate and one Economic and Social Councillor, all chosen on the basis of universal adult suffrage.

Defence

France has been testing nuclear weapons at Mururoa Atoll, in the Tuamotu Archipelago, since 1966 and was maintaining a force of 5,400 military personnel in the territory in July 1986.

Economic Affairs

In 1984, according to estimates by the World Bank, the territory's gross domestic product (GDP), measured at average 1982–84 prices, was US $1,300m. ($8,190 per head). The influx of large numbers of French military personnel, in connection with the testing of nuclear weapons in the territory since the mid-1960s, has, by creating new opportunities for employment, distorted the economy, to the extent that many islanders believe that a French withdrawal from Tahiti would mean economic disaster. The initial demand for labour diverted large numbers of the work-force from the coconut and vanilla plantations to construction work for the French, causing a steady migration from outer islands into Tahiti and the military bases. However, the gradual decline of this demand has led to the existence of a large group of people who no longer possess the agricultural subsistence skills of previous generations, and has resulted in a growth in the rate of unemployment. Coconuts are the principal cash crop, and copra the major export commodity, but the territory's total earnings from exports were less than 25% of the cost of imports in the mid-1980s, compared with 83% before the nuclear tests began. Other export commodities include vanilla, black pearls and, since 1986, shark meat.

Tourism is an important and developed industry, particularly on Tahiti, and helps to offset a persistent trade deficit, which in 1984 was 80,538m. francs CFP. The tourist industry accounts for some 7% of the territory's GDP, and its contribution to the economy is estimated to be at least three times that of total exports. In 1985 an extensive programme for expansion in this sector included a huge combined tourism and agriculture project at Aimaono, on the south coast of Tahiti, involving an investment of 20,000m. francs CFP, and plans for a luxury hotel on the island of Huahine, to be built with private US investment of 1,400m. francs CFP. The total number of hotel rooms in the territory was expected to increase from 2,100 in 1985 to 4,000 by 1989.

The annual rate of inflation declined from 16% in 1982 to 8% in 1985. A five-year development plan (1984–88) stressed increased primary production, especially in agriculture, forestry and fishing, the development of hydroelectric schemes, improved social services and the expansion of the tourist industry. Proposed budget expenditure for 1985, totalling 45,189m. francs CFP, was to be financed mainly by indirect taxation, which was to account for 78% of the projected revenues, with income tax being levied only on commercial firms. Customs duties payable on materials imported in connection with the nuclear tests were to be the only direct contribution from France; in an attempt to increase the territory's economic independence, 700m. francs CFP was to be allocated to the promotion of tourism, and 590m. francs CFP to exploration of the sea-bed. In 1986 rich, exploitable deposits of cobalt were discovered on the outer slopes of several atolls in the Tuamotu Archipelago.

Social Welfare

In 1980 there were 31 hospitals in French Polynesia, with a total of 982 beds, and there were 143 physicians working in the territory.

Education

Education is compulsory for eight years between six and 14 years of age. It is free of charge for day pupils in government schools. Primary education, lasting six years, is financed by the territorial budget, while secondary and technical education are supported by state funds. There are 210 government primary schools and kindergartens, while secondary education is provided by both government and church schools. In 1984/85 there were 11,937 pupils attending kindergartens, 28,866 at primary schools, 12,970 at secondary schools, and 3,822 at technical institutions. In 1986 France announced plans to build a university on Tahiti.

Tourism

Tourism is an important and developed industry in French Polynesia, particularly on Tahiti, and 101,595 people visited the territory in 1984, excluding cruise passengers and excursionists.

Public Holidays

1987: 1 January (New Year's Day), 20 April (Easter Monday), 1 May (Labour Day), 8 May (Liberation Day), 28 May (Ascension Day), 8 June (Whit Monday), 14 July (Fall of the Bastille), 11 November (Armistice Day), 25 December (Christmas Day).
1988: 1 January (New Year's Day), 4 April (Easter Monday), 2 May (for Labour Day), 8 May (Liberation Day), 12 May (Ascension Day), 23 May (Whit Monday), 14 July (Fall of the Bastille), 11 November (Armistice Day), 25 December (Christmas Day).

Weights and Measures

The metric system is in force.

Currency and Exchange Rates

100 centimes = 1 franc de la Communauté française du pacifique (franc CFP or Pacific franc).

Exchange rates (30 September 1986):
 £1 sterling = 174.77 francs CFP;
 US $1 = 120.77 francs CFP.

Statistical Survey

Source (unless otherwise indicated): Institut Territorial de la Statistique, BP 395, Papeete; tel. 37196.

AREA AND POPULATION

Area: 4,200 sq km (1,622 sq miles).
Population: 166,753 (census of 15 October 1983); 172,080 (official estimate for 31 December 1984); *Capital:* Papeete, population 23,496 (1983).
Births and Deaths (1984): Live births 5,130 (birth rate 29.9 per 1,000 in 1983); Deaths 878 (death rate 5.5 per 1,000 in 1983).
Employment (census of 15 October 1983): Civilians 54,599 (males 36,392, females 18,207); Police and armed forces 3,264 (males 3,166, females 98).

AGRICULTURE, ETC.

Principal Crops (1985, metric tons): Vegetables and melons 6,000 Roots and tubers 13,000 (estimate), Fresh fruit 4,000, Coconuts 110,000 (estimate), Copra 14,000 (unofficial figure). Source: FAO, *Production Yearbook*.
Livestock (FAO estimates, year ending September 1985): Cattle 10,000, Horses 2,000, Pigs 34,000, Goats 3,000, Sheep 2,000. Source: FAO, *Production Yearbook*.

FRENCH OVERSEAS TERRITORIES   *French Polynesia*

Fishing (metric tons, live weight): Total catch 2,299 in 1982; 2,400 in 1983 (estimate); 3,506 in 1984 (estimate). Source: FAO, *Yearbook of Fishery Statistics*.

INDUSTRY

Production: Coconut oil 6,155 metric tons (1984), Beer 100,000 hectolitres (1980), Printed cloth 200,000 m (1979), Japanese sandals 600,000 pairs (1979), Electric energy (Tahiti) 193.7m. kWh (1984).

FINANCE

Currency and Exchange Rates: 100 centimes = 1 franc de la Communauté française du pacifique (franc CFP or Pacific franc). *Coins:* 50 centimes; 1, 2, 5, 10, 20 and 50 francs CFP. *Notes:* 100, 500, 1,000 and 5,000 francs CFP. *Sterling, Dollar and French Franc Equivalents* (30 September 1986): £1 sterling = 174.77 francs CFP; US $1 = 120.77 francs CFP; 1 French franc = 18.182 francs CFP; 1,000 francs CFP = £5.722 = $8.280 = 55 French francs.

Budget (million francs CFP, 1984 estimates): *Revenue:* Ordinary receipts 32,973, Extraordinary receipts 4,618, Total 37,591; *Expenditure:* Ordinary expenditure 26,443, Extraordinary expenditure 4,558, Total 31,001; Estimated total expenditure in 1985: 45,189m. francs CFP.

Aid from France (1981, million francs CFP): 37,300; also subsidies to local authorities, of which 660 to general expenses, 381 to FIDES, 2,500 (1978) to public funds; loans at low interest rates 2,500.

Cost of Living (Consumer Price Index for December; base: December 1980 = 100): 133.6 (1982), 151.9 (1983), 168.1 (1984).

Gross Domestic Product (million francs CFP at current prices): 108,291 in 1981; 136,953 in 1982; 132,000 in 1984.

EXTERNAL TRADE

1984 (million francs CFP): *Imports:* 85,475 (mainly cereals, petroleum products, metal manufactures); principal suppliers: France 39,994, USA 11,108. *Exports:* 5,084 (mainly copra oil (863), cultured pearls (481), trochus shells, vanilla, fresh fruit); principal customer: France.

TRANSPORT

Shipping (1984): ships entered 1,772; goods loaded 14,400 metric tons, unloaded 578,000 metric tons (international freight); passenger arrivals 155,100, departures 168,900.

Civil Aviation (International traffic only, Faaa airport, Papeete, 1984): aircraft arrivals 1,055, aircraft departures 1,055, freight handled 5,422 metric tons, passenger arrivals ('000) 135.8, passenger departures ('000) 135.6.

TOURISM

Visitors (1984): 101,595, excluding cruise passengers and excursionists.

EDUCATION

1984/85: Pupils: Kindergarten 11,937; Primary 28,866; Secondary 12,970; Technical 3,822; Teachers (total, 1982/83): 3,215.
Source: Service de l'Education, Papeete.

Directory

The Government
(February 1987)

High Commissioner: Pierre Angéli.
Secretary-General: Bertrand Labarthe.

COUNCIL OF MINISTERS

The Council of Ministers is formed of a President, who is elected by the Territorial Assembly (see below) from among its members, and between six and nine other members of the Assembly, chosen by the President and approved by the Assembly, to serve as Ministers.

President: (vacant).
Vice-President, and Minister for the Economy, Planning, Tourism, Maritime Affairs, Industry and Foreign Trade: Alexandre Léontieff.

Minister for Education, Culture and Relations with the South Pacific Commission, and Government Spokesman: Jacques Teuira.
Minister for Agriculture: Sylvain Millaud.
Minister for Finance and Internal Affairs: Patrick Peaucellier.
Minister for Equipment, Development, Energy and Mines: Edouard Fritch.
Minister for Social Affairs, Unity, the Family, Relations with the Territorial Assembly and Relations with the Economic and Social Committee: Mme Huguette Hong-Kiou.
Minister for Health, Scientific Research and the Environment: Lysis Lavigne.
Minister for Youth, Sport, Popular Education and Traditional Crafts: Georges Kelly.
Minister for Transport, Ports and Posts and Telecommunications: Alban Ellacott.
Minister for Works, Employment, Housing and Vocational Education: Michel Buillard.

MINISTRIES

All Ministries are in Papeete.

Legislature

ASSEMBLÉE TERRITORIALE

The Territorial Assembly is elected for a five-year term on the basis of universal adult suffrage. It has 41 members.

President: Jacques Teuira.
Vice-President: Henri Marere.

Election, 16 March 1986

Party	Seats
Tahoeraa Huiraatira/RPR	24*
Amuitahiraa Mo Porinesia†	6
Pupu Here Ai'a	4
Ia Mana Te Nunaa	3
Front de Libération	2
Others	2
Total	41

* Increased from preliminary result of 21 seats, following a recount in one constituency and the decision of two members, elected as independents, to join the ruling party.

† A coalition of parties under the leadership of Emile Vernaudon and Enrique ('Quito') Braun-Ortega.

Deputies to the French National Assembly: Alexandre Léontieff (RPR), Edouard Fritch (RPR).

Representative to the French Senate: Daniel Millaud (Union centriste des Démocrates de Progrès).

Economic and Social Councillor: Raymond Desclaux.

Political Organizations

Ai'a Api (New Land): Papeete; tel. 481135; f. 1982 after split in Te E'a Api; Leader Emile Vernaudon.

Front de Libération de la Polynésie: advocates independence; Leader Oscar Temaru.

Ia Mana Te Nunaa: rue du Commandant Destrémau, BP 1223, Papeete; tel. 426699; f. 1976; advocates 'socialist independence'; Sec.-Gen. Jacques Drollet.

Pupu Here Ai'a Te Nunaa Ia Ora: BP 3195, Papeete; tel. 420766; f. 1965; advocates autonomy; 8,000 mems; Pres. Jean Juventin.

Pupu Taina/Rassemblement des Libéraux: rue Cook, BP 169, Papeete; tel. 429880; f. 1976; seeks to retain close links with France; associated with the French Union pour la Démocratie Française (UDF); Leader Michel Law.

FRENCH OVERSEAS TERRITORIES   French Polynesia

Taatiraa Polynesia: BP 283, Papeete; tel. 428619; f. 1976; Leader ARTHUR CHUNG.

Tahoeraa Huiraatira/Rassemblement pour la République—RPR: rue du Commandant Destrémeau, BP 471, Papeete; tel. 429898; telex 249; f. 1958; supports links with France but advocates internal autonomy; Pres. GASTON FLOSSE.

Te E'a Api (United Front Party): Papeete; tel. 420366; advocates increased autonomy; Leader FRANCIS SANFORD.

Judicial System

Court of Administrative Law: BP 4522, Papeete; tel. 422482; Pres. PIERRE DAVIN; Cllr BERNARD LEPLAT.

Court of Appeal: Papeete; tel. 420117; telex 308; Pres. HENRI DE LABRUSSE; Attorney-General PAUL MARCHAUD.

Court of the First Instance: Papeete; tel. 420116; telex 308; Pres. ALAIN LE GALL; Procurator JEAN-YVES DUVAL; Clerk of the Court DANIEL SALMON.

Religion

About 55% of the population are Protestant Christians.

CHRISTIANITY
Protestant Church

L'Eglise évangélique: BP 113, Papeete; tel. 420029; f. 1963; Pres. of Council MARURAI UTIA; Sec.-Gen. JOHN DOOM.

The Roman Catholic Church

French Polynesia comprises the archdiocese of Papeete and the suffragan diocese of Taiohae o Tefenuaenata. At 31 December 1984 there were an estimated 58,600 adherents in the territory, representing about 34% of the total population. The Archbishop and the Bishop participate in the Episcopal Conference of the Pacific, based in Fiji.

Archbishop of Papeete: Most Rev. MICHEL COPPENRATH, Archevêché, BP 94, Papeete; tel. 420251.

Other Christian Churches

There are small Sanito, Church of Jesus Christ of Latter-day Saints (Mormon), and Seventh-day Adventist missions.

The Press

Le Canard Tahitien: rue Clapier, Papeete; weekly; French; satire.

La Dépêche de Tahiti: Société Polynésienne de Presse, BP 50, Papeete; tel. 424343; f. 1964; daily; Dir MICHEL ANGLADE; Man. PHILIPPE MAZELLIER; circ. 14,000.

Le Journal de Tahiti: BP 6000, Papeete; daily; French.

Les Nouvelles: BP 629, Papeete; tel. 429556; f. 1956; daily; French; Editor MICHEL FRANÇOIS.

Sports Tahiti: rue des Ramparts, BP 600, Papeete; 2 a week.

Tahiti Bulletin: BP 912, Papeete; daily; French and English.

Tahiti Sun Press: BP 887, Papeete; tel. 426850; f. 1980; weekly; English; Man. Editor G. WARTI; circ. 4,000.

Foreign Bureaux

Agence France-Presse (AFP): BP 2679, Papeete; tel. 482121; Correspondent JEAN-PAUL PERÉA.

Associated Press (AP) (USA): BP 912, Papeete; tel. 437562; telex 537; Correspondent AL PRINCE.

Reuters (UK): BP 6144, Faaa, Tahiti; tel. Papeete 424343; Correspondent PHILIPPE MAZELLIER.

United Press International (UPI) (USA): BP 50, Papeete; tel. 424343; Correspondent MICHEL ANGLADE.

Publisher

Haere: BP 1958, Papeete; travel and local interest.

Radio and Television

In 1985 there were an estimated 80,000 radio receivers and 26,000 television receivers in use, of which about 1,500 were colour receivers.

Radio-Télé-Tahiti: 410 rue Dumont d'Urville, BP 125, Papeete; tel. 439212; telex 200; f. 1951 as Radio-Tahiti; television service began 1965; run by Société Nationale de Radio-Télévision Française d'Outre-Mer (RFO), Paris; daily programmes in French and Tahitian; Dir MARCEL BEAUBZA.

Finance

(cap. = capital; res = reserves; dep. = deposits; m. = million; brs = branches; amounts in CFP francs)

BANKING
Commercial Banks

Banque Indosuez (France): 2 place Notre-Dame, Papeete; tel. 427526; telex 395; Dir YVES CEVAERT; brs in Papeete, Faaa, Pirae and Uturoa.

Banque Paribas (France): Papeete; telex 392.

Banque de Polynésie SA: blvd Pomare, BP 530, Papeete; tel. 428688; telex 230; f. 1973; cap. 500m., res 181.5m., dep. 18,279m. (Dec. 1984); Pres. JACQUES DE MALEVILLE; Gen. Man. MICHEL OTTAVIANI; 10 brs.

Banque de Tahiti SA: rue Paul Gauguin, BP 1602, Papeete; tel. 425389; telex 237; f. 1969; affil. to Bank of Hawaii, Honolulu, and Crédit Lyonnais, Paris; cap. 600m., dep. 23,374m. (Dec. 1985); Pres. CHARLES GIORDAN; Dirs MICHEL DUPIEUX, FRANCIS FORTLACROIX, GERARD E. SEIDL; 12 brs.

Trade and Industry

Chambre de Commerce et d'Industrie de la Polynésie Française: BP 118, Papeete; tel. 420344; telex 274; f. 1880; 27 mems; Pres. CHARLES T. POROÏ.

Chambre d'Agriculture et d'Elevage (CAEP): route de l'Hippodrome, BP 5383, Pirae; tel. 425393; f. 1886; 10 mems; Pres. SYLVAIN MILLAUD.

Association pour la Formation et le Développement en Polynésie (AFODEP): Immeuble FARA, rue E. Ahnne, BP 455, Papeete; tel. 426683; f. 1983; Pres. H. DEVAY; Dir-Gen. J. WILD.

EMPLOYERS' ORGANIZATIONS

Chambre Syndicale des Entrepreneurs du Bâtiment et des Travaux Publics: BP 2218, Papeete; tel. 425309; Pres. CLAUDE GUTIERREZ.

Conseil des Employeurs: Immeuble FARA, rue E. Ahnne, BP 972, Papeete; tel. 438898; f. 1983; Pres. J. E. ANESTIDES; Sec.-Gen. NICOLE VINCENTI.

Fédération Polynésienne de l'Agriculture et de l'Elevage: Papara, Tahiti; Pres. MICHEL LEHARTEL.

Fédération Polynésienne de l'Hôtellerie et des Industries Touristiques: BP 118, Papeete; f. 1967; Pres. ALBERT MOUX.

Syndicat des Importateurs et des Négociants: BP 1607, Papeete; Pres. JULES CHANGUES.

Union Interprofessionnelle du Tourisme de la Polynésie Française: BP 1588, Papeete; f. 1973; 1,200 mems; Pres. PAUL MAETZ; Sec.-Gen. JEAN CORTEEL.

Union Patronale: BP 317, Papeete; tel. 420257; f. 1948; 51 mems; Pres. HENRI DEVAY.

TRADE UNIONS

Confédération des Syndicats Indépendants de Polynésie: Papeete; Sec.-Gen. STANLEY CROSS.

Fédération des Syndicats de la Polynésie Française: BP 1136, Papeete; Pres. MARCEL AHINI.

Fédération Inter-Iles des Syndicats des Travailleurs de Polynésie Française: Papeete; Pres. CHARLES TAUFA.

Syndicat de la Solidarité des Travailleurs Polynésiens: Papeete; Pres. JEAN-MARC PAMBRUN.

Syndicat des Cadres de la Fonction Publique: Papeete; Pres. PIERRE ALLAIN.

FRENCH OVERSEAS TERRITORIES   *French Polynesia, French Southern and Antarctic Territories*

Syndicat Territorial des Instituteurs et Institutrices de Polynésie: BP 3007, Papeete; Sec.-Gen. WILLY URIMA.

Union des Syndicats Autonomes des Travailleurs de Polynésie: BP 1201, Papeete; Pres. COCO TERAIEFA CHANG; Sec.-Gen. THÉODORE CÉRAN JÉRUSALEMY.

Union des Syndicats de l'Aéronautique: Papeete; Pres. JOSEPH CONROY.

Union des Syndicats des Dockers Polynésiens: BP 3366, Papeete; Pres. FELIX COLOMBEL.

Union des Travailleurs de Tahiti et des Iles: rue Albert Leboucher, BP 3366, Papeete; tel. 437369; Pres. JOHN TEFATUA-VAIHO.

Transport

ROADS

French Polynesia has 243.8 km of bitumen-surfaced and 497 km of stone-surfaced roads.

SHIPPING

The principal port is Papeete, on Tahiti.

Agence Tahiti Poroi: Fare Ute, BP 83, Papeete; tel. 420070; telex 211; f. 1958; travel agents, tour operators.

Columbus Line: Agents: Agence Maritime Internationale de Tahiti, BP 274, Papeete; tel. 428972; telex 227; services every 45 days to the South Pacific and Europe.

Compagnie Générale Maritime: ave du Général de Gaulle, PB 96, Papeete; tel. 420-0890; telex 259; shipowners and agents; freight services between Europe and many international ports; agents in French Polynesia for Shell, Chevron, Total, Morflot, Cunard Line, Holland America Line and Sitmar Cruises, Norwegian American Cruises, Hapag Lloyd; Dir HUBERT PARISIS.

Polynesia Line: Agents: Agence Maritime Internationale de Tahiti, BP 274, Papeete; tel. 428972; telex 227; services every four weeks to American Samoa, Western Samoa and the USA.

Other companies operating services to, or calling at, Papeete are: Daiwa Line, Karlander, Hamburg-Sued, China Navigation Co, Nedlloyd, Shipping Corpn of New Zealand Ltd, Bank Line and Kyowa Line.

CIVIL AVIATION

There is one international airport, Faaa airport, on Tahiti and there are about 40 smaller airstrips.

Air Polynésie: BP 314, Papeete; tel. 422333; f. 1953; inter-islands services to Anaa, Makemo, Hao, Gambier-Mangareva, Ua Pou, Mataiva, Tikehau, Huahine, Raiatea, Bora Bora, Rangiroa, Manihi, Ua-Huka, Moorea, Maupiti, Tubuai, Takapoto, Rurutu, Napuka, Apataki, Hiva-oa, Kaukura, Nuku Hiva, Fakarava, Pukarua, Tatakoto, Pukapuka, Fangatau, Arutua, Reao and Nukutavake; since 1985 the company has been 68% govt-owned, with 15% being retained by the French airline UTA; Chair. CHRISTIAN VERNAUDON; Gen. Man. MARCEL GALENON; fleet of 2 Fairchild F-27, 2 ATR-42, 1 Twin Otter DHC-6.

Air Tahiti: BP 6019, Papeete; tel. 424834; telex 314; f. 1968; operates internal services between Tahiti and Moorea Island and some inter-territorial services; since 1985 the airline has been 90% govt-owned; Dir-Gen. JEAN GILLOT; fleet of 6 Britten Norman Islander, 2 Piper Aztec, 1 Twin Otter.

Tourism

Office de Promotion et d'Animation Touristiques de Tahiti et ses Iles: Fare Manihini, blvd Pomare, BP 65, Papeete; tel. (689) 429626; telex 254; f. 1966; Dir CHRISTIAN VERNAUDON.

Service du Tourisme: Fare Manihini, blvd Pomare, BP 4527, Papeete; tel. (689) 429330; telex 254; Dir GÉRARD VANIZETTE.

Syndicat d'Initiative de la Polynésie Française: BP 326, Papeete; Pres. Mme PIU BAMBRIDGE.

FRENCH SOUTHERN AND ANTARCTIC TERRITORIES

The French Southern and Antarctic Territories (Terres Australes et Antarctiques françaises) form an Overseas Territory but are administered under a special statute. The territory comprises Adélie Land, a narrow segment of the mainland of Antarctica, and several islands (the Kerguelen and Crozet Archipelagos, St Paul and Amsterdam) in the southern Indian Ocean.

Statistical Survey

Area (sq km): Kerguelen Archipelago 7,000, Crozet Archipelago 500, Amsterdam Island 60, St Paul Island 7, Adélie Land (Antarctica) 500,000.

Population (the population, comprising members of scientific missions, fluctuates according to season, being higher in the summer; the figures given are approximate): Kerguelen Archipelago, Port-aux-Français 100; Amsterdam Island at Martin de Viviès 40; Adélie Land at Base Dumont d'Urville 30; the Crozet Archipelago at Alfred-Faure 40; St Paul Island is uninhabited. Total population (January 1985): 210.

Fishing: (catch in metric tons): Crayfish in Amsterdam and St Paul: 600 (1982); fishing by French and foreign fleets in the Kerguelen Archipelago: 40,000 annually.

Currency: French currency is used (see French Guiana).

Budget: Balanced at approx. 160m. francs annually.

External Trade: Exports consist mainly of crayfish and other fish going to France and Réunion.

Directory

Government: Chief Administrator Adm. CLAUDE PIERI; there is a Central Administration in Paris (34 rue des Renaudes, 75017 Paris, France; telex 640980).

Consultative Council: composed of 7 members appointed by the Secrétariat d'Etat aux Départments et Territoires d'Outre-Mer, Ministries of National Education, Scientific Research, Merchant Marine, National Meteorology, National Defence and scientists; Pres. CLAUDE FREJACQUES.

Transport: Shipping: A charter vessel calls four times a year in the Antarctic islands, and another calls twice a year in Adélie Land. Civil Aviation: a landing strip is being built to serve the research station on Adélie Land.

Research Stations: There are meteorological stations and geophysical research stations on Kerguelen, Amsterdam, Adélie Land and Crozet.

NEW CALEDONIA

Introductory Survey

Location, Climate, Language, Religion, Capital

The territory of New Caledonia comprises one large island and several smaller ones, lying in the south Pacific Ocean, about 1,500 km (930 miles) east of Queensland, Australia. The main island, New Caledonia, is long and narrow, and has a total area of 16,750 sq km; rugged mountains divide the west of the island from the east, and there is little flat land. The nearby Loyalty Islands, which are administratively part of the territory, are 2,353 sq km in area, and a third group of islands, the uninhabited Chesterfield Islands, lies about 400 km north-west of the main island. The climate is generally a mild one, with an average temperature of about 23°C (73°F) and a rainy season between December and March. The average rainfall in the east of the main island is about 2,000 mm (80 in) per year, and in the west about 1,000 mm (40 in). French is the official language, but Polynesian and Melanesian languages are also spoken by the indigenous population. New Caledonians are almost all Christians; about 65% are Roman Catholics, and there is a substantial Protestant minority. The capital is Nouméa, on the main island.

Recent History

New Caledonia became a French possession in 1853, when the island was annexed as a dependency of Tahiti. In 1884 a separate administration was established, and in 1946 it became an overseas territory of the French Republic. Early European settlers on New Caledonia, supported by legislation, quickly set about alienating Melanesian land, which provoked a number of rebellions by the indigenous population, the last being in 1917.

In 1956 the first Territorial Assembly, with 30 members, was elected by universal adult suffrage, although the French Governor effectively retained control of the functions of government. New Caledonian demands for a measure of self-government were answered in December 1976 by a new statute, which gave the Council of Government, elected from the Territorial Assembly, responsibility for certain internal affairs. The post of Governor was replaced by that of French High Commissioner to the territory. In 1978 the pro-independence parties obtained a majority of the posts in the Council of Government but, in March 1979, the French Government dismissed the Council, following its failure to support a proposal for a 10-year 'contract' between France and New Caledonia, because the plan did not acknowledge the possibility of New Caledonian independence. The territory was then placed under the direct authority of the High Commissioner. A general election was held in July, but a new electoral law, which affected mainly the Melanesian-supported, pro-independence parties, ensured that minor parties were not represented in the Assembly. Two parties loyal to France together won 22 of the 36 seats.

Tension grew sharply in September 1981 after the assassination of Pierre Declercq, Secretary-General of the pro-independence party Union calédonienne, and in November President Mitterrand of France called an urgent meeting of ministers in Paris to discuss the situation. Recognizing the need for major reforms, Henri Emmanuelli, the Secretary of State for Overseas Departments and Territories, outlined in December the immediate aims of the French Government, including fiscal reform, equal access for all New Caledonians to positions of authority, land reforms, the wider distribution of mining revenue and the fostering of Melanesian cultural institutions. To assist in effecting these reforms, the French Government simultaneously announced that it would rule by decree for a period of at least one year. In June 1982, accusing its partner in the ruling coalition of 'active resistance to evolution and change' in New Caledonia, the Fédération pour une nouvelle société calédonienne (FNSC) joined with the opposition Front indépendantiste (FI) to form a government which was more favourable to the proposed reforms.

In July 1983 the French Government held a meeting in Paris with representatives of the territory's main political groupings, and drew up a statute, providing for a five-year period of increased autonomy from July 1984 and a referendum in 1989 to determine New Caledonia's future, with independence as one of the options to be offered. The statute was opposed in New Caledonia, both by parties in favour of independence (because five years was considered too long to wait, given the possibility that a less sympathetic government might take over in France before 1989) and by those against, and it was rejected by the Territorial Assembly in April 1984. However, it was approved by the French National Assembly in September 1984. Under the provisions of the statute, the territorial Council of Ministers was responsible for many internal matters of government, its President henceforth being an elected member instead of the French High Commissioner; a second legislative chamber, with the right to be consulted on development planning and budgetary issues, was created at the same time. All of the main parties seeking independence, except the Libération kanake socialiste (LKS) party, which left the FI, boycotted elections for a new Territorial Assembly in November 1984 and, following the dissolution of the FI, formed a new movement called the Front de libération nationale kanake socialiste (FLNKS), whose congress instituted a 'provisional government', headed by Jean-Marie Tjibaou, on 1 December. The elections to the Territorial Assembly attracted only 50.12% of electors, and the anti-independence party Rassemblement pour la Calédonie dans la République (RPCR) won 34 of the 42 seats and 70.9% of the total vote. An escalation of violence by both kanaks (Melanesians) and caldoches (French settlers) began in November but, after a number of deaths had resulted, political leaders successfully appealed for peace.

In January 1985 Edgard Pisani, the new High Commissioner, announced a plan by which the territory might become independent 'in association with' France on 1 January 1986, subject to the result of a referendum in July 1985, in which all adults resident in the territory for at least three years would have the right to vote. A major obstacle to the success of such a plan was the fact that Melanesians constituted only 43% of the population of the territory, with people of European (37%) and other, mainly Asian and Pacific, origin accounting for the balance; Melanesian groups seeking independence had hitherto insisted that the indigenous population be allowed to determine its own fate. A resurgence of violence followed the announcement of Pisani's plan for a referendum on independence, and a state of emergency was declared after Eloi Machoro, a leading member of the FLNKS, was shot dead by police in an incident at La Foa, 65 km west of Nouméa. The renewed violence prompted President Mitterrand to make a brief visit to the territory later in the month.

In April 1985 the French Prime Minister, Laurent Fabius, announced a new plan for the future of New Caledonia, whereby the referendum on independence, formerly scheduled for July 1985, was deferred until an unspecified date not later than the end of December 1987. Meanwhile, the territory was to be divided into four regions, each to be governed by its own elected autonomous council, which would have extensive powers in the spheres of planning and development, education, health and social services, land rights, transport and housing. The elected members of all four councils together would serve as regional representatives in a territory-wide Congress (to replace the Territorial Assembly).

The new set of proposals (known as the 'Fabius plan') was well received by the FLNKS, which, at its third Congress in May 1985, voted in favour of participating in the regional elections, although it reaffirmed the ultimate goal of independence. It was also decided to maintain the 'provisional government' under Tjibaou at least until the end of December. The RPCR, however, condemned the plan, pointing out that the envisaged distribution of seats would give a more favourable ratio of seats to voters in the pro-independence regions, and the proposals were rejected by the predominantly anti-independence Territorial Assembly at the end of May. However, the necessary legislation was approved by the French National Assembly in Paris in July, and the Fabius plan came into force.

The parties opposing independence finally also consented to take part in the elections, although the extreme right-wing Front National later decided to withdraw its candidates from the marginal Centre region, in a bid to avoid splitting the French loyalist vote against Melanesian militants demanding independence. The elections were held in September, and, as expected, only in the Centre region around Nouméa, where the bulk of the population is non-Melanesian, was an anti-independence majority recorded. However, the pro-independence Melanesians, in spite of their majorities in the three non-urban regions, would be in a minority in the Territorial Congress. Although the elections took place without disruption, there were subsequent fears that the feelings that had been aroused by right-wing anti-independence campaigners might result in resistance to the new political arrangements.

The FLNKS boycotted the general election to the French National Assembly in March 1986, in which the Socialists were defeated by a conservative alliance, including the Rassemblement

FRENCH OVERSEAS TERRITORIES

New Caledonia

pour la République (RPR), led by Jacques Chirac, who became Prime Minister of France. Only about 50% of the eligible voters in New Caledonia participated in the election, at which the territory's two seats in the Assembly were won by RPR candidates.

In May 1986 the French Council of Ministers approved a draft law providing for a referendum to be held in New Caledonia within 12 months, whereby a choice would be offered between independence and a further extension of regional autonomy. Chirac indicated that he was confident that the populace would vote to remain part of the French Republic. The proposal was opposed by the Socialist President, François Mitterrand, but was approved by the French National Assembly.

Chirac visited New Caledonia in August 1986, when he outlined a proposed development programme, costing an estimated $A80m., to be implemented during 1986/87. He also indicated to the New Caledonian political groups that the conduct of the referendum was open to negotiation.

At the 17th meeting of the South Pacific Forum in Suva, Fiji, in September 1986, representatives of the 13 member countries condemned the Chirac programme and expressed support for measures to hasten New Caledonia's independence from France, voting to refer the issue to the UN Committee on Decolonization.

In November 1986 Chirac cancelled a meeting in Paris with Tjibaou, following an outbreak of violence in Thio, New Caledonia, in which one loyalist militant was shot dead. Discussions on the question of self-determination were resumed in Nouméa in December, when the French Minister for Overseas Departments and Territories, Bernard Pons, acceded to the request of the FLNKS that the electorate eligible to participate in the referendum on independence be limited to those who had been resident in New Caledonia for at least three years. Subsequently, however, the discussions reached a deadlock. In December, in spite of strong French diplomatic opposition, the UN General Assembly voted to reinscribe New Caledonia on the UN list of non-self-governing territories. In January 1987 Pons announced that the referendum would be held in July or August of that year.

Government

The French Government is represented in New Caledonia by its High Commissioner to the territory, and controls a number of important spheres of government, including defence, foreign diplomacy and justice. Pending the referendum on the question of independence for New Caledonia, to be held in mid-1987, the territory is divided into four regions—North, Centre, South and the Loyalty Islands—which have the status of self-governing territorial units. Each is governed by a regional council, which is elected by direct universal suffrage and has its own elected President. The four regional councils together form the Territorial Congress, which, in turn, has its own elected President.

An executive council, comprising the Presidents of the four regional councils and headed by the President of the Territorial Congress, has a consultative role in the discussion of proposals submitted to the Congress.

In each region there is a 'customary' consultative council, charged with giving an opinion on all matters submitted to it by the regional authorities, while the members of all four consultative councils together constitute a territorial 'customary' council, which has an advisory role in the consideration of all questions submitted to it by the High Commissioner.

In addition, New Caledonia elects two deputies to the French National Assembly in Paris (under a system of proportional representation in March 1986), one representative to the French Senate and one Economic and Social Councillor, all chosen on the basis of universal adult suffrage.

Defence

France was maintaining a force of 4,900 military personnel in New Caledonia in July 1986.

Economic Affairs

New Caledonia possesses about 30% of the world's known reserves of nickel, and is the third largest producer of the metal, after the USSR and Canada. Production of nickel ore totalled 86,592 metric tons (metal content) in 1980, declining to 46,162 tons in 1983. Other metals present in the territory include chromium cobalt, iron, manganese, lead and zinc, but these are mined only spasmodically.

Nickel is the principal export commodity, accounting for 97% of total export revenue in 1984, the main customers being France (which took 45.4% of total exports in 1983) and Japan. Copra and coffee are also exported, and other important crops are cereals, potatoes, sweet potatoes, bananas and other fruits and vegetables. Cattle-farming is often able to satisfy entirely the territory's demand for beef.

New Caledonia's considerable dependence on the nickel industry has led to periods of economic depression, such as occurred in 1973, when demand for the product is low. Political unrest during 1984 and 1985 led to enormous financial losses; sabotage and strike action at New Caledonia's main nickel mine, at Thio, in early 1985 stopped production for three months, and resulted in a reduction in output of more than 40%, so that the 1985 production forecast was cut from 960,000 to 550,000 metric tons.

In an effort to diversify the economy, the production of import substitutes, together with other enterprises not based on nickel, are being encouraged by grants, subsidies and tax concessions, and the territory's 1984 budget provided for considerable expenditure on regional development, with particular emphasis on agriculture, forestry and fishing. In January 1985 the French President, François Mitterrand, announced plans to strengthen French military bases in New Caledonia and to build a major naval base in Nouméa.

In mid-1985 a million-dollar campaign was launched in an attempt to revive the tourist industry, one of the mainstays of the territory's economy, which had also been severely affected by the recent political strife. The French Government agreed to subsidize the wages of staff at hotels and restaurants that would otherwise have been faced with the prospect of closure, and to provide funding for a large-scale development programme to improve tourist facilities. However, in spite of these measures and plans for an extensive television advertising campaign in Australia, New Zealand and Japan, the number of visitors to the territory, which in 1984 exceeded 92,000, declined to 51,000 in 1985.

The annual rate of inflation averaged 12.3% in 1983, falling to 8.7% in 1984 and to 5.2% in the year ending April 1985. According to estimates by the World Bank, the territory's gross national product (at average 1982–84 prices) was US $920m. ($6,240 per head) in 1984.

Social Welfare

In 1981 there were 38 hospitals in New Caledonia, with a total of 1,536 beds, and there were 168 physicians working in the territory.

Education

Education is compulsory for 10 years between six and 16 years of age. Schools are operated by both the State and churches, under the supervision of the Department of Education. The French Government finances the state secondary system. In 1984 there were 278 primary schools (with 33,884 pupils), 41 secondary schools (with 12,481 pupils), 32 technical institutions (with 5,264 students) and five institutions of higher education (with 660 students). Work began in 1981 on a new university of technology in Nouméa, due eventually to serve 1,500 students. About 100 students attend universities in France.

Tourism

New Caledonia earned almost $A40m. from tourism in 1983, when 91,775 people visited the territory. The total increased to 92,982 in 1984, but fell to 51,000 in 1985, owing to the political unrest.

Public Holidays

1987: 1 January (New Year's Day), 20 April (Easter Monday), 1 May (Labour Day), 8 May (Liberation Day), 28 May (Ascension Day), 8 June (Whit Monday), 14 July (Fall of the Bastille), 11 November (Armistice Day), 25 December (Christmas Day).

1988: 1 January (New Year's Day), 4 April (Easter Monday), 2 May (for Labour Day), 8 May (Liberation Day), 12 May (Ascension Day), 23 May (Whit Monday), 14 July (Fall of the Bastille), 11 November (Armistice Day), 25 December (Christmas Day).

Weights and Measures

The metric system is in force.

Currency and Exchange Rates

100 centimes = 1 franc de la Communauté française du pacifique (franc CFP or Pacific franc).

Exchange rates (30 September 1986):
 £1 sterling = 174.77 francs CFP;
 US $1 = 120.77 francs CFP.

FRENCH OVERSEAS TERRITORIES

Statistical Survey

Source (unless otherwise stated): Direction Territoriale de la Statistique et des Etudes Economiques, BP 823, Nouméa; tel. 275481.

AREA AND POPULATION

Area: 19,103 sq km (7,376 sq miles).
Population: 145,368 (census of April 1983); *Capital:* Nouméa, population 60,112 (1983 census).
Ethnic Groups (census of 1983): Melanesians 61,870, Europeans 53,974, Wallisians 12,174, Polynesians 5,570, Others 11,780.
Births and Deaths (1984): Live births 3,360, deaths 775.
Economically Active Population (census of 1983, excluding 3,497 unemployed): Agriculture 4,727, Total (incl. others) 44,842.

AGRICULTURE, ETC.

Principal Crops (FAO estimates, metric tons, 1985): Maize 2,000, Wheat 1,000, Taro 3,000, Potatoes 2,000, Sweet potatoes 4,000, Yams 11,000, Coconuts 11,000, Cassava 3,000, Vegetables and melons 5,000, Fresh fruit 9,000. Source: FAO, *Production Yearbook.*
Livestock (FAO estimates, '000 head, 1985): Horses 10, Cattle 122, Pigs 40, Sheep 3, Goats 18. Source: FAO, *Production Yearbook.*
Forestry ('000 cu m): *Roundwood removals:* 12 in 1979. Source: FAO, *Yearbook of Forest Products.*
Fishing (FAO estimates, metric tons, 1984): Marine fishes 3,095; Crustaceans and molluscs 115; Trochus shells 296; Total catch 3,506. Source: FAO, *Yearbook of Fishery Statistics.*

MINING

Production (metric tons): Nickel ore (metal content) 78,090 in 1981; 60,101 in 1982; 46,162 in 1983.

INDUSTRY

Production ('000 metric tons, 1983): Ferro-nickel 71.

FINANCE

Currency and Exchange Rates: see French Polynesia.
Budget (1985, million francs CFP): Expenditure: Ordinary expenditure 29,765, Extraordinary expenditure 860, Total 30,625; Revenue: Ordinary receipts 29,765, Extraordinary receipts 860, Total 30,625. Direct aid from France in 1985 amounted to 8,631m. francs CFP.
Aid from France (francs CFP, FIDES 1982): Local section 153m.; General section 1,018m.
Gross Domestic Product (million francs CFP at current prices): 96,304 in 1981; 108,093 in 1982; 114,161 in 1983.
Cost of Living (Consumer Price Index at 1 April 1985; August 1975 = 100): 238.

EXTERNAL TRADE

1984 (million francs CFP): *Imports:* 49,605 (of which 39.9% from France); *Exports:* 33,452 (of which 57.9% to France).

TRANSPORT

Road Traffic (1982): Motor vehicles (incl. tractors) 36,035, Motor cycles 4,215.
Shipping (1984): Vessels entered 391; Freight entered 675,300 metric tons.
Civil Aviation (La Tontouta airport, Nouméa, 1984): Passengers arriving 118,774, Passengers departing 119,307; Freight unloaded 1,670 metric tons, Freight loaded 3,811 metric tons.

TOURISM

Visitors (1984): 92,982. (Source: Police de l'Air et des Frontières.)

EDUCATION

Primary (1984): 278 schools, 33,884 pupils, 1,589 teachers.
Secondary (1984): 41 schools, 12,481 pupils, 976 teachers.
Technical (1984): 32 institutions, 5,264 students, 309 teachers.
Higher (1984): 5 institutions, 660 students, 59 teachers.

New Caledonia

Directory

The Government
(January 1987)

High Commissioner: JEAN MONTPEZAT.
Secretary-General: CHRISTIAN BLANC.

Legislature

CONGRÈS TERRITORIAL

The Territorial Congress, with 46 members, is the aggregate of four autonomous elected regional councils. It comprises nine councillors from the North region, nine from the Centre region, 21 from the South and seven from the Loyalty Islands.

President: DICK UKEIWÉ (RPCR).

Election, 29 September 1985

Party	Votes	%	Seats
RCPR	37,148	52.00	25
FLNKS	20,545	28.76	16
LKS	4,594	6.43	1
FN	5,263	7.37	3
RPC	1,058	1.48	1
Others	2,833	3.97	—
Total	71,441	100.00	46

The regional distribution of seats was as follows:

	North	Centre	South	Loyalty Islands
RCPR	2	4	17	2
FLNKS	6	5	1	4
LKS	—	—	—	1
FN	—	—	3	—
RPC	1	—	—	—

Each regional council (conseil de région) has its own elected President:
North region: JEAN-MARIE TJIBAOU (FLNKS).
Centre region: LÉOPOLD JORÉDIÉ (FLNKS).
South region: JEAN LEQUES (RPCR).
Loyalty Islands: YEIWENÉ YEIWENÉ (FLNKS).

An executive council (conseil exécutif), comprising the Presidents of the four regional councils and headed by the President of the Territorial Congress, has a consultative role in the discussion of proposals submitted to the Congress.
In each region a 'customary' consultative council (conseil consultatif coutumier) is charged with giving an opinion on all matters submitted to it by the regional authorities. A territorial 'customary' council (conseil coutumier territorial), composed of all four consultative councils, gives advice on all questions submitted to it by the High Commissioner.

Deputies to the French National Assembly: JACQUES LAFLEUR (RPR), MAURICE NÉNOU-PWATAHO (RPR).
Representative to the French Senate: DICK UKEIWÉ (RPR).
Economic and Social Councillor: GUY MENNESSON.

Political Organizations

Parties in favour of retaining the status quo or of New Caledonia's becoming a department of France:
Front National (FN): Nouméa; extreme right-wing.
Rassemblement pour la Calédonie dans la République (RPCR): Conseil de la Région Sud, BP 4142, Nouméa; f. 1977; Leader JACQUES LAFLEUR; a coalition of the following parties:
    Centre des Démocrates Sociaux (CDS): Nouméa; f. 1971; Leader JEAN LEQUES.

FRENCH OVERSEAS TERRITORIES
New Caledonia

Parti Républicain (PR): Nouméa; Leader Pierre Maresca.
Rassemblement pour la République (RPR): Nouméa; f. 1977; Leaders Jacques Lafleur, Dick Ukeiwé.

Parties in favour of internal autonomy:

Fédération pour une nouvelle société calédonienne (FNSC): Nouméa; f. 1979; Leader Jean-Pierre Aïfa; a coalition of the following parties:

    Mouvement wallisien et futunien: f. 1979; Pres. Finau Melito.
    Parti républicain calédonien (PRC): 8 rue Gagarine, Nouméa; tel. 252395; f. 1979; Leader Lionel Cherrier.
    Union démocratique (UD): Nouméa; f. 1968; Leader Gaston Morlet.
    Union nouvelle calédonienne (UNC): Nouméa; f. 1977; Leader Jean-Pierre Aïfa.

Parties in favour of independence:

Front de libération nationale kanake socialiste (FLNKS): Nouméa; f. 1984 (following dissolution of Front indépendantiste); Leaders Jean-Marie Tjibaou, Yeiwené Yeiwené; a grouping of the following parties:

    Front uni de libération kanak (FULK): Nouméa; f. 1974; Leader Yann Céléné Uregei.
    Parti socialiste calédonien (PSC): Nouméa; f. 1975; Leader M. Violette.
    Union calédonienne (UC): 8 rue Gambetta, 1° Vallée du Tir, Nouméa; f. 1952; 5,000 mems; Pres. Roch Pidjot; Sec.-Gen. Léopold Jorédié.
    Union progressiste mélanésienne (UPM): Nouméa; f. 1974 as the Union progressiste multiraciale; 2,300 mems; Leader Edmond Nékiriaï.

Libération kanake socialiste (LKS): Nouméa; Leader Nidoïsh Naisseline.

Judicial System

Court of Appeal: Palais de Justice, BP F4, Nouméa; First Pres. G. Goudot; Procurator-Gen. J. Dufour.
Court of the First Instance: Nouméa; Pres. J. L. Siband; Procurator of the Republic J. Santarelli.

Religion

The population is overwhelmingly Christian, with Roman Catholics comprising about 65% of the total. There is a substantial Protestant minority.

CHRISTIANITY
The Roman Catholic Church

The territory comprises a single archdiocese, with an estimated 93,500 adherents in 1984. The Archbishop participates in the Episcopal Conference of the Pacific, based in Fiji.

Archbishop of Nouméa: Most Rev. Michel-Marie-Bernard Calvet, Archevêché, BP 3, Nouméa; tel. 273149.

BAHÁ'Í FAITH

National Spiritual Assembly: BP 1564, Nouméa; tel. 275624; mems resident in 13 localities in New Caledonia and 16 localities in the Loyalty Is.

The Press

L'Avenir Calédonien: 10 rue Gambetta, Nouméa; organ of the Union calédonienne; Dir Païta Gabriel.
Le Devenir Calédonien: 7 rue Mascart, Rivière Salée, BP 4481, Nouméa; monthly; social, cultural and economic news of New Caledonia.
Dixit: BP 370, Nouméa; tel. 286631; telex 078; f. 1984; annual; French (circ. 12,000) and English (circ. 8,000); Dir Hubert Chavelet.
Eglise de Nouvelle-Calédonie: BP 170, Nouméa; f. 1976; fortnightly; official bulletin of the Roman Catholic Church in New Caledonia; circ. 450.
La France Australe: 5 rue de la Somme, BP 25, Nouméa; tel. 274444; daily.
Le Journal Calédonien: BP 3002, Nouméa; weekly.
Les Nouvelles Calédoniennes: 34 rue de la République, BP 179, Nouméa; tel. 272584; telex 812; f. 1971; daily; Publr J. P. Leyraud; Dir Edouard Ventrillon; Editors Henri Lepot, Jacques D'André circ. 16,000.
La Presse Calédonienne: 14 rue de Sebastopol, BP 4034, Nouméa; tel. 285055; daily; circ. 8,000.

NEWS AGENCY

Agence France-Presse (AFP): 29 rue Tindale, Nouméa; tel. 263033; telex 826; Correspondent Michel Conrath.

Publisher

Editions d'Art Calédoniennes: 40 rue de Paris, BP 1626, Nouméa; tel. 261184; telex 048; art, reprints, travel.

Radio and Television

In 1985 there were an estimated 80,000 radio receivers and 32,000 television receivers in use, of which about 21,000 were colour receivers.

RADIO

Radiodiffusion Française d'Outre-mer (RFO): BP G3, Nouméa; tel. 274327; telex 052; f. 1942; 20 hours of daily programmes in French; Dir Fred Jouhaud.
Radio Rythme Bleu: BP 1390, Nouméa; tel. 283357.

TELEVISION

Télé Nouméa: Société Nationale de Radio-Télévision Française d'Outre-mer, BP G3, Nouméa; tel. 274327; telex 052; f. 1965; transmits 10 hours daily; Dir Fred Jouhaud.

Finance

(cap. = capital; res = reserves; m. = million; brs = branches; amounts in CFP francs)

BANKING

Banque Indosuez (France): angle rue de l'Alma et ave Foch, BP G5, Nouméa; tel. 272212; telex 023.
Banque Nationale de Paris Nouvelle Calédonie (France): 37 R.T. 13, BP K3, Nouméa; tel. 275555; telex 022; f. 1969 as Banque Nationale de Paris; present name adopted in 1978; cap. 30m., res 38m., dep. 811m. (Dec. 1984); Pres. Edouard Finot; Gen. Man. Jacques Lobinger; 8 brs.
Banque de Nouvelle-Calédonie (BNC)/Crédit Lyonnais: 13 ave de la Victoire, BP L3, Nouméa; tel. 285069; telex 091; f. 1974; cap. 150m. (1986); Pres. Bernard Thiolon; Gen. Man. Robert Sabatier.
Banque Paribas Pacifique (Nouvelle-Calédonie): 33 rue de l'Alma, BP 777, Nouméa; tel. 275181; telex 086; cap. 400m., res 70m. (Dec. 1985); Chair. Pierre Decker; Gen. Man. Christian de Bernede.
Société Générale Calédonienne de Banque: 56 ave de la Victoire, BP G2, Nouméa; tel. 272264; telex 067; f. 1981; cap. 275m. (1985); Gen. Man. Raymond Clavier; 6 brs.

Trade and Industry

Chambre d'Agriculture: BP 111, Nouméa; tel. 272056; f. 1909; 46 mems; Pres. Roger Pene.
Chambre de Commerce et d'Industrie: BP 10, Nouméa; tel. 272551; telex 045; f. 1879; 20 mems; Pres. Arnold Daly; Gen. Man. Georges Giovannelli.

FRENCH OVERSEAS TERRITORIES   *New Caledonia*

EMPLOYERS' ORGANIZATION

Fédération Patronale de Nouvelle-Calédonie et Dépendances: 13 rue de Verdun, BP 466, Nouméa; tel. 273525; f. 1936; represents the leading companies of New Caledonia in the defence of professional interests, co-ordination, documentation and research in socio-economic fields; Pres. DIDIER LEROUX; Sec.-Gen. ANNIE BEUSTES.

TRADE UNIONS

Confédération des Travailleurs Calédoniens: Nouméa; Sec.-Gen. R. JOYEUX; grouped with:

Fédération des Fonctionnaires: Nouméa; Sec.-Gen. GILBERT NOUVEAU.

Syndicat Général des Collaborateurs des Industries de Nouvelle Calédonie: Sec.-Gen. H. CHAMPIN.

Syndicat des Travailleurs canaques exploités: Nouméa; Leader LOUIS UREGEÏ.

Union des Syndicats Ouvriers et Employés de Nouvelle-Calédonie: Nouméa; Sec.-Gen. GUY MENNESSON.

Union Territoriale Force Ouvrière: 13 rue Jules Ferry, BP 4773, Nouméa; tel. 274950; f. 1982; Sec.-Gen. BERNARD CHENAIE.

Transport

ROADS

In 1983 there was a total of 5,980 km of roads in New Caledonia; 766 km were bitumen-surfaced, 589 km unsealed, 1,618 km stone-surfaced and 2,523 km tracks in 1980. The outer islands had a total of 470 km of roads and tracks in 1980.

SHIPPING

Most traffic is through the port of Nouméa. Passenger and cargo services, linking Nouméa to other towns and islands, are regular and frequent.

Shipping companies operating cargo services include Hamburg-Sued, Nedlloyd and Bank Line (which connect Nouméa with European ports), Kyowa Line (with Hong Kong, Taiwan, the Republic of Korea and Japan), Somacal (with Sydney, Australia), Sofrana-Unilines (with various Pacific islands and ports on the west coast of Australia), Daiwa Line (with Sydney, Australia, Japan, and various Pacific Islands), Compagnie des Chargeurs Calédoniens (with Sydney, Australia, and European and Mediterranean ports) and the China Navigation Co (with New Zealand, Fiji and Japan).

CIVIL AVIATION

There is an international airport at Nouméa, and an internal network provides air services linking Nouméa to other towns and islands.

Air Calédonie: BP 212, Nouméa; tel. 252339; telex 112; f. 1955; services throughout New Caledonia and to the Loyalty Islands; Chair. CÉSAR QENEGEI; Man. Dir DOMINIQUE LEONARDON; fleet of 3 Twin Otter, 1 ATR 42-300, 1 Cessna 310P.

Air Calédonie International: Nouméa; tel. 283333; telex 048; f. 1983; services to Brisbane and Melbourne (Australia), Fiji, Wallis Island and Vanuatu; Man. Dir D. FAMIN.

Tourism

Office Territorial du Tourisme de Nouvelle-Calédonie: 25 ave Maréchal Foch, BP 688, Nouméa; tel. 272632; telex 063; f. 1960; Dir MICHEL DOPPLER.

WALLIS AND FUTUNA ISLANDS

Introductory Survey

Location, Climate, Language, Religion, Capital

The territory of Wallis and Futuna comprises two groups of islands: the Wallis Islands, including Wallis Island (also known as Uvea) and 22 islets on the surrounding reef, and, to the south-east, Futuna (or Hooru), comprising the two small islands of Futuna and Alofi. The islands are located north-east of Fiji and west of Western Samoa. Temperatures are generally between about 23°C (73°F) and 30°C (86°F), and there is a cyclone season between October and March. French and Wallisian, the indigenous Polynesian language, are spoken in the territory, and the entire population is nominally Roman Catholic. The capital is Mata-Utu, on Wallis Island.

Recent History

The first Europeans to discover Futuna and Alofi were Dutch navigators (in 1616) who named them the Hoorn Islands after the town from which they had sailed. The Wallis Islands were discovered by a British expedition, led by Samuel Wallis, in 1767. A French protectorate since 1888, the islands chose by referendum in December 1959 to become an overseas territory. In July 1961 they were granted this status.

Although there is no movement in Wallis and Futuna seeking secession of the territory from France (in contrast with the situation in the other French Pacific territories, French Polynesia and New Caledonia), the two kings whose kingdoms share the island of Futuna requested in November 1983, through the Territorial Assembly, that the island groups of Wallis and Futuna become separate overseas territories of France, arguing that the administration and affairs of the territory had become excessively concentrated on Wallis Island.

At elections to the 20-member Territorial Assembly in March 1982, the Rassemblement pour la République (RPR) and its allies won 11 seats, while the remaining nine went to candidates belonging to, or associated with, the Union pour la Démocratie Française (UDF). Later in 1982 one member of the Lua kae tahi, a group affiliated to the metropolitan UDF, defected to the RPR group, thereby strengthening the RPR's majority. In November 1983, however, three of the 12 RPR members joined the Lua kae tahi, forming a new majority. In the subsequent election for President of the Territorial Assembly, this 11-strong block of UDF-associated members supported the ultimately successful candidate, Falakiko Gata, even though he had been elected to the Territorial Assembly in 1982 as a member of the RPR.

In April 1985 Gata formed a new political party, the Union populaire locale (UPL), which was committed to giving priority to local, rather than metropolitan, issues. At a meeting with the French Prime Minister in Paris in June, Gata reaffirmed that it was in the territory's interests to remain French and not to seek independence.

In March 1986 Benjamin Brial, the candidate of the RPR, was re-elected as the territory's deputy to the French National Assembly, obtaining 2,798 votes (44.4%) of the total 6,302 votes cast in the second ballot. On 29 October 1986 the islands' Chief Administrator, Jacques Le Hénaff, declared a state of emergency in the territory, following a stone-throwing incident during a display of unrest among some local chiefs. The latter had expressed dissatisfaction with the French Secretary-General of the territory, Georges Jaymes, and requested his removal and repatriation, owing to his transfer of a number of highly-respected French civil servants from their posts in the territory. As a precautionary measure, 30 gendarmes were brought in from New Caledonia to restore order, but the disturbance was not renewed, and the state of emergency was lifted on the following day.

Government

The territory of Wallis and Futuna is administered by a representative of the French Government, the Chief Administrator, who is assisted by a Territorial Assembly. The Assembly has 20 members and is elected for a five-year term. The three traditional kingdoms, from which the territory was formed, one on Wallis and two sharing Futuna, have equal rights, although the kings' powers are limited. In addition, the territory elects one deputy to the French National Assembly in Paris and one representative to the French Senate.

Economic Affairs

Most monetary income in Wallis and Futuna is derived from government employment and remittances sent home by islanders employed in New Caledonia. Copra and handicrafts are the only significant export commodities. Yams, taro, bananas, coconuts, cassava and other food crops are also cultivated.

During his visit to Paris in June 1985, Falakiko Gata, the President of the Territorial Assembly, told the French Prime Minister that the policies relating to agricultural and fisheries development since 1960 had been a complete failure. It was hoped that these areas of the economy could be improved through new administrative arrangements, whereby development funding would be channelled through traditional chiefs.

In December 1986 almost all the cultivated vegetation on the island of Futuna, notably the banana plantations, was destroyed by a cyclone.

Social Welfare

In 1981 there were three state hospitals in Wallis and Futuna, with a total of 93 beds, and there were four physicians working in the islands.

Education

In 1983 there were 13 state-financed primary and lower-secondary schools in Wallis and Futuna, with a total of 3,962 pupils.

Tourism

There are three small hotels on Wallis Island.

Public Holidays

1987: 1 January (New Year's Day), 20 April (Easter Monday), 1 May (Labour Day), 8 May (Liberation Day), 28 May (Ascension Day), 8 June (Whit Monday), 14 July (Fall of the Bastille), 11 November (Armistice Day), 25 December (Christmas Day).

1988: 1 January (New Year's Day), 4 April (Easter Monday), 2 May (for Labour Day), 8 May (Liberation Day), 12 May (Ascension Day), 23 May (Whit Monday), 14 July (Fall of the Bastille), 11 November (Armistice Day), 25 December (Christmas Day).

Weights and Measures

The metric system is in force.

Currency and Exchange Rates

100 centimes = 1 franc de la Communauté française du Pacifique (franc CFP or Pacific franc).

Exchange rates (30 September 1986):
£1 sterling = 174.77 francs CFP;
US $1 = 120.77 francs CFP.

Statistical Survey

AREA AND POPULATION

Area (sq km): Wallis Island 159, Futuna Island and Alofi Island 115, total of all islands 274.

Population (1983): 12,391; Wallis Island 8,072 (chief town Mata-Utu), Futuna Island 4,319; Alofi Island uninhabited; about 11,000 Wallisians and Futunians live in New Caledonia and in Vanuatu.

AGRICULTURE, ETC.

Principal Crops (FAO estimates, '000 metric tons, 1985): Cassava 2, Yams 1, Taro (Coco yam) 2, Coconuts 3, Bananas 4, Other fruit 5, Vegetables and melons 1. Source: FAO, *Production Yearbook*.

Livestock (FAO estimates, year ending September 1985): Pigs 26,000, Goats 7,000. Source: FAO, *Production Yearbook*.

FINANCE

Currency and Exchange Rates: see French Polynesia.
Budget (1983): 20,350,000 French francs.
Aid from France (1982): 55,000,000 French francs.

FRENCH OVERSEAS TERRITORIES

EXTERNAL TRADE

1981: *Imports:* 667m. francs CFP. *Exports:* n.a.

TRANSPORT

Civil Aviation: Wallis Island (1980): aircraft arrivals and departures 581; freight handled 171 metric tons; passenger arrivals 4,555, passenger departures 4,300; mail loaded and unloaded 72 metric tons.

EDUCATION

Primary and lower secondary (1983): 13 state-financed schools, 3,962 pupils.

Directory

The Government

(January 1987)

The territory is administered by a French-appointed Chief Administrator who is assisted by a Territorial Assembly (see below).

Chief Administrator: JACQUES LE HÉNAFF.

All government offices are in Mata-Uta, Wallis Island.

Legislature

ASSEMBLÉE TERRITORIALE

The Territorial Assembly is elected for a five-year term on the basis of universal adult suffrage. It has 20 members. The Assembly, together with a member of the French Senate and a deputy to the French National Assembly, are elected locally on a common roll. At the election of 21 March 1982 the Rassemblement pour la République (RPR) and its affiliates won 11 seats, and the Union pour la Démocratie Française (UDF) and its affiliates won nine seats. As a result of subsequent changes of allegiance by various members of the Assembly, the UDF block obtained a majority.

President of the Territorial Assembly: FALAKIKO GATA.

Deputy to the French National Assembly: BENJAMIN BRIAL (RPR).

Representative to the French Senate: SOSEFO MAKAPE PAPILIO (RPR).

Political Organizations

Lua kae tahi: affiliated to UDF.

Rassemblement pour la République (RPR): Gaullist.

Union populaire locale (UPL): f. 1985; emphasizes importance of local issues; Leader FALAKIKO GATA.

Union pour la Démocratie Française (UDF).

Religion

Almost all of the inhabitants profess Christianity and are adherents of the Roman Catholic Church.

CHRISTIANITY

The Roman Catholic Church

The territory comprises a single diocese, suffragan to the archdiocese of Nouméa (New Caledonia). In 1984 an estimated 98.5% of the population were adherents. The Bishop participates in the Episcopal Conference of the Pacific, based in Fiji.

Bishop of Wallis and Futuna: Mgr LOLESIO FUAHEA, Lano, BP 15, Mata-Utu, Wallis Island; tel. 22283.

Radio and Television

Radiodiffusion Française d'Outre-mer (RFO): BP 102, Mata-Utu, Iles de Wallis et Futuna (par Nouméa); tel. 19681; transmitters at Mata-Utu (Wallis) and Alo (Futuna); programmes in Wallisian and French; a television service, transmitting for three hours daily, began operation in September 1986; Man. R. CIPOLIN.

Transport

ROADS

Wallis Island has a few kilometres of road, one route circling the island, and there is also a road circling the island of Futuna; the only surfaced roads are in Mata-Utu.

SHIPPING

Mata-Utu serves as the seaport of Wallis Island, while Sigave is the only port on Futuna. Services to Nouméa (New Caledonia), Suva (Fiji), Port Vila and Santo (Vanuatu), are operated by the Compagnie Wallisienne de Navigation.

CIVIL AVIATION

There is an international airport on Wallis Island. Air Calédonie (New Caledonia) operates three flights a week from Wallis to Futuna, and one flight a week from Wallis to Nouméa; Air Calédonie International also serves Wallis Island.

GABON

Introductory Survey

Location, Climate, Language, Religion, Flag, Capital
The Gabonese Republic is an equatorial country on the west coast of Africa, with Equatorial Guinea and Cameroon to the north and the Congo to the south and east. The climate is tropical, with an average annual temperature of 26°C (79°F) and an average annual rainfall of 2,490 mm (98 in). The official language is French, but Fang (in the north) and Bantu dialects (in the south) are also widely spoken. About 60% of the population are Christians, mainly Roman Catholics. Most of the remainder follow animist beliefs. The national flag (proportions 4 by 3) has three equal horizontal stripes, of green, yellow and blue. The capital is Libreville.

Recent History
Formerly a province of French Equatorial Africa, Gabon gained internal autonomy in 1957. It achieved self-government, within the French Community, in November 1958 and attained full independence on 17 August 1960.

At the time of independence, there were two main political parties: the Bloc démocratique gabonaise (BDG), led by Léon M'Ba, and the Union démocratique et sociale gabonaise (UDSG), led by Jean-Hilaire Aubame. The two parties were almost evenly matched in support and neither had a majority in the National Assembly. However, with the backing of independent deputies, M'Ba became Prime Minister in 1958 and Head of State at independence. He favoured close relations with France, and his rule was generally conservative. Members of the UDSG joined the Council of Ministers after independence, and the two parties agreed on a joint list of candidates for elections in February 1961, when a new constitution came into effect. M'Ba was elected Gabon's first President, with 99.6% of the votes cast, and Aubame, his long-standing rival, became Minister for Foreign Affairs. The BDG wanted the two parties to merge but the UDSG resisted this proposal. As a result, all the UDSG ministers were forced to resign in February 1963. President M'Ba dissolved the National Assembly in January 1964, in preparation for new elections.

In February 1964, shortly before the planned elections, President M'Ba was deposed by a military coup, staged by army supporters of Aubame. However, French forces immediately intervened, and the M'Ba Government was restored. Aubame was found guilty of treason, and sentenced to 10 years' imprisonment. The elections were postponed until April 1964, when the BDG won 31 of the 47 seats in the National Assembly. The UDSG was formally outlawed and, over the next two years, almost all of the opposition members in the Assembly joined the BDG.

In February 1967, with President M'Ba in poor health, the Constitution was revised to provide for the succession of a Vice-President if the President died or resigned. At the next elections, in March, there were no opposition candidates and the BDG was returned to power. President M'Ba was re-elected for a seven-year term, with Albert-Bernard Bongo, previously Deputy Prime Minister, as Vice-President. M'Ba died in November 1967 and was succeeded by Bongo, then aged 31. On 12 March 1968 the Parti démocratique gabonais (PDG) was established, and one-party government was formally instituted.

In February 1973 Bongo was re-elected President. In September he announced his conversion to Islam, adopting the forename Omar. In April 1975 President Bongo abolished the Vice-Presidency, replacing it by a new post of Prime Minister. Accordingly, Léon Mébiame, who had been Vice-President since 1968, took office as Prime Minister. At the same time, local administration was reorganized to confer considerable autonomous powers on the provinces.

In 1977 President Kerekou of Benin accused Gabon of having aided an airborne mercenary attack on Cotonou. President Bongo strongly denied these accusations, and ordered the expulsion of all nationals of Benin from Gabon. Altogether, about 6,000 Beninois were expelled. In May 1981 several thousand Cameroonians resident in Gabon were airlifted back to Cameroon following violence against the Cameroonian communities in Libreville and Port-Gentil.

At a meeting of the PDG Congress in January 1979, elections were held to the party's Central Committee, thus introducing the first element of democracy into Gabon's political system. Following his nomination by the PDG, President Bongo stood as the sole candidate in the presidential election held in December 1979, and was re-elected for another seven-year term. Legislative and municipal elections were held in early 1980; for the first time since 1960, independents were free to stand against party candidates. All seats in the National Assembly were, none the less, won by members of the PDG. In a government reshuffle in November 1981, Bongo relinquished his ministerial posts and the title of Head of Government, thereafter conferred upon the Prime Minister, Léon Mébiame. Two further technical government reshuffles, in March 1984 and December 1985, resulted in the expansion to 58 of the number of ministerial posts. PDG candidates received 99.5% of the total votes at a general election in February 1985 for an enlarged National Assembly, and at the party's third ordinary congress, held in September 1986, the memberships of the Central Committee and Political Bureau were also increased. At the next presidential election, held in November, Bongo (the sole candidate) received an estimated 99.97% of the votes. In January 1987 the Council of Ministers was reshuffled, and its membership reduced to 46.

President Bongo has adopted stern measures against any form of protest or dissent in the country. An illegal opposition group, the Mouvement de redressement national (MORENA), emerged in November 1981, advocating the establishment of a multi-party system in Gabon. In November 1982 a total of 29 MORENA sympathizers, including a former government minister, were found guilty of endangering state security, and received prison sentences, some with hard labour. Although they were all subsequently released, with the last group being granted clemency in May 1986, Bongo's firm line against any opposition movement has been maintained. When MORENA announced the formation of a government-in-exile in Paris during August 1985, Bongo applied pressure on the French Government to deny any form of recognition to the new grouping. Six soldiers were arrested in August for allegedly plotting a coup, and their leader was executed in September 1985.

Under Gabon's liberal economic system, efforts have been made to attract foreign companies and investors to the country. However, since January 1974 all companies operating in Gabon are required to have their headquarters there, and the State must be given a 10% share in all new foreign enterprises setting up in the country. Deteriorating economic conditions led to the imposition of controls on immigrant workers in May 1986. Bongo has pursued a policy of close co-operation with France in the fields of economic and foreign affairs. Relations with France became strained in October 1983, however, as a result of the publication in Paris of a book which was critical of the Bongo regime, and a six-week ban on news pertaining to France was imposed on the Gabonese media. Tension was reduced following a visit to Libreville in April 1984 by the French Prime Minister, Pierre Mauroy, and relations between the two countries were finally restored in October 1984, when Bongo paid a three-day state visit to Paris. The President has, nevertheless, attempted to diversify Gabon's external relations, and in September 1984 he visited Japan, the Republic of Korea and Thailand, with a view to strengthening economic and political links with Asian countries.

Government
The 1961 Constitution, as subsequently revised, vests executive power in the President, elected by universal adult suffrage for

seven years. The President appoints, and presides over, a Council of Ministers. The legislative organ is the unicameral National Assembly, with a term of five years. The Assembly has 120 members, of whom 111 are chosen by election and nine by nomination. Gabon became a one-party state in 1968. The Parti démocratique gabonais (PDG) is the only legal party. The PDG's highest authority is the Party Congress which, in September 1986, elected 186 of the 297 members of the Central Committee, the remaining members being appointed by the President, to supervise Party work. To direct its policy, the Central Committee has a Political Bureau of 44 members. The country is divided into nine provinces, each under an appointed Governor, and 37 prefectures.

Defence

In July 1986 the army consisted of 1,900 men, the air force of 600 men, and the navy of 200 men. Paramilitary forces numbered at least 4,800. Military service is voluntary. France maintains a military detachment of 600 in Gabon. Estimated defence expenditure for 1985 was 35,500m. francs CFA.

Economic Affairs

With abundant mineral resources and a relatively small population, Gabon is the richest country in sub-Saharan Africa, measured in terms of average income. In 1984, according to estimates by the World Bank, Gabon's GNP per head was US $4,100 (at average 1982–84 prices), having increased at an average rate of 5.9% annually, in real terms, since 1965. However, the World Bank estimates assume that Gabon's total population is considerably less than the official assessment.

More than one-half of the working population are engaged in subsistence agriculture, largely untouched by the expansion of the market economy. There is a little commercial agricultural production, the main crops being the oil palm, coffee, cocoa and bananas. The agricultural sector contributed only 4% of Gabon's GDP in the mid-1980s, compared with 14% in 1966. Government plans to develop the rural sector are intended to halt the drift of population to urban areas and to reduce Gabon's dependence on imported foodstuffs, which supply about 85% of the country's needs. Imports of food and agricultural products in 1984, which were valued at nearly 72,000m. francs CFA, represented an estimated 22.5% of the total import bill in that year, compared with 11.7% in 1981.

Forests cover 82% of Gabon's land area, and for many years the economy was largely dependent upon forestry, particularly production of okoumé, a wood used in the making of plywood. Exports of okoumé rose by 2.3%, to 1,011,830 cu m, in 1984, while shipments of another tropical softwood, ozigo, fell to 45,278 cu m. Although wood remains Gabon's second most important export commodity (providing 6.4% of total export earnings in 1985), the country's production of timber has been declining since 1977, and several forestry companies were in financial difficulties in the early 1980s. The lack of internal outlets, and international competition, as well as transport difficulties, mean that the wood industry is underdeveloped. The Transgabon railway, currently under construction, will allow previously inaccessible areas of forest to be exploited.

The economy is heavily dependent on petroleum, which provided 83% of export earnings and 65% of government revenue in 1984. The petroleum price rises of 1974 coincided with peak production from Gabon's oilfields, but in 1977 output began to level off and recession set in, as economic expansion had proceeded more rapidly than the availability of finance. Gabon's annual output of crude petroleum was the fifth highest in Africa in 1976, at 11.3m. metric tons, but subsequently declined, reaching a low of 7.6m. tons in 1981. Production recovered following a period of increased exploration; reaching a peak of 8.6m. tons in 1985, it was expected to stabilize at around 8m. tons per year during the late 1980s. However, earnings from the petroleum sector were sharply reduced as a result of the decline in world oil prices in 1985 and 1986; the value of the Government's oil receipts fell to about 285,000m. francs CFA in 1986, compared with 400,000m. francs CFA in 1985, and was expected to total only 60,000m. francs CFA in 1987.

Gabon is the world's fourth largest producer of manganese, and it has been estimated that the deposits at Moanda constitute around one-quarter of the world's known reserves (excluding the USSR). An estimated 1.17m. tons of manganese (figures refer to the metal content of the ore) were produced in 1980, but output fell to less than 800,000 tons per year in 1981 and 1982, following the recession in the world's steel industries, which utilize 95% of world manganese production in the manufacture of various alloys. Production increased to 947,000 tons in 1983. There are plans for the exploitation of major iron ore deposits at Belinga, in the north-east, on completion of the Transgabon rail link to the coast. The deposits contain an estimated 850m. tons of ore, with 64.5% metal content.

The exploitation of uranium deposits at Mounana began in 1961. Known reserves amount to 20 years' output at recently-achieved rates, and new deposits have been discovered at Boyindzi and Oklo. Production was 970 tons of uranium metal in 1982, rising to 1,006 tons in 1983 before declining slightly to total 918 tons in 1985. The ore is extracted and concentrated by the Compagnie des Mines d'Uranium de Franceville (COMUF), a consortium largely controlled by French interests but with a 25% interest held by the Gabonese Government. New deposits of barytes, talc, lead, zinc, copper, gold and diamonds have also been discovered. A complete geological survey of the interior is to be carried out as part of a mineral development project.

Gabon's manufacturing sector is relatively restricted, though it is being expanded, and accounted for 3.6% of GDP in 1984. However, shortage of labour and a high minimum wage, together with inadequate infrastructure, have prevented further expansion. There are petroleum refineries at Port-Gentil and tanker facilities for vessels of up to 25,000 tons. Since July 1972 the 'Gabonization' of the economy has been undertaken. Foreigners have been replaced by Gabonese in positions of authority, and the state has taken a share in the capital of foreign companies.

An ambitious five-year plan was launched in 1976, of which the most important part was the Transgabon railway, the total construction cost of which was estimated at nearly 500,000m. francs CFA. The 340-km first stage, from Owendo to Booué, was opened in 1983, and the second stage, a line of 330 km from Booué to Franceville, was inaugurated in December 1986, ahead of schedule. A final stage would connect Booué to Belinga. Development of the railway is essential if Gabon is to be able to exploit efficiently the mineral deposits inland (uranium, manganese and iron ore) when petroleum reserves are exhausted. The development of both forestry and mining has been hampered by a lack of transport facilities. There is considerable potential for hydroelectric power in Gabon, and three hydroelectric power stations are currently in operation. An electricity and water supply programme was launched in 1984, with financial assistance from France and Canada. Proposals for the construction of a 300-MW nuclear power station, to be financed by France, were abandoned in May 1986, following the nuclear accident at Chernobyl in the USSR.

Gabon's valuable natural resources have not prevented the accumulation of a large foreign debt, which was estimated by the World Bank to total US $724.5m. at the end of 1984. This has necessitated a policy of budgetary restraint. Following the implementation of an IMF stabilization plan in 1978, the total debt, then estimated at 1,600m. French francs, fell by 15.5% in 1979: the cost of debt servicing has remained heavy, however, and was assigned 147,500m. francs CFA out of total planned expenditure of 624,000m. francs CFA in 1984. The collapse of world oil prices in 1985 and 1986, and the subsequent decline in Gabon's total export revenue, led the Government to suspend payments on both official and commercial debt in September 1986, and to seek a rescheduling of its debt commitments. In December the IMF granted Gabon a medium-term stand-by arrangement worth $118.3m. In 1984 the balance of payments showed a current surplus of $83.9m., compared with $72.0m. in 1983, $309.4m. in 1982 and $403.3m. in 1981. The total value of annual imports rose by more than 40% over the period 1982–85, to an estimated 362,000m. francs CFA, while that of petroleum exports increased by only 1% over the same period, to around 550,000m. francs CFA. The trade surplus was estimated at just over 500,000m. francs CFA in 1985, and was expected to decline in 1986. Gabon's gross domestic product (GDP) increased from 1,320,000m. francs CFA in 1983 to 1,455,600m. francs CFA in 1984; however, it stagnated in 1985 and was expected to decline by approximately 1.5% in 1986.

The fifth Five-Year Plan (1984–88) aimed to stabilize growth under a liberal but planned economy. Almost one-half of the proposed investment of 1,228,478m. francs CFA over the Plan period was allocated to infrastructure projects. Several of these, including the proposed construction of a new terminal to handle mineral ore at the port of Owendo, were suspended in June 1986, following overall reductions of 140m. francs CFA in the investment budget for that year: these were imposed, along with public-sector wage 'freezes', in an effort to offset the expected decline in export revenue from oil. Under the 1984–88 Plan, high priority was to be given to diversification of the country's productive sector, and in March 1986 the African Development Bank (ADB) agreed to part-finance the first phase of a US $117m. rubber development project. In July 1986 the Government announced plans to 'privatize' some state-owned companies.

Social Welfare

There is a national Fund for State Insurance, and a guaranteed minimum wage. In 1984 Gabon had 22 hospitals, 113 medical centres and 284 dispensaries. There were 5,774 hospital beds and 300 physicians. Maternal and infant health is a major priority.

Education

Education is officially compulsory for 10 years between six and 16 years of age: in 1982 70% of children in the relevant age-group attended primary and secondary schools (73% of boys; 67% of girls). Primary and secondary education is provided by state and mission schools. There is a university in Libreville, and a second is planned for Franceville. Primary education begins at the age of six and lasts for six years. Secondary education, beginning at 12 years of age, lasts for up to seven years, comprising a first cycle of four years and a second of three years. The university has more than 2,000 students. In addition, many students go to France for university and technical training. In 1985, according to estimates by UNESCO, adult illiteracy averaged 38.4% (males 29.8%; females 46.6%). Education is a major priority, and the 1983 budget allocated 32,800m. francs CFA to expenditure on primary and secondary education.

Tourism

Tourism is being extensively developed, with new hotels and several important projects, including a 'holiday village' near Libreville (opened in 1973), reorganization of Pointe-Denis tourist resort, and the promotion of national parks. There are approximately 2,000 hotel rooms. There were 16,000 tourist arrivals in 1982, when tourist receipts totalled about US $9m.

Public Holidays

1987: 1 January (New Year's Day), 12 March (Anniversary of Renovation, foundation of the Parti démocratique gabonais), 20 April (Easter Monday), 1 May (Labour Day), 30 May* (Id al-Fitr, end of Ramadan), 8 June (Whit Monday), 6 August* (Id al-Adha, feast of the Sacrifice), 17 August (Anniversary of Independence), 1 November (All Saints' Day), 25 December (Christmas).

1988: 1 January (New Year's Day), 12 March (Anniversary of Renovation, foundation of the Parti démocratique gabonais), 4 April (Easter Monday), 1 May (Labour Day), 18 May* (Id al-Fitr, end of Ramadan), 23 May (Whit Monday), 25 July* (Id al-Adha, feast of the Sacrifice), 17 August (Anniversary of Independence), 1 November (All Saints' Day), 25 December (Christmas).

* These holidays are dependent on the Islamic lunar calendar and may vary by one or two days from the dates given.

Weights and Measures

The metric system is in official use.

Currency and Exchange Rates

100 centimes = 1 franc de la Coopération financière en Afrique centrale (CFA).

Exchange rates (30 September 1986):
 1 franc CFA = 2 French centimes;
 £1 sterling = 480.625 francs CFA;
 US $1 = 332.125 francs CFA.

GABON

Statistical Survey

Source (unless otherwise stated): Direction Générale de la Statistique et des Etudes Economiques, BP 179, Libreville; tel. 72-13-69; telex 5370.

Area and Population

AREA, POPULATION AND DENSITY

Area (sq km)	267,667*
Population (census results)†	
8 October 1960–May 1961	
Males	211,350
Females	237,214
Total	448,564
Population (UN estimates at mid-year)‡	
1982	1,108,000
1983	1,127,000
1984	1,146,000
Density (per sq km) at mid-1984	4.3

* 103,347 sq miles.
† The results of a census in August 1980 were officially repudiated and a decree in May 1981 declared a population of 1,232,000, including 122,000 Gabonese nationals resident abroad.
‡ Source: UN, *World Population Prospects: Estimates and Projections as Assessed in 1982*. These estimates represented a considerable upward revision from the UN Population Division's previous (1980) assessment. In its 1984 assessment, the UN estimated Gabon's mid-1984 population at 1,131,000. Other sources continue to quote lower estimates, e.g. the World Bank has assessed Gabon's mid-year population as: 797,000 in 1983; 812,000 in 1984.

BIRTHS AND DEATHS

Average annual birth rate 31.0 per 1,000 in 1970–75, 32.9 per 1,000 in 1975–80; death rate 20.2 per 1,000 in 1970–75, 19.2 per 1,000 in 1975–80 (UN estimates).

REGIONS

Region	Population (1976 estimate)	Chief town
Estuaira	311,300	Libreville
Haut-Ogooué	187,500	Franceville
Moyen-Ogooué	50,500	Lambaréné
Ngounie	122,600	Mouila
Nyanga	89,000	Tchibanga
Ogooué-Ivindo	56,500	Makokou
Ogooué-Lolo	50,500	Koula-Moutou
Ogooué-Maritime	171,900	Port-Gentil
Woleu-Ntem	162,300	Oyem
Total	**1,202,100**	

PRINCIPAL TOWNS (population in 1975)

Libreville (capital)	251,400	Lambaréné	22,682
Port-Gentil	77,611		

ECONOMICALLY ACTIVE POPULATION
(ILO estimates, '000 persons at mid-1980)

	Males	Females	Total
Agriculture, etc.	205	174	379
Industry	49	5	54
Services	50	19	69
Total	**305**	**198**	**502**

Source: ILO, *Economically Active Population Estimates and Projections, 1950–2025*.

Agriculture

PRINCIPAL CROPS (FAO estimates, '000 metric tons)

	1982	1983	1984
Maize	10	10	10
Cassava (Manioc)	250	260	265
Yams	85	85	90
Taro (Coco yam)	55	55	60
Vegetables	24	25	26
Bananas	8	8	8
Plantains	165	170	170
Cocoa beans*	3	3	2
Groundnuts (in shell)	9	9	10
Sugar cane	150	170	155

* Unofficial estimates.
Source: FAO, *Production Yearbook*.

LIVESTOCK
(FAO estimates, '000 head, year ending September)

	1982*	1983	1984
Cattle	6	7	7
Pigs	140	145	150
Sheep	77	80	80
Goats	59	60	60

* Unofficial estimates.

Poultry (FAO estimates, million): 2 in 1982; 2 in 1983; 2 in 1984.
Source: FAO, *Production Yearbook*.

LIVESTOCK PRODUCTS

1984 (FAO estimates, '000 metric tons): Meat 22; Hen eggs 1.

Forestry

ROUNDWOOD REMOVALS ('000 cubic metres)

	1982	1983	1984
Industrial wood	1,260†	1,303	1,484†
Fuel wood*	1,222	1,222	1,222
Total	2,482	2,525	2,706

* FAO estimates (assumed to be unchanged since 1981).
† Unofficial estimate.
Source: FAO, *Yearbook of Forest Products*.

Fishing

('000 metric tons, live weight)

	1980	1981	1982
Inland waters	0.4	4.9	2.6
Atlantic Ocean	26.4	38.7	50.0
Total catch	26.8	43.6	52.6

1983 and 1984: Annual catch as in 1982 (FAO estimates).
Source: FAO, *Yearbook of Fishery Statistics*.

Mining

		1981	1982	1983
Crude petroleum	'000 metric tons	7,600	7,748	7,920*
Natural gas*	petajoules	62	60	58
Uranium ore†	'000 metric tons	1,020	970	1,042*
Manganese ore†	'000 metric tons	758.6	771.3	947.1*
Gold	kilograms	18	17	17

* Provisional or estimated data.
† Figures refer to the metal content of ores and concentrates.
Source: UN, *Industrial Statistics Yearbook*.

Industry

PETROLEUM PRODUCTS ('000 metric tons)

	1981	1982	1983
Liquefied petroleum gas*	5	6	5
Motor spirit (petrol)	120	120	110
Kerosene	25	26	25
Jet fuel	92	90	87
Distillate fuel oils	348	360	350
Residual fuel oil	630	620	471
Bitumen (asphalt)	13	14	12

* Provisional or estimated data.
Source: UN, *Industrial Statistics Yearbook*.

SELECTED OTHER PRODUCTS

	1981	1982	1983
Palm oil (metric tons)*	2,000	2,000	2,000
Beer ('000 hectolitres)	600	n.a.	n.a.
Wheat flour (sales) ('000 metric tons)	16	15*	15*
Cement ('000 metric tons)†	150	172	179
Plywood ('000 cu metres)*	39	39	39
Veneer sheets ('000 cu metres)*	60	60	60
Electric energy (million kWh)	535	530	535

* FAO estimates.   † Provisional or estimated data.
Source: UN, *Industrial Statistics Yearbook*.

Finance

CURRENCY AND EXCHANGE RATES

Monetary Units
100 centimes = 1 franc de la Coopération financière en Afrique centrale (CFA).

Denominations
Coins: 1, 2, 5, 10, 25, 50 and 100 francs CFA.
Notes: 100, 500, 1,000, 5,000 and 10,000 francs CFA.

French Franc, Sterling and Dollar Equivalents (30 September 1986)
1 French franc = 50 francs CFA;
£1 sterling = 480.625 francs CFA;
US $1 = 332.125 francs CFA;
1,000 francs CFA = £2.081 = $3.011.

Average Exchange Rate (francs CFA per US $)
1983   381.06
1984   436.96
1985   449.26

CENTRAL BANK RESERVES
(US $ million at 31 December)

	1983	1984	1985
Gold*	4.86	3.97	4.16
IMF special drawing rights	0.44	5.70	2.28
Reserve position in IMF	7.36	0.03	0.03
Foreign exchange	179.10	193.72	190.23
Total	191.76	203.42	196.71

* Valued at market-related prices.
Source: IMF, *International Financial Statistics*.

BUDGET ESTIMATES (million francs CFA)

Revenue	1980	1981	1982
Income from petroleum	187,300	271,500	308,500
Other revenue	122,800	136,700	154,600
Tax receipts	n.a.	127,400	145,700
Customs duties	63,240	69,509	77,000
Turnover tax	11,503	14,837	18,000
Non-tax revenue	n.a.	9,300	8,900
Total	310,100	408,200	463,100

Expenditure	1980	1981	1982
Current budget	110,000	134,800	150,800
Personnel	45,600	52,500	n.a.
Transfers and interventions	n.a.	16,600	19,300
Public debt	132,100	155,000	131,000
Development expenditure	92,000	134,200	175,400
Manufacturing sector	8,828	13,655	17,374
Infrastructure	51,698	73,526	99,686
Social services	7,396	14,577	25,640
Research	792	920	1,870
Participation	1,290	4,685	2,600
Administrative and other supplies	14,452	24,014	24,275
Total	334,100	424,800	457,200

1983 Budget (million francs CFA): balanced at 562,000 (income from petroleum 309,200).
1984 Budget (million francs CFA): balanced at 624,000 (income from petroleum 357,000, public debt expenditure 147,500, recurrent expenditure 195,000, development expenditure 280,000).
1985 budget estimates (million francs CFA): Revenue 594,000 (income from petroleum 375,000, external financing 85,000); Expenditure 679,000 (public debt 135,000, recurrent expenditure 219,000, development expenditure 325,000).
1986 budget estimates (million francs CFA): Revenue 603,000 (income from petroleum 285,000); Expenditure 670,000 (recurrent expenditure 232,000, development expenditure 279,000).
1987 draft budget (million francs CFA): Revenue 276,000 (income from petroleum 60,000); Expenditure 360,000 (public debt interest 64,000, recurrent expenditure 196,000, development expenditure 100,000).

MONEY SUPPLY ('000 million francs CFA at 31 December)

	1983	1984	1985
Currency outside banks	48.39	52.64	55.79
Demand deposits at commercial and development banks	92.57	113.16	119.33
Checking deposits at post office	1.63	1.95	1.45
Total money	142.59	167.76	176.56

Source: IMF, *International Financial Statistics*.

FIFTH DEVELOPMENT PLAN, 1984–88
(proposed expenditure, million francs CFA at 1983 prices)

Productive sector	239,054
Infrastructure	595,662
Social services and education	213,972
General investments	162,520
Total	1,228,478

Source: *Annuaire National de la République Gabonaise 1983–84*.

COST OF LIVING (Retail Price Index for African families in Libreville; base: 1980 = 100)

	1983	1984	1985
All items	140.0	148.2	159.1

NATIONAL ACCOUNTS (million francs CFA at current prices)
National Income and Product

	1977	1978	1979
Compensation of employees	199,749	182,835	186,774
Operating surplus	257,984	166,320	231,527
Domestic factor incomes	457,733	349,155	418,301
Consumption of fixed capital	94,105	85,430	90,079
Gross domestic product at factor cost	551,838	434,585	508,380
Indirect taxes	140,976	107,545	117,923
Less subsidies	2,643	2,924	4,088
GDP in purchasers' values	690,171	539,206	622,215
Factor income from abroad	9,169	5,488	1,561
Less Factor income paid abroad	47,974	64,768	78,463
Gross national product	651,366	479,926	545,313
Less Consumption of fixed capital	94,105	85,430	90,079
National income in market prices	557,261	394,496	455,234
Other current transfers from abroad	13,759	13,390	15,365
Less Other current transfers paid abroad	20,430	17,467	39,921
National disposable income	550,590	390,419	430,678

GDP in purchasers' values ('000 million francs CFA at current prices): 904.5 in 1980; 1,049.6 in 1981; 1,188.9 in 1982; 1,320.0 in 1983; 1,455.6 in 1984.

Expenditure on the Gross Domestic Product

	1977	1978	1979
Government final consumption expenditure	124,926	73,817	77,922
Private final consumption expenditure	162,123	196,600	213,038
Increase in stocks	62,827	−35,201	6,833
Gross fixed capital formation	338,045	224,030	181,822
Total domestic expenditure	687,921	459,246	479,615
Exports of goods and services	356,104	332,992 ⎱	142,600
Less Imports of goods and services	353,854	253,032 ⎰	
GDP in purchasers' values	690,171	539,206	622,215

BALANCE OF PAYMENTS (US $ million)

	1982	1983	1984
Merchandise exports f.o.b.	2,160.4	2,000.1	2,017.8
Merchandise imports f.o.b.	−722.6	−725.5	−733.2
Trade balance	1,437.8	1,274.6	1,284.6
Exports of services	190.3	218.1	156.8
Imports of services	−1,259.4	−1,331.3	−1,290.4
Balance on goods and services	368.7	161.4	151.0
Private unrequited transfers (net)	−83.6	−95.1	−92.5
Government unrequited transfers (net)	24.3	5.6	25.3
Current balance	309.4	72.0	83.9
Direct capital investment (net)	127.0	106.1	4.8
Other long-term capital (net)	−42.7	−62.4	103.3
Short-term capital (net)	−204.4	−163.4	−188.4
Net errors and omissions	−42.8	−41.9	7.6
Total (net monetary movements)	146.5	−89.5	11.2
Valuation changes (net)	−30.8	−27.3	1.4
Official financing (net)	0.2	0.2	1.9
Changes in reserves	115.9	−116.6	14.5

Source: IMF, *International Financial Statistics*.

External Trade

Note: Figures exclude trade in gold and trade with other countries in the Customs and Economic Union of Central Africa (UDEAC): Cameroon, the Central African Republic and the Congo.

PRINCIPAL COMMODITIES (million francs CFA)

Imports	1980	1981	1982
Food products	22,700	26,500	42,200
Mineral products	3,700	4,000	6,600
Manufactured products	20,600	23,700	41,000
Construction materials	5,200	6,200	3,400
Chemical products	14,000	16,500	19,000
Metal and metal products	21,200	28,100	42,200
Equipment and tools	49,600	64,600	70,900
Transport equipment	15,600	20,600	30,500
Total (incl. others)	152,600	226,800	253,000

1983: Total imports 261,000m. francs CFA.
1984 (estimates): Total imports 320,350m. francs CFA.
1985 (estimates): Total imports 362,000m. francs CFA.

Exports	1980	1981	1982
Crude petroleum	413,300	485,200	544,300
Timber	49,900	47,000	52,000
Manganese ores and concentrates	32,200	27,600	33,000
Agricultural products	700	1,700	20,000
Total (incl. others)	511,000	578,400	669,300

Source: *Marchés Tropicaux et Méditerranéens*.
1983: Total exports 562,300m. francs CFA.
1984 (estimates): Total exports 881,500m. francs CFA.
1985 (estimates): Total exports 862,500m. francs CFA.

GABON *Statistical Survey*

PRINCIPAL TRADING PARTNERS (million francs CFA)

Imports	1982	1983
Belgium/Luxembourg	3,900	4,700
France	135,000	141,500
Germany, Fed. Republic	16,000	13,300
Italy	7,200	8,200
Japan	18,000	19,300
Netherlands	6,700	9,900
Spain	4,700	6,500
United Kingdom	7,400	9,400
USA	40,000	28,800
Total (incl. others)	253,000	261,200

Exports	1983
Brazil	24,900
Canada	24,900
France	171,000
Italy	30,800
Netherlands	26,900
Spain	37,600
United Kingdom	22,900
USA	144,100
Total (incl. others)	562,300

Source: Centre Gabonais du Commerce Extérieur.

Transport

RAILWAYS (traffic)

	1983	1984	1985
Passengers carried	102,283	135,913	137,111
Freight carried (metric tons)	620,203	664,605	723,034

Source: Ministry of Rail, Road and Inland Water Transport.

ROAD TRAFFIC (motor vehicles in use)

	1983	1984	1985
Passenger cars	15,150	15,650	16,093
Buses and coaches	479	508	546
Goods vehicles	9,240	9,590	9,960

Source: Ministry of Rail, Road and Inland Water Transport.

CIVIL AVIATION (traffic on scheduled services)

	1980	1981	1982
Kilometres flown ('000)	6,400	6,600	5,800
Passengers carried	331,000	340,000	421,000
Passenger-kilometres ('000)	374,000	394,000	430,000
Freight ton-kilometres ('000)	26,500	26,700	27,300
Mail ton-kilometres ('000)	600	700	800

Source: UN, *Statistical Yearbook*.

INTERNATIONAL SEA-BORNE SHIPPING
Port of Libreville-Owendo

	1980	1981	1982*
Ships entered	986	n.a.	n.a.
Goods loaded ('000 metric tons)	476.8	324	243
Goods unloaded ('000 metric tons)	440.0	468	538

Port-Gentil

	1980	1981	1982*
Goods loaded ('000 metric tons)	9,618.6	6,526	6,524
Goods unloaded ('000 metric tons)	176.8	174	195

* Estimates.

Source: *Annuaire National de la République Gabonaise 1983–84*.

Education

	Schools (1982)	Teachers (1982)	Pupils (1983)
Primary	886	3,526	148,520
Secondary	64	1,222	22,148
Technical	11	368	5,864
University	1	295	2,350

Source: Ministère de l'Education Nationale.

Directory

The Constitution

The Constitution of the Gabonese Republic was adopted on 21 February 1961. It was revised in February 1967, April 1975, August 1981 and September 1986.

PREAMBLE

Upholds the Rights of Man, liberty of conscience and of the person, religious freedom and freedom of education. Sovereignty is vested in the people, who exercise it through their representatives or by means of referenda. There is direct, universal and secret suffrage.

HEAD OF STATE

The President is elected by direct suffrage for a seven-year term and is eligible for re-election. He is Head of State, of the administration and of the Armed Forces. The President may, after consultation with his Ministers and leaders of the National Assembly, order a referendum to be held. There is a Prime Minister appointed by the President.

EXECUTIVE POWER

Executive power is vested in the President and the Council of Ministers, who are appointed by the President and are responsible to him. The President presides over the Council.

LEGISLATIVE POWER

The National Assembly is elected by direct suffrage for a five-year term and normally holds two sessions a year. It may be dissolved or prorogued for up to 18 months by the President, after consultation with the Council of Ministers and President of the Assembly. The President may return a Bill to the Assembly for a second reading when it must be passed by a majority of two-thirds of the members. If the President dissolves the Assembly, elections must take place within 40 days.

JUDICIAL POWER

The President guarantees the independence of the Judiciary and presides over the Conseil Supérieur de la Magistrature. There is a Supreme Court and a High Court of Justice. The High Court, which is composed of deputies of the National Assembly elected from among themselves, has power to try the President or members of the government.

The Government

HEAD OF STATE

President: El Hadj OMAR (ALBERT-BERNARD) BONGO (took office 2 December 1967).

COUNCIL OF MINISTERS
(February 1987)

Prime Minister: LÉON MÉBIAME.

First Deputy Prime Minister, Minister of Rail, Road and Inland Water Transport, Water and Forest Resources and Social Communications: GEORGES RAWIRI.

Second Deputy Prime Minister, Minister of Mines and Hydrocarbons: ETIENNE-GUY MOUVAGHA TCHIOBA.

Third Deputy Prime Minister, Minister of Public Administration and Administrative Reforms: EMILE KASSA-MAPSI.

Fourth Deputy Prime Minister, Minister of Town Planning, Housing and Habitation: SIMON ESSIMENGANE.

Minister of State for Foreign Affairs and Co-operation: MARTIN BONGO.

Minister of State for Public Land, Land Registration and the Law of the Sea: HENRY MINKO.

Minister of State, Secretary-General at the Presidency: RENÉ RADEMBINO-CONIQUET.

Minister of State for Higher Education and Scientific Research: JULES BOURDES-OGOULIGUENDE.

Minister of State for Industry and Consumption: ETIENNE MOUSSIROU.

Minister of State for Territorial Administration, Local Collectives and Immigration: RICHARD NGUEMA BEKALE.

Minister of State for Trade, Transfer of Technologies and Rationalization: JEAN-FRANÇOIS NTOUTOUME-EMANE.

Minister of State for Culture, Arts and Popular Education: FRANÇOIS OWONO-NGUEMA.

Minister of National Defence, Veterans' Affairs and Public Security: JULIEN MPOUNA-EPIGAT.

Minister of Justice and Keeper of the Seals: Mme SOPHIE NGWAMASSANA.

Minister of Information, Posts and Telecommunications: ZACHARIE MYBOTO.

Minister of Finance, the Budget and State Shareholdings: JEAN-PIERRE LEMBOUMBA LEPANDOU.

Minister of Public Works, Equipment, Construction and Territorial Development: Gen. JEAN-BONIFACE ASSELE.

Minister of Planning and the Economy: PASCAL NZÉ.

Minister of Agriculture, Livestock and Rural Development: MICHEL ANCHOUEY.

Minister of National Education: ALEXANDRE SAMBAT.

Minister of Labour, Employment and Human Resources: LOUIS-GASTON MAYILA.

Minister of Civil and Commercial Aviation: MICHEL ESSONGHE.

Minister of Public Health and Population: Dr JEAN-PIERRE OKIAS.

Minister of Social Affairs, Natural Disasters and Social Security: SILVESTRE OYOUOMI.

Minister of Youth and Sports: VICTOR AFFENE.

Minister in charge of State Control: JEAN-EMILE MBOT.

Minister of Professional Training and Handicrafts: JOSÉ JOSEPH AMIAR-NGANGA.

Minister of Energy and Hydraulic Resources: DIVUNGI DI-NDINGUE.

Minister of Small and Medium-sized Enterprises: EMMANUEL NZÉ-BEKALE.

Minister of the Environment and Nature Protection: HERVÉ MOUTSINGA.

Minister-delegate to the Prime Minister in charge of the Merchant Navy: MATHIEU NGUEMA.

Minister-delegate to the First Deputy Prime Minister: Dr PAULIN OBAME-NGUEMA.

Minister-delegate to the Second Deputy Prime Minister: BONJEAN FRANÇOIS ONDO.

Minister-delegate to the Third Deputy Prime Minister: ANTOINE MBOUMBOU-NIYAKOU.

Minister-delegate to the Fourth Deputy Prime Minister: GUY NZOUBA-NDAMA.

There are 10 Secretaries of State.

MINISTRIES

Office of the Prime Minister: BP 546, Libreville; telex 5409.

Ministry of Culture and Arts: Libreville; telex 5625.

Ministry of Economy and Finance: BP 165, Libreville; tel. 72-12-10; telex 5238.

Ministry of Energy and Hydraulic Resources: Libreville; tel. 72-31-96; telex 5629.

Ministry of Foreign Affairs and Co-operation: BP 2245, Libreville; tel. 76-22-70; telex 5255.

Ministry of Higher Education and Scientific Research: BP 496, Libreville; tel. 72-21-75.

Ministry of Information, Posts and Telecommunications: BP 3127, Libreville; tel. 76-16-92; telex 5361.

Ministry of Justice: Libreville; tel. 72-26-95.

Ministry of Livestock, Agriculture and Rural Development: BP 551, Libreville; tel. 76-29-43; telex 5587.

GABON — Directory

Ministry of Mines and Hydrocarbons: Libreville; tel. 74-06-00; telex 5499.
Ministry of National Defence, Veterans' Affairs and Public Security: Libreville; tel. 76-25-95; telex 5453.
Ministry of National Education: BP 6, Libreville; tel. 72-17-41; telex 5501.
Ministry of Planning: Libreville; tel. 72-14-32; telex 5417.
Ministry of Public Health and Population: Libreville; tel. 76-30-32; telex 5385.
Ministry of Public Land, Registration, Urban Affairs and the Law of the Sea: Libreville; tel. 72-10-39.
Ministry of Public Works, Equipment and Construction: BP 371, Libreville; tel. 76-14-87.
Ministry of Rail, Road and Inland Water Transport and Social Communications: BP 3974, Libreville; tel. 72-11-62; telex 5479.
Ministry of Social Affairs, Social Security and Welfare: Libreville; tel. 72-42-22.
Ministry of Territorial Administration and Local Collectives: Libreville; tel. 74-00-21; telex 5638.
Ministry of Trade and Industry: BP 3906, Libreville; tel. 76-30-55.
Ministry of Training and Crafts: BP 3919, Libreville; tel. 72-38-81.
Ministry of Water Resources and Forests: Libreville; tel. 73-31-91; telex 5583.
Ministry of Youth and Sports: Libreville; tel. 76-35-76; telex 5642.

Legislature

ASSEMBLÉE NATIONALE

At the most recent general election, held in March 1985, all 111 elective seats were won by the sole legal political organization, the Parti démocratique gabonais. A further nine members of the Assembly are appointed by the Head of State.
President: AUGUSTIN BOUMAH.
Secretary-General: PIERRE N'GUEMA-MVÉ.

Political Organizations

Parti démocratique gabonais (PDG): Libreville; f. 1968 to replace the Bloc démocratique gabonais; sole political party since March 1968; congress is highest party authority; there is a permanent cttee of 13 mems, a political bureau of 44 mems and a cen. cttee of 297 mems; the political bureau may issue decrees without reference to the government; the cen. cttee acts in an advisory capacity; there are nine regional delegates, numerous local cttees and four specialized organs: Ecole des cadres du parti, Union des jeunes (UJPDG), Union des femmes du PDG (UFPDG) and Fédération des syndicats gabonais (FESYGA); Founding Chair. El Hadj OMAR BONGO; First Sec. LÉON MÉBIAME.

Mouvement de redressement national (MORENA): Paris, France; f. 1981; advocates multi-party politics in Gabon; formed government-in-exile in August 1985; Pres. PAUL MBA-ADESSOLE.

Diplomatic Representation

EMBASSIES IN GABON

Algeria: BP 4008, Libreville; tel. 73-23-18; telex 5313; Ambassador: SAMIR IMALHAYEN.
Angola: BP 4884, Libreville; tel. 73-04-26; telex 5565; Ambassador: DOMBELE M'BALA BERNARDO.
Argentina: BP 4065, Libreville; tel. 74-05-49; telex 5611; Ambassador: JOSÉ H. LEDESMA.
Belgium: BP 4079, Libreville; tel. 73-29-92; telex 5273; Ambassador: JACQUES-BENOÎT FOBE.
Brazil: BP 3899, Libreville; tel. 76-05-35; telex 5492; Ambassador: JOÃO LUÍS AREIAS NETTO.
Cameroon: BP 14001, Libreville; tel. 73-28-00; telex 5396; Ambassador: DOMINIQUE YONG.
Canada: BP 4037, Libreville; telex 5527; Ambassador: BERNARD DUSSAULT.
Central African Republic: BP 2096, Libreville; tel. 72-12-28; telex 5323; Ambassador: ALPHONSE-GABRIEL NDOTAH.
Chile: BP 736, Libreville; tel. 73-19-53; telex 5670; Chargé d'affaires: HERNÁN TASSARA.
China, People's Republic: BP 3914, Libreville; tel. 72-44-11; telex 5376; Ambassador: TIAN YIMIN.
Congo: BP 269, Libreville; tel. 72-23-14; telex 5541; Ambassador: ROGER ISSOMBO.
Egypt: BP 4240, Libreville; tel. 73-25-38; telex 5425; Ambassador: AHMED NAZMY.
Equatorial Guinea: BP 4262, Libreville; tel. 76-30-15; Chargé d'affaires: MARÍA RESURRECCIÓN BITA BORIESA.
France: BP 2125, Libreville; tel. 76-20-31; telex 5249; Ambassador: LOUIS DOMINICI.
Germany, Federal Republic: BP 299, Libreville; tel. 76-01-88; telex 5248; Ambassador: GERMAN HAUPTMANN.
Haiti: BP 3864, Libreville; tel. 73-04-78; Ambassador: (vacant).
Iran: BP 2158, Libreville; tel. 73-05-33; telex 5502; Ambassador: Dr ABBASSE SAFARIAN.
Italy: BP 2251, Immeuble Personnaz et Gardin, rue de la Mairie, Libreville; tel. 72-10-93; telex 5287; Chargé d'affaires a.i.: NICOLA MARIA D'ERCOLE.
Ivory Coast: BP 3861, Libreville; tel. 72-05-96; telex 5317; Ambassador: (vacant).
Japan: BP 2259, Libreville; tel. 73-22-97; telex 5428; Ambassador: HIDEO KARINUMA.
Korea, Democratic People's Republic: BP 4012, Libreville; tel. 72-22-93; telex 5486; Ambassador: TCHA-SUN GON.
Korea, Republic: BP 2620, Libreville; tel. 72-36-44; telex 5356; Ambassador: NAM-CHA HWANG.
Lebanon: BP 3341, Libreville; tel. 73-14-77; telex 5547; Ambassador: MAMLOUK ABDELLATIF.
Mauritania: BP 3917, Libreville; tel. 72-32-38; telex 5570; Ambassador: El Hadj THIAM.
Morocco: BP 3983, Libreville; tel. 73-31-03; telex 5434; Ambassador: MOULAYE DRISS ALAOUI.
Nigeria: BP 1191, Libreville; tel. 73-22-03; telex 5605; Ambassador: MUHAMMADU DAN-HAMIDU.
Philippines: BP 1198, Libreville; tel. 72-34-80; telex 5279; Chargé d'affaires: MARCIANO A. RAYNOR.
Romania: BP 557, Libreville; tel. 73-27-87; telex 5359; Chargé d'affaires: NICOLAE MANASOIU.
São Tomé and Príncipe: BP 489, Libreville; tel. 72-15-46; telex 5557; Chargé d'affaires: ORLANDO FERNANDEZ.
Senegal: BP 3856, Libreville; tel. 74-11-36; telex 5332; Ambassador: OUSMANE CAMARA.
Spain: BP 1157, Libreville; tel. 72-12-64; telex 5258; Ambassador: JOAQUÍN PÉREZ GÓMEZ.
Togo: BP 14160, Libreville; tel. 72-40-81; telex 5490; Chargé d'affaires: ZAKARI PAGNANI.
USSR: BP 3963, Libreville; tel. 73-27-46; Ambassador: LATIF MAKSOUDOV.
United Kingdom: BP 476, immeuble CK2, blvd de l'Indépendance, Libreville; tel. 72-29-85; telex 5538; Ambassador: MARK AUBREY GOODFELLOW.
USA: BP 4000, Libreville; tel. 72-20-03; telex 5250; Ambassador: LARRY WILLIAMSON.
Uruguay: BP 5556, Libreville; tel. 72-40-24; telex 5646; Chargé d'affaires a.i.: ALICIA P. DE DUMONT.
Venezuela: BP 3859, Libreville; tel. 73-31-18; telex 5264; Ambassador: ROY CHADERTON-MATOS.
Yugoslavia: BP 930, Libreville; tel. 73-30-05; telex 5329; Ambassador: NIKOLA SKRELJI.
Zaire: BP 2257, Libreville; tel. 72-02-56; telex 5335; Ambassador: BOMINA-N'SONI LANGANGE N'GOMBA.

GABON

Directory

Judicial System

Supreme Court: BP 1043, Libreville; tel. 76-09-68; has four chambers: constitutional, judicial, administrative, and accounts; Pres. (vacant).

High Court of Justice: Libreville; mems appointed by and from the deputies of the National Assembly; Pres. MARCEL SANDOUNGOUT.

Court of Appeal: Libreville-Franceville.

Cour de Sûreté de l'Etat: Libreville; 13 mems; Pres. VICTOR DIEUDONNÉ MOUCKEYTOU.

Conseil Supérieur de la Magistrature: Libreville; Pres. El Hadj OMAR BONGO; Vice-Pres. Minister of Justice (ex officio).

There are also Tribunaux de Première Instance (County Courts) at Libreville-Port-Gentil, Franceville, Lambaréné, Mouila, Oyem, Koulamoutou, Makokou and Tchibanga.

Religion

About 60% of Gabon's population are Christians, mainly adherents of the Roman Catholic Church. About 40% are animists, and fewer than 1% are Muslims.

CHRISTIANITY
The Roman Catholic Church

Gabon comprises one archdiocese and three dioceses. At 31 December 1984 there were an estimated 580,000 adherents in the country.

Bishops' Conference: Conférence Episcopale du Gabon, BP 230, Franceville; tel. 67-71-83; f. 1973; Pres. FÉLICIEN-PATRICE MAKOUAKA, Bishop of Franceville.

Archbishop of Libreville: Mgr ANDRÉ FERNAND ANGUILÉ, Archevêché Sainte-Marie, BP 2146, Libreville; tel. 72-20-73.

Protestant Churches

Christian and Missionary Alliance: active in the south of the country; 16,000 mems.

Eglise Evangélique du Gabon: BP 80, Libreville; f. 1842; c. 60,000 mems; Pres. Pastor S. SIMA NDONE, Pastor S. NANG ESSONO.

The Press

Bulletin Evangélique d'Information et de Presse: BP 80, Libreville; monthly; religious.

Bulletin Mensuel de la Chambre de Commerce, d'Agriculture, d'Industrie et des Mines: BP 2234, Libreville; tel. 72-20-64; telex 5554; monthly.

Bulletin Mensuel de Statistique de la République Gabonaise: BP 2081, Libreville; monthly bulletin of the National Service of Statistics.

Dialogue: Maison du PDG, BP 213, Libreville; f. 1969; organ of the PDG; monthly; Chief Editor J.-J. BOUCAVEL; circ. 3,000.

L'Economiste Gabonais: BP 3906, Libreville; quarterly; publ. by the Centre gabonais du commerce extérieur.

Gabon d'Aujourd'hui: BP 750, Libreville; weekly; publ. by the Ministry of Information.

Gabon-Matin: BP 168, Libreville; daily; publ. by the Agence Gabonaise de Presse; Man. MENGUE BA N'NA; circ. 18,000.

Journal Officiel de la République Gabonaise: BP 563, Libreville; f. 1959; twice monthly; Man. Dir HENRI WALKER-DEEMIN.

Ngondo: BP 168, Libreville; monthly; publ. by Agence Gabonaise de Presse.

Promex: BP 3906, Libreville.

Sept Jours: BP 213, Libreville; weekly.

L'Union: BP 3849, Libreville; f. 1975; weekly; official govt publication; 75% state-owned; Man. Dir ALBERT YANGARI; Dirs J.-M. CORVOL, NDONG ONDO; circ. 15,000.

NEWS AGENCIES

Agence Gabonaise de Presse (AGP): BP 168, Libreville; tel. 21-26; telex 5628.

Foreign Bureau

Agence France-Presse (AFP): BP 788, Villa 32, Borne 2, Cité du 12 mars, Libreville; tel. 76-14-36; telex 5239; Correspondent BERNARD APFELDORFER.

Publishers

Imprimerie Centrale d'Afrique (IMPRIGA): BP 154, Libreville; tel. 70-22-55; f. 1973; Chair. JOSEPH VIAL; Dir M. CAUVIN.

Multipress Gabon: BP 3875, blvd Président-Léon-M'Ba, Libreville; tel. 73-22-33; telex 5389; f. 1973; Chair. LÉON AUGE; Man. Dir P. SAINT-BLANCARD.

Société Imprimerie de l'Ogooué (SIMO): BP 342, Port-Gentil; f. 1977; Man. Dir URBAIN NICOUE.

Government Publishing House

Société Nationale de Presse et d'Edition (SONAPRESSE): BP 3849, Libreville; tel. 73-21-84; telex 5391; f. 1975; Chair. LÉON AUGE; Man. Dir ALBERT YANGARI; Dir NDONG ONDO.

Radio and Television

In 1983 there were an estimated 102,000 radio receivers and 20,000 television receivers in use.

RADIO

The national network, 'La Voix de la Rénovation', and a provincial network broadcast for 24 hours each day in French and local languages.

Africa No. 1: BP 1, Libreville; tel. 76-00-01; telex 5588; f. 1980; French-built international commercial radio station; broadcasts began in February 1981; will eventually broadcast for 18 hours each day in French; Pres. LUC MVOULA; Man. Dir JACQUES BARBIER-DECROZES.

TELEVISION

Television transmissions can be received as far inland as Kango and Lambaréné; in 1986, proposals were announced for the extension and modernization of the network to cover the whole of Gabon. Programmes are also transmitted by satellite to other African countries. Colour broadcasts began in December 1975.

Radiodiffusion-Télévision Gabonaise (RTG): BP 10150, Libreville; tel. 73-27-84; telex 5342; govt-controlled; Man. Dir JACQUES ADIAHENOT; Dir of Broadcasting R. MOUBOUYI.

Finance

(cap. = capital; res = reserves; dep. = deposits; brs = branches; m. = million; amounts in francs CFA)

BANKING
Central Bank

Banque des Etats de l'Afrique Centrale (BEAC): BP 112, Libreville; tel. 72-13-52; telex 5215; Headquarters in Yaoundé, Cameroon; f. 1972; central bank of issue for mem. states of the Customs and Economic Union of Central Africa (UDEAC), comprising Cameroon, the Central African Republic, Chad, the Congo, Equatorial Guinea and Gabon; cap. and res 92,485m. (June 1983); Gov. CASIMIR OYE MBA; Dir in Gabon J. P. LEYIMANGOYE.

Commercial Banks

Banque du Gabon et du Luxembourg: BP 3879, Libreville; tel. 72-28-62; telex 5344; f. 1974; cap. 1,200m.; 51% owned by Société Intercontinentale de Participations (Luxembourg); Pres. JULIEN MPOUHO-EPIGAT; Man. Dir JEAN-MARIE CLAUDEL.

Banque Intercontinentale du Gabon (INTERBANQUE): BP 4013, Libreville; tel. 76-11-13; telex 5482; f. 1979; cap. 750m.; Chair. GEORGES RAWIRI; Man. Dir MAXIMILIAN J. SENYI.

Banque Internationale pour le Commerce et l'Industrie du Gabon SA (BICIG): BP 2241, ave du Colonel Parant, Libreville; tel. 76-26-13; telex 5226; f. 1973; cap. 3,000m., res 3,922m., dep. 85,954m. (Dec. 1984); 27.7% state-owned, 26% Société Financière pour les Pays d'Outre-Mer, 25% Banque Nationale de Paris; Pres. ETIENNE GUY MOUVAGHA TCHIOBA; Man. Dir EMILE DOUMBA; 9 brs.

Banque Internationale pour le Gabon (BIPG): BP 106, immeuble Concorde, blvd de l'Indépendance, Libreville; tel. 76-26-26; telex 5221; f. 1975; cap. 900m.; 90% owned by Banque Internationale pour l'Afrique Occidentale (France); Pres. MOUAPA BEOTSA; Man. Dir SAMSON NGOMO; 6 brs.

Banque Paribas Gabon: BP 2253, blvd de l'Indépendance, Libreville; tel. 76-40-35; telex 5265; f. 1971; cap. 2,892m.; res 1,289m.; 32.9% state-owned; Pres. EDOUARD MBOUY BOUTZIT; Man. Dir CHRISTIAN COURTOIS; br. at Port-Gentil.

Crédit Foncier du Gabon (CREFOGA): BP 3905, Libreville; tel. 72-47-45; telex 5450; f. 1976; cap. 1,500m.; Man. Dir A. NKOGHE ESSINGONE.

Union Gabonaise de Banque SA (UGB): BP 315, ave du Colonel Parant, Libreville; tel. 76-15-14; telex 5232; f. 1962; cap. 2,000m., res 696m., dep. 53,340m. (Dec. 1984); Pres. PIERRE CLAVER DIVOUNGUY; Gen. Man. MARCEL DOUPAMBY MATOKA; 6 brs.

Development Banks

Banque Gabonaise de Développement (BGD): BP 5, rue Alfred Marche, Libreville; tel. 76-24-29; telex 5430; f. 1960; cap. 7,000m.; 69% state-owned; Pres. MICHEL ANCHOUEY; Man. Dir JEAN-FÉLIX MAMALEPOT; brs in Franceville, Port-Gentil.

Caisse Centrale de Coopération Economique (CCCE) (France): BP 64, Libreville; tel. 72-23-89; telex 5362; Dir JACQUES ALBUGUES.

Caisse Nationale de Crédit Rurale (CNCR): BP 1120, Libreville; govt-owned; Dir ERNEST MICKALA DOUKAGA.

Société Gabonaise de Participations et de Développement (SOGAPAR): BP 1624, blvd de l'Indépendance, Libreville; tel. 76-23-26; telex 5265; f. 1971; 64% owned by Paribas International; studies and promotes projects conducive to Gabon's economic development; cap. 2,063m.; Pres. DANIEL BEDIN; Man. Dir JEAN-YVES COCHET.

Société Nationale d'Investissements du Gabon (SONADIG): BP 479, Libreville; tel. 72-19-07; f. 1968; govt-owned investment company; cap. 100m.; Dir-Gen. SIMON EDOU-EYENNE.

INSURANCE

Assurances Générales Gabonaises (AGG): BP 2148, Libreville; tel. 76-09-73; telex 5473; cap. 26.5m.; Chair. and Man. Dir JEAN DENDE.

Assureurs Conseils Franco-Africains du Gabon (ACFRA-GABON): BP 1116, Libreville; tel. 72-32-83; telex 5485; cap. 43.4m.; Chair. EMILE CASALEGNO; Dir M. GARNIER.

Assureurs Conseils Gabonais-Faugère, Jutheau et Cie: BP 2138, Immeuble Shell-Gabon, Libreville; tel. 72-04-36; telex 5435; cap. 10m.; represents foreign insurance companies; Dir GÉRARD MILAN.

Mutuelle Gabonaise d'Assurances: BP 2225, ave du Colonel Parant, Libreville; tel. 72-13-91; telex 5240; Sec.-Gen. M. YENO-OLINGOT.

Omnium Gabonais d'Assurances et de Réassurances (OGAR): BP 201, blvd Triomphal Omar Bongo, Libreville; tel. 72-04-95; telex 5505; f. 1976; 10% govt-owned; general; cap. 340m.; Man. Dir EDOUARD VALENTIN; brs in Oyem, Port-Gentil, Franceville.

Société Nationale Gabonaise d'Assurances et de Réassurances (SONAGAR): BP 3082, Libreville; tel. 76-28-97; telex 5366; f. 1974; cap. 300m.; 36% govt-owned; privatization plans announced 1986; Dir-Gen. JEAN-LOUIS MESSAN.

SOGERCO-Gabon: BP 2102, Libreville; tel. 76-09-34; telex 5224; f. 1975; cap. 10m.; general; Dir J. MOURARET.

L'Union des Assurances du Gabon (UAG): BP 131, Libreville; tel. 72-22-52; telex 5404; f. 1976; cap. 280.5m.; 72% owned by L'Union des Assurances de Paris; Chair. ALBERT ALEVINA-CHAVIHOT; Dir EDOUARD DELOUVRIER.

Trade and Industry

GOVERNMENT ADVISORY BODY

Conseil Economique et Social de la République Gabonaise: BP 1075, Libreville; tel. 76-26-68; comprises representatives from salaried workers, employers and govt; commissions on economic and financial affairs, social affairs and forestry and agriculture; Pres. M. BOUCKAT-BOU-NZIENGUI; Vice-Pres. M. RICHEPIN EYOGO EDZANG.

CHAMBER OF COMMERCE

Chambre de Commerce, d'Agriculture, d'Industrie et des Mines du Gabon: BP 2234, Libreville; tel. 72-20-64; telex 5554; f. 1935; regional offices at Port-Gentil and Franceville; Pres. EDOUARD ALEXIS M'BOUY-BOUTZIT; Sec.-Gen. DOMINIQUE MANDZA.

EMPLOYERS' FEDERATIONS

Confédération Patronale Gabonaise: BP 84, Libreville; tel. 72-26-11; f. 1959; represents the principal industrial, mining, petroleum, public works, forestry, banking, insurance, commercial and shipping concerns; Pres. M. PAUL-APANDINA; Sec.-Gen. M. E. MESSERSCHMITT.

Conseil National du Patronat Gabonais (CNPG): Libreville; Pres. RAHANDI CHAMBRIER; Sec.-Gen. THOMAS FRANCK EYA'A.

Syndicat des Entreprises Minières du Gabon (SYNDIMINES): BP 260, Libreville; telex 5388; Pres. ANDRÉ BERRE; Sec.-Gen. SERGE GREGOIRE.

Syndicat des Importateurs Exportateurs du Gabon (SIMPEX): BP 1743, Libreville; Pres. ALBERT JEAN; Sec.-Gen. R. TYBERGHEIN.

Syndicat National des Transporteurs Urbains et Routiers du Gabon (SYNTRAGA): BP 1025, Libreville; Pres. LAURENT BIBANG-BI-EDZO; Sec.-Gen. MARTIN KOMBILA-MOMBO.

Syndicat des Producteurs et Industriels du Bois du Gabon: BP 84, Libreville; tel. 72-26-11; Pres. CLAUDE MOLENAT; Sec.-Gen. JACQUES KIEFFER.

Syndicat Professionnel des Usines de Sciages et Placages du Gabon: BP 417, Port-Gentil; f. 1956; Pres. PIERRE BERRY.

Union des Représentations Automobiles et Industrielles (URAI): BP 1743, Libreville; Pres. M. MARTINENT; Sec. R. TYBERGHEIN.

PRINCIPAL DEVELOPMENT ORGANIZATIONS

Agence Nationale de Promotion de la Petite et Moyenne Entreprise (PROMO-GABON): BP 3939, Libreville; tel. 72-41-04; f. 1964; govt-owned; promotion of and assistance to small and medium-sized industries; Man. Dir JEAN-FIDÈLE OTANDO.

Centre Gabonais de Commerce Extérieur (CGCE): BP 3906, Libreville; tel. 76-11-67; telex 5347; promotion of foreign trade and investment; Man. Dir MICHEL LESLIE TEALE.

Commerce et Développement (CODEV): BP 2142, Libreville; tel. 76-06-73; telex 5214; f. 1976; cap. 2,000m. francs CFA; 95% govt-owned; privatization plans announced 1986; import and distribution of capital goods and food products; Chair. and Man. Dir JÉRÔME NGOUA-BEKALE.

Mission Française de Coopération: BP 2105, Libreville; administers bilateral aid from France; Dir FRANÇOIS CHAPPELET.

Office Gabonais d'Amélioration et de Production de Viande (OGAPROV): BP 245, Moanda; f. 1971 to improve the quality of meat production; govt-owned; manages ranches at Okouma and Ekedi; Dir ANDRÉ NGUEMA-NDONG.

Palmiers et Hévéas du Gabon (PALMÉVÉAS): BP 75, Libreville; f. 1956; cap. 145m. francs CFA; govt-owned; palm oil development.

Société de Développement de l'Agriculture au Gabon (AGROGABON): BP 2248, Libreville; tel. 76-40-82; telex 5468; f. 1976; cap. 7,355m. francs CFA; 96% govt-owned; Man. Dir ANDRÉ LE ROUX.

Société de Développement de l'Hévéaculture (HÉVÉGAB): BP 316, Libreville; tel. 70-03-48; telex 5615; f. 1981; cap. 1,999m. francs CFA; 99.8% govt-owned; development of rubber plantations; Chair. E. ONDO-METHOGO; Man. Dir P.-Y. WINTREBERT.

Société Gabonaise de Recherches et d'Exploitations Minières (SOGAREM): BP 976, blvd de Nice, Libreville; govt-owned; research and development of gold mining; Chair. ARSÈNE BOUNGUENZA; Man. Dir SERGE GASSITA.

Société Nationale de Développement des Cultures Industrielles (SONADECI): BP 256, Libreville; tel. 76-33-97; telex 5362; f. 1978; cap. 600m. francs CFA; govt-owned; agricultural development; Chair. PAUL KOUNDA KIKI; Man. Dir GEORGES BEKALE.

Société Nationale Pétrolière Gabonaise (PETROGAB): BP 564, Libreville; tel. 72-31-23; telex 5578; f. 1979; cap. 20,000m. francs CFA; govt-owned; prospecting for and exploitation of hydrocarbons and their processing and storage; financial and commercial operations relating to petroleum industry; Man. Dir FAUSTIN BANGOLE YENVOU.

GABON

TRADE UNIONS

Confédération Syndicale Gabonaise (COSYGA): BP 14017, Libreville; telex 5623; f. 1969 by the govt as a specialized organ of the PDG to organize and educate workers, to contribute to social peace and economic development and to protect the rights of trade unions; Pres. MARTIN ALLINI.

Transport

RAILWAYS

The Transgabon railway, which will eventually open up the densely-forested interior, was begun in 1974. The first phase, from Owendo (the port of Libreville) to Booué (340 km), was inaugurated in January 1983, and the second phase, from Booué to Franceville (330 km), in December 1986. The construction of a 235-km spur from Booué to Belinga, to serve future iron ore mines in the north-east, is planned for the 1990s. At present, the manganese mine at Moanda is connected with Pointe-Noire (Congo) by a 76-km cableway and a 296-km railway.

Office du Chemin de Fer Transgabonais (OCTRA): BP 2198, Libreville; tel. 70-24-78; telex 5307; f. 1972; cap. 231,243m. francs CFA; govt-owned; Man. Dir CHARLES TSIBAH.

ROADS

In 1984 there were 7,500 km of roads, of which 6,400 km were maintained and 577 km bituminized. A large-scale programme of road development is in progress; a further 500 km are expected to be macadamized and 1,121 km of secondary roads improved.

Société Africaine de Transit et d'Affrètement Gabon (SATA-GABON): BP 2258, blvd de l'Indépendance, Libreville; tel. 76-11-28; telex 5439; f. 1961; cap. 300m. francs CFA; freight; Man. Dir MATHIEU VALENZA.

Société de Transports des Villes (SOTRAVIL): BP 1148, Libreville; tel. 72-07-29; cap. 1,065m. francs CFA; 93% govt-owned, privatization plans announced 1986; urban transport; Chair. PAUL ENENGBE; Man. Dir PAUL JAMES.

INLAND WATERWAYS

The most important river is the Ogooué, navigable from Port-Gentil to Ndjolé (310 km) and serving the towns of Lambaréné, Ndjolé and Sindara.

Compagnie Nationale de Navigation Intérieure (CNI): BP 3982, Libreville; tel. 72-39-28; telex 5289; f. 1978; cap. 500m. francs CFA; govt-owned; has four vessels for transport on inland waterways; agencies at Port-Gentil, Mayumba and Lambaréné; Dir MATHURIN ANOTHO-ONANGA.

SHIPPING

The principal deep-water ports are Port-Gentil, which handles chiefly petroleum exports, and Owendo, 15 km from Libreville, which handles mainly barge traffic. Facilities for handling timber came into operation at Owendo in 1979. There are also timber ports at Mayumba and Nyanga. A new terminal for the export of minerals was opened at Owendo in March 1985, and is expected to be able to handle up to 2m. metric tons of manganese ore annually. The construction of a deep-water port at Mayumba is planned. At mid-1982 the merchant shipping fleet had a total displacement of 78,000 grt, of which 74,000 grt were oil tankers.

Compagnie de Manutention et de Chalandage d'Owendo (COMACO): BP 2131, Libreville; tel. 70-26-35; telex 5208; f. 1974; cap. 1,500m. francs CFA; Pres. GEORGES RAWIRI; Dir. in Libreville M. HERBUEL.

Office des Ports et Rades du Gabon (OPRAG): BP 1051, Libreville; tel. 70-17-97; telex 8312; govt-owned; Pres. JEAN-FELIX ONTALA M'BAYE; Man. Dir MARIUS FOUNGUES.

Société Nationale d'Acconage et de Transit (SNAT): BP 3897, Libreville; tel. 72-04-04; telex 5420; f. 1976; cap. 600m. francs CFA; 51% govt-owned; freight transport; Chair. JULES BOURDES OGOULIGUENDE; Man. Dir JEAN-CLAUDE MOULOUNGUY.

Société Nationale de Transports Maritimes (SONA-TRAM): BP 3841, Libreville; tel. 76-39-51; telex 5289; f. 1976; cap. 1,500m. francs CFA; 51% govt-owned; river and ocean cargo transport; Man. Dir LUDOVIC OGNAGNA OCKOGHO.

Société Ouest Africaine d'Entreprises Maritimes (SOAEM-GABON): BP 518, Port-Gentil; tel. 75-21-71; telex 5205; shipping freight; Chair. RENÉ KOLOWSKI; Man. Dir T. DE PONTBRIAND.

SOCOPAO-Gabon: BP 4, Libreville; tel. 70-21-40; telex 5212; f. 1963; cap. 120m. francs CFA; Dir H. LECORDIER.

CIVIL AVIATION

There are international airports at Libreville, Port-Gentil and Franceville, 65 other public and 50 private airfields linked mostly with forestry and oil industries. Extension work costing 10,000m. francs CFA is being carried out at Libreville's Léon M'Ba airport, with completion expected in 1987.

Air Affaires Gabon: BP 3962, Libreville; tel. 73-20-10; telex 5360; f. 1975; domestic passenger and cargo chartered and scheduled flights; Chair. M. BELLANGER; Man. Dir D. BOMPARD; fleet of 1 King Air F90, 1 E90, 2 Super King 200, 2 Bandeirante E 110, 3 Lama SA 315, 1 Alouette III, 1 Lear 35, 1 HS 125-600, 4 B-58.

Air Gabon: BP 2206, Libreville; tel. 73-21-97; telex 5213; f. 1951; cap. 6,500m. francs CFA; 70% govt-owned; internal and international cargo and passenger services; Chair. ETIENNE MBOUMA-MOUDOUNGA; Man. Dir FABIEN OWONDO-ESSONO; fleet of 1 Boeing 747-200B, 1 Boeing 737-200C, 2 Fokker F-28-2000, 1 F28-1000, 1 F28-1000C, 1 Lockheed C-130.

Air Service Gabon (ASG): BP 2232, Libreville; tel. 73-24-07; telex 5263; f. 1965; charter flights; Gen. Man. ALAIN REGOURD.

Tourism

Secrétariat d'État au Tourisme et aux Loisirs: BP 403, Libreville; tel. 72-42-29.

Société Nationale d'Hôtellerie (SNH): BP 2085, Libreville; tel. 72-42-29; telex 5373; f. 1978; cap. 200m. francs CFA; govt-owned; Chair. VINCENT MAVOUNGOU; Man. Dir SIDOINE ONGAYE.

THE GAMBIA

Introductory Survey

Location, Climate, Language, Religion, Flag, Capital

The Republic of The Gambia is a narrow territory around the River Gambia on the west coast of Africa. The country has a short coastline on the Atlantic Ocean but is otherwise surrounded by Senegal. The climate is tropical and, away from the river swamps, most of the terrain is covered by savanna bush. The average annual temperature in the capital, Banjul, is 27°C (80°F). English is the official language, while the principal vernacular languages are Mandinka, Fula and Wolof. About 85% of the inhabitants are Muslims, and most of the remainder are Christians, with some adherents of animism. The national flag (proportions 3 by 2) has red, blue and green horizontal stripes, with two narrow white stripes bordering the central blue band. The capital is Banjul (formerly called Bathurst).

Recent History

The Gambia was formerly a British dependency. It became a separate colony in 1888, having previously been united with Sierra Leone. The principle of election was introduced for the first time in the 1946 constitution. Political parties were formed in the 1950s, and another constitution was adopted in 1960. This was amended in April 1962, when the office of Premier was created. Following elections in May, the leader of the People's Progressive Party (PPP), Dr (later Sir) Dawda Kairaba Jawara, took office as Premier in June 1962. Full internal self-government followed in October 1963.

On 18 February 1965 The Gambia became an independent country within the Commonwealth, with Dr Jawara as Prime Minister. On 24 April 1970 the country became a republic, with Sir Dawda Jawara (as he had become in 1966) taking office as President. He was re-elected in 1972 and again in April 1977, as a result of PPP victories in legislative elections. In September 1978 the only United Party member remaining in the House of Representatives, following a by-election defeat in May 1977, joined the PPP, leaving only the five members of the National Convention Party (NCP) as opposition.

In October 1980 the Government was obliged to ask neighbouring Senegal to dispatch troops to The Gambia to assist in maintaining internal security under the terms of a mutual defence pact. A more serious threat was posed in July 1981, when a coup was staged during President Jawara's absence. Left-wing rebels formed a 12-man National Revolutionary Council and proclaimed their leader, Kukoi Samba Sanyang, as Head of State. Senegalese troops again entered Banjul and quickly crushed the rebellion. A state of emergency was announced, and more than 1,000 people were arrested. During the resulting trials, held in subsequent months, more than 60 people were sentenced to death, but by late 1986 the majority of the sentences had been commuted to life imprisonment and no executions had taken place. The state of emergency was finally lifted in February 1985.

Plans were announced in August 1981 for the merger of The Gambia and Senegal, which had always had close links, in a confederation to be called Senegambia. These proposals were approved by the Gambian House of Representatives in December, and came into effect on 1 February 1982 (see p. 1139). The first Confederal Council of Ministers, headed by President Abdou Diouf of Senegal (with President Jawara as his deputy), was announced in November 1982. The two most important institutions of the Confederation, the Council of Ministers and the Confederal Assembly, held their inaugural meetings in January 1983. Subsequent meetings have led to agreements on co-ordination of foreign policy, communications, defence and security; negotiations on economic and monetary union were in progress in 1986. There is some disillusion, particularly in Senegal, over President Jawara's apparent reluctance to complete the process of confederation, in the interests of minimizing the economic cost to The Gambia. Meanwhile, Gambian critics have felt that the country's political autonomy has been sacrificed to ensure the Government's survival.

The holding of legislative and presidential elections in May 1982 helped to restore The Gambia's democratic image in the aftermath of the 1981 coup attempt. The PPP won 27 of the 35 elective seats in the House of Representatives, and Bakary Darbo, former High Commissioner to Senegal, was appointed Vice-President. President Jawara was re-elected, this time by universal suffrage, gaining 137,020 votes compared with 52,136 for the leader of the NCP, Sherif Mustapha Dibba, at that time in detention for his alleged involvement in the abortive coup; he was acquitted and released in June 1982. Following the elections, the PPP sought to restore further its public standing by bringing a number of younger, reformist Ministers into the Cabinet. However, the resignation of the Minister of Justice, Fafa M'Bai, in June 1984, amid unconfirmed reports of financial misconduct, and the dismissal of the Minister of Economic Planning, Dr M. S. K. Manneh, in January 1985, following allegations of abuse of power, served to illustrate that corruption remained a major problem. In 1986 two new opposition parties were formed: the socialist Gambian People's Party (GPP), led by a former PPP government minister, Hassan Musa Camara; and the People's Democratic Organisation for Independence and Socialism, a group that is strongly opposed to what it regards as the unequal relationship of The Gambia with Senegal, negotiated by the PPP. Both parties were expected to present candidates in the general election that was scheduled to be held in March 1987.

Government

Legislative power is held by the unicameral House of Representatives, with 49 members: 35 directly elected by universal adult suffrage for five years; five Chiefs' Representatives Members, elected by the Chiefs in Assembly; eight non-voting nominated members; and the Attorney-General. The President is elected by direct universal suffrage for a five-year term. He is Head of State and appoints a Vice-President (who is leader of government business in the House) and a Cabinet consisting of elected members of the House or other nominees.

Defence

Under the terms of the Senegambia confederation pact, which came into effect in February 1982, Confederal units were to be formed, comprising members of the Senegalese and Gambian defence forces. However, both countries were also to maintain separate armies. Confederal defence expenditure in 1985/86 was 3,274m. francs CFA. By July 1986 the Gambian armed forces comprised 600 men (army 125, gendarmerie 400, marine 50, air 25). Military service is voluntary. The Gambia's defence budget for 1985/86 was estimated at 7.8m. dalasi.

Economic Affairs

The economy is based on peasant cultivation of groundnuts, which normally provide more than 90% of export earnings. The Gambia is therefore particularly vulnerable to fluctuations in groundnut harvests and to changes in international prices. More than 80% of the working population are engaged in agriculture, and the sector provided 29% of gross domestic product (GDP) in 1984/85. The major cash crops are groundnuts and cotton. In January 1985 the official prices payable to groundnut producers were increased, to bring them into line with price levels in Senegal, and so reduce smuggling. Industrial activity is largely based on the processing of groundnuts, while beverages and construction materials are also produced. The Government has attempted to diversify the industrial sector in recent years, and in 1983 the Kanifing industrial estate was established outside Banjul. The fishing and livestock industries are being developed, with financial assistance from the African Development Bank. 'Gambianization' has gradually been introduced into all sectors of the economy except tourism, which remains almost exclusively under foreign control. Since 1981, however, foreign investment has been encouraged in other sectors, particularly horticulture and light industry. Food, machinery and other manufactured goods constitute the country's main import requirements.

Between 1977 and 1981 erratic rainfall and pest infestation had an adverse effect on the output of crops, so that foreign aid, in the form of emergency food supplies, had to be provided. By 1980/81 groundnut production had fallen to its lowest level for 30 years. It recovered again, to 151,000 tons, in 1982, but renewed drought in 1983 severely affected the agricultural sector, and President Jawara appealed for aid from the international community to alleviate the food shortfall. Gross output of food grains declined from 104,000 tons in 1982/83 to 68,000 tons in 1983/84: the consequent fall in export revenue brought about a trade deficit of 132.7m. dalasi in 1982/83, which increased to 180.8m. dalasi in 1983/84, owing mainly to higher prices for imported petroleum and the increased need for food imports, which totalled 34% of total imports in that year, compared with 25% in 1982/83. Groundnut production was severely reduced in 1984/85, to only 45,000 tons, with a trade deficit in that year of 235.1m. dalasi and an estimated foodgrain shortfall of 44,000 tons.

In February 1984 the dalasi was devalued by 25% against the pound sterling, in order to arrest increases in prices of imports from non-sterling sources. A series of austerity measures, including a 'freeze' on wages, reductions in planned government spending and an increase in prices for basic commodities, was implemented in accordance with a 15-month IMF stand-by arrangement, agreed in May 1984 and authorizing purchases by The Gambia of up to 12.83m. SDRs. This was suspended in April 1985, however, after only one instalment had been drawn, because The Gambia owed substantial arrears to the Fund. At the end of 1984 the country's total external public debt was estimated at US $161m. In June 1985 the Government launched an Economic Recovery Programme, which aimed to increase agricultural output and gave rise to austerity measures such as an increase in import duties and the eventual retrenchment of over 3,000 public-sector workers, and the IMF loan was restored. In January 1986 a 'floating' exchange rate was adopted, and in the same month a balance-of-payments support grant of £6m. was agreed with the UK. In August formal agreement was reached on a structural adjustment credit of $16.9m. from the World Bank, and in September the IMF agreed to provide $14.62m., of which $6.65m. was available immediately. Disbursement of the remainder was to be conditional upon the implementation of certain reforms, reflected in the 1986/87 budget proposals, which were announced in June 1986. These combined a projected 22% increase in revenue (based on improved tax collection methods) with continuing cost-cutting efforts. In October 1986 the African Development Bank announced a loan of $10.8m. to support The Gambia's recovery programme.

The annual rate of inflation, estimated at 10.2% in 1982/83, rose to 27.4% in 1983/84 and was estimated to be running at around 42% in September 1986. According to World Bank estimates, GNP per head (at average 1982–84 prices) was US $260 in 1984, showing an average annual real growth rate of only 1.0% over the period 1965–84. In 1984/85 The Gambia's GDP per head declined, in real terms, compared with 1983/84.

Development programmes have been concerned mainly with improving and diversifying The Gambia's infrastructure. A five-year project, begun in 1976, emphasized rural development, irrigation, increased production of subsistence crops, including the Jahaly and Patcharr swamp rice project (which produced one-quarter of The Gambia's rice requirement in 1984), and the expansion of education and health facilities. By 1981 projects to increase cotton, livestock and fish production had come into effect, while studies for a joint desalination bridge-barrage with Senegal over the River Gambia were under way in 1983. By 1982 a total of US $51m. had been pledged for finance of the bridge-barrage by international agencies and the Federal Republic of Germany. The project will extend irrigated cultivation in The Gambia to 24,000 ha, and it is hoped that, as a result, the country will become a net exporter of rice. The Gambia currently produces only one-half of its requirements, and imported around 50,000 tons of rice in 1982/83. The Second Five-Year Plan (1981/82–1985/86) strongly emphasized agricultural development and improvements in transport and communications. The Economic Recovery Programme, launched in 1985, aimed to raise real economic growth to 3–3.5% per year by 1989/90 and to reduce the deficit on the current account of the balance of payments to 15% of GDP by 1990/91. In 1984 the Government launched a five-year urban renewal project, aiming to upgrade around 450 ha of land in Banjul and neighbouring areas.

The Senegambian Confederation, inaugurated in February 1982 (see Recent History), is intended eventually to produce an economic and monetary union between Senegal and The Gambia, and the possible absorption of The Gambia into the West African Monetary Union (see p. 155).

Social Welfare

In 1978 The Gambia had 16 hospital establishments, with a total of 699 beds. At the end of 1980 there were 43 government physicians, 23 private practitioners and five dentists. There were four hospitals and a network of 12 health centres, 17 dispensaries and 68 maternity and child welfare clinics throughout the country. A mother-and-child health scheme, primary health care, immunization and leprosy control programmes are being developed.

Education

Primary education, beginning at eight years of age, is free but not compulsory and lasts for six years. On completion of this period, pupils may sit a common entrance examination, leading either to five years of secondary high school or to four years of secondary technical school. High schools offer an academic-based curriculum leading to examinations at the 'Ordinary' level of the General Certificate of Education (GCE), under the auspices of the West African Examinations Council. Two of the high schools provide two-year courses leading to GCE 'Advanced' level. Gambia College, at Brikama, offers post-secondary courses in teacher-training, agriculture and health; other post-secondary education is provided by technical training schools. Non-formal education services are being expanded to offer increased educational opportunities in rural areas, and to provide for primary school leavers who are unable to continue their studies. University education must be obtained abroad. In 1982 an estimated 53% of children in the primary age-group (67% of boys; 38% of girls) were enrolled at primary schools. Secondary enrolment in 1982 was equivalent to only 12% of children aged between 14 and 19 (17% of boys; 7% of girls). According to UNESCO estimates, adult illiteracy in 1985 averaged 74.9% (males 64.4%, females 84.9%). In 1977 The Gambia introduced Koranic studies at all stages of education.

Tourism

Tourism has been a major industry in The Gambia since 1971, and the Government is committed to its further expansion. It is now the second largest earner of foreign exchange, after agriculture. In 1980/81 The Gambia received 21,327 foreign visitors, but in 1981/82 arrivals fell to 16,962, owing to the world recession and the coup attempt in July 1981. A record 77,039 tourists visited the country in 1985/86, when receipts from tourism totalled an estimated US $21.8m. There is a haven for bird watchers, and more than 400 species of birds have been recorded.

Public Holidays

1987: 1 January (New Year's Day), 1 February (Senegambia Confederation Day), 18 February (Independence), 17–20 April (Easter), 1 May (Labour Day), 30 May* (Id al-Fitr, end of Ramadan), 6 August* (Id al-Adha, feast of the Sacrifice), 15 August (Assumption), 4 November* (Mouloud, birth of the Prophet), 25 December (Christmas).

1988: 1 January (New Year's Day), 1 February (Senegambia Confederation Day), 18 February (Independence), 1–4 April (Easter), 1 May (Labour Day), 18 May* (Id al-Fitr, end of Ramadan), 25 July* (Id al-Adha, feast of the Sacrifice), 15 August (Assumption), 23 October* (Mouloud, birth of the Prophet), 25 December (Christmas).

* These holidays are dependent on the Islamic lunar calendar and may vary by one or two days from the dates given.

Weights and Measures

Imperial weights and measures are used. Importers and traders also use the metric system.

Currency and Exchange Rates

100 butut = 1 dalasi.

Exchange rates (30 September 1986):
  £1 sterling = 10.58 dalasi;
  US $1 = 7.31 dalasi.

THE GAMBIA

Statistical Survey

Source (unless otherwise stated): Directorate of Information and Broadcasting, Apollo Extension, Orange St, Banjul; tel. 8472.

AREA AND POPULATION

Area: 11,295 sq km (4,361 sq miles).

Population: 493,499 (census of 23–30 April 1973); 695,886 (estimate based on preliminary figures from census of 24 April 1983, excluding seasonal farming immigrants). *Principal ethnic groups* (April 1963 census): Mandinka (40.8%), Fula (13.5%), Wolof (12.9%), Jola (7.0%), Serahuli (6.7%).

Density: 61.6 per sq km (April 1983).

Principal Towns (1973 census): Banjul (capital) 39,476, Serrekunda/Bakau 34,382, Gunjur 4,677, Sukuta 3,844, Farafenni 3,778.

Births and Deaths (1975–80): Average annual birth rate 48.3 per 1,000; death rate 30.4 per 1,000 (UN estimates).

Economically Active Population (estimates, '000 persons at mid-1980): Agriculture, etc. 243 (males 129, females 114); Industry 19 (males 17, females 2); Services 27 (males 21, females 6); Total 289 (males 167, females 122) (Source: ILO, *Economically Active Population Estimates and Projections, 1950–2025*).

Employment (March 1984): 30,802 employees (males 26,208; females 4,594).

AGRICULTURE, ETC.

Principal Crops ('000 metric tons, 1984): Millet and sorghum 33, Rice (paddy) 22, Maize 11 (FAO estimate), Cassava (Manioc) 6 (FAO estimate), Palm kernels 2 (FAO estimate), Groundnuts (in shell) 114 (Source: FAO, *Production Yearbook*).

Livestock (FAO estimates, '000 head, year ending September 1984): Cattle 280, Sheep 175, Goats 185, Pigs 11, Asses 4 (Source: FAO, *Production Yearbook*).

Livestock Products (FAO estimates, '000 metric tons, 1984): Meat 7, Cows' milk 5 (Source: FAO, *Production Yearbook*).

Forestry (FAO estimates, 1984): *Roundwood removals* ('000 cu m): Sawlogs, veneer logs and logs for sleepers 14, Other industrial wood 7, Fuel wood 756; Total 777 (Source: FAO, *Yearbook of Forest Products*).

Fishing ('000 metric tons, live weight, 1984): Inland waters 3.5; Atlantic Ocean 9.2; Total catch 12.7 (Source: FAO, *Yearbook of Fishery Statistics*).

INDUSTRY

Production ('000 metric tons, 1983): Palm oil 3.0 (FAO estimate), Salted, dried or smoked fish 4.0 (FAO estimate), Electric energy 40 million kWh.
Source: UN, *Industrial Statistics Yearbook*.

FINANCE

Currency and Exchange Rates: 100 butut = 1 dalasi (D). *Coins:* 1, 5, 10, 25 and 50 butut; 1 dalasi. *Notes:* 1, 5, 10 and 25 dalasi. *Sterling and Dollar Equivalents* (30 September 1986): £1 sterling = 10.58 dalasi; US $1 = 7.31 dalasi; 1,000 dalasi = £94.54 = $136.80. *Average Exchange Rate* (US $ per dalasi): 0.3792 in 1983; 0.2791 in 1984; 0.2593 in 1985. Note: On 20 January 1986 a 'floating' rate of exchange was introduced.

Budget ('000 dalasi, year ending 30 June): 1985/86 revised estimates: Recurrent revenue 247,250; Recurrent expenditure 182,100; Development expenditure 83,500. 1986/87 budget proposal: Recurrent revenue 296,700; Recurrent expenditure 262,530; Development expenditure 201,200.

Second National Development Plan (proposed investment, '000 dalasi, 1981/82–1985/86): Agriculture and natural resources 131,300, Industry 29,200, Public utilities 67,300, Transport and communications 143,900, Tourism, trade and finance 7,300, Education, youth, sports and culture 37,000, Health, labour and social welfare 15,000, Housing 21,000, Total (incl. others) 475,000 (Source: *National Development Plan, 1981/82–1985/86*).

International Reserves (US $ million at 31 December 1985): Reserve position in IMF 0.04, Foreign exchange 1.69, Total 1.73 (Source: IMF, *International Financial Statistics*).

Money Supply (million dalasi at 31 December 1985): Currency outside banks 85.67, Demand deposits at commercial banks 74.98 (Source: IMF, *International Financial Statistics*).

Cost of Living (Consumer price index for Banjul and Kombo St Mary, year ending 30 June; base: 1974 = 100): 289.0 in 1983/84; 351.9 in 1984/85; 475.1 in 1985/86.

Gross Domestic Product by Economic Activity ('000 dalasi at constant prices, year ending 30 June 1985): Agriculture, etc. 105,100; Industry 38,200; Trade 91,700; Other services 125,600; GDP at factor cost 360,600; Indirect taxes *less* subsidies 34,500; GDP at market prices 395,100.

Balance of Payments (US $ million, year ending 30 June 1983): Merchandise exports f.o.b. 54.55, Merchandise imports f.o.b. −89.69, *Trade Balance* −35.15; Export of services 27.41, Import of services −47.58, *Balance on Goods and Services* −55.32; Private unrequited transfers (net) 2.69, Government unrequited transfers (net) 19.65, *Current Balance* −32.98; Long-term capital (net) −5.51, Short-term capital (net) 6.36, Net errors and omissions 10.06, *Total (net monetary movements)* −22.07; Valuation changes (net) 0.16, Exceptional financing (net) 13.58, *Changes in Reserves* −8.33. Source: IMF, *International Financial Statistics*.

EXTERNAL TRADE

Principal Commodities ('000 dalasi, year ending 30 June): *Imports* (1985/86): Food and live animals 175,280, Beverages and tobacco 27,881, inedible crude materials (except fuels) 8,167, Mineral fuels, lubricants, etc. 56,630, Animal and vegetable oils and fats 3,146, Chemicals 34,008, Basic manufactured goods 113,916 Machinery and transport equipment 97,850, Miscellaneous and manufactured articles 27,322, Total (incl. others) 557,643. *Exports* (1979/80, excl. re-exports): Groundnuts (shelled) 35,799, Groundnut meal and cake 5,098, Groundnut oil 14,732, Fish and fish preparations 6,601, Total (incl. others) 64,819. *Re-exports* (1985/86): 18,245.

Principal Trading Partners ('000 dalasi, 1985/86): *Imports:* Belgium 18,998, People's Republic of China 31,157, France 81,457, Federal Republic of Germany 28,835, Japan 22,096, Malawi 6,439, Netherlands 30,135, Thailand 32,409, United Kingdom 64,294, USA 26,633. *Exports:* Belgium 3,334, France 8,123, Guinea 4,654, Guinea-Bissau 16,959, Mali 8,807, Netherlands 30,263, Nigeria 918, Sweden 1,579, Switzerland 46,706, United Kingdom 13,686.

TRANSPORT

Road Traffic (motor vehicles in use, estimates 31 December 1985): Passenger cars 5,200; Buses and coaches 100; Goods vehicles 600; Motorcycles, scooters and mopeds 2,000 (Source: IRF, *World Road Statistics*).

Shipping (international sea-borne freight traffic, estimates in '000 metric tons, 1983): Goods loaded 88; Goods unloaded 188.

Civil Aviation (1983/84): 1,700 aircraft landed.

EDUCATION

Primary (1984/85): 189 schools, 2,640 teachers, 66,257 pupils (25,083 girls).

Secondary Technical (1984/85): 16 schools, 502 teachers, 10,102 pupils (3,119 girls).

Secondary High (1984/85): 8 schools, 235 teachers, 4,348 pupils (1,180 girls).

Post-secondary (1984/85): 9 schools, 177 teachers, 1,489 pupils.

Directory

The Constitution

The Gambia's present Constitution took effect on 24 April 1970, when the country became a republic. Its major provisions are summarized below:

Executive power is vested in the President, who is Head of State and Commander-in-Chief of the armed forces. The President is elected by direct universal suffrage, following a constitutional amendment in March 1982, and serves a five-year term. The President appoints a Vice-President, who is leader of government business in the House of Representatives, and other Cabinet Ministers from members of the House.

Legislative power is vested in the unicameral House of Representatives, with 49 members: 35 elected by universal adult suffrage, five Chiefs (elected by the Chiefs in Assembly), eight non-voting nominated members and the Attorney-General.

The Government

HEAD OF STATE

President: Alhaji Sir Dawda Kairaba Jawara (took office 24 April 1970; re-elected 1972, 1977 and 1982).

CABINET
(December 1986)

President and Minister of Defence: Alhaji Sir Dawda Kairaba Jawara.
Vice-President: Bakary B. Darbo.
Minister of Education, Youth and Sports: Louise N'Jie.
Minister of Justice and Attorney-General: Hassan Jallow.
Minister of External Affairs: Alhaji Lamin Kitty Jabang.
Minister of the Interior: Alhaji A. E. W. F. Badji.
Minister of Finance and Trade: Sheriff Sisay.
Minister of Information, Broadcasting and Tourism: Landing Jallow Sonko.
Minister of Health, Labour and Social Welfare: Alhaji Muhamadu Cherno Jallow.
Minister of Agriculture and Natural Resources: Saikou Sabally.
Minister of Economic Planning and Industrial Development: Alhaji Abdoulie K. N'Jie.
Minister of Local Government and Lands: Amulai Janneh.
Minister of Works and Communications: Lamin Bora M'Boge.
Minister of Water Resources and of the Environment: Omar Amadu Jollow.

MINISTRIES

Office of the President: The Quadrangle, Banjul; tel. 8291; telex 2204.
Ministry of Agriculture and Natural Resources: Central Bank Bldg, Banjul; tel. 8147.
Ministry of Economic Planning and Industrial Development: Central Bank Bldg, Banjul; tel. 8229; telex 2293.
Ministry of Education, Youth and Sports: Bedford Place Bldg, Banjul; tel. 8231.
Ministry of External Affairs: The Quadrangle, Banjul; tel. 8291; telex 2254.
Ministry of Finance and Trade: The Quadrangle, Banjul; tel. 8291; telex 2264.
Ministry of Health, Labour and Social Welfare: Central Bank Bldg, Banjul; tel. 223.
Ministry of Information, Broadcasting and Tourism: Apollo Extension, Orange St, Banjul; tel. 8472; telex 2204.
Ministry of the Interior: 71 Dobson St, Banjul; tel. 8611.
Ministry of Justice: Marina Parade, Banjul; tel. 8181.
Ministry of Local Government and Lands: The Quadrangle, Banjul; tel. 8291.
Ministry of Water Resources and the Environment: 5 Marina Parade, Banjul; tel. 431.
Ministry of Works and Communications: Half-Die, Banjul; tel. 449.

President and Legislature

PRESIDENT
Presidential Election, 4–5 May 1982

	Votes
Alhaji Sir Dawda Jawara	137,020
Sherif Mustapha Dibba	52,136
Total	189,156

HOUSE OF REPRESENTATIVES
Speaker: Alhaji Momodou B. N'Jie.

Election, 4–5 May 1982

	Votes	Seats
People's Progressive Party	102,545	27
National Convention Party	32,634	3
United Party*	4,782	0
Independent	26,141	5
Total	166,102	35

* Although the United Party no longer existed as an organized political entity, candidates were entered under the former party name.

In addition to the 35 members directly elected, the House has 14 other members: the Attorney-General, five Chiefs and eight nominated (non-voting) members.

Political Organizations

Gambia People's Party (GPP): Banjul; f. 1986 by fmr mems of the PPP; socialist; Leader Hassan Musa Camara.

National Convention Party (NCP): 4 Fitzgerald St, Banjul; f. 1975; advocates a fairer society and more equitable distribution of national wealth; 50,000 mems; Leader Sherif Mustapha Dibba.

People's Democratic Organisation for Independence and Socialism: Banjul; f. 1986; aims to safeguard economic and political independence of The Gambia.

People's Progressive Party (PPP): 21 Leman St, Banjul; f. 1959; merged in 1965 with Democratic Congress Alliance, and in 1968 with Gambia Congress Party; ruling party; favours continued membership of the Commonwealth; Leader Alhaji Sir Dawda Kairaba Jawara.

The following self-styled Marxist opposition groups were banned in November 1980:

Gambia Socialist Revolutionary Party (GSRP).

Movement for Justice in Africa (MOJA): Leader Koro Sallah.

Diplomatic Representation

EMBASSIES AND HIGH COMMISSIONS IN THE GAMBIA

China, People's Republic: 23 Wellington St, Banjul; tel. 8384; Chargé d'affaires: Zhao Wei.

Mauritania: 284 Kanifing South, Banjul; tel. 93-2886; Ambassador: Ould Chein.

Nigeria: 61 Buckle St, Banjul; tel. 561; High Commissioner: F. C. Nwoko.

THE GAMBIA   Directory

Senegal: 10 Cameron St, Banjul; tel. 469; High Commissioner: IBRA DGUENE KA.
Sierra Leone: Leman St, Banjul; tel. 8206; High Commissioner: DENNIS WOODE.
USSR: 7 Buckle St, Banjul; tel. 8282.
United Kingdom: 48 Atlantic Rd, Fajara, POB 507, Banjul; tel. 93-2133; telex 2211; High Commissioner: JOHN DONALD GARNER.
USA: Pipe Line Rd, Banjul; tel. 526; Ambassador: HERBERT E. HOROWITZ.

Judicial System

The judicial system of The Gambia is based on English Common Law and legislative enactments of the Republic's Parliament which include an Islamic Law Recognition Ordinance by which an Islamic Court exercises jurisdiction in certain cases between, or exclusively affecting, Muslims.
The Supreme Court consists of the chief justice and puisne judges; has unlimited jurisdiction; appeal lies to the Court of Appeal.
   Chief Justice: EMMANUEL OLAYINKA AYOOLA.
The Gambia Court of Appeal is the Superior Court of Record and consists of a president, justices of appeal and other judges of the Supreme Court ex officio. Final appeal, with certain exceptions, to the Judicial Committee of the Privy Council in the United Kingdom.
   President: S. J. FORSTER (acting).
The Banjul Magistrates Court, the Kanifing Magistrates Court and the **Divisional Courts** are courts of summary jurisdiction presided over by a magistrate or in his absence by two or more lay justices of the peace. In 1974 a system of travelling magistrates was introduced to help promote more effective administration of justice in the provinces. They have limited civil and criminal jurisdiction, and appeal lies from these courts to the Supreme Court.
Islamic Courts have jurisdiction in matters between, or exclusively affecting, Muslim Gambians and relating to civil status, marriage, succession, donations, testaments and guardianship. The Courts administer Islamic Law. A cadi, or a cadi and two assessors, preside over and constitute an Islamic Court. Assessors of the Islamic Courts are Justices of the Peace of Islamic faith.
District Tribunals are appeal courts which deal with cases touching on customs and traditions. Each court consists of three district tribunal members, one of whom is selected as president, and other court members from the area over which it has jurisdiction.

Religion

About 85% of the people are Muslims. The remainder are mainly Christians, and there are a few animists, mostly of the Jola tribe.

ISLAM
Imam of Banjul: Alhaji ABDOULIE JOBE, 39 Lancaster St, Banjul; tel. 369.

CHRISTIANITY
The Anglican Communion
Anglicans in The Gambia are adherents of the Church of the Province of West Africa.
Bishop of The Gambia: Rt Rev. J. RIGAL ELISEE.

The Roman Catholic Church
The Gambia comprises a single diocese, directly responsible to the Holy See. At 31 December 1984 there were an estimated 14,000 adherents in the country. The Bishop of Banjul is a member of the Inter-territorial Catholic Bishops' Conference of the Gambia, Liberia and Sierra Leone (based in Freetown, Sierra Leone).
Bishop of Banjul: Most Rev. MICHAEL J. CLEARY, Bishop's House, POB 165, Banjul; tel. 2343.

Other Christian Churches
Methodist Church: Rev. ERNEST B. STAFFORD, POB 288, Banjul; tel. 425.

The Press

Gambia News Bulletin: Bedford Place Bldgs, Banjul; f. 1943; 3 a week; govt newspaper; Editor A. A. N'JIE; circ. 2,500.
The Gambia Onward: 48 Grant St, Banjul; 3 a week; Editor RUDOLPH ALLEN.
The Gambia Outlook: 29 Grant St, Banjul; 3 a week.
The Gambian: 60 Lancaster St, Banjul; 3 a week.
The Gambian Times: 21 Leman St, POB 698, Banjul; tel. 445; f. 1981; 4 a week; organ of People's Progressive Party; Editor JAY SAIDY.
The Nation: People's Press Printers, 3 Box Bar Rd, POB 334, Banjul; fortnightly; Editor W. DIXON-COLLEY.
The Torch: 59 Gloucester St, Banjul; f. 1984; 3 a week; Editor SANA MANNEH.
The Worker: 6 Albion Place, POB 508, Banjul; 3 a week; publ. by the Gambia Labour Congress; Editor M. M. CEESAY.

NEWS AGENCY
Foreign Bureau
Agence France-Presse (AFP): 6 Allen St, POB 279/280, Banjul; tel. 8170; Correspondent DEYDA HYDARA.

Publisher

Government Printer: MacCarthy Sq., Banjul; tel. 399.

Radio

There were an estimated 100,000 radio receivers in use in 1984. There is no national television service, but transmissions can be received from Senegal.
Radio Gambia: Mile 7, Banjul; tel. 93-2101; telex 2204; f. 1962; non-commercial govt service of information, education and entertainment; one transmitting station of two 10 kW transmitters broadcasting about 15 hours daily in English, French, Mandinka, Wolof, Fula, Jola, Serer and Serahuli; two channels in operation, providing English programmes and schools broadcasting on Channel One, and vernacular languages and rural broadcasting on Channel Two; Dir SWAEBOU CONATEH.
Radio Syd: POB 279/280, Banjul; tel. 8170; commercial station broadcasting 20 hours a day, mainly music; programmes in English, French, Wolof, Mandinka, Fula, Jola and Serahuli; tourist information in Swedish; Dir CONSTANCE W. ENHÖRNING.

Finance

(cap. = capital; res = reserves; dep. = deposits; br. = branch; m. = million; amounts in dalasi unless otherwise stated)

BANKING
Central Bank
Central Bank of The Gambia: 1–2 Buckle St, Banjul; tel. 8103; telex 2218; f. 1971; bank of issue; cap. 1m.; res 7.5m.; dep. 161m. (June 1983); Gov. TOM SENGHORE; Gen. Man. A. A. FAAL.

Other Banks
Agricultural Development Bank: 10 Cameron St, Banjul; tel. 8721; telex 2273; cap. 3m.; Man. Dir SIDIN SAGUIA.
The Gambia Commercial and Development Bank: 3–4 Buckle St, POB 666, Banjul; tel. 8651; telex 2221; f. 1972; 51% state-owned; cap. 1m., res 2.8m., dep. 136m. (1981); Chair. C. L. CARAYOL; Man. Dir HOUSAINOU N'JAI; 3 brs.
Standard Chartered Bank Gambia Ltd: 8 Buckle St, POB 259, Banjul; tel. 8681; telex 2210; f. 1978 to acquire Gambian brs of Standard Bank of West Africa Ltd; cap. 2.5m., res 5.1m., dep. 95.6m. (1985); 15% state-owned; Chair. H. LLOYD-EVANS; Man. Dir M. INMAN; 4 brs.

INSURANCE
Capital Insurance Co. Ltd: 7 Buckle St, POB 485, Banjul; tel. 8544; telex 2255; f. 1986; Man. Dir MOMODOU M. TAAL.

THE GAMBIA

The Gambia National Insurance Corporation: 78 Wellington St, POB 750, Banjul; tel. 8412; telex 2268; f. 1979; Man. Dir OMAR B. Y. DIBBA.

Senegambia Insurance Co Ltd: 23 Buckle St, Banjul; tel. 8866; f. 1984; Gen. Man. BABOU CEESAY.

Trade and Industry

CHAMBER OF COMMERCE

Gambia Chamber of Commerce and Industry: 78 Wellington St, Banjul; tel. 765; f. 1961; Exec. Sec. P. W. F. N'JIE.

TRADE AND MARKETING ORGANIZATIONS

Gambia Produce Marketing Board: Marina Foreshore, Banjul; tel. 572; telex 2205; govt-controlled; Chair. M. M. JALLOW; Man. Dir KABBA JALLOW.

National Trading Corporation of The Gambia: 1–3 Wellington St, POB 61, Banjul; tel. 8395; telex 2252; f. 1973; Chair. M. B. N'JIE; Man. Dir ALIEU MBOGE; 15 brs.

EMPLOYERS' ASSOCIATION

Gambia Employers' Association: POB 333, Banjul; f. 1961; Vice-Chair. G. MADI; Sec. P. W. F. N'JIE.

TRADE UNIONS

Gambia Labour Congress: 6 Albion Place, POB 508, Banjul; tel. 641; f. 1935; Pres. B. B. KEBBEH; Gen. Sec. MOHAMED CEESAY.

The Gambia Trades Union Congress: POB 307, Banjul; Sec.-Gen. SAM THORPE.

The Gambia Workers' Union: Banjul; Sec.-Gen. M. E. JALLOW.

Transport

RAILWAYS

There are no railways in The Gambia.

ROADS

In 1985 there were 2,358 km of roads in The Gambia. Of this total, 757 km were main roads, and 452 km were secondary roads. Some roads are impassable in the rainy season, as only 21% of the road network is paved. The South Bank Trunk Road links Banjul with the Trans-Gambian Highway, which intersects it at Mansakonko. The South Bank Trunk Road is bituminized as far as Basse, about 386 km from Banjul. The North Bank Trunk Road connects Barra with Georgetown. A major highways maintenance project, expected to cost US $16.4m., was announced in 1986.

Gambia Public Transport Corporation: POB 801, Banjul; tel. 93-2501; telex 2243; f. 1979 as Gambian-Libyan Public Transport Corpn; fleet of 50 buses; Chair. Alhaji A. J. SENGHORE; Man. Dir ARTHUR CARROL.

SHIPPING

The River Gambia is well suited to navigation. The port of Banjul receives about 300 ships annually, and there are intermittent sailings to and from North Africa, the Mediterranean and the Far East. A weekly river service is maintained between Banjul and Basse, 390 km above Banjul, and a ferry plies between Banjul and Barra. Construction of a barrage across the river at Balingho is planned. Small ocean-going vessels can reach Kaur, 190 km above Banjul, throughout the year.

Gambia Ports Authority: Wellington St, POB 617, Banjul; tel. 266; telex 2235; administers Banjul port, which was substantially expanded in 1974; further improvements were completed in 1984; Man. Dir MOMODOU GAYE.

The **Organisation pour la Mise en Valeur du Fleuve Gambie** (Gambia River Basin Development Organization), a joint project with Senegal, Guinea and Guinea-Bissau to develop the river and its basin, was founded in 1978 and is based in Dakar, Senegal (see p. 217).

Regular shipping services to Banjul are maintained by **Elder Dempster Agencies.** Other British and Scandinavian lines run occasional services. The Gambia is also served by **Nigerian National** and **Black Star** (Ghana) Lines.

CIVIL AVIATION

There is an international airport at Yundum, 27 km from Banjul.

Gambia Airways: City Terminal, Wellington St, POB 268, Banjul; tel. 778; f. 1964; handling agency only; operated by Gambian govt, which holds 60% of shares, in partnership with British Caledonian Airways; owns no aircraft; Gen. Man. S. M. JALLOW.

Tourism

Over 77,000 tourists visited The Gambia in 1985/86. Tourists come mainly from the United Kingdom, Scandinavia and the Federal Republic of Germany. In 1985/86 there were 4,100 hotel beds in resort areas.

Ministry of Information, Broadcasting and Tourism: Apollo Extension, Orange St, Banjul; tel. 8472; telex 2204.

SENEGAMBIA

The Confederation of Senegambia came into being on 1 February 1982. The following is a summary of its general principles:

The Confederation shall be based on the integration of the armed and security forces of The Gambia and Senegal; economic and monetary union; co-ordination of policy in the fields of external relations and communications, and in all other fields where the Confederal State may agree to exercise joint jurisdiction.

The institutions shall be the President and the Vice-President of the Confederation; the Confederal Council of Ministers; and the Confederal Assembly. The President of Senegal shall be President of the Confederation; the President of The Gambia shall be Vice-President of the Confederation.

Each of the Confederal States shall maintain its independence and sovereignty.

The official languages are to be the African languages chosen by the Confederal President and Vice-President, along with English and French; the Confederal President is to be in charge of the armed and security forces of the Confederation, the Gambian President remaining Commander-in-Chief of the Gambian armed forces.

The Government

COUNCIL OF MINISTERS
(December 1986)

President: Abdou Diouf.
Vice-President: Alhaji Sir Dawda Kairaba Jawara.
Minister of Foreign Affairs: Ibrahima Fall.
Deputy Minister of Foreign Affairs: Alhaji Lamin Kitty Jabang.
Minister of Defence: Medoune Fall.
Minister of Security: Ibrahim Wone.
Deputy Minister of Security: Alhaji A. Badji.
Minister of Finance: Sheriff Sisay.
Minister of Economic Affairs: Alhaji Abdoulie K. N'Jie.
Minister of Transport: Robert Sagna.
Minister of Information and Telecommunications: Djibo Ka.

Legislature

CONFEDERAL ASSEMBLY

The Confederal Assembly consists of 60 members, of whom one-third are chosen by the Gambian House of Representatives and two-thirds by the Senegalese National Assembly. The Assembly meets twice a year.

Speaker: Alhaji Mamadou Baboucar N'Jie.
Deputy Speaker: Habib Thiam.

THE GERMAN DEMOCRATIC REPUBLIC

Introductory Survey

Location, Climate, Language, Religion, Flag, Capital

The German Democratic Republic lies in Eastern Europe. It is bounded to the north by the Baltic Sea, to the west, south-west and south by the Federal Republic of Germany, to the south-east by Czechoslovakia and to the east by Poland along the line of the rivers Oder and Neisse. The climate is temperate. The mean annual temperature is 8.5°C (47.3°F), with an average of −0.7°C (30.7°F) for January and 18.1°C (64.6°F) for July. The official language is German, spoken by an overwhelming majority of the population. There is a small Sorbian-speaking minority. Most of the inhabitants profess Christianity: about 50% are Protestants (mainly belonging to the Evangelical Church) and 8% Roman Catholics. The national flag (proportions 5 by 3) has three equal horizontal stripes, of black, red and gold, bearing, in the centre, the state emblem (a hammer and a pair of compasses, encircled by a wreath of grain). The capital is Berlin (the German Democratic Republic having jurisdiction only in the eastern section of the city).

Recent History

At the Potsdam Conference in July 1945 it was decided that the former German territories east of the Oder and Neisse rivers, with the city of Danzig, should become part of Poland, and that the northern part of East Prussia should become a part of the USSR. Germany was divided into British, French, Soviet and US occupation zones, as was Berlin. The whole country was placed under Allied Administration but, after the failure of negotiations to form a unified German administration, the zones that were occupied by the Western allies merged to form the Federal Republic of Germany in September 1949. On 7 October the Soviet zone proclaimed itself the German Democratic Republic (GDR), with Wilhelm Pieck as President and Otto Grotewohl as Prime Minister. These two men were joint chairmen of the Sozialistische Einheitspartei Deutschlands (SED, Socialist Unity Party of Germany), which had been formed in April 1946 by the merger of the Communist Party and the Social Democratic Party in the Soviet zone. The USSR granted complete sovereignty to the GDR on 27 March 1954.

In the immediate post-war period, the USSR compensated for a small part of its wartime losses with equipment, money and livestock from the Soviet zone. More than 200 industrial concerns became Soviet joint-stock companies and were returned, after reconstruction, to the GDR in 1953. In comparison with the reparations paid by the GDR, the Federal Republic escaped relatively lightly. Soviet policy also involved the creation of a Communist economic and political system. As early as 1945 the large agricultural estates were broken up and nationalized. In July 1946 all large-scale industrial concerns became state-owned. The policy of nationalization was continued by the SED regime as the USSR gradually transferred control. The increasing 'Sovietization' of administrative and economic affairs, coupled with severe food shortages, led to uprisings and strikes in June 1953. These were forcibly suppressed by Soviet troops. In 1960 it was announced that 50% of those farms which remained outside state control were to be nationalized. This measure led to a sudden rush of refugees to West Berlin, which, in turn, was the main reason for the construction by GDR 'shock troops' of a wall between East and West Berlin in August 1961.

The first elections, which were local ones, took place in September 1946, when the SED gained 57.1% of the vote, the Christian Democrat and Liberal Democrat parties together 39.9% and others 3.0%. The composition of the National Front, an umbrella organization formed in January 1950 for the various political parties and mass organizations, effectively gave the SED and its partners an overall majority. The SED has been the dominant political force since that time.

Walter Ulbricht took office as Secretary-General (later restyled First Secretary) of the SED in 1950, and was Chairman of the Council of State (Head of State) from September 1960 until his death in August 1973. He had been replaced by Erich Honecker as First Secretary of the SED in May 1971. The ninth congress of the SED (the highest party authority), held in May 1976, approved a revised party statute, under which the leader was restyled General (rather than First) Secretary. In October 1976 Honecker was also named Chairman of the Council of State, replacing Willi Stoph, who was reappointed Chairman of the Council of Ministers, the post that he had held from 1964 to 1973.

The 11th SED congress took place in April 1986. It was reported that 63,000 party members had been expelled in the five years preceding the congress. A new Central Committee and Politburo (differing little from their predecessors) were elected, and Honecker was unanimously re-elected General Secretary of the party. The congress endorsed a mandate to continue existing policies, approved the draft of a new five-year economic plan, and reaffirmed the GDR's allegiance to the USSR, whose leader, Mikhail Gorbachev, attended the congress. Elections to the Volkskammer (People's Chamber) were held in June, when the National Front candidates won 99.94% of the vote. The United Kingdom, France, the USA and the Federal Republic of Germany protested at the direct election of 66 deputies to represent East Berlin, which violated the 1971 Quadripartite Agreement on the status of Berlin. Honecker was formally reaffirmed as Head of State on 16 June.

In 1970, with the adoption by the Government of the Federal Republic of a new policy towards Eastern Europe (Ostpolitik), talks were held for the first time since the division of Germany between representatives of the two German states. Further such talks, following a Quadripartite Agreement on West Berlin in September 1971, clarified the details of access rights to West Berlin and also allowed West Berliners to visit the GDR. The two states signed a Basic Treaty in December 1972, agreeing to develop normal good-neighbourly relations with each other, on the basis of equality of rights, and to be guided by the United Nations Charter. In March 1974 a further agreement was signed in Bonn, implementing Article 8 of the Basic Treaty, to set up Permanent Representative Missions in Bonn and East Berlin. These agreements opened the way for many Western countries to establish diplomatic relations with the GDR, and for the GDR and the Federal Republic to join the UN in September 1973.

In October 1980 relations with the Federal Republic deteriorated when the GDR Government raised the minimum exchange requirement for foreign visitors and renewed its old demands for recognition as an independent state. By December 1981, however, the situation had improved enough to allow the first official meeting between the two countries' leaders for 11 years, when Chancellor Helmut Schmidt of the Federal Republic travelled to the GDR for talks with Honecker. In April 1983, however, Honecker cancelled a proposed visit to Bonn, following a sharp deterioration in inter-German relations after the death of three West Germans at a border checkpoint. The situation was further threatened by the deployment in late 1983 of US nuclear missiles in the Federal Republic, and by the subsequent siting of additional Soviet missiles in the GDR. Despite this, however, inter-German relations improved steadily under the new Federal German Chancellor, Dr Helmut Kohl, and in 1983–84 there was a series of meetings between East and West German politicians.

The inter-German *rapprochement* suffered a serious set-back in September 1984, however, when Honecker again abruptly cancelled a scheduled visit to the Federal Republic, apparently under pressure from the USSR. During 1984–85 relations between the two German governments were strained by the issue of the numerous East German refugees who sought asylum in the West German permanent mission in East Berlin and in West German embassies in Eastern Europe. However, contacts

GERMAN DEMOCRATIC REPUBLIC

between the two states gradually resumed during 1985; Honecker and Kohl met in Moscow in March, following the funeral of the Soviet President, Konstantin Chernenko, and there were hopes that Honecker's long-awaited visit to the Federal Republic might be rearranged. It did not take place during 1986, but the President of the Volkskammer, Horst Sindermann, did visit Bonn in February. He was the most senior GDR politician to visit the Federal Republic for 15 years, and he confirmed that Honecker still intended to visit Chancellor Kohl 'at a time to be agreed by both'. In May 1986 the two German states signed a wide-ranging cultural agreement, with the aim of furthering academic and sporting co-operation. However, inter-German relations were strained in the same month by the GDR's sudden demand that diplomats who were based in East Berlin should show passports to cross to the West (instead of the previously acceptable identity cards). This demand was seen by the Western powers as an attempt to alter the complex status of Berlin (by implying that the Berlin Wall was an international frontier, a view rejected by the West). Eventually the GDR compromised by agreeing to issue a new type of identity card, not a passport, for the purpose. The Federal Republic also protested at the number of refugees, mainly from developing countries, who were allowed to reach the West via East Berlin. The number was expected to reach 50,000 in 1986. This was again seen as an attempt by the GDR to compel the FRG to impose border controls, thus implicitly recognizing the border as international. In September 1986, however, the GDR agreed to impose a visa requirement before allowing the refugees to cross into West Berlin.

The 25th anniversary of the initial construction of the Berlin Wall, in August 1986, was marked by demonstrations and protest rallies in the West of the city, while the GDR organized a parade and speeches to commemorate the erection of the 'anti-fascist protective barrier'.

The GDR has sought to improve relations with other Western European states, and established a dialogue with ministers from several countries during 1985. Honecker's visit to Italy in April marked his first visit to a NATO country. However, the GDR's celebration in May of the 40th anniversary of the capitulation of Nazi Germany proved to be controversial, owing to the strong emphasis that was placed on the Soviet role in the defeat of Nazism. During 1986 relations with the People's Republic of China were upgraded, apparently with the approval of the USSR. In May a Chinese Government delegation visited Berlin, and in October Honecker visited China (as well as Mongolia and the Democratic People's Republic of Korea), when it was announced that links between the Chinese Communist Party and the SED were to be restored.

The GDR became a member of the Council for Mutual Economic Assistance (CMEA, see p. 126) in 1950 and signed the Warsaw Pact (see p. 206) in 1955. A Treaty of Friendship and Mutual Assistance between the GDR and the USSR, concluded in 1964, was renewed for 25 years in 1975. Similar treaties exist between the GDR and other East European countries.

Government

Under the 1968 constitution, the supreme organ of state power is the Volkskammer (People's Chamber), a unicameral body of 500 members, including 66 representatives of East Berlin. Since June 1979, when East Berlin was fully incorporated, all members of the Chamber have been directly elected for five years by universal adult suffrage. The Chamber elects a Staatsrat (Council of State) to be its permanent organ. The Council of State functions collectively but its Chairman deals with all foreign relations as effective Head of State.

The executive branch of government is the Ministerrat (Council of Ministers), headed by a Chairman (Minister-President) who is appointed by the Chamber, which also approves his appointed Ministers. The Chairman directs the activities of the Council of Ministers and its Presidium.

Political power is held by the Socialist Unity (Communist) Party of Germany, the SED, which dominates the National Front of the German Democratic Republic (including four minor parties and four mass organizations). The SED's highest authority is the Party Congress, which elects the Central Committee to supervise Party work. The Central Committee elects a Political Committee (Politbüro) to direct its policy.

For local government, the country is divided into 14 districts (Bezirke) and the city of East Berlin.

Defence

A National People's Army, comprising land, sea and air forces, was created out of the People's Police in 1956. In July 1986, according to Western estimates, the total strength of the armed forces was 179,000, comprising: army 123,000, navy 16,000, air force 40,000. Military service lasts 18 months in the army and air force, and 36 months in the navy. There are also 49,000 border troops, 13,000 special police units and 15,000 combat groups of the Workers' Militia. Defence expenditure for 1986 was estimated at 19,430m. DDR-Marks. The GDR is a member of the Warsaw Pact (see p. 206), and there are some 380,000 Soviet troops stationed in the country.

Economic Affairs

The GDR has been a member of the Council for Mutual Economic Assistance (CMEA, see p. 126) since 1950, and the economy of the country is closely linked with that of the USSR and other CMEA member-states. The GDR's economy is one of the healthiest in the Soviet bloc, and ambitious economic targets have been set in a series of successive Five-Year Plans. The 1976–80 Plan achieved an increase of 25.4% in net material product (NMP); industrial production rose by 32%, and construction by 27%, while foreign trade increased by 61%. During the 1981–85 Plan, the country's NMP (at 1980 prices) for the five-year period totalled 1,087,000m. DDR-Marks, an increase of around 33% over the comparable total during the previous Plan. Labour productivity was reported to have increased by 38% during 1981–85. In the agricultural sector, crop production increased by 11%, while livestock production rose by 5.4%. Foreign trade turnover increased by 50%. The 1986–90 Five-Year Plan set further ambitious targets in many sectors. The Plan's aim was to improve living standards through continued high growth, increased efficiency and scientific and technological progress. It was envisaged that NMP would increase by 24%–26%, to total more than 1,300,000m. Marks during the Plan period. Net production in the sectors of the industrial ministries was to be increased by 46%–51%, while the production of manufactured goods was to be increased by 22%–24%. Proposed investment during the five years was set at 346,000m. Marks, to be concentrated in the area of micro-electronics, computers, automation technology and bio-technology. Exports to socialist countries were planned to increase by 29% (30% to the USSR), and it was envisaged that trade with the West would also expand, and would achieve a significant export surplus.

NMP expanded, in real terms, by 2.6% in 1982, and by 4.4% in 1983. In 1984 NMP rose by 5.5%, while labour productivity grew by 5%. These trends continued during 1985: NMP increased by 4.8%, spurred by an 8.4% rise in labour productivity. In the first half of 1986, NMP increased by 4.3% (compared with January–June 1985), while industrial labour productivity grew by 8.6%. As a result of heavy expenditure on imports of industrial machinery during the 1970s, debts to Western countries amounted to US $12,800m. at the end of 1981. However, by December 1983 the GDR's outstanding debt to Western banks had fallen to US $4,700m., and successful debt management was reported to have raised significantly the GDR's credit-worthiness with international banks. By December 1985 the debt had fallen to around $6,000m.

By 1972 99% of the GDR's industry was state-owned. In 1984 industrial activities employed 41% of the labour force and contributed about 74% of NMP. More than 90% of employees working in state-owned industry are concentrated in large Kombinate, which have a degree of autonomy in production and trade. There is, however, a small private sector, mainly limited to trades and services, which, since 1976, has benefited from a relaxation of trade policy and from increased state support for private initiative. The private sector accounted for only 2% of total industrial output in 1983, but represented 11.7% of total retail turnover. In terms of production, the GDR is one of the world's leading industrial nations. Output grew by

GERMAN DEMOCRATIC REPUBLIC

5.3% in 1979 but the growth rate had slowed to 4.1% by 1983. Industrial production grew by 4.2% in 1984, and by 4.4% in 1985. The machine, chemical and heavy engineering industries are leading exporters (with chemical products accounting for almost 20% of national industrial output), but, in addition to these traditional areas, emphasis is being laid on the development of new high-technology industries. The electronics industry has developed rapidly since the 1970s, and priority is being given to the expansion of industrial automation, in an attempt to modernize the manufacturing sector.

All farmers are members of agricultural production co-operatives. The number employed in agriculture has remained steady and is around 10% of the working population. The economic importance of agriculture is gradually declining, and the sector provided only 8.6% of NMP in 1984. The 1983 harvest of grain (cereals and pulses) produced more than 10m. tons, but this failed to meet the planned annual target. Agriculture showed good results in 1984, however, with a record grain harvest of 11.5m. tons, and continued sparing use of scarce raw materials and fuel. The 1985 harvest reached 11.6m. tons.

The only major natural resource is lignite (a low-grade form of brown coal), which supplies more than 60% of the GDR's basic energy. Annual production is being expanded from 258m. metric tons in 1980 to a long-term target of 315m. tons per year by the year 2000, but in recent years the mining of lignite has become increasingly expensive, owing to less favourable geological conditions. Output of lignite for 1986 was targeted at a record 314m. tons. The GDR relies heavily on coal from Poland and on petroleum from the USSR, which is supplied by pipeline, and which meets about 80% of the country's oil requirements; a five-year trade agreement, signed in 1985, provided for the delivery of 17.1m. metric tons of Soviet oil per year, compared with 19.2m. tons in 1981. The GDR has had to import petroleum from the Federal Republic of Germany and the Middle East in order to meet its needs. The USSR also agreed to increase supplies of natural gas from 1986. There are two nuclear power plants in operation, and the GDR is continuing to develop the use of nuclear energy, which generated about 12% of the country's electricity in 1982; in 1984, however, nuclear power decreased as a proportion of total generation, falling to 10.7%, but it was announced that after 1988 the GDR's rising demand for electricity was to be met only through the development of nuclear power.

Foreign trade turnover, which grew at around 14% annually from 1971 to 1976, rose by only 7% in 1977 and by 12% in 1979. In 1984 it increased by 8%, and in 1985 it expanded by 3.5% (thus failing to meet the target of 8% growth). About 63% of GDR trade in 1984 was with the USSR and other CMEA countries (trade with the USSR accounted for 39% of the total in 1984). Between 1976 and 1983 the GDR had an accumulated trade deficit of about $4,500m. with the USSR. This figure is largely attributable to the increases in the price of petroleum and other raw materials imported from the USSR. In an attempt to counteract this, the GDR has agreed to supply goods and technical expertise in return for Soviet supplies of petroleum and natural gas. In 1984 the GDR became the first CMEA country to achieve a surplus in trade with the USSR, thus enabling it to begin reducing its debt. The Federal Republic of Germany remains the most important trading partner outside the Eastern bloc, accounting for around 8% of total trade in 1984: in 1981 the GDR achieved its first favourable balance of trade with the Federal Republic since 1965, a surplus of DM 221m., but in 1982 and 1983 the Federal Republic again achieved small surpluses. In 1984 the GDR achieved a small surplus, but in 1985 the trend was again reversed, when the Federal Republic achieved a surplus of DM 430m. Trade between the two states virtually stagnated in 1984, after growing by 8% in 1983, but in 1985 overall trade rose by 8%, to reach DM 16,700m. The GDR's imports from the Federal Republic rose by 18%, while its exports fell by 1%. In the first half of 1986 intra-German trade fell by 7%, largely owing to the effects of the fall in world petroleum prices. Intra-German trade operates under a system of 'swing' loans, providing the GDR with interest-free credit from the Federal Republic; in 1985 this facility was increased from DM 600m. to DM 850m. for the period 1986-90 (although, in practice, the facility is not usually drawn upon to the full amount). The Federal Republic is seeking a wider role in the GDR economy, and in 1984 the two states reached agreements on economic co-operation, including one allowing West German companies to process East German steel, and a contract providing for the production under licence of Volkswagen engines in the GDR. In 1980 a five-year trade agreement was signed between the GDR and France, designed to establish France as the GDR's second largest Western trading partner; this was extended by an agreement in 1985 to expand trade between France and the GDR five-fold by 1990.

Social Welfare

State social insurance is compulsory for all employees. It also covers their dependants and special categories such as students. The scheme is administered by the Confederation of Free German Trades Unions (FDGB; see p. 1161) and provides for medical and dental treatment, sickness benefits, maternity grants and pensions for retirement, disability and bereavement. There are communal medical centres (Polyklinik), all physicians and nurses are employed by the state health service and medical treatment is free. In 1984 the GDR had 170,389 hospital beds (equivalent to one for every 98 inhabitants) and 37,057 physicians. There is a comprehensive scheme of family allowances and places in crèches are available for 60% of children under three years of age. Total expenditure on social insurance was 27,700m. DDR-Marks in 1985. A five-day working week is now constitutionally enforced, and the paid annual holiday of between 18 and 24 days may be spent at one of the GDR's 1,200 vacation centres. Youth services and sport receive large state subsidies.

Education

Education in the GDR plans to cater for children from early childhood to the completion of a university course. Children attend nursery schools from the age of three to six years. In 1975 the replacement of elementary and secondary schools by comprehensive schools was completed. The 10-year course, beginning at six years of age, is free and officially compulsory. In 1983 the total enrolment at comprehensive schools was equivalent to 95% of all children in the relevant age-group.

After attendance at a comprehensive school, a pupil may apply to stay for a further two years to take the advanced level examination (Abitur), which is necessary for admission to establishments of higher education. Enrolment in this two-year course in 1983 was equivalent to 88% of children in the appropriate age-group. Those leaving school after 10 years may serve either a two- or a three-year apprenticeship, thus qualifying for enrolment respectively at a technical school or at a university or college.

Courses at technical schools are generally of three years' duration and lead to professional qualifications. Courses at institutions of university status (these include colleges of technology, engineering and agriculture, teacher training colleges and art schools as well as seven actual universities) last for either four or five years, the first two years being dedicated to basic and general study, and the remainder to specialization. Day-release, correspondence and evening courses are designed to allow people to obtain a degree without interrupting their career.

Tourism

Tourism is promoted by the State Travel Bureau. The island of Rügen, off the Baltic coast, has considerable tourist traffic. The mountains of Thuringia and the Erzgebirge, on the Czech frontier, are much visited, both in summer and winter. In 1982 there were 1.5m. tourist arrivals at all accommodation establishments. In 1983 933,889 tourists visited the GDR through the State Travel Bureau.

Public Holidays

1987: 1 January (New Year's Day), 17 April (Good Friday), 1 May (May Day), 8 June (Whit Monday), 7 October (National Day), 25, 26 December (Christmas), 31 December (half-day, New Year's Eve).

1988: 1 January (New Year's Day), 1 April (Good Friday), 1 May (May Day), 23 May (Whit Monday), 7 October (National

Day), 25, 26 December (Christmas), 31 December (half-day, New Year's Eve).

Weights and Measures
The metric system is in force.

Currency and Exchange Rates
100 Pfennige = 1 Mark der Deutschen Demokratischen Republik (DDR-Mark).

Exchange rates (31 August 1986):
£1 sterling = 3.030 DDR-Marks;
US $1 = 2.050 DDR-Marks.

GERMAN DEMOCRATIC REPUBLIC

Statistical Survey

Source (unless otherwise stated): Panorama DDR, Auslandspresseagentur GmbH, 1054 Berlin, Wilhelm-Pieck-Str. 49; tel. 230; telex 114872; and *Statistisches Jahrbuch 1985 der DDR*.

Area and Population

AREA, POPULATION AND DENSITY

Area (sq km)	108,333*
Population (census results)	
1 January 1971	17,068,318
31 December 1981	
Males	7,849,112
Females	8,856,523
Total	16,705,635
Population (official estimates at mid-year)	
1983	16,698,555
1984	16,670,767
1985	16,644,000
Density (per sq km) at mid-1985	153.6

* 41,828 sq miles.

PRINCIPAL TOWNS
(estimated population at 31 December 1984)

East Berlin (capital)	1,196,900	Erfurt		215,000
Leipzig	555,800	Potsdam		137,700
Dresden	520,100	Gera		131,300
Karl-Marx-Stadt (Chemnitz)	317,200	Schwerin		126,400
		Cottbus		122,900
Magdeburg	288,900	Zwickau		120,100
Rostock	241,900	Jena		107,100
Halle an der Saale	236,500	Dessau		103,800

BIRTHS, MARRIAGES AND DEATHS

	Registered live births		Registered marriages		Registered deaths	
	Number	Rate (per 1,000)	Number	Rate (per 1,000)	Number	Rate (per 1,000)
1977	223,152	13.3	147,402	8.8	226,233	13.5
1978	232,151	13.9	141,063	8.4	232,332	13.9
1979	235,233	14.0	136,884	8.2	232,742	13.9
1980	245,132	14.6	134,195	8.0	238,254	14.2
1981	237,543	14.2	128,174	7.7	232,244	13.9
1982	240,102	14.4	124,890	7.5	227,975	13.7
1983	233,756	14.0	125,429	7.5	222,695	13.3
1984*	228,135	13.7	133,898	8.0	221,204	13.3

* Provisional figures.

EMPLOYMENT ('000 persons at 30 September each year)*

	1982	1983	1984
Industry†	3,439	3,460	3,483
Agriculture and forestry	889	901	914
Construction	585	583	583
Commerce	853	856	861
Transport and communications	620	625	627
Others	1,982	2,020	2,031
Total	8,368	8,445	8,499

* Excluding apprentices, numbering (at 30 September each year): 445,000 in 1982; 426,000 in 1983; 417,000 in 1984.
† Including fishing and handicraft.

GERMAN DEMOCRATIC REPUBLIC

Statistical Survey

DISTRICTS (each district is named after its capital)

	Area (sq km)	Population (31 Dec. 1982—'000) Male	Female	Total	Density (per sq km)
Berlin (city)	403	544.8	628.3	1,173.0	2,911
Cottbus	8,262	423.4	461.2	884.5	107
Dresden	6,738	835.8	964.1	1,799.9	267
Erfurt	7,349	585.2	652.9	1,238.2	168
Frankfurt (a.d. Oder)	7,186	339.9	367.2	707.1	98
Gera	4,004	349.4	392.6	741.9	185
Halle (a.d. Saale)	8,771	856.3	959.9	1,816.2	207
Karl-Marx-Stadt	6,009	884.6	1,026.5	1,911.1	318
Leipzig	4,966	645.7	749.9	1,395.6	281
Magdeburg	11,526	593.6	666.4	1,259.9	109
Neubrandenburg	10,948	299.7	320.9	620.6	57
Potsdam	12,568	531.7	588.4	1,120.2	89
Rostock	7,074	429.6	463.9	893.5	126
Schwerin	8,672	281.8	309.1	590.9	68
Suhl	3,856	260.5	288.9	549.5	143
Total	108,333	7,862.1	8,840.2	16,702.3	154

Agriculture

PRINCIPAL CROPS ('000 metric tons)

	1982	1983	1984*
Wheat	2,739	3,550	4,100
Rye	2,119	2,092	2,300
Barley	4,055	3,882	4,400
Oats	848	498	700
Sugar beet	7,193	5,711	6,500
Potatoes	8,883	7,063	8,000
Carrots	217	249	261
Onions	99	108	100
Tomatoes	59	65	65
Cabbages	409	353	321
Cauliflowers	134	125	125
Green beans	24	20	20
Green peas	19	19	20
Cucumbers and gherkins	95	93	94
Apples	780	784	500
Pears	73	100	61
Plums	31	56	72
Currants	19	24	29
Strawberries	36	37	42

* FAO estimates.
Source: FAO, *Production Yearbook*.

LIVESTOCK ('000 head recorded at December)

	1982	1983	1984
Cattle	5,690	5,768	5,848
Pigs	12,107	13,058	13,191
Sheep	2,198	2,359	2,528
Goats	22	24	21
Horses	81	88	101
Poultry	51,356	53,018	51,317
Beehives	473	524	527

LIVESTOCK PRODUCTS ('000 metric tons)

	1982	1983	1984
Beef and veal	385*	367*	405†
Mutton and lamb	14*	12*	13†
Pig meat*	1,155	1,196	1,220
Poultry meat	147	153	152†
Other meat*	22	22	22
Edible offals	98	102	100
Cows' milk	7,678	8,203	8,750*
Goats' milk†	19	19	19
Butter	266.2	290.8	297.0*
Cheese	222.6*	225.2*	227.0†
Condensed and evaporated milk†	123.0	125.0	126.7
Dried milk	144.3	144.1	145.0†
Hen eggs	336.1	345.2	350.0†
Honey	7.2	8.9	9.0†
Wool (clean)	6.1	5.9	6.1†
Cattle hides and calf skins†	53.7	50.0	50.1
Sheep skins†	1.5	1.4	1.5

* Unofficial figure. † FAO estimate.
Source: FAO, mainly *Production Yearbook*.

Forestry

ROUNDWOOD REMOVALS
('000 cubic metres, excluding private consumption)

	1982	1983	1984
Industrial wood	9,600	9,763	10,315
Fuel wood	748	669	669*
Total	10,348	10,432	10,984*

* FAO estimate.

SAWNWOOD PRODUCTION ('000 cubic metres)

	1982	1983	1984
Coniferous (softwood)	1,879	1,900	1,983
Broadleaved (hardwood)	447	447	497
Total	2,326	2,347	2,480

Source: FAO, *Yearbook of Forest Products*.

Fishing

('000 metric tons, live weight)

	1982	1983	1984
Common carp	10.0	12.0	12.9
Atlantic cod	12.0	11.1	10.6
Jack and horse mackerels	98.3	89.1	74.1
Atlantic herring	50.9	52.0	50.1
Sardinellas	9.9	13.1	11.1
Other fishes	54.6	58.7	54.9
Crustaceans and molluscs	0.6	1.3	9.6
Total catch	236.3	237.4	223.3
Inland waters	17.2	19.3	18.1
Atlantic Ocean	218.5	217.4	204.5
Indian Ocean	0.6	0.6	0.7

Source: FAO, *Yearbook of Fishery Statistics*.

Mining

('000 metric tons)

	1981	1982	1983
Brown coal (incl. lignite)[1]	266,734	276,038	277,968
Iron ore[2]	9	9	9
Copper ore (metric tons)[2,4]	12,000	13,000	12,000
Tin ore (metric tons)[2,3]	1,600	1,700	1,800
Nickel ore (metric tons)[2,4]	2,700	2,500	2,200
Salt (unrefined)	3,112	2,978	2,907
Potash[5]	3,460	3,434	3,431
Sulphur			
(a)[6,7]	10	8	8
(b)[6]	80	92	97
Silver (metric tons)[7]	45	45	45
Natural gas (million cu m.)[8]	8,999	9,250	11,100
Crude petroleum	54	57	60

[1] Gross weight.
[2] Figures refer to the metal content of ores.
[3] Estimated production (Source: *World Metal Statistics*).
[4] Estimated production (Source: Metallgesellschaft Aktiengesellschaft, Frankfurt am Main).
[5] Figures refer to the K_2O content or equivalent of potash salts mined.
[6] Figures refer to (a) the sulphur content of iron and copper pyrites, including pyrite concentrates obtained from copper, lead and zinc ores; and (b) sulphur recovered as by-products in the purification of coal-gas, petroleum refineries, gas plants and from copper, lead and zinc sulphide ores.
[7] Estimated production (Source: Bureau of Mines, US Department of the Interior).
[8] Net calorific value 3,120 kilocalories per cubic metre.

Source: mainly UN, *Industrial Statistics Yearbook*.

1984 ('000 metric tons): Brown coal 296,341; Potash 3,465.
1985: Brown coal 312,150,000 metric tons.

Industry

SELECTED PRODUCTS

		1982	1983	1984
Flour[1]	'000 metric tons	1,373	1,363	1,402
Refined sugar	'000 metric tons	896	846	870
Margarine	'000 metric tons	180.5	177.3	180
Spirits	'000 hectolitres	2,234	2,496	2,521
Beer	'000 hectolitres	24,404	25,313	24,500
Non-alcoholic beverages	'000 hectolitres	14,832	14,862	14,121
Cigarettes	million	25,695	27,387	28,018
Cigars and cigarillos	million	532	530	521
Cotton yarn (pure and mixed)[2]	metric tons	135,300	134,700	n.a.
Woven cotton fabrics	'000 sq metres	287,778	298,000	n.a.
Wool yarn (pure and mixed)[2]	metric tons	75,800	76,400	n.a.
Woven woollen fabrics	'000 sq metres	39,600	39,000	n.a.
Non-cellulosic discontinuous fibres	'000 metric tons	148.6	150.5	n.a.
Rayon and acetate fabrics	'000 sq metres	50,400	48,600	n.a.
Leather footwear	'000 pairs	42,627	43,230	n.a.
Other footwear	'000 pairs	39,485	38,453	n.a.
Cellulose wood pulp	'000 metric tons	512	520	511
Newsprint and other paper	'000 metric tons	857	860	871
Paperboard and products	'000 metric tons	404	384	422
Synthetic rubber	metric tons	147,000	150,000	n.a.
Rubber tyres[3]	'000	7,051	7,380	7,784
Ethyl alcohol	'000 hectolitres	383	413	n.a.
Sulphuric acid	'000 metric tons	920	926	885
Caustic soda	metric tons	694,639	687,000	694,000
Soda ash	metric tons	882,405	887,000	890,000
Ammonia	metric tons	1,418,900	1,471,000	1,467,000
Calcium carbide	'000 metric tons	1,179	1,176	1,177
Nitrogenous fertilizers (a)[4]	metric tons	948,432	968,300	959,100
Phosphate fertilizers (b)[4]	metric tons	286,236	315,000	308,400
Plastics and synthetic resins	'000 metric tons	990	1,045	1,057
Motor spirit (petrol)[5]	'000 metric tons	3,891	3,955	4,140
Kerosene and distillate fuel oils[5]	'000 metric tons	6,142	6,054	6,132
Residual fuel oils[5]	'000 metric tons	8,500	8,500	n.a.
Lubricating oils	'000 metric tons	437	463	n.a.
Petroleum bitumen (asphalt)	'000 metric tons	520	510	n.a.
Liquefied petroleum gas	'000 metric tons	276	275	n.a.
Coke-oven coke (incl. gas coke)	'000 metric tons	1,226	1,193	n.a.
Brown coal coke	'000 metric tons	5,511	5,711	5,790
Cement	'000 metric tons	11,721	11,782	11,555
Pig-iron and ferro-alloys	'000 metric tons	2,149	2,207	2,357
Crude steel	'000 metric tons	7,169	7,219	7,573
Radio receivers	number	899,800	976,000	1,110,000
Television receivers	number	652,300	667,000	639,000
Vacuum cleaners	number	1,223,518	1,206,000	1,248,000
Domestic refrigerators	number	700,446	763,000	895,000
Domestic washing machines	number	485,288	504,000	525,000
Merchant ships launched	'000 grt	328	343	n.a.
Passenger motor cars	number	182,930	188,000	202,000
Lorries	number	38,763	40,000	43,000
Motor cycles (all types)	number	81,000	80,000	84,000
Bicycles	'000	631	651	664
Sewing machines	'000	272	282	292
Construction:				
New dwellings completed[6]	number	122,417	123,000	122,000
Electric energy	million kWh	102,906	104,928	110,093
Manufactured gas	million cu metres	6,348	7,230	7,722

[1] Flour from wheat, rye and semolina.
[2] Including thread and (for cotton) tyre cord yarn.
[3] Tyres for passenger motor cars, commercial motor vehicles and motor cycles.
[4] Fertilizer production is measured in terms of (a) nitrogen or (b) phosphoric acid. Output of phosphate fertilizers includes ground rock phosphate.
[5] Including products made from coal.
[6] Dwellings in residential buildings only.

Finance

CURRENCY AND EXCHANGE RATES

Monetary Units
100 Pfennige = 1 Mark der Deutschen Demokratischen Republik (DDR-Mark).

Denominations
Coins: 1, 5, 10, 20 and 50 Pfennige; 1, 2, 5, 10 and 20 DDR-Marks.
Notes: 5, 10, 20, 50 and 100 DDR-Marks.

Sterling and Dollar Equivalents (31 August 1986)
£1 sterling = 3.030 DDR-Marks;
US $1 = 2.050 DDR-Marks;
100 DDR-Marks = £33.00 = $48.78.

COST OF LIVING
(Index of Retail Prices and Service Charges. Base: 1970 = 100)

	1982	1983	1984
Food (incl. drinks)	99.6	99.6	99.6
Fuel, light and water	100.0	100.0	100.0
Clothing (excl. footwear) and household linen	87.9	87.9	87.9
Rent	99.0	98.8	98.8
All items (incl. others)	99.1	99.1	99.1

BUDGET ESTIMATES (million DDR-Marks)

Revenue	1985*	1986	1987
State economy	184,099.7	193,148.9	191,080.6
Taxes and dues	17,151.6	18,107.8	19,662.4
Health care and social care	8,053.7	8,427.8	8,888.4
Social insurance, etc.	17,231.7	17,554.5	18,017.3
Total (including others)	231,084.0	263,750.7	276,779.1

Expenditure	1985*	1986	1987
State economy	72,423.0	73,527.9	76,677.0
Housing construction	13,232.2	15,370.7	15,834.5
Price support	40,049.0	46,224.5	48,820.4
Public education	8,524.0	8,844.7	9,280.6
Health care and social care	12,251.6	12,726.8	14,889.4
Social insurance, etc.	32,354.5	33,553.4	34,985.6
National defence	13,041.2	14,045.4	15,140.9
Total (including others)	230,944.0	263,590.9	276,614.1

* Actual figures were: Revenue 235,534m. DDR-Marks, Expenditure 234,392m. DDR-Marks.

NATIONAL ACCOUNTS
Net Material Product* (million DDR-Marks at 1980 prices)

Activities of the Material Sphere	1982	1983	1984
Agriculture and forestry	16,715	17,540	19,190
Industry and productive crafts	148,641	156,730	165,280
Construction	12,360	12,980	13,770
Trade, restaurants and hotels	20,100	20,478	21,250
Transport, post and telecommunications	8,825	9,205	9,620
Others	6,500	6,710	6,990
Sub-total	213,141	223,643	236,100
Statistical discrepancy†	−12,001	−13,213	−14,010
Total	201,140	210,430	222,090

* Defined as the total net value of goods and 'productive' services, including turnover taxes, produced by the economy. This excludes economic activities not contributing directly to material production, such as public administration, defence and personal and professional services.
† Relating to intermediate consumption.

External Trade

COMMODITY GROUPS (% of trade in effective prices)

Imports	1980	1981	1982
Machinery, equipment and means of transport	30.8	32.0	32.3
Fuels, mineral raw materials, metals	36.7	36.8	39.9
Other raw materials and semi-manufactured goods for industrial purposes, raw materials and products of the food industry	18.9	17.8	16.3
Durable consumer goods	5.0	4.9	4.1
Chemical products, fertilizers, synthetic rubber, building materials and other goods	8.6	8.5	7.4

Exports	1980	1981	1982
Machinery, equipment and means of transport	51.3	48.9	48.5
Fuels, mineral raw materials, metals	14.8	16.8	18.5
Other raw materials and semi-manufactured goods for industrial purposes, raw materials and products of the food industry	6.4	7.5	6.9
Durable consumer goods	14.8	14.1	14.2
Chemical products, fertilizers, synthetic rubber, building materials and other goods	12.7	12.7	11.9

PRINCIPAL TRADING PARTNERS
(turnover in million DDR Valuta-Marks, valued f.o.b.)*

	1982	1983	1984
Austria	3,020.9	4,694.3	4,698.8
Belgium/Luxembourg	1,972.7	3,146.6	3,764.3
Bulgaria	4,568.7	4,830.5	4,900.5
Cuba	1,430.8	1,814.4	2,027.5
Czechoslovakia	10,499.4	11,854.9	12,834.6
France	2,673.7	2,963.0	2,286.2
Germany, Federal Republic, and West Berlin	12,527.4	13,559.6	13,791.6
Hungary	7,630.2	8,231.3	8,579.3
Japan	1,318.0	2,473.0	1,529.7
Netherlands	1,213.9	1,731.4	2,080.3
Poland	7,205.0	7,912.0	8,740.6
Romania	4,408.6	4,222.9	4,628.2
Sweden	2,224.5	1,633.4	1,931.7
Switzerland†	2,500.1	2,607.3	4,239.8
USSR	55,164.3	60,821.3	67,107.8
United Kingdom	2,255.7	2,930.4	2,523.3
Yugoslavia	2,950.2	3,134.1	3,039.1
Total (incl. others)‡	145,109.3	160,423.7	173,902.5

* For 1982 the exchange rate was US $1 = 3.46 DDR Valuta-Marks; for 1983 it was $1 = 3.54 DDR Valuta-Marks; and for 1984 and 1985 it was $1 = 3.64 DDR Valuta-Marks.
† Including Liechtenstein.
‡ Separate figures for imports and exports by countries are not available. The totals (in million DDR Valuta-Marks) were: Imports 69,878 in 1982, 76,197 in 1983, 83,501 in 1984; Exports 75,231 in 1982, 84,227 in 1983, 90,402 in 1984.

1985 (million DDR Valuta-Marks): Imports 91,975; Exports 93,490.

Transport

RAILWAYS (millions)

	1983	1984	1985
Number of passengers	620	628	623
Passenger-km	22,605	22,919	22,451
Freight ton-km	54,884	56,654	58,668

ROAD TRAFFIC (licensed vehicles)

	1983	1984	1985
Passenger cars	3,019,875	3,157,077	3,306,230
Lorries	352,797	355,337	360,821
Omnibuses	53,178	53,595	55,698

CIVIL AVIATION

	1983	1984	1985
Kilometres flown ('000)	33,605	34,442	34,173
Passengers carried	1,358,700	1,419,600	1,446,000
Passenger-km ('000)	2,307,100	2,469,500	2,541,000
Freight ton-km ('000)*	72,120	75,535	71,643

* Figures refer to both cargo and mail.

SHIPPING
Inland Waterways (million)

	1983	1984	1985
Number of passengers	7	6	7
Passenger-km	164	176	188
Freight ton-km	2,424	2,642	2,437

Merchant Fleet (at 31 December)

	1983	1984	1985
Number of ships	174	172	171
Displacement (grt)	1,223,865	1,201,575	1,222,410

International Sea-borne Freight Traffic ('000 metric tons)

	1983	1984	1985
Goods loaded and unloaded	23,100	24,700	25,100

Tourism

FOREIGN TOURIST ARRIVALS*

Country of Origin	1981	1982	1983
Bulgaria	11,264	12,477	12,235
Czechoslovakia	145,147	146,951	133,356
Hungary	29,990	22,651	17,370
Poland	41,014	13,348	43,597
Romania	7,301	7,546	7,530
USSR	73,752	81,243	89,637
Total (incl. others)	858,224	891,636	933,889

* Visits arranged by the State Travel Bureau.

Communications Media

	1980	1981	1982
Radio licences	6,409,200	6,459,100	6,439,500
Television licences	5,730,900	5,811,100	5,847,200
Telephones in use	3,155,733	3,251,950	3,344,263
Book production: titles	6,109	6,180	6,130
Newspapers and magazines:			
Number	523	519	521
Circulation (total, million)	255.2	262.3	n.a.

1983: Radio licences 6,415,000; Television licences 5,970,000.

Education

(1984)

	Institutions	Students
Infant schools*	12,793	784,884
General polytechnic schools	5,171	1,950,908
Extended polytechnic schools	213	44,266
Vocational schools	965	391,626
Technical schools	240	163,573
Universities (incl. technical)	54	129,628

* 1983 figures.

Directory

The Constitution

The Constitution of the German Democratic Republic was promulgated on 9 April 1968, replacing the original Constitution which came into force when the Republic was founded in 1949. It was amended on 7 October 1974. A summary is given below.

I. FOUNDATIONS OF THE SOCIALIST SOCIAL AND STATE ORDER

Political Foundations

Articles 1–8. The German Democratic Republic is a socialist state of workers and farmers. It is the political organization of the working people in towns and countryside who are jointly implementing socialism under the leadership of the working class and its Marxist-Leninist party. The capital is Berlin; the State flag is black, red, and gold, and bears the State coat of arms. All political power in the Republic is exercised by the working people and all power serves their welfare. The National Front of the German Democratic Republic unites all political parties and mass organizations working for the development of the socialist state. Citizens exercise their political power through democratically elected people's representatives. The Republic pursues a peaceful foreign policy and is linked irrevocably and permanently with the USSR and other socialist states.

Economic Foundations, Science, Education and Culture

Articles 9–18. The national economy is based on the socialist ownership of the means of production and is a socialist planned economy. All foreign economic relations are the monopoly of the state. All large industrial enterprises, mineral resources, banks and means of transport are nationally owned and private ownership of these facilities is not allowed. All installations, machinery and livestock in agricultural co-operatives and profits derived from co-operative use of the soil are co-operative property. The personal property of citizens and the right of inheritance are guaranteed.

The Republic promotes culture, the arts and science and assures all citizens a high standard of education.

II. CITIZENS AND ORGANIZATIONS IN SOCIALIST SOCIETY

Basic Rights and Basic Duties of Citizens

Articles 19–40. The Republic respects the dignity and freedom of the individual and guarantees to all citizens the exercise of their rights. The conditions for acquiring and losing citizenship of the German Democratic Republic are stipulated by law. All citizens are equal before the law. Men and women have equal rights and the same legal status. Every citizen who has reached the age of 18 on election day has the right to vote and may be elected to the People's Chamber (Volkskammer) and to local people's representative bodies. Every citizen is obliged to serve in defence of his country. The Republic can grant political asylum to citizens of other states in certain circumstances.

Freedom of speech, the press, radio and television are guaranteed, as is the right to peaceful demonstration and assembly. Personal liberty is inviolable and everyone has the right to move freely within the state territory within the framework of the law. Postal and telecommunication privacy is assured and may be limited only for purposes of state security or criminal prosecution. Every citizen has the right to legal protection by the organs of the state when he is abroad.

The right to work is guaranteed and every citizen is free to select his own job. Everyone has the same right to education and attendance at secondary school is obligatory. All citizens are entitled to leisure time and annual paid holidays, to medical and other social welfare benefits. Social care is provided for the elderly and disabled. Housing is under public control and there is legal protection against eviction. Every citizen has the right of the inviolability of his home. Marriage, motherhood and the family have the special protection of the state and provision is made for large families, fatherless families, etc. Religious freedom is assured. Citizens of the German Democratic Republic of Sorb nationality have the right to cultivate their mother tongue and culture.

Enterprises, Towns and Local Communities in Socialist Society

Articles 41–43. Enterprises, towns, villages and communal associations are entities with responsibilities of their own in which citizens work and shape their social relations. They safeguard the basic rights of citizens and are protected by the constitution. The local representative bodies are elected by the people and are responsible for local affairs. The working people also co-operate in the management of enterprises both directly and with the help of their elected organs.

The Trades Unions and Their Rights

Articles 44–45. The free trades unions are united in the Confederation of Free German Trades Unions. They are independent bodies, are represented at all levels of the social system and play a decisive part in the solution of problems. They conclude agreements with government authorities and enterprise managements on all questions concerning the working and living conditions of the people. They take part in the shaping of the socialist legal system and administer the social insurance system of the workers.

Socialist Production Co-operatives and Their Rights

Article 46. These are voluntary associations of farmers for the purpose of joint production and receive government assistance. They are represented in the state organs and take an active part in the state planning. Production co-operatives on the same lines also exist among fishermen, craftsmen and market gardeners.

III. STRUCTURE AND SYSTEM OF STATE MANAGEMENT

Democratic Centralism

Article 47. The structure and activities of the state organs are determined by the aims and tasks of state power, as stipulated in this Constitution. The sovereignty of the working people, which is implemented on the basis of democratic centralism, is the fundamental principle of the state structure.

The People's Chamber (Volkskammer)

Articles 48–65. The People's Chamber is the supreme organ of state power and guarantees the enforcement of its laws. It is composed of 500 deputies elected by the people in a free, general, equal and secret ballot for a period of five years. It is convened not later than the 30th day after the election. It elects its Presidium to conduct the plenary sessions for the legislative period. The People's Chamber can be dissolved before the expiry of the legislative period only on its own decision.

Committees are formed from among the members of the People's Chamber to discuss bills and to co-operate in submitting them to the voters for popular discussion. They then submit their comments to the plenary session of the People's Chamber. Laws passed are proclaimed in the Law Gazette by the Chairman of the Council of State within one month and come into force on the 14th day after their proclamation.

The People's Chamber decides on the proclamation of war and the holding of referenda.

The Council of State (Staatsrat)

Articles 66–75. The Council of State is the organ of the People's Chamber, operating between sessions of the latter, and fulfils all fundamental tasks resulting from its laws and decisions. It is elected by the People's Chamber at its first session and is responsible to it for its activities. It deals with bills to be submitted to the People's Chamber and with all basic tasks arising from its laws and decisions. It makes fundamental decisions on defence matters and exercises control over the constitutionality and legality of the activities of the Supreme Court and the Prosecutor General. The Council of State represents the GDR internationally and ratifies and abrogates international treaties. It determines military and diplomatic ranks and other special titles and establishes state honours. It also exercises the right of amnesty and pardon.

The Council of Ministers (Ministerrat)

Articles 76–80. The Council of Ministers, the Government of the GDR, is an organ of the People's Chamber. Acting on its behalf, it directs government policy, economic affairs and foreign policy in accordance with the provisions of the Constitution. It prepares international treaties, draws up bills, directs and co-ordinates the Ministries and other government bodies. It is answerable to the People's Chamber.

Local People's Representative Bodies and Their Organs

Articles 81–85. The elected organs of state power in the districts, towns, regions, municipal boroughs and local communities are responsible for deciding on all local issues on the basis of law. The local people's representative bodies draw up and implement the economic plan and budget for their areas, and have their own income. Their decisions are binding and must be published. All such bodies elect their own councils and committees.

IV. SOCIALIST LEGALITY AND THE ADMINISTRATION OF JUSTICE

Articles 86–104. The Constitution has the force of law and legal regulations may not contradict it. Details of all laws and binding regulations are published. The citizens' participation in the administration of justice is guaranteed and it is the declared aim of socialist society to combat all violations of the law. Laws on the punishment of war crimes and of crimes against peace and humanity correspond to the generally recognized norms of international law.

The administration of justice in the Republic is exercised by the Supreme Court, the District Courts, the Regional Courts and the social (lay) courts. In military matters jurisdiction is exercised by the Supreme Court, military tribunals and military courts. The Supreme Court is the highest organ of the administration of justice and is responsible to the People's Chamber. All judges are democratically elected by the people's representative bodies or by the citizens themselves and must be men of knowledge and experience who are loyally devoted to the socialist state. The public prosecutors' office safeguards socialist legality and ensures that persons who have commmitted crimes are called to account before the court. The public prosecutors' office is directed by the Prosecutor General and the public prosecutors of the districts and regions are appointed by him and subordinate to him.

An act is punishable only if it contravened penal law at the time of its commission, if the offender has acted in a culpable way and if his guilt is proved beyond doubt. Persons under arrest must be brought before a judge within 24 hours of their arrest and only judges are authorized to judge the admissibility of detention on remand. Nobody may be denied the right to appear before his lawful judge and special courts are inadmissible. Every citizen has the right to be heard in court and the right to be defended by a counsel is guaranteed throughout the whole criminal procedure. Any citizen or organization has the right to submit suggestions or grievances to the authorities and may suffer no disadvantages as a result. Damages inflicted on a citizen or his personal property as a result of unlawful measures by government officials are to be compensated by the authority concerned.

CONCLUDING PROVISIONS

Articles 105–106. The Constitution may be amended only through a law of the People's Chamber of the German Democratic Republic which expressly amends or supplements the text of the Constitution.

The Government

(December 1986)

COUNCIL OF STATE

Chairman: Erich Honecker.

Vice-Chairmen: Willi Stoph, Horst Sindermann, Dr Manfred Gerlach, Gerald Götting, Prof. Dr Heinrich Homann, Egon Krenz, Dr Ernst Mecklenburg, Dr Günter Mittag.

Members: Eberhard Aurich, Fritz Dallmann, Werner Felfe, Prof. Kurt Hager, Brunhilde Hanke, Leonhard Helmschrott, Friedrich Kind, Eveline Klett, Prof. Dr Lothar Kolditz, Peter Moreth, Margarete Müller, Alois Pisnik, Bernhardt Quandt, Dr Klaus Sorgenicht, Paul Strauss, Ilse Thiele, Harry Tisch, Prof. Dr Johanna Töpfer, Rosel Walther, Monika Werner.

Secretary: Heinz Eichler.

COUNCIL OF MINISTERS

Presidium

Chairman (Prime Minister): Willi Stoph.

First Deputy Chairmen: Alfred Neumann, Werner Krolikowski, Horst Sölle.

Deputy Chairman and Chairman of the National Arbitration Board: Manfred Flegel.

Deputy Chairman and Minister of Justice: Hans-Joachim Heusinger.

GERMAN DEMOCRATIC REPUBLIC

Deputy Chairman and Permanent Representative to the CMEA: Günther Kleiber.

Deputy Chairman and Minister for the Supply of Materials: Wolfgang Rauchfuss.

Deputy Chairman and Minister for Environmental Protection and Water Resources: Dr Hans Reichelt.

Deputy Chairman and Chairman of the State Planning Commission: Gerhard Schürer.

Deputy Chairman and Minister for Posts and Telecommunications: Rudolph Schulze.

Deputy Chairman and Minister for Science and Technology: Dr Herbert Weiz.

Members

Minister of Transport: Otto Arndt.
State Secretary for Labour and Wages: Wolfgang Beyreuther.
Minister of Geology: Dr Manfred Bochmann.
Minister of Finance: Ernst Höfner.
Minister for Higher and Technical Education: Prof. Hans-Joachim Böhme.
Minister of Trade and Supply: Gerhard Briksa.
Minister of Light Industry: Werner Buschmann.
Minister of the Interior and Chief of People's Police: Col-Gen. Friedrich Dickel.
Minister of Foreign Affairs: Oskar Fischer.
Minister of Machine Tools and Processing Machines: Dr Rudi Georgi.
Minister of the Glass and Ceramics Industry: Prof. Dr Karl Grünheid.
State Secretaries in the State Planning Commission: Heinz Klopfer, Wolfgang Gress.
Minister and Head of the Price Office: Walter Halbritter.
Minister of Culture: Hans-Joachim Hoffmann.
Minister of National Defence: Gen. Heinz Kessler.
Minister of Education: Dr h.c. Margot Honecker.
Minister of Construction: Wolfgang Junker.
President of the State Bank of the German Democratic Republic: Horst Kaminski.
Lord Mayor of the GDR Capital, Berlin: Erhard Krack.
Minister of Agriculture, Forestry and Food Economy: Bruno Lietz.
Minister of General and Agricultural Machinery and Vehicle Construction: Gerhard Tautenhahn.
Minister of Health: Prof. Dr Ludwig Mecklinger.
Minister of State Security: Gen. Erich Mielke.
Minister of Coal and Power: Wolfgang Mitzinger.
Minister of Ore Mining, Metallurgy and Potash: Dr-Ing. Kurt Singhuber.
Minister of Foreign Trade: Dr Gerhard Beil.
Minister of Electrical Engineering and Electronics: Felix Meier.
Minister and Chairman of the Committee of the Workers' and Farmers' Inspectorate: Dr Albert Stief.
Minister of County-Controlled and Food Industries: Dr Udo-Dieter Wange.
Minister of the Chemical Industry: Günther Wyschofsky.
Minister of Heavy Engineering and Plant Construction: Hans-Joachim Lauck.
State Secretary for Religious Affairs: Klaus Gysi.

MINISTRIES

Council of Ministers: 1020 Berlin, Klosterstr. 47; tel. 223; telex 1152337.

Ministry of Agriculture, Forestry and Food Economy: 1157 Berlin, Köpenicker Allee 39-57; tel. 25007; telex 112584.

Ministry of the Chemical Industry: 1086 Berlin, Leipziger Str. 5-7; tel. 232; telex 1152311.

Ministry of Coal and Power: 102 Berlin, Karl-Liebknecht-Str. 34; tel. 235; telex 114528.

Ministry of Construction: 102 Berlin, Scharrenstr. 2-3; tel. 223; telex 61523.

Ministry of County-Controlled and Food Industries: 1086 Berlin, Leipziger Str. 5-7; tel. 232; telex 1152311.

Ministry of Culture: 1020 Berlin, Molkenmarkt 1-3; tel. 230; telex 115230.

Ministry of Education: 1086 Berlin, Unter den Linden 69-73; tel. 232; telex 1152345.

Ministry of Electrical Engineering and Electronics: 102 Berlin, Alexanderplatz 6; tel. 218; telex 1152417.

Ministry of Environmental Protection and Water Resources: 1026 Berlin, Hans-Beimler-Str. 70-72; tel. 235.

Ministry of Finance: 1086 Berlin, Leipziger Str. 5-7; tel. 232; telex 1152331.

Ministry of Foreign Affairs: 102 Berlin, Marx-Engels-Platz 2; tel. 223; telex 114621.

Ministry of Foreign Trade: 108 Berlin, Unter den Linden 44-60; tel. 2330; telex 114437.

Ministry of General and Agricultural Machinery and Vehicle Construction: 1086 Berlin, Leipziger Str. 5-7; tel. 232; telex 1152311.

Ministry of Geology: 104 Berlin, Invalidenstr. 44; tel. 236; telex 1152251.

Ministry of the Glass and Ceramics Industry: 1086 Berlin, Leipziger Str. 5-7; tel. 232; telex 1152311.

Ministry of Health: 102 Berlin, Rathausstr. 3; tel. 235.

Ministry of Heavy Engineering and Plant Construction: 1086 Berlin, Leipziger Str. 5-7; tel. 232.

Ministry of Higher and Technical Education: 102 Berlin, Marx-Engels-Platz 2; tel. 223; telex 1152415.

Ministry of the Interior: 1086 Berlin, Mauerstr. 29-32; tel. 222; telex 112255.

Ministry of Justice: 108 Berlin, Clara-Zetkin-Str. 93; tel. 237; telex 113155.

Ministry of Light Industry: 1086 Berlin, Leipziger Str. 5-7; tel. 232; telex 1152311.

Ministry of Machine Tools and Processing Machines: 1086 Berlin, Leipziger Str. 5-7; tel. 232; telex 1152311.

Ministry of National Defence: 119 Berlin, Schnellerstr. 1-4; tel. 6352881; telex 112582.

Ministry of Ore Mining, Metallurgy and Potash: 102 Berlin, Karl-Liebknecht-Str. 34; tel. 235; telex 1152371.

Ministry of Posts and Telecommunications: 1066 Berlin, Mauerstr. 69-75; tel. 2312101; telex 112558.

Ministry of Science and Technology: 1170 Berlin, Köpenicker Str. 325A; tel. 65760; telex 113070.

Ministry of State Security: 113 Berlin, Normannenstr. 22; tel. 5509991; telex 112726.

Ministry of Supply of Materials: 1086 Berlin, Leipziger Str. 5-7; tel. 232; telex 1152342.

Ministry of Trade and Supply: 1026 Berlin, Hans-Beimler-Str. 70-72; tel. 235; telex 1152421.

Ministry of Transport: 1086 Berlin, Voss Str. 33; tel. 490; telex 112564.

POLITBÜRO OF THE SOCIALIST UNITY PARTY CENTRAL COMMITTEE

Members: Hermann Axen, Hans-Joachim Böhme, Horst Dohlus, Werner Eberlein, Werner Felfe, Prof. Kurt Hager, Joachim Herrmann, Erich Honecker (General Secretary of the Central Committee), Dr Werner Jarowinsky, Gen. Heinz Kessler, Günther Kleiber, Egon Krenz, Werner Krolikowski, Siegfried Lorenz, Gen. Erich Mielke, Günter Mittag, Erich Mückenberger, Alfred Neumann, Günter Schabowski, Horst Sindermann, Willi Stoph, Harry Tisch.

Candidate Members: Ingeburg Lange, Margarete Müller, Gerhard Schürer, Werner Walde.

Legislature

VOLKSKAMMER
(People's Chamber)

Presidium

President: Horst Sindermann (SED).
Vice-President: Gerald Götting.

GERMAN DEMOCRATIC REPUBLIC

Members: Dr Rudolf Agsten (LDPD), Eberhard Aurich (FDJ), Heinz Eichler (SED), Werner Heilemann (FDGB), Wolfgang Heyl (CDU), Ernst Mecklenburg (DBD), Erich Mückenberger (SED), Wolfgang Rösser (NDPD), Rudi Rothe (DBD), Wilhelmine Schirmer-Pröscher (DFD), Dr Karl-Heinz Schulmeister (KB).

The most recent election for the Volkskammer was held on 8 June 1986. The candidates nominated by the National Front obtained 99.94% of the total vote. The Chamber has 500 members, including 66 representatives of East Berlin.

Political Organizations

Nationale Front der Deutschen Demokratischen Republik (National Front): combines the political organizations listed below, which issue a joint programme before elections; Pres. Prof. Dr Lothar Kolditz.

Christlich-Demokratische Union Deutschlands (CDU) (Christian Democratic Union of Germany): 1080 Berlin, Otto-Nuschke-Str. 59–60; telex 112240; f. 1945; 130,000 mems (1985); Chair. Gerald Götting; Vice-Chair. Wolfgang Heyl, Max Sefrin, Dr Heinrich Toeplitz.

Demokratische Bauernpartei Deutschlands (DBD) (Democratic Farmers' Party): 1080 Berlin, Behrenstr. 47-48; telex 114801; f. 1948; 92,000 mems; Chair. Dr Ernst Mecklenburg; Deputy Chair. Paul Scholz, Dr Hans Reichelt.

Demokratischer Frauenbund Deutschlands (DFD) (Democratic Women's League of Germany): 1080 Berlin, Clara-Zetkin-Str. 16; f. 1947; 1.4m. mems; Chair. Ilse Thiele.

Freie Deutsche Jugend (FDJ) (Free German Youth): 1086 Berlin, Unter den Linden 36-38; f. 1946; 2.3m. mems; First Sec. Eberhard Aurich.

Freier Deutscher Gewerkschaftsbund (FDGB) (Confederation of Free German Trades Unions): see p. 1161.

Kulturbund der DDR (KB) (GDR League of Culture): 1080 Berlin, Otto-Nuschke-Str. 1; tel. 2202991; telex 114630; f. 1945; 260,000 mems; Pres. Prof. Dr Hans Pischner.

Liberal-Demokratische Partei Deutschlands (LDPD) (Liberal Democratic Party of Germany): 1086 Berlin, Johannes-Dieckmann-Str. 48-49; telex 114800; f. 1945; 100,000 mems (1986); Chair. Prof. Dr Manfred Gerlach.

National-Demokratische Partei Deutschlands (NDPD) (National Democratic Party of Germany): 108 Berlin, Friedrichstr. 65; telex 112293; f. 1948; Chair. Prof. Dr Heinrich Homann.

Sozialistische Einheitspartei Deutschlands (SED) (Socialist Unity Party of Germany): 1020 Berlin, Am Marx-Engels-Platz 2; tel. 2020; telex 113090; formed in 1946 as a result of a unification of the Social Democratic Party and the Communist Party in Eastern Germany; 2.3m. mems (1986); Gen. Sec. Erich Honecker; Chair. of Central Control Commission Erich Mückenberger; Chair. of Central Auditing Commission Kurt Seibt.

There are no opposition parties.

Diplomatic Representation

EMBASSIES IN THE GERMAN DEMOCRATIC REPUBLIC

Afghanistan: 1080 Berlin, Otto-Grotewohl-Str. 3a/III; tel. 2202071; Ambassador: Abdul Wahed Baba Jan.

Albania: 1100 Berlin, Florastr. 94; tel. 4825435; Chargé d'affaires: Dhimiter Karanxha.

Algeria: 1100 Berlin, Esplanade 23; tel. 4722043; Ambassador: Youcef Kraïba.

Angola: 1080 Berlin, Clara-Zetkin-Str. 89/II; tel. 2202031; Ambassador: Agostinho André Mendes de Carvalho.

Argentina: 1080 Berlin, Clara-Zetkin-Str. 89, IV/Links; tel. 2202621; telex 113018; Ambassador: Alfredo Cipriano Pons Benítez.

Australia: 1110 Berlin, Grabbeallee 34-40; tel. 4800126; telex 112460; Ambassador: Donald William Witheford.

Austria: 1080 Berlin, Otto-Grotewohl-Str. 5; tel. 2291031; telex 114275; Ambassador: Dr Franz Wunderbaldinger.

Bangladesh: 1080 Berlin, Clara-Zetkin-Str. 97/V; tel. 2292434; telex 114272; Ambassador: Mufleh Rahman Osmany.

Belgium: 1100 Berlin, Esplanade 13; tel. 4723102; telex 113153; Ambassador: Roger Prues.

Bolivia: 1080 Berlin, Leipziger Str. 61; tel. 4895684; telex 114140; Ambassador: (vacant).

Brazil: 1110 Berlin, Esplanade 11; tel. 4723002; telex 113123; Ambassador: Vasco Mariz.

Bulgaria: 1100 Berlin, Berliner Str. 127; tel. 4800171; telex 112907; Ambassador: Peter Meschduretschki.

China, People's Republic: 1110 Berlin, Heinrich-Mann-Str. 9; tel. 4800161; telex 112474; Ambassador: Ma Xusheng.

Colombia: 1080 Berlin, Clara-Zetkin-Str. 89/V; tel. 2292669; telex 114221; Ambassador: Dr Ramses Hakim-Murad.

Congo: 1080 Berlin, Clara-Zetkin-Str. 97/III; tel. 2202021; telex 114088; Ambassador: Justin Ballay-Megot.

Cuba: 1100 Berlin, Berliner Str. 120–121; tel. 4800216; telex 112449; Ambassador: Ramiro del Río Pérez Terán.

Czechoslovakia: 1080 Berlin, Otto-Grotewohl-Str. 21; tel. 2200481; telex 114026; Ambassador: Pavel Sadovský.

Denmark: 1080 Berlin, Unter den Linden 41; tel. 2202916; telex 114220; Ambassador: Erik Herluf Krog-Meyer.

Ecuador: 1080 Berlin, Clara-Zetkin-Str. 89/V; tel. 2291367; telex 112755; Ambassador: Alfonso Barrera Valverde.

Egypt: 1100 Berlin, Str. 22, 3; tel. 4825095; telex 113014; Ambassador: Mustafa Ahmed Hannafi.

Ethiopia: 1100 Berlin, Arnold-Zweig-Str. 19; tel. 4700117; telex 114286; Ambassador: Lemma Gutema.

Finland: 1080 Berlin, Schadowstr. 6; tel. 2202521; telex 114029; Ambassador: Arto Tanner.

France: 1080 Berlin, Unter den Linden 40; tel. 2202101; Ambassador: Joëlle Timsit.

Germany, Federal Republic: 1040 Berlin, Hannoversche Str. 30; tel. 2825261; telex 113244; Head of Permanent Representation: Dr Hans Otto Bräutigam.

Ghana: 1110 Berlin, Waldstr. 10; tel. 4827893; telex 112405; Ambassador: Kwame Sanaa-Poku Jantuah.

Greece: 1080 Berlin, Otto-Grotewohl-Str. 3a; tel. 2291922; telex 112464; Ambassador: Antonios J. Coundakis.

Guinea: 1110 Berlin, Heinrich-Mann-Str. 32; tel. 4829488; telex 112473; Ambassador: Mouctar Touré.

Guinea-Bissau: 1080 Berlin, Clara-Zetkin-Str. 97/11; tel. 2292661; Ambassador: Ensa Mahatma Djandy.

Hungary: 1080 Berlin, Unter den Linden 76; tel. 2202561; telex 114201; Ambassador: István Roska.

India: 1080 Berlin, Clara-Zetkin-Str. 89/VI; tel. 2292213; Ambassador: Prem Kumar Budhwar.

Indonesia: 1100 Berlin, Esplanade 9; tel. 4722002; telex 112652; Ambassador: M. P. Azhari Boer.

Iran: 1071 Berlin, Stavanger Str. 23; tel. 4720002; telex 113085; Ambassador: Dr Hamid Reza Assefi.

Iraq: 1110 Berlin, Tschaikowskistr. 51; tel. 4800501; telex 114056; Ambassador: Riyadh Ali Saba al-Azzawi.

Italy: 1080 Berlin, Unter den Linden 40; tel. 2202601; telex 113262; Ambassador: Carlo Albertario.

Japan: 1080 Berlin, Otto-Grotewohl-Str. 5/1; tel. 2202481; telex 114053; Ambassador: Keizo Kimura.

Kampuchea: 1100 Berlin, Str. 22, 2; tel. 4828853; telex 113228; Ambassador: Meas Sip.

Korea, Democratic People's Republic: 1080 Berlin, Glinkastr. 7; tel. 2298013; telex 113039; Ambassador: Pak Yong Chan.

Laos: 1100 Berlin, Esplanade 17; tel. 4722052; telex 113167; Ambassador: Vanheuang Vongvichit.

Lebanon: 1080 Berlin, Clara-Zetkin-Str. 89/IV; tel. 2202921; telex 114048; Ambassador: Joseph Akl.

Libya: 1157 Berlin, Hermann-Duncker-Str. 26; tel. 5090951; Secretary of the People's Bureau: Dr Mabruk Ali Elgayed.

Mali: 1110 Berlin, Heinrich-Mann-Str. 22; tel. 4824751; telex 112988; Ambassador: Souleymane Sidibé.

Mexico: 1110 Berlin, Homeyerstr. 40; tel. 4829492; telex 112977; Ambassador: Rogelio Martínez Aguilar.

Mongolia: 1157 Berlin, Fritz-Schmenkel-Str. 81; tel. 5090119; telex 112736; Ambassador: Ragtschaabasaryn Shamz.

GERMAN DEMOCRATIC REPUBLIC

Mozambique: 1080 Berlin, Clara-Zetkin-Str. 97/IV; tel. 2291751; telex 115074; Ambassador: Júlio Gonçalo Braga.

Netherlands: 1080 Berlin, Otto-Grotewohl-Str. 5/II; tel. 2292057; Ambassador: Carel J. Schneider.

Nicaragua: 1080 Berlin, Clara-Zetkin-Str. 97/IV; tel. 2202156; telex 113292; Ambassador: Rodrigo Cardenal Martínez.

Nigeria: 1100 Berlin, Platanenstr. 98a; tel. 4828580; telex 112741; Chargé d'affaires: James Afolabi.

Norway: 1080 Berlin, Otto-Grotewohl-Str. 5/IV; tel. 2292489; Ambassador: Erik Christian Selmer.

Pakistan: 1080 Berlin, Otto-Grotewohl-Str. 3a/II; tel. 2292428; telex 114020; Ambassador: A. A. Chowdhury.

Panama: 1156 Berlin, Ho-Chi-Minh-Str. 2; tel. 3720093; Chargé d'affaires: Dr Humberto Jaén Castillo.

Peru: 1080 Berlin, Schadowstr. 6/IV; tel. 2291455; telex 114274; Ambassador: Ricardo Walter Stubbs Vega.

Philippines: 1080 Berlin, Otto-Grotewohl-Str. 3a; tel. 2202136; telex 112810; Ambassador: Rafael A. Gonzales.

Poland: 1080 Berlin, Unter den Linden 72–74; tel. 2202551; Ambassador: Janusz Obodowski.

Portugal: 1080 Berlin, Otto-Grotewohl-Str. 3a/V; tel. 2291388; telex 112406; Ambassador: Dr Augusto Henrique de Almeida Coelho Lopes.

Romania: 1100 Berlin, Parkstr. 23; tel. 4825594; Ambassador: Gheorghe Caranfil.

Somalia: 1080 Berlin, Clara-Zetkin-Str. 97/I; tel. 2202006; telex 112411; Ambassador: Basi Mohamed Sufi.

Spain: 1080 Berlin, Clara-Zetkin-Str. 97/II; tel. 2292586; telex 113296; Ambassador: Alonso Alvarez de Toledo y Merry del Val.

Sudan: 1080 Berlin, Clara-Zetkin-Str. 97; telex 114009; Ambassador: Omar Muhammad Babiker Shouna.

Sweden: 1080 Berlin, Otto-Grotewohl-Str. 3a; tel. 2202146; Ambassador: Carl Henrik Sihver Liljegren.

Switzerland: 1100 Berlin, Esplanade 21; tel. 4724002; telex 112430; Ambassador: Peter Dietschi.

Syria: 1080 Berlin, Otto-Grotewohl-Str. 3a; tel. 2202046; Ambassador: Fayssal Sammak.

Tunisia: 1100 Berlin, Esplanade 12; tel. 4722064; telex 114019; Ambassador: Jameleddine Gordah.

Turkey: 1080 Berlin, Schadowstr. 6/IV; tel. 2202471; Ambassador: Hikmet Özkan.

USSR: 1080 Berlin, Unter den Linden 63-65; tel. 2291110; telex 114045; Ambassador: Vyacheslav Ivanovich Kochemasov.

United Kingdom: 1080 Berlin, Unter den Linden 32-34; tel. 2202431; telex 113171; Ambassador: Timothy John Everard.

USA: 1080 Berlin, Neustädtische Kirchstr. 4-5; tel. 2202741; telex 112479; Ambassador: Francis Joseph Meehan.

Uruguay: 1080 Berlin, Clara-Zetkin-Str. 97/V, rechts; tel. 2291424; telex 112413; Ambassador: Leslie Close-Pozzo.

Venezuela: 1080 Berlin, Otto-Grotewohl-Str. 5/IV; tel. 2292111; telex 114058; Ambassador: Dr Rodolfo Molina-Duarte.

Viet-Nam: 1157 Berlin, Hermann-Duncker-Str. 125; tel. 5098262; telex 112416; Ambassador: Tran Hoai Nam.

Yemen Arab Republic: 1110 Berlin, Waldstr. 15; tel. 4800391; telex 112857; Ambassador: (vacant).

Yemen, People's Democratic Republic: 1100 Berlin, Str. 22, 1; tel. 4800206; telex 113119; Ambassador: Ali Ismail Sayf.

Yugoslavia: 1040 Berlin, Albrechtstr. 26; tel. 2825446; Ambassador: Milan Predojević.

Zaire: 1080 Berlin, Otto-Grotewohl-Str. 3a; tel. 2291347; telex 112490; Ambassador: Ikolo Bolelema.

Zimbabwe: 1080 Berlin, Otto-Grotewohl-Str. 3a/IV; tel. 2202056; Ambassador: Moses Jackson Mvenge.

Judicial System

The principles on which the legal system functions are embodied in the Constitution. Jurisdiction is exercised by the Supreme Court, the County Courts (Bezirksgerichte), the District Courts (Kreisgerichte) and the Social Courts. There are also Military Courts. The Supreme Court is the highest organ of justice and supervises the work of the other courts. It is responsible to the People's Chamber.

Cases in the first instance are dealt with in the County and District Courts with one presiding judge and two lay judges. In a District Court one judge may preside and pass sentence. Cases in the second instance are dealt with by three judges in the County Courts and in the Supreme Court. However, cases are handled to an increasing extent by the Social Courts and, in the case of minor civil offences and labour disputes, by the disputes commissions.

All judges and members of the Social Courts are independent in their administration of justice. They can be recalled by their electors only if they violate the Constitution or the law or commit a serious breach of their duties.

According to the Constitution, all judges and members of the Social Courts are elected either by popular representative bodies (People's Chamber, County Parliaments, Town Assembly, etc.) or by direct popular vote. Candidates are submitted by the Minister of Justice after consultations with the relevant committees of the National Front. Candidates for the Labour Courts are submitted to the Minister of Justice by the Confederation of Free German Trades Unions (FDGB). The members of the disputes commissions are elected by the workers in their organizations. The State Prosecutors are appointed by the Prosecutor-General.

Attached to the People's Chamber is the Constitutional and Legislature Commission in which all parties are represented according to their size. All members of the Commission are appointed by the People's Chamber. Three members of the Supreme Court and three State Law Teachers, who may not be members of the People's Chamber, also serve on the Commission.

A new Criminal Code was introduced in January 1968, replacing the German Criminal Code of 1871. Amendments to this were made in December 1974 and January 1976. Similarly, a new Civil Code of January 1976 replaced the German Civil Code of 1896. A new Labour Code came into force on 1 January 1978.

Oberstes Gericht der Deutschen Demokratischen Republik (Supreme Court of the GDR): 1026 Berlin, Littenstr. 13; Pres. Dr Günter Sarge.

Generalstaatsanwalt der Deutschen Demokratischen Republik (Prosecutor-General of the GDR): Günter Wendland; 1040 Berlin, Hermann-Matern-Str. 33–34.

Ministerium der Justiz der Deutschen Demokratischen Republik (Ministry of Justice of the GDR): 108 Berlin, Clara-Zetkin-Str. 93; tel. 237; telex 113155; Minister Hans-Joachim Heusinger.

Religion

CHRISTIANITY

Protestant Churches

(For the origin, constitutional structure, and recent development of the Evangelical Churches, see the corresponding section in the chapter on the Federal Republic of Germany.)

Bund der Evangelischen Kirchen in der Deutschen Demokratischen Republik (BEKDDR) (Federation of Evangelical Churches): 1040 Berlin, Augustr. 80; tel. 28860; some 5m. people, about 30% of the population of the GDR, belong to one of the Territorial Churches united in the BEKDDR, compared with an estimated 70% in the 1950s; Pres. of Synod Dr Rainer Gaebler; Exec. Sec. Oberkirchenrat Martin Ziegler.

Arbeitsgemeinschaft Christlicher Kirchen in der DDR (Association of Christian Churches in the GDR): 1040 Berlin, Augustr. 80; tel. 28860; f. 1970; unites member churches of BEKDDR with other churches; Chair. Eberhard Natho.

Konferenz der Evangelischen Kirchenleitungen in der DDR (Conference of Evangelical Church Leaders in the GDR): 1040 Berlin, Augustr. 80; Chair. Landesbischof Dr Werner Leich.

Affiliated to the BEKDDR

Vereinigte Evangelisch-Lutherische Kirche in der Deutschen Demokratischen Republik (VELKDDR) (United Evangelical-Lutheran Church): Chancellery: 1040 Berlin, Auguststr. 80; tel. 2828969; Pres. Dr Helmut Zeddies.

Presiding Bishop: Landesbischof Christoph Stier, 2751 Schwerin, Münzstr. 8.

Evangelische Kirche der Union (EKU): Kirchenkanzlei (Chancellery): Bereich DDR, 1040 Berlin, Auguststr. 80; tel. 28860; (see the corresponding section in the chapter on the Federal Republic of Germany for details); Pres. Dr Friedrich Winter.

†**Evangelical Church of Anhalt:** Kirchenpräsident: Eberhard Natho (4500 Dessau, Otto-Grotewohl-Str. 22; tel. 7247).

GERMAN DEMOCRATIC REPUBLIC

†**Evangelical Church in Berlin-Brandenburg** (in the GDR): 1020 Berlin, Neue Grünstr. 19; tel. 20030; Bischof Dr GOTTFRIED FORCK (1120 Berlin-Weissensee, Parkstr. 21).

†**Evangelical Church of the Church Region of Görlitz:** 8900 Görlitz, Berliner Str. 62; tel. 5412; formerly Church Province of Silesia; Bischof Dr Dr JOACHIM ROGGE.

†**Evangelical Church of Greifswald:** 2200 Greifswald, Bahnhofstr. 35–36; tel. 5261; formerly Evangelical Church of Pomerania; Bischof Dr HORST GIENKE.

‡**Evangelical-Lutheran Church of Mecklenburg:** 2751 Schwerin, Münzstr. 8; tel. 864165; Landesbischof CHRISTOPH STIER.

†**Evangelical Church of the Church Province of Saxony:** 3010 Magdeburg, Am Dom 2; tel. 31881; Bischof Dr CHRISTOPH DEMKE.

‡**Evangelical-Lutheran Church of Saxony:** 8032 Dresden, Lukasstr. 6; tel. 475841; Landesbischof Dr JOHANNES HEMPEL.

‡**Evangelical-Lutheran Church in Thuringia:** 5900 Eisenach, Dr-Moritz-Mitzenheim Str. 2A; tel. 5226; Landesbischof Dr WERNER LEICH.

(† Member of the EKU; ‡ Member of the VELKDDR)

Other Protestant Churches

Bund Evangelisch-Freikirchlicher Gemeinden in der DDR (Union of Evangelical Free Church Congregations): 1034 Berlin, Gubener Str. 10; tel. 5891832; Pres. Rev. MANFRED SULT; Gen. Sec. Rev. ROLF DAMMANN.

Bund Freier evangelischer Gemeinden in der DDR (Federation of Free Evangelical Congregations): 1199 Berlin, Handjerystr. 29-31; tel. 6762665; Federal Chair. JOHANNES SCHMIDT.

Evangelische Brüder-Unität, Distrikt Herrnhut (Unitas Fratrum-Moravian Church in the District of Herrnhut); 8709 Herrnhut, Zittauer Str. 20; tel. 258; Pres. Rev. CHRISTIAN MÜLLER.

Evangelisch-Lutherische (altlutherische) Kirche in der DDR (Evangelical Lutheran—Old Lutheran—Church): 1020 Berlin, Annenstr. 53; tel. 2793583; f. 1830; c. 8,000 mems; Sec. Kirchenrat JOHANNES ZELLMER.

Evangelisch-Methodistische Kirche in der DDR (United Methodist Church): 8020 Dresden, Wiener Str. 56; tel. 477441; Bischof Dr RÜDIGER MINOR.

Kirchenbund Evangelisch-Reformierter Gemeinden in der DDR (Church Federation of Evangelical Reformed Congregations): 7010 Leipzig, Tröndlinring 7; tel. 291079; Pastor HANS-JÜRGEN SIEVERS.

Mennonitengemeinde in der DDR (Mennonite Congregation): 1174 Berlin, Donizettistr. 47; tel. 5275028; Dir Pastor KNUTH HANSEN.

The Roman Catholic Church

It is estimated that about 1.2 million people (1984) are Roman Catholics.

Römisch-katholische Kirche in der DDR: 1086 Berlin, Französische Str. 34; tel. 2000281; supervises the activities of Roman Catholic churches in the GDR and organizes the Berlin Bishops' Conference of GDR Bishops.

Bishops' Conference: Berliner Bischofskonferenz, 1086 Berlin, Französische Str. 34; f. 1984; Pres. Cardinal JOACHIM MEISNER, Bishop of Berlin.

Bishop of Berlin: Cardinal JOACHIM MEISNER, 1086 Berlin, Französische Str. 34; tel. 2000281.

Bishop of Dresden-Meissen: GERHARD SCHAFFRAN, 8053 Dresden, Käthe-Kollwitz-Ufer 84; tel. 34161.

Apostolic Administrator of Görlitz: BERNHARD HUHN (Titular Bishop of Tasaccora), 8900 Görlitz, Carl-von-Ossietzky-Str. 41; tel. 4630.

Apostolic Administrator in Erfurt-Meiningen: Dr JOACHIM WANKE (Titular Bishop of Castellum in Mauretania), 5010 Erfurt, Herrmannsplatz 9; tel. 24595.

Apostolic Administrator in Magdeburg: JOHANNES BRAUN (Titular Bishop of Putia in Byzacena), 3010 Magdeburg, Max-Josef-Metzger Str. 1; tel. 33991.

Apostolic Administrator in Schwerin: HEINRICH THEISSING (Titular Bishop of Mina), 2762 Schwerin, Lankower Str. 14; tel. 44025.

Other Christian Churches

Apostelamt Jesu Christi in der DDR: 7500 Cottbus, Otto-Grotewohl-Str. 57; tel. 713297; Pres. WALDEMAR ROHDE.

Gemeindeverband der Altkatholischen Kirche in der DDR (Union of the Old Catholic Church): 3720 Blankenburg, Georgstr. 7; tel. 2297; Deaconess URSULA BUSCHLÜTER.

Gemeinschaft der Siebenten-Tags-Adventisten in der DDR (Seventh-day Adventist Church): 1160 Berlin, Helmholtzstr. 1; tel. 6351320; Pres. LOTHAR REICHE.

Religiöse Gesellschaft der Freunde (Quäker) in der DDR (Society of Friends): 1086 Berlin, Planckstr. 20; tel. 2071525; f. 1969; 51 mems; Sec. HEINRICH BRÜCKNER.

Russische Orthodoxe Kirche—Mitteleuropäisches Exarchat (Russian Orthodox Church): 1157 Berlin, Wildensteiner Str. 10; tel. 5099191; Archbishop GERMAN.

JUDAISM

It is estimated that the Jewish Community in the Democratic Republic numbers about 5,000.

Verband der Jüdischen Gemeinden in der DDR (Union of Jewish Communities): 806 Dresden, Bautzner Str. 20; tel. 55491; Pres. HELMUT ARIS.

Jüdische Gemeinde Berlin (Jewish Community in Berlin): 1040 Berlin, Oranienburgerstr. 28; tel. 2823327; Pres. Dr PETER KIRCHNER.

The Press

The 1968 Constitution of the German Democratic Republic guarantees the freedom of the press, radio and television, and states that every citizen of the GDR has the right, 'in accordance with the spirit and aims of the Constitution, to express his opinion freely and publicly. This right is not limited by any service or employment relationship. No person may be placed at a disadvantage for exercising this right'. There is thus no formal censorship but editors are personally responsible for the content of their papers which are expected to reflect the social and political system of the GDR.

All newspapers and periodicals are owned and managed by political or independent organizations such as party committees, trade unions, cultural associations, youth organizations, etc. Almost all dailies are controlled by or affiliated to a political party, such as *Neues Deutschland* (Socialist Unity party), *Der Morgen* (Liberal Democratic Party), *National-Zeitung* (National Democratic Party) and *Neue Zeit* (Christian Democratic Union). *Tribüne* is the organ of the Confederation of Free German Trades Unions and *Bauern-Echo* of the Democratic Farmers' Party. The Free German Youth publishes the daily *Junge Welt*. The official news agency, the *Allgemeiner Deutscher Nachrichtendienst*, became a state monopoly in 1946.

In 1986 39 dailies appeared in the GDR, with a total circulation of 9.3m. copies per issue. There are 32 weeklies, with a circulation of 9.4m., and 522 periodicals and illustrated magazines, with a combined average circulation of 21.1m. According to the Press Association of the GDR, each family buys on average at least one daily newspaper, one weekly and three periodicals. In 1982 the GDR ranked third in the world in terms of daily newspaper circulation (535 per 1,000 of population).

The most important and influential dailies are those published by the Socialist Unity Party, headed by *Neues Deutschland* in Berlin, and by the Berlin organs of the other parties mentioned above. Though circulation figures are often not disclosed, a very popular paper is *Berliner Zeitung am Abend* (circulation 198,961 in 1986). Leading dailies outside Berlin are *Freie Presse* (Karl-Marx-Stadt), *Freiheit* (Halle), *Sächsische Zeitung* (Dresden), *Leipziger Volkszeitung* (Leipzig), *Ostsee Zeitung* (Rostock) and *Freies Wort* (Suhl).

The most widely-read periodicals are the weeklies *FF-dabei*, an illustrated radio and television magazine, *Wochenpost*, and the women's magazine *Für Dich*. Other high-circulation weeklies are the illustrated popular magazines *Neue Berliner Illustrierte* and *Freie Welt*, and the satirical weekly *Eulenspiegel*.

PRINCIPAL DAILIES

Bautzen

Nowa Doba: 8600 Bautzen, Tuchmacher Str. 27; tel. 511316; telex 287220; morning; Sorbian language paper; Editor SIEGHARD KOSEL; circ. 1,750.

Berlin

Bauern-Echo: 1040 Berlin, Reinhardtstr. 14; tel. 28930; telex 114424; f. 1948; morning; organ of the DBD; Editor LEONHARD HELMSCHROTT; circ. 91,546.

GERMAN DEMOCRATIC REPUBLIC

Berliner Zeitung: 1026 Berlin, Karl-Liebknecht-Str. 29; tel. 2440; telex 114854; f. 1945; morning; SED; Editor Dieter Kerschek; circ. 393,000.

Berliner Zeitung (BZ) am Abend: 1026 Berlin, Karl-Liebknecht-Str. 29; tel. 2440; telex 114854; evening; Editor Horst Hertelt; circ. 198,961.

Deutsches Sport-Echo: 1086 Berlin, Neustädtische Kirchstr. 15; sports; Editor Dieter Wales; circ. 181,916.

Junge Welt: 1026 Berlin, Karl-Liebknecht-Str. 29; tel. 2440; telex 114857; morning; FDJ; Editor Hans-Dieter Schütt; circ. 1,263,376.

Der Morgen: 1086 Berlin, Johannes-Dieckmann-Str. 47; tel. 2202181; telex 112704; f. 1945; morning; LDPD; Editor Gerhard Fischer; circ. 53,738.

National-Zeitung: 1055 Berlin, Prenzlauer Allee 36; tel. 4300215; telex 112714; f. 1948; morning; NDPD; Editor Diethard Wend; circ. 54,685.

Neue Zeit: 1086 Berlin, Mittelstr. 2–4; tel. 2000421; telex 112536; f. 1945; morning; CDU; Editor Dr Dieter Eberle; circ. 99,018.

Neues Deutschland: 1017 Berlin, Franz-Mehring-Platz 1; tel. 5850; telex 112051; f. 1946; morning; SED; Editor Herbert Naumann; circ. 1,093,234.

Tribüne: 1193 Berlin, Am Treptower Park 28–30; tel. 27100; telex 112611; f. 1945; morning; FDGB; Editor Günter Simon; circ. 410,964.

Cottbus

Lausitzer Rundschau: 7500 Cottbus, Str. der Jugend 54; tel. 625231; telex 17210; SED; morning; Editor Joachim Telemann; circ. 282,473.

Dresden

Märkische Union: 8000 Dresden, Str. der Befreiung 21; f. 1948; morning; CDU; Editor Friedrich Eismann; circ. 3,872.

Sächsische Neueste Nachrichten: 8060 Dresden, Antonstr. 8; morning; NDPD; Editor Siegmar Hofmann; circ. 29,226.

Sächsische Zeitung: 8010 Dresden, Julian-Grimau-Allee; tel. 4864240; telex 2251; f. 1946; morning; SED; Editor Johannes Schulz; circ. 554,972.

Die Union: 8000 Dresden, Str. der Befreiung 21; f. 1946; morning; CDU; Editor Friedrich Eismann; circ. 61,114.

Erfurt

Das Volk: 5010 Erfurt, Juri-Gagarin-Ring 113–117; tel. 530316; telex 61212; f. 1946; morning; SED; Editor Werner Herrmann; circ. 391,897.

Frankfurt a.d. Oder

Neuer Tag: 1200 Frankfurt a.d. Oder, Karl-Marx-Str. 23; tel. 311211; telex 16288; morning; SED; Editor Herbert Thieme; circ. 201,591.

Gera

Volkswacht: 6500 Gera, Julius-Fucik-Str. 18; tel. 612262; telex 58227; morning; SED; Editor Lothar Oberück; circ. 233,023.

Halle

Freiheit: 4020 Halle, Str. der DSF 76; tel. 38461; telex 4265; f. 1946; morning; SED; Editor Dr Hans-Dieter Krüger; circ. 574,255.

Liberal-Demokratische Zeitung: 4000 Halle, Gr. Brauhausstr. 16–17; f. 1945; morning; LDPD; Editor Hans-Herbert Biermann; circ. 57,101.

Der Neue Weg: 4000 Halle, Klement-Gottwald-Str. 61; telex 4417; f. 1946; morning; CDU; Editor Klaus-Peter Bigalke; circ. 37,443.

Karl-Marx-Stadt

Freie Presse: 9010 Karl-Marx-Stadt 1, Karl-Marx Allee 15-19; tel. 656280; telex 7233; SED; morning; Editor Dietmar Griesheimer; circ. 652,278.

Leipzig

Leipziger Volkszeitung: 7010 Leipzig, Peterssteinweg 19; tel. 7154327; telex 51495; f. 1894; morning; SED; Editor Rudi Röhrer; circ. 479,350.

Mitteldeutsche Neueste Nachrichten: 7010 Leipzig, Thomasiusstr. 2; morning; NDPD; Editor Rainer Duclaud; circ. 20,047.

Sächsisches Tageblatt: 7010 Leipzig, Neumarkt 6; tel. 295251; telex 512236; f. 1946; morning; LDPD; Editor Armin Hopf; circ. 63,994.

Magdeburg

Volksstimme: 3010 Magdeburg, Bahnhofstr. 17; tel. 388240; telex 8462; morning; SED; Editor Heinz Wiese; circ. 442,203.

Neubrandenburg

Freie Erde: 2080 Neubrandenburg, Str. der Befreiung 27; tel. 585440; telex 33211; f. 1945; morning; SED; Editor Gerhard Schiedewitz; circ. 195,501.

Potsdam

Brandenburgische Neueste Nachrichten: 1500 Potsdam, Leninallee 185; morning; NDPD; Editor Georg Jopke; circ. 22,701.

Märkische Volksstimme: 1500 Potsdam, Friedrich-Engels-Str. 24; tel. 3240; telex 15333; morning; SED; Editor Dr Peter Trommer; circ. 333,542.

Rostock

Der Demokrat: 2500 Rostock, Kröpelinerstr. 44–47; telex 31205; f. 1945; CDU; Editor Xaver Kugler; circ. 18,207.

Norddeutsche Neueste Nachrichten: 2500 Rostock, Kröpelinerstr. 21; tel. 94161; telex 031105; f. 1953; morning; NDPD; Editor Wolf-Dietrich Gehrke; circ. 35,026.

Ostsee-Zeitung: 2500 Rostock, Richard-Wagner-Str. 1A; tel. 3650; telex 31317; f. 1952; morning; SED; Editor Dr Siegbert Schütt; circ. 284,998.

Schwerin

Norddeutsche Zeitung: 2751 Schwerin, Graf-Schack-Allee 11; tel. 865091; telex 32238; f. 1946; morning; LDPD; Editor Günter Grasmeyer; circ. 22,100.

Schweriner Volkszeitung: 2791 Schwerin, Hermann-Duncker-Str. 27; tel. 3530; telex 32420; f. 1946; SED; Editor Hans Brandt; circ. 199,000.

Suhl

Freies Wort: 6000 Suhl, Wilhelm-Pieck-Str. 6; tel. 5130; telex 62205; morning; SED; Editor Helmut Linke; circ. 173,316.

Weimar

Thüringer Neueste Nachrichten: 5300 Weimar, Goetheplatz 9A; tel. 4192; telex 618924; f. 1951; NDPD; Editor Klaus-Rainer Lorenz; circ. 31,431.

Thüringer Tageblatt: 5300 Weimar, Coudraystr. 6; telex 618922; f. 1951; morning; CDU; Editor Franz Gerth; circ. 31,443.

Thüringische Landeszeitung: 5300 Weimar, Marienstr. 14; tel. 3201; telex 618937; f. 1945; morning; LDPD; Editor H.-D. Woithon; circ. 69,000.

SELECTED POPULAR PERIODICALS

Bild und Ton: 7031 Leipzig, Karl-Heine-Str. 16; tel. 49500; telex 51451; f. 1947; special photographic and cinematographic monthly; Editor Dr Walter.

Deine Gesundheit: 1020 Berlin, Neue Grünstr. 18; tel. 2000621; popular monthly dealing with health and welfare; circ. 242,700.

Einheit: 1020 Berlin, Am Marx-Engels-Platz; monthly; circ. 250,000.

Eulenspiegel: 1026 Berlin, Karl-Liebknecht-Str. 29; tel. 2440; telex 114854; political satirical weekly; Editor Gerd Nagel; circ. 490,000.

FF-dabei: 1026 Berlin, Karl-Liebknecht-Str. 29; tel. 2440; telex 114854; weekly; Editor Osmund Schwab; circ. 1,480,000.

Filmspiegel: 1040 Berlin, Oranienburger Str. 67–68; fortnightly; films and cinematography; circ. 300,000.

Fotografie: 7031 Leipzig, Karl-Heine-Str. 16; tel. 49500; telex 51451; f. 1946; special photographic monthly; Editor Dr Walter.

Fotokino-Magazin: 7031 Leipzig, Karl-Heine-Str. 16; tel. 49500; telex 51451; f. 1962; popular photographic monthly; Editor Dr Walter.

Freie Welt: 1026 Berlin, Karl-Liebknecht-Str. 29; tel. 2440; telex 114854; weekly; international politics; Editor Günter Bonow; circ. 360,000.

Für Dich: 1026 Berlin, Karl-Liebknecht-Str. 29; tel. 2440; telex 114854; women's weekly; Editor Dr Marlis Allendorf; circ. 943,616.

FUWO—Die Neue Fussballwoche: 1086 Berlin, Neustädtische Kirchstr. 15; tel. 2212420; telex 2853; weekly; football; Editor Jürgen Nöldner; circ. 300,000.

Guter Rat: 7010 Leipzig, Friedrich-Ebert-Str. 76–78; quarterly for women and home; circ. 446,700.

GERMAN DEMOCRATIC REPUBLIC

Horizont: 1026 Berlin, Karl-Liebknecht-Str. 29; tel. 2440; telex 114854; monthly; international politics and economics; Editor Ernst-Otto Schwabe; circ. 130,000.

Illustrierter Motorsport: 1086 Berlin, Neustädtische Kirch-Str. 15; monthly; cars, motorcycles and motor-boats; Editor Eberhard Pester.

Jugend + Technik: 1026 Berlin, Postfach 43, Mauerstr. 39–40; tel. 2233427; telex 114483; f. 1953; popular scientific/technological monthly for young people; circ. 205,000.

Die Kirche: 1020 Berlin, Sophienstr. 3; f. 1945; organ of the Protestant Church in Berlin-Brandenburg; Editor Pastor Gerhard Johann; circ. 42,000.

Das Magazin: 1026 Berlin, Karl-Liebknecht-Str. 29; tel. 2440; telex 114854; monthly; Editor Manfred Gebhardt; circ. 565,000.

Modische Maschen: 7010 Leipzig, Friedrich-Ebert-Str. 76–78; popular women's quarterly for fashion and knitting.

Neue Berliner Illustrierte: 1026 Berlin, Karl-Liebknecht-Str. 29; tel. 2440; telex 114854; f. 1945; weekly; Editor Wolfgang Nordalm; circ. 772,656.

neues leben: 1080 Berlin, Mauerstr. 39–40; monthly; youth; circ. 542,955.

Pramo: 7010 Leipzig, Friedrich-Ebert-Str. 76–78; monthly; practical fashion for women and children; circ. 753,100.

Saison: 7010 Leipzig, Friedrich-Ebert-Str. 76–78; quarterly; fashion; circ. 209,500.

St Hedwigsblatt: 1086 Berlin, Hinter der Katholischen Kirche 3, Postfach 1343; tel. 2071754; f. 1954; weekly; organ of the Catholic Church, Berlin diocese; circ. 25,000.

Sibylle: 7010 Leipzig, Friedrich-Ebert-Str. 76–78; 6 a year; women's fashion magazine.

Sonntag: 1086 Berlin, Niederwallstr. 39; cultural weekly; Editor Dr Wilfried Geissler; circ. 22,252.

Standpunkt: 1190 Berlin, Fennstr. 16; tel. 6351024; Protestant monthly; circ. 3,000.

Urania: 1080 Berlin, Otto-Nuschke-Str. 28; tel. 2071632; popular scientific monthly; circ. 116,600.

Die Weltbühne: 1026 Berlin, Karl-Liebknecht-Str. 29; tel. 2443301; telex 114854; weekly; politics, art, economics; Editor Peter Theek; circ. 31,000.

Wochenpost: 1026 Berlin, Karl-Liebknecht-Str. 29; tel. 2440; telex 114854; weekly; Editor Brigitte Zimmermann; circ. 1,255,328.

SELECTED SPECIALIST PERIODICALS

Ärztliche Jugendkunde: 7010 Leipzig, Salomonstr. 18B, Postfach 109; tel. 70131; f. 1888; 5 a year; medical; Editors Prof. Dr Dr H. Grimm, Prof. Dr H. Patzer; circ. 750.

Bildende Kunst: 1040 Berlin, Oranienburger Str. 67–68; tel. 2879306; telex 112302; f. 1953; monthly; painting, sculpture and graphics; Editor Dr Peter Michel; circ. 19,100.

Biologische Rundschau: 6900 Jena, Villengang 2; tel. 27332; telex 058 86176; 6 a year; all fields of biology; Editor F. W. Stöcker; circ. 1,300.

Chemische Technik: 7031 Leipzig, Karl-Heine-Str. 27; monthly; chemistry, chemical engineering.

Deutsche Lehrerzeitung: 1086 Berlin, Krausenstr. 50, Am Spittelmarkt; weekly for teachers; Editor Otto Pfeiffer; circ. 155,520.

Deutsche Nationalbibliographie und Bibliographie des im Ausland erschienenen deutschsprachigen Schrifttums: 7010 Leipzig, Deutscher Platz 1; tel. 88120; telex 51562; register of all German language publications all over the world; published by the Deutsche Bücherei, Leipzig, in three sections: Series A: New publications of the book trade (weekly); Series B: New publications not for general sale (fortnightly); Series C: Theses and Inaugural Dissertations (monthly).

Elektrie: 1020 Berlin, Oranienburger Str. 13–14; tel. 28700; telex 112228; f. 1947; monthly for electrical trade; circ. 5,000.

Film und Fernsehen: 1040 Berlin, Oranienburger Str. 67–68; tel. 2879265; telex 112302; f. 1973; monthly; organ of the Union of Film and TV Artists; Editor Günter Netzeband; circ. 10,000.

Fremdsprachen: 7010 Leipzig, Gerichtsweg 26, Postfach 130; quarterly dealing with interpreting, translating, etc. in Russian, English, French and Spanish; circ. 3,200.

Handelswoche/Konsum-Genossenschafter: 1055 Berlin, Am Friedrichshain 22; tel. 43870; telex 114566; fortnightly for trade and business.

Das Hochschulwesen: 1080 Berlin, Friedrichstr. 167–168; monthly; education; circ. 3,500.

Humanitas: 1020 Berlin, Neue Grünstr. 18; fortnightly for medical and social welfare; circ. 48,331.

Informatik: 1055 Berlin, Am Friedrichshain 22; tel. 43870; telex 114566; 6 a year; scientific journal.

Junge Generation: 1026 Berlin, Postfach 43, Mauerstr. 39–40; tel. 2233321; f. 1947; monthly; youth; circ. 72,000.

Die Mode: 7010 Leipzig, Friedrich-Ebert-Str. 76–78; 2 a year; fashion; circ. 23,300.

Neue Deutsche Bauernzeitung: 1017 Berlin, Franz-Mehring-Platz 1; tel. 5852191; telex 112728; agricultural weekly; Editor Dr Udo Augustin; circ. 225,130.

Neue Deutsche Literatur: 1086 Berlin, Friedrichstr. 169; tel. 2335059; f. 1953; monthly; review of literature; Editor Walter Nowojski.

Neue Deutsche Presse: 1086 Berlin, Friedrichstr. 101; tel. 2000106; telex 114947; f. 1946; monthly; journalist affairs, press, radio, television; Editor Erika Gelhaar; circ. 5,000.

Das neue Handwerk: 1055 Berlin, Am Friedrichshain 22; tel. 43870; telex 114566; monthly; circ. 236,625.

Neue Werbung: 1055 Berlin, Am Friedrichshain 22; tel. 43870; telex 114566; 6 a year; advertising.

Plaste und Kautschuk: 7031 Leipzig, Karl-Heine-Str. 27; monthly; chemistry, physics, processing and application.

Radio Fernsehen Elektronik: 1020 Berlin, Oranienburger Str. 13–14; tel. 28700; telex 772228; f. 1952; monthly; theory and practice of electronics; circ. 85,000.

Sozialistische Finanzwirtschaft: 1055 Berlin, Am Friedrichshain 22; 6 a year; finance and economics; circ. 42,000.

Technische Gemeinschaft: 1080 Berlin, Kronenstr. 18; monthly; technology; circ. 208,000.

Theater der Zeit: 1040 Berlin, Oranienburger Str. 67; tel. 2879259; f. 1946; monthly; theatre, drama, opera, operetta, musical, puppet theatre, ballet; Editor Hans-Rainer John; circ. 12,000.

Wirtschaftswissenschaft: 1055 Berlin, Am Friedrichshain 22; tel. 43870; telex 114566; monthly; economic science, socialist economy.

Zahntechnik: 1020 Berlin, Neue Grünstr. 18; every 2 months; dentistry; circ. 5,350.

ZAMM: 1080 Berlin, Leipziger Str. 3–4; monthly; applied mathematics and mechanics; circ. 1,900.

Zeitschrift für Chemie: 7031 Leipzig, Karl-Heine-Str. 27; monthly; chemistry.

Zeitschrift für Geschichtswissenschaft: 1080 Berlin, Glinkastr. 13–15; monthly; history and historiography; circ. 4,500.

Zeitschrift für Klinische Medizin (Das deutsche Gesundheitswesen): 1020 Berlin, Neue Grünstr. 18; fortnightly for the medical profession.

Zeitschrift für Psychologie mit Zeitschrift für angewandte Psychologie: 7010 Leipzig, Salomonstr. 18B, Postfach 109; tel. 70131; f. 1890; 4 a year; psychology and applied psychology; Editors Prof. Dr H. D. Schmidt, Dr H. Sydow, Prof. Dr F. Klix, Prof. Dr F. Kukla; circ. 1,300.

Zentralblatt für Neurochirurgie: 7010 Leipzig, Salomonstr. 18B, Postfach 109; tel. 70131; f. 1936; 4 a year; neuro-surgery; Editors Prof. Dr H. G. Niebeling, Dr W. E. Goldhahn; circ. 850.

NEWS AGENCIES

Allgemeiner Deutscher Nachrichtendienst (ADN): 1026 Berlin, Mollstr. 1; tel. 230; telex 1146010; f. 1946; official news agency of the GDR; has 42 offices and additional correspondents abroad; maintains a press photo dept, 'Zentralbild', and provides daily news service in German as well as radio teletype casts in English, French, Spanish, Portuguese and Arabic, and radio photo services; Dir-Gen. Günter Pötschke.

Foreign Bureaux

Agence Arabe Syrienne d'Information: 1136 Berlin, Volkradstr. 8.

Agence Belga (BRT) (Belgium): 1006 Berlin, Koppenstr. 59, Postfach 37-05; tel. 6816468; Correspondent Dr R. Mondelaers.

Agence Congolaise d'Information (ACI) (Congo): 1156 Berlin, Rudolf-Seiffert-Str. 60; tel. 3729137.

GERMAN DEMOCRATIC REPUBLIC

Agence France-Presse (AFP): 1020 Berlin, Karl-Liebknecht-Str. 11; tel. 2123549; telex 114001; Correspondent KARL-HEINZ BAAB.

Agenzia Nazionale Stampa Associata (ANSA) (Italy): 1020 Berlin, Karl-Liebknecht-Str. 11; tel. 2123662; telex 114049; Correspondent RICCARDO EHRMAN.

Bulgarian Telegraph Agency (BTA): 102 Berlin, Alexanderstr. 5; telex 114227.

Československá tisková kancelář (ČTK) (Czechoslovakia): 1100 Berlin, Max-Lingner-Str. 12A; tel. 4721015; telex 114269.

Deutsche Presse Agentur (dpa) (Federal Republic of Germany): 1080 Berlin, Clara-Zetkin-Str. 89; tel. 2291109; telex 114038.

Iraqi News Agency (INA): 1156 Berlin, Leninallee 175; Correspondent SA'ID AL-FAHDI.

Magyar Távirati Iroda (MTI) (Hungary): 1020 Berlin, Mollstr. 12; telex 114081; Correspondent FERENC PACH.

Novinska Agencija Tanjug (Yugoslavia): 1017 Berlin, Lichtenbergerstr. 13.

Polska Agencja Prasowa (PAP) (Poland): 1086 Berlin, Neustädtische Kirchstr. 3; telex 114060.

Prensa Latina (Cuba): 1080 Berlin, Mohrenstr. 36–37; tel. 2080257; telex 114284; Correspondent MERCEDES RAMOS CHAVIANO.

Reuters (UK): 1058 Berlin, Schönhauser Allee 27; tel. 4485706; telex 114049.

Telegrafnoye Agentstvo Sovetskovo Soyuza (TASS) (USSR): 1080 Berlin, Mohrenstr. 36–37; Correspondent ANATOLY TUPAEV.

Viet-Nam News Agency (VNA): 1017 Berlin, Leninplatz 27; telex 114008.

Xinhua (New China) News Agency (People's Republic of China): 1110 Berlin, Pfeilstr. 17; tel. 4824396; telex 112231; Correspondent XING GUIMIN.

PRESS ASSOCIATION

Verband der Journalisten der DDR: 1086 Berlin, Friedrichstr. 101; tel. 2000106; telex 114974; f. 1946; Chair. EBERHARD HEINRICH; 8,500 mems.

Publishers

Akademie-Verlag: 1080 Berlin, Leipziger Str. 3–4, Postfach 1233; tel. 22360; telex 114420; f. 1946; books and periodicals on scientific theory and practice; Dir Prof. Dr L. BERTHOLD.

Akademische Verlagsgesellschaft Geest & Portig K.-G.: 7010 Leipzig, Sternwartenstr. 8, Postfach 106; tel. 293158; telex 512381; f. 1906; mathematics, physics, science, engineering, history of science; Dir H. KRATZ.

Altberliner Verlag: 1020 Berlin, Neue Schönhauser Str. 8; tel. 2826749; f. 1945; books for children; Dir Dr G. DAHNE.

Aufbau-Verlag Berlin und Weimar: 1080 Berlin, Französische Str. 32; tel. 2202421; telex 4739; f. 1945; literature, German and foreign, classical literature and criticism; Dir ELMAR FABER.

Johann Ambrosius Barth: 7010 Leipzig, Salomonstr. 18B, Postfach 109; tel. 70131; f. 1780; textbooks, monographs and periodicals, medicine, stomatology, physics, chemistry, astronomy and psychology; Dir K. WIECKE.

VEB Verlag für Bauwesen: 1086 Berlin, Französische Str. 13–14; tel. 20410; telex 112229; building; Dir S. SEELIGER.

VEB Bibliographisches Institut Leipzig: 7010 Leipzig, Gerichtsweg 26; tel. 7801; telex 512773; f. 1826; encyclopaedias, German language books, reference books, bibliographies, biographies, information and documentation; Dir H. BÄHRING.

Hermann Böhlaus Nachf. Verlag: 5300 Weimar, Meyerstr. 50A; tel. 2071; f. 1624; literary history and criticism, history, law; Man. Dir Prof. Dr LOTHAR BERTHOLD.

VEB Breitkopf & Härtel Musikverlag: 7010 Leipzig, Karlstr. 10; tel. 7351; f. 1719; classical music, contemporary and vocal music and literature on music; Dir Dr G. HEMPEL.

VEB F. A. Brockhaus Verlag Leipzig: 7010 Leipzig, Postfach 19; tel. 7846; f. 1805; travel books, reference books, picture books, popular science, calendars; Dir A. NEUMANN.

VEB Deutscher Landwirtschaftsverlag: 1040 Berlin, Reinhardstr. 14; tel. 28930; f. 1960; agriculture; Dir G. HOLLE.

VEB Deutscher Verlag der Wissenschaften: 1080 Berlin, Johannes-Dieckmann-Str. 10; tel. 22900; telex 114390; f. 1954; mathematics, physics, chemistry, philosophy, psychology, history; Dir Dr L. WALTER.

VEB Deutscher Verlag für Grundstoffindustrie: 7031 Leipzig, Karl-Heine-Str. 27; tel. 44441; telex 51451; f. 1960; technical books and journals for science and industry; Dir H. BROMMA.

VEB Deutscher Verlag für Musik: 7010 Leipzig, Karlstr. 10; tel. 7351; f. 1954; classical and contemporary and vocal music and literature on music; Dir Dr G. HEMPEL.

Dieterich'sche Verlagsbuchhandlung: 7022 Leipzig, Mottelerstr. 8; tel. 58726; f. 1766; literature; Dir R. LINKS.

Dietz Verlag Berlin: 1020 Berlin, Wallstr. 76–79; tel. 27030; telex 114741; f. 1945; social science, politics, history, philosophy, political economy, cultural policy, memoirs, periodicals; Dir Dr G. HENNIG.

VEB Domowina-Verlag: 8600 Bautzen, Tuchmacherstr. 27; tel. 511316; telex 287220; f. 1958; books in Sorbian and in German on Sorbian culture, children's books, belles-lettres; Dir M. BENAD.

Edition Leipzig—Verlag für Kunst und Wissenschaft: 7030 Leipzig, Karl-Liebknecht-Str. 77; tel. 312412; telex 512918; f. 1960; arts and history of civilization, scientific and bibliophilic reprints, science and technics, general; Dir Dr D. NADOLSKI.

VEB Edition Peters: 7010 Leipzig, Talstr. 10, Postfach 746; tel. 7721; telex 512381; f. 1800; classical and contemporary music, music books: *Musikwissenschaftliche Studienbibliothek Peters, Peters-Textbücher;* Dir N. MOLKENBUR.

VEB Verlag Enzyklopädie Leipzig: 7010 Leipzig, Gerichtsweg 26; tel. 7801; telex 512773; f. 1956; dictionaries, foreign language text-books, German for foreigners; Dir H. BÄHRING.

Eulenspiegel, Verlag für Satire und Humor: 1080 Berlin, Kronenstr. 73–74; tel. 2202126; f. 1954; humour, satire, caricature, cartoons; Dir W. SELLIN.

Evangelische Haupt-Bibelgesellschaft zu Berlin: 1017 Berlin, Krautstr. 52; f. 1814; tel. 2792902; religion; Dir K. WEBER.

Evangelische Verlagsanstalt GmbH: 1017 Berlin, Krautstr. 52; tel. 2700521; f. 1946; religion; Dirs Dr S. BRÄUER, Dr G. GRAU.

VEB Fachbuchverlag Leipzig: 7031 Leipzig, Karl-Heine-Str. 16, Postfach 67; tel. 49500; telex 51451; f. 1949; mathematics, physics and technical, basic sciences, textiles, commerce, printing, catering, etc, and technical periodicals; Dir Dr E. WALTER.

VEB Gustav Fischer Verlag: 6900 Jena, Villengang 2; tel. 27332; telex 5886176; f. 1878; biological science, human and veterinary medicine; Dir H. SCHUSTER.

VEB Fotokinoverlag Leipzig: 7031 Leipzig, Karl-Heine-Str. 16, Postfach 67; tel. 49500; telex 51451; f. 1957; books on photography, cinematography and periodicals; Dir Dr E. WALTER.

Verlag für die Frau: 7010 Leipzig, Friedrich-Ebert-Str. 76–78; tel. 71790; telex 51773; f. 1946; women's magazines and books, fashion, household, family, hobby, hand-coloured art prints; Dir E. KONECNY.

Greifenverlag: 6820 Rudolstadt, Heidecksburg, Postfach 142; tel. 2085; f. 1919; belles-lettres; Dir Dr URSULA STEINHAUSSEN.

VEB Harth Musik Verlag: 7010 Leipzig, Karl-Liebknecht-Str. 12; tel. 312612; f. 1946; Dir RITA PREISS.

Henschelverlag Kunst und Gesellschaft: 1040 Berlin, Oranienburgerstr. 67; tel. 28790; telex 112302; f. 1945; stage, music, literature, film, art; Dir K. MITTELSTÄDT.

VEB Hermann Haack Geographisch-Kartographische Anstalt Gotha: 5800 Gotha, Justus-Perthes-Str. 3–9; tel. 3872; telex 6185333; f. 1785; maps, atlases, geographical and cartographical books and periodicals; Dir M. HOFFMANN.

VEB Hinstorff Verlag Rostock: 2500 Rostock, Kröpelinerstr. 25; tel. 34441; f. 1831; German and north European literature, regional literature, maritime literature; Dir H. FAUTH.

S. Hirzel Verlag: 7010 Leipzig, Sternwartenstr. 8; tel. 282263; f. 1853; medicine, veterinary medicine, natural sciences, agronomic sciences, intellectual sciences, periodicals, review, *Deutsches Wörterbuch* von J. und W. Grimm; Dir H. KRATZ.

VEB Friedrich Hofmeister Musikverlag: 7010 Leipzig, Karlstr. 10; tel. 7357; f. 1807; classical, contemporary, vocal and folk music; Dir Dr G. HEMPEL.

Insel-Verlag Anton Kippenberg: 7022 Leipzig, Mottelerstr. 8; tel. 58726; f. 1899; Insel library; world literature, classics, arts; Dir R. LINKS.

Verlag Junge Welt: 1026 Berlin, Postfach 43; tel. 2233; telex 114483; f. 1952; books and periodicals for children and young people; Dir M. RUCHT.

Gustav Kiepenheuer Verlag: 7022 Leipzig, Mottelerstr. 8; tel. 58726; f. 1909; general; Gustav-Kiepenheuer library; literature, history, arts; Dir R. LINKS.

Kinderbuchverlag: 1080 Berlin, Behrenstr. 40–41; tel. 20932765; Postfach 1225; f. 1949; children's books; Dir A. HEMPEL.

Koehler & Amelang (VOB): 7010 Leipzig, Hainstr. 2; tel. 282379; f. 1925; history, history of culture and art, literary history, theology; Dir Prof. Dr H. FAENSEN.

VEB Verlag der Kunst: 8019 Dresden, Spenerstr. 21; tel. 34486; f. 1952; art books and reproductions; Dir Prof. Dr H. JÄHNER.

VEB Lied der Zeit, Musikverlag: 1020 Berlin, Rosa-Luxemburgstr. 41; tel. 2825081; f. 1954; dance, brass band and light music, sheet-music, musical comedies, books on music, children's books, almanacs, posters; autographs; Dir KLAUS DAEHN.

Paul List Verlag: 7022 Leipzig, Mottelerstr. 8; tel. 58726; f. 1894; literature; Dir R. LINKS.

Militärverlag der DDR: 1055 Berlin, Storkower Str. 158, Postfach 46 551; tel. 4300618; telex 112673; f. 1956; military topics, fiction.

Mitteldeutscher Verlag Halle-Leipzig: 4010 Halle/Saale, Postfach 295, Thälmannplatz 2; tel. 873544; f. 1946; general fiction and non-fiction; Man. Dir Dr EBERHARD GÜNTHER.

Buchverlag Der Morgen: 1170 Berlin, Seelenbinderstr. 152; tel. 6504151; telex 6504151; f. 1958; belles-lettres, politics; Dir Dr W. TENZLER.

Verlag der Nation: 1040 Berlin, Friedrichstr. 113; tel. 28390; f. 1948; literature, politics, biographies, paperbacks; Dir H.-O. LECHT.

Verlag Das Neue Berlin: 1080 Berlin, Kronenstr. 73–74; tel. 2202126; f. 1946; crime, adventure, science fiction; Dir W. SELLIN.

Verlag Neues Leben: 1080 Berlin, Behrenstr. 40–41; tel. 20932765; telex 114781; f. 1946; books for young people and fiction; Dir RUDOLF CHOWANETZ.

Verlag Neue Musik: 1086 Berlin, Leipziger Str. 26; tel. 2202051; f. 1957; music and literature on music; Dir FERDINAND HIRSCH.

Neumann Verlag: 7010 Leipzig, Salomonstr. 26–28; tel. 7426; f. 1946; books on gardening, forestry, agriculture, fishing, nature.

VEB Postreiter-Verlag: 4020 Halle/Saale, Ernst-Toller-Str. 18; tel. 28097; f. 1947; children's books; Dir CH. KUPFER.

Prisma-Verlag Zenner und Gürchott: 7010 Leipzig, Leibnizstr. 10; tel. 281411; f. 1957; popular science, art history, novels; Dirs KLAUS ZENNER, FRITZ GÜRCHOTT.

VEB Pro Musica Verlag: 7010 Leipzig, Karl-Liebknecht-Str. 12; tel. 312612; f. 1946; Dir RITA PREISS.

VEB Räthgloben-Verlag Leipzig: 7033 Leipzig, Raimundstr. 14; tel. 45169; telex 512923; f. 1917; Dir H. GOESCHEL.

Verlag Philipp Reclam Jun.: 7031 Leipzig, Nonnenstr. 38; tel. 44501; f. 1828; Reclam's *Universal-Bibliothek:* pocket-book series (including philosophy, history and culture, language and literature, biographies) and works of world literature in attractive format; Dir Dr H. MARQUARDT.

Rütten & Loening Berlin: 1080 Berlin, Französische Str. 32; f. 1844; tel. 2202421; telex 4739; belles-lettres, literary criticism magazines; Dir ELMAR FABER.

VEB E. A. Seemann, Buch- und Kunstverlag: 7010 Leipzig, Jacobstr. 6; tel. 7736; f. 1858; art books and reproductions; Dir Dr G. KEIL.

St Benno Verlag GmbH: 7033 Leipzig, Thüringerstr. 1–3; tel. 44161; f. 1951; Catholic publications; Dirs F.-J. CORDIER, C. BOCKISCH.

Seven Seas Publishers: 1086 Berlin, POB 1221, Glinkastr. 13–15; tel. 2202851; paperbacks, books by English language writers, and English translations of modern GDR authors.

Sportverlag: 1086 Berlin, Neustädtische Kirchstr. 15, Postfach 1218; tel. 22120; telex 112853; f. 1947; sports, recreation, technical, sport education, reports; Dir H. SCHUBERT.

VEB Verlag Technik: 1020 Berlin, Oranienburgerstr. 13–14, Postfach 201; tel. 28700; telex 112228; f. 1946; technical books, dictionaries and periodicals; Dir K. HIERONIMUS.

BSB B.G. Teubner Verlagsgesellschaft Leipzig: 7010 Leipzig, Sternwartenstr. 8, Postfach 930; tel. 293158; telex 512381; f. 1811; mathematics, physics, science, technology, classical philology, biography, history of science; Dir H. KRATZ.

VEB Georg Thieme: 7010 Leipzig, Hainstr. 17–19; tel. 27332; telex 5886176; f. 1886; medicine, bioscience; Dir H. SCHUSTER.

VEB Tourist Verlag: 1020 Berlin, Neue Grünstr. 17; tel. 2071018; telex 114488; f. 1977; maps, tourist guides and travel books; Dir Dr R. PUSTKOWSKI.

Transpress VEB Verlag für Verkehrswesen: 1086 Berlin, Französische Str. 13–14; tel. 20410; telex 112229; f. 1960; specialized literature on transport, telecommunications, philately, numismatics; Dir Dr H. BÖTTCHER.

Tribüne, Verlag und Druckereien des FDGB: 1193 Berlin, Am Treptower Park 28–30; tel. 27100; telex 112611; f. 1945; trade union publications, general literature; Dir F. MÖLLER.

Union Verlag VOB: 1080 Berlin, Charlottenstr. 79; tel. 2202711; telex 114767; f. 1951; publications of the Christlich-Demokratische Union Deutschlands; literature, art; Dir KLAUS-PETER GERHARDT.

Urania-Verlag Leipzig/Jena/Berlin: 7010 Leipzig, Salomonstr. 26–28, Postfach 969; tel. 7426; f. 1924; natural and social sciences, cultural history, hobbies; Dir H. BULLAN.

VEB Verlag Volk und Gesundheit: 1020 Berlin, Neue Grünstr. 18; tel. 2000621; telex 114488; f. 1952; medicine; Dir H. SCHUSTER.

Verlag Volk und Welt: 1086 Berlin, Postfach 1221, Glinkastr. 13–15; tel. 2202851; f. 1947; 20th-century international fiction, drama and poetry; Dir J. GRUNER.

Volk und Wissen Volkseigener Verlag: 1086 Berlin, Krausenstr. 50, Am Spittelmarkt; tel. 204330; telex 112181; f. 1945; adult education; Dir R. WEBER.

Verlag die Wirtschaft: 1055 Berlin, Am Friedrichshain 22; tel. 43870; telex 114566; f. 1946; specialist books, brochures and periodicals on economics, industrial management, economic planning, data processing, work study, trade; Dir D. GRÜNEBERG.

Verlag Zeit im Bild: 8012 Dresden, Postfach 61; tel. 48640; telex 2291; f. 1946; periodicals, politics, economics, foreign language; Man. K.-H. KAMENZ.

Zentralantiquariat der DDR, Reprint-Abteilung: 7010 Leipzig, Talstr. 29; tel. 295808; telex 512684; f. 1964; reprints; Dir H. KAZIMIREK.

A. Ziemsen Verlag: 4600 Wittenberg Lutherstadt, Lucas-Cranach-Str. 21; tel. 2528; f. 1902; works on biology.

Government Publishing House

Staatsverlag der DDR: 1086 Berlin, Otto-Grotewohl-Str. 17; tel. 2336336; telex 1152344; f. 1963; official publications, law, history, economics, politics; Dir R. TIETZ.

PUBLISHERS' ORGANIZATION

Börsenverein der Deutschen Buchhändler zu Leipzig (Association of German Democratic Republic Publishers and Booksellers in Leipzig): 7010 Leipzig, Gerichtsweg 26, POB 146; tel. 293851; telex 512773; f. 1825; Chair. JÜRGEN GRUNER; Dir H. BAIER.

Radio and Television

Radio licences issued totalled 6,415,000 and television licences 5,970,000 in 1983.

RADIO

Staatliches Komitee für Rundfunk beim Ministerrat der DDR (State Committee for Radio Broadcasting): 1160 Berlin, Nalepastr. 18–50; tel. 6320; telex 112276; Dir-Gen. A. BECKER; the co-ordinating body of all radio organizations in the GDR.

Home Service

Berliner Rundfunk: 1160 Berlin, Nalepastr. 18–50; tel. 6320; telex 112276; 16 medium wave and 11 VHF transmitters broadcasting 142 hours a week; Dir HANNES POTTHAST.

Radio DDR: 1160 Berlin, Nalepastr. 18–50; tel. 6320; telex 112276; 11 medium wave and VHF transmitters, broadcasting 168 hours a week on Programme I, 104 hours a week on Programme II and 329 hours a week on regional programmes; Dir ROLF SCHMIDT.

Stimme der DDR: 1160 Berlin, Nalepastr. 18–50; tel. 6360; telex 112276; one long wave, two medium wave, two short wave and 10 VHF transmitters broadcasting 168 hours a week; Dir MARTIN RADMANN.

External Service

Radio Berlin International: 1160 Berlin, Nalepastr. 18–50; tel. 6360; telex 112276; broadcasts in 11 languages (Arabic, Danish, English, French, German, Hindi, Italian, Portuguese, Spanish, Swahili and Swedish) on one medium wave and 11 short wave transmitters; Dir KLAUS FISCHER.

GERMAN DEMOCRATIC REPUBLIC

Radio Volga: 15 Potsdam, Menzelstr. 5; operates one 200 kW transmitter on 1141 metres for Soviet forces in the GDR; broadcasts for 18 hours a day with its own Russian language programmes and relays from Radio Moscow.

TELEVISION

About 80% of East Germans live in areas where they can receive television programmes from the Federal Republic. It is estimated that West German current affairs programmes are seen by about 40%, some light entertainment by 70% and news programmes by as many as 80% of East German viewers.

Staatliches Komitee für Fernsehen (State Committee for Television Broadcasting): 1199 Berlin-Adlershof; tel. 6310; telex 112885; Chair. HEINZ ADAMECK; supervises:

Fernsehen der DDR: 1199 Berlin-Adlershof, Rudower Chaussee 3; tel. 6310; telex 112885; member of International Radio and Television Organization since 1960. There are 13 transmitters, which in 1984 broadcast 96 hours a week on Programme I (90 hours in colour) and 61 hours a week on Programme II (54 hours in colour); Programme Dir HORST SAUER; Technical Dir ROLF KRAMER; Dir of International Relations Dr KURT OTTERSBERG.

Finance

(cap. = capital; res = reserves; m. = million; M. = Marks)

BANKS
Central Bank

Staatsbank der Deutschen Demokratischen Republik (State Bank of the GDR): 1086 Berlin, Charlottenstr. 33–33A; tel. 23230; telex 114671; f. 1948; capital stock 1,500m. M.; Pres. HORST KAMINSKY; Vice-Pres. HANS TAUT.

Other Banks

Bank für Landwirtschaft und Nahrungsgüterwirtschaft der DDR: 108 Berlin, Clara-Zetkin-Str. 37; f. 1951; cap. 250m. M.; credits for agricultural and co-operative organizations; Pres. GÜNTHER SCHMIDT; Vice-Pres. HANS WOLFF.

Deutsche Aussenhandelsbank AG: 1080 Berlin, Unter den Linden 24–30; tel. 22870; telex 114411; f. 1966; responsible for the carrying out of all business connected with export, import and transit trade; cap. 800m. M., res 2,055m. M., dep. 62,631m. M. (Dec. 1985); Pres. Dr WERNER POLZE; Vice-Pres. Prof. Dr FRIEDMAR JOHN.

Deutsche Handelsbank AG: 1080 Berlin, Behrenstr. 22; tel. 2202911; telex 114665; f. 1956; cap. and res 256.1m. M.; conducts banking business with regard to import, export and transit trade; Gen. Man. FEODOR ZIESCHE; Deputy Gen. Mans INGEBORG KLEIN, HEINRICH GRAMER.

INSURANCE

Auslands- und Rückversicherungs-AG der DDR (DARAG): 1020 Berlin, Inselstr. 1B; tel. 2700522; telex 114402; f. 1958; marine and general insurances of all kinds, re-insurance, non-payment insurance; Chair. GÜNTER HEIN; Gen. Man. L. THOMAS.

Staatliche Versicherung der DDR: 1026 Berlin, Breite Str. 30–31; tel. 21620; telex 115043; f. 1952; State organization for property, liability, and personal insurance; Gen. Man. GÜNTER HEIN.

Trade and Industry

Ministerium für Aussenhandel (Ministry of Foreign Trade): 1080 Berlin, Unter den Linden 44/60; tel. 2330; telex 114437.
Foreign trade is a state monopoly. Trade organizations conduct import and export transactions for particular sectors of industry.

TRADE CENTRE

Internationales Handelszentrum (International Trade Centre): 1086 Berlin, Friedrichstr.; tel. 20960; telex 114381; opened 1978; offices of foreign enterprises accredited in the GDR; seat of the GDR Association of Foreign Trade Agencies and Brokers and its member organizations; provision of rooms and services for conferences, symposia, exhibitions and negotiations for the promotion of international trade.

CHAMBER OF FOREIGN TRADE

Kammer für Aussenhandel der Deutschen Demokratischen Republik: 1100 Berlin, Schönholzer Str. 10–11; tel. 48220; telex 114840; f. 1952; members of the Chamber are the foreign trade corporations and the major industrial enterprises; Pres. HANS-JOACHIM LEMNITZER.

FOREIGN TRADE ORGANIZATIONS

Baukema Export/Import: 1080 Berlin, Mohrenstr. 53–54; tel. 2240; telex 112248; building machines, cranes, machinery and equipment for the production of building material machines.

Berliner Import-Export-Gesellschaft mbH: 1185 Berlin, Bruno-Taut-Str. 8; tel. 68120; telex 113282; consumer goods, metal processing industry and building industry products.

Buchexport: 7010 Leipzig, Leninstr. 16; tel. 71370; telex 51678; books, periodicals, music, records, reproductions, calendars, globes, maps, atlases, etc.

Chemieanlagen Export/Import: 1055 Berlin, Storkower Str. 120; tel. 43520; telex 112916; export of plant and machinery for the chemical industry, equipment for special fields of foodstuffs sector.

Chemie-Export-Import: 1055 Berlin, Storkower Str. 133; tel. 43220; telex 112171; chemicals, incl. household chemicals and plastics, photographic materials, tyres, etc.

DEFA Aussenhandel: 1058 Berlin, Milastr. 2; tel. 4400801; telex 114511; films.

Demusa: 9652 Klingenthal, Leninstr. 133; tel. 2341; telex 77920; musical instruments, toys, paint brushes, writing equipment, artists' materials, jewellery, fancy goods, arts and crafts.

Elektronik Export-Import: 1026 Berlin, Alexanderplatz 6; tel. 2183001; telex 114721; time-measuring and meteorological instruments, electronic components, freeze drying.

Elektrotechnik Export-Import: 1026 Berlin, Alexanderplatz 6; tel. 2180; telex 115061; electrical installations for industry, radio, railways.

Fischimpex Rostock: 2510 Rostock 5, Postfach 42; tel. 8100; telex 31309; export and import of fish and fish products; commercial relations in all fields of the fishing industry, fishing operations, scientific-technical services, licences.

Fortschritt Landmaschinen Export-Import: 1185 Berlin, Bruno-Taut-Str. 4; tel. 68220; telex 112522; agricultural machinery, machines for foodstuffs industry.

Fruchtimex: 1020 Berlin, Schicklerstr. 7; tel. 21480; telex 114684; fresh fruit and vegetables, raw products for children's food.

Genussmittel Import-Export: 1086 Berlin, Thälmannplatz 2; tel. 2202811; telex 112353; exports and imports foodstuffs, spices, brewing malt, wines and spirits; also imports coffee, cocoa, tea, tobacco.

GERMED-export-import: 1199 Berlin, Glienicker Weg 125–127; tel. 6790; telex 112740; medicines, drugs, dressing materials, plaster, chemicals.

GISAG Export-Import: 1020 Berlin, Köpenicker Str. 127–129; tel. 27020; telex 114163; foundry plant, foundry goods.

Glas-Keramik: 1080 Berlin, Kronenstr. 19–19A; tel. 20570; telex 114661; glass and glass products, porcelain, earthenware.

Heim-Electric Export-Import: 1026 Berlin, Alexanderplatz 6; tel. 2180; telex 114555; electric household appliances, equipment for engineering, electronics and electric industry, cameras, entertainment electronics, electroceramics, electric installation material, light fittings, electrical equipment for motor vehicles and bicycles.

Holz und Papier Export-Import: 1080 Berlin, Krausenstr. 35–36; tel. 20750; telex 112235; exports paper, furniture; imports timber, veneers, wicker, cellulose, paper.

Industrieanlagen-Import: 1086 Berlin, Mauerstr. 83–84; tel. 22890; telex 112214; import of complete plant and processes for chemical industry, metallurgy, power generation, glassware, ceramics, building materials, process instrumentation, control engineering, electronics and telecommunication engineering, automotive industry.

Intercontrol GmbH: 1080 Berlin, Clara-Zetkin-Str. 112–114; tel. 22860; telex 114852; controls commercial goods of all types, inspection, supervision, expert opinions, analyses.

Interpelz: 7010 Leipzig, Nikolaistr. 13–25; tel. 71330; telex 51477; leather goods, shoes, furs and hides.

Interwerbung GmbH: 1157 Berlin, Hermann-Duncker-Str. 89, Postfach 230; tel. 5090981; telex 112106; advisory organization for advertising, including exhibitions for foreigners in the GDR.

Intrac Handelsgesellschaft mbH: 1100 Berlin, Pestalozzistr. 5–8; tel. 4840; telex 114923; metals, ores, mineral oil and oil products.

Isocommerz GmbH: 1115 Berlin, Lindenberger Weg 70; tel. 3400111; telex 113148; f. 1964; export of radioactive and stable isotopes, phosphors, special inorganic chemicals; Dir Dr G. Ewald.

Kali-Bergbau: 1080 Berlin, Otto-Nuschke-Str. 55; tel. 20450; telex 114471; export of fertilizers, agricultural chemicals and mineral salts; imports of barytes, etc.

Kohle-Energie Export-Import: 1080 Berlin, Johannes-Dieckmann-Str. 26; tel. 20450; telex 114470; export and import of coal, natural gas, lignite and mixed fuels, electric energy.

Kunst und Antiquitäten GmbH: 1080 Berlin, Französische Str. 15; tel. 2202671; telex 112962; art and antiquities.

Limex-Bau-Export-Import: 1040 Berlin, Allee der Kosmonauten 26; tel. 5400131; telex 114968; metal and concrete constructions and building material; responsible for scientific-technological co-operation with socialist and developing countries on the basis of state orders.

Metallurgiehandel: 1054 Berlin, Brunnenstr. 188–190; tel. 28920; telex 115123; steel and other metals.

MLW intermed-export-import: 1020 Berlin, Schicklerstr. 5–7; Postfach 17; tel. 21480; telex 114571; medical equipment and supplies (including public health service), technical education equipment, equipment for industrial and agricultural research.

Nahrung Export-Import: 1020 Berlin, Schicklerstr. 5–7; tel. 21480; telex 114892; seeds, sugar, starch, dairy products, meat, fish, live animals.

VEB Philatelie Wermsdorf: 7264 Wermsdorf, Gruner Weg 4A, Postfach; tel. 216; telex 518871; wholesale import and export of stamps, stamp collections and special issues.

Polygraph Export/Import: 1080 Berlin, Friedrichstr. 61; tel. 2000601; telex 112310; machinery for the printing industry.

Robotron Export/Import: 1140 Berlin, Allee der Kosmonauten 24; tel. 5400130; telex 112311; exports data-processing systems.

Schienenfahrzeuge Export/Import: 1100 Berlin, Ötztalerstr. 5; tel. 48040; telex 114322; passenger coaches, compartment wagons, sleeping-cars, restaurant cars, luggage vans, long distance carriages, etc.

Schiffscommerz: 2501 Rostock, Doberaner Str. 44–47; tel. 3670; telex 31355; cargo vessels, fishing vessels, special ships and marine machinery and equipment.

SKET Export/Import: 1080 Berlin, Johannes-Dieckmann-Str. 7–9; tel. 2240; telex 112693; cement plants and equipment, plants for the production of cables and wire ropes.

Spielwaren und Sportartikel Export/Import: 1080 Berlin, Charlottenstr. 46; tel. 22830; telex 112797; export and import of boats, camping, sports and fishing equipment, arts and craft products, toys and prams.

TAKRAF Export/Import: 1080 Berlin, Mohrenstr. 53–54; tel. 2240; telex 112347; cranes, open-cast mining equipment, equipment for power plants.

Technocommerz: 1086 Berlin, Johannes-Dieckmann-Str. 11–13; tel. 2240; telex 114977; technical equipment including air-conditioning, refrigeration plants, pumps, compressors, diesel engines and diesel-driven generating sets, ventilation, hydraulic sets and equipment, gearings, couplings, fittings and valves for all branches of industry.

Textil Commerz: 1080 Berlin, Unter den Linden 62–68, Postfach 1206; tel. 2200301; telex 112816; fabrics, clothing, household linen, carpets, upholstery, haberdashery.

Textima-Export/Import: 1086 Berlin, Johannes-Dieckmann-Str. 11–13; tel. 2240; telex 114118; machinery and plants for the textile industry.

Transportmaschinen Export-Import: 1086 Berlin, Johannes-Dieckmann-Str. 11–13; tel. 2240; telex 114494; catering, agricultural machinery and small motor vehicles, spare parts and accessories.

Union Haushaltgeräte Export/Import: 1080 Berlin, Wilhelm-Külz-Str. 46, Postfach 1203; tel. 2200101; telex 112538; f. 1965; tools, metalware, household appliances.

Verpackung und Bürobedarf Export/Import: 7010 Leipzig, Nikolaistr. 15–25, Postfach 806; tel. 79740; telex 512594; export and import of packing materials, cardboard, paper, foil, wallpapers, labels, office stationery, painting and drawing paper.

WMW Export-Import: 1040 Berlin, Chausseestr. 111–112; tel. 28900; telex 112804; exports machine tools.

WUNEX Wälzlager und Normteile Export/Import: 9022 Karl-Marx-Stadt, Reichenhainer Str. 31–33, Postfach 1045; tel. 57060; telex 07279; export and import of roller bearings, fasteners and wire products.

Kombinat VEB Carl Zeiss Jena: 6900 Jena, Carl-Zeiss-Str. 1; tel. 832246; telex 5886242; exports instruments and instrument systems for industrial research, particularly in optics.

Zellstoff und Papier Export/Import: 1080 Berlin, Mauerstr. 77; tel. 20750; telex 114523; paper, carton, cellulose.

Zentral-Kommerz GmbH: 1100 Berlin, Pestalozzistr. 5–8; tel. 4840; telex 114981; agricultural products, foodstuffs, secondary raw materials.

Zimex GmbH: 7010 Leipzig, Goldschmidtstr. 29; tel. 71870; telex 51492; exports books, brochures, greetings cards, prints, philatelic items, folders, albums, playing cards, etc.

NATIONALIZED INDUSTRY

The greater part of industry is organized in Volkseigene Betriebe (VEBs—nationally-owned enterprises). About 80% of workers are employed in state enterprises, 15% in co-operatives, 1% in semi-state enterprises and less than 5% in private concerns. The following are some of the major industrial combines:

VEB Kombinat Luft- und Kältetechnik: 8000 Dresden; telex 2414; aero-technical plant and equipment.

VEB Kombinat NAGEMA: 8045 Dresden; telex 33341; food processing machinery; about 30 factories and 21,000 employees.

VEB Leuna-Werke 'Walter Ulbricht': Leuna; telex 4221; chemicals; about 30,000 employees.

VEB Schwermaschinenbau-Kombinat 'Ernst Thälmann' Magdeburg (SKET): 3000 Magdeburg; telex 28824; rolling mills, cement, wire and cables, vegetable oil, minerals; about 28,000 employees.

VEB WMW-Kombinat 'Fritz Heckert': 9030 Karl-Marx-Stadt, Jagdschänkenstr. 17; tel. 860; telex 75031; machine tools, machining systems, lubricators, fixtures, castings, industrial plants.

MANUFACTURERS' ASSOCIATIONS

Vereinigungen volkseigener Betriebe der DDR (Associations of Nationally Owned Enterprises): each major industry has its own Association, and the foreign trade enterprises co-operate closely with them. The managements of the Associations share responsibility with the foreign trade enterprises for the export of modern and top quality products, for market research, for advising customers and for organizing a number of services.

TRADE UNIONS

Freier Deutscher Gewerkschaftsbund (FDGB) (Confederation of Free German Trades Unions): 1026 Berlin, Fritz-Heckert-Str. 70; tel. 27010; telex 113011; f. 1945; Chair. Harry Tisch; 9.5m. mems.

The following unions are affiliated to the FDGB:

Agricultural, Food Processing and Forestry Workers' Union: 1086 Berlin, Unter den Linden 15; tel. 2000131; f. 1968; Pres. Horst Zimmermann; 650,000 mems.

Industrial Union of Building and Wood Workers: 1026 Berlin, Wallstr. 61–65; tel. 27410; f. 1950; Pres. Lothar Lindner; 960,000 mems.

Union of Central and Local Government Employees and Municipal Workers: 1026 Berlin, Am Köllnischen Park 3; tel. 2700543; f. 1945; Pres. Rolf Hösselbarth; 670,000 mems.

Industrial Union of Chemical, Glass and Ceramic Workers: 4020 Halle/Saale, Rudolf-Breitscheid-Str. 9; tel. 38011; f. 1946; Pres. Edith Weber; 520,000 mems.

Cultural Workers' Union: 1026 Berlin, Am Köllnischen Park 3; tel. 2700543; f. 1949; Pres. Herbert Bischoff; 74,000 mems.

Union of Distributive, Catering, Food and Allied Products Workers: 1086 Berlin, Unter den Linden 15; tel. 2000131; f. 1958; Pres. Hannelore Schulz; 1.1m. mems.

Health Workers' Union: 1081 Berlin, Mauerstr. 53; tel. 2202161; f. 1949; Pres. Dr Elfriede Gerboth; 590,000 mems.

Trade Union of Instruction and Education: 1086 Berlin, Unter den Linden 13–15; tel. 2000131; f. 1946; teachers and educational workers; Pres. Helga Labs; 560,000 mems.

Industrial Union of Metal Workers: 1086 Berlin, Unter den Linden 13; tel. 2000131; f. 1946; Pres. Reinhard Sommer; 1.8m. mems.

GERMAN DEMOCRATIC REPUBLIC

Industrial Union of Mine and Power Workers: 4011 Halle/Saale, Merseburger Str. 135; tel. 48272; telex 04337; f. 1963; Pres. GÜNTER WOLF; 460,000 mems.

Industrial Union of Printing and Paper Workers: 1086 Berlin, Unter den Linden 15; tel. 2000131; f. 1946; Pres. WERNER PEPLOWSKI; 160,000 mems.

Scientific Workers' Union: 1086 Berlin, Unter den Linden 15; tel. 2000131; f. 1953; Pres. Prof. Dr ROLF RINKE; 170,000 mems.

Industrial Union of Textile, Clothing and Leather Workers: 1086 Berlin, Unter den Linden 15; tel. 2000131; f. 1950; Pres. ANNELIE UNGER; 610,000 mems.

Industrial Union of Transport and Communications Workers: 1086 Berlin, Unter den Linden 15; tel. 2000131; f. 1963; Pres. KARL KALAUCH; 780,000 mems.

TRADE FAIR

International Leipzig Trade Fair: 7010 Leipzig, Leipziger Messeamt, Markt 11–15, Postfach 720; tel. 71810; telex 512294; 9,000 exhibitors from all over the world in spring, 6,000 exhibitors in autumn; 200 issuing offices for Fair tickets in principal cities of the world; capital and consumer goods; twice a year in March and September; Dir-Gen. SIEGFRIED FISCHER.

Transport

Ministerium für Verkehrswesen (Ministry of Transport): Ministerrat der DDR, 1086 Berlin, Vossstr. 33; tel. 490; telex 112564; controls all transport.

RAILWAYS

In 1985 there were 14,054 km of normal gauge track, of which some 2,523 km were electrified. There were also 285 km of narrow gauge.

Deutsche Reichsbahn: 1086 Berlin, Vossstr. 33; under the auspices of the Ministry of Transport.

ROADS

In 1985 there were 1,850 km of motorways, 11,251 km of trunk roads, 34,040 km of district roads and 77,400 km of roads in towns and villages (Kommunalstrassen).

Hauptverwaltung Strassenwesen (Dept of Public Roads and Motorways): 1086 Berlin, Vossstr. 33.

Hauptverwaltung des Kraftverkehrs (Dept of Public Passenger and Goods Road Transport): 1086 Berlin, Vossstr. 33.

INLAND WATERWAYS

Hauptabteilung Binnenschiffahrt und Wasserstrassen (Dept of Inland Shipping and Waterways): 1086 Berlin, Vossstr. 33; controls all inland navigation; there were 2,319 km of navigable waterways in 1985.

Wasserstrassenaufsichtsamt der DDR (Supervisory Board of Inland Navigation and Waterways): 1020 Berlin, Poststr. 21–22; telex 114967; Dir ADOLF MEIER.

VE Kombinat Binnenschiffahrt und Wasserstrassen: 1017 Berlin, Alt Stralau 55–58; telex 112703; Dir-Gen. Dr WOLFGANG HETTLER.

Affiliated:

    VEB Binnenhäfen 'Mittelelbe': 3010 Magdeburg, Wittenberger Str. 17.

    VEB Binnenhäfen 'Oberelbe': 8012 Dresden, Magdeburger Str. 58.

    VEB Binnenhäfen 'Oder': 1220 Eisenhüttenstadt, Glashüttenstr.; telex 168444.

    VEB Binnenreederei im VE Kombinat Binnenschiffahrt und Wasserstrassen (Inland Shipping Company): 1017 Berlin, Alt Stralau 55–58; tel. 5523; telex 112703.

    VEB Forschungsanstalt für Schiffahrt, Wasser- und Grundbau: 1017 Berlin, Alt Stralau 44; tel. 5523; telex 112703.

    VEB Schiffsreparaturwerften: 1017 Berlin, Alt Stralau 55–58.

    VEB Wasserstrassenbau: 1160 Berlin, Goethestr. 16.

    VEB Wasserstrassenbetrieb und -unterhaltung Eberswalde: 1300 Eberswalde/Finow, Hans-Beimler-Str. 1.

    VEB Wasserstrassenbetrieb und -unterhaltung Magdeburg: 3010 Magdeburg, Wallstr. 19–20.

SHIPPING

Rostock is the principal seaport. In 1985 the GDR's merchant fleet had 171 ships (excluding passenger vessels), with a total displacement of about 1.2m. grt.

DDR-Schiffs-Revision und -Klassifikation: 1615 Zeuthen, Eichenallee 12; tel. 2633; telex 158721; f. 1950; registration of shipping, survey of the technical safety of ships and classification; Dir Prof. Dr GÜNTER BOSSOW.

Hauptverwaltung des Seeverkehrs (Dept of Merchant Fleet and Sea-Ports): 1086 Berlin, Vossstr. 33.

Seefahrtsamt der DDR (Board of Navigation and Maritime Affairs of the GDR): 2500 Rostock, Patriotischer Weg 120; telex 31134; Dir Capt. GERD HAUSSMANN.

Seekammer der DDR (Naval Court of the GDR): 2500 Rostock, Patriotischer Weg 120; tel. 3832363; Chair. Capt. DIETER RAPPHAHN.

Tallierungs-GmbH—Ladungskontrollunternehmen der DDR: 2500 Rostock-Überseehafen; tallying, checking, weighing, surveying, draught measurement, inspection and expertise; Dir MARGOT RECKLING.

VE Kombinat Deutrans: 1086 Berlin, Otto-Grotewohl-Str. 25, Postfach 1243; tel. 2200121; telex 114631; international forwarding enterprise; Dir-Gen. RAINER SCHWABE.

VE Kombinat Seeverkehr und Hafenwirtschaft—Deutfracht/Seereederei: 2500 Rostock-Überseehafen; tel. 3660; telex 31381; comprises various shipping and harbour enterprises; Dir-Gen. ARTUR MAUL.

VEB Bagger-, Bugsier- und Bergungsreederei: 2530 Rostock, Am Seekanal 14; telex 318845; dredging, towage, salvage; Dir WOLFGANG SOYK.

VEB Deutfracht/Seereederei: 2500 Rostock-Überseehafen; telex 31139; shipping company; 173 ships with about 1.6m. dwt, bulk carriers, liner ships, cargo trailer ships, refrigeration ships, tankers; Dir-Gen. ARTUR MAUL.

VEB Schiffsmaklerei: 2500 Rostock, Strandstr. 86; tel. 383365; telex 31265; f. 1958; international clearing and liner agency; agencies at Rostock, Wismar, Stralsund; branch office in Berlin; Dir PETER BEUCH.

VEB Schiffsversorgung Rostock: 2500 Rostock-Überseehafen; tel. 3667000; telex 31114; f. 1959; general ship supplies, provisions, technical equipment, nautical charts and handbooks, duty-free goods; Dir GERHARD BECKMANN.

VEB Seehafen Rostock (Overseas port, Rostock): 2500 Rostock-Überseehafen; telex 31264; Dir DIETER NOLL.

VEB Seehafen Stralsund (Stralsund seaport): 2300 Stralsund, Hafenstr. 15; tel. 692360; telex 317350; Dir HEINZ HAPP.

VEB Seehafen Wismar (Wismar seaport): 2400 Wismar; telex 318882; Dir KLAUS BODDIN.

CIVIL AVIATION

Interflug, Gesellschaft für internationalen Flugverkehr mbH: 1189 Berlin-Schönefeld; tel. 6720; telex 112893; f. 1954; flights throughout Europe and to the Middle, Near and Far East, Africa and Central America; Dir-Gen. Dr KLAUS HENKES; fleet of 11 IL-62, 13 IL-18, 37 TU-134.

There are international airports at Berlin-Schönefeld, Dresden, Erfurt and Leipzig.

Tourism

Reisebüro der Deutschen Demokratischen Republik: 1026 Berlin, Alexanderplatz 5; tel. 2150; telex 114648; f. 1958; branches in every town of 40,000 inhabitants or over; Dir-Gen. HORST DANNAT.

Atomic Energy

There were two nuclear power plants in operation in 1986, and nuclear power accounted for 10.7% of total electricity generation in 1984.

Arbeitsstelle für Molekularelektronik (Institute for Molecular Electronics): 808 Dresden, Königsbrücker Landstr. 159; f. 1961; Dir Prof. Dr-Ing. WERNER HARTMANN.

Institut für Hochenergiephysik der Akademie der Wissenschaften der DDR (Research Institute of High Energy Physics of the GDR Academy of Sciences): 1615 Zeuthen, Platanenallee 6; tel. 6858001; telex 158770; f. 1952; Dir Prof. Dr K. LANIUS.

GERMAN DEMOCRATIC REPUBLIC

Isocommerz GmbH (Import and Export of Radioactive and Stable Isotopes): 1115 Berlin, Lindenberger Weg 70; telex 113148; f. 1964; Dir Dr G. EWALD.

Ministerium für Wissenschaft und Technik (Ministry of Science and Technology): 1170 Berlin, Köpenickerstr. 325A; tel. 65760; telex 113070; f. 1955.

Staatliches Amt für Atomsicherheit und Strahlenschutz der DDR (Board of Nuclear Safety and Radiation Protection of the GDR): 1157 Berlin-Karlshorst, Waldowallee 117; f. 1962; theoretical problems of radiation protection and nuclear safety; medical, biological and technical research; legislation and licensing; radiation protection monitoring in working areas and medical supervision; environmental protection including radioactive waste processing and disposal; nuclear safeguards; training courses for health physicists and physicians; Pres. Prof. Dr GEORG SITZLACK.

VEB Kernkraftwerk (VEB Atomic Power Station): Rheinsberg/Mark; telex 318322; f. 1961; Dir Prof. KARL RAMSBUSCH; Technical Centre: Berlin-Pankow, Görschstr. 45–46; Dir Dipl.-Ing. GERHARD TEICHLER.

VEB RFT Messelektronik 'Otto Schön' Dresden: 8012 Dresden, Postfach 211; tel. 4870; telex 260068; Dir D. HANKE.

VEB Vakutronik WIB Dresden: 8021 Dresden 21, Dornblüthstr. 14; f. 1955; Dir Ing. FELIX WIECZOREK.

Zentralinstitut für Festkörperphysik und Werkstofforschung der Akademie der Wissenschaften (Central Institute for Solid State Physics and Raw Materials Research of the Academy of Sciences): 8027 Dresden, Helmholtzstr. 20; tel. 46590; telex 2131; f. 1969; Dir Prof. Dr JOHANNES BARTHEL.

Zentralinstitut für Isotopen- und Strahlenforschung der Akademie der Wissenschaften (Central Institute of Isotope and Radiation Research of the AdW): 7050 Leipzig, Permoserstr. 15; tel. 2392308; telex 51536; f. 1969; Dir Prof. Dr Dr KLAUS WETZEL.

Zentralinstitut für Kernforschung der Akademie der Wissenschaften (Central Institute for Nuclear Research of the Academy of Sciences): 8051 Dresden, Postfach 19; tel. 5910; telex 2167; f. 1956; Dir Prof. Dr-Ing. GÜNTER FLACH.

THE FEDERAL REPUBLIC OF GERMANY AND WEST BERLIN

Introductory Survey

Location, Climate, Language, Religion, Flag, Capital

The Federal Republic of Germany lies in the heart of Europe. Its neighbours to the west are the Netherlands, Belgium, Luxembourg and France, to the south Switzerland and Austria, to the east Czechoslovakia and the German Democratic Republic, and to the north Denmark. The climate is temperate, with an average annual temperature of 9°C (48°F), although there are considerable variations between the North German lowlands and the Bavarian Alps. The language is German. Almost all citizens of the Federal Republic profess Christianity, and adherents are about equally divided between Protestants and Roman Catholics. The national flag (proportions 5 by 3) consists of three equal horizontal stripes, of black, red and gold. The seat of government is Bonn.

Recent History

After the defeat of the Third Reich in 1945, Germany was divided, according to the Berlin Agreement, into US, Soviet, British and French occupation zones. Berlin was similarly divided. After the failure of negotiations to establish a unified German administration, the three Western-occupied zones were integrated economically in 1948. A provisional constitution, the Grundgesetz (Basic Law), came into force in the three zones (excluding Saarland) in May 1949. The first federal elections were held in August 1949, when the Christian Democratic Union/Christian Social Union (CDU/CSU) and the Social Democratic Party (SPD) emerged as the two largest political parties. The Federal Republic of Germany (FRG) was established on 21 September 1949, although its sovereignty was limited by the continuing Allied military occupation. The first President of the Republic was Theodor Heuss. In October 1949 the Soviet-occupied zone of Germany declared itself the German Democratic Republic (GDR), with the Soviet-occupied zone of Berlin as its capital. This left the remainder of Berlin, known as West Berlin, as an 'island' of the FRG in GDR territory. Following the establishment of the Federal Republic, the military occupation was converted into a contractual defence relationship. The Paris Agreement of 1954 gave full sovereign status to the Federal Republic from 5 May 1955, and also gave it membership of NATO. In 1957 the Bundestag (Federal Assembly) declared Berlin the capital of Germany, and the Federal Republic continues to aim for a united Germany. Until such time, the seat of the Federal Government is Bonn. Saarland, under French occupation, was reunited with the FRG administratively in January 1957 and became economically incorporated in July 1959. The isolation of West Berlin was increased in August 1961, when the GDR constructed a wall along the boundary between the eastern and western sectors of the city.

Under the chancellorship of Dr Konrad Adenauer (1949–63) and the direction of Economics Minister Dr Ludwig Erhard, who succeeded Adenauer as Chancellor until 1966, the Federal Republic rebuilt itself rapidly to become one of the most affluent and economically dynamic states of Europe, allying itself with the West, to avoid the threat of 'expansionist' communism, and becoming a founder member of the European Communities. Owing to the Government's insistence on reunification, maintaining that the 1937 borders of the Reich remained legally valid until the signing of a peace treaty by the government of a united Germany, the Federal Republic became completely cut off from eastern Europe.

The CDU/CSU, which had formed the government from 1949, ruled in coalition with the SPD from 1966 to 1969, under the chancellorship of Dr Kurt Kiesinger. After the general election of October 1969, a new coalition of the SPD and the Free Democratic Party (FDP) formed the government, under the chancellorship of Willy Brandt, adopting a fresh policy towards eastern Europe (Ostpolitik) and particularly towards the GDR.

Following elections in November 1972, the SPD became, for the first time, the largest party in the Bundestag. Chancellor Brandt resigned in May 1974, after the discovery that his personal assistant had been working for the GDR, and was succeeded by Helmut Schmidt, previously Minister of Finance. In the same month Walter Scheel, Brandt's Vice-Chancellor and Foreign Minister, was elected Federal President in place of Gustav Heinemann.

A deteriorating economic situation was accompanied by a decline in the popularity of the Government and increasing tension between the coalition partners. In the general election of October 1976 the SPD lost its position as largest party in the Bundestag, but the SPD-FDP coalition retained a slender majority. Traditional partnerships between parties became less certain; the Bavarian CSU split from, and then rejoined, the CDU in 1976. In July 1979 Dr Karl Carstens of the CDU, President of the Bundestag, succeeded Walter Scheel as President of the Federal Republic.

In the general election of October 1980 the SPD-FDP coalition achieved a majority of 45 seats in the Bundestag: the greatest gains were made by the FDP, whereas the SPD made almost negligible gains. At local elections in 1981 and 1982 the SPD-FDP coalition suffered severe set-backs and became increasingly unstable, while disputes over nuclear power, defence policy and economic measures continued to divide the parties. By September 1982 the two parties were disagreeing openly and the FDP eventually withdrew from the coalition, marking the long-expected end of the 13-year partnership. On 1 October, after a 'constructive vote of no confidence', Schmidt was replaced as Chancellor by the CDU leader, Dr Helmut Kohl, and the FDP agreed to form a coalition with the CDU/CSU. This partnership was confirmed by the results of the general election held in March 1983, when the CDU/CSU substantially increased their share of the vote, winning 48.8% of the total, while the SPD, led by Hans-Jochen Vogel after Helmut Schmidt's retirement, gained only 38.8%. The environmentalist Green Party entered the Bundestag for the first time, after obtaining 5.6% of the vote.

During 1983–84 the Government suffered a series of domestic crises. There was disunity between the coalition partners over several questions of policy, while in November 1983 the deployment of US missiles in the FRG provoked a large-scale confrontation with the country's anti-nuclear movement. In May–June 1984 the Government faced the first major industrial conflict since 1978 when trade union demands for a shorter working week led to a seven-week strike in the engineering and metal industry, which brought the country's production of motor cars almost to a standstill. In July Dr Richard von Weizsäcker, the former Governing Mayor of West Berlin, became Federal President, succeeding Dr Karl Carstens.

In November 1984, following continuing differences within the coalition, Dr Kohl appointed Wolfgang Schäuble as Head of the Chancellery. The new post carried responsibility for the co-ordination of government policy, and its creation was seen as an attempt to improve the efficiency of the Government. Three important regional elections, which were considered to be vital mid-term tests for the Government, were held in 1985: in March the SPD won an absolute majority in Saarland, gaining control of the regional government for the first time; an election in West Berlin on the same day, however, led to a disappointing result for the SPD, as the CDU and FDP, the existing coalition partners in the city, increased their representation at the SPD's expense. In May the SPD won an overwhelming victory in the North Rhine-Westphalia local election. This result represented a personal victory for Johannes Rau, the local SPD leader, who in August 1986 was officially confirmed as the SPD's candidate for Chancellor at the 1987 general election.

Investigations into a long-running scandal over allegations of bribery and irregular political campaign funds, obtained from the Flick industrial holding company, led to the resignation in June 1984 of the Minister of Economics, Dr Otto Graf Lambsdorff, followed in October by that of Dr Rainer Barzel, President of the Bundestag; the 'Flick affair' threatened still wider repercussions, as it appeared to have undermined the credibility of the established political parties. Several leading politicians, including Dr Kohl, Willy Brandt and Franz Josef Strauss (Minister-President of Bavaria), appeared before an all-party committee of enquiry, and investigations suggested that the Flick concern had made illegal donations to all parties in the Bundestag, except the Green Party. In May 1986 the last two charges against Chancellor Kohl were withdrawn, because of insufficient evidence. In April the West Berlin Senate was restructured, when three of the city's senators resigned, following allegations of corruption.

The Government was encouraged by the results of three important local elections during 1986. In June the CDU lost its absolute majority in the Lower Saxony assembly, but retained control by forming a coalition with the FDP. This result also meant that the CDU majority in the Bundesrat (Federal Council) was preserved. In October the CSU retained control, as expected, in Bavaria, but the SPD lost some of its support to the Green Party, whose representatives entered the local parliament for the first time. At elections in November, for the city parliament in Hamburg (a traditional SPD stronghold), the SPD's share of the vote fell from 51.3% to 41.4%, while the CDU received 42.4%, the largest proportion of the vote. This result encouraged the Government coalition during the run-up to the general election of January 1987. The general election campaign was dominated by environmental issues, as the local elections had been. The nuclear accident at Chernobyl, in the USSR, in April 1986 had extensive environmental repercussions in the Federal Republic, and brought new emphasis to the controversial issue of nuclear power there. Anti-nuclear protests took place throughout the country, and in June Chancellor Kohl acknowledged public concern by creating a new ministry, of the Environment, Conservation and Reactor Safety.

Despite disunity between the coalition partners (principally the CSU and FDP) in late 1986, over the issue of proposed new legislation on law and order, the Government faced the forthcoming general election to the Bundestag with confidence, boosted by the strong economy. At the election, held on 25 January 1987, the CDU/CSU received 44.3% of the votes, 4.5% less than in 1983, while the FDP's share rose by 2.1%, to 9.1%. The SPD received 37% of votes cast, while the Green Party increased its share of support from 5.6% to 8.3%. The CDU/CSU/FDP coalition returned to power, although with a reduced majority.

During 1970 formal talks were conducted for the first time between the Federal Republic and the GDR, and there was a marked increase in diplomatic contacts between the Federal Republic and the other Communist countries of Europe. Treaties were signed with the USSR on the Renunciation of Force, and with Poland, recognizing the Oder/Neisse Line as the border between Germany (actually the GDR) and Poland. The Federal Republic also renounced German claims on the eastern territories of the old Reich. In 1971 the Quadripartite Agreement of the four powers on the position of West Berlin provided that there should be unimpeded access from the Federal Republic to West Berlin and that citizens of West Berlin should be allowed to visit the GDR. In 1972 the two German states concluded a Basic Treaty governing their relationship, and in September 1973 they became members of the United Nations. Between 1974 and 1979 Permanent Representative Missions were set up in Bonn and East Berlin, and access for West Germans to the GDR was made easier.

In October 1980, however, relations between the two countries deteriorated when the GDR Government raised the minimum exchange requirement for foreign visitors and renewed its demands for full diplomatic recognition by the FRG. The situation has since gradually improved, despite the second abrupt cancellation in two years by Erich Honecker, the GDR leader, of a proposed visit to the FRG. Inter-German relations suffered a set-back in August 1985, when a new espionage scandal emerged: several suspected GDR agents, including Bonn's senior counter-intelligence official, defected to the GDR, seriously undermining West German security. In 1986 relations with the GDR were again strained, when a large number of refugees, mainly from developing countries, were allowed by the GDR to cross into West Berlin. The issue was resolved in September, when the GDR agreed to restrict access for the refugees. In March 1986 Chancellor Kohl announced his Government's support for the USA's 'Strategic Defense Initiative' (SDI), a plan, first announced by President Ronald Reagan in March 1983, to assess the feasibility of creating a space-based 'shield' against attack by ballistic missiles. However, West German participation in SDI was to be restricted to low-level research, in an attempt to limit any damage to the Federal Republic's Ostpolitik.

Government

The Federal Republic is composed of 10 Länder (states) —each Land having its own constitution, parliament and government—plus West Berlin, which retains a separate status.

The country has a parliamentary regime, with a bicameral legislature. The Upper House is the Bundesrat (Federal Council), with 45 seats, including 41 members of Land governments (which appoint and recall them) and four representatives, with limited voting rights, appointed by the West Berlin Senate. The term of office of Bundesrat members varies with Land election dates. The Lower House, and the country's main legislative organ, is the Bundestag (Federal Assembly), with 519 deputies, including 497 elected for four years by universal adult suffrage (using a mixed system of proportional representation and direct voting) and 22 members, with limited voting rights, elected by the West Berlin House of Representatives.

Executive authority rests with the Federal Government, led by the Federal Chancellor, who is elected by an absolute majority of the Bundestag and appoints the other Ministers. The Federal President is elected by a Federal Convention (Bundesversammlung) which meets only for this purpose and consists of the Bundestag and an equal number of members elected by Land parliaments. The President is a constitutional Head of State with little influence on government.

Each Land has its own legislative assembly, with the right to pass laws except on matters which are the exclusive right of the Federal Government, such as defence, foreign affairs and finance. Education, police, culture and environmental protection are in the control of the Länder. Local responsibility for the execution of Federal and Land laws is undertaken by the city boroughs and counties.

Defence

The Federal Republic is a member of NATO. Conscription has been in force since 1956 and lasts for 15 months (to be extended to 18 months from 1989). In July 1986 the armed forces totalled 485,800, including 228,850 conscripts. The strength of the army stood at 340,800, including 181,300 conscripts. The navy numbered 36,300 (including 9,450 conscripts), and there were 108,700 in the air force (38,100 conscripts). Defence expenditure for 1986 was estimated at DM49,911m.

Economic Affairs

After the destruction caused by the Second World War, the Federal Republic, containing most of the principal industrial areas of Germany, made a remarkable economic recovery which was sustained over a number of years and has often been described as Germany's 'Wirtschaftswunder' (economic miracle). In 1984, according to estimates by the World Bank, the Federal Republic's gross national product (GNP) per head (at average 1982–84 prices) was US $11,130, having increased at an average rate of 2.7% annually, in real terms, since 1965. The average annual increase in overall gross domestic product (GDP), measured in constant prices, was 4.6% in 1965–73, slowing to 2.0% in 1973–84. West Germany is now one of the world's major economic powers, and its people enjoy a high standard of living.

The basis of the country's prosperity has been the industrial sector, which (with construction) provided 42.6% of gross domestic product (GDP) in 1985, compared with 53.5% in 1960. The principal manufacturing sectors are mechanical engineering, electrical engineering and electronics, vehicles, chemicals and food processing. The mechanical engineering industry is heavily export-oriented, with around two-thirds of output being sold abroad. High-technology industries are developing rapidly, especially micro-electronics, communications and computer industries, and traditional engineering products, such as machine tools and locomotives, have been largely overtaken in importance by the office and information equipment sector, which increased by 350% between 1970 and 1985. The chemical industry (particularly plastics and synthetic fibres) has shown steady growth in recent years, with output from the sector increasing by 7.3% in 1983 and 5.2% in 1984, and has been among the main contributors to the Federal Republic's economic growth since 1983. After experiencing recession in the early 1980s, the steel industry achieved an export-led recovery in 1984 and 1985, but output in 1986 was expected to fall by 6%, as exports again decreased. The manufacture of vehicles is very important; in 1985 output of cars increased by 10% over 1984, to reach 4.45m. vehicles, of which around 62% were exported. Industrial output as a whole increased by 3.2% in 1984, despite a protracted strike in the metal-working industry which adversely affected the year's output. In 1985 industrial output rose by 4.7%, but during 1986 output levelled off, and in October it fell for the third consecutive month, to 1.2% below its level of a year earlier. Agriculture contributed only 1.7% of GDP in 1985 (down from 5.8% in 1960) and employed just under 6% of the working population. In May 1986 the Government announced a new programme of farming subsidies, totalling DM 575m., which were intended partially to offset reductions in the price of some agricultural produce, as agreed by the EEC in April. The contribution of trade and transport to GDP has also declined (from 18.3% to 15.4% between 1960 and 1985), but that of other services (including restaurants and hotels) rose from 22.5% in 1960 to 40.2% in 1985.

The Federal Republic has relatively few natural resources; hard coal, lignite (low-grade brown coal) and salt are the only mineral deposits of any size. Mining of hard coal in the Ruhr area has been declining, with production falling from 87,146,000 metric tons in 1980 to 82,398,000 tons in 1985. The Government is strongly committed to the nuclear energy programme (which provided 32% of total electricity output in 1985), and has shifted its priorities away from coal production. Nuclear energy's share of total electricity output is expected to increase to 34.7% by the year 2000. A trade agreement on supplies of natural gas from the USSR, to meet some 30% of gas requirements, was signed in November 1981. Dependence on petroleum was expected to fall from 45% of energy requirements in 1982 to 41% in 1990.

The Federal Republic is the world's second largest exporter, after the USA, and regularly achieves a large trade surplus. In 1986, however, the Federal Republic was expected to replace the USA as the largest exporter, in US dollar terms, owing to the steep decline in the value of the dollar in relation to the Deutsche Mark. In 1984 the trade surplus reached a record DM 54,000m. (compared with DM 42,000m. in 1983), owing largely to an increase in demand from the US market. Since 1970 about 50% of trade has been with other EEC countries, especially the Netherlands and France, but in 1984, as the US dollar rose against the Deutsche Mark, German exports to the USA increased by 42.6%, making the USA West Germany's second most important foreign market (after France). This trend continued in 1985, when total imports rose by 6.8%, while exports increased by 10%. The trade surplus amounted to DM 73,600m. in 1985, and was expected to reach around DM 110,000m. in 1986, as the Federal Republic benefited from favourable terms of trade: advantageous exchange rates brought higher export prices, while the decline in international prices for commodities reduced the cost of imports, especially petroleum. The Federal Republic's current account registered a surplus of DM 17,700m. in 1984, and in 1985 this figure increased to DM 39,800m. As the surplus continued to rise during 1986, the Federal Republic came under increasing pressure from abroad (especially the USA) to adopt a more expansionist economic policy, in order to stimulate growth in the world market.

GNP increased by 2.4% in 1985, and was expected to grow by 3.4% in 1986, after recovering from a slight fall in the first quarter. During 1986 the stimulus for economic growth shifted from the export sector to the home market, as domestic demand increased by around 4%. The annual inflation rate averaged 2.2% in 1985, but continued to decline in 1986: by October the consumer price index had fallen by nearly 1% from the year before. Tax cuts which were introduced in January 1986 further boosted consumer spending.

Unemployment represents the Government's most pressing problem: the unemployment rate rose from 3.8% of the labour force in 1979 to 9.1% in 1983 and 1984. In 1985 the rate averaged 9.3%. By November 1986 2.1m. people were out of work (8.3% of the work-force). The construction industry was particularly badly affected, owing to large reductions in the public-sector construction programme. In response to the problem, the Government introduced legislation allowing workers to retire at 59 years of age, and encouraging employers to engage temporary workers, and also announced a scheme of repatriation grants to encourage some of the country's 4.7m. foreign workers (Gastarbeiter) to leave the FRG. The shipbuilding industry, faced with increasing competition from the Far East, has also been affected by unemployment: it was estimated in 1986 that one-quarter of the remaining 40,000 people employed in the sector (compared with 54,000 in 1982) would lose their jobs over the next few years. In October 1986 the Government announced a plan to allocate DM 420m. in regional aid to the shipbuilding areas, to provide alternative work on infrastructural projects.

Since taking office, the Kohl Government has adopted a stringent fiscal policy, and has reduced the federal budget deficit from DM 31,500m. to DM 22,700m. in 1985. The 1987 budget aimed to keep the growth in expenditure below 3%, for the fifth consecutive year. The Government has pledged to cut federal subsidies to industry, as part of its policy of reducing state involvement in the economy, and is also undertaking a controversial programme of 'privatization' of state enterprises. An income of DM 4,700m. is expected in 1987–88 from the sale of the government holding in various large companies (including the national airline, Lufthansa, the motor company Volkswagen, and other transport firms). The first stage of a two-part programme of tax cuts was implemented in 1986, with the second stage scheduled for 1988, in an attempt to strengthen domestic consumer demand and to boost economic growth.

Social Welfare

Social legislation has established comprehensive insurance cover for sickness, accidents, retirement, disability and unemployment. The insurance schemes for disability, retirement and unemployment are compulsory for all employees, and more than 80% of the population is covered. Insurance is administered by autonomous regional and local organizations. Pensions are the highest in Europe; the amount is based on contributions paid, is related to national average earnings and regularly adjusted. Sickness insurance pays for all medical attention and provides a benefit of 85% to 90% of the normal wage. There is no national health service, but in 1984 the country had 3,106 hospital establishments, with a total of 678,708 beds (equivalent to one for every 90 inhabitants). In 1984 there were 153,895 physicians working in the Federal Republic. About 35% of the expenditure of the Federal budget is allocated to social security payments.

Education

The Basic Law gives the control of education entirely to the Land governments. They do, however, co-operate quite closely to ensure a large degree of conformity in the system.

Education is compulsory for children aged six to 18 years. At least nine years of education must be full-time. Primary education is free, and grants are made for secondary education wherever fees are payable. Attendance at the Grundschule (elementary school) is obligatory for all children during the

FEDERAL REPUBLIC OF GERMANY

first four years of their school life, after which they go on to one of three other types of school. Approximately one-half of this age-group attend the Hauptschule (general school) for five or six years, after which they go into employment, but continue their education part-time for three years at a vocational school. Alternatively, pupils may attend the Realschule (intermediate school) for six years, or the Gymnasium (grammar school) for nine years. The Abitur (grammar school leaving certificate) is a necessary prerequisite for university education. In addition to the three main types of post-elementary school, all Länder have, mostly on an experimental basis, Gesamtschulen (comprehensive schools). In 1981 the total enrolment at primary and secondary schools was equivalent to 79% of the school-age population.

In the 1970s the Federal Republic's 48 universities and nine technical universities suffered a severe crisis of space. A university building programme, started in 1971, failed to keep up with demand and the number of students at universities and colleges rose from 585,000 in 1971 to 1,338,042 in 1985/86. Legislation now limits the length of study and numbers of students, especially in such subjects as medicine.

Tourism

Germany's tourist attractions include spas, summer and winter resorts, mountains, medieval towns and villages. The North Sea coast, the Rhine Valley, the Black Forest and Bavaria are the most popular areas. In 1985 there were around 1.8m. beds available for tourists. Overnight stays by foreign tourists totalled nearly 28m. in 1985, when the total number of foreign tourists visiting the Federal Republic was 12.6m.

Public Holidays

1987: 1 January (New Year's Day), 6 January (Epiphany)*, 2 March (Carnival/Rose Monday), 17 April (Good Friday), 20 April (Easter Monday), 1 May (Labour Day), 28 May (Ascension Day), 8 June (Whit Monday), 17 June (Day of German Unity, anniversary of 1953 uprising in the GDR), 18 June (Corpus Christi)*, 15 August (Assumption)*, 1 November (All Saints' Day)*, 18 November (Repentance Day), 25–26 December (Christmas).

1988: 1 January (New Year's Day), 6 January (Epiphany)*, 15 February (Carnival/Rose Monday), 1 April (Good Friday), 4 April (Easter Monday), 1 May (Labour Day), 12 May (Ascension Day), 23 May (Whit Monday), 2 June (Corpus Christi)*, 17 June (Day of German Unity, anniversary of 1953 uprising in the GDR), 15 August (Assumption)*, 1 November (All Saints' Day)*, 16 November (Repentance Day), 25–26 December (Christmas).

* Religious holidays observed in certain Länder only.

Weights and Measures

The metric system is in force.

Currency and Exchange Rates

100 Pfennige = 1 Deutsche Mark.

Exchange rates (30 September 1986):
  £1 sterling = 2.9325 DM;
  US $1 = 2.027 DM.

FEDERAL REPUBLIC OF GERMANY

Statistical Survey

Source (unless otherwise stated): Statistisches Bundesamt, 6200 Wiesbaden 1, Gustav-Stresemann-Ring 11, Postfach 5528; tel. (06121) 7051; telex 4-86511.
(All statistical data relate to the Federal Republic of Germany, including West Berlin, except where indicated.)

Area and Population

AREA, POPULATION AND DENSITY

Area (sq km)	248,717*
Population (census results)	
6 June 1961	56,174,826
27 May 1970	
Males	28,866,724
Females	31,783,875
Total	60,650,599
Population (official estimates at mid-year)	
1983	61,420,700
1984	61,181,100
1985	61,015,300
Density (per sq km) at mid-1985	245

* 96,030 sq miles.

BIRTHS, MARRIAGES AND DEATHS (Federal Republic)

	Registered live births Number	Rate (per 1,000)	Registered marriages Number	Rate (per 1,000)	Registered deaths Number	Rate (per 1,000)
1978	576,468	9.4	328,215	5.4	723,218	11.8
1979	581,984	9.5	344,823	5.6	711,732	11.6
1980	620,657	10.1	362,408	5.9	714,117	11.6
1981	624,557	10.1	359,658	5.8	722,192	11.7
1982	621,173	10.1	361,966	5.9	715,857	11.6
1983	594,177	9.7	369,963	6.0	718,337	11.7
1984	584,157	9.5	364,140	5.9	696,118	11.3
1985*	586,155	9.6	364,684	6.0	704,296	11.5

* Provisional figures.

PRINCIPAL TOWNS (estimated population at 30 June 1985)

West Berlin	1,852,700	Gelsenkirchen	286,500
Hamburg	1,585,900	Münster	273,000
München (Munich)	1,266,100	Karlsruhe	268,400
Köln (Cologne)	919,300	Wiesbaden	267,000
Essen	622,000	Mönchengladbach	255,100
Frankfurt am Main	598,000	Braunschweig	
Dortmund	575,200	(Brunswick)	250,700
Düsseldorf	563,000	Kiel	245,300
Stuttgart	561,200	Augsburg	244,200
Bremen	528,900	Aachen (Aix-la-Chapelle)	239,200
Duisburg	520,200	Oberhausen	223,000
Hannover (Hanover)	510,800	Krefeld	217,000
Nürnberg (Nuremberg)	466,100	Lübeck	211,000
Bochum	383,200	Hagen	206,700
Wuppertal	378,100	Mainz	188,200
Bielefeld	300,800	Saarbrücken	187,600
Mannheim	295,200	Kassel	184,500
Bonn (capital)	292,600	Freiburg im Breisgau	182,200

EMPLOYMENT
(civilian labour force employed, '000)

	1982	1983	1984
Agriculture, hunting, forestry and fishing	1,381	1,372	1,370
Mining and quarrying	329	323	318
Manufacturing	8,318	8,007	7,923
Electricity, gas and water	248	245	240
Construction	1,826	1,783	1,773
Trade, restaurants and hotels	3,775	3,706	3,717
Transport, storage and communications	1,538	1,517	1,502
Financing, insurance, real estate and business services	1,569	1,584	1,596
Community, social and personal services	6,116	6,153	6,210
Total	25,100	24,690	24,649
Males	15,408	15,116	15,074
Females	9,692	9,574	9,575

Source: ILO, *Year Book of Labour Statistics*.

STATES (30 June 1985)

	Area (sq km)	Population ('000)	Density (per sq km)	Capital	Population of capital ('000)
Schleswig-Holstein	15,726.7	2,613.7	166	Kiel	245.3
Hamburg	754.7	1,585.9	2,101	Hamburg	1,585.9
Niedersachsen (Lower Saxony)	47,450.0	7,203.5	152	Hannover (Hanover)	510.8
Bremen	404.2	663.4	1,641	Bremen	528.9
Nordrhein-Westfalen (North Rhine-Westphalia)	34,067.9	16,684.4	490	Düsseldorf	563.0
Hessen (Hesse)	21,114.1	5,530.6	262	Wiesbaden	267.0
Rheinland-Pfalz (Rhineland-Palatinate)	19,847.2	3,619.2	182	Mainz	188.2
Baden-Württemberg	35,751.4	9,252.6	259	Stuttgart	561.2
Bayern (Bavaria)	70,552.9	10,961.0	155	München (Munich)	1,266.1
Saarland	2,567.9	1,048.3	408	Saarbrücken	187.6
West Berlin	480.1	1,852.7	3,859	West Berlin	1,852.7
Total	248,717.2	61,015.3	245	Bonn	292.6

FEDERAL REPUBLIC OF GERMANY

Agriculture

PRINCIPAL CROPS ('000 metric tons)

	1983	1984	1985
Wheat	8,998	10,223	9,866
Rye	1,599	1,931	1,821
Barley	8,944	10,284	9,691
Oats	2,068	2,507	2,807
Maize	934	1,026	1,204
Mixed grain	469	518	527
Sugar beets	16,295	20,060	20,813
Potatoes	6,299	8,050	8,704
Rapeseed	599	662	803
Cabbages	412	517	602
Carrots	119	149	173
Grapes	1,739	1,145*	780*
Apples	1,313	1,799	1,500
Pears	380	449	335
Plums	379	488	481
Currants	130	134	n.a.

* Unofficial estimate.

LIVESTOCK ('000 head at December)

	1983	1984	1985
Horses	353.6	370.2	n.a.
Cattle	15,551.9	15,688.0	15,626.6
Pigs	23,449.3	23,616.8	24,282.1
Sheep	1,217.8	1,299.6	1,295.8
Chickens	75,088.2	78,708.2	71,057.1
Geese	352.5	377.1	346.4
Ducks	956.2	1,087.1	1,382.5
Turkeys	1,907.5	2,122.4	2,209.5

LIVESTOCK PRODUCTS ('000 metric tons)

	1982	1983	1984
Beef and veal	1,432.4	1,447.7	1,567.1
Mutton and lamb	27.0	27.9	27.2
Pig meat	3,150	3,218	3,232
Poultry meat	395	358	365*
Edible offals	302	308	320
Lard	407	418	422
Tallow	74	74	81
Cows' milk	25,464.9	26,913.2	26,151.1
Butter[1]	555.6	627.2	572.2
Cheese[1,2]	839.1	846.7	878.2
Hen eggs	787	782	800*

* FAO estimate.
[1] Excluding West Berlin.
[2] Factory production only. Total production (in '000 metric tons) was: 840.1 in 1982; 847.7 in 1983.

Source: Mainly FAO, *Production Yearbook*.

Forestry

ROUNDWOOD REMOVALS
('000 cubic metres, excluding bark)

	1982	1983	1984
Industrial wood	26,805	24,360	22,978
Fuel wood	4,200	3,800	3,800*
Total	31,005	28,160	26,778

* FAO estimate.
Source: FAO, *Yearbook of Forest Products*.

SAWNWOOD PRODUCTION
('000 cubic metres, including boxboards)

	1982	1983	1984
Coniferous (softwood)	7,038	7,818	8,321
Broadleaved (hardwood)	1,557	1,488	1,602
Total	8,595	9,306	9,923

Railway sleepers ('000 cu metres): 119 in 1982; 107 in 1983; 93 in 1984.

Fishing

('000 metric tons, live weight)

	1983	1984	1985
Deep-sea trawlers and luggers	161.7	151.6	103.0
Others	111.9	141.6	87.7
Total	273.6	293.2	190.7

Mining

('000 metric tons)

	1983	1984	1985
Hard coal	82,202	79,426	82,398
Brown coal	124,281	126,739	120,667
Iron ore*	279	293	309
Crude petroleum	4,116	4,055	4,105

* Metal content.

Industry

SELECTED PRODUCTS

		1983	1984	1985
Electricity	million kWh	373,813	394,884	409,000
Manufactured gas from gas works	terajoules	76,066	n.a.	n.a.
Manufactured gas from cokeries	terajoules	186,433	n.a.	n.a.
Hard coal briquettes	'000 metric tons	1,244	1,437	1,511
Hard coal coke	'000 metric tons	22,425	20,586	22,331
Brown coal briquettes	'000 metric tons	3,568	3,818	4,068
Pig-iron	'000 metric tons	26,598	30,203	31,531
Steel ingots	'000 metric tons	35,346	38,991	38,794
Motor spirit (petrol)	'000 metric tons	20,104	20,074	20,387
Diesel oil	'000 metric tons	11,676	11,842	11,637
Cement	'000 metric tons	30,466	28,909	25,758
Potash (K_2O)	'000 metric tons	2,419	2,645	2,583
Sulphuric acid	'000 metric tons	3,543	3,518	3,428
Soda ash	'000 metric tons	1,218	1,364	1,412
Caustic soda	'000 metric tons	3,350	3,611	3,697
Chlorine	'000 metric tons	3,136	3,426	3,493
Nitrogenous fertilizers (N)	'000 metric tons	1,071	1,172	1,161
Phosphatic fertilizers (P_2O_5)	'000 metric tons	547	519	490
Artificial resins, plastics	'000 metric tons	7,100	7,505	7,666
Primary aluminium (unwrought)	'000 metric tons	743	777	745
Refined copper (unwrought)	'000 metric tons	420.3	n.a.	n.a.
Zinc (unwrought)	'000 metric tons	349.7	n.a.	n.a.
Refined lead (unwrought)	'000 metric tons	261.5	n.a.	n.a.
Rubber tyres	'000	37,878	39,253	40,475
Wool yarn	'000 metric tons	46	49	42
Cotton yarn	'000 metric tons	n.a.	n.a.	131
Machine tools	'000 metric tons	312	300	336
Agricultural machinery	'000 metric tons	364	366	372
Textile machinery	'000 metric tons	140	189	202
Passenger cars and minibuses	'000	3,568	3,505	3,867
Motor cycles	'000	139	119	n.a.
Bicycles	'000	3,334	3,024	2,891
Radio receivers	'000	3,292	3,031	3,376
Television receivers	'000	4,705	3,917	3,738
Clocks and watches	'000	27,643	30,682	33,979
Footwear	'000 pairs	91,717	89,826	83,504
Cameras	'000	1,427	1,126	863
Dwellings completed	number	312,217	366,816	n.a.

FEDERAL REPUBLIC OF GERMANY

Statistical Survey

Finance

CURRENCY AND EXCHANGE RATES

Monetary Units
100 Pfennige = 1 Deutsche Mark (DM).

Denominations
Coins: 1, 2, 5, 10 and 50 Pfennige; 1, 2, 5 and 10 DM.
Notes: 5, 10, 20, 50, 100, 500 and 1,000 DM.

Sterling and Dollar Equivalents (30 September 1986)
£1 sterling = 2.9325 DM;
US $1 = 2.027 DM;
100 DM = £34.10 = $49.33.

Average Exchange Rate (DM per US $)
1983 2.5533
1984 2.8459
1985 2.9440

INTERNATIONAL RESERVES*
(US $ million at 31 December)

	1983	1984	1985
Gold†	5,026	4,349	5,562
IMF special drawing rights	1,613	1,362	1,547
Reserve position in IMF	3,748	3,750	3,808
Foreign exchange	37,313	35,028	39,025
Total	47,700	44,489	49,942

* Data on gold and foreign exchange holdings exclude deposits made with the European Monetary Co-operation Fund.
† National valuation.
Source: IMF, *International Financial Statistics*.

MONEY SUPPLY (million DM at 31 December)

	1983	1984	1985
Currency outside banks	96,428	99,804	103,870

COST OF LIVING (Consumer Price Index. Base: 1980 = 100)

	1983	1984	1985
Food	114.3	116.0	116.9
Clothes and shoes	113.0	115.7	118.4
Rent	115.6	120.0	123.9
Energy	124.5	128.8	133.4
Furniture, domestic appliances and other household expenses	113.7	115.9	117.7
Transport and communications	117.1	120.1	123.2
Health	115.6	118.0	119.7
Entertainment and culture	111.4	114.2	116.2
Personal expenses	118.5	120.8	125.7
Total	115.6	118.4	121.0

BUDGET* (million DM)

Revenue	1983	1984	1985
Current receipts	480,887	502,905	530,517
Taxes and similar revenue	383,477	401,022	422,943
Income from economic activity	36,544	37,976	40,885
Interest	4,213	3,040	3,410
Allocations and grants for current purposes	90,313	95,830	99,701
Other receipts	49,640	52,082	54,213
Less Deductible payments on the same level	83,300	87,045	90,635
Capital receipts	18,551	17,476	17,305
Sale of property	6,570	6,600	5,317
Loans and grants for investment	25,745	25,660	25,470
Repayment of loans	7,702	7,375	8,596
Public sector borrowing	2,158	2,370	2,785
Less Deductible payments on the same level	23,624	24,529	24,863
Total	499,438	520,381	547,822

Expenditure	1983	1984	1985
Current expenditure	461,667	473,161	491,697
Personnel expenses	181,323	184,293	190,682
Goods and services	88,586	92,799	96,498
Interest	51,438	53,684	56,222
Allocations and grants for current purposes	223,620	229,429	238,930
Less Deductible payments on the same level	83,300	87,045	90,635
Capital expenditure	92,388	92,805	94,215
Construction	37,280	36,195	36,926
Purchase of property	10,626	11,142	12,574
Allocations and grants for investment	45,929	44,064	44,010
Loans	17,377	20,763	20,329
Sale of shares	3,484	3,821	3,793
Repayment expenses in the public sector	1,316	1,349	1,446
Less Deductible payments on the same level	23,624	24,529	24,863
Total	554,055	565,966	585,912

* Figures represent a consolidation of the accounts of all public authorities, including the Federal Government and state administrations.

FEDERAL REPUBLIC OF GERMANY — Statistical Survey

NATIONAL ACCOUNTS (million DM at current prices, excluding trade with the GDR)

National Income and Product

	1983	1984	1985
Compensation of employees	918,490	950,470	986,870
Operating surplus*	357,680	387,060	419,820
Domestic factor incomes	1,276,170	1,337,530	1,406,690
Consumption of fixed capital	210,760	220,720	230,270
Gross domestic product at factor cost	1,486,930	1,558,250	1,636,960
Indirect taxes	214,450	226,310	229,820
Less Subsidies	31,820	36,420	36,350
GDP in purchasers' values	1,669,560	1,748,140	1,830,430
Factor income from abroad	40,940	47,320	49,390
Less Factor income paid abroad	36,400	38,560	41,920
Gross national product	1,674,100	1,756,900	1,837,900
Less Consumption of fixed capital	210,760	220,720	230,270
National income in market prices	1,463,340	1,536,180	1,607,630
Other current transfers from abroad	13,310	12,910	12,900
Less Other current transfers paid abroad	39,640	44,820	44,890
National disposable income	1,437,010	1,504,270	1,575,640

* Obtained as a residual.

Expenditure on the Gross Domestic Product

	1983	1984	1985
Government final consumption expenditure	336,530	350,490	365,730
Private final consumption expenditure	958,540	990,300	1,027,290
Increase in stocks	−2,000	11,200	14,200
Gross fixed capital formation	344,120	354,580	359,320
Total domestic expenditure	1,637,190	1,706,570	1,766,540
Exports of goods and services	485,430	541,020	598,010
Less Imports of goods and services	453,060	499,450	534,120
GDP in purchasers' values	1,669,560	1,748,140	1,830,430
GDP at constant 1980 prices	1,489,550	1,531,390	1,569,740

Gross Domestic Product by Economic Activity

	1983	1984	1985
Agriculture and livestock	28,500 ⎫	34,800	30,870
Forestry and fishing	3,910 ⎭		
Mining[1]	17,420 ⎫	66,130	71,010
Electricity, gas and water	45,270 ⎭		
Manufacturing[1,2,3]	524,480	549,200	595,770
Construction[2]	97,190	99,960	93,290
Wholesale and retail trade	158,280	166,790	170,940
Transport, storage and communications	96,510	99,520	103,690
Finance, insurance and dwellings[4]	203,950	214,750	225,020
Restaurants and hotels	21,340 ⎫	233,900	247,980
Community, social and personal services[3,5]	200,230 ⎭		
Less Imputed bank service charges	81,480	83,680	85,350
Domestic product of industries	1,315,600	1,381,370	1,453,220
Government services	195,790	200,030	207,570
Private non-profit services to households	31,190	32,780 ⎫	36,580
Domestic services of households	1,480	1,530 ⎭	
Sub-total	1,544,060	1,615,710	1,697,370
Non-deductible sales tax	109,390	116,160	116,460
Import duties	16,110	16,270	16,600
GDP in purchasers' values	1,669,560	1,748,140	1,830,430

[1] Quarrying is included in manufacturing.
[2] Structural steel erection is included in manufacturing.
[3] Publishing is included in community, social and personal services.
[4] Including imputed rents of owner-occupied dwellings.
[5] Business services and real estate, except dwellings, are included in community, social and personal services.

BALANCE OF PAYMENTS (million DM)

	1982	1983	1984
Merchandise exports f.o.b.	412,920	417,641	467,053
Merchandise imports f.o.b.	−348,182	−358,245	−400,738
Trade Balance	64,738	59,396	66,315
Exports of services	116,052	117,240	129,527
Imports of services	−144,467	−139,117	−146,422
Balance of goods and services	36,323	37,519	49,420
Unrequited transfers:			
Foreign workers' remittances*	−7,550	−7,500	−7,900
Other private transfers (net)	−4,342	−4,418	−4,020
Government transfers (net)	−16,231	−15,093	−19,694
Current balance	8,201	10,507	17,807
Long-term capital (net):			
Private	−19,052	−12,519	−12,395
Government	4,842	5,107	−2,634
Short-term capital (net):			
Private	1,510	−7,222	−14,650
Government	737	−3,263	−1,780
Net errors and omissions	−1,249	1,541	10,499
Total (net monetary movements)	−5,011	−5,849	−3,153

* Estimates.

DEVELOPMENT AID (public and private development aid to developing countries and multilateral agencies, million DM)

	1983	1984	1985
Public development co-operation	8,116	7,916	8,657
Bilateral	5,368	5,315	5,826
Multilateral	2,748	2,601	2,831
Other public transactions	1,541	2,831	2,699
Bilateral	1,523	2,859	2,731
Multilateral	18	−28	−32
Private development aid	947	1,088	1,247
Other private transactions	7,300	6,681	4,314
Bilateral	6,244	5,722	3,194
Multilateral	1,056	959	1,120
Total	17,904	18,516	16,917

FEDERAL REPUBLIC OF GERMANY   *Statistical Survey*

External Trade

Note: Figures include trade in second-hand ships, and stores and bunkers for foreign ships and aircraft. Imports also exclude military supplies under the off-shore procurement programme and exports exclude war reparations and restitutions, except exports resulting from the Israel Reparations Agreement. Official figures exclude trade with the German Democratic Republic, which is compiled separately (see table below).

PRINCIPAL COMMODITIES (distribution by SITC, million DM)

Imports c.i.f.	1983	1984	1985
Food and live animals	38,554.8	41,948.8	44,320.2
Meat and meat preparations	5,253.5	5,472.5	5,845.0
Fresh, chilled or frozen meat	4,499.3	4,723.9	n.a.
Dairy products and birds' eggs	4,204.2	4,134.4	4,422.5
Cereals and cereal preparations	3,108.4	3,395.4	4,373.9
Vegetables and fruit	12,171.5	13,573.1	13,759.8
Fresh and dried fruit and nuts (excl. oil nuts)	4,703.4	5,115.8	n.a.
Coffee, tea, cocoa and spices	5,973.1	7,489.9	8,244.9
Coffee and coffee substitutes	3,945.5	4,673.3	n.a.
Animal feeding stuff (excl. cereals)	4,163.2	4,012.2	3,354.1
Beverages and tobacco	4,209.4	4,113.5	4,602.2
Crude materials (inedible) except fuels	27,116.4	31,006.2	31,881.1
Oilseeds and oleaginous fruit	3,710.7	3,729.9	4,382.2
Cork and wood	3,065.4	2,986.0	2,579.2
Metalliferous ores and metal scrap	7,043.9	8,745.3	9,236.6
Mineral fuels, lubricants, etc.	82,690.6	88,533.9	92,181.9
Petroleum, petroleum products, etc.	64,304.8	69,393.0	70,956.9
Crude petroleum oils, etc.	37,771.3	41,663.0	n.a.
Refined petroleum products	24,708.7	25,822.0	n.a.
Motor spirit and other light oils	8,516.3	8,271.7	n.a.
Gas oils	10,294.9	10,903.4	n.a.
Gas (natural and manufactured)	15,452.4	16,387.3	18,010.4
Petroleum gases, etc. in the gaseous state	14,978.0	15,918.1	n.a.
Animal and vegetable oils, fats and waxes	1,858.7	2,954.8	2,754.7
Chemicals and related products	31,882.6	37,082.4	41,259.6
Organic chemicals	9,113.7	10,502.6	11,735.3
Inorganic chemicals	4,080.5	5,138.9	5,697.9
Artificial resins and plastic materials, etc.	8,237.6	9,606.4	10,512.6
Basic manufactures	63,447.5	71,258.6	74,921.5
Paper, paperboard and manufactures	6,900.0	8,210.4	8,662.7
Paper and paperboard (not cut to size or shape)	5,693.2	6,856.3	n.a.
Textile yarn, fabrics, etc.	12,925.6	14,089.1	14,972.5
Non-metallic mineral manufactures	6,047.6	6,381.2	6,189.1
Iron and steel	13,121.2	14,273.1	16,005.6
Non-ferrous metals	10,460.7	12,970.0	12,838.6
Other metal manufactures	6,575.2	7,206.7	7,788.9
Machinery and transport equipment	85,094.9	95,109.8	105,954.4
Power generating machinery and equipment	5,417.1	6,106.4	7,059.8
Machinery specialized for particular industries (excl. metalworking)	5,950.9	6,395.4	7,479.9
General industrial machinery, equipment and parts	8,780.3	9,654.9	10,933.6
Office machines and automatic data processing equipment	10,563.6	13,507.4	16,343.9
Telecommunications and sound equipment	7,326.0	8,013.0	8,282.2
Other electrical machinery, apparatus and appliances	13,847.7	17,446.1	19,329.1
Road vehicles (incl. air-cushion vehicles) and parts[1]	19,360.2	20,480.8	21,838.9
Passenger motor cars (excl. buses)	11,449.7	12,298.9	n.a.
Motor vehicle parts and accessories[1]	5,182.7	5,498.4	n.a.
Other transport equipment	11,968.4	11,441.4	11,922.6
Aircraft and associated equipment	11,159.2	10,453.6	n.a.
Miscellaneous manufactured articles	43,721.5	49,553.2	52,904.4
Furniture and parts	3,233.7	3,540.9	3,634.9
Articles of apparel and clothing accessories (excl. footwear)	17,098.4	19,777.4	20,562.0
Footwear	3,979.1	4,461.9	4,804.4
Professional, scientific and controlling instruments, etc.	4,608.4	5,362.7	6,204.1
Photographic apparatus, optical goods, watches and clocks	4,139.6	4,491.3	5,139.1
Other commodities and transactions[2]	11,615.5	12,695.8	13,031.1
Special transactions[3]	8,878.1	9,627.9	n.a.
Total[2]	390,192.0	434,256.9	463,811.0

[1] Excluding tyres, engines and electrical parts.
[2] Including monetary gold (million DM): 476.2 in 1983; 429.2 in 1984.
[3] Including government imports. Also included are returns and replacements, not allocated to their appropriate headings.

FEDERAL REPUBLIC OF GERMANY — Statistical Survey

Exports f.o.b.	1983	1984	1985
Food and live animals	18,886.2	20,925.4	21,540.6
Dairy products and birds' eggs	4,821.1	5,316.5	5,292.5
Beverages and tobacco	2,836.4	3,097.8	3,510.9
Crude materials (inedible) except fuels	8,100.1	9,806.6	10,727.9
Mineral fuels, lubricants, etc.	14,630.9	16,104.8	15,284.1
Coal, coke and briquettes	3,851.2	4,869.6	4,360.1
Petroleum, petroleum products, etc.	6,370.8	6,809.1	6,850.7
Animal and vegetable oils, fats and waxes	1,732.9	2,570.7	2,795.3
Chemicals and related products	56,696.9	66,261.9	71,143.3
Organic chemicals	15,309.9	18,157.8	19,158.0
Inorganic chemicals	4,877.4	5,965.4	6,132.9
Dyeing, tanning and colouring materials	5,516.0	6,101.3	6,619.2
Medicinal and pharmaceutical products	5,424.8	6,126.7	6,938.8
Artificial resins and plastic materials, etc.	13,909.2	16,340.5	17,673.3
Basic manufactures	80,119.7	91,117.3	100,311.3
Rubber manufactures	3,635.5	4,035.9	4,465.8
Paper, paperboard and manufactures	7,429.5	9,037.0	10,152.4
Textile yarn, fabrics, etc.	13,926.4	16,073.5	17,836.3
Non-metallic mineral manufactures	7,471.9	8,063.2	8,858.3
Iron and steel	20,346.6	24,079.0	27,510.2
Bars, rods, angles, shapes and sections	2,659.2	3,151.4	n.a.
Universals, plates and sheets	6,087.2	6,866.7	n.a.
Tubes, pipes and fittings	5,710.7	6,296.5	n.a.
Non-ferrous metals	9,532.6	10,924.3	10,883.2
Other metal manufactures	14,080.7	14,885.7	16,398.2
Machinery and transport equipment	196,370.9	218,802.2	246,715.2
Power generating machinery and equipment	12,530.7	13,940.4	14,796.2
Internal combustion piston engines and parts	6,546.0	7,173.8	n.a.
Machinery specialized for particular industries (excl. metalworking)	25,366.7	28,536.9	33,127.7
Textile and leather machinery	4,980.6	5,880.3	n.a.
Metalworking machinery	7,024.8	7,155.7	8,059.9
Machine-tools for working metal, etc.	5,723.6	5,859.2	n.a.
General industrial machinery and equipment	25,861.9	28,443.3	32,748.5
Mechanical handling equipment	3,882.6	4,035.7	n.a.
Office machines and automatic data processing equipment	9,248.0	11,114.1	14,168.4
Telecommunications and sound equipment	7,997.5	8,964.1	10,022.7
Other electrical machinery, apparatus and appliances	23,429.7	27,023.9	30,582.1
Switchgear, etc.	5,574.1	6,225.3	n.a.
Road vehicles (incl. air-cushion vehicles) and parts[1]	67,959.8	74,754.9	86,392.8
Passenger motor cars (excl. buses)	41,410.8	47,097.1	n.a.
Motor vehicles for goods transport, etc.	6,924.5	6,052.2	n.a.
Goods vehicles	5,758.7	5,193.3	n.a.
Motor vehicle parts and accessories[1]	15,331.0	17,080.7	n.a.
Other transport equipment	12,404.5	14,514.1	12,946.9
Miscellaneous manufactured articles	40,489.5	46,385.8	53,625.2
Furniture and parts	4,238.0	4,721.9	5,396.8
Articles of apparel and clothing accessories (excl. footwear)	6,453.8	7,399.1	8,381.0
Professional scientific and controlling instruments, etc.	8,928.4	10,459.1	12,508.4
Measuring, checking, analysing and controlling instruments	6,379.6	7,545.6	n.a.
Photographic apparatus, optical goods, watches and clocks	4,743.5	5,432.4	6,138.3
Other commodities and transactions[2]	12,417.6	13,150.5	11,510.3
Special transactions[3]	10,527.4	10,907.8	n.a.
Total[2]	432,281.1	488,223.0	537,164.2

[1] Excluding tyres, engines and electrical parts.
[2] Including monetary gold (million DM): 341.9 in 1983; 402.6 in 1984.
[3] Including returns and replacements, not allocated to their appropriate headings.

FEDERAL REPUBLIC OF GERMANY

PRINCIPAL TRADING PARTNERS*
(million DM, including gold)

Imports c.i.f.	1983	1984	1985
Algeria	3,167.2	2,797.5	4,111.8
Austria	12,603.7	13,726.9	15,350.5
Belgium/Luxembourg	28,092.6	28,833.8	29,112.0
Brazil	4,310.1	5,547.2	6,365.4
Canada	3,316.8	4,056.5	3,845,5
Denmark	6,983.2	7,111.0	8,017.7
Finland	3,626.1	4,386.5	4,295.0
France	44,566.8	45,839.6	49,279.8
Greece	2,751.0	3,078.9	3,259.2
Hong Kong	3,564.7	3,958.9	3,709.2
Ireland	2,193.5	2,666.1	3,141.5
Italy	31,570.2	34,173.1	37,154.8
Japan	14,819.1	18,306.2	20,719.8
Libya	6,316.5	6,166.1	6,274.7
Netherlands	48,143.0	53,047.0	58,277.1
Nigeria	4,677.0	6,237.4	6,343.1
Norway	10,808.5	10,545.5	11,006.6
Poland	2,184.0	2,766.2	3,080.4
Saudi Arabia	4,000.9	2,828.3	2,185.6
South Africa	2,741.8	2,973.5	3,162.7
Spain	5,793.7	7,018.4	7,672.1
Sweden	8,427.6	9,929.3	10,870.0
Switzerland	13,971.4	15,636.3	17,164.3
Taiwan	2,556.7	2,991.7	2,968.7
Turkey	1,837.4	2,485.0	2,907.7
USSR	11,788.4	14,391.6	13,628.5
United Kingdom	27,137.7	33,285.5	37,163.9
USA	27,711.7	31,097.2	32,341.5
Venezuela	3,114.3	2,746.1	3,494.2
Yugoslavia	3,555.2	4,120.7	4,773.8
Total (incl. others)	390,192.0	434,256.9	463,811.0

Exports f.o.b.	1983	1984	1985
Argentina	3,056.2	2,225.7	1,463.7
Australia	2,762.7	3,691.4	4,587.2
Austria	22,123.3	24,333.8	27,394.6
Belgium/Luxembourg	31,849.4	34,017.6	36,967.2
Canada	3,103.8	4,320.6	5,474.6
China, People's Repub.	2,751.5	2,975.2	6,428.8
Denmark	8,582.8	10,029.5	11,810.2
Egypt	2,952.1	3,213.9	3,149.9
Finland	4,185.7	4,748.8	5,547.2
France	55,563.8	61,336.2	64,000.8
Greece	4,612.7	4,945.9	5,454.3
Hungary	2,439.0	2,743.7	3,062.6
India	2,117.2	2,621.8	3,377.3
Iran	7,720.5	6,524.1	4,841.7
Iraq	3,684.4	2,449.3	2,452.4
Italy	32,088.0	37,663.0	41,794.9
Japan	5,602.8	6,918.2	7,888.4
Netherlands	37,857.3	42,124.9	46,254.5
Norway	5,027.4	5,484.2	6,797.3
Saudi Arabia	7,606.3	6,306.9	5,235.4
South Africa	4,982.0	6,648.7	4,997.2
Spain	7,587.1	8,629.8	9,755.8
Sweden	11,271.1	12,975.6	14,733.6
Switzerland	22,376.0	25,872.1	28,855.7
Turkey	2,970.4	3,390.1	4,212.4
USSR	11,244.8	10,766.8	10,527.2
United Kingdom	35,400.9	40,579.4	45,967.4
USA	32,847.0	46,834.3	55,533.4
Yugoslavia	5,140.0	5,512.9	6,215.1
Total (incl. others)	432,281.1	488,223.0	537,164.2

* Imports by country of production; exports by country of consumption. Totals exclude trade with the German Democratic Republic (see below). The distribution by countries excludes stores and bunkers for ships and aircraft (million DM): Imports 251.5 in 1983, 234.0 in 1984, 280.9 in 1985; Exports 1,377.8 in 1983, 1,505.8 in 1984, 1,629.5 in 1985.

TRADE WITH THE GERMAN DEMOCRATIC REPUBLIC (million DM)

	1983	1984	1985
Purchases	6,878	7,744	7,636
Deliveries	6,947	6,408	7,903

FEDERAL REPUBLIC OF GERMANY

Transport

FEDERAL RAILWAYS (million)

	1983	1984	1985*
Passengers	1,124	1,105	1,103
Passenger-km	39,097	39,575	41,202
Freight net ton-km	57,334	61,471	65,443

* Provisional figures.

ROAD TRAFFIC ('000 licensed vehicles at July each year)

	1983	1984	1985
Passenger cars	24,580.5	25,217.8	25,844.5
Lorries	1,277.5	1,277.9	1,280.8
Buses	71.3	70.3	69.4
Motor cycles	1,243.0	1,355.6	1,406.9
Trailers	1,592.3	1,677.7	1,763.2

CIVIL AVIATION (million)

	1982	1983	1984
Kilometres flown	538	551	584
Passenger-km	64,038	67,072	73,280
Freight ton-km	2,597	2,884	3,276
Mail ton-km	231	246	274

SHIPPING
Inland Waterways

	1983	1984	1985*
Freight ton-km (million)	49,087	51,996	48,183

* Provisional figure.

Sea-borne Shipping

	1982	1983	1984
Merchant fleet (gross registered tons)*	6,671,196	6,308,017	5,932,694
Vessels entered ('000 net registered tons)†			
Domestic (coastwise)	16,702	15,189	15,036
International	139,486	135,040	136,819
Vessels cleared ('000 net registered tons)†			
Domestic	16,108	14,907	14,979
International	119,300	115,983	119,243
Freight unloaded ('000 metric tons)‡			
International	88,864	81,178	84,984
Freight loaded ('000 metric tons)‡			
International	42,975	40,855	43,601
Total domestic freight ('000 metric tons)	5,209	4,242	4,105

* Vessels of more than 100 grt at 31 December.
† Loaded vessels only.
‡ Including transhipments.

Tourism

FOREIGN TOURIST ARRIVALS

Country of Residence	1983	1984	1985
Austria	403,149	426,294	450,574
Belgium and Luxembourg	403,948	454,708	458,593
Canada	129,221	193,400	205,038
Denmark	469,189	550,178	614,839
France	508,761	617,894	651,717
Italy	454,419	512,886	542,130
Japan	354,876	410,296	488,582
Netherlands	1,559,521	1,699,965	1,706,906
Norway	192,007	210,794	266,705
Spain	140,622	166,108	188,199
Sweden	465,355	565,420	611,682
Switzerland	465,690	511,249	544,827
United Kingdom	969,644	1,142,233	1,179,126
USA	1,827,080	2,498,993	2,630,553
Total (incl. others)	9,829,617	11,866,420	12,605,695

Communications Media

	1982	1983	1984
Radio receivers in use	24,158,000	24,299,855	24,856,997
Television receivers in use	21,834,000	21,959,483	22,340,623
Telephones	31,370,000	35,137,000	36,582,000
Book titles	61,332	60,598	51,733
Daily newspaper circulation	25,882,000	25,834,000	26,800,000

1985: Telephones 37,899,000.

Education

	Institutions 1984	Institutions 1985	Teachers 1984	Students ('000) 1984	Students ('000) 1985
Primary	19,325	19,280	234,549	4,005.6	3,827.9
General Secondary:					
Intermediate schools	2,628	2,617	63,164	1,132.2	1,049.0
Grammar schools	2,487	2,486	125,517	1,852.7	1,750.3
Comprehensive schools	301	314	28,533	220.9	217.5
Special	2,819	2,826	41,273	284.6	271.4
Vocational secondary*	5,847	5,328	80,065	2,554.9	2,544.6
Trade and technical	2,932	2,896	9,990	207.6	213.8
Higher:					
Universities, etc.†	93	93	108,456	1,001.1	1,015.1
Colleges of art and music	26	26	4,685	21.0	21.7
Vocational	119	122	21,425	292.1	301.3

* Including part-time students.
† Universities and other institutions of similar standing, including colleges of theology and colleges of education.

Directory

The Constitution

The Basic Law (Grundgesetz), which came into force in the British, French and US Zones of Occupation in Germany (excluding Saarland) on 23 May 1949, was and is intended as a provisional Constitution to serve until a permanent one for Germany as a whole can be drawn up. The Parliamentary Council which framed it set out to continue the tradition of the Constitution of 1848–49, and to preserve some continuity with subsequent German constitutions (with Bismarck's Constitution of 1871, and with the Weimar Constitution of 1919) while avoiding the mistakes of the past. It contains 146 articles, divided into 11 sections, and introduced by a short preamble.

I. BASIC RIGHTS

The opening articles of the Constitution guarantee the dignity of man, the free development of his personality, the equality of all men before the law, and freedom of faith and conscience. Men and women shall have equal rights, and no one may be prejudiced because of sex, descent, race, language, homeland and origin, faith or religion or political opinion.

No one may be compelled against his conscience to perform war service as a combatant (Article 4). All Germans have the right to assemble peacefully and unarmed and to form associations and societies. Everyone has the right freely to express and to disseminate his opinion through speech, writing or pictures. Freedom of the press and freedom of reporting by radio and motion pictures are guaranteed (Article 5). Censorship is not permitted.

The State shall protect marriage and the family property and the right of inheritance. The care and upbringing of children is the natural right of parents. Illegitimate children shall be given the same conditions for their development and their position in society as legitimate children. Schools are under the supervision of the State. Religion forms part of the curriculum in the State schools, but parents have the right to decide whether the child shall receive religious instruction (Article 7).

A citizen's dwelling is inviolable; house searches may be made only by Court Order. No German may be deprived of his citizenship if he would thereby become stateless. The politically persecuted enjoy the right of asylum (Article 16).

II. THE FEDERATION AND THE LÄNDER

Article 20 describes the Federal Republic (Bundesrepublik Deutschland) as a democratic and social federal state. The colours of the Federal Republic are to be black-red-gold, the same as those of the Weimar Republic. Each Land within the Federal Republic has its own Constitution, which must, however, conform to the principles laid down in the Basic Law. All Länder, districts and parishes must have a representative assembly resulting from universal, direct, free, equal and secret elections (Article 28). The exercise of the power of state is the concern of the Länder, in so far as the Basic Law does not otherwise prescribe. Where there is incompatibility, Federal Law supersedes Land Law (Article 31). Every German has in each Land the same civil rights and duties.

Political parties may be freely formed in all the states of the Federal Republic, but their internal organization must conform to democratic principles, and they must publicly account for the sources of their funds. Parties which seek to impair or abolish the free and democratic basic order or to jeopardize the existence of the Federal Republic of Germany are unconstitutional (Article 21). So are activities tending to disturb the peaceful relations between nations, and, especially, preparations for aggressive war, but the Federation may join a system of mutual collective security in order to preserve peace. The rules of International Law shall form part of Federal Law and take precedence over it and create rights and duties directly for the inhabitants of the Federal territory (Article 25).

The territorial composition of the Länder may be reorganized by Federal law, subject to plebiscite and with due regard to regional unity, territorial and cultural connections, economic expediency and social structure.

III. THE BUNDESTAG

The Federal Assembly or Bundestag is the Lower House. Its members are elected by the people in universal, free, equal, direct and secret elections, for a term of four years.* Any person who has reached the age of 18 is eligible to vote and any person who has reached the age of 18 is eligible for election (Article 38). A deputy may be arrested for a punishable offence only with the permission of the Bundestag, unless he be apprehended in the act or during the following day.

The Bundestag elects its President and draws up its Standing Orders. Most decisions of the House require a majority vote. Its meetings are public, but the public may be excluded by the decision of a two-thirds majority. Upon the motion of one-quarter of its

* The elections of 1949 were carried out on the basis of direct election, with some elements of proportional representation. In January 1953 the draft of a new electoral law was completed by the Federal Government and passed shortly before the dissolution. The new law represents a compromise between direct election and proportional representation, and is designed to discourage the rise of many small parties.

members the Bundestag is obliged to set up an investigation committee.

IV. THE BUNDESRAT

The Federal Council or Bundesrat is the Upper House, through which the Länder participate in the legislation and the administration of the Federation. The Bundesrat consists of members of the Land governments, which appoint and recall them (Article 51). Each Land has at least three votes; Länder with more than two million inhabitants have four, and those with more than six million inhabitants have five. The votes of each Land may only be given as a block vote. The Bundesrat elects its President for one year. Its decisions are taken by simple majority vote. Meetings are in public, but the public may be excluded. The members of the Federal Government have the right, and, on demand, the obligation, to participate in the debates of the Bundesrat.

V. THE FEDERAL PRESIDENT

The Federal President or Bundespräsident is elected by the Federal Convention (Bundesversammlung), consisting of the members of the Bundestag and an equal number of members elected by the Länder Parliaments (Article 54). Every German eligible to vote in elections for the Bundestag and over 40 years of age is eligible for election. The candidate who obtains an absolute majority of votes is elected, but if such majority is not achieved by any candidate in two ballots, whoever receives most votes in a further ballot becomes President. The President's term of office is five years. Immediate re-election is admissible only once. The Federal President must not be a member of the Government or of any legislative body or hold any salaried office. Orders and instructions of the President require the counter-signature of the Federal Chancellor or competent Minister, except for the appointment or dismissal of the Chancellor or the dissolution of the Bundestag.

The President represents the Federation in International Law and accredits and receives envoys. The Bundestag or the Bundesrat may impeach the President before the Federal Constitutional Court on account of wilful violation of the Basic Law or of any other Federal Law (Article 61).

VI. THE FEDERAL GOVERNMENT

The Federal Government (Bundesregierung) consists of the Federal Chancellor (Bundeskanzler) and the Federal Ministers (Bundesminister). The Chancellor is elected by an absolute majority of the Bundestag on the proposal of the Federal President (Article 63). Ministers are appointed and dismissed by the President upon the proposal of the Chancellor. Neither he nor his Ministers may hold any other salaried office. The Chancellor determines general policy and assumes responsibility for it, but within these limits each Minister directs his department individually and on his own responsibility. The Bundestag may express its lack of confidence in the Chancellor only by electing a successor with the majority of its members; the President must then appoint the person elected (Article 67). If a motion of the Chancellor for a vote of confidence does not obtain the support of the majority of the Bundestag, the President may, upon the proposal of the Chancellor, dissolve the House within 21 days, unless it elects another Chancellor within this time (Article 68).

VII. THE LEGISLATION OF THE FEDERATION

The right of legislation lies with the Länder in so far as the Basic Law does not specifically accord legislative powers to the Federation. Distinction is made between fields of exclusive legislation of the Federation and fields of concurrent legislation of Bund and Länder. In the field of concurrent legislation the Länder may legislate so long and so far as the Federation makes no use of its legislative right. The Federation has this right only in so far as a matter cannot be effectively regulated by Land legislation, or the regulation by Land Law would prejudice other Länder, or if the preservation of legal or economic unity demands regulation by Federal Law. Exclusive legislation of the Federation is strictly limited to such matters as foreign affairs, citizenship, migration, currency, copyrights, customs, railways, post and telecommunications. In most other fields, as enumerated (Article 74), concurrent legislation exists.

The legislative organ of the Federation is the Bundestag, into which Bills are introduced by the Government, by members of the Bundestag or by the Bundesrat (Article 76). After their adoption they must be submitted to the Bundesrat, which may demand, within three weeks, that a committee of members of both houses be convened to consider the Bill (Article 77). In so far as its express approval is not needed, the Bundesrat may veto a law within two weeks.

An alteration of the Basic Law requires a majority of two-thirds in both houses, but an amendment by which the division of the Federation into Länder and the basic principles contained in Articles 1 and 20 would be affected, is inadmissible (Article 79).

The Federal Government or the Länder Governments may be authorized by law to issue ordinances. A state of legislative emergency for a Bill can be declared by the President on the request of the Government with the approval of the Bundesrat. If then the Bundestag again rejects the Bill, it may be deemed adopted nevertheless in so far as the Bundesrat approves it. An emergency may not last longer than six months and may not be declared more than once during the term of office of any one Government (Article 81).

VIII. THE EXECUTION OF FEDERAL LAWS AND THE FEDERAL ADMINISTRATION

The Länder execute the Federal Laws as their own concern in so far as the Basic Law does not otherwise determine. In doing so, they regulate the establishment of the authorities and the administrative procedure, but the Federal Government exercises supervision in order to ensure that the Länder execute the Federal Laws in an appropriate manner. For this purpose the Federal Government may send commissioners to the Land authorities (Article 84). Direct Federal administration is foreseen for the Foreign Service, Federal finance, Federal railways, postal services, Federal waterways and shipping.

In order to avert imminent danger to the existence of the democratic order, a Land may call in the police forces of other Länder; and if the Land in which the danger is imminent is itself not willing or able to fight the danger, the Federal Government may place the police in the Land, or the police forces in other Länder, under its instructions (Article 91).

IX. THE ADMINISTRATION OF JUSTICE

Judicial authority is invested in independent judges, who are subject only to the law and who may not be dismissed or transferred against their will (Article 97).

Justice is exercised by the Federal Constitutional Court, by the Supreme Federal Courts and by the Courts of the Länder. The Federal Constitutional Court decides on the interpretation of the Basic Law in cases of doubt, on the compatibility of Federal Law or Land Law with the Basic Law, and on disputes between the Federation and the Länder or between different Länder. Supreme Federal Courts are to be established for the spheres of ordinary, administrative, finance, labour and social jurisdiction. If a Supreme Federal Court intends to judge a point of law in contradiction to a previous decision of another Supreme Federal Court, it must refer the matter to a special senate of the Supreme Courts. Extraordinary courts are inadmissible.

The freedom of the individual may be restricted only on the basis of a law. No one may be prevented from appearing before his lawful judge (Article 101). Detained persons may be subjected neither to physical nor to mental ill-treatment. The police may hold no one in custody longer than the end of the day following the arrest without the decision of a court. Any person temporarily detained must be brought before a judge who shall either issue a warrant of arrest or set him free, at the latest on the following day. A person enjoying the confidence of the detainee must be notified forthwith of any continued duration of a deprivation of liberty. An act may be punished only if it was punishable by law before the act was committed, and no one may be punished more than once on account of the same criminal act. The death sentence shall be abolished.

X. FINANCE

The Federation has the right of exclusive legislation only on customs and financial monopolies; on most other taxes, especially on income, property and inheritance, it has concurrent legislation rights with the Länder (see VII above).

Customs, financial monopolies, excise taxes (with exception of the beer tax), the transportation tax, the value added tax and property dues serving non-recurrent purposes, are administered by Federal finance authorities, and the revenues thereof accrue to the Federation. The remaining taxes are administered, as a rule, by the Länder and the Gemeinden to which they accrue. The Federation and the Länder shall be self-supporting and independent of each other in their budget economy (Article 109). In order to ensure the working efficiency of the Länder with low revenues and to equalize their differing burden of expenditure, there exists a system of revenue sharing among the Länder; in addition, the Federation may take grants, out of its own funds, to the poorer Länder. All revenues and expenditures of the Federation must be estimated for each fiscal year and included in the budget, which must be established by law before the beginning of the fiscal year. Decisions of

FEDERAL REPUBLIC OF GERMANY

the Bundestag or the Bundesrat which increase the budget expenditure proposed by the Federal Government require its approval (Article 113).

XI. TRANSITIONAL AND CONCLUDING PROVISIONS

The Articles 116–146 regulate a number of disconnected matters of detail, such as the relation between the old Reich and the Federation, the Federal Government and Allied High Commission, the expenses for occupation costs which have to be borne by the Federation, and the status of former German nationals who now may regain their citizenship. Article 143 contains the threat of severe punishment to those who attempt to change by force the constitutional order of the Federation or of a Land, or to prevent the Federal President by force or the threat of danger from exercising his powers.

Major Constitutional Amendments

I. SOVEREIGNTY AND RESPONSIBILITY

An amending bill of 1954:

(1) Laid down under an amendment to Article 73 of the Basic Law that the Federal Parliament had full powers to legislate in all matters relating to national defence 'including obligatory national service for men over 18 years of age';

(2) Introduced a new article (142A) which declared that 'the treaties signed in Bonn and Paris on 26 and 27 May 1952 (i.e. the Bonn Conventions and European Defence Community Treaty) were not contrary to the Federal Constitution'.

Until September 1954 the operation of the Basic Law was conditioned by two further instruments: the first, the Occupation Statute of 1949 (with subsequent amendments) defining the rights and obligations of the United States, Great Britain and France with respect to Germany; and the second, the Bonn Conventions, designed to replace the Occupation Statute and to grant almost full sovereignty to the German people.

The Bonn Conventions, 1952

(1) The Occupation Statute was abolished, and the Federal Government inherited full freedom in so far as the international situation permits.

(2) Allied forces in Germany were no longer occupation forces, but part of 'the defence of the free world, of which the Federal Republic and West Berlin form a part'.

(3) A number of problems which would normally be settled by a Peace Treaty were resolved; the Conventions were in effect a provisional treaty to end the war between the Federal Republic and the Three Powers, pending a final treaty between the whole of Germany and the Four. Under this heading the following provisions were made:

(a) The Federal Republic would have full control over its internal and foreign affairs and relations with the Three Powers would be conducted through ambassadors.

(b) Only because of the international situation would the Three Powers claim their rights regarding the stationing of armed forces on German soil, matters concerning Berlin, the reunification of Germany and the final Peace Treaty.

(c) The Federal Republic undertook to conduct its policy according to the principles of the United Nations.

(d) In their negotiations with states with which the Federal Republic has no relations, the Three Powers would consult with the Federal Government.

(e) The Federal Republic would participate in the European Defence Community.

(f) The Three Powers and the Federal Republic agreed that a freely negotiated peace settlement for the whole of Germany was their common aim, and that determination of the final boundaries of Germany must await such a treaty.

The Conventions also included supplementary contractual agreements concerning the rights and obligations of foreign troops in Germany, taxation of the armed forces, a Finance Convention, and a Convention on the settlement of matters arising out of the war and the occupation.

The London and Paris Agreements

The terms of the London Agreement of 1954 were that Germany and Italy should enter an expanded Brussels Treaty Organization; that German sovereignty should be restored and that Germany should, on agreed terms, enter NATO, and that an Agency for the control of armaments on the continent of Europe should be set up. The Paris Agreement later that year established the details of the points agreed in London.

German Sovereignty

On 5 May 1955, with the depositing of the instruments of ratification of the London and Paris Agreements, the Federal Republic of Germany attained its sovereignty. The three-power status continues for the time being in West Berlin, but is modified by a declaration by the American, French and British Commandants.

II. OTHER AMENDMENTS

In June 1968 legislation was finally passed providing for emergency measures to be taken during a time of crisis.

The main provisions of this, the 17th Amendment to the Constitution, were to allow the authorities to place certain restrictions on the secrecy of correspondence and telecommunications, to conscript men into the armed forces and to use the armed forces to fight armed insurgents if the free democratic status of the Federal Republic or of any Land was threatened. A new Article 53A provided for the establishment of a committee of 33 members, two-thirds members of the Bundestag and one-third members of the Bundesrat, which must be informed by the Federal Government of any plans in the event of a defence emergency. The life of parliamentary bodies and the terms of office of the Federal President and his deputy might be extended during a defence emergency.

The Government

(December 1986)

HEAD OF STATE

Federal President: Dr RICHARD VON WEIZSÄCKER (took office 1 July 1984).

THE FEDERAL GOVERNMENT

A coalition of the Christian Democratic Union (CDU)/Christian Social Union (CSU) and the Free Democratic Party (FDP).

Federal Chancellor: Dr HELMUT KOHL (CDU).
Vice-Chancellor and Minister for Foreign Affairs: HANS-DIETRICH GENSCHER (FDP).
Head of the Chancellery: WOLFGANG SCHÄUBLE (CDU).
Minister of the Interior: Dr FRIEDRICH ZIMMERMANN (CSU).
Minister of Justice: HANS A. ENGELHARD (FDP).
Minister of Finance: Dr GERHARD STOLTENBERG (CDU).
Minister of Economics: Dr MARTIN BANGEMANN (FDP).
Minister of Food, Agriculture and Forestry: IGNAZ KIECHLE (CSU).
Minister of Labour and Social Affairs: DR NORBERT BLÜM (CDU).
Minister of Defence: Dr MANFRED WÖRNER (CDU).
Minister for Youth, Family and Health Affairs: Prof. Dr RITA SÜSSMUTH (CDU).
Minister of Transport: Dr WERNER DOLLINGER (CSU).
Minister for the Environment, Conservation and Reactor Safety: Dr WALTER WALLMANN (CDU).
Minister of Posts and Telecommunications: Dr CHRISTIAN SCHWARZ-SCHILLING (CDU).
Minister for Regional Planning, Construction and Urban Development: Dr OSCAR SCHNEIDER (CSU).
Minister for Intra-German Relations: HEINRICH WINDELEN (CDU).
Minister of Research and Technology: Dr HEINZ RIESENHUBER (CDU).
Minister for Education and Science: Frau Dr DOROTHEE WILMS (CDU).
Minister for Economic Co-operation: Dr JÜRGEN WARNKE (CSU).

MINISTRIES

Office of the Federal President: 5300 Bonn 1, Kaiser-Friedrich-Str. 16; tel. (0228) 2001; telex 886393.
Office of the Federal Chancellor: 5300 Bonn 1, Adenauerallee 141; tel. (0228) 561; telex 886750.

FEDERAL REPUBLIC OF GERMANY

Ministry of Defence: 5300 Bonn 1, Hardthöhe, Postfach 1328; tel. (0228) 121; telex 886575.

Ministry of Economic Co-operation: 5300 Bonn 1, Karl-Marx-Str. 4–6; tel. (0228) 5351; telex 8869452.

Ministry of Economics: 5300 Bonn 1, Villemombler Str. 76; tel. (0228) 6151; telex 886747.

Ministry of Education and Science: 5300 Bonn 2, Heinemannstr. 2; tel. (0228) 571; telex 885666.

Ministry of the Environment, Conservation and Reactor Safety: 5300 Bonn 1, Adenauerallee 139; tel. (0228) 561; telex 886750.

Ministry of Finance: 5300 Bonn 1, Graurheindorfer Str. 108; tel. (0228) 6821; telex 886645.

Ministry of Food, Agriculture and Forestry: 5300 Bonn 1, Rochusstr. 1; tel. (0228) 5291; telex 886844.

Ministry of Foreign Affairs: 5300 Bonn 1, Adenauerallee 99–103; tel. (0228) 171; telex 886591.

Ministry of the Interior: 5300 Bonn 1, Graurheindorfer Str. 198; tel. (0228) 6811; telex 886896.

Ministry for Intra-German Relations: 5300 Bonn 2, Godesberger Allee 140; tel. (0228) 3061; telex 885673.

Ministry of Justice: 5300 Bonn 2, Heinemannstr. 6, Postfach 200650; tel. (0228) 581; telex 8869679.

Ministry of Labour and Social Affairs: 5300 Bonn 1, Rochusstr. 1, Postfach 140280; tel. (0228) 5271; telex 886641.

Ministry of Posts and Telecommunications: 5300 Bonn 2, Heinrich-von-Stephan-Str. 1; tel. (0228) 140; telex 886707.

Ministry of Regional Planning, Construction and Urban Development: 5300 Bonn 2, Deichmannsaue; tel. (0228) 3371; telex 885462.

Ministry of Research and Technology: 5300 Bonn 2, Heinemannstr. 2; tel. (0228) 591; telex 885674.

Ministry of Transport: 5300 Bonn 2, Kennedyallee 72; tel. (0228) 3001; telex 885700.

Ministry of Youth, Family and Health Affairs: 5300 Bonn 2, Kennedyallee 105–107; tel. (0228) 3381; telex 885700.

Legislature

BUNDESTAG
(Federal Assembly)

President: Dr Philipp Jenninger (CDU).

Vice-Presidents: Annemarie Renger (SPD), Dieter Julius Cronenberg (FDP), Richard Stücklen (CSU), Heinz Westphal (SPD).

General Election, 25 January 1987

	Votes	%	Seats*
Social Democratic Party (SPD)	14,023,407	37.0	186
Christian Democratic Union (CDU)	13,045,540	34.5	174
Christian Social Union (CSU)	3,715,660	9.8	49
Free Democratic Party (FDP)	3,439,686	9.1	46
Green Party	3,124,657	8.3	42

* In addition to the 497 directly elected members, the Bundestag has 22 members, with limited voting powers, elected by the West Berlin House of Representatives.

BUNDESRAT
(Federal Council)

President: Holger Börner.

The Bundesrat has 45 members. Each Land has three, four or five votes, depending on the size of its population, and sends as many members to the sessions as it has votes. As in the Bundestag, representatives from West Berlin have no voting power in plenary sessions. The head of government of each Land is automatically a member of the Bundesrat. Ministers and Members of the Federal Government attend the sessions, which are held every two to three weeks.

Länder	Seats
North Rhine-Westphalia	5
Bavaria	5
Baden-Württemberg	5
Lower Saxony	5
Hesse	4
Rhineland-Palatinate	4
Schleswig-Holstein	4
Hamburg	3
Saarland	3
Bremen	3
Berlin (West)	4

The Land Governments

The ten Länder of the Federal Republic are autonomous but not sovereign states, enjoying a high degree of self-government and wide legislative powers.

SCHLESWIG-HOLSTEIN

The Provisional Constitution was adopted by the Diet on 13 December 1949. The Land Government consists of the Minister-President and the Ministers appointed by him. It is formed from the majority party (CDU).

Minister-President: Dr Dr Uwe Barschel (CDU).

The Diet was elected on 13 March 1983 and is composed as follows:

President of Diet: Rudolf Tizzck.

Party	Seats
Christian Democratic Union	39
Social Democratic Party	34
Südschleswigscher Wählerverband	1

HAMBURG

The Constitution of the 'Free and Hanseatic City of Hamburg' was passed in June 1952. There is complete parity between the Town Assembly and the Land Diet on the one hand and between the Mayor and the President on the other. The members of the Senate are elected by the City Council. The Senate in turn elects the President and his deputy from its own ranks. The President remains in office for one year, but may offer himself for re-election. The Senate has a minority Government formed by the SPD.

President of Senate and First Bürgermeister: Dr Klaus von Dohnanyi (SPD).

The City Council was elected on 9 November 1986, and is composed as follows:

President: Peter Schulz (SPD).

Party	Seats
Christian Democratic Union	54
Social Democratic Party	53
Green Alternative List	13

LOWER SAXONY

The Provisional Constitution was passed by the Diet on 13 April 1951, and came into force on 1 May 1951. The Land Government is formed from a coalition of the CDU and the FDP.

Minister-President: Dr Ernst Albrecht (CDU).

As a result of elections held on 15 June 1986, the Diet is composed as follows:

President of the Diet: Dr Edzard Blanke (CDU).

FEDERAL REPUBLIC OF GERMANY

Party	Seats
Christian Democratic Union	69
Social Democratic Party	66
Green Party	11
Free Democratic Party	9

Lower Saxony is divided into four governmental districts: Brunswick, Hanover, Lüneburg and Weser-Ems.

BREMEN

The Constitution of the Free Hanseatic City of Bremen was sanctioned by referendum of the people on 12 October 1947. The main constitutional organs are the City Council, the Senate and the Constitutional Court. The Senate is the executive organ elected by the Council for the duration of its own tenure of office. The Senate elects from its own ranks two Bürgermeister, one of whom becomes President of the Senate. The Senators cannot be simultaneously members of parliament. A vote of no-confidence can only be given under special conditions. Decisions of the Council are subject to the delaying veto of the Senate. The Senate is formed from the majority party (SPD).

First Bürgermeister and President of the Senate: KLAUS WEDEMEIER (SPD).

The Council consists of 100 members elected for four years. The election of 25 September 1983 resulted in the following composition:
President of the Bürgerschaft: Dr DIETER KLINK (SPD).

Party	Seats
Social Democratic Party	58
Christian Democratic Union	37
Green List	5

NORTH RHINE-WESTPHALIA

The present Constitution was passed by the Diet on 6 June 1950, and was endorsed by the electorate in the elections held on 18 June. The Land Government is presided over by the Minister-President who appoints his Ministers. It is formed from the majority SPD.

Minister-President: JOHANNES RAU (SPD).

The Diet, elected on 12 May 1985, is composed as follows:
President of Diet: KARL-JOSEF DENZER (SPD).

Party	Seats
Social Democratic Party	125
Christian Democratic Union	88
Free Democratic Party	14

The state is divided into five governmental districts: Düsseldorf, Münster, Arnsberg, Detmold and Cologne.

HESSE

The Constitution of this Land dates from 11 December 1946. The Minister-President is elected by the Diet and he appoints and dismisses his Ministers with its consent. The Diet can force the resignation of the State Government by a vote of no-confidence. The Government was formed from a coalition of the SPD and the Green Party, until its collapse in February 1987 (see Late Information).

Minister-President: HOLGER BÖRNER (SPD).

The Diet, elected on 25 September 1983, is composed as follows:
President of Diet: Dr ERWIN LANG (SPD).

Party	Seats
Social Democratic Party	51
Christian Democratic Union	44
Free Democratic Party	8
Green Party	7

Hesse is divided into two governmental districts: Kassel and Darmstadt. The districts are divided into urban and rural districts.

RHINELAND-PALATINATE

The three chief agencies of the Constitution of this Land are the Diet, the Government and the Constitutional Court. The Minister-President is elected by the Diet, with whose consent he appoints and dismisses his Ministers. The Government, which is dependent on the confidence of the Diet, is made up from the majority party (CDU).

Minister-President: Dr BERNHARD VOGEL (CDU).

The members of the Diet are elected according to a system of proportional representation. Its composition, as the result of elections held on 6 March 1983, is as follows:
President of Diet: Dr HEINZ PETER VOLKERT (CDU).

Party	Seats
Christian Democratic Union	57
Social Democratic Party	43

Rhineland-Palatinate is divided into three districts: Koblenz, Rheinhessen-Palatinate and Trier.

BADEN-WÜRTTEMBERG

The Constitution was passed by the Land Assembly in Stuttgart on 19 November 1953. The Minister-President is elected by the Diet. He appoints and dismisses his Ministers. The Government, which is responsible to the Diet, is formed by the majority party (CDU).

Minister-President: Dr LOTHAR SPÄTH (CDU).

The Diet, elected on 25 March 1984, is composed as follows:
President of Diet: ERICH SCHNEIDER (CDU).

Party	Seats
Christian Democratic Union	68
Social Democratic Party	41
Green Party	9
Free Democratic Party	8

The Land is divided into four administrative districts: Stuttgart, Karlsruhe, Tübingen and Freiburg.

BAVARIA

The Constitution of Bavaria allows for a two-chamber Parliament and a Constitutional Court. Provision is also made for a popular referendum. The Minister-President is elected by the Diet for four years. He appoints the Ministers and Secretaries of State with the consent of the Diet. The State Government is formed from the majority party (CSU).

Minister-President: Dr FRANZ JOSEF STRAUSS (CSU).

The composition of the Diet, as a result of elections held on 12 October 1986, is as follows:
President of Diet: Dr FRANZ HEUBL (CSU).

Party	Seats
Christian Social Union	128
Social Democratic Party	61
Green Party	15

The Senate, or second chamber, consists of 60 members, divided into 10 groups representing professional interests, e.g. agriculture, industry, trade, free professions and religious communities. Every two years one-third of the Senate is replaced by elections.

President of the Senate: HIPPOLYT Freiherr VON POSCHINGER.

Bavaria is divided into seven districts: Mittelfranken, Oberfranken, Unterfranken, Schwaben, Niederbayern, Oberpfalz and Oberbayern. Each district is subdivided into a number of urban and rural districts.

SAARLAND

By the Constitution which came into force on 1 January 1957, Saarland became politically integrated with the Federal Republic as a Land. It became economically integrated with the Federal Republic in July 1959. The Minister-President is elected by the Diet. The Government is formed by the SPD.

FEDERAL REPUBLIC OF GERMANY

Minister-President: Oskar Lafontaine (SPD).

The Diet, elected on 10 March 1985, is composed as follows:
President of the Diet: Albrecht Herold (SPD).

Party	Seats
Social Democratic Party	27
Christian Democratic Union	19
Free Democratic Party	5

West Berlin

On 4 August 1950, the Berlin City Assembly passed a constitution defining its special position under technical three-power control. Under German Constitutional Law Berlin is a Land of the Federal Republic but this law is at present suspended by three-power reservations. Nevertheless West Berlin sends representatives to the Bundestag and Bundesrat in Bonn, but these representatives have no vote in the plenary sessions of either House. To be valid in West Berlin, Federal Law has to be specially adopted there. The Constitution came into force on 1 October 1950.

The House of Representatives (Abgeordnetenhaus) is the legislative body, and has 133 members. The executive agency is the Senate, which is composed of the Governing Mayor (Regierender Bürgermeister), his deputy, and at the most 16 Senators. The Governing Mayor is elected by a majority of the House of Representatives. The Senate is responsible to the House of Representatives and dependent on its confidence.

Regierender Bürgermeister: Eberhard Diepgen (CDU).

Bürgermeisterin and Senator for Education, Vocational Training and Sport: Dr Hanna-Renate Laurien (CDU).

SENATORS

Economics and Labour: Elmar Pieroth (CDU).

Justice and Federal Affairs: Dr Rupert Scholz (CDU).

Finance: Dr Günter Rexrodt (FDP).

Cultural Affairs: Dr Volker Hassemer (CDU).

Interior: Dr Wilhelm Kewenig (CDU).

Public Health and Social Affairs: Ulf Fink (CDU).

Building and Housing: Georg Wittwer (CDU).

Urban Development and Environment: Dr Jürgen Starnick (Independent).

Transport and Public Utilities: Edmund Wronski (CDU).

Youth and Family Affairs: Cornelia Schmalz-Jacobsen (FDP).

Science and Research: Dr George Turner (Independent).

The state of parties in the House, as the result of elections held on 10 March 1985, is as follows:

President of House of Representatives: Peter Rebsch (CDU).

Party	Seats
Christian Democratic Union	69
Social Democratic Party	48
Alternative List	15
Free Democratic Party	12

Political Organizations

Christlich-Demokratische Union (in Bavaria: **Christlich-Soziale Union**) **(CDU/CSU)** (Christian Democratic and Christian Social Union): CDU: 5300 Bonn 1, Konrad-Adenauer-Haus, Friedrich-Ebert-Allee 73-75; tel. (0228) 5441; telex 886804; f. 1945; became a federal party in 1950; stands for the united action between Catholics and Protestants for rebuilding German life on a Christian basis, while guaranteeing private property and the freedom of the individual and for a 'free and equal Germany in a free, politically united and socially just Europe'; other objectives are to guarantee close ties with allies within NATO and the principle of self-determination; 715,037 mems (1986); Chair. Dr Helmut Kohl; Sec.-Gen. Dr Heiner Geissler; CSU: 8000 Munich 2, Nymphenburger Str. 64; tel. (089) 1243; telex 522278; f. 1946; Christian Democratic, anti-socialist party, aiming for a free market economy 'in the service of man's economic and intellectual freedom'; also combines national consciousness with support for a united Europe; 186,000 mems; Chair. Dr Franz Josef Strauss; Sec.-Gen. Gerold Tandler.

Deutsche Kommunistische Partei (DKP) (German Communist Party): 4000 Düsseldorf, Prinz-Georg-Str. 79; telex 8584387; 49,000 mems; Chair. Herbert Mies.

Freie Demokratische Partei (FDP) (Free Democratic Party): Bonn, Baunscheidtstr. 15, Thomas-Dehler-Haus; tel. (0228) 5470; telex 886580; f. 1948; represents democratic and social liberalism and makes the individual the focal point of the state and its laws and economy; approx. 70,000 mems (1986); Chair. Martin Bangemann; Deputy Chair. Wolfgang Mischnick, Gerhart Rudolf Baum, Wolfgang Gerhardt; Chair. in Bundestag Wolfgang Mischnick; Sec.-Gen. Dr Helmut Haussmann.

Die Grünen (Green Party): 5300 Bonn 1, Colmantstr. 36; tel. (0228) 692021; telex 886330; f. 1980; largely comprised of the membership of the Grüne Aktion Zukunft, the Grüne Liste Umweltschutz and the Aktionsgemeinschaft Unabhängiger Deutscher, also includes groups of widely varying political views; essentially left-wing party programme includes ecological issues, dissolution of NATO and Warsaw Pact military blocs, breaking down of large economic concerns into smaller units, 35-hour week and unlimited right to strike; approx. 39,000 mems (1986); Exec. Rainer Trampert, Lukas Beckmann, Jutta Ditfurth.

Nationaldemokratische Partei Deutschlands (NPD) (National Democratic Party of Germany): 7000 Stuttgart 1, Postfach 2881; tel. (0711) 610605; telex 244012; f. 1964; right-wing; 15,000 mems; youth organization Junge Nationaldemokraten (JN), 6,000 mems; Chair. Martin Mussgnug.

Sozialdemokratische Partei Deutschlands (SPD) (Social Democratic Party of Germany): 53 Bonn, Ollenhauerstr 1; tel. (0228) 5321; telex 886306; the party maintains that a vital democracy can be built only on the basis of social justice; advocates for the economy as much competition as possible, as much planning as necessary to protect the individual from uncontrolled economic interests; a positive attitude to national defence, while favouring controlled disarmament; a policy of religious toleration; rejects any political ties with Communism; approx. 919,000 mems (1986); Chair. of SPD Willy Brandt; Deputy Chair. Johannes Rau, Dr Hans-Jochen Vogel; Chair. of Parliamentary Party Dr Hans-Jochen Vogel; Deputy Chair. Dr Hans Apel, Dr Herta Däubler-Gmelin, Prof. Dr Horst Ehmke, Dr Alfred Emmerlich, Anke Fuchs, Dr Volker Hauff, Wolfgang Roth, Dr Willfried Penner.

There are also numerous other small parties, none of them represented in the Bundestag, covering all shades of the political spectrum and various regional interests.

Diplomatic Representation

EMBASSIES IN THE FEDERAL REPUBLIC OF GERMANY

Afghanistan: 5300 Bonn 1, Liebfrauenweg 1a; tel. (0228) 251927; Chargé d'affaires: Taher Nangialai.

Algeria: 5300 Bonn 2, Rheinallee 32; tel. (0228) 356054; telex 885723; Ambassador: Amor Benghezal.

Argentina: 5300 Bonn 1, Adenauerallee 50–52; tel. (0228) 222011; telex 886478; Ambassador: Hugo Boatti Ossorio.

Australia: 5300 Bonn 2, Godesberger Allee 107; tel. (0228) 81030; telex 885466; Ambassador: Charles Robin Ashwin.

Austria: 5300 Bonn 1, Johanniterstr. 2; tel. (0228) 230051; telex 886780; Ambassador: Dr Willibald Pahr.

Bangladesh: 5300 Bonn 2, Bonner Str. 48; tel. (0228) 352525; telex 885640; Ambassador: Muzammel Hussain.

Belgium: 5300 Bonn 1, Kaiser-Friedrich-Str. 7; tel. (0228) 212001; telex 886777; Ambassador: Michel J. M. M. G. van Ussel.

Benin: 5300 Bonn 2, Rüdigerstr. 10; tel. (0228) 344031; telex 885594; Ambassador: Guy Boukary-Mory.

Bolivia: 5300 Bonn 2, Konstantinstr. 16; tel. (0228) 362038; telex 885785; Ambassador: Dr Vicente Mendoza Nava.

Brazil: 5300 Bonn 2, Kennedyallee 74; tel. (0228) 376976; telex 885471; Ambassador: Jorge de Carvalho e Silva.

Bulgaria: 5300 Bonn 2, Auf der Hostert 6; tel. (0228) 363061; telex 885739; Ambassador: Georgi Evtimov.

Burkina Faso: 5300 Bonn 2, Wendelstadtallee 18; tel. (0228) 332063; telex 885508; Ambassador: Gomtirbou Anatole Tiendrebeogo.

FEDERAL REPUBLIC OF GERMANY

Burma: 5300 Bonn 1, Schumann Str. 112; tel. (0228) 210091; telex 8869560; Ambassador: U MAUNG MAUNG THAN TUN.

Burundi: 5307 Wachtberg-Niederbachem, Drosselweg 2; tel. (0228) 345032; telex 885745; Ambassador: EGIDE NKURIYINGOMA.

Cameroon: 5300 Bonn 2, Rheinallee 76; tel. (0228) 356037; telex 885480; Ambassador: JEAN MELAGA.

Canada: 5300 Bonn 1, Friedrich-Wilhelm-Str. 18; tel. (0228) 231061; telex 886421; Ambassador: DONALD S. MCPHAIL.

Central African Republic: 5300 Bonn 2, Dürenstr. 12; tel. (0228) 354077; telex 8861166; Ambassador: NESTOR KOMBOT-NAGUEMON.

Chad: 5300 Bonn 2, Basteistr. 80; tel. (0228) 356025; Ambassador: Dr ISSA HASSAN KHAYAR.

Chile: 5300 Bonn 2, Kronprinzenstr. 20; tel. (0228) 363089; telex 885403; Ambassador: VASCO UNDURRAGA GAUCHE.

China, People's Republic: 5300 Bonn 2, Kurfürstenallee 12; tel. (0228) 361095; telex 885655; Ambassador: GUO FENGMIN.

Colombia: 5300 Bonn 1, Friedrich-Wilhelm-Str. 35; tel. (0228) 234565; telex 886305; Ambassador: Dr LUIS GONZÁLEZ BARROS.

Congo: 5300 Bonn 2, Rheinallee 45; tel. (0228) 357085; telex 886690; Ambassador: GÉRARD-FRANÇOIS YANDZA.

Costa Rica: 5300 Bonn 1, Borsigallee 2; tel. (0228) 252940; telex 8869961; Ambassador: (vacant).

Cuba: 5300 Bonn 2, Kennedyallee 22–24; tel. (0228) 3091; telex 885733; Ambassador: LUIS GARCÍA PERAZA.

Cyprus: 5300 Bonn 2, Kronprinzenstr. 58; tel. (0228) 363336; telex 885519; Ambassador: COSTAS PAPADEMAS.

Czechoslovakia: 5300 Bonn 1, Im Rheingarten 7; tel. (0228) 284765; telex 8869322; Ambassador: Dr DUŠAN SPÁČIL.

Denmark: 5300 Bonn 1, Pfälzer Str. 14; tel. (0228) 729910; telex 886892; Ambassador: Dr PAUL HENNING FISCHER.

Dominican Republic: 5300 Bonn 2, Burgstr. 87; tel. (0228) 223160; Ambassador: Dr MANUEL RAFAEL GARCÍA LIZARDO.

Ecuador: 5300 Bonn 2, Koblenzer Str. 37; tel. (0228) 352544; telex 8869527; Ambassador: Dr JULIO ANÍBAL MORENO ESPINOSA.

Egypt: 5300 Bonn 2, Kronprinzenstr. 2; tel. (0228) 364008; telex 885719; Ambassador: ABDEL-HAMID SHAFFIE.

El Salvador: 5300 Bonn 1, Burbacherstr. 2; tel. (0228) 221351; telex 8869692; Ambassador: Dr JUAN RICARDO RAMÍREZ RAUDA.

Ethiopia: 5300 Bonn 1, Brentanostr. 1; tel. (0228) 233041; telex 8869498; Ambassador: TADESSE TERREFE.

Finland: 5300 Bonn 2, Friesdorfer Str. 1; tel. (0228) 311033; telex 885626; Ambassador: ANTTI KARPPINEN.

France: 5300 Bonn 2, Kapellenweg 1A; tel. (0228) 362031; telex 885445; Ambassador: SERGE BOIDEVAIX.

Gabon: 5300 Bonn 2, Kronprinzenstr. 52; tel. (0228) 354084; telex 885520; Ambassador: JEAN-ROBERT FANGUINOVENY.

German Democratic Republic: 5300 Bonn 2, Godesberger Allee 18; tel. (0228) 379051; telex 885645; Head of Permanent Representation: EWALD MOLDT; also in Düsseldorf.

Ghana: 5300 Bonn 2, Rheinallee 58; tel. (0228) 352011; telex 885660; Ambassador: KWAME SAMUEL ADUSEI-POKU.

Greece: 5300 Bonn 2, Koblenzerstr. 103; tel. (0228) 355036; telex 885636; Ambassador: NICOLAS KATAPODIS.

Guatemala: 5300 Bonn 2, Ziethenstr. 16; tel. (0228) 351579; telex 8869983; Ambassador: ANTONIO CARRERA MOLINA.

Guinea: 5300 Bonn 1, Rochusweg 50; tel. (0228) 231097; telex 886448; Ambassador: ALKHALY BANGOURA.

Haiti: 5300 Bonn 2, Schlossallee 10; tel. (0228) 340351; Ambassador: WILLIAM CAMBRONNE.

Holy See: 5300 Bonn 2, Turmstr. 29; tel. (0228) 376901; Apostolic Nuncio: Mgr GIUSEPPE UHAČ.

Honduras: 5300 Bonn 2, Ubierstr. 1; tel. (0228) 356394; telex 889496; Ambassador: ALEX MAYR.

Hungary: 5300 Bonn 2, Turmstr. 30; tel. (0228) 376797; telex 886501; Ambassador: Dr ISTVÁN HORVÁTH.

Iceland: 5300 Bonn 2, Kronprinzenstr. 6; tel. (0228) 364021; telex 885690; Ambassador: Dr HANNES JONSSON.

India: 5300 Bonn 1, Adenauerallee 262–264; tel. (0228) 54050; telex 8869301; Ambassador: JAGDISH CHAND AJMANI.

Indonesia: 5300 Bonn 1, Bernkasteler Str. 2; tel. (0228) 310091; telex 886352; Ambassador: ASHADI TJAHJADI.

Iran: 5300 Bonn 2, Godesberger Allee 133–137; tel. (0228) 37810050; telex 885697; Ambassador: DJRVAD SALARI.

Iraq: 5300 Bonn 2, Dürenstr. 33; tel. (0228) 82031; telex 8869471; Ambassador: (vacant).

Ireland: 5300 Bonn 2, Godesberger Allee 119; tel. (0228) 376937; telex 885588; Ambassador: JOHN CAMPBELL.

Israel: 5300 Bonn 2, Simrockallee 2; tel. (0228) 8231; telex 885490; Ambassador: JITZHAK BEN-ARI.

Italy: 5300 Bonn 2, Karl-Finkelnburg-Str. 51; tel. (0228) 364015; telex 885450; Ambassador: Prof. LUIGI VITTORIO FERRARIS.

Ivory Coast: 5300 Bonn 1, Königstr. 93; tel. (0228) 212098; telex 886524; Ambassador: DIEUDONNÉ ESSIENNE.

Jamaica: 5300 Bonn 2, Am Kreuter 1; tel. (0228) 354045; telex 885493; Ambassador: GLAISTER GEORGE DUNCAN.

Japan: 5300 Bonn 1, Bonn-Center, H1 701, Bundeskanzlerplatz; tel. (0228) 5001; telex 886878; Ambassador: HIROMICHI MIYAZAKI.

Jordan: 5300 Bonn 2, Beethovenallee 21; tel. (0228) 357046; telex 885401; Ambassador: FAWAZ SHARAF.

Kenya: 5300 Bonn 2, Villichgasse 17: tel. (0228) 353066; telex 885570; Ambassador: MAURICE PETER OMWONY.

Korea, Republic: 5300 Bonn 1, Adenauerallee 124; tel. (0228) 218095; telex 8869508; Ambassador: CHUNG SOON-KUN.

Kuwait: 5300 Bonn 2, Godesberger Allee 77-81; tel. (0228) 378081; telex 886525; Ambassador: CHALID AL-BABTAIN.

Lebanon: 5300 Bonn 2, Rheinallee 27; tel. (0228) 352075; telex 8869339; Ambassador: SOUHEIL CHAMMAS.

Lesotho: 5300 Bonn 2, Godesberger Allee 50; tel. (0228) 376868; telex 8869370; Ambassador: MOKHESENG REGINALD TEKATEKA.

Liberia: 5300 Bonn 1, Hohenzollernstr. 73; tel. (0228) 351810; telex 886637; Ambassador: NATHANIEL EASTMAN.

Libya: 5300 Bonn 2, Beethovenallee 12A; tel. (0228) 362041; telex 885738; Secretary of the People's Committee: ELMAHDI M. IMBERESH.

Luxembourg: 5300 Bonn 1, Adenauerallee 110; tel. (0228) 214008; telex 886557; Ambassador: ADRIEN FERDINAND JOSEF MEISCH.

Madagascar: 5300 Bonn 2, Rolandstr. 48; tel. (0228) 331057; telex 885781; Ambassador: SALOMON RAHATOKA.

Malawi: 5300 Bonn 1, Bonn-Center, HI 1103, Bundeskanzlerplatz; tel. (0228) 213050; telex 8869689; Ambassador: LINNAEUS STEPHEN KAUTA MSISKA.

Malaysia: 5300 Bonn 2, Mittelstr. 43; tel. (0228) 376803; telex 885683; Ambassador: Dato' ABDUL MAJID BIN MUHAMMAD.

Mali: 5300 Bonn 2, Bassteistr. 86; tel. (0228) 357048; telex 885680; Ambassador: SEKOU ALMAMY KOREISSI.

Malta: 5300 Bonn 2, Viktoriastr. 1; tel. (0228) 363017; telex 885748; Ambassador: ALBERT FRIGGIERI.

Mauritania: 5300 Bonn 2, Bonnerstr. 48; tel. (0228) 364024; telex 885550; Ambassador: NALLA OUMAR KANE.

Mexico: 5300 Bonn 1, Oxfordstr. 12–16; tel. (0228) 631226; telex 886819; Ambassador: CÉSAR SEPÚLVEDA.

Monaco: 5300 Bonn 1, Zitelmannstr. 16; tel. (0228) 232007; Ambassador: RENE BOCCA.

Morocco: 5300 Bonn 2, Gotenstr. 7–9; tel. (0228) 355044; telex 885428; Ambassador: ABDELKADER BEN SLIMANE.

Nepal: 5300 Bonn 2, Im Hag 15; tel. (0228) 343097; telex 8869297; Ambassador: SIMHA PRATAP SHAH.

Netherlands: 5300 Bonn 1, Strässchensweg 10; tel. (0228) 238091; telex 886826; Ambassador: JAN GERARD VAN DER TAS.

New Zealand: 5300 Bonn 1, Bonn-Center, HI 902, Bundeskanzlerplatz; tel. (0228) 214021; telex 886322; Ambassador: EDWARD FARNON.

Nicaragua: 5300 Bonn 2, Konstantinstr. 41; tel. (0228) 362505; telex 885734; Ambassador: HEBERTO INCER.

Niger: 5300 Bonn 2, Dürenstr. 9; tel. (0228) 356057; telex 885572; Ambassador: IDRISSA AROUNA.

Nigeria: 5300 Bonn 2, Goldbergweg 13; tel. (0228) 322071; telex 885522; Ambassador: ABBA ZORU.

Norway: 5300 Bonn 2, Gotenstr. 163; tel. (0228) 374055; telex 885491; Ambassador: SVERRE JULIUS GJELLUM.

Oman: 5300 Bonn 2, Lindenallee 11; tel. (0228) 357031; telex 885688; Ambassador: NAZAR MOHAMED ALI.

Pakistan: 5300 Bonn 2, Rheinallee 24; tel. (0228) 352004; telex 885787; Ambassador: ABDUL WAHEED.

Panama: 5300 Bonn 2, Lützowstr. 1; tel. (0228) 361036; telex 885600; Ambassador: ANGEL ERNESTO RIERA-DÍAZ.

FEDERAL REPUBLIC OF GERMANY

Papua New Guinea: 5300 Bonn 2, Gotenstr. 163; tel. (0228) 376855; Ambassador: (vacant).
Paraguay: 5300 Bonn 2, Plittersdorfer Str. 121; tel. (0228) 356727; Ambassador: Dr Víctor Manuel Godoy.
Peru: 5300 Bonn 1, Mozartstr. 34; tel. (0228) 638012; telex 886325; Ambassador: Enrique Fernández de Paredes.
Philippines: 5300 Bonn 1, Argelanderstr. 1; tel. (0228) 213071; telex 8869571; Ambassador: (vacant).
Poland: 5000 Cologne 51, Lindenallee 7; tel. (0221) 380261; telex 8881040; Ambassador: Tadeusz Nestorowicz.
Portugal: 5300 Bonn 2, Ubierstr. 78; tel. (0228) 363011; telex 885577; Ambassador: Fernando Manuel da Silva Marques.
Qatar: 5300 Bonn 2, Brunnenallee 6; tel. (0228) 351074; telex 885476; Ambassador: Ahmed Abdulla al-Khal.
Romania: 5300 Bonn 1, Legionsweg 14; tel. (0228) 678697; telex 8869792; Ambassador: Marcel Dinu.
Rwanda: 5300 Bonn 2, Beethovenallee 72; tel. (0228) 355058; telex 885604; Ambassador: Juvénal Renzaho.
Saudi Arabia: 5300 Bonn 2, Godesberger Allee 40–42; tel. (0228) 379013; telex 885442; Ambassador: Sheikh Rasahd Mussallam Nuweilati.
Senegal: 5300 Bonn 1, Argelanderstr. 3; tel. (0228) 218008; telex 8869644; Ambassador: Cheikh Lèye.
Singapore: 5300 Bonn 2, Südstr. 133; tel. (0228) 312007; telex 885642; Ambassador: See Chak Mun.
Somalia: 5300 Bonn 2, Hohenzollernstr. 12; tel. (0228) 355084; telex 885724; Ambassador: Dr Hassan Sheikh Hussein.
South Africa: 5300 Bonn 2, Auf der Hostert 3; tel. (0228) 821010; telex 885720; Ambassador: Willem Retief.
Spain: 5300 Bonn 1, Schlossstr. 4; tel. (0228) 217094; telex 886792; Ambassador: Eduardo Foncillas.
Sri Lanka: 5300 Bonn 2, Rolandstr. 52; tel. (0228) 332055; telex 885612; Ambassador: Stanley Jayaweera.
Sudan: 5300 Bonn 2, Koblenzerstr. 99; tel. (0228) 363074; telex 885478; Ambassador: Mirghani Suleiman Khalil.
Sweden: 5300 Bonn 1, Allianzplatz, Haus I, An der Heussallee 2–10; tel. (0228) 260020; telex 886667; Ambassador: Lennart Eckerberg.
Switzerland: 5300 Bonn 2, Gotenstr. 156; tel. (0228) 376655; telex 885646; Ambassador: Charles Müller.
Syria: 5300 Bonn 2, Am Kurpark 2; tel. (0228) 363091; telex 885757; Ambassador: Shtewi Seifou.
Tanzania: 5300 Bonn 2, Theaterplatz 26; tel. (0228) 353477; telex 885569; Ambassador: Ahmed Hassan Diria.
Thailand: 5300 Bonn 2, Ubierstr. 65; tel. (0228) 355065; telex 886574; Ambassador: Kosol Sindhvananda.
Togo: 5300 Bonn 2, Beethovenallee 13; tel. (0228) 355091; telex 885595; Ambassador: Nepo Ali.
Tunisia: 5300 Bonn 2, Godesberger Allee 103; tel. (0228) 376981; telex 885477; Ambassador: Mongi Sahli.
Turkey: 5300 Bonn 2, Ute Str. 47; tel. (0228) 346052; telex 885521; Ambassador: Oktay Işcen.
Uganda: 5300 Bonn 2, Dürenstr. 44; tel. (0228) 355027; telex 885578; Ambassador: Perezi Karukubiro Kamunanwire.
USSR: 5300 Bonn 2, Waldstr. 42; tel. (0228) 312086; Ambassador: Yuli A. Kvitsinsky.
United Arab Emirates: 5300 Bonn 1, Erste Fährgasse 6; tel. (0228) 223021; telex 885741; Ambassador: Rashid A. al-Mukhawi.
United Kingdom: 5300 Bonn 1, Friedrich-Ebert-Allee 77; tel. (0228) 234061; telex 886887; Ambassador: Sir Julian Bullard.
USA: 5300 Bonn 2, Deichmanns Aue 29; tel. (0228) 3391; telex 885452; Ambassador: Richard R. Burt.
Uruguay: 5300 Bonn 2, Gotenstr. 1–3; tel. (0228) 356570; telex 885708; Ambassador: Julio Lacarte Muró.
Venezuela: 5300 Bonn 2, Godesberger Allee 119; tel. (0228) 376631; telex 885447; Ambassador: Humberto Enrique Alcalde Alvarez.
Viet-Nam: 5300 Bonn 2, Konstantinstr. 37; tel. (0228) 357022; telex 8861122; Ambassador: (vacant).
Yemen Arab Republic: 5300 Bonn 2, Godesberger-Allee 125–127; tel. (0228) 376851; telex 885765; Ambassador: Muhammad Abdulla al-Eriani.
Yugoslavia: 5300 Bonn 2, Schlossallee 5; tel. (0228) 344051; telex 885530; Ambassador: Dragutin Rozman.
Zaire: 5300 Bonn 2, Im Meisengarten 133; tel. (0228) 346071; telex 885573; Ambassador: Mabolia Inengo Tra Bwato.
Zambia: 5300 Bonn 2, Mittelstr. 39; tel. (0228) 376811; telex 885511; Ambassador: Putteho Muketoi Ngonda.
Zimbabwe: 5300 Bonn 2, Viktoriastr. 28; tel. (0228) 356071; telex 885580; Ambassador: Eubert Paul Tayireva Mashaire.

Judicial System

Judges are not removable except by the decision of a court. Half of the judges of the Federal Constitutional Court are elected by the Bundestag and half by the Bundesrat. A committee for the selection of judges participates in the appointment of judges of the Superior Federal Courts.

FEDERAL CONSTITUTIONAL COURT

Bundesverfassungsgericht (Federal Constitutional Court): 7500 Karlsruhe, Schlossbezirk 3; tel. (0721) 1491; telex 7826749.

President: Prof. Dr Wolfgang Zeidler.

Vice-President: Prof. Dr Roman Herzog.

Judges: Prof. Dr Herman Heussner, Dr Karin Grasshof, Dr Helmut Simon, Prof. Dr Konrad Hesse, Prof. Dr Engelbert Niebler, Dr Dietrich Katzenstein, Prof. Dr Helmut Steinberger, Dr Gisela Niemeyer, Ernst Träger, Dr Ernst Gottfried Mahrenholz, Dr Otto Seidl, Dr Johann Friedrich Henschel, Prof. Dr Ernst-Wolfgang Böckenförde, Prof. Dr Hans Hugo Klein.

SUPERIOR FEDERAL COURTS

Bundesgerichtshof (Federal Court of Justice): 7500 Karlsruhe, Herrenstr. 45A; tel. (030) 32021; telex 7825828.

President: Prof. Dr Gerd Pfeiffer.

Vice-President: Dr Ludwig Thumm.

Presidents of the Senate: Dr Dieter Hoegen, Dr Otto Friedrich Freiherr von Gamm, Hannskarl Salger, Horst Herrmann, Hans Wolfgang Schmidt, Wolfram Braxmaier, Dr Alfred Kellermann, Dr Wolfgang Girisch, Friedrich Lohmann, Gerhard Herdegen, Dr Günter Krohn, Franz Merz, Dr Erich Steffen, Dr Horst Schauenburg, Dr Karl Bruchhausen.

Federal Solicitor-General: Prof. Dr Kurt Rebmann.

Federal Prosecutors: Dr Heinrich Wunder, Gerhard Löchner, Helmut Lunz.

Bundesverwaltungsgericht (Federal Administrative Court): 1000 Berlin 12, Hardenbergstr. 31; tel. (089) 301081.

President: Prof. Dr Horst Sendler.

Vice-President: Dr Günter Zehner.

Presidents of the Senate: Prof. Dr Horst Gützkow, Jürgen Saalmann, Prof. Dr Wilhelm Dodenhoff, Dr Herbert Heinrich, Prof. Dr Felix Weyreuther, Dr Günter Korbmacher, Alfred Fischer, Dr Paul Schwarz, Helmut Hacker, Prof. Dr Otto Schlichter.

Bundesfinanzhof (Federal Financial Court): 8000 Munich 80, Ismaningerstr. 109.

President: Prof. Dr Franz Klein.

Vice-President: Karl-Heinz Nissen.

Presidents of the Senate: Dr Kurt Messmer, Prof. Heinrich Beisse, Dr Georg Döllerer, Dr Max Rid, Dr Claus Grimm, Heinz Schellenberger, Anton Erdweg.

Religion

CHRISTIANITY

Arbeitsgemeinschaft christlicher Kirchen in der Bundesrepublik Deutschland und Berlin (West) eV (Council of Christian Churches in the Federal Republic of Germany and West Berlin): 6000 Frankfurt/Main 1, Neue Schlesingergasse 22–24; tel. (069) 20334; f. 1948; 15 Churches are affiliated to this Council including the Roman Catholic Church and the Greek Orthodox Metropoly; Pres. Dr Heinz Joachim Held.

The Roman Catholic Church

It is estimated that about 45% of the population of the Federal Republic are adherents of the Roman Catholic Church, which is strongest in the South.

Archbishop of Bamberg: Dr ELMAR MARIA KREDEL.
   Bishop of Eichstätt: Dr KARL HEINRICH BRAUN.
   Bishop of Speyer: Dr ANTON SCHLEMBACH.
   Bishop of Würzburg: Prof. Dr PAUL-WERNER SCHEELE.
Archbishop of Munich and Freising: Cardinal FRIEDRICH WETTER.
   Bishop of Augsburg: Dr JOSEPH STIMPFLE.
   Bishop of Passau: Dr FRANZ EDER.
   Bishop of Regensburg: Dr MANFRED MÜLLER.
Archbishop of Freiburg: Dr OSKAR SAIER.
   Bishop of Mainz: Dr KARL LEHMANN.
   Bishop of Rottenburg-Stuttgart: Dr GEORG MOSER.
Archbishop of Cologne: Cardinal JOSEPH HÖFFNER (also Chair. German Conference of Bishops).
   Bishop of Aachen: Dr KLAUS HEMMERLE.
   Bishop of Münster: Dr REINHARD LETTMANN.
   Bishop of Osnabrück: Dr HELMUT HERMANN WITTLER.
   Bishop of Limburg: Dr FRANZ KAMPHAUS.
   Bishop of Trier: Dr HERMANN JOSEF SPITAL.
   Bishop of Essen: Dr FRANZ HENGSBACH.
Archbishop of Paderborn: Dr JOHANNES JOACHIM DEGENHARDT.
   Bishop of Hildesheim: Dr JOSEF HOMEYER.
   Bishop of Fulda: Dr JOHANNES DYBA.
   Bishop of Berlin: Cardinal JOACHIM MEISNER.
Apostolic Nuncio in Germany: Mgr GIUSEPPE UHAČ.
Secretariat of the German Conference of Bishops: 5300 Bonn 1, Kaiserstr. 163; tel. (0228) 1030; telex 8869438; Sec. Prälat WILHELM SCHÄTZLER.
Commissariat of German Bishops—Catholic Office: 53 Bonn, Kaiser-Friedrich-Str. 9; tel. 218015; (represents the German Conference of Bishops before the Federal Government on political issues); Leader Prälat PAUL BOCKLET.
Central Committee of German Catholics: 53 Bonn-Bad Godesberg, Hochkreuzallee 246; tel. (0228) 316056; telex 885696; f. 1868; summarizes the activities of Catholic laymen and lay-organizations in the Federal Republic; Pres. Prof. Dr HANS MAIER; Gen. Sec. Dr FRIEDRICH KRONENBERG.

Protestant Churches

Until 1969 the Protestant churches in both the Federal and Democratic Republics were united in the Evangelische Kirche in Deutschland (EKD), a federation established at the Conference of Eisenach (Thuringia) in 1948. In 1969, however, the churches in the Democratic Republic declared themselves organizationally independent and established the Bund der Evangelischen Kirchen in der DDR. Consequently the EKD is now restricted to the Federal Republic and Berlin (West) only, but maintains links with the churches in the Democratic Republic.

The Vereinigte Evangelisch-Lutherische Kirche Deutschlands (VELKD), one of the federations within the EKD, also divided in 1968 and is paralleled in the Democratic Republic by the VELKDDR. The Evangelische Kirche der Union (EKU) is partly divided and spans both the Federal and the Democratic Republics (see the chapter on the German Democratic Republic).

About 41.6% of the population of the Federal Republic (25.5m.) are members of the Protestant Church, the great majority belonging to churches forming the EKD. The total membership of the Lutheran churches is almost 10m., of the United Churches about 13.5m., and of the Reformed Churches about 448,000.

Outside the EKD are numerous small Protestant Free Churches, such as the Baptists, Methodists, Mennonites and the Lutheran Free Church, with a membership of approximately 400,000 in all.

Evangelische Kirche in Deutschland (EKD) (Protestant Church in Germany): 3000 Hanover 21, Herrenhäuserstr. 12; tel. (0511) 71110; telex 923445; Berlin Office: 1000 Berlin 12, Jebensstr. 3. The governing bodies of the EKD are its Synod of 120 clergy and lay members which meets at regular intervals, the Conference of member churches, and the Council, composed of 15 elected members; the EKD has an ecclesiastical secretariat of its own (the Protestant Church Office), including a special office for foreign relations; Chair. of the Council Bischof Dr MARTIN KRUSE; Pres. of the Office WALTER HAMMER.

Synod of the EKD: 3000 Hanover 21, Herrenhäuserstr. 12; tel. (0511) 71110; telex 923445; Pres. Dr JÜRGEN SCHMUDE.

Deutscher Evangelischer Kirchentag (German Protestant Church Assembly): 6400 Fulda, Magdeburgerstr. 59; tel. (0661) 601091; Pres. ELEONORE VON ROTENHAN.

Churches and Federations within the EKD:

Vereinigte Evangelisch-Lutherische Kirche Deutschlands (VELKD) (The United Protestant-Lutheran Church of Germany): 3000 Hanover 1, Richard-Wagner-Str. 26; tel. (0511) 62611; telex 922673; f. 1949; mems 10m.; a body uniting all but two of the Lutheran territorial Churches within the Protestant Church in Germany; Presiding Bishop Bischof KARLHEINZ STOLL (2380 Schleswig, Plessenstr. 5A).

Evangelische Kirche der Union (EKU) (Protestant Church of the Union): Chancellery, Western Region: 1000 Berlin 12, Jebensstr. 3; Eastern Region: 104 Berlin, Auguststr. 80; tel. (030) 319001-0; composed of Lutheran and Reformed elements; includes the Protestant Churches of Berlin-Brandenburg, Westphalia and the Rhineland (Western Region), Berlin-Brandenburg, Saxony, Greifswald (Pomerania), Görlitz (Silesia) and Anhalt (Eastern Region); Chair. of Council Präses D. GERHARD BRANDT (Western Region), Bischof Dr FORCK (Eastern Region); Chair of Synod Präses CHRISTOF KARZIG (1000 Berlin 31, Hohenzollerndamm 130A) (Western Region), Präses HERBERT KARPINSKI (Eastern Region); Pres. of Administration PETER KRASKE (Western Region), Dr FRIEDRICH WINTER (Eastern Region).

Arnoldshainer Konferenz: 1000 Berlin 12, Jebensstr. 3; tel. (030) 319001-0; f. 1967; a loose federation of the church governments of one Lutheran, one Reformed Territorial and all United Churches, aiming at greater co-operation between them; Chair. of Council Landesbischof Prof. Dr KLAUS ENGELHARDT.

Reformierter Bund (Reformed League): 4444 Bad Bentheim, Klapperstiege 13; tel. (05922) 1234; f. 1884; unites the Reformed Territorial Churches and Congregations of Germany. The central body of the Reformed League is the 'Moderamen', the elected representation of the various Reformed Congregations; Moderator Prof. Dr HANS-JOACHIM KRAUS (5600 Wuppertal 23, Zur Gloria 25); Gen. Sec. Pfarrer JOACHIM GUHRT.

Affiliated to the EKD:

Bund Evangelisch-Reformierter Kirchen (Association of Protestant Reformed Churches): 2000 Hamburg 1, Ferdinandstr. 21; tel. (040) 332760; Chair. Präses P. HERMANN KELLER.

Herrnhuter Brüdergemeine or **Europäisch-Festländische Brüder-Unität** (Moravian Church): f. 1457; there are 24 congregations in the Federal Republic, the Democratic Republic, Switzerland, Denmark and the Netherlands with approximately 30,000 mems; Chair. of Western District Rev. Dr HELMUT BINTZ (7325 Bad Boll, Badwasen 6; tel. (07164) 2047).

   †**Protestant Church in Baden:** 7500 Karlsruhe 1, Blumenstr. 1; tel. (147) 234; Landesbischof Prof. Dr KLAUS ENGELHARDT.

   ***Protestant-Lutheran Church in Bavaria:** 8000 Munich 2, Meiserstr. 13; tel. (089) 55951; telex 529674; Landesbischof D. Dr phil., Mag. theol. JOHANNES HANSELMANN DD.

   †**Protestant Church in Berlin-Brandenburg (Berlin West):** Konsistorium: 1000 Berlin 21, Bachstr. 1–2; tel. (030) 390910; telex 181241; Bischof Dr MARTIN KRUSE.

   †**Protestant Church of Bremen:** 2800 Bremen 1, Franziuseck 2–4, Postfach 10 69 29; tel. (0421) 55970; Pres. ECKART RANFT.

   ***Protestant-Lutheran Church in Brunswick:** 3340 Wolfenbüttel, Neuer Weg 88–90; tel. (05331) 8020; Landesbischof Prof. Dr GERHARD MÜLLER DD.

   ***Protestant-Lutheran Church of Hanover:** 3000 Hanover 1, Haarstr. 6; tel. (0511) 12411; Landesbischof Prof. D. EDUARD LOHSE.

   †**Protestant Church in Hesse and Nassau:** 6100 Darmstadt, Paulusplatz 1; tel. (06151) 4050; Pres. Rev. HELMUT SPENGLER.

   †**Protestant Church of Kurhessen-Waldeck:** 3500 Kassel-Wilhelmshöhe, Wilhelmshöher Allee 330; tel. (0561) 30831; Bischof Dr HANS-GERNOT JUNG.

   †**Church of Lippe:** 4930 Detmold 1, Leopoldstr. 27; tel. (05231) 74030; Landessuperintendent Dr AKO JAARBECK.

   ***Protestant-Lutheran Church of North Elbe:** Bischof D. KARLHEINZ STOLL (2380 Schleswig, Plessenstr. 5A; tel. (04621) 24622); Bischof Prof. Dr ULRICH WILCKENS (2400 Lübeck, Bäckerstr. 3–5; tel. (0451) 797176); Bischof Prof. D. PETER KRUSCHE (2000 Hamburg 11, Neue Burg 1; tel. (040) 3689-216); Pres. of North Elbian Church Administration Dr KLAUS BLASCHKE (2300 Kiel, Dänische Str. 21–35; tel. (0431) 991-1).

†**Protestant-Reformed Church in North-West Germany:** 2950 Leer, Saarstr. 6; tel. (0491) 8030; Provincial Superintendent Dr Gerhard Nordholt; Pres. of the Territorial Church Council Rev. Hinnerk Schröder.

†**Protestant-Lutheran Church in Oldenburg:** 2900 Oldenburg, Philosophenweg 1; tel. (0441) 77010; Bischof D. Dr H. H. Harms.

†**Protestant Church of the Palatinate:** 6720 Speyer, Domplatz 5; tel. (06232) 1091; Pres. Heinrich Kron.

†**Protestant Church in the Rhineland:** 4000 Düsseldorf 30, Hans-Böckler-Str. 7; tel. (0211) 45621; Pres. D. Gerhard Brandt.

***Protestant-Lutheran Church of Schaumburg-Lippe:** 3062 Bückeburg, Herderstr. 27; tel. (05722) 25021); Landesbischof Prof. Dr Joachim Heubach; Pres. Dr Michael Winckler.

†**Protestant Church of Westphalia:** 4800 Bielefeld 1, Altstädter Kirchplatz 5; tel. (0521) 5941; Präses Hans-Martin Linnemann.

†**Protestant-Lutheran Church of Württemberg:** 7000 Stuttgart 1, Gänsheidestr. 2 and 4, Postfach 92; tel. (0711) 21491; Landesbischof D. Hans von Keler.

(* Member of the VELKD; † member of the EKU)

Other Protestant Churches

Bund Evangelisch-Freikirchlicher Gemeinden (Union of Protestant Free Church Congregations; Baptists): 6380 Bad Homburg v. d. H. 1, Friedberger Str. 101; tel. (06172) 80040; f. 1849; Pres. Rev. Günter Hitzemann; Dirs Rev. Manfred Otto, Rev. Gerd Rudzio.

Bund Freier evangelischer Gemeinden (Covenant of Free Evangelical Churches in Germany): 5810 Witten (Ruhr), Goltenkamp 4; tel. (02302) 39901; f. 1854; Pres. Karl H. Knöppel; Sec. Assessor Heinz-Adolf Ritter; 24,100 mems.

Evangelisch-methodistische Kirche (United Methodist Church): 6000 Frankfurt/Main 1, Wilhelm-Leuschner-Str. 8; tel. (069) 250012; f. 1968 when the former Evangelische Gemeinschaft and Methodistenkirche united; Bishop Hermann L. Sticher.

Selbständige Evangelisch-Lutherische Kirche (Independent Evangelical-Lutheran Church): Schopenhauerstr. 7, 3000 Hanover 61; tel. (0511) 557808; f. 1972; Bishop Dr Jobst Schöne, D.D.

Vereinigung der deutschen Mennonitengemeinden (Union of German Mennonite Congregations): 2970 Emden, Brückstr. 74; tel. (04921) 22966; f. 1886; Chair. Dr Heinold Fast.

Other Christian Churches

Alt-Katholische Kirche (Old Catholic Church): 5300 Bonn 1, Gregor-Mendelstr. 28; seceded from the Roman Catholic Church as a protest against the declaration of Papal infallibility in 1870; belongs to the Utrecht Union of Old Catholic Churches; in full communion with the Anglican Communion; Pres. Bischof Dr Sigisbert Kraft (Bonn); 28,000 mems.

JUDAISM

The Jewish community in Germany is estimated to number about 35,000, of whom more than 30,000 live in the Federal Republic and West Berlin.

Zentralrat der Juden in Deutschland (Central Council of Jews in Germany): 5300 Bonn 2, Rüngsdorfer Str. 6; tel. (0228) 357023; Pres. Board of Dirs Werner Nachmann; Sec.-Gen. Alexander Ginsburg.

The Press

Article 5 of the 1949 Basic Law of the Republic stipulates: 'Everyone has the right freely to express or to disseminate his opinion by speech, writing and pictures and freely to inform himself from generally accessible sources. Freedom of the press and freedom of reporting by radio and motion pictures are guaranteed. There shall be no censorship. These rights are limited by the provisions of the general laws, the provisions of the law for the protection of youth, and by the right to inviolability of personal honour.' These last qualifications refer to the Federal law penalizing the sale to young people of literature judged to endanger morality, and to articles in the Penal Code relating to defamation, in particular Article 187A concerning defamation of public figures.

There is no Federal Press Law, all legal action being normally referred back to the Constitution. But the press is subject to general items of legislation, some of which may significantly limit press freedom. Article 353C of the Penal Code, for example, dating from the Nazi period, prohibits the publication of official news supposed to be secret; under it a journalist may be required to reveal his sources. The Code of Criminal Procedure also constitutes a danger in that it authorizes the Government to confiscate objects potentially important as evidence in a legal investigation, which may be construed to include papers, print, etc.

Freedom of the press is stipulated in each of the Constitutions of the individual Länder. Many Länder have enacted laws defining the democratic role of the press and some give journalists access to sources of government information; some authorize the journalist to refuse to disclose his sources; others qualify, and even withhold this right. Some permit printed matter to be confiscated on suspicion of an indictable offence only if authorized by an independent judge; others allow a district attorney or even the police to give this authorization.

The German Press Council was founded in 1956 and is composed of publishers and journalists. It lays down guidelines, investigates complaints against the press and enjoys considerable standing.

The Federal German press is quite free of government control. No daily is directly owned by a political party, and though some 10% of papers support a party line, the majority of newspapers, including all the major dailies, are politically independent.

The political and economic conditions since 1949 have fostered the rapid development of a few large publishing groups.

In 1968 a government commission laid down various limits on the proportions of circulation one group should be allowed to control: (1) 40% of the total circulation of newspapers or 40% of the total circulation of magazines; (2) 20% of the total circulation of newspapers and magazines together; (3) 15% of the circulation in one field if the proportion owned in the other field is 40%. At that time the Springer Group's estimated ownership was 39.2% of newspaper circulation (65–70% in Berlin) and 17.5% of magazine circulation. In June 1968 Springer reduced his share of the periodical market to around 11%.

In 1986 there were 382 daily newspapers, with a combined circulation of 20.9m. copies. There were 4 Sunday papers, with a circulation of 3.7m., and 45 weekly papers, with a circulation of 1.9m. The most important and influential national dailies include *Frankfurter Allgemeine Zeitung, Süddeutsche Zeitung* (Munich) and *Die Welt* (Hamburg). The newspaper with the largest circulation is *Bild Zeitung* (circ. 5,400,000) which is printed in eight different provincial centres. The most influential weekly newspapers include *Die Zeit* and the Sundays *Bild am Sonntag* and *Welt am Sonntag*. In 1981 about 9,400 periodicals were published, with a total circulation of over 200m. copies. Those with circulations of over 1m. included the illustrated news weeklies *Der Spiegel, Stern* and *Quick*, the TV and Radio magazine *HÖRZU* and women's magazines *Brigitte, Burda-moden, Frau im Spiegel* and *Für Sie*.

The principal newspaper publishing groups are:

Axel Springer Group: 1000 Berlin 61, Kochstr. 50; tel. (030) 25-91-0; telex 184257; and 2000 Hamburg 36, Kaiser-Wilhelm-Str. 6; tel. (040) 3-47-1; telex 403242; the largest newspaper publishing group in continental Europe; includes five major dailies *(Die Welt, Hamburger Abendblatt, Bild Zeitung, Berliner Morgenpost, BZ)*, two Sunday papers *(Welt am Sonntag, Bild am Sonntag)*, three radio, television and family magazines *(HÖRZU, Funk Uhr, Bildwoche)*, two women's journals *(JOURNAL für die Frau, Bild der Frau)*, the weekly motoring magazine *Auto-Bild*, and the book publishing firm Verlag Ullstein GmbH; Propr Axel Springer Verlag AG.

Gruner und Jahr AG & Co Druck- und Verlagshaus: 2210 Itzehoe, Am Vossbarg, Posfach 1240; telex 28289; and 2000 Hamburg 36, Postfach 302040; telex 2195213; owns *Stern, Brigitte, Essen und Trinken, Geo, Capital, Eltern, Nicole, Häuser, Yps, Schöner Wohnen, Hamburger Morgenpost*.

Süddeutscher-Verlag: 8000 Munich 2, Sendlingstr. 80; tel. (089) 21830; telex 523426; owns *Süddeutsche Zeitung*; Mans Dr Jörn Könke, Günther Viertler, Klaus Wagner, Manfred Winterbach.

Jahreszeiten-Verlag GmbH: 2000 Hamburg 60, Possmoorweg 1; tel. (040) 27170; telex 213214; owns amongst others the periodicals *Für Sie* and *Moderne Frau;* Pres. Helmut Ganske.

Heinrich-Bauer-Verlag: 2000 Hamburg 1, Burchardstr. 11 and 8000 Munich 2, Augustenstr. 10; telex 524350; owns 25 popular illustrated magazines, including *Quick* (Munich), *Neue Revue* (Hamburg), *Praline, Neue Post, Das Neue Platt* and *Bravo;* Pres. Heinrich Bauer.

Burda GmbH: 7600 Offenburg, Postfach 1230; tel. (0781) 8401; telex 528000; owns *Bunte, Bild+Funk, Freundin, Pan, Freizeit Revue, Meine Familie und ich, Mein Schöner Garten, Das Haus,*

FEDERAL REPUBLIC OF GERMANY

Architectural Digest (Deutsch) and *Ambiente;* Mans. Dr Franz Burda, Frieder Burda, Dr Hubert Burda, Karl-Heinz Hiller, Peter Boenisch, Gerd Spraul, Herbert Warth.

PRINCIPAL DAILIES

Aachen

Aachener Nachrichten: 5100 Aachen, Dresdner Str. 3, Postfach 110; tel. (0241) 5101-1; telex 832851; f. 1872; Publrs Zeitungsverlag Aachen; Edited by Verlagsanstalt Cerfontaine GmbH & Co., 5100 Aachen, Theaterstr. 24-34; circ. 60,000.

Aachener Volkszeitung: 5100 Aachen, Dresdner Str. 3, Postfach 110; tel. (0241) 51011; telex 832851; f. 1946; Publishers Zeitungsverlag Aachen; Editor-in-Chief Dr Anton Sterzl; circ. 106,000.

Ansbach

Fränkische Landeszeitung: 8800 Ansbach, Nürnberger Str. 9–17, Postfach 1362; tel. (0981) 95000; telex 61815; Editors-in-Chief Gerhard Egetemayer, Peter M. Szymanowski; circ. 50,000.

Aschaffenburg

Main-Echo: 8750 Aschaffenburg (Main), Goldbacher Str. 25–27, Postfach 548; tel. (06021) 3961; telex 4188837; Editors Gerold Martin, Franz Niessner, Dr Helmut Teufel; circ. 80,000.

Augsburg

Augsburger Allgemeine: 8900 Augsburg 1, Curt-Frenzel-Str. 2, Postfach 100054; tel. (0821) 70071; telex 53837; Editor Günter Holland; circ. 340,000.

Baden-Baden

Badisches Tagblatt: 7570 Baden-Baden, Stefanienstr. 1–3, Postfach 120; tel (07221) 2151; telex 781158; Editor Udo F. A. Rotzoll; circ. 40,000.

Bamberg

Fränkischer Tag: 8600 Bamberg, Gutenbergstr. 1; tel. (0951) 1880; telex 662426; Publr Karl Weber; circ. 71,000.

Berlin

Berliner Morgenpost: 1000 Berlin 61, Kochstr. 50, Postfach 110303; tel. (030) 25910; telex 183132; f. 1898; published by Ullstein GmbH; Editor Johannes Otto; circ. 182,000.

BZ (Berliner Zeitung): 1000 Berlin 61, Kochstr. 50; tel. (030) 25910; telex 183132; f. 1877; published by Ullstein GmbH; Editor Wilhelm Pannier; circ. 307,000.

Der Tagesspiegel: 1000 Berlin 30, Potsdamer Str. 87; tel. (030) 26931; telex 183773; f. 1945; circ. 120,000.

Bielefeld

Neue Westfälische: 4800 Bielefeld 1, Niedernstr. 23–27, Postfach 26; tel. (0521) 5550; telex 932799; f. 1967; Editors Tim Arnold, Dr Heinz Epping; circ. 213,256.

Westfalen-Blatt: 4800 Bielefeld, Südbrackstr. 14–18, Postfach 8740; tel. (0521) 5850; f. 1946; Editor Carl-W. Busse; circ. 147,000.

Bonn

Bonner Rundschau: 5300 Bonn, Thomas-Mann-Str. 51–53, Postfach 1248; tel. (0228) 7211; telex 886702; f. 1946; Dir Dr Heinrich Heinen; circ. 50,700.

General-Anzeiger: 5300 Bonn, Justus von Liebig-Str. 15, Postfach 1609; tel. (0228) 66880; f. 1725; independent; Publrs Hermann Neusser, Hermann Neusser Jr; Editor Friedhelm Kemna; circ. 85,000.

Die Welt: 5300 Bonn, Godesberger Allee 99; tel. (0228) 3041; telex 885714; f. 1946; published by Axel Springer Verlag; Publr Dr Herbert Kremp; Editors Peter Gillies, Manfred Schell; circ. 210,000.

Bremen

Bremer Nachrichten: 2800 Bremen, Martinistr. 43; tel. (0421) 3671-1; telex 244720; f. 1743; Publr Herbert C. Ordemann; Editors Dietrich Ide, Volker Weise; circ. 44,000.

Weser-Kurier: 2800 Bremen 1, Martinistr. 43, Postfach 107801; tel. (0421) 3671-11; telex 244530; f. 1945; Publr Herbert C. Ordemann; circ. 185,000.

Bremerhaven

Nordsee-Zeitung: 2850 Bremerhaven 1, Hafenstr. 140; tel. (0471) 597-0; telex 238761; Chief Editor Hans-Dieter Hamboch; circ. 80,000.

Brunswick

Braunschweiger Zeitung: 3300 Brunswick, Hamburger Str. 277 (Pressehaus), Postfach 3263; tel. (0531) 39000; telex 952722; Editor Dr Arnold Rabbow; circ. 167,000.

Cologne

Express: 5000 Cologne 1, Breite Str. 70, Postfach 100410; tel. (0221) 2240; telex 8882965; f. 1964; Publr Alfred Neven Dumont; Editor Michael Spreng; circ. 450,000.

Kölner Stadt-Anzeiger: 5000 Cologne 1, Breite Str. 70, Postfach 100410; tel. (0221) 2240; telex 8882965; f. 1876; Publr Alfred Neven Dumont; Editor Hans Schmitz; circ. 263,000.

Kölnische Rundschau: 5000 Cologne 1, Stolkgasse 25–45, Postfach 101910; tel. (0221) 16320; telex 8882687; f. 1946; Publr Dr Heinrich Heinen; Editor-in-Chief Jürgen C. Jagla; circ. 160,000.

Darmstadt

Darmstädter Echo: 6100 Darmstadt, Holzhofallee 25–31, Postfach 110269; tel. (06151) 3871; telex 419363; f. 1945; Publrs Max Bach, Horst Bach; Editor-in-Chief Roland Hof; circ. 100,000.

Dortmund

Ruhr-Nachrichten: 4600 Dortmund 1, Pressehaus, Westenhellweg 68-88, Postfach 282; telex 822106; f. 1949; Editor Florian Lensing-Wolff; circ. 253,000.

Westfälische Rundschau: 4600 Dortmund 1, Brüderweg 9; tel. (0231) 54941; telex 822460; Editor Günter Hammer; circ. 250,000.

Düsseldorf

Handelsblatt: 4000 Düsseldorf 1, Kasernenstr. 67, Postfach 1102; tel. (0211) 8388-0; telex 17211308; 5 a week; only economics, business and finance newspaper with national circulation; Man. Dir Dr Pierre Gerckens; Editor-in-Chief Klaus Bernhardt; circ. 110,000.

Rheinische Post: 4000 Düsseldorf, Schadowstr. 11, Postfach 1135; tel. (0211) 5050; telex 8581901; f. 1946; Dirs Dr J. Schaffrath; Editor Dr Joachim Sobotta; circ. 395,000.

Westdeutsche Zeitung: 4000 Düsseldorf 1, Königsallee 27, Postfach 1132; tel. (0211) 8382-0; Editor-in-Chief Paulheinz Grupe; Publisher and Editor Dr M. Girardet; circ. 216,000.

Essen

Neue Ruhr Zeitung: 4300 Essen, Friedrichstr. 34–38, Postfach 104161; tel. (0201) 20640; telex 8579951; Editor-in-Chief Jens Feddersen; circ. 215,000.

Westdeutsche Allgemeine Zeitung: 4300 Essen, Friedrichstr. 34–38, Postfach 104161; tel. (0201) 20640; telex 8579951; Editor Siegfried Maruhn; circ. 660,000.

Frankfurt am Main

Frankfurter Allgemeine Zeitung: 6000 Frankfurt a.M., Hellerhofstr. 2-4, Postfach 100808; tel. (069) 75910; telex 41223; f. 1949; Editors Bruno Dechamps, Fritz Ullrich Fack, Joachim C. Fest, Jürgen Jeske, Johann Georg Reissmüller; circ. 350,000.

Frankfurter Neue Presse: 6000 Frankfurt a.M., Frankenallee 71–81, Postfach 100801; tel. (069) 75011; telex 411054; independent; Editor Werner Wirthle; circ. 129,000.

Frankfurter Rundschau: 6000 Frankfurt a.M., Grosse Eschenheimer Str. 16–18, Postfach 100660; tel. (069) 21991; telex 411651; Editor Werner Holzer; circ. 196,000.

Freiburg

Badische Zeitung: 7800 Freiburg i. Br., Basler Landstr. 3; tel. (0761) 4961; telex 772820; f. 1946; Editor Dr Ansgar Fürst; circ. 170,000.

Göttingen

Göttinger Tageblatt: 3400 Göttingen, Dransfelder Str. 1, Postfach 1953; tel. (0551) 9011; telex 96800; f. 1889; Man. Dir Manfred Dallmann; Editor-in-Chief Dr Rainer Wiese; circ. 48,000.

Hagen

Westfalenpost: 5800 Hagen, Mittelstr. 22; tel. (02331) 2041; telex 823861; f. 1946; Chief Editor Robert Schmelzer; circ. 157,000.

Hamburg

Bild Zeitung: 2000 Hamburg 36, Kaiser-Wilhelm-Str. 6; tel. (040) 3471; telex 2170010; f. 1952; published by Axel Springer Verlag; Chief Editor Horst Fust; circ. 5,400,000.

Hamburger Abendblatt: 2000 Hamburg 36, Kaiser-Wilhelm-Str. 6, Postfach 304630; tel. (040) 3471; telex 2170010; published by

FEDERAL REPUBLIC OF GERMANY

Axel Springer Verlag; Editor-in-Chief Klaus Korn; circ. 280,000 (Saturdays 358,000).
Hamburger Morgenpost: 2000 Hamburg 50, Griegstr. 75; tel. (040) 883031; telex 2161168; Editor Nils von der Heyde; circ. 236,000.

Hanover
Hannoversche Allgemeine Zeitung: 3000 Hanover 1, Bemeroder Str. 58, Postfach 209; tel. (0511) 5180; telex 923911-15; Editor Luise Madsack; circ. 208,000.

Heidelberg
Rhein-Neckar-Zeitung: 6900 Heidelberg, Hauptstr. 23, Postfach 104560; telex 461751; Publrs Dr Ludwig Knorr, Winfried Knorr, Dr Dieter Schulze; circ. 100,000.

Heilbronn
Heilbronner Stimme: 7100 Heilbronn, Hochhaus Allee 2, Postfach 1940; tel. (07131) 615-1; telex 728729; f. 1946; Editor-in-Chief Werner Thunert; circ. 104,000.

Hof-Saale
Frankenpost: 8670 Hof-Saale, Poststr. 11, Postfach 1320; tel. (09281) 8161; telex 643601; Publr Frankenpost Verlag GmbH; Editor-in-Chief Heinrich Giegold; circ 72,000.

Ingolstadt
Donau-Kurier: 8070 Ingolstadt, Stauffenbergstr. 2, Postfach 340; tel. (0841) 6801; telex 55845; f. 1872; Publr and Dir Dr W. Reissmüller; circ. 75,000.

Karlsruhe
Badische Neueste Nachrichten: 7500 Karlsruhe 1, Lammstr. 1-5, Postfach 1469; tel. (0721) 1441; telex 7826960; Publr and Editor Hans W. Baur; circ. 167,000.

Kassel
Hessische/Niedersächsische Allgemeine: 3500 Kassel, Frankfurter Str. 168, Postfach 101009; tel. (0561) 2030; telex 99635; f. 1959; independent; Editor-in-Chief Achim von Roos; circ. 230,000.

Kempten
Allgäuer Zeitung: 8960 Kempten, Kotternerstr. 64, Postfach 1129; tel. (0831) 2061; telex 54871; f. 1968; Publrs Georg Fürst von Waldburg-Zeil, Günter Holland; Editor-in-Chief Günter Holland; circ. 110,000.

Kiel
Kieler Nachrichten: 2300 Kiel 1, Fleethörn 1-7, Postfach 1111; tel. (0431) 9030; telex 292716; Chief Editor Karlheinz Vater; circ. 111,969.

Koblenz
Rhein-Zeitung: 5400 Koblenz, August-Horch-Str. 28, Postfach 1540; tel. (0261) 8921; telex 862611; Editor Hans Peter Sommer; circ. 223,000.

Konstanz
Südkurier: 7750 Konstanz, Marktstätte 4, Postfach 4300; tel. (07531) 2820; telex 733231; f. 1945; Editor J. Weyl; circ. 137,000.

Leutkirch
Schwäbische Zeitung: 7970 Leutkirch 1, Rudolf-Roth-Str. 18, Postfach 1145; tel. (07561) 800; telex 7321915; f. 1945; Editor Chrysostomus Zodel; circ. 190,000.

Lübeck
Lübecker Nachrichten: 2400 Lübeck, Königstr. 53-57; tel. (0451) 1441; telex 26801; f. 1945; Chief Editor Klaus J. Groth; circ. 112,337.

Ludwigshafen
Die Rheinpfalz: 6700 Ludwigshafen/Rhein, Amtsstr. 5-11, Postfach 211147; tel. (0621) 590201; telex 464624; Dir Dr Dieter Schaub; circ. 240,000.

Mainz
Allgemeine Zeitung: 6500 Mainz, Grosse Bleiche 44-50, Postfach 3120; tel. (06131) 1441; telex 4187753; part of the Zeitungsgruppe Rhein-Main-Nahe; circ. 128,000.

Mannheim
Mannheimer Morgen: 6800 Mannheim 1, Am Marktplatz, Postfach 1503; tel. (0621) 17020; telex 462171; Publrs Dr K. Ackermann, R. v. Schilling; Chief Editors Sigmar Heilmann, Horst-Dieter Schiele; circ. 182,700.

Munich
Abendzeitung/8-Uhr-Blatt: 8000 Munich 2, Sendlingerstr. 79; tel. (089) 23770; f. 1948; Publr Anneliese Friedmann; Editor-in-Chief Wolfhart Berg; circ. 270,000.
Münchner Merkur: 8000 Munich 2, Bayerstr. 57-67, Pressehaus; tel. (089) 53060; Publr Dr Dirk Ippen; Editor Alfons Döser; circ. 167,000.
Süddeutsche Zeitung: 8000 Munich 2, Sendlingerstr. 80, Postfach 20220; tel. (089) 21830; telex 523426; f. 1945; Editor-in-Chief Dieter Schröder; circ. 370,000.

Münster
Münstersche Zeitung: 4400 Münster, Neubrückenstr. 8-11, Postfach 5560; tel. (0251) 592-0; f. 1870; independent; Editor Dr Ralf Richard Koerner; circ. 61,000.
Westfälische Nachrichten: 4400 Münster, Soester Str. 13, Postfach 8680; tel. (0251) 6900; telex 892830; Chief Editor Bertram von Hobe; circ. 204,000.

Nuremberg
Nürnberger Nachrichten: 8500 Nuremberg, Marienplatz 1/5; tel. (0911) 2160; telex 622339; f. 1945; Editor Bruno Schnell; circ. 340,000.

Oberndorf-Neckar
Schwarzwälder Bote: 7238 Oberndorf-Neckar, Postfach 1380; tel. (07423) 780; telex 762814; circ. 96,000.

Oelde
Die Glocke: 4740 Oelde, Engelbert-Holterdorf-Str. 4-6; tel. (02522) 3111; telex 89543; f. 1880; Editors Karl Friedrich Gehring, Engelbert Holterdorf; circ. 64,000.

Offenbach
Offenbach-Post: 6050 Offenbach, Grosse Marktstr. 36-44, Postfach 100263; tel. (069) 80630; telex 4152864; f. 1947; Publr Udo Bintz; circ. 54,000.

Oldenburg
Nordwest-Zeitung: 2900 Oldenburg, Peterstr. 28-34, Postfach 2525; tel. (0441) 2391; telex 441102; published by the Druck- und Pressehaus GmbH; Editor B. Schulte; circ. 122,000.

Osnabrück
Neue Osnabrücker Zeitung: 4500 Osnabrück, Grosse Str. 17/19, Postfach 4260; tel. (0541) 3250; telex 944841; f. 1967 from merger of *Neue Tagespost* and *Osnabrücker Tageblatt*; Chief Editor F. Schmedt; circ. 183,000.

Passau
Passauer Neue Presse: 8390 Passau, Neuburger Str. 28, Postfach 2040; tel. (0851) 5020; telex 57879; f. 1946; Man. Dirs Dr W. J. Grau, K. Haack; Editor-in-Chief Ulrich Zimmermann; circ. 155,100.

Regensburg
Mittelbayerische Zeitung: 8400 Regensburg 1, Kumpfmühler Str. 11; tel. (0941) 2071; telex 65841; f. 1945; Editor Karlheinz Esser; circ. 100,000.

Saarbrücken
Saarbrücker Zeitung: 6600 Saarbrücken, Gutenbergstr. 11-23, Postfach 296; tel. (0681) 5020; telex 4421262; f. 1761; Editors Dr Hans Stiff, Uwe Jacobsen; circ. 205,000.

Stuttgart
Stuttgarter Nachrichten: 7000 Stuttgart 80, Plieninger Str. 150, Postfach 550; tel. (0711) 72051; telex 7255395; f. 1946; Editor-in-Chief Jürgen Offenbach; circ. 260,000.
Stuttgarter Zeitung: 7000 Stuttgart 80, Plieninger Str. 150, Postfach 150; tel. (0711) 72051; telex 7255395; Chief Editor Dr Thomas Löffelholz; circ. 160,000.

FEDERAL REPUBLIC OF GERMANY
Directory

Trier
Trierischer Volksfreund: 5500 Trier, Nikolaus-Koch-Platz 1–3, Postfach 3770; tel. (0651) 45091; telex 472860; Chief Editor ALLRICH EDEN; circ. 94,000.

Ulm
Südwest Presse: 7900 Ulm, Frauenstr. 77, Postfach 3333; tel. (0731) 15601; telex 712461; circ. 356,500.

Weiden
Der Neue Tag: 8480 Weiden, Weigelstr. 16, Postfach 1340; tel. (0961) 851; telex 63880; Editor-in-Chief HORST HOMBERG; circ. 76,000.

Wetzlar
Wetzlarer Neue Zeitung: 6330 Wetzlar, Elsa-Brandström-Str. 18, Postfach 2940; tel. (06441) 7010; telex 483883; f. 1945; Editor JANOS BARDI; circ. 70,000.

Wiesbaden
Wiesbadener Kurier: 6200 Wiesbaden 1, Langgasse 21, Postfach 6029; tel. (06221) 3550; telex 4186244; Chief Editor HILMAR BÖRSING; circ. 65,000.

Würzburg
Main-Post: 8700 Würzburg, Berner Str. 2; tel. (0931) 60010; f. 1883; independent; Publrs JOHANNES VON GUTTENBERG, GERHARD WIESEMANN; Editor-in-Chief BRUNO WALTERT; circ. 155,000.

SUNDAY AND WEEKLY PAPERS

Bayernkurier: 8000 Munich 19, Nymphenbürger Str. 64; tel. (089) 120041; weekly; organ of the CSU; Chief Editor W. SCHARNAGL; circ. 170,000.

Bild am Sonntag: 2000 Hamburg 36, Kaiser-Wilhelm-Str. 6, Postfach 566; tel. (040) 3471; telex 403242; f. 1956; Sunday; Published by Axel Springer Verlag; Chief Editor EWALD STRUWE; circ. 2,400,000.

Deutsches Allgemeines Sonntagsblatt: 2000 Hamburg 13, Mittelweg 111; tel. (040) 447011; telex 212973; Sunday; circ. 129,000.

Rheinischer Merkur: 5400 Koblenz, Görgenstr. 11, Pressehaus; tel. (0261) 12303-06; f. 1946; weekly; Editor Dr ALOIS RUMMEL; circ. 133,000.

Vorwärts: 5300 Bonn 2, Am Michaelshof 8; tel. (0228) 820050; telex 885603; f. 1876; weekly; organ of the SPD.

Welt am Sonntag: 2000 Hamburg 36, Kaiser-Wilhelm-Str. 1; tel. (040) 3471; telex 403242; Sunday; published by Axel Springer Verlag; Editors CLAUS JACOBI, MANFRED GEIST; circ. 336,000.

Die Zeit: 2000 Hamburg 1, Postfach 10 68 20, Speersort 1, Pressehaus; tel. (040) 3280-0; telex 886433; f. 1946; weekly; Publrs HILDE VON LANG, HELMUT SCHMIDT; Editor-in-Chief Dr THEO SOMMER; circ. 452,000.

SELECTED PERIODICALS
Agriculture

Agrar Praxis: 43 Essen, Girardetstr. 2–36; tel. (0201) 7996-418; telex 857888; f. 1882; monthly; Editor-in-Chief KLAUS NIEHÖRSTER; circ. 60,250.

Agrarwirtschaft: 6000 Frankfurt 1, Schumannstr. 27; tel. (069) 7433-1; telex 4170335; f. 1952; monthly; agricultural management, market research and agricultural policy; Publr ALFRED STROTHE; circ. 3,000.

Bayerisches Landwirtschaftliches Wochenblatt: 8000 Munich 2, Postfach 200509, Lothstr. 29; f. 1810; weekly; organ of the Bayerischer Bauernverband; Editor LUDWIG M. GAUL; circ. 110,000.

Eisenbahn-Landwirt: 43 Essen 11, Am Ellenbogen 12, Postfach 110664; tel. (0201) 670525; f. 1918; monthly; Dir HANS HÜSKEN; circ. 125,000.

Land und Garten: 3 Hanover, Bemeroder Str. 58, Postfach 3720; f. 1920; weekly; agriculture and gardening; Editor LUISE MADSACK; circ. 80,000.

Das Landvolk: 3000 Hanover, Kabelkamp 6, Postfach 160; telex 921169; fortnightly; issued by Landbuch-Verlag GmbH; Chief Editor WALDEMAR FRITZ; circ. 104,000.

Die Landpost: 7000 Stuttgart 70, Wollgrasweg 31; tel. (0711) 451091; telex 111092; f. 1945; weekly; agriculture and gardening; Editors Dr KONRAD BINKERT, ERICH REICH.

Art, Drama, Architecture and Music

AIT Architektur, Innenarchitektur, Technischer Ausbau: 7000 Stuttgart 1, Postfach 3081; f. 1890; every two months; Editors E. HOEHN, R. SELLIN; circ. 10,000.

Die Kunst: 8000 Munich 90, Pilgersheimer Str. 38; telex 523981; f. 1885; monthly; arts and antiques; published by Karl Thiemig AG München; circ. 6,500.

Das Kunstwerk: 7000 Stuttgart 80, Hessbrühlstr. 69; tel. (0711) 7863-1; telex 7-255820; f. 1946; every two months; modern art.

Musica: 3500 Kassel, Postfach 10 03 29; Editor Prof. Dr CLEMENS KÜHN; circ. 8,000.

Theater heute: 1000 Berlin 30, Lützowplatz 7; tel. (030) 2617002; monthly; Editors Dr HENNING RISCHBIETER, Dr PETER VON BECKER, Dr MICHAEL MERSCHMEIER.

Economics, Finance and Industry

Absatzwirtschaft: 4000 Düsseldorf 1, Kasernenstr. 67, Postfach 1102; tel. 8388493/4; f. 1958; monthly; journal for marketing; Dir UWE HOCH; Editor FRIEDHELM PÄLIKE; circ. 13,000.

Atomwirtschaft-Atomtechnik: 4000 Düsseldorf 1, Kasernenstr. 67, Postfach 1102; tel. (0211) 8388-498; telex 17211308; f. 1956; monthly; technical, scientific and economic aspects of nuclear engineering and technology; Editors Dipl.-Ing. R. HOSSNER, Dipl.-Ing. W.-M. LIEBHOLZ; circ. 5,000.

Baurundschau: 2 Hamburg 11, Gr. Burstah 49; monthly; published by Robert Mölich Verlag; Editor ROBERT MÖLICH.

Der Betrieb: 4000 Düsseldorf 1, Kasernenstr. 67, Postfach 1102; tel. (0211) 83880; telex 11308; weekly; business administration, revenue law, labour and social legislation; circ. 24,500.

Capital: 2000 Hamburg, Postfach 302040; telex 2195213; f. 1956; business and economics; circ. 248,876.

Creditreform: Düsseldorf, Kasernenstr. 67, Postfach 1102; f. 1879; 11 a year; Editor WERNER A. MERKES; circ. 88,000.

Getränketechnik, Zeitschrift für Industrie und Handel: 8500 Nuremberg 1, Breite Gasse 58–60; tel. (0911) 203831; telex 623081; 6 a year; trade journal for the brewing and beverage industries; circ. 205,113.

Der Handelsvertreter und Handelsmakler: 6 Frankfurt a.M., Grosse Eschenheimer Str. 16, Postfach 101937, Siegel-Verlag Otto Müller; telex 411699; f. 1949; fortnightly; Editor HEINZ VOSS; circ. 24,000.

Haustechnik: 43 Essen, Girardetstr. 2; tel. (0202) 7966-0; telex 857888; f. 1970; monthly; Editor Dr B. JANSSEN; circ. 16,200.

Industrie-Anzeiger: 43 Essen, Girardetstr. 2; tel. (0202) 7996-0; telex 857888; f. 1879; 2 a week; Editor W. GIRARDET; circ. 26,000.

Management International Review: 6200 Wiesbaden, Taunusstr. 54; tel. (06121) 53435; telex 4186567; f. 1960; quarterly; issued by Betriebswirtschaftlicher Verlag Dr Th. Gabler; English; Editor Prof. Dr K. MACHARZINA (Stuttgart-Hohenheim).

VDI Nachrichten: 4000 Düsseldorf 1, Graf-Recke-Str. 84; tel. (0211) 62141; telex 8586525; f. 1946; weekly; circ. 125,000.

Versicherungswirtschaft: 7500 Karlsruhe 1, Klosestr. 22; tel. (0721) 30811; telex 7826943; f. 1946; monthly; Editor KARL-HEINZ REHNERT; circ. 11,600.

Wirtschaft und Statistik: 6500 Mainz 42, Postfach 421120; tel. (06131) 59094; telex 4187768; monthly; organ of the Federal Statistical Office; published by Verlag W. Kohlhammer GmbH; Editor Dr GÜNTER HAMER; circ. 5,000.

Wirtschaftswoche: 4000 Düsseldorf, Postfach 3734; telex 8582917; weekly; business; circ. 118,882.

Education and Youth

Bravo: 8000 Munich 2, Postfach 201728; telex 524350; weekly; for young people; circ. 1,301,440.

Erziehung und Wissenschaft: 4300 Essen, Goldammerweg 16; tel. (0201) 41757; telex 8579801; f. 1948; monthly; Editor-in-Chief STEFFEN WELZEL; circ. 194,000.

Geographische Rundschau: 3300 Brunswick, Georg-Westermann-Allee 66; tel. (0531) 708235; f. 1949; monthly; Man. Editor Dr KLAUS ADAM.

Praxis Deutsch: 3016 Seelze, Postfach 100150; telex 922923; 6 a year; German language and literature; circ. 28,786.

Rocky-Das Freizeit Magazine: 8000 Munich 19, Arnulfstr. 197; monthly; pop music magazine for young people; circ. 475,662.

Westermanns Pädagogische Beiträge: 3300 Brunswick, Georg-Westermann-Allee 66, Postfach 3320; telex 952841; f. 1949;

monthly; Editors R. TESKE, Prof. Dr H. GUDJONS, Prof. Dr R. WINKEL; circ. 7,320.

Law

Deutsche Richterzeitung: 5300 Bonn-Bad Godesberg, Seufertstr. 27; f. 1909; monthly; Editor PETER MARQUA; circ. 11,000.

Juristenzeitung: 7400 Tübingen, Wilhelmstr. 18, Postfach 2040; tel. (07071) 26064; telex 7262872; fortnightly; circ. 6,000.

Juristische Rundschau: 1000 Berlin 30, Genthiner Str. 13; tel. (030) 26005-0; telex 184027; monthly; Editor Dr HELWIG HASSENPFLUG.

Neue Juristische Wochenschrift: 6 Frankfurt 1, Palmengartenstr. 14, and 8 Munich 40, Wilhelmstr. 5–9; tel. (069) 742636; telex 412472; f. 1947; weekly; Editors Dr ALFRED FLEMMING, Dr W. LEWALD, Prof. Dr R. NIRK, Dr FRITZ OSTLER, Prof. Dr KONRAD REDEKER; circ. 55,000.

Rabels Zeitschrift für ausländisches und internationales Privatrecht: 2000 Hamburg 13, Mittelweg 187; tel. 41271; telex 212893; f. 1927; quarterly; Editors ULRICH DROBNIG, HEIN KÖTZ, ERNST-JOACHIM MESTMÄCKER; Man. Editor JÜRGEN THIEME.

Versicherungsrecht: 7500 Karlsruhe 1, Klosestr. 22; tel. (0721) 30811; telex 7826943; f. 1950; 4 a month; Editors Prof. Dr ERNST KLINGMÜLLER, KARL-HEINZ REHNERT; circ. 7,750.

Zeitschrift für die gesamte Strafrechtswissenschaft: 1000 Berlin 30, Genthiner Str. 13; tel. (030) 26005-0; telex 184027; f. 1881; quarterly; Chief Editor Prof. Dr HANS-HEINRICH JESCHECK.

Politics, Literature, Current Affairs

Akzente: 8000 Munich 86, Kolbergerstr. 22; tel. (089) 92694-0; f. 1954; Editor MICHAEL KRÜGER.

Buch Aktuell: 4600 Dortmund 1, Westfalendamm 67, Postfach 1305; tel. (0231) 4344-0; telex 822214; 3 a year.

Europa-Archiv, Zeitschrift für internationale Politik: 5300 Bonn, Adenauerallee 131; tel. (0228) 217021; telex 886822; f. 1946; 2 a month; journal of the German Society for Foreign Affairs; published by the Verlag für Internationale Politik GmbH, Bonn; Editor WOLFGANG WAGNER; Man. Editor JOCHEN THIES; circ. 4,600.

Die Fackel: 5300 Bonn 2, Wurzerstr. 2–4; tel. (0228) 364061; telex 885464; f. 1950; monthly; Publr Verband der Kriegs- und Wehrdienstopfer, Behinderten und Sozialrentner Deutschlands eV; Editor JOACHIM FAUSTMANN; circ. 850,000.

Gegenwartskunde: Leske Verlag + Budrich GmbH, 5090 Leverkusen-Opladen, Postfach 300406; tel. (02171) 2079; quarterly; economics, politics, education; Editors W. GAGEL, H.-H. HARTWICH, W. HILLIGEN, B. SCHÄFERS.

Geist und Tat: 6 Frankfurt a.M., Elbestr. 46; Bonn, Postfach 364; monthly; political, cultural; Editor W. EICHLER; circ. 3,500.

Merian: 2000 Hamburg 13, Harvestehuder Weg 45; tel. (040) 441881; telex 214259; f. 1948; monthly; every issue deals with a country or a city; Chief Editor FERDINAND RANFT; circ. 250,000.

Merkur (Deutsche Zeitschrift für europäisches Denken): 8000 Munich 2, Sonnenstr. 10; tel. (089) 555681; f. 1947; monthly; literary, political; Editor KARL HEINZ BOHRER; circ. 6,000.

Die Neue Gesellschaft—Frankfurter Hefte: 5300 Bonn 2, Godesberger Allee 143; tel. (0228) 378021; telex 885479; f. 1946; monthly; cultural, political; Dirs Prof. Dr WALTER DIRKS, Prof. Dr EUGEN KOGON; circ. 11,000.

Neue Rundschau: 6000 Frankfurt a.M. 70, Postfach 700480, Geleitsstr. 25; tel. (069) 60620; telex 412410; f. 1890; quarterly; literature and essays; Editors THOMAS BECKERMANN, GÜNTHER BUSCH; circ. 6,000.

Politik und Kultur: 5300 Bonn 1, Remigiusstr. 1; f. 1983; quarterly; Editor Dr W. W. SCHUTZ.

Sozialdemokrat Magazin: 5300 Bonn 2, Am Michaelshof 8; tel. (0228) 361011; telex 885603; Publisher Vorwärts Verlag GmbH; circ. 888,938.

Universitas: 7000 Stuttgart 1, Birkenwaldstr. 44, Postfach 40; tel. (0711) 2582-0; f. 1946; monthly; scientific, literary and philosophical; Editors GÜNTER FÖRSTER, CHRISTIAN ROTTA; circ. 7,200; quarterly editions in English and Spanish (circ. 4,800).

Welt des Buches: 53 Bonn 2, Godesberger Allee 99; telex 885714; f. 1971; weekly; literary supplement of *Die Welt*.

Westermanns Monatshefte: 3300 Brunswick, Georg-Westermann-Allee 66; telex 952973; f. 1856; monthly; circ. 100,000.

Wille und Weg: 8000 Munich 34, Postfach 340144; tel. (089) 2117-0; telex 5212394; monthly; published by VdK-Deutschland, Landesverband Bayern eV; circ. 320,000.

Popular

Anna: 7600 Offenburg, Am Kestendamm 2; tel. (0781) 8402; telex 752804; f. 1974; knitting and needlecrafts; Editor AENNE BURDA.

Das Beste aus Readers Digest: 7000 Stuttgart, PO Box 178, Augustenstr. 1; tel. (0711) 66020; telex 723539; magazines, books and recorded music programmes; Man. Dir WERNER WEIDMANN; circ. 1,350,000.

Bild + Funk: 8000 Munich 81, Arabellastr. 23; tel. (089) 9250-0; telex 522043; radio and television weekly; Editor GÜNTER VAN WAASEN; circ. 1,219,038.

Brigitte: Gruner und Jahr AG, 2 Hamburg 36, Postfach 302040; tel. (040) 41182550; telex 2195228; f. 1866; fortnightly; women's magazine; circ. 1,631,667.

Bunte Illustrierte: 7600 Offenburg, Burda-Hochhaus, Hauptstr. 130; tel. (0781) 8402; telex 528000; f. 1948; weekly family illustrated; circ. 1,350,530.

burdamoden: 7600 Offenburg, Am Kestendamm 2; tel. (0781) 8402; telex 752804; f. 1949; Editor AENNE BURDA; circ. 2,300,000.

Eltern: 2000 Hamburg 1, Postfach 302040; Pressehaus Gruner und Jahr; telex 2195213; f. 1966; monthly; for young parents; Editor OTTO SCHUSTER; circ. 511,680.

Frau aktuell: 4000 Düsseldorf 1, Adlerstr. 22; tel. (0211) 36661; telex 8587669; f. 1965; Editor UDO BELING; circ. 340,872.

Frau im Spiegel: 2400 Lübeck, Julius Leber Str. 3-7, Postfach 2139; tel. (0451) 1410; telex 26864; women's magazine; circ. 1,006,846.

Freundin: 8000 Munich 81, Arabellastr. 23; telex 528143; f. 1948; fortnightly for young women; Chief Editor ELISABETH BÄR.

Funk Uhr: 2000 Hamburg 36, Kaiser-Wilhelm-Str. 6, Postfach 304630; tel. (040) 3471; telex 403242; radio and television weekly; published by Axel Springer Verlag AG; Editor WERNER PIETSCH; circ. 2,200,000.

Für Sie: 2000 Hamburg 60, Possmoorweg 5; telex 213214; women's magazine; circ. 959,838.

Gong: 8500 Nuremberg, Luitpoldstr. 5; telex 9118134; f. 1948; radio and TV weekly; Editor HELMUT MARKWORT; circ. 1,054,000.

Heim und Welt: 3000 Hanover, Am Jungfernplan 3; tel. (0511) 855757; telex 921158; weekly; Editors WERNER A. TÖNJES, H. G. BRÜNEMANN; circ. 300,000.

Hörzu: 2 Hamburg 36, Kaiser-Wilhelm-Str. 6, Postfach 304630; tel. (040) 3471; telex 217001210; f. 1946; radio and television; published by Axel Springer Verlag; Editor FELIX SCHMIDT; circ. 4,300,000.

Kicker-Sportmagazin: 85 Nuremberg 81, Badstr. 4–6; tel. (911) 2160; telex 622906; f. 1946; sports weekly illustrated; published by Olympia Verlag; Man. Dir HERMANN KRAEMER; circ. 300,000.

Meine Familie & ich: 8000 Munich 81, Arabellastr. 23; tel. (089) 9250-0; telex 528143; circ. 787,690.

Neue Post: 2000 Hamburg 1, Postfach 100444; telex 2163701; weekly; circ. 1,995,000.

Neue Revue: 2000 Hamburg 1, Burchardstr. 11, Postfach 100406; tel. (040) 3019-0; telex 2161821; f. 1946; illustrated weekly; Editor-in-Chief RICHARD MAHKORN; circ. 1,250,000.

Neue Welt: 4000 Düsseldorf 1, Adlerstr. 22; telex 8587669; f. 1932; weekly; Editors PETER PREISS, GÜNTHER GROTKAMP; circ. 445,397.

Pardon: 6000 Frankfurt a.M., Oberweg 157, Postfach 180426; f. 1962; satirical monthly; Editor HANS A. NIKEL; circ. 70,000.

Petra: Jahreszeiten-Verlag, 2000 Hamburg 60, Possmoorweg 1; telex 213214; monthly; circ. 507,245.

Praline: 2000 Hamburg 1, Burchardstr. 11; telex 2163770; fortnightly; women's magazine; circ. 731,000.

Quick: 8000 Munich 83, Charles-de-Gaulle Str. 8; tel. (089) 67860; telex 523600; f. 1948; illustrated weekly; Editor GERT BRAUN; circ. 842,235.

Scala: 6000 Frankfurt a.M. 1, Frankenallee 71–81; tel. (069) 75010; telex 411655; 6 a year; independent; Editor WERNER WIRTHLE; circ. 330,000; editions in German, English, French, Spanish, Portuguese.

Schöner Wohnen: 2000 Hamburg 36, Warburgstr. 50, Postfach 302040; telex 2195213; monthly; homes and gardens; Editor HOLGER SCHNITGERHANS; circ. 365,000.

7 Tage: 6720 Speyer, Wormser Landstr.; telex 465126; f. 1843; weekly; Editor FRANZ HELLEBRAND; circ. 425,902.

Der Spiegel: 2000 Hamburg 11, Brandstwiete 19/Ost-West-Str., Postfach 110420; telex 2162477; f. 1947; weekly; political, general; Publr RUDOLF AUGSTEIN; Editors-in-Chief ERICH BOEHME, JOHANNES K. ENGEL, Dr WERNER FUNK; circ. 940,751.

Stern: Gruner und Jahr AG, 2000 Hamburg 36, Postfach 302040; tel. (040) 41181; telex 2195213; illustrated weekly; Publr Dr PETER SCHOLL-LATOUR; Editors-in-Chief HEINER BREMER, MICHAEL JÜRGS, KLAUS LIEDTKE; circ. 1,426,414.

TV Hören+Sehen: 2000 Hamburg 1, Burchardstr. 11; tel. (040) 30490; telex 12161102; Chief Editor HAJO PAUS; circ. 2,600,000.

Wochenend: 2000 Hamburg 1, Burchardstr. 2, Postfach 10044; telex 2163770; f. 1948; weekly; Editor GERD ROHLOF; circ. 695,346.

Religion and Philosophy

Christ in der Gegenwart: 7800 Freiburg i. Br., Hermann-Herder-Str. 4; f. 1948; weekly; Editor MANFRED PLATE; circ. 40,000.

Die Christliche Familie: 43 Essen-Werden, Ruhrstr. 52–60; f. 1885; weekly; Publisher Dr ALBERT E. FISCHER; Editor Dr HEINRICH HÖPKER; circ. 88,000.

Der Dom: 4790 Paderborn, Liboristr. 1–3; telex 936807; weekly; Catholic; Publr Bonifatius-Druckerei GmbH; circ. 128,695.

Europa: 8000 Munich 5, Ickstattstr. 7, Postfach 140620; tel. (089) 2015505; telex 5215020; Publr VZV Zeitschriften-Verlags-GmbH; circ. 15,800.

Evangelischer Digest: 7000 Stuttgart 1, Postfach 56; tel. (0711) 610551; telex 722985; Publr Verlag Axel B. Trunkel; circ. 15,000.

Evangelische Theologie: 8000 Munich 40, Isabellastr. 20; 6 a year; f. 1934; Editor GERHARD SAUTER; circ. 3,400.

Katholischer Digest: 7000 Stuttgart 1, Postfach 56; tel. (0711) 610551; telex 722985; Publr Verlag Axel B. Trunkel; circ. 46,500.

Katholisches Sonntagsblatt: 7302 Ostfildern 1, Senefelderstr. 12; telex 723556; weekly; Publr Schwabenverlag AG; circ. 120,000.

Kirche und Leben: 4400 Münster, Antoniuskirchplatz 21; tel. (0251) 55400; telex 892888; f. 1945; weekly; Catholic; Chief Editor Dr GÜNTHER MEES; circ. 215,542.

Kirchenzeitung für das Erzbistum Köln: 5 Cologne, Ursulaplatz 1; tel. (0221) 134960; telex 8881128; weekly; Editor Dr HAJO GOERTZ; circ. 130,000.

Philosophisches Jahrbuch: 78 Freiburg i. Breisgau, Hermann-Herder Str. 4; f. 1893; 2 a year; Editors Prof. Dr H. KRINGS, Prof. Dr L. OEING-HANHOFF, Prof. Dr H. ROMBACH, Prof. Dr A. HALDER, Prof. Dr A. BARUZZI.

Der Weg: 4000 Düsseldorf, Postfach 6409; tel. (0211) 3610-1; telex 8582627; weekly; protestant; Editor Dr GERHARD E. STOLL; circ. 70,000.

Weltbild: 89 Augsburg, Frauentorstr. 5; telex 533715; 2 a week; Catholic; Editor EUGEN GEORGE SCHWARZ; circ. 350,000.

Science, Medicine

Angewandte Chemie: VCH Verlagsgesellschaft mbH, 6940 Weinheim, Postfach 1260/1280; tel. (06201) 602315; telex 465516; f. 1888; monthly; circ. 5,000; monthly international edition in English, f. 1962, circ. 2,800.

Archiv der Pharmazie: 694 Weinheim/Bergstr., Pappelallee 3; f. 1822; monthly; Editor Prof. Dr J. KNABE; circ. 1,000.

Ärztliche Praxis: 8032 München-Gräfelfing, Hans-Cornelius-Str. 4; 2 a week; Editor Dr EDMUND BANASCHEWSKI; circ. 49,000.

Atomkernenergie-Kerntechnik: 8000 Munich 80, Kolbergerstr. 22; tel. (089) 92694-0; telex 522837; f. 1958; published by Carl Hanser GmbH; 8 a year; independent journal on energy systems and radiation; circ. 1,200.

Berichte der Bunsen-Gesellschaft für physikalische Chemie: VCH Verlagsgesellschaft mbH 6940 Weinheim/Bergstr., Pappelallee 3; tel. (06201) 6020; telex 465516; f. 1894; monthly; Editors K. G. WEIL, A. WEISS; circ. 2,300.

Chemie-Ingenieur-Technik: VCH Verlagsgesellschaft mbH, 6940 Weinheim, Pappelallee 3, Postfach 1260; tel. (06201) 6020; telex 465516; f. 1928; monthly; Editor G. WELLHAUSEN; circ. 8,000.

Chemische Industrie: 4000 Düsseldorf 1, Kasernenstr. 67, Handelsblatthaus, Postfach 1102; tel. (211) 83880; telex 17211308; f. 1949; review for chemical engineering and industrial chemistry; Dir UWE HOCH; Editor Dr E. KOCH; circ. 5,000.

Der Chirurg: 6900 Heidelberg 1, Postfach 105280; tel. (06621) 487387; telex 461723; f. 1929; monthly; Editors Prof. Ch. HERFARTH, Prof. Dr G. HEBERER, Prof. Dr E. KERN; circ. 6,500.

Deutsche Apotheker Zeitung: 7000 Stuttgart 1, Birkenwaldstr. 44, Postfach 40; tel. (0711) 25820; telex 723636; f. 1861; weekly; Editor Dr WOLFGANG WESSINGER; circ. 18,000.

Deutsche Automobil-Revue: 6 Frankfurt a.M., Städelstr. 19; f. 1926; Editor Dr JÜRGEN CHRIST.

Deutsche Medizinische Wochenschrift: 7000 Stuttgart 30, Rüdigerstr. 14; weekly; Editors F. KÜMMERLE, P. C. SCRIBA, W. SIEGENTHALER, A. STURM, R. H. ROSIE, W. KUHN.

Deutsche Zahnärztliche Zeitschrift: 8 Munich 86, Kolbergerstr. 22; monthly; dental medicine; Editors Prof. Dr A. KRÖNCKE, Dr G. MASCHINSKI.

Deutsche Zeitschrift für Mund-, Kiefer- und Gesichtschirurgie: 8 Munich 86, Kolbergerstr. 22; quarterly; oral and maxillofacial surgery and oral pathology; Editors Dr R. BECKER, Dr H. SCHEUNEMANN, Dr G. SEIFERT.

Elektro-Anzeiger: 43 Essen, Girardetstr. 2; telex 857888; f. 1948; 24 a year; Editor Dr B. JANSSEN; circ. 12,000.

euromed: 8032 München-Gräfelfing, Hans-Cornelius-Str. 4; monthly; Editor Dr EDMUND BANASCHEWSKI.

Europa Chemie: 4000 Düsseldorf 1, Kasernenstr. 67, Handelsblatthaus, Postfach 1102; tel. (211) 83880; telex 17211308; topical news service of the review *Chemische Industrie;* Dir UWE HOCH; Editor Dipl. Chem. H. SEIDEL; circ. 5,200.

Geologische Rundschau: Geologische Vereinigung eV, 5442 Mendig, Postfach 249; tel. (02652) 1508; general, geological; circ. 3,000.

Handchirurgie, Mikrochirurgie, Plastische Chirurgie: 7000 Stuttgart 30, Rüdigerstr. 14; 6 a year; Editors Prof. Dr med. D. BUCK-GRAMCKO, Prof. Dr H. MILLESI, Prof. Dr Dr P. ZELLNER.

Historisches Jahrbuch: 78 Freiburg i. Breisgau, Hermann-Herder Str. 4; f. 1879; 2 double vols a year; Editor Prof. Dr J. SPÖRL.

Journal of Neurology/Zeitschrift für Neurologie: Springer-Verlag, 1000 Berlin 33, Heidelberger Platz 3; f. 1891; continuation of *Deutsche Zeitschrift für Nervenheilkunde;* Editor-in-Chief Prof. Dr M. MUMENTHALER.

Kosmos: 7 Stuttgart 1, Pfizerstr. 5–7, Postfach 640; tel. (0711) 21910; telex 721669; f. 1904; monthly; popular scientific journal; Editor Dr RAINER KÖTHE; circ. 102,925.

Medizinische Klinik: 8000 Munich 2, Lindwurmstr. 95; tel. (089) 514150; telex 521701; f. 1905; fortnightly; Editor Dr HELGA SCHICHTL; circ. 13,500.

Mikrokosmos: 7000 Stuttgart 1, Pfizerstr. 5–7; tel. (0711) 2191214; f. 1906; monthly; microscopical studies; Editor D. KRAUTER; circ. 3,000.

Nachrichten aus Chemie, Technik und Laboratorium: 6940 Weinheim, Pappelallee 3; tel. (06201) 602316; telex 465516; f. 1953; monthly; circ. 22,000.

Naturwissenschaftliche Rundschau: 7000 Stuttgart 1, Birkenwaldstr. 44, Postfach 40; tel. (0711) 2582-0; f. 1948; monthly; scientific; Editors HANS ROTTA, ROSWITHA SCHMID; circ. 7,600.

Planta medica: 7000 Stuttgart 30, Rüdigerstr. 14; f. 1952; every 2 months; Editor E. REINHARD.

Pro Medico: 8032 München-Gräfelfing, Hans-Cornelius-Str. 4; monthly; Editor Dr EDMUND BANASCHEWSKI; circ. 6,000.

Therapie der Gegenwart: 8000 Munich 2, Lindwurmstr. 95; tel. (089) 51415-0; telex 521701; f. 1890; monthly; Chief Editor INGO DERIS; circ. 35,000.

Zahnärztliche Praxis: 8032 München-Gräfelfing, Hans-Cornelius-Str. 4; monthly; Editor Dr EDMUND BANASCHEWSKI; circ. 12,000.

Zeitschrift für Allgemeinmedizin: 7000 Stuttgart 30, Rüdigerstr. 14; tel. (0711) 89310; f. 1924; 3 a month; general medicine; Editors Dr W. MAHRINGER, Prof. Dr P. DOENECKE, Dr M. KOCHEN, Dr G. VOLKERT, Dr W. HARDINGHAUS.

Zeitschrift für Kinderchirurgie: 7000 Stuttgart 30, Rüdigerstr. 14; f. 1964; 6 a year; Editors Prof. Dr A. M. HOLSCHNEIDER; Dr M. BETTEX.

Zeitschrift für Klinische Psychologie u. Psychotherapie: 78 Freiburg i. Breisgau, Hermann-Herder-Str. 4; f. 1952; quarterly; Editor Dr W. J. REVERS.

Zeitschrift für Metallkunde: 7000 Stuttgart 80, Heisenbergstr. 5; tel. (0711) 681476; telex 725555; f. 1911; monthly; metal research; Editors G. PETZOW, P. HAASEN, V. SCHUMACHER.

Zeitschrift für Physik: 6900 Heidelberg 1, Philosophenweg 19; 20 a year; Co-ordinating Editor Prof. Dr O. HAXEL; Editors-in-Chief (Atoms and Nuclei) Prof. Dr H. A. WEIDENMÜLLER, (Condensed Matter) Prof. Dr H. HORNER, Prof. Dr M. CAMPAGNA, (Particles and Fields) Prof Dr G. KRAMER, Prof. Dr W. SATZ.

NEWS AGENCIES

dpa Deutsche Presse-Agentur GmbH: 2000 Hamburg 13, Mittelweg 38; tel. (040) 41131; telex 212995; f. 1949; supplies all the

FEDERAL REPUBLIC OF GERMANY

daily newspapers, broadcasting stations and some 1,000 further subscribers in the Federal Republic of Germany and West Berlin with its national and regional news service. English, Spanish, Arabic and German language news is also transmitted regularly to 550 press agencies, newspapers, radio and television stations and ministries of information in over 85 countries. The dpa Television News Service 'e-te-s' delivers news films in several languages to television stations abroad; Dir Gen. Dr WALTER RICHTBERG; Editor-in-Chief Dr HANS BENIRSCHKE.

VWD: 6236 Eschborn 1, Niederurseler Allee 8–10, Postfach 6105; tel. (06196) 405-0; telex 4072895; economic news.

Foreign Bureaux

Agence France-Presse (AFP): 53 Bonn, Friedrich-Wilhelm-Str. 5; tel. (0228) 234051; telex 886898; Man. PIERRE LEMOINE.

Agencia EFE (Spain): 5300 Bonn 1, Heussallee 2–10, Pressehaus II/12–14; tel. (0228) 214058; telex 886556; Reps JUAN CARLOS BARRENA, RAFAEL GOLÁS, ROBERTO DE LA CRUZ, HANS-JÜRGEN PLOENES; Bureau Chief JOAQUÍN RABAGO.

Agenzia Nazionale Stampa Associata (ANSA) (Italy): 5300 Bonn 1, Dahlmannstr. 36; tel. (0228) 214770; telex 886857; Correspondent SANDRO DE ROSA.

Allgemeiner Deutscher Nachrichtendienst (ADN) (German Democratic Republic): 5300 Bonn, Allianzplatz, Pressehaus I/15; Correspondent RALF BACHMANN.

Associated Press (AP) (USA): 5300 Bonn 12, Heussallee 2-10; tel. (0228) 213091; telex 886301; also in Frankfurt, Hamburg, Berlin, Munich and Düsseldorf; Correspondent ERICH ESIH.

Central News Agency (Republic of China): 5307 Wachtberg-Pech, Auf dem Girzen 4; tel. (0228) 324972; Correspondent FRANCIS FINE.

Československá tisková kancelář (ČTK) (Czechoslovakia): 5300 Bonn, Heussallee 2–10, Pressehaus I/207; tel. (0228) 215811; telex 886772.

Inter Press Service (IPS) (Italy): 5300 Bonn 1, Heussallee 2–10, Pressehaus II/205; tel. (0228) 219138; telex 886331; Correspondent JORGE GILLIES.

Jiji Tsushin-sha (Japan): 2000 Hamburg 13, Mittelweg 38; tel. (040) 445553; telex 211470; Correspondent EIICHI NAKAMURA.

Kyodo Tsushin (Japan): 5300 Bonn, Reuterstr. 124-132, Bonn-Center; tel. (0228) 225543; telex 886308; Man. JUICHI OTSUKA.

Magyar Távirati Iroda (MTI) (Hungary): 5300 Bonn 1, Heussallee 2–10, Pressehaus I; telex 8869652; Correspondent JÁNOS FOLLINUS.

Prensa Latina (Cuba): 5300 Bonn 1, Heussallee 2–10, Pressehaus II/201; tel. (0228) 211330; telex 886517; Man. VICTORIO MANUEL COPA.

Reuters (UK): 5300 Bonn, Bonn-Center, Reuterstr. 124/132, Postfach 120324; tel. (0228) 225021; telex 886677; Chief Correspondent M. WOOD.

Telegrafnoye Agentstvo Sovetskovo Soyuza (TASS) (USSR): 5300 Bonn, Heussallee 2–10, Pressehaus I/133; telex 886472; Chief Correspondent ALEXEY GRIGORIEV.

United Press International (UPI) (USA): 5300 Bonn, Heussallee 2–10, Pressehaus I; tel. (0228) 215031; telex 886538; Chief Correspondent J. B. FLEMING.

Xinhua (New China) News Agency (People's Republic of China): 5300 Bonn 2, Lyngsbergstr. 33; tel. (0228) 331845; telex 885531; Correspondent XIA ZHIMIAN.

APN (USSR) is also represented.

PRESS AND JOURNALISTS' ASSOCIATIONS

Bundesverband Deutscher Zeitungsverleger eV (Association of Newspaper Publishers): 5300 Bonn 2, Riemenschneiderstr. 10, Postfach 205002; tel. (0228) 810040; telex 885461; there are nine affiliated Land Associations; Pres. ROLF TERHEYDEN; Chief Sec. RÜDIGER NIEMANN.

Deutscher Journalisten-Verband (German Journalists' Association): 5300 Bonn, Bennauerstr. 60; tel. (0228) 219093; telex 886567; Chair. WERNER RUDOLPH; Sec. HUBERT ENGEROFF; 12 Land Associations.

Deutscher Presserat (German Press Council): 5300 Bonn 2, Wurzerstr. 46, Postfach 200783; tel. (0228) 351846; telex 885407; 20 mems; Sec. HEIDI A. JÄGER.

Verband Deutscher Zeitschriftenverleger eV (Association of Publishers of Periodicals): 5300 Bonn 2, Winterstr. 50; tel. (0228) 311046; telex 8869391; there are six affiliated Land Associations; Man. Dir WINFRIED RESKE.

Verein der Ausländischen Presse in der BRD (VAP) (Foreign Press Association): 5300 Bonn 1, Heussallee 2–10, Pressehaus I/35; tel. (0228) 210885; f. 1951; Chair. MARCEL LINDEN.

Publishers

There are about 1,850 publishing firms in the Federal Republic of Germany, of which nearly 80% produce fewer than 10 books per year. There is no national publishing centre.

ADAC Verlag: 8000 Munich 70, Am Westpark 8; tel. (089) 76760; telex 528404; f. 1958; travel, guidebooks, legal brochures, technical manuals, maps, magazines ADAC-Motorwelt, Deutsches Autorecht; Man. Dir MANFRED M. ANGELE.

Karl Alber Verlag GmbH: 7800 Freiburg i.Br., Hermann-Herder-Str. 4; tel. (0761) 273495; telex 7721440; f. 1939; philosophy, history and theory of science, psychology, sociology, political science, communications; Man. Dir Dr MEINOLF WEWEL.

Arani-Verlag GmbH: 1000 Berlin 31, Kurfürstendamm 126, Postfach 31 0829; tel. (030) 8911008; f. 1947; fiction, general; Man. HORST MEYER.

Arena-Verlag AG & Co: 8700 Würzburg 1, Rottendorfer Str. 16; tel. (0931) 75011; telex 68833; f. 1949; books for children and juveniles, non-fiction; Dir HANS-GEORG NOACK.

Artemis und Winkler Verlag GmbH: 8000 Munich 44, Martiusstr. 8; tel. (089) 348074; telex 5215517; f. 1957; literature, encyclopaedias; Dir HANS-JÜRGEN SCHMIDT.

Aschendorffsche Verlagbuchhandlung: 4400 Münster/Westfalen, Soesterstr. 13, Postfach 1124; tel. (0251) 6900; telex 892830; f. 1720; Catholic theology, philosophy, psychology, education, jurisprudence, general and church history, philology; Dirs MAXIMILIAN F. HÜFFER, Dr ANTON WILHELM HÜFFER.

Athenäum Verlag: 6000 Frankfurt a.M., Savignystr. 53, Postfach 170101; tel. (069) 7560950; telex 414531; f. 1973; literary sciences, languages, social sciences, general trade and non-fiction, education, Judaism; Publisher AXEL RÜTTERS.

Aussaat- und Schriftenmissions-Verlag: 4390 Gladbeck, Humboldtstr. 15, Postfach 548; tel. (02043) 28028; f. 1978; religion, juveniles; Dir THOMAS VON PUSKAS.

Badenia Verlag und Druckerei GmbH: 7500 Karlsruhe 21, Rudolf-Freytag-Str. 6, Postfach 210248; tel. (0721) 578041; telex 7826726; f. 1874; religion, text-books, school books, fiction; Dir Dr HELMUT WALTER.

Friedrich Bahn Verlag GmbH: 7750 Konstanz, Zasiusstr. 8; tel. (07531) 23054; f. 1891; religion, literature; Dir HERBERT DENECKE.

Bardtenschlager Verlag GmbH: 8000 Munich 81, Oberfoehringerstr. 105A; tel. (089) 952043; f. 1852; juvenile literature, pedagogics; Dir PETER EISMANN.

Otto Wilhelm Barth Verlag: 8000 Munich 19, Stievestr. 9; tel. (089) 172237; telex 5215282; f. 1924; a division of Scherz Verlag; Far East religions and philosophy, meditation, healing, mysticism, etc.; Dir RUDOLF STREIT-SCHERZ; Editor STEPHAN SCHUHMACHER.

Bastei-Verlag: 5060 Bergisch Gladbach 2, Scheidtbachstr. 23–31; tel. (02202) 1210; telex 887922; f. 1949; paperbacks; Man. Dir GUSTAV LÜBBE.

Bayerische Verlagsanstalt GmbH: 8600 Bamberg, Laubange 23; tel. (0951) 7902-0; telex 662860; f. 1949; Dir KURT KIENING.

Bechtle-Verlag: 7300 Esslingen, Zeppelinstr. 116; tel. (0711) 3108-1; telex 7-256487; f. 1868; biography, history, literature, humour, poetry; Man. Dir OTTO W. BECHTLE.

Verlag C. H. Beck: 8000 Munich 40, Wilhelmstr. 9; tel. (089) 381891; telex 5215085; f. 1763; law, science, theology, archaeology, philosophy, philology, history, politics, art, literature; Dirs Dr HANS DIETER BECK, WOLFGANG BECK.

Beltz Verlag: 6940 Weinheim, Am Hauptbahnhof 10, Postfach 1120; tel. (06201) 63071; telex 465500; f. 1841; textbooks; Man. Dir Dr MANFRED BELTZ-RÜBELMANN.

Berghaus Verlag: 8347 Kirchdorf/Inn, Ramerding 18; tel. (08571) 2042; f. 1973; art; Man. Dir URSULA BADER.

Verlagsgruppe Bertelsmann: 4830 Gütersloh 1, Carl-Bertelsmann-Str. 270; tel. (05241) 801; telex 933646; f. 1970; general, reference; Man. Dirs Dr H. BENZING, F. FREIBERG, O. PAESCHKE, K. PORADA, Dr U. WECHSLER.

Beuroner Kunstverlag GmbH: 7782 Beuron 1; tel. (07466) 264; f. 1898; fine art, religion, calendars; Dir LEO P. GABRIEL GAWLETTA.

Bibliographisches Institut AG: 6800 Mannheim 1, Dudenstr. 6, Postfach 311; tel. (0621) 39010; telex 462107; f. 1826; encyclo-

FEDERAL REPUBLIC OF GERMANY

paedia, reference books, scientific books, atlases; Man. Dirs KARL FELDER, CLAUS W. GREUNER, Dr MICHAEL WEGNER.

Biederstein Verlag: 8000 Munich 40, Wilhelmstr. 9; tel. (089) 381891; telex 05-215085; f. 1946; belles-lettres, non-fiction; Man. Dir WOLFGANG BECK.

Georg Bitter Verlag KG: 4350 Recklinghausen, Herner Str. 62; tel. (02361) 25888; f. 1968; children's books; Dir Dr GEORG BITTER.

Blanvalet Verlag: 8000 Munich 80, Neumarkter Str. 18, Postfach 800 360; tel. (089) 41730; telex 523259; fiction; Man. Dirs WOLFGANG KURTH, MICHAEL MELLER.

BLV Verlagsgesellschaft mbH: 8000 Munich 40, Lothstr. 29; tel. (089) 127050; telex 5215087; f. 1946; cookery, reference, crafts, nature, motoring, education, etc.; Man. Dir Dr A. EGGER.

Böhlau-Verlag: 5000 Cologne 60, Niehlerstr. 272–274; tel. (0221) 769340; f. 1951; history, music, art; Man. Dir Dr GÜNTER J. HENZ.

Boje-Verlag GmbH: 8520 Erlangen, Am Pestalozziring 14, Postfach 2829; tel. (09131) 6060-0; telex 629766; f. 1947; children's books; Man. Dir HILDEGARD FISCHER.

Harald Boldt Verlag GmbH: 5407 Boppard am Rhein, Postfach 1110; tel. (06742) 2511; f. 1951; history, reference, general and social science, demography; Man. Dirs HARALD BOLDT, PETER BOLDT.

Gebrüder Borntraeger Verlagsbuchhandlung: 7000 Stuttgart 1, Johannesstr. 3A; tel. (0711) 625001; f. 1790; geology, palaeontology, mineralogy, biology, botany, oceanography, meteorology, geophysics, geomorphology, geography, metallography, periodicals; Proprs Dr E. NÄGELE, KLAUS OBERMILLER.

Verlag G. Braun: 7500 Karlsruhe, Karl-Friedrich-Str. 14–18; tel. (0721) 1651; telex 7826904; f. 1813; physics, mathematics, flow mechanics, medicine; Dirs Dr EBERHARD KNITTEL, HANS LÜCK, HELLO Graf VON RITTBERG.

Braun & Schneider: 8000 Munich 2, Maximiliansplatz 9; tel. (089) 555580; f. 1843; children's literature, fiction; Dirs Dr J. SCHNEIDER, FRIEDRICH SCHNEIDER.

Breitkopf & Härtel: 6200 Wiesbaden 1, Walkmühlstr. 52, Postfach 1707; tel. (06121) 402031; telex 4182647; f. 1719; music and music books; Dirs LIESELOTTE SIEVERS, GOTTFRIED MÖCKEL.

F. A. Brockhaus GmbH: 6800 Mannheim 1, Dudenstr. 6, Postfach 5303; tel. (0621) 390101; telex 462107; f. 1805; encyclopaedias, dictionaries, travel, natural sciences, memoirs, archaeology; Dirs U. PORAK, HUBERTUS BROCKHAUS, Dr MICHAEL WEGNER.

Verlag Bruckmann München: 8 Munich 20, Nymphenburgerstr. 86, Postfach 27; tel. (089) 125701; telex 523739; f.1858; art; Man. Dir ERHARDT D. STIEBNER.

Buchhändler-Vereinigung GmbH: 6000 Frankfurt a.M.1, Grosser Hirschgraben 17-21; tel. (069) 1306282; telex 413573; f. 1846; publishing dept of Börsenverein des Deutschen Buchhandels eV (German Book Trade Asscn); Dir W. ROBERT MÜLLER.

Verlag Busse und Seewald GmbH: 4900 Herford, Ahmser Str. 190, Postfach 1344; tel. (05221) 7750; telex 934717; politics, economics, contemporary history, biography, sociology, wine, interior decoration, carpets, etc.

Butzon & Bercker GmbH: 4178 Kevelaer 1, Postfach 215; tel. (02832) 2908; telex 812207; f. 1870; Catholic religion and theology, meditation, prayers, liturgy, children's books; Dirs KLAUS BERCKER, Dr EDMUND BERCKER.

Verlag Georg D. W. Callwey GmbH & Co: 8000 Munich 80, Streitfeldstr. 35; tel. (089) 433096; telex 5216752; f. 1884; history, cultural history, architecture, sculpture, painting, gardens, art restoration; Man. Dirs HELMUTH BAUR-CALLWEY, Dr VERONIKA BAUR-CALLWEY.

Verlag Hans Carl GmbH & Co KG: 8500 Nuremberg 1, Breite Gasse 58–60; tel. (0911) 203831; telex 623081; f. 1861; technical, scientific and general literature; Man. Dir GÜNTER SCHMIEDEL.

Carlsen Verlag GmbH: 2057 Reinbek, Dieselstr. 6, Postfach 1169; tel. (040) 7224051; telex 217879; f. 1953; children's books; Dirs CARL-JOHAN BONNIER, VIKTOR NIEMANN.

Christliche Verlagsanstalt GmbH: 7750 Konstanz, Zasiusstr. 8; tel. (07531) 23054; f. 1892; religion, children's books, literature; Dir HERBERT DENECKE.

Colloquium Verlag GmbH: 1000 Berlin 45, Unter den Eichen 93; tel. (030) 8328085; f. 1948; biography, history, political and social science, Latin-American studies; Dirs OTTO H. HESS, STEFAN HESS; Editor Dr GABRIELE PANGRATZ.

Columbus Verlag Paul Oestergaard GmbH: 7056 Weinstadt 1, Postfach 1180, Columbus Haus; tel. (07151) 68011; telex 724382; f. 1909; maps, globes, atlases; Dir PETER OESTERGAARD.

Deutsche Verlags-Anstalt GmbH: 7000 Stuttgart 1, Neckarstr. 121, Postfach 209; tel. (0711) 26310; telex 722503; f. 1831; general; Dirs ULRICH FRANK-PLANITZ, Dr HANS GLÜCKER.

Deutscher Apotheker Verlag: 7000 Stuttgart 1, Birkenwaldstr. 44, Postfach 40; tel. (0711) 25820; telex 723636; f. 1861; pharmacy; Dirs Dr WOLFGANG WESSINGER, VINCENT SIEVEKING, REINHOLD HACK.

Deutscher Instituts-Verlag: 5000 Cologne 51, Gustav-Heinemann-Ufer 84–88; tel. (0221) 37041; telex 8882768; f. 1951; economic, literature; attached to Institut der deutschen Wirtschaft, Cologne (German Economics Institute); Man. Dir Prof. Dr GERHARD FELS.

Deutscher Kunstverlag GmbH: 8000 Munich 21, Vohburgerstr. 1; tel. (089) 568145; f. 1921; art books.

Deutscher Verlag für Kunstwissenschaft GmbH: 1000 Berlin 61, Lindenstr. 76; tel. (030) 25913864; telex 183723; f. 1964; German art; Dirs H. PETERS, H. BOCK.

Deutscher Taschenbuch Verlag (dtv): 8000 Munich 40, Friedrichstr. 1A; tel. (089) 397031; telex 5215396; f. 1960; general fiction, history, music, art, reference, children, general and social science, medicine, textbooks; Man. Dir HEINZ FRIEDRICH.

Eugen Diederichs Verlag: 5000 Cologne 1, Merlostr. 8; tel. (0221) 720672; f. 1896; literature, cultural sciences, psychology, sociology, philosophy; Dirs KLAUS DIEDERICHS, ULF DIEDERICHS.

Verlag Moritz Diesterweg: 6000 Frankfurt a.M. 1, Hochstr. 29–31, Postfach 110651; tel. (069) 13010; telex 413234; f. 1860; text books, economics, social sciences, sciences, pedagogics; Dir DIETRICH HERBST.

Droemersche Verlagsanstalt Th. Knaur Nachf GmbH & Co: 8000 Munich 80, Rauchstr. 9–11; tel. (089) 92710; telex 522707; f. 1901; general literature, non-fiction, art books, paperbacks; Man. Dirs RÜDIGER HILDEBRANDT, Dr KARL H. BLESSING.

Droste Verlag GmbH: 4000 Düsseldorf 11, Druckzentrum Düsseldorf, Zülpicher Str. 10, Postfach 1135; tel. (0211) 5050; telex 8582495; f. 1711; fiction, non-fiction, German and foreign literature; Publ. Dr M. LOTSCH.

Duncker & Humblot GmbH: 1000 Berlin 41, Dietrich-Schäfer-Weg 9; tel. (030) 7912026; f. 1798; economics, sociology, law, science, history, philosophy, political sciences.

Econ Verlagsgruppe: 4000 Düsseldorf 1, Grupellostr. 28, Postfach 9229; tel. (0211) 360516; telex 8587327; general fiction and non-fiction; Publr Dr HERO KIND; Man. Dir PETER SCHAPER.

Ehrenwirth Verlag GmbH: 8000 Munich 80, Vilshofenerstr. 8; tel. (089) 989025; telex 529667; f. 1945; general literature, fiction, education, textbooks, periodicals; Dirs MARTIN EHRENWIRTH, FRANK AUERBACH.

N. G. Elwert Verlag: 3550 Marburg/Lahn, Reitgasse 7–9; tel. (06421) 25024; f. 1726; history, religion, law, social science; Man. Dir Dr W. BRAUN-ELWERT.

Ferdinand Enke Verlag: 7000 Stuttgart 1, Postfach 1304, and 7000 Stuttgart 30, Rüdigerstr. 14; tel. (0711) 89310; telex 7252275; f. 1837; medicine, veterinary medicine, sciences (geosciences), psychology, social sciences; books and periodicals; Man. Dr MARLIS KUHLMANN.

Ernst & Sohn: 1000 Berlin 31, Hohenzollerndamm 170; tel. (030) 860003-0; telex 184143; f. 1851; architecture, technology.

Europäische Verlagsanstalt GmbH: 6000 Frankfurt a.M. 1, Savignystr. 53; tel. (069) 7560950; telex 414531; f. 1946; social sciences, politics, culture, history, economics, education; Publr AXEL RÜTTERS.

Fackelträger-Verlag GmbH: 3000 Hanover 1, Goseriede 10–12; tel. (0511) 14648; f. 1949; Man. Dirs SIEGFRIED LIEBRECHT, PETER SEIFRIED.

Fackelverlag: 7000 Stuttgart 1, Herdweg 29-31; tel. (0711) 20171; telex 722875; f. 1919; popular literature; Man. DIETER BOWITZ.

S. Fischer Verlag GmbH: 6000 Frankfurt a.M. 70, Geleitsstr. 25; tel. (069) 60620; telex 412410; f. 1886; general, paperbacks; Publr MONIKA SCHOELLER; Man. Dirs KARL-MICHAEL MEHNERT, Dr EMMANUEL A. WIEMER.

Fleischhauer & Spohn Verlag: 7000 Stuttgart 30, Maybachstr. 18, Postfach 301160; tel. (0711) 89340; telex 723113; f. 1830; fiction, literature.

Focus-Verlag: 6300 Giessen, Grünbergerstr. 16; tel. (0641) 34760; f. 1971; history, reference, social science; Man. Dirs JOCHEN MENDE, HELMUT SCHMIDT.

Franckh'sche Verlagshandlung, W. Keller & Co: 7000 Stuttgart 1, Pfizerstr. 5–7, Postfach 640; tel. (0711) 21910; telex 721669;

FEDERAL REPUBLIC OF GERMANY

f. 1822; science, natural history, railway books, field guides, children's books; Dirs R. KELLER, E. NEHMANN, C. KELLER.

Verlag Frauenoffensive: 8000 Munich 80, Kellerstr. 39; tel. (089) 485102; f. 1976; feminist publs; Dirs INGE JAKOB, SUSANNE KAHN-ACKERMANN, GERLINDE KOWITZKE, REGINA GUCKERT.

Friedrich Frommann Verlag, Günther Holzboog GmbH & Co: 7000 Stuttgart 50 (Bad Cannstatt), König-Karlstr. 27, Postfach 500460; tel. (0711) 569039; telex 7254754; f. 1727; philosophy, theology, sociology, politics, linguistics, mathematics, history of science; Man. GÜNTHER HOLZBOOG.

Dr Th. Gabler Betriebswirtschaftlicher Verlag GmbH: 6200 Wiesbaden 1, Taunusstr. 54, Postfach 1546; tel. (06121) 5341; telex 4186567; f. 1928; business, industry, banking, insurance; Dirs Dr FRANK LUBE, Dr HANS-DIETER HAENEL.

Dr Rudolf Georgi Verlag: 5100 Aachen, Theaterstr. 77; tel. (0241) 477910; telex 832337; f. 1932; history, calendars, art, general science; Man. Dirs WERNER, MANFRED GEORGI.

Wilhelm Goldmann Verlag: 8000 Munich 80, Neumarkter Str. 18; tel. (089) 43180-0; telex 529965; f. 1922; fiction, non-fiction, paperbacks; Man. Dir JÜRGEN KREUZHAGE.

Gräfe und Unzer GmbH: 8000 Munich 40, Isabellastr. 32; tel. (089) 272720; telex 5216929; f. 1722; cookery, health, nature; Man. Dirs KURT PRELINGER, CHRISTIAN STRASSER, DIETER BANZHAF.

G. Grote'sche Verlagsbuchhandlung KG: 5000 Cologne 40, Max-Planck-Str. 12, Postfach 400263; tel. (02234) 1060; telex 8882662; f. 1861; social and political science, history, law, economics, administration, periodicals; Dir F. PLAGGE.

Matthias Grünewald-Verlag GmbH: 6500 Mainz 1, Max-Hufschmidt-Str. 4A, Postfach 3080; tel. (06131) 839055; f. 1918; theology, philosophy, history, children's books; Dir Dr JAKOB LAUBACH.

Walter de Gruyter & Co Verlag: 1000 Berlin 30, Genthinerstr. 13; tel. (030) 260050; telex 184027; f. 1919; humanities and theology, law, science, medicine, mathematics, economics, data processing, general; Man. Dirs Dr KURT LUBASCH, Dr KURT-GEORG CRAM, Dr HELWIG HASSENPFLUG.

Gütersloher Verlagshaus Gerd Mohn: 4830 Gütersloh 1, Königstr. 23–25, Postfach 1343; tel. (05241) 862-0; telex 933868; f. 1959; theology, politics, paperbacks; Man. HANS-JÜRGEN MEURER.

Verlag Anton Hain: 6000 Frankfurt a.M., Savignystr. 53, Postfach 170101; tel. (069) 7560950; telex 414531; f. 1946; philosophy, psychology, politics, sociology, economics, quarterly periodicals; Publr AXEL RÜTTERS.

Carl Hanser Verlag: 8000 Munich 80, Kolbergerstr. 22; tel. (089) 92694-0; telex 522837; f. 1928; modern literature, plastics, technology, chemistry, science, dentistry; Man. Dirs JOACHIM SPENCKER, CHRISTOPH SCHLOTTERER, F.-J. KLOCK.

Peter Hanstein Verlag GmbH: 6000 Frankfurt a.M., Savignystr. 53, Postfach 170101; tel. (069) 7560950; telex 414531; f. 1878; religion, economics; Publr AXEL RÜTTERS.

Verlag Otto Harrassowitz: 6200 Wiesbaden 1, Postfach 2929; tel. (06121) 521046; telex 4186135; f. 1872; oriental studies, linguistics, history of Eastern Europe, education in Eastern Europe, librarianship.

Verlag Gerd Hatje: 7000 Stuttgart 50, Wildungerstr. 83, Postfach 500468; tel. (0711) 561109; f. 1945; modern art, architecture and design, general; Propr GERD HATJE.

Karl F Haug Verlag: 6900 Heidelberg 1, Fritz-Frey-Str. 21; tel. (06221) 49974; telex 461683; f. 1903; medicine; Man. Dir Dr E. FISCHER.

Dr Ernst Hauswedell & Co: 7000 Stuttgart 1, Rosenberg Str. 113; tel. (0711) 638265; f. 1927; bibliographies, book trade, fine arts, humanities, literature, illustrated periodicals, collecting.

Henssel Verlag: 1000 Berlin 39 (West), Glienicker Str. 12; tel. (030) 8051493; f. 1938; poetry, literature, general fiction, travel, humour; Man. Dir KARL-HEINZ HENSSEL.

F. A. Herbig Verlagsbuchhandlung: 8000 Munich 22, Thomas-Wimmer-Ring 11; tel. (089) 2350080; telex 5215045; f. 1821; fine arts, popular sciences, fiction, hobbies; Man. Dir Dr HERBERT FLEISSNER.

Verlag Herder GmbH & Co KG: 7800 Freiburg i. Br., Hermann-Herder-Str. 4; tel. (0761) 27171; telex 7721440; f. 1801; religion, philosophy, history, education, art, music, encyclopaedias, children's books; Propr Dr H. HERDER.

Carl Heymanns Verlag KG: 5000 Cologne 41, Luxemburger Str. 449; tel. (0221) 460100; telex 8881888; brs at Berlin, Bonn and Munich; f. 1815; law, political science and administration; periodicals; Man. Dir BERTRAM GALLUS.

Anton Hiersemann Verlag: 7000 Stuttgart 1, Rosenbergstr. 113; tel. (0711) 638264; f. 1884; library, documentation, history, philology, literature, theatre, religion, art, bibliography; Pres. KARL G. HIERSEMANN.

Hirschgraben-Verlag GmbH: 6000 Frankfurt 1, Fürstenbergerstr. 223, Postfach 180 245; tel. (069) 550491; telex 176997604; f. 1946; school books; Dirs Dr F. LÖFFELHOLZ, WERNER THIELE.

S. Hirzel Verlag GmbH & Co: 7000 Stuttgart 1, Birkenwaldstr. 44, Postfach 347; tel. (0711) 25820; telex 723636; f. 1853; chemistry, physics, philosophy, psychology; Dirs Dr WOLFGANG WESSINGER, VINCENT SIEVEKING, REINHOLD HACK.

Julius Hoffmann Verlag: 7000 Stuttgart 1, Pfizerstr. 5–7; tel. (0711) 2191320; f. 1826; architecture, art, technology, handbooks; Propr KURT HOFFMANN.

Hoffmann & Campe Verlag: 2000 Hamburg 13, Harvestehuderweg 45; tel. (040) 441881; telex 2214259; f. 1781; biography, fiction, history, economics, science, also magazine *Merian*; Man. Dir THOMAS GANSKE.

Insel Verlag: 6000 Frankfurt 1, Lindenstr. 29, Suhrkamp Haus, Postfach 101130; tel. (069) 756010; telex 413972; f. 1899; literature, general; Dir Dr SIEGFRIED UNSELD.

Axel Juncker-Verlag: 8000 Munich 40, Neusser Str. 3; tel. (089) 360960; f. 1902; dictionaries, phrase-books; Man. Dir Dr FLORIAN TIELEBIER-LANGENSCHEIDT.

Chr. Kaiser Verlag: 8000 Munich 40, Isabellastr. 20, Postfach 509; tel. (089) 2712097; telex 529649; f. 1845; theological; Dir MANFRED WEBER.

Hermann Kessler Verlag für Sprachmethodik: 5300 Bonn 2, Plittersdorfer Str. 91; tel. (0228) 363004; f. 1953; German, English and Chinese language; Publr HANS-PETER DÜRR-AUSTER.

Verlag Kiepenheuer & Witsch & Co: 5000 Cologne 51, Rondorferstr. 5; tel. (0221) 380004; telex 8881142; f. 1948; general fiction, biography, history, sociology, politics; Man. Dir Dr REINHOLD NEVEN DU MONT.

Kindler Verlag GmbH: 8000 Munich 40, Leopoldstr. 54; tel. (089) 394041; telex 5215678; f. 1951; biography, literature, psychology, fiction.

Kirchheim & Co GmbH: 6500 Mainz 1, Kaiserstr. 41; tel. (06131) 671081; telex 4187521; f. 1736; science, law, medicine, periodicals; Dir KARLHEINZ ICKRATH.

Verlag Ernst Klett: 7000 Stuttgart 1, Rotebühlstr. 77; tel. (0711) 66720; telex 722225; f. 1844; secondary school and university textbooks (especially German as a foreign language), dictionaries, atlases, teaching aids; Dirs MICHAEL KLETT, ROLAND KLETT, Dr THOMAS KLETT.

Klett-Cotta Verlagsgemeinschaft: 7000 Stuttgart 1, Rotebühlstr. 77; tel. (0711) 66720; telex 722225; f. 1977; literature, linguistics, education, humanities, social sciences, psychology, history, philosophy, fine arts; Dirs MICHAEL KLETT, ROLAND KLETT, Dr THOMAS KLETT.

Erika-Klopp-Verlag GmbH: 1000 Berlin 31, Postfach 310829, Kurfürstendamm 126; tel. (030) 8911008; f. 1925; children's books; Man. HORST MEYER.

Vittorio Klostermann GmbH Verlag: 6000 Frankfurt a.M. 90, Frauenlobstr. 22; tel. (069) 774011; f. 1930; bibliography, philosophy, literature, history, law, periodicals; Man. Dirs MICHAEL and VITTORIO E. KLOSTERMANN.

Verlag Josef Knecht: 6000 Frankfurt a.M. 1, Liebfrauenberg 37; tel. (069) 281767; f. 1946; politics, religion, arts; Propr Erbengemeinschaft Dr BRUNO UND CLEMENS KNECHT, Verlag Herder GmbH & Co KG.

Knorr & Hirth Verlag GmbH: 3167 Burgdorf/Hanover, Alt-Ahrbeck 1; tel. (05136) 5501; f. 1894; art, travel, guide-books, postcards; Dir BERTHOLD FRICKE.

K. F. Koehler Verlag: 7000 Stuttgart 80, Schockenriedstr. 39; tel. (0711) 7860; telex 7255684; f. 1789; biography, history, sociology, political science, law, geography; Publr TILL GRUPP.

Koehlers Verlagsgesellschaft mbH: 4900 Herford, Steintorwall 17, Postfach 2352; tel. (05221) 59910; telex 934801; f. 1789; international shipping, marine reference books.

W. Kohlhammer GmbH: 7000 Stuttgart 80, Hessbrühlstr. 69, Postfach 800430; tel. (0711) 7863-1; telex 7255820; f. 1866; publishers of the Federal Statistical Office; general textbooks; Man. Dirs Dr JÜRGEN GUTBROD, GÜNTER HABERLAND, HANS-JOACHIM NAGEL.

Kommentator Verlag: 6000 Frankfurt a.M. 1, Zeppelinallee 43, Postfach 970148; tel. (069) 793009-0; telex 4189621; f. 1947; law; Man. Dir Dr C. J. B. SANDMANN.

FEDERAL REPUBLIC OF GERMANY

Konradin-Fachzeitschriften-Verlag GmbH: 7022 Leinfelden-Echterdingen, Ernst-Mey-Str. 8; tel. (0711) 7594-0; telex 7255421; f. 1865; technical and agricultural trade journals; Publr Konrad Kohlkammer.

Kösel-Verlag: 8000 Munich 19, Flüggenstr. 2; tel. (089) 175077; telex 5215492; f. 1593; philosophy, religion, literature, history, education; Dir Dr Christoph Wild.

Kreuz Verlag GmbH: 7000 Stuttgart 80, Breitwiesenstr. 30, Postfach 800669; tel. (0711) 7800281; f. 1983; theology, psychology, pedagogics; Man. Dir Dieter Breitsohl.

Alfred Kröner Verlag: 7000 Stuttgart 1, Reinsburgstr. 56, Postfach 1109; tel. (0711) 620221; f. 1904; humanities, handbooks, reference; Man. Dirs Arno Klemm, Walter Kohrs.

Kyrios-Verlag GmbH: 8050 Freising, Luckengasse 8/10; tel. (08161) 5527; f. 1916; religion, meditation, calendars, periodicals; Dir Ursula Blum.

Lambertus-Verlag: 7800 Freiburg i. Br., Wölflinstr. 4, Postfach 1026; tel. (0761) 31566; f. 1898; social work, social sciences, education, periodicals; Dirs Fritz Boll, Gerhild Neugart.

Landbuch Verlag GmbH: 3000 Hanover 1, Kabelkamp 6; tel. (0511) 67806-0; telex 921169; f.1945; agriculture, animal breeding, forestry, hunting, gardening, nature; Dir Friedrich Butenholz.

Langenscheidt-Verlag: 1000 Berlin 62, Crellestr. 29–30; 8000 Munich 40, Neusser Str. 3; tel. (089) 360960; telex 183175; f. 1856; foreign languages, German for foreigners, dictionaries, textbooks, records, tapes, cassettes; Man. Dir Karl Ernst Tielebier-Langenscheidt.

Karl Robert Langewiesche Nachfolger Hans Köster KG: 6240 Königstein im Taunus, Am grünen Weg 6, Postfach 1327; tel. (06174) 7333; f. 1902; art, literature, music, history, monographs; Owner and Man. Hans-Curt Köster.

Leske Verlag & Budrich GmbH: 5090 Leverkusen 3, Gerhart-Hauptmann-Str. 27, Postfach 300 406; tel. (02171) 45525; f. 1820; economics, politics, educational and school books; Man. Dir Edmund Budrich.

Lichtenberg Verlag GmbH: 8000 Munich 40, Leopoldstr. 54; tel. (089) 394041; telex 5215678; f. 1962; popular fiction, non-fiction; Dir Peter Nikel.

Limes Verlag: 8000 Munich 22, Thomas-Wimmer-Ring 11; tel. (089) 235008-0; telex 5215045; f. 1945; poetry, essays, novels, art, contemporary history, translations; Dir M. Schlüter.

Paul List Verlag GmbH & Co KG: 8000 Munich 2, Goethestr. 43; tel. (089) 51480; telex 522405; school books, atlases; Man. Dir Michael Ziegenbein.

Hermann Löffler: 1000 Berlin 49, Schillerstr. 115; tel. (030) 7425818; f. 1903; music; Propr H. Löffler.

Hermann Luchterhand Verlag GmbH & Co: 5450 Neuwied, Heddesdorfer Str. 31, Postfach 1780; tel. (06151) 33521; telex 419310; f. 1924; insurance, law, taxation, labour; Man. Dirs Fritz Berger, Dr Hans Altenheim.

Otto Maier Verlag GmbH: 7980 Ravensburg, Marktstr. 22–26, Postfach 1860; tel. (0751) 861; telex 732926; f. 1883; games, puzzles, hobbies, children's crafts, art, design, educational; Man. Dir Claus Runge.

Gebr. Mann Verlag GmbH & Co: 1000 Berlin 61, Lindenstr. 76; tel. (030) 25913864; telex 183723; f. 1917; archaeology, art; Dir H. Peters.

Maximilian-Verlag: 4900 Herford, Steintorsall 17, Postfach 2352; tel. (05221) 59910; telex 934801; textbooks, history, social sciences, law, administration.

Felix Meiner Verlag GmbH: 2000 Hamburg 76, Richardstr. 47; tel. (040) 294870; f. 1911; re-f. 1951 in Hamburg; humanities, especially philosophy; Dirs R. Meiner, M. Meiner.

J. B. Metzlersche Verlagsbuchhandlung und C.E. Poeschel Verlag GmbH: 7000 Stuttgart 1, Postfach 529; tel. (0711) 223067; telex 7262891; literature, pedagogics, linguistics, history, economics, commerce, textbooks; Dir Günther Schweizer.

Alfred Metzner Verlag: 6000 Frankfurt a.M. 1, Postfach 970148, Zeppelinallee 43; tel. (069) 739009-0; telex 4189621; f. 1909; law; Man. Dir Dr C. J. B. Sandmann.

Gertraud Middelhauve Verlag GmbH & Co KG: 5000 Cologne 80, Wiener Platz 2; tel. (0221) 614982; f. 1947; children's and picture books; Dir Gertraud Middelhauve.

Verlag E. S. Mittler & Sohn GmbH: 4900 Herford, Steintorwall 17, Postfach 2352; tel. (05221) 59910; telex 934801; also 5300 Bonn 1, Austr. 19; military sciences, aviation, philosophy, history.

Verlag Moderne Industrie AG: 8910 Landsberg, Justus-von-Liebig-Str. 1; tel. (08191) 125-1; telex 527114; f. 1952; management, investment, technical; Man. Dir Dr Reinhard Möstl.

Verlag Modernes Lernen Borgmann KG: 4600 Dortmund, Hohe Str. 39; tel. (0231) 128008; telex 8227208; f. 1969; modern learning and educational books; Dir D. Borgmann.

J. C. B. Mohr (Paul Siebeck): 7400 Tübingen, Wilhelmstr. 18; tel. (07071) 26064; telex 7262872; f. 1801; religion, philosophy, law, economics, sociology, history, political science; Propr G. Siebeck.

C. F. Müller Juristischer Verlag: 6900 Heidelberg 1, Im Weiher 10, Postfach 102640; tel. (06221) 489267; telex 461727; f. 1973; periodicals, humanities, insurance, law, science, technology; Dir Dr Hans Windsheimer.

Muster-Schmidt-Verlag Christian Hansen-Schmidt: 3400 Göttingen 1, Grünberger Weg 6; tel. (0551) 71741; telex 96704; f. 1905; history, scientific works; Dirs Hans Hansen-Schmidt, Frau E. Gerhardy.

Verlag Neue Wirtschafts-Briefe: 4690 Herne 1, Eschstr. 22; tel. (02323) 141-0; telex 8229870; f. 1947; accountancy, industrial management, political economics; Man. Dir E.-O. Kleyboldt.

Verlag Günther Neske: 7417 Pfullingen, Kloster, Postfach 7240; tel. (07121) 71339; telex 729790; f. 1951; poetry, psychiatry, philosophy, theology, jurisprudence, picture books; Propr Günther Neske.

Max Niemeyer Verlag: 7400 Tübingen, Pfrondorferstr. 4; tel. (07071) 81104; f. 1870; scholarly books on philology, philosophy, history, linguistics; Dir R. Harsch-Niemeyer.

Nymphenburger Verlagshandlung: 8000 Munich 22, Thomas-Wimmer-Ring 11; tel. (089) 235008-0; telex 5215045; f. 1946; politics, belles lettres, history, science, travel, adventure, sports and music; Dir Dr Herbert Fleissner.

R. Oldenbourg Verlag GmbH: 8000 Munich 80, Rosenheimerstr. 145; tel. (089) 41120; telex 529296; f. 1858; technology, science, history, textbooks, mathematics, economics, dictionaries, periodicals; Dirs Dr T. von Cornides, G. Ohmeyer, Johannes Oldenbourg.

Paul Parey: 2000 Hamburg 1, Spitalerstr. 12; tel. (040) 339690; telex 2161391; and 1000 Berlin 61, Lindenstr. 44–47; tel. (030) 2599040; telex 184777; f. 1848; biology, botany, zoology, ethology, veterinary science, laboratory animals science, food technology and control, agriculture, starch research and technology, brewing and distilling, forestry, horticulture, phytomedicine, plant and environment protection, water management, hunting, fishing, dogs, equitation; technical and scientific journals; Dirs Dr Friedrich Georgi, Dr Rudolf Georgi.

Paul Pattloch Verlag: 8750 Aschaffenburg, Goldbacherstr. 6, Postfach 549; tel. (06021) 21187; telex 4188517; f. 1827; theology; Dir Clemens Pattloch.

Paulinus-Verlag: 5500 Trier, Fleischstr. 62/65, Postfach 3040; tel. (0651) 4604-34; telex 472735; f. 1875; religious literature and theology, periodicals; Dir Siegfried Fäth.

Physik Verlag GmbH: 6940 Weinheim/Bergstr., Pappelallee 3; tel. (06201) 602-0; telex 465516; f. 1947; physics, journals, textbooks, monographs; Man. Dirs Prof. Dr H. Grünewald, Hans Dirk Köhler.

R. Piper GmbH & Co KG Verlag: 8000 Munich 40, Georgenstr. 4, Postfach 430120; tel. (089) 381801-0; telex 5215385; f. 1904; literature, philosophy, arts, psychology, natural sciences, biographies, music, education, biology, theology; Dirs Klaus Piper, Dr Ernst R. Piper.

Polyglott-Verlag: 8000 Munich 40, Neusser Str. 3; tel. (089) 36096-0; telex 5215379; f. 1902; travel guides, dictionaries, phrasebooks.

Prestel-Verlag: 8000 Munich 40, Mandlstr. 26; tel. (089) 381709-0; telex 5216366; fine arts, arts and crafts, art history, travel; Dirs Georgette Capellmann, Gustav Stresow, Jürgen Tesch.

Verlag Friedrich Pustet: 8400 Regensburg 11, Gutenbergstr. 8, Postfach 110441; tel. (0941) 96044; telex 65672; f. 1826; religion, art, liturgical books, folklore; also periodical *Liturgie Konkret*; Man. Dir Dr Friedrich Pustet.

Quell Verlag: 7000 Stuttgart 1, Furtbachstr. 12A, Postfach 897; tel. (0711) 60100-0; f. 1830; Protestant literature; Dirs Dr Wolfgang Reister, Walter Waldbauer.

Quelle & Meyer Verlag: 6200 Wiesbaden, Luisenplatz 2, Postfach 4747; tel. (06121) 373071; f. 1906; religion, natural and social science, textbooks; Man. Dirs Günther Fertig, Gerhard Stahl.

FEDERAL REPUBLIC OF GERMANY

Walter Rau Verlag: 4000 Düsseldorf 12, Benderstr. 168A, Postfach 120407; tel. (0211) 283095; telex 8586682; literature, magazines, translations, chess; Dir GISELA RAU.

Karl Rauch Verlag KG: 4000 Düsseldorf 1, Grafenberger Allee 100; tel. (0211) 360301; telex 8586707; history, translations, art; Dir HARALD EBNER.

Ravenstein Verlag: 6232 Bad Soden, Auf der Krautweide 24; tel. (06196) 29040; telex 4072538; f. 1830; maps and atlases; Man. Dirs RÜDIGER BOSSE, HELGA RAVENSTEIN.

Philipp Reclam jun. Verlag GmbH: 7257 Ditzingen bei Stuttgart, Siemensstr. 32, Postfach 1149; tel. (07156) 5021; telex 7266704; f. 1828; literature, literary criticism, fiction, history of culture and literature, philosophy and religion, biography, fine arts, music; Acting Partner Dr DIETRICH BODE.

Regensbergsche Buchhandlung und Buchdruckerei GmbH & Co: 4400 Münster, Daimlerweg 58, Postfach 6748; tel. (0251) 717061; f. 1591; Catholic and scientific books; Dir Dr BERNHARD LUCAS.

Dietrich Reimer Verlag: 1000 Berlin 45, Unter den Eichen 57; tel. (030) 8314081; f. 1845; geography, ethnology, sociology, scientific, archaeology, history of civilization, art; Propr Dr FRIEDRICH KAUFMANN.

Verlag Ernst Reinhardt GmbH & Co: 8000 Munich 19, Kemnatenstr. 46; tel. (089) 1783005; f. 1899; psychology, education, philosophy, psychotherapy, social sciences; Man. KARL MÜNSTER.

Dr Riederer Verlag GmbH: 7000 Stuttgart 1, Gutbrodstr. 9, Postfach 447; tel. (0711) 639797; technology; Dir H. SCHNEIDER.

Rowohlt Verlag GmbH and Rowohlt Taschenbuch Verlag GmbH: 2057 Reinbek bei Hamburg, Hamburgerstr. 17; tel. (040) 72721; telex 217854; f. 1908/1953; politics, science, fiction, translations of international literature; Dirs Dr MICHAEL NAUMANN, HORST VARRELMANN, Dr HELMUT DÄHNE, ERWIN STEEN.

K.G. Saur Verlag: 8000 Munich 71, Heilmannstr. 17, Postfach 711009; tel. (089) 791040; telex 5212067; f. 1949; library science, reference, dictionaries, microfiches; brs in New York, London, Oxford and Paris; Propr K. G. SAUR.

Moritz Schauenburg Verlag GmbH & Co: 7630 Lahr 1, Schillerstr. 13, Postfach 2120; tel. (07821) 2783-0; telex 754943; f. 1794; fiction, literature, linguistics, philosophy, music; Dir Dipl.-Kfm. JÖRG SCHAUENBURG.

Fachverlag Schiele & Schön GmbH: 1000 Berlin 61, Markgrafenstr. 11; tel. (030) 2516029; telex 181470; f. 1946; technology, telecommunications, textile and clothing industry, biomedical engineering, optics, reference; Dir PETER SCHÖN.

Schlütersche Verlagsanstalt und Druckerei: 3000 Hanover 1, Georgswall 4, Postfach 5440; tel. (0511) 12360; telex 923978; f. 1747; non-fiction, periodicals, Yellow Pages; Man. Dir HORST DRESSEL.

Erich Schmidt Verlag GmbH: 1000 Berlin 30, Genthinerstr. 30G; tel. (030) 250085-0; telex 183671; law, economics, philology, technology; Man. CLAUS-MICHAEL RAST.

Wilhelm Schmitz Verlag: 6301 Wettenberg 2, Wissmar auf der Heide 5; tel. (06406) 2324; f. 1847; German studies, East European studies, Slavonic folklore; Dir S. SCHMITZ.

Franz Schneekluth Verlag: 8000 Munich 22, Widenmayerstr. 34; tel. (089) 221391; telex 529070; f. 1949; general literature; Publr ULRICH STAUDINGER.

Franz Schneider Verlag: 8000 Munich 46, Frankfurter Ring 150; tel. (089) 381910; telex 5215804; f. 1913; children's books; Publr GERT FREDERKING.

Verlag Lambert Schneider GmbH: 6900 Heidelberg, Hausackerweg 16; tel. (06221) 21354; f. 1925; literature, philosophy, religion, Judaism (especially the publications of Martin Buber); Dir L. STIEHM.

Verlag Schnell & Steiner: 8000 Munich 60, Paganinistr. 92, Postfach 112; tel. (089) 8112015; f. 1933; art, travel, history; Man. Dir KARL A. STICH.

B. Schott's Söhne: 6500 Mainz 1, Weihergarten, Postfach 3640; tel. (06131) 246-0; telex 4187 821; f. 1770; sheet music, music books, records, music periodicals; Man. Dirs Dr PETER HANSER-STRECKER, LUDOLF Freiherr VON CANSTEIN, JÜRGEN M. LUCZAK.

Verlag J. F. Schreiber: 7300 Esslingen, Postfach 285; tel. (07153) 22011; telex 7266880; f. 1831; children's books, juveniles; Publrs GERHARD SCHREIBER, HEINZ STÜHMER.

Carl Ed. Schünemann KG: 2800 Bremen 1, 2 Schlachtpforte 7, Postfach 106067; tel. (0421) 36903-0; telex 244397; f. 1810; art, periodicals; Dirs CARL SCHÜNEMANN, CARL FRITZ SCHÜNEMANN.

Schwabenverlag AG: 7302 Ostfildern 1; tel. (0711) 4406-0; telex 723556; f. 1848; regional history, literature, theology, picture books; Man. Dir DIETER HIRSMÜLLER.

Pädagogischer Verlag Schwann-Bagel GmbH: 4000 Düsseldorf 1, Postfach 7640, Am Wehrhahn 100; tel. (0211) 360301; telex 8581345; f. 1821; pedagogics, languages, art, history, children's books, textbooks, records; Dir Dr HANS WEYMAR.

E. Schweizerbart'sche Verlagsbuchhandlung: 7000 Stuttgart 1, Johannesstr. 3A; tel. (0711) 625001; f. 1826; geology, palaeontology, mineralogy, hydrobiology, limnology, botany, zoology, fisheries, anthropology; periodicals; Proprs KLAUS OBERMILLER, Dr E. NÄGELE.

Societäts-Verlag: 6000 Frankfurt a.M. 1, Frankenallee 71–81, Postfach 100801; tel. (069) 75011; telex 411655; f. 1921; literature, art, economics; Publr W. WIRTHLE.

Sonnenweg-Verlag: 7750 Konstanz, Raitenaugasse 11; tel. (07531) 23054; f. 1922; religion, literature; Dir HERBERT DENECKE.

W. Spemann Verlag: 7000 Stuttgart 1, Pfizerstr. 5/7; tel. (0711) 21910; telex 721669; f. 1873; history, culture, art, military; Dirs C. KELLER, R. KELLER, E. NEHMANN.

Adolf Sponholtz Verlag: 3250 Hameln, Osterstr. 19; tel. (05151) 200310; telex 92859; f. 1894; literature, poetry; Publ. Dir HANS FREIWALD.

Springer-Verlag Berlin, Heidelberg, New York KG: 1000 Berlin 33, Heidelberger Platz 3; tel. (06221) 4870; telex 461723; f. 1842; medicine, biology, mathematics, physics, chemistry, psychology, engineering, geosciences, philosophy, law, economics; Proprs Dr Dres. h.c. HEINZ GÖTZE, Dr KONRAD F. SPRINGER, Dipl.-Kfm. CLAUS MICHALETZ, Prof. Dr DIETRICH GÖTZE, JOLANDA L. VON HAGEN.

Franz Steiner Verlag GmbH: 7000 Stuttgart, Birkenwaldstr. 44, Postfach 347; tel. (0711) 25820; telex 723636; f. 1949; archaeology, linguistics and philology, classical and oriental studies, history, geography, history of arts and sciences; periodicals; Man. Dirs HANS ROTTA, VINCENT SIEVEKING.

Dr Dietrich Steinkopf Verlag: 6100 Darmstadt 11, Saalbaustr. 12, Postfach 111008; tel. (06151) 26538; f. 1908; medical and science books and periodicals; Dir BERNHARD LEWERICH.

Lothar Stiehm Verlag GmbH: 6900 Heidelberg 1, Hausackerweg 16; tel. (06221) 21354; f. 1966; literature, bibliography; Dir L. STIEHM.

Süddeutscher Verlag: 8000 Munich 2, Goethestr. 43; tel. (089) 5148; telex 522405; f. 1945; fiction, non-fiction, history, art, religion; Man. Dir Dr WOLFGANG REISTER.

Suhrkamp Verlag KG: 6000 Frankfurt a.M. 1, Lindenstr. 29–35, Suhrkamp Haus, Postfach 101945; tel. (069) 756010; telex 413972; f. 1950; modern German and foreign literature, philosophy, poetry; Dir SIEGFRIED UNSELD.

B. G. Teubner GmbH: 7000 Stuttgart 80, Industriestr. 15, Postfach 801069; tel. (711) 789010; f. 1811; physics, mathematics, engineering, biology, geography, philology, sociology; Man. Dir HEINRICH KRÄMER.

Georg Thieme Verlag: 7000 Stuttgart 30, Rüdigerstr. 14; tel. (0711) 89310; telex 7252275; f. 1886; medicine and natural science; Man. Dirs Dr GÜNTHER HAUFF, Dr ALBRECHT GREUNER.

K. Thienemanns Verlag: 7000 Stuttgart 1, Blumenstr. 36; tel. (0711) 210550; telex 723933; f. 1849; diet cookery books, picture books, children's books, juveniles; Dirs HANSJÖRG WEITBRECHT, RICHARD WEITBRECHT, GUNTER EHNI.

Jan Thorbecke Verlag: 7480 Sigmaringen, Karlstr. 10; tel. (07571) 3016; f. 1946; reference books; Dir GEORG BENSCH.

Verlag Ullstein GmbH: 1000 Berlin 61, Lindenstr. 76; tel. (030) 25911; telex 183723; f. 1877; belles-lettres, biography, history, art, general and social science, politics; Man. Dir Dr HERBERT FLEISSNER.

Buchverlag Ullstein Langen Müller: 8000 Munich 22, Thomas-Wimmer-Ring 11; tel. (089) 235008-0; telex 5215045; f. 1894; literature, art, music, theatre, contemporary history, biography; Man. Dir Dr HERBERT FLEISSNER.

Verlag Eugen Ulmer GmbH & Co: 7000 Stuttgart 70, Wollgrasweg 41, Postfach 700561; tel. (0711) 45070; telex 723634; f. 1868; agriculture, horticulture, science, periodicals; Dir ROLAND ULMER.

Umschau-Verlag Breidenstein GmbH: 6000 Frankfurt a.M. 1, Stuttgarter Str. 18–24, Postfach 110262; tel. (069) 26001; telex 411964; f. 1850; picture books, non-fiction, biology, chemistry, geography, films, food, military affairs, travel; Man. Dir HANS JÜRGEN BREIDENSTEIN.

FEDERAL REPUBLIC OF GERMANY

Universitas Verlag: 8000 Munich 22, Thomas-Wimmer-Ring 11; tel. (089) 177041; f. 1920; travel, history, fiction, biography; Dir Dr HERBERT FLEISSNER.

Urban & Schwarzenberg GmbH: 8000 Munich 2, Pettenkoferstr. 18; tel. (089) 5383-0; telex 523864; f. 1866; medicine, natural sciences; Man. Dir MICHAEL URBAN; brs in Munich, Vienna, Baltimore.

VCH Verlagsgesellschaft mbH: 6940 Weinheim, Pappelallee 3; tel. (06201) 602-0; telex 465516; f. 1921; natural sciences, especially chemistry, biotechnology and physics, medicine, history, philosophy, art, architecture, scientific software, civil engineering; Man. Dirs Prof. Dr HELMUT GRÜNEWALD, HANS DIRK KÖHLER.

Verlag Franz Vahlen GmbH: 8000 Munich 40, Wilhelmstr. 9; tel. (089) 381891; telex 5215085; f. 1870; law, economics; Man. Dir Dr HANS DIETER BECK.

Vandenhoeck & Ruprecht Verlag: 3400 Göttingen, Theaterstr. 13; tel. (0551) 54031; telex 965226; f. 1735; Protestant theology, economics, medical psychology, mathematics, philosophy, linguistics, history, classical studies, secondary school books; Dirs Dr ARNDT RUPRECHT, Dr DIETRICH RUPRECHT.

Friedr. Vieweg & Sohn VerlagsgmbH: 6200 Wiesbaden 1, Faulbrunnenstr. 13, Postfach 5829; tel. (06121) 5341; telex 4186928; f. 1786; books on mathematics, natural sciences, architecture, medicine, philosophy, microcomputers, technics; scientific and technical periodicals; Man. Dir Dr FRANK LUBE.

Vincentz-Verlag: 3000 Hanover 1, Schiffgraben 41–43; tel. (0511) 3499944; telex 923846; f. 1893; science, trade, building, social welfare; Dir Dr LOTHAR VINCENTZ.

Verlag Klaus Wagenbach: 1000 Berlin 30, Ahornstr. 4; tel. (030) 2115060; f. 1964; literature, politics, periodicals, paperbacks; Dir Dr KLAUS WAGENBACH.

Ernst Wasmuth Verlag GmbH & Co: 7400 Tübingen, Fürststr. 133; tel. (07071) 33658; f. 1872; architecture, archaeology, art, history of art; Dir ELSE WASMUTH.

A. Weichert Verlag: 3000 Hanover 1, Tiestestr. 14; tel. (0511) 813068; telex 923872; f. 1872; children's books; Man. Dir ALFRED TRIPPO.

Weidmannsche Verlagsbuchhandlung: 3200 Hildesheim, Hagentorwall 7; tel. (05121) 37007; telex 927454; f. 1945; history, art, study of languages and literature, classics, pedagogy, law; Publr W. GEORG OLMS, Dr E. MERTENS.

Weiss Verlag: 6072 Dreieich 3, Wildscheuerweg 1; tel. (030) 7817725; telex 4185381; f. 1945; fiction, popular science, children's books, science fiction, paperbacks; Propr. ABRAHAM MELZER.

Westdeutscher Verlag GmbH: 6200 Wiesbaden 1, Faulbrunnenstr. 13, Postfach 160210; tel. (06121) 5341; telex 4186928; f. 1947; history, economics, sociology, politics, psychology, law, periodicals; Man Dir Dr FRANK LUBE.

Georg Westermann Verlag: 3300 Brunswick, Georg-Westermann-Allee 66; tel. (0531) 7081; telex 952841; f. 1838; cartography, education, science, technology, fiction, periodicals; Dirs Dr JÜRGEN MACKENSEN, DIRCK TEBBENJOHANNS, GERD MACKENSEN.

Bruno Wilkens Verlag KG: 3000 Hanover 51, Postfach 510308; tel. (0511) 6498811; f. 1922; medicine; Dir HELGA HOFMEISTER-WILKENS.

Carl Winter Universitätsverlag GmbH: 6900 Heidelberg, Lutherstr. 59; tel. (06221) 49111; telex 461660; f. 1822; university textbooks; Publr Dr CARL WINTER.

Verlag Wissenschaft und Politik: 5000 Cologne 1, Salierring 14–16; tel. (0221) 312878; f. 1961; politics, sociology, history, law, periodicals; Dirs BEREND VON NOTTBECK, SIEGMUND MINDT, CLAUS-PETER VON NOTTBECK.

Wissenschaftliche Verlagsgesellschaft mbH: 7000 Stuttgart 1, Birkenwaldstr. 44, Postfach 40; tel. (0711) 25820; telex 723636 daz; science, medicine, pharmacy; Dirs Dr WOLFGANG WESSINGER, VINCENT SIEVEKING, REINHOLD HACK.

Friedrich Wittig Verlag: 2000 Hamburg 61, In der Masch 6; tel. (040) 580358; f. 1946; religion, art books; Man. Dir FRIEDRICH HOLST.

Rainer Wunderlich Verlag Hermann Leins: 7400 Tübingen 1, Eduard-Haber-Str. 15, Postfach 2740; tel. (0711) 223067; telex 7262891; f. 1926; fiction, biography, music, politics, history, poetry; Man. Dir Dipl. Kfm. GÜNTHER SCHWEIZER.

Paul Zsolnay Verlag GmbH: 2000 Hamburg 50, Stresemannstr. 300; tel. (040) 85431; f. 1948; poetry, non-fiction, fiction; Dirs HANS W. POLAK, KURT LINGENBRINK.

PRINCIPAL ASSOCIATION OF BOOK PUBLISHERS AND BOOKSELLERS

Börsenverein des Deutschen Buchhandels eV: 6000 Frankfurt a.M. 1, Postfach 100442, Grosser Hirschgraben 17–21; tel. (069) 1306-0; telex 413573; f. 1825; Chair. GÜNTHER CHRISTIANSEN; Man. Dir Dr HANS-KARL VON KUPSCH (see Buchhändler-Vereinigung GmbH under Publishers).

Radio and Television

In June 1986 there were 25,737,837 radio receivers and 22,908,293 television receivers in use in the Federal Republic.

Arbeitsgemeinschaft der öffentlich-rechtlichen Rundfunkanstalten der Bundesrepublik Deutschland (ARD) (Association of Public Law Broadcasting Organizations): 6 Frankfurt a.M., Bertramstr 8, Postfach 101001; tel. (069) 590607; telex 411127; Chair. Intendant WILLIBALD HILF; the co-ordinating body of the Federal German Radio and Television organizations: Bayerischer Rundfunk, Hessischer Rundfunk, Norddeutscher Rundfunk, Radio Bremen, Saarländischer Rundfunk, Sender Freies Berlin, Süddeutscher Rundfunk, Südwestfunk, Westdeutscher Rundfunk, Deutsche Welle, Deutschlandfunk; RIAS is represented on the Council by an observer.

RADIO

Each of the members of ARD broadcasts 2-3 channels. Deutsche Welle and Deutschlandfunk broadcast programmes for Europe and overseas.

Deutsche Welle: 5000 Cologne 1, Raderberggürtel 50, Postfach 100444; tel. (0221) 3890; telex 888485; German short-wave service; broadcasts 93 programmes daily in 34 languages; Dir-Gen. KLAUS SCHÜTZ; Editor-in-Chief JOSEF M. GERWALD; Tech. Dir GÜNTER ROESSLER; Dir of Public Relations LOTHAR SCHWARTZ.

Deutschlandfunk: 5 Cologne 51, Raderberggürtel 40; tel. (0221) 3451; telex 8884920; 24 hours daily broadcasting from eight stations for the Federal Republic and Europe; Dir-Gen. RICHARD BECKER; Administrative Dir KLAUS PRISSOK; Technical Dir W. HINZ.

RIAS Berlin (Rundfunk im amerikanischen Sektor): 1000 Berlin 62, Kufsteiner Str. 69; tel. (030) 85030; telex 183790; Chair. of US Supervisory Board WILLIAM W. MARSH; Dir Dr PETER SCHIWY.

TELEVISION

There are three television channels. The nine autonomous regional broadcasting organizations combine to provide material for the First Programme which is produced by ARD. The Second Programme (Zweites Deutsches Fernsehen/ZDF) is completely separate and is controlled by a public corporation of all the Länder. It is partly financed by advertising. The Third Programme provides a cultural and educational service in the evenings only with contributions from several of the regional bodies.

Zweites Deutsches Fernsehen (ZDF): 6500 Mainz 1, Postfach 4040; tel. (06131) 701; telex 4187661; f. 1961 by the Länder Governments as a second television channel; 90 main transmitters; Dir-Gen. Prof. DIETER STOLTE; Dir of Programmes ALOIS SCHARDT; Editor-in-Chief REINHARD APPEL; Dir, International Affairs HANS KIMMEL.

REGIONAL BROADCASTING ORGANIZATIONS

Bayerischer Rundfunk: 8000 Munich 2, Rundfunkplatz 1; tel. (089) 59001; telex 521070; Chair. Dr FRANZ HEUBL; Dir-Gen. REINHOLD VÖTH; Admin. Dir OSKAR MAIER.

Radio Bremen: 28 Bremen 33, Heinrich-Hertz-Str. 13; tel. (0421) 2460; telex 245181; Dir-Gen. KARL-HEINZ KLOSTERMEIER.

Hessischer Rundfunk: 6000 Frankfurt a.M. 1, Bertramstr. 8; tel. (069) 1551; telex 411127; Dir-Gen. Dr HARTWIG KELM; Chair. Admin. Council EITEL-OSKAR HÖHNE; Chair. Broadcasting Council GÜNTER E. TH. BEZZENBERGER.

Norddeutscher Rundfunk (NDR): 2 Hamburg 13, Rothenbaumchaussee 132–134; tel. (040) 4131; telex 219891; Dir-Gen. FRIEDRICH WILHELM RÄUKER.

Saarländischer Rundfunk: 6600 Saarbrücken, Funkhaus Halberg, Postfach 1050; tel. (0681) 6021; telex 4428977; Chair. FRANZ SCHLEHOFER; Dir-Gen. Prof. Dr HUBERT ROHDE; Admin. Dir Dr FRIEDRICH FELDBAUSCH.

Sender Freies Berlin: 1 Berlin 19, Masurenallee 8–14; tel. (030) 30310; telex 182813; Chair. HELMUT EICHMEYER; Dir-Gen. Dr GÜNTER HERRMANN; Admin. Dir DIRK JENS RENNEFELD.

FEDERAL REPUBLIC OF GERMANY

Süddeutscher Rundfunk: 7000 Stuttgart 1, Neckarstr. 230, Postfach 837; tel. (0711) 2881; telex 723456; f. 1924; Chair. WALTER AYASS; Dir-Gen. Prof. Dr HANS BAUSCH; Admin. Dir HERMANN FÜNFGELD.

Südwestfunk (SWF): 7570 Baden-Baden, Hans-Bredow-Str., Postfach 820; tel. (07221) 2761; telex 787810; Chair. Admin. Council JULIUS SAXLER; Dir-Gen. WILLIBALD HILF; Admin. Dir Dr HANS-JOACHIM LEHMANN.

Westdeutscher Rundfunk (WDR): 5000 Cologne 1, Appellhofplatz 1; tel. (0221) 2201; telex 8882575; Chair. REINHARD GRÄTZ (Broadcasting Council), Dr THEODOR SCHWEFER (Admin. Council); DORIS EMONS (School Broadcasting); Dir-Gen. FRIEDRICH NOWOTTNY; Admin. Dir Dr NORBERT SEIDEL.

Europe 1: Europäische Rundfunk und Fernseh AG, Europe 1, 6600 Saarbrücken, Postfach 111; tel. (0681) 30782; telex 4421166; broadcasts in French; Dir CLAUDE FABRE.

FOREIGN RADIO STATIONS

American Forces Network: 6000 Frankfurt/Main, Bertramstr. 6; tel. (069) 1516101; telex 413201; f. 1943; 10 stations, 52 AM/FM transmitters and four TV studios; Commanding Officer Lt-Col SONNY CRAVEN; Programme Dir PAUL D. VAN DYKE.

British Forces Broadcasting Service, Germany: 5 Cologne-Marienburg, Parkstr. 61, BFPO 19; tel. (0221) 376990; telex 8881329; since April 1982 a division of the newly-formed Services Sound and Vision Corporation; 10 VHF radio transmitters and 45 low-powered TV transmitters; Regional Dir (Broadcasting) RICHARD C. S. NORTON.

Radio Free Europe/Radio Liberty Inc: Oettingenstr. 67, 8000 Munich 22; tel. (089) 21021; a non-profit-making private corporation, operating under American management and funded by congressional grants supplied through the Board for International Broadcasting, which also oversees the operations of both stations; transmitter facilities in Spain, Portugal and the Federal Republic of Germany. Radio Free Europe broadcasts to Bulgaria, Czechoslovakia, Estonia, Hungary, Latvia, Lithuania, Poland and Romania. Radio Liberty broadcasts to the USSR in Russian, Armenian, Azeri, Byelorussian, Georgian, Kazakh, Kirghiz, Tadzhik, Tatar-Bashkir, Turkestani, Ukrainian, Uzbek; Pres. E. EUGENE PELL; Dirs GREGORY WIERZYNSKI (RFE Div.), NICHOLAS VASLEF (Radio Liberty Div.).

Voice of America (Relay Station and European Correspondents' Bureau): 8000 Munich 22, Ludwigstr. 2; telex 524434; controlled by the US Information Agency, Washington, DC; one Medium Wave and five Short Wave transmitters broadcasting in Russian, English, Polish, Hungarian, Czech, Lithuanian, Estonian, Latvian, Bulgarian, Georgian, Armenian, Ukrainian, Albanian and Slovene. The Correspondents' Bureau provides VOA Washington headquarters with reports and feature programmes in English and other languages on newsworthy developments in Eastern and Western Europe and the USSR.

VOA—Europe: 8000 Munich; telex 524326; f. 1985; 24-hour a day broadcasts in English of news, commentary, music and entertainment; Dir FRANK SCOTT.

Finance

(cap. = capital; p.u. = paid up; brs = branches; dep. = deposits; DM = Deutsche Mark; m. = million; res = reserves)

The Deutsche Bundesbank, the central bank of the Federal Republic of Germany, consists of the central administration in Frankfurt (considered to be the financial capital of the country), 11 main offices (Landeszentralbanken) in the Länder and Berlin, and over 200 branches. In carrying out its functions as determined by law, the Bundesbank is independent of the Federal Government, but is required to support the government's general economic policy. All other credit institutions are subject to governmental supervision through the Federal Banking Supervisory Office (Bundesaufsichtsamt für das Kreditwesen) in Berlin.

Banks outside the central banking system are divided into three groups: private commercial banks, credit institutions incorporated under public law and co-operative credit institutions. All these commercial banks are 'universal banks', conducting all kinds of customary banking business. There is no division of activities. As well as the commercial banks there are a number of specialist banks, such as private or public mortgage banks.

The group of private commercial banks includes: those known as the 'Big Three' (the Deutsche Bank, the Dresdner Bank and the Commerzbank); all banks incorporated as a company limited by shares (Aktiengesellschaft—AG, Kommanditgesellschaft auf Aktien—KGaA) or as a private limited company (Gesellschaft mit beschränkter Haftung—GmbH) and those which are known as 'regional banks' because they do not usually function throughout the Federal Republic; and the private banks, which are established as sole proprietorships or partnerships and mostly have no branches outside their home town. Foreign banks are classed as regional banks. The main business of all private commercial banks is short-term lending. The private bankers fulfil the most varied tasks within the banking system.

The public law credit institutions are the savings banks (Sparkassen) and the Landesbanken. The latter act as central banks and clearing houses on a national level for the savings banks. Laws governing the savings banks limit them to certain sectors—credits, investments and money transfers—and they concentrate on the areas of home financing, municipal investments and the trades. In December 1984 there were 591 savings banks and 11 Landesbanken.

The head institution of the co-operative system is the Deutsche Genossenschaftsbank. At the end of 1984 there were 3,707 industrial and agricultural credit co-operatives, with a total of 19,587 offices.

Banking federations were set up in 1948. The federal association for the private commercial banks is the German Bankers' Association (Bundesverband deutscher Banken), which consists of 11 provincial associations, the Association of German Mortgage Banks (Verband deutscher Hypothekenbanken) and the Association of German Shipping Banks (Verband deutscher Schiffsbanken). Other federal banking associations are the German Savings Banks Association (Deutscher Sparkassen- und Giroverband), the Association of German Industrial and Agricultural Credit Co-operatives (Bundesverband der Deutschen Volksbanken und Raiffeisenbanken) and the Association of Public-Law Credit Institutions (Verband öffentlicher Banken).

BANKS
The Central Banking System

Deutsche Bundesbank: 6000 Frankfurt 50, Wilhelm-Epstein-Str. 14; tel. (069) 1581; telex 414431; f. 1957; to issue bank notes, to regulate note and coin circulation and supply of credit; maintains head offices (Hauptverwaltungen) in each Land, known as Landeszentralbanken; required to support government economic policy, although it is independent of instructions from the government. The Bank may advise on important monetary policy, and members of the Federal Government may take part in the deliberations of the Central Bank Council but may not vote; Pres. KARL OTTO PÖHL; Vice-Pres. Dr HELMUT SCHLESINGER.

Landeszentralbank in Baden-Württemberg: 7000 Stuttgart 1, Marstallstr. 3; tel. (0711) 20741; telex 723512; Pres. Board of Management Prof. Dr Dr h.c. NORBERT KLOTEN.

Landeszentralbank in Bayern: 8000 Munich 2, Postfach 20 16 05, Ludwigstr. 13; tel. (089) 23700-1; telex 522890; Pres. Board of Management LOTHAR MÜLLER.

Landeszentralbank in Berlin: 1000 Berlin 12, Leibnizstr. 9–10; tel. (030) 3404-1; telex 181653; Pres. Board of Management Dr DIETER HISS.

Landeszentralbank in Bremen: 2800 Bremen 1, Kohlhökerstr. 29; tel. (0421) 3291-0; telex 244810; Pres. Board of Management Dr KURT NEMITZ.

Landeszentralbank in der Freien und Hansestadt Hamburg: 2000 Hamburg 11, Ost-West-Str. 73; tel. (040) 3707-0; telex 2174645; Pres. Board of Management Dr WILHELM NÖLLING.

Landeszentralbank in Hessen: 6 Frankfurt a.M., Neue Mainzer Str. 47; tel. (069) 2561-1; telex 411070; Pres. Board of Management Dr ALFRED HÄRTL.

Landeszentralbank in Niedersachsen: 3 Hanover, Georgsplatz 5; tel. (0511) 1933-1; telex 923583; Pres. Board of Management Dr JULIA DINGWORT-NUSSECK.

Landeszentralbank in Nordrhein-Westfalen: 4000 Düsseldorf, Berliner Allee 14; tel. (0211) 874-1; telex 8582774; Pres. HANS WERTZ.

Landeszentralbank in Rheinland-Pfalz: 6500 Mainz, Kaiserstr. 50-52; tel. (06131) 602-1; telex 4187544; Pres. Board of Management JOHANN WILHELM GADDUM.

Landeszentralbank im Saarland: 66 Saarbrücken 1, Keplerstr. 18; tel. (0681) 5802-0; telex 4421258; Pres. HANS GLIEM.

Landeszentralbank in Schleswig-Holstein: 2300 Kiel, Fleethörn 26; tel. (0431) 990-0; telex 299803; Pres. Board of Management Dr JOHANN B. SCHÖLLHORN.

FEDERAL REPUBLIC OF GERMANY

Private Commercial Banks

Baden-Württembergische Bank AG: 7000 Stuttgart 1, Kleiner Schlossplatz, Postfach 142; tel. (0711) 2094-0; telex 721881; f. 1977 by merger of Badische Bank, Handelsbank Heilbronn and Württembergische Bank; cap. DM 108m., dep. DM 10,146m. (Dec. 1985); Mans Dr Otto K. Deutelmoser, Dr Walter Küster, Dieter Maier, Dr Helmut Mattes, Dr Harro Petersen, Dr Manfred Prechtl; 87 brs and 48 agencies.

Bank für Gemeinwirtschaft AG: 6000 Frankfurt a.M. 1, Theaterplatz 2; tel. (069) 2580; telex 4122154; f. 1958; cap. and res DM 2,000m. (Dec. 1985); Chair. Ernst Breit; over 250 brs.

Bank für Handel und Industrie AG: 1 Berlin 12, Uhlandstr. 9/11; tel. (030) 3196-1; telex 1-83875; f. 1949; subsidiary of Dresdner Bank AG; cap. DM 125m., dep. DM 9,747m. (Dec. 1985); Man. Dirs Dr Joachim Meyer-Blücher, Dr Wolfgang Poeck, Rudi Puchta, Manfred Tüngler; 80 brs.

Bankers Trust GmbH: 6000 Frankfurt a.M. 1, Bockenheimer Landstr. 39, Postfach 2665; f. 1889; tel. (069) 71321; telex 411500; formerly Deutsche Unionbank GmbH, name changed in 1980; cap. DM 22.7m., dep. DM 1,876m. (Dec. 1984); Man. Dirs Dr Wolfgang Dietrich Kunz, K. H. Coonley, J. Lindemann, A. R. Montemurno; 3 brs.

Bankhaus H. Aufhäuser: 8000 Munich 2, Löwengrube 18; tel. (089) 2393-1; telex 523154; f. 1870; cap. DM 45m., dep. DM 1,083.3m. (Dec. 1984); Partners Rudolf Bayer, Dr Wolfgang Wunder, Dipl.-Kfm. Dirk Freiherr von Dörnberg, Rüdiger von Michaelis.

Bankhaus Bensel GmbH: 6800 Mannheim 1, Postfach 210; tel. (0621) 24866; telex 463271; f. 1936; cap. DM 6m., dep. DM 117m. (Dec. 1984); Partner and Gen. Man. Wolfgang Köhn, Dr Harro Petersen; Partner Baden-Württembergische Bank AG.

Bankhaus Gebrüder Bethmann: 6000 Frankfurt 1, Bethmannhof, Bethmannstr. 7–9; tel. (069) 21771; telex 413033; f. 1748; foreign trade bank; total assets DM 974.8m. (Dec. 1984); Partners Matthias von Oppen, Dr Wilhelm Pigorsch, Dr Walter Schorr; 8 brs.

Bankhaus J. A. Krebs: 7800 Freiburg i. Br., Münsterplatz 4; tel. (0761) 31466; telex 772807; f. 1721; Proprs Adolf Krebs, Heinz Krebs, Dr Walter Krämer.

Bankhaus Gebr. Martin: 7320 Göppingen (Württemberg), Kirchstr. 35; tel. (07161) 77644; telex 727880; f. 1912; Partners Dr Renate Hees, Susanne Martin.

Bankhaus Neelmeyer AG: 2800 Bremen 1, Am Markt 14/16; tel. (0421) 36030; telex 244866; f. 1907; cap. DM 18m., dep. DM 882.0m. (Dec. 1984); Gen. Mans Wilhelm Kröncke, Dr Rolf Lattreuter, Dr Hans Eberhard Menges, Dr Helmut Landswehr; 9 brs.

Bankhaus Carl F. Plump & Co: 2800 Bremen 1, Am Markt 19, Postfach 102507; tel. 36851; telex 244756; f. 1828; foreign trade bank; Partners Fr. Hoffmann, Jan Freysoldt.

Bankverein Bremen AG: 2800 Bremen 1, Wachtstr. 16; tel. (0421) 3684-1; telex 244816; f. 1863; cap. DM 11.5m., dep. DM 573m. (Dec. 1985); Mans Günther Kück, Heiko E. Dettmers, Dr W. J. Roelants; 1 br.

Bayerische Hypotheken- und Wechsel-Bank AG (Hypo-Bank): 8000 Munich 2, Theatinerstr. 11 Postfach 200527; tel. (089) 23661; telex 52865-0; f. 1835; cap. DM 620m., dep. DM 69,300m. (Dec. 1985); Chair. Dr Klaus Götte; 486 brs.

Bayerische Vereinsbank AG: 8000 Munich 2, Kardinal-Faulhaber-Str. 1 and 14, Postfach 1; tel. (089) 21321; telex 529921; f. 1869; cap. 522m., dep. 72,081m. (Dec. 1985); Chair. (Board of Dirs) Dr Werner Premauer.

Bayerische Volksbanken AG: 8000 Munich 22, Triftstr. 6; tel. (089) 23050; telex 5286421; f. 1903; cap. DM 50m., res DM 68m., dep. 4,475m. (Dec. 1985); Man. Dirs Dr A. Herrmann, Dr S. Lorenz, A. Pelzer.

Joh. Berenberg, Gossler & Co: 2000 Hamburg 36, Neuer Jungfernstieg 20; tel. (040) 34960; telex 215781; f. 1590; cap. DM 80m., dep. 1,308m. (Dec. 1984); Partners Joachim H. Wetzel, Peter Freiherr von Kap-Herr, Joachim von Berenberg-Consbruch.

Berliner Bank AG: 1000 Berlin 12, Hardenbergstr. 32, Postfach 12 17 09; tel. (030) 3109-0; telex 182010; f. 1950; total assets DM 27,000m. (Dec. 1985); Chair. Edzard Reuter; Man. Dir (International) Günther Bernt; Chief Man. (International) Klaus A. Heiliger; 83 brs in West Berlin, brs in Düsseldorf, Frankfurt, Hamburg, Hanover, Stuttgart and Munich, London, subsidiary in Luxembourg.

Berliner Commerzbank AG: 1000 Berlin 30, Potsdamerstr. 125, Postfach 110420; tel. (030) 26971; telex 183862; f. 1949; wholly-owned subsidiary of Commerzbank AG; cap. DM 72.5m., dep. DM 5,048m. (Dec. 1985); Mans Siegfried Ernst, Dr Hans Strathus, Peter von Jena; 60 brs in West Berlin.

Berliner Handels- und Frankfurter Bank (BHF-Bank): 6000 Frankfurt a.M. 1, Bockenheimer Landstr. 10; tel. (069) 718-0; telex 411026; f. 1856; cap. DM 176m., dep. DM 11,464m. (Dec. 1985); Partners Dr W. Graebner, Dr W. Rupf, W. Strutz, K. Subjetzki, R. v. Tresckow.

Berliner Volksbank (West) EG: 1000 Berlin 19, Kaiserdamm 86; tel. 3006-1; telex 186024; f. 1946; cap. DM 38.0m., dep. DM 2,593m. (Dec. 1984); Chair. Hans-Dieter Blaese; 29 brs in West Berlin.

Commerzbank AG: 6000 Frankfurt a.M., Postfach 100505; tel. (069) 13621; telex 4152530; f. 1870; cap. and res DM 4,237m., dep. DM 77,915m. (June 1986); Chair. (Supervisory Board) Paul Lichtenberg; Chair. Board of Man. Dirs Dr Walter Seipp; 780 domestic and 13 foreign brs.

Delbrück & Co: 1000 Berlin 30, Rankestr. 13; tel. (030) 8842880; 5000 Cologne 1, Gereonstr. 15–23; tel. (0221) 16241; telex 8882605; f. 1854; cap. DM 40m., dep. DM 751m. (Dec. 1984); Man. Partners A. Ratjen, Dr Jürgen Frese, A. Momm, Dr G. Ernst, H. Cadenbach, P. von der Heydt, C. Graf von Pourtales, Georg Georgius, Christian Ratjen, Jörg Frese, E. Diehl.

Deutsch-Skandinavische Bank AG: 6000 Frankfurt a.M., Alte Rothofstr. 8; tel. (069) 2983-0; telex 413413; f. 1976; cap. DM 65m., dep. DM 1,600m. (Dec. 1984); Chair. Alf Åkerman.

Deutsch-Südamerikanische Bank AG (Banco Germánico de la América del Sud): 2000 Hamburg 36, Neuer Jungfernstieg 16, Postfach 301246; tel. (040) 341070; telex 2142360; f. 1906; cap. DM 178m., dep. DM 5,933m. (Dec. 1985); Chair. Jürgen Sarrouzin; Gen. Mans Albrecht C. Rädecke, Helmut Fröhlich, Ernst-Günther Lipkau, Dr Herbert Mittendorff.

Deutsche Bank AG: Central Office: 6000 Frankfurt a.M., Grosse Gallusstr. 10–14; tel. (069) 2141; telex 417300; f. 1870; cap. DM 1,599m., dep. DM 124,242m. (Dec. 1985); Hon. Pres. Hermann J. Abs; Chair. Franz Heinrich Ulrich; 1,162 brs.

Deutsche Bank (Asia): 2000 Hamburg 36, Neuer Wall 50; tel. (040) 361460; telex 2152240; f. 1972; cap. DM 196m., dep. DM 8,351m. (Dec. 1984); Chair. Dr Ulrich Cartellieri.

Deutsche Bank Berlin AG: 1000 Berlin 10, Otto-Suhr-Allee 6/16; tel. (030) 34070; telex 181433; f. 1949; wholly-owned subsidiary of Deutsche Bank AG; cap. DM 80m., dep. DM 6,364m. (Dec. 1985); Chair. Supervisory Board Dr Klaus Mertin.

Deutsche Länderbank AG: 1000 Berlin 15, Kurfüstendamm 42; tel. (030) 8822011; telex 184479; 6000 Frankfurt, Bockenheimer Landstr.23; tel. (069) 71431; telex 312194; f. 1909; merchant bank; subsidiary of Bank für Handel und Industrie AG; cap. DM 45m., dep. DM 2,908m. (Dec. 1984); Man. Dirs Klaus Garde, Manfred G. Schneider-Rothhaar.

Dresdner Bank AG: 6000 Frankfurt a.M. 11, Jürgen-Ponto-Platz 1; tel. (069) 263-0; telex 415240; f. 1872; cap. DM 1,138m., dep. DM 61,168m. (Dec. 1985); Chair. Board of Man. Dirs Dr Wolfgang Röller; 953 brs.

Grunelius & Co: 6000 Frankfurt a.M. 16, Untermainkai 26; tel. (069) 234141; telex 411723; f. 1824; Partners Dr Ernst Max von Grunelius, Edmund Knapp.

Georg Hauck & Sohn Bankiers KGaA: 6000 Frankfurt a.M. 1, Kaiserstr. 24; tel. (069) 21611; telex 411061; f. 1796; cap. DM 18.4m., res DM 19.6m. (Dec. 1985); Partners M. Hauck, Dr Burkhard Kopf, A. Schütz.

Hesse Newman AG & Co: 2000 Hamburg 1, Ferdinandstr. 25-27, Postfach 103020; tel. (040) 339620; telex 2161942; f. 1777; cap. DM 25m., dep. DM 188m. (June 1985); Man. Peter C. Queitsch.

Von der Heydt-Kersten & Söhne: 5600 Wuppertal-Elberfeld 1, Neumarkt 5–13; tel. (0202) 4871; telex 8591824; f. 1754; wholly-owned subsidiary of Commerzbank AG; Partners Dr Kurt Vollmer, Gerhard Wichelhaus.

Ibero-Amerika Bank AG: 2800 Bremen 1, Domshof 14/15; tel. (0421) 36300-0; telex 244899; f. 1949; cap. DM 10m., res DM 31.0m. (Dec. 1985); br. in Hamburg; Gen. Mans Klaus F. Müller-Leiendecker, Rolf E. Beisser, Herbert Schoennagel.

Kleinwort, Benson (Deutschland) GmbH & Co: 2800 Bremen 1, Langenstr. 15-21; tel. (0421) 36660; telex 244812; f. 1872, fmrly Bankhaus Martens & Weyhausen, name changed 1983; cap. DM 35m., res DM 7,037m., dep. DM 576m. (Dec. 1982); Mans Wolfgang Kunze, Jens-Peter Knoblauch.

Marcard & Co: 2000 Hamburg 1, Ballindamm 36; tel. (040) 30990; telex 2165032; f. 1893; cap. DM 50.35m., dep. DM 716m. (Dec. 1985); Partners Dieter Witt, Walter Krusemark, Enno-Edzard von Marcard.

FEDERAL REPUBLIC OF GERMANY

Merck Finck & Co: 8000 Munich 2, Pacellistr. 4; tel. (089) 21041; telex 522303; f. 1870; cap. DM 75m., dep. DM 2,908m. (Dec. 1985); Partners August von Finck, Wilhelm von Finck, Adolf Kracht, Dr iur. Wilhelm Winterstein, Agricola Verwaltungsgesellschaft KG.

Metallbank GmbH: 6000 Frankfurt a.M. 1, Reuterweg 14, Postfach 101501; telex 416341; f. 1980; cap. DM 36.5m., dep. DM 443.3m. (Sept. 1984); Mans Günter Janik, Dr Joachim Steck, Curt Cleres; 2 brs.

B. Metzler seel. Sohn & Co Bankers: 6000 Frankfurt a.M. 1, Grosse Gallusstr. 18; tel. (069) 21041; telex 412724; f. 1674; cap. DM 20m., dep. DM 500m. (Dec. 1985); Partners Christoph von Metzler, Friedrich von Metzler, Hans Hermann Reschke.

National-Bank AG: 4300 Essen 1, Theaterplatz 8; tel. (0201) 1721; telex 857811; f. 1921; cap. DM 22m., dep. DM 1,386m. (Dec. 1985); Mans Günter Ehlen, Dr Hans Braun, Gunther Lange, Gerhard Leppelmann.

Norddeutsche Genossenschaftsbank AG: 3000 Hanover, Rathenaustr. 5–6, Postfach 249; tel. (0511) 19271; telex 922751; f. 1982 by merger; cap. DM 180m., dep. DM 13,500m. (Dec. 1984); Chair. Karl-Heinz Scharmann.

Oldenburgische Landesbank AG: 2900 Oldenburg, Stau 15; tel. (0441) 2211; telex 25882; f. 1868; cap. DM 52.2m., dep. DM 4,213m. (Dec. 1984); Chair. Dr jur. Carl S. Gross; Mans Hermann Conring, Dr Hubert Forch, H.-D. von Laue.

Sal. Oppenheim Jr & Cie: 5 Cologne 1, Unter Sachsenhausen 4; tel. (0221) 16511; telex 8882547; 6 Frankfurt/M., Bockenheimer Landstr. 20; tel. (069) 71341; telex 411016; f. 1789; cap. DM 150m., dep. DM 2,830m. (Dec. 1985); Partners Will Marx, Alfred Freiherr von Oppenheim, Manfred Freiherr von Oppenheim, Dr Nikolaus Graf Strasoldo, Hans-Ulrich Trippen, Dr Karl Heinz Wessel, Dr Thomas Bscher, Matthias Graf von Krockow.

Reuschel & Co: 8000 Munich 2, Maximiliansplatz 13; tel. (089) 2395-1; telex 523690; f. 1947; cap. DM 35m., dep. DM 2,140m. (Dec. 1985); Partners Dr Ernst Thiemann, Dr Bernd Voss, Walter Schertel.

Karl Schmidt Bankgeschäft: 8670 Hof/Saale, Ernst-Reuter-Str. 119, Postfach 1629, 1649; tel. (09281) 6011; telex 643880; f. 1828; cap. DM 93.6m., dep. DM 2,056.5m. (Dec. 1984); Partners Dr Karl-Gerhard Schmidt, Georg Becher, Werner Schmidt, Dr Reiner Schmidt, Dr Klaus Becher; 90 brs.

Otto M. Schröder: 2000 Hamburg 36, Alsterarkaden 27; tel. (040) 363141; telex 211119; f.1932; Owner Otto M. Schröder.

Schröder, Münchmeyer, Hengst & Co: 2000 Hamburg 1, Postfach 105903, 38 Ballindamm; tel. (040) 32950; telex 2162151; f. 1969 by merger, 1983 became wholly-owned subsidiary of the Lloyds Bank group; cap. DM 140m. (March 1985); CEO John Hobley.

Schweizerische Kreditanstalt (Deutschland) AG: 6000 Frankfurt a.M., Kaiserstr. 30; tel. (069) 2691-1; telex 412127; f. 1970; cap. DM 125m., dep. DM 3,536.5m. (April 1986); Mans B. A. Brandt, K. Miesel, H. Clavadetscher, R. J. Schmölz.

Simonbank AG: 4000 Düsseldorf 1, Martin-Luther-Platz 32; tel. (0211) 87931; telex 8587931; f. 1960; cap. DM 30m., dep. DM 1,512.4m. (Dec. 1984); Chair. Dr Maximilian Hackl; Man. Dirs Günter Daniel, Peter Klever, Klaus Lichtenauer, Manfred Seidel.

J. H. Stein: 5000 Cologne 1, Unter Sachsenhausen 10–20, Postfach 101748; telex 8882506; f. 1790; Partners Johann Heinrich von Stein, Dr Gerd Hollenberg, Dr Hans Kaspar Freiherr von Rheinbaben.

Trinkaus & Burkhardt: 4000 Düsseldorf 1, Königsallee 21–23; tel. (0211) 831-1; telex 8581436; f. 1785; cap. DM 90m., dep. DM 3,921m. (Dec. 1985); Chair. Herbert H. Jacobi.

Vereins- und Westbank: 2000 Hamburg 11, Alter Wall 22; tel. (040) 3692-01; telex 2151640; f. 1974 by merger; cap. and res DM 484m., dep. DM 11,005m. (Dec. 1985).

M. M. Warburg-Brinckmann, Wirtz & Co: 2000 Hamburg 1, Ferdinandstr. 75; tel. (040) 32821; telex 2162211; f. 1798; cap. DM 110m., dep. DM 2,338m. (Dec. 1985); Partners Dr C. Brinckmann, Dr C. Olearius, Dipl. Kfm. H.-D. Sandweg, Dr Hans Stracke, Max A. Warburg.

Westfalenbank AG: 4630 Bochum 1, Huestr. 21–25; tel. (0234) 6160; telex 825825; f. 1921; cap. DM 224m., dep. DM 3,994m. (1985); Dirs Dr H.-H. Friedl, J. Kleppa, C. Schmidt.

Public-Law Credit Institutions

Bayerische Landesbank Girozentrale: 8000 Munich 2, Brienner Str. 20; tel. (089) 217101; telex 5286270; f. 1972; cap. DM 850m., dep. DM 77,767m. (Dec. 1985); Chair. Dr Ludwig Huber.

Deutsche Girozentrale-Deutsche Kommunalbank: 6000 Frankfurt a.M. 1, Taunusanlage 10, Postfach 110542; tel. (069) 26931; telex 414168; and 1000 Berlin 15, Kurfürstendamm 32; tel. (030) 8812606; telex 183353; f. 1918; cap. and res DM 615m. (Dec. 1985); Chair. Board of Management Ernst-Otto Sandvoss; Mans Dr Wiegand Hennicke, Manfred Zass, Dr Eberhard Zinn.

Hamburgische Landesbank-Girozentrale: 2000 Hamburg 1, Gerhart-Hauptmann-Platz 50, Postfach 102820; tel. (040) 3333-0; telex 2161632; f. 1938; cap. DM 446m., res DM 426.5m. (Dec. 1985); Chair. Dr H. Fahning.

Hessische Landesbank Girozentrale: 6000 Frankfurt a.M., Junghofstr. 18–26; tel. (069) 132-01; telex 415291-0; cap. and res DM 1,341m. (Dec. 1985); CEO Dr Herbert Kazmierzak.

Landesbank Rheinland-Pfalz Girozentrale: 6500 Mainz, Grosse Bleiche 54–56; tel. (06131) 130; telex 4187858; cap. and res DM 759m., total assets DM 37,600m. (Dec. 1985); Chair. Dr Paul Wieandt.

Landesbank Stuttgart: 7000 Stuttgart 1, Lautenschlagerstr. 2; tel. (0711) 2049-0; telex 725190; cap. and res DM 541m., total assets DM 31,836m. (1985); Chair. Dr Gerhard Volz; Deputy Chair. Werner Schmidt; Mans Alfred Baumann, Dr Ulrich Gekeler, Rolf Limbach.

Norddeutsche Landesbank Girozentrale (NORD/LB): 3000 Hanover 1, Georgsplatz 1; tel. (511) 103-0; telex 921620; f. 1970 by merger of several north German banks; cap. and res DM 1,644m., total assets DM 92,615m. (Dec. 1985); Chair. Dr Bernd Thiemann; 224 brs.

Westdeutsche Landesbank Girozentrale (WestLB): 4000 Düsseldorf 1, Herzogstr. 15, Postfach 1128; tel. (0211) 826-01; telex 8588216; f. 1969; cap. DM 1,815m., res DM 2,217m., dep. DM 133,209m. (1985); Chair. F. Neuber.

Central Bank of Co-operative Banking System

Deutsche Genossenschaftsbank: 6000 Frankfurt a.M. 1, Am Platz der Republik, Postfach 100651; tel. (069) 744701; telex 412291; f. 1949; cap. and res DM 2.3m., total assets DM 103,745m. (Dec. 1985); supports more than 3,600 local and seven regional banks; Chair. H. Guthardt; Vice-Chair. Karl Fehrenbach, R. Bergsträsser, Dr A. Humpert, Dr J. Remmers, Dr W. von Schimmelmann, G. Schmidt-Weyland, Dr K.-H. Schneider-Gädicke.

Specialist Banks

Bayerische Hypotheken- und Wechsel-Bank AG: 8000 Munich 2, Theatinerstr. 11; tel. (089) 2366-1; telex 52865-0; f. 1835; cap. DM 620m., res DM 3,038m. (Dec. 1985); Chair. (Supervisory Board) Dr Klaus Götte; Chair. (Board of Management) Dr Wilhelm Arendts.

Deutsche Verkehrs-Kredit-Bank AG: 6000 Frankfurt a.M., Untermainkai 23–25; tel. (069) 26481; telex 411956; f. 1923; cap. p.u. DM 65m., dep. DM 4,912m., res DM 159m. (Dec. 1984); Mans K.-H. Boldt, Dr K. Menche, Dr F. Schlossnikl.

Frankfurter Hypothekenbank AG: 6000 Frankfurt a.M., Junghofstr. 5–7; tel. (069) 29898-0; telex 411608; f. 1862; mortgage bank; cap. DM 70.4m.; Gen. Mans Dr Bernt W. Rohrer, Dr Hans Schuck, Dr Klaus Ullmann.

Industriekreditbank AG-Deutsche Industriebank: 4000 Düsseldorf 1, Karl-Theodor-Str. 6; tel. (0211) 8221-1; telex 8582791; and 1000 Berlin 12, Bismarckstr 105; tel. (030) 31009-0; telex 184376; f. 1949; cap. DM 733.5m. (1986); Chair. (Supervisory Board) Dr Dieter Spethmann.

Kreditanstalt für Wiederaufbau: 6000 Frankfurt a.M. 11, Postfach 111141; tel. (069) 74310; telex 411352; f. 1948; cap. DM 1,000m., total assets DM 87,769m. (Dec. 1985); Chair. Bd of Dirs Dr Gerhard Stoltenberg; Vice-Chair. Dr Martin Bangemann.

Bankers' Organizations

Bundesverband deutscher Banken eV: 5000 Cologne 1, Mohrenstr. 35–41, Postfach 100246; tel. (0221) 16631; telex 8882730; f. 1948; Pres. Dr Hanns C. Schroeder-Hohenwarth.

Bundesverband der Deutschen Volksbanken und Raiffeisenbanken eV: 5300 Bonn 1, Heussallee 5, Postfach 120440; tel. (0228) 509-0; telex 886779; f. 1971; Pres. Bernhard Schramm; 3,600 mems.

Deutscher Sparkassen- und Giroverband eV; 5300 Bonn, Simrockstr. 4, Postfach 1429; tel. (0228) 204-0; telex 886709; Pres. Dr Helmut Geiger; Mans Gustav Schröder, Wolfgang Starke.

STOCK EXCHANGES

Arbeitsgemeinschaft der deutschen Wertpapierbörsen (Association of German Stock Exchanges): 6000 Frankfurt a.M. 1,

FEDERAL REPUBLIC OF GERMANY

Börsenplatz 6; tel. (069) 21970; telex 411412; f. 1986; supervisory board of regional exchanges; Pres. GERNOT ERNST.

Frankfurt-am-Main: 6000 Frankfurt a.M., Wertpapierbörse, Postfach 100811; tel. (069) 21970; telex 411412; f. 1585; mems 177; Chair. MICHAEL HAUCK; Man. HANS-JOACHIM SCHWARZE.

Berlin: Börse, 1000 Berlin 12, Hardenbergstr. 16–18; tel. (030) 31800; telex 183663; f. 1685; Pres. Dr GERNOT ERNST.

Bremen: Bremer Wertpapierbörse, 2800 Bremen 1, Domshof 12, Postfach 10 07 26; tel. (0421) 323037; telex 245958; mems 19 credit institutes; Pres. Dr MANFRED SCHRÖDER; Man. AXEL H. SCHUBERT.

Düsseldorf: Rheinisch-Westfälische Börse zu Düsseldorf, Ernst-Schneider-Platz 1; tel. (0211) 8621; telex 8582600; f. 1935; 98 mem. firms; Pres. ALFRED Freiherr VON OPPENHEIM.

Hamburg: 2000 Hamburg 11, Börse; tel. (040) 367444; telex 213228; 96 mem. firms; Pres. HANS-DIETER SANDWEG.

Hanover: Niedersächsische Börse zu Hannover, 3000 Hanover 1, Rathenaustr. 2; tel. (0511) 327661; telex 5118444; f. 1787; mems 27; Pres. HORST RISSE; Man. Dr HANS HEINRICH PETERS.

Munich: Bayerische Börse, 8 Munich 2, Lenbachplatz 2A/1; tel. (089) 59900; telex 523515; f. 1548; mems 68; Chair. of Council RUDOLF BAYER; Mems of Council Dr RUDOLF BAUR, WILHELM PFEIFFER, HANS SIEGBURG, Prof. Dr GERHARD TREMER; Syndic R. A. KLAUS LECKEBUSCH.

Stuttgart: Baden-Württembergische Wertpapierbörse zu Stuttgart, 7 Stuttgart 1, Hospitalstr. 12; tel. (0711) 290183; telex 721514; f. 1861; mems 44; Pres. GERHARD BURK; Man. Dir Rechtsanwalt HANS-JOACHIM FEUERBACH.

INSURANCE

German law specifies that property- and accident insurance may not be jointly underwritten with life-, sickness-, legal protection- or credit- insurance by the same company. Insurers are therefore obliged to establish separate companies to cover the different classes of insurance.

Aachener und Münchener Lebensversicherung AG: 5100 Aachen, Robert-Schumann-Str. 51, Postfach 26; tel. (0241) 6001-0; telex 832346; f. 1868; Chair. Dr HELMUT GIES; Gen. Man. W.-D. BAUMGARTL.

Aachener und Münchener Versicherung AG: 5100 Aachen, Aureliusstr. 2, Postfach 10; tel. (0241) 456-1; telex 832872; f. 1825; Chair. Prof. Dr jur. Dr-Ing. E.h. R. SCHMIDT; Gen. Man. Dr HELMUT GIES.

Albingia Versicherungs-AG: 2000 Hamburg 1, Ballindamm 39; tel. (040) 30220; telex 2161774; f. 1901; Chair. C. Prinz WITTGENSTEIN; Gen. Man. H. SINGER.

Allianz AG Holding: 8000 Munich 44, Postfach 440124; tel (089) 38001; telex 523011; f. 1985; Chair. Supervisory Bd Dr H. GRÜNEWALD; Chair. Bd of Mans Dr W. SCHIEREN.

Allianz Lebensversicherungs-AG: 7000 Stuttgart 1, Postfach 534; tel. (0711) 663-0; telex 723571; f. 1922; Chair. Bd of Mans Dr U. HAASEN; Chair. Supervisory Bd Dr W. SCHIEREN.

Colonia Lebensversicherung AG: 5000 Cologne 80, Postfach 805060; tel. (0221) 690-02; telex 881585; f. 1853; Chair. Dr N. Graf STRASOLDO; Gen. Man. D. WENDELSTADT.

Colonia Versicherung AG: 5000 Cologne 80, Postfach 805050; tel. (0221) 69001; telex 8815-0; f. 1838; Chair. Dr N. Graf STRASOLDO; Gen. Man. D. WENDELSTADT.

Continentale Krankenversicherung auf Gegenseitigkeit: 4600 Dortmund 1, Postfach 1343; tel. (0231) 12011; telex 822515; f. 1926; Chair. Dr J. LORSBACH; Gen. Man. Dr H. HOFFMANN.

Debeka Krankenversicherungsverein auf Gegenseitigkeit: 5400 Koblenz, Ferdinand-Sauerbruch-Str. 18, Postfach 460; tel. (0261) 4980; f. 1905; Chair. H. LANGE; Gen. Man. P. GREISLER.

Deutsche Beamten-Versicherung öffentlichrechtliche Lebens- und Renten-Versicherungsanstalt: 6200 Wiesbaden 1, Postfach 2109; tel. (06121) 3631; telex 4186705; f. 1872; Chair. Dr W. HESSELBACH; Gen. Man. F. BODE.

Deutsche Krankenversicherung AG: 5000 Cologne 41, Aachener Str. 300, Postfach 100588; tel. (0221) 5781; telex 8881634; f. 1927; Chair. K. WESSELKOCK; Gen. Man. H. G. TIMMER.

Deutscher Herold Lebensversicherungs-AG: 5300 Bonn 1, Postfach 1448; tel. (0228) 26801; telex 886653; f. 1921; Chair. W. SOBOTA; Speaker H. D. RITTERBEX, W. EWERT.

Frankfurter Versicherungs-AG: 6000 Frankfurt 1, Postfach 2142; tel. (069) 71261; telex 411376; f. 1929; Chair. Dr W. SCHIEREN; Gen. Man. P. Graf zu CASTELL-CASTELL.

Gerling-Konzern Allgemeine Versicherungs-AG; 5000 Cologne 1, Postfach 100808; tel. (0221) 144-1; telex 88110; f. 1918; Chair. G. VOGELSANG; Speaker A. WEILER.

Gothaer Versicherungsbank Versicherungsverein auf Gegenseitigkeit: 5000 Cologne 1, Kaiser-Wilhelm-Ring 23-25, Postfach 108026; tel. (0221) 5746-00; telex 221305; f. 1820; direct and indirect underwriting of all classes of insurance in Germany and abroad; Chair. Dr H. VOSSLOH; Gen. Man. Prof. A. W. KLEIN.

Haftpflicht-Unterstützungs-Kasse kraftfahrender Beamter Deutschlands auf Gegenseitigkeit in Coburg (HUK-Coburg): 8630 Coburg, Postfach 402; tel. (09561) 96-1; telex 663414; f. 1933; Chair. Dr B. SCHRÖDER.

Haftpflichtverband der Deutschen Industrie Versicherungsverein auf Gegenseitigkeit: 3000 Hanover 51, Postfach 510369; tel. (0511) 645-1; telex 922678; f. 1903; Chair. Prof. Dr F. THOMÉE; Gen. Man. Dipl. Ing. A. MORSBACH.

Hamburg-Mannheimer Versicherungs-AG: 2000 Hamburg 60, Postfach 601060; tel. (040) 6376-1; telex 2174600; f. 1899; Chair. Dr H. K. JANNOTT; Gen. Man. K. WESSELKOCK.

Iduna Vereinigte Lebensversicherung auf Gegenseitigkeit für Handwerk, Handel und Gewerbe: 2000 Hamburg 36, Postfach 302721; tel. (040) 441841; telex 211397; f. 1914; Chair. G. WÄGER; Gen. Man. H. BECKER.

Landwirtschaftlicher Versicherungsverein auf Gegenseitigkeit: 4400 Münster, Postfach 6145; tel. (0251) 7020; telex 892560; f. 1896; Chair. H. OSTROP; Gen. Man. K.-A. LOSKANT.

Nordstern Allgemeine Versicherungs-AG: 5000 Cologne 1, Postfach 101368; tel. (0221) 148-1; telex 8882714; f. 1866; direct and indirect underwriting of all classes of private insurance in Germany and abroad; life-, health-, credit- and legal protection-insurance through reinsurance only; Chair. Dr N. Graf STRASOLDO; Gen. Man. C. KLEYBOLDT.

R+V Allgemeine Versicherung AG: 6200 Wiesbaden, Taunusstr. 1, Postfach 4840; tel. (06121) 533-0; telex 4186819; f. 1922; Chair. W. CROLL; Gen. Man. Dr P. C. VON HARDER.

R+V Lebensversicherung auf Gegenseitigkeit: 6200 Wiesbaden, Taunusstr. 1, Postfach 4840; tel. (06121) 533-0; telex 4186803; f. 1922; Chair. W. CROLL; Gen. Man. Dr P. C. VON HARDER.

Signal Krankenversicherung auf Gegenseitigkeit: 4600 Dortmund 1, Joseph-Scherer-Str. 3, Postfach 237; tel. (0231) 135-0; telex 822231; f. 1907; Chair. G. SCHULHOFF; Gen. Man. H. FROMMKNECHT.

Vereinigte Krankenversicherung AG: 8000 Munich 2, Postfach 202522; tel. (089) 6785-0; telex 5215721; f. 1925; Chair. Dr R. HEDINGER; Gen. Man. Dr H. K. JÄKEL.

Victoria Feuer-Versicherungs-AG: 4000 Düsseldorf 1, Postfach 1116; tel. (0211) 82801; telex 8582984; f. 1904; Chair. Dr E. OVERBECK; Gen. Man. Dr E. JANNOTT.

Victoria Lebens-Versicherungs-AG: 4000 Düsseldorf 1, Postfach 1116; tel. (0211) 82801; telex 8582984; f. 1853; Chair. Dr E. OVERBECK; Gen. Man. Dr E. JANNOTT.

Volksfürsorg Deutsche Lebensversicherung AG: 2000 Hamburg 1, Postfach 106420; tel. (040) 2865-0; telex 402002; f. 1912; Chair. G. FEHRENBACH; Gen. Man. W. SCHULZ.

Württembergische Feuerversicherung AG; 7000 Stuttgart 1, Johannesstr. 1–7, Postfach 60; tel. (0711) 6621; telex 723553; f. 1828; Chair. R. KLETT; Gen. Man. Dr G. BÜCHNER.

Reinsurance

Aachener Rückversicherungs-Gesellschaft AG: 5100 Aachen, Schloss-Rahe-Str. 15, Postfach 25; tel. (0241) 186-0; telex 832629; f. 1853; Chair. Supervisory Bd Prof. Dr HELMUT GIES; Chair. Bd of Mans Dr A. MORENZ.

Bayerische Rückversicherung AG: 8000 Munich 22, Postfach 220106; tel. (089) 3844-1; telex 5215247; f. 1911; Chair. Prof. Dr B. BÖRNER; Gen Man Dr P. FREY.

Deutsche Rückversicherung AG: 2000 Hamburg 13, Postfach 2622; tel. (040) 4106055; telex 214950; f. 1952; Chair. Dr W. RIEGER; Gen. Man. G. HASSE.

Frankona Rückversicherungs-AG: 8000 Munich 86, Postfach 860380; tel. (089) 9228-0; telex 522531; f. 1886; Chair. Dr M. GÜNTHER; Gen. Man. Dr A. KANN.

Gerling-Konzern Globale Rückversicherungs-AG: 5000 Cologne 1, Postfach 100808; tel. (0221) 144-1; telex 88110; f. 1954; Chair. R. SCHLENKER; Speaker Dr R. WOLTERECK.

Hamburger Internationale Rückversicherung AG: 2000 Hamburg 11, Postfach 111522; tel. (040) 37008-1; telex 2162938; f. 1965; Chair. W. SCHULZ.

FEDERAL REPUBLIC OF GERMANY
Directory

Hannover Rückversicherungs-AG: 3000 Hanover 61, Karl-Wiechert-Allee 50, Postfach 610369; tel (0511) 5604-0; telex 922599; f. 1966; Chair. Supervisory Board A. MORSBACH; Chair. Board of Mans R. C. BINGEMER.

Kölnische Rückversicherungs-Gesellschaft AG: 5000 Cologne 1, Theodor-Heuss-Ring 11, Postfach 108016; tel. (0221) 7759-0; telex 8885231-0; f. 1846; Chair. Dr N. Graf STRASOLDO; Gen. Man. Dr J. ZECH.

Münchener Rückversicherungs-Gesellschaft: 8000 Munich 40, Postfach 401320; tel. (089) 3891-0; telex 5215233-0; f. 1880; Chair. Supervisory Bd Dr D. SPETHMANN; Chair. Bd of Mans Dr H. K. JANNOTT.

Rhein-Main-Rückversicherungs-Gesellschaft AG: 6200 Wiesbaden 1, Sonnenberger Str. 44; tel. (06121) 525001; telex 4186473; f. 1935; all classes of reinsurance; Chair. W. CROLL; Gen. Man. Dr P. C. VON HARDER.

Principal Insurance Association

Gesamtverband der Deutschen Versicherungswirtschaft eV: 5000 Cologne 1, Ebertplatz 1; tel. (0221) 7764-0; telex 8885255; f. 1948; affiliating 5 mem. asscns and 415 mem. companies; Pres. Dr GEORG BÜCHNER (Stuttgart); Vice-Pres. Dr U. HAASEN (Stuttgart), D. WENDELSTADT (Cologne).

Trade and Industry

CHAMBERS OF INDUSTRY AND COMMERCE

Deutscher Industrie- und Handelstag (Association of German Chambers of Industry and Commerce): 5300 Bonn 1, Adenauerallee 148; tel. (0228) 1040; telex 886805; Pres. OTTO WOLFF VON AMERONGEN; Sec.-Gen. Dr FRANZ SCHOSER; affiliates 69 Chambers of Industry and Commerce.

There are Chambers of Industry and Commerce in all the principal towns and also nine regional associations as follows:

Arbeitsgemeinschaft der Industrie- und Handelskammern in Baden-Württemberg, Vorort: Industrie- und Handelskammer Mittlerer Neckar Sitz Stuttgart: 7000 Stuttgart 1, Jägerstr. 30, Postfach 84; tel. (0711) 2005-0; telex 722031; Chair. Dipl.-Ing. BERTHOLD LEIBINGER; Sec. PETER KISTNER.

Arbeitsgemeinschaft der Bayerischen Industrie- und Handelskammern: 8000 Munich 34, Max-Joseph-Str. 2; tel. (089) 51160; telex 523678; Chair. Prof. Dr ROLF RODENSTOCK; Sec. Dr WILHELM WIMMER; 10 mems.

Arbeitsgemeinschaft Hessischer Industrie- und Handelskammern: 6000 Frankfurt a.M. 1, Börsenplatz; tel. (069) 21970; telex 411255; Chair. Dr HANS MESSER; Sec. RICHARD SPEICH; 12 mems.

Vereinigung der Niedersächsischen Industrie- und Handelskammern: 3000 Hanover 1, Königstr. 19, Postfach 3029; tel. (0511) 3481565; telex 922769; f. 1899; Pres. GUSTAV HEBOLD; Man. Dir Dr CHRISTIAN AHRENS; 7 mems.

Vereinigung der Industrie- und Handelskammern des Landes Nordrhein-Westfalen: 4000 Düsseldorf 1, Postfach 240120; tel. (0211) 352091; telex 8582363; Chair. Dr HEINZ MALANGRÉ; Sec. Ass. HANS G. CRONE-ERDMANN; 16 mems.

Kammergemeinschaft Öffentlichkeitsarbeit der Nordrhein-Westfälischen Industrie- und Handelskammern: 5000 Cologne 1, Unter Sachsenhausen 10–26; tel. (0221) 1640-157; telex 8881400; Chair. Dr HEINZ MALANGRÉ; Sec. GÜNTER BOCK; 14 mems.

Arbeitsgemeinschaft der Industrie- und Handelskammern Rheinland-Pfalz: 6500 Mainz, Schillerplatz 7; tel. (06131) 2620; telex 4187886; Sec. ERNST THÖNE; 4 mems.

Verband der Industrie- und Handelskammern des Landes Schleswig-Holstein: 2300 Kiel, Lorentzendamm 24; tel. (0431) 59041; telex 299864; Chair. Dr FRITZ SÜVERKRÜP; Sec. WOLF-RÜDIGER JANZEN; 3 mems.

Arbeitsgemeinschaft Öffentlichkeitsarbeit der Norddeutschen Industrie- und Handelskammern: 2000 Hamburg 11, Börse; tel. (040) 366382; telex 211250; Chair. GUSTAV G. HEBOLD; Sec. Dr UWE CHRISTIANSEN.

EXPORT AND TRADE ASSOCIATIONS

Arbeitsgemeinschaft Aussenhandel der Deutschen Wirtschaft: 5000 Cologne 51, Gustav-Heinemann-Ufer 84–88; Dir HEINZ TEMBRINK.

Bundesstelle für Aussenhandelsinformation (German Foreign Trade Information Office): 5000 Cologne, Blaubach 13, Postfach 108007; tel. (0221) 2057-1; telex 8882735.

Bundesverband des Deutschen Gross- und Aussenhandels eV: 5300 Bonn, Kaiser-Friedrichstr. 13, Postfach 1349; tel. (0228) 26004-0; telex 886783; Pres. Konsul KLAUS RICHTER; 82 mem. asscns.

Hauptgemeinschaft des Deutschen Einzelhandels eV: 5000 Cologne, Sachsenring 89; tel. (0221) 33980; telex 8881443; f. 1947; Chair. WOLFGANG HINRICHS; Exec. Dir GÜNTHER WASSMANN.

Zentralverband der Genossenschaftlichen Grosshandels- und Dienstleistungsunternehmen eV (Central Association of Co-operative Wholesale and Service Trade): 53 Bonn 1, Postfach 120220; tel. (0228) 210011; Pres. HANS-JÜRGEN KLUSSMANN; c. 250,000 mems; 880 primary co-operatives; 13 central co-operatives.

INDUSTRIAL ASSOCIATIONS

Bundesverband der Deutschen Industrie eV (Federation of German Industry): 5000 Cologne 51, Gustav-Heinemann-Ufer 84–88; tel. (0221) 3708-1; telex 8882601; Pres. Dr TYLL NECKER; Dir-Gen. Dr SIEGFRIED MANN; mems include some of the following asscns:

Arbeitsgemeinschaft Industriengruppe (General Industry): 8500 Nuremberg 1, Messezentrum; tel. (0911) 86688; telex 626271; Chair. GEORG MEIDENBAUER; Dir Dr BENNO KORBMACHER.

Arbeitsgemeinschaft Keramische Industrie eV (Ceramics): 6000 Frankfurt a.M. 97, Friedrich-Ebert-Anlage 38, Postfach 970171; tel. (069) 740617; telex 4189085; Chair. ROLAND DORSCHNER; Dir R. A. REINFRIED VOGLER; 6 mem. asscns.

Bundesverband Bekleidungsindustrie eV (Clothing): 5000 Cologne 1, Mevissenstr. 15; tel. (0221) 77440; telex 8883363; Pres. GERD SOMBERG; Dirs-Gen. Dipl.-Kfm. WALTER F. HERPELL, RAINER MAUER.

Bundesvereinigung der Deutschen Ernährungsindustrie eV (Food): 5300 Bonn 2, Rheinallee 18; tel. (0228) 351051; telex 885679; f. 1949; Chair. HERMANN BAHLSEN; Chief Gen. Man. Dr GERHARD HEIN; 37 branch-organizations.

Bundesverband der Deutschen Luftfahrt-, Raumfahrt- und Ausrüstungsindustrie eV (BDLI) (Aerospace Industries): 5300 Bonn 2, Konstantinstr. 90; tel. (0228) 330011; telex 885528; Pres. Dr OTTO GREVE; Dir ARNO L. SCHMITZ.

Bundesverband Druck eV (Printing): 6200 Wiesbaden 1, Postfach 1869, Biebricher Allee 79; tel. (06121) 8030; telex 4186888; f. 1947; Pres. FRANZ JOSEF WEIXLER; Dir Dipl.-Vw. HUBERTUS LOSS; 11 mem. asscns.

Bundesverband Glas- und Mineralfaserindustrie eV (Glass): 4000 Düsseldorf 1, Stresemannstr. 26, Postfach 8340; tel. (0211) 16894-0; telex 8587686; Chair. Dr H. J. KLEIN; Dirs JOHANN-FRIEDRICH HÜNERÖDER, Dipl.-Vw. NORBERT ELL; 6 mem. asscns.

Bundesverband Steine und Erden eV (Building): 6000 Frankfurt a.M., Friedrich-Ebert-Anlage 38, Postfach 970171; tel. (069) 740617; telex 4189085; f. 1948; Pres. Dipl.-Kfm. PETER SCHUHMACHER; Chief Dir Dipl.-Volksw. HANS-JÜRGEN REITZIG.

Deutscher Giessereiverband (Foundries): 4000 Düsseldorf 1, Sohnstr. 70, Postfach 8709; tel. (0211) 68711; telex 8586885; Pres. Dipl.-Ing. EBERHARD MÖLLMANN; Man. Dir Dr HORST BERMIG.

Deutsche Verbundgesellschaft eV (Electricity): 6900 Heidelberg 1, Ziegelhäuser Landstr. 5; tel. (06221) 4037-0; telex 461849; Chair. Dr-Ing. WILHELM KIWIT, Dr-Ing. GÜNTER KLÄTTE; Dir-Gen. Dipl.-Ing. HANS-GÜNTER BUSCH.

Gesamtverband kunststoffverarbeitende Industrie eV (GKV) (Plastics): 6000 Frankfurt a.M. 1, Am Hauptbahnhof 12; tel. (069) 271050; f. 1949; Chair. LUDWIG EBERHARD; Sec.-Gen. HORST PRIEPNITZ; 900 mems.

Gesamtverband der Textilindustrie in der BRD (Gesamttextil) eV (Textiles): 6000 Frankfurt a.M. 70, Schaumainkai 87; tel. (069) 633040; telex 411034; Pres. ERNST-GÜNTER PLUTTE; Dir-Gen. Dr KONRAD NEUNDÖRFER.

Hauptverband der Deutschen Bauindustrie eV (Building): 6200 Wiesbaden, Abraham-Lincoln-Str. 30, Postfach 2966; tel. (06121) 7720; telex 4186147; 5300 Bonn 1, Am Hofgarten 9; tel. (0228) 225055; telex 886881; f. 1948; Pres. Dr-Ing. GÜNTHER HERION; Dir-Gen. Dr HORST FRANKE; 16 mem. asscns.

Hauptverband der Deutschen Holzindustrie und verwandter Industriezweige eV (Woodwork): 6200 Wiesbaden 1, An den Quellen 10, Postfach 2928; tel. (06121) 39305; telex 4186631;

FEDERAL REPUBLIC OF GERMANY

f. 1948; Pres. Dr Manfred Thome; Dir Hans Helmut Kalbe; 28 mem. asscns, 4,000 mems.

Hauptverband der Papier, Pappe und Kunststoffe verarbeitenden Industrie eV (HPV) (Paper, Board and Plastic): 6000 Frankfurt a.M. 1, Arndtstr. 47; tel. (069) 740311; telex 411925; f. 1948; 11 regional groups, 18 production groups; Pres. Richard Dohse; Dirs-Gen. Dr Horst Kohl, Dieter von Tein; 1,300 mems.

Mineralölwirtschaftsverband eV (Petroleum): 2000 Hamburg 1, Steindamm 71; tel. (040) 2854-1; telex 2162257; f. 1946; Chair. Wolfgang Oehme; Man. Dir Dr Frank Schmidt.

Verband der Automobilindustrie eV (Motor Cars): 6000 Frankfurt a.M. 17, Westendstr. 61, Postfach 170563; tel. (069) 7570-1; telex 411293; Pres. Hans-Erdmann Schönbeck; Man. Dirs Dr Achim Diekmann, Dr Erhard Bieger, Dipl.-Ing. Peter v. Manteuffel.

Verband der Cigarettenindustrie (Cigarettes): 2000 Hamburg 13, Harvestehuder Weg 88; tel. (040) 414009-0; telex 215044; Chair. Dieter von Specht; Dir-Gen. Dr Harald König.

Verband der Chemischen Industrie eV (Chemical Industry): 6000 Frankfurt a.M. 1, Karlstr. 21; telex 6997654; f. 1877; Pres. Dr Hans Albers; Dir-Gen. Dr Wolfgang Munde; 1,500 mems.

Verband der deutschen feinmechanischen und optischen Industrie eV (Optical and Precision Instruments): 5000 Cologne 1, Pipinstr. 16; tel. (0221) 219458; telex 8882226; f. 1949; Chair. Dr Georg-Wilhelm Oetjen; Dir Dipl.-Kfm. Harald Russegger.

Verband Deutscher Maschinen- und Anlagenbau eV (VDMA) (Machinery and Plant Manufacture): 6000 Frankfurt a.M. 71 (Niederrad), Lyoner Str. 18, Postfach 710864; tel. (069) 66030; telex 411321; f. 1892; Pres. Dr-Ing. Otto H. Schiele; Gen. Man. Dr Justus Fürstenau.

Verband Deutscher Papierfabriken eV (Paper): 5300 Bonn 1, Adenauerallee 55; tel. (0228) 26705-0; telex 886767; Pres. Carl-Ludwig Graf von Deym; Dir-Gen. Dr Oskar Haus.

Verband der Deutschen Schiffbauindustrie eV (Shipbuilding): 2000 Hamburg 1, An der Alster 1; tel. (040) 246205; telex 2162496; Pres. Dr jur. Michael Budczies; Gen. Man. Dipl.-Kfm. Werner Fante.

Verein der Zuckerindustrie (Sugar): 5300 Bonn 1, Am Hofgarten 8, Postfach 2545; tel. (0228) 22850; telex 886718; f. 1850; Chair. Jaspar Freiherr von Maltzan; Dir-Gen. Dr Konrad Dankowski.

Vereinigung Deutscher Sägewerksverbände eV (Sawmills): Mainzer Str. 64, Postfach 61 28, 6200 Wiesbaden 1; tel. (06121) 300020; Chair. Eugen Decker; Man. Dr Ernst-Jürgen Neuser.

Wirtschaftsverband der Deutschen Kautschukindustrie eV (W.d.K.) (Rubber): 6000 Frankfurt a.M. 90, Zeppelinallee 69; tel. (069) 79360; telex 411254; f. 1894; Pres. Helmut Werner; Man. Klaus Mocker; 94 mems.

Wirtschaftsverband Eisen, Blech und Metall verarbeitende Industrie eV (Metal Goods): 4000 Düsseldorf 30, Kaiserswerther Str. 135, Postfach 321230; tel. (0211) 454930; telex 8584985; Pres. Günter Becker; Gen.-Man. Dipl.-Vw. Klaus Bellwinkel.

Wirtschaftsverband Erdöl- und Erdgasgewinnung eV (Association of Crude Oil and Gas Producers): 3000 Hanover, Brühlstr. 9; tel. (0511) 327648; telex 921462; f. 1945; Pres. Prof. Dr-Ing. Heino Lübben; Gen. Man. Dr Günter Fuchs.

Wirtschaftsverband Stahlbau und Energietechnik (SET) (Steel and Energy): 5000 Cologne 1, Ebertplatz 1; tel. (0221) 7731117; telex 8885373; Chair. Dipl.-Ing. Fritz Adrian; Dir-Gen. Dr rer. pol. Hans-Georg Kiera.

Wirtschaftsverband Stahlverformung eV (Steelworks): 5800 Hagen-Emst, Goldene Pforte 1, Postfach 4009; tel. (02331) 51041; telex 823806; Pres. Dr-Ing. Jochen F. Kirchhoff; Dir-Gen. Dr Hermann Hassel.

Wirtschaftsvereinigung Bergbau eV (Mining): 5300 Bonn 1, Zitelmannstr. 9–11, Postfach 120280; tel. (0228) 540020; telex 8869566; Pres. Dr-Ing. Rudolf Lenhartz; Gen. Mans Karl-Heinrich Jakob, Dr-Ing. Harald Kliebhan; 16 mem. asscns.

Wirtschaftsvereinigung Eisen- und Stahlindustrie (Iron and Steel): 4000 Düsseldorf 1, Breitestr. 69, Postfach 8705; tel. (0211) 8291; telex 8582286; Chair. Dr Heinz Kriwet; Dir Dr Ruprecht Vondran.

Wirtschaftsvereinigung Metalle eV (Metal): 4000 Düsseldorf 30, Tersteegenstr. 28, Postfach 8706; tel. (0211) 45471-0; telex 8584721; Pres. Dr Jürgen Heraeus; Dir-Gen. Jürgen Ulmer.

Wirtschaftsvereinigung Ziehereien und Kaltwalzwerke eV (Metal): 4000 Düsseldorf 30, Drahthaus, Kaiserwerther Str. 137; tel. (0211) 4564-246; Chair. Hans Martin Wälzholz-Junius; Gen.-Man. Günter Müller.

Zentralverband der Elektrotechnik und Elektronik Industrie (ZVEI) eV (Electrical and Electronic Equipment): 6000 Frankfurt a.M. 70, Stresemannallee 19, Postfach 700969; tel. (069) 6302-1; telex 411035; f. 1918; Chair. Dr Helmut Lohr; Dirs Prof. Dr Rudolf Scheid, Dr Bodo Böttcher (Economic and Commercial), Rudolf Winckler (Technical); 1,500 mems.

CONSULTATIVE ASSOCIATIONS

(See also under Bankers' Organizations, Chambers of Industry and Commerce, etc.)

Gemeinschaftsausschuss der Deutschen gewerblichen Wirtschaft (Joint Committee for German Industry and Commerce): 5300 Bonn 1, Adenauerallee 148; tel. (0228) 1040; telex 886805; f. 1950; a discussion forum for the principal industrial and commercial organizations; Pres. Otto Wolff von Amerongen; 15 mem. organizations, including:

Centralvereinigung Deutscher Handelsvertreter- und Handelsmakler-Verbände (CDH): 5000 Cologne 41, Geleniusstr. 1; tel. (0221) 514043; telex 8881743; Pres. Norbert Hopf; Gen. Sec. Ernst H. Haumann; 31,000 mems in all brs.

Deutscher Hotel- und Gaststättenverband eV: 5300 Bonn 2, Kronprinzenstr. 46; tel. (0228) 820080; telex 885489; f. 1949; Pres. Leo Imhoff; over 100,000 mems.

Zentralverband des Deutschen Handwerks: 5300 Bonn 1, Haus des Deutschen Handwerks, Johanniterstr. 1; tel. (0228) 545-1; telex 886338; f. 1949; Pres. P. Schnitker; Gen. Sec. Dr Klaus-Joachim Kübler; 42 mem. chambers, 52 asscns.

EMPLOYERS' ASSOCIATION

Bundesvereinigung der Deutschen Arbeitgeberverbände (Confederation of German Employers' Associations): 5000 Cologne 51, Postfach 510508, Gustav-Heinemann Ufer 72; tel. (0221) 37950; telex 8881466; Pres. Otto Esser; Dirs Dr Ernst-Gerhard Erdmann, Dr Fritz-Heinz Himmelreich, Dr Werner Doetsch; affiliates 12 regional associations, and 46 trade associations, of which some are listed under industrial associations (see above).

Affiliated associations:

Arbeitgeberkreis Gesamttextil im Gesamtverband der Textilindustrie in der Bundesrepublik Deutschland eV (General Textile Employers' Organization): 6000 Frankfurt a.M. 70, Schaumainkai 87; tel. (069) 63304-0; telex 411034; Chair. Peter Frowein; Dir Dr Klaus Schmidt; 7 mem. asscns.

Arbeitgeberverband der Cigarettenindustrie (Employers' Association of Cigarette Manufacturers): 2 Hamburg 13, Harvestehuder Weg 88; tel. (040) 41400918; telex 215044; f. 1949; Pres. Prof. Dr Ernst Zander; Dir Dr Joachim Schwahn.

Arbeitgeberverband der Deutschen Binnenschiffahrt eV (General Employers' Association for Shipping on the River Rhine): 4100 Duisburg 13, Dammstr. 15–17; tel. (0203) 82001; telex 855692; Pres. Dr G. W. Hulsman; Dir G. Dütemeyer.

Arbeitgeberverband Deutscher Eisenbahnen eV (German Railway Employers' Association): 5000 Cologne, Volksgartenstr. 54A; tel. (0221) 313980; Pres. Hansjörg Kraft; Dir Dr Helmut Depenheuer.

Arbeitgeberverband des Privaten Bankgewerbes eV (Private Banking Employers' Association): 5 Cologne, Andreaskloster 5–11; tel. (0221) 131024; f. 1954; 155 mems; Pres. Dr Horst Burgard; Dir Dr Klaus Dutti.

Arbeitgeberverband der Versicherungsunternehmen in Deutschland (Employers' Association of Insurance Companies): 8000 Munich 22, Bruderstr. 9; tel. (089) 2368080; telex 524713; Pres. Dr Peter von Blomberg; Dir-Gen. Dr Jürgen Willich.

Bundesarbeitgeberverband Chemie eV (Federation of Employers' Associations in the Chemical Industry): 6200 Wiesbaden, Abraham-Lincoln-Str. 24, Postfach 1280; tel. (06121) 719016; telex 4186646; Pres. Dr Dieter Schlemmer; Dir Dr Karl Molitor; 12 mem. asscns.

Bundesvereinigung der Arbeitgeber im Bundesverband Bekleidungsindustrie eV (Confederation of Employers of the Clothing Industry): 5 Cologne 1, Mevissenstr. 15; tel. (0221) 77440; telex 8883363; Dir Rainer Mauer; 11 mem. asscns.

Gesamtverband der Deutschen Land- und Forstwirtschaftlichen Arbeitgeberverbände eV (Federation of Agricultural and Forestry Employers' Associations): 53 Bonn 2, Godesberger Allee 142–148, Postfach 20 09 28; tel. (0228) 376955;

FEDERAL REPUBLIC OF GERMANY

telex 885586; Pres. ODAL VON ALTEN-NORDHEIM; Dir Dipl.-Volksw. Dipl.-Landw. MARTIN MALLACH; 13 mem. asscns.

Gesamtverband der metallindustriellen Arbeitgeberverbände eV (Federation of the Metal Trades Employers' Associations): 5000 Cologne 1, Volksgartenstr. 54A; tel. (0221) 33990; telex 8882583; Pres. Dr WERNER STUMPFE; Dir Dr DIETER KIRCHNER; 13 mem. asscns.

Vereinigung der Arbeitgeberverbände der Deutschen Papierindustrie eV (Federation of Employers' Associations of the German Paper Industry): 5300 Bonn, Adenauerallee 55; tel. (0228) 222066; telex 886767; Pres. Dr WOLFGANG FROMEN; Dir RA. ANSGAR PAWELKE; 8 mem. asscns.

Vereinigung der Arbeitgeberverbände energie- und versorgungswirtschaftlicher Unternehmungen (Employers' Federation of Energy and Power Supply Enterprises): 3000 Hanover, Kurt Schumacher-Str. 24; tel. (0511) 323405; f. 1962; Pres. Dr DAVID BEICHTER; Dir GERHARD M. MEYER; 6 mem. asscns.

Regional employers' associations:

Landesvereinigung Baden-Württembergischer Arbeitgeberverbände eV: 7000 Stuttgart 1, Hölderlinstr. 3A, Postfach 527; tel. (0711) 294753; telex 723651; Pres. HELMUT EBERSPÄCHER; Dir HERFRIED HEISLER; 44 mem. asscns.

Vereinigung Badischer Unternehmerverbände eV (Association of Industry in Baden): 7800 Freiburg i. Br., Lerchenstr. 6; tel. (0761) 31734; telex 772876; Pres. RICHARD H. CLASS; Dir WERNER RUDOLPH; 17 mem. asscns.

Vereinigung der Arbeitgeberverbände in Bayern (Federation of Employers' Associations in Bavaria): 8000 Munich 2, Brienner Str. 7, Postfach 202527; tel. (089) 228211; telex 523457; f. 1949; Pres. HUBERT STÄRKER; Dir WOLF MOSER; 80 mem. asscns.

Zentralvereinigung Berliner Arbeitgeberverbände (Federation of Employers' Associations in Berlin): 1000 Berlin 12, Am Schillertheater 2; tel. (030) 310050; telex 184366; Pres. KLAUS OSTERHOF; Dir Dr HARTMANN KLEINER; 50 mem. asscns.

Vereinigung der Arbeitgeberverbände im Lande Bremen eV (Federation of Employers' Associations in the Land of Bremen): 2800 Bremen, Schillerstr. 10; tel. (0421) 36802-0; telex 244577; Pres. PETER-OTTO ENGISCH; Dir Dr jur. EBERHARD WEHR; 14 mem. asscns.

Landesvereinigung der Arbeitgeberverbände in Hamburg eV (Federation of Employers' Associations in Hamburg): 2 Hamburg 13, Feldbrunnenstr. 56; tel. (040) 447486; telex 214333; Pres. ALEXANDER SCHÖN; Gen. Man. JÜRGEN MEINEKE; 21 mem. asscns.

Vereinigung der Hessischen Unternehmerverbände eV (Federation of Employers' Associations in Hesse): 6000 Frankfurt a.M. 90, Lilienthalallee 4; tel. (069) 79050; telex 412136; f. 1947; Pres. HERMANN HABICH; Dir and Sec. Dr HUBERT STADLER; 52 mem. asscns.

Unternehmerverbände Niedersachsen eV: (Federation of Employers' Associations in Lower Saxony): 3000 Hanover 1, Schiffgraben 36; tel. (0511) 85051; telex 922912; Pres. HERMANN BAHLSEN; Mans GERNOT PREUSS, GÜNTER SEIDE, Dr JÜRGEN WOLFSLAST; 56 mem. asscns.

Landesvereinigung der Arbeitgeberverbände Nordrhein-Westfalens eV (North Rhine-Westphalia Federation of Industrial Employers' Associations): 4000 Düsseldorf 30, Uerdingerstr. 58–62; tel. (0211) 45731; telex 8586864; Pres. Dr Ing. JOCHEN F. KIRCHHOFF; 86 mem. asscns.

Landesvereinigung Rheinland-Pfälzischer Unternehmerverbände eV (Federation of Employers' Associations in the Rhineland Palatinate): 6500 Mainz, Schillerplatz 7; tel. (06131) 232715; telex 4187741; f. 1963; Pres. Dipl.-Ing. EDGAR GEORG; Man. Dr GÜNTHER HERZOG; 13 mem. asscns.

Vereinigung der Arbeitgeberverbände des Saarlandes eV (Federation of Employers' Associations in Saarland): 6600 Saarbrücken 6, Harthweg 15; tel. (0681) 51061; telex 4421229; Pres. Dr PAUL WEBER; Dir Dr KURT PHIELER; 18 mem. asscns.

Vereinigung der Schleswig-Holsteinischen Unternehmensverbände eV (Federation of Employers' Associations in Schleswig-Holstein): 2370 Rendsburg, Adolf-Steckel-Str. 17; tel. (04331) 5232; telex 29640; Pres. Dr KLAUS MURMANN; Dir Dr WOLFGANG DE HAAN; 37 mem. asscns.

TRADE UNIONS

Deutscher Gewerkschaftsbund (DGB): 4 Düsseldorf 30, Hans-Böckler-Str. 39, Postfach 2601; tel. (0211) 43010; telex 8584819; f. 1949; Pres. ERNST BREIT; Vice-Pres. GERD MUHR, GUSTAV FEHRENBACH.

The following unions, with a total of 7,719,468 (Dec. 1985) members, are affiliated to the DGB:

Industriegewerkschaft Bau-Steine-Erden (Building and Construction Trade): 6000 Frankfurt a.M., Bockenheimer Landstr. 73–77; tel. (069) 7437-0; telex 412826; Pres. KONRAD CARL; 486,000 mems (Aug. 1986).

Industriegewerkschaft Bergbau und Energie (Mining and Energy): 463 Bochum, Alte Hattingerstr. 19; tel. (0234) 3190; telex 825809; f. 1889; Pres. HEINZ-WERNER MEYER; 356,706 mems (Dec. 1985).

Industriegewerkschaft Chemie- Papier- Keramik (Chemical, Paper and Ceramics): 3 Hanover, Konigsworther Platz 6; telex 922608; Pres. HERMANN RAPPE; 649,569 mems (Dec. 1985).

Industriegewerkschaft Druck und Papier (Printing and Paper): 7000 Stuttgart 1, Friedrichstr. 15; tel. (0711) 20181; telex 723146; Pres. ERWIN FERLEMANN; 140,725 mems. (Dec. 1985).

Gewerkschaft der Eisenbahner Deutschlands (Railwaymen): 6 Frankfurt a.M., Beethovenstr. 12–16; tel. 75360; telex 411715; Pres. ERNST HAAR; 354,180 mems (Dec. 1985).

Gewerkschaft Erziehung und Wissenschaft (Education and Sciences): 6 Frankfurt a.M., Unterlindau 58; tel. (069) 720096; telex 412989; Pres. Dr DIETER WUNDER; 194,028 mems (Dec. 1985).

Gewerkschaft Gartenbau, Land- und Forstwirtschaft (Horticulture, Agriculture and Forestry): 3500 Kassel 1, Druseltalstr. 51, Postfach 410180; tel. (0561) 34060; telex 99630; f. 1909; Pres. WILLI LOJEWSKI; 42,450 mems (Dec. 1985).

Gewerkschaft Handel, Banken und Versicherungen (Commerce, Banks and Insurance): 4 Düsseldorf 30, Tersteegenstr. 30; telex 8584653; f. 1973; Pres. GÜNTER VOLKMAR; 371,238 mems (Dec. 1985).

Gewerkschaft Holz und Kunststoff (Wood and Plastic-work): 4000 Düsseldorf, Sonnenstr. 14; tel. (0211) 786461; telex 2114218; f. 1945; Pres. HORST MORICH; 142,780 mems (Aug. 1986).

Gewerkschaft Kunst (Art): 4000 Düsseldorf 30, Hans-Böckler-Str. 39; tel. (0211) 4301-334; Pres. ALFRED HORNE; 27,019 mems (Dec. 1985).

Gewerkschaft Leder (Leather): 7000 Stuttgart 1, Willi-Bleicher-Str. 20; tel. (0711) 295555; Pres. WERNER DICK; 48,725 mems (Dec. 1985).

Industriegewerkschaft Metall (Metal Workers' Union): 6 Frankfurt a.M., Wilhelm-Leuschner-Str. 79–85; tel. (069) 26471; telex 411115; Chair. FRANZ STEINKÜHLER; 2,553,041 mems (Dec. 1985).

Gewerkschaft Nahrung- Genuss- Gaststätten (Food, Delicacies and Catering): 2 Hamburg 1, Gertrudenstr. 9; telex 2161884; f. 1949; Pres. GÜNTER DÖDING; 267,158 mems (Dec. 1985).

Gewerkschaft Öffentliche Dienste, Transport und Verkehr (Public Services and Transport Workers' Union): 7000 Stuttgart 1, Theodor Heuss-Str. 2; telex 723302; Chair. Dr MONIKA WULF-MATHIES; 1,179,396 mems (Dec. 1985).

Gewerkschaft der Polizei (Police Union): 4010 Hilden, Forststr. 3A; tel. (0211) 71040; telex 8581968; f. 1950; Chair. GÜNTER SCHRÖDER; Sec. W. DICKE; 163,590 mems (Dec. 1985).

Deutsche Postgewerkschaft (Postal Union): 6000 Frankfurt a.M. 71, Rhonestr. 2; tel. (069) 66951; telex 412112; Pres. KURT VAN HAAREN; 460,626 mems (Dec. 1985).

Gewerkschaft Textil-Bekleidung (Textiles and Clothing): 4 Düsseldorf 30, Ross Str. 94; Pres. BERTHOLD KELLER; 258,846 mems (Dec. 1985).

The following are the largest unions outside the DGB:

Deutsche Angestellten-Gewerkschaft (DAG) (Clerical, Technical and Administrative Workers): 2 Hamburg 36, Karl-Muck-Platz 1; tel. (040) 349150; telex 211642; f. 1945; Chair. HERMANN BRANDT; 500,922 mems (1985).

Deutscher Beamtenbund (Federation of Civil Servants): 5300 Bonn 2, Dreizehnmorgenweg 36; tel. (0228) 8110; telex 885457; f. 1918; Pres. ALFRED KRAUSE; 796,254 mems (1986).

TRADE FAIRS

More than 80 trade fairs take place annually in the Federal Republic. Fair organizers include:

Berlin: AMK Berlin Ausstellungs-Messe-Kongress-GmbH, Messedamm 22, 1000 Berlin 19; tel. (030) 30381; telex 182908; Man. Dirs Dr MANFRED BUSCHE, Dr WOLFGANG WEGMANN.

FEDERAL REPUBLIC OF GERMANY

Cologne: Messe- und Ausstellungs GmbH, 5000 Cologne 21, Postfach 210760; tel. (0221) 821-1; telex 8873426.

Düsseldorf: Düsseldorfer Messe GmbH—NOWEA, Postfach 320203, 4000 Düsseldorf 30; tel. (0211) 45601; telex 8584853.

Essen: Messe Essen GmbH, Norbertstr., Postfach 100165, 4300 Essen 1; tel. (0201) 7244-0; telex 8579647.

Frankfurt: Messe Frankfurt GmbH, Postfach 970126, 6000 Frankfurt a.M. 1; tel. (069) 7575 0; telex 411558; f. 1907; Chair. Dr HORSTMAR STAUBER.

Friedrichshafen: Internationale Bodensee-Messe GmbH, Messegelände, 7990 Friedrichshafen 1; tel. (07541) 708-0; telex 734315.

Hamburg: Hamburg Messe und Congress GmbH, Jungiusstr. 13, 2000 Hamburg 36; tel. (040) 35691; telex 212609; f. 1973; multipurpose congress centre with 17 halls and conference rooms; Dir Conventions AXEL DAVID.

Hanover: Deutsche Messe- und Ausstellungs-AG, Messegelände, 3000 Hanover 82; tel. (0511) 891; telex 922728.

Karlsruhe: Karlsruher Kongress- und Ausstellungs GmbH, Postfach 1208, 7500 Karlsruhe 1; tel. (0721) 37200; telex 721157.

Munich: Münchener Messe- und Ausstellung GmbH, Messegelände, Postfach 121009, 8000 Munich 12; tel. (089) 51070; telex 5212086.

Nuremberg: NMA Nürnberger Messe- und Ausstellungs GmbH, Messezentrum, 8500 Nuremberg 50; tel. (0911) 8606-0; telex 623613; f. 1974; Dir Dr HARTWIG HAUCK.

Offenbach: Offenbacher Messe GmbH, Postfach 101423, 6050 Offenbach/M. 1; tel. (069) 817091; telex 411298.

Saarbrücken: Saarmesse GmbH, Messegelände, 6600 Saarbrücken; tel. (0681) 53056.

Stuttgart: Stuttgarter Messe- und Kongress-GmbH, Am Kochenhof 16, Postfach 990, 7000 Stuttgart 1; tel. (0711) 25981; telex 722584.

Wiesbaden: Heckmann GmbH, Kapellenstr. 47, 6200 Wiesbaden; tel. (06121) 524071; telex 4186518.

Transport

RAILWAYS

In 1984 German Federal Railways controlled 27,784 km of standard gauge track, of which 11,272 km were electrified.

Deutsche Bundesbahn (DB) (German Federal Railways): 6 Frankfurt a.M., Friedrich-Ebert-Anlage 43–45; tel. 2651; telex 414087; Pres. Dr.-Ing. REINER GOHLKE; Dirs HEINZ FRIESER, HANS-JOACHIM GRÖBEN, HEMJÖ KLEIN, WILHELM PÄLLMANN, Dipl.-Ing. HANS WIEDEMANN, KNUT REIMERS.

Metropolitan Railway

Berliner Verkehrs-Betriebe (Berlin Transport Authority —West Berlin): 1000 Berlin 30, Potsdamer Str. 188; tel. (030) 2561; telex 302020; operates 105.5 km of underground railway and 71.5 km of 'S-Bahn' railway; also runs bus services; Mans HELMUT DÖPFER, WILLI DIEDRICH, HARRO SACHSSE.

Stadtwerke München: 8000 Munich 80, Einsteinstr. 28, Postfach 202222; tel. (089) 2191-1; telex 522063; underground (40.9 km), tramway (87.4 km), omnibus (395.4 km); Dir Dipl.-Ing. DIETER BUHMANN.

Associations

Bundesverband Deutscher Eisenbahnen (BDE) (Union of Non-Federal Railways, Bus-Services and Cable-Ways): 5000 Cologne 1, Hülcrather Str. 17; tel. (0221) 730021; Pres. DIETER LUDWIG; Dir MANFRED MONTADA.

Verband Öffentlicher Verkehrsbetriebe eV (VÖV) (Association of Public Transport): 5000 Cologne 1, Kamekestr. 37–39; telex 8881718; f. 1895; Pres. Dir Dr SATTLER; Sec. Prof. Dr-Ing. GIRNAU.

ROADS

In December 1984 there were 490,045 km of classified roads, including 8,198 km of motorway, 31,485 km of other main roads and 63,306 km of secondary roads.

Zentralarbeitsgemeinschaft des Strassenverkehrsgewerbes eV (ZAV) (Central Association of the Road Transport Industry): 6 Frankfurt a.M. 93, Breitenbachstr. 1, Haus des Strassenverkehrs; tel. (069) 775719; telex 411627; Pres. HEINZ HERZIG; Gen. Sec. W. NEUMANN.

INLAND WATERWAYS

There are about 4,430 km of navigable inland waterways, and the Rhine-Main-Danube Canal, linking the North Sea and the Black Sea, is expected to be completed by 1992. Inland shipping accounts for more than 20% of total freight traffic.

Abteilung Binnenschiffahrt und Wasserstrassen (Federal Ministry of Transport, Inland Waterways Dept): 5300 Bonn 2, Kennedyallee 72; tel. (0228) 3001; telex 885700; deals with construction, maintenance and administration of federal waterways and with national and international inland water transport.

Associations

Bundesverband der deutschen Binnenschiffahrt eV: 4100 Duisburg 13, Dammstr. 15–17; tel. (0203) 82001; telex 855692; f. 1948; central Inland Waterway Association to further the interests of operating firms; Pres. Dr KARL-HEINZ KÜHL; Mans JÖRG ARTL, Dr HEINZ DURGELOH, Rechtsanwalt Dr HERMANN-ULRICH PABST.

Hafenschiffahrtverband Hamburg eV: 2000 Hamburg 11, Mattentwiete 2; tel. 36128-0.

Verein für Binnenschiffahrt und Wasserstrassen eV (VBW): 4100 Duisberg 13, Dammstr. 15–17, Postfach 130 960; tel. (0203) 83740; formerly Zentral-Verein für deutsche Binnenschiffahrt eV and Verein zur Wahrung der Rheinschiffahrtsinteressen eV; an organization for the benefit of all branches of the inland waterways; Pres. D. WILLERS; Dirs Dr H.-J. GUSCHALL, D. WILLUHN, Dr W. MÜLLER, C. MEISTERMANN; Man. Dr H.-U. PABST.

SHIPPING

The principal seaports for freight are Bremen, Hamburg and Wilhelmshaven. Some important shipping companies are:

Christian F. Ahrenkiel: 2000 Hamburg 1, An der Alster 45; tel. (040) 28680; telex 213812; tramp, shipowners and managers; 45 vessels, 500,000 grt.

Argo Reederei Richard Adler & Söhne: 28 Bremen, Argo-Haus, Postfach 107529; tel. (0421) 363070; telex 245206; Finland, United Kingdom, Mediterranean; Propr MAX ADLER; 6 vessels, 23,500 grt.

Aug. Bolten Wm. Miller's Nachfolger: 2 Hamburg 11, Mattentwiete 8; tel. (040) 3601-1; telex 211431; tramp; 6 vessels, 105,700 grt.

Bugsier-Reederei- und Bergungs-AG: 2 Hamburg 11, Johannisbollwerk 10, Postfach 112273; tel. (040) 31110; telex 211228; salvage, towage, tugs, ocean-going heavy lift cranes, submersible pontoons, harbour tugs; liner services between continent/Denmark and UK and Ireland; Chief Officers Capt. K.-G. MEYER, H. BENECKE; 6 vessels, 26,500 grt.

DAL Deutsche Afrika-Linien GmbH & Co: 2000 Hamburg, Palmaille 45, Postfach 500 369; tel. (040) 380160; telex 212897-0; Europe, West, South and East Africa; Man. Dirs R. BRENNECKE, H. VON RANTZAU, Dr E. VON RANTZAU.

Deutsche Shell Tanker GmbH: 2000 Hamburg 60, Ueberseering 35, Postfach 600 440; tel. (040) 6341; telex 2163091; 8 vessels; 467,665 grt.

Dohle, Peter, Schiffahrts-KG (GmbH & Co): 2000 Hamburg 50, Palmaille 33, Postfach 500440; tel. (040) 381080; telex 214444; Man. Dirs PETER DOHLE, H.-G. HÖLCK, JOCHEN DÖHLE; chartering agent for about 110 vessels.

John T. Essberger: 2000 Hamburg 50, Palmaille 49, Postfach 500429; tel. (040) 380160; telex 212852; f. 1924; Man. Dirs L. v. RANTZAU-ESSBERGER, L. BIELENBERG, Dr E. VON RANTZAU, H. VON RANTZAU; 9 tankers, 12,792 grt.

Esso Tankschiff Reederei GmbH: 2000 Hamburg 60, Postfach 600640, Kapstadtring 2; tel. (040) 6331; telex 2174151; f. 1928; 13 tank barges.

Fisser & v. Doornum: 2 Hamburg 13, Feldbrunnenstr. 43, Postfach 132265; tel. (040) 44186-0; telex 212671; f. 1879; tramp; Man. Dirs Dr FRANK FISSER, WULF V. MOLTKE; 22 vessels, 79,600 grt.

Johs. Fritzen & Sohn GmbH: 2970 Emden 1, Neptunhaus; tel. (04921) 20011; telex 27821; port agents, tug service, Lloyd's sub-agents, bunker agents.

Hamburg-Sudamerikanische Dampfschifffahrts-Gesellschaft Eggert & Amsinck: 2000 Hamburg 11, Ost-West-Str. 59, Hamburg-Süd-Haus; tel. (040) 37050; telex 21321699; worldwide service; 19 vessels, 342,697 grt.

Hapag-Lloyd AG: 2000 Hamburg 1, Ballindamm 25 and 2800 Bremen, Gustav-Deetjen-Allee 2–6; tel. (040) 3030; telex 217002; f. 1970; USA East Coast, Canada, North Pacific (Euro-Pacific), US Gulf/South Atlantic (Combi Line), West Indies (Carol), Mexico,

FEDERAL REPUBLIC OF GERMANY

Venezuela, Colombia and Costa Rica (Euro-Caribbean), Central America/West Coast (German Central America Service), Northern Brazil, South America/West Coast, Far East (Trio Service), Indonesia, Australia, New Zealand (Australia, New Zealand, Europe Container Service), the Canary Islands, also a Trans-Pacific service between USA West Coast and the Far East; Chair. Dr C. U. D. DECKEN; 40 vessels, 696,000 grt.

F. Laeisz SchiffahrtsgmbH & Co: 2 Hamburg 11, Trostbrücke 1; tel. (040) 36881; telex 215741; Dir NIKOLAUS W. SCHÜES; Dir G. HEYENGA; 3 refrigerated vessels, 4 containers, 2 bulk carriers, 2 bulk-container vessels, 178,000 grt.

Moller, Walther & Co: 2000 Hamburg 50, Thedestr. 2; tel. (040) 389931; telex 211523; 30 vessels.

Sloman Neptun Schiffahrts-AG: 2800 Bremen 1, Langenstr. 52+54, Postfach 1014 69; tel. (0421) 17631; telex 244421; f. 1873; Scandinavia, Baltic, Western Europe, North and West Africa and North Pacific; Mans JÜRGEN WILLHÖFT, WERNER KRIEGER, HERBERT JUNIEL; 17 vessels, 54,417 grt.

Oldenburg-Portugiesische Dampfschiffs-Rhederei GmbH: 2000 Hamburg 11, Postfach 110869; tel. (040) 361580; telex 211110; f. 1882; Spain, Portugal, Mediterranean, Madeira, Algeria, Tunisia, Morocco, Canary Isles; Man. Dirs P. T. HANSEN, A. OTTO; 3 vessels, 6,000 grt.

Egon Oldendorff: 24 Lübeck, Fünfhausen 1; tel. (0451) 15000; telex 26411; Dirs H. OLDENDORFF, H. E. HELLMANN, G. ARNDT, E. L. GIERMANN, W. SCHARNOWSKI, K. WEIDEMANN; tramp; 29 vessels, 550,000 gross tonnage.

Rhein Maas und See-Schiffahrtskontor GmbH: 4100 Duisburg 13, Krausstr. 1A, Postfach 130780; tel. (0203) 8041; telex 855700; 68 vessels.

Ernst Russ: 2000 Hamburg 36, Alsterarkaden 27; tel. (040) 36840; telex 2150090; f. 1893; Europe, Scandinavia, worldwide; tramps; Dir ERNST-ROLAND LORENZ-MEYER; 8 vessels, 213,268 grt.

Schlüssel Reederei KG: 2800 Bremen 1, Am Wall 58/60, Postfach 10 18 47; tel. (0421) 170561; telex 244520; f. 1950; tramps; 3 vessels, 86,158 grt.

H. Schuldt: 2000 Hamburg 1, Ballindamm 8; tel. (040) 309050; telex 161900; f. 1868; reefers; services to the USA; Gen. Mans E. SIEH, B. TODSEN; 4 vessels, 21,000 grt.

Seereederei "Frigga" AG: 2000 Hamburg 1, Ballindamm 17; tel. (040) 335782; telex 2161345; f. 1921; tramps; Dirs E. EBERS, Dr N. ROTHER; 2 vessels, 79,695 grt.

Hugo Stinnes Transozean Schiffahrt GmbH: 4330 Mülheim (Ruhr), Weseler Str. 60; telex 856714; liner service; Continent-West Africa; 9 vessels, 40,867 grt.

Thode, Johs.: 2000 Hamburg 50, Kohlbrandtreppe 2; tel. (040) 3802040; telex 211375; 50 vessels.

Tietjen, Wilhelm: 2000 Hamburg 50, Palmaille 35; tel. (040) 381171; telex 211342; 43 vessels.

Unterweser Reederei GmbH: 2800 Bremen 1, Blumenthalstr. 16, Postfach 100867; tel. (0421) 340085; telex 244179; f. 1890; Man. Dirs K. ESAU, M. SCHROIFF; 2 a.h. tug/supply vessels, 2 reduced draft supply vessels; 27 tugs.

Shipping Organizations

Verband Deutscher Küstenschiffseigner (German Coastal Shipowners Association): 2000 Hamburg-Altona, Grosse Elbstr. 36; tel. (040) 313435; telex 214444; f. 1896; Pres. Dr H. J. STÖCKER; Man. Dipl. sc. pol. KLAUS LUTH.

Verband Deutscher Reeder eV (German Shipowners' Association): 2000 Hamburg 36, Esplanade 6, Postfach 305580; tel. (040) 350970; telex 211407; Dirs Dr BERND KRÖGER, Dipl.-Kfm. HERBERT HOLST.

Verband der Deutschen Schiffbauindustrie eV: 2000 Hamburg 1, An der Alster 1; tel. (040) 246205; telex 2162496; Pres. Dr jur. MICHAEL BUDCZIES; Gen. Man. Dipl.-Kfm. WERNER FANTE.

Zentralverband der Deutschen Seehafenbetriebe eV (Federal Association of German Seaport Operators): 2000 Hamburg 50, Grosse Elbstr. 14; tel. (040) 311561; f. 1932; Chair. WERNER SCHRÖDER; Man. Dr LOTHAR L. V. JOLMES; approx. 850 mems.

CIVIL AVIATION

The major international airports are at Berlin (West), Cologne-Bonn, Düsseldorf, Frankfurt, Hamburg, Hanover, Munich and Stuttgart. Lufthansa has no landing rights at Berlin (West). More than 80 foreign airlines operate scheduled services to the Federal Republic and West Berlin.

Aero Lloyd Flugreisen GmbH & Co: Luftverkehrs KG, 6000 Frankfurt a.M. 1, Wilhelm-Leuschner-Str. 25, Postfach 160152; tel. (069) 25731; telex 4189372; f. 1981; charter services; Man. Dr W. SCHNEIDER; Dir Dr M. AKSMANOVIĆ; fleet of 3 Caravelle SE 210-10 BIR, 3 DC 9-32, 2 MD83.

Condor Flugdienst GmbH: Hans-Boeckler-Str. 7, 6078 Neu-Isenburg 1; tel. (06102) 2451; telex 417697; f. 1955, wholly-owned subsidiary of Lufthansa; charter and inclusive-tour services; fleet of 3 DC-10-30, 8 727-230, 4 737-230, 3 Airbus A310; Man. Dirs Dr MALTE BISCHOFF, Dr CLAUS GILLMANN, Capt. STEFAN HESS.

Deutsche Lufthansa AG: 5000 Cologne 21, Von-Gablenz-Str. 2-6; tel. (0221) 8261; telex 8873531; f. 1953; extensive world-wide network; Chair. Exec. Board HEINZ RUHNAU; Deputy Chair. Exec. Board Dipl. Ing. REINHARDT ABRAHAM; Chair. Supervisory Board GERD LAUSEN; fleet of 13 Boeing 747-230SCD, 4 747-230, 3 747-230F, 28 727-230, 38 737-230, 2 737-230C, 11 McDonnell Douglas DC10-30, 5 Airbus A300B4, 10 Airbus A310.

DLT Deutsche Luftverkehrs-GmbH: 6000 Frankfurt a.M. 75, Flughafen; tel. (069) 6905664; telex 411643; scheduled services; Mans PETER ORLOVIUS, G. H. EBERHARD SCHMIDT; fleet of 6 HS 748 2 B, 2 Embraer 120.

GCS German Cargo Services GmbH: Lufthansa Cargo Centre, Airport, Postfach 750271, 6000 Frankfurt a.M. 75; tel. (069) 6905427; telex 4189142; f. 1977; wholly-owned subsidiary of Lufthansa; freight-charter world-wide; Mans W. ALTHEN, S. KOEHLER; fleet of 5 DC8-73.

Germania Flug-GmbH: 5000 Cologne 90, Flughafen; tel. (02203) 401; telex 8873712; f. 1978; charter and inclusive-tour services; Man. Dr BISCHOFF; fleet of 2 Boeing 727-100.

Hapag-Lloyd Flug-GmbH: 3000 Hanover 42, Flughafen; tel. (0511) 73030; telex 9230136; f. 1972; charter and inclusive-tour services; Man. Dir CLAUS WÜLFERS; fleet of 4 Airbus A 300B4, 1 A300C4, 4 Boeing 737-200, 2 Boeing 727-200, 1 727-100.

Jet Air Luftfahrt-Verwaltungs-GmbH: 8000 Munich 87, Flughafen, Postfach 870349; tel. (089) 92118700; telex 5214377; charter and inclusive-tour services; Mans WOLFGANG JÜNGERAND, MICHAEL VOGEL; fleet of 2 Boeing 727.

LTS Lufttransport Süd AG & Co Fluggesellschaft: 8000 Munich 87, Flughafen Müncher-Riem; tel. (089) 9211-8950; telex 5214762; f. 1983; charter; Man. WOLFGANG KRAUSS; fleet of 2 Boeing 757.

LTU Lufttransport-Unternehmen KG: 4000 Düsseldorf 30, Flughafen Halle 8; tel. (0211) 41521; telex 8585573; f. 1955; charter; Mans WOLFGANG KRAUS, WERNER HÜHN; fleet of 8 TriStar.

Tourism

Deutsche Zentrale für Tourismus eV (DZT) (German National Tourist Board): 6000 Frankfurt a.M. 1, Beethovenstr. 69; tel. (069) 75720; telex 4189178; f. 1948; Dir-Gen. GÜNTHER SPAZIER.

Atomic Energy

Bundesministerium für Forschung und Technologie (Federal Ministry for Research and Technology): 5300 Bonn 2, Heinemannstr. 2, Postfach 200706; tel. (0228) 591; telex 885674; f. 1955; Minister Dr HEINZ RIESENHUBER.

The Ministry is divided into five departments, the first dealing with administration and establishment, the second with basic research, co-ordination of research, and international co-operation, the third with energy, biology and ecology, the fourth with information and production engineering and research on working conditions, and the fifth with aerospace, raw materials and geosciences.

The Ministry's responsibility in the nuclear energy field is to promote nuclear research and nuclear engineering as well as to plan and co-ordinate the activities of all of these bodies within the framework of the German Energy Research and Energy Technology Programme.

Nuclear research and development is carried out by the research centres of the following institutions in co-operation with universities and industry:

1. Kernforschungszentrum Karlsruhe GmbH, Karlsruhe (KfK).

2. Kernforschungsanlage Jülich GmbH, Jülich (KFA).

3. Max-Planck-Institut für Plasmaphysik (IPP) Garching bei München.

FEDERAL REPUBLIC OF GERMANY

4. Gesellschaft für Strahlen- und Umweltforschung mbH, Munich (GSF).

5. GKSS-Forschungszentrum, Geesthacht GmbH.

6. Hahn-Meitner Institut für Kernforschung GmbH, Berlin (HMI).

7. Deutsches Elektronen-Synchrotron (DESY), Hamburg.

8. Gesellschaft für Schwerionenforschung mbH, Darmstadt (GSI).

In December 1985 there were 19 nuclear power stations in operation, with a total generating capacity of 17m. kW.

Nuclear power stations in operation in 1986 were: the AVR Project at Jülich (North Rhine-Westphalia), with a capacity of 15 MW; the VAK Project at Kahl/Main (Bavaria), with a capacity of 17 MW; the KWO Project at Obrigheim/Neckar (Baden-Württemberg), with a capacity of 345 MW; the KWW Project at Würgassen/Weser (North Rhine-Westphalia), with a capacity of 670 MW; the KKS Project at Stade/Elbe (Lower Saxony), with a capacity of 662 MW; the Biblis A and Biblis B Projects at Biblis/Rhein (Hessen), with respective capacities of 1,204 MW and 1,300 MW; the KKP Project at Philippsburg (Baden-Württemberg), with a capacity of 960 MW; the KKB Project at Brunsbuttel/Elbe (Schleswig-Holstein), with a capacity of 805 MW; the GKN I Project at Neckarwestheim/Neckar (Baden-Württemberg), with a capacity of 855 MW; the KNK II Project at Karlsruhe (Baden-Württemberg), with a capacity of 21 MW; the KKU Project at Esenshamm (Lower Saxony), with a capacity of 1,300 MW; the KKI I Project at Ohu/Isar (Bavaria), with a capacity of 907 MW; the KKK Project at Krümmel (Schleswig-Holstein), with a capacity of 1,316 MW; the KWG Project at Grohnde (Lower Saxony), with a capacity of 1,361 MW; the KKG Project at Grafenrheinfeld (Bavaria), with a capacity of 1,229 MW; the KRB IIB and C Projects at Gundremmingen (Bavaria), with a capacity of 1,310 MW each; and the KBR Project at Brokdorf (Schleswig-Holstein), with a capacity of 1,365 MW.

Nuclear power made a contribution of about 32% to electricity supply in 1985. This proportion is to rise to 34.7% by the year 2000.

Three nuclear power plants were under construction in 1986: the THTR-300 Project at Hamm-Uentrop (North Rhine Westphalia), with a capacity of 308 MW; the SNR-300 Project at Kalkar (North Rhine-Westphalia), with a capacity of 327 MW; and the Mulheim-Kärlich Project (Rhineland Palatinate), with a capacity of 1,308 MW.

The construction of the KWS I Project at Wyhl (Baden-Württemberg), with a capacity of 1,362 MW, has been halted by a court ruling.

In addition, nine more nuclear power plants are due to be constructed and start operation by the year 2000. Sites have been chosen at Biblis, Neupotz (two plants), Neckarwestheim, Hamm, Ohu, Vahnum (two plants) and Borken. These will have a total capacity of about 15,600 MW. The following nuclear power stations, which were demonstration plants and started operation in the mid-1960s, have been closed down: the KRB Project at Gundremmingen (Bavaria), with a capacity of 250 MW; the KWL Project at Lingen (Lower Saxony), with a capacity of 268 MW; and the VAK Project at Kohl/Main, with a capacity of 17 MW.

The use of nuclear energy has given rise to much controversy in the Federal Republic and various protest groups have been formed. In 1975 the Government started an information campaign, which aims to provide the public with information on nuclear energy and all related energy questions, including energy conservation. The Government of Chancellor Helmut Kohl is strongly in favour of the continuation of the nuclear energy programme, and several new projects have been proposed.

GHANA

Introductory Survey

Location, Climate, Language, Religion, Flag, Capital

The Republic of Ghana lies on the west coast of Africa, with the Ivory Coast to the west and Togo to the east. It is bordered by Burkina Faso to the north. The climate is tropical, with temperatures generally between 21°C and 32°C (70°–90°F) and average annual rainfall of 2,000 mm (80 in) on the coast, decreasing inland. English is the official language, but there are eight major national languages. Many of the inhabitants follow traditional beliefs and customs. Christians make up an estimated 42% of the population. The national flag (proportions 3 by 2) has three equal horizontal stripes, of red, gold and green, with a five-pointed black star in the centre of the gold stripe. The capital is Accra.

Recent History

Ghana was formed by a merger of the Gold Coast, a former British colony, and the British-administered part of Togoland, a UN Trust Territory.

In the Gold Coast a new constitution was issued in December 1950. The first general election to the new Legislative Assembly, held in February 1951, resulted in an overwhelming victory for the Convention People's Party (CPP), led by Dr Kwame Nkrumah, who became Prime Minister in March 1952. The CPP retained power in the 1954 and 1956 elections. In May 1956, by a UN-supervised plebiscite, British Togoland voted to join the Gold Coast in an independent state. Ghana was duly granted independence, within the Commonwealth, on 6 March 1957, and Dr Nkrumah continued in power. The country was the first British dependency in sub-Saharan Africa to become independent under majority rule. Dr Nkrumah established an authoritarian regime, aiming to lead Ghana towards 'African socialism', and played a leading role in the Non-Aligned Movement. Ghana became a republic on 1 July 1960, with Dr Nkrumah as President. In February 1964 the country became a one-party state, with the CPP as the sole authorized party. President Nkrumah modified his previous policy of non-alignment and established close relations with the USSR and other communist countries.

On 24 February 1966 President Nkrumah, whose repressive policies and financial mismanagement had caused increasing resentment, was deposed by the army and police while he was visiting the People's Republic of China. The coup leaders established the National Liberation Council (NLC), led by Gen. Joseph Ankrah. The NLC released many political prisoners, carried out a purge of CPP supporters in positions of authority, and took rigorous measures to cope with economic problems. In April 1969, following disputes within the ruling NLC, Gen. Ankrah was replaced by Brig. (later Lt-Gen.) Akwasi Afrifa, who implemented plans for a return to civilian government. After the introduction of a new constitution, which established a non-executive presidency, an election for a new National Assembly was held in August 1969. Of the 140 seats in the Assembly, 105 were won by the Progress Party (PP), led by Dr Kofi Busia, who was appointed Prime Minister in September. Although military rule ended and the PP Government took office on 1 October 1969, presidential power was held by a three-man commission, formed by NLC members, until 31 August 1970, when Edward Akufo-Addo was inaugurated as civilian President.

In the wake of increasing economic and political difficulties, the army seized power again in January 1972. The Constitution was abolished and all political institutions were replaced by a National Redemption Council (NRC) under the chairmanship of Lt-Col (later Gen.) Ignatius Acheampong. In October 1975 supreme legislative and administrative authority was transferred from the NRC to a Supreme Military Council (SMC), also led by Gen. Acheampong.

In 1976 Gen. Acheampong put forward plans for a return to civilian rule without political parties, in the form of 'union' government, in which it was envisaged that the military should continue to play a role. Fears that this would amount only to a continuation of military rule, combined with increasing dissatisfaction with the economic situation and the prevalence of smuggling and profiteering, led to unrest. In response, the Government announced a definite programme for return to civilian government by July 1979, beginning with a referendum held in March 1978, which resulted in a vote of 54% in favour of Union Government. This result was, however, largely discredited.

In July 1978 Acheampong's deputy, Lt-Gen. Frederick Akuffo, assumed power in a bloodless coup and declared that the return to a popularly elected government would take place in July 1979, as planned. He introduced a number of civilians into the NRC and freed many political prisoners. In December a Constituent Assembly was set up to decide on the form of the new constitution. The six-year ban on party politics was lifted in January 1979, and 16 new parties were subsequently registered.

Only a fortnight before the elections were due to take place, a coup was staged by junior officers of the armed forces, led by Flight-Lt Jerry Rawlings. Their main grievance was the fact that Ghana's military, past and present, were evidently not going to be held responsible for the economic mismanagement and widespread corruption of recent times: the new draft constitution granted former rulers immunity from financial investigation. Under Rawlings, an Armed Forces Revolutionary Council (AFRC) took over power and began a 'house-cleaning exercise' to stamp out kalabule (corruption) at all levels. A 'Revolutionary Court' found Acheampong, Akuffo, Afrifa and six other senior officers guilty of corruption, and they were executed. Although the return to civilian rule was postponed until September 1979, the elections took place in June as planned. The People's National Party (PNP) gained a majority of parliamentary seats, and its leader, Dr Hilla Limann, was elected President, taking office on 24 September 1979.

During the next two years the Government took measures to improve the chronic food shortages, to stamp out corruption and smuggling at all levels and to stem civil and tribal unrest. In October 1980, however, the United National Convention (UNC) ended its alliance with the PNP, accusing the latter of ineptitude. As a result, the PNP had a majority of only one seat in Parliament. In June 1981 the UNC joined three other parties to form the All People's Party, a viable alternative to the PNP.

Dissatisfaction with the Government came to a head in December 1981, when Flight-Lt Rawlings once again took power in a military coup and established a Provisional National Defence Council (PNDC), with himself as Chairman. The Council of State was abolished, the Constitution suspended, Parliament dissolved and political parties banned. City and district councils were dissolved in March 1982 and replaced by People's Defence Committees (PDCs), designed to give the people a voice in the government of Ghana. The PDCs aimed to expose and deal with corruption, to maintain discipline and to 'protect the aims of the revolution'. They were renamed Committees for the Defence of the Revolution (CDRs) in December 1984.

The PNDC's policies initially received strong support from students and industrial workers, but discontent with the regime and the apparent ineffectiveness of its economic policies took the form of a series of attempted coups, all involving military personnel. In 1983 students became increasingly dissatisfied with the regime, and a number of violent street demonstrations took place. Legon University was occupied in May, and subsequently closed by pro-Government workers, and Kumasi University was also shut, following clashes between workers and students who were protesting about price rises. Both universities remained closed until March 1984.

Opposition to the PNDC became more active in 1985–86. Joseph Mensah, the chairman of the London-based Ghana Democratic Movement (GDM), was arrested in the USA in December 1985, and was accused of participating in a conspiracy to purchase weapons for shipment to dissidents in Ghana. In March 1986 a number of people were charged with conspiracy to overthrow the Government, which linked the plot with the discovery in Brazil of weapons aboard a ship destined for Ghana. In May nine people were sentenced to death for their involvement in the plot, seven of whom were executed in June. In August a former minister and presidential candidate, Victor Owusu (leader of the disbanded Popular Front Party), was arrested for alleged subversion.

In the early months of 1983 an estimated 1m. Ghanaians returned from Nigeria, following a mass expulsion of illegal immigrants. This sudden influx of homeless and unemployed persons placed a considerable strain on the already ailing economy—their evacuation alone cost the Government about 45m. cedis—but this was partly offset by foreign aid in the form of food and medical supplies. Refugees were encouraged to return to their home villages, and to take up agricultural occupations, in order to avoid increased overcrowding in the urban centres. Nigeria again expelled illegal immigrants in May 1985, when an estimated 300,000 Ghanaians were forced to return home.

Since the 1983 coup in Upper Volta (now Burkina Faso), which brought Capt. Thomas Sankara to power, the Ghanaian Government has forged close links with the neighbouring state. During 1984 a series of co-operation and security agreements were signed, and in April 1985 the Ghana-Burkina Faso Joint Commission issued a communiqué announcing that the two countries were exploring the means to integrate politically in order to consolidate the revolutions undertaken by both states. In August 1986 Ghana and Burkina Faso agreed to establish a high-level political body, which would be responsible for preparing a 10-year timetable for the political union of the two countries. The countries also agreed to harmonize their currencies, energy, transport, trade and educational systems, and in September and October 1986 a joint military exercise, 'Teamwork 1986', was held.

Relations with Togo deteriorated in 1986. In recent years the two countries had co-operated over border security, smuggling and tribal clashes. In May 1986, however, Ghanaian security forces captured a group of armed dissidents crossing the border from Togo. The Secretary for Foreign Affairs, Dr Obed Asamoah, protested over the use of neighbouring territories as bases for subversive activities against Ghana. In September there was an attempted coup in Togo, and the Togolese Government claimed that the plotters came from Ghanaian territory, and were trained in Ghana and Burkina Faso. In Lomé, the Togolese capital, there was growing tension between Ghanaian immigrants and the Togolese, and between October and early December 233 Ghanaians were deported from Togo. In October Ghana and Togo closed their common border.

Government

Upon its accession to power on 31 December 1981, the PNDC dissolved Parliament, abolished the Council of State and suspended the 1979 Constitution. Executive and legislative powers are vested in the PNDC, which rules by decree. Local government is by Committees for the Defence of the Revolution. Plans for the holding of local elections were announced in December 1986.

Defence

In July 1986 Ghana had total armed forces of 11,200 (army 9,000, navy 1,200 and air force 1,000). There is a paramilitary force of 5,000 and three Border Guard battalions. The defence budget for 1985 was 325m. cedis. The headquarters of the Defence Commission of the OAU is in Accra.

Economic Affairs

In 1984, according to estimates by the World Bank, Ghana's gross national product (GNP) per head, measured at average 1982–84 prices, was US $350. It was estimated that GNP per head declined, in real terms, at an average rate of 1.9% per year between 1965 and 1984. Ghana's overall gross domestic product (GDP), measured in constant prices, increased at an average of 3.4% annually in 1965–73 but declined by 0.9% per year in 1973–84.

Ghana is primarily an agricultural country. Agriculture employs nearly 70% of the working population and accounts for over one-half of the country's GDP. Only 11% of the land area is cultivated, half of which is used to grow cocoa, the country's principal commercial crop, which generally provides around 60% of export earnings. Ghana's harvest of cocoa beans declined from the early 1970s: estimated annual output fell from 470,000 metric tons in 1971/72 to about 250,000 tons in 1982/83, owing to ageing and diseased trees, poor transport facilities, and considerable smuggling across Ghana's borders. The price at which cocoa is purchased from producers was tripled in 1981 as an incentive to farmers, and in the following year the Rawlings Government formed a student task force to evacuate cocoa from the interior, and closed land borders to prevent smuggling. In 1983 the cocoa crop was ravaged by drought and fires: 35%–40% of the farms were destroyed, and the crop for 1983/84 was 158,000 tons. In response, the Government announced a plan to encourage the redevelopment of the cocoa industry: farmers were offered cash incentives to replant crops, the producer price was raised by 67%, and new crop-spraying machinery and insecticides were imported. The Government estimated that the scheme would increase cocoa output by 25% in its first year and by 40% in its second year. The crop for 1984/85 was estimated at only 175,000 tons, but in 1985/86 the crop increased to about 210,000 tons. It was expected to reach 230,000 tons in 1986/87. Cocoa plantations are being rehabilitated with financial assistance from the World Bank, and in May 1985 the Government announced new production incentives, including a rise of 90% in the guaranteed prices payable to growers. There has also been a campaign to curb cocoa smuggling to neighbouring countries, which formerly accounted for up to 50,000 tons of the annual crop. By 1985 it was estimated that only 10,000–20,000 tons of cocoa were being lost through smuggling. The 1986–88 Economic Recovery Programme aimed to increase cocoa production to more than 350,000 tons per year. The Government increased incentives to cocoa producers by increasing the producer price of cocoa to 85,000 cedis per ton, with a bonus of 500 cedis per ton where production targets were exceeded, by devaluing the cedi, by improving the transport system and by increasing the use of pesticides. The Ghana Cocoa Board designated 320,000 ha of cocoa-farming land as special zones for rehabilitation, and in 1986 a Secretariat for Cocoa Affairs was established as an intermediary between the Government and the Ghana Cocoa Board.

In the early 1980s production of foodstuffs suffered from adverse weather conditions and economic mismanagement. In 1983 and 1984 the Government was forced to appeal to the international community for emergency food aid to overcome the shortfall in food production. Donor countries supplied 192,000 metric tons of cereals in 1983, and 257,000 tons in 1984. However, in the 1984/85 season there was an excellent harvest, and by May 1986 rice imports were banned, as 30,000 tons of rice had already been produced, which was enough to meet the national requirement. The Government continued to encourage self-sufficiency in foodstuffs by implementing a programme to provide pricing, marketing and credit incentives to farmers, fishermen and agro-industries.

There is considerable state participation in the major sectors of the economy. In 1986 the Government reorganized and partly 'privatized' some state enterprises, in an attempt to increase efficiency in production and marketing, and introduced legislation allowing the Government the right to acquire land for mineral exploration. The timber and mining industries are next in importance after agriculture, with hardwoods, gold, bauxite, manganese and diamonds as major sources of foreign exchange. Earnings from exports of logs and sawn timber rose from 333m. cedis in 1984 to 1,412m. cedis in 1985. In 1981 a project was adopted to revitalize the ailing gold-mining industry, as production had slumped to 5,000 troy ounces per month from 15,000 in the 1970s. By 1985 production had recovered to reach 327,000 troy ounces. Ghana is seeking to develop its energy resources: offshore petroleum was discovered in 1970, and natural gas in 1980. Extraction of petroleum began from the Saltpond oilfield in January 1979, and by 1984 production of crude oil had reached 1,200 barrels per day, equivalent to 7%

GHANA

of the country's needs. The Ghana National Petroleum Corporation was established in 1983 to explore areas not covered by agreement with foreign companies. In 1984 the Government announced that the country's largest petroleum refinery, at Tema, was to be rehabilitated and enlarged to cope with increased petroleum production.

Political instability and general mismanagement have had a disastrous effect on the economy. In the early 1980s there were large current deficits on the balance of payments, a rapidly increasing money supply (rising by 64.7% in 1981) and a high rate of inflation, averaging 22.3% in 1982 and 122.9% in 1983. Contributory factors included an artificially high exchange rate, over-reliance on imports (especially petroleum), shortages of raw materials and spare parts, the decline in world prices and markets, inadequate marketing, storage and distribution facilities and smuggling. However, the rate of inflation decreased to 39.7% in 1984 and to about 12% in 1985, one of the lowest recorded levels since the mid-1970s. The balance-of-payments deficit has also fallen in recent years, owing to the provisions of the 1983–85 Economic Recovery Programme (see below).

The Rawlings Government introduced price controls in February 1982 and suspended the 1981/82 budget, since a deficit of 8,000m. cedis was foreseen. Government spending was severely curtailed. By June 1982 the foreign debt stood at 1,555m. cedis, with foreign exchange reserves totalling only 271.4m. Negotiations for IMF assistance were resumed in October, but the Government was unwilling to accept a further devaluation of the cedi, which was being sold on the 'black market' at only one-twentieth of its official value. A 'Green Revolution' was launched to reduce Ghana's dependence on imported foodstuffs, while foreign-exchange earners were to be rehabilitated and imports severely restricted.

In the 1983 budget the Government announced a new system of bonuses and surcharges on foreign exchange transactions. Users of foreign exchange were to be taxed in order to finance bonuses for earners of foreign exchange, but the system amounted to a multiple exchange rate for the cedi. Ghana continued to negotiate for IMF aid in 1983, and an agreement was eventually reached in August of that year. Ghana was granted $253.6m. in stand-by payments and $128.1m. from the compensatory financing facility to make up for the fall in export earnings. A compromise was reached on the question of the devaluation of the cedi. The IMF provisionally accepted Ghana's new foreign exchange system, but insisted that Ghana should unify the exchange rate and devalue the cedi within a year of the agreement. The cedi was subsequently devalued by more than 90% in November 1983. Three further devaluations were made in 1984, and three in 1985. The IMF authorized a further stand-by arrangement of SDR 180m. in August 1984. Ghana also received some $270m. from the World Bank between 1982 and 1985, $73m. in 1985, and a further estimated $150m. in 1986. In January 1986 the Government devalued the cedi by 33.3%, with the exchange rate adjusted from 60 to 90 cedis per US dollar. A weekly auction of foreign exchange to purchase imports was operated from September 1986. However, purchases of crude petroleum and essential drugs, debt servicing and cocoa revenue were to be excluded from the auction, and continued to be traded at the fixed rate of US $1 = 90 cedis. In December 100% of the value of transactions were carried out in cedis, compared with 20% in October. By January 1987 crude petroleum imports and cocoa export earnings were included in the auction, and the IMF provided stand-by funds to make oil purchases possible at the floating rate. The foreign exchange market aimed to stimulate exports and domestic production. In October 1986, in order to expand Ghana's export base and to offset the adverse effects of unfavourable terms of trade on traditional exports, the Government selected seven non-traditional commodities, including copra, furniture and liquefied petroleum gas, to be exported under a new counter-trade scheme.

In late 1982 the Government launched the 1983–85 Economic Recovery Programme (ERP), for which it required US $700m. in external aid. The programme consisted of a wide-ranging set of reforms, including movement towards a more realistic exchange rate and gradual easing of price controls. In November 1983 an international donors' conference was held in Paris, at which pledges for $150m. were received for 1984; further conferences were held in December 1984 and November 1985, and raised pledges for $450m. and $517.3m. respectively. In November 1985 the Government announced the second three-year ERP (1986–88), which aimed to achieve a significant rate of export growth, and included measures to rationalize the use of the labour force. By 1985 there was considerable evidence that the Government's austerity measures were beginning to show results: the rate of inflation had been drastically reduced, there were increases in production of all the major crops, the value of exports had risen by 29% in 1984, and in the same year the budget deficit, as a percentage of GDP, fell to 1.5%. This recovery continued into 1986, and the targets of the 1986–88 ERP were being achieved: although imports were 2.4% higher than projected (at $745m.), exports (at $633m.) exceeded the ERP target by 3.7%, resulting in a trade deficit of $112m., $4m. below the level set by the ERP. The budget deficit in 1985 was held within the ERP limit, at 7,500m. cedis, and GDP growth in 1985 reached 5.3%. Foreign exchange reserves in 1986 were estimated at $1,400m. Ghana's external debt at the end of 1986 stood at an estimated $1,800m. In July 1986 the IMF agreed to provide a stand-by facility of SDR 90m. In October the IMF endorsed Ghana's economic measures, and agreed to provide a stand-by arrangement of SDR 81.1m. over the next 12 months, although negotiations continued over the provision of a three-year extended Fund facility, allowing drawings of 95% of Ghana's quota of SDR 204.5m. annually, to replace stand-by arrangements.

The good performance of the economy in 1985 allowed the Government to propose a more ambitious budget for 1986/87, aiming for increased economic growth by tripling capital expenditure. This was to be funded, in order to remain within the ERP target for the budget deficit, by a projected increase in total revenue of 115%, to 85,200m. cedis, of which 34,400m. cedi would come from taxes on international trade. Total expenditure was projected to rise by 88%, to about 90,000m. cedis, of which 26,100m. cedis was allocated to development projects, especially the improvement of roads. The budget deficit would be reduced by 37%, to about 4,700m. cedis. In July 1986, however, the original budget proposals were modified, as the Government envisaged an increase in current expenditure, with reduced targets for development expenditure and revenue. An import levy of 10% on all goods except petroleum products was introduced in July.

Ghana is a member of ECOWAS (see p. 133). Overseas aid comes mainly from the EEC, particularly the United Kingdom and the Federal Republic of Germany, and also the UN, the People's Republic of China, Canada and the USA.

Social Welfare

The Government provides hospitals and medical care at nominal rates, and there is a government pension scheme. There were 293 hospitals, health centres and posts and 60 private clinics in 1982. There were 1,665 physicians working in Ghana in 1981. Over the period 1974–84 there was a decline in expenditure on health services, and by 1984 the World Bank estimated that the number of doctors in Ghana had fallen to 817. Ghana's shortage of foreign exchange has limited imports of medical equipment. The 1986–88 Economic Recovery Programme was to provide 7,126m. cedis to expand health services, and aimed to make these services accessible to all Ghanaians by the year 2000. Of total expenditure by the central government in 1984, 2,270m. cedis (8.5%) was for health, and a further 1,131m. cedis (4.2%) for social security and welfare.

Education

In April 1974 the NRC announced the introduction of a new educational structure, consisting of an initial phase of six years' primary education (beginning at six years of age), followed by three years' junior secondary education. All this schooling is free and, officially, compulsory. At the junior secondary schools a selection is made between senior secondary school courses, leading to examinations at the 'Ordinary' level of the General Certificate of Education, and technical and vocational courses. However, this system is being operated on an experimental basis, and over 90% of children still follow the old educational system, consisting of six years' primary education and four years at a middle school. In 1983 enrolment at primary schools was equivalent to 79% of children in the relevant age-group (89% of boys; 70% of girls), while the comparable ratio at

GHANA

middle schools was 38% of children (48% of boys; 28% of girls). There are three universities. The military regime that assumed power in December 1981 stressed the need for education to be geared more closely to the country's practical needs. Expenditure on education by the central government in 1984 was 5,387m. cedis, representing 20.2% of total spending. The 1986–88 Economic Recovery Programme allocated 1,167m. cedis to education, to be invested mainly in primary education, literacy programmes and the expansion of technical and scientific education. According to UNESCO estimates, the adult illiteracy rate in 1985 was 46.8% (males 35.9%; females 57.2%).

Tourism

Ghana's tourist industry is expanding. The attractions include fine beaches, game reserves, traditional festivals and old trading forts and castles. In 1980 Ghana had 2,220 hotel beds. In 1982 there were about 44,000 tourist arrivals, excluding visits by Ghanaian nationals residing abroad.

Public Holidays

1987: 1 January (New Year's Day), 6 March (Independence Day), 17–20 April (Easter), 1 July (Republic Day), 25–26 December (Christmas), 31 December (Revolution Day).

1988: 1 January (New Year's Day), 6 March (Independence Day), 1–4 April (Easter), 1 July (Republic Day), 25–26 December (Christmas), 31 December (Revolution Day).

Weights and Measures

The metric system is in force.

Currency and Exchange Rates

100 pesewas = 1 new cedi.

Exchange rates (30 September 1986):
 £1 sterling = 130.23 cedis;
 US $1 = 90.00 cedis.

GHANA

Statistical Survey

Statistical Survey

Source (except where otherwise stated): Central Bureau of Statistics, POB 1098, Accra; tel. 66512.

Area and Population

AREA, POPULATION AND DENSITY

Area (sq km)	238,537*
Population (census results)	
1 March 1970	8,559,313
18 March 1984	12,205,575†
Population (official estimates at mid-year)	
1980	11,100,000
1982	11,690,000
1983	11,990,000
Density (per sq km) at March 1984	51.2†

* 92,100 sq miles.   † Preliminary figures.

POPULATION BY REGION (1984 census*)

Western	1,116,930
Central	1,145,520
Greater Accra	1,420,065
Eastern	1,697,483
Volta	1,201,095
Ashanti	2,089,683
Brong-Ahafo	1,179,407
Northern	1,162,645
Upper East	771,584
Upper West	439,161
Total	**12,205,574**

* Preliminary figures.

Principal Ethnic Groups (1960 census, percentage of total population): Akan 44.1, Mole-Dagbani 15.9, Ewe 13.0, Ga-Adangbe 8.3, Guan 3.7, Gurma 3.5.

PRINCIPAL TOWNS (population at 1984 census)

Accra (capital)	964,879
Kumasi	348,880
Tamale	136,828
Tema	99,608
Takoradi	61,527
Cape Coast	57,700
Sekondi	32,355

BIRTHS AND DEATHS

Average annual birth rate 47.2 per 1,000 in 1970–75, 47.1 per 1,000 in 1975–80; death rate 17.4 per 1,000 in 1970–75, 15.9 per 1,000 in 1975–80 (UN estimates).

ECONOMICALLY ACTIVE POPULATION (1970 census*)

	Males	Females	Total
Agriculture, hunting, forestry and fishing	1,038,468	773,634	1,812,102
Mining and quarrying	29,075	2,385	31,460
Manufacturing	168,918	214,761	383,679
Electricity, gas and water	11,984	459	12,443
Construction	73,495	2,708	76,203
Trade, restaurants and hotels	68,496	370,852	439,348
Transport, storage and communications	84,212	2,325	86,537
Financing, insurance, real estate and business services	7,651	1,877	9,528
Community, social and personal services	272,770	52,578	325,348
Total	**1,755,069**	**1,421,579**	**3,176,648**

* Figures exclude persons seeking work for the first time, totalling 154,970 (males 104,326; females 50,644), but include other unemployed persons, numbering 43,601 (males 37,141; females 6,460).

Agriculture

PRINCIPAL CROPS ('000 metric tons)

	1983	1984	1985
Maize	172	575	460†
Millet	40	90†	54
Sorghum	56	140†	62
Rice (paddy)	40	66	64
Sugar cane*	100	100	110
Cassava (Manioc)	1,729	4,083	2,373
Yams	866	880*	850*
Taro (Coco yam)	720	730*	600*
Onions*	26	27*	28*
Tomatoes	250*	300*	375
Eggplants (Aubergines)*	20	21	22
Pulses	12	11*	11*

* FAO estimate.   † Unofficial figure.
Source: FAO, *Production Yearbook*.

	1983	1984	1985
Oranges*	35	35	35
Lemons and limes*	30	30	30
Bananas	10*	15*	22
Plantains	342	650*	677†
Pineapples*	5	5	6
Palm kernels*	30	30	30
Groundnuts (in shell)	91	90*	128
Coconuts	140*	120*	108
Copra*	7	7	7
Coffee (green)	1†	2†	2*
Cocoa beans†	160	175	200
Tobacco (leaves)	2*	2*	3

* FAO estimate.   † Unofficial figure.
Source: FAO, *Production Yearbook*.

LIVESTOCK
(FAO estimates, '000 head, year ending September)

	1983	1984	1985
Horses	4	4	4
Asses	25	25	25
Cattle	800	810	820
Pigs	375	375	375
Sheep	2,000	2,000	2,000
Goats	2,000	2,000	2,000

Poultry (FAO estimates, million): 13 in 1983; 13 in 1984; 14 in 1985.
Source: FAO, *Production Yearbook*.

LIVESTOCK PRODUCTS (FAO estimates, '000 metric tons)

	1983	1984	1985
Beef and veal	12	12	12
Mutton and lamb	6	6	6
Goat meat	6	6	6
Pig meat	8	8	8
Poultry meat	15	16	17
Other meat	94	91	89
Cows' milk	7	7	7
Hen eggs	15.9	16.2	16.5
Cattle hides	1.5	1.5	1.5

Source: FAO, *Production Yearbook*.

Forestry

ROUNDWOOD REMOVALS ('000 cubic metres)

	1980	1981	1982
Sawlogs, veneer logs and logs for sleepers	600	550	410
Other industrial wood*	381	381	381
Fuel wood*	7,058	7,284	7,284
Total	8,039	8,215	8,075

* FAO estimates.
1983-84: Annual output as in 1982 (FAO estimates).
Source: FAO, *Yearbook of Forest Products*.

SAWNWOOD PRODUCTION ('000 cubic metres)

	1982	1983	1984
Total (incl. boxboards)	150	150*	174

* FAO estimate.
Source: FAO, *Yearbook of Forest Products*.

Fishing

('000 metric tons, live weight)

	1982	1983	1984*
Inland waters	40.0	40.0	40.0
Atlantic Ocean	196.8	203.4	198.4
Total catch	236.8	243.4	238.4

* FAO estimates.
Source: FAO, *Yearbook of Fishery Statistics*.

Mining

	1983	1984	1985
Gold ore ('000 kg)	8.6	8.9	9.3
Diamonds ('000 carats)	339	345	366
Manganese ore ('000 tons)	173	287	316
Bauxite ('000 tons)	70	49	170

Crude petroleum: 70,000 metric tons (estimate) in 1983.

Industry

SELECTED PRODUCTS

		1983	1984	1985
Wheat flour	'000 metric tons	18.0	39.6	45.3
Beer	'000 hectolitres	310	452	429
Soft drinks	'000 crates	382	553	718
Cigarettes	millions	1,074	2,008	1,942
Motor spirit (petrol)	'000 metric tons	153.0	172.0	216.0
Kerosene	'000 metric tons	77.0	86.0	120.0
Diesel and gas oil	'000 metric tons	164.0	218.0	278.0
Cement	'000 metric tons	278.0	235.0	356.0
Electric energy	million kWh	2,547.8	1,798.7	2,996.2

Aluminium (unwrought): 42,500 metric tons (primary metal) in 1983.

GHANA

Statistical Survey

Finance

CURRENCY AND EXCHANGE RATES

Monetary Units
100 pesewas = 1 new cedi.

Denominations
Coins: ½, 1, 2½, 5, 10, 20 and 50 pesewas; 1 and 5 cedis.
Notes: 1, 2, 5, 10, 50, 100 and 200 cedis.

Sterling and Dollar Equivalents (30 September 1986)
£1 sterling = 130.23 cedis;
US $1 = 90.00 cedis;
1,000 cedis = £7.679 = $11.111.

Average Exchange Rate (cedis per US dollar)
1983   3.45
1984   35.34
1985   54.05

INTERNATIONAL RESERVES
(US $ million at 31 December)

	1983	1984	1985
Gold*	72.5	91.7	46.1
IMF special drawing rights	2.2	0.1	18.9
Foreign exchange	142.6	301.5	459.6
Total	217.3	393.3	524.6

* National valuation.
Source: IMF, *International Financial Statistics*.

MONEY SUPPLY (million new cedis at 31 December)

	1983	1984	1985
Currency outside banks	10,036.6	13,943.3	21,896.9
Offical entities' deposits with monetary authorities	539.3	135.9	784.5
Demand deposits at commercial banks	8,194.2	12,564.2	20,789.7
Total money	18,770.1	26,507.4	42,686.6

Source: Research Dept, Bank of Ghana.

COST OF LIVING (Consumer Price Index for Accra; average of monthly figures. Base: 1977 = 100)

	1983	1984	1985
Food	2,358.8	2,629.4	2,407.3
Clothing	1,441.1	2,605.9	3,859.2
Rent, fuel and light	863.8	1,364.7	1,947.5
All items (incl. others)	1,877.5	2,729.8	3,282.7

GENERAL BUDGET (million cedis)

Revenue*	1982	1983	1984
Taxes on production and expenditure	2,465.8	6,704.4	13,816.7
Taxes on income and property	1,502.3	1,729.8	4,013.6
Fines, penalties and forfeitures	17.3	48.6	13.5
Sales and fees	186.5	213.6	722.4
Interests, profits and dividends	385.0	906.3	2,500.0
Rent of government lands, buildings and houses	6.1	8.4	9.0
Others	27.5	572.9	651.8
Total	4,592.5	10,184.0	21,727.0

* Excluding grants received from abroad (million cedis): 52 in 1982; 57 in 1983; 914 in 1984.

1985 (million cedis): Revenue 38,692, excluding grants (1,620).

Expenditure†	1982	1983	1984
General services	2,123.9	4,108.6	7,450.9
General administration	1,322.9	2,889.1	4,669.7
Defence	463.8	672.9	1,605.2
Justice and police	337.2	546.6	1,176.0
Community services	578.9	—	—
Roads and waterways	384.7	917.3	1,890.7
Housing and community services	194.2	243.9	590.8
Other	4.6	209.7	566.3
Social services	3,158.5	4,548.8	9,386.8
Education	1,793.8	3,013.5	5,386.9
Health	538.7	646.9	2,270.4
Social security and welfare	744.2	628.6	1,131.2
Other	81.8	259.8	598.3
Economic services	1,216.6	2,269.1	3,161.2
Agriculture and non-mineral resources	962.5	1,536.6	1,320.6
Fuel and power	3.3	24.8	93.7
Other mineral, manufacturing and construction	125.7	251.6	663.9
Transport, storage and communications	120.6	246.4	516.7
Other	4.6	209.7	566.3
Unallocable	2,700.1	2,667.6	4,213.6
Interest on general debt	2,168.1	2,204.0	5,425.0
General transfers to local government	313.4	463.6	788.6
Other	218.6	—	—
Total	9,778.1	14,755.3	26,694.0

† Excluding net lending (million cedis): 420 in 1983; 791 in 1984.
1985 (million cedis): Total expenditure 45,764, excluding net lending (2,127).

NATIONAL ACCOUNTS (million new cedis at current prices)
National Income and Product

	1982	1983	1984
GDP in purchasers' values	86,450.8	184,038.4	272,297.2
Net factor income from abroad	−224.7	−1,640.0	−2,890.0
Gross national product	86,226.1	182,398.4	269,407.2
Less Consumption of fixed capital	2,628.4	4,196.9	7,247.9
National income in market prices	83,597.7	178,201.5	262,159.3
Other current transfers from abroad (net)	236.6	2,200.0	5,135.8
National disposable income	83,824.3	180,401.5	267,295.1

Expenditure on the Gross Domestic Product

	1982	1983	1984
Government final consumption expenditure	5,602.9	10,787.0	17,050.0
Private final consumption expenditure	77,619.3	172,140.1	243,971.8
Increase in stocks	−132.9	−20.8	55.0
Gross fixed capital formation	3,053.0	6,922.1	18,541.7
Total domestic expenditure	86,142.3	189,828.4	279,618.5
Exports of goods and services	2,886.2	11,239.0	21,593.0
Less Imports of goods and services	2,577.8	17,029.0	28,914.3
GDP in purchasers' values	86,450.8	184,038.4	272,297.2
GDP at constant 1975 prices	4,974.1	4,733.3	5,242.3

Source: Bank of Ghana.

BALANCE OF PAYMENTS (US $ million)

	1983	1984	1985
Merchandise exports f.o.b.	439.1	565.9	632.4
Merchandise imports f.o.b.	−499.7	−533.0	−668.7
Trade balance	−60.6	32.9	−36.3
Export of services	38.5	45.8	38.3
Import of services	−224.4	−289.3	−304.0
Balance of goods and services	−246.5	−210.6	−302.0
Private unrequited transfers (net)	−1.8	8.1	31.9
Government unrequited transfers (net)	74.2	141.2	104.6
Current balance	−174.1	−61.3	−165.5
Direct capital investment (net)	2.4	2.0	5.6
Other long-term capital (net)	31.4	201.1	32.3
Short-term capital (net)	85.3	2.7	31.4
Net errors and omissions	−125.8	−110.0	94.8
Total (net monetary movements)	−180.8	34.5	−1.4
Monetization of gold (net)	3.7	19.2	−45.6
Valuation changes (net)	2.8	36.5	−71.7
Exceptional financing (net)	−74.9	−101.8	61.8
Changes in reserves	−249.1	−11.7	−56.9

Source: IMF, *International Financial Statistics*.

External Trade

PRINCIPAL COMMODITIES ('000 cedis)

Imports	1980	1981	1982
Food and live animals	241,530	247,309	275,317
Beverages and tobacco	43,046	29,321	11,560
Crude materials (inedible) except fuels	56,881	63,829	29,939
Mineral fuels, lubricants, etc.	827,418	1,056,169	990,693
Animal and vegetable oils and fats	28,386	30,796	9,153
Chemicals	482,703	413,256	305,176
Basic manufactures	380,483	394,851	299,937
Machinery and transport equipment	922,818	950,476	577,511
Miscellaneous manufactured articles	64,512	120,078	134,170
Other commodities and transactions	55,805	178,225	147,176
Total	3,103,584	3,484,310	2,781,626

Total imports (million cedis): 8,740 in 1983; 20,871 in 1984.

Exports	1983	1984	1985
Cocoa	3,989,166	12,391,272	19,904,089
Logs	75,949	113,973	576,116
Sawn timber	136,099	218,964	835,445
Bauxite	42,254	39,143	147,802
Manganese ore	127,919	329,966	487,779
Diamonds	64,020	93,239	280,919
Gold	2,112,445	3,629,786	5,010,746
Total (incl. others)	8,851,000	20,161,000	33,185,000

PRINCIPAL TRADING PARTNERS ('000 cedis)

Imports	1980	1981	1982
Canada	30,287	57,783	24,053
China, People's Republic	48,528	25,019	12,915
France	95,086	88,479	67,677
Germany, Federal Republic	292,397	371,176	184,275
Italy	74,015	80,760	75,626
Japan	116,573	123,333	70,283
Libya	86,882	495	298,158
Netherlands	87,623	111,004	44,726
Nigeria	630,252	859,136	564,740
Norway	33,847	12,860	35,462
United Kingdom	677,858	563,280	396,102
USA	375,922	387,206	428,270
Total (incl. others)	3,103,584	3,484,310	2,781,626

Exports	1980	1981	1982
Australia	28,170	31,730	12,623
Germany, Federal Republic	198,981	218,103	201,780
Ireland	34,792	n.a.	n.a.
Italy	32,263	17,271	6,658
Japan	245,669	309,930	158,937
Netherlands	480,403	306,835	335,644
Spain	51,289	55,832	29,495
USSR	461,541	168,918	128,501
United Kingdom	558,502	258,672	295,127
USA	258,205	538,893	415,235
Yugoslavia	4,954	39,320	12,497
Total (incl. others)	3,157,765	2,685,633	2,211,729

Source: Bank of Ghana.

Transport

RAILWAYS (traffic)

	1983	1984	1985
Passengers carried ('000)	3,395	1,379	2,115
Freight carried ('000 metric tons)	357.1	370.0	509.6
Passenger-km (million)	380.0	157.4	190.3
Net ton-km (million)	59.8	43.5	77.2

ROAD TRAFFIC ('000 motor vehicles*)

	1979	1980	1981
Passenger cars	85.1	75.2	109.1
Commercial vehicles	34.7	33.2	41.5

* Including vehicles no longer in circulation.
Source: UN, *Statistical Yearbook*.

SHIPPING (sea-borne freight traffic)

	1979	1980	1981
Vessels entered:			
Number	782	698	775
Displacement ('000 net reg. tons)	3,439	3,063	3,265
Vessels cleared:			
Number	790	627	775
Displacement ('000 net reg. tons)	3,443	2,657	3,234
Goods ('000 metric tons):			
Loaded	1,072	903	1,251
Unloaded	1,947	2,450	2,968

CIVIL AVIATION (traffic on scheduled services)

	1980	1981	1982
Kilometres flown (million)	4.3	3.1	3.0
Passengers carried ('000)	361	245	230
Passenger-km (million)	324	321	291
Freight ton-km (million)	2.8	5.7	4.6
Mail ton-km (million)	0.8	0.5	0.6
Total ton-km (million)	32	35	31

Source: UN, *Statistical Yearbook*.

Tourism

	1980	1981	1982
Tourist arrivals ('000)*	40	42	44

* Excluding arrivals of Ghanaian nationals residing abroad (16,069 in 1979).

Source: Ghana Tourist Board, Accra.

Education

(1984/85)

	Institutions	Teachers†	Students
Primary	8,965	47,921	1,464,624
Middle	5,242	22,541	579,981
Junior secondary*	118	1,461	17,745
Secondary	229	6,034	125,659
Teacher training	39	890	14,880
Technical and vocational	22	837	9,947
University	3	1,041	7,878

* The Junior Secondary schools are being run on an experimental basis.
† 1980/81 figures.

Source: Ghana Education Service, Planning Division, POB K451, Accra.

Directory

The Constitution

Following the coup in December 1981, the 1979 Constitution was suspended.

The Government

HEAD OF STATE

Chairman of the Provisional National Defence Council: Flight-Lt JERRY RAWLINGS (took power 31 December 1981).

PROVISIONAL NATIONAL DEFENCE COUNCIL
(January 1987)

Flight-Lt JERRY RAWLINGS (Chairman and Chief of Defence Staff).
Mrs AANAA ENIN.
EBO TAWIAH.
Justice D. F. ANNAN.
Alhaji IDDRISU MAHAMA.
Capt. KOJO TSIKATA.
P. V. OBENG.
Maj.-Gen. ARNOLD QUAINOO.
Brig. W. M. MENSA-WOOD.

CABINET
(February 1987)

Secretary for Fuel and Power: APPEA KORANG.
Secretary for Trade and Tourism: KOFI DJIN.
Secretary for Local Government and Rural Development: Dr E. ATO AYIREBI-ACQUAH (acting).
Secretary for Cocoa Affairs: Dr ADJEI MARFO.
Secretary for Internal Affairs: Brig. W. M. MENSA-WOOD.
Secretary for Education and Culture: Dr MUHAMMAD BEN ABDALLAH.
Secretary for Youth and Sports: ATO AUSTIN.
Secretary for Foreign Affairs: Dr OBED ASAMOAH.
Secretary for Information: KOFI TOTOBI QUAKYI.
Secretary for Transport and Communications: KWAME PEPRAH.
Secretary for Works and Housing: Dr KOFI SAM.
Secretary for Industry, Science and Technology: Dr FRANCIS ACQUAH.
Secretary for Justice and Attorney General: G. E. K. AIKINS.
Secretary for Agriculture: Cdre STEVE OBIMPEH.
Secretary for Roads and Highways: Dr E. O. DONKOR.
Secretary for Finance and Economic Planning: Dr KWESI BOTCHWEY.
Secretary for Health: Air Cdre F. W. KLUTSE.
Secretary for Lands and Natural Resources: GEORGE ADAMU.
Secretary for Mobilization and Productivity: WILLIAM YEBOAH.
Secretary for Defence: MAHAMA IDDRISSU.
Secretary of Chieftaincy Affairs: EMMANUEL TANOH.
Secretary for the National Defence Committee (NDC): YAW AKRASI-SARPONG.
Chairman of the Committee of Secretaries: P. V. OBENG.

GHANA
Directory

REGIONAL SECRETARIES
(January 1987)

Greater Accra: SELINA TAYLOR.
Eastern: KOFI ACQUAAH-HARRISON.
Volta: RICHARD SEGLAH.
Brong Ahafo: Col (retd) ALEX ANTWI.
Ashanti: Col (retd) OSEI OWUSO.
Central: Lt-Col (retd) E. A. BAIDOO.
Northern: HUDU YAHAYA.
Upper East: J. E. SAKYI.
Upper West: SALIFU BAWA DY-YAKAH.
Western Region: Lt-Col (retd) W. A. THOMSON.

SECRETARIATS

Secretariat for Agriculture: POB M37, Accra; tel. 665421.
Secretariat for Cocoa Affairs: Accra.
Secretariat for Defence: Burma Camp, Accra; tel. 777611; telex 2077.
Secretariat for Education and Culture: POB M45, Accra; tel. 665421.
Secretariat for Finance and Economic Planning: POB M40, Accra; tel. 665421.
Secretariat for Foreign Affairs: POB M53, Accra; tel. 665421; telex 2001.
Secretariat for Fuel and Power: POB M212, Accra; tel. 665421.
Secretariat for Health: POB M44, Accra; tel. 665421.
Secretariat for Industry, Science and Technology: POB M47, Accra; tel. 665421.
Secretariat for Information: POB 745, Accra; tel. 228011; telex 2201.
Secretariat for Internal Affairs: POB M42, Accra; tel. 665421.
Secretariat for Lands and Natural Resources: POB M212, Accra; tel. 665421.
Secretariat for Local Government and Rural Development: POB M50, Accra; tel. 665421.
Secretariat for Mobilization and Productivity: POB M84, Accra; tel. 665421.
Secretariat for Roads and Highways: POB M43, Accra.
Secretariat for Trade and Tourism: POB M47, Accra; tel. 665421; telex 2105.
Secretariat for Transport and Communications: POB M38, Accra; tel. 665421.
Secretariat for Works and Housing: POB M43, Accra; tel. 665421.
Secretariat for Youth and Sports: Accra; tel. 665421.

Legislature

Parliament was dissolved and the Council of State abolished after the December 1981 coup.

Political Organizations

Following the coup in December 1981, all political parties were proscribed, as they had been in 1966–69 and 1972–79. However, there are several opposition groups operating outside Ghana. These include the **Ghana Democratic Movement (GDM,** f. 1983), led by JOSEPH H. MENSAH, which is based in London and advocates the restoration of a liberal democratic system.

Diplomatic Representation

EMBASSIES AND HIGH COMMISSIONS IN GHANA

Algeria: House No. F606/1, off Cantonments Rd, Christiansborg, POB 2747, Accra; tel. 776828; Ambassador: ABDELHAMID SEMICHI.
Austria: 32 Independence Ave, POB 564, Accra; tel. 225716; telex 2115.
Benin: C175 Odoi Kwao Crescent, POB 7871, Accra; tel. 225701; Chargé d'affaires: CYRILLE OGUIN.
Brazil: 5 Volta St, Airport Residential Area, POB 2918, Accra; tel. 777154; telex 2081; Ambassador: AGENOR SOARES DOS SANTOS.
Bulgaria: 3 Kakramadu Rd, East Cantonments, POB 3193, Accra; tel. 774231; Ambassador: KOSTADIN GEORGIEV GYAUROV.
Burkina Faso: House No. 772/3, Asylum Down, off Farrar Ave, POB 651, Accra; tel. 221988; telex 2108; Ambassador: JEAN-PAUL T. BAMOGHO.
Canada: No. 46, Independence Ave, POB 1639, Accra; tel. 228555; telex 2024; High Commissioner: AUBREY L. MORANTZ.
China, People's Republic: No. 7, Agostinho Neto Rd, Airport Residential Area, POB 3356, Accra; tel. 777073; Ambassador: GU XINER.
Cuba: 10 Ridge Rd, Roman Ridge, Airport Residential Area, POB 9163 Airport, Accra; tel. 775842; Ambassador: NIEL RUIZ GUERRA.
Czechoslovakia: C260/5, Kanda High Rd No. 2, POB 5226, Accra-North; tel. 223540; Ambassador: LADISLAV SOBR.
Egypt: 3 Jawaharlal Nehru Ave, POB 2508, Accra; Ambassador: FATHI EL-GEWELY.
Ethiopia: House No. 6, Adiembra Rd, East Cantonment, POB 1646, Accra; tel. 775928; Ambassador: Ato ASSEFAW LEGGESSE.
France: 12th Rd, off Liberation Ave, POB 187, Accra; tel. 228571; telex 2101; Ambassador: JEAN MICHEL AUCHÈRE.
German Democratic Republic: House No. 40, Liberation Rd, Airport Residential Area, POB 2348, Accra; tel. 776861; telex 2142; Ambassador: FRANZ EVERHARTZ.
Germany, Federal Republic: Valldemosa Lodge, Plot No. 18, North Ridge Residential Area, 7th Ave Extension, POB 1757, Accra; tel. 221311; telex 2025; Ambassador: GOTTFRIED FISCHER.
Guinea: 11 Osu Badu St, Dzorwulu, POB 5497, Accra-North; tel. 777921; Ambassador: DORE DIALE DRISS.
Holy See: 1 Noi Fetreke St, Airport Residential Area, POB 9675, Accra; Apostolic Pro-Nuncio: Archbishop IVAN DIAS.
Hungary: House No. F582 A/1, Salem Rd, Christiansborg, POB 3027, Accra; tel. 774917; Ambassador: LÁSZLÓ SZIKRA.
India: 12 Mankata Ave, Airport Residential Area, POB 3040, Accra; tel. 775601; telex 2154; High Commissioner: GURCHARAN SINGH.
Italy: Jawaharlal Nehru Rd, POB 140, Accra; tel. 775621; telex 2039; Ambassador: LUIGI DURANTE.
Ivory Coast: House No. 9, 8th Lane, off Cantonments Rd, POB 3445, Christiansborg, Accra; tel. 774611; telex 2131; Ambassador: KONAN NDA.
Japan: 8 Rangoon Ave, off Switchback Rd, POB 1637, Accra; tel. 775616; telex 2068; Ambassador: MASATADA HIGAKI.
Korea, Democratic People's Republic: 139 Roman Ridge, Ambassadorial Estate, Nortei Ababio Estate, POB 13874, Accra; tel. 777825; Ambassador: CHANG DU HO.
Korea, Republic: 3 Abokobi Rd, East Cantonments, POB 13700, Accra; tel. 777533; Ambassador: NAM HONG-WOO.
Lebanon: 2 Rangoon Ave, POB 562, Accra; tel. 776727; telex 2118; Ambassador: Dr ASSEM JABER.
Liberia: F675/1, off Cantonments Rd, Christiansborg, POB 895, Accra; tel. 775641; telex 2071; Ambassador: WEAHPLAH WILSON.
Libya: 14 Sixth St, Airport Residential Area, POB 6995, Accra; tel. 774820; telex 2179; Secretary of People's Bureau: ABDULLAH MUJADIAN (acting).
Mali: Crescent Rd, Block 1, POB 1121, Accra; tel. 666421; telex 2061; Ambassador: DIALLO DEMBA.
Netherlands: 89 Liberation Rd, National Redemption Circle, POB 3248, Accra; tel. 221655; telex 2128; Chargé d'affaires a.i.: (vacant).
Niger: E104/3, Independence Ave, POB 2685, Accra; tel. 224962; telex 2141; Chargé d'affaires: MOUSSA YERIMA.
Nigeria: Rangoon Ave, POB 1548, Accra; tel. 776158; telex 2051; High Commissioner: Brig. HARRIS O. D. EGHAGHA.
Pakistan: 11 Ring Rd East, Accra; tel. 776059; Ambassador: Miss SALMA KISHWAR JAN.
Poland: House No. F820/1, off Cantonments Rd, Christiansborg, POB 2552, Accra; tel. 774711; Chargé d'affaires a.i.: KAZIMIERZ DABROWSKI.
Romania: North Labone, Ward F, Block 6, House 262, POB M112, Accra; tel. 774076; telex 2027; Chargé d'affaires: ILIE VINCENTIU.

Saudi Arabia: F868/1, off Cantonments Rd, OSU RE, Accra; tel. 776651; Chargé d'affaires: ABDUL HAMEE AL-GAREE.

Spain: Airport Residential Area, Lamptey Ave Extension, POB 1218, Accra; tel. 774004; Ambassador: JOSÉ MARÍA SIERRA.

Switzerland: 9 Water Rd S.I., North Ridge Area, POB 359, Accra; tel. 228125; telex 2197; Chargé d'affaires a.i.: WALTER BAUMANN.

Togo: Togo House, near Cantonments Circle, POB 4308, Accra; tel. 777950; telex 2166; Ambassador: NAMPOUGUINI LARE.

USSR: F856/1, Ring Rd East, POB 1634, Accra; tel. 775611; Ambassador: VYACHESLAV M. SEMYONOV.

United Kingdom: Osu Link, POB 296, Accra; tel. 664651; telex 2323; High Commissioner: ARTHUR H. WYATT.

USA: Ring Road East, POB 194, Accra; tel. 775346; Ambassador: STEVEN R. LYNE.

Yugoslavia: 10 West Cantonments, off Jawaharlal Nehru Rd, POB 1629, Accra; tel. 776868; Ambassador: LAZAR COVIĆ.

Zaire: 58 Third Rangoon Close E/1, POB 5448, Accra; tel. 775837; telex 2188; Ambassador: MUTUALE KIKANYE.

Judicial System

The civil law in force in Ghana is based on the Common Law, doctrines of equity and general statutes which were in force in England in 1874, as modified by subsequent Ordinances. Ghanaian customary law is, however, the basis of most personal, domestic and contractual relationships. Criminal Law is based on the Criminal Code, enacted in 1960 and dependent on English Criminal Law, and since amended at intervals. The Superior Court of Judicature consists of the Supreme Court, the Court of Appeal and the High Court of Justice; the Inferior Courts include the Circuit Courts, the District Courts and such other inferior courts as may be provided by law.

Supreme Court: The Supreme Court consists of the Chief Justice and not fewer than four other Justices of the Supreme Court. It is the final court of appeal in Ghana and has jurisdiction in matters relating to the enforcement or interpretation of the Constitution.

Chief Justice: E. N. P. SOWAH.

The Court of Appeal: The Court of Appeal consists of the Chief Justice and not fewer than five Judges of the Court of Appeal. It has jurisdiction to hear and determine appeals from any judgment, decree or order of the High Court.

The High Court: The High Court of Ghana consists of the Chief Justice and not fewer than twelve Justices of the High Court and has an original jurisdiction in all matters, civil and criminal, other than those for offences involving treason. Trial by jury is practised in criminal cases in Ghana and the Criminal Procedure Code, 1960, provides that all trials on indictment shall be by a jury or with the aid of Assessors.

The Circuit Court: Circuit Courts were created in 1960, and the jurisdiction of a Circuit Court consists of an original jurisdiction in civil matters where the amount involved does not exceed C100,000. It also has jurisdiction with regard to the guardianship and custody of infants, and original jurisdiction in all criminal cases, except offences where the maximum punishment is death or the offence, treason. Finally it has appellate jurisdiction from decisions of any District Court situated within its circuit.

District Courts: To each magisterial district is assigned at least one District Magistrate who has original jurisdiction to try civil suits in which the amount involved does not exceed C50,000. District Magistrates also have jurisdiction to deal with all criminal cases, except first-degree felonies, and commit cases of a more serious nature to either the Circuit Court or the High Court. A Grade I Circuit Court can impose a fine not exceeding C1,000 and sentences of imprisonment of up to two years and a Grade II Circuit Court may impose a fine not exceeding C500 and a sentence of imprisonment of up to 12 months. A District Court has no appellate jurisdiction, except in rent matters under the Rent Act.

Juvenile Courts: Empowered to hear charges against juveniles, persons under 17 years, except where the juvenile is charged jointly with an adult. They consist of a Chairman who must be either the District Magistrate or a lawyer, and not fewer than two other members appointed by the Chief Justice in consultation with the Judicial Council. The public is excluded from proceedings of Juvenile Courts which can make orders as to the protection and supervision of a neglected child and can negotiate with parents to secure the good behaviour of a child.

National Public Tribunal: Set up by the PNDC in 1984 to hear appeals from the Regional Public Tribunals. Its decisions are final and are not subject to any further appeal. The Tribunal consists of at least three members and not more than five, one of whom acts as Chairman.

Regional Public Tribunals: Set up by the PNDC in 1982 to judge criminal offences relating to prices, rent or exchange control, theft, fraud, forgery, corruption or any offence under any enactment which may be referred to them by the PNDC.

Special Military Tribunal: Set up by the PNDC in 1982 to judge crimes committed by members of the armed forces. It consists of between five and seven members.

Religion

According to the 1960 census, the distribution of religious groups was: Christians 42.8%, traditional religions 38.2%, Muslims 12.0%, unclassified 7.0%.

CHRISTIANITY

Christian Council of Ghana: POB 919, Accra; f. 1929; advisory body comprising 13 Protestant churches.

The Anglican Communion

Anglicans in Ghana are adherents of the Church of the Province of West Africa.

Bishop of Accra: Rt Rev. FRANCIS W. B. THOMPSON; Bishopscourt, POB 8, Accra; tel. 662292.

Bishop of Cape Coast: Rt Rev. JOHN ACKON.

Bishop of Koforidua: Rt Rev. ROBERT OKINE.

Bishop of Kumasi: Rt Rev. E. K. YEBOAH.

Bishop of Sekondi: Rt Rev. T. ANNOBIL.

Bishop of Sunyani and Tamale: Rt Rev. JOSEPH DADON.

The Roman Catholic Church

Ghana comprises two archdioceses and seven dioceses. At 31 December 1984 there were an estimated 1,575,000 adherents in the country.

Ghana Bishops' Conference: POB 42, Tamale; tel. 2425; f. 1980; Pres. Most Rev. PETER POREKU DERY, Archbishop of Tamale.

Archbishop of Cape Coast: Most Rev. JOHN KODWO AMISSAH, Archbishop's House, POB 112, Cape Coast; tel. 2593.

Archbishop of Tamale: Most Rev. PETER POREKU DERY, POB 42, Tamale; tel. 2425.

Other Christian Churches

African Methodist Episcopal Zion Church: POB 239, Sekondi.

Christian Methodist Episcopal Church: POB 3906, Accra.

Evangelical-Lutheran Church: POB 197, Kaneshie; Pres. Rev. PAUL K. FLYNN; Sec. Rev. V. SCHINDLER; 2,500 mems.

Evangelical-Presbyterian Church: POB 18, Ho; tel. 755; f. 1847; Moderator Rt Rev. Prof. N. K. DZOBO; 185,000 mems.

Ghana Baptist Convention: POB 1979, Kumas; Pres. L. SARPONG-MENSAH.

Ghana Conference of Seventh-day Adventists: Cape Coast; 24,100 mems.

Mennonite Church: POB 5485, Accra; f. 1957; Moderator Rev. E. A. GALBAH-NUSETOR; Sec. ABRAHAM K. WETSEH; 800 mems.

Methodist Church of Ghana: Liberia Rd, POB 403, Accra; tel. 228120; fully autonomous since 1961; Pres. Rt Rev. Dr JACOB S. A. STEPHENS; Sec. Rev. JOSEPH K. TEKYI-ANSAH; 290,642 mems.

Presbyterian Church of Ghana: POB 1800, Accra; tel. 662511; f. 1828; Moderator Rt Rev. D. A. KORANTENG; 422,438 mems.

Western African Union of Seventh-day Adventists: POB 1016, Accra; tel. 223720; telex 2119; f. 1943; Pres. P. K. ASAREH; Sec. SETH A. LARYEA.

The African Methodist Episcopal Church and the Feden Church are also active in Ghana.

ISLAM

There are a considerable number of Muslims in the Northern Region. The majority are Malikees.

Chief Imam: Alhaji MUKITAR ABASS.

GHANA
Directory

The Press

NEWSPAPERS

Daily

Daily Graphic: Graphic Rd, POB 742, Accra; tel. 228911; f. 1950; state-owned; Editor SAM CLEGG; circ. 200,000.

The Ghanaian Times: Ring Rd West, POB 2638, Accra; tel. 228282; f. 1958; state-owned; Editor K. GYAWU-KYEM; circ. 100,000.

People's Evening News: POB 7505, Accra; tel. 229416; Man. Editor OSEI POKU; circ. 60,000.

The Pioneer: Abura Printing Works Ltd, POB 325, Kumasi; tel. 2204; f. 1939; English; Man. J. K. TSIBOE; Editor BAFFOUR ANKOMAH; circ. 100,000.

Weekly

Believer: POB 6828, Accra-North; Man. Dir MARK D. N. ADDY; Editor GAB KOFI AKRONG; publication suspended.

Business Weekly: POB 2351, Ring Rd Industrial Area South, Accra; tel. 226037; f. 1966; Man. Editor MARK BOTSIO; circ. 5,000.

The Catholic Standard: POB 765, Accra; f. 1938; Roman Catholic; Editor ANTHONY BONNAH KOOMSON; circ. 30,400; (licence revoked Dec. 1985).

Champion: POB 6828, Accra-North; tel. 229079; Man. Dir MARK D. N. ADDY; Editor FRANK CAXTON WILLIAMS; circ. 300,000.

Echo: POB 5288, Accra; f. 1968; Sundays; Man. Editor J. K. TSIBOE; circ. 30,000.

The Mirror: Graphic Rd, POB 742, Accra; f. 1953; state-owned; Sundays; Editor K. GYAN APPENTENG; circ. 180,000.

New Nation: POB 6828, Accra-North; Man. Dir MARK D. N. ADDY; Editor S. N. SASRAKU; circ. 300,000.

The Palaver Tribune: POB 5018, Accra; f. 1970; Editor-in-Chief CHRISTIAN ASHER; Editor BENJAMIN BAAH ARMAH; circ. 100,000; publication suspended.

Punch: POB 6828, Accra-North; f. 1976; Man. Dir MARK D. N. ADDY; Editor PRINCE K. GOSWIN; circ. 280,000; publication suspended.

Sporting News: POB 5481, Accra-North; f. 1967; Man. Editor J. OPPONG-AGYARE.

Star: Accra; Editor J. W. DUMOGA.

The Statesman: Accra; Man. Editor W. K. DUMOGA (acting).

Weekly Spectator: New Times Corpn, Ring Road West, POB 2638, Accra; state-owned; f. 1963; Sundays; Editor J. D. ANDOH KESSON; circ. 165,000.

PERIODICALS

Fortnightly

Legon Observer: POB 11, Legon; f. 1966; publ. by Legon Society on National Affairs; Chair. J. A. DADSON; Editor EBOW DANIEL.

New Ghana: Information Services Dept, POB 745, Accra; English; political, economic and cultural affairs for international dissemination.

Monthly

African Woman: Ring Rd West, POB 1496, Accra.

Armed Forces News: Ghana Armed Forces, Burma Camp, Accra.

Boxing and Football Illustrated: POB 8392, Accra; f. 1976; Editor NANA O. AMPOMAH; circ. 10,000.

Chit Chat: POB 7043, Accra; Editor ROSEMOND ADU.

Christian Messenger: Presbyterian Depot Bldg, POB 3075, Accra; tel. 662415; f. 1883; English, Twi and Ga editions; Editor G. B. K. OWUSU; circ. 60,000.

Drum: POB 1197, Accra; general interest.

Ghana Journal of Science: Ghana Science Asscn, POB 7, Legon; Editor Dr A. K. AHAFIA.

Ideal Woman (Obaa Sima): POB 5737, Accra; Editor KATE ABBAM.

Police News: Police HQ, Accra; Editor S. S. APPIAH; circ. 20,000.

Students World: POB M18, Accra; tel. 774248; telex 2171; f. 1974; educational magazine for African students; Man. Editor ERIC OFEI; circ. 10,000.

The Symbol: POB 8162, Tema; Editor EMMANUEL DOE ZIORKLUI; circ. 10,000.

The Teacher: Ghana National Union of Teachers, POB 209, Accra; tel. 221515; f. 1931.

The Ghana Information Services (POB 745, Accra; tel. 228011) publish the following periodicals:

Akwansosem: Akwapim Twi; Editor FOSTER APPIAH.

Ghana Digest: UN, OAU and agency reports; Editor S. IKOI-KWAKU; circ. 12,000.

Ghana News Bulletin: f. 1974; Editor E. A. AFRO; circ. 8,000.

Ghana Review: f. 1961; economic, social and cultural affairs; Editor J. OPPONG-AGYARE; circ. 18,000.

Kabaare: f. 1967; edited by ISD; circ. 2,000.

Kakyevole: Nzema; Editor T. E. KWESI; circ. 10,500.

Kasem Labie (Kasem): POB 57, Tamale; Editor A. C. AZIIBA.

Lahabili Tsugu: POB 57, Tamale; Dagbani; Editor T. T. SULEMANA.

Mansralo: Ga; Editor MARTIN NII-MOI.

Motabiala: Ewe; Editor K. GROPONE; circ. 10,000.

Nkwantabisa: Asante, Twi and Fante; Editors FOSTER APPIAH (Twi), E. N. S. EDUFUL (Fante); circ. 20,000.

The Post: f. 1980; govt publication; current affairs and analysis; circ. 25,000.

Volta Review: f. 1976; edited by ISD; circ. 3,000.

Quarterly

Ghana Enterprise: Ghana National Chamber of Commerce, POB 2325, Accra; f. 1976; Editor J. B. K. AMANFU.

Ghana Manufacturer: Asscn of Ghana Industries, POB 8624, Accra-North; tel. 777283; f. 1974; Editor (vacant); circ. 1,500.

Insight and Opinion: POB 5446, Accra; Editorial Sec. W. B. OHENE.

Kpodoga: Tsito; f. 1976; rural community newspaper publ. by the Inst. of Adult Education of Univ. of Ghana; Ewe; Editor YAO ADUAMAH; circ. 5,000.

Radio and T.V. Times: POB 1633, Accra; tel. 221161; telex 2114; f. 1960; Editor ERNEST ASAMOAH; circ. 5,000.

Others

Economic Bulletin of Ghana: Economic Society of Ghana, POB 22, Legon; Editor Prof. JOHN COLEMAN DE GRAFT-JOHNSON.

Health Digest: POB 5446, Accra; every 2 months; Editorial Sec. W. B. OHENE.

NEWS AGENCIES

Ghana News Agency: POB 2118, Accra; tel. 665135; telex 2400; f. 1957; Gen. Man. (vacant); 9 regional offices, 30 district offices and 4 overseas offices.

Foreign Bureaux

Agence France-Presse (AFP): POB 9110, Accra; Bureau Chief GILBERT AYITTEY.

Associated Press (AP) (USA): POB 6172, Accra; Bureau Chief P. K. COBBINAH-ESSEM.

Telegrafnoye Agentstvo Sovetskovo Soyuza (TASS) (USSR): POB 9141, Accra; Agent IGOR AGEBEKOV.

United Press International (UPI) (USA): POB 9715, Accra; tel. 225436; telex 2340; Bureau Chief R. A. QUANSAH.

Xinhua (New China) News Agency (People's Republic of China): 35 Sir Arku Korsah Rd, Airport Residential Area, POB 3897, Accra.

Deutsche Presse-Agentur (Federal Republic of Germany) is also represented.

Publishers

Advance Publishing Co Ltd: New Town Rd, POB 2317, Accra New Town; tel. 21577; general non-fiction, paperbacks; Man. Dir A. O. MILLS.

Advent Press: POB 0102, Accra; telex 2119; Press Man. SETH A. ARMAH.

Adwinsa Publications (Ghana) Ltd: POB 92, Legon; tel. 74248; telex 2171; f. 1977; general, educational; Man. Dir KWABENA AMPONSAH.

Afram Publications: 72 Ring Rd East, POB M18, Accra; tel. 774248; telex 2171; f. 1973; textbooks and general; Man. Dir KWESI SAM-WOODE.

Africa Christian Press: POB 30, Achimota; tel. 225554; f. 1964; religious fiction and non-fiction, biography, paperbacks; Gen. Man. RICHARD A. B. CRABBE.

Anowuo Educational Publications: 2R McCarthy Hill, POB 3918, Accra; tel. 24910; f. 1966; educational, fiction and poetry in English and nine Ghanaian languages; Publr SAMUEL ASARE KONADU.

Asempa Publishers: POB 919, Accra; tel. 221706; f. 1973; religion, social questions, African music, fiction, children's books; Gen. Man. Rev. EMMANUEL A. B. BORTEY (acting).

Benibengor Book Agency: POB 40, Aboso; fiction, biography, children's books and paperbacks; Man. Dir J. BENIBENGOR BLAY.

Black Mask Ltd: POB 252, Kumasi; tel. 6454; f. 1979; educational textbooks, plays, novels; Man. Dir YAW OWUSU ASANTE.

Bureau of Ghana Languages: POB 1851, Accra; tel. 64130; f. 1951; educational and general in 11 Ghanaian languages; research and translation agency; Dir D. E. K. KRAMPAH; 96 mems.

Editorial and Publishing Services: POB 5743, Accra; general, reference; Man. Dir M. DANQUAH.

Emmanuel Publishing Services: POB 5282, Accra; tel. 25238; f. 1978; educational and children's books; Dir EMMANUEL K. NSIAH.

Encyclopaedia Africana Project: POB 2797, Accra; tel. 76939; f. 1962; reference; Dir E. T. ASHONG.

Frank Publishing Ltd: POB M414, Accra; tel. 29510; f. 1976; secondary school textbooks; Man. Dir FRANCIS K. DZOKOTO.

Ghana Publishing Corpn: PMB Tema; tel. 2921; f. 1965; textbooks and general fiction and non-fiction; Man. Dir F. K. NYARKO.

Ghana Universities Press: POB 4219, Accra; tel. 25032; f. 1962; scholarly and academic; Dir A. S. K. ATSU.

Moxon Paperbacks: Barnes Rd, POB M160, Accra; tel. 65397; f. 1967; travel and guide books, Africana, fiction and poetry; quarterly catalogue of Ghanaian books and periodicals in print; Man. Dir JAMES MOXON.

Sedco Publishing Ltd: Sedco House, Tabon St, North Ridge, POB 2051, Accra; tel. 221332; f. 1977; educational; Man. Dir COURAGE KWAMI SEGBAWU.

Unlit Publishing Co: POB 4432, Accra; tel. 22689; f. 1970; religion, politics, economics, science, fiction; Publr RONALD MENSAH.

Waterville Publishing House: POB 195, Accra; tel. 63124; f. 1963; general fiction and non-fiction, textbooks, paperbacks, Africana; Man. Dir A. S. OBUAM.

PUBLISHERS' ASSOCIATIONS

Ghana Book Development Council: POB M430, Accra; tel. 29178; agency of Ministry of Education; promotes and co-ordinates writing, production and distribution of books; Dep. Exec. Dir ANNOR NIMAKO.

Ghana Book Publishers' Association: c/o Ghana Universities Press, POB 4219, Accra.

Radio and Television

In 1985 there were an estimated 2.5m. radio receivers in use. There are internal radio broadcasts in English, Akan, Dagbani, Ewe, Ga, Hausa and Nzema; there is an external service in English, French and Hausa. There are two sound transmitting stations and 53 relay stations. In 1986 a new radio station was constructed at Bolgatanga.

The television service came into operation in 1965; there are two studios in Accra and four transmission stations: Ajangote about 32 km from Accra, Kissi in the Central Region, Jamasi in Ashanti and Tamale in the Northern Region. In 1987 new colour television equipment was commissioned in Accra. In 1985 there were an estimated 140,000 television receivers in use.

Ghana Broadcasting Corporation: Broadcasting House, POB 1633, Accra; tel. 221161; telex 2114; f. 1935; Dir of TV DAVID GHARTEY-TAGOE; Dir of Radio FELIX SEDZIATA; Dir of News DAVID ANAGLATE.

Finance

(cap. = capital; p.u. = paid up; auth. = authorized; res = reserves; dep. = deposits; m. = million; brs = branches; amounts in cedis)

BANKING

Central Bank

Bank of Ghana: POB 2674, Thorpe Rd, Accra; tel. 666902; telex 2052; f. 1957; auth. cap. 100m. (Dec. 1985); Gov. JOHN SACKAH ADDO; Dep. Govs SAMUEL KYE APEA, EMMANUEL OSSEI-KUMAH.

State Banks

Agricultural Development Bank: POB 4191, Accra; tel. 228453; telex 2295; f. 1965; cap. 60m.; state-owned; credit facilities for farmers and commercial banking; Chair. and Man. Dir SAMUEL ODAME-LABI.

Bank of Credit and Commerce Ghana: POB 11011, 4 Graphic Rd, Accra; tel. 220788; telex 2208; cap. 2m. (Dec. 1983); Chair. Dr J. L. S. ABBEY; Man. S. M. K. AIDAM.

Bank for Housing and Construction: Mobil House, POB MI, Accra; tel. 666143; telex 2096; f. 1973; cap. 20m. (June 1984); Chair. S. Q. DUNCAN; Man. Dir YAW OSAFO-MAAFO.

Ghana Commercial Bank: POB 134, Accra; tel. 664914; telex 2034; f. 1953; state-owned; cap. p.u. 270., dep. 7,759m. (1983); 141 brs; Man. Dir KOFI AGYEMAN.

Ghana Co-operative Bank: Liberty Ave, POB 5292, Accra-North; f. 1974; cap. p.u. 102,315, dep. 9m. (Dec. 1983); Man. Dir Dr A. K. APPIAH.

National Investment Bank: 37 Kwame Nkrumah Ave, POB 3726, Accra; tel. 221312; telex 2161; f. 1963; provides long-term investment capital and consultancy, joint venture promotion, consortium finance management and commercial banking services; cap. p.u. 39m.; Chair. and Man. Dir E. M. K. AIDAM.

National Savings and Credit Bank: Kwame Nkrumah Ave, Accra; tel. 228322; f. 1888; state-owned; cap. p.u. 6m. (March 1983); dep. 189.2m. (1981); Man. Dir J. A. NUAMAH.

National Trust Holding Co: Dyson House, Liberty Ave, POB 9563, Airport, Accra; f. 1976 to finance company takeovers by Ghanaians under the 1976 indigenization decree; finances investment in Ghanaian companies and assists in their development and expansion; carries out trusteeship business; cap. p.u. 3.3m.; Man. Dir W. COOKE.

Social Security Bank: POB 13119, Accra; tel. 221726; telex 2209; f. 1976; cap. p.u. 10m.; Chair. NANA ADDO DANKWA III; Man. Dir J. BENTUM-WILLIAMS.

There are rural banks at Asiama, Agona, Biriwa and Afosu.

Merchant Bank

Merchant Bank (Ghana) Ltd: Swannmill, Kwame Nkrumah Ave, POB 401, Accra; tel. 666331; telex 2191; f. 1972; 30% state-owned; cap. 100m.; dep. 946m. (Dec. 1985); Chair. Y. M. SARPONG; Man. Dir K. AGYEI-GYAMFI.

Foreign Banks

Barclays Bank of Ghana Ltd (UK): High St, Accra, POB 2949; tel. 664901; f. 1971; 40% state-owned; cap. 100m. (1985); Chair. Prof. S. SEY; Man. Dir CHARLES M. MABON; 41 brs.

Standard Chartered Bank Ghana Ltd (UK): High St, POB 768, Accra; tel. 664591; f. 1896 (as Bank of British West Africa); ownership: Standard Chartered Bank 60%, govt 27.5%, public 12.5%; cap. and res 668.6m. (1985); Chair. KWAME A. KWATENG; Man. Dir J. R. GILBERT; 25 brs, 14 sub-brs.

INSURANCE

The State Insurance Corporation of Ghana: POB 2363, Accra; tel. 666961; telex 2171; f. 1962; state-owned; undertakes all lines of insurance, invests in real estate and provides other investments to support the economy.

Social Security and National Insurance Trust: POB M149, Accra; f. 1972; covers over 1.25m. employees; Chief Admin. A. AWUKU.

Vanguard Assurance Co Ltd: Post Office Sq., Insurance Hall, POB 1868, Accra; f. 1975; general accident, marine and motor insurance.

Several foreign insurance companies operate in Ghana.

Trade and Industry

PUBLIC BOARDS AND CORPORATIONS

Bast Fibres Development Board: POB 1992, Kumasi; f. 1970; promotes the commercial cultivation of bast fibres and their processing, handling and grading.

Food Production Corporation: POB 1853, Accra; f. 1971; state corpn providing employment for youth in large scale farming enterprises; controls 76,900 ha of land with 16,200 ha under cultivation; operates 87 food farms on a co-operative and self-supporting basis, and rears poultry and livestock.

GHANA

Directory

Ghana Cocoa Board: POB 933, Accra; telex 2082; f. 1947 as Gold Coast Marketing Board; responsible for purchase, grading and export of cocoa, coffee and shea nuts, and encourages production and scientific research aimed at improving quality and yield of cocoa, coffee and shea nuts; Chief Exec. HARRY DODOO; Deputy Chief Execs Flight-Lt (rtd) JOE B. ATIEMO, Dr A. ASARE NYAKO, K. N. OWUSU.

Ghana Consolidated Diamond Co Ltd: POB M108, Accra; telex 2058; f. 1986, to replace Diamond Marketing Corpn, to grade, value and process diamonds, buy all locally won, produced or processed diamonds, promote the industry; responsible for securing the most favourable terms for purchase, grading, valuing, export and sale of local diamonds; Chair. KOFI AGYEMAN.

Ghana Cotton Co Ltd: f. 1986 to replace Cotton Development Board; ownership: govt 70%, private textile cos 30%; 15 regional offices; Chair. HARRY GANDA.

Ghanaian Enterprises Development Commission: Accra; f. 1975; assists the indigenization of the economy; especially small and medium-scale industrial and commercial enterprises, by providing loans and advisory services.

Ghana Food Distribution Corporation: POB 4245, Accra; tel. 228428; f. 1971 by merger of Food Marketing Corpn and Task Force Food Distribution unit; buys, stores, preserves, distributes and sells foodstuffs throughout the country; 10 regional centres for preservation, storage, distribution and sales; Man. Dir Dr P. A. KURANCHIE.

Ghana Industrial Holding Corporation (GIHOC): POB 2784, Accra; tel. 664998; telex 2109; f. 1967; manages 26 state enterprises, including the steel, paper, bricks, paint, pharmaceuticals, electronics, metals, canneries, distilleries and boat-building factories; also has three wholly-owned subsidiaries and four joint ventures; in 1979 it was decided to convert all divisions into wholly-owned limited liability companies; Chair. J. E. K. MOSES; Man. Dir J. K. WILLIAMS.

Ghana Investment Centre: Central Ministerial Area, POB M193, Accra; tel. 665125; telex 2229; f. 1981 to replace Capital Investments Board; negotiates new investments, approves projects, registers foreign capital and decides extent of govt participation; Chair. Secretary for Finance and Economic Planning.

Ghana National Manganese Corporation: POB M. 183, Ministry Post Office, Accra; telex 2046; f. 1975 following govt takeover of African Manganese Co mine at Nsuta; Chair. P. O. AGGREY; Man. Dir Dr A. O. BARNAFO.

Ghana National Petroleum Corporation: Accra; f. 1984; develops petroleum potential; Chair. Alhaji IDDRISU MAHAMA; Man. Dir. Dr A. K. ADDAE (acting).

Ghana National Trading Corporation: POB 67, Accra; tel. 664871; f. 1961; organizes exports and imports of commodities determined by the Corporation; over 500 retail outlets in 14 admin. dists.

Ghana Standards Board: c/o POB M245, Accra; tel. 662606; telex 2041; f. 1967; establishes and promulgates standards; promotes standardization, industrial efficiency and development and industrial welfare, health and safety; operates certification mark scheme; 285 mems; Dir Dr L. TWUM-DANSO; Sec. F. K. DONKOR.

Ghana Water and Sewerage Corporation: POB M194, Accra; f. 1966 to provide, distribute and conserve water for public, domestic and industrial use, and to establish, operate and control sewerage systems.

Grains and Legumes Development Board: Kumasi; f. 1970; main govt organ developing and promoting grain and legume industry.

Minerals Commission: State House, 2nd Floor, 2nd Bay, POB M248, Accra; tel. 664143; f. 1984; fmrly Aluminium Industries Commission; monitors, promotes and co-ordinates the minerals industry.

Posts and Telecommunications Corporation: Posts and Telecommunications Bldg, Accra-North; f. 1974; provides both internal and external postal and telecommunication services.

State Construction Corporation: Ring Rd West, Industrial Area, Accra; f. 1966; state corpn with a labour force of 7,000; construction plans are orientated to aid agricultural production; Man. Dir J. A. DANSO, Jr.

State Farms Corporation: Accra; undertakes agricultural projects in all regions but Upper Region; Man. Dir E. N. A. THOMPSON (acting).

State Fishing Corporation: POB 211, Tema; telex 2043; f. 1961; govt-sponsored deep-sea fishing, distribution and marketing (including exporting) org.; owns 12 deep-sea fishing trawlers.

State Gold Mining Corporation: POB 109, Tarkwa; Accra Office, POB 3634; tel. 775376; telex 2348; f. 1961; manages four gold mines; CEO F. AWUA-KYEREMATEN.

State Hotels Corporation: POB 7542, Accra-North; f. 1965; responsible for all state-owned hotels, restaurants, etc.; provides such facilities in 13 major centres; Man. Dir Col W. A. ODJIDJA; Gen. Man. FRANCIS ADU.

State Housing Construction Company: POB 2753, Accra; f. 1982 by merger of State Housing Corpn and Tema Development Corpn; oversees govt housing programme.

Timber Export Development Board: POB 515, Takoradi; tel. 2921; telex 2189; f. 1985 in place of Ghana Timber Marketing Board; promotes the sale and export of timber; CEO J. F. BAIDOO.

CHAMBER OF COMMERCE

Ghana National Chamber of Commerce: POB 2325, Accra; tel. 662427; f. 1961; promotes trade and commerce, organizes trade fairs; 1,500 individual mems and 13 mem. chambers; Pres. ISAAC D. ADADE; Exec. Sec. JOHN B. K. AMANFU.

COMMERCIAL AND INDUSTRIAL ORGANIZATIONS

Ghana Export Promotion Council: POB M146, Accra; telex 2076; f. 1972; Chair. and mems appointed by Ghana Mfrs' Asscn, Ghana National Chamber of Commerce, Ghana Export Co, Capital Investments Board, Ministries for Agriculture, Foreign Affairs, Information, Industries, Trade and Tourism, Bank of Ghana, and the Ghana Standards Board.

The Indian Association of Ghana: POB 2891, Accra; f. 1939; Pres. HEMANT DADLANI; Sec. K. N. IYER.

EMPLOYERS' ASSOCIATION

Ghana Employers' Association: Kojo Thompson Rd, POB 2616, Accra; tel. 228455; f. 1959; 353 mems; Pres. E. DARKO-OWIREDU; Vice-Pres. J. A. HICKIN; Exec. Dir F. BANNERMAN-MENSON.

Affiliated Bodies

Association of Ghana Industries: POB 8624, Accra-North; tel. 777283; telex 3027; f. 1957; Pres. A. APPIAH-MENKA; Exec. Sec. EDDIE IMBEAH-AMOAKUH.

Ghana Booksellers' Association: POB 10367, Accra-North; tel. 227148; Pres. SAMPSON BRAKO; Gen. Sec. FRED J. REMMER.

Ghana Chamber of Mines: POB 991, Accra; tel. 662719; telex 2036; f. 1928; promotes mining interests; Exec. Dir SAM POKU.

Ghana Electrical Contractors' Association: POB 1858, Accra.

Ghana National Contractors' Association: c/o J. T. Osei and Co, POB M11, Accra.

Ghana Port Employers' Association: c/o Ghana Cargo Handling Co Ltd, POB 488, Tema.

Ghana Timber Federation: POB 246, Takoradi; f. 1952; promotes, protects and develops timber industry; Chair. H. WALTERS.

CO-OPERATIVES

The co-operative movement began in Ghana in 1928 among cocoa farmers, and grew into the largest farmers' organization in the country. In 1944 the Department of Co-operatives, known then as the Department of Co-operation, was established as the controlling body of co-operative societies. The movement was dissolved by the Nkrumah government in 1960, but was re-established after the coup in 1966. It is now under the direction of a government-appointed secretary-general. There are 1,261 co-operative societies and 43 co-operative produce marketing unions. The structure of the movement places the co-operative associations at the top, co-operative unions in a secondary position of seniority in the towns, and village co-operative societies at the base.

Department of Co-operatives: POB M150, Accra; tel. 666212; f. 1944; govt-supervised body, responsible for registration, auditing and supervision of co-operative societies; Registrar R. BUACHIE-APHRAM; Sec.-Gen. J. M. APPIAH.

Ghana Co-operatives Council: Accra; co-ordinates activities of all co-operative societies; over 100,000 mems.

The co-operative associations are:

Ghana Co-operative Credit Association: POB 3040, Accra.

Ghana Co-operative Fisheries Association: Accra; f. 1967; includes over 200 fish marketing societies; Gen. Sec. WILLIAM BUCKMAN.

GHANA

Ghana Co-operative Marketing Association: POB 832, Accra; f. 1944.

Ghana Co-operative Poultry Farmers' Association: Accra.

Ghana Co-operative Transport Association: Accra; f. 1960; comprises 28 primary societies with seven regional unions; especially involved with cocoa exporting.

TRADE UNIONS

Ghana Trades Union Congress: Hall of Trade Unions, POB 701, Accra; f. 1945; all chairmen, general secretaries and vice-chairmen of 17 affiliated unions, and the constitution of the TUC were suspended in March 1982; Chair. Interim Man. Cttee Mr ABOAGYE; Sec.-Gen. AUGUSTUS YANKEY.

The following Unions are affiliated to the Congress (figures refer to membership in 1979):

Construction and Building Workers' Union (46,000); General Agricultural Workers' Union (127,000); General Transport, Petroleum and Chemical Workers' Union (12,504); Private Road Transport Workers' Union (21,700); Health Services Workers' Union (12,000); Industrial and Commercial Workers' Union (115,052); Local Government Workers' Union (38,933); Maritime and Dockworkers' Union (23,720); Mine-workers' Union (22,000); National Union of Seamen (5,000); Post and Telecommunications Workers' Union (11,500); Public Services Workers' Union (45,000); Public Utility Workers' Union (25,000); Railway Enginemen's Union (701); Railway and Port Workers' Union (13,216); Teachers' and Educational Workers' Union (34,000); Timber and Woodworkers' Union (22,000).

Transport

Department of Transport and Communications: POB M38, Accra.

State Transport Corporation: Accra; f. 1901 as Govt Transport Dept, name changed in 1965; Man. Dir Lt-Col AKYEA-MENSAH.

RAILWAYS

There were 953 km of railways in 1985, connecting Accra, Kumasi and Takoradi.

Ghana Railway Corporation: POB 251, Takoradi; tel. 2181; telex 2297; f. 1977; responsible for the operation and maintenance of all railways; Gen. Man. S. S. NAYAK.

ROADS

In 1985 there were about 28,300 km of classified roads in Ghana. Of this total, 14,140 km were trunk roads, managed by the Ghana Highway Authority. A further 14,160 km were feeder roads, managed by the Department of Feeder Roads. These two agencies are under the control of the Secretariat for Roads and Highways. There were also some 6,000 km of tracks, owned and managed by private mining and timber companies. These are not classified. Only roads managed by the Ghana Highway Authority are paved. Of the total length of roads, 5,782 km were paved in 1985, including 150 km of motorway. A major rehabilitation programme to improve the quality of the road network is under way.

Ghana Highway Authority: POB 1641, Accra; f. 1974 to plan, develop, classify and maintain roads and ferries; CEO B. T. K. ADADEVOH.

The **Ghana-Burkina Faso Road Transport Commission** was set up to implement the 1968 agreement to improve communications between the two countries. Work commenced in 1982 on a road between Accra and Abidjan, Ivory Coast, as part of the planned West African Highway.

SHIPPING

The two main ports are Tema (near Accra) and Takoradi, both of which are linked with Kumasi by rail. In 1985 it was announced that Tema and Takoradi ports were to be expanded and modernized at a cost of around US $50m., with assistance from the World Bank and other donors. The work will involve a major rehabilitation of the ports' infrastructure, facilities and equipment. In 1981 goods loaded totalled 1.25m. metric tons, and goods unloaded 2.97m. tons.

Alpha (West Africa) Line Ltd: POB 451, Tema; telex 2184; operates regular cargo services to West Africa, the UK, the USA, the Far East and northern Europe; agents for Mercandia (West Africa) Line, Cameroon National Line, Pakistan National Lines, Uiterwyk West Africa Lines and Great South America Line; Man. Dir E. COLLINGWOODE-WILLIAMS; Gen. Mans E. T. ADDY, E. P. O. KWAFO.

Black Star Line Ltd: 4th Lane, Kuku Hill Osu, POB 2760, Accra; tel. 776161; telex 2019; f. 1957; state-owned; operates passenger and cargo services to Europe, the UK, Canada, the USA, the Mediterranean and west Africa; agents for Gold Star Line, Woermann Line, Zim West Africa Lines, Compagnie Maritime Belge, Seven Stars (Africa) Line, Société Ivoirienne de Transport Maritime (SITRAM), and Compagnie Maritime Zaïroise (CMZ); fleet of 7 freighters; displacement 96,912 g.r.t.; Man. Dir CHRISTOPH JOCHEN BENE.

Holland West-Afrika Lijn N.V.: POB 269, Accra; POB 216, Tema; and POB 18, Takoradi; cargo services to and from North America and the Far East; agents for Royal Interocean Lines and Dafra Line.

Liner Agencies (Ghana) Ltd: POB 66, Accra; telex 2009; POB 210, Takoradi; POB 214, Tema; freight services to and from UK, Europe, USA, Canada, Japan and Italy; intermediate services between West African ports; freight services from India and Pakistan; agents for Barber Line, Elder Dempster Lines, Guinean Gulf Line, Kawasaki Kisen Kaisha, Mitsui OSK Lines, Nigerian National Shipping Line, Marine Chartering of San Francisco, A/S Bulkhandling of Oslo, Botany Bay Shipping Co, SITRAM, CMZ and Palm Line; Man. Dir M. N. ANKUMA; Agent (Takoradi) I. K. NKETIA; Agent (Tema) J. OSSEI-YAW.

Remco Shipping Lines Ltd: POB 3898, Accra; tel. 23385; displacement 5,012 g.r.t.

Scanship (Ghana) Ltd: CFAO Bldg, High St, POB 1705, Accra; tel. 664314; telex 2181; agents for Maersk Line, Splosna Plovba Line, Hoegh Line, Jadranska Slobodna Plovidba-Split, Keller Shipping, Prompt Shipping, Polish Ocean Line, DSR Line, EAC Line, Estonian Shipping Co, Shipping Corpn of India, US Africa Line.

CIVIL AVIATION

The main international airport is at Kotoka (Accra). There are also airports at Takoradi, Kumasi, Sunyani and Tamale.

Gemini Airlines Ltd: America House, POB 7328, Accra-North; tel. 665785; f. 1974; operates once-weekly cargo flight between Accra and London; fleet of one B-707F; Dir V. OWUSU; Gen. Man. P. F. OKINE.

Ghana Airways Corporation: Ghana House, POB 1636, Accra; tel. 664856; f. 1958; state-owned; operates domestic services and international routes to West African destinations, Italy, the Federal Republic of Germany and the UK; fleet of one DC-10-30, two Fokker F28, one DC 9-50; Chair. A. W. ADDA; Man. Dir Wing-Commdr J. B. AZARIAH.

Tourism

Ghana Tourist Board: State House Complex, 6th Floor, Bay 2, POB 3106, Accra; tel. 665461; telex 2143; f. 1968; Chair. Dr KOFI AFFRIFAH; Exec. Dir Dr ADJEI-BARWUAH.

Ghana Association of Tourist and Travel Agencies: Ramia House, Kojo Thompson Rd, POB 7140, Accra; Pres. JOSEPH K. ANKUMAH; Sec. JOHNNIE MOREAUX.

Ghana Tourist Development Co Ltd: Ridge near old EEC Office, POB 8710, Accra; tel. 228138; Man. Dir ABEL EDUSEI.

Atomic Energy

Atomic Energy Commission: POB 80, Legon/Accra; construction of a nuclear reactor at Kwabenya, near Accra, which was begun in 1964, was temporarily halted between 1966 and 1974; the Commission's present activities are mainly concerned with the applications of radio-isotopes in agriculture and medicine; Chair. Dr A. K. AHAFIA.

GREECE

Introductory Survey

Location, Climate, Language, Religion, Flag, Capital

The Hellenic Republic lies in south-eastern Europe. The country consists mainly of a mountainous peninsula between the Mediterranean Sea and the Aegean Sea, bounded to the north by Albania, Yugoslavia and Bulgaria, and to the east by Turkey. To the south, east and west of the mainland lie numerous Greek islands, of which the largest is Crete. The climate is Mediterranean, with mild winters and hot summers. The language is Greek, of which there are two forms—the formal language (katharevoussa) and the language commonly spoken and taught in schools (demotiki). Almost all of the inhabitants profess Christianity, and the Greek Orthodox Church, to which about 97% of the population adhere, is the established religion. The national flag (proportions 3 by 2) displays a white cross on a blue background. The capital is Athens.

Recent History

The liberation of Greece from the German occupation was followed by a civil war which lasted until 1949. The Communist forces were defeated, and the constitutional monarchy re-established. King Constantine came to the throne on the death of his father, King Paul, in 1964. A succession of weak governments and conflicts between the King and his ministers, and an alleged conspiracy involving military personnel who supported the Centre Union Party, resulted in a coup, led by right-wing army officers, in April 1967. An attempted counter-coup, led by the King, failed, and he went into exile. Colonel George Papadopoulos emerged as the dominant personality in the new regime, becoming Prime Minister in December 1967 and Regent in March 1972. The regime produced nominally democratic constitutional proposals, but all political activity was banned and opponents of the regime were expelled from all positions of power or influence.

Following an abortive naval mutiny, said to be supported by the exiled King, Greece was declared a republic in June 1973. Papadopoulos was appointed President in July. Martial law was ended, and a civilian Cabinet was appointed in preparation for a general election to be held by the end of 1973. A student uprising at the Athens Polytechnic in November 1973 was bloodily repressed by the army, and another military coup overthrew Papadopoulos. Lieut-Gen. Phaidon Ghizikis was appointed President, and a mainly civilian Cabinet, led by Adamantios Androutsopoulos, was installed, but effective power lay with a small group of officers and the military police under Brig.-Gen. Demetrios Ioannides. As a result of the failure of the military junta's attempt to overthrow President Makarios of Cyprus and its inability to prevent the Turkish invasion of the island (see chapter on Cyprus), the Androutsopoulos Cabinet disintegrated in July 1974. President Ghizikis called Constantine Karamanlis, a former Prime Minister, back from exile to form a civilian Government of National Salvation. Martial law was ended, the press was freed from state control, and political parties, including the Communists, were allowed to emerge. A general election in November 1974 resulted in a decisive victory for Karamanlis' New Democracy (ND) party, which gained 54% of the votes cast and won 220 of the 300 seats in Parliament. A referendum in December 1974 rejected proposals for a return to constitutional monarchy, and in June 1975 a new republican constitution, providing for a parliamentary democracy, was promulgated. In the same month Prof. Constantine Tsatsos, a former cabinet minister, was elected President.

In the general election of November 1977 ND was re-elected with a reduced majority. In May 1980 Karamanlis was elected President and resigned as Prime Minister. The new leader of ND, George Rallis, formed a government, reshuffling the previous Cabinet. He faced a growing challenge from the rising Panhellenic Socialist Movement (PASOK). In the general election of October 1981 PASOK gained an absolute majority in Parliament. Its leader, Andreas Papandreou, became Prime Minister of the first socialist government in Greek history, initially committed to withdrawal from the EEC, removal of US military bases, and to implementing a sweeping programme of reform. By the end of 1982 domestic reforms included the lowering of the voting age to 18; legalization of civil marriage and divorce, while adultery was no longer a criminal offence; overhauling the university system; replacement of officers in the armed forces, bankers and other leading figures; and the abolition of school uniforms. In January 1983 a general amnesty was granted to the Communist exiles from the period of the civil war. A major cabinet reshuffle in July 1982 represented a renewed attempt to deal with continuing economic problems, creating a new Ministry of National Economy, to include industrial and commercial affairs. Proposed radical 'socialization' of industry faced widespread opposition and was largely limited to the introduction of worker participation in supervisory councils, although state control was imposed in the pharmaceutical industry in 1982, and in 1983 the Government nationalized one of Greece's largest and most successful companies, the Heracles Cement Co. Index-linking of wage increases to the rate of inflation, one of the first measures that the PASOK Government had introduced, was modified at the end of 1982 in an attempt to reduce inflation, and a 'freeze' on wages was imposed from January 1983. After a series of strikes in the first half of 1983, a controversial law was adopted in June, increasing worker participation in the public sector, but also limiting the right to strike: this measure was strongly opposed by the Communist Party, which had hitherto generally supported the Government's domestic policy. The Government's relations with trade unions were expected to improve following gains made by PASOK-affiliated unions in elections for the leadership of the General Confederation of Greek Workers in December 1983. A prices and incomes policy, announced in December, provided for wage indexation in the public sector in 1984, and for price controls. The unions withdrew their demands for wage indexation in the private sector, and a back-dated general wage increase was agreed in February 1984. In the elections to the European Parliament, held in June 1984, PASOK slightly increased its percentage of the votes in comparison with the 1981 election, winning 10 of the 24 seats, while ND won nine.

In March 1985 Papandreou unexpectedly withdrew support for President Karamanlis' candidature for a further five-year term in office. The Prime Minister planned to amend the 1975 constitution, proposing to relieve the President of all executive power and transfer it to the legislature, thus reducing the head of state to a purely ceremonial figure. President Karamanlis resigned in protest at the proposed changes, and Parliament elected Christos Sartzetakis, a judge, as President, in a vote that was widely considered to be unconstitutional. In April the proposed amendments to the Constitution achieved the first of three required votes of parliamentary approval by the necessary three-fifths majority, and a similar vote was recorded at the legislation's second presentation to Parliament in May. A general election was held in June to enable the Government to secure support for the proposed constitutional changes. PASOK was returned to power, receiving 45.8% of the total votes (compared with 48% in 1981) and winning 161 seats in the 300-member Parliament. The main opposition party, ND, received 41% of the votes and secured 126 seats.

In October Papandreou introduced a stringent two-year programme of economic austerity, including the devaluation of the drachma by 15% and a two-year 'freeze' on wages, to combat inflation and a soaring deficit on the current account of the balance of payments. In response to these measures, a series of strikes took place throughout Greece, culminating in November in a one-day general strike, called by the militant left wing and the majority of the trade unions (a minority remained loyal to the Government). Later in the month there were two days of rioting in Athens during the commemoration of the 12th anniversary of the student uprising in 1973. The young demonstrators used the commemorative events to express their opposition to the Government's economic measures. Anti-austerity protests and strikes (dismissed by the Government as politically-motivated) continued throughout Greece in 1986.

In March 1986 the Greek Parliament approved a series of constitutional amendments (denounced by ND as 'a step towards autocratic rule') limiting the powers of the President. The President was divested of his executive powers, which were transferred to the legislature. The amendments limited the President's power to call a referendum and transferred to Parliament the right to declare a state of emergency. The President lost the right to dismiss the Prime Minister, and may dissolve Parliament only if the resignation of two Governments in quick succession demonstrates the absence of political stability. Although the President has become a figurehead, he may continue to play a substantial moderating role by the use of his right to object to legislation and to request Parliament to reconsider it or to approve it with an enlarged majority.

In an extensive government reshuffle in April 1986, Papandreou relinquished the portfolio of Defence, and the Ministries of the Interior and of Public Order reverted to their separate status. At the local elections held throughout Greece in October 1986, the ruling PASOK lost substantial support to both ND and the Communist KKE. Despite Papandreou's attempt to operate a tactical alliance between PASOK and the Communists, three ND candidates were elected as mayors in Greece's three largest cities—Athens, Piraeus and Thessaloniki. A government reshuffle in October, which reduced the Cabinet from 48 to 36 members, was widely criticized for failing to remove those ministers generally considered to be most responsible for PASOK's decline in popularity. By the end of 1986 there were some doubts as to whether the PASOK Government would be able to retain power for the remainder of its second term, due to end in mid-1989.

The treaty of accession to the European Communities was signed in May 1979 and Greece became a full member in January 1981. Although originally critical of Greece's membership, the Socialist Government confined itself to seeking modification of the terms of accession, in order to take into account the under-developed Greek economy, and gave qualified assent to concessions proposed by the EEC in April 1983. Greece's independent attitude within the Community was shown in October 1984, when Papandreou became the first EEC leader to visit Poland since martial law was declared there in 1981. This independent stance was upheld in 1986, when the Greek Government initially refused to implement the EEC measures to restrict Libyan diplomats, following several terrorist attacks in Europe in December 1985, for which Libya was widely believed to be responsible, and when it refused to join the EEC in condemning Syria's alleged links with terrorism.

In September 1983, despite its pledge to remove American military bases, the Government signed a five-year agreement on defence and economic co-operation with the USA: the four existing US bases were to remain, and Greece was to receive US $500m. worth of military aid in 1984/85. In March 1986 Greece and the USA agreed to hold talks, by early 1987, concerning the future of the four US bases. In November 1986 a Greek-US agreement on defence and industrial co-operation was signed. Under this five-year agreement, the USA agreed to help Greece to modernize its military industry and armed forces. A 10-year economic co-operation agreement with the USSR was signed in 1983. Proposals for the establishment of a Balkan nuclear-free zone were made by Greece in 1983, and talks with neighbouring states continued in 1984. During a visit to Bulgaria in September 1986, both Papandreou and President Todor Zhivkov reiterated their countries' determination to work actively towards the elimination of nuclear and chemical weapons from the Balkan region. In the same month a security agreement was signed by Greece and Italy to enhance co-operation against terrorism, drug trafficking and other organized crime.

Relations with Turkey have been characterized by longstanding disputes concerning Cyprus (q.v.) and sovereignty over the continental shelf beneath the Aegean Sea. Having left the military structure of NATO in 1974, in protest at the Turkish occupation of northern Cyprus, Greece rejoined in 1980, but in 1981 the new Government demanded that NATO should guarantee protection against possible Turkish aggression, as a condition of continuing Greek membership; disputes with Turkey over air-space continued, and talks between the two countries' Ministers of Foreign Affairs made little progress. The difficulties in relations with Turkey were exacerbated by the unilateral declaration of an 'independent' Turkish-Cypriot state in Cyprus in November 1983, together with various minor sovereignty disputes over islands in the Aegean Sea, which led to Greece's withdrawal from NATO exercises in August 1984 and to a boycott of them in 1985 and 1986. A new position of Minister for the Aegean was created in 1985 to deal with Greece's various disputes with Turkey. Relations between the two countries did not improve in 1986. Greece remained determined to obstruct Turkey's full membership of the EEC. In June another UN peace initiative for Cyprus collapsed, and a further round of UN talks was held in Cyprus in November. Also in November, the Greek Government accused Turkey of helping Iranian refugees to enter Greece illegally across the Evros River. The situation worsened in December when one Greek soldier and two Turkish military personnel were killed in an incident along the Evros frontier. The USA and the UK were expected to increase their efforts to encourage the two countries to resume a diplomatic dialogue.

In August 1985 Greece and Albania reopened their borders, which had remained closed since 1940, and Greece formally annulled claims to North Epirus (southern Albania), where there is a sizeable Greek minority. The main highway between Greece and Albania was reopened at Kakavia in January 1985. In May 1986 Greece prepared to put a formal end to a legal vestige of the Second World War by proclaiming that it no longer considered itself at war with Albania. This proposal was opposed by ND, which accused the Government of failing to ensure the rights of Albania's Greek minority in return for ending the state of war.

Government

Under the Constitution of June 1975, the President is Head of State and is elected by Parliament for a five-year term. The President appoints the Prime Minister and, upon his recommendation, the other members of the Cabinet. In March 1986 Parliament approved a series of constitutional amendments limiting the powers of the President and, thus, reducing him to a ceremonial figure. The amendments basically divested the President of his executive powers and transferred them to the legislature (see Recent History). The unicameral Parliament has 300 members, directly elected by universal adult suffrage for four years. In 1983 measures were introduced to devolve powers of local government (formerly confined almost exclusively to 55 representatives of the central government) to local councils, which were eventually to be directly elected.

Defence

Greece returned to the military structure of NATO in October 1980, after an absence of six years. Military service is compulsory and lasts 21–25 months. In 1978 women were given the right to volunteer for military service of 30–50 days' basic training and for specialized training. In July 1986 the armed forces numbered 209,000, of whom 136,500 were conscripts, and consisted of an army of 165,500, a navy of 19,500 and an air force of 24,000; there was a gendarmerie of 25,000 and also a National Guard of 100,000. Estimated defence expenditure for 1985 totalled 281,713m. drachmae.

Economic Affairs

Greece has traditionally been an agricultural nation, producing most of its own needs and exporting a considerable amount of produce. The country produces large quantities of wheat, barley, maize, tobacco, sugar beet, tomatoes and dried and fresh fruit. Since 1960, however, there has been a rapid increase in the importance of industry. The annual rate of expansion of agricultural output slowed from about 2.5% in the 1970s to about 1% in 1986. Agricultural products accounted for 91.45% of all exports in 1960, but in 1984 they accounted for only 22%, while manufacturing provided 48%. Agriculture provided an estimated 17.4% of gross domestic product (GDP), and manufacturing an estimated 17.9%, in 1985. In 1986, however, 29.4% of the working population were engaged in agriculture, compared with an EEC average of 7.6%. About one-third of the population and 57% of industrial production is situated in the area around Athens, and this creates serious environmental problems. Nevertheless, Greece is generally regarded as only semi-industrialized, and its average income is lower than that of other EEC countries. In 1984, according to estimates by the World Bank, Greece's gross national product (GNP) per head, measured at average 1982–84 prices, was US $3,770. Between 1965 and 1984, it was estimated, GNP per head increased, in real terms, at an average rate of 3.8% per year: the third highest rate of growth for any non-communist European country. It was estimated that the average annual increase of overall GDP, measured in constant prices, was 7.5% in 1965–73, slowing to 2.7% in 1973–84.

Mineral resources are intensively exploited, and a major development has been the processing of an expanding proportion of the ores in Greece, rather than exporting raw materials. In 1982 Greece was dependent on petroleum for 73% of its energy requirements. Petroleum and petroleum products accounted for 28.5% of the value of imports in 1985. Hydroelectric power resources are being developed, and in June 1981 the production of crude petroleum began from the Prinos oilfield, off the northern Aegean island of Thassos. Output from Prinos was expected to provide an estimated 13% of Greece's annual requirements. To replace power generated from lignite deposits, which are expected to be exhausted by the 1990s, the Greek Government had planned to construct nuclear power stations, but the project was temporarily halted in 1981, owing partly to a series of unusually severe and widespread earthquakes. Industry is being encouraged to switch from petroleum to alternative sources of power, principally coal. In 1979 uranium deposits were discovered in northern Greece, and in 1981 a natural gas field was discovered off the western Peloponnese. In March 1984 agreement was reached with the USSR on the joint construction of a plant on the Gulf of Corinth for the processing of Greek bauxite, with the aim of exporting 600,000 metric tons of alumina annually to Bulgaria and the USSR. The last major detail in negotiations for the $450m. project was resolved in November 1986.

The military regime, which relinquished power in 1974, left behind a stagnant economy, restricted by bureaucratic controls, and severe inflation. By 1975, however, the Karamanlis Government had restored confidence in the economy, and foreign investment rose considerably. The inflation rate averaged 12.1% in 1977, but had increased to over 20% by 1985. The rate of inflation was expected to exceed the 16% target set for 1986. The annual growth of GDP in Greece fluctuated between 0.2% and 2.4% in the years 1980–84. The growth of GDP was 1.8% in 1985, but only 0.5% in 1986. GDP was expected to decline marginally in 1987. Unemployment rose from 4.1% of the labour force in 1982 to an estimated 9.3% in 1986. In January 1983 the drachma was devalued by 15.5%, with the aim of stimulating income from exports and tourism by restoring price competitiveness.

Industrialization and the expansion of exports, which increased more than 11-fold between 1970 and 1980, have not saved Greece from a large deficit on the current account of its balance of payments, exacerbated in 1978–80 by a sharp rise in the cost of petroleum imports. In 1979 the deficit totalled US $1,886m., and in 1985 it reached a record $3,276m. (equivalent to about 8% of GDP). The target for the deficit in 1986 was set at $1,700m. but it was projected in late 1986 that the actual deficit would be $1,800m. In the first seven months of 1985 imports rose by 6.3% and exports fell by 7.9%, while external borrowing reached $1,840m., compared with a total of $1,530m. for 1984. The record deficit in 1985 reflected a decline in earnings from tourism, shipping and workers' remittances from abroad. Private capital inflows, which had covered about 90% of the deficit until 1979, fell to around 40%. This contributed to a virtual trebling of the foreign debt between 1978 and the end of 1984, to around $18,000m. In October 1986 it was estimated that Greece's debt to foreign institutions was about $15,300m. (roughly equivalent to 39% of annual GNP). It was projected that, by the end of 1986, the year's foreign borrowing would reach US $2,200m., bringing Greece's overall foreign debt to more than $17,000m. The level of foreign debt repayment over the period 1986–90 is expected to average $1,700m. per annum. The trade deficit rose from 212,582m. drachmae in 1979 to 541,203m. drachmae in 1984 and to 783,712m. drachmae in 1985, as the industrial sector, in particular, was adversely affected by competition from other countries in the EEC. The public-sector deficit has also risen because of mismanagement and indirect financing of consumption. In January 1986 the Ministry of National Economy established a 50-member secretariat to monitor public-sector bodies, with the aim of improving their efficiency and ensuring that they adhere to the Government's stringent targets for wage levels and public spending. In November the authorities expected to meet the public-sector deficit target comfortably, with a reduction of the public-sector borrowing requirement to about 14% of GDP, from 17.8% in 1985. The Government aimed to reduce the public-sector borrowing requirement to below 10% of GDP in 1987. The worsening economic crisis fuelled inflation, which remained at about 20% annually in the years 1980–85. In the 12 months to November 1986, at 19.8%, Greece had the highest annual rate of inflation in the EEC.

In October 1985 the Papandreou Government introduced a programme of austerity measures, aiming to reduce the current account deficit to $1,700m. in 1986 and to $1,600m. in 1987. The main measures were a 15% devaluation of the drachma; a two-year 'freeze' on wages, with extensive deregulation of the system of wage indexation; an import deposit scheme on about 40% of total imports; higher taxes and prices; and reductions in planned government spending. Plans to stimulate Greece's deteriorating economy, announced by the Government in August 1986, included the linking of wages to productivity rather than to inflation (effective from January 1988, when the virtual 'freeze' on wages was due to end) and, in an effort to reduce unemployment, the introduction of strict controls on the holding of second jobs by workers in both the public and private sectors. In late 1985 the EEC granted Greece a further one-year extension, to January 1987, of the deadline for the introduction of value-added tax (VAT) and deregulation of the petroleum market, and for ending the tax rebates on exports, as well as continuing to restrict the movement of capital. In late 1985 Greece decided to end restrictions on the repatriation of foreign capital brought into the country by EEC residents, and profits deriving from it, at the beginning of 1986. This liberalization was to be extended to residents of all foreign countries shortly thereafter. In November 1986 the Government ordered a three-month 'freeze' on the prices of all domestic and imported goods and services, in an attempt to discourage profiteering, upon the introduction of VAT on 1 January 1987. Products and services are subject to three basic VAT rates: of 6%, 18% and 36%. The 1986 budget proposals envisaged a 31.8% increase in total revenue, to 1,642,500m. drachmae, and a 20.3% increase in expenditure, to 2,212,000m. drachmae. This would result in an overall deficit of 569,500m. drachmae, 4% lower than the 1985 deficit and equivalent to 10.6% of GDP, compared with 13.1% in 1985. Provisional figures for the 1986 budget showed that the target of a 4% reduction in the budget deficit, compared with 1985, would not be met. This was due to excess spending of some 100,000m. drachmae, and in spite of slightly higher revenue than expected. The decrease in the deficit was projected at 1.4%. The budget for 1987 envisaged total expenditure of US $15,000m. It maintained high defence and welfare spending, while seeking to reduce the inflation rate. The 1987 budget deficit was forecast to widen by 5.2%, to 688,000m. drachmae. In November 1985 the EEC approved a loan of ECU 1,750m. (US $1,535m. at November 1985 values) for Greece to help the country to overcome its balance-of-payments problems, but linked the two-part loan to the implementation of strict economic conditions. The first instalment was made available immediately, but in December 1986 the disbursement of the second instalment was not approved at a meeting of the EEC monetary committee in Brussels.

The major part of Greece's external trade is with other members of the EEC. Under the transitional arrangements, subsequent to joining the EEC in January 1981, Greece agreed to remove all remaining tariff and quantitative controls by 1986. Greek agriculture was to be aligned with EEC policy over a period of seven years, with farm prices being raised gradually

GREECE

to meet the higher levels prevailing in other EEC countries. In 1981, for the first time, Greece had a trade deficit in agricultural products with EEC member states, while the total trade deficit with the EEC rose by 94%. In March 1982 the Government asked for special arrangements, pointing out that EEC rules on competition, subsidies and the protection of new industries were hindering Greek development, while the EEC's common agricultural policy, designed to assist the more advanced northern members, had brought no benefit to Greece. In response, the European Commission offered special assistance in the areas of transport, agriculture, employment, pollution and taxation reform, while Greece's share of Community aid under the 1985–91 Integrated Plan for the Mediterranean Region was to amount to 2,542m. ECUs (US $2,460m. at December 1982 values), of which 49% was for development and diversification of agriculture. The Commission insisted, however, that Greece should operate within existing Community rules, and refused to allow more than one-half of the import restrictions which had been proposed by Greece in January 1983. The agricultural trade deficit with the EEC showed an improvement in 1983, when it fell to 8,400m. drachmae from 19,700m. drachmae in 1982, owing to a drop in cereal imports and a rise in exports of olive oil, fruit and vegetables. In March 1985 the EEC agreed to grant Greece 2,000m. ECUs of development finance over the next seven years.

Social Welfare

There is a state social insurance scheme for wage-earners. Salaried staff are provided for by voluntary or staff insurances. Every citizen is entitled to an old-age pension and sickness benefit. In 1981 Greece had 688 hospital establishments, with a total of 59,914 beds, equivalent to one for every 162 inhabitants, and there were 24,724 physicians working in the country. Of total expenditure by the central government in 1981, about 86,700m. drachmae (10.1%) was for health, and a further 251,900m. drachmae (29.3%) for social security and welfare.

Education

Education is available free of charge at all levels, and is officially compulsory for all children between the ages of six and 15 years. Primary education begins at the age of six and lasts for six years. Secondary education, beginning at the age of 12, is generally for six years, divided into two equal cycles. In 1979 an estimated 93% of children in the relevant age-group attended primary schools, while secondary enrolment averaged 73% (boys 76%; girls 68%). Primary enrolment rose to 96% in 1980. Expenditure on education by the central government in 1981 was about 79,000m. drachmae (9.2% of total spending). Between 1951 and 1981 the average rate of adult illiteracy declined from 72% to 10%. In 1985, according to estimates by UNESCO, the rate was only 7.7% (males 2.9%; females 12.2%).

The vernacular language (demotiki) has replaced the formal version (katharevoussa) in secondary education, and a system of technical lycées is being expanded.

Tourism

The sunny climate, the natural beauty of the country and its great history and traditions have made Greece a magnet for tourists. There are numerous islands and other sites of archaeological interest. Tourism is expanding rapidly, with the improvement of transport and accommodation facilities. The number of tourists visiting Greece increased from 1m. in 1968 to 6m. in 1984 and 7m. in 1985. Earnings from tourism, which totalled US $120m. in 1968, amounted to $1,313m. in 1984 and $1,428m. in 1985.

Public Holidays

1987: 1 January (New Year's Day), 6 January (Epiphany), 2 March (Clean Monday), 25 March (Independence Day), 17–20 April (Greek Orthodox Easter), 1 May (Labour Day), 8 June (Holy Spirit Day), 15 August (Assumption of the Virgin Mary), 28 October ('Ochi' Day, anniversary of Greek defiance of Italy's 1940 ultimatum), 25–26 December (Christmas).

1988: 1 January (New Year's Day), 6 January (Epiphany), 22 February (Clean Monday), 25 March (Independence Day), 8–11 April (Greek Orthodox Easter), 1 May (Labour Day), 30 May (Holy Spirit Day), 15 August (Assumption of the Virgin Mary), 28 October ('Ochi' Day, anniversary of Greek defiance of Italy's 1940 ultimatum), 25–26 December (Christmas).

Weights and Measures

The metric system is in force.

Currency and Exchange Rates

100 leptae (singular: lepta) = 1 drachma.
Exchange rates (30 September 1986):
　£1 sterling = 193.82 drachmae;
　US $1 = 135.205 drachmae.

Statistical Survey

Source (unless otherwise stated): National Statistical Service of Greece, Odos Lycourgou 14–16, Athens; tel. (21) 3249302; telex 216734.

Area and Population

AREA, POPULATION AND DENSITY

Area (sq km)	131,957*
Population (census results)	
14 March 1971	8,768,641
5 April 1981	9,740,417
Population (official estimates at mid-year)	
1983	9,846,627
1984	9,895,801
1985	9,934,796
Density (per sq km) at mid-1985	75.3

* 50,949 sq miles.

PRINCIPAL TOWNS (population at 1981 census)

Athinai (Athens, the capital)	885,737		Larissa	102,426
Thessaloniki (Salonika)	406,413		Iraklion	102,398
			Volos	71,378
Piraeus	196,389		Kavala	56,705
Patras	142,163		Canea	47,451
			Serres	46,317

BIRTHS, MARRIAGES AND DEATHS

	Registered live births		Registered marriages		Registered deaths	
	Number	Rate (per 1,000)	Number	Rate (per 1,000)	Number	Rate (per 1,000)
1978	146,588	15.7	72,523	7.8	81,615	8.7
1979	147,965	15.7	79,023	8.4	82,338	8.7
1980	148,134	15.4	62,352	6.5	87,282	9.1
1981	140,953	14.5	71,178	7.3	86,261	8.9
1982	137,275	14.0	67,784	6.9	86,345	8.8
1983	132,608	13.5	71,143	7.2	90,586	9.2
1984	125,724	12.7	54,793	5.6	88,397	8.9
1985	116,481	11.7	63,709	6.4	92,886	9.3

ECONOMICALLY ACTIVE POPULATION
(estimates, June 1983*)

	Males	Females	Total
Agriculture, hunting, forestry and fishing	597,500	457,100	1,054,600
Mining and quarrying	28,500	2,000	30,500
Manufacturing	507,600	209,600	717,200
Electricity, gas and water	26,000	3,700	29,700
Construction	297,900	4,100	302,000
Trade, restaurants and hotels	355,400	195,700	551,100
Transport, storage and communications	240,500	26,500	267,000
Finance, insurance, real estate and business services	79,700	46,200	125,900
Community, social and personal services	316,200	248,400	564,600
Activities not adequately defined	22,500	36,200	58,700
Total	2,471,800	1,229,500	3,701,300

* Figures are based on a labour force sample survey (excluding institutional households) and relate to persons aged 14 years and over, excluding persons on compulsory military service. The data exclude persons seeking work for the first time, numbering 106,900 (males 37,700; females 69,200), but include other unemployed persons, numbering 192,400 (males 109,100; females 83,300).

1984 (labour force sample survey): Employed 3,500,500 (males 2,341,100; females 1,159,300); Unemployed 310,300 (males 150,100; females 160,200); Total labour force 3,810,700 (males 2,491,200; females 1,319,500).

Agriculture

PRINCIPAL CROPS ('000 metric tons)

	1983	1984*	1985*
Wheat	2,059	2,309	1,790
Rice (paddy)	86	92	103
Barley	624	890	606
Maize	1,758	2,091	1,948
Oats	62	67	65
Potatoes	1,135	1,053	1,009
Dry beans	32	32	31
Other pulses	23	19	18
Sunflower seed	27	69	—
Cottonseed	274	294	336
Cotton (lint)	128†	138	157
Olives	1,430	1,307	—
Cabbages	176	174	—
Tomatoes	1,869	2,345	2,238
Cucumbers and gherkins	141	140	—
Onions (dry)	136	130	144
Watermelons	609	571	598
Melons	110‡	117	126
Grapes	1,706†	1,565‡	1,568
Sugar beet	2,413	1,789	2,506
Apples	308	305	267
Pears	145	130	139
Peaches and nectarines	495	561	532
Oranges	663	757	608
Lemons and limes	190	171	192
Apricots	137	95	128
Nuts	90	81‡	85
Tobacco (leaves)	116	142	150

* Estimates.
† Unofficial estimate.
‡ FAO estimate.

LIVESTOCK ('000 head at December)

	1982	1983	1984*
Asses	209	199	188
Buffaloes	1	1	1
Cattle	792	755	725
Goats	4,637	4,744	4,816
Horses	86	80	74
Mules	99	94	89
Pigs	1,059	1,065	1,061
Sheep	8,227	8,252	8,258
Chickens	30,253	29,082	29,137
Ducks	108	105	107
Geese	43	44	44
Turkeys	149	158	149

* Estimates.

LIVESTOCK PRODUCTS (metric tons)

	1982	1983	1984†
Beef, veal and buffalo meat	98,514	95,404	91,517
Mutton, lamb and goat meat	122,203	123,686	126,631
Pig meat	146,115	146,896	148,048
Poultry meat*	131,756	124,137	120,971
Edible pig fat	4,699	4,760	4,286
Cows' milk	612,553	610,072	574,817
Buffaloes' milk	229	191	159
Sheep's milk	619,690	612,160	621,981
Goats' milk	445,763	456,103	462,822
Butter	5,665	5,462	5,591
Cheese:			
hard	35,063	34,942	34,901
soft	105,161	107,320	105,636
Fresh cream	3,378	3,410	3,460
Hen eggs	127,291	124,608	120,550
Honey	11,349	10,902	11,958
Raw silk	71	65	67
Wool: greasy	10,213	9,286	9,320
Hides and skins ('000 pieces):			
from small animals	7,472	7,565	7,559
from large animals	288	280	260

* Including meat from other small animals.
† Estimates.

GREECE

Forestry

ROUNDWOOD REMOVALS ('000 cubic metres, excl. bark)

	1982	1983	1984
Sawlogs, veneer logs and logs for sleepers	615	446	407
Pulpwood	141	170	142
Other industrial wood	23	226	219
Fuel wood	1,628	2,072	1,915
Total	2,407	2,914	2,683

Source: FAO, *Yearbook of Forest Products*.

SAWNWOOD PRODUCTION ('000 cubic metres, incl. boxboards)

	1982	1983	1984
Coniferous (softwood)	178	191	191
Broadleaved (hardwood)	185	132	130
Total	363	323	321

Source: FAO, *Yearbook of Forest Products*.

Fishing

('000 metric tons, live weight)

	1982	1983	1984
Inland waters	9.1	8.4	8.6†
Atlantic Ocean	9.6	8.6	9.0
Mediterranean*	84.3	80.9	88.1
Total catch*	103.0	97.9	105.7

* Excluding catches from vessels of less than 19 hp, estimated at 26,000 metric tons in 1981.
† Estimate.

Mining

('000 metric tons)

	1981	1982	1983
Lignite	27,303.7	27,326.2	30,705.5
Crude petroleum	196	1,120	1,330
Iron ore*	1,279.1	520	1,330
Bauxite	3,248.8	2,887.8	2,435.2
Zinc concentrates†	24.1	19.9	21.4
Lead concentrates†	22.3	18.9	19.4
Chromium ore†	20.8	23.2	n.a.
Magnesite	817.4	902.0	858.8
Kaolin (raw)	31.9	44.7	42.4
Perlite (raw)	57.1	88.0	32.0
Bentonite (raw)	102.6	121.9	144.1
Salt (unrefined)	130.6	105.4	147.7
Marble ('000 cubic metres)	216.4	211.3	207.4
Natural gas ('000 terajoules)	n.a.	4	3

* The estimated iron content is 43%.
† Figures refer to the metal content of ores and concentrates.

Industry

SELECTED PRODUCTS

		1981	1982	1983
Margarine	'000 metric tons	39.8	41.0	42.8
Olive oil (crude)	'000 metric tons	294.8	343.8	293.3
Wheat flour	'000 metric tons	885.1	860.6	n.a.
Raw sugar	'000 metric tons	322.6	229.5	297.5
Wine	'000 metric tons	259	275	305
Beer	'000 hectolitres	3,104	2,929	2,847
Cigarettes	metric tons	22,861	27,382	26,207
Cotton yarn (pure)	'000 metric tons	118.2	119.4	128.7
Woven cotton fabrics (pure and mixed)	metric tons	35,873	35,575	39,693
Flax, hemp and jute yarn (pure and mixed)	metric tons	2,403	2,226	1,801
Linen fabrics	metric tons	2,910	3,000	n.a.
Wool yarn (pure)	metric tons	13,299	11,404	11,068
Woven woollen fabrics (pure and mixed)[1]	metric tons	3,431	3,779	3,344
Non-cellulosic continuous filaments[2]	metric tons	8,869	9,506	n.a.
Woven fabrics of non-cellulosic fibres	metric tons	11,019	10,251	n.a.
Footwear (excl. rubber and plastic)	'000 pairs	16,141	13,134	12,599
Rubber footwear	'000 pairs	1,402	1,250	919
Paper and paperboard	'000 metric tons	284	273	270.6
Sulphuric acid	'000 metric tons	980	1,000	1,016
Hydrochloric acid (21° Bé)	'000 metric tons	49.7	40.1	40.5
Nitric acid (54% or 36.3° Bé)	'000 metric tons	274	395	440
Ammonia	'000 metric tons	284.1	271.5	275.9
Caustic soda (Sodium hydroxide)	'000 metric tons	33	33	30
Nitrogenous fertilizers (a)[3]	'000 metric tons	311.3	306.8	364.4
Phosphate fertilizers (b)[3]	'000 metric tons	170.4	143.4	166.7
Polyvinyl chloride	'000 metric tons	49.4	40.9	50.7
Liquefied petroleum gas	'000 metric tons	265	177	180
Naphthas	'000 metric tons	907.8	790.1	830.5
Motor spirit (petrol)	'000 metric tons	1,456	1,616	1,575
Jet fuels	'000 metric tons	1,783	1,619	1,608
Distillate fuel oils	'000 metric tons	4,099	4,014	3,901
Residual fuel oils	'000 metric tons	7,012	7,720	5,456
Coke-oven coke	'000 metric tons	47	—	—
Cement	'000 metric tons	13,366	13,297	14,196.3
Pig-iron	'000 metric tons	91	—	—
Crude steel (incl. alloys)	'000 metric tons	812	831	754.6
Aluminium (unwrought)	'000 metric tons	185.6	173.4	157.9
Refined lead (unwrought)	'000 metric tons	20.2	4.2	—
Refrigerators (household)	'000	227	185.4	149.8
Washing machines (household)	'000	84	77	88
Television receivers	'000	179	215	177
Lorries (Trucks)[4]	number	13,005	11,232	7,552
Electric energy	million kWh	21,657	21,554	22,048

[1] After undergoing finishing processes.
[2] Source: Textile Economic Bureau, New York.
[3] Production during 12 months ending 30 June of year stated. Figures are in terms of (a) nitrogen or (b) phosphoric acid.
[4] Assembled wholly or mainly from imported parts.

Finance

CURRENCY AND EXCHANGE RATES

Monetary Units
100 leptae (singular: lepta) = 1 drachma.

Denominations
Coins: 10, 20 and 50 leptae; 1, 2, 5, 10 and 20 drachmae.
Notes: 50, 100, 500 and 1,000 drachmae.

Sterling and Dollar Equivalents (30 September 1986)
£1 sterling = 193.82 drachmae;
US $1 = 135.205 drachmae;
1,000 drachmae = £5.159 = $7.396.

Average Exchange Rate (drachmae per US $)
1983   88.06
1984   112.72
1985   138.12

MONEY SUPPLY ('000 million drachmae at 31 December)

	1983	1984	1985
Currency outside banks	348.2	408.2	513.5
Private sector deposits at Bank of Greece	55.0	56.9	31.3
Demand deposits at commercial banks	122.4	166.5	199.4
Total money	525.6	631.6	744.2

Source: IMF, *International Financial Statistics*.

COST OF LIVING (Consumer Price Index. Base: 1982 = 100)

	1983	1984	1985
Foodstuffs	118.0	139.6	166.8
Alcohol, beverages and tobacco	118.6	141.5	162.4
Clothing and footwear	122.3	154.3	188.4
Housing	113.7	130.5	152.8
Household equipment	125.5	149.5	180.1
Medical and personal care	121.6	145.1	166.7
Education and recreation	126.2	152.4	188.7
Transport and communications	121.0	135.1	157.8
Miscellaneous	134.0	161.6	199.0
All items	120.2	142.4	169.9

BUDGET ESTIMATES (million drachmae)

Revenue	1983	1984	1985
Ordinary budget:			
Direct taxes	245,200	276,600	378,420
Excise duties	13,200	11,200	9,770
Indirect taxes	487,650	565,250	721,865
European Community	18,700	25,800	25,000
Other	35,550	56,150	79,945
Sub-total	800,300	935,000	1,215,000
Extraordinary budget:			
Revenue from investments	3,800	5,000	8,000
Aid and loans from abroad	82,450	106,100	127,000
Revenue from NATO works	3,660	5,392	6,730
Increase in national debt	89,700	110,000	140,000
Total	979,910	1,161,492	1,496,730

Expenditure	1983	1984	1985
Ordinary budget:			
Political ministries	672,488	814,352	1,093,211
Defence	146,033	176,546	204,319
European Community	22,400	34,200	36,750
Police and other sectors	40,633	46,732	55,020
Sub-total	881,554	1,071,830	1,389,300
Provision for increase	48,743	30,500	20,000
Sub-total	930,297	1,102,330	1,409,300
Extraordinary budget:			
Expenditure on NATO works	3,313	4,862	4,800
Investments	175,000	220,000	275,000
Total	1,108,610	1,327,192	1,689,100

INTERNATIONAL RESERVES
(US $ million at 31 December)

	1983	1984	1985
Gold*	142.2	140.9	862.8
IMF special drawing rights	0.6	1.1	—
Reserve position in IMF	90.2	79.8	82.4
Foreign exchange	809.7	873.3	785.6
Total	1,042.7	1,095.1	1,730.8

* Valued at 35 SDRs per troy ounce in 1983 and 1984. Beginning in December 1985, gold reserves are valued at market-related prices.

Source: IMF, *International Financial Statistics*.

NATIONAL ACCOUNTS (million drachmae at current prices)

	1983	1984*	1985†
Gross domestic product at factor cost	2,706,100	3,317,770	4,025,537
of which:			
Agriculture	462,769	593,421	700,237
Manufacturing	491,571	601,761	720,300
Wholesale and retail trade (incl. banking, insurance, etc.)	419,159	512,640	617,750
Public administration and defence	291,340	361,340	1,987,250
Other activities	1,041,261	1,248,608	
Income from abroad	30,408	1,865	−33,800
Gross national product (GNP) at factor cost	2,736,508	3,319,635	3,991,737
Less depreciation allowances	−272,598	−329,253	−402,550
National income at factor cost	2,463,910	2,990,382	3,589,187
Indirect taxes, less subsidies	345,934	452,058	501,608
National income in market prices	2,809,844	3,442,440	4,090,795
Depreciation allowances	272,598	329,253	402,550
GNP in market prices	3,082,442	3,771,693	4,493,345
Balance of exports and imports of goods and services, and borrowing‡	285,465	312,592	569,690
Available resources	3,367,907	4,084,285	5,063,035
of which:			
Private consumption expenditure§	2,135,777	2,580,545	3,230,655
Government consumption expenditure	579,370	724,490	900,680
Fixed capital formation‡	624,000	698,500	859,800
Change in stocks	28,760	80,750	71,900

* Provisional.   † Estimates.   ‡ Excluding ships operating overseas.
§ Including statistical discrepancies (million drachmae): 117,853 in 1983; 149,803 in 1984; 264,372 in 1985.

BALANCE OF PAYMENTS (US $ million)

	1983	1984	1985
Merchandise exports f.o.b.	4,106	4,394	4,293
Merchandise imports f.o.b.	−8,400	−8,624	−9,346
Trade balance	−4,294	−4,230	−5,053
Exports of services	3,060	2,939	2,818
Imports of services	−2,411	−2,473	−2,707
Balance of goods and services	−3,645	−3,764	−4,942
Private unrequited transfers (net)	931	917	797
Government unrequited transfers (net)	836	715	869
Current balance	−1,878	−2,132	−3,276
Direct capital investment (net)	439	485	447
Other long-term capital (net)	1,671	1,288	2,396
Short-term capital (net)	181	732	413
Net errors and omissions	−313	−242	563
Total (net monetary movements)	100	131	543
Valuation changes (net)	−60	−69	80
Changes in reserves	39	62	623

Source: IMF, *International Financial Statistics*.

External Trade

PRINCIPAL COMMODITIES (million drachmae)

Imports c.i.f.	1983	1984	1985
Food and live animals	99,778	124,613	161,844
Meat and meat preparations	45,886	51,334	60,961
Fresh, chilled or frozen meat	43,999	48,890	58,173
Crude materials (inedible) except fuels	52,183	63,189	80,708
Textile fibres and waste	14,784	18,395	23,948
Mineral fuels, lubricants, etc.	232,440	295,916	416,522
Petroleum and petroleum products	221,965	277,165	402,538
Crude petroleum	211,171	253,046	363,927
Petroleum products*	8,631	21,815	34,986
Chemicals	70,829	96,998	121,036
Chemical elements and compounds	20,395	29,059	35,181
Plastic materials, etc.	18,192	24,065	29,913
Basic manufactures	140,615	171,054	224,365
Textile yarn, fabrics, etc.	26,958	11,612	15,128
Iron and steel	38,707	42,924	59,268
Machinery and transport equipment	210,444	278,064	333,852
Non-electric machinery	80,003	99,730	114,411
Electrical machinery, apparatus, etc.	19,898	24,411	33,367
Transport equipment	99,863	140,891	165,351
Road motor vehicles and parts (excl. tyres, engines and electrical parts)	50,826	52,783	79,893
Ships and boats	47,141	81,448	77,321
Miscellaneous manufactured articles	29,775	42,409	56,555
Total (incl. others)	848,295	1,083,880	1,412,797

Exports f.o.b.	1983	1984	1985
Food and live animals	86,417	119,445	134,142
Fruit and vegetables	56,964	76,048	95,824
Fresh fruit and nuts (excl. oil nuts)†	17,683	20,493	30,946
Dried fruit†	10,301	14,980	16,947
Dried grapes (raisins)	8,683	12,705	14,839
Preserved or prepared vegetables	15,441	20,826	22,933
Beverages and tobacco	21,089	25,115	28,651
Tobacco and manufactures	17,410	20,664	21,202
Unmanufactured tobacco	17,135	20,423	20,792
Crude materials (inedible) except fuels	26,286	38,998	46,666
Mineral fuels, lubricants, etc.	27,192	54,909	75,780
Petroleum products*	25,397	45,787	62,231
Chemicals	16,779	21,544	25,469
Basic manufactures	118,443	161,472	180,991
Textile yarn, fabrics, etc.	38,845	52,213	57,407
Textile yarn and thread	24,373	34,184	37,159
Non-metallic mineral manufactures	26,927	28,094	31,254
Lime, cement, etc.	23,641	24,913	27,545
Cement	20,467	20,739	22,414
Iron and steel	17,026	35,295	40,576
Non-ferrous metals	16,027	22,574	24,125
Aluminium and aluminium alloys	13,376	19,084	19,718
Machinery and transport equipment	13,585	13,760	18,351
Miscellaneous manufactured articles	57,008	83,109	104,471
Clothing (excl. footwear)	46,832	68,119	87,052
Total (incl. others)	392,652	542,677	629,085

* Including partly refined petroleum.
† Dried citrus fruit and dried tropical fruit are included with 'fresh fruit and nuts'.

PRINCIPAL TRADING PARTNERS* (million drachmae)

Imports c.i.f.	1983	1984	1985
Austria	12,386.9	10,094.9	14,864.3
Belgium/Luxembourg	27,292.6	26,844.9	39,532.4
Brazil	7,188.2	8,230.0	9,677.7
Denmark	8,189.0	10,059.9	15,324.0
Egypt	544.1	1,653.4	9,454.0
France	57,745.7	74,607.2	90,924.8
German Democratic Republic	4,130.8	10,315.5	8,856.9
Germany, Federal Republic	146,390.2	180,336.9	240,359.5
Iran	9,067.1	7.0	7,704.5
Iraq	42,074.4	38,102.5	66,048.7
Italy	75,379.3	104,442.6	131,962.9
Japan	57,202.4	82,350.6	89,733.6
Netherlands	54,799.5	66,475.1	82,409.4
Romania	8,937.7	6,511.7	7,795.8
Saudi Arabia	104,715.6	73,411.0	113,583.1
Spain	5,842.0	14,627.5	17,928.5
Sweden	8,548.8	14,629.9	14,149.3
Switzerland	10,052.7	12,655.1	18,601.1
USSR	21,729.1	57,259.0	73,545.3
United Kingdom	34,945.8	42,811.2	53,411.5
USA	31,038.9	31,755.2	44,437.3
Yugoslavia	6,454.3	11,752.9	14,711.6
Total (incl. others)	848,294.8	1,083,940.4	1,412,797.3

Exports f.o.b.	1983	1984	1985
Belgium/Luxembourg	7,079.4	9,554.5	11,791.8
Bulgaria	4,580.8	4,637.9	6,091.6
Cyprus	6,078.1	9,167.1	11,649.9
Egypt	13,894.7	18,399.6	19,801.5
France	29,231.1	46,829.5	50,226.9
Germany, Federal Republic	78,809.9	106,600.1	126,292.7
Hungary	3,149.0	2,720.3	2,141.1
Iraq	4,735.4	6,048.6	6,282.9
Italy	53,050.3	73,257.8	71,195.9
Japan	2,310.1	6,072.9	5,890.8
Lebanon	4,384.2	5,824.0	5,758.6
Libya	9,125.9	9,886.9	6,533.9
Netherlands	15,032.3	18,354.6	25,534.1
Romania	4,580.8	4,276.6	5,419.3
Saudi Arabia	28,556.2	27,636.0	24,990.4
Sweden	1,673.3	3,498.0	5,047.7
Syria	3,107.1	3,862.5	4,981.6
USSR	1,624.5	13,662.7	19,528.2
United Kingdom	19,010.2	34,062.1	43,602.8
USA	24,640.4	45,093.3	51,267.7
Yugoslavia	5,633.8	7,176.5	10,303.9
Total (incl. others)	392,652.1	542,676.6	629,084.8

* Imports by country of first consignment; exports by country of consumption.

Transport

RAILWAYS (millions)

	1983	1984	1985*
Passenger-kilometres	1,628.7	1,541.1	1,501.8
Net ton-kilometres	670.1	769.6	733.0

* Estimates.

ROAD TRAFFIC (motor vehicles in use at 31 December)

	1983*	1984*	1985*
Passenger cars	1,070,352	1,155,946	1,264,375
Buses and coaches	17,992	18,242	18,638
Goods vehicles	538,669	572,210	602,086
Motorcycles, etc.	140,104	154,539	169,024

* Estimates.

CIVIL AVIATION
(domestic and foreign flights of Olympic Airways)

	1983	1984	1985
Kilometres flown ('000)	41,692	47,660	52,918
Passenger-kilometres ('000)	5,323,748	6,311,774	7,468,306
Freight ton-kilometres ('000)	65,477	73,767	103,246
Mail ton-kilometres ('000)	8,484	10,490	11,744

SHIPPING
Merchant fleet (at 1 July)

	1985 Vessels	1985 Gross reg. tons	1986 Vessels	1986 Gross reg. tons
Cargo boats	1,610	18,796,073	1,339	16,097,464
Passenger boats	328	618,360	340	600,543
Tankers	367	9,988,755	347	10,740,908
Others	281	83,941	286	84,038

Freight traffic

	1982	1983	1984†
Vessels entered ('000 net reg. tons)	146,397	148,006	141,608
Goods loaded ('000 metric tons)*	19,627	19,729	20,326
Goods unloaded ('000 metric tons)*	29,200	27,087	28,226

* International sea-borne shipping. † Provisional.

Tourism

FOREIGN TOURIST ARRIVALS

	1983	1984	1985
Cruise passengers	479,895	504,074	465,435
Other tourists	4,778,477	5,523,192	6,573,993
Total	5,258,372	6,027,266	7,039,428
Earnings (US $'000)	1,175,727	1,312,751	1,428,030

TOURISTS BY COUNTRY OF ORIGIN
(foreign citizens, excluding cruise passengers)

Country	1983	1984	1985
Australia	83,230	96,953	121,894
Austria	195,381	237,918	282,468
Canada	72,540	82,226	102,552
Denmark	148,626	124,037	160,792
France	299,506	405,907	441,141
German Democratic Republic			
Germany, Federal Republic	728,478	864,000	1,050,078
Italy	327,610	328,598	364,177
Netherlands	153,672	192,879	280,309
Sweden	189,921	194,356	223,956
Switzerland	173,830	156,995	205,662
United Kingdom	888,991	1,043,363	1,329,259
USA	406,887	474,845	466,155
Yugoslavia	55,375	263,209	350,735
Others	1,050,767	1,055,746	1,194,319
Unspecified	3,663	2,160	496
Total	4,778,477	5,523,192	6,573,993

Communications Media

	1979	1980	1981
Radio receivers ('000 in use)	2,900	3,310	3,400
Television receivers ('000 licensed)	1,385	1,500	1,550
Telephones ('000 in use)	2,664	2,796	2,943
Book titles published*	4,664	4,048	n.a.
Newspapers:			
Daily	116	n.a.	n.a.
Non-daily	871	n.a.	n.a.
Other periodicals	868	n.a.	n.a.

* Figures include pamphlets (647 in 1979; 430 in 1980).

Television receivers: 1.7 million in 1982.
Telephones: 3,100,749 in 1982; 3,302,355 in 1983; 3,520,674 in 1984; 3,714,752 in 1985.
Newspapers, etc: daily 131 in 1982, 143 in 1984; non-daily 875 in 1982, 872 in 1984; periodicals 858 in 1984.

Education

(1983/84)

	Institutions	Teachers	Students
Pre-primary	5,003	7,132	158,816
Primary	9,234	34,958	896,339*
Secondary:			
General	2,399	37,882	690,382
Vocational	605	7,886	99,984
Higher:			
Universities	13	7,836	100,254
Other	94	4,231	48,261

* Provisional.

Directory

The Constitution

A new constitution for the Hellenic Republic came into force on 11 June 1975. The main provisions of this Constitution, as subsequently amended, are summarized below.

Greece shall be a parliamentary democracy with a President as Head of State. All powers are derived from the people and exist for the benefit of the people. The established religion is that of The Eastern Orthodox Church of Christ.

EXECUTIVE AND LEGISLATIVE

The President

In March 1986 a series of amendments to the Constitution was approved by a majority vote of Parliament, which relieved the President of his executive power and transferred such power to the legislature, thus reducing the Head of State to a purely ceremonial figure.

The President is elected by Parliament for a period of five years. The re-election of the same person shall be permitted only once. The President represents the State in relations with other nations, is Supreme Commander of the armed forces and may declare war and conclude treaties. The President shall appoint the Prime Minister and, on the Prime Minister's recommendation, the other members of the Government. The President shall convoke Parliament once every year and in extraordinary session whenever he deems it reasonable. In exceptional circumstances the President may preside over the Cabinet, call the Council of the Republic, and suspend Parliament for a period not exceeding 30 days. In the amendment of March 1986, the President lost the right to dismiss the Prime Minister, his power to call a referendum was limited, and the right to declare a state of emergency was transferred to Parliament. The President can now dissolve Parliament only if the resignation of two Governments in quick succession demonstrates the absence of political stability. If no party has a majority in Parliament, the President must offer an opportunity to form a government to each of the four biggest parties' leaders in turn, strictly following the order of their parliamentary strengths. If no party leader is able to form a government, the President may try to assemble an all-party government; failing that, the President must appoint a caretaker Cabinet, led by a senior judge, to hold office until a fresh election takes place. The Constitution continues to reserve a substantial moderating role for the President, however, in that he retains the right to object to legislation and may request Parliament to reconsider it or to approve it with an enlarged majority.

The Government

The Government consists of the Cabinet which comprises the Prime Minister and Ministers. The Government determines and directs the general policy of the State in accordance with the Constitution and the laws. The Cabinet must enjoy the confidence of Parliament and may be removed by a vote of no confidence. The Prime Minister is to be the leader of the party with an absolute majority in Parliament, or, if no such party exists, the leader of the party with a relative majority.

The Council of the Republic

The Council of the Republic shall be composed of all former democratic Presidents, the Prime Minister, the leader of the

GREECE

Opposition and the parliamentary Prime Ministers of governments which have enjoyed the confidence of Parliament, presided over by the President. It shall meet when the largest parties are unable to form a government with the confidence of Parliament and may empower the President to appoint a Prime Minister who may or may not be a member of Parliament. The Council may also authorize the President to dissolve Parliament.

Parliament

Parliament is to be unicameral and composed of not fewer than 200 and not more than 300 deputies elected by direct, universal and secret ballot for a term of four years. Parliament shall elect its own President, or Speaker. It must meet once a year for a regular session of at least five months. Bills passed by Parliament must be ratified by the President and the President's veto can be nullified by an absolute majority of the total number of deputies. Parliament may impeach the President by a motion signed by one-third and passed by two-thirds of the total number of deputies. Parliament is also empowered to impeach present or former members of the Government. In these cases the defendant shall be brought before an *ad hoc* tribunal presided over by the President of the Supreme Court and composed of twelve judges. Certain legislative work, as specified in the Constitution, must be passed by Parliament in plenum, and Parliament cannot make a decision without an absolute majority of the members present, which under no circumstances shall be less than one-quarter of the total number of deputies. The Constitution provides for certain legislative powers to be exercised by not more than two Parliamentary Departments. Parliament may revise the Constitution in accordance with the procedure laid down in the Constitution.

THE JUDICIAL AUTHORITY

Justice is to be administered by courts of regular judges, who enjoy personal and functional independence. The President, after consultations with a judicial council, shall appoint the judges for life. The judges are subject only to the Constitution and the laws. Courts are divided into administrative, civil and penal and shall be organized by virtue of special laws. They must not apply laws which are contrary to the Constitution. The final jurisdiction in matters of judicial review rests with a Special Supreme Tribunal.

Certain laws, passed before the implementation of this constitution and deemed not contrary to it, are to remain in force. Other specified laws, even if contrary to the Constitution, are to remain in force until repealed by further legislation.

INDIVIDUAL AND SPECIAL RIGHTS

All citizens are equal under the Constitution and before the law, having the same rights and obligations. No titles of nobility or distinction are to be conferred or recognized. All persons are to enjoy full protection of life, honour and freedom, irrespective of nationality, race, creed or political allegiance. Retrospective legislation is prohibited and no citizen may be punished without due process of law. Freedom of speech, of the Press, of association and of religion are guaranteed under the Constitution. All persons have the right to a free education, which the state has the duty to provide. Work is a right and all workers, irrespective of sex or other distinction, are entitled to equal remuneration for rendering services of equal value. The right of peaceful assembly, the right of a person to property and the freedom to form political parties are guaranteed under the Constitution. The exercise of the right to vote by all citizens over 18 years of age is obligatory. No person may exercise his rights and liberties contrary to the Constitution.

MOUNT ATHOS

The district of Mount Athos shall, in accordance with its ancient privileged status, be a self-governing part of the Greek State and its sovereignty shall remain unaffected.

The Government

HEAD OF STATE

President: Christos Sartzetakis (took office 30 March 1985).

THE CABINET
(February 1987)

Prime Minister: Andreas Papandreou.
Deputy Prime Minister and Minister of Defence: Yannis Charalambopoulos.

Minister in charge of the Prime Minister's Office: Apostolos Kaklamanis.
Minister of the Interior: Emmanouil Papastefanakis.
Minister of Public Order: Antonis Drossoyannis.
Minister of Foreign Affairs: Karolos Papoulias.
Minister of National Economy: Costas Simitis.
Minister of Health, Welfare and Social Services: Yeorgios Alexandros Mangakis.
Minister of Justice: Elevtherios Verivakis.
Minister of Education and Religion: Antonios Tritsis.
Minister of Culture: Melina Mercouri.
Minister of Finance: Dimitris Tsovolas.
Minister of Northern Greece: Stilianos Papathemelis.
Minister of the Aegean: Petros Valvis.
Minister of Agriculture: Yannis Pottakis.
Minister of the Environment, Town Planning and Public Works: Evangelos Kouloumbis.
Minister of Labour: Konstandinos Papanayiotou.
Minister of Industry, Energy and Technology: Anastasios Peponis.
Minister of Commerce: Panayiotis Roumeliotis.
Minister of Transport and Communications: Konstandinos Bandouvas.
Minister of Merchant Marine: Stathis Alexandris.
Minister without Portfolio: Athanasios Filippopoulos.

There are also 19 Deputy Ministers and two Alternate Ministers.

MINISTRIES

Ministry to the President: Odos Zalokosta 10, Athens; tel. (01) 3630911; telex 216325.
Ministry to the Prime Minister: Leoforos Vassilissis Sophias 15, 106 74 Athens; tel. (01) 3646350; telex 214333.
Ministry of Agriculture: Odos Aharnon 2–6, Athens; tel. (01) 3291206; telex 215308.
Ministry of Commerce: Kanningos Sq., Athens; tel. (01) 3616251; telex 215282.
Ministry of Communications: Leoforos Syngrou 49, Athens; tel. (01) 9233941; telex 216369.
Ministry of Culture and Sciences: Odos Aristidou 14, Athens; tel. (01) 3243015; telex 222156.
Ministry of Defence: Holargos, Athens; tel. (01) 6465201.
Ministry of Education and Religion: Odos Metropoleos 15, Athens; tel. (01) 3230461; telex 216059.
Ministry of Finance: Odos Karageorgi Servias 10, Athens; tel. (01) 3224071; telex 216373.
Ministry of Foreign Affairs: Odos Zalokosta 2, Athens; tel. (01) 3610581.
Ministry of Health, Welfare and Social Security: Odos Zalokosta 10, Athens; tel. (01) 3630911; telex 21625.
Ministry of Industry, Energy and Technology: Odos Zalokosta 10, Athens; tel. (01) 3630911; telex 216325.
Ministry of the Interior: Odos Stadiou 27, Athens; tel. (01) 3223521; telex 215776.
Ministry of Justice: Odos Zinonos 12, Athens; tel. (01) 5225903; telex 216352.
Ministry of Labour: Odos Pireos 40, Athens; tel. (01) 5233110; telex 216608.
Ministry of Merchant Shipping: Odos Vas. Sophias 150, Piraeus; tel. (01) 4121211; telex 211232.
Ministry of National Economy: Syntagma Sq., Athens; tel. (01) 3230911; telex 221086.
Ministry of Natural Resources: Odos Mihalakopoulou 80, Athens; tel. (01) 215811; telex 215811.
Ministry of Northern Greece: Odos El. Venizelou 48, Thessaloniki; tel. (31) 264321.
Ministry of Physical Planning, Housing and Environment: Odos Amaliados 17, Athens; tel. (01) 6431461; telex 216374.
Ministry of Public Order: Odos 3rd September 48, Athens; tel. (01) 8236011; telex 216353.
Ministry of Public Works: Odos Har Trikoupi 182; tel. (01) 3618311; telex 216353.

GREECE

Legislature

VOULI

President of Parliament: IOANNIS ALEVRAS.

General Election, 2 June 1985

	Votes	%	Seats
Panhellenic Socialist Movement (PASOK)	2,916,450	45.82	161
New Democracy (ND)	2,599,949	40.85	126
Communist Party (KKE—Exterior)	629,518	9.89	12
Communist Party (KKE—Interior)*	117,050	1.84	1
Others	102,072	1.60	—

* Renamed New Hellenic Left Party in May 1986.

Political Organizations

Communist Party of Greece—Exterior (Kommunistiko Komma Ellados—KKE—Exterior) ('Orthodox', 'of the Exterior'): Odos Kapodistriou 16, 147 Athens; f. 1918; banned 1947, reappeared 1974; Moscow-line communist party; Gen. Sec. CHARILAOS FLORAKIS.

Democratic Centre Union (Enosi Demokratikou Kentrou—EDIK): Odos Charilaou Trikoupi 18, 106 79 Athens; tel. (01) 3612792; telex 216689; f. 1974; democratic socialist party, merging Centre Union (f. 1961 by GEORGIOS PAPANDREOU) and New Political Forces (f. 1974 by Prof. IOANNIS PESMAZOGLOU and Prof. G. A. MANGAKIS); favours membership of the EEC; Leader Dr IOANNIS G. ZIGHDIS.

Democratic Renewal: Athens; f. 1985 by former ND deputies; populist; advocates Greek independence from NATO; Leader KOSTIS STEFANOPOULOS.

Democratic Socialist Party (KODISO): Odos Mavromichali 9, Athens; tel. (01) 3600724; f. March 1979 by former EDIK deputies; liberal; favours membership of the EEC and political wing of NATO, decentralization and a mixed economy; Sec.-Gen. CH. PROTOPAPAS.

Greek National Political Society (EPEN): Athens; f. 1984; right-wing; Leader GEORGIOS PAPADOPOULOS.

Liberal Party: Vissarionos 1, Athens; f. 1981; aims to revive political heritage of fmr Prime Minister, Eleftherios Venizelos; Leader NIKITAS VENIZELOS.

New Democracy Party (Nea Demokratia—ND): Odos Rigillis 18, 106 74 Athens; tel. (01) 7290071; telex 210856; f. 1974 by CONSTANTINE KARAMANLIS; broadly-based party with policy of pragmatic social and economic reform, Greek sovereignty and military independence; favours membership of the EEC; Leader CONSTANTINE MITSOTAKIS.

New Hellenic Left Party (formerly known as the Greek Communist Party of the Interior): 1 Eleftherias Sq., Athens; tel. (01) 3217516; f. 1968 after split from pro-Soviet Communist Party of Greece as liberal Marxist movement, free from Soviet domination; renamed in May 1986 when it also discarded Marxism-Leninism from its ideological charter and reconstituted itself as a broader party of the left; Pres. LEONIDAS KYRKOS; Sec. YANNIS BANIAS.

Panhellenic Socialist Movement (Panellinion Socialistikou Kinema—PASOK): Odos Charilaou Trikoupi 50, Athens; tel. (01) 3232049; telex 218763; f. 1974; incorporates Democratic Defence and Panhellenic Liberation Movement resistance organizations; favours socialization of the means of production, decentralization and self-management, aims at a Mediterranean socialist development through international co-operation; 500 local organizations, 30,000 members; Leader ANDREAS PAPANDREOU.

Progressive Party: Odos Panepistimiou 6, Athens; tel. (01) 3636513; f. 1979; right-wing; Leader PAPAGEORGIOU APOSTOLOS.

United Democratic Left (Eniaia Demokratike Aristerá—EDA): Odos Academias 62, Athens; tel. (01) 3238615; f. 1951; banned 1967-74; broad left-wing parliamentary group, acted as front for banned Communist Party 1951-67; Leader MANOLIS GLEZOS.

Other parties include the People's Militant Unity Party (f. 1985 by PASOK splinter group), the (Maoist) Revolutionary Communist Party of Greece (EKKE) and the left-wing United Socialist Alliance of Greece (ESPE, f. 1984).

Diplomatic Representation

EMBASSIES IN GREECE

Albania: Odos Karachristou 1, Athens; tel. (01) 7234412; Ambassador: KSENOFON NUCHI.

Algeria: Leoforos Vassileos Konstantinou 14, Athens; tel. (01) 7513560; Chargé d'affaires a.i.: ABDERRAHM ABOURA.

Argentina: Leoforos Vassilissis Sofias 59, Athens; tel. (01) 7224753; telex 215218; Ambassador: HIPÓLITO JESÚS PAZ.

Australia: Leoforos Messoghion 15, Athens; tel. (01) 7757650; telex 215815; Ambassador: DONALD JOHNSON KINGSMILL.

Austria: Leoforos Alexandras 26, 106 83 Athens; tel. (01) 8211036; telex 215938; Ambassador: Dr HELLMUTH STRASSER.

Belgium: Odos Sekeri 3, Athens; tel. (01) 3617886; Chargé d'affaires a.i.: MARC M. L. THUNUS.

Brazil: Platia Philikis Etairias 14, Athens; tel. (01) 7213039; telex 216604; Ambassador: ALARICO SILVEIRA JUNIOR.

Bulgaria: Odos Akademias 12, Athens; tel. (01) 3609411; Ambassador: PETAR ILIEV SLAVTCHEV.

Canada: Odos Ioannou Ghennadiou 4, 115 21 Athens; tel. (01) 7239511; Ambassador: ANDRÉ COUVRETTE.

Chile: Leoforos Vasilissis Sofias 96, Athens; tel. (01) 7775017; Chargé d'affaires a.i.: MANUEL ATRIA.

China, People's Republic: Odos Krinon 2, Palaio Psychico, Athens; tel. (01) 6723282; Ambassador: CHANG HONGSHENG.

Cuba: Odos Davaki 10, Athens; tel. (01) 6925367; Ambassador: M. F. ALFONSO RODRÍGUEZ.

Cyprus: Odos Herodotou 16, Athens; tel. (01) 7237883; Ambassador: DEMOS HADJIMILTIS.

Czechoslovakia: Odos Georges Seferis 6, Palaio Psychico, Athens; tel. (01) 6713755; Ambassador: JOZEF NALEPKA.

Denmark: Platia Philikis Etairias 15, 106732 Athens; tel. (01) 7249315; telex 215586; Chargé d'affaires a.i.: OTTO SCHEPELERN.

Egypt: Leoforos Vassilissis Sofias 3, Athens; tel. (01) 3618612; Chargé d'affaires a.i.: SAID ABDEL FATTAH RAGAB.

Ethiopia: Odos Davaki 10, Erythros, 115 26 Athens; tel. (01) 6920483; telex 218548; Ambassador: SAMUEL TEFERRA.

Finland: Odos Eratosthenous 1, 116 35 Athens; tel. (01) 7011775; Ambassador: PAUL GEORGE TYRKAENKALLIO.

France: Leoforos Vassilissis Sofias 7; tel. (01) 3611663; Ambassador: PIERRE LOUIS BLANC.

German Democratic Republic: Vassileos Pavlou 7, Palaio Psychico, Athens; tel. (01) 6725160; telex 214544; Ambassador: HORST BRIE.

Germany, Federal Republic: POB 3071, Odos Caraoli Dimitriou 3, 102 10 Athens; tel. (01) 36941; Ambassador: Dr RÜDIGER VON PACHELBEL.

Honduras: Leoforos Vassilissis Sofias 86, Athens; tel. (01) 7775802; Chargé d'affaires a.i.: TEODOLINDA DE MAKRIS.

Hungary: Odos Kalvou 16, Palaio Psychico, Athens; tel. (01) 6714889; Ambassador: IMRE HOLLAI.

India: Odos Meleagrou 4, Athens; tel. (01) 7216481; Ambassador: BENI PRASAD AGARWAL.

Iran: Odos Kalari 16, Palaio Psychico, Athens; tel. (01) 6471436; Ambassador: AHMAD AJALLOOEIAN.

Iraq: Odos Mazaraki 4, Palaio Psychico, Athens; tel. (01) 6715012; Ambassador: NABIL NAJIM.

Ireland: Leoforos Vassileos Konstantinou 7, Athens; tel. (01) 7232771; telex 218111; Ambassador: CHARLES V. WHELAN.

Israel: Odos Marathonodromou 1, Palaio Psychico, 154 52 Athens; tel. (01) 6719530; Chargé d'affaires a.i.: ARIE TENNE.

Italy: Odos Sekeri 2, Athens; tel. (01) 3611722; Ambassador: MARCO PISA.

Japan: 21st Floor, Athens A Tower, Leoforos Messoghion 2-4, Ambelokipi, 115 27 Athens; tel. (01) 7758101; telex 214460; Ambassador: TSUNEO TANAKA.

Jordan: Odos Palaio Zervou 30, Palaio Psychico, 154 52 Athens; tel. (01) 6474161; telex 219366; Ambassador: Lt-Col AWWAD AL-KHALDI.

GREECE

Korea, Republic: Odos Eratosthenous 1, Athens; tel. (01) 7012122; telex 216202; Ambassador: SHIM KI-CHUL.

Kuwait: Odos Alex. Papanastassiou, Athens; tel. (01) 6473593; Ambassador: MOHAMAD SALEM AL-BALHAN.

Lebanon: Leoforos Kifissias 26, Athens; tel. (01) 7785158; Ambassador: CHAWKI CHOUERI.

Libya: Odos Vironos 13, Paleo Psychico, Athens; tel. (01) 6472120; Ambassador: ABDALLA ABUMAHARA.

Mexico: Leoforos Vassileos Konstantinou 5–7, 106 74 Zappio, Athens; tel. (01) 7230754; telex 216172; Ambassador: OLGA PELLICER.

Morocco: Odos Mousson 14, Paleo Psychico, Athens; tel. (01) 6474209; Ambassador: MUHAMMAD FASSI FIHRI.

Netherlands: Leoforos Vassileos Konstantinou 5–7, 106 74 Athens; tel. (01) 7239701; telex 215971; Ambassador: G. W. VAN BARNEVELD KOOY.

New Zealand: An. Tsoha 15–17, Ambelokipi, 115 21 Athens; tel. (01) 6410311; telex 216630; Ambassador: DONALD HARPER.

Norway: Leoforos Vassileos Konstantinou 7, 106 74 Athens; tel. (01) 7246173; telex 215109; Ambassador: KJELL RASMUSSEN.

Pakistan: Odos Loukianou 6, Athens; tel. (01) 790122; Ambassador: MUZAFFAR KHAN MALIK.

Panama: Leoforos Vassilissis Sofias 21, Athens; tel. (01) 3631847; Ambassador: MARÍA LAKAS BAHAS.

Poland: Odos Chryssanthemon 22, Palaio Psychico, Athens; tel. (01) 6716917; Ambassador: JÓZEF TEJCHMA.

Portugal: Odos Loukianou 19, Athens; tel. (01) 790096; Ambassador: JOÃO MORAIS DA CUNHA MATOS.

Romania: Odos Emmanuel Benaki 7, Palaio Psychico, Athens; tel. (01) 6718008; Ambassador: NICOLAE ECOBESCU.

Saudi Arabia: Odos Marathonodromou 71, Palaio Psychico, 154 52 Athens; tel. (01) 6716911; Ambassador: Sheikh ABDULLAH ABDUL-RAHMAN AL-MALHOOQ.

South Africa: Leoforos Kifissias 124, Athens; tel. (01) 6922125; telex 218165; Ambassador: JOHN FRANS JOHANNES CRONJE.

Spain: Leoforos Vassilissis Sofias 29, Athens; tel. (01) 7214885; telex 215860; Ambassador: ENRIQUE MAHOU STAUFFER.

Sweden: Leoforos Vassileos Konstantinou 7, 106 74 Athens; tel. (01) 7224504; telex 215646; Ambassador: HANS COLLIANDER.

Switzerland: Odos Iassiou 2, 115 21 Athens; tel. (01) 7230364; telex 216230; Ambassador: CHARLES STEINHÄUSLIN.

Syria: Odos Marathonodromou 79, Palaio Psychico, Athens; tel. (01) 6725577; Ambassador: M. ALI AL-MADANI.

Thailand: Leoforos Amalias 26, Athens; tel. (01) 3223428; Chargé d'affaires a.i.: SANGKATE KLAIPAKSEE.

Tunisia: Odos Ethnikis Antistaseos, Chalandri, Athens; tel. (01) 6717590; Ambassador: SALAH LADGHAM.

Turkey: Odos Vassileos Gheorghiou II 8, Athens; tel. (01) 7245915; Ambassador: NAZMI AKIMAN.

USSR: Odos Papanastassiou, Palaio Psychico, Athens; tel. (01) 711261; Ambassador: VIKTOR FYODOROVICH STUKALIN.

United Kingdom: Odos Ploutarchou 1, 106 75 Athens; tel. (01) 7236211; telex 216440; Ambassador: Sir JEREMY CASHEL THOMAS.

USA: Leoforos Vassilissis Sofias 91, Athens; tel. (01) 7212951; Ambassador: ROBERT VOSSLER KEELEY.

Uruguay: Odos Licavitou I G, 106 72 Athens; tel. (01) 3613549; Ambassador: CARLOS A. DUARTE.

Venezuela: Leoforos Vassilissis Sofias 112, Athens; tel. (01) 7708769; Ambassador: JOSÉ RAMÓN MEDINA.

Yugoslavia: Leoforos Vassilissis Sofias 106, Athens; tel. (01) 7774344; Ambassador: VLADIMIR SULTANOVÍC.

Zaire: Odos Vassileos Constantinou 2, 116 35 Athens; tel. (01) 7016171; Ambassador: BOMOLO LOKOKA.

Judicial System

The Constitution of 1975 provides for the establishment of a Special Supreme Tribunal. Other provisions in the Constitution provided for a reorganization of parts of the judicial system to be accomplished through legislation.

SUPREME ADMINISTRATIVE COURTS

Special Supreme Tribunal: Odos Patision 30, Athens; this court has final jurisdiction in matters of constitutionality.

Council of State: Old Palace Bldg, Athens; the Council of State has appellate powers over acts of the administration upon application by civil servants or other civilians.

SUPREME JUDICIAL COURT

Supreme Court: Leoforos Alexandros 121, Athens; this is the supreme court in the State, having also appellate powers. It consists of six sections, four Civil and two Penal, and adjudicates in quorum; Pres. Supreme Court GEORGE KONSTAS.

COURTS OF APPEAL

These are 12 in number. They have jurisdiction in cases of Civil and Penal Law of second degree, and, in exceptional penal cases, of first degree.

COURTS OF FIRST INSTANCE

There are 59 Courts of First Instance with jurisdiction in cases of first degree, and in exceptional cases, of second degree. They function both as Courts of First Instance and as Criminal Courts. For serious crimes the Criminal Courts function with a jury.

In towns where Courts of First Instance sit there are also Juvenile Courts. Commercial Tribunals do not function in Greece, and all commercial cases are tried by ordinary courts of law. There are however, Tax Courts in some towns.

OTHER COURTS

There are 360 Courts of the Justice of Peace throughout the country. There are 48 Magistrates' Courts (or simple Police Courts).

In all the above courts, except those of the Justice of Peace, there are District Attorneys, In Courts of the Justice of Peace the duties of District Attorney are performed by the Public Prosecutor.

Religion

CHRISTIANITY

The Orthodox Church of Greece

The Greek branch of the Holy Eastern Orthodox Church is the officially established religion of the country, to which nearly 97% of the population profess adherence. The administrative body of the Church is the Holy Synod of 12 members, elected by the 78 bishops of the Hierarchy.

Primate of Greece: Archbishop SERAPHIM of Athens.

Within the Greek State there is also the semi-autonomous Church of Crete, composed of seven Metropolitans and the Holy Archbishopric of Crete. The Church is administered by a Synod consisting of the seven Metropolitans under the Presidency of the Archbishop; it is under the spiritual jurisdiction of the Oecumenical Patriarchate of Constantinople, which also maintains a degree of administrative control.

Archbishop of Crete: Archbishop TIMOTHEOS (whose See is in Heraklion).

There are also four Metropolitan Sees of Dodecanese, which are spiritually and administratively dependent on the Oecumenical Patriarchate and, finally, the peninsula of Athos, which constitutes the region of the Holy Mountain (Mount Athos) and comprises twenty monasteries. These are dependent on the Oecumenical Patriarchate of Constantinople, but are autonomous and are safeguarded constitutionally.

The Roman Catholic Church

Latin Rite

Greece comprises four archdioceses (including two directly responsible to the Holy See), four dioceses and one Apostolic Vicariate. In 1985 there were about 50,000 adherents in the country.

Archdiocese of Athens: Archbishopric, Odos Omirou 9, 106 72 Athens; tel. (01) 3624311; Archbishop Most Rev. NICOLAUS FOSCOLOS.

Archdiocese of Rhodes: Archbishopric, Odos Dragoumi 43, Rhodes; tel. 21845; Apostolic Administrator Fr MICHEL PIERRE FRANZIDIS.

Metropolitan Archdiocese of Corfu, Zante and Cefalonia: Catholic Archbishopric, 49100 Kerkyra; tel. 30277; Archbishop Mgr ANTONIO VARTHALITIS.

Metropolitan Archdiocese of Naxos, Andros, Tinos and Myconos: Archbishopric, Tinos (summer residence); Naxos (winter residence); also responsible for the suffragan dioceses of Candia (Crete), Chios, Santorini and Syros and Milo; Archbishop Mgr GIOVANNI PERRIS.

Apostolic Vicariate of Salonika (Thessaloniki): Leoforos Vassilissis Olgas 120B, 546 45 Thessaloniki; tel. 835780; Apostolic Administrator Fr DEMETRIO ROUSSOS.

Byzantine Rite

Apostolic Exarchate for the Byzantine Rite in Greece: Odos Acharnon 246, 112 53 Athens; tel. (01) 8677039; 2 parishes (Athens and Jannitsa, Macedonia); 12 secular priests, 18 religious sisters, 2,300 adherents (1986 est.); Exarch Apostolic Mgr ANARGHYROS PRINTESIS, Titular Bishop of Gratianopolis.

Armenian Rite

Episcopacy of the Armenian Rite in Greece: Odos René Piot 2, 117 44 Athens; tel. (01) 9014089; 650 adherents (1984); Bishop HOVANNES KOYOUNIAN.

Protestant Church

Greek Evangelical Church (Presbyterian): Odos Markon Botsari 24, 117 41 Athens; f. 1886; comprises 30 organized churches; embraces about 0.1% of population; Moderator Rev. PHAEDON CAMBOUROPOULOS.

ISLAM

The law provides as religious head of the Muslims a Chief Mufti; the Muslims in Greece possess a number of mosques and schools.

JUDAISM

The Jewish population of Greece, estimated in 1943 at 75,000 people, was severely reduced as a result of the German occupation. In 1973 there were about 5,000 Jews in Greece.

Rabbi of Athens: JACOB D. ARAR, Odos Melidoni 5, 105 53 Athens; tel. (01) 3252773.

Central Board of the Jewish Communities of Greece: Odos Sourmeli 2, Athens 104 39; tel. (01) 8839953; telex 225110; f. 1945; officially recognized representative body of the community; Pres. JOSEPH LOVINGER.

The Press

In 1983 total newspaper circulation for the year was 276.2m. in Athens and 30.7m. in Thessaloniki. Afternoon papers are more popular than morning ones; in the Athens area in 1983 about 141,071 papers were sold each morning and up to 771,516 each afternoon.

PRINCIPAL DAILY NEWSPAPERS

Morning papers are not published on Mondays, nor afternoon papers on Sundays.

Athens

Acropolis: Odos Fidiou 12, 106 78 Athens; tel. (01) 3618811; telex 215733; f. 1881; morning; Independent-Conservative; Acropolis Publications SA; Publr G. LEVIDES; Dir MARNIS SKOUNDRIDAKIS; circ. 50,819 (1981).

Apogevmatini (The Afternoon): Odos Fidiou 12, 106 78 Athens; tel. (01) 3618811; telex 215733; f. 1956; independent; Publr GEORGIOS HATZIKONSTANTINOU; Editor J. MOSCHOVITIS; circ. 130,000 (1984).

Athens Daily Post: Odos Stadiou 57, Athens; tel. (01) 3249504; f. 1952; morning; English; Owner G. SKOURAS.

Athens News: Odos Lekka 23–25, 105 62 Athens; tel. (01) 3224253; f. 1952; morning; English; Publr-Propr JOHN HORN; circ. 10,000 (1983).

Athlitiki Icho (Athletics Echo): Odos Voulgari 11, 104 37 Athens; tel. (01) 5222524; f. 1945; morning; Editors and Proprs ATHAN SEMBOS, G. GEORGALAS; circ. 24,117 (1981).

Avgi (Dawn): Ag. Constantiou 12, 104 31 Athens; tel. (01) 5231831; telex 222671; f. 1952; morning; New Hellenic Left Party; Dir GRIGORIS GIANNAROS; Editor L. VOUTSAS; circ. 55,000 (1986).

Avriani: Odos Dimitros 11, 177 78 Athens; tel. (01) 3471443; telex 218440; f. 1980; evening; Dir DINOS KOUTSOUMIS; Publr and Editor G. COURIS; circ. 65,000 (1986).

Eleftheros Kosmos: Ekdotikai Epichiriseis, Odos Panepistimiou 58, Athens; tel. (01) 3619511; morning; Propr A. E. LOGOS.

Eleftheri Ora: Odos Akadimias 32, 106 72 Athens; tel. (01) 3644128; f. 1981; evening; Publr J. MICHALOPOULOS; Dir G. MICHALOPOULOS; circ. 5,239 (1984).

Eleftherotypia: Odos Panepistimiou 57; f. 1974; evening; Publr CHR. TEGOPOULOS; Dir S. FYNTANIDIS; circ. 85,000 (1986).

Estia (Vesta): Odos Anthinou Gazi 7, 105 61 Athens; tel. (01) 3220631; f. 1898; afternoon; Publr and Editor ADONIS K. KYROU; circ. 7,978 (1984).

Ethnos (Nation): Odos Benaki, Metamorfosi Chalandriou, 152 35 Athens; tel. (01) 6580640; telex 2104415; f. 1981; evening; Publr G. BOBOLAS; Dir A. FILIPOPOULOS; circ. 203,216 (1984).

Express: Odos Halandriou 39, Paradissos Amaroussiou, 151 25 Athens; tel. (01) 6827582; morning, financial; Publr Hellenews Publications; Gen. Man. D. KALOFOLIAS; Editor-in-Chief T. MATSOUKIS; circ. 22–25,000 (1986).

Imerissia: Odos Geraniou 7A, 105 52 Athens; tel. (01) 5232159; f. 1947; morning; Publr A. MOTHONIOS and Co; circ. 11,000.

Kathimerini: Odos Socratous 57, 104 31 Athens; tel. (01) 5239315; telex 214877; f. 1919; morning; Conservative; Publr K. D. LOUNDRAS; Editor Mrs HELEN VLACHOS; circ. 80,000 (1986).

Mesimvrini (Midday): Odos Panepistimiou 10, 106 71 Athens; tel. (01) 3646010; telex 216495; f. 1980; evening; Publr ATHAN SEKERIS; Dir CH. PASSALARIS; circ. 24,701.

Naftemboriki (Daily Journal): Odos Piraeus 9–11, Athens; tel. (01) 5246711; f. 1923; morning; non-political journal of finance, commerce and shipping; Dir N. ATHANASSIADIS; circ. 33,000 (1986).

Rizospastis (Radical): Leoforos N. Ionias 13B, Perissos, Athens; tel. (01) 2526434; telex 216156; morning; pro-Soviet Communist; Dir GRIGORIS FARAKOS; Editor G. TRIKALINOS; circ. 48,513 (1984).

Ta Nea (News): Odos Christou Lada 3, 102 39 Athens; tel. (01) 3230221; telex 210608; f. 1944; Liberal; evening; Publr CHRISTOS LAMBRAKIS; Dir L. KARAPANAGIOTIS; circ. 155,000 (1985).

Vradyni (Evening Press): Odos Piraeus 9–11, 105 52 Athens; tel. (01) 5231001; telex 215354; f. 1923; evening; right-wing; Gen. Man. H. ATHANASIADOU; circ. 71,914.

Patras

Peloponnesos: Odos Alex. Ipsilandou 177, 26225 Patras; tel. (61) 272452; f. 1886; independent conservative; Publr and Editor S. DOUCAS; circ. 6,000.

Thessaloniki

Ellinikos Vorras (Greek North): Odos Grammou-Vitsi 19, 55134 Thessaloniki; tel. (31) 416621; telex 412213; f. 1935; morning; Publr TESSA LEVANTIS; Dir N. MERGIOS; circ. 14,467.

Makedonia: Odos Monastiriou 85, 54627; Thessaloniki; tel. (31) 521621; f. 1911; morning; Propr Publishing Co. of Northern Greece SA; Dir K. DIMADIS; Editor KATERINA VELIDES; circ. 47,989 (1984).

Thessaloniki: Odos Monastiriou 85, 54627; Thessaloniki; tel. (31) 521621; f. 1963; evening; Propr Publishing Co of Northern Greece SA; Editor KATERINA VELIDES; circ. 36,040 (1984).

SELECTED PERIODICALS

Aktines: Odos Karytsi 14, 105 61 Athens; tel. (01) 3235023; f. 1938; monthly; current affairs, science, philosophy, arts; aims to promote a Christian civilization; Publr Christian Union; circ. 10,000.

The Athenian: Odos Daedalou 20, 105 58 Athens; f. 1974; monthly; English; Publr and Editor SLOANE ELLIOTT; circ. 13,200 (1984).

Cosmopolitan: Leoforos Marathonas 14, Pallini, 153 00 Athens; tel. (01) 6665706; f. 1979; monthly; women's magazine; Publr P. ROKANAS; Dir K. KOSTOULIAS.

Deltion Diikiseos Epichiriseon (Business Administration Bulletin): Odos Rigilis 26, 106 74; Athens; tel. (01) 7235736; telex 29006; monthly; Editor J. PAPAMICHALAKIS; circ. 26,000 (1985).

Economicos Tachydromos (Financial Courier): Odos Christou Lada 3, 102 37 Athens; tel. (01) 3230221; telex 210608; f. 1926; weekly; Dir JOHN MARINOS; circ. 17,000 (1986).

Embros (Forward): Odos Christou Lada 7, Athens; tel. (01) 3228656; f. 1896; weekly; independent; Editor A. E. PARASCHOS.

Epikaira: Odos Voulis 17, Athens; Amaroussion Papyros Press Ltd; weekly; circ. 35,274 (1981).

Fantazio: Odos Ermou 8, Athens; f. 1969; weekly; Publr E. TERZOPOULOS; circ. 70,722 (1981).

Gynaika (Women): Fragoklissias 7, Marousi 151 25 Athens; (01) 6826680; f. 1950; fortnightly; fashion, beauty, handicrafts, cookery, social problems, fiction, knitting, embroidery; Publr EVANGELOS TERZOPOULOS SA; circ. 94,654 (1984).

GREECE

Hellenews: Odos Halandriou 39, Paradissos Amaroussiou 151 25 Athens; tel. (01) 6827582; telex 219746; weekly; English; finance and business; Publr Hellenews Publications; Editor G. V. PAVLIDES; Dir D. KALOFOLIAS.

Ikogeniakos Thesavros (Family Treasure): Odos Halkokondili 36, 104 38 Athens; tel. (01) 5231033; f. 1967; weekly; women's and social matters; Publr COSTANTINOS PAPACRISTOPHILOU; Editor TAKIS AGELOPOULOS; circ. 31,180 (1983).

Makedoniki Zoi (Macedonian Life): Odos Mitropoleos 70, 546 22 Thessaloniki; tel. (31) 277700; monthly; Editor N. J. MERTZOS.

Pantheon: Odos Anaksagora 5, Athens; tel. (01) 5245433; fortnightly; Publr and Dir N. THEOFANIDES; circ. 74,141 (1981).

Politica Themata: Odos Ipsilantou 25, 106 75 Athens; tel. (01) 7218421; weekly; Publr J. CHORN; Dir C. KYRKOS; circ. 2,544 (1984).

Tachydromos (The Courier): Odos Christou Lada 3, 102 37 Athens; tel. (01) 3250810; telex 215904; f. 1953; weekly; illustrated magazine; Publr C. LAMBRAKIS SA; Dir ROULA MITROPOULOU; circ. 177,182 (1984).

Technika Chronika (Technical Times): Odos Carageorgi Servias 4, 105 62 Athens; tel. (01) 3234751; f. 1952; monthly; general edition on technical and economic subjects; Editor D. ROKOS; circ. 12,000.

To Vima (Tribune): Odos Christou Lada 3, 107 32 Athens; tel. (01) 3230221; telex 215904; f. 1922; weekly; Liberal; Dir and Editor STAVROS P. PSYCHARIS; circ. 35,000 (1984).

Viomichaniki Epitheorissis (Industrial Review): Odos Zalokosta 4, 106 71 Athens; f. 1934; monthly; industrial and economic review; Publr S. VOVOLINIS; Editor D. KARAMANOS; circ. 25,000.

NEWS AGENCIES

Athenagence (ANA): Odos Pindarou 6, 106 71 Athens; tel. (01) 3639816; telex 215300; f. 1896; correspondents in leading capitals of the world and towns throughout Greece; Gen. Dir ANDREAS CHRISTODOULIDES.

Foreign Bureaux

Agence France-Presse (AFP): POB 3392, Odos Voukourestiou 18, 106 71 Athens; tel. (01) 3633388; telex 215595; Bureau Chief FRANCIS CAMOIN.

Agencia EFE (Spain): Odos Zalokosta 4, Athens; tel. (01) 3635826; telex 219561; Bureau Chief D. MARÍA-LUISA RUBIO.

Agentstvo Pechati Novosti (APN) (USSR): Odos Irodotou 9, Athens; Bureau Chief BORIS KOROLYOV.

Agenzia Nazionale Stampa Associata (ANSA) (Italy): Odos Valaoritou 9B, 106 71 Athens; tel. (01) 3605285; telex 221860; Correspondent NICOLA RIENZI.

Allgemeiner Deutscher Nachrichtendienst (ADN) (German Democratic Republic): POB 30057, 100 33 Athens; Correspondent HANS-JOACHIM THEBUD.

Anatolian News Agency (Turkey): Athens; Correspondent AHMET URAN BARAN.

Associated Press (AP) (USA): Odos Akadimias 27A, 106 71 Athens; tel. (01) 3602755; telex 215133; Correspondent KERIN HOPE.

Bulgarian Telegraph Agency (BTA): Odos Adifilou 2, Ilissia, 115 28 Athens; tel. (01) 7245020; Bureau Chief BOYKO BORISOV.

Deutsche Press-Agentur (dpa) (Federal Republic of Germany): Odos Achaeou 8, Athens 139; tel. (01) 7230290; telex 215839; Correspondent URSULA DIEPGEN.

Prensa Latina (Cuba): Erifilis 1, Pangrati, Athens; tel. (01) 7291826; Chief TSALAPATI KISMET.

Reuters (UK): Odos Pindarou 7, Athens 134; Correspondent NEOKOSMOS TZALLAS.

Telegrafska Agencija Nova Jugoslavija (Tanjug) (Yugoslavia): Evrou 94–96, Ambelokipi, Athens; tel. (01) 7791545.

Telegrafnoye Agentstvo Sovetskovo Soyuza (TASS) (USSR): Odos Gizi 44, Palaio Psychico, Athens; Correspondent ANATOLI TKACHUK.

United Press International (UPI) (USA): Odos Valaritou 12, 10671 Athens; tel. (01) 3633807; telex 215572; Correspondent JAMES DORSEY.

Xinhua (New China) News Agency (People's Republic of China): Odos Amarilidos 19, Palaio Psychico, Athens; tel. (01) 6724997; telex 216235; Bureau Chief XIE CHENGHAO.

PRESS ASSOCIATIONS

Enossis Syntakton Imerission Ephimeridon Athinon (Journalists' Union of the Athens Daily Newspapers): Odos Akademias 20, Athens; f. 1914; Pres. VAS. KORAHAIS; Gen. Sec. DIMITRIOS MATHIOPOULOS; 918 mems.

Enossis Syntakton Periodikou Typou (Journalists' Union of the Periodical Press): Odos Valaoritou 9, Athens; Pres. ANDREAS KALOMARIS; 220 mems.

Foreign Press Association of Greece: Odos Academias 23, 134 Athens.

Publishers

Angyra Ekdotikos Oikos: Odos Piraeus 18, 101 Athens; tel. (01) 5223694; telex 210804; f. 1932; general; Man. Dir DIMITRIOS PAPADIMITRIOU.

John Arsenides Ekdotis: Odos Akademias 57, 143 Athens; tel. (01) 618707; biography, history, philosophy, social sciences; Man. Dir JOHN ARSENIDES.

Ekdotike Athenon SA: Vissariones 1, 135 Athens; tel. (01) 3608911; f. 1961; history, archaeology, art; Man. Dirs GEORGE A. CHRISTOPOULOS, JOHN C. BASTIAS.

Bergadi Editions: Odos Mavromichali 4, Athens; tel. (01) 3614263; academic, children's books; Dir MICHAEL BERGADIS.

Boukoumanis Editions: Odos Mavromichali 1, 106 79 Athens; tel. (01) 3618502; f. 1967; history, politics, sociology, psychology, belles lettres, educational, arts, children's books, ecology; Man. ELIAS BOUKOUMNAIS.

Dimitrios Dimitrakos: Odos Metropoleos 3, Athens; f. 1896; general, school equipment, *Great Dictionary of the Greek Language;* Dirs D., P., L. and SP. DIMITRAKOS.

G. C. Eleftheroudakis SA: Odos Nikis 4, and Odos Sinopis 2, 10563 Athens; tel. (01) 3222255; telex 219410; f. 1915; general, technical and scientific; Man. Dir VIRGINIA ELEFTHEROUDAKIS-GREGOU.

Etairia Ellinikon Ekdoseon: Odos Akademias 84, 142 Athens; tel. (01) 3630282; f. 1958; fiction, academic, educational; Man. Dir STAVROS TAVOULARIS.

Kassandra M. Grigoris: Odos Solonos 71, 106 79 Athens; tel. (01) 3629684; f. 1967; Greek history, Byzantine archaeology, literature, theology; Man. Dir MICHEL GRIGORIS.

Denise Harvey and Company: Lambrou Fotiadi 6, Mets, 11636 Athens; tel. (01) 9233547; f. 1972; modern Greek literature and poetry, translations, selected general list (English and Greek); Man. Dir DENISE HARVEY; Editor PHILIP SHERRARD.

I.D. Kollaros & Co: Odos Solonos 60, 135 Athens; tel. (01) 3635970; f. 1885; literature, textbooks, general; Gen. Dir MARINA KARAITIDES.

Papazissis Publishers: Nikitara 2, 106 78 Athens; tel. (01) 3622496; telex 219807; f. 1929; economics, politics, law, history, school books; Man. Dir VICTOR PAPAZISSIS.

D. and B. Saliveros: Arcadias and Teftidos 1, Peristeri, Athens; f. 1893; general and religious books, maps, diaries and calendars; Chair. D. SALIVEROS.

John Sideris: Odos Stadiou 44, Athens; tel. (01) 3229638; f. 1898; school textbooks, general; Man. J. SIDERIS.

J. G. Vassiliou: Odos Hippocratous 15, 106 79 Athens; tel. (01) 3623382; f. 1913; fiction, history, philosophy, dictionaries and children's books.

Government Publishing House

Government Printing House: Odos Kapodistriou 34, 104 32 Athens; tel. (01) 5248320.

PUBLISHERS' ASSOCIATION

Publishers' and Booksellers' Association of Athens: Odos Themistocleus 54, 106 81 Athens; tel. (01) 3630029; Pres. D. PANTELESKOS; Sec. STEPHANOS PATAKIS.

Radio and Television

A television network of 17 transmitters is in operation. In 1984 there were an estimated 4m. radio receivers and 1,710,000 television receivers in use.

The Constitution of June 1975 placed radio and television under the direct supervision of the State.

Elliniki Radiophonia Tileorassi (Hellenic National Radio-Television): POB 19, Aghia Paraskevi, Attikis, Athens; tel. (01)

GREECE
                                                                                            Directory

6595970; telex 216066; state controlled since 1939; Pres. of the Admin. Council K. BEIS; Dir-Gen. G. ROMEOS; Dir Radio I. KAMBANELLIS.

Ypiressia Enimerosseos Enoplon Dhynameon (YENED) (Greek Armed Forces Radio and Television): 'ERT 2', Katehaki and Messogion St, 136 Athens; f. 1967; tel. (01) 701911; radio broadcasts from Heraklion, Pyrgos, Larissa, Athens, Thessaloniki, Tripolis, Kojani, Ioannina, Serres, Orestias and Kavala; television broadcasts from Athens; retransmission from 28 stations; Chair. CHRISTOS APOSTOLOPOULOS.

Finance

(cap. = capital; p.u. = paid up; res = reserves; dep. = deposits; drs = drachmae; m. = million; br. = branch)

BANKING

Central Bank

Bank of Greece: Odos El. Venizelou 21, POB 105, 102 50 Athens; tel. (01) 3201111; telex 215102; f. 1928; State Bank of Issue; cap. drs 3,876.9m., res drs 7,572.3m., dep. drs 556,688.9m. (Dec. 1985); Gov. DEMETRIOS CHALIKIAS; 27 brs.

Commercial Banks

Agricultural Bank of Greece: Odos El. Venizelou 23, Athens; tel. (01) 3222252; telex 222160; f. 1929; a state agricultural bank; cap. drs 33,593m., dep. drs 237,216m. (Dec. 1983); Gov. and Chair. VASILIS KAFIRIS; 400 brs.

Bank of Attica: Odos Omirou 23, 106 72 Athens; tel. (01) 3646910; telex 223344; f. 1925; affiliated to Commercial Bank of Greece; cap. drs 431.9m., res drs 73m., dep. drs 5,784m. (Dec. 1983); Chair. and Gen. Man. COSTAS KALYVIANAKIS; 10 brs.

Bank of Crete: Odos Voukourestiou 22, 106 71 Athens; tel. (01) 3606511; telex 218633; f. 1924 (reformed 1974); cap. drs 964.5m., res drs 416.3m., dep. drs 28,181.5m. (Dec. 1985); Chair. and Man. Dir Dr G. KOSKOTAS; Vice-Chair. and Gen. Man. PANOS VAKALIS; 50 brs.

Bank of Piraeus: Odos Stadiou 34, 132 Athens; f. 1916; cap. drs 83.2m., res drs 193.5m., dep. drs 2,694.6m. (Dec. 1979); Chair. of Bd, Pres. and Gen. Man. KOSTAS LAMBRAKIS; Vice-Pres. CONSTANTINE A. CATSIAMBAS; Man. PETROS S. GREGOROPOULOS; 8 brs.

Commercial Bank of Greece: POB 16, Odos Sophocleous 11, 122 Athens; tel. (01) 3210911; telex 216545; f. 1907; total cap. p.u. drs 4,203.1m., res drs 12,578.2m., dep. drs 234,082.9m. (Dec. 1982); Chair. ANDREAS BOUMIS; Man. Dir S. KAPARIS; 237 brs.

Credit Bank: Odos Stadiou 40, 102 52 Athens; tel. (01) 3245111; telex 218691; f. 1879, renamed 1972; cap. drs 2,640m., res drs 2,460.6m., dep. drs 214,818m. (Dec. 1985); Chair. and Gen. Man. YANNIS S. COSTOPOULOS; 92 brs.

Ergobank SA: Odos Panepistimiou 36, 106 79 Athens; tel. (01) 3601011; telex 218826; f. 1975; cap. drs 1,034.4m. (1982); Chair. and Man. Dir C. S. CAPSASKIS; Gen. Mans A. G. BIBAS, X. C. NICKITAS, P. P. HAGGIPAVLOU; 36 brs.

General Hellenic Bank: Odos Panepistimiou 9, 102 29 Athens; tel. (01) 3250301; telex 219841; f. 1937 as Bank of the Army Share Fund, renamed 1966; cap. drs 1,375.1m., res drs 1,005.2m., dep. drs 76,180m. (Dec. 1985); Chair. DIMOSTHENIS DIMOSTHENOPOULOS; Gen. Man. PANAGIS BENETATOS; 70 brs.

Investment Bank, SA: Odos Omirou 8, 133 Athens; f. 1974; cap. drs 300m.

Ionian and Popular Bank of Greece: Leoforos El. Venizelou 45. 132 Athens; tel. (01) 3225501; telex 215269; f.1958; cap. drs 2,301.2m., res drs 7,596.1m., dep. drs 204,047m. (Dec. 1985); Chair. PANAYOTIS KORLIRAS; Gen. Man. EUGENE CALAFATIS; 152 brs.

National Bank of Greece, SA: Odos Aeolou 86, 102 32 Athens; tel. (01) 3210411; telex 214931; f. 1841; cap. drs 19,635.9m., res drs 32,115.5m., dep. drs 840,349.1m. (Dec. 1982); Gov. STELIOS PANAGOPOULOS; 472 brs in Greece, 22 abroad.

National Mortgage Bank of Greece: Odos El. Venizelou 40, POB 667, Athens; tel. (01) 7799301; telex 215026; f. 1927; share cap. drs 2,349m., res drs 5,078m., dep. drs 215,545.1m. (Dec. 1985); Chair. and Gov. NICHOLAS G. SKOULAS; Man. CONSTANTINE E. PAVLIDIS; 40 brs.

Traders' Credit Bank: Odos Santaroza 3, 131 Athens; tel. (01) 3212371; telex 215481; f. 1924; cap. drs 339.2m., res drs 287.3m. (Dec. 1982); Chair. CONST. SIETOS; Dir and Gen. Man. NICHOLAS BOUROPOULOS; 14 brs.

Development Banks

Hellenic Industrial Development Bank: Odos El. Venizelou 18, 106 72 Athens; tel. (01) 3237981; telex 215203; f. 1964; cap. drs 7,200m.; state-owned limited liability banking company; the major Greek institution in the field of industrial investment; Gov. NIKOS KOUMBIS.

National Investment Bank for Industrial Development, SA: Leoforos Amalias 14, 102 36 Athens; tel. (01) 3242915; telex 2166113; f. 1963; cap. drs 1.4m.; res drs 5.2m.; long-term loans, equity participation, promotion of co-operation between Greek and foreign enterprises; Man. Dir THEODOROS B. KARATZAS.

PRINCIPAL INSURANCE COMPANIES

Aeolis: Odos Voukourestiou 11, 106 71 Athens; tel. (01) 3607311; telex 214325; f. 1972; Gen. Man. J. DELENDAS.

Alfa: Leoforos Kifissias 252–254, 152 31 Halandri; tel. (01) 6472411; telex 222693; f. 1977; Gen. Man. DEM. ATHINEOS.

Apollon: Leoforos Syngrou 39, 117 43 Athens; tel. (01) 9236362; Gen. Man. A. M. APOSTOLATOS.

Aspis Pronia: Odos Othonos 4, 105 57 Athens; tel. (01) 3224023; telex 215350; f. 1945; Man. Dir A. TAMBOURAS.

Astir: Odos Merlin 6, 106 71 Athens; tel. (01) 3604111; telex 215383; f. 1930; Gen. Man. N. OTHONEOS.

Athinaiki: Odos Panepistimiou 34, 106 79 Athens; tel. (01) 3615774; f. 1917; Dir C. PAPACONSTANTIOU.

Atlantiki Enosis: Odos Messoghion 71, 115 26 Athens; tel. (01) 7799211; telex 216822; f. 1970; Gen. Man. N. LAPATAS.

Atlas: Odos Stadiou 24, 105 64 Athens; tel. (01) 3254971; telex 216635; f. 1941; Gen. Man. A. COOK.

Attiki: Odos Akti Miaouli 81, Piraeus; f. 1973; Gen. Man. D. SAHINIS.

Balkan Union: Odos Dimosthenous 1, Piraeus; Gen. Man. MARAGHIOS-XIFIOS.

Cigna Hellas A.A.E.: Odos Fidippidou 2, 115 26 Athens; tel. (01) 7754731; telex 218339; Gen. Man. CHR. ATHANASSIADES.

Commercial and Industrial Union Assurance SA: Odos Karageorghi Servias 4, 105 62 Athens; tel. (01) 3230981; telex 215379; f. 1940; Gen. Man. V. PLYTA.

Continental Hellas: Leoforos Syngrou 253, 17122 Athens; tel. (01) 9429021; telex 222746; f. 1942; incorporating Plioktitai SA; Man. Dir MANOLIS VALAVANIS.

Cosmos: Odos Panepistimiou 25, 105 64 Athens; tel. (01) 3229273; f. 1942; Gen. Man. N. PLACIDIS.

Diana: Odos Tsimiski and I. Dragoumi 6, 54624 Thessaloniki; tel. (31) 263729; telex 412526; f. 1975; Gen. Man. D. SPYRTOS.

Doriki: Odos Panepistimiou 58, 106 78 Athens; tel. (01) 36358121; telex 214326; f. 1972; Gen. Man. SPYROS NIKOLAIDES.

Dynamis SA: Leoforos Syngrou 106, 117 41 Athens; tel. (01) 9227255; telex 216678; f. 1977; Man. Dir NICOLAS STAMATOPOULOS.

Economiki: Odos Capodistriou 38, 104 32 Athens; tel. (01) 5243374; Rep. N. NICOLAYDIS.

Elliniki Etairia Plion Kai Aeroskaphon: Odos Stadiou 24, 105 64 Athens; tel. (01) 3233376; f. 1964; Gen. Man. D. FITIZAS.

Emporiki: Odos Philhellinon 6, 105 57 Athens; tel. (01) 3240093; telex 219218; f. 1940; Chair. PHOTIS P. COSTOPOULOS; Exec. Dir MICHAEL P. PSALIDAS.

Estia Insurance and Reinsurance Co SA: Leoforos Syngrou 255, 171 22 Athens; tel. (01) 9425513; telex 215833; f. 1943; Chair. DIONYSIOS VRACHAS; Gen. Man. STAVROULA VAVAS-POLYCHRONOPOULOS.

Ethniki: Odos Karageorgi Servias 8, 105 62 Athens; tel. (01) 3222121; telex 215400; f. 1891; Man. Dir P. NICOLAIDIS.

Ethnikon Idrima Asphalion tis Ellados: Odos Agiou Constantinou 6, 101 Athens; tel. (01) 3221411; f. 1933; Gen. Man. J. KYRIAKOS.

Europi: Leoforos Syngrou 70, 117 45 Athens; tel. (01) 9226077; Rep. I. MORFINOS.

Evropaiki Enosis: Odos Nikis 10, 105 63 Athens; tel. (01) 3249234; f. 1973; Gen. Man. P. VAPHIADIS.

Galaxias: Odos Panepistimiou 56, 106 78 Athens; tel. (01) 3639370; f. 1967; Gen. Man. I. TSOUPRAS.

General Insurance of Athens: Odos Zalokosta 8, 106 71 Athens; tel. (01) 3605343; Rep. D. A. LONG.

Geniki Epagelmatiki: Odos Panepistimiou 56, 106 78 Athens; tel. (01) 3636910; f. 1967; Gen. Man. G. GIATRAKOS.

1243

GREECE — Directory

Gothaer Hellas: Odos Michalakopoulou 174, 115 27 Athens; tel. (01) 7750801; Gen. Man. S. GALANIS.

Halkyon: Odos Philonos 107–109, Piraeus; Man. Dir K. MARTINOS.

Hellas: Leoforos Kifissias 119, 15124 Marousi; tel. (01) 8068501; telex 215226; f. 1973; Gen. Man. N. ADAMANTIADIS.

Hellenic Reliance Insurances S.A.: Odos Mavromichali 3, 18503 Piraeus; tel. (01) 4115311; telex 212679; f. 1972; Gen. Man. M. N. LOURIDAS.

Hellinoelvetiki: Odos Hermou 6, 105 63 Athens; tel. (01) 3252106; telex 216936; f. 1943; Gen. Man. J. DELENDAS.

Hellinokypriaki A.E.G.A.: Leoforos Syngrou 102, 117 41 Athens; tel. (01) 9226094; telex 218722; Gen. Man. K. SAKELLAROPOULOS.

Hellinovretanniki: Odos Messoghion 2–4, 115 27 Athens; tel. (01) 7755301; telex 216448; f. 1974; Gen. Man. J. PALEOLOGOS.

Hermes: Odos Christou Lada 2, 105 61 Athens; tel. (01) 3225602; f. 1940; general insurance; Gen. Man. N. NEGAS.

Horizon: Leoforos Amalias 26A, 105 57 Athens; tel. (01) 3227932; telex 216158; f. 1965; Gen. Mans G. AHIS and CH. AHIS.

Hydrogios: Odos Lagoumigi 6, 176 71 Athens; tel. (01) 9222749; Gen. Man. A. CASCARELIS.

Ikonomiki: Odos Kapodistriou 38, 102 Athens; f. 1968; Gen. Man. D. NIKOLAIDIS.

Ikostos Aion: Odos Kapodistriou 38, 104 32 Athens; tel. (01) 5243544; f. 1972; Gen. Man. N. KYLPASIS.

Ilios: Odos Mavromichali 10, 106 79 Athens; tel. (01) 3606411; telex 215834; f. 1941; Man. Dir P. J. TOWNSEND; Chair C. A. POTHITAKIS.

Imperial Hellas: Odos Veranzerou 5, 106 77 Athens; tel. (01) 3630600; f. 1971; Gen. Man. SAVVAS TZANNIS.

Interamerican Insurance Co: Interamerican Tower, Leoforos Syngrou 350, 17674 Kallithea; tel. (01) 9421222; telex 214685; f. 1971; Gen. Man. DIMITRI KONTOMINAS.

Intertrust Insurance Co: Odos Doiranis 240, 176 74 Kallithea; tel. (01) 9422701; telex 214685; f. 1975; Man. Dir G. ANTONIADIS.

Ioniki: Odos Korai 1, 105 64 Athens; tel. (01) 3236901; f. 1939; Gen. Man. N. CRONTIRAS.

Kykladiki: Odos Panepistimiou 59, 105 64 Athens; tel. (01) 3219184; telex 218560; f. 1919; Gen. Man. PAN. KATSICOSTAS.

Laiki: Leoforos Syngrou 135, and Odos Kratitos 2, 17121 N. Smyrni; tel. (01) 9332911; telex 215403; f. 1942; Gen. Man. N. MOURTZOUKOS.

Lloyd Hellenique SA: Odos Panepistimiou 59, 102 10 Athens; tel. (01) 3219825; f. 1942; Dir ROGER SEILLIER.

Makedonia Insurance Co: Odos Egnatia 1, 546 30 Thessaloniki; tel. (31) 526133; Gen. Man. K. EFTHIMIADIS.

Merimna: Odos Voulis 45–47, 105 57 Athens; tel. (01) 3235553; f. 1943; Man. Dir E. BALA-HILL.

Messoghios: Leoforos Syngrou 165, Athens; f. 1942; Gen. Man. E. TSAOUSIS.

National Insurance Institution of Greece: Odos Agiou Constantinou 6, 104 31 Athens; tel. (01) 5223300; Rep. J. KYRIAKOS.

Olympic Ins. Co SA: Odos Tsimiski 21, 54624 Thessaloniki; tel. (31) 239331; telex 415251; f. 1962; Man. Dir G. TARNATOROS-ANAGNOSTOU.

Omonia: Odos Agiou Constantinou 2, Athens; Pres. F. TSOUKALAS.

Pangosmios Asphalistiki: Leoforos Syngrou 194, 176 71 Athens; tel. 9581341; f. 1975; Chair. E. KAMMENOS; Vice-Chair. S. CHARAMIS; Gen. Man. P. IATROPOULOS.

Panellinios: Leoforos Syngrou 171, 171 21 Athens; tel. (01) 9352003; f. 1918; Gen. Man. A. VALYRAKIS.

Parthenon: Odos Hippokratous 2, 143 Athens; tel. (01) 3606711; f. 1972; Gen. Man. P. GERMANACOS.

Pegasus Insurance Co: Odos Voucourestiou 16, 106 71 Athens; tel. (01) 3607863; telex 214188; Gen. Man. M. PARASKAKIS.

Phoenix-General Insurance Company of Greece SA: Odos Omirou 2, 105 64 Athens; tel. (01) 322951; f. 1928; general insurance; Chair. S. P. KAPARIS; Gen. Man. STELIOS TOKKAS.

Piraiki: Odos Georges 10, 106 77 Athens; tel. (01) 3624868; telex 225921; f. 1943; Dir Gen. K. PAPAGEORGIOU.

Poseidon: Odos Karaiskou 163, 18535 Piraeus; tel. (01) 4522685; f. 1972; Gen. Man. E. SARANTOU.

Promitheus: Odos 3rd September 84, 104 Athens; tel. (01) 8827085; f. 1941; Gen. Man. C. GHONIS.

Proodos: Leoforos Syngrou 196, 17671 Kallithea; tel. (01) 9593302; telex 214364; f. 1941; Gen. Man. N. DOIMAS.

Propontis: Odos Agiou Constantinou 6, 104 31 Athens; tel. (01) 522300; f. 1917; Gen. Man. J. KYRIAKOS.

Prostasia: Leoforos Syngrou 253, 176 72 Athens; tel. (01) 9427091; Rep. A. PALMOS.

Scourtis GH: Odos Panepistimiou 58, 106 78 Athens; tel. (01) 3626081; Gen. Man. G. SCOURTIS.

Syneteristiki: Odos Gennadiou and Akadimias 8, 115 24 Athens; tel. (01) 3642611; Gen. Man. N. GEORGAKOPOULOS.

Transatlantic: Leoforos Syngrou 102, Athens; f. 1975; Gen. Man. G. DIAMANTOPOULOS.

A large number of foreign insurance companies also operate in Greece.

Insurance Associations

Insurers' Union of Greece: Odos Voulis 22, 105 63 Athens; tel. (01) 3229395; 39 mems; Pres. J. KYRIAKOS; Man. CH. TSOUPIS.

Association of Greek Insurance Companies: Odos Solonos 14, 106 73 Athens; tel. (01) 3610287; f. 1907; 26 mems; Chair. P. NICOLAIDES.

Association of Insurance Companies: Odos Xenophontos 10, 105 57 Athens; tel. (01) 3236733; 94 mems.

Trade and Industry

CHAMBERS OF COMMERCE

Athens Chamber of Commerce & Industry: Odos Akademias 7, 106 71 Athens; tel. (01) 3604815; telex 215707; f. 1919; Pres. LAZAROS EFRAIMOGLOU; Sec.-Gen. DIM. DANILATOS; 37,500 mems.

Handicraft Chamber of Athens: Odos Akademias 18, 106 71 Athens; tel. (01) 3630253; Pres. G. KYRIOPOULOS; Sec.-Gen. S. PAPAGELOU; c. 60,000 mems.

Handicraft Chamber of Piraeus: Odos Karaiscou 111, 18532 Piraeus; tel. (01) 4174152; f. 1925; Pres. EVAG. MYTILINEOS; Sec.-Gen. ATHAN. MYSTAKIDIS; 18,500 mems.

Piraeus Chamber of Commerce & Industry: Odos Loudovicou, 18531 Piraeus; tel. (01) 4177241; telex 212970; f. 1919; Pres. MANOLIS NIADAS; Dir JOHN KALOMIRIS; Sec.-Gen. GEORGE KASSIMATIS.

Thessaloniki Chamber of Commerce and Industry: Odos Tsimiski 29, 54624 Thessaloniki; tel. (31) 220920; telex 412115; f. 1919; Pres. VAS. PETRIDIS; Sec.-Gen. JOHN MITATOS; 8,450 mems.

INDUSTRIAL ASSOCIATIONS

Association of Industries of Northern Greece: POB 10709, 1 Morihovou Sq., 54110 Thessaloniki; tel. (31) 539817, telex 418310; f. 1914; Pres. ALEXANDROS BAKATSELOS.

Federation of Greek Industries: Odos Xenophontos 5, 105 57 Athens; f. 1907; Pres. THEODORE PAPALEXOPOULOS; 950 mems.

Hellenic Cotton Board: Leoforos Syngrou 150, 176 71 Athens; tel. (01) 9225011; telex 214556; state organization; Pres. ANASTASIOS LEKKAS.

Hellenic Organization of Small and Medium-size Industries and Handicrafts: Odos Xenias 16, 115 28 Athens; tel. (01) 7715002; telex 218819.

TRADE UNIONS

There are about 5,000 registered trade unions, grouped together in 77 federations and 85 workers' centres, which are affiliated to the General Confederation of Greek Workers (GSEE).

General Confederation of Greek Workers (GSEE): Odos Patision 69, Athens; tel. (01) 8834611; f. 1918; Pres. GEORGE RAFTOPOULOS; Gen. Sec. D. KOSTOPOULOS; 600,000 mems.

Pan-Hellenic Seamen's Federation: Livaros Building, Akti Miaouli 47–49, Piraeus; tel. (01) 4523589; f. 1920; confederation of 14 marine unions; Gen. Sec. MICHEL ZENZEFILIS.

TRADE FAIR

Hellexpo: Odos Egnatia 154, 54621 Thessaloniki; tel. (31) 239221; telex 412291; f. 1929; official organizer of international fairs, exhibitions, festivals and congresses (most notably the annual International Fair of Thessaloniki, which takes place over three weeks starting on the first Sunday in September); Pres. VASILIS DOLMAS.

Transport

RAILWAYS

Ilektriki Sidirodromi Athinon–Pireos (ISAP) (Athens–Piraeus Electric Railways): Odos Athinas 67, 105 52 Athens; tel. (01) 3248311; telex 219998; Gen. Dir G. Bousbouras.

Organismos Sidirodromon Ellados (OSE) (Hellenic Railways Organization Ltd): Odos Karolou 1, 104 37 Athens; tel. (01) 3624402; telex 215187; f. 1971; state railways. Total length of track: 2,557 km (1986); Pres. P. Kontogeorgis; Dir Gen. A. Lambrinopoulos.

In early 1987 work was to commence on a supplementary 27 km metropolitan network in Athens (in addition to the already existing 25.8 km). The new network is expected to be in full operation by 1996.

ROADS

In 1985 there were 34,492 km of roads in Greece. Of this total, 8,700 km were main roads, and 92 km were motorways.

INLAND WATERWAYS

There are no navigable rivers in Greece.

Corinth Canal: built 1893; over six km long, links the Corinthian and Saronic Gulfs. The Canal shortens the journey from the Adriatic to the Piraeus by 325 km; it is spanned by three single-span bridges, two for road and one for rail. The canal can be used by ships of a maximum draught of 22 ft and a width of 60 ft. During 1976, 9,438 ships with a total tonnage of 4,616,852 nrt passed through the Corinth Canal.

SHIPPING

In June 1986 the Greek merchant fleet totalled 2,312 vessels, compared with 2,586 ships in June 1985. The principal ports are Piraeus, Patras and Thessaloniki.

Union of Greek Shipowners: Karageorgis Bldg, Akti Kondyli, Piraeus; Pres. Stathis Gourdomichalis.

Among the largest shipping companies are:

Chandris Cruise Lines: 95 Akti Miaouli, 185 38 Piraeus; tel. (01) 4120932; telex 212327; Man. Dir D. S. Sarandis; 5 cruise liners.

Hellenic Lines, Ltd: Odos Filonos 61–65, 185 35 Piraeus; tel. (01) 4171541; telex 212514; US Atlantic and Mexican Gulf ports; Mediterranean, Red Sea, Persian Gulf, India, south and east Africa; Black Sea and Mediterranean–UK and north European ports; Adriatic ports; Dir G. R. Callimanopulos; 34 cargo vessels, 3 roll-on, roll-off, 2 fully cellular container vessels.

Hellenic Mediterranean Lines Co Ltd: Electric Railway Station Building, POB 80057, 185 10 Piraeus; tel. (01) 4174341; telex 212517; f. 1929; Chair. Const. A. Ringas; Man. Dir A. G. Yannoulatos; 7 passenger and car ferries.

Michail A. Karageorgis SA: 26–28 Karageorgis Bldg, Akti Kondyli, 185 03 Piraeus; tel. (01) 4122670; telex 212660; Chair. M. A. Karageorgis; Man. Dirs S. F. Triantfyllakis, G. Tegopoulos; 8 passenger and car ferries, 21 tankers.

John S. Latsis: POB 203, Odos Othonos 8–10, 105 57 Athens; tel. (01) 3230151; telex 215456; passenger and cargo services; Pres. J. S. Latsis; fleet of 50 vessels, including 28 tankers.

Varnima Corporation International SA: Marine Enterprises Bldg, Akti Miaouli 53–55, 185 36 Piraeus; tel. (01) 4522911; telex 212461; worldwide oil transportation; Chair. Vardis J. Vardinoyannis; Man. Dir G. J. Vardinoyannis; 21 tankers, cargo vessel.

CIVIL AVIATION

There are international airports at Athens, Thessaloniki, Alexandroupolis, Corfu, Lesbos, Andravida, Rhodes, Kos and Heraklion/Crete, and 25 domestic airports. There are plans for a new international airport to be built at Spatsa, 48 km east of Athens, to be completed by 1987.

Olympic Airways SA: Leoforos Syngrou 96–100, 117 41 Athens; tel. (01) 9292111; telex 215134; f. 1957; state-owned; domestic services linking principal cities and islands in Greece, and international services to Albania, Australia, Austria, Belgium, Canada, Cyprus, Denmark, Egypt, France, Germany, Israel, Italy, Jordan, Kenya, Kuwait, Libya, the Netherlands, Saudi Arabia, Singapore, South Africa, Spain, Switzerland, Syria, Turkey, the United Kingdom, the United Arab Emirates and the USA; fleet of 3 Boeing 747-212B, 1 Boeing 747-284B, 6 Boeing 707, 6 Boeing 727-284, 11 Boeing 737-284, 8 Airbus A300B4, 6 SD330-200, 7 Dornier DO228-201, and light aircraft. Chair. and Dir-Gen. Alexandros D. Akrivakis.

Tourism

Ellinikos Organismos Tourismou (National Tourist Organization of Greece): Odos Amerikis 2B, 101 10 Athens; tel. (01) 3223111; telex 215832; Pres. K. Kyriazis; Dir Prof. P. Lazaridis.

Atomic Energy

Elliniki Epitropi Atomikis Energias (Greek Atomic Energy Commission): Aghia Paraskevi, Attikis; tel. (01) 6513111; telex 216199; f. 1954; seven-member administrative cttee; Pres. Prof. Th. Yannakopoulos; Vice-Pres. Prof. C. Papathanassopoulos; Scientific Dir Prof. N. Antoniou.

'Demokritos' National Research Centre for Physical Sciences: Aghia Paraskevi, Attikis, near Athens; tel. (01) 6513111; telex 216199; laboratories for: physics, electronics, chemistry, biochemistry, experimental medicine, soil science, environmental radioactivity, radio-isotope production, biology, technology, health physics, radioactive waste treatment installations; also reactor, linear accelerator and computer centre; Pres. Prof. Th. Yannakopoulos; Scientific Dir Prof. N. Antoniou.

GRENADA

Introductory Survey

Location, Climate, Language, Religion, Flag, Capital

Grenada, a mountainous, heavily-forested island, is the most southerly of the Windward Islands, in the West Indies. The country also includes some of the small islands known as the Grenadines, which lie to the north of Grenada. The largest of these is the low-lying island of Carriacou. The climate is semi-tropical, with an average annual temperature of 28°C (82°F) in the lowlands. Annual rainfall averages about 1,500 mm (60 in) in the coastal area and 3,800 mm to 5,100 mm (150–200 in) in mountain areas. Most of the rainfall occurs between June and December. The majority of the population speak English, although a French patois is also spoken. The main religion is Roman Catholicism but other Christian churches are also represented. The national flag (proportions 2 by 1) consists of a diagonally-quartered rectangle (yellow in the upper and lower segments, green in the right and left ones) surrounded by a red border bearing six five-pointed yellow stars (three at the upper edge of the flag, and three at the lower edge). There is a red disc, containing a large five-pointed yellow star, in the centre, and a representation of a nutmeg (in yellow and red) on the green segment near the hoist. The capital is St George's.

Recent History

Grenada was initially colonized by the French but was captured by the British in 1762. British control was recognized in 1783 by the Treaty of Versailles. Grenada continued as a British colony until 1958, when it joined the Federation of the West Indies, remaining a member until the dissolution of the Federation in 1962. Full internal self-government and statehood in association with the United Kingdom were achieved in March 1967. During this period, the political life of Grenada was dominated by Eric Gairy, a local trade union leader, who in 1950 founded the Grenada United Labour Party (GULP), with the support of an associated trade union. In 1951 GULP won a majority of the elected seats on the Legislative Council but in 1957 it was defeated by the Grenada National Party (GNP), led by Herbert Blaize. Gairy was Chief Minister in 1961–62 but was removed from office by the British, and the Constitution suspended, after allegations of corruption. In the subsequent elections the GNP gained a majority of the elected seats, and Blaize became Chief Minister again. Gairy became Premier after the elections of 1967 and again after those of 1972, which he fought chiefly on the issue of total independence. Grenada became independent, within the Commonwealth, on 7 February 1974, with Gairy as Prime Minister. Opposition to Gairy within the country was expressed in demonstrations and a general strike, and the formation, by the three opposition parties, of the People's Alliance, which contested the 1976 general elections and reduced GULP's majority in the Lower House. The alliance comprised the GNP, the United People's Party and the New Jewel Movement (NJM).

The rule of Sir Eric Gairy, who was knighted in June 1977, was regarded by the opposition as increasingly autocratic and corrupt, and on 13 March 1979 he was replaced in a bloodless coup by the leader of the left-wing NJM, Maurice Bishop. The new People's Revolutionary Government (PRG) suspended the 1974 Constitution and announced the imminent formation of a People's Consultative Assembly to draft a new constitution. Meanwhile, Grenada remained a monarchy, with the British Queen as Head of State, represented in Grenada by a Governor-General. General elections were promised, and detainees, including former ministers from the Gairy administration, were to be tried as soon as possible. The PRG pledged a non-aligned foreign policy and committed itself to solving the country's economic problems. In June 1980 a coup plot was discovered, followed by an assassination attempt against Maurice Bishop and other members of the PRG and an escalation of anti-Government violence. Restrictions against the privately-owned press were imposed, and in 1979 and 1981 two newspapers were closed down by the Government, which accused the owners of involvement in a destabilization campaign. Bishop appealed for help to the UN and foreign governments in July 1981, when he became convinced that manoeuvres by US forces off Puerto Rico were part of US preparations for an invasion of Grenada; this was strongly denied by the USA.

By mid-1982 relations with the USA, the United Kingdom and the more conservative members of CARICOM were becoming increasingly strained: elections had not been arranged, many detainees were still awaiting trial, and Grenada was aligning more closely with Cuba and the USSR. Cuba was supplying about 40% of the funds, and several hundred construction workers, for the airport at Point Salines, a project which further fuelled the USA's insistence that Grenada was to become a major staging-post for Soviet manoeuvres in the area.

In March 1983 the PRG again announced its fears that the USA was planning an invasion, and the armed forces were put on alert. The USA strenuously denied these allegations. In June Maurice Bishop sought to improve relations with the USA, and announced the appointment of a commission to draft a new constitution. This conciliation attempt was not popular with the more left-wing members of the PRG regime, who regarded Bishop's actions as an ideological betrayal. This division within the Government erupted in October into a power struggle between Bishop and his deputy, Bernard Coard, the Minister of Finance and Planning. On 13 October Bishop was placed under house arrest, allegedly for his refusal to share power with Coard. Four days later, Gen. Hudson Austin, the commander of the People's Revolutionary Army (PRA), announced that Bishop had been expelled from the NJM. On 19 October thousands of Bishop's supporters, incensed by this news, stormed the house, freed Bishop from imprisonment, and demonstrated outside the PRA headquarters. Violence ensued, with PRA forces firing into the crowd. Later in the day, Bishop, three of his ministers and three trade union spokesmen were all executed. A military coup had taken place, and the Government was replaced by a 16-man Revolutionary Military Council (RMC), led by Gen. Austin. The remaining NJM ministers were arrested and imprisoned, and a total curfew was imposed.

Regional and international outrage at the assassination of Bishop, plus fears of a US military intervention, were so intense that, after four days, the RMC relaxed the curfew, reopened the airport and promised to return to civilian rule as soon as possible. However, the Organization of Eastern Caribbean States (OECS, see p. 109) decided to intervene in an attempt to restore democratic order, and asked for help from the USA, which, already concerned for the safety of some 1,000 US citizens on the island and convinced that Cuba and the USSR were behind the RMC's actions, readily complied. (It is unclear whether the decision to intervene preceded or followed a request for help to the OECS by the Grenadian Governor-General, Sir Paul Scoon.) On 25 October about 1,900 US military personnel invaded the island, accompanied by 300 troops from Jamaica, Barbados and member-countries of the OECS. Fighting continued for some days, and the USA gradually increased its troop strength, with further reinforcements waiting off shore with a US naval task force. The RMC's forces were defeated, while Bernard Coard, Gen. Hudson Austin and others who had been involved in the coup were captured and imprisoned on the island, to await trial.

On 9 November Sir Paul Scoon appointed a non-political interim council to assume responsibility for the government of the country until elections could be held. Nicholas Braithwaite, a former Commonwealth official, was appointed Chairman in December. The 1974 Constitution was reinstated, and an electoral commission was created to prepare for elections. The USA began a gradual withdrawal of troops in mid-November, and by mid-December only 300 support troops were left, comprising military police and technicians who were to help the 430 members of Caribbean forces who remained on the island. These numbers were maintained throughout 1984. A 550-member police force, trained by the USA and the United Kingdom, was to be established, including a paramilitary element which was to be the new defence contingent.

Several political parties, which had gone underground or into exile during the rule of the PRG, re-emerged and announced their intention of contesting the elections for a new House of Representatives. Sir Eric Gairy returned to Grenada in January 1984 to lead his GULP, although he stated that he would not stand as a candidate himself. In May three former NJM ministers formed the Maurice Bishop Patriotic Movement (MBPM) to contest the elections. A number of parties emerged, broadly occupying the centre of the political spectrum, including the Grenada National Party (GNP), led by Herbert Blaize, the former Premier; the Grenada Democratic Movement (GDM), led by Dr Francis Alexis; the National Democratic Party (NDP), led by George Brizan; and the Christian Democratic Labour Party (CDLP), led by Winston Whyte. Fears that a divided opposition would allow GULP to win a majority of seats in the new House led to negotiations between the centre parties to form an electoral alliance. In April the GNP, NDP and GDM agreed to form an informal coalition. However, subsequent disagreements over the leadership and the selection of candidates led to the break-up of the alliance a month later. In response to US apprehension over growing support for GULP, a meeting between the GNP, GDM, NDP and CDLP was arranged at the end of August 1984 on Union Island, and attended by the Prime Ministers of Barbados, Saint Lucia and Saint Vincent and the Grenadines. The result was the agreed merger of the parties to form the New National Party (NNP), to be led by Herbert Blaize. The CDLP, however, soon left the new party, and there were some fears over the cohesion of the new grouping.

In the general election, held on 3 December, the NNP achieved a convincing victory over its opponents by winning 14 of the 15 seats in the House of Representatives, and 59% of the popular vote. Both Sir Eric Gairy and the MBPM claimed that the poll had been fraudulent, and the one successful GULP candidate initially refused to take his seat in protest. He subsequently accepted the seat but was expelled from the party. Blaize became Prime Minister, and announced a seven-member Cabinet, which included Brizan and Alexis. He also asked the remaining US and Caribbean troops on the island to stay, at least until March 1985, and stressed the need for national reconciliation. The last contingents of US and Caribbean troops left the island in September.

The trial before the Grenada High Court of 19 detainees (including Coard, his wife and Austin), accused of murder and conspiracy against Bishop and six of his associates, had opened in November 1984. However, repeated adjournments prevented the start of proceedings. The approval by the House of Representatives of all the legislation that had been enacted during the rule of the PRG prevented an appeal by the detainees to the judicial committee of the British Privy Council, and, in response to requests from the defence lawyers, further adjournments postponed the trial of 18 of the detainees until April 1986. One of the detainees agreed to give evidence for the State in return for a pardon. The defence lawyers withdrew from the trial in April, at the request of their clients, after challenging the constitutionality of the Grenada High Court. Although the Appeal Court issued a ruling in July ordering the High Court to hear the defence appeal, a request for the trial to be delayed was refused. Following the presentation of the case for the prosecution, some charges against two of the defendants were withdrawn. Proceedings were repeatedly interrupted and criticized by the defendants, but verdicts on 196 charges of murder and conspiracy to murder were returned by the jury in December. Fourteen of the defendants were sentenced to death, three were given prison sentences of between 30 and 45 years, and one was found not guilty. The accused were expected to appeal.

The divisions between the different groupings that comprise the NNP remained during 1985 and 1986, and were expressed in frequent disagreements between Cabinet members and in resentment at Blaize's style of leadership. The issue of leadership assumed greater importance following successive visits by Blaize to the USA for medical treatment. The NNP's first convention was held in December 1985, and Dr Francis Alexis, the Minister of Labour, was elected deputy leader of the party. In May 1986 the junior Education Minister, Kenny Lalsingh, withdrew from the party, and in August he formed the Democratic Labour Congress. In September the Deputy Speaker of the House of Representatives also resigned, reducing the NNP's parliamentary strength to 12 seats.

Government

Grenada has dominion status within the Commonwealth. The British monarch is Head of State and is represented locally by a Governor-General. Executive power is held by the Cabinet, led by the Prime Minister. Parliament comprises the Senate, made up of 13 Senators appointed by the Governor-General on the advice of the Prime Minister and the Leader of the Opposition, and the 15-member House of Representatives, elected by universal adult suffrage. The Cabinet is responsible to Parliament.

Defence

A police force was set up in late 1983, modelled on the British system and trained by British officers. It was expected that there would be about 600 fully-trained officers by 1986. A paramilitary element, known as the Special Service Unit and trained by US advisers, acts as the defence contingent and participates in the regional defence pact with other East Caribbean states.

Economic Affairs

According to estimates by the World Bank, Grenada's GNP per head (at average 1982–84 prices) was US $860 in 1984. Between 1965 and 1984, it was estimated, the country's GNP per head increased, in real terms, by an average of 1.7% annually. For the 1970–80 decade alone, however, it fell by 0.6% per year.

The economy of Grenada is essentially agricultural and centres on the traditional production of spices, particularly nutmeg. The principal exports are nutmeg, cocoa and bananas, although mace, cotton, coffee, coconuts, citrus fruit and minor spices are also significant. Agriculture contributes about 30% of GDP. Since the early 1970s, however, Grenada's agricultural exports have been seriously affected by a combination of natural disasters and low international commodity prices. The ravages since 1978 of the banana disease, moko, combined with flooding in 1979 and hurricane and storm damage in 1980 and 1981, have damaged the plantations, while export shipments were suspended in 1983 because of the political crisis. Banana exports fell from 12,200 metric tons in 1980 to 8,858 tons in 1984, while the value of earnings fell from EC $11m. to EC $8.2m. Earnings from cocoa exports fell from EC $18m. in 1981 to EC $12.5m. in 1982, and to EC $11m. in 1983, although there was a modest recovery in production during 1984, when export earnings rose to EC $12.1m. The recovery continued during 1985, and it was announced that the Canadian International Development Agency (CIDA) was to help to finance a multi-year rehabilitation project.

In 1983 nutmeg provided 35% of income, helped by a five-year trade agreement with the USSR, signed in 1982. However, this agreement was subsequently broken by the Interim Government that took office in November 1983, following the US-led invasion, and low prices and the Indonesian monopoly of the market led to the stockpiling of 6m. lb during 1984, representing six months' production. Nutmeg exports totalled 4.9m. lb in 1984, earning only EC $5.7m. Although exports declined in volume in 1985, a rise in world prices increased export earnings to EC $9m. In 1986 exports increased to 7.5m. lb, earning EC $16.8m. Sugar cane and a wide variety of fruit and vegetables are also grown for local consumption, and exports of fresh fruit and vegetables rose steadily during 1984 and 1985. There are extensive forested areas in the interior of the country. Land tenure is based on privately-owned smallholdings and local co-operative ventures, and a number of the loss-making state-run farms are being returned to private ownership. Livestock production is important for local consumption, though meat and milk still have to be imported. Cuba and the USSR provided some equipment and expertise to develop Grenada's fishing industry. In 1980 a fish-processing plant was established, and in 1981 the Government formed a National Fishing Company.

The development of manufacturing industries has not kept pace with other activities, owing mainly to the limited local market. Industry centres on the processing of agricultural products, and cottage industries producing garments and spice-based goods for the export market. By May 1986, although more than 80 projects, involving planned investment in excess of EC $180m., had been approved by the Industrial Development Corporation (established in January 1985), anticipated investment by American businessmen in light industry on the island, taking advantage of the benefits of the US Government's Caribbean Basin Initiative (CBI), had failed to materialize. Taxes on company profits and customs duties remain high when compared with rates of taxation in other Caribbean islands, and Grenada's infrastructure is poor. However, it was announced in mid-1986 that a US company was to invest more than US $70m. in a series of projects, including an aircraft repair station, a hotel and an electricity-generating plant.

Tourism is an important sector of the economy but, because of political upheaval, tourist arrivals slumped between 1978 and 1983. Only 82,676 tourists arrived in 1983, compared with 148,667 in 1978. However, the completion of the new Point Salines Airport, opened in 1984, and the refurbishment and expansion of the island's hotels stimulated a revival in the tourist trade. Although the number of cruise ship passenger arrivals declined by 32% during 1984, the number of stop-over arrivals increased by 21%, to a total of 39,503, and earnings from tourism totalled EC $45m. In 1985 the number of stop-over arrivals increased by a further 32%, to total 51,979, and there were 90,701 cruise ship passengers, an increase of 165.5%.

Unemployment fell from 49% in 1979 to 35% in 1980, and to 22% in 1982, mainly as a consequence of the PRG's expansion of the armed forces, and the development of youth and community projects. The disbanding of the army, and the suspension of the projects by the Interim Government, helped to cause a rise in unemployment, estimated to be over 30% by the end of 1984. The trade deficit rose from EC $109m. in 1981 to EC $124.7m. in 1982, as a result of the low prices for Grenada's agricultural exports. A reduction in imports, however, helped to reduce the trade deficit to EC $105.1m. in 1984, despite another fall in the value of the country's exports. In 1985 the trade deficit increased to EC $127m.

The construction of roads, buildings and other infrastructural necessities, and the development of the agricultural and industrial sectors, is heavily dependent on foreign aid and loans. Expenditure of EC $70m. in 1981 on capital projects was raised largely from foreign aid donors, and the IMF granted a one-year stand-by credit of 3,425,000 SDRs to support the Government's financial programme. Major co-operation agreements were signed with Canada and Mexico in 1981, and substantial Cuban and Soviet aid for 1982 was directed primarily at development of infrastructure. In 1983 the IMF agreed further funds of US $14.1m. but this was withdrawn because of political instability in late 1983. Heavy expenditure on the new airport had pushed the level of capital expenditure to EC $145m. in the 1983 budget, and funds for recurrent expenditure were diverted towards the airport project, producing an increased burden of debt and interest payments, which rose from an equivalent of 16.5% of GDP in 1980 to 42% by the end of 1983. Total national debt had reached more than EC $168m. by December 1985. Expenditure was reduced by 17% in the 1984/85 budget, introduced by the Interim Government. The projected budget deficit of EC $31.8m., however, was largely offset by US aid, totalling US $57.2m. for the 1984/85 financial year. In addition, US $3m. was provided in November 1983 as emergency aid, and $6m. as compensation for war damage. The 1986/87 budget proposals envisaged total expenditure of EC $236.2m., or EC $13.5m. less than in 1985/86. Capital expenditure was projected at EC $110.4m. A total of 17 taxes were abolished, the most significant of which was income tax. A value-added tax of 20% was introduced and was expected to yield EC $50m. during the financial year. However, in September 1986 the Government was forced to reduce planned expenditure in its capital budget by more than EC $10m., to postpone debt repayments of EC $13.4m. and to reduce recurrent expenditure, owing to a shortfall in revenue from the new tax system and a reduction in US budgetary support.

Canada, the United Kingdom, the EEC and the USA have been among those aid donors contributing to Grenada's reconstruction and development, by financing various projects. US aid during 1984 and 1985 totalled US $74m. However, aid was reduced in 1986 to US $20m., and was expected to total $15m. in 1987. In February 1984 the US Government agreed to provide US $21m. towards the completion of the Point Salines Airport, and further sums for the repair of roads and the telephone system, damaged during the fighting. Canada's aid has included US $6m. for the new airport and C $7.5m. for the modernization of the telephone system, while the United Kingdom has provided US $2.5m. in loans, partly for the improvement of the island's electricity generating capacity, the inadequacy of which causes frequent power cuts.

Social Welfare

There was no system of social security payments in Grenada prior to March 1979. New initiatives which were launched in 1979 included the Youth for Reconstruction Programme, to provide basic paramedical services and assistance to the elderly and disabled, a national milk distribution programme and the establishment of community-directed day care centres. A national insurance scheme began in 1983. In 1984 there were 32 physicians working in Grenada and the country had three hospitals, with a total of 360 beds. There are local health centres situated in the main towns. A mental hospital, destroyed by military action in October 1983, was to be rebuilt with US financial aid.

Education

Education is free and compulsory between the ages of six and 14 years. The standard of education is high, and the system is modelled, to a large extent, on the British pattern. Primary education begins at five years of age and lasts for seven years. Secondary education, beginning at the age of 12, lasts for a further seven years, comprising a first cycle of five years and a second of two years. In 1984 there were 58 primary schools and 20 secondary schools. In 1970 only 2.2% of the adult population had received no schooling. Technical Centres have been set up in each parish, and there is a Technical and Vocational Institute in St George's. The Extra-Mural Department of the University of the West Indies has a branch in St George's, and there is also a Teachers' Training College. A School of Medicine has been established at St George's, a School of Agriculture at Mirabeau and a School of Fishing at Victoria.

Tourism

The colonial architecture of the capital, the excellent yachting facilities and Grand Anse beach are the major tourist attractions. In 1984 there were 15 hotels, providing a total of 504 beds. A five-year tourism development plan, introduced in 1985, aimed to increase the number of hotel rooms to 1,500 by the end of 1987. In 1985 Grenada received 142,680 foreign visitors (including 90,701 cruise ship passengers), compared with a total of 72,669 visitors in 1984.

Public Holidays

1987: 1–2 January (New Year), 7 February (Independence Day), 17–20 April (Easter), 1 May (Labour Day), 8 June (Whit Monday), 18 June (Corpus Christi), 3 August (for Emancipation Day), 29 November (Thanksgiving), 25–26 December (Christmas).

1988: 1–2 January (New Year), 7 February (Independence Day), 1–4 April (Easter), 2 May (for Labour Day), 23 May (Whit Monday), 2 June (Corpus Christi), 1 August (Emancipation Day), 29 November (Thanksgiving), 25–26 December (Christmas).

Weights and Measures

The metric system is in use.

Currency and Exchange Rates

100 cents = 1 East Caribbean dollar (EC $).
Exchange rates (30 September 1986):
  £1 sterling = EC $3.907;
  US $1 = EC $2.700.

Statistical Survey

Source (unless otherwise stated): Central Statistical Office, Government of Grenada, Church Street, St George's; tel. 3034.

AREA AND POPULATION

Area: 344 sq km (133 sq miles).
Population: 93,858 (census of 7 April 1970); 89,088 (census of 30 April 1981).
Principal Town: St George's (capital), population 7,500 (1980 estimate).
Births and Deaths (1982): Registered live births 2,614; Registered deaths 721.

AGRICULTURE, ETC.

Principal Crops ('000 metric tons, 1984): Roots and tubers 4, Bananas 14, Coconuts 8, Sugar cane 6, Cocoa beans 3 (FAO estimate), Mangoes 2, Avocados 2. Source: FAO, *Production Yearbook*.
Livestock (FAO estimates, year ending September 1984): Cattle 6,000, Pigs 11,000, Sheep and goats 29,000, Asses 1,000. Source: FAO, *Production Yearbook*.
Fishing (metric tons, live weight): Total catch 1,801 in 1982; 630 in 1983; 567 in 1984. Source: FAO, *Yearbook of Fishery Statistics*.

INDUSTRY

Production (1983): Rum 2,000 hectolitres (1982); Beer 10,000 hectolitres (estimate); Cigarettes 98 metric tons (1981); Electric energy 25 million kWh. Source: UN, *Industrial Statistics Yearbook*.

FINANCE

Currency and Exchange Rates: 100 cents = 1 East Caribbean dollar (EC $). *Coins:* 1, 2, 5, 10, 25 and 50 cents. *Notes:* 1, 5, 20 and 100 dollars. *Sterling and US Dollar Equivalents* (30 September 1986): £1 sterling = EC $3.907; US $1 = EC $2.700; EC $100 = £25.60 = US $37.04.
Budget (estimates, EC $ million, 1984): Expenditure 211 (current 113, capital 98).
International Reserves (US $ million at 31 December 1985): IMF special drawing rights 0.01; Foreign exchange 20.80; Total 20.81. Source: IMF, *International Financial Statistics*.
Money Supply (EC $ million at 31 December 1985): Currency outside banks 25.07; Demand deposits at deposit money banks 29.05; Total money 54.12; Source: IMF, *International Financial Statistics*.
Gross Domestic Product (EC $ million in current purchasers' values): 232.2 in 1980; 258.8 in 1981; 290.5 in 1982. Source: IMF, *International Financial Statistics*.

Balance of Payments (US $ million, 1985): Merchandise exports f.o.b. 22.12; Merchandise imports f.o.b. −62.59; *Trade balance* −40.47; Exports of services 28.01; Imports of services −21.67; *Balance on goods and services* −34.13; Private unrequited transfers (net) 9.75; Government unrequited transfers (net) 29.22; *Current balance* 4.84; Long-term capital (net) −4.34; Short-term capital (net) 1.08; Net errors and omissions 4.56; *Total* (net monetary movements) 6.15; Valuation changes (net) −0.37; Exceptional financing (net) 3.42; *Changes in reserves* 9.20. Source: IMF, *International Financial Statistics*.

EXTERNAL TRADE

Principal Commodities (EC $ million, 1983): *Imports:* Food and live animals 35.4; Beverages and tobacco 3.3; Crude materials (inedible) except fuels 8.4; Mineral fuels, lubricants, etc. 17.2; Chemicals 12.1; Basic manufactures 39.2; Machinery and transport equipment 17.1; Total (incl. others) 154.5. *Exports:* Food and live animals 46.6 (Cocoa 11.0, Nutmeg 9.5, Bananas 8.7, Mace 2.3, Fresh fruit 12.8); Clothing 3.5; Total (incl. others) 50.7 (excl. re-exports 1.1).
Principal Trading Partners (EC million, 1984): *Imports:* Japan 10.4; Trinidad and Tobago 22.5; United Kingdom 27.6; USA 37.2; Total (incl. others) 151.1. *Exports* (incl. re-exports): Federal Republic of Germany 4.5; Netherlands 3.5; Trinidad and Tobago 16.7; United Kingdom 15.6; USA 2.4; Total (incl. others) 46.0.

TRANSPORT

Road Traffic (1984): Vehicles registered 7,741.
International Sea-borne Shipping (estimated freight traffic, '000 metric tons, 1983): Goods loaded 20; Goods unloaded 50. Source: UN, *Monthly Bulletin of Statistics*.

TOURISM

Visitor Arrivals (1985): 142,680 (incl. 90,701 cruise ship passengers).

COMMUNICATIONS MEDIA

Radio Receivers (1983): 38,000 in use. Source: UNESCO *Statistical Yearbook*.
Telephones (1984): 3,432 in use.
Book Production (1979): 10 titles (11,000 copies).

EDUCATION

Primary (1984): 58 schools; 735 teachers; 19,736 pupils.
Secondary (1984): 20 schools; 311 teachers; 6,686 pupils.

Directory

The Constitution

The 1974 independence Constitution was suspended in March 1979, following the coup, and restored in November 1983 after the overthrow of the People's Revolutionary Government. The main provisions of this Constitution are summarized below:

The Head of State is the British monarch, represented in Grenada by an appointed Governor-General. Legislative power is vested in the bicameral Parliament, comprising a Senate and a House of Representatives. The Senate consists of 13 Senators, seven of whom are appointed on the advice of the Prime Minister, three on the advice of the Leader of the Opposition and three on the advice of the Prime Minister after he has consulted interests which he considers Senators should be selected to represent. The House of Representatives consists of 15 members elected from single-member constituencies on the basis of universal adult suffrage.

The Cabinet consists of a Prime Minister, who must be a member of the House of Representatives, and such other Ministers as the Governor-General may appoint on the advice of the Prime Minister.

There is a Supreme Court and, in certain cases, a further appeal lies to Her Majesty in Council.

The Government

Head of State: HM Queen ELIZABETH II.
Governor-General: Sir PAUL SCOON (took office 1978).

THE CABINET
(December 1986)

Prime Minister and Minister of Finance, Security and Home Affairs: HERBERT BLAIZE.
Minister of Agriculture, Forestry, Lands, Fisheries and Tourism: GEORGE BRIZAN.
Minister of Legal and External Affairs: BEN JONES.
Minister of Health, Housing, Community Development and Women's Affairs: DANNY WILLIAMS.

GRENADA

Minister of Labour, Co-operatives, Social Security and Local Government: Dr Francis Alexis.
Minister of Works, Communications, Public Utilities, Civil Aviation and Energy: Dr Keith Mitchell.
Minister of Education, Culture, Youth Affairs and Sport: George McGuire.

MINISTRIES
All Ministries are in St George's.
Office of the Prime Minister: St George's; tel. 2225; telex 3457.

Legislature

PARLIAMENT
Senate
President: Larry Joseph.
There are 13 appointed members.

House of Representatives
Speaker: Sir Hudson Scipio.

General Election, 3 December 1984

Party	Votes	%	Seats
New National Party	23,984	58.64	14*
Grenada United Labour Party	14,677	35.88	1†
Maurice Bishop Patriotic Movement	2,022	4.94	—
Others	220	0.54	—
Total	40,903	100.00	15

* In 1986 the NNP's seats were reduced to 12, following the resignations of two members, one of whom formed the Democratic Labour Congress.
† The Grenada United Labour Party member at first refused to take his seat. When he did so, however, he was expelled from the party. He subsequently formed his own party, the Grenada Democratic Labour Party.

Political Organizations

Christian Democratic Labour Party (CDLP): St George's; f. 1984; Leader Winston Whyte.
Democratic Labour Congress: St George's; f. 1986; Leader Kenny Lalsingh.
Grenada Democratic Labour Party (GDLP): St George's; f. 1985; Leaders Marcel Peters, Oliver Raeburn, Albert Forsythe.
Grenada United Labour Party (GULP): St George's; f. 1950; right-wing party; Leader Sir Eric Gairy.
Maurice Bishop Patriotic Movement (MBPM): St George's; f. 1984; socialist party; Leader Kenrick Radix.
New National Party (NNP): St George's; f. 1984; centre party; merger of Grenada Democratic Movement, Grenada National Party and National Democratic Party; Leader Herbert Blaize; Deputy Leader Dr Francis Alexis; Gen. Sec. Keith Mitchell.

Diplomatic Representation

EMBASSIES IN GRENADA
USA: Belmont St, St. George's; tel. 1731; Chargé d'affaires: Roy Haverkamp.
Venezuela: Scott St, St George's; tel. 1721; telex 3414; Ambassador: Hermes José Salas Rivero.

Judicial System

Justice is administered by the Grenada Supreme Court, composed of a High Court of Justice and a two-tier Court of Appeal. The Court of Magisterial Appeals is presided over by the Chief Justice. The Itinerant Court of Appeal consists of three judges and sits twice a year; it hears appeals from the High Court and is the final court of appeal. There are also Magistrates' Courts which administer summary jurisdiction.

Directory

Chief Justice: Denis Byron.
Puisne Judge: James A. Patterson.
Registrar of the Supreme Court: Christian St Louis (acting).

Religion

CHRISTIANITY
The Anglican Communion
Anglicans in Grenada are adherents of the Church in the Province of the West Indies. The country forms part of the diocese of the Windward Islands (the Bishop resides in Kingstown, Saint Vincent).

The Roman Catholic Church
Grenada comprises a single diocese, suffragan to the archdiocese of Castries (Saint Lucia). The Bishop participates in the Antilles Episcopal Conference (based in Kingston, Jamaica).
Bishop of St George's in Grenada: Rt Rev. Sydney Charles, Bishop's House, Morne Jaloux, POB 375, St George's; tel. 5299.

Other Christian Churches
The Presbyterian, Methodist, Plymouth Brethren, Baptist and Seventh-day Adventist faiths are also represented.

The Press

NEWSPAPERS
Grenada Guardian: St George's; weekly; organ of GULP.
The Grenadian Voice: St George's; weekly; Editor Leslie Pierre.
Government Gazette: St George's; weekly; official.
The Informer: St George's; weekly; Editor York Marryshow.
The West Indian: 45 Hillsborough St, St George's.

PRESS ASSOCIATION
Press Association of Grenada: St George's; f. 1986; Pres. George Worme.

Publisher

Grenada Publishers Ltd: Torchlight Melville St, St George's; tel. 2305.

Radio and Television

In 1983 there were an estimated 38,000 radio receivers in use.
The radio station, known as Radio Free Grenada between 1979 and 1983, was destroyed during the military intervention in October 1983, and is at present housed in temporary studios.
Radio Grenada: POB 34, St George's; tel. 3033; f. 1983; state-owned; Man. (vacant).

Between 1980 and 1983 television broadcasts were provided by Free Grenada Television, which was owned and operated by the Government. Television programmes from Trinidad and from Barbados can be received on the island.

Finance

BANKING
Grenada Bank of Commerce Ltd: Cross and Halifax Sts, POB 4, St George's; tel. 3521; telex 3467; Man. M. Mathlin.
Grenada Co-operative Bank Ltd: 8 Church St, St George's; tel. 2111; f. 1932; Man. Dir and Sec. G. V. Steele; brs in St Andrew's and St Patrick's.
Grenada Development Bank: The Carenage, St George's; tel. 2382; f. 1976 after merger of the Grenada Agricultural Bank and the Grenada Development Corporation; Chair. Samuel Graham; Man. Ronald Charles.
National Commercial Bank of Grenada Ltd: Corner of Halifax and Hillsborough Sts, POB 57, St George's; tel. 3566; telex 3413; f. 1979; state-owned; Gen. Man. M. B. Archibald; 5 brs.

GRENADA

Foreign Banks

Bank of Nova Scotia (Canada): POB 194, Halifax St, St George's; tel. 3274; telex 3452; Man. C. A. S. HINKSON.

Barclays Bank (UK): POB 37, Church and Halifax Sts, St George's; tel. 3232; telex 3421; Man. L. E. POLLARD; 2 sub-brs in Carriacou and Grenville.

INSURANCE

Several locally-owned and foreign insurance companies operate in Grenada and the other islands of the group.

Trade and Industry

Grenada Chamber of Industry and Commerce, Inc: POB 129, St George's; tel. 2937; telex 3469; f. 1921, incorporated 1947; 148 mems; Pres. BRIAN PITT; Exec. Dir JENNI KILLAM.

Grenada Cocoa Association: Scott St, St George's; tel. 2234; telex 3444; f. 1964; controls cocoa marketing throughout Grenada; Chair. L. A. PURCELL.

Grenada Co-operative Banana Society: Scott St, St George's; tel. 2486; f. 1955; a statutory body to control production and marketing of bananas; Chair. (vacant).

Grenada Co-operative Nutmeg Association: POB 160, St George's; tel. 2117; telex 3454; f. 1947; processes and markets all the nutmeg and mace grown on the island; Gen. Man. R. S. RENWICK.

Grenada Electricity Services Ltd (Grenlec): POB 381, St George's; tel. 2097; telex 3472; Man. G. C. BOWEN.

Grenada Hotel and Tourism Association: POB 440, St George's; tel. 1590; telex 3425; f. 1961; Pres. ANDRÉ CHERMAN.

Grenada Industrial Development Corporation: Archibald Ave, St George's; tel. 3909; f. 1985.

Grenada Manufacturers' Association: St George's; f. 1986; Pres. JAMES ANTOINE; Sec. PETER JOSEPH.

Marketing and National Importing Board: Young St, St George's; tel. 3191/3111/1791-3; telex 3435; f. 1974; state-owned; imports basic food items, incl. sugar, rice and milk; Chair. MICHAEL ARCHIBALD; Gen. Man. ANDY MITCHELL.

EMPLOYERS' ORGANIZATION

Employers' Federation: Mt Gay, St George's; tel. 1832.

TRADE UNIONS

Agricultural and General Workers' Union: St George's; Pres. GODWIN THOMAS.

Bank and General Workers' Union: St George's; Pres. DEREK ALLARD.

Commercial and Industrial Workers' Union: St George's; 400 mems; Pres. A. DEBOURG.

Directory

Grenada Manual, Maritime and Intellectual Workers' Union: St George's; Pres. Sir ERIC GAIRY.

Grenada Union of Teachers: Marine Villa, St George's; f. 1913; Pres. DAWNE LETT; 1,300 mems.

Seamen and Waterfront Workers' Union: Carenage St, POB 154, St George's; tel. 2573; f. 1952; Pres. ARTHUR RAMSEY; Gen. Sec. ERIC PIERRE; 500 mems.

Technical and Allied Workers' Union: POB 405, Green St, St George's; tel. 2231; f. 1958; Pres. WILFRED HAYES; about 1,400 mems.

Transport

RAILWAYS

There are no railways in Grenada.

ROADS

In 1983 there were approximately 980 km (610 miles) of roads, of which 766 km (476 miles) were suitable for motor traffic. Many of these were severely damaged by military action in October 1983, and US aid was provided in 1984 for their repair. The 1986/87 budget allocated EC $29m. for road repair and construction. In 1984 there were 7,741 vehicles registered. Public transport is provided by small private operators, with a system covering the entire country.

SHIPPING

The main port is St George's, with accommodation for two ocean-going vessels of up to 500 ft. A number of shipping lines call at St George's. Grenville, on Grenada, and Hillsborough, on Carriacou, are used mostly by small craft.

CIVIL AVIATION

The airfield at Pearls, 30 km (18 miles) from St George's, is served by Air Martinique, Inter Island Air Services (subsidiary of LIAT) and LIAT (Antigua). Lauriston Airport, on the island of Carriacou, offers regular scheduled services to Grenada, Saint Vincent and Palm Island (Grenadines of Saint Vincent). The Point Salines International Airport was opened in October 1984, and is served by LIAT, BWIA (Trinidad and Tobago) and Grenada Airways.

Grenada Airways: St George's; f. 1985; charter flights to Miami and New York, USA.

Tourism

There were 504 hotel beds in 1984.

Grenada Hotel and Tourism Association: POB 440, St George's; tel. 1590; telex 3425.

Grenada Tourist Department: POB 293, St George's; tel. 2001; telex 3422; Chair. JOHN WATTS; Dir of Tourism JIMMY EMMANUEL.

GUATEMALA

Introductory Survey

Location, Climate, Language, Religion, Flag, Capital

The Republic of Guatemala lies in the Central American isthmus, bounded to the north and west by Mexico, with Honduras and Belize to the east and El Salvador to the south. It has a long coastline on the Pacific Ocean and a narrow outlet to the Caribbean Sea. The climate is tropical in the lowlands, with an average temperature of 28°C (83°F), and more temperate in the central highland area, with an average temperature of 20°C (68°F). The official language is Spanish, but more than 20 indigenous languages are also spoken. Almost all of the inhabitants profess Christianity: the majority are Roman Catholics, while about 25% are Protestants. The national flag (proportions 3 by 2) has three equal vertical stripes, of blue, white and blue, with the national coat of arms (depicting a quetzal, the 'bird of freedom', and a scroll, superimposed on crossed rifles and sabres, encircled by a wreath) in the centre of the white stripe. The capital is Guatemala City.

Recent History

Under Spanish colonial rule, Guatemala was part of the Viceroyalty of New Spain. Independence was obtained from Spain in 1821, from Mexico in 1824 and from the Federation of Central American States in 1838. Subsequent attempts to revive the Federation failed and, under a series of dictators, there was relative stability, tempered by periods of disruption. A programme of social reform was begun by Juan José Arévalo (President in 1944–50) and his successor, Col Jacobo Arbenz Guzmán, whose policy of land reform evoked strong opposition from landowners. In 1954 President Arbenz was overthrown in a coup led by Col Carlos Castillo Armas, who invaded the country with US assistance. Castillo became President but was assassinated in July 1957. The next elected President, Gen. Miguel Ydigoras Fuentes, took office in March 1958 and ruled until he was deposed in March 1963 by a military coup, led by Col Enrique Peralta Azurdia. He assumed full powers as Chief of Government, suspended the Constitution and dissolved the legislature. A Constituent Assembly, elected in 1964, produced a new constitution in 1965. Dr Julio César Méndez Montenegro was elected President in 1966, and in 1970 the candidate of the Movimiento de Liberación Nacional (MLN), Col (later Gen.) Carlos Araña Osorio, was elected President after a turbulent campaign. Despite charges of fraud in the elections of March 1974, Gen. Kjell Laugerud García of the MLN took office as President in July.

President Laugerud sought to discourage extreme right-wing violence and claimed some success, although in September 1979 Amnesty International estimated the number of lives lost in political violence since 1970 at between 50,000 and 60,000. In February 1976 a series of earthquakes in central Guatemala resulted in 23,000 dead, 77,000 injured and about 1m. homeless. In March 1978 Gen. Fernando Romeo Lucas García was elected President. The guerrilla movement increased in strength in 1980 and 1981, while the Government was accused of the murder and torture of civilians and, particularly, persecution of the country's indigenous Indian inhabitants, who make up 60% of the population. An estimated 11,000 civilians were killed in 1981.

In the presidential and congressional elections of 7 March 1982, from which the left-wing parties were absent, the largest number of votes was awarded to the Government's candidate, Gen. Angel Aníbal Guevara, who was later confirmed as President by Congress. The other presidential candidates denounced the elections as fraudulent. Guevara was prevented from taking office in July by a coup on 23 March, in which a group of young right-wing military officers installed Gen. Efraín Ríos Montt (a candidate in the 1974 presidential elections) as leader of a three-man junta. Congress was closed, and the Constitution and political parties suspended. In June Gen. Ríos Montt dissolved the junta and assumed the Presidency. He attempted to fight corruption, reorganized the judicial system and disbanded the secret police. The number of violent deaths diminished. However, after initially gaining the support of the national university, the Roman Catholic Church and the labour unions and hoping to enter into dialogue with the guerrillas, who refused to respond to an amnesty declaration in June, President Ríos Montt declared a state of siege, and imposed censorship of the press, in July.

The war against the guerrillas intensified, and a civil defence force of Indians was established. The efficiency of the army increased. Whole villages were burnt, and many inhabitants killed, in order to deter the Indians from supporting the guerrillas. Up to 500,000 Indians have been displaced by the war, and many have escaped across the border to Mexico, where refugee camps have been established. President Ríos Montt's increasingly corporatist policies alienated all groups, and his fragile hold on power was threatened in 1982 by several attempted coups, which he managed to forestall.

President Ronald Reagan of the USA was eager to renew sales of armaments and the provision of economic and military aid to Guatemala, which had been suspended in 1977 as a result of serious violations of human rights. Several sales of spare parts for military equipment were made to Guatemala in 1982, despite restrictions by the US Congress. In January 1983 the US Government, satisfied that there had been a significant decrease in the abuse of human rights during Gen. Ríos Montt's presidency, announced the resumption of arms sales to Guatemala. However, independent reports claimed that the situation had deteriorated, and revealed that 2,600 people had been killed during the first six months of President Ríos Montt's rule. An estimated 100,000 refugees fled to Mexico during early 1983, and relations between Guatemala and Mexico were strained, following further incursions into Mexican territory by Guatemalan security forces, which resulted in the deaths of several refugees. In March the army was implicated in the massacre of 300 Indian peasants at Nahulá, and there was a resurgence in the activity of both left- and right-wing 'death squads'. The President declared a 30-day amnesty for guerrillas and political exiles, and lifted the state of siege which had been imposed in July 1982. Furthermore, he announced the creation of an electoral tribunal to organize and oversee a proposed transfer from military rule to civilian government. In April the army launched a new offensive, which made significant gains against the guerrillas, principally in the rebel stronghold of Petén and the province of El Quiché. In response, the URNG (the main guerrilla grouping) announced a major change in tactics, which gave priority to attacks on economic targets instead of to direct confrontation with the army. The Government's pacification programme comprised three phases of aid programmes, combined with the saturation of the countryside by anti-guerrilla units. The 'guns and beans' policy provided food and medicine in exchange for recruitment to the PAC, a pro-Government peasant militia. The 'roofs, bread and work' phase involved the development of 'model villages', and the 'Aid Programme for Areas in Conflict' (PAAC) was an ambitious rural development scheme.

By June 1983 opposition to the President was widespread, and several attempted coups were reported. Gen. Ríos Montt had alienated the most influential groups within Guatemalan society by his dependence upon a group of advisers which consisted of six young army officers and fellow members of his fundamentalist Protestant church. The President no longer enjoyed the support of the Roman Catholic Church, the conservative hierarchy and the business community, who were angered by his evangelical doctrines, austerity measures and proposed agrarian reform. The increasing abuses of human rights and the continuing existence of secret tribunals had provoked international criticism and damaged US-Guatemalan relations. The shift in power towards the lower ranks of the armed forces had created divisions within the officer corps, and led to dissension. On 29 June the air force and four army garrisons rebelled against the President. They called for a return to constitutional rule and for the dismissal of the President's advisers. Gen. Ríos Montt agreed to both demands but remained unconvincing on the issue of electoral reform. On 8 August 1983 Gen. Oscar Humberto Mejía Victores, the Minister of Defence, led a successful coup against President Ríos Montt.

The new President announced the abolition of the secret tribunals and ended press censorship. In addition, the Council of State was abolished. A 90-day amnesty for guerrillas was announced in October. The amnesty was extended throughout 1984. Urban and rural terrorism continued to escalate, however, and in November 1983 the Government was accused of directing a campaign of kidnappings against the Roman Catholic Church. Following the murder of six USAID workers in northern Guatemala, the US House of Representatives suspended the $50m. in aid which President Reagan had requested for Guatemala in 1984. Nevertheless, the US Administration resolved to provide $24m. in economic aid during 1984. Israel continued to supply weapons to Guatemala, and Israeli military advisers were reported to be active in the country. In October Gen. Mejía Victores acted to strengthen his position after rumours of his unpopularity among high-ranking officers. Supporters of Gen. Ríos Montt were sent into exile, and in January 1984 new army reforms were introduced. In accordance with the President's assurance of electoral reform, elections for a Constituent Assembly were scheduled for July 1984.

The start of campaigning for elections to the Constituent Assembly heralded a new wave of political violence. By March 1984 the number of weekly political assassinations had risen to an average of 145. It was estimated that more than 50 people were abducted each week. Fifteen political parties planned to contest the election in July. Contrary to public forecasts, the centre groups, including the newly formed Unión del Centro Nacional (UCN), obtained the greatest number of votes. Under the system of proportional representation, however, the rightwing coalition of the MLN and the Central Auténtica Nacionalista (CAN) together obtained a majority of seats in the Assembly. In August a directive board, composed of representatives from the three major political parties, began drafting the Constitution.

In 1984 the Government continued to develop its controversial strategy of 'model villages', which entailed the construction of new settlements in isolated locations for Indian communities. Relations with neighbouring Mexico deteriorated in 1984, following an attack in April on a Guatemalan refugee camp situated in Mexico, during which six people were killed. By August 1984 the Organización del Pueblo en Armas (ORPA) had emerged as the most active of the guerrilla groups, operating in San Marcos and Quezaltenango. In October an upsurge of violence in Guatemala City, coupled with unrest in the business sector, gave rise to rumours of government instability and encouraged scepticism at the Government's commitment to holding the forthcoming presidential election. Under Gen. Mejía Victores, it was estimated that more than 100 political assassinations and 40 abductions occurred each month.

Guatemala's new constitution was promulgated in May 1985. In June President Mejía Victores confirmed that elections for the presidency, the National Congress and 331 mayoralties would be held in November. Prior to the elections, there was a substantial increase in rebel activity and political assassinations by 'death squads'. However, the principal threat to internal security before the elections occurred in September, when violent protests, led by students and trade unionists, broke out in reaction to a series of price increases which had been authorized by the Government in August. In the course of the protests, several people were reported to have been killed and hundreds of demonstrators were arrested. In addition, the University of San Carlos in Guatemala City was temporarily occupied by soldiers.

Eight candidates participated in the presidential election in November 1985, but the main contest was between Jorge Carpio Nicolle, candidate of the Unión del Centro Nacional, and Mario Vinicio Cerezo Arévalo, candidate of the Partido Democracia Cristiana Guatemalteca (PDCG). As neither of the leading candidates obtained the requisite majority, a second round of voting was held in December, at which Vinicio Cerezo secured 68% of the votes cast. The PDCG formed the majority party in the new National Congress and won the largest proportion of mayoralties. Vinicio Cerezo was thought to enjoy the backing of the US administration, which increased its allocation of economic aid to $104.4m. in 1986, and resumed military aid (of $5.1m.) to Guatemala in support of the new civilian Government.

Immediately prior to the transfer of power in January 1986, the outgoing military Government decreed a general amnesty to encompass those suspected of involvement in murders and other abuses of human rights since March 1982. In February 1986, however, in an attempt to curb the continuing violence and to improve the country's bad record for the observance of human rights, President Cerezo instigated a raid on the headquarters of the secret police, the Department of Technical Investigations (DIT), which had been accused of numerous kidnappings and murders of citizens. About 600 members were detained, and 115 officers against whom evidence of human rights violations was found were to be tried. The DIT was dissolved and replaced by a new criminal investigations unit. Cerezo's action was welcomed by the Grupo Apoyo Mutuo (GAM), a grouping of the relatives of victims of repression, and by Amnesty International. Violence continued unabated, however, with 700 killings being recorded by human rights groups in the first six months of 1986 alone. President Cerezo claimed that not all murders were politically motivated, while his relations with the armed forces remained precarious. Meanwhile, the GAM attracted increasing support, and in August about 3,000 demonstrators took part in a protest to demand information on the fate of the thousands of 'disappeared'. By late 1986 the accused DIT agents, arrested in February, had yet to be put on trial.

Until the return to civilian government in 1986, Guatemala remained steadfast in its claims to the neighbouring territory of Belize, a former British dependency. In protest at the United Kingdom's decision to grant independence to Belize, in accordance with a UN resolution of November 1980, Guatemala severed diplomatic relations with the United Kingdom. An agreement between Guatemala and the United Kingdom, signed in March 1981, was rejected by Guatemala in July 1982. Talks resumed in January 1983 but, despite a modification in Guatemalan demands, the negotiations broke down. In November Guatemala announced its support for the maintenance of a British presence in Belize as 'insurance' against a possible take-over by guerrilla forces. Tripartite talks were held in May 1984. Guatemala's new constitution, promulgated in May 1985, did not include Belize in its delineation of Guatemalan territory. Upon taking office in 1986, President Cerezo showed a desire to end his country's diplomatic isolation. He expressed willingness to recognize the people of Belize as a distinct community and to resume good relations with the United Kingdom. In July Congress voted to repeal the 1963 decree that severed diplomatic relations with the United Kingdom, and in August consular links between the two countries were restored. In December full diplomatic relations were resumed, and a British Embassy was to be opened in Guatemala City in 1987. The United Kingdom was to retain a garrison of 1,600 soldiers in Belize.

The attempt to settle the dispute over Belize is important, both economically and politically, for Guatemala. The lifting of economic sanctions and trade restrictions from Belize in late 1986 opened the way to Guatemalan investment in that territory and to the possibility of joint development projects. As much of Guatemala's foreign debt is owed to EEC members, President Cerezo was anxious to remain on good terms with the EEC countries. A settlement of the dispute is also important for Guatemala's Central American policy and for hopes of achieving peace in the region. Neighbouring countries did not support Guatemala in its claims to Belize. At a summit meeting of Central American leaders, held in Guatemala in May 1986, the Presidents committed themselves to a continuation of peace negotiations. The formation of a Central American parliament was also agreed.

Government

Guatemala is a republic comprising 22 departments. Under the new constitution, which took effect in January 1986, legislative

GUATEMALA

Introductory Survey

power is vested in the unicameral National Congress, with 100 members elected for five years by universal adult suffrage. Of the total seats, 75 are filled by direct election and 25 on the basis of proportional representation. Executive power is held by the President (also directly elected for five years), assisted by a Vice-President and an appointed Cabinet.

Defence

In July 1986 the armed forces totalled 32,000, of whom 30,300 were in the army, 1,000 in the navy (including 650 marines) and 700 in the air force. There were paramilitary forces of 9,500. Military service is by conscription for at least two years. In the early 1980s the Patrullas de Autodefensa Civil (PAC), an anti-guerrilla peasant militia, was established. By 1985 these self-defence patrols numbered 900,000 men. Defence expenditure in 1985 was estimated to be 198.4m. quetzales.

Economic Affairs

The economy is predominantly agricultural, with more than one-half of the country's active population working in agriculture, forestry and fishing. The agricultural sector usually provides more than 25% of Guatemala's gross domestic product (GDP) and over 60% of export earnings. In 1984, according to estimates by the World Bank, the country's gross national product (GNP) per head, measured at average 1982–84 prices, was US $1,160. Between 1965 and 1984, it was estimated, GNP per head increased, in real terms, at an average rate of 2.0% per year. The average annual growth of overall GDP, in constant prices, was 6.0% in 1965–73, slowing to 3.1% in 1973–84. Guatemala is Central America's second most important coffee producer. Coffee is the country's leading export commodity, generating an estimated 42.6% of total export earnings in 1985. Following a fall in production in 1983, the 1984 harvest increased to 2.34m. bags (each of 60 kg). Production declined by 7% in 1985, but was expected to rise by 20% in 1986. Export earnings increased from US $361m. in 1984 to an estimated $451.6m. in 1985. Coffee exports in 1986 were estimated at $440m. Other major crops are sugar cane, bananas, cardamom and cotton. Production of sugar cane fell from a record 6.2m. metric tons in 1982 to 5.5m. tons in 1983. Exports of sugar were worth an estimated $46.5m. in 1985, compared with $71.3m. in 1984. Unfavourable weather conditions during 1985 depressed production (estimated at 5.5m. tons), but output was expected to rise again in 1986. Cotton provided 13.3% of export income in 1981 but only 6.2% in 1983, owing to high costs, low world prices, lack of domestic credit and the guerrilla war. Production of cotton lint increased from 60,000 tons in 1983 to an estimated 67,000 tons in 1985, when exports of cotton rose to $73m. In 1986 the Cerezo administration promised $10m. in loans to aid the cotton industry. In March 1983 high winds caused $60m. in damage to banana plantations. Agricultural production declined by 6% in 1983. A further threat to the agricultural sector was the guerrilla campaign against economic targets, launched in 1983. Attempts to diversify agricultural production initially resulted in increased exports of tobacco, vegetables, fruit and beef. Between 1981 and 1985, however, Guatemala's exports of fresh meat declined from $29.3m. to $10.0m., owing to the suspension of sales to Mexico and a fall in domestic beef production. Under the 'Aid Programme for Areas in Conflict' (PAAC), inaugurated in 1983, the Government hoped to transform the mainly Indian-populated highlands by establishing extensive plantations for the cultivation of fruit and vegetables, which were to provide new agricultural products for export. Additional funding for agricultural development projects has been provided by the IMF and the IDB. Extensive forests provide timber and chicle.

Guatemala's industrial sector is the largest in Central America. Manufacturing contributes about 16% of GDP and provides employment for 16% of the working population. The main branches of industry are food processing, rubber, textiles, paper and pharmaceuticals. Exports of manufactured goods more than trebled between 1972 and 1978, but in 1982 the Central American market collapsed. Subsequently, priority has been given to trade with the USA. A shortage of domestic credit and lack of external demand, principally from other CACM members, have cut the sector's growth rate. Private investment has declined because of social unrest, and public investment has been curtailed by austerity measures and the scarcity of foreign exchange. Following the closure of 185 businesses in 1982, more factories were expected to go bankrupt. In 1984 an estimated 44% of the labour force were unemployed. In 1985 the industrial sector was operating at only 60% of its installed capacity.

Commercial quantities of petroleum were discovered in 1974 and 1975, and the Rubelsanto and West Chinajá fields have reserves estimated at 127m. barrels. In 1985 their output averaged 6,600 barrels per day (b/d). Further deposits were found in 1981 in Alta Verapaz and the Petén Basin: these are being exploited by Texaco, Amoco and Hispanoil. A 50,000 b/d pipeline, linking Rubelsanto and the Caribbean coastline, was completed in 1981. Guatemala's earnings from exports of petroleum declined from US $60m. in 1983 to barely $12m. in 1985. New wells were discovered in 1981 and 1982, and the find at Tierra Blanca is expected to produce as much as 6,000–6,500 b/d. Guatemala remains a marginal producer; average output declined from over 6,000 b/d in 1982 to 3,000 b/d in 1986. Domestic consumption was averaging 12,000 b/d during 1985–86. A new oilwell in Petén, which started producing 2,000 b/d, increased Guatemala's oil production by 30% in 1986. Proven reserves total 22m. barrels, while potential reserves are believed to be 800m.–1,000m. barrels. Although foreign companies were reluctant to invest in Guatemala, owing to the unfavourable terms offered by the Government and to the guerrilla war, new legislation was introduced in October 1983 to encourage foreign investment in exploration for petroleum. There were plans to build a state-owned petroleum refinery with a capacity of 30,000 b/d, despite an existing surplus of refining capacity. In 1985 Guatemala experienced severe fuel shortages as a result of its inability to raise foreign exchange to pay for imports of petroleum, costing an estimated $22m. per month. In July the Government sold one-fifth of Guatemala's reserves of gold in order to finance petroleum imports. However, the cost of such imports in 1986 was considerably lower, owing to the fall in world oil prices and to increased domestic production. A 300-MW hydroelectric project at Chixoy was inaugurated in 1986. There were plans to construct a geothermal generating plant, to be known as Zunil 1.

The Exmibal consortium has invested 224m. quetzales in exploiting the deposits of nickel ore, estimated at 60m. tons, near Lake Izabal at Chalac-El Estor. A refining plant began operating in mid-1977 and, at full capacity, was to have produced 28m. lb. (12,700 metric tons) of nickel per year, but in November 1981 it was decided to close down the mine indefinitely, as falling sales, the rising cost of fuel and new taxation had made the venture financially unviable. In July 1986 plans to revive the small-scale mining industry were announced. Minas de Guatemala was expected to reopen small lead, antimony and tungsten mines.

Despite the earthquake, Guatemala's GDP rose by 9% in 1976. By 1981, however, the growth rate had dropped to 1%, as a result of low world prices for export crops, and in 1982 GDP fell by 3%. A further fall of 2.5% was recorded in 1983, and, although there was a slight positive growth in 1984, the negative trend continued in 1985. Tourism, once the third largest exchange earner, had virtually ceased by 1983, with a drop in revenue from $82m. in 1979 to $8m. in 1983. Total export earnings fell by 7.7%, to US $1,260m., in 1982. Imports increased by 11%, to $1,774m., in 1981. The current deficit on the balance of payments, which had been $573m. in 1981, declined to $246m. in 1985. Official reserves of foreign exchange fell from $653.5m. at the end of 1979 to only $65m. in April 1983. By the end of 1984 foreign exchange reserves had increased to $272m. Readily available reserves of convertible currency were estimated at between $25m. and $50m. in 1983. A flight of capital and an increase in service payments on Guatemala's external debt were responsible for the sharp drop in reserves. Net reserves were in deficit. In 1983, in response to increasing economic difficulties, the Government implemented a series of austerity measures. Planned budget expenditure was reduced by 20%, about 3,000 employees were made redundant, and the price of petrol was increased. In September the Government reached agreement with the IMF on a stand-by arrangement allowing Guatemala to obtain up to the equivalent of 114.8m. SDRs ($109.6m.) over a period of 16 months. Under the terms of the agreement, the Government undertook to reduce the budget deficit and to introduce a programme of tax reforms. Following protests at the 10% rate of value-added tax (VAT), the rate was reduced to 7% in October. This decision prompted the IMF to suspend its agreement with the Government. In addition, credit amounting to $360m. was withdrawn by international financing agencies. A resumption of negotiations appeared to be unlikely, following the Government's reluctance to implement further increases in taxation, including VAT. The existing tax programme was regarded as a failure, having yielded only 40% of the expected revenue. In July 1984 the IMF suspended disbursement of $60m. from the original credit. In September the Government was forced to enact changes in the tax programme to compensate for tax evasion amounting to 100m. quetzales since 1983. In November, after many years of being at parity with the US dollar, the quetzal was partially devalued, when a 'parallel' exchange rate of 1.60 quetzales per US dollar, applicable to non-essential imports and to some exports, was introduced. Following the introduction of a 'parallel' rate, the cost of importing basic foods and other goods increased by between 25% and 50%. By mid-1985 the 'parallel' exchange rate stood at US $1 = 3.04 quetzales.

In April 1985 the Government introduced a series of tax increases which were immediately rejected by Guatemala's powerful business sector. In compliance with the sector's demands, the Ministers of Finance and of the Economy were dismissed by President Mejía Victores. In August the Government announced increases of up to 50% in the cost of public transport fares and basic foods. In the face of widespread public protests at the price rises, the Government rescinded the increases in September.

In early 1986 President Cerezo outlined plans to improve the standard of living in Guatemala, where an estimated 63% of the population were living in conditions inferior to the officially-defined level of poverty. A programme of road-building and improvement to the water system was expected to generate 3,000–4,000 new jobs. A World Bank loan of $81m. was secured in 1986 to finance the expansion of electric services and the improvement of power distribution, a project costing an estimated $133.2m. in total. A further loan of $23m. was granted to finance a water supply rehabilitation project.

In 1984 and 1985 the Guatemalan economy was in decline. GDP grew, in real terms, by only 0.2% in 1984, and fell by about 1.5% in 1985. The budget deficit was expected to be US $343m. in 1985. The annual rate of inflation increased from 22.5% in 1984 to 57% in the year to May 1985, while unemployment remained a serious problem, affecting at least 40% of the labour force. Debt servicing on Guatemala's foreign debt of $3,000m. was expected to absorb 36% of export earnings in 1985. Following the transfer of power to a civilian government in January 1986, a programme of austerity measures and financial reform was implemented, and, as a result, the economy started to show signs of revival. By 1986 Guatemala's foreign debt had fallen to about $2,400m., and inflation fell to an average of 24% for the first three months of the year. In July the country's reserves of foreign exchange amounted to about $240m., and, for the first time in four years, they were adequate to cover import needs. The devaluation of the quetzal in March and the doubling of international coffee prices were believed to have helped in generating these reserves. It was hoped that 1986 would mark the end of the recession in Guatemala's economy. The 1987 budget envisaged expenditure of 2,550m. quetzales, of which more than 20% was to be allocated to debt servicing.

Social Welfare

Social security is compulsory, and all employers with five or more workers are required to enrol with the State Institute of Social Security, which came under army control in 1983. Benefits are available to registered workers for industrial accidents, sickness, maternity, disability, widowhood and hospitalization. In 1979 there were 819 physicians working in the government health service. A $51m. project to improve health services, including two new hospitals in Guatemala City and one in Antigua, was announced in 1980. In 1986 a vaccination programme to benefit more than 1m. children was announced, in a campaign to combat infant mortality

Education

Elementary education is free and, in urban areas, compulsory between seven and 14 years of age. Primary education begins at the age of seven and lasts for six years. Secondary education, beginning at 13 years of age, lasts for up to six years, comprising two cycles of three years each. In 1982 an estimated 56% of children in the relevant age-group (boys 59%; girls 53%) attended primary schools, while the comparable figure for secondary education was only 13%. In 1983 the level of enrolment at primary schools increased to 60%. In 1984 the total enrolment at primary and secondary schools was equivalent to 48% of the school-age population. There are five universities. In 1981 a 'national literacy crusade' was launched by the Government, but in 1985, according to estimates by UNESCO, the average rate of adult illiteracy was 45% (males 37.4%; females 52.9%), the second highest level in the Western hemisphere.

Tourism

The main attractions lie in the mountain regions, with their volcanoes, lakes and mountain villages which remain much the same as in the days of the Maya Empire. The old capital, Antigua, retains the ruins of buildings wrecked in the great earthquake of 1773. The Government is expanding tourist facilities in the Izabal-El Petén region. There are significant Mayan ruins at Tikal, Yaxhá, Nakum and El Mirador. The tourist industry has been devastated by the recent violence within Guatemala, and the annual total of tourist arrivals declined from 504,000 in 1979, when tourist receipts were US $201m., to 192,000 in 1984 (receipts $56.6m.). In 1985, however, arrivals rose to an estimated 251,946, while receipts increased to $67.2m.

Public Holidays

1987: 1 January (New Year's Day), 6 January (Epiphany), 17–20 April (Easter), 1 May (Labour Day), 30 June (Anniversary of the Revolution), 15 August (Assumption, Guatemala City only), 15 September (Independence Day), 12 October (Columbus Day), 20 October (Revolution Day), 1 November (All Saints' Day), 24–25 December (Christmas), 31 December (New Year's Eve).

1988: 1 January (New Year's Day), 6 January (Epiphany), 1–4 April (Easter), 1 May (Labour Day), 30 June (Anniversary of the Revolution), 15 August (Assumption, Guatemala City only), 15 September (Independence Day), 12 October (Columbus Day), 20 October (Revolution Day), 1 November (All Saints' Day), 24–25 December (Christmas), 31 December (New Year's Eve).

Weights and Measures

The metric system is in official use.

Currency and Exchange Rates

100 centavos = 1 quetzal.

Exchange rates (30 September 1986):
  £1 sterling = 1.447 quetzales;
  US $1 = 1.000 quetzal (official rates).

Statistical Survey

Sources (unless otherwise stated): Banco de Guatemala, 7a Avda 22-01, Zona 1, Guatemala City; Dirección General de Estadística, Edif. América 4°, 8a Calle 9-55, Zona 1, Guatemala City; tel. 26136.

Area and Population

AREA, POPULATION AND DENSITY

Area (sq km)	
Land	108,429
Inland water	460
Total	108,889*
Population (census results)†	
26 March 1973	5,160,221
26 March 1981	
Males	3,015,826
Females	3,038,401
Total	6,054,227
Population (official estimates at mid-year)	
1983	7,926,728
1984	8,161,403
1985	8,403,025
Density (per sq km) at mid-1985	77.2

* 42,042 sq miles.
† Excluding adjustments for underenumeration.

DEPARTMENTS (estimated population at mid-1985)

Alta Verapaz	393,446	Jutiapa	348,032
Baja Verapaz	160,567	Quezaltenango	478,080
Chimaltenango	283,887	Retalhuleu	228,563
Chiquimula	220,067	Sacatepéquez	148,574
El Petén	118,116	San Marcos	590,152
El Progreso	106,115	Santa Rosa	263,060
El Quiché	460,956	Sololá	181,816
Escuintla	565,215	Suchitepéquez	327,763
Guatemala	2,050,673	Totonicapán	249,067
Huehuetenango	571,292	Zacapa	155,496
Izabal	330,546		
Jalapa	171,542	**Total**	8,403,025

PRINCIPAL TOWNS (population at 1981 census)

Guatemala City (capital)	754,243	Puerto Barrios	46,882
Escuintla	75,442	Retalhuleu	46,652
Quezaltenango	72,922	Chiquimula	42,571
		Mazatenango	38,181

Source: CELADE.

BIRTHS, MARRIAGES AND DEATHS

	Registered live births		Registered marriages		Registered deaths	
	Number	Rate (per 1,000)	Number	Rate (per 1,000)	Number	Rate (per 1,000)
1980	303,443	41.8	31,230	4.3	71,383	9.8
1981	308,413	41.2	32,398	4.3	75,658	10.1
1982	311,978	40.5	31,233	4.1	76,267	9.9
1983	288,502	36.4	30,422	3.8	74,462	9.4
1984	302,961	37.1	31,351	3.8	75,462	9.2
1985	322,994	38.4	38,199	4.5	68,955	8.2

ECONOMICALLY ACTIVE POPULATION
(official estimates for 1985)

	Males	Females	Total
Agriculture, forestry, hunting and fishing	1,397,374	25,206	1,422,580
Mining and quarrying	2,414	35	2,449
Manufacturing	257,309	75,687	332,996
Construction	99,837	551	100,388
Electricity, gas, water and sanitary services	7,138	207	7,345
Commerce	120,478	58,263	178,741
Transport, storage and communications	59,698	1,515	61,213
Services	122,301	171,519	293,820
Activities not adequately described	37,607	11,363	48,970
Total	2,104,156	344,346	2,448,502

Source: Secretaría General del Consejo Nacional de Planificación Económica.

Agriculture

PRINCIPAL CROPS ('000 metric tons)

	1983	1984	1985*
Sugar cane	5,450	5,459	5,492
Cotton (lint)	60	61	67
Maize	998	1,137	1,096
Rice	45	44	38
Dry beans	92	104	114
Wheat	53	54	44
Coffee	166	174	164
Bananas ('000 stems)	13,492	13,538	15,773

* Preliminary.
Source: *Cuentas Nacionales,* Banco de Guatemala.

LIVESTOCK ('000 head, year ending September)

	1983	1984	1985
Horses*	100	100	100
Cattle	2,185	2,605	2,587†
Sheep	657	660	670*
Pigs	806	810	832*
Goats	73	76	76*

Chickens (million): 15* in 1983; 15* in 1984; 15* in 1985.
* FAO estimates. † Unofficial figure.
Source: FAO, *Production Yearbook.*

LIVESTOCK PRODUCTS ('000 metric tons)

	1983	1984	1985
Beef and veal*	63	64	57
Pig meat	17†	17†	16
Poultry meat†	50	50	55
Cheese†	15.2	14.6	14.9
Butter and ghee†	4.7	4.5	4.5
Hen eggs	40.1*	40.5*	41.5†
Cattle hides†	10.0	10.0	8.4

* Unofficial figure. † FAO estimates.
Source: FAO, *Production Yearbook.*

Forestry

ROUNDWOOD REMOVALS
('000 cubic metres, excluding bark)

	1982	1983	1984
Sawlogs, veneer logs and logs for sleepers	184	148	146
Other industrial wood*	10	10	10
Fuel wood*	6,457	6,648	6,844
Total	6,651	6,806	7,000

* FAO estimates.
Source: FAO, *Yearbook of Forest Products.*

SAWNWOOD PRODUCTION ('000 cubic metres)

	1982	1983	1984
Coniferous sawnwood	74	72	77
Broadleaved sawnwood	55	32	26
Sub-total	129	104	103
Railway sleepers	1	—	—
Total	130	104	103

Source: FAO, *Yearbook of Forest Products.*

Fishing

(metric tons, live weight)

	1982	1983	1984
Total catch	4,284	2,376	2,963

Source: FAO, *Yearbook of Fishery Statistics.*

Mining

SELECTED PRODUCTS (metric tons)

	1983	1984	1985
Antimony ore	n.a.	160	1,324
Petroleum	342,188	230,228	143,384
Iron ore	1,159	1,100	2,333
Lead ore	100	100	100

Source: Ministry of Energy and Mines.

Industry

SELECTED PRODUCTS

	1983	1984	1985
Cement ('000 metric tons)	466	401	526
Sugar ('000 metric tons)	525	508	542
Electricity (million kWh)	1,430	1,504	1,568
Cigarettes (million)	2,136	2,008	1,936

Source: *Cuentas Nacionales,* Banco de Guatemala.

Finance

CURRENCY AND EXCHANGE RATES

Monetary Units
100 centavos = 1 quetzal.

Denominations
Coins: 1, 5, 10 and 25 centavos.
Notes: 50 centavos; 1, 5, 10, 20, 50 and 100 quetzales.

Sterling and Dollar Equivalents (30 September 1986)
£1 sterling = 1.447 quetzales;
US $1 = 1.000 quetzal;
100 quetzales = £69.11 = $100.00.

Note: The foregoing data refer to the official market rate, whereby the quetzal is fixed at par with the US dollar. However, a multiple exchange rate system is in effect. The official rate is applicable to essential imports (as defined by the Government) and to certain other transactions. There is also a banking market rate (introduced in 1984) and an auction market rate (introduced in 1985). The banking market rate was US $1 = 2.86 quetzales at 30 September 1986, and its average level in 1985 was $1 = 2.77 quetzales.

INTERNATIONAL RESERVES
(US $ million at 31 December)

	1983	1984	1985
Gold*	22.1	22.1	22.1
IMF special drawing rights	0.6	2.0	—
Reserve position in IMF	8.2	—	—
Foreign exchange	201.2	272.4	300.9
Total	232.1	296.5	323.0

* Valued at US $42.22 per troy ounce.
Source: IMF, *International Financial Statistics*.

BUDGET (million quetzales)

Revenue	1983	1984	1985*
Taxation	572.8	497.9	679.3
Treasury bills and foreign loans	391.0	293.2	441.3
Other receipts	170.9	170.7	187.1
Total	1,134.7	961.8	1,307.7

Expenditure	1983	1984	1985*
Education	134.9	137.9	137.9
Health	73.6	85.7	78.8
Agriculture	51.4	42.5	33.9
Defence	162.7	181.1	196.8
Communications and public works	141.8	81.0	77.4
Transportation	95.8	92.0	72.8
Other items	437.1	511.4	589.8
Total	1,097.3	1,131.6	1,187.4

* Preliminary.
Source: Ministry of Finance.

MONEY SUPPLY (million quetzales at 31 December)

	1984	1985	1986*
Currency outside banks	460.9	697.8	682.3
Private sector deposits at Bank of Guatemala	58.8	65.0	60.1
Demand deposits at deposit money banks	402.1	642.3	636.6
Total money	921.8	1,405.1	1,379.0

* At July.

NATIONAL ACCOUNTS (million quetzales in current prices)

	1983	1984	1985*
Government final consumption expenditure	687.9	725.9	774.8
Private final consumption expenditure	7,500.7	7,855.9	9,261.4
Increase in stocks	52.3	183.5	46.4
Gross fixed capital formation	950.2	912.4	1,226.8
Total domestic expenditure	9,191.1	9,677.7	11,309.4
Exports of goods and services	1,175.8	1,262.9	2,036.0
Less Imports of goods and services	1,317.0	1,454.8	2,290.8
Gross domestic product	9,049.9	9,485.8	11,054.6
Factor income from abroad	29.1	−202.7	−165.0
Less Factor income paid abroad	142.6		
Gross national product	8,936.5	9,283.1	10,889.6

* Preliminary.
Source: *Cuentas Nacionales*, Banco de Guatemala.

GUATEMALA

BALANCE OF PAYMENTS (US $ million)

	1983	1984	1985
Merchandise exports f.o.b.	1,091.7	1,132.2	1,059.7
Merchandise imports f.o.b.	−1,056.0	−1,182.2	−1,076.7
Trade balance	35.7	−50.0	−17.0
Exports of services	113.3	129.0	131.6
Imports of services	−403.5	−485.1	−380.6
Balance on goods and services	−254.5	−406.1	−266.0
Private unrequited transfers (net)	29.8	28.0	18.9
Government unrequited transfers (net)	0.8	0.7	0.8
Current balance	−223.9	−377.4	−246.3
Direct capital investment (net)	45.0	38.0	61.8
Other long-term capital (net)	−16.2	−86.1	−133.1
Short-term capital (net)	117.6	−61.3	−57.1
Net errors and omissions	−37.1	15.5	43.7
Total (net monetary movements)	−114.6	−471.3	−331.0
Valuation changes (net)	5.5	10.3	−14.2
Exceptional financing (net)	124.2	487.9	438.2
Official financing (net)	41.4	−6.0	4.0
Changes in reserves	56.4	20.9	97.0

Source: IMF, *International Financial Statistics*.

External Trade

PRINCIPAL COMMODITIES ('000 quetzales)

Imports c.i.f.	1983	1984	1985*
Basic manufactures	232,591	236,195	195,288
Machinery and transport equipment	167,291	210,258	222,831
Chemicals and products	257,436	297,292	269,840
Food products	77,107	84,142	81,883
Mineral fuels, lubricants, etc.	256,651	303,123	271,296
Crude materials (inedible) except fuels	31,939	28,687	29,642
Total (incl. others)	1,134,995	1,278,496	1,174,811

Exports f.o.b.	1983	1984	1985*
Coffee, incl. soluble	309,146	360,731	451,582
Cotton	67,691	72,353	73,063
Fresh meat	15,593	12,689	9,964
Bananas	55,100	55,289	71,455
Sugar	95,342	71,340	46,455
Vegetables	26,721	24,136	21,124
Cardamom	59,414	100,257	60,691
Petroleum	60,033	34,000	11,954
Total (incl. others)	1,091,679	1,132,190	1,059,671

* Preliminary.
Source: *Balanza de Pagos*, Banco de Guatemala.

PRINCIPAL TRADING PARTNERS ('000 quetzales)

Imports c.i.f.	1983	1984	1985*
Costa Rica	81,976	63,878	31,150
El Salvador	103,840	97,592	47,717
Germany, Federal Republic	56,561	75,596	86,550
Honduras	26,885	10,111	4,198
Italy	11,634	11,282	12,084
Japan	55,714	70,906	67,835
Mexico	89,045	116,515	124,273
Netherlands	5,689	16,586	14,676
Netherlands Antilles	68,552	92,224	53,978
Trinidad and Tobago	2,413	3,024	3,149
United Kingdom	12,655	16,509	22,075
USA	358,803	395,566	435,097
Venezuela	102,163	103,990	78,726

Exports f.o.b.	1983	1984	1985*
China, People's Republic	812	n.a.	343
Costa Rica	52,428	54,528	45,208
El Salvador	163,424	176,641	120,239
Germany, Federal Republic	63,637	58,511	59,161
Honduras	54,284	34,253	26,538
Italy	38,517	35,992	47,717
Japan	49,216	49,841	35,522
Mexico	13,786	12,294	10,979
Netherlands	31,539	28,318	19,858
Nicaragua	50,789	26,010	15,772
United Kingdom	12,927	12,011	4,368
USA	350,880	400,245	406,586
Venezuela	133	6,978	89

* Preliminary.
Source: *Balanza de Pagos*, Banco de Guatemala.

Transport

ROAD TRAFFIC ('000 motor vehicles in use)

	1981	1982	1983
Passenger cars	166.6	176.6	188.1
Commercial vehicles	50.1	54.5	58.5

Source: Ministerio de Finanzas Públicas.

SHIPPING ('000 metric tons)

	1983	1984	1985*
Goods loaded	1,865	1,499	1,546
Goods unloaded	1,849	2,245	2,098

* Preliminary.

CIVIL AVIATION (traffic on scheduled services)

	1980	1981	1982
Passengers carried ('000)	119	124	115
Passenger-km (million)	159	174	160
Freight ton-km (million)	6.4	4.9	5.2

Tourism

	1983	1984	1985*
Tourist arrivals	235,166	191,934	251,946
Expenditure (US $ million)	61.7	56.6	67.2

* Preliminary.
Source: Instituto Guatemalteco de Turismo (INGUAT).

Education

(1986)

	Schools	Teachers	Pupils
Pre-primary	2,896	4,341	130,964
Primary	7,979	29,320	1,073,756
Secondary	1,390	16,608	223,473

Source: Instituto Nacional de Estadística/USIPE, Ministerio de Educación.

Directory

The Constitution

In December 1984 the Constituent Assembly drafted a new constitution (based on that of 1965), which was approved in May 1985 and came into effect in January 1986. Its main provisions are summarized below:

Guatemala has a republican representative democratic system of government and power is exercised equally by the legislative, executive and judicial bodies. The official language is Spanish. Suffrage is universal and secret, obligatory for those who can read and write and optional for those who are illiterate. The free formation and growth of political parties whose aims are democratic is guaranteed. There is no discrimination on grounds of race, colour, sex, religion, birth, economic or social position or political opinions.

The State will give protection to capital and private enterprise in order to develop sources of labour and stimulate creative activity.

Monopolies are forbidden and the State will limit any enterprise which might prejudice the development of the community. The right to social security is recognized and it shall be on a national, unitary, obligatory basis.

Constitutional guarantees may be suspended in certain circumstances for up to 30 days (unlimited in the case of war).

CONGRESS

Legislative power rests with Congress, which is made up of 100 deputies, 75 of whom are elected directly by the people through universal suffrage. The remaining 25 deputies are elected on the basis of proportional representation. Congress meets on 15 June each year and ordinary sessions last four months; extraordinary sessions can be called by the Permanent Commission or the Executive. All Congressional decisions must be taken by absolute majority of the members, except in special cases laid down by law. Deputies are elected for five years; they may be re-elected after a lapse of one session, but only once. Congress is responsible for all matters concerning the President and Vice-President and their execution of their offices; for all electoral matters; for all matters concerning the laws of the Republic; for approving the budget and decreeing taxes; for declaring war; for conferring honours, both civil and military; for fixing the coinage and the system of weights and measures; for approving, by two-thirds majority, any international treaty or agreement affecting the law, sovereignty, financial status or security of the country.

PRESIDENT

The President is elected by universal suffrage, by absolute majority for a non-extendable period of five years. Re-election or prolongation of the presidential term of office are punishable by law. The President is responsible for national defence and security, fulfilling the Constitution, leading the armed forces, taking any necessary steps in time of national emergency, passing and executing laws, international policy, nominating and removing Ministers, officials and diplomats, co-ordinating the actions of Ministers of State. The Vice-President's duties include presiding over Congress and taking part in the discussions of the Council of Ministers.

ARMY

The Guatemalan Army is intended to maintain national independence, sovereignty and honour, territorial integrity and peace within the Republic. It is an indivisible, apolitical, non-deliberating body and is made up of land, sea and air forces.

LOCAL ADMINISTRATIVE DIVISIONS

For the purposes of administration the territory of the Republic is divided into Departments and these into Municipalities, but this division can be modified by Congress to suit interests and general development of the Nation without loss of municipal autonomy.

JUDICIARY

Justice is exercised exclusively by the Supreme Court of Justice and other tribunals. Administration of Justice is obligatory, free and independent of the other functions of State. The President of the Judiciary, judges and other officials are elected by Congress for four years. The Supreme Court of Justice is made up of at least seven judges. The President of the Judiciary is also President of the Supreme Court. The Supreme Court nominates all other judges. Under the Supreme Court come the Court of Appeal, the Administrative Disputes Tribunal, the Tribunal of Second Instance of Accounts, Jurisdiction Conflicts, First Instance and Military, the Extraordinary Tribunal of Protection. There is a Court of Constitutionality presided over by the President of the Supreme Court.

GUATEMALA

The Government

HEAD OF STATE

President: Mario Vinicio Cerezo Arévalo (took office 14 January 1986).

Vice-President: Roberto Carpio Nicolle.

THE CABINET
(February 1987)

Minister of Foreign Affairs: Mario Rafael Quiñónez Amezquita.
Minister of the Interior: Juan José Rodil Peralta.
Minister of National Defence: Gen. Héctor Gramajo.
Minister of Economy: Lizardo Arturo Sosa López.
Minister of Finance: Rodolfo Paiz Andrade.
Minister of Public Health and Social Assistance: Carlos Armando Soto.
Minister of Communications and Public Works: Eduardo Goyzueta.
Minister of Agriculture: Rodolfo Estrada.
Minister of Education: Eduardo Meyer Maldonado.
Minister of Labour and Social Welfare: Catalina Soberanis.
Minister of Energy and Mines: Roland Castillo Contoux.
Minister of Culture and Sport: Elmar René Rojas.
Minister of Development: René Armando de León Schlotter.

MINISTRIES

All Ministries are situated in the Palacio Nacional, Guatemala City.

President and Legislature

PRESIDENT
Election, 3 November 1985

	Votes cast	Percentage of votes cast
Mario Vinicio Cerezo Arévalo (PDCG)	648,681	38.65
Jorge Carpio Nicolle (UCN)	339,552	20.23
Jorge Serrano Elías (PDCN/PR coalition)	231,397	13.78
Mario Sandóval Alarcón (MLN/PID coalition)	210,806	12.56
Mario David García (CAN)	105,473	6.28
Mario Solórzano Martínez (PSD)	57,362	3.41
Alejandro Maldonado Aguirre (PNR)	52,941	3.15
Leonel Sisniega Otero (PUA/FUN/MEC coalition)	32,118	1.91

Since no candidate achieved the required overall majority, a second round of voting was held on 8 December 1985. At this election, Mario Vinicio Cerezo Arévalo (PDCG) received 68% of the valid votes cast, while Jorge Carpio Nicolle (UCN) won the remaining 32%.

CONGRESO NACIONAL

President: Alfonso Cabrera.

At elections on 3 November 1985 the PDCG secured an absolute majority in the National Congress by winning 51 of the 100 seats. The National Congress took office on 14 January 1986, replacing the previous legislative body, the Asamblea Nacional Constituyente.

Political Organizations

Following the introduction of new legislation in 1983, all political parties were required to disband and reapply for registration. All political parties were legalized in May 1985.

Alianza Democrática: Guatemala City; f. 1983; centre party; Leader Leopoldo Urrutia.

Directory

Central Auténtica Nacionalista (CAN): Guatemala City: f. 1980 from the CAO (Central Arañista Organizado); Leader Carlos Araña Osorio.

Comité Guatemalteca de Unidad Patriota (CGUP) (Guatemalan Committee of Patriotic Unity): f. 1982; opposition coalition consisting of:

Frente Democrático contra la Represión (FDCR): Leader Rafael García.

Frente Popular 31 de Enero (FP-31): f. 1980; left-wing amalgamation of student, peasant and trade union groups; seized Brazilian Embassy, May 1982.

Frente Cívico Democrático (FCD): Guatemala City; Leaders Danilo Barillas, Jorge González del Valle; formed electoral alliance with PDCG, January 1985.

Frente Demócrata Guatemalteco: Leader Clemente Marroquín Rojas.

Frente de Trabajadores: workers' front.

Frente Unido Revolucionario (FUR): f. 1985; electoral alliance formed by parties of the democratic left and consisting of:

Fuerza Nueva: Leader Carlos Rafael Soto.

Movimiento Humanista de Integración Demócrata: Guatemala City; f. 1983; Leader Victoriano Alvarez.

Movimiento 20 de Octubre: Leader Marco Antonio Villamar Contreras.

Partido Socialista Democrático (PSD): Guatemala City; Pres. Carlos Gallardo Flores; Sec.-Gen. Mario Solórzano Martínez.

Frente de Unidad Nacional (FUN): 7a Avda Sta Cecilia 27-51, Zona 8, Guatemala City; tel. 714048; f. 1971; nationalist group; Leaders Col Enrique Peralta Azurdia, Gabriel Girón Ortiz.

Fuerza Democrática Popular: 11a Calle 4-13, Zona 1, Guatemala City; f. 1983; democratic popular force; Sec. Lic. Francisco Reyes Ixcamey.

Fuerza Popular Organizada: popular organized force.

Movimiento Emergente de Concordia (MEC): Guatemala City; f. 1983; Leaders Darío Chávez, Arturo Ramírez.

Movimiento de Liberación Nacional (MLN): 5a Calle 1–20, Zona 1, Guatemala City; f. 1960; extreme right-wing; 95,000 mems; Leader Lic. Mario Sandóval Alarcón.

Pantinamit: f. 1977; represents interests of Indian population; Leader Fernando Tezahuic Tohón.

Partido Democracia Cristiana Guatemalteca (PDCG): 8a Avda 14-53, Zona 1, Guatemala City; f. 1968; 89,000 mems; Sec.-Gen. Alfonso Cabrera; right-wing faction led by Dr Francisco Villagrán Kramer.

Partido Democrático de Cooperación Nacional (PDCN): 4a Avda 4-05, Zona 1, Guatemala City; tel. 24848; f. 1985; Sec.-Gen. Lic. Rolando Baquiax Gómez.

Partido Institucional Democrático (PID): 2a Calle 10–73, Zona 1, Guatemala City; f. 1965; 60,000 mems; moderate conservative; Leader Jorge Lamport Rodil; Dir Donaldo Alvarez Ruiz.

Partido Nacionalista Renovador (PNR): Guatemala City; first granted legal status in August 1979; 72,000 mems; Leader Alejandro Maldonado Aguirre; Sec.-Gen. Mario Castejón.

Partido Petenero: Guatemala City; f. 1983; defends regional interests of El Petén.

Partido Populista: populist party.

Partido Revolucionario (PR): Guatemala City; f. 1957; democratic party; 100,000 mems; Leaders Jorge García Granados, Mario Fuentes Pieruccini.

Partido Revolucionario de los Trabajadores Centroamericanos (PRTC): Guatemala City.

Partido Socialista: Guatemala City; f. 1980.

Partido Social Cristiano: Guatemala City; f. 1983.

Partido de Unificación Anticomunista (PUA): Guatemala City; right-wing party; Leader Leonel Sisniega Otero.

Unidad Revolucionaria Demócrata (URD).

Unión del Centro Nacional (UCN): f. 1984; centre party; Leader Jorge Carpio Nicolle; Sec.-Gen. Ramiro de León Carpio.

Unión Popular: popular union.

In February 1982 the principal guerrilla groups unified to form the **Unidad Revolucionaria Nacional Guatemalteca (URNG)** (Guatemalan National Revolutionary Unity), which has links with the PSD. The political wing of the URNG is the **Representación**

GUATEMALA

Unitaria de la Oposición Guatemalteca (RUOG): Leader RAÚL MOLINA MEJÍA. The URNG consists of:

Ejército Guerrillero de los Pobres (EGP): f. 1972; draws main support from Indians of western highlands; works closely with the Comité de Unidad Campesina (CUC) (Committee of Peasant Unity) and radical Catholic groups; mems 4,000 armed, 12,000 unarmed.

Fuerzas Armadas Rebeldes (FAR): formed early 1960s; originally military commission of CGT; associated with the CNT and CONUS trade unions; based in Guatemala City, Chimaltenango and El Petén; Commander NICOLÁS SIS.

Organización del Pueblo en Armas (ORPA): f. 1979; military group active in San Marcos province; originally part of FAR; Leader RODRIGO ILOM ('GASPAR ILOM').

Partido Guatemalteco del Trabajo (PGT): communist party; divided into three armed factions: PGT-Camarilla (began actively participating in war in 1981); PGT-Núcleo de Conducción y Dirección; PGT-Comisión Nuclear; Gen. Sec. CARLOS GONZÁLEZ.

Other guerrilla groups are:

Comando de las Fuerzas Populares: f. 1981; left-wing.

Comando Guerrilleros del Pueblo (CGP): f. 1985; left-wing.

Ejército Secreto Anticomunista (ESA): right-wing guerrilla group.

Escuadrón de la Muerte (EM): right-wing death squad.

Fuerza de Guerrilleros de los Pobres (FGP).

Diplomatic Representation

EMBASSIES IN GUATEMALA

Argentina: 2a Avda 11-04, Zona 10, Guatemala City; telex 5285; Ambassador: Dr ANGEL FERNANDO GIRARDI.

Austria: 6a Avda 20-25, Zona 10, Guatemala City; telex 5224; Chargé d'affaires a.i.: Dr HANS KAUFMANN.

Belgium: Avda Reforma 13-70, Apdo 687-A, Zona 9, Guatemala City; tel. 315608; telex 5137; Ambassador: PIETER O. MADDENS.

Bolivia: Guatemala City; Chargé d'affaires a.i.: Dr JOSÉ GABINA VILLANUEVA G.

Brazil: Edif. El Cortez 5°, 5a Avda 12-31, Apdo 196-A, Zona 9, Guatemala City; telex 5200; Ambassador: HEITOR PINTO DE MOURA.

Canada: Galería España, 7 Avda y 12 Calle, Zona 9, Guatemala City; telex 5206; Ambassador: PIERRE TANGUAY.

Chile: Avda Reforma 13-70, Zona 9, Guatemala City; telex 6162; Ambassador: SILVIO SALGADO RAMÍREZ.

China (Taiwan): Edif. Torrecafe, Of. 1030, 7a Avda 1-20, Zona 4, Guatemala City; telex 5107; Ambassador: MAO CHI-HSIEN.

Colombia: Edif. Ejecutivo 5°, 7 Avda 15-13, Zona 1, Guatemala City; Ambassador: LAURA OCHOA DE ARDILLA.

Costa Rica: 24a Calle 16-09, Zona 10, Guatemala City; Chargé d'affaires: ROBERTO CHÁVEZ LIZANO.

Dominican Republic: 7a Calle 'A' 4-28, Zona 10, Guatemala City; Ambassador: PEDRO PABLO ALVAREZ BONILLA.

Ecuador: Diagonal 6, 13-08, Zona 10, Guatemala City; telex 6218; Ambassador: LUIS ORTIZ TERÁN.

Egypt: 12a Calle 6-15, Zona 9, Guatemala City; telex 5157; Ambassador: MAHMOUD ABBAS.

El Salvador: 3a Calle 6-09, Zona 9, Guatemala City; telex 5418; Ambassador: AGUSTÍN MARTÍNEZ VARELA.

France: Edif. Marbella 11°, 16a Calle 4-53, Zona 10, Guatemala City; tel. 374080; telex 5963; Ambassador: ANDRÉ LE GUEN.

Germany, Federal Republic: Edif. Plaza Maritima, 6 Avda 20-25, Zona 10, Guatemala City; tel. 370028; telex 5209; Ambassador: Dr PETER BENSCH.

Holy See: 10a Calle 4-47, Zona 9, Guatemala City; tel. 324274; Apostolic Nuncio: Mgr ORIANO QUILICI.

Honduras: 12a Calle 6-14, Zona 9, Guatemala City; Ambassador: OSCAR COLINDRES COARRALES.

Israel: 13a Avda 14-07, Zona 10, Guatemala City; telex 5218; Ambassador: ELIEZER ARMON.

Italy: 8a Calle 3-14, Zona 10, Guatemala City; tel. 65432; telex 5129; Ambassador: GIUSEPPE AVITABILE.

Japan: Ruta 6, 8-19, Apdo 531, Zona 4, Guatemala City; telex 5926; Ambassador: FUJIO HARA.

Directory

Korea, Republic: 16a Calle 3-38, Zona 10, Guatemala City; telex 5369; Ambassador: MOON CHANG-HWA.

Mexico: 16a Calle 0-51, Zona 14, Guatemala City; tel. 680769; telex 5961; Ambassador: ABRAHAM TALAVERA LÓPEZ.

Nicaragua: 2a Calle 15-95, Zona 13, Guatemala City; telex 5653; Chargé d'affaires: LEONEL ROSALES MANZANARES.

Peru: 2a Avda 9-58, Zona 9, Guatemala City; Ambassador: ANDRÉS ARAMBURU ALVAREZ-CALDERÓN.

Spain: Guatemala City; telex 5393; Ambassador: JOSÉ LUIS CRESPO DE VEGA.

Sweden: 4a Avda 12-70, Zona 10, Guatemala City; telex 5916; Ambassador: CARL-ERHARD LINDAHL.

Switzerland: 4a Calle 7-73, Apdo 1426, Zona 9, Guatemala City; tel. 65726; telex 5257; Ambassador: FRANÇOIS NORDMANN.

USA: Avda La Reforma 7-01, Zona 10, Guatemala City; tel. 311541; Ambassador: Dr ALBERTO M. PIEDRA.

Uruguay: 20a Calle 8-00, Apdo 2b, Zona 10, Guatemala City; Chargé d'affaires: HÉCTOR L. PEDETTI A.

Venezuela: 8a Calle 0-56, Zona 9, Guatemala City; telex 5317; Ambassador: Dr ROGELIO ROSAS GIL.

Judicial System

Corte Suprema: Centro Cívico, 21 Calle y 7a Avda, Guatemala City; tel. 84323.

President of the Supreme Court: BAUDILLO NAVARRO.

Civil Courts of Appeal: 10 courts, 5 in Guatemala City, 2 in Quezaltenango, 1 each in Jalapa, Zacapa and Antigua. The two Labour Courts of Appeal are in Guatemala City.

Judges of the First Instance: 7 civil and 10 penal in Guatemala City, 2 civil each in Quezaltenango, Escuintla, Jutiapa and San Marcos, 1 civil in each of the 18 remaining Departments of the Republic.

Religion

Almost all of the inhabitants profess Christianity, with a majority belonging to the Roman Catholic Church. In recent years the Protestant Churches have attracted a growing number of converts.

CHRISTIANITY
The Roman Catholic Church

Guatemala comprises one archdiocese, eight dioceses, the Territorial Prelature of Escuintla, the Apostolic Vicariate of El Petén and the Izabal region, under the jurisdiction of an Apostolic Administrator.

Bishops' Conference: Conferencia Episcopal de Guatemala, Secretariado General del Episcopado, 26a Calle 8-90, Zona 12, Guatemala City; tel. 764171; f. 1973; Pres. PRÓSPERO PEÑADOS DEL BARRIO, Archbishop of Guatemala City.

Archbishop of Guatemala City: PRÓSPERO PEÑADOS DEL BARRIO, Arzobispado, Apdo 723, Guatemala City; tel. 29707.

Protestant Churches

The Baptist Church: Convention of Baptist Churches of Guatemala, 12a Calle 9-54, Zona 1, Apdo 322, Guatemala City; tel. 514516; Pres. Rev. JUAN MANUEL NÚÑEZ.

The Episcopal Church: Avda Castellana 40-06, Zona 8, Guatemala City; tel. 720764; diocese founded 1967; Bishop: Rt Rev. ARMANDO GUERRA; Cathedral Church of St James and six missions in Guatemala City, three missions in Quezaltenango, three missions in El Quiché and 13 rural missions in the Departments of Izabal and Zacapa.

Church of Jesus Christ of Latter-day Saints: 12a Calle 3-37, Zona 9, Guatemala City; 17 bishoprics, 9 chapels; Regional Rep. GUILLERMO ENRIQUE RITTSCHER.

The Lutheran Church: Consejo Nacional de Iglesias Luteranas, Apdo 1111, Guatemala City; tel. 23401; 2,522 mems; Pres. HÉCTOR CANJURA GUZMÁN.

The Presbyterian Church: Iglesia Evangélica Presbiteriana Central, 6a Avda 'A' 4-68, Zona 1, Apdo 655, Guatemala City; tel. 538532; f. 1882; 36,000 mems; Pastors: Rev. SAMUEL REINOSO DE LEÓN, Rev. MARDOQUEO MUÑOZ C., Rev. JULIO CÉSAR PAZ PORTILLO, Rev. DAVID VELÁSQUEZ.

GUATEMALA

The Union Church: 12 Calle 7–37, Plazuela España, Zona 9, Apdo 150A; Guatemala City; tel. 316904; f. 1943.

BAHÁ'Í FAITH

National Spiritual Assembly of the Bahá'ís: 3a Calle 4–54, Zona 1, Guatemala City; tel. 29673; mems resident in 385 localities.

The Press

PRINCIPAL DAILIES

Diario de Centroamérica: 18a Calle 6–72, Zona 1, Guatemala City; tel. 24418; f. 1880; morning; official; Dir DANILO DE LÉON; circ. 12,000.

El Gráfico: 14a Avda 9–18, Zona 1, Guatemala City; tel. 510021; f. 1963; morning; Dir JORGE CARPIO NICOLLE; circ. 60,000.

La Hora: 9a Calle 'A' 1–56, Zona 1, Guatemala City; tel. 26864; f. 1944; evening; independent; Dir OSCAR MARROQUÍN ROJAS; circ. 20,000.

La Palabra: 1a Avda 4–33, Zona 1, Guatemala City; tel. 28568; f. 1983; morning; Dir JAIME F. OSORIO; circ. 7,000; publication suspended in 1986, owing to financial problems.

Prensa Libre: 13a Calle 9–13, Zona 1, Guatemala City; tel. 511838; f. 1951; morning; independent; Dir and Gen. Man. PEDRO JULIO GARCÍA; circ. 68,500.

PERIODICALS

AGA: 9a Calle 3–43, Zona 1, Guatemala City; monthly; agricultural.

Gerencia: 10a Calle 3–17, Zona 10, Guatemala City; tel. 311564; fmrly Otra Revista; official organ of the Association of Guatemalan Managers; Dir RICHARD AITKENHEAD CASTILLO.

Industria: Ruta 6 No 9–21, Zona 4, Guatemala City; monthly; official organ of the Chamber of Industry.

Inforpress Centroamericana: 9a Calle 'A' 3–56, Zona 1, Guatemala City; tel. 29432; f. 1972; weekly; published in Spanish and English; regional political and economic news and analysis.

PRESS ASSOCIATIONS

Asociación de Periodistas de Guatemala (APG): 14 Calle 3–29, Zona 1, Guatemala City; tel. 21813; Pres. MARIO ANTONIO SANDÓVAL SAMAYOA.

Cámara Guatemalteca de Periodismo (CGP): Guatemala City; Pres. TERESA BOLAÑOS DE ZARCO.

Círculo Nacional de Prensa (CN): Guatemala City; Pres. EDUARDO SORIA S.

NEWS AGENCIES

Inforpress Centroamericana: 9a Calle 'A' 3–56, Zona 1, Guatemala City; tel. 29432; f. 1972; independent news agency.

Foreign Bureaux

ACAN-EFE (Central America): Edif. El Centro, 9a Calle y 7a Avda, Zona 1, Guatemala City; tel. 519484; Dir LUIS MARROQUÍN GODOY.

Agencia EFE (Spain): Edif. El Centro, 7a Avda 8–56, Zona 1, Guatemala City; tel. 519454; Bureau Chief (vacant).

Agenzia Nazionale Stampa Associata (ANSA) (Italy): 2a Calle 761, Zona 9, Guatemala City; tel. 62802; telex 5251; Chief ALFONSO ANZUETO LÓPEZ.

Deutsche Presse-Agentur (dpa) (Federal Republic of Germany): 5a Calle No 4–30, Apdo 2333, Zona 1, Guatemala City; tel. 517505; telex 5227; Correspondent JULIO CÉSAR ANZUETO.

Inter Press Service (IPS) (Italy): Avda Juan Chapin 3–61, Zona 1, Guatemala City; tel. 517271; telex 9246; Correspondent FÉLIX LOARCA GUZMÁN.

United Press International (UPI) (USA): 7a Calle 10–54, Zona 1, Guatemala City; tel. 535815.

Publishers

Editorial del Ministerio de Educación: 15a Avda 3–22, Zona 1, Guatemala City.

Editorial Universitaria: Universidad de San Carlos de Guatemala, Edif. de Recursos Educativos, Ciudad Universitaria, Zona 12, Guatemala City; tel. 760790; literature, social sciences, health, pure and technical sciences, humanities, secondary and university educational textbooks; Editor Lic. OSCAR GUILLERMO LÓPEZ.

Piedra Santa: 7a Avda 4–45, Zona 1, Guatemala City; tel. 510231; f. 1947; educational textbooks for all levels, science and technology, literature, philosophy and sport; Man. Dir ORALIA DÍAZ DE PIEDRA SANTA.

Seminario de Integración Social Guatemalteco: 11a Calle 4–31, Zona 1, Guatemala City; tel. 29754; f. 1956; sociology, anthropology, social sciences, educational textbooks.

Radio and Television

In 1985 there were an estimated 325,000 radio receivers and 207,000 television receivers in use.

Dirección General de Radiodifusión y Televisión Nacional: 5a Avda 13–18, Zona 1, Guatemala City; tel. 25045; f. 1931; government supervisory body; Dir-Gen. MARIO MONTERROSO MIRÓN.

RADIO

There are five government and six educational stations, including:

La Voz de Guatemala: 5a Avda 13–18, Zona 1, Guatemala City; Government station; Dir MARIO MONTERROSO MIRÓN.

Radio Cultural TGN: 4a Avda 30–09, Zona 3, Apdo 601, Guatemala City; tel. 714378; f. 1950; religious and cultural station; programmes in Spanish and English, Cakchiquel, Kekchí and Mam; Dir ESTEBAN SYWULKA; Man. JULIÁN LLORET.

There are 77 commercial stations of which the most important are:

Emisoras Unidas de Guatemala: 7a Avda 6–45, Zona 9, Guatemala City; Dirs CARLOS ARCHILA, JORGE EDGARDO ARCHILA, ROLANDO ARCHILA.

La Voz de las Américas: 11a Calle 2–43, Zona 1, Guatemala City; Dir AUGUSTO LÓPEZ S.

Radio Cinco Sesenta: 8a Calle 1–11, Zona 11, Guatemala City; Dir EDNA CASTILLO OBREGÓN.

Radio Continental: 15a Calle 3–45, Zona 1, Guatemala City; Dir R. VIZCAÍNO R.

Radio Nuevo Mundo: 6a Avda 10–45, Zona 1, Apdo 281, Guatemala City; Man. H. GONZÁLEZ G.

Radio Panamericana: 1a Calle 35–48, Zona 7, Guatemala City; Dir M. V. DE PANIAGUA.

TELEVISION

Canal 3—Radio-Televisión Guatemala, SA: 30a Avda 3–40, Zona 11, Apdo 1367, Guatemala City; tel. 922491; telex 5253; f. 1956; commercial station; Pres. Lic. MAX KESTLER FARNÉS; Vice-Pres. J. F. VILLANUEVA.

Tele Once: 20a Calle 5–02, Zona 10, Guatemala City; tel. 682165; commercial; Dir A. MOURRA.

Televisiete, SA: 3a Calle 6–24, Zona 9, Apdo 1242, Guatemala City; tel. 62216; f. 1964; commercial station channel 7; Dir Dr J. VILLANUEVA P.

Televisión Cultural Educativa: 4a Calle 18–38, Zona 1, Guatemala City; tel. 531913; government station.

Trecevisión SA: 3a Calle 10–70, Zona 10, Guatemala City; tel. 316023; telex 6070; commerical; Dir Ing. PEDRO MELGAR R.; Gen. Man. GILDA VALLADARES ORTIZ.

Finance

(cap. = capital; p.u. = paid up; res = reserves; dep. = deposits; m. = million; brs = branches; amounts in quetzales)

BANKING

Superintendencia de Bancos: 7a Avda 22–01, Zona 1, Apdo 2306, Guatemala City; tel. 534243; telex 5231; f. 1946; Superintendent Lic. JOSÉ MIGUEL GAITÁN ALVAREZ; Gen. Sec. Lic. WILLIAM GARCÍA.

Central Bank

Banco de Guatemala: 7a Avda 22–01, Zona 1, Apdo 365, Guatemala City; tel. 534053; telex 5231; f. 1946; guarantee fund 94.8m. (Sept. 1986); Pres. Lic. FEDERICO LINARES; Man. Lic. FERNANDO FIGUEROA AMADO.

GUATEMALA

State Commercial Bank

Crédito Hipotecario Nacional de Guatemala: 7a Avda 22–77, Zona 1, Apdo 242, Guatemala City; tel. 82041; telex 4139; f. 1930; government-owned; cap. p.u. 11.5m., res 6.2m., dep. 161.8m. (Sept. 1986); Pres. Luis Mario Montúfar Luna; Gen. Man. Lic. Ricardo Contreras Cruz; 2 brs.

Private Commercial Banks

Guatemala City

Banco Agrícola Mercantil, SA: 7a Avda 9–11, Zona 1, Guatemala City; tel. 21601; telex 5347; f. 1946; cap. 5m., res 11.7m., dep. 255.9m. (Sept. 1986); Man. Lic. Armando González Campo; 1 br.

Banco del Agro, SA: 9a Calle 5–39, Zona 1, Apdo 1443, Guatemala City; tel. 22541; telex 4167; f. 1958; cap. 4.7m., res 7.8m., dep. 184.3m. (Sept. 1986); Pres. Ricardo Rodríguez Paúl; Man. Lic. Manuel Méndez Escobar.

Banco del Café, SA: Avda La Reforma 9–00, Zona 9, Apdo 831, Guatemala City; tel. 311311; telex 5123; f. 1978; cap. 9.1m., res 0.3m., dep. 210.5m. (Sept. 1986); Pres. Eduardo M. González Rivera; Gen. Man. Lic. Roberto Mazariegos Godoy.

Banco de la Construcción, SA: 12a Calle 4–17, Zona 1, Apdo 999, Guatemala City; tel. 23041; telex 5308; f. 1983; cap. 6.1m., dep. 82.5m. (Sept. 1986); Pres. Arq. Héctor Quezada; Man. Lic. Oscar Alvarez Marroquín.

Banco del Ejército, SA: 5a Avda 6–06, Zona 1, Apdo 1797, Guatemala City; tel. 532146; telex 4197; f. 1972; cap. 9.3m., res 5.1m., dep. 133.2m. (Sept. 1986); Pres. Lic. Carlos Arroyave Castillo; Man. Lic. Máximino Ruano Ayala.

Banco de Exportación, SA: Avda La Reforma II-49, Zona 10, Guatemala City; tel. 373861; telex 5896; f. 1985; cap. 5.0m., res 0.1m., dep. 70.8m. (Sept. 1986); Pres. Benancio Botrán Borja; Man. Ing. Rafael Viejo Rodríguez.

Banco Granai y Townson, SA: 7a Avda 1–86, Zona 4, Apdo 654, Guatemala City; tel. 312333; telex 5159; f. 1962; cap. 11.0m., res 2.6m., dep. 300.9m. (Sept. 1986); Pres. Mario Granai Arévalo; Man. Lic. Mario Asturias Arévalo; 22 brs.

Banco Industrial, SA: 7a Avda 5–10, Zona 4, Apdo 744, Guatemala City; tel. 312323; telex 5236; f. 1968 to promote industrial development; cap. 25m., res 4.5m., dep. 417.4m. (Sept. 1986); Pres. Ing. Ramiro Castillo Love; Man. Lic. Norberto Rodolfo Castellanos Díaz.

Banco Inmobilario, SA: 8a Avda 10–57, Zona 1, Apdo 1181, Guatemala City; tel. 516093; telex 4117; f. 1958; cap. 25m., res 0.4m., dep. 204.8m. (Sept. 1986); Pres. Jorge Hasbun; Man. Lic. Mario Orrego Estrada.

Banco Internacional, SA: 7a Avda 11–20, Zona 1, Apdo 2588, Guatemala City; tel. 512021; telex 4178; f. 1976; cap. 8m., res 1.6m., dep. 152.4m. (Sept. 1986); Pres. Lic. Jorge Skinner-Kléen; Man. Julio Vielman Pineda.

Banco Metropolitano, SA: 5a Avda 8–24, Zona 1, Apdo 2688, Guatemala City; tel. 25360; telex 5188; f. 1978; cap. 9.4m., res 0.3m., dep. 117.7m. (Sept. 1986); Pres. Ing. Francisco Alvarado Macdonald; Man. Heberto César Siguenza López.

Banco Promotor, SA: 10 Calle 6-47, Zona 1, Apdo 930, Guatemala City; tel. 512928; telex 9238; f. 1986; cap. 3.1m., dep. 1.2m. (Sept 1986); Pres. Lic. Julio Valladares Castillo; Man. Lic. Raúl Monterroso Rivera.

Banco del Quetzal, SA: Edif. Plaza 6–26, Zona 9, Apdo 1002, Guatemala City; tel. 318333; telex 5893; f. 1984; cap. 3.2m., dep. 42.5m. (Sept. 1986); Pres. Lic. Mario Roberto Leal Pivaral; Man. Ing. Juan Carlos Vercesi Galeani.

Banco de los Trabajadores: 8a Avda 9–41, Zona 1, Apdo 1956, Guatemala City; tel. 24341; telex 9212; f. 1966; cap. 15.4m., res 0.0m., dep. 70.9m. (Sept. 1986); deals with loans for establishing and improving small industries as well as normal banking business; Pres. Lic. Juan José Alonzo Estrada; Man. Lic. Oscar H. Andrade Elizondo.

Quezaltenango

Banco de Occidente, SA: 4a Calle 11–38, Zona 1, Apdo 228, Quezaltenango; tel. 0612861; telex 5455; f. 1881; cap. 5.0m., res 13.4m., dep. 339.8m. (Sept. 1986); Pres. Lic. Luis Miguel Aguirre Fernández; Man. Lic. Mario Antonio Mejía González; 1 br.

State Development Banks

Banco Nacional de Desarrollo Agrícola—BANDESA: 9a Calle 9–47, Zona 1, Apdo 350, Guatemala City; tel. 535222; telex 4122; f. 1971; cap. 10.4m., dep. 69.3m. (Sept. 1986); agricultural development bank; Pres. Ing. Rodolfo Estrada Hurtarte; Man. Lic. Gustavo Adolfo Leal Castellanos.

Banco Nacional de la Vivienda—BANVI: 6a Avda 1–22, Zona 4, Apdo 2632, Guatemala City; tel. 325777; telex 5371; f. 1973; cap. 30.6m., dep. 40.2m. (Sept. 1986); Pres. Arq. Rafael Escobar Donis.

Finance Corporations

Corporación Financiera Nacional—CORFINA: 8a Avda 10–43, Zona 1, Guatemala City; tel. 83331; telex 5186; f. 1973; provides assistance for the development of industry, mining and tourism; cap. 34.3m., res 0.2m. (Sept. 1986); Pres. Lic. Elizardo Sosa; Gen. Man. Lic. Carlos Alberto Molina Woolford.

Financiera Guatemalteca, SA—FIGSA: 1a Avda 11–50, Zona 10, Apdo 2460, Guatemala City; tel. 316051; f. 1962; cap. 4.1m., res 0.4m. (Sept. 1986); Pres. Carlos González Barrios; Man. Lic. José Roberto Ortega Herrera.

Financiera Industrial y Agropecuaria, SA (FIASA): Avda La Reforma 10–00, Zona 9, Guatemala City; tel. 310303; telex 5958; f. 1969; private development bank; medium- and long-term loans to private industrial enterprises in Central America; cap. 2.5m., res 9.1m. (Sept. 1986); Pres. Jorge Castillo Love; Gen. Man. Lic. Federico Linares Martínez.

Financiera Industrial, SA (FISA): Torre No. 2 Centro Financiero, 7a Avda 5–10, Zona 4, Apdo 744, Guatemala City; tel. 312323; telex 5236; f. 1981; cap. 3m., res 0.2m. (Sept. 1986); Pres. Carlos Arías Masselli; Man. Lic. Carlos Humberto Alpírez Pérez.

Financiera de Inversión, SA: 10a Calle 3–17, Zona 10, Guatemala City; tel. 311266; f. 1981; cap. 1.5m. (Sept. 1986); Pres. Antonio Guirola Batres; Man. Lic. Mario Augusto Porras G.

Foreign Banks

Bank of America, NT & SA: 11a Calle 5–07, Zona 1, Apdo 1335, Guatemala City; tel. 512266; telex 5205; f. 1957; cap. 3m., res 2.9m., dep. 73.1m. (Sept. 1986); Man. Michael Suárez.

Lloyds Bank International Ltd: POB 1106, 8a Avda 10–67, Zona 1, Guatemala City; tel. 24651; telex 5263; f. 1959; cap. 5.2m., res 0.4m., dep. 124.5m. (Sept. 1986); Man. Philip Coggins Long; 6 brs.

Banking Association

Asociación de Banqueros de Guatemala: Edif. Quinta Montúfar 2°, 12a Calle 4–74, Zona 9, Guatemala City; tel. 318211; f. 1961; represents all state and private banks; Pres. Ing. Rafael Viejo Rodríguez; Vice-Pres. Julio Vielman Pineda.

INSURANCE

National Companies

La Alianza, Cía Anglo-Centroamericana de Seguros, SA: Edif. Etisa 6°, Plazuela España, Zona 9, Guatemala City; tel. 316593; telex 5551; f. 1968; Pres. F. Antonio Gándara García; Man. Francisco Catalán Molina.

Aseguradora General, SA: 10a Calle 3–17, Zona 10, Guatemala City; tel. 325933; telex 5441; f. 1968; Pres. Juan O. Nieman; Man. Enrique Neutze.

Aseguradora Guatemalteca de Transportes, SA: 5a Avda 6-06, Zona 1, Guatemala City; tel. 519794; telex 4197; f. 1978; Pres. Lic. Maximino Ruano Ayala; Man. César A. Ruano Sandóval.

Cía de Seguros Generales Granai & Townson, SA: 7a Avda 1–82, Zona 4, Guatemala City; tel. 61361; telex 5955; f. 1947; Pres. Ernesto Townson R; Gen. Man. Mario Asturias Arévalo.

Cía de Seguros Panamericana, SA: Avda La Reforma 9–00, Zona 9, Guatemala City; tel. 325922; telex 5925; f. 1968; Pres. G. Frank Purvis, Jr.; Gen. Man. J. Antonio González A.

Cía de Seguros El Roble, SA: 7a Avda 5–10, Zona 4, Guatemala City; tel. 321702; telex 6094; f. 1973; Pres. Federico Köng Vielman; Man. Ing. Ricardo Erales Cóbar.

Comercial Aseguradora Suizo-Americana, SA: 7a Avda 7-07, Zona 9, Apdo Postal 132, Guatemala City; tel. 61661; telex 5502; f. 1946; Pres. Sam W. Scales; Gen. Man. Ernesto A. Piñero.

Departamento de Seguros y Previsión del Crédito Hipotecario Nacional: 7a Avda 22–77, Zona 1, Guatemala City; tel. 82041; telex 6065; f. 1935; Pres. Lic. Luis M. Montúfar Luna; Man. Lic. Ricardo Contreras Cruz.

La Seguridad de Centroamérica, SA: Avda La Reforma 12–01, Zona 10, Guatemala City; tel. 317566; telex 5243; f. 1967; Pres. Carlos Talavera Klingensuss; Gen. Man. Edgardo Wagner D.

Seguros Cruz Azul, SA: Edif. Plaza Marítima 10, 6a Avda 20-25, Zona 10; tel. 372285; telex 5204; Gen. Man. Brian Murphy.

GUATEMALA   Directory

Seguros de Occidente, SA: 7a Calle 'A' 7–14, Zona 9, Guatemala City; tel. 311222; telex 5605; f. 1979; Pres. Ing. HERCULANO AGUIRRE MONTALVO; Gen. Man. Lic. PEDRO AGUIRRE.

Seguros Universales, SA: 4a Calle 7–73, Zona 9, Guatemala City; tel. 66156; telex 6104; f. 1962; Pres. FRANCISCO JAVIER VALLS PLANAS; Man. NOLASCO SICILIA GARCÍA.

Insurance Association

Asociación Guatemalteca de Instituciones de Seguros —AGIS: Guatemala City; f. 1953; 8 mems; Pres. ENRIQUE NEUTZE AYCINENA; Man. Lic. FEDERICO PIÑOL.

Trade and Industry

CHAMBERS OF COMMERCE AND INDUSTRY

Comité Coordinador de Asociaciones Agrícolas, Comerciales, Industriales y Financieras (CACIF): Edif. Cámara de Industria de Guatemala, Ruta 6, No 9–21, Zona 4, Guatemala City; tel. 310651; co-ordinates work on problems and organization of free enterprise; mems: 9 chambers; Pres. Ing. ALVARO CASTILLO MONGE.

Cámara de Comercio de Guatemala: 10a Calle 3–80, Zona 1, Guatemala City; tel. 82681; telex 5478; f. 1894; Pres. PEDRO MIGUEL LAMPORT KELSALL; Man. JONÁS VÁSQUEZ ALVARADO.

Cámara de Industria de Guatemala: Ruta 6, 9–21, Zona 4, Apdo 214, Guatemala City; tel. 317069; telex 5402; f. 1958; Pres. Ing. ALVARO CASTILLO MONGE; Exec. Dir Ing. LIONEL TORIELLO NÁJERA.

DEVELOPMENT ORGANIZATIONS

Comisión Nacional del Petróleo: Diagonal 17, 29-78, Zona 11, Guatemala City; tel. 460111; f. 1983; awards petroleum exploration licences.

Consejo Nacional de Planificación Económico: Ministry of Finance, Palacio Nacional, Guatemala City; prepares and supervises the implementation of the national economic development plan; Sec. LEONEL HERNÁNDEZ CÁRDENA.

Corporación Financiera Nacional (Corfina): see under Finance.

Dirección General de Hidrocarburos: Diagonal 17, 29-78, Zona 11, Guatemala City; tel. 460111; f. 1983; control and supervision of petroleum and gas development.

Empresa Nacional de Fomento y Desarrollo Económico de El Petén (FYDEP): 11a Avda 'B' 32–46, Zona 5, Guatemala City; attached to the Presidency; economic development agency for the Department of El Petén; Dir Col JORGE MARIO REYES PORRAS.

Instituto de Fomento de Hipotecas Aseguradas (FHA): 6a Avda 0–60, Zona 4, Guatemala City; f. 1961; insured mortgage institution for the promotion of house construction; Pres. Lic. OSCAR GONZALO OSORIO MOLINA; Gen. Man. Col Lic. RAÚL REINA ROSAL.

Instituto Nacional de Administración para el Desarrollo (INAD): 5a Avda 12–65, Zona 9, Guatemala City; tel. 66339; f. 1964; provides technical experts to assist all branches of the Government in administrative reform programmes; administers co-operative farms; provides in-service training for local and central government staff; has research programmes in administration, sociology, politics and economics; provides postgraduate education; Gen. Man. Dr ARIEL RIVERA IRÍAS.

Instituto Nacional de Transformación Agraria (INTA): 14 Calle 7–14, Zona 1, Guatemala City; f. 1962 to carry out agrarian reform; current programme includes development of the 'Faja Transversal del Norte'.

PRODUCERS' ASSOCIATIONS

Asociación de Azucareros de Guatemala (ASAZGUA): Edif. Tívoli Plaza, 6a Calle 6–38, Zona 9, Guatemala City; telex 5248; f. 1957; sugar producers' asscn; 19 mems; Gen. Man. Lic. OSCAR GUILLERMO ZÚASTEGUI.

Asociación de Exportadores de Café: 11a Calle 5–66 3°, Zona 9, Guatemala City; telex 5368; coffee exporters' asscn; 29 mems; Pres. EDUARDO GONZÁLEZ RIVERA.

Asociación General de Agricultores: 9a Calle 3–43, Zona 1, Guatemala City; f. 1920; general farmers' asscn; 350 mems; Man. PEDRO ARRIVILLAGA RADA.

Asociación Nacional de Avicultores (ANAVI): Apdo 83-A, Guatemala City; telex 6215; f. 1964; national asscn of poultry farmers; 60 mems; Gen. Man. Dr MARIO A. MOTTA G.

Asociación Nacional de Fabricantes de Alcoholes y Licores (ANFAL): Avda La Reforma 6–39, Apdo 2065, Zona 10, Guatemala City; f. 1947; distillers' asscn; Pres. RENÉ GONZÁLEZ BARRIOS; Man. Lic. CARLOS RIVERA CIFUENTES.

Asociación Nacional del Café—Anacafé: Edif. Etisa, Plazuela España, Zona 9, Guatemala City; tel. 67180; telex 5915; f. 1960; national coffee asscn; Pres. RODOLFO FERNÁNDEZ DE LA VEGA; Man. Lic. OSCAR G. ZUÁSTEGUI.

Asociación de Agricultores Productores de Aceites Esenciales: 6a Calle 1–36, Zona 10, Apdo 272, Guatemala City; tel. 313855; telex 5316; f. 1948; essential oils producers' asscn; 40 mems; Man. Ing. LUIS ALBERTO ASTURIAS.

Cámara del Agro: 15a Calle 'A', No 7–65, Zona 9, Guatemala City; tel. 317824; f. 1973; Man. CÉSAR BUSTAMANTE ARAÚZ.

Consejo Nacional del Algodón: Avda de las Américas 13–08, Zona 13, Guatemala City; f. 1965; consultative body for cultivation and classification of cotton; 125 mems; Man. AMÍLCAR ALVAREZ.

Gremial de Huleros de Guatemala: 7a Avda 7-78 4°, Zona 4, Guatemala City; telex 5114; f. 1970; union of rubber producers; 125 mems; Pres. FRANCISCO BENECKE; Man. Lic. JOSÉ BUITRÓN ESPINOZA.

CO-OPERATIVES

The following federations group all Guatemalan co-operatives:

Federación de Cooperativas Artesanales.

Federación Guatemalteca de Cooperativas de Consumo.

Federación Nacional de Cooperativas de Ahorro y Crédito.

Federación Nacional de Cooperativas de Vivienda y Servicios Varios.

TRADE UNIONS

Trade union activity can now take place freely, having been severely restricted after repression in 1979 and 1980.

Frente Nacional Sindical—FNS (National Trade Union Front): Guatemala City; f. 1968, to achieve united action in labour matters; affiliated are two confederations and 11 federations, which represent 97% of the country's trade unions and whose General Secretaries form the governing council of the FNS. The affiliated organizations include:

Comité Nacional de Unidad Sindical Guatemalteca (CONUS): Leader MIGUEL ANGEL SOLÍS; Sec.-Gen. GERÓNIMO LÓPEZ DÍAZ.

Confederación General de Sindicatos (General Trade Union Confederation): 18a Calle 5–50, Zona 1, Apdo 959, Guatemala City.

Confederación Nacional de Trabajadores (National Workers' Confederation): Guatemala City; Sec.-Gen. MIGUEL ANGEL ALBIZÚREZ.

Confederación de Unidad Sindical: Guatemala City; f. 1983; under government control.

Consejo Sindical de Guatemala (Guatemalan Trade Union Council): 18a Calle 5–50, Zona 1, Apdo 959, Guatemala City; f. 1955; admitted to ICFTU and ORIT; Gen. Sec. JAIME V. MONGE DONIS; 30,000 mems in 105 affiliated unions.

Federación Autónoma Sindical Guatemalteca (Guatemalan Autonomous Trade Union Federation): Guatemala City; Gen. Sec. MANUEL CONTRERAS.

Federación de Obreros Textiles (Textile Workers' Federation): Edif. Briz, Of. 503, 6a Avda 14–33, Zona 1, Guatemala City; f. 1957; Sec.-Gen. FACUNDO PINEDA.

Federación de Trabajadores de Guatemala (FTG) (Guatemalan Workers' Federation): 5a Calle 4–33, Zona 1, Guatemala City; Sec.-Gen. JUAN FRANCISCO CALDERÓN.

A number of unions exist without a national centre, including the Union of Chicle and Wood Workers, the Union of Coca-Cola Workers and the Union of Workers of the Enterprise of the United Fruit Company.

Central Nacional de Trabajadores (CNT): 9a Avda 4–29, Zona 1, Apdo 2472, Guatemala City; f. 1972; cover all sections of commerce, industry and agriculture including the public sector; clandestine since June 1980; Sec.-Gen. JULIO CELSO DE LEÓN; 23,735 mems.

GUATEMALA

Transport

RAILWAYS

Ferrocarriles de Guatemala—FEGUA: 9a Avda 18–03, Zona 1, Guatemala City; telex 5342; f. 1968; government-owned; 819 km open from Puerto Barrios and Santo Tomás de Castilla on the Atlantic coast to Tecún Umán on the Mexican border, via Zacapa, Guatemala City and Santa María. Branch lines: Santa María–San José; Las Cruces–Champerico. From Zacapa another line branches southward to Anguiatú, on the border with El Salvador; owns the ports of Barrios (Atlantic) and San José (Pacific); Chair. of Board J. A. PILONA CORDERO.

There are 148 km of plantation lines.

ROADS

In 1984 there were 17,315 km of roads, of which 2,887 km were asphalted and 6,576 km gravel. The Guatemala section of the Pan-American highway is 824 km long, including 552 km of paved roads. The construction of a 1,500-km network of new highways, including a four-lane motorway from the capital to San José, began in 1981. A 44-km toll road linking Escuintla with San José was due to be built in the mid-1980s, at a cost of US $18m.

SHIPPING

Guatemala's major ports are Puerto Barrios, San José, Santo Tomás de Castilla and Champerico. A major port reconstruction and expansion programme began in 1976, and in March 1983 the extension to the port of San José was opened.

Armadora Marítima Guatemalteca, SA: 14a Calle 8–14, Zona 1, Apdo 1008, Guatemala City; tel. 537243; telex 5214; cargo services; Pres. and Gen. Man. J. L. CORONADO ALVAREZ.

Flota Mercante Gran Centroamericana, SA: Edif. Canella 5°, 1a Calle 7–21, Zona 9, Guatemala City; tel. 316666; telex 5211; f. 1959; services from Europe (in association with WITASS), Gulf of Mexico, US Atlantic and East Coast Central American ports; Pres. R. S. RAMÍREZ; Gen. Man. J. E. A. MORALES.

Líneas Marítimas de Guatemala, SA: 7a Avda 7–78 11°, Zona 4, Guatemala City; cargo services; Pres. J. R. MATHEU ESCOBAR; Gen. Man. F. HERRERAS E.

Several foreign lines link Guatemala with Europe, the Far East and North America.

CIVIL AVIATION

In 1982 a new international airport was completed at Santa Elena Petén.

AVIATECA—Empresa Guatemalteca de Aviación: Avda Hincapié, Aeropuerto 'La Aurora', Zona 13, Guatemala City; telex 5960; f. 1945; internal services and external services to the USA; Pres. Capt. JORGE ADRIÁN SOLARES CARRANZA; Vice-Pres. CARLOS BORGES; fleet: 2 Boeing 727-100C, 1 DC-3.

Tourism

Guatemala Tourist Commission: 7a Avda 1–17, Centro Cívico, Zona 4, Guatemala City; tel. 311333; telex 1967; f. 1971; policy and planning council: 13 mems representing the public and private sectors; Dir CLAUDIA ARENAS BIANCHI.

Asociación Guatemalteca de Agencias de Viajes (AGAV) (Guatemalan Association of Travel Agencies): 6a Avda 9–62, Zona 1, Apdo 67, Guatemala City; tel. 510522; Pres. FRANCISCO SANDÓVAL.

Atomic Energy

Dirección General de Energía Nuclear: Diagonal 17 29–78, Zona 11, Apdo 1421, Guatemala City; tel. 760679; telex 5516; programmes include the application of nuclear energy in agriculture and industry, nuclear medicine and radiation protection; Dir Ing. RAÚL EDUARDO PINEDA GONZÁLEZ.

GUINEA

Introductory Survey

Location, Climate, Language, Religion, Flag, Capital

The Republic of Guinea lies on the west coast of Africa, with Sierra Leone and Liberia to the south, Senegal to the north, and Mali and the Ivory Coast inland to the east. The climate on the coastal strip is hot and moist, with temperatures ranging from about 17°C (62°F) in the dry season to about 30°C (86°F) in the wet season. The interior is higher and cooler. The official language is French, but Soussou, Manika and six other national languages are widely spoken. Most of the inhabitants are Muslims but some still adhere to traditional animist beliefs. Around 1% are Roman Catholics. The national flag (proportions 3 by 2) consists of three equal vertical stripes, of red, yellow and green. The capital is Conakry.

Recent History

Guinea was formerly French Guinea, part of French West Africa. It became the independent Republic of Guinea on 2 October 1958, after 95% of voters had rejected the Constitution of the Fifth Republic under which the French colonies became self-governing within the French Community. The new state was the object of punitive reprisals by the outgoing French authorities: all aid was withdrawn, and the government infrastructure destroyed. The administration was rebuilt on the basis of the Guinean Confédération Général du Travail, which had organized a series of strikes culminating in a general strike in 1953, and the Parti démocratique de Guinée (PDG), which won 58 of the 60 seats in the Territorial Assembly in 1957. Its leader, Ahmed Sekou Touré, became President, and the PDG the sole political party. President Sekou Touré vigorously pursued a policy of socialist revolution, with emphasis on ideology and popular political participation.

There were attempted coups in 1961, 1965 and 1967. An abortive invasion by Portuguese troops and Guinean exiles in 1970 was followed by the arrest of prominent Guineans and foreigners, suspected of involvement. Many executions took place, and, as a result, diplomatic relations with Senegal and the Federal Republic of Germany were broken off in 1971, and with the Ivory Coast in 1973. This led to the country's virtual isolation, as dealings with the USSR had declined since the early 1960s. Reports of a 'permanent conspiracy' by foreign powers to overthrow the Government continued to circulate, but in 1975 Guinea resumed normal relations with its African neighbours, France and the Western powers, signing the Lomé Convention (see p. 149) and joining ECOWAS (see p. 133).

All private trade was forbidden in 1975, and transactions were conducted through official co-operatives under the supervision of an 'economic police'. In September 1977 demonstrations against the abolition of the traditional market, and the abuse of power by the 'economic police', were held by women in Conakry, and rioting broke out in other towns. Three state governors were killed. As a result, Sekou Touré yielded to many of the demands expressed, disbanded the 'economic police' and allowed private trading to recommence in July 1979.

Under Sekou Touré's regime, opposition was ruthlessly crushed and by 1983 almost 2m. Guineans were estimated to have fled abroad. Allegations of widespread violations of human rights were repeatedly denied by the Government. However, between 1977 and 1978 nearly 1,000 prisoners were released, while Guinean exiles were encouraged to return. In November 1978, at the 11th Congress of the PDG, the membership of the central organs of the party was increased to allow the expression of new opinion, and the merging of the functions of party and state was announced. The country was renamed the Popular and Revolutionary Republic of Guinea. The President reiterated Guinea's commitment to socialist aims but expressed its desire for co-operation with Western investors. In December 1978 President Giscard d'Estaing made the first visit by a French President to independent Guinea, and plans for economic co-operation between the two countries were discussed. During 1979 Guinea furthered relations with other countries, and there was a general move away from rigid Marxism.

In legislative elections, held in January 1980, the voters approved the PDG's list of 210 candidates to the National Assembly. Sekou Touré was returned unopposed for a fourth seven-year term of office as President at an election in May 1982, with a reported 100% of the votes cast, and was re-elected Secretary-General of the PDG during the Party Congress of November 1983. A *rapprochement* with France resulted from the President's visit to Paris in 1982, despite protests by various groups of Guinean exiles. Sekou Touré also visited the USA and Canada during that year.

In January 1984 a plot to overthrow the Government was discovered when a group of 20 mercenaries were arrested in southern Senegal. It was reported that thousands of Guineans were subsequently detained, accused of complicity in the coup plot. In March 1984, however, Sekou Touré died while undergoing heart surgery in the USA. On 3 April, before a permanent successor had been chosen by the PDG, the Guinean armed forces seized power in a bloodless coup. A Comité Militaire de Redressement National (CMRN) was appointed, headed by Col (later Gen.) Lansana Conté. The PDG and the National Assembly were dissolved, and the Constitution was suspended. The CMRN affirmed Guinea's support for the OAU and the country's principles of non-alignment, and pledged to restore democracy and to respect human rights. Hundreds of political prisoners were released, and a lifting of press restrictions was announced. The country's original name was restored, replacing the 'Popular and Revolutionary Republic' which had been adopted as a title in 1978. A delegation led by the Prime Minister, Col Diarra Traoré, toured West African states to rally support from Guinea's neighbours, and in June Col Traoré visited several European countries in an effort to attract foreign investment and to consolidate relations, particularly with France. By July 1984 an estimated 200,000 Guinean exiles had returned to the country.

Trials of former politicians, most of whom had been detained since the coup in April, began in November 1984. Following allegations of corruption and rivalry within the CMRN, President Conté extensively reshuffled his government in December 1984, personally taking over the posts of Head of Government and Minister of Defence. The post of Prime Minister was abolished, and Diarra Traoré was demoted to Minister of National Education. While President Conté was chairing a summit conference of ECOWAS in Togo, ex-Prime Minister Traoré staged an attempted coup on 4 July 1985, seizing the radio station in Conakry. Troops loyal to Conté suppressed the revolt, during which 18 people were killed. Traoré was later arrested, along with many members of his family and more than 200 suspected sympathizers and followers. A series of attacks was subsequently aimed at the Malinké ethnic group, of which both Traoré and the late Sekou Touré were members. A Court of State Security and a military tribunal were created in August in order to try the detainees, amid allegations that Traoré and others had already been executed.

In October 1985 President Conté began to implement the radical economic reforms that the World Bank and IMF had demanded as preconditions for the provision of structural aid (see Economic Affairs), and in December the Council of Ministers was reshuffled to include a majority of civilians. Its size was reduced from 20 to 17 members, and a CMRN Executive Committee was created. In addition, resident ministries were set up in Guinea's four main natural regions. Conté visited Morocco in May 1986, and in November a visit to Guinea by President Mitterrand of France consolidated the improved relations between the two nations.

Government

The 1982 Constitution, providing for a National Assembly elected by universal adult suffrage, was suspended following the coup in April 1984. A Comité Militaire de Redressement National (CMRN—Military Committee for National Recovery), with 25 (later 17) members, assumed power. The President of the Republic is assisted by a Council of Ministers. In December 1984 the President also became Head of Government, and in 1985 an eight-member CMRN Executive Committee was created. Local administration is based on eight provinces, each under the authority of a provincial governor; there are 33 provincial prefectures. Provincial administrative councils meet every three months. Elections to district councils in the Conakry area were held in April 1986.

Defence

In July 1986 Guinea had an army of 8,500, a navy of 600 and an air force of 800. Paramilitary forces numbered 9,600, including a People's Militia of about 7,000. It was announced in March 1985 that the Militia was to be dissolved and assigned to the army. Military service is compulsory and lasts for two years. Defence expenditure in 1982 was 1,850m. sylis. In August 1986 the Federal German Government agreed a US $2.4m. loan for the purchase of engineering equipment for the Guinean army. In September 1986 a non-aggression pact was signed with Sierra Leone and Liberia, Guinea's partners in the Mano River Union (see Economic Affairs).

Economic Affairs

Following Guinea's independence in 1958, a centralized socialist economy was set up, with direct state control of production and consumption in every sector except mining. However, the loss of French aid, technology and export markets was not easily overcome, and the economy did not perform well during the 1960s and 1970s, with many industrial units operating at below 25% capacity. Under the Lansana Conté Government, extensive efforts have been made to liberalize the economy and to increase participation by both local and foreign private investors.

Guinea's agricultural sector employs more than 80% of the labour force and contributed an estimated 41% of GDP in 1984. The principal export crops are bananas, groundnuts, oil palm, citrus fruits, pineapples and coffee. The output of major food crops in 1984 was estimated at 400,000 metric tons of paddy rice, 650,000 tons of cassava and 56,000 tons of maize. Food grain imports averaged around 100,000 tons per year during the early 1980s, accounting for some 25% of total food requirements and 30% of export revenue. Since July 1984, the Government has attempted to boost agricultural production by progressively increasing the official prices payable to agricultural producers. A programme has been launched to develop rice-growing in the Siguiri area; the scheme includes rehabilitation of 7,000 ha of rice fields and aims at least to double the current annual yield of 700 kg per ha. Under the 1985–87 Interim Programme for National Recovery, foreign investment is being sought for various agro-industrial projects, aimed at promoting rural development while building up essential infrastructures. Particular emphasis is to be given to the rehabilitation of the fisheries sub-sector: it is planned to construct a deep-water port at Conakry. Industry is based mainly on the processing of local raw materials, and in 1984 contributed around 21% of GDP.

Guinea's most important foreign-currency earner is mining, which provides over 90% of export receipts. The country possesses large bauxite deposits, accounting for an estimated one-third of the world's high-grade reserves. Output of crude bauxite rose from 2.6m. tons in 1972 to an estimated 13.9m. tons in 1980, and was scheduled to reach 20m. tons per year by the late 1980s. A slump in world demand for aluminium during the early 1980s had a slightly depressive effect on Guinea's bauxite production, which declined to 11.8m. tons in 1982 before recovering to average 13m. tons per year in 1983 and 1984. The main sites under exploitation in 1986 were Boké, Fria-Kimbo and Kindia-Debele. Bauxite is processed into alumina by a Fria-based company, Friguia. Production of alumina rose from 489,000 tons in 1963 to 708,000 tons in 1980, but declined in subsequent years, to an estimated 600,000 tons in 1983. An upgrading programme, scheduled for completion in 1986, aims to increase annual capacity to more than 1m. tons. At present, Cameroon processes much of Guinea's alumina to produce aluminium.

Following the exhaustion of iron-ore deposits at Kaloum, near Conakry, in 1969, government efforts have been directed towards obtaining international financial support for the exploitation of the estimated 1,500m. tons of reserves at Mount Nimba. In August 1986 the World Bank agreed to co-finance a scaled-down version of the project, which has been developed jointly with the Government of Liberia. The revised scheme aims to extract some 8m. tons of ore per year, commencing in the late 1980s, at an estimated total cost of US $330m. The original investment target was $1,000m. It is eventually hoped to construct a railway to connect with the proposed deep-water port at Conakry. Meanwhile, the ore is to be exported through the Liberian port of Buchanan.

Diamond mining was suspended in the late 1970s, owing to smuggling and theft from the mines, but resumed in 1980, when the Government allowed investment by two multinational companies. In May 1984 the Aredor diamond mine, in south-east Guinea, came into production: annual output was expected to total around 250,000 carats, rising to 1m. carats from 1987. A new company, the Société de Diamant de Guinée (jointly owned by the Government and private investors), was formed in November 1984 to exploit diamond mining in Kouroussa province. In January 1985 private diamond prospecting was suspended, and land was transferred to Aredor, while a loan of US $230m. was granted by the USSR towards restoring the diamond mines. Later in the same year, two joint-venture companies were formed to conduct exploration of gold deposits. Production was expected to commence before the end of 1986.

Guinea also has considerable hydroelectric resources. The Yugoslav Government has financed the construction of a dam on the Bafing river, with a hydroelectric generating capacity of 100 MW, and there are plans to build a 350 MW complex on the Konkouré river. Meanwhile, the World Bank and international aid agencies have agreed to finance an electricity supply management scheme at an estimated total cost of US $20m. In 1982 an international consortium was formed to study Guinea's uranium deposits, and there has also been exploration for petroleum off shore.

Despite its mineral wealth, Guinea remains one of the world's poorest countries. In 1984, according to World Bank estimates, Guinea's GNP per head was US $330 (at average 1982–84 prices), having increased at an average rate of only 1.1% annually, in real terms, since 1965. Overall GDP, which totalled an estimated $2,100m. in 1984, rose by an average of 3.1% per year between 1973 and 1984. The first development plan (1960–64) was largely financed by Eastern bloc countries, but since then more assistance has been given by the West. At the end of 1984 Guinea's total foreign debt was $1,170m., equal to 64.6% of annual GNP. Export earnings were estimated to be $504m. in 1984, while the cost of imports amounted to $382m. in the same year. Annual debt service payments averaged an estimated $83.5m. in 1982–84. In April 1986, subsequent to the implementation of the IMF-backed Interim Programme for National Recovery (see below), the 'Paris Club' of Western creditor nations rescheduled US $200m. of Guinea's official external debt. Discussions on rescheduling were also reported to have begun with Eastern bloc creditors.

Guinea's potential richness in terms of mineral and agricultural resources has helped the Conté Government to secure substantial overseas financial support for its liberalization programme. In February 1986 the IMF approved a 13-month stand-by credit arrangement, valued at US $36m., and the World Bank agreed to provide a structural adjustment loan worth $42.6m. Prior to, and as a precondition for, the granting of these loans, a radical restructuring of the banking sector was implemented, with the six principal state-owned banks being dissolved and replaced, in December 1985, by Guinean subsidiaries of French banks. In October 1985 a dual exchange rate for the syli was established, and in January 1986 the currency was further devalued, when the syli was abolished and replaced by a revived Guinea franc, the unit that the syli replaced in 1972. The dual exchange rate was abolished in June 1986. It was widely expected in 1986 that Guinea would eventually return to the Franc Zone (see p. 155). Further elements of the 1985–87 reform programme, which aims to create the conditions for an annual growth rate of 5% before 1990, included the continued improvement of price incentives to producers, the reform of tariffs and the reduction of the role of the State throughout the economy. In addition to radical 'privatization' measures, the size of the civil service work-force, which had increased to 84,000 employees under Sekou Touré, was to be reduced by 30% in 1986, by means of various incentives.

In 1980 Guinea became a member of both the Mano River Union (with Sierra Leone and Liberia) and the Gambia River Development Organization (with Senegal and The Gambia), thus strengthening economic links with the rest of West Africa. Sekou Touré's policy of 'positive neutrality' has been continued by the Conté Government: since 1984, agreements on aid and co-operation have been signed with a number of countries, including the USSR, the People's Republic of China, Morocco and Saudi Arabia. US aid totalled $9m. in 1984, and France provided 630m. French francs in 1985, mainly in support of education, agriculture and transport projects.

Social Welfare

Wages are fixed according to the Government Labour Code. A maximum working week of 48 hours is in force for industrial workers. In 1979 there were 248 hospitals and dispensaries, with a total of 6,858 beds. In 1981 there were only an estimated 100 physicians working in official medical services. Private medical care has been legally available since July 1984.

Education

Education is free at every level. Primary education, beginning at seven years of age and lasting for six years, is officially compulsory. However, estimated enrolment at primary schools in 1984 was equivalent to only 36% of the relevant age-group (boys 49%; girls 23%). Secondary education, from the age of 13, lasts for a further six years, comprising two cycles of three years each. In 1983 the estimated enrolment at secondary schools was equivalent to only 15% of children (21% of boys; 8% of girls) in the appropriate age-group. Education at the country's one university, in Conakry, is divided into two stages of two and three years, often interrupted for periods of practical experience in the chosen field. In 1985, according to estimates by UNESCO, the average rate of adult illiteracy was 71.7% (males 60.3%; females 82.8%). Under the six-year transitional education plan that the Government announced in June 1984, political education was eliminated and French was adopted as the language of instruction in schools. Teaching of the eight national languages was to continue, however. Private schools were legalized in 1984, after 23 years of being banned under the regime of the late President Sekou Touré.

Tourism

Guinea is noted for the beauty of its scenery, especially in the mountains of the Futa Djalon, but the country receives few tourists.

Public Holidays

1987: 1 January (New Year), 20 March (Easter Monday), 1 May (Labour Day), 30 May* (Id al-Fitr, end of Ramadan), 27 August (Anniversary of Women's Revolt), 28 September (Referendum Day), 2 October (Republic Day), 1 November (All Saints' Day), 4 November* (Mouloud, birth of Muhammad), 22 November (Day of 1970 Invasion), 25 December (Christmas).

1988: 1 January (New Year), 4 April (Easter Monday), 1 May (Labour Day), 18 May* (Id al-Fitr, end of Ramadan), 27 August (Anniversary of Women's Revolt), 28 September (Referendum Day), 2 October (Republic Day), 23 October* (Mouloud, birth of Muhammad), 1 November (All Saints' Day), 22 November (Day of 1970 Invasion), 25 December (Christmas).

* These holidays are determined by the Islamic lunar calendar and may vary by one or two days from the dates given.

Weights and Measures

The metric system is in force.

Currency and Exchange Rates

100 centimes = 1 franc guinéen (FG or Guinea franc).

Exchange rates (30 September 1986):
 £1 sterling = 520.92 Guinea francs;
 US $1 = 360.00 Guinea francs.

Statistical Survey

Source (unless otherwise stated): Service de la Statistique Générale, Bureau du Premier Ministre, Conakry; tel. 44-21-48.

Area and Population

AREA, POPULATION AND DENSITY

Area (sq km)	245,857*
Population (census results)	
15 January–31 May 1955	2,570,219†
4–17 February 1983	5,781,014‡
Population (UN estimates at mid-year)§	
1984	5,931,000
1985	6,075,000
Density (per sq km) at February 1983	23.5‡

* 94,926 sq miles.
† Estimates for African population, based on results of sample survey.
‡ Provisional figures.
§ Not revised to take account of the 1983 census results.

PRINCIPAL TOWNS (population at December 1972)
Conakry (capital) 525,671 (later admitted to be overstated); Kankan 60,000.

BIRTHS AND DEATHS

Average annual birth rate 46.9 per 1,000 in 1970–75 and in 1975–80; death rate 26.8 per 1,000 in 1970–75, 25.3 per 1,000 in 1975–80 (UN estimates).

ECONOMICALLY ACTIVE POPULATION
(ILO estimates, '000 persons at mid-1980)

	Males	Females	Total
Agriculture, etc.	1,153	966	2,119
Industry	183	54	237
Services	196	74	270
Total	**1,532**	**1,094**	**2,626**

Source: ILO, *Economically Active Population Estimates and Projections, 1950–2025.*
Mid-1985 (estimates in '000): Agriculture, etc. 2,222; Total 2,846 (Source: FAO, *Production Yearbook*).

REGIONS (population at mid-1963)

Region	Area (sq km)	Population ('000)
Beyla	17,542	170
Boffa	6,003	90
Boké	11,053	105
Conakry	308	172
Dabola	6,000	54
Dalaba	5,750	105
Dinguiraye	11,000	67
Dubréka	5,676	86
Faranah	12,397	94
Forécariah	4,265	98
Fria	n.a.	27
Gaoual	11,503	81
Guéckédou	4,157	130
Kankan	27,488	176
Kindia	8,828	152
Kissidougou	8,872	133
Kouroussa	16,405	93
Labé	7,616	283
Macenta	8,710	123
Mali	8,800	152
Mamou	6,159	162
N'Zérékoré	10,183	195
Pita	4,000	154
Siguiri	23,377	179
Télimelé	8,155	147
Tougué	6,200	75
Youkounkoun	5,500	55
Total	**245,857**	**3,360**

Agriculture

PRINCIPAL CROPS (FAO estimates, '000 metric tons)

	1983	1984	1985
Maize	39*	42*	43
Sorghum	3*	3*	3
Rice (paddy)	396*	403*	470*
Other cereals	70*	70*	72
Sweet potatoes	69*	70*	70
Cassava (Manioc)	494*	496*	500
Yams	59*	60*	61
Taro (Coco yam)	31*	32*	32
Pulses	45	45	45
Coconuts	15	15	15

	1983	1984	1985
Vegetables	410	420	420
Sugar cane	225	225	225
Citrus fruits	157	160	160
Bananas	103	104	104
Plantains	350	350	350
Pineapples	18	20	20
Other fruits	35	36	36
Palm kernels	35	35	35
Groundnuts (in shell)	75	75	75
Coffee (green)	15	15	15

* Official estimate.
Source: FAO, *Production Yearbook.*

GUINEA

LIVESTOCK
(FAO estimates, '000 head, year ending September)

	1983	1984	1985
Cattle	1,900	1,850	1,800
Sheep	450	455	460
Goats	440	450	460
Pigs	44	45	47
Asses	3	3	3

Poultry (FAO estimates, million): 9 in 1983; 10 in 1984; 11 in 1985.
Source: FAO, *Production Yearbook*.

LIVESTOCK PRODUCTS (FAO estimates, metric tons)

	1983	1984	1985
Beef and veal	19,000	19,000	18,000
Poultry meat	13,000	14,000	15,000
Other meat	7,000	6,000	7,000
Cows' milk	44,000	43,000	42,000
Goats' milk	4,000	4,000	4,000
Hen eggs	9,765	10,710	11,550
Cattle hides	3,384	3,330	3,240

Source: FAO, *Production Yearbook*.

Forestry

ROUNDWOOD REMOVALS
(FAO estimates, '000 cubic metres, excluding bark)

	1982	1983	1984
Sawlogs, veneer logs and logs for sleepers*	180	180	180
Other industrial wood	353	361	370
Fuel wood†	3,085	3,085	3,085
Total	3,618	3,626	3,635

*Assumed to be unchanged since 1972.
† Assumed to be unchanged since 1981.
Source: FAO, *Yearbook of Forest Products*.

SAWNWOOD PRODUCTION
Total (incl. boxboards): 90,000 cubic metres per year in 1972–84 (FAO estimates).

Fishing

('000 metric tons, live weight)

	1977*	1978*	1979
Inland waters	1.0	1.0	1.0*
Atlantic Ocean	8.1	9.0	17.5
Total catch	9.1	10.0	18.5

*FAO estimates.
1980–84: Annual catch as in 1979 (FAO estimates).
Source: FAO, *Yearbook of Fishery Statistics*.

Mining

	1981	1982	1983
Bauxite ('000 metric tons)	12,822	11,828	12,986
Diamonds ('000 carats)*	38	40	45

* Estimates by the US Bureau of Mines.
Source: UN, *Industrial Statistics Yearbook*.
Bauxite (1984): Production as in 1983 (Source: *World Metal Statistics*, London).

Industry

SELECTED PRODUCTS
(estimated production)

	1981	1982	1983
Electric energy (million kWh)	498	498	499
Raw sugar ('000 metric tons)	22	22	14
Palm oil ('000 metric tons)*	42	45	45
Plywood ('000 cubic metres)*	2	2	2
Alumina (calcined equivalent, '000 metric tons)†	608	549	600

* FAO estimates.
† Estimates by the US Bureau of Mines.
Source: UN, *Industrial Statistics Yearbook*.

Finance

CURRENCY AND EXCHANGE RATES

Monetary Units
100 centimes = 1 franc guinéen (FG or Guinea franc).

Sterling and Dollar Equivalents (30 September 1986)
£1 sterling = 520.92 Guinea francs;
US $1 = 360.0 Guinea francs;
1,000 Guinea francs = £1.920 = $2.778.

Note: The Guinea franc was re-introduced in January 1986, replacing (at par) the syli. At the same time, the currency was devalued by more than 90%. The syli had been introduced in October 1972, replacing the original Guinea franc (at 10 francs per syli). In June 1975 the syli's value was linked to the IMF special drawing right at an exchange rate of SDR 1 = 24.6853 sylis. This remained in force until the syli's abolition. The average exchange rate of sylis per US dollar was: 22.366 in 1982; 23.095 in 1983; 24.090 in 1984. Some of the figures in this Survey are still in terms of sylis.

BUDGET* (million sylis)

	1975/76	1976/77
Ordinary budget:		
Revenue	4,312	5,283
Expenditure	3,047	3,904
Capital budget	1,614	3,089

*Unofficial estimates.

1979 (million sylis): Balanced at 11,250 (Current Budget 6,790, Capital Budget 4,460).

NATIONAL ACCOUNTS (estimates, million sylis at current prices)

Expenditure on the Gross Domestic Product

	1980	1981	1982
Government final consumption expenditure	5,430	6,350	7,510
Private final consumption expenditure	22,640	26,470	31,550
Increase in stocks	5,140	6,440	7,230
Gross fixed capital formation			
Total domestic expenditure	33,210	39,260	46,290
Exports of goods and services	8,810	9,190	10,430
Less Imports of goods and services	8,280	9,460	11,060
GDP in purchasers' values	33,740	38,990	45,660

Gross Domestic Product by Economic Activity

	1980	1981	1982
Agriculture, hunting, forestry and fishing	13,440	15,450	17,790
Mining and quarrying	4,600	5,400	5,560
Manufacturing	900	1,050	1,280
Electricity, gas and water	90	110	130
Construction	790	970	1,060
Trade, restaurants and hotels	3,910	4,600	5,430
Transport, storage and communications	730	880	1,040
Finance, insurance, real estate and business services	610	720	840
Public administration and defence	3,730	4,470	5,290
Other services	250	290	340
GDP at factor cost	29,050	33,940	38,760
Indirect taxes, *less* subsidies	4,690	5,050	6,900
GDP in purchasers' values	33,740	38,990	45,660

Source: UN Economic Commission for Africa, *African Statistical Yearbook*.

External Trade

PRINCIPAL COMMODITIES (million sylis)

Imports	1978	1979	1980
Food	123	628	389
Beverages	277	4	n.a.
Petroleum products	3	720	1,173
Building materials	2	106	117
Agricultural equipment	85	197	153
Textiles	291	221	117
Pharmaceutical products	115	99	92
Industrial processing equipment	548	841	1,087
Total (incl. others)	2,411	4,568	3,877

Exports	1978	1979	1980
Bauxite	4,728	7,082	8,571
Alumina	1,740		
Pulses and oilseeds	n.a.	257	253
Fresh fruit	n.a.	27	11
Total (incl. others)	6,567	7,383	8,852

Source: Ministère des Finances et Direction des Douanes.

PRINCIPAL TRADING PARTNERS

Imports (14 months, 1975–76): EEC 2,301 million sylis; USA 743 million sylis.

Exports (1973): EEC 1,260 million sylis, USA 545 million sylis.

Transport

RAILWAYS (traffic)

	1980	1981	1982
Freight ton-km (million)	498	521	550

Source: UN Economic Commission for Africa, *African Statistical Yearbook*.

INTERNATIONAL SEA-BORNE SHIPPING
(estimated freight traffic, '000 metric tons)

	1981	1982	1983
Goods loaded	11,540	9,375	10,403
Goods unloaded	587	673	666

Source: UN, *Monthly Bulletin of Statistics*.

ROAD TRAFFIC (motor vehicles in use)

1978: Passenger cars 92,000, Commercial vehicles 98,000. (Source: UN Economic Commission for Africa, *African Statistical Yearbook*).

CIVIL AVIATION ('000)
Traffic on Scheduled Services*

	1981	1982
Kilometres flown	3,100	3,100
Passengers carried	128	131
Passenger-km	142,000	144,000
Freight ton-km	600	700

* UN estimates.

Source: UN, *Statistical Yearbook*.

Communications Media

	1981	1982	1983
Radio receivers ('000 in use)	144	153	160
Television receivers ('000 in use)	7	8	8

Daily newspapers (1979): 1 (average circulation 20,000 copies).
Source: UNESCO, *Statistical Yearbook*.

Education

(1983)

	Institutions	Teachers	Pupils
Primary	2,635*	7,867	246,129
Secondary			
General	n.a.	5,091	89,756
Teacher training	n.a.	103*	997
Vocational	n.a.	641*	6,966
University and equivalent	n.a.	614*	3,750*
Other higher education	n.a.	759*	9,432*

* 1982 figures.
1984: Primary: 284,386 pupils.
Source: UNESCO, *Statistical Yearbook*.

Directory

The Constitution

The Constitution of the Popular and Revolutionary Republic of Guinea, adopted in May 1982, was suspended in April 1984 by the Military Committee for National Recovery, which had assumed power in a coup. The country's former name, the Republic of Guinea, was subsequently restored.

The Government

HEAD OF STATE
President: Gen. LANSANA CONTÉ (took office 4 April 1984).

COUNCIL OF MINISTERS
(January 1987)

Head of Government, Minister of Defence, Security, Planning and Co-operation, and Information: Gen. LANSANA CONTÉ.
Minister delegated to the Presidency for National Defence: Lt-Col SORY DOUMBOUYA.
Minister delegated to the Presidency for the Interior and Decentralization: Maj. ALPHA OUMAR DIALLO.
Minister delegated to the Presidency for Planning and Co-operation: EDOUARD BENJAMIN.
Minister delegated to the Presidency for Information and Culture: ZAINOUL ABIDINE SANOUSSI.
Minister of Justice: BASSIROU BARRY.
Minister of Foreign Affairs: Maj. JEAN TRAORÉ.
Minister of Economy and Finance: LAMINE BOLIVOGUI.
Minister of Rural Development: Maj. ALHOUSSENY FOFANA.
Minister of Natural Resources, Energy and the Environment: Dr OUSMANE SYLLA.
Minister of Human Resources, Industry, and Minister of Small and Medium Enterprises: KEMOKO KEITA.
Minister of Equipment and Town Planning: MBAYA SIDIBE.
Minister of National Education: SALIOU KOUMBASSA.
Minister of Health and Social Affairs: PATHE DIALLO.
Minister of Religious Affairs: El Hadj ABDOURAHMANE BAH.
Resident Minister for Maritime Guinea (Kindia): Maj. JEAN KOLIPÉ LAMA.
Resident Minister for Middle Guinea (Labé): Maj. MANKAN CAMARA.
Resident Minister for Upper Guinea (Kankan): Capt. MAMADOU BALDET.
Resident Minister for Forest Guinea (N'Zérékoré): Capt. FACINÉ TOURÉ.

There are also 11 Secretaries of State.

MINISTRIES

Office of the President: Conakry; tel. 44-11-47; telex 623.
Ministry of Economy and Finance: Conakry; tel. 44-21-62; telex 601.
Ministry of Foreign Affairs and International Co-operation: Conakry; tel. 40-50-55; telex 634.
Ministry of Industrial Development: Conakry; tel. 44-38-95; telex 2171.
Ministry of Justice: Conakry; tel. 44-16-04.
Ministry of Labour and Social Affairs: Conakry; tel. 44-33-05.
Ministry of National Education: Conakry; tel. 44-19-01; telex 631.
Ministry of Religious Affairs: Conakry; tel. 44-23-38.
Ministry of Rural Development: BP 576, Conakry; tel. 44-19-66.
Ministry of Trade: Conakry; tel. 44-45-12; telex 652.

Legislature

ASSEMBLÉE NATIONALE
The National Assembly was dissolved by the Military Committee for National Recovery on 3 April 1984, following the military coup.

Political Organizations

Following the military coup of April 1984, the country's sole political party since independence, the Parti démocratique de Guinée (PDG), was dissolved. Although no political organizations have been formally active in Guinea since the coup, there still exist several groups, formed by Guineans in exile to oppose the regime of the late President Sekou Touré:

Mouvement pour le renouveau en Guinée: fmrly the Union du peuple guinéen (UPG); Pres. Maj. DIALLO THIERNO.
Organisation unifiée pour la libération de la Guinée (OULG): based mainly in the Ivory Coast; Pres. IBRAHIMA KAKE.

Six other groups are based in France: **Association de la jeunesse guinéenne en France (AJGF); Groupe de réflexion des Guinéens (GRG); Ligue guinéenne des droits de l'homme (LGDHC); Regroupement de Guinéens de l'exterieur (RGE); Solidarité guinéenne (SG); Union des forces patriotiques guinéennes (UFPG).**

Diplomatic Representation

EMBASSIES IN GUINEA

Algeria: BP 1004, Conakry; tel. 44-15-03; Chargé d'affaires a.i.: BOUCHERIT NACEUR.
Benin: BP 787, Conakry; Ambassador: JONAS GBOHOUNDADA.
China, People's Republic: BP 714, Conakry; Ambassador: YU HUIMIN.
Congo: BP 178, Conakry; Ambassador: Mme C. ECKOMBAND.
Cuba: BP 71, Conakry; Ambassador: COLMAN FERREI.
Czechoslovakia: BP 1009 bis, Conakry; tel. 46-14-37; Ambassador: Dr ZDENKO HRČKA.
Egypt: BP 389, Conakry; Ambassador: HUSSEIN EL-NAZER.
France: BP 373, Conakry; tel. 44-16-55; telex 600; Ambassador: HENRI RÉTHORÉ.
German Democratic Republic: Conakry; tel. 44-15-16; Ambassador: Dr WOLFGANG KUBISCH.
Germany, Federal Republic: BP 540, Conakry; telex 779; Ambassador: Dr PETER TRUHART.
Ghana: BP 732, Conakry; Ambassador: LARRY BIMI.
Guinea-Bissau: BP 298, Conakry; Ambassador: ARAFAN ANSU CAMARA.
Hungary: BP 1008 bis, Conakry; Ambassador: RAYMOND TÓTH.
India: BP 186 bis, Conakry; telex 659; Ambassador: Mr BALACHANDRA.
Iraq: Conakry; telex 2162; Chargé d'affaires: MUNIR CHIHAB AHMAD.
Italy: BP 84, Village Camayenne, Conakry; tel. 46-23-32; telex 636; Ambassador: ROBERTO ROSSELINI.
Ivory Coast: Conakry; telex 2126; Chargé d'affaires: ATTA YACOUBA.
Japan: BP 895, Conakry; tel. 46-14-38; telex 782; Chargé d'affaires: TERUO OKADA.
Korea, Democratic People's Republic: BP 723, Conakry; Ambassador: KIM CHIN-KI.
Lebanon: BP 342, Conakry; telex 2106; Ambassador: MOHAMED ISSA.
Liberia: BP 18, Conakry; telex 2105; Chargé d'affaires: ANTHONY ZEZO.
Libya: BP 1183, Conakry; telex 645; Chargé d'affaires: MUFTAH MADI.

GUINEA

Mali: Conakry; telex 2154; Ambassador: KIBILI DEMBA DIALLO.
Morocco: BP 193, Conakry; telex 2122; Ambassador: TAYEB BELLARBI.
Nigeria: BP 54, Conakry; telex 633; Ambassador: GBOKO YOUGH.
Romania: BP 348, Conakry; Ambassador: PETRU DESPOT.
Saudi Arabia: BP 611, Conakry; telex 2146; Chargé d'affaires: WAHEEB SHAIKHON.
Sierra Leone: BP 625, Conakry; Ambassador: Mrs MARIAM KAMARA.
Switzerland: BP 720, Conakry; tel. 46-26-12; telex 2116; Chargé d'affaires: SIEGFRIED BRAZEROL.
Syria: BP 609, Conakry; tel. 46-13-20; Chargé d'affaires: BECHARA KHAROUF.
Tanzania: BP 189, Conakry; tel. 46-13-32; telex 2104; Ambassador: NORMAN KIONDO.
USSR: BP 329, Conakry; Ambassador: VLADIMIR N. RAYEVSKY.
USA: BP 603, Conakry; tel. 44-15-20; telex 2103; Chargé d'affaires: WILLIAM C. MITHOEFER.
Viet-Nam: BP 551, Conakry; Ambassador: PHAM VAN SON.
Yugoslavia: BP 1154, Conakry; Ambassador: LJILJANA TODOROVA.
Zaire: BP 880, Conakry; telex 632; Ambassador: B. KALUBYE.

Judicial System

There is a High Court whose jurisdiction extends to political cases. The Cour d'appel, the Chambre des mises en accusation and the Tribunal supérieur de cassation are at Conakry. A Court of State Security and a military tribunal were established in August 1985 to try cases of crime against the internal and external security of the state.

Tribunaux du premier degré exist at Conakry and Kankan and have jurisdiction over civil and criminal cases and also act as industrial courts. A justice of the peace sits at N'Zérékoré.

Président, Cour d'Appel: FODÉ MAMADOU TOURÉ.

Religion

It is estimated that 95% of the population are Muslims and 1.5% Christians. There were an estimated 50,000 Roman Catholics at 31 December 1977. In May 1967 President Sekou Touré ordered that all priests should be Guinea nationals.

CHRISTIANITY

The Anglican Communion

Anglicans in Guinea are adherents of the Church of the Province of West Africa.

Bishop of Guinea: Rt Rev. W. Y. MACAULEY.

The Roman Catholic Church

Guinea comprises the archdiocese of Conakry, the diocese of N'Zérékoré and the apostolic prefecture of Kankan (of which the Archbishop of Conakry is Apostolic Administrator).

Bishops' Conference: Conférence Episcopale de la Guinée, BP 1006 bis, Conakry; Pres. Mgr ROBERT SARAH, Archbishop of Conakry.

Archbishop of Conakry: Mgr ROBERT SARAH, Archevêché, BP 1006 bis, Conakry; tel. 436-27.

There are also six Protestant mission centres active in Guinea: four run by British and two by US societies.

The Press

Ecole Nouvelle: Conakry; monthly; education.
Fonike: BP 341, Conakry; sport and general; Dir IBRAHIMA KALIL DIARE.
Horoya (Liberty): BP 191, Conakry; weekly; Man. Dir MOHAMED MOUNIR CAMARA.
Journal Officiel de Guinée: BP 156, Conakry; fortnightly; govt.

Directory

La Guinéenne: Conakry; monthly; women's interest.
Le Travailleur de Guinée: Conakry; monthly; trade union organ.

NEWS AGENCIES

Agence Guinéenne de Presse: BP 1535, Conakry; tel. 46-54-14; f. 1960; Man. Dir MOHAMED CONDÉ.

Foreign Bureaux

Agentstvo Pechati Novosti (APN) (USSR): c/o USSR Embassy, BP 329, Conakry; Dir NIKOLAI A. SOLOGUBOVSKY.
Xinhua (New China) News Agency (People's Republic of China): BP 455, Conakry; tel. 46-13-47; telex 2128; Correspondent ZHANG ZHENYI.

TASS (USSR) is also represented.

Publisher

Editions du Ministère de l'Education Nationale: Secrétariat à la Recherche scientifique, BP 561, Conakry; general and educational.

Radio and Television

In 1983 there were an estimated 160,000 radio receivers and 8,000 television receivers in use. In June 1986 the construction of a new satellite station, at an estimated cost of 23m. FG, was announced.

Radiodiffusion-Télévision Guinéenne (RTG): BP 391, Conakry; telex 640; programmes in French, English, Créole-English, Portuguese, Arabic and local languages; colour; Man. Dir EMMANUEL KATTY.

Finance

(cap. = capital; m. = million; amounts in Guinea francs unless otherwise stated)

BANKING

Central Bank

Banque Centrale de la République de Guinée: BP 692, 12 blvd du Commerce, Conakry; tel. 44-26-28; telex 635; f. 1960; controls all banking activity; Gov. KERFALLA YANSANE.

Commercial Banks

As part of the economic reform programme that the Government implemented during the latter part of 1985 and in 1986, all existing state-owned banks were liquidated, and the following joint-venture institutions were established in their place.

Banque Internationale pour l'Afrique en Guinée (BIAG): BP 1419, ave de la République, Conakry; f. 1985; 'offshore' banking services; 51% state-owned, 49% owned by Banque Internationale pour l'Afrique de l'Ouest (France); cap. 500m.; Man. Dir YVES DURAND.

Banque Internationale pour le Commerce et l'Industrie de la Guinée (BICI-GUI): BP 1484, route du Niger, Carrefour Moukarim, Conakry 1; tel. 44-37-84; telex 2175; f. 1985; 51% state-owned, 20% by Banque Nationale de Paris (BNP), 14% by Caisse Centrale de Coopération Economique, 7% by European Investment Bank, 8% by Société Financière des Pays d'Outre-Mer (comprises BNP, Dresdner Bank, Banque Bruxelles Lambert).

Société Générale de Banques en Guinée: BP 1514, ave de la République, Conakry 1; tel. 44-17-41; telex 622; f. 1985; cap. 2,500m.; 34% owned by Société Générale (France); Man. Dir M. VERCHÈRE.

Other banks operating in Guinea include:

Banque Islamique de Guinée: BP 1247, ave de la République, Conakry; tel. 44-50-73; telex 2184; f. 1983; cap. US $1.4m.; 51% owned by Dar al-Maal al-Islami (DMI); provides Islamic banking services; Pres. MOHAMED FOUAD EL SARRAF; Man. MOHAMED Y. KOROMA.

Caisse Centrale de Coopération Economique (CCCE) (France): Conakry; telex 780; development bank.

INSURANCE

Société Nationale d'Assurances et de Réassurances de la République de Guinée (SNAR): BP 179, Conakry; has monopoly of insurance in Guinea; Man. Dir OUSMANE SANOKO.

Trade and Industry

CHAMBER OF COMMERCE

Chambre de Commerce, d'Industrie et d'Agriculture de Guinée: Conakry; f. 1986.

TRADE ORGANIZATION

Entreprise Nationale Import-Export (IMPORTEX): BP 152, Conakry; tel. 44-28-13; telex 625; state-owned import and export agency; Dir MAMADOU BOBO DIENG.

NATIONALIZED INDUSTRIES

Under the regime of the late President Sekou Touré, a total of 35 state companies, responsible for all sectors of the economy, were established. In 1986 it was announced that all but 11 of these were to be either dissolved, restructured or privatized under new names, as part of the Conté Government's economic and financial reform programme.

TRADE UNIONS

The Comité Militaire pour le Redressement National has announced the legalization of free trade unions.

Confédération des travailleurs de Guinée: Conakry; f. 1984 to replace the Confédération nationale des travailleurs de Guinée, which had formed part of the structure of the Parti démocratique de Guinée; Sec.-Gen. Dr MOHAMED SAMBAS KEBE.

Transport

RAILWAYS

There are 662 km of 1-m gauge track from Conakry to Kankan in the east of the country, crossing the Niger at Kouroussa. Three lines for the transport of bauxite link Sangaredi with the port of Kamsar in the west, and Conakry with Kindia and Fria, a total of 376 km. Arrangements have been made with the Liberian authorities for the use of the line linking the Nimba iron ore deposits with the port of Buchanan, and rehabilitation work is being carried out.

Office National des Chemins de Fer de Guinée (ONCFG): BP 581, Conakry; Gen. Man. SEKOU CAMARA.

ROADS

There are approximately 14,000 km of classified roads and tracks, of which 3,467 km are all-weather routes and 1,100 km are tarred. An 895-km cross-country road links Conakry to Bamako, in Mali, and the main highway connecting Dakar (Senegal) to Abidjan (Ivory Coast) also crosses Guinea.

The second phase of a rehabilitation and maintenance project, covering 54% of Guinea's paved roads, began in 1984, financed by a loan of US $14m. from the International Development Association. The construction of a 303-km bituminized road from Guekédou to N'Zérékoré, scheduled for completion in 1988, will connect the forested south-eastern region to the internal road network.

Office du Projet Routier: BP 581, Conakry.

Société Générale des Transports de Guinée (SOGETRAG): Conakry; f. 1984.

SHIPPING

Conakry and Kamsar are the international shipping ports. In 1982 2.4m. tons of bauxite were exported through Conakry and 9m. tons through Kamsar. Port development projects in progress in 1982 included the construction of 15,000 sq m of warehousing as well as a fruit quay and a container terminal, the construction of secondary ports along the coast and the construction of a naval repair dockyard at Conakry, where a new deep-water port was also to be built. The merchant fleet (13 vessels in 1981) was also to be expanded. There are 2,450 m of quays providing nine alongside berths for ocean-going ships at Conakry.

Port de Conakry: BP 534, Conakry.

ENTRAT: BP 315, Conakry; state-owned stevedoring and forwarding co; Dir-Gen. DAOUDA DIAWARA.

Société Navale Guinéenne: BP 522, Conakry; telex 644; f. 1968; state-owned shipping co; agents for Cie Maritime des Chargeurs Réunis, Cie de Navigation Fraissinet et Cyprien Fabre, Delta Steamship Lines Inc, Elder Dempster Line, Hanseatic Africa Line, Leif Hoëgh and Co A/S, Lloyd Triestino, Nouvelle Compagnie de Paquebots (NCP), Palm Line Ltd, Scandinavian West Africa Line, Société Navale de l'Ouest, United West Africa Service; Dir-Gen. NABY SYLLA.

SOTRAMAR: Kamsar; f. 1971; bauxite export from mines at Boké through port of Kamsar.

CIVIL AVIATION

There is an international airport at Conakry, and smaller airfields at Labé, Kankan and Faranah.

Air Guinée: BP 12, ave de la République, Conakry; f. 1960; international and internal services; flights to Bamako, Dakar, Freetown and Monrovia; Dir-Gen. NFA MOUSSA DIANE; fleet of 1 Ilyushin Il-18, 2 Antonov An-12B, 4 An-24, 1 Boeing 707-320C, 1 727-100C, 1 737-200C, 1 Yak-40, 1 Dash-7.

Tourism

Office National du Tourisme et de l'Hotellerie (ONATHOL): Conakry; state tourist office.

GUINEA-BISSAU

Introductory Survey

Location, Climate, Language, Religion, Flag, Capital

The Republic of Guinea-Bissau lies on the west coast of Africa, with Senegal to the north and Guinea to the east and south. The climate is tropical, although maritime and Sahelian influences are felt. The average temperature is 20°C (68°F). The official language is Portuguese, of which the locally spoken form is Creole (Crioulo). Other dialects are also widely spoken. The principal beliefs are animism and Islam. There is a small minority of Roman Catholics and other Christian groups. The national flag (proportions 2 by 1) has two equal horizontal stripes, of yellow and green, and a red vertical stripe, with a five-pointed black star at its centre, at the hoist. The capital is Bissau.

Recent History

Portuguese Guinea (Guiné) was settled by the Portuguese in the 15th century. Small nationalist groups began to form in the 1950s, and the Partido Africano da Independência da Guiné e Cabo Verde (PAIGC) was formed in 1956. Fighting broke out in the early 1960s, and by 1972 the PAIGC was in control of two-thirds of the country. In 1973 a National People's Assembly was elected in 'liberated' areas, and the independence of the Republic of Guinea-Bissau was proclaimed in September, with Luiz Cabral as President of the State Council. To combat the PAIGC's guerrilla campaign, about 40,000 Portuguese troops were operating in the territory. Portuguese forces began to sustain heavy losses in 1973–74, and this may have been a factor in the military coup in Portugal in April 1974. This coup brought the fighting to an end, and in August the new Portuguese Government and the PAIGC negotiated an agreement to end Portuguese rule. Accordingly, on 10 September 1974, Portugal recognized the independence of Guinea-Bissau.

The PAIGC regime introduced measures to lay the foundations for a socialist state. At elections in December 1976 and January 1977 voters chose regional councils from which a new National People's Assembly was later selected. In July 1978 Francisco Mendes, who had been Chief State Commissioner since 1973, died; he was replaced by Commander João Vieira, the former State Commissioner for the Armed Forces and President of the National People's Assembly.

Until 1980 the PAIGC supervised both Cape Verde and Guinea-Bissau, the two constitutions remaining separate, but with a view to eventual unification. However, on 14 November, four days after the Government had approved a new constitution which gave President Cabral almost total control and, some claimed, gave unfair preference to Cape Verdeans (who were permitted to hold senior administrative and government posts), Cabral was deposed in a coup and Vieira was installed as Chairman of the Council of the Revolution. The National People's Assembly was dissolved.

At the PAIGC Congress in November 1981 it was decided to preserve the single-party status of the PAIGC, with Vieira as Secretary-General, despite Cape Verde's withdrawal. Diplomatic relations between the two countries were restored after the release of Cabral from detention in January 1982. Vítor Saúde Maria, former Minister of Foreign Affairs and Vice-Chairman of the Council of Ministers, was appointed Prime Minister in a government reshuffle in May, the post having been vacant since the 1980 coup; several ministers who were regarded as left-wing lost their portfolios.

In March 1983 President Vieira set up a commission, headed by the Minister of Justice, to examine plans for the revision of the Constitution and the electoral law. In March 1984 President Vieira dismissed the Prime Minister, Vítor Saúde Maria. Although the reason given for his dismissal was alleged involvement in a planned coup, the differences between Vieira and Saúde Maria appeared to centre on the proposed constitutional changes, which would abolish the post of Prime Minister and concentrate more power in the hands of the President. Several other senior party members were subsequently accused of colluding with Saúde Maria and were expelled from the PAIGC. In April President Vieira formally assumed the role of Head of Government. Elections to the regional councils were held in April, and the National People's Assembly was re-established in May, its members being chosen from the regional councillors. The 15-member Council of State, which replaced the Council of the Revolution, was selected from the members of the National People's Assembly. Vieira was elected as President of the Council of State and Head of State. The National People's Assembly immediately ratified the new constitution, and formally abolished the position of Prime Minister.

In August 1985 President Vieira launched a campaign against corruption, and many senior officials were dismissed or arrested. This campaign was apparently the cause of an attempted military coup which took place in November, led by Col Paulo Correia, the First Vice-President of the Council of State, and several senior army officers. Although the coup was swiftly foiled and its leaders were arrested, the involvement of so many senior figures seriously undermined the Vieira government. By July 1986 six people who had been accused of involvement in the coup attempt had died in prison, leading to claims that they had been murdered. At the trial of the surviving defendants, which concluded in July, 12 alleged plotters were sentenced to death and 41 were sentenced to hard labour. Later in the month, six of those condemned to death, including Correia, were executed, but the six other plotters had their death sentences commuted, following appeals for clemency from the President of Portugal, the Pope and the Association of African Jurists.

The attempted coup had posed a serious threat to President Vieira, and in July 1986 he announced a major government reshuffle, aiming to increase government security. The Super-Ministries of Justice and Local Power, Economic Co-ordination and Planning, and International Co-operation were abolished in favour of smaller ministries. The Council of Ministers was enlarged from 15 to 19 members, and the posts of three resident Ministers for the Provinces were created. During the fourth PAIGC congress, held in November, delegates supported the liberalization of the economy (see Economic Affairs), and re-elected President Vieira as secretary-general of the PAIGC for a further four years.

Government

The Constitution of 1984 states that the PAIGC is the leading force in society and in the nation. The PAIGC's highest authority is the Party Congress, convened every five years. The Congress elects a Central Committee (70 members in November 1986) to supervise the Party's work. To direct its policy, the Central Committee elects from its members a Political Bureau (12 full members and four alternate members in November 1986). Legislative power is vested in the National People's Assembly, which has 150 members, chosen by the eight directly-elected regional councils from among their own members. The National People's Assembly, in turn, elects from among its members the 15-member Council of State, which assumes legislative functions between sessions of the National People's Assembly. The regional councils also elect, for a five-year term, the President of the Council of State (a post corresponding to that of President of the Republic), in whom executive power is vested. The President of the Council of State is also Head of Government, and appoints the Ministers and Secretaries of State.

Defence

In July 1986 the armed forces totalled 8,550 men (army 6,200, navy 275, and air force 75). The army is supported by a militia,

GUINEA-BISSAU

the Forças Armadas da Libertação, which totalled 2,000. The estimated defence budget for 1982 was 375m. pesos.

Economic Affairs

Subsistence agriculture is the mainstay of the economy, engaging about 80% of the population. Rice is the staple food, and maize, beans, cassava and sweet potatoes are also grown. Groundnuts, cashew nuts and palm kernels are exported, providing more than 68% of export earnings in 1983. Cattle-breeding is important in the interior. In 1983 agricultural exports earned 71.3% of total export earnings, but the value of agricultural imports was double that of exports. In March 1986 Guinea-Bissau appealed for international food aid to offset the anticipated shortfall of 28,000 tons, as agricultural production in 1985 had reached only 119,000 tons, well below the national cereal consumption of about 147,000 tons per year. The Government plans to make the country self-sufficient in essential foods, to increase production for export and to diversify crops; tobacco, cotton and sugar cane are being grown experimentally. Co-operative farming methods are being introduced. The fishing industry is being modernized and has expanded rapidly; in 1983 fish products provided 24% of export earnings, and it has been estimated that the potential annual catch in Guinea-Bissau's waters is up to 200,000 tons of fish. The Government has also signed fishing agreements with Spain, the EEC and the USSR, permitting foreign vessels to fish in Guinea-Bissau's maritime zone in return for aid to the country's own fishing industry.

Industry, based on the processing of food and raw materials, is being developed in order to provide employment, to reduce imports and to satisfy consumer demand; however, only timber is exported. The agro-industrial complex at Cumeré is capable of processing 50,000 metric tons of rice and 70,000 tons of groundnuts annually. A sugar refinery that is being built at Gambiel will be capable of producing 10,000 tons of refined sugar per year. Following the Government's encouragement of the private sector in November 1986, a car assembly plant was reopened. The factory had opened in 1979, but was forced to close in 1984, owing to a lack of components and low productivity. The mining sector has still to be developed: the exploitation of bauxite, phosphates and petroleum deposits is being studied. In 1984 the Government reached agreement with a group of foreign oil companies concerning petroleum prospecting in an offshore concession covering 4,500 sq km. In 1985, following the relaxation of the country's hydrocarbons law to attract foreign companies, licences for exploration of some 40 offshore blocks were offered on very favourable terms, and several major oil companies were expected to bid in 1986.

There is a serious lack of basic infrastructure and transport facilities. Owing to persistent shortages of foreign exchange, Guinea-Bissau has been unable to import sufficient quantities of petroleum and spare parts. Guinea-Bissau relies heavily on water transport, and in 1983 the World Bank granted a loan of US $16m. to finance the modernization of the port of Bissau and the rehabilitation of four river stations. In September 1986 construction of a new river port at N'Pangda was initiated, to improve the transport of rice to northern Guinea-Bissau. Other plans include the construction of a dam on the Corrubal river, to supply hydroelectric power for the development of a modern aluminium industry, the renovation of the Bissau thermal power station, the development of a new telecommunications network and a major road rehabilitation project. In 1983 Guinea-Bissau joined the Organisation pour la Mise en Valeur du Fleuve Gambie (OMVG, see p. 217), in the hope of benefiting from integrated development projects in the Gambia river basin.

Since independence, the country has had a serious trade deficit, which has increased since 1977, because of the effects of the drought on crops, rising oil prices and world inflation, and stood at $33.4m. in 1982. In 1983 exports covered only 16% of imports, leaving a trade imbalance of $44.5m., and in 1984 the trade deficit totalled $15.2m. In 1985 export earnings were equivalent to 25% of the value of imports. The annual rate of inflation rose from an estimated 9% in 1977 to 30% in 1981. Between 1973 and 1983, according to estimates by the World Bank, Guinea-Bissau's gross national product (GNP), measured in constant prices, expanded at an average rate of 2.1% per year, while annual population growth averaged 4.3%. As a result, real GNP per head declined by 2.1% annually over the period. In 1984 GNP per head (at average 1982–84 prices) was an estimated $190, among the 15 lowest national levels in the world.

Commander Vieira's Government had originally aimed to downgrade many of the prestigious projects that had been started during the regime of President Cabral, and to emphasize rural development. The need for co-ordination was recognized, and the first development plan (1983–86) was drawn up in 1982. An international donors' conference on Guinea-Bissau, held in May 1984, raised US $60m. towards projects in the development plan. In December 1983 the peso was devalued by 50% as part of an economic stabilization programme launched by the Government. The programme aimed to liberalize trade and to increase activity in the private sector.

In early 1986 the IMF proposed a further drastic devaluation of the peso, redundancies in the civil service and the introduction of an austerity programme. Trade restrictions were lifted in August, allowing private traders to import and export goods, although the two state-owned enterprises continued to control trading of rice, petroleum products, pesticides and various other articles. Pressure increased on the Government to liberalize trade, from farmers who had benefited from the Government's agricultural policy. In September the World Bank agreed on the outline of a structural adjustment programme, and for this purpose proposed a loan of about $25m. During the fourth PAIGC congress in November, Vieira introduced a new policy of economic liberalization, with the aim of disengaging state control over most economic sectors and trading activities. Various incentives were offered to encourage foreign businesses to invest in Guinea-Bissau, including devaluation of the peso, and measures allowing foreign companies to retain 75% of their foreign currency earnings. The programme is to be wholly financed through external aid. By late 1986 Guinea-Bissau's total foreign debt had exceeded $270m. ($50m. of which was owed to Portugal), and had thus almost doubled in two years. Guinea-Bissau receives many foreign loans and credits, and is a member of ECOWAS (see p. 133).

Social Welfare

Medical services are limited, owing to a severe shortage of facilities. The Government aims to set up one regional hospital in each of the eight regions. In 1981 there were 1,532 hospital beds. In 1982 there were about 100 physicians and 360 nurses working in the country.

Education

Education is officially compulsory only for the period of primary schooling, which begins at seven years of age and lasts for six years. Secondary education, beginning at the age of 13, lasts for up to five years (a first cycle of three years and a second of two years). In 1982 the enrolment ratio at primary schools of children in the relevant age-group was estimated to be 100% for boys but only 49% for girls. The comparable figures for secondary schools in 1981 were 8% for boys and 2% for girls. Mass literacy campaigns have been launched: according to UNESCO estimates, the average rate of adult illiteracy in 1980 was 81.1% (males 75.4%; females 86.6%), but by 1985 the rate had declined to 68.6% (males 53.8%; females 82.7%).

Tourism

There is very little tourism in Guinea-Bissau, but the island of Bubaque is being developed as a resort. A new 180-bed hotel was planned to open in June 1987.

Weights and Measures

The metric system is used.

Currency and Exchange Rates

100 centavos = 1 Guinea peso.

Exchange rates (30 September 1986):
 £1 sterling = 308.42 pesos;
 US $1 = 213.14 pesos.

Statistical Survey

AREA AND POPULATION

Area: 36,125 sq km (13,948 sq miles).

Population: 487,448 (census of 15 December 1970, which covered only those areas under Portuguese control); 767,739 (males 370,225; females 397,514) at census of 16–30 April 1979; 810,000 (official estimate for mid-1981). *By Region* (1979 census, provisional): Bafatá 116,032, Biombo 56,463, Bissau 109,214, Bolama/Bijagos 25,743, Cacheu 130,227, Gabú 104,315, Oio 135,114, Quinara 35,532, Tombali 55,099.

Density (mid-1981): 22.4 per sq. km.

Principal Towns: Bissau (capital) 109,214, Bafatá 13,429, Gabú 7,803, Mansôa 5,390, Catió 5,170, Cantchungo 4,965, Farim 4,468 (census of April 1979).

Births and Deaths (UN estimates, 1975–80): Average annual birth rate 40.9 per 1,000; Death rate 21.9 per 1,000.

Economically Active Population (ILO estimates, '000 persons at mid-1980): Agriculture, etc. 332 (males 174, females 158); Industry 14 (males 12, females 3); Services 57 (males 46, females 11); Total 403 (males 231, females 172). Source: ILO, *Economically Active Population Estimates and Projections, 1950–2025*.

AGRICULTURE, ETC.

Principal Crops (FAO estimates, '000 metric tons, 1985): Rice (paddy) 110, Maize 15, Millet 25, Sorghum 15, Roots and tubers 40, Groundnuts (in shell) 30, Coconuts 25, Copra 5, Palm kernels 11, Palm oil 2.8, Vegetables and melons 20, Plantains 25, Other fruits 15, Sugar cane 5.

Livestock (FAO estimates, '000 head, year ending September 1985): Cattle 225, Pigs 133, Sheep 65, Goats 150.

Livestock Products (FAO estimates, '000 metric tons, 1985): Beef and veal 3; Pig meat 4; Cow's milk 7; Goat's milk 2.

Forestry (FAO estimates, '000 cubic metres, 1984): Roundwood removals 558 (sawlogs, etc. 40, other industrial wood 96, fuel wood 422); Sawnwood production 16.

Fishing (metric tons, live weight, 1984): Fishes 2,466; Crustaceans and molluscs 230; Total catch 2,696.

INDUSTRY

Electric energy (1983): 13 million kWh.

FINANCE

Currency and Exchange Rates: 100 centavos = 1 Guinea peso. *Coins:* 5, 10, 20 and 50 centavos; 1, 2½, 5, 10 and 20 pesos. *Notes:* 50, 100 and 500 pesos. *Sterling and Dollar Equivalents* (30 September 1986): £1 sterling = 308.42 pesos; US $1 = 213.14 pesos; 1,000 Guinea pesos = £3.242 = $4.692. *Average Exchange Rate* (Guinea pesos per US dollar): 39.87 in 1982; 42.10 in 1983; 105.29 in 1984. Note: Between May 1978 and December 1983 the currency was tied to the IMF's special drawing right at a mid-point exchange rate of SDR1 = 44 Guinea pesos.

Budget (US $ million, 1982): *Revenue:* Direct taxes 5.2, Indirect taxes 13.7, Other recurrent revenue 4.5, Capital receipts 0.1, Total 23.5; *Expenditure:* Total 59.9.

Gross Domestic Product (estimates, million Guinea pesos at current prices): 5,204 in 1980; 5,888 in 1981; 6,490 in 1982. Source: UN Economic Commission for Africa, *African Statistical Yearbook*.

EXTERNAL TRADE

Principal Commodities (US $ million 1983): *Imports:* Food, beverages and tobacco 11.9, Fuels and lubricants 7.5, Machinery and equipment 2.6, Transport equipment 7.1, Total (incl. others) 54.9. *Exports:* Palm kernels 1.3, Groundnuts (shelled) 3.4, Cashew nuts 1.2, Fish 2.1, Timber 0.4, Total (incl. others) 8.6.

Principal Trading Partners (million pesos): *Imports* (1984): France 232.7, Germany, Fed. Repub. 213.7, Italy 110.4, Netherlands 215.6, Portugal 924.0, Senegal 362.0, Sweden 70.2, USSR 462.7, USA 192.4, Total (incl. others) 3,230.7. Source: Ministry of Planning, Bissau.
Exports (1980): Cape Verde 23.0, China, People's Repub. 14.6, Guinea 10.3, Netherlands 20.9, Portugal 101.3, Senegal 5.5, Spain 95.2, Switzerland 87.5, Total (incl. others) 382.3. Source: Direcção-Geral de Estatística, Bissau.

TRANSPORT

Road Traffic (vehicles in use, 1972): Cars 3,268, Lorries and buses 1,098, Motor cycles 758, Total 5,124.

International Sea-borne Shipping (estimated freight traffic, '000 metric tons, 1983): Goods loaded 35; Goods unloaded 100. Source: UN, *Monthly Bulletin of Statistics*.

Civil Aviation (1979): Passengers embarked 11,916, Passengers disembarked 9,879, Freight loaded 102,406 kg, Freight unloaded 364,276 kg.

EDUCATION

Pre-School (1984/85): 6 schools, 736 pupils, 38 teachers.

Basic 1st cycle (1984/85): 640 schools, 67,818 pupils, 2,435 teachers.

Basic 2nd cycle (1984/85): 28 schools, 13,626 pupils, 718 teachers.

Secondary (1984/85, *liceus*): 12 schools, 11,710 pupils, 650 teachers.

Teacher Training (1984/85): 2 schools, 594 pupils, 38 teachers.

Technical (1984/85): 2 schools, 433 pupils, 69 teachers.

Source: Ministério da Educação Nacional, Bissau.

Directory

The Constitution

A new constitution for the Republic of Guinea-Bissau was approved by the National People's Assembly on 16 May 1984. Its main provisions are summarized below:

The Constitution defines Guinea-Bissau as an anti-colonialist and anti-imperialist Republic and a State of revolutionary national democracy, based on the people's participation in carrying out, controlling and directing public activities. The Constitution states that the party that fought against Portuguese colonialism, the Partido Africano da Independência da Guiné e Cabo Verde (PAIGC), shall be the leading political force in society and in the State. The PAIGC shall define the general bases for policy in all fields.

The economy of Guinea-Bissau shall be organized on the principles of state direction and planning. The State shall control the country's foreign trade.

The representative bodies in the country are the National People's Assembly and the regional councils. Other state bodies draw their powers from these. The members of the regional councils shall be directly elected. Members of the councils must be more than 18 years of age. The National Assembly shall have 150 members, who are to be elected by the regional councils from among their own members. All members of the National Assembly must be more than 21 years of age.

The National Assembly shall elect a 15-member Council of State, to which its powers are delegated between sessions of the Assembly. The Assembly also elects the President of the Council of State, who is also automatically Head of the Government and Commander-in-Chief of the Armed Forces. The Council of State will later elect two Vice-Presidents and a Secretary. The President and Vice-Presidents of the Council of State form part of the Government, as do Ministers, Secretaries of State and the Governor of the National Bank.

The Constitution can be revised at any time by the National People's Assembly on the initiative of the deputies themselves, or of the Council of State or the Government.

The Government

HEAD OF STATE

Head of Government, President of the Council of State and Commander-in-Chief of the Armed Forces: Commdr João Bernardo Vieira (assumed power 14 November 1980; elected President of the Council of State 16 May 1984).

COUNCIL OF STATE
(January 1987)

Commdr João Bernardo Vieira (President).
Col Iafai Camara (Vice-President).
Dr Vasco Cabral (Secretary).
Carlos Correia.
José Pereira.
Filinto Barros.
Tiago Alelua Lopes.
Buato Na Batcha.
Bengate Na Beate.
Júlio Semedo.
Francisca Pereira.
Mário Mendes.
Teoboldo Barboza.
Bana Match.

COUNCIL OF MINISTERS
(January 1987)

Head of Government, President of the Council of State, Commander-in-Chief of the Armed Forces, Minister of Defence and of the Interior: Commdr João Bernardo Vieira.
Vice-President of the Council of State and Minister of State for the Armed Forces: Col Iafai Camara.
Minister of State for Justice: Dr Vasco Cabral.
Minister of State at the Presidency: Tiago Alelua Lopes.
Minister of State for Rural Development and Fisheries: Carlos Correia.
Minister of Education, Culture and Sport: Fidelis Cabral d'Almada.
Minister of Social Affairs: Avito da Silva.
Minister of National Security and Public Order: José Pereira.
Minister of Natural Resources and Industry: Filinto de Barros.
Minister of Foreign Affairs: Júlio Semedo.
Minister of Finance: Vítor Freire Monteiro.
Minister of Public Health: Alexandre Nunes Correia.
Minister of Trade and Tourism: Col Manuel dos Santos.
Minister of Economic Planning: Bartolomeu Simões Pereira.
Minister for the Civil Service, Labour and Social Security: Henriqueta Godinho Gomes.
Minister-Governor of the National Bank: Dr Pedro A. Godinho Gomes.
Minister of Information and Telecommunications: Mussa Djassi.
Minister for the Northern Province: Mario Cabral.
Minister for the Eastern Province: Malam Bacai Sanha.
Minister for the Southern Province: Luís Oliveira Sanca.
There are eight Secretaries of State.

MINISTRIES
All Ministries are in Bissau.

Legislature

NATIONAL PEOPLE'S ASSEMBLY

A new National People's Assembly was inaugurated on 14 May 1984. Its 150 members were selected from among the members of the eight directly-elected regional councils. All members are nominees of the PAIGC.

President: Carmen Pereira.

Political Organization

Partido Africano da Independência da Guiné e Cabo Verde (PAIGC): CP 106, Bissau; f. 1956 by Dr Amílcar Cabral; fmrly the ruling party in both Guinea-Bissau and Cape Verde; although Cape Verde withdrew from the PAIGC following the coup in Guinea-Bissau in November 1980, Guinea-Bissau decided to retain the party name and initials; the PAIGC is 'the leading force in society and in the nation'; cen. cttee of 70 mems (60 full and 10 alternate mems) and political bureau of 16 mems (12 full and four alternate); Sec.-Gen. Commdr João Bernardo Vieira; Perm. Sec. of Cen. Cttee Dr Vasco Cabral.

In November 1986 an opposition party, the **Guinea-Bissau Bafata Resistance Movement,** was founded in Lisbon, and advocates a pluralist democratic system.

Diplomatic Representation

EMBASSIES IN GUINEA-BISSAU

Algeria: Rua 12 de Setembro 12, CP 350, Bissau; tel. 211522; Ambassador: R. Benchikh el Fegoun.
Brazil: Rua São Tomé Esquina/Avda Francisco Mendes, Bissau; tel. 212648; telex 245; Ambassador: Affonso Celso de Ouro-Preto.
Cape Verde: Bissau; Ambassador: António Lima.
China, People's Republic: Rua Eduardo Mondlane 33–35, Bissau; tel. 212908; Ambassador: Hu Jingrui.
Cuba: Rua Joaquim N'Com 1, Bissau; tel. 213579; Ambassador: Dr Armando Torres Santrayll.
Egypt: Avda Domingos Ramos 24-B, Bissau; tel. 213642; Ambassador: Muhammad Abdo Hassanein Makhlouf.
France: Rua Eduardo Mondlane 67-A, Bissau; tel. 212633; Ambassador: Louis Bouroux.
German Democratic Republic: Avda Osvaldo Vieira 28, Bissau; tel. 212992; Ambassador: Erich Meske.
Guinea: Rua 14 no. 9, CP 396, Bissau; tel. 212681; Ambassador: Guirane Ndiaye.
Korea, Democratic People's Republic: Avda Domingos Ramos 42, Bissau; tel. 212885; Ambassador: Mun Song-Kuk.
Libya: Rua 16, CP 362, Bissau (People's Bureau); tel. 212006; Representative: Dokali Ali Mustafa.
Portugal: Rua de Lisboa, no. 6, Bissau; tel. 213009; telex 248; Ambassador: Manuel Barreiros Martins.
Senegal: Bissau; tel. 2636; Ambassador: Ibrahima Diengo.
USSR: Rua Rui Djassi 17, Bissau; tel. 213535; Ambassador: Lev Vladislavovich Krylov.
USA: Avda Domingos Ramos, CP 297, Bissau; Ambassador: John Blacken.

Judicial System

Under the provisions of the 1984 constitution, judges of the Supreme Court are appointed by the President of the Council of State.

Attorney-General: Joseph Turpin.

Religion

About 60% of the population are animists, 35% are Muslims and 5% are Christians, mainly Roman Catholics.

CHRISTIANITY
The Roman Catholic Church

Guinea-Bissau comprises a single diocese, directly responsible to the Holy See. At 31 December 1984 there was an estimated 44,350 adherents in the country.

Bishop of Bissau: Mgr Settimio Arturo Ferrazzetta, CP 20, Bissau; tel. 212469.

The Press

Nô Pintcha: Bissau; 3 a week; official govt publ.; Dir Sra CABRAL; circ. 6,000.

Radio

There were an estimated 25,000 radio receivers in use in 1985. There is no television service.

Radiodifusão Nacional da República da Guiné-Bissau: CP 191, Bissau; govt-owned; broadcasts on short-wave, medium-wave and FM in Portuguese; Dir FRANCISCO BARRETO.

Finance

(cap. = capital; m. = million; brs = branches; amounts in Guinea pesos)

BANKING

Banco Nacional da Guiné-Bissau: Avda Amílcar Cabral, CP 38, Bissau; tel. 215433; telex 969249; central and commercial bank; f. 1976; cap. 100m.; Gov. Dr PEDRO A. GODINHO GOMES; 3 brs.

Caixa de Crédito da Guiné: Bissau; govt savings and loan institution.

Caixa Económica Postal: Avda Amílcar Cabral, Bissau; tel. 212999; telex 979; postal savings institution.

INSURANCE

In June 1979 it was announced that a single state-owned insurer would be set up to replace the Portuguese company Ultramarina.

Trade and Industry

Since independence the Government has been actively pursuing a policy of small-scale industrialization to compensate for the almost total lack of manufacturing capacity. It has adopted an elaborate state control programme and in late 1976 acquired 80% of the capital of a Portuguese company, **Ultramarina**, a large firm specializing in a wide variety of trading, ship-repairing and agricultural processing. The Government has also acquired major interests in the **CICER** brewery and created a joint venture company with the Portuguese concern **SACOR** to sell petroleum products after the construction of new storage facilities. Since 1975 three fishing companies have been set up with foreign participation: **GUIALP** (with Algeria), **Estrela do Mar** (with the USSR) and **SEMAPESCA** (with France). In December 1976 **SOCOTRAM**, an enterprise for the sale and processing of timber, was inaugurated. It operates a new factory in Bissau for the production of wooden tiles and co-ordinates sawmills and carpentry shops all over the country. In 1979 the **Empresa de Automóveis da Guiné** opened an assembly plant at Bissau, capable of producing 500 cars a year.

Empresa Nacional de Pesquisas e Exploração Petrolíferas e Mineiras (PETROMINAS): Rua Eduardo Mondlane 58, Bissau; tel. 212279; state-owned company; regulates all mineral prospecting; Dir-Gen. PIO GOMES CORREIA.

TRADE UNION

National Union of Workers (UNTG): 13 Avda Ovai di Vievra, BP 98, Bissau; Sec.-Gen. MÁRIO MENDES.

Transport

RAILWAYS

The construction of a railway from Boé to Buba is planned.

ROADS

In 1983 there were 2,500 km of roads, of which 400 km were tarred. A major road rehabilitation scheme is under way, and by the end of 1983, 522 km of roads had been rehabilitated. In 1984 the International Development Association committed US $7m. to Guinea-Bissau for the rehabilitation of a further 920 km of roads An international road is planned, which would link Guinea-Bissau with The Gambia and Senegal.

SHIPPING

Work started in 1984 on a major port modernization project, due to be completed in 1987. The main port at Bissau was to be renovated and expanded, and four river ports were to be upgraded to enable barges to load and unload at low tide. The total cost of the project was estimated at US $47.4m., and finance was provided by the World Bank and Arab funds. In 1986 work began on a new river port at N'Pungda, which will be partly funded by the Netherlands.

Empresa Nacional de Agências e Transportes Marítimos (Guinémar): Sociedade de Agências e Transportes da Guiné Lda, Rua Guerra Mendes, 4-4A, CP 244, Bissau; tel. 212675; telex 240; nationalized 1976; shipping agents and brokers; Gen. Man. MARCOS T. LOPES, Asst Gen. Man. NOËL CORREIA.

CIVIL AVIATION

There is an international airport at Bissalanca, which there are plans to expand, and 10 smaller airports serving the interior.

Linhas Aéreas da Guiné-Bissau (LIA): Aeroporto Craviero Lopes, CP 111, Bissau; f. 1977; domestic services and flights to Guinea, Cape Verde and Senegal; Gen. Man. Capt. JOSÉ POMBO; fleet of 1 HS-748, 1 Dornier 28 Sky-servant, 2 Dornier 27, 1 Cessna 206.

Tourism

The island of Bubaque is being developed as a tourist resort, with 110 rooms in 1979. Work began in 1985 on a 180-room luxury hotel in Bissau which was planned to open in June 1987.

Centro de Informação e Turismo: CP 294, Bissau; state tourism and information service.

GUYANA

Introductory Survey

Location, Climate, Language, Religion, Flag, Capital

The Co-operative Republic of Guyana lies on the north coast of South America, between Venezuela to the west and Suriname to the east, with Brazil to the south. The narrow coastal belt has a moderate climate with two wet seasons, from April to August and from November to January, alternating with two dry seasons. Inland, there are tropical forests and savannah, and the dry season lasts from September to February. The average annual temperature is 27°C (80°F), with average rainfall of 1,520 mm (60 in) per year inland, rising to between 2,030 mm (80 in) and 2,540 mm (100 in) on the coast. English is the official language but Hindi, Urdu and Amerindian dialects are also spoken. The principal religions are Christianity, Hinduism and Islam. The national flag (proportions 5 by 3 when flown on land, but 2 by 1 at sea) is green, with a white-bordered yellow triangle (apex at the edge of the fly) on which is superimposed a black-bordered red triangle (apex in the centre). The capital is Georgetown.

Recent History

Guyana was formerly British Guiana, a colony of the United Kingdom, formed in 1831 from territories finally ceded to Britain by the Dutch in 1814. A new constitution, providing for universal adult suffrage, was introduced in 1953. The elections of April 1953 were won by the left-wing People's Progressive Party (PPP), led by Dr Cheddi Jagan. In October, however, the United Kingdom Government, claiming that a communist dictatorship was threatened, suspended the Constitution. An interim administration was appointed. The PPP split in 1955, and in 1957 some former members founded a new party, the People's National Congress (PNC), under the leadership of Forbes Burnham. The PNC draws its support mainly from the African-descended population, while PPP support comes largely from the (Asian-descended) Indian community. Both parties adhere to Marxist-Leninist ideology.

A revised constitution was introduced in December 1956 and fresh elections held in August 1957. The PPP won and Dr Jagan became Chief Minister. Another constitution, providing for internal self-government, was adopted in July 1961. The PPP won the elections in August and Dr Jagan was appointed Premier in September. In the election of December 1964, held under the system of proportional representation that had been introduced in the previous year, the PPP won the largest number of seats in the Legislative Assembly, but not a majority. A coalition government was formed by the PNC and the United Force, with Burnham as Prime Minister. This coalition led the colony to independence, as Guyana, on 26 May 1966.

The PNC won elections in December 1968 and in July 1973, although the results of the latter were disputed by the opposition parties. Guyana became a Co-operative Republic on 23 February 1970, and Arthur Chung was elected non-executive President in March. In May 1976 the PPP, which had boycotted the National Assembly since 1973, offered the Government its 'critical support'. Following a referendum in July 1978, which gave the Assembly power to amend the Constitution, elections to the Assembly were postponed for 15 months. The legislature assumed the role of a Constituent Assembly, established in November 1978, to draft a new constitution. In October 1979 elections were postponed for a further year. In October 1980 Forbes Burnham declared himself executive President of Guyana, a new constitution was promulgated, and elections were announced for December. Internal opposition to the PNC Government increased after the assassination in June 1980 of Dr Walter Rodney, leader of the Working People's Alliance (WPA), as the Government was widely believed to have been involved in the incident. After all opposition parties except the PPP and United Force called for a boycott of the December elections to the National Assembly, the PNC, under Burnham, received 77.7% of the votes, according to official results, and won 41 of the 53 elective seats, although allegations of substantial electoral malpractice were made. On the basis of the voting for the Assembly, Burnham was declared to have been elected President. He was formally inaugurated in January 1981. The Government's international reputation was further diminished when an international observer team denounced the elections as fraudulent. In 1981 arrests and trials of opposition leaders continued, and in 1982 the Government's relations with human rights groups, and especially the Christian churches, deteriorated further. Editors of opposition newspapers were threatened, political violence increased, and the Government was accused of interference in the legal process. Popular passive resistance to the Government took the form of economic non-co-operation, while the Government gave much publicity to rumours of an imminent invasion by Venezuela, in an attempt to divert attention from the internal crisis.

In 1983 Guyana's worsening economic situation increased public opposition to the Government, and led to growing disaffection within the trade union movement and the PNC. In June the shortage of basic foodstuffs, created by the Government's ban on the import of such staples as wheat flour and powdered milk, resulted in a wave of public unrest. In July 4,000 bauxite workers at the principal mining centre of Linden undertook a six-week strike in protest at food shortages. A further source of popular discontent was the Government's severe response to the thriving 'black market' in banned foodstuffs, which operated between Guyana and Venezuela, Brazil and Suriname. A virtual 'freeze' on wages since 1979 has resulted in a fall in income, in real terms, for government employees, and during 1984 anti-Government trade unions conducted strikes in the sugar industry, protesting at wage levels and food shortages. In December 1984 Burnham announced an amelioration of the Government's austerity measures by raising the daily minimum wage, and by promising that more basic consumer items would become available. Speculation about a possible government of national unity, formed by the PNC and the PPP to counter the threat of a right-wing military coup, increased after a series of talks between the two parties.

Guyana condemned the US-led invasion of Grenada in October 1983, a move which, although popular in Guyana, led to rapid deterioration in relations with the USA, which had worsened after the US Government had vetoed anticipated loans to Guyana in September. Guyana's decision to dispense with seeking IMF financial support further compounded the country's increasing isolation among Western nations. In response, Guyana sought to improve relations with socialist countries, such as Cuba, Libya, the Democratic People's Republic of Korea and Yugoslavia, to compensate for the decline in Western aid.

Forbes Burnham died in August 1985 and was succeeded as President by Desmond Hoyte, hitherto the First Vice-President and Prime Minister. President Hoyte's former posts were filled by Hamilton Green, previously the First Deputy Prime Minister. At a general election, held in December, the PNC won 78% of the votes and 42 of the elective seats in the National Assembly. Desmond Hoyte was declared elected as President. Opposition groups, including the PPP and WPA, denounced the poll as fraudulent, and made allegations of widespread electoral malpractice. In January 1986 five of the six opposition parties formed the Patriotic Coalition for Democracy.

President Hoyte's Government announced that its chief priority would be the revitalization of Guyana's rapidly deteriorating economy. Efforts were also made during 1986 to improve foreign relations, in particular with the USA and other Western countries, and in March the Government announced legislative proposals to provide tax benefits and investment opportunities in an attempt to encourage 'offshore' banking and business in Guyana. The ban on the import of wheat flour, imposed in 1982, was lifted, and the first shipments of flour from the USA arrived in September, as part of a new agreement on food aid. Further restrictions on several food items were lifted in November. In December the Cabinet resigned, at the request of President Hoyte, to enable him to reorganize his Government. Cabinet changes were announced in January 1987.

Guyana has border disputes with its neighbours, Venezuela and Suriname, although relations with Brazil have continued to improve through trade and military agreements. In 1962 Venezuela renewed its claim to 130,000 sq km (50,000 sq miles) of land west of the Essequibo river (nearly two-thirds of Guyanese territory). The area was accorded to Guyana in 1899, and the Port of Spain Protocol of 1970 put the issue in abeyance until 1982. Venezuela based its claim on a papal bull of 1493, referring to Spanish colonial possessions. Several border incidents were reported in 1982. Direct negotiations in June failed, and in October Venezuela rejected Guyana's proposal to resolve the dispute through international arbitration. In March 1983 Guyana and Venezuela referred the dispute to the UN, but no further progress was made. A meeting between the Ministers of Foreign Affairs of the two countries in February 1985 led to a series of agreements on trade and the exchange of information and assistance. A UN special envoy was asked to mediate in the border dispute, and, following talks held in March, it was announced that some progress had been made towards a reconciliation. Suriname restored diplomatic representation in Guyana in 1979, and bilateral talks were resumed at the end of the year. In 1983 relations improved further as a result of increased trade links between the countries. An EEC grant was provided in 1985 for a new ferry service between the two countries. It was hoped that this would be in operation by 1988.

Government

Under the 1980 Constitution, legislative power is held by the unicameral National Assembly, with 65 members: 53 elected for five years by universal adult suffrage, on the basis of proportional representation, and 12 regional representatives. Executive power is held by the President, who leads the majority party in the Assembly and holds office for its duration. The President appoints and leads a Cabinet, which includes a Prime Minister, and may include Ministers who are not elected members of the Assembly. The Cabinet is collectively responsible to the National Assembly. Guyana comprises 10 regions, each having a Regional Democratic Council which returns a representative to the National Assembly.

Defence

The armed forces are combined in a single service, the Guyana Defence Force, consisting of 5,450 men in July 1986. Paramilitary forces total 5,000. Estimated defence expenditure in 1985 was US $45m. National Service was established in 1974.

Economic Affairs

The economy is based mainly on agriculture and the production of bauxite. Bauxite, sugar and rice usually account for about 70% of total export earnings. In 1984, according to estimates by the World Bank, Guyana's gross national product (GNP) per head, measured at average 1982–84 prices, was US $590, the third poorest in the Western hemisphere. GNP per head was estimated to have increased at an average rate of only 0.5% per year, in real terms, between 1965 and 1984. The principal crops are sugar cane and rice, while other important agricultural products are citrus fruits, coconuts, groundnuts, oil palms and a variety of vegetables. Since 1982 the agricultural sector has suffered from low productivity and the effects of the ending of government price subsidies. The Government has invested US $45m. in the Mahaica-Mahaicony-Abary agricultural development scheme, which will, the Government hopes, enable Guyana to supply both itself and other CARICOM countries with food. A four-year agricultural development plan, announced in October 1985, aimed to achieve a gross annual export total of $G900m. by 1989, with an increase in productivity of 31%.

By 1979 Guyana had become self-sufficient in sugar, rice, vegetables, fish, meat, poultry and fruit. Sugar accounts for about 30% of export earnings, but since 1982 revenue has fallen because of poor harvests. Production of raw sugar rose from 273,000 metric tons in 1980 to 306,000 tons in 1981, but was still below target levels and far short of the processing capacity of 450,000 tons. Strikes and adverse weather caused the worst first-crop sugar harvest for three years in 1982, and the final production total was 292,000 tons. Two of Guyana's 10 sugar mills were closed in 1982. In 1983 production of raw sugar declined to 251,870 tons. The industry was again affected by strikes during 1984, when output was only 241,861 tons. Output rose to 242,990 metric tons in 1985, but was still 9% below the planned target, and the state sugar corporation, Guysuco, recorded operating losses of US $18.25m. In March 1986 the Government introduced a restructuring plan for the sugar sector, in an effort to improve the efficiency of the industry. One factory was to be closed, the area planted with sugar cane was to be reduced, and production of raw sugar was to be stabilized at 250,000 tons per year. Cane plantations were also to be used for the cultivation of other crops, including rice and fruit.

The cultivation of rice in Guyana is highly mechanized but the crop is farmed in uneconomic units of an average of 11 acres (4.5 ha). In 1981 only about one-half of the land available for rice was cultivated, and it was thought that, when subsidies were removed and fuel prices increased, farmers had ceased planting. Production of milled rice in 1981 was 169,000 metric tons, up from 163,000 tons in 1980, but 48,000 tons below target. In 1982 production increased to 182,224 tons, but export sales fell by 50%. Disease and adverse weather severely damaged the 1983 harvest, which, at 80,139 tons, was 107,000 tons below the target. Of the 1983 output, 41,715 tons were exported, an increase from 34,831 tons in 1982. Output increased by 24% in 1984, but fell by 13%, to 156,124 tons, in 1985, when export sales were only 50% of the planned target. Rice flour was promoted as a substitute to imported wheat flour, but continued poor harvests and the export of some of the crop caused domestic shortages. However, the lifting of the import ban on wheat flour in 1986 reduced the pressure on rice production, and it was hoped that an increase in the prices payable to rice farmers would stimulate exports.

More than 80% of Guyana is covered by tropical forest, and the estimated annual volume of marketable timber is 1m. cu m, of which 25% is accessible. The annual production of logs is about 150,000 cu m, taken from an area of 7,000 ha. In November 1985 the Government signed an agreement with private-sector sawmilling companies for the commercial exploitation of around 1m. acres (400,000 ha) of state-owned forest, and in October 1986 a separate Ministry of Forestry was established. Guyana's fishing fleet has been improved with the assistance of foreign countries, but has suffered from the illegal sale of shrimps, the main catch, to foreign ships at sea.

Bauxite is Guyana's principal source of export earnings. By the end of 1975 the whole bauxite industry had been nationalized. Production fell from 3.6m. tons in 1973–74 to 1.8m. tons in 1980, and to 1.68m. tons in 1981, 30% below target. In 1982 the industry began to experience difficulties as the price of bauxite collapsed on the world market. In 1982 production fell to 1.43m. tons, but in 1983 output recovered to 1.97m. tons. In 1983 about 1,700 workers were laid off, and the country's only refinery was closed. Exports of alumina fell in 1982, owing to reduced demand, and the alumina plant was temporarily closed in June. The state-owned mining company, Guymine, registered a loss of $G131m. in 1983. Production of bauxite in 1984 was 1.55m. tons, achieving output targets. As part of the Government's plan to revitalize the bauxite industry, the US company, Reynolds, was invited back to Guyana in 1985 to provide technical and marketing assistance, and to rehabilitate the country's bauxite refinery. Plans to revitalize the industry by 1989 and to increase the production of calcined bauxite by 40%, at a cost of around US $22m., were announced in 1986. It was hoped that Guyana would be able to start marketing a new refractory-grade bauxite in 1987.

Plans to expand the gold-mining industry, with the assistance of companies from North and South America, were announced in February 1986. A US $5m. mining operation was begun at Omai by a Canadian company, and it was estimated that, when operations began in 1987, the mine would produce around 20,000 troy ounces of gold per year. The company intended to develop four other mining sites. The average annual output being declared to the Geology and Mines Commission in the mid-1980s was 10,000 ounces, but officials estimated in 1986 that annual output could reach 200,000 ounces by 1988. It has been estimated that less than 25% of the gold and diamonds that are mined in Guyana are declared and sold to the Government, the sole legal buyer. In 1984 an IMF report claimed that the country was losing US $1.7m. per week through the smuggling of gold and diamonds. In an effort to prevent the smuggling of gold out of the country, the Government announced in October 1986 that miners would be paid 132% more per ounce of raw gold declared.

Industry is based on mineral processing, agro-industries (such as the production of rum, beer and cigarettes) and light industry, principally textiles and clothing. The manufacture of pharmaceutical products was expected to begin by early 1988 at a factory being built with Argentine assistance and for which Barbados and Trinidad and Tobago were to supply the raw materials. Industrial development depends on the expansion of energy sources, and the 750 MW hydroelectric project on the Upper Mazaruni river, scheduled for completion in 1986, should make possible the construction of a local aluminium smelter. In February 1986 the results of a petroleum exploration study of Guyana were presented to several foreign oil companies. Information packs were purchased by four major companies, and in July discussions on possible bids for exploration licences began.

The economy, in a crisis since the mid-1970s, was on the point of collapse by 1982, as inefficiency, corruption and a decline of managerial and technical skills (as a result of emigration, mainly from the Asian sector) were added to low world prices. The collapse of popular morale was also widely regarded as a fundamental cause of the country's failure to produce. Guyana's relations with other CARICOM members had deteriorated, following its violation of a CARICOM trade agreement and its failure to repay large debts to the organization. Guyana's GDP declined by 12.4%, in real terms, in 1982, and by a further 9.6% in 1983. GDP rose by 5% during 1984, mainly as the result of improved production by the mining sector, and grew by 4% in 1985. The country's total debt stood at $ G2,625m. in September 1983, and was expected to rise still further to finance the growing budget deficit, which totalled $ G392m. in 1985 and was expected to reach $ G417m. in 1986. Debt servicing in 1986 was expected to require around 42% of projected export receipts, necessitating debt rescheduling. Imports of cheese, split peas and cooking oil have been prohibited since 1982, while shortages of basic commodities, including eggs, fish, chicken, kerosene, rice and sugar, produced long queues outside shops. Foreign exchange reserves fell from US $12.7m. at the end of 1980 to $5.85m. by the end of 1984. In August 1986 foreign exchange dealings by the Guyana Central Bank were suspended, owing to a shortage of convertible currency, and were not expected to resume until revenue entered the banking system from exports of sugar to Europe. The acute shortage of foreign currency provoked an extension of import controls and a thriving illegal trade in the smuggling of foodstuffs and other goods from neighbouring countries. In 1982 the official inflation rate was 25%, but 100% increases of prices on the 'parallel' market occurred between January and June alone. Illegal trading in foreign currency was widely practised in order to pay rapidly-increasing prices. The restriction of imports, however, has been successful in curbing the trade deficit, which fell from US $53.2m. in 1980 to $32.4m. in 1983, although the widespread smuggling of goods, both in and out of the country, makes reliable trade statistics impossible to evaluate.

The economy is 80% state-controlled, but in May 1982 the Government began a programme of privatization, although this was officially denied. In 1983 and 1984 co-operation agreements were signed with several foreign companies, including Canadian, Yugoslav and Brazilian mining firms, granting them rights to explore for gold and other minerals in the north-east of the country. In June 1983 the Government expressed its willingness to engage in non-monetary transactions in order to secure vital products. Guyana agreed to barter goods with Suriname and Japan, and made further trade deals with Yugoslavia, Trinidad and Tobago, the People's Republic of China, Cuba, Brazil and other countries, exchanging bauxite and rice for petroleum, machinery and other essential goods. In 1986 President Hoyte stressed the need for greater private-sector involvement in the economy, and in March he introduced legislation to encourage overseas banks and businesses to invest in the country. Several trade agreements were signed in 1986. A barter agreement with Trinidad and Tobago, whereby rice had been exchanged for petroleum, was suspended in December 1985, however, because of Guyana's inability to repay debts of TT $400m. Shortages of petroleum led to fuel rationing in February 1986. However, an agreement for the exchange of bauxite for oil was signed with Venezuela, thus easing the fuel shortage, and a further agreement with Trinidad and Tobago was signed in May.

The IMF has provided balance-of-payments support and other facilities since 1979, but agreements have lapsed, owing to Guyana's failure to meet IMF conditions. Credits were finally suspended in June 1982. In 1983 the USA vetoed $ G224.4m. in potential aid funds from the US Government and the IDB. Guyana attempted to raise a loan from the IMF in excess of US $176m. Negotiations broke down in May 1984 as Guyana refused to agree to the conditions laid down by the IMF, which included a currency devaluation of 40%–60%, the 'freezing' of wage levels in the public sector and the implementation of large cuts in the Government's current and capital spending, including the removal of food subsidies. By January 1984 the crisis had become so severe that the Government was forced to devalue the Guyana dollar by 20%, and a further devaluation of 8.9% occurred in October. In May 1985 the IMF formally declared Guyana ineligible for further assistance until outstanding debts to the Fund had been cleared. Discussions continued, however, in order to find measures, acceptable both to Guyana and to the Fund, to allow the Government to borrow money for debt rescheduling and balance-of-payments support. In September 1986 a group from the IMF, the World Bank and the Inter-American Development Bank visited Guyana for talks. In January 1987 the Guyana dollar was devalued by 56%.

Guyana is a founder member of the Caribbean Common Market (CARICOM, see p. 108) and the International Bauxite Association (p. 222), and in May 1986 joined the Inter-American Investment Corporation (p. 157).

Social Welfare

Improved water supplies, anti-tuberculosis campaigns and the control of malaria have steadily improved general health. A National Insurance scheme, compulsory for most workers and employers, was established in 1969, and was subsequently extended to cover self-employed people. In 1979 there were 85 physicians in government service. In 1981 Guyana had 29 hospitals and 149 health centres. Of total expenditure by the central government in 1984, $ G51.5m. (3.7%) was for health, and a further $ G36.8m. (2.7%) for social security and welfare.

Education

Education is officially compulsory, and is provided free of charge, for eight years between six and 14 years of age. In 1976 the Government assumed responsibility for all church and private schools. In 1983 Guyana had 368 nursery, 423 primary, 30 secondary and community high, and 58 general secondary schools. Primary education begins at six years of age and lasts for at least six years. Children receive secondary education either in a general secondary school for five years or stay on at primary school for a further three years. Enrolment at all primary and secondary schools in 1981 was equivalent to 80% of the school-age population. Primary enrolment in 1981 included an estimated 90% of children in the relevant age-group. The total number of pupils in all schools was 233,723 in 1983. There are also 15 technical, vocational, special and higher educational institutions. These include the University of Guyana in Georgetown and three teacher training colleges. A loan of US $14.4m. was received in 1985 for improvements in the higher education system. Expenditure on education by the central government in 1984 was $ G102.5m., representing 7.4% of total spending. In 1985, according to estimates by UNESCO, the average rate of adult illiteracy was only 4.1% (males 3.0%; females 5.2%), one of the lowest in the Western hemisphere.

Tourism

Despite the beautiful scenery in the interior of the country, Guyana does little to encourage tourism. Tours to the interior, including the famous Kaieteur falls (with a drop of 741 ft or 226 m) and the diamond fields at Kurupung on the Mazaruni river, may be arranged.

GUYANA

Public Holidays

1987: 1 January (New Year's Day), 23 February (Republic Day), 17–20 April (Easter), 1 May (Labour Day), 30 May (Id al-Fitr, end of Ramadan), 1 July (Caribbean Day), 3 August (Freedom Day), 6 August (Id al-Adha, feast of the Sacrifice), 4 November (Yum an-Nabi, birth of the Prophet), 25–26 December (Christmas).

1988: 1 January (New Year's Day), 23 February (Republic Day), 1–4 April (Easter), 2 May (for Labour Day), 18 May (Id al-Fitr, end of Ramadan), 1 July (Caribbean Day), 25 July (Id al-Adha, feast of the Sacrifice), 23 October (Yum an-Nabi, birth of the Prophet), 25–26 December (Christmas).

Divali (October) are celebrated. These festivals are dependent on sightings of the moon and their precise date is not known until two months before they take place.

Weights and Measures

The metric system has been introduced.

Currency and Exchange Rates

100 cents = 1 Guyana dollar ($ G).

Exchange rates (30 September 1986):
 £1 sterling = $ G6.222;
 US $1 = $ G4.300.

Statistical Survey

Sources (unless otherwise stated): Bank of Guyana, POB 1003, Georgetown; tel. 63251; telex 2267; Ministry of National Development, Georgetown.

AREA AND POPULATION

Area: 214,969 sq km (83,000 sq miles).

Population: 758,619 (males 375,481, females 382,778) at census of 12 May 1980; 790,000 (official estimate for mid-1985).

Density: 3.7 per sq km (mid-1985).

Ethnic Groups (1970 census, *de jure* population): 'East' Indians 362,735, Africans 218,400, Europeans 7,849, Chinese 3,402, Amerindians 34,302, Mixed 72,316, Others 844; Total 699,848.

Capital: Georgetown, population 72,049 (metropolitan area 187,056) at mid-1976 (estimate).

Births and Deaths (1978 registrations, provisional): 23,200 live births (birth rate 28.3 per 1,000); 6,000 deaths (death rate 7.3 per 1,000).

Economically Active Population (persons between 15 and 65 years of age, 1980 census): Agriculture, forestry and fishing 48,603; Mining and quarrying 9,389; Manufacturing 27,939; Electricity, gas and water 2,772; Construction 6,574; Trade, restaurants and hotels 14,690; Transport, storage and communications 9,160; Financing, insurance, real estate and business services 2,878; Community, social and personal services 57,416; Activities not adequately defined 15,260; Total employed 194,681 (males 153,645; females 41,036); Unemployed 44,650 (males 26,439, females 18,211); Total labour force 239,331 (males 180,084, females 59,247).

AGRICULTURE, ETC.

Principal Crops (FAO estimates, '000 metric tons, 1985): Rice (paddy) 300, Maize 1, Roots and tubers 18, Coconuts 40, Sugar cane 3,520, Oranges 11, Bananas 5, Plantains 15. Source: FAO, *Production Yearbook*.

Livestock (FAO estimates, '000 head, year ending September 1985): Cattle 140, Pigs 148, Sheep 118, Goats 76. Source: FAO, *Production Yearbook*.

Livestock Products (FAO estimates, '000 metric tons, 1985): Beef and veal 2, Pig meat 1, Poultry meat 19, Cows' milk 15, Hen eggs 4.2. Source: FAO, *Production Yearbook*.

Forestry ('000 cubic metres, FAO estimates 1984): Roundwood removals: Sawlogs, veneer logs and logs for sleepers 179, Other industrial wood 10, Fuel wood 12, Total 201; Sawnwood production: Total (incl. boxboards) 70. Source: FAO, *Yearbook of Forest Products*.

Fishing ('000 metric tons, live weight): Total catch 25.8 in 1982; 27.6 in 1983; 32.4 in 1984. Source: FAO, *Yearbook of Fishery Statistics*.

MINING

Production (1983): Bauxite 1,791,000 metric tons; Gold 167 kg; Diamonds (industrial) 5,000 metric carats, Diamonds (gem) 4,000 metric carats. Source: UN, *Industrial Statistics Yearbook*.

INDUSTRY

Selected Products (1983): Wheat flour ('000 metric tons) 10 (provisional figure), Raw sugar ('000 metric tons) 265, Rum ('000 hectolitres) 133, Beer (1980, '000 hectolitres) 130, Cigarettes (million) 408, Electric energy (million kWh) 435. Source: UN, *Industrial Statistics Yearbook*.

FINANCE

Currency and Exchange Rates: 100 cents = 1 Guyana dollar ($ G). *Coins:* 1, 5, 10, 25 and 50 cents. *Notes:* 1, 5, 10 and 20 dollars. *Sterling and US Dollar Equivalents* (30 September 1986): £1 sterling = $ G6.222; US $1 = $ G4.300; $ G100 = £16.07 = US $23.26. *Exchange Rate:* US $1 = $ G2.55 between October 1975 and June 1981; US $1 = $ G3.00 between June 1981 and January 1984; US $1 = $ G3.75 between January and October 1984. The average rates ($ G per US $) were: 3.8316 in 1984; 4.2519 in 1985.

Budget ($ G million, 1985): *Revenue:* 642. *Expenditure:* Current expenditure on goods and services 1,034, Capital expenditure 523; Total 1,557.

International Reserves (US $ million at 31 December 1984): Foreign exchange 5.85; Total 5.85.

Money Supply ($ G million at 31 December 1985): Currency outside banks 421.7, Demand deposits at commercial banks 311.5; Total money (including also private sector deposits at the Bank of Guyana) 739.7.

Cost of Living (Urban Consumer Price Index; base: 1970 = 100): 322.7 in 1981; 390.2 in 1982; 448.5 in 1983.

Gross Domestic Product ($ G million at current prices): 1,468 in 1983; 1,700 in 1984; 1,964 in 1985.

Balance of Payments (US $ million, 1985): Merchandise exports f.o.b. 214.0, Merchandise imports f.o.b. −209.1, *Trade Balance* 4.9; Exports of services 48.0, Imports of services −144.3, *Balance on Goods and Services* −91.4; Private unrequited transfers (net) −2.0, Government unrequited transfers (net) −3.2, *Current Balance* −96.6; Long-term capital (net) −36.0, Short-term capital (net) −1.5, Net errors and omissions −4.3, *Total* (net monetary movements) −138.5; Valuation changes (net) −8.5, Exceptional financing (net) 143.0, *Changes in Reserves* −4.0. Source: IMF, *International Financial Statistics*.

EXTERNAL TRADE

Principal Commodities ($ G million, 1983): *Imports c.i.f.:* Consumer goods 65.2 (Food 17.9); Intermediate goods 534.7 (Fuels and lubricants 319.5, Chemicals 50.2); Capital goods 131.3 (Building materials 33.5, Machinery 67.9, Transport equipment 21.8); Total (incl. others) 738.3. *Exports f.o.b.* (excl. re-exports): Bauxite 218.9; Sugar 214.6; Rice 64.9; Total (incl. others) 548.7.

Principal Trading Partners (US $ million, 1982): *Imports:* Canada 11.4; Trinidad and Tobago 122.8; United Kingdom 25.5; USA 55.2; Total (incl. others) 290.2. *Exports:* Trinidad and Tobago 27.6; United Kingdom 79.4; USA 93.6; Venezuela 56.0; Total (incl. others) 388.1.

TRANSPORT

Road Traffic ('000 vehicles in use, 1976): Passenger cars 27.5, Lorries and vans 7.5, Tractors and trailers 9.5, Motor cycles 20.1.

Shipping (international sea-borne freight traffic, estimates in '000 metric tons, 1983): Goods loaded 1,200; Goods unloaded 625. Source: UN, *Monthly Bulletin of Statistics*.

Civil Aviation (1975): Passenger arrivals 42,210, departures 59,364; Freight loaded 2,438 tons, unloaded 1,297 tons.

COMMUNICATIONS MEDIA

Radio Receivers (1983): 350,000 in use.

Telephones (1 January 1978): 27,000 in use.

Book Titles (production, 1983): 55 (17 books, 38 pamphlets).

EDUCATION

Pre-primary (1981): Institutions 368, Teachers 1,783, Students 29,958.

Primary (1981): Institutions 423, Teachers 3,493, Students 130,003.

Secondary (1981): Teachers 3,797, Students 73,762.

Higher (1983): Teachers 534, Students 2,111. Source: UNESCO, *Statistical Yearbook*.

Directory

The Constitution

Guyana became a republic, within the Commonwealth, on 23 February 1970. A new constitution was promulgated on 6 October 1980. Its main provisions are summarized below:

The Constitution declares the Co-operative Republic of Guyana to be an indivisible, secular, democratic sovereign state in the course of transition from capitalism to socialism. The bases of the political, economic and social system are political and economic independence, involvement of citizens and socio-economic groups, such as co-operatives and trade unions, in the decision-making processes of the State and in management, social ownership of the means of production, national economic planning and co-operativism as the principle of socialist transformation. Personal property, inheritance, the right to work, with equal pay for men and women engaged in equal work, free medical attention, free education and social benefits for old age and disability are guaranteed. Individual political rights are subject to the principles of national sovereignty and democracy, and freedom of expression to the State's duty to ensure fairness and balance in the dissemination of information to the public. Relations with other countries are guided by respect for human rights, territorial integrity and non-intervention.

THE PRESIDENT

The President is the supreme executive authority, Head of State and Commander-in-Chief of the armed forces, elected for a term of office, usually of five years' duration, with no limit on re-election. The successful presidential candidate is the nominee of the party with the largest number of votes in the legislative elections. The President may prorogue or dissolve the National Assembly (in the case of dissolution, fresh elections must be held immediately) and has discretionary powers to postpone elections for up to one year at a time for up to five years. The President may be removed from office on medical grounds, or for violation of the Constitution (with a two-thirds majority vote of the Assembly), or for gross misconduct (with a three-quarters majority vote of the Assembly if allegations are upheld by a tribunal).

The President appoints a First Vice-President and Prime Minister who must be an elected member of the National Assembly, and a Cabinet of Ministers, which includes non-elected members and is collectively responsible to the legislature. The President also appoints a Minority Leader, who is the elected member of the Assembly deemed by the President most able to command the support of the opposition.

THE LEGISLATURE

The legislative body is a unicameral National Assembly of 65 members; 53 members are elected by universal adult suffrage in a system of proportional representation, 10 members are elected by the 10 Regional Democratic Councils and two members are elected by the National Congress of Local Democratic Organs. The Assembly passes bills, which are then presented to the President, and may pass constitutional amendments.

LOCAL GOVERNMENT

Guyana is divided into 10 Regions, each having a Regional Democratic Council elected for a term of up to five years and four months, although it may be prematurely dissolved by the President. Local councillors elect from among themselves deputies to the National Congress of Democratic Organs. This Congress and the National Assembly together form the Supreme Congress of the People of Guyana, a deliberative body which may be summoned, dissolved or prorogued by the President and is automatically dissolved along with the National Assembly.

OTHER PROVISIONS

Impartial commissions exist for the judiciary, the public service and the police service. An Ombudsman is appointed, after consultation between the President and the Minority Leader, to hold office for four years.

The Government

HEAD OF STATE

President: HUGH DESMOND HOYTE (assumed office 6 August 1985; sworn in as elected President 12 December 1985).

CABINET
(January 1987)

President and Minister of Home Affairs, Co-operatives and Agriculture: HUGH DESMOND HOYTE.

Vice-Presidents

Prime Minister and First Vice-President: HAMILTON GREEN.

First Deputy Prime Minister, Vice-President, Attorney-General and Minister of Justice: Dr MOHAMMED SHAHABUDDEEN.

Deputy Prime Minister and Vice-President for Education and Social Development: VIOLA BURNHAM.

Deputy Prime Minister and Vice-President for National Development: RANJI CHANDISINGH.

Senior Ministers

Deputy Prime Minister and Minister of Planning and Development: WILLIAM HASLYN PARRIS.

Deputy Prime Minister and Minister of Public Utilities: ROBERT CORBIN.

Minister of Agriculture: PAT MACKENZIE.

Minister of Communications and Works: JULES RANENBURG.

Minister of Education: DERYCK BERNARD.

Minister of Finance: CARL B. GREENIDGE.

Minister of Foreign Affairs: RASHLEIGH E. JACKSON.

Minister of Health: NOEL BLACKMAN.

Minister of Education, Environment and Food Policy: Dr RICHARD VAN WEST CHARLES.

Minister of Trade: WINSTON MURRAY.

Ministers

Minister of Agriculture: VIBERT PARVATTAN.

Minister of Forestry: SHARAMDHEO SAWH.

Minister of Information and Public Service: YVONNE HAREWOOD-BENN.

Minister of Manpower, Housing and Environment: SEERAM PRASHAD.

Minister of Medical Education, Environment and Food Policy: JAILLAL KISSOON.

Minister of Regional Development: JEFFREY THOMAS.

Minister in the Ministry of National Development: URMIA E. JOHNSON.

Minister in the Office of the President: PANDIT CHINTAMAN GOWKARRAN SHARMA.

Ministers of State

Ministry of Home Affairs: STELLA ODIE-ALLI.

Ministry of Manpower, Housing and Environment: DONALD AINSWORTH.

Ministry of Planning and Development: Dr FAITH HARDING.

MINISTRIES

Office of the President: New Garden St, Georgetown; tel. 51330; telex 2205.

Ministry of Agriculture: Regent and Vlissingen Rds, Georgetown; tel. 68714.

Ministry of Education and Social Development: 26 Brickdam, Georgetown; tel. 56329/54163.

Ministry of Energy and Mines: 41 Brickdam, Georgetown; tel. 66549.

Ministry of Finance: Ave of the Republic and Brickdam, Georgetown; tel. 72360.

Ministry of Foreign Affairs: Georgetown; telex 2220.

Ministry of Forestry: 1 Water St and Battery Rd, Kingstown, Georgetown.

Ministry of Health and Public Welfare: Homestretch Ave, D'Urban Park, Georgetown; tel. 65861.

Ministry of Home Affairs: 6 Brickdam, Georgetown; tel. 63310.

Ministry of Information: 18–20 Brickdam, Georgetown.

GUYANA

Ministry of Internal Trade and Consumer Protection: 95 Carmichael St, Georgetown; tel. 62505; telex 2288.

Ministry of Justice: 95 Carmichael St, Georgetown; tel. 62616.

Ministry of Manpower: Homestretch Ave, D'Urban Park, Georgetown; tel. 64021.

Ministry of National Development: Sophia, Georgetown.

Ministry of National Mobilization: Homestretch Ave, D'Urban Park, Georgetown.

Ministry of Transport: Wight's Lane, Kingston, Georgetown; tel. 62217.

Legislature

NATIONAL ASSEMBLY

Speaker: SASE NARAIN.

Election, 9 December 1985

Party	Votes	%	Seats
People's National Congress	228,718	78.55	42
People's Progressive Party	45,926	15.77	8
United Force	9,810	3.37	2
Working People's Alliance	4,176	1.43	1
Democratic Labour Movement	2,157	0.74	—
People's Democratic Movement	232	0.08	—
National Democratic Front	156	0.05	—
Total	291,175	100.00	53

In addition to the 53 elected members, the Assembly has 12 regional representatives.

Political Organizations

Patriotic Coalition for Democracy (PCD): Georgetown; f. 1986; comprising:

Democratic Labour Movement (DLM): Georgetown; f. 1982; small centre party; Leader PAUL TENNASSEE.

National Democratic Front (NDF): Georgetown; f. 1985; Leader JOSEPH BACCHUS.

People's Democratic Movement (PDM): Georgetown; f. 1973; small centre party; Leader LLEWELLEN JOHN.

People's Progressive Party (PPP): 41 Robb St, Georgetown; tel. 72095; f. 1950; Marxist-Leninist mass party; Gen. Sec. Dr CHEDDI B. JAGAN.

Working People's Alliance (WPA): Walter Rodney House, 45 Croal St, Stabroek, Georgetown; originally popular pressure group, became political party 1979; independent Marxist; Collective Leadership: EUSI KWAYANA, Dr RUPERT ROOPNARINE.

People's National Congress (PNC): POB 10330, Congress Place, Sophia, Georgetown; tel. 57850; f. 1957 after a split with the PPP in 1955; Marxist-Leninist; Leader HUGH DESMOND HOYTE; Deputy Leader RANJI CHANDISINGH.

United Force (UF): 96 Robb St, Bourda, Georgetown; right-wing; advocates rapid industrialization through government partnership and private capital; Leader MARCELLUS FEILDEN SINGH.

Diplomatic Representation

EMBASSIES AND HIGH COMMISSIONS IN GUYANA

Brazil: 308 Church St, Queenstown, POB 10489, Georgetown; tel. 57970; telex 2246; Ambassador: OCTAVIO GOULART.

Canada: High and Young Streets, POB 10880, Georgetown; tel. 72081; telex 2215; High Commissioner: JOHN MACLACHLAN.

China, People's Republic: 108 Duke St, Kingston, Georgetown; tel. 71651; tel. 2251; Ambassador: NI ZHENGJIAN.

Colombia: 306 Church and Peter Rose Sts, Queenstown, Georgetown; tel. 71410; telex 2206; Ambassador: REYNALDO OSPINA CAICEDO.

Cuba: 46 High St, Kingston, Georgetown; tel. 66732; telex 2272; Ambassador: (vacant).

Directory

German Democratic Republic: 176 Middle St, POB 10308, Georgetown; tel. 66755; telex 2230; Chargé d'affaires a.i.: GÜNTER MÄSER.

India: 10 Ave of the Republic, Georgetown; tel. 63996; High Commissioner: P. SOMARI.

Korea, Democratic People's Republic: 88 Premniranjan Place, Georgetown; tel. 60266; telex 2228; Ambassador: CHONG JON-GYU.

Libya: 375 Ganges St, Prashad Nagar, Georgetown; tel. 61697; telex 2259; Chargé d'affaires: AHMED IBRAHIM EHIWASS.

Suriname: 304 Church St, POB 10508, Georgetown; tel. 67844; telex 2282; Ambassador: JOHN KOLANDER.

Trinidad and Tobago: 91 Middle St, POB 101029, Georgetown; tel. 72061; telex 2287; High Commissioner: TERRENCE BADEN-SEMPER (acting).

USSR: 48 Chandra Nagar St, Prashad Nagar, Georgetown; tel. 72975; telex 2277; Ambassador: ANATOLY ULANOV.

United Kingdom: 44 Main St, POB 10849, Georgetown; tel. 65881; telex 2221; High Commissioner: JOHN D. MASSINGHAM.

USA: 31 Main St, Georgetown; tel. 54900; telex 2213; Ambassador: CLINT A. LAUDERDALE.

Venezuela: 296 Thomas St, Georgetown; tel. 61543; telex 2237; Ambassador: ENRIQUE PEINADO BARRIOS.

Yugoslavia: 72 Brickdam, POB 256, Georgetown; tel. 71136; telex 2231; Ambassador: MARIN GERSKOVIĆ.

Judicial System

The Judicature of Guyana comprises the Supreme Court of Judicature, which consists of a Court of Appeal and a High Court (both of which are superior courts of record), and a number of Courts of Summary Jurisdiction.

The Court of Appeal consists of the Chancellor as President, the Chief Justice, and such number of Justices of Appeal as may be prescribed by the National Assembly. This Court came into operation in June 1966.

The High Court of the Supreme Court consists of the Chief Justice as President of the Court and Puisne Judges. Its jurisdiction is both original and appellate. It has criminal jurisdiction in matters brought before it on indictment. A person convicted by the Court has a right of appeal to the Guyana Court of Appeal. The High Court of the Supreme Court has unlimited jurisdiction in civil matters and exclusive jurisdiction in probate, divorce and admiralty and certain other matters. Under certain circumstances, appeal in civil matters lies either to the Full Court of the High Court of the Supreme Court, which is composed of not less than two judges, or to the Guyana Court of Appeal.

A magistrate has jurisdiction to determine claims where the amount involved does not exceed $ G1,500. Appeal lies to the Full Court.

Chancellor: KEITH STANISLAUS MASSIAH.

Chief Justice: KENNETH M. GEORGE.

Appeal Court Judges: R. H. LUCKHOO, K. S. MASSIAH, C. J. E. FUNG-A-FATT.

High Court Judges: F. VIEIRA, R. H. HARPER, G. A. G. POMPEY, A. F. R. BISHOP, C. C. KENNARD, C. BABURAM, DESIRÉE P. BERNARD, L. L. PERRY.

Attorney-General: Dr MOHAMMED SHAHABUDDEEN.

Religion

The principal Christian religious bodies with places of worship are Anglican, Roman Catholic, Presbytery of Guyana, Guyana Presbyterian, Methodist, Congregational Union, Moravian, Lutheran, Seventh-day Adventists and Jehovah's Witnesses. Hindus and Muslims also maintain places of worship.

CHRISTIANITY

The Anglican Communion

Anglicans in Guyana are adherents of the Church in the Province of the West Indies. In 1985 the estimated membership in the country was 170,000.

Bishop of Guyana: Rt Rev. RANDOLPH GEORGE, Austin House, Georgetown.

GUYANA   Directory

The Baptist Church
The Baptist Convention of Guyana: POB 101030, Georgetown; tel. 60428; Chair. Rev. ALFRED JULIEN.

The Lutheran Church
The Lutheran Church in Guyana: 28–29 North and Alexander Sts, Lacytown, Georgetown; tel. 64227; 14,147 mems; Pres. JAMES LOCHAN.

The Roman Catholic Church
Guyana comprises the single diocese of Georgetown, suffragan to the archdiocese of Port of Spain, Trinidad and Tobago. At 31 December 1984 there were an estimated 94,000 adherents in the country. The Bishop participates in the Antilles Episcopal Conference, based in Kingston, Jamaica.

Bishop of Georgetown: G. BENEDICT SINGH, Bishop's House, POB 10720, 27 Brickdam, Georgetown; tel. 64469.

HINDUISM
The Hindu religious centre is Maha Sabha, 162 Lamaha St, Georgetown; tel. 57443; Hindus number about 390,000; Pres. SASE NARAIN.

ISLAM
Guyana United Sad'r Islamic Anjuman Inc.: POB 101175, 157 Alexander St, Kitty, Greater Georgetown; f. 1936; 120,000 mems; Pres. MOHAMED YACOOB ALLY; Sec. MOHAMED ISHMAEL (acting).

The Press

The Constitution does not provide for complete freedom of expression, and indirect press censorship is exercised by the state control of newsprint.

DAILY
Guyana Chronicle: POB 11, Lama Ave, Bel Air Park, Georgetown; tel. 67461; f. 1881; state-owned; Gen. Man. COURTNEY GIBSON; Editor FRANK CAMPBELL; circ. 60,000 (weekdays), 100,000 (Sundays).

WEEKLIES AND PERIODICALS
The Catholic Standard: Catholic Centre, Brickdam, POB 10720, Georgetown; tel. 67461; f. 1905; weekly; Editor Rev. ANDREW MORRISON; circ. 10,000.

Diocesan Magazine: Carmichael and Church Streets, Georgetown; weekly.

Guyana Business: 156 Waterloo St, Georgetown; f. 1889; organ of the Georgetown Chamber of Commerce and Industry; quarterly; Editor C. D. KIRTON.

Guymine News: Linden, Georgetown; f. 1971; organ of Guymine; quarterly; Editor LOUIS LONDON; circ. 8,000 (local and overseas).

Guynews: 18 Brickdam, Georgetown; monthly.

Labour Advocate: 61 Hadfield St, Werkenrust, Georgetown; weekly.

Mirror: Lot 8, Industrial Estate, Ruimveldt, Greater Georgetown; tel. 62471; owned by the New Guyana Co Ltd; Sundays; Editor JANET JAGAN; circ. 20,000.

New Nation: Sophia Exhibition Site, Georgetown; tel. 68520; f. 1955; organ of the People's National Congress; weekly; Editor ADAM E. HARRIS; circ. 26,000.

The Official Gazette of Guyana: Ministry of Information, 18-20 Brickdam, Georgetown; weekly; circ. 1,156.

Ratoon: 215 King St, Georgetown; monthly.

Sugar News: 201 Camp St, Georgetown; f. 1955; monthly; house journal of the Guyana Sugar Corporation; Editor A. B. POOLE; circ. 15,000.

Sunday Chronicle: POB 11, Lama Ave, Bel Air Park, Georgetown; tel. 63243; f. 1881; Editor HANK F. HARPER; circ. 75,000.

Thunder: 41 Robb St, Georgetown; f. 1950; organ of the People's Progressive Party; quarterly; Editor CLINTON COLLYMORE; circ. 10,000.

Weekend Post and Sunday Argosy: La Penitence, East Bank, Demerara, Georgetown.

NEWS AGENCIES
Guyana News Agency: Lama Ave, Bel Air Park, Georgetown; tel. 53105; telex 2210; f. 1981; state-run; Editor-in-Chief COURTNEY E. GIBSON.

Foreign Bureaux
Inter Press Service (Italy): Zaman Ali Bldg, Lot 8, Croal St, Stabroek; tel. 025-3213; Correspondent HUGH HAMILTON.

Prensa Latina (Cuba): Georgetown; Correspondent JORGE LUNA.

Telegrafnoye Agentstvo Sovetskovo Soyuza (TASS) (USSR): Bo Kaieteur Rd and Eping Ave, Bel Air Park, Georgetown; Correspondent ALEKSANDR KAMISHEV.

Xinhua (New China) News Agency (People's Republic of China): 52 Brickdam, Stabroek, Georgetown; tel. 69965; Correspondent CHEN JING.

Associated Press (USA) is also represented.

Publisher

Guyana National Printers Ltd: 1 Public Rd, La Penitence, Georgetown; tel. 62651; state-owned printers and publishers (member of Guystac).

Radio

In 1983 there were an estimated 350,000 radio receivers in use.

Guyana Broadcasting Corporation: POB 10760, St Phillips Green and High Sts, Georgetown; tel. 69231; f. 1979; formed from the Guyana Broadcasting Service and the Broadcasting Co Ltd (Radio Demerara) when the Government took over the assets of the latter; Exec. Chair. J. L. PHILADELPHIA.

Plans to set up a national television network have been shelved.

Finance

(dep. = deposits; m. = million; brs = branches; amounts in Guyana dollars)

BANKING
Central Bank
Bank of Guyana: 1 Church St and Ave of the Republic, POB 1003, Georgetown; tel. 63251; telex 2267; f. 1965; assets $ G2,663.7m. (Dec. 1984); Central Bank of note issue; Gov. PATRICK E. MATTHEWS; Man. IVAN HAMILTON.

Local Banks
Guyana Co-operative Agricultural and Industrial Development Bank: Lot 126, Parade and Barrack Sts, Kingston, Georgetown; tel. 58808; f. 1973; Man. Dir JOHN C. YATES; 10 brs.

Guyana Co-operative Mortgage Finance Bank: 46 Main St, POB 1083, Georgetown; tel. 68415; f. 1973; Man. Dir ALFRED E. O. BOBB.

Guyana National Co-operative Bank: 1 Lombard and Cornhill Sts, POB 242, Georgetown; tel. 57810; telex 2235; f. 1979; dep. $ G132m. (1976); Man. Dir STEPHEN BAKKER; 7 brs and 3 agencies.

National Bank of Industry and Commerce: 38–39 Water St, POB 10440, Georgetown; tel. 63231; 7 brs.

Foreign Banks
Bank of Baroda (India): 10 Regent St and Ave of the Republic, POB 10768, Georgetown; tel. 64005; telex 2243; f. 1908; Vice-Pres. G. S. JAIN; 2 brs.

Bank of Nova Scotia (Canada): POB 10631, Alico Bldg, Regent and Hincks Sts, Georgetown; tel. 64301; Man. CHESTER HINCKSON.

Barclays Bank (UK): POB 10280, Water St, Georgetown; tel. 68431; telex 2248; Man. R. E. SHIPMAN; 2 brs.

INSURANCE
Demerara Mutual Life Assurance Society Ltd: 61 Ave of the Republic and Robb St, POB 10409, Georgetown; tel. 58994; f. 1891; Chair. C. B. REIS; Gen. Man. and Dir HUGH K. GEORGE.

Guyana Co-operative Insurance Service: 47 Main St, Georgetown; tel. 68421; telex 2207; f. 1976; Chair. B. CLAUDE BONE; Gen. Man. HAROLD WILSON; Sec. D. COLE.

Guyana and Trinidad Mutual Life Insurance Co Ltd: Lots 27–29, Robb and Hincks Sts, Georgetown; tel. 57912; telex 2207; f. 1925; Chair. ERIC S. STOBY; Man. Dir R. E. CHEONG; affiliated company: Guyana and Trinidad Mutual Fire Insurance Co Ltd.

GUYANA

Hand-in-Hand Mutual Fire Insurance Co Ltd, Hand-in-Hand Mutual Life Assurance Co Ltd: 1–3 Ave of the Republic, Georgetown; tel. 51867; telex 2211; f. 1965; Chair. J. A. Chin; Gen. Man. F. W. Spooner.

Trade and Industry

CHAMBER OF COMMERCE

Georgetown Chamber of Commerce and Industry: 156 Waterloo St, Cummingsburg, POB 10110, Georgetown; tel. 56451; f. 1889; 104 mems; Pres. Wainwright McKenzie; Chief Exec. G. C. Fung-On.

PRODUCERS' ORGANIZATIONS

Consultative Association of Guyanese Industry Ltd: 78 Church St, POB 10730, Georgetown; tel. 57170; f. 1962; 6 mem. asscns, 12 assoc. mems; Chair. H. B. Davis.

Forest Products Association of Guyana: 6 Croal St and Manget Place, Georgetown; tel. 69848; f. 1944; 43 mems; Pres. David Persaud (acting); Exec. Officer F. E. Dalzell.

Guyana Manufacturers' Association: 8 Church St, Company Path, Georgetown; tel. 66791; Pres. Brian Gittens; Exec. Sec. Shiek Amir.

Guyana Rice Producers' Association: Lot 104 Regent St, Lacytown, Georgetown; tel. 64411; f. 1946; c. 35,000 families; Pres. Budram Mahadeo; Gen. Sec. Pariag Sukhai.

STATE INDUSTRIES AND MARKETING ORGANIZATIONS

Guyana's major industrial companies were nationalized during the 1970s, and the state sector predominates in the economy.

Bauxite Industry Development Company Ltd: 71 Main St, Georgetown; tel. 57780; telex 2244; f. 1976; holding company of Guyana Mining Enterprise Ltd.

Guyana Mining Enterprise Ltd (Guymine): Georgetown; tel. 57780; telex 2244; f. 1977 by merger of Guyana Bauxite Co (Guybau) and Berbice Mining Enterprises; Exec. Chair. Bernard Crawford.

Guyana Rice Board: 1–2 Water St, Georgetown; tel. 59453; telex 2266; f. 1973 to develop the rice industry and promote the expansion of its export trade, and to engage in industrial, commercial and agricultural activities necessary for the development of the rice industry; Exec. Chair. O. E. Clarke.

Guyana Sugar Corporation (Guysuco): 22 Church St, Georgetown; tel. 66171; telex 2265; f. 1976; Chair. Harold B. Davis; Sec. C. J. Lawrence.

Guyana State Corporation (Guystac): 45-47 Water St, Georgetown; tel. 60530; holding company for state enterprises; includes the following:

Guyana Fisheries Ltd: Georgetown; tel. 58960-9; telex 2286; owners of 22 trawlers, landing and processing facilities; Man. Dir Mike E. Davis.

Guyana Forestry Commission: Georgetown; development and management of forestry resources; Sr Assistant Commr Balkaran Udit.

Guyana Liquor Corporation: 61 Ave of the Republic, Georgetown; tel. 53904; telex 2284; Exec. Chair. Yesu Persaud.

Guyana Marketing Corporation: 1 Lombard St, Georgetown; tel. 65846; Chair. Wilfred Lee; Gen. Man. Dr T. Richmond.

Guyana National Engineering Corporation: 2-9 Lombard St, Georgetown; tel. 63291; telex 2218; metal foundry, ship building and repair, shipping agents; Exec. Chair. Claude Saul.

Guyana National Trading Corporation Ltd: 45-47 Water St, Georgetown; tel. 66191; telex 2214; importers and distributors; Exec. Chair. F. A. Griffith.

Guyana Oil Co Ltd: Providence, East Bank Demerara; tel. 62877; telex 2291.

Guyana Pharmaceutical Corporation Ltd: 1 Public Rd, La Penitence, Georgetown; tel. 63281; telex 2203; pharmaceuticals, chemicals and cosmetics; Exec. Chair. W. A. Lee.

Guyana Stockfeeds Ltd: Ruimveldt, Gr. Georgetown; tel. 63402; telex 2203.

Guyana Stores Ltd: 19 Water St, Georgetown; tel. 66171; retailers and wholesalers; Chair. Paul Chin-A-Sue.

Guyana Transport Services: 45 Urquhart St, Georgetown; tel. 60511.

Livestock Development Co Ltd: 58 High St, Georgetown; tel. 61601.

DEVELOPMENT AGENCIES

Guyana-Libya Fishing Co: Houston, East Bank Demerara; tel. 54382; joint venture between the Governments of Guyana and Libya to develop fishing potential; Chair. Gavin Kennard.

Mahaica-Mahaicony-Abary Agricultural Development Authority: Onverwagt, West Coast Berbice; tel. 03-3117; telex 2268; aims to bring Berbice-Abary region into full agricultural production.

CO-OPERATIVE SOCIETIES

Chief Co-operatives Development Officer: Georgetown; tel. 54312; M. G. Edghill.

In January 1982 there were 1,509 registered co-operative societies, mainly agricultural credit societies, with a total membership of approx. 144,200.

TRADE UNIONS

Trades Union Congress: Nonpareil Park, Georgetown; tel. 61493; national trade union body; 23 affiliated unions; Pres. George Daniels; Gen. Sec. Joseph Pollydore; 75,262 mems.

Amalgamated Transport and General Workers' Union: 46 Urquhart St, Georgetown; tel. 66243.

Clerical and Commercial Workers' Union: 140 Murray St, Georgetown; tel. 52822.

General Workers' Union: 106–107 Lamaha St, Georgetown; tel. 61185.

Guyana Agricultural and General Workers' Union: 104–106 Regent St, Georgetown; tel. 72091.

Guyana Labour Union: 198 Camp St, Georgetown; tel. 63275.

Guyana Mine Workers' Union: 784 Determa St, Linden; tel. 04-3146.

Guyana Postal and Telecommunication Workers' Union: 310 East St, Georgetown; tel. 65255.

Guyana Public Service Union: 160 Regent Rd and New Garden Sts, Georgetown; tel. 61770.

Transport

RAILWAYS

There are two railways in Guyana. One between Ituni and Linden is used for the transport of bauxite. The other, between Matthews Ridge and Port Kaituma in the north-west of the country, is also used for minerals. Neither caters for passengers.

ROADS

The coastal strip has a well-developed road system. There are more than 3,000 miles (4,830 km) of paved and good-weather roads and trails. In 1982 a road linking Linden to Mabura was officially opened. A floating two-lane bridge to replace ferry services on the Demerara River to Georgetown was opened in July 1978. A road project linking Guyana with Brazil was resumed in 1986 after being suspended in 1980.

SHIPPING

Guyana's principal ports are at Georgetown and New Amsterdam. A ferry service is operated between Springlands, Guyana, and Nieuw Nickerie, Suriname, and it was hoped that a new ferry service would be in operation by 1988. Communications with the interior are chiefly by river, although access is hindered by rapids and falls. The main rivers are the Mazaruni, the Potaro, the Essequibo, the Demerara and the Berbice.

John Fernandes Ltd: 24 Water St, Georgetown; tel. 56294; telex 2226; containerized and break bulk cargo; reps for West Indies Shipping Corpn (WISCO), Bernuth Lines, Suriname Line, Caribbean Liners and Carib Services Ltd; Man. B. A. Fernandes.

Shipping Association of Georgetown: 28 Main and Holmes Sts, Georgetown; tel. 62632; f. 1952; Chair. F. A. Griffith; Sec. and Man. W. V. Bridgemohan; members:

Caribbean Molasses Co Ltd: POB 10208, Mud Lots 1-2, Water St, Kingston, Georgetown; tel. 69238; telex 2274; exporters of molasses in bulk; Man. Dir N. F. Cooper.

Guyana National Engineering Corporation Ltd: 2–9 Lombard St, POB 10520, Charlestown, Georgetown; tel. 63291; telex 2218; agents for Saguenay Shipping Ltd, Tec Lines Ltd, W.I. Shipping Co Inc, Ivaran Lines, Linhas Brasileiras de Navegação, SA, Shipping Corpn of India Ltd, Flota Mercante Grancolombiana, SA; Exec. Chair. CLAUDE SAUL.

Guyana National Shipping Corporation Ltd: 5–9 Lombard St, La Penitence, Georgetown; tel. 66171; telex 2232; reps for Harrison and Mitsui OSK Lines, Samba and Resolve Maritime Corpn, airline reservations, and Lloyd Agencies; Exec. Chair. P. A. CHAN-A-SUE.

Guyana National Trading Corporation Ltd: 45–47 Water St, Georgetown; tel. 66191; importers and distributors of a wide range of goods; reps for Royal Netherlands Steamship Co, Suriname Navigation Co, Himmelman Supply Co, Smit-Lloyd and K-Line; travel agents for British Airways and British West Indian Airways; Exec. Chair. F. A. GRIFFITH.

CIVIL AVIATION

The main airport is Timehri International, 42 km (26 miles) from Georgetown. The more important settlements in the interior have airstrips.

Guyana Airways Corporation: 32 Main St, POB 10223, Georgetown; tel. 67201; telex 2242; f. 1939; state-owned; operates internal scheduled services and to the Caribbean and the USA; Exec. Chair. D. I. YANKANA; Gen. Man. R. L. ABRAHAMS; fleet of 2 Twin Otters, 1 DC-6BF, 2 HS-748, 1 Boeing 707, 1 Tupolev Tu-154 B.

A twice-weekly service operates between Georgetown and Boa Vista in Brazil.

Tourism

Guyana Overland Tours: 6 Ave of the Republic, POB 10173, Robbstown, Georgetown; tel. 69876; f. 1968.

HAITI

Introductory Survey

Location, Climate, Language, Religion, Flag, Capital

The Republic of Haiti occupies the western part of the Caribbean island of Hispaniola (the Dominican Republic occupies the remaining two-thirds) and some smaller offshore islands. Cuba, to the west, is less than 80 km away. The climate is tropical but the mountains and fresh sea winds mitigate the heat. Temperatures vary little with the seasons, and the annual average in Port-au-Prince is about 27°C (80°F). The rainy season is from May to November. The official language is French but a creole dialect is generally spoken. In early 1987 the question of whether French should remain the official language was under discussion. About 80% of the population belong to the Roman Catholic Church, the country's official religion, and other Christian churches are also represented. A form of witchcraft, known as voodoo, is the folk religion. The national flag (proportions 2 by 1) has two equal vertical stripes, of blue and red. The state flag has, in addition, a white rectangular panel, containing the national coat of arms (a palm tree, surmounted by a Cap of Liberty and flanked by flags and cannons), in the centre. The capital is Port-au-Prince.

Recent History

Haiti was first colonized in 1659 by the French, who named the island Saint-Domingue. A successful uprising between 1791 and 1803 by African-descended slaves established the country in 1804 as an independent state, ruled by Jean-Jacques Dessalines, who proclaimed himself Emperor of Haiti. Hostility between the negro population and the mulattos continued throughout the 19th century until, after increasing political instability, the USA intervened militarily and ruled the country from 1915 to 1934. Thereafter, mulatto presidents were in power until 1946, when a negro president, Dusmarsais Estimé, was elected. He was overthrown in 1950 by a military coup, led by another negro, Gen. Paul Magloire, who was himself forced to resign in 1956. In 1957 Dr François Duvalier, a country physician, was elected President.

Despite a promising start, the Duvalier administration soon became a dictatorship, maintaining its authority by means of a notorious private army, popularly called the Tontons Macoutes (creole for 'Bogeymen'), who used extortion and intimidation to crush all possible opposition to the President's rule. In 1964 Duvalier's tenure was changed to that of President-for-Life, and he retained almost total power over the country, by means of violence and voodoo threats, until his death in April 1971. In January 1971 the Constitution was amended to allow Duvalier to nominate his successor. He promptly named his son, Jean-Claude Duvalier, who became President, at 19 years of age, on the day of his father's death.

The release of political prisoners and an amelioration of conditions, including the appointment of more moderate Cabinet ministers, indicated that the regime was slightly more humane than its predecessor, with the increasing need for international aid pressuring the Government to take notice of human rights agencies and critical donor countries. As a consequence, the regime was characterized by frequent Cabinet changes and alternating policies of tentative liberalization and subsequent repression. Elections took place in February 1979 for the 58-seat National Assembly. As 57 of the seats were won by the official government party, the Parti de l'Unité Nationale (PUN), demonstrations took place against alleged electoral malpractice.

In mid-1979 three illegal Christian Democratic opposition parties were formed by critics of the Duvalier regime. In October 1979 a new press law was introduced, banning any criticism of the President, or of government or security officials, and any articles or broadcasts deemed to be subversive. The rearrest in October 1980 of Sylvio Claude, the leader of the Parti Démocratique Chrétien d'Haïti (PDCH), for alleged subversion was followed in November and December by more than 400 arrests of opposition politicians, journalists and broadcasters. Leading opponents of the regime were deported. Claude was sentenced to 15 years' hard labour in August 1981. Foreign criticism forced a retrial at which the sentence was reduced to six years, and in September 1982 Claude was released into house arrest, from which he subsequently escaped.

The first municipal elections for 25 years were held in 1983. President Duvalier had promised in April 1982 that they would be 'free, honest and democratic'. In the event, all the opposition candidates for the politically sensitive Port-au-Prince posts were arrested just before the polls. In the provincial constituencies allegations of electoral fraud were made. On 27 August the Assembly was dissolved when the Constitution was amended, reaffirming, however, the Presidency-for-Life and Duvalier's right to name his successor. Elections for the Assembly were held on 12 February 1984. All 59 seats were won by the pro-Duvalier party, PUN, as no opposition candidates were allowed. Although, during March and April, President Duvalier had publicized his intention of observing human rights and the freedom of the press, a decree of 10 May subsequently banned all political activity and opposition newspapers. Several journalists who had prepared publications critical of the Government were arrested, and their printing presses closed down. Opposition politicians went into hiding or were placed under house arrest. In May and June there were spontaneous outbreaks of rioting in the northern towns of Cap Haïtien and Gonaïves, and in a number of other rural towns, provoked by government corruption and the failure to distribute food aid. A Cabinet reshuffle at the end of May resulted in the dismissal of Ministers who were held responsible for the rioting, and a further reshuffle in August helped to strengthen the power of 'hard-line' elements within the Government, especially that of Dr Roger Lafontant, the Minister of State for the Interior and National Defence. More arrests were made in November, in response to an alleged plot against the Government.

Demonstrations were organized by the Roman Catholic Church and other religious groups to protest at poverty and corruption within the country. In April 1985 Duvalier announced a programme of constitutional reforms, including the eventual appointment of a Prime Minister and the formation of political parties, subject to certain limiting conditions. A popular referendum, held in June, to endorse these changes and the concept of the Life Presidency resulted in a 99.98% vote in favour. Opposition leaders alleged widespread electoral fraud, and denounced the Government's liberalization measures as an insincere gesture, designed for the benefit of foreign aid donors. In September Roger Lafontant, the minister most closely identified with the Government's acts of repression, was dismissed in a Cabinet reshuffle. Unrest in the northern areas of Haiti was again reported in December, after the deaths of four students in an anti-Government demonstration in Gonaïves. Duvalier dismissed four of his principal ministers and reduced the prices of basic commodities in an attempt to prevent an escalation of the disturbances. Further measures to curb continued disorder were taken in January 1986. The university and schools were closed indefinitely, and radio stations were forbidden to report on current events. Finally, Duvalier imposed a state of siege and declared martial law. Following intensified popular protests at the end of January, it was reported that more than 50 people had died in the disturbances, mostly as a result of reprisal killings by the Tontons Macoutes.

On 7 February Duvalier and his family fled from Haiti to exile in France, leaving a five-member National Council of Government, led by the army chief of staff, Gen. Henri Namphy, to succeed him and to lead Haiti towards eventual democracy. The interim military-civilian Council announced the appointment of a new Cabinet. The National Assembly was dissolved, and the Constitution was suspended. Later in the month, the Tontons Macoutes were disbanded, educational establishments were reopened, the traditional blue and red flag was restored, and plans were made to recover and nationalize Duvalier's vast assets. Prisoners from Haiti's largest gaol were freed under a general amnesty. In March US $26m. of US aid, which had been withheld since January in protest against abuses of human rights, was released.

However, after the initial euphoria following the downfall of Duvalier, renewed rioting occurred to protest against the inclusion in the new Government of known supporters of the former dictatorship. Curfews lasting 16 hours per day were imposed to quell the disturbances. In March there was a Cabinet reshuffle, following the resignations of three Duvalierist members of the National Council of Government (only one of whom was replaced). The new three-member National Council of Government comprised Gen. Namphy, Col William Regala (Minister of the Interior and National Defence) and Jacques François (then Minister of Finance). Appeals for a national strike failed in March, but demonstrations in protest at the failure of the Government to deal with the country's problems, and persistent demands for the resignation of certain ministers, continued.

In April Gen. Namphy showed signs of positive action in the announcement, firstly, of a road-building programme, expected to provide 6,000 jobs, and, secondly, of a proposed time-table for elections. In October a Constituent Assembly was to be elected to prepare a revised Constitution, which would then be submitted to the electorate for approval in a referendum in February 1987. Municipal elections would follow in July 1987, with presidential and legislative elections scheduled for November 1987. The new President would take office in February 1988. Gen. Namphy also announced that he would not be standing as a candidate in the presidential election. The first of these elections, to select 41 people (from 101 candidates) who would form part of the 61-member Constituent Assembly which was to revise the Constitution, took place in October 1986. However, the level of participation at the election was only about 5%, owing to the absence of democratic tradition in Haiti and to the lack of adequate organization and publicity.

In November and December, further strikes indicated continuing public discontent with the Government, and an opposition coalition, demanding the Government's resignation, was formed. The securing of a further US $10m. of aid (enabling Haitians to train in the USA as technicians, administrators and medical personnel), during a visit by Gen. Namphy to the USA, prevented a planned five-day general strike, aimed at forcing the Government to resign.

International relations, although improved after 1971, continued to be strained until 1986 because of Haiti's unpopular political regime and government corruption. The country's reputation was expected to improve under the new Government. Relations between Haiti and its neighbour on the island of Hispaniola, the Dominican Republic, have traditionally been tense because of the use of the border area by anti-Government guerrillas, smugglers and illegal emigrants, resulting in the periodic closure of the border. Haiti is a member of the OAS (see p. 189).

Government

The Constitution of 1950, providing for a unicameral legislative chamber of 59 members (elected for six years by universal adult suffrage), was suspended in February 1986, upon the downfall of Life President Jean-Claude Duvalier. Executive and legislative powers were assumed by a National Council of Government, comprising five members, subsequently reduced to three members. In October 1986 a 61-member Constituent Assembly was formed to draw up a new constitution, which was to be submitted to the electorate for approval in a referendum in early 1987. Presidential and legislative elections were scheduled for late 1987. There are nine Départements, subdivided into arrondissements and communes.

Defence

In July 1986 Haiti had a defence force with a total strength of about 6,900, including a battalion of commando-type troops known as the Léopards. The army of 6,400 men includes a Presidential Guard. The navy comprises a coastguard patrol of 300 men and 14 vessels, and there is an air force of about 200.

There is also a paramilitary police force of 14,900. Estimated defence expenditure in 1984 was US $30m.

Economic Affairs

In terms of average income, Haiti is the poorest country in the Western hemisphere. In 1984, according to estimates by the World Bank, Haiti's gross national product (GNP) per head, measured at average 1982–84 prices, was US $320, well below the level of any other country in Latin America. Even this low income is unevenly distributed. In the mid-1970s the richest 5% of the population accounted for about 50% of Haiti's total GNP. It is estimated that the average annual growth of GNP per head, in real terms, was only 1.0% between 1965 and 1984. In the 1970–80 decade alone, however, it increased by 1.8% annually. The overall growth of gross domestic product (GDP) averaged 1.7% per year in 1965–73, but the average annual growth rate rose to 2.7% in 1973–84. Pressures on the economy led to a decline in GDP, in real terms, of 2.9% in the year to September 1981 (following growth of 7.4% in 1979/80), and a further fall, of 3.4%, in 1981/82. In subsequent years there was some recovery (with growth of 0.8% in 1982/83 and 0.3% in 1983/84), although many sectors of the economy, including agriculture, remained stagnant. GDP growth rose to 1.1% in 1984/85.

In 1982/83 an estimated 65% of the working population were engaged in agriculture, forestry and fishing, although this sector provided only 33.2% of the country's GDP in that year. Agricultural production meets only about 60% of Haiti's domestic needs. The amount spent on food imports increased from US $16m. in 1970 to $77m. in 1983. Haiti's principal commercial crop, and its major export commodity, is coffee. However, the yields from coffee have been poor in recent years. Efforts to increase agricultural productivity, through the improvement of power, transportation and irrigation, are hindered by deforestation and soil erosion. Reductions in public spending have caused the suspension of many rural development projects. In 1982/83 Haiti's exports of coffee were valued at $51m., providing 26.9% of total export earnings. The destruction of more than one-half of the coffee crop by Hurricane Allen in 1980, coinciding with falling world prices, led to a decline of 61% in export earnings between September 1980 and September 1981. Coffee production rose during 1983, but failed to reach pre-1980 levels. The value of coffee exports declined to $47.4m. in 1984, and further declined, to $35m., in 1985.

Drought in 1982 and 1983 affected the production of important staple food crops, such as maize, rice and beans, although the output of sugar cane and sweet potatoes increased. Cocoa and sisal are the other major crops grown for export. Livestock is raised for internal consumption, and for limited export, but the country's entire population of black pigs was destroyed because of infection by African swine fever. Restocking, with the American pink pig (which costs more to feed), has been gradual. The use of charcoal, which accounts for about 75% of Haiti's energy consumption, is rapidly causing the deforestation of mountain sides, leading to serious problems of soil erosion. Two hydroelectric dams have been been built in the Artibonite valley, but they supply electricity only to Port-au-Prince.

The mining of bauxite in Haiti, which used to produce about 600,000 metric tons annually, ceased in 1983, owing to the low international demand for aluminium. In 1982/83 the manufacturing sector employed 6.5% of the working population and contributed 18.2% of GDP. An industrial zone has been established outside Port-au-Prince, and more than 300 companies, mostly from the USA, have built factories there. Processing industries, attracted by a cheap labour force (minimum daily wage US $3 in 1985) and the lack of legislation to protect workers, include the assembly of sophisticated electronic equipment, toys, sports equipment, clothes and other goods for the US market. Trade is largely with the USA, although the EEC countries, especially France, are now significant trading partners. The benefits for US companies of the US Government's Caribbean Basin Initiative (CBI) have provided an additional incentive: the value of exports of assembled goods to the USA increased from $107m. in 1978/79 to $187.4m. in 1982/83. The value of exports of light manufactured goods totalled $390m. in 1985, a slight increase on previous years. Tourism was formerly a major source of foreign exchange, and an important sector of the economy. In 1982/83 the total number of arrivals, including cruise passengers, was 221,094, a rise after the decline of the previous two years. By 1985, however, the number of visitors had declined to fewer than 100,000, partly because of reports that Haiti was one of the sources of the incurable disease AIDS, and partly because of the current unrest in the country. Unemployment is widespread, especially in the rural areas, causing migration to the towns, in particular to Port-au-Prince, where the population has doubled in 10 years, placing a severe strain on the capital's resources. In 1986 unemployment was estimated at between 50% and 70% of the work-force. In October 1986 President Namphy announced a $40m. emergency development programme, to be financed by foreign aid.

Haiti is a major beneficiary of international aid organizations, and up to 75% of its budget is financed by foreign donors. Between 1981 and 1986 disbursement of aid was increasingly accompanied by demands for an end to administrative corruption and for an improvement in social and political conditions. The US Government provided US $44.6m. in aid (representing 24% of Haiti's budget), half of which was in the form of food aid, in 1983/84, and $45m. for 1984/85. The latter figure was $9m. less than the amount requested by the Duvalier Government. France, the Federal Republic of Germany and Canada are the other major aid donors to Haiti. Food aid is constantly supplied by the FAO, and some 'food for work' schemes have been introduced. Commitments of foreign aid for 1986/87 reached record levels.

Haiti has recorded a deficit on merchandise trade in every year since 1965. In the year to September 1981 this was extremely high (US $209m.), owing to the fall in exports after Hurricane Allen. The IMF provided compensatory financing, and in 1982 agreed to provide support of SDR 34.5m. over a two-year period. In 1983 this facility was extended to provide a $60m. stand-by loan for a further two years. The conditions that were imposed by the IMF included reductions in government expenditure. In December 1986 the IMF approved a three-year structural adjustment facility of SDR 20.7m. Haiti's trade deficit declined to $124.8m. in 1981/82, owing to curbs on imports, but rose to $139.3m. in 1982/83. It eased to $115m. in 1984. In the year to September 1986 the overall balance of payments registered a surplus for the first time in many years.

About one-half of government revenue, which totalled US $169.2m. in 1982/83, derives from customs duties. Haiti's public debt is low in comparison with other Latin American countries, since a large proportion of the budget is provided by grant aid and concessionary loans. The budget proposals for 1986/87 envisaged total expenditure of $258m., 70% of which would be financed by foreign aid. The average annual rate of inflation rose from 7.4% in 1982 to 10.2% in 1983, but it declined to 6.4% in 1984, helped by the recovery of the US economy. However, inflation averaged 10.6% in 1985. It has been calculated that remittances from Haitians living and working abroad contribute about $100m. annually to the economy. In 1986 one of Haiti's main economic problems was the shortage of foreign exchange to finance imports of fuel, food and spare parts. The country's reserves of foreign exchange declined from $10.9m. at mid-1985 to only $2.7m. at mid-1986.

Social Welfare

Industrial and commercial workers are provided with free health care. In 1980 Haiti had 52 hospital establishments, with a total of only 3,964 beds, equivalent to one for every 1,264 inhabitants: the lowest level of provision in any country of the Western hemisphere. In 1979 there were 600 physicians in government service. Public health received an allocation of 89.5m. gourdes for 1984/85. Religious and other voluntary groups provide medical services in rural areas and in Port-au-Prince.

Education

Education is officially compulsory for children between the ages of seven and 13 years, but, owing to the lack of facilities and staff, only about 40% of children in this age-group attended school in 1981. Education is provided by the State, by the Roman Catholic Church and by other religious organizations, but many schools charge for tuition, books or uniforms. Learning is based on the French model, and French is used as the language of instruction. Secondary education, beginning at 13 years of age and usually lasting for six years, is provided by 21 public lycées and by a number of private and religious schools. Enrolment at secondary schools in 1981 was equivalent to only 13% of children in the relevant age-group. In 1985, according to estimates by UNESCO, the average rate of adult illiteracy was 62.4% (males 59.9%; females 64.7%), the highest national level in the Western hemisphere. The rate is even higher in rural areas (about 85%), where creole is the popular language. Some basic adult education programmes, with instruction in creole, have been created in an attempt to redress this. Higher education is provided by technical, vocational and domestic science schools, and by the Université d'Etat d'Haiti, which has faculties of law, medicine, dentistry, science, agronomy and ethnology. Government expenditure on education in 1982 was 87.1m. gourdes, representing 9.5% of total expenditure.

Tourism

Haiti's bays, beaches, mountains, folklore and primitive art are of interest to tourists. Another attraction is the magnificent 19th-century citadel and palace of King Henri Christophe. Tourism was formerly Haiti's second largest source of foreign exchange. In 1982/83 the number of visitors totalled 221,094, including 99,738 cruise passengers. In 1985 there were fewer than 100,000 visitors. About 45% of tourists are from the USA.

Public Holidays

1987: 1 January (Independence Day), 2 January (Heroes of Independence), 2 March (Shrove Monday, half day), 3 March (Shrove Tuesday), 17 April (Good Friday), 1 May (Labour Day), 18 May (Flag Day), 22 May (National Sovereignty), 2 November (All Souls' Day, half day), 18 November (Army Day and Commemoration of the Battle of Vertières), 5 December (Discovery Day), 25 December (Christmas Day).

1988: 1 January (Independence Day), 2 January (Heroes of Independence), 15 February (Shrove Monday, half day), 16 February (Shrove Tuesday), 1 April (Good Friday), 1 May (Labour Day), 18 May (Flag Day), 22 May (National Sovereignty), 2 November (All Souls' Day, half day), 18 November (Army Day and Commemoration of the Battle of Vertières), 5 December (Discovery Day), 25 December (Christmas Day).

Weights and Measures

Officially the metric system is in force but many US measures are also used.

Currency and Exchange Rates

100 centimes = 1 gourde.

Exchange rates (30 September 1986):
 £1 sterling = 7.235 gourdes;
 US $1 = 5.000 gourdes.

HAITI   Statistical Survey

Statistical Survey

Sources (unless otherwise stated): Banque de la République d'Haïti, Angle rue du Magasin d'État et rue des Miracles, Port-au-Prince; tel. 2-4142; telex 2030394; Ministère de l'Economie, des Finances et de l'Industrie, Port-au-Prince.

Area and Population

AREA, POPULATION AND DENSITY

Area (sq km)	27,750*
Population (census results)	
31 August 1971	4,329,991
30 August 1982	
Males	2,448,370
Females	2,605,422
Total	5,053,792
Population (official estimates at mid-year)	
1983	5,119,000
1984	5,184,680
Density (per sq km) at mid-1984	186.8

* 10,714 sq miles.

PRINCIPAL TOWN

Port-au-Prince (capital), population 719,617 in 1982.

BIRTHS AND DEATHS

Average annual birth rate 36 per 1,000; death rate 17 per 1,000 (estimates).

ECONOMICALLY ACTIVE POPULATION
(1982 census*)

	Males	Females	Total
Agriculture, hunting, forestry and fishing	848,958	373,901	1,222,859
Mining and quarrying	9,425	9,835	19,260
Manufacturing	65,556	55,653	121,209
Electricity, gas and water	1,295	762	2,057
Construction	18,588	3,604	22,192
Trade, restaurants and hotels	64,335	221,392	285,727
Transport, storage and communications	14,072	2,313	16,385
Financing, insurance, real estate and business services	2,733	1,297	4,030
Community, social and personal services	64,544	59,931	124,475
Activities not adequately defined	26,555	24,706	51,261
Total employed	1,116,065	753,392	1,869,457
Unemployed	141,351	118,853	260,204
Total labour force	1,257,416	872,245	2,129,661

* Figures are based on a 2.5% sample of census returns. Owing to independent estimation, the totals shown may differ from the sum of the component parts.

Source: ILO, *Year Book of Labour Statistics*.

Agriculture

PRINCIPAL CROPS (FAO estimates, '000 metric tons)

	1983	1984	1985
Rice (paddy)	113*	124*	125
Maize*	171	180	90
Sweet potatoes	346	350	350
Beans	50	52	52
Sugar cane	3,000	3,000	3,000
Bananas	230	235	235
Coffee (green)*	40	38	39
Cocoa beans	3*	3*	3

* Unofficial figure.

Source: FAO, *Production Yearbook*.

LIVESTOCK
(FAO estimates, '000 head, year ending September)

	1982	1983	1984
Horses	420	425	425
Mules	82	83	83
Asses	210	212	212
Cattle	1,200*	1,300	1,350
Pigs	600*	500	500
Sheep	91	92	92
Goats	1,000	1,100	1,100

* Unofficial figure.
Chickens (FAO estimates, million): 6 in 1982; 7 in 1983; 8 in 1984.
1985: Livestock numbers as in 1984 (FAO estimates).
Source: FAO, *Production Yearbook*.

LIVESTOCK PRODUCTS (FAO estimates, '000 metric tons)

	1982	1983	1984
Beef and veal	30	32	33
Goats' meat	4	4	4
Pig meat	8	7	9
Horse meat	5	5	5
Poultry meat	7	8	9
Cows' milk	20	21	22
Goats' milk	27	27	28
Cheese	1.7	1.7	1.7
Hen eggs	3.1	3.3	3.3
Cattle hides	3.6	4.0	4.0

1985: Production as in 1984 (FAO estimates).
Source: FAO, *Production Yearbook*.

HAITI

Forestry

ROUNDWOOD REMOVALS
(FAO estimates, '000 cubic metres)

	1982	1983	1984
Sawlogs, veneer logs and logs for sleepers*	224	224	224
Other industrial wood*	15	15	15
Fuel wood	5,248	5,385	5,522
Total	5,487	5,624	5,761

* Assumed to be unchanged since 1971.

Sawnwood production (FAO estimates): 12,000 cubic metres per year (1973–84).

Source: FAO, *Yearbook of Forest Products*.

Fishing

(FAO estimates, '000 metric tons, live weight)

	1982	1983	1984
Freshwater fishes	0.3	0.3	0.3
Marine fishes	3.8	3.9	4.0
Caribbean spiny lobster	0.1	0.1	0.1
Total catch	4.2	4.3	4.4

Source: FAO, *Yearbook of Fishery Statistics*.

Mining

('000 metric tons)

	1980	1981	1982
Bauxite	477	488	431

Note: The mining of bauxite ceased in 1983.
Source: UN, *Industrial Statistics Yearbook*.

Industry

SELECTED PRODUCTS (year ending 30 September)

		1980/81	1981/82	1982/83
Cottonseed oil (refined)	'000 metric tons	24.4	17.1	12.7
Wheat flour	'000 metric tons	120.8	88.4	118.4
Raw sugar	'000 metric tons	51.6	50.4	48.9
Cigarettes	million	1,043.3	964.6	932.2
Footwear	'000 pairs	528.4	588.3	519.2
Soap	'000 metric tons	11.7	12.8	12.8
Cement	'000 metric tons	240.7	206.0	224.5
Electric energy	million KwH	355.4	377.8	393.1*

* Estimate.

Finance

CURRENCY AND EXCHANGE RATES

Monetary Units
  100 centimes = 1 gourde.

Denominations
  Coins: 5, 10, 20 and 50 centimes.
  Notes: 1, 2, 5, 10, 50, 100, 250 and 500 gourdes
  (US currency notes also circulate).

Sterling and Dollar Equivalents (30 September 1986)
  £1 sterling = 7.235 gourdes;
  US $1 = 5.000 gourdes;
  100 gourdes = £13.82 = $20.00.

Exchange Rate
  Fixed at US $1 = 5 gourdes.

INTERNATIONAL RESERVES
(US $ million at 31 December)

	1983	1984	1985
Gold	6.2	6.2	n.a.
IMF special drawing rights	1.0	—	—
Reserve position in IMF	0.1	0.1	0.1
Foreign exchange	7.9	12.9	6.3
Total	15.2	19.2	n.a.

Source: IMF, *International Financial Statistics*.

MONEY SUPPLY (million gourdes at 31 December)

	1982	1983	1984
Currency outside banks	565.6	599.5	691.0
Demand deposits at commercial banks	318.2	357.2	396.4

Source: IMF, *International Financial Statistics*.

HAITI

BUDGET (million gourdes, year ending 30 September)

Revenue*	1980/81	1981/82	1982/83
Tax revenue	650.0	928.4†	822.3
Taxes on income	136.0	181.9	152.2
Excises	115.8	151.1	167.6
Other taxes on goods and services	51.1	43.7	131.7
Import duties	247.0	216.9	229.4
Export duties	45.6	49.5	73.4
Other revenue	n.a.	89.0	n.a.
Total	n.a.	1,017.4	n.a.

* Excluding grants from abroad (million gourdes): 178.4 in 1980/81; 95.9 in 1981/82; n.a. in 1982/83.
† Including unallocable tax revenue of 223.2 million gourdes.

Expenditure	1979/80	1980/81	1981/82
Goods and services		1,191.0	802.4
Interest payments	1,012.5	36.0	58.7
Other current expenditure		72.7	344.3
Capital expenditure	265.7	160.4	144.2
Total	1,268.2	1,460.1	1,349.6

1982/83 (total expenditure): 1,418.4 million gourdes.
Source: IMF, *Government Finance Statistics Yearbook*.

BALANCE OF PAYMENTS (US $ million, year ending 30 September)

	1981/82	1982/83	1983/84
Merchandise exports f.o.b.	177.1	186.6	206.6
Merchandise imports f.o.b.	−301.9	−325.9	−337.9
Trade balance	−124.8	−139.3	−131.3
Exports of services	101.3	108.0	108.2
Imports of services	−189.5	−193.1	−211.7
Balance on goods and services	−213.0	−224.4	−234.8
Private unrequited transfers (net)	49.7	46.4	45.0
Government unrequited transfers (net)	62.0	64.0	78.0
Current balance	−101.3	−114.1	−111.7
Direct capital investment (net)	7.1	8.4	4.5
Other long-term capital (net)	38.4	37.6	59.6
Short-term capital (net)	−8.1	−5.6	−8.2
Net errors and omissions	17.7	40.5	26.6
Total (net monetary movements)	−46.3	−33.1	−29.2
Valuation changes (net)	2.4	1.1	4.6
Changes in reserves	−43.9	−32.0	−24.6

Source: IMF, *International Financial Statistics*.

External Trade

PRINCIPAL COMMODITIES
(million gourdes, year ending 30 September)

Imports c.i.f.	1980/81	1981/82	1982/83
Food and live animals	359.5	341.0	353.0
Beverages and tobacco	33.4	34.3	38.2
Mineral fuels, lubricants, etc.	246.8	234.0	242.0
Crude materials (inedible) except fuels	53.2	51.7	53.9
Animal and vegetable oils and fats	137.7	130.0	134.6
Chemicals	175.6	166.0	171.0
Basic manufactures	376.8	357.0	369.0
Machinery and transport equipment	375.0	355.0	367.0
Total (incl. others)	1,922.6	1,825.0	1,890.0

Exports f.o.b.*	1980/81	1981/82	1982/83
Coffee	165.7	179.4	255.7
Cocoa	17.1	11.1	20.1
Meat	20.8	8.6	2.6
Essential oils	24.5	28.4	35.0
Light industrial products	108.3	178.7	203.6
Manufactured articles	274.2	241.7	275.5
Bauxite	83.1	106.8	—
Sisal	2.3	8.6	0.4
Sugar	—	—	6.4
Molasses	4.6	2.5	3.7
Rope and cord	34.0	39.8	24.4
Total (incl. others)	775.5	906.6	951.8

* Excluding re-exports.

PRINCIPAL TRADING PARTNERS
(million gourdes, year ending 30 September)

Imports c.i.f.	1976/77	1977/78	1978/79
Argentina	0.2	8.3	15.3
Belgium/Luxembourg	12.8	13.0	15.5
Brazil	10.2	10.9	22.0
Canada	72.0	84.3	80.4
China, People's Republic	17.2	22.2	26.6
Dominican Republic	12.0	19.4	19.8
France	33.4	37.4	43.8
Germany, Federal Republic	41.3	50.2	39.6
Italy	12.3	9.6	11.5
Jamaica	10.8	14.5	7.9
Japan	73.0	97.3	106.0
Netherlands	22.3	23.5	35.6
Netherlands Antilles	104.5	108.3	163.8
United Kingdom	24.8	30.3	26.8
USA/Puerto Rico	566.5	528.6	613.3
Total (incl. others)	1,041.2	1,103.4	1,330.7

Source: Administration Générale des Douanes.

Exports f.o.b.*	1976/77	1977/78	1978/79
Belgium/Luxembourg	58.4	46.5	34.0
Canada	8.8	10.4	12.1
Denmark	7.5	4.3	4.3
Ecuador	1.5	5.4	—
France	91.2	106.2	91.2
French Guiana	5.5	3.3	1.3
Germany, Federal Republic	13.7	5.5	9.8
Guadeloupe	0.9	4.3	6.9
Honduras	9.8	0.0	—
Ireland	4.5	35.2	—
Italy	44.4	55.6	46.0
Netherlands	19.2	22.2	14.8
USA/Puerto Rico	418.6	465.8	490.5
Total (incl. others)	587.7	716.5	741.9

* Excluding re-exports.

Transport

ROAD TRAFFIC ('000 motor vehicles in use)

	1978	1979	1980
Passenger cars	24.3	24.9	23.3
Commercial vehicles	6.5	8.3	5.2

Source: UN, *Statistical Yearbook*.
1984: 50,000 vehicles.

INTERNATIONAL SEA-BORNE SHIPPING
(freight traffic, '000 metric tons)

	1981	1982	1983
Goods loaded	264	374	328
Goods unloaded	506	662	886

Source: UN, *Monthly Bulletin of Statistics*.

CIVIL AVIATION
International Flights, 1976: Passengers arriving 217,657; Passengers departing 147,668.

Tourism

VISITORS (year ending 30 September)

	1980/81	1981/82	1982/83
Arrivals	134,129	115,250	121,356
Cruise passengers	149,011	94,720	99,738
Total	283,140	209,970	221,094

Education
(1981/82)

	Schools	Teachers	Students
Primary	3,321	14,927	658,102
Secondary:			
general	n.a.	4,034*	98,562
teacher-training	n.a.	123*	833
vocational	n.a.	235*	2,124

* 1980 figures.
University of Haiti: 4,500 students (1985).

Directory

The Constitution

The Constitution for the Republic of Haiti, promulgated in 1950 and subsequently revised, was suspended by the National Council of Government which assumed power in February 1986, following the downfall of President Jean-Claude Duvalier. In October 1986 a 61-member Constituent Assembly was formed in order to prepare a draft constitution, which was to be submitted to the electorate for approval in a referendum, scheduled for February 1987. It was envisaged that henceforth each elected President of the Republic would serve a five-year term.

The Government

HEAD OF STATE
President: Gen. HENRI NAMPHY (assumed power 7 February 1986).

NATIONAL COUNCIL OF GOVERNMENT
President: Gen. HENRI NAMPHY.
Members: Col WILLIAM REGALA, JACQUES FRANÇOIS.

CABINET
(January 1987)

Minister of the Interior and National Defence: Col WILLIAM REGALA.
Minister for Information and Public Relations: JACQUES LORTHE.
Minister of Finance and the Economy: LESLIE DELATOUR.
Minister of Industry and Commerce: MARIO CÉLESTIN.
Minister of Planning: JACQUES VILGRAIN.
Minister of Justice: FRANÇOIS SAINT-FLEUR.
Minister of Education, Youth and Sports: PATRICE DALENCOUR.
Minister of Foreign Affairs and Worship: Col HÉRARD ABRAHAM.
Minister of Social Affairs: GÉRARD NOEL.
Minister of Public Works, Transport and Communications: Col JACQUES JOACHIM.
Minister of Health and Population: Lt-Col JEAN VERLY.
Minister of Agriculture: GUSTAVE MENAGER.
Minister without Portfolio: ALIX CINÉAS.

MINISTRIES

Office of the President: Palais National, Port-au-Prince; tel. 2-4020; telex 2030068.
Ministry of Agriculture, Natural Resources and Rural Development: Damien, Port-au-Prince; tel. 2-3457.
Ministry of Education: Port-au-Prince; tel. 2-1036.
Ministry of Finance, the Economy and Industry: 311 rue Legitime, Port-au-Prince; tel. 2-1628; telex 2030207.
Ministry of Foreign Affairs and Worship: Cité de l' Exposition, Port-au-Prince; tel. 2-1647.
Ministry of Health and Population: Palais des Ministères, Port-au-Prince; tel. 2-1248.
Ministry of Information and Public Relations: Palais National, Port-au-Prince; tel. 2-4020; telex 2030068.
Ministry of the Interior and National Defence: Palais des Ministères, Port-au-Prince; tel. 2-1714.
Ministry of Justice: Cité de l'Exposition, Port-au-Prince; tel. 2-0718.
Ministry of Mines and Energy Resources: Port-au-Prince; tel. 6-2853; telex 2030246.
Ministry of Planning: Port-au-Prince; tel. 2-1027.
Ministry of Public Works, Transport and Communications: Palais des Ministères, Port-au-Prince; tel. 2-2164.
Ministry of Social Affairs: rue de la Révolution, Port-au-Prince; tel. 2-2450.
Ministry of Youth and Sports: rue Camille Léon, Port-au-Prince; tel. 5-3415.

Legislature

The 59-member National Assembly was dissolved in February 1986. A 61-member Constituent Assembly, comprising 41 elected members and 20 appointees of the National Council of Government, was formed in October 1986 to draw up a new constitution. Presidential and legislative elections were scheduled for November 1987.

Political Organizations

Many political leaders returned to Haiti from exile, following the downfall of President Duvalier in February 1986. In August 1986 the National Council of Government issued a decree granting legal recognition to political parties on condition that they had at least 20 founding members and 2,000 sponsors. Many new parties were formed prior to local elections, due to be held in July 1987.

Mouvement pour l'Instauration de la Démocratie en Haïti (MIDH): Pres. MARC BAZIN.
Parti démocratique Chrétien d'Haïti (PDCH): f. 1979; Christian Democrat party; Leader SYLVIO CLAUDE.
Parti démocratique Chrétien d'Haïti de 27 juin (PDCH-27 juin): f. 1979; also known as Parti Social Chrétien (PSC); Christian Democrat party; Leader GRÉGOIRE EUGÈNE.
Parti National Progressiste (PNP): Port-au-Prince; f. 1985; supported the policies of fmr President Jean-Claude Duvalier.
Parti Nationaliste Progressiste Révolutionnaire (PANPRA): f. 1986; Leader SERGE GILLES.
Parti Unifié des Communistes Haïtiens (PUCH): f. 1968; Sec.-Gen. RENÉ THÉODORE.
Union des Forces Patriotiques et Démocratiques Haïtiennes (UFOPADA): socialist.

Diplomatic Representation

EMBASSIES IN HAITI

Argentina: impasse Géraud, 20 Bourdon, Port-au-Prince; tel. 2-2063; telex 0176; Chargé d'affaires: ANTONIO MERI.
Brazil: 107 ave John Brown, Bourdon, Port-au-Prince; tel. 2-2328; telex 0096; Ambassador: PAOLO FRASSINETTI.
Canada: 18 route de Delmas, Port-au-Prince; tel. 2358; telex 0069; Ambassador: ANTHONY MALONE.
Chile: 384 route de Delmas entre rues 42 et 44, Port-au-Prince; Ambassador: AGUSTÍN RODRÍGUEZ PULGAR.
China (Taiwan): 2 rue Rivière, Port-au-Prince; Ambassador: LEE NAN HSING.
Colombia: 384 route de Delmas, entre rues 42 et 44, Port-au-Prince; tel. 6-2599; Ambassador: JUAN ZAPATA OLIVELLA.
Dominican Republic: Port-au-Prince; Ambassador: OSCAR PAVILLA MEDRANO.
Ecuador: 81 impasse Cicéron, Bourdon, Port-au-Prince; tel. 2-4576; Chargé d'affaires: FRANCISCO TOBAR GARCÍA.
France: Champ de Mars, Port-au-Prince; tel. 2-0951; telex 0049; Ambassador: MICHEL DE LA FOURNIÈRE.
Germany, Federal Republic: 14 ave Marie Jeanne, Port-au-Prince; tel. 2-0634; telex 0072; Ambassador: Dr KARL-FRIEDRICH GANSÄUER.
Holy See: Morne Calvaire, Pétionville, BP 326, Port-au-Prince; tel. 7-3411; Apostolic Nuncio: Mgr PAOLO ROMEO.
Israel: 8 rue Berthé, Pétionville; tel. 7-2008; telex 0096; Ambassador: JACQUES DECKEL.
Italy: 18 route de Delmas, Port-au-Prince; tel. 2-2649; telex 0447; Ambassador: SERGIO EMINA.

HAITI

Japan: Villa Bella Vista, 2 impasse Tulipe, Desprez, Port-au-Prince; tel. 5-3333; telex 0368; Ambassador: Mussoro Ossada.
Liberia: 37 rue Lamarre, Pétionville, Port-au-Prince; tel. 7-0692; Ambassador: Henry T. Hoff.
Mexico: Maison Roger Esper, 57A route de Delmas, Port-au-Prince; tel. 6-2215; telex 0217; Ambassador: Mario Armando Amador.
Panama: 29 rues Met. and Chavannes, Pétionville; tel. 7-2260; Ambassador: Alejaniro Cuéllar.
Peru: 38 Débussy, Port-au-Prince; tel. 55-425; Ambassador: Julio Balbuena.
Spain: 11 rue Oscar, Desprez, Port-au-Prince; tel. 5-4411; Ambassador: José Francisco de Castro.
USA: blvd Harry Truman, Cité de l'Exposition, Port-au-Prince; tel. 2-0200; telex 0157; Ambassador: Brunson McKinley.
Venezuela: blvd Harry Truman, Cité de l'Exposition, BP 2158, Port-au-Prince; tel. 2-0973; telex 0413; Ambassador: José Gregorio González-Rodríguez.

Judicial System

Law is based on the French Napoleonic Code, substantially modified during the presidency of Dr François Duvalier.

Courts of Appeal and Civil Courts sit at Port-au-Prince and the three provincial capitals: Gonaïves, Cap Haïtien and Port de Paix. In principle each commune has a Magistrates' Court.

Court of Cassation: Port-au-Prince; Pres. Pierre Gonzales.

Courts of Appeal. Civil Courts. Magistrates' Courts. Judges of the Supreme Courts and Courts of Appeal appointed by the President.

Religion

Roman Catholicism is the official religion, followed by 80% of the population. The folk religion is voodoo.

CHRISTIANITY
The Roman Catholic Church

Archbishop of Haiti: François-Wolff Ligondé, Archevêché, BP 538, Port-au-Prince; tel. 2-2043.

In addition to the Archbishopric of Port-au-Prince, there are also six Suffragan Bishoprics.

Bishop of Cap Haïtien: François Gayot; Evêché, BP 22, Cap Haïtien; tel. 2-0071.
Bishop of Hinche: Léonard Petion Laroche; c/o BP 1594, Port-au-Prince; tel. 2-0452.
Bishop of Jérémie: Willy Romélus; Evêché, Brouette, Jérémie; tel. 4-5167.
Bishop of Les Cayes: Jean-Jacques Claudius Angénor; Evêché, rue Toussaint-Louverture, Les Cayes; tel. 6-0131.
Bishop of Les Gonaïves: Emmanuel Constant; Evêché, 89 ave des Dattes, Les Gonaïves; tel. 4-0146.
Bishop of Port-de-Paix: Frantz Colimon; Evêché, Port-de-Paix; tel. 8-6134.

Other Christian Churches

The Episcopal (Anglican) Church is strong and its first Haitian bishop was consecrated in 1971. Other sects are well represented, including Methodists, Baptists and many American missionary churches. There are an estimated 1m. Protestants in Haiti.

Baptist Convention: BP 20, Cap-Haïtien; tel. 2-0567; Pres. Rev. André Jean.
Lutheran Church: Petite Place Cuzeau, BP 13147, Delmas, Port-au-Prince; tel. 6-3179; Minister Rodrigue Ben Bichotte.

The Press

Following the downfall of President Duvalier in 1986, numerous new newspapers were established.

DAILIES

Artibonite Journal: Les Gonaives.
Le Courier du Sud: Les Cayes.
Le Journal Sud-Ouest: Jacmel.
Le Matin: 88 rue du Quai, Port-au-Prince; tel. 2-2040; f. 1908; French; independent; Dir Frank Magloire; circ. 5,000.
Le Nouveau Monde: ave Pie XII, Port-au-Prince; tel. 2-0323; Dir Jean Magloire; circ. 6,500; temporarily closed by interim Government, 1986.
Le Nouvelliste: 198 rue du Centre, BP 1013, Port-au-Prince; tel. 2-2114; f. 1896; evening; French; independent; Editor Lucien Montas; circ. 6,000.
Panorama: 27 rue du Peuple, Port-au-Prince; tel. 2-2625; French; Dir Paul Blanchet; circ. 2,500.

PERIODICALS

L'Assaut: Port-au-Prince; monthly; French; government-owned; Dir Dr Rony Gilot.
Convictions: Port-au-Prince; weekly.
Dialogue: Port-au-Prince; monthly; French and English; government-owned.
Haiti Herald: Port-au-Prince; monthly; tourist information.
Hebdo Jeune Presse: Port-au-Prince; weekly.
Le Messager du Nord-Ouest: Port de Paix; weekly.
Le Moniteur: BP 214 bis, Port-au-Prince; tel. 2-1026; 2 a week; French; the official gazette; Dir Marcel Elibert; circ. 2,000.
Optique: French Institute, BP 1316, Port-au-Prince; monthly; arts.
Le Petit Samedi Soir: Fontamara, Port-au-Prince; tel. 4-0144; weekly; French; independent; Editor Dieudonné Fardin; circ. 10,000.
Revue de la Société Haïtiene d'Histoire: Port-au-Prince; f. 1925; quarterly; Editor Henock Trouillot.
Le Septentrion: Cap Haïtien; weekly; Editor Nelson Bell; circ. 2,000.

NEWS AGENCIES

Haitian News Service: Port-au-Prince; f. 1981; government-owned; Dir Guy Meyer.

Foreign Bureaux

Agence France-Presse (AFP): 72 rue Pavée, Bldg Electrotostore, BP 62, Port-au-Prince; tel. 2-3759; telex 2030379; Bureau Chief Dominique Levanti.
Associated Press (AP) (USA): BP 2443, Port-au-Prince; tel. 2-0062; telex 2030277; Dir Arthur Candell.
United Press International (UPI) (USA) and **Agencia EFE** (Spain): 21 rue Gabart, Pétionville; tel. 7-1628; telex 3490480; Reps Sondra Singer Beaulieu, Serge Beaulieu.

Publishers

Editions Caraïbes: Lalve, BP 2013, Port-au-Prince; tel. 2-3179; telex 0198.
Editions du Soleil: BP 2471, rue du Centre, Port-au-Prince; tel. 2-3147; telex 0001; education.
Maison Henri Deschamps: Grand rue, BP 164, Port-au-Prince; Man. Dir Jacques Deschamps.
Theodor: Imprimerie, rue Dantes, Destouches, Port-au-Prince.

Radio and Television

In 1985 there were an estimated 120,000 radio receivers and 75,000 television receivers in use. There are 25 radio stations and one television station.

Conseil National des Télécommunications (CONATEL): BP 2002, Port-au-Prince; government communications licensing authority; Dir-Gen. Fritz A. Michel.

RADIO

La Voix du Peuple: 21 Bizoton, Port-au-Prince; independent.
Radio Antilles: 170 rue du Centre, Port-au-Prince; independent.
Radio Cacique: 5 Bellevue, Port-au-Prince; independent.
Radio Caraïbes: 23 ruelle Chavannes, Port-au-Prince; independent.

HAITI

Radio Haïti Inter: rue du Quai, BP 737, Port-au-Prince; Dir Jean L. Dominique.

Radio Lumière: BP 1050, Port-au-Prince; tel. 4-0330; f. 1959; Protestant; independent; Pres. Brezil St Germain; Dir-Gen. Emmanuel Blaise.

Radio MBC: 86 rue Américaine, Port-au-Prince; independent.

Radio Métropole: rue Pavée, BP 62, Port-au-Prince; independent; Dir H. Widmaer.

Radio Nationale: rue du Magasin de l'Etat, Port-au-Prince; government-operated; Dir Charles Abellard.

Radio Nouveau Monde: Port-au-Prince; Dir Webert Guerrir.

Radio Port-au-Prince: Stade Sylvio Cator, Port-au-Prince; independent.

Radio Soleil: BP 1362, Port-au-Prince; tel. 2-3073; Catholic; independent; educational; broadcasts in creole; Man. Fr Hugo Trieste.

TELEVISION

Télé Haïti: blvd J. J. Dessalines, BP 1126, Port-au-Prince; telex 0189; f. 1959; independent; pay-cable station with 4 channels; in French and English; Gen. Man. Philip Bayard.

Télévision Nationale d'Haïti: BP 13400, Delmas 31, Port-au-Prince; tel. 6-0200; telex 0416; government-owned; cultural; Gen. Man. Jacques Lemaire.

Finance

(cap. = capital; m. = million; dep. = deposits; amounts in gourdes; brs = branches)

BANKING

Banque de la République d'Haïti: Angle rue du Magasin de l'Etat et rue des Miracles, BP 1570, Port-au-Prince; tel. 2-4700; telex 0317; f. 1911; fmrly Banque Nationale de la République d'Haïti; the central bank and bank of issue; cap. 50m., dep. 859.8m. (Nov. 1984); Gov. Karl Voltaire; 12 brs.

Banque Nationale de Crédit: Angle rue du Quai et rue des Miracles, Port-au-Prince; tel. 2-0800; telex 0196; f. 1979; cap. 25m., dep. 548.2m. (Sept. 1982); Pres. Edouard Raciné.

Banque Populaire Haïtienne: Angle rue Américaine et Fort Per, Port-au-Prince; tel. 2-1800; telex 0406; f. 1955; state bank; cap. 5m.

Banque de l'Union Haïtienne: Angle rue du Quai et rue Bonne Foi, Port-au-Prince; cap. 15m.; tel. 2-1300; telex 0173; Pres. and Dir-Gen. Marcel Leger; 5 brs.

Foreign Banks

Bank of Nova Scotia (Canada): rue des Miracles, Port-au-Prince; tel. 2-4461; telex 0155.

Banque Nationale de Paris (France): ave John Brown, Port-au-Prince; tel. 2-2908; telex 0191.

Citibank, NA (USA): BP 1688, route de Delmas, Port-au-Prince; tel. 6-0985; telex 0124; Vice-Pres. Gladys M. Coupet.

First National Bank of Boston (USA): BP 2216, rue des Miracles, Port-au-Prince; tel. 2-1900; telex 0163; 3 brs.

Development Banks

Banque Nationale de Développement Agricole et Industriel: rue de Quai, Port-au-Prince; tel. 2-1969; Dir-Gen. Jean Michel Ligonde.

Fonds de Développement Industriel: 43 rue des Miracles, BP 2597, Port-au-Prince; tel. 2-7852; telex 0432; f. 1981; Dir Léonce Thelusma.

Société Financière Haïtienne de Développement (SOFIHDES): BP 1399, blvd Harry S. Truman, Port-au-Prince; tel. 2-8628.

INSURANCE

North American and European insurance companies have branches in Haiti.

Trade and Industry

Chambre de Commerce d'Haïti: BP 982, Port-au-Prince; tel. 2-0281; Pres. Louis A. Desrouleaux; Exec. Sec. Paula A. Mevs.

Association des Industries d'Haiti: 100 Delmas 31, BP 2568, Port-au-Prince; tel. 6-4509; telex 2030071; Exec. Dir Claude Levy.

TRADE UNIONS

Central Autonome des Travailleurs Haïtiens: Port-au-Prince; f. 1980; Sec. Yves Antoine Richard.

Fédération Haïtienne de Syndicats Chrétiens (Haitian Federation of Christian Unions): BP 416, Port-au-Prince; Pres. Léonvil Leblanc.

Union Nationale des Ouvriers d'Haïti—UNOH (National Union of Workers of Haiti): BP 276, Port-au-Prince; f. 1951; admitted to ORIT; Pres. Marcel Vincent; Sec.-Gen. Fritzner St Vil; 3,000 mems from 8 affiliated unions.

A number of unions are non-affiliated and without a national centre, including those organized on a company basis.

Transport

RAILWAYS

The only railway is used to transport sugar cane.

ROADS

There are 4,000 km of roads, of which about 600 km are paved; a construction and repair programme is being undertaken. An all-weather road from Port-au-Prince to Cap Haïtien, on the northern coast, has been completed with finance from the World Bank. Another major road, connecting Port-au-Prince with Jacmel, has been built and financed by France. Haiti has also received a $15m. credit from the IDA towards the reconstruction and upgrading of roads and the rebuilding of two major bridges.

SHIPPING

Many European and American shipping lines call at Haiti. The two principal ports are Port-au-Prince and Cap Haïtien. The development of port facilities at Port-au-Prince and two other ports is being financed by the IDA.

CIVIL AVIATION

The international airport, situated 16 km outside Port-au-Prince, is the country's principal airport, and is served by many international airlines linking Haiti with the USA and other Caribbean islands. The airport at Cap Haïtien is used by Turks and Caicos Airways, and there are smaller airfields at Jacmel, Jérémie and Port-de-Paix.

Air Haiti: 35 ave Marie-Jeanne, Port-au-Prince; f. 1969; began cargo charter operations 1970; scheduled cargo and mail services from Port-au-Prince to Cap Haïtien, San Juan (Puerto Rico), Miami and New York; Gen. Man. Ernest Cineas; fleet of 1 Boeing 737-200.

Internal services are at present operated by the Government, using military aircraft.

Tourism

Office National du Tourisme d'Haïti: ave Marie-Jeanne, Port-au-Prince; tel. 2-1729; telex 0206; Dir (vacant).

Association Hotelière et Touristique d'Haïti: Port-au-Prince; tel. 5-2551.

HONDURAS

Introductory Survey

Location, Climate, Language, Religion, Flag, Capital

The Republic of Honduras lies in the middle of the Central American isthmus. It has a long northern coastline on the Caribbean Sea and a narrow southern outlet to the Pacific Ocean. Its neighbours are Guatemala to the west, El Salvador to the south-west and Nicaragua to the south-east. The climate ranges from temperate in the mountainous regions to tropical in the coastal plains. The rainy season is from May to November. The national language is Spanish. Almost all of the inhabitants profess Christianity, and the overwhelming majority are adherents of the Roman Catholic Church. The national flag (proportions 3 by 2) has three horizontal stripes, of blue, white and blue, with five blue five-pointed stars, arranged in a diagonal cross, in the centre of the white stripe. The capital is Tegucigalpa.

Recent History

Honduras was ruled by Spain from the 16th century until independence in 1821, when the Federation of Central America was formed. Honduras emerged as an independent state in 1838. Between 1939 and 1949 the country was ruled as a dictatorship by Gen. Tiburcio Carías Andino, leader of the Partido Nacional (PN). He was succeeded by Juan Manuel Gálvez. In 1954 the leader of the Partido Liberal de Honduras (PLH), Dr José Ramón Villeda Morales, was elected President but was immediately deposed by Julio Lozano Díaz, himself overthrown by a military junta in 1956. The junta organized elections in 1957, when the PLH secured a majority in Congress and Dr Villeda Morales was re-elected President for a six-year term. He was overthrown in 1963 by Col (later Brig.-Gen.) Oswaldo López Arellano, the Minister of Defence, who, following elections held on the basis of a new constitution, was appointed President in June 1965.

A presidential election in March 1971 was won by Dr Ramón Ernesto Cruz Uclés, the PN candidate, who took office in June. However, popular discontent over government austerity measures and delayed land reforms culminated in a bloodless coup, led by the former President, Gen. López Arellano, in December 1972. A group of young army officers, in favour of social reform, took control of the Supreme Council of the Armed Forces, and in March 1974 replaced President López Arellano as Commander-in-Chief of the Army by Col (later Gen.) Juan Melgar Castro, who was appointed President in April 1975. In 1976 the President postponed the 1977 elections until 1979. He was forced to resign by the Supreme Council of the Armed Forces in August 1978, being replaced by a military junta comprising the commanders-in-chief of the army, air force and national police. The army commander, Gen. Policarpo Paz García, assumed the role of Head of State, and the junta promised that elections would be held.

Military rule was ended officially when, in April 1980, elections to a Constituent Assembly were held. The PLH won 52% of the votes but was unable to assume power. General Paz was appointed interim President for one year and, as the armed forces were allowed to nominate four members of the coalition Cabinet, the PLH was in a minority. A general election in November 1981 resulted in a victory for the PLH, led by Dr Roberto Suazo Córdova, which gained an absolute majority in the National Assembly. Dr Suazo was sworn in as President in January 1982. However, the country's military leaders retained control of security decisions and were able to veto Cabinet appointments. Real power rested in the hands of Gen. Gustavo Alvarez, the Commander-in-Chief of the Armed Forces, who rejected the previous policy of neutrality regarding regional conflicts, and engaged his troops in operations against guerrilla forces in El Salvador. His plans for a major offensive against Nicaragua in August 1982 were thwarted by US opposition. In November Gen. Alvarez succeeded in amending the Constitution in order to diminish government control over the armed forces. Political unrest increased, trade union activists and left-wing sympathizers were arrested, and the appearance of 'death squads' was reported. Several power stations were damaged by bombs.

Political tensions were increased by the presence of about 35,000 refugees from neighbouring countries in 1982. It was thought that Honduran troops were responsible for the deaths of several hundred Salvadorean refugees, and that refugee camps for Miskito Indians from Nicaragua were being used by former Nicaraguan National Guards, regarded by the left-wing Sandinista Government of Nicaragua as counter-revolutionaries ('Contras'), as bases for attacks on Nicaragua.

In January 1983 President Suazo survived a major challenge to his administration, following the defection of six PLH deputies to a new alliance grouping within the National Assembly. Three deputies were persuaded to return to the PLH and another was dismissed, thereby narrowly averting a defeat for the ruling party. As a result of this incident, public support for the administration was thought to be in decline. By contrast, Gen. Alvarez continued to enjoy extensive influence over the Government. He keenly supported US policy in Central America and favoured further Honduran involvement in the conflict along the border with Nicaragua. In September an air and sea battle with Nicaraguan forces was reported, and there were frequent accusations from both sides of cross-border incursions. In an attempt to eradicate all forms of internal dissent, Gen. Alvarez organized a campaign of repression against trade unions and small left-wing parties. By June, 11 people had been murdered and four had disappeared. The army won an important victory over left-wing guerrilla forces in October, when 100 guerrillas were killed in an ambush at Olancho.

Throughout 1983, US involvement in Honduras increased substantially. In February the USA and Honduras began a series of joint manoeuvres, known as 'Big Pine', which were expected to continue until 1988. The manoeuvres were considered to be a cover to enable the USA to construct permanent military installations in Honduras. A naval base was under construction at Puerto Castilla, while a further two airstrips and radar stations were built in 1983. The US Central Intelligence Agency continued to be active in both covert and overt operations against the Nicaraguan Government, and there was clear evidence that Honduras and the USA provided assistance to Nicaraguan counter-revolutionaries who were based in Honduras. In January 1984 a US military helicopter was shot down in the border zone.

In March 1984 Gen. Alvarez was ousted from power by a group of junior officers. He was subsequently sent into exile. His dismissal was thought to be the result of growing disenchantment among the armed forces with the General's authoritarian policies. Several other high-ranking officers were also sent abroad. The appointment of Gen. Walter López Reyes as his successor was approved by the National Assembly. For the US Government, the departure of Gen. Alvarez represented the loss of its main ally within the Honduran administration. In response to mounting public opposition to the US military presence, the Government indicated its intention to examine its role within the US Government's policy towards Central America. In August the Government suspended the training of Salvadorean troops by US military advisers in Honduras, pending agreement with El Salvador on disputed territory. In addition, the Government called for the establishment of a joint US-Honduran commission to review military and economic co-operation, and to revise the 1954 military agreement between the two countries. In December the US Government, prompted by the deterioration in its relations with Honduras, held talks with the Honduran Government. In 1985 the US administration

HONDURAS

declined to enter into a security pact with Honduras, but confirmed that it would take 'appropriate measures' to defend Honduras against 'Communist aggression'.

In May 1984 relations with Nicaragua reached their lowest level, following the shooting-down over Nicaraguan territory of a Honduran helicopter. In the following months, however, the Government indicated its concern at the disruptive presence of the Contras, who were held responsible by the authorities for violations of human rights within Honduras. In January 1985 Steadman Fagoth Müller, a Miskito Indian leader from Nicaragua, was deported from Honduras. Reports that the Government was planning to deport Contras based in Honduras were denied by the Government. In September relations between Honduras and Nicaragua again deteriorated, following a clash on the border between members of the Honduran and Sandinista armed forces. The Honduran armed forces were placed on the alert and 2,000 troops were dispatched to secure the border zone.

In August 1984 division within the PLH, coupled with the continuing economic decline, resulted in a Cabinet reshuffle in which four Ministers were replaced. In November a plot by exiled Honduran businessmen to assassinate President Suazo and to overthrow his Government was uncovered in the USA. A more serious threat to the President emerged in March 1985, when a constitutional crisis developed. The crisis was ostensibly caused by the National Assembly's decision to replace five Supreme Court judges with its own appointees. This act was deemed to be a technical coup d'état by the President, who ordered the arrest of the Assembly's appointees. However, the real cause of the crisis was the conflict between opposing factions within the PLH over the selection procedure for the party's presidential candidate for the elections due to be held in November 1985. The main protagonists in the dispute were the President himself and Efraín Bu Girón, President of the National Assembly, whose candidacy President Suazo refused to support. In the ensuing disorder rumours of an imminent coup circulated and trade unions threatened to call a general strike. In the President's absence, an agreement was reached in May between representatives of the trade unions and the Assembly and members of the armed forces. Under the terms of the accord, the Government's original appointees were permitted to complete their four-year term of office and the President's prerogative to designate the ruling party's presidential candidate was abolished.

Nine candidates contested the presidential election held in November 1985. Elections were also held for 134 seats in the National Assembly and 284 mayoralties. The PLH presented four presidential candidates and the PN presented three candidates. Although there were no reports of electoral malpractice, considerable confusion was caused by uncertainty over the electoral procedure. The 1982 Constitution established that the election of the President would be by a simple majority of the voters, but, prior to the elections, the electoral tribunal ruled that the presidency would be assumed by the leading candidate of the party receiving the most votes. Although the leading candidate of the PN, Rafael Leonardo Callejas, obtained 42% of the individual votes cast, the leading candidate of the PLH, José Simeón Azcona del Hoyo (who had obtained only 27% of the individual votes cast), was declared the winner because the combined votes of the PLH's candidates secured the requisite majority of 51% of the total votes cast. The result led to some dissent, but the transfer of power took place in January 1986, as planned. Upon taking office, President Azcona promised to work towards social and economic development. The new Cabinet contained two PN members. The powerful Commander-in-Chief of the Armed Forces, Gen. Walter López Reyes, unexpectedly announced his retirement, and was replaced by Brig.-Gen. Humberto Regalado Hernández.

Renewed fighting on the border with Nicaragua occurred during 1986, and the increasing involvement of the USA in the conflict gave rise to growing concern in the region. In March it was reported that Sandinista troops had crossed into Honduran territory, near Las Trojes, with the intention of destroying base camps of the Nicaraguan Contras. In response to this, the USA pledged $20m. in emergency aid to Honduras, and US Army helicopters were used to transport Honduran troops to the combat zone. The USA also promised that it would grant further aid in the event of any further incursions. The contin-

Introductory Survey

uation of US military manoeuvres, and the rise in the number of US troops stationed in Honduras placed Honduras in an increasingly precarious position. In December 1986 US aircraft were again used to transport Honduran forces to the border area in order to repulse Sandinista troops who had repeatedly crossed the frontier in pursuit of the US-backed Contras. The decision by Honduras to curb border violations by Nicaraguan government forces marked a serious escalation in the conflict. Following revelations that the USA had secretly sold weapons to Iran and that the proceeds had been used to finance the activities of the Contras, and fearing the withdrawal of aid from the USA, President Azcona requested the removal of Nicaraguan Contra rebels from Honduras. Their presence in an area that had become known as 'Nueva Nicaragua' (New Nicaragua) was also adversely affecting the Honduran economy, as the region contained important coffee-growing land.

Honduras has a border dispute with El Salvador over the island of Meanguera, in the Gulf of Fonseca, and several small stretches of the land border covering some 400 sq km. In 1969 the dispute provoked a four-day war between the two countries. In 1980 a peace treaty was drawn up, but the 1983 Salvadorean Constitution renews El Salvador's claim to Meanguera. In 1986 President Azcona of Honduras and President José Napoleón Duarte of El Salvador signed an agreement to refer the dispute to the International Court of Justice at the Hague.

Government

Under the provisions of the new Constitution, approved by the National Assembly in 1982, the President is elected by a simple majority of the voters. However, at the presidential and general elections in November 1985, the leading candidate of the political party that received the most votes was appointed President. The President holds executive power and has a four-year mandate. Legislative power is vested in the National Assembly, with 134 members elected by universal adult suffrage for a term of four years.

Defence

Military service is by conscription. Active service lasts eight months, with subsequent reserve training. In July 1986 the armed forces totalled 19,200 men, of whom 17,000 were in the army, 700 in the navy and 1,500 in the air force. Paramilitary forces numbered 5,000 men. Defence expenditure in 1984 was 180m. lempiras. In 1986/87 Honduras was to receive foreign military aid amounting to US $87m.

Economic Affairs

In 1984, according to estimates by the World Bank, the country's gross national product (GNP) per head, measured at average 1982–84 prices, was US $700. Apart from Haiti and Bolivia, Honduras had the lowest level of average income in Latin America. Between 1965 and 1984, it was estimated, GNP per head increased, in real terms, at an average rate of only 0.5% annually. The overall increase in gross domestic product (GDP) averaged 4.5% per year in 1965–73, slowing to 3.8% per year in 1973–84.

Agriculture is the principal sector of the economy, accounting for 31.4% of the country's GDP in 1985. More than one-half of the country's working population are engaged in the agricultural sector. Agriculture has suffered from low world prices for principal exports, but since 1982 a modest recovery has been taking place. The sector grew by 2.5% in both 1983 and 1984. Bananas are the leading export and, together with coffee, timber and meat, account for 65% of all export earnings. In April 1985 the Government introduced a banana export incentive scheme, with the aim of increasing production by 20%. The banana crop had an export value of US $179.2m. in 1985. Low world prices and reduced export quotas led to a decline in coffee earnings by 36% in 1981, when exports fell to $172m. Exports continued to decline in 1982 and 1983. Honduras' export quota was cut by 16.3% in 1983. Output declined from 1.5m. bags (each of 60 kg) in 1983/84 to 1.28m. bags in 1984/85. In 1984 fears were expressed that the coffee industry was facing a severe crisis, as 90% of plantations were affected by coffee rust. Nevertheless, export earnings increased to $169m. in 1984. In 1986, owing to a disastrous slump in Brazil's coffee harvest, all export restrictions were lifted and international coffee prices rose sharply at the beginning of the year. The sugar industry has been operating at less than 60% of capacity, and export earnings fell from $25.6m. in 1984 to $10.4m. in 1985.

Forests cover nearly 45% of the land area, and wood is the fourth largest export. A forestry project at Olancho, involving the construction of three sawmills and a pulp and paper plant, has been completed at a cost of US $600m. The project was adversely affected in 1980 by fires which destroyed a total of 44,000 ha of woodland throughout the country. The mining and quarrying sector contributed only 2.2% to GDP in 1984, a fractional increase on previous years. Zinc, lead, gold and silver are mined, and there are deposits of copper and low-grade iron ore. Petroleum output in the mid-1980s averaged about 14,000 barrels per day, and small quantities of petroleum derivatives are exported. Foreign companies are undertaking exploration work. The 292,000 kW hydroelectric plant at El Cajón came into operation in late 1985. In 1985 domestic consumption of petroleum fell to 4.1m. barrels, and imports were reduced by 9%, to 4.52m. barrels.

Although industrial activity is still a small part of the economy, the sector grew by 20% in 1979, with development mainly in the San Pedro Sula area. By 1982, however, industry was contracting rapidly and growth had fallen to 1.7%. From the record figure of US $319.5m. in 1980, industrial exports fell by 8.6% in 1981 and by 14.6% in 1982. In 1983 the manufacturing sector accounted for 15.2% of GDP and employed 13.3% of the country's work-force. In 1985 this sector accounted for 14.1% of GDP. Most factories operate at 60% of capacity. Industry has suffered from insufficient investment, a shortage of foreign exchange, a lack of spare parts, and depressed overall demand from the Central American Common Market (CACM, see p. 110), which Honduras joined in 1960. In 1985 Puerto Cortés was designated a free-trade zone. A further free-trade zone was planned at La Ceiba.

In January 1975 Honduras adopted a new law concerning agrarian reform, aiming at the distribution of 600,000 ha of land to 100,000 families by 1980. However, only about one-third of the land had actually been expropriated, and still less redistributed, by 1979, when lack of funds and pressure from landowners virtually halted the programme. The programme was renewed in 1982, but was hampered by insufficient funding. There are still an estimated 200,000 landless peasant families in Honduras. In 1986 peasants staged land invasions in protest at delays in implementation of a land reform programme.

Increased agricultural production accounted for average real growth in GDP of about 7% per year between 1975 and 1980, but in 1981 low commodity prices and high petroleum prices and interest rates resulted in growth of only 0.5%. GDP declined by 1.7% in 1982, and by a further 0.5% in 1983. However, GDP expanded by 2.8% in 1984, and by 2.6% in 1985. In real terms, average wages fell by 4.5% in 1984 and by 3.3% in 1985. Consumer prices rose by 4.7% in 1984, by 3.4% in 1985, and by an estimated 5% in 1986. Living standards fell sharply as the population continued to expand by more than 2.9% annually. In 1985 unemployment was estimated to be 29%; under-employment was estimated to be 52%.

Political developments in the region have eroded the confidence of the private sector and discouraged foreign creditors. The flight of capital from Honduras amounted to US $1,128m. between 1979 and 1984. Reserves of foreign exchange declined from $237.8m. in March 1980 to $71.8m. in July 1982. By May 1986 they stood at $131.8m. The scarcity of foreign exchange resulted in fuel shortages. The budget deficit increased from $39.6m. in 1979 to $193.3m. in 1985. The current deficit on the balance of payments in 1980 and 1981 was more than $300m., but it fell substantially to $228m. in 1982 and $219m. in 1983, principally as a result of reduced imports. In 1984 the deficit rose to $302m. In that year imports increased by 10.6%, to $989m., and exports increased by 9.9%, to $850m. In 1985 exports reached $943.5m. The foreign debt was $1,600m. in 1983 and increased to $2,441m. in 1985. Debt servicing was absorbing about 30% of export earnings by 1985. In 1986 about 11.7% of total foreign debt was owed to foreign commercial banks.

A stand-by arrangement, over a period of 14 months, was agreed with the IMF in November 1982. Under the terms of the agreement, strict controls were to be imposed on mismanaged state-owned corporations, and incentives were to be given to the private sector and to attract foreign capital. In November 1983 the IMF suspended the disbursement of credit amounting to $15.3m., as Honduras had failed to meet the terms of the 1982 agreement. In May 1984, following further negotiations with the IMF, the Government announced a programme of austerity measures, including increases in direct taxes and reductions in planned expenditure. As a result of the Government's action, the US Government disbursed $65m. in aid. In June, however, public protests at the austerity measures, coupled with the threat of a general strike, prompted the Government to suspend its programme. In March 1985 the Government reached a preliminary agreement with 40 foreign creditor banks on the rescheduling of $220m. of debts. However, further talks on rescheduling were suspended in September, when the Government refused to comply with the banks' demand for Honduras to reach a settlement with the IMF. An agreement with the IMF would have been conditional upon a substantial devaluation of the lempira and the introduction of austerity measures to reduce the annual public-sector deficit, which had risen to $350m. The Liberal administration of José Azcona, which took office in early 1986, was also opposed to devaluation of the lempira. Rescheduling negotiations recommenced in mid-1986, when the requirement first to normalize relations with the IMF was abandoned. However, the talks ended without agreement. In 1986 financing of $97m. was obtained from the IDB. Economic aid from the USA totalled $120.2m. in 1986.

Social Welfare

The state-run system of social security provides benefits for sickness, maternity, orphans, unemployment and accidents. It also provides family and old-age allowances. A Labour Code affords guarantees for employees. In 1980 Honduras had 1,141 physicians and 35 hospitals. In 1979 there were 449 rural health centres. There was a total of 4,723 hospital beds available. The 1986 budget allocated 239.5m. lempiras to the health sector.

Education

Primary education, beginning at seven years of age and lasting for six years, is officially compulsory and is provided free of charge. Secondary education, which is not compulsory, begins at the age of 13 and lasts for up to five years, comprising a first cycle of three years and a second of two years. In 1983 the enrolment at primary schools included an estimated 86% of children in the relevant age-group (compared with 76% in 1980), while the comparable ratio for secondary enrolment was only 24%. On completion of the first period of compulsory education, every adult must teach at least two illiterate adults to read and write. In 1985 there were 6,492 primary schools and 452 secondary and technical schools. There is an autonomous national university in Tegucigalpa, and private universities were opened in San Pedro and Tegucigalpa in 1978. In 1985, according to official estimates, adult illiteracy averaged 40.5% (males 39.3%; females 41.6%).

Tourism

The ruins of Copán, second largest city of the old Mayan Empire, attract tourists and archaeologists. Lake Yojoa, near San Pedro Sula, and Trujillo Bay provide fishing and boating, and there is bathing on the Bay Islands and along the beaches of the northern coast. A number of new hotels, forming part of a tourist complex (costing 50m. lempiras) in the San Pedro Sula-Tela area, were completed in 1981. Honduras received 154,599 tourists in 1985.

Public Holidays

1987: 1 January (New Year's Day), 14 April (Pan-American Day/Bastilla's Day), 16–19 April (Easter), 1 May (Labour Day), 15 September (Independence Day), 3 October (Morazán Day), 12 October (Discovery Day), 21 October (Army Day), 25 December (Christmas).

1988: 1 January (New Year's Day), 31 March–3 April (Easter), 14 April (Pan-American Day/Bastilla's Day), 1 May (Labour Day), 15 September (Independence Day), 3 October (Morazán Day), 12 October (Discovery Day), 21 October (Army Day), 25 December (Christmas).

HONDURAS

Weights and Measures
The metric system is in force, although some old Spanish measures are used, including: 25 libras = 1 arroba; 4 arrobas = 1 quintal (46 kg).

Currency and Exchange Rates
100 centavos = 1 lempira.

Exchange rates (30 September 1986):
£1 sterling = 2.894 lempiras;
US $1 = 2.000 lempiras.

Statistical Survey

Source (unless otherwise stated): Department of Economic Studies, Banco Central de Honduras, 1a Calle, 6a y 7a Avda, Tegucigalpa; tel. 22-2270; telex 1121.

Area and Population

AREA, POPULATION AND DENSITY

Area (sq km)	
Land	111,888
Inland water	200
Total	112,088*
Population (census results)†	
17 April 1961	1,884,765
6 March 1974	
Males	1,317,307
Females	1,339,641
Total	2,656,948
Population (official estimates at mid-year)	
1983	3,612,200
1984	3,717,300
1985	3,826,200
Density (per sq km) at mid-1985	34.0

* 43,277 sq miles.
† Excluding adjustments for underenumeration.

BIRTHS AND DEATHS

(1980 estimates): Birth rate 49.2 per 1,000; death rate 14.2 per 1,000.

Expectation of life at birth: Males 53.4 years; females 56.9 years (1973–75).

PRINCIPAL TOWNS
(Preliminary mid-1985 population estimate, excluding suburbs)

Tegucigalpa	571,400	Tela	26,700	
San Pedro Sula	372,800	Siguatepeque	24,100	
La Ceiba	61,900	Santa Rosa de		
Choluteca	57,200	Copán	19,400	
El Progreso	55,500	Danlí	18,200	
Puerto Cortés	39,900	Juticalpa	13,800	
Comayagua	28,800	Olanchito	12,400	

EMPLOYMENT ('000)

	1983	1984	1985
Agriculture, forestry, hunting and fishing	552.4	568.5	584.8
Mining and quarrying	5.0	5.1	5.3
Manufacturing	138.4	142.4	146.6
Construction	45.3	46.6	47.9
Electricity, gas, water and sanitary services	3.8	3.9	4.0
Transport, storage and communications	41.7	42.9	44.1
Wholesale and retail trade	100.8	103.7	106.9
Banking, insurance, etc.	12.2	12.5	12.9
Other services	144.2	148.4	152.7
Total	1,043.8	1,074.0	1,105.2

Agriculture

PRINCIPAL CROPS ('000 quintals*)

	1983	1984	1985†
Maize	8,557	9,481	9,438
Rice	912	841	757
Dry beans	988	1,098	1,122
Sorghum	980	1,081	852
Cotton	283	395	325
Tobacco	163	170	167
Coffee	1,752	1,638	1,718
Bananas	19,292	21,862	22,650
Sugar cane	69,448	71,840	70,117
Plantains	3,572	3,615	3,704
African palm	3,777	5,715	6,426

* Figures are in terms of the old Spanish quintal, equal to 46 kg (101.4 lb).
† Preliminary.

LIVESTOCK ('000 head)

	1983	1984	1985
Cattle	2,219	2,277	2,371
Pigs	711	714	717
Horses and mules	302	300	298
Chickens	6,942	7,346	7,778

LIVESTOCK PRODUCTS ('000 metric tons)

	1983	1984	1985
Beef and veal	61	63	66
Pig meat	9	9	9
Cows' milk ('000 litres)	231	237	248
Hen eggs ('000 eggs)	514	538	559

Forestry

ROUNDWOOD REMOVALS
('000 cubic metres, excluding bark)

	1982	1983	1984*
Sawlogs, veneer logs and logs for sleepers	947	529	529
Other industrial wood*	15	15	15
Fuel wood*	4,107	4,249	4,393
Total	5,069	4,793	4,937

* FAO estimates.
Source: FAO, *Yearbook of Forest Products*.

SAWNWOOD PRODUCTION
('000 cubic metres)

	1983	1984	1985
Coniferous (softwood)	852	800	811
Broadleaved (hardwood)	21	18	21
Total	873	818	832

Fishing

(metric tons, live weight)

	1983	1984	1985*
Fishes	4,141	4,232	4,362
Shrimps and lobsters	4,505	4,180	4,064
Others	198	184	179
Total catch	8,844	8,596	8,605

* Preliminary.

Mining

	1983	1984	1985
Lead (metric tons)	13,553	15,863	15,601
Zinc (metric tons)	28,176	31,275	36,176
Silver (metric tons)	78	78	80
Gold (kg)	6	17	16

Industry

SELECTED PRODUCTS

		1983	1984	1985
Raw sugar	'000 quintales	4,638	4,801	4,687
Cement	'000 bags of 42.5 kg	11,422	12,569	8,177
Cigarettes	'000 packets of 20	101,221	106,936	115,594
Matches	'000 boxes of 50	64,081	60,016	65,166
Beer	'000 12 oz bottles	131,160	142,398	132,204
Soft drinks	'000 6 oz bottles	489,606	516,093	477,647
Wheat flour	'000 quintales	1,359	1,388	1,475
Fabric	'000 yards	14,311	16,206	13,883
Rum	'000 litres	1,705	1,716	1,553
Other alcoholic drinks	'000 litres	4,882	4,484	4,375

Finance

CURRENCY AND EXCHANGE RATES

Monetary Units
100 centavos = 1 lempira.

Denominations
Coins: 1, 2, 5, 10, 20 and 50 centavos.
Notes: 1, 2, 5, 10, 20, 50 and 100 lempiras.

Sterling and Dollar Equivalents (30 September 1986)
£1 sterling = 2.894 lempiras;
US $1 = 2.000 lempiras;
100 lempiras = £34.55 = $50.00.

Exchange Rate
The official rate is fixed at US $1 = 2.00 lempiras.

CENTRAL BANK RESERVES
(US $ million at 31 December)

	1983	1984	1985
Gold	1.05	1.05	1.05
IMF special drawing rights	2.22	0.16	—
Reserve position in IMF	4.40	—	—
Foreign exchange	107.00	128.00	105.80
Total	114.67	129.21	106.85

Source: IMF, *International Financial Statistics*.

MONEY SUPPLY (million lempiras at 31 December)

	1983	1984	1985
Currency outside banks	361.9	383.5	410.2
Private sector deposits at Central Bank	19.5	16.0	18.6
Demand deposits at commercial banks	433.5	446.5	426.8
Total money	814.9	846.0	855.6

Source: IMF, *International Financial Statistics*.

COST OF LIVING
(Consumer Price Index for Urban Centres. Base: 1978 = 100)

	1983	1984	1985
Food	157.4	158.1	160.5
Housing	172.3	188.6	198.5
Clothing	217.2	228.3	234.9
Medical care	177.4	186.0	189.9
Personal care	173.0	181.0	178.4
Beverages and tobacco	200.5	206.6	220.3
Transport	156.4	158.6	161.9
Miscellaneous	170.8	187.8	200.6
All items	170.9	178.9	184.9

BUDGET (million lempiras)

Revenue	1983	1984	1985
Current revenue	1,409.9	1,653.2	1,837.5
Taxes	746.0	917.7	1,023.6
Income tax	190.3	233.9	240.6
Property tax	17.4	23.3	23.6
Tax on production, internal commerce and transactions	258.3	313.6	349.4
Import taxes and duties	201.5	258.8	316.6
Export taxes and duties	77.8	87.3	92.5
Other taxes	0.7	0.8	0.9
Non-tax revenue	512.2	568.0	615.2
Transfers	9.5	16.1	14.9
Other receipts	142.2	151.4	183.8
Capital revenue	1,066.6	1,283.5	1,166.3
Internal debt	576.4	533.4	523.9
External debt	445.7	628.0	525.6
Capital transfers	44.5	122.1	116.8
Total	2,476.5	2,936.7	3,003.8

Expenditure	1983	1984	1985
Current expenditure	1,453.4	1,597.5	1,777.6
Consumption expenditure	1,384.6	1,544.5	1,685.7
of which wages and salaries	737.5	774.7	851.3
Current transfers	68.8	53.0	91.9
Capital expenditure	734.2	816.4	666.8
Direct investment	691.9	816.4	648.7
of which real investment	608.8	725.5	577.7
Indirect investment	30.8	—	18.1
Pre-investment and development	11.5	—	—
Net allowance on loans	104.1	94.3	82.4
Public debt servicing	303.8	408.9	551.4
Internal	244.2	331.3	432.5
External	59.6	77.6	118.9
Total	2,595.5	2,917.1	3,078.2

1986 (estimate, million lempiras): Current expenditure 1,886.1.

NATIONAL ACCOUNTS (million lempiras at current prices)
Expenditure on the Gross Domestic Product

	1983	1984	1985*
Government final consumption expenditure	889	960	1,065
Private final consumption expenditure	4,326	4,527	4,797
Increase in stocks	−130	75	134
Gross fixed capital formation	1,060	1,193	1,164
Total domestic expenditure	6,145	6,755	7,160
Exports of goods and services	1,556	1,658	1,848
Less Imports of goods and services	1,810	2,116	2,289
GDP in purchasers' values	5,891	6,297	6,719

* Preliminary.

Gross Domestic Product by Economic Activity

	1983	1984	1985*
Agriculture, hunting, forestry and fishing	1,450	1,527	1,607
Mining and quarrying	114	132	132
Manufacturing	785	831	838
Electricity, gas and water	128	137	148
Construction	320	342	356
Wholesale and retail trade	692	728	786
Transport, storage and communications	403	425	450
Finance, insurance and real estate	252	269	294
Owner-occupied dwellings	377	405	437
Public administration and defence	276	298	323
Other services	476	507	548
GDP at factor cost	5,273	5,601	5,919
Indirect taxes, less subsidies	618	696	800
GDP in purchasers' values	5,891	6,297	6,719

* Preliminary.

BALANCE OF PAYMENTS (US $ million)

	1983	1984	1985
Merchandise exports f.o.b.	698.7	745.7	835.1
Merchandise imports f.o.b.	−756.3	−879.6	−954.4
Trade balance	−57.6	−133.9	−119.3
Exports of services	116.3	126.3	131.4
Imports of services	−322.4	−374.2	−398.4
Balance on goods and services	−263.7	−381.8	−386.3
Private unrequited transfers (net)	9.7	10.3	12.4
Government unrequited transfers (net)	34.8	69.7	111.1
Current balance	−219.2	−301.9	−262.8
Direct capital investment (net)	21.0	20.5	27.5
Other long-term capital (net)	108.9	234.7	194.5
Short-term capital (net)	−20.7	16.8	−3.6
Net errors and omissions	12.7	−30.3	10.7
Total (net monetary movements)	−97.4	−60.2	−33.6
Valuation changes (net)	8.2	16.4	−29.9
Exceptional financing (net)	54.0	45.2	44.9
Official financing (net)	−4.2	25.5	—
Changes in reserves	−39.4	26.8	−18.6

Source: IMF, *International Financial Statistics*.

External Trade

PRINCIPAL COMMODITIES (million lempiras)

Imports c.i.f.	1983	1984	1985*
Food and live animals	146.5	154.3	159.7
Mineral fuels, lubricants, etc.	327.6	359.2	327.3
Chemicals	337.6	336.0	352.9
Basic manufactures	379.0	404.5	386.6
Machinery and transport equipment	297.2	387.1	406.3
Miscellaneous manufactured articles	79.3	90.3	99.2
Total (incl. others)	1,605.2	1,776.2	1,776.2

* Preliminary.

Exports f.o.b.	1983	1984	1985*
Bananas	406.3	462.0	547.0
Coffee	302.4	338.2	370.4
Wood	80.8	69.7	68.2
Lead and zinc	49.6	76.1	93.9
Silver	35.1	31.0	32.0
Frozen meat	62.7	42.4	36.3
Shellfish	71.9	99.6	81.9
Soap	22.0	12.1	11.6
Cotton	8.5	15.4	13.6
Tobacco	21.6	16.7	17.3
Total (incl. others)	1,343.6	1,450.7	1,560.1

* Preliminary.

PRINCIPAL TRADING PARTNERS (million lempiras)

Imports c.i.f.	1983	1984	1985
Brazil	20.1	28.6	29.4
Canada	19.8	42.0	19.4
Costa Rica	68.5	89.2	75.0
France	45.1	22.9	27.1
Germany, Federal Republic	55.9	73.2	68.6
Guatemala	117.4	82.5	87.5
Japan	73.4	87.3	103.5
Mexico	57.1	105.5	81.9
Netherlands	45.8	33.8	41.6
Trinidad and Tobago	65.4	63.5	3.7
United Kingdom	30.4	30.4	31.0
USA	596.5	642.5	635.8
Venezuela	137.4	177.1	231.0

Exports f.o.b.	1983	1984	1985*
Belgium	57.1	74.5	102.2
Costa Rica	19.3	15.3	14.3
Germany, Federal Republic	68.3	65.7	117.5
Guatemala	56.6	23.3	7.9
Italy	28.4	67.0	121.1
Japan	79.8	116.5	102.8
Netherlands	30.1	47.8	47.3
Nicaragua	19.3	29.2	12.6
Spain	40.0	37.2	40.7
Trinidad and Tobago	31.3	28.7	20.4
United Kingdom	21.3	31.9	40.0
USA	725.1	755.8	738.4

* Preliminary.

Transport

ROAD TRAFFIC (motor vehicles in use)

	1983	1984	1985
Passenger cars	32,605	32,149	32,748
Lorries and buses	46,857	49,868	52,677

INTERNATIONAL SEA-BORNE SHIPPING
(freight traffic in '000 metric tons)

	1983	1984	1985*
Goods loaded	1,214	1,207	1,382
Goods unloaded	1,424	1,324	1,703

* Provisional figures.

CIVIL AVIATION (traffic on scheduled services)

	1983	1984	1985*
Passengers ('000)	301	307	313
Passenger-km (million)	329	388	458
Freight-km (million)	13	17	22

* Provisional figures.

Tourism

	1983	1984	1985
Number of visitors	157,715	144,232	154,599

Education

(1985)

	Institutions	Teachers	Pupils
Primary	6,492	20,724	765,296
Secondary	452	6,799	130,277
Teachers' training college	1	299	4,336
Universities	3	2,272	30,616

Directory

The Constitution

Following the elections of April 1980, the 1965 Constitution was revised. The new Constitution was approved by the National Assembly in November 1982. The following are some of its main points:

Honduras is constituted as a democratic Republic. All Hondurans over the age of 18 are citizens.

THE SUFFRAGE AND POLITICAL PARTIES

The vote is direct and secret. Any political party which proclaims or practises doctrines contrary to the democratic spirit is forbidden. A National Electoral Council will be set up at the end of each Presidential term. Its general function will be to supervise all elections and to register political parties. A proportional system of voting will be adopted for the election of Municipal Corporations.

INDIVIDUAL RIGHTS AND GUARANTEES

The right to life is declared inviolable; the death penalty is abolished. The Constitution recognizes the right of habeas corpus and arrests may be made only by judicial order. Remand for interrogation may not last more than six days, and no-one may be held incommunicado for more than 24 hours. The Constitution recognizes the rights of free expression of thought and opinion, the free circulation of information, of peaceful, unarmed association, of free movement within and out of the country, of political asylum and of religious and educational freedom. Civil marriage and divorce are recognized.

WORKERS' WELFARE

All have a right to work. Day work shall not exceed eight hours per day or 44 hours per week; night work shall not exceed six hours per night or 36 hours per week. Equal pay shall be given for equal work. The legality of trades unions and the right to strike are recognized.

EDUCATION

The State is responsible for education, which shall be free, lay, and, in the primary stage, compulsory. Private education is liable to State inspection and regulation.

LEGISLATIVE POWER

Deputies are obliged to vote, for or against, on any measure at the discussion of which they are present. The National Assembly has power to grant amnesties to political prisoners; approve or disapprove of the actions of the Executive; declare part or the whole of the Republic subject to a state of siege; declare war; approve or withhold approval of treaties; withhold approval of the accounts of public expenditure when these exceed the sums fixed in the Budget; decree, interpret, repeal and amend laws, and pass legislation fixing the rate of exchange or stabilizing the national currency. The National Assembly may suspend certain guarantees in all or part of the Republic for 60 days in the case of grave danger from civil or foreign war, epidemics or any other calamity. Deputies are elected in the proportion of one deputy and one substitute for every 35,000 inhabitants, or fraction over 15,000. Congress may amend the basis in the light of increasing population.

EXECUTIVE POWER

The Executive Power is exercised by the President of the Republic, who is elected for four years, by a simple majority of the people. No President may serve more than one term.

JUDICIAL POWER

The Judiciary consists of the Supreme Court, the Courts of Appeal and various lesser tribunals. The nine judges and seven substitute judges of the Supreme Court are elected by the National Assembly for a period of four years. The Supreme Court is empowered to declare laws unconstitutional.

THE ARMED FORCES

The armed forces are declared by the Constitution to be essentially professional and non-political. The President exercise military power through a Commander-in-Chief who is designated for a period of three years by the National Assembly, and may be dismissed only by it by a two-thirds majority. Military service is obligatory.

LOCAL ADMINISTRATION

The country is divided into 18 Departments for purposes of local administration, and these are subdivided into autonomous Municipalities; the functions of local offices shall be only economic and administrative.

The Government

HEAD OF STATE

President: José Simeón Azcona del Hoyo (assumed office 27 January 1986).

CABINET
(February 1987)

Minister of the Interior and Justice: Raúl Elvir Colindres.
Minister of Foreign Affairs: Carlos López Contreras*.
Minister of Public Education: Elisa Estela Valle de Martines Pavetti.
Minister of Finance: José Efraín Bu Girón.
Minister of Economy and Commerce: Reginaldo Panting Penalba.
Minister of Health and Social Security: Dr Rubén Antonio Villeda Bermúdez.
Minister of Natural Resources: Rodrigo Castillo.
Minister of Labour and Social Affairs: Adalberto Discua Rodríguez*.
Minister of Defence and Public Security: Luis Alonso Cardona Macias.
Minister of Communications, Public Works and Transport: Juan Fernando López.
Minister of Culture, Tourism and Information: Arturo Rendon Pineda.
Secretary for Economic Planning: Francisco Figueroa Zúñiga.
Director of the National Agricultural Institute: Mario Espinal Zelaya.
Secretary of State to the Presidency: Celeo Arias Moncacada.

* Member of Partido Nacional (PN).

MINISTRIES

Office of the President: Casa Presidencial, 6a Avda, 1a Calle, Tegucigalpa; tel. 22-8287.
Ministry of Communications, Public Works and Transport: Barrio La Bolsa, Comayagüela, Tegucigalpa; tel. 33-7690.
Ministry of Culture, Tourism and Information: Costado Este del Palacio Legislativo, Tegucigalpa; tel. 22-9721.
Ministry of Defence and Public Security: Palacio de los Ministerios, Tegucigalpa; tel. 22-9521.
Ministry of Economy and Commerce: Edif. Salame, 5a Avda, 4a Calle, Tegucigalpa; tel. 22-3251; telex 1396.
Ministry of Finance: Palacio de Hacienda, Avda Cervantes, Tegucigalpa; tel. 22-8452.
Ministry of Foreign Affairs: Palacio de los Ministerios, Tegucigalpa; tel. 22-8540; telex 1129.
Ministry of Health and Social Security: 4a Avda, 3a Calle, Tegucigalpa; tel. 22-1386.
Ministry of the Interior and Justice: Palacio de los Ministerios 2°, Tegucigalpa; tel. 22-8604.
Ministry of Labour and Social Affairs: 2a y 3a Avda, 7a Calle, Comayagüela, Tegucigalpa; tel. 22-8527.
Ministry of Natural Resources: Blvd Miraflores, Tegucigalpa; tel. 32-3141.
Ministry of Public Education: 1a Avda, 2a y 3a Calle, No 201, Comayagüela, Tegucigalpa; tel. 22-8573.

President and Legislature

PRESIDENT

A presidential election was held on 24 November 1985. Nine candidates contested the election: four candidates of the PLH, three candidates of the PN, one candidate of the PINU and one candidate of the PDC. The two leading candidates, RAFAEL LEONARDO CALLEJAS (PN) and JOSÉ SIMEÓN AZCONA DEL HOYO (PLH), obtained 639,000 votes and 416,000 votes respectively. However, as the combined votes for the candidates of the PLH amounted to 51% of the total votes cast, whilst the combined votes for the candidates of the PN were only 45% of the total votes cast, JOSÉ SIMEÓN AZCONA DEL HOYO was declared President-elect, in accordance with the new electoral law. The transfer of power took place on 27 January 1986.

ASAMBLEA NACIONAL

President: CARLOS ORBIN MONTOYA.

General Election, 24 November 1985

Party	Seats
Partido Liberal de Honduras (PLH)	67
Partido Nacional (PN)	63
Partido Demócrata Cristiano (PDC)	2
Partido de Innovación y Unidad (PINU)	2
Total	**134**

Political Organizations

Asociación para el Progreso de Honduras (APROH): right-wing grouping of business interests and members of the armed forces; Vice-Pres. MIGUEL FACUSSÉ; Sec. OSWALDO RAMOS SOTO.

Frente Patriótico Hondureño (FPH): left-wing alliance comprising:

  Partido Comunista de Honduras (PCH): f. 1954; gained legal status 1981; linked with DNU; Leader RIGOBERTO PADILLA RUSH.

  Partido Comunista Marxista-Leninista.

  Partido Socialista (Paso): Leaders MARIO VIRGILIO CARAS, ROGELIO MARTÍNEZ REINA.

Partido Demócrata Cristiano (PDC): legally recognized in 1980; Pres. EFRAÍN DÍAZ ARRIVILLAGA; Leader Dr HERNÁN CORRALES PADILLA.

Partido de Innovación y Unidad (PINU): Apdo 105, Tegucigalpa; f. 1970; legally recognized in 1978; Leader Dr MIGUEL ANDONIE FERNÁNDEZ.

Partido Liberal de Honduras (PLH): Tegucigalpa; f. 1980; Liberal Party; Pres. JUAN DE LA CRUZ AVELAR; Leader Dr ROBERTO SUAZO CÓRDOVA; internal opposition tendencies include:

  Alianza Liberal del Pueblo (ALIPO): f. 1978; comprises:

    Izquierda Democrática: Tegucigalpa.

    Movimiento Villeda Morales: San Pedro Sula.

  Frente de Unidad Liberal (FUL).

  Movimiento Liberal Democrático Revolucionario (M-líder): f. 1984; Pres. JORGE ARTURO REINA; Sec.-Gen. ARMANDO AGUILAR CRUZ.

  Roldista tendency: conservative.

Partido Nacional (PN): Tegucigalpa; f. 1923; traditional right-wing party; internal opposition tendencies include Movimiento Democratizador Nacionalista (Modena), Movimiento de Unidad y Cambio (MUC), Movimiento Nacional de Reivindicación Callejista (MONARCA) and Tendencia Nacionalista de Trabajo; Sec.-Gen. Gen. JUAN ALBERTO MELGAR CASTRO.

Partido Revolucionario Hondureño (PRH): Apdo 1319, San Pedro Sula; f. 1977; not legally recognized; 8,300 mems; Sec.-Gen. FRANCISCO RODOLFO JIMÉNEZ CABALLERO.

Unión Revolucionaria del Pueblo (URP): f. 1980 from split in Communist Party; left-wing group, with peasant support; Leaders TOMÁS NATIVI, FIDEL MARTÍNEZ (in 1981 Nativi and Martínez were reported killed, but the URP maintained that they were alive and held by the armed forces).

In 1985 a broad-based opposition alliance, the Coordinadora Opositora Democrática Constitucional—Codeco, was formed by members of the PDC, PLH and PN.

In 1983 the guerrilla forces united to form the Directorio Nacional Unido (DNU), consisting of the following groups:

Fuerzas Populares Revolucionarias (FRP) Lorenzo Zelaya.

Frente Morazanista para la Liberación de Honduras (FMLH).

Froylan Turcios.

Movimiento Popular de Liberación Cinchonero (MPLC).

Movimiento de Unidad Revolucionaria (MUR).

Partido Revolucionario de los Trabajadores Centroamericanos de Honduras (PRTCH).

Diplomatic Representation

EMBASSIES IN HONDURAS

Argentina: 3a Avda 308, 2a Calle, Colonia Palmira, Tegucigalpa; telex 1120; Ambassador: Dr ARTURO OSSORIO ARANA.

Brazil: Costado Poniente del Parque San Martín 208, Colonia Palmira, Apdo 341, Tegucigalpa; telex 1151; Ambassador: JOÃO CABRAL DE MELONETO.

Chile: Avda República de Panamá 1925, Colonia Palmira, Apdo 222, Tegucigalpa; telex 1195; Ambassador: HOSMÁN A. PÉREZ SEPÚLVEDA.

China (Taiwan): Avda República de Panamá 303, Colonia Palmira, Apdo 6-C, Tegucigalpa; telex 1383; Ambassador: HUANG CHUAN-LI.

Colombia: Edif. Condominio 8°, Apdo 468, Tegucigalpa; tel. 22-0287; telex 1336; Ambassador: Gen. JOSÉ GONZALO FORERO D.

Costa Rica: Blvd Morazán, Costado Oeste de Reasa, Apdo 512, Tegucigalpa; telex 1154; Ambassador: RAFAEL LÓPEZ GARRIDO.

Dominican Republic: Casa 3215, 2a Calle, Colonia Florencia Sur, Apdo 1460, Tegucigalpa; Ambassador: PABLO GIUDICELLI VELÁZQUEZ.

Ecuador: Colonia Palmira, junto al Parque Benito Juárez, Apdo 358, Tegucigalpa; telex 1471; Ambassador: MANUEL IGNACIO CORNEJO-QUIROZ.

El Salvador: 2a Avda 205, Colonia San Carlos, Tegucigalpa; tel. 32-5045; telex 1301; Ambassador: SALVADOR TRIGUEROS.

France: Avda Juan Lindo, Apdo 14-C, Colonia Palmira, Tegucigalpa; telex 1180; Ambassador: EDOUARD AUBIN DE BLANPRÉ.

Germany, Federal Republic: Edif. Paysen 3°, Blvd Morazán, Apdo C-38, Tegucigalpa; tel. 32-3161; telex 1118; Ambassador: Dr ECKEHARD SCHOBER.

Guatemala: 4a Calle 12-50, Las Minitas, Apdo 34-C, Tegucigalpa; Ambassador: MARÍA MERCEDES MARROQUÍN MILLA.

Holy See: Palacio de la Nunciatura Apostólica, Colonia Palmira 401, Apdo 324, Tegucigalpa; tel. 32-8280; Apostolic Nuncio: Mgr ANDRES CORDERO LANZA DI MONTEZEMOLO.

Israel: Edif. Midence Soto 4°, Apdo 1187, Tegucigalpa; Ambassador: MOSHE DAYAN.

Italy: Avda Principal Colonia Reforma 2602, Apdo 317, Tegucigalpa; telex 1332; Ambassador: Dr MARIO ALBERTO MONTECALVO.

Japan: 2a Avda, Colonia Reforma, Apdo 125-C, Tegucigalpa; telex 1141; Ambassador: KENJI ISHIKAWA.

Mexico: Avda República del Brasil 2028, Apdo 769, Tegucigalpa; tel. 32-4039; telex 1143; Ambassador: Lic FRANCISCO CORREA VILLALOBOS.

Nicaragua: Colonia Rubén Darío 110, Apdo 392, Tegucigalpa; tel. 32-1209; telex 1274; Ambassador: DANIEL ABUD VIVAS.

Panama: Colonia Matamoros, Apdo 397, Tegucigalpa; Ambassador: SALVADOR DE LA IGLESIA.

Peru: Edif. Fiallos Soto, Apdo 64-C, Tegucigalpa; Ambassador: Dr JORGE CÉSAR CORDILLO BARRETO.

Spain: Colonia Matamoros 103, Apdo 114-C, Tegucigalpa; telex 1142; Ambassador: FERNANDO GONZÁLEZ CAMINO.

United Kingdom: Edif. Palmira 3°, Avda República de Chile, 4a Calle, Apdo 290, Tegucigalpa; tel. 32-5429; telex 1234; Ambassador: B. O. WHITE.

USA: Avda La Paz, Apdo 26-C, Tegucigalpa; Ambassador: EVERETT E. BRIGGS.

HONDURAS

Directory

Uruguay: Edif. Midence Soto 4°, Apdo 329, Tegucigalpa; Ambassador: Julián Olascoaga Casas.
Venezuela: Blvd Morazán, Apdo 775, Tegucigalpa; telex 1238; Ambassador: Dionísio Mariano.

Judicial System

There is a Supreme Court with nine judges. In addition, there are five Courts of Appeal, and departmental courts which have their own local jurisdiction.

Tegucigalpa has two Courts of Appeal which have jurisdiction (1) in the department of Francisco Morazán, and (2) in the departments of Choluteca Valle, El Paraíso and Olancho.

The Appeal Court of San Pedro Sula has jurisdiction in the department of Cortés. That of Comayagua has jurisdiction in the departments of Comayagua, La Paz and Intibucá; that of Santa Bárbara in the departments of Santa Bárbara, Lempira, Copán.
Supreme Court: 10a y 11a Avda, 3a Calle, Tegucigalpa; tel. 22-8790.
President of the Supreme Court of Justice: Salomon Jiménez.

Religion

The majority of the population are Roman Catholics; the Constitution guarantees toleration to all forms of religious belief.

CHRISTIANITY
The Roman Catholic Church

Honduras comprises one archdiocese, four dioceses and one territorial prelature. At 31 December 1984 an estimated 93% of the population were adherents.
Bishops' Conference: Conferencia Episcopal de Honduras, Arzobispado, Apdo 106, Tegucigalpa; tel. 22-0353; f. 1972; Pres. Héctor Enrique Santos Hernández, Archbishop of Tegucigalpa.
Archbishop of Tegucigalpa: Héctor Enrique Santos Hernández, Arzobispado, Apdo 106, Tegucigalpa; tel. 22-0353.

The Baptist Church
Baptist Convention of Honduras: Apdo 868, Tegucigalpa; tel. 22-7392; Pres. Alexis Vides.

BAHÁ'Í FAITH
National Spiritual Assembly: Apdo 273, Tegucigalpa; tel. 33-1182; mems resident in 560 localities.

The Press

DAILIES

El Cronista: Apdo 432, Tegucigalpa; f. 1912; Dir Antonio J. Valladres; circ. 35,000.
El Faro Porteño: Puerto Cortés.
La Gaceta: Tegucigalpa; f. 1830; morning; official government paper; Dir Rodolfo Heriberto Gómez; circ. 3,000.
El Heraldo: Avda los Próceres, Frente Instituto del Tórax, Tegucigalpa; f. 1979; morning; independent; Dir José Francisco Morales Cálix; circ. 35,000.
La Prensa: 3a Avda No 34, Apdo 143, San Pedro Sula; f. 1964; Dir Gen. Ramón Murillo Cantoral; circ. 50,000.
El Tiempo: Barrio La Fuente 809, Tegucigalpa; f. 1970; liberal; Dir Edmond L. Bográn; circ. 50,000.
El Tiempo: 7a Avda No 6, Calle S.O. 55, Apdo 450, San Pedro Sula; f. 1970; left-of-centre; Dir Edmond L. Bográn; Ed. Manuel Gamero; circ. 70,000.
La Tribuna: Apdo 1501, Tegucigalpa; f. 1977; morning; Dir Oscar A. Flores; circ. 50,000.

PERIODICALS

Alcaraván: Apdo 1843, Tegucigalpa; bi-monthly; political and literary review; Publr Guayamures.
El Alfiler: San Pedro Sula; weekly.
Ariel: Tegucigalpa; monthly.
El Comercio: Cámara de Comercio e Industrias de Tegucigalpa, Bulevar Centroamérica, Apdo 17-C, Tegucigalpa; tel. 32-8110; f. 1970; monthly; commercial and industrial news.
Cultura para Todos: San Pedro Sula; monthly.
El Expectador: San Pedro Sula; weekly.
Extra: Apdo 54-C, Tegucigalpa; monthly; current affairs; Dir Vincente Machado Valle.
Impacto: Tegucigalpa; weekly; Gen. Man. Raúl Barnica López.
Panorama Económico: San Pedro Sula; monthly; economics.
Presente: Tegucigalpa; monthly.
Revista Ideas: Tegucigalpa; 6 a year; women's interest.
Semáforo: Tegucigalpa; weekly.
Social: El Progreso, Yoro; fortnightly.
Sucesos: Tegucigalpa; monthly.
Tribuna Gráfica: Tegucigalpa; fortnightly.
Tribuna Sindical: Tegucigalpa; monthly.
El Trópico: Avda Atlántida, 3a Calle, La Ceiba; f. 1938; weekly; independent; general news; Dir Rodolfo Zavala.

PRESS ASSOCIATION
Asociación de Prensa Hondureña: 6a Calle (altos), Barrio Guanacaste, Tegucigalpa; Pres. Guillermo Pagan Solórzano.

FOREIGN NEWS AGENCIES
Agencia EFE (Spain): Edif. Jiménez Castro, 50°, of. 505, Tegucigalpa; tel. 22-0493; Bureau Chief Armando Enrique Cerrato Cortés.
Agenzia Nazionale Stampa Associata (ANSA) (Italy): 2a Avda B 434, Barrio Morazán, Tegucigalpa; Correspondent Raúl Moncada.
Deutsche Presse-Agentur (dpa) (Federal Republic of Germany): Apdo 1501, Tegucigalpa; tel. 22-8883; Correspondent Paulino Medina.
Inter Press Service (IPS) (Italy): Apdo 228, Tegucigalpa; tel. 32-5342; Correspondent Juan Ramón Durán.
Reuters (UK): Edif. Jiménez Castro 503, Tegucigalpa; tel. 22-2450.

Publishers

Compañía Editora Nacional, SA: 5a Calle Oriente No 410, Tegucigalpa.
Editora Cultural: 6a Avda Norte, 7a Calle, Comayagüela, Tegucigalpa.
Editorial Nuevo Continente: Avda Cervantes 123, Tegucigalpa; tel. 22-5073; Dir Leticia Silva de Oyuela.
Editorial Paulino Valladares, Carlota Vda de Valladares: 5a Avda, 5a y 6a Calle, Tegucigalpa.
Guayamures: Apdo 1843, Tegucigalpa.
Industria Editorial Lypsa: Apdo 167-C, Tegucigalpa; tel. 22-9775; Man. José Bennaton.
Universidad Nacional Autónoma de Honduras: Oficina de Relaciones Públicas, Tegucigalpa.

Radio and Television

In 1985 there were 209 radio stations, four main television stations, and an estimated 20,000 radio receivers and 140,000 television sets in use.

RADIO

Empresa Hondureña de Telecomunicaciones (Hondutel): Apdo 1794, Tegucigalpa; tel. 22-2101; telex 1220; Gen. Man. Col Roberto Ortiz Alméndarez.
Radio América: Apdo 259, Tegucigalpa; commercial station; 13 relay stations; Gen. Man. Rodrigo Wong Arévalo.
Radio Honduras: official station, operated by the Government; tel. 22-8042; telex 1147; f. 1976; Dir Alexis Zúñiga Alemán.
La Voz de Centroamérica: El Progreso; commercial station; Gen. Man. Jorge Sikaffi.
La Voz de Honduras: Apdo 642, Tegucigalpa; commercial station; 23 relay stations; Gen. Man. Nahún Valladares.

HONDURAS												Directory

TELEVISION

Compañía Televisora Hondureña, SA: Apdo 734, Tegucigalpa; tel. 32-1475; telex 1126; f. 1967; main station Channel 5; nine relay stations; Gen. Man. JOSÉ RAFAEL FERRARI.

Telesistema Hondureño, SA: Blvd Suyapa, Apdo 734, Tegucigalpa; f. 1959; main station Channel 3; four relay stations; Gen. Man. MANUEL VILLEDA TOLEDO; Man. CARLOS EDUARDO RIEDEL.

Telsat, SA: Tegucigalpa; subscriber TV; one relay station in San Pedro Sula; Gen. Man. RAFAEL H. NODARSE.

TVS: Tegucigalpa; subscriber TV; one relay station in San Pedro Sula; Gen. Man. SEMIR KAWAS.

Finance

(cap. = capital; p.u. = paid up; res = reserves; dep. = deposits; m. = million; amounts in US dollars unless otherwise stated)

BANKING
Central Bank

Banco Central de Honduras—BANTRAL: 6a y 7a Avda, 1a Calle, Tegucigalpa; tel. 22-2270; telex 1121; f. 1950; cap. and res $75.4m., dep. $108.3m. (June 1984); bank of issue; Pres. GONZALO CARÍAS PINEDA; Man. RIGOBERTO PINEDA S.; 5 brs.

Commercial Banks

Banco de El Ahorro Hondureño, SA (BANCAHORRO): Apdo 78-C, Tegucigalpa; tel. 22-5161; f. 1960; cap. and res $5.3m., dep. $83.3m. (June 1984); Pres. and Gen. Man. FRANCISCO VILLARS; 8 brs.

Banco Atlántida, SA (BANCATLAN): Blvd Miraflores, Plaza Bancatlán, Apdo 57-C, Tegucigalpa; tel. 32-1050; telex 1106; f. 1913; cap. and res $9.1m., dep. $152.1m. (June 1984); First Pres. Lic. PAUL VINELLI; 16 brs.

Banco La Capitalizadora Hondureña, SA (BANCAHSA): Apdo 344, Tegucigalpa; tel. 22-1171; telex 1162; f. 1948; cap. and res $5.5m., dep. $100.3m. (June 1984); Pres. and Gen. Man. Lic. JORGE ALBERTO ALVARADO; 37 brs.

Banco de Comercio, SA (BANCOMER): 6a Avda, 1-2 Calle SO, San Pedro Sula; tel. 54-3600; cap. and res $6.5m., dep. $28.3m. (June 1984); Exec. Pres. RODOLFO CÓRDOBA; 4 brs.

Banco Continental, SA (BANCON): Apdo 390, San Pedro Sula, Cortés; tel. 53-2622; telex 5648; f. 1974; cap. and res $10m., dep. $31.9m. (June 1986); Pres. Ing. JAIME ROSENTHAL OLIVA; 2 brs.

Banco de Honduras, SA: Edif. Midence Soto, Apdo 7-C, Tegucigalpa; tel. 22-1152; telex 1116; f. 1889; cap. and res $3.8m., dep. $31.3m. (June 1984); Pres. and Gen. Man. Lic. MARÍA LIDIA SOLANO; 3 brs.

Banco de las Fuerzas Armadas, SA (BANFFAA): Apdo 877, Tegucigalpa; tel. 22-8131; telex 1245; f. 1979; cap. and res $4m., dep. $40.5m. (June 1984); Pres. Brig.-Gen. HUMBERTO REGALADO HERNÁNDEZ; Exec. Pres. ARMANDO SAN MARTÍN.

Banco de Occidente, SA (BANCOCCI): Apdo 208, Santa Rosa de Copán; tel. 62-0232; f. 1951; cap. and res $5.1m., dep. $68.9m. (June 1984); Pres. and Gen. Man. Lic. JORGE BUESO ARIAS; 14 brs.

Banco Sogerin, SA: Plaza Sogerin 1, Apdo 440, San Pedro Sula; tel. 53-0085; telex 5526; f. 1969; cap. and res $5.2m., dep. $54.4m. (June 1986); Pres. EDMOND L. BOGRÁN; 23 brs.

Banco de los Trabajadores, SA (BANCOTRAB): 3a Avda, 13a Calle, El Obelisco, Apdo 139-C, Comayagüela; tel. 22-6476; telex 1202; f. 1967; cap. and res $7.1m., dep. $28.0m. (June 1984); Pres. ROLANDO DEL CID V.; Man. RAÚL SOLÍS DACOSTA; 13 brs.

Development Banks

Banco Centroamericano de Integración Económica: Apdo 772, Tegucigalpa; tel. 22-2230; telex 1269; f. 1961 to finance the economic development of the Central American Common Market and its member countries; mems Guatemala, El Salvador, Honduras, Nicaragua, Costa Rica; cap. and res $324.9m. (June 1983); Pres. Lic. DANTE GABRIEL RAMÍREZ.

Banco Hondureño del Café (BANHCAFE, SA): 6a Avda, 5a Calle, Tegucigalpa; tel. 22-4219; telex 1278; f. 1981 to help finance coffee production; cap. and res $16.9m., dep. $35.0m. (July 1986); owned principally by private coffee producers; Gen. Man. Lic. ROGER MARÍN NEDA.

Banco Municipal Autónomo (BANMA): 6a Avda, 6a Calle, Tegucigalpa; tel. 22-5963; f. 1963; cap. and res $25.2m., dep. $1.4m. (June 1984); Pres. Lic. JUSTO PASTOR CALDERÓN; 2 brs.

Banco Nacional de Desarrollo Agrícola (BANADESA): Apdo 212, Comayagüela; f. 1980; cap. and res $38.8m., dep. $27.3m. (June 1984); government development bank; loans to agricultural sector; Pres. ROBERTO ZELAYA ECHEVERRÍA.

Financiera Centroamericana, SA (FICENSA): Apdo 1432, Tegucigalpa; tel. 22-1035; telex 1200; f. 1974; private finance organization giving loans to industry, commerce and transport; cap. and res $3.9m., dep. $41.1m. (Dec. 1984); Pres. OSWALDO LÓPEZ ARELLANO; Gen. Man. JOSÉ ARTURO ALVARADO.

Financiera Nacional de la Vivienda—FINAVI: Apdo 1194, Tegucigalpa; f. 1975; housing development bank; cap. and res $5.3m. (July 1984); Exec. Pres. Lic. ELMAR LIZARDO.

Foreign Banks

Bank of America NT & SA (USA): Edif. Centro Comercial Los Castaños, Blvd Morazán, Apdo 199, Tegucigalpa; tel. 32-7350; telex 1101; cap. and res $1.5m., dep. $10.8m. (July 1983); Gen. Man. VÍCTOR PAZ.

Bank of London and Montreal Ltd (Bahamas): 5a Avda, 4a Calle, Apdo 29-C, Tegucigalpa; tel. 22-5151; telex 1117; Man. JULES P. GENASI; 5 brs.

Banking Association

Asociación Hondureña de Instituciones Bancarias (AHIBA): Edif. Bancahsa 5°, Pieza 505, Tegucigalpa; tel. 22-7336; f. 1956; 15 mem. banks.

INSURANCE

El Ahorro Hondureño, SA, Compañía de Seguros: Edif. Trinidad, 5a Calle, 11a Avda, Tegucigalpa; tel. 22-8219; telex 1122; f. 1917; Pres. Dr ROBERTO RAMÍREZ; Gen. Man. RAÚL A. RAUDALES.

Aseguradora Hondureña, SA: Centro Comercial Plaza Miraflores 3°, Col. Miraflores, Apdo 613, Tegucigalpa; tel. 32-2729; telex 1246; f. 1954; Pres. and Gen. Man. ALBERTO AGURCIA.

Compañía de Seguros Interamericana, SA: Apdo 593, Colonia Los Castaños, Tegucigalpa; tel. 32-7614; telex 1362; f. 1957; Pres. SALOMÓN D. KAFATI; Gen. Man. RUBÉN ALVAREZ H.

The Hanover Insurance Co: Edif. Los Castaños 4°, Blvd Morazán, Apdo 113-C, Tegucigalpa; tel. 32-2152; telex 1228; f. 1933; Gen. Man. O. REYNALDO RAMÍREZ.

Pan American Life Insurance Co: Edif. PALIC, Avda República de Chile 804, Tegucigalpa; tel. 32-8774; telex 1237; f. 1944; Gen. Man. Lic. FERNANDO RODRÍGUEZ.

Previsión y Seguros, SA: Apdo 770, Colonia Sabana-Grande y Avda Los Próceres, Tegucigalpa; tel. 32-4834; telex 1392; f. 1981; Gen. Man. EDGARDO ZAPATA C.

Seguros Continental, SA: Edif. Continental 4°, 3a Avda SO 7, Apdo 320, San Pedro Sula; tel. 53-1821; telex 5561; f. 1968; Pres. Ing. JAIME ROSENTHAL OLIVA; Man. MARIO R. SOLÍS.

Insurance Association

Cámara Hondureña de Aseguradores (CAHDA): Apdo 183-C, Tegucigalpa; tel. 32-6020; Pres. O. REYNALDO RAMÍREZ C.; Sec. LILA A. DE MONTES.

Trade and Industry

CHAMBERS OF COMMERCE

Cámara de Comercio e Industrias de Cortés: 17a Avda, 10a y 12a Calle, Apdo 14, San Pedro Sula; f. 1931; 680 mems; Pres. Ing. FELIPE ARGUELLO C.

Federación de Cámaras de Comercio e Industrias de Honduras (Fedecámara): Blvd Centroamérica, Apdo 17-C, Tegucigalpa; tel. 32-8110; f. 1985; 2,000 mems; Man. Lic. J. SAÚL CARRASCO O.

DEVELOPMENT ORGANIZATIONS

Consejo Hondureño de la Empresa Privada (COHEP): Avda Los Próceres 505, Apdo Postal 133-C, Tegucigalpa; f. 1968; comprises 23 organizations; private enterprise organization; Pres. (vacant); Exec. Sec. Ing. JOAQUÍN LUNA MEJÍA.

Corporación Financiera de Olancho: f. 1977 to co-ordinate and manage all financial aspects of the Olancho forests project; Pres. RAFAEL CALDERÓN LÓPEZ.

Corporación Hondureña del Banano—COHBANA (Banana Corporation of Honduras): Tegucigalpa; tel. 53-2868; f. 1975; autonomous organization in charge of all operations concerned with bananas; Gen. Man. CARLOS D. CABRERA.

HONDURAS

Corporación Hondureña de Desarrollo Forestal (COHDEFOR): Salida Carretera del Norte, Zona El Carrizal, Apdo 1378, Comayagüela; telex 1172; f. 1974 to encourage the development of forestry and agrarian reform; Gen. Man. RAFAEL CALDERÓN LÓPEZ.

Corporación Nacional de Inversiones (CONADI): Apdo 842, Tegucigalpa; telex 1192; f. 1974; industrial development investment corporation; Exec. Pres. EDUARDO RAMOS; Exec. Vice-Pres. Lic. LEMPIRA BONILLA.

Dirección General de Minas e Hidrocarburos (General Directorate of Mines and Hydrocarbons): Tegucigalpa.

Fondo Cafetelero Hondureño: f. 1977 to manage the distribution of excess foreign exchange earned from coffee.

Instituto Hondureño del Café—IHCAFE: POB 40-C, Tegucigalpa; telex 1167; f. 1970; coffee development programme; Gen. Man. ARMANDO ZELAYA.

Instituto Hondureño de Mercadeo Agrícola (IHMA): POB 727, Tegucigalpa; telex 1138; Gen. Man. DARÍO HUMBERTO HERNÁNDEZ.

Instituto Nacional Agrario (INA): Tegucigalpa; telex 1218; agricultural development programmes; Dir M. ESPINAL ZELAYA.

Secretaría Técnica del Consejo Superior de Planificación Económica (CONSUPLANE): Edif. Bancatlán 3°, Apdo 1327, Comayagüela; tel. 22-8738; telex 1222; f. 1965; national planning office; Exec. Sec. FRANCISCO FIGUEROA ZÚÑIGA.

PRODUCERS' ASSOCIATIONS

Asociación de Bananeros Independientes—ANBI (National Association of Independent Banana Producers): POB 421, San Pedro Sula; tel. 22-7336; f. 1964; 62 mems; Pres. Ing. JORGE ALBERTO ALVARADO; Sec. CECILIO TRIMINIO TURCIOS.

Asociación Hondureña de Productores de Café (Coffee Producers' Association): 10a Avda, 6a Calle, Apdo 959, Tegucigalpa.

Asociación Nacional de Exportadores de Honduras (ANEXHON): Tegucigalpa; comprises 104 private enterprises; Pres. Dr RICHARD ZABLAH.

Asociación Nacional de Industriales (ANDI) (National Association of Manufacturers): Blvd Los Próceres No 505, Apdo 20-C, Tegucigalpa; Pres. Ing. LEONEL Z. BENDECK; Exec. Sec. DORCAS DE GONZALES.

Asociación Nacional de Pequeños Industriales (ANPI) (National Association of Small Industries): Apdo 730, Tegucigalpa; Pres. JUAN RAFAEL CRUZ.

Federación Hondureña de Cooperativas Cafetaleras (Fehcocal) (Federation of Coffee Co-operatives of Honduras): Tegucigalpa; f. 1969.

Federación Nacional de Agricultores y Ganaderos de Honduras (FENAGH) (Farmers and Livestock Breeders' Association): Colonia Palmira, Tegucigalpa; Pres. Ing. FERNANDO LARDIZÁBAL.

Federación Nacional de Cooperativas Cañeras (Fenacocal) (National Federation of Sugar Cane Co-operatives): Tegucigalpa.

TRADE UNIONS

Confederación de Trabajadores de Honduras—CTH (Workers' Confederation of Honduras): Barrio La Fuente, Calle Lempira, Casa 515, Apdo 720, Tegucigalpa; f. 1964; affiliated to CTCA, ORIT and ICFTU; Pres. MARIANO DE JESÚS GONZÁLEZ; Sec.-Gen. ANDRÉS VÍCTOR ARTILES; 150,000 mems; comprises the following federations:

Federación Central de Sindicatos Libres de Honduras (FECESITLIH) (Federation of Free Trade Unions): 1a Avda, 1a Calle, No 102, Apdo 621, Comayagüela; Pres. EMILIO GONZALES GARCÍA.

Federación Sindical de Trabajadores Nacionales de Honduras (FESITRANH) (Honduran Federation of Farmworkers): 9a Avda, 3a Calle SO, No 65, Apdo 245, San Pedro Sula, Cortés; f. 1957; Pres. FRANCISCO GUERRERO.

Sindicato Nacional de Motoristas de Equipo Pesado de Honduras (SINAMEQUIP) (National Union of HGV Drivers): Tegucigalpa.

Central General de Trabajadores (CGT) (General Confederation of Labour): Apdo 1236, Tegucigalpa; attached to Partido Demócrata Cristiano; Sec.-Gen. FELICITO ÁVILA.

Federación Auténtica Sindical de Honduras (FASH): 1a Avda, 11a Calle No 1102, Comayagüela.

Directory

Federación de Trabajadores del Sur (FETRASUR) (Federation of Southern Workers): Choluteca.

Federación Unitaria de Trabajadores de Honduras (FUTH): Tegucigalpa; f. 1981; linked to left-wing electoral alliance Frente Patriótico Hondureño; Pres. NAPOLEÓN ACEVEDO GRANADOS; 50,000 mems.

Frente de Unidad Nacional Campesino de Honduras (FUNACAMH): f. 1980; group of farming co-operatives and six main peasant unions as follows:

Asociación Nacional de Campesinos de Honduras (ANACH) (National Association of Honduran Farmworkers): 8a Avda, 9a Calle SO, No 36, Blvd Lempira, San Pedro Sula, Cortés; f. 1962; affiliated to ORIT; Pres. ANTONIO JULÍN MÉNDEZ; 80,000 mems.

Federación de Cooperativas Agropecuarias de la Reforma Agraria de Honduras (FECORAH).

Frente Nacional de Campesinos Independientes de Honduras.

Unión Nacional de Campesinos (UNC) (National Union of Farmworkers): Tegucigalpa; linked to CLAT; Leader ADÁN PALACIOS; Sec.-Gen. MARCEL CABALLERO; c. 25,000 mems.

Unión Nacional de Campesinos Auténticos de Honduras (UNCAH).

Unión Nacional de Cooperativas Populares de Honduras (UNACOOPH).

Transport

RAILWAYS

In 1984 there were 1,780 km of railways, all of which are in the north of the country and most of which are used for fruit cargo. A 97-km rail link is being built between La Ceiba and San Pedro Sula, and there are plans to construct a 250-km railway line to link Sonaguera with Bonito Oriental.

Ferrocarril Nacional de Honduras (National Railway of Honduras): Apdo Postal 496, San Pedro Sula; tel. 52-1266; f. 1870; government-owned; 128 km of track open; Gen. Man. C. QUIÑÓNEZ.

Tela Railroad Co: La Lima; tel. (504) 56-2018; telex 8305; 344 km of track open; Pres. RONALD F. WALKER; Gen. Man. JOHN A. ORDMAN.

Vaccaro Railway: La Ceiba; 447 km of track open; Gen. Man. D. DEHORENZO.

ROADS

In 1985 there were 12,986 km of roads in Honduras, including 2,078 km of paved roads. Roads are being constructed by the Instituto Hondureño del Café and COHDEFOR in order to facilitate access to coffee plantations and forestry development areas.

Dirección General de Caminos: Tegucigalpa; highways board.

SHIPPING

Empresa Nacional Portuaria (National Port Authority): Apdo 18, Puerto Cortés; telex 8007; f. 1965; has jurisdiction over all ports in Honduras; manages Puerto Cortés, Tela, La Ceiba, Trujillo/Castilla, Roatán, Amapala and San Lorenzo; an improvement programme costing US $10m. has increased the container traffic at Puerto Cortés and San Lorenzo; a network of paved roads connects Puerto Cortez and San Lorenzo with the main cities of Honduras, and with the principal cities of Central America; the new deep-water Pacific port at San Lorenzo began operating in January 1979; in 1978 works to the port of Castilla began at a cost of US $25m.; Gen. Man. Lic. JERÓNIMO SANDÓVAL.

There are several minor shipping companies. A number of foreign shipping lines call at Honduran ports.

CIVIL AVIATION

Local airlines in Honduras compensate for the deficiencies of road and rail transport, linking together small towns and inaccessible districts. There are three international airports and a fourth is under consideration at Talanga.

Servicio Aéreo de Honduras, SA (SAHSA): Apdo 129, Tegucigalpa; telex 321-1146; f. 1944; private company; operates domestic flights and also to the USA, Colombia, Nicaragua, Guatemala, Belize, Costa Rica and Panama; Pres. Gen. OSWALDO LÓPEZ; Gen. Man. Capt. ROLANDO FIGUEROA; fleet: 1 Electra, 3 DC-3, 2 Boeing 727-100, 1 Boeing 737-200.

Aerovías Nacionales de Honduras, SA (ANHSA): c/o SAHSA; f. 1950; a local airline which serves the north coast and the east of the country; fleet: 2 DC-3.

Transportes Aéreos Nacionales, SA (TAN): Edif. TAN, Apdo 628, Tegucigalpa; telex 848-5909; f. 1947; operates passenger and cargo services, internal and international to Belize, Mexico and the USA; Pres. Gen. OSWALDO LÓPEZ; Gen. Man. Capt. ROLANDO FIGUEROA; fleet: 1 Boeing 737-200, 1 L-188 Electra.

Líneas Aéreas Nacionales, SA (LANSA): Apdo Postal 35, La Ceiba; f. 1971; scheduled services within Honduras and to Islas de Bahía; Gen. Man. OSCAR M. ELVIR; fleet: 1 F27J, 4 DC-3, 1 Cessna 182, 1 Cessna 206.

Tourism

Instituto Hondureño de Turismo: Apdo 154-C, Tegucigalpa; tel. 22-1181; telex 1322; f. 1971; department of the Secretaría de Cultura y Turismo; Dir-Gen. Lic. DEBORAH MILLS DE GOLDNER.

Atomic Energy

Comisión Hondureña de Energía Atómica: Apdo 104, Tegucigalpa; Pres. Dr RAFAEL TORRES FIALLOS.

HUNGARY

Introductory Survey

Location, Climate, Language, Religion, Flag, Capital

The Hungarian People's Republic lies in Eastern Europe, bounded to the north by Czechoslovakia, to the east by the USSR and Romania, to the south by Yugoslavia and to the west by Austria. Its climate is continental, with long, dry summers and severe winters. Temperatures in Budapest are generally between −3°C (27°F) and 28°C (82°F). The language is Hungarian (Magyar). Most of the inhabitants profess Christianity, and the largest single religious denomination is the Roman Catholic Church, claiming more than 6m. adherents. Other Christian groups are the Hungarian Reformed Church (a Presbyterian sect with about 2m. members), the Lutheran Church and the Hungarian Orthodox Church. The national flag (proportions 3 by 2) consists of three equal horizontal stripes, of red, white and green. The capital is Budapest.

Recent History

Hungary allied itself with Nazi Germany before the Second World War and obtained additional territory when Czechoslovakia was partitioned in 1938 and 1939. Having sought to break the alliance in 1944, Hungary was occupied by German forces. In January 1945 Hungary was liberated by Soviet troops and signed an armistice, restoring the pre-1938 frontiers. It became a republic in February 1946. Meanwhile, land distribution, under the March 1945 land reform, continued. Nationalization measures began in December 1946, despite opposition from the Roman Catholic Church under Cardinal József Mindszenty. In the 1947 elections the Communists became the largest single party, with 22.7% of the vote. By the end of that year the Communist Party had emerged as the leading political force. The Communists merged with the Social Democrats to form the Hungarian Workers' Party in June 1948. A People's Republic was established in August 1949.

Mátyás Rákosi became the leading figure as First Secretary of the Workers' Party. Opposition was subsequently removed by means of purges and political trials. Rákosi became Prime Minister in 1952 but, after the death of Stalin a year later, lost this post to the more moderate Imre Nagy, and a short period of liberalization followed. Rákosi, however, remained as First Secretary of the Party, and in 1955 Nagy was forced to resign. András Hegedüs, sponsored by Rákosi, was appointed Prime Minister. In-fighting between the Rákosi and Nagy factions increased in 1956 after the condemnation of Stalinism at the 20th CPSU Congress in Moscow; in July Rákosi was forced to resign but was replaced by a close associate, Ernő Gerő.

The consequent discontent led to demonstrations, and in October 1956 fighting broke out. Nagy was returned as Prime Minister and headed a series of governments. He promised various controversial reforms, but fighting continued. In November a new Soviet-backed government, headed by János Kádár, was set up. Soviet troops, stationed in Hungary under the 1947 peace treaty, were asked to intervene and the uprising was suppressed. Kádár also took over as head of the newly-formed Hungarian Socialist Workers' Party (HSWP). He held the premiership until January 1958 and from September 1961 to July 1965 but, even when not formally in the Government, his Party leadership makes him dominant in political life.

In April 1978 Béla Biszku, who had been regarded as Kádár's deputy, was retired from the Secretariat of the Central Committee of the HSWP. At the Party Congress in March 1980 Kádár was re-elected First Secretary of the Central Committee; five Politburo members were not reappointed. The June 1980 general election resulted in a 99.3% vote in favour of the Patriotic People's Front (dominated by the HSWP). An extensive government reshuffle followed. Changes included the election of six new members to the Presidential Council and the removal of two Deputy Chairmen from the Council of Ministers. In January 1981 three industrial ministries were merged into a single Ministry of Industry to improve co-ordination. A minor reshuffle took place in June 1982. In July 1983 Péter Várkonyi replaced Frigyes Puja as Foreign Minister. László Kapolyi was appointed Minister of Industry in December 1983. In June 1984 László Somogyi became Minister of Construction and Lajos Urbán was appointed Minister of Communications. In December 1984 three new Deputies of the Chairman of the Council of Ministers were appointed. Col-Gen. István Oláh became Minister of Defence but died a year later, and was replaced by Gen. Ferenc Karpati. János Kamara was appointed Minister of the Interior in March 1985.

The 13th HSWP Congress was held in March 1985. János Kádár was re-elected leader of the Party, taking the new title of General Secretary of the Central Committee. Károly Németh, a member of the HSWP Politburo and of the Presidential Council, was elected to the newly-created post of Deputy General Secretary of the Party Central Committee. A new Politburo and Central Committee Secretariat were chosen, each containing three members elected for the first time. The Congress also reaffirmed the commitment to the country's economic reforms.

The legislative elections of June 1985 were the first to be held under the revised electoral law, giving voters a wider choice of candidates under the system of mandatory multiple nominations. The National Assembly again re-elected Pál Losonczi as President of the Presidential Council, which included seven new members.

In February 1986 up to 100 Hungarian and Austrian environmentalists attempted to stage a demonstration in Budapest to protest against the construction in northern Hungary of the Gabcikovo-Nagymaros hydroelectric dam across the River Danube, but the demonstration was halted by the police. In March, during celebrations in Budapest to mark the anniversary of the 1848 Hungarian uprising, disturbances broke out when hundreds of disenchanted young people took part in a protest march. The police used force to stop the marchers, and the incident was reportedly the worst display of public disorder in the country for many years. Criminal proceedings, on charges of breach of the peace, were instigated against 11 of the demonstrators. The 30th anniversary of the 1956 uprising, in October, passed off peacefully.

In December 1986 a Deputy Chairman of the Council of Ministers was replaced, and a new Minister of Finance, Peter Medgyessy, was appointed. The Presidents of the National Planning Office and of the Central People's Control Commission were also replaced.

Hungary is closely aligned with the countries of Eastern Europe through its membership of the Warsaw Pact (see p. 206). However, Hungary's relations with Romania and, to a lesser extent, with Czechoslovakia have been strained by the issue of the position of the large Hungarian minorities resident in these countries. Hungary pursues an active foreign policy, and relations with the West, particularly Austria, France, the Federal Republic of Germany and the United Kingdom, are improving steadily. János Kádár paid an official visit to France in October 1984, and in late 1985 visited the United Kingdom and Austria. The US Secretary of State, George Shultz, visited Hungary for talks in December 1985, and in June 1986 the Soviet leader, Mikhail Gorbachev, had talks in Budapest with Kádár.

Government

Under the 1949 Constitution, the highest organ of state power is the unicameral National Assembly, with 387 members (expanded from 352 in 1985) elected for five years by universal adult suffrage. Since 1971 the electorate has had the right to nominate two or more candidates for a constituency, thus providing wider representation in the National Assembly. At the elections of June 1985 the system of multiple candidacy was extended to all the original 352 constituencies, in 78 of which there were more than two candidates. The additional 35 members were elected unopposed on a new national list of prominent politicians (including nine members of the HSWP Politburo), trade unionists, clergymen, etc. The Assembly elects from its members a Presidential Council (21 members were elected in 1985) to be its permanent organ and the state's executive authority, responsible to the Assembly. The Council, led by a President, collectively acts as the Head of State. The Council of Ministers, the highest organ of state administration, is elected by the Assembly on the recommendation of the Presidential Council.

Political power is held by the Communist HSWP, the only legal party, which dominates the Patriotic People's Front. The Front presents an approved list of candidates, nominated at public meetings, for elections to representative bodies. No other candidates are permitted. Any individual or body may nominate a candidate, but must receive the backing of at least one-third of those at the meeting for the nomination to be valid. The HSWP's highest authority is the Party Congress, which elects a Central Committee (105 members were elected in March 1985) to supervise Party work. The Central Committee elects a Political Committee (Politburo) of 13 members to direct policy. For local administration Hungary is divided into 19 counties and the capital city with 22 districts.

Defence

Hungary was a founder member of the Warsaw Pact in 1955, and in 1969 joined the Geneva Disarmament Commission. Military service starts at the age of 18 years and normally lasts for 18 months in the army and 24 months in the air force. According to Western estimates, the total regular forces in July 1986 numbered 105,000 (including 58,000 conscripts): army 83,000 (including the Danube Flotilla of 700) and air force 22,000. There is also an armed force of 16,000 border guards and a Workers' Militia with 60,000 members. The 1986 defence budget totalled an estimated 40,745m. forint.

Economic Affairs

In 1968 a new system of economic management was introduced, known as the 'new economic mechanism' (NEM). The official definition of the plan was to 'harmonize state planning and market development'. Until then the economy had been based on the standard Soviet central planning system. Under the new scheme, industry has been decentralized to a certain extent, with the aim of evolving a socialist market economy, with emphasis on monetarist policies. The reforms initially brought a rapid improvement in the standard of living in Hungary.

Various measures to encourage the further development of private enterprise have been implemented since 1982. In January 1982 new regulations were introduced to give more scope to small private and co-operative ventures, including the opportunity to lease machinery from state concerns. In 1983, in order to attract foreign investment, new measures permitted the establishment of customs-free zones for joint ventures between Hungarian enterprises and foreign companies. In January 1986 taxes on the profits of joint ventures were reduced and the licensing system was simplified. By early 1987 more than 70 joint ventures had been agreed with Western companies, mostly from Austria and the Federal Republic of Germany. Negotiations for the formation of a further 30 joint companies were in progress.

In 1985 radical reforms in the system of management, giving enterprises more autonomy, were introduced. In about 80% of companies managers are to be elected: in large and medium companies election will be by newly-formed enterprise councils, representing workers and officials; in small companies managers will be elected directly by employees. New regulations, aimed at improving efficiency and profitability, allow successful enterprises to pay higher wages and to streamline the labour force if necessary, while loss-making companies face the possibility of liquidation. Between 1980 and 1985 the State provided 80,000m. forint in subsidies to unprofitable enterprises. A new bankruptcy law, applicable to both companies and co-operatives, took effect in September 1986. Henceforth, state aid to loss-making organizations will be offered only in exceptional circumstances.

Reforms in the financial sector include the restructuring of the banking system. In January 1985 the issue and credit functions of the National Bank were formally separated, and in January 1987 five commercial banks were established, in order to improve efficiency in the allocation of financial resources. Since 1984 a domestic 'bond market' has been in existence, the money raised by the issue of bonds (both to enterprises and to private individuals) being used to finance housing and infrastructural schemes.

The Hungarian foreign trade organizations are being reorganized, and by 1985 over 250 companies had acquired foreign trade rights. New regulations in 1985 also allowed foreign trade organizations to become 'trading houses', thus extending their sphere of activity. The economy is heavily dependent on foreign trade, which usually amounts to about 50% of net material product (NMP). The most important industries are engineering and chemicals, the engineering sector employing 32% of those engaged in industry in 1984. Higher quality goods that are competitive on the world market are now being produced, in a bid to boost exports. Hungary is an exporter of rolled steel, engineering products, machine tools, buses, telecommunications and electrical equipment, electronic instruments, pharmaceuticals, clothing and footwear. Meat, fruit, vegetables and wine are also significant exports. The country's principal imports are crude petroleum, iron ore, copper and copper products, raw materials for the plastics industry, chemical fibres, artificial fertilizers, paper, cotton, animal foodstuffs and capital and consumer goods.

In 1986 20% of the economically active population were employed in agriculture and forestry. More than 50% of the total area is arable land, most of which is state or co-operatively owned. In 1984 there were 129 state and complex farms. In 1986 the 1,270 co-operative farms cultivated a total of 5.8m. ha and accounted for 70% of the country's agricultural production. The household plots of co-operative members make a significant contribution to total agricultural output. The principal crops include wheat, maize, sunflowers, sugar beet and potatoes. Vineyards covered a total of 159,000 ha in 1982 and forests a total of 1,723,000 ha in 1985.

With the exception of rich deposits of bauxite, production of which totalled almost 3m. metric tons in 1985, Hungary is not well-endowed with natural resources. The country's oil consumption fell from 12.5m. metric tons in 1979 to 9.1m. tons in 1985. Domestic output of crude petroleum, from the Pannonian Basin, totalled 2m. tons in 1986. In 1984 the cost of imports of petroleum and petroleum products (mostly from the USSR) reached 60,572.6m. forint, almost double that of 1981, but in 1985 fell to 51,728.4m. forint. Output of hard coal in 1984 fell to 2.6m. metric tons, and by late 1985 a serious shortage of coal had developed, necessitating additional imports. By late 1986, however, the power stations' coal stocks had improved and totalled 1.2m. tons. It was envisaged that during 1986–90 total coal production (hard coal, brown coal and lignite) would remain at 24m. tons annually. Output of natural gas totalled 7,456m. cu m in 1985. Gas imports from the USSR, by pipeline, were to total 4,500m. cu m in 1986. The Paks nuclear power station project was inaugurated in 1983 and by 1986 was producing one-third of the country's electricity. When fully operational the plant will supply about 17% of Hungary's total energy. Hungary's uranium reserves are sufficient to supply the Paks station until the year 2020. In 1985 Hungary decided to proceed with the Gabcikovo (Boes)-Nagymaros Danube barrage scheme, a joint project with Czechoslovakia. Austrian participation in the scheme was agreed in 1986. Scheduled for completion in 1993, the project's two hydroelectric power stations are expected to supply a total of 3,600m. kWh per year. The total cost of the project is estimated at 70,000m. forint.

During the fourth Five-Year Plan (1971–75) Hungary's NMP rose by 35% over the previous five-year period, industrial production increased by 38%, and agricultural output by 18%. Investment expanded by 40%, and foreign trade turnover went up by 60%. The 1976–80 Plan laid emphasis on the modernization of industry. As a result of higher costs for raw materials and less favourable conditions of trade, the targets of this Plan were scaled down. NMP increased by 20% instead of 30%–32%. Industrial production rose by 18%–19%, and agricultural output by 13%. Investment, originally scheduled to increase by 25%, was severely curtailed.

The sixth Five-Year Plan (1981–85) called for continued austerity and stressed the need for greater efficiency and profitability. Over the Plan period, an increase of 14%–17% in NMP was envisaged, but growth of only 7% was achieved. Industrial production rose by 12%, compared with a target of 19%–22%. The engineering and chemical industries recorded increases in output of 18% and 11.8% respectively over the five-year period. As a percentage of the 1976–80 average, agricultural output went up by 12%. Per caput real income rose by 7%–8% during the 1981–85 period, slightly more than planned. Total exports were set to increase by 37%–39%, and imports by 18%–19%, but went up by 27% and 6%, respectively. Between 1980 and 1983 the volume of investments fell annually by about 5%.

The seventh Five-Year Plan (1986–90) projects growth of 15%–17% in NMP, compared with the level of 1985. Industrial production is planned to increase by 14%–16%. Agricultural output (compared to the 1981–85 period) is expected to rise by 7%–10%. It is envisaged that domestic consumption will go up by 13%–16% and real income per head by 9%–11%. Total exports are planned to grow by 16%–18% and imports by the same percentage. Investments in the socialist sector will approach 1,500,000m. forint.

In 1984 NMP expanded by almost 3% over the previous year, but in 1985 it contracted by 1.4%. NMP rose by 0.5% in 1986, compared with the target of 2.3%–2.7%. An increase of at least 2% was envisaged in 1987. Per caput real income rose by 1%–1.5% in 1985 and by 3% in 1986. Industrial production rose by 1% in 1985 and by 1.8% in 1986. The value of the Hungarian chemical industry's exports to the convertible currency area declined substantially in 1986, owing to the fall in international prices for petroleum and consequently for petrochemical products. It was hoped to offset this shortfall by increasing exports of other chemical products. Hungary's newly-established microelectronics industry suffered a major set-back in May 1986, when the industry's main plant in Budapest was almost totally destroyed by fire. Agricultural output increased by almost 3% in 1984. The severe weather of early 1985 and the fall in world market prices created serious problems in the agricultural sector, with production declining by 6% in 1985. The sector's difficulties were compounded in 1986 by the nuclear power station accident at Chernobyl, in the USSR, and the West's introduction of restrictions on agricultural imports from Hungary, and also by drought, which resulted in serious shortfalls in crop production and further export losses. Total exports increased by 10.6% in 1984 and by 2.6% in 1985, while imports rose by 6.9% in 1984 and by 4.7% in 1985.

A uniform exchange rate for the forint was introduced in 1981. The forint has been successively devalued against major Western currencies. From 1986 the forint was to be allowed to move freely on a daily basis in relation to 20 Western currencies, thus becoming the first CMEA currency to have a flexible exchange rate, but the innovation was postponed. In September 1986 the forint was devalued by an average of 8% against Western currencies.

In January 1985 there were further steep rises in the prices of basic foods, domestic fuels and public transport fares. Consumer prices rose by 39% between 1981 and 1985. The inflation rate was expected to average 7% in 1987, slightly higher than the 1986 level. Wages were planned to rise by 5.0%–5.5% in 1987. In December 1986 a four-month wage 'freeze' was declared. The 1987 budget deficit was estimated at 43,800m. forint, compared with 23,000m. in 1986.

Hungary is a member of the Council for Mutual Economic Assistance (CMEA, see p. 126) and of GATT (p. 59), and in 1982 joined the IMF and the World Bank. In July 1983 Hungary and the World Bank concluded an agreement on two loans, totalling US $239.4m., for the financing of the 1981–85 energy programme and for the implementation of a programme for the production and storage of wheat. In January 1984 the IMF granted Hungary a seven-year credit of $450m. In April 1984 the World Bank approved further loans totalling $200m. for the development of industrial exports and for research and production in the oil and gas industries. In June 1985 Hungary obtained a loan of $300m., co-financed by the World Bank and commercial banks, for the implementation of projects in the livestock, chemical and transport sectors. In December 1985 Hungary made an early repayment to the IMF of SDR88.3m., having been granted a two-year stand-by loan of SDR375m. in 1982 and a one-year stand-by loan of SDR425m. in 1984. In May 1986 the World Bank approved a $100m. loan towards industrial restructuring to help Hungary achieve international competitiveness. Loans of $64m. and of $25m. were also granted for the renovation of Hungary's power stations and for the energy rationalization programme. In 1986 Hungary obtained an eight-year loan of $300m. from an international banking consortium for the financing of foreign trade. Hungary's convertible currency reserves rose to a record $3,800m. in the first quarter of 1986. The country's gross debt in convertible currency, however, increased from $8,840m. in 1985 to $11,760m. in 1986.

Trade with other members of the CMEA, mainly the USSR, accounted for 56% of total foreign trade in 1985. The EEC accounted for 22%. The Federal Republic of Germany is Hungary's second largest trading partner. In 1980 Hungary achieved a surplus in its balance of payments with the West, the first since 1973. In order to maintain this surplus, temporary import quotas for raw materials and industrial components were introduced in 1982. The trade surplus on transactions in convertible currencies fell to US $303m. in 1985, compared with $720m. in 1984. The deficit on trade with CMEA countries was eliminated in 1985: Hungary's exports to these countries increased by 8% and imports by only 3.2% over 1984, resulting in a surplus of 255m. roubles.

Social Welfare

The national insurance scheme is based largely on non-state contributions. Employees contribute between 3% and 15% of their earnings to the pension fund. Employers usually pay 40% of the earnings of each person employed. Publicly-financed employers pay 10%. The cost of health services and other social services is met by state subsidies and contributions from the place of work. The 1985 state budget allotted 35,000m. forint to health and social welfare.

The implementation of the five-day working week was completed by 1985. A uniform system of retirement pensions was introduced in 1975: workers draw between 33% and 75% of their earnings, according to the number of years of service. Male workers are usually entitled to retirement pensions at the age of 60 and women at 55. There are also invalidity pensions, widows' pensions and orphans' allowances. Social insurance covers sickness benefits. Patients are entitled to sick pay, usually for one year, or two years in the case of tuberculosis, occupational disease and industrial accident. All medical consultation and treatment is free, although a very small charge is generally made for medicines and between 15% and 50% for medical appliances. In 1985 there were almost 33 physicians and 95.9 hospital beds per 10,000 of the population. The social insurance scheme also covers maternity benefits. Women are entitled to 24 weeks' maternity leave on full pay. A new child-care payment, in addition to the child-care allowance, was made available in 1985. In 1984 there were more than 3,600 private medical practices in Hungary, one-third of which were in Budapest.

Education

Children under the age of three years attend crèches (bölcsődék), and those between the ages of three and six years attend kindergartens (óvodák). They are not compulsory, but in 1985 about 91% of children in this age-group were attending. Compulsory education begins at six years of age, with the basic school (általános iskola). Basic education, comprising general subjects together with some practical training, continues until the child is 14. Provision is made in the basic school for talented children, particularly those who are linguistically inclined. In southern Hungary bilingual schools are being established to promote the languages of the national minorities. Children attend school until the age of 16 years. There are four types of secondary school, excluding special schools for the very gifted or, alternatively, the backward or abnormal child. The majority of children continue with their education after 16 years of age. The most popular types of secondary school are the grammar school (gimnázium) and the secondary vocational schools (technikum). The gimnázium provides a four-year course of mainly academic studies, although some vocational training does figure on the curriculum. The technikum offers full vocational training together with a general education, emphasis being laid on practical work. Apprentice training schools (ipari tanulók gyak-

HUNGARY

orló iskolai) are attached to factories, agricultural co-operatives, etc., and lead to full trade qualifications. General education is less important as part of the curriculum in this type of school. Further education reform is being directed at revising the curricula and the method of assessing pupils. There are 58 higher institutes, including nine universities and nine technical universities.

Tourism

Tourism has developed rapidly and is an important source of foreign exchange. Earnings from tourism in 1985 totalled 25,280m. forint, 15% higher than 1984. Lake Balaton is the main holiday centre for boating, bathing and fishing. The cities have great historical and recreational attractions. The annual Budapest Spring Festival is held in March. Budapest has numerous swimming pools watered by thermal springs, which are equipped with modern physiotherapy facilities. The first Budapest Grand Prix, the only Formula-1 motor race to be held in Eastern Europe, took place in August 1986. In 1985 there were 15.1m. foreign visitors, 13% more than in the previous year. In 1986 the number of visitors rose to 16.6m. There were 43,719 hotel beds in 1985.

Public Holidays

1987: 1 January (New Year's Day), 4 April (Liberation Day), 20 April (Easter Monday), 1 May (Labour Day), 20 August (Constitution Day), 7 November (October Revolution Day), 25–26 December (Christmas).

1988: 1 January (New Year's Day), 4 April (Liberation Day, Easter Monday), 1 May (Labour Day), 20 August (Constitution Day), 7 November (October Revolution Day), 25–26 December (Christmas).

Weights and Measures

The metric system is in force.

Currency and Exchange Rates

100 fillér = 1 forint.

Exchange rates (30 September 1986):
 £1 sterling = 67.69 forint;
 US $1 = 46.78 forint.

Statistical Survey

Source (unless otherwise stated): Központi Statisztikai Hivatal (Hungarian Central Statistical Office), 1525 Budapest, Keleti Károly u. 5–7; tel. 358-530; telex 22-4308.

Area and Population

AREA, POPULATION AND DENSITY

Area (sq km)	93,036*
Population (census results)	
1 January 1970	10,322,099
1 January 1980	
Males	5,188,709
Females	5,520,754
Total	10,709,463
Population (official estimates at 1 January)	
1984	10,679,000
1985	10,657,000
1986	10,640,000
Density (per sq km) at 1 January 1986	114.4

* 35,920 sq miles.

Languages (1980 Census): Magyar (Hungarian) 98.8%; German 0.3%; Slovak 0.1%; Romany 0.3%; Croatian 0.2%; Romanian 0.1%.

PRINCIPAL TOWNS (population at 1 January 1986)

Budapest (capital)	2,075,990	Nyíregyháza	116,782
Debrecen	211,823	Székesfehérvár	111,478
Miskolc	211,660	Kecskemét	102,889
Szeged	182,137	Szombathely	86,013
Pécs	177,104	Szolnok	80,461
Győr	129,116	Tatabánya	76,465

ADMINISTRATIVE DIVISIONS (1 January 1986)

	Area (sq km)	Resident Population ('000)	Density (per sq km)	County Town (with population)
Counties:				
Baranya	4,487	432	96	Pécs (177,104)
Bács-Kiskun	8,362	559	67	Kecskemét (102,889)
Békés	5,632	422	75	Békéscsaba (70,441)
Borsod-Abaúj-Zemplén	7,248	791	109	Miskolc (211,660)
Csongrád	4,263	456	107	Szeged (182,137)
Fejér	4,374	426	97	Székesfehérvár (111,478)
Győr-Sopron	4,012	428	107	Győr (129,116)
Hajdú-Bihar	6,212	551	89	Debrecen (211,823)
Heves	3,637	341	94	Eger (65,156)
Komárom	2,250	321	143	Tatabánya (76,465)
Nógrád	2,544	233	92	Salgótarján (49,424)
Pest	6,394	985	154	Budapest* (2,075,990)
Somogy	6,036	353	58	Kaposvár (73,990)
Szabolcs-Szatmár	5,938	584	98	Nyíregyháza (116,782)
Szolnok	5,608	436	78	Szolnok (80,461)
Tolna	3,704	266	72	Szekszárd (38,364)
Vas	3,337	280	84	Szombathely (86,013)
Veszprém	4,689	388	83	Veszprém (64,071)
Zala	3,784	313	83	Zalaegerszeg (61,456)
Capital City				
Budapest*	525	2,076	3,954	—
Total	93,036	10,640	114	—

* Budapest has separate County status. The area and population of the city are not included in the larger County (Pest) which it administers.

HUNGARY

Statistical Survey

BIRTHS, MARRIAGES AND DEATHS

	Registered live births		Registered marriages		Registered deaths	
	Number	Rate (per 1,000)	Number	Rate (per 1,000)	Number	Rate (per 1,000)
1978	168,160	15.8	92,438	8.7	140,121	13.1
1979	160,364	15.0	87,172	8.1	136,829	12.8
1980	148,673	13.9	80,331	7.5	145,355	13.6
1981	142,890	13.3	77,131	7.2	144,757	13.5
1982	133,559	12.5	75,550	7.1	144,318	13.5
1983	127,258	11.9	75,969	7.1	148,643	13.9
1984	125,359	11.8	74,951	7.0	146,709	13.8
1985	130,200	12.2	73,238	6.9	147,614	13.9

ECONOMICALLY ACTIVE POPULATION*
('000 persons at January each year)

	1984	1985	1986
Agriculture and forestry	1,072.0	1,035.1	986.1
Manufacturing, mining, electricity and water	1,622.1	1,617.7	1,615.2
Construction	363.2	356.4	347.5
Commerce	503.8	508.8	508.8
Transport and communications	397.0	396.1	400.5
Services (incl. gas and sanitary services)	981.9	998.8	1,034.4
Total	**4,940.0**	**4,912.9**	**4,892.5**

* Excluding persons seeking work for the first time.

Agriculture

PRINCIPAL CROPS ('000 metric tons)

	1983	1984	1985
Wheat	5,985	7,392	6,578
Rice (paddy)	47	33	38
Barley	1,013	1,220	1,046
Maize	6,426	6,686	6,818
Rye	138	193	166
Oats	124	156	133
Potatoes	1,234	1,551	1,378
Pulses*	154	225	211
Sunflower seed*	592	600	672
Rapeseed*	93	92	85
Sugar beet	3,783	4,360	4,073
Grapes	979	800	466
Apples*	1,141	1,088	n.a.
Tobacco (leaves)*	21	20	19

* Source: FAO, *Production Yearbook*.

LIVESTOCK (at December each year)

	1983	1984	1985
Cattle	1,907,000	1,901,000	1,766,000
Pigs	9,844,000	9,237,000	8,280,000
Sheep	2,977,000	2,832,000	2,465,000
Horses	110,770	101,559	97,856
Goats	15,754	n.a.	n.a.
Chickens	59,155,000	57,756,000	56,686,000
Ducks	2,073,000	1,938,000	1,946,000
Geese	1,002,000	1,150,000	1,402,000
Turkeys	1,046,000	1,202,000	1,536,000
Bee colonies	385,273	n.a.	n.a.

LIVESTOCK PRODUCTS (metric tons)

	1983	1984	1985
Beef and veal	127,400	131,800	145,500
Mutton and lamb	7,000	8,100	8,800
Pig meat	1,049,300	1,123,500	1,011,100
Poultry meat	402,300	402,500	402,000
Edible offal	49,000	52,300	49,000
Edible pig fat	357,500	384,400	346,000
Cows' milk	2,806,544	2,797,480	2,710,033
Sheep's milk	8,009	8,536	7,960
Goats' milk	2,903	2,699	2,995
Butter*	32,729	32,482	31,110
Cheese:			
from cows' milk*	33,289	34,616	35,693
from other milk*	898	1,568	1,169
Dried milk	43,786	40,748	32,747
Hen eggs	247,092	240,594	235,090
Honey	15,619	14,048	15,388
Wool:			
greasy	12,720	12,214	11,118
clean†	5,364	5,107	5,100
Cattle hides	14,026	14,338	15,858
Pig skins	13,185	13,494	15,451

* Factory production only, i.e. butter and cheese produced at milk plants, excluding farm production.
† Source: FAO, *Production Yearbook*.

Forestry

ROUNDWOOD REMOVALS ('000 cu metres)

	1983	1984	1985
Industrial wood	3,661	3,755	3,782
Fuel wood	2,771	2,503	2,503
Total	6,432	6,258	6,285

SAWNWOOD PRODUCTION ('000 cu metres)

	1983	1984	1985
Coniferous (soft wood)	323	394	352
Broadleaved (hard wood)	387	332	327
Total	710	726	719

Fishing

(metric tons, live weight)

	1983	1984	1985
Total catch	43,857	38,976	36,927

Mining

	1983	1984	1985
Hard coal ('000 metric tons)	2,827	2,573	2,639
Brown coal ('000 metric tons)	14,406	14,448	14,016
Lignite ('000 metric tons)	7,980	8,026	7,387
Crude petroleum ('000 metric tons)	2,004	2,012	2,012
Iron ore:			
gross weight ('000 metric tons)	441	383	311
metal content ('000 metric tons)	96	82	68
Bauxite ('000 metric tons)	2,917	2,994	2,815
Natural gas (million cu metres)	6,510	6,911	7,456

Industry

SELECTED PRODUCTS

		1983	1984	1985
Pig iron	'000 metric tons	2,047	2,097	2,095
Crude steel	'000 metric tons	3,616	3,750	3,646
Rolled steel	'000 metric tons	2,815	2,953	2,863
Aluminium	'000 metric tons	74.0	74.2	73.9
Cement	'000 metric tons	4,243	4,145	3,678
Nitrogenous fertilizers*	'000 metric tons	684.7	674.8	685.3
Phosphatic fertilizers†	'000 metric tons	285.4	285.8	253.4
Refined sugar	'000 metric tons	476.8	406.8	483.2
Buses and lorries	number	12,376	13,241	13,990
Cotton fabrics	'000 sq metres	306,859	302,934	309,715
Leather footwear	'000 pairs	43,627	44,569	45,169
Electric power	million kWh	25,713	26,239	26,725
Woollen cloth	'000 sq metres	37,310	38,554	36,100
Television receivers	'000	363	370	407

* Production in terms of nitrogen.
† Production in terms of phosphoric acid.

Finance

CURRENCY AND EXCHANGE RATES

Monetary Units
100 fillér = 1 forint.

Denominations
Coins: 10, 20 and 50 fillér; 1, 2, 5, 10 and 20 forint.
Notes: 10, 20, 50, 100, 500 and 1,000 forint.

Sterling and Dollar Equivalents (30 September 1986)
£1 sterling = 67.69 forint;
US $1 = 46.78 forint;
1,000 forint = £14.77 = $21.38.

Average Exchange Rate (forint per US dollar)
1983 42.67
1984 48.04
1985 50.12

NATIONAL ACCOUNTS

Net Material Product* ('000 million forint at current prices)

Activities of the Material Sphere	1983	1984	1985
Industry†	276.9	301.9	329.7
Construction	77.6	84.5	86.2
Agriculture and forestry	97.8	105.6	100.3
Transport and communications	57.8	58.8	60.6
Wholesale and retail trade	81.3	93.0	101.1
Other material activities	8.9	10.8	12.8
Taxes on commodities (net) and price differences	104.6	114.5	114.1
Non-material services purchases by material sphere	33.4	35.0	37.5
Total	738.1	804.1	842.3

* Defined as the total net value of goods and 'productive' services, including turnover taxes, produced by the economy. This excludes economic activities not contributing directly to material production, such as public administration, defence and personal and professional services.
† Manufacturing, mining, electricity and gas.

BALANCE OF PAYMENTS (US $ million)

	1983	1984	1985
Merchandise exports f.o.b.	8,881	8,836	8,935
Merchandise imports f.o.b.	−8,453	−8,024	−8,324
Trade balance	427	812	610
Exports of services	1,409	1,619	1,472
Imports of services	−1,859	−2,228	−2,203
Balance on goods and services	−23	203	−121
Unrequited transfers (net)	56	66	69
Current balance	33	269	−52
Long-term capital (net)	83	856	1,709
Short-term capital (net)	337	−942	−488
Net errors and omissions	99	14	28
Total (net monetary movements)	552	197	1,198
Valuation changes (net)	−99	131	−121
Changes in reserves	453	328	1,077

Source: IMF, *International Financial Statistics*.

STATE BUDGET ('000 million forint)

Revenue	1983	1984	1985
Payments made by enterprises (co-operatives)	289.6 ⎱	294.9	286.7
Payments made by agricultural co-operatives	16.5 ⎰		
Consumers' turnover tax	82.7	87.3	92.2
Payments made by the population	14.2	16.8	22.0
Social security payments	86.7	120.2	135.0
Other receipts	54.0	53.7	57.3
Total revenue	543.7	572.9	593.5

Expenditure	1983	1984	1985
Investment	57.3	58.9	61.8
Industrial enterprises (co-operatives)	86.2 ⎱	93.2	102.7
Agricultural co-operatives	9.7 ⎰		
Supplement to consumers' prices	66.5	53.5	50.2
Budgetary institutions	172.4	183.8	206.9
Health and social welfare	28.6	31.4	35.0
Culture	51.1	55.8	62.8
Defence	21.9	22.7	23.8
Legal and security order	13.7	14.7	16.5
Administration	6.8	7.4	8.7
Economic tasks	38.1	40.9	48.9
Others	12.2	10.9	11.2
Social security	107.2	120.0	131.5
Others	50.5	67.2	56.2
Total expenditure	549.8	576.6	609.3

External Trade

PRINCIPAL COMMODITIES (distribution by SITC, million forint)

Imports c.i.f.	1983	1984	1985
Food and live animals	22,496.3	24,460.1	24,017.4
Coffee, tea, cocoa and spices	4,092.3	6,307.9	6,759.9
Animal feeding-stuff (excl. cereals)	11,759.5	11,455.2	9,244.0
Crude materials (inedible) except fuels	25,766.0	28,873.5	28,396.2
Cork and wood	3,843.5	4,913.3	5,349.0
Textile fibres and waste	6,654.5	7,308.1	7,362.3
Mineral fuels, lubricants, etc.	83,386.0	87,896.3	90,365.7
Coal, coke and briquettes	6,944.1	7,198.6	14,410.0
Petroleum, petroleum products, etc.	56,837.7	60,572.6	51,728.4
Gas (natural and manufactured)	12,167.9	11,985.9	14,494.2
Chemicals and related products	48,118.9	53,591.2	54,921.4
Organic chemicals	7,868.0	8,767.0	9,113.4
Inorganic chemicals	5,775.4	7,006.3	8,580.0
Artificial resins and plastic materials, etc.	7,684.5	8,463.0	8,286.0
Basic manufactures	59,689.4	65,251.8	67,580.0
Paper, paperboard and manufactures	7,015.1	6,635.6	6,763.9
Textile yarn, fabrics, etc.	10,590.3	13,015.2	12,662.4
Iron and steel	12,301.5	12,895.1	13,772.0
Non-ferrous metals	11,290.4	12,107.8	11,170.7
Other metal manufactures	6,103.5	5,785.1	6,535.7
Machinery and transport equipment	99,260.9	101,710.1	112,352.8
Machinery specialized for particular industries	24,057.5	26,244.7	30,513.1
Metalworking machinery	5,292.1	5,499.8	5,738.5
Road vehicles and parts (excl. tyres, engines and electrical parts)	22,305.4	22,980.2	25,520.3
Miscellaneous manufactured articles	19,558.9	21,847.1	24,938.1
Total (incl. others)	364,963.1	390,511.2	410,127.5

Exports f.o.b.	1983	1984	1985
Food and live animals	70,162.9	73,704.7	71,354.9
Live animals	11,553.4	10,394.6	8,907.7
Meat and meat preparations	24,970.4	27,229.6	23,586.6
Cereals and cereal preparations	10,097.0	11,354.2	15,497.6
Vegetables and fruit	13,856.4	13,805.6	1,362.0
Beverages and tobacco	9,279.2	10,046.3	10,127.6
Crude materials (inedible) except fuels	14,965.7	16,311.8	17,215.7
Mineral fuels, lubricants, etc.	34,578.3	35,732.2	21,692.6
Petroleum, petroleum products, etc.	33,152.5	34,635.7	19,731.1
Chemicals and related products	37,887.3	45,154.3	48,876.0
Organic chemicals	8,426.4	9,606.3	11,584.8
Medicinal and pharmaceutical products	13,925.1	15,597.7	17,341.4
Basic manufactures	46,745.3	54,442.5	52,195.1
Textile yarn, fabrics, etc.	9,385.6	10,837.6	10,534.1
Iron and steel	11,076.8	14,732.1	14,478.6
Non-ferrous metals	7,301.2	9,421.0	7,496.2
Machinery and transport equipment	113,689.5	124,614.7	142,094.5
Machinery specialized for particular industries	25,944.7	26,557.9	29,855.8
Telecommunications and sound equipment	15,429.3	16,669.7	20,273.0
Other electrical machinery, apparatus, etc.	14,523.0	16,932.6	17,334.5
Road vehicles and parts (excl. tyres, engines and electrical parts)	32,642.2	37,267.2	42,311.2
Miscellaneous manufactured articles	36,858.9	41,528.2	47,849.2
Clothing and accessories (excl. footwear)	11,753.1	13,321.4	14,799.6
Footwear	6,174.9	6,510.5	7,196.3
Professional, scientific and controlling instruments and apparatus	8,265.9	9,817.3	12,414.4
Total (incl. others)	374,107.9	413,956.9	424,600.6

HUNGARY

PRINCIPAL TRADING PARTNERS* (million forint)

Imports c.i.f.	1983	1984	1985
Austria	17,162.0	19,940.2	26,313.6
Belgium and Luxembourg	3,816.1	3,719.6	4,391.5
Brazil	10,034.3	12,077.6	6,854.8
Bulgaria	5,770.9	5,558.0	6,080.9
China, People's Republic	1,295.3	2,214.2	3,524.3
Czechoslovakia	18,711.0	19,600.2	20,311.8
Finland	1,985.5	2,579.8	2,542.8
France	6,857.2	6,750.8	7,555.9
German Democratic Republic	24,399.9	24,862.9	26,550.2
Germany, Federal Republic	37,271.1	41,766.9	46,830.0
Iran	9,109.2	8,461.3	2,978.6
Italy	8,471.2	9,474.9	11,466.6
Japan	4,282.5	4,216.9	6,887.7
Libya	15,535.0	10,457.2	2,430.7
Netherlands	4,571.4	5,026.0	5,329.7
Poland	15,948.3	17,332.9	19,209.1
Romania	6,673.5	6,895.9	7,185.8
Sweden	3,226.4	3,725.4	4,364.9
Switzerland and Liechtenstein	7,888.4	7,823.4	8,098.9
USSR	104,186.4	113,655.2	123,186.1
United Kingdom	7,792.2	7,072.5	7,857.6
USA	9,584.3	9,599.8	12,292.1
Yugoslavia	13,284.8	15,260.4	14,470.5
Total (incl. others)	364,963.1	390,511.2	410,127.5

Exports f.o.b.	1983	1984	1985
Algeria	5,919.8	6,991.7	5,372.7
Austria	16,315.6	21,883.3	22,854.6
Bulgaria	6,650.7	5,995.3	6,080.2
China, People's Republic	1,974.3	3,198.9	5,608.4
Cuba	2,744.3	3,681.2	3,807.0
Czechoslovakia	18,036.0	21,489.3	24,039.5
Egypt	1,608.3	2,572.7	3,858.4
Finland	1,999.6	1,940.4	2,269.5
France	5,774.1	6,905.2	5,714.2
German Democratic Republic	21,949.1	24,500.7	25,805.2
Germany, Federal Republic	27,544.0	30,704.7	33,186.6
Greece	1,729.4	1,819.3	2,126.8
Iran	7,433.6	4,268.5	5,342.4
Iraq	7,652.0	5,752.3	5,112.6
Italy	12,428.3	13,535.1	12,496.2
Libya	4,407.5	4,157.0	4,551.8
Netherlands	3,624.5	4,528.0	3,883.4
Nigeria	1,618.5	2,001.5	3,190.6
Poland	14,754.3	17,564.7	16,289.2
Romania	4,827.5	6,039.0	7,248.8
Sweden	2,397.4	2,964.0	3,127.5
Switzerland and Liechtenstein	5,524.1	9,268.9	8,507.4
Turkey	1,667.9	2,113.0	2,472.0
USSR	118,104.1	124,664.1	142,749.1
United Kingdom	4,171.6	6,182.6	6,154.9
USA	7,608.6	11,071.8	9,830.7
Yugoslavia	12,807.1	14,218.6	15,166.4
Total (incl. others)	374,107.9	413,956.9	424,600.6

* Imports by country of production; exports by country of last consignment.

Transport

RAILWAYS (traffic)

	1983	1984	1985
Passengers carried (million)	337.3	338.5	334.4
Passenger-kilometres (million)	12,026	12,198	12,130
Net ton-kilometres (million)	23,076	22,844	22,306

ROAD TRAFFIC (motor vehicles in use at 31 December)

	1983	1984	1985
Passenger cars	1,258,496	1,344,101	1,435,937
Goods vehicles	144,509	157,797	167,136
Buses	24,387	24,946	24,854
Motor cycles*	422,012	393,759	395,622

* Excluding mopeds and motor cycles with an engine capacity of less than 125 c.c.

CIVIL AVIATION (traffic)

	1983	1984	1985
Kilometres flown	20,119,400	20,994,400	22,287,100
Passengers carried	999,268	1,072,895	1,159,773
Passenger-km ('000)	1,180,941	1,238,833	1,332,984
Cargo carried: metric tons	13,472	12,944	15,946
Cargo ton-km	22,933,000	21,835,000	25,905,000

INLAND WATERWAYS (traffic)

	1983	1984	1985
Freight carried ('000 metric tons)	3,229	3,251	3,300
Freight ton-km (million)	1,737	1,805	1,623

Tourism

('000 arrivals)

	1983	1984	1985
Foreign tourists	6,764	8,731	9,724
Foreign visitors in transit	3,699	4,698	5,402
Total	10,463	13,429	15,126

TOURISTS BY COUNTRY OF ORIGIN
(including visitors in transit)

	1983	1984	1985
Austria	1,604.9	1,948.9	2,024.3
Bulgaria	308.5	374.9	462.2
Czechoslovakia	3,096.7	4,503.3	5,449.2
German Democratic Republic	1,032.6	1,262.7	1,314.4
Germany, Federal Republic	703.3	816.1	898.8
Poland	1,431.1	1,817.0	1,892.0
Romania	482.7	557.7	623.5
USSR	426.3	402.2	451.2
Yugoslavia	732.3	979.0	1,171.0
Total (incl. others)	10,462.5	13,428.8	15,126.5

Communications Media

	1983	1984	1985
Television receivers*	373	372	385
Radio receivers†	534	545	560
Books titles (including translations)	8,241	9,128	8,015
Daily newspapers	29	29	29
Average daily circulation	2,937,000	3,000,407	2,992,894

* Estimated number of television receivers per 1,000 inhabitants.
† Estimated number of radio receivers per 1,000 inhabitants.
Telephone subscribers (1985): 499,000.

Education

(1985/86)

	Institutions	Teachers	Students
Nursery	4,823	33,548	424,678
Primary	3,546	88,066	1,297,818
Secondary	561	17,899	320,708
Higher	58	14,850	99,344

Directory

The Constitution

A new constitution was introduced on 18 August 1949, and the Hungarian People's Republic was established two days later. The Constitution was amended in April 1972 and December 1983. The following is a summary of its main provisions:

NATIONAL STATUS

Hungary is a People's Republic, a state of workers and working peasants, in which all power belongs to the working people and is exercised through elected representatives. The Republic defends the power and liberty of the working people and the independence of the country and opposes the exploitation of man.

SOCIAL STRUCTURE

The bulk of the means of production is owned by the State, by public bodies or by co-operative organizations, and state and co-operative ownership enjoy equal status. Means of production may also be privately owned. The national economy is directed by the state power of the people. The economic life of the Republic is determined by a state national economic plan in which the State strives to expand the forces of production, increase national wealth, raise material and cultural standards and strengthen the defences of the country. All natural resources, means of communication, banks, mines and major industrial plants are the property of the State. Foreign trade is carried out both by state trading companies and by companies and enterprises with export-import rights.

The Republic recognizes and guarantees the right of the working peasants to the land and regards it as its duty to assist the socialist development of agriculture. The State supports every genuine co-operative movement of the workers that is directed against exploitation. The Constitution recognizes and protects all property acquired by labour and guarantees the right of inheritance. Private enterprise is not allowed to run counter to the public interest.

Labour is the base of the social order and every able-bodied citizen has the right and the duty to work to the best of his ability. By their labour, the workers serve the cause of socialist construction.

GOVERNMENT

National Assembly

The highest organ of state authority in the Hungarian People's Republic is the National Assembly which exercises all the rights deriving from the sovereignty of the people and determines the organization, direction and conditions of government. The National Assembly enacts laws, determines the state budget, decides the national economic plan, elects the Presidential Council and the Council of Ministers, directs the activities of ministries, decides upon declaring war and concluding peace and exercises the prerogative of amnesty.

The National Assembly is elected for a term of five years and members enjoy immunity from arrest and prosecution without parliamentary consent. It meets at least twice a year and is convened by the Presidential Council or by a written demand of one-third of its members. It elects a President, two Deputy Presidents and six recorders from among its own members, and it lays down its own rules of procedure and agenda. As a general rule, the sessions of the National Assembly are held in public.

The National Assembly has the right of legislation which can be initiated by the Presidential Council, the Council of Ministers or any member of the National Assembly. Decisions are valid only if at least half of the members are present, and they require a simple majority. Constitutional changes require a two-thirds majority. Acts of the National Assembly are signed by the President and the Secretary of the Presidential Council. The National Assembly may set up committees.

The National Assembly may pronounce its dissolution before the expiration of its term, and in the event of an emergency may prolong its mandate or may be reconvened after dissolution. A new National Assembly must be elected within three months of dissolution and convened within one month of polling day. At its first sitting the National Assembly elects from among its members the Presidential Council, consisting of a President, two Vice-Presidents, a Secretary and 17 members. The Chairman of the Council of Ministers, its Deputy Chairmen and its members are ineligible for election to the Presidential Council.

Members of the National Assembly are elected on the basis of universal, equal and direct suffrage by secret ballot, and they are accountable to their constituents, who may recall them. All citizens

HUNGARY

of eighteen years and over have the right to vote, with the exception of those who are unsound of mind, and those who are deprived of their civil rights by a court of law.

Presidential Council

The Presidential Council may issue the writ for a general election, convene the National Assembly, initiate legislation, hold plebiscites, direct local government, conclude international treaties, appoint diplomatic representatives, ratify international treaties, appoint higher civil servants and officers of the armed forces, award orders and titles, and exercise the prerogative of mercy. It may annul or modify by-laws, dissolve local organs of government and, when the National Assembly is not in session, may enact laws. The Presidential Council is responsible to the National Assembly, which can recall it.

Council of Ministers

The highest organ of state administration is the Council of Ministers, responsible to the National Assembly and consisting of a Chairman, Deputy Chairmen, Ministers of State and other Ministers who are elected by the National Assembly on the recommendation of the Presidential Council. The Council of Ministers directs the work of the ministries (listed in a special enactment) and ensures the enforcement of laws and the fulfilment of economic plans; it may issue decrees and annul or modify measures taken by any central or local organ of government.

Local Administration

The local organs of state power are the county, town, borough and town precinct councils, whose members are elected for a term of five years by the voters in each area. Local councils direct economic, social and cultural activities in their area, prepare local economic plans and budgets and supervises their fulfilment, enforce laws, supervise subordinate organs, maintain public order, protect public property and individual rights, direct local economic enterprises and support co-operatives. They may issue regulations and annul or modify those of subordinate councils. Local Councils are administered by an Executive Committee elected by and responsible to them.

JUDICATURE

Justice is administered by the Supreme Court of the Hungarian People's Republic, county and district courts. The Supreme Court exercises the right of supervising in principle the judicial activities and practice of all other courts.

All judicial offices are filled by election; Supreme Court, county and district court judges are all elected for an indefinite period; the President of the Supreme Court is elected by the National Assembly. All court hearings are public unless otherwise prescribed by law, and those accused are guaranteed the right of defence. An accused person must be considered innocent until proved guilty.

Public Prosecutor

The function of the Chief Public Prosecutor is to watch over the observance of the law. He is elected for a period of five years by the National Assembly, to whom he is responsible. The organization of public prosecution is under the control of the Chief Public Prosecutor, who appoints the public prosecutors.

RIGHTS AND DUTIES OF CITIZENS

The Hungarian People's Republic guarantees for its citizens the right to work and to remuneration, the right of rest and recreation, the right to care in old age, sickness or disability, the right to education, and equality before the law; women enjoy equal rights with men. Discrimination on grounds of sex, religion or nationality is a punishable offence. The State also ensures freedom of conscience, religious worship, speech, the Press and assembly. The right of workers to organize themselves is stressed in order to promote democracy, socialist construction, cultural and educational development and international solidarity. The freedom of the individual, and the privacy of the home and of correspondence are inviolable. Freedom for creative work in the sciences and the arts is now guaranteed by the Constitution under the amendments adopted in 1972.

The basic freedoms of all workers are guaranteed and foreign citizens enjoy the right of asylum.

It is the fundamental duty of all citizens to defend the property of the people, consolidate social assets, increase economic strength, raise the living standards and cultural levels of the workers, and strengthen the people's democratic system. Military service and the defence of their country are the duties of all citizens.

AMENDMENTS

Amendments to the Constitution were approved by the National Assembly in December 1983. These included the setting up of an independent Council for Constitutional Law to examine legislation; the inclusion of the President of the Central People's Control Commission in the Council of Ministers; and the abolition of administrative districts within the counties, coupled with an increase in the authority of local town councils.

Amendments to the electoral law, approved at the same session, provided for all seats in the National Assembly and local councils to be contested in future elections.

The Government

(February 1987)

PRESIDENTIAL COUNCIL

President: PÁL LOSONCZI.

Vice-Presidents: SÁNDOR GÁSPÁR, Dr REZSŐ TRAUTMANN.

Secretary: IMRE KATONA.

Members: ERZSÉBET BÁNATI, SÁNDOR BARCS, Dr TIBOR BARTHA, IMRE BIRÓ, REZSŐ BOGNAR, MÁRIA DUSCHEK, JÁNOS ELEKI, ISTVÁN GAJDOCSI, ERZSÉBET HORVÁTH, JÁNOS KÁDÁR, GYULA KÁLLAI, TEREZ KREMER, MARIN MANDITY, KÁROLY NÉMETH, GÉZA SZALAI, JÁNOS SZENTAGOTHAY, Dr MIKLÓS VIDA.

COUNCIL OF MINISTERS

Chairman: GYÖRGY LÁZÁR.

Deputies of the Chairman: FRIGYES BERECZ, Dr JUDIT CSEHÁK, LAJOS CZINEGE, JÓZSEF MARJAI, Dr LÁSZLÓ MARÓTHY.

Minister of Foreign Affairs: Dr PÉTER VÁRKONYI.

Minister of the Interior: DR JÁNOS KAMARA.

Minister of Defence: FERENC KARPATI.

Minister of Agriculture and Food: JENŐ VÁNCSA.

Minister of Finance: PETER MEDGYESSY.

Minister of Health: Dr LÁSZLÓ MEDVE.

Minister of Culture and National Education: BÉLA KÖPECZI.

Minister of Internal Trade: Dr ZOLTÁN JUHÁR.

Minister of Industry: Dr LÁSZLÓ KAPOLYI.

Minister of Foreign Trade: PÉTER VERESS.

Minister of Construction and Town Planning: LÁSZLÓ SOMOGYI.

Minister of Justice: Dr IMRE MARKÓJA.

Minister of Communications: LAJOS URBÁN.

President of the National Planning Office: Dr LÁSZLÓ MARÓTHY.

President of the Central People's Control Commission: LÁSZLÓ BÁLLAI.

MINISTRIES

Council of Ministers (Secretariat): 1055 Budapest, Kossuth Lajos tér 1/3; tel. 120-600; telex 22-5541.

Ministry of Agriculture and Food: 1055 Budapest, Kossuth Lajos tér 11; tel. 113-000; telex 22-5445.

Ministry of Communications: 1077 Budapest, Dob u. 75/81; tel. 220-220; telex 22-5729.

Ministry of Construction and Town Planning: 1054 Budapest, Beloiannisz u. 2/4; tel. 532-200; telex 22-4204.

Ministry of Culture and National Education: 1055 Budapest, Szalay u. 10/14; tel. 530-600; telex 22-5935.

Ministry of Defence: 1055 Budapest, Pálffy György u. 7/11; tel. 322-500; telex 22-5424.

Ministry of Finance: 1051 Budapest, József Nádor tér 2/4; tel. 182-066.

Ministry of Foreign Affairs: 1027 Budapest, Bem rkp. 47; tel. 350-100; telex 22-5571.

Ministry of Foreign Trade: 1055 Budapest, Honvéd u. 13/15; tel. 530-000; telex 22-5578.

Ministry of Health: 1051 Budapest, Arany János u. 6/8; tel. 323-100; telex 22-4337.

Ministry of Industry: 1024 Budapest, Mártírok u. 85; tel. 326-570; telex 22-5376.

HUNGARY

Ministry of the Interior: 1051 Budapest, József Attila u. 2/4; tel. 121-710; telex 22-5216.

Ministry of Internal Trade: 1051 Budapest, Vigadó u. 6; tel. 185-044; telex 22-5182.

Ministry of Justice: 1055 Budapest, Szalay u. 16; tel. 325-330.

National Planning Office: 1051 Budapest, Roosevelt tér 7/8; tel. 110-200; telex 22-4993.

Central People's Control Commission: 1052 Budapest, Apáczai Csere János u. 10; tel. 319-170; telex 22-4308.

POLITICAL COMMITTEE (POLITBURO) OF THE HUNGARIAN SOCIALIST WORKERS' PARTY

János Kádár (General Secretary), Károly Németh (Deputy General Secretary), György Aczél, Sándor Gáspár, Károly Grósz, Csaba Hámori, Ferenc Havasi, György Lázár, Pál Losonczi, Dr László Maróthy, Miklós Óvári, István Sarlós, István Szabó.

Legislature

ORSZÁGGYÜLÉS
(National Assembly)

The National Assembly consists of a single chamber of 387 members, elected every five years; 352 members are elected on a territorial basis and the 35 additional members are elected unopposed on a national list which includes leading politicians, trade unionists, clergymen and prominent members of the national minority groups. The national list was introduced at the most recent elections, held on 8 June 1985, when all territorial constituencies were contested. About 7.7m. people were entitled to vote and take part in the nomination meetings; 873 candidates were put forward for the 352 territorial constituencies—795 proposed by the Patriotic People's Front and 78 direct from the floor of the nomination meetings, 43 of whom were elected. There were more than two candidates in 78 constituencies. A total of 244 members were elected for the first time. On 22 June 1985 a second round of voting was held in over 40 constituencies where no candidate had obtained the requisite absolute majority, this time the candidate receiving the largest number of votes being elected. Turn-out was 93.9% at the first round and 83% at the second round of voting.

President of the National Assembly: István Sarlós.

Deputy Presidents: János Péter, Ilona Cservenka.

Political Organizations

In Hungary there is no parliamentary opposition. Opposition parties have been either absorbed in the Patriotic People's Front or dissolved.

Magyar Szocialista Munkáspárt (Hungarian Socialist Workers' Party—HSWP): 1054 Budapest, Széchenyi rkp. 19; f. 1956 to replace the Workers' Party (merger of the Communist and Social Democratic Parties); 871,000 mems (March 1985); Gen. Sec. of Central Committee János Kádár; Deputy Gen. Sec. Károly Németh; Mems of Secretariat: János Berecz, Ferenc Havasi, István Horváth, Miklós Óvári, Lénárd Pál, Mátyás Szürös.

Hazafias Népfront (Patriotic People's Front): 1056 Budapest, Belgrád rkp. 24; f. 1954; socio-political mass movement formed as a successor to the Hungarian Independent People's Front; composed of Party and non-Party people, and represents mass organizations such as trade unions, peasants, youth movements, the churches and national minorities; compiles the lists of candidates, on the basis of nominations from public meetings, for national and local elections; 3,000 committees with 85,000 elected mems; Pres. Gyula Kállai; Sec.-Gen. Imre Pozsgay.

Magyar Kommunista Ifjúsági Szövetség—KISZ (Communist Youth Union of Hungary): 1388 Budapest, Kun Béla rkp. 37–38; tel. 403-940; telex 22-4244; f. 1957 to replace the Union of Working Youth—DISZ; 926,000 mems (1986); First Sec. of Central Committee Csaba Hámori.

Magyar Nők Országos Tanácsa—MNOT (National Council of Hungarian Women): 1062 Budapest, Népköztársaság u. 124; tel. 317-529; f. 1957 to replace Hungarian Democratic Women's Union; 32,000 stewards, 160,000 activists; Pres. Mária Duschek.

Diplomatic Representation

EMBASSIES IN HUNGARY

Afghanistan: 1062 Budapest, Lendvay u. 23; tel. 126-896; Ambassador: Sarwar Mangal.

Albania: Budapest VI, Munkácsy Mihály u. 6; tel. 229-278; Chargé d'affaires: Shpetim Çaushi.

Algeria: Budapest I, Disz tér 6; tel. 360-550; telex 22-6916; Ambassador: Mostepha Boutaieb.

Argentina: 1068 Budapest, Rippl-Rónai u. 1; tel. 228-467; telex 22-4128; Ambassador: (vacant).

Australia: 1052 Budapest, Fórum Hotel, Apáczai-Csere János u. 12–14; tel. 188-100; telex 22-7708; Ambassador: Oliver Cordell.

Austria: Budapest VI, Benczúr u. 16; tel. 229-467; telex 22-4447; Ambassador: Dr Arthur Agster.

Belgium: Budapest I, Donáti u. 34; tel. 153-099; telex 22-4664; Ambassador: Maurice Vaisière.

Bolivia: Budapest II, Mártírok u. 43–45; tel. 163-019; Chargé d'affaires: Dr Mario Paz-Zamora.

Brazil: Budapest XI, Somlói u. 3; tel. 666-992; telex 22-5795; Ambassador: Celso Diniz.

Bulgaria: Budapest V, Népköztársaság u. 115; tel. 220-836; telex 22-5441; Ambassador: Venelin Todorov.

Canada: 1021 Budapest, Budakeszi u. 32; tel. 387-312; telex 22-4588; Ambassador: Robert Elliott.

China, People's Republic: Budapest VI, Benczúr u. 17; tel. 224-872; Ambassador: Zu Ankang.

Colombia: 1024 Budapest, Mártírok u. 43–45; tel. 352-534; telex 22-6012; Ambassador: Enrique Parejo González.

Cuba: Budapest VI, Benczúr u. 26; tel. 214-039; telex 22-4388; Ambassador: Euclides Vázquez Candela.

Czechoslovakia: Budapest XIV, Népstadion u. 22; tel. 636-600; telex 22-4744; Ambassador: Ondrej Durej.

Denmark: 1023 Budapest, Vérhalom u. 12–16b; tel. 152-066; telex 22-4137; Ambassador: Hans Kuhne.

Egypt: Budapest I, Bérc u. 16; tel. 668-060; telex 22-5184; Ambassador: (vacant).

Finland: Budapest II, Vérhalom u. 12–16b; tel. 150-600; telex 22-4710; Ambassador: Arto Mansala.

France: Budapest VI, Lendvay u. 27; tel. 128-268; telex 22-5143; Ambassador: Christiane Malitchenko.

German Democratic Republic: 1143 Budapest, Népstadion u. 101–103; tel. 635-275; telex 22-5954; Ambassador: Karl-Heinz Lugenheim.

Germany, Federal Republic: Budapest XIV, Izsó u. 5; tel. 224-204; telex 22-5951; Ambassador: Dr Ernst-Friedrich Jung.

Greece: Budapest VI, Szegfű u. 3; tel. 228-004; telex 22-4113; Ambassador: Pantelis Economou.

India: 1025 Budapest, Buzavirág u. 14; tel. 153-243; telex 22-6374; Ambassador: Satinder Kumar Lambah.

Indonesia: Budapest VI, Gorkij fasor 26; tel. 428-508; telex 22-5263; Ambassador: Kasman Pahala Haodjahan Siahaan.

Iran: Budapest VI, Délibáb u. 29; tel. 225-038; telex 22-4129; Ambassador: (vacant).

Iraq: Budapest XIV, Szántó Béla u. 13; tel. 226-418; telex 22-6058; Ambassador: Dr Arif Eisa al-Rawi.

Italy: Budapest XIV, Népstadion u. 95; tel. 225-077; telex 22-5294; Ambassador: Emilio Paolo Bassi.

Japan: Budapest II, Rómer Flóris u. 58; tel. 150-043; telex 22-5048; Ambassador: Ryozo Mogi.

Kampuchea: Budapest XII, Rath György u. 48; tel. 151-878; Ambassador: Chim Nguon.

Korea, Democratic People's Republic: Budapest VI, Benczúr u. 31; tel. 425-174; telex 22-6721; Ambassador: Yi Yong-Kol.

Libya: Budapest XIV, Népstadion u. 111; tel. 226-076; Ambassador: Mohamed Ali Zintani.

Mexico: Budapest II, Budakeszi u. 55/D; tel. 767-906; telex 22-6633; Ambassador: José Caballero Bazán.

Mongolia: Budapest XII, Istenhegyi u. 59–61; tel. 151-412; Ambassador: Dangasurengin Saldan.

Netherlands: Budapest XIV, Abonyi u. 31; tel. 228-432; telex 22-5562; Ambassador: G. W. Baron de Vos van Steenwijk.

Norway: Budapest XII, Határőr u. 35; tel. 665-161; telex 22-5867; Ambassador: Per Naevdal.

HUNGARY

Peru: Budapest II, Mártírok u. 43–45; tel. 150-292; Ambassador: José Pablo Morán Val.

Poland: Budapest VI, Gorkij fasor 16; tel. 228-437; Ambassador: Tadeusz Czechowicz.

Portugal: Budapest II, Mártírok u. 43–45; tel. 155-602; Ambassador: Zozimo de Silva.

Romania: Budapest XIV, Thököly u. 72; tel. 426-944; telex 22-5847; Ambassador: Nicolae Vereş.

Spain: Budapest VI, Eötvös u. 11b; tel. 428-580; telex 22-4130; Ambassador: Francisco Javier Rubio.

Sweden: Budapest XIV, Ajtósi Dürer sor 27/a; tel. 229-880; telex 22-5647; Ambassador: Anders Ragnar Dromberg.

Switzerland: Budapest XIV, Népstadion u. 107; tel. 229-491; Ambassador: Paul Wipfli.

Syria: 1026 Budapest, Harangvirág u. 3; tel. 387-186; telex 22-6605; Ambassador: Abdul Aziz Masharika.

Turkey: Budapest I, Úri u. 45; tel. 161-497; Ambassador: Asaf Inhan.

USSR: Budapest VI, Bajza u. 35; tel. 320-911; Ambassador: Boris Stukalin.

United Kingdom: Budapest V, Harmincad u. 6; tel. 182-888; telex 22-4527; Ambassador: Leonard Appleyard.

USA: Budapest V, Szabadság tér 12; tel. 124-224; telex 22-4222; Ambassador: Mark Palmer.

Uruguay: Budapest II, Vérhalom u. 12–16; tel. 368-333; Ambassador: Dr Gualberto Talamas.

Venezuela: Budapest II, Vérhalom u. 12–16; tel. 353-562; telex 22-6666; Ambassador: Antonio Casas Salvi.

Viet-Nam: Budapest VI, Benczúr u. 18; tel. 429-943; Ambassador: Nguyen Lung.

Yemen, People's Democratic Republic: Budapest II, Budakeszi u. 55/d; tel. 164-259; Ambassador: Mohammed Saed Abdullah Mohsen.

Yugoslavia: Budapest VI, Dózsa György u. 92/b; tel. 420-566; Ambassador: Milovan Zidar.

Judicial System

The system of court procedure in Hungary is based on an Act that was promulgated in 1954 and updated in 1972. The system of jurisdiction is based on the local courts (district courts in Budapest, city courts in other cities), labour courts, county courts, the Metropolitan Court and the Supreme Court. In the legal remedy system of two instances, appeals against the decisions of city and district courts can be lodged with the competent county court and the Metropolitan Court of Budapest respectively. Against the judgment of first instance of the latter, appeal is to be lodged with the Supreme Court. The Chief Public Prosecutor and the President of the Supreme Court have the right to submit a protest on legal grounds against the final judgment of any court.

By virtue of the 1973 Act, effective 1974 and modified in 1979, the procedure in criminal cases is differentiated for criminal offences and for criminal acts. In the first instance, criminal cases are tried, depending on their character, by a professional judge; where justified by the magnitude of the criminal act, by a council composed of three members, a professional judge and two lay assessors, while in major cases the court consists of five members, two professional judges and three lay assessors. In the Supreme Court, second instance cases are tried only by professional judges. The President of the Supreme Court is elected by the National Assembly for a period of five years. Judges are elected by the Presidential Council for an indefinite period. Assessors, in turn, are elected by the local municipal councils.

In the interest of ensuring legality and a uniform application of the Law, the Supreme Court exercises a principled guidance over the jurisdiction of courts. In the Hungarian People's Republic judges are independent and subject only to the Law and other legal regulations.

The Minister of Justice supervises the general activities of courts. The Chief Public Prosecutor is elected by the National Assembly for a period of five years. The Chief Public Prosecutor and the Prosecutor's Office provide for the consistent prosecution of all acts violating or endangering the legal order of society, the safety and independence of the state, and for the protection of citizens.

The Prosecutors of the independent prosecuting organization exert supervision over the legality of investigations and the implementation of punishments, and assist with specific means in ensuring that legal regulations should be observed by state, economic and other organs and citizens, and they support the legality of court procedures and decisions.

President of the Supreme Court: Dr Jenő Szilbereky.

Chief Public Prosecutor: Dr Károly Szijártó.

Religion

Állami Egyházügyi Hivatal (State Office for Church Affairs): 1062 Budapest, Lendvay u. 28; f. 1951; deals with Church-State relations; Chair. Imre Miklós.

CHRISTIANITY

Magyarországi Egyházak Ökuménikus Tanácsa (Ecumenical Council of Churches in Hungary): 1054 Budapest, Szabadság tér 2; tel. 114-862; f. 1943; member churches: Reformed Church, Evangelical Lutheran, Baptist, Methodist, Hungarian Orthodox, Romanian Orthodox and Council of Free Churches; Pres. Bishop Dr Tibor Bartha; Gen. Sec. Rev. Dr Tibor Görög.

The Roman Catholic Church

Hungary comprises three archdioceses, eight dioceses (including one for Catholics of the Byzantine rite) and one territorial abbacy (directly responsible to the Holy See). In 1985 the Church had 6,365,976 adherents in Hungary.

Bishops' Conference: Magyar Püspöki Kar Konferenciája, 6301 Kalocsa, Szabadság tér 1; tel. 155; f. 1969; Pres. László Paskai, Coadjutor-Archbishop of Kalocsa.

Latin Rite

Archbishop of Eger: (vacant), 3301 Eger, Széchenyi u. 1; tel. 13-259.

Archbishop of Esztergom: (vacant), Primate of Hungary, 2500 Esztergom, Berenyi Zsigmond u. 2; tel. 330-511.

Archbishop of Kalocsa: Dr József Ijjas, 6301 Kalocsa, Szabadság tér 1; tel. 155.

Byzantine Rite

Bishop of Hajdudorog: Imre Timkó, 4400 Nyíregyháza, Bethlen u. 5; tel. 17-397; about 250,000 adherents; the Bishop is also Apostolic Administrator of the Apostolic Exarchate of Miskolc, with an estimated 22,800 Catholics of the Byzantine rite (31 December 1984).

Protestant Churches

Evangélikus Egyház (Lutheran Church in Hungary) (Evangelical): 1088 Budapest, Puskin u. 12; tel. 13-86-56; 430,000 mems; Presiding Bishop Dr Zoltán Káldy; Gen. Sec. Dr Agoston Karner.

Magyarországi Baptista Egyház (Baptist Union of Hungary): 1062 Budapest, Aradi u. 48; tel. 322-332; f. 1846; 12,250 mems; Pres. Rev. János Viczián; Sec. Rev. Emil Kiss.

Magyarországi Református Egyház (Reformed Church in Hungary) (Presbyterian): 1146 Budapest, Abonyi u. 21; 2 m. mems (1981); Pres. of Gen. Synod Bishop Dr Tibor Bartha.

Magyarországi Szabadegyházak Tanácsa (Council of Free Churches in Hungary): 1062 Budapest, Aradi u. 48; tel. 310-194; co-operative organization of Baptists, Methodists, Adventists, Evangelical Christians, Pentecostalists, and other smaller denominations; Chair. Dr József Szakács; Gen. Sec. Rev. Oliver Szebeni.

Orthodox Churches

Magyar Orthodox Egyház (Hungarian Orthodox Church): 1052 Budapest, Petőfi tér 2.1.2.; tel. 184-813; Administrator Archpriest Dr Feriz Berki.

Görögkeleti Szerb Egyházmegye (Serbian-Orthodox Diocese): Szentendre; Parochus Dusán Vujicsics.

The Russian (6,000 mems), Bulgarian and Romanian Orthodox Churches are also represented.

JUDAISM

The first synagogue to be built in Hungary since 1945 opened at Siofok in 1986.

Magyar Izraeliták Országos Képviselete (Central Board of Hungarian Jews); **Budapesti Izraelita Hitközség** (Jewish Community of Budapest): 1079 Budapest, Síp u. 12; 80,000 mems;

HUNGARY

Orthodox and Conservative; Pres. Dr András Losonci; Gen. Sec. Ilona Seifert; Chief Rabbi of Budapest Dr Alfréd Schőner.

The Press

The Hungarian Constitution guarantees freedom of the press and freedom of speech, but the press is in fact constrained to promote the ideological aims of the Hungarian Socialist Workers' Party and fundamental criticism of the political system is not permitted. On the other hand, failures in public administration, economic, cultural and other fields, are commonly criticized in editorials and grievances publicized in letters from members of the public. Since 1963 all official institutions so criticized have been legally obliged to investigate the matter promptly.

Conversely, considerable legislation is designed to prevent the abuse of press rights; Article 127 of the penal code penalizes the provoking of hatred of minorities by the press; incitement and libel are similarly dealt with. Since a decree in 1959, persons and institutions victimized by false press reports may claim rectification which a government minister is empowered to enforce.

No organization has the right to exercise censorship. The Government Information Office has nation-wide authority over the press, including the right to grant licences and ensure newsprint distribution, and the task of seeing that all government decrees and decisions are made available to the press. The national news agency, Magyar Távirati Iroda (MTI), handles the bulk of foreign news and has bilateral agreements with the major world agencies.

As in many East European countries most papers are the organs of political parties, trade unions, youth and social organizations. A wide range of specialist periodicals is published by societies, factories, scientific institutions, etc. There is no private ownership of publications but since 1957 independent commercial organizations have received publishing licences.

The high circulation of daily papers enables publishing houses to produce specialized periodicals of a high standard. Moreover, the State gives direct subsidies to certain educational, medical and literary publications, to the religious press and to the four minority language papers. Some 80% of newspapers are sold by subscription.

There are 28 dailies with an average total circulation of 3,008,000 (1984). These include 21 provincial dailies which have a combined daily circulation of about 1,328,000. Budapest dailies circulate nationally. In order of popularity they are: *Népszabadság, Népszava*, the evening *Esti Hirlap* and *Magyar Nemzet*. *Népszabadság*, the most important daily, is the central organ of the Socialist Workers' Party. Otherwise the paper most respected for the quality of its news coverage and commentary is *Magyar Nemzet*.

Weekly newspapers and periodicals number 56; there are 111 fortnightly journals and 490 monthlies. Among the most popular are the illustrated weeklies, which include the satirical *Ludas Matyi*, the women's magazine *Nők Lapja*, the illustrated news journal *Képes Ujság* and the political paper *Szabad Föld*. A news magazine giving a high standard of reporting and political discussion is *Magyarország*. Specialized periodicals include 42 cultural publications, 35 medical journals, 108 scientific papers, 24 agricultural and 16 religious publications. Of this last category *Új Ember, Evangélikus Élet* and *Új Élet* for Catholic, Lutheran and Jewish congregations respectively, are representative.

PRINCIPAL DAILIES

Daily News: 1016 Budapest, Fém u. 5–7; tel. 756-722; telex 22-4371; f. 1967; published by the Hungarian News Agency; in English and German; Editor-in-Chief Tamás Kocsis; circ. 15,000.

Esti Hirlap (Evening Journal): 1085 Budapest, Blaha Lujza tér 1–3; tel. 336-130; telex 22-7040; Editor Gábor Paizs; circ. 200,000.

Magyar Hirlap (Hungarian Journal): 1393 Budapest, POB 305; tel. 222-400; telex 22-4268; f. 1968; Editor-in-Chief Zsolt Bajnok; circ. 55,000.

Magyar Nemzet (Hungarian Nation): 1073 Budapest, Lenin krt 9–11; tel. 222-400; telex 22-4269; Patriotic People's Front; Editor István Soltesz; circ. 105,000.

Népsport (People's Sport): 1085 Budapest, Somogyi Béla u. 6; tel. 130-460; telex 22-5245; Editor József Varga; circ. 275,000.

Népszabadság (People's Freedom): 1960 Budapest, Blaha Lujza tér 3; tel. 336-130; telex 22-5551; f. 1942; Hungarian Socialist Workers' Party; Editor-in-Chief Gabor Borbely; circ. 705,000.

Népszava (Voice of the People): 1203 Budapest, Rákóczi u. 54; tel. 224-810; telex 22-4101; Hungarian Trades Union Council; Editor László Fodor; circ. 295,000.

WEEKLIES

Élet és Irodalom (Life and Literature): 1054 Budapest, Széchenyi u. 1; tel. 533-122; f. 1957; literary and political; Editor Imre Bata; circ. 60,000.

Élet és Tudomány (Life and Science): 1073 Budapest, Lenin krt 5; tel. 215-290; f. 1946; popular science; Editor-in-Chief László Ludas; circ. 85,000.

Evangélikus Élet: 1088 Budapest, Puskin u. 12; tel. 142-074; f. 1933; church affairs; Editor László Lehel; circ. 12,000.

Figyelő (Observer): 1355 Budapest, Alkotmány u. 10; tel. 127-664; telex 22-6613; weekly; f. 1957; economic policy and management; Editor-in-Chief Dr György Varga; circ. 24,000.

Film, Szinház, Muzsika (Films, Theatre, Music): 1073 Budapest, Lenin krt 9–11; tel. 222-400; Editor Zoltán Iszlai; circ. 70,000.

Heti Világgazdaság (World Economics Weekly): 1133 Budapest, Vág u. 13; tel. 408-776; telex 22-6676; f. 1979; Editor-in-Chief Mátyás Vince; circ. 110,000.

Képes Újság (Illustrated News): 1085 Budapest, Gyulai Pál u. 14; tel. 137-660; Patriotic People's Front; Editor Mihaly Kovács; circ. 558,000.

Ludas Matyi: 1077 Budapest, Gyulai Pál u. 14; tel. 335-718; satirical; Editor József Árkus; circ. 352,000.

L'udové Noviny: 1065 Budapest, Nagymező u. 49; tel. 319-184; for Slovaks in Hungary; Editor Pál Kondács; circ. 1,700.

Magyar Ifjúság (Hungarian Youth): 1085 Budapest, Somogyi Béla u. 6; tel. 130-460; telex 22-6423; Editor Lajos Gubcsi; circ. 207,000.

Magyarország (Hungary): 1085 Budapest, Gyulai Pál u. 14; tel. 137-660; telex 22-6351; f. 1964; news magazine; Editor Dr József Pálfy; circ. 200,000.

Narodne Novine: 1396 Budapest, POB 495; tel. 124-869; f. 1945; for Yugoslavs in Hungary; in Serbo-Croat and Slovene; Chief Editor Marko Marković; circ. 2,800.

Neue Zeitung: 1391 Budapest, Nagymező u. 49, Pf. 224; tel. 326-334; for Germans in Hungary; Editor Peter Leipold; circ. 4,500.

Nők Lapja (Women's Journal): 1085 Budapest, Blaha Lujza tér 3; tel. 336-130; f. 1961; Editor-in-Chief Irén Németi; circ. 975,000.

Ország-Világ (Land and World): 1073 Budapest, Lenin krt 9–11; tel. 222-400; f. 1957; Editor András Gál; circ. 208,000.

Rádió és Televízióújság (Radio and TV News): POB 6, 1801 Budapest; tel. 330-536; f. 1956; Editor János Boros; circ. 1,350,000.

Reformátusok Lapja: 1395 Budapest, POB 424; tel. 176-809; f. 1957; Reformed Church paper for the laity; Editor-in-Chief and Publr Attila P. Komlós; circ. 40,000.

Szabad Föld (Free Soil): 1085 Budapest, Somogyi Béla u. 6; tel. 138-821; Patriotic People's Front; Editor Gyula Eck; circ. 530,000.

Szövetkezet (Co-operative): 1054 Budapest, Szabadság tér 14; tel. 313-132; National Council of Hungarian Consumer Co-operative Societies; Editor-in-Chief Attila Kovács; circ. 85,000.

Új Ember (New Man): 1053 Budapest, POB 111; tel. 173-638; religious weekly of the Actio Catholica; Editor Ferenc Magyar; circ. 100,000.

Új Tükör (New Mirror): 1073 Budapest, Lenin krt 9–11; tel. 223-058; illustrated cultural and sociological magazine; Editor-in-Chief Sandor Fekete; circ. 101,000.

Vasárnapi Hirek (Sunday News): 1979 Budapest, POB 14; tel. 134-460; political; Editor Dr Zoltán Lőkös; circ. 303,000.

FORTNIGHTLIES

Foaia Noastra (Our Leaf): 1055 Budapest, Bajcsy Zs. u. 78; for Romanians in Hungary; Editor Sándor Hocopán; circ. 1,500.

Magyar Hirek (Hungarian News): 1905 Budapest, Benczúr u. 15; tel. 225-616; illustrated magazine published by World Asscn of Hungarians; primarily for Hungarians living abroad; Editor György Halász; circ. 80,000.

Magyar Mezőgazdaság (Hungarian Agriculture): 1053 Budapest, Kossuth Lajos tér 11; tel. 122-433; Editor Károly Fehér; circ. 24,000.

Szövetkezeti Hírlap (Co-operative Herald): 1052 Budapest, Pesti Barnabás u. 6; tel. 170-181; National Union of Artisans; Editor Mária Dolezsal; circ. 12,000.

Új Élet (New Life): 1075 Budapest, Síp u. 12; tel. 222-829; for Hungarian Jews; Editor Dr István Domán; circ. 7,000.

OTHER PERIODICALS

(Published monthly unless otherwise indicated)

Állami Gazdaság (State Farming): General Direction of State Farming, 1054 Budapest, Akadémia u. 1–3; tel. 323-934; f. 1946; 12 a year; Editor Mrs P. GÖRGÉNYI.

Business Partner Hungary: Budapest; f. 1986; quarterly; Hungarian, German and English; economic journal published by Institute for Economic and Market Research.

Cartactual: 1367 Budapest, POB 76; tel. 126-480; telex 22-4964; f. 1965; every 2 months; map service periodical with supplement *Cartinform* (map bibliography); published in English, French, German and Hungarian; Editor-in-Chief ERNŐ CSÁTI.

Egyházi Krónika (Church Chronicle): 1052 Budapest, Petőfi tér 2.1.2; tel. 184-813; f. 1952; every 2 months; Eastern Orthodox Church journal; Editor Archpriest Dr FERIZ BERKI.

Elektrotechnika: 1055 Budapest, Kossuth Lajos tér 6–8; tel. 120-488; f. 1908; electrical engineering; Editor TIBOR KELEMEN.

Élelmezési Ipar (Food Industry): 1361 Budapest, POB 5; tel. 122-859; f. 1947; Scientific Society for Food Industry; Editor Dr ÖDÖN VAJDA.

Energia és Atomtechnika (Energy and Nuclear Technology): 1054 Budapest, Kossuth Lajos tér 6–8; tel. 328–989; Scientific Society for Energy Economy; Editor ISTVÁN VARGA.

Energiagazdálkodás (Energy Economy): 1055 Budapest, Kossuth Lajos tér 6; tel. 532-894; Scientific Society for Energetics; Editor Dr TAMÁS RAPP.

Építésügyi Szemle (Building Review): 1054 Budapest, Beloiannisz u. 2–4; tel. 313-180; building; Editor Dr JÓZSEF KÁDÁR.

Ezermester (The Handyman): 1051 Budapest, Münnich F. u. 15; tel. 125-245; f. 1957; do-it-yourself magazine; Editor J. SZŰCS; circ. 135,000.

Gép (Machinery): 1055 Budapest, Kossuth Lajos tér 6–8; tel. 329-999; telex 22-5792; f. 1949; monthly; Society of Mechanical Engineers; Editor Dr KORNÉL LEHOFER.

Hungarian Book Review: 1051 Budapest, Vörösmarty tér 1.X.1010; tel. 176-222; f. 1958; quarterly review of Hungarian Publishers' and Booksellers' Association; in English, French and German; Editor-in-Chief GYULA KURUCZ.

Hungarian Business Herald: 1054 Budapest, Lengyel Gyula u. 6; tel. 533-522; f. 1970; quarterly review published in English and German by the Hungarian Chamber of Commerce; Editor-in-Chief Dr GERD BÍRÓ; circ. 4,000.

Hungarian Digest: 1073 Budapest, Lenin krt 9–11; tel. 451-580; f. 1980; every 2 months; illustrated review with articles from Hungarian press, short stories etc.; English; also in French as Revue de Hongrie; Editor TIBOR ZÁDOR; circ. 15,000.

Hungarian Economy: 1355 Budapest, POB 18; tel. 322-186; telex 22-6613; quarterly; economic and business review; English edn of weekly Figyelő; Editor-in-Chief Dr JÁNOS FOLLINUS.

Hungarian Trade Union News: 1415 Budapest, Dózsa György u. 84/B; tel. 428-313; f. 1957; in six languages including English; Editor-in-Chief JÁNOS SIKLÓS.

Hungarian Travel Magazine: 1088 Budapest, Muzeum u. 11; tel. 339-995; quarterly in English and German, 2 a year in a third language; illustrated journal of the Tourist Board for the visitor to Hungary; Managing Editor JÚLIA SZ. NAGY.

Ipargazdaság (Industrial Economy): 1368 Budapest, POB 240; tel. 354-529; f. 1948; Editor Dr ISTVÁN HARSÁNYI; circ. 4,000.

Jogtudományi Közlöny (Law Gazette): 1250 Budapest, Pf. 25, Országház u. 30; tel. 759-011; f. 1866; law; Editor-in-Chief Dr JÓZSEF HALÁSZ; Editor Dr IMRE VÖRÖS; circ. 2,500.

Kortárs (Contemporary): 1054 Budapest, Széchenyi u. 1; tel. 121-240; literary gazette; Editor GYÖRGY SZÁRAZ; circ. 11,000.

Könyvtáros (The Librarian): 1051 Budapest, Alpári Gyula u. 2; tel. 189-895; monthly; Editor LÁSZLÓ BERECZKY; circ. 6,000.

Közgazdasági Szemle (Economic Review): 1112 Budapest, Budaörsi u. 43–45; tel. 850-777; f. 1954; monthly; published by Cttee for Economic Sciences of Academy of Sciences; Editor KATALIN SZABÓ; circ. 15,000.

Look at Hungary: 1906 Budapest, POB 223; tel. 860-133; f. 1980; quarterly photomagazine in English, Arabic, French and Portuguese; Editor-in-Chief GÁBOR VAJDA.

Made in Hungary: 1426 Budapest, POB 3; every 2 months; economics and business magazine published in English by MTI; Editor GYÖRGY BLASITS.

Magyar Jog (Hungarian Law): 1055 Budapest, Szalay u. 16; tel. 326-170; law; Editor Dr PÉTER BÖŐR.

Magyar Közlöny (Official Gazette): 1055 Budapest, Bajcsy Zs. u. 78; tel. 121-236; Editor Dr ELEMÉR KISS; circ. 90,000.

Magyar Tudomány (Hungarian Science): Hungarian Academy of Sciences, 1051 Budapest, Münnich Ferenc u. 7; tel. 179-524.

Méhészet (Beekeeping): Budapest; tel. 331-141; apiculture; Editor ANTAL NIKOVITZ; circ. 16,000.

Muzsika: 1073 Budapest, Lenin krt 9–11; tel. 426-139; f. 1958; musical review; Editor-in-Chief MÁRIA FEUER; circ. 7,500.

Nagyvilág (The Great World): 1054 Budapest, Széchenyi u. 1; tel. 321-160; f. 1956; review of world literature; Editor LÁSZLÓ KÉRY; circ. 12,000.

Nemzetközi Szemle (International Review): 1054 Budapest, Steindl u. 6; tel. 110-697; f. 1957; Editor-in-Chief LÁSZLÓ FENCSIK; circ. 32,000.

Népfront (People's Front): 1054 Budapest, Belgrád rkp. 24; published by the Patriotic People's Front; Editor ISTVÁN HAJDUSKA; circ. 18,000.

New Hungarian Exporter: 1073 Budapest, Lenin krt 9–11; tel. 221-285; telex 22-6207; Hungarian Chamber of Commerce; monthly in English; fortnightly in other languages; quarterly technical issues in English; Editor-in-Chief MÁRIA MURAI; circ. 18,000.

New Hungarian Quarterly: 1088 Budapest, Rákóczi u. 17; tel. 136-857; f. 1961; illustrated quarterly in English; politics, economics, philosophy, education, culture, poems, short stories, etc.; Editor IVÁN BOLDIZSÁR; circ. 5,400.

Református Egyház: 1146 Budapest, Abonyi u. 21; tel. 227-870; f. 1949; official journal of the Hungarian Reformed Church; Editor-in-Chief FERENC DUSICZA; circ. 1,600.

Rubik's Logic and Fantasy: 1906 Budapest, POB 223; international games quarterly published in English and Hungarian; Editor-in-Chief ERNŐ RUBIK.

Statisztikai Szemle (Statistical Review): 1525 Budapest, POB 51; tel. 155-208; f. 1923; Editor-in-Chief Dr FERENC GYULAY; circ. 3,500.

Társadalmi Szemle (Social Review): 1358 Budapest, Széchenyi rkp. 19; tel. 114-400; theoretical-political review; Editor VALÉRIA BENKE; circ. 45,000.

Technika (Technology): 1055 Budapest, Néphadsereg u. 7; tel. 327-332; f. 1957; general technical review; monthly in Hungarian, annually in English, German and Russian; Editor GYULA SIMON; circ. 20,000.

Turizmus (Tourism): 1088 Budapest, Muzeum u. 11; tel. 138-625; Editor ZSOLT SZEBENI; circ. 8,000.

Új Technika (New Technology): 1014 Budapest, Szentháromság tér 1; tel. 557-122; telex 22-6490; f. 1967; popular industrial quarterly; circ. 35,000.

Vigilia (Vigil): 1364 Budapest, POB 111; tel. 177-246; f. 1935; monthly; Catholic; Editor LÁSZLÓ LUKÁCS; circ. 12,000.

Villamosság (Electricity): 1055 Budapest, Kossuth Lajos tér 6–8; tel. 120-488; Electrotechnical Association; Gen. Editor FERENC KOVÁCS; circ. 3,000.

NEWS AGENCIES

Magyar Távirati Iroda (MTI) (Hungarian News Agency): 1016 Budapest, Fém u. 5–7; tel. 756-722; telex 22-4371; f. 1880; 19 brs in Hungary; 23 bureaux abroad; Pres., Man. Dir SÁNDOR BURJÁN.

Foreign Bureaux

Agence France-Presse (AFP): c/o MTI, 1016 Budapest, Fém. u. 5–7; tel. 159-490; telex 22-4371; Correspondent PAUL HERSKOVITS.

Agentstvo Pechati Novosti (APN) (USSR): 1056 Budapest, Március 15 tér 1; Bureau Chief YURI AKIMOV.

Agenzia Nazionale Stampa Associata (ANSA) (Italy): 1024 Budapest, Mártírok u. 43/45; tel. 352-323; telex 22-4711; Bureau Chief ROBERTO PAPPI.

Allgemeiner Deutscher Nachrichtendienst (ADN) (German Democratic Republic): 1146 Budapest, Zichy Géza u. 5; telex 22-4674; Bureau Chief KLAUS RIEMANN.

Associated Press (AP) (USA): Budapest II, Riado u. 12; tel. 159-490; Rep. ANDY TIMAR.

Bulgarian Telegraph Agency (BTA): 1016 Budapest, Flat 10, Lisznyai u. 15; Bureau Chief GEORG VEDRODENSZKI.

Československá tisková kancelář (ČTK) (Czechoslovakia): 1146 Budapest, Zichy Géza u. 5; tel. 427-115; telex 22-5367; Correspondent STEFAN NÉMETH.

Inter Press Service (IPS) (Italy): 1026 Budapest, Filler u. 26; tel. 363-903; telex 22-4371; Rep. CATALINA WEINER.

HUNGARY

Prensa Latina (Cuba): 1021 Budapest, Budakeszi u. 55/D, 7 p.; tel. 387-474; telex 22-4800; Correspondent HUGO LUIS SÁNCHEZ GONZÁLEZ.

Reuters (UK): c/o Magyar Távirati Iroda, 1426 Budapest, POB 3.

Telegrafnoye Agentstvo Sovetskovo Soyuza (TASS) (USSR): 1023 Budapest, Vérhalom u. 12–16; Correspondent YEVGENI POPOV.

United Press International (UPI) (USA): 1137 Budapest, Pozsonyi u. 14; telex 22-5649; Bureau Chief Dr ANDREW L. SÜMEGHI.

Xinhua (New China) News Agency (People's Republic of China): 1068 Budapest, Benczur u. 39/A.1.4; tel. 228-420; telex 22-5447; Chief Correspondent HOU FENGQING.

PRESS ASSOCIATIONS

Magyar Újságírók Országos Szövetsége (MUOSZ) (National Association of Hungarian Journalists): 1062 Budapest, Népköztársaság u. 101; tel. 221-699; telex 22-5045; Pres. JÓZSEF PÁLFY; Gen. Sec. KÁROLY MEGYERI; 4,700 mems.

Union of Hungarian Newspaper Publishers: Budapest; f. 1986 by four newspaper publishing companies.

Publishers

PRINCIPAL PUBLISHING HOUSES

Akadémiai Kiadó: 1054 Budapest, Alkotmány u. 21; tel. 111-010; telex 22-6228; f. 1828; Publishing House of the Hungarian Academy of Sciences; humanities, social, natural and technical sciences, dictionaries, encyclopaedias, periodicals of the Academy and other institutions, issued partly in foreign languages; Pres. GYÖRGY HAZAI; Man. Dir PÉTER INKEI.

Corvina Kiadó: 1051 Budapest, Vörösmarty tér 1; tel. 176-222; telex 22-4440; f. 1955; Hungarian works translated into foreign languages, art and educational books, fiction and non-fiction, tourist guides, cookery books, sport, musicology, juvenile and children's literature; Man. Dir ISTVÁN BART; Editorial Dir KÁROLY VÉBER.

Editio Musica Budapest: 1051 Budapest, Vörösmarty tér 1; tel. 184-228; telex 22-5500; f. 1950; sheet music and books on musical subjects; Dir ISTVÁN HOMOLYA.

Európa Könyvkiadó: 1055 Budapest, Kossuth Lajos tér 13–15; tel. 312-700; telex 22-5645; f. 1945; world literature translated into Hungarian; Man. JÁNOS DOMOKOS.

Gondolat Könyvkiadó: 1088 Budapest, Bródy Sándor u. 16; tel. 343-380; popular scientific publications on natural and social sciences, art, encyclopaedic handbooks; Dir Dr MARGIT SIKLÓS.

Helikon Kiadó: 1053 Budapest, Eötvös L. u. 8; tel. 174-765; bibliophile books; Dir MAGDA MOLNAR.

Képzőművészeti Alap Kiadóvállalata: 1051 Budapest, Vörösmarty tér 1; tel. 176-222; telex 22-4405; fine arts; Man. Dr LÁSZLÓ SERES.

Kossuth Könyvkiadó Vállalat: 1054 Budapest, Steindl u. 6; tel. 117-440; f. 1944; political, historical, economic and philosophical publications; Man. Dr GYÖRGY NONN.

Közgazdasági és Jogi Könyvkiadó: 1054 Budapest, Nagy Sándor u. 6; tel. 126-430; telex 22-6511; f. 1955; economic, sociological and juridical; Man. VILMOS DALOS.

Magvető Könyvkiadó: 1806 Budapest, Vörösmarty tér 1; tel. 185-109; literature; Man. MIKLÓS JOVÁNOVICS.

Medicina Könyvkiadó: 1054 Budapest, Beloiannisz u. 8; tel. 122-650; f. 1957; books on medicine, sport, tourism; Man. Prof. Dr ISTVÁN ÁRKY.

Mezőgazdasági Könyvkiadó: 1054 Budapest, Báthory u. 10; tel. 116-650; agricultural; Man. Dr PÁL SÁRKÁNY.

Móra Ferenc Gyermek és Ifjúsági Könyvkiadó: 1146 Budapest, Május 1 u. 57–59; tel. 212-390; telex 22-7027; f. 1950; children's books, science fiction; Man. JÁNOS SZILÁDI.

Műszaki Könyvkiadó: 1014 Budapest, Szentháromság tér 1; tel. 160-860; telex 22-6490; f. 1955; technical; Man. HERBERT FISCHER.

Népszava Lap-és Könyvkiadó Vállalat: 1553 Budapest, Rákóczi u. 54; tel. 224-810; Hungarian Trade Union Council Press; Man. Dr JENŐ KISS.

Statisztikai Kiadó Vállalat: 1033 Budapest, Kaszásdűlő u. 2; tel. 803-311; telex 22-6699; f. 1954; publications on statistics, system-management and computer science; Dir JÓZSEF KECSKÉS.

Szépirodalmi Könyvkiadó: 1073 Budapest, Lenin krt 9–11; tel. 221-285; telex 22-6754; f. 1950; modern and classical Magyar literature; Man. ENDRE ILLÉS.

Tankönyvkiadó Vállalat: 1055 Budapest, Szalay u. 10–14; tel. 530-600; f. 1949; school and university textbooks, pedagogical literature and language books; Man. ANDRÁS PETRÓ.

Zrinyi Katonai Kiadó: 1087 Budapest, Kerepesi u. 29; tel. 334-750; military literature; Man. LÁSZLÓ NÉMETH.

CARTOGRAPHERS

Országos Földügyi és Térképészeti Hivatal (National Office of Lands and Mapping): 1055 Budapest, Kossuth Lajos tér 11; tel. 311-349; telex 22-5445; f. 1954; Pres. ISTVÁN HOFFER.

Cartographia (Hungarian Company for Surveying and Mapping): 1443 Budapest, POB 132; tel. 634-639; telex 22-6218; f. 1954; Dir GYÖRGY DOMOKOS.

PUBLISHERS' ASSOCIATION

Magyar Könyvkiadók és Könyvterjesztők Egyesülése (Hungarian Publishers' and Booksellers' Association): 1051 Budapest, Vörösmarty tér 1; tel. 184-758; f. 1878; most Hungarian publishers are members of the Association; Pres. ANDRÁS PETRÓ; Sec.-Gen. FERENC ZÖLD.

WRITERS' UNION

Magyar Írók Szövetsége (Association of Hungarian Writers): 1062 Budapest, Bajza u. 18; tel. 228-840; f. 1945; Pres. TIBOR CSERES; Sec.-Gen. MIKLÓS VERESS.

Radio and Television

Radio licences (1979): 2,608,000. Radio licences were abolished in 1980. Television licences (1984): 2,895,000. Cable television systems are expanding, and in early 1985 were operating in 12 cities. In 1986 Hungary completed negotiations to receive TV programmes from a Western European satellite network. Reception will be limited initially to hotels in Budapest and other Hungarian cities.

RADIO

Magyar Rádió: 1800 Budapest, Brody Sándor u. 5–7; tel. 338-330; telex 22-5188; f. 1924; stations: Radio Kossuth (Budapest); Radio Petőfi (Budapest); Radio 3 (Budapest, mainly music); external broadcasts: in English, German, Hungarian, Italian, Spanish and Turkish; Pres. Dr ISTVÁN HÁRS.

Radio Danubius: f. 1986; commercial station; broadcasts news, music and information in German 11 hours a day in summer to tourists in Lake Balaton region; Dir GYÖRGY VARGA.

TELEVISION

Magyar Televízió: 1810 Budapest, Szabadság tér 17; tel. 533-200; telex 22-5568; f. 1957; first channel broadcasts about 66 hours a week and the second channel about 20 hours a week, mostly colour transmissions; no broadcasts on Mondays; Pres. Dr MIHÁLY KORNIDESZ; Vice-Pres FERENC GERENCSÉR, GYÖRGY MURAI, PÉTER NEMES.

Finance

The Hungarian financial system is being restructured. In January 1985 the functions of issue and credit at the National Bank were separated. Under reforms implemented in January 1987, the central banking and commercial banking functions were separated, and the banking system is now organized on three levels. The National Bank of Hungary, as the bank of issue, continues to participate in the formulation of economic policy. The 1987 reforms did not affect the National Bank's foreign exchange authority, nor alter substantially the Bank's total assets. At the second level are the commercial banks. These institutions have general and nation-wide authority, keep the accounts of enterprises, accept their deposits and extend credits to them. The commercial banks may participate in ventures and may provide banking services for their clients. They establish their own business policy and the terms and conditions of their contracts, within the limits of central banking regulations. The commercial banks (established from the units seceding from the National Bank of Hungary, the reorganization of the State Development Bank and the Creditbank of Budapest, and the General Banking and Trust Co Ltd) are: The General Banking and Trust and Co Ltd; Budapest Bank Rt.; Hungarian Creditbank Ltd; Hungarian Foreign Trade Bank; Commercial and Creditbank Ltd. At the third level of the banking system are the so-called specialized financial institutions. These small banks may establish deposit and credit links with economic entities, may participate in ventures and may provide banking services. Unlike the commercial banks, the specialized financial institutions may not keep the accounts of their clients.

The Savings Co-operatives (Takarékszövetkezet) operate at the local level. Their main activity is the collection of deposits and the provision of credit to their members. Since January 1985, these co-operatives have been able to maintain accounts for small enterprises and private entrepreneurs, and can extend credit to them. They are also empowered to provide mortgage facilities to individuals. Minimum registered capital is 2,000m. forint at each co-operative. In early 1987 there were 260 such co-operatives in Hungary. Their interests are represented by SZÖVOSZ (National Council of Hungarian Consumer Co-operative Societies—see p. 1337).

Financial institutions with foreign capital shares may be founded with government permission. The first bank in Hungary to be founded with foreign capital involvement was the Central European International Bank (CIB), established in 1979. In 1985 a joint Hungarian-US commercial bank was established by the Central Exchange and Credit Bank of Budapest and Citibank of New York. It began operations in 1986, under the supervision of the National Bank of Hungary. Unicbank Rt., founded with 45% foreign capital, commenced operations in January 1987.

The issue of bonds, in order to finance housing and infrastructural projects, is of increasing significance. Offering a higher rate of interest than that of the National Savings Bank, bonds were first issued on a large scale in early 1983, available initially only to enterprises but later also to private individuals. In September 1984 the State Development Bank (now State Development Institution) began repurchasing and reselling bonds, thus giving rise to the existence of a domestic 'bond market'. By mid-1986 local councils and enterprises had issued 130 bonds to a total value of 8,000m. forint (equivalent to almost 3% of total Hungarian investment in 1985), about 70% of which had been purchased by private citizens. By late 1986 there were 150 bonds, worth over 9,000m. forint, in circulation. Budapest Bank Rt. was to establish an independent office for securities transactions.

BANKING

(cap. = capital; res = reserves; dep. = deposits; m. = million; Ft = forint; brs = branches)

Central Bank
Magyar Nemzeti Bank (National Bank of Hungary): 1850 Budapest, Szabadság tér 8; tel. 532-600; telex 22-5755; f. 1924; cap. 10,000m. Ft, res 8,403m. Ft, dep. 470,718m. Ft (Dec. 1985); issue of bank notes; transacts international payments business; supervises banking system; 18 brs; Pres. Dr Mátyás Timár; First Vice-Pres. János Fekete.

Commercial Banks
Általános Értékforgalmi Bank Rt. (General Banking and Trust Co Ltd): 1431 Budapest, Szamuely U. 38; tel. 171-255; telex 22-6548; f. 1952; general banking activities, transactions in securities, management of real estate and other assets; Dir-Gen. Dr Antal Beszedes.

Budapest Bank Rt.: 1052 Budapest, Deák Ferenc u. 5; tel. 181-200; telex 22-3013; f. 1986; cap. 3,524m. Ft; Dir-Gen. Oszkár Hegedűs.

Magyar Hitelbank Rt. (Hungarian Creditbank Ltd): 1051 Budapest, Szabadság tér 5–6; tel. 532-600; telex 22-5671; f. 1986; cap. 8,983m. Ft; Dir-Gen. Sándor Demján.

Magyar Külkereskedelmi Bank Rt. (Hungarian Foreign Trade Bank Ltd): 1821 Budapest, Szt. István tér 11; tel. 329-360; telex 22-6941; f. 1950; cap. 3,500m. Ft; Gen. Dir Sándor Demcsák.

Országos Kereskedelmi és Hitelbank Rt. (Commercial and Creditbank Ltd): 1850 Budapest, Arany János u. 24; tel. 532-052; f. 1986; cap. 6,590m. Ft; Pres.-Gen. Dir Dr Pál Kis.

Development Financial Institution
Állami Fejlsztési Intézet (State Development Institution): 1052 Budapest, Deák F. u. 5; tel. 181-200; telex 22-5672; f. 1987 to succeed the State Development Bank; management and control of development projects financed partly from the state budget; Gen. Dir Dr Borbála Báger.

Specialized Financial Institutions
AGRIT—Agrár Innovációs Bank Rt. (AGRIT—Agricultural Innovation Bank Ltd): 1054 Budapest, Széchenyi rkp. 6; tel. 114-732; telex 22-7434; f. 1984; joint-stock company; cap. 600m. Ft; Dir Miklós Szigethy.

Általános Vállalkozási Bank Rt. (General Bank for Venture Financing Ltd): 1055 Budapest, Stollár B. u. 3A; tel. 326-590; f. 1985; joint-stock company; cap. 2,200m. Ft; Gen. Man. Géza Lenk.

Építőipari Innovációs Bank Rt. (Innovation Bank for Construction Industry Ltd): 1139 Budapest, Teve u. 8–10; tel. 298-044; telex 22-533; f. 1985; joint stock company; cap. 744m. Ft; Man. Dir Tamás Varga.

INNOFINANCE—Általános Innovációs Pénzintézet (INNOFINANCE—General Financial Institution for Innovation): 1061 Budapest, Paulay Ede u. 13; tel. 421-762; telex 22-5260; f. 1980; joint-stock company; registered cap. 500m. Ft; Man. Dir Erzsébet Birmann.

INTERINVEST—Külkereskedelmi Fejlesztési Hitelbank (INTERINVEST—Development Credit Corporation for the Development of Foreign Trade-deposit Association): 1051 Budapest, Dorottya u. 8, 5th Floor; tel. 186-427; telex 22-7879; f. 1980; cap. 2,074m. Ft; Man. Dir György Iványi.

INVESTBANK—Műszaki Fejlesztési Bank (Bank for Technical Development-deposit Association): 1052 Budapest, Deák F. u. 5; tel. 184-917; telex 22-5672; f. 1983; cap. 620m. Ft; Dir Dr Anna Temesi.

Ipari Szövetkezeti Fejlesztési Bank (Development Bank of Industrial Co-operatives-deposit Association): 1397 Budapest, Semmelweis u. 21; tel. 182-209; telex 22-5990; f. 1984; cap. 300m. Ft; Dir Béla Seydl.

Kisvállalkozási Bank (Bank for Small Ventures): 1876 Budapest, Münnich F. u. 16; tel. 316-940; telex 22-4280; f. 1986; affiliated to NSB; cap. 673m. Ft; Dir Árpád Bacsóka.

TECHNOVA—Ipari Fejlesztési Bank BT (TECHNOVA—Industrial Development Bank-deposit Association): 1051 Budapest, Október 6 u. 7; tel. 180-173; telex 22-7351; f. 1986; cap. 504m. Ft; Dir Gyula Pázmándi.

Consortium Banks
Central European International Bank Ltd—CIB: 1052 Budapest, Váci u. 16B; tel. 188-377; telex 22-4759; f. 1979; shareholders: National Bank of Hungary (34%), Banca Commerciale Italiana, Bayerische Vereinsbank, Creditanstalt Bankverein, Long-Term Credit Bank of Japan, Société Générale, Taiyo Kobe Bank (11% each); an offshore bank conducting international banking business of all kinds; share cap. US $38.793m.; dep. US $342m., total resources $385.7m. (Dec. 1985); Chair. Dr Arno Puhlmann; Deputy Chair. János Fekete; Man. Dir Dr Lajos Komár.

Citibank Budapest: 1052 Budapest, Váci u. 19–21; tel. 382-666; telex 22-7822; f. 1986; joint-stock company; share cap. 1,000m. Ft; Gen. Man. Robin M. Winchester.

Unicbank Rt.: 1052 Budapest, Váci u. 19-21; tel. 182-088; telex 22-3172; f. 1986; cap. 1,000m. Ft; Man. Dir Dr Ágnes Cseresnyés; Deputy Man. Dir Dr Rudolf Pfletschinger; Shareholders: International Finance Corporation (IFC) (15%); Genossenschaftliche Zentralbank AG (GZB), Vienna (15%); Deutsche Genossenschaftsbank AG (DG Bank), Frankfurt (15%); Central Bank of Exchange and Credit Ltd (20%); National Savings Bank (11%); Association of Agricultural Co-operatives (6%); Association of Industrial Co-operatives (6%); Association of Service Co-operatives (6%); Association of Private Artisans (6%).

Savings Bank
Országos Takarékpénztár—OTP (National Savings Bank—NSB): 1876 Budapest, Münnich Ferenc u. 16; tel. 531-444; telex 22-4280; f. 1949; cap. 1,300m. Ft, dep. 213,942m. Ft (1985); savings deposits, credits, foreign transactions, lotteries; acts as estate agent; 598 brs; Gen. Man. Dr László Tisza.

Central Corporation
Pénzintézeti Központ (Central Corporation of Banking Companies): 1431 Budapest, Szamuely u. 38; tel. 171-255; f. 1916; banking, property, rights and interests, deposits, securities, and foreign exchange management; Dir-Gen. Mihály Biró.

INSURANCE
The state monopoly in insurance ended in July 1986, when the state insurance enterprise was divided into two companies, one of which retained the name of the former Állami Biztosító.

HUNGARY

Állami Biztositó—AB (State Insurance Co): 1813 Budapest, Üllői u. 1–3; tel. 181-866; telex 22-4550; f. 1949, reorganized 1986; handles life and property insurance, insurance of agricultural plants, co-operatives, etc.; Gen. Man. ANDREA DEÁK.

Hungária Biztositó (Hungária Insurance, Reinsurance and Export Credit Insurance Co): 1014 Budapest, Dísz tér 4–5; tel. 759-211; telex 22-3199; f. 1986; handles international insurance, insurance of state companies and motor-car insurance; Gen. Man. TAMÁS UZONYI.

Trade and Industry

CHAMBER OF COMMERCE

Magyar Kereskedelmi Kamara (Hungarian Chamber of Commerce): 1389 Budapest, POB 106; tel. 533-333; telex 22-4745; f. 1948; develops trade with other countries; mediates between companies, etc.; mems: 1,100 industrial and foreign trade organizations; Pres. TAMÁS BECK; Gen. Sec. PETER LŐRINCZE.

SELECTED FOREIGN TRADE ORGANIZATIONS

Since 1980 the foreign trade organizations have been undergoing modernization. By 1985 over 250 enterprises had acquired foreign trade rights. Also, radical reforms in 1985 permitted the foreign trade organizations to become 'trading houses', widening their sphere of activity by extending the range of goods available, supplying capital to producers and commissioning manufacture of the goods required by the foreign market. Among the first foreign trade organizations to announce their conversion in 1985 were Transelektro, Konsumex, Hungarotex and Skála Coop.

AÉV No 31: 1364 Budapest, POB 83; tel. 180-511; telex 22-4928; f. 1951; state building factory; construction of industrial units, power plants, chemical combines, cement plants, etc.; undertakes building work abroad.

Agrária-Bábolna: 2943 Bábolna; tel. 34-11118; telex 22-6555; f. 1789; turn-key poultry and pig farms with breeding stock and feed premixes; hatching eggs, breeding poultry, pigs, sheep and breeding jumping and riding horses; processed chicken, rodent and insect extermination services, etc.

Agrimpex: 1392 Budapest, POB 278; tel. 113-800; telex 22-5751; f. 1948; agricultural products.

Agrober: 1502 Budapest, POB 93; tel. 260-640; telex 22-5868; consultant engineers for agriculture and food.

Agrotek: 1388 Budapest, POB 66; tel. 530-555; telex 22-5651; import of agricultural machinery, including machinery for livestock breeding, and forestry equipment.

Artex: 1390 Budapest, POB 167; tel. 530-222; telex 22-4951; furniture, carpets, porcelain, ceramics, gold and silver ware, applied arts, household and sports goods.

BHG: 1509 Budapest, POB 2; tel. 453-300; telex 22-5933; telecommunications.

Bivimpex: 1325 Budapest, POB 55; tel. 690-614; telex 22-4279; f. 1971; raw hide and leather; Dir JÓZSEF KEZTYŰS.

Bőrker: 1391 Budapest, POB 215; tel. 210-760; telex 22-5543; trading company for basic materials and accessories for shoes, fancy leather goods, garments and furniture.

BRG: 1300 Budapest, POB 43; tel. 682-080; telex 22-5928; radio engineering.

Budaprint: 1036 Budapest, POB 111; tel. 889-780; telex 22-4576; textile printing.

Budavox: 1392 Budapest, POB 267; tel. 221-015; telex 22-5077; f. 1956; telecommunications.

Chemokomplex: 1389 Budapest, POB 141; tel. 329-980; telex 22-5158; machines and equipment for the chemical industry; Man. Dir ISTVÁN KOVÁCS.

Chemolimpex: 1805 Budapest, POB 121; tel. 183-970; telex 22-4351; chemicals, agrochemicals, plastics, paints; Gen. Man. Dr PÉTER DOBROVITS.

Chinoin: 1325 Budapest, POB 110; tel. 690-900; telex 22-4236; pharmaceutical and chemical works.

Compack: 1441 Budapest, POB 42; tel. 211-520; telex 22-4846; trading and packing company.

Datorg Foreign Trade Data Processing and Organizing Co Ltd: 1396 Budapest, POB 479; tel. 184-055; telex 22-5191.

Délker: 1366 Budapest, POB 70; tel. 185-888; telex 22-4428; company for trading of citrus fruits, foodstuffs, cosmetics and household goods.

Elektroimpex: 1392 Budapest, POB 296; tel. 328-300; telex 22-5771; telecommunication and precision articles.

Elektromodul: 1390 Budapest, POB 158; tel. 495-940; telex 22-5154; electro-technical components; Gen. Man. GÁBOR IKLODY.

ERBE: 1361 Budapest, POB 17; tel. 116-460; telex 22-5442; power plant investment company.

Factory and Machinery Erecting Enterprise: 1394 Budapest, POB 384; tel. 327-360; telex 4783.

Fékon: 1475 Budapest, POB 67; tel. 572-447; telex 22-5527; clothing company.

Ferunion: 1829 Budapest, POB 612; tel. 172-611; telex 22-5054; tools, glassware, building materials, hardware.

FMV: 1475 Budapest, POB 215; tel. 640-200; telex 22-4409; precision mechanics.

Folkart: 1364 Budapest, POB 20; tel. 184-840; telex 22-6814; foreign trade office of the Cooperative Enterprise for Folk Art and Handicraft.

Gábor Áron Works: 1440 Budapest, POB 39; tel. 335-986; telex 22-4127; engineering works.

Gamma Művek: 1509 Budapest, POB 1; tel. 853-144; telex 22-4946; f. 1920; medical instruments, deep-bore logging and process control systems; Gen. Dir JÁNOS HENZ..

Ganz Electric Works: 1525 Budapest, POB 63; tel. 158-210; telex 22-5363; f. 1878; heavy machinery.

Ganz-MÁVAG: 1967 Budapest, POB 136; tel. 335-950; telex 22-5575; f. 1844; railway rolling stock, hydraulic equipment, lifts, compressors, diesel engines, steel structures; Gen. Man. Dr ADÁM JUHÁSZ.

Ganz Measuring Instrument Works: 1701 Budapest, POB 58; tel. 271-025; telex 22-4395; all types of electrical measuring instrument.

Generalimpex: 1518 Budapest, POB 168; tel. 260-200; telex 22-6758; f. 1980; permitted to import or export any product; Dir LÁSZLÓ NAGY.

Geominco: 1525 Budapest, POB 92; tel. 354-580; telex 22-4442; geological and mining engineering; undertakes exploration and research.

Hungagent Ltd: 1374 Budapest, POB 542; tel. 886-180; telex 22-4526; foreign representations agency; export-import co-operation.

Hungarian Aluminium Corporation (HUNGALU): 1387 Budapest, POB 30; tel. 494-750; telex 22-5471; Gen. Man. Dr LAJOS DÓZSA.

Hungarian Deepfreezing Industry: 1364 Budapest, POB 12; tel. 183-900; telex 22-4579.

Hungarian Shipyards and Crane Factory: 1904 Budapest, POB 280; tel. 496-370; telex 22-5047; f. 1835.

Hungarocoop: 1370 Budapest, POB 334; tel. 531-711; telex 22-4859; Hungarian Co-operative Foreign Trading Company; import and export of consumer goods.

Hungarofilm: 1363 Budapest, POB 39; tel. 116-650; telex 22-5768; f. 1956; films; Sales Man. ISTVÁN VÁRADI.

Hungarofruct: 1394 Budapest, POB 386; tel. 317-120; telex 22-5351; f. 1953; fresh, preserved and dehydrated fruit and vegetables.

Hungarotex: 1804 Budapest, POB 100; tel. 174-555; telex 22-4751; f. 1953; textiles and garments; Gen. Dir ÉVA SZABÓ.

Hungexpo (Hungarian Foreign Trade Office for Fairs and Publicity): 1441 Budapest, POB 44; tel. 225-008; telex 22-4525; advertising, publicity, public relations; printing; fairs, exhibitions.

Hunicoop: 1367 Budapest, POB 111; tel. 424-950; telex 22-4435; foreign trade office for co-operation and purchasing of licences in industry.

Ikarus: 1630 Budapest, POB 3; tel. 636-440; telex 22-4766; export of buses in complete state or in sets for assembly; Man. Dir GÁBOR NAGY.

Industria Ltd: 1117 Budapest, POB 272; commercial representation of foreign firms, technical consulting service, market research etc.

Industrialexport: 1251 Budapest, POB 24; tel. 150-090; telex 22-4541; complete factory equipment.

Interag Co Ltd: 1390 Budapest, POB 184; tel. 326-770; telex 22-4776; negotiates trade agreements, undertakes market research, handles consignment stocks and operates service stations.

Intercooperation Co Ltd: 1253 Budapest, POB 23; tel. 152-220; telex 22-4242; establishment and carrying out of co-operation agreements, joint ventures and import and export deals.

HUNGARY

Interinvest: 1051 Budapest, Dorottya u. 8; tel. 186-427; telex 22-7879; foreign trade promotion; Man. Dir GYÖRGY IVÁNYI.

IPV (Publishing and Promotion Co for Tourism): 1140 Budapest, POB 164; tel. 633-652; telex 22-6074; publishing, publicity, filmmaking, exhibitions, advertising; Gen. Man JÓZSEF TESZÁR.

KGyV Metallurgical Engineering Corpn: 1553 Budapest, POB 23; tel. 112-274; telex 22-5920; metallurgical engineering.

Komplex: 1807 Budapest, POB 125; tel. 117-010; telex 22-5957; f. 1953; agricultural machinery, plant and equipment for food industry; Man. Dir ADOLF FÉDERER.

Konsumex: 1441 Budapest, POB 58; tel. 530-511; telex 22-5151; consumer goods, household articles, etc.

Kultura: 1389 Budapest, POB 149; tel. 359-370; telex 22-4441; books, periodicals, posters, postcards, slides, works of art, sheet music, teaching aids.

Labor MIM: 1450 Budapest, POB 73; tel. 144-396; telex 22-4162; f. 1899; scientific instruments, laboratory equipment and engineering; Gen. Man. M. MÓDI; Trade Man. G. HARSÁNYI.

Lampart: 1475 Budapest, POB 41; tel. 570-111; telex 22-5365; f. 1883; glass-lined processing equipment.

Lehelex: 5101 Jászberény, POB 64; tel. 12611; telex 02-3341; export of domestic refrigerators.

Licencia: 1368 Budapest, POB 207; tel. 181-111; telex 22-5872; f. 1950; purchase and sale of patents and inventions; Dir Dr LAJOS VÉKONY.

Lignimpex: 1393 Budapest, POB 323; tel. 129-850; telex 22-4251; timber, paper and fuel.

Magnesite Industry: 1475 Budapest, POB 11; tel. 571-378; telex 22-5644; f. 1892; refractory products; Dir B. HAZAI.

Magyar Media Advertising Agency: 1392 Budapest 62, POB 279; tel. 325-176; telex 22-3040.

MAHIR Hungarian Publicity Company: 1818 Budapest, POB 367; tel. 183-444; telex 22-5341; advertising agency.

Masped: 1364 Budapest, POB 104; tel. 182-922; telex 22-4471; international forwarding and carriage.

Medicor: 1389 Budapest, POB 150; tel. 495-130; telex 22-5051; medical instruments, X-ray apparatus and complete hospital installations; Pres. Dr ISTVÁN MARTOS.

Medimpex: 1808 Budapest; tel. 183-955; telex 22-5477; export and import of pharmaceutical and biological products, veterinary drugs, laboratory chemicals.

Mert: 1397 Budapest, POB 542; tel. 325-300; telex 22-5777; f. 1951; quality control of import and export goods.

Metalimpex: 1393 Budapest, POB 330; tel. 187-611; telex 22-5251; metals and metal products.

Metrimpex: 1391 Budapest, POB 202; tel. 125-600; telex 22-5451; electronic measuring instruments and equipment.

Mezőgép: 6001 Kecskemét, POB 43; tel. (76) 27-666; telex 22-5517; Budapest office: 1364 Budapest 4, POB 167; tel. 189-557; telex 22-5517; engineering and servicing for agriculture and food processing.

Mineralimpex: 1389 Budapest, POB 130; tel. 116-470; telex 22-4651; oils and mining products; Dir-Gen. JÓZSEF TÓTH.

Modex: 1804 Budapest, POB 100; tel. 174-555; telex 22-4751; ready-made clothing.

Mogürt: 1391 Budapest, POB 249; tel. 184-133; telex 22-5357; f. 1949; motor vehicles; Gen. Man. LÁSZLÓ PÁL TÓTH.

MOM: 1525 Budapest, POB 52; tel. 158-090; telex 22-4151; optical instruments.

Monimpex: 1392 Budapest, POB 268; tel. 531-222; telex 22-5371; wines, spirits, paprika, honey, sweets, ornamental plants.

MVMT: 1251 Budapest, POB 34; tel. 152-600; telex 22-4382; electricity.

Nádex: 1525 Budapest, POB 14; tel. 350-365; telex 22-6767; reed farming.

Nikex: 1809 Budapest, POB 128; tel. 851-122; telex 22-6406; heavy industry.

Novex: 1364 Budapest, POB 62; tel. 184-022; telex 22-6054; deals with transfer of technology to and from Hungary; Man. Dir JUDITH SALUSINSZKY.

Ofotért: 1917 Budapest; tel. 203-669; telex 22-4418; f. 1949; optical and photographic articles; Gen. Dir JÁNOS SZILÁGYI.

OMIKK Technoinform: 1428 Budapest, POB 12; tel. 138-247; telex 22-4944; technical and economic information services including translations, studies, conferences, periodicals and documentation, software programmes.

OMKER: 1367 Budapest, POB 91; tel. 123-000; telex 22-4683; f. 1950; medical instruments; Gen. Dir RÓBERT ZENTAI.

ORION: 1475 Budapest, POB 84; tel. 284-830; telex 22-5798; radios, televisions and electrical goods.

Pannonia (Foreign Trade Company of Cespel Works): 1394 Budapest, POB 354; tel. 212-450; telex 22-5128; metallurgical materials, welding electrodes, cast iron fittings, steel tubes and cylinders, bicycles, industrial sewing and pressing machinery and laundry equipment, complete tube manufacturing plants, bottle plants, etc.

Patentbureau Danubia: 1368 Budapest, POB 198; tel. 181-111; telex 22-5872; f. 1951; patent services; Dir Dr L. VÉKONY.

Pharmatrade: 1367 Budapest, POB 126; tel. 185-966; telex 22-6650; medicinal plants, cosmetics, medicinal muds and waters, food and feed additives, radioactive products.

Philatelia Hungarica: 1373 Budapest, POB 600; tel. 316-146; telex 22-6508; stamps; wholesale only.

Phylaxia: 1486 Budapest, POB 23; tel. 575-311; telex 22-4549; vaccines, veterinary products.

Precision Fittings Factory: 3301 Eger, POB 2; tel. 11-911; telex 63-331.

Prodinform: 1372 Budapest, POB 453; tel. 323-770; telex 22-7750; technical and scientific information, technical consultations.

RÁBA (Hungarian Railway Carriage and Machine Works): 9002 Győr, POB 50; tel. 12-111; telex 02-4255; rolling stock; Gen. Man. EDE HORVÁTH.

Rekard: 9027 Győr, Kandó Kálmán u. 5–7; tel. (96) 13-122; telex 24-360; farm equipment.

Skála-Coop: 1450 Budapest, POB 60; tel. 336-770; telex 22-5135; national co-operative company for purchase and disposal of goods including fine ceramics and glassware, industrial, agricultural and household metal ware, hand tools, electronic games, rubber and plastic products, cosmetics and chemicals, wood and paper industry products, leather and textile industry products, ready-to-wear clothing, vegetables and other foodstuffs; Gen. Man. ISTVÁN IMRE.

Tannimpex: 1395 Budapest, POB 406; tel. 123-400; telex 22-4557; hides, leather shoes, gloves, fancy goods and furs.

Tatabánya Coal Mines: 2803 Tatabánya, POB 323; tel. (34) 10-144; telex 22-6206; f. 1894; technologies, machines and turn-key installations for processing of refuse dumps (coal, iron ore, etc.), preparation of industrial and drinking water, purification of waste waters, dewatering of sludges, tunnelling; Gen. Man. LAJOS FEKETE.

Taurus: 1440 Budapest, POB 25; tel. 341-140; telex 22-5312; rubber; Chief Exec. ILONA TATAI.

Technoimpex: 1390 Budapest, POB 183; tel. 184-055; telex 22-4171; assembly and construction, conservation projects, equipment for the oil and gas industries, agricultural equipment and plant; Gen. Man. ISTVÁN MÁTYÁS.

Temaforg: 1361 Budapest, POB 8; tel. 118-450; telex 22-4663; textile and synthetic wastes, industrial wipers, geotextiles for agriculture, road and railway construction.

Terimpex: 1825 Budapest, POB 251; tel. 175-011; telex 22-4551; cattle and agricultural products; Gen. Man. Dr LÁSZLÓ RÁNKY.

TERTA: 1956 Budapest, POB 16; tel. 634-240; telex 22-4087; telecommunications and data transmission equipment.

Tesco: 1367 Budapest, POB 101; tel. 110-850; telex 22-4642; f. 1962; organization for international technical and scientific cooperation; export and import of technical services world-wide.

Transelektro: 1394 Budapest, POB 377; tel. 320-100; telex 22-4571; generators, power stations, cables, lighting, transformers, household appliances, catering equipment, etc.; Dir Gen. PÁL KERTÉSZ.

TSZKER (Trading Company for Agricultural Cooperatives): 1445 Budapest, POB 354; tel. 340-900; telex 22-4147; industrial metal constructions, pottery ware and ornaments, plastics for household purposes, wooden products and toys, charcoal, fancy goods, canned fruits and vegetables, dried and fresh fruits, poppy seeds, walnuts and other nuts, ornamental shrubs, seedlings and stock.

TUNGSRAM Co Ltd: 1340 Budapest, Újpest 4; tel. 692-800; telex 22-5058; f. 1896; light sources, lighting systems, vacuum engineering machinery, vacuum electronics, electronics and components, etc.; Gen. Man. ANDRÁS GÁBOR.

Vegyépszer: 1379 Budapest, POB 540; tel. 666-497; telex 22-6017; building and assembling of chemical plant, supply of complete equipment.

HUNGARY

VEPEX Contractor Ltd: 1370 Budapest, POB 308; tel. 425-534; telex 22-4208; vegetable protein extract.

Videoton Rt: 1398 Budapest, POB 557; tel. 210-520; telex 22-4763; TV sets, tape recorders, computer systems and peripherals, software; Man. Dir ISTVÁN PAPP.

Volánpack: 1431 Budapest, POB 115; tel. 335-980; telex 22-6404; forwarding and transport, packaging, warehousing, etc.

Vörös Október MGTSZ, Ócsa: 1734 Budapest, POB 26; tel. 279-654; telex 22-6156; agricultural co-operative.

TRADE FAIRS

Budapest International Fairs: Hungexpo, 1441 Budapest, POB 44; tel. 573-555; telex 22-4188; f. 1968; technical goods (spring), consumer goods (autumn), and other specialized exhibitions and fairs; Dir FERENC SCHRIFFERT.

CO-OPERATIVE ORGANIZATIONS

Fogyasztási Szövetkezetek Országos Tanácsa (SZÖVOSZ) (National Council of Hungarian Consumer Co-operative Societies): 1054 Budapest, Szabadság tér 14; tel. 123-857; telex 22-4862; safeguards interests of Hungarian consumer, housing and saving co-operative societies, co-owner of co-op foreign trading companies and joint ventures; Pres. JÓZSEF HARTMANN; Gen. Sec. Dr ISTVÁN SZLAMENICKY; 3.5m. mems.

Ipari Szövetkezetek Országos Tanács (OKISZ) (National Council of Industrial Co-operatives): 1146 Budapest, Thököly u. 58–60; tel. 415-140; telex 22-7576; Pres. LAJOS KÖVESKUTI.

Országos Szövetkezeti Tanács (OSzT) (National Co-operative Council): 1373 Budapest, Szabadság tér 14; tel. 127-467; telex 22-4862; Pres. Dr ISTVÁN SZABÓ.

Termelőszövetkezetek Országos Tanácsa (TOT) (National Council of Agricultural Co-operatives): 1054 Budapest, Akadémia u. 1–3; tel. 328-167; telex 22-6810; f. 1967; Pres. ISTVÁN SZABÓ; Gen. Sec. Dr JÁNOS ELEKI; 1,280 co-operatives with 816,000 mems.

TRADE UNIONS

Magyar Szakszervezetek Országos Tanácsa (SZOT) (Central Council of Hungarian Trade Unions): 1415 Budapest, Dózsa György u. 84B; tel. 532-900; telex 22-5861; f. 1898; Pres. SÁNDOR GÁSPÁR; Gen. Sec. TIBOR BARANYAI; nearly 5m. mems.

Affiliated Unions

Magyar Bányaipari Dolgozók Szakszervezete (Hungarian Union of Mineworkers): 1068 Budapest, Gorkij fasor 46–48; tel. 221-226; telex 22-7499; f. 1913; Pres. ISTVÁN HAVRÁN; Gen. Sec. LÁSZLÓ KOVÁKS; 168,092 mems.

Magyar Bőripari Dolgozók Szakszervezete (Hungarian Union of Leather Trade Workers): 1062 Budapest, Bajza u. 24; tel. 429-970; f. 1868; Gen. Sec. PÁL CSIKOS; 49,499 mems.

Magyar Egészégügyi Dolgozók Szakszervezete (Hungarian Union of Medical and Health Workers): 1363 Budapest, Münnich F. u. 32; tel. 327-530; f. 1945; Pres. Dr ZOLTÁN SZABÓ; Gen. Sec. Dr ISTVÁN FÜZI; 267,581 mems.

Magyar Élelmezésipari Dolgozók Szakszervezete (Hungarian Union of Food Industry Workers): 1068 Budapest, Gorkij fasor 44; tel. 225-880; f. 1905; Gen. Sec. ELISABETH BALOGH; 221,216 mems.

Magyar Építő-, Fa- és Építőanyagipari Dolgozók Szakszervezete (Hungarian Union of Building, Woodworking and Building Materials Industries): 1068 Budapest, Dózsa György u. 84A; tel. 425-760; f. 1906; Pres. FERENC RESZEGI; Gen. Sec. ISTVÁN GYÖNGYÖSI; 388,251 mems.

Magyar Helyiipari és Városgazdasági Dolgozók Szakszervezete (Hungarian Union of Municipal Workers and Local Industries): 1391 Budapest, Benczur u. 43; tel. 116-950; f. 1952; Pres. ZOLTAN FABOK; Gen. Sec. Dr FERENC SALI; 284,642 mems.

Magyar Kereskedelmi, Pénzügyi és Vendéglátóipari Dolgozók Szakszervezete (Hungarian Union of Distributive, Clerical and Catering Workers): 1066 Budapest, Jókai u. 6; tel. 318-970; f. 1948; Pres. JÁNOS TAUSZ; Gen. Sec. JÁNOS VAS; 542,789 mems.

Magyar Közalkalmazottak Szakszervezete (Hungarian Union of Civil Service Workers): 1088 Budapest, Puskin u. 4; tel. 141-640; f. 1945; Pres. Dr OLGA PRIESZOL; Gen. Sec. ENDRE SZABÓ; 237,050 mems.

Magyar Közlekedési és Szállítási Dolgozók Szakszervezete (Hungarian Union of Road Haulage and Transport Workers): 1081 Budapest, Köztársaság tér 3; tel. 138-468; f. 1898; Gen. Sec. GYULA MOLDOVAN; 192,203 mems.

Directory

Magyar Mezőgazdasági, Erdészeti és Vizügyi Dolgozók Szakszervezete (MEDOSZ) (Hungarian Union of Agricultural, Forestry and Water Supply Workers): 1066 Budapest, Jókai u. 2–4; tel. 314-550; f. 1906; Pres. ISTVÁN HUNYA; Gen. Sec. Dr FERENC DOBI; 401,331 mems.

Magyar Művészeti Szakszervezetek Szövetsége (Association of Hungarian Art Workers' Unions): 1068 Budapest, Gorkij fasor 38; tel. 211-120; f. 1957; Pres. IMRE VASS; Gen. Sec. TIBOR SIMÓ; 41,568 mems.

Magyar Nyomda- és Papíripar és a Sajtó Dolgozóinak Szakszervezete (Hungarian Printing, Paper and Press Workers' Union—renamed Printing, Paper Industry, Press and Book Publishing Industry Union in 1986): 1085 Budapest, Kölcsey u. 2; tel. 338-185; f. 1862; Pres. LÁSZLÓ TERÉNYI; Gen. Sec. JÁNOS LUX; 53,662 mems.

Magyar Pedagógusok Szakszervezete (Hungarian Union of Teachers): 1068 Budapest, Gorkij fasor 10; tel. 228-456; f. 1945; Pres. Dr LÁSZLÓ SZÜCS; Gen. Sec. Dr JÓZSEF VOKSÁN; 293,287 mems.

Magyar Postások Szakszervezete (Hungarian Union of Post Office Workers): 1146 Budapest, Cházár András u. 13; tel. 428-777; f. 1945; Pres. GÉZÁNÉ BENKE; Gen. Sec. GRICSER ENIKŐ HENSZKY; 83,830 mems.

Magyar Ruházatipari Dolgozók Szakszervezete (Hungarian Union of Clothing Workers): 1077 Budapest, Almássy tér 1; tel. 229-843; f. 1892; Pres. JULIANNA TÓTH; Gen. Sec. Dr MARGIT CZERVÁN; 39,840 mems.

Magyar Textilipari Dolgozók Szakszervezete (Hungarian Union of Textile Workers): 1068 Budapest, Rippl-Rónai u. 2; tel. 221-626; f. 1905; Pres. JÓZSEF APRÓ; Gen. Sec. Mrs ISTVÁN MARTOS; 141,450 mems.

Magyar Vas- Fém- és Villamosenergiaipari Dolgozók Szakszervezete (Hungarian Union of Iron, Metal and Electric Energy Workers): 1086 Budapest, Koltói Anna u. 5–7; tel. 135-200; f. 1877; Pres. AMBRUS BOROWSZKY; Gen. Sec. KÁROLY HERCZEG; 656,773 mems.

Magyar Vasutasok Szakszervezete (Hungarian Union of Railway Workers): 1068 Budapest, Benczúr u. 41; tel. 221-895; f. 1945; Pres. JENŐ GYÓCSI; Gen. Sec. FERENC KOSZORUS; 195,513 mems.

Magyar Vegyipari Dolgozók Szakszervezete (Hungarian Union of Chemical Workers): 1068 Budapest, Benczúr u. 45; tel. 421-778; f. 1897; Pres. SÁNDOR TAKÁCS; Gen. Sec. FERENC DAJKA; 155,366 mems.

Transport

Raabersped: 1525 Budapest, POB 241; tel. 388-777; telex 22-4249; international transport management.

RAILWAYS

Magyar Államvasutak (MÁV) (Hungarian State Railways): 1940 Budapest, Népköztarsaság u. 73–75; tel. 220-660; telex 22-4342; state-owned since 1868; total network 7,617 km, including 1,917 km of electrified lines; in the 1986–90 period 354 km of lines were to be electrified; Dir-Gen. Dr GYULA VÁRSZEGI.

There is an underground railway in Budapest, with a network of 28 km in 1985; 328.5m. passengers were carried in 1984.

ROADS

In 1985 the road network totalled 90,696 km, including 324 km of motorways, 6,385 km of main or national roads and 22,987 km of secondary roads. Construction of the Budapest ring motorway was due to start in 1987, with financial assistance from the World Bank. There are extensive long-distance bus services. Road passenger and freight transport is provided by the state-owned VOLÁN companies and by individual (own account) operators.

Hungarocamion: 1442 Budapest, POB 108; tel. 415-165; telex 22-5489; international road freight transport company; 16 offices in Europe and the Middle East; fleet of 1,700 articulated lorries; Gen. Man. IMRE TORMA.

SHIPPING AND INLAND WATERWAYS

In 1986 the Hungarian merchant fleet comprised 20 vessels totalling 100,000 dwt.

MAHART—Magyar Hajózási Rt. (Hungarian Shipping Co): 1052 Budapest, Apáczai Csere János u. 11; tel. 181-880; telex 22-5258; carries goods and passengers on the Danube and Lake Balaton;

maintains regular cargo traffic between Budapest and the Middle East ports, and between Adriatic and Mediterranean ports, including North Africa; operates Continental/Far East/India and Red Sea service via Suez; operates the Hungarian merchant fleet as well as public ports including container-terminal and ship-repairing yards; Dir-Gen. JÓZSEF SCHUSTER.

MAFRACHT: 1364 Budapest, POB 105, Kristóf tér 2; tel. 185-276; telex 22-4471; shipping agency.

CIVIL AVIATION

The international airport is at Ferihegy, 16 km from the centre of Budapest. An expansion and development programme began in 1977, and the reconstruction work on the runways was scheduled for completion in 1987. Ferihegy-2 opened in 1985. There are no public internal air services.

Légügyi Főigazgatóság (Hungarian Air Authority): 1077 Budapest, Dob u. 75–81; tel. 422-544; General Directorate of Civil Aviation, Ministry of Transport; controls civil aviation; Dir-Gen. ENDRE FARKAS.

Magyar Légiközlekedési Vállalat (MALÉV) (Hungarian Airlines): 1051 Budapest, Roosevelt tér 2; tel. 189-033; telex 22-4954; f. 1946; regular services from Budapest to Europe, North Africa and the Middle East; Gen. Dir LAJOS JAHODA; fleet of 4 Il-18, 8 TU-134 and 10 TU-154.

Tourism

Országos Idegenforgalmi Hivatal (Hungarian Tourist Board): 1051 Budapest, Dorottya u. 4; tel. 186-354; telex 22-5182; f. 1968; Head Dr ISTVÁN MEGGYES.

Budapest Tourist—Budapesti Idegenforgalmi Vállalat (Budapest Travel Company): 1051 Budapest, Roosevelt tér 5-7; tel. 186-663; telex 22-6448; f. 1972; runs tours, congresses, owns four hotels, two camping sites; Dir ISTVÁN CSABAI.

Co-optourist—Magyar Szövetkezetek Utazási Irodája (Travel Bureau of Hungarian Co-operatives): 1055 Budapest, Kossuth Lajos tér 13–15; tel. 121-017; telex 22-4741; f. 1969; services for businessmen include accommodation, car rental, programme organization, etc.; branch offices throughout the country; Gen. Dir Dr SÁNDOR SIPOS.

DANUBIUS—Danubius Travels: 1138 Budapest, Margitsziget; tel. 173-652; telex 22-6342; Dir IMRE GELLAI.

Express Ifjusági és Diák Utazási Iroda (Express Youth and Student Travel Bureau): 1054 Budapest, Szabadság tér 16; tel. 530-660; telex 22-5384; f. 1957; specializes in tours and services for young people; Gen. Man. Dr GYULA TARCSI.

Hungar Hotels—Hungarian Hotel and Restaurant Company: 1052 Budapest, Petőfi Sándor u. 16, POB 106; tel. 182-033; telex 22-4209; f. 1956; Pres. Dr GYULA GYÖKÖSSY.

IBUSZ—Idegenforgalmi, Beszerzési, Utazási és Szállitási Rt. (Hungarian Travel Agency): 1364 Budapest, Felszabadulás tér 5; tel. 186-866; telex 22-4976; f. 1902; 24-hour service for individual travellers at: 1052 Budapest, Petőfi tér 3; tel. 185-707; telex 22-4941; IBUSZ has 118 brs throughout Hungary; Gen. Man. ZOLTÁN HARSÁNYI.

Malév Air-Tours: 1051 Budapest, Roosevelt tér 2; Dir TAMÁS DÉRI.

Pannónia—Hotel and Catering Company: 1088 Budapest, Puskin u. 6, POB 159; tel. 341-518; telex 22-4561; f. 1949; owns 41 hotels; organizes through its Tourist Service Bureau tours, programmes, conferences etc. in Hungary, and Hungarian gastronomic festivals abroad; Gen. Man. JENŐ SOMOGYI.

Pegazus Tours: 1053 Budapest, Károlyi Mihály u. 5; Dir MAUSZ GOTTHARD.

Volántourist Vállalat: 1051 Budapest, Oktober 6 u. 11/13; tel. 123-410; telex 22-6181; f. 1971; Dir GÉZA MESZLÉNYI.

Atomic Energy

Hungary's first nuclear power station at Paks (on the Danube, south of Budapest), built with Soviet assistance, began trial operations in December 1982, and was formally inaugurated in November 1983. Three units, each of 440 MW, were in operation by 1986. Total capacity was scheduled to reach 1,760 MW in 1987, upon completion of the fourth unit. Two 1,000-MW blocks are due to be put into operation in 1994 and 1996. Agreements have been signed for co-operation in the peaceful uses of atomic energy with Cuba, Czechoslovakia, France, the German Democratic Republic, India, Italy, Romania and the USSR. Hungary is a member of the International Atomic Energy Agency, Vienna, the Joint Institute for Nuclear Research, Dubna, near Moscow, and the CMEA Standing Committee on the Peaceful Uses of Atomic Energy.

Országos Atomenergia Bizottság (National Atomic Energy Commission): 1374 Budapest, POB 565; tel. 327-172; telex 22-4907; f. 1956; Pres. PÁL TÉTÉNYI.

Kossuth Lajos Tudományegyetem Kisérleti Fizikai Intézete (Institute for Experimental Physics of the Kossuth Lajos University): 4001 Debrecen, POB 105; tel. 15-222; telex 72-200; f. 1923; Dir Prof. Dr J. CSIKAI.

Magyar Tudományos Akadémia Atommag Kutató Intézete—ATOMKI (Institute of Nuclear Research of the Hungarian Academy of Sciences): 4026 Debrecen, Bem tér 18/C; tel. 17-266; telex 72-210; f. 1954; research in nuclear structure, reaction, ion-atom collisions, etc.; Dir Prof. Dr D. BERÉNYI.

Magyar Tudományos Akadémia Izotóp Intézete (Institute of Isotopes of the Hungarian Academy of Sciences): 1525 Budapest, POB 77, Konkoly Thege u.; tel. 696-687; telex 22-5360; f. 1959; Dir Dr A. VERES.

Magyar Tudományos Akadémia Központi Fizikai Kutató Intézete—KFKI (Central Research Institute for Physics of the Hungarian Academy of Sciences): 1525 Budapest, POB 49; tel. 698-566; telex 22-4722; f. 1950; 7 organizational units; Dir-Gen. Dr FERENC SZABÓ.

Országos 'Frédéric Joliot-Curie' Sugárbiológiai és Sugáregészségügyi Kutató Intézet (National Research Institute for Radiobiology and Radiohygiene): 1775 Budapest, POB 101; f. 1957; tel. 385-954; telex 22-5103; research on effects of ionizing and non-ionizing radiations; Dir Dr L. B. SZTANYIK.

Paksi Atomerőmű Vállalat—PAV: Paks, POB 71; tel. (75) 11-222; telex 14-440; f. 1976; foreign trade org.; training of nuclear power plant specialists, licences and auxiliary equipment for nuclear power plants; exports spent nuclear fuel; imports fresh nuclear fuel, nuclear power plant mountings.

ICELAND

Introductory Survey

Location, Climate, Language, Religion, Flag, Capital

The Republic of Iceland comprises one large island and numerous smaller ones, situated near the Arctic Circle in the North Atlantic Ocean. The main island lies about 300 km south-east of Greenland, about 1,000 km west of Norway and about 800 km north of Scotland. The Gulf Stream keeps Iceland warmer than might be expected, with average temperatures ranging from 10°C (50°F) in the summer to 1°C (34°F) in winter. Icelandic is the official language. Almost all of the inhabitants profess Christianity: the Evangelical Lutheran Church is the established church and embraces 93% of the population. The national flag (proportions 25 by 18) displays a red cross, bordered with white, on a blue background, the upright of the cross being to the left of centre. The capital is Reykjavík.

Recent History

Iceland became independent on 17 June 1944, when the Convention that linked it with Denmark, under the Danish throne, was terminated. Iceland is a founder member of the Nordic Council (1953) and has belonged to both NATO and the Council of Europe since 1949.

From 1959 to 1971 Iceland was governed by a coalition of the Independence and Social Democratic Parties. In the general election of June 1971 there was a swing to the left, and Olafur Jóhannesson, the leader of the Progressive Party, formed a coalition government with the People's Alliance and the Union of Liberals and Leftists. Elections held in June 1974 showed a swing back to the right, and in August the Independence and Progressive Parties formed a coalition led by Geir Hallgrímsson. Loss of popularity through its treatment of Iceland's economic problems, such as the perpetuation of rampant inflation by index-linked wage settlements, led to the Government's resignation in June 1978, following extensive election gains by the left-wing People's Alliance and Social Democratic Party. Disagreements over economic measures, and over the People's Alliance's policy of withdrawal from NATO, led to two months of negotiations before a new government was formed. In September 1978 Jóhannesson, the former Prime Minister, formed a coalition of his own Progressive Party with the People's Alliance and the Social Democrats, but this government, after dealing with immediate economic necessities, resigned in October 1979, when the Social Democrats withdrew. A caretaker administration was formed by Benedikt Gröndal, the Social Democratic leader. General elections held in December were inconclusive, and in February 1980 Gunnar Thoroddsen of the Independence Party formed a coalition with the People's Alliance and Progressive Party.

In June 1980 Vigdís Finnbogadóttir, a non-political candidate who was favoured by left-wing groups because of her opposition to the US military airbase in Iceland, achieved a narrow victory in the election for the mainly ceremonial office of President. She took office on 1 August 1980, becoming the world's first popularly-elected female Head of State, and began a second four-year term (unopposed and without an election) in August 1984.

The coalition government lost its majority in the Lower House of the Althing in September 1982, and a general election was held in April 1983. The Independence Party received the largest share (38.7%) of the votes, but there was a swing away from traditional parties, with two new parties (the Social Democratic Alliance and the Women's Alliance) together winning nearly 13% of the votes. A centre-right coalition was formed between the Independence and Progressive Parties, with Steingrímur Hermannsson, the Progressive Party leader and former Minister of Fisheries and Communications, as Prime Minister, and Geir Hallgrímsson, Prime Minister from 1974 to 1978 and leader of the Independence Party, as Minister for Foreign Affairs. In an attempt to halt spiralling inflation (see Economic Affairs), the Government discontinued wage indexation, extended existing wage agreements and devalued the króna in May 1983. Although this brought inflation down to an average of about 18% in the year to August 1984, a strike by over 11,000 public-sector employees, concerned at the fall in their real incomes over the past three years and demanding wage increases of 30%, paralysed the country's economy for a month in October. The Government eventually agreed to wage increases of about 22% over the next 14 months, but refused to reintroduce wage indexation. In November 1984 the króna was again devalued. In March 1985, after a two-week strike, Iceland's fishermen were awarded a 30% wage increase. Real wages had fallen below the levels of late 1983 and of most of 1984. The wage contracts between the Government and the trade unions could be repealed from September 1985 onwards, and, to forestall the threat of further strikes, in June 1985 the private-sector employers secured with the Icelandic Federation of Labour a no-strike agreement, valid for 18 months, in return for a 15% increase in wages. In February 1986 a further wage settlement was agreed by the Government, the trade unions and the employers, providing for a four-tier pay increase of 13% during 1986. These increases were based on the premise that the increase in the cost of living would not exceed 6.1% between January and November.

The importance of fishing to Iceland's economy, and fears of excessive exploitation of the fishing grounds near Iceland by foreign fleets, caused the Icelandic Government to extend its territorial waters to 12 nautical miles (22 km) in 1964 and to 50 nautical miles (93 km) in September 1972. British opposition to these extensions produced two 'cod wars'. In October 1975 Iceland unilaterally introduced a fishing limit of 200 nautical miles (370 km), both as a conservation measure and to protect important Icelandic interests. The 1973 agreement on fishing limits between Iceland and the United Kingdom expired in November 1975 and failure to reach a new agreement led to the third and most serious 'cod war'. Casualties occurred, and in February 1976 Iceland temporarily broke off diplomatic relations with Britain, the first ever diplomatic break between two NATO countries. In June 1976 the two countries reached an agreement, and in December the British trawler fleet withdrew from Icelandic waters. In June 1979 Iceland declared its exclusive rights to the 200-mile fishing zone. Relations between Iceland and the USA were strained during July 1986, when the USA argued that, by approving the catch of 80 fin whales and 40 sei whales, Iceland was acting against a moratorium imposed by the International Whaling Commission, and threatened to impose a boycott on Icelandic fish products. Iceland declared that the catch of whales was for scientific purposes only, and, after a halt during August for conservation talks, whaling was resumed.

In May 1985 the Althing unanimously approved a resolution declaring the country a 'nuclear-free zone', i.e. banning the entry of nuclear weapons. Iceland was host to a US-Soviet summit meeting in October 1986.

Government

According to the Constitution, executive power is vested in the President (elected for four years by universal adult suffrage) and the Cabinet, consisting of the Prime Minister and other Ministers appointed by the President. In practice, however, the President performs only nominally the functions ascribed in the Constitution to this office, and it is the Cabinet alone which holds real executive power. Legislative power is held jointly by the President and the Althing (Parliament), with 60 members elected by universal suffrage for four years (subject to dissolution by the President), using a mixed system of proportional representation. The Althing chooses 20 of its members to form

ICELAND

the Upper House, the other 40 forming the Lower House. For some purposes the two Houses sit jointly as the United Althing. Electoral reforms, approved by the Althing in 1983 (subject to approval by the next Althing, in accordance with the Constitution), include the creation of three new seats and the lowering of the minimum voting age from 20 to 18 years. The Cabinet is responsible to the Althing. Iceland has seven administrative districts.

Defence

Iceland has no defence forces of its own but is a member of the North Atlantic Treaty Organization (NATO, see p. 179). There are units of US forces at Keflavík air base, which is used for observation of the North Atlantic Ocean, under an agreement made in 1951 between Iceland and NATO. The airfield at Keflavík is a base for the new US airborne early warning system. An agreement between Iceland and the USA in October 1974 limited US troops stationed in Iceland to 2,900. In July 1983 Iceland agreed to the construction of a military and civilian air-terminal at Keflavík, funded by the USA at a cost of US $120m.

Economic Affairs

The Icelandic economy is excessively dependent on fishing, which provided 67% of total visible export receipts in 1984, and 75% in 1985. Iceland is, therefore, very susceptible to movements in world prices of fish products and to fluctuations in the size of its catches. The modernized trawler fleet supplies about 80 freezing plants, which produce white fish fillets, frozen prawns, scallops, Norway lobster (scampi) and capelin. Other fish products, such as oil, meal and salted fish, are major exports. During the 1970s, an increase in fisheries production was made possible by Iceland's exclusive rights over an extended fishing zone (see Recent History). Iceland's total annual catch rose from 681,000 metric tons in 1971 to 1,641,000 tons in 1979. In 1981, however, there was a decline in catches of herring, halibut and capelin, the last of which had accounted for up to 15% of total exports. The total catch slumped from 1,435,000 tons in 1981 to 786,000 tons in 1982, mainly because of a temporary ban on capelin fishing, to preserve stocks. Catches of capelin were only 13,200 tons in 1982, compared with more than 640,000 tons in 1981. The total catch rose to 835,000 tons (including 133,500 tons of capelin) in 1983, and to 1,525,100 tons (including 864,800 tons of capelin) in 1984. Catches of cod, the most valuable part of the total, declined from 461,000 tons in 1981 to 281,500 tons in 1984. However, 1985 was one of the best years in Icelandic fishing history, with a total catch of 1,672,300 tons (including 993,000 tons of capelin and 322,800 tons of cod), an increase of nearly 10% over the 1984 total. Between January and September 1986 the catch was 1,086,200 tons, compared with 976,000 tons in the first nine months of 1985. All fishing was temporarily halted in January 1987, when 5,000 fishermen staged a 15-day strike, demanding a higher share of the catch. Despite an agreement by the fishermen to return to work, exports continued to be delayed by a walk-out of 250 seamen, which prevented cargo ships from leaving the country.

Very little land is arable, but good grazing keeps Iceland self-sufficient in meat and milk products. Production costs are high and exports have to be subsidized. In recent years the wool industry has developed rapidly, a total of 1,533 metric tons being produced in 1983, when exports of woollen products earned 653m. krónur. Exports in 1985 totalled 1,099m. krónur.

Iceland's only significant natural resource, apart from fish, is its potential for cheap hydroelectric and geothermal power production. Geothermal energy is used for home heating and in diatomite production, and may be more fully exploited as a substitute for imported petroleum products, of which 60% come from the USSR. In 1984 Iceland's economically harnessable hydroelectric power was estimated at 64,000 GWh per annum, of which only about 6% was being utilized. Total installed capacity was 750 MW in 1983; a new plant with capacity of 150 MW was due to begin operating in 1987. Cheap hydroelectricity is used by the aluminium plant owned by the Swiss Alusuisse group. At this plant imported ore is processed, producing ingots and rolling slabs for export. Aluminium exports contributed 17.6% of total visible export receipts in 1983, 14.6% in 1984 and 9.9% in 1985, when production fell by 9.5%. Other foreign companies have shown an interest in the establishing of plants in Iceland for energy-intensive processes. Norway owns a 45% share in Iceland's first ferro-silicon plant in Whale Bay, which began exporting in 1979, when exports earned a total of 33m. krónur. In 1985 exports of ferro-silicon earned 1,220m. krónur.

In 1985 the principal sources of imports to Iceland were the Federal Republic of Germany, the United Kingdom, Denmark and the Netherlands; its main export markets were the USA, the United Kingdom, the Federal Republic of Germany and the USSR. Iceland joined EFTA in 1970, and negotiated a trade agreement with the EEC in 1972. Tariffs on Icelandic fish exports to the EEC were reduced after the settlement of the fisheries dispute with the United Kingdom. The final abolition of tariffs between Iceland and the EEC and EFTA took place on 1 January 1980. In 1985 EFTA countries took 14.2% of exports and provided 22.0% of imports, while EEC members accounted for 39.3% of exports and 49.4% of imports; the USA took 27% of exports.

In recent years the Icelandic economy has experienced the difficulties resulting from severe inflation, which rose from an annual average of 33% during 1971–80 to averages of 52% in 1981, 49% in 1982 and 87% in 1983. Large pay rises, accompanied by the index-linking of wages to the price level, kept inflation high. Government economic policy was mainly directed towards maintaining full employment, reducing inflation and minimizing borrowing abroad. In May 1983 the Government announced that the policy of wage indexation was to be discontinued; the rate of inflation subsequently fell, averaging about 18% in the 12 months to August 1984, but rose again after a serious strike in the public sector in October, which resulted in wage increases of about 22% until the end of 1985. By December 1985, after falling to an average of about 13% in May, the annual inflation rate had risen to 30%. A new wage agreement, signed in 1986, provided for an overall pay increase of 13%, based on the premise that the exchange rate would be kept stable and that price increases between January and November would be limited to 6.1%. This, combined with improvements in trade, reduced inflation during 1986, and it was hoped that, by the end of the year, the annual rate of inflation would be below 10% for the first time since 1971. Price rises have forced repeated devaluation of the currency to maintain competitive pricing of fish exports: the value of the króna depreciated by 57% between 1973 and 1977. Three devaluations in 1981 were followed by devaluations of 12% and 14.3% in 1982, of 9% in January 1983 and of 14.6% in May 1983. In November 1984 the króna was devalued by 12%. In January 1981 a 'new' króna was introduced, equivalent to 100 'old' krónur. Controls on interest rates were abolished in August 1984, and in October rates reached about 28%, among the highest, in real terms, in the world. Although interest rates reached 32% in February 1986, they were reduced in March, to 20% (following the new wage settlements), and again in April, to 15.5%.

The trade deficit increased from 949m. krónur in 1981 to 3,168m. in 1982, owing to falling fish catches and depressed world demand for aluminium and ferro-silicon. Exports of these metals improved, however, in 1983 and 1984. The trade deficit fell to 1,973m. krónur in 1983, but rose to 3,187m. krónur in 1984. Exports of marine products rose from 15,833m. krónur in 1984 to 25,226m. krónur in 1985. Despite an increase in total export earnings during 1985, the trade deficit also increased, to 3,850m. krónur. The decline in international petroleum prices in 1986 considerably reduced the import bill, and this development, combined with increased demand for exports, was expected to produce a significant improvement in the trade balance for 1986 and a reduction in the current account deficit, which was equivalent to 4.3% of gross domestic product (GDP) in 1985.

Iceland's inhabitants enjoy a high standard of living. In 1984, according to estimates by the World Bank, the country's gross national product (GNP) per head, at average 1982–84 prices, was US $11,020, one of the highest national levels in Europe. Between 1965 and 1984, it was estimated, GNP per head, measured in constant prices, increased at an average rate of 2.6% per year. Total GNP (in 1980 prices) increased by 2.1% in 1981, compared with a 5.4% rise in 1980, but it fell by 0.9% in 1982 and by a further 5.7% in 1983. However, real GNP increased by 2.8% per year in 1984 and 1985, and was expected to increase by 5.2% in 1986. Iceland's long-term foreign debt was equivalent to 40.4% of annual GDP at the end of 1982, and had risen to 55% of GDP by the end of 1985. Unemployment averaged 1% of the labour force in 1983, remained below 2% during 1984, in spite of the Government's anti-inflationary measures, and was reduced to an average of 0.9% in 1985.

Social Welfare

There is a comprehensive system of social security, providing a wide range of insurance benefits, including old-age pensions, family allowances, maternity grants, widows' pensions, etc. Contributions to the scheme are compulsory. Pensions and health insurance now apply to the whole population. Accident insurance applies to all wage and salary earners and self-employed persons—unless they request exemption—and unemployment insurance to the unions of skilled and unskilled workers and seamen in all towns and villages of over 300 inhabitants, as well as to several unions in villages of less than 300 inhabitants. In 1980 there were 488 physicians working in Iceland, and the country had 46 hospital establishments, with a total of 3,730 beds, equivalent to one for every 61 inhabitants: one of the best ratios in the world. Of total expenditure by the central government in 1982, 2,197.2m. krónur (21.0%) was for health, and a further 1,700.2m. krónur (16.3%) for social security and welfare.

Education

Education is compulsory and free for nine years between seven and 16 years of age. Primary education, beginning at the age of seven and lasting for six years, is available in day schools in urban regions, while in the more remote country districts pupils attend a state boarding-school. The total enrolment at primary schools in 1982 was equivalent to 99% of children in the relevant age-group. Secondary education begins at 13 years of age and lasts for up to seven years, comprising a first cycle of three years and a second of four years. Enrolment at secondary schools in 1982 was equivalent to 87% of children in the appropriate age-group. In 1974 the primary and lower secondary schools were formed into basic schools, leading to a national examination which gives access to further education. The matriculation examination at the end of four years at upper secondary school or at comprehensive school provides the qualification for university entrance. Iceland has three institutions of higher learning. Expenditure on education by the central government in 1982 was 1,357.3m. krónur, representing 13.0% of total spending.

Tourism

Iceland's main attraction for tourists lies in the ruggedness of the interior, with its geysers and thermal springs. Following a period of rapid growth between 1968 and 1971, when the number of foreign visitors to Iceland increased by 50%, the rate of expansion slowed. Tourist arrivals fell from about 76,900 in 1979 to 65,900 in 1980, recovering to 77,600 in 1983, 85,200 in 1984 and 97,443 in 1985. Receipts from foreign visitors totalled 1,462m. krónur in 1983, 2,030m. in 1984 and 3,101m. in 1985.

Public Holidays

1987: 1 January (New Year's Day), 16 April (Maundy Thursday), 17 April (Good Friday), 20 April (Easter Monday), 28 May (Ascension Day), 8 June (Whit Monday), 17 June (National Day), 8 August (Bank Holiday), 24–26 December (Christmas), 31 December (New Year's Eve).

1988: 1 January (New Year's Day), 31 March (Maundy Thursday), 1 April (Good Friday), 4 April (Easter Monday), 12 May (Ascension Day), 23 May (Whit Monday), 17 June (National Day), 8 August (Bank Holiday), 24–26 December (Christmas), 31 December (New Year's Eve).

Weights and Measures

The metric system is in force.

Currency and Exchange Rates

100 aurar = 1 new Icelandic króna.

Exchange rates (30 September 1986):
  £1 sterling = 58.46 krónur;
  US $1 = 40.40 krónur.

ICELAND

Statistical Survey

Sources (unless otherwise stated): Statistical Bureau of Iceland, Reykjavík; tel. (1) 26699; National Economic Institute of Iceland, Reykjavík; tel. (1) 26699; Seðlabanki Islands (Central Bank of Iceland), Hafnarstraeti 10, POB 160, 121 Reykjavík; tel. (1) 20500; telex 2020.

AREA AND POPULATION

Area: 103,000 sq km (39,769 sq miles).

Population: 204,930 (males 103,621; females 101,309) at census of 1 December 1970; 242,089 registered at 1 December 1985.

Density (per sq km): 2.4 (1985).

Births, Marriages and Deaths (1984): Live births 4,113 (birth rate 17.2 per 1,000); Marriage rate 5.9 per 1,000; Deaths 1,853 (death rate 7.1 per 1,000).

Employment* (1984): Agriculture, forestry and fishing 23,726; Mining, quarrying and manufacturing 27,813; Construction 11,614; Trade, restaurants and hotels 16,866; Community, social and personal services 27,813; Total (incl. others) 116,559.

* Figures refer to the working population covered by compulsory social insurance.

AGRICULTURE, ETC.

Principal Crops (metric tons, 1985): Potatoes 12,818; Turnips 498.

Livestock (December 1985): Cattle 72,900; Sheep 709,300; Horses 54,100; Pigs 2,575; Poultry 322,600.

Livestock Products (metric tons, 1985): Mutton and lamb 12,200; Milk 119,400; Wool (unwashed) 1,490; Sheep skins 2,612; Eggs 2,612.

Fishing ('000 metric tons, live weight, 1985): Atlantic cod 322.8; Haddock 49.6; Saithe 55.1; Atlantic redfishes 91.4; Capelin 993.0; Atlantic herring 49.4; Crustaceans 27.3; Total (incl. others) 1,672.3.

INDUSTRY

Selected Products ('000 metric tons, 1985): Frozen fish 122; Salted, dried or smoked fish 75; Cement 117; Ferro-silicon 57.7; Aluminium (unwrought) 73.4; Electric energy 3,837 million kWh.

FINANCE

Currency and Exchange Rates: 100 aurar (singular: eyrir) = 1 new Icelandic króna (plural: krónur). *Coins:* 5, 10 and 50 aurar; 1 and 5 krónur. *Notes:* 10, 50, 100 and 500 krónur. *Sterling and Dollar equivalents* (30 September 1986): £1 sterling = 58.46 krónur; US $ = 40.40 krónur; 1,000 new krónur = £17.11 = $24.75. *Average Exchange rate* (new krónur per US $): 24.843 in 1983; 31.694 in 1984; 41.508 in 1985.

Note: The new króna, equal to 100 old krónur, was introduced on 1 January 1981.

Budget (million new krónur, 1985): *Revenue:* Direct taxes 8,395 (taxes on income and wealth 7,071); Indirect taxes 26,341 (sales tax 11,906, taxes on alcohol and tobacco 1,925, excise tax 1,495, import duties 3,939, other indirect taxes 7,076); Non-tax revenue 2,176; Total 36,912. *Expenditure* (excluding net lending): General administration 3,381; Education 5,746; Health and welfare 14,299; Subsidies 2,856; Agriculture 841; Fisheries 432; Manufacturing 185; Power 799; Communications 3,696; Other purposes 6,471; Total 38,706.

International Reserves (US $ million at 31 December 1985): Gold 1.8; IMF special drawing rights 0.4; Reserve position in IMF 4.4; Foreign exchange 200.0; Total 206.6.

Money Supply (million new krónur at 31 December 1985): Currency outside banks 1,226; Demand deposits at commercial and savings banks 5,529; Total money 6,755.

Cost of Living (consumer price index for Reykjavík; average of monthly figures; base: 1 February 1984 = 100): 83.02 in 1983; 107.25 in 1984; 141.97 in 1985.

Gross Domestic Product in purchasers' values (million new krónur at current prices): 62,656 in 1983; 81,532 in 1984; 110,523 in 1985.

Balance of Payments (US $ million, 1985): Merchandise exports f.o.b. 814.0, Merchandise imports f.o.b. −814.3, *Trade balance* −0.3; Exports of services 410.3, Imports of services −525.4, *Balance of goods and services* −115.3; Private unrequited transfers (net) 1.3, Government unrequited transfers (net) −1.1, *Current balance* −115.1; Direct capital investment (net) 24.1, Other long-term capital (net) 131.1, Short-term capital (net) 77.2, Net errors and omissions −46.7, *Total* (net monetary movements) 70.6; Valuation change (net) −6.5, *Changes in reserves* 64.1.

EXTERNAL TRADE

Principal Commodities (million new krónur, distribution by SITC, 1982): *Imports c.i.f.:* Food and live animals 940.7; Crude materials (inedible) except fuels 738.6; Petroleum, petroleum products, etc. 1,738.0 (Refined petroleum products 1,688.1); Chemicals and related products 805.7; Basic manufactures 2,254.5; Machinery and transport equipment 3,173.0 (Road vehicles and parts, excl. tyres, engines and electrical parts, 733.7); Miscellaneous manufactured articles 1,663.5; Total (incl. others) 11,644.8. *Exports f.o.b.:* Fish, crustaceans, molluscs and preparations 5,996.0 (Fresh, chilled or frozen fish 3,224.9, Dried, salted or smoked fish 2,207.7); Basic manufactures 1,446.1 (Unwrought aluminium and alloys 852.2); Total (incl. others) 8,478.8.

Principal Trading Partners (million new krónur, country of consignment, 1985): *Imports c.i.f.:* Australia 1,315, Denmark 3,412, France 1,081, Federal Republic of Germany 4,985, Japan 1,632, Netherlands 3,356, Norway 2,855, Sweden 2,995, USSR 3,016, United Kingdom 3,592, USA 2,559; Total (incl. others) 37,600. *Exports f.o.b.:* France 1,346, Federal Republic of Germany 2,810, Japan 1,672, Portugal 1,909, Spain 1,309, Switzerland 1,082, USSR 2,272, United Kingdom 6,315, USA 9,118; Total (incl. others) 33,750.

TRANSPORT

Road Traffic (registered motor vehicles at 31 December 1985): Passenger cars 102,954; Buses and coaches 1,422; Goods vehicles 12,741.

Shipping: *Merchant fleet* (registered vessels, 1985): Fishing vessels 832 (displacement 112,954 grt); Passenger ships, tankers and other vessels 131 (displacement 73,408 grt). *International freight traffic* ('000 metric tons, 1985): Goods loaded 943; Goods unloaded 1,565.

Civil Aviation (scheduled external Icelandic traffic, '000, 1985): Kilometres flown 13,425, Passenger-kilometres 2,102,245, Cargo ton-kilometres 15,823, Mail ton-kilometres 4,365.

TOURISM

Foreign Visitors By Country of Origin (1985): Denmark 9,946, France 4,483, Federal Republic of Germany 9,419, Norway 7,665, Sweden 8,167, United Kingdom 9,720, USA 31,633; Total (incl. others) 97,443.

COMMUNICATIONS MEDIA

Radio Receivers (1985): 72,965 licensed.

Television Receivers (1985): 68,848 licensed.

Telephones (1985): 105,407 in use.

Books (production, 1982): 1,200 titles (incl. new editions).

Daily Newspapers (1982): 5 (combined circulation 114,000 copies per issue).

EDUCATION

1982: Pre-primary and primary: 216 institutions, 3,220 staff (incl. part-time teachers), 4,235 pre-primary students, 25,018 Primary students; Secondary: 115 institutions, 1,450 staff (incl. part-time teachers), 28,700 students; Universities and colleges: 3 institutions, 280 Staff (incl. part-time teachers), 4,600 students.

Source: Ministry of Education and Culture.

Directory

The Constitution

A new constitution came into force on 17 June 1944, when Iceland declared its full independence. The main provisions of the Constitution are summarized below:

GOVERNMENT

The President is elected for four years by universal suffrage. All those qualified to vote who have reached the age of 35 years are eligible for the Presidency.

Legislative power is jointly vested in the Althing and the President. Executive power is exercised by the President and other governmental authorities in accordance with the Constitution and other laws of the land.

The President summons the Althing every year and determines when the session shall close. The President may adjourn meetings of the Althing but not for more than two weeks nor more than once a year. The President appoints the Ministers and presides over the State Council. The President may be dismissed only if a resolution supported by three-quarters of the Althing is approved by a plebiscite.

The President may dissolve the Althing. Elections must be held within two months and the Althing must reassemble within eight months.

The Althing is composed of 60 members, 49 of whom are elected by eight proportionately represented constituencies for a period of four years, while 11 supplementary seats are allotted to the parties for equalization, intended to achieve as near a truly proportional representation with regard to the total of votes gained by each party as possible, without raising the total number of members above 60. Substitute members are elected at the same time and in the same manner as Althing members. The Althing is divided into two houses, the Upper House (efri deild) and the Lower House (nedri deild); but sometimes both Houses work together as a United Althing. The Upper House consists of one-third of the members, whom the United Althing chooses from among the representatives, the remaining two-thirds forming the Lower House. Each House and the United Althing elects its own Speaker. The minimum voting age, both for local administrative bodies and for the Althing is 20 years and all citizens domiciled in Iceland may vote, provided they are of unblemished character and financially responsible.

The budget must be introduced in the United Althing but other bills may be introduced into either House. They must, however, be given three readings in each house and be approved by a simple majority before they are submitted to the President. If the President disapproves a bill, it nevertheless becomes valid but must be submitted to a plebiscite. Ministers may speak in either House, but may vote only in that of which they are members. The Ministers are responsible to the Althing and may be impeached by that body, in which case they are tried by the Court of Impeachment.

LOCAL GOVERNMENT

For purposes of local government, the country is divided into Provinces, Districts and Municipalities. The eight Urban Municipalities are governed by Town Councils, which possess considerable autonomy. The Districts also have Councils and are further grouped together to form the Provinces, over each of which a centrally appointed Chief Official presides. The franchise for municipal purposes is universal above the age of 20 years, and elections are conducted on a basis of proportional representation.

The Government

HEAD OF STATE

President: Vigdís Finnbogadóttir (took office 1 August 1980; began a second term 1 August 1984).

THE CABINET
(January 1987)

A coalition of the Independence Party (IP) and the Progressive Party (PP).

Prime Minister: Steingrímur Hermannsson (PP).
Minister for Foreign Affairs: Matthías A. Matthiesen (IP).
Minister of Agriculture, Justice and Ecclesiastical Affairs: Jón Helgason (PP).
Minister of Culture and Education: Sverrir Hermannsson (IP).
Minister of Fisheries: Halldór Ásgrímsson (PP).
Minister of Trade and Commerce: Matthías Bjarnason (IP).
Minister of Health, Social Security, and Communications: Ragnhildur Helgadóttir (IP).
Minister of Finance: Thorsteinn Pálsson (IP).
Minister of Energy and Industry: Albert Guðmundsson (IP).
Minister of Social Affairs: Alexander Stefánsson (PP).

MINISTRIES

Prime Minister's Office: Stjórnarráðshúsið v/Lækjartorg, 150 Reykjavík; tel. (1) 25000.
Ministry of Agriculture: Arnarhváli, 150 Reykjavík; tel. (1) 25000.
Ministry of Commerce: Arnarhváli, 150 Reykjavík; tel. (1) 25000; telex 2092.
Ministry of Communications: Hafnarhúsinu við Tryggvagötu, 150 Reykjavík; tel. (1) 25000.
Ministry of Education: Hverfisgötu 6, 150 Reykjavík; tel. (1) 25000; telex 2111.
Ministry of Finance: Arnarhváli, 150 Reykjavík; tel. (1) 25000.
Ministry of Fisheries: Lindargötu 9, 150 Reykjavík; tel. (1) 25000; telex 2342.
Ministry of Foreign Affairs: Hverfisgötu 115, 150 Reykjavík; tel. (1) 25000; telex 2225.
Ministry of Health and Social Security: Laugavegi 116, 150 Reykjavík; tel. (1) 25000.
Ministry of Industry: Arnarhváli, 150 Reykjavík; tel. (1) 25000.
Ministry of Justice and Ecclesiastical Affairs: Arnarhváli, 150 Reykjavík; tel. (1) 25000.
Ministry of Social Affairs: Hafnarhúsinu við Tryggvagötu, 150 Reykjavík; tel. (1) 25000.

President

Presidential Election, 29 June 1980*

	Votes
Vigdís Finnbogadóttir	43,530
Guðlaugur Thorvaldsson	41,624
Albert Guðmundsson	25,567
Pétur Thorsteinsson	18,124

* The presidential election that had been scheduled for 30 June 1984 was not held, as President Finnbogadóttir was the only candidate.

Legislature

ALTHING

Speaker of the United Althing: Thorvaldur G. Kristjánsson (IP).
Speaker of the Upper House: Salome Thorkelsdóttir (IP).
Speaker of the Lower House: Ingvar Gislason (PP).
Secretary-General (Clerk) of the Althing: Fridjón Sigurdsson.

General Election, 23 April 1983

	Votes	%	Seats
Independence Party	50,251	38.7	23
Progressive Party	24,095	18.5	14
People's Alliance	22,490	17.3	10
Social Democratic Party	15,214	11.7	6
Social Democratic Alliance	9,489	7.3	4
Women's Alliance	7,125	5.5	3
Others	1,298	1.0	—
Total	129,962	100.0	60

ICELAND

Political Organizations

Althýdubandalag (People's Alliance): Hverfisgötu 105, 101 Reykjavík; tel. (1) 17500; f. 1956 by amalgamation of a section of the Social Democratic Party and the Socialist Unity Party, reorganized as a Socialist party 1968; Chair. SVAVAR GESTSSON; Parliamentary Leader RAGNAR ARNALDS.

Althýduflokkurinn (Social Democratic Party): Althyduhusid, Hverfisgata 8–10, Reykjavík; tel. (1) 29244; f. 1916 with a moderate Socialist programme; Chair. JÓN BALDVIN HANNIBALSSON; Parliamentary Leader EIÐUR GUÐNASON.

Bandalag Jafnadarmanna (Social Democratic Alliance): Templarasund 3, Reykjavík; tel. (1) 21833; f. 1983; liberal-socialist programme; Party Leader GUÐMUNDUR EINARSSON; Parliamentary Leader STEFÁN BENEDIKTSSON.

Framsóknarflokkurinn (Progressive Party): POB 5531, Rauðarárstígur 18, 125 Reykjavík; tel. (1) 24480; f. 1916 with a programme of social and economic amelioration and co-operation; Chair. STEINGRÍMUR HERMANNSSON; Parliamentary Leader PÁLL PÉTURSSON; Sec. GUÐMUNDUR BJARNASON.

Samtoek um Kvennalista (Women's Alliance): Hotel Vik, Reykjavík; f. 1983; to promote the interests of women and children; Parliamentary Leader GUDRUN AGNARSDÓTTIR.

Sjálfstaedisflokkurinn (Independence Party): Háaleitisbraut 1, Reykjavík; tel. (1) 82900; f. 1929 by an amalgamation of the Conservative and Liberal Parties; its programme is social reform within the framework of private enterprise and the furtherance of national and individual independence; Leader THORSTEINN PÁLSSON.

Diplomatic Representation

EMBASSIES IN ICELAND

China, People's Republic: Viðimelur 29, Reykjavík; telex 2148; Chargé d'affaires: ZHAI SHIXIONG.

Czechoslovakia: POB 1443, Smáragata 16, 101 Reykjavík; tel. (1) 19823; Chargé d'affaires a.i.: (vacant).

Denmark: Hverfisgata 29, Reykjavík; telex 2008; Ambassador: HANS ANDREAS DJURHUUS.

Finland: Reykjavík; telex 2373; Ambassador: ANDERS HULDEN.

France: Túngata 22, Reykjavík; tel. (1) 17621; telex 2063; Ambassador: YVES MAS.

German Democratic Republic: Ægissiða 78, Reykjavík; telex 2002; Chargé d'affaires: KLAUS BREDOW.

Germany, Federal Republic: Túngata 18, Reykjavík; tel. (1) 19535; Ambassador: HANS HERMANN HAFERKAMP.

Norway: Fjólugata 17, Reykjavík; telex 2163; Ambassador: NIELS L. DAHL.

Sweden: Fjólugata 9, Reykjavík; telex 2087; Ambassador: GUNNAR-AXEL DAHLSTROM.

USSR: Garðastraeti 33, Reykjavík; telex 2200; Ambassador: IGOR NIKOLAYEVICH KRASAVIN.

United Kingdom: POB 460, Laufásvegur 49, Reykjavík; tel. (1) 15883; telex 2037; Ambassador: MARK F. CHAPMAN.

USA: Laufásvegur 21, Reykjavík; tel. (1) 29100; telex 3044; Ambassador: NICHOLAS RUWE.

Judicial System

All cases are heard in Ordinary Courts except those specifically within the jurisdiction of Special Courts. The Ordinary Courts include both a lower division of urban and rural district courts presided over by the district magistrates, and the Supreme Court.

Justices of the Supreme Court are appointed by the President and cannot be dismissed except by the decision of a court. The Justices elect the Chief Justice for a period of two years.

SUPREME COURT

Chief Justice: MAGNÚS THORODDSEN.

Justices: BJARNI K. BJARNASON, GUÐMUNDUR JÓNSSON, GUÐMUNDUR SKAFTASON, GUÐRÚN ERLENDSDÓTTIR, HALLDÓR THORBJÖRNSSON, MAGNÚS TH. TORFASON, THOR VILHJÁLMSSON.

Religion

There is complete religious freedom in Iceland.

CHRISTIANITY
Protestant Churches

Evangelical Lutheran Church: Biskupsstofa, Suðurgata 22, Reykjavík 101; tel. (1) 621500; telex 3014; the national Church, endowed by the State; more than 93% of the population are members; Iceland forms one diocese, Reykjavík, with two suffragan sees; 299 congregations and 122 pastors; Bishop PÉTUR SIGURGEIRSSON.

Frikirkjani i Reykjavík (Free Church of Reykjavík): POB 1671, 121 Reykjavík; tel. (1) 14579; f. 1899; Free Lutheran denomination; 7,000 mems; Head Rev. GUNNAR BJÖRNSSON.

Ohádi Frikirkusöfnudurinn (Independent Congregation): Reykjavík; Free Lutheran denomination; 2,000 mems; Head Rev. EMIL BJÖRNSSON.

Seventh-day Adventists: POB 262, 121 Reykjavík.

The Roman Catholic Church

Iceland comprises a single diocese, directly responsible to the Holy See. In 1985 there were an estimated 1,800 adherents in the country.

Bishop of Reykjavík: (vacant), Hávallagata 14, 101 Reykjavík; tel. (1) 11423; Vicar-Gen. Rev. AUGUSTINUS GEORGE.

The Press

PRINCIPAL DAILIES

Althýdubladid (The Labour Journal): Armúli 38, Reykjavík; tel. (1) 81866; f. 1916; organ of the Social Democratic Party; Editor GUÐMUNDUR ARNI STEFÁNSSON; circ. 5,000.

DV (Dagbladid-Visir): Síðumúli 12–14, Reykjavík; tel. (1) 27022; telex 2214; f. 1910; independent; Editors JONAS KRISTJANSSON, ELLERT B. SCHRAM; circ. 39,000.

Morgunbladid (Morning News): Adalstræti 6, POB 1555, Reykjavík; tel. (1) 691100; telex 2127; f. 1913; Independent; Editors MATTHÍAS JOHANNESSEN, STYRMIR GUNNARSSON; circ. 46,000.

Thjódviljinn (Will of the Nation): Skolavordustig 19, Reykjavík; tel. (1) 17500; telex 2178; f. 1936; organ of socialism, labour movement and national independence; Editors ARNI BERGMANN, EINAR KARL HARALDSSON, KJARTAN OLAFSSON; circ. 12,000.

Timinn (The Times): Síðumúli 15, Box 370, Reykjavík; tel. (1) 86300; f. 1917; organ of the Progressive Party; Editors ELIAS SNAELAND JONSSON, THORARINN THORARINSSON; circ. 17,000.

Visir (Indicator): Sídumuli 14, Reykjavík; tel. 86611; weekly; conservative.

WEEKLIES

Althýdumadurinn (Commoner): Strandgata 9, Akureyri; f. 1931; weekly; organ of Social Democratic Party; Editor BJARNI SIGTRYGGSSON; circ. 3,500.

Einherji: Siglufjorður; weekly; organ of the Progressive Party.

Íslendingur-Isafold (Icelander-Icecountry): Kaupangi v/Mýrarveg, 600 Akureyri; tel. (6) 21500; f. 1915; for North and East Iceland; Editor STEFÁN SIGTRYGGSSON.

Mánudagsbladid (Monday Paper): Tjarnargata 39, Reykjavík.

Siglfirdingur: Siglufjorður; weekly; organ of the Independence Party.

Skutull: Isafjörður; weekly; organ of the Social Democratic Party.

Vikan (The Week): Thverholt 11, 105 Reykjavík; tel. (1) 27022; telex 3079; f. 1938; illustrated weekly; Editor THORUNN GESTSDÓTTIR; circ. 8,000.

PERIODICALS

Aegir (The Sea): c/o Fiskifélag Íslands, Reykjavík; f. 1905; published by the Fisheries Asssociation, Reykjavík; monthly; Editors THORSTEINN GÍSLASON, JÓNAS BLÖNDAL; circ. 2,400.

Æskan (The Youth): POB 523, 121 Reykjavík; f. 1897; 9 per year; children's magazine.

Atlantica: Hoefdabakki 9, POB 93, Reykjavík 121; tel. (1) 84966; telex 2121; quarterly; in-flight magazine of Icelandair.

Dagur (The Day): Strandgata 31, POB 58, Akureyri; f. 1918; 3 a week; organ of the Progressive Party; Editor H. SVEINBJÖRNSSON; circ. 6,100.

ICELAND

Economic Statistics: POB 160, 101 Reykjavík; f. 1980; quarterly; published by the Economic Department of the Central Bank of Iceland.

Eimreidin (Progress): Síðumúli 12, Reykjavík; f. 1895; quarterly; literary and critical review.

Freyr: POB 7080, 127 Reykjavík; tel. (1) 19200; f. 1904; fortnightly; organ of the Icelandic Agriculture Society and the Farmers' Union; Editors MATTHÍAS EGGERTSSON, JÚLÍUS DANIELSSON; circ. 4,100.

Frjáls verzlun (Free Trade): Ármúli 18, POB 1193, Reykjavík; f. 1939; 8 a year; news and business magazine; Editor SIGHVATUR BLÖNDAHL.

Gródur and Gardar: Ármúli 18, Reykjavík; 2 a year; gardening; Editor SIGHVATUR BLÖNDAHL.

Hagtidindi: published by the Statistical Bureau of Iceland, Hverfisgata 8–10, 101 Reykjavík; tel. (1) 26699; f. 1914; monthly; Dir-Gen. HALLGRÍMUR SNORRASON.

Heima Er Bezt: Tryggvabraut 18–20, Akureyri; f. 1951; monthly; literary; circ. 4,200.

Helgafell: Reykjavík; quarterly; literary review; Editor TÓMAS GUÐMUNDSSON.

Iceland Review: Hoefdabakki 9, POB 8576, Reykjavík 121; tel. (1) 84966; telex 2121; 4 a year; English; general.

Iceland: Yearbook of Trade and Industry: Hoefdabakki 9, Reykjavík 121; tel. (1) 84966; telex 2121; annual; English.

Idnadarbladid: Ármúli 18, 105 Reykjavík; 6 a year; news and industry magazine; Editor J. STEINAR LUÐVIGSSON; circ. 6,400.

Íslenzk Fyrirtaeki (Icelandic Firms): Ármúli 18, Reykjavík; tel. (1) 82300; annually; business and industrial directory; Editor ERLA EINARSDÓTTIR.

Ithróttabladid: Ármúli 18, Reykjavík; monthly; sport; Editor J. STEINAR LUÐVIGSSON.

News from Iceland: Hoefdabakki 9, POB 8576, Reykjavík; tel. (1) 84966; telex 2121; 10 a year; English.

Nýtt Líf: Ármúli 18, Reykjavík; 6 a year; fashion; Editor GULLVEIG SÆMUNDSDÓTTIR.

Rjettur: Reykjavík; monthly; left-wing magazine on politics and social problems; Editor EINAR OLGEIRSSON.

Samvinnan: Suðurlandsbraut 32, Reykjavík; monthly; publ. by the Federation of Icelandic Co-operative Societies; Editor GYLFI GRÖNDAL; circ. 6,000.

Sjávarfréttir: Ármúli 18, Reykjavík; monthly; fishing and fishing-industry; Editor SIGHVATUR BLÖNDAHL.

Úrval (Digest): Síðumúli 33, Reykjavík; monthly; Editor SIGURÐUR HREIÐAR HREIÐARSSON; circ. 4,000.

Vikungur (Seaman): Barugata 11, Reykjavík; 10 a year.

Vinnan (Work): Grensásvegur 16, 108 Reykjavík; tel. (1) 83044; f. 1943; publ. by Icelandic Federation of Labour; Editor SVERRIR ALBERTSSON; circ. 5,000.

NEWS AGENCY
Foreign Bureau

Agence France-Presse (AFP): Bragattagata 3A, 101 Reykjavík; tel. 2066; Correspondent GÉRARD LEMARQUIS.

Publishers

Aegisútgáfan: Sólvallagötu 74, Reykjavík; Man. GUÐMUNDUR JAKOBSSON.

Akranesútgáfan: Deildartúni 8, Akranes.

Almenna Bókafélagid: Austurstraeti 18, Reykjavík; tel. (1) 25544; telex 2046; f. 1955; general; book club editions; Man. Dir KRISTJÁN JOHANNSSON.

Bókaforlag Odds Björnssonar: POB 558, Tryggvabraut 18–20, 600 Akureyri; tel. (6) 22500; f. 1897; general; Dir GEIR S. BJÖRNSSON.

Bókaútgáfa Æskunnar: POB 523, 121 Reykjavík; tel. (1) 10248.

Bókaútgáfa Gudjóns O. Gudjónssonar: Thverholti 13, Reykjavík; tel. (1) 27233.

Bókaútgáfa Thorsteins M. Jónssonar: Eskihlid 21, 105 Reykjavík.

Bókaútgáfan Björk: Háholti 7, Akranes; Man. DANIEL AGÚSTÍNUSSON.

Bókaútgáfan Hildur: Fögrubrekku 47, Kópavogi; tel. 76700; Man. GUNNAR THORLEIFSSON.

Bókaútgáfan Hlidskjálf: Ingólfsstraeti 22, 101 Reykjavík; tel. (1) 17520.

Bókaverzlun Sigfúsar Eymundssonar: Austurstraeti 18, Reykjavík; f. 1872; educational and general, import and export of books, maps of Iceland; Man. EINAR ÓSKARSSON.

Fjölvi: Hjallalandi 28, Reykjavík.

Forni: Kleppsvegi 4, 105 Reykjavík.

Fródi, hf: Ármúla 21, Reykjavík; Man. GISSUR EGGERTSSON.

Heimskringla: Laugavegi 18, Reykjavík, POB 392; tel. (1) 15199; telex 2265; f. 1932; Man. ÁRNI EINARSSON.

Helgafell: Veghúsastíg 7, Reykjavík; tel. (1) 16837; Dir RAGNAR JÓNSSON.

Hid islenzka bokmenntafélag: Thingholtsstræti 3, 101 Reykjavík, POB 1252; tel. (1) 21960; f. 1816; general; Pres. SIGURDUR LÍNDAL.

Hörpuútgáfan: Stekkjarholt 8-10, POB 25, 300 Akranes; Dir BRAGI THORDARSON.

Idunn: Braeðraborgarstígur 16, POB 294, 121 Reykjavík; tel. (1) 28555; telex 2308; general; f. 1945; Man. Dir ANNA VALDIMARSDÓTTIR.

Hladbud, hf: Braeðraborgarstígur 16, POB 294, 121 Reykjavík; tel. (1) 28555; telex 2308; f. 1944; mainly school books; Dir VALDIMAR JÓHANNSSON.

Ísafoldarprentsmidja, hf: Thingholtsstraeti 5, Reykjavík; tel. (1) 17165; f. 1877; Chair. and Gen. Man. LEÓ E. LÖVE.

Íslenzka Fornritafélag, Hid: Austurstraeti 18, Reykjavík; f. 1928; Pres. J. NORDAL.

Jonsonn & Co (The English Bookshop): Hafnarstr 4/9, POB 1131, Reykjavík 101; tel. (1) 13133; f. 1927; general; Man. Dir BENEDIKT KRISTJÁNSSON.

Kynning: POB 1238, Reykjavík; tel. (1) 38456; f. 1966; natural science, books on Iceland, art, history; Man. H. HANNESSON.

Leiftur, hf: Höfðatúni 12, Reykjavík; tel. (1) 17554; Man. HJÖRTUR THORDARSON.

Litbrá-Offset: Höfðatúni 12, POB 999, 121 Reykjavík.

Ljódhus Ltd.: Laufásvegi 4, POB 1506, Reykjavík; Man. SIGFÚS DAÐASON.

Mál og Menning (Literary Book Club): Laugavegi 18, Reykjavík; tel. (1) 15199; telex 2265; f. 1937; 4,600 mems; Chair. THORLEIFUR EINARSSON; Man. ÁRNI EINARSSON; Editor HALLDOR GUÐMUNDSSON.

Menningarsjódur og Thjódvinafélagi: POB 1398, Reykjavík; tel. (1) 621822; f. 1940; publishing dept of Cultural Fund; Dir. HRÓLFUR HALLDÓRSSON.

Námsgagnastofnun (National Centre for Educational Materials): POB 5192, Reykjavík 125; tel. (1) 28088; telex 3000; f. 1979; Dir (Publishing House) ASGEIR GUÐMUNDSSON.

Örn og Örlygur, hf: Síðumúli 11, 108 Reykjavík; tel. (1) 84866; telex 2197; f. 1966; general; book club editions; Owner and Man. Dir ÖRLYGUR HÁLFDANARSON.

Prenthusid: Barónsstíg 11B, Reykjavík.

Prentsmidja Árna Valdimarssonar: Brautarholti 16, Reykjavík.

Prentsmidjan Oddi, hf: Höfðabakka 7, POB 1305, 121 Reykjavík.

Rökkur: Flókagötu 15, Reykjavík; tel. (1) 18768.

Setberg: Freyjugötu 14, 101 Reykjavík; tel. (1) 17667; publisher and printer; Dir ARNBJÖRN KRISTINSSON.

Siglufjardardrentsmidja: Suðurgötu 16, Siglufirði.

Skjaldborg Ltd: Hafnarstraeti 67, POB 218, 600 Akureyri; tel. 11024.

Skuggsjá: Strandgötu 31, 220 Hafnarfjörður; tel. 50045; general fiction; Dirs JÓHANNES OLIVERSSON, LILJA OLIVERSDÓTTIR.

Snaefell: Álfaskeiði 58, 220 Hafnarfirði; Man. THORKELL JOHANNESSON.

Stafafell: Laugavegi 1, Reykjavík; Man. MAGNÚS BRYNJÓLFSSON.

Steindórsprent, hf: Ármúla 5, Reykjavík.

Sudri: Kleppsvegi 2, 105 Reykjavík; tel. (1) 36384; Man. GUDJÓN ELÍASSON.

Thjódsaga: Thingholtsstraeti 27, Reykjavík; tel. (1) 13510; Dir HAFSTEINN GUÐMUNDSSON.

Valafell: Thykkvabae 16, Reykjavík; tel. (1) 84179; school books.

Vikingsútgáfan: Veghúsastíg 7, Reykjavík; Dir RAGNAR JONSSON.

Vikurútgáfan: Kleppsvegi 2, Reykjavík.

ICELAND   *Directory*

PUBLISHERS' ASSOCIATION

Félag íslenskra bókaútgefenda: Laufásvegi 12, 101 Reykjavík; tel. (1) 27820; Pres. Eyjólfur Sigurdsson; Man. Björn Gíslason.

Radio and Television

In 1986 there were 73,000 radio receivers and 65,200 television receivers in use.

RADIO

Ríkisútvarpið (Icelandic State Broadcasting Service): Skúlagata 4, POB 120, Reykjavík; tel. (1) 22260; telex 2066; f. 1930; Dir-Gen. Markús Örn Antonsson; Chair. of Programme Board Inga Jóna Thordardóttir; Dir Radio Elfa-Björk Gunnarsdóttir.

Programme 1: Skúlagata 4, POB 120, Reykjavík; tel. (1) 22260; telex 2066; Head of Programmes Gunnar Stefánsson; there are two long wave, 8 medium wave and 63 FM transmitters broadcasting 121 hours a week.

Programme 2: Efstaleiti 1, 108 Reykjavík; tel. (1) 38500; telex 2066; Head of Programmes Thorgeir Ástvaldsson; there are 38 FM transmitters broadcasting 63 hours a week.

Radio Bylgjan: Snorrabraut 54, 105 Reykjavík; privately-owned.

TELEVISION

Rikisútvarpid-Sjónvarp (Icelandic State Broadcasting Service—Television): Laugavegur 176, 105 Reykjavík; tel. (1) 38800; telex 2035; f. 1966; covers 98% of the population; broadcasts daily except on Thursdays, total 35 hours a week; Dir Pétur Guðfinnsson; Head of Programmes Hrafn Gunnlaugsson.

Stöð 2: Krókhálsi 6, 110 Reykjavík; privately-owned.

The US Navy operates a radio station (24 hours a day), and a television service (80 hours a week), on the NATO base at Keflavík.

Finance

(cap. = capital; p.u. = paid up; res = reserves; dep. = deposits; m. = million; kr = krónur; brs = branches)

BANKING
Central Bank

Seðlabanki Íslands (Central Bank of Iceland): Hafnarstræti 10, POB 160, 121 Reykjavík; tel. (1) 20500; telex 2020; f. 1961 to take over central banking activities of Landsbanki Íslands; cap. 1m. kr, res 3,004m. new kr, dep. 16,898m. kr (1985); Govs Dr Jóhannes Nordal, Tómas Arnason, Geir Hallgrímsson.

Commercial Banks

Althydubankinn hf (The Union Bank Ltd): Laugavegur 31, Reykjavík; telex 94620; f. 1976; cap. and res 86m. new kr, dep. 975m. kr; Gen. Man. Stefán Gunnarsson; 3 brs.

Búnaðarbanki Íslands (Agricultural Bank of Iceland): Austurstræti 5–7, 101 Reykjavík, POB 1720; tel. (1) 25600; telex 2383; f. 1929; independent state-owned bank; res 830.3m. new kr, dep. 7,059m. kr (1985); Gov. Stefán Valgeirsson; Man. Dirs Stefán Hilmarsson, Stefán Pálsson, Jón Adolf Gudjonsson; 20 brs.

Idnadarbanki Íslands (Industrial Bank of Iceland): Laekjargotu 12, 101 Reykjavík; f. 1953; tel. (1) 20580; telex 3003; cap. and res 241m. new kr, dep. 2,837m. kr; Dirs Bragi Hannesson, Valur Valsson, Ragnar Önundarson; 9 brs.

Landsbanki Íslands (National Bank of Iceland): Austurstræti 11, POB 700, 101 Reykjavík; tel. (1) 27722; telex 2030; f. 1885; cap. and res 2,072m. new kr, dep. 12,662m. kr (1985); Gen. Mans Björgvin Vilmundarson, Jónas H. Haralz, Helgi Bergs; 30 brs.

Samvinnubanki Íslands hf (Co-operative Bank of Iceland): Bankastræti 7, Reykjavík; tel. (1) 20700; f. 1962; cap. and res 279m. new kr, dep. 2,578m. kr; Man. Geir Magnússon; 18 brs.

Útvegsbanki Íslands (Fisheries Bank of Iceland): POB 190, Austurstræti 19, 101 Reykjavík; tel. (1) 17060; telex 2047; f. 1930; converted into independent government institution in 1957; cap. and res 90m. new kr, dep. 3,748m. kr (1985); Gen. Mans Halldór Guðbjörnsson, Olafur Helgason, Lárus Jónsson; 13 brs.

Verzlunarbanki Íslands hf: (Iceland Bank of Commerce Ltd): Bankastræti 5, POB 790, 121 Reykjavík; tel. (1) 27200; telex 3027; f. 1961; cap. and res 238m. new kr, dep. 1,758m. kr; Chair. Árni Gestsson; Gen. Mans Kristján Oddsson, Höskuldur Olafsson; 8 brs.

INSURANCE

Tryggingastofnun Ríkisins (State Social Security Institution): Laugavegi 114, 105 Reykjavík; tel. (1) 19300; f. 1936; Man. Dir Eggert G. Thorsteinsson; Chair. of Tryggingaráð (Social Security Board) Ólafur G. Einarsson.

Private Companies

Almennar Tryggingar Ltd (General Insurance): Síðumúla 39, 105 Reykjavík; tel. (1) 82800; telex 2086; f. 1943; cap. p.u. 46.8m. new kr (1986); Gen. Man. Olafur B. Thors.

Brunabótafélag Íslands (Iceland Fire Insurance Society): Laugavegi 103, Reykjavík; tel. (1) 26055; f. 1915; net assets 121.7m. new kr (1983); Man. Dir I. R. Helgason.

Íslenzk Endurtrygging (National Icelandic Reinsurance Co): Suðurlandsbraut 6, 108 Reykjavík; tel. (1) 681444; telex 2153; f. 1939; cap. 37.7m. new kr (1985); Gen. Man. Bjarni Thordarson.

Líftryggingafélagid Andvaka (Andvaka Mutual Life Insurance Co): Ármúla 3, 105 Reykjavík; f. 1949; Man. Dir Hallgrímur Sigurðsson.

Samábyrgd Íslands á Fiskiskipum (Icelandic Mutual Fishing Craft Insurance): Lágmuli 9, 108 Reykjavík; tel. (1) 81400; f. 1909; Man. Dir Páll Sigurdsson.

Samvinnutryggingar (Co-operative Insurance Co): Ármúla 3, 105 Reykjavík; tel. (1) 681411; f. 1946; Chair. E. Einarsson; Man. Dir H. Sigurdsson.

Sjóvátryggingarfélag Íslands hf (Iceland Marine Insurance Co): POB 5300, Suðurlandsbraut 4, 125 Reykjavík; tel. (1) 82500; telex 2051; f. 1918; share cap. 50.2m. kr, res fund 741.9m. kr (1985); Chair. Benedikt Sveinsson; Gen. Man. Einar Sveinsson.

Trade and Industry

CHAMBER OF COMMERCE

Verzlunarrád Íslands (Chamber of Commerce); House of Commerce, 108 Reykjavík; tel. (1) 83088; telex 2316; f. 1917; Chair. Jóhann J. Ólafsson; Gen. Sec. Arni Arnason; 530 mems.

EMPLOYERS' ORGANIZATIONS

Federation of Icelandic Industries: POB 1407, Reykjavík; tel. (1) 27577; f. 1933; Chair. Viglundur Thorsteinsson; Gen. Man. Olafur Davidsson; 300 mems.

Vinnuveitendasamband Íslands (Employers' Federation): Garðastræti 41, 101 Reykjavík; f. 1934; Chair. G. J. Friðriksson; Man. Dir Thorarinn V. Thorarinsson.

FISHING INDUSTRY ASSOCIATIONS

Félag Íslenzkra Botnvörpuskipaeigenda (Steam Trawler Owners' Association): Hafnarhuoll, Tryggvagötu, Reykjavík; tel. (1) 29500; telex 2090; f. 1916; Chair. Thorhallur Helgason; Sec.-Gen. Ágúst Einarsson.

Fiskifélag Íslands (Fisheries Association): Reykjavík; f. 1911; conducts technical and economic research and services for fishing vessels; performs various functions for the fishing industry in accordance with Icelandic law or by arrangement with the Ministry of Fisheries; Man. Már Elísson.

Fiskveidasjódur Íslands (Fisheries Loan Fund of Iceland): Reykjavík; f. 1905; lends money for construction and purchase of fishing vessels, equipment and plant; financed by interest charges; loans granted 1,121m. new kr (1985); Chair. Björgvin Vilmundarson; Gen. Man. Már Elísson.

Landssamband Islenzkra Utvegsmanna (Fishing Vessel Owners' Federation): POB 893, Reykjavík; f. 1939; Chair. K. Ragnarsson; Man. Kristjan Ragnarsson.

Sölusamband Íslenzkra Fiskframleidenda (Union of Fish Producers): Adalstræti 6, POB 889, 121 Reykjavík; tel. (1) 11480; telex 2041; Dir Magnús Gunnarsson.

CO-OPERATIVE ASSOCIATION

Samband Íslenskra Samvinnufélaga (Federation of Icelandic Co-operative Societies): Sölvhólsgata 4, 101 Reykjavík; tel. (1) 28200; telex 2023; f. 1902; links 42 co-operative societies; Chair. Valur Arnthórsson; Dir-Gen. Gudjón B. Ólafsson; 46,657 mems.

ICELAND — Directory

TRADE UNIONS

Althýdusamband Íslands (Icelandic Federation of Labour): Grensásveg 16, 108 Reykjavík; f. 1916; affiliated to ICFTU; Pres. Ásmundur Stefánsson; 59,000 mems.

Menningar- og Fraedslusamband Althýdu (MFA) (Workers' Educational Association): Grensásveg 16, 108 Reykjavík; Chair. Helgi Gudmundsson; Gen. Sec. Tryggvi Thór Adalsteinsson.

Bandalag Starfsmanna Rikis og Baeja (Municipal and Government Employees' Association): Grettisgötu 89, 105 Reykjavík; f. 1942; Chair. Kristjan Thorlacius; 13,600 mems.

Bladamannafélag Íslands (Union of Icelandic Journalists): Sídumúli 23, Reykjavík; tel. (1) 39155; f. 1897; Chair. Omar Valdimarsson; Sec. Frída Björnsdottir; 310 mems.

Landssamband Idnadarmanna (Federation of Icelandic Crafts and Industries): Hallveigarstigur 1, Reykjavík; tel. (1) 621590; telex 2085; f. 1932; non-party; Chair. Haraldur Sumarlidason; Gen. Sec. Thórleifur Jónsson; 3,200 mems.

Transport

RAILWAYS

There are no railways in Iceland.

ROADS

Much of the interior is uninhabited and the main road follows the coastline. Regular motor coach services link the main settlements. Development plans provide for new roads and harbour installations. At 31 December 1985 Iceland had 11,569 km of roads, of which 3,771 km were main roads.

Umferdarmáladeild (Transport Department): Umferdarmidstödin, Vatnsmýrarvegi 10, 101 Reykjavík; tel. (1) 19220; f. 1935; supervises passenger transport (coaches).

Félag Sérleyfishafa (Icelandic Bus Routes Union): BSI bus terminal, Umferdarmidstödinni, Vatnsmýrarveg 10, 101 Reykjavík; tel. (1) 22300; telex 3082; f. 1936; scheduled bus services throughout Iceland; also operates sightseeing tours and excursions; Chair. Ágúst Hafberg.

SHIPPING

Heavy freight is carried by coastal shipping. The principal seaport for international shipping is Reykjavík.

Hf. Eimskipafélag Íslands (Iceland Steamship Co.): POB 220, Pósthússtraeti 2, 101 Reykjavík; tel. (1) 21460; telex 2022; f. 1914; liner trade, general and bulk cargo between Iceland and the UK, Scandinavia, the Continent, the Baltic and the USA; also operates coastal services; Man. Dir Hördur Sigurgestsson; 20 vessels totalling 29,246 grt.

Hafskip Ltd: POB 524, 121 Reykjavík; tel. (1) 21160; telex 2034; f. 1958; liner services to Scandinavia, Hamburg, Antwerp, Rotterdam, UK, Baltic and USA; Chair. R. Kjartansson; Man. Dir Björgólfur Gudmundsson; Gen. Man. B. Gudmundsson; 6 cargo vessels.

Nesskip Ltd: Nesskip's House, 170 Seltjarnarnes; tel. (1) 625055; telex 2256; contract and tramp service; Man. Dir G. Asgeirsson; 5 vessels totalling 28,250 dwt (1986).

Skipaútgerd Ríkisins (Icelandic Shipping Dept): Hafnarhúsinu V, Tryggvagötu, Reykjavík 101; tel. (1) 28822; telex 3008; f. 1930; passenger and freight service round Iceland all the year; Gen. Man. Gudmundur Einarsson.

Samband Islenskra Samvinnufélaga (Samband Line): POB 1480, Sölvholsgata 4, 101 Reykjavík; tel. (1) 28200; telex 2101; Iceland-Europe-USA; Dir Omar Johannsson; 8 cargo vessels, 1 tanker.

CIVIL AVIATION

Air transport is particularly important to Iceland and is used, for example, to transport agricultural produce from remote districts. There are regular air services between Reykjavík and outlying townships. There is an international airport at Keflavík, 47 km from Reykjavík.

Eagle Air (Arnarflug): POB 1046, Lágmúli 7, 121 Reykjavík; telex 2183; f. 1976; 40% owned by Icelandair; internal network to 11 domestic airfields; external service to Amsterdam; summer flights to Düsseldorf and Zürich; Chair. of Board Haukur Björnsson; Man. Dir Agnar Fridriksson; fleet of 1 Boeing 707-320C, 1 Boeing 727-200C, 1 Boeing 707-320B, 1 Cessna 402C, 1 Twin Otter, 1 Cheyenne 11.

Icelandair (Flugleidir): Reykjavík Airport; tel. (1) 690100; telex 2021; f. 1973 as the successor to the two principal Icelandic airlines Flugfélag Íslands (f. 1937) and Loftleidir (f. 1944); in 1979 all licences, permits and authorizations previously held by Flugfélag Íslands and Loftleidir were transferred to it; internal network centred on Reykjavík to 10 domestic airfields; external year-round services to Scandinavia, the United Kingdom, Luxembourg and the USA, and summer flights to Austria, France, Greenland and the Federal Republic of Germany; Pres. and CEO Sigurdur Helgason; fleet of 4 DC-8-63, 1 DC-8-55, 1 Boeing 727-100C, 1 Boeing 727-200ADV, 1 Fokker F27-500, 4 Fokker F27-200.

Tourism

Iceland Tourist Bureau: Skogarhlid 6, Reykjavík; tel. (1) 25855; telex 2049; Gen. Man. Kjartan Lárusson.

INDIA

Introductory Survey

Location, Climate, Language, Religion, Flag, Capital

The Republic of India forms a natural sub-continent, with the Himalaya mountain range to the north. Two sections of the Indian Ocean, the Arabian Sea and the Bay of Bengal, lie to the west and east, respectively. India's neighbours are the People's Republic of China, Bhutan and Nepal to the north, Pakistan to the north-west and Burma to the north-east, while Bangladesh is surrounded by Indian territory except for a short frontier with Burma in the east. Near India's southern tip, across the Palk Strait, is Sri Lanka. India's climate ranges from temperate to tropical, with an average summer temperature on the plains of approximately 27°C (85°F). Annual rainfall varies widely, but the summer monsoon brings heavy rain over much of the country in June and July. The official language is Hindi, spoken by about 30% of the population. English is used as an associate language for many official purposes. The Indian Constitution also recognizes 16 regional languages, of which the most widely spoken are Telugu, Bengali, Marathi, Tamil, Urdu and Gujarati. Many other local languages are also used. According to the 1971 census, about 83% of the population are Hindus and 11% Muslims. There are also Christians, Sikhs, Buddhists, Jains and other minorities. The national flag (proportions 3 by 2) has three equal horizontal stripes, of saffron, white and green, with the Dharma Chakra (Wheel of the Law), in blue, in the centre of the white stripe. The capital is New Delhi.

Recent History

After a prolonged struggle against British colonial rule, India became independent, within the Commonwealth, on 15 August 1947. The United Kingdom's Indian Empire was partitioned, broadly on a religious basis, between India and Pakistan (then in two sections, of which the eastern wing became Bangladesh in 1971). The principal nationalist movement opposing British rule was the Indian National Congress (later known as the Congress Party). At independence the Congress leader, Jawaharlal Nehru, became India's first Prime Minister. Sectarian violence, the movement of 12m. refugees, the integration of the former princely states into the Indian federal structure and a dispute with Pakistan over Kashmir presented major problems.

India became independent as a dominion, with the British monarch as Head of State, represented locally by an appointed Governor-General. In November 1949, however, the Constituent Assembly approved a republican constitution, providing for a President (with mainly ceremonial functions) to be Head of State. Accordingly, India became a republic on 26 January 1950, although remaining a member of the Commonwealth. France transferred sovereignty of Chandernagore to India in May 1950, and ceded its four remaining Indian settlements in November 1954.

Nehru established the dominance of the Congress Party. The lack of effective opposition aided the process of social reform and industrialization. In December 1961 Indian forces successfully invaded the Portuguese territories of Goa, Daman and Diu, which were immediately annexed by India. Border disputes with the People's Republic of China escalated into a brief military conflict in October 1962. Nehru died in May 1964 and was succeeded by Lal Bahadur Shastri, a former Minister of Home Affairs. India and Pakistan fought a second major war over Kashmir in August–September 1965. Following mediation by the USSR, Shastri and President Ayub Khan of Pakistan signed a joint declaration, aimed at a peaceful settlement of the Kashmir dispute, on 10 January 1966. Shastri died on the next day, however, and Nehru's daughter, Mrs Indira Gandhi, formerly Minister of Information and Broadcasting, became Prime Minister.

In the 1967 general elections the Congress Party's majority was reduced. After the presidential election of August 1969, when two wings of Congress supported different candidates, the success of Indira Gandhi's candidate split the party. The Organization (Opposition) Congress, led by Morarji Desai, a former Deputy Prime Minister, was formed in November 1969. However, at the next general election to the Lok Sabha, held in March 1971, Indira Gandhi's wing of Congress won 350 of the 515 elective seats where polling took place.

Border incidents led to a 12-day war with Pakistan in December 1971. The Indian army rapidly occupied East Pakistan, which India recognized as the independent state of Bangladesh. Indira Gandhi and President Zulfiqar Ali Bhutto of Pakistan held a summit conference at Simla, India, in June–July 1972, when the two leaders agreed that their respective forces should respect the cease-fire line in Kashmir, and that India and Pakistan should resolve their differences through bilateral negotiations or other peaceful means. As a result of legislation approved in April–May 1975, the former protectorate of Sikkim became the 22nd state of the Indian Union, a constitutional change which soured India's relations with Nepal.

In 1975 Indira Gandhi was found guilty of electoral malpractice in the 1971 elections and was barred from holding elective office for six years. She then declared a state of emergency, and arrested more than 900 political opponents. In November the Supreme Court cleared her of electoral malpractice. A general election to the Lok Sabha was held in March 1977, when the number of elective seats was increased to 542. The election resulted in victory for the Janata (People's) Party, chaired by Morarji Desai, who became Prime Minister. Janata and an allied party, the Congress for Democracy, together received 43.2% of the total votes and won 298 of the 540 seats where polling took place. Congress received 34.5% of the votes and won 153 seats.

In January 1978 Indira Gandhi became leader of a new political group, the Congress (Indira) Party, known as Congress (I). A commission of inquiry, investigating the alleged excesses of her regime, found her guilty of corruption. In June Charan Singh, the Home Minister, and Raj Narain, the Health Minister, were dismissed for their criticism of Desai's Government. In November Indira Gandhi was elected to the Lok Sabha, but the House found her guilty of breach of privilege during the emergency rule, and she was expelled from the Lok Sabha.

In January 1979 Charan Singh returned to the Government as Minister of Finance and Desai's deputy. The Government's inability to handle the worsening domestic situation provoked a wave of defections by Lok Sabha members of the Janata Party. Many joined Narain, who formed a new party, the Lok Dal, based on secularism. Congress (I) lost its position as official opposition party after defections from its ranks to the then official Congress party by members who objected to Indira Gandhi's authoritarianism. The resignation of Desai's Government was followed by the resignation from the party of Singh, who became the leader of the Lok Dal and, shortly afterwards, Prime Minister in a coalition with both Congress parties. When Congress (I) withdrew its support in August, Singh's 24-day Government fell and Parliament was dissolved. A general election to the Lok Sabha was held in January 1980, when polling took place in 525 of the 542 elective seats. Two more seats were decided in February. Altogether, Congress (I) received 42.7% of the total votes but won an overwhelming majority (352) of the seats. Janata, with 18.9% of the votes, won only 31 seats, while the Lok Dal (9.4%) won 41 seats. Indira Gandhi was reinstated as Prime Minister. Presidential rule was imposed in nine states, ruled by opposition parties, in February. At elections in June, Congress (I) gained majorities in eight of the nine states.

By-elections in June 1981 for the Lok Sabha and state assemblies were notable because of the landslide victory which Rajiv Gandhi, the Prime Minister's son and a former airline pilot, obtained in the former constituency of his late brother, Sanjay (who had been killed in an air crash in June 1980) and because of the failure of the fragmented Janata party to win any seats. In January 1982 Indira Gandhi reshuffled the Council of Ministers, appointing a new Minister of Defence, a portfolio that she had previously held. In September there was a major reshuffle when Indira Gandhi appointed eight new Ministers, including five followers of the late Sanjay Gandhi. In February 1983 Rajiv Gandhi became a General Secretary of Congress (I).

Indira Gandhi's Government faced serious problems, as disturbances in several states, particularly in Assam, continued in 1982 and 1983, with violent protests against the presence of Bengali immigrants. Presidential rule in Assam was replaced by a Congress (I) Government in February 1982, in an effort to quell dissent. To avoid a constitutional crisis, further elections were held in Assam (and Meghalaya) in February 1983, amid scenes of great intercommunal violence, leading to several thousand deaths. In an effort to curtail the flow of Bengali immigrants, it was decided in July that the Assam/Bangladesh border should be fenced. There was also unrest in Jammu and Kashmir during local elections there in June 1983, and in July 1984 when the Chief Minister was deposed. Alleged police corruption and the resurgence of caste violence (notably in Bihar and Gujarat) caused further problems for the Government. The election defeats in Andhra Pradesh, Karnataka and Tripura in January 1983 represented a set-back for Indira Gandhi, who then reshuffled her Council of Ministers.

Another major problem was the widespread unrest in the Sikh community of Punjab, despite the election to the Indian presidency in July 1982 of Giani Zail Singh, the first Sikh to hold the position. There were demands for greater religious recognition, for the settlement of grievances over land and water rights, and over the sharing of the state capital at Chandigarh with Haryana, and also demands from a small minority for a separate Sikh state ('Khalistan'). In October 1983 the Punjabi Government was dismissed and the state was brought under presidential control, to prevent an escalation of violence between the Sikh and Hindu populations. However, the violence continued, and followers of an extremist Sikh leader, Jarnail Singh Bhindranwale, established a terrorist stronghold inside the Golden Temple (the Sikh holy shrine) at Amritsar. In June 1984 the Government sent in troops to dislodge the extremists. The armed assault on the Golden Temple resulted in the death of Bhindranwale and hundreds of his supporters, and serious damage to sacred buildings. A curfew was imposed in Punjab, and army personnel blockaded Amritsar. There were mutinies among Sikh troops in various parts of India. The situation remained tense throughout the summer.

In October 1984 Indira Gandhi was assassinated by militant Sikh members of her personal guard. Her son, Rajiv Gandhi, was immediately sworn in as Prime Minister, despite his lack of previous ministerial experience. There was widespread communal violence throughout India, with more than 2,000 deaths, which was curbed by the prompt action of the Government.

A general election to the Lok Sabha, which was due in January 1985 under the Constitution, was held in December 1984 throughout the country, apart from the states of Assam and Punjab (together having 27 seats), which were deemed by the Government to be too disturbed, as well as in two snowbound constituencies and five in which voting was postponed until January 1985. Congress (I), aided by the youthfulness of the electorate (68% of whom were between 21 and 40 years of age), the total disunity of the opposition and a large sympathy vote for Rajiv Gandhi, achieved a decisive victory, gaining the largest parliamentary majority in India's history. Including the results of the January 1985 polling, the party received 49.2% of the total votes and won 403 of the 513 contested seats. Rajiv Gandhi announced his Council of Ministers on 31 December, and pledged to continue most of his mother's policies. At the state assembly elections of March 1985, however, Congress (I) performed less well than expected, suffering heavy defeats in Andhra Pradesh, Karnataka and Sikkim, and reduced majorities in other states. In September 1985 Rajiv Gandhi carried out his first government reshuffle, bringing in 15 new Ministers.

In January 1986, in an attempt to revitalize Congress (I), Rajiv Gandhi appointed Arjun Singh, a former Governor of Punjab and hitherto Minister of Commerce, to the newly-created post of Vice-President of the party (the post being abolished in October 1986), and two other senior Ministers as General Secretaries. In February there were mass demonstra-tions and strikes throughout India, in protest against government-imposed increases in the prices of basic commodities such as petroleum products, fertilizers, rice and wheat. The opposition parties united against Rajiv Gandhi's policies, and the entire parliamentary opposition boycotted the President's traditional address on the opening day of the budget session in Parliament. Congress (I) suffered considerable setbacks in the indirect elections to the Rajya Sabha in March, when its overall strength in the House declined to considerably less than the two-thirds majority necessary to enable constitutional amendments to be approved without the support of opposition members. In April Rajiv Gandhi expelled one senior member and suspended three others from Congress (I), in an attempt to purge the party of critics calling themselves 'Indira Gandhi loyalists'. In a major government reshuffle in May, the Prime Minister appointed Sikhs to two senior positions. Rajiv Gandhi survived an assassination attempt by three Sikhs in New Delhi in October.

Mizoram became India's 23rd state in June 1986, when Lal Denga, the leader of the Mizo National Front (MNF), signed a peace agreement with Rajiv Gandhi, thus ending Mizoram's 25 years of rebellion. The accord also granted Mizoram limited autonomy in the drafting of local laws, independent trade with neighbouring foreign countries and a general amnesty for all Mizo rebels. Lal Denga was to lead an interim coalition government, formed by the MNF and Congress (I). In December the Rajya Sabha gave final approval to measures establishing Arunachal Pradesh as India's 24th state. At local elections in Karnataka in January 1987, the ruling Janata Party gained control in 17 out of 19 districts.

Intercommunal violence continued throughout 1985 and 1986. The violence in Goa, Assam, Karnataka and Tamil Nadu arose as a result of agitation over the official languages, and in Gujarat, Uttar Pradesh and Madhya Pradesh as a result of Hindu–Muslim tension. Caste violence continued to be a problem in Bihar. After its failure to curb the Hindu–Muslim violence, the elected Government of Jammu and Kashmir was dismissed, and the state was placed first under Governor's rule in March 1986, and then under President's rule in September. In November an agreement was reached by Rajiv Gandhi and Dr Farook Abdullah, the leader of the Jammu and Kashmir National Conference Party (F), whereby an interim government—a coalition of Congress (I) and the National Conference Party (F), with Dr Abdullah as Chief Minister—was installed in the state. In 1986 the Gurkhas (of Nepalese stock) resident in West Bengal launched a campaign for a separate autonomous homeland and the recognition of Nepali as an official language (the latter point was also demanded by the Chief Minister of Sikkim). The separatist campaign, led by the Gurkha National Liberation Front, was activated by the eviction, in March, of about 10,000 Nepalis from the state of Meghalaya, where the native residents had feared that they were becoming outnumbered by immigrants. In 1986 also, the Tribal National Volunteers demanded an autonomous tribal state in Tripura.

The situation in Punjab showed little sign of improvement in 1985 and 1986. In September 1985 Rajiv Gandhi achieved a temporary solution to the unrest when a general election for the state assembly was held, following an agreement, signed in July, between the Government and Harchand Singh Longowal, the moderate president of the main Sikh party, Akali Dal. Despite the assassination of Longowal by Sikh extremists in August, the election was peaceful and resulted in a victory for Akali Dal, which assumed power in the state after two years of presidential rule. On the same day as the state election, polling also took place for Punjab's 13 seats in the Lok Sabha, postponed from December 1984. An important element in the agreement that Rajiv Gandhi and the late Longowal negotiated in July 1985 was the transfer of Chandigarh, since 1966 the joint capital of Punjab and Haryana, to Punjab alone. In return, Haryana was to benefit from the completion of the Sutlej–Yamuna canal, to bring irrigation water from Punjab to the dry south of the state, and the transfer of a number of Hindi-speaking border villages from Punjab to Haryana. Four commissions were set up to organize the transfer, but each one of them failed to carry out its task, and by early 1987 the transfer had still not taken place. Hindu–Sikh violence continued throughout 1986 (it was estimated that about 650 people were killed during the year) despite the replacement of the

Governor of Punjab, after only three months in office, in April 1986, the drafting in of thousands of paramilitary reinforcements from New Delhi and the considerable improvement in the efficiency of the Punjab police force. A worrying development was that, after years of comparative quiescence among Punjab's Hindu minority, the extremist Hindu Shiv Sena ('Army of Shiva') group began to organize resistance against Sikh terrorism. Many Hindu families, on the other hand, began to leave Punjab for Haryana, to escape the unrest. A steady flow of Sikh families began to enter Punjab from Haryana, where they feared retaliation from the Hindu majority. In January 1986 the Sikh extremist groups re-established a terrorist stronghold inside the Golden Temple complex at Amritsar. In April the extremists announced that they had formed the independent Sikh state of 'Khalistan' and appealed for foreign recognition. This declaration led the moderate Akali Dal Government of Punjab to order a raid by the security forces on the complex a few days later, aiming to dislodge the extremists. As a result of this raid, there was a split in the ruling Akali Dal; the militant dissidents formed a separate party, with Prakash Singh Badal, a former Chief Minister of the state, as president. In December it was decided that parts of Punjab, to be identified as 'disturbed', were to be placed under the control of the army. Despite demands by opposition leaders for the imposition of President's rule in Punjab, Rajiv Gandhi continued to maintain that the central Government should not intervene directly while the state continued to be administered by an elected government. There was another raid on the Golden Temple complex by the police and paramilitary forces in January 1987. In February the five high priests of the Sikh faith, with extremist backing, demanded the resignation of the Punjab state government, and excommunicated the Chief Minister, Surjit Singh Barnala, when he refused to comply.

In December 1985 an election for the state assembly in Assam took place, following an accord, reached after five years of sectarian violence, which limited the voting rights of immigrants to Assam: those foreigners (mainly Bangladeshis) who had arrived before 1966 were to be accorded full voting rights; those who had arrived between 1966 and 1971 were to be disenfranchized for 10 years; and those who had arrived after 1971 (the proclamation date of the independence of Bangladesh) were to be expelled from Assam. The election result was a victory for the Asom Gana Parishad (Assam People's Council), a newly-formed local party, which won a clear majority over its nearest rival, Congress (I). The delayed voting for Assam's 14 seats in the Lok Sabha took place on the same day. Plans were revived in 1985 to erect a fence along the Assam/Bangladesh border, in an attempt to curb illegal immigration from Bangladesh. When the accord was announced in December, Bangladesh stated that it would not take back Bengali immigrants from Assam and denied that it had allowed any illegal refugees to cross its borders into Assam.

In foreign affairs, the Janata Government of 1977-80 had embarked on a policy of improving relations with all neighbouring countries, which the Congress (I) Government continued. In 1982 India made an interim agreement with Bangladesh over the sharing of the Ganges waters, and in 1985 an interim agreement was reached which guaranteed Bangladesh's share of the Ganges' dry-season flow. In December 1986 India and Bangladesh signed an agreement on measures aimed at preventing cross-border terrorism.

Relations with Pakistan had deteriorated in the late 1970s and early 1980s, owing to Pakistan's potential capability for the development of nuclear weapons and major US deliveries of armaments to that country. The Indian Government believed that such deliveries would upset the balance of power in the region and would precipitate an arms race. Talks between Pakistan's President, Gen. Mohammad Zia ul-Haq, and Indira Gandhi in November 1982 eased the tension. On the death of Indira Gandhi, Pakistan immediately assured India of its continued peaceful intentions, and President Zia ul-Haq, along with many other world leaders, attended her funeral. President Zia ul-Haq visited India again in December 1985, when he and Rajiv Gandhi announced their mutual commitment not to attack each other's nuclear installations and to negotiate the sovereignty of the disputed Siachin glacier region in northern Kashmir. Relations between the two countries continued to improve when they signed a document on bilateral economic co-operation in January 1986. By March, however, relations had deteriorated again, and the two countries had resumed the exchange of widely-publicized diplomatic attacks (including India's allegations that Pakistan was harbouring and training Sikh extremists to infiltrate Punjab). A trip by Rajiv Gandhi to Islamabad, planned for April, was postponed, but further talks on the Siachin region were held in New Delhi in June. In November Pakistan was continuing to demand a settlement of the Kashmir problem in accordance with earlier UN resolutions, prescribing a plebiscite in the two parts of the state, now divided between India and Pakistan. India, however, argued that the problem should be settled in accordance with the Simla agreement of 1972, which required that all Indo-Pakistani disputes be resolved through bilateral negotiations. Tension increased between December 1986 and February 1987, when both countries conducted extensive military exercises near their common border in the sensitive Punjab region. A Pakistani delegation arrived in Delhi in late January to hold talks with the Indian Foreign Ministry about reversing the military build-up. In early February it was reported that thousands of Indian families were fleeing from villages along the border, in fear of a confrontation between the Indian and Pakistani armies. On 4 February Pakistan and India agreed on measures to defuse tension on their border, including the withdrawal of all troops to peace-time positions.

In December 1985 the South Asian Association for Regional Co-operation (SAARC, see p. 218) held its inaugural meeting in Dhaka, Bangladesh. The second summit meeting, chaired by Rajiv Gandhi, was held in Bangalore in November 1986. India and Sri Lanka took the opportunity to discuss the latter's Tamil ethnic crisis (in which India is playing the role of arbitrator). Problems had arisen throughout the year over the Tamil demand that Sri Lanka's northern and eastern districts, where the Tamil presence is strong, should be merged. Raids by the Indian police on Tamil guerrillas, sheltering in and around Madras, in November were regarded as an indication that India was hardening its attitude towards the Tamil militants.

During 1981 there was a marked improvement in India's relations with the People's Republic of China, which had suffered a set-back after India's recognition of the Heng Samrin Government of Kampuchea in July 1980. Both countries agreed to find an early solution to their border dispute (over about 128,000 sq km of land) and to seek to normalize relations. No substantial progress was made during the seventh round of Sino-Indian talks, held in Beijing in July 1986. China was displeased when Arunachal Pradesh was granted full statehood in December.

The USSR is a major contributor of economic and military assistance to India (in 1986 it was estimated that about 70% of India's defence equipment was supplied by the USSR). In 1973 a 15-year agreement was concluded between the two countries, and in 1981 India became the USSR's leading trade partner in the developing world. Indira Gandhi visited Moscow for talks in September 1982. The Indo-Soviet Chamber of Commerce and Industry was formally inaugurated in Delhi, to expand bilateral trade between the two countries, in June 1986, and Mikhail Gorbachev, the Soviet leader, held a successful series of meetings during a visit to India in November. There are close ties between the USA and India in economic and scientific affairs, and political ties were strengthened after Indira Gandhi's visit to the USA in July 1982, when a compromise was agreed on the question of nuclear fuel for India's atomic reactor at Tarapur. India remains uneasy over the continued support, in aid and armaments, which is given to Pakistan by the USA, while the USA, in turn, remains worried lest its military or dual-use technology be 'leaked' to the USSR through India, or diverted to an Indian programme to produce nuclear weapons.

Government

India is a federal republic. Legislative power is vested in Parliament, consisting of the President and two Houses. The Council of States (Rajya Sabha) has 244 members, most of whom are indirectly elected by the State Assemblies for six years (one-third retiring every two years), the remainder (seven in 1986) being nominated by the President for six years. The House of the People (Lok Sabha) has 544 members, serving for five years (subject to dissolution). Two members of the Lok

Sabha are nominated by the President to represent the Anglo-Indian community, while 542 members are directly elected by universal adult suffrage in single-member constituencies. The President is a constitutional Head of State, elected for five years by an electoral college comprising elected members of both Houses of Parliament and the state legislatures. The President exercises executive power on the advice of the Council of Ministers, which is responsible to Parliament. The President appoints the Prime Minister and, on the latter's recommendation, other Ministers.

India contains 24 self-governing states, each with a Governor (appointed by the President for five years), a legislature (elected for five years) and a Council of Ministers headed by the Chief Minister. Andhra Pradesh, Bihar, Jammu and Kashmir, Karnataka, Madhya Pradesh, Maharashtra, Tamil Nadu and Uttar Pradesh have bicameral legislatures, the other 16 state legislatures being unicameral. Each state has its own legislative, executive and judicial machinery, corresponding to that of the Indian Union. In the event of the failure of constitutional government in a state, presidential rule can be imposed by the Union. There are also seven Union Territories, administered by Chief Commissioners, Lieutenant-Governors or Administrators, all of whom are appointed by the President.

Defence

In July 1986 the estimated strength of India's armed forces was 1,260,000: an army of 1,100,000, a navy of 47,000 and an air force of 113,000. Military service has been voluntary but, under the amended Constitution, it is the fundamental duty of every citizen to perform national service when called upon. Net defence expenditure for 1985/86 was estimated at 77,471m. rupees.

Economic Affairs

On the basis of aggregate gross national product (GNP), India ranks among the 15 largest economies in the world. However, with its vast population (second only to the People's Republic of China), the country remains among the 20 poorest in terms of average income. In 1984, according to estimates by the World Bank, India's GNP per head was US $260 (at average 1982–84 prices), having increased by 1.6% annually, in real terms, since 1965. The growth in GNP was 3.7% in 1984/85, and was expected to increase to 4.5%–5% in 1985/86: close to the 5% target annual rate set by the seventh Five-Year Plan (1985–90). The average annual growth of overall gross domestic product (GDP), measured in constant prices, was 3.9% in 1965–73, rising to 4.1% in 1973–84. During the sixth Five-Year Plan (1980–85) the average annual growth of GDP was 5.2%. Growth in 1985/86 was nearly 5%, but it was estimated that growth in 1986/87 would not exceed 4.2%.

About 65% of the working population are engaged in agriculture, which accounts for more than one-third of GDP. The major part of the sown area is taken up by cereals, the staple crops. Extensive plantations produce tea, rubber and coffee, while cotton, jute, sugar, oilseeds, tobacco and other cash crops are also grown. Crops are frequently damaged by drought and floods. Since 1975/76 improved irrigation, the increased use of chemical fertilizers and the introduction of high-yield strains of rice and wheat, as well as favourable monsoons, have led to record harvests. Owing to a poor monsoon, agricultural production recorded a decline of 0.9% in 1984/85, compared with growth of 13.7% in the previous year. Agricultural production was expected to increase by 3% in 1985/86, despite drought in several regions. The area under irrigation was expected to expand from 63.3m. ha in 1983/84 to 68m. ha in 1984/85. India's production of food grains (cereals and pulses), after two poor harvests in 1980 and 1981, reached a record 133.3m. metric tons (including rice on a milled basis) in 1981/82, which was surpassed by a harvest of 152.4m. tons in 1983/84, but in 1984/85 output declined to 145.5m. tons. The annual output of food grains increased by 14% in the period 1979–84, representing an average annual increase of 2.6%; a rate which exceeded the 2% annual population growth. In spite of extremely adverse weather in many areas during 1985/86, production of food grains was estimated at 150.5m. tons. The target for 1986/87 was set at 160m. tons. Under the seventh Five-Year Plan, India's annual output of food grains is expected to reach 183m. tons by 1990.

While concentrating on increasing the production of wheat and rice, however, other crops have been neglected with the result that food still has to be imported.

India has the fourth largest coal reserves in the world, and in 1985/86 output totalled an estimated 155m. metric tons. Coal is India's prime source of commercial energy, and new production targets for the industry (set in 1986) envisaged output of 226m. tons per year by 1989/90. There are large reserves of iron ore in Bihar and Orissa, as well as bauxite, titanium ore, manganese, mica and rare metals. In 1981 the Government negotiated a large foreign loan to finance construction of new aluminium and steel plants in Orissa. The state-owned Hindustan Copper Ltd planned to increase copper production at its Malanjkhard copper project in Madhya Pradesh in 1987, and to carry out further exploration. In 1986 the Malanjkhard copper project was India's largest open-cast mine. In 1983 India became the world's leading exporter of cut diamonds, and placed 5.6m. carats on the international market. Total output of uncut diamonds reached an estimated 16,284 carats in 1985.

Inshore deposits of petroleum have been found in Assam, Gujarat and Nagaland, and offshore oilfields have been discovered in the Western continental shelf off the Maharashtra and Gujarat coasts, in the Cauvery basin and in the Bay of Bengal. In 1980 it was announced that foreign oil companies would be allowed to explore for petroleum, both onshore and offshore. In 1986 India invited bids from international oil companies for exploring 27 offshore blocks. Production at the Bassei offshore gas field (one of the largest in the world) began in 1985. In 1985 the Government planned to construct a gas pipeline of 1,800 km, from near Bombay to Bareilly, to tap the reserves of the Bombay offshore fields. In 1986 an ambitious gas pipeline project was instigated, involving the laying of a 1,730-km pipeline from Hazira, in Gujarat, to Jagdishpur, in Uttar Pradesh, to carry natural gas from two offshore fields to six fertilizer plants in northern India. Petroleum from India's own resources is playing a growing role in the economy. India produced about 70% of its petroleum requirements in 1986, compared with 50% in 1983 and 34% in 1980. Output of crude petroleum was 26m. tons in 1983/84, and increased to 29m. tons in 1984/85. In 1985/86, as there was no significant addition to the recoverable reserves, production reached its peak level of about 30.4m. tons. Production was expected to fall to 27.4m. tons in 1986/87. As a result of increased production, imports (in value terms) of iron and steel, crude petroleum and petroleum products declined by around 25% in the fiscal year 1984. The Government aims to spend Rs 1,272,767m. on the petroleum industry during the seventh Five-Year Plan (1985–90), drilling more than 2,500 new oil wells and increasing annual refining capacity to 45m. tons, in an attempt to become self-sufficient in petroleum by 1990.

India ranks among the 10 leading industrial nations in the world, although manufacturing employs only about 10% of the country's workers. New industries, such as heavy engineering, iron and steel, chemicals and electronics, have expanded rapidly, and by 1978 machinery and transport equipment had superseded tea or jute as India's largest single earner of foreign currency. In 1983/84 the value of tea exports was Rs 5,013.7m. and jute exports totalled Rs 1,645.2m., while sales of machinery and transport equipment earned Rs 4,939.8m. Annual growth in industrial production reached a peak of 10.6% in 1976/77. The increase in 1978/79 was only 2% below this, but in 1979/80 India's industrial output fell by 1.4%, mainly as a result of drought and a shortage of power and coal. The position improved slightly in 1980/81, when overall industrial growth was estimated at 4.1%. Various measures have been introduced to try to improve both power generation and industrial relations, the two main hindrances to increased production. During the sixth Five-Year Plan (1980–85) the average annual increase in industrial output was 5.6%. There was a small improvement in 1985/86, when industrial growth reached 6.3%.

Aided by a favourable monsoon, the Indian economy recovered in the fiscal year 1984, after a disappointing performance in the previous two years, and GNP rose by 7%, compared with growth of 2.6% in 1983 and 5.9% in 1982, while inflation fell to around 6.3% from 10% in 1982/83 and 8% in 1981/82. Inflation continued to fall in 1984/85 when it was 5.6%, and in 1985/86, when it was 3.8%. The trade deficit, which had widened from Rs 25,630m. in 1979/80 to Rs 58,496m. in 1980/81 (owing to the rising cost of imports), declined marginally, to Rs 58,017m., in 1981/82 and fell to Rs 54,480m. in 1982/83. However, the deficit rose to Rs 58,977m. in 1983/84 (despite a drop in the oil-import bill), mainly because of a prolonged strike in India's ports. In 1984/85 the trade deficit fell again slightly, to Rs 54,352m. (imports Rs 170,921m., exports Rs 116,569m.), but in 1985/86 it soared to a record Rs 81,400m. (imports Rs 179,200m., exports Rs 97,800m.), owing to a drastic decrease in exports of crude petroleum. Official reserves of foreign exchange fell from US $6,731m. at the end of 1979 to $3,442m. in September 1982, but they recovered to $5,697m. in April 1985. In 1986 reserves were at an adequate level, despite the record trade deficit. In 1981 the IMF sanctioned a loan of US $5,760m., the largest single borrowing by India, as part of an attempt to overcome balance-of-payments difficulties and to restructure the economy. The overall strengthening of India's economy was indicated by the waiving of $360m. of the loan in June 1983. In 1986 India secured from its Western aid consortium new financial aid commitments totalling US $4,500m. for 1987 (16% higher than the aid commitments granted in 1985). It was estimated that the current deficit on the balance of payments would be $3,159m. in 1985/86, compared with $2,753m. in 1984/85 and $2,863m. in 1982/83.

In 1985 the seventh Five-Year Plan (1985–90) was announced. It allows for a total investment of Rs 3,220,000m. (double that of the sixth Plan) and aims at an average annual GDP growth rate of around 5%. The plan projects an average annual growth of 5.8% in imports and of 6.8% in exports. Growth rates of 4% for agriculture and 8% for industry are envisaged. The main emphasis is on improving the energy sector, which is to receive 30% of the total outlay in an attempt to reduce the crippling power shortages; and on reducing the number of people below the 'poverty line' from 273m. (37% of the total population) in 1985 to 211m. (26%) by 1990. The Plan also aims to develop the infrastructure and make better use of existing capital investment while increasing employment. The sixth Five-Year Plan (1980–85) achieved its target of an annual growth rate of 5.2%. The budget proposals for 1986/87 envisaged increases of 65% in public expenditure on agricultural and rural development programmes, along with adjustments to income tax provisions and other measures to help the poor. The other major priority was to curb the rising revenue deficit.

Social Welfare

Health programmes are primarily the responsibility of the State Governments, but the Union Government provides finance for improvements in public health services. The structure of the health system is based on a network of primary health centres. In 1977 there were 5,372 such centres and 37,745 sub-centres in rural areas. In 1981 India had 1,066,164 hospital beds and 268,712 physicians. Various national health programmes aim to combat leprosy, malaria and tuberculosis. Smallpox was declared eradicated in 1977. The family planning programme was launched in 1952 and was allocated Rs 10,000m. under the 1980–85 Five-Year Plan. The emphasis now is on advice and education through Family Welfare Centres. A new approach to family planning was being developed in 1986, with the aim of reducing India's rate of population growth from 2.3% to 1.2% per year, so that the population does not exceed 1,000m. by the year 2000.

Education

Education is primarily the responsibility of the individual State Governments. Elementary education for children up to 14 years of age is theoretically compulsory in all states except Nagaland and Himachal Pradesh. Lower primary education, for children aged six to 11, is free in all states. Upper primary education, for children aged 11–14, is free in 12 states. Enrolment at the first level of education in 1982 was equivalent to 85% of children aged five to nine (100% of boys; 68% of girls). Secondary enrolment in 1982 was 34% of those aged 10 to 15 (44% of boys; 24% of girls). A new pattern of education, consisting of 10 years' elementary education, two years at higher secondary level and three years for the first degree course, was planned to be introduced in all states by 1980. It is hoped that universal free and compulsory education up to the age of 14 can be achieved by 1990. In 1978 the National Board for Adult Education launched a massive programme to combat illiteracy. Of the total population, 36.17% were literate in 1981, compared with 15.67% in 1961. However, female literacy was only 24.88% in 1981, and women's education, especially in rural areas, has made few advances.

Tourism

The tourist attractions of India include its scenery, its historic forts, palaces and temples, and its rich variety of wild life. Tourist infrastructure has recently been expanded by the provision of more luxury hotels and improved means of transport. In 1985 there were 836,908 foreign visitors to India.

Public Holidays

The public holidays observed in India vary locally. The dates given below apply to Delhi. As religious feasts depend on astronomical observations, holidays are usually declared at the beginning of the year in which they will be observed. It is not possible, therefore, to indicate more than the month in which some of the following holidays will occur.

1987: January (Pongal), 26 January (Republic Day), 26 February (Maha Shrivratri), March (Holi), 12 April (Ram Navami and Mahabir Jayanti), 17 April (Good Friday), 13 May (Buddha Purnima), 30 May (Rath Yatra and Id al-Fitr, end of Ramadan), 6 August (Id-uz-Zuha), 15 August (Independence Day), 20 August (Janmashtami), 26 August (Muharram, Islamic New Year), 28 August (Onam), 2 October (Mahatma Gandhi's Birthday), 18–20 October (Durga Puja-Dussehra), 22 October (Diwali), 1 November (Guru Nanak Jayanti), 25–26 December (Christmas).

1988: January (Pongal), 26 January (Republic Day), February (Maha Shrivratri), March (Holi), April (Ram Navami and Mahabir Jayanti), 1 April (Good Friday), May (Buddha Purnima), 18 May (Rath Yatra and Id al-Fitr, end of Ramadan), 25 July (Id-uz-Zuha), 14 August (Muharram, Islamic New Year), 15 August (Independence Day), 20 August (Janmashtami), 28 August (Onam), 2 October (Mahatma Gandhi's Birthday), October (Diwali), 18–20 October (Durga Puja-Dussehra), 1 November (Guru Nanak Jayanti), 25–26 December (Christmas).

Weights and Measures

The metric system has been officially introduced. The imperial system is also still in use, as are traditional Indian weights and measures, including:
1 tola = 11.66 grams
1 seer = 933.1 grams
1 maund = 37.32 kg
1 lakh = (1,00,00) = 100,000
1 crore = (1,00,00,000) = 10,000,000

Currency and Exchange Rates

100 paisa = 1 Indian rupee (R).

Exchange rates (30 September 1986):
£1 sterling = 18.400 rupees;
US $1 = 12.716 rupees.

Statistical Survey

Source (unless otherwise stated): Central Statistical Organization, Ministry of Planning, Sardar Patel, Bhavan, Parliament St, New Delhi 110001; tel. (11) 353626.

Area and Population

AREA, POPULATION AND DENSITY*

Area (sq km)	3,287,263†
Population (census results)‡	
1 April 1971	548,159,652
1 March 1981§	
Males	354,397,884
Females	330,786,808
Total	685,184,692
Population (official estimates at mid-year)	
1983	720,300,000
1984	735,600,000
1985	750,900,000
Density (per sq km) at mid-1985	228.4

* Including Sikkim (incorporated into India on 26 April 1975) and the Indian-held part of Jammu and Kashmir.
† 1,269,219 sq miles.
‡ Excluding adjustment for underenumeration, estimated at 1.67% in 1971.
§ Including estimates for Assam.

Source: Registrar General of India.

PRINCIPAL TOWNS (population at 1981 census*)

Greater Bombay	8,243,405	Hubli-Dharwar	527,108
Delhi	4,884,234	Cochin	513,249
Calcutta	3,288,148	Sholapur	511,103
Madras	3,276,622	Jodhpur	506,345
Bangalore	2,476,355	Ranchi	489,626
Hyderabad	2,187,262	Trivandrum	483,086
Ahmedabad	2,059,725	Vijaywada	
Kanpur (Cawnpore)	1,481,789	(Vijayavada)	454,577
Nagpur	1,219,461	Rajkot	445,076
Pune (Poona)	1,203,351	Mysore	441,754
Jaipur (Jeypore)	977,165	Jamshedpur	438,385
Lucknow	895,721	Meerut	417,395
Indore	829,327	Jalandhar	408,196
Madurai	820,891	Kozhikode (Calicut)	394,447
Surat	776,583	Bareilly	386,734
Patna	776,371	Ajmer	375,593
Howrah	744,429	Chandigarh	373,789
Vadodara (Baroda)	734,473	Guntur	367,699
Varanasi (Banaras)	708,647	Tiruchirapalli	362,045
Coimbatore	704,514	Salem	361,394
Agra	694,191	Kota	358,241
Bhopal	671,018	Kolhapur	340,625
Allahabad	616,051	Raipur	338,245
Jabalpur		Warangal	335,150
(Jubbulpore)	614,162	Faridabad	330,864
Ludhiana	607,052	Moradabad	330,051
Amritsar	594,844	Aligarh	320,861
Srinagar	594,775	Durgapur	311,798
Visakhapatnam	565,321	Thane	309,897
Gwalior	539,015	Bhavnagar	307,121

* Figures refer to the city proper in each case. For urban agglomerations, the following populations were recorded: Calcutta 9,194,018; Delhi 5,729,283; Madras 4,289,347; Bangalore 2,921,751; Ahmedabad 2,548,057; Hyderabad 2,545,836; Pune (Poona) 1,686,109; Kanpur 1,639,064; Nagpur 1,302,066; Jaipur 1,015,160; Lucknow 1,007,604; Coimbatore 920,355; Patna 918,903; Surat 913,806; Madurai 907,732; Varanasi (Banaras) 797,162; Jabalpur 757,303; Agra 747,318; Vadodara (Baroda) 744,881; Cochin 685,836; Dhanbad 678,069; Jamshedpur 669,580; Allahabad 650,070; Ulhasnagar 648,671; Tiruchirapalli 609,548; Srinagar 606,022; Visakhapatnam 603,630; Gwalior 555,862; Kozhikode (Calicut) 546,058; Vijaywada 543,008; Meerut 536,615; Trivandrum 520,125; Salem 518,615; Sholapur 514,860; Ranchi 502,771.

Capital: New Delhi, population 273,036 in 1981.

BIRTHS AND DEATHS
(estimates, based on Sample Registration Scheme)

	1982	1983	1984*
Birth rate (per 1,000)	33.8	33.7	33.8
Death rate (per 1,000)	11.9	11.9	n.a.

* Provisional.

ECONOMICALLY ACTIVE POPULATION
(1981 census, excluding Assam)*

	Males	Females	Total
Agriculture, hunting, forestry and fishing	116,482,682	36,532,504	153,015,187
Mining and quarrying	1,100,931	163,158	1,264,089
Manufacturing	21,480,943	3,662,094	25,143,037
Electricity, gas and water	949,663	24,135	973,799
Construction	3,207,287	358,121	3,565,408
Trade, restaurants and hotels	11,356,083	808,674	12,164,757
Transport, storage and communications	5,898,901	170,432	6,069,332
Finance, insurance, real estate and business services	1,656,407	107,830	1,764,237
Community, social and personal services	15,410,505	3,146,217	18,556,722
Activities not adequately defined†	3,536,806	18,551,606	22,088,411
Total	181,080,208	63,524,771	244,604,979

* Figures are based on a 5% sample tabulation of census returns. As each figure is estimated independently, the totals shown may differ from the sum of the component parts.
† The figures refer to marginal workers and persons who were unemployed or seeking work for the first time.

STATES AND TERRITORIES

	Capital	Area (sq km)	Population April 1971	Population March 1981
States				
Andhra Pradesh	Hyderabad	275,068	43,502,708	53,549,673
Assam	Dispur	78,438	14,625,152	19,896,843‡
Bihar	Patna	173,877	56,353,369	69,914,734
Gujarat	Gandhinagar	196,024	26,697,475	34,085,799
Haryana	Chandigarh†	44,212	10,036,808	12,922,618
Himachal Pradesh	Simla	55,673	3,460,434	4,280,818
Jammu and Kashmir*	Srinagar	222,236	4,616,632	5,987,389
Karnataka	Bangalore	191,791	29,299,014	37,135,714
Kerala	Trivandrum	38,863	21,347,375	25,453,680
Madhya Pradesh	Bhopal	443,446	41,654,119	52,178,844
Maharashtra	Bombay	307,690	50,412,235	62,784,171
Manipur	Imphal	22,327	1,072,753	1,420,953
Meghalaya	Shillong	22,429	1,011,699	1,335,819
Nagaland	Kohima	16,579	516,449	774,930
Orissa	Bhubaneswar	155,707	21,944,615	26,370,271
Punjab	Chandigarh†	50,362	13,551,060	16,788,915
Rajasthan	Jaipur	342,239	25,765,806	34,261,862
Sikkim	Gangtok	7,096	209,843	316,385
Tamil Nadu	Madras	130,058	41,199,168	48,408,077
Tripura	Agartala	10,486	1,556,342	2,053,058
Uttar Pradesh	Lucknow	294,411	88,341,144	110,862,013
West Bengal	Calcutta	88,752	44,312,011	54,580,647
Territories				
Andaman and Nicobar Islands	Port Blair	8,249	115,133	188,741
Arunachal Pradesh	Itanagar	83,743	467,511	631,839
Chandigarh†	Chandigarh	114	257,251	451,610
Dadra and Nagar Haveli	Silvassa	491	74,170	103,676
Delhi	Delhi	1,483	4,065,698	6,220,406
Goa, Daman and Diu	Panaji	3,814	857,771	1,086,730
Lakshadweep	Kavaratti	32	31,810	40,249
Mizoram§	Aizawl	21,081	332,390	493,757
Pondicherry	Pondicherry	492	471,707	604,471

* The area figure refers to the whole of Jammu and Kashmir State, of which 78,114 sq km is occupied by Pakistan. The population figures refer only to the Indian-held part of the territory.
† Chandigarh forms a separate Union Territory, not within Haryana or Punjab. As part of a scheme for a transfer of territory between the two states, Chandigarh was due to be incorporated into Punjab on 26 January 1986.
‡ Estimate.
§ Mizoram was granted statehood in August 1986.

Source: *Census of India*, Part II—B(i) Primary Census Abstract of General Population 1981.

Agriculture

PRINCIPAL CROPS ('000 metric tons, year ending 30 June)

	1983/84	1984/85	1985/86
Rice (milled)	60,100	58,337	64,153
Sorghum (Jowar)	11,920	11,402	10,123
Cat-tail millet (Bajra)	7,720	6,046	3,684
Maize	7,924	8,442	6,890
Finger millet (Ragi)	2,830	2,530	2,522
Small millets	1,676	1,194	1,297
Wheat	45,480	44,069	46,885
Barley	1,830	1,556	1,952
Total cereals	139,480	133,576	137,506
Chick-peas (Gram)	4,755	4,561	5,683
Pigeon-peas (Tur)	2,580	2,585	2,426
Dry beans, dry peas, lentils and other pulses	5,560	4,816	4,855
Total food grains	152,370	145,538	150,470

	1983/84	1984/85	1985/86
Groundnuts (in shell)	7,090	6,436	5,547
Sesame seed	560	521	496
Rapeseed and mustard	2,610	3,073	2,639
Linseed	440	389	373
Castor beans	400	470	305
Total oil seeds (incl. others)	12,690	12,946	11,154
Cotton lint*	6,390	8,507	8,612
Jute†	6,320	6,531	10,952
Kenaf (Mesta)†	1,400	1,256	1,776
Tea (made)	588	625	657
Sugar cane:			
production gur	18,000	17,100	17,200
production cane	174,080	170,319	171,681
Tobacco (leaves)	490	470	n.a.
Potatoes	12,150	12,571	10,696
Chillies (dry)	566	605	n.a.

Source: Directorate of Economics and Statistics, Ministry of Agriculture and Rural Development.

* Production in '000 bales of 170 kg each.
† Production in '000 bales of 180 kg each.

LIVESTOCK (FAO estimates, '000 head year ending September)

	1983	1984	1985
Cattle	181,850	182,160	182,410
Sheep	40,820	40,890	41,300
Goats	79,850	80,800	81,500
Pigs	8,600	8,650	8,826
Horses	900	900	910
Asses	1,000	1,000	1,000
Mules	130	130	135
Buffaloes	64,500	64,000	64,500
Camels	1,050	1,050	1,100

Poultry (FAO estimates, million): 150 in 1983; 160 in 1984; 161 in 1985.

Source: FAO, *Production Yearbook*.

LIVESTOCK PRODUCTS (FAO estimates, '000 metric tons)

	1983	1984	1985
Beef and veal	80	86	89
Buffalo meat	132	134	135
Mutton and lamb	134	134	135
Goats' meat	302	305	315
Pig meat	80	82	85
Poultry meat	137	150	158
Cows' milk*	16,400	17,100	18,500
Buffaloes' milk*	19,587	20,439	21,270
Goats' milk*	1,113	1,161	1,230
Butter and ghee	730	740	750
Hen eggs	704.6	756	812
Wool:			
greasy	38	38	38
clean	25.4*	25.4	25.4
Cattle and buffalo hides (fresh)	810	817	823
Sheep skins (fresh)	37.1	37.4	37.6
Goat skins (fresh)	72.9	73.4	75.6

* Unofficial estimate(s).

Source: FAO, *Production Yearbook*.

Forestry

ROUNDWOOD REMOVALS (FAO estimates, '000 cu metres)

	1982	1983	1984
Sawlogs, veneer logs and logs for sleepers*	14,551	14,551	14,551
Pulpwood†	1,208	1,208	1,208
Other industrial wood	4,120	4,178	4,236
Fuel wood	210,370	214,622	218,866
Total	230,249	234,559	238,861

* Assumed to be unchanged since 1980.
† Assumed to be unchanged since 1978.

Source: FAO, *Yearbook of Forest Products*.

SAWNWOOD PRODUCTION ('000 cu metres)

	1978	1979	1980*
Coniferous sawnwood (incl. boxboards)	1,225	1,347*	1,480
Broadleaved sawnwood (incl. boxboards)	7,650	8,410*	9,244
Sub-total	8,875	9,757	10,724
Railway sleepers	124	252	252
Total	8,999	10,009	10,976

* FAO estimates.

1981–84: Annual production as in 1980 (FAO estimates).

Source: FAO, *Yearbook of Forest Products*.

Fishing

('000 metric tons, live weight)

	1982	1983	1984*
Indian Ocean:			
Bombay-duck (Bummalo)	82.9	91.0	116.4
Marine catfishes	53.2	62.9	70.8
Croakers and drums	116.6	91.2	137.4
Indian oil-sardine (sardinella)	260.7	255.4	291.1
Anchovies	76.7	125.1	118.1
Hairtails and cutlass fishes	61.9	65.3	62.2
Indian mackerel	27.9	32.2	54.6
Other marine fishes (incl. unspecified)	508.1	572.4	680.9
Total sea-fish	1,188.0	1,295.5	1,513.6
Shrimps and prawns	209.7	192.3	203.0
Other marine animals	29.8	31.5	42.4
Total sea catch	1,427.5	1,519.3	1,777.0
Inland waters:			
Freshwater fishes	939.6	987.4	1,081.9
Total catch	2,367.1	2,506.7	2,858.9

*Provisional.

1985 (estimates, '000 metric tons): Total sea catch 1,692.9; Total catch 2,810.6.

Source: Ministry of Agriculture and Rural Development.

Mining

		1983	1984	1985
Coal	'000 metric tons	136,212	144,768	149,259
Lignite	'000 metric tons	7,344	7,644	7,774
Iron ore*	'000 metric tons	38,672	42,000	42,036
Manganese ore*	'000 metric tons	1,277	1,128	1,236
Bauxite	'000 metric tons	1,929	2,076	4,016
Chalk (Fireclay)	'000 metric tons	700	648	540
Kaolin (China clay)	'000 metric tons	583	624	720
Dolomite	'000 metric tons	2,165	2,304	2,208
Gypsum	'000 metric tons	988	1,248	1,260
Limestone	'000 metric tons	38,336	45,132	48,492
Crude petroleum	'000 metric tons	25,148	27,936	29,883
Sea salt	'000 metric tons	7,005	7,656'	9,876
Chromium ore*	'000 metric tons	365	456	552
Phosphorite	'000 metric tons	776	868	900
Kyanite	'000 metric tons	42	38	30
Magnesite	'000 metric tons	436	418	420
Steatite	'000 metric tons	284	346	336
Copper ore*	'000 metric tons	3,437	3,894	4,152
Lead concentrates*	metric tons	32,244	34,248	35,400
Zinc concentrates*	metric tons	75,574	85,259	88,692
Mica (crude)	metric tons	8,400	6,000	4,800
Gold	kg	2,156	1,988	1,824
Diamonds	carats	14,286	14,412	16,284
Natural gas†	million cu m	3,000	3,236	3,782

* Figures refer to gross weight. For 1983 the estimated metal content (in '000 metric tons) was: Iron 24,359; Manganese 488.8; Chromium 108; Copper 46.9; Lead 20.7; Zinc 40.4.
† Figures refer to gas utilized.

Source: Indian Bureau of Mines.

Industry

SELECTED PRODUCTS

		1983	1984	1985
Refined sugar*	'000 metric tons	8,238	5,916	7,980
Cotton cloth	million metres	8,522	8,828	9,289
Jute manufactures	'000 metric tons	1,335	1,154	1,223
Paper and paper board	'000 metric tons	1,138	1,358	1,463
Sulphuric acid	'000 metric tons	2,409	2,076	n.a.
Soda ash	'000 metric tons	752	828	814
Fertilizers	'000 metric tons	4,338	5,172	5,580
Petroleum products	'000 metric tons	32,268	33,360	38,256
Cement	'000 metric tons	30,432	29,016	31,080
Pig iron	'000 metric tons	9,087	9,382	9,701
Finished steel	'000 metric tons	6,196	6,564	7,841
Aluminium	metric tons	203,796	268,176	260,016
Diesel engines (stationary)	number	149,292	167,664	168,408
Sewing machines	number	342,000	326,400	333,600
Radio receivers	number	1,236,000	1,356,000	1,212,000
Electric fans	number	4,272,000	4,608,000	5,064,000
Passenger cars and jeeps	number	68,496	87,960	117,156
Passenger buses and trucks	number	85,730	93,348	105,324
Motor cycles and scooters	number	429,276	474,648	666,192
Bicycles	number	5,343,600	5,884,800	5,646,000

* Figures relate to crop year (beginning November) and are in respect of cane sugar only.

Source: Ministry of Industry and Company Affairs.

Finance

CURRENCY AND EXCHANGE RATES

Monetary Units
100 paise (singular: paisa) = 1 Indian rupee.

Denominations
Coins: 5, 10, 20, 25 and 50 paise; 1 and 2 rupees.
Notes: 1, 2, 5, 10, 20, 50 and 100 rupees.

Sterling and Dollar Equivalents (30 September 1986)
£1 sterling = 18.400 rupees;
US $1 = 12.716 rupees;
1,000 Indian rupees = £54.35 = US $78.64.

Average Exchange Rate (rupees per US $)
1983   10.099
1984   11.363
1985   12.369

INTERNATIONAL RESERVES
(US $ million at 31 December)

	1983	1984	1985
Gold	215	184	203
IMF special drawing rights	110	331	336
Reserve position in IMF	510	477	535
Foreign exchange	4,318	5,034	5,549
Total	5,153	6,026	6,623

Source: IMF, *International Financial Statistics*.

MONEY SUPPLY (million rupees, last Friday of the year)

	1983	1984	1985
Currency with the public	180,700	217,420	239,410
Demand deposits with banks	137,610	158,410	182,710
Other deposits with reserve bank	1,570	3,020	2,890
Total money	319,880	378,850	425,010

Source: Reserve Bank of India.

COST OF LIVING
(Consumer Price Index for industrial workers. Base: 1970 = 100)

	1982	1983	1984
Food	249.0	282.0	302.0
Fuel and light	370.1	405.4	456.9
Clothing	321.4	347.2	363.5
Rent	181.1	198.5	221.2
All items (incl. others)	258.2	289.1	313.0

BUDGET (estimates, million rupees, year ending 31 March)

Revenue	1985/86*	1986/87
Tax revenue	266,048.2	289,248.0
Customs	92,960.0	104,068.1
Union excise duties	129,200.2	141,061.9
Corporation tax	31,180.0	31,330.0
Income tax	5,510.2	5,650.5
Estate duty	46.9	33.9
Wealth taxes	1,100.0	1,000.0
Interest tax	600.0	100.0
Gift tax	105.0	110.0
Others	5,345.9	5,893.6
Non-tax revenue	166,693.6	178,667.4
Interest receipts	48,022.6	55,212.0
Dividends and profits	4,770.3	4,556.4
Others	113,900.7	118,899.0
Total	432,741.8	467,915.4

* Revised budget.

Expenditure	1985/86*	1986/87
General services	183,108.1	208,616.3
Organs of states	1,936.8	1,991.7
Fiscal services	10,112.4	11,505.5
Interest payments	74,000.0	87,500.0
Administrative services	11,780.0	14,945.4
Pensions and miscellaneous services	13,309.0	13,524.7
Defence (net)	71,969.9	79,149.0
Social and community services	24,698.1	26,819.1
Economic services	154,368.0	162,512.1
General economic services	7,707.2	7,763.5
Agriculture and allied services	23,682.4	25,621.7
Industry and minerals	27,022.1	27,111.7
Water and power development	4,820.5	5,204.9
Transport and communications	5,776.8	5,407.5
Railways	64,866.2	69,966.9
Postal services	6,892.9	7,736.0
Telecommunication services	13,600.0	13,700.0
Aid and contributions	129,967.2	138,703.9
Total	492,141.4	536,651.3

* Revised budget.

Source: Government of India, Annual Budget Papers, 1986/87.

Seventh Five-Year Plan, 1985–90 (estimates, million rupees): total expenditure 3,200,000; public sector outlay 1,800,000; private sector outlay 650,000.

NATIONAL ACCOUNTS ('000 million rupees at current prices, year ending 31 March)
National Income and Product (provisional)

	1982/83	1983/84	1984/85
Compensation of employees	558.49	646.00	n.a.
Operating surplus*	782.89	942.05	n.a.
Domestic factor incomes	1,341.38	1,588.05	1,741.82
Consumption of fixed capital	114.27	133.71	152.52
Gross domestic product at factor cost	1,455.65	1,721.76	1,894.34
Indirect taxes	229.82	267.72	237.49
Less Subsidies	38.07	51.07	
GDP in purchasers' values	1,647.40	1,938.41	2,131.83
Factor income from abroad	5.25	−9.75	−9.75
Less Factor income paid abroad	12.06		
Gross national product	1,640.59	1,928.66	2,122.08
Less Consumption of fixed capital	114.27	133.71	152.52
National income in market prices	1,526.32	1,794.95	1,969.56
Other current transfers from abroad	25.41	27.74	30.50
Less Other current transfers paid abroad	0.14		
National disposable income	1,551.59	1,822.69	2,000.06

* Including mixed income of self-employed ('000 million rupees): 532.14 in 1982/83; 661.56 in 1983/84.

Expenditure on the Gross Domestic Product (provisional)

	1982/83	1983/84	1984/85
Government final consumption expenditure	180.23	208.61	245.00
Private final consumption expenditure	1,102.64	1,337.05	n.a.
Increase in stocks	51.49	64.03	72.73
Gross fixed capital formation	347.75	401.78	449.54
Total domestic expenditure	1,682.11	2,011.47	n.a.
Exports of goods and services	116.68	132.42	n.a.
Less Imports of goods and services	158.06	176.32	n.a.
Sub-total	1,640.73	1,967.57	n.a.
Statistical discrepancy	6.67	−29.16	n.a.
GDP in purchasers' values	1,647.40	1,938.41	2,131.83

Gross Domestic Product by Economic Activity (at current factor cost)

	1983/84*	1984/85*	1985/86†
Agriculture	589.08	601.47	640.01
Forestry and logging	13.41	15.37	17.62
Fishing	12.83	15.77	17.97
Mining and quarrying	50.33	58.29	64.78
Manufacturing	275.43	310.81	357.98
Electricity, gas and water	31.14	37.20	47.19
Construction	85.74	100.40	116.30
Trade, restaurants and hotels	255.74	285.35	318.53
Transport, storage and communications	109.22	125.63	149.16
Banking and insurance	61.74	76.25	90.83
Real estate and business services	60.77	70.33	81.61
Public administration and defence	85.74	101.58	117.92
Other services	95.87	110.43	130.34
Total	1,727.04	1,908.88	2,150.24

* Provisional. † Estimates.

INDIA *Statistical Survey*

BALANCE OF PAYMENTS (US $ million)

	1981	1982	1983
Merchandise exports f.o.b.	8,437	9,226	9,770
Merchandise imports f.o.b.	−14,149	−14,046	−13,868
Trade balance	**−5,711**	**−4,820**	**−4,098**
Exports of services	3,769	3,541	3,770
Imports of services	−3,762	−4,162	−4,687
Balance on goods and services	**−5,704**	**−5,441**	**−5,015**
Private unrequited transfers (net)	2,281	2,599	2,650
Government unrequited transfers (net)	725	318	411
Current balance	**−2,698**	**−2,524**	**−1,953**
Long-term capital (net)	779	1,116	1,532
Short-term capital (net)	66	−659	510
Net errors and omissions	−325	369	−824
Total (net monetary movements)	**−2,178**	**−1,698**	**−736**
Allocation of IMF special drawing rights	148	—	—
Valuation changes (net)	−604	−196	−19
Exceptional financing (net)	4	—	—
Changes in reserves	**−2,629**	**−1,894**	**−755**

Source: IMF, *International Financial Statistics*.

External Trade

PRINCIPAL COMMODITIES (million rupees, year ending 31 March)

Imports c.i.f.	1982/83	1983/84	1984/85
Wheat	2,922.7	5,071.2	1,074.1
Milk and cream	598.7	148.5	961.6
Fruit and nuts (excl. cashew nuts)	227.3	389.7	389.9
Textile yarn, fabrics, etc.	1,125.9	1,250.5	898.5
Synthetic and regenerated fibres	1,247.3	1,025.6	488.1
Crude rubber (incl. synthetic and reclaimed)	540.8	806.2	706.9
Crude fertilizers	555.1	807.2	1,110.2
Manufactured fertilizers	1,456.4	1,124.8	7,510.2
Sulphur and unroasted iron pyrites	693.3	633.0	1,106.5
Other crude minerals	408.9	517.6	630.3
Metalliferous ores and metal scrap	1,522.2	1,445.7	1,132.1
Iron and steel	11,459.6	9,629.0	7,773.3
Non-ferrous metals	2,790.6	3,690.8	3,451.4
Other metal manufactures	1,364.7	1,477.7	1,295.6
Edible vegetable oil	2,262.7	5,409.8	8,301.9
Mineral fuels, lubricants, etc.	56,049.6	48,301.1	53,820.8
Organic chemicals	2,381.4	3,970.4	3,893.3
Inorganic chemicals	1,488.9	2,126.1	3,798.0
Chemical materials and products	732.3	1,228.5	1,117.0
Artificial resins, plastic materials	1,257.1	1,890.2	1,823.6
Medicinal and pharmaceutical products	805.8	1,317.2	1,292.9
Paper, paperboard and manufactures	1,474.7	1,725.9	1,751.2
Pulp and waste paper	271.9	823.0	1,426.0
Pearls, precious and semi-precious stones	6,774.3	10,823.8	10,277.2
Other non-metallic mineral manufactures	1,413.9	1,752.2	1,305.2
Non-electric machinery	13,831.1	19,738.4	18,723.3
Electrical machinery, apparatus, etc.	2,481.9	4,035.6	4,611.4
Transport equipment	6,004.9	4,562.4	2,841.1
Professional, scientific and controlling instruments, photographic and optical goods, watches and clocks	1,898.4	2,806.9	2,404.7
Wool (raw)	385.4	430.9	549.6
Total (incl. others)	**143,557.6**	**157,629.5**	**170,921.2**

Source: Ministry of Commerce, *Annual Report, 1983/84, 1984/85, 1985/86*.

Exports f.o.b.	1982/83	1983/84	1984/85*
Fish, crustaceans, molluscs and preparations	3,494.5	3,273.0	3,358.2
Meat and meat preparations	805.7	683.2	759.8
Rice	1,995.0	1,471.3	1,216.8
Wheat	—	12.9	110.9
Cashew kernels	1,339.7	1,566.2	1,744.8
Other vegetables and fruit	1,588.0	1,551.6	1,617.8
Crude vegetable materials	810.2	968.9	1,364.8
Sugar and sugar preparations	623.5	1,398.6	217.4
Coffee and coffee substitutes	1,842.0	1,832.6	1,981.3
Tea and maté	3,675.3	5,013.7	7,078.6
Spices	889.3	1,092.6	1,740.6
Oil cakes	1,493.5	1,462.9	1,328.1
Unmanufactured tobacco, tobacco refuse	2,085.4	1,496.1	1,486.3
Cotton (raw)	1,011.6	1,489.5	568.0
Cotton fabrics	2,655.2	2,776.0	4,128.7
Ready-made garments	5,275.0	6,095.9	8,578.4
Jute manufactures	2,027.6	1,645.2	3,410.7
Carpets (hand-made)	1,685.7	1,940.4	2,270.7
Leather and leather manufactures	3,458.8	3,499.3	4,252.4
Pearls, precious and semi-precious stones	8,249.1	12,139.9	11,946.8
Works of art	1,096.1	1,166.4	1,347.7
Iron ore	3,737.9	3,853.4	4,472.3
Other ores and minerals	321.5	368.1	451.8
Iron and steel	557.5	464.3	620.5
Metal manufactures (excl. iron and steel)	2,015.6	1,944.1	1,834.5
Machinery and transport equipment	5,846.0	4,969.8	5,549.4
Chemicals and allied products	3,082.0	2,777.1	3,705.9
Cotton articles	970.1	763.0	920.3
Total (incl. others)	89,077.5	98,721.0	116,569.3

* Provisional.

Source: Ministry of Commerce, *Annual Report 1983/84, 1984/85, 1985/86*.

PRINCIPAL TRADING PARTNERS
(million rupees, year ending 31 March)

Imports c.i.f.	1982/83	1983/84	1984/85
Australia	2,787.2	1,447.7	1,924.1
Belgium	6,176.2	6,716.5	7,930.1
Brazil	1,768.3	2,803.0	2,940.3
Canada	2,510.0	3,423.9	5,083.7
France	4,137.8	3,075.7	3,518.9
Germany, Federal Republic	8,012.9	11,204.2	12,977.5
Iran	7,826.6	7,815.0	5,101.6
Iraq	8,840.7	7,910.4	6,743.7
Italy	2,412.3	2,707.4	2,887.4
Japan	10,699.8	14,555.3	12,404.1
Korea, Republic	t2,249.0	1,463.5	1,473.0
Kuwait	2,824.3	2,614.0	3,681.3
Malaysia	2,084.0	3,582.7	5,484.8
Netherlands	2,548.7	2,507.4	2,887.4
Saudi Arabia	14,962.4	10,782.1	12,494.8
Singapore	3,619.3	4,058.1	5,420.7
Switzerland	1,111.8	1,543.7	1,682.2
USSR	15,134.4	16,585.8	18,033.8
United Arab Emirates	3,651.2	2,753.0	3,589.8
United Kingdom	8,855.8	11,430.8	10,188.3
USA	13,706.6	17,908.6	16,666.0

Exports f.o.b.	1982/83	1983/84	1984/85
Australia	1,023.5	947.6	1,485.0
Belgium	2,110.2	2,072.0	1,856.3
Egypt	840.5	1,160.9	1,052.0
France	1,483.1	1,565.0	2,089.2
Germany, Federal Republic	3,431.5	3,752.8	4,709.2
Hong Kong	1,916.8	2,165.0	1,737.4
Iran	740.4	1,194.5	1,340.3
Italy	1,418.5	1,639.2	2,031.6
Japan	7,946.3	8,256.8	10,609.7
Kuwait	1,290.1	1,170.6	1,159.0
Nepal	838.9	1,079.2	1,810.8
Netherlands	1,157.5	1,954.0	1,821.2
Romania	1,182.7	646.6	637.8
Saudi Arabia	2,272.9	2,449.0	2,450.0
Singapore	1,941.9	1,969.2	1,912.3
Sri Lanka	973.3	1,077.2	1,142.3
Switzerland	956.3	1,210.9	1,187.4
USSR	15,583.0	13,058.7	16,545.9
United Arab Emirates	2,192.1	2,292.3	2,687.8
United Kingdom	4,571.6	5,560.8	6,700.6
USA	9,502.5	13,955.5	17,684.8

Source: Ministry of Commerce, *Annual Report 1983/84, 1984/85, 1985/86*.

INDIA

Transport

RAILWAYS (million, year ending 31 March)

	1982/83	1983/84	1984/85
Passengers	3,655.4	3,325.2	3,333.0
Passenger-km	226,930.5	222,935.1	226,582.0
Freight (metric tons)	256.0	258.0	264.8
Freight (metric ton-km)	177,766.5	178,446.4	182,161.0

Source: Ministry of Railways.

ROAD TRAFFIC ('000 motor vehicles in use at 31 March)

	1982	1983	1984
Private cars	947	1,061	1,092
Jeeps	141	154	179
Taxis	119	136	142
Buses and coaches	164	177	200
Goods vehicles	629	696	773
Motor cycles and scooters	2,963	3,512	4,234
Others	882	982	1,118
Total	5,845	6,718	7,738

Source: Transport Wing, Ministry of Shipping and Transport.

INTERNATIONAL SEA-BORNE SHIPPING
(year ending 31 March)

	1980/81	1981/82‡	1982/83‡
Vessels* ('000 net reg. tons):			
Entered	25,204	25,913	25,767
Cleared	23,025	24,709	25,300
Freight† ('000 metric tons):			
Loaded	29,040	30,709	21,258
Unloaded	38,740	38,068	36,375

* Excluding minor and intermediate ports.
† Including bunkers.   ‡ Provisional.
Source: Directorate General of Commercial Intelligence and Statistics.

CIVIL AVIATION ('000)

	1983	1984	1985
Kilometres flown	97,680	103,000	104,904
Passenger-km	14,081,484	14,749,177	14,762,304
Freight ton-km	489,204	577,080	513,960
Mail ton-km	37,128	35,200	33,144

Source: Directorate General of Civil Aviation.

Tourism

FOREIGN VISITORS BY COUNTRY OF ORIGIN*

	1983	1984	1985
Australia	23,436	24,546	22,047
Canada	29,857	25,135	29,022
France	50,158	47,148	44,091
Germany, Federal Republic	51,087	47,913	44,790
Iran	n.a.	15,302	23,305
Italy	27,947	23,570	23,187
Japan	26,662	29,566	30,573
Malaysia	25,796	22,993	23,265
Saudi Arabia	25,121	22,449	20,728
Sri Lanka	81,716	92,449	69,063
United Kingdom	136,823	124,205	119,544
USA	95,847	95,651	95,920
Total (incl. others)	884,731	852,503	836,908

* Figures exclude nationals of Bangladesh and Pakistan. Including these, the totals were: 1,304,976 in 1983; 1,193,752 in 1984; 1,259,384 in 1985.
Source: Ministry of Tourism.

Communications Media

	1981	1982	1983
Radio receivers*	10,178,555	12,201,000	n.a.
Television receivers*	1,672,628	2,196,000	n.a.
Telephones*	2,785,000	2,982,000	3,215,000
Daily newspapers*	1,264	1,334	1,423
Non-daily newspapers* Other periodicals	17,880	18,603	19,335

* Figures refer to year ending 31 March.
Sources: Ministry of Communications; Registrar of Newspapers for India; Ministry of Information and Broadcasting.

Education

(1983/84)

	Institutions	Teachers	Students
Primary	509,143	1,391,912	81,096,807
Middle	126,345	878,562	24,584,552
Secondary (High School)	44,951	602,535	10,155,488
Higher secondary (Old course)	6,973	202,877	3,699,322
Higher secondary (New pattern)	6,407	226,807	1,815,959

Source: Ministry of Education.

Directory

The Constitution

The Constitution of India, adopted by the Constituent Assembly on 26 November 1949, was inaugurated on 26 January 1950. The Preamble declares that the People of India solemnly resolve to constitute a Sovereign Democratic Republic and to secure to all its citizens justice, liberty, equality and fraternity. There are 397 articles and nine schedules, which form a comprehensive document.

UNION OF STATES

The Union of India comprises 24 states and seven Union Territories. There are provisions for the formation and admission of new states.

The Constitution confers citizenship on a threefold basis of birth, descent, and residence. Provisions are made for refugees who have migrated from Pakistan and for persons of Indian origin residing abroad.

FUNDAMENTAL RIGHTS AND DIRECTIVE PRINCIPLES

The rights of the citizen contained in Part III of the Constitution are declared fundamental and enforceable in law. 'Untouchability' is abolished and its practice in any form is a punishable offence. The Directive Principles of State Policy provide a code intended to ensure promotion of the economic, social and educational welfare of the State in future legislation.

THE PRESIDENT

The President is the head of the Union, exercising all executive powers on the advice of the Council of Ministers responsible to Parliament. He is elected by an electoral college consisting of elected members of both Houses of Parliament and the Legislatures of the States. The President holds office for a term of five years and is eligible for re-election. He may be impeached for violation of the Constitution. The Vice-President is the ex officio Chairman of the Rajya Sabha and is elected by a joint sitting of both Houses of Parliament.

THE PARLIAMENT

The Parliament of the Union consists of the President and two Houses: the Rajya Sabha (Council of States) and the Lok Sabha (House of the People). The Rajya Sabha consists of 244 members, of whom a number are nominated by the President. One-third of its members retire every two years. Elections are indirect, each state's legislative quota being elected by the members of the state's legislative assembly. The Lok Sahba has 542 members elected by adult franchise; not more than 17 represent the Union Territories. It may also include a number of members nominated by the President.

GOVERNMENT OF THE STATES

The governmental machinery of states closely resembles that of the Union. Each of these states has a governor at its head appointed by the President for a term of five years to exercise executive power on the advice of a council of ministers. The states' legislatures consist of the Governor and either one house (legislative assembly) or two houses (legislative assembly and legislative council). The term of the assembly is five years, but the council is not subject to dissolution.

LANGUAGE

The Constitution provides that the official language of the Union shall be Hindi. (The English language will continue to be an associate language for many official purposes.)

LEGISLATION—FEDERAL SYSTEM

The Constitution provides that bills, other than money bills, can be introduced in either House. To become law, they must be passed by both Houses and receive the assent of the President. In financial affairs, the authority of the Lower House is final. The various subjects of legislation are enumerated on three lists in the seventh schedule of the Constitution: the Union List, containing nearly 100 entries, including external affairs, defence, communications and atomic energy; the State List, containing 65 entries, including local government, police, public health, education; and the Concurrent List, with over 40 entries, including criminal law, marriage and divorce, labour welfare. The Constitution vests residuary authority in the Centre. All matters not enumerated in the Concurrent or State Lists will be deemed to be included in the Union List, and in the event of conflict between Union and State Law on any subject enumerated in the Concurrent List the Union Law will prevail. In time of emergency Parliament may even exercise powers otherwise exclusively vested in the states. Under Article 356, 'If the President on receipt of a report from the government of a state or otherwise is satisfied that a situation has arisen in which the Government of the state cannot be carried on in accordance with the provisions of this Constitution, the President may by Proclamation: (a) assume to himself all or any of the functions of the government of the state and all or any of the powers of the governor or any body or authority in the state other than the Legislature of the state; (b) declare that the powers of the Legislature of the state shall be exercisable by or under the authority of Parliament; (c) make such incidental provisions as appear to the President to be necessary': provided that none of the powers of a High Court be assumed by the President or suspended in any way. Unless such a Proclamation is approved by both Houses of Parliament, it ceases to operate after two months. A Proclamation so approved ceases to operate after six months, unless renewed by Parliament. Its renewal cannot be extended beyond a total period of three years. An independent judiciary exists to define and interpret the Constitution and to resolve constitutional disputes arising between states, or between a state and the Government of India.

OTHER PROVISIONS

Other Provisions of the Constitution deal with the administration of tribal areas, relations between the Union and states, inter-state trade and finance.

AMENDMENTS

The Constitution is flexible in character, and a simple process of amendment has been adopted. For amendment of provisions concerning the Supreme Courts and the High Courts, the distribution of legislative powers between the Union and the states, the representation of the states in Parliament, etc., the amendment must be passed by both Houses of Parliament and must further be ratified by the legislatures of not less than half the states. In other cases no reference to the state legislatures is necessary.

Numerous amendments were adopted in August 1975, following the declaration of a state of emergency in June. The Constitution (39th Amendment) Bill laid down that the President's reasons for proclaiming an emergency may not be challenged in any court. Under the Constitution (40th Amendment) Bill, 38 existing laws may not be challenged before any court on the ground of violation of fundamental rights. Thus detainees under the Maintenance of Internal Security Act could not be told the grounds of their detention and were forbidden bail and any claim to liberty through natural or common law. The Constitution (41st Amendment) Bill provided that the President, Prime Minister and state Governors should be immune from criminal prosecution for life and from civil prosecution during their term of office.

In November 1976 a 59-clause Constitution (42nd Amendment) Bill was approved by Parliament and came into force in January 1977. Some of the provisions of the Bill are that the Indian Democratic Republic shall be named a 'Democratic Secular and Socialist Republic'; that the President 'shall act in accordance with' the advice given to him by the Prime Minister and the Council of Ministers, and, acting at the Prime Minister's direction, shall be empowered for two years to amend the Constitution by executive order, in any way beneficial to the enforcement of the whole; that the term of the Lok Sabha and of the State Assemblies shall be extended from five to six years; that there shall be no limitation on the constituent power of Parliament to amend the Constitution, and that India's Supreme Court shall be barred from hearing petitions challenging Constitutional amendments; that strikes shall be forbidden in the public services and the Union Government have the power to deploy police or other forces under its own superintendence and control in any state. Directive Principles are given precedence over Fundamental Rights: 10 basic duties of citizens are listed, including the duty to 'defend the country and render national service when called upon to do so'.

The Janata Party government, which came into power in March 1977, promised to amend the Constitution during the year, so as to 'restore the balance between the people and Parliament, Parliament and the judiciary, the judiciary and the executive, the states and the centre, and the citizen and the Government that the founding fathers of the Constitution had worked out'. The Constitution (43rd Amendment) Bill, passed by Parliament in December 1977, the Constitution (44th Amendment) Bill, passed by Parliament in December 1977 and later redesignated the 43rd Amendment, and the Constitution (45th Amendment) Bill, passed by Parliament in December 1978 and later redesignated the 44th Amendment, reversed most of the changes enacted by the Constitution (42nd Amendment) Bill. The 44th Amendment is particularly detailed on emergency provisions: An emergency may not be proclaimed unless 'the security of India or any part of its territory was threatened by war or external aggression or by armed rebellion.' Its introduction must be approved by a two-thirds majority of Parliament within a month, and after six months the emergency may be continued only with the approval of Parliament. Among the provisions left unchanged after these Bills were a section subordinating Fundamental Rights to Directive Principles and a clause empowering the central government to deploy armed forces under its control in any state without the state government's consent. In May 1980 the Indian Supreme Court repealed sections 4 and 55 of the 42nd Amendment Act, thus curtailing Parliament's power to enforce directive principles and to amend the Constitution. The death penalty was declared constitutionally valid. The 53rd Amendment to the Constitution, approved by Parliament in August 1986, granted statehood to the Union Territory of Mizoram. (In December 1986 Parliament approved the establishment of the Union Territory of Arunachal Pradesh as the 24th state of India. The Constitution was to be amended accordingly).

THE PANCHAYAT RAJ SCHEME

This scheme is designed to decentralize the powers of the Union and state governments. It is based on the Panchayat (Village Council) and the Gram Sabha (Village Parliament) and envisages the gradual transference of local government from state to local authority. Revenue and internal security will remain state responsibilities at present. By 1978 the scheme had been introduced in all the states except Meghalaya, Nagaland and 23 out of 31 districts in Bihar. The Panchayat operated in all the Union Territories except Lakshadweep, Mizoram (which became India's 23rd state in June 1986) and Pondicherry.

The Government

President: Giani ZAIL SINGH (sworn in 25 July 1982).
Vice-President: RAMASWAMY VENKATARAMAN.

COUNCIL OF MINISTERS
(February 1987)

Prime Minister and Minister of Finance, Science and Technology, Planning, Atomic Energy and Space: RAJIV GANDHI.
Minister of Agriculture and Rural Development: GURDIAL SINGH DHILLON.
Minister of Commerce: P. SHIV SHANKAR.
Minister of Communications: ARJUN SING.
Minister of Defence: VISHWANATH PRATAP SINGH.
Minister of Energy: VASANT SATHE.
Minister of the Environment and Forests: BHAJAN LAL.
Minister of External Affairs: NARAYAN DUTT TIWARI.
Minister of Home Affairs: BUTA SINGH.
Minister of Human Resources Development and Health and Family Welfare: P. V. NARASIMHA RAO.
Minister of Industry: J. VENGAL RAO.
Minister of Law and Justice: ASHOKE KUMAR SEN.
Minister of Parliamentary Affairs, Food and Civil Supplies: HAR KISHAN LAL BHAGAT.
Minister of Programme Implementation: A. B. A. GHANI KHAN CHOUDHURY.
Minister of Steel and Mines: KRISHNA CHANDRA PANT.
Minister of Tourism: MUFTI MOHAMMED SYED.
Minister of Urban Development: MOHSINA KIDWAI.
Minister of Water Resources: B. SHANKARANAND.
Minister of State for Information and Broadcasting: AJIT PANJA.
Minister of State for Textiles: RAM NIWAS MIRDHA.
Minister of State for Labour: P. A. SANGMA.
Minister of State for Welfare: Dr RAJENDRA KUMARI BAJPAI.
Minister of State for Railways: MADHAVRAO SCINDIA.
Minister of State for Civil Aviation: JAGDISH TYTLER.
Minister of State for Surface Transport: RAJESH PILOT.
Minister of State for Petroleum and Natural Gas: BRAHM DUTT.

In addition, there are 29 Ministers of State, without independent charges, and three Deputy Ministers.

MINISTRIES

President's Office: Rashtrapti Bhavan, New Delhi 110004; tel. (11) 3015321.
Prime Minister's Office: South Block, New Delhi 110011; tel. (11) 3012312; telex 3165705.
Ministry of Agriculture and Rural Development: Krishi Bhavan, Dr Rajendra Prasad Rd, New Delhi 110001; tel. (11) 382651; telex 3166489.
Ministry of Atomic Energy: South Block, New Delhi 110011; tel. (11) 3011773; telex 66182.
Ministry of Commerce: Udyog Bhavan, New Delhi 110011; tel. (11) 3016664; telex 312558.
Ministry of Communications: Sanchar Bhavan, 20 Asoka Rd, New Delhi 110001; tel. (11) 381209; telex 314422.
Ministry of Defence: South Block, New Delhi 110011; tel. (11) 3012380; telex 314729.
Ministry of Electronics: Lok Nayak Bhavan, New Delhi 110003; tel. (11) 698713.
Ministry of Energy: Shram Shakti Bhawan, Rafi Marg, New Delhi 110001; tel. (11) 382966.
Ministry of the Environment and Forests: Bikaner House, Shahjahan Rd, New Delhi 110011; tel. (11) 387497.
Ministry of External Affairs: South Block, New Delhi 110011; tel. (11) 3012318; telex 3161876.
Ministry of Finance: North Block, New Delhi 110001; tel. (11) 3012611; telex 312282.
Ministry of Food and Civil Supplies: Krishi Bhavan, New Delhi 110001; tel. (11) 382349; telex 3166505.
Ministry of Health and Family Welfare: Nirman Bhavan, New Delhi 110011; tel. (11) 3018863.
Ministry of Home Affairs: North Block, New Delhi 110001; tel. (11) 3011989.
Ministry of Human Resources Development: Shastri Bhavan, New Delhi 110001; tel. (11) 381298.
Ministry of Industry: Udyog Bhavan, New Delhi 110011; tel. (11) 3011815; telex 314994.
Ministry of Information and Broadcasting: Shastri Bhavan, New Delhi 110001; tel. (11) 383513; telex 3166349.
Ministry of Labour: Shram Shakti Bhavan, Rafi Marg, New Delhi 110001; tel. (11) 382945; telex 3161253.
Ministry of Law and Justice: Shastri Bhavan, Dr Rajendra Prasad Rd, New Delhi 110001; tel. (11) 384777.
Ministry of Parliamentary Affairs: Parliament House, New Delhi 110001; tel. (11) 3017663.
Ministry of Petroleum and Natural Gas: Shastri Bhavan, New Delhi 110001; tel. (11) 383501; telex 3166235.
Ministry of Planning: Yojana Bhavan, Parliament St, New Delhi 110001; tel. (11) 386354.
Ministry of Programme Implementation: Nirman Bhavan, New Delhi 110011; tel. (11) 3012787.
Ministry of Science and Technology: Technology Bhavan, New Mehrauli Rd, New Delhi 110016; tel. (11) 661439.
Ministry of Social and Women's Welfare: Shastri Bhavan, Dr Rajendra Prasad Rd, New Delhi 110001; tel. (11) 386317; telex 314410.
Ministry of Steel and Mines: Udyog Bhavan, New Delhi 110011; tel. (11) 3014096; telex 312801.
Ministry of Textiles: Udyog Bhavan, New Delhi 110011; tel. (11) 3011769.
Ministry of Tourism: Transport Bhavan, Parliament St, New Delhi 110001; tel. (11) 381995; telex 312827.
Ministry of Transport (Railways): Rail Bhavan, New Delhi 110001; tel. (11) 384010.
Ministry of Transport (Shipping and Surface): Transport Bhavan, Sansad Marg, New Delhi 110001; tel. (11) 384938.
Ministry of Transport (Civil Aviation): Transport Bhavan, Sansad Marg, New Delhi 110001; tel. (11) 351700.
Ministry of Urban Development: Nirman Bhavan, New Delhi 110011; tel. (11) 3018377.
Ministry of Water Resources: Shram Shakti Bhavan, Rafi Marg, New Delhi 110001; tel. (11) 383098.

INDIA

Ministry of Welfare: Shram Shakti Bhavan, Rafi Marg, New Delhi 110001; tel. (11) 382683.

Legislature

PARLIAMENT

Rajya Sabha
(Council of States)

Most of the members of the Rajya Sabha are indirectly elected by the State Assemblies for six years, with one-third retiring every two years. The remaining members are nominated by the President.

Chairman: RAMASWAMY VENKATARAMAN.

Distribution of Seats, January 1987

Party	Seats
Congress (I)	150
Communist (CPM—Marxist)	14
All India Anna Dravida Munnetra Kazhagam	11
Janata Party	10
Telugu Desam	10
Bharatiya Janata Party	9
Lok Dal	8
Communist (CPI)	4
Dravida Munnetra Kazhagam	3
Congress (S)	2
Shiromani Akali Dal	2
Forward Bloc	2
Asom Gana Parishad	2
Jammu and Kashmir National Conference (F)	1
Independents and others	9
Nominated	7
Total	**244**

Lok Sabha
(House of the People)

Speaker: BALRAM JHAKHAR.

General Election, 24, 27 and 28 December 1984*

Party	Percentage of votes	Seats at Dec. 1984	Seats at Jan. 1987
Congress (I)	49.17	400	412
Telugu Desam	4.12	28	30
Communist (CPM—Marxist)	5.80	22	22
All India Anna Dravida Munnetra Kazhagam (ADMK)	1.72	12	11
Janata	7.03	10	13
Shiromani Akali Dal	—	—	7
Asom Gana Parishad	—	—	7
Communist (CPI)	2.73	6	6
Congress (S)	n.a.	4	4
Jammu and Kashmir National Conference (F)	n.a.	3	3
Revolutionary Socialist Party	n.a.	3	3
Lok Dal	5.91	3	2
Forward Bloc	n.a.	2	2
Bharatiya Janata Party	7.71	2	2
Muslim League	—	—	2
Kerala Congress	—	—	2
Dravida Munnetra Kazagam	—	—	2
Unattached, independents and others	15.80†	12	9
Nominated	—	2‡	2‡
Vacant	—	35	3
Total	**100.00**	**542**	**544**

* Polling was postponed until 28 January 1985 in two constituencies in Andhra Pradesh, one in Uttar Pradesh, one in Tamil Nadu and also in Bhopal, in Madhya Pradesh. Ladakh, in Jammu and Kashmir, and Mandi, in Himachal Pradesh, went to the polls on 24 April and 24 May respectively. Polling took place in Punjab on 25 September, and in Assam on 16 December 1985.

† Including the parties listed above for which voting figures are not available.

‡ These members are nominated by the President to represent the Anglo-Indian community.

State Governments
(February 1987)

ANDHRA PRADESH
(Capital—Hyderabad)

Governor: KUMUDBEN JOSHI.
Chief Minister: N. T. RAMA RAO (Telugu Desam).
Legislative Assembly: 294 seats (Telugu Desam Party 201, Congress—I 50, Janata 3, Communist—CPM 11, Communist—CPI 11, Majlis-Ittehad-ul-Muslimeen 3, Bharatiya Janata Party 8, independents and others 7).
Legislative Council: 90 seats.

ARUNACHAL PRADESH
(Capital—Itanagar)

Governor: SHIVA SWAROOP.
Chief Minister: GAGONG APANG (Congress—I).
Legislative Assembly: 30 seats (Congress—I 26, People's Party of Arunachal 2, independent and others 2).

In December 1986 Arunachal Pradesh became the 24th state of India through comprehensive legislation.

ASSAM
(Capital—Dispur)

Governor: BHISHMA NARAIN SINGH.
Chief Minister: PRAFULLA KUMAR MAHANTA (Asom Gana Parishad).
Legislative Assembly: 126 seats (Asom Gana Parishad 69, Congress—I 25, United Minorities Front 17, Congress—S 4, Plains Tribal Council of Assam 3, Communist—CPM 2, independents and others 6).

BIHAR
(Capital—Patna)

Governor: PONDAKAINTI VENKATASUBBAIAH.
Chief Minister: BINDESWARI DUBEY (Congress—I).
Legislative Assembly: 324 seats (Congress—I 196, Lok Dal 48, Communist—CPI 12, Bharatiya Janata Party 13, Janata 13, Jharkhand Party 11, independents and others 31).
Legislative Council: 90 seats.

GUJARAT
(Capital—Gandhinagar)

Governor: R. K. TRIVEDI.
Chief Minister: AMARSINH CHAUDHARI (Congress—I).
Legislative Assembly: 182 seats (Congress—I 149, Janata 14, Bharatiya Janata Party 11, independents and others 8).

HARYANA
(Capital—Chandigarh)

Governor: S. M. H. BURNEY.
Chief Minister: BANSI LAL (Congress—I).
Legislative Assembly: 92 seats (Congress—I 60, Lok Dal Party 15, Bharatiya Janata Party 5, Janata Party 6, Congress (J) 2, vacant 4).

HIMACHAL PRADESH
(Capital—Simla)

Governor: Vice-Adm. (retd) RUSTOM KHUSRO SHAMPOORJEE GANDHI.
Chief Minister: VIR BHADRA SINGH (Congress—I).
Legislative Assembly: 68 seats (Congress—I 56, Bharatiya Janata Party 7, Lok Dal 1, independents and others 4).

JAMMU AND KASHMIR
(Capitals—Srinagar (Summer), Jammu (Winter))

Governor: JAGMOHAN (MALHOTRA).
Chief Minister: Dr FAROOK ABDULLAH (Coalition of Jammu and Kashmir National Conference Party—F and Congress—I).
Legislative Assembly: 78 seats (National Conference Party—F 34, Congress—I 27, National Conference Party—K 16, others 1).
Legislative Council: 36 seats.

Jammu and Kashmir was placed under Governor's rule in March 1986, and under President's rule in September, since when the Assembly has been suspended. President's rule was terminated in November, and a coalition government installed.

KARNATAKA
(Capital—Bangalore)
Governor: A. N. Banerjee.
Chief Minister: Rama Krishna Hegde (Janata).
Legislative Assembly: 224 seats (Congress—I 66, Janata 141, independents and others 9, Bharatiya Janata Party 2, Communist—CPI 4, Communist—CPM 2).
Legislative Council: 63 seats.

KERALA
(Capital—Trivandrum)
Governor: P. Ramachandran.
Chief Minister: K. Karunakaran (Congress—I).
Legislative Assembly: 140 seats (Communist—CPM 31, Communist—CPI 13, Congress—I 35, Muslim League 18, Kerala Congress 5, Kerala Congress (Joseph Group) 8, Congress—S 6, Janata 4, Revolutionary Socialist Party 3, Janata—G 4, National Democratic Party 4, independents and others 9).

MADHYA PRADESH
(Capital—Bhopal)
Governor: K. M. Chandy.
Chief Minister: Motilal Vora (Congress—I).
Legislative Assembly: 320 seats (Congress—I 251, Bharatiya Janata 58, Janata 5, independents and others 6).
Legislative Council: 90 seats.

MAHARASHTRA
(Capital—Bombay)
Governor: Dr Shankar Dayal Sharma.
Chief Minister: Shankarrao B. Chavan (Congress—I).
Legislative Assembly: 288 seats (Congress—I 161, Congress—S 56, Janata 20, Bharatiya Janata Party 16, independents and others 19, People and Workers' Party 12, Communist—CPI 2, Communist—CPM 2).
Legislative Council: 78 seats.

MANIPUR
(Capital—Imphal)
Governor: Gen. (retd) K. V. Krishna Rao.
Chief Minister: Rishang Keishing (Congress—I).
Legislative Assembly: 60 seats (Congress—I 32, Janata 4, Manipur People's Party 3, independents and others 21).

MEGHALAYA
(Capital—Shillong)
Governor: Bhishma Narain Singh.
Chief Minister: Capt. Williamson Sangma (Meghalaya Democratic Front).
Legislative Assembly: 60 seats (Congress—I 37, Hills State People's Democratic Party 13, All Party Hill leaders Conference 9, independent 1).

MIZORAM
(Capital—Aizawl)
Governor: Hiteswar Saikia.
Chief Minister: Lal Denga (Mizo National Front).
Legislative Assembly: 40 seats (Mizo National Front 25, Congress—I 12, People's Conference 2, vacant 1).
Mizoram became the 23rd state of India through an amendment to the Constitution in August 1986.

NAGALAND
(Capital—Kohima)
Governor: Gen. (retd) K. V. Krishna Rao.
Chief Minister: Hokishe Sema (Congress—I).
Legislative Assembly: 60 seats (Naga National Democratic Party 24, Congress—I 25, Unattached 11).

ORISSA
(Capital—Bhubaneswar)
Governor: Bishambhar N. Pande.
Chief Minister: Janaki Ballabh Patnaik (Congress—I).
Legislative Assembly: 147 seats (Congress—I 117, Janata 21, independents and others 9).

PUNJAB
(Capital—Chandigarh)
Governor: Sidhartha Shankar Ray.
Chief Minister: Surjit Singh Barnala (Shiromani Akali Dal).
Legislative Assembly: 117 seats (Shiromani Akali Dal 73, Congress—I 32, Bharatiya Janata Party 6, Communist 1, Janata 1, others 4).

RAJASTHAN
(Capital—Jaipur)
Governor: Vasant Rao Patil.
Chief Minister: Harideo Joshi (Congress—I).
Legislative Assembly: 200 seats (Congress—I 115, Bharatiya Janata Party 38, Janata 10, Lok Dal 27, Congress—S 3, independents and others 10).

SIKKIM
(Capital—Gangtok)
Governor: T. V. Rajeshwar.
Chief Minister: Nar Bahadur Bhandari (Sikkim Samgram Parishad).
Legislative Assembly: 32 seats (Sikkim Samgram Parishad 30, Congress—I 1, Independent 1).
Sikkim was placed under President's rule in May 1984, since when the Assembly has been suspended.

TAMIL NADU
(Capital—Madras)
Governor: Sundar Lal Khurana.
Chief Minister: M. G. Ramachandran (ADMK).
Legislative Assembly: 234 seats (ADMK 133, DMK 10, Congress—I 62, Communist—CPM 5, Communist—CPI 2, Gandhi-Kamaraj National Congress 2, Janata 3, independents and others, vacant 10).
Legislative Council: 63 seats.

TRIPURA
(Capital—Agartala)
Governor: Gen. (retd) K. V. Krishna Rao.
Chief Minister: Nripen Chakrabarty (Communist—CPM).
Legislative Assembly: 60 seats (Communist—CPM 37, Congress—I 12, Tripura Upajati Juba Samity 6, independents and others 5).

UTTAR PRADESH
(Capital—Lucknow)
Governor: Mohd Usman Arif.
Chief Minister: Veer Bahadur Singh (Congress—I).
Legislative Assembly: 425 seats (Congress—I 269, Lok Dal 84, Bharatiya Janata Party 16, Janata 20, Communist—CPI 6, Communist—CPM 2, Congress—J 3, independents and others 25).
Legislative Council: 108 seats.

WEST BENGAL
(Capital—Calcutta)
Governor: Syed Nurul Hassan.
Chief Minister: Jyoti Basu (Communist—CPM).
Legislative Assembly: 294 seats (Communist—CPM 168, Congress—I 54, Forward Bloc 27, Revolutionary Socialist 18, Communist—CPI 7, others 20).

UNION TERRITORIES

Andaman and Nicobar Islands (Headquarters—Port Blair):
Lt-Gov.: Tirath Singh Oberoi.
Chandigarh (Headquarters—Chandigarh):
Administrator: Sidhartha Shankar Ray.
Chandigarh was to be incorporated into Punjab state on 26 January 1986, but the transfer was postponed.
Dadra and Nagar Haveli (Headquarters—Silvassa):
Administrator: Gopal Singh.
Delhi (Headquarters—Delhi):
Lt-Gov.: Air Marshal H. K. L. Kapur.
Metropolitan Council: 56 seats (Congress—I 33, Bharatiya Janata Party 20, Lok Dal 2, Janata 1, vacant 3).

INDIA   Directory

Goa, Daman and Diu (Capital—Panaji):
Lt-Gov.: GOPAL SINGH.
Chief Minister: PRATAP SINGH RANE (Congress—I).
Assembly: 30 seats (Congress—I 18, Maharashtrawadi Gomantak Party 8, independents and others 4).
Lakshadweep (Headquarters—Kavaratti):
Administrator: P. M. NAIR.
Pondicherry (Capital—Pondicherry):
Administrator: Lt-Gov. TRIBHUVAN PRASAD TEWARY.
Chief Minister: M. O. H. FAROOK (Congress—I).
Assembly: 30 seats (DMK 5, ADMK 6, Congress—I 15, Janata 2, others 2).

Pondicherry was placed under President's rule in June 1983, since when the Assembly has been suspended.

Political Organizations

Prior to independence, the leading nationalist group was the Congress Party, established in 1885. In 1907 Congress split into two factions: the Extremists and the Moderates. In 1969 Congress again split into two distinct organizations, with Indira Gandhi's Government continuing in office while the Indian National Congress (Organization) became India's first recognized opposition party. Further splits occurred in January 1978, when Indira Gandhi formed a breakaway group, the Indian National Congress (I), and again in 1981, when the Indian National Congress (Socialist) was formed. In July 1981 a Supreme Court ruling confirmed Congress (I) as the official Congress party. Congress (J) broke away in August 1981, but rejoined Congress (I) in 1986. Breakaway parties from Congress (I) were formed by 'Indira loyalists' in August 1986 and again in January 1987. In December 1986 Congress (S) split, the majority faction voting to rejoin Congress (I) while the remaining members decided to continue as Congress (S).

All India Congress Committee (I): 24 Akbar Rd, New Delhi 110011; tel. (11) 384422; f. 1978, as Indian National Congress (I), as a breakaway group under Indira Gandhi; Pres. RAJIV GANDHI; Gen. Secs G. KARUPPIAH MOOPANAR, A. K. ANTHONY, R. L. BHATIA, NAWAL KISHORE SHARMA, Mrs NAJMA HEPTULLA, (vacant).

  Congress (J): 6 Krishna Menon Marg, New Delhi 110011; tel. (11) 3012963; f. 1981 as a breakaway group from the main Congress party; formerly led by Jagjivan Ram (who died in 1986); Pres. INDIRA RAM; Gen. Sec. H. S. BALLA; 2m. mems; rejoined Congress (I) in 1986.

Indian National Congress (S): 3 Raisina Rd, New Delhi 110001; tel. (11) 382478; f. 1981; aims include the establishment by peaceful means of a socialist, co-operative commonwealth; advocates govt control of large-scale industries and services; co-operative industry and agriculture; a neutral foreign policy; Pres. SARAT CHANDRA SINHA; Gen. Secs K. P. UNNIKRISHNAN, V. KISHORE CHANDRA, S. DEO; 4m. mems.

India's other major national political organizations are:

Akhil Bharat Hindu Mahasabha: Hindu Mahasabha Bhavan, Mandir Marg, New Delhi 110001; tel. (11) 343105; f. 1915; aims to establish a democratic Hindu state; Pres. VIKRAM SAVARKAR; Gen. Sec. MADHAV DUTTATRAYA PATHAK; 500,000 mems.

All India Forward Bloc: 128 North Ave, New Delhi 110001; tel. (11) 376904; f. 1940 by Netaji Subhash Chandra Boase; socialist aims, including nationalization of key industries, land reform and redistribution; Chair. P. D. PALIWAL; Gen. Sec. CHITTA BASU; 900,000 mems.

Bharatiya Janata Party (BJP): (Indian People's Party): 11 Ashok Rd, New Delhi 110001; tel. (11) 383349; f. 1980; breakaway group from main Janata Party after the Janata exec. decided to ban dual membership of Janata and the Rashtriya Swayam Sewak Sangh; an extremist body, based on right-wing Hindu Jana Sangh party; Pres. LALKRISHNA ADVANI.

Communist Party of India (CPI): Ajoy Bhavan, Kotla Marg, New Delhi 110002; tel. (11) 3315546; f. 1925; advocates the establishment of a socialist society led by the working class, and ultimately of a communist society; Leaders INDRAJIT GUPTA, N. E. BALARAM; Sec.-Gen. C. RAJENSWARA RAO; 445,987 mems.

Communist Party of India—Marxist (CPM): 14 Ashoka Rd, New Delhi 110001; tel. (11) 382870; f. 1964 as pro-Beijing breakaway group from the CPI; declared its independence of Beijing in 1968 and is managed by a politbureau of 9 mems; Leaders JYOTI BASU, P. RAMAMURTI; Gen. Sec. E. M. SANKARAN NAMBOODIRIPAD; 369,000 mems.

Janata Party (People's Party): 7 Jantar Mantar Rd, New Delhi 110001; tel. (11) 383981; f. May 1977 by the merger of the Indian National Congress (Organization), the Bharatiya Lok Dal (BLD), the Bharatiya Jan Sangh (People's Party of India) and the Socialist Party, which had combined as the Janata Party to contest the March 1977 general election; Congress for Democracy, a party formed in February 1977, merged into the Janata Party in May 1977; aims to achieve by democratic and peaceful means a socialist society, free from social, political and economic exploration; Leaders Prof. MADHU DANDAVATE (Lok Sabha), M. S. GURUPADASWAMY (Rajya Sabha); Pres. CHANDRA SHEKHAR; Gen. Secs INDUBHAI PATEL, ANANTRAM JAISWAL, YASHWANT SINHA, BHAI VAIDYA, S. JAIPAL REDDY; 3m. mems.

Lok Dal (People's Party): 15 Windsor Place, New Delhi 110001; tel. (11) 388925; f. 1984 by merger of the Lok Dal (a splinter group from the Janata Party) with the Democratic Socialist Party and the Janavadi Dal; advocates secularism, the primacy of agriculture and small industry; Pres. CHAUDHARY CHARAN SINGH; Gen. Secs B. P. MAURYA, RASHEED MASUD, AJIT SINGH, SHARAD YADAV, SATYA PRAKASH MALAVIYA, TARAKESWARI SINHA; 6m. mems.

National Socialist Congress Party: f. 1987 as a breakaway group from Congress (I); promotes the programmes and policies of Indira Gandhi; Pres. PRANAB MUKHERJEE.

Peasants' and Workers' Party of India: Mahatma Phule Rd, Naigaum, Bombay 400014; f. 1949; Marxist; seeks to nationalize all basic industries, to promote industrialization, and to establish a unitary state with provincial boundaries drawn on a linguistic basis; Gen. Sec. DAJIBA DESAI; c. 10,000 mems.

Republican Party of India (RPI): Azad Maidan, Fort, Bombay 400001, Maharashtra; main aim is to realize the aims and objects set out in the preamble to the 1950 Constitution; Pres. BALA SAHIB PRAKASH; Gen. Sec. Mrs J. ISHWARIBAI.

Shiromani Akali Dal: Baradan Shri Dabar Sahib, Amritsar; f. 1920; merged with Congress Party 1958–62; moderate; Sikh party; opposes govt interference in Sikh affairs; seeks autonomy for all states, equal rights for all and safeguards for minorities; Pres. SURJIT SINGH BARNALA; Gen. Sec. HARBHAJAN SINGH SANDU; 1m. mems. (In 1986 the Akali Dal split into various factions, one of the most militant groups being led by PRAKASH SINGH BADAL.)

India's major regional political organizations are:

All-India Anna Dravida Munnetra Kazhagam (ADMK) (All-India Anna Dravidian Progressive Asscn): 156 Lloyds Rd, Madras 600004; f. 1972; splinter group of the DMK; Leader M. G. RAMACHANDRAN.

Asom Gana Parishad (AGP) (Assam People's Council): Golaghat, Assam; f. 1985; draws support from the All-Assam Gana Sangram Parishad and the All-Assam Students' Union; campaigning for unity of India in diversity and a united Assam; Leader PRAFULLA KUMAR MAHANTA.

Dravida Munnetra Kazhagam (DMK): Royapuram, Madras 600013; f. 1949; aims at full autonomy for Tamil Nadu within the Union, to establish regional languages as State languages and English as the official language; Pres. Dr M. KARUNANIDHI; Gen. Sec. K. ANBAZHAGAN; over 1.6m. mems.

Jammu and Kashmir National Conference Party (JKNC): Mujahid Manzil, Srinagar; tel. (11) 71500; fmrly All Jammu and Kashmir Muslim Conference, f. 1931, renamed 1938, revived 1975; state-based party campaigning for responsible self-govt; split into two rival sections in 1984: JKNC (F), led by Dr FAROOK ABDULLAH, Gen. Sec. SHEIKH NAZIR AHMAD, and JKNC (K) led by BEGUM KHALIDA SHAH. (The latter section is not recognized by the Election Commission of India.)

Telugu Desam (Telugu Nation): 3-5-910, Himayatnagar, Hyderabad 500029; tel. (842) 227070; f. 1982; state-based party (Andhra Pradesh) campaigning against rural poverty and social prejudice; Founder and Pres. N. T. RAMA RAO; Gen.-Sec. P. UPENDRA; 1,184,595 mems.

Diplomatic Representation

EMBASSIES AND HIGH COMMISSIONS IN INDIA

Afghanistan: Shanti Path, Chanakyapuri, New Delhi 110021; tel. (11) 603331; Ambassador: ABDOL SAMAD AZHAR.

Algeria: 15, Anand Lok, New Delhi 110049; tel. (11) 655216; telex 31-4548; Ambassador: ABDER RAHMANE BENSID.

Argentina: B-8/9 Vasant Vihar, Paschimi Marg, New Delhi 110057; tel. (11) 671345; telex 31-61642; Ambassador: TERESA HOTENCIA INÉS FLOURET.

Australia: 1/50-G Shanti Path, Chanakyapuri, New Delhi 110021; tel. (11) 601336; telex 31-61156; High Commissioner: GRAHAM BARTON FEAKES.
Austria: EP/13 Chandragupta Marg, New Delhi 110021; tel. (11) 601555; telex 31-61699; Ambassador: Dr BENNO KOCH.
Bangladesh: 56 Ring Rd, Lajpat Nagar-III, New Delhi 110024; tel. (11) 615668; telex 31-65218; High Commissioner: FARUQ AHMED CHOUDHURY.
Belgium: 50N, Plot 4, Shantipath, Chanakyapuri, New Delhi 110021; tel. (11) 608295; telex 31-61487; Ambassador: CHRISTIAN L. C. FELLENS.
Bhutan: Chandragupta Marg, Chanakyapuri, New Delhi 110021; tel. (11) 609217; Ambassador: LYONPO TASHI TOBGYEL.
Brazil: N-90 Panchshila Park, New Delhi 110017; tel. (11) 6436791; telex 31-65277; Ambassador: JORGE D' ESCRAGNOLLE TAUNAY.
Bulgaria: 16/17 Chandragupta Marg, Chanakyapuri, New Delhi 110021; tel. (11) 607411; telex 31-2545; Ambassador: TOCHO KIRYAKOV TOCHEV.
Burma: Burma House, 3/50-F Nyaya Marg, Chanakyapuri, New Delhi 110021; tel. (11) 600251; Ambassador: U KO KO LAY.
Canada: 7/8 Shanti Path, Chanakyapuri, New Delhi 110021; tel. (11) 608161; telex 31-66346; High Commissioner: JAMES C. HARRIS.
Chile: 1/13 Shanti Niketan, New Delhi 110021; tel. (11) 671363; telex 31-4197; Ambassador: MARCELO PADILLA MINVIELLE.
China, People's Republic: 50D Shanti Path, Chanakyapuri, New Delhi 110021; tel. (11) 600328; telex 31-62250; Ambassador: LI LIANQING.
Colombia: 82D Malcha Marg, Chanakyapuri, New Delhi 110021; tel. (11) 3012771; Ambassador: Dr NELLY TURBAY DE MUÑOZ.
Cuba: D-5 South Extension, Part II, New Delhi 110049; tel. (11) 6442897; telex 31-66286; Ambassador: JOSÉ PÉREZ NOVOA.
Cyprus: 52 Jor Bagh, New Delhi 110003; tel. (11) 697503; telex 31-61788; High Commissioner: ANTONIOS J. VAKIS.
Czechoslovakia: 50M Niti Marg, Chanakyapuri, New Delhi 110021; tel. (11) 608382; telex 31-2386; Ambassador: JAROMIR NEHERA.
Denmark: 2 Golf Links, New Delhi 110003; tel. (11) 616273; telex 31-3166160; Ambassador: KAJ BAAGOE.
Egypt: 55–57 Sunder Nagar, New Delhi 110003; tel. (11) 619081; telex 031-4211; Ambassador: AMRE MOUSSA.
Ethiopia: 7/50-G Satya Marg, Chanakyapuri, New Delhi 110021; tel. (11) 604407; telex 31-4429; Ambassador: Brig.-Gen. AMDEMIKAEL BELAGHEW.
Finland: Nyaya Marg, Chanakyapuri, New Delhi 110021; tel. (11) 605409; telex 31-65030; Ambassador: JAN GROOP.
France: 2/50E, Shantipath, New Delhi 110021; tel. (11) 604004; telex 31-2277; Ambassador: JEAN-BERNARD MÉRIMÉE.
German Democratic Republic: 2 Nyaya Marg, Chanakyapuri, New Delhi 110021; tel. (11) 3014204; telex 031-2245; Ambassador: Dr BERND BIEDERMANN.
Germany, Federal Republic: 6 Block 50G, Shanti Path, Chanakyapuri, New Delhi 110021; tel. (11) 604861; telex 031-65670; Ambassador: GÜNTHER SCHÖDEL.
Ghana: A-42 Vasant Marg, Vasant Vihar, New Delhi 110057; tel. (11) 670716; High Commissioner: KWAME SAARAH-MENSAH.
Greece: 16 Sundar Nagar, New Delhi 110003; tel. (11) 617800; telex 31-65232; Ambassador: GEORGE SIORIS.
Guyana: 85 Poorvi Marg, Vasant Vihar, New Delhi 110057; tel. (11) 674194; telex 31-3246; High Commissioner: S. S. NARAINE.
Holy See: 50C Niti Marg, Chanakyapuri, New Delhi 110021 (Apostolic Nunciature); tel. (11) 606520; Pro-Nuncio: Most Rev. AGOSTINO CACCIAVILLAN.
Hungary: Plot 2, 50M Niti Marg, Chanakyapuri, New Delhi 110021; tel. (11) 608414; telex 31-4718; Ambassador: JÓZSEF OLÁH.
Indonesia: 50A Chanakyapuri, New Delhi 110021; tel. (11) 602352; telex 31-65709; Ambassador: R. TAMTOMO.
Iran: 5 Barakhamba Road, New Delhi 110001; tel. (11) 385491; telex 31-3921; Ambassador: EBRAHIM BENHAM DEHKORDY.
Iraq: 169 Jor Bagh, New Delhi 110003; tel.(11) 618011; telex 31-3353; Ambassador: ABDU WADOOD ABDUL AL-SHEIKHLI.
Ireland: 13 Jor Bagh, New Delhi 110003; tel. (11) 617435; telex 31-3766; Ambassador: PAUL DEMPSEY.
Italy: 13 Golf Links, New Delhi 110003; tel. (11) 618311; telex 31-66020; Ambassador: Dr RINIERI PAULUCCI DI CALBOLI BARONE.
Japan: Plot Nos 4 and 5, 50G, Shanti Path, Chanakyapuri, New Delhi 110021; tel. (11) 604071; Ambassador: TAKUMI HOSAKI.
Jordan: 35 Malcha Marg, Chanakyapuri, New Delhi 110021; tel. (11) 3013495; telex 31-61963; Ambassador: JAMAL KHUTAT.
Kampuchea: C4/4 Paschimi Marg, Vasant Vihar, New Delhi 110057; tel. (11) 608595; Ambassador: THEAM CHUNY.
Kenya: E-66 Vasant Marg, Vasant Vihar, New Delhi 110057; tel. (11) 672303; telex 31-2797; High Commissioner: TIREITO KIMUNAI.
Korea, Democratic People's Republic: 42/44 Sundar Nagar, New Delhi 110003; tel. (11) 616889; telex 31-4259; Ambassador: SOK AN.
Korea, Republic: 9 Chandragupta Marg, Chanakyapuri, New Delhi 110021; tel. (11) 601601; telex 315537; Ambassador: DONG WON SHIN.
Kuwait: 5A Shanti Path, Chanakyapuri, New Delhi 110021; tel. (11) 600791; telex 31-4332; Ambassador: ALI ZAKURIA AL-ANSARI.
Laos: 20 Jor Bagh, New Delhi 110003; tel. (11) 616187; telex 31-65128; Ambassador: SALY KHAMSY.
Lebanon: 10 Sardar Patel Marg, Chanakyapuri, New Delhi 110021; tel. (11) 3013174; Ambassador: RABIA HAIDAR.
Liberia: New Delhi.
Libya: 22 Golf Links, New Delhi 110003; tel. (11) 697717; telex 031-3901; Secretary of People's Bureau: OMAR AHMAD JADOLLAH AL- AUKALI.
Malaysia: 50M Satya Marg, Chanakyapuri, New Delhi 110021; tel. (11) 601291; telex 31-65096; High Commissioner: MOHAMED HARON.
Maldives: New Delhi; High Commissioner: MOHAMED MUSTHAFA HUSSAIN.
Mauritius: 5 Kautilya Marg, Chanakyapuri, New Delhi 110021; tel. (11) 3011112; telex 31-2945; High Commissioner: ANUND PRIYA NEEWOOR.
Mexico: 10 Jor Bagh, New Delhi 110003; tel. (11) 697991; telex 31-2821; Ambassador: GRACIELA DE LA LAMA.
Mongolia: 34 Archbishop Makarios Marg, New Delhi 110003; tel. (11) 618921; Ambassador: OYUNY HOSBAYAR.
Morocco: 33 Archbishop Makarios Marg, New Delhi 110003; tel. (11) 611588; telex 31-66118; Chargé d'affaires: ALAOUI M'HAMEDI MOUSTAPHA.
Nepal: Barakhamba Rd, New Delhi 110001; tel. (11) 381484; Ambassador: RANA JAGDISH SHUMSHER.
Netherlands: 6/50 F Shanti Path, Chanakyapuri, New Delhi 110021; tel. (11) 609571; telex 31-65070; Ambassador: A. VAN DER WILLIGEN.
New Zealand: 25 Golf Links, New Delhi 110003; tel. (11) 697592; telex 65100; High Commissioner: Sir EDMUND HILLARY.
Nigeria: 21 Palam Marg, Vasant Vihar, New Delhi 110057; tel. (11) 670405; telex 31-2595; High Commissioner: Rear-Adm. (retd) DENSON ERE OKUJAGU.
Norway: 50C Shantipath, Chanakyapuri, New Delhi 110021; tel. (11) 605982; telex 31-65397; Ambassador: KAARE DAEHLEN.
Oman: 16 Palam Marg, New Delhi 110057; tel. (11) 671575; telex 31-2889; Ambassador: AHMED YOUSUF AL-HARITHY.
Pakistan: 2/50 G Shanti Path, Chanakyapuri, New Delhi 110021; tel. (11) 600601; Ambassador: Dr M. HUMAYUN KHAN.
Panama: S-260 Greater Kailash, Part II, New Delhi 110048; tel. (11) 6413884; Ambassador: HORACIO J. BUSTAMANTE.
Peru: A 15/27, Vasant Vihar, New Delhi 110057; tel. (11) 673937; telex 31-3164; Ambassador: FERNANDO GUILLÉN.
Philippines: 50N Nyaya Marg, Chanakyapuri, New Delhi 110021; tel. (11) 608842; Ambassador: ROSALINDA V. TIRONA.
Poland: 50M, Shanti Path, Chanakyapuri, New Delhi 110021; tel. (11) 608321; telex 31-2539; Ambassador: JANUSZ SWITOWSKI.
Portugal: A-24 West End Colony, New Delhi 110021; tel. (11) 674568; telex 031-3608; Ambassador: ANTÓNIO TELCO DE ALMEIDA DE MAGHALHÃES COLACO.
Qatar: A-3 West End Colony, New Delhi 110021; tel. (11) 673745; telex 31-65170; Ambassador: Dr HASSAN ALI HUSSAIN AL-NI'MAH.
Romania: A-52 Vasant Marg, Vasant Vihar, New Delhi 110057; tel. (11) 676111; telex 31-2287; Ambassador: N. FINANTU.
Saudi Arabia: 1 Ring Rd, Kilokri, New Delhi 110014; tel. (11) 632081; Ambassador: Shaikh FOUAD S. MOUFTI.
Singapore: E-6 Chandragupta Marg, Chanakyapuri, New Delhi 110021; tel. (11) 604162; telex 31-61494; High Commissioner: CHAN KENG HOWE.

INDIA

Somalia: 12A Golf Links, New Delhi 110003; tel. (11) 619559; telex 31-65010; Ambassador: Brig.-Gen. MOHAMAD FARAH ALDID.

Spain: 12 Prithviraj Rd, New Delhi 110011; tel. (11) 3013834; telex 31-61488; Ambassador: CARLOS FERNÁNDEZ ESPESO.

Sri Lanka: 27 Kautilya Marg, Chanakyapuri, New Delhi 110021; tel. (11) 3010201; telex 31-61162; High Commissioner: BERNARD P. TILAKARATNA.

Sudan: 6 Jor Bagh, New Delhi 110003; tel. (11) 660434; telex 31-3728; Ambassador: ABDEL MONEIM MUSTAFA.

Sweden: Nyaya Marg, Chanakyapuri, New Delhi 110021; tel. (11) 604051; telex 31-2415; Ambassador: AXEL EDELSTAM.

Switzerland: Nyaya Marg, Chanakyapuri, New Delhi 110021; tel. (11) 604225; telex 31-3156; Ambassador: JEAN CUENDET.

Syria: 28 Vasant Marg, Vasant Vihar, New Delhi 110057; tel. (11) 670233; telex 031-4348; Ambassador: MOHAMMAD KHODAR.

Tanzania: 27 Golf Links, New Delhi 110003; tel. (11) 694351; High Commissioner: MOHAMMED RAMIA ABDIWAWA.

Thailand: 56N Nyaya Marg, Chanakyapuri, New Delhi 110021; tel. (11) 607289; Ambassador: BIRATH ISRASENA.

Trinidad and Tobago: 131 Jor Bagh, New Delhi 110003; tel. (11) 618186; telex 31-62481; High Commissioner: Dr H. E. MAJOR.

Tunisia: B 9/22, Vasant Vihar, New Delhi 110057; tel. (11) 676174; telex 31-61465; Ambassador: ABDERRAOUF OUNAIES.

Turkey: 50N Nyaya Marg, Chanakyapuri, New Delhi 110021; tel. (11) 601921; Ambassador: ILDENIZ DIVANLIOGLU.

Uganda: 61 Golf Links, New Delhi 110003; tel. (11) 693584; telex 31-2243; High Commissioner: Dr CHEBROT STEPHEN CHEMOIKO.

USSR: Shanti Path, Chanakyapuri, New Delhi 110021; tel. (11) 606026; telex 31-2802; Ambassador: VASSILY N. RYKOV.

United Arab Emirates: A-7 West End, New Delhi 110021; tel. (11) 670651; telex 31-2184; Ambassador: (vacant).

United Kingdom: Shanti Path, Chanakyapuri, New Delhi 110021; tel. (11) 601371; telex 31-65125; High Commissioner: DAVID GOODALL.

USA: Shanti Path, Chanakyapuri, New Delhi 110021; tel. (11) 600651; telex 31-65269; Ambassador: JOHN GUNTHER DEAN.

Venezuela: 114N Panchshila Park, New Delhi 110017; tel. (11) 6436783; telex 31-4674; Ambassador: BERNARDE BRICENE.

Viet-Nam: 2 Navjivan Vihar, New Delhi 110017; tel. (11) 669843; Ambassador: HOANG ANH TUAN.

Yemen Arab Republic: 55B Paschimi Marg, Vasant Vihar, New Delhi 110057; tel. (11) 674064; telex 31-5266; Ambassador: YEHYA ZAID AL- RADHI.

Yemen, People's Democratic Republic: B-70 Greater Kailash-I, New Delhi 110048; tel. (11) 6414623; telex 31-65567; Chargé d'affaires: MOHAMED NASSER ALI.

Yugoslavia: 3/50 G Niti Marg, Chanakyapuri, New Delhi 110021; tel. (11) 604311; telex 31-4554; Ambassador: ZIVOJIN JAZIĆ.

Zaire: 160 Jor Bagh, New Delhi 110003; tel. (11) 619455; telex 31-2775; Ambassador: (vacant).

Zambia: 14 Jor Bagh, New Delhi 110003; tel. (11) 619115; telex 31-3084; High Commissioner: MARTIN CHIBULU MUBANGA.

Zimbabwe: B-1/42, Safdarjung Enclave, New Delhi 110029; tel. (11) 677460; High Commissioner: Dr N. G. G. MAKURA.

Judicial System

THE SUPREME COURT

The Supreme Court, consisting of a Chief Justice and not more than 17 judges appointed by the President, exercises exclusive jurisdiction in any dispute between the Union and the states (although there are certain restrictions where an acceding state is involved). It has appellate jurisdiction over any judgment, decree or order of the High Court where that Court certifies that either a substantial question of law or the interpretation of the Constitution is involved.

Provision is made for the appointment by the Chief Justice of India of judges of High Courts as ad hoc judges at sittings of the Supreme Court for specified periods, and for the attendance of retired judges at sittings of the Supreme Court. The Supreme Court has advisory jurisdiction in respect of questions which may be referred to it by the President for opinion. The Supreme Court is also empowered to hear appeals against a sentence of death passed by a State High Court in reversal of an order of acquittal by a lower court, and in a case in which a High Court has granted a certificate of fitness.

The Supreme Court also hears appeals which are certified by High Courts to be fit for appeal, subject to rules made by the Court. Parliament may, by law, confer on the Supreme Court any further powers of appeal.

Chief Justice of India: RAGHUNANDAN SWARUP PATHAK.

Judges of the Supreme Court: G. J. OTHA, O. CHINNAPPA REDDY, A. P. SEN, E. S. VENKATARAMIAH, B. C. RAY, V. BALAKRISHNA ERADI, RAMBRIKSH MISRA, SABYASACHI MUKHERJEE, D. P. MADON, MANHARIAL PRANLAL THAKKAR, RANGANATH MISRA, V. KHALID, MURARI MOHAN DUTT, KAMAL NARAIN SINGH, SIVASANKAR NATARAJAN.

HIGH COURTS

The High Courts are the Courts of Appeal from the lower courts, and their decisions are final except in cases where appeal lies to the Supreme Court.

LOWER COURTS

Provision is made in the Code of Criminal Procedure for the constitution of lower criminal courts called Courts of Session and Courts of Magistrates. The Courts of Session are competent to try all persons duly committed for trial, and inflict any punishment authorized by the law. The President and the local government concerned exercise the prerogative of mercy.

The constitution of inferior civil courts is determined by regulations within each state.

Religion

INDIAN FAITHS

Buddhism: The Buddhists in Ladakh (Jammu and Kashmir) owe allegiance to the Dalai Lama. Head Lama of Ladakh: KAUSHAK SAKULA, Dalgate, Srinagar, Kashmir. In 1981 there were 4.72m. Buddhists in India (0.70% of the population).

Hinduism: 549.8m. Hindus (1981 census), representing 80.25% of the population.

Islam: Muslims are divided into two main sects, Shi'as and Sunnis. Most of the Indian Muslims are Sunnis. In 1986 the Muslim population numbered about 85m.

Jainism: 3.2m. adherents (1981 census), 0.46% of the population.

Sikhism: 13.1m. Sikhs (comprising 1.91% of the population at the 1981 census), the majority living in the Punjab.

Zoroastrians: More than 120,000 Parsis practise the Zoroastrian religion.

CHRISTIANITY

In 1986 there were about 27m. Christians in India, of whom 11.7m. were Roman Catholics.

National Council of Churches in India: Christian Council Lodge, Nagpur, Maharashtra 440001; tel. (712) 31312; mems: 22 reformed and 3 orthodox churches, 14 regional Christian councils, 15 All-India ecumenical organizations and 6 related agencies; represents total membership of 8m.; Pres. Rt Rev. S. K. PARMAR; Gen. Sec. MATHAI ZACHARIAH.

Protestant Churches

Church of North India: Moderator Most Rev. DIN DAYAL, Bishop's House, 25 Mahatma Gandhi Marg, Allahabad 211001; the Church has 23 dioceses with 23 Bishops and Diocesan Councils and a Synod; 700,000 mems.; Gen. Sec. Rev. PRITAM B. SANTRAM, CNI Bhavan, 16 Pandit Pant Marg, New Delhi 110001; tel. 386513; telex 3166736.

Church of South India: Moderator Most Rev. Dr SOLOMON DORAISAWMY, 8 Racquet Court Lane, POB 31, Tiruchirapalli 620001; c. 1.8m. mems.

Malankara Orthodox Syrian Church: Catholicate Palace, Kottayam-4, Kerala; Catholicos of the East and Malankara Metropolitan: HH BASELIUS MAR THOMA MATHEWS I; Sec. Metropolitan DANIEL MAR PHILOXENOS; 1.5m. mems.

Mar Thoma Syrian Church of Malabar: Mar Thoma Sabha Office, Tiruvalla 689101, Kerala; tel. (47811) 2449; Metropolitan: Most Rev. Dr ALEXANDER MAR THOMA; Sec. Rev. C. G. ALEXANDER; 550,000 mems.

United Church of North India and Pakistan: Church House, Mhow, Madhya Pradesh; Sec. (vacant).

INDIA

United Evangelical Lutheran Churches in India: 1 First St, Haddows Rd, Madras 600006; tel. (44) 471676; telex 41-6613; f. 1975 nine member churches; Pres. Rev. K. NATHANIEL; Exec. Sec. Dr K. RAJARATNAM; 1.5m. mems.

The Baptist and Methodist Churches are also represented.

The Roman Catholic Church

India comprises 19 archdioceses, 92 dioceses and two Apostolic Prefectures. These include two archdioceses and 17 dioceses of the the Syro-Malabarese rite, and one archdiocese and two dioceses of the Syro-Malankarese rite. The archdiocese of Goa and Damão, the seat of the Patriarch of the East Indies, is directly responsible to the Holy See. The remaining archdioceses are metropolitan sees. One of the Apostolic Prefectures is Jammu and Kashmir, including the Pakistani-held portion of this disputed territory. In 1986 there were an estimated 11.7m. adherents in the country.

Catholic Bishops' Conference of India (CBCI): CBCI Centre, Goldakkhana, New Delhi 110001; tel. (11) 322064; f. 1976; Pres. Most Rev. SIMON IGNATIUS PIMENTA, Archbishop of Bombay.

Latin Rite

Patriarch of the East Indies: Most Rev. RAUL NICOLAU GONSALVES (Archbishop of Goa and Damão), Paço Patriarcal, POB 216, Pangim, Goa 403001; tel. 3353.

Archbishop of Agra: Most Rev. CECIL DE SA, Archbishop's House, Wazirpura Rd, Agra 282003, Uttar Pradesh; tel. (562) 72407.

Archbishop of Bangalore: Most Rev. PACKIAM AROKIASWAMY, Archbishop's House, Miller's Rd, Bangalore 560026, Karnataka; tel. (812) 55438.

Archbishop of Bhopal: Most Rev. EUGENE D'SOUZA, Archbishop's House, 33 Ahmedabad Palace Rd, Bhopal 492001, Madhya Pradesh; tel. (755) 73619.

Archbishop of Bombay: Most Rev. SIMON IGNATIUS PIMENTA, Archbishop's House, 21 Nathalal Parekh Marg, Bombay 400039, Maharashtra; tel. (22) 2021093.

Archbishop of Calcutta: Cardinal LAWRENCE TREVOR PICACHY, Archbishop's House, 32 Park St, Calcutta 700016; tel. (33) 444666.

Archbishop of Cuttack-Bhubaneswar: Most Rev. RAPHAEL CHEENATH, Archbishop's House, Satya Nagar, Bhubaneswar 751007, Orissa; tel. 52234.

Archbishop of Delhi: Most Rev. ANGELO INNOCENT FERNANDES, Archbishop's House, Ashok Place, New Delhi 110001; tel. (11) 333457.

Archbishop of Hyderabad: Most Rev. SAMININI ARULAPPA, Archbishop's House, Sardar Patel Rd, Secunderabad 500003, Andhra Pradesh; tel. 75545.

Archbishop of Madras and Mylapore: Most Rev. RAYAPPA ARULAPPA, Archbishop's House, 21 San Thome High Rd, Madras 600004, Tamil Nadu; tel. (44) 71102.

Archbishop of Madurai: Most Rev. CASIMIR GNANADICKAM, Archdiocesan Curia, Madurai 625008, Tamil Nadu; tel. (452) 41408.

Archbishop of Nagpur: Most Rev. LEOBARD D'SOUZA, Archbishop's House, Mohan Nagar, Nagpur 440001, Maharashtra; tel. (712) 33239.

Archbishop of Pondicherry and Cuddalore: Most Rev. VENMANI SELVANATHAR, Archbishop's House, POB 2, Pondicherry 605001; tel. 4748.

Archbishop of Ranchi: Most Rev. TELESPHORE TOPPO, Archbishop's House, POB 5, Ranchi 834001, Bihar; tel. 22226.

Archbishop of Shillong-Gauhati: Most Rev. HUBERT D'ROSARIO, Archbishop's House, POB 37, Shillong 793003, Meghalaya; tel. 23355.

Archbishop of Verapoly: Most Rev. JOSEPH KELANTHARA, Latin Archbishop's House, POB 2581, Cochin 682031, Kerala; tel. 32892

Syro-Malabarese Rite

Archbishop of Changanacherry: Most Rev. JOSEPH POWATHIL, Metropolitan Curia, POB 20, Changanacherry 686101, Kerala; tel. 40.

Archbishop of Ernakulam: Most Rev. ANTHONY PADIYARA, Archdiocesan Curia, POB 2580, Ernakulam, Cochin 682031, Kerala; tel. 32629.

Syro-Malankarese Rite

Archbishop of Trivandrum: Most Rev. BENEDICT VARGHESE GREGORIOS THANGALATHIL, Archbishop's House, Trivandrum 695004, Kerala; tel. (487) 67642.

BAHÁ'Í FAITH

National Spiritual Assembly: POB 19, New Delhi 110001; tel. (11) 389326; telex 31-63171.

The Press

Freedom of the Press was guaranteed under articles 13 and 19 of the Constitution. A measure giving the Press the right to publish proceedings of Parliament without being subjected to censorship or the fear of civil or criminal action was popularly known as the 'Feroz Gandhi Act'. This privilege was withdrawn when the Government declared a state of emergency in June 1975 and article 19 of the Constitution, which guaranteed the right to freedom of speech and expression, was suspended. In order to facilitate censorship of all news, a merger of the existing news agencies was enforced in January 1975, and Samachar, the state news agency, was established. However, pre-censorship was declared illegal by the courts in September 1975, and censorship of foreign correspondents ended in September 1976, but the Prevention of Publication of Objectionable Matter Act, passed by Parliament in early 1976, still greatly restricted press freedom. In April 1977 the new Government introduced bills to repeal the Prevention of Publication of Objectionable Matter Act and to restore the rights of the 'Feroz Gandhi Act', which were both subsequently approved by Parliament. The right to report Parliamentary proceedings was further guaranteed under the Constitution (45th amendment) Bill of December 1978, later redesignated the 44th amendment. In April 1978 Samachar was disbanded and the original agencies were re-established.

In March 1979 a Press Council was set up (its predecessor was abolished in 1975). Its function is to uphold the freedom of the Press and maintain and improve journalistic standards. In 1980 a second Press Commission was appointed to inquire into the growth and status of the press since the first commission gave its report, and suggest how best it should develop in the future.

The growth of a thriving press has been made difficult by cultural barriers caused by religious, caste and language differences. Consequently the English-language press, with its appeal to the educated middle-class urban readership throughout the states, has retained its dominance. The English metropolitan dailies, such as the *Times of India* (published in six cities), *Indian Express* (published in 11 cities), the *Hindu* (published in six cities) and the *Statesman* (published in two cities), are some of the widest circulating and most influential newspapers. In 1982 there were 19,937 newspapers and magazines: 1,334 were dailies, 5,898 weeklies and 12,705 other periodicals. More were published in Hindi than in English, and the combined circulation for Hindi papers was 13,763,000 copies per issue, while the English language press had a total circulation of 9,722,000. The readership of daily newspapers is just over 21 per thousand, and in 1985 they were published in 85 languages. There were 21,784 newspapers on 31 December 1984. There were 605 government publications in 1982.

The main Indian language dailies, such as the *Navbharat Times* (Hindi), *Malayala Manorama* (Malayalam), the *Jugantar* (Bengali) and *Ananda Bazar Patrika* (Bengali), by paying attention to rural affairs, cater for the increasingly literate non-anglophone provincial population. Most Indian-language papers have a relatively small circulation.

The more popular weekly and fortnightly periodicals include the cultural Tamil publications *Kumudam*, *Kalki*, *Rani* and *Ananda Vikatan*, the Malayalam weekly *Vanitha*, the English *Illustrated Weekly of India*, *India Today*, *Sunday* and the sensationalist *Blitz*, published in English, Hindi and Urdu. The main monthly periodicals are the *Reader's Digest* and the Hindi *Manohar Kahaniyan*.

The majority of publications in India are under individual ownership (66% in 1982), while newspapers owned by joint stock companies claim the largest part of the total circulation (40.3% in 1982). The most powerful groups own most of the large English dailies and frequently have considerable private commercial and industrial holdings. Four of the major groups are as follows:

Times of India Group (controlled by ASHOK JAIN and family): dailies: the *Times of India*, *Economic Times*, the *Evening News of India* (Bombay), the Hindi *Navbharat Times*, the *Sandhya Times*, the *Maharashtra Times* (Bombay); periodicals: the *Illustrated Weekly of India*, *Career and Competition Times*, the Hindi weeklies *Dharmayug* and *Dinaman*, the English fortnightlies *Femina* and *Filmfare* and Hindi pubs including *Parag*, *Sarita*, *Khel Bharati* and *Vama*.

Indian Express Group (controlled by the RAMNATH GOENKA family): publishes nine dailies including the *Indian Express*, the Marathi *Loksatta*, the Tamil *Dinamani*, the Telugu *Andhra*

INDIA   *Directory*

Prabha, the Kannada *Kannada Prabha* and the English *Financial Express*; six periodicals including the English weeklies the *Indian Express* (Sunday edition), *Screen*, *Cinema Express* (fortnightly), the Telugu *Andhra Prabha Illustrated Weekly* and the Tamil *Dinamani Kadir* (weekly).

Hindustan Times Group (controlled by the K. K. BIRLA family): dailies: the *Hindustan Times* (Delhi and Patna), *Pradeep* (Patna), the Hindi *Hindustan* (Delhi) and *Bharat* (Allahabad); periodicals: the weeklies the *Overseas Hindustan Times*, *Week End Review*, the Hindi *Saptahik Hindustan* (Delhi) and the Hindi monthly *Nandan* and *Kadambini* (New Delhi).

Ananda Bazar Patrika Group (controlled by AVEEK SARKAR and family): dailies: the *Ananda Bazar Patrika* (Calcutta), the English *Business Standard*, *The Telegraph*; periodicals include the English weeklies *Sunday* and *Sports World*, the English fortnightly *Business World*, Bengali weekly *Desh*, Hindi weekly *Ravivar*, Bengali monthly *Anandamela*, Bengali fortnightly *Anandlok* and the Bengali monthly *Sananda*.

PRINCIPAL DAILIES
Delhi (incl. New Delhi)

Daily Milap: 8A Bahadur Shah Zafar Marg, Delhi 110002; tel. (11) 3317737; f. 1923; Urdu; nationalist; also publ. from Jullundur and Hyderabad; Man. Editor PUNAM SURI; Chief Editor NAVIN SURI; combined circ. 52,000.

Daily Pratap: Pratap Bhawan, 5 Bahadur Shah Zafar Marg, Delhi 110002; tel. (11) 3317938; f. 1919; Urdu; Editor K. NARENDRA; circ. 28,000.

The Economic Times: Bahadur Shah Zafar Marg, Delhi 110002; tel. (11) 3312277; telex 031-73300; f. 1961; English; also publ. from Calcutta, Bangalore and Bombay; circ. (Delhi) 24,512.

The Financial Express: Bahadur Shah Zafar Marg, Delhi 110002; tel. (11) 3311111; telex 031-65803; f. 1961; morning; English; also publ. from Bombay and Madras; circ. (national) 41,695.

Hindustan: 18/20 Kasturba Gandhi Marg, Delhi 110001; tel. (11) 3318201; telex 031-66310; f. 1936; morning; Hindi; also publ. from Patna; Editor VINOD KUMAR MISHRA; circ. 170,000.

Hindustan Times: 18/20 Kasturba Gandhi Marg, Delhi 110001; tel. (11) 3318201; telex 031-66310; f. 1923; morning; English; also publ. from Patna; Editor PREM SHANKAR JHA; circ. 260,000.

Indian Express: Bahadur Shah Zafar Marg, Delhi 110002; tel. (11) 3311111; telex 031-6909; f. 1953; English; also publ. from Bombay, Chandigarh, Cochin, Bangalore, Ahmedabad, Madras, Madurai, Hyderabad, Vizianagaram and Vijayawada; Chief Editor SUMAN DUBEY; combined circ. 600,000; circ. (Delhi and Chandigarh) 172,660.

Janasatta: Bahadur Shah Zafar Marg, New Delhi 110002; f. 1983; Hindi; tel. (11) 3311111; telex 031-6908; Editor-in-Chief PRABHASH JOSHI; circ. 117,402.

National Herald: Herald House, Bahadur Shah Zafar Marg, Delhi 110002; tel. (11) 275722; telex 31-3041; English; nationalist; also publ. from Lucknow; Editor YASHPAL KAPOOR.

Navbharat Times: 7 Bahadur Shah Zafar Marg, Delhi 110002; tel. (11) 3318365; f. 1947; Hindi; also publ. from Bombay; Editor RAJENDRA MATHUR; circ. (national) 382,857, (Delhi) 289,242.

Patriot: Link House, Bahadur Shah Zafar Marg, Delhi 110002; tel. (11) 3311056; f. 1963; English; Chair. of Editorial Board ARUNA ASAF ALI; Editor R. K. MISHRA; circ. 33,000.

Statesman: Connaught Circus, Delhi 110001; tel. (11) 3315911; telex 31-2683; f. 1875; morning; English; Delhi Editor S. SAHAY; also publ. from Calcutta; combined circ. 214,463.

Times of India: 7 Bahadur Shah Zafar Marg, Delhi 110002; tel. (11) 3312277; telex 031-2155; English; also publ. from Bombay, Jaipur, Bangalore, Ahmedabad, Lucknow and Patna; circ. (Delhi) 210,972.

Andhra Pradesh
Hyderabad

Deccan Chronicle: 36 Sarojini Devi Rd, Hyderabad 500003; tel. (0842) 72126; telex 0155-6644; f. 1938; English; Editor T. VENKATRAM REDDY; circ. 47,893.

Eenadu: Somajiguda, Hyderabad 500001; tel. (0842) 223422; telex 0155-521; f. 1974; Telugu; also publ. from Tirupati, Visakhapatnam and Vijayawada; Chief Editor RAMOJI RAO; circ. 301,435.

Newstime: 6-3-570 Somajiguda, Hyderabad 500482; tel. (0842) 223422; telex 0155-521; f. 1984; Editor RAMOJI RAO; circ. 60,000.

Rahnuma-e-Deccan: 1810 Afzalgunj, Hyderabad 500012; tel. (0842) 43210; f. 1949; morning; Urdu; independent; Editor SYED VICARUDDIN; circ. 23,000.

Siasat Daily: Jawaharlal Nehru Rd, Hyderabad 500001; tel. (0842) 44180; f. 1949; morning; Urdu; Editor ABID ALI KHAN; circ. 40,898.

Vijayawada

Andhra Jyoti: Andhra Jyoti Bldg, Vijayawada 520010; tel. (866) 74532; telex 475217; f. 1960; Telugu; Editor NANDURI RAMAMOHANA RAO; circ. 71,827.

Andhra Patrika: POB 534, Gandhinagar, Vijayawada 520003; tel. (866) 61247; f. 1914; Telugu; also publ. from Hyderabad; Editor S. RADHAKRISHNA; circ. 26,036.

Andhra Prabha: 16-1-28, Kolandareddy Rd, Vijayawada 520003; tel. (866) 61351; telex 475231; f. 1935; Telugu; also publ. from Bangalore, Hyderabad and Vijianagram; Editor P. V. RAO (acting); circ. (national) 98,148.

Indian Express: George Oakes Building, Besant Rd, Vijayawada 520003; English; circ. (Vijayawada, Bangalore, Madras, Cochin, Hyderabad, Vijianagram and Madurai) 291,174.

Assam
Guwahati

Assam Tribune: Tribune Bldgs, Guwahati 781003; tel. 23251; f. 1938; English; Editor R. N. BOROOAH; circ. 37,241.

Dainik Assam: Tribune Bldgs, Guwahati 781003; tel. 23251; f. 1965; Assamese; Editor K. N. HAZARIKA; circ. 59,924.

Bihar
Patna

Aryavarta: Mazharul Haque Path, Patna 800001; tel. (612) 22130; telex 267; f. 1940; morning; Hindi; Editor H. JHA SHASHTRI; circ. 71,548.

Hindustan Times: Buddha Marg, Patna 800001; tel. (612) 23434; f. 1918; fmrly *Searchlight*; morning; English; Editor PREM SHANKAR JHA; circ. 26,000.

The Indian Nation: Mazharul Haque Path, Patna 800001; tel. (612) 22130; telex 267; f. 1930; morning; English; Editor DEENA NATH JHA; circ. 40,050.

Pradeep: Buddha Marg, Patna 800001; tel. (612) 23413; f. 1947; morning; Hindi; Editor PARAS NATH SINGH; circ. 34,000.

Goa
Panaji

Gomantak: Gomantak Bhavan, St Inez, Goa 403001; tel. 3212; f. 1962; morning; Marathi; Editor NARAYAN G. ATHAWALAY; circ. 15,000.

Navhind Times: Dempo House, Campal, Goa 403001; tel. 5684; f. 1963; morning; English; Editor (vacant); circ. 20,000.

Gujarat
Ahmedabad

Gujarat Samachar: Gujarat Samachar Bhavan, Khanpur, Ahmedabad 380001; tel. (272) 22821; telex 642; f. 1932; morning; Gujarati; also publ. from Surat and Bombay; Editor SHANTILAL A. SHAH; circ. 296,854.

Indian Express: Janasatta Bldg, Mirzapur Rd, Ahmedabad; f. 1968; English; circ. (Ahmedabad) 16,691.

Lokasatta—Janasatta: PB 188, Mirzapur Rd, Ahmedabad 380001; tel. (272) 26300; f. 1953; morning; Gujarati; also publ. from Rajkot and Vadodara; Editor Dr KANTI RAMI; circ. (national) 96,000.

Sandesh: Sandesh Bldg, Cheekanta Rd, Ahmedabad 380001; tel. (272) 25920; f. 1923; Gujarati; also publ. from Vadodara; Editor C. S. PATEL; circ. 203,718.

Times of India: POB 4046, 139 Ashram Rd, Ahmedabad 380009; tel. (272) 402151; telex 0121490; f. 1968; English; also publ. from Bombay, Delhi, Bangalore, Jaipur, Patna and Lucknow; Editor P. G. MAHADEVAN; circ. (Ahmedabad) 50,308.

Western Times: Gujarat Samachar Bhavan, Khanpur, Ahmedabad 380001; tel. (272) 26762; f. 1967; English; Man. Editor NIKUNJ PATEL; circ. 14,000.

Rajkot

Jai Hind: POB 59, Sharda Baug, Rajkot 360001; tel. (281) 40511; f. 1948; morning and evening (in Rajkot); Gujarati; also publ. from Ahmedabad; Editor N. L. SHAH; circ. (Rajkot, morning) 40,000, (Rajkot, evening) 40,000, (Ahmedabad) 20,000.

Phulchhab: Phulchhab Bhavan, Mahatma Gandhi Rd, Rajkot; tel. (281) 44611; f. 1950; morning; Gujarati; Editor HARSUKH M. SANGHANI; circ. 101,161.

INDIA   Directory

Surat

Gujaratmitra and Gujaratdarpan: Gujaratmitra Bhavan, nr Old Civil Hospital, Sonifalia, Surat 395003; tel. (261) 23284; telex 0178261; f. 1863; morning; Gujarati; Editor B. P. RESHAMWALA; circ. 79,529.

Pratap: Pratap Sadan, Nanavat, POB 242, Surat 395003; tel. (261) 23251; f. 1926; morning and evening; Gujarati; Man. KIRIT D. SHUKLA; Editor JAGDISH R. SHAH; circ. 13,932.

Jammu and Kashmir

Jammu

Kashmir Times: Residency Rd, Jammu 180001; tel. 44777; f. 1955; morning; English; Editor V. BHASIN; circ. 21,775.

Srinagar

Srinagar Times: Badshah Bridge, Srinagar; f. 1969; Urdu; circ. 14,000.

Karnataka

Bangalore

Deccan Herald: 75 Mahatma Gandhi Rd, Bangalore 560001; tel. (812) 573291; telex 0845339; f. 1948; morning; English; Editor M. P. YASHWANTH KUMAR; circ. 143,720.

Indian Express: 1 Queen's Rd, Bangalore 560001; tel. (812) 76894; telex 845597; f. 1965; English; circ. (Bangalore, Cochin, Hyderabad, Madras, Madurai, Vijayawada and Vizianagaram) 291,174.

Kannada Prabha: 1 Queen's Rd, Bangalore 56001; tel. (812) 76893; Kannada; Editor KHADRI SHAMANNA; circ. 84,586.

Prajavani: 75 Mahatma Gandhi Rd, Bangalore 560001; tel. (812) 53291; telex 0845339; f. 1948; morning; Kannada; Editor-in-Chief K. N. HARIKUMAR; Editor M. B. SINGH; circ. 192,707.

Kerala

Calicut

Deshabhimani: 11/127 Convent Rd, Calicut 673032; tel. (495) 77286; f. 1946; morning; Malayalam; also publ. from Cochin; Chief Editor E. K. NAYANAR; circ. 56,344.

Mathrubhumi: Mathrubhumi Bldgs, Robinson Rd, Calicut 673001; tel. (495) 63651; f. 1923; Malayalam; Editor M. D. NALAPAT; also publ. from Trivandrum and Cochin; circ. 432,000.

Kottayam

Deepika: PB 7, Kottayam 686001; tel. (481) 3706; telex 0888203; f. 1887; Malayalam; independent; also publ. from Trichur; Editor VICTOR Z. NARIVELY; circ. 54,684.

Malayala Manorama: Malayala Manorama, Kottayam 686001; tel. (481) 3615; telex 888201; f. 1887; also publ. from Kozhikode and Cochin; morning; Malayalam; Chief Editor K. M. MATHEW; circ. 645,605.

Trichur

Express: PB 15, Trichur 680001; tel. 23631; f. 1944; Malayalam; Editor K. BALAKRISHNAN; circ. 54,343.

Trivandrum

Kerala Kaumudi: PB 77, Pettah, Trivandrum 695024; tel. (487) 71050; telex 0884214; f. 1911; Malayalam; Editor M. S. MADHUSOODANAN; circ. 104,859.

Madhya Pradesh

Bhopal

Dainik Bhaskar: Agrawal Bhawan, Sultania Rd, Bhopal; tel. (755) 75144; f. 1958; morning; Hindi; also publ. from Indore and Gwalior; Editor R. C. AGRAWAL; circ. (national) 109,248.

Indore

Nai Duniya: 60/1 Babu Labhchand, Chajlani Marg, Indore 452009; tel. (731) 62061; telex 0735342; f. 1947; morning; Hindi; Man. Editor BASANTILAL SETHIA; circ. 134,699.

Maharashtra

Bombay

Bombay Samachar: Red House, Syed Abdulla Brelvi Rd, Fort, Bombay 400001; tel. (22) 2045531; telex 11-4237; f. 1822; morning and Sunday; Gujarati; political and commercial; Editor JEHAN D. DARUWALA; circ. 136,857.

The Economic Times: Head Office, POB 213, Bombay 400001; tel. (22) 4150271; f. 1961; also publ. from New Delhi, Calcutta and Bangalore; English; Editor MANU SHROFF; circ. (national) 78,273.

Evening News of India: Dr Dadabhai Naoroji Rd, Bombay 400001; tel. (22) 4150271; telex 11-2504; f. 1923; evening; English; Editor PRITISH NANDY; circ. 12,837.

The Financial Express: Express Towers, Nariman Point, Bombay 400021; tel. (22) 2022627; telex 112585; f. 1961; morning; English; also publ. from New Delhi and Madras; Editor N. S. JAGANNATHAN; circ. (national) 41,695.

Free Press Journal: Free Press House, 215 Free Press Journal Rd, Nariman Point, Bombay 400021; tel. (22) 274143; telex 0112570; f. 1930; English; also publ. from Indore; Editor VIRENDRA KAPOOR; circ. 40,000.

Indian Express: Express Towers, Nariman Point, Bombay 400021; tel. (22) 2022627; telex 112276; f. 1940; English; Editor-in-Chief SUMAN DUBEY; circ. 112,425.

Inquilab: 156D J. Dadajee Rd, Tardeo, Bombay 400034; tel. (22) 494256; telex 1175624; f. 1938; Urdu; Man. Editor KHALID ANSARI; circ. 23,913.

Jam-e-Jamshed: Ballard House, Mangalore St, Bombay 400038; tel. (22) 262571; f. 1832; English and Gujarati; Chair. NANABHOY JEEJEEBHOY; Editor ADI MARZBAN; circ. 8,000 (daily), 12,000 (Sunday).

Janmabhoomi: Janmabhoomi Bhavan, Ghoga St, Fort, Bombay 400001; tel. (22) 255831; telex 116859; f. 1934; evening; Gujarati; Propr Saurashtra Trust; Editor HARINDRA J. DAVE; circ. 36,388.

Lokasatta: Express Towers, Nariman Point, Bombay 400021; tel. (22) 2022627; f. 1948; morning (except Sunday); Marathi; Editor MADHAVRAO GADKARI; circ. 248,386.

Maharashtra Times: The Times of India Press, POB 213, Bombay 400001; tel. (22) 4150271; telex 11-2504; Dr Dadabhai Naoroji Rd; f. 1962; Marathi; Editor G. S. TALWALKAR; circ. 173,885.

Mid-Day: 156D J. Dadajee Rd, Tardeo, Bombay 400034; tel. (22) 4942586; telex 11-75624; f. 1979; daily and Sunday; English; also publ. from New Delhi; Man. Editor KHALID A. H. ANSARI; circ. 45,000.

Mumbai Sakal: N. B. Parulekar Rd, Prabhadevi, Bombay 400025; f. 1970; daily and Sunday; Marathi; also publ. from Pune.

Navbharat Times: Dr Dadabhai Naoroji Rd, Bombay 400001; tel. (22) 4150271; telex 11-2504; f. 1950; Hindi; also publ. from New Delhi; circ. (Bombay) 93,615.

Navshakti: 215, Free Press Journal Rd, Bombay 400021; tel. (22) 274143; telex 11-2570; f. 1932; Marathi; Editor P. R. BEHERE; circ. 28,000.

Pravasi: Janmabhoomi Bhavan, Ghoga St, Fort, Bombay 400001; tel. (22) 255831; telex 116859; f. 1979; morning; Gujarati; Propr Saurashtra Trust; Editor HARINDRA J. DAVE; circ. 32,456.

Times of India: Dr Dadabhai Naoroji Rd, Bombay 400001; telex 112204; f. 1838; morning; English; publ. from Delhi, Ahmedabad, Bangalore, Jaipur, Patna and Lucknow; Editor GIRILAL JAIN; circ. (Bombay) 297,411.

Nagpur

Hitavada: Wardha Rd, Nagpur; tel. (712) 23155; f. 1911; morning; English; also publ. from Bhopal; Editor M. Y. BODHANKAR; circ. 27,552.

Maharashtra: House No. 510, Ogale Rd, Mahal, Nagpur; f. 1941; Marathi; nationalist; Editor M. R. DANGRE; circ. 17,000.

Nagpur Times: 37 Farmland, Ramdaspeth, Nagpur 440010; tel. (712) 22935; telex 0715235; f. 1933; English; Editor M. V. PADALKAR; circ. 21,000.

Nava Bharat: Cotton Market, Nagpur 440018; tel. (712) 46145; f. 1938; morning; Hindi; also publ. from Bhopal, Jabalpur, Bilaspur, Indore and Raipur; Editor-in-Chief R. G. MAHESWARI; circ. (national) 105,106.

Tarun Bharat: 28 Farmland, Ramdaspeth, Nagpur 440010; f. 1944; Marathi; independent; also publ. from Pune; Editor M. G. VAIDYA; circ. 46,000.

Pune

Kesari: 568 Narayan Peth, Pune 411030; tel. (212) 449250; f. 1881; Marathi; also publ. from Solapur; Editor CHANDRAKANT GHORPADE; circ. 77,501.

Sakal: 595 Budhwar Peth, Pune 411002; tel. (212) 448402; f. 1932; daily and Sunday; Marathi; Editor S. K. KULKAMI; Gen. Man. K. M. BHIDE; circ. daily (Pune, Bombay and Kolhapur) 166,652.

Orissa

Cuttack

Samaj: Gopabandhu Bhawan, Buxibazar, Cuttack 753001; tel. (671) 20994; f. 1919; Oriya; Editor R. N. RATH; circ. 109,309.

INDIA   Directory

Punjab
Jalandhar

Ajit: Ajit Bhavan, Nehru Garden Rd, Jalandhar 144001; f. 1955; Punjabi; tel. 75961; telex 0385-265; Man. Editor S. BARJINDER SINGH; circ. 104,583.

Hind Samachar: Pacca Bagh, Jalandhar 144001; tel. 75951; telex 0385-221; f. 1948; morning; Urdu; Editor VIJAY KUMAR CHOPRA; circ. 73,869.

Jag Bani: Pacca Bagh, Jalandhar 144001; tel. 75951; telex 0385-221; f. 1978; morning; Punjabi; publ. by Hind Samachar Ltd; Editor VIJAY KUMAR CHOPRA; circ. 54,563.

Punjab Kesari: Civil Lines, Jalandhar 144001; tel. 75951; telex 0385-221; f. 1965; morning; Hindi; Editor VIJAY KUMAR CHOPRA; circ. 311,217.

Chandigarh

The Tribune: 29-C Chandigarh 160020; tel. (172) 28461; telex 395-285; f. 1881; English, Hindi and Punjabi; Editor (English edn) V. N. NARAYANAN; Editor (Hindi edn) RADHE SHYAM SHARMA; Editor (Punjabi edn) GULZAR SINGH SANDHU; circ. 147,479 (English), 28,941 (Hindi), 64,000 (Punjabi).

Rajasthan
Jaipur

Rajasthan Chronicle: A-31, 'Rajhut', Nehrunagar, Jaipur (141) 302016; tel. 75414; f. 1951; English; Editor K. S. NARANG.

Rajasthan Patrika: Kesargarh, Jawahar Lal Nehru Marg, Jaipur 302004; tel. (141) 61321; telex 0365-435; f. 1956; Hindi; English; also publ. from Jodhphur, Udaipur and Kota; Editor VIJAY BHANDARI; circ. (Hindi) 188,415.

Rashtradoot: HO, POB 30, M.I. Rd, Jaipur 302001; tel. (141) 72634; f. 1951; Hindi; also publ. from Kota and Bikaner; Chief Editor RAJESH SHARMA; circ. (Jaipur) 104,000, (Kota) 42,000, (Bikaner) 30,000.

Tamil Nadu
Madras

Daily Thanthi: 46 E.V.K. Sampath Rd, Madras 600007; tel. (44) 31331; telex 041366; f. 1942; Tamil; also publ. from Bangalore, Coimbatore, Cuddalore, Madurai, Salem, Tiruchi, Tirunelveli and Vellore; Editor R. S. RATHNAM; circ. 292,717.

Dinakaran: 106–107 Kutchery Rd, Mylapore, Madras 600004; tel. (44) 71006; telex 041-6065; f. 1977; Tamil; also publ. from Madurai, Trichy, Salem and Coimbatore; Editor K. P. KANDASAMY; circ. 165,000.

The Hindu: 859/860 Anna Rd, Madras 600002; tel. (44) 846567; telex 041-358; f. 1878; morning; English; independent; also publ. from Bangalore, Coimbatore, Hyderabad, New Delhi and Madurai; Editor G. KASTURI; circ. 401,577.

Indian Express: Express Estate, Mount Rd, Madras 600002; tel. (44) 810551; telex 041-222; also publ. from Delhi, Bombay, Chandigarh, Cochin, Bangalore, Ahmedabad, Madurai, Hyderabad and Vijayawada; Editor-in-Chief S. MULGAOKAR; circ. (Madras, Madurai, Bangalore, Cochin, Hyderabad, Vijayawada and Vijianagram) 291,174.

Murasoli: 93 Kodambakkam High Rd, Madras 600034; tel. (44) 470044; f. 1960; Tamil; Editor MURASOLI MARAN; circ. 54,000.

Madurai

Dinamani: 137 Ramnad Rd, Madurai 625009; tel. (452) 23221; f. 1951; morning; Tamil; Editor A. N. SIVRARAMAN; circ. (Madurai and Madras) 192,000.

Uttar Pradesh
Agra

Amar Ujala: Sikandara Rd, Agra 282007; tel. (562) 72408; telex 565225; also 19 Civil Lines, Bareilly; f. 1948 (Agra), 1969 (Bareilly); Hindi; Editors ANIL K. AGARWAL (Agra), ASHOK K. AGARWAL (Bareilly); circ. (Agra) 67,757, (Bareilly) 46,281.

Sainik: Sainik Bhavan, Moti Katra, Agra 282003; f. 1925; Hindi; Editor R. S. SHARMA; circ. 16,000.

Allahabad

Amrita Prabhat: 10 Edmonstone Rd, Allahabad 211001; tel. (532) 52620; f. 1977; Hindi; also publ. from Lucknow; Chief Editor TUSHAR KANTI GHOSH; Editor KAMLESH BIHARI MATHUR; Gen. Man. TARAK NATH BHATTACHARYA; circ. 42,374.

Bharat: Leader Bldg, 3 Leader Rd, Allahabad 211001; f. 1928; Hindi; Chief Editor Dr M. D. SHARMA; circ. 15,000.

Northern India Patrika: 10 Edmonstone Rd, Allahabad 211001; tel. (532) 52665; f. 1959; English; also publ. from Lucknow; Chief Editor TUSHAR KANTI GHOSH; Editor S. K. BOSE; circ. 46,410.

Kanpur

Daily Jagran: 2 Sarvodaya Nagar, Kanpur 208005; tel. 216161; telex 325-285; f. 1942; Hindi; also publ. from Gorakhpur, Jhansi, Lucknow, Meerut and Varanasi; Man. Editor RAJENDRA GUPTA; circ. 349,987.

Daily Veer Bharat: 48/15 Lathi Mohal, Kanpur 208001; f. 1926; Hindi; Editor A. K. PANDEY; circ. 15,000.

Pratap: 22/120 Shri Ganesh Shankar Vidyarathi Rd, Kanpur; f. 1932; Hindi; Editor SURESH CHANDRA BHATTACHARYA; circ. 16,000.

Vyapar Sandesh: 48/12 Lathi Mohal Lane, Kanpur, 208001; tel. (512) 69889; f. 1958; Hindi; commercial news and economic trends; Editor HARI SHANKAR SHARMA; circ. 13,000.

Lucknow

National Herald: 1 Bisheshwar North Rd, Lucknow 226001; f. 1938 Lucknow, 1968 Delhi; English; Man. Editor YASHPAL KAPOOR.

The Pioneer: 20 Vidhan Sabha Marg, Lucknow 226001; tel. (522) 31291; f. 1865; English; also publ. from Varanasi; Editor SOMNATH SAPRU; combined circ. 91,463.

Swatantra Bharat: Pioneer House, 20 Vidhan Sabha Marg, Lucknow 226001; tel. (522) 31292; f. 1947; Hindi; Editor VIRENDRA SINGH; circ. 82,133.

Varanasi

Aj: Sant Kabir Rd, Kabirchaura, POB 7 & 52, Varanasi 221001; tel. (542) 62061; f. 1920; Hindi; also publ. from Gorakhpur, Patna, Allahabad, Ranchi and Kanpur; Chief Editor S. K. GUPTA; circ. 114,263 (Varanasi, Allahabad and Gorakhpur), 53,624 (Kanpur), 106,354 (Patna and Ranchi).

West Bengal
Calcutta

Aajkaal: 96 Raja Rammohan Sarani, Calcutta 700009; tel. (33) 363630; telex 021-2216; f. 1981; morning; Bengali; Editor P. K. ROY; circ. 125,000.

Amrita Bazar Patrika: 14 Ananda Chatterji Lane, Calcutta 700003; tel. (33) 555231; telex 0217245; f. 1868; morning; English; Nationalist; also published from Jamshedpur (Bihar); Editor T. K. GHOSH; circ. 128,101.

Ananda Bazar Patrika: 6 Prafulla Sarkar St, Calcutta 700001; tel. (33) 274880; telex 021-5468; f. 1922; morning; Bengali; Editor AVEEK SARKAR; circ. 407,508.

Bartaman: 76A Acharya J.C. Bose Rd, Calcutta 700014; tel. (33) 213939; telex 0217380; f. 1984; Editor BARUN SENGUPTA; circ. 75,413.

Business Standard: 6 Prafulla Sarkar St, Calcutta 700001; tel. (33) 274880; telex 0215468; f. 1975; morning; English; Editor AVEEK SARKAR; circ. 21,471.

Dainik Basumati: 166 Bepin Behari Ganguly St, Calcutta 700012; tel. (33) 359462; f. 1914; Bengali; independent nationalist; Editor RANAJIT ROY; circ. 30,494.

The Economic Times: 105/7A, S. N. Banerjee Rd, Calcutta; tel. (33) 244243; telex 021-7580; English; also publ. from Delhi, Bangalore and Bombay; circ. (Calcutta) 16,900.

Jugatar: 72/1 Baghbazar St, Calcutta 700003; tel. (33) 555231; telex 0217245; f. 1936; Bengali; Editor T. K. GHOSH; circ. 301,759.

Paigam: 26/1 Market St, Calcutta 700087; tel. (33) 246040; f. 1948; Bengali; morning; Editor MARJINA TARAFDAR; circ. 28,000.

Sanmarg: 160C Chittaranjan Ave, Calcutta 700007; tel. (33) 342836; f. 1948; Hindi; nationalist; Editor RAMAWTAR A. GUPTA; circ. 68,000.

Satyajug: 13 Prafulla Sarkar St, Calcutta 700072; tel. (33) 278836; f. 1972; Bengali; morning; Editor JIBANLAL BANERJEE; circ. 16,000.

Statesman: Statesman House, 4 Chowringhee Sq., Calcutta 700001; tel. (33) 271000; telex 021-4509; f. 1875; morning; English; independent; also publ. from New Delhi; Editor (vacant); circ. 214,463.

Vishwamitra: 74 Lenin Sarani, Calcutta 700013; tel. (33) 249567; telex 0213370; f. 1916; morning; Hindi; commercial; also publ. from Bombay and Kanpur; Editor KRISHNA CHANDRA AGRAWALLA; circ. 90,000.

SELECTED PERIODICALS
Delhi and New Delhi

Akashvani: PTI Bldg, 2nd Floor, New Delhi 110001, POB 12; tel. (11) 382249; f. 1936; All-India Radio programmes; English, Hindi and Urdu edns; Chief Editor V. B. SINHA; circ. 15,000 (English), 3,000 (Hindi), 3,000 (Urdu).

Bal Bharati: Patiala House, Publications Division, Ministry of Information and Broadcasting, Delhi; tel. (11) 387038; f. 1948; monthly; Hindi; for children; Editor P. K. BHARGAVA; circ. 30,000.

Biswin Sadi: POB 7013, 3583 Netaji Subash Marg, Darya Ganj, New Delhi 110002; tel. (11) 271637; f. 1937; monthly; Urdu; Editor Z. REHMAN NAYYAR; circ. 34,823.

Caravan: Delhi Press Bldg, E-3, Jhandewala Estate, Rani Jhansi Rd, Delhi 110055; tel. (11) 526222; f. 1940; fortnightly; English; political and cultural; Editor VISHWA NATH; circ. 20,191.

Careers and Courses: 94 Baird Rd, Delhi; tel. (11) 526222; f. 1949; monthly; English; Editor A. C. GOYLE; circ. 44,000.

Careers Digest: 21 Shankar Market, Delhi 110001; tel. (11) 44726; f. 1963; monthly; English; Editor O. P. VARMA; circ. 35,000.

Champak: Delhi Press Bldg, E-3, Jhandewala Estate, Rani Jhansi Rd, Delhi 110055; tel. (11) 526222; f. 1969; fortnightly; Hindi, also in English, Gujarati and Marathi; Editor VISHWA NATH; circ. 85,396.

Children's World: Nehru House, 4 Bahadur Shah Zafar Marg, Delhi 110002; tel. (11) 3316970; f. 1968; monthly; English; Editor K. RAMAKRISHNAN; circ. 25,000.

Competition Success Review: 604 Prabhat Kiran, Rajendra Place, Delhi 110008; tel. (11) 5712898; monthly; English; f. 1963; Editor S. K. SACHDEVA; circ. 290,678.

Dinaman: 10 Daryaganj, New Delhi 110002; tel. (11) 271911; f. 1965; Hindi news weekly; Editor SATISH JHA; circ. 28,996.

Ekta Sandesh: 8/818 Ajmeri Gate, Delhi 110006; f. 1963; weekly; Hindi; Editor PREM CHAND VERMA; circ. 12,000.

Employment News: Government of India, East Block IV, level 7, R. K. Puram, New Delhi 110066; tel. (11) 615605; f. 1976; weekly; Hindi, Urdu and English edns; Editor (English edn) N. N. SHARMA; circ. 290,000.

Film Mirror: 26F Connaught Place, Delhi 110001; tel. (11) 3312329; f. 1964; monthly; English; Editor HARBHAJAN SINGH; circ. 24,900.

Filmi Duniya: 16 Darya Ganj, Delhi 110002; tel. (11) 278087; telex 031-66205; f. 1958; monthly; Hindi; Chief Editor NARENDRA KUMAR; circ. 144,404.

Filmi Kaliyan: 16/39 Subhash Nagar, New Delhi 110027; tel. (11) 272080; f. 1969; monthly; English; cinema; Editor-in-Chief V. S. DEWAN; circ. 121,219.

Grih Shobha: Delhi Press Bldg, E-3 Jhandelwala Estate, Rani Jhansi Rd, New Delhi 110055; tel. (11) 526222; f. 1979; monthly; Hindi; Editor VISHWA NATH; circ. 234,237.

India Today: F 14/15, Connaught Place, Delhi 110001; tel. (11) 3315801; telex 031-61245; f. 1975; fortnightly; English and Hindi; Editor AROON PURIE; circ. 317,627.

Indian Observer: 26-F Connaught Place, Delhi 110001; tel. (11) 3314455; f. 1958; monthly; English; Editor HARBHAJAN SINGH; circ. 19,700.

Indian and Foreign Review: Shastri Bhavan, Delhi 110001; f. 1963; fortnightly; review of politics, socio-economics and culture; Chief Editor SWAGATH GHOSH; circ. 35,000.

Indian Horizons: Azad Bhavan, Indraprastha Estate, New Delhi 110002; tel. (11) 262052; telex 031-4904; f. 1951; quarterly; English; publ. by the Indian Council for Cultural Relations; Editor A. SRINIVASAN; circ. 5,000.

Indian Railways: POB 467, New Delhi 110001; tel. (11) 383000; telex 031-3561; f. 1956; monthly; English; publ. by the Department of Railways (Railway Board), Ministry of Transport; Editor S. K. AHUJA; circ. 12,000.

Intensive Agriculture: Ministry of Agriculture and Rural Development, Directorate of Extension, New Delhi 110066; tel. (11) 600591; f. 1955; monthly; English; Editor SHUKLA HAZRA; circ. 15,000.

Jagat (Hindi) Monthly: 8/818 Ajmeri Gate, Delhi 110006; f. 1958; Hindi; popular and family magazine; Editor PREM CHAND VERMA; circ. 18,000.

Jagat Weekly: 8/818 Ajmeri Gate, Delhi 110006; tel. (11) 664847; f. 1956; Urdu; progressive; Editor PREM CHAND VERMA; circ. 11,000.

Journal of Industry and Trade: Ministry of Commerce and Supply, Delhi 110011; tel. (11) 3016664; f. 1952; monthly; English; Man. Dir A. C. BANERJEE; circ. 2,000.

Kadambini: Hindustan Times House, Kasturba Gandhi Marg, Delhi 110001; tel. (11) 3318201; telex 031-66310; f. 1960; monthly; Hindi; Editor RAJENDRA AWASTHY; circ. 100,000.

Krishak Samachar: A-1 Nizamuddin West, New Delhi 110013; f. 1957; monthly; English, Hindi, Marathi; agriculture; Editor Dr D. A. BHOLAY; circ. (English) 10,000, (Hindi) 11,000, (Marathi) 12,000.

Kurukshetra: Krishi Bhavan, Delhi 110001; monthly; English; rural development; Editor RATNA JUNEJA; circ. 13,000.

Lalita: 92 Daryaganj, Delhi 110002; tel. (11) 272482; f. 1959; monthly; Hindi; Editor L. RANIGUPTA; circ. 20,000.

Link Indian News Magazine: Link House, Bahadurshah Zafar Marg, Delhi 110002; tel. (11) 3311056; telex 62384; f. 1958; weekly; independent; Editor R. K. MISHRA; circ. 10,801.

Mayapuri Weekly: A-5, Mayapuri, Delhi 110064; tel. (11) 591439; telex 031-63231; f. 1974; weekly; Hindi; Editor A. P. BAJAJ; circ. 261,027.

Nandan: Hindustan Times House, New Delhi 110001; tel. (11) 3318201; telex 031-66327; f. 1963; monthly; Hindi; Editor JAI PRAKASH BHARTI; circ. 210,000.

Nav Chitrapat: 92 Daryaganj, Delhi 110002; tel. (11) 272482; f. 1932; monthly; Hindi; Editor SATYENDRA SHYAM; circ. 36,000.

New Age: 15 Kotla Rd, Delhi 110002; tel. (11) 3310762; telex 313882; f. 1953; main organ of the Communist Party of India; weekly; English; Editor INDRADEEP SINHA; circ. 205,000.

Organiser: 29 Rani Jhansi Rd, Delhi 110055; tel. (11) 529595; f. 1947; weekly; English; Editor V. P. BHATIA; circ. 66,000.

Overseas Hindustan Times: Hindustan Times House, Kasturba Gandhi Marg, Delhi 110001; weekly; English.

Panchajanya: 29 Rani Jhansi Marg, New Delhi 110055; tel. (11) 529595; f. 1947; weekly; Hindi; Editor R. S. AGNIHOTRI; circ. 34,000.

Parag: 10 Daryaganj, New Delhi 110002; tel. (11) 277360; f. 1958; children's monthly; Hindi; Editor HARI KRISHNA DEVSARE; circ. 68,030.

Priya: 92 Daryaganj, Delhi 110002; f. 1960; monthly; Hindi; Editor SATYENDRA SMYAM; circ. 28,000.

Punjabi Digest: 209 Hemkunt House, 6 Rajindera Place, POB 2549, New Delhi 110008; tel. (11) 575225; f. 1971; literary monthly; Gurmukhi; Chief Editor Sardar S. B. SINGH; circ. 57,161.

Rang Bhumi: 5A/15 Ansari Rd, Darya Ganj, Delhi 110002; f. 1941; Hindi; films; Editor S. K. GUPTA; circ. 30,000.

Ruby Magazine: POB 7014, 3583 Netaji-Subash Marg, Darya Ganj, New Delhi 110002; tel. (11) 271637; f. 1966; monthly; Urdu; Editor REHMAN NAYYAR; circ. 23,000.

Sainik Samachar: Block L-1, Church Rd, Delhi 110001; tel. (11) 3019668; f. 1909; pictorial weekly for Indian armed forces; English, Hindi, Urdu, Tamil, Punjabi, Telugu, Marathi, Gorkhali, Malayalam, Bengali, Assamese, Oriya and Kannada edns; Editor-in-Chief BIBEKANANDA RAY; circ. 18,000.

Saptahik Hindustan: 18–20 Kasturba Gandhi Marg, Delhi 110001; tel. (11) 3311617; f. 1950; weekly; Hindi; Editor RAJENDRA AWASTHY; circ. 100,000.

Sarita: Delhi Press Bldg, E-3, Jhandewala Estate, Rani Jhansi Rd, Delhi 110055; tel. (11) 526222; f. 1946; fortnightly; Hindi; Editor VISHWA NATH; circ. 263,408.

Shama: 13/14 Asaf Ali Rd, Delhi 110002; tel. (11) 272077; telex 3161601; f. 1939; monthly; Urdu; Editors M. YUSUF DEHLVI, M. YUNUS DEHLVI, IDREES DEHLVI, ILYAS DEHLVI; circ. 73,178.

Sher-i-Punjab: Hemkunt House, 6 Rajindera Place, New Delhi 110005; tel. (11) 575225; f. 1911; weekly news magazine; Chief Editor Sardar JANG BAHADUR SINGH; circ. over 15,000.

Sun Weekly: 8B Bahadur Shah Zafar Marg, POB 7164, Delhi 110002; tel. (11) 273737; telex 314531; f. 1977; weekly; English; Editor V. B. GUPTA; circ. 41,025.

Surya India: Kanchenjunga Bldg, 18 Barakhamba Rd, Delhi; tel. (11) 3310102; telex 31-62399; f. 1977; monthly; English; political and social news; Editors Dr J. K. JAIN, KHUSHWANT SINGH, M. V. KAMATH, G. S. BHARGAVA.

Sushama: 13/14 Asaf Ali Rd, Delhi 110002; tel. (11) 732666; telex 3161601; f. 1959; monthly; Hindi; Editors IDREES DEHLVI, ILYAS DEHLVI, YUNUS DEHLVI; circ. 75,000.

Vigyan Pragati: PID Bldg, Hillside Rd, Delhi 110012; f. 1952; monthly; Hindi; popular science; Editor SHYAM SUNDER SHARMA; circ. 100,000.

Woman's Era: Delhi Press Bldg, E-3, Jhandewala Estate, Rani Jhansi Rd, Delhi 110055; tel. (11) 526222; f. 1973; fortnightly; English; Editor VISHWA NATH; circ. 70,189.

Yojana: Planning Commission, Yojana Bhavan, Parliament St, Delhi 110001; tel. (11) 383655; f. 1957; fortnightly; English, Tamil, Bengali, Marathi, Gujarati, Assamese, Malayalam, Telugu, Kannada, Punjabi, Urdu and Hindi edns; Chief Editor R. THUKRAL; circ. 90,000.

Andhra Pradesh
Hyderabad
Islamic Culture: POB 171, Hyderabad; f. 1927; quarterly; English; Editor Dr M. A. MUID KHAN; circ. 11,000.

Vijayawada
Andhra Jyoti Sachitra Vara Patrika: Labbipet, Vijayawada 520010; tel. (866) 74532; f. 1967; weekly; Telugu; Editor P. S. SARMA; circ. 85,966.

Bihar
Patna
Anand Digest: POB 5, Govind Mitra Rd, Patna 800004; tel. 50341; f. 1981; monthly; Hindi; family magazine; Editor Dr S. S. SINGH; circ. 60,426.

Balak: POB 5, Govind Mitra Rd, Patna 800004; tel. 50341; f. 1926; monthly; Hindi; children's; Editor S. R. SARAN; circ. 31,848.

Jyotsana: Rajendranagar, Patna; f. 1947; monthly; Hindi; Editor S. NARAYAN; circ. 11,000.

Nar Nari: Nari Prakashan, Patna 800004; f. 1949; monthly; Hindi; Editor V. VATSYAYAN; circ. 10,000.

Gujarat
Ahmedabad
Aaspas: Nr Khanpur Gate, Khanpur, Ahmedabad 380001; tel. (272) 391131; f. 1976; weekly; Gujarati; Editor GUNVANT C. SHAH; circ. 100,373.

Akhand Anand: Swami Akhandanand Marg, POB 50, Bhadra, Ahmedabad; tel. (272) 391798; f. 1947; monthly; Gujarati; Pres. H. M. PATEL; Editor T. K. THAKKAR; circ. 34,654.

Chitralok: Gujarat Samachar Bhavan, Khanpur, POB 254, Ahmedabad; f. 1952; weekly; Gujarati; films; Editor SHREYANS SHAH; circ. 23,265.

Sakhi: Sakhi Publications, Jai Hind Press Bldg, nr Gujarat Chamber, Ashram Rd, Navrangpura, Ahmedabad 380009; tel. (272) 407052; f. 1984; monthly; Gujarati; women's; Editor Y. N. SHAH; circ. 20,000.

Stree: POB 151, Sandesh Bhavan, Gheekanta, Ahmedabad 380001; tel. (272) 24243; telex 121-532; f. 1962; weekly; Gujarati; Editor LILABEN PATEL; circ. 78,048.

Zagmag: Gujarat Samachar Bhavan, Khanpur, Ahmedabad 380001; tel. (272) 22821; telex 0121-642; f. 1952; weekly; Gujarati; for children; Editor BAHUBALI S. SHAH; circ. 12,000.

Rajkot
Amruta: Sharda Baug, Rajkot 360001; tel. (281) 40513; f. 1967; weekly; Gujarati; films; Editor Y. N. SHAH; circ. 45,000.

Niranjan: Niranjan Publications, Jai Hind Press Bldg, Sharda Baug, Rajkot 360001; tel. (281) 40513; f. 1971; fortnightly; Gujarati; children's; Editor N. R. SHAH; circ. 25,000.

Parmarth: Sharda Baug, Rajkot 360001; tel. (281) 40511; monthly; Gujarati; philosophy and religion; Editor N. L. SHAH; circ. 30,000.

Phulwadi: Sharda Baug, Rajkot 360001; tel. (281) 40513; weekly; Gujarati; for children; Editor Y. N. SHAH; circ. 80,000.

Karnataka
Bangalore
Mysindia: 38A Mahatma Gandhi Rd, Bangalore; f. 1939; weekly; English; news and current affairs; Editor D. N. HOSALI; circ. 14,000.

New Leader: 93 North Rd, St Mary's Town, Bangalore 560005; f. 1887; weekly; English; Editor Rt Rev. HERMAN D'SOUZA; circ. 10,000.

Prajamata: North Anjaneya Temple Rd, Basavangudi, Bangalore; f. 1931; weekly; Kannada; news and current affairs; Chief Editor H. V. NAGARAJA RAO; circ. 92,850.

Kerala
Calicut
Mathrubhumi Illustrated Weekly: Mathrubhumi Bldg, Calicut 673001; tel. 63651; f. 1923; weekly; Malayalam; Editor M. D. NALAPAT; circ. 73,000.

Cochin
The Week: POB 2314, Manorama Bldgs, Panampilly Nagar, Cochin 682016; tel. 366285; telex 885696; f. 1982; weekly; Editor T. V. R. SHENOY; circ. 82,000.

Kottayam
Balarama: POB 226, Kottayam 686001; tel. (481) 5380; telex 0888-201; f. 1972; children's monthly; Malayalam; Chief Editor MAMMEN MATHEW; circ. 244,348.

Malayala Manorama: Malayala Manorama, Kottayam 686001; tel. (481) 3615; telex 0888-201; f. 1937; weekly; Malayalam; Editor MAMMEN VERGHESE; circ. 546,445.

Manorama Year Book: Malayala Manorama, Kottayam 686001; tel. (481) 3615; telex 0888-201; f. 1965; annually; English; Chief Editor K. M. MATHEW; circ. 75,000.

Vanitha: POB 226, Kottayam 686001; tel.(481) 5380; telex 0888-201; f. 1975; women's monthly; Malayalam; Editor Mrs K. M. MATHEW; circ. 275,182.

Madhya Pradesh
Krishak Jagat: POB 3, Bhopal 462001; tel. (755) 73466; f. 1946; weekly; Hindi; also Marathi edn; agriculture; Chief Editor S. C. GANGRADE; Editor V. K. BONDRIYA; circ. 11,775.

Maharashtra
Bombay
Beautiful Working Woman: 34 Mittal Chambers, Nariman Point, Bombay 400021; tel. (22) 2022830; f. 1974; monthly; English; Editor LYNN DEAS; circ. 55,000.

Bhavan's Journal: Bharatiya Vidya Bhavan, Bombay 400007; tel. (22) 351461; f. 1954; fortnightly; English; literary; Man. Editor J. H. DAVE; Editor S. RAMAKRISHNAN; circ. 25,000.

Blitz News Magazine: 17/17-H Cawasji Patel St, Bombay 400001; tel. (22) 2043546; f. 1941; weekly; English, Hindi and Urdu edns; Editor-in-Chief R. K. KARANJIA; combined circ. 425,000.

Bombay: 28 A&B Jolly Maker Chambers-II, Nariman Point, Bombay 400021; tel. (22) 2026152; telex 115373; f. 1979; fortnightly; English; Editor MOHINI BHULLAR; circ. 51,000.

Business India: Wadia Bldg, 17/19 Dalal St, Bombay 400023; tel. (22) 274161; telex 113557; f. 1978; fortnightly; English; Publr ASHOK H. ADVANI; Editor RUSI ENGINEER; circ. 63,844.

Business World: 145 Atlanta, 209 Ceremonial Blvd, Nariman Point, Bombay 400021; tel. (22) 241083; telex 0112354; f. 1980; fortnightly; English; Editor DILIP THAKORE; circ. 59,000.

Chitralekha: 62 Vaju Kotak Marg, Fort, Bombay 400001; tel. (22) 261526; telex 78298; f. 1950; weekly; Gujarati; Editors Mrs M. V. KOTAK, H. MEHTA; circ. 247,374.

Cine Blitz: 17/17-H Cowasji Patel St, Bombay 400001; tel. (22) 2044143; telex 0116801; f. 1974; monthly; English; films; Editor RITA K. MEHTA; circ. 118,000.

Commerce: N.K.M. International House, 178 Backbay Reclamation, Bombay 400020; tel. (22) 2024505; telex 011-6915; f. 1910; weekly; English; Editor SUBHASHCHANDRA SARKER; circ. 7,000.

Current: 15th Floor, Nariman Bhavan, Nariman Point, Bombay 400021; tel. (22) 2024067; f. 1949; weekly; English; also publ. from New Delhi; Editor AYUB SYED; circ. 80,000.

Dharmayug: Dr Dadabhai Naoroji Rd, Bombay 400001; tel. (22) 4150271; telex 112504; f. 1950; weekly; Hindi; Editor D. V. BHARATI; circ. 120,918.

Eve's Weekly: J. K. Somani Bldg, Bombay Samachar Marg, Bombay 400023; tel. (22) 271444; f. 1947; English; Editor GULSHAN EWING; circ. 40,000.

Femina: Times of India Bldg, Dr D. N. Rd, Bombay 400001; tel. (22) 4150271; telex 73504; f. 1959; fortnightly; English; Editor VIMLA PATIL; circ. 63,628.

Filmfare: Times of India Bldg, Dr D. N. Rd, Bombay 400001; tel. (22) 4150271; telex 112504; f. 1952; fortnightly; English; Editor RAUF AHMED; circ. 72,767.

Illustrated Weekly of India: Dr Dadabhai Naoroji Rd, Bombay 400001; tel. (22) 4150271; telex 112504; f. 1929; weekly; English; Editor PRITISH NANDY; circ. 105,343.

Imprint: Maker Towers E, 18th Floor, Cuffe Parade, Bombay 400005; f. 1961; monthly, English; Editor DOM MORAES; circ. 31,724.

Indian and Eastern Engineer: Piramal Mansion, 235 Dr Dadabhai Naoroji Rd, Bombay 400001; tel. (22) 261322 f. 1858; monthly; English; Editors MICK DE SOUZA, S. K. GHASWALA; circ. 7,000.

Indian PEN: Theosophy Hall, 40 New Marine Lines, Bombay 400020; tel. (22) 292175; f. 1934; 6 a year; organ of Indian Centre of the International PEN; Assoc. Editor NISSIM EZEKIEL.

Janmabhoomi Panchang: Janmabhoomi Bhavan, Ghoga St, Fort, Bombay 400001; tel. (22) 255831; telex 116859; f. 1943; annual almanac; Gujarati; Propr Saurashtra Trust; Editor JYOTI BHATT; circ. 50,000.

Mirror: J. K. Somani Bldg, Samachar Marg, Bombay 400023; tel. (22) 271444; f. 1961; monthly; English; Editor PRABHA GOVIND; circ. 54,000.

Onlooker: Free Press House, 215 Free Press Journal Marg, Nariman Point, Bombay 400021; tel. (22) 234143; telex 011-2570; f. 1939; fortnightly; English; news magazine; Editor RAJAT SHARMA; circ. 61,000.

Pravasi: Janmabhoomi Bhavan, Ghoga St, Fort, Bombay 400001; f. 1939; weekly; Gujarati; Propr Saurashtra Trust; Editor HARINDRA J. DAVE; circ. 98,534.

Reader's Digest: Orient House, Mangalore St, Ballard Estate, Bombay 400038; tel. (22) 267291; telex 011-73389; f. 1954; monthly; English; Man. Dir and Publr ANIL GORE; Editor ASHOK MAHADEVAN; circ. 289,962.

Screen: Express Towers, Nariman Point, Bombay 400021; tel. (22) 2022627; f. 1951; film weekly; English; Editor B. K. KARANJIA; circ. 114,420.

Shree: 40 Cawasji Patel St, Bombay 400023; tel. (22) 292381; telex 01171529; f. 1967; weekly; Marathi; Editor KAMLESH D. MEHTA; circ. 105,708.

Shreewarsha: 40 Cawasji Patel St, Bombay 400023; f. 1980; weekly; Hindi; Editor and Man. Dir R. M. BHUTTA; circ. 50,000.

Sportsweek: 156D J. Dadajee Rd, Tardeo, Bombay 400034; tel. (22) 4942586; telex 1175624; f. 1968; weekly; English; Man. Editor KHALID ANSARI; circ. 51,000.

Star and Style: J. K. Somani Bldg, Bombay Samachar Marg, Bombay 400023; tel. (22) 271444; f. 1965; fortnightly; English; film and fashion; Editor GULSHAN EWING; circ. 87,000.

Stardust: Lana Publishing Co, 14 Advent, 1st Floor; 12A Gen. J. Bhonsale Marg, Bombay 400021; tel. (22) 234135; telex 0112029; f. 1971; monthly, English; Editor VANITA GHOSH; circ. 144,730.

Sunday Loksatta: Express Towers, Nariman Point, Bombay 400021; tel. (22) 232627; f. 1948; Marathi; Editor V. S. GOKHALE; Gen. Man. N. M. DUGAR; circ. 277,000.

Sunday Mid-Day: 156D J. Dadajee Rd, Tardeo, Bombay 400034; tel. (22) 4942586; telex 1175624; f. 1980; Man. Editor KHALID ANSARI; circ. 140,000.

Vyapar: Janmabhoomi Bhavan, Ghoga St, Fort, Bombay 400001; tel. (22) 255831; telex 116859; f. 1949; Gujarati; fortnightly; commerce; Propr Saurashtra Trust; Editor S. J. VASANI; circ. 39,301.

Yuvdarhsan: c/o Warsha Publications Pvt Ltd, Warsha House, 6 Zakaria Bunder Rd, Sewri, Bombay 400015; tel. (22) 441843; f. 1975; weekly; Gujarati; Editor and Man. Dir R. M. BHUTTA; circ. 39,012.

Nagpur

All India Reporter: AIR Ltd, POB 209, Congress Nagar, Nagpur 440012; tel. (712) 34321; f. 1914; monthly; English; law journal; Chief Editor V. R. MANOHAR; circ. 36,000.

Pune (Poona)

Swaraj: Bombay Papers Ltd, 595 Budhawar Peth, Pune 411002; tel. (212) 448403; f. 1936; weekly; Marathi; Gen. Man. K. M. BHIDE; Editor D. P. LELE; circ. (Pune) 51,142.

Rajasthan
Jaipur

Rashtradoot Saptahik: HO, POB 30, M.I.Rd, Jaipur 302001; tel. (141) 72634; f. 1983; Hindi; Editor RAJESH SHARMA; circ. 124,000.

Tamil Nadu
Madras

Ambulimama: 188 Arcot Rd, Vadapalani, Madras 600026; f. 1947; monthly; Tamil; Editor NAGI REDDI; circ. 78,000.

Ambuli Ammavan: 188 Arcot Rd, Vadapalani, Madras 600026; f. 1970; children's monthly; Malayalam; Editor NAGI REDDI; circ. 35,000.

Ananda Vikatan: 757 Mount Rd, Madras 600002; tel. (44) 83084; f. 1924; weekly; Tamil; Editor S. BALASUBRAMANIAN; circ. 200,729.

Andhra Prabha Illustrated Weekly: Express Estates, Mount Rd, Madras 600002; f. 1952; weekly; Telugu; Editor POTTURI VENKATESWARA RAO; circ. 85,000.

Chandamama: 188 Arcot Rd, Vadapalani, Madras 600026; f. 1947; children's monthly; Hindi, Gujarati, Telugu, Kannada, English, Bengali, Punjabi, Assamese; Editor NAGI REDDI; combined circ. 462,000.

Chandoba: 188 Arcot Rd, Vadapalani, Madras 600026; f. 1952; monthly; Marathi; Editor NAGI REDDI; circ. 114,000.

Dinamani Kadir: Express Estate, Mount Rd, Madras 600002; weekly; Editor G. KASTURI RANGAN (acting); circ. 55,000.

Jahnamamu (Oriya): 188 Arcot Rd, Vadapalani, Madras 600026; f. 1972; children's monthly; Editor NAGI REDDI; circ. 90,000.

Kalai Magal: POB 604, Madras 600004; tel. (44) 76011; f. 1932; monthly; Tamil; literary and cultural; Editor R. NARAYANASWAMY; circ. 34,198.

Kalkandu: 151 Purasawalkam High Rd, Madras; f. 1948; weekly; Tamil; Editor TAMIL VANAN; circ. 202,274.

Kalki: 84/1C Race Course Rd, Guindy, Madras 600032; tel. (44) 431543; f. 1941; weekly; Tamil; literary and cultural; Editor K. RAJENDRAN; circ. 69,000.

Kumudam: 151 Purasawalkam High Rd, Madras 600010; tel. (44) 662146; telex 41-462; f. 1947; weekly; Tamil; Editor S. A. P. ANNAMALAI; circ 607,517.

Malai Mathi: 50 Edward Elliots Rd, Madras; f. 1958; weekly; Tamil; Editor P. S. ELANGO; circ. 98,843.

Pesum Padam: 325 Arcot Rd, Madras 600024; tel. (44) 422064; f. 1942; monthly; Tamil; films; Man. Editor K. NATARAJAN; circ. 25,802.

Picturpost: 325 Arcot Rd, Madras 600024; tel. (44) 422064; f. 1943; monthly; English; films; Man. Editor K. NATARAJAN; circ. 13,908.

Puthumai: 101 Purasawalkam High Rd, Madras; f. 1957; monthly; Tamil; Editor K. T. KOSALRAM; circ. 27,000.

Rani Weekly: 1091 Periyar E.V.R. High Rd, Madras 600007; tel. (44) 38471; f. 1962; Tamil; Managing Partner B. S. ADITYAN; circ. 350,119.

Sunday Times: 69 Peters Rd, Madras; f. 1956; weekly; English; Editor S. V. S. VINOD; circ. 50,000.

Thayaga Kural: 2-16 Mount Rd, Madras; f. 1961; weekly; Tamil; Editor A. MA. SAMY; circ. 50,000.

Vani: Madras; f. 1949; fortnightly; Telugu; All India Radio journal; circ. 18,000.

Other Towns

Mathajothidam: 3 Arasamaram, Vellore; f. 1949; monthly; Tamil; astrology; Editor V. K. V. SUBRAMANYAM; circ. 28,000.

Uttar Pradesh
Allahabad

Alokpaat: Mitra Prakashan (Pvt) Ltd, 281 Muthiganj, Allahabad 211003; tel. (532) 51042; telex 540280; f. 1986; Bengali; Editor ALOKE MITRA; circ. 139,243.

Jasoosi Duniya: 5 Kolhan Tola St, Allahabad; f. 1953; monthly; Urdu and Hindi edns; Editor S. ABBAS HUSAINY; combined circ. 70,000.

Manohar Kahaniyan: Mitra Prakashan (Pvt) Ltd, 281 Muthiganj, Allahabad 211003; tel. (532) 51042; telex 540280; f. 1940; monthly; Hindi; Editor ALOKE MITRA; circ. 373,203.

Manorama: Mitra Parkashan (Pvt) Ltd, 281 Muthiganj, Allahabad 211003; tel. (532) 51042; telex 540280; f. 1924; fortnightly; Hindi; Editor ALOKE MITRA; circ. 183,066.

Maya: Mitra Prakashan (Pvt) Ltd, 281 Muthiganj, Allahabad 211003; tel. (532) 51042; telex 540280; f. 1929; monthly; Hindi; Editor ALOKE MITRA; circ. 227,089.

Probe India: Mitra Prakashan (Pvt) Ltd, 281 Muthiganj, Allahabad 211003; tel. (532) 53681; telex 540280; f. 1978; monthly; English; Editor ALOKE MITRA; circ. 58,819.

Satyakatha: Mitra Prakashan (Pvt) Ltd, 281 Muthiganj, Allahabad 211003; tel (532) 51042; telex 540280; f. 1974; monthly; Hindi; Editor ALOKE MITRA; circ. 173,329.

Kanpur

Kanchan Prabha: Rajendra Nagar (East), Kanpur 226004; f. 1974; Hindi; monthly; Man. Editor P. C. GUPTA; Editor Y. M. GUPTA; circ. 26,000.

Lucknow

Rashtra Dharma: POB 207, Dr Raghubir Nagar, Lucknow; tel. (522) 42901; f. 1964; monthly; Hindi; Editor VEERESHWAR DWIVEDI; Man. M. R. GUPTA; circ. 15,000.

INDIA

Other Towns

Current Events: 15 Rajpur Rd, Dehra Dun; f. 1955; quarterly review of national and international affairs; English; Editor DEV DUTT; circ. 5,000.

West Bengal
Calcutta

All India Appointment Gazette: 7 Old Court House St, Calcutta 700001; tel. (33) 226485; f. 1973; weekly; English; Editor S. C. TALUKDAR; circ. 156,000.

Anandalok: 6 Prafulla Sarkar St, Calcutta 700001; tel. (33) 278000; telex 0215468; f. 1975; fortnightly; Bengali; film; Editor SEVABRATA GUPTA; circ. 52,547.

Anandamela: 6 Prafulla Sarkar St, Calcutta 700001; tel. (33) 232283; telex 0217321; f. 1975; monthly; Bengali; juvenile; Editor NIRENDRANATH CHAKRAVARTI; circ. 66,225.

Capital: POB 14, 1/2 Old Court House Corner, Calcutta 700001; tel. (33) 200099; telex 7172; f. 1888; fortnightly; English; financial; Editor V. DUDEJA, (acting); circ. 8,250.

Competition Leader: 7 Old Court House St, Calcutta 700001; f. 1977; monthly; English; Editor S. C. TALUKDAR; circ. 97,000.

Desh: 6 Prafulla Sarkar St, Calcutta 700001; tel. (33) 274880; telex 021-5468; f. 1933; weekly; Bengali; literary; Editor S. GHOSH; circ. 104,540.

Economic Age: P-36 India Exchange Place, 2nd Floor, Calcutta 700001; tel. (33) 277860; f. 1988; monthly; English; economics and business; Editor SIB BANERJEE; circ. 8,000.

Engineering Times: Wachel Molla Mansion, 8 Lenin Sarani, Calcutta 700072; f. 1955; weekly; English; Editor E. H. TIPPOO; circ. 19,000.

Khela: 96 Raja Rammohan Sarani, Calcutta 700009; tel. (33) 355302; telex 021-2216; f. 1981; weekly; Bengali; sports; Editor ASOKE DASGUPTA; circ. 29,293.

Naba Kallol: 11 Jhamapooker Lane, Calcutta 700009; tel. (33) 354294; f. 1960; monthly; Bengali; Editor P. K. MAZUMDAR; circ. 80,000.

Neetee: 4 Sukhlal Johari Lane, Calcutta; f. 1955; weekly; English; Editor M. P. PODDAR.

Ravivar: 6 Prafulla Sarkar St, Calcutta 700001; tel. (33) 278000; telex 0215468; f. 1977; weekly; Hindi; Editor UDAYAN SHARMA; circ. 54,954.

Screen: P-5, Kalakar St, Calcutta 700070; f. 1960; weekly; Hindi; Editor M. P. PODDAR; circ. 58,000.

Sportsworld: 6 Prafulla Sarkar St, Calcutta 700001; tel. (33) 278000; telex 0215468; weekly; English; Editor MANSUR ALI KHAN PATAUDI; circ. 46,106.

Statesman: 4 Chowringhee Sq., Calcutta 700001; tel. (33) 271000; telex 021-5303; f. 1875; overseas weekly; English; Editor SUNANDA KUMAR DUTTA ROY.

Suktara: 11 Jhamapooker Lane, Calcutta 700009; tel. (33) 355294; f. 1948; monthly; Bengali; juvenile; Editor M. MAJUMDAR; circ. 150,000.

Sunday: 6 Prafulla Sarkar St, Calcutta 700001; tel. (33) 232283; telex 0217321; f. 1973; weekly; English; Editor AVEEK SARKAR; circ. 126,189.

NEWS AGENCIES

Press Trust of India Ltd: 357 Dr Dadabhai Naoroji Rd, Bombay 400001; tel. (22) 252371; telex 011-2343; f. 1947, re-established 1978; Chair. RAMNATH GOENKA; Gen. Man. P. UNNIKRISHNAN.

United News of India (UNI): 9 Rafi Marg, New Delhi 110001; tel. (11) 383845; telex 031-2505; f. 1961; Indian language news; special services covering banking, business, economic affairs, agriculture, overseas news and features; brs in over 90 centres in India; Chair. K. K. PAI; Gen. Man. and Chief Editor U. R. KALKUR.

Foreign Bureaux

Agence France-Presse (AFP): Room 20, PTI Bldg, 4 Parliament St, New Delhi 110001; tel. (11) 384292; telex 65075; Bureau Chief YVES DE SAINT-JACOB.

Agentstvo Pechati Novosti (USSR): 2/8 Shantiniketan, New Delhi, 110021; tel. (11) 674347; Correspondent Dr SERGEI L. ZIMIN.

Agenzia Nazionale Stampa Associata (ANSA) (Italy): A-293, New Friends Colony, New Delhi, 110065; tel. (11) 634402; telex 65381; Chief Rep. ELIO CRISCUOLI.

Allgemeiner Deutscher Nachrichtendienst (ADN) (German Democratic Republic): C-64, Annand Niketan, New Delhi 110021; tel. (11) 671864; telex 66860; Correspondent KLAUS-DIETER PFLAUM.

Associated Press (AP) (USA): 19 Narendra Place, Sansad Marg, New Delhi 110001; tel. (11) 310377; telex 65932; Bureau Chief VICTORIA A. GRAHAM.

Československá tisková kancelář (ČTK) (Czechoslovakia): C-59, Annand Niketan, New Delhi 110021; tel. (11) 672276; telex 314389; Correspondent JIŘÍ MAJSTR.

Deutsche Presse-Agentur (dpa) (Federal Republic of Germany): E 14/3 Vasant Vihar, New Delhi 110057; tel. (11) 671663; telex 2809; Chief Rep. CHRISTIAN FURST.

Inter Press Service (IPS) (Italy): C-13 1st Fl. East Nizamuddin, New Delhi 110013; tel. (11) 615992; Correspondent M. VENUGOPALA RAO.

Jiji Tsushin-sha (Japan): N-50 Panchsila Park, New Delhi 110017; tel. (11) 666619; Correspondent SHINJI YAMAZAKI.

Kyodo Tsushin (Japan): 1st Floor, PTI Bldg, 4 Parliament St, New Delhi, 110001; tel. (11) 381954; telex 4716; Chief MASAMICHI FUJITSUKA.

Novinska Agencija Tanjug (Yugoslavia): 14 Palam Marg, Vasant Vihar, New Delhi 110057; tel. (11) 672649; Correspondent SRETEN PETROVIĆ.

Prensa Latina (Cuba): C-105 Anand Niketan, New Delhi 110021; tel. (11) 675015; telex 66532; Correspondent EDEL SUÁREZ.

Reuters (UK): G-6, 6th Fl., Hansalaya Bldg, 15 Barakhamba Rd, New Delhi 110001; tel. (11) 3313525; telex 2323; Correspondent H. PAIN.

Telegrafnoye Agentstvo Sovetskovo Soyuza (TASS) (USSR): A-32 West End Colony, New Delhi 110021; tel. (11) 672351; telex 66092; Bureau Chief VLADIMIR G. BAIDASHIN.

United Press International (UPI) (USA): Ambassador Hotel, Suite 204, Sujan Singh Park, New Delhi 110003; tel. (11) 698991; telex 4515; Bureau Chief JONATHAN LANDAY.

Xinhua (New China) News Agency (People's Republic of China): 50D, Shanti Path, Chanakyapuri, New Delhi 110021; tel. (11) 611394; telex 3162250; Chief TAN RENXIA.

The following agencies are also represented: Associated Press of Pakistan, Bangladesh Sangbad Sangsta, BTA (Bulgaria), PAP (Poland) and Viet-Nam News Agency.

CO-ORDINATING BODIES

Press Information Bureau: Shastri Bhavan, Dr Rajendra Prasad Rd, New Delhi 110001; tel. (11) 383643; f. 1946 to co-ordinate press affairs for the govt; represents newspaper managements, journalists, news agencies, parliament; has power to examine journalists under oath and may censor objectionable material; Prin. Information Officer I. RAMAMOHAN RAO.

Registrar of Newspapers for India: Ministry of Information and Broadcasting, West Block, No.8, Wing 2, Ramakrishna Puram, New Delhi 110066; tel. (11) 698758; f. 1956 as a statutory body to collect press statistics; maintains a register of all Indian newspapers; Registrar KRIPA SAGAR.

PRESS ASSOCIATIONS

All-India Newspaper Editors' Conference: 36–37 Northend Complex, Rama Krishna Ashram Marg, New Delhi 110001; tel. (11) 344519; f. 1940; 450 mems; Pres. VISHWA BANDHU GUPTA; Sec.-Gen. M. S. MADHUSOODANAM.

The Foreign Correspondents' Association of South Asia: c/o Los Angeles Times, F 160 Malcha Marg, New Delhi 110021; tel. (11) 3011374; 116 mems; Pres. ERIC SILVER; Sec. S. GOPAL.

Indian and Eastern Newspaper Society: IENS Bldgs, Rafi Marg, New Delhi 110001; tel. (11) 385401; f. 1939; 536 mems; Pres. RUSI M. CAMA; Sec. S. C. RAO.

Indian Federation of Working Journalists: Flat 29, New Central Market, Connaught Circus, New Delhi 110001; tel. (11) 3310459; f. 1950; 13,000 mems; Pres. K. VIKRAM RAO; Sec.-Gen. K. MATHEW ROY.

Indian Languages Newspapers' Association: Janmabhoomi Bhavan, Ghoga St, Fort, Bombay 400001; tel. (22) 310537; f. 1941; 265 mems; Pres. K. S. DESHPANDE; Gen. Secs L. P. KUNTE, KIRAN SHETH, V. S. SWAMI RENAPURKAR.

National Union of Journalists (India): 7 Jantar Mantar Rd, New Delhi 110001; tel. (11) 351610; f. 1972; 4,000 mems; Pres. ARUN BAGCHI; Sec.-Gen. JITENDRA KUMAR GUPTA.

INDIA   *Directory*

Press Institute of India: Sapru House Annexe, Barakhamba Rd, New Delhi 110001; tel. (11) 3318066; f. 1963; 29 mem. newspapers and other orgs; Chair. G. KASTURI; Dir S. PRAKASA RAO.

Publishers

Delhi and New Delhi

Affiliated East West Press (Pvt) Ltd: G-1/16 Ansari Rd, New Delhi 110002; tel. (11) 279113; textbooks; Man. Dir K. S. PADMANABHAN.

Amerind Publishing Co (Pvt) Ltd: 66 Janpath, New Delhi 110001; tel. (11) 344578; f. 1970; offices at Calcutta, Bombay and New York; scientific and technical; Dirs G. PRIMLANI, R. PRIMLANI.

Arnold Heinemann Publishers India (Pvt) Ltd: AB/9 Safdarjung Enclave, New Delhi 110029; tel. (11) 607806; literature and general; Man. Dir G. A. VAZIRANI.

Atma Ram and Sons: POB 1429, Kashmere Gate, Delhi 110006; tel. (11) 2518139; f. 1909; scientific, technical, humanities, medical; Man. Dir ISH K. PURI.

B.R. Publishing Corporation: 461 Vivekanand Nagar, Delhi 110052; Partner PARMIL MITTAL.

Cambridge Publishing House: D-36 South Extension, Part 1, New Delhi 110049; tel. (11) 619125; juvenile; Dir RAM AVTAR GUPTA.

S. Chand and Co Ltd: POB 5733, Ram Nagar, New Delhi 110055; tel. (11) 772080; telex 031-2185; f. 1917; educational and general in English and Hindi; also book exports and imports; Man. Dir SHYAM LAL GUPTA.

Children's Book Trust: Nehru House, 4 Bahadur Shah Zafar Marg, New Delhi 110002; tel. 3316970; children's books in several languages; Dir G. M. R. SHANKAR.

Concept Publishing Co: H-13 Bali Nagar, New Delhi 110015; tel. (11) 503967; f. 1975; agriculture, geography, history, rural and urban development, education, sociology, economics, commerce, anthropology, psychology, political science; Man. Dir NAURANG RAI; Man. Editor ARVIND K. MITTAL.

Eurasia Publishing House (Pvt) Ltd: Ram Nagar, New Delhi 110055; tel (11) 772080; f. 1964; educational in English and Hindi; Man. Dir S. L. GUPTA.

Heritage Publishers: 4C Ansari Rd, Darya Ganj, New Delhi 110002; tel. (11) 269333; economics, commerce, literature; Dir B. R. CHAWLA.

Hind Pocket Books (Pvt) Ltd: G. T. Rd, Shahdara, Delhi 110032; tel. (11) 202332; f. 1958; fiction and non-fiction paperbacks in English, Hindi, Punjabi and Urdu; Man. Dir DINANATH MALHOTRA.

Hindustan Publishing Corporation: 6 U.B. Jawahar Nagar, Delhi 110007; tel. (11) 2915059; archaeology, pure and applied sciences, sociology, anthropology, economics; Dir S. K. JAIN.

Inter-India Publications: D-17, Raja, Garden Extension, New Delhi 110015; tel. (11) 5413145; f. 1977; academic; Dir MOOL CHAND MITTAL.

Lancers Books: POB 4236, 46 Ajit Arcade, New Delhi 110048; tel. (11) 6414617; f. 1977; politics with special emphasis on northeast India; Propr S. KUMAR.

Macmillan India Ltd: 2/10 Ansari Rd, Daryaganj, New Delhi 110002; tel. (11) 273814; telex 31-62718; f. 1970; textbooks; Man. Dir S. G. WASANI; Vice-Pres. VINOD JAIN; Chief Editor RAVI VYAS; Adviser S. D. BHASIN.

Motilal Banarsidass: 41-UA Bungalow Rd, Jawahar Nagar, Delhi 110007; tel. (11) 2911985; f. 1903; Indology, in English and Sanskrit; Dirs N. P. JAIN, J. P. JAIN, R. P. JAIN.

Neel Kamal Prakashan: Raj Bhawan, 4/C Daryaganj, Delhi; educational; Propr S. K. AGGARWAL.

Oxford and IBH Publishing Co (Pvt) Ltd: 66 Janpath, New Delhi 110001; tel. (11) 344578; f. 1964; science, technology and reference in English; Dirs GULAB PRIMLANI, MOHAN PRIMLANI.

Oxford University Press: POB 43, YMCA Library Bldg, Jai Singh Rd, New Delhi 110001; tel. (11) 322769; telex 31-61108; educational, scientific, medical and reference; Gen. Man. R. DAYAL.

People's Publishing House (Pvt) Ltd: 5E Rani Jhansi Rd, Delhi 110055; tel. (11) 529823; f. 1943; paperbacks, textbooks, general; Gen. Man. P. P. G. JOSHI.

Rajkamal Prakashan (Pvt) Ltd: 8 Netaji Subhas Marg, Delhi 110002; tel. (11) 274463; f. 1946; Hindi; literary; also literary journal, monthly trade journal; Man. Dir SHEILA SANDHU.

Rajpal and Sons: 1,590 Madarsa Rd, Kashmere Gate, Delhi 110006; tel. (11) 2519104; f. 1891; humanities, social sciences, art, juvenile; Hindi; Man. Partner VISHWANATH MALHOTRA.

Sahgal, N. D., and Sons: Dariba Kalan, Delhi; f. 1917; politics, history, general knowledge, sport, fiction and juvenile in Hindi; Man. G. SAHGAL.

Shiksha Bharati: Madrasa Rd, Kashmere Gate, Delhi 110006; tel. (11) 2523904; f. 1955; textbooks, popular science and juvenile in Hindi and English; Man. Partner VEENA MALHOTRA.

Sterling Publishers (Pvt) Ltd: L-10 Green Park Extension, New Delhi 110016; tel. (11) 669560; telex 31-61443; f. 1965; academic books on the humanities and social sciences, paperbacks; Chair. O. P. GHAI; Man. Dir S. K. GHAI.

Technical and Commercial Book Co: 75 Gokhale Market, Tis Hazari, Delhi 110054; tel. (11) 228315; telex 011-2651; f. 1913; technical; Propr D. N. MEHRA; Man. RAMAN MEHRA.

Thomson Press (India) Ltd: 9K Connaught Circus, New Delhi 110001; tel. (11) 353808; juvenile; Dir AROON PURIE.

Vikas Publishing House (Pvt) Ltd: 5 Ansari Rd, New Delhi 110002; tel. (11) 866536; telex 592-262; medicine, sciences, engineering, textbooks, academic, fiction, women's studies; Man. Dir NARENDRA KUMAR.

Bombay

Allied Publishers (Pvt) Ltd: 15 J. N. Heredia Marg, Ballard Estate, Bombay 400038; tel. (22) 261959; telex 112090; f. 1934; economics, politics, history, philosophy; Man. Dir R. N. SACHDEV.

Asia Publishing House (Pvt) Ltd: 18/20 K. Dubash Marg, Bombay 400023; tel. (22) 5353; telex 1171665; f. 1981; humanities, social sciences, science and general; English; Man. Dir ANANDA JAISINGH.

Bharatiya Vidya Bhavan: Munshi Sadan, Kulapati Munshi Marg, Bombay 400007; tel. (22) 351461; f. 1938; art, literature, culture, philosophy, religion, history of India in English, Hindi, Sanskrit and Gujarati; various periodicals; Pres. GIRDHARILAL MEHTA; Vice-Pres C. SUBRAMANIAM, PRAVINCHANDRA V. GANDHI.

Blackie and Son (Pvt) Ltd: Blackie House, 103–105 Walchand Hirachand Marg, POB 381, Bombay 400001; tel. (22) 261410; f. 1901; educational, scientific and technical, general and juvenile; Man. Dir D. R. BHAGI.

Chetana (Pvt) Ltd: 34 Rampart Row, Bombay 400023; f. 1948; religion, philosophy; Dir S. DIKSHIT.

Himalaya Publishing House: 'Ramdoot', Dr Bhalerao Marg (Kelevadi), Girgaon, Bombay 400004; tel. (22) 360170; f. 1976; textbooks; Gen. Man. D. P. PANDEY.

Hind Kitab Ltd: 32–34 Veer Nariman Rd, Bombay 400001; f. 1940; English, Hindi, Gujarati and Kannada.

India Book House (Pvt) Ltd: 412 Tulsiani Chambers, Nariman Point, Bombay 400021; tel. (22) 240626; telex 011-6297; Chair. G. L. MIRCHANDANI.

International Book House (Pvt) Ltd: Indian Mercantile Mansions Extension, Madame Cama Rd, Bombay 400039; tel. (22) 2021634; f. 1941; general, educational, scientific and law; Man. Dir S. K. GUPTA; Gen. Man. C. V. THAMBI.

Jaico Publishing House: 121 Mahatma Gandhi Rd, Bombay 400023; tel. (22) 270621; f. 1947; general paperbacks; imports scientific, technical and educational; Man. Dir JAMAN SHAH.

Mid-Day Publications (Pvt) Ltd: 156D J. Dadajee Rd, Tardeo, Bombay 400034; tel. (22) 4942586; telex 117-5624; newspapers and periodicals; Editor KHALID ANSARI.

Popular Prakashan (Pvt) Ltd: 35c Pandit Madan Mohan Malaviya Marg, Tardeo, Popular Press Bldg, opp. Roche, Bombay 400034; tel. (22) 4941656; f. 1968; sociology, biographies, current affairs, medicine, history, politics and administration in English and Marathi; Man. Dir R. G. BHATKAL; Jt Dir S. G. BHATKAL.

Somaiya Publications (Pvt) Ltd: 172 Mumbai Marathi Grantha Sangrahalaya Marg, Dadar, Bombay 400014; tel. (22) 8820230; telex 011-2723; f. 1967; economics, sociology, history, politics, mathematics, sciences; Chair. S. K. SOMAIYA.

Taraporevala, Sons and Co (Pvt) Ltd: 210 Dr D. Naroji Rd, Fort, Bombay 400001; tel. (22) 261433; f. 1864; Indian art, culture, history, sociology, scientific, technical and general in English; Dirs M. J. TARAPOREVALA, S. J. TARAPOREVALA.

N. M. Tripathi (Pvt) Ltd: 164 Samaldas Gandhi Marg, Bombay 400002; tel. (22) 313651; f. 1888; law and general in English and Gujarati; Chair. D. M. TRIVEDI.

INDIA — Directory

Calcutta

Academic Publishers: POB 12341, 5A Bhawani Dutta Lane, Calcutta 700073; tel. (33) 324697; f. 1958; textbooks; Man. Partner B. K. Dhur.

Allied Book Agency: 18/A Shyama Charan De St, Calcutta 700073; tel. (33) 341815; general and academic; Dir B. Sarkar.

Ananda Publishers (Pvt) Ltd: 45 Beniatola Lane, Calcutta 700009; tel. (33) 314352; literature, general; Dir A. Sarkar.

Assam Review Publishing Co: 29 Waterloo St, Calcutta 700001; tel. (33) 232251; f. 1926; tea publs directory; Partners G. L. Banerjee, S. Banerjee.

Book Land (Pvt) Ltd: 1 Shankar Ghosh Lane, Calcutta 700007; economics, politics, history and general; Man. Dir J. N. Basu.

Chuckerverty, Chatterjee and Co Ltd: 15 College Sq., Calcutta 700012; Dir Binodelal Chakravarti.

Eastern Law House (Pvt) Ltd: 54 Ganesh Chunder Ave, Calcutta 700013; tel. (33) 274989; f. 1918; legal, commercial and accountancy; Dir Asok De.

Firma KLM Private Ltd: 257B B. B. Ganguly St, Calcutta 700012; tel. (33) 274391; f. 1950; Indology, scholarly in English, Bengali, Sanskrit and Hindi; Man. Dir R. N. Mukerji.

Intertrade Publications (India) (Pvt) Ltd: 55 Gariahat Rd, POB 10210, Calcutta; tel. (33) 474872; f. 1954; economics, medicine, law, history and trade directories; Man. Dir Dr K. K. Roy.

A. Mukherjee and Co (Pvt) Ltd: 2 Bankim Chatterjee St, Calcutta 700012; tel. (33) 341606; f. 1940; educational and general in Bengali and English; Man. Dir Rajeev Neogi.

New Era Publishing Co: 31 Gauri Bari Lane, Calcutta 700004; f. 1944; Propr Dr P. N. Mitra; Man. S. K. Mitra.

W. Newman and Co Ltd: 3 Old Court House St, Calcutta 700069; f. 1851; general; Man. Dir P. N. Bhargava.

Oriental Publishing Co: f. 1910; Propr D. N. Bose; Man. D. P. Bose.

Renaissance Publishers (Pvt) Ltd: 15 Bankim Chatterjee St, Calcutta 700012; f. 1949; politics, philosophy, history; Man. Dir J. C. Goswami.

M. C. Sarkar and Sons (Pvt) Ltd: 14 Bankim Chatterjee St, Calcutta 700012; tel. (33) 341782; f. 1910; reference; Dirs Supriya Sarkar, Samit Sarkar.

Thacker's Press and Directories: M.P. Works Pvt Ltd, 6-B, Bentinck St, POB 2512, Calcutta 700001; industrial publs and directories; Chair. Juthika Roy; Dirs B. B. Roy, A. Bose.

Madras

Higginbothams Ltd: 814 Anna Salai, Madras 600002; tel. (44) 811841; f. 1844; general; Gen. Man. S. Chandrasekhar.

B. G. Paul and Co: 4 Francis Joseph St, Madras; f. 1923; general, educational and oriental; Man. K. Nilakantan.

Srinivasa Varadachari and Co: 2–16 Mount Rd, Madras; f. 1879; educational; Prop G. Venkatachari.

Thompson and Co (Pvt) Ltd: 33 Broadway, Madras 600001; f. 1890; directories in English, Tamil, Telugu and Malayalam; Man Dir K. M. Cherian.

Other Towns

Bharat Bharti Prakashan: Western Kutchery Rd, Meerut 250001; tel. 73748; f. 1952; textbooks; Man. Dir Rajendra Agarwal.

Bharati Bhawan: Govind Mitra Rd, Patna 800004; tel. (612) 50325; f. 1942; educational and juvenile; other brs in Muzaffarpur, Ranchi, Darbhanga and Calcutta; Partners T. K. Bose, Dolly Bose, Surojit Bose and Sanjib Bose.

Bishen Singh Mahendra Pal Singh: 23A Connaught Place, POB 137, Dehradun 248001; tel. (935) 24048; f. 1957; botany; Dir Gajendra Singh.

Catholic Press: Ranchi 834001 Bihar; f. 1928; books and periodicals; Dir William Tigga.

Chugh Publications: POB 101, 2 Strachey Rd, Allahabad; tel. (532) 21589; sociology, economics, history, general; Propr Ramesh Kumar.

Geetha Book House: K. R. Circle, Mysore 570001; tel. (821) 33589; f. 1959; general; Dirs M. Gopala Krishna, M. Gururaja Rao.

Goel Publishing House: Subhash Bazar, Meerut 250001; tel. 27843; textbooks; Dir Kamal K. Rastogi.

Kalyani Publishers: 1/1 Rajinder Nagar, Ludhiana, Punjab; tel. (161) 20221; textbooks; Dir Raj Kumar.

Kitabistan: 30 Chak, Allahabad 211003; tel. (532) 51885; f. 1932; general, agriculture, govt publs in Urdu, Farsi and Arabic; Partners A. U. Khan, Sultan Zaman, Naseem Farooqi.

Law Book Co (Pvt) Ltd: POB 1004, Sardar Patel Marg, Allahabad 211001; tel. (532) 2415; f. 1929; legal texts in English; Man. Dir L. R. Bagga; Dirs Rajesh Bagga, Deepak Bagga, Anil Bagga, Rakesh Bagga.

Macmillan India Ltd: 248 Upper Palace Orchards, Bangalore 560080; tel. (532) 53807; telex 0845-615; scholarly monographs in English and Hindi, textbooks and general; Pres. and Man. Dir S. G. Wasani.

Navajivan Publishing House: PO Navajivan, Ahmedabad 380014; tel. (272) 4473295; f. 1919; Gandhiana and related social science; in English, Hindi and Gujarati; Man. Trustee Jitendra Desai.

Nem Chand and Bros: Civil Lines, Roorkee 247667; tel. 2258; f. 1951; engineering textbooks and journals.

Orient Longman Ltd: 5-9-41/1 Bashir Bagh, Hyderabad 500029; tel. (842) 230343; f. 1948; educational, technical, general and children's in almost all Indian languages; Chair. J. Rameshwar Rao.

Pioneer Publishing Co: 42 Lal Bahadur Shastri Marg, Allahabad 211001; tel. (532) 2415; f. 1971; law books; Partners A. Bagga, R. Bagga, D. Bagga, Mrs R. Bagga, Mrs S. Bagga.

Publication Bureau: Punjab University, Chandigarh 160014; tel. (172) 22782; f. 1948; textbooks and general; Head of Bureau and Sec. R. K. Malhotra.

Ram Prasad and Sons: Hospital Rd, Agra 282003; tel. (562) 72935; f. 1905; agricultural, arts, commerce, education, general, pure and applied science, economics, sociology; Dirs H. N., R. N., B. N. and Y. N. Agarwal; Mans S. N. Agarwal and R. S. Tandon.

Upper India Publishing House (Pvt) Ltd: Aminabad, Lucknow 226018; tel. (522) 42711; f. 1921; Indian history, religion, art and science; English and Hindi; Man. Dir S. Bhargava.

Government Publishing House

Publications Division: Ministry of Information and Broadcasting, Govt of India, Patiala House, New Delhi 110001; tel. (11) 387321; f. 1941; culture, art, literature, planning and development, general; also 21 magazines in English and several Indian languages; Dir Dr S. S. Shashi.

PUBLISHERS' ASSOCIATIONS

All India Booksellers' and Publishers' Association: 17-L Connaught Circus, POB 328, New Delhi 110001; tel. (11) 42166; Pres. A. N. Varma.

Federation of Indian Publishers: Federation House, 18/1-C Institutional Area, JNU Rd, New Delhi 110000; tel. (11) 654847; 10 affiliated asscns; 152 mems; Pres. S. K. Sachdeva; Exec. Sec. H. L. Luthra; Sec.-Gen. S. K. Bhatia.

Federation of Publishers and Booksellers Associations in India: 1st Floor, 4833/24 Govind Lane, Ansari Rd, New Delhi 110002; tel. (11) 272845; 16 affiliated asscns; 589 mems; Pres. C. M. Chawla; Sec. Bhupinder Chowdhri.

Radio and Television

Radio broadcasting in India began in 1927 and came under government control in 1930. Commercial television began in 1976, and by 1981 it covered 18% of the population, spread over 6.5% of the country. In 1978 it was decided that All India Radio and Doordarshan India should become autonomous corporations. To maximize broadcasting coverage, the Government installs and maintains radio and television sets in community centres. Both radio and television carry commercial advertising.

In 1983 there were an estimated 45m. radio receivers and 2.1m. television receivers in use.

RADIO

All India Radio (AIR): Akashvani Bhavan, Parliament St, New Delhi 110001; tel. (11) 382021; telex 0313225; broadcasting is controlled by the Ministry of Information and Broadcasting and govt-financed; operates a network of 88 broadcasting centres, covering 89% of the population and 78% of the total area of the country; proposes to cover 97.5% of the population and 91% of the total area of the country through 200 radio stations by March 1990; Dir-Gen. Suresh Mathur.

The News Services Division of AIR, centralized in New Delhi, is one of the largest news organizations in the world. It has 41 regional news units, which broadcast 269 bulletins daily in 24 languages and 36 dialects. Eighty-one bulletins in 19 languages are broadcast in the Home Services and 64 bulletins in 24 languages in the External Services.

Radio broadcasting stations are grouped into five zones:

East: Agartala, Aizawl, Bhagalpur, Calcutta, Cuttack, Darbhanga, Dibrugarh, Gangtok, Guwahati, Imphal, Jeypore, Kohima, Kurseong, Pasighat, Patna, Ranchi, Sambalpur, Shillong, Silchar, Siliguri, Tawang, Tezu and Tura.

North: Ajmer, Allahabad, Bikaner, Chandigarh, Delhi, Gorakhpur, Jaipur, Jodhpur, Jullundur, Kanpur, Lucknow, Mathura, Najibabad, Rampur, Rohtak, Simla, Udaipur and Varanasi.

South: Alleppey, Bangalore, Bhadravati, Coimbatore, Cuddapah, Dharwar, Gulbarga, Hyderabad, Calicut, Madras, Mangalore, Mysore, Pondicherry, Port Blair, Tiruchirapalli, Tirunelveli, Trichur, Trivandrum, Vijayawada and Vishakhapatnam.

West: Ahmedabad, Ambikapur, Aurangabad, Bhopal, Bhuj, Bombay, Chhatarpur, Gwalior, Indore, Jabalpur, Jagdalpur, Jalgaon, Nagpur, Panaji, Parbhani, Pune, Raipur, Rajkot, Ratnagiri, Rewa, Sangli, Suratgarh and Vadodara (Baroda).

Kashmir: Jammu, Leh and Srinagar.

TELEVISION

Doordarshan India (Television India): Mandi House, Copernicus Marg, New Delhi 110001; tel. (11) 387786; telex 031-4413; f. 1976, when television broadcasting became independent of All India Radio; 8 centres, 3 base production centres, 6 Satellite Instructional Television Experiment (SITE) on-going transmitters and 5 relay centres; programmes: 280 hours weekly; colour transmission began in 1981. While only 0.2% of India's 685m. inhabitants owned a television receiver in 1981, 15% (102m.) had access to television through community centres. In 1985 an estimated 36% of the country's area and 58% of the population were covered by the TV network. There were 186 transmitters in operation in March 1986, and by the end of the seventh Five-Year Plan (1985–90) 80% of the population should be covered by the TV network; Dir-Gen. BHASKAR GHOSH.

Principal television stations are located at:

Amritsar: began transmissions in 1973.
Bangalore: began transmissions in 1981.
Bombay: began transmissions in 1972; TV studio at Worli and relay transmitters at Sinhagarh, Pune and Nagpur.
Calcutta: began transmissions in 1975.
Delhi: began transmissions in 1959; relay centre at Mussoorie.
Gulbarga: began transmissions in 1977.
Hyderabad: began transmissions in 1977.
Jaipur: began transmissions in 1977.
Jalandhar: began transmissions in 1977; relay centre at Amritsar.
Kanpur: began transmissions in 1979.
Lucknow: began transmissions in 1975; relay installation at Kanpur.
Madras: began transmissions in 1975 with relay centre at Bangalore.
Mussoorie: began transmissions in 1977.
Muzaffarpur: began transmissions in 1978.
Nagpur: began transmission in 1982.
Panaji: began transmissions in 1986.
Pij (Ahmedabad): began transmissions in 1976.
Pune: began transmissions in 1973.
Raipur: began transmissions in 1977.
Sambalpur: commissioned in 1978.
Srinagar: began transmissions in 1973 in Urdu and Kashmiri.

Finance

(cap.=capital; p.u.=paid up; auth.=authorized; dep.=deposits; m.=million; res=reserves; brs=branches; amounts in rupees, unless otherwise stated)

BANKING
State Banks

Reserve Bank of India: Central Office, Mint Rd, Bombay 400001; tel. (22) 295000; telex 115673; f. 1935; nationalized 1949; sole bank of issue; cap. 50m.; res 1,500m. (1986); Gov. R. N. MALHOTRA; Exec. Dirs T. N. ANANTHARAM IYER, U. K. SHARMA, A. HASIB; 11 brs.

State Bank of India: POB 10121, Madame Cama Rd, Bombay 400021; tel. (22) 2022426; telex 0112995; f. 1955; cap. and res 5,784m., dep. 298,076m. (1986); subsidiaries in Bikaner and Jaipur, Hyderabad, Indore, Mysore, Patila, Saurashtra and Travancore; there are 28 state co-operative banks and 349 district co-operative banks; 34 private-sector banks and 194 regional rural banks; representative offices and branches worldwide; Chair. DHRUBA NARAYAN GHOSH; Man. Dir. C. S. KALYANASUNDARAM; 10,838 brs.

Commercial Banks

Fourteen of India's major commercial banks were nationalized in July 1969 and a further six in April 1980. They are managed by 15-mem. boards of directors (two directors to be appointed by the central government, one employee director, one representing employees who are not workmen, one representing depositors, three representing farmers, workers, artisans, etc., five representing persons with special knowledge or experience, one Reserve Bank of India official and one Government of India official). The Department of Banking of the Ministry of Finance controls all banking operations.

There were 52,936 branches of public sector and other commercial banks in March 1986.

Aggregate deposits of all scheduled commercial banks amounted to Rs 1,020,598m. in January 1987.

Allahabad Bank: 2 Netaji Subhas Rd, Calcutta 700001; tel. (532) 292310; telex 21-7106; f. 1865; cap. p.u. 160m., res 93.4m., dep. 25,000m. (1986); Chair. and Man. Dir R. SRINIVASAN; Exec. Dir. R. L. WADHWA; Gen. Man. M. V. KULKARNI; 1,303 brs.

Andhra Bank: Andhra Bank Bldg, Sultan Bazar, Hyderabad 500001; tel. (842) 40141; telex 015283; f. 1923; nationalized 1980; cap. p.u. 120m., dep. 17,139m. (1985); Chair. and Man. Dir M. VENKATARATNAM; Exec. Dir K. RAMACHANDRA NAYAK; 852 brs.

Bank of Baroda: 3 Walchand Hirachand Marg, Ballard Pier, Bombay 400038; tel. (22) 260341; telex 011-6345; f. 1908; cap. p.u 520m., res. 353m., dep. 61,867m. (1985); Chair. and Man. Dir PREMJIT SINGH; Exec. Dir Dr A. C. SHAH; 1,870 brs.

Bank of India: POB 234, Express Towers, Nariman Point, Bombay 400021; tel. (22) 2023020; telex 0112281; f. 1906; cap. p.u. 140m., dep. 75,790m. (1985); Chair. and Man. Dir (vacant); Exec. Dir N. S. PARULEKAR; 1,925 brs (worldwide).

Bank of Maharashtra: Lokmangal, 1501 Shivajinagar, Pune 411005; tel. (212) 52731; telex 0145207; f. 1935; cap. 24.2m., dep. 15,663m. (1984); Chair. and Man. Dir P. S. DEPANDE; Exec. Dir R. K. GUPTE; 953 brs.

Canara Bank: POB 6648, 112 Jayachamarajendra Rd, Bangalore 560002; tel. (812) 76851; telex 0845205; f. 1906; cap. p.u. 295m., dep. 56,282m. (1985); Chair. and Man. Dir B. RATNAKAR; Exec. Dir N. D. PRABHU; 1,841 brs.

Central Bank of India: Chandermukhi, Nariman Point, Bombay 400021; telex 0112589; f. 1911; cap. p.u. 72.5m., res. 206.1m., dep. 60,963m. (1985); Chair. and Man. Dir M. N. GOIPORIA; Exec. Dir D. K. CONTRACTOR; 2,468 brs (worldwide).

Corporation Bank: Mangaladevi Temple Rd, POB 88; Mangalore 575001; tel. (824) 26416; telex 842-228; f. 1906; nationalized 1980, cap. 60m., dep. 7,907m. (1985); Chair. and Man. Dir Y. S. HEDGE; Gen. Mans U. NARAYAN NAYAK, T. V. RAO; 400 brs.

Dena Bank: POB 6058, Maker Towers 'E', Cuffe Parade, Bombay 400005; tel. 211231; telex 11-3567; f. 1938; cap. 150m., res 42.3m., dep. 16,541m. (1985); Chair. and Man. Dir B. K. GHOSH; Exec. Dir G. S. DAHOTRE; 1,000 brs.

Indian Bank: POB 1384, 31 Rajaji Salai, Madras 600001; tel. (22) 514151; telex 41307; f. 1907; cap. p.u. 270m., dep. 31,643m. (1985); Chair. and Man. Dir M. G. K. NAIR; Exec. Dir A. SANKARALINGAM; Gen. Man M. GOPALAKRISHNAN; 1,102 brs.

Indian Overseas Bank: POB 3765, 762 Anna Salai, Madras 600002; tel. (44) 82041; telex 41290; f. 1937; cap. p.u. 130m., res. 197.2m., dep. 32,292m. (1984); Chair. and Man. Dir S. PADMANABHAN; Exec. Dir R. RAMACHANDRAN; 1,033 brs.

The New Bank of India: 1 Tolstoy Marg, New Delhi 110001; tel. (11) 33114521; telex 313220; f. 1936; nationalized April 1980; cap. p.u. 90m., dep. 11,371m. (1985); Chair. and Dir R. C. SUNEJA; 525 brs.

Oriental Bank of Commerce: POB 329, E Block, Connaught Place, New Delhi 110001; tel. (11) 351021; telex 31-65462; f. 1943; nationalized April 1980; cap. p.u. 80m.; dep. 10,196m. (1985); Chair. and Man. Dir P. S. GOPALAKRISHNAN; Exec. Dir S. P. TALWAR; Gen. Mans S. K. SONI, R. C. KAPOOR; 454 brs.

INDIA *Directory*

Punjab and Sind Bank: 21 Bank House, Rajendra Place, New Delhi 110008; tel. (11) 321658; telex 313684; f. 1908; nationalized April 1980; cap. 8.9m., dep. 13,505m. (1985); Chair. and Man. Dir S. Autar Singh Bagga; Exec. Dir M. S. Chahal; 638 brs.

Punjab National Bank: POB 274, 5 Sansad Marg, New Delhi 110001; tel. (11) 382061; telex 312330; f. 1895; cap. p.u. 100m., dep. 58,081m. (1985); Chair. and Man. Dir J. S. Varshneya; 2,262 brs (worldwide).

Syndicate Bank: Manipal, Karnataka State 576119; tel. 8261; telex 082242; f. 1925; cap. 330m., dep. 48,000m. (1986); Chair. and Man. Dir P. S. V. Mallya; 1,439 brs.

UCO Bank (United Commercial Bank): 10 Biplabi Trailokya Maharaj Sarani (Brabourne Rd), Calcutta 700001; tel. (33) 260120; telex 214323; f. 1943; cap. p.u. 325m., res 105m., dep. 33,678m. (1985); Chair. and Man. Dir K Manmohan Shenoi; Gen. Mans H. N. Vohra, C. T. Thakur, M. V. Ramaseshan, Dr A. C. Parikh; 1,722 brs.

Union Bank of India: 239 Backbay Reclamation, Nariman Point, Bombay 400021; tel. (22) 2024647; telex 11-4208; f. 1919; cap. p.u. 300m., res 102.7m., dep. 33,148m. (1985); Chair. and Man. Dir J. S. Bhatnagar; Exec. Dir M. U. Kini; 1,619 brs.

United Bank of India: 16 Old Court House St, Calcutta 700001; tel. (33) 237471; telex 0217387; f. 1950; cap. p.u. 26.9m., dep. 27,073m. (1985); Chair. and Man. Dir K. D. Nayyar; Exec. Dir K. B. Damle; 947 brs.

Vijaya Bank: 2 Residency Rd, Bangalore 560025; f. 1931; nationalized 1980; cap. p.u. 11.8m., dep. 8,740m. (1984); Chair. and Man. Dir R. Vijayaraghavan; Exec. Dir K. Sadananda Shetty; 637 brs.

Principal Private Banks

Bank of Madura Ltd: 33 North Chitrai St, Madurai 625001; cap. p.u. 10m.; dep. 2,029m. (1985); Chair. S. Kumarasundaram.

Bombay Mercantile Co-operative Bank Ltd: 78 Mohamedali Rd, Bombay 400003; tel. (22) 325961; telex 011-75424; f. 1939; cap. p.u. 20m., dep. 2,144m. (June 1986); Chair. Ghulam Ghouse; Man. Dir Zain G. Rangoonwala; 32 brs.

Karnataka Bank Ltd: Dongerkery, Mangalore 3; f. 1924; cap. p.u. 5m., dep. 1,342.7m. (1981); Chair. P. Raghuram; 249 brs.

The Sangli Bank Ltd: Rajwada Chowk, POB 158, Sangli 416416; tel. 3611; telex 0193211; f. 1916; cap. p.u. 4.3m., dep. 2,041m. (1985); Chair. and CEO A. R. Pradhan; Gen. Man. A. K. Chatterjee; 167 brs.

United Western Bank Ltd: POB 2, 172–4 Raviwar Peth, Shivaji Circle, Satara 415001; tel. 2523; f. 1936; cap. 5m., dep. 2,037m. (1984); Chair. A. G. Pandit; Gen. Man. S. T. Modak; 166 brs.

Foreign Banks

There are 21 foreign banks (with 136 branches) operating in India, of which the most important are:

Abu Dhabi Commercial Ltd (UAE): Rehmat Manzil, 75 Veer Nariman Rd, Bombay 40020; Man. Ebrahim Abdul Rahman.

Algemene Bank Nederland NV (Netherlands): 14 Veer Nariman Rd, Bombay 400023; tel. (22) 2642331; telex 113246; Gen. Man. (India) A. Oortman Gerlings; 3 brs.

American Express International Banking Corpn (USA): Dalamal Towers, First Floor 211, Nariman Point, Bombay 400021; tel. (22) 233230; telex 11-3808; Vice-Pres. (India) T. R. Collins; 3 brs.

Bank of America National Trust and Savings Association (USA): Express Towers, Air India Bldg, 16th Fl., Nariman Point, Bombay 400021; tel. (22) 2023431; telex 2152; Regional Vice-Pres. N. Venkateswaran; 4 brs.

Bank of Credit and Commerce International (Overseas) Ltd (Cayman Islands): Marker Chambers III, Nariman Point, Bombay 400021; tel. (22) 241091; telex 11-5839; Regional Gen. Man. Krishan Murari.

Bank of Oman Ltd: 4–6 Maker Arcade, Cuffe Parade, Bombay 400005.

Bank of Tokyo Ltd (Japan): Jeevan Prakash, Sir P. Mehta Rd, Bombay 400001; tel. (22) 259664; telex 2155; Gen. Man. K. Hanaoka; 3 brs.

Banque Nationale de Paris (France): French Bank Bldg, POB 45, 62 Homji St, Fort, Bombay 400001; tel. (22) 255943; telex 6044; Man. P. Grandamy; 5 brs.

Barclays Bank PLC (UK): 67 Maker Towers 'F', Cuffe Parade, Bombay 400005; Rep. Noel Davenport.

British Bank of the Middle East (Hong Kong): 16 Veer Nariman Rd, Fort, Bombay 400023; tel. (22) 258203; telex 011-5956; Man. S. Daulet Singh.

Citibank (USA): POB 1672, 293 Dr D.N. Rd, Bombay 400021; tel. (22) 258792; telex 2288; Vice-Pres. David H. Roberts; 5 brs.

Deutsche Bank (Asia) (Federal Republic of Germany): Tulsiani Chambers, PO 9995, Nariman Point, Bombay 400021; tel. (22) 223262; telex 114042; CEO Heinz Poehlsen.

Grindlays Bank (UK): POB 725, 90 Mahatma Gandhi Rd, Bombay 400023; tel. (22) 271295; telex 011-4792; Regional Dir George Cunningham; 54 brs.

Hongkong and Shanghai Banking Corpn (Hong Kong): POB 128, 52/60 Mahatma Gandhi Rd, Bombay 400001; tel. (22) 274921; telex 011-2223; CEO Colin Selby; 21 brs.

Midland Bank (UK): 152 Maker Chamber No. IV, 14th Floor, 222 Nariman Point, Bombay 400021.

Mitsui Bank Ltd. (Japan): 6 Wallace St, Bombay 400001; tel. (22) 2043931; telex 11-2987; Gen. Man. and CEO Kiybo Matsumoto; 1 br.

Oman International Bank (Oman): 1A Mittal Court, Nariman Point, Bombay 400021; tel. (22) 2047444; CEO V. V. Chandy.

Royal Bank of Canada: c/o 410 The Taj Mahal Hotel, 1 Man Singh Rd, New Delhi 110011; tel. (11) 386162; telex 31-3604; Regional Rep. Colin D. Liptrot.

Société Générale (France): Maker Chambers IV, Nariman Point, Bombay 400021; tel. (22) 243547; telex 11-2635; Gen. Man. Gerard Hannotin.

Sonali Bank (Bangladesh): 15 Park St, Calcutta 700016; tel. (33) 297998; telex 21-2727; Dep. Gen. Man. Md. Sanaul Haque; 1 br.

Standard Chartered Bank (UK): POB 558, 23–25 Mahatma Gandhi Rd, Fort, Bombay 400023; tel. (22) 257198; telex 011-2230; Chief Man. R. J. Guthrie; 24 brs.

Banking Organizations

Indian Banks' Association: Stadium House, 81–83 Veer Nariman Rd, Bombay 400020; tel. (22) 222365; telex 011-5146; 84 mems; Chair. M. N. Goiporia; Sec. N. S. Pradhan.

Indian Institute of Bankers: 'The Arcade', World Trade Centre, Second Floor, East Wing, Cuffe Parade, Bombay 400005; tel. (22) 217746; f. 1928; 248,577 mems; Pres. R. N. Malhotra; Chief Sec. R. D. Pandya.

National Institute of Bank Management: Kondhwe Khurd, Pune 411022; tel. (212) 69080; telex 145-256; f. 1968; Dir Dr R. Bandyopadhyay.

DEVELOPMENT FINANCE ORGANIZATIONS

Agricultural Finance Corpn Ltd: Dhanraj Mahal, 1st Floor, Chatrapati Shivaji Maharaj Marg, Bombay 400039; tel. (22) 2028924; telex 0115849; f. 1968; a consortium of commercial banks, set up to help member commercial banks participate in agriculture and rural development projects; provides project consultancy services to commercial banks, Union and State govts, public sector corpns, the World Bank, the ADB, FAO, the International Fund for Agricultural Development and other institutions and to individuals; undertakes techno-economic and investment surveys in agriculture and agro-industries etc.; project office in New Delhi; regional offices in Calcutta, Lucknow and Madras; brs in Ahmedabad, Bhopal, Chandigarh, Hyderabad, Patna, Shillong and Trivandrum; cap. p.u. 50m.; Chair. Dr. G. V. K. Rao; Man. Dir B. Venkata Rao.

Credit Guarantee Corpn of India Ltd: Vidyut Bhavan, 3rd Floor, BEST Bldg, Pathakwadi, Bombay 400002; f. 1971; promoted by the Reserve Bank of India; guarantees loans and other credit facilities extended by (i) scheduled and non-scheduled commercial banks to small traders, farmers and self-employed persons and small borrowers under a differential interest rates scheme; (ii) scheduled and non-scheduled commercial banks and state financial corpns to small transport and business enterprises; (iii) scheduled commercial banks and certain state and central co-operative banks to service co-operative socs assisting their mems engaged in industrial activity; Chair. Dr R. K. Hazari; Man. C. S. Subramaniam.

Industrial Credit and Investment Corpn of India Ltd: 163 Backbay Reclamation, Bombay 400020; tel. (22) 2022535; telex 0113062; f. 1955 to assist industrial enterprises by providing finance in both rupee and foreign currencies in the form of long- or medium-term loans or equity participation, sponsoring and underwriting new issues of shares and securities, guaranteeing loans from other private investment sources, furnishing managerial, tech. and admin. advice to industry; also offers merchant banking and equip-

INDIA   Directory

ment leasing; regional offices at Calcutta, Madras and New Delhi; share cap. 495m.; res 1,255m. (1985); Chair. and Man. Dir N. VAGHUL.

Industrial Development Bank of India (IDBI): Nariman Bhavan, 227 Vinay K. Shah Marg, Nariman Point, Bombay 400021; telex 0112193; f. 1964, reorg. 1976; the main financial institution for co-ordinating and supplementing the working of other financial institutions and also for promoting and financing industrial development; 5 regional offices and 11 br. offices; cap. p.u. 4,150m., res 3,284m. (June 1985); Chair. and Man. Dir SURESH S. NADKARNI.

Industrial Finance Corpn of India: Bank of Baroda Bldg, 16 Sansad Marg, POB 363, New Delhi 110001; tel. (11) 2027012; telex 031-2623; f. 1948 to provide medium- and long-term finance to cos and co-operative socs in India, engaged in manufacture, preservation or processing of goods, shipping, mining, hotels and power generation and distribution; promotes industrialization of less developed areas, and sponsors training in management techniques and development banking; cap. p.u. 450m.; res 1,450m. (1985/86); Chair. D. N. DAVAR; Exec. Dir R. N. SAHOO; 8 regional offices and 10 br. offices.

National Bank for Agriculture and Rural Development: POB 6552, Garment House, Shivsagar Estate, Dr Annie Besant Rd, Worli, Bombay 400018; tel. (22) 369930; telex 115529; f. 1982 to provide credit for agricultural and rural development through commercial, co-operative and regional rural banks; cap. p.u. 1,000m. held 50% each by the central govt and the Reserve Bank; Chair. R. K. KAUL; Man. Dir G. P. BHAVE; 16 regional offices and 7 sub-offices.

STOCK EXCHANGES

There are 14 stock exchanges in India, including:

Ahmedabad Share and Stock Brokers' Association: Manekchowk, Ahmedabad 380001; tel. (272) 347149; f. 1894; 299 mems; Pres. NARESHBHAI LALBHAI PARIKH; Exec. Dir J. C. PANDYA; Sec. D. M. PANCHAL.

Bangalore Stock Exchange: Indian Bank Bldg, Kempegowda Rd, Bangalore 560009; tel. 227238; 36 mems; Pres. L. K. SRINIVASAMURTHY; Sec. M. RAGHAVENDRA.

Bombay Stock Exchange: Phiroze Jeejeebhoy Towers, Dalal St, Bombay 400023; tel. (22) 272720; telex 5925; f. 1875; 504 mems; Pres. RAMDAS LALLUBHAIDALAL; Exec. Dir M. R. MAYYA; Sec. A. J. SHAH.

Calcutta Stock Exchange Association Ltd: 7 Lyons Range, Calcutta 700001; f. 1908; 643 mems; Pres. S. L. BARDHAN; Exec. Dir S. R. BASU; Sec. P. K. DE.

Delhi Stock Exchange Association Ltd: 3 & 4/4B Asaf Ali Rd, New Delhi 110002; tel. (11) 271302; telex 31-65317; f. 1947; 125 mems; Pres. PREM CHAND JAIN; Exec. Dir R. K. PANDEY.

Madras Stock Exchange Ltd: POB 183, Exchange Bldg, 11 Second Line Beach, Madras 600001; tel. 512237; telex 041-8059; f. 1937; 81 mems; Pres. S. RAMASWAMI; Exec. Dir E. R. KRISHNAMURTI; Sec. S. RAMANATHAN.

INSURANCE

In January 1973 all Indian and foreign insurance companies were nationalized. The general insurance business in India is now transacted by only four companies, subsidiaries of the General Insurance Corpn of India.

Deposit Insurance Corpn: Vidyut Bhavan, Pathakwadi, Bombay 400002; provides insurance of up to Rs 10,000 to a depositor with funds in any of the 956 banks insured by the corpn; cap. 20m.; Chair. K. R. PURI; Man. V. S. MOHARIR.

General Insurance Corpn of India (GIC): Industrial Assurance Bldg, 4th Floor, Churchgate, Bombay 400020; tel. (22) 220046; telex 0113833; f. 1973 when 106 private life and non-life insurance cos were grouped under the four cos listed below: Man. Dirs C. N. S. SHASTRI, S. K. SETH, ASHOK GOENKA; subsidiaries:

National Insurance Co Ltd: 3 Middleton St, Calcutta 700071; telex 217074; cap. p.u. 80m.; res 348m.; Chair. and Man. Dir N. N. LAHIRI.

New India Assurance Co Ltd: New India Assurance Bldg, Mahatma Gandhi Rd, Fort, Bombay 400023; tel. (22) 274617; telex 112423; Chair. and Man. Dir K. C. PONNAPPA.

Oriental Fire and General Insurance Co Ltd: Oriental House, A-25/27 Asaf Ali Rd, New Delhi 110002; telex 313743; Chair. and Man. Dir H. J. SEQUERA.

United India Insurance Co Ltd: 24 Whites Rd, Madras 600014; tel. (44) 810061; telex 6141; cap. p.u. 200m.; res 684m.; Chair. and Man. Dir G. C. BHATTACHARJYA; Gen. Mans S. KRISHNAMURTHY, M. V. S. APPA RAO, C. B. KARIAPPA, Y. D. PATIL.

Life Insurance Corpn of India: Jeevan Bima Marg, Bombay 400021; tel. (22) 2021383; telex 0112327; f. 1956; cap. 50m.; life insurance fund 126,600m.; controls all life insurance business; Chair. R. NARAYANAN; Man. Dir C. R. THAKORE; 1,197 brs.

Insurance Association

Indian Insurance Companies' Association: Co-operative Insurance Bldg, Sir P. Mehta Rd, Fort, Bombay; f. 1928 to represent the interests of the insurance industry; 43 mems.

Trade and Industry

CHAMBERS OF COMMERCE

There are chambers of commerce in most commercial and industrial centres. The following are among the most important:

Associated Chambers of Commerce and Industry of India: 2nd Floor, Allahabad Bank Bldg, 17 Parliament St, New Delhi 110001; tel. (11) 310704; telex 31-2537; f. 1921; a central org. of chambers of commerce and industry representing over 6,000 cos throughout India; six industrial asscns, over 200 assoc. mems and 17 constituent chambers; Pres. B. R. SULE; Dir-Gen. AROON K. BASAK.

Federation of Indian Chambers of Commerce and Industry: Federation House, Tansen Marg, New Delhi 110001; tel. (11) 3319251; telex 03162521; 507 mem. bodies and 1,679 assoc. mems; Pres. K. S. G. HAJA SHAREEFF; Sec.-Gen. D. H. PAI PANANDIKER.

Indian National Committee of International Chamber of Commerce: Federation House, Tansen Marg, New Delhi 110001; tel. (11) 3319251; telex 0312546; f. 1979; 45 org. mems, 180 assoc. mems, 67 cttee mems; Pres. B. M. KHAITAN; Sec.-Gen. D. H. PAI PANANDIKER.

Bengal Chamber of Commerce and Industry: 6 Netaji Subhas Rd, Calcutta 700001; tel. (33) 228393; telex 217369; f. 1853; 215 mems; Pres. R. S. SIKAND; Sec. P. DAS GUPTA.

Bengal National Chamber of Commerce and Industry: 23 R. N. Mukherjee Rd, Calcutta 700001; telex 212189; f. 1887; 340 mems and 30 industrial and trading asscns are affiliated, some having common working arrangements; Pres. B. N. BHATTACHARJEE; Sec. SUNIL BANIK.

Bharat Chamber of Commerce: 28 Hernanta Basu Sarani, Calcutta 700001; tel. (33) 230023; f. 1900; 900 mems, 39 asscn mems; Pres. DHIRENDRA KUMAR; Sec. B. S. SARKAR (acting).

Bihar Chamber of Commerce: Judges' Court Rd, POB 71, Patna 800001; tel.(612) 53505; f. 1926; 800 mems, 150 asscn mems; Pres. R. K. P. N. SINGH; Sec.-Gen. S. N. PATWARI.

Bombay Chamber of Commerce and Industry: Mackinnon Mackenzie Bldg, 4 Shoorji Vallabhdas Marg, Ballard Estate, POB 473, Bombay 400001; tel. (22) 264681; telex 011-73571; f. 1836; 1,123 mems, 1,112 ordinary and 11 asscn mems; Pres. N. M. DESAI; Sec. B. P. GUNAJI.

Calcutta Chamber of Commerce: 18-H Park St, Stephen Court, Calcutta 700071; tel. (33) 240500; 375 mems; Pres. S. S. SWAIKA; Sec. P. K. JALAN.

Cocanada Chamber of Commerce: Commercial Rd, Kakinada 533007, Andhra Pradesh; tel. 6239; f. 1868; 42 mems; Chair. D. SURYA RAO; Sec. D. RADHA KRISHNA MURTY.

Gujarat Chamber of Commerce and Industry: Gujarat Chamber Bldg, Ranchhodlal Rd, POB 4045, Ahmedabad 380009; tel. (272) 402301; f. 1949; 5,979 mems; Pres. GAUTAMBHAI V. SHAH; Vice-Pres. DEEPAK NAVANITLAL; Hon. Sec. THAKORBHAI P. AMIN.

Indian Chamber of Commerce: India Exchange, 4 India Exchange Place, Calcutta 700001; tel. (33) 223242; telex 21-7432; f. 1925; 68 assoc. mems, 343 ordinary mems; Pres. SAROJ KUMAR PODDAR; Sec. B. K. AGRAWAL.

Indian Merchants' Chamber: 76 Veer Nariman Rd, Bombay 400020; tel. (22) 2046633; telex 015195; f. 1907; 159 asscn mems, 2,122 mem. firms, 38 assoc. mems; Pres. NALIN K. VISSANJI; Sec.-Gen. RAMU PANDIT.

Madras Chamber of Commerce and Industry: 41 Kasturi Ranga Rd, Alwarpet, Madras 600018; tel. (44) 451452; telex 041-536; f. 1836; 183 mem. firms, 22 assoc., 7 affiliated and 11 hon.; Chair. N. SANKAR; Sec. C. S. KRISHNASWAMI.

INDIA   Directory

Maharashtra Chamber of Commerce: K. Dubhash Marg, Bombay 400023; tel. (22) 244548; telex 113527; f. 1927; over 2,000 mems; Pres. PADMAKAR DHAMDHERE; Sec.-Gen. S. S. PINGLE.

Merchants' Chamber of Uttar Pradesh: 14/76 Civil Lines, Kanpur; tel. (532) 210617; f. 1932; 170 mems, 60 industrial category mems and 170 traders' category mems; Pres. K. B. AGARWAL; Sec. B. K. PARIEK.

North India Chamber of Commerce and Industry: 9 Gandhi Rd, Dehra Dun, Uttar Pradesh; tel. (935) 23479; f. 1967; 102 mems, 29 asscn mems, 5 mem. firms, 91 assoc. mems; Pres. DEV PANDHI; Hon. Sec. ASHOK K. NARANG; Sec.-Gen. B. L. JAIN.

Oriental Chamber of Commerce: 6 Dr Rajendra Prasad Sarani (Clive Row), Calcutta 700001; tel. (33) 203609; f. 1932; 276 mems, five assoc. mems; Pres. SYED ZAFAR ALI; Joint Sec. KAZI ABU ZOBER.

PHD Chamber of Commerce and Industry: PHD House, 4/2 Siri Institutional Area, opp. Asian Games Village, POB 130, New Delhi 110016; tel. (11) 665425; telex 031-61958; f. 1905; 1,005 mems; Pres. K. P. SINGH; Sec.-Gen. M. L. NANDRAJOG.

Southern India Chamber of Commerce and Industry: Indian Chamber Bldgs, Esplanade, Madras 600108; tel. (44) 562228; telex 41-6689; f. 1909; 1,000 mems; Pres. A. C. MUTHIAH; Sec. J. PRASAD DAVIDS.

United Chamber of Trade Associations: Amirchand Marg, Katra Rathi, Delhi 110006; tel. (11) 238444; 107 assoc. mems; Pres. MAHESHAWR DAYAL; Sec.-Gen. P. R. MITTAL.

Upper India Chamber of Commerce: POB 63, 14/113 Civil Lines; Kanpur 208001; tel. (512) 210684; f. 1888; 136 mems; Pres. GOKUL DAS NAGORY; Sec. K. K. GANGADHARAN.

Uttar Pradesh Chamber of Commerce: 15/197 Civil Lines, Kanpur 208001; tel. 62321; f. 1914; 200 mems; Pres. V. K. SRIVASTAVA; Sec. AFTAB SAMI.

FOREIGN TRADE CORPORATIONS

Export Credit Guarantee Corpn of India Ltd: POB 373, Express Towers, 10th Floor, Nariman Point, Bombay 400021; tel. (22) 2023023; telex 0113231; f. 1964 to insure for risks involved in exports on credit terms and to supplement credit facilities by issuing guarantees, etc.; cap. p.u. Rs25m.; res 231.3m.; Chair. and Man. Dir M. K. VENKATESHAN; Gen. Man. K. G. KRISHNA.

Minerals and Metals Trading Corpn of India Ltd: POB 7051, Express Bldg, 9 and 10, Bahadur Shah Zafar Marg, New Delhi 110002; tel. (11) 3319448; telex 31-2285; f. 1963; export of iron and manganese ore, ferro-manganese, finished stainless steel products, mica, coal and other minor minerals; import of steel, non-ferrous metals, rough diamonds, fertilizers, etc. for supply to industrial units in the country; auth. cap. Rs500m.; 10 regional offices in India; foreign offices in Japan and Romania; Chair. S. V. S. RAGHAVAN; Exec. Dirs R. GANAPATHY, I. P. HAZARIKA, S. K. AGARWAL, BHUPINDER SINGH.

State Trading Corpn of India Ltd: Chandralok, 36 Janpath, New Delhi 110001; tel. (11) 353164; telex 31-65180; f. 1956; govt undertaking dealing in exports and imports; 17 regional brs and 17 offices overseas; Chair. SUDHIR JAYANTILAL MULJI; Exec. Dirs S. JAYARAMAN, Dr T. PRAKASH, B. K. SHROFF, A. SAHAY.

Cashew Corpn of India Ltd: POB 1019, Ernakulam, Mahatma Gandhi Rd, Cochin 682011; tel. (484) 32177; telex 885202; imports raw cashew nuts for distribution to the export-orientated sector of the cashew processing industry; also undertakes exports of cashew kernels; Chair. A. S. BHATIA.

Handicrafts and Handloom Export Corpn of India Ltd: Lok Kalyan Bhavan, 11A Rouse Ave Lane, New Delhi 110002; tel. (11) 3311086; telex 31-61522; f. 1958; undertakes export of handicrafts, handloom goods, ready-to-wear clothes, carpets and precious jewellery while promoting exports and trade development; auth. cap. Rs75m.; Chair. and Man. Dir M. P. PINTO; Gen. Man. J. C. SARIN.

Projects and Equipment Corpn of India Ltd: Hansalaya, 15 Barakhamba Rd, New Delhi 110001; tel. (11) 3313351; telex 31-65256; f. 1971; export of engineering, industrial and railway equipment; undertakes turnkey and other projects and management consultancy abroad; Chair. and Man. Dir Col R. M. SINGH.

Trade Development Authority: POB 767, Bank of Baroda Bldg, 16 Parliament St, New Delhi 110001; tel. (11) 310214; telex 031-65155; f. 1970 to promote selective development of exports of high quality products; arranges investment in export-oriented ventures undertaken by India with foreign collaboration; brs in Frankfurt, New York, Tokyo, Harare, Abu Dhabi, (Los Angeles and Kuala Lumpur from April 1987); Chair. PREM KUMAR; Exec. Dir K. OBAYYA.

INDUSTRIAL AND AGRICULTURAL ORGANIZATIONS

Organizations engaged in the financing of agricultural and industrial development are listed under Finance. There are also industrial development corporations in the separate states. The following are among the more important industrial and agricultural organizations.

Coal India Ltd: 10 Netaji Subhas Rd, Calcutta 700001; tel. (33) 239101; telex 021-7180; Govt of India holding company with five subsidiaries; responsible for planning and production of coal mines; Chair. and Man. Dir GULSHAN LAL TANDON.

Cotton Corpn of India Ltd: Air India Bldg, 12th Floor, Nariman Point, Bombay 400021; tel. (22) 2024363; telex 0113463; f. 1970 to act as an agency in the public sector for the purchase, sale and distribution of home-produced cotton and imported cotton staple fibre; exports long staple cotton; Chair. and Man. Dir N. JAYARAMAN.

Fertilizer Corpn of India Ltd: Madhuban, 55 Nehru Place, New Delhi 110019; tel. (11) 6439694; telex 031-5197; f. 1961; two operating fertilizer factories at Sindri and Gorakhpur; two at Talcher and Ramagundam, producing nitrogenous, phosphatic and some industrial products; Chair. and Man. Dir R. GUPTA.

Food Corpn of India: 16–20 Barakhamba Lane, New Delhi 110001; tel. (11) 3310551; telex 31-2418; f. 1965 to undertake trading in food-grains on a commercial scale but within the framework of an overall govt policy; to provide the farmer an assured price for his produce, supply food-grains to the consumer at reasonable prices; also purchases, stores, distributes and sells food-grains and other foodstuffs and arranges imports and handling of food-grains and fertilizers at the ports; distributes sugar in a number of states and has set up rice mills; Chair. T. C. DUTT; Man. Dir AJIT SINGH.

Forest Development Corpn of Maharashtra Ltd: 6A Nawab Layout, Tilak Nagar, Nagpur 440010; f. 1974 to undertake large-scale forest redevelopment, by felling areas of uneconomic forest and planting them with teak to increase the income from timber and provide employment; Man. Dir M. Y. SOWANI.

Housing and Urban Development Corpn Ltd: HUDCO House, Lodhi Rd, New Delhi 110003; tel. (11) 693022; telex 013-61037; f. 1970; to finance and undertake housing and urban development programmes including the setting-up of new or satellite towns and building material industries; auth. cap. Rs810m. (1986); six brs; Chair. and Man. Dir S. K. SHARMA.

Indian Dairy Corpn: Suraj Plaza II, Sayajigunj, Baroda 390005; tel. (265) 66637; telex 0175239; objects: to promote dairying in India; to execute the IDA/EEC/Govt of India dairy development programme 'Operation Flood' which aims at covering 155 districts for dairy development to link them to major urban centres for milk marketing to enable the organized dairy sector to obtain a commanding share of these markets, to set up a national milk herd and a national milk network; Chair. Dr V. KURIEN; Man. Dir G. M. JHALA.

Jute Corpn of India Ltd: 1 Shakespeare Sarani, Calcutta 700071; telex 213266; f. 1971; objects: (i) to undertake price support operations in respect of raw jute; (ii) to ensure remunerative prices to producers through efficient marketing; (iii) to operate a buffer stock to stabilize raw jute prices; (iv) to handle the import and export of raw jute; (v) to promote the export of jute goods; Chair. and Man. Dir B. K. BHATTACHARYA.

National Co-operative Development Corpn: 4 Siri Institutional Area, Hauz Khas, New Delhi 110016; tel. (11) 669246; telex 31-66359; f. 1962 to plan and promote country-wide programmes through co-operative societies for the production, processing, marketing, storage, export and import of agricultural produce, foodstuffs and notified commodities; also programmes for the development of poultry, dairy, fish products, coir, handlooms, distribution of consumer articles in rural areas and minor forest produce in the co-operative sector; seven regional and seven project offices; Pres. S. GURDIAL SINGH DHILLON; Man. Dir R. V. GUPTA.

National Industrial Development Corpn Ltd: Chanakya Bhavan, Africa Ave, Chanakyapuri, POB 5212, New Delhi 110021; tel. (11) 670154; telex 031-62891; f. 1954; auth. cap. Rs10m.; consultative engineering services to central and state govts, public and private sector enterprises, the UN and overseas investors; Chair. and Man. Dir R. C. BAJPAI; Technical Dir R. S. TYAGI.

National Mineral Development Corpn Ltd: POB 52, Khanÿ Bhavan, 10-3-311/A Castle Hills, Masab Tank, Hyderabad 500028; tel. (842) 222071; telex 155-6452; f. 1958; central govt undertaking under the Ministry of Steel and Mines; to exploit minerals (excluding coal, atomic minerals, lignite, petroleum and natural gas) in public sector; may buy, take on lease or otherwise acquire mines for prospecting, development and exploitation; iron ore mines at Bailadila-11C, Bailadila-14 and Bailadila-5 in Madhya Pradesh, and at Donimalai in Karnataka State, and diamond mines at Panna in Madhya Pradesh; research and development laboratories and consultancy wing at Hyderabad; investigates mineral projects; iron ore production in 1984/85 was 6.92m. metric tons, diamond production 14,978 carats; Chair. and Man. Dir P. C. GUPTA.

National Productivity Council: Productivity House, Lodi Rd, New Delhi 110003; tel. (11) 690331; f. 1958 to increase productivity and to improve quality by improved techniques which aim at efficient and proper utilization of available resources; autonomous body representing national orgs of employers and labour, govt ministries, professional orgs, local productivity councils, small-scale industries and other interests; 75 mems; Chair. D. V. KAPUR; Dir-Gen. Dr G. K. SURI.

National Research Development Corpn of India: 20–22, Zamroodpur Community Centre, Kailash Colony Extension, New Delhi 110048; tel. (11) 6432121; telex 31-65094; f. 1953 to stimulate development and commercial exploitation of new inventions with financial and technical aid; finances development projects to set up demonstration units in collaboration with industry; exports technology; Man. Dir N. K. SHARMA.

National Seeds Corpn Ltd: Beej Bhavan, Pusa, New Delhi 110012; tel. (11) 569712; telex 31-3705; f. 1963 to improve and develop the seed industry; Chair. K. P. A. MENON; Man. Dir Dr S. K. SENGUPTA.

National Small Industries Corpn Ltd: Near Industrial Estate, Okhla, New Delhi 110020; tel. (11) 632874; telex 31-62131; f. 1955 to aid, advise, finance, protect and promote the interests of small industries; auth. cap. Rs300m., issued Rs208m., all shares held by the govt; Chair. J. S. JUNEJA.

Rehabilitation Industries Corpn Ltd: 25 Free School St, Calcutta 700016; f. 1959 to create employment opportunities through industries for refugees from Bangladesh and migrants from West Pakistan, repatriates from Burma and Sri Lanka, and other immigrants of Indian extraction; Chair. B. K. DASCHOWDHURY; Man. Dir A. R. KOHLI.

State Farms Corpn of India Ltd: Farm Bhavan, 14–15 Nehru Place, New Delhi 110019; tel. (11) 6413125; f. 1969 to administer the central state farms; activities include the production of quality seeds of high-yielding varieties of wheat, paddy, maize, bajra and jowar; advises on soil conservation, reclamation and development of waste and forest land; consultancy services on farm mechanization; auth. cap. Rs150m.; Chair. A. R. MALLU; Man. Dir T. S. G. NAIR.

Steel Authority of India Ltd: Ispat Bhawan, Lodi Rd, New Delhi 110003; tel. (11) 690481; telex 31-2979; f. 1973 to provide co-ordinated development of the steel industry in both the public and private sectors; steel plants at Bhilai, Bokaro, Durgapur, Rourkela, Salem; alloy steel plant at Durgapur; subsidiaries Indian Iron and Steel Corpn Ltd, Burnpur; combined ingot steel capacity is 10.2m. metric tons annually; cap. p.u. Rs37,136.5m.; res Rs731.8m.; Chair. V. KRISHNAMURTI.

Tea Board of India: POB 2172, 14 Brabourne Rd, Calcutta 700001; tel. (33) 260210; telex 021-4527; f. to provide financial assistance to tea research stations; sponsors and finances independent research projects in universities and tech. institutions to supplement the work of tea research establishments; also promotes tea producion and export; Chair. R. K. TRIPATHY.

PRINCIPAL INDUSTRIAL ASSOCIATIONS

Ahmedabad Textile Mills' Association: Ranchhodlal Marg, Navrangpura, Ahmedabad 380009; tel. (272) 408927; telex 121-227; f. 1891; 48 mems; Pres. MANUBHAI H. PATEL; Exec. Dir M. D. RAJPAL.

Bharat Krishak Samaj (Farmers' Forum, India): A-1 Nizamuddin West, New Delhi 110013; tel. (11) 619508; f. 1954; national farmers' org.; Pres. (Ex-Officio) Minister of Agriculture and Rural Development; over 1m. ordinary mems; 40,000 life mems; Chair. Dr BALRAM JAKHAR; Sec.-Gen. Dr D. A. BHOLAY.

Bombay Millowners' Association: POB 95, Elphinstone Bldg, 10 Veer Nariman Rd, Fort, Bombay 400001; tel. (22) 2040411; f. 1875; 46 mem. cos; Chair. SUDHIR K. THACKERSEY; Sec.-Gen. R. L. N. VIJAYANAGAR.

Bombay Motor Merchants' Association Ltd: Sukh Sagar, 3rd Floor, Sandhurst Bridge, Bombay 400007; tel. (22) 356669; 495 mems; Pres. S. PRABHJOT SINGH CHANDHOK; Gen. Sec. SANMUKH SINGH SETHI.

Bombay Piece-Goods Merchants' Mahajan: Shaikh Memon St, Bombay 400002; tel. (22) 255750; f. 1881; 1,752 mems; Pres. SURENDRA TULSIDAS SAVAI; Secs PRAMOD P. NARSANA, PRASANNA M. SHAH.

Bombay Presidency Association: 107 M. Gandhi Rd, Bombay 400023; f. 1886; Pres. NAUSHIR BHARUCHA.

Bombay Textile and Engineering Association: 343 Sattar Bldg, Grant Rd, Bombay 400007; f. 1900; Pres. N. F. BHARUCHA.

Calcutta Baled Jute Association: 6 Netaji Subhas Rd, Calcutta 700001; tel. (22) 208393; telex 217369; f. 1892; 49 mems; Chair. PURANMULL KANKARIA; Sec. A. E. SCOLT.

Calcutta Flour Mills Association: 6 Netaji Subhas Rd, Calcutta 700001; tel. (33) 208393; telex 21-7369; f. 1932; 22 mems; Chair. R. C. PAROLIA (acting); Sec. PROSENJIT DAS GUPTA.

Confederation of the Engineering Industry—CEI (Association of the Indian Engineering Industry—AIEI): 172 Jor Bagh, New Delhi 110003; tel. (11) 615115; telex 031-66655; f. 1974 by merger of Engineering Asscn of India and Indian Engineering Asscn; 1,900 mem. companies, 35 affiliated asscns; Pres. K. N. SHENOY; Sec. TARUN DAS.

East India Cotton Association Ltd: Cotton Exchange, Marwari Bazar, Bombay 400002; tel. (22) 314876; f. 1921; 335 mems; Pres. CHANDRASINH H. MIRANI; Sec. V. M. UNCHAGAONKAR.

Federation of Gujarat Mills and Industries: Federation Bldg, R. C. Dutt Rd, Baroda 390005; tel. (265) 65101; f. 1918; 281 mems; Pres. VIREN PATEL; Sec. P. J. SATHE.

Federation of Indian Export Organizations: 4/2 SIRI Institutional Area, Hauz Khas, New Delhi 110016; tel. (11) 666582; telex 031-065194; f. 1965; 1,968 mems; Pres. VIRENDARA P. PUNJ; Sec. Gen. CHANDRAKANT G. RAO.

Grain, Rice and Oilseeds Merchants' Association: Grain-seeds House, 72/80 Yusef Meheralli Rd, Bombay 400003; tel. (22) 324021; f. 1899; 967 mems; Pres. RAICHAND LILADHAR SHAH; Sec. R. J. BHATT.

Indian Chemical Manufacturers' Association: India Exchange, 4 India Exchange Place, Calcutta 700001; tel. (33) 203242; telex 0217432; f. 1938; 245 mems; Pres. K. R. V. SUBRAHMANIAN; Sec. B. K. AGRAWAL.

Industries and Commerce Association: ICO Association Rd, POB 70, Dhanbad 826001 (Bihar); tel. (326) 2639; f. 1933; 79 mems; Pres. HARSUKH WORAH; Asst Sec. D. D. BANERJEE.

Indian Jute Mills Association: Royal Exchange, 6 Netaji Subhas Rd, Calcutta 700001; tel. (33) 209918; telex 217369; sponsors and operates export promotion, research and product development; regulates labour relations; Chair. B. K. JALAN.

Indian Mining Association: 6 Netaji Subhas Rd, Calcutta 700001; tel. (33) 263861; telex 217369; f. 1892; 50 mems; Sec. K. MUKERJEE.

Indian Mining Federation: 135 Biplabi Rashbehari Basu Rd, Calcutta 700001; tel. (33) 250484; f. 1913 to aid and stimulate mining, particularly coal, and to protect the commercial interests; 65 mems; Chair. H. S. CHOPRA; Sec. S. K. GHOSE.

Indian National Shipowners' Association: 22 Maker Tower F, Cuffe Parade, Bombay 400005; tel. (22) 211268; telex 011-4611; f. 1929; 30 mems; Pres. Capt. R. D. KOHLI; Sec. B. V. NILKUND.

Indian Paper Mills Association: India Exchange, 8th Floor, India Exchange Place, Calcutta 700001; f. 1939; 40 mems; Pres. SHANKAR GHOSH; Asst Sec. B. GHOSH.

Indian Sugar Mills Association: Sugar House, 39 Nehru Place, New Delhi 110019; tel. (11) 6416601; f. 1932; 168 mems; Pres. DHRUV M. SAWHNEY; Sec.-Gen. J. S. MEHTA.

Indian Tea Association: Royal Exchange, 6 Netaji Subhas Rd, Calcutta 700001; tel. (33) 208393; telex 217369; f. 1881; 219 mems; 456 tea estates; Chair. R. L. RIKHYE; Sec. Y. K. VOHRA.

Jute Balers' Association: 12 India Exchange Place, Calcutta 700001; tel. (33) 221491; f. 1909; 265 mems; represents all Indian jute balers; Chair. HAJARIMALL PANDYA; Sec. SUJIT CHOUDHURY.

Master Stevedores' Association: Royal Exchange, 6 Netaji Subhas Rd, Calcutta 700001; tel. (33) 208393; telex 217369; f. 1934; 11 mems; Pres. D. S. BOSE; Sec. ALBAN E. SCOLT.

Silk and Art Silk Mills' Association Ltd: Resham Bhavan, 78 Veer Nariman Rd, Bombay 400020; tel. (22) 2041006; telex 11-4685; f. 1939; 667 mems; Chair. M. H. DOSHI; Sec. D. A. JOSHI.

Southern India Mills' Association: Racecourse, Coimbatore 641018, Tamil Nadu; f. 1933; 200 mems; Chair. D. LAKSHMINARAYANASWAMY; Sec. T. RANGASWAMY.

INDIA — Directory

EMPLOYERS' FEDERATIONS

Council of Indian Employers: Federation House, Tansen Marg, New Delhi 110001; tel. (11) 3319252; telex 031-2546; f. 1956; Sec. R. C. Pande; comprises:

All-India Organization of Employers (AIOE): Federation House, Tansen Marg, New Delhi 110001; tel. (11) 3315292; telex 031-2546; f. 1932; mems 8 industrial asscns and 8 corporate cos; Pres. A. S. Kasliwal; Sec.-Gen. D. H. Pai Panandikar; Sec. R. C. Pande.

Employers' Federation of India (EFI): Army and Navy Bldg, 148 Mahatma Gandhi Rd, Bombay 400023; tel. (22) 245070; telex 0112529; f. 1933; 228 mems; Pres. Keshub Mahindra; Sec. V. B. Mahatme.

Standing Conference of Public Enterprises (SCOPE): 7 Pragati Vihar, Lodi Estate, New Delhi 110003; tel. (11) 362604; telex 031-3857; f. 1973; representative body of all central public enterprises in India; advises the govt and public enterprises on matters of major policy and co-ordination; 200 mems; Chair. S. P. Wahi; Sec. Waris Rasheed Kidwai.

Employers' Association of Northern India: 14/69 Civil Lines, POB 344, Kanpur 208001; tel. (512) 48185; f. 1937; 126 mems; Chair. R. C. Agarwal; Sec. D. Massey (acting).

Employers' Federation of Southern India: 41 Kasturi Ranga Rd, Alwarpet, Madras 600018; tel. (44) 451452; telex 41536; f. 1920; 241 mem. firms; Pres. C. Rajagopalan; Sec. C. S. Krishnaswami.

TRADE UNIONS

In the absence of compulsory registration and the need to file returns, a precise estimate of the aggregate trades-union membership in India is not available, but in 1986 it was believed that only about 10m. workers, out of a labour force of 222.5m., belonged to unions.

Indian National Trade Union Congress (INTUC): 1B Maulana Azad Rd, New Delhi 110011; tel. (11) 3018150; f. 1947; the largest and most representative trade union org. in India; 4,298 affiliated unions with a total membership of 3,957,660; affiliated to ICFTU; 26 state brs and 25 national industrial federations; Pres. G. Ramanujan; Gen. Sec. Kanti Mehta.

Centre of Indian Trade Unions: 6 Talkatora Rd, New Delhi 110001; tel. (11) 384071; f. 1970; 1.8m. mems; over 3,000 affiliated unions; Pres. B. T. Ranadive; Gen. Sec. Samar Mukherjee.

National industrial federations:

All India Council of Atomic Energy Employees: Tel Rasayan Bhavan, Tilak Rd, Dadar, Bombay 400014; f. 1981; 3,000 mems; Pres. Raja Kulkarni; Gen. Sec. Mary Emmanuel.

Indian National Cement and Allied Workers' Federation: Mazdoor Karyalaya, Congress House, Bombay 400004; tel. (22) 351809; 52,800 mems; Pres. H. N. Trivedi; Gen. Sec. N. Nanjappan.

Indian National Chemical Workers' Federation: Tel Rasayan Bhavan, Tilak Rd, Dadar, Bombay 400014; Pres. Raja Kulkarni; Gen. Sec. K. H. Dastoor.

Indian National Defence Workers' Federation: 25/19 Karachi Khana, Kanpur; Pres. Kali Mukherjee.

Indian National Electricity Workers' Federation: 19 Mazdoor Maidan, Power House, Jaipur 302006; tel. (141) 76175; 124,600 mems; 17 affiliated unions; Pres. Dalip Singh Azad; Gen. Sec. Damodar Maurya.

Indian National Metal Workers' Federation: 26 K Rd, Jamshedpur 831001; tel. (657) 3506; Pres. V. G. Gopal; Gen. Sec. S. Gopeshwar.

Indian National Mineworkers' Federation: Michael John Smriti Bhawan, Rajendra Path, Dhanbad, Bihar; tel. 3506; f. 1949; 364,151 mems in 155 affiliated unions; Pres. Kanti Mehta; Gen. Sec. S. Das Gupta.

Indian National Paper Mill Workers' Federation: Ballarpur, Chanda; Pres. G. Sanjeeva Reddy; Gen. Sec. P. J. Nair.

Indian National Port and Dock Workers' Federation: PB 87, Vasco-da-Gama 403802, Goa; f. 1954; 18 affiliated unions; 81,000 mems; Pres. Mohan Nair; Gen. Sec. Janaki Mukherjee.

Indian National Press Workers' Federation: 162 South Ave, New Delhi 110011; Pres. S. W. Dhabe.

Indian National Sugar Mills Workers' Federation: 19 Lajpatrai Marg, Lucknow; tel. (522) 47638; 100 affiliated unions; 40,000 mems; Pres. C. Singh; Gen. Sec. Ram Yash Singh.

Indian National Textile Workers' Federation: Mazdoor Manzil, G. D. Ambekar Marg, Parel, Bombay 400012; tel. (22) 4123713; f. 1948; 403 affiliated unions; 532,295 mems; Pres. P. L. Subbaiha; Gen. Sec. H. J. Naik.

Indian National Transport Workers' Federation: Sham Shivir, Tansen Marg, Gwalior 474002; Pres. T. S. Viyogi; Gen. Sec. K. S. Verma.

National Federation of Petroleum Workers: Tel Rasayan Bhavan, Tilak Rd, Dadar, Bombay 400014; f. 1959; 22,340 mems; Pres. Raja Kulkarni.

Assam Chah Karmachari Sangha: POB 13, Dibrugarh 786001; tel. (33) 20870; 10,703 mems; 20 brs; Pres. Bijoy Chandra Bhagavati; Gen. Sec. A. K. Bhattacharya.

All-India Trade Union Congress: 24 Canning Lane, New Delhi 110001; tel. (11) 386427; f. 1920; affiliated to WFTU; 3.03m. mems, 3,229 affiliated unions; 19 state brs, eight national federations; Pres. Chaturanan Mishra; Gen. Sec. Indrajit Gupta.

Major affiliated unions:

Annamalai Plantation Workers' Union: Valparai, Via Pollachi, Tamil Nadu; over 21,000 mems.

Zilla Cha Bagan Workers' Union: Malabar, Jalpaiguri, West Bengal; 21,000 mems.

United Trades Union Congress (UTUC): 249 Bepin Behari Ganguly St, Calcutta 700012; f. 1949; 608,052 mems from 607 affiliated unions; 10 state brs; Pres. N. Srikantan Nair; Sec.-Gen. P. Chowdhury.

Major affiliated unions:

All-India Farm Labour Union: c/o UTUC Jakkanpur New Area, Patna 800001, Bihar; over 35,000 mems (est.).

Bengal Provincial Chatkal Mazdoor Union: 64 Chittarajan Ave, Calcutta 700012; textile workers; 28,330 mems.

Hind Mazdoor Sabha (HMS): Nagindas Chambers, 167 P. D'Mello Rd, Bombay 400038; tel. (22) 262185; f. 1948; affiliated to ICFTU; 2.1m. mems from 1,300 affiliated unions; 18 regional brs; Pres. Rajkishore Samantrai; Gen. Sec. Umraomal Purohit.

Major affiliated unions:

Bombay Port Trust Employees Union: Pres. Dr Shanti Patel; Gen. Sec. S. K. Shetye.

Colliery Mazdoor Congress (Coalminers' Union) **and Koyala Ispat Mazdoor Panchayat Jharia-Asansol:** coal and steel workers; Working Pres. P. Tiwari; Gen. Sec. Jayanta Podder.

Oil and Natural Gas Commission Employees Mazdoor Sabha: Vododara; 4,000 mems; Pres. R. Dulare; Gen. Sec. G. G. Paradkar.

South Central Railway Mazdoor Union: 7C, Railway Bldg, Accounts Office Compound, Secunderabad 500025 AP; tel. (842) 77823; f. 1966; 71,572 mems; Pres. K. S. N. Murthy; Gen. Sec. A. V. K. Chaitanya; 118 branches.

West Bengal Chah Sramik Union: Jalpaiguri, West Bengal; tel. 156; 40,025 mems; Pres. B. D. Rai; Gen. Sec. Deven Sarkar.

Confederation of Central Government Employees' Unions: New Delhi; c. 700,000 mems; Pres. M. Bhakta; Sec.-Gen. R. K. Sangle.

Affiliated union:

National Federation of Post, Telephone and Telegraph Employees (NFPTTE): C-1/2 Baird Rd, New Delhi 110001; tel. (11) 322545; f. 1954; 221,880 mems (est.); Pres. R. G. Sharma; Gen. Sec. O. P. Gupta.

All-India Bank Employees' Association (AIBEA): 10/9 East Patel Nagar, New Delhi; Pres. D. P. Chadda; Gen. Sec. Tarakeswar Chakravarty.

All-India Defence Employees' Federation (AIDEF): 70 Market Rd, Pune 411003; tel. (212) 58761; 298 affiliated unions; 350,000 mems; Pres. S. M. Banerjee; Gen. Sec. K. M. Mathew.

All-India Port and Dock Workers' Federation: 9 Second Line Beach, Madras, 600001; tel. (44) 25983; f. 1948; 100,000 mems in 26 affiliated unions; Pres. S. R. Kulkarni; Gen. Sec. S. C. C. Anthony Pillai.

All-India Railwaymen's Federation (AIRF): 4 State Entry Rd, New Delhi 110055; tel. (11) 322993; f. 1924; 747,372 mems; 13 affiliated unions; Pres. U. M. Purohit; Gen. Sec. J. P. Chaubey.

National Federation of Indian Railwaymen (NFIR): 3 Chelmsford Rd, New Delhi 110055; f. 1952; 15 affiliated unions; 600,162 mems; Pres. T. V. Anandan; Gen. Sec. Keshav H. Kulkarni.

Transport

RAILWAYS

India's railway system is the largest in Asia and the fourth largest in the world. The total length of Indian railways in March 1984 was 61,460 route-km. The Government exercises direct or indirect control over all railways through the Railway Board.

A 16.43-km underground railway for Calcutta is scheduled for completion by 1988. In 1986 the underground network covered a total of 10.6 km, in two sections. It is expected to carry more than 1m. people daily.

Indian Government Administration (Ministry of Transport, Railway Board): Rail Bhawan, Raisina Rd, New Delhi; tel. (11) 388931; telex 31-3561; Chair. PRAKASH NARAIN.

Zonal Railways

The railways are grouped into nine zones:

Central: Victoria Terminus, Bombay; tel. (22) 268041; Gen. Man. VIJAYA SINGH.

Eastern: 17 Netaji Subhas Rd, Calcutta 700001; tel. (33) 226811; Gen. Man. HRISHIKESH BANDOPADHYAY.

North Eastern: Gorakhpur 273012; tel. (551) 3041; Gen. Man. Y. B. L. MATHUR.

Northeast Frontier: Maligaon, Guwahati 781011; tel. 88422; Gen. Man. P. S. CHOUDHURI.

Northern: Baroda House, New Delhi 110001; tel. (11) 387227; Gen. Man. S. K. DATTA.

South Central: Rail Nilayam, Secunderabad 500371; tel. (842) 74848; Gen. Man. P. K. SRINIVASAN.

South Eastern: Calcutta 700043; tel. (33) 451741; Gen. Man. ANUP SINGH.

Southern: Park Town, Madras 600003; tel. (44) 33157; Gen. Man. K. VISWANATHAN.

Western: Churchgate, Bombay 400020; tel. (22) 298016; Gen. Man. RANJIT MATHUR.

ROADS

In March 1983 there were 1,554,000 km of roads in India, 31,710 km of which were national highways and 95,369 km state highways. Total outlay on roads and bridges in the sixth Five-Year Plan (1980–1985) was Rs34,389.6m., and the proposed total outlay in the seventh Five-Year Plan (1985–90) was Rs52,000m. Proposed expenditure on roads in the 1986/87 budget was Rs6,180m.

Ministry of Shipping and Transport (Roads Wing): Transport Bhawan No. 1, Parliament St, New Delhi 110001; tel. (11) 385047; telex 31-2448; responsible for the maintenance of India's system of national highways, with a total length of about 31,710 km in 1984, connecting the state capitals and major ports and linking with the highway systems of neighbouring countries. This system includes 63 highways which constitute the main trunk roads of the country.

Border Roads Development Board: f. 1960 to accelerate the economic development of the north and north-eastern border areas; it has constructed and improved 17,895 km of existing roads and surfaced 13,850 (1985).

Central Road Transport Corpn Ltd: 4 Fairlie Place, Calcutta 700001; f. 1964 to supplement the transport capacity in the eastern sector of the country; fleet of over 200 trucks; Chair. Commdr K. CHELLIAH; Man. Dir M. YUSUF KHAN.

INLAND WATERWAYS

About 16,180 km of rivers are navigable by power-driven craft, and 3,631 km by large country boats. Services are mainly on the Ganga and Brahmaputra and their tributaries, the Godavari, the Mahanadi, the Narmada, the Tapi and the Krishna.

Central Inland Water Transport Corpn Ltd: 4 Fairlie Place, Calcutta 1; tel. (33) 222321; telex 212779; f. 1967; inland water transport services in Bangladesh and the north-east Indian states; also shipbuilding and repairing, general engineering, dredging, lightening of ships and barge services; Chair. and Man. Dir S. K. BHOSE.

SHIPPING

In July 1984 India was 16th on the list of principal merchant fleets of the world. In March 1986 the fleet had 362 vessels totalling 9.5m. dwt. There are some 53 shipping companies in India. The major ports are Bombay, Calcutta, Cochin, Kandla, Madras, Mangalore, Mormugao, Pradip (Paradeep), Tuticorin and Vishakhapatnam (Visakhapatnam). An auxiliary port to Calcutta at Haldia was opened to international shipping in 1977 and has since undergone further modernization. An auxiliary port to Bombay at Nhavasheva was due to be completed by 1985. Provision of Rs12,610m. was made in the seventh Five-Year Plan for development of ports.

Bombay

Bharat Line Ltd: Bharat House, 104 Apollo St, Fort, Bombay 400001; Chair. and Man. Dir GUNVANTRAI T. KAMDAR; brs in Calcutta, Bhavnagar and Madras.

Great Eastern Shipping Co Ltd: Hong Kong Bank Bldg, 60 Mahatma Gandhi Rd, Bombay 400023; tel. (22) 274869; telex 2824; f. 1948; cargo services; 23 vessels; Chair. VASANT J. SHETH; Dep. Chair. and Man. Dir K. M. SHETH; office in New Delhi.

Malabar Steamship Co Ltd, The: 4th Floor, Express Towers, Nariman Point, Bombay 400021, POB 34; f. 1935; cargo and transport services; three vessels; Gen. Man. R. H. NARECHANIA; brs in Calcutta and Cochin.

Scindia Steam Navigation Co Ltd: Scindia House, Narottam Morarjee Marg, Ballard Estate, Bombay 400038; tel. (22) 268161; telex 011-73519; f. 1919; cargo services; 28 vessels totalling 424,408 grt; Chair. Mrs SUMATI MORARJEE; brs at Calcutta, Gandhidham, Mangalore and London.

Shipping Corpn of India Ltd: Shipping House, 245 Madame Cama Rd, Bombay 400021; tel. (22) 2022653; telex 011-2371; f. 1961 as a govt undertaking; took over Jayanti Shipping Co Ltd in 1973 and Mogul Line Ltd in 1986; fleet of 146 vessels of 5.36m. dwt, consisting of tankers, freighters, VLCCs, combination carriers, product carriers, passenger-cum-cargo ships, bulk carriers; operates 24 services; brs in Calcutta, New Delhi, Mombasa, Rameshwaram and London; Chair. and Man. Dir L. M. S. RAJWAR.

South-East Asia Shipping Co Ltd: 402–406 Himalaya House, Dr Dadabhoy Naoroji Rd, Bombay 400001; tel. (22) 269231; telex 112753; f. 1948; world-wide cargo services; five vessels of 61,259 dwt; Chair. N. H. DHUNJIBHOY; CEO D. P. ADENWALLA.

Calcutta

India Steamship Co Ltd: 21 Old Court House St, POB 2090, Calcutta 700001; tel. (33) 231171; telex 0212549; cargo services; 20 vessels; Chair. K. K. BIRLA; CEO Cdre A. K. SARKAR; brs in Bombay, Kakinada, Visakhapatnam, Delhi and London.

Ratnakar Shipping Co Ltd: 14–15 Old Court House St, Calcutta 700001; tel. (33) 228901; telex 217659; world-wide tramping services; eight vessels (six cargo vessels and two tankers); Chair. K. K. BIRLA; Gen. Man. K. C. MATHUR.

Surrendra Overseas Ltd: Apeejay House, 15 Park St, Calcutta 700016; tel. (33) 246881; telex 0213485; cargo services; five vessels (three bulk carriers and two cargo vessels); Chair. JIT PAUL; CEO Capt. B. S. KUMAR.

Goa

Chowgule Steamships Ltd: Chowgule House, Mormugao Harbour, Goa 403803; tel. (22) 2026822; telex 112409; f. 1963; six bulk carriers, of 305,415 dwt (1985); Chair. VISHWASRAO DATTAJI CHOWGULE; Man. Dir SHIVAJIRAO DATTAJI CHOWGULE.

Madras

South India Shipping Corpn Ltd: Chennai House, 7 Esplanade Rd, POB 234, Madras 600108; tel. (44) 560141; telex 41371; 10 bulk carriers; Chair. J. H. TARAPORE; Man. Dir F. G. DASTUR.

CIVIL AVIATION

There are four international airports in India: Bombay Airport, Calcutta Airport, Delhi Airport and Madras Airport. There are 90 other airports.

Air India: Air-India Bldg, Nariman Point, Bombay 400021; tel. (22) 2024142; telex 0112427; f. 1932 (as Tata Airlines; renamed Air India in 1946), in 1953 became a state corpn responsible for international flights; services to 38 countries covering five continents; Chair. RATAN TATA; Man. Dir DHRUBA BOSE; fleet of 9 Boeing 747-237B, 1 Boeing 747 freighter, 3 Boeing 707-337B, 2 Boeing 707-337C, 3 Airbus A300-B4, 6 A310-300, 2 DC8-63F, 1 IL-76.

Indian Airlines: Airlines House, 113 Gurudwara Rakab Ganj Rd, New Delhi 110001; tel. (11) 386370; telex 31-2810; f. 1943; state corpn responsible for regional and domestic flights; services throughout India and to Afghanistan, Bangladesh, Maldives, Nepal, Pakistan, Sri Lanka, Thailand; unduplicated route length: 51,000 km; Chair. RAHUL BAJAJ; Man. Dir KAMINI CHADHA; fleet of 25 Boeing 737, 11 HS-748, 8 F-27, 10 Airbus.

Vayudoot Private Ltd: Safdarjung Airport, New Delhi 110003; tel. (11) 693851; telex 61052; f. 1981 to connect the smaller towns of north-eastern India; links 78 airfields with Calcutta, Delhi, Hyderabad and Bombay; jtly owned by Indian Airlines and Air India; Chair. S. S. Sidhu; Gen. Man. Harsh Vardhan; fleet of 3 HS-748, 2 F-27, 4 Dornier 228.

Tourism

Department of Tourism of the Government of India: Ministry of Tourism, Transport Bhavan, Parliament St, New Delhi 110001; tel. (11) 384111; telex 031-2827; formulates and administers govt policy for promotion of tourism; plans the organization and development of tourist facilities; operates tourist information offices in India and overseas; Dir-Gen. Dr N. K. Sengupta.

India Tourism Development Corpn Ltd: Jeevan Vihar, 3 Sansad Marg, New Delhi 110001; tel. (11) 310923; telex 031-63361; f. 1966; operates hotels (largest hotel chain owner), resort accommodation, tourist transport services, duty-free shops and a travel agency and provides consultancy and management services; Chair. A. M Sethna; Man. Dir Rajan Jetley.

Atomic Energy

There are three operating nuclear power stations, at Tarapur near Bombay, at Kalpahkam (Tamil Nadu) and at Kota (Rajasthan). A fourth one is being built at Narora (Uttar Pradesh) and there are plans to set up a fifth at Kakrapar (Surat). India has five heavy water plants in operation and three more have been sanctioned.

Atomic Energy Commission: Chhatrapati Shivaji Maharaj Marg, Bombay 400039; organizes research on the use of atomic energy for peaceful purposes; Chair. and Sec. M. R. Srinivasan.

Bhabha Atomic Research Centre (BARC): Trombay, Bombay 400085; tel. (22) 5512791; telex 011-71017; f. 1957; national centre for research in and development of nuclear energy for peaceful uses; Dir Dr P. K. Iyengar; seven reactors:

APSARA: 100 MW, research and isotope production, criticality 1956.

CIRUS: 40 MW, isotope production and material testing, criticality 1960.

ZERLINA: Zero Energy Reactor for Lattice Investigations and New Assemblies, decommissioned 1983.

PURNIMA: criticality 1972, originally Plutonium Oxide fuelled fast critical facility, modified as PURNIMA II with Uranium 233 in the form of Uranyl nitrate solution as fuel, criticality 1984.

DHRUVA: 100 MW, research isotope production, material and reactor components testing, criticality 1985.

ISOMED: for radiation sterilization of medical products.

MOX: fuel fabrication facility to make uranium oxide and plutonium oxide fuel.

INDONESIA

Introductory Survey

Location, Climate, Language, Religion, Flag, Capital

The Republic of Indonesia consists of a group of about 13,700 islands, lying between the mainland of South-East Asia and Australia. The archipelago is the largest in the world, and it stretches from the Malay peninsula to New Guinea. The principal islands are Java, Sumatra, Kalimantan (Borneo), Sulawesi (Celebes), Irian Jaya (West New Guinea), the Moluccas and Timor. Indonesia's only land frontiers are with Papua New Guinea, to the east of Irian Jaya, and with the Malaysian states of Sarawak and Sabah, which occupy northern Borneo. The climate is tropical, with an average annual temperature of 26°C (79°F) and heavy rainfall during most seasons. The official language is Bahasa Indonesia (a form of Malay) but some 25 local languages (mainly Javanese) and more than 250 dialects are also spoken. An estimated 78% of the inhabitants profess adherence to Islam, and Indonesia has more Muslims than any other country. About 11% of the population are Christians, while most of the remainder are either Hindus or Buddhists. The national flag (proportions 3 by 2) has two equal horizontal stripes, of red and white. The capital is Jakarta, on the island of Java.

Recent History

Indonesia was formerly the Netherlands East Indies, except for the former Portuguese colony of East Timor (see below).

Dutch occupation began in the 17th century and was gradually extended to the whole archipelago. Nationalist opposition to colonial rule began in the early 20th century. During the Second World War the territory was occupied by Japanese forces from March 1942. On 17 August 1945, three days after the Japanese surrender, a group of nationalists proclaimed the independence of Indonesia. The first President of the self-proclaimed republic was Dr Sukarno, a leader of the nationalist movement since the 1920s. The declaration of independence was not recognized by the Netherlands, which attempted to restore its pre-war control of the islands. After four years of intermittent warfare and negotiations between the Dutch authorities and the nationalists, agreement was reached on a formal transfer of power. On 27 December 1949 the United States of Indonesia became legally independent, with Dr Sukarno continuing as President. The first Vice-President was Dr Mohammed Hatta, Sukarno's closest collaborator in the nationalist movement. Initially, the country had a federal constitution which gave limited self-government to the 16 constituent regions. In August 1950, however, the federation was dissolved and the country became the unitary Republic of Indonesia. The abandonment of regional autonomy met some resistance, particularly among the Christian population of the South Moluccas. The 1949 independence agreement excluded West New Guinea (now Irian Jaya), which remained under Dutch control until October 1962; following a brief period of UN administration, however, it was transferred to Indonesia in May 1963.

President Sukarno followed a policy of extreme nationalism, and his regime became increasingly dictatorial. His foreign policy was sympathetic to the People's Republic of China but he also played a leading role in the Non-Aligned Movement. Vice-President Hatta, alienated by Sukarno's one-man rule, resigned in 1956. President Sukarno bitterly opposed the establishment of the Federation of Malaysia (q.v.) in 1963. Inflation, widespread corruption and Sukarno's Marxist tendencies provoked opposition to his regime from students, the armed forces and Islamic groups. In September–October 1965 there was an attempted military coup, in which the Indonesian Communist Party (PKI) was strongly implicated. The attempt failed, and a mass slaughter of alleged PKI members and supporters ensued. In March 1966, as a consequence of the abortive coup, President Sukarno was forced to transfer emergency executive powers to military commanders, led by Gen. Suharto, Chief of Staff of the Army, who outlawed the PKI. The policy of 'confrontation' with Malaysia ended in August 1966, and Indonesia rejoined the UN (which it had left in 1965 in protest against Malaysia's membership of the Security Council). In February 1967 President Sukarno transferred full power to Gen. Suharto. In March the People's Consultative Assembly removed Sukarno from office and named Gen. Suharto acting President. He became Prime Minister in October 1967 and, after his election by the Assembly, he was inaugurated as President in March 1968. Meanwhile, Indonesia's relations with China had deteriorated drastically and were formally suspended in October 1967. In July 1971, in the first general election since 1955, the government-sponsored Sekber Golongan Karya (Joint Secretariat of Functional Groups), known as Golkar, won a majority of seats in the House of Representatives. President Suharto was re-elected in March 1973.

Under Suharto's 'New Order', real power passed from the legislature and Cabinet to a small group of army officers and to Kopkamtib, the chief security organization. Left-wing movements were suppressed, and a liberal economic policy adopted. A general election in May 1977 gave Golkar a majority in the legislature, and Suharto was re-elected President (unopposed) in March 1978. Between 1977 and 1979 the Government released political prisoners who had been detained since the 1965 coup attempt. In 1980 a petition criticizing the Government was channelled constitutionally through the People's Consultative Assembly. The 50 signatories, known as the Petition of 50, comprised generals, academics, former politicians and other prominent citizens. Further petitions followed. Throughout 1981 there were a number of anti-Chinese disturbances. Golkar won an increased majority in the elections in May 1982, but the campaign was marred by considerable violence. New legislation, approved in July, confirmed the 'dual (i.e. military and socioeconomic) function' of the armed forces. In March 1983 Suharto was re-elected, again unopposed, as President, and in October 1986 he announced his intention to seek a fifth five-year term as President, upon the expiry of his present term in March 1988.

President Suharto's announcement in 1986 was made at a time when there was widespread criticism of Suharto and his government within Indonesia and from abroad, following the publication, in an Australian newspaper, of a report accusing the Suharto family of corrupt practices, and amid further allegations of abuses of human rights in East Timor (see below). The ruling party, Golkar, nevertheless appeared confident of retaining its majority in the House of Representatives at the forthcoming general election, scheduled for April 1987, partly as a result of divisions within the leadership of the Partai Persatuan Pembangunan, the largest opposition group in the House.

During 1984 Suharto's attempt to introduce legislation requiring all political, social and religious organizations to adopt Pancasila, the state philosophy, as their only ideology, met with opposition, particularly from the Petition of 50. In September serious rioting, apparently started by Muslim activists, took place in the port area of Tanjung Priok, near Jakarta, when an estimated 18 people died and more than 50 were injured, following clashes between Muslim rioters and troops. The disturbances that followed, including a spate of bombings and arson attempts in Jakarta, were thought to have been instigated by Muslim opponents of the proposed legislation. Among those tried and sentenced to imprisonment for their part in the bombings (mostly Muslims) was Muhammad Sanusi, a former minister, who received a 19-year sentence. In 1986 Sanusi received a second sentence of 20 years' imprisonment for his part in an alleged plot to kill Suharto. Hartono Dharsono, a former Secretary-General of ASEAN and a member of the Petition of 50, received a 10-year sentence, reduced to seven

INDONESIA

years upon appeal. The law concerning mass organizations was enacted in June 1985, and all the political parties had accepted Pancasila by July.

In 1975 Portugal withdrew from its colony of East Timor. The territory's capital, Dili, was occupied by the forces of the left-wing Frente Revolucionário de Este Timor Independente (Fretilin), which advocated independence for East Timor. To prevent Fretilin from gaining full control, Indonesian troops intervened and set up a provisional government. In July 1976 East Timor was fully integrated as the 27th province of Indonesia. Although the UN does not yet recognize Indonesia's absorption of the territory, the issue has not been debated at the UN General Assembly since 1982. In February 1983 the UN Commission on Human Rights adopted a resolution affirming East Timor's right to independence and self-determination. In September 1983, following a five-month cease-fire during which talks took place between Fretilin and the Government, the armed forces launched a major new offensive. During 1984 it was reported that conditions in East Timor had worsened, with widespread hunger, disease and repression among civilians, and continuing battles between rebels and Indonesian troops. Fighting continued in the area during 1985 and 1986, and there were reports of atrocities against the population by government forces. The rebels suffered a serious set-back in August 1985, when the Australian Government recognized Indonesia's incorporation of East Timor. In early 1986 Fretilin leaders announced that they were about to engage in joint diplomatic and military initiatives with the Timorese Democratic Union (UDT), following reports that a new Indonesian offensive was to be launched against them in May. There were at least 7,000 Indonesian troops in the area in 1985, compared with about 1,000 Fretilin guerrillas. It has been estimated that the population of the region declined by one-third between 1975 and 1985.

In May 1977 there was a rebellion in Irian Jaya, said to have been organized by the Organisasi Papua Merdeka (OPM), or Free Papua Movement, which seeks unification with Papua New Guinea. Fighting continued until 1979, when, in December, Indonesia and Papua New Guinea finalized a new border administrative agreement. Since then, however, there have been frequent border incidents, and in early 1984 fighting broke out in Jayapura, the capital of Irian Jaya. As a result, about 10,000 refugees fled over the border into Papua New Guinea. Discussions between the Governments of Indonesia and Papua New Guinea concerning the return of the refugees took place during 1984, following a low point in diplomatic relations when Indonesian troops crossed into Papua New Guinea in pursuit of OPM rebels, and when Papua New Guinea's air space was violated by two aircraft of the Indonesian air force. In October the two countries signed a five-year agreement which established a joint border security committee; by the end of 1985 Indonesians were continuing to cross into Papua New Guinea, but a limited number of repatriations took place in 1986. There was also concern among native Irian Jayans (who are of Melanesian origin) at the introduction of large numbers of Javanese into the province, under the Government's transmigration scheme. This has been interpreted as an attempt to reduce the Melanesians to a minority and thus to stifle opposition. In 1986 it was announced that the Government intended to resettle 65m. people over 20 years, and that the World Bank had granted $2,500m. per year in aid, in spite of protests from human rights and conservation groups that the scheme would cause ecological damage and interfere with the rights of the native Irian Jayans.

Under President Suharto, Indonesia's foreign policy is one of non-alignment, although the country maintains close relations with the West. Indonesia is a member of ASEAN and supports that organization's opposition to Viet-Nam's continuing military presence in Kampuchea. In April 1986 US President Reagan visited Indonesia to discuss with the Foreign Ministers of ASEAN member-states various issues, including the problem of Kampuchea. His arrival was accompanied by criticism of human rights abuses and press censorship in Indonesia, following the expulsion of a number of foreign journalists from the country.

In July 1985 the trade organizations of Indonesia and the People's Republic of China signed a memorandum of understanding on the resumption of direct trade links between the two countries, which had been suspended since 1967. Indonesia subsequently improved its relations with the USSR, and the two countries signed an agreement to exchange economic information and to increase contacts, following the visit, in May 1986, of a delegation from the Soviet Chamber of Commerce.

Government

The highest authority of the state is the People's Consultative Assembly, with 920 members who serve for five years. The Assembly includes 460 members of the House of Representatives, the country's legislative organ. The House has 96 appointed members and 364 directly elected representatives. The remaining 460 seats in the Assembly are allocated to government appointees, delegates of regional assemblies and to representatives of parties and groups in proportion to their elected seats in the House. Owing to an increase in the electorate, the House of Representatives was to expand to 500 members at the elections in April 1987. Of the total members, 100 would be nominated by the President, with the remaining 400 directly elected. The People's Consultative Assembly was consequently to expand from 920 to 1,000 members in 1987. Executive power rests with the President, elected for five years by the Assembly. He governs with the assistance of an appointed Cabinet, responsible to him.

There are 27 provinces, and local government is through a three-tier system of Provincial, Regency and Village Assemblies. Provincial Governors are appointed by the President.

Defence

Military service is selective. In July 1986 the total strength of the armed forces was 281,000 men: army 216,000, navy 38,000 and air force 27,000. There were also a Police Mobile Brigade of 12,000 and about 70,000 militia. Defence expenditure for 1986/87 was budgeted at 2,318,000m. rupiahs.

Economic Affairs

Indonesia has extensive natural wealth but, with a large and rapidly increasing population, it remains a relatively poor country in terms of average income. The fertile island of Java is one of the most densely populated areas in the world, but some of the other large islands are sparsely inhabited. In 1984, according to estimates by the World Bank, Indonesia's gross national product (GNP), measured at average 1982–84 prices, was US $85,400m., equivalent to $540 per head. Between 1965 and 1984, it was estimated, GNP per head expanded, in real terms, at an average rate of 4.9% per year. The average annual increase in overall gross domestic product (GDP), measured in constant prices, was 8.1% in 1965–73, slowing to 6.8% in 1973–84.

The economy is predominantly agricultural. More than one-half of the working population are employed in agriculture, forestry and fishing, which together provided 24.9% of Indonesia's GDP in 1984. The staple crop is rice; in 1985 production of milled rice was estimated at a record 26.3m. metric tons. A total of 25.8m. tons of milled rice was produced in 1984, when Indonesia finally became self-sufficient in the cereal, following several years as the world's largest importer of rice. Imports of 390,000 tons were required in 1984, however, in order to maintain stockpile levels. The situation improved in 1985, when rice imports of only about 30,000 tons were necessary. Oil palm, coconuts, sugar cane and coffee are among the country's principal cash crops. Indonesia is the world's second largest producer of natural rubber (after Malaysia); production was estimated at 1.1m. metric tons in 1985, compared with 997,000 tons in 1983.

About two-thirds of Indonesia's land area is covered by tropical rain forests, and output of industrial logs was 26m. cu m in 1983/84. Since 1980 the country's exports of forest products have slumped, owing to falling demand and restrictions on exporting unprocessed timber (all log exports have been banned since January 1985), and earnings declined from $1,710m. in 1979 to $504m. in 1981/82, and to only $221m. in 1983/84. However, production of plywood has increased significantly since 1975, rising from 107,000 cu m to almost 5m. cu m in 1985, and Indonesia is now the world's largest exporter, accounting for about 70% of the total world market. Export earnings from plywood were estimated at $1,000m. in 1985.

Indonesia's principal mineral resource is petroleum, of which it produced a record 615.1m. barrels in 1977. Output fell to

INDONESIA

Introductory Survey

490.5m. barrels in 1983, restricted by an OPEC production limit of 1.3m. barrels per day, but rose to 516.9m. barrels in 1984, although the OPEC restriction was still in force. Production declined to 483.6m. barrels in 1985. Revenue from exports of crude petroleum declined from $11,021m. in 1984, to $8,251m. in 1985, owing to the reduction in international oil prices and a fall in the value of the US dollar. The increasing production of liquefied natural gas (LNG) is a significant development, and Indonesia is the world's leading exporter. Exports of gas were valued at $3,541.1m. in 1984, and at $3,634.5m. in 1985. In terms of volume, 15.0m. metric tons were exported in 1984, and 16.7m. tons in 1985. Output of LNG is projected to triple between 1980 and 1990, when LNG will, it is planned, become Indonesia's prime earner of revenue. Work on the expansion of two LNG plants was completed in 1984. Virtually all LNG exports went to Japan until 1986, when the first shipments to the Republic of Korea were made. In late 1986 Indonesia also completed negotiations for the export of LNG to Taiwan; shipments were due to begin in 1990. Tin, bauxite, nickel, copper and coal are also mined. Output of tin was 22,413 metric tons in 1985, making Indonesia the world's second largest producer (after Malaysia). The manufacturing sector developed slowly, contributing only 12% of GDP in 1984, in spite of a rapid growth rate (nearly 21% in 1984). By 1986, however, the sector had begun to experience recession. Major branches of manufacturing include petroleum refining and the production of fertilizers, pharmaceuticals, cement and textiles. The Government needs to create an additional 17m. new jobs between the mid-1980s and the mid-1990s, as the labour force is expanding by 2.3% per annum. The industrial sector, in particular, required significant investment to meet this demand, and in 1986 (when oil export revenues were declining) changes in investment and export regulations were announced, in order to encourage foreign investors.

Repelita III (1979–84), the third Five-Year Plan, recorded an average annual growth rate of 8%, except for 1982/83, when economic growth was only 2.25%. In 1983/84 growth in GDP was 4.2% in real terms, and in 1984/85 the rate of growth increased to 6.5%. Repelita IV (1984–89) emphasizes expansion of the industry sector and non-oil exports, and forecasts an annual growth rate of 5% (at 1973 prices). Indonesia's foreign reserves reached a record $12,000m. in April 1981. In May 1983 the Government cancelled or rescheduled 48 major projects, involving planned expenditure of about $21,000m., in order to save foreign reserves and to reduce the balance-of-payments deficit. Foreign reserves fell to $4,810m. in 1983, but by 1986 they had recovered to $10,700m. Indonesia's development plans have been financed largely by foreign aid. The country receives continuous aid from the Inter-Governmental Group for Indonesia (IGGI). For the fiscal year 1985/86, donor countries pledged $2,149m. Other foreign investment, approved by the Capital Investment Co-ordinating Board, has fallen, from $1,110m. in 1984 to $859m. in 1985, partly as a result of the bombings and riots, as well as the new tax laws. In September 1986 the rupiah was devalued by 30.7% against the US dollar, in order to bolster foreign exchange reserves, to maintain the balance of payments, and to mitigate the effect of the decline in petroleum revenues. The deficit on the current account of the balance of payments fell from 8.4% of GDP in 1983/84 to 2.4% in 1984/85. The overall balance of payments showed a surplus of only $38m. in 1985/86, compared with $667m. in 1984/85. The current account of the balance of payments recorded a deficit of $4,200m. in 1983/84, easing to $1,900m. in 1984/85. In 1985/86, however, the deficit rose to $2,079m., owing to a decline in export earnings from petroleum and gas and a decrease in non-petroleum exports. In late 1986 the foreign debt was estimated at $36,800m., compared with $28,400m. at the end of 1985. Inflation reached 21.8% in 1979 and fell to 7.1% in 1981, rising to 11.5% in 1983. It subsequently fell to 8.8% in 1984, and to 4.3% in 1985.

Since the early 1970s Indonesia has had a surplus on the balance of trade, amounting to $4,799.9m., in 1983 and rising to $8,005.7m. in 1984. The surplus rose only marginally in 1985, to $8,327.6m., owing to a decline of 26% in the value of imports. A loss of export earnings from crude petroleum in 1984 was offset by an increase of 37.1% in LNG exports and a rise in non-oil and -gas exports. As a result of earlier increases in the price of petroleum and the growth of LNG exports, export trade more than doubled in value between 1977 and 1984, from $10,853m. to $21,888m. Total exports in 1985/86 declined by 9.1%, to $18,100m., owing to an unexpected fall in world petroleum prices. Sales of petroleum and natural gas contributed 66% of total export revenue in 1985, compared with 70% in 1984. Non-petroleum exports increased only slightly in value, in spite of a considerable rise in volume, as commodity prices generally declined in 1985. Indonesia's inadequate refining capacity has meant that, until recently, much of the country's consumption of refined petroleum products has been imported. However, following the completion of a new hydrocracker plant and refinery in 1984, Indonesia can now produce all its own requirements of refined petroleum. The 1986/87 budget extended the programme of austerity and reduced total expenditure by 7%. Development expenditure fell by 22%.

Indonesia's principal trading partner is Japan, accounting for 25.7% of imports and 46.2% of exports in 1985, followed by the USA and Singapore, which, respectively, accounted for 19.2% and 8.4% of total trade. Indonesia's main imports are machinery, fuel, foodstuffs and transport equipment.

Social Welfare

About 10% of the population benefit from a state insurance scheme. Benefits include life insurance and old-age pensions. In addition, there are two social insurance schemes, administered by state corporations, providing pensions and industrial accident insurance. Expenditure on health by the central government in 1983/84 was about 362,500m. rupiahs, representing 2.2% of total spending. In 1984/85 Indonesia had 1,306 hospitals (with a total of 106,035 beds), 5,453 community health centres and more than 18,000 other health centres. About one-half of the hospitals are privately administered. In 1985 there were 18,447 physicians working in the country.

Education

Education is mainly under the control of the Ministry of Education and Culture, but the Ministry of Religion is in charge of Islamic religious schools at the primary level. Primary education, beginning at seven years of age and lasting for six years, is officially compulsory; it was hoped to implement universal compulsory primary education by 1987. Secondary education, which is not compulsory, begins at the age of 13 and lasts for a further six years, comprising two cycles of three years each. Enrolment at primary schools in 1984 included about 97% of children in the appropriate age-group, while secondary enrolment was about 44% for children aged 13 to 15, and about 25% for children aged 16 to 18. In 1983/84 25.8m. pupils were enrolled at primary schools, while 6.4m. were receiving general secondary education. There were 1,023,000 students in higher education in 1984/85. In 1986 there were 512,000 secondary school-leavers seeking 90,000 places in government tertiary education establishments; there were 43 state universities and teacher-training colleges, and 360 private universities and colleges, of which 10 were recognized by the Government as 'centres of excellence'. Expenditure on education by the central government in 1983/84 was 1,544,900m. rupiahs, representing 9.4% of total spending. The average rate of adult illiteracy declined from 43.4% in 1971 to 32.7% (males 22.5%; females 42.3%) in 1980. According to estimates by UNESCO, the rate in 1985 was 25.9% (males 17.0%; females 34.6%).

Tourism

Indonesia's tourist industry is based mainly on the islands of Java, famous for its volcanic scenery and religious temples, and Bali, renowned for its traditional dancing and religious festivals. In 1984 700,910 tourists visited Indonesia. It is hoped to achieve 1.2m. tourists annually by the end of Repelita IV (1989).

Public Holidays

1987: 1 January (New Year's Day), 28 March (Ascension of the Prophet Muhammad), 17 April (Good Friday), 28 May (Ascension Day), 30 May (Id al-Fitr, end of Ramadan), 6 August (Id al-Adha), 17 August (Indonesian National Day), 26 August (Islamic New Year), 4 November (Mouloud, Prophet Muhammad's Birthday), 25 December (Christmas Day).

1988: 1 January (New Year's Day), 16 March (Ascension of the Prophet Muhammad), 1 April (Good Friday), 12 May

INDONESIA

(Ascension Day), 18 May (Id al-Fitr, end of Ramadan), 25 July (Id al-Adha), 14 August (Islamic New Year), 17 August (Indonesian National Day), 23 October (Mouloud, Prophet Muhammad's Birthday), 25 December (Christmas Day).

Weights and Measures
The metric system is in force.

Currency and Exchange Rates
100 sen = 1 rupiah.
Exchanges rates (30 September 1986):
£1 sterling = 2,362.95 rupiahs;
US $1 = 1,633.00 rupiahs.

Statistical Survey

Source (unless otherwise stated): Central Bureau of Statistics, 8 Jalan Dokter Sutomo, POB 3, Jakarta; tel. (021) 363366; telex 45159.
Note: Unless otherwise stated, figures for the disputed former Portuguese territory of East Timor (annexed by Indonesia in July 1976) are not included in the tables.

Area and Population

AREA, POPULATION AND DENSITY

Area (sq km)	
Indonesia	1,904,569*
East Timor	14,874†
Population (census results)	
24 September 1971	
Indonesia	119,208,229
31 October 1980	
Indonesia	
Males	73,049,264
Females	73,885,684
Total	146,934,948
East Timor	
Males	283,280
Females	272,070
Total	555,350
Population (official estimates at 31 December)‡	
Indonesia	
1981	150,790,400
1982	154,148,700
1983	157,557,900
East Timor	
1981	571,200
1982	585,300
1983	599,800
Density (per sq km) at 31 December 1983‡	
Indonesia	82.7
East Timor	40.3

* 735,358 sq miles.
† 5,743 sq miles.
‡ The estimated total population (including East Timor) was 161,632,000 at 31 December 1984, rising to 165,155,000 (density 86.0 per sq km.) at 31 December 1985.

PRINCIPAL ISLANDS*
(estimated population at 31 December 1983)

	Area (sq km)	Population	Density (per sq km)
Jawa (Java) and Madura	132,187	96,892,900	733.0
Sumatera (Sumatra)	473,606	30,928,500	65.3
Kalimantan (Borneo)	539,460	7,350,000	13.6
Sulawesi (Celebes)	189,216	11,112,200	58.7
Bali		2,593,900	
Maluku (Moluccas)		1,534,300	
Irian Jaya (West New Guinea)	570,100	1,268,600	19.7
Others		5,814,600	
Indonesia	1,904,569	157,495,000	82.7
East Timor	14,874	587,700	39.5
Total	1,919,443	158,082,700	82.4

* Figures for population and density are provisional. For revised totals, see previous table.

PRINCIPAL TOWNS (population)

	1980 Census	1983*
Jakarta (capital)	6,503,449	7,347,800
Surabaya	2,027,913	2,223,600
Bandung	1,462,637	1,566,700
Medan	1,378,955	1,805,500
Semarang	1,026,671	1,205,800
Palembang	787,187	873,900
Ujung Pandang (Makassar)	709,038	840,500
Malang	511,780	547,100
Padang	480,922	656,800
Surakarta	469,888	490,900
Yogyakarta	398,727	420,700
Banjarmasin	381,286	423,600
Pontianak	304,778	342,700

* Revised official estimates for 31 December.

BIRTHS AND DEATHS

Average annual birth rate 41.4 per 1,000 in 1970–75, 36.4 per 1,000 in 1975–80; death rate 17.3 per 1,000 in 1970–75, 15.1 per 1,000 in 1975–80 (UN estimates). Estimates for 1984: birth rate 33.5 per 1,000; death rate 11.7 per 1,000.

ECONOMICALLY ACTIVE POPULATION
(household survey, persons aged 10 years and over, 1982)

	Males	Females	Total
Agriculture, hunting, forestry and fishing	20,443,213	11,150,101	31,593,314
Mining and quarrying	323,851	66,810	390,661
Manufacturing	3,138,871	2,883,058	6,021,929
Electricity, gas and water	54,569	7,097	61,666
Construction	2,103,007	43,203	2,146,210
Trade, restaurants and hotels	4,328,750	4,225,169	8,553,919
Transport, storage and communications	1,778,628	17,484	1,796,112
Financing, insurance, real estate and business services	92,386	20,473	112,859
Community, social and personal services	4,800,947	2,324,472	7,125,419
Activities not adequately described	382	330	712
Total employed	37,064,604	20,738,197	57,802,801
Unemployed	1,022,771	773,054	1,795,825
Total labour force	38,087,375	21,511,251	59,598,626

Agriculture

PRINCIPAL CROPS ('000 metric tons)

	1983	1984	1985
Rice (paddy)	35,303	38,136	38,660†
Maize	5,087	5,228	5,300†
Potatoes	217	180*	190*
Sweet potatoes	2,044	2,257	2,300†
Cassava (Manioc)	12,229	14,205	14,500†
Other roots and tubers	222	215	210
Pulses	452	299*	303*
Soybeans	568	743	825†
Groundnuts (in shell)	793	747†	800†
Coconuts*	10,097	10,355	10,754
Copra	1,070	1,101	1,160†
Palm kernels	155.3	176.0	214.0†
Vegetables	3,054	2,439*	2,457*
Bananas	2,320	2,000†	2,085*
Other fruit	2,765	2,223	2,273*
Sugar cane	24,470†	23,726*	24,901*
Coffee (green)	236	276	327
Tea (made)	110	119	129
Tobacco (leaves)	130	109	128†
Natural rubber	997	1,115†	1,125*

* FAO estimate.   † Unofficial estimate.
Source: FAO, *Production Yearbook*.

LIVESTOCK ('000 head, year ending September)

	1983	1984	1985*
Cattle	6,650*	6,800	6,859
Sheep	4,300	4,790	4,958
Goats	7,900	10,969	11,173
Pigs	3,600	4,065	4,050
Horses	660*	527	527
Buffaloes	2,500*	2,391	2,424

Chickens (million): 132 in 1983; 133 in 1984; 144* in 1985.
Ducks (million): 17 in 1983; 17 in 1984; 18* in 1985.
* FAO estimate.
Source: FAO, *Production Yearbook*.

LIVESTOCK PRODUCTS ('000 metric tons)

	1983	1984	1985
Beef and veal	122	135*	135
Buffalo meat	32	35*	35
Mutton and lamb	20	24*	24
Goats' meat	39	38*	38
Pig meat*	85	87	90
Poultry meat	191*	195*	209
Cows' milk	135	153†	162
Hen eggs	235.0	230.0*	240.0
Other poultry eggs	80.0	80.0	84.8
Cattle and buffalo hides*	25.9	27.5	27.5

Note: Figures for meat refer to inspected production only, i.e. from animals slaughtered under government supervision.
* FAO estimate.   † Unofficial estimate.
Source: FAO, *Production Yearbook*.

Forestry

ROUNDWOOD REMOVALS
('000 cubic metres, excluding bark)

	1982	1983	1984
Sawlogs, veneer logs and logs for sleepers:			
Coniferous	325	363*	370*
Non-coniferous	22,448†	25,470†	26,000
Pulpwood	172†	242†	242*
Other industrial wood*	2,438	2,481	2,523
Fuel wood*	115,021	117,052	119,059
Total	140,404	145,608	148,194

* FAO estimate.   † Unofficial estimate.
Source: FAO, *Yearbook of Forest Products*.

SAWNWOOD PRODUCTION ('000 cubic metres)

	1981	1982	1983
Coniferous sawnwood*	12†	13†	14†
Non-coniferous sawnwood*	5,250‡	6,798	6,296
Railway sleepers†	7	7	7
Total	5,269	6,818	6,317

* Including boxboards.   † FAO estimate.
‡ Unofficial estimate.
1984: Production as in 1983 (FAO estimates).
Source: FAO, *Yearbook of Forest Products*.

INDONESIA

Fishing

('000 metric tons, live weight)

	1982	1983	1984
Carps, barbels, etc.	111.1	120.3	115.5
Other freshwater fishes (incl. unspecified)	272.4	283.9	282.3
Milkfish	73.3	81.5	91.7
Other diadromous fishes	13.7	19.0	21.1
Scads	77.4	91.9	94.1
Indian oil-sardine	57.0	90.9	105.7
Fringescale sardinella	99.0	104.6	16.2
'Stolephorus' anchovies	104.6	104.7	104.5
Tunas, bonitos, billfishes, etc.	244.0	261.2	289.6
Indian mackerels	99.3	95.7	97.8
Other marine fishes (incl. unspecified)	637.5	705.9	739.0
Total fish	1,789.3	1,959.5	1,957.4
Marine shrimps, prawns, etc.	130.5	138.2	122.0
Other crustaceans	20.4	21.6	23.3
Molluscs	45.7	60.0	73.1
Other aquatic animals	4.2	25.6	41.3
Total catch	1,990.1	2,204.9	2,217.2
Inland waters	506.8	532.5	538.0
Indian Ocean	148.4	172.0	191.6
Pacific Ocean	1,334.9	1,500.4	1,487.6

Aquatic plants ('000 metric tons): 7.5 in 1982; 9.6 in 1983; 10.8 in 1984.

Source: FAO, *Yearbook of Fishery Statistics*.

Mining

	1983	1984	1985
Crude petroleum ('000 barrels)	490,491	516,990	483,645
Natural gas ('000 million cu ft)	1,184,671	1,520,441	1,577,790
Bauxite (metric tons)	777,869	1,003,087	830,471
Coal (metric tons)	485,669	1,085,000	1,491,652
Nickel ore (metric tons)*	1,298,031	1,066,816	955,604
Copper (metric tons)*	205,008	190,349	233,446
Tin (metric tons)	26,553	23,223	22,413
Gold (kg)	259.5	239.1	234.4
Silver (kg)	1,793.7	1,999.7	2,151.8

* Figures refer to gross weight. In 1983 the metal content (in metric tons) was: Nickel 31,153; Copper 65,400.

Source: Ministry of Mines and Energy.

Industry

PETROLEUM PRODUCTS ('000 barrels)

	1981	1982	1983*
Motor spirit (petrol)	25,048.5	15,653.5	13,577.8
Kerosene	36,025.9	33,340.9	30,443.7
Jet fuel	1,655.1	1,826.9	2,760.8
Distillate fuel oils	32,263.6	35,315.1	37,631.3
Residual fuel oils	75,838.5	67,027.0	65,287.7

* Preliminary figures.

OTHER PRODUCTS

	1982	1983	1984
Wheat flour ('000 metric tons)	1,076	1,234	1,074
Refined sugar ('000 metric tons)	1,361	1,590	1,573
Cotton yarn ('000 bales)*	870	847	1,281
Nitrogenous fertilizers ('000 metric tons)	2,160	2,426	2,462
Cement ('000 metric tons)	5,832	6,150	6,693
Cigarettes (million)	85,068	91,463	102,897
Tyres ('000)†	3,102	3,387	3,336
Radio receivers ('000)	1,199	1,045	933
Television receivers ('000)	604	517	517
Motor vehicles (assembly) ('000)	196	165	167

* Including synthetic yarn.
† For motor cars only.

Palm oil ('000 metric tons): 824.0 in 1982; 972.1 in 1983; 1,086.7 in 1984 (Source: FAO).

Tin (primary metal, metric tons): 29,755 in 1982; 28,390 in 1983 (Source: International Tin Council).

Finance

CURRENCY AND EXCHANGE RATES

Monetary Units
100 sen = 1 rupiah (Rp.).

Denominations
Coins: 5, 10, 25, 50 and 100 rupiahs.
Notes: 100, 500, 1,000, 5,000 and 10,000 rupiahs.

Sterling and Dollar Equivalents (30 September 1986)
£1 sterling = 2,362.95 rupiahs;
US $1 = 1,633.00 rupiahs;
10,000 rupiahs = £4.232 = $6.124.

Average Exchange Rate (rupiahs per US $)
1983   909.3
1984   1,025.9
1985   1,110.6

BUDGET ESTIMATES
('000 million rupiahs, year ending 31 March)

Revenue	1984/85	1985/86
Petroleum	8,895.1 ⎫	11,159.7
Natural gas	1,471.5 ⎭	
Other tax receipts	5,167.8	6,786.3
Income tax	2,451.1	3,074.0
Sales tax	958.2	1,666.4
Import tax	681.4 ⎫	1,680.4
Excise tax	727.5 ⎭	
Export tax	123.6	101.7
Other taxes	75.4	96.4
Regional development tax (Ipeda)	150.6	167.4
Non-tax receipts	615.0	731.9
Total domestic receipts	16,149.4	18,677.9
Foreign aid receipts	4,411.0	4,368.1
Programme aid	39.5	70.9
Project aid and export credits	4,371.5	4,297.2
Total	20,560.4	23,046.0

Expenditure	1984/85	1985/86
Personal emoluments	3,189.5	4,117.3
Salaries and pensions	2,307.9	3,115.8
Rice allowances	415.7	482.5
Food allowances	286.6	313.3
Other remunerations	99.9	116.6
Missions abroad	79.4	89.1
Purchases of goods	1,263.9	1,529.9
Domestic products	1,207.8	1,451.8
Foreign products	56.1	78.1
Regional subsidies	1,784.6	2,590.4
Personal	n.a.	2,349.0
Non-personal	n.a.	241.4
Debt servicing	2,686.1	3,559.1
Domestic debts	30.0	30.0
Foreign debts	2,656.1	3,529.1
Others	1,177.0	602.3
Fuel oil subsidy	1,147.0	532.3
Miscellaneous	30.0	70.0
Total ordinary budget	10,101.1	12,399.0
Total development budget	10,459.3	10,647.0
Locally financed	6,087.8	6,349.8
Project aid	4,371.5	4,297.2
Total	20,560.4	23,046.0

Source: Ministry of Finance.

DEVELOPMENT EXPENDITURE
('000 million rupiahs, year ending 31 March)*

	1983/84	1984/85	1985/86
Agriculture	829.0 ⎫	1,401.7	1,430.3
Irrigation	494.8 ⎭		
Industry	448.1	650.0	655.1
Mining	235.5 ⎫	1,300.9	1,301.7
Energy	880.5 ⎭		
Tourism and communications	1,307.3	1,392.1	1,425.4
Manpower and transmigration	621.9	675.1	676.8
Regional, rural and urban development	783.0	809.9	868.2
Education	1,329.3	1,501.9	1,510.8
Health, social welfare, women's affairs and family planning	344.0	408.0	413.4
Housing accommodation and settlement	297.1	432.7	437.7
National defence and security	574.0	697.7	714.1
Total (incl. others)	9,290.3	10,459.3	10,647.0

* Planned.
Source: Ministry of Finance.

INTERNATIONAL RESERVES
(US $ million at 31 December)

	1983	1984	1985
Gold*	1,096	947	906
IMF special drawing rights	4	1	56
Reserve position in IMF	76	71	80
Foreign exchange	3,639	4,702	4,838
Total	4,815	5,721	5,880

* Valued at market-related prices.
Source: IMF, *International Financial Statistics*.

FOREIGN AID (US $ million)*

	1984/85	1985/86
Soft loans from IGGI	2,335.0	2,148.8
Bilateral	727.7	601.4
Australia	—	9.5
Belgium	—	6.0
Canada	21.7	—
France	42.0	23.3
Germany, Fed. Repub.	75.0	29.8
Italy	8.0	—
Japan	406.4	489.2
Netherlands	24.0	22.4
Switzerland	—	—
USA	78.6	—
Multilateral (international agencies)	1,607.3	1,547.4
IBRD	1,053.9	1,234.1
ADB	553.4	313.3
Semi-concessionary loans and commercial loans, including export credit for projects	1,278.3	1,013.1
Cash loans	1,105.1	1,867.1
Total	4,718.4	5,029.0

* Figures refer to agreed commitments to provide aid, rather than to actual disbursements.
Source: Bank Indonesia.

INDONESIA

Statistical Survey

MONEY SUPPLY ('000 million rupiahs at 31 December)

	1983	1984	1985
Currency outside banks	3,340	3,712	4,460
Demand deposits at deposit money banks	4,177	4,817	5,560

Source: IMF, *International Financial Statistics*.

COST OF LIVING (Consumer Price Index—average of monthly figures. Base: April 1977–March 1978 = 100)

	1983	1984	1985
Food	202.8	222.8	232.3
Fuel and light	223.7	256.9	284.3
Clothing	210.0	217.8	229.2
Rent	216.7	239.7	254.9
All items	214.7	237.2	248.4

NATIONAL ACCOUNTS ('000 million rupiahs at current prices)

National Income and Product

	1982	1983	1984
Domestic factor incomes*	53,624.0	68,874	80,405
Consumption of fixed capital	3,876.1	3,658	4,150
Gross domestic product at factor cost	57,500.1	72,532	84,555
Indirect taxes, *less* subsidies	2,132.5	1,166	1,359
GDP in purchasers' values	59,632.6	73,698	85,914
Net factor income from abroad	−1,957.5	−3,643	−4,990
Gross national product	57,675.1	70,055	80,924
Less Consumption of fixed capital	3,876.1	3,658	4,150
National income in market prices	53,799.0	66,397	76,774

* Compensation of employees and the operating surplus of enterprises. The amount is obtained as a residual.

Expenditure on the Gross Domestic Product

	1982	1983	1984
Government final consumption expenditure	6,831.7	8,077	8,937
Private final consumption expenditure	41,670.3	44,739	51,399
Increase in stocks	13,467.1	2,695	3,251
Gross fixed capital formation		18,974	19,315
Total domestic expenditure	61,969.1	74,485	82,902
Exports of goods and services	13,345.2	20,448	23,380
Less Imports of goods and services	15,681.7	21,235	20,368
GDP in purchasers' values	59,632.6	73,698	85,914

Gross Domestic Product by Economic Activity

	1982	1983	1984
Agriculture, forestry and fishing	15,668.3	17,696	21,424
Mining and quarrying	11,707.8	13,652	15,218
Manufacturing	7,680.7	8,528	10,318
Electricity, gas and water	380.3	524	700
Construction	3,507.2	4,597	4,883
Wholesale and retail trade	8,865.1	12,009	13,372
Transport and communications	2,795.2	3,978	5,003
Finance, insurance, real estate, etc.	3,306.5		
Government services	4,428.7	12,714	14,996
Other services (incl. restaurants and hotels)	1,292.8		
Total	59,632.6	73,698	85,914

BALANCE OF PAYMENTS (US $ million)

	1983	1984	1985
Merchandise exports f.o.b.	18,689	20,754	18,459
Merchandise imports f.o.b.	−17,726	−15,254	−12,583
Trade balance	963	5,500	5,876
Exports of services	1,217	1,418	1,552
Imports of services	−8,622	−9,146	−9,231
Balance of goods and services	−6,442	−2,228	−1,803
Unrequited transfers (net)	104	114	171
Current balance	−6,338	−2,114	−1,632
Long-term capital (net)	5,323	3,027	1,522
Short-term capital (net)	731	401	380
Net errors and omissions	462	−400	201
Total (net monetary movements)	178	914	471
Valuation changes (net)	−7	25	57
Changes in reserves	172	940	528

Source: IMF, *International Financial Statistics*.

External Trade

PRINCIPAL COMMODITIES (US $ million)

Imports c.i.f.	1983	1984	1985
Food and live animals	1,134.5	676.2	556.1
Cereals and cereal preparations	744.9	433.9	296.1
Rice	384.0	132.1	8.8
Beverages and tobacco	27.8	29.1	20.9
Crude materials (inedible) except fuels	675.6	883.4	129.0
Mineral fuels, lubricants, etc.	4,149.9	2,705.1	1,287.7
Petroleum and petroleum products	4,144.2	2,696.7	1,275.5
Crude and partly refined petroleum	986.9	1,392.0	928.0
Crude petroleum	893.7	1,320.7	846.5
Petroleum products	3,157.2	1,304.7	347.6
Animal and vegetable oils, fats and waxes	12.1	51.7	35.6
Chemicals and related products	1,893.0	2,137.3	1,916.6
Chemical elements and compounds	812.3	1,005.4	820.9
Basic manufactures	2,351.5	1,885.1	1,717.9
Iron and steel	1,072.4	882.4	717.8
Universals, plates and sheets	499.4	413.5	379.2
Machinery and transport equipment	5,684.0	5,036.9	3,617.0
Non-electric machinery	3,529.8	2,828.5	2,335.6
Electrical machinery, apparatus, etc.	722.8	638.6	419.7
Transport equipment	1,431.4	1,569.9	861.6
Road motor vehicles and parts*	721.0	794.8	390.0
Lorries and trucks (incl. ambulances)	344.4	369.2	132.7
Miscellaneous manufactured articles	358.8	378.6	331.9
Other commodities and transactions	64.6	98.6	46.5
Total	16,351.8	13,882.1	10,259.1

* Excluding tyres, engines and electrical parts.

Exports f.o.b.	1983*	1984	1985
Food and live animals	1,093.1	1,368.5	1,383.1
Coffee, tea, cocoa and spices	687.8	959.2	900.9
Coffee (incl. extracts, etc.)	429.9	567.6	561.9
Beverages and tobacco	49.8	43.5	48.7
Crude materials (inedible) except fuels	1,649.7	1,761.9	1,403.1
Crude rubber, etc.	847.9	951.9	718.4
Wood, lumber and cork	347.8	365.8	243.7
Rough or roughly squared wood	286.1	170.1	6.8
Metalliferous ores and metal scrap	280.2	274.2	266.4
Non-ferrous ores and concentrates	279.7	272.7	266.0
Mineral fuels, lubricants, etc.	16,152.0	16,044.6	12,757.3
Petroleum and petroleum products	13,557.9	12,477.0	9,083.4
Crude petroleum	12,600.0	11,021.4	8,251.3
Petroleum products	957.9	1,455.6	832.0
Residual fuel oils	947.4	1,075.7	424.1
Gas (natural and manufactured)	2,582.8	3,541.1	3,634.5
Animal and vegetable oils, fats and waxes	148.7	174.9	414.1
Chemicals and related products	119.0	169.7	210.0
Basic manufactures	1,349.7	1,565.3	1,804.4
Wood and cork manufactures (excl. furniture)	745.5	802.3	952.3
Non-ferrous metals	442.5	491.1	505.6
Tin	309.4	269.8	240.5
Machinery and transport equipment	133.3	223.2	98.0
Miscellaneous manufactured articles	213.2	372.2	437.0
Other commodities and transactions	238.4	164.0	30.9
Total	21,145.9	21,887.8	18,586.7

* Figures are provisional. Revised total is $21,151.7 million.

PRINCIPAL TRADING PARTNERS (US $ million)

Imports	1983	1984	1985
Australia	402.3	372.0	460.5
Canada	186.0	318.8	198.1
China, People's Republic	204.0	224.4	248.9
France	591.1	431.9	284.4
Germany, Fed. Republic	741.4	820.1	677.1
Japan	3,793.1	3,307.7	2,644.4
Korea, Republic	387.5	212.4	205.0
Netherlands	257.3	266.1	215.1
Philippines	181.6	15.0	23.0
Saudi Arabia	905.4	1,344.6	882.4
Singapore	3,464.5	1,791.4	839.1
Taiwan	510.5	387.3	290.7
Thailand	208.7	55.4	47.9
United Kingdom	364.4	297.2	300.4
USA	2,533.7	2,559.9	1,720.9
Total (incl. others)	16,351.8	13,882.1	10,259.1

Exports	1983	1984	1985
Australia	208.4	275.2	149.2
Bahamas	139.7	174.5	0.0
Germany, Fed. Republic	252.4	246.3	254.9
Hong Kong	181.7	261.3	348.4
Italy	120.5	167.3	152.0
Japan	9,678.2	10,352.5	8,593.5
Korea, Republic	326.7	594.8	656.2
Netherlands	289.2	331.9	392.0
New Zealand	215.0	220.4	n.a.
Philippines	241.9	166.1	198.6
Singapore	3,131.0	2,125.5	1,625.6
Taiwan	218.5	323.1	353.7
Trinidad and Tobago	847.0	829.2	311.5
United Kingdom	199.0	167.7	191.4
USA	4,267.3	4,504.7	4,040.2
Total (incl. others)	21,151.7	21,887.8	18,586.7

Transport

RAILWAYS (traffic)

	1982	1983	1984
Passenger-km (million)	6,293	6,105	6,379
Freight ton-km (million)	885	916	1,173

ROAD TRAFFIC (motor vehicles registered at 31 December)

	1983	1984	1985
Passenger cars	865,940	925,335	987,099
Lorries and trucks	717,873	787,717	845,338
Buses and coaches	160,260	190,808	231,463
Motor cycles	4,135,677	4,550,742	4,765,067

INTERNATIONAL SEA-BORNE SHIPPING

	1981	1982	1983
Goods loaded ('000 metric tons)	97,353	98,456	88,687
Goods unloaded ('000 metric tons)	18,632	23,468	56,944
Merchant shipping fleet* ('000 grt)	1,745	1,847	1,950

* At 30 June.

CIVIL AVIATION (traffic on scheduled services)

	1983	1984	1985
Kilometres flown (million)	129.7	142.0	120.0
Passengers carried ('000)	6,205	6,694	6,285
Passenger-km (million)	8,419	9,402	9,529
Freight ton-km (million)	167.2	169.8	146.2

Tourism

	1982	1983	1984
Visitors ('000)	592.0	638.9	683.0
Receipts (US $ million)	358.8	440.0	519.0

Source: Directorate General of Tourism.

Communications Media

	1982	1983	1984
Television receivers (registered)	2,936,979	5,273,450	5,699,487
Telephones (registered)	669,301	717,660	788,365

Education

(1983/84)

	Schools	Teachers	Pupils and Students
Primary	129,388	925,834	25,804,380
General secondary	18,630	384,219	6,447,030
Technological	966	29,464	315,688

Source: Department of Education and Culture.

Directory

The Constitution

Indonesia had three provisional constitutions: in August 1945, February 1950 and August 1950. In July 1959 the Constitution of 1945 was re-enacted by presidential decree. The General Elections Law of 1969 supplemented the 1945 Constitution, which has been adopted permanently by the People's Consultative Assembly. The following is a summary of its main provisions:

GENERAL PRINCIPLES

The 1945 Constitution consists of 37 articles, four transitional clauses and two additional provisions, and is preceded by a preamble. The preamble contains an indictment of all forms of colonialism, an account of Indonesia's struggle for independence, the declaration of that independence and a statement of fundamental aims and principles. Indonesia's National Independence, according to the text of the preamble, has the state form of a Republic, with sovereignty residing in the People, and is based upon the *Pancasila*:

1. Belief in the One Supreme God.
2. Just and Civilized Humanity.
3. The Unity of Indonesia.
4. Democracy led by the wisdom of deliberations (*musyawarah*) among representatives.
5. Social Justice for all the people of Indonesia.

STATE ORGANS

Majelis Permusyawaratan Rakyat—MPR (People's Consultative Assembly)

Sovereignty is in the hands of the People and is exercised in full by the People's Consultative Assembly as the embodiment of the whole Indonesian People. The Consultative Assembly is the highest authority of the State, and is to be distinguished from the legislative body proper (Dewan Perwakilan Rakyat, see below) which is incorporated within the Consultative Assembly. The Consultative Assembly, with a total of 920 members (to increase to 1,000 members in 1987), is composed of all members of the Dewan, augmented by delegates from the regions and representatives of the functional groups in society (farmers, workers, businessmen, the clergy, intelligentsia, armed forces, students, etc.). The Assembly sits at least once every five years, and its primary competence is to determine the constitution and the broad lines of the policy of the State and the Government. It also elects the President and Vice-President, who are responsible for implementing that policy. All decisions are taken unanimously in keeping with the traditions of *musyawarah*.

The President

The highest executive of the Government, the President, holds office for a term of five years and may be re-elected. As Mandatory of the MPR he must execute the policy of the State according to the Decrees determined by the MPR during its Fourth General and Special Sessions. In conducting the administration of the State, authority and responsibility are concentrated in the President. The Ministers of the State are his assistants and are responsible only to him.

Dewan Perwakilan Rakyat—DPR (House of Representatives)

The legislative branch of the State, the House of Representatives, sits at least once a year. It has 460 members: 364 elected, 96

INDONESIA

appointed from Functional Groups (to increase to 500 members in 1987: 100 nominated by the President and 400 directly elected). Every statute requires the approval of the DPR. Members of the House of Representatives have the right to submit draft bills which require ratification by the President, who has the right of veto. In times of emergency the President may enact ordinances which have the force of law, but such Ordinances must be ratified by the House of Representatives during the following session or be revoked.

Dewan Pertimbangan Agung—DPA (Supreme Advisory Council)
The DPA is an advisory body assisting the President who chooses its members from political parties, functional groups and groups of prominent persons.

Mahkamah Agung (Supreme Court)
The judicial branch of the State, the Supreme Court and the other courts of law are independent of the Executive in exercising their judicial powers.

Badan Pemeriksa Keuangan (Supreme Audit Board)
Controls the accountability of public finance, enjoys investigatory powers and is independent of the Executive. Its findings are presented to the DPR.

The Government

HEAD OF STATE

President: SUHARTO (inaugurated 27 March 1968; re-elected March 1973, March 1978 and March 1983).
Vice-President: Gen. UMAR WIRAHADIKUSUMAH.

CABINET
(January 1987)

Minister of Home Affairs: Gen. SUPARDJO RUSTAM.
Minister of Foreign Affairs: Prof. Dr MOCHTAR KUSUMAATMADJA.
Minister of Defence and Security: Gen. S. PONIMAN.
Minister of Justice: ISMAIL SALEH.
Minister of Information: HARMOKO.
Minister of Finance: Drs RADIUS PRAWIRO.
Minister of Trade: RACHMAT SALEH.
Minister of Co-operatives: BUSTANIL ARIFIN.
Minister of Agriculture: ACHMAD AFFANDI.
Minister of Forestry: SUJARWO.
Minister of Industry: HARTARTO.
Minister of Mining and Energy: Prof. Dr SUBROTO.
Minister of Public Works: SUYONO SOSRODARSONO.
Minister of Communications: RUSMIN NURJADIN.
Minister of Tourism, Post and Telecommunications: Gen. ACHMAD TAHIR.
Minister of Manpower: Adm. SUDOMO.
Minister of Transmigration: MARTONO.
Minister of Education and Culture: Prof. FUAD HASSAN.
Minister of Health: Dr SUWARDJONO SURJANINGRAT.
Minister of Religious Affairs: Haji MUNAWIR SJADZALI.
Minister of Social Affairs: Mrs NANI SUDARSONO.
Minister-Co-ordinator for Political Affairs and Security: Gen. SURONO REKSODIMEDJO.
Minister-Co-ordinator for the Economy, Finance, Industry and Development Supervision: Prof. Dr ALI WARDHANA.
Minister-Co-ordinator for Public Welfare: Gen. ALAMSJAH RATU PERWIRANEGARA.
Minister of State and State Secretary: Gen. SUDHARMONO.
Minister of State for National Development Planning, concurrently Chairman of the National Development Planning Board: Prof. Dr JOHANNES B. SUMARLIN.
Minister of State for Research and Technology, concurrently Chairman of the Board for the Study and Application of Technology: Prof. Dr BUCHARUDDIN JUSUF HABIBIE.
Minister of State for Population and the Environment: Prof. Dr EMIL SALIM.

Minister of State for Public Housing: Drs COSMAS BATUBARA.
Minister of State for Youth and Sports: Dr ABDUL GAFUR.
Minister of State for State Administrative Reforms, concurrently Vice-Chairman of the National Development Planning Board: Dr SALEH AFIF.
Minister of State for Women's Affairs: Mrs LASIYAH SUTANTO.
Junior Minister and Cabinet Secretary: MURDIONO.
Junior Minister for Promotion of the Use of Domestic Products: Dr GINANDJAR KARTASASMITA.
Junior Minister for Development of Food Production: Dr WARDOYO.
Junior Minister for Development of Tree Crops: Dr HASRUL HARAHAP.
Junior Minister for Development of Fisheries and Animal Husbandry: Prof. Dr J. H. HUTASOIT.
Officials with the rank of Minister of State:
Attorney-General: Maj.-Gen. HARI SUHARTO.
Chairman of the Audit Board: Gen. M. YUSUF.
Governor of Bank Indonesia: Dr ARIFIN M. SIREGAR.
Commander-in-Chief of the Indonesian Armed Forces: Gen. L. B. MURDANI.

MINISTRIES

Office of the President: Istana Merdeka, Jakarta; tel. (021) 331097.
Office of the Vice-President: Jalan Merdeka Selatan 6, Jakarta; tel. (021) 363539.
Ministry of Agriculture: Jalan Imam Bonjol 29, Jakarta; tel. (021) 334648.
Office of the Attorney-General: Jalan Sultan Hasanuddin 1, Jakarta; tel. (021) 773557.
Office of the Audit Board: Bapeka Bldg, 9th Floor, Rm 908, Jalan Jenderal Gatot Subroto, Jakarta; tel. (021) 584880.
Office of the Cabinet Secretary: Jalan Veteran 18, Jakarta Pusat; tel. (021) 348531.
Ministry of Communications: Jalan Merdeka Barat 8, Jakarta 10110; tel. (021) 366332; telex 46116.
Ministry of Co-operatives: Jalan Mohd Ikhwan Ridwan Rais 5, Jakarta; tel. (021) 357758.
Ministry of Defence and Security: Jalan Merdeka Barat 13, Jakarta Pusat; tel. (021) 374408.
Ministry for Development of Fisheries and Animal Husbandry: Jalan Imam Bonjol 29, Jakarta; tel. (021) 337137.
Ministry for Development of Food Production: Jalan Imam Bonjol 29, Jakarta; tel. (021) 337178.
Ministry for Development of Tree Crops: Jalan Imam Bonjol 29, Jakarta; tel. (021) 337156.
Ministry of the Economy, Finance, Industry and Development Supervision: Jalan Lapangan Banteng Timur 4, Jakarta; tel. (021) 365079.
Ministry of Education and Culture: Jalan Jenderal Sudirman, Senayan, Jakarta Pusat; tel. (021) 581618.
Ministry of Finance: Jalan Lapangan Banteng Timur 4, Jakarta Pusat; tel. (021) 348938.
Ministry of Foreign Affairs: Jalan Taman Pejambon 6, Jakarta Pusat; tel. (021) 368014.
Ministry of Forestry: Gedung Pusat Kehutanan, Senayan, Jakarta Selatan; tel. (021) 581820.
Ministry of Health: Jalan Prapatan 10, Jakarta Pusat; tel. (021) 349801.
Ministry of Home Affairs: Jalan Merdeka Utara 7, Jakarta Pusat; tel. (021) 373908.
Ministry of Industry: Jalan Jenderal Gatot Subroto Kav. 52-53, Jakarta; tel. (021) 511661.
Ministry of Information: Jalan Merdeka Barat 9, Jakarta Pusat; tel. (021) 377408; telex 44264.
Ministry of Justice: Jalan Hayam Wuruk 7, Jakarta Pusat; tel. (021) 342083.
Ministry of Manpower: Jalan Jenderal Gatot Subroto, Jakarta Pusat; tel. (021) 515717.
Ministry of Mining and Energy: Jalan Merdeka Selatan 18, Jakarta Pusat; tel. (021) 360232.

INDONESIA

Ministry of National Development Planning: Jalan Taman Suropati 2, Jakarta Pusat; tel. (021) 336207; telex 61623.

Ministry of Political Affairs and Security: Jalan Merdeka Barat 15, Jakarta; tel. (021) 376004.

Ministry for Population and the Environment: Jalan Medan Merdeka Barat 15, Jakarta Pusat; tel. (021) 371295; telex 46143.

Ministry for Promotion of the Use of Domestic Products: Jalan Veteran 17, Jakarta; tel. (021) 349063.

Ministry of Public Housing: Jalan Kebon Sirih 31, Jakarta Pusat; tel. (021) 333649.

Ministry of Public Welfare: Jalan Merdeka Barat 3, Jakarta Pusat; tel. (021) 353055.

Ministry of Public Works: Jalan Pattimura 20, Kebayoran Baru, POB 21/KBY Jakarta Selatan; tel. (021) 717564; telex 47247.

Ministry of Religious Affairs: Jalan M. H. Thamrin 6, Jakarta Pusat; tel. (021) 320135.

Ministry of Research and Technology: Gedung Menara Patra, 3rd Floor, Jalan M. H. Thamrin 8, Jakarta Pusat; tel. (021) 324767.

Ministry of Social Affairs: Jalan Ir H. Juanda 36, Jakarta Pusat; tel. (021) 341329.

Ministry for State Administrative Reforms: Jalan Taman Suropati 2, Jakarta; tel. (021) 334811.

Office of the State Secretary: Perpustakaan, Dewan Perwakilan Rakyat-R.I., Jalan Jenderal Gatot Subroto, Senayan, Jakarta.

Ministry of Tourism, Posts and Telecommunications: Jalan Kebon Sirih 36, Jakarta; tel. (021) 346855.

Ministry of Trade: Jalan Mohd Ikhwan Ridwan Rais 5, Jakarta; tel. (021) 348667.

Ministry of Transmigration: Jalan Letjen. Haryono MT, Cikoko, Jakarta Selatan; tel. (021) 794682.

Ministry of Women's Affairs: Jalan Merdeka Barat 3, Jakarta Pusat; tel. (021) 376431.

Ministry of Youth and Sports: Jalan Jenderal Sudirman, Senayan, Jakarta Pusat; tel. (021) 581986.

Legislature

MAJELIS PERMUSYAWARATAN RAKYAT—MPR
(People's Consultative Assembly)

The Assembly consists of the members of the House of Representatives, regional delegates, members of Golkar and the Armed Forces, and of the two parties appointed in proportion to their share of DPR seats. In 1986 the total membership was 920, but in 1987 the Assembly was to be enlarged to 1,000 members.

Chairman: AMIR MACHMUD.

	Seats
Golkar	461
Armed forces	230
Partai Persatuan Pembangunan	148
Partai Demokrasi Indonesia	43
Non-affiliated regional representatives	34
Members from East Timor	4
Total	920

Dewan Perwakilan Rakyat—DPR
(House of Representatives)

In March 1960 a presidential decree prorogued the elected Council of Representatives and replaced it by a nominated House of 283 members (increased to 460 in 1968). Subsequently, the number of appointed members was reduced to 96. The remaining 364 were directly elected. In July 1986, as a result of an increase in the size of the electorate, it was announced that the House of Representatives would expand from 460 to 500 members in the April 1987 elections. The President would nominate 100 members and the remaining 400 members would be directly elected.

Speaker: AMIR MACHMUD.

Directory

General Election, 4 May 1982

	Seats
Golkar	246
Partai Persatuan Pembangunan	94
Partai Demokrasi Indonesia	24
Appointed members*	96
Total	460

*Members of the political wing of the Indonesian Armed Forces (ABRI).

Political Organizations

A presidential decree of January 1960 enables the President to dissolve any party whose membership does not cover one-quarter of Indonesia, or whose policies are at variance with the aims of the State.

The following parties and groups participated in the general election held in May 1982:

Partai Demokrasi Indonesia (PDI) (Indonesian Democratic Party): Jakarta; f. 1973 by the merger of five nationalist and Christian parties; Gen. Chair. SURYADI.

Partai Persatuan Pembangunan (PPP) (United Development Party): Jalan Diponegoro 60, Jakarta; tel. 356381; f. 1973 by the merger of four Islamic parties (Nahdlatul Ulama—NU, Sarikat Islam, Perti and Muslimin Indonesia—MI); Pres. SOEDARDJI; Sec.-Gen. MARDINSYAH.

Sekber Golongan Karya (Golkar) (Joint Secretariat of Functional Groups): Jakarta; f. 1964, reorganized 1971; the governing alliance of groups representing farmers, fishermen and the professions; Pres. and Chair. of Advisory Board SUHARTO; Gen. Chair. Gen. SUDHARMONO; Sec.-Gen. SARWONO KUSUMAATMADJA.

The following groups are in conflict with the Government:

Frente Revolucionário de Este Timor Independente (Fretilin): based in East Timor; f. 1974; desires self-government and independence in East Timor; entered into alliance with the UDT in 1986; International Relations Sec. JOSÉ RAMOS HORTA.

Organisasi Papua Merdeka (OPM) (Free Papua Movement): based in Irian Jaya; f. 1963; seeks unification with Papua New Guinea; Leader ELKY BEMEI.

União Democrática Timorense (UDT): based in Dili, East Timor; f. 1974; advocates self-determination for East Timor through a gradual process in which ties with Portugal would be maintained; formed a coalition with Fretilin in 1986.

Diplomatic Representation

EMBASSIES IN INDONESIA

Afghanistan: Jalan Dr Kusuma Atmaja 15, Jakarta; tel. (021) 333169; Chargé d'affaires: ABDUL AZIZ ELYASSI.

Algeria: Jl. H. R. Rasuna Said Kav. 10-1, Kuningan, Jakarta; tel. 514719; Ambassador: MUHAMMAD KESSOURI.

Argentina: Jalan Panarukan 17, Jakarta 10310; tel. (021) 338088; telex 45529; Ambassador: Dr TOMÁS ALVA NEGRI.

Australia: Jalan M. H. Thamrin 15, Jakarta; tel. (021) 323109; Ambassador: BILL MORRISON.

Austria: Jalan Diponegoro 44, Jakarta; tel. (021) 338101; telex 46387; Ambassador: Dr ERNST ILLSINGER.

Bangladesh: Jalan Mendut 3, Jakarta; tel. (021) 324850; Ambassador: Maj.-Gen. MOINUL HUSSEIN CHOWDHURY.

Belgium: Jalan Cicurug 4, Jakarta; tel. (021) 348719; telex 44413; Ambassador: JAN HELLEMANS.

Brazil: Jalan Cik Ditiro 39, Menteng, Jakarta; tel. (021) 358378; telex 45657; Ambassador: JORGE DE SÁ ALMEIDA.

Bulgaria: Jalan Imam Bonjol 34/36, Jakarta 10310; tel. (021) 346725; telex 45106; Ambassador: YULI BAHNEV.

Burma: Jalan Haji Agus Salim 109, Jakarta; tel. (021) 320440; Ambassador: U THAN HLA.

Canada: 5th Floor, Wisma Metropolitan, Jalan Jendral Sudirman 29, POB 52/JKT, Jakarta; tel. (021) 510709; telex 62131; Ambassador: JACK WHITTLETON.

Chile: 14th Floor, Arthaloka Bldg, Jalan Jendral Sudirman 2, Jakarta; tel. (021) 584308; telex 46533; Ambassador: THOMAS AMENABAR.

INDONESIA

Czechoslovakia: Jalan Prof. Mohd Yamin 29, POB 319, Jakarta; tel. (021) 346480; telex 45139; Ambassador: RICHARD KRAL.
Denmark: Denmark House, Jalan Abdul Muis 34, POB 2329, Jakarta Pusat; tel. (021) 346615; telex 44188; Ambassador: ANDERS BRANDSTRUP.
Egypt: Jalan Teuku Umar 68, Jakarta; tel. (021) 331141; Ambassador: MUHAMMAD ALI KAMEL.
Finland: Bina Mulia Bldg, 10th Floor, Jalan H. R. Rasuna Said Kav. 10, Kuningan, Jakarta 12950; tel. (021) 516980; telex 48280; Ambassador: ERIK HEINRICHS.
France: Jalan M. H. Thamrin 20, Jakarta; tel. (021) 332807; Ambassador: LOÏC HENNEKINNE.
German Democratic Republic: Jalan Raden Saleh 56, POB 2252, Jakarta; tel. (021) 349547; telex 46463; Ambassador: SIEGFRIED KÜHNEL.
Germany, Federal Republic: Jalan M. H. Thamrin 1, Jakarta; tel. (021) 323908; telex 44333; Ambassador: Dr HELMUT MATTHIAS.
Holy See: Jalan Merdeka Timur 18, POB 4227, Jakarta (Apostolic Nunciature); tel. (021) 341142; Apostolic Pro-Nuncio: PABLO PUENTE.
Hungary: 36 Jalan Rasuna Said, Kav. 3 Kuningan, Jakarta; tel. (021) 587521; telex 46839; Ambassador: GYULA BARANYI.
India: Jalan H. R. Rasuna Said 51, Kuningan, Jakarta; tel. (021) 518150; telex 44260; Ambassador: VINOD C. KHANNA.
Iran: Jalan Hos Cokroaminoto 110, Jakarta; tel. (021) 330623; Ambassador: ABDOLAZIM HASHEMI-NIK.
Iraq: Jalan Teuku Umar 38, Jakarta; tel. (021) 355017; telex 46280; Ambassador: ZAKI ABDULHAMID AL-HABBA.
Italy: Jalan Diponegoro 45, Jakarta; tel. (021) 348339; telex 44118; Ambassador: GIORGIO VECCHI.
Japan: Jalan Mohammad Hoesni Thamrin 24, Jakarta; tel. (021) 324308; Ambassador: TOSHIO YAMAZAKI.
Korea, Democratic People's Republic: Jalan Teuku Umar 72/74, Jakarta; tel. (021) 346457; Ambassador: CHO SONG-BOM.
Korea, Republic: Jalan Jendral Gatot Subroto 57, Jakarta Selatan; tel. (021) 512309; Ambassador: CHOI SANG-SUP.
Malaysia: Jalan Imam Bonjol 17, Jakarta 10310; tel. (021) 336438; telex 44445; Ambassador: Tuan Haji MUHAMMAD KHATIB BIN ABDUL HAMID.
Mexico: Jalan M. H. Thamrin 59, Jakarta; tel. (021) 337974; Ambassador: GUILLERMO CORONA MUÑOZ.
Netherlands: Jalan H. R. Rasuna Said, Kav. S-3, Kuningan, Jakarta 12950; tel. (021) 511515; Ambassador: FRANS VAN DONGEN.
New Zealand: Jalan Diponegoro 41, Menteng, Jakarta; tel. (021) 330552; telex 46109; Ambassador: GORDON PARKINSON.
Nigeria: 34 Jalan Diponegoro, Jakarta; tel. (021) 345484; telex 44580; Ambassador: (vacant).
Norway: Jalan Padalarang 4, Jakarta; tel. (021) 354556; Ambassador: KNUT BERGER.
Pakistan: Jalan Teuku Umar 50, Jakarta; tel. (021) 350576; Ambassador: MATAHAR HUSEIN.
Papua New Guinea: Panin Bank Centre, 1 Jalan Jendral Sudirman, Jakarta; tel. (021) 711225; Ambassador: BRIAN K. AMINI.
Philippines: Jalan Imam Bonjol 6–8, Jakarta; tel. (021) 346786; Ambassador: Brig.-Gen. RAMON FAROLAN.
Poland: Jalan Diponegoro 65, Jakarta; tel. (021) 320509; Ambassador: CZESŁAW MUSZALSKI.
Romania: Jalan Cik Ditiro 42A, Jakarta; tel. (021) 354847; telex 61208; Ambassador: VALERIU GEORGESCU.
Saudi Arabia: Jalan Imam Bonjol 3, Jakarta; tel. (021) 346342; Ambassador: MUHAMMAD SAID BASRAWI.
Singapore: Jalan Proklamasi 23, Jakarta; tel. (021) 348761; Ambassador: J. F. CONCEICAO.
Spain: Wisma Kosgoro, 14th Floor, Jalan M. H. Thamrin 53, Jakarta; tel. (021) 325996; Ambassador: JOSÉ ANTONIO ACEVAL (designate).
Sri Lanka: Jalan Diponegoro 70, Jakarta; tel. (021) 321018; Ambassador: D. SERASINGHE.
Sweden: Jalan Taman Cut Mutiah 12, POB 2824, Jakarta 10001; tel. (021) 333061; telex 61452; Ambassador: KARL GÖRAN ENGSTRÖM.
Switzerland: Jalan H. R. Rasuna Said, Blok X 3/2, Kuningang, Jakarta Selantan; tel. (021) 516061; telex 44113; Ambassador: GÉRARD FRANEL.
Syria: Jalan Gondangdia Lama 38, Jakarta; tel. (021) 359261; Ambassador: NADIM DOUAY.
Thailand: Jalan Imam Bonjol 74, Jakarta; tel. (021) 343762; Ambassador: RONGPET SUBHARITIKUL.
Turkey: Jalan R. S. Kuningan Kav. I, Kuningan, Jakarta; tel. (021) 516258; Ambassador: AYDIN ALACKAPTAN.
USSR: Jalan M. H. Thamrin 13, Jakarta; tel. (021) 322162; Ambassador: STANISLAV I. SEMIVOLOS.
United Kingdom: Jalan M. H. Thamrin 75, Jakarta 10310; tel. (021) 330904; telex 61166; Ambassador: ALAN DONALD.
USA: Jalan Merdeka Selatan 5, Jakarta; tel. (021) 360360; Ambassador: PAUL WOLFOWITZ.
Venezuela: 17th Floor, Central Plaza Bldg, Jl. Sudirman, Jakarta; tel. (021) 516885; telex 62701; Ambassador: JESÚS GARCÍA CORONADO.
Viet-Nam: Jalan Teuku Umar 25, Jakarta; tel. (021) 347325; Ambassador: TRINH XUAN LANG.
Yugoslavia: Jalan Hos Cokroaminoto 109, Jakarta; tel. (021) 333593; Ambassador: Dr DJORDJE JAKOVLJEVIĆ.

Judicial System

There is one codified criminal law for the whole of Indonesia. Europeans are subject to the Code of Civil Law published in the State Gazette in 1847. For Indonesians the civil law is the uncodified customary law (*Hukum Adat*) which varies from region to region. Alien orientals (i.e. Arabs, Indians, etc.) and Chinese are subject to certain parts of the Code of Civil Law and the Code of Commerce. The work of codifying this law has started but in view of the great complexity and diversity of customary law it may be expected to take a considerable time to achieve.

Supreme Court: The final court of appeal (cassation).
Chief Justice: Lt-Gen. ALI SAID.
  High Courts in Jakarta, Surabaya, Medan, Ujungpandang (Makassar), Banda Aceh, Padang, Palembang, Bandung, Semarang, Banjarmasin, Menado, Denpasar, Ambon and Jayapura deal with appeals from the District Courts.
  District Courts deal with marriage, divorce and reconciliation.

Religion

In 1984 an estimated 78% of the population were Muslims, while 11% were Christians, 2% were Hindus and 5% professed adherence to tribal religion.

ISLAM

Indonesian Ulama Council (MUI): Central Muslim organization; Chair. (vacant).

CHRISTIANITY

The Roman Catholic Church

Indonesia (excluding East Timor) comprises seven archdioceses and 26 dioceses. At 31 December 1984 there were an estimated 3,930,000 adherents in the country, representing about 2.5% of the total population. East Timor comprises the single diocese of Dili, directly responsible to the Holy See. At 31 December 1984 the territory had an estimated 470,737 Roman Catholics (about 75% of the total population).

Bishops' Conference: Majelis Agung Waligeraja Indonesia, Taman Cut Mutiah 10, Jakarta 11/14; tel. (021) 356452; f. 1973; Pres. Mgr FRANCIS XAVIER SUDARTANTO HADISUMARTA, Bishop of Malang.
Archbishop of Ende: Most Rev. DONATUS DJAGOM, Agung-Ende, Ndona-Ende-Flores, Tromol Pos 210, Surabaya; tel. 176.
Archbishop of Jakarta: Most Rev. LEO SOEKOTO, Jalan Katedral 7, Jakarta 10710; tel. (021) 362392.
Archbishop of Medan: Most Rev. ALFRED GONTI PIUS DATUBARA, Jalan Imam Bonjol 39, 20152 Medan, Sumatra Utara; tel. (061) 516647.
Archbishop of Merauke: Most Rev. JACOBUS DUIVENVOORDE, Keuskupan Agung, Merauke, Irian Jaya; tel. (0971) 21011.
Archbishop of Pontianak: Most Rev. HIERONYMUS HERCULANUS BUMBUN, POB 120, Jalan A.R. Hakim 92A, Pontianak, Kalimantan Barat; tel. (0561) 2382.

INDONESIA

Archbishop of Semarang: Most Rev. JULIUS RIYADI DARMAATMADJA, Jalan Pandanaran 13, 50231 Semarang; tel. (024) 313025.

Archbishop of Ujung Pandang: (vacant), Keuskupan Agung, Jalan Thamrin 5-7, Ujung Pandang; tel. (0411) 5744.

Other Christian Churches

Indonesian Christian Church: Gen. Sec. Rev. J. H. WIRAKOTAN; Jalan Panglima Polim 1/51A, Kebayoran Baru, Jakarta 12160; tel. (021) 712040; Reformed Presbyterian Church; 77,170 mems, 119 congregations and 177 ministers in 1985.

Indonesian Lutheran Church: Rev. DIPNA PANDJI TISNA, Jakarta Selatan.

Methodist Church of Indonesia: Bishop J. GULTOM; Methodist Headquarters, Jalan Hang Tuah 8, Medan; tel. 510570.

Union of Indonesian Baptist Churches: Pres. WIM H. THEORNPUN; Sec. Rev. DAVID SUMARTO; POB 2474, Jakarta Pusat; tel. (021) 356584.

The Press

PRINCIPAL DAILIES

Java

Berita Buana: Jalan Tanah Abang Dua 33-35, Jakarta Pusat 10110; tel. (021) 340011; telex 46472; f. 1970; Indonesian; Editor SUKARNO HADI WIBOWO; circ. 150,000.

Berita Yudha: Jalan Bangka II/2, 2nd Floor, Kebayoran Baru, Jakarta; tel. (021) 75286; f. 1971; Indonesian; Editor SUNARDI; circ. 50,000.

Harian Indonesia (Indonesia Rze Pao): Jalan Toko Tiga Seberang 21, POB 534, Jakarta Kota; f. 1966; Chinese; Editors Drs T. W. SLAMET, HADI WIBOWO; circ. 40,000.

Harian Umum AB: CTC Bldg, 2nd Floor, Kramat Raya 94, Jakarta Pusat; f. 1965; official armed forces journal; Dir GOENARSO; Editor-in-Chief N. SOEPANGAT; circ. 80,000.

The Indonesia Times: Jalan Letjen. S. Parman Kav. 72, POB 224, Slipi, Jakarta; tel. (021) 592403; telex 46968; f. 1974; English; Chief Editor R. P. HENDRO; circ. 35,000.

Indonesian Daily News: Surabaya; f. 1957; English; Editor HOS. NURYAHYA; circ. 10,000.

Indonesian Observer: Jalan A. M. Sangaji 11, Jakarta; tel. (021) 43334; f. 1955; English; independent; Editor GANIS HARSONO; circ. 25,000.

Jakarta Post: Jalan Palmerah Selatan 15B/C, Jakarta Pusat 10270; tel. (021) 5483948; telex 46327; f. 1983; English; Gen. Man. MOHAMED CHUDORI; Editor SABAM SIAGIAN; circ. 16,400.

Jawa Pos: Jalan Kembang Jepun 167, Surabaya; tel. (031) 22778; telex 31988; f. 1949; Indonesian; Chief Editor DAHLAN ISKAN; circ. 52,000.

Kedaulatan Rakyat: Jalan P. Mangkubumi 40-42, Yogyakarta; f. 1945; Indonesian; independent; Editor IMAN SUTRISNO; circ. 50,000.

Kompas: Jalan Palmerah Selatan 20-28, POB 615/DAK, Jakarta Pusat; tel. (021) 543008; telex 46327; f. 1965; Indonesian; Editor Drs JAKOB OETAMA; circ. 415,000.

Masa Kini: Jalan Mayor Suryotomo 23, Yogyakarta; f. 1966; Chief Editor H. ACHMAD BASUNI; circ. 25,000.

Merdeka: Jalan A. M. Sangaji 11, Jakarta; tel. (021) 364858; f. 1945; Indonesian; independent; Dir and Chief Editor B. M. DIAH; circ. 130,000.

Pelita (Torch): Jalan Diponegoro 60, Jakarta; f. 1974; Indonesian; Muslim; Editor AKBAR TANJUNG; circ. 80,000.

Pewarta Surabaya: Jalan Karet 23, POB 85, Surabaya; f. 1905; Indonesian; Editor RADEN DJAROT SOEBIANTORO; circ. 10,000.

Pikiran Rakyat: Jalan Asia-Afrika 77, Bandung; f. 1950; independent; Editor ATANG ROSWITA; circ. 80,000.

Pos Kota: Jalan Gajah Mada 63, Jakarta; f. 1970; Indonesian; Editor H. SOFYAN LUBIS; circ. 250,000.

Pos Sore: Jalan Asemka 29/30, Jakarta; tel. (021) 24039; f. 1971; Indonesian; Editor S. ABIJASA; circ. 40,000.

Sinar Harapan (Ray of Hope): Jalan Dewi Sartika 136-D, Cawang, Jakarta 13630; tel. (021) 803208; telex 48202; f. 1961; independent; Publr H. G. RORIMPANDEY; Editor SUBAGYO PR; circ. 300,000.

Sinar Pagi: Jalan Letjen. Haryono MT 22, Jakarta Selatan; f. 1971; Indonesian; Editor C. T. SIAHAAN; circ. 25,000.

Directory

Suara Karya: Jalan Bangka 11/2, Kebayoran Baru, Jakarta; f. 1971; Indonesian; Editor SYAMSUL BASRI; circ. 100,000.

Suara Merdeka: Jalan Kaligawe Km 5, Semarang; tel. (024) 21480; telex 22269; f. 1950; Indonesian; Publr Ir BUDI SANTOSO; Editor SUWARNO; circ. 145,000.

Surabaya Post: Jalan AIS Nasution 1, Surayaba; tel. (031) 45523; telex 31158; f. 1953; independent; Publr Mrs TUTY AZIS; Editor A. AZIS; circ. 85,000.

Kalimantan

Banjarmasin Post: Jalan Pasar Baru 222, Banjarmasin; f. 1971; Indonesian; Chief Editor H. J. DJOK MENTAYA; circ. 50,000.

Gawi Manuntung: Jalan Pangeran Samudra 97B, Banjarmasin; f. 1972; Indonesian; Editor M. ALI SRI INDRADJAYA; circ. 5,000.

Sulawesi

Pedoman Rakyat: Jalan H. A. Mappanyukki 28, Ujungpandang; f. 1947; independent; Editor M. BASIR; circ. 30,000.

Sumatra

Analisa: Jalan Jend. A. Yani 37-43, Medan; tel. (061) 326655; telex 51326; f. 1972; Indonesian; Editor SOFFYAN; circ. 75,000.

Haluan: Jalan Damar 57 C/F, Padang; f. 1948; Editor-in-Chief RIVAI MARLAUT; circ. 40,000.

Mimbar Umum: 30A Jalan Palang, Merah; tel. (061) 517807; telex 51905; f. 1947; Indonesian; independent; Editor MOHD LUD LUBIS; circ. 55,000.

Sinar Indonesia Baru: Jalan Brigjen. Katamso 54, ABCD Medan; f. 1970; Indonesian; Chief Editor G. M. PANGGABEAN; circ. 60,000.

Suara Rakyat Semesta: Jalan K. H. Ashari 52, Palembang; Indonesian; Editor DJADIL ABDULLAH; circ. 10,000.

Waspada: Jalan Suprapto/Katamso 1, Medan; f. 194.; Indonesian; Editors PRABUDI SAID, AMMARY IRABI; circ. 55,000 (daily), 50,000 (Sunday).

PRINCIPAL PERIODICALS

Basis: POB 20, Yogyakarta; tel. (0274) 88283; f. 1951; monthly; cultural; Editor DICK HARTOKO; circ. 3,000.

Berita Negara: Jalan Pertjetakan Negara 21, Kotakpos 2111, Jakarta; f. 1960; 3 a week; official gazette.

Bobo: Jalan Palmerah Selatan 22, Jakarta; tel. (021) 534008; telex 41216; f. 1973; weekly; children's magazine; Editor TINEKE LATUMETEN; circ. 160,000.

Buana Minggu: Jalan Tanah Abang Dua 33, Jakarta Pusat 10110; tel. (021) 364190; telex 46472; weekly; Sunday; Indonesian; Editor WINOTO PARARTHO; circ. 193,450.

Budaja Djaja: Jalan Gajah Mada 104-110A, Jakarta Barat; f. 1968; cultural; independent; Editor AJIP ROSIDI; circ. 4,000.

Business News: Jalan H. Abdul Muis 70, Jakarta; tel. (021) 348207; f. 1956; 3 a week (Indonesian edn), 2 a week (English edn); Chief Editor SANJOTO SASTROMIHARDJO; circ. 15,000.

Depthnews Indonesia: Jalan Jatinegara Barat III/6, Jakarta Timur; tel. (021) 814994; f. 1972; weekly; publ. by Press Foundation of Indonesia; Editor SUMONO MUSTOFFA.

Dunia Wanita: Jalan Brigjen. Katamso 1, Medan; f. 1949; fortnightly; Indonesian; women's magazine; Chief Editor Mrs PRAPUDI SAID; circ. 10,000.

Economic Review: c/o BNI 1946, Jalan Lada 1, POB 1946 KB, Jakarta 11001; tel. (021) 672075; f. 1947; quarterly; English.

Economics and Finance in Indonesia: Institute for Economic and Social Research, University of Indonesia, Jalan Raya Salemba 4, POB 295/JKT, Jakarta; quarterly; circ. 4,000.

Ekonomi Indonesia: Indonesian Economic Journal, Metraco Bldg, Jalan Enggano 15, Jakarta 14310; tel. (021) 494458; fortnightly; English; Editor Z. ACHMAD; circ. 20,000.

Femina: Jalan H. R. Rasuna Said, Blok B, Kav. 32-33, Jakarta Selatan; tel. (021) 513816; telex 62338; f. 1972; weekly; women's magazine; Publisher SOFJAN ALISJAHBANA; circ. 130,000.

Fokus: Jakarta; f. 1982; Editor H. S. WARDOYO; circ. 10,000.

Gema Jusani: Jalan Salemba Tengah 47, Jakarta Pusat; f. 1981; monthly; Indonesian; journal of Corps of Invalids; Editor H. ANWAN BEY; circ. 20,000.

Hai: Jalan Palmerah Selatan 22, Jakarta 10270; tel. 5483008; telex 41216; f. 1973; weekly; youth magazine; Editor ARSWENDO ATMOWILOTO.

INDONESIA

Harian Pagi Umum (Bali Post): Jalan Kepudang 67A, Denpasar; f. 1948; weekly (Indonesian edn), monthly (English edn); Editor RAKA WIRATMA; circ. 5,000.

Horison: Jalan Gajah Mada 104–110A, Jakarta Barat; f. 1966; monthly; literary and cultural; independent; Editors MOCHTAR LUBIS, H. B. JASSIN, TAUFIC ISMAEL; circ. 4,000.

Hukum & Keadilan: Jalan Gajah Mada 110A, Jakarta Barat; f. 1974; fortnightly; independent law journal; Editors SUARDI TASRIF, SOENARDI, ADNAN BUYUNG NASUTION; circ. 3,000.

Indonesia Magazine: 20 Jalan Merdeka Barat, Jakarta; tel. (021) 352015; telex 46655; f. 1969; monthly; English; Chair. G. DWIPAYANA; Editor-in-Chief HADELY HASIBUAN; circ. 15,000.

Intisari (Digest): Jalan Palmerah Selatan 26–28, POB 615/DAK, Jakarta; tel. (021) 5483008; telex 46327; f. 1963; monthly; investment and trading; Editors IRAWATI, Drs J. OETAMA; circ. 141,000.

Keluarga: Jalan Sangaji 9–11, Jakarta; monthly; women's and family magazine; Editor D. S. MULYANTO.

Majalah Ekonomis: POB 4195, Jakarta; monthly; English; business; Chief Editor S. ARIFIN HUTABARAT; circ. 20,000.

Majalah Kedokteran Indonesia (Journal of the Indonesian Medical Asscn): Jalan Kesehatan 111/29, Jakarta 11/16; f. 1951; monthly; Indonesian, English.

Manglé: Jalan Lodaya 19–21, Bandung; tel. (022) 411438; f. 1957; weekly; Sundanese; Chief Editor Drs OEJANG DARAJATOEN; circ. 74,000.

Matra: Jakarta; f. 1986; monthly; men's magazine; general interest and current affairs; Editor-in-Chief FIKRI JUFRI; circ. 100,000.

Mimbar Kabinet Pembangunan: Jalan Merdeka-Barat 7, Jakarta; f. 1966; monthly; Indonesian; publ. by Dept of Information.

Mimbar Pembangunan: Jalan Merdeka-Barat 7, Jakarta; f. 1968; quarterly; Indonesian; publ. by Dept of Information.

Mimbar Penerangan: Jalan Merdeka-Barat 7, Jakarta; f. 1950; quarterly; Indonesian; publ. by Dept of Information.

Mutiara: Jalan Dewi Sartika 136-D, Cawang, Jakarta Timur; general interest; Publr H. G. RORIMPANDEY.

Peraba: Bintaran Kidul 5, Yogyakarta; weekly; Indonesian and Javanese; Roman Catholic; Editor W. KARTOSOEHARSONO.

Pertani PT: Jalan Pasar Minggu, Kalibata, POB 247 KBY, Jakarta Selatan; tel. (021) 793108; telex 47249; f. 1974; monthly; Indonesian; agricultural; Pres. Dir Ir RUSLI YAHYA.

Rajawali: Jakarta; monthly; Indonesian; civil aviation and tourism; Dir R. A. J. LUMENTA; Man. Editor KARYONO ADHY.

Selecta: Kebon Kacang 29/4, Jakarta; fortnightly; illustrated; Editor SAMSUDIN LUBIS; circ. 80,000.

Sinar Jaya: Jalan Sultan Agung 67A, Jakarta Selatan; bi-weekly; agriculture; Chief Editor Ir SURYONO PROJOPRANOTO.

Tempo: Pusat Perdagangan Senen, Blok II, Lantai III, Jakarta; tel. (021) 343561; telex 46777; f. 1971; weekly; Indonesian; current affairs; Editor GOENAWAN MOHAMAD; circ. 150,000.

Topik: Jalan A. M. Sangaji 9–11, Jakarta; f. 1972; monthly; Indonesian; Editor B. M. DIAH; circ. 10,000.

NEWS AGENCIES

Antara (Indonesian National News Agency): Wisma Antara, 19th and 20th Floors, 17 Merdeka Seletan, POB 257, Jakarta 1002; tel. (021) 344379; telex 44305; f. 1937; state radio, TV and 52 newspaper subscribers in 1985; 27 brs in Indonesia, two overseas brs; connected with 37 foreign agencies; mem. of ASEAN news exchange network, Organization of Asia-Pacific News Agencies, International Islamic News Agency, OPEC News Agency and Non-Aligned Press Agencies Pool; 8 bulletins in Indonesian and 7 in English; one European edn, one Asian edn; monitoring service of stock exchanges world-wide; Gen. Man. BAKIR HASAN; Editor-in-Chief BAKIR HASAN.

Kantorberita Nasional Indonesia (KNI News Service): Jalan Jatinegara Barat III/6, Jakarta Timur; tel. (021) 811003; f. 1966; independent national news agency; foreign and domestic news in Indonesian and English; Dir and Editor-in-Chief Drs SUMONO MUSTOFFA; Exec. Editor SUDJARWO.

Foreign Bureaux

Agence France-Presse (AFP): Jalan Indramayu 18, Jakarta Pusat; tel. (021) 334877; Chief Correspondent JACQUES GUILLON.

Agencia EFE (Spain): J. L. Cilandak VI/37, Kebayoran Baru, Jakarta-Selantan, Jakarta; Bureau Chief MIRIAM PADILLA.

Agenzia Nazionale Stampa Associata (ANSA) (Italy): Jalan Mesjid 11/8, Pejompongan, Jakarta; tel. (021) 587422; Correspondent PAUL HANDLEY.

Associated Press (AP) (USA): Jalan Kebon Sirih 40 (Flat 30), POB 2056, Jakarta; tel. (021) 360234; Correspondent GHAFUR FADYL.

Jiji Tsushin-sha (Japan): Jalan Situbondo 10, Menteng, Jakarta; tel. (021) 343594; Correspondent SHIGEKI YAMASHITA.

Kyodo Tsushin (Japan): Skyline Bldg, 11th Floor, M. H. Thamrin 9, Jakarta Pusat; tel. (021) 345012; Correspondent MASAYUKI KITAMURA.

Reuters (UK): 17th Floor, Wisma Antara, Jalan Medan Merdeka Selatan 17, POB 2318, Jakarta Pusat; tel. (021) 345011; telex 45373; Correspondent PETER MILLERSHIP.

Telegrafnoye Agentstvo Sovetskovo Soyuza (TASS) (USSR): 7 Surabaya, Jakarta; Correspondent YURI SAGAJDA.

United Press International (UPI) (USA): Wisma Antara, 14th Floor, Jalan Medan Merdeka Selatan 17, Jakarta; tel. (021) 341056; Bureau Chief JOHN HAIL.

PRESS ASSOCIATIONS

Persatuan Wartawan Indonesia (Indonesian Journalists' Asscn): Gedung Dewan Pers, 4th Floor, 34 Jalan Kebon Sirih, Jakarta 10110; tel. (021) 353131; f. 1946; 4,000 mems (Aug. 1984); Exec. Chair. ZULHARMANS; Gen. Sec. ATANG RUSWITA.

Serikat Penerbit Suratkabar (SPS) (Indonesian Newspaper Publishers' Asscn): Gedung Dewan Pers, Floor 6, Jalan Kebonsirih 34, Jakarta Pusat; f. 1946; tel. (021) 359671; Chair. D. M. SUNARDI; Sec.-Gen. MUHAMMAD CHUDORI.

Yayasan Pembina Pers Indonesia (Press Foundation of Indonesia): Jalan Jatinegara Barat III/6, Jakarta Timur; tel. (021) 814994; f. 1967; Chair. SUGIARSO SUROYO, MOCHTAR LUBIS.

Publishers

Jakarta

Akadoma: Jalan Proklamasi 61, Jakarta Pusat; tel. (021) 882328; Dir ADAM SALEH.

Aksara Baru: 5 Jalan Jend. Sudirman, Kav. 46A, Blok B, Bendungan Hilir, Jakarta Pusat; tel. (021) 586640; f. 1972; general science and university texts; Dir Drs SOFJAN AHMAD.

Aries Lima: Komplex Maya Indah II, Blok B/2, Jalan Kramat Raya 3E, Jakarta Pusat; tel. (021) 367038; f. 1974; general and children's; Pres. TUTI SUNDARI AZMI.

Balai Pustaka: Jalan Dr Wahidin 1, POB 29, Jakarta; tel. (021) 361701; telex 45905; f. 1908; children's, literary, scientific publs and periodicals; CEO Drs SOETOJO GONDO.

Bhratara Karya Aksara: Jalan Rawabali II/5, Kawasan Industri Pulogadung, Jakarta Timur; tel. (021) 4890280; telex 49283; f. 1958; university and educational textbooks; Man. Dir AHMAD JAYUSMAN.

Bulan Bintang: Jalan Kramat Kwitang 1/8, Jakarta 10420; tel. (021) 342883; f. 1954; religious, social science, natural and applied sciences, art; Pres. AMRAN ZAMZAMI; Man. Dir FAUZI AMELZ.

Djambatan: Jalan Kramat Raya 152, Tromolpos 116, Jakarta Pusat; tel. (021) 345131; f. 1954; children's, textbooks, social sciences, fiction; Dir ROSWITHA PAMOENTJAK SINGGIH.

Dunia Pustaka Jaya: Jalan Kramat Raya 5K, Jakarta 10450; tel. (021) 367339; f. 1971; fiction, religion, essays, poetry, drama, criticism, art, philosophy and children's; Man. YUS RUSAMSI and SUMARYOTO.

Erlangga: Jalan Kramat IV/II, Jakarta Pusat; tel. (021) 356593; f. 1952; secondary school and university textbooks; Man. Dir M. HUTAURUK.

Gaya Favorit Press: Jalan H. Rasuna Said, Blok B Kav. 32–33, Jakarta 12910; tel. (021) 513816; telex 62338; f. 1971; fiction, popular science and children's; Man. Dir SOFJAN ALISJAHBANA.

Ghalia Indonesia: Jalan Pramuka Raya 4, Jakarta Timur; tel. (021) 884814; f. 1972; children's and general science, textbooks; Man. Dir LUKMAN SAAD.

Gramedia: Jalan Palmerah Selatan 22, Lantai IV, POB 615, Jakarta Pusat; tel. (021) 5483008; telex 46327; f. 1970; university textbooks, general non-fiction, children's and magazines; Gen. Man. Y. ADISUBRATA.

Gunung Agung: Jalan Kwitang 8, POB 145, Jakarta 10002; tel. (021) 362909; telex 44359; f. 1953; general, textbooks, science; Pres. H. MASAGUNG.

INDONESIA

Gunung Mulia: Jalan Kwitang 22, Jakarta Pusat; tel. (021) 372208; f. 1951; general, children's, religious, home economics; Man. W. H. SIMANJUTAK.

Hidakarya Agung PT: Jalan Kebon Kosong F74, Kemayoran, Jakarta Pusat; tel. (021) 411074; Dir CHAIRI MACHMUD.

Ichtiar: Jalan Majapahit 6, Jakarta Pusat; tel. (021) 341226; f. 1957; textbooks, law, social sciences, economics; Dir JOHN SEMERU.

Indira PT: Jalan Borobudur 20, Jakarta Pusat; tel. (021) 882754; telex 48211; f. 1953; general science and children's; Man. Dir WAHYUDI DJOJOADINOTO.

Kinta PT: Jalan Cik Ditiro 54A, Jakarta Pusat; tel. (021) 350221; f. 1950; textbooks, social science, general; Man. Drs MOHAMAD SALEH.

Mutiara Sumber Widya PT: Jalan Pulokambing 9, Industrial Estate Pulogadung, Jakarta Timur; tel. (021) 4893810; telex 46709; f. 1951; textbooks, religious, social sciences, general and children's; Pres. and Dir H. OEMAR BAKRI TAN BESAR.

Pembangunan PT: Jalan Grinting I/15, Kebayoram Baru, Jakarta Selantan; tel. (021) 770039; f. 1953; textbooks, children's; Mans SUMANTRI, SUWEDO.

Penerbit Universitas Indonesia: Jalan Salemba Raya 4, Jakarta; tel. (021) 335373; f. 1969; science; Man. Dr EDI SWASONO.

Pradnya Paramita PT: Jalan Kebon Sirih 46, POB 146/JKT, Jakarta 10002; tel. (021) 360411; f. 1973; children's, general, educational, technical and social science; Dir SADONO DIBYOWIROYO.

Pustaka Antara PT: Jalan Majapahit 28, Jakarta Pusat 10160; tel. (021) 341321; f. 1952; textbooks, political, religious, children's and general; Man. Dir H. M. JOESOEF AHMAD.

Pustaka Sinar Harapan: Jalan Dewi Sartika 136D, Jakarta 13630; tel. (021) 803208; telex 48202; f. 1981; general science, fiction, children's; Dir ARISTIDES KATOPPO.

Sastra Hudaya: Jalan Proklamasi 61, Jakarta Pusat; tel. (021) 882328; f. 1967; religious, textbooks, children's and general; Man. ADAM SALEH.

Tintamas Indonesia: Jalan Kramat Raya 60, Jakarta Pusat 10420; tel. (021) 346186; f. 1947; biography, history, modern science and culture, especially Islamic; Man. Miss MARHAMAH DJAMBEK.

Widjaya: Jalan Pecenongan 48C, Jakarta Pusat; tel. (021) 363446; f. 1950; textbooks, children's, religious and general; Man. NAZAR YAHYA.

Yasaguna: Jalan Minangkabau 44, POB 422, Jakarta Selatan; tel. (021) 820422; f. 1964; agricultural, children's, handicrafts; Dir HILMAN MADEWA.

Bandung

Alma'arif: Jalan Tamblong 48–50, Bandung; tel. (022) 50708; f. 1949; textbooks, religious and general; Man. H. M. BAHARTHAH.

Alumni: Jalan Dr. Djundjunan 190, POB 272, Bandung; tel. (022) 87672; telex 28460; f. 1968; university and school textbooks; Dir EDDY DAMIAN.

Angkasa: Jalan Merdeka 6, POB 354, Bandung; tel. (022) 51795; telex 28530; Dir FACHRI SAID.

Binacipta: Jalan Ganesya 4, Bandung; tel. (022) 84319; f. 1967; textbooks, scientific and general; Man., Pres. and Dir Mrs R. BARDIN; Gen. Man. A. BARDIN.

Diponegoro Publishing House: Jalan Mohamed Toha 44–46, Bandung 40252; tel. (022) 59395; f. 1963; religious, textbooks, fiction, non-fiction, general; Man. IDA HAMIDAH DAHLAN.

Eresco PT: Jalan Hasanudin 9, Bandung 40132; tel. (022) 82311; f. 1957; scientific and general; Man. Mrs H. P. ROCHMAT SOEMITRO.

Orba Sakti: Jalan Pandu Dalam 3/67, Bandung; tel. (022) 614718; Dir H. HASULLOH.

Pelita Masa: Jalan Lodaya 25, Bandung; tel. (022) 50823; f. 1973; reference and children's; Man. ROCHDI PARTAATMADJA.

Remaja Karya: Jalan Ciateul 34–36, POB 284, Bandung; tel. (022) 58226; textbooks and children's fiction; Man. ROZALI USMAN.

Rosda: Jalan Raya Cimahi-Padalarang Km 12.5, 858, Bandung; tel. (022) 56627; f. 1969; school textbooks, children's; Dir NY H. MURSYIDAH.

Tarsito: Jalan Guntur 20, Bandung; tel. (022) 421915; Dir T. SITORUS.

Tira Pustaka: Jalan Cemara Raya 1, Kav. 10D, Jaka Permai Jakasampurna, Bekasi Jawa Barat, Bandung; tel. (99) 71276; telex 62612; Dir WILLIE KOEN.

Flores

Nusa Indah: Jalan Katedral 5, Ende, Flores; tel. 198; f. 1973; religious, general and periodicals; Man. ALEXANDER BEDING.

Kudus

Menara Kudus: Jalan Menara 2, Kudus; tel. 143527; f. 1958; religious; Man. HILMAN NAJIB.

Medan

Hasmar: Jalan Letjen Haryono M.T. 1, POB 446, Medan; tel. (061) 24181; primary school textbooks; Dir HASBULLAH LUBIS; Man. AMRAN SAID RANGKUTI.

Islamiyah: Jalan Sutomo 328–329, Kotakpos 11, Medan; tel. (061) 25426; f. 1954.

Madju: Jalan Sutomo P342, Medan; f. 1950; textbooks, children's and general; Pres. and Dir H. MOHAMED ARBIE.

Semarang

Effhar COY PT: Jalan Dorang 7, Semarang; tel. (024) 23518; f. 1974; school books; Dir DARADJAT HARAHAP.

Intan: Jalan Bhayangkara II/20, Klaten, Semarang; tel. (024) 21883; Dir EDY WIDYANTO.

Surabaya

Airlangga University Press: Dharmahusada 47, Surabaya; tel. (031) 472719; Dir Drs SOEDHARTO.

Assegaff: Jalan Panggung 136, Surabaya; tel. (031) 22971; f. 1951; religion, languages, primary school textbooks; Man. HASSAN ASSEGAFF.

Bina Ilmu PT: Jalan Tunjungan 53E, Surabaya; tel. (031) 472214; f. 1973; school textbooks; Pres. ARIEFIN NOOR.

Bintang: Jalan Putroagung III/1A, Surabaya; tel. (031) 315941; Dir AGUS WINARNO.

Grip: Jalan Kawung 2, POB 129, Surabaya; tel. (031) 22564; f. 1958; textbooks and general; Man. Mrs SURIPTO.

Institut Dagang Muchtar: Jalan Embong Wungu 8, Surabaya; tel. (031) 42973; textbooks for business colleges; Pres. Z. A. MOECHTAR.

Jaya Baya: Jalan Embong Malang 6gH, POB 250, Surabaya; tel. (031) 41169; f. 1945; religion, philosophy and ethics; Man. TADJIB ERMADI.

Karunia: Jalan Peneleh 18, Surabaya; tel. (031) 44120; f. 1970; textbooks and general; Man. HASAN ABDAN.

Marfiah: Jalan Kalibutuh 131, Surabaya; reference and primary school textbooks; Man. S. WAHYUDI.

Sinar Wijaya: Komplek Terminal Jembatan Merah, Stand C33-37, Surabaya; tel. (031) 270284; Dir DULRADJAK.

Ujungpandang

Bhakti Centra Baru PT: Jalan Jend. Akhmad Yani 15, Ujungpandang; tel. (0411) 5192; telex 71156; f. 1972; textbooks, religion and general; Gen. Man. MOHAMMAD ALWI HAMU.

Yogyakarta

Indonesia UP: Jalan Sultan Agung 57, Yogyakarta; tel. 3010; f. 1950; general science; Dir H. KARKONO KAMAJAYA.

Kedaulatan Rakyat PT: Jalan P. Mangkubumi 40–42, Yogyakarta; tel. (0274) 2163; telex 25176; Dir DRONO HARDJUSUWONGSO.

Yayasan Kanisius: Jalan Panembahan Senopati 24, Yogyakarta; tel. (0274) 2309; telex 25143; f. 1922; textbooks, religious and general; Man. R. P. S. PADMOBUSONO.

Government Publishing House

Balai Pustaka (State Publishing and Printing House): Jalan Dr Wahadin 1, Jakarta; history, anthropology, politics, philosophy, medical, arts and literature.

PUBLISHERS' ASSOCIATION

Ikatan Penerbit Indonesia (IKAPI) (Asscn of Indonesian Book Publishers): Jalan Kalipasir 32, Jakarta Pusat 10330; tel. (021) 321907; f. 1950; 271 mems; Pres. Drs AZMI SYAHBUDDIN; Sec.-Gen. Drs ARSELAN HARAHAP.

Radio and Television

In 1984 there were an estimated 6.6m. radio receivers and 5.4m. registered television receivers in use. Three new TV transmitters were expected to be in operation by early 1987.

INDONESIA   Directory

Directorate-General of Posts and Telecommunications: Jalan Kebon Sirih 37, Jakarta; tel. (021) 346000; telex 44407; Dir-Gen. S. ABDULRACHMAN.

RADIO

Radio Republik Indonesia (RRI): Jalan Merdeka Barat 4–5, POB 157, Jakarta; tel. (021) 349091; telex 44349; f. 1945; 49 stations; Dir Ir ISKANDAR ARFAN; Dep. Dirs JUL CHAIDIR (Overseas Service), I. M. P. TANTRAWAN (Domestic Service), UTIEK RUKTININGSIH (News).

Voice of Indonesia: POB 157, Jakarta; foreign service; daily broadcasts in Arabic, English, French, German, Indonesian, Japanese, Bahasa Malaysia, Mandarin, Spanish and Thai.

TELEVISION

Yayasan Televisi Republik Indonesia (TVRI): Senayan, Kebayoran Baru, Jakarta; tel. (021) 581125; telex 46154; f. 1962; state-controlled; Gen. Man. M. SUMADI.

Finance

(cap. = capital; res = reserves; dep. = deposits; p.u. = paid up; auth. = authorized; m. = million; brs = branches; amounts in rupiahs)

BANKING

In addition to the five state commercial banks and one state savings bank, there were 69 private national banks, one national development bank, 27 regional development banks, two private savings banks, 11 foreign banks and 13 non-bank financial institutions in 1986.

Central Bank

Bank Indonesia: Jalan M. H. Thamrin 2, Jakarta; tel. (021) 372408; telex 44164; f. 1828; nationalized 1951; became the central bank in 1953; cap. and res 447,000m., dep. 3,406,000m. (March 1986); Gov. ARIFIN M. SIREGAR; Pres. T. M. ZAHIRSJAH.

State Banks

Bank Bumi Daya: Jalan Imam Bonjol 61, POB 106, Jakarta; tel. (021) 333721; telex 61117; f. 1959; commercial and foreign exchange bank, specializes in credits to the plantation and forestry sector; cap. p.u. 300m., dep. 5,716,728m. (March 1986); Pres. OMAR ABDALLA; 81 brs.

Bank Dagang Negara: Jalan M. H. Thamrin 5, POB 338/JKT, Jakarta; tel. (021) 321707; telex 44721; f. 1960; auth. foreign exchange bank; specializes in credits to the mining sector; cap. p.u. 250m., dep. 5,141,631m. (March 1986); Pres. H. M. WIDARSADIPRADJA; 86 brs, 2 overseas brs.

Bank Ekspor Impor Indonesia: Jalan Lapangan Setasiun 1, POB 32, Jakarta Kota; tel. (021) 673122; telex 42702; f. 1968; commercial and foreign exchange bank; specializes in credits for manufacture and export; cap. 200m., dep. 5,276,080m. (March 1986); Pres. MOELJOTO DJOJOMARTONO; 56 brs.

Bank Negara Indonesia 1946: Jalan Lada 1, Jakarta Kota 11001; tel. (021) 672075; telex 42704; f. 1946; commercial and foreign exchange bank; specializes in credits to the industrial sector; cap. and res 500m., dep. 8,202,295m. (March 1986); Pres. H. SOMALA WIRIA; 253 domestic brs, 6 overseas brs.

Bank Rakyat Indonesia; Jalan Veteran 8, POB 94, Jakarta; tel. (021) 374208; telex 44300; f. 1895, present name since 1946; commercial and foreign exchange bank; specializes in credits to cooperatives in agriculture and fisheries, in rural credit generally and international business; cap. 300m., dep. 5,276,080m. (March 1986); Pres. KARMADY ARIEF; 295 brs.

Bank Tabungan Negara (State Savings Bank): Jalan Gajah Mada 1, Jakarta; tel. (021) 360237; telex 45272; f. 1964; savings bank; cap. p.u. 100m., dep. 810,033m. (June 1986); Pres. SASONOTOMO; 12 brs.

Selected National Private Banks

PT Bank Bali: Jalan Hayam Wuruk 84–85, Jakarta 11160; tel. (021) 848006; telex 42724; f. 1954; foreign exchange bank; cap. p.u. 7,088m., dep. 255,871m. (March 1986); Pres. G. KARYADI; Chair. P. H. SUGIRI; 5 brs, 3 sub-brs.

PT Bank Buana Indonesia: Jalan Asemka 32–35, Jakarta; tel. (021) 672901; telex 42042; f. 1956; foreign exchange bank; cap. p.u. 7,500m., dep. 261,896m. (June 1986); Pres. HENDRA SURYADI; 11 brs, 10 sub-brs.

PT Bank Central Asia: Jalan Asemka 27–30, Jakarta; tel. (021) 671771; telex 42860; f. 1957; cap. p.u. 32,000m., dep. 594,227m. (June 1986); Pres. A. ALI; CEO Dir MOCHTAR RIADY; 20 brs, 15 sub-brs, repr. office 1.

PT Bank Duta: Jalan Kebon Sirih 12, Jakarta 10110; tel. (021) 3800900; telex 48308; f. 1966; foreign exchange bank; cap. p.u. 10,000m., dep. 352,104m. (March 1986); Pres. ABDULGANI; Dirs BEY YOESOEF, MUCHTAR MANDALA, DICKY ISKANDAR DI NATA; 7 brs, 2 sub-brs.

PT Bank Niaga: Jalan Gajah Mada 18, Jakarta; tel. (021) 377809; telex 45894; f. 1955; foreign exchange bank; cap. p.u. 9,896m., dep. 271,515m. (March 1986); Pres. Dir ROBBY DJOHAN; Man. Dirs I. JONOSEWOJO, WIJATNO SOEPENADIE; 16 brs, 4 sub-brs.

PT Bank NISP: Jalan Taman Cibeunying Selatan 31, Bandung; tel. (022) 57926; telex 28269; f. 1941; cap. p.u. 4,200m., dep. 67,193m. (Aug. 1986); Pres. KARMAKA SURJAUDA; Man. Dirs PETER EKO SUTIOSO, ANWARY SURJAUDAJA; 6 brs.

PT Bank Pacific: Jalan K. H. Samanhudi 17–19, Jakarta; tel. (021) 376408; telex 44818; f. 1958; foreign exchange bank; cap. p.u. 12,000m., dep. 82,974m. (March 1986); Pres. M. HATTA ABDULAH; Man. Dirs OEMAR SAID, ABDUL FIRMAN, H. P. TOAR; 5 brs, 3 sub-brs.

PT Bank Perdania: Jalan Raya Mangga Besar 7–11, Jakarta; tel. (021) 621708; telex 41120; f. 1956; foreign exchange bank; Pres. ISMED SIREGAR. 1 br., 1 sub-br.

PT Bank Umum Nasional: Jalan Prapatan 50, Jakarta; tel. (021) 365563; telex 46034; f. 1952; private national foreign exchange bank; cap. p.u. 9,100m., dep. 295,989m. (March 1986); Pres. Dir KAHARUDIN ONGKO, S. RANTY, V. U. KULIH; Exec. Dir M. DJAILANI; 15 brs, 4 sub-brs.

PT Overseas Express Bank: Jalan Pecenongan 84, Jakarta; tel. (021) 358103; telex 46350; f. 1974; foreign exchange bank; cap. p.u. 6,000m., dep. 171,033m. (June 1986); Chair. SOETIANTO SOEMALI; 8 brs.

PT Pan Indonesia (Panin) Bank: Panin Bldg, Jalan Jen. Sudirman, Senayan, Jakarta; tel. (021) 734545; telex 47394; f. 1971; foreign exchange bank; cap. p.u. 16,000m., dep. 403,504m. (March 1986); Pres. H. ANDI GAPPA; Exec. Vice-Pres MU'MIN ALI G., TIDJAN ANANTO; 12 brs, 10 sub-brs.

PT Sejahtera Bank Umum: Jalan Tiang Bendera 15, Jakarta Barat; tel. (021) 673804; telex 42760; f. 1952; cap. p.u. 3,650m., dep. 69,446m. (June 1986); Pres. LESMANA BASUKI; Man. Dir STEPHANUS SOEARTO; 4 brs, 2 sub-brs.

PT South East Asia Bank Ltd: Jalan Asemka 16–17, Jakarta; tel. (021) 672197; telex 42731; f. 1957; cap. p.u. 4,000m., dep. 24,110m. (June 1986); Pres. Dir AGUS SALIM; Man. Dirs Drs B. SURYADI, TRISNO HARIANTO, HARIONO; 2 brs.

PT United City Bank: Jalan Hayam Wuruk 121, Jakarta; tel. (021) 623508; telex 41165; f. 1968; cap. p.u. 4,053m., dep. 62,915m. (March 1986); Pres. AGUS ANANDATIO; 3 brs, 2 sub-brs.

Development Bank

Bank Pembangunan Indonesia (BAPINDO) (Development Bank of Indonesia): Jalan Gondangdia Lama 2–4, POB 140, Jakarta 10002; tel. (021) 321908; telex 44214; f. 1960; state bank; financial assistance to govt enterprises and privately-owned industrial and other productive enterprises; helps in development or establishment of new industries and other productive ventures, or expansion and modernization of existing enterprises; conducts feasibility studies of state projects; auth. cap. 50,000m., cap. p.u. 49,981m., total resources 1,389,037m. (March 1986); Pres. SUBEKTI ISMAUN; 21 brs.

Selected Finance Corporations

PT Bahana Pembinaan Usaha Indonesia (BAHANA): Jalan Teuku Cik Ditiro 23, Jakarta; tel. (021) 325207; telex 45332; f. 1973; cap. p.u. 6,000m.; Pres. BAHAUDDIN DARUS.

PT Inter-Pacific Financial Corpn: Jalan Jenderal Sudirman Kav. 31, Jakarta; tel. (021) 5781118; telex 46289; f. 1973; cap. p.u. 1,500m.; Pres. and Dir S. R. DWIANTO.

PT Multinational Finance Corpn (MULTICOR): Wisma BCA, 12th Floor, Jalan Jenderal Sudirman Kav. 22-23, Jakarta 12920; tel. (021) 5781450; telex 44932; f. 1974; cap. p.u. 1,000m.; Pres. and Dir K. R. WYNN.

PT Mutual International Finance Corpn: Nusantara Bldg, 17th Floor, Jalan M. H. Thamrin 59, Jakarta; tel. (021) 331108; telex 46259; f. 1973; cap. p.u. 1,000m.; Pres. Dir RACHMAT TANUSAPUTRA.

INDONESIA
Directory

PT Private Development Finance Co of Indonesia: Jalan Abdul Muis 60, Jakarta; tel. (021) 366608; telex 46778; f. 1973; cap. p.u. 4,539m.; Chair. and CEO Sudiarso.

PT Usaha Pembiayaan Pembangunan Indonesia (PT Indonesia Development Finance Co): UPPINDO Bldg, Jalan Abdul Muis 28, POB 24, Jakarta 10002; tel. (021) 354621; telex 46349; f. 1972; cap. p.u. 16,000m. (June 1986); Chair. Hendrobudiyanto; Pres. and Dir G. L. S. Kapitan; Man. Dir Sarwono Wishnuwardhana.

Foreign Banks

Algemene Bank Nederland NV (Netherlands): Jalan Ir H. Juanda 23–24, POB 2950, Jakarta 10001; tel. (021) 362309; telex 44124; Man. H. J. Buss.

Bangkok Bank Ltd (Thailand): Jalan M. H. Thamrin 3, Jakarta; tel. (021) 366008; telex 46193; Gen. Man. and Sr Vice-Pres. Adisorn Tantimedh.

Bank of America NT & SA (USA): Wisma Antara, 1st Floor, Jalan Medan Merdeka Selatan 17, POB 195, Jakarta; tel. (021) 348031; telex 44374; f. 1978; Vice-Pres. and Man. P. E. Yoomans.

Bank of Tokyo Ltd (Japan): Nusantara Bldg, Jalan M. H. Thamrin 59, POB 2711, Jakarta 10001; tel. (021) 333409; telex 44325; Gen. Man. Shigeyoshi Akaike.

The Chase Manhattan Bank, NA (USA): Chase Plaza, Jalan Jenderal Sudirman, Kav. 21, POB 311/JKT, Jakarta; tel. (021) 5782213; telex 44369; Country Man. Francis X. Shea.

Citibank, NA (USA): Jalan M. H. Thamrin 55, Jakarta 10001; tel. (021) 330507; telex 44368; f. 1912; Vice-Pres A. R. Batubara, M. M. Mistri.

Deutsche Bank (Asia) (Federal Republic of Germany): Jalan Imam Bonjol 80, POB 135, Jakarta 10002; tel. (021) 331092; telex 44114; Man. Dr Klaus Zeidler.

Hongkong and Shanghai Banking Corpn (Hong Kong): Jalan Hayam Wuruk 8, POB 2307, Jakarta 10001; tel. (021) 377808; telex 44160; br. at Jalan Pintu Besar Seletan 109b, Jakarta; tel. 672380; Man. K. R. Whitson.

Standard Chartered Bank (UK): Wisma Kosgoro, Jalan M. H. Thamrin 53, POB 57/JKWK, Jakarta 10350; tel. (021) 325008; telex 61179; Man. B. R. Knight.

Westpac Banking Corpn (Australia): 5th Floor, Bangkok Bank Bldg, Jalan M. H. Thamrin 3, Jakarta; tel. (021) 353758; telex 46125; f. 1972; Chief Rep. P. R. Milton.

Banking Association

Indonesian National Private Banks Association (Perhimpunan Bank-Bank Nasional Swasta—PERBANAS): Jalan Sindanglaya 1, Jakarta Pusat; tel. (021) 351939; telex 41513; f. 1952; 67 mems; Chair. Nyoman Moena; Sec.-Gen. Jusuf Wantah.

STOCK EXCHANGES

Badan Pelaksana Bursa Komoditi (Indonesian Commodity Exchange Board—ICEB): Jakarta; tel. 371918; telex 44194; trades in rubber and coffee; Chair. Paian Nainggolan.

Badan Pelaksana Pasar Modal (BAPEPAM) (Capital Market Executive Agency): Jalan Medan Merdeka Selatan 14, Jakarta; tel. (021) 365509; telex 45604; Chair. Prof Drs Barli Halim; Exec. Sec. Jusuf Anwar.

INSURANCE

In accordance with Ministry of Finance regulations, all 12 non-life foreign insurance companies had merged by 1980 with one or more domestic companies to form joint ventures. In 1982 a new regulation allowed foreign companies to form joint ventures in the life insurance sector.

In 1986 there were 93 insurance companies, comprising 12 non-life joint venture companies, 54 non-life companies, 19 life companies, 3 reinsurance companies, 5 social insurance companies, and 1 life joint venture company.

Insurance Supervisory Authority of Indonesia: Directorate of Financial Institutions, Ministry of Finance, Jalan Lapangan Banteng Timur 2–4, Jakarta Pusat; tel. (021) 360298; telex 46415; Dir Marzuki Usman.

Selected Life Insurance Companies

PT Asuransi Jiwa Buana Putra: Jalan Salemba Raya 23, Jakarta Pusat; tel. (021) 884116; telex 44338; f. 1974; Pres. Soebagyo Soetjitro.

PT Asuransi Jiwa Central Asia Raya: Jalan Gajah Mada 3–5, Jakarta; tel. (021) 348512; Pres. Wardoyo, S. H.

PT Asuransi Jiwa Ikrar Abadi: Jalan Letjen. Jend. S. Parman 108, Slipi, Jakarta Barat; tel. (021) 591335; f. 1975; Pres. Dir Harry Harmain Diah.

PT Asuransi Jiwa Iman Adi: Jalan Matraman Raya 102, Slipi, Jakarta; Man. B. W. Dumalang.

PT Asuransi Jiwa 'Panin Putra': Jalan Pintu Besar Selatan 52a, Jakarta Barat; tel. (021) 672586; telex 42881; f. 1974; Pres. Dir Achmad Danuningrat; Chair. Norman Batubara.

PT Asuransi Jiwa Jiwasraya: Jalan H. Juanda 34, POB 240, Jakarta Pusat; tel. (021) 345031; telex 45601; f. 1959; Pres. Alibasya Satari.

PT Asuransi Pensiun Bumiputera 1974: Jalan HOS Cokroaminoto 85, POB 3504, Jakarta; tel. (021) 344347; telex 44494; f. 1974; Gen. Man. Sudibyo Sutowibowo.

Bumi Asih Jaya Life Insurance Co: Jatinegara Barat 144, Jakarta; tel. 8190408; telex 48278; f. 1967; Pres. K. M. Sinaga.

Bumiputera 1912 Mutual Life Insurance Co: Wisma Bumiputera Jalan Jend. Sudirman Kav. 75, Jakarta; tel. (021) 575853; telex 44494; f. 1912; Pres. Sumardi Silvester.

PT Mahkota Jaya Abadi (Life Insurance Ltd): Jalan Sisingamangaraja 11, Jakarta Selatan; Man. Widodo Sukarno.

Selected Non-Life Insurance Companies

PT Asuransi Bintang: Jalan Hayam Wuruk 4cx, Jakarta Pusat; tel. (021) 372908; telex 45648; f. 1955; general insurance; Man. Dir B. Munir Syamsuddin; Gen. Mans Oloan Harahap, Pratyakso Hardjono.

PT Asuransi Central Asia: Jalan Gajah Mada 3, Jakarta Pusat; tel. (021) 373073; telex 46569; Pres. Anthony Salim.

PT Asuransi Indrapura: Wisma Metropolitan 2, 11th Floor, Jalan Jenderal Sudirman, Jakarta 12920; tel. 5780660; telex 62641; f. 1954; Pres. Dir Ruchimat Bratasasmita.

PT Asuransi Jasa Indonesia: Jalan Letjen. M. T. Haryono, Kav. 61, Jakarta Selatan; tel. (021) 794508; telex 42743; Pres. Iwa Sewaka.

PT Asuransi 'Ramayana': Jalan Kebon Sirih 49, Jakarta Pusat; tel. (021) 337148; telex 61670; f. 1956; Pres. R. G. Doeriat; Dirs Sadijono Harjokusumo, F. X. Widiastanto.

PT Asuransi Tugu Pratama Indonesia: Gedung Patra, 1st Floor, Jalan Gatot Subroto, Kav. 32–34, Jakarta 12950; tel. (021) 512041; telex 62800; Pres. Sonni Dwi Harsono.

PT Asuransi Wahana Tata: Jalan Roa Malaka Selatan 6, Jakarta 11230; tel. (021) 670123; telex 42937; Pres. Rudy Wanandi.

PT Maskapai Asuransi Indonesia: Jalan Sultan Hasannuddin 53-54, Kebayoran Baru, Jakarta Selatan; tel. (021) 710708; telex 47290; Pres. Z. U. Salawati.

PT Perusahaan Maskapai Asuransi Murni: Jalan Roa Malaka Selatan 21–23, Jakarta; tel. (021) 671826; telex 42851; f. 1953; Dirs H. Ninkeula, Soegiatna Probopinilih.

PT Maskapai Asuransi Timur Jauh: Jalan Medan Merdeka Barat 1, Jakarta Pusat; tel. (021) 375408; telex 44202; f. 1954; Pres. Dir Tantio A. P. Sudharmono; Dirs V. H. Kolondam, Mustafa Kamal.

Joint Ventures

PT Asuransi Jayasraya: Jl. M. H. Thamrin 9, Jakarta; tel. (021) 324207; Dirs Supartono, Sadao Suzuki.

PT Asuransi Insindo Taisho: Jl. M. H. Thamrin 59, Jakarta; tel. (021) 330246; Dirs Putu Widnyana, Reiso Haze.

PT Asuransi New Hampshire Agung: Jl. KH. Hasyim Ashari 35 Jakarta; tel. (021) 356581; Dirs Luis Le Fevre, Nani Kaudin.

PT Asuransi Royal Indrapura: Jl. M. H. Thamrin 53, Jakarta; tel. (021) 323709; Dirs F. Lamury, R. E. Hughes.

Insurance Association

Dewan Asuransi Indonesia (Insurance Asscn of Indonesia): Jalan Majapahit 34, Blok V/29, Jakarta; tel. (021) 363264; telex 44981; f. 1957; Chair. Sidharta; Exec. Sec. Bambang Hadikusumo.

Trade and Industry

National Development Planning Agency (Bappenas): Jalan Taman Suropati 2, Jakarta; tel. (021) 348990; drafts Indonesia's national economic development plans; Chair. Prof. Dr J. B. Sumarlin; Vice-Chair. Dr Saleh Afiff.

INDONESIA

CHAMBER OF COMMERCE

Kamar Dagang dan Industri Indonesia (KADIN) (Indonesian Chamber of Commerce and Industry): Jalan Merdeka Timur 11, Jakarta Pusat; tel. (021) 367096; telex 45977; f. 1966; 27 regional offices throughout Indonesia; Pres. SUKAMDANI S. GITOSARDJONO; Sec.-Gen. SOEKAMTO SAJIDIMAN.

TRADE ORGANIZATIONS

Association of State-Owned Companies: CTC Bldg, Jalan Kramat Raya 94–96, Jakarta; tel. (021) 346071; telex 44208; co-ordinates the activities of state-owned enterprises; Pres. ODANG.

Badan Koordinasi Penanaman Modal (BKPM) (Investment Co-ordinating Board): Jalan Jenderal Gatot Subroto 6, POB 3186, Jakarta; tel. (021) 512008; telex 45651; f. 1976; Chair. GINANDJAR KARTASASMITA.

CAFI (Commercial Advisory Foundation in Indonesia): Jalan Probolinggo 5, POB 249, Jakarta 10002; f. 1958; information, consultancy and translation services; Chair. Dr R. Ng. S. SOSROHADIKOESOEMO; Man. Dir DICK HAGE.

Export Arbitration Board: Jalan Kramat Raya 4–6, Jakarta; Chair. Ir R. M. SOSROHADIKUSUMO; Vice-Chair. SANUSI.

Gabungan Perusahaan Ekspor Indonesia (Indonesian Exporters' Federation): Jalan Kramat Raya 4–6, Jakarta; Pres. NAAFII; Sec. A. SOFYAN MUNAF.

GINSI (Importers' Asscn of Indonesia): Pintu Timur, Jalan Kesejahteraan, Arena Pekan Raya, POB 2744/JKT, Jakarta Pusat 10110; tel. (021) 377008; telex 46793; f. 1956; 2,360 mems; Chair. ZAHRI ACHMAD; Sec. Gen. K. S. OETOMO.

Indonesian Textile Products Traders Association: Wisma Fairbanks, Rooms A1–J1, Pintu Satu Senayan, Jakarta 10270; tel. (021) 581291; telex 46389.

Indonesian Tobacco Association: Jalan Kramat Raya 4–6, Jakarta; tel. (021) 320627; Pres. H. A. ISMAIL.

Masyarakat Perhutanan Indonesia (MPI) (Indonesian Forestry Association): Gedung Manggala Wanabakti, 9th Floor, Wing C/Blok IV, Jalan Jenderal Gatot Subroto, Jakarta Pusat 10270; tel. (021) 583010; telex 46977; f. 1974; 8 mems; Pres. SUKAMDANI SAHID GITOSARDJONO; Sec. Gen. H. A. RUSTAM EFFENDI.

National Board of Arbitration (BANI): Jalan Merdeka Timur 11, Jakarta; f. 1977; resolves company disputes; Chair. Prof. R. SUBEKTI.

Shippers' Council of Indonesia: Jalan Kramat Raya 4–6, Jakarta; Pres. R. S. PARTOKUSUMO.

STATE TRADING ORGANIZATIONS

General Management Board of the State Trading Corporations (BPU-PNN): Jakarta; f. 1961; Pres. Col SUHARDIMAN.

PT Aneka Tambang: Jalan Bungur Besar 24, POB 2513, Jakarta; tel. (021) 410108; telex 49147; f. 1968; minerals; Pres. Ir KOSIM GANDATARUNA.

PT Dharma Niaga Ltd: Jalan Abdul Muis 6/8/10, POB 2028, Jakarta; tel. (021) 349978; telex 44312; f. 1970; import, export, distribution, installation, after sales service; Pres. Drs ABU SADIKIN.

PT Indosat: Wisma Antara Bldg, 3rd Floor, Jalan Merdeka Selatan 17, Jakarta; telecommunications.

PT Nurtanio: BPP Teknologi Bldg, Jalan M. H. Thamrin 8, Jakarta; tel. (021) 322395; telex 44331; aerospace; Chair. Dr B. J. HABIBIE.

Perum Perhutani (State Forest Corpn): Gedung Manggala Wanabakti, Blok IV/Lantai 4, Jalan Gatot Subroto Senayan, POB 19 JKWB, Jakarta Pusat; tel. (021) 587090; telex 46283; f. 1973; Pres. Dir Ir HARTONO WIRJODARMODJO.

Perum Telekomunikasi (Perumtel): Jalan Ciasanggarang 2, Bandung; tel. (022) 59100; telex 28220; telephone and telegraphic services; CEO Ir W. MOENANDIR.

Perusahaan Pertambangan Minyak dan Gas Bumi Negara (PERTAMINA): Jalan Merdeka Timur 1, POB 12, Jakarta; tel. (021) 3032300; telex 44152; f. 1957; petroleum and natural gas; Pres. and Dir Maj.-Gen. ABDUL RAHMAN RAMLI.

PN Pos dan Giro: Jalan Cilaki 73, Bandung 40115; tel. (022) 58100; telex 28174; provides postal and giro services; CEO MOELJOTO.

PN Tambang Batubara: Jalan Prof. Supomo 10, Jakarta; tel. (021) 825608; telex 48203; f. 1968; coal-mining; Pres. ACHMAD PRIYONO.

PT Tambang Timah Persero: Jalan Jenderal Gatot Subroto, Jakarta; tel. (021) 510731; telex 44401; tin; Gen. Man. SUDJATMIKO.

Directory

PT Tjipta Niaga: Jalan Kalibesar Timur IV/1, POB 1213/DAK, Jakarta; tel. (021) 673923; telex 42747; f. 1964; import and distribution of basic goods, bulk articles, sundries, provisions and drinks, and export of Indonesian produce; Pres. Drs E. SIMANDJUNTAK.

TRADE UNION FEDERATION

All-Indonesia Union of Workers (SPSI): Jalan Tanah Abang III/21, Jakarta; tel. (021) 349197; f. 1973, renamed 1985; comprises 10 national industrial unions; Chair. IMAM SUDARWO; Vice-Chair. Drs SUKARNO; Gen. Sec. ADOLF RACHMAN.

Transport

RAILWAYS

There are railways on Java, Madura and Sumatra, totalling 6,444 km (4,004 miles) in 1985.

Perusahaan Jawatan Kereta Api (Indonesian State Railways): Jalan Perintis Kermedekaan 1, Bandung; tel. (021) 58001; telex 28263; six regional offices; controls 6,969.5 km of track on Java, Madura and Sumatra, of which 85 km are electrified (1985); Chief Dir Ir SUDJONO KRAMADIBRATA.

ROADS

There are adequate roads in Java, but on most of the other islands traffic is by jungle track or river boat. Total length of roads in 1984 was 177,896 km (110,539 miles), of which 12,235 km (7,602 miles) were motorways. A five-year road development programme, begun in 1982 to construct and repair roads and bridges, was to include a three-island tunnel and bridge link-up between Java, Bali and Sumatra. The cost of the project was estimated at US $520m. in 1986/87, of which $300m. was financed by the World Bank and $220m. by the Government.

Directorate General of Highways: Ministry of Public Works, Jalan Pattimura 20, Kebayoran Baru, POB 181/KBY, Jakarta; tel. (021) 772908; Dir Gen. Ir SURYATIN.

SHIPPING

The Ministry of Communications controls 336 ports, of which the four main ports of Tanjung Priok, near Jakarta, Tanjung Perak near Surabaya, Belawan near Medan and Ujungpandung in South Sulawesi have been designated gateway ports for nearly all international shipping to deal with Indonesia's exports and are supported by 15 collector ports. A major development programme for Jakarta's Tanjung Priok port to make it Indonesia's first container terminal was completed in 1979. A six-year port modernization programme, costing $186.5m., began in 1985. Among the ports which will be upgraded is Surabaya's Tanjung Perak, which will have expanded container facilities. In 1985 the total merchant fleet (inter-island and ocean-going) was 7,400 vessels, including 35 ocean-going cargo vessels and 78 bulk carriers.

Inter-island shipping is conducted by state-owned and private shipping lines, and there are many small craft.

Indonesian National Ship Owners' Association (INSA): Jalan Tanah Abang III/10, Jakarta; tel. (021) 375682; telex 46428; Pres. BOED IHAROJO SASTROHADIWIRJO.

Indonesian Oriental Lines, PT Perusahaan Pelayaran Nusantara: Jalan Raya Pelabuhan Nusantara, POB 2062, Jakarta 10001; tel. (021) 494344; telex 44233; 6 ships; Pres. Dir A. J. SINGH.

PT Jakarta Lloyd: Jalan Haji Agus Salim 28, Jakarta Pusat 10340; tel. (021) 331301; telex 44375; f. 1950; services to USA, Europe, Japan, Australia and the Middle East; 4 semi containers, 3 full containers, 3 general cargo vessels; Pres. Dir BAMBANG WAHYUDIONO.

PT Karana Line: Jalan Kali Besar Timur 30, POB 81, Jakarta Kota; tel. (021) 679103; telex 42727; 6 ships; Pres. Dir HAPOSAN PAN GABEAN.

PT Pelayaran Bahtera Adhiguna: Jalan Kalibesar Timur 10–12, Jakarta Kota; tel. (021) 676547; telex 42854; f. 1971; 7 ships; Pres. Drs ROESMAN ANWAR.

PT Pelayaran Nasional Indonesia (PELNI): Jalan Angkasa 18, POB 115, Jakarta; tel. (021) 417817; telex 44301; state-owned national shipping company; 4 passenger ships, 34 cargo vessels; Pres. Dir SOEDHARNO MUSTAFA.

PT Pelayaran Nusantara Sriwidjaya Raya: Jalan Tiang Bendera 52, Jakarta Kota; tel. (021) 675862; telex 42745; inter-island cargo and passenger services; 10 cargo vessels; Dirs SJAHRUL GHOZI BAJUMI, ROSIHAN NUCH BAJUMI.

INDONESIA

PT Pengembangan Armada Niaga Nasional: 4th Floor, Graha Purna Yudha Bldg, Jalan Jendral Sudirman 50, Jakarta; tel. (021) 515086; telex 515086; state-controlled; 24 ships; Pres. A. NAZAHAR.

PT Perusahaan Pelayaran Nusantara 'Nusa Tenggara': Kantor Pusat, Jalan Diponegoro 115 Atas, POB 69, Denpasar 80001, Bali; tel. (0361) 27720; telex 35210; 5 ships; Man. Dir KETUT DERESTHA.

PT Perusahaan Pelayaran Samudera Admiral Lines: Jalan Gunung Sahari 79-80, POB 476, Jakarta Pusat; tel. (021) 417908; telex 49122; 9 ships; Pres. H. SJOFJAN AFFANDIE.

PT Perusahaan Pelayaran Samudera Gesuri Lloyd: Gesuri Lloyd Bldg, Jalan Tiang Bendera 45, POB 289/JKT, Jakarta 11220; tel. (021) 675870; telex 42043; f. 1964; 7 cargo vessels, 5 charter ships; Pres. Dir ADIL NURIMBA.

PT Perusahaan Pelayaran Samudera Samudera Indonesia: Jalan Kali Besar Barat 43, POB 1244, Jakarta Kota; tel. (021) 671093; telex 42753; 4 ships; CEO H. S. SASTROSATAMO.

PT Perusahaan Pelayaran Samudera Trikora Lloyd: Jalan Malaka 1, POB 1076/JAK, Jakarta 11001; tel. (021) 671751; telex 42061; f. 1964; 5 ships; Pres. Dir B. SASTROHADIWIRYO; Man. Dir M. HARJONO KARTOHADIPRODJO.

PT Perusahaan Pertambangan Minyak dan Gas Bumi Negara (PERTAMINA): Jalan Jos Sudarso 32-34, POB 265, Tanjung Priok, Jakarta; tel. (021) 671093; telex 42753; state-owned; tanker services; 43 ships; Pres. and Chair. ABDUL RACHMAN RAMLY.

CIVIL AVIATION

The first stage of a new international airport, the Sukarno-Hatta Airport, at Cengkareng, near Jakarta, was opened in April 1985, to replace Halim Perdanakusuma Airport and Kemayoran Airport in Jakarta. Other international airports include Polonia Airport in Medan, Sumatra, Ngurah Rai Airport in Bali, Juanda Airport near Surabaya, Sam Ratulangi Airport, in Manado and Hasanuddin Airport near Ujung Pandang. Domestic air services link the major cities, and international services are provided by the state airline, PT Garuda Indonesian Airways, and by many foreign airlines.

PT AOA Zamrud Aviation Corpn: Jalan Dr Wahidin, Denpasar; f. 1969; domestic pasenger and cargo services and charter flights; Pres. UTOJO UTOMO; Dir DJOEBER AFFANDI; fleet of 3 DC-3.

PT Bali International Air Service: Jalan Angkasa 1-3, POB 2965, Jakarta; tel. (021) 625388; telex 41247; f. 1970; private company; subsidiary of BIA; charter services; Pres. J. A. SUMENDAP; Gen. Man. G. B. RUNGKAT; fleet of 4 Trislander, 4 BN Islander, 1 Cessna 404.

PT Bouraq Indonesia Airlines (BIA): Jalan Angkasa 1-3, POB 2965, Jakarta; tel. (021) 625364; telex 41247; f. 1970; private company; scheduled domestic passenger and cargo services linking Jakarta with points in Java, Kalimantan, Sulawesi, Bali, Timor and Tawau (Malaysia); Pres. J. A. SUMENDAP; Vice-Pres. Finance H. A. TUCUNAN; Exec. Vice-Pres. G. B. RUNGKAT; fleet of 16 HS-748, 4 VC8, 3 NC12 Aviocar.

PT Garuda Indonesian Airways: Jalan Ir Haji Juanda 15, Jakarta; tel. (021) 370709; telex 49113; f. 1950; state airline; operates domestic, regional and international services to Australia, France, the Federal Republic of Germany, Guam, Hong Kong, Italy, Japan, Malaysia, the Netherlands, New Zealand, the Philippines, Saudi Arabia, Singapore, Switzerland, Thailand, Taiwan, the United Arab Emirates and the United Kingdom; Pres. Dir R. A. J. LUMENTA; Gen. Man. SUPARNO; fleet of 6 Boeing 747, 34 Fokker-28, 19 DC-9, 6 DC-10, 9 Airbus A-300.

PT Mandala Airlines: Jalan Veteran I/34, POB 3706, Jakarta; tel. (021) 368107; f. 1969; private company; passenger and cargo services from Jakarta to Medan, Padang, Semarang, Surabaya, Ujungpadang, Ambon, Denpasar and Menado; Pres. Dir SANTOSO; fleet of 2 Vickers Viscount, 6 Lockheed Electra.

PT Merpati Nusantara Airlines: Jalan Angkasa 2, POB 323, Kemayoran, Jakarta; tel. (021) 413608; telex 49154; f. 1962; subsidiary of PT Garuda Indonesian Airways; domestic and regional services to Australia and Malaysia; Pres. SOERATMAN; fleet of 1 Vanguard 953, 2 Viscount 828, 14 F-27, 2 HS-748, 17 Twin Otter, 22 CASA CN-212, 2 L-300.

PT Sempati Air Transport: Jalan Medan Merdeka Timur 7, POB 2068, Jakarta; tel. (021) 343323; telex 45132; f. 1968; subsidiary of PT Tri Usaha Bhakti; passenger and cargo services throughout ASEAN countries; Pres. Capt. DOLF LATUMAHINA; fleet of 6 Fokker F-27.

Tourism

Dewan Pariwisata Indonesia (Indonesian Council for Tourism): 81 Jalan Kramat Raya, Jakarta; tel. (021) 343150; telex 45625; f. 1957; private body to promote national and international tourism; Chair. HAMENGKU BUWONO; Vice-Chair. Sri BUDOYO; Dir-Gen. JOOP AVE.

Atomic Energy

In 1986 the Government was conducting research on the construction of Indonesia's first nuclear power plant, in central Java, but a decision to build a plant was postponed, owing to the scarcity of government funds and to considerations of safety.

National Atomic Energy Agency (Badan Tenaga Atom Nasional—BATAN): Jalan K. H. Abdul Rachim, Kuningan Barat, Mampang Prapatan, POB 85/KBY, Jakarta Selatan; tel. (021) 511109; f. 1958; Dir-Gen. Ir DJALI AHIMSA.

IRAN

Introductory Survey

Location, Climate, Language, Religion, Flag, Capital

The Islamic Republic of Iran lies in western Asia, bordered by the USSR to the north, by Turkey and Iraq to the west, by the Persian (Arabian) Gulf and the Gulf of Oman to the south, and by Pakistan and Afghanistan to the east. The climate is one of great extremes. Summer temperatures of more than 55°C (131°F) have been recorded, but in the winter the great altitude of much of the country results in temperatures of −18°C (0°F) and below. The principal language is Farsi (Persian), spoken by about 50% of the population. Turkic-speaking Azerbaizhanis form about 27% of the population, and Kurds, Arabs, Baluchis and Turkomans form less than 25%. The great majority of Persians and Azerbaizhanis are Shi'i Muslims, while the other ethnic groups are mainly Sunni Muslims. There are also small minorities of Christians (mainly Armenians), Jews and Zoroastrians. The Bahá'í faith, which originated in Iran, has been severely persecuted. The national flag (proportions 3 by 1) has three horizontal stripes, of green, white and red, with the emblem of the Islamic Republic centrally positioned in red and the inscription 'Allaho Akbar' ('God is Great') repeated 22 times at the top and bottom. The capital is Teheran.

Recent History

Iran, called Persia until 1935, was formerly a monarchy, ruled by a Shah (Emperor). The country adopted its first imperial constitution in 1906, when the Qajar dynasty was in power. In 1921 Reza Khan, a Cossack officer, staged a military coup and became Minister of War. In 1923 he became Prime Minister, and in 1925 the National Assembly deposed the Shah and handed full power to Reza Khan. He was subsequently elected Shah, taking the title Reza Shah Pahlavi, and began the modernization of the country. During the Second World War Reza Shah favoured Nazi Germany. British and Soviet forces entered Iran in 1941, forcing the Shah to abdicate in favour of his son, Mohammed Reza Pahlavi.

After the war, British and US forces left Iran, although Soviet forces remained in Azerbaizhan until 1946. The Majlis (National Consultative Assembly) approved the nationalization of the petroleum industry in March 1951. The leading advocate of this measure was Dr Mohammed Mussadeq, leader of the National Front, who became Prime Minister in April 1951. After internal disturbances, Mussadeq was deposed in August 1953 in a coup supported by the USA and other Western countries. The dispute over nationalization was settled in August 1954, when an agreement was reached with foreign interests whereby concessions for petroleum drilling were granted to a consortium of eight companies. The Shah assumed total control of government in 1963, when he began an extensive redistribution of large estates to small farmers. In 1965 the Prime Minister, Hassan Ali Mansur, was assassinated, reportedly by a follower of the Ayatollah Ruhollah Khomeini, a Shi'i Muslim religious leader (exiled in 1964) who opposed the Shah's 'White Revolution' because it conflicted with traditional Islamic customs. The next Prime Minister was Amir Abbas Hoveida, who held office until 1977.

Between 1965 and 1977 Iran enjoyed political stability and considerable economic growth, based on revenue from petroleum. In March 1975 the Shah introduced a single-party system, based on the Iran National Resurgence Party (Rastakhiz). Opposition became increasingly evident, however, and during 1977 and 1978 demonstrations and strikes against the Shah and, in particular, against his secret police (SAVAK) rose to crisis level. The most effective opposition came from the exiled religious leader, Ayatollah Khomeini, who conducted his campaign from France, where he had arrived in October 1978 after 14 years of exile in Iraq. Khomeini demanded a return to the principles of Islam, and the response to this call in Iran was so great that the Shah felt compelled to leave the country in January 1979. Khomeini arrived in Teheran shortly afterwards, quickly overcame opposition from Dr Shapour Bakhtiar (appointed Prime Minister by the Shah in January) and took power on 11 February. Both houses of the legislature requested their own dissolution. Khomeini appointed a provisional government, with Dr Mehdi Bazargan as Prime Minister, but power rested with the 15-member Islamic Revolutionary Council. Dr Bazargan resigned in November.

Iran quickly cut its ties with the Central Treaty Organization (CENTO) and aligned itself with the Arab world against Israel. Khomeini declared Iran an Islamic Republic on 1 April, and a new constitution, prepared by an elected Council of Experts, was approved by referendum in December. According to the principle propounded in Khomeini's book *Wilayat e Faqih* ('Rule of the Theologian'), the Constitution vests supreme authority in the Wali Faqih, a religious leader (initially Khomeini) appointed by the Shi'ite clergy, with no fixed term of office, while the elected President is chief executive. A presidential election in January 1980 resulted in a convincing win for Abolhasan Bani-Sadr, with about 75% of the votes. In February he was sworn in as President, and also became Chairman of the Revolutionary Council. Elections to the 270-seat Majlis (National Assembly) were held in two rounds in March and May 1980, and resulted in a clear win for the Islamic Republican Party (IRP), which was identified with Khomeini.

After the Majlis began its first session in May 1980, the Islamic Revolutionary Council was dissolved. It was clear that a rift was developing between President Bani-Sadr and the more extreme element in the IRP. Bani-Sadr distrusted the Prime Minister, Muhammad Ali Rajai, whom he had reluctantly appointed in August. In March 1981 Ayatollah Khomeini appointed a three-man commission to resolve these differences, but in the space of a few days in June Khomeini dismissed Bani-Sadr as Commander-in-Chief of the Armed Forces and as President. Bani-Sadr fled to France, where he formed a 'National Council of Resistance' in alliance with Massoud Rajavi, the former leader in Iran of the Mujaheddin Khalq (an Islamic guerrilla group), who had also fled to France. Bani-Sadr left the council in April 1984 because of his objection to Rajavi's increasing co-operation with the Iraqi Government. Rajavi himself left Paris in June 1986 for Baghdad, Iraq.

Iran's relations with the USA received a severe setback in November 1979, when Iranian students seized 63 hostages in the US Embassy in Teheran. The original purpose of the seizure was to give support to a demand for the return of the Shah (then in the USA) to Iran to face trial. The problem was not resolved by the death of the Shah in Egypt in July 1980, as the Iranians made other demands. Most important of the new demands was one for a US undertaking not to interfere in the affairs of Iran. Intense diplomatic activity finally resulted in the release of the 52 remaining US hostages in January 1981.

Meanwhile, political chaos developed. A three-man Presidential Council replaced Bani-Sadr after his dismissal, until a new presidential election could be held in July 1981. In late June, however, a bomb exploded at the headquarters of the IRP, killing Ayatollah Beheshti (the Chief Justice of Iran and leader of the IRP), four government ministers, six deputy ministers and 20 members of the Majlis.

On 24 July a presidential election took place, as arranged, and resulted in a win for the Prime Minister, Muhammad Ali Rajai. Muhammad Javad Bahonar then became Prime Minister in a new administration, introduced to the Majlis on 13 August. A further bomb outrage occurred in late August, this time killing both the President (Rajai) and the Prime Minister (Bahonar). Ayatollah Muhammad Reza Mahdavi Kani became Prime Minister in September 1981, and another presidential election took place on 2 October. Hojatoleslam Ali Khamenei, a leading figure in the IRP, was elected President, winning more than 16m. of the 16.8m. votes cast. Later in October, Mir Hussein Moussavi, who had been Minister of Foreign Affairs since July, was appointed Prime Minister. A Council of Experts was elected in December 1982 to choose a successor to Ayatollah Khomeini.

Internal political strife has not been the only problem of post-revolutionary Iran. War broke out with Iraq in September 1980, when Iraq invaded Iran over a front of 500 km (300 miles) after a border dispute. The port of Khorramshahr was lost and retaken before Iranian counter-attacks forced the Iraqis to withdraw to their own territory in mid-1982. The Gulf War, as it became known, then degenerated into a conflict of attrition, with neither side apparently able to launch a decisive offensive. When, beginning in October 1983, Iran staged a series of offensives across its northern border with Iraq, threatening what was, at the time, the only remaining outlet for Iraqi exports of petroleum through the Kirkuk pipeline, Iraq intensified its attacks, with missiles and aircraft, against Iranian towns and petroleum installations. With French-built Super Etendard fighter aircraft and Exocet missiles, Iraq threatened to destroy Iran's petroleum industry, centred on Kharg Island in the Gulf. Iran countered by promising to make the Gulf impassable to all shipping if Iraqi military action destroyed its ability to export oil by that route.

In retaliation for the sale of five Super Etendard fighters to Iraq in 1983, Iran severed most of its economic ties with France: French imports were banned, and French banks were excluded from financing Iranian oil sales.

In February and March 1984 a further Iranian offensive resulted in the capture of marshlands around the Majnoun Islands in southern Iraq, the site of significant petroleum deposits. Iraq failed to recapture all of the lost territory and was censured internationally for its alleged use of mustard gas in the fighting. A long hiatus ensued, during which Iran was believed to be preparing a massive offensive, involving more than 500,000 men (including thousands of volunteers), in the region of the southern Iraqi port of Basra. Preparations were hampered by renewed fighting with Kurdish separatists, which led, in August 1984, to an assault by government forces in north-west Iran, which diverted men and equipment, and by apparent disagreements in the Government as to the long-term conduct of the war. (There is also the generally accepted fact of Iran's military inferiority to Iraq in the quantity and sophistication of its armaments.) Iraq exploited the delay to construct a formidable defensive network along the southern front.

Although it had declared a maritime exclusion zone at the north-east end of the Persian Gulf, enclosing Kharg Island, in August 1982 and made spasmodic attacks against shipping (not only oil tankers but, in some cases, ships well outside the zone), Iraq refrained from attacking tankers using the Kharg terminal until May 1984. Iran retaliated by attacking Saudi Arabian and Kuwaiti tankers in the Gulf. A sporadic series of attacks on shipping by both Iran and Iraq continued, while Iraqi fighter aircraft inflicted damage on the Kharg Island oil terminal in occasional raids, dating from the end of February 1984. Syria, anxious over supplies of discounted oil from Iran and concerned that the extension of hostilities to the Gulf might draw other contiguous states into the conflict (as Iraq hoped it would), tried, unsuccessfully, to use its influence with Iran to curb attacks on shipping. Despite the relative escalation of the war, however, it remained doubtful whether either Iran or Iraq possessed the capability respectively to close the Strait of Hormuz (between Iran and Oman) to shipping or to destroy Iran's oil export industry, and, if so, whether it was ultimately in either country's interest to exploit such a capability.

Two peace formulas that were proposed in 1984 by President Mubarak of Egypt, as well as attempts at mediation by Saudi Arabia and Japan, were rejected by Iran, which continues to refuse to negotiate with the Iraqi regime of Saddam Hussain. With the success of a limited offensive in the central sector of the war front in October 1984, Iran expelled the Iraqis from all of its territory. On the other hand, Iran is second only to Pakistan in the number of refugees that it accommodates. By the end of 1985 it was estimated that Iran was host to 1m.–2m. of its own citizens who had been displaced by the Gulf War, 500,000 Iraqis (expelled from their own country) and 2m. Afghans fleeing from the Soviet intervention in Afghanistan.

Tension over Iran's ethnic, religious and political minorities, either not in evidence or stifled under the Shah, has been a recurring problem since the revolution. Most serious has been the demand for autonomy from the Kurds in the north-west, which has often led to open warfare in that area. From July 1983, government forces combined a series of offensives against Iraq, across Iran's northern border, with operations to suppress renewed activity by Kurdish guerrillas in the area. According to Amnesty International, at least 470 people were executed in Iran in 1985, bringing the total to 6,377 since the Revolution. The Mujaheddin Khalq assess the number of executions at 40,000 since June 1981, and in September 1985 published the names of 12,028 people who had allegedly been executed by the Islamic regime. The Iranian Communist Party (the Tudeh Party) was banned in April 1983, its leaders were arrested and forced to appear on television to confess to having worked for the Soviet Union, and 18 Soviet diplomats were expelled from the country.

In August 1983 the resignation of the Ministers of Commerce and of Labour, followed shortly afterwards by the dismissal of three other Ministers, was the result of factional strife within the Government. The outgoing Ministers were right-wing 'bazaaris', the merchant class, who oppose, on grounds of religion and self-interest, the programme of nationalization and land reform that is advocated by the technocrats in the Council of Ministers. Prime Minister Moussavi nominated five replacements from the latter group but only two of them were acceptable to the Majlis, which gave Moussavi three months from September to make alternative choices. New Ministers of Mines and Metals and of Agriculture were finally approved by the Majlis in December, though the Prime Minister's choice of Housing Minister did not receive the necessary support, and the vacancy was not filled until August 1984. The predominantly conservative, clerical Majlis also blocked basic policy initiatives, particularly in the field of economic reform.

Elections to the second Majlis were held on 15 April and 17 May 1984, significantly altering the distribution of influence within the assembly. A high proportion of the 1,230 or more candidates who contested the elections were professional people, such as doctors, scientists and engineers. The elections were boycotted by the Liberation Movement (the sole officially-recognized opposition party) of the former Prime Minister, Dr Mehdi Bazargan, in protest against the allegedly undemocratic conditions prevailing in Iran. Some 60%–70% of the electorate (totalling 24m.–25m.) voted in the elections. Polling had to be repeated in 20 constituencies, owing to irregularities, but the second Majlis was opened on 28 May. It was estimated that more than 50% of the seats in the assembly were filled by new members, and this gave rise to speculation that, with a theoretically more radical and sympathetic Majlis, Prime Minister Moussavi might have greater success in implementing his economic programme. However, the Council of Guardians, which exists to determine whether legislation that has been approved by the Majlis is both constitutional and conforms to Islamic law, is of a conservative, clerical cast and may continue to be an obstacle to socialist economic reform.

In August 1984 Ayatollah Khomeini intervened in the long-standing debate on the question of the nationalization of foreign trade. Before the Revolution, the 'bazaaris' handled about two-thirds of Iran's domestic trade and one-third of all imports. The Government, which had already curtailed the bazaaris' share of trade, proposed to nationalize foreign trade (partly in order to reduce Iran's growing import bill). Khomeini, contrary to the Constitution (which stipulates the nationalization of foreign trade), spoke in favour of free enterprise and a greater role for the merchants in the economy. He intervened in a similar manner in 1980 to suspend radical reform of land ownership, involving the redistribution of land among peasants.

Moussavi's Council of Ministers suffered a reverse in August 1984, when, under the provisions of new legislation requiring a separate vote of confidence for each Minister, five of its members failed to win the approval of the Majlis. Those who were rejected included the Minister of Defence, Col Muhammad Salimi, and the Minister of Education, Ali Akbar Parvaresh, both believed to belong to the right-wing Hojjatieh group.

Widespread active popular opposition to the Islamic regime in Teheran was not conspicuous until 1985. Dissatisfaction with the conduct of the war with Iraq, and with austere economic conditions, sparked off demonstrations and rioting in several Iranian cities, including Teheran. Bombings, carried out by guerrilla groups, are a frequent occurrence in Teheran, and three weeks of civil disturbance were reported in the capital in April and May. The Government has staged a number of counter-demonstrations.

Islamic codes of correction were introduced in 1983, including the amputation of a hand or fingers for theft; flogging for fornication and violations of the strict code of dress for women; and stoning for adultery. These began to be more rigidly enforced in 1985, in response to demonstrations in April by young Muslim fundamentalists demanding stricter adherence to Islamic law.

President Ali Khamenei was due to complete his four-year term of office in September 1985, and a presidential election was held on 16 August, with only three candidates, including Ali Khamenei, taking part. The Council of Guardians rejected the candidacy of nearly 50 people who had applied to stand in the election, including Dr Mehdi Bazargan, leader of the Liberation Movement of Iran, the only legally-recognized opposition party, who opposed the continuation of the war with Iraq. Ali Khamenei was re-elected President for a second four-year term, with 85.7% of the 14,244,630 votes being cast in his favour.

Although 99 deputies either voted against him or abstained, Hussein Moussavi was confirmed as Prime Minister by the Majlis on 13 October. A dispute over the composition of Moussavi's new Council of Ministers, which President Khamenei considered to be too radical (withholding his approval from half of Moussavi's appointees), was not resolved until the intervention of Ayatollah Khomeini on Moussavi's behalf. On 28 October the Majlis approved 22 of the 24 nominations that had been submitted by Moussavi, rejecting only the candidates for the portfolios of economic affairs and finance, and mines and metals. Ministers for these posts were finally approved in January 1986. All but seven of the 24 members of the new Council of Ministers had served in the previous government.

The death toll in the continuing Gulf War was estimated at more than 1m. (including civilians) in 1986, while damage to property and industry amounts to thousands of millions of dollars, but Iran has ignored Iraqi terms for a cease-fire, insisting that nothing less than the removal of the regime of Saddam Hussain, the withdrawal of all Iraqi forces from Iran (this has been achieved by Iranian military action) and Iraqi settlement of Iranian claims for US $350,000m. in war damages (as calculated in March 1985) can bring an end to hostilities. Iran's apparent plan to prolong the war until the Iraqi economy collapses completely, bringing Hussain down with it, depends for its success on the extent to which Iraq manages to rehabilitate its oil export industry and on the continuing willingness of Iraq's principal financial backers, Saudi Arabia and Kuwait, to maintain their support. There were indications in 1984 that they were not prepared to do so indefinitely.

Iran mounted an assault in the region of the al-Hawizah marshes in southern Iraq, east of the Tigris, in March 1985. It was not of the proportions of the long-promised decisive thrust, involving only some 50,000 troops at most. The attack succeeded in pushing the Iraqis back across the Tigris, and, for a time, Iranian forces closed the main road between Baghdad and Basra. The Iraqis launched a successful counter-offensive, repulsing the Iranian attack.

The UN had painstakingly engineered an agreement between Iran and Iraq in June 1984, suspending attacks on civilian targets, but, after the failure of the Iranian offensive in March 1985 (and with the war on the ground once more in a state of deadlock), Iraq declared Iranian airspace a war zone and resumed its bombardment of Iranian cities from the ground and from the air. The first Iraqi raid on Teheran in four years took place in March. Iran retaliated, shelling Basra and other Iraqi towns, and attacking Baghdad with ground-launched missiles. Iraq, in this instance making full use of its superiority in the air, struck more than 30 Iranian population centres in the first half of 1985, killing hundreds of civilians, though it was initially claimed that only government, economic and military sites were the targets. President Saddam Hussain's stated intention was to carry the war to every part of Iran until the Iranian leadership decided to begin negotiating.

The UN Secretary-General, Javier Pérez de Cuéllar, visited both Teheran and Baghdad in April, in an attempt to establish a basis for peace negotiations, but Iran continued to insist on Iraq's payment of war reparations and that Iraq admit responsibility for starting the war. There was less official insistence on the removal of Saddam Hussain and his Baathist regime from power as a condition of peace, but it was accepted that, if the other conditions were met, he would fall anyway.

On two occasions Hussain suspended Iraqi air raids on Iranian towns to give Iran the opportunity to begin peace talks. However, the moratoriums, of six weeks in April and May, and of 16 days in June, met with no response from Iran.

Iraqi raids on petroleum installations and on tankers carrying Iranian oil in the Gulf from May 1984 onwards reduced the level of Iran's exports, but until mid-1985 Iraq had failed to launch attacks against the main oil terminal on Kharg Island of sufficient frequency or intensity seriously to threaten the continuation of oil exports, and the terminal remained largely undamaged. Between August 1985 and January 1986, however, Iraq made a concentrated series of some 60 raids on Kharg Island and oil shipments from the terminal were reduced to a trickle, while the overall rate of exports of crude petroleum fell to 1.2m. b/d in February. In the latter month Iraq announced an expansion of the area of the Gulf from which it would try to exclude Iranian shipping. Previously confined to the waters around Iran's Gulf ports, the area was broadened to include the coast of Kuwait. Attacks on tankers and other commercial vessels in the Gulf were increased by both sides during 1986, and Iran intensified its practice of intercepting merchant vessels in the Gulf and confiscating goods which it believed to be destined for Iraq. Iraq was successful in damaging the alternative oil export facilities which Iran established at the islands of Sirri and Larak (as the Kharg terminal was progressively rendered more ineffective, despite their remoteness at the mouth of the Persian Gulf (see Economic Affairs).

In the land war, Iran launched limited offensives in the region of the Hawizah marshes and in the north, in Kurdistan, in July 1985, and again in Kurdistan in September. However, the next important engagement, in terms of land changing control, did not occur until 1986. In February 1986 Iran began the Wal-Fajr (Dawn) 8 offensive, so called to commemorate the month of Ayatollah Khomeini's return to Iran in 1979. Iranian forces (some 85,000 troops were thought to be involved in the operation) crossed the Shatt al-Arab waterway and occupied the disused Iraqi port of Faw, on the Persian Gulf, and, according to Iran, about 800 sq km of the Faw peninsula. From this position, within sight of the Kuwaiti island of Bubiyan (commanding the Khawr Abdullah channel between the peninsula and the island), Iran threatened Iraq's only access to the Gulf. However, the difficulty of the terrain to the west was not conducive to further Iranian gains, and the position on the Faw peninsula was not easily defensible, in view of the problem of maintaining supply lines across the Shatt al-Arab. To divert Iraqi forces, Iran had begun a complementary assault along the Faw–Basra road. When Iraq launched a counter-offensive on Faw in mid-February, Iran opened up a second front (the Wal-Fajr 9 offensive) in Iraqi Kurdistan, several hundred kilometres to the north. Iraq's counter-offensive failed to dislodge an estimated 30,000 Iranian troops from in and around Faw. At the end of February the UN Security Council, while urging the combatants to agree on a cease-fire, implicitly blamed Iraq for starting the war.

In May 1986 Iraq made its first armed incursions into Iran since withdrawing its forces from Iranian territory in 1982. About 150 sq km of land, including the deserted town of Mehran (some 105 km east of Baghdad), were occupied until July, when Iranian forces counter-attacked and drove the Iraqis out of the country. Also in May, Iraqi aircraft raided Teheran for the first time since June 1985, initiating a new wave of reciprocal attacks on urban and industrial targets in Iran and Iraq, in particular on petroleum-related installations.

From mid-1986 onwards, Iran was reported to be massing troops (many of them Basij-'mobilization'-volunteers) along the entire length of the 1,100-km war-front in preparation for a major assault. On 24 December Iran mounted an offensive (Karbala-4) in the region of Basra (as anticipated, though the scale and ultimate effect of the attack was disputed by the two sides), but failed to penetrate Iraqi defences on four islands in the Shatt al-Arab waterway. On 8 January 1987 a two-pronged offensive, Karbala-5, was launched towards Basra. Iranian forces, attacking from the east, established a bridgehead inside Iraq, between the Shatt al-Arab and the artificial Fish Lake, and advanced gradually towards Basra, sustaining heavy casualties (an estimated 40,000 Iranians died between 24 December 1986 and 20 January 1987); while an attack from the south-east secured a group of islands in the Shatt al-Arab. Iran opened a second front, 400 km to the north, with the Karbala-6 offensive on 13 January. By mid-February, Iranian forces from the east had advanced to within about 10 km of Basra.

Although it is denied in Beijing, it is believed that the People's Republic of China has been Iran's main supplier of military equipment during the Gulf War, while Israel is also thought to have made deliveries of weapons and spare parts. In November 1986 it emerged that the USA, despite its discouragement of arms sales to Iran by other countries, had been conducting secret negotiations with the Islamic Republic since July 1985 and had made several shipments of weapons and spare parts to Iran through Israeli intermediaries, allegedly in exchange for Iranian assistance in releasing American hostages who had been detained by Shi'ite extremists in Lebanon, and an Iranian undertaking to abstain from involvement in international terrorism. The talks were reportedly conducted by the Speaker of the Majlis, Hojatoleslam Hashemi Rafsanjani, with Ayatollah Khomeini's consent but without the knowledge of other senior government figures, including the Prime Minister and the President.

Government

Legislative power is vested in the Islamic Consultative Assembly (Majlis), with 270 members. The chief executive of the administration is the President. The Majlis and the President are both elected by universal adult suffrage for a term of four years. A 12-member Council of Guardians supervises elections and ensures that legislation is in accordance with the Constitution and with Islamic precepts. The executive, legislative and judicial wings of state power are subject to the authority of the Wali Faqih. Ayatollah Hussain Ali Montazari was chosen as eventual successor to the Wali Faqih in November 1985 by the Council of Experts, which had been appointed to determine the succession in December 1982.

Defence

In July 1986 Iran's regular armed forces totalled 704,500 (army 305,000, Revolutionary Guard Corps (Pasdaran) 350,000, navy 14,500, air force 35,000). Including active paramilitary forces, however, the total strength could be up to 2m. There were 350,000 reserves and more than 2.5m. in paramilitary forces, including 2.5m. in the Home Guard (Hezbollahi, 'of the party of God'). There is a two-year period of military service. Defence expenditure for 1985/86 was estimated at IR 1,295,000m.

Economic Affairs

Before the Islamic Revolution and the Gulf War, Iran was one of the world's leading producers of petroleum, and massive government revenues from the petroleum industry stimulated the rest of the economy. Although industrial activity now predominates over agriculture in the formation of the gross national product (GNP), agriculture still occupies the largest proportion of the total labour force. However, in spite of official claims of increases in agricultural output, estimates by the US Department of Agriculture reveal that imports of foodstuffs reached $3,670m. in 1984, and were only slightly reduced in 1985. With the decline in income from sales of petroleum, the high level of food imports is causing concern in Iran. Rice imports are to be reduced in 1986/87, and additional aid is to be given to rice growers. However, there are doubts that significant increases in agricultural productivity can be achieved in the short term. Agriculture has suffered massive losses of labour (an estimated 5m. workers reportedly left the sector between 1982 and 1986); the issue of land ownership, raised by the revolution, remains unresolved; provision of farm inputs is inadequate, and the state marketing system is ineffective. Cereals, sugar beet, fruits, nuts and vegetables are grown. Dairy produce, wool, hair and hides are also produced. There is a small fishing industry, both in the Caspian Sea, where caviar (Iran's biggest export earner after petroleum) is obtained, and in the Persian Gulf. Forests cover more than 20m. ha. There are considerable deposits of copper and iron ore. A major copper complex at Sar Cheshmeh opened in May 1982, and by the end of 1984 was only 5,000 tons short of its operating capacity of 145,000 tons per year.

The Islamic revolution of 1978–79, the Gulf War which began in 1980, and the political troubles of 1981 have hampered the economy considerably. Petroleum remains predominant, and sales of oil account for about 80% of government revenue and some 95% of foreign exchange earnings, but production, which averaged about 6m. barrels per day (b/d) in 1976, fell to 5.2m. b/d in 1978 and to 3.1m. b/d in 1979. It was generally accepted that production was recovering in 1980, but the onset of the Gulf War in September 1980 seriously affected output, and production in 1980/81 averaged only 1.5m. b/d, falling to 1.3m. b/d in 1981/82, and to 400,000 b/d in 1982/83. However, the average rate of production rose to 1.7m. b/d in 1983/84. Government revenue from petroleum fell from US $23,000m. in 1977/78 to $8,500m. in 1981/82, but recovered to $23,000m. in 1982/83 and $21,500m. in 1983/84. In 1984/85 oil exports of 1.68m. b/d were worth $17,000m., 5% less than had been forecast, and in 1985/86 the value of oil exports declined to between $13,000m. and $15,000m., compared with the Government's forecast of $19,700m. The most important buyers of Iranian oil are Japan (which accounts for about 20% of oil exports), Italy, Romania and the Federal Republic of Germany.

Iran managed to maintain its exports of petroleum at a comparatively high level in spite of the damage to oilwells, refineries and export terminals that had been caused in the first two years of the war. Iran's largest refinery, at Abadan, was destroyed in the early days of the war. However, so successful was Iran in raising its production after the low point of 1982 that in November 1983 it was demanding a 33% increase in its official OPEC production quota, from 2.4m. b/d to 3.2m. b/d, though it subsequently agreed to abide by the OPEC allocation.

Potentially as great a threat to oil exports as actual damage to facilities has been the effect of the war on tanker insurance in the Gulf. Charges on vessels destined for Iran's main export terminal at Kharg Island rose to 7.5% of hull value in mid-1984 (10 times the premium at the beginning of the year), and in May Japan instructed its tankers not to use Kharg Island, both developments coinciding with the initiation of Iraqi attacks on tankers using the terminal there. As a consequence, exports in May were 1m. b/d, compared with an OPEC quota of 1.7m. b/d. Iran was forced to reduce its prices to retain its customers, ignoring the official OPEC price ($29 per barrel in 1984). Although, in March 1983, OPEC had given tacit approval to prices up to $1.50 per barrel below official levels, Iran was reportedly offering oil at $25.40 per barrel in September and October 1984, as well as undertaking to pay shipping and insurance costs. Insurance premiums for war risk dropped to 3% of hull value in August 1984, and Japanese tankers returned to Kharg Island after a three-month absence, as the frequency of Iraqi attacks on the terminal declined. In the periods when customers have been available, Iran has flouted OPEC quotas in order to maximize its earnings of foreign exchange while the Kharg Island terminal remains operational. Exports increased to 2.3m. b/d in July, when domestic consumption was estimated at 800,000 b/d, putting total output at some 3.1m. b/d. Production was cut by about 50% in September and October, not (according to the Minister of Oil) owing to the effects of the war but in order to prevent a collapse in oil prices and to strengthen OPEC during the world oil glut. Subsequently, Iran agreed to a reduction in its OPEC production quota from 2.4m. b/d to 2.3m. b/d. In November 1984, after a three-month period during which Iran had refused to offer large discounts to all but its most important customers, and as reserves of foreign exchange were declining, an export drive was launched, and price discounts (of up to $3 per barrel) returned. At the beginning of December oil exports were up to more than 2m. b/d. The export drive coincided with a seven-week lull in Iraqi attacks on shipping from 19 October, and, at the end of November, the minimum war risk insurance rate for vessels bound for Kharg Island was reduced to 2%. The Kharg Island jetty which serves the largest tankers became operational again in November, having been out of action since June, when it was damaged in an air raid.

A resumption of Iraqi attacks on shipping in December 1984 had the effect of reducing Iran's oil exports to an estimated 1.1m. b/d and caused the Government to suspend imports temporarily while there was a shortage of foreign exchange. Iran responded to these renewed attacks by deciding to offer rebates for increased shipping costs for transporting its oil, rather than simple discounts, and in January 1985 Iran increased its oil prices, realigning them more closely with those of other OPEC producers. Prices of light crude were cut by $1.05, to $28.05, per barrel in February, when OPEC's 'marker' price for Arabian Light was reduced by $1 to $28 per barrel. By mid-1985 Iran was once again offering discounts on its oil. Barter deals (oil for goods) helped to increase exports of oil to more than 2.3m. b/d in April 1985, with overall production reaching about 3m. b/d. In 1984 25% of all oil exports were in the form of barter exchanges or under bilateral trade agreements. Emphasis on this aspect of trade was reduced in mid-1985, but bartering returned to favour with the appointment of a new Council of Ministers in January 1986.

A short-term solution to the problem of Iraqi air raids on Kharg Island involved the establishment of a tanker shuttle service between Kharg and a makeshift floating oil terminal, 450 km to the south-east, at Sirri Island (close to the mouth of the Gulf and, in theory, safer from Iraqi attack), where Iran would not have to offer expensive discounts for tankers loading oil. The Sirri facility began operating in March 1985, with an export capacity of up to 1.5m. b/d. Initially based on three tankers anchored off the island, and employing a fleet of 11 supertankers to transport oil from Kharg, the terminal was believed to comprise six ultra-large crude oil carriers, capable of storing 2.2m. tons of oil, in March 1986. Floating terminals were also being established between Kharg Island and the mainland, to provide additional export capacity of 300,000–400,000 b/d by the end of 1985.

Between August 1985 and January 1986 Iraq launched a series of some 60 attacks against the Kharg Island terminal (which was still responsible for more than 80% of Iran's oil exports). At the beginning of October, as a result of damage caused by these attacks, exports were reported to be of the order of only 750,000–800,000 b/d, compared with an average rate of about 1.5m. b/d in the months preceding the new wave of air raids. However, by dint of rapid repairs, the ample spare capacity available at Kharg, and alternative means of export, such as the shuttle to Sirri (despite Iraqi attacks on tankers shuttling oil), Iran was able to claim that exports in October finally averaged 1.7m. b/d. Average oil production in Iran at the end of 1985 was between 2.2m. and 2.5m. b/d, while exports were about 1.6m. b/d. Iraqi attacks on Kharg were reported to have reduced exports from the terminal to a trickle by January 1986, and the overall rate of export fell from about 1.5m. b/d in January to 1.2m. b/d in February. In August an Iraqi raid demonstrated that the Sirri oil export facility was vulnerable to attack; two supertankers, used for oil storage, were destroyed, and Iran was forced to transfer more of its export operations to the floating terminal at Larak Island (250 km east of Sirri, in the Strait of Hormuz), which had been established in June. The terminal at Larak was itself attacked in November. Further Iraqi attacks on Kharg Island in September and October left only three out of 16 oil-loading berths at the terminal operational, and Iran's oil exports averaged only 800,000 b/d in the latter month, while total production reached 1.4m. b/d.

At the end of January 1986 Iran offered to halve its oil production and, in February, pressed OPEC to suspend oil exports for two weeks, in an attempt to force up international prices, which were falling more quickly than hitherto, following the decision of OPEC, in December 1985, to increase production in pursuit of a 'fair' share of an already glutted market. In July the world price of crude petroleum declined to less than $10 per barrel, and in August OPEC members, at Iranian instigation, agreed to reduce their output and to revert to earlier production quotas (imposed in October 1984) for two months from 1 September. Iran concurred in the exemption of Iraq from the new agreement but averred that military action in the Gulf War would effectively limit Iraqi oil production. In October, when the price of oil had risen to about $15 per barrel, OPEC members agreed to increase collective production by some 200,000 b/d. In December all OPEC members, with the exception of Iraq, accepted a 7.25% reduction in their output for the first half of 1987, which, it was hoped, would enable the organization to support a fixed price of $18 per barrel in that period. The reduction gave Iran a production quota of 2.26m. b/d, compared with 2.32m. b/d in November and December.

Plans for three oil pipelines were abandoned during 1986, although there is continuing speculation concerning a 1,100-km pipeline from Gurreh (the main pumping station to Kharg) to Jask, outside the Persian Gulf, and well out of range of Iraqi aircraft. In July 1986 Iran and Turkey signed an agreement for the construction of a 1,900-km pipeline from the southern Iranian province of Khuzestan to the Turkish port of Iskenderun, on the Mediterranean coast. The pipeline will have a capacity of 1m. b/d and is scheduled for completion in late 1990, at an expected cost of $4,300m.

Iran has apparently budgeted at least $15,000m. for the expansion of the petroleum and petrochemical industries during the five years from 1984/85, the first stage of a 20-year plan. There are plans for five new petroleum refineries. With the destruction of the main Abadan refinery (capacity 628,000 b/d), Iran's refining capacity fell to 555,000 b/d in 1980. This figure rose to 574,000 b/d in mid-1985, and could reach between 1m. b/d and 1.5m. b/d when the planned refineries come into operation in the early 1990s. The average production of Iran's refineries was 642,000 b/d in 1983/84, rising to 685,310 b/d in 1984/85, and at the end of 1985 it was reported that the refineries were operating at 31% above design capacity, giving a total output of 728,000 b/d. Iran is preparing to exploit petroleum reserves (estimated at 8,000m. barrels) in deposits around the Majnoun Islands, captured from Iraq in February 1984. The joint Iran/Japan petrochemicals complex at Bandar Khomeini, construction of which was originally projected to cost $4,000m., has repeatedly been suspended, owing to Iraqi air raids, which have caused considerable damage. After renewed Iraqi bombing in September 1984, however, the Iran Chemical Development Company, the Japanese-led partner in the joint venture, withdrew all its technicians, and the company is apparently determined not to return until the end of the war. In February 1986 Iran decided to end all repayments on credits and loans that it had received from Japan, and this suggests that the project will be either abandoned or restructured.

According to Prime Minister Moussavi, some 30% of the budget for the year 1983/84 (21 March–20 March), totalling an estimated IR 3,600,000m. ($42,400m.), was spent on the war effort. This expenditure rose in 1984/85 to IR 1,303,000m., or 31% of the budget. For 1985/86 IR 400,000m. were allocated to basic war expenditure, with other war-related allocations set at IR 785,500m. (a total of IR 1,185,500m., or 30.6% of the proposed budget of IR 3,868,700m.). The official Iranian assessment of the cost of war damage was $350,000m. in March 1985. Owing to the cost of the war, and the effect of economic boycotts and of internal troubles since the Islamic revolution, the Iranian economy declined in 1979/80 and 1980/81. These factors notwithstanding, according to Moussavi, Iran's GNP increased, in real terms, by 15.2% in 1982/83, when growth in the industrial sector was 14.8%. In the same year, Iran had a currency surplus of about $6,000m. and total foreign reserves of $9,500m. at March 1983. The National Iranian Industries Organization claimed that industrial output rose by 23% during 1983/84. However, this year was acknowledged as the most successful for the economy since the revolution. As a result of the continuing fall in the price of oil, government income was seriously reduced during 1985/86, and the prospects for 1986/87 appeared to be even worse. Oil revenues were expected to fall to $9,000m.–$11,000m., compared with an estimated $13,000m.–$15,000m. in 1985/86. Observers believe that Iran may soon be unable to finance its war effort while simultaneously maintaining import levels at an essential minimum. In mid-1986 reserves of foreign exchange (which fluctuate according to the level of petroleum sales) were independently estimated at $3,000m.–$4,000m., compared with government estimates of $6,000m.–$8,000m. There is evidence that economic growth declined to less than 10% in 1984/85, and may have fallen to zero in 1985/86. With oil revenues declining, a decline in real GNP (the first since 1980/81) may be recorded in 1986/87. The cost of fighting the Gulf War was estimated at $6,500m. for the period 1980–85, and at $1,000m. in 1985 alone. The decline in Iran's foreign debt to between $500m. and $1,000m., from $15,000m. at the time of the revolution, indicated that the war with Iraq had been pursued without recourse to foreign borrowing. However, Iran may soon be forced to raise money abroad, or to impose restrictions on the domestic economy, if it is not to slacken the war effort.

Despite efforts to reduce the import bill and conserve foreign exchange, the value of imports rose from $11,845m. in 1982/83 to $18,103m. in 1983/84, although they declined to about $15,485m. in 1984/85. The import bill fell by 13% in 1985/86, with the tightening of import controls, to $13,500m., including military purchases. Observers predict another round of austerity measures in 1986/87, as oil revenues fall, and a further decline in the value of trade. Trade with the West is now increasing steadily, and the Federal Republic of Germany remains Iran's leading supplier (a position which it shared with the USA before the revolution). As a result of the suspension of US imports and the imposition of EEC and Japanese sanctions, in the years after the revolution Iran found new sources of supply in the Third World and among non-aligned countries in Western Europe. The Ministry of Commerce claimed that the Third World's share of imports by Iran rose to 21% in 1983/84, compared with 8% before the revolution. A protocol which envisages the development of economic relations between Iran and the USSR was signed in Moscow in September 1985. Relations between the two countries had been steadily deteriorating since July 1983, when the Iranian Communist Party, Tudeh, was banned. With the cost of the war and a burgeoning 'black market', inflation has been a persistent problem for the economy. The official rate of inflation actually fell from 32.5% in 1980/81 to 17% in 1983/84, and to 7.6% in 1984/85. In October 1985, however, the rate of inflation was believed to be considerably higher than the officially quoted figure of 5.5%. Proposed expenditure in the budget for 1984/85 was cut by the Majlis, partly in an attempt to reduce inflation and an anticipated budget deficit of $10,000m. The budget for 1985/86 envisaged a 25% fall in the deficit, compared with the projected level for 1984/85. The plan and budget committee of the Majlis reduced budget expenditure from a proposed $42,000m. to $38,300m., with almost the entire reduction being made in current expenditure, to bring it into line with the anticipated fall in revenue from lower oil exports. The value of oil exports for 1985/86 was estimated at $19,700m. for budget purposes, but they eventually realized only $13,000m.–$15,000m. The budget for 1986/87, which was presented to the Majlis in December 1985, envisaged total expenditure of IR 4,049,700m. ($50,600m.) and provided for an increase of 12.5% in defence spending, while allocations to all other sectors were to be reduced, compared with those for 1985/86. In a debate in February 1986 the Government was criticized for failing to allow for the rapid fall in oil prices, and the consequent decline in oil revenues, in preparing the budget. Contrary to expectations, however, in March 1986 the Majlis increased planned expenditure for 1986/87 to IR 4,249,700m. ($53,100m.), though projected oil revenue was revised downwards to IR 1,500,000m. ($18,600m.). Most of the spending increase was allocated to defence and the steel and nuclear industries.

The Islamic Republic's first five-year development plan was announced in August 1983. It is intended as the first step towards quadrupling the annual level of the gross domestic product (GDP) from IR 8,800,000m. ($103,000m.) in 1982/83 to IR 34,000,000m. ($400,000m.) in 2002/03. The aims of the plan, covering the years 1983/84–1987/88, were stated to be the expansion of education and culture, securing the interests of the *mostazafin* (the deprived or downtrodden people), and the development of the agricultural sector, its proportion of GDP being envisaged to grow at an average annual rate of 7%, with total investment of $26,400m. over the period of the plan. The Government's long-term objective is to secure economic independence for Iran by achieving self-sufficiency in food and by reducing dependence on the petroleum sector. (Crude oil's share of GNP was 20% in 1982/83, and oil exports accounted for 97% of all sales by value in 1983/84.) The value of non-oil exports (mainly carpets, caviar, pistachio nuts, hides, cotton and sulphur) rose from $283.7m. in 1982/83 to an estimated $525m. in 1985/86 (itself an increase of about 25% compared with 1984/85) but this constituted a negligible proportion of total exports including oil.

The Five-Year Plan was criticized for being too optimistic. Projected oil revenues were based on a price of $33.25 per barrel at a time when the price of Iranian crude had fallen to $28. The Majlis forced a revision of the Plan, which cut total expenditure by 10% and increased agriculture's share of investment to 16.7%, while the share of non-oil industry fell to around 50%. The Plan was returned to the Plan and Budget Organization again in early 1984. In January 1985 the Majlis approved legislation that transformed the Plan and Budget Organization into a ministry, though it remains to be seen whether this will result in a stronger commitment to the process of economic planning. In January 1986 the Majlis approved the outline of the revised Five-Year Development Plan, which had been redrafted by the Ministry of Planning and Budget. However, the acute economic problems resulting from the Gulf War and falling oil prices suggest that implementation of the Plan is unlikely in the immediate future. According to the Ministry of Planning and Budget, Iran sustained losses amounting to an estimated $309,000m. during the first five years of the Gulf War, including $160,000m. in the oil sector.

Following the June 1979 nationalization of banking and insurance, the Government announced in 1980 the establishment of an Islamic banking system, which officially came into force from 21 March 1984. Interest on loans is to be replaced by a 4% commission and interest on deposits with profits (estimated to be a minimum of 7%–8.5%), though it seems unlikely that the new system will be fully implemented for several years.

Social Welfare

Under Article 29 of the 1979 Constitution, the Government has a duty to provide every citizen with insurance benefits covering illness, unemployment and retirement. In 1984 Iran had 589 hospital establishments, with a total of 70,000 beds. In 1981 there were 15,182 physicians working in the country. Of total expenditure by the central government in 1983/84, about IR 220,300m. (5.7%) was for health, and a further IR 407,800m. (10.6%) for social security and welfare.

Education

Education is officially compulsory for eight years, between six and 14 years of age, but this has not been fully implemented in rural areas. Primary education, which is provided free of charge, begins at the age of six and lasts for five years. Secondary education, from the age of 11, lasts for up to seven years: a first cycle of three years and a second of four years. As a proportion of school-age children, the total enrolment at primary and secondary schools in 1982 was 67% (boys 78%; girls 55%). There are 22 universities, including eight in Teheran, which were closed by the Government in 1980 but have been reopened gradually since 1983. About 45,000 students were admitted to colleges and universities for the academic year 1984/85. In 1976 adult illiteracy averaged 63.8% (males 52.4%; females 75.7%). According to the census of October 1986, the rate of illiteracy was 38% among Iranians aged over six years, compared with 52.5% in 1976. Expenditure on education by the central government in 1983/84 was about IR 535,200m., representing 13.9% of total spending. Post-revolutionary policy has been to eliminate mixed-sex schools and to reduce instruction in art and music, while greater emphasis has been placed on agricultural and vocational programmes in higher education. According to the Government, 24,000 new schools were built between the Revolution, in 1979, and 1984.

Tourism

Tourism has been adversely affected by the political upheaval. Iran's chief attraction for the tourist is its wealth of historical sites, notably Isfahan, Rasht, Tabriz, Susa and Persepolis. There were 62,373 visitors to Iran in 1982, compared with 185,756 in 1981. It was provisionally estimated that 157,000 people visited Iran in 1984.

Public Holidays

The Iranian year 1366 runs from 21 March 1987 to 20 March 1988, and the year 1367 runs from 21 March 1988 to 20 March 1989.

1987: 11 February (National Day—Fall of the Shah), 20 March (Oil Nationalization Day), 21–24 March (Now Ruz, the Iranian New Year), 28 March (Leilat al-Meiraj, ascension of Muhammad), 1 April (Islamic Republic Day), 2 April (Revolution Day), 30 May (Id al-Fitr, end of Ramadan), 9 June (Birthday of Twelfth Imam), 14 July (Martyrdom of Imam Ali), 6 August

IRAN

(Id al-Ådha, feast of the Sacrifice), 4 September (Ashoura), 4 November (Mouloud, Birth of Muhammad).

1988: 11 February (National Day—Fall of the Shah), 16 March (Leilat al-Meiraj), 20 March (Oil Nationalization Day), 21–24 March (Now Ruz, the Iranian New Year), 1 April (Islamic Republic Day), 2 April (Revolution Day), 18 May (Id al-Fitr), 9 June (Birthday of Twelfth Imam), 14 July (Martyrdom of Imam Ali), 25 July (Id al-Adha), 23 August (Ashoura), 23 October (Mouloud).

Weights and Measures

The metric system is in force, but some traditional units are still in general use.

Currency and Exchange Rates

100 dinars = 1 Iranian rial (IR).

Exchange rates (30 September 1986):
 £1 sterling = 110.325 rials;
 US $1 = 76.244 rials.

Statistical Survey

The Iranian year runs from 21 March to 20 March.

Source (except where otherwise stated): Statistical Centre of Iran, Dr Fatemi Ave, Cnr Rahiye Moayeri, Opposite Sazeman-e-Ab, Teheran; tel. 655061; telex 213233.

Area and Population

AREA, POPULATION AND DENSITY

Area (sq km)	1,648,000*
Population (census results)†	
1 November 1976	
Males	17,356,347
Females	16,352,397
Total	33,708,744
8 October–1 November 1986	48,181,463
Density (per sq km) at 1986 census	29.2

* 636,296 sq miles.
† Excluding adjustment for underenumeration, estimated to have been 2.28% in 1976.

PRINCIPAL TOWNS (estimated population, spring 1982)

Tehran (Teheran)	5,770,000*	Abadan	294,068‡
Mashad (Meshed)	1,119,748	Orumiyeh	262,588
Isfahan	926,601	Rasht	259,638
Tabriz	852,296	Qazvin	244,265
Shiraz	800,416	Kerman	238,777
Bakhtaran		Hamadan	234,473
(Kermanshah)	531,350	Ardebil	221,970
Karaj	526,272†	Arak	209,970
Ahwaz	470,927	Yazd	193,282
Qom	424,048	Khorramshahr	140,490‡

* Population at October–November 1986 census, including suburbs.
† Including suburbs.
‡ Population at November 1976 census.

BIRTHS AND DEATHS

Average annual birth rate 45.5 per 1,000 in 1970–75, 42.3 per 1,000 in 1975–80; death rate 13.5 per 1,000 in 1970–75; 11.7 per 1,000 in 1975–80 (UN estimates).

ECONOMICALLY ACTIVE POPULATION*
(November 1976 census)

	Males	Females	Total
Agriculture, forestry, hunting and fishing	2,763,934	227,935	2,991,869
Mining and quarrying	86,604	3,284	89,888
Manufacturing	1,032,960	639,099	1,672,059
Construction	1,180,913	7,807	1,188,720
Electricity, gas, water supply	59,716	1,917	61,633
Commerce	656,177	12,317	668,494
Transport, storage and communications	422,647	8,824	431,471
Services	1,324,586	296,011	1,620,597
Others (not adequately defined)	59,863	14,826	74,689
Total in employment	7,587,400	1,212,020	8,799,420
Unemployed	759,650	236,986	996,636
Total	8,347,050	1,449,006	9,796,056

* Including nomadic tribes and other unsettled population.

1984/85: Total in employment 11m.; Unemployed 1.7m.; Total economically active population 12.7m.

Agriculture

PRINCIPAL CROPS (estimates, '000 metric tons)

	1981/82	1982/83	1983/84
Wheat	6,610	6,660	5,956
Barley	1,700	1,903	2,034
Rice (paddy)	1,624	1,605	1,215
Maize	60	n.a.	n.a.
Sugar beet	3,231	4,321	3,648
Sugar cane	1,677	1,810	2,053
Tea (green leaves)*	147	157	162
Oil seeds†	105	138	188
Cotton (lint)	275	358	300
Tobacco	27	25	21
Pulses	290	296	290
Potatoes	1,540	1,814	1,740
Onions	675	965	736
Pistachios	122	95	84

* Production of made tea is assumed to be 22.5%.
† Sunflower seeds and soybeans.

Source: Ministry of Agriculture and Rural Development.

LIVESTOCK
(FAO estimates, '000 head, year ending September)

	1983	1984	1985
Horses	316	316	316
Mules	123	123	123
Asses	1,800	1,800	1,800
Cattle	8,600	8,200	8,350
Buffaloes	228	230	230
Camels	30	27	27
Pigs	30	20	n.a.
Sheep	34,500	34,000	34,500
Goats	13,550	13,600	13,600

Chickens (FAO estimates, million): 85 in 1983; 90 in 1984; 95 in 1985.

Source: FAO, *Production Yearbook*.

LIVESTOCK PRODUCTS (FAO estimates, '000 metric tons)

	1983	1984	1985
Beef and veal	165	165	168
Buffalo meat	10	10	10
Mutton and lamb	230	234	234
Goats' meat	45	45	45
Poultry meat	230	235	240
Other meat	17	18	18
Cows' milk	1,650	1,650	1,700
Buffaloes' milk	39	39	39
Sheep's milk	705	705	715
Goats' milk	223	223	223
Cheese	103.8	104.4	106.4
Butter	69.7	69.7	71.4
Hen eggs	200	210	220
Honey	6	6	6
Wool:			
greasy	16.2	16.2	16.3
clean	8.9	8.9	9.0
Cattle and buffalo hides	34.4	34.4	35.1
Sheep skins	38.4	39.0	39.0
Goat skins	9.0	9.1	9.1

Source: FAO, *Production Yearbook*.

Forestry

ROUNDWOOD REMOVALS (FAO estimates, '000 cu metres)

	1982	1983	1984
Sawlogs, veneer logs and logs for sleepers*	369	369	369
Other industrial wood†	4,007	4,007	4,007
Fuel wood	2,339	2,351	2,363
Total	6,715	6,727	6,739

* Assumed to be unchanged since 1977.
† Assumed to be unchanged since 1974.
Source: FAO, *Yearbook of Forest Products*.

SAWNWOOD PRODUCTION ('000 cu metres)

	1975	1976	1977
Sawnwood (incl. boxboards)*	90	90	90
Railway sleepers	80	54	73
Total	170	144	163

* FAO estimate (production assumed to be unchanged since 1974).
1978–84: Annual production as in 1977 (FAO estimate).
Source: FAO, *Yearbook of Forest Products*.

Fishing

(FAO estimates, '000 metric tons, live weight)

	1982	1983	1984
Inland waters	4.6	4.5	4.0
Marine fishes	33.1	37.6	35.4
Marine crustaceans	2.0	2.0	2.0
Total catch	39.7	44.1	41.4

* FAO estimates.
Source: FAO, *Yearbook of Fishery Statistics*.
Production of caviar (metric tons): 234 in 1981/82; 204 in 1982/83; 225 in 1983/84 (Source: Iran Fishery Co).

Mining

CRUDE PETROLEUM (net production, '000 barrels per day)

	1981/82	1982/83	1983/84
Southern Oilfields	1,255	2,437	2,454
Naftshahr Oilfield	0	0	0
Offshore oilfields	186	242	255
Doroud-Forouzan-Abouzar-Soroush	7	60	63
Bahregansar–Nowruz	0	0	0
Salman–Rostam	154	160	172
Sirri	25	22	20
Total	1,441	2,679	2,709

NATURAL GAS (million cu metres)

	1981/82	1982/83	1983/84
Consumption (Domestic)	9,700	18,000	15,500
Flared	6,000	12,400	12,300
Total production	15,700	30,400	27,800

Source: Bank Markazi Iran, *Economic Report and Balance Sheet 1362*.

OTHER MINERALS*
('000 metric tons, year ending 20 March)

	1981/82	1982/83	1983/84
Hard coal	700	800	800
Iron ore†	366	406	340
Copper ore†	2.0	43.0	48.5
Lead ore†	20	25	26
Zinc ore†	35.0	40.0	39.9
Chromium ore†	10	13	17
Magnesite (crude)	4	3	3
Native sulphur	50	50	50
Salt (unrefined)	600	700	753

* Estimated production, based on data from the US Bureau of Mines.
† Figures refer to the metal content of ores.
Source: UN, *Industrial Statistics Yearbook*.

IRAN

Statistical Survey

Industry

PETROLEUM PRODUCTS ('000 metric tons)

	1981	1982	1983
Liquefied petroleum gas*†	1,049	1,073	1,080
Naphtha	91	124	430
Motor spirit (petrol)	3,065	3,368	3,400
Aviation gasoline	60	70	60
Kerosene	3,536	4,112	4,120
White spirit*	70	70	70
Jet fuel	380	400	490
Distillate fuel oils	6,412	6,977	7,100
Residual fuel oils	8,856	8,923	9,020
Lubricating oils*	130	130	140
Petroleum bitumen (asphalt)*	1,038	1,136	1,140

* Estimated production.
† Includes production from natural gas plants ('000 metric tons): 500 in 1981, 1982 and 1983; and from petroleum refineries: 549 in 1981; 573 in 1982; 580 in 1983.
Source: UN, *Industrial Statistics Yearbook*.

OTHER PRODUCTS*

	1981	1982	1983
Refined sugar ('000 metric tons)	565	672	986
Cigarettes (million)	12,549	13,546	15,104
Paints ('000 metric tons)	46.6	44.6	58.7
Cement ('000 metric tons)	9,319	10,356	11,093
Refrigerators ('000)	524	541	671
Kitchen stoves ('000)	285	277	1,066
Household ovens ('000)	629	689	1,306
Radio receivers (sales) ('000)	43	19	171
Television receivers ('000)	346	401	585
Motor vehicles (assembled) ('000)	202	206	319

* Source: UN, *Industrial Statistics Yearbook*, except 1983 (Source: Statistical Centre of Iran).

Production of Electricity (million kWh): 24,906 in 1981/82; 28,823 in 1982/83; 33,010 in 1983/84 (Source: Ministry of Energy).

Finance

CURRENCY AND EXCHANGE RATES

Monetary Units
100 dinars = 1 Iranian rial (IR).

Denominations
Coins: 1, 2, 5, 10, 20 and 50 rials.
Notes: 100, 200, 500, 1,000, 2,000, 5,000 and 10,000 rials.

Sterling and Dollar Equivalents (30 September 1986)
£1 sterling = 110.325 rials;
US $1 = 76.244 rials;
1,000 Iranian rials = £9.064 = $13.116.

Average Exchange Rate (rials per US $)
1983   86.358
1984   90.030
1985   91.052

Note: The data on exchange rates refer to the official rate of the Central Bank, applicable to all foreign exchange transactions since December 1984, and to almost all transactions prior to that date. Since 22 May 1980 this valuation of the Iranian rial has been linked to the IMF's special drawing right (SDR) at a mid-point rate of SDR 1 = 92.30 rials. Prior to December 1984, a system of multiple exchange rates was in operation, with a preferential rate, applicable to proceeds from non-oil exports, and another rate applicable to sales of foreign exchange for tourism.

GOVERNMENT BUDGET ESTIMATES
(million rials, year ending 20 March)

Revenue	1985/86	1986/87
General revenue	3,780,400	3,574,700
Income from taxation	1,138,200	1,169,800
Oil	1,867,000	1,600,000
Sales of foreign exchange	119,000	111,000
Other	396,300	424,200
Special income	259,900	269,700
Deficit finance	354,400	475,000
Total	4,134,800	4,049,700

Expenditure	1985/86	1986/87
Expenditure	3,874,900	3,780,000
War expenditure	400,000	430,000
War reconstruction	50,000	35,000
Fixed investment	1,085,800	949,200
Repayment of foreign loans	33,800	24,500
Current expenditure	2,305,300	2,341,300
From special income	259,900	269,700
Total	4,134,800	4,049,700

IRAN

CENTRAL BANK RESERVES
(US $ million at 31 December)

	1980	1981	1982
Gold*	220	247	229
IMF special drawing rights	307	339	331
Reserve position in IMF	299	165	84
Foreign exchange*	9,617	1,102	5,287
Total	10,443	1,853	5,931

* Figures refer to 20 December. Gold is valued at 35 SDRs per troy ounce.

Source: IMF, *International Financial Statistics*.

MONEY SUPPLY ('000 million rials at 20 December)

	1981	1982	1983
Currency outside banks	1,248.30	1,465.40	1,756.90
Official entities' deposits at Central Bank	166.50	329.10	335.00
Demand deposits at commercial banks	1,222.10	1,498.20	1,830.10
Total	2,636.90	3,292.70	3,922.00

Source: IMF, *International Financial Statistics*.

BALANCE OF PAYMENTS (US $ million)

	1975	1976	1977
Merchandise exports f.o.b.	20,432	23,960	24,356
Merchandise imports f.o.b.	−12,898	−15,972	−15,824
Trade balance	7,534	7,988	8,532
Exports of services	2,472	2,887	3,628
Imports of services	−5,280	−6,138	−7,070
Balance on goods and services	4,725	4,737	5,090
Unrequited transfers (net)	−18	−20	−9
Current balance	4,707	4,717	5,081
Direct capital investment (net)	141	743	802
Other long-term capital (net)	−3,010	−2,580	−442
Short-term capital (net)	−1,079	−3,239	−2,960
Net errors and omissions	−659	800	924
Total (net monetary movements)	100	441	3,406
Valuation changes (net)	420	−503	19
Changes in reserves	520	−62	3,425

Source: IMF, *International Financial Statistics*.

External Trade

PRINCIPAL COMMODITIES
(US $ million, year ending 20 March)

Imports c.i.f.	1981/82	1982/83	1983/84
Food and live animals	2,161	2,164	2,368
Beverages and tobacco	482	351	530
Crude materials (inedible) except fuels	667	461	802
Mineral fuels, lubricants, etc.	214	207	205
Animal and vegetable oils and fats	294	192	338
Chemicals and chemical products	2,180	1,679	2,084
Basic manufactures	3,986	3,507	5,326
Machinery and transport equipment	3,527	3,331	6,317
Miscellaneous manufactured articles	393	284	530
Other commodities and transactions	5	13	43
Total	13,515	11,485	18,103

Exports f.o.b. (excl. petroleum and gas)	1981/82	1982/83	1983/84
Agricultural and traditional goods	321.3	255.3	318.1
Carpets	149.4	67.0	88.9
Fruit (fresh and dried)	58.4	78.8	125.5
Animal skins and hides, and leather	53.4	40.6	34.6
Caviar	15.3	18.9	19.0
Casings	20.3	17.6	13.6
Others	24.5	32.4	36.5
Metal ores	5.0	7.1	12.5
Industrial manufactures	13.2	21.3	26.0
Shoes	0.5	1.7	2.8
Biscuits and pastries	0.6	—	1.3
Textile manufactures	8.9	9.6	10.0
Cements	—	3.4	3.1
Motor vehicles	0.3	1.5	1.4
Others	2.9	5.1	7.4
Total	339.5	283.7	356.6

PETROLEUM EXPORTS
('000 barrels per day, year ending 20 March)

	1981/82	1982/83	1983/84
Crude petroleum	791	1,889	2,045
Refined oil products	140	181	57

Source: Ministry of Oil.

Value of crude petroleum exports ('000 million rials, year ending 20 December; estimates): 731.5 in 1981; 1,508.3 in 1982; 1,621.0 in 1983; 1,065.9 in 1984; 1,156.7 in 1985 (Source: IMF, *International Financial Statistics*).

Total Exports ('000 million rials, year ending 20 December; estimates): 980.8 in 1981; 1,632.4 in 1982; 1,684.7 in 1983; 1,127.8 in 1984; 1,218.6 in 1985 (Source: IMF, *International Financial Statistics*).

PERCENTAGE GEOGRAPHICAL DISTRIBUTION OF CRUDE PETROLEUM EXPORTS

	1981	1982	1983
Western Europe	43.1	50.8	48.4
Japan	18.0	14.6	20.2
Asia (excluding Japan)	23.0	24.3	21.7
Africa	—	0.2	0.1
South America	—	1.0	1.8
Other regions*	15.9	9.1	7.8

* Includes Eastern European countries, Australia and New Zealand.

Source: Ministry of Oil.

IRAN

PRINCIPAL TRADING PARTNERS
(US $ million, year ending 20 March)

Imports c.i.f.	1981/82	1982/83	1983/84
Argentina	62	152	421
Belgium	318	338	417
Brazil	84	222	425
France	456	382	291
Germany, Fed. Republic	2,252	1,936	3,442
Italy	715	552	839
Japan	1,619	1,250	3,022
Korea, Republic	614	400	503
Netherlands	444	312	404
Romania	301	463	313
Spain	412	359	384
Sweden	256	210	492
Switzerland	530	296	356
Turkey	292	774	853
United Arab Emirates	404	127	335
United Kingdom	852	709	1,087
Total (incl. others)	13,515	11,845	18,103

Exports f.o.b.*	1981/82	1982/83	1983/84
Czechoslovakia	8.1	7.9	5.1
France	8.0	9.9	7.9
German Democratic Republic	8.9	4.4	5.8
Germany, Fed. Republic	108.2	53.3	73.4
Hungary	1.2	1.4	10.7
Italy	46.3	35.6	33.0
Japan	1.2	7.0	8.4
Kuwait	11.8	15.2	9.4
Lebanon	5.9	5.5	2.8
Netherlands	2.6	4.3	3.8
Saudi Arabia	22.4	9.0	4.5
Switzerland	26.3	9.8	13.2
USSR	39.8	55.5	40.0
United Arab Emirates	4.1	18.1	50.2
United Kingdom	9.2	8.6	16.3
Total (incl. others)	339.5	283.7	356.6

* Excluding petroleum products and hydrocarbon solvents obtained from petroleum.

Transport

RAILWAYS (traffic)

	1981	1982	1983
Passenger journeys ('000)	4,320	4,344	6,441
Freight ('000 metric tons)	6,741	7,903	9,927

MERCHANT SHIPPING FLEET
('000 gross registered tons at 30 June)

	1980	1981	1982
Oil tankers	666	632	631
Other vessels	618	570	682
Total	1,284	1,202	1,313

INTERNATIONAL SEA-BORNE SHIPPING
(estimated freight traffic, '000 metric tons)

	1981	1982	1983
Goods loaded	36,365	81,145	93,780
Goods unloaded	10,312	10,297	12,280

Source: UN, *Monthly Bulletin of Statistics*.

ROAD TRAFFIC ('000 vehicles in use)

	1981	1982	1983
Cars	1,540	1,604	1,694
Buses	48	71	57
Trucks	281	293	332
Ambulances	366	425	575
Motor cycles	435	472	475

CIVIL AVIATION (traffic on scheduled services)

	1980	1981	1982
Kilometres flown (million)	15.6	10.6	14.9
Passengers carried ('000)	1,998	1,540	2,009
Passenger-km (million)	2,071	1,611	1,852
Freight ton-km (million)	20.3	35.6	42.1

Source: UN, *Statistical Yearbook*.

Tourism

	1980	1981	1982
Visitors	156,380	185,756	62,373

1984: Total number of visitors 157,000 (estimate).

Education

('000 students)

	1982/83*	1983/84*
Kindergartens	177	203
Primary schools	5,593	5,994
Junior high schools	1,717	1,818
High schools	849	867
Technical and vocational schools	127	148
Colleges and teacher training colleges	19	36
Others†	218	183
Total	8,700	9,249
Number of institutions	61,967	65,361
Number of teachers‡	425,600	432,822

* The Iranian year runs from 21 March to 20 March. The year 1982/83 corresponds to the Iranian year 1361; 1983/84 to 1362.
† Includes students at schools for exceptional children and on general adult courses.
‡ Includes kindergartens, primary, junior high, and high schools.
Source: Ministry of Education.

Directory

The Constitution

A draft constitution for the Islamic Republic of Iran was published on 18 June 1979. It was submitted to a 'Council of Experts', elected by popular vote on 3 August 1979, to debate the various clauses and to propose amendments. The amended Constitution was approved by a referendum on 2–3 December 1979.

The Constitution states that the form of government of Iran is that of an Islamic Republic, and that the spirituality and ethics of Islam are to be the basis for political, social and economic relations. Persians, Turks, Kurds, Arabs, Baluchis, Turkomans and others will enjoy completely equal rights.

The Constitution provides for a President to act as chief executive. The President is elected by universal adult suffrage for a term of four years. Legislative power is held by the Majlis (Islamic Consultative Assembly), with 270 members who are similarly elected for a four-year term. Provision is made for the representation of Zoroastrians, Jews and Christians.

All legislation passed by the Islamic Consultative Assembly must be sent to the Council for the Protection of the Constitution (Article 94), which will ensure that it is in accordance with the Constitution and Islamic legislation. The Council for the Protection of the Constitution consists of six religious lawyers appointed by the Faqih (see below) and six lawyers appointed by the High Council of the Judiciary and approved by the Islamic Consultative Assembly. Articles 19–42 deal with the basic rights of individuals, and provide for equality of men and women before the law and for equal human, political, economic, social and cultural rights for both sexes.

The press is free, except in matters that are contrary to public morality or insult religious belief. The formation of religious, political and professional parties, associations and societies is free, provided they do not negate the principles of independence, freedom, sovereignty and national unity, or the basis of Islam.

The amended Constitution contains a significant change from the earlier draft. It provides for a Wali Faqih (religious leader) who, in the absence of the Imam Mehdi (the hidden Twelfth Imam), carries the burden of leadership. Article 107 gives Ayatollah Khomeini these powers for the rest of his natural life. Thereafter, an elected Council of Experts will choose an individual or three or five people to form a council of leadership, and the choice must be 'approved by the nation'. According to Article 57 the executive, legislative and judicial branches of state power are under the authority of the Faqih. Among the extensive powers reserved to the Faqih is the right to appoint half the members of the Council for the Protection of the Constitution (see above). He is also Supreme Commander of the Armed Forces and can appoint the Joint Chiefs of Staff and the Head of the Revolutionary Guard. He appoints four of the seven members of the National Defence Council and, on their recommendation, appoints the senior commanders of the armed forces. He also has power to declare war and make peace on the recommendation of the National Defence Council. The first Faqih has the right to vet all candidates for the presidency (a right which was exercised by Ayatollah Khomeini). The Faqih can also dismiss the President on the basis of a Supreme Court decision or a vote of no confidence by the Islamic Consultative Assembly.

PROVINCIAL DIVISIONS

According to the state division of May 1977, Iran was divided into 23 provinces (Ostans), 472 counties (shahrestan) and 499 municipalities (bakhsh).

The Government

WALI FAQIH (RELIGIOUS LEADER)

Ayatollah SAYED RUHOLLAH MOUSSAVI KHOMEINI (formally designated in Constitution adopted by referendum on 2–3 December 1979).

HEAD OF STATE

President: Hojatoleslam SAYED ALI KHAMENEI (took office 13 October 1981).

COUNCIL OF MINISTERS
(January 1987)

Prime Minister: MIR HOSSEIN MOUSSAVI.

Deputy Prime Minister in charge of Political Affairs: ALI REZA MOAYERI.

Minister of Foreign Affairs: Dr ALI AKBAR VELAYATI.

Minister of Education and Training: SAYED QASSEM AKRAMI.

Minister of Culture and Islamic Guidance: Hojatoleslam Dr SAYED MUHAMMAD KHATAMI.

Minister of the Islamic Revolutionary Guards Corps: MOHSEN RAFIQDUST.

Minister of Commerce: HASSAN ABEDI JAAFARI.

Minister of Health: Dr ALI REZA MARANDI.

Minister of Posts, Telegraphs and Telephones: Eng. SAYED MUHAMMAD GHARAZI.

Minister of Justice: Dr HASSAN HABIBI.

Minister of Defence: Col MUHAMMAD HUSSEIN JALALI.

Minister of Roads and Transport: Eng. MUHAMMAD SAYEDIKIYA.

IRAN

Minister of Industries: Eng. GHOLAM REZA SHAFEI.
Minister of Heavy Industry: Eng. BEHZAD NABAVI.
Minister of Higher Education and Culture: Dr MUHAMMAD FARHADI.
Minister of Mines and Metals: MUHAMMAD REZA AYATOLLAHI.
Minister of Labour and Social Affairs: ABOLQASSEM SARHADIZADEH.
Minister of the Interior: Hojatoleslam SAYED ALI AKBAR MOHTASHAMI.
Minister of Agriculture: ABBAS ALI ZELLI.
Minister of Housing and Urban Development: Eng. SERAGEDDIN KAZEROUNI.
Minister of Energy: Dr MUHAMMAD TAQI BANKI.
Minister of Oil: GHOLAMREZA AQAZADEH.
Minister of Economic Affairs and Finance: MUHAMMAD JAVAD IRAVANI.
Minister of Information: Hojatoleslam MUHAMMAD MUHAMMADI REYSHAHRI.
Minister of Construction Jihad: Eng. BIJAN NAMDAR ZANGANEH.
Minister of Planning and Budget: MASSOUD ZANJANI.
Minister of State and Head of State Welfare Organization: JAVAD EZHEH'I.
Minister of State for Executive Affairs and Supervisor of Prime Minister's Office: (vacant).

MINISTRIES
All ministries are in Teheran.

President and Legislature

PRESIDENTIAL ELECTION
16 August 1985

Candidates	Votes	%
Hojatoleslam SAYED ALI KHAMENEI	12,203,870	85.7
MAHMOUD MOSTAFAVI KASHANI	1,402,416	9.8
HABIBOLLAH ASGAR-OWLADI	283,297	2.0
Invalid	355,047	2.5
Total	14,244,630	100.0

MAJLIS-E-SHURA E ISLAMI—ISLAMIC CONSULTATIVE ASSEMBLY

Elections to the second Majlis took place in two rounds, on 15 April and 17 May 1984. Re-elections took place on 9 August 1984 in 20 constituencies in which irregularities caused the results to be nullified. The 270 seats were contested by about 1,230 candidates. The Islamic Republican Party won a clear majority of the seats, as it had done in the first elections to the Assembly, held in 1980.

Speaker: Hojatoleslam HASHEMI RAFSANJANI..
Deputy Speakers: MAHDI KARRUBI, MUHAMMAD YAZDI.

COUNCIL OF EXPERTS

Elections were held on 10 December 1982 to appoint a Council of Experts which was to choose an eventual successor to the Wali Faqih, Ayatollah Khomeini, after his death. Elections for 10 seats on the Council were held on 15 April 1984. The Council comprises 83 clerics. (In November 1985 it was announced that the Council had elected Ayatollah Hossein Ali Montazari to be Ayatollah Khomeini's successor.)

Chairman: Ayatollah ALI MESHKINI.
Deputy Chairman: Hojatoleslam HASHEMI RAFSANJANI.

SHURA-E-NIGAHBAN—COUNCIL OF GUARDIANS

The Council of Guardians, composed of six qualified jurists and six lay Muslim lawyers, appointed by Ayatollah Khomeini and the Supreme Judicial Council respectively, was established in 1980 to supervise elections and to examine legislation, ensuring that it accords with the Constitution and with Islamic precepts.
Chairman: Ayatollah MAHDAVI-KANI.

Political Organizations

Islamic Republican Party: Dr Ali Shariati Ave, Teheran; tel. 319934; telex 21-5869; f. 1978; party founded to bring about the Islamic Revolution under the leadership of Ayatollah KHOMEINI; Sec.-Gen. Hojatoleslam SAYED ALI KHAMENEI; Central Cttee: Pres. SAYED ALI KHAMENEI; mems Hojatoleslam HASHEMI RAFSANJANI, MUHAMMAD HEHDI RABBANI-AMLASHI, ABBAS YA'EZ-TABAS, MOVAHEDI KERMANI.

Iran is fundamentally a one-party state. Of the parties listed below, only the Nelzat-Azadi (Liberation Movement of Iran) has official recognition and is allowed to participate in elections.

Democratic Party of Iranian Kurdistan: Mahabad; f. 1945; seeks autonomy for Kurdish area; mem. of the National Council of Resistance; 54,000 mems; Sec.-Gen. Dr ABD AR-RAHMAN QASSEMLOU.

Fedayeen-el-Khalq: urban Marxist guerrillas.

Hezb-e-Komunist Iran (Communist Party of Iran): f. 1979 on grounds that Tudeh Party was Moscow-controlled; Sec.-Gen. 'AZARYUN'.

Komala: f. 1969; Kurdish wing of the Communist Party of Iran; Marxist-Leninist; Leader IBRAHIM ALIZADEH.

Mujaheddin-e-Khalq: Islamic guerrilla group; mem. of the National Council of Resistance; Leader MASSOUD RAJAVI (fmrly in Paris; in Baghdad 1986–); Leader (in Iran) Eng. ALI ZARKESH.

Muslim People's Republican Party: Tabriz; over 3.5m. members (2.5m. in Azerbaizhan); Sec.-Gen. HOSSEIN FARSHI.

National Democratic Front: f. March 1979; Leader HEDAYATOLLAH MATINE-DAFTARI (in Paris, January 1982–).

National Front (Union of National Front Forces): comprises Iran Nationalist Party, Iranian Party, and Society of Iranian Students.

Nelzat-Azadi (Liberation Movement of Iran): f. 1961; emphasis on basic human rights as defined by Islam; Gen. Sec. Dr MEHDI BAZARGAN; Principal Officers Prof. SAHABI, Dr YAZDI, S. SADR, Dr SADR, Eng. SABAGHIAN, Eng. TAVASSOLI.

Pan-Iranist Party: extreme right-wing; calls for a Greater Persia; Leader MOHSEN PEZESHKPOUR.

Sazmane Peykar dar Rahe Azadieh Tabaqe Kargar (Organization Struggling for the Freedom of the Working Class): Marxist-Leninist.

Tudeh Party (Communist): f. 1941; declared illegal 1949; came into open 1979, banned again April 1983; pro-Moscow; First Sec. ALI KHAVARI.

The National Council of Resistance was formed in Paris in October 1981 by former President ABOLHASAN BANI-SADR and MASSOUD RAJAVI, the former leader of the Mujaheddin Khalq in Iran. In 1984 the Council comprised 15 opposition groups, operating either clandestinely in Iran or from exile abroad. BANI-SADR left the Council in 1984 because of his objection to RAJAVI's growing links with the Iraqi Government. RAJAVI left Paris in June 1986 and is now based in Baghdad, Iraq. There is also a National Movement of Iranian Resistance, led by a former Prime Minister, Dr SHAPOUR BAKHTIAR.

Diplomatic Representation

EMBASSIES IN IRAN

Afghanistan: Abbas Abad Ave, Pompe Benzine, Corner of 4th St, Teheran; Chargé d'affaires a.i.: Dr BASSIR RANJBAR.

Algeria: Vali Asr Ave, Ofogh St, No. 26, Teheran; tel. 857222; Ambassador: ABD AL-HAMID ADJALI.

Argentina: POB 98–164, Ave Mossadegh, Blvd Nahid, No. 35, Tajrish, Teheran; Chargé d'affaires a.i.: EDELBERTO J. LEMOS.

Australia: Khaled al-Islambuli Ave, No. 123, POB 3408, Teheran; tel. 835047; Ambassador: (vacant).

Austria: Taleghani Ave, Corner Forsat Ave No. 140, Teheran; tel. 828431; telex 212872; Ambassador: Dr MANFRED KIEPACH.

Bahrain: Park Ave, 31st St, No. 16, Teheran; Ambassador: (vacant).

Bangladesh: Gandhi Ave, 5th St, Building No. 14, POB 11365-3711, Teheran; tel. 682979; telex 212303; Chargé d'affaires a.i.: ASHFAQUR RAHMAN.

Belgium: Fereshteh Ave, Shabdiz Lane, 3 Babak St, POB 11365-115, Teheran 19659; tel. 294574; telex 212446; Ambassador: VICTOR ALLARD.

Brazil: 58 Vanak Sq., Vanak Ave, Teheran 19964; tel. 683498; telex 212392: Ambassador: LANDULPHO V. BORGES DA FONSECA.

Bulgaria: Vali Asr Ave, Tavanir St, Nezami Ganjavi St No. 82, POB 11365-7451, Teheran; tel. 685662; telex 212789; Ambassador: STEFAN POLENDAKOV.
China, People's Republic: Pasdaran Ave, Golestan Ave 1 No. 53, Teheran; Ambassador: WANG BENZUO.
Colombia: Bihaghi Ave, 14th St, No. 15, POB 41-3315, Teheran; Ambassador: ANTONIO BAYONA.
Cuba: Africa Ave, Amir Parviz St No. 1/28, Teheran; tel. 632953; Ambassador: LUIS MARISY FIGUEREDO.
Czechoslovakia: Enghelab Ave, Sarshar St No. 61, POB 1500, Teheran; tel. 828168; Ambassador: MILAN MACHA.
Denmark: Intersection Africa and Modaress Expressway, Bidar St No. 40, POB 11365-158, Teheran; tel. 297371; telex 212784; Ambassador: IB ANDREASEN.
Finland: Gandhi Ave, 19th St, No. 26, POB 15875-4734, Teheran; tel. 684985; telex 212930; Ambassador: TIMO JALKANEN.
France: ave de France No. 85, Teheran; Chargé d'affaires a.i.: PIERRE LAFRANCE.
Gabon: POB 337, Teheran; tel. 823828; telex 215038; Ambassador: J. B. ESSONGUE.
German Democratic Republic: Mirza-ye Shirazi Ave, Ali Mirza Hassani St 15, Teheran; tel. 627858; telex 212453; Ambassador: GÜNTHER FRITSCH.
Germany, Federal Republic: 324 Ferdowsi Ave, POB 11365-179, Teheran; tel. 314111; telex 2488; Ambassador: Dr JENS PETERSEN.
Ghana: Ghaem Magham Farahani Ave, Varahram St No. 12, Teheran; Chargé d'affaires a.i.: HUMPHREY OKPOTI LARSEY.
Greece: Park Ave, 35th St No. 20, Teheran; tel. 686096; Ambassador: DMITRI FRANTZESKAKIS.
Holy See: Razi Ave, No. 97, ave de France Crossroad, POB 11365-178, Teheran (Apostolic Nunciature); tel. 643574; Apostolic Pro-Nuncio: Mgr GIOVANNI DE ANDREA.
Hungary: Abbas Abad Park Ave, 13th St, No. 18, Teheran; tel. 622800; Ambassador: Dr ZSIGMOND KÁZMÉR.
India: Saba Shomali Ave, No. 166, POB 11365-6573, Teheran; tel. 894554; telex 212858; Ambassador: A. B. GHOKALE.
Indonesia: Ghaem Magham Farahani Ave, No. 210, POB 11365-4564, Teheran; tel. 626865; telex 212049; Ambassador: MOHAMMAD SABIR.
Ireland: Mirdamad Ave, Khiaban Razane, Shomali, No. 8, Teheran; tel. 222731; telex 213865; Chargé d'affaires a.i.: NIALL HOLOHAN.
Italy: ave de France No. 81, Teheran; tel. 672107; telex 214171; Ambassador: GIUSEPPE BALDOCCI.
Japan: Bucharest Ave, N.W. Corner of 5th St, POB 11365-814, Teheran; tel. 623396; telex 212757; Ambassador: YUTAKA NOMURA.
Korea, Democratic People's Republic: Fereshteh Ave, Sarvestan Ave, No. 11, Teheran; Ambassador: CHO KYU-IL.
Korea, Republic: 37 Bucharest Ave, Teheran; tel. 621125; Chargé d'affaires a.i.: SUNG KU KANG.
Kuwait: Dehkadeh Ave, 3–38 Sazman-Ab St, Teheran; tel. 636712; Ambassador: AHMED ABD AL-AZIZ AL-JASSIM.
Lebanon: Bucharest Ave, 16th St, No. 43, Teheran; Ambassador: JA'FAR MA'AWI.
Libya: Motahhari Ave, No. 163, Teheran; Head of Committee of People's Bureau: SAAD MOSTAPHA MOJBER.
Malaysia: Bucharest Ave, No. 8, Teheran; tel. 629523; Chargé d'affaires a.i.: SOPIAN BIN AHMAD.
Mauritania: Africa Ave, Sayeh St, No. 78, Teheran; tel. 623655; telex 213524; Ambassador: ALI THIERNO BARO.
Netherlands: Vali Asr Ave, Ostad Motahari Ave, Sarbederan St, Jahansouz Alley No. 36, Teheran; tel. 896012; telex 212788; Ambassador: EDUARD VAN DER PALS.
New Zealand: Mirza-ye-Shirazi Ave, Kucheh Mirza Hassani, No. 29, POB 11365-436, Teheran; tel. 625061; telex 212078; Ambassador: E. RICHARD WOODS.
Nicaragua: Teheran; Ambassador: GONZALO MURILLO.
Nigeria: Jomhoori Islami Ave, 31st St, No. 9, POB 11365-7148, Teheran; tel. 684934; Ambassador: A. AL-GAZALI.
Norway: Bucharest Ave, 6th St, No. 23, POB 6747-11356, Teheran; tel. 624644; telex 213009; Ambassador: NIKOLAI ALFRED FOUGNER.
Oman: Pasdaran Ave, Golestan 9, No. 5 and 7, POB 41-1586, Teheran; tel. 243199; telex 212835; Chargé d'affaires a.i.: HASSAN MOHSEN ALI.
Pakistan: Dr Fatemi Ave, Jamshidabad Shomali, Mashal St No. 1, Teheran; tel. 934331; Ambassador: ABD AL-MALIK KHATTAK.
Philippines: Bucharest Ave, No. 6, POB 14155-5337, Teheran; tel 625392; Chargé d'affaires a.i.: OSCAR G. ORCINE.
Poland: Africa Expressway, Piruz St No. 1/3, Teheran; tel. 227262; Ambassador: TADEUSZ KOHOREWICZ.
Portugal: Mossadegh Ave, Tavanir Ave, Nezami Ghanjavi Ave, No. 30, Teheran; tel. 681380; telex 212588; Ambassador: FERNANDO PINTO DOS SANTOS.
Qatar: Africa Expressway, Golazin Ave, Parke Davar No. 4, Teheran; tel. 221255; telex 212375; Chargé d'affaires a.i.: I. MUHAMMAD AL-QAYED.
Romania: Fakhrabad Ave 22–28, Teheran; tel. 759841; telex 212791; Ambassador: NICOLAE STEFAN.
Saudi Arabia: Bucharest Ave, No. 59, POB 2903, Teheran; tel. 624297; Chargé d'affaires a.i.: MARVAN BASHIR AR-ROOMI.
Senegal: Vozara Ave, 4 8th St, BP 3217, Teheran; tel. 624142.
Somalia: Shariati Ave, Soheyl Ave No. 20, Teheran; Chargé d'affaires a.i.: MUHAMMAD SHEIKH AHMAD.
Spain: Ghaem Magham Farahani Ave, Varahram St No. 14, Teheran; tel. 624575; telex 212980; Ambassador: JAVIER OYARZUN.
Sudan: Gandhi Ave, 21st St, No. 5, Teheran.
Sweden: Taleghani Ave, Forsat Ave, Teheran; tel. 828305; telex 212822; Ambassador: GORAN BUNDY; British interests section at Royal Swedish Embassy, 143 Ferdowsi Ave, POB 11365-4474, Teheran 11344; tel. 675011; telex 212493; Head of Section: CHRISTOPHER MACRAE.
Switzerland: Boustan Ave, POB 11365-176; Teheran; tel. 268226; telex 212851; Ambassador: SERGE SALVI.
Syria: Bucharest Ave, 10th St, No. 42, Teheran; Ambassador: IBRAHIM YUNIS.
Thailand: Baharestan Ave, Parc Amin ed-Doleh No. 4, POB 11495-111, Teheran; tel. 301433; telex 214140; Ambassador: PHAIBULYA MAOLANON.
Turkey: Ferdowsi Ave No. 314, Teheran; tel. 315299; Ambassador: VULKAN VURAL.
USSR: Neauphle-le-Château Ave, Teheran; Ambassador: VIL KONSTANTINOVICH BOLDYREV.
United Arab Emirates: Zafar Ave, No. 355–7, Teheran; tel. 221333; telex 212697; Chargé d'affaires a.i.: T. AHMAD AL-HAIDAN.
Venezuela: Bucharest Ave, 9th St, No. 31, Teheran; tel. 625185; telex 213790; Ambassador: Dr JOSÉ RAFAEL ZANONI.
Yemen Arab Republic: Bucharest Ave, No. 26, Teheran; Chargé d'affaires a.i.: ABDULLAH AR-RAZI.
Yemen, People's Democratic Republic: Bucharest Ave, 10th St, No. 41, Teheran; Ambassador: KHADIR SALIH AL-HAMZAH.
Yugoslavia: Vali Asr Ave, Fereshteh Ave, Amir Teymour Alley, No. 12, Teheran; tel. 294127; telex 214235; Ambassador: MIRKO ZARIĆ.
Zaire: Vali Asr Ave, Chehrazi St, No. 68, POB 11365-3167, Teheran; tel. 222199; Chargé d'affaires a.i.: N'DJATE ESELE SASA.

Judicial System

In August 1982 the Supreme Court revoked all laws dating from the previous regime which did not conform with Islam. In October 1982 all courts set up prior to the Islamic Revolution were abolished. A new system of *qisas* (retribution) is being established, where the emphasis is on speedy justice. Islamic codes of correction were introduced in 1983, including the amputation of a hand or fingers for theft, flogging for fornication and violations of the strict code of dress for women, and stoning for adultery. One hundred and nine offences carry the death penalty. More than a thousand itinerant justices have been set up to tour the country, deciding cases on the spot and dispensing immediate punishment. The aim is to keep imprisonment to a minimum. In January 1983, however, investigative teams were set up to ensure that the judiciary did not exceed its authority. In 1984 there was a total of 2,200 judges. The new Supreme Court has 16 branches.

SUPREME COURT

Chief Justice: Ayatollah ABD AL-KARIM MOUSSAVI ARDEBILI.

Prosecutor-General: MUHAMMAD MOUSSAVI KHOENIHA.

Head of Military Revolutionary Courts and Head of Drug Offences Court: Hojatoleslam MOKHDAI.

IRAN

Islamic Revolutionary Prosecutor: Hojatoleslam RAAZINI.
Administrative Tribunal: President MUHAMMAD YAZDI.

Religion

According to the 1979 Constitution, the official religion is Islam of the Ja'fari sect (Shi'ite), but other Islamic sects, including Zeydi, Hanafi, Maleki, Shafe'i and Hanbali, will be valid and respected. Zoroastrians, Jews and Christians will be recognized as official religious minorities. According to the 1976 census, there were then 310,000 Christians (mainly Armenian), 80,000 Jews and 30,000 Zoroastrians.

ISLAM

The great majority of the Iranian people are Shi'i Muslims, but there is a minority of Sunni Muslims. Persians and Azerbaizhanis are mainly Shi'i, while the other ethnic groups are mainly Sunni.

During 1978 there was a revival of the influence of the Ayatollahs (or senior Shi'ite divines). Ayatollah Ruhollah Khomeini of Qom, who had been exiled to Iraq in 1964 and moved to near Paris in October 1978, conducted a campaign of opposition to the Shah, returning to Iran in February 1979 and bringing about the downfall of the Shah's regime. Other important Ayatollahs include Ayatollah ABD AL-KARIM MOUSSAVI ARDEBILI, Ayatollah HOSSEIN ALI MONTAZARI of Teheran, Ayatollah ABOLGHASSEM KHOI of Najaf, and the Ayatollahs Shahaboldin NAJAFI MARASHI and MUHAMMAD REZA GOLPAYEGHANI of Qom.

CHRISTIANITY
The Roman Catholic Church

At 31 December 1984 there were an estimated 18,000 adherents in Iran, including 12,000 of the Chaldean Rite and 3,000 each of the Armenian and Latin Rites.

Armenian Rite

Bishop of Isfahan: VARTAN TEKEYAN, Armenian Catholic Bishopric, Khiaban Ghazzali 22, Teheran; tel. 677204.

Chaldean Rite

Archbishop of Ahwaz: HANNA ZORA, Archbishop's House, POB 61956, Zahedi St, Ahwaz; tel. 24980.

Archbishop of Teheran: YOUHANNAN SEMAAN ISSAYI, Archevêché, Forsat Ave 91, Teheran 15819; tel. 823549.

Archbishop of Urmia (Rezayeh) and Bishop of Salmas (Shahpour): THOMAS MERAM, Khalifagari Kaldani Katoliq, POB 338, Orumiyeh 57135; tel. (0441) 22739.

Latin Rite

Archbishop of Isfahan: (vacant), Consolata Church, POB 11365-445, Teheran; tel. 673210; Apostolic Administrator: Fr JEAN-BAPTISTE DARRIBAT.

The Anglican Communion

Anglicans in Iran are adherents of the Episcopal Church in Jerusalem and the Middle East. The Rt Rev. HASSAN DEHQANI-TAFTI, the Bishop in Iran since 1961, was President-Bishop of the Church from 1976 to 1986. Following an assassination attempt against him in October 1979, the Bishop went into exile (he now resides in England and has been Assistant Bishop of Winchester since 1982).

Bishop in Iran: Rt Rev. HASSAN BARNABA DEHQANI-TAFTI, Bishop's House, POB 12, Isfahan; diocese founded 1912.

Presbyterian Church

Synod of the Evangelical (Presbyterian) Church in Iran: Assyrian Evangelical Church, Khiaban-i Hanifnejad, Khiaban-i Aramanch, Teheran; Moderator Rev. ADLE NAKHOSTEEN.

ZOROASTRIANS

There are about 30,000 Zoroastrians, a remnant of a once widespread sect. Their religious leader is MOUBAD.

OTHER COMMUNITIES

Communities of Armenians, and somewhat smaller numbers of Jews (an estimated 30,000 in 1986), Assyrians, Greek Orthodox Christians, Uniates and Latin Christians are also found as officially recognized faiths. The Bahá'í faith, which originated in Iran, has about 300,000 Iranian adherents, although at least 10,000 are believed to have fled since 1979 in order to escape persecution. The Government banned all Bahá'í institutions in August 1983.

The Press

Teheran dominates the press scene as many of the daily papers are published there and the bi-weekly, weekly and less frequent publications in the provinces generally depend on the major metropolitan dailies as a source of news. A press law which was announced in August 1979 required all newspapers and magazines to be licensed and imposed penalties of imprisonment for insulting senior religious figures. Offences against the Act will be tried in the criminal courts. In the Constitution which was approved in December 1979, the press is free, except in matters that are contrary to public morality, insult religious belief or slander the honour and reputation of individuals. Many of the papers which were published under the Shah's regime ceased publication after the revolution. In August 1980 Ayatollah Khomeini issued directives which indicated that censorship would be tightened up, and several papers were closed down in 1981. The radical daily *Azadegan* was closed by the Prosecutor-General in June 1985 and reappeared under a different title, *Abrar* (Rightly Guided), after complaints from deputies in the Majlis of its criticism of conservative members of the assembly. Later in 1985, however, a policy of relative liberalization of the press was introduced. Ayatollah Khomeini told journalists in September and October that criticism of the government was permissible, provided that it was constructive and not designed to arouse dissent.

PRINCIPAL DAILIES

Abrar (Rightly Guided): Apadan Ave 198, Abbasabad, Teheran; tel. 859971; f. 1985 after closure of *Azadegan* by order of the Prosecutor-General; morning; Farsi.

Alik: POB 11365-953, Jomhoori Islami Ave, Alik Alley, Teheran 11357; tel. 676671; f. 1931; afternoon; political and literary; Armenian; Propr A. AJEMIAN.

Bahari Iran: Khayaban Khayham, Shiraz; tel. 33738.

Bamdadan: Teheran.

Ettela'at (Information): Khayyam St, Teheran; tel. 311071; telex 212336; f. 1925; evening; Farsi; political and literary; owned and managed by Mostazafin Foundation from October 1979 until 1 January 1987, when it was placed under the direct supervision of Wilayat e Faqih (religious jurisprudence); Editor Mr SHIRANI; circ. 250,000.

Jomhoori Islami (Islamic Republic): Teheran; organ of Islamic Republican Party; Farsi.

Kayhan (Universe): Ferdowsi Ave, Teheran; tel. 310261; telex 213863; f. 1941; evening; Farsi; political; also publishes *Kayhan International* (daily; English), *Kayhan Arabic* (daily; Arabic), *Kayhan Turkish* (weekly; Turkish), *Kayhan Havaie* (weekly for Iranians abroad; Farsi), *Zan-e-Ruz* (Woman Today; weekly; Farsi), *Kayhan Varzeshi* (World of Sport; weekly; Farsi), *Kayhan Bacheha* (Children's World; weekly; Farsi), *Kayhan Farhangi* (World of Culture; monthly; Farsi); owned and managed by Mostazafin Foundation from October 1979 until 1 January 1987, when it was placed under the direct supervision of Wilayat e Faqih (religious jurisprudence); Chief Editor SAYED HASSAN SHAH-SHERAGI; circ. 350,000.

Khalqa-Musalman: Teheran; Farsi.

Khorassan: Meshed; Head Office: Khorassan Daily Newspapers, 14 Zohre St, Mobarezan Ave, Teheran; f. 1948; Propr MUHAMMAD SADEGH TEHERANIAN; circ. 40,000.

Mojahed: POB 64–1551, Teheran; organ of the Mujaheddin Khalq.

Rahnejat: Darvazeh Dowlat, Isfahan; political and social; Propr N. RAHNEJAT.

Risala'at (The Message): Teheran; Propr Hojatoleslam AHMAD AZARI-QOMI.

Teheran Times: Iranshahr Ave, Homa St, Block 2, Teheran 15836; tel. 824199; telex 213662; f. 1979; independent; English; Editor-in-Chief M. B. ANSARI.

PRINCIPAL PERIODICALS

Acta Medica Iranica: Faculty of Medicine, Enghelab Ave, Teheran Univ., Teheran 14; tel. 6112743; f. 1960; quarterly; English, French, German; under the supervision of the Educational Vice-Chancellor (M. PAZHUHI) and the Editorial Board; circ. 2,000.

Al-Akha: Khayyam Ave, Tehran; telex 212336; f. 1960; weekly; Arabic; Editor NAZIR FENZA.

Akhbar-e-Pezeshki: 86 Ghaem Magham Farahani Ave, Teheran; weekly; medical; Propr Dr T. FORUZIN.

IRAN
Directory

Armaghan: Baghe Saba, 127 Salim Street, Teheran 16137; tel. 750698; f. 1910; monthly; literary and historical; Propr Dr Muhammad Vahid-Dastgerdi; circ. 3,000.

Ashur: Ostad Motahhari Ave, Teheran; Assyrian; monthly; Propr Dr V. Bitmansur.

Auditor: 77 Ferdowsi Ave North, Teheran; quarterly; financial and managerial studies.

Ayandeh: POB 19575-583, Niyavaran, Teheran; tel. 283254; monthly; Iranian literary, historical and book review journal; Editor Prof. Iraj Afshar.

Daneshkadeh Pezeshki: Faculty of Medicine, Teheran University; tel. 6112743; f. 1947; 10 a year; medical magazine; Propr Dr Hossein Saadatzadeh; circ. 1,500.

Daneshmand: 447 Baharestan St, Teheran; monthly; scientific and technical magazine; Editor A. Mirzai.

Dokhtaran and Pesaran: Khayyam Ave, Teheran; f. 1947; weekly teenage magazine; Editor Nader Akhavan Haydari.

Donaye Varzesh: Khayyam Ave, Ettela'at Bldg, Teheran; telex 212336; weekly; sport; Editor Mr Samimi.

Echo of Islam: POB 14155-3987, Teheran; monthly; English; published by Ministry of Islamic Guidance.

Ettela'at Banovan: 11 Khayyam St, Teheran; telex 212336; weekly; women's magazine; Editor Mrs Rahnaward; circ. 85,000.

Ettela'at Haftegi: 11 Khayyam St, Teheran; telex 212336; weekly; Editor Mr Nayyeri; circ. 60,000.

Farhang-e-Iran Zamin: POB 19575-583, Niyavaran, Teheran; tel. 283254; annual; Iranian studies; Editor Prof. Iraj Afshar.

Faza: Enghelab Ave, Teheran; aviation; Propr H. Kamali-Taqari.

Film va Honar: Mobarezan Ave, Teheran; weekly; Editor A. Ramazani.

Honar va Memar: Enghelab Ave No. 256, Teheran; monthly; scientific and professional; Propr A. H. Echragh.

Iran Press Digest (Economic): Hafiz Ave, 4 Kucheh Hurtab, POB 11365-5551, Teheran; tel. 668114; telex 212300; weekly; Editor J. Behrouz.

Iran Press Digest (Political): Hafiz Ave, 4 Kucheh Hurtab, POB 11365-5551, Teheran; tel. 668114; telex 212300; weekly.

Iran Trade and Industry: POB 1228, Hafiz Ave, Teheran; monthly; English.

Iran Tribune: POB 111244, Teheran; monthly; English.

Jam: POB 1871, Jomhoori Islami Ave, Sabuhi Bldg, Teheran; monthly; arts; Propr A. Vakili.

Jame'e Dandan-Pezeshki Iran: 2 Ex-Shahi Alley, Shahid Dr Abbaspour St, Vali Asr Ave, POB 14155-3695, Teheran; tel. 686508; telex 212918; monthly; medical; organ of Iranian Dental Assen; Propr Dr Hamid Adeli-Nadjafi.

Javanan Emrooz: 11144 Khayyam Ave, POB 11335-9365, Ettela'at, Teheran; tel. 311205, telex 212336; f. 1966; weekly; youth; Editor Ali Agha Muhammadi.

Javaneh: POB 15875-1163, Motahhari Ave, Cnr Mofatteh St, Tajrish, Teheran; tel. 839051; published by Soroush Press; quarterly.

Kayhan Bacheha (Children's World): Ferdowsi Ave, Teheran; tel. 310251; telex 212467; weekly; Editor Amir Hossein Fardi; circ. 150,000.

Kayhan Varzeshi (World of Sport): Ferdowsi Ave, Teheran; tel. 310251; telex 212467; weekly; Dir Mahmad Monseti; circ. 125,000.

Mahjubah: POB 14155-3987, Teheran; Islamic women's magazine; published by the Islamic Thought Foundation.

Majda: 2 Ex-Shahi Alley, Shahid Dr Abaspour St, Vali-Asr Ave, Teheran; tel. (021) 686508; telex 212918; f. 1963; three a year; medical; journal of the Iranian Dental Association.

Mokhtarein va Mobtakerin: Motahhari Ave, Cnr Mofatteh St, POB 15875-1163, Teheran; tel. 839051; quarterly; Farsi; published by Soroush Press; Iranian technological innovations.

Music Iran: 1029 Amiriye Ave, Teheran; f. 1951; monthly; Editor Bahman Hirbod; circ. 7,000.

Nameh-e-Mardom: Teheran; organ of the Tudeh Party.

Neda-e-Nationalist: W. Khayaban Hafiz (Khayaban Rish Kutcha Bostan), POB 1999, Teheran.

Negin: Vali Asr Ave, Adl St 52, Teheran; monthly; scientific and literary; Propr and Dir M. Enayat.

Pars: Alley Dezhban, Shiraz; f. 1941; irregular; Propr and Dir F. Sharghi; circ. 10,000.

Pezhuhshgar: Vali Asr Ave, Teheran; scientific; Propr Dr R. Olumi.

Salamate Fekr: M.20, Kharg St, Teheran; tel. 223034; f. 1958; monthly; organ of the Mental Health Soc.; Editors Prof. E. Tchehrazi, Ali Reza Shafai.

Sepid va Siyah: Ferdowsi Ave, Teheran; monthly; popular; Editor Dr A. Behzadi; circ. 30,000.

Setareye Esfahan: Isfahan; weekly; political; Propr A. Mihankhah.

Sokhan: Hafiz Ave, Zomorrod Passage, Teheran; f. 1943; Khanlari; monthly; literary and art; Propr Parviz Natel-Khanlary.

Soroush: Motahhari Ave, Corner Mofatteh St, POB 15875-1163, Teheran; tel. 839051; f. 1972; weekly in Farsi, monthly in English, French and Arabic; cultural magazine.

Tarikh-e-Islam: Amiriyeh 94 Ku, Ansari, Teheran; monthly; religious; Propr A. A. Tashayyod.

Tebb-o-Daru: POB 3033, Inqilab Ave, Teheran; medical; Man. Dr Sh. Assadi Zadeh.

Teheran Mossavar: Lalezar Ave, Teheran; weekly; political and social.

Vahid: 55 Jomhoori Islami Ave, Jam St, Teheran; weekly; literature; Propr Dr S. Vahidnia.

Yaghma: 15 Khanequah Ave, Teheran; tel. 305344; f. 1948; monthly; literature; Propr Habib Yaghmaie.

Zan-e-Ruz (Woman Today): Ferdowsi Ave, Teheran; telex 212467; weekly; women's; circ. over 100,000.

NEWS AGENCIES

Islamic Republic News Agency (IRNA): 873 Vali Asr Ave, POB 764, Teheran; tel. 892050; telex 212827; f. 1936; Man. Dir Dr Kamal Kharrazi.

Foreign Bureaux

Agence France-Presse (AFP): POB 1535, Ghaen St, Teheran; tel. 314190; telex 2479; Correspondent Jacques Charmelot.

Agenzia Nazionale Stampa Associata (ANSA) (Italy): 7 East Africa St, Nahid Blvd 7, Teheran; tel. 009821; telex 213629; Correspondent (vacant).

Kyodo Tsushin (Japan): No. 23, First Floor, Couche Kargozar, Couche Sharsaz Ave, Zafar, Teheran; tel. 220448; telex 214058; Correspondent Masaru Imai.

Reuters (UK): POB 15875-1193, Teheran; tel. 847700; telex 211634; (Correspondent, Hugh Pope, expelled from Iran in July 1986 for allegedly revealing military secrets).

Telegrafnoye Agentstvo Sovetskovo Soyuza (TASS) (USSR): Kehyaban Hamid, Kouche Masoud 73, Teheran; Correspondent (vacant).

Xinhua (New China) News Agency (People's Republic of China): 75 Golestan 2nd St, Pasdaran Ave, Teheran; tel. 241852; telex 212399; Correspondent Xu Boyuan.

Publishers

Ali Akbar Elmi: Jomhoori Islami Ave, Teheran; Dir Ali Akbar Elmi.

Amir Kabir: 28 Vessal Shirazi St, Teheran; f. 1950; historical, social, literary and children's books; Dir Abd ar-Rahim Jafari.

Boroukhim: Ferdowsi Ave, Teheran; dictionaries.

Danesh: 357 Nasser Khosrow Ave, Teheran; f. 1931 in India, transferred to Iran in 1937; literary and historical (Persian); imports and exports books; Man. Dir Noorouah Iranparast.

Ebn-e-Sina: Meydane 25 Shahrivar, Teheran; f. 1957; educational publishers and booksellers; Dir Ebrahim Ramazani.

Eghbal Printing & Publishing Organization: 15 Booshehr St, Dr Shariati Ave, Teheran; tel. 768113; f. 1903; Man. Dir Djavad Eghbal.

Iran Chap Co: Khayyam Ave, Teheran; f. 1966; newspapers, books, magazines, colour printing and engraving; Man. Dir Dr Ali-Reza Shirami.

Kanoon Marefat: 6 Lalezar Ave, Teheran; Dir Hassan Marefat.

Khayyam: Jomhoori Islami Ave, Teheran; Dir Mohammad Ali Taraghi.

Majlis Press: Baharistan Ave, Teheran.

Safiali Shah: Baharistan Sq., Teheran; Dir Mansour Moshfegh.

Sahab Geographic and Drafting Institute: 30 Somayeh St, Hoquqi Crossroad, Dr Ali Shariati Ave, POB 11365-617, Teheran; tel. 765691; maps, atlases, and books on geography, science, history and Islamic art; Founder and Pres. ABBAS A. SAHAB.

Scientific and Cultural Publications Co: Ministry of Higher Education and Culture, POB 5433-5437, Teheran; tel. 686317; f. 1974; Iranian and Islamic studies and scientific and cultural books; Pres. M. BOROUJERDI.

Taban Press: Nassir Khosrow Ave, Teheran; f. 1939; Propr A. MALEKI.

Teheran Economist: 99 Sargord Sakhaie Ave, Teheran-11.

Teheran University Press: 16 Kargar Shomali Ave, Teheran; tel. 632062; f. 1944; university textbooks; Man. Dir Dr FIRUZ HARIRCHI.

Towfigh: Jomhoori Islami Ave, Teheran; publishes humorous Almanac and pocket books; distributes humorous and satirical books; Dir Dr FARIDEH TOWFIGH.

Zawar: Jomhoori Islami Ave, Teheran; Dir AKBAR ZAWAR.

Radio and Television

There were over 10m. radio receivers and 2.1m. television sets in use in 1985.

Islamic Republic of Iran Broadcasting (IRIB): Mossadegh Ave, Jame Jam St, POB 19395-1774, Teheran; tel. 21961; telex 212431; semi-autonomous government authority; non-commercial; operates two national television and three national radio channels, as well as local provincial radio stations throughout the country; Dir-Gen. MUHAMMAD HASHEMI.

RADIO

Radio Network 1 (Voice of Islamic Republic of Iran): there are three national radio channels: Radio Networks 1 and 2 and Radio Quran, which broadcasts recitals of the Quran (Koran) and other programmes related to it; covers whole of Iran and reaches whole of Europe, SW USSR, whole of Asia, Africa and part of USA; medium-wave regional broadcasts in local languages; Arabic, Armenian, Assyrian, Azerbaizhani, Baluchi, Bandari, Dari, Farsi, Kurdish, Mazandarani, Pashtu, Turkoman, Turkish and Urdu; external broadcasts in English, French, German, Spanish, Turkish, Arabic, Kurdish, Urdu, Pashtu, Armenian, Bengali, Russian and special overseas programme in Farsi; 53 transmitters.

TELEVISION

Television: 625-line, System B; Secam colour; two production centres in Teheran producing for two networks and 28 local TV stations; Dir-Gen. M. HASHEMI.

Finance

(cap. = capital; p.u. = paid up; dep. = deposits; res = reserves; brs = branches; m. = million; amounts in rials)

BANKING

Banks were nationalized in June 1979 and a revised banking system has been introduced consisting of nine banks. Three banks were reorganized, two (Bank Tejarat and Bank Mellat) resulted from mergers of 22 existing small banks, three specialize in industry and agriculture and one, the Islamic Bank (now Islamic Economy Organization) set up in May 1979, was exempt from nationalization. A change-over to an Islamic banking system, with interest being replaced by a 4% commission on loans, began on 21 March 1984 and will take several years to complete.

Although the number of foreign banks operating in Iran has fallen dramatically since the Revolution, some 30 are still represented. Since the exclusion of French banks from the Iranian market at the end of 1983, Federal German, Swiss, Japanese and British banks have been responsible for about 30% of total trade financing.

Central Bank

Bank Markazi Islamic Republic of Iran (Central Bank): Ferdowsi Ave, Teheran; tel. 310100; telex 212503; f. 1960; Bank Markazi Iran until Dec. 1983; central note-issuing bank of Iran, government banking; cap. 125,000m., govt dep. 872,338m., bank dep. 1,171,430m., res 69,023m. (1982); Gov. MAJID QASSEMI.

Commercial Banks

Bank Keshavarzi (Agricultural Bank): 129 Patrice Lumumba St, Jalal al-Ahmad Expressway, POB 14155-6395, Teheran; tel. 9121; telex 212058; f. 1979 as merger of the Agricultural Development Bank of Iran and the Agricultural Co-operative Bank of Iran; cap. 132,270.6m., dep. 103,534m. (August 1986); 306 brs; Man. Dir ALI-REZA TALAYI.

Bank Mellat (Nation's Bank): 4 Dameshgh St, Vali Asr Ave, POB 11365-5964, Teheran; tel. 891021; telex 213251; State-owned bank; f. 1979 as merger of the following: National Bank of Iran, Bank Bimeh Iran, Bank Dariush, Distributors' Co-operative Credit Bank, Iran Arab Bank, Bank Omran, Bank Pars, Bank of Teheran, Foreign Trade Bank of Iran; cap. p.u. 33,500m., dep. 797,743m., res 23,754m. (March 1985); 764 brs throughout Iran; Chair. and Man. Dir VALIOL-LAH SEIF.

Bank Melli Iran (The National Bank of Iran): Ferdowsi Ave, POB 11365-171, Teheran; tel. 3231; telex 212890; f. 1928; State-owned bank; cap. and res 32,198m., dep. 2,223,584m., total assets 3,304,825m. (March 1985); 1,600 brs throughout Iran, 24 brs abroad; Chair. and Man. Dir KAZEM ELMI.

Bank Saderat Iran (The Export Bank of Iran): 124 Jomhoori Islami Ave, POB 11365-7168, Teheran; tel. 670041; telex 212352; f. 1952, reorganized 1979; cap. and res. 21,908.2m., dep. 1,347,898.9m. (Dec. 1985); 3,000 brs in Iran, brs throughout Middle East and Europe; Man. Dir SAYED SHARIF RAZAVI FALLAHIEH.

Bank Sepah (Army Bank): Imam Khomeini Sq, Teheran; tel. 311091; telex 212462; f. 1925, reorganized 1979; cap. p.u. 8,000m., dep. 386,666m. (March 1980); 670 brs throughout Iran and 4 brs abroad; Pres. MUHAMMAD MEHDI JAHANBIN.

Bank Tejarat: 184 Taleghani Ave, POB 11365-5416, Teheran; tel. 892071; telex 212077; f. 1979 as merger of the following: Irano-British Bank, Bank Etebarate Iran, The Bank of Iran and the Middle East, Mercantile Bank of Iran and Holland, Bank Barzagani Iran, Bank Iranshahr, Bank Sanaye Iran, Bank Shahriar, Iranians' Bank, Bank Kar, International Bank of Iran and Japan, Bank Russo-Iran; cap. p.u. 39,200m., dep. 589,156m., res 159,204m. (1985); 667 brs throughout Iran and brs in London and Paris; Man. Dir JAVAD BOSTANIAN.

Islamic Economy Organization (formerly Islamic Bank of Iran): Ferdowsi Ave, Teheran; f. February 1980; cap. 2,000m.; provides interest-free loans and investment in small industry.

Development Bank

Bank Sanat and Madan (Bank of Industry and Mines): 593 Hafiz Ave, POB 11365/4978, Teheran; tel. 893271; telex 212816; f. 1979 as merger of the following: Industrial Credit Bank (ICB), Industrial and Mining Development Bank of Iran (IMDBI), Development and Investment Bank of Iran (DIBI), Iranian Bankers Investment Company (IBICO); cap. p.u. 40,980m. (1984); Chair. and Man. Dir MORTEZA ARAMY PARCHEBAF.

STOCK EXCHANGE

Teheran Stock Exchange: 521 Taghinia Bldg, South Saadi Ave, Teheran 11447; tel. 311149; f. 1966; Chair. of Council M. NOURBAKHSH.

INSURANCE

The nationalization of insurance companies was announced on 25 June 1979.

Bimeh Iran (Iran Insurance Co): Saadi Ave, Teheran; tel. 304026; telex 212782; f. 1935; state-owned insurance company; all types of insurance; cap. p.u. 3,500m.; Man. Dir AMIR SADEGHI NESHAT.

Bimeh Markazi Iran (Central Insurance Co): 149 Taleghani Ave, Teheran; Pres. AHMAD GERANMAYEH.

Dana Insurance Co Ltd: POB 2868, Enghelab Ave, Teheran; in association with Commercial Union Assurance Co. Ltd.

Hafez Insurance Co: Ostad Motahhari Ave, 44 Daraye Noor St, Teheran; f. 1974; most classes of insurance; Man. Dir K. HELMI.

Iran-American International Insurance Co: Ave Zohre, Teheran.

Pars, Société Anonyme d'Assurances: Avenue Saadi, Teheran; f. 1955; fire, marine, motor vehicle, third party liability, personal accident, group, life, contractor's all-risk and medical insurance.

Shirkat Sahami Bimeh Arya (Arya Insurance Co Ltd): 202 Soraya Ave, Teheran; f. 1952; nationalized 1979; cap. 300m.; Man. Dir KHALIL KARIMABADI.

IRAN

Shirkat Sahami Bimeh Asia (Asia Insurance Co Ltd): Asia Insurance Bldg, Taleghani Ave, Teheran; tel. 836040; telex 213664; f. 1960; Man. Dir Masoum Zamiri.

Shirkat Sahami Bimeh Iran and America: 8 Apartments Kavah, 20 Mitu Zohra, Mobarezan Ave, Teheran; f. 1974; cap. 1,000m.; Man. Dir Khosrow Shabai.

Shirkat Sahami Bimeh Melli (The National Insurance Co Ltd): Ayatollah Taleghani Ave, Rasekh St, POB 1786, Teheran; f. 1956; all classes of insurance; Man. Dir Reza Fatemi.

Shirkat Sahami Bimeh Omid: Boulevard Karimkhan Zand, Kheradniand Jonoubi Ave 99, Teheran; f. 1960.

Shirkati Sahami Bimeh Sakhtiman Va Kar (Construction and Labour): Apartments Bank Kar, Khayaban-i-Hafiz; f. 1964; cap. 200m.; Man. Dir Samad Taheri.

Shirkat Sahami Bimeh Shargh: North Saadi Ave, Teheran; f. 1950; cap. 200m.; Man. Dir M. Kashanian.

Shirkat Sahami Bimeh Teheran: 43 Khayaban Khushbin Villa, Teheran; f. 1974; cap. 500m.; Man. Dir Eraj Ali Abadi.

Shirkat-i-Sahami Bimeh Dan: 315 Enghelab Ave, Teheran; f. 1974; cap. 500m.; joint venture between Iranian interests and Commercial Union Insurance Co, London; Man. Dir Mansoor Akhwan.

Trade and Industry

CHAMBER OF COMMERCE

Iran Chamber of Commerce, Industries and Mines: 254 Taleghani Ave, Teheran; tel. 836031; telex 213382; supervises the affiliated 20 Chambers in the provinces.

STATE ENTERPRISES

National Iranian Oil Company (NIOC): Taleghani Ave (POB 1863), Teheran; a state organization controlling all petroleum, petrochemical and natural gas operations in Iran; incorporated April 1951 on nationalization of oil industry to engage in all phases of oil operations; in February 1979 it was announced that in future Iran would sell oil direct to the oil companies and in September 1979 the Ministry of Oil took over control of the National Iranian Oil Company, and the Minister of Oil took over as Chairman and Managing Director; Chair. of Board and Gen. Man. Dir Gholam-reza Aqazadeh (Minister of Oil); Directors: Ehsanollah Butorabi (Engineering), Muhammad Reza Kadivar (Refining), Heydar Ali Alizadeh (Distribution and Pipelines), Sayed Kazem Vaziri Hamaneh (Administration), Sayed Mostafa Zeinedin (Legal Affairs), Allahkaram Mirzai (International Affairs), Morteza Nassir (Corporate Planning Affairs), Mostafa Kalmor (Commercial Affairs), Muhammad Hasan Tavalai (Oil Production).

Iranian National Drilling Co: Chair. Mansour Parvinian.

Iranian Offshore Oil Company (IOOC): 339 Dr Beheshti Ave, POB 1434, Teheran; tel. 624102; telex 212707; wholly-owned subsidiary of NIOC; f. 1980; development, exploitation and production of crude oil, natural gas and other hydrocarbons in all offshore areas of Iran in Persian Gulf; Chair. Muhammad Hadi Nejad Hoseynihan; Man. Dir M. Aghaee.

CO-OPERATIVES

Central Organization for Co-operatives of Iran: Teheran; in October 1985 there were 4,598 labour co-operatives, with a total membership of 703,814 and capital of 2,184.5m. rials, and 9,159 urban non-labour co-operatives, with a total membership of 262,118 and capital of 4,187.5m. rials.

Central Organization for Rural Co-operatives of Iran (CORC): Teheran; Man. Dir Sayed Hassan Motevalli-zadeh.

The CORC was founded in 1963, and the Islamic Government of Iran has pledged that it will continue its educational, technical, commercial and credit assistance to rural co-operative societies and unions. At the end of the Iranian year 1362 (1983/84) there were 3,084 Rural Co-operative Societies with a total membership of 3,839,000 and share capital of 22,872m. rials. There were 174 Rural Co-operative Unions with capital of 6,700m. rials. The number of member Co-operative Societies of the Unions was 3,080.

TRADE FAIR

Export Promotion Centre of Iran: POB 11-48, Tajrish, Teheran; tel. 2199; telex 212896; international trade fairs and exhibitions; Pres. Hossein Khabbazan.

Transport

RAILWAYS

Iranian State Railway: Rahe-Ahan Sq., Teheran; tel. 555120; telex 213103; f. 1938; Pres. Eng. Sayed Abulhassan Khamoushi; Vice-Pres. Hossein Teherani (Admin. and Finance), Eng. Sadegh Afshar (Technical and Operations), Hamid Mehrazma (Planning and Technical Studies), Eng. Muhammad Sayedikiya (Construction and Renovation).

The Iranian railway system, which is generally single-tracked, includes the following main routes:

Trans-Iranian Railway runs 1,392 km from Bandar Turkman on the Caspian Sea in the north, through Teheran, and south to Bandar Imam Khomeini on the Persian Gulf.

Southern Line links Teheran to Khorramshahr via Qom, Arak, Dorood, Andimeshk and Ahwaz; 937 km.

Northern Line links Teheran to Gorgan via Garmsar, Firooz Kooh and Sari; 499 km.

Teheran-Kerman Line via Kashan, Yazd and Zarand; 1,106 km.

Teheran-Tabriz Line linking with the Azerbaizhan Railway; 736 km.

Tabriz-Djulfa Electric Line: 146 km.

Garmsar-Meshed Line connects Teheran with Meshed via Semnan, Damghan, Shahrud and Nishabur; 812 km.

Qom-Zahedan Line when completed will be an intercontinental line linking Europe and Turkey, through Iran, with India. Zahedan is situated 91.7 km west of the Baluchistan frontier, and is the end of the Pakistani broad gauge railway. The section at present links Qom to Kerman via Kashan, Sistan, Yazd, Bafq and Zarand; 1,005 km. A branch line from Sistan was opened in 1971 via Isfahan to the steel mill at Folad Shahr; 112 km.

Ahwaz-Bandar Khomeini Line connects Bandar Khomeini with the Trans-Iranian railway at Ahwaz; this line is due to be double-tracked; 112 km.

Azerbaizhan Railway extends from Tabriz to Djulfa (146.5 km), meeting the Caucasian railways at the Soviet frontier. Electrification works for this section have been completed and the electrified line was opened in April 1982. A standard gauge railway line (139 km) extends from Tabriz (via Sharaf-Khaneh) to the Turkish frontier at Razi.

A 730-km line to link Bandar Abbas and Bafq has been under construction since 1982. The total length of main lines is 4,567 km. There are plans to add 1,300 km to the system by 1989.

Underground Railway. An agreement was signed in March 1976 between the Municipality of Teheran and French contractors for the construction of a subway. Four lines are to be built with a total length of 143 km. Construction began during 1978, but the project was suspended after the revolution in 1979, and work was not resumed until September 1986.

ROADS

In 1985 there were 490 km of motorways, 16,551 km of paved main roads, 23,025 km of paved feeder roads, 46,866 km of gravel roads and 49,440 km of earth roads. There is a paved highway (A1) from Bazargan on the Turkish border to the Afghanistan border. The A2 highway runs from the Iraqi border to Mir Javeh on the Pakistan border; 2,220 km of the A2 has been completed, and the remaining 80 km are under construction.

Ministry of Roads and Transport: Ministry of Roads and Transport, 49 Taleghani Ave, Teheran; tel. 646770.

INLAND WATERWAYS

Principal waterways:

Lake Rezaiyeh (Lake Urmia) 80 km west of Tabriz in North-West Iran; and River Karun flowing south through the oilfields into the River Shatt el-Arab, thence to the head of the Persian Gulf near Abadan.

Lake Rezaiyeh: From Sharafkhaneh to Golmankhaneh there is a twice-weekly service of tugs and barges for transport of passengers and goods.

River Karun: Regular cargo service is operated by the Mesopotamia-Iran Corpn Ltd. Iranian firms also operate daily motor-boat services for passengers and goods.

SHIPPING

Persian Gulf: The main oil terminal is at Kharg Island. The principal commercial non-oil ports are Bandar Shahid Rajai (which was officially inaugurated in 1983 and handles 9m. of the 12m. tons of cargo passing annually through Iran's Persian Gulf ports), Bandar Khomeini, Bushehr, Bandar Abbas and Chah Bahar. A project to develop Bandar Abbas port, which pre-dates the Islamic Revolution and was originally to cost IR 1,900,000m., is now in progress. Khorramshahr, Iran's biggest port, was put out of action in the Gulf War, and Bushehr and Bandar Khomeini also sustained war damage, which has restricted their use. Iran was to spend IR 24,000m. on expanding eight ports in the Persian Gulf during 1985, including Bandar Khomeini, Shahid Rajai and six smaller ports. Nine floating jetties are under construction to connect Iran's islands with ports on the mainland. Six of these jetties have been built at Abu Musa, Lavan, Kish, Qeshm, Hormuz and Larak. The remaining three are being built at Kong, Bushehr and Bandar Abbas.

Caspian Sea: Principal port Bandar Anzali (formerly Bandar Pahlavi) and Bandar Nowshahr.

Iranian National Tanker Co: 67 Shahid Atefi St, Africa Ave, POB 16765-947, Teheran; tel. 296041; telex 213938; fleet of 11 vessels; Chair. and Man. Dir MUHAMMAD SOURI.

Irano–Hind Shipping Co: 265 Ostad Motahhari Ave, Teheran; tel. 628176; telex 215233; joint venture with the Shipping Corpn of India; fleet of 8 ocean liners and two refrigerated cargo ships; Chair. Adm. R. K. S. GHANDI; Vice-Chair. MUHAMMAD SOURI; Man. Dir A. KOOHESTANI.

Islamic Republic of Iran Shipping Lines (IRISL): POB 353, Arya Building, 127 Ghaem Magham Farahani Ave, Teheran; tel. 833061; telex 212794; f. 1967; affiliated to the Ministry of Commerce March 1984; fleet of 68 ocean liners, 5 passenger and cargo ships and 10 service ships; liner services between the Persian Gulf and Europe, the Far East and South America; Chair. and Man. Dir MUHAMMAD HOSSEIN DAHMER.

Ports and Shipping Organization: 751 Enghelab Ave, Teheran; tel. 837041; telex 212271; Man. Dir M. MADAD.

CIVIL AVIATION

The two main international airports are Mehrabad (Teheran) and Abadan. An international airport was opened at Isfahan in July 1984 and the first international flight took place in March 1986. Work on a new international airport, 40 km south of Teheran, abandoned in 1979, was due to be resumed in the mid-1980s. An international airport is to be built near Gorgan, east of the Caspian Sea. A new runway was opened at Kerman airport in January 1986, and the terminal was to be expanded by 1987. Six airports have been added to the national network since the Islamic Revolution. In addition, airports at Ardebil, Sari and Meshed are to be expanded to take heavy aircraft.

Airline of the Islamic Republic of Iran (Iran Air): Iran Air Bldg, Mehrabad Airport, Teheran; telex 212975; f. 1962; Man. Dir MUHAMMAD REZA MAJIDI; serves Persian Gulf area, Athens, Beijing, Bombay, Damascus, Frankfurt, Geneva, Istanbul, Karachi, London, Madrid, Paris, Rome, Tokyo, Vienna; fleet of 2 Boeing 747-200B, 1 Boeing 747-100B, 2 Boeing 747-200F, 4 Boeing 747-SP, 1 Boeing 707-320B, 4 Boeing 707-320C, 6 Airbus A300B2-203, 5 Boeing 727-200, 2 Boeing 727-100, 2 Boeing 737-200, 2 Boeing 737-200C.

Iranian Asseman Airlines: POB 13145-1476; Mehrabad Airport, Teheran; tel. (021) 661967; telex 212575; f. after Islamic Revolution as result of merger of Air Taxi Co (f. 1958), Pars Air (f. 1969), Air Service Co (f. 1962) and Hoor Asseman; Man. Dir M. H. SHAHANGIAN; domestic routes and charter services; fleet of 1 Fokker F27-600, 2 Fokker F28-4000, 2 FH 227B, 4 Falcon 20F, 7 Turbo Commander, 12 Aero Commander, 3 Piper Chieftain, 3 Islander.

Tourism

Tourism has suffered considerably from the disturbances caused by the revolution and the war with Iraq. The Islamic element in Iranian cultural life is now encouraged, and Western influences are discouraged.

Atomic Energy

Atomic Energy Organization of Iran: POB 14155-1339, Teheran; tel. 638025; telex 213383; f. 1973; originally set up to produce nuclear power to provide for the base load electricity needs of the country; main aim now is the exploration and exploitation of uranium (deposits have been found in several regions of Iran in commercially viable quantities); to secure fuel needs of Iran's nuclear energy programme; to utilize nuclear energy in industry, agriculture and medicine; to provide research and development work and training for greater national self-sufficiency in nuclear science technology; Bushehr nuclear power plant, a pressurized water reactor (two 1,200 MW units), being built by Kraftwerk Union AG of the Federal Republic of Germany, is scheduled for completion by 1988; Pres. REZA AMROLLAHI.

Isfahan Nuclear Technology Centre (INTC): Isfahan; f. pre-Revolution; technological assistance to industry; a sub-critical research reactor was scheduled to begin operation in March 1985; a zero-power reactor is planned.

Teheran University Nuclear Centre: Institute of Nuclear Science and Technology, POB 2989, Teheran; f. 1958; research in nuclear physics, electronics, nuclear chemistry, radiobiology and nuclear engineering; training and advice on nuclear science and the peaceful applications of atomic energy; a 5-MW pool-type research reactor on the new campus of Teheran University went critical in November 1967; a 3-MeV Van de Graaff-type accelerator became operational in 1972; Dir Dr J. MOGHIMI.

IRAQ

Introductory Survey

Location, Climate, Language, Religion, Flag, Capital

The Republic of Iraq is an almost land-locked state in western Asia, with a narrow outlet to the sea on the Persian (Arabian) Gulf. Its neighbours are Iran to the east, Turkey to the north, Syria and Jordan to the west, and Saudi Arabia and Kuwait to the south. The climate is extreme, with hot, dry summers, when temperatures may exceed 43°C (109°F), and cold winters, especially in the highlands. Summers are humid near the Persian Gulf. The official language is Arabic, spoken by about 80% of the population. About 15% speak Kurdish, while there is a small Turkoman-speaking minority. About 95% of the population are Muslims, of whom more than 50% belong to the Shi'i sect. However, the regime that came to power in 1968 has been dominated by members of the Sunni sect. The national flag (proportions 3 by 2) has three equal horizontal stripes, of red, white and black, with three five-pointed green stars on the central white stripe. The capital is Baghdad.

Recent History

Iraq was formerly part of Turkey's Ottoman Empire. During the First World War (1914–18), when Turkey was allied with Germany, the territory was captured by British forces. In 1920 Iraq was placed under a League of Nations mandate, administered by the United Kingdom. In 1921 Amir Faisal ibn Hussain, a member of the Hashimi (Hashemite) dynasty of Arabia, was proclaimed King. In the same year, his brother, Abdullah, was proclaimed Amir (Emir) of neighbouring Transjordan (later renamed Jordan), also administered by the United Kingdom under a League of Nations mandate. The two new monarchs were sons of Hussain (Hussein) ibn Ali, the Sharif of Mecca, who had proclaimed himself King of the Hijaz (now part of Saudi Arabia) in 1916. The British decision to nominate Hashemite princes to be rulers of Iraq and Transjordan was a reward for Hussain's co-operation in the wartime campaign against Turkey.

During its early years the new kingdom was faced by Kurdish revolts (1922–32) and by border disputes in the south. The leading personality in Iraqi political life under the monarchy was Gen. Nuri as-Said, who became Prime Minister in 1930 and held the office for seven terms, over a period of 28 years. He strongly supported Iraq's friendship with the United Kingdom and with the West in general. After prolonged negotiations, a 25-year Anglo-Iraqi Treaty of Alliance was signed in 1930. The British mandate ended on 3 October 1932, when Iraq became fully independent.

King Faisal I died in 1933 and was succeeded by his son, Ghazi. In 1939, however, King Ghazi was killed in a motor accident. The new king, Faisal II, was only three years old at the time of his accession, and his uncle, Prince Abd al-Ilah, acted as regent until 1953, when the king assumed full powers. Like Gen. Nuri, Prince Abd al-Ilah was pro-Western in outlook. An attempted pro-Nazi coup in May 1941 was thwarted by the intervention of British forces. Despite nationalist opposition, Iraq declared war on Germany and Italy in January 1943. British troops were withdrawn in October 1947, although a British air base remained until 1959. Iraqi forces participated in the Arab–Israeli war of 1948–49. The Constitutional Union Party, founded by Gen. Nuri in 1949, became the sole legal party in 1953, after all opposition groups were banned. In 1955 Iraq signed the Baghdad Pact, an agreement on collective regional security against a possible threat from the USSR.

In February 1958 Iraq and Jordan formed an Arab Federation, with King Faisal of Iraq as its Head of State. In March Gen. Nuri resigned as Iraqi Prime Minister to become Prime Minister of the new union. On 14 July, however, a military revolution overthrew the Iraqi monarchy. King Faisal, Prince Abd al-Ilah and Gen. Nuri were all killed. The victorious rebels abolished the 1925 Constitution, dissolved the legislature and proclaimed a republic, with Brig. (later Lt-Gen.) Abd al-Karim Kassem at the head of a left-wing nationalist regime. Iraq withdrew from the Baghdad Pact in March 1959. For more than four years, Kassem maintained a precarious and increasingly isolated position, opposed by Pan-Arabs, Kurds and other groups. In February 1963 the Pan-Arab element in the armed forces staged a coup in which Kassem was killed. A new government was set up under Col (later Field Marshal) Abd as-Salem Muhammad Aref, who had briefly held office as Deputy Prime Minister after the 1958 revolution. President Aref initiated a policy of closer relations with the United Arab Republic (Egypt). Martial law, in force since 1958, was brought to an end in January 1965, and a purely civilian government was inaugurated in September 1965. President Aref was killed in an air accident in March 1966, and was succeeded by his brother, Major-Gen. Abd ar-Rahman Muhammad Aref. Iraq declared war on Israel at the outbreak of the Six-Day War in June 1967, but Iraqi forces were not involved in the conflict. The second President Aref was ousted by members of the Arab Socialist Renaissance (Baath) Party on 17 July 1968. Major-Gen. (later Field Marshal) Ahmad Hassan al-Bakr, a former Prime Minister, became President and Prime Minister, and supreme authority was vested in the Revolutionary Command Council (RCC), of which President al-Bakr was also Chairman. Provisional constitutions, proclaiming socialist principles, were introduced in September 1968 and July 1970. A National Charter, to be the basis of a permanent constitution, was issued in November 1971. This envisaged an elected National Assembly but, until the Assembly's formation, power remained with the RCC.

Relations with the Syrian Government deteriorated after a younger generation of Baathists seized power in Syria in 1970. Except for a period in 1978–79, bitter rivalry has existed between Syrian and Iraqi Baathists. Relations with Syria dramatically improved in October 1978, when President Assad of Syria visited Baghdad. Plans were announced for eventual complete political and economic union of the two countries. Economic difficulties, such as the dispute over water from the Euphrates river, were soon settled but progress on political union was slow. On 16 July 1979 the Vice-Chairman of the RCC, Saddam Hussain, who had long been the real power in Iraq, replaced Bakr as Chairman, and also as President of Iraq. A few days later, an attempted coup was reported and several members of the RCC were executed for their alleged part in the plot. The suspicion of Syrian implication put an end to all further talk of political union between Iraq and Syria, but economic co-operation continued.

During 1979 the National Progressive Front, an alliance of Baathists and Communists, broke up amid accusations from communist sources that the Baathists were conducting a 'reign of terror'. In February 1980 President Hussain announced his 'National Charter', reaffirming the principles of non-alignment. In June elections, the first since the 1958 revolution, were held for a 250-member National Assembly (to perform legislative duties alongside the RCC), followed in September by elections for a 50-member Kurdish Legislative Council.

Relations with Iran, precarious for many years, developed into full-scale war in September 1980. Prior to 1975, Iran had been supporting a rebellion by Kurds in northern Iraq. An agreement between Iran and Iraq, signed in 1975, defined the border between the two countries as running down the middle of the Shatt al-Arab waterway, and also virtually ended the Kurdish rebellion by depriving it of Iranian support. In the years after 1975, however, Iraq grew increasingly dissatisfied with the 1975 agreement. Iraq also wanted the withdrawal of Iranian forces from Abu Musa and Tumb islands, which Iran occupied in 1971.

The Iranian revolution of 1979 exacerbated these grievances.

Conflict soon developed over Arab demands for autonomy in Iran's Khuzestan region (named 'Arabistan' by Arabs), which Iran accused Iraq of encouraging. Iraq's Sunni leadership was suspicious of Shi'ite Iran, and feared that trouble might arise from its own Shi'ites, who form more than 50% of the population. Border squabbling took place between Iraq and Iran in the summer of 1980, and more extensive fighting began after Iran ignored Iraqi diplomatic efforts, demanding the withdrawal of Iranian forces from the border area of Zain ul-Qos in Diali province. Iraq maintained that this area should have been returned under the 1975 agreement, which Iraq then abrogated on 16 September 1980. Iraqi advances into Iran began on 22 September along a front of 500 km (300 miles). Fierce Iranian resistance brought about a stalemate, which lasted until the spring of 1982, when Iranian counter-offensives led to the retaking of the port of Khorramshahr in May and the withdrawal of Iraqi troops from the territory which they had taken in 1980. In July 1982 the Iranian army crossed into Iraq.

The Gulf War, as it is known, has since degenerated into a conflict of attrition, with Iraq holding an advantage in terms of the quantity and sophistication of its armaments, and Iran having a greater supply of manpower but being, as yet, unable to stage a decisive offensive. While Iran launched a series of attacks across its northern border with Iraq in October 1983, threatening the last outlet for Iraqi exports of petroleum through the Kirkuk pipeline, Iraq intensified missile attacks and bombing raids against Iranian towns and petroleum installations. During the autumn of 1983 Iraq took delivery of five French-built Super Etendard fighter aircraft. With these and with the Exocet missiles which it already possessed, Iraq threatened to destroy Iran's oil industry, centred on Kharg Island in the Gulf. Iran, in turn, has said that it will block the Gulf at the Straits of Hormuz to all traffic (including exports of one-sixth of the West's petroleum requirements) if Iraqi military action makes it impossible to export its oil by that route.

The military and civilian death toll in the war was estimated at more than 1m. in 1986, while the cost of the damage to industry and property amounts to thousands of millions of dollars. Iraq has accepted UN terms for a cease-fire but Iran insists that nothing less than the removal of the Hussain regime, the withdrawal of Iraqi troops from Iranian territory and the agreement to pay US $350,000m. in war reparations (as calculated in March 1985) can bring an end to hostilities. Further approaches to Iran in 1984 by Egypt, Saudi Arabia and Japan, among others, were met with the stubborn refusal to negotiate with Iraq while Saddam Hussain is in power there.

In February 1984 a further Iranian offensive resulted in the capture of marshlands around the Majnoun Islands in southern Iraq, the site of rich petroleum deposits. Iraq failed to recapture all the lost territory, and was censured internationally for its alleged use of mustard gas in the fighting. A long hiatus ensued, during which Iran was believed to be preparing a massive offensive, involving more than 500,000 men, in the region of the southern Iraqi port of Basra, but no attack of such magnitude had materialized by the end of 1986. While the Iranians delayed, Iraq constructed a formidable defensive network, including dams and a huge artificial lake, along the southern front.

In 1984 the balance of military power moved in Iraq's favour, and its financial position improved as the USA and the USSR, both officially neutral in the war with Iran, provided aid. The USSR, having already sold SS-12 missiles to Iraq, increased its military aid following a *rapprochement* in March, precipitated by Iran's anti-Soviet stance, and is responsible for providing an estimated two-thirds of Iraq's total armaments and much of its ammunition. The USA is assisting Iraq with the financing of crucial oil export pipeline projects and an increasing allocation of commodity credits, which totalled $2,500m. between 1981 and 1985. (Iraq and the USA re-established full diplomatic relations on 26 November 1984, more than 17 years after they had been broken off by Iraq following the Arab–Israeli war of 1967.) Egypt is estimated to have provided ammunition and military spare parts worth US $1,300m. since the beginning of the war, and Brazil, Chile and the People's Republic of China have also sold arms to Iraq. The delivery of eight French Mirage F-1 EQ5 fighter aircraft in October 1984 brought the Iranian Levan Island oil terminal within Iraq's range and underlined its superiority in the air. An Iranian offensive would lack vital air cover, while on the ground Iraq's tank force is superior in numbers and sophistication.

Although it had declared a maritime exclusion zone at the north-east end of the Persian Gulf, enclosing Kharg Island, in August 1982 and made spasmodic attacks against shipping (not only tankers but, in some cases, ships well outside the zone), Iraq refrained from attacking tankers using the Kharg Island oil terminal until May 1984. After the first series of attacks on some dozen vessels, regardless of nationality, Iran retaliated by attacking Saudi Arabian and Kuwaiti tankers in the Gulf. It was apparently Iraq's intention to extend the conflict and to bring other Gulf states into the war. Saudi Arabia and Kuwait continue to support Iraq financially, so, to Iran, their vessels were legitimate targets and attacking them was a means of exerting pressure on Gulf states to dissuade Iraq from continuing to raid Iranian oil installations. A sporadic series of Iraqi attacks on Gulf tanker traffic, and on the Kharg Island terminal itself, continued, but the success of these tactics was limited. The attacks were not sufficiently intensive or destructive to starve Iran of vital oil revenues. Rates of insurance for tankers using Kharg Island and other Iranian terminals have risen sharply during periods of Iraqi raids, deterring customers for Iranian oil, but have fallen equally sharply when the attacks cease for a time, encouraging the tankers, also attracted by Iran's oil price discounts, to return. Saudi Arabia (apart from an incident in June 1984, in which an Iranian fighter aircraft encroaching on its airspace was shot down) and Kuwait have remained militarily aloof from the war.

In spite of setbacks in the war, Saddam Hussain retained his positions as Chairman of the RCC and Regional Secretary of the Baath Party, following its regional Congress in June 1982. In fact, a subsequent purge throughout the administration left him more firmly in control than before. In August, however, the Baathist regime suffered a disappointment when Iraq had to abandon arrangements to host a summit conference of non-aligned countries in September. Kurdish rebels (known as *peshmergas*; literally, 'those who confront death') have also become active again in northern Iraq, occasionally supporting Iranian forces. Another threat is posed by the Supreme Council of Iraqi Opposition Groups, formed in Teheran in November 1982 by the exiled Shi'ite leader, Hojatoleslam Muhammad Baqir al-Hakim.

An attempted coup is believed to have taken place in Baghdad in October 1983, led by the recently dismissed head of intelligence, Barzan Takriti, the President's half-brother, and a number of senior army officers, who were later reported to have been executed.

Hussain has largely managed to retain his authority. Iraq's Shi'ite community (about 55% of the total population) is evidently not attracted by Khomeini's brand of fundamentalism and has remained loyal to Iraq and its Sunni President, while the opposition of Iranian-backed terrorist groups (such as the Shi'ite fundamentalist Dawa group, which has repeatedly attempted to assassinate Hussain) has had no significant effect.

The problem of autonomy for Iraq's 2.5m.–3m. Kurds (currently in limited operation in three provinces) has a particular significance for Saddam Hussain, as costly equipment and manpower has been repeatedly diverted from critical areas in the war with Iran to control Kurdish rebellion in the north-east of the country. Unable to fight wars on two fronts, Hussain has sought an accommodation with the Kurds. A series of talks began in December 1983 after a cease-fire had been agreed with Jellal Talibani, leader of the main Kurdish opposition party in Iraq, the Patriotic Union of Kurdistan (PUK), and of an estimated 40,000 Kurdish soldiers. The success of these talks would provide only a partial solution to the problem as they do not include the other main Kurdish group, the Democratic Party of Kurdistan (DPK), led by Idris and Masoud Barzani, which is antipathetic towards the PUK and seeks to further the cause of Kurdish autonomy by siding with Iran. Hopes for a government of national unity, including the PUK and the Communist Party of Iraq, have so far been frustrated. Hussain's conciliatory attitude appeared to change, possibly owing to the greater international support for Iraq which was forthcoming in 1984, and the talks broke down in May 1984. However, it was reported that Hussain persisted, informally, in trying to persuade the PUK to join the National Progressive Front. It was clear that, in order to win its support, Hussain would have to make major concessions to the PUK, such as granting Kurdish control of Kirkuk province, where some of Iraq's main oilfields are situated, and giving the Kurds a fixed share of national oil revenues (reportedly 20%-30%), and this he was unlikely to do. Negotiations on Kurdish autonomy collapsed again in January 1985. After a cease-fire lasting 14 months, fighting broke out in Kurdistan between PUK guerrillas and government troops. The PUK blamed the Government's continued persecution and execution of Kurds; its refusal to permit consideration in autonomy talks of the one-third of Kurdistan which contains the Kirkuk oilfields; and an agreement with Turkey to act jointly to quell Kurdish resistance, which had been made in October 1984. The PUK then rejected the offer of an amnesty for President Hussain's political opponents, at home and abroad, in February, and fighting has continued, with Kurdish and Iranian forces repeatedly collaborating in raids against Iraqi military and industrial targets. In May 1986 Kurdish guerrillas were reported to have captured the northern Iraqi town of Mangesh, which is situated close to a major international road and Iraq's oil pipeline to Turkey from Kirkuk.

An Iraqi ground attack in January 1985, in the region of the Majnoun Islands, made no progress. In March Iran mounted an assault, involving some 50,000 troops, in the area of the Hawizah marshes, east of the Tigris, in southern Iraq. The Tigris was crossed and, for a time, the Iranians succeeded in closing the main road connecting Baghdad and Basra. An Iraqi counter-offensive repulsed the Iranian attack. Iraqi losses were estimated at 10,000, while the Iranians were thought to have lost between 20,000 and 30,000 dead or wounded. Iraq was again accused of using chemical weapons during this engagement.

In June 1984 the UN had engineered an agreement between Iran and Iraq, suspending attacks on civilian targets. However, in March 1985, with the war on the ground in a state of deadlock, Iraq resorted to air raids on Iranian towns and declared Iranian airspace a war zone. Saddam Hussain's stated intention was to carry the war to every part of Iran until the Iranian leadership should decide to begin negotiating. The first Iraqi air raid on Teheran in four years took place in March. Although Iraq initially identified its targets as industrial, government and military installations only, thousands of civilians were killed in attacks on more than 30 Iranian towns and cities between March and May. Iran retaliated with shelling and air raids on Iraqi cities, including Basra and Baghdad (which was struck by ground-launched missiles), though Iran lacked the power in the air to reply with such force as Iraq could command.

In March 1985 King Hussein of Jordan and President Mubarak of Egypt made an unexpected visit to Baghdad to demonstrate their support for Saddam Hussain, despite the fact that full diplomatic relations have not existed between Egypt and Iraq since Egypt's signing of the peace treaty with Israel in 1979.

The UN Secretary-General, Javier Pérez de Cuéllar, visited both Teheran and Baghdad in April, to try to establish a basis on which peace negotiations could begin. Iraq made it clear that it was interested only in a permanent cease-fire and immediate, direct negotiations with Iran; while Iran, though placing less official emphasis on the removal of Saddam Hussain's regime as a pre-condition of peace, acknowledged that an acceptance by him of Iran's other conditions (including an Iraqi admission of responsibility for starting the war, and the payment of reparations) would be sufficient to ensure his fall from power.

On two occasions, for six weeks in April and May and 16 days in June, Hussain ordered the suspension of Iraqi air raids on Iranian towns, to allow Iran the opportunity of opening negotiations. Neither moratorium produced the desired response, and raids were resumed, though Iraq subsequently turned its attention to attacks on Iran's oil installations.

In response to a joint Irano-Libyan strategic alliance which was becoming more open in character, Iraq withdrew its diplomatic mission from Tripoli in June 1985, and asked the Libyans to withdraw theirs from Baghdad.

Until mid-1985 Iraq had failed to launch attacks against the main Iranian oil terminal on Kharg Island of sufficient frequency or intensity seriously to threaten the continuation of oil exports, and the terminal remained largely undamaged. Between August 1985 and January 1986, however, Iraq made a concentrated series of some 60 air raids on Kharg Island. Despite rapid repair work and the taking up of spare capacity by Iran, the cumulative effect of the raids was to reduce oil exports from the terminal to a trickle by the beginning of 1986, by which time Iraq had already turned its attention to attacks on tankers shuttling oil from Kharg to the makeshift floating terminal at Sirri Island, 450 km to the south-east, for transhipment.

In February 1986 Iraq announced an expansion of the area of the Gulf from which it would try to exclude Iranian shipping. Previously confined to the waters around Iran's Gulf ports, the area was extended to include the coast of Kuwait. Attacks on tankers and other commercial vessels in the Gulf were increased by both sides during 1986, so that, by mid-year, they numbered more than the 46 recorded in the whole of 1985. In August 1986 an Iraqi air raid demonstrated that the Sirri oil export facility was vulnerable to attack, and Iran was forced to transfer more of its export operations to the floating terminal at Larak Island (250 km east of Sirri, at the mouth of the Strait of Hormuz), which had been established in June. However, even the Larak facility proved to be within the range of Iraqi aircraft, and was itself attacked in November. Further Iraqi attacks on Kharg Island in September and October left only three out of 16 oil-loading berths at the terminal operational.

In the land war, Iran launched limited offensives in the region of the Hawizah marshes and in the north, in Kurdistan, in July 1985, and again in Kurdistan in September. Iraq mounted an assault on Kurdish rebels in December, but the next important engagement, in terms of land changing control, did not occur until 1986. In February Iran began the Wal-Fajr (Dawn) 8 offensive. Some 85,000 Iranian troops (leaving about 400,000 uncommitted on the southern front) crossed the Shatt al-Arab waterway and occupied the disused Iraqi oil port of Faw, on the Persian Gulf, and, according to Iran, about 800 sq km of the Faw peninsula. From this position, within sight of the Kuwaiti island of Bubiyan (commanding the Khor Abdullah channel between the Faw peninsula and the island), Iran threatened Iraq's only access to the Gulf and, if it could extend the offensive to the north-west, Iraq's Umm Qasr naval base. However, the difficulty of the terrain to the west was not conducive to further Iranian gains, and the position on the Faw peninsula was not easily defensible in view of the difficulty of maintaining supply lines across the Shatt al-Arab. To divert Iraqi forces, Iran had begun a complementary assault along the Faw-Basra road. When Iraq mounted a counter-offensive on Faw in mid-February, Iran opened up a second front with the Wal-Fajr 9 offensive in Iraqi Kurdistan, several hundred kilometres to the north. At the beginning of 1987 Iran retained its foothold on the Faw peninsula, but the difficulties of supply and reinforcement make it doubtful that further significant territorial gains could be made from this position.

In May 1986 Iraq made its first armed incursions into Iran since withdrawing its forces from Iranian territory in 1982. About 150 sq km of land, including the deserted town of Mehran (some 105 km east of Baghdad), were occupied until July, when an Iranian counter-attack forced the Iraqis back across the border. Also in May, Iraqi aircraft raided Teheran for the first time since June 1985, initiating a new wave of reciprocal attacks on urban and industrial targets in Iran and Iraq (in particular on petroleum-related installations), which continued for the remainder of the year, and caused hundreds of civilian casualties. For perhaps the first time in the war, Iraq made full use of its aerial superiority to damage Iranian industry and further to limit Iranian oil production, with numerous raids on oil refineries, pumping stations and export terminals.

From mid-1986 onwards, Iran was reported to be reinforcing its army along the entire length of the 1,100-km war-front in preparation for a major assault. When an Iranian offensive (Karbala-4) was launched on 24 December, it came, as anticipated, in the region of Basra, and was directed against Iraqi positions on islands in the Shatt al-Arab waterway. However, the attack was repulsed by the Iraqis, and the Iranians suffered heavy casualties. The offensive followed a series of Iraqi air raids on Iranian towns and military targets, which may have been designed to disrupt Iranian plans for a major attack in early 1987. The scale of the December offensive was disputed by Iran and Iraq, the Iraqi Government maintaining that it had been a major undertaking, with Basra as its goal.

On 8 January 1987 a two-pronged offensive, Karbala-5, was

launched by Iran towards Basra. Iranian forces, attacking from the east, established a bridgehead inside Iraq, between the Shatt al-Arab and the artificial Fish Lake, and advanced gradually towards Basra, sustaining heavy casualties (an estimated 40,000 Iranians died between 24 December 1986 and 20 January 1987); while an attack from the south-east secured a group of islands in the Shatt al-Arab. Iran opened a second front, 400 km to the north, with the Karbala-6 offensive on 13 January. By mid-February, Iranian forces from the east had advanced to within about 10 km of Basra, but, confronted by the city's main network of defensive fortifications, had apparently decided to consolidate their hold on the territory that they had occupied before mounting a further assault.

On 25 December 1986 a Boeing 737 airliner of Iraqi Airways, travelling from Baghdad to Amman in Jordan, crashed in Saudi Arabia, killing 62 people, after a gun battle between security guards and hijackers who were believed to belong to the dissident Iraqi group, Dawa.

In July 1986 the ruling Arab Baath Socialist Party held an extraordinary regional conference, the first since June 1982. Three new members were elected to the party's Regional Command (RC), increasing its number to 17. Naim Haddad, who had been a member of the RC and of the ruling Revolutionary Command Council (RCC) since their formation in 1968, was not re-elected to the RC, and was subsequently removed from the RCC, on which he was replaced by Sa'adoun Hammadi, the Chairman, or Speaker, of the National Assembly. These changes effectively strengthened Saddam Hussain's position as leader of the party.

Government

Power rests with the President and a Revolutionary Command Council (RCC), which in December 1986 comprised nine members (including the Chairman and Vice-Chairman). Considerable influence is wielded by the Iraq Regional Command of the Baath Party, while the routine administration of the country is carried out by an appointed Council of Ministers. Legislative responsibility is shared between the RCC and the National Assembly, with 250 members elected by universal adult suffrage for four years. The country is divided into 15 Provinces and three Autonomous Regions. A Kurdish autonomous area has been set up, and elections to a 50-member Kurdish Legislative Council were held in September 1980 and August 1986.

Defence

Military service is compulsory for all men at the age of 18 years, and lasts between 21 months and two years, extendable in wartime. In July 1986 the armed forces totalled 845,000 regular members; the army had a total strength of 800,000 (including an estimated 230,000 active reserves); the air force had a strength of 40,000, and the navy 5,000. In order to wage the Gulf War, these forces are supplemented by a 650,000-strong popular army and possibly 10,000 volunteers from Arab countries. Estimated defence expenditure in 1985 was ID 4,000m. (US $12,866m.).

Economic Affairs

Prior to the discovery of petroleum in Iraq, agriculture was the dominant sector of the economy, and dates were the most lucrative export commodity. Dates remain Iraq's second most valuable export, but petroleum is now the most important sector of the economy, and by 1979 Iraq had outstripped Iran as the largest oil producer in the Middle East after Saudi Arabia. Iraq officially assessed its total reserves of crude petroleum at 145,000m. barrels in 1985, which, if correct, would place Iraq second only to Saudi Arabia in the extent of reserves. Discovered and proven reserves were reported to total 65,000m. barrels. Average output of crude petroleum increased from 2.21m. barrels per day (b/d) in 1977 to 2.6m. b/d in 1978, and to 3.45m. b/d in 1979, while annual government revenues from the petroleum sector rose from US $9,500m. to $21,200m. over the same period. Because of the outbreak of the Gulf War, which caused the loss of refinery capacity and export facilities, and a lower world demand for oil, production in 1980 fell by 23.7% to 2.64m. b/d, but higher prices meant that government revenues from the petroleum industry rose to US $26,500m. Production in 1981 fell to 900,000 b/d, with revenues of only $9,198m. Oil exports were a record 3.2m. b/d in 1980 but, because of the Gulf War, Iraq could export only about 650,000 b/d in 1983 through the 980-km (610-mile) pipeline across Turkey, its only remaining normal outlet for oil exports, plus 50,000–60,000 b/d by road.

The severe burden which has been imposed on the economy by the war (estimated to be costing Iraq $600m.–$1,000m. per month at the begining of 1986) emerged as the most critical concern for President Hussain in 1983. The Iraqi Government's revenue from oil had been reduced to a level that was insufficient to cover war expenses, following the destruction of Iraq's oil terminals on the Gulf, the closure of the pipeline across hostile Syria (with a capacity of 650,000 to 700,000 b/d) in April 1982, and the decline in international prices for petroleum, owing to the existence of a large surplus of oil supplies on the world market. Iraq's oil revenues were in the range $9,000m.–$11,000m. per year in 1981–85, and were expected to be worth only between $5,000m. and $8,000m. in 1986. The country's main port, Basra, has been closed since 1980 because of the war and no attempt has been made to restore it, because of its vulnerability to attack. The 1981–85 Five-Year Development Plan had to be abandoned, and planning is now done on a yearly basis, though a new Five-Year Plan, running from 1986 to 1990, was to be instituted, with the aim of improving the country's social services and infrastructure. Countries that had been eager to invest in Iraq and to bid for lucrative construction contracts even after the war with Iran had begun, when Iraq was an oil-rich country committed to an ambitious programme of development, are now faced with the problem of obtaining payment. Foreign contractors have been asked to defer receipt of payments, to refinance the foreign currency portion of outstanding payments, or to accept part-payment in oil, owing to a shortage of 'hard' currency in Iraq. Iraq's reserves of foreign exchange, which had been some $35,000m. at the beginning of the war in 1980, fell below $5,000m. by mid-1983. Little new information is available, and estimates in 1986 assessed the level of reserves at anywhere between zero and $5,000m. The value of exports fell from $26,278m. in 1980 to $9,785m. in 1983. Import costs increased from $13,642m. in 1980 to in excess of $19,000m. in 1982. As a result of efforts to restrict purchases, the cost of imports was reduced to an estimated $12,000m. per year in 1983, 1984 and 1985, and was expected to fall to $9,000m. in 1986.

Iraq's total GNP was estimated at $30,000m. in 1984, rising to $33,000m. in 1985, with large increases in agricultural and industrial productivity. In 1986, however, the precipitate fall in oil prices during the first half of the year and the decline in the value of the dollar frustrated hopes that the economy would make a significant recovery. Although the Government was able to reduce public spending in most sectors, the continuing Gulf War necessitated an increase in expenditure on weapons and military equipment. As a result of the continuing and increasing shortage of foreign exchange, the Government was unable to meet instalments due in 1985 and 1986 on payments to foreign contractors that had been deferred in 1983 and 1984. Iraq's total foreign debt was estimated at up to $50,000m. in 1986. Of this total, $25,000m.–$30,000m. was in the form of loans from neighbouring Gulf states; about $9,330m. is civil debt guaranteed by export credit agencies for payment between 1985–90; and a further $6,000m. is owed to Western companies and is not covered by export credit guarantees. Italy is the largest creditor (with up to $2,200m. owing), followed by Japan and the Federal Republic of Germany. Iraq's civil and military debt to France total an estimated $1,350m. and $1,750m. respectively. Some $3,000m. per year is required merely to service the Western portion of the foreign debt. In October 1985 the Rafidain Bank raised a $500m. Euroloan. The five-year loan will be used to finance foreign trade and development projects, similar to the $500m. Euroloan that was obtained in 1983, on which Baghdad is up to date with its payments. Saudi Arabia and Kuwait loaned about $26,000m. to Iraq in the first year of the war, and, since then, through the Arabian Oil Co (which operates in the Neutral Zone), have provided some $3,000m. per year in revenues from up to 310,000 b/d of oil (250,000 b/d from the Neutral Zone and the remainder from Saudi Arabia, sold on Iraq's behalf to compensate it for lost export capacity. The arrangement was renewed in 1986.

The Euroloan that Iraq secured in 1983 was used to finance

the expansion of its sole functioning oil pipeline from Kirkuk to Cayhan in Turkey. The capacity of the pipeline reached 1m. b/d in August 1984, and further expansion work will increase its capacity to 1.5m. b/d by mid-1987. In addition, Iraq has two new pipeline projects in train, which could double its annual oil revenues to about $20,000m. by 1987. In August 1984 it was decided to construct a new pipeline, 980 km in length, running parallel to the existing one from Kirkuk to Yumurtalik in Turkey. Construction work on the pipeline began in February 1986 and was expected to take 18 months to complete, at a cost of $550m. The combined export capacity of the two lines will be about 1.5m. b/d by about mid-1987. However, an existing plan for Iraq and Turkey to co-operate in the construction of a pipeline to carry 3m. tons of liquefied petroleum gas per year from Kirkuk to Yumurtalik was abandoned in 1984, owing to the cost of the project, weak world prices and insufficient gas reserves to make it economic. Notwithstanding this decision, Iraq began exporting 5.7m. cu m (200m. cu ft) of natural gas per day to Kuwait in September 1986. The daily rate of export is scheduled to rise to 11.3m. cu m (400m. cu ft) in early 1987. A refinery to process Iraqi crude oil is to be built in Turkey. A two-stage oil pipeline project, agreed with Saudi Arabia in November 1983, should increase Iraq's export capacity by 1.6m. b/d by 1988. The first stage, of 640 km (398 miles), was opened in September 1985 and links Iraqi oilfields in the south with the Saudi Petroline. The line's capacity is 500,000 b/d, but it was pumping at a rate of 350,000 b/d–400,000 b/d during 1986. Work on the second stage, which was offered for tender in mid-1986, involves the laying of a 970-km independent Iraqi pipeline parallel to the Saudi line, terminating at Yanbu, on the Red Sea, and providing a total throughput of 1.6m. b/d by mid-1987 or the beginning of 1988. A third project was to have been a joint venture with Jordan to build a pipeline 1,650 km long from western Iraq to Aqaba on Jordan's Red Sea coast. The pipeline was to have had a capacity of 1m. b/d, but the project was suspended in 1984, as Iraq could secure no guarantee of compensation from the US Bechtel Corporation, the projects managing contractor, for Israeli sabotage of the pipeline, which would have terminated close to Jordan's border with Israel.

The pipeline from Iraq to Banias, in Syria, is likely to remain closed for the duration of the war with Iran, from which Syria is receiving subsidized oil for blending at Banias. With its promised new export capacity, however, Iraq has no interest in the Syrian pipeline. When the new line across Turkey and the two phases of the trans-Saudi Arabia development are in full operation, Iraq's pipeline export capacity will total about 3.1m. b/d. The facilities in the south, which have been put out of action by the war, could provide another 3m. b/d in exports when the war is over, and to this can be added the 80,000 b/d–100,000 b/d of petroleum products that are transported by road through Jordan and Turkey. Iraq's production quota was fixed at 1.2m. b/d, as part of an OPEC agreement, in March 1982. Iraq was not required to make a reduction in its output in October 1984, when OPEC cut production by 1.5m. b/d, in order to prevent a further fall in prices on the world market, which was over-supplied with oil. With new export outlets becoming available, Iraq has been campaigning for an increase in its OPEC production quota, although it has already consistently exceeded its allocation. During 1986 oil prices continued to decline, largely owing to the decision by the members of OPEC, in December 1985, to increase production in order to secure a 'fair' share of the market, despite the existing oil glut. In July 1986 the international price of crude petroleum declined to less than $10 per barrel. When, in August, at Iran's suggestion, OPEC agreed to reduce its members' aggregate production to a maximum of 16.7m. b/d for two months (effectively reverting to the quota restrictions that had been imposed in October 1984), Iraq was the only member permitted to maintain production at existing levels (about 2m. b/d in July 1986). Iran asserted that Iraqi production would be curtailed by military action in the Gulf War. The effect of the two months of production restraint was to stabilize oil prices at about $15 per barrel, and in October OPEC agreed to raise production by 200,000 b/d. Iraq renewed its demand for a production quota equivalent to that allotted to Iran when OPEC met to set its members output levels for 1987 in December. Alone of the organization's 13 members, Iraq refused to accept a 7.25% reduction in its output for the first half of 1987, which it was hoped would enable OPEC to support a fixed price of $18 per barrel during that period. Under the new arrangement, Iraq was being asked to observe a quota of 1.47m. b/d, compared with 2.26m. b/d for Iran (and Iraq's actual production rate of about 1.7m. b/d in December 1986).

Even before the re-establishment of diplomatic relations with the USA in November 1984, trade between the USA and Iraq had been increasing. The value of commodity credits granted to Iraq by the US Department of Agriculture in the fiscal year 1984 was a record $633m. In fiscal 1983 Iraq actually purchased US produce worth $681.8m., although its initial allocation under the credit guarantee scheme was only about $500m. US exports to Iraq totalled $511.7m. in 1983, rose to $664m. in 1984 but fell to $427m. in 1985. Total Iraqi exports to the USA rose from $39.3m. in 1982 to $491m. in 1985, when the USA resumed purchase of oil from Iraq. Trade with the USSR consists mainly of Soviet military supplies. In line with its political support for Iraq in the Gulf War, the USSR virtually ceased purchases of oil from Iran and turned to Iraq and Saudi Arabia for its main Gulf supplies, after the signing of an accord with Iraq in April 1984 to increase co-operation in oil production. In July Iraq obtained a $2,000m. credit from the USSR for a number of development projects, including oil exploration and production, dam construction and energy use. Iraq's principal trading partner in 1985 was Turkey, which imported $1,136m. worth of Iraqi goods (mainly oil) and exported $961m. worth of goods to Iraq.

Social Welfare

A limited Social Security Scheme was introduced in 1957 and extended in 1976. Benefits are given for old age, sickness, unemployment, maternity, marriage and death. Health services are free. Many of the new health facilities that were scheduled under the 1981–85 Five-Year Plan have been completed in spite of the war. More than $1,500m. has been spent on building more than 30 new hospitals, which will provide about 11,500 beds. These additions meant that in 1985 Iraq had an estimated 230 hospital establishments, with a total of 37,000 beds. There were reportedly about 6,000 physicians working in the country in 1985.

Education

Education is free, and primary education, beginning at six years of age and lasting for six years, has been made compulsory in an effort to reduce illiteracy. Enrolment at primary schools of children in the relevant age-group reached 100% in 1978, but the proportion had fallen to 94% by 1982. Secondary education begins at 12 years of age and lasts for up to six years, divided into two cycles of three years each. An estimated 49% of children in the appropriate age-group (64% of boys; 33% of girls) attended secondary schools in 1981. An anti-illiteracy campaign, costing US $22m., began in December 1978, and has been encouraged by President Hussain. There are seven teacher-training institutes, 19 technical institutes and six universities.

Tourism

Iraq is the ancient Mesopotamia of early history, and one of the oldest centres of civilization. The ruins of Ur of the Chaldees, Babylon, Nineveh and other relics of the Sumerian, Babylonian, Assyrian and Persian Empires are of interest to the tourist. Hatra and Ctesiphon represent the early medieval period. In spite of the Gulf War, the number of visitor arrivals to Iraq increased from 1,222,000 in 1980 (when tourist receipts were an estimated US $ 170m.) to 2,020,000 in 1982.

Public Holidays

1987: 1 January (New Year's Day), 6 January (Army Day), 8 February (14 Ramadan Revolution, anniversary of the 1963 coup), 28 March* (Leilat al-Meiraj, ascension of Muhammad), 1 May (Labour Day), 30 May* (Id al-Fitr, end of Ramadan), 14 July (Republic Day, anniversary of the 1968 coup), 6 August* (Id al-Adha, feast of the Sacrifice), 26 August* (Islamic New Year), 4 September* (Ashoura), 4 November* (Mouloud, Birth of Muhammad).

1988: 1 January (New Year's Day), 6 January (Army Day), 8 February (14 Ramadan Revolution, anniversary of the 1963 coup), 16 March* (Leilat al-Meiraj), 18 May* (Id al-Fitr), 14 July (Republic Day, anniversary of the 1968 coup), 25 July* (Id al-Adha), 14 August* (Islamic New Year), 23 September* (Ashoura), 23 October* (Mouloud).

* These holidays are dependent on the Islamic lunar calendar and may vary by one or two days from the dates given.

Weights and Measures

The metric system is in force. Some local measurements are also used, e.g. 1 meshara or dunum = 2,500 sq metres (0.62 acre).

Currency and Exchange Rates

1,000 fils = 20 dirhams = 1 Iraqi dinar (ID).

Exchange rates (30 September 1986):
 £1 sterling = 449.81 fils;
 US $1 = 310.86 fils.

IRAQ

Statistical Survey

Source: Central Statistical Organization, Ministry of Planning, Karradat Mariam, Ash-Shawaf Sq., Baghdad; tel. 537-0071; telex 212218.

Area and Population

AREA, POPULATION AND DENSITY

Area (sq km)	438,317*
Population (census results)†	
14 October 1965	8,047,415
17 October 1977	
Males	6,182,898
Females	5,817,599
Total	12,000,497
Population (official estimates at October)†	
1980	13,238,000
1981	13,669,000
1982	14,110,425
Density (per sq km) at October 1982	32.2

* 169,235 sq miles. This figure includes 924 sq km (357 sq miles) of territorial waters but excludes the Neutral Zone, of which Iraq's share is 3,522 sq km (1,360 sq miles). The Zone lies between Iraq and Saudi Arabia, and is administered jointly by the two countries. Nomads move freely through it but there are no permanent inhabitants.

† Excluding Iraqis abroad, estimated at 129,000 in 1977.

ECONOMICALLY ACTIVE POPULATION (1977 census)

	Males	Females	Total
Agriculture, forestry and fishing	591,066	352,824	943,890
Mining and quarrying	34,716	2,119	36,835
Manufacturing	235,777	48,618	284,395
Electricity, gas and water	22,241	949	23,190
Construction	316,560	5,136	321,696
Trade, restaurants and hotels	207,949	16,155	224,104
Transport, storage and communications	172,814	4,985	177,799
Financing, insurance, real estate and business services	26,023	5,066	31,089
Community, social and personal services	871,879	86,100	957,979
Activities not adequately defined	46,258	11,979	58,237
Total employed	2,525,283	533,931	3,059,214
Unemployed	64,278	10,447	74,725
Total labour force	2,589,561	544,378	3,133,939

GOVERNORATES (estimated population at October 1982)

	Area* (sq km)	Population ('000)	Density (per sq km)
Nineveh	38,430	1,258	32.7
Salah ad-Din	29,004	412	14.2
At-Ta'meem	9,659	587	60.8
Diala	19,292	650	33.7
Baghdad	5,159	4,038	782.8
Al-Anbar	137,723	536	3.9
Babylon	5,258	681	129.5
Karbala	5,034	306	60.7
An-Najaf	27,844	439	15.8
Al-Qadisiya	8,507	476	55.9
Al-Muthanna	51,029	239	4.7
Thi-Qar	13,626	683	50.2
Wasit	17,308	456	26.3
Maysan	14,103	396	28.1
Basrah	19,070	1,184	62.1
Autonomous Regions:			
D'hok	6,120	296	48.4
Arbil	14,471	657	45.4
As-Sulaimaniya	15,756	816	51.8
Total	437,393	14,110	32.3

* Excluding territorial waters.

PRINCIPAL TOWNS (population at 1977 census)

Baghdad (capital)	3,236,000	Mosul	1,220,000
Basrah (Basra)	1,540,000	Kirkuk	535,000

BIRTHS AND DEATHS

Average annual birth rate 47.4 per 1,000 in 1970–75, 47.0 per 1,000 in 1975–80; death rate 14.6 per 1,000 in 1970–75, 13.0 per 1,000 in 1975–80 (UN estimates).

Agriculture

PRINCIPAL CROPS ('000 metric tons)

	1983	1984	1985
Wheat	841	471	650*
Rice (paddy)	111	109	105*
Barley	836	482	700*
Maize	28	31	32*
Sorghum	5†	1†	1†
Potatoes	105	120	115*
Dry beans	3	4	4*
Dry broad beans	7	8	8*
Chick-peas	13	9	12*
Lentils	4	3	5*
Sunflower seed	6	10	10*
Sesame seed	6	6	7*
Cottonseed	8*	5*	7*
Olives	12†	11†	12†
Cabbages	7	15	10*
Tomatoes	439	531	540
Pumpkins, etc.	46	69	70
Cucumbers and gherkins	284	358	300*
Aubergines	112	177	150*
Chillies and peppers	27	37	37*
Onions (dry)	72	97	90
Carrots	8	20	17*
Watermelons	583	571	630†
Melons	270	302	250*
Grapes	419†	425†	440†
Dates	345	251	100†
Sugar cane	82	86	85
Apples	112†	116†	120†
Peaches and nectarines	28*	30*	30*
Plums	30*	29*	30*
Oranges	155†	153†	157*
Tangerines, etc.	46*	45*	46*
Lemons and limes	8*	8*	8*
Apricots	32*	31*	32*
Tobacco (leaves)	14	14	14†
Cotton (lint)	4*	2*	4*

* FAO estimates.   † Unofficial figure.
Source: FAO, mainly *Production Yearbook*.

LIVESTOCK
(FAO estimates, '000 head, year ending September)

	1983	1984	1985
Horses	50	50	50
Mules	28	25	28
Asses	450	400	450
Cattle	1,450	1,550	1,500
Buffaloes	145	150	145
Camels	50	50	55
Sheep	8,500	8,300	8,500
Goats	2,200	2,300	2,350

Poultry (FAO estimates, million): 45 in 1983; 55 in 1984; 65 in 1985.
Source: FAO, *Production Yearbook*.

LIVESTOCK PRODUCTS ('000 metric tons)

	1983	1984	1985*
Beef and veal	34*	40*	35
Buffalo meat	3*	3*	3
Mutton and lamb	48*	55*	50
Goats' meat	11*	12*	11
Poultry meat	113	125	150
Cows' milk	319†	336†	300
Buffalo milk	24†	25†	25
Sheep's milk	165*	165*	168
Goats' milk	69*	69*	70
Cheese	33.1*	33.6*	32.9
Butter	8.1*	8.3*	7.9
Hen eggs	41.2*	40.7*	45
Wool:			
greasy	16†	19†	20
clean	7.5*	8.0*	8.7
Cattle and buffalo hides	5.0*	5.8*	5.1
Sheep skins	9.0*	10.4*	9.3
Goat skins	2.3*	2.5*	2.3

* FAO estimates.   † Unofficial figure.
Source: FAO, *Production Yearbook*.

Fishing

(FAO estimates, '000 metric tons, live weight)

	1982	1983	1984
Inland waters	17.0	16.5	16.0
Indian Ocean	7.0	6.0	5.0
Total catch	24.0	22.5	21.0

Source: FAO, *Yearbook of Fishery Statistics*.

Mining

	1981	1982	1983
Crude petroleum ('000 metric tons)	43,949	49,629	46,819
Natural gas ('000 terajoules)	157	164	167*

* Estimate.
Source: UN, *Industrial Statistics Yearbook*.

Industry

PETROLEUM PRODUCTS ('000 metric tons)

	1981	1982	1983
Liquefied petroleum gas*†	360	360	260
Naphtha	460	500	460
Motor spirit (petrol)	1,340	1,350	1,300
Kerosene	550	620	570
Jet fuel	360	400	360
Distillate fuel oils	2,398	2,400	2,400
Residual fuel oils	2,100	2,970	2,700
Lubricating oils	60	60	70
Paraffin wax	20	20*	20*
Petroleum bitumen (asphalt)	280	280	280

* Estimated production.

† Includes production ('000 metric tons) from natural gas plants: 260 in 1981; 260 in 1982; 160 in 1983; and from petroleum refineries: 100 in 1981; 100 in 1982; 100 in 1983.

Source: UN, *Yearbook of Industrial Statistics*.

OTHER PRODUCTS ('000)

	1973	1974	1975
Leather tanning:			
Upper leather (sq ft)	11,001.1	11,658.2	10,169.2
Toilet soap (tons)	35.4	43.6	28.0
Vegetable oil (tons)	89.3	92.7	90.9
Woollen textiles:			
Cloth (metres)	1,112.4	1,187.9	n.a.
Blankets (number)	724.4	710.1	654.0
Cotton textiles (metres)	76,031.8	71,844.9	n.a.
Beer (litres)	12,723.1	12,321.4	19,297.0
Matches (gross)	2,101.3	2,253.1	n.a.
Cigarettes (million)	7.3	6.4	9.9
Shoes (pairs)	4,597.4	5,820.6	8,321.3

1981: Toilet soap (tons) 7,062; Vegetable oil (tons) 109,230; Woollen cloth (metres) 2,906; Beer (litres) 66,939,000; Matches ('000) 540,720; Cigarettes (million) 7.7; Shoes (pairs) 7,334,000.

Finance

CURRENCY AND EXCHANGE RATES

Monetary Units
1,000 fils = 20 dirhams = 1 Iraqi dinar (ID).

Denominations
Coins: 1, 5, 10, 25, 50 and 100 fils; 1 dinar.
Notes: 250 and 500 fils; 1, 5 and 10 dinars.

Sterling and Dollar Equivalents (30 September 1986)
£1 sterling = 449.81 fils;
US $1 = 310.86 fils;
100 Iraqi dinars = £222.32 = $321.69.

Exchange Rate
From February 1973 to October 1982 the Iraqi dinar was valued at US $3.3862. Since October 1982 it has been valued at $3.2169. The dinar's average value in 1982 was $3.3513.

CENTRAL BANK RESERVES
(US $ million at 31 December)

	1975	1976	1977
Gold	168.0	166.7	176.1
IMF special drawing rights	26.9	32.5	41.5
Reserve position in IMF	31.9	31.7	33.4
Foreign exchange	2,500.5	4,369.8	6,744.7
Total	2,727.3	4,600.7	6,995.7

1982 ((US $ million): IMF special drawing rights 81.9; Reserve position in IMF 123.5.
1983 (US $ million): IMF special drawing rights 9.0.

Note: No figures for gold or foreign exchange have been available since 1977.

Source: IMF, *International Financial Statistics*.

BUDGET ESTIMATES (ID million)

Revenue	1981	1982
Ordinary	5,025.0	8,740.0
Economic development plan	6,742.8	7,700.0
Autonomous government agencies	7,667.8	n.a.
Total	19,434.9	n.a.

Petroleum revenues (estimates, US $ million): 9,198 in 1981; 10,250 in 1982; 9,650 in 1983; 10,000 in 1984.

Expenditure	1981	1982
Ordinary	5,025.0	8,740.0
Economic development plan	6,742.0	7,700.0
Autonomous government agencies	7,982.4	n.a.
Total	19,750.2	n.a.

CONSUMER PRICES INDEX (IFS) (1975 = 100)

	1976	1977	1978
All items	112.8	123.1	128.8

External Trade

PRINCIPAL COMMODITIES (ID million)

Imports c.i.f.	1976	1977*	1978
Food and live animals	159.6	154.0	134.5
Cereals and cereal preparations	70.0	79.9	74.9
Sugar, sugar preparations and honey	37.2	24.1	10.2
Crude materials (inedible) except fuels	33.7	20.5	25.1
Chemicals	58.5	47.4	58.7
Basic manufactures	293.3	236.7	285.2
Textile yarn, fabrics, etc.	44.3	69.4	72.7
Iron and steel	127.5	44.3	73.2
Machinery and transport equipment	557.4	625.8	667.4
Non-electric machinery	285.4	352.5	368.1
Electrical machinery, apparatus, etc.	106.9	120.2	160.5
Transport equipment	165.2	153.1	138.8
Miscellaneous manufactured articles	33.2	49.4	51.7
Total (incl. others)	1,150.9	1,151.3	1,244.1

* Provisional. Revised total is ID 1,323.2 million.

Total imports (estimates, ID million): 1,738.9 in 1979; 2,208.1 in 1980; 2,333.8 in 1981.

Exports f.o.b.*	1976	1977	1978
Mineral fuels, lubricants, etc.	2,595.6	2,557.3	3,223.1
Petroleum and petroleum products	2,595.6	2,557.3	3,222.9
Crude and partly refined petroleum	2,564.2	2,541.1	3,204.4
Petroleum products	31.4	16.2	18.5
Total (incl. others)	2,626.5	2,583.8	3,267.3

* Figures are provisional. Revised totals (ID million) are: 2,738.1 in 1976; 2,849.6 in 1977; 3,266.4 in 1978; 6,329.0 in 1979.

Total exports (estimates, ID million): 7,760.4 in 1980; 3,109.7 in 1981; 3,055.7 in 1982; 3,041.8 in 1983.

Exports of crude petroleum (estimates, ID million) were: 2,691.6 in 1976; 2,806.9 in 1977; 3,204.2 in 1978; 6,287.0 in 1979; 7,718.4 in 1980; 3,067.7 in 1981; 3,013.7 in 1982; 2,999.8 in 1983; 3,494.6 in 1984.

Source: IMF, *International Financial Statistics*.

PRINCIPAL TRADING PARTNERS (ID million)

Imports	1979	1980	1981
Austria	27.3	32.9	33.7
Belgium/Luxembourg	78.5	73.0	46.4
France	119.4	127.5	127.1
Germany, Fed. Republic	176.4	359.2	371.9
Italy	124.7	179.8	180.9
Japan	345.7	451.8	710.4
Jordan	10.0	23.0	30.3
Netherlands	47.9	50.8	30.1
Spain	21.9	29.8	37.2
Sweden	51.1	62.5	57.8
Switzerland	100.8	67.8	35.6
USSR	35.0	13.6	9.0
United Kingdom	84.0	122.2	131.5
USA	81.5	94.1	81.2
Total (incl. others)	1,738.9	2,208.1	2,333.8

Note: Since 1975 no official figures have been available for the destination of petroleum exports.

Transport

RAILWAYS (traffic)

	1980	1981	1982
Passenger-km ('000)	918	1,215	1,482
Freight ton-km ('000)	3,112	2,081	1,192

SHIPPING OF CRUDE PETROLEUM
(Export by tankers from all ports)

	1973	1974	1975
Total ('000 metric tons)	26,669	35,710	37,052

SHIPPING (movement of cargo vessels in Iraqi ports)

	1978	1979	1980
Number of vessels			
Entered	1,127	1,664	1,446
Cleared	1,136	1,124	1,485
Gross registered tons ('000)			
Entered	13,841	14,006	18,187
Cleared	13,871	n.a.	n.a.
Cargo ('000 metric tons, excl. crude petroleum)			
Entered	4,191	6,717	6,535
Cleared	897	1,335	1,097

ROAD TRAFFIC ('000 licensed motor vehicles)

	1974	1975	1982
Passenger cars	85.7	118.3	229.5
Goods vehicles	49.1	65.5	118.7
Buses	16.4	19.6	26.5
Motor cycles	8.9	9.4	n.a.

Source: International Road Federation.

CIVIL AVIATION (revenue traffic on scheduled services)

	1980	1981	1982
Kilometres flown (million)	12.6	10.4	13.3
Passengers carried ('000)	620	457	481
Passenger-km (million)	1,161	1,289	1,470
Freight ton-km (million)	52.0	49.2	53.7

Source: UN, *Statistical Yearbook*.

Tourism

ARRIVALS OF VISITORS BY COUNTRY OF ORIGIN
('000)

	1978	1979	1980
Egypt	109.8	190.2	229.7
Jordan	63.6	86.6	108.3
Kuwait	160.1	191.3	137.6
Saudi Arabia	102.8	142.0	105.5
Syria	26.4	207.4	248.0
Turkey	59.8	56.2	84.5
Total (incl. others)	719.8	1,168.0	1,212.8

Total arrivals ('000): 1,564 in 1981; 2,020 in 1982.

Education

(1982/83)

	Schools	Pupils	Teachers
Primary	10,223	2,614,927	107,364
Secondary (General)	1,977	971,827	32,556
Vocational	157	61,383	4,733
Teacher training	43	32,674	1,241
Universities	6	85,573	4,624
Colleges and technical institutes	19	30,687	2,050

1985/86: Technical institutes: 14,800 pupils.

Directory

The Constitution

The following are the principal features of the Provisional Constitution, issued on 22 September 1968:

The Iraqi Republic is a popular democratic and sovereign state. Islam is the state religion.

The political economy of the state is founded on socialism.

The state will protect liberty of religion, freedom of speech and opinion. Public meetings are permitted under the law. All discrimination based on race, religion or language is forbidden. There shall be freedom of the Press, and the right to form societies and trade unions in conformity with the law is guaranteed.

The Iraqi people is composed of two main nationalities: Arabs and Kurds. The Constitution confirms the nationalistic rights of the Kurdish people and the legitimate rights of all other minorities within the framework of Iraqi unity.

The highest authority in the country is the Council of Command of the Revolution (or Revolutionary Command Council—RCC), which will promulgate laws until the election of a National Assembly. The Council exercises its prerogatives and powers by a two-thirds majority.

Two amendments to the Constitution were announced in November 1969. The President, already Chief of State and head of the government, also became the official Supreme Commander of the Armed Forces and President of the Command Council of the Revolution. Membership of the latter body was to increase from five to a larger number at the President's discretion.

Earlier, a Presidential decree replaced the 14 local government districts by 16 governorates, each headed by a governor with wide powers. In April 1976 Tekrit (Saladin) and Karbala became separate governorates, bringing the number of governorates to 18, although three of these are designated Autonomous Regions.

The 15-article statement which aimed to end the Kurdish war was issued on 11 March 1970. In accordance with this statement, a form of autonomy was offered to the Kurds in March 1974, but some of the Kurds rejected the offer and fresh fighting broke out. The new Provisional Constitution was announced in July 1970. Two amendments were introduced in 1973 and 1974, the 1974 amendment stating that 'the area whose majority of population is Kurdish shall enjoy autonomy in accordance with what is defined by the Law'.

The President and Vice-President are elected by a two-thirds majority of the Council. The President, Vice-President and members of the Council will be responsible to the Council. Vice-Presidents and Ministers will be responsible to the President.

In July 1973 President Bakr announced a National Charter as a first step towards establishing the Progressive National Front. A National Assembly and People's Councils are features of the Charter. A law to set up a 250-member National Assembly and a 50-member Kurdish Legislative Council was adopted on 16 March 1980, and the two Assemblies were elected in June and September 1980 respectively.

The Government

HEAD OF STATE

President: SADDAM HUSSAIN (assumed power 16 July 1979).
Vice-President: TAHA MOHI ED-DIN MARUF.

REVOLUTIONARY COMMAND COUNCIL

Chairman: SADDAM HUSSAIN.
Vice-Chairman: IZZAT IBRAHIM.
Secretary-General: KHALED ABD AL-MONEIM RASHID.
Members:
TAHA YASSIN RAMADAN
ADNAN KHAIRALLAH
SA'ADOUN SHAKER MAHMOUD
TAREQ AZIZ ISA
HASSAN ALI NASSAR AL-AMIRI
SA'ADOUN HAMMADI
TAHA MOHIEDDIN MAROUF

COUNCIL OF MINISTERS
(March 1987)

President and Prime Minister: SADDAM HUSSAIN.
First Deputy Prime Minister: TAHA YASSIN RAMADAN.
Deputy Prime Minister and Minister of Foreign Affairs: TAREQ AZIZ.
Deputy Prime Minister and Minister of Defence: Gen. ADNAN KHAIRALLAH.
Minister of Transport and Communications: ABD AL-JABBAR ABD AR-RAHIM AL-ASADI.
Head of Presidency Diwan (Presidential Cabinet): AHMAD HUSSAIN AS-SAMARRAI.
Minister of the Interior: SA'ADOUN SHAKER MAHMOUD.
Minister of Education: ABD AL-QADIR IZZUDIN HAMMUDI.
Minister of Higher Education and Scientific Research: SAMIR MUHAMMAD ABD AL-WAHHAB.
Minister of Justice: Dr MUNDHIR IBRAHIM.
Minister of Finance: HISHAM HASSAN TAWFIQ.
Minister of Housing and Construction: MUHAMMAD FADEL.
Minister of Planning: SAMAL MAJID FARAJ.
Minister of Health: Dr SADIQ HAMID ALLUSH.
Minister of Industry and Minerals: SUBHI YASIN KHUDAYR.
Minister of Oil: QASIM AHMAD TAQI AL-URAIBI.
Minister of Trade: HASSAN ALI.
Minister of Youth Affairs: ABD AL-FATAH MUHAMMAD AMIN.
Minister of Agriculture and Agrarian Reform: AZIZ SALIH HASSAN AN-NUMAN.
Minister of Culture and Information: LATIF NASIF AL-JASIM.
Minister of Irrigation: ABD AL-WAHAB MAHMOUD ABDULLA.
Minister of Labour and Social Affairs: BAKR MAHMOUD RASOUL.
Minister of Awqaf (Religious Endowments) and Religious Affairs: ABDULLAH FADEL-ABBAS.
Minister of Local Government: ADNAN DAHWOUD SALMAN.
Minister of Light Industries: HATEM ABD AR-RASHID.
Minister of State for Foreign Affairs: (vacant).
Minister of State for Military Affairs: Gen. ABD AL-JABBAR SHANSHAL.

Minister of State at the President's Office: HASHIM SUBHI.
Advisers to President (with status of Minister): MUHAMMAD HAMZAH AZ-ZUBAYDI, ABD AL-GHANI ABD AL-GHAFUR, SAMIR MUHAMMAD ABD AL-WAHHAB, ABD AL-HASAN RAHI FIR'AWN, SAADI MAHDI SALIH, MAZBAN KADR HADI, KHALED ABD AL-MONEIM.
Ministers of State: HASHIM HASSAN, ABDULLAH ISMAIL AHMAD, ARSHAD AHMAD MUHAMMAD AZ-ZIBARI.

MINISTRIES

Office of the President: Presidential Palace, Karradat Mariam, Baghdad.
Office of the First Deputy Prime Minister: Karradat Mariam, Baghdad.
Ministry of Agriculture and Agrarian Reform: Khulafa St, Khullani Sq., Baghdad; tel. 887-3251; telex 212222.
Ministry of Awqaf and Religious Affairs: North Gate, St opposite College of Engineering, Baghdad; tel. 888-9561; telex 212785.
Ministry of Culture and Information: Nr An-Nusoor Sq., fmrly Qasr as-Salaam Bldg, Baghdad; tel. 551-4333; telex 212800.
Ministry of Defence: North Gate, Baghdad; tel. 888-9071; telex 212202.
Ministry of Education: POB 258, Baghdad; tel. 886-0000; telex 2259.
Ministry of Finance: Khulafa St, Nr Ar-Russafi Sq., Baghdad; tel. 887-4871; telex 212459.
Ministry of Foreign Affairs: Opposite State Org. for Roads and Bridges, Karradat Mariam, Baghdad; tel. 537-0091; telex 212201.
Ministry of Light Industries: Nidhal St, Nr Sa'adoun Petrol Station, Baghdad; tel. 887-2006; telex 212205.
Ministry of Labour and Social Affairs: Khulafa St, Khullani Sq., Baghdad; tel. 887-1881; telex 212621.
Ministry of Local Government: Karradat Mariam, Baghdad; tel. 537-0031; telex 212568.
Ministry of Oil: POB 6178, Al-Mansour, Baghdad; tel. 5410031; telex 212216.
Ministry of Planning: Karradat Mariam, Ash-Shawaf Sq., Baghdad; tel. 537-0071; telex 212218.
Ministry of Trade: Khulafa St, Khullani Sq., Baghdad; tel. 887-2682; telex 212206.
Ministry of Transport and Communications: Nr Martyr's Monument, Karradat Dakhil, Baghdad; tel. 776-6041; telex 212020.
Ministry of Youth: Al-Muthanna St, Opposite Officers' City, Baghdad; tel. 774-8261; telex 212502.

KURDISH AUTONOMOUS REGION

Executive Council: Acting Chair. MUHAMMAD AMIN MUHAMMAD.
Legislative Council: Chair. AHMAD ABD AL-QADIR AN-NAQSHABANDI.

Legislature

NATIONAL ASSEMBLY

No form of National Assembly existed in Iraq between the 1958 revolution, which overthrew the monarchy, and June 1980. The existing provisional constitution contains provisions for the election of an assembly at a date to be determined by the Government. The members of the Assembly are to be elected from all political, social and economic sectors of the Iraqi people. In December 1979 the RCC invited political, trade union and popular organizations to debate a draft law for setting up a 250-member National Assembly (elected from 56 constituencies) and a 50-member Kurdish Legislative Council, both to be elected by direct, free and secret ballot. Elections for the first National Assembly took place on 20 June 1980, and for the Kurdish Legislative Council on 11 September 1980 and 13 August 1986. The Assembly is dominated by members of the ruling Baath Party.

Elections for the second National Assembly were held on 20 October 1984. The total number of votes cast was 7,171,000 and Baath Party candidates won 73% (183) of the 250 seats, compared with 75% in the previous Assembly. The number of women elected rose to 33.

Chairman: Dr SA'ADOUN HAMMADI.
Chairman of the Kurdish Legislative Council: AHMAD ABD AL-QADIR AN-NAQSHABANDI.

Political Organizations

National Progressive Front: Baghdad; f. July 1973, when Arab Baath Socialist Party and Iraqi Communist Party signed a joint manifesto agreeing to establish a comprehensive progressive national and nationalistic front. In 1975 representatives of Kurdish parties and organizations and other national and independent forces joined the Front; the Iraqi Communist Party left the National Progressive Front in mid-March 1979; Sec.-Gen. NAIM HADDAD (Baath).

Arab Baath Socialist Party: POB 6012, Al-Mansour, Baghdad; revolutionary Arab socialist movement founded in Damascus in 1947; has ruled Iraq since July 1968, and between July 1973 and March 1979 in alliance with the Iraqi Communist Party in the National Progressive Front; Sec.-Gen. MICHAEL AFLAQ; Regional Command Sec. SADDAM HUSSAIN; Deputy Regional Command Sec. IZZAT IBRAHIM; mems. of Regional Command: TAHA YASSIN RAMADAN, HASSAN ALI AL-AMIRI, SA'ADOUN SHAKER, TAREQ AZIZ, ADNAN KHAIRALLAH, MUHAMMAD HAMZAH AZ-ZUBAYDI, ABD AL-GHANI ABD AL-GHAFUR, SAMIR MUHAMMAD ABD AL-WAHHAB, ABD AL-HASSAN RAHI FIR'AWN, SAADI MAHDI SALIH, SA'ADOUN HAMMADI MAZBAN KHADR HADI, ALI HASSAN AL-MAJID, KAMIL YASSIN RASHID and LATIF NASIF AL-JASIM; approx. 100,000 mems.

Iraqi Communist Party: Baghdad; f. 1934; became legally recognized in July 1973 on formation of National Progressive Front; left National Progressive Front March 1979; First Sec. AZIZ MUHAMMAD.

Kurdistan Democratic Party: Aqaba bin Nafi's Sq., Baghdad; f. 1946; Kurdish Party; supports the National Progressive Front; Sec.-Gen. AZIZ AQRAWI.

Kurdistan Revolutionary Party: f. 1972; succeeded Democratic Kurdistan Party; admitted to National Progressive Front 1974; Sec.-Gen. ABD AS-SATTAR TAHER SHAREF.

There is also a Democratic Party of Kurdistan (DPK; f. 1946) in opposition to the Iraqi Government (Leader MASOUD BARZANI); a Patriotic Union of Kurdistan (PUK; f. 1975; Leader JELLAL TALIBANI), a Socialist Party of Kurdistan (SPK) (Leader RASSOUL MARMAND); a United Socialist Party of Kurdistan (USPK) (Leader MAHMOUD OSMAN), a breakaway group from the PUK; and the Kurdish Hezbollah (party of God; f. 1985; Leader Sheikh MUHAMMAD KALED) a breakaway group from the DPK and a member of the Supreme Council of the Islamic Revolution, based in Teheran.

Various alliances of political groups have been formed to oppose the regime of Saddam Hussein in recent years. In November 1980 eight organizations, including the PUK, the USPK, the Iraqi Communist Party (IRC) and the Damascus-based faction of the Baath Party, formed the National Democratic Patriotic Front. Only a fortnight later, the IRC left this grouping to form the National Democratic Front, with the DPK and the SPK. In the spring of 1981 a third (Islamic) front, comprising Iraqi Shi'ite groups, dissident Baath Party members and the DPK, was formed. The first-named front no longer exists for practical purposes, having been reduced to the PUK alone. The second is still active and based in Iraqi Kurdistan, while the third now comprises only the Shi'ite element and, known as the Supreme Council of the Islamic Revolution of Iraq, is based in Teheran under the exiled Iraqi Shi'ite leader, Hojatoleslam Muhammad Baqir al-Hakim.

Diplomatic Representation

EMBASSIES IN IRAQ

Afghanistan: Maghrib St, Ad-Difa'ie, 27/1/12 Waziriyah, Baghdad; tel. 422-9986; Ambassador: ABD AL-HADI MOKAMMEL.

Algeria: Ash-Shawaf Sq., Karradat Mariam, Baghdad; tel. 537-2181; Ambassador: MUHAMMAD AL-HAJI HAMDADOU.

Argentina: Hay al-Jamia District 915, St 24, No. 142, POB 2443, Baghdad; tel. 776-8140; telex 3500; Ambassador: A. H. PIÑEIRO.

Australia: Al-Karada ash-Sharqiya Masbah 39B/35, POB 661, Baghdad; tel. 719-3423; telex 212148; Ambassador: M. KUPA.

Austria: POB 294, Hay Babel 929/2/5 Aqaba bin Nafi's Sq., Masbah, Baghdad; tel. 719-9033; telex 212383; Ambassador: Dr GEORG POTYKA.

Bahrain: 44/7/605 Hay al-Mutanabi, Al-Mansour, Baghdad; tel. 542-8945; telex 213304; Ambassador: ABD AR-RAHMAN SELMAN KAMEL.

Bangladesh: 75/17/929 Hay Babel, Baghdad; tel. 718-4143; telex 2370; Ambassador: Brig. AHM ABD AL-MOMEN.

Belgium: Hay Babel 929/27/25, Baghdad; tel. 719-8297; telex 212450; Ambassador: Count ALBERT DE BORCHGRAVE D'ALTENA.

Brazil: 609/16 Al-Mansour, Houses 62/62-1, Baghdad; tel. 551-1365; telex 2240; Ambassador: A. F. WERNER.

Bulgaria: 9/12 Harthiya, Baghdad; tel. 542-0049; Ambassador: ANGEL GEORGIEV ANGELOV.

Canada: 47/1/7 Al-Mansour, Baghdad; tel. 542-1459; telex 212486; Ambassador: A. PERCY SHERWOOD.

Central African Republic: 208/406 Az-Zawra, Harthiyah, Baghdad; tel. 551-6520; Ambassador: Col FRANÇOIS DIALLO.

Chad: 97/4/4 Karradat Mariam, POB 8037, Baghdad; tel. 537-6160; Ambassador: HAMID MUHAMMAD ISHAQ.

China, People's Republic: New Embassy Area, International Airport Rd, Baghdad; tel. 556-2740; telex 212195; Ambassador: ZHANG JUNHUA.

Cuba: St 7, District 929 Hay Babel, Al-Masbah Arrasat al-Hindi; tel. 719-5177; telex 212389; Ambassador: ARGILES PÉREZ.

Czechoslovakia: Dijlaschool St, No. 37, Mansour, Baghdad; tel. 541-7136; Ambassador: MIROSLAV KOTORA.

Denmark: Zukak No. 34, Mahallat 902, Hay al-Wahda, House No. 18/1, POB 2001, Alwiyah, Baghdad; tel. 719-3058; telex 212490; Ambassador: TORBEN G. DITHMER.

Djibouti: POB 6223, Al-Mansour, Baghdad; tel. 551-3805; Ambassador: ABSEIA BOOH ABDULLA.

Egypt: Baghdad; Chargé d'affaires: ABD AL-MONEIM M. GHONEIM.

Finland: POB 2041, Alwiyah, Baghdad; tel. 719-6174; telex 212454; Ambassador: HAAKAN KROGIUS.

France: 102/55/7 Abu Nawas, Baghdad; tel. 719-6061; telex 212160; Ambassador: MAURICE COURAGE.

German Democratic Republic: 12/10/929 Hay Babel, Baghdad; tel. 719-0071; Ambassador: GUENTHER SCHARFENBERG.

Germany, Federal Republic: Zukak 2, Mahala 929 Hay Babel (Masbah Square), Baghdad; tel. 719-2037; telex 212262; Ambassador: Dr HEINZ FIEDLER.

Greece: 63/3/913 Hay al-Jamia, al-Jadiriya, Baghdad; tel. 776-9511; telex 212479; Ambassador: ANTONIOS EXARCHOS.

Holy See: As-Sa'adoun St 904/2/46, POB 2090, Baghdad (Apostolic Nunciature); tel. 719-5183; Apostolic Pro-Nuncio: Mgr LUIGI CONTI.

Hungary: Abu Nuwas St, Az-Zuwiya, POB 2065, Baghdad; tel. 776-5000; telex 212293; Ambassador: TAMÁS VARGA.

India: Taha St, Najib Pasha, Adhamiya, Baghdad; tel. 422-2014; Ambassador: (vacant).

Indonesia: 906/2/77 Hay al-Wahda, Baghdad; tel. 719-8677; telex 2517; Ambassador: ABD AR-RACHMAN GUNADIRDJA.

Italy: 1 Zukak, 73 Mahalla, 913 Hay al-Jamia (University Circle), Jadiriya, Baghdad; tel. 776-5058; telex 212242; Ambassador: Dr ANTONIO NAPOLITANO.

Japan: 929/17/70 Hay Babel, Masbah, Baghdad; tel. 719-3840; telex 212241; Ambassador: KEIZO KIMURA.

Jordan: House 200/406, St 11, Area 213, Hay al-Hindi, Baghdad; tel. 541-2892; telex 2805; Ambassador: SALEH KABARITI.

Kuwait: 35/5/915 Hay al-Jamia, Baghdad; tel. 776-3151; telex 212108; Ambassador: ABD AR-RAZZAQ AL-BAIJAN.

Lebanon: Iwadia Askary St, House 5, Baghdad; tel. 416-8092; telex 2263; Ambassador: (vacant).

Malaysia: 6/14/929 Hay Babel, Baghdad; tel. 719-2048; telex 2452; Ambassador: ANAITULLAH KARIM.

Mauritania: Al-Mansour, Baghdad; tel. 551-8261; Ambassador: MUHAMMAD YEHYA WALAD AHMAD AL-HADI.

Mexico: 601/11/45 Al-Mansour, Baghdad; tel. 719-8039; telex 2582; Chargé d'affaires: VICTOR M. DELGADO.

Morocco: Hay al-Mansour, POB 6039, Baghdad; tel. 552-1779; Ambassador: ABOLESLAM ZENINED.

Netherlands: 29/35/915 Jadiriya, POB 2064, Baghdad; tel. 776-7616; telex 212276; Ambassador: C. J. VREEDENBURGH.

New Zealand: 2D/19 Az-Zuwiyah, Jadiriya, Baghdad; POB 2350, Alwiyah, Baghdad; tel. 776-8177; telex 212433; Ambassador: JOHN G. CARTER.

Nigeria: 2/3/603 Al-Mansour, Baghdad; tel. 5421750; Ambassador: ALI GOMBE.

Norway: 20/3/609 Hay al-Mansour, Baghdad; tel. 5410097; telex 212715; Ambassador: TOROLF RAA.

Oman: POB 6180, 213/36/15 Al-Harthiya, Baghdad; tel. 551-8198; telex 212480; Ambassador: BASHIR BIN-SALEEM BINFARGI.

Pakistan: 14/7/609 Al-Mansour, Baghdad; tel. 541-5120; Ambassador: KHALID MAHMOUD.

Philippines: Hay Babel, Baghdad; tel. 719-3228; telex 3463; Ambassador: C. C. PASTORES.

Poland: 30/13/931 Hay Babel, Baghdad; tel. 719-0296; Ambassador: WITOLD JURASZ.

Portugal: 66/11 Al-Karada ash-Sharqiya, Hay Babel, Sector 925, St 25, No. 79, POB 2123, Alwiyah, Baghdad; tel. 776-4953; telex 212716; Ambassador: ZÓZIMO DA SILVA.

Qatar: 152/406 Harthiya, Hay al-Kindi, Baghdad; tel. 551-2186; telex 2391; Ambassador: MOHAMMAD RASHID KHALIFA AL-KHALIFA.

Romania: Arassat al-Hindia, Hay Babel, Mahalla 929, Zukak 31, No 452/A, Baghdad; tel. 7762860; telex 2268; Ambassador: IONEL MIHAIL CETATEANU.

Saudi Arabia: 48A/1/7, 609 Al-Mansour, Baghdad; tel. 551-3566; Ambassador: TARAD IBN ABDULLAH AL-HARITHI.

Senegal: Jadiriya 75G 31/15, POB 565, Baghdad; tel. 776-7636; Ambassador: Y. BARRO.

Somalia: 603/1/5 Al-Mansour, Baghdad; tel. 551-0088; Ambassador: YASIN SHIRE FARAH.

Spain: Ar-Riad Quarter, District 929, Street No. 1, No. 21, POB 2072, Alwiyah, Baghdad; tel. 719-0176; telex 2239; Ambassador: ALVARA DEL CASTILLO.

Sri Lanka: 19/16/906 Hay al-Wahda, Baghdad; tel. 719-3040; Ambassador: N. NAVARATNARAJAH.

Sudan: 38/15/601 Al-Imarat, Baghdad; tel. 542-4889; Ambassador: ALI ADAM MUHAMMAD AHMAD.

Sweden: 15/41/103 Hay an-Nidhal, Baghdad; tel. 719-5361; telex 212352; Ambassador: ARNE THORÉN.

Switzerland: Al-Karada Sharqiya Masbah, House No. 41/5/929, POB 2107, Baghdad; tel. 719-3091; telex 212243; Ambassador: M. SCHURTENBERGER.

Thailand: 1/4/609, POB 6062, Al-Mansour, Baghdad; tel. 5418798; telex 213345; Ambassador: CHEUY SUETRONG.

Tunisia: Mansour 34/2/4, POB 6057, Baghdad; tel. 551-7786; Ambassador: HABIB NOUIRA.

Turkey: 2/8 Waziriyah, POB 14001, Baghdad; tel. 422-2768; Ambassador: ABD AL-MONEIM M. GHONEIM; Egyptian interests section: tel. 537-7347; Head of Section: AHMAD KAMIL.

Uganda: 41/1/609 Al-Mansour, Baghdad; tel. 551-3594; Ambassador: SWAIB M. MUSOKE.

USSR: 4/5/605 Al-Mutanabi, Baghdad; tel. 541-4749; Ambassador: VIKTOR J. MININ.

United Arab Emirates: Al-Mansour, 50 Al-Mansour Main St, Baghdad; tel. 551-7026; telex 2285; Ambassador: MUHAMMAD ABD AL-LATIF RASHID.

United Kingdom: Zukak 12, Mahala 218, Hay al-Khelood, Baghdad; tel. 537-2121; telex 213414; Ambassador: T. J. CLARK.

USA: 929/7/57 Hay Babel, Masbah, POB 2447, Alwiyah, Baghdad; tel. 719-6138; telex 212287; Ambassador: DAVID G. NEWTON.

Venezuela: Al-Mansour, House No. 12/79/601, Baghdad; tel. 552-0965; telex 2173; Ambassador: FREDDY RAFAEL ALVAREZ YANES.

Viet-Nam: 29/611 Hay al-Andalus, Baghdad; tel. 551-1388; Ambassador: TRAN KY LONG.

Yemen Arab Republic: Jadiriya 923/28/29, Baghdad; tel. 776-0647; Ambassador: AHMAD MUHAMMAD AR-RAWDHI.

Yemen, People's Democratic Republic: 906/16/8, Hay Al-Wahdah, Baghdad; tel. 719-6027; Ambassador: AHMAD ALI MAISARI.

Yugoslavia: 16/35/923 Babel Area, Jadiriya, POB 2061, Baghdad; tel. 776-7887; telex 213521; Ambassador: DZEVAD MUJEZINOVIĆ.

Judicial System

Courts in Iraq consist of the following: The Court of Cassation, Courts of Appeal, First Instance Courts, Peace Courts, Courts of Sessions, Shari'ah Courts and Penal Courts.

The Court of Cassation: This is the highest judicial bench of all the Civil Courts; it sits in Baghdad, and consists of the President and a number of vice-presidents and not fewer than 15 permanent judges, delegated judges and reporters as necessity requires. There are four bodies in the Court of Cassation, these are: (a) the General body, (b) Civil and Commercial body, (c) Personal Status body, (d) the Penal body.

Courts of Appeal: The country is divided into five Districts of Appeal: Baghdad, Mosul, Basra, Hilla, and Kirkuk, each with its Court of Appeal consisting of a president, vice-presidents and not fewer than three members, who consider the objections against the decisions issued by the First Instance Courts of first grade.

Courts of First Instance: These courts are of two kinds: Limited and Unlimited in jurisdiction.

Limited Courts deal with Civil and Commercial suits, the value of which is five hundred Dinars and less; and suits, the value of which cannot be defined, and which are subject to fixed fees. Limited Courts consider these suits in the final stage and they are subject to Cassation.

Unlimited Courts consider the Civil and Commercial suits irrespective of their value, and suits the value of which exceeds five hundred Dinars with first grade subject to appeal.

First Instance Courts consist of one judge in the centre of each *Liwa*, some *Qadhas* and *Nahiyas*, as the Minister of Justice judges necessary.

Revolutionary Courts: These deal with major cases that would affect the security of the state in any sphere: political, financial or economic.

Courts of Sessions: There is in every District of Appeal a Court of Sessions which consists of three judges under the presidency of the President of the Court of Appeal or one of his vice-presidents. It considers the penal suits prescribed by Penal Proceedings Law and other laws. More than one Court of Sessions may be established in one District of Appeal by notification issued by the Minister of Justice mentioning therein its headquarters, jurisdiction and the manner of its establishment.

Shari'ah Courts: A Shari'ah Court is established wherever there is a First Instance Court; the Muslim judge of the First Instance Court may be a *Qadhi* to the Shari'ah Court if a special *Qadhi* has not been appointed thereto. The Shari'ah Court considers matters of personal status and religious matters in accordance with the provisions of the law supplement to the Civil and Commercial Proceedings Law.

Penal Courts: A Penal Court of first grade is established in every First Instance Court. The judge of the First Instance Court is considered as penal judge unless a special judge is appointed thereto. More than one Penal Court may be established to consider the suits prescribed by the Penal Proceedings Law and other laws.

One or more Investigation Court may be established in the centre of each *Liwa* and a judge is appointed thereto. They may be established in the centres of *Qadhas* and *Nahiyas* by order of the Minister of Justice. The judge carries out the investigation in accordance with the provisions of Penal Proceedings Law and the other laws.

There is in every First Instance Court a department for the execution of judgments presided over by the Judge of First Instance if a special president is not appointed thereto. It carries out its duties in accordance with the provisions of Execution Law.

Religion

ISLAM

About 95% of the population are Muslims, more than 50% of whom are Shi'ite. The Arabs of northern Iraq, the Bedouins, the Kurds, the Turkomans and some of the inhabitants of Baghdad and Basra are mainly of the Sunni sect, the remaining Arabs south of the Diyali belong to the Shi'i sect.

CHRISTIANITY

There are Christian communities in all the principal towns of Iraq, but their principal villages lie mostly in the Mosul district. The Christians of Iraq fall into three groups: (a) the free Churches, including the Nestorian, Gregorian, and Jacobite; (b) the churches known as Uniate, since they are in union with the Roman Catholic Church including the Armenian Uniates, Jacobite Uniates, and Chaldeans; (c) mixed bodies of Protestant converts, New Chaldeans, and Orthodox Armenians.

Roman Catholic Church:

Latin Rite: Archbishop of Baghdad: HE Mgr PAUL DAHDAH, Wahdah 904/8/44, POB 2090, Baghdad; tel. 719-9537; approx. 3,500 adherents.

IRAQ
Directory

Armenian Rite: Archbishop of Baghdad: Most Rev. PAUL COUSSA, POB 2344, Baghdad; tel. 91827.

Chaldean Rite: Archbishop of Mosul: Most Rev. GEORGE GARMO; Patriarch of Babylon of the Chaldeans: His Beatitude PAUL II CHEIKHO, with 18 archbishops and bishops in Iraq, Iran, Syria, Turkey, Egypt, USA and Lebanon; approx. 475,000 adherents.

Syrian Rite: Archbishop of Mosul: Most Rev. CYRIL EMANUEL BENNI; Archbishop of Baghdad: Most Rev. MAR T. M. SHABA MATOKA; approx. 35,000 adherents.

Orthodox Syrian Community: 12,000 adherents.

Armenian Orthodox (Apostolic) **Community:** Bishop AVAK ASADOURIAN, Primate of the Armenian Diocese of Iraq, Younis as-Saba'awi Sq., Baghdad; tel. 887-3637; nine churches (four in Baghdad); 23,000 adherents mainly in Baghdad.

JUDAISM

Unofficial estimates put the present size of the community at 2,500, almost all living in Baghdad.

OTHERS

About 30,000 Yazidis and a smaller number of Turkomans, Sabeans and Shebeks make up the rest of the population.

Sabean Community: 20,000 adherents; Head Sheikh DAKHIL, Nasiriyah; Mandeans, mostly in Nasiriyah.

Yazidis: 30,000 adherents; Leader TASHIN BAIK, Ainsifni.

The Press

DAILIES

Al-Baath ar-Riyadhi: Baghdad; sports; Propr and Editor UDAI SADDAM HUSSAIN.

Baghdad Observer: POB 624, Karantina, Baghdad; f. 1967; English; State-sponsored; Editor-in-Chief NAJI AL-HADITHI; circ. 22,000.

Al-Iraq: POB 5717, Baghdad; f. 1976; Kurdish; formerly *Al-Ta'akhi*; organ of the National Progressive Front; Editor-in-Chief SALAHUDIN SAEED; circ. 30,000.

Al-Jumhuriya (The Republic): POB 491, Waziriyah, Baghdad; f. 1963, re-founded 1967; Arabic; Editor-in-Chief SAMI MAHDI; circ. 220,000.

Ar-Riyadhi (Sportsman): POB 58, Jadid Hassan Pasha, Baghdad; f. 1971; Arabic; published by Ministry of Youth; circ. 30,000.

Tariq Ash-Sha'ab (People's Path): As-Sa'adoun St, Baghdad; Arabic; organ of the Iraqi Communist Party; Editor ABD AR-RAZZAK AS-SAFI.

Ath-Thawra (Revolution): Aqaba bin Nafi's Square, POB 2009, Baghdad; tel. 96161; f. 1968; Arabic; organ of Baath Party; Editor-in-Chief HAMEED SAEED; circ. 22,000.

WEEKLIES

Alif Baa (Alphabet): POB 491, Karantina, Baghdad; Arabic; Editor-in-Chief KAMIL ASH-SHARQI; circ. 150,000.

Al-Idaa'a wal-Television (Radio and Television): Iraqi Broadcasting and Television Establishment, Karradat Mariam, Baghdad; tel. 537-1161; telex 212246; radio and television programmes and articles; Arabic; Editor-in-Chief KAMIL HAMDI ASH-SHARQI; circ. 40,000.

Al-Mizmar: Children's Culture House, POB 14176, Baghdad; telex 2606; Arabic; children's newspaper; Editor-in-Chief AMAL ASH-SHARQI; circ. 50,000.

Ar-Rased (The Observer): Baghdad; Arabic; general.

Sabaa Nisan: Baghdad; f. 1976; Arabic; organ of the General Union of the Youth of Iraq.

Sawt al-Fallah (Voice of the Peasant): Karradat Mariam, Baghdad; f. 1968; Arabic; organ of the General Union of Farmers Societies; circ. 40,000.

Waee ul-Ummal (The Workers' Consciousness): Headquarters of General Federation of Trade Unions in Iraq, Gialani St, Senak, POB 2307, Baghdad; Arabic; Iraq Trades Union organ; Chief Editor KHALID MAHMOUD HUSSEIN; circ. 25,000.

PERIODICALS

Afaq Arabiya (Arab Horizons): Aqaba bin Nafi's Sq., POB 2009, Baghdad; monthly; Arabic; literary and political; Editor-in-Chief Dr MUHSIN J. AL-MUSAWI.

Al-Aqlam (Pens): Adamiya, POB 4032, Baghdad; tel. 443-6044; telex 214135; f. 1964; publ. by the Ministry of Culture and Information; monthly; Arabic; literary; Editor-in-Chief Dr ALI J. AL-ALLAQ; circ. 7,000.

Bagdad: Dar al-Ma'mun for Translation and Publishing, Karradat Mariam, POB 24015, Baghdad; tel. 538-3171; telex 212984; fortnightly; French; cultural and political.

Al-Funoon al-Ida'iya (Fields of Broadcasting): Cultural Affairs House, Karradat Mariam, Baghdad; quarterly; Arabic; supervised by Broadcasting and TV Training Institute; engineering and technical; Chief Editor MUHAMMAD AL-JAZA'RI.

Gilgamesh: Dar al-Ma'mun for Translation and Publishing, Karradat Mariam, POB 24015, Baghdad; tel. 538-3171; telex 212984; quarterly; English; cultural.

Hurras al-Watan: Baghdad; Arabic.

L'Iraq Aujourd'hui: Aqaba bin Nafi's Sq, POB 2009, Baghdad; f. 1976; bi-monthly; French; cultural and political; Editor NADJI AL-HADITHI; circ. 12,000.

Iraq Oil News: Al-Mansour, POB 6178, Baghdad; tel. 541-0031; telex 2216; f. 1973; monthly; English; publ. by the Information and Public Relations Div. of the Ministry of Oil.

Journal of the Faculty of Medicine, The: College of Medicine, University of Baghdad, Jadiriya, Baghdad; tel. 93091; f. 1935; quarterly; Arabic and English; medical and technical; Editor Prof. YOUSIF D. AN-NAAMAN.

Majallat al-Majma' al-'Ilmi al-'Iraqi (Iraqi Academy Journal): Iraqi Academy, Waziriyah, Baghdad; f. 1947; quarterly; Arabic; scholarly magazine on Arabic Islamic culture; Gen. Sec. Dr NURI HAMMOUDI AL-QAISI.

Majallat ath-Thawra az-Ziraia (Magazine of Iraq Agriculture): Baghdad; quarterly; Arabic; agricultural; published by the Ministry of Agriculture.

Al-Masrah wal-Cinema: Iraqi Broadcasting, Television and Cinema Establishment, Salihiya, Baghdad; monthly; Arabic; artistic, theatrical and cinema.

Al-Mawrid: Aqaba bin Nafi's Sq, POB 2009, Baghdad; f. 1971; monthly; Arabic; cultural.

Al-Mu'allem al-Jadid: Ministry of Education, Al-Imam al-A'dham St, A'dhamaiya, Nr Antar Sq., Baghdad; tel. 422-5081; telex 212259; f. 1935; quarterly; Arabic; educational, social, and general; Editor KHALIL AS-SAMARRAI; circ. 105,000.

An-Naft wal-Aalam (Oil and the World): publ. by the Ministry of Oil, POB 6178, Baghdad; f. 1973; monthly; Arabic; Editor-in-Chief QASIM AHMAD TAQI AL-URAIBI (Minister of Oil).

Sawt at-Talaba (The Voice of Students): Al-Maghreb St, Waziriyah, Baghdad; f. 1968; monthly; Arabic; organ of National Union of Iraqi Students; circ. 25,000.

As-Sina'a (Industry): POB 5665, Baghdad; every 2 months; Arabic and English; publ. by Ministry of Industry and Minerals; Editor-in-Chief ABD AL-QADER ABD AL-LATIF; circ. 16,000.

Sumer: State Organization of Antiquities and Heritage, Karkh, Salihiya, St, Baghdad; tel. 537-6121; f. 1945; annually; archaeological, historical journal; Chair. of Ed. Board Dr MUAYAD SA'ID DAMERJI.

Ath-Thaqafa (Culture): Place at-Tahrir, Baghdad; f. 1970; monthly; Arabic; cultural; Editor-in-Chief SALAH KHALIS; circ. 5,000.

Ath-Thaqafa al-Jadida (The New Culture): Baghdad; f. 1969; monthly; pro-Communist; Editor-in-Chief SAFA AL-HAFIZ; circ. 3,000.

At-Turath ash-Sha'abi (Popular Heritage): Aqaba bin Nafi's Sq., POB 2009, Baghdad; monthly; Arabic; specializes in Iraqi and Arabic folklore; Editor-in-Chief LUTFI AL-KHOURI; circ. 15,000.

Al-Waqai al-Iraqiya (Official Gazette of Republic of Iraq): Ministry of Justice, Baghdad; f. 1922; Arabic and English weekly editions; circ. Arabic 13,000, English 1,000; Dir AMER HASSAN FAHD.

NEWS AGENCIES

Iraqi News Agency (INA): Zaytoon St, POB 3084, Baghdad; tel. 887-5661; telex 212267; f. 1959; Dir-Gen. TAHA YASSIN HASSAN AL-BASRI.

IRAQ   Directory

Foreign Bureaux

Agence France-Presse (AFP): Apt 761-91-97, POB 190, Baghdad; tel. 5514333; Corresp. FAROUK SHOUKRI.

Allgemeiner Deutscher Nachrichtendienst (ADN) (German Democratic Republic): Zukak 24, Mahalla 906, Hay al-Wahda, Beit 4, Baghdad; Correspondent HUBERT BERG.

Associated Press (AP) (USA): Al-Khadra Quarters 629, Lane No. 23, Baghdad; tel. 5559041; Corresp. SAMIR F. GHATTAS.

Deutsche Presse-Agentur (dpa) (Federal Republic of Germany): POB 5699, Baghdad; Correspondent NAJHAT KOTANI.

Reuters (UK): House No. 8, Zukak 75, Mahalla 903, Hay al-Karada, Baghdad; tel. 7191843; telex 213777.

Telegrafnoye Agentstvo Sovetskovo Soyuza (TASS) (USSR): 67 Street 52, Alwiyah, Baghdad; Correspondent ANDREI OSTALSKY.

Xinhua (New China) News Agency (People's Republic of China): Al-Mansour, Adrus District, 611 Small District, 5 Lane No. 8, Baghdad; tel. 5418904; telex 213253; Corresp. SHEN ZHAODU.

ANSA (Italy) also has an office in Baghdad.

Publishers

National House for Publishing, Distribution and Advertising: Ministry of Culture and Information, Al-Jumhuriya St, POB 624, Baghdad; tel. 425-1846; telex 212392; f. 1972; publishes books on politics, economics, education, agriculture, sociology, commerce and science in Arabic and other Middle Eastern languages; sole importer and distributor of newspapers, magazines, periodicals and books; controls all advertising activities, inside Iraq as well as outside; Dir-Gen. M. A. ASKAR.

Afaq Arabiya Publishing House: Adamiya, POB 4032, Baghdad; tel. 443-6044; telex 214135; publisher of literary monthly, *Al-Aqlam*.

Dar al-Ma'mun for Translation and Publishing: Karradat Mariam, POB 24015, Baghdad; tel. 538-3171; telex 212984; publisher of newspapers and magazines including: *The Baghdad Observer* (daily newspaper), *Bagdad* (fortnightly magazine), *Gilgamesh* (quarterly magazine).

Al-Hurriyah Printing Establishment: Karantina, Sarrafia, Baghdad; tel. 69721; telex 212228; f. 1970; largest printing and publishing establishment in Iraq; State-owned; controls *Al-Jumhuriya* (see below).

Al-Jamaheer Press House: Sarrafia, Baghdad; f. 1963; publisher of a number of newspapers and magazines, *Al-Jumhuriyah, Baghdad Observer, Alif Baa, Yord Weekly*; Pres. SAAD QASSEM HAMMOUDI.

Al-Ma'arif Ltd: Mutanabi St, Baghdad; f. 1929; publishes periodicals and books in Arabic, Kurdish, Turkish, French and English.

Al-Muthanna Library: Mutanabi St, Baghdad; f. 1936; booksellers and publishers of books in Arabic and oriental languages; Man. MUHAMMAD K. M. AR-RAJAB.

An-Nahdah: Mutanabi St, Baghdad; politics, Arab affairs.

Kurdish Culture Publishing House: Baghdad; f. 1976; attached to the Ministry of Culture and Information.

Ath-Thawra Printing and Publishing House: Aqaba bin Nafi's Sq., POB 2009, Baghdad; tel. 96161; telex 212215; f. 1970; state-owned; Chair. TARIQ AZIZ.

Thnayan Printing House: Baghdad.

Radio and Television

In 1985 there were an estimated 2.2m. radio receivers and 600,000 television receivers in use.

RADIO

State Organization for Broadcasting and Television: Broadcasting and Television Bldg, Salihiya, Karkh, Baghdad; tel. 537-1161; telex 212246.

Iraqi Broadcasting and Television Establishment: Salihiya, Baghdad; tel. 537-1161; telex 212446; home service broadcasts in Arabic, Kurdish, Syriac and Turkoman; foreign service in French, German, English, Russian, Swahili, Turkish and Urdu; there are 16 medium wave and 30 short wave transmitters; Dir-Gen. Dr MAJID AHMAD AS-SAMARRIE; Dir of Engineering and Technical Affairs MUHAMMAD FAKHRI RASHID.

Idaa'a Baghdad (Radio Baghdad): f.1936; 22 hours daily.

Idaa'a Sawt al-Jamahir: f. 1970; 24 hours.

Other stations include **Idaa'a al-Kurdia, Idaa'a al-Farisiya** (Persian).

TELEVISION

Baghdad Television: Ministry of Culture and Information, Iraqi Broadcasting and Television Establishment, Salihiya, Karkh, Baghdad; tel. 537-1161; telex 212446; f. 1956; government station operating daily on two channels for 9 hours and 8 hours respectively; Dir-Gen. Dr MAJID AHMAD AS-SAMARRIE.

Kirkuk Television: f. 1967; government station; 6 hours daily.

Mosul Television: f. 1968; government station; 6 hours daily.

Basra Television: f. 1968; government station; 6 hours daily.

Missan Television: f. 1974; government station; 6 hours daily.

Kurdish Television: f. 1974; government station; 8 hours daily.

There are 18 other TV stations operating in the Iraqi provinces.

Finance

(cap. = capital; p.u. = paid up; dep. = deposits; res = reserves; brs = branches; m. = million; amounts in Iraqi dinars)

All banks and insurance companies, including all foreign companies, were nationalized in July 1964. The assets of foreign companies were taken over by the State.

BANKING

Central Bank

Central Bank of Iraq: Banks St, POB 64, Baghdad; tel. 887-1101; telex 212203; f. 1947 as National Bank of Iraq; has the sole right of note issue; cap. and res 125m. (1983); Gov. HIKMAT IBRAHIM AL-AZZAWI; brs in Mosul and Basra.

Commercial Bank

Rafidain Bank: New Banks' St, POB 11360 Massarif, Baghdad; tel. 886-1496; telex 212211; f. 1941; cap. p.u. 50m., res 341.4m., dep. 8,394.3m. (Dec. 1984); Chair. TARIQ TALIB AT-TUKMAJI; 228 brs.

Specialized Banks

Agricultural Co-operative Bank of Iraq: Rashid St, Baghdad; tel. 888-4191; f. 1936; cap. p.u. 280.6m.; Gen. Man. BHNAM AZIZ BUNNI; 47 brs.

Industrial Bank of Iraq: Al-Khullani Sq., POB 5025, Baghdad; tel. 887-2181; telex 212224; f. 1940; cap. p.u. 75m., dep. 3.3m. (Dec. 1982); Dir-Gen. Dr ABDEL-WAHAB AN-NAJAR; 8 brs.

Real Estate Bank of Iraq: Hasan bin Thabit St, POB 14185, Baghdad; tel. 89091; f. 1949; 27 brs; gives loans to assist the building industry; cap. p.u. 600m.; acquired the Co-operative Bank in 1970; Gen. Man. KADHIM AR-RUBAI.

INSURANCE

Iraqi Life Insurance Co: 25/5/21 Curd Al-Pasha, Al-Karada Ash-Sharqiya, POB 989, Baghdad; telex 213818; f. 1959; Chair. and Gen. Man. ABD AL-KHALIQ RA'OOF KHALIL.

Iraq Reinsurance Company: Aqaba bin Nafi's Sq., Khalid bin Al-Waleed St, POB 297, Baghdad; tel. 719-5131; telex 212233; f. 1960; transacts reinsurance business on the international market; Chair. and Gen. Man. K. M. AL-MUDARIES.

National Insurance Co: Al-Aman Bldg, Al-Khullani St, POB 248, Baghdad; telex 2397; f. 1950; cap. p.u. 20m.; state monopoly for all direct non-life insurance; Chair. and Gen. Man. MOWAFAQ H. RIDHA.

Trade and Industry

CHAMBERS OF COMMERCE

Federation of Iraqi Chambers of Commerce: Mustansir St, Baghdad; tel. 888-6111; f. 1969; all Iraqi Chambers of Commerce are affiliated to the Federation; Chair. ABD AL-MOUHSEN A. ABU ALKAHIL; Sec.-Gen. FUAD H. ABD AL-HADI.

IRAQ

EMPLOYERS' ORGANIZATION

Iraqi Federation of Industries: Iraqi Federation of Industries Bldg, Al-Khullani Sq., Baghdad; f. 1956; 6,000 mems; Pres. HATAM ABD AR-RASHID.

INDUSTRIAL ORGANIZATIONS

There are numerous State organizations responsible to government ministries for all aspects of planning, production, marketing, distribution and sales in every sector of Iraqi industry. The following are some of the principal bodies:

Iraqi Dates Corporation: Museum Sq., Gamal Abd an-Nasir St, Baghdad; tel. 381-6110; telex 212231; sole body for the marketing and export of dates; Dir. GEORGE BATTAH.

State Enterprise for Sea Fisheries: POB 260, Basra; telex 7011; Baghdad office: POB 3296, Baghdad; tel. 92023; telex 2223; fleet of 12 vessels (incl. 8 fish factories, 2 fish carriers, 1 fishing boat, 1 refrigerated ship).

State Organization for Chemical Industries: Al-Jumhuria St, Al-Khullani Sq., POB 5424, Baghdad; tel. 888-9121; telex 212205.

State Organization for Construction Industries: POB 2102, Baghdad; tel. 776-2651; telex 212236.

State Organization for Electricity: Off Al-Jumhuriya St, Bldg No. 166, Nafoora Sq., POB 5796, Baghdad; tel. 888-0051; telex 212220.

State Organization for Engineering Industries: Ministry of Industry Bldg, An-Nidhal St, POB 3093, Baghdad; tel. 887-2006; telex 212226.

State Organization for Exports: As-Sa'adoun St, POB 5670, Baghdad; tel. 887-6605; telex 212649; Chair. FAROUK AL-UBAIDI.

State Organization for Food Industries: Camp Sarah Khatoon, POB 2301, Baghdad; tel. 771-5713; telex 212205.

State Organization for Grains: Karada ash-Sharqiya, Rakhaita, Alwiyah, POB 2261, Baghdad; tel. 776-0090; telex 212588; Chair. GHANIM AZIZ.

State Organization for Industrial Development: Samaramis Sq., POB 5736, Baghdad; tel. 888-1990; telex 212224; Chair. NAJI EZZAT.

State Organization for Minerals: As-Sa'adoun St, Alwiyah, POB 2330, Baghdad; tel. 887-2006; telex 212292; f. 1969; responsible for exploiting all minerals in Iraq, except petroleum; Pres. Dr ABD AR-RAZZAK AL-HASHIMI.

State Organization for Oil Projects: See Petroleum and Gas.

State Organization for Technical Industries: Al-Khullani St, Baghdad; tel. 888-7141.

State Organization for Textile Industries: An-Nidhal St, Al-Khullani Sq., Baghdad; tel. 887-2006; telex 212249.

TRADE UNIONS

General Federation of Trade Unions of Iraq: POB 3049, Aleppo Sq., Baghdad; tel. 537-8151; telex 212457; f. 1959; 7 general unions and 18 local trade union federations in the governorates of Iraq. Number of workers in industry is 536,245, in agriculture 150,967 (excluding peasants) and in other services 476,621; GFTU is a member of the International Confederation of Arab Trade Unions and of the World Federation of Trade Unions; Pres. AHMAD MUHSEN ALDILIMY; Sec.-Gen. FADHIL MAHMOOD GHAREB.

Union of Teachers: Al-Mansour, Baghdad; Pres. Dr ISSA SALMAN HAMID.

Union of Palestinian Workers in Iraq: Baghdad; Sec.-Gen. SAMI ASH-SHAWISH.

There are also unions of doctors, pharmacologists, jurists, artists, and a General Federation of Iraqi Women (Chair. MANAL YOUNIS).

CO-OPERATIVES

At the end of 1982 there were 1,976 agricultural and 66 consumer co-operatives with 394,755 and 167,638 members, respectively.

PEASANT SOCIETIES

General Federation of Peasant Societies: Baghdad; f. 1959; has 734 affiliated Peasant Societies.

PETROLEUM AND GAS

Ministry of Oil: POB 6178, Al-Mansour City, Baghdad; tel. 551-0031; telex 2216; solely responsible for petroleum sector and activities relevant to it; Minister of Oil QASIM AHMAD TAQI AL-URAIBI; controls the following:

Iraq National Oil Company (INOC): Al-Khullani Sq., POB 476, Baghdad; tel. 887-1115; telex 212204; f. in 1964 to operate the petroleum industry at home and abroad; when Iraq nationalized its petroleum, structural changes took place in INOC and it has become solely responsible for exploration, production, transportation and marketing of Iraqi crude petroleum and petroleum products. The Iraq Company for Oil Operations (ICOO) has become the Northern Petroleum Organization (NPO) and is under the control of INOC; Chair. ESSAM ABD AR-RAHIM.

Central Petroleum Organization: POB 5271, Al-Khullani Sq., Baghdad; tel. 443-3521; telex 212831; responsible for carrying out petroleum operations in the central area of the country; Chair. ALI HUMMADI.

Northern Petroleum Organization (NPO): POB 1, At-Ta'meem Governorate; established to carry out petroleum operations in northern area of Iraq; Chair. Dr SAMI SHARIF.

Southern Petroleum Organization (SPO): POB 240, Basra; similar to the Northern Petroleum Organization, it was established to undertake petroleum operations in southern area of Iraq; Chair. MOOJID ABD AZ-ZAHRA.

State Organization for Oil Projects (SOOP): POB 198, As-Sa'adoun St, Baghdad; tel. 776-3250; telex 212230; responsible for construction of petroleum projects, mostly inside Iraq through direct execution, and also for design supervision of the projects and contracting with foreign enterprises, etc.; Chair. RAJIH MOHIEDDIN.

State Organization for Distribution of Oil Products and Gas: Rashid St, POB 3, South Gate, Baghdad; tel. 888-9911; telex 212247; responsible for distribution, marketing and selling of all distillates, lubricating oils, greases, natural gas, liquid gas and others in Iraq. It supplies ships and tankers entering Iraqi waters and the Arabian Gulf with fuels by means of a special fleet of 6 tankers and 6 coasters. It also supplies aircraft in Iraqi airports; and has a network of pipelines, the most important of which is the pipeline for transporting oil products between Baghdad and Basra; Chair. HAZIM ALI AT-TALIB.

State Organization for Oil Refining and Gas Processing: POB 3069, As-Sa'adoun St, Baghdad; tel. 888-6071; telex 212229; responsible for oil refining and gas processing in Iraq. It operates 8 oil refineries (1981). A number of plants for gas production were established to use the gas as fuel, etc.; two major projects for exploitation of northern and southern gas are being executed; and after inauguration all the associated gas will no longer be flared; Chair. SA'AD ALLUH AL-FATHI.

State Organization for Oil Marketing: Baghdad; is responsible for marketing of crude oil, negotiation and contracting with foreign enterprises; Chair. Dr RAMZI SALMAN.

State Establishment for Oil Exploration and Gas: INOC Building, POB 476, Al-Khullani Sq, Baghdad; responsible for exploration and operations in difficult terrain such as marshes, swamps, deserts, valleys and in mountainous regions; Chair. HASHIM AL-KHIRSAN.

State Establishment for Oil Tankers: POB 37, Basra; tel. 219990; telex 207007; responsible for operating Iraq's fleet of 16 oil tankers; Chair. ADNAN ABD AL-HAMID NASIR.

State Establishment for Oil Training: POB 37, Waziriyah, Baghdad; responsible for training and distribution of personnel to provide the oil sector with its specialist needs, in addition to those provided by the universities; Chair. KHADIM TURKI.

Transport

RAILWAYS

The metre-gauge line runs from Baghdad, through Khanaqin and Kirkuk, to Erbil. The standard gauge line covers the length of the country, from Rabia, on the Syrian border, via Mosul, to Baghdad, and from Baghdad to Basra and Umm Qasr, on the Arabian Gulf. A 404-km standard gauge line linking Baghdad to Husaibah, near the Iraqi-Syrian frontier, was completed in 1983. The 550-km line from Baghdad to Qaim (on the Syrian border) and the 273-km Kirkuk-Baiji-Haditha line were opened in 1986. The 150-km line linking the Akashat phosphate mines and the fertilizer complex at Qaim was formally opened in January 1986 but had already been in use for two years. Lines totalling some 2,400 km, are planned. All standard gauge trains are now hauled by diesel-electric locomotives. There are plans to replace all existing narrow gauge (one metre) line with standard gauge (1,435 mm). As well as the internal service, there is a regular international service between Baghdad and Istanbul.

IRAQ

Iraqi Republic Railways: Baghdad Central Station Bldg, Damascus Sq., Baghdad; tel. 537-30011; telex 212272; under the supervision of State Org. for Iraqi Railways; total length of track (1981): 2,439 km, consisting of 1,906 km of standard gauge, 533 km of one-metre gauge; Pres. T. T. ABD AR-RAZZAK; Dir-Gen. K. S. AMMAR.

New Railways Implementation Authority: POB 17040, Al-Hurriya, Baghdad; tel. 537-0021; telex 2906; f. to design and construct railways to augment the standard-gauge network and to replace the metre-gauge network; Sec.-Gen. R. A. AL-UMARI.

ROADS

According to the Ministry of Housing and Construction, there were 25,385 km of main roads in 1984.

The most important roads are: Baghdad–Mosul–Tel Kotchuk (Syrian border), 521 km; Baghdad–Kirkuk–Arbil–Zakho (border with Turkey), 544 km; Kirkuk–Sulaimaniya, 109 km; Baghdad–Amara–Basra–Safwan (Kuwaiti border), 595 km; Baghdad–Rutba–Syrian border (to Damascus), 555 km; Baghdad–Babylon–Diwaniya, 181 km. Work is in progress on the Baghdad–Babylon section of a six-lane 1,205-km Express Highway which will link Iraq with Syria, Jordan and Kuwait via Baghdad and Basra. The entire project is scheduled for completion in 1988. Studies have been completed for a second, 525-km Express Highway linking Baghdad and Zakho on the Turkish border. The estimated cost of the project is more than $3,000m. and is likely to preclude its implementation in the immediate future.

State Organization for Roads and Bridges: Karradat Mariam, Karkh, POB 917, Baghdad; tel. 32141; telex 212282; responsible for road and bridge construction projects to the Ministry of Housing and Construction.

SHIPPING

The ports of Basra and Umm Qasr are usually the commercial gateway of Iraq. They are connected by various ocean routes with all parts of the world, and constitute the natural distributing centre for overseas supplies. The Iraqi State Enterprise for Maritime Transport maintains a regular service between Basra, the Gulf and north European ports. The Port of Basra is closed because of the Gulf War (between Iraq and Iran). There is also a port at Khor az-Zubair, which came into use during 1979.

At Basra there is accommodation for 12 vessels at the Maqal Wharves and accommodation for 7 vessels at the buoys. There are 1 silo berth and 2 berths for oil products at Muftia and 1 berth for fertilizer products at Abu Flus. There is room for 8 vessels at Umm Qasr. There are deep-water tanker terminals at Faw and Khor al-Amaya for 4 and 3 vessels respectively.

For the inland waterways, which are now under the control of the State Organization of Iraqi Ports, there are 1,036 registered river craft, 48 motor vessels and 105 motor boats.

State Organization of Iraqi Ports: Maqal, Basra; tel. 413211; telex 207008; fleet of 33 vessels (incl. 20 dredgers, 6 crane ships, 2 tugs, 2 research ships, 2 pilot ships and 1 cargo/training ship); Acting Pres. FALEH MAHMOUD EL-MOOSA.

State Organization for Iraqi Water Transport: As-Sa'adoun St, Alwiyah, POB 3052, Baghdad; tel. 888-5164; telex 212207; responsible for the planning, supervision and control of six nat. water transportation enterprises incl:

Iraqi State Enterprise for Maritime Transport (Iraqi Line): Al-Jadiriya al-Hurriyah Ave, POB 13038; Baghdad; tel. 776-3201; telex 2565; Basra office: 14 July St, POB 766, Basra; tel. 210206; telex 207052; f. 1952; 14 general cargo vessels; Dir-Gen. JABER Q. HASSAN; Operations Man. M. A. ALI.

CIVIL AVIATION

There are international airports near Baghdad, at Bamerni, and at Basra. A new Baghdad International Airport is under construction. Internal flights connect Baghdad to Basra and Mosul.

State Organization for Civil Aviation: Al-Mansour, Baghdad; tel. 551-9443; telex 212662; responsible to the Ministry of Transport and Communications for the supervision of airports and airways.

Iraqi Airways: Saddam International Airport, Baghdad; tel. 551-9999; telex 28906; f. 1946; Dir-Gen. Iz AD-DIN MAHMOUD MUHAMMAD; regular services from Baghdad to Abu Dhabi, Algiers, Amman, Amsterdam, Athens, Bahrain, Bangkok, Basra, Beirut, Belgrade, Berlin, Bombay, Bucharest, Budapest, Cairo, Casablanca, Copenhagen, Damascus, Dhahran, Doha, Dubai, Frankfurt, Geneva, Istanbul, Jeddah, Karachi, Khartoum, Kuala Lumpur, Kuwait, London, Madrid, Moscow, Mosul, Munich, New Delhi, Paris, Prague, Rome, Sofia, Tripoli, Tunis, Vienna, Warsaw; fleet: 3 Boeing 747-200C, 2 Boeing 707-320C, 6 Boeing 727-200, 3 Boeing 737-200, 1 Boeing 747SP, 20 Ilyushin Il-76T/M, 6 Antonov An-12, 3 Antonov An-24, 6 JetStar II, 4 Falcon 50, 2 Falcon 20F, 4 Piaggio P.166.

Tourism

State Organization for Tourism: As-Sa'adoun St, Karrada Al-Basra, Alwiyah, POB 2387, Baghdad; tel. 95051; telex 212265; plans state tourist policies and building and man. of tourist establishments.

General Establishment for Travel and Tourism Services; Al-Kodwa Sq., Khalid bin al-Waleed St, Baghdad; tel. 776-0026.

Ministry of Culture and Information: Tourism and Resorts Administration: Aqaba bin Nafi's Sq., Baghdad; f. 1956; Dir-Gen. Dr ALI GHALIB AL-ANI.

Atomic Energy

A French-built research reactor at Tamuz, near Baghdad, was destroyed in an Israeli air raid in June 1981. Israel claimed that the reactor was part of an Iraqi programme to construct nuclear weapons. The war with Iran has delayed a French commitment to rebuild the reactor.

In March 1984 it was reported that the Soviet Union had agreed to build a nuclear power station in Iraq.

IRELAND

Introductory Survey

Location, Climate, Language, Religion, Flag, Capital

The Republic of Ireland consists of 26 of the 32 counties which comprise the island of Ireland. The remaining six counties, in the north-east, form Northern Ireland, which is part of the United Kingdom. Ireland lies in the Atlantic Ocean, about 80 km (50 miles) west of Great Britain. The climate is mild and equable, with temperatures generally between 0°C (32°F) and 21°C (70°F). Irish is the official first language, but its use as a vernacular is now restricted to certain areas, collectively known as the Gaeltacht, mainly in the west of Ireland. English is universally spoken. Official documents are printed in English and Irish. Almost all of the inhabitants profess Christianity: about 95% are Roman Catholics and 5% Protestants. The national flag (proportions 2 by 1) consists of three equal vertical stripes, of green, white and orange. The capital is Dublin.

Recent History

The whole of Ireland was formerly part of the United Kingdom. In 1920 the island was partitioned, the six north-eastern counties remaining part of the United Kingdom, with their own government. On 6 December 1922 the 26 southern counties achieved dominion status, under the British Crown, as the Irish Free State. The dissolution of all remaining links with Great Britain culminated in the adoption, by plebiscite, of a new constitution, which gave the Irish Free State full sovereignty within the Commonwealth as from 29 December 1937. Formal ties with the Commonwealth were ended on 18 April 1949, when the 26 southern counties became a republic. The partition of Ireland remains a contentious issue, and the Provisional wing of the Irish Republican Army (IRA) has mounted a violent campaign to achieve reunification.

In the general election of February 1973, Fianna Fáil, Ireland's traditional ruling party with 44 years in office, was defeated. Jack Lynch, who had been Prime Minister since 1966, resigned, and Liam Cosgrave formed a coalition between his own party, Fine Gael, and the Labour Party. The Cosgrave Government, in an attempt to find reconciliation with Northern Ireland (see Northern Ireland in United Kingdom chapter), considered constitutional changes which would involve the Republic's renunciation of territorial claims in Northern Ireland. The Irish Government remained committed to power-sharing in the six counties, but resisted any British military withdrawal from Northern Ireland.

Following the assassination of the British Ambassador to Ireland by the Provisional IRA in July 1976, the Irish Government introduced stronger measures against terrorism. President Carroll O'Daly resigned in October 1976, and Dr Patrick Hillery of Fianna Fáil, the only candidate nominated for the presidency, took office in December. Fianna Fáil won the general election of June 1977 and Jack Lynch again became Prime Minister, maintaining the improved relations with the British Government which had been achieved by the Cosgrave administration; he aimed at devolved government in Northern Ireland, rather than a totally united Ireland, a policy which aroused criticism from within Fianna Fáil. After the murder by the IRA in August 1979 of Admiral of the Fleet the Earl Mountbatten of Burma, a prominent British public figure, at Mullaghmore, County Sligo, and the massacre on the same day of 18 British soldiers at Warrenpoint in Northern Ireland, Lynch agreed to increase border security. In December Lynch resigned as Prime Minister and was succeeded by Charles Haughey, formerly Minister for Health, who pursued the aim of a united Ireland with a measure of autonomy for the six northern counties, provided that a power-sharing executive be maintained.

In June 1981, following an early general election, Dr Garret FitzGerald, who had been Minister for Foreign Affairs in 1973–77, became Prime Minister. He formed a coalition government between his own party, Fine Gael, and the Labour Party. However, the rejection by the Dáil of the coalition's budget proposals brought another general election in February 1982. Haughey was returned to power, with the support of three Workers' Party members and two independents. The worsening economic situation, however, made the Fianna Fáil government increasingly unpopular, and in November Haughey lost the support of the independents over proposed public expenditure cuts. In the subsequent general election Fianna Fáil failed to gain an overall majority and Dr FitzGerald again became Prime Minister. In December he formed a coalition with the Labour Party, and included four of its members in the Cabinet. The coalition's proposed programme included raising extra revenue by an income-related property tax and heavier capital taxation; special measures to create employment; a review of the social welfare system; and reforms of the civil service. In September 1983 a controversial referendum approved a constitutional amendment to ban abortion. In the elections to the European Parliament, held in June 1984, Fianna Fáil won eight of the 15 seats allotted to Ireland, while Fine Gael won six; the Labour Party lost all four of the seats that it had previously held.

By 1986 Dr FitzGerald's government was declining in popularity, partly due to the formation, in December 1985, of a new party, the Progressive Democrats. In February 1986 Dr FitzGerald carried out a major Cabinet reshuffle, in an attempt to restore confidence in his government. A controversial government proposal to end a 60-year constitutional ban on divorce was defeated by national referendum in early June, and shortly afterwards, as a result of a series of defections, the Government lost its parliamentary majority. Although it survived a Fianna Fáil motion of 'no confidence' in October, Dr FitzGerald's coalition collapsed in January 1987, when Labour members refused to support Fine Gael's budget proposals envisaging reductions in planned public expenditure. At a general election held on 17 February, Fianna Fáil, led by Charles Haughey, won 81 of the 166 seats in the Dáil, with 44% of the first-preference votes, while the Progressive Democrats, contesting their first election, won 14 seats. Fine Gael's strength declined from 68 to 51 seats.

Regular discussions between the British and Irish heads of government, initiated in May 1980, led to the formation in November 1981 of an Anglo-Irish Inter-Governmental Council, intended to meet at ministerial and official levels. Anglo-Irish relations were damaged by Ireland's neutral stance over the Argentine invasion of the Falkland Islands in 1982, but formal discussions by the heads of government were resumed in November 1983.

In May 1983 representatives of the three main political parties in the Republic, and of the Social Democratic and Labour Party of Northern Ireland, initiated the New Ireland Forum to discuss the future of Ireland and Northern Ireland. The Forum's report, published in May 1984, had a mixed reception. It concluded that peace and stability in Ireland could be achieved only with the consent of the people of both the Republic of Ireland and Northern Ireland, with due regard to the preservation of their two identities and democratic rights. In particular, the Northern Ireland Unionists wished to maintain their loyalty to the British Crown and to retain the advantageous economic link with the rest of the United Kingdom. The report was rejected by the British Government, but discussions between Great Britain and Ireland continued, and in November 1985 resulted in the signing of the Anglo-Irish Agreement. The Agreement provided for regular participation in Northern Ireland by the Irish Government on political, legal, security and cross-border matters. The involvement of the Government of Ireland was to be through an Intergovernmental Conference. The Agreement maintained that no change in the status of Northern Ireland would be made without the assent of the majority of its population. The terms of the Agreement were approved by a majority in both chambers of the Irish Parliament, and by the British Parliament, but in

IRELAND

Northern Ireland many Protestants expressed strong disapproval, which continued throughout 1986.

Under the provisions of the Anglo-Irish Agreement, the Irish Government had pledged co-operation in the implementation of new measures to improve cross-border security, in order to suppress IRA operations; several significant discoveries of concealed weapons in the Republic followed. At the time of the Anglo-Irish Agreement, the Irish Government promised to participate in the European Convention on the Suppression of Terrorism, which it subsequently signed in February 1986. The Convention had not been signed by the Irish Government previously, because it was thought to contravene a provision in the Constitution which prevented extradition for political offences.

In November 1986, following an announcement by Sinn Fein (the political wing of the IRA) that it had abandoned its policy of abstentionism from Parliament for the first time since 1922, Dr FitzGerald urged all Irish 'democratic' parties to do their utmost to ensure that no Sinn Fein representatives were elected to Parliament.

Government

Legislative power is vested in the bicameral National Parliament, comprising a Senate (with restricted powers) and a House of Representatives. The Senate (Seanad Eireann) has 60 members, including 11 nominated by the Prime Minister and 49 indirectly elected for five years. The House (Dáil Eireann) has 166 members, elected by universal adult suffrage for five years (subject to dissolution) by means of the single transferable vote, a form of proportional representation. A referendum in June 1984 approved a proposal to allow non-Irish residents to vote in national elections.

The President is a constitutional Head of State, elected by direct popular vote for seven years. Executive power is effectively held by the Cabinet, led by the Taoiseach (Prime Minister), who is appointed by the President on the nomination of the Dáil. The President appoints other Ministers on the nomination of the Prime Minister with the previous approval of the Dáil. The Cabinet is responsible to the Dáil.

Defence

In July 1986 the regular armed forces totalled 14,115. The army comprised 12,282, the navy 943 and the air force 890. There was also a regular reserve of 1,070, and a territorial army reserve of 14,564. The defence budget for 1986 was I£284m. Military service is voluntary.

Economic Affairs

Agriculture, formerly the most important sector of the Irish economy, is now dwarfed by the industrial sector; in 1984 industrial goods accounted for nearly 80% of total export earnings. In 1985 agriculture, forestry and fishing accounted for 15.7% of employment, 11.5% of gross domestic product (GDP) and 22.6% of total exports. Ireland's accession to the EEC in 1973 provided a larger market for agricultural exports: farmers' incomes rose by 142% during the first five years of EEC membership, but dropped by more than 30% during 1979–84. In 1985 the real income of farmers declined by 17%, as a result of adverse weather and the imposition of price reductions by the EEC.

Tourism has become an important sector of the economy. There were 2,423,000 foreign visitors to Ireland in 1985, when revenue from tourism amounted to I£464m.

Major industrial expansion has taken place since 1960, and is promoted by the Industrial Development Authority (IDA), which has created about 40,000 jobs since 1973. The USA, with about 325 companies based in Ireland, is the principal foreign investor, followed by the United Kingdom and Canada, attracted by tax relief on exports. Companies producing computers and electronic equipment are important targets of IDA efforts. The electronics sector has created about 20,000 jobs, and in 1984 provided 18.6% of total export earnings. As one of the less-developed members of the EEC, Ireland has received substantial assistance from the Community's Regional Fund: in 1984 payments of 101.5m. ECUs (I£1 = 1.399 ECUs at 31 December 1984) were approved, while total assistance receiving approval between 1975 and 1984 amounted to 713m. ECUs for 938 investment projects. In 1985 net EEC transfers to Ireland amounted to I£1,128m.—a subsidy of I£320 per head. The principal manufacturing sectors are food and beverages, metals and engineering, electronics, chemicals, textiles and tobacco. In 1984 the mining, manufacturing and construction sectors together accounted for 33.9% of GDP.

Ireland's principal exports are machinery, food, live animals and chemical products. In 1985 the value of Ireland's exports increased by 8.6%, compared with an increase of 28.1% in 1984, while imports increased by 5.4% in 1985, compared with 21% in 1984. The trade deficit was I£1,124.7m. in 1982, falling to I£14.6m. in 1984; in 1985 there was a surplus of I£312m., and in 1986 a surplus of I£700m., was predicted. The United Kingdom remains the principal foreign trade partner, accounting for 42.6% of imports and 32.9% of exports in 1985. In recent years Ireland has diversified its external trade and, since its accession to the EEC, has improved its European trade links, particularly with France and the Federal Republic of Germany. In 1983 62% of Ireland's energy requirements were imported. In 1982 imported fuels cost I£1,009m., or 14.8% of total imports by value, but in 1983 this amount declined to I£993m., or 13.4% of total imports; the proportion fell again in 1984, to 12.4%. In 1986, however, exports declined by 5%, compared with 1985.

There have been four discoveries of petroleum offshore. The largest, announced in July 1983, is off the southern coast, with a flow of approximately 10,000 barrels per day. There are substantial reserves of natural gas in the Kinsale field, and a further discovery was made in 1985. In August 1984 an agreement in principle to build a pipeline to Northern Ireland, to supply natural gas to the north, collapsed after the Irish government rejected the United Kingdom's requests for a reduction in costs. Gas is the principal source of energy, providing 54% of total requirements in 1984, while oil provided 20%, peat 18%, hydroelectric power 7% and coal 1%. A programme for further exploitation of the limited low-grade coal deposits is under way. Europe's largest lead-zinc mines are at Navan. Production began in 1983 at an alumina plant in County Limerick, processing imported bauxite. The full capacity of the plant is 800,000 metric tons per year. In 1979 the first drilling for uranium took place in County Donegal.

In 1978 the growth rate of GNP was 6% in real terms, but output declined by 1.3% in 1982, and by a further 0.2% in 1983. However, growth of 2.2% was recorded in 1984. In 1985 GNP was estimated at about 2.5% in real terms, and for 1986 it was projected to remain at this level. In spite of the creation of jobs by the IDA, the unemployment rate rose sharply, from 7.4% of the labour force in 1979 to 19.3% in December 1986. Unemployment among people under 25 years of age had reached 27.4% by this time. Heavy government investment led to a borrowing requirement amounting to 17.0% of GDP in 1984; in 1986 the borrowing requirement was 13% of GNP, higher than the Government's target of 11.8%. The Government has made efforts to reduce massive foreign borrowing, which reached I£1,255m. in 1981. By 1983 this figure had been reduced significantly, to I£828m.; in 1986 foreign borrowing totalled I£812m. The rate of inflation has been successfully brought down from its peak of 20.4% in 1981, reaching 3.1% in the year to September 1986, its lowest level for 20 years. Owing to a large influx of capital in 1984–85, Ireland's reserves of foreign exchange nearly tripled, to reach I£3,120m. at the end of June 1985.

In 1979 Ireland joined the European Monetary System (EMS), ending the punt's alignment with sterling. The punt remained stable in comparison with the pound sterling until 1985, and the realignment amounted to a devaluation against the pound, which was beneficial to exporters. In 1986, however, a decline in international prices for petroleum resulted in the rapid appreciation of the punt against sterling, and in August, in an attempt to increase exports, the Irish Government devalued the punt by 8% against other currencies in the EMS.

The budget proposals for 1986 envisaged reductions of I£55m. in expenditure and an increase of I£54m. in revenue. Indirect taxation was projected to increase from 35.7% to 36.6% of GNP. Attempts to reduce the budget deficit to 7.4% of annual GNP failed in 1986, when the deficit reached I£1,300m. (equivalent to 8% of GNP).

In January 1987 Dr Fitzgerald's Government foundered over a series of budget proposals, which again aimed at reducing the deficit to I£1,200m., or 7.4% of GNP, and which involved

IRELAND

stringent reductions in public expenditure. Spending on social services, including unemployment benefits, had rapidly increased between 1980 and 1984, from 28.9% to 35.6% of GNP. In an effort to reduce the public-sector borrowing requirement from I£2,500m. in 1986 to I£2,300m. in 1987, and to reduce the national debt (which in 1986 amounted to I£24,000m.), the Government proposed reductions in spending on social services totalling I£210m. Labour Party ministers in the coalition fiercely rejected these budget proposals; the Government collapsed, and a general election was called.

Social Welfare

Social welfare benefits in Ireland fall into two general categories: (1) those received under compulsory insurance schemes by contributors and their dependants; and (2) those received on a non-contributory basis by people of inadequate means. Child benefit is also paid to all households for each child.

Social Welfare Insurance is compulsory for both manual and non-manual workers. The social insurance scheme provides for widows', retirement and old-age pensions; unemployment, disability, maternity and invalidity benefits; and death grants. The cost is shared by the employer, the employee and the state. An occupational injuries benefit scheme is also in operation.

People of inadequate means who are not entitled to benefit under these contributory schemes may receive non-contributory pensions or other benefits from the state or other public funds. These benefits include widows' pensions, deserted wives' allowances, old-age and blindness pensions, supplementary welfare allowance and unemployment assistance. Expenditure on social insurance and assistance for 1986 was about I£2,500m.

Health services are provided by eight health boards, under the administration of the Department of Health. There are three categories of entitlement. Category I covers people on a low income who qualify for the full range of health services free of charge: the services of a general medical practitioner, drugs and medicines, hospital and specialist services, and dental, aural and optical services. Maternity care and infant welfare services are also provided. About 39% of the population are in this category. There is provision for hardship cases. Category II includes people whose annual income in 1984/85 was under I£13,500. They and their dependants are entitled to free hospital services (in-patient and out-patient), a full maternity and infant welfare service and assistance towards the cost of prescriptions. This category involves about 46% of the population. Category III covers people whose annual income was I£13,500 or more in 1984/85. They are entitled to in-patient and out-patient hospital services, and assistance towards the costs of prescriptions. This group represents about 15% of the population.

Drugs and medicines are available free of charge to all people suffering from specified long-term ailments. Hospital in-patient and out-patient services are free of charge to all children under 16 years of age, suffering from specified long-term ailments. Immunization and diagnostic services, as well as hospital services, are free of charge to everyone suffering from an infectious disease. A maintenance allowance is also payable in certain cases. Government expenditure on health was estimated at I£1,030m. in 1986. In addition, there are various community welfare services for the chronically sick, the elderly, the disabled and families under stress. In 1980 Ireland had 209 hospital establishments, with a total of 33,028 beds, and in 1981 there were 4,443 physicians working in the country.

Education

Education in Ireland is compulsory for nine years between six and 15 years of age. Primary education begins at the age of six and lasts for six years. Most children attend a national school until the age of 12, when they transfer to a post-primary school. In 1981 the total enrolment at primary and secondary schools was equivalent to 95% of the school-age population. In 1985 there were 3,387 primary schools, with a total of 566,289 pupils.

Post-primary education takes place in four sorts of school and lasts for up to five years, comprising a first cycle of three years and a second of two years. Secondary schools are private institutions, administered by boards of governors or religious communities, but they are subsidized by the Department of Education. Pupils take the Intermediate Certificate at 15 or 16 years of age, and may proceed to a two-year course leading to the Leaving Certificate at 17 or 18. Enrolment at the 507 secondary schools numbered 212,342 pupils in 1985. The 250 vocational schools provide primary school leavers with a general course which is similar to that for pupils in secondary schools, but with a greater emphasis on non-academic subjects. There were 15 state comprehensive schools in 1985, offering academic and technical subjects, structured to the needs, abilities and interests of the pupils, and leading to examinations for the Intermediate Certificate or the Leaving Certificate. The 43 community schools offer a similar curriculum. They were originally intended to replace existing vocational and secondary schools in rural areas, but by 1985 they were also being established in new city areas. In 1981 an estimated 79% of children in the secondary age-group were receiving secondary education.

Nine Technical Colleges provide post-primary apprenticeship, technical, professional and other courses. A further four colleges are planned for the Dublin area.

The gaining of certain successes in the Leaving Certificate examination qualifies for entrance to the two universities: the University of Dublin (Trinity College), which offers a full range of courses; and the National University of Ireland, which comprises the University Colleges of Cork, Dublin and Galway. They are both self-governing, though they receive annual state grants. The National Institutes for Higher Education, at Limerick and Dublin, offer degree courses of a largely technological nature, although the humanities are represented. The Department of Education provides grants to about one-third of students in further education.

In the 1986 budget an estimated I£927m. was allocated to education.

Tourism

Intensive marketing campaigns have been undertaken in recent years to develop new markets for Irish tourism. The country has numerous beauty spots, notably the Killarney Lakes and the west coast. In 1985 2,423,000 foreign tourists (excluding excursionists) visited the Republic.

Public Holidays

1987: 1 January (New Year), 17 March (St Patrick's Day), 17 April (Good Friday), 20 April (Easter Monday), 1 June (June Bank Holiday), 3 August (August Bank Holiday), 26 October (October Bank Holiday), 25–26 December (Christmas).

1988: 1 January (New Year), 17 March (St Patrick's Day), 1 April (Good Friday), 4 April (Easter Monday), 6 June (June Bank Holiday), 1 August (August Bank Holiday), 31 October (October Bank Holiday), 25–26 December (Christmas).

Weights and Measures

The imperial system of weights and measures is in force, but metrication is being introduced gradually.

Currency and Exchange Rates

100 pence = 1 Irish pound (I£ or punt).

Exchange rates (30 September 1986):
  £1 sterling = I£1.0700;
  US $1 = 73.96 pence.

IRELAND

Statistical Survey

Source (unless otherwise stated): Central Statistics Office, St Stephen's Green House, Earlsfort Terrace, Dublin 2; tel. (01) 767531.

Area and Population

AREA, POPULATION AND DENSITY

Area (sq km)	
Land	68,895
Inland waters	1,388
Total	70,283*
Population (census results)	
5 April 1981	3,443,405
13 April 1986†	
Males	1,767,499
Females	1,769,696
Total	3,537,195
Population (official estimates at 15 April)	
1983	3,508,000
1984	3,529,000
1985	3,540,000
Density (per sq km) at April 1986	50.3

* 27,136 sq miles.
† Source: *Census of the Population of Ireland, 1986—Preliminary Figures.*

PROVINCES (1986 census)*

	Land area (sq km)	Population	Density (per sq km)
Connaught	17,122	430,726	25.2
Leinster	19,633	1,851,134	94.3
Munster	24,127	1,019,694	42.3
Ulster (part)	8,012	235,641	29.4
Total	68,895	3,537,195	51.3

* Source: *Census of the Population of Ireland, 1986—Preliminary Figures.*

PRINCIPAL TOWNS
(population, including suburbs or environs, at 1981 census)

Dublin (capital)*	915,115		Galway	41,861
Cork	149,792		Waterford	39,636
Limerick	75,520			

* Greater Dublin area, including Dún Laoghaire (population 54,496 in 1981).

BIRTHS, MARRIAGES AND DEATHS (rates per 1,000)

	Birth rate	Marriage rate	Death rate
1978	21.2	6.4	10.2
1979	21.5	6.2	10.0
1980	21.8	6.4	9.8
1981	21.0	6.0	9.6
1982	20.4	5.8	9.3
1983	19.2	5.6	9.4
1984*	18.2	5.2	9.1
1985*	17.6	5.2	9.4

* Provisional figures.

ECONOMICALLY ACTIVE POPULATION
(estimates, '000 persons, excluding unemployed, at April 1985)

Agriculture, forestry and fishing	169
Mining, quarrying and turf production	10
Manufacturing	204
Construction	76
Electricity, gas and water	15
Commerce, insurance and finance	209
Transport and communications	68
Public administration and defence	73
Other economic activity	250
Total	1,074

Agriculture

PRINCIPAL CROPS ('000 metric tons)

	1983	1984	1985
Wheat	387	602	495
Oats	101	141	106
Barley	1,503	1,770	1,494
Potatoes	661	870	686
Sugar beet*	1,630	1,694	1,309

* Figures relate to quantities delivered to factories.

LIVESTOCK ('000 head)

	1983	1984	1985
Cattle	6,859	6,872	6,907
Sheep	3,583	3,698	3,989
Pigs	1,081	1,036	1,004

IRELAND	Statistical Survey

LIVESTOCK PRODUCTS ('000 metric tons)

	1983	1984	1985
Beef and veal	352	401	448
Mutton and lamb	40	41	48
Pig meat	161	144	135
Poultry meat	55	53	56
Edible offals	63*	64	n.a.
Cows' milk†	5,341	5,585	5,682
Butter	158	165	160
Cheese	52	55	78
Dry milk	192	211	190
Hen eggs	35.5	37.2	36.6
Wool: greasy	7.0	6.7	n.a.
Wool: clean (equivalent)	5.8	5.6	n.a.
Cattle hides	32.1	n.a.	n.a.
Sheep skins	5.3	n.a.	n.a.

* FAO estimate.   † Excluding milk fed to animals.

Fishing

SEA FISH (landings in metric tons)

	1983	1984	1985
Brill	91	110	121
Common sole	411	313	348
Turbot	216	208	178
Atlantic cod	6,781	5,464	6,523
Haddock	3,838	3,766	3,472
European hake	986	1,066	1,050
Atlantic herring	32,026	31,622	31,716
Atlantic mackerel	65,537	53,212	60,700
European plaice	2,223	2,420	3,043
Ray	1,852	2,112	2,553
Whiting	8,312	8,813	9,111
Others	31,898	31,898	45,935
Total catch	154,170	141,004	164,750

INLAND FISH (catch in metric tons)

	1983	1984	1985
Atlantic salmon	1,515	839	1,493
Sea trout	22	25	22
European eel	n.a.	89	n.a.

Mining

	1983	1984	1985
Coal ('000 metric tons)	75	70	57
Natural gas (terajoules)	82,609	87,794	90,394
Copper ('000 metric tons)*	—	—	—
Lead ('000 metric tons)*	33.6	37.2	35
Zinc ('000 metric tons)*	185.9	205.9	192
Silver (metric tons)*	10	9	8,600
Peat ('000 metric tons)	5,713	7,933	3,336

* Figures refer to the metal content of ores mined.

Industry

SELECTED PRODUCTS

	1983	1984	1985
Flour ('000 metric tons)	164	187	174
Margarine ('000 metric tons)	16	16.9	18.0
Cigarettes (million)	7,531	7,289	8,037
Wool yarn ('000 metric tons)	7.4	8.0	8.5
Woven cotton fabrics (million sq m)	36	34	30
Woven woollen fabrics (million sq m)	2.5	3.2	3.3
Footwear ('000 pairs)	3,030	2,715	n.a
Nitrogenous fertilizers ('000 metric tons)*	235	265	260
Phosphate fertilizers ('000 metric tons)*	12.6	15.3	8.0
Motor spirit ('000 metric tons)	314	307	317
Distillate fuel oils ('000 metric tons)	383	417	434
Residual fuel oils ('000 metric tons)	443	457	487
Cement ('000 metric tons)	1,483	1,377	1,457
Passenger cars (assembled) ('000)	22.2	n.a.	n.a.
Electric energy (million kWh)	11,039	11,424	11,919
Manufactured gas (terajoules)	2,914	2,798	2,293

* Source: FAO, *Monthly Bulletin of Statistics*. Figures are in terms of nitrogen or phosphoric acid, and refer to estimated production during the 12 months ending 30 June of the year stated.

Finance

CURRENCY AND EXCHANGE RATES

Monetary Units:
100 pence = 1 Irish pound (I£ or punt).

Denominations:
Coins: ½, 1, 2, 5, 10, 20 and 50 pence.
Notes: 1, 5, 10, 20, 50 and 100 pounds.

Sterling and Dollar Equivalents (30 September 1986)
£1 sterling = I£1.0700;
US $1 = 73.96 pence;
I£100 = £93.46 sterling = $135.20.

Average Exchange Rate (US $ per Irish pound)
1983   1.2482
1984   1.0871
1985   1.0656

GOLD RESERVES AND CURRENCY IN CIRCULATION
(I£ million at 31 December)

	1983	1984	1985
Official gold reserves	93.3	88.3	76.4
Coin and bank notes in circulation	973.2	1,048.6	1,081.0

COST OF LIVING
(Consumer Price Index. Base: November 1968 = 100)

	1984	1985	1986 (August)
Food	650.3	675.1	708.9
Alcoholic drink	754.6	759.8	829.3
Tobacco	616.1	698.2	773.7
Clothing and footwear	546.4	581.0	600.8
Fuel and light	973.4	1,072.8	1,026.3
Housing	409.6	444.0	465.1
Durable household goods	551.8	565.2	572.5
Other goods	758.4	781.2	818.1
Transport	900.2	964.5	956.7
Services and related expenditure	828.9	885.9	950.0
All items	696.9	734.8	765.3

BUDGET (I£ million)

Revenue	1985*	1986†
Customs	96.8	104.0
Excise	1,316.1	1,377.7
Capital taxes	32.6	35.0
Income tax	2,103.1	2,356.4
Corporation tax, etc.	217.2	249.9
Motor vehicle duties	122.1	130.7
Stamp duties	119.5	167.0
Value added tax	1,402.3	1,562.4
Youth employment levy	82.9	87.0
EEC agricultural levies	14.5	13.0
Total (incl. others)	6,330.9	6,792.1

* Out-turn.   † Estimate.

Expenditure	1985*	1986†
Debt service	1,967	2,020
Agriculture, fisheries and forestry	320	325
Defence	274	284
Justice (incl. police)	325	347
Education	890	927
Social welfare	1,431	1,596
Health	995	1,030
Housing	202	207
Industry and labour	222	254
Total (incl. others)	7,615	8,042

* Out-turn.   † Estimate.

IRELAND

Statistical Survey

NATIONAL ACCOUNTS (I£ million at current prices)
National Income and Product

	1983	1984	1985
Gross domestic product at factor cost	12,761.2	14,226	15,458
Net factor income from the rest of the world*	−1,183.9	−1,660	−1,992
Gross national product at factor cost	11,577.3	12,566	13,466
Less Consumption of fixed capital	1,424.0	1,498	1,600
Net national product at factor cost	10,153.3	11,068	11,866
of which:			
Compensation of employees	8,160.1	8,979	9,447
Other domestic income	1,993.2	2,089	2,419
Indirect taxes, less subsidies	1,779.4	1,880	1,796
Net national product at market prices	11,932.7	12,948	13,662
Consumption of fixed capital	1,424.0	1,498	1,600
Gross national product at market prices	13,356.7	14,446	15,262
Less Net factor income from the rest of the world*	−1,183.9	−1,660	−1,992
Gross domestic product at market prices	14,540.6	16,106	17,254
Balance of exports and imports of goods and services*	412.5	47	−393
Available resources	14,953.1	16,153	16,861
of which:			
Private consumption expenditure	8,659.3	9,256	9,797
Government consumption expenditure	2,864.5	3,080	3,290
Gross fixed capital formation	3,335.3	3,422	3,597
Increase in stocks	94.0	395	177

* Excludes transfers between Ireland and the rest of the world.

Gross Domestic Product by Economic Activity (at factor cost)

	1983	1984	1985
Agriculture, forestry and fishing	1,551.0	1,774	1,660
Mining, manufacturing and construction	4,480.7	4,953	5,519
Public administration and defence	906.6	992	1,063
Transport, communications and trade	2,232.1	2,609	2,943
Other services	4,266.2	4,642	5,068
Adjustment for financial services	−675.4	−744	−795
Total	12,761.2	14,226	15,458

BALANCE OF PAYMENTS (I£ million)

	1983	1984	1985
Current Receipts:			
Merchandise exports (f.o.b.)*	6,812.7	8,695.7	9,527
Tourism and travel	390.0	441.5	518
Trading and investment income	549.1	628.2	722
International transfers	901.8	1,071.4	1,338
Other items	561.4	644.0	709
Total	9,215.0	11,481.1	12,814
Current Expenditure:			
Merchandise imports (c.i.f.)*	7,334.2	8,892.8	9,372
Tourism and travel	363.0	378.3	399
Foreign trading and investment income	1,745.4	2,300.2	2,728
International transfers	230.6	253.4	288
Other items	467.0	345.9	576
Total	10,140.2	12,370.6	13,363
Current balance	−925.2	−889.5	−549

* Adjusted for balance-of-payments purposes.

External Trade

PRINCIPAL COMMODITIES (distribution by SITC, I£'000)

Imports c.i.f.	1983	1984	1985†
Food and live animals	845,198	932,970	994,440
Cereals and cereal preparations	159,976	173,551	172,675
Vegetables and fruit	146,242	172,964	179,473
Animal feeding-stuff (excl. cereals)	152,058	141,128	147,902
Crude materials (inedible) except fuels	221,177	295,802	297,350
Mineral fuels, lubricants, etc.	993,019	1,106,718	1,122,027
Petroleum, petroleum products, etc.	864,386	977,140	944,990
Crude petroleum oils, etc.	198,143	239,694	254,340
Refined petroleum products	645,327	713,351	668,465
Motor spirit (petrol) and other light oils	181,761	165,555	155,607
Motor spirit (incl. aviation spirit)	152,995	154,407	146,517
Gas oils (distillate fuels)	200,053	214,142	224,099
Other fuel oils	162,308	222,924	175,306
Chemicals and related products	843,484	1,031,930	1,103,240
Organic chemicals	144,706	194,136	200,636
Medicinal and pharmaceutical products	135,059	153,228	167,443
Manufactured fertilizers	126,149	167,780	183,087
Artificial resins and plastic materials, etc.	164,542	205,786	213,785
Products of polymerization, etc.	117,803	145,749	147,715
Basic manufactures	1,172,668	1,369,690	1,415,039
Paper, paperboard, etc.	214,601	247,263	265,265
Paper and paperboard	132,056	152,971	161,881
Textile yarn, fabrics, etc.	281,339	320,324	343,890
Non-metallic mineral manufactures	113,180	128,284	126,714
Iron and steel	138,748	164,599	170,973
Machinery and transport equipment	2,119,807	2,778,477	2,945,834
Power generating machinery and equipment	111,522	116,308	142,738
Machinery specialized for particular industries	219,145	259,671	295,851
General industrial machinery, equipment and parts	248,676	264,631	290,063
Office machines and automatic data processing equipment	582,506	958,637	988,193
Parts and accessories for office machines, etc.	429,828	765,151	756,931
Telecommunications and sound equipment	127,614	143,824	172,062
Other electrical machinery, apparatus, etc.	394,750	544,261	557,359
Road vehicles and parts (excl. tyres, engines and electrical parts)	369,500	373,281	402,875
Passenger motor cars (excl. buses)	231,043	222,372	238,260
Miscellaneous manufactured articles	892,498	1,031,807	1,090,507
Clothing and accessories (excl. footwear)	292,291	325,475	344,551
Total (incl. others)*	7,366,775	8,912,170	9,430,492

* Including transactions not classified by commodity (I£'000): 167,334 in 1983; 221,003 in 1984; 277,246 in 1985. These amounts include imports through Shannon Free Airport (I£'000): 92,520 in 1983; 112,592 in 1984; 112,570 in 1985. The total also includes imports of non-monetary gold (I£'000): 4,413 in 1983; 3,609 in 1984; 5,788 in 1985.
† Provisional.

Exports f.o.b.	1983	1984	1985†
Food and live animals	1,743,792	2,064,174	2,204,972
Live animals	234,391	256,692	251,515
Bovine animals	193,547	206,488	180,132
Meat and meat preparations	555,202	535,930	608,830
Fresh, chilled or frozen meat	501,818	490,704	568,602
Meat of bovine animals	385,579	378,584	445,974
Dairy products and birds' eggs	395,076	585,278	536,224
Milk and cream	121,666	224,708	195,928
Preserved, concentrated or sweetened milk and cream	114,436	218,382	189,287
Butter	178,775	249,172	207,651
Beverages and tobacco	183,374	208,113	236,383
Beverages	150,998	172,478	197,364
Crude materials (inedible) except fuels	284,381	505,117	450,071
Chemicals and related products	963,619	1,236,289	1,406,424
Organic chemicals	509,664	633,362	742,316
Organo-inorganic and heterocyclic compounds	419,949	445,214	550,344
Heterocyclic compounds (incl. nucleic acids)	376,578	394,118	511,061
Basic manufactures	725,442	845,106	904,082
Textile yarn, fabrics, etc.	267,798	295,354	298,261
Machinery and transport equipment	1,814,153	2,550,254	2,889,335
General industrial machinery, equipment and parts	159,007	178,804	221,671
Office machines and automatic data processing equipment	961,192	1,536,261	1,826,588
Automatic data processing machines and units	689,243	1,051,764	1,288,515
Complete digital data processing machines	443,189	690,532	965,303
Electrical machinery, apparatus, etc.	398,720	539,187	566,464
Miscellaneous manufactured articles	831,748	991,166	1,080,402
Clothing and accessories (excl. footwear)	141,568	166,294	187,407
Professional, scientific and controlling instruments and apparatus	236,383	309,994	334,052
Total (incl others)*	6,943,836	8,897,525	9,743,029

* Including transactions not classified by commodity (I£'000): 306,802 in 1983; 372,800 in 1984; 425,201 in 1985. These amounts include exports through Shannon Free Airport (I£'000): 240,597 in 1983; 282,639 in 1984; 293,748 in 1985. The total also includes exports of non-monetary gold (I£'000): 1,358 in 1983; 1,833 in 1984; 1,655 in 1985.
† Provisional.

PRINCIPAL TRADING PARTNERS* (I£'000)

Imports c.i.f.	1983	1984	1985†
Belgium/Luxembourg	155,650	190,573	205,547
Canada	91,854	100,052	83,889
Denmark	73,997	82,254	96,689
Finland	60,586	81,039	77,289
France	343,315	429,307	456,296
Germany, Federal Republic	586,733	677,646	729,566
Italy	176,387	215,595	214,021
Japan	244,122	299,570	334,350
Netherlands	272,157	335,003	356,225
Spain	85,291	100,835	101,023
Sweden	112,172	145,731	148,696
Switzerland	77,008	87,036	95,329
United Kingdom	3,338,851	3,822,004	4,026,046
USA	1,082,770	1,465,922	1,603,221
Total (incl. others)	7,366,775	8,912,170	9,430,492

Exports f.o.b.	1983	1984	1985†
Belgium/Luxembourg	274,708	382,589	396,389
Canada	80,586	150,206	171,852
Denmark	55,409	67,672	88,527
Egypt	88,102	95,273	109,002
France	572,156	745,785	821,440
Germany, Federal Republic	686,647	902,867	985,746
Italy	208,692	278,848	363,919
Netherlands	405,481	621,789	663,725
Nigeria	67,446	55,680	105,506
Spain	79,166	94,309	111,216
Sweden	106,701	136,437	170,868
United Kingdom	2,562,120	3,064,465	3,211,477
USA	564,790	866,003	953,309
Total (incl. others)	6,943,836	8,897,525	9,743,029

* Imports by country of origin; exports by country of final destination. The distribution excludes trade through Shannon Free Airport (see previous tables) except for Canada, the USA and the EEC.
† Provisional.

IRELAND

Statistical Survey

Transport

RAILWAYS (traffic, '000)

	1983	1984	1985
Passengers carried	13,027	15,560	20,090
Passenger train-km	7,963	8,273	9,336
Freight tonnage	3,319	3,383	3,379
Freight train-km	4,464	4,411	4,305

ROAD TRAFFIC (licensed motor vehicles at 30 September)

	1983	1984	1985
Private cars	719,877	712,479	710,933
Goods vehicles	69,978	84,103	93,369
Public service vehicles	6,909	7,436	7,653
Motor cycles	25,208	26,305	26,025

SHIPPING (sea-borne freight traffic, displacement of vessels, '000 net registered tons)

	1982	1983	1984
International trade	14,890	15,993	17,997
Coastal trade	489	1,067	908

CIVIL AVIATION (traffic of Aer Lingus)

	1983/84	1984/85	1985/86
Miles flown ('000)	16,735	16,480	15,883
Passengers carried	2,212,963	2,194,626	2,267,145
Freight carried (tons)	55,792	58,484	50,978
Mail carried (tons)	2,606	2,434	2,253
Passenger-miles ('000)*	1,320,618	1,360,364	1,568,432
Freight ton-miles ('000)	66,682	68,134	59,433

* Scheduled services only.

Tourism

FOREIGN TOURIST ARRIVALS ('000)

	1983	1984	1985
Long-stay visitors:			
Great Britain	1,049	1,120	1,119
Northern Ireland	543	590	479
France	81	87	95
Germany, Federal Republic	92	89	98
Netherlands	29	32	33
Other continental Europe	93	97	108
United States	286	318	392
Canada	24	26	30
Other areas	60	69	69
Sub-total	2,257	2,428	2,423
Day-trippers	7,542	7,486	7,502
Total	9,799	9,914	9,925

Communications Media

	1983	1984	1985
Television licences	721,147	742,730	755,095
Telephones in use	823,875	894,000	942,000
Daily newspapers	7	7	7

Radio receivers: 1.6 million in use (1983).

Education

(1984/85)

	Institutions	Teachers (full-time)	Students (full-time)
Primary schools	3,387	20,933	566,289
Secondary schools	507	11,902	212,342
Vocational schools	250	4,949	79,930
Comprehensive schools	15	536	8,787
Community schools	43	1,640	28,124
Teacher (primary) training colleges	6	177	1,957
Preparatory colleges	1		13
Technical colleges*	9	1,094	9,885
Technology colleges*	9	871	7,306
Universities and Institutes	7	n.a.	31,425

* Third-level pupils only.

Sources: Department of Education, Dublin 1; Higher Education Authority.

Directory

The Constitution

The original Constitution of the Irish Free State came into operation on 6 December 1922. Certain provisions which were regarded as contrary to national sentiments were gradually removed by successive amendments, with the result that by 1937 the text differed considerably from that of the original document. It was superseded by an entirely new Constitution, which was approved by Parliament on 14 June 1937, and enacted by the people by means of a plebiscite on 1 July. This new Constitution came into operation on 29 December 1937. Ireland became a republic on 18 April 1949. The following is a summary of the Constitution's main provisions:

TITLE OF THE STATE

The title of the State is Éire or, in the English language, Ireland.

NATIONAL STATUS

The Constitution declares that Ireland is a sovereign, independent, democratic State. It affirms the inalienable, indefeasible and sovereign right of the Irish nation to choose its own form of government, to determine its relations with other nations, and to develop its life, political, economic and cultural, in accordance with its own genius and traditions.

The Constitution applies to the whole of Ireland, but, pending the re-integration of the national territory, the laws enacted by the Parliament established by the Constitution have the same area and extent of application as those of the Irish Free State.

THE PRESIDENT

At the head of the State is the President, elected by direct suffrage, who holds office for a period of seven years. He, on the advice of the Government or its head, summons and dissolves Parliament, signs and promulgates laws and appoints judges; on the nomination of the Dáil he appoints the Prime Minister and, on the nomination of the Prime Minister with the previous approval of the Dáil, he appoints the other members of the Government. The supreme command of the Defence Forces is vested in him, its exercise being regulated by law.

In addition, the President has the power to refer certain Bills to the Supreme Court for decision on the question of their constitutionality; and also, at the instance of a prescribed proportion of the members of both Houses of Parliament to refer certain Bills to the people for decision at a referendum.

The President, in the exercise and performance of certain of his constitutional powers and functions, has the aid and advice of a Council of State.

PARLIAMENT

The Oireachtas, or National Parliament, consists of the President and two Houses, viz. a House of Representatives called Dáil Éireann, and a Senate, called Seanad Éireann. The Dáil consists of 166 members, who are elected for a five-year term by adult suffrage on the system of proportional representation by means of the single, transferable vote. Of the 60 members of the Senate, 11 are nominated by the Prime Minister, six are elected by the universities, and 43 are elected from five panels of candidates established on a vocational basis, representing: National language and culture, literature, art, education and such professional interests as may be defined by law for the purpose of this panel; Agriculture and allied interests, and fisheries; Labour, whether organized or unorganized; Industry and commerce, including banking, finance, accountancy, engineering and architecture; Public administration and social services, including voluntary social activities.

A maximum period of 90 days is afforded to the Senate for the consideration or amendment of Bills sent to that House by the Dáil, but the Senate has no power to veto legislation.

EXECUTIVE

The Executive Power of the State is exercised by the Government, which is responsible to the Dáil and consists of not fewer than seven and not more than 15 members. The head of the Government is the Prime Minister.

FUNDAMENTAL RIGHTS

The State recognizes the family as the natural, primary and fundamental unit group of Society, possessing inalienable and imprescriptible rights antecedent and superior to all positive law. It acknowledges the right to life of the unborn and guarantees in its laws to defend and vindicate that right. It acknowledges the right and duty of parents to provide for the education of their children, and, with due regard to that right, undertakes to provide free education. It pledges itself also to guard with special care the institution of marriage.

The Constitution contains special provision for the recognition and protection of the fundamental rights of citizens, such as personal liberty, free expression of opinion, peaceable assembly, and the formation of associations and unions.

Freedom of conscience and the free practice and profession of religion are, subject to public order and morality, guaranteed to every citizen. No religion may be endowed or subjected to discriminatory disability. Since December 1972, when a referendum was taken on the issue, the Catholic Church is no longer granted a special, privileged position.

SOCIAL POLICY

Certain principles of social policy intended for the general guidance of Parliament, but not cognizable by the courts, are set forth in the Constitution. Among their objects are the direction of the policy of the State towards securing the distribution of property so as to subserve the common good, the regulation of credit so as to serve the welfare of the people as a whole, the establishment of families in economic security on the land, and the right to an adequate means of livelihood for all citizens.

The State pledges itself to safeguard the interests, and to contribute where necessary to the support, of the infirm, the widow, the orphan and the aged, and shall endeavour to ensure that citizens shall not be forced by economic necessity to enter occupations unsuited to their sex, age or strength.

AMENDMENT OF THE CONSTITUTION

No amendment to the Constitution can be effected except by the decision of the people given at a referendum.

The Government
(January 1987)

HEAD OF STATE

President: Dr PATRICK HILLERY (PÁDRAIG Ó HIRIGHILE) (assumed office 3 December 1976; re-elected 21 October 1983).

THE CABINET

A coalition between Fine Gael (FG) and the Irish Labour Party (LP), formed in December 1982; a new Cabinet was to be announced in March 1987, following the general election.

Taoiseach (Prime Minister): Dr GARRET FITZGERALD (FG).

Tánaiste (Deputy Prime Minister) and Minister for Energy: RICHARD SPRING (LP).

Minister for Foreign Affairs: PETER BARRY (FG).

Minister for Industry and Commerce: MICHAEL NOONAN (FG).

Minister for the Environment: JOHN BOLAND (FG).

Minister for Defence and Minister for the Gaeltacht: PATRICK O'TOOLE (FG).

Minister for Tourism, Fisheries and Forestry: LIAM KAVANAGH (LP).

Minister for Communications: JAMES MITCHELL (FG).

Minister for Finance: JOHN BRUTON (FG).

Minister for Health: GEMMA HUSSEY (FG).

Minister for Social Welfare: BARRY DESMOND (LP).

Minister for Agriculture: AUSTIN DEASY (FG).

Minister for Justice: ALAN DUKES (FG).

Minister for Education: PATRICK COONEY (FG).

Minister for Labour and Minister for the Public Service: RUAIRI QUINN (LP).

Attorney-General (not in the Cabinet): JOHN ROGERS.

IRELAND

MINISTRIES

Office of the President: Áras an Uachtaráin, Phoenix Park, Dublin 8; tel. (01) 772815.

Office of the Prime Minister: Government Bldgs, Upper Merrion St, Dublin 2; tel. (01) 689333; telex 25800.

Department of Agriculture: Agriculture House, Kildare St, Dublin 2; tel. (01) 789011; telex 93607.

Department of Communications: Kildare St, Dublin 2; tel. (01) 789522; telex 24651.

Department of Defence: Parkgate, Dublin 8; tel. (01) 771881; telex 25250.

Department of Education: Marlborough St, Dublin 1; tel. (01) 717101; telex 31136.

Department of Energy: 25 Clare St, Dublin 2; tel. (01) 715233; telex 90335;

Department of the Environment: Custom House, Dublin 1; tel. (01) 793377; telex 31014.

Department of Finance: Government Bldgs, Upper Merrion St, Dublin 2; tel. (01) 767571; telex 30357.

Department of Foreign Affairs: 80 St Stephen's Green, Dublin 2; tel. (01) 780822; telex 25300.

Department of the Gaeltacht: 1 Lower Grand Canal St, Dublin 2; tel. (01) 764751; telex 30782.

Department of Health: Custom House, Dublin 1; tel. (01) 735777; telex 24894.

Department of Industry and Commerce: Kildare St, Dublin 2; tel. (01) 614444; telex 93478.

Department of Justice: 72–76 St Stephen's Green, Dublin 2; tel. (01) 789711; telex 90495.

Department of Labour: Davitt House, 50–60 Mespil Rd, Dublin 4; tel. (01) 765861; telex 24534.

Department the Public Service: 36–42 Kildare St, Dublin 2; tel. (01) 779601; telex 24806.

Department of Social Welfare: Áras Mhic Dhiarmada, Dublin 1; tel. (01) 786444; telex 24704.

Department of Tourism, Fisheries and Forestry: Leeson Lane, Dublin 2; tel. (01) 600444; telex 90253.

Legislature

OIREACHTAS (PARLIAMENT)

Parliament comprises two Houses—Dáil Éireann (House of Representatives), with 166 members, and Seanad Éireann (Senate), with 60 members, of whom 11 are nominated by the Taoiseach and 49 elected (six by the universities and 43 from specially constituted panels).

Dáil Éireann

Speaker: (vacant).

General Election, 17 February 1987

Party	Votes	% of votes	Seats
Fianna Fáil	784,606	44.15	81
Fine Gael	481,137	27.07	51
Progressive Democrats	210,587	11.85	14
Labour Party	114,553	6.45	12
Workers' Party	67,263	3.78	4
Sinn Fein	32,933	1.85	—
Others	86,163	4.85	4

Seanad Éireann

Speaker: Patrick J. Reynolds.

Election, January 1983 (11 members nominated)

Party	Seats at election	Seats at Nov. 1986
Fine Gael	25	25
Fianna Fáil	19	19
Labour	10	9
Independent*	6	6
Progressive Democrats	—	1

* University representatives.

Political Organizations

Communist Party of Ireland: James Connolly House, 43 East Essex St, Dublin 2; tel. (01) 711943; f. 1933; its aim is a united, socialist Ireland; Chair. Michael O'Riordan; Gen. Sec. James Stewart.

Democratic Socialist Party: POB 806, Dublin 8; tel. (01) 309892; f. 1982 following merger of Socialist Party (f. 1970) and Limerick Socialist Organization; aims to create a democratic socialist Ireland, opposes Irish nationalist claim to Northern Ireland; Pres. James Kemmy; Chair. Michael Conaghan; Sec. Martin McGarry.

Fianna Fáil (literally, Soldiers of Destiny—The Republican Party): 13 Upper Mount St, Dublin 2; tel. (01) 761551; telex 32559; f. 1926; supports the peaceful reunification of Ireland; Pres. Charles Haughey; Gen. Sec. Frank Wall.

Fine Gael (United Ireland Party): 51 Upper Mount St, Dublin 2; tel. (01) 761573; telex 31569; f. 1933; mem. of the European People's Party (Christian Democratic Group) in the European Parliament; Pres. and Leader Dr Garret FitzGerald; Nat. Exec. Chair. Peter Barry; Gen. Sec. Finbarr Fitzpatrick.

Irish Republican Socialist Party: 34 Upper Gardiner St, Dublin 1; tel. (01) 721175; f. 1974; political wing of INLA (see Northern Ireland, Vol. II); aims to establish a united 32-county democratic socialist republic in Ireland; Chair. Jim Laine; Gen. Sec. Francis Barry.

The Labour Party: 16 Gardiner Place, Dublin 1; tel. (01) 788411; telex 90570; originated with the addition of political functions to the Trade Union Congress in 1912; at the end of 1930 it was decided to separate the political and industrial functions of the Party, and the TUC and the Labour Party became separate bodies; Chair. Michael D. Higgins; Vice-Chair. Mervyn Taylor; Leader of Parl. Labour Party Richard Spring; Gen. Sec. Raymond Kavanagh.

Progressive Democrats: 25 South Frederick St, Dublin 2; tel. (01) 794399; f. 1985; represents a break with Fianna Fáil and Fine Gael; desires a peaceful approach to the Northern Ireland situation; tax reforms; the encouragement of private enterprise; a clear distinction between church and state; and the removal of a constitutional ban on divorce; Leader Desmond O'Malley; Gen. Sec. Patrick Cox.

Republican Sinn Fein: f. 1986 by disaffected members of Sinn Fein; supports military resistance to British rule in Northern Ireland; Chair. Daithi O'Connell.

Sinn Fein ('Ourselves Alone'): 44 Parnell Sq., Dublin 1; tel. (01) 726932; f. 1905; advocates the complete overthrow of British rule in Ireland; seeks the reunification of Ireland by revolutionary means, and the establishment of a 32-county democratic socialist republic; Pres. Gerard Adams.

The Workers' Party (WP): 30 Gardiner Place, Dublin 1; tel. (01) 740716; telex 31490; f. 1905; formerly Sinn Fein The Workers' Party; aims to establish an All Ireland Unitary Socialist State; Pres. Tomas MacGiolla; Gen. Sec. Sean Garland.

Diplomatic Representation

EMBASSIES IN IRELAND

Argentina: 15 Ailesbury Drive, Dublin 4; tel. (01) 691546; Ambassador: Federico Diego Erhart del Campo.

Australia: 6th Floor, Fitzwilton House, Wilton Terrace, Dublin 2; tel. (01) 761517; telex 25762; Ambassador: F. W. S. Milne.

Austria: 15 Ailesbury Court, 93 Ailesbury Rd, Dublin 4; tel. (01) 694577; telex 30366; Ambassador: Dr Gerhard W. Rainer.

Belgium: 2 Shrewsbury Rd, Dublin 4; tel. (01) 692082; telex 24351; Ambassador: André Rahir.

Canada: 65–68 St Stephen's Green, Dublin 2; tel. (01) 781988; telex 25488; Ambassador: Dennis McDermott.

China, People's Republic: 40 Ailesbury Rd, Dublin 4; tel: (01) 691707; telex 30626; Ambassador: Xing Zhongxiu.

Denmark: 121–122 St Stephen's Green, Dublin 2; tel. (01) 756404; telex 93523; Ambassador: Vagn Korsbæk.

Egypt: 12 Clyde Rd, Ballsbridge, Dublin 4; tel. (01) 606566; telex 33202; Ambassador: Abd el-Hamid Abd el-Aziz Onsi.

France: 36 Ailesbury Rd, Dublin 4; tel. (01) 694777; Ambassador: Bernard Guitton.

IRELAND

Germany, Federal Republic: 31 Trimleston Ave, Booterstown, Blackrock, Co Dublin; tel. (01) 693011; telex 25311; Ambassador: HORST GRABERT.

Greece: 1 Upper Pembroke St, Dublin 2; tel. (01) 767254; telex 30878; Ambassador: PANAYOTIS A. TSOUNIS.

Holy See: 183 Navan Rd, Dublin 7 (Apostolic Nunciature); tel. (01) 309344; Papal Nuncio: Most Rev. GAETANO ALIBRANDI.

India: 6 Leeson Park, Dublin 6; tel. (01) 970843; telex 30670; Ambassador: PREM SHUNKER.

Iran: 72 Mount Merrion Ave, Blackrock, Co Dublin; tel. 880252; telex 90336; Ambassador: BAHRAM GHASEMI.

Italy: 63/65 Northumberland Rd, Dublin 4; tel. (01) 601744; telex 93950; Ambassador: Dr LORENZO TOZZOLI.

Japan: 22 Ailesbury Rd, Dublin 4; tel. (01) 694244; Ambassador: YOSHINAO ODAKA.

Netherlands: 160 Merrion Rd, Ballsbridge, Dublin 4; tel. (01) 693444; telex 24849; Ambassador: A. B. HOYTINK.

Nigeria: 56 Leeson Park, Dublin 6; tel. (01) 604366; telex 24163; Ambassador: Prof. SALIHU SULEIMAN.

Norway: Hainault House, 69/71 St Stephen's Green, Dublin 2; tel. (01) 783133; telex 90173; Ambassador: ROLF TRYGVE BUSCH.

Portugal: Knocksinna House, Knocksinna, Foxrock, Dublin 18; tel. (01) 893375; telex 30777; Ambassador: LUÍS ALBERTO DE VASCONCELOS GOIS FERNANDES FIGUEIRA.

Spain: 17A Merlyn Park, Dublin 4; tel. (01) 691640; telex 25549; Ambassador: ANTONIO FOURNIER.

Sweden: Sun Alliance House, 13–17 Dawson St, Dublin 2; tel. (01) 715822; telex 93341; Ambassador: ILMAR BERKERIS.

Switzerland: 6 Ailesbury Rd, Ballsbridge, Dublin 4; tel. (01) 692515; telex 93299; Ambassador: RENÉ SEREX.

Turkey: 60 Merrion Rd, Dublin 4; tel. (01) 685240; telex 31563; Ambassador: SELÇUK NAHIT TOKER.

USSR: 184–186 Orwell Rd, Rathgar, Dublin 6; tel. (01) 975748; telex 33622; Ambassador: GENNADI VASILEVICH URANOV.

United Kingdom: 33 Merrion Rd, Dublin 4; tel. (01) 695211; telex 25296; Ambassador: NICHOLAS MAXTED FENN.

USA: 42 Elgin Rd, Ballsbridge, Dublin 4; tel. (01) 688777; telex 93684; Ambassador: MARGARET HECKLER.

Judicial System

Justice is administered in public by Judges appointed by the President on the advice of the Government. The Judges of all Courts are completely independent in the exercise of their judicial functions. The jurisdiction and organization of the Courts are dealt with in the Courts (Establishment and Constitution) Act, 1961, and the Courts (Supplemental Provisions) Acts, 1961 to 1981.

SUPREME COURT

The Supreme Court, consisting of the Chief Justice and five other Judges, has appellate jurisdiction from all decisions of the High Court. The President of Ireland may, after consultation with the Council of State, refer a Bill which has been passed by both Houses of the Oireachtas (other than a Money Bill or certain others), to the Supreme Court to establish whether it or any other provisions thereof are repugnant to the Constitution.

Chief Justice: THOMAS A. FINLAY.

Judges:
BRIAN WALSH.
SEAMUS HENCHY.
FRANCIS GRIFFIN.
ANTHONY HEDERMAN.
NIALL MCCARTHY.

COURT OF CRIMINAL APPEAL

The Court of Criminal Appeal, consisting of the Chief Justice or an ordinary Judge of the Supreme Court and two Judges of the High Court, deals with appeals by persons convicted on indictment, where leave to appeal has been granted. The decision of this Court is final unless the Court or Attorney-General or the Director of Public Prosecutions certifies that a point of law involved should, in the public interest, be taken to the Supreme Court.

HIGH COURT

The High Court, consisting of the President of the High Court and 15 ordinary Judges, has full original jurisdiction in, and power to determine, all matters and questions whether of law or fact, civil or criminal. The High Court on circuit acts as an appeal court from the Circuit Court. The Central Criminal Court sits as directed by the President of the High Court to try criminal cases outside the jurisdiction of the Circuit Court. The duty of acting as the Central Criminal Court is assigned, for the time being, to a Judge of the High Court.

President: LIAM HAMILTON.

Judges:
SEAN GANNON, DECLAN COSTELLO, JAMES D'ARCY, RONAN KEANE, DONAL BARRINGTON, MELLA CARROLL, RORY O'HANLON, HENRY D. BARRON, FRANCIS D. MURPHY, KEVIN LYNCH, SEAMUS EGAN, ROBERT BARR, GERARD LARDNER, JOHN J. BLAYNEY, JOHN J. P. MACKENZIE.

CIRCUIT AND DISTRICT COURTS

The civil jurisdiction of the Circuit Court is limited to £15,000 in contract and tort and in actions founded on hire-purchase and credit-sale agreements and to a rateable value of £200 in equity, and in probate and administration, but where the parties consent the jurisdiction is unlimited. In criminal matters the Court has jurisdiction in all cases except murder, treason, piracy and allied offences. One Circuit Judge is permanently assigned to each circuit outside Dublin and five to the Dublin circuit. In addition there is one permanently unassigned Judge. The Circuit Court acts as an appeal court from the District Court, which has a summary jurisdiction in a large number of criminal cases where the offence is not of a serious nature. In civil matters the District Court has jurisdiction in contract and tort (except slander, libel, seduction, slander of title, malicious prosecution and false imprisonment) where the claim does not exceed £2,500 and in actions founded on hire-purchase and credit-sale agreements.

All criminal cases except those dealt with summarily by a Justice in the District Court are tried by a Judge and a jury of 12 members. Juries are also used in very many civil cases in the High Court. In a criminal case the jury must be unanimous in reaching a verdict but in a civil case the agreement of nine members is sufficient.

Religion

CHRISTIANITY

The organization of the churches takes no account of the partition of Ireland into two separate political entities. Thus the Republic of Ireland and Northern Ireland are subject to a unified jurisdiction for ecclesiastical purposes. The Roman Catholic Primate of All Ireland and the Church of Ireland (Protestant Episcopalian) Primate of All Ireland now have their seats in Northern Ireland, at Armagh, and the headquarters of the Presbyterian Church in Ireland is at Belfast, Northern Ireland.

At the end of 1984 the Roman Catholic population of Ireland was 2,465,868, while people belonging to the Presbyterian Church numbered just over 347,000.

The Roman Catholic Church

Ireland (including Northern Ireland) comprises four archdioceses and 22 dioceses.

Archbishop of Armagh and Primate of All Ireland: HE Cardinal TOMÁS Ó FIAICH, Ara Coeli, Armagh, BT61 7QY, Northern Ireland; tel. (0861) 522045.

Archbishop of Cashel and Emly: Most Rev. THOMAS MORRIS, Archbishop's House, Thurles, Co Tipperary; tel. (0504) 21512.

Archbishop of Dublin and Primate of Ireland: Most Rev. KEVIN MCNAMARA, Archbishop's House, Dublin 9; tel. (01) 373732.

Archbishop of Tuam: Most Rev. JOSEPH CUNNANE, St Jarlath's, Tuam, Co Galway; tel. (093) 24166.

Besides the hierarchy, the Roman Catholic Church has numerous religious orders strongly established in the country. These play an important role, particularly in the sphere of education, health and social welfare.

Church of Ireland
(The Anglican Communion)

Ireland (including Northern Ireland) comprises two archdioceses and 10 dioceses.

Central Office of the Church of Ireland: Church of Ireland House, Church Ave, Rathmines, Dublin 6; tel. (01) 978422; 379,211 mems; Chief Officer and Sec. to the Representative Church Body H. R. ROBERTS.

IRELAND

Archbishop of Armagh and Primate of All Ireland: Most Rev. ROBERT HENRY ALEXANDER EAMES, The See House, Cathedral Close, Armagh, BT61 7EE, Northern Ireland; tel. (0861) 522851.

Archbishop of Dublin and Primate of Ireland: Most Rev. DONALD CAIRD, The See House, 17 Temple Rd, Milltown, Dublin 6; tel. (01) 977849.

Protestant Churches

Lutheran Church: 21 Merlyn Park, Dublin 4; tel. 692529; Rev. PAUL G. FRITZ.

Methodist Church: 3 Upper Malone Rd, Belfast, BT9 6TD; tel. (0232) 668458; Sec. Rev. CHARLES G. EYRE; Pres. Rev. SYDNEY FRAME, 43 Rosetta Park, Belfast BT6 0DL; tel. (0232) 694108.

Presbyterian Church: Church House, Fisherwick Place, Belfast, BT1 6DW; tel. (0232) 322284; Moderator Rt Rev. Dr JOHN THOMPSON; Clerk of Assembly and Gen. Sec. Very Rev. Dr T. J. SIMPSON.

JUDAISM

Chief Rabbi: Very Rev. EPHRAIM MIRVIS, Herzog House, Zion Rd, Rathgar, Dublin 6; tel. (01) 967351.

The Press

The Constitution of Ireland provides for the recognition and protection of the fundamental rights of the citizen, including free expression of opinion. Despite the powerful position of the Roman Catholic Church in Ireland there is open discussion on controversial issues. The right of a journalist's professional secrecy is not recognized by the Irish Courts.

Ireland has seven daily newspapers, five in Dublin and two in Cork, including four morning papers which are distributed nationally. There are four national Sunday papers.

DAILIES

Cork

Cork Evening Echo: 95 Patrick St, Cork; tel. (021) 963300; telex 6014; f. 1892; Editorial Dir D. CROSBIE; Editor JAMES O'SULLIVAN; circ. 36,250.

Cork Examiner: 95 Patrick St, Cork; tel. (021) 963300; telex 6014; f. 1841; national; Editor T. CREAMER; circ. 63,560.

Dublin

Evening Herald: Independent House, 90 Middle Abbey St, Dublin 1; tel. (01) 731333; f. 1891; independent national; Editor BRIAN QUINN; circ. 132,314.

Evening Press: Tara House, Tara St, Dublin 2; tel. (01) 713333; f. 1954; Editor SEAN WARD; circ. 129,695.

Irish Independent: Independent House, 90 Middle Abbey St, Dublin 1; tel. (01) 731666; telex 25133; f. 1905; non-party; Editor VINCENT DOYLE; circ. 174,788.

Irish Press: Tara House, Tara St, Dublin 2; tel. (01) 713333; telex 25353; f. 1931; independent; Editor T. P. COOGAN; circ. 86,655.

The Irish Times: 13 D'Olier St, Dublin 2; tel. (01) 792022; telex 25167; f. 1859; independent national; Editor CONOR BRADY; circ. 85,420.

WEEKLY AND OTHER NEWSPAPERS

Anglo-Celt: Anglo-Celt Place, Cavan; tel. (049) 31100; telex 31959; f. 1846; Friday; nationalist; Editor E. T. O'HANLON; circ. 18,868 (incl. USA and Canada).

Argus: Argus Newspapers Ltd, Jocelyn St, Dundalk; tel. (042) 31500; f. 1835; Thursday; Editor JIM SMYTH; circ. 7,931.

Clare Champion: O'Connell St, Ennis, Co Clare; tel. (065) 28105; f. 1903; Thursday; independent; Editor J. F. O'DEA; Man. Dir F. GALVIN; circ. 21,040.

Connacht Tribune: Market St, Galway; tel. (091) 67251; telex 50066; f. 1909; Friday; nationalist; Editor J. CUNNINGHAM; circ. 29,085.

Connaught Telegraph: Ellison St, Castlebar, Co Mayo; tel. (094) 21711; f. 1828; Wednesday; Man. Dir J. CONNOLLY; Editor TOM COURELL; circ. 12,000.

Derry People and Donegal News: Crossview House, High Rd, Letterkenny, Co Donegal; tel. (074) 21014; f. 1902; Saturday; nationalist; Editor T. QUIGLEY.

Donegal Democrat: Donegal Rd, Ballyshannon, Co Donegal; tel. (072) 51201; telex 40507; f. 1919; Friday; republican; Man. Dir CECIL J. KING; Editor A. G. KING; circ. 18,411.

Drogheda Independent: 9 Shop St, Drogheda, Co Louth; tel. (041) 38658; f. 1884; Thursday; Editor L. B. CONYNGHAM; circ. 16,491.

Dundalk Democrat: 3 Earl St, Dundalk, Co Louth; tel. (042) 34058; f. 1849; Saturday; independent; Editor T. P. ROE; circ. 18,400.

East Cork News: Industrial Estate, Waterford; tel. (051) 74951; f. 1981; Wednesday; Editor PETER DOYLE.

Echo and South Leinster Advertiser: Mill Park Rd, Enniscorthy, Co Wexford; tel. (054) 33231; f. 1902; Saturday; independent; Man. Editor DICK ROCHE; circ. 18,600.

The Guardian: The People Newspapers Ltd, 1A North Main St, Wexford; tel. (053) 22155; f. 1881; Friday; Man Dir RAY DOYLE; Editor G. BREEN; circ. 35,407.

Ireland's Catholic Standard: 55 Lower Gardiner St, Dublin 1; tel. (01) 747538; f. 1938; Friday; Gen. Man. GERARD CROWLEY; circ. 9,000.

Iris Oifigiuil (Dublin Gazette): Stationery Office, Dublin 4; tel. (01) 689066; f. 1922; Tuesday and Friday; official paper publ. under government authority; Editor The Controller.

The Kerryman: Clash Industrial Estate, Tralee, Co Kerry; tel. (066) 21666; telex 28100; f. 1904; Thursday; independent; Editor S. MCCONVILLE; circ. 41,185.

Kilkenny People: 34 High St, Kilkenny; tel. (056) 21015; telex 80214; f. 1892; independent nationalist weekly; Editor and Man. Dir JOHN E. KERRY KEANE; circ. 17,825.

Leinster Express: Dublin Rd, Portlaoise, Co Laois; tel. (0502) 21666; telex 60024; f. 1831; Wednesday for Saturday; Editor TEDDY FENNELLY; circ. 16,245.

Leinster Leader: 19 South Main St, Naas, Co Kildare; tel. (045) 97302; f. 1880; Saturday; nationalist; Editor W. J. RALPH; circ. 14,000.

Leitrim Observer: St George's Terrace, Carrick-on-Shannon, Co Leitrim; tel. (078) 20025; f. 1889; Saturday; national; Editor G. DUNNE; circ. 8,522.

Limerick Chronicle: 54 O'Connell St, Limerick; tel. (061) 315233; f. 1766; Tuesday; independent; Editor BRENDAN HALLIGAN; circ. 8,000.

Limerick Echo and Shannon News: 51 O'Connell St, Limerick; tel. (061) 49966; f. 1897; Thursday; independent; Editor MARTIN BYRNES; circ. 18,000.

Limerick Leader: 54 O'Connell St, Limerick; tel. (061) 315233; f. 1889; 3 a week; independent; Editor BRENDAN HALLIGAN; circ. Monday and Wednesday 3,788, Friday 33,901.

Longford Leader: Market Sq., Longford; tel. (043) 45241; telex 31901; f. 1897; Friday; independent; Editor VINCENT KELLY; circ. 19,500.

Mayo News: James's St, Westport, Co Mayo; tel. (098) 25365; f. 1892; Wednesday; independent; Editor MARTIN CURRY; circ. 11,500.

Meath Chronicle: 12 Market Sq., Navan, Co Meath; tel. (046) 21442; f. 1897; weekly; Man. Dir JOHN T. DAVIS; Editor JAMES DAVIS; circ. 17,500.

Midland Tribune: Emmet St, Birr, Co Offaly; tel. (0509) 20003; f. 1881; Wednesday; national; Editor J. I. FANNING; circ. 10,000.

The Munster Express: 37 The Quay and 1–6 Hanover St, Waterford; tel. (051) 72141; f. 1859; independent; 3 a week; Editor and Gov. Dir J. J. WALSH; circ. 18,265.

Nationalist and Leinster Times: 42 Tullow St, Carlow, Co Carlow; tel. (0503) 31731; f. 1883; Wednesday for Friday; independent; Editor DESMOND FISHER; circ. 18,909.

Nationalist and Munster Advertiser: Nationalist Newspaper Co Ltd, Queen St, Clonmel, Tipperary; tel. (052) 22211; f. 1890; Thursday for Saturday; nationalist; Editor BRENDAN LONG; circ. 14,484.

New Ross Standard: 1A North Main St, Wexford; tel. (053) 22155; f. 1880; Friday; Proprs The People Newspapers Ltd; Man. Dir RAY DOYLE; Editor G. BREEN; circ. 35,407.

The Northern Standard: The Diamond, Monaghan; tel. (047) 82188; f. 1839; weekly; county newspaper of Co Monaghan; Editor P. SMYTH; circ. 13,250.

Offaly Independent: Tullamore, Co Offaly; tel. (0506) 51398 (news), 21403 (advertising); Thursday; Editor MARGARET GRENNAN; circ. 12,000.

Portlaoise News and Weekender: Pepper's Lane, Portlaoise; tel. (0502) 21673.

Roscommon Champion: Castle St, Roscommon; tel. (0903) 6186; f. 1927; weekly; news, features and sport; Editor JAMES QUIGLEY; circ. 10,000.

Sligo Champion: Wine St, Sligo; tel. (071) 3440; f. 1836; Wednesday; nationalist; Editor S. FINN; circ. 26,473.

Southern Star: Skibbereen, Co Cork; tel. (028) 21200; f. 1889; Friday; non-political; Editor W. J. O'REGAN; circ. 17,408.

Sunday Independent: Independent House, 90 Middle Abbey St, Dublin; tel. (01) 731333; telex 25133; f. 1905; non-party; Editor AENGUS FANNING; circ. 236,566.

The Sunday Press: Tara House, Tara St, Dublin 2; tel. (01) 713333; telex 25353; f. 1949; independent; Editor VINCENT JENNINGS; circ. 266,019.

Sunday Tribune: 8–11 Lower Baggot St, Dublin 2; tel. (01) 607777; telex 90995; f. 1980; Editor VINCENT BROWNE.

Sunday World: Newspaper House, 18 Rathfarnham Rd, Terenure, Dublin 6; tel. (01) 901980; telex 24886; f. 1973; Editor COLIN MCCLELLAND; circ. 361,422.

Tipperary Star: Friar St, Thurles, Co Tipperary; tel. (0504) 21122; f. 1909; Saturday; independent; Editor GERARD O'GRADY; circ. 10,923.

Tullamore Tribune: Church St, Tullamore, Co Offaly; tel. (0506) 21152; f. 1978; Wednesday; Editor G. V. OAKLEY; circ. 5,000.

Waterford News and Star: Industrial Estate, Waterford; tel. (051) 74951; f. 1848; Thursday; Editor PETER DOYLE; circ. 16,000.

Western People: Francis St, Ballina, Co Mayo; tel. (096) 21188; telex 40787; f. 1883; Tuesday; independent nationalist; Man. Editor TERENCE REILLY; Dir and Sec. P. A. MAGUIRE; circ. 28,242.

Westmeath Examiner: Dominick St, Mullingar, Co Westmeath; tel. 48426; f. 1882; weekly; Man. Dir NICHOLAS J. NALLY; circ. 12,800.

Westmeath Independent: Gleeson St, Athlone, Co Westmeath; tel. (0902) 72003; telex 53005; f. 1846; Thursday; Editor J. A. SPOLLEN; circ. 12,000.

Wicklow People: Fitzwilliam Sq., Wexford, Co Wicklow; tel. (0404) 2198; f. 1883; Friday; Proprs The People Newspapers Ltd; Man. Dir RAY DOYLE; Editor G. BREEN; circ. 35,407.

SELECTED PERIODICALS

Amarách (Tomorrow): 51 Mountjoy St, Dublin 7; f. 1956; news and articles in Irish; weekly; Editor P. O'CEALLAIGH.

Aspect: POB 15, New Rd, Greystones, Co Wicklow; tel. (0404) 875514; f. 1982; monthly; current affairs; Editor JOHN O'NEILL.

Business & Finance: 50 Fitzwilliam Sq. West, Dublin 2; tel. (01) 764587; telex 93374; f. 1964; weekly; Editor J. DUNNE; Man. Editor W. AMBROSE; circ. 11,299.

Caritas (1934) Ireland: St Augustine's, Blackrock, Co Dublin; tel. (01) 885518; quarterly; publ. by The Hospitaller Brothers of St John of God; covers the Order's health services in Ireland.

Hi-Fi and Video Review: 59 Upper Georges St, Dun Laoghaire, Co Dublin; tel. (01) 800692; telex 30547; monthly.

Horizon: 2–6 Tara St, Dublin 2; tel. (01) 713500; publ. by Jude Publications Ltd; circ. 8,000.

Hot Press: 6 Wicklow St, Dublin 2; tel. (01) 795077; fortnightly; music, leisure, current affairs; Editor NIALL STOKES; circ. 21,500.

In Dublin: 40 Lower Ormond Quay, Dublin 1; tel. (01) 726622; f. 1976; fortnightly; listings and reviews of theatre, music, restaurants, exhibitions and other events in Dublin; Editor DAVID MCKENNA; circ. 15,000.

Industry and Commerce: 2–6 Tara St, Dublin 2; tel. (01) 713500; publ. by Jude Publications Ltd; circ. 11,900.

Ireland of the Welcomes: Baggot St Bridge, Dublin 2; tel. (01) 765871; f. 1952; every 2 months; publ. by Irish Tourist Board; Irish cultural items; Dir THOMAS F. BEHAN; Editor ELIZABETH HEALY; circ. 125,000.

Ireland's Own: North Main St, Wexford; tel. 22155; f. 1902; weekly; stories, articles, serials, cartoons, family reading; Man. Dir A. CHANNING; Editor J. MCDONNELL; circ. 64,687.

Ireland Today: Dept of Foreign Affairs, 80 St Stephen's Green, Dublin 2; tel. (01) 780822; Editor BILL NOLAN; circ. 20,500.

Irish Arts Review: Carrick-on-Suir; tel. (0353) 5140524; f. 1984; quarterly.

Irish Boats & Yachting: 59 Upper Georges St, Dun Laoghaire, Co Dublin; tel. (01) 800692; telex 30547; monthly; Man. Editor NORMAN BARRY.

Irish Builder & Engineer: 59 Upper Georges St, Dun Laoghaire, Co Dublin; tel. (01) 800692; telex 30547; monthly; Editor NORMAN BARRY; circ. 5,020.

Irish Business: 126 Lower Baggot St, Dublin 2; tel. (01) 608264; f. 1975; monthly; Editor FRANK FITZGIBBON; circ. 10,760.

Irish Catholic: 55 Lower Gardiner St, Dublin 1; tel. (01) 742795; f. 1888; weekly; Editor NICK LUNDBERG; circ. 40,000.

The Irish Exporter: 2–6 Tara St, Dublin 2; tel. (01) 713500; publ. by Jude Publications Ltd; circ. 9,500.

Irish Farmers' Journal: The Irish Farm Centre, Bluebell, Dublin 12; tel. (01) 501166; telex 33338; f. 1948; weekly; Editor PATRICK O'KEEFFE; circ. 70,354.

Irish Field: POB 74, 11–15 D'Olier St, Dublin 2; tel. (01) 792022; telex 93639; f. 1870; Saturday; horse-racing, show-jumping and breeding; Proprs The Irish Times Ltd; Man. Editor V. LAMB; circ. 10,854.

Irish Journal of Medical Science: Royal Academy of Medicine in Ireland, 6 Kildare St, Dublin 2; tel. (01) 767650; f. 1832; monthly; organ of the Royal Academy; Editor Dr JOHN F. MURPHY.

Irish Law Reports Monthly: The Round Hall Press, Kill Lane, Blackrock, Co Dublin; tel. 850922; f. 1981; Sr Editor BART DALY.

Irish Law Times: The Round Hall Press, Kill Lane, Blackrock, Co Dublin; tel. 850922; f. 1867; monthly; Editor BART DALY.

Irish Marketing Journal: 59 Upper Georges St, Dun Laoghaire, Co Dublin; tel. (01) 800692; telex 30547; f. 1974; monthly; Editor NORMAN BARRY; circ. 5,300.

Irish Medical Update: 2–6 Tara St, Dublin 2; tel. (01) 713500; publ. by Medical Press Ltd; circ. 6,000.

IT-Irish Tatler: The Village Centre, Ballybrack, Co Dublin; tel. 826411; f. 1890; Editor NOELLE CAMPBELL-SHARP; circ. 27,138.

Journal of the Institute of Bankers in Ireland: Nassau House, Nassau St, Dublin 2; tel. (01) 777199; f. 1898; quarterly; Editor DERMOT FINUCANE; circ. 13,000.

Magill: Dublin; f. 1977; 14 issues a year; deals with Irish current affairs; Publr VINCENT BROWNE; Editor FINTAN O'TOOLE; circ. 33,000.

Management: Jemma Publications Ltd, 22 Brookfield Ave, Blackrock, Co Dublin; tel. (01) 886946; telex 90169; f. 1954; monthly; Editor FRANK CORR; circ. 7,500.

Motoring Life: G. P. Publications, 48 North Great George's St, Dublin 1; tel. (01) 721636; f. 1946; monthly; Editor DERMOT GILLEECE; circ. 10,000.

The Pioneer: 27 Upper Sherrard St, Dublin 1; tel. (01) 749464; f. 1948; monthly; official organ of Pioneer Total Abstinence Association of the Sacred Heart; Editor Rev. W. J. REYNOLDS; circ. 25,000.

RTE Guide: Radio Telefís Éireann, Donnybrook, Dublin 4; tel. (01) 693111; weekly programme of the Irish broadcasting service; Editor (vacant); circ. 125,522.

Reality: Redemptorist Publications, 75 Orwell Rd, Dublin 6; tel. (01) 961488; f. 1936; Christian monthly; Editor Rev. KEVIN DONLON; circ. 30,000.

Rosc: 6 Straid Fhearchair, Dublin 2; tel. (01) 757401; f. 1951; 6 a year; current affairs; bilingual; Gen. Man. DONNCHADH Ó HAODHA; Editor SEÁN MAC MATHÚNA; circ. 2,000.

Social and Personal: The Village Centre, Ballybrack, Co. Dublin; tel. 826411; Editor NOELLE CAMPBELL-SHARP; circ. 10,500.

Studies: 35 Lower Leeson St, Dublin 2; tel. (01) 766785; f. 1912; quarterly review of letters, history, religious and social questions; Editor BRIAN LENNON.

Success Magazine: The Village Centre, Ballybrack, Co Dublin; tel. (01) 826411; f. 1982; Man. Dir and Editor-in-Chief NOELLE CAMPBELL-SHARP; circ. 10,500.

Timire an Chroí Naofa (Gaelic Messenger): 28 Upper Sherrard St, Dublin; tel. (01) 745953; f. 1911; Irish religious quarterly; circ. 2,000.

U Magazine: Smurfit Publications, 4 South Great George's St, Dublin 2; tel. (01) 779321; f. 1979; monthly; women's interest; Editor MARLENE LYNG.

Woman's Way: 126 Lower Baggot St, Dublin 2; tel. (01) 608264; f. 1963; Editor CELINE NAUGHTON; circ. 70,800.

NEWS AGENCIES

There is no national news agency.

IRELAND

Foreign Bureaux

Agenzia Nazionale Stampa Associata (ANSA) (Italy): 4 Idrone Close, Templeogue, Dublin 16; tel. 941389; Bureau Chief ENZO FARINELLA.

Reuters Ltd (UK): Elm House, Clanwilliam Court, Lower Mount St, Dublin 2; tel. (01) 603377; Correspondent B. MOONEY.

Telegrafnoye Agentstvo Sovetskovo Soyuza (TASS) (USSR): 59 Glenbrook Park, Dublin 14; Correspondent IGOR PONOMAREV.

PRESS ORGANIZATION

Provincial Newspapers Association of Ireland: 24 Dame St, Dublin 2; tel. (01) 793679; f. 1917; 37 mems; association of Irish provincial newspapers; Pres. W. P. O'HANLON; Sec. UNA SHERIDAN.

Publishers

Anvil Books Ltd: 90 Lower Baggot St, Dublin 2; tel (01) 762359; f. 1964; imprint: The Children's Press; biography, Irish history, folklore, sociology, children's; Man. Dir R. DARDIS.

Arlen House Ltd: Kinnear Court, 16-20 Cumberland St, Dublin 2; tel. (01) 717383; f. 1977; imprint: The Women's Press; Chief Exec. CATHERINE ROSE.

The Blackwater Press: Airton Rd, Tallaght, Co Dublin; tel. (01) 515311; non-fiction, history, Irish studies; Editor ANNE SENIOR.

Boole Press Ltd: POB 5, 51 Sandycove Rd, Dún Laoghaire, Co Dublin; tel. (01) 808025; telex 30547; f. 1979; scientific, technical, medical, scholarly; Chair M. O'REILLY.

Comhairle Bhéaloideas Éireann: University College, Belfield, Dublin 4; University College Dublin Press.

Co-op Books (Publishing) Ltd: 16 Lower Liffey St, Dublin 1; tel. 726329; f. 1976; fiction, drama; Dirs L. BARDWELL, A. CRONIN.

The Dolmen Press Ltd: The Lodge, Mountrath, Portlaoise; tel. (0502) 32213; f. 1951; poetry, literary; Publr LIAM MILLER.

Duffy, James & Co Ltd: 21 Shaw St, Dublin 2; f. 1830; official Catholic publications, religious books, works of Irish interest, plays; Man. Dir EOIN O'KEEFFE.

Dundalgan Press (W. Tempest) Ltd: Francis St, Dundalk; tel. (042) 34013; f. 1859; historical and biographical works; Man. Dir J. V. MCQUAID; Sec. BRIAN A. MCQUAID.

Eason & Son Ltd: 66 Middle Abbey St, Dublin 1; tel. (01) 733811; telex 32566; f. 1886; general Irish interest; Chair. W. H. CLARKE.

Educational Co of Ireland Ltd: POB 43A, Ballymount Rd, Walkinstown, Dublin 12; tel. (01) 500611; f. 1877, inc. 1910; school textbooks; Dirs F. MAGUIRE, J. M. DAVIN, S. O'NEILL, URSULA NÍ DHÁLAIGH.

C. J. Fallon Ltd: POB 1054, Lucan Rd, Palmerstown, Dublin 20; tel. (01) 265777; f. 1927; educational; Man. Dir H. J. MCNICHOLAS.

Folens and Co Ltd: Airton Rd, Tallaght, Co Dublin; tel. (01) 515311; educational; Man. Dir D. FOLENS.

Four Courts Press: Kill Lane, Blackrock, Co Dublin; tel. (01) 850922; f. 1977; philosophy, theology; Man. Dir MICHAEL ADAMS.

Gallery Press: 19 Oakdown Rd, Dublin 14; tel. (01) 985161; f. 1970; poetry, plays, prose, drawings; Chief Exec. PETER FALLON.

Gill and Macmillan Ltd: Goldenbridge, Inchicore, Dublin 8; tel. (01) 531005; telex 92197; f. 1968; literature, biography, history, social sciences, theology, philosophy and textbooks; Man. Dir M. H. GILL.

Hodges, Figgis and Co Ltd: 56 Dawson St, Dublin 2; tel. (01) 774754; publrs to Dublin University and the Chester Beatty Library; Man. Dir WALTER POHLI.

Irish Academic Press: Kill Lane, Blackrock, Co Dublin; tel. (01) 850922; f. 1974; imprints: Irish University Press, Irish Academic Press, Ecclesia Press; history, travel, literature, bibliography; Man. Dir MICHAEL ADAMS.

Mercier Press Ltd: 4 Bridge St, POB 5, Cork; tel. (021) 504022; telex 75463; f. 1946; Irish folklore, history, music, bibliography, religious; Man. Dir JOHN SPILLANE.

The O'Brien Press: 20 Victoria Rd, Rathgar, Dublin 6; tel. (01) 979598; f. 1974; fiction, biography, history, general, children's; Man. Dir MICHAEL O'BRIEN; Gen. Editor IDE NÍ LAOGHAIRE.

Phoenix Publishing Co Ltd: 20 Parnell Sq., Dublin 1; tel. (01) 749215; educational; Dirs W. SHORTLAND, R. WALKER.

Poolbeg Press Ltd: Knocksedan House, Forrest Great, Swords, Co Dublin; tel. (01) 401133; telex 32895; f. 1976; fiction; Man. Dirs P. MACDERMOTT, D. MARCUS.

The Round Hall Press: Kill Lane, Blackrock, Co Dublin; tel. (01) 850922; law books and journals; Man. Dir BART DALY.

Runa Press: 2 Belgrave Terrace, Monkstown, Co Dublin; tel. (01) 801869; f. 1942; belles-lettres, educational (university), essays, poetry, science, philosophy; Dir RHODA HANAGHAN.

Talbot Press Ltd: POB 43A, Ballymount Rd, Walkinstown, Dublin 12; tel. (01) 500611; f. 1913; books on Ireland, Irish history, Irish literature; Dirs J. M. DAVIN, S. O'NEILL, F. MAGUIRE.

Veritas Publications: Veritas House, 7-8 Lower Abbey St, Dublin 1; tel. (01) 788177; f. 1900; general, religion, school and University textbooks, audio, video tapes, multi-media education kits; Dir MARTIN TIERNEY.

Ward River Press: Knocksedan House, Forrest Great, Swords, Co Dublin; tel. (01) 401133; telex 24639; f. 1980; general; Man. Dir P. MACDERMOTT.

Wolfhound Press: 68 Mountjoy Sq., Dublin 1; tel. 740354; f. 1974; literature, biography, art, children's, fiction, history; Publr SEAMUS CASHMAN.

Government Publishing House

Stationery Office: Bishop St, Dublin 8; tel. (01) 781666; Controller P. HOWARD.

PUBLISHERS' ASSOCIATION

Cumann Leabharfhoilsitheoirí Éireann (CLÉ) (Irish Book Publishers' Association): Book House Ireland, 65 Middle Abbey St, Dublin 1; tel. (01) 730108; f. 1970; 65 mems; Pres. MICHAEL ADAMS (until February 1987); Admin. CLARA CLARK.

Radio and Television

In 1983 there were about 1.6 million radio receivers in use. In 1986 there were 918,000 television receivers in use, including 740,000 colour sets.

Radio Telefís Éireann (RTE): Donnybrook, Dublin 4; tel. (01) 693111; telex 93700; autonomous statutory corporation, f. 1960 under the Broadcasting Authority Act; controls and operates radio and television in the Republic. Operations are financed by repayable state loans to a permitted limit of I£25m. and surpluses earned on the operating account, and the current expenditure by net licence revenue and sale of advertising time. Governed by Authority of nine, appointed by the government; Chair. of Authority JAMES P. CULLITON; Dir-Gen. VINCENT FINN; Dir of Programmes (Television) BOB COLLINS; Dir of Programmes (Radio) M. CARROLL.

RADIO

RTE broadcasts on two channels (Radio 1 and Radio 2) approx. 262 hours a week, Cork local radio 13 hours a week and community radio 8-9 hours a week. Advertising is limited to 10% of transmission time.

Raidió na Gaeltachta: Casla, Connemara, Co Galway; tel. (091) 62161; telex 28315; f. 1972; broadcasts c. 38 hours a week for Irish-speaking communities; financed by RTE; Controller BREANDÁN FEIRITÉAR; c. 60,000 listeners.

TELEVISION

Reception of both RTE-1, from seven main transmitters, and of RTE-2 is available to 98% of the population. Advertising is limited to 10% of transmission time. Regular transmissions: c. 3,400 hours yearly on RTE-1, 2,300 hours on RTE-2.

Finance

(cap. = capital; p.u. = paid up; auth. = authorized; res = reserves; dep. = deposits; m. = million; brs = branches; amounts in Irish pounds unless otherwise stated)

BANKING

Bank Ceannais na hÉireann (Central Bank of Ireland): POB 559, Dame St, Dublin 2; tel. (01) 716666; telex 31041; f. 1942; sole issuer of Irish currency in the State; cap. and res I£827m., dep. I£1,176m. (Dec. 1985); Gov. T. F. Ó COFAIGH; Gen. Man. and Sec. TIMOTHY O'GRADY-WALSHE.

IRELAND

Principal Banks

Algemene Bank Nederland (Ireland) Ltd: 121–122 St Stephen's Green, Dublin 2; tel. (01) 717333; telex 24857; f. 1972; wholly-owned subsidiary of Algemene Bank Nederland NV, Amsterdam; assets 42,000m. (Dec. 1984); Chair. D. E. WILLIAMS; Gen. Man. J. SLOTEMA; Man. Dir C. V. REILLY.

Allied Irish Banks plc: POB 452, Bankcentre, Ballsbridge, Dublin 4; tel. (01) 600311; telex 25232; f. 1966; mem. of Associated Banks; cap. issued 41.9m., dep. 6.9m. (1985); Chair. NIALL CROWLEY; Group CEO GERALD B. SCANLAN; 500 brs and sub-brs in the Republic of Ireland, 70 brs in Northern Ireland, and Great Britain, 6 overseas brs and 1 rep. office.

Allied Irish Investment Bank plc: Bankcentre, Ballsbridge, Dublin 4; tel. (01) 604733; telex 93917; f. 1966; merchant banking, corporate finance and investment management; cap. auth. 10m., cap. p.u. I£8m., dep. 1,138m., total assets I£1,213m. (1986); Chair. NIALL CROWLEY; Man. Dir PATRICK M. DOWLING; Sec. B. CULLEN.

Anglo Irish Bank Ltd: Stephen Court, 18–21 St Stephen's Green, Dublin 2; tel. (01) 684100; f. 1964; merchant bank concerned primarily with industrial lending, bill discounting, hire purchase, investment management and advice; service to depositors; acquired by City of Dublin Bank Group 1978; cap. auth. 1m., dep. 6m. (Dec. 1980); Chair. A. GERARD MURPHY; Gen. Man. S. P. FITZPATRICK.

Ansbacher & Co Ltd: 52 Lower Leeson St, Dublin 2; tel. (01) 613699; telex 93241; f. 1950; dep. 69.1m. (Dec. 1985); Chair. D. W. O'GRADY; Man. Dir G. J. MOLONEY.

Bank of America NT & SA: Russell Court, St Stephen's Green, Dublin 2; tel. (01) 781222; telex 25795.

Bank of Ireland: Head Office: Lower Baggot St, Dublin 2; tel. (01) 785744; telex 25573; Donegal Place, Belfast BT1 5BX; tel. (0232) 244901; telex 74327; 2 Lombard St, London, EC3P 3EU; tel. (01) 626-2575; telex 8813504; f. 1783; cap. auth. 100m., issued 80m.; dep. 5,785m.; mem. of Associated Banks; Gov. Dr W. J. L. RYAN; CEO M. HELY HUTCHINSON; brs in Britain, Northern Ireland, Jersey, New York and Cayman Islands, rep. offices in Chicago and Frankfurt.

Banque Nationale de Paris (Ireland) Ltd: 111 St Stephen's Green West, Dublin 2; tel. (01) 712811; telex 90641; Chair. E. PHILIPPON; Gen. Man. G. MUGUET.

Barclays Bank plc: 47/48 St Stephen's Green, Dublin 2; tel. (01) 600688; telex 30427; Gen. Man. for Ireland T. S. JONES.

Chase Bank (Ireland) plc: Stephen Court, 18–21 St Stephen's Green, Dublin 2; tel. (01) 785111; telex 93644; wholly-owned subsidiary of Chase Manhattan Overseas Banking Corpn; cap. auth. 2.5m., issued 2m.; Man. Dir DOUGLAS K. BONNAR; Sec. L. CONNICK.

Cuideachta an Cháirde Thionnscail, Teoranta (Industrial Credit Co Ltd): 32–34 Harcourt St, Dublin 2; tel. (01) 720055; telex 24140; f. 1933; state-owned; industrial and commercial financing; cap. 27m., dep. 278m. (October 1983); Chair. J. T. BARTON; Man. Dir F. A. CASEY.

Guinness and Mahon Ltd: 17 College Green, Dublin 2; tel. (01) 796944; telex 93667; f. 1836; affiliated to Guinness, Mahon and Co Ltd, London; cap. auth. 1.5m., issued 1m.; Non-Exec. Dirs J. H. GUINNESS (Pres.), MICHAEL MURPHY (Chair.), B. A. URSELL (Deputy Chair.); Exec. Dirs MICHAEL J. PENDER (Man. Dir), GERALD C. J. MCCRACKEN (Sec.).

Hill Samuel & Co (Ireland) Ltd: Hill Samuel House, Adelaide Rd, Dublin 2; tel. (01) 764396; telex 93760; f. 1964; subsidiary co of Hill Samuel Group PLC; merchant bank providing full banking services, investment portfolio management services and corporate finance services; cap. 2.5m., res 6.0m., dep. 205m. (Oct. 1986); Chair. BRIAN QUICK; Man. Dir HENRY MCCORMICK; Exec. Dir SEAMUS O'SHEA.

Investment Bank of Ireland Ltd: 26 Fitzwilliam Place, Dublin 2; tel. (01) 686433; telex 25505; f. 1966; merchant bank; subsidiary of Bank of Ireland; auth. cap. 10m., issued cap. 6m., dep. 873m. (March 1985); Chair. T. P. HARDIMAN; Man. Dir K. WYLIE.

Irish Bank of Commerce Ltd: 52/53 Harcourt St, Dublin 2; tel. (01) 756411; telex 90880; f. 1973; merchant bank; subsidiary of Crédit Commercial de France; cap. 2m., res 977,000, dep. 76.1m. (September 1983); Chair. A. G. MURPHY; Man. Dir MICHAEL SHEEHAN.

Irish Intercontinental Bank Ltd: 91 Merrion Sq., Dublin 2; tel. (01) 760291; telex 25781; f. 1973; subsidiary of Kredietbank NV, Antwerp, Belgium; merchant bank; cap. issued 4m.; dep. 231m. (December 1983); Chair. D. MCALEESE; Man. Dir PATRICK MCEVOY.

Northern Bank Finance Corpn Ltd: Griffin House, 7/8 Wilton Terrace, Dublin 2; tel. (01) 785066; telex 24403; f. 1969; merchant bank; subsidiary of Northern Bank Ltd; cap. issued 8m. (Dec. 1983); Chair. C. BARNES; Man. Dir M. K. CONDELL.

Northern Bank Trust Corpn Ltd: 27 College Green, Dublin 2; tel. (01) 798788; subsidiary of Northern Bank (Ireland) Ltd, Dublin; nominal cap. 250,000; Chair. A. S. PARK.

Smurfit Paribas Bank Ltd: 94 St Stephen's Green, Dublin 2; tel. (01) 774573; telex 90951; f. 1983; merchant bank; Chair. IVOR KENNY; CEO PATRICK MILLER.

Standard Chartered Bank Ireland Ltd: 18 Dawson St, Dublin 2; tel. (01) 776951; telex 25770; f. 1978; cap. 2.5m.; Chair. D. COAKLEY; Man. Dir J. C. RYAN.

Trinity Bank: 40 Dame St, Dublin 2; tel. (01) 796811; telex 93243; f. 1972; merchant bank; subsidiary of Brown Shipley and Co Ltd and asscd with the Philadelphia National Bank; cap. p.u. I£1.3m., res 536,520 dep. 40.6m. (March 1986); Chair. Lord FARNHAM; Jt Man. Dirs PAUL A. CRAN, JOHN MCGILLIGAN.

UDT Bank Ltd: 13–16 Fleet St, Dublin 2; tel. (01) 713311; telex 24146; Chair. DON C. MCCRICKARD.

Ulster Bank Ltd: 33 College Green, Dublin 2; tel. (01) 777623; telex 25166; and 47 Donegall Place, Belfast, BT1 5AU; tel. (0232) 220222; telex 747334; subsidiary of National Westminster Bank PLC (United Kingdom); issued and p.u. cap. £4.25m., dep. £1,387m.; Chair. F. J. O'REILLY; CEO V. CHAMBERS; 157 brs.

Ulster Investment Bank Ltd: 2 Hume St, Dublin 2; tel. (01) 613444; telex 93980; f. 1973; mem. of National Westminster Bank Group; cap. 27.211m.; res 19.1m.; Chair. MARTIN RAFFERTY; CEO DAVID WENT.

Savings Banks

Post Office Savings Bank: College House, Townsend St, Dublin 2; tel. (01) 728888; telex 33444; dep. I£388m. (Dec. 1985); f. 1861; Man. of Savings J. COSGRAVE; over 1,400 brs.

Association of Trustee Savings Banks in Ireland: Administration Centre, Douglas, Cork; tel. (021) 361301; telex 75347; f. 1817; total assets exceed I£650m.; Pres. T. A. RICHARDS; CEO M. N. CONLON.

Banking Associations

The Institute of Bankers in Ireland: Nassau House, Nassau St, Dublin 2; tel. (01) 793311; f. 1898; Pres. GERALD C. J. MCCRACKEN; CEO and Sec. PATRICK J. ROCK.

Irish Bankers' Federation: Nassau House, Nassau St, Dublin 2; tel. (01) 715311; telex 25843; Sec.-Gen. BRIAN FOLEY; Pres. W. D. FINLAY.

STOCK EXCHANGE

The Stock Exchange (Irish Unit): 24–28 Anglesea St, Dublin 2; tel. (01) 778808; telex 93437; f. 1799 as the Dublin Stock Exchange; merged in 1971 with the Cork Stock Exchange to form the Irish Stock Exchange; amalgamated in 1973 with the United Kingdom stock exchanges to form The Stock Exchange, centred in London; Pres. A. C. A. MCDONNELL; Gen. Man. P. J. GOWRAN; 87 mems.

INSURANCE
Principal Companies

Abbey Life Assurance (Ireland) Ltd: Abbey Life House, Temple Rd, Blackrock, Co Dublin; tel. (01) 832377; f. 1981; Chair. M. L. HEPHER.

Cornhill Insurance plc: Russell Court, St Stephen's Green, Dublin 2; tel. (01) 730622; Man. S. B. HEHIR.

Eagle Star Insurance Co Ltd: Shield House, 45–47 Pembroke Rd, Ballsbridge, Dublin 4; tel. (01) 683943; telex 30737.

Guardian Assurance plc: 35–38 St Stephen's Green, Dublin 2; tel. (01) 609000; f. 1821; Chair. J. E. H. COLLINS; Man. Dir P. R. DUGDALE.

Guardian Royal Exchange Assurance plc: 35–38 St Stephen's Green, Dublin 2; tel. (01) 609000; f. 1968; issued cap. 34.7m. (1978); Chair. J. E. H. COLLINS; Man. Dir P. R. DUGDALE.

Hibernian Insurance Co Ltd: Haddington Rd, Dublin 4; tel. (01) 608288; telex 30872; f. 1908; Hibernian Fire and General Insurance Co Ltd; fire and general; cap. p.u. 2m.; Chair. PATRICK A. DUGGAN; Dir and Gen. Man. E. F. WALSH.

Irish Life Assurance plc: Irish Life Centre, Lower Abbey St, Dublin 1; tel. (01) 720288; telex 24206; f. 1939; cap. p.u. 500,000; industrial and life assurance, annuity group assurance and pension schemes; Chair. JOHN REIHILL; Man. Dir T. D. KINGSTON; Sec. M. D. MCGUANE.

Irish National Insurance Co plc: 9–10 Dawson St, Dublin 2; tel. (01) 776881; telex 30460; f. 1919; fire, engineering, third party, employers' liability, motor, general, accident, burglary, bonds, livestock, reinsurance, contractors all risks; brs in London and Paris; wholly-owned subsidiary of New Ireland Assurance Co PLC; Chair. MAIRTIN MCCULLOUGH; Man. Dir A. B. O'TIGHEARNAIGH.

Irish Public Bodies Mutual Insurances Ltd: 1 Westmoreland St, Dublin 2; tel. (01) 778000; telex 93290; f. 1926; fire and accident; Chair. PATRICK MCAULIFFE; Gen. Man. G. J. BRENNAN; Sec. and Asst Gen. Man. EAMON SMYTH; Asst Gen. Man. BRENDAN DOYLE.

New Ireland Assurance Co plc: 11–12 Dawson St, Dublin 2; tel. (01) 717077; telex 30460; f. 1924; auth. cap. 1m.; Chair. EOIN RYAN; Man. Dir T. KEVIN O'DONNELL; Sec. J. C. BRESLIN.

Norwich Union Life Insurance Society and **Norwich Union Fire Insurance Society Ltd:** 60/63 Dawson St, Dublin 2; tel. (01) 717181; telex 93426; f. 1797, in Ireland 1816; Chair. M. D. CORBETT.

Phoenix Assurance plc: Phoenix House, 7/9 South Leinster St, Dublin 2; tel. (01) 764091; f. 1782; fire, accident, motor, marine and aviation; cap. p.u. 61m.; Man. J. E. DOHERTY.

PMPA Insurance Co Ltd: Wolfe Tone House, 39–52 Wolfe Tone St, Dublin 1; tel. (01) 726444; telex 31003; Exec. Chair. JOSEPH MOORE; CEO A. J. HATCH.

Shield Insurance Co Ltd: Shield House, 45–47 Pembroke Rd, Ballsbridge, Dublin 4; tel. (01) 683943; telex 30737; f. 1950; general, excluding life; Chair. S. F. THOMPSON.

Standard Life Assurance Co: 90 St Stephen's Green, Dublin 2; tel. (01) 757411; est. in Scotland 1825, operating in Ireland since 1834; life assurance and annuities; assets exceed I£11,000m.; Chair. (in Edinburgh) R. C. SMITH; Man. Dir G. D. GWILT.

Zurich Insurance Co: Stephen Court, 18–21 St Stephen's Green, Dublin 2; tel. (01) 764276; Man. E. O. BAILY.

Insurance Associations

Insurance Institute of Ireland: Office and Library: 32 Nassau St, Dublin 2; tel. 772753; f. 1885; Pres. A. J. KIRWAN; Sec.-Gen. M. D. MATSON; 3,035 mems.

Life Offices Association of Ireland: 32 Nassau St, Dublin 2; tel. (01) 720288; Chair. M. F. DOERR; Deputy Chair. T. D. KINGSTON; Hon. Sec. C. LONG.

Trade and Industry

CHAMBERS OF COMMERCE

Association of Western Chambers of Commerce of Ireland: James St, Westport; mem. chambers: Ballina, Ballyshannon, Castlebar, Ennis, Galway, Letterkenny, Limerick, Sligo, Westport; Chair. CHARLES N. RABBITT; Sec. MICHAEL BROWNE.

The Chambers of Commerce of Ireland: 7 Clare St, Dublin 2; tel. (01) 612888; telex 90716; f. 1923; Pres. G. EATON; Deputy Pres. J. D. COYLE; Sec.-Gen. M. F. BRADLEY; 52 mems.

EMPLOYERS' ASSOCIATIONS

Confederation of Irish Industry: Confederation House, Kildare St, Dublin 2; tel. (01) 779801; telex 93502; f. 1932; 2,000 mems; Pres. TERENCE LARKIN; Dir-Gen. LIAM CONNELLAN; Sec. GERARD SHEEHY.

Federated Union of Employers: Baggot Bridge House, 84–86 Lower Baggot St, Dublin 2; tel. (01) 601011; telex 25493; 3,500 mems; Pres. D. F. QUIRKE; Dir-Gen. D. J. MCAULEY; Sec. JOHN CASEY.

TRADE UNIONS

Irish Congress of Trade Unions: 19 Raglan Rd, Dublin 4; tel. (01) 680641; f. 1959; represents 666,000 workers in the Republic and Northern Ireland; Gen. Sec. DONAL NEVIN; 83 affiliated unions (July 1986).

Principal affiliated unions:

*These unions have their head office in the United Kingdom and the membership figure given is for the Republic of Ireland and Northern Ireland together.

*Amalgamated Transport and General Workers' Union: Transport House, 102 High St, Belfast, BT1 2DL; tel. (0232) 232381; telex 747202; Irish Sec. J. FREEMAN; 100,000 mems.

*Amalgamated Union of Engineering Workers— Engineering Section: 26–34 Antrim Rd, Belfast, BT15 2AA; tel. (0232) 743271; Sec. J. BLAIR; 26,812 mems (1983).

*Amalgamated Union of Engineering Workers, Technical and Supervisory Section: 26-34 Antrim Rd, Belfast, BT15 2AA; tel. (0232) 746189; Irish Rep. J. BOWERS; 6,350 mems.

*Association of Professional, Executive, Clerical and Computer Staff: 291 Antrim Rd, Belfast, BT15 2GZ; tel. (0232) 748678; Area Sec. P. A. MCCARTAN; 4,000 mems.

*Association of Scientific, Technical and Managerial Staffs: R. JEARY, New Forge Lane, Malone Rd, Belfast, BT9 5NW; Irish Rep. R. MURPHY, 38 Lower Leeson St, Dublin 2; tel. (01) 762306; 20,000 mems.

Bakery and Food Workers' Amalgamated Union: Four Provinces House, 46–48 Harcourt St, Dublin 2; tel. (01) 752446; f. 1889; Gen. Sec. PATRICK SHANLEY; 4,000 mems.

Civil and Public Services Staff Association: 72 Lower Leeson St, Dublin 2; tel. (01) 765394; Gen. Sec. W. A. LYNCH; 12,003 mems.

Civil Service Executive Union: 30 Merrion Square, Dublin 2; tel. (01) 764315; f. 1893; Gen. Sec. D. MURPHY; 4,500 mems.

Communications Union of Ireland: 575–577 North Circular Rd, Dublin 1; tel. (01) 743402; f. 1922; Gen. Sec. SEAMUS DEPAOR; 9,000 mems (1985).

*Confederation of Health Service Employees: 37 Ulsterville Ave, Lisburn Rd, Belfast, BT9 7AS; tel. (0232) 662994; Irish Rep. W. F. JACKSON; 19,000 mems.

Electrical Trades Union: 5 Cavendish Row, Dublin 1; tel. (01) 747047; f. 1923; Gen. Sec. T. HEERY; 9,602 mems.

*Electrical, Electronic, Telecommunication and Plumbing Union: Yorkshire House, 10 Donegall Sq., Belfast, BT1 5JD; tel. (0232) 221752; Nat. Officer J. COSBY.

Electricity Supply Board Officers' Association: 43 East James's Place, Lower Baggot St, Dublin 2; tel. (01) 767444; f. 1959; Gen. Sec. JOHN HALL; Pres. EAMON KELLY; 3,035 mems.

Federated Workers' Union of Ireland: 29/30 Parnell Sq., Dublin 1; tel. (01) 748711; f. 1924; merged with Federation of Rural Workers 1981; Gen. Sec. WILLIAM A. ATTLEY; 52,000 mems.

*Furniture, Timber and Allied Trades Union: 52 Peter's Hill, Belfast, BT13 2AB; tel. (0232) 243588; District Organizer J. WILLEY; 1,458 mems (1985).

*General, Municipal, Boilermakers and Allied Trades Union: 102 Lisburn Rd, Belfast, BT9 6AG; tel. (0232) 681421; T. D. DOUGLAS; 8,001 mems.

Ireland Association of Secondary Teachers: 36 Lower Baggot St, Dublin 2; tel. (01) 607444; f. 1909; Gen. Sec. KIERAN MULVEY; 12,000 mems.

Irish Distributive and Administrative Trade Union (IDATU): O'Lehane House, 9 Cavendish Row, Dublin 1; tel. (01) 746321; f. 1901; Gen. Sec. JOHN MITCHELL; 21,000 mems.

Irish Federation of Musicians and Associated Professions: Cecilia House, 63 Lower Gardiner St, Dublin 1; tel. (01) 744645; Gen. Sec. (vacant); 1,000 mems.

Irish Medical Organization: 10 Fitzwilliam Place, Dublin 2; tel. (01) 767273; Sec. Gen. MICHAEL B. MCCANN; Deputy Sec.-Gen. ED MADDEN; 4,000 mems.

Irish Municipal Employees' Trade Union: 8 Gardiner Place, Dublin 1; tel. (01) 743362; Gen. Sec. SEAN REDMOND; 3,000 mems.

Irish National Painters and Decorators' Trade Union: 76 Aungier St, Dublin 2; tel. (01) 751720; Gen. Sec. GERARD FLEMING; 3,010 mems.

Irish National Teachers' Organization: 35 Parnell Sq., Dublin 1; tel. (01) 746381; f. 1868; Pres. S. PUIRSÉIL; Sec. E. G. QUIGLEY; 25,000 mems (1986).

Irish National Union of Vintners', Grocers' and Allied Trades Assistants: 20 Parnell Sq., Dublin 1; tel. (01) 746634; f. 1917; Gen. Sec. J. CAGNEY; 4,680 mems.

Irish Shoe and Leather Workers' Union: St Crispin Hall, Seatown, Dundalk, Co Louth; Gen. Sec. M. BELL; 2,000 mems.

Irish Transport and General Workers' Union: Liberty Hall, Dublin 1; tel. (01) 749731; f. 1909; Gen. Pres. JOHN F. CARROLL; Gen. Sec. CHRIS KIRWAN; 160,000 mems.

Irish Women Workers' Union: 48 Fleet St, Dublin 2; tel. (01) 778069; f. 1917; Gen. Sec. PADRAIGIN NI MHURCHU; 3,000 mems.

Local Government and Public Services Union: 9 Gardiner Place, Dublin 1; tel. (01) 728899; Gen. Sec. P. FLYNN; 18,000 mems (1985).

IRELAND   Directory

Marine, Port and General Workers' Union: 14 Gardiner Place, Dublin 1; tel. (01) 726566; Gen. Sec. SEAMUS REDMOND; 7,000 mems.

National Association of Transport Employees: 33 Parnell Sq., Dublin 1; tel. (01) 743971; Gen. Sec. M. COX; 3,445 mems.

National Engineering and Electrical Trade Union: 6 Gardiner Row, Dublin 1; tel. (01) 745935; f. 1966 as result of merger between National Engineering Union, National Union of Scalemakers and Irish Engineering Industrial and Electrical Trade Union; Jt Gen. Secs K. M. P. MCCONNELL (Financial), I. J. MONELEY (Industrial); 10,000 mems.

*__National Graphical Association (1982):__ Graphic House, 107 Clonskeagh Rd, Dublin 6; tel. (01) 697788; Gen. Sec. A. D. DUBBINS; Regional Officer N. S. BROUGHALL; 4,550 mems.

*__National Union of Journalists (Irish Council):__ Liberty Hall, Dublin 1; tel. (01) 748694; Chair. RAY MCGUIGAN; National Exec. mems RAY MCGUIGAN (Republic of Ireland), PAUL MCGILL (Northern Ireland); 2,904 mems (1986).

*__National Union of Public Employees:__ 523 Antrim Rd, Belfast, BT15 3BS; tel. (0232) 770813; Irish Rep. Ms I. MCCORMACK; 12,000 mems.

*__National Union of Tailors and Garment Workers:__ Irish Divisional Office, 44 Elmwood Ave, Belfast, BT9 6BB; tel. (0232) 662942; Irish Rep. MARTIN DUMMIGAN; 9,165 mems.

National Union of Woodworkers and Woodcutting Machinists: 'Arus Hibernia', 13 Blessington St, Dublin 7; tel. (01) 304869; f. 1921; Gen. Secs G. WALL, G. J. LAMON; 2,600 mems.

Postal and Telecommunications Workers' Union: 53 Parnell Sq., Dublin 1; tel. (01) 745881; f. 1923; Gen. Sec. DAVID T. BEGG; 11,500 mems.

Teachers' Union of Ireland: 73 Orwell Rd, Rathgar, Dublin 6; tel. (01) 961588; Gen. Sec. JAMES DORNEY; 7,000 mems.

*__Transport Salaried Staffs' Association:__ 7 Gardiner Place, Dublin 1; tel. (01) 743467; f. 1897; Sec. D. CASEY; 3,025 mems.

*__Union of Construction, Allied Trades and Technicians:__ 56 Parnell Sq. West, Dublin 1; tel. (01) 746687; Republic of Ireland Rep. R. P. RICE; 18,178 mems.

Union of Professional and Technical Civil Servants: 16 Earlsfort Terrace, Dublin 2; tel. (01) 789855; f. 1919; Gen. Sec. G. MAXWELL; 6,000 mems.

*__Union of Shop, Distributive and Allied Workers:__ 1st Floor, Leicester House, 61–63 Royal Ave, Belfast, BT1 1FX; tel. (0232) 241851; Sec. ALAN WHITE; 6,905 mems.

Principal unaffiliated unions:

Automobile, General Engineering and Mechanical Operatives' Union: 22 North Frederick St, Dublin 1; tel. (01) 744233; Gen. Sec. LAURENCE DOYLE; 7,000 mems.

Institute of Journalists (Irish Region): The Lodge, Glendalough, Co Wicklow; tel. (0404) 5196; Chair. GEORGE PECHE; Education Officer VALERIE COX.

Irish Bank Officials' Association: 93 St Stephen's Green, Dublin 2; tel. (01) 722255; telex 90746; f. 1917; Gen. Sec. JOB M. STOTT.

National Busworkers' Union: 54 Parnell Sq., Dublin 1; tel. (01) 744205; Gen. Sec. THOMAS DARBY.

Post Office Officials' Association: Lismullen, Navan; tel. (046) 23266; Gen. Sec. L. MCCARTHY.

DEVELOPMENT ORGANIZATIONS

Córas Tráchtála (Irish Export Board): Merrion Hall, Strand Rd, Sandymount, Dublin 4; tel. (01) 695011; telex 93678; f.1959; promotion and development of exports and aid for Irish exporters and a comprehensive service to foreign buyers, financed by a grant-in-aid; 25 overseas offices; Chair. D. E. WILLIAMS; Chief Exec. A. P. MCCARTHY.

Industrial Development Authority of Ireland: Lansdowne House, Lansdowne Rd, Dublin 4; tel. (01) 686633; telex 24525; f. 1949; autonomous state-sponsored organization with national responsibility for industrial development; administers financial incentive schemes for new industrial investment; divisions: marketing services, press and public liaison, natural resources, electronics and international services, engineering, organization, planning and accounts, development co-operation, pharmaceuticals, health care, paper and print, consumer products, small industries, building operations; 21 overseas offices; Man. Dir PADRAIC WHITE.

Irish Co-operative Organization Society Ltd: The Plunkett House, 84 Merrion Sq., Dublin 2; tel. (01) 764783; telex 30379; f. 1894 as co-ordinating body for agricultural co-operative movement; Pres. MICHAEL GIBBONS; Dir-Gen. J. C. MOLONEY; mems: 200 co-operatives, approx. 140,000 farmers.

Irish Goods Council: Merrion Hall, Strand Rd, Dublin 4; tel. (01) 696011; serves industry in the home market; Chair. TOM HARDIMAN; CEO VIVIAN MURRAY.

PRINCIPAL NATIONALIZED INDUSTRIES

(Information about Aer Lingus, B + I Lines, Córas Iompair Éireann and Irish Shipping Ltd will be found in the section on Transport, Bord Fáilte Éireann (Irish Tourist Board) in the section on Tourism.)

An Post (The Post Office): GPO, Dublin 1; tel. (01) 728888; telex 33444; f. 1984; provides national postal services through 2,200 outlets; 8,948 employees; Chair. FEARGAL QUINN; CEO GERARD P. HARVEY.

Bord Gais Éireann (BGE) (The Irish Gas Board): POB 51, Inchera, Little Island, Co Cork; tel. (021) 509199; telex 75087; 25 St Stephen's Green, Dublin 2; tel. (01) 604377; telex 90794; f. 1975; state gas transmission company; Chair. P. J. DINEEN; CEO N. O. DOWLING.

Bord na Móna (Irish Peat Board): Lower Baggot St, Dublin 2; tel. (01) 688555; telex 30206; f. 1946; develops Ireland's peat resources, produces milled peat and machine turf for electricity generation and general domestic and industrial use and horticultural moss peat products for gardeners; 5,937 employees; Chair. B. HALLIGAN; Man. Dir P. MACEVILLY.

Bord Solathair an Leictreachais (Electricity Supply Board): 27 Lower Fitzwilliam St, Dublin 2; tel. (01) 771821; telex 25313; f. 1927; controls 11 generating stations operating on peat, 2 oil stations, 2 oil or gas stations, 2 gas stations, 10 hydro stations and 2 coal-fired stations; 12,454 employees; Chair. Prof. C. T. G. DILLON; CEO P. J. MORIARTY.

Ceimici Teoranta (Irish Chemical Co): Fitzwilton House, Wilton Place, Dublin 2; tel. (01) 764341; telex 25464; f. 1938; produces industrial and potable alcohol; two factories with 80 employees; Exec. Chair. R. A. RUTLEDGE.

Cómhlucht Groighe Náisiúnta Na h-Éireann Teoranta (Irish National Stud Co Ltd): Tully, Kildare; tel. (045) 21251; telex 60706; f. 1946 primarily for the running of a stud farm for thoroughbred horses at the National Stud and in particular to provide the services of first-class stallions; advisory service to breeders; farming activities such as raising cattle, hay etc.; cap. issued I£3.4m. held by minister of finance; 62 employees; Chair. JOHN M. OXX; Man. JOHN CLARKE.

Irish Steel Ltd: Haulbowline, Cobh, Co Cork; tel. (021) 811731; telex 26123; 25 St Stephen's Green, Dublin; tel. (01) 600200; telex 30774; f. 1947; steelmaking, rolling and galvanized sheetmaking; auth. cap. I£120m.; 633 employees; Chair. K. C. MCCOURT; CEO L. S. COUGHLAN.

Nitrigin Éireann Teoranta (NET): 60 Northumberland Rd, Dublin 4; tel. (01) 689833; telex 93977; f. 1961; production of nitrogenous fertilizers and complete fertilizers; cap. auth. I£77.5m.; 800 employees; Chair. S. MACHALE; Man. Dir T. A. JAGO.

Siúicre Éireann Cpt (Irish Sugar plc): St Stephen's Green House, Dublin 2; tel. (01) 767501; telex 25352; f. 1933; processing of sugar beet grown by 7,000 Irish farmers for domestic and industrial purposes, processing of vegetables for human consumption and formulation of other food products, production of animal feedstuffs, manufacture of specialized machinery, and production and distribution of ground limestone; 2,864 employees; Chair. JAMES E. FITZPATRICK; Man. Dir MAURICE SHEEHY.

> **Erin Foods Ltd:** St Stephen's Green House, Dublin 2; tel. (01) 767501; telex 25352; f. 1958; a division of Irish Sugar PLC; processing of vegetables, manufacture of soups and formulated products; Group Chair. JAMES E. FITZPATRICK; Man. Dir MAURICE SHEEHY.

Telecom Éireann: St Stephen's Green West, Dublin 2; tel. (01) 714444; telex 91119; f. 1984; provides telecommunications services; 18,000 employees; Chair. M. W. J. SMURFIT.

In addition to these there exist numerous smaller state-sponsored bodies. Among those not mentioned elsewhere in this chapter are: The Irish Livestock and Meat Board, The Voluntary Health Insurance Board, The Hospitals Trust Board and the Institute for Industrial Research and Standards.

Transport

Córas Iompair Éireann (CIE) (The Irish Transport Co): Heuston Station, Dublin 8; tel. (01) 771871; telex 25153; f. 1945; government-appointed; controls the railways, inland waterways and road transport services; Chair. G. T. PAUL CONLON; Gen. Man. JOHN F. HIGGINS.

RAILWAYS

There were 1,876 km (1,166 miles) of track in 1984, controlled by Córas Iompair Éireann (see above). The electrification of 30 km of railway track and the modernization and construction of 25 stations was begun in 1979 and came into service in July 1984. The Dublin Area Rapid Transit (DART) was built at a cost of I£113m., to provide extra passenger capacity.

INLAND WATERWAYS

The commercial canal services of CIE have been discontinued. However, the Grand Canal and the canal link into the Barrow Navigation System are maintained by the CIE for use by pleasure craft. The River Shannon is navigable for 241 km (150 miles). Other inland waterways are estimated at 188 km (117 miles).

ROADS

At 31 December 1984 there were 92,303 km (57,354 miles) of roads of which 5,255 km (3,265 miles) were main roads. About 94% of all roads were surfaced.

SHIPPING

The principal sea ports are Dublin, Dún Laoghaire, Cork, Waterford, Rosslare, Limerick, Foynes, Galway, New Ross, Drogheda, Dundalk, Fenit and Whiddy Island.

B+I Line (British & Irish Steam Packet Co Ltd): North Wall House, 12 North Wall, Dublin 1; tel. (01) 788266; telex 25356; f. 1836; drive on/drive off car ferry and roll on/roll off freight services between Dublin and Liverpool, Dublin and Holyhead, and Rosslare and Pembroke; roll-on/roll-off freight service between Dublin and Fleetwood; groupage and roll-on/roll-off from all parts of Britain to and from Ireland; unit load freight service between Dublin and Le Havre, Rotterdam and Antwerp; agents in Ireland for Sealand Inc., C.M.A. and Isle of Man Steam Packet Co; Chair. FRANK BOLAND; Chief Exec. W. B. MULLIGAN; Sec. C. O'SULLIVAN; 6 vessels and other vessels on charter.

Celtic Coasters Ltd: Beech Hill, Clonskeagh, Dublin 4; tel. (01) 694300; telex 25467; f. 1958; also in Cork; Chair. L. ST J. DEVLIN; Gen. Man. E. CONNOR; 2 tankers.

Dublin Shipping Ltd: 6 Beech Hill, Clonskeagh, Dublin 4; tel. (01) 696477; telex 25467; Chair. L. ST J. DEVLIN; Man. Dir E. CONNOR; 4 tankers.

Irish Shipping Ltd: Merrion Hall, Strand Rd, Dublin 4; tel. (01) 695522; telex 25126; f. 1941; world-wide tramping service; Dir and Gen. Man. W. A. O'NEILL; 10 carriers.

Sealink British Ferries: Adelaide House, 7 Haddington Terrace, Dun Laoghaire, Co Dublin; tel. (01) 807777; telex 30847; services between Dún Laoghaire and Holyhead, Rosslare and Fishguard, passengers, drive-on/drive-off car ferry, roll-on/roll-off services; Dublin (North Wall) and Holyhead containers and freight.

CIVIL AVIATION

There are international airports at Shannon, Dublin, Cork and Knock, but only Shannon is used for transatlantic flights. The national airline is Aer Lingus. In 1986 Knock International Airport was opened in Co Mayo.

Aer Rianta (Irish Airports): Dublin Airport, Dublin; tel. (01) 379900; telex 31266; responsible for the management and development of Dublin, Shannon and Cork airports; Chair. P. J. HANLEY; CEO MARTIN DULLY.

Airlines

Aer Lingus: POB 180, Dublin Airport, Dublin; tel. (01) 370011; telex 25101; f. 1936; incorporated Aerlinte Eireann 1947; regular services to 29 cities in Europe and the USA; Chair. BRIAN A. SLOWEY; CEO DAVID KENNEDY; fleet of 3 Boeing 747, 14 Boeing 737, 4 BAC 1-11 and 4 Short-360.

Aer Turas Teoranta: Corballis Rd South, Dublin Airport, Dublin; tel. (01) 379131; telex 33393; f. 1962; worldwide cargo charter services; CEO P. J. COUSINS; fleet of 1 Douglas DC8-63F QN, 2 Canadair CL-44J.

Tourism

Bord Fáilte Éireann (Irish Tourist Board): Baggot St Bridge, Dublin 2; tel. (01) 765871; telex 93755; f. 1955; Chair. P. V. DOYLE; Dir-Gen. MICHAEL MACNULTY; Sec. TREVOR BYNE.

Dublin and Eastern Regional Tourism Organization Ltd: 1 Clarinda Park North, Dun Laoghaire, Co Dublin; tel. (01) 808571; telex 24846; Chair. P. J. BYRNE; Man. MATT MCNULTY.

ISRAEL

Introductory Survey

Location, Climate, Language, Religion, Flag, Capital

The State of Israel lies in western Asia, occupying a narrow strip of territory on the eastern shore of the Mediterranean Sea. The country also has a narrow outlet to the Red Sea at the northern tip of the Gulf of Aqaba. All of Israel's land frontiers are with Arab countries, the longest being with Egypt to the west and with Jordan to the east. Lebanon lies to the north, and Syria to the north-east. The climate is Mediterranean, with hot, dry summers, when the maximum temperature in Jerusalem is generally between 30°C and 35°C (86°F to 95°F), and mild, rainy winters, with a minimum temperature in Jerusalem of about 5°C (41°F). The climate is sub-tropical on the coast but more extreme in the Negev Desert, in the south, and near the shores of the Dead Sea (a lake on the Israeli-Jordanian frontier), where the summer temperature may exceed 50°C (122°F). The official language of Israel is Hebrew, spoken by about two-thirds of the population, including most Jews. About 15% of Israeli residents, including Muslim Arabs, speak Arabic (which is also the language spoken by the inhabitants of the 'occupied areas'), while many European languages are also spoken. About 85% of the population profess adherence to Judaism, the officially recognized religion of Israel, while about 13% are Muslims. The national flag (proportions 250 by 173) has a white background, with a six-pointed blue star composed of two overlapping triangles (the 'Shield of David') between two horizontal blue stripes near the upper and lower edges. The Israeli Government has designated the city of Jerusalem (part of which is Jordanian territory annexed by Israel in 1967) as the country's capital, but this is not recognized by the United Nations, and most foreign governments maintain their embassies in Tel-Aviv.

Recent History

The Zionist movement, launched in Europe in the 19th century, aimed at the re-establishment of an autonomous community of Jews in their historic homeland of Palestine (the 'Promised Land'). The growth of Zionism was partly due to the insecurity that was felt by Jewish minorities in many European countries as a result of racial and religious hostility, known as anti-semitism, which sometimes included discrimination, persecution and even massacre.

Palestine, for long inhabited by Arabs, became a part of Turkey's Ottoman Empire in the 16th century. During the First World War (1914–18), when Turkey was allied with Germany, the Arabs under Ottoman rule rebelled. Palestine was occupied by British forces in 1917–18, when the Turks withdrew. Meanwhile, in November 1917, the British Foreign Secretary, Arthur Balfour, declared British support for the establishment of a Jewish national home in Palestine, providing that the rights of 'the existing non-Jewish communities' there were safeguarded. The Balfour Declaration, as it is known, was confirmed by the governments of other countries then at war with Turkey.

British occupation of Palestine continued after the war, when the Ottoman Empire was dissolved. In 1920 the territory was formally placed under British administration by a League of Nations mandate, which incorporated the Balfour Declaration. British rule in Palestine was hampered by the conflict between the declared obligations to the Jews and the rival claims of the indigenous Arab majority. In accordance with the mandate, Jewish settlers were admitted to Palestine (whose population in 1919 was almost entirely Arab), but only on the basis of limited annual quotas. Serious anti-Jewish rioting by Arabs occurred in 1921 and 1929. Attempts to restrict immigration led to Jewish-sponsored riots in 1933. The extreme persecution of Jews by Nazi Germany caused an increase in the flow of Jewish immigrants, both legal and illegal, but this intensified the unrest in Palestine. In 1937 a British proposal to establish separate Jewish and Arab states, while retaining a British-mandated area, was accepted by most of the Zionists but rejected by the Arabs, and by the end of that year the conflict between the two communities had developed into open warfare, which continued throughout 1938. A British offer of eventual independence for a bi-communal Palestinian state, made in 1939, led to further incidents, but the scheme was postponed because of the Second World War (1939–45). During the war the Nazis caused the deaths of an estimated 6m. Jews in central and eastern Europe, more than one-third of the world's total Jewish population. The enormity of this massacre, known to Jews as the Holocaust, greatly increased international sympathy for Jewish claims to a homeland in Palestine.

After the war, there was strong opposition by Palestinian Jews to continued British occupation. Numerous terrorist attacks were made by Jewish groups against British targets. In November 1947 the UN approved a plan for the partition of Palestine into two states, one Jewish (covering about 56% of the area) and one Arab. The plan was, however, rejected by Arab states and by the leadership of the Palestinian Arabs. Meanwhile, the conflict between the two communities in Palestine escalated into full-scale war.

On 14 May 1948 the United Kingdom terminated its Palestine mandate, and Jewish leaders immediately proclaimed the State of Israel, with David Ben-Gurion as Prime Minister. Although the new nation had no agreed frontiers, it quickly received wide international recognition. However, the neighbouring Arab states sent forces into Palestine in an attempt to crush Israel. Fighting continued until January 1949. The cease-fire agreements left Israel in control of 75% of Palestine, including West Jerusalem. The *de facto* territory of Israel was thus nearly one-third greater than the area that had been assigned to the Jewish state under the UN partition plan. Most of the remainder of Palestine was controlled by Jordanian forces. This area, known as the West Bank (or, to Israelis, as Judaea and Samaria), was annexed by Jordan in December 1949 and, following a referendum, fully incorporated in April 1950. No independent Arab state was established in Palestine, and the independence of Israel was not recognized by any Arab government until 1980, when Egypt and Israel established diplomatic relations.

When the British mandate ended, the Jewish population of Palestine was about 650,000 (or 40% of the total), compared with 56,000 in 1920. With the establishment of Israel, the new state encouraged further Jewish immigration. The Law of Return, adopted in July 1950, established a right of immigration for all Jews. The rapid influx of Jewish settlers (2m. Jews had arrived by May 1962) enabled Israel to consolidate its specifically Jewish character. At the same time, many former Arab residents of Palestine had become refugees in neighbouring countries, mainly Jordan and Lebanon. About 400,000 Arabs had evacuated their homes prior to May 1948, and another 400,000 fled subsequently. In 1964 some exiled Palestinian Arabs formed the Palestine Liberation Organization (PLO), aimed at the overthrow of Israel.

In July 1956 the Egyptian Government announced the nationalization of the company that operated the Suez Canal. In response, Israel launched an attack on Egypt in October, occupying the Gaza Strip (part of Palestine under Egyptian occupation since 1949) and the Sinai Peninsula. After pressure from the UN and the USA, Israeli forces evacuated these areas in 1957, when a UN Emergency Force (UNEF) was established in Sinai. In May 1967 the United Arab Republic (Egypt) secured the withdrawal of UNEF from its territory. Egyptian forces immediately reoccupied the garrison at Sharm esh-Sheikh, near the southern tip of Sinai, and closed the Straits of Tiran to Israeli shipping, effectively blockading the Israeli port of Eilat, situated at the head of the Gulf of Aqaba. In retaliation, Israel attacked Egypt and other Arab countries in June. Israeli forces quickly overcame opposition and made substantial territorial gains. The Six-Day War, as it is known, left Israel in possession of all Jerusalem, the West Bank area of Jordan, the Sinai Peninsula in Egypt, the Gaza Strip and the Golan Heights in Syria. East Jerusalem was almost immediately integrated into the State of Israel, while the other conquered territories were regarded as 'occupied areas'.

Ben-Gurion resigned in June 1963 and was succeeded by Levi Eshkol, formerly Minister of Finance. Three of the parties in the ruling coalition merged to form the Israel Labour Party in 1968. On the death of Eshkol in February 1969, Golda Meir, a former Minister of Foreign Affairs, was elected Prime Minister by the Labour Party executive. She continued in office following the general elections of October 1969 and December 1973. A cease-fire between Egypt and Israel was arranged in August 1970, so ending the two years of war of attrition in the Suez Canal zone, but other Arab states and Palestinian Arab guerrilla groups, mainly PLO forces, continued their hostilities. Another war between the Arab states and Israel broke out on 6 October 1973, coinciding with Yom Kippur (the Day of Atonement), the holiest day of the Jewish year. In simultaneous attacks on Israeli-held territory, Egyptian forces crossed the Suez Canal and reoccupied part of Sinai, while Syrian troops launched an equally strong offensive on the Golan Heights. After extremely bitter fighting, involving heavy losses of men and material, Israel made cease-fire agreements with Egypt and Syria on 24 October. A disengagement agreement with Syria was signed in May 1974. A further disengagement agreement between Israel and Egypt was signed in September 1975.

Internally, Gen. Itzhak Rabin had succeeded Golda Meir as Prime Minister of a Labour Alignment coalition after her resignation in June 1974. In December 1976 Rabin lost the support of the National Religious Party (NRP) and subsequently resigned, continuing in office in a caretaker capacity until May 1977, when the Labour Alignment was unexpectedly defeated in a general election. The Likud (Consolidation) bloc, led by Menachem Begin of the Herut (Freedom) Party, was able to form a government in June 1977 with the support of minority parties.

In November 1977 President Anwar Sadat of Egypt visited Israel, indicating a tacit recognition by Egypt of the State of Israel. In September 1978 President Carter of the USA, President Sadat and Prime Minister Begin met at Camp David, in the USA, and drew up two agreements. The first was a 'framework for peace in the Middle East', providing for autonomy for the West Bank and the Gaza Strip after a transitional period of five years, and the second was a 'framework for the conclusion of a peace treaty between Egypt and Israel', which was subsequently signed in Washington on 26 March 1979. In February 1980 Israel and Egypt exchanged ambassadors. Egypt thus became the first Arab country to grant diplomatic recognition to Israel. Israel's phased withdrawal from Sinai was completed in April 1982. Little progress has been made on Palestinian autonomy. The approval in July 1980 of legislation which stated explicitly that Jerusalem should be for ever the undivided capital of Israel, and Israel's formal annexation of the Golan Heights in December 1981, have inhibited prospects for advances on this issue.

In June 1982 a major crisis developed when Israeli forces launched 'Operation Peace for Galilee', advanced through Lebanon and surrounded West Beirut, trapping 6,000 PLO fighters. Egypt withdrew its ambassador from Tel-Aviv in protest at the Israeli action. Intensive diplomatic efforts, led by the US Special Envoy, Philip Habib, resulted in the evacuation of 14,000–15,000 PLO and Syrian fighters from Beirut to various Arab countries at the end of August 1982. With Israeli troops in effective control of Beirut, a horrific massacre took place in the Palestinian refugee camps of Sabra and Chatila in mid-September; Israel finally acknowledged a figure of 700–800 dead, but denied responsibility for the massacre. The Israeli Government instituted an enquiry, chaired by the Chief Justice of the Supreme Court, Itzhak Kahan. Published in February 1983, the report of the enquiry blamed Lebanese Phalangists for the actual killing, but concluded that Israel's political and military leaders bore indirect responsibility through their negligence. General Ariel Sharon was forced to resign as Minister of Defence, but remained in the Cabinet as Minister without Portfolio.

Lengthy talks between Israel and Lebanon, begun in December 1982, culminated in the signing on 17 May 1983 of a 12-article agreement, formulated by the US Secretary of State, George Shultz, declaring an end to hostilities and calling for the withdrawal of all foreign forces from Lebanon within three months. Syria rejected the agreement, leaving some 30,000 troops and 7,000 PLO men in the north-east of Lebanon, and Israel consequently refused to withdraw from the south. In September 1983 Israel redeployed its forces south of Beirut along the Awali river.

Meanwhile, Begin's inability to withstand pressure from the Gush Emunim movement to foster Jewish settlements on the West Bank caused several resignations from his coalition. Rampant inflation further weakened Begin's position, and in January 1981 he decided to call an early general election in June. Begin's belligerent stance over the threat of Syrian missiles in Lebanon in June, and the efforts of a new Minister of Finance, Yoram Aridor, to curb the rise in the cost of living, resulted in an unexpected swing in his favour; and, although the election results were close, by making an agreement with the religious parties, Begin was able to present a new coalition to the Knesset in early August. When Israeli forces moved into Lebanon in June 1982, support for Begin continued until the operation, which initially had the limited objective of removing the threat to Galilee from the PLO, escalated into a full-scale war.

By the summer of 1983, the Government's prestige had been damaged both by the Beirut massacres and by a capitulation to wage demands by the country's doctors. Already depressed by the death of his wife in November 1982, Begin announced his resignation on 30 August 1983. Itzhak Shamir, the Minister of Foreign Affairs since 1980, was elected leader of the Likud bloc on 2 September. Begin withheld his formal resignation until 15 September. Shamir was asked to form a government on 21 September, his Likud grouping having a theoretical majority of seven seats with the support of minority religious parties. Shamir pronounced himself committed to the Israeli presence in Lebanon, to the continuation of the West Bank settlement programme and to tackling the country's economic problems.

During the second half of 1983 the monetary crisis (see Economic Affairs) emerged as the main cause of the Government's declining popularity. In October the Finance Minister, Yoram Aridor, resigned. The austerity measures of Aridor's successor, Yigal Cohen-Orgad, threatened to alienate elements of Shamir's fragile coalition (who were concerned over the effects of cuts in social services) and were the cause of growing labour unrest. The Government narrowly survived a vote of 'no confidence' in the Knesset in January 1984. Its position was further weakened by the resignation from the Cabinet (and the loss of the guaranteed vote) of the Minister without Portfolio, Mordechai Ben-Porat. Finally, in March, the Government failed to prevent the passage of legislative proposals, sponsored by the Labour Party, calling for the dissolution of the Knesset prior to a general election.

In July the election produced no conclusive result. The Labour Alignment received 34.9% of the total votes and won 44 of the 120 seats in the Knesset, while Likud, with 31.9% of the votes, won 41 seats. The balance of power lay, once again, with the smaller parties. Neither Labour nor Likud, however, was able to gain sufficient support to form a viable coalition government. The President, Gen. Chaim Herzog, nominated the Labour leader, Shimon Peres, as Prime Minister-designate on 5 August, and invited him to form a 'government of national unity'. After six weeks of negotiation between Peres and Itzhak Shamir the new Government, whose component parties accounted for 97 of the 120 Knesset seats, was formed on 13 September. It contained representatives of the two major party groupings (Labour and Likud), four religious parties (the NRP, Shas, Agudat Israel and Morasha) and the Shinui, Yahad and Ometz parties. Under the terms of the coalition agreement, Shimon Peres was to hold the premiership for the first two years and one month of the Government, while Itzhak Shamir was to serve as Deputy Prime Minister and Minister of Foreign Affairs, after which time they were to exchange their respective posts for a further period of two years and one month. Within the Cabinet of 25 Ministers, an inner Cabinet of 10 (including five members each from Labour and Likud) was formed.

The withdrawal in September 1983 of Israeli forces in Lebanon to the Awali river produced a *de facto* partition of the country and, as the move was unco-ordinated with the Lebanese armed forces, left a military vacuum which was filled by civil war between Druzes and Christians in the Chouf Mountains. Increasing responsibility for the policing of the occupied southern area fell upon the Israeli-controlled militia, the so-called 'South Lebanon army' (SLA), led by Maj. Sa'ad Haddad, until his death in December 1983, and subsequently by Maj.-Gen. Antoine Lahad, who was appointed in March 1984. In the latter month, under the influence of Syria, President Gemayel of Lebanon abrogated the 17 May (1983) agreement with Israel. The agreement was already effectively a 'dead letter' but the Israeli Government of Itzhak Shamir was committed not to withdraw the Israeli Defence Forces (IDF) while Syrian forces remained in the north of Lebanon.

The Government of National Unity, formed in September 1984, pledged itself to withdrawing the IDF from Lebanon, and to tackling the problems of the economy. To ensure the security of its northern border, Israel sought Syrian commitments not to redeploy its forces in areas evacuated by the IDF; to prevent the infiltration of PLO terrorists into the south of Lebanon; to grant freedom of operation to the SLA; and to allow the UN Interim Force in Lebanon (UNIFIL), a peace-keeping body operating in southern Lebanon since 1978, to deploy north of the SLA area up to Syrian lines in the Beka'a valley. Lebanon demanded $10,000m. in reparations, and the unconditional withdrawal of the IDF. Israel dropped its demand for simultaneous Syrian withdrawal, and Syria approved a series of talks, under UN auspices, between Lebanese and Israeli army representatives, to agree the terms of the IDF's withdrawal. The talks began in Naqoura (Lebanon) in November and repeatedly foundered on the question of which forces should take the place of the IDF. The Lebanese, influenced by Syria, wanted UNIFIL to police the Israel-Lebanon border (as it had been mandated to do in 1978), and the Lebanese Army to deploy north of the Litani river, between UNIFIL and the Syrians. Israel wanted UNIFIL to be deployed north of the Litani while the SLA patrolled the southern Lebanese border. Israel withdrew from the talks, and on 14 January 1985 the Israeli Cabinet voted to take unilateral steps towards withdrawal, arousing fears of outright civil war in southern Lebanon. The Cabinet agreed a three-phase withdrawal plan whose final aim was the return of the IDF to the international border within nine months. The cost of the withdrawal plan was put at $100m. and that of the entire 'Operation Peace for Galilee' at $3,500m.

The first phase of the withdrawal took place in February 1985 and involved the evacuation of the IDF from the western occupied sector, around Sidon, to the Litani river area, around Nabatiyah. The UN force was asked to police the vacated area with the Lebanese Army. The second phase, in which the IDF was to evacuate the occupied central and eastern sector (including the southern Beka'a valley), began on 3 March, with no fixed duration. Guerrilla groups from the majority Shi'ite population of southern Lebanon, who had resisted the Israeli occupation, now attacked the IDF with greater frequency in retreat. Israel responded by adopting an 'Iron Fist' policy, purging Shi'ite villages of suspected guerrillas or attacking them indiscriminately, causing the deaths of innocent inhabitants. Instead of decreasing, the number of attacks on Israeli forces, organized by the Shi'ite National Resistance Movement, Amal and Hezbollah (the Party of God), multiplied. Israel accelerated the process of withdrawal, and the second stage was completed with the evacuation of Tyre on 29 April.

On 4 April, prior to withdrawing from that part of western Lebanon, Israel released 750 Shi'ite prisoners, detained during the 'Iron Fist' operation, from Ansar Camp. At the same time, contrary to international conventions (as they were not prisoners of war), 1,200 Lebanese and Palestinian detainees were transferred to prisons in Israel. On 20 May 1,150 Lebanese and Palestinian prisoners were exchanged for three Israeli prisoners of war. The release of 766 Shi'ite prisoners, transferred from Lebanon to Atlit prison in Israel, became the central demand of members of the extremist Shi'ite Hezbollah who hijacked a US airliner in June and held its largely American crew and passengers hostage at Beirut airport and subsequently at secret locations in the city. Israel refused to release the prisoners unless requested to do so by the USA. Some 450 were freed at the end of June and in early July, although Israel denied that their release was related to the Beirut hostage crisis, which ended on 30 June with the release of the hostages. All the Shi'ite prisoners had been released by mid-September.

The third and final stage of the IDF's withdrawal, taking it behind Israel's northern border and leaving a buffer strip (between 10 km and 20 km wide) along the Lebanese side of the border, controlled by the SLA, was completed on 10 June, three months ahead of the original schedule. However, about 500 Israeli troops remained inside Lebanon to assist the SLA in their policing role, which is not recognized by the UN or the Lebanese Government. The invasion of Lebanon had cost the lives of nearly 700 Israelis. With the Israeli presence in Lebanon reduced to a token force, Syria withdrew about 10,000 troops from the Beka'a valley, leaving about 25,000 in position. After the Israeli evacuation was completed, Shi'ite guerrilla attacks on the SLA gradually increased, and UNIFIL has been impotent to prevent the fighting. A potentially more significant development, as regards Israeli security, was the resurgence of the PLO in refugee camps in southern Lebanon. Israel made bombing raids on PLO bases during 1986, in direct retaliation for rocket attacks on Israeli border towns, and in an attempt to hinder the PLO's revival.

In 1984 Israel rejected a call by King Hussein of Jordan for a Middle East peace conference involving all the interested parties in the Arab–Israeli conflict, preferring talks to be confined to itself, Jordan, Egypt and the USA. The formal establishment by King Hussein and Yasser Arafat of a joint position on future peace talks (on 23 February 1985 in Amman), providing for a combined Jordanian-Palestinian delegation to such talks and foreseeing the creation of a confederation of Jordan and a Palestinian state on the West Bank, gave new impetus to the search for a diplomatic solution to the Palestinian question. Israel supports the involvement of the five permanent members of the UN Security Council in the peace process and the need for talks to proceed on the basis of UN Security Council Resolutions 242 and 338, but, after the Amman accord, it rejected King Hussein's reiterated proposal of an international peace conference, under UN auspices, and the suggestion of preliminary talks between the USA and a joint Jordanian-Palestinian delegation containing members of the PLO. Israel remained interested only in direct talks with a delegation containing 'authentic Palestinian representatives' from the Occupied Territories, while the USA is committed not to hold talks with members of the PLO until it recognizes Israel's right to exist, renounces terrorism and, in effect, accepts UN Security Council Resolution 242. The PLO has consistently refused to recognize this resolution as a basis for negotiation, as it makes mention only of a Palestinian 'refugee problem' and not of the right of Palestinians to self-determination. In July Israel rejected a list of seven Palestinians, five of whom were members of the PLO loyal to Arafat or had links with the Palestine National Council, whom King Hussein had presented to the USA as candidates for membership of a joint Jordanian-Palestinian delegation to preliminary peace talks. Shimon Peres subsequently approved the nomination of the two Palestinians on the list who lived in the West Bank, but Richard Murphy, the US Assistant Secretary of State, refused to meet a Jordanian-Palestinian delegation while on a tour of the Middle East in September. Further progress was then hampered by a series of terrorist incidents in which the PLO was implicated.

Firstly, in September, three Israelis were murdered by terrorists in Larnaca, Cyprus. Israel held the PLO's élite Force 17 responsible and, at the beginning of October, bombed the organization's headquarters in Tunis, killing about 70 people, including a dozen Tunisian civilians. Then, in October, the Italian cruise ship the *Achille Lauro* was 'hijacked' in the eastern Mediterranean by members of a wing of the Palestine Liberation Front, led by Abu Abbas, which is nominally loyal to Yasser Arafat. They killed a Jewish American passenger before surrendering in Port Said, Egypt.

These incidents gave Israel further cause to reject the PLO as a prospective partner in peace negotiations, though they may have been inspired by Syria to discredit Arafat. Meanwhile, Jewish settlers in the Occupied Territories had made it clear that any attempt to negotiate Israeli sovereignty of the disputed areas would be greeted by a campaign of civil disobedience.

In September 1985, while reiterating the need for talks to take place in the framework of an international conference involving all the interested parties (including the USSR and

Syria), King Hussein suggested modified preliminary meetings between the USA and a Jordanian delegation excluding Palestinians, to be followed by Israeli recognition of the PLO and talks between Israel and a joint Jordanian-Palestinian delegation. King Hussein and Shimon Peres met secretly in the south of France in October, and later, in a speech at the UN, Peres intimated that he would not rule out an international conference. Rumours of a further secret meeting between the two leaders were followed at the end of October by the calculated 'leaking' to the Israeli press of a document drawn up by the Prime Minister's office, which purported to summarize the state of negotiations between Israel and Jordan and the points of agreement and dispute in a list of peace proposals. The document suggested the establishment of an interim Israeli-Jordanian condominium over the West Bank, granting a form of Palestinian autonomy, and recorded mutual agreement on the desirability of an international forum for peace talks, with Israel agreeing to the participation of the USSR (provided that it re-established diplomatic relations with Israel) and Syria (with which Jordan was improving relations) but not the PLO. These reports led to considerable criticism of Peres by Likud. Ariel Sharon, the Ministry of Industry and Trade, was particularly outspoken. Peres demanded a public apology, threatening to dismiss Sharon from the Cabinet. With the coalition government in danger of collapse if he refused, Sharon grudgingly apologized. In December 1985 17 people were killed when terrorists, believed to belong to Abu Nidal's anti-Arafat Fatah Revolutionary Council, attacked passengers at the desks of the Israeli state airline, El Al, in Rome and Vienna airports.

King Hussein of Jordan formally severed political links with the PLO in February 1986. It emerged that, in January, the USA (without Israel's knowledge) had undertaken to invite the PLO to an international peace conference, on condition that the PLO publicly accepted UN Security Council Resolutions 242 and 338 as the basis for negotiation. Arafat refused to make such a commitment without a similar acknowledgement by the USA of the Palestinians' right to self-determination.

Since February 1986 King Hussein has resisted Israeli requests for direct talks excluding the PLO. However, Jordan and Israel appear to have a common interest in fostering a Palestinian constituency in the West Bank, which is independent of the PLO and with which they can deal, and, to this extent, their policy in the region has coincided since the demise of the joint Jordanian/PLO peace initiative. Israel revived a programme of limited Palestinian autonomy, with the appointment of Palestinians to replace Israeli officials in municipal government, though this has resulted in civil protest by pro-PLO Palestinians and the intimidation or assassination of Israeli appointees. Jordan has begun a major investment programme in the West Bank and gave its approval to an Israeli proposal for the establishment of a branch of the Amman-based Cairo-Amman Bank in Nablus, under dual Jordanian/Israeli authority, to provide financial services to the Palestinian community. The branch was opened in November 1986.

A meeting took place between Shimon Peres and King Hassan of Morocco in Ifrane (Morocco) in July 1986, the first direct contact between an Israeli leader and the head of an Arab state other than Egypt. The meeting was condemned by Syria and Libya, and welcomed only by President Mubarak of Egypt.

In January 1985, in an attempt to improve relations with Egypt, Israel took part in the first talks for two years on the question of the sovereignty of the tiny Taba area, on the Red Sea, which Israel did not vacate when it left Sinai in 1982. The question of relations with Egypt in general and of the Taba issue in particular threatened the survival of the fragile Israeli Government of National Unity on several occasions during 1985. In particular, Shimon Peres and Itzhak Shamir were divided over the repeated Egyptian demand that the matter of sovereignty over Taba should be taken to international arbitration. Peres approved the proposal, as he regards the Taba issue as the key to a general improvement in Israeli-Egyptian relations and to progress on broader issues affecting the Middle East, while to Egypt a settlement of the Taba dispute is an absolute condition for the normalization of relations. In January 1986 the Israeli Cabinet agreed to submit the case to international arbitration, provided that this procedure was preceded by an eight-month period of conciliation (for which Shamir had argued) during which the chosen arbitrators would attempt to secure a compromise solution before delivering a binding decision. In August the terms of this process were finally agreed, and a list of potential arbitrators was submitted to both countries by the USA. After the appointment of the arbitration committee (consisting of three independent members and one each from Egypt and Israel) and the demarcation of the Taba enclave had been concluded, final approval was granted to the arbitration document by both countries on 10 September 1986, and the process of arbitration began in December.

On 11 September 1986 President Mubarak of Egypt and Prime Minister Peres of Israel met in Alexandria, Egypt, to discuss ways of reviving the Middle East peace process. They agreed to form a committee to prepare for an international peace conference, but failed to agree on the nature of the Palestinian representation at such a conference. Following the 'summit' meeting (the first between Egypt and Israel since August 1981) and the signing of the Taba arbitration agreement, President Mubarak appointed Muhammad Bassiouni as Egyptian ambassador to Israel. The previous ambassador had been recalled from Israel in 1982, following the Israeli invasion of Lebanon.

Apart from the Taba issue, a number of disagreements threatened the survival of the coalition government during 1986. A difference of opinion between Prime Minister Peres and Itzhak Modai, the Minister of Finance, over the management of the economy culminated, in April, with Modai's accusing Peres of having no understanding of economics. Peres demanded Modai's resignation as Minister of Finance, but the Likud members of the Cabinet threatened to resign *en masse* if Modai was replaced or dismissed, despite Modai's offer to resign. The crisis was resolved after 10 days, when a compromise solution was agreed, whereby Modai exchanged Cabinet portfolios with Moshe Nissim, the Minister of Justice.

The activities of Shin Bet, the Israeli internal security service, came under scrutiny in 1986, when it was suggested that the deaths of two Palestinians under interrogation, following the 'hijacking' of an Israeli bus in April 1984, had been deliberately concealed. Two official inquiries, between April 1984 and August 1985, confirmed that the two terrorists had 'died at a later stage' (contrary to the evidence of Shin Bet agents, who maintained that they had died at the scene of the 'hijacking') and identified Brig.-Gen. Itzhak Mordechai as the prime suspect in their deaths. Mordechai was acquitted by a military court in August 1985, and the Attorney-General, Itzhak Zamir, initiated investigations into the affair. He was told by leading Shin Bet officials that Avraham Shalom, the director of the agency, had ordered the prisoners' execution and had falsified evidence and suborned witnesses at the two official inquiries. In May 1986 the Cabinet refused to suspend Shalom, and rejected Zamir's recommendation of a police inquiry. On 1 June Zamir, who had wanted to resign in February, was replaced as Attorney-General by Josef Harish. At the end of June Shalom resigned as director of Shin Bet, after he and three of his deputies had been assured of a pardon and immunity from prosecution by the President of Israel, Chaim Herzog. In a letter to President Herzog, Shalom stated that his actions had been taken 'on authority and with permission', presumably from Itzhak Shamir, to whom, as Prime Minister at the time of the killings and the cover-up, he was responsible.

In July the Cabinet voted, by a narrow margin, in favour of holding a police inquiry into the affair, rather than the full judicial inquiry which was advocated by the Labour group. Later that month, having criticized Shimon Peres for his handling of the Shin Bet controversy, Itzhak Modai resigned from the Cabinet. The inquiry, which reported in December, found that there was no case to answer against Shamir.

In accordance with the terms of the agreement under which the coalition Government of National Unity was formed in September 1984, Shimon Peres, the leader of the Labour Party, resigned as Prime Minister on 10 October 1986, to allow Itzhak Shamir, the Minister of Foreign Affairs and the leader of Likud (the other main party grouping in the coalition), to assume the premiership on 14 October. The transfer of power was delayed while the coalition parties negotiated the composition of the new Cabinet, which was approved by the Knesset on 20 October. The Labour group had objected to the reinstatement of Itzhak Modai, but his name was finally included in the Cabinet, in which he was one of five ministers without portfolio. The only unscheduled changes in the Cabinet were the replacement of Dr Josef Burg, who resigned as Minister of Religious Affairs, by Zvulun Hammer, and the naming of Shoshana Arbeli-Almoslino as Minister of Health, instead of Mordechai Gur, who refused to serve under Itzhak Shamir. The composition of the inner Cabinet was unchanged. Peres and Shamir duly exchanged posts on 20 October.

In October 1986, using information supplied by Mordechai Vanunu, a former technician at Israel's nuclear research establishment at Dimona, *The Sunday Times* of London claimed that Israel had succeeded in developing thermonuclear weapons and was stockpiling them at Dimona. Vanunu subsequently disappeared from London, and at the end of October Israeli authorities admitted that he was in their custody and would be tried for breaching national security.

Following the revelation in a Lebanese magazine, in November 1986, that the USA had made several deliveries of military equipment to Iran during the preceding year, it emerged that the sale of weapons and spare parts had been effected through Israeli intermediaries. According to some reports, Israel had itself been supplying armaments to Iran since the outbreak of the Iran–Iraq war in 1980.

Government

Supreme authority in Israel rests with the Knesset (Assembly), with 120 members elected by universal suffrage for four years (subject to dissolution), on the basis of proportional representation. The President, a constitutional Head of State, is elected by the Knesset for five years. Executive power lies with the Cabinet, led by the Prime Minister. The Cabinet takes office after receiving a vote of confidence in the Knesset, to which it is responsible. Ministers are usually members of the Knesset, but non-members may be appointed.

The country is divided into six administrative districts. Local authorities are elected at the same time as elections to the Knesset. There are 31 municipalities (including two Arab towns), 115 local councils (46 Arab and Druze) and 49 regional councils (one Arab) comprising representatives of 700 villages.

Defence

The Israel Defence Forces consist of a small nucleus of commissioned and non-commissioned regular officers, a contingent called up for national service, and a large reserve. Men are called up for 36 months of military service, and women for 24 months. Military service is compulsory for Jews and Druzes, but voluntary for Christians and Arabs. Total regular armed forces numbered 149,000 (including 93,300 conscripts) in July 1986, and full mobilization to 700,000 can be quickly achieved with reserves of 554,000. The armed forces are divided into an army of 112,000, a navy of 9,000 and an air force of 28,000. The defence budget for 1986/87 was 8,030m. new shekels (US $5,378m.).

Economic Affairs

Of the total labour force of about 1,460,000, about 6% are employed in agriculture and about 30% in industry (manufacturing, mining and construction). Continuous immigration and an economic boycott by Arab countries have obliged Israel to develop agriculture and industry on an intensive scale and to seek far afield for international trade. Citrus fruit is the main export crop and the oldest export industry. However, sales are declining in both volume and value, owing to competition (particularly from Spain), adverse weather and fluctuating exchange rates. Earnings from exports of citrus fruit declined from US $256m. in 1978/79 to $186m. in 1981/82 and are not believed to have exceeded $125m. in 1983/84. Agriculture is the second largest export-earner, after cut diamonds, which earn more than $1,000m. per year. Israel is second only to Belgium in processing diamonds. The value of all exports rose by 80% between 1977 and 1981 but declined in 1982 and 1983.

During 1983 a major economic crisis developed. The shekel (which replaced the Israeli pound in 1980) was being supported at an artificially high level in 1982 and 1983 as part of a strategy to curb an inflation rate which exceeded 100% every year in 1980–83. Israel's gross domestic product grew in real terms, by only 1.0% in 1982, and by 1.8% in 1983. Meanwhile, exports continued a two-year decline while imports rose; Israel's foreign debt was $24,200m. in 1983, the highest per caput in the world; the cost of servicing this debt amounted to the total amount of US aid for the 1984 fiscal year—$2,400m. (Israel is the largest recipient of US military and economic aid); the trade deficit was $3,470m. in 1983, a 17% increase compared with 1982; the deficit on the current balance of payments exceeded $5,000m. in 1983; defence expenditure, already absorbing more than one-quarter of the country's gross national product, increased as a result of commitments in Lebanon, costing an estimated $1m. per day; the programme for establishing Jewish settlements on the occupied West Bank, and the costly settlement of a strike by the nation's doctors in July 1983, added to the economic burden. From September 1982 the Treasury had made the reduction of inflation its priority, using heavy subsidization in an attempt to keep increases in the price of basic commodities down to 5% per month, and allowing a gradual, monthly depreciation of the shekel of no more than 5% against the US dollar. Any impact which these measures may have had on inflation was effectively dissipated by the quarterly cost-of-living increment which is received by every salaried employee as a result of the indexation of wages to inflation. At the same time, the artificially high exchange rate of the shekel was making exports unprofitable and imports more attractive.

The shekel was devalued by 7.5% in August, and Yoram Aridor, the Minister of Finance, announced cuts in government spending, with the heaviest reductions intended for the defence budget, but he managed to obtain Cabinet approval for only two-thirds of the proposed $1,000m. in cuts. With a major devaluation of the shekel apparently inevitable, Israelis rushed to buy dollars, selling even their bank shares. This trend continued during the political uncertainty following Begin's resignation in September, and trading on the stock exchange was suspended for two weeks in October. The shekel was devalued by 23% in October, and food subsidies were reduced by 50%, followed by cuts in support for electricity, water and public transport. Aridor, in proposing the temporary use of the US dollar as legal tender (to undercut the system of cost-of-living increments and to give his austerity measures a chance to reduce inflation), was forced to resign. His replacement, Yigal Cohen-Orgad, made a reduction in the balance-of-payments deficit his priority, and embarked on pruning $2,000m. from current budget expenditure before the end of the year.

Labour unrest grew as inflation accelerated at the end of 1983 to 190%. A new round of price increases in January 1984, coupled with the reduction of food subsidies, meant that food prices had trebled in three months. To avert a wave of strikes, the Government approved a 46.5% cost-of-living increment for wage-earners in January, amounting to 85% of the increase in inflation during the preceding quarter. The Cabinet decided that some 10% (more than US $600m.) would be cut from the defence budget for 1984/85, though $300m. of this would be redistributed US defence aid. The total budget was to be $22,700m., while cuts in departmental appropriations amounted to $800m. In response to Cohen-Orgad's economies, the real value of wages fell by 25% in the year to March 1984. He allowed the shekel to depreciate in line with inflation, the control of which was no longer the Government's principal aim. As a result, the annual rate of inflation rose from 150% in October 1983, when Cohen-Orgad took office, to about 400% in July 1984. Valuable time for dealing with the problems of the economy was wasted while a new coalition pact was worked out after the July general election.

The new Government (which included a new Minister of Finance, Itzhak Modai) immediately requested more aid from the USA, including $1,000m., unrelated to Israel's annual grant (set at $2,600m. in fiscal 1985 and comprising $1,200m. in economic and $1,400m. in military aid), to be paid at once. The US Government, in turn, refused to give extra aid until Israel reduced spending and introduced a thoroughgoing economic austerity programme to curb inflation. Such a programme required the agreement of the employers' organizations and of the Histadrut (the General Federation of Labour in Israel), and negotiations were not initially successful. The Histadrut opposed a planned 'freeze' of wages and prices, and refused to accept a reduction in the cost-of-living increment, which stood at 80% of inflation. Planned expenditure cuts of $1,000m. were whittled down to $250m. by dissenting ministers. The Government did devalue the shekel by 9% in September but the principal effect of the removal of subsidies on oil, the cutting of those on electricity and foodstuffs, and consequent price increases was that inflation rose even more sharply than before. The retail price index rose by 21.4% in September, the highest rise for any month in Israel's history until October, when the rate was 24.3% (equivalent to an annual inflation rate of 1,260%). A decision to cut subsidies on basic foods by a further 24%–95% had to be reversed in October, when a number of ministers protested that they had not been consulted.

The Government's economic programme was approved by employers and unions in November 1984. To last for three months, the aim of the package was to cut the standard of living by 10%–12%, and to reduce inflation to a monthly rate of 10% (still equivalent to an annual rate of 200%). Prices, wages, taxes and profits were 'frozen', while the shekel was maintained at its existing value against the US dollar. In addition, one-third was cut from the cost-of-living increment, reducing it to 55% of inflation, and it was decided to shed 14,000 jobs from the public sector (10% of its work-force). The negative effects of these measures were that unemployment, traditionally 2%–3% of the labour force, rose to almost 6%, a degree of social unrest was discernible, and special courts had to be established to enforce the 'freeze'. However, this monetary policy had an almost immediate effect. Inflation fell to 19.5% in November (equivalent to an annual rate of 486%), and to only 3.7% in December, though it rose to 5.3% in January 1985. Inflation in the year to December 1984 was 444.9%, compared with 190% in 1983. The gross national product (GNP), which had not risen at all during 1982, rose by less than 1% during 1983 and 1984.

Lengthy negotiations between government, unions and employers led to the signing of an agreement for a second economic programme, which was to come into operation for eight months when the term of its predecessor expired on 31 January 1985. In anticipation of the second package (and with a view to saving $1,000m.), subsidies on many essential goods were heavily cut. The eight-month plan aimed to allow prices of unsubsidized goods to rise by an average of 3%–5% per month, while prices of most subsidized goods would not be allowed to rise by more than 13%. Subsidies on oil, electricity and water were either to be reduced or removed altogether, so that prices would rise by between 25% and 50%. To offset these increases, wage-earners were to receive a flat-rate cash compensation and 5% monthly tax relief, but the cost-of-living increment was not to take into account increases in the price of subsidized goods.

The austerity programme had been intended to clear the way for substantial reductions in government expenditure. The Cabinet agreed a budget for 1985/86, involving planned expenditure of $23,300m., somewhat more than that for 1984/85, with cuts in spending ($1,300m.) which were considerably less than the amount for which Itzhak Modai, the Minister of Finance, had argued.

Since July 1984 Israel's reserves of foreign exchange have been well below the $3,000m. regarded by the Bank of Israel as the minimum acceptable working level and less than the cost of three months of essential imports. The inability to implement a policy of strict budgetary control did not assist Israel's cause in securing increased aid from the US Government, which repeatedly stressed the need for more stringent economic measures. For the year beginning in October 1985 Israel was seeking an increase in US aid to $4,100m. (comprising $1,900m. in economic aid and $2,200m. in military aid). President Reagan gained the approval of Congress for military aid of $1,800m. but any increase in economic aid remained conditional on concerted action to reform the economy.

The second 'package' of economic measures was introduced on 4 February 1985. However, consumer prices rose by 13.5% in February, 12.1% in March, 19% in April, 6.8% in May and 14.9% in June, equivalent to an annual rate of more than 300%. The country's reserves of foreign exchange, which fell to $2,300m. in January 1985, continued to dwindle. In March the US Government agreed to provide economic aid of $1,200m. in 1985/86, and in June the US House of Representatives approved additional emergency aid of $1,500m. to be spread over 1985/86 and 1986/87 to shore up Israel's foreign currency reserves.

The sharp rise in inflation recorded in April prompted the Government to implement a new set of austerity measures in May. Value added tax, the tax on foreign travel and the purchase tax on foreign goods were all increased; wages and contracts in the public sector were 'frozen' for three months; and a law was approved which limited the Government's power to cover the budget deficit by ordering the Central Bank to print money, a practice which the Government undertook to phase out entirely within two years. Then, at the end of May, controversial increases were announced in the prices of goods (those of basic subsidized foods were increased by 25%) and many services. The Histadrut opposed any attempt to alter the existing arrangement of wages indexation, which continued, though to a lesser degree than previously, to undercut government attempts to reduce spending.

A wave of strikes hit the country in June but a new three-month economic stabilization programme, to reduce proposed government expenditure, was approved by the Cabinet at the beginning of July. Food subsidies were cut so that prices rose by an average of 25%, and the shekel was devalued by 18.8% to US $1 = 1,500 shekels, at which point most prices, the currency exchange rate and wages were to be 'frozen' until October. Health, education and welfare spending were reduced and ministry budgets were cut by a total of $750m., despite strong opposition in the Cabinet. The Knesset approved the measures, and on the same day more than 1m. Israelis participated in a 24-hour general strike in protest against them.

Two weeks of negotiation produced a compromise agreement between the Government, the employers and the Histadrut on 16 July and averted a prolonged general strike. Salaried employees were to receive an 18% increase in pay, after which their earnings were to be 'frozen', though from October they would be compensated for every cumulative rise in the consumer price index of 4% or more, or after every two months. (Under the previous arrangement, compensation was for every rise of 12% in inflation.) On 24 July, after further negotiations, the Cabinet abandoned its attempt to cut public-sector wages by 3%.

The rate of inflation in July was, at 27.5%, a new record for a single month, corresponding to an annual rate of 380% and a cumulative rate for 1985 of 150%. In August, the first month of the three-month programme, the rate of inflation fell to 3.9%, while in September it was a mere 3%, the lowest monthly figure for four years. The trade deficit for August fell to $213m., down 10.7% compared with the corresponding month in 1984. However, the Government was engaged upon a cost-saving programme which involved the shedding of more than 26,000 public sector jobs, while about 1,000 companies were believed to be in serious financial difficulties, placing a further 40,000 jobs at risk. Unemployment rose by 2% during the July–September plan, and by November some 120,000 people, or 8.3% of the working population (above the 7.5% 'ceiling' which, at the beginning of 1985, the Government had announced to be acceptable), were out of work, compared with about 72,000 in April.

At the end of September the three-month price 'freeze' was extended until the end of June 1986. The Histadrut was opposed to the further suspension of wage indexation but offered to forego all pay increases until April 1986, in return for the preservation of the principle of free collective bargaining. A new shekel, worth 1,000 of the old units, was officially introduced on 1 January 1986, partly as a financial practicality (the old shekel had become unwieldy in calculation, owing to inflation) and to restore faith in the currency in the face of the widespread use of the US dollar as an alternative currency in barter and on the 'black market'. The Cabinet cut the budget for the fiscal year 1986/87 by $580m. in December 1985. The proposed budget totalled $21,200m. (30,300m. new shekels), with defence spending claiming the biggest share, after the Minister of Defence had resisted Finance Ministry demands for reductions in its allowance. Subsidies on basic foodstuffs, public transport and services were to be cut by $120m.

The economic stabilization programme, launched in July 1985, continued to contribute to low monthly rates of inflation: in October the rate was 4.7%; in November 0.5%; and in December 1.4% (giving an overall rate for 1985 of 185.2%). In January 1986 consumer prices actually fell by 1.3% (the first monthly decline for more than a decade), though in February they rose by 1.6%. Between July 1985 and the end of the year the real value of wages fell by about 25%, and in February 1986 the Histadrut called a strike of public-sector employees to protest against the continuation of stringent monetary policy in the 1986/87 budget.

The monthly rate of inflation remained below 2% from March until the end of June, and in July no rise in prices was recorded. The success of the economic programme was indicated by the announcement of a surplus (the first ever) of $1,100m. on the current account of the balance of payments in fiscal 1985; an achievement that was only in part due to emergency economic aid of $750m. from the USA. Israel's reserves of foreign exchange increased by 60% between July 1985 and July 1986, to about $3,500m., and the trade deficit declined by 17% during 1985.

In June 1986 the Knesset approved an extension of the price 'freeze' until the end of the year, while the Government sought the co-operation of the Histadrut in 'freezing' public-sector wages for a further 12 months. During 1986, with lower inflation, compensation payments, and the partial indexation that was still in operation, wages rose to be higher than they had been prior to the introduction of the economic austerity programme in July 1985. A combination of wage rises, a 10% fall in exports during the last quarter of 1986, and an increase in the level of imported consumer goods, threatened to offset the benefits of the Government's austerity measures. The rate of inflation rose to 2.4% in October, and to 2.9% in November; it fell to 1.5% in December, but rose to 2.1% in January 1987. (The overall rate for 1986 was 19%.) After initial opposition, a new programme of measures was introduced in January 1987, with the approval of the manufacturers' association and the Histadrut. The new 10-point programme was devised by Moshe Nissim, the Minister of Finance. A proposed reduction of 180m. new shekels in the defence budget was successfully resisted in the Cabinet. Total recommended reductions of planned expenditure by 500m. new shekels in the 1987/88 budget were restricted to 400m. new shekels, but they included a cut of more than 100m. new shekels in government subsidies on basic commodities. In addition there were to be large cut-backs in spending on health, education and social welfare; a major reform of the tax system; a wages 'freeze'; a two-month postponement of cost-of-living payments, which were to be cut by 2.7%; and reductions in the public-sector work-force. The programme was to be introduced in two stages, in January and on 1 April. On 12 January the Cabinet approved a budget of 34,000m. new shekels for fiscal 1987/88, incorporating spending cuts which still left a substantial deficit. Two days later, the shekel was devalued by 10.2% in relation to a 'basket' of international currencies. (The shekel, which had formerly been aligned with the US dollar, was linked with a 'basket' of currencies in July 1986, in an attempt to prevent wide fluctuations in the exchange rate and to stabilize returns from foreign trade.)

Social Welfare

There is a highly advanced system of social welfare. Under the National Insurance Law, the state provides retirement pensions, benefits for industrial injury and maternity, and allowances for large families. The Histadrut (General Federation of Labour), to which more than 90% of all Jewish workers in Israel belong, provides sickness benefits and medical care. The Ministry of Social Welfare provides for general assistance, relief grants, child care and other social services. In 1983 Israel had 11,895 physicians, equivalent to one for every 339 inhabitants, one of the best doctor-patient ratios in the world. In 1985 there were 151 hospitals (of which 60 were private) and 27,500 beds.

Education

Israel has European standards of literacy and educational services. Free compulsory primary education is provided for all children between five and 15 years of age. There is also secondary, vocational and agricultural education. Post-primary education is also free, and it lasts six years, of which four are compulsory. Enrolment at primary and secondary schools in 1981 was equivalent to 89% of children aged six to 17. There are six universities, one institute of technology and one institute of science (the Weizmann Institute), which incorporates a graduate school of science.

Tourism

Israel's tourist attractions include biblical sites, places holy to three religions, sunny beaches and kibbutzim (collective settlements). The Government maintains 20 tourist offices abroad. In 1985 1,264,367 tourists visited Israel.

Public Holidays

The Sabbath starts at sunset on Friday and ends at nightfall on Saturday. The Jewish year 5748 begins on 24 September 1987, and the year 5749 on 12 September 1988.

1987: 15 March (Purim), 14–20 April (Passover), 4 May (Independence Day), 3 June (Shavuot), 24 September (Rosh Hashanah, Jewish New Year), 3 October (Yom Kippur), 8–15 October (Succot—half-day holidays), 16 October (Simhat Torah).

1988: 3 March (Purim), 2–8 April (Passover), 21 April (Independence Day), 22 May (Shavuot), 12 September (Rosh Hashanah, Jewish New Year), 21 September (Yom Kippur), 26 September–3 October (Succot—half-day holidays), 4 October (Simhat Torah).

(The Jewish festivals and fast days commence in the evening of the dates given.)

Islamic holidays are observed by Muslim Arabs, and Christian holidays by the Christian Arab community.

Weights and Measures

The metric system is in force.

1 dunum = 1,000 sq metres.

Currency and Exchange Rates

100 new agorot (singular: agora) = 1 new shekel (sheqel).

Exchange rates (30 September 1986):
£1 sterling = 2.1575 new shekels;
US $1 = 1.4910 new shekels.

Note: The new shekel, worth 1,000 of the former units, was introduced on 1 January 1986.

Statistical Survey

Source: Central Bureau of Statistics, Hakirya, Givat Ram, POB 13015, Jerusalem 91130; tel. (02) 211400.

Area and Population

AREA, POPULATION AND DENSITY

Area (sq km)	
Land	21,501
Inland water	445
Total	21,946*
Population (*de jure*; census results)†	
20 May 1972	3,147,683
4 June 1983	
Males	2,011,590
Females	2,026,030
Total	4,037,620
Population (*de jure*; official estimates at mid-year)†	
1983	4,076,200
1984	4,159,100
1985	4,233,000
Density (per sq km) at mid-1985	192.9

* 8,473.4 sq miles. Area includes East Jerusalem, annexed by Israel in June 1967.
† Including the population of East Jerusalem and Israeli residents in certain other areas under Israeli military occupation since June 1967. Beginning in December 1981, figures also include non-Jews in the Golan sub-district, an Israeli-occupied area of Syrian territory. Census results exclude adjustment for under-enumeration.

ADMINISTERED TERRITORIES*

	Area (sq km)	Population (31 December 1984)
Golan	1,176	21,400
Judaea and Samaria	5,879	793,400
Gaza Area†	n.a.	509,900
Total	n.a.	1,324,700

The area figures in this table refer to 1 October 1973. No later figures are available.
* The area and population of the Administered Territories have changed as a result of the October 1973 war.
† Not including El-Arish and Sinai which, as of April 1979 and April 1982 respectively, were returned to Egypt.

POPULATION BY RELIGION (census of 4 June 1983)

	Males	Females	Total	%
Jews	1,662,725	1,687,272	3,349,997	82.97
Muslims	268,644	257,995	526,639	13.04
Christians	45,897	48,260	94,157	2.33
Druze	33,833	32,028	65,861	1.63
Others	491	475	966	0.02
Total	2,011,590	2,026,030	4,037,620	100.00

PRINCIPAL TOWNS (population at 4 June 1983)

Jerusalem (capital)	428,668*	Petach-Tikva	123,868
Tel-Aviv—Jaffa	327,625	Ramat Gan	117,072
Haifa	235,775	Beersheba	110,813
Holon	133,460	Bene Beraq	96,150

* Including East Jerusalem, annexed in June 1967.

BIRTHS, MARRIAGES AND DEATHS*

	Registered live births		Registered marriages		Registered deaths	
	Number	Rate (per 1,000)	Number	Rate (per 1,000)	Number	Rate (per 1,000)
1978	92,602	25.1	29,379	7.9	25,153	6.8
1979	93,710	24.7	29,924	7.9	25,700	6.7
1980	94,321	24.3	29,592	7.6	26,325	6.8
1981	93,308	23.6	29,652	7.5	26,024	6.6
1982	96,695	24.0	29,555	7.3	27,714†	6.9
1983	98,724	24.0	31,096	7.6	27,824	6.8
1984	98,478	23.7	29,871	7.2	27,931	6.6
1985	99,376	23.5	29,158	6.9	n.a.	n.a.

* Including East Jerusalem.
† Excluding casualties of war.

IMMIGRATION*

	1983	1984	1985
Immigrants:			
on immigrant visas	5,711	11,974	4,665
on tourist visas†	1,516	1,070	802
Potential immigrants:			
on potential immigrant visas	7,658	5,519	4,240
on tourist visas†	2,021	1,418	935
Total	16,906	19,981	10,642

* Excluding immigrating citizens (693 in 1983; 446 in 1984) and Israeli residents returning from abroad.
† Figures refer to tourists who changed their status to immigrants or potential immigrants.

ECONOMICALLY ACTIVE POPULATION
(annual averages, '000 persons aged 14 and over)

	1983	1984	1985
Agriculture, forestry and fishing	73.7	72.1	78.1
Mining and quarrying	5.0	5.6	6.2
Manufacturing	298.4	306.1	307.4
Electricity and water	12.7	12.8	11.7
Construction	86.2	79.1	72.3
Trade, restaurants and hotels	169.9	169.9	169.5
Transport, storage and communications	87.0	89.6	86.4
Financing and business services	126.5	129.5	131.6
Public and community services	392.6	398.3	405.0
Personal and other services	77.4	86.2	90.9
Activities not adequately defined	9.6	9.8	9.1
Total employed	1,339.4	1,359.0	1,368.3
Unemployed	63.2	85.1	98.5
Total civilian labour force	1,402.6	1,444.1	1,466.8

Agriculture

PRINCIPAL CROPS (metric tons, year ending August)

	1982/83	1983/84	1984/85
Wheat	335,000	130,000	127,700
Barley	38,000	8,500	6,500
Sorghum	25,300	6,700	8,200
Groundnuts	23,100	21,500	22,900
Cotton lint	92,700	87,600	99,000
Cottonseed	153,100	136,500	163,400
Watermelons	78,200	90,000	91,200
Melons	42,300	40,500	40,800
Vegetables	764,500	767,200	762,700
Potatoes	199,300	198,200	204,400
Grapefruit	457,700	407,700	374,900
Lemons	72,000	58,000	66,000
Oranges:			
Shamouti	528,300	617,900	601,400
Lates	315,400	284,900	273,800
Other citrus fruit	149,000	154,500	170,900
Other fruit	470,400	458,600	470,400

LIVESTOCK ('000 head, in Jewish farms)

	1982/83	1983/84	1984/85
Cattle	279	288	294.5
Poultry*	17,500	15,000	12,200
Sheep	93	97	112
Goats	19	23	27.5

* Except broilers.

Milk production (million litres): 800.7 in 1982/83; 832.2 in 1983/84; 823.5 in 1984/85.

Fishing

('000 metric tons, live weight)

	1982	1983	1984
Inland waters	13.5	12.9	13.2
Mediterranean and Black Sea	4.1	4.2	4.6
Atlantic Ocean	6.0	5.3	5.0
Indian Ocean	0.1	0.1	0.1
Total catch	23.7	22.4	23.0

Source: FAO, *Yearbook of Fishery Statistics*.

Mining

	1983	1984	1985
Crude petroleum (million litres)	13	19	10
Natural gas (million cu m)	66	53	53
Phosphate rock ('000 metric tons)	1,966	2,065	2,195
Potash	1,518	1,795	1,953

Industry

SELECTED PRODUCTS

		1983	1984	1985
Wheat flour	'000 metric tons	506	516	507
Refined vegetable oils	metric tons	84,055	89,462	72,279
Margarine	'000 metric tons	33.2	34.2	32.7
Wine	'000 litres	16,509	17,584	18,348
Beer	'000 litres	40,805	41,525	51,066
Cigarettes	metric tons	6,373	6,714	6,709
Cotton yarn	metric tons	16,450	16,492	15,235
Newsprint	metric tons	2,014	772	819
Writing and printing paper	metric tons	53,583	64,875	63,944
Other paper	metric tons	28,904	32,131	29,334
Rubber tyres	'000	1,045	1,009	930
Ammonia	metric tons	97,411	101,064	106,424
Ammonium sulphate	metric tons	49,291	42,155	60,389
Sulphuric acid	'000 metric tons	171	189	178
Caustic soda	metric tons	30,974	28,501	31,248
Polyethylene	metric tons	62,500	73,953	73,879
Cement	'000 metric tons	2,058	1,889	1,596
Commercial vehicles	number	n.a.	2,146	1,130
Electricity	million kWh	14,042	14,346	15,010

ISRAEL *Statistical Survey*

Finance

CURRENCY AND EXCHANGE RATES

Monetary Units
100 agorot (singular: agora) = 1 new shekel (sheqel).

Denominations
Notes: 5, 10, 50 and 100 new shekels.

Sterling and Dollar Equivalents (30 September 1986)
£1 sterling = 2.1575 new shekels;
US $1 = 1.4910 new shekels;
100 new shekels = £46.35 = $67.07.

Average Exchange Rate (new shekels per US $)
1983   0.0562
1984   0.2932
1985   1.1788

Note: The new shekel, worth 1,000 of the former units, was introduced on 1 January 1986.

ORDINARY AND DEVELOPMENT BUDGET (million new shekels, year ending 31 March)

Actual revenue 1,494.6 in 1983/84; 8,220.6 in 1984/85. Actual expenditure 1,451.5 in 1983/84; 8,681.3 in 1984/85.

CENTRAL BANK RESERVES (US $ million at 31 December)

	1983	1984	1985
Gold*	37.2	34.9	39.1
IMF special drawing rights	1.7	0.1	0.1
Reserve position in IMF	36.4	—	—
Foreign exchange	3,613.1	3,060.2	3,680.1
Total	3,688.4	3,095.2	3,719.3

* Valued at 35 SDRs per troy ounce.
Source: IMF, *International Financial Statistics*.

MONEY SUPPLY (million new shekels at 31 December)

	1983	1984	1985
Currency outside banks	25	123	481
Demand deposits	38	153	508
Total money	63	276	989

COST OF LIVING
(Consumer Price Index, annual averages. Base: 1980 = 100)

	1982	1983	1984
All items	477.8	1,173.5	5,560.4

NATIONAL ACCOUNTS ('000 new shekels at current prices)
National Income and Product

	1981	1982	1983
Compensation of employees	132,090	298,755	762,718
Operating surplus	79,886	168,431	390,038
Domestic factor incomes	211,976	467,186	1,152,756
Consumption of fixed capital	34,309	77,111	187,209
Statistical discrepancy	−2,035	−12,401	−16,439
Gross domestic product at factor cost	244,250	531,896	1,323,526
Indirect taxes	28,504	64,940	176,894
Less Subsidies	23,448	39,223	86,401
GDP in purchasers' values	249,306	557,613	1,414,019
Net factor income from abroad	−7,701	−21,116	−54,325
Gross national product	241,605	536,497	1,359,694
Less Consumption of fixed capital	34,309	77,111	187,209
National income in market prices	207,296	459,386	1,172,485

Expenditure on the Gross Domestic Product

	1981	1982	1983
Government final consumption expenditure	91,419	190,553	451,286
Private final consumption expenditure	152,680	352,930	919,040
Increase in stocks	−5,223	−222	−9,852
Gross fixed capital formation	57,219	131,369	335,801
Total domestic expenditure	296,095	674,630	1,696,275
Exports of goods and services	113,517	228,302	550,097
Less Imports of goods and services	160,306	345,319	832,353
GDP in purchasers' values	249,306	557,613	1,414,019
GDP at constant 1980 prices	110,291	111,447	113,497

ISRAEL Statistical Survey

BALANCE OF PAYMENTS (US $ million)

	1983	1984	1985
Merchandise exports f.o.b.	5,538	6,187	6,601
Merchandise imports f.o.b.	−8,753	−8,790	−9,013
Trade balance	−3,215	−2,603	−2,412
Export of services	4,430	4,302	4,089
Import of services	−6,196	−6,462	−5,644
Balance on goods and services	−4,981	−4,763	−3,967
Private unrequited transfers (net)	926	818	871
Government unrequited transfers (net)	1,932	2,534	4,196
Current balance	−2,123	−1,411	1,100
Long-term capital (net)	2,344	1,261	−5
Short-term capital (net)	−340	−202	−479
Net errors and omissions	−443	−211	72
Total (net monetary movements)	−562	−563	688
Valuation changes (net)	4	43	−141
Changes in reserves	−557	−520	547

Source: IMF, *International Financial Statistics*.

External Trade

PRINCIPAL COMMODITIES (US $ '000)

Imports	1983	1984	1985
Diamonds, rough	719,466	818,400	1,098,600
Machinery and parts	1,455,100	1,272,100	1,250,800
Electrical machinery and parts	391,800	402,500	418,800
Iron and steel	266,600	291,700	268,200
Vehicles	574,500	319,500	411,300
Chemicals	574,100	620,800	609,500
Crude petroleum and petroleum products	1,495,300	1,455,300	1,352,000
Cereals	278,000	312,600	277,100
Textiles and textile articles	220,900	198,100	222,700
Ships, boats, aircraft etc.	195,400	159,500	1,000
Total (incl. others)	8,663,200	8,344,000	8,319,600

Exports	1983	1984	1985
Diamonds, worked	1,207,658	1,212,600	1,432,700
Clothing	208,400	217,700	218,300
Textiles and textile articles	117,000	132,900	135,800
Fruit and vegetables	459,800	475,100	541,900
Fertilizers	141,600	170,600	159,800
Organic chemicals	165,500	200,000	238,700
Inorganic chemicals	141,033	170,800	174,500
Transport equipment	230,100	200,900	316,200
Non-electric machinery	441,000	570,600	661,700
Electrical machinery and parts	184,500	250,700	216,900
Total (incl. others)	5,111,700	5,807,300	6,256,400

PRINCIPAL TRADING PARTNERS (US $ '000)

Imports	1983	1984	1985
Argentina	66,900	26,500	16,900
Australia	46,200	48,600	45,500
Austria	41,000	43,100	45,200
Belgium/Luxembourg	582,800	769,300	991,000
Brazil	29,300	56,000	37,800
Canada	104,700	94,800	103,500
Denmark	41,900	37,100	36,400
Finland	56,300	53,900	44,300
France	406,100	320,400	303,200
Germany, Fed. Rep.	1,040,400	941,700	898,300
Hong Kong	36,800	23,200	25,200
Italy	471,300	395,100	411,000
Japan	273,700	190,400	186,200
Netherlands	233,900	260,000	221,000
Romania	31,400	26,300	20,300
South Africa	169,600	165,100	174,700
Spain	124,700	84,200	77,100
Sweden	117,200	84,100	74,300
Switzerland	522,700	455,200	545,900
United Kingdom	667,300	695,300	753,900
USA	1,722,900	1,756,000	1,679,000
Yugoslavia	35,000	20,900	11,300

Exports	1983	1984	1985
Australia	47,500	62,000	58,500
Austria	35,100	32,700	31,100
Belgium/Luxembourg	251,200	231,000	235,400
Canada	42,600	59,700	65,300
France	248,700	236,200	262,500
Germany, Fed. Rep.	355,700	359,700	329,400
Greece	33,700	79,600	53,000
Hong Kong	148,700	156,100	190,100
Italy	194,500	212,000	249,100
Japan	188,600	189,700	210,000
Netherlands	231,500	257,600	276,100
Nigeria	32,300	20,000	11,500
Romania	13,000	25,400	10,000
Singapore	59,100	46,600	53,600
South Africa	82,800	104,400	63,800
Spain	27,000	29,500	29,900
Sweden	33,400	28,000	34,900
Switzerland	164,700	163,800	133,300
Turkey	26,800	28,700	34,400
United Kingdom	411,300	481,300	477,000
USA	1,329,200	1,644,600	2,138,000
Yugoslavia	24,700	22,200	23,600

Transport

RAILWAYS (traffic)

	1983	1984	1985
Passengers ('000)	2,790	3,002	2,814
Freight ('000 metric tons)	5,698	5,798	6,016

ROAD TRAFFIC, 1985 (motor vehicles)

Private cars (incl. station wagons)	613,680
Trucks, trailers	114,696
Buses	8,519
Taxis	7,150
Motor cycles, motor scooters	28,663
Other vehicles	3,509
Total	776,217

SHIPPING
(international sea-borne freight traffic, '000 metric tons)*

	1983	1984	1985
Goods loaded	6,456	7,085	9,205
Goods unloaded	8,862	9,283	7,088

* Excluding petroleum.

CIVIL AVIATION (El Al revenue flights only, '000)

	1983	1984	1985
Kilometres flown	28,103	36,360	40,152
Revenue passenger-km	5,303,000	6,302,000	6,608,000
Mail (tons)	1,070	1,150	1,046

Tourism

	1983	1984	1985
Tourist arrivals	1,166,820	1,259,200	1,264,367

Communications Media

(at December each year)

	1983	1984	1985
Telephones in use	1,527,000	1,625,000	n.a.
Daily newspapers	40	n.a.	21
Periodicals	n.a.	n.a.	890

Radio receivers: an estimated 3m. in 1983.
TV receivers: 582,000 in 1983.

Education

(1985/86, provisional figures)

	Schools	Pupils
Jewish		
Kindergarten	n.a.	256,700
Primary schools	1,307	470,746
Intermediate schools	283	107,624
Secondary schools	519	184,744
Vocational schools	306	89,132
Agricultural schools	26	4,924
Teacher training colleges	33	11,601
Others (handicapped)	206	11,963

	Schools	Pupils
Arab		
Kindergarten	n.a.	20,500
Primary schools	314	138,325
Intermediate schools	55	22,357
Secondary schools	79	33,537
Vocational schools	35	5,444
Agricultural schools	2	627
Teacher training colleges	2	420
Others (handicapped)	16	1,022

Directory

The Constitution

There is no written Constitution. In June 1950 the Knesset voted to adopt a State Constitution by evolution over an unspecified period. A number of laws, including the Law of Return (1950), the Nationality Law (1952), the State President (Tenure) Law (1952), the Education Law (1953) and the 'Yad-va-Shem' Memorial Law (1953), are considered as incorporated into the State Constitution. Other constitutional laws are: The Law and Administration Ordinance (1948), the Knesset Election Law (1951), the Law of Equal Rights for Women (1951), the Judges Act (1953), the National Service and National Insurance Acts (1953), and the Basic Law (The Knesset) (1958). The provisions of constitutional legislation that affect the main organs of government are summarized below:

THE PRESIDENT

The President is elected by the Knesset for five years.

Ten or more Knesset Members may propose a candidate for the Presidency.

Voting will be by secret ballot.

The President may not leave the country without the consent of the Government.

The President may resign by submitting his resignation in writing to the Speaker.

The President may be relieved of his duties by the Knesset for misdemeanour.

The Knesset is entitled to decide by a two-thirds majority that the President is incapacitated owing to ill health to fulfil his duties permanently.

The Speaker of the Knesset will act for the President when the President leaves the country, or when he cannot perform his duties owing to ill health.

THE KNESSET

The Knesset is the parliament of the State. There are 120 members.

It is elected by general, national, direct, equal, secret and proportional elections.

Every Israeli national of 18 years or over shall have the right to vote in elections to the Knesset unless a court has deprived him of that right by virtue of any law.

Every Israeli national of 21 and over shall have the right to be elected to the Knesset unless a court has deprived him of that right by virtue of any law.

The following shall not be candidates: the President of the State; the two Chief Rabbis; a judge (shofet) in office; a judge (dayan) of a religious court; the State Comptroller; the Chief of the General Staff of the Defence Army of Israel; rabbis and ministers of other religions in office; senior State employees and senior Army officers of such ranks and in such functions as shall be determined by law.

The term of office of the Knesset shall be four years.

The elections to the Knesset shall take place on the third Tuesday of the month of Cheshven in the year in which the tenure of the outgoing Knesset ends.

Election day shall be a day of rest, but transport and other public services shall function normally.

Results of the elections shall be published within 14 days.

The Knesset shall elect from among its members a Chairman and Vice-Chairman.

The Knesset shall elect from among its members permanent committees, and may elect committees for specific matters.

The Knesset may appoint commissions of inquiry to investigate matters designated by the Knesset.

The Knesset shall hold two sessions a year; one of them shall open within four weeks after the Feast of the Tabernacles, the other within four weeks after Independence Day; the aggregate duration of the two sessions shall not be less than eight months.

The outgoing Knesset shall continue to hold office until the convening of the incoming Knesset.

The members of the Knesset shall receive a remuneration as provided by law.

THE GOVERNMENT

The Government shall tender its resignation to the President immediately after his election, but shall continue with its duties until the formation of a new government. After consultation with representatives of the parties in the Knesset, the President shall charge one of the Members with the formation of a government. The government shall be composed of a Prime Minister and a number of ministers from among the Knesset Members or from outside the Knesset. After it has been chosen, the government shall appear before the Knesset and shall be considered as formed after having received a vote of confidence. Within seven days of receiving a vote of confidence, the Prime Minister and the other ministers shall swear allegiance to the State of Israel and its Laws and undertake to carry out the decisions of the Knesset.

The Government

HEAD OF STATE

President: Gen. CHAIM HERZOG (took office 5 May 1983).

THE CABINET
(January 1987)

Prime Minister: ITZHAK SHAMIR* (Likud-Herut).

Deputy Prime Minister and Minister of Foreign Affairs: SHIMON PERES* (Labour).

Vice-Premier and Minister of Education and Culture: ITZHAK NAVON* (Labour).

Vice-Premier and Minister of Housing and Construction: DAVID LEVI* (Likud-Herut).

Minister of Defence: ITZHAK RABIN* (Labour).

Minister of Finance: MOSHE NISSIM (Likud-Liberal).

Minister of Economics and Planning: GAD Y'ACOBI (Labour).

Minister of Agriculture: AYREH NEAHAMKIN (Labour).

Minister of Communications: Prof. AMNON RUBINSTEIN (Shinui).

Minister of Transport: CHAIM CORFU (Likud-Herut).

Minister of Energy and Infrastructure: MOSHE SHAHAL (Labour).

Minister of Justice and of Tourism: AVRAHAM SHARIR (Likud-Liberal).

Minister of Industry and Trade: ARIEL SHARON* (Likud-Herut).

Minister of Health: SHOSHANA ARBELI-ALMOSLINO (Labour).

Minister of the Interior: (vacant).

Minister of Religious Affairs: ZVULUN HAMMER (National Religious Party).

Minister of Labour and Social Affairs: MOSHE KATZAV (Likud-Herut).

Minister of Police Affairs: CHAIM BAR-LEV* (Labour).

Minister of Immigration and Absorption: YAACOV TSUR (Labour).

Minister of Science and Development: GIDEON PATT (Likud-Liberal).

Ministers without Portfolio: MOSHE ARENS* (Likud-Herut), JOSEF SHAPIRA (Morasha/National Religious Party), YIGAEL HURWITZ (Ometz), ITZHAK MODAI (Likud-Liberal), EZER WEIZMANN* (Yahad).

* Members of the inner Cabinet.

MINISTRIES

Office of the Prime Minister: Hakirya, Ruppin St, Jerusalem.

Ministry of Agriculture: POB 7011, Hakirya, Tel-Aviv 61070; tel. 03-255473; telex 361496.

Ministry of Defence: Hakirya, Tel-Aviv.

Ministry of Education and Culture: Hakirya, 14 Klausner St, Tel-Aviv; tel. 03-414155.

ISRAEL

Ministry of Energy and Infrastructure: Hakirya, Jerusalem.
Ministry of Finance: Hakirya, Ruppin St, Jerusalem; tel. 02-522205; telex 25216.
Ministry of Foreign Affairs: Hakirya, Romema, Jerusalem; tel. 02-235111.
Ministry of Health: 2 Ben Tabai St, Jerusalem; tel. 02-638212.
Ministry of Housing and Construction: Hakirya, 23 Hillel St, Jerusalem.
Ministry of the Interior: POB 6158, Jerusalem 91061; tel. 02-660151; telex 26162.
Ministry of Religious Affairs: Hakirya, 30 Jaffo St, Jerusalem.
Ministry of Tourism: POB 1018, 24 King George St, Jerusalem; tel. 02-237311.
Ministry of Transport: Klal Bldg, 97 Jaffa Rd, Jerusalem; tel. 02-229211.

Legislature

KNESSET

President: ABBA EBAN (acting).
Speaker: SHLOMO HILEL.

General Election, 23 July 1984

Party	Votes	Seats
Labour Alignment	724,074	44*
Likud	661,302	41
Tehiya	88,037	5
National Religious Party	73,530	4
Hadash (New Communist Party, Black Panthers)	69,815	4
Shas	63,605	4
Shinui	54,747	3
Citizens' Rights	49,698	3
Yahad	46,302	3
Progressive List for Peace	38,012	2
Agudat Israel	36,079	2
Morasha (Heritage)	33,287	2
Tami	31,103	1
Kach	25,907	1
Ometz	23,845	1
Others (11 parties)	53,978	—
Total	**2,078,321**	**120**

* The six deputies of the United Workers' Party (Mapam) who were elected on 23 July withdrew their support from the Labour Alignment when the Israel Labour Party formed the government of national unity with Likud. One Labour deputy crossed the floor to join the Citizens' Rights party.

Political Organizations

Agudat Israel: Jerusalem; ultra-orthodox Jewish party; stands for strict observance of Jewish religious law; Leader AVRAHAM SHAPIRA.

Agudat Israel World Organization (AIWO): Hacherut Sq., POB 326, Jerusalem 91002; tel. 02-223357; f. 1912 at Congress of Orthodox Jewry, Kattowitz, Germany (now Katowice, Poland), to help solve the problems facing Jewish people all over the world; more than 500,000 mems in 25 countries; Pres. Rabbi Dr I. LEWIN (New York); Chair. Rabbi J. M. ABRAMOWITZ (Jerusalem), Rabbi M. SHERER (New York); Gen. Sec. ABRAHAM HIRSCH (Jerusalem).

Centre Liberal Party: f. 1986 by members of the Liberal Party of Israel; Leader ARYE DULZIN.

Citizens' Rights Party (Ratz): f. 1973; breakaway movement from Labour Party; Leader Mrs SHULAMIT ALONI.

Gush Emunim (Bloc of the Faithful): f. 1967; engaged in unauthorized establishment of Jewish settlements in the occupied territories; Leader Rabbi MOSHE LEVINGER.

Independent Liberal Party: 48 King George St, POB 23076, Tel-Aviv; f. 1965 by 7 Liberal Party Knesset members after the formation of the Herut Movement and Liberal Party Bloc; 20,000 mems; Chair. MOSHE KOL; Gen. Sec. NISSIM ELIAD.

Israel Labour Party: 110 Ha'yarkon St, Tel-Aviv; tel. 03-209222; f. 1968 as a merger of the three Labour groups, Mapai, Rafi and Achdut Ha'avoda; a Zionist democratic socialist party, was in government from 1948 to 1977; with the United Workers' Party (Mapam), formed the main opposition bloc under name of Labour-Mapam Alignment until elections of July 1984; Chair. of Israel Labour Party SHIMON PERES; Sec.-Gen. UZI BARAM.

Kach (Thus): 111 Agripas St, Jerusalem; tel. 02-247202; f. 1977; right-wing religious nationalist party; advocates creation of a Torah state and expulsion of all Arabs from Israel and the occupied territories; Leader Rabbi MEIR KAHANE.

Likud (Consolidation): Tel-Aviv; f. September 1973; is a parliamentary bloc of Herut (Freedom; f. 1948; Leader ITZHAK SHAMIR), the Liberal Party of Israel (f. 1961; Chair. AVRAHAM SHARIR), Laam (For the Nation; f. 1976; fmrly led by YIGAEL HURWITZ, who left the coalition to form his own party, Ometz, before the 1984 general election) and Ahdut (a one-man faction, HILLEL SEIDEL); aims: territorial integrity (advocates retention of all the territory of post-1922 mandatory Palestine); absorption of newcomers; a social order based on freedom and justice, elimination of poverty and want; development of an economy that will ensure a decent standard of living; improvement of the environment and the quality of life. Likud was the sole government party from June 1977 until September 1984; Leader of Likud ITZHAK SHAMIR.

Morasha (Heritage): Tel-Aviv; merged with National Religious Party faction in the Knesset July 1986.

National Religious Party: 166 Ibn Gavirol St, Tel-Aviv; f. 1956; stands for strict adherence to Jewish religion and tradition, and strives to achieve the application of religious precepts of Judaism in everyday life; it is also endeavouring to establish the Constitution of Israel on Jewish religious law (the Torah); withdrew from (Labour) government coalition in December 1976 and before the 1984 general election supported the Likud coalition; 135,000 mems; Leader ZVULUN HAMMER.

New Communist Party of Israel (Rakah): POB 26205, Tel-Aviv; descended from the Socialist Workers' Party of Palestine (f. 1919); renamed Communist Party of Palestine 1921, Communist Party of Israel (Maki) 1948; pro-Soviet anti-Zionist group formed Rakah 1965; Jewish Arab membership; aims for a socialist system in Israel, a lasting peace between Israel and the Arab countries and the Palestinian Arab people, favours full implementation of UN Security Council Resolutions 242 and 338, Israeli withdrawal from all Arab territories occupied since 1967, formation of a Palestinian Arab state in the West Bank and Gaza Strip, recognition of national rights of State of Israel and Palestine people, democratic rights and defence of working class interests, and demands an end of discrimination against Arab minority in Israel and against oriental Jewish communities. Fought 1984 general election as Hadash (Democratic Front for Peace and Equality), an alliance with the Black Panther movement of Oriental Jews, winning 4 seats in the Knesset; Sec.-Gen. MEIR VILNER.

Poale Agudat Israel: f. 1924; working-class Orthodox Judaist party; Leader Dr KALMAN KAHANE.

Political Zionist Opposition (Ometz): f. 1982; one-man party, YIGAEL HURWITZ.

Progressive List for Peace: f. 1984; Jewish Arab; advocates recognition of the PLO and the establishment of a Palestinian state in the West Bank and the Gaza Strip; Leader MOHAMMED MU'ARI.

Religious Zionism Party (Matzad): Tel-Aviv; f. 1983; breakaway group from the National Religious Party; also known as Morasha (Heritage); Leader Rabbi HAIM DRUCKMAN.

Shas (Sephardic Torah Guardians): f. 1984 by splinter groups from Agudat Israel; ultra-orthodox Jewish party; Leader Rabbi ITZHAK PERETZ.

Shelli Party Peace and Equality: 4 Dizengoff Sq., POB 46109, Tel-Aviv 61460; tel. 03-284733; f. 1977; advocates a peace settlement with the Arab peoples and the Palestinians; an alliance of patriotic socialist groups, which included Mokked (Focus), the Independent Socialists, Uri Avnery's Ha'olam Hazeh party and others; in February 1979 these united; in 1983 Uri Avnery left the party; Shelli fought 1984 general election as the Democratic Party; 1,600 mems; Exec. Cttee: Chair. RAN COHEN, NAGIB ABU-RAKIA, A. BURSHAI, DAN DARIN, Y. SILBER, MUHAMED TABAKH, Dr B. TEMKIN, Dr MEIR LAM, M. PHANUS, JOE FUCHS, YONATHAN PELED, A. PAPOVICZ, AVI RYBNICKI.

Shinui-Movement for Change: f. 1974 and restored 1978 when Democratic Movement for Change split into two parties; centrist party; left Begin's coalition in Sept. 1978 at time of split; Leaders AMNON RUBINSTEIN and MORDECAI VIRSHUBSKY.

Tami: f. 1981; represents the interests of Sephardic Jews; Leader AHARON UZAN.

ISRAEL

Tehiya—Zionist Revival Movement: 4 King David St, Jerusalem; tel. 02-244281; f. September 1979; aims: Israeli sovereignty over Judaea, Samaria, Gaza; extensive settlement programme; economic independence; uniting of religious and non-religious camps; opposes Camp David accords; Leaders YUVAL NE'EMAN, RAFAEL EITAN, GEULA COHEN, Rabbi ELIEZER WALDMAN.

Telem—State Renewal Movement: f. 1981 by the late MOSHE DAYAN; proposes the administration of a unilateral Palestinian autonomy in Judaea and Samaria, against the annexation of territories to Israel; supports Likud coalition; Leader MORDECHAI BEN-PORAT.

United Arab List: Arab party affiliated to Labour Party.

United Workers' Party (Mapam): POB 1777, Tel-Aviv 61016; tel. 03-266245; telex 33499; f. 1948; left-wing socialist-Zionist Jewish-Arab party; grouped in Labour-Mapam Alignment with Israel Labour Party from January 1969 until Sept. 1984 when it withdrew in protest over Labour's formation of a national government with Likud; 45,000 mems; Sec.-Gen. ELAZAR GRANOT.

Yahad (Together): f. 1984; advocates a peace settlement with the Arab peoples and the Palestinians; Leader EZER WEIZMANN.

Diplomatic Representation

EMBASSIES IN ISRAEL

Argentina: 112 Rehov Hayarkon, 2nd Floor, Tel-Aviv; tel. 03-293411; telex 33730; Ambassador: ALBERTO DUMONT.

Australia: 37 Shaul Hamelech Blvd, Tel-Aviv 64928; tel. 03-250451; telex 33777; Ambassador: Dr ROBERT STUART MERRILLEES.

Austria: 11 Rehov Herman Cohen, Tel-Aviv; tel. 03-246186; telex 33435; Ambassador: Dr OTTO PLEINERT.

Belgium: 266 Rehov Hayarkon, Tel-Aviv 63504; tel. 03-454164; telex 342211; Ambassador: BOB J. L. LEBACQ.

Bolivia: 73A Rehov Nordau, Herzliya 'B'; tel. 052-72261; Ambassador: ALFREDO VILLARROEL.

Brazil: 14 Hei Beiyar, Tel-Aviv; tel. 03-219292; telex 33752; Ambassador: Dr LAMO SOUTELLO ALVES.

Burma: 19 Rehov Yona, Ramat Gan; Chargé d'affaires a.i.: U SOE MYINT.

Canada: 220 Rehov Hayarkon, Tel-Aviv 63405; tel. 03-228122; telex 341293; Ambassador: JAMES K. BARTLEMAN.

Chile: 54 Rehov Pinkas, Apt 45, Tel-Aviv; tel. 03-440414; telex 342189; Chargé d'affaires a.i.: LUIS PALMA.

Colombia: 52 Rehov Pinkas, Tel-Aviv; tel. 03-449616; telex 342165; Ambassador: LAZAR GILINSKI.

Costa Rica: 13 Diskin St, Apt 1, Jerusalem; tel. 02-660674; telex 26319; Ambassador: EDUARDO JENKINS DOBLES.

Denmark: 23 Rehov Bnei Moshe, POB 21080, Tel-Aviv 61210; tel. 03-440405; telex 33514; Ambassador: SVEN A. NIELSEN.

Dominican Republic: 32 Zamenhoff St, 46592 Herzliya Bet; tel. 052-72422; Ambassador: Dr ENRIQUILLO ROJAS ABREU.

Ecuador: 'Asia House', 4 Rehov Weizman, POB 34002, Tel-Aviv; tel. 03-258764; telex 342179; Ambassador: LUIS ORTIZ-TERAN.

Egypt: 54 Rehov Bezel, Tel-Aviv; telex 361289; Ambassador: MUHAMMAD BASSIOUNI.

El Salvador: 16 Kovshei Katamon, POB 4005, Jerusalem 91039; Ambassador: Col ENRIQUE GUTTFREUND.

Finland: Beith Eliahu, 2 Rehov Ibn Gvirol, Tel-Aviv; telex 33552; Ambassador: (vacant).

France: 112 Tayelet Herbert Samuel, Tel-Aviv; tel. 03-245371; telex 33662; Ambassador: ALAIN PIERRET.

Germany, Federal Republic: 16 Rehov Soutine, Tel-Aviv; telex 33621; Ambassador: Dr NIELS HANSEN.

Greece: 65 Shderot Shaul Hamelech, Tel-Aviv; tel. 03-259704; telex 341227; Ambassador: EMMANUEL GHIKAS.

Guatemala: 1 Bernstein Cohen, 47227 Ramat Hasharon, Tel-Aviv; tel. 03-490456; Ambassador: Col RAMIRO GEREDA ASTURIAS.

Haiti: 14 Tevuot Haaretz, Shikun Dan, Tel-Aviv; tel. 03-496222; Ambassador: FRANCK M. JOSEPH.

Honduras: 46 Rehov Hei Beiyar, Apt 3, Kikar Hamedina, Tel-Aviv 62093; tel. 03-218015; telex 361499; Ambassador: MOISES STARKMAN.

Italy: 'Asia House', 4 Rehov Weizman, Tel-Aviv; tel. 03-264223; telex 342664; Ambassador: GIOVANNI DOMINEDÒ.

Directory

Ivory Coast: Tel-Aviv; telex 25240; Ambassador: JEAN-PIERRE BONI.

Japan: 'Asia House', 4 Rehov Weizman, Tel-Aviv; tel. 342202; Ambassador: SHOZO KADOTA.

Liberia: 119 Shderot Rothschild, Tel-Aviv; tel. 03-203191; telex 361637; Ambassador: Maj. SAMUEL B. PEARSON, Jr.

Malawi: Tel-Aviv; Ambassador: MCLEEN WONGA MACHINJILI.

Mexico: 14 Rehov Hei Beiyar, Tel-Aviv; telex 32352; Ambassador: RAÚL VALDÉS AGUILAR.

Netherlands: 'Asia House', 4 Rehov Weizman, Tel-Aviv 61333; tel. 03-257377; telex 342180; Ambassador: J. H. R. D. VAN ROIJEN.

Norway: 10 Rehov Hei Beiyar, Tel-Aviv; tel. 03-295207; telex 33417; Ambassador: TORLEIV ÅNDA.

Panama: 28 Rehov Hei Beiyar, Kikar Hamedina, Tel-Aviv; tel. 03-256711; Ambassador: Maj. EDUARDO HERRERA HASSAN.

Peru: 52 Rehov Pinkas, Apt 31, 8th Floor, Tel-Aviv 62261; tel. 03-454065; telex 371351; Ambassador: GUILLERMO FERNÁNDEZ-CORNEJO.

Philippines: 12 Rehov Hei Beiyar, Tel-Aviv; telex 32104; Ambassador: ETTA C. ENRIQUEZ.

Romania: 24 Rehov Adam Hacohen, Tel-Aviv; Ambassador: CONSTANTIN VASILIU.

South Africa: 2 Rehov Kaplan, Tel-Aviv; telex 361208; Ambassador: E. A. LOUBSER.

Spain: Tel-Aviv; Ambassador: PEDRO LÓPEZ DE AGUIRREBENGOA.

Sweden: 'Asia House', 4 Rehov Weizman, Tel-Aviv; telex 33650; Ambassador: SVEN HIRDMAN.

Switzerland: 228 Rehov Hayarkon, Tel-Aviv; telex 342237; Ambassador: PIERRE-YVES SIMONIN.

Thailand: Tel-Aviv; Ambassador: SUCHINDA YONGSUNTHON.

Turkey: 34 Rehov Amos, Tel-Aviv; tel. 03-454155; Chargé d'affaires a.i.: BULENT MERIC.

United Kingdom: 192 Rehov Hayarkon, Tel-Aviv; tel. 03-249171; telex 33559; Ambassador: C. WILLIAM SQUIRE.

USA: 71 Rehov Hayarkon, Tel-Aviv; tel. 03-654338; telex 33376; Ambassador: THOMAS R. PICKERING.

Uruguay: 52 Rehov Pinkas, Tel-Aviv; tel. 03-440411; telex 342669; Ambassador: Dr AGUSTÍN ESPINOSA L.

Venezuela: Textile Center, 2 Rehov Kaufmann, Tel-Aviv; tel. 03-656287; telex 342172; Ambassador: NESTOR COLL BLASINI.

Zaire: 60 Hei Beiyar, Kikar Hamedina, Tel-Aviv; tel. 03-452681; telex 371239; Ambassador: Vice-Admiral LOMPONDA WA BOTENDE.

The Jewish Agency for Israel

POB 92, Jerusalem 91920; tel. 02-202211; telex 25236.

Organization: The governing bodies are the Assembly which determines basic policy, the Board of Governors which sets policy for the Agency between Assembly meetings and the Executive responsible for the day to day running of the Agency.

Chairman of Executive: ARYE L. DULZIN.

Chairman of Board of Governors: JEROLD C. HOFFBERGER.

Director-General: Maj.-Gen. (retd) SHLOMO GAZIT.

Secretary-General: HOWARD WEISBAND.

Functions: According to the Agreement of 1971, the Jewish Agency undertakes the immigration and absorption of immigrants in Israel, including absorption in agricultural settlement and immigrant housing; social welfare and health services in connection with immigrants; education, youth care and training; neighbourhood rehabilitation through project renewal.

Budget (1985/86): US $429m.

Judicial System

The law of Israel is composed of the enactments of the Knesset and, to a lesser extent, of the acts, orders-in-council and ordinances that remain from the period of the British Mandate in Palestine (1922–48). The pre-1948 law has, largely, been replaced, amended or reorganized, in the interests of codification, by Israeli legislation. This legislation generally follows a pattern which is very similar to that operating in England and the USA.

Attorney-General: JOSEPH HARISH.

ISRAEL

CIVIL COURTS

The Supreme Court is the highest judicial instance in the State. It has jurisdiction as an Appellate Court from the District Courts in all matters, both civil and criminal (sitting as a Court of Civil Appeal or as a Court of Criminal Appeal), and as a Court of First Instance (sitting as a High Court of Justice) in matters in which it considers it necessary to grant relief in the interests of justice and which are not within the jurisdiction of any other court or tribunal. This includes applications for orders in the nature of *habeas corpus*, *mandamus*, prohibition and *certiorari*, and enables the court to review the legality of acts of administrative authorities of all kinds.

President of the Supreme Court: MEIR SHAMGAR.

Vice-President of the Supreme Court: MIRIAM BEN-PORAT.

Justices of the Supreme Court: M. EYLON, A. BARAK, M. BEJSKI, SH. LEVIN, D. LEVIN, G. BACH, S. NETANYAHU, A. HALIMA, E. GOLDBERG.

Chief Registrar: Judge S. TZUR (magistrate).

The District Courts: Jerusalem, Tel-Aviv, Jaffa, Haifa, Beersheba, Nazareth. They have unlimited jurisdiction as Courts of First Instance in all civil and criminal matters not within the jurisdiction of a Magistrates' Court, all matters not within the exclusive jurisdiction of any other tribunal, and matters within the concurrent jurisdiction of any other tribunal so long as such tribunal does not deal with them, and as an Appellate Court in appeals from judgments and decisions of Magistrates' Courts and judgments of Municipal Courts and various administrative tribunals.

Magistrates' Courts: There are 28 Magistrates' Courts, having criminal jurisdiction to try contraventions, misdemeanours and certain felonies, and civil jurisdiction to try actions concerning possession or use of immovable property, or the partition thereof whatever may be the value of the subject matter of the action, and other civil actions on a limited basis.

Labour Courts: Established in 1969. Regional Labour Courts in Jerusalem, Tel-Aviv, Haifa and Beersheba, composed of Judges and representatives of the public. A National Labour Court in Jerusalem, presided over by Judge Z. Bar-Niv. The Courts have jurisdiction in all matters arising out of the relationship between employer and employee; between parties to a collective labour agreement; matters concerning the National Insurance Law and the Labour Law and Rules.

RELIGIOUS COURTS

The Religious Courts are the Courts of the recognized religious communities. They are competent in certain defined matters of personal status concerning members of their community. Where any action of personal status involves persons of different religious communities the President of the Supreme Court will decide which Court shall have jurisdiction. Whenever a question arises as to whether or not a case is one of personal status within the exclusive jurisdiction of a Religious Court, the matter must be referred to a Special Tribunal composed of two Justices of the Supreme Court and the President of the highest court of the religious community concerned in Israel. The judgments of the Religious Courts are executed by the process and offices of the Civil Courts.

Jewish Rabbinical Courts: These Courts have exclusive jurisdiction in matters of marriage and divorce of Jews in Israel who are Israeli citizens or residents. In all other matters of personal status they have concurrent jurisdiction with the District Courts with the consent of all parties concerned.

Muslim Religious Courts: These Courts have exclusive jurisdiction in matters of marriage and divorce of Muslims who are not foreigners, or who are foreigners subject by their national law to the jurisdiction of Muslim Religious Courts in such matters. In all other matters of personal status they have concurrent jurisdiction with the District Courts with the consent of all parties concerned.

Christian Religious Courts: The Courts of the recognized Christian communities have exclusive jurisdiction in matters of marriage and divorce of members of their communities who are not foreigners. In all other matters of personal status they have concurrent jurisdiction with the District Courts with the consent of all parties concerned. But neither these Courts nor the Civil Courts have jurisdiction to dissolve the marriage of a foreign subject.

Druze Courts: These Courts, established in 1963, have exclusive jurisdiction in matters of marriage and divorce of Druze in Israel, who are Israeli citizens or residents, and concurrent jurisdiction with the District Courts in all other matters of personal status of Druze with the consent of all parties concerned.

Religion

JUDAISM

Judaism, the religion of the Jews, is the faith of the great majority of Israel's inhabitants. According to the census of June 1983, Judaism's adherents totalled 3,349,997, equivalent to 83% of the country's population. Its basis is a belief in an ethical monotheism.

There are two main Jewish communities: the Ashkenazim and the Sephardim. The former are the Jews from Eastern, Central, or Northern Europe, while the latter originate from the Balkan countries, North Africa and the Middle East.

There is also a community of about 10,000 Falashas (Ethiopian Jews) who have been airlifted to Israel at various times since the fall of Emperor Haile Selassie in 1974. Between 1980 and 1982 some 2,000 were brought to Israel. The majority of the Falashas (about 7,000) were secretly flown from Sudan to Israel, via Europe, between October 1984 and January 1985, with the co-operation of international Jewish organizations. Thousands of Falashas had entered Sudan to escape the famine in Ethiopia. When the operation was revealed by the world press the Sudanese Government suspended the airlift. The USA secretly completed the airlift of the 1,000 Falashas stranded in Sudan in March 1985.

The supreme religious authority is vested in the Chief Rabbinate, which consists of the Ashkenazi and Sephardi Chief Rabbis and the Supreme Rabbinical Council. It makes decisions on interpretation of the Jewish law, and supervises the Rabbinical Courts. There are 8 regional Rabbinical Courts, and a Rabbinical Court of Appeal presided over by the two Chief Rabbis.

According to the Rabbinical Courts Jurisdiction Law of 1953, marriage and divorce among Jews in Israel are exclusively within the jurisdiction of the Rabbinical Courts. Provided that all the parties concerned agree, other matters of personal status can also be decided by the Rabbinical Courts.

There are 195 Religious Councils, which maintain religious services and supply religious needs, and about 405 religious committees with similar functions in smaller settlements. Their expenses are borne jointly by the State and the local authorities. The Religious Councils are under the administrative control of the Ministry of Religious Affairs. In all matters of religion, the Religious Councils are subject to the authority of the Chief Rabbinate. There are 365 officially appointed rabbis. The total number of synagogues is about 7,000, most of which are organized within the framework of the Union of Israel Synagogues.

Head of the Ashkenazi Community: The Chief Rabbi AVRAHAM SHAPIRO.

Head of the Sephardic Community: Jerusalem; tel. 02-244785; The Chief Rabbi MORDECHAI ELIAHU.

Two Jewish sects still loyal to their distinctive customs are:

The Karaites, a sect which recognizes only the Jewish written law and not the oral law of the Mishna and Talmud. The community of about 12,000, many of whom live in or near Ramla, has been augmented by immigration from Egypt.

The Samaritans, an ancient sect mentioned in 2 Kings xvii, 24. They recognize only the Torah. The community in Israel numbers about 500; about half of them live in Holon, where a Samaritan synagogue has been built, and the remainder, including the High Priest, live in Nablus, near Mt Gerizim, which is sacred to the Samaritans.

ISLAM

The Muslims in Israel are mainly Sunnis, and are divided among the four rites of the Sunni sect of Islam: the Shafe'i, the Hanbali, the Hanafi and the Maliki. Before June 1967 they numbered approx. 175,000; in 1971, approx. 343,900. At the census of June 1983 the total Muslim population of Israel was 526,639 (including some 110,000 in East Jerusalem).

Mufti of Jerusalem: POB 20002, Jerusalem; tel. 02-285994; Sheikh SAAD ED-DIN AL-ALAMI.

There was also a total of 65,861 Druzes in Israel at the census of June 1983.

CHRISTIANITY

The total Christian population of Israel at the census of June 1983 was 94,157 (including some 13,000 in East Jerusalem).

The Roman Catholic Church

Armenian Rite

The Armenian Catholic Patriarch of Cilicia is resident in Beirut, Lebanon.

ISRAEL

Patriarchal Vicariate of Jerusalem: Via Dolorosa 41, POB 19546, Jerusalem; Vicar Patriarchal Fr JOSEPH CHADEREVIAN.

Chaldean Rite

The Chaldean Patriarch of Babylon is resident in Baghdad, Iraq.

Patriarchal Vicariate of Jerusalem: Chaldean Patriarchal Vicariate, Saad and Said Quarter, Nablus Rd, Jerusalem; Vicar Patriarchal HENRI GOUILLON.

Latin Rite

The Patriarchate of Jerusalem covers Palestine, Jordan and Cyprus. At 31 December 1984 there were an estimated 61,713 adherents.

Bishops' Conference: Conférence des Evêques Latins dans les Régions Arabes, Patriarcat Latin, POB 14152, Jerusalem; tel. 02-282323; f. 1967; Pres. His Beatitude GIACOMO GIUSEPPE BELTRITTI, Patriarch of Jerusalem.

Patriarchate of Jerusalem: Patriarcat Latin, POB 14152, Jerusalem; tel. 02-282323; Patriarch: His Beatitude GIACOMO GIUSEPPE BELTRITTI; Vicar General for Israel: Mgr HANNA KALDANY (Titular Bishop of Gaba), Vicariat Patriarcal Latin, Nazareth.

Maronite Rite

The Maronite community, under the jurisdiction of the Maronite Patriarch of Antioch (resident in Lebanon), has about 6,350 members.

Patriarchal Vicariate of Jerusalem: Vicariat Maronite, Maronite St 25, Jerusalem; tel. 02-282158; Vicar Patriarchal AUGUSTIN HARFOUCHE (also representing the Archbishop of Tyre, Lebanon, as Vicar General for Israel).

Melkite Rite

The Greek-Melkite Patriarch of Antioch is resident in Damascus, Syria.

Patriarchal Vicariate of Jerusalem: Vicariat Patriarcal Grec-Melkite Catholique, POB 14130, 0091141 Jerusalem; tel. 02-282023; about 3,000 adherents (1984); Vicars Patriarchal Mgr HILARION CAPUCCI (Titular Archbishop of Caesarea in Palestine), Mgr LOUTIF LAHAM (Titular Archbishop of Tarsus).

Archbishop of Akka (Acre): Most Rev. MAXIMOS SALLOUM, Archevêché Grec-Catholique, POB 279, Haifa; tel. 04-523114; about 42,000 adherents (1984).

Syrian Rite

The Syrian Catholic Patriarch of Antioch is resident in Beirut, Lebanon.

Patriarchal Vicariate of Jerusalem: Vicariat Patriarcal Syrien Catholique, Nablus Rd, POB 19787, Jerusalem; tel. 02-282657; about 1,000 adherents in Palestine and Jordan (1983); Vicar Patriarchal Mgr PIERRE ABD AL-AHAD.

The Greek Orthodox Church

The Patriarchate of Jerusalem contains an estimated 260,000 adherents throughout the Middle East.

Patriarch of Jerusalem: DIODOROS I, Greek Orthodox Patriarchate St, Old City, POB 19632, Jerusalem; tel. 02-284917.

The Anglican Communion

Episcopal Church in Jerusalem and the Middle East: St George's Close, POB 1248, Jerusalem; President-Bishop Rt Rev. SAMIR KAFITY, Bishop in Jerusalem.

Other Christian Churches

Other denominations include the Armenian Orthodox Church (900 members), the Coptic Orthodox Church (700 members), the Russian Orthodox Church (which maintains an Ecclesiastical Mission), the Ethiopian Church, and the Baptist Lutheran and Presbyterian Churches.

The Press

Tel-Aviv is the main publishing centre. Largely for economic reasons there has developed no local press away from these cities; hence all papers regard themselves as national. Friday editions, Sabbath eve, are increased to up to twice the normal size by special weekend supplements, and experience a considerable rise in circulation. No newspapers appear on Saturday.

Most of the daily papers are in Hebrew, and others appear in Arabic, English, French, Polish, Yiddish, Hungarian and German. The total daily circulation is 500,000–600,000 copies, or 21 papers per hundred people, although most citizens read more than one daily paper.

Most Hebrew morning dailies have strong political or religious affiliations. *Al-Hamishmar* is affiliated to Mapam, *Hatzofeh* to the National Religious Front—World Mizrahi. *Davar* is the long-established organ of the Histadrut. Mapai publishes the weekly *Ot*. Most newspapers depend on subsidies from political parties, religious organizations or public funds. The limiting effect on freedom of commentary entailed by this party press system has provoked repeated criticism.

The Jerusalem Arabic daily *Al-Anba* has a small circulation (10,000) but an increasing number of Israeli Arabs are now reading Hebrew dailies. The daily, *Al-Quds*, was founded in 1968 for Arabs in Jerusalem and the West Bank; the small indigenous press of occupied Jordan has largely ceased publication or transferred operations to Amman. Two of the four Arabic newspapers which are published in occupied East Jerusalem, the daily, *Al-Mithaq*, and the weekly, *Al-Ahd*, were closed by the Israeli authorities in August 1986. It was alleged that they were financed and managed by the Popular Front for the Liberation of Palestine.

There are around 400 other newspapers and magazines including some 50 weekly and 150 fortnightly; over 250 of them are in Hebrew, the remainder in eleven other languages.

The most influential and respected dailies, for both quality of news coverage and commentary, are *Ha'aretz* and the trade union paper, *Davar*, which frequently has articles by government figures. These are the most widely read of the morning papers, exceeded only by the popular afternoon press, *Ma'ariv* and *Yedioth Aharonoth*. The *Jerusalem Post* gives detailed and sound news coverage in English.

The Israeli Press Council (Chair. JOSHUA ROTENSTREICH), established in 1963, deals with matters of common interest to the Press such as drafting the code of professional ethics which is binding on all journalists.

The Daily Newspaper Publishers' Association represents publishers in negotiations with official and public bodies, negotiates contracts with employees and purchases and distributes newsprint, of which Israel now manufactures 75% of its needs.

DAILIES

Al-Anba (The News): POB 428, 37 Hillel St, Beit Agron, Jerusalem; f. 1968; Arabic; published by Jerusalem Publications Ltd; Editor and Man. Dir OVADIA DANON; circ. 10,000.

Chadshot Hasport: Tushia St, POB 20011, Tel-Aviv 61200; f. 1954; Hebrew; sports; independent; circ. 30,000.

Davar (The Word): POB 199, 45 Sheinkin St, Tel-Aviv; f. 1925; morning; official organ of the General Federation of Labour (Histadrut); Editor HANNAH ZEMER; circ. 39,000; there are also weekly magazine editions.

Al-Fajr (The Dawn): Jerusalem; Arabic; Publr PAUL AJILOUNY; Editor HANNAH SINIORA.

Ha'aretz (The Land): 21 Salman Schocken St, Tel-Aviv; tel. 03-824261; telex 33748; f. 1918; morning; Hebrew; liberal, independent; Editor GERSHOM G. SCHOCKEN; circ. 55,000 (weekdays), 75,000 (weekends).

Al-Hamishmar (The Guardian): Al-Hamishmar House, 4 Ben Avigdor St, Tel-Aviv; tel. 03-57171; f. 1943; morning; Hebrew; organ of the United Workers' Party (Mapam); Editor MARK GEFEN; circ. 25,000.

Hamodia: Kikar Hacheruth, POB 1306, Jerusalem; morning; organ of Agudat Israel; Editor YEHUDA L. LEVIN; circ. 8,000.

Hatzofeh: 66 Hamasger St, Tel-Aviv; f. 1938; morning; organ of the National Religious Front; Editor M. ISHON; circ. 16,000.

Israel Nachrichten: 52 Harakevet St, Tel-Aviv; tel. 03-370011; f. 1974; morning; German; Editor S. HIMMELFARB; circ. 20,000.

Israelski Far Tribuna: 113 Givat Herzl St, Tel-Aviv; tel. 03-3700; f. 1952; Bulgarian; circ. 6,000.

Al-Ittihad (Unity): POB 104, Haifa; tel. 04-511296; f. 1944; Arabic; organ of the Israeli Communist Party; Chief Editor EMILE HABIBY.

The Jerusalem Post: POB 81, Romema, 91000, Jerusalem; tel. 02-551616; telex 26121; f. 1932; morning; English; independent; Editor and Man. Dir ARI RATH; Editor ERWIN FRENKEL; circ. 30,000 (weekdays), 47,000 (weekend edition); there is also a weekly international edition, circ. 55,000.

Le Journal d'Israel: 26 Agra St, POB 28330, Tel-Aviv; f. 1971; French; independent; Chief Editor J. RABIN; circ. 10,000; also overseas weekly selection; circ. 15,000.

Letzte Nyess (Late News): 52 Harakevet St, POB 28034, Tel-Aviv; f. 1949; morning; Yiddish; Editor S. HIMMELFARB; circ. 23,000.

Ma'ariv: 2 Carlebach St, Tel-Aviv 67132; tel. 03-439111; f. 1948;

ISRAEL

mid-morning; independent; Editor IDO DISSENTCHIK; circ. daily 147,000, Friday 245,000.

Mabat: 56 Wolfson St, Tel-Aviv; f. 1971; morning; economic and social; Editor S. YARKONI.

Al-Mawqif: Jerusalem; Arabic; owned by the Arab Council for Public Affairs.

Al-Mithaq (The Covenant): Jerusalem; Arabic; Editor MAHMOUD KHATIB; (closed down by Israeli authorities August 1986).

Nowiny i Kurier: 52 Harakevet St, Tel-Aviv; f. 1952; morning; Polish; Editor S. HIMMELFARB; circ. 15,000.

Al-Quds (Jerusalem): POB 19788, Jerusalem; tel. 02-284061; telex 02-282475; f. 1968; Arabic; Publr MAHMOUD ABU ZALAF; Editor-in-Chief WALID ABU ZALAF; circ. 40,000.

Ash-Sha'ab (The People): Jerusalem; f. 1972; Arabic; circ. 15,000; Editor (vacant).

Sha'ar: 52 Harakevet St, Tel-Aviv 64284; Hebrew; economy and finance; Editor S. HIMMELFARB.

Shearim: 64 Frishman St, Tel-Aviv; tel. 03-242126; organ of Poale Agudat Israel; Editor MAIER HALACHMI; circ. 12,000.

Uj Kelet: 52 Harakevet St, Tel-Aviv; f. 1918; morning; Hungarian; independent; Editor S. HIMMELFARB; circ. 20,000.

Viata Noastra: 52 Harakevet St, Tel-Aviv; f. 1950; morning; Romanian; Editor ADRIAN ZAHAREANU; circ. 30,000.

Yedioth Aharonoth: 138 Petah Tikva Rd, Tel-Aviv; f. 1939; evening; independent; Editor Dr H. ROSENBLUM; circ. 180,000, Friday 280,000.

Yom Yom: POB 1194, 34–36 Itzhak Sadeh St, Tel-Aviv; f. 1964; morning; Yiddish; economy and finance; Editor S. HIMMELFARB.

WEEKLIES AND FORTNIGHTLIES

Al-Ahd (Sunday): Jerusalem; Arabic; weekly; (closed down by Israeli authorities August 1986).

Bama'alah: POB 303, Tel-Aviv; journal of the young Histadrut Movement; Editor N. ANAELY.

Bamahane: Military POB 1013, Tel-Aviv; f. 1948; military, illustrated weekly of the Israel Armed Forces; Editor-in-Chief YOSSEF ESHKOL; circ. 70,000.

Bitaon Heyl Ha'avir (Air Force Magazine): Doar Zwai 1560, Zahal; tel. 03-260948; f. 1948; fortnightly; Man. Editor D. MOLAD; Editor-in-Chief AHARON LAPIDOT; Technical Editor RAM AVRAHAMI; circ. 30,000.

Davar Hashavua: 45 Sheinkin St, Tel-Aviv; f. 1946; weekly; popular illustrated; published by Histadrut, General Federation of Labour; Editor O. ZMORA; circ. 43,000.

Ethgar: 75 Einstein St, Tel-Aviv; twice weekly; Editor NATHAN YALIN-MOR.

Gesher (The Bridge): Jerusalem; fortnightly; Hebrew; Editor ZIAD ABU ZAYAD.

Glasul Populurui: 37 Eilath St, POB 2675, Tel-Aviv; weekly of the Communist Party of Israel; Romanian; Editor MEÏR SEMO.

Haolam Hazeh: POB 136, 3 Gordon St, Tel-Aviv; tel. 03-232262; f. 1937; weekly; independent; illustrated news magazine; Editor-in-Chief URI AVNERY.

Harefuah: 39 Shaul Hamelech Blvd, Tel-Aviv 64928; f. 1920; fortnightly journal of the Israeli Medical Association; with English summaries; Editor I. SUM; circ. 7,500.

Hotam: Al-Hamishmar House, Choma U'Migdal St, Tel-Aviv; weekly of the United Workers' Party (Mapam).

Al-Hurriya (Freedom): 38 King George St, Tel-Aviv; Arabic weekly of the Herut Party.

Illustrirte Weltwoch: Tel-Aviv; f. 1956; weekly; Yiddish; Editor M. KARPINOVITZ.

Jerusalem Post International Edition: POB 81, Romema, Jerusalem 91000; tel. 02-551616; telex 26121; f. 1959; weekly; English; Overseas edition of the *Jerusalem Post* (q.v.); circ. 55,000 to 95 countries.

Kol Ha'am (Voice of the People): 37 Eilath St, POB 2675, Tel-Aviv; f. 1947; organ of the Communist Party of Israel; Editor B. BALTI.

Laisha: POB 28122, 7 Fin St, Tel-Aviv 67132; f. 1946; Hebrew; women's magazine; Editor ZVI ELGAT.

Ma'ariv Lanoar: 2 Carlebach St, Tel-Aviv 67132; tel. 03-439111; f. 1957; weekly for youth; Editor AMNON BEI-RAV; circ. 100,000.

Magallati: Arabic Publishing House, POB 28049, Tel-Aviv; tel. 03-371438; f. 1960; young people's fortnightly; Man. JOSEPH ELIAHOU; Editor-in-Chief IBRAHIM MUSA IBRAHIM; Editors GAMIL DAHLAN, MISHEL HADDAD; circ. 10,000.

MB (Mitteilungsblatt): POB 1480, Tel-Aviv; tel. 03-664461; f. 1932; German monthly journal of the Irgun Olei Merkas Europa (Settlers from Central Europe); Editor Dr HANS CAPELL.

Al-Mirsad (The Telescope): POB 1777, Tel-Aviv; tel. 03-266244; f. 1948; Arabic; Mapam.

Reshumot: Ministry of Justice, Jerusalem; f. 1948; Hebrew, Arabic and English; official Government gazette.

Sada at-Tarbia (The Echo of Education): published by the Histadrut and Teachers' Association, POB 2306, Rehovot; f. 1952; fortnightly; Arabic; educational; Editor TUVIA SHAMOSH.

OTHER PERIODICALS

Ariel: Cultural and Scientific Relations Division, Ministry for Foreign Affairs, Jerusalem; Publishers, Editorial and Distribution: Jerusalem Post Publications Ltd, POB 3349, Jerusalem 91002; tel. 02-223766 (editorial); f. 1962; quarterly review of the arts and letters in Israel; regular edns in English, Spanish, French and German; occasional edns in several other languages; Editor ASHER WEILL; circ. 20,000.

Avoda Urevacha Ubituach Leumi: POB 915, Jerusalem; f. 1949; monthly review of the Ministry of Labour and Social Affairs, and the National Insurance Institute, Jerusalem; Chief Editor AVNER MICHAELI; Editor MICHAEL KLODOVSKY; circ. 2,500.

Bakalkala Uvems'har (Economics and Trade): POB 20027, Tel-Aviv; tel. 03-288224; telex 33484; f. 1919; monthly; Hebrew; published by Federation of Israeli Chambers of Commerce; Editor Z. AMIT.

Al-Bushra (Good News): POB 6088, Haifa; f. 1935; monthly; Arabic; organ of the Ahmadiyya movement; Editor FALAHUD DIN O'DEH.

Business Diary: 37 Hanamal St, Haifa; f. 1947; weekly; English, Hebrew; shipping movements, import licences, stock exchange listings, business failures, etc.; Editor G. ALON.

Christian News from Israel: 30 Jaffa Rd, Jerusalem; f. 1949; half-yearly; English, French, Spanish; issued by the Ministry of Religious Affairs; Editor SHALOM BEN-ZAKKAI; circ. 10,000.

Di Goldene Keyt: 30 Weizmann St, Tel-Aviv; f. 1949; literary quarterly; Yiddish; published by the Histadrut; Editor A. SUTZKEVER; Co-Editor ALEXANDER SPIEGELBLATT; Man. Editor MOSHE MILLIS.

Divrei Haknesset: c/o The Knesset, Jerusalem; f. 1949; records of the proceedings of the Knesset; published by the Government Printer, Jerusalem; Editor LIORA SEGEV (acting); circ. 350.

Doing Business with Israel: POB 20027, Tel-Aviv; published by Federation of Israeli Chambers of Commerce; Editor ZVI SEGAL.

The Family Physician: 101 Arlosoroff St, POB 16250, Tel-Aviv; tel. 03-433387; f. 1970; three times a year; Hebrew with English summaries; medical; Editor Prof. MAX R. POLLIACK; circ. 4,500.

Folk un Zion: POB 92, Jerusalem; tel. 02-533123; f. 1950; bi-monthly; current events relating to Israel and World Jewry; circ. 3,000; Editor MOSHE KALCHHEIM.

Frei Israel: POB 8512, Tel-Aviv; progressive monthly, published by Asscn for Popular Culture; Yiddish.

Gazit: 8 Zvi Brook St, POB 4190, Tel-Aviv; f. 1932; monthly; Hebrew and English; art, literature; Publisher G. TALPHIR.

Hameshek Hahaklai: 21 Melchett St, Tel-Aviv; f. 1929; agricultural; Editor ISRAEL INBARI.

Al-Hamishmar (The Guardian): 4 Ben Avigdor St, Tel-Aviv; Bulgarian monthly of United Workers' Party.

Hamizrah Hehadash (The New East): Israel Oriental Society, The Hebrew University, Mount Scopus, Jerusalem 91905; tel. 02-883633; f. 1949; annual of the Israel Oriental Society; Middle Eastern, Asian and African Affairs; Hebrew with English summary; Editor AHARON LAYISH; circ. 1,500–2,000.

Hamionai (The Hotelier): POB 11586, Tel-Aviv; f. 1962; monthly of the Israel Hotel Association; Hebrew and English; Editor Z. PELTZ.

Hapraklit: 8 Wilson St, POB 14152, Tel-Aviv; tel. 03-625477; f. 1943; quarterly; published by the Israel Bar Association; Editor-in-Chief A. POLONSKI; Editor ARNAN GAVRIELI; circ. 9,000.

Hassadeh: 8 Shaul Hamelech Blvd, POB 40044, Tel-Aviv 61400; tel. 03-252171; f. 1920; monthly; review of settlement and agriculture; English summaries; Editor J. M. MARGALIT; circ. 10,000.

Hed Hagan: 8 Ben Saruk St, Tel-Aviv; f. 1935; educational; Editor Mrs ZIVA PEDAHZUR; circ. 3,500.

ISRAEL

Hed Hahinukh: 8 Ben Saruk St, Tel-Aviv; tel. 03-260211; f. 1926; monthly; Hebrew; educational; published by the Israeli Teachers' Union; Editor Ora Gadell; circ. 24,000.

Innovation: POB 7422, 31070 Haifa; tel. 04-255104; f. 1975; monthly; English; industrial research and development in Israel; published by A. G. Publications Ltd; Editor A. Greenfield.

Israel Business: POB 7422, 31070 Haifa; tel. 04-255104; f. 1961; monthly; English; business news and economic devt; published by A.G. Publications Ltd; Editor A. Greenfield.

Israel Economist: 6 Hazanowitz St, POB 7052, Jerusalem 91070; tel. 02-234131; f. 1945; monthly; English; independent; political and economic; Man. Editor Pinchas Levinson; Editor J. Kollek; also publishes *Keeping Posted* (diplomatic magazine), *Mazel and Brucha* (jewellers' magazine); annuals: *Travel Agents' Manual, Electronics, International Conventions in Israel, Arkia, In Flight,* various hotel magazines.

Israel Environment Bulletin: Hakirya, Ruppin St, Jerusalem; tel. 02-660151; telex 26162; quarterly; published by the Ministry of the Interior.

Israel Export and Trade Journal: POB 11586, Tel-Aviv; f. 1949; monthly; English; commercial and economic; published by Israel Periodicals Co Ltd; Man. Dir Zalman Peltz.

Israel Journal of Medical Sciences: POB 1435, Jerusalem 91013; tel. 02-227085; f. 1965; monthly; Editor-in-Chief Dr M. Prywes; Man. Mrs S. Toledano; circ. 5,500.

Israel Journal of Psychiatry and Related Sciences: Israel Science Publishers, POB 3115, Jerusalem 91030; f. 1963; quarterly; Editor-in-Chief E. L. Edelstein.

Israel Journal of Veterinary Medicine: POB 3076, Rishon Le-Zion 75130; f. 1943; quarterly of the Israel Veterinary Medical Asscn; formerly *Refuah Veterinarith*; Editor Prof. M. Torten.

Israel Scene: POB 92, Jerusalem 91920; tel. 02-533123; telex 26436; f. 1980 as continuation of Israel Digest; monthly; English; published by the World Zionist Organization; news, features and analysis; circ. 20,000; Editor Asher Weill.

Israel-South Africa Trade Journal: POB 11587, Tel-Aviv; f. 1973; bi-monthly; English; commercial and economic; published by Israel Publications Corpn Ltd; Man. Dir Z. Peltz.

Israel Tax Law Letter: POB 7422, Haifa 31070; tel. 04-255104; f. 1980; English; irregular; new developments in Israel tax law; Editor A. Greenfield.

Israels Aussenhandel: POB 11586, Tel-Aviv 61114; tel. 03-280215; f. 1967; monthly; German; commercial; published by Israel Periodicals Co Ltd; Editor Gabriela Blum; Man. Dir Zalman Peltz.

Al-Jadid (The New): POB 104, Haifa; literary monthly; Arabic; Editor Emile Touma.

Kalkalan: 8 Akiva St, POB 7052, Jerusalem; f. 1952; monthly; independent; Hebrew commercial and economic; Editor J. Kollek.

Kiryat Sefer: POB 503, Jerusalem; tel. 02-585019; f. 1924; bibliographical quarterly of the Jewish National and University Library, Jerusalem; Editor Dr A. Shinan.

Labour in Israel: 93 Arlosorof St, POB 303, Tel-Aviv 61002; tel. 03-431624; telex 342488; quarterly; English, French, German and Spanish; bulletin of the Histadrut (General Federation of Labour in Israel); circ. 28,000.

Leshonenu: Academy of the Hebrew Language, POB 3449, Jerusalem 91034; tel. 02-632242; f. 1929; 4 a year; for the study of the Hebrew language and cognate subjects; Editor J. Blau.

Leshonenu La'am: Academy of the Hebrew Language, POB 3449, Jerusalem 91034; tel. 02-632242; f. 1945; popular Hebrew philology; Editors E. Etan, M. Medan.

Ma'arachot (Campaigns): Hakirya, 3 Mendler St, POB 7026, Tel-Aviv; tel. 03-268426; f. 1939; military and political bi-monthly; periodical of Israel Defence Force; Editors Col U. Dromi, Maj. R. Rojanski.

Mada (Science): Weizmann Science Press of Israel, POB 801, Jerusalem 91007; tel. 02-663203; telex 26144; f. 1956; popular scientific bi-monthly in Hebrew; Editor-in-Chief Kapai Pines; circ. 11,000.

Melaha Vetaassiya (Trade and Industry): POB 11587, Tel-Aviv; f. 1969; bi-monthly review of the Union of Artisans and Small Manufacturers of Israel; Man. Dir Z. Peltz.

Mibifnim (From Within): 3 Ta'as St, Ramath-Gan, POB 40015, Tel-Aviv 61400; tel. 03-7514938; f. 1923; quarterly of the United Kibbutz Movement (TKM); Editor Dani Hadazi; circ. 5,000.

Molad: POB 1165, Jerusalem; f. 1948; 2 a year; Hebrew; independent political and literary periodical; published by Miph'ale Molad Ltd; Editor Ephraim Broido.

Monthly Bulletin of Statistics: Israel Central Bureau of Statistics, POB 13015, Jerusalem 91130; f. 1949.

    Foreign Trade Statistics: f. 1950; Hebrew and English; appears annually, 2 vols; imports/exports.

    Judea, Samaria and Gaza Area Statistics: f. 1971; Hebrew and English.

    Tourism and Hotel Services Statistics Quarterly: f. 1973; Hebrew and English.

    Price Statistics Monthly: f. 1959; Hebrew.

    Foreign Trade Statistics Quarterly: f. 1950; Hebrew and English.

    Transport Statistics Quarterly: f. 1974; Hebrew and English.

    Agricultural Statistics: f. 1970; quarterly; Hebrew and English.

    New Statistical Projects: quarterly.

Moznayim (Balance): POB 7098, Tel-Aviv; f. 1929; monthly; literature and culture; Editors Chaim Pessah, Asher Reich; circ. 3,000.

Na'amat-Urim Lahorim: 5 Ben-Shaprut St, POB 303, Tel-Aviv; tel. 03-269747; f. 1934; monthly journal of the Council of Women Workers of the Histadrut; Hebrew; Editor Zivia Cohen; circ. 16,500.

Nekuda: organ of the Jewish settlers of the West Bank and Gaza Strip.

New Outlook: 9 Gordon St, Tel-Aviv 63458; tel. 03-236496; f. 1957; monthly; Israeli and Middle Eastern Affairs; dedicated to the quest for Arab-Israeli peace; Editor-in-Chief Chaim Shur; Man. Editor Liora Barash; circ. 10,000.

Poetics Today: Israel Science Publishers, POB 3115, Jerusalem; f. 1979; quarterly; Editor-in-Chief B. Hrushovski.

Proche-Orient Chrétien: POB 19079, Jerusalem 91190; tel. 02-283285; f. 1951; quarterly on churches and religion in the Middle East; circ. 800.

Quarterly Review of the Israel Medical Association (Mif'al Haverut Hutz—World Fellowship of the Israel Medical Association): 39 Shaul Hamelech Blvd, Tel-Aviv 64928; quarterly; English; also published in French; Editors Dr S. Erdman, Dr S. Tyano.

La Revue de l'A.M.I. (World Fellowship of the Israel Medical Association): 39 Shaul Hamelech Blvd, Tel-Aviv 64928; quarterly; French and English; Editors Dr S. Erdman, Dr S. Tyano.

Scopus: Hebrew University of Jerusalem, Mount Scopus, Jerusalem 91905; tel. 02-882812; telex 26458; f. 1946; two a year; English; published by Department of Press and Publications, Hebrew University of Jerusalem; Editors V. London and I. Black.

The Sea: Hane'emanim 8, POB 33706, Haifa; tel. 04-529818; every six months; published by Israel Maritime League; review of marine problems; Pres. M. Pomrock; Sec.-Gen. Zadok Eshel; Chief Editor M. Litovski; circ. 5,000.

Shdemot: 10 Dubnov, Tel-Aviv 64732; tel. 03-251465; three a year; journal of the Kibbutz Movement; Editor Shalom Lilker; circ. 2,500.

Shituf (Co-operation): 24 Ha'arba St, POB 7151, Tel-Aviv; f. 1948; bi-monthly; economic, social and co-operative problems in Israel; published by the Central Union of Industrial, Transport and Service Co-operative Societies; Editor L. Losh; circ. 12,000.

Sillages: POB 92, Jerusalem; tel. 02-527156; f. 1980; published by Inf. Dept of World Zionist Org.; literary and political; French; Editor-in-Chief Katy Bisraor.

Sinai: POB 642, Jerusalem; tel. 02-526231; f. 1937; Torah science and literature; Editor Dr Yitzchak Raphael.

Sindibad: POB 28049, Tel-Aviv; f. 1970; children's monthly; Man. Joseph Eliahou; Editors Walid Hussein, Jamil Dahlan; circ. 10,000.

Spectrum: Jerusalem; monthly of the Israel Labour Party; Editor David Twersky.

At-Ta'awun (Co-operation): POB 303, Tel-Aviv; tel. 03-431836; telex 342488; f. 1961; published by the Arab Workers' Dept of the Histadrut; co-operatives irregular; Editor Muhammad Ghanayim.

Terra Santa: POB 186, Jerusalem; tel. 02-282354; f. 1921; monthly; published by the Custody of the Holy Land (the official custodians of the Holy Shrines); Italian, Spanish, French, English and Arabic editions published in Jerusalem, by the Franciscan

ISRAEL

Printing Press, German edition in Vienna, Maltese edition in Valletta.

Tmuroth: 48 Hamelech George St, POB 23076, Tel-Aviv; f. 1960; monthly; organ of the Liberal Labour Movement; Editor S. MEIRI.

WIZO Review: Women's International Zionist Organization, 38 Sderoth David Hamelekh, Tel-Aviv; tel. 03-257321; telex 35770; English, Spanish and German editions; Editor SYLVIA SATTEN BANIN; circ. 20,000.

Zion: POB 4179, Jerusalem; f. 1935; quarterly; Hebrew, with English summaries; research in Jewish history; Editors H. BEINART, S. ETTINGER, M. STERN.

Zraim: 7 Dubnov St, POB 40027, Tel-Aviv; f. 1953; journal of the Bnei Akiva (Youth of Tora Va-avoda) Movement; Editor ELYAHU DAVID.

Zrakor: Haifa; f. 1947; monthly; Hebrew; news digest, trade, finance, economics, shipping; Editor G. ALON.

The following are all published by Weizmann Science Press of Israel, 8A Horkania St, POB 801, Jerusalem 91007; tel. 02-663203; telex 26144; Editor P. GREENBERG.

Israel Journal of Botany: f. 1951; quarterly; Editor Prof. A. HALEVI.

Israel Journal of Chemistry: f. 1951; quarterly; Editor Prof. S. SAREL.

Israel Journal of Earth Sciences: f. 1951; quarterly; Editor Dr C. BINYAMINI.

Israel Journal of Mathematics: f. 1951; monthly, 3 vols of 4 issues per year; Editor Prof. H. M. FARKAS.

Israel Journal of Technology: f. 1951; quarterly; Editor Prof. D. ABIR.

Israel Journal of Zoology: f. 1951; quarterly; Editor Prof. Y. L. WERNER.

Journal d'Analyse Mathématique: f. 1955; one or two vols per year; Editor Prof. H. FURSTENBERG.

PRESS ASSOCIATIONS

Daily Newspaper Publishers' Association of Israel: POB 2251, 4 Kaplan St, Tel-Aviv 64734; safeguards professional interests and maintains standards, supplies newsprint to dailies; negotiates with trade unions, etc.; mems all daily papers; affiliated to International Federation of Newspaper Publishers; Pres. SHABTAI HIMMELFARB; Gen. Sec. BETZALEL EYAL.

Israel Press Association: Sokolov House, 4 Kaplan St, Tel-Aviv.

NEWS AGENCIES

Jewish Telegraphic Agency (JTA): Israel Bureau, Jerusalem Post Building, Romema, Jerusalem; Dir DAVID LANDAU.

ITIM, News Agency of the Associated Israel Press: 10 Tiomkin St, Tel-Aviv; f. 1950; co-operative news agency; Dir and Editor ALTER WELNER.

Foreign Bureaux

Agence France-Presse: 16 Hatikva Yemin Moshe St, POB 1507, Jerusalem; Correspondent PIERRE LEMOINE.

Agencia EFE (Spain): POB 3279, Avizohar 2, Apt 9, Bet Ha'Kerem, Jerusalem 91032; tel. 02-528658; telex 26446; Correspondent ELÍAS-SAMUEL SCHERBACOVSKY.

Agenzia Nazionale Stampa Associata (ANSA) (Italy): POB 21342, Tel-Aviv 61212; tel. 03-251672; telex 341704; Bureau Chief VITTORIO FRENQUELLUCCI: 10 Marcus St, Jerusalem 92233; tel. 02-666098; telex 26420; Correspondent GIORGIO RACCAH.

Associated Press (AP) (USA): 30 Ibn Gavirol St, POB 20220, Tel-Aviv 61201; tel. 03-262283; telex 341411; Chief of Bureau NICHOLAS TATRO; Beit Agron, Hilel St, Jerusalem; tel. 02-224632; telex 25258; Chief Correspondent ARTHUR MAX.

Deutsche Presse-Agentur (dpa) (Federal Republic of Germany): 30 Ibn Gavirol St, POB 16231, Tel-Aviv; tel. 03-254268; telex 33416; Correspondents LASZLO TRANKOVITS and GIDEON BERU.

Jiji Tsushin-Sha (Japan): 7/B/23 Etzel French Hill, Jerusalem; tel. 02-812727; Correspondent HIROKAZU OIKAWA.

Kyodo Tsushin (Japan): 19 Lessim St, Tel-Aviv; tel. 03-258185; telex 361568; Correspondent RYUICHI KAWAKAMI.

Reuters (UK): 38 Hamasger St, Tel-Aviv 67211; tel. 03-335176; telex 361567.

United Press International (UPI) (USA): 138 Petah Tikva Rd, Tel-Aviv; Bureau Man. BROOKE W. KROEGER.

The following are also represented: North American Newspaper Alliance and TASS (USSR).

Publishers

Achiasaf Ltd: 13 Yosef Hanassi St, POB 4810, Tel-Aviv; tel. 03-283339; f. 1933; general; Man. Dirs SCHACHNA ACHIASAF, MATAN ACHIASAF.

Am Hassefer Ltd: 9 Bialik St, Tel-Aviv; tel. 03-53040; f. 1955; Man. Dir DOV LIPETZ.

'Am Oved' Ltd: 22 Mazah St, POB 470, Tel-Aviv; tel. 03-291526; f. 1942; fiction, biography, history, social science; reference books, school and university textbooks, technical and professional works, juvenile, poetry, essays, science fiction; Man. Dir AHARON KRAUS.

Amichai Publishing House Ltd: 5 Yosef Hanassi St, Tel-Aviv; tel. 03-284990; f. 1948; Man. Dir YEHUDA ORLINSKY.

Arabic Publishing House: 17A Hagra St, POB 28049, Tel-Aviv; tel. 03-371438; f. 1960; established by the Histadrut (trade union) organization; periodicals and books; Dir JOSEPH ELIAHOU; Editor-in-Chief IBRAHIM M. IBRAHIM.

Carta, The Israel Map and Publishing Co Ltd: Yad Haruzim St, POB 2500, Jerusalem 91024; tel. 02-713536; telex 26587; f. 1958; the principal cartographic publisher; Pres. EMANUEL HAUSMAN; Man. Dir SHAY HAUSMAN.

Dvir Publishing Co Ltd, The: 58 Mazah St, POB 149, Tel-Aviv; tel. 03-622991; f. 1924; literature, science, art, education; Publrs O. ZMORA, A. BITAN.

Eked Publishing House: 29 Bar-Kochba St, POB 11138, Tel-Aviv; tel. 03-283648; f. 1959; poetry, belles lettres, fiction; Man. Dir MARITZA ROSMAN.

Encyclopedia Publishing Co: 46 Beit Lehem Rd, Jerusalem; tel. 02-719441; telex 26144; f. 1947; Hebrew Encyclopedia and other encyclopaedias; Chair. Mrs BRACHA PELI; Pres. ALEXANDER PELI.

Rodney Franklin Agency: 5 Karl Netter St, POB 37727, Tel-Aviv; tel. 03-288948; telex 341118; exclusive representative of various British and USA publishers; Dir RODNEY FRANKLIN.

G.G. The Jerusalem Publishing House Ltd: 39 Tchernechovski St, POB 7147, Jerusalem; tel. 02-636511; telex 26144; f. 1967; biblical research, history, encyclopaedias, archaeology, arts of the Holy Land, cookbooks, guide books, economics, politics; Dir SHLOMO S. GAFNI; Man. Editor RACHEL GILON.

Gazit: 8 Zvi Brook St, POB 4190, Tel-Aviv; tel. 03-53730; art publishers; Editor GABRIEL TALPHIR.

Hakibbutz Hameuchad Publishing House Ltd: 15 Nehardea St, POB 40015, Tel-Aviv; tel. 03-751483; f. 1940; general; Dir UZI SHAVIT.

Israeli Music Publications Ltd: 25 Keren Hayesod St, POB 7681, Jerusalem 91076; tel. 02-241377; f. 1949; books on music and musical works; Dir STANLEY SIMMONDS.

Izre'el Publishing House Ltd: 76 Dizengoff St, Tel-Aviv; tel. 03-285350; f. 1933; Man. ALEXANDER IZRE'EL.

Jewish History Publications (Israel 1961) Ltd: 46 Beit Lehem Rd, Jerusalem; tel. 02-719441; telex 26144; f. 1961; encyclopaedias, World History of the Jewish People series; Chair. ALEXANDER PELI; Man. Dir IDIT REGEV; Editor-in-Chief Prof. J. PRAWER.

Karni Publishers Ltd: 58 Mazeh St, POB 149, Tel-Aviv 61001; tel. 03-622991; f. 1951; children's and educational books; Publrs O. ZMORA, A. BITAN.

Keter Publishing House Jerusalem Ltd: POB 7145, Givat Shaul B, Jerusalem; tel. 02-523261; f. 1959; original and translated works in all fields of science and humanities, published in English, French, German, other European languages and Hebrew; publishing imprints: Israel Program for Scientific Translations, Israel Universities Press, Keter Books, Encyclopedia Judaica; Man. Dir ELIAV COHEN.

Kiryat Sefer: 15 Arlosoroff St, Jerusalem; tel. 02-521141; f. 1933; concordances, dictionaries, textbooks, maps, scientific books; Dir AVRAHAM SIVAN.

Magnes Press, The: The Hebrew University, Jerusalem; tel. 02-660341; f. 1929; biblical studies, Judaica, and all academic fields; Dir BEN-ZION D. YEHOSHUA.

Rubin Mass Ltd: 11 Marcus St, POB 990, Jerusalem 91009; tel. 02-632565; telex 26144; f. 1927; Hebraica, Judaica; Dir OREN MASS.

Massada Press Ltd: 46 Beit Lehem Rd, Jerusalem; tel. 02-719441; telex 26144; f. 1961; encyclopaedias, Judaica, the arts, educational material, children's books; Chair. ALEXANDER PELI; Man. Dir NATHAN REGEV.

Ministry of Defence Publishing House: 27 David Elazar St, Hakiriya, Tel-Aviv 67673; tel. 03-217940; f. 1939; military literature, Judaism, history and geography of Israel; Dir SHALOM SERI.

ISRAEL

M. Mizrachi Publishers: 67 Levinsky, Tel-Aviv; tel. 03-625652; f. 1960; children's books, novels; Dir MEIR MIZRACHI.

Mosad Harav Kook: POB 642, Jerusalem; tel. 02-526231; f. 1937; editions of classical works, Torah and Jewish studies; Dir Rabbi M. KATZENELENBOGEN.

Otsar Hamoreh: 8 Ben Saruk, POB 303, Tel-Aviv; tel. 03-260211; f. 1951; educational.

Alexander Peli Jerusalem Publishing Co Ltd: 46 Beit Lehem Rd, Jerusalem; tel. 02-719441; telex 26144; f. 1977; encyclopaedias, Judaica, history, the arts, educational material; Chair. ALEXANDER PELI; Man. Dir NATHAN REGEV.

Schocken Publishing House Ltd: POB 2316, Tel-Aviv 61022; tel. 03-650961; telex 341118; f. 1938; general; Dir Mrs RACHELI EDELMAN.

Shikmona Publishing Co Ltd: 33 Herzog St, POB 4044, Jerusalem; tel. 02-660188; f. 1965; Zionism, archaeology, art, fiction and non-fiction.

Sifriat-Ma'ariv Ltd: Derech Petach Tikva 72A, POB 20208, Tel-Aviv 61201; f. 1954; Man. Dir IZCHAK YACHIN; Editor-in-Chief ARIE NIR.

Sifriat Poalim Ltd: 2 Choma Umigdal St, Tel-Aviv 67771; tel. 03-376845; f. 1939; general literature; Gen. Man. NATHAN SHAHAM.

Sinai Publishing Co: 72 Allenby St, Tel-Aviv; tel. 03-663672; f. 1853; Hebrew books and religious articles; Dir MOSHE SCHLESINGER.

World Zionist Organization Torah Education Dept: POB 7044, Jerusalem; tel. 02-632584; f. 1945; education, Jewish philosophy, children's books published in Hebrew, English, French and Spanish.

Weizmann Science Press of Israel: 8A Horkanya St, POB 801, Jerusalem 91007; tel. 02-663203; f. 1955; publishes scientific books and periodicals; Man. Dir RAMI MICHAELI; Exec. Editor L. LESTER.

Yachdav United Publishers Co Ltd: 29 Carlebach St, POB 20123, Tel-Aviv; tel. 03-284191; telex 341118; f. 1960; educational; Chair. EPHRAIM BEN-DOR; Exec. Dir ARIE FRIEDLER.

Yavneh Publishing House Ltd: 4 Mazeh St, Tel-Aviv 65213; tel. 03-297856; telex 35770; f. 1932; general; Dir AVSHALOM ORENSTEIN.

S. Zack and Co: 2 King George St, Jerusalem; tel. 02-227819; f. c. 1930; fiction, science, philosophy, religion, children's books, educational and reference books; Dir MICHAEL ZACK.

PUBLISHERS' ASSOCIATION

Israel Book Publishers Association: 29 Carlebach St, POB 20123, Tel-Aviv 67132; tel. 03-284191; telex 341118; f. 1939; mems: 84 publishing firms; Chair. RACHELI EIDELMAN; Exec. Dir ARIE FRIEDLER.

Radio and Television

In 1983 there were an estimated 3m. radio receivers and 582,000 TV receivers in use.

RADIO

Israel Broadcasting Authority (IBA) (Radio): POB 6387, Jerusalem; tel. 02-222121; telex 26488; f. 1948; station in Jerusalem with additional studios in Tel-Aviv and Haifa. IBA broadcasts six programmes for local and overseas listeners on medium, shortwave and VHF/FM in 16 languages; Hebrew, Arabic, English, Yiddish, Ladino, Romanian, Hungarian, Moghrabit, Persian, French, Russian, Bucharian, Georgian, Portuguese, Spanish and Ethiopian; Dir-Gen. URI PORAT.

Galei Zahal: POB MPO 01005, Zahal; tel. 814888; f. 1951; Israeli defence forces broadcasting station, Tel-Aviv, with studios in Jerusalem; broadcasts music, news and other programmes on medium-wave and FM stereo in Hebrew; Dir NACHMAN SHAI; Dir of Engineering S. KASIF.

TELEVISION

Israel Broadcasting Authority (IBA): POB 7139, Jerusalem; tel. 02-557111; telex 25301; broadcasts began in 1968; station in Jerusalem with additional studios in Tel-Aviv; one black and white network (VHF with UHF available in some areas); broadcasts in Hebrew and Arabic; Dir-Gen. JOSEPH LAPID; Dir of Engineering G. FISCHER.

Instructional Television Centre: Ministry of Education and Culture, 14 Klausner St, Tel-Aviv; tel. 03-414155; telex 34118; f. 1966 by Hanadiv (Rothschild Memorial Group) as Instructional Television Trust; began transmission in 1966; school programmes form an integral part of the syllabus in a wide range of subjects; also adult education; Gen. Man. YA'AKOV LORBERBAUM; Dir of Engineering A. KAPLAN.

In September 1986 the Government approved the establishment of a commercial radio and television network to be run in competition with the state system.

Finance

(cap. = capital; p.u. = paid up; dep. = deposits; m. = million; res = reserves; brs = branches)

BANKING

Central Bank

Bank of Israel: Bank of Israel Bldg, Kiryat Ben Gurion, POB 780, Jerusalem 91007; tel. 02-552211; telex 25213; f. 1954 as the Central Bank of the State of Israel; cap. 200m. shekels, res 800m. shekels, dep. 1,000m. shekels (Dec. 1984); Gov. Prof. MICHAEL BRUNO; Deputy Gov. Dr Y. PLESSNER; Mans M. FRAENKEL, S. PELED, G. MAOR, M. LAHAV, O. HEZRONI, F. WIEDER, V. MEDINA, S. BILITZKI, M. HERZBERG, I. IGRA, M. RABOY; 2 brs.

Principal Israeli Banks

American Israeli Bank Ltd: 28A Rothschild Blvd, POB 1346, Tel-Aviv 61013; tel. 03-614656; telex 33710; f. 1975; subsidiary of Bank Hapoalim BM; cap. and res 19.2m. new shekels, dep. 622.9m. new shekels (Dec. 1985); Chair. M. AMIT; Man. Dir A. SCHER; 20 brs.

Bank Hapoalim BM: 50 Rothschild Blvd, Tel-Aviv 65124; tel. 03-673333; telex 32121; f. 1921; cap. and res 344,024m. shekels, dep. 8,700,290m. shekels (Dec. 1984); Chair. Bd of Man. AMIRAM SIVAN; Man. Dirs J. GEVA, G. GIL, M. OLENIK; 370 brs and offices.

Bank Leumi le-Israel BM: 24–32 Yehuda Halevi St, Tel-Aviv 65546; tel. 03-648111; telex 33586; f. 1902; total assets US $22,200m., dep. US $14,700m. (Dec. 1985); Chair. Dr MEIR HETH; Man. Dir ZADIK BINO; 245 brs.

Finance and Trade Bank Ltd: 14 Rothschild Blvd, POB 937, Tel-Aviv 61008; tel. 03-629756; telex 33520; f. 1979; subsidiary of United Mizrahi Bank Ltd; cap. and res 13.4m. new shekels, dep. 44.3m. new shekels (Dec. 1985); Chair. MOSHE MANN; Man. Dir DAVID BLUMBERG.

First International Bank of Israel Ltd: Shalom Mayer Tower, 9 Ahad Ha'am St, POB 29036, Tel-Aviv 61290; tel. 03-636111; telex 341252; f. 1972 as a result of a merger between The Foreign Trade Bank Ltd and Export Bank Ltd; cap. and res 6,398m. shekels, dep. 166,871m. shekels (Dec. 1983); Chair. YIGAL ARNON; Deputy Chair. and Chief Exec. Officer DAVID GOLAN; Man. Dir SHALOM SINGER; 87 brs.

Industrial Development Bank of Israel Ltd: 2 Dafna St, Tel-Aviv 61334; tel. 03-430611; telex 033646; f. 1957; cap. and res 58,161m. shekels, dep. 361,465m. shekels; Chair. A. FRIEDMANN; Man. Dir JOSEPH SARIG.

Israel Ampal Industrial Development Bank Ltd: 111 Arlosoroff St, POB 27, Tel-Aviv 61000; f. 1956; cap. p.u. 3,034.7m. shekels, dep. 155,213m. shekels (Dec. 1984); Chair. M. OLENIK; Man. Dirs M. BACHAR, M. JAFFE.

Israel Bank of Agriculture Ltd: 83 Hahashmonaim St, POB 2440, Tel-Aviv 61024; f. 1951; cap. p.u. 1,547m. shekels, dep. 46.7m. shekels (March 1984); Chair. G. MAKOFF; Gen. Man. I. RAUCH.

Israel Continental Bank Ltd: 65 Rothschild Blvd, POB 37406, Tel-Aviv 61373; tel. 03-204148; telex 341447; f. 1973; capital held jointly by Bank Hapoalim BM and Bank für Gemeinwirtschaft AG; cap. p.u. 7,185m. shekels, dep. 108,390m. shekels (Dec. 1984); Chair. Dr WALTER HESSELBACH; Man. Dir MOSHE GOLDNER; 3 brs.

Israel Discount Bank Ltd: 27-31 Yehuda Halevi St, Tel-Aviv 65546; tel. 03-637111; telex 33724; f. 1935; cap. p.u. 920,000 new shekels (Dec. 1985); dep. 14,834m. new shekels (Dec. 1985); Chair. JOSEF GECHANOVER; more than 270 brs in Israel and abroad.

Israel General Bank Ltd: 38 Rothschild Blvd, POB 677, Tel-Aviv 61006; tel. 03-645645; telex 33515; f. 1964; Chair. Baron EDMOND DE ROTHSCHILD; Man. Dir ABRAHAM BIGGER; 3 brs.

Leumi Agricultural Development Bank Ltd: 19 Rothschild Blvd, POB 2, Tel-Aviv 65121; tel. 03-632111; telex 33586; f. 1922; subsidiary of Bank Leumi le-Israel BM; cap. and res 19.3m. new shekels, dep. 945.5m. new shekels (Dec. 1985); Chair. G. LEV; Man. Dir L. MALOWANCZYK.

ISRAEL — *Directory*

Leumi Industrial Development Bank Ltd: 19 Rothschild Blvd, POB 2, Tel-Aviv 65121; tel. 03-632111; telex 33586; f. 1944; subsidiary of Bank Leumi le-Israel BM; cap. and res 13.0m. new shekels, dep. 1,308.4m. new shekels (Dec. 1985); Chair. J. ERTEL; Man. Dir L. MALOWANCZYK.

Maritime Bank of Israel Ltd: 16 Ahad ha'am St, POB 29373, Tel-Aviv 61293; f. 1962; cap. and res 1,553m. shekels, dep. 18,167m. shekels (June 1984); Chair. I. FLAXMAN; Man. Dir H. DUVSHANI.

North American Bank Ltd: 116 Allenby St, POB 30218, Tel-Aviv 61301; f. 1978; cap. and res 1,473m. shekels, dep. 9,807m. shekels (Dec. 1983); Man. Dir. D. ZAFRIR; 4 brs.

Union Bank of Israel Ltd: 6–8 Ahuzat Bayit St, POB 2428, Tel-Aviv 65143; tel. 03-631631; telex 033493; f. 1951; subsidiary of Bank Leumi le-Israel BM; Chair. E. I. JAPHET; Man. Dir M. M. MAYER; Gen. Man. S. SOROKER; 27 brs.

United Mizrahi Bank Ltd: 13 Rothschild Blvd, Tel-Aviv 65121; tel. 03-629211; telex 36125; f. 1923; Chair. ITZHAK YAGER; Man. Dir MICHAEL ZVINERI; 85 brs.

Mortgage Banks

Israel Development and Mortgage Bank Ltd: 16–18 Simtat Beit Hashoeva, Tel-Aviv 65814; f. 1959; subsidiary of Israel Discount Bank Ltd; cap. p.u. 879.4m., res 5,305.7m. shekels (Dec. 1984); Chair. M. B. GITTER; Man. Dir KARL REICH.

Leumi Mortgage Bank Ltd: 31–37 Montefiore St, POB 69, Tel-Aviv 65201; tel. 03-202444; f. 1921; subsidiary of Bank Leumi le-Israel BM; total assets 1,319.8m. new shekels (Dec. 1985); Chair. J. ROSH; Man. Dir Z. BIRNBAUM; 4 brs.

Merav Mortgage and Savings Bank Ltd: 49 Rothschild Blvd, POB 116, Tel-Aviv 61000; f. 1922; subsidiary of First International Bank of Israel Ltd; cap. and res 1,558m. shekels (Dec. 1983); Chair. A. SACHAROV; Man. Dir E. SHANOON.

Mishkan-Hapoalim Mortgage Bank Ltd: 2 Ibn Gvirol St, Tel-Aviv 64077; f. 1950; subsidiary of Bank Hapoalim BM; cap. and res 762m. shekels (Dec. 1983); dep. 14,635m. shekels (1983); Chair. M. OLENIK; Man. Dir A. KROIZER.

Tefahot, Israel Mortgage Bank Ltd: 9 Heleni Hamalka St, POB 93, Jerusalem 91000; tel. 02-219111; f. 1945; subsidiary of United Mizrahi Bank Ltd; cap. and res 38,092m. shekels; total assets 925,297m. shekels (March 1984); Chair. A. MEIR; Man. Dir MOSHE MANN; affiliated Bank: **Carmel Mortgage and Investment Bank Ltd,** 9 Heleni Hamalka St, POB 93, Jerusalem 91000; cap. and res 2,320m. shekels (March 1985); Chair. MOSHE MANN; Man. Dir A. DICK.

Foreign Banks

Barclays Discount Bank Ltd: 103 Allenby Rd, POB 1292, Tel-Aviv 61012; tel. 03-643333; telex 33550; f. 1971 by Barclays Bank International Ltd and Israel Discount Bank Ltd to incorporate Israel brs of Barclays; cap. and res 58.2m. new shekels, dep. 776.6m. new shekels (Dec. 1985); Chair. GIDEON LAHAV; Gen. Man. MOSHE NEUDORFER; 71 brs; wholly owned subsidiary: **Mercantile Bank of Israel Ltd,** POB 512, 24 Rothschild Blvd, Tel-Aviv; f. 1924; cap. and res 3.7m. new shekels, dep. 27.3m. new shekels (Dec. 1985); Chair. and Man. Dir S. MAGRISO.

A branch of the Jordan-based Cairo-Amman Bank was opened in Nablus, in the occupied West Bank, in November 1986 to provide financial services to the Palestinian community. The branch will operate in both Jordanian dinars and Israeli shekels and be subject to dual Jordanian and Israeli regulatory authority. The manager of the branch was named as JAUDAT SHA'SHA.

STOCK EXCHANGE

Tel-Aviv Stock Exchange: 54 Ahad Ha'am St, POB 29060, Tel-Aviv 61290; tel. 03-627411; telex 342112; f. 1953; Chair. HAIM STOESSEL; Gen. Man. J. NITZANI.

INSURANCE

The Israel Insurance Association lists 35 companies, a selection of which are listed below; not all companies are members of the association.

Ararat Insurance Co Ltd: Ararat House, 13 Montefiore St, Tel-Aviv 65164; tel. 03-640888; telex 341484; f. 1949; cap. p.u. 9.1m. new shekels; Co-Chair. AHARON DOVRAT, PHILIP ZUCKERMAN; Gen. Man. PINCHAS COHEN.

Aryeh Insurance Co Ltd: 9 Ahad Ha'am St, Tel-Aviv 65251; tel. 03-652671; telex 342125; f. 1948; Chair. AVINOAM M. TOCATLY.

Clal Insurance Co Ltd: 42 Rothschild Blvd, POB 326, Tel-Aviv 61002; tel. 03-627711; telex 341701; f. 1962; Man. Dir R. BEN-SHAOUL.

Hassneh Insurance Co of Israel Ltd: 115 Allenby St, POB 805, Tel-Aviv 61007; f. 1924; Man. Dir EITAN AVNEYON.

Israel Phoenix Assurance Co Ltd, The: 30 Levontin St, Tel-Aviv 65116; tel. 03-620111; telex 341199; f. 1949; Chair. of Board DAVID J. HACKMEY; Man. Dir JOSEPH D. HACKMEY.

Israel Reinsurance Co Ltd, The: 5 Drujanov St, POB 11589, Tel-Aviv 61114; tel. 03-296141; telex 342677; f. 1951; Chair. N. MISHOR; Man. Dir S. JANNAI.

Maoz Insurance Co Ltd: 10 Betzalel-Yafe St, Tel-Aviv 65204; f. 1945; formerly Binyan Insurance Co Ltd; Chair. B. YEKUTIELI.

Menorah Insurance Co Ltd: Menorah House, 73 Rothschild Blvd, Tel-Aviv 65786; tel. 03-294771; telex 341433; f. 1935; Pres. DAVID HIRSCHFELD.

Migdal Insurance Co Ltd: 26 Sa'adiya Ga'on St, POB 37633, Tel-Aviv 61375; tel. 03-298129; telex 342331; part of Bank Leumi Group; f. 1934; Chair. B. YEKUTIELI; Gen. Mans U. E. LEVY, M. ZANGEN.

Palglass Palestine Plate Glass Insurance Co Ltd: 30 Achad Ha'am St, Tel-Aviv 65541; f. 1934; Gen. Man. AKIVA ZALZMAN.

Sahar Insurance Co Ltd: Sahar House, 23 Ben-Yehuda St, POB 26222, Tel-Aviv 63806; tel. 03-630311; telex 33759; f. 1949; Chair. A. SACHAROV; Man. Dir AL. SACHAROV.

Samson Insurance Co Ltd: Aviv Bldg, 5 Jabotinski Rd, Ramat-Gan 52520, POB 33678, Tel-Aviv; f. 1933; Chair. A. GOLZ; Gen. Man. D. SERR.

Sela Insurance Co Ltd: 53 Rothschild Blvd, Tel-Aviv 65124; tel. 03-61028; telex 35744; f. 1938; Man. Dir E. SHANI.

Shiloah Co Ltd: 2 Pinsker St, Tel-Aviv 63322; f. 1933; Gen. Man. Dr S. BAMIRAH; Man. Mme BAMIRAH.

Yardenia Insurance Co Ltd: 22 Maze St, Tel-Aviv 65213; f. 1948; Man. Dir H. LEBANON.

Zion Insurance Co Ltd: 120 Allenby Rd, Tel-Aviv 65128; f. 1935; Chair. A. R. TAIBER.

The Histadrut

Hahistadrut Haklalit shel Haovdim Beeretz Israel (General Federation of Labour in Israel): 93 Arlosoroff St, Tel-Aviv 62098.

The General Federation of Labour in Israel, usually known as the Histadrut, is the largest voluntary organization in Israel, and the most important economic body in the state. It is open to all workers, including members of co-operatives and of the liberal professions, who join directly as individuals. The Histadrut engages in four main fields of activity: trade union organization; economic development; social insurance based on mutual aid; and educational and cultural activities. Dues—3.9% of wages—cover all its trade union, health and social services activities. The Histadrut was founded in 1920.

Secretary-General: ISRAEL KAISSAR.

ORGANIZATION

In 1983 the Histadrut had a membership of 1,600,000, including over 160,000 in collective, co-operative and private villages (kibutzim and moshavim) affiliated through the Agricultural Workers' Union, and 360,000 wives (who have membership status); 170,000 of the members were Arabs. In addition some 110,000 young people under 18 years of age belong to the Organization of Working and Student Youth, a direct affiliate of the Histadrut. The main religious labour organizations, Histadrut Hapoel Hamizrahi and Histadrut Poalei Agudat Israel, belong to the trade union section and welfare services, which thus extend to 85% of all workers in Israel.

All members take part in elections to the Histadrut Convention (Veida), which elects the General Council (Moetsa) and the Executive Committee (Vaad Hapoel). The latter elects the 43-member Executive Bureau (Vaada Merakezet), which is responsible for day-to-day implementation of policy. The Executive Committee also elects the Secretary-General, who acts as its chairman as well as head of the organization as a whole and chairman of the Executive Bureau. Nearly all political parties are represented on the Histadrut Executive Committee. Throughout Israel there are 72 local Labour Councils.

The Executive Committee has the following departments: Trade Union, Integration of Arab Members, Mutual Security Centre,

Organization, International, Finance, Legal, Employment, Vocational Training, Absorption and Development, Academic Workers, Culture and Education, Institute of Economic and Social Research, Diaspora Communities, Youth and Sport, Consumers' Authority, Industrial Democracy, Religious Affairs and Higher Education.

TRADE UNION ACTIVITIES

Collective agreements with employers fix wage scales, which are linked with the retail price index; provide for social benefits, including paid sick leave and employers' contributions to sick and pension and provident funds; and regulate dismissals. Dismissal compensation is regulated by law. The Histadrut actively promotes productivity through labour management boards and the National Productivity Institute, and supports incentive pay schemes.

There are unions for the following groups: clerical workers, building workers, teachers, engineers, agricultural workers, technicians, textile workers, printing workers, diamond workers, metal workers, food and bakery workers, wood workers, government employees, seamen, nurses, civilian employees of the armed forces, actors, musicians and variety artists, social workers, watchmen, cinema technicians, institutional and school staffs, pharmacy employees, medical laboratory workers, X-ray technicians, physiotherapists, social scientists, microbiologists, psychologists, salaried lawyers, pharmacists, physicians, occupational therapists, truck and taxi drivers, hotel and restaurant workers, workers in Histadrut-owned industry, garment, shoe and leather workers, plastic and rubber workers, editors of periodicals, painters and sculptors and industrial workers.

ECONOMIC ACTIVITIES AND SOCIAL SERVICES

These include Hevrat Ovdim (Economic Sector, employing 260,000 workers in 1983), Kupat Holim (the Sick Fund, covering almost 77% of Israel's population), seven pension funds, and NA'AMAT (women's organization which runs nursery homes and kindergartens, organizes vocational education and promotes legislation for the protection and benefit of working women).

Trade and Industry

CHAMBERS OF COMMERCE

Federation of Israeli Chambers of Commerce: 84 Hahashmonaim St, POB 501, Tel-Aviv; tel. 03-288224; telex 33484; co-ordinates the Tel-Aviv, Jerusalem, Haifa and Beersheba Chambers of Commerce; Dir ZVI AMIT.

Jerusalem Chamber of Commerce: POB 183, 10 Hillel St, Jerusalem 91000; tel. 02-224333; f. 1908; about 300 mems; Pres. JOSEPH PERLMAN; Vice-Pres HAIM COHEN, AVRAHAM DASKAL, SHALOM P. DORON, AVNER PEREZ, JOSEPH PINCHASSOF, ADIN TALBAR; Dir-Gen. SHLOMO NAHMIAS.

Haifa Chamber of Commerce and Industry (Haifa and District): POB 33176, 53 Haatzmaut Rd, Haifa 31331; tel. 04-663471; telex 46653; f. 1921; 700 mems; Pres. GAD SASSOWER; Gen. Sec. A. MEHULAL.

Chamber of Commerce, Tel-Aviv-Jaffa: 84 Hahashmonaim St, POB 20027, Tel-Aviv 67011; tel. 03-288224; telex 33484; f. 1919; 1,800 mems; Pres. DAN GILLERMAN; Man. Dir ZVI AMIT; Dept Dirs BARRY PINTOW, J. SHOSTAK.

Federation of Bi-National Chambers of Commerce with and in Israel: 84 Hahashmonaim St, POB 1127, Tel-Aviv; federates: Israel-America Chamber of Commerce and Industry; Israel-British Chamber of Commerce; Australia-Israel Chambers of Commerce; Chamber of Commerce and Industry Israel-Africa; Chamber of Commerce Israel-Belgique-Luxembourg; Canada-Israel Chamber of Commerce and Industry; Israel-Danish Chamber of Commerce; Chambre de Commerce Israel-France; Chamber of Commerce and Industry Israel-Germany; Camera di Commercio Israeli-Italia; Israel-Japan Chamber of Commerce; Israel-Latin America, Spain and Portugal Chamber of Commerce; Netherlands-Israel Chamber of Commerce; Israel-Norway Chamber of Commerce; Handelskammer Israel-Schweiz; Israel-South Africa Chamber of Commerce; Israel-Sweden Chamber of Commerce; also incorporates Bi-National Chamber of Commerce existing in 20 foreign countries with Israel.

Israel-British Chamber of Commerce: POB 16065, Tel-Aviv 61160; tel. 03-259732; telex 342315; f. 1951; 440 mems; Gen. Sec. FELIX KIPPER; Chair. S. EYAL.

TRADE AND INDUSTRIAL ORGANIZATIONS

The Agricultural Union: Tchlenov 20, Tel-Aviv; consists of more than 50 agricultural settlements and is connected with marketing and supplying organizations, and Bahan Ltd, controllers and auditors.

Central Union of Artisans and Small Manufacturers: POB 4041, Tel-Aviv 61040; f. 1907; has a membership of over 40,000 divided into 70 groups according to trade; the union is led by a seventeen-man Presidium; Chair. JACOB FRANK; Sec. ITZHAK HASSON; 30 brs.

Citrus Marketing Board: 6 Wissotzky St, POB 21371, Tel-Aviv 61213; the growers' institution for the control of the Israel citrus industry; Board made up of representatives of the Government and the growers. Functions: control of plantations, supervision of picking and packing operations, marketing of the crop overseas and on the home markets; shipping; supply of fertilizers, insecticides, equipment for orchards and packing houses and of packing materials, technical research and extension work; long-term financial assistance to growers.

Farmers' Union of Israel: 8 Kaplan St, POB 209, Tel-Aviv; tel. 03-252227; f. 1913; membership of 7,000 independent farmers, citrus and winegrape growers; Pres. ELIAHU IZAKSON; Chair. Council IZCHAK-ZIV-AV; Dir-Gen. SHLOMO REISMAN.

General Association of Merchants in Israel: 6 Rothschild Blvd, Tel-Aviv; the organization of retail traders; has a membership of 30,000 in 60 brs.

Israel Diamond Exchange Ltd: POB 3222, Ramat-Gan; tel. 03-214211; f. 1937; production, export, import and finance facilities; estimated exports (1985) US $1,433m.; Pres. MOSHE SCHNITZER.

Israel Journalists' Association Ltd: 4 Kaplan St, Tel-Aviv; Sec. MOSHE RON.

Manufacturers' Association of Israel: 29 Hamered St, POB 50022, Tel-Aviv 61500; tel. 03-650121; telex 342651; 1,200 mem.-enterprises employing nearly 72% of industrial workers in Israel; Pres. DOV LAUTMAN; Dir-Gen. ARNON TIBERG.

TRADE UNIONS

Histadrut Haovdim Haleumit (National Labour Federation): 23 Sprintzak St, Tel-Aviv 64738; tel. 03-258351; f. 1934; 150,000 mems.

Histadrut Hapoel Hamizrahi (National Religious Workers' Party): 166 Even Gavirol St, Tel-Aviv; 125,000 mems in 81 settlements.

Histadrut Poale Agudat Israel (Agudat Israel Workers' Organization): 64 Frishman St, POB 11044, Tel-Aviv; tel. 03-242126; has 33,000 members in 16 settlements and 8 educational insts.

Transport

RAILWAYS

Freight traffic consists mainly of grain, phosphates, potash, containers, oil and building materials. Rail service serves Haifa and Ashdod, ports on the Mediterranean Sea, while a combined railroad service extends to Eilat port on the Red Sea. Work is in progress on a 173-km extension of the network to Eilat. Passenger services operate between the main towns: Nahariya, Haifa, Tel-Aviv and Jerusalem.

Israel State Railways: Central Station, POB 44, Haifa; tel. 04-531211; telex 46570; all lines are managed and operated from Haifa. The total length of main line is 573 km; gauge 1,435 mm; Gen. Man. ELIAHU BARAK; Deputy Gen. Man. (Admin.) DAVID GUY; Deputy Gen. Man. (Tech.) LEON HEYMAN.

Underground Railway

Haifa Underground Funicular Railway: 12 Hanassi Ave, Haifa; opened 1959; 2 km in operation; Man. D. SCHARF.

ROADS

At the beginning of 1985 there were 13,280 km of paved roads. There are 4,600 km of metalled inter-urban highways not including roads in towns and settlements.

Ministry of Housing and Construction: Public Works Dept, Jerusalem.

SHIPPING

In 1984 Israel had a merchant fleet of 88 ships.

Haifa and Ashdod are the main ports in Israel. The former is a natural harbour, enclosed by two main breakwaters and dredged to 39 ft below mean sea-level. In 1965 the new deep water port was completed at Ashdod which had a capacity of about 7.3m. tons in 1985.

The port of Eilat is Israel's gate to the Red Sea. It is a natural harbour, operated from a wharf. A new port, to the south of the original one, started operating in 1965.

The Israel Ports Authority: Maya Building, 74 Petach Tikva Rd, POB 20121, Tel-Aviv; tel. 03-338911; telex 33677; f. 1961; to plan, build, develop, administer, maintain and operate the ports. In 1985/86 investment plans amounted to US $57.8m. for the development budget in Haifa, Ashdod and Eilat ports. Cargo traffic April 1985–March 1986 amounted to 13.3m. tons (oil excluded); Chair. Zvi Keinan; Dir-Gen. Ing. Shaul Raziel.

ZIM Israel Navigation Co Ltd: 7–9 Pal-Yam Ave, POB 1723, Haifa 31016; tel. 04-652111; telex 46501; f. 1945; runs cargo and container services in the Mediterranean and to N Europe, N and S America, Far East, Africa and Australia; operates 32 ships; Chair. Haim Stoessel; Man. Dir Matty Morgenstern.

CIVIL AVIATION

El Al Israel Airlines Ltd: POB 41, Ben Gurion Airport, Lod, Tel-Aviv; tel. 03-9716111; telex 31107; f. 1948; the Government is the major stockholder; daily services to most capitals of Europe; over 20 flights weekly to New York; services to the USA, Canada, Egypt, Kenya, South Africa and Turkey; fleet of 4 Boeing 747-200B, 2 Boeing 747-200B Combi, 1 Boeing 747-200F, 1 Boeing 747-100F, 5 Boeing 707, 2 Boeing 737-200, 4 Boeing 767-200; Chair. Nachman Perel; Pres. Rafael Har-Lev.

Arkia Israeli Airlines Ltd: Sde-Dov Airport, POB 39301, Tel-Aviv 61392; tel. 03-422777; telex 341749; f. 1980 through merger of Kanaf-Arkia Airlines and Aviation Services; scheduled passenger services linking Tel-Aviv, Jerusalem, Haifa, Eilat, Rosh Pina and Luxor (Egypt); cargo services to European destinations; fleet of 2 De Havilland Dash-7, 5 Navajo Chieftain, 2 Islander, 1 Aero Commander, 2 Cessna 337 (2 Boeing 707 leased from El Al); Pres. Joseph Rosen; Man. Dir David Borovitz.

Tourism

Ministry of Tourism: Hakirya, POB 1018, Jerusalem; tel. 02-237311; Minister of Tourism Avraham Sharir; Dir-Gen. Rafael Farber.

Atomic Energy

Israel Atomic Energy Commission: 26 Rehov Hauniversita, Ramat Aviv, POB 7061, Tel-Aviv; tel. 03-415111; telex 33450; f. 1952; advises the government on long term policies and priorities in the advancement of nuclear research and development; supervises the implementation of policies approved by the government, including the licensing of nuclear power plants and the promotion of technological and industrial applications; represents Israel in its relations with scientific institutions abroad and international organizations engaged in nuclear research and development (Israel is a member of IAEA); Chair. The Prime Minister; Dir-Gen. David Peleg (acting).

The Atomic Energy Commission has two research and development centres: the Nahal Soreq Nuclear Research Centre and the Negev Nuclear Research Centre near Dimona. The main fields of research are: nuclear physics and chemistry, plasma physics, solid state physics and chemistry, optics and electro-optics, reactor physics and engineering, radiation chemistry and biology, metallurgy and materials engineering, nuclear medicine and radiopharmaceutics, non-destructive testing and environmental studies. Research and development projects and work with industrial applications include studies in isotopes, radiopharmaceuticals, medical and solid state lasers, crystal growth, high-tech. materials (including ceramics, ultra-pure electro-optical materials, infra-red glasses), mineral prospecting and the recovery of uranium from phosphates, use of intense sources of radiation in the medical, chemical and food industries, and the engineering and design of equipment for use in highly corrosive environments. The centres also provide national services: radiation protection, production and distribution of radioactive and stable isotopes, molecule and radiopharmaceutical labelling, high vacuum engineering, training of personnel, information and documentation, etc.

Negev Nuclear Research Centre: Dimona; equipped with a natural uranium-fuelled and heavy water-moderated reactor IRR-2 of 25 MW thermal; Dir Abraham Seroussi.

Soreq Nuclear Research Centre: Yavne 70600; tel. 08-484211; telex 341955; f. 1954; equipped with a 'swimming pool' type research reactor IRR-1 of 5 MW thermal; Dir G. Frank.

Weizmann Institute of Science: POB 26, Rehovot; tel. 08-482111; telex 361900; f. 1949; incorporates the Daniel Sieff Research Institute (f. 1934); includes 21 research units grouped into 5 faculties (Mathematical Sciences, Physics, Chemistry, Biophysics-Biochemistry, Biology), and a department of science teaching within the Feinberg Graduate School; 12 research centres have been established; the scientific staff numbers about 630, including 390 resident scientists, some 120 long-term visiting scientists, and 120 research assistants; there are about 400 students studying at the Feinberg Graduate School and doing research in the Institute's laboratories; there is also a Department of Isotope Research (Head: S. Vega); the technical staff numbers 830 and there are 540 administrative and service personnel; Chair. Bd of Govs Lord Sieff of Brimpton; Pres. Prof. Michael Sela; Chair. Scientific Council Prof. A. Friesem.

Estimated Defence Expenditure (1985): 3,600,000m. shekels (US $3,621m.).

Military Service (Jewish and Druze population only; Christians may volunteer): Men under 29 and some unmarried women under 26 are called for regular service of up to 39 months for men and 24 months for women. Physicians may be called up to the age of 34.

Total Armed Forces (July 1985): 142,000: including 93,300 conscripts; this can be raised to 500,000 by mobilizing reservists within 48–72 hours; army 104,000 (88,000 conscripts); navy 10,000 (3,300 conscripts); air force 28,000 (2,000 conscripts).

Paramilitary Forces (July 1985): 4,500.

ITALY

Introductory Survey

Location, Climate, Language, Religion, Flag, Capital
The Italian Republic comprises a peninsula, extending from southern Europe into the Mediterranean Sea, and a number of adjacent islands. The two principal islands are Sicily, to the south-west, and Sardinia, to the west. The Alps form a natural boundary to the north, where the bordering countries are France to the north-west, Switzerland and Austria to the north and Yugoslavia to the north-east. The climate is temperate in the north and Mediterranean in the south, with mild winters and long, dry summers. The average temperature in Rome is 7.4°C (45.3°F) in January and 25.7°C (78.3°F) in July. The principal language is Italian. German is spoken in the Alto Adige region on the Austrian border, and French in the Valle d'Aosta region (bordering France and Switzerland), while in the Basilicata region of south-eastern Italy there is an Albanian-speaking minority. Almost all of the inhabitants profess Christianity: more than 90% are adherents of the Roman Catholic Church. There is freedom of expression for other Christian denominations and for non-Christian religions. The national flag (proportions 3 by 2) has three equal vertical stripes, of green, white and red. The capital is Rome.

Recent History
The Kingdom of Italy, under the House of Savoy, was proclaimed in 1861 and the country was unified in 1870. Italy subsequently acquired an overseas empire, comprising the African colonies of Eritrea (now part of Ethiopia), Italian Somaliland and Libya. Benito Mussolini, leader of the Fascist Party, became Prime Minister in October 1922 and assumed dictatorial powers in 1925–26. Relations between the Italian state and the Roman Catholic Church, a subject of bitter controversy since Italy's unification, were codified in 1929 by a series of agreements, including the Lateran Treaty, which recognized the sovereignty of the State of the Vatican City (q.v.), a small enclave within the city of Rome, under the jurisdiction of the Pope. Italian forces from Eritrea and Somaliland attacked and occupied neighbouring Ethiopia in 1935–36. Under Mussolini's rule, Italy also supported the Fascist forces in the Spanish Civil War of 1936–39, and annexed Albania in April 1939. From June 1940, Italy supported Nazi Germany in the Second World War. Italian forces from Albania attacked Greece in October 1940, but were defeated and forced to withdraw. In 1941 British forces captured Eritrea and Italian Somaliland, and ended Italy's occupation of Ethiopia, and in 1942 British and French forces occupied Libya. As forces from the allied powers invaded Italy, the Fascist regime crumbled. King Victor Emmanuel III dismissed Mussolini, and the Fascist Party was dissolved, in July 1943. With Italy's effective withdrawal from the war, German forces assumed the occupation of Albania. In Italy itself, anti-Fascist partisans joined allied forces in resisting the occupation by the remaining German troops. German forces in Italy surrendered, and Mussolini was killed, in April 1945. The war had caused the dissolution of Italy's overseas empire, although in 1950 the British military administration of Italian Somaliland ended and the pre-war colony became a UN Trust Territory, with Italy returning as the administering power, until its merger with neighbouring British Somaliland, to form the independent state of Somalia, in 1960.

In May 1946 King Victor Emmanuel abdicated in favour of his son, Umberto II. However, he reigned for only one month. On 10 June, following a referendum, the monarchy was abolished and Italy became a republic. Between 1946 and 1984 there were 44 administrations within nine parliaments. Until 1963 the Christian Democrats' monopoly of power was unchallenged; industry expanded rapidly in a liberal economic system supported by capital from the USA. By 1963, however, low wage rates and lack of social reforms had increased discontent, and in the elections of that year the Communist Party, together with other parties of the extreme right and left, made considerable gains at the expense of the Christian Democrats. The result of these losses was a rapid succession of mainly coalition governments involving the Christian Democrats and one or more of the other major parties. The failure of these successive governments to cope with economic decline, corruption and the increasing problem of terrorism led to further discontent among the electorate.

Aldo Moro's coalition government of Christian Democrats and Republicans, formed in November 1974, resigned in January 1976 after the withdrawal of support by the Socialists. Moro formed a minority Christian Democratic administration in February, but this government was forced to resign in April. General elections for both Houses of Parliament were held in June, when the Communists won 34.4% of the votes for the Chamber of Deputies. Although the Christian Democrats still led the poll with 38.7% (the same as in the 1972 election), support for the Communists was significantly greater than in the previous poll, and they increased their strength in the 630-member Chamber from 179 to 228 seats. The Communists continued to press for the 'historic compromise', a plan for a broad-based government with representatives from the Christian Democratic, Socialist and Communist parties, based on an alliance between Communism and Roman Catholicism. This was rejected by the Christian Democrats, who insisted on excluding the Communists from power, although they could no longer govern against Communist opposition in Parliament. In July a minority government of Christian Democrats was formed by Giulio Andreotti, a former Prime Minister, with the assurance of the abstention of the Communist deputies, and proceeded to introduce severe austerity measures to cope with the continuing economic crisis. In July 1977 the Communists, after four months of negotiations, were allowed a voice in policy-making but no direct role in the Government. The minority government was forced to resign in January 1978, owing to pressure from the Communists, who wanted a more active participation in government, but Andreotti formed a new, almost identical administration in March, with Communist support. The first crisis faced by this government was the murder in May 1978 of Aldo Moro, the former Prime Minister, by the Brigate Rosse (Red Brigades), a terrorist group. The second came in June, when the President, Giovanni Leone, resigned as a result of allegations of corruption. A series of inconclusive ballots finally ended with the inauguration in July of Alessandro Pertini, a former President of the Chamber of Deputies, as the first Socialist President of the Republic.

The Andreotti administration collapsed in January 1979, when the Communists withdrew from the official parliamentary majority, subsequently renewing their claim to posts in the Council of Ministers. After protracted negotiations, a new coalition government was formed by Andreotti in March, only to be defeated within 10 days on a vote of confidence. Parliamentary elections in June did not relieve the stalemate. However, the Communists' share of the vote for the Chamber of Deputies dropped to 30.4%. This unprecedented loss of support prompted the Communists to return to the role of opposition in the next Parliament.

In August 1979 Francesco Cossiga, a former Minister of the Interior, formed a minority 'government of truce', composed of Christian Democrats, Liberals and Social Democrats, relying on the abstention of the Socialists. In spite of its mandate, the new government's initiatives were repeatedly thwarted by obstructionism in Parliament. Cossiga's second administration, formed in April 1980, admitted the Socialists to the Government for the first time in six years in a majority coalition with the Christian Democrats and the Republicans. The deliberate exclusion of the Communists led to an open campaign by their representatives in Parliament to bring down the new coalition.

In September the Government was forced out of office in a secret ballot on its economic programme. In October 1980 Arnaldo Forlani, the chairman of the Christian Democratic party, assembled a coalition of Christian Democrats, Socialists, Republicans and Social Democrats. The new administration's integrity was damaged by a series of scandalous allegations, and it was finally forced to resign in May 1981, after it had been made known that more than 1,000 of Italy's foremost establishment figures belonged to a secret masonic lodge named P-2 ('Propaganda Due') which had extensive criminal connections, both in Italy and abroad. The lodge was linked with many political and financial scandals and even right-wing terrorism, culminating in the summer of 1982 with the collapse of one of the leading Italian banks, Banco Ambrosiano, and the death of its president, Roberto Calvi.

In June 1981 Senator Giovanni Spadolini, leader of the small Republican party, formed a majority coalition of Socialists, Republicans, Christian Democrats, Social Democrats and Liberals, thus becoming the first non-Christian Democratic Prime Minister since 1946. This government fell in August 1982, after the defection of the Socialists, but was reconstituted later that month with the same ministers. In November Spadolini resigned, following a quarrel between Christian Democratic and Socialist ministers concerning the worsening economic situation. A new government was formed in December by Amintore Fanfani, a former Christian Democratic Prime Minister, leading a coalition of Christian Democrats, Socialists, Social Democrats and Liberals, committed to controlling the economy by increasing taxes and reducing public expenditure. This administration lasted until April 1983, when the Socialists withdrew their support and called for a general election. Parliament was dissolved in May, despite attempts by President Pertini to secure the formation of a new government. In the elections held in June, the Christian Democrats, who had rarely won less than 38% of the total vote in any poll since 1946, received only 32.9% of valid votes for the Chamber of Deputies. This loss of support meant that several of the smaller parties increased their shares of the vote. The Socialists made a small advance, taking 11.4% of the total vote. This increase, combined with the loss of support for the Christian Democrats, resulted in the accession of Bettino Craxi, the leader of the Socialist Party, as the first Socialist Prime Minister in the history of the republic. The new administration, a five-party coalition of Christian Democrats, Socialists, Republicans, Social Democrats and Liberals, took office in August, committed to cutting the budget deficit and to economic reform. Its anti-inflation measures included a government decree, imposed in February 1984, to reduce automatic index-linked wage increases (the 'scala mobile'). Despite strikes, demonstrations and fierce parliamentary delaying tactics by the Communist opposition, the decree became law in June.

The sympathy evoked by the sudden death of the Communists' leader, Enrico Berlinguer, in June 1984 assisted a revival in the party's electoral fortunes in the elections to the European Parliament in the same month, when (in alliance with the small Democratic Party for Proletarian Unity) its share of the total vote was 33.3%, surpassing the Christian Democrats' 33.0%. The repercussions of the P-2 scandals (see above) continued in 1984, when Pietro Longo, leader of the Social Democrats in the coalition government, resigned from his post as Budget Minister in July, after allegations that he was a member of the P-2 lodge. This, combined with growing misgivings among some members of the coalition over Craxi's uncompromising style of leadership, created tensions within the Government; the lack of any viable alternative, however, persuaded the leaders of the five coalition parties to agree, in discussions held at the end of July, to avoid a government collapse by continuing to support Craxi as Prime Minister. Craxi continued to consolidate his position by winning votes of confidence in the Senate and the Chamber of Deputies for his programme of economic reforms. In local and regional elections, held in May 1985, the Communists' hopes of electoral advances were unfulfilled, as their share of the vote fell sharply, to 30.2%, while support for the Christian Democrat and Socialist parties increased. The result of a referendum, held in June and sponsored by the Communists, on the Government's decree of the previous year reducing the 'scala mobile', further vindicated the coalition's policies, when 54.3% of votes cast supported the Government.

In July 1985 Francesco Cossiga, President of the Senate and a former Christian Democratic Prime Minister, succeeded Alessandro Pertini as President of the Republic, having been elected on the first ballot of the electoral college. The seizure of an Italian cruise ship, the *Achille Lauro*, in the eastern Mediterranean by Palestinian terrorists in October, and the subsequent repercussions, led to the collapse of the Government when the Republicans withdrew from the coalition, claiming that they had not been fully consulted on policy decisions. A reconciliation was achieved within a few days, and Craxi's resignation as Prime Minister was revoked.

Regional elections were held in Sicily in June 1986, when the Christian Democrats obtained 38% of the votes and the Communists 19%. The extreme left-wing Proletarian Democracy party also gained its first seat in the regional assembly. Later in the same month, Bettino Craxi resigned as Prime Minister, following a vote of 'no confidence' in the Chamber of Deputies, thus bringing to an end Italy's longest administration (1,060 days) since the Second World War. President Cossiga subsequently nominated Giulio Andreotti, the Christian Democrat Minister of Foreign Affairs, to form a new government. However, the refusal of the other coalition parties to support his nomination led to Craxi's return to power in July, on condition that he would transfer the premiership to a Christian Democrat in March 1987. Craxi's new Council of Ministers included five new ministers and two ministers who had changed posts. By November 1986 the Government again appeared to be dangerously weakened as a result of a series of parliamentary defeats on the 1987 budget. Craxi resigned in March 1987.

In February 1986 the biggest trial of Mafia suspects ever held, in which 474 defendants (121 of whom were absent) were being tried in connection with 450 alleged offences (including 97 murders), opened in Palermo, Sicily.

Italy's foreign policy has traditionally been governed by its firm commitment to Europe, through participation in the EEC, and by its role in NATO. In 1983 Italian troops played an important part in the multinational peace-keeping force in Beirut, Lebanon. As a consequence of the US air raid on Libya in April 1986, Italian armed forces took control of Lampedusa island, lying south of Sicily (of which region it forms a part) and about 300 km north of Tripoli, following an unsuccessful Libyan attack on the island's US radar facilities. In May eight Libyan diplomats were expelled from Italy in response to Libya's expulsion of 25 Italian diplomats from Tripoli earlier in the month.

In December 1985 Arab terrorists, belonging to the Palestinian Abu Nidal group, attacked Rome airport, killing 17 people and wounding 75. (A simultaneous attack took place at Vienna airport in Austria.)

Government

Under the 1948 Constitution, legislative power is held by the bicameral Parliament, elected by universal suffrage for five years (subject to dissolution) on the basis of proportional representation. The Senate has 315 elected members (seats allocated on a regional basis) and seven life Senators. The Chamber of Deputies has 630 members. The minimum voting age is 25 years for the Senate and 18 years for the Chamber. The two houses have equal power.

The President of the Republic is a constitutional Head of State elected for seven years by an electoral college comprising both Houses of Parliament, and 58 regional representatives. Executive power is exercised by the Council of Ministers. The Head of State appoints the President of the Council (Prime Minister) and, on the latter's recommendation, other Ministers. The Council is responsible to Parliament.

The country is divided into 20 regions, of which five (Sicily, Sardinia, Trentino-Alto Adige, Friuli-Venezia Giulia and Valle d'Aosta) enjoy a special status. There is a large degree of regional autonomy. Each region has a regional council elected every five years by universal suffrage and a Giunta regionale responsible to the regional council. The regional council is a legislative assembly, while the Giunta holds executive power.

Defence

Italy has been a member of NATO since 1949. In July 1986 it maintained armed forces totalling 387,800 (including 274,500 conscripts): an army of 270,000, a navy of 47,200 and an air force of 70,600. Military service lasts 12 months in the army and air force, and 18 months in the navy. In 1985 defence expenditure was an estimated 16,380,000m. lire, and the defence budget for 1986 was 17,600,000m. lire.

Economic Affairs

After the Second World War, Italy experienced rapid economic development and was transformed from a mainly rural country into a modern industrial power. Between 1950 and 1980 the average income per head increased by more than 200% in real terms. Despite such gains, Italy's standard of living is generally below that of other countries in the EEC. In 1984, according to estimates by the World Bank, Italy's GNP per head (in average 1982–84 prices) was US $6,420, having increased since 1965 at an average real rate of 2.7% per year. The average annual increase in overall gross domestic product (GDP), measured in constant prices, was 5.2% in 1965–73, slowing to 2.1% in 1973–84.

Although agriculture has always represented an important part of the Italian economy, a substantial advance has taken place since the war in the proportion of the GDP contributed by industrial activity, particularly in engineering and other manufacturing sectors. This change has been far more pronounced in the northern part of the country, with its proximity to the rest of Europe. The long-term economic problem, therefore, remains the integration of the southern half of Italy, where the average annual income is still substantially less than that in the north, and where employment and production lag far behind. There are several development agencies and banks which attempt to increase investment in the south, to improve infrastructure and communications and to promote the region's industrialization.

In 1983 agriculture employed only 12.2% of the working population; only 6% of GDP was provided by agriculture, compared with 40% by industry. Plans to improve and modernize the agricultural sector have been thwarted by increased consumption and the inadaptability of many small farms to mechanization. The principal crops, by volume, in 1985 were sugar beet, wheat, maize, olives, grapes and tomatoes. Until 1986, Italy was also the leading producer and exporter of wine in the world, exporting 18m. hl, almost a quarter of its total production, in the year to August 1985. However, it was believed that the discovery, in March 1986, that a small minority of Italian wine producers had added synthetic methanol to their output would reduce exports by at least one-third. In September 1986 Italian exports of live animals and some meat to other EEC countries were banned, for an indefinite period, as the result of an outbreak of foot-and-mouth disease. The Ministry of Agriculture announced an emergency plan to compensate farmers who were affected by the ban.

Tourism is an important source of income, with 53.6m. foreign visitors in 1985, spending a total of 16,721,973m. lire. There are more than 5m. Italians living abroad and their remittances form a valuable source of income. The flourishing 'submerged economy', operating outside government control, is estimated to account for as much as one-third of the national income.

Industrial growth in Italy has, in the past, concentrated on the development of heavy industry, in which the State plays an important part through the large holding companies, IRI, ENI and EFIM. However, many of these industries, such as steel and shipbuilding, are now in decline, leading to the closure of plant and redundancies among the work-force. As the result of a limited 'privatization' programme (introduced in 1983), ENI became profitable for the first time in 12 years, recording a net profit of more than 800,000m. lire in 1985, following a loss of 64,000m. lire in the previous year. The joint turnover of IRI, ENI and EFIM in 1985 was estimated to be in excess of 100,000,000m. lire, following overall losses recorded by IRI and EFIM of 6,000,000m. lire in 1983. Industrial production (excluding construction) grew by 5% in 1980, but fell by 2.2% in 1981, by 3.1% in 1982 and by 2.4% in 1983. However, improvements in labour costs, together with increased investment and the adoption of new technologies, has resulted in higher productivity and manufacturing output in a wide range of industries, including motor cars, textiles, clothing, electronics and consumer goods. Industrial production rose by 4.1% in the year to June 1986, and by 5.1% in the second half of that year. The employers' association, Confindustria, predicted that industrial production would increase by 2.2% in 1987 and by 2.9% in 1988. Investment in manufacturing industry was expected to rise by 9.6% in 1987 and by 6% in the following year.

Italy depended on imported petroleum for 57.4% of its energy requirements in 1984, and in 1985 imports of crude petroleum accounted for 14.7% of total imports. Since the sharp increases in international petroleum prices in 1973–74, measures have been taken to diversify Italy's energy sources. These include a rapid expansion of gas consumption. In June 1983 a natural gas pipeline from Algeria came 'on stream', and was expected to supply 12,000m. cu m of methane in 1986. In May 1984 agreement was reached with the USSR whereby Italy would receive up to 6,000m. cu m of gas per year through the Siberian pipeline. Italy's nuclear power resources remain small. The country currently has four completed nuclear power stations, providing 3.8% of total electricity requirements in 1984.

The Italian economy relies heavily on the export of its manufactured goods to pay for essential imports of petroleum, raw materials and food. Recession in Europe and the rising cost of petroleum, coupled with high inflation and undiminished internal demand, led to annual trade deficits after 1978. Modest economic growth during 1984 caused a rapid rise in the level of imports, while exports were constrained by the overvaluation of the Italian currency within the European Monetary System (EMS). As a result, by 1984 the annual trade deficit had reached a record 19,200,000m. lire and in 1985 grew to 23,023,000m. lire, mainly as the result of a deficit of 39,000,000m. lire on trade in petroleum. The trade deficit for the first seven months of 1986 was 5,524,000m. lire, compared with 16,372,000m. lire in the corresponding period of 1985. The current account of the balance of payments, which had been transformed from a deficit of US $9,747m. in 1980 to a small surplus of $555m. in 1983, was in deficit by $2,821m. in 1984, and by $4,653m. in 1985. According to provisional figures, the deficit was 2,087,000m. lire in the first half of 1986, compared with 5,743,000m. lire in the corresponding period of 1985. The lira was devalued against the EEC currencies within the EMS several times between 1981 and 1983. However, continuing concern over the disparity between Italy's rate of inflation and large trade and public sector deficits, and those of other member countries, prompted a further devaluation of 8% in July 1985. Real GDP fell by 0.4% in 1982 and by 1.2% in 1983, but grew by 2.6% during 1984, by an estimated 2.4% in 1985 and 2.7% in 1986.

Since the early 1970s, increased spending on social services and industry has caused high levels of government expenditure and a public sector deficit far in excess of those of Italy's European competitors. The failure of revenue and taxation to equal this growth has produced a large budget deficit, financed by government borrowing, interest payments for which further fuel the public borrowing requirement. Government spending, measured as a proportion of GDP, reached 58% in 1983 and the public sector deficit rose to 16.8% of GDP. Recent governments have tried to limit this deficit by cuts in public spending, measures against tax evasion and by increases in indirect taxation. Measures introduced by the Craxi Government succeeded in limiting the annual deficit to 95,350,000m. lire in 1984, or 15.4% of GDP. Further restraints on spending were expected to reduce the deficit to 14.8% of GDP in 1985. However, preliminary estimates suggested an acceleration in the growth of the deficit, caused by the need to pay interest on short-term government bonds used to finance the growing national debt. Accumulated government debt in 1984 totalled 93% of GDP, and interest payments represented 9.6% of GDP. In 1986 the national debt increased to the equivalent of 95.9% of annual GDP, or 684,900,000m. lire at current prices, and was expected to exceed 100% of GDP by the end of 1987.

The high public sector deficit was one of the main causes of inflation, which averaged 17.8% in 1981. It fell slightly in 1982, to 16.5%, and agreement between employers and trade unions in January 1983, to reduce quarterly inflation-linked wage increases (the seven-year-old 'scala mobile'), helped to bring inflation down to an average of 14.6% in 1983. Reduced price rises for energy and raw materials, and the Government's success in curtailing the 'scala mobile' (see Recent History), together with measures designed to cut public spending in health services and pensions, had brought inflation down to 10.4% by August 1984. A target of 7% was set for 1985, but by July inflation had only fallen to 9.4%. In the year to November

1986 the annual inflation rate reached its lowest level in 15 years, falling to 4.7%. Plans to introduce the 'lira nuova', to be worth 1,000 of the existing unit (and giving Italy one of the larger currency units in the world), were postponed in late 1986, owing to conflicts between parliamentary finance and budget commissions. Unemployment increased gradually from an average of 8% of the labour force in 1980 to 11.8% in 1983 and to an estimated 12.6% in 1984. In December 1985 the unemployment rate reached 13.2%, the highest level since the Second World War. The rate fell to 11.1% in October 1986. During 1986 the Government announced plans to spend 7,500,000m. lire, over the next three years, on the creation of more than 500,000 new jobs in the south, where the unemployment rate was about double that of the north.

Draft proposals for the 1987 budget envisaged a reduction in the public sector borrowing requirement to 100,000,000m. lire, or 12.2% of GDP, compared with an expected deficit in 1986 of 110,000,000m. lire, or 14.3% of GDP. A GDP growth rate of 3.5% was predicted, and annual inflation was expected to fall to less than 4%. The economy was helped greatly in 1986 by the fall in international petroleum prices and by the weakness of the US dollar in relation to the lira. A current deficit of 66,200,000m. lire was envisaged in the 1987 budget proposals, compared with a deficit of 68,700,000m. lire projected for 1986. In November 1986 the Government averted a general strike by negotiating a series of concessions with the trade unions. The agreements envisaged additional social costs for employees, totalling 880,000m. lire, to be included in the 1987 budget, and the provision of an extra 1,500,000m. lire, over the next three years, to finance the implementation of a new agreement on wages for 3.5m. public-sector workers who had been adversely affected by the flat-rate indexed pay rises of recent years.

Social Welfare

Italy has a comprehensive system of social benefits covering unemployment and disability as well as retirement pensions and family allowances. These benefits are all provided by the social security system (Istituto Nazionale della Previdenza Sociale). There is also an industrial injuries scheme, operated by the Istituto Nazionale per l'Assicurazione contro gli Infortuni sul Lavoro.

A comprehensive national health service, aiming to provide free medical care for all citizens, was introduced in 1980. However, minimum charges are still made for essential medicines, medical examinations and hospital treatment. All workers will be eligible for benefits under a unified national medical insurance scheme. In 1979 Italy had 1,832 hospital establishments, with a total of 554,595 beds: equivalent to one for every 103 inhabitants. In 1979 there were 164,555 registered physicians, not all resident and working in Italy. Expenditure by the central government in 1984 included 38,511,000m. lire for health and 104,489,000m. lire for social security and welfare.

Education

Education is free and compulsory between the ages of six and 14 years. The curricula of all Italian schools are standardized by the Ministry of Education. After primary school, for children aged six to 11 years, the pupil enters the lower secondary school (scuola media unificata). An examination at the end of three years leads to a lower secondary school certificate, which gives access to all higher secondary schools. Pupils wishing to enter a classical lycée (liceo classico) must also pass an examination in Latin.

Higher secondary education is provided by classical, artistic and scientific lycées, training schools for elementary teachers and technical and vocational institutes (industrial, commercial, nautical, etc.). After five years at a lycée, the student sits an examination for the higher secondary school certificate (maturità), which allows automatic entry into any university faculty. Special four-year courses are provided at the teachers' training schools and the diploma obtained permits entry to a special university faculty of education, the magistero, and a few other faculties. The technical institutes provide practical courses which prepare students for a specialized university faculty.

University courses last for a minimum of four years. Study allowances are awarded to students according to their means and merit. Expenditure on education by the central government was 27,418,000m. lire in 1984.

Tourism

With Alpine and Mediterranean scenery, a sunny climate, Roman buildings, medieval and Baroque churches, Renaissance towns and palaces, paintings and sculpture and famous opera houses, Italy attracts great numbers of tourists. In 1985 more than 53.6m. foreign visitors (including excursionists) arrived in Italy. There are about 4m. tourist beds.

Public Holidays

1987: 1 January (New Year's Day), 6 January (Epiphany), 20 April (Easter Monday), 25 April (Liberation Day), 1 May (Labour Day), 12 May (Festival of the Tricolour), 15 August (Assumption), 1 November (All Saints' Day), 8 December (Immaculate Conception), 25 December (Christmas Day), 26 December (St Stephen).

1988: 1 January (New Year's Day), 6 January (Epiphany), 4 April (Easter Monday), 25 April (Liberation Day), 1 May (Labour Day), 12 May (Festival of the Tricolour), 15 August (Assumption), 1 November (All Saints' Day), 8 December (Immaculate Conception), 25 December (Christmas Day), 26 December (St Stephen).

There are also numerous local public holidays, held on the feast day of the patron saint of each town.

Weights and Measures

The metric system is in force.

Currency and Exchange Rates

The Italian lira (nominally of 100 centesimi).
Exchange rates (30 September 1986):
 £1 sterling = 2,028.0 lire;
 US $1 = 1,401.5 lire.

ITALY

Statistical Survey

Source (unless otherwise stated): Istituto Centrale di Statistica, Via Cesare Balbo 16, 00100 Rome; tel. (06) 4673; telex 610338.

Area and Population

AREA, POPULATION AND DENSITY

Area (sq km)	301,277*
Population (census results)	
24 October 1971	54,136,547
25 October 1981	
Males	27,506,354
Females	29,050,557
Total	56,556,911
Population (official estimates at 31 December)	
1983	56,929,101
1984	57,080,498
1985	57,202,345
Density (per sq km) at 31 December 1985	190

* 116,324 sq miles.

EMIGRATION

Destination	1982	1983	1984
Belgium	2,981	3,060	2,891
France	6,113	5,326	4,708
Germany, Federal Repub.	34,437	29,524	27,609
Switzerland	26,359	21,352	18,892
United Kingdom	2,311	2,004	2,653
Other European Countries	3,126	3,429	3,789
Argentina	940	811	830
Brazil	751	640	475
Canada	2,455	1,785	1,432
USA	5,022	4,555	3,959
Venezuela	1,502	1,124	930
Australia	1,799	1,477	1,282
Other Countries	9,855	10,051	7,868
Total	**98,241**	**85,138**	**77,318**

PRINCIPAL TOWNS (population at 31 December 1985)

Roma (Rome, the capital)	2,826,488	Salerno	155,755
Milano (Milan)	1,515,233	Ferrara	145,703
Napoli (Naples)	1,206,010	Perugia	145,062
Torino (Turin)	1,035,383	Ravenna	136,347
Genova (Genoa)	735,600	Pescara	131,543
Palermo	719,755	Reggio nell' Emilia	130,344
Bologna	437,203	Rimini	130,174
Firenze (Florence)	430,748	Monza	122,287
Catania	376,312	Bergamo	120,949
Bari	365,630	Sassari	119,871
Venezia (Venice)	334,107	Siracusa (Syracuse)	119,427
Messina	267,264	Vicenza	111,302
Verona	259,992	La Spezia	111,119
Trieste	244,506	Terni	110,730
Taranto	241,386	Forlì	110,117
Padova (Padua)	227,528	Piacenza	106,365
Cagliari	223,487	Cosenza	106,001
Brescia	200,790	Ancona	105,091
Modena	178,190	Torre del Greco	104,917
Parma	178,051	Pisa	104,244
Livorno (Leghorn)	176,575	Bolzano (Bozen)	103,177
Reggio di Calabria	175,104	Novara	102,619
Prato	163,736	Catanzaro	102,111
Foggia	158,681	Udine	100,469

REGIONS (31 December 1985)

Region	Area ('000 hectares)	Population	Regional capital	Population of capital
Abruzzi	1,079	1,250,057	L'Aquila	66,097
Basilicata	999	618,647	Potenza	66,519
Calabria	1,508	2,131,412	Catanzaro	103,177
Campania	1,360	5,651,200	Napoli (Naples)	1,206,010
Emilia-Romagna	2,212	3,939,289	Bologna	437,203
Friuli-Venezia Giulia	785	1,219,526	Trieste	241,386
Lazio	1,720	5,101,641	Roma (Rome)	2,826,488
Liguria	542	1,771,319	Genova (Genoa)	735,600
Lombardia (Lombardy)	2,386	8,881,683	Milano (Milan)	1,515,233
Marche	969	1,425,734	Ancona	104,917
Molise	444	333,502	Campobasso	50,478
Piemonte (Piedmont)	2,540	4,394,312	Torino (Turin)	1,035,383
Puglia	1,935	4,005,226	Bari	365,630
Sardegna (Sardinia)	2,409	1,638,172	Cagliari	223,487
Sicilia (Sicily)	2,571	5,084,311	Palermo	719,755
Toscana (Tuscany)	2,299	3,576,508	Firenze (Florence)	430,748
Trentino-Alto Adige	1,362	878,590	Bolzano (Bozen)*	102,111
			Trento (Trent, Trient)*	99,983
Umbria	846	816,939	Perugia	145,703
Valle d'Aosta	326	113,714	Aosta	37,038
Veneto	1,836	4,370,533	Venezia (Venice)	334,107

* Joint regional capitals.

ITALY

Statistical Survey

BIRTHS, MARRIAGES AND DEATHS

	Registered live births Number	Rate (per 1,000)	Registered marriages Number	Rate (per 1,000)	Registered deaths Number	Rate (per 1,000)
1978	709,043	12.5	336,417	5.9	540,671	9.5
1979	670,221	11.8	323,930	5.7	538,352	9.5
1980	640,401	11.2	316,953	5.7	554,510	9.7
1981*	623,103	11.0	316,953	5.6	545,291	9.7
1982*	617,507	10.9	312,494	5.5	531,632	9.4
1983*	600,218	10.6	300,855	5.3	561,214	9.9
1984*	585,972	10.3	298,028	5.2	531,899	9.3
1985*	575,495	10.1	295,990	5.2	544,811	9.5

* Provisional.

Average expectation of life (1977–79): Males 70.61 years; females 77.19 years.

ECONOMICALLY ACTIVE POPULATION*
(annual averages, '000 persons aged 14 years and over)

	1983	1984	1985
Agriculture, forestry, hunting and fishing	2,526	2,426	2,296
Energy and water	210	206	209
Manufacturing	5,080	4,881	4,766
Construction	2,063	1,956	1,921
Commerce (excl. banking and insurance)	4,100	4,293	4,365
Transport, storage and communications	1,114	1,069	1,091
Other services	5,466	5,816	6,093
Total employed	20,559	20,647	20,742
Persons seeking work for the first time	1,291	1,167	1,250
Other unemployed	974	1,223	1,222
Total labour force	22,821	23,038	23,213
Males	14,952	14,986	15,040
Females	7,869	8,052	8,173

* Excluding persons on compulsory military service.

Agriculture

PRINCIPAL CROPS ('000 metric tons)

	1983	1984	1985
Wheat	8,833.5	10,226.9	8,602.0
Barley	1,200.2	1,640.5	1,642.7
Oats	317.3	439.7	388.4
Rice (paddy)	1,030.6	1,018.0	1,130.0
Maize	6,752.1	6,857.4	6,336.3
Dry broad beans	170.8	201.9	183.9
Green broad beans	124.6	124.0	120.6
Dry beans	72.4	73.2	61.1
Green beans	279.5	283.6	254.1
Green peas	236.0	235.3	218.9
Potatoes	2,574.3	2,503.4	2,494.8
Onions	504.4	505.8	489.4
Carrots	274.8	286.2	312.9
Turnips	59.5	67.3	62.6
Artichokes	552.1	534.2	502.8
Fennel	336.4	338.7	355.0
Celery	135.2	147.2	147.2
Cabbages	543.5	534.9	502.1
Cauliflowers	444.5	383.3	405.6
Endives, lettuces, radishes	847.7	860.8	839.4
Spinach	101.2	97.7	89.2
Aubergines (Egg-plants)	319.0	312.5	299.4
Tomatoes	5,994.0	6,774.2	6,311.0
Pumpkins	357.8	352.4	337.4
Water melons	823.6	830.2	813.4
Melons	370.1	363.8	366.0
Sugar beet	10,242.8	11,597.9	9,606.0
Tobacco	156.0	163.1	166.5
Grapes	13,176.3	11,108.3	9,774.4
Olives	4,553.3	1,973.2	3,520.0
Oranges	2,378.6	1,768.8	2,233.1
Lemons	889.0	732.2	776.3
Apples	2,056.8	2,240.5	2,038.4
Pears	1,213.7	1,071.7	808.8
Peaches	1,645.1	1,585.7	1,444.5
Fresh figs	49.8	54.0	52.5
Dried figs	4.8	5.3	6.3
Almonds (unshelled)	131.4	103.5	109.0

LIVESTOCK ('000 head)

	1983	1984	1985
Cattle	9,113	9,106	9,009
Buffaloes	108	100	
Sheep	10,745	11,098	11,293
Goats	1,088	1,089	1,089
Pigs	9,187	9,041	9,169
Horses	253	246	
Mules	59	57	398
Asses	101	98	

Chickens: (FAO estimates, million, year ending September): 110 in 1983; 111 in 1984; 112 in 1985.

LIVESTOCK PRODUCTS ('000 metric tons)

	1983	1984	1985
Beef and veal	1,149	1,182	1,205
Mutton and lamb	63	67	66
Goats' meat	4	4	4
Pig meat	1,166	1,218	1,187
Horse meat	48	52	55
Poultry meat	1,043	1,019	996
Other meat	194	197	200
Edible offals	206	213	214
Lard	209	210	224
Cows' milk	10,858	10,901	n.a.
Buffaloes' milk	68	70	n.a.
Sheep's milk	597	599	n.a.
Goats' milk	126	126	n.a.
Butter	78	81	n.a.
Cheese	631	661	n.a.
Hen eggs	617	603	612
Wool: greasy	12.7	12.7	12.9
clean	6.1	n.a.	n.a.

1496

Forestry

ROUNDWOOD REMOVALS ('000 cubic metres, excl. bark)

	1982	1983	1984
Sawlogs, veneer logs and logs for sleepers	2,525	2,266	2,333
Pulpwood	909	807	980
Other industrial wood	1,184	1,092	1,102
Fuel wood	4,098	4,211	4,844
Total	8,716	8,376	9,259

Source: FAO, *Yearbook of Forest Products*.

SAWNWOOD PRODUCTION ('000 cubic metres)

	1982	1983	1984
Coniferous (soft wood)	1,070	920	1,003
Broadleaved (hard wood)	1,196	1,043	1,179
Total	2,266	1,963	2,182

Railway sleepers ('000 cubic metres): 64 in 1982; 62 in 1983; 52 in 1984.
Source: FAO, *Yearbook of Forest Products*.

Fishing

('000 metric tons, live weight)

	1982	1983	1984
Trouts	31.4	32.5	35.8
European hake	16.4	22.5	29.6
Surmullets (Red mullets)	8.9	10.0	11.9
Jack and horse mackerels	8.4	9.3	10.6
European sardine (pilchard)	72.4	60.2	45.8
European anchovy	54.0	54.4	43.7
Atlantic mackerel	13.9	3.1	3.9
Other fishes (incl. unspecified)	150.8	157.1	181.2
Total fish	356.2	349.2	362.4
Shrimps, prawns, etc.	10.3	12.7	18.0
Other crustaceans	10.6	11.4	12.8
Striped venus	33.3	34.9	38.9
Cuttlefishes	14.5	15.6	13.1
Squids	16.4	12.1	12.3
Octopuses	11.6	13.9	12.9
Other molluscs	23.1	28.6	24.7
Total catch	476.0	478.4	495.0
Inland waters	39.8	41.3	43.8
Mediterranean and Black Sea	390.4	398.6	409.4
Atlantic Ocean	45.5	37.0	41.0
Indian Ocean	0.4	1.4	0.7

Source: FAO, *Yearbook of Fishery Statistics*.

Mining

('000 metric tons)

	1983	1984	1985
Bauxite	3	n.a.	n.a.
Iron ore*	n.a.	273.7	n.a.
Lead concentrates*	19.6	35.0	25.7
Zinc concentrates*	46.7	50.7	86.8
Barytes	135.4	106.4	127.2
Fluorspar	177.7	188.3	152.9
Pyrites	646.2	442.7	690.4
Petroleum	2,197.6	2,236.2	2,342.5
Asphalt and bituminous rock	93.3	92.0	88.7
Lignite	1,736.6	1,806.1	1,892.4
Crude sulphur	40.9	20.6	4.9

* Figures refer to gross weight of ores and concentrates. In 1983 the metal content (in '000 metric tons) was: Lead 12.1; Zinc 21.0.

ITALY — Statistical Survey

Industry

SELECTED PRODUCTS

		1983	1984	1985
Wine	'000 hectolitres	82,200	70,900	62,577
Pig iron	'000 metric tons	10,312.7	11,631.0	12,062.5
Steel	'000 metric tons	21,805.2	24,038.3	23,897.6
Rolled iron	'000 metric tons	18,928.7	20,308.3	20,350.0
Other iron and steel-finished manufactures	'000 metric tons	697.1	755.6	795.4
Iron alloys and *spiegel-eisen* special pig irons	'000 metric tons	205.1	264.0	282.7
Fuel oil	'000 metric tons	25,852.7	23,279.8	20,065.8
Synthetic ammonia	'000 metric tons	11,335.4	14,693.8	14,771.8
Sulphuric acid at 50° Bé	'000 metric tons	4,123.4	4,259.1	4,358.2
Synthetic organic dyes	'000 metric tons	10.2	8.2	15.0
Tanning materials	'000 metric tons	40.1	52.4	53.9
Caustic soda	'000 metric tons	1,008.8	1,072.3	1,031.1
Rayon and acetate filament yarn	'000 metric tons	29.0	30.9	30.3
Cotton yarn	'000 metric tons	216.6	230.1	221.1
Natural methane gas	million cu m	12,990.7	13,901.7	14,158.1
Sewing machines	'000	439.2	460.9	425.3
Typewriters	'000	391.6	578.7	482.3
Passenger motor cars	'000	1,393.9	1,438.7	1,384.2
Lorries (Trucks)	'000	179.3	159.7	184.5
Hydroelectric power*	million kWh	43,940	44,903	44,056
Thermoelectric power*	million kWh	130,540	128,537	132,198

* Net production.

Finance

CURRENCY AND EXCHANGE RATES

Monetary Units
100 centesimi = 1 Italian lira (plural: lire)

Denominations
Coins: 5, 10, 20, 50, 100, 200 and 500 lire.
Notes: 1,000, 2,000, 5,000, 10,000, 20,000, 50,000 and 100,000 lire.

Sterling and Dollar Equivalents (30 September 1986)
£1 sterling = 2,028.0 lire;
US $1 = 1,401.5 lire;
10,000 lire = £4.931 = $7.135.

Average Exchange Rate (lire per US $)
1983   1,518.8
1984   1,757.0
1985   1,909.4

INTERNATIONAL RESERVES
(US $ million at 31 December)*

	1983	1984	1985
Gold†	26,152	21,637	23,558
IMF special drawing rights	591	633	326
Reserve position in IMF	990	1,074	1,160
Foreign exchange	18,259	19,089	14,029
Total	45,992	42,433	39,073

* Excluding deposits made with the European Monetary Co-operation Fund.
† Valued at market-related prices.
Source: IMF, *International Financial Statistics*.

MONEY SUPPLY ('000 million lire at 31 December)

	1983	1984	1985
Currency outside banks	37,787	42,542	46,329
Demand deposits at commercial banks	202,274	227,668	250,279

Source: IMF, *International Financial Statistics*.

COST OF LIVING (Consumer Price Index; base: 1980 = 100)

	1983	1984	1985
Food	152.0	165.9	180.3
Fuel and light	181.7	201.9	219.8
Clothing	154.4	171.9	190.4
Rent	160.4	196.2	207.9
All items (incl. others)	157.3	174.3	190.3

Source: ILO, *Year Book of Labour Statistics*.

ITALY
Statistical Survey

STATE BUDGET (million lire—1984)

Revenue	
Property and income taxes	88,918,662
Business taxation and duties	48,111,637
Customs and frontier charges	} 15,265,025
Taxes on manufacturing and consumption	
Public lottery and sweepstakes	965,348
State monopolies	4,299,115
Other ordinary revenue	42,481,799
Total real revenue	200,041,586
Capital movements	583,519
General total	200,625,105

Expenditure	
Ministry of the Treasury	154,864,141
Ministry of Finance	10,255,599
Ministry of Justice	2,233,816
Ministry of Education	25,438,015
Ministry of the Interior	29,131,606
Ministry of Public Works	3,404,011
Ministry of Agriculture and Forests	2,873,791
Ministry of Defence	14,145,299
Ministry of Labour and Social Welfare	22,719,108
Other Ministries	29,188,477
General total	294,253,863

NATIONAL ACCOUNTS ('000 million lire)

	1981	1982	1983
Gross domestic product at factor cost	372,024	437,432	489,253
of which:			
Agriculture, forestry and fisheries	25,057	28,490	32,747
Industry	148,901	173,032	188,003
Other activities	161,516	190,738	217,948
Less imputed bank service charge	−18,341	−19,579	−24,728
Public administration	54,891	64,751	75,283
Income from abroad	−2,434	−3,806	−4,265
Gross national product at factor cost	369,590	433,626	484,988
Less depreciation allowance	−40,667	−48,909	−56,724
National income at factor cost	328,923	384,717	428,264
Indirect taxes less subsidies	29,555	33,958	46,651
National income in market prices	358,478	418,675	474,915
Depreciation allowances	40,667	48,909	56,724
Gross national product in market prices	399,145	467,584	531,639
Balance of exports and imports of goods and services	16,490	17,024	11,523
Available resources	415,635	484,608	543,162
of which:			
Private consumption expenditure	254,661	299,545	342,753
Government consumption expenditure	75,293	90,171	107,377
Gross fixed capital formation	81,149	89,560	96,268
Increase in stocks	4,532	5,332	−3,236

BALANCE OF PAYMENTS (US $ million)

	1983	1984	1985
Merchandise exports f.o.b.	72,025	72,982	77,681
Merchandise imports f.o.b.	−75,240	−78,968	−85,207
Trade balance	−3,215	−5,986	−7,526
Exports of services	25,397	26,080	28,035
Imports of services	−22,832	−24,189	−26,254
Balance on goods and services	−650	−4,097	−5,745
Private unrequited transfers (net)	1,406	1,454	1,419
Government unrequited transfers (net)	−201	−179	−327
Current balance	555	−2,821	−4,653
Direct capital investment (net)	−945	−687	−938
Other long-term capital (net)	1,477	2,082	2,992
Short-term capital (net)	3,839	1,575	−2,405
Net errors and omissions	466	2,434	−2,890
Total (net monetary movements)	5,391	2,583	−7,894
Valuation changes (net)	−1,927	−1,460	215
Exceptional financing	422	61	457
Changes in reserves	3,885	1,183	−7,223

Source: IMF, *International Financial Statistics*.

External Trade

Note: Data refer to the trade of Italy (excluding the communes of Livigno and Campione) and San Marino, with which Italy maintains a customs union. The figures include trade in second-hand ships, and stores and bunkers for foreign ships and aircraft, but exclude manufactured gas, surplus military equipment, war reparations and repayments and gift parcels by post. Also excluded are imports of military goods and exports of fish landed abroad directly from Italian vessels. Figures include gold ingots for non-monetary uses.

PRINCIPAL COMMODITIES (distribution by SITC, '000 million lire)

Imports c.i.f.	1983	1984	1985
Food and live animals	14,541.0	15,906.5	20,130.5
Live animals	1,837.9	1,784.2	2,253.5
Bovine cattle	1,440.5	1,386.8	1,682.1
Meat and meat preparations	3,458.9	3,333.7	4,281.3
Fresh, chilled or frozen meat	3,336.8	3,196.4	4,117.6
Meat of bovine cattle	2,092.6	1,923.1	2,461.2
Dairy products and eggs	2,315.0	2,482.8	3,296.5
Cereals and cereal preparations	1,933.5	2,992.1	2,638.7
Maize (unmilled)	463.8	502.4	403.6
Beverages and tobacco	1,072.2	1,139.1	1,719.8
Crude materials (inedible) except fuels	10,302.6	14,484.3	15,811.3
Wood, lumber and cork	1,731.1	2,156.6	2,088.1
Shaped or simply worked wood	1,181.8	1,469.3	1,365.1
Textile fibres and waste	2,083.2	2,993.0	3,406.0
Metalliferous ores and metal scrap	1,862.2	2,834.1	3,204.2
Mineral fuels and lubricants	38,047.7	42,048.5	46,596.0
Petroleum and petroleum products	32,204.6	33,308.5	37,015.9
Crude petroleum	24,143.1	23,290.8	25,472.0
Animal and vegetable oils and fats	845.2	899.3	1,306.9
Chemicals	11,092.2	13,724.8	16,186.1
Chemical elements and compounds	4,353.1	5,164.0	6,190.1
Organic chemicals	3,294.8	4,141.3	5,068.7
Plastic materials, etc.	2,701.4	3,569.7	4,095.5
Basic manufactures	14,569.6	19,211.4	22,005.3
Textile yarn, fabrics, etc.	3,310.2	4,420.2	5,235.7
Iron and steel	3,161.6	4,331.6	4,967.8
Non-ferrous metals	2,768.2	3,568.8	3,708.1
Copper and copper alloys	1,152.2	1,367.9	1,572.9
Machinery and transport equipment	21,461.6	28,366.9	34,655.6
Non-electric machinery / Electrical machinery, apparatus, etc.	13,708.6	18,104.5	22,264.7
Transport equipment	7,753.0	10,262.4	12,390.9
Road motor vehicles and parts	6,570.6	8,442.6	10,231.4
Passenger cars (excl. buses)	4,365.9	5,750.3	6,972.5
Miscellaneous manufactured articles	6,100.4	7,433.2	9,043.0
Scientific instruments, watches, etc.	2,769.4	3,317.4	3,970.6
Other commodities and transactions	3,969.1	4,963.8	5,361.9
Total	122,001.9	148,177.8	172,816.4

Exports f.o.b.	1983	1984	1985
Food and live animals	5,706.5	6,673.5	8,522.4
Fruit and vegetables	3,279.5	3,613.6	4,254.4
Fresh fruit and nuts	1,738.9	1,619.0	2,007.3
Beverages and tobacco	1,477.3	1,781.2	2,058.1
Crude materials (inedible) except fuels	1,807.4	2,315.0	2,515.3
Mineral fuels, lubricants, etc.	6,128.3	6,022.8	7,093.5
Petroleum products	5,678.4	5,598.1	6,673.6
Animal and vegetable oils and fats	267.9	447.8	571.3
Chemicals	7,834.8	9,982.7	11,447.4
Chemical elements and compounds	2,524.4	3,341.8	3,811.7
Plastic materials, etc.	2,347.8	3,014.7	3,317.2
Basic manufactures	25,631.3	30,122.1	34,104.6
Textile yarn, fabrics, etc.	6,438.6	7,753.3	8,989.5
Textile yarn and thread	1,711.1	2,060.3	2,312.8
Woven non-cotton fabrics (excl. narrow or special fabrics)	3,127.4	3,877.3	4,709.5
Non-metallic mineral manufactures	4,275.5	4,849.5	5,226.7
Iron and steel	5,010.7	5,948.9	6,728.7
Machinery and transport equipment	35,866.8	40,199.7	47,295.0
Non-electric machinery } Electric machinery, apparatus, etc.	25,962.8	29,491.5	35,330.6
Domestic electrical equipment	2,022.6	2,222.1	2,461.8
Transport equipment	9,904.0	10,708.2	11,964.4
Road motor vehicles and parts	7,148.2	8,046.4	9,024.9
Passenger cars (excl. buses)	2,543.5	2,844.0	3,107.1
Miscellaneous manufactured articles	24,442.8	29,788.6	34,733.9
Clothing (excl. footwear)	6,844.8	8,435.0	10,086.9
Clothing not of fur	6,323.6	7,804.4	9,381.4
Footwear	5,243.9	6,160.0	7,106.2
Other commodities and transactions	1,373.3	1,681.2	1,359.5
Total	110,537.2	129,014.6	149,701.0

PRINCIPAL TRADING PARTNERS* ('000 million lire)

Imports c.i.f.	1983	1984	1985
Algeria	2,053.3	4,787.1	3,064.9
Argentina	597.4	951.4	775.7
Australia	648.7	1,079.1	990.7
Austria	2,147.3	3,084.0	2,704.8
Belgium/Luxembourg	4,127.6	6,416.4	5,451.7
Brazil	1,531.2	2,660.7	2,164.3
Canada	793.7	1,004.1	1,025.0
Denmark	1,111.7	1,464.0	1,120.9
Egypt	2,398.5	3,057.7	2,663.5
France	15,362.3	21,541.0	18,398.5
Germany, Federal Republic	19,371.8	25,743.4	23,564.9
Iran	4,000.9	2,848.8	3,270.0
Iraq	1,801.0	2,196.8	1,837.1
Japan	1,688.4	2,828.0	2,367.9
Kuwait	1,596.3	2,724.1	2,041.5
Libya	4,088.3	6,811.3	4,853.5
Netherlands	5,941.6	8,795.6	7,233.2
Saudi Arabia	4,503.6	2,783.4	3,375.9
South Africa	1,975.1	3,508.3	3,024.4
Spain (excl. Canary Is.)	1,708.6	3,334.5	2,436.9
Sweden	1,316.2	1,985.2	1,810.5
Switzerland	4,734.3	6,665.3	6,093.5
USSR	5,456.8	5,690.5	7,096.7
United Kingdom	4,749.5	8,540.7	6,444.6
USA	7,246.0	10,295.3	9,041.5
Yugoslavia	1,538.6	2,197.3	1,935.1
Total (incl. others)	122,001.9	172,816.4	148,177.8

Exports f.o.b.	1983	1984	1985
Algeria	1,303.7	1,369.3	1,803.7
Austria	2,601.3	2,911.5	3,293.8
Belgium/Luxembourg	3,176.7	3,734.0	4,442.5
Canada	967.5	1,419.6	1,868.2
Denmark	812.7	978.7	1,236.6
France	16,253.7	18,078.1	21,003.8
Germany, Federal Republic	18,331.4	20,781.4	24,169.7
Greece	1,852.9	2,207.0	2,619.4
Iran	1,366.7	1,669.1	1,159.2
Japan	1,201.8	1,481.6	1,765.3
Libya	3,192.7	2,919.7	2,401.2
Netherlands	3,308.1	3,708.1	4,630.2
Nigeria	722.5	636.6	661.5
Saudi Arabia	4,557.3	4,190.8	3,504.9
Spain (excl. Canary Is.)	1,857.5	1,952.6	2,445.9
Sweden	1,079.5	1,352.3	1,647.8
Switzerland	4,578.5	5,245.2	6,070.4
Turkey	840.6	1,160.0	1,346.1
USSR	2,850.3	2,786.1	2,917.6
United Kingdom	7,019.3	8,714.4	10,423.1
USA	8,526.1	14,050.1	18,348.5
Venezuela	497.6	718.2	827.7
Yugoslavia	1,517.3	1,699.0	2,262.9
Total (incl. others)	110,537.2	129,014.6	149,701.0

* Imports by country of production; exports by country of consumption.

ITALY — *Statistical Survey*

Transport

STATE RAILWAYS (traffic)

	1983	1984	1985*
Passenger journeys ('000)	388,602	385,516	388,700
Passenger-km (million)	38,840	39,045	39,194
Freight ton-km (million)	16,746	17,870	18,024

* Provisional figures.

ROAD TRAFFIC (licensed vehicles at 31 December)

	1983	1984	1985
Passenger motor cars	20,388,599	20,888,210	22,398,000
Buses and coaches	71,017	71,981	75,250
Goods vehicles	1,653,537	1,683,218	1,788,000
Tractors (non-agricultural)	37,824	38,227	38,600
Trailers and semi-trailers	398,936	408,810	450,000
Motorcycles and scooters	1,585,001	1,696,325	1,796,000
Mopeds	3,646,471	3,767,654	3,877,000

Source: IRF, *World Road Statistics*.

SHIPPING
Merchant Fleet ('000 gross registered tons)

	1982	1983	1984
Total	10,341	9,620	9,117

Sea-borne Freight Traffic (international and coastwise)

	1982	1983	1984
Vessels entered ('000 n.r.t)	299,289	295,223	304,365
Vessels cleared ('000 n.r.t.)	298,704	294,019	303,421
Goods loaded ('000 metric tons)	86,916	85,297	88,292
Goods unloaded ('000 metric tons)	252,345	238,792	248,480

CIVIL AVIATION (traffic on scheduled services)

	1982	1983	1984
Passengers carried ('000)	11,211.0	11,996.6	12,593.6
Passenger-km (million)	14,786.5	14,983.6	16,077.0
Freight ton-km (million)	566.1	614.4	689.4

Tourism

	1983	1984	1985
Foreign tourist arrivals*	46,576,801	49,150,736	53,634,408
Amount spent (million lire)	13,721,232	15,098,723	16,721,973

* Including excursionists and cruise passengers. Arrivals at accommodation establishments were 18,483,325 in 1983; 19,279,279 in 1984; 19,960,692 in 1985.

Number of hotel beds: (31 December 1984) 1,617,211.

TOURIST ARRIVALS BY COUNTRY OF ORIGIN
(including excursionists)

	1983	1984	1985
Austria	4,621,900	4,981,180	5,265,085
Belgium	855,000	880,558	795,832
France	7,891,900	8,462,438	8,708,159
Germany, Federal Republic	10,366,000	10,812,412	11,717,155
Netherlands	1,704,500	1,763,087	1,660,220
Switzerland	10,022,900	10,750,203	12,465,534
United Kingdom	1,890,200	1,788,371	1,770,713
USA	1,717,400	1,774,821	1,834,420
Yugoslavia	1,147,000	1,820,682	3,075,251
Total (incl. others)	46,576,800	49,150,736	53,634,408

Communications Media

	1983	1984	1985
Telephones in use	22,292,000	24,331,000	n.a.
Radio licences	14,212,781	14,319,493	14,223,345
Television licences	13,831,260	13,951,161	13,915,813
Book titles produced*	13,718	14,312	15,545

* Excluding reprints.

Education

1983/84

	Schools	Teachers	Students
Pre-school	29,473	108,207	1,695,911
Primary	28,727	281,311	4,062,756
Secondary:			
Scuola Media	10,050	282,135	2,815,922
Secondaria Superiore	7,546	251,842	2,508,800
of which:			
Technical	2,685	117,713	1,129,207
Vocational	1,668	55,870	494,569
Teacher training	907	21,932	222,376
Art Licei	248	10,191	64,883
Classical, linguistic and scientific Licei	2,038	51,136	597,765
Higher	796	49,015	744,970

Directory

The Constitution

The Constitution of the Italian Republic was approved by the Constituent Assembly on 22 December 1947 and came into force on 1 January 1948. The fundamental principles are set out in Articles 1–12, as follows:

Italy is a democratic republic based on the labour of the people.

The Republic recognizes and guarantees as inviolable the rights of its citizens, either as individuals or in a community, and it expects, in return, devotion to duty and the fulfilment of political, economic and social obligations.

All citizens shall enjoy equal status and shall be regarded as equal before the law, without distinction of sex, race, language or religion, and without regard to the political opinions which they may hold or their personal or social standing.

It shall be the function of the Republic to remove the economic and social inequalities which, by restricting the liberty of the individual, impede the full development of the human personality, thereby reducing the effective participation of the citizen in the political, economic and social life of the country.

The Republic recognizes the right of all citizens to work and shall do all in its power to give effect to this right.

The Republic, while remaining one and indivisible, shall recognize and promote local autonomy, fostering the greatest possible decentralization in those services which are administered by the State, and subordinating legislative methods and principles to the exigencies of decentralized and autonomous areas.

The State and the Catholic Church shall be sovereign and independent, each in its own sphere. Their relations shall be governed by the Lateran Pact ('Patti Lateranensi'), and any modification in the pact agreed upon by both parties shall not necessitate any revision of the Constitution.

All religious denominations shall have equal liberty before the law, denominations other than the Catholic having the right to worship according to their beliefs, in so far as they do not conflict with the common law of the country.

The Republic shall do all in its power to promote the development of culture and scientific and technical research. It shall also protect and preserve the countryside and the historical and artistic monuments which are the inheritance of the nation.

The juridical system of the Italian Republic shall be in conformity with the generally recognized practice of international law. The legal rights of foreigners in the country shall be regulated by law in accordance with international practice.

Any citizen of a foreign country who is deprived of democratic liberty such as is guaranteed under the Italian Constitution, has the right of asylum within the territory of the Republic in accordance with the terms of the law, and his extradition for political offences will not be granted.

Italy repudiates war as an instrument of offence against the liberty of other nations and as a means of resolving international disputes. Italy accepts, under parity with other nations, the limitations of sovereignty necessary for the preservation of peace and justice between nations. To that end, it will support and promote international organizations.

The Constitution is further divided into Parts I and II, in which are set forth respectively the rights and responsibilities of the citizen and the administration of the Republic.

PART ONE

Civic Clauses

Section I (Articles 13–28). The liberty of the individual is inviolable and no form of detention, restriction or inspection is permitted unless it be for juridical purposes and in accordance with the provisions of the law. The domicile of a person is likewise inviolable and shall be immune from forced inspection or sequestration, except according to the provisions of the law. Furthermore, all citizens shall be free to move wheresoever they will throughout the country, and may leave it and return to it without let or hinderance. Right of public meeting, if peaceful and without arms, is guaranteed. Secret organizations of a directly or indirectly political or military nature are, however, prohibited.

Freedom in the practice of religious faith is guaranteed.

The Constitution further guarantees complete freedom of thought, speech and writing, and lays down that the Press shall be entirely free from all control or censorship. No person may be deprived of civic or legal rights on political grounds.

The death penalty is not allowed under the Constitution except in case of martial law. The accused shall be considered 'not guilty' until he is otherwise proven. All punishment shall be consistent with humanitarian practice and shall be directed towards the re-education of the criminal.

Ethical and Social Clauses

Section II (Articles 29–34). The Republic regards the family as the fundamental basis of society and considers the parents to be responsible for the maintenance, instruction and education of the children. The Republic shall provide economic assistance for the family, with special regard to large families, and shall make provision for maternity, infancy and youth, subject always to the liberty and freedom of choice of the individuals as envisaged under the law.

Education, the arts and science shall be free, the function of the State being merely to indicate the general lines of instruction. Private entities and individuals shall have the right to conduct educational institutions without assistance from the State, but such non-state institutions must ensure to their pupils liberty and instruction equal to that in the state schools. Institutions of higher culture, universities and academies shall be autonomous within the limitations prescribed by the law.

Education is available to all and is free and obligatory for at least eight years. Higher education for students of proven merit shall be aided by scholarships and other allowances made by the Republic.

Economic Clauses

Section III (Articles 35–47). The Republic shall safeguard the right to work in all its aspects, and shall promote agreement and co-operation with international organizations in matters pertaining to the regulation of labour and the rights of workers. The rights of Italian workers abroad shall be protected.

All workers shall be entitled to remuneration proportionate to the quantity and quality of their work, and in any case shall be ensured of sufficient to provide freedom and a dignified standard of life for themselves and their families.

The maximum working hours shall be fixed by law, and the worker shall be entitled to a weekly day of rest and an annual holiday of nine days with pay.

Women shall have the same rights and, for equal work, the same remuneration as men. Conditions of work shall be regulated by their special family requirements and the needs of mother and child. The work of minors shall be specially protected.

All citizens have the right to sickness, unemployment and disability maintenance.

Liberty to organize in trade unions is guaranteed and any union may register as a legal entity, provided it is organized on a democratic basis. The right to strike is admitted within the limitations of the relevant legislation.

Private enterprise is permitted in so far as it does not run counter to the well-being of society nor constitute a danger to security, freedom and human dignity.

Ownership of private property is permitted and guaranteed within the limitations laid down by the law regarding the acquisition, extent and enjoyment of private property. Inheritance and testamentary bequests shall be regulated by law.

Limitation is placed by law on private ownership of land and on its use, with a view to its best exploitation for the benefit of the community.

The Republic recognizes the value of mutual co-operation and the right of the workers to participate in management.

The Republic shall encourage all forms of saving, by house purchase, by co-operative ownership and by investment in the public utility undertakings of the country.

Political Clauses

Section IV (Articles 48–54). The electorate comprises all citizens, both men and women, who have attained their majority. Voting is free, equal and secret, and its exercise is a civic duty. All citizens have the right to associate freely together in political parties, and may also petition the Chambers to legislate as may be deemed necessary.

ITALY

All citizens of both sexes may hold public office on equal terms.

Defence of one's country is a sacred duty of the citizen, and military service is obligatory within the limits prescribed by law. Its fulfilment shall in no way prejudice the position of the worker nor hinder the exercise of political rights. The organization of the armed forces shall be imbued with the spirit of democracy.

All citizens must contribute to the public expenditure, in proportion to their capacity.

All citizens must be loyal to the Republic and observe the terms of the law and the Constitution.

PART TWO

Sections I, II and III (Articles 55–100). These sections are devoted to a detailed exposition of the Legislature and legislative procedure of the Republic.

Parliament shall comprise two Chambers, namely the Chamber of Deputies (Camera dei Deputati) and the Senate of the Republic (Senato).

The Chamber of Deputies is elected by direct universal suffrage, the number of Deputies being 630. All voters who on the day of the elections are 25 years of age, may be elected Deputies.

Seats are apportioned by dividing the number of inhabitants of the Republic, as shown in the last general census by 630, and allocating the seats proportionally to the population of each constituency.

The Senate of the Republic is elected on regional basis, the number of eligible Senators being 315. No region shall have less than seven Senators. Valle d'Aosta has only one Senator.

Seats are allocated proportionally among the Regions in the same way as the Chamber of Deputies.

The Chamber of Deputies and the Senate of the Republic are elected for five years.

The term of each House cannot be extended except by law and only in the case of war.

Members of Parliament shall receive remuneration fixed by law.

The President of the Republic must be a citizen of at least fifty years of age and in full enjoyment of all civic and political rights. The person shall be elected for a period of seven years (Articles 84–85).

The Government shall consist of the President of the Council and the Ministers who themselves shall form the Council. The President of the Council, or Prime Minister, shall be nominated by the President of the Republic, who shall also appoint the ministers on the recommendation of the Prime Minister (Article 92).

Section IV (Articles 101–113). Sets forth the judicial system and procedure.

Section V (Articles 114–133). Deals with the division of the Republic into regions, provinces and communes, and sets forth the limits and extent of autonomy enjoyed by the regions. Under Article 131 the regions are enumerated as follows:

Piemonte (Piedmont)	Marche
Lombardia (Lombardy)	Lazio
Veneto	Abruzzi
Liguria	Molise
Emilia-Romagna	Campania
Toscana (Tuscany)	Puglia
Umbria	Basilicata
Calabria	Trentino-Alto Adige*
Sicilia (Sicily)*	Friuli-Venezia Giulia*
Sardegna (Sardinia)*	Valle d'Aosta*

*These five regions have a wider form of autonomy based on constitutional legislation specially adapted to their regional characteristics (Article 116). Each region shall be administered by a Regional Council, in which is vested the legislative power and which may make suggestions for legislation to the Chambers, and the Giunta regionale which holds the executive power (Article 121).

The final articles provide for the establishment of the Corte Costituzionale to deal with constitutional questions and any revisions which may be found necessary after the Constitution has come into operation.

The Government

(February 1987)

HEAD OF STATE

President of the Republic: Francesco Cossiga (took office 3 July 1985).

COUNCIL OF MINISTERS

A coalition of Christian Democrats (DC), Socialists (PSI), Social Democrats (PSDI), Liberals (PLI) and Republicans (PRI).

Prime Minister: Bettino Craxi (PSI); resigned March 1987.
Deputy Prime Minister: Arnaldo Forlani (DC).
Minister of Foreign Affairs: Giulio Andreotti (DC).
Minister of the Interior: Oscar Luigi Scalfaro (DC).
Minister of Justice: Virginio Rognoni (DC).
Minister of the Treasury: Giovanni Giuseppe Goria (DC).
Minister of Finance: Bruno Visentini (PRI).
Minister of the Budget: Pier Luigi Romita (PSDI).
Minister of Defence: Giovanni Spadolini (PRI).
Minister of Education: Franca Falcucci (DC).
Minister of Public Works: Franco Nicolazzi (PSDI).
Minister of Transport: Claudio Signorile (PSI).
Minister of Agriculture and Forests: Filippo Maria Pandolfi (DC).
Minister of Posts and Telecommunications: Antonio Gava (DC).
Minister of Industry: Valerio Zanone (PLI).
Minister of Labour and Social Security: Gianni de Michelis (PSI).
Minister of State Industry: Clelio Darida (DC).
Minister of Foreign Trade: Salvatore Formica (PSI).
Minister of Health: Carlo Donat Cattin (DC).
Minister of Tourism: Nicola Capria (PSI).
Minister of the Cultural Heritage: Antonino Gullotti (DC).
Minister of the Merchant Navy: Costante Degan (DC).
Minister of Southern Development: Salverino de Vito (DC).
Minister of Regional Affairs: Carlo Vizzini (PSDI).
Minister of Relations with Parliament: Oscar Mammi (PRI).
Minister of Civil Defence: Giuseppe Zamberletti (DC).
Minister of Public Administration: Remo Gaspari (DC).
Minister of European Affairs: Loris Fortuna (PSI).
Minister of Scientific Research: Luigi Granelli (DC).
Minister of the Environment: Francesco de Lorenzo (PLI).

MINISTRIES

Office of the President: Palazzo del Quirinale, 00187 Rome; tel. (06) 4699; telex 611440.
Office of the Prime Minister: Palazzo Chigi, Piazza Colonna 370, 00100 Rome; tel. (06) 6779; telex 613199.
Ministry of Agriculture and Forests: Via XX Settembre, 00100 Rome; tel. (06) 4665; telex 610148.
Ministry of the Budget: Via XX Settembre 97, 00100 Rome; tel. (06) 4761; telex 612431.
Ministry of the Cultural Heritage: Via del Collegio Romano 27, 00100 Rome; tel. (06) 6723.
Ministry of Defence: Palazzo Baracchini, Via XX Settembre, 00100 Rome; tel. (06) 4759841.
Ministry of the Environment: Piazza Venezia 11, 00187 Rome; tel. (06) 6797124.
Ministry of Education: Viale Trastevere 76A, 00100 Rome; tel. (06) 58491; telex 613181.
Ministry of Finance: Viale America, EUR, 00100 Rome; tel. (06) 5997.
Ministry of Foreign Affairs: Piazzale della Farnesina 1, 00194 Rome; tel. (06) 36911; telex 610611.
Ministry of Foreign Trade: Viale America 341, EUR, 00100 Rome; tel. (06) 5993; telex 610083.
Ministry of Health: Viale dell'Industria 20, 00100 Rome; tel. (06) 5994.
Ministry of Industry: Via Vittorio Veneto 33, 00100 Rome; tel. (06) 4705.
Ministry of the Interior: Piazza Viminale, Palazzo Viminale, Via Depretis, 00100 Rome; tel. (06) 46671.
Ministry of Justice: Via Arenula 70, 00186 Rome; tel. (06) 65101; telex 65101.
Ministry of Labour and Social Security: Via Flavia 6, 00187 Rome; tel. (06) 4683; telex 626144.

ITALY

Ministry of the Merchant Navy: Viale dell'Arte 16, EUR, 00144 Rome; tel. (06) 5908.

Ministry of Posts and Telecommunications: Viale America, EUR, 00144 Rome; tel. (06) 54601.

Ministry of Public Works: Piazza Porta Pia 1, 00100 Rome; tel. (06) 8482.

Ministry of State Industry: Via Sallustiana 53, 00187 Rome; tel. (06) 4750420.

Ministry of Tourism: Via della Ferratella in Laterano 51, 00184 Rome; tel. (06) 77321; telex 616400.

Ministry of Transport: Piazza della Croce Rossa 1, 00161 Rome; tel. (06) 84901; telex 613111.

Ministry of the Treasury: Via XX Settembre 97, 00187 Rome; tel. (06) 47611; telex 623139.

Legislature

PARLAMENTO
(Parliament)

Senato
(Senate)

President: AMINTORE FANFANI (Christian Democrat).

General Election, 26–27 June 1983

Parties	Votes	%	Seats
Christian Democrats (DC)	10,076,141	32.4	120
Communists (PCI)	9,579,964	30.8	107
Socialists (PSI)	3,541,218	11.4	38
Italian Social Movement– National Right (MSI-DN)	2,283,691	7.3	18
Republicans (PRI)*	1,452,359	4.7	10
Social Democrats (PSDI)*	1,186,271	3.8	8
Liberals (PLI)*	834,235	2.7	6
Radicals (PR)	551,644	1.8	1
Proletarian Democracy (DP)	327,564	1.1	—
South Tyrol People's Party (SVP)	157,427	0.5	3
Others	1,104,797	3.6	4
Total	**31,095,311**	**100.0**	**315**

* Senate election results exclude votes for the 'Alleanza laica', formed by the PRI, PSDI and PLI.

Camera dei Deputati
(Chamber of Deputies)

President: Mrs NILDE JOTTI (Communist).

General Election, 26–27 June 1983

Parties	Votes	%	Seats
Christian Democrats (DC)	12,145,800	32.9	225
Communists (PCI)	11,028,158	29.9	198
Socialists (PSI)	4,222,487	11.4	73
Italian Social Movement– National Right (MSI-DN)	2,511,722	6.8	42
Republicans (PRI)	1,872,536	5.1	29
Social Democrats (PSDI)	1,507,431	4.1	23
Liberals (PLI)	1,065,833	2.9	16
Radicals (PR)	809,672	2.2	11
Proletarian Democracy (DP)	541,493	1.5	7
South Tyrol People's Party (SVP)	184,892	0.5	3
Others	1,000,257	2.7	3
Total	**36,890,281**	**100.0**	**630**

Political Organizations

Movimento Sociale Italiano-Destra Nazionale (MSI-DN) (Italian Social Movement-National Right): Via della Scrofa 39, 00186 Rome; tel. (06) 6543014; f. 1946; right-wing party; Pres. PINO ROMUALDI; Sec.-Gen. GIORGIO ALMIRANTE; 400,000 mems.

Partito Comunista Italiano (PCI) (Communist Party): Central Office: Via delle Botteghe Oscure 4, 00186 Rome; tel. (06) 6711; f. 1921; the largest Communist Party in Western Europe; advocates far-reaching economic, social and democratic reforms, to be implemented by a broad coalition of democratic forces; programme includes development of the South, democratic planning, agrarian reform, democratic reform of the State and social services, and other policies leading to an original Italian path towards socialism; advocates an independent foreign policy for peace and international détente and co-operation; Gen. Sec. ALESSANDRO NATTA; 1.50m. mems (1985).

Partito della Democrazia Cristiana (DC) (Christian Democrat Party): Central Office: Piazza Don Luigi Sturzo, EUR, 00144 Rome; tel. (06) 5901; f. 1943, the successor to the pre-Fascist Popular Party; while extending its appeal to voters of all classes, the party attempts to maintain a centre position; it is openly and militantly anti-communist; Pres. (vacant); Sec.-Gen. CIRIACO DE MITA; Admin. Sec. GIUSEPPE TONUTTI.

Partito Liberale Italiano (PLI) (Liberal Party): Via Frattina 89, 00187 Rome; tel. (06) 6796951; f. 1848 by Cavour, its chief aim is the realization of the principle of freedom in all public and private matters; Pres. ALDO BOZZI; Sec. RENATO ALTISSIMO; 153,000 mems.

Partito Radicale (PR) (Radical Party): Via Torre Argentina 18, 00186 Rome; tel. (06) 6547168; telex 610495; campaigns on civil rights issues; Pres MARCO PANNELLA, DOMENICO MODUGNO; Sec.-Gen. GIOVANNI NEGRI; 5,382 mems.

Partito Repubblicano Italiano (PRI) (Republican Party): Piazza dei Caprettari 70, 00186 Rome; tel. (06) 6544641; f. 1897; followers of the principles of Mazzini (social justice in a modern free society) and modern liberalism; Pres. BRUNO VISENTINI; Political Sec. GIOVANNI SPADOLINI; 110,000 mems.

Partito Socialista Democratico (PSDI) (Social Democrat Party): Via Santa Maria in Via 12, 00187 Rome; tel. (06) 6797851; f. 1969 after breaking away from the former United Socialist Party, of which it had been part since 1966; composed of former Social Democrats and stands to the right of the PSI; Pres. GIUSEPPE SARAGAT; Sec. FRANCO NICOLAZZI; 200,000 mems.

Partito Socialista Italiano (PSI) (Socialist Party): Via del Corso 476, 00186 Rome; tel. (06) 67781; telex 616300; f. 1892; in 1921 a group broke away to found Italian Communist Party; a further rift in 1947 led to the foundation of the Italian Social Democrat Party; in 1966 merged with the Democratic Socialist Party to form the United Socialist Party, but in 1969 the Democratic Socialists broke away; a centre-left party at the service of the workers and of the civil life of the nation, aiming to create conditions for greater prosperity, freedom and social justice in the country; it adheres to the Socialist International and believes that socialism is inseparable from democracy and individual freedom; Sec.-Gen. BETTINO CRAXI.

Südtiroler Volkspartei (SVP) (South Tyrol People's Party): Brennerstrasse 7A, 39100 Bozen/Bolzano; tel. (0471) 24484; regional party of the German-speaking people in the South Tyrol; Pres. SILVIUS MAGNANO; Gen. Sec. Dr BRUNO HOSP.

There are also numerous small political parties, including the following: Union Valdôtaine (regional party for the French minority in the Valle d'Aosta); the 'Green' party (campaigning on environmental and anti-nuclear issues); Partito Sardo d'Azione (Sardinian autonomy party); Democrazia Proletaria (left-wing); and Lotta Continua (left-wing).

Diplomatic Representation

EMBASSIES IN ITALY

Afghanistan: Via Carlo Fea 1, 00161 Rome; tel. (06) 856898; Chargé d'affaires a.i.: MUHAMMAD NAZIR FEDAIY.

Albania: Via Asmara 9, 00199 Rome; tel. (06) 8380725; telex 614169; Ambassador: BASHKIM DINO.

Algeria: Via Barnaba Oriani 26, 00161 Rome; tel. (06) 879369; telex 680846; Ambassador: ABDERRAHMANE CHERIET.

Angola: Via Filippo Bernardini 21, 00165 Rome; tel. (06) 6374325; telex 614505; Ambassador: (vacant).

Argentina: Piazza dell'Esquilino 2, 00185 Rome; tel. (06) 482551; telex 610386; Ambassador: ALFREDO E. ALLENDE.

Australia: Via Alessandria 215, 00198 Rome; tel. (06) 841241; telex 610165; Ambassador: DANIEL GERALD NUTTER.

Austria: Via G.B. Pergolesi 3, 00198 Rome; tel. (06) 868241; telex 610139; Ambassador: Dr FRIEDRICH FRÖLICHSTHAL.

ITALY

Bangladesh: Via Antonio Bertoloni 14, 00197 Rome; tel. (06) 803595; telex 614615; Ambassador: Waliur Rahman.

Belgium: Via dei Monti Parioli 49, 00197 Rome; tel. (06) 3609441; telex 610425; Ambassador: Marcel van de Kerkchove.

Bolivia: Via Archimede 143, 00197 Rome; tel. (06) 804228; Ambassador: Walter Rios Gamboa.

Brazil: Palazzo Pamphil, Piazza Navona 14, 00186 Rome; tel. (06) 650841; telex 610099; Ambassador: Carlos Ouro-Preto.

Bulgaria: Via Pietro P. Rubens 21, 00197 Rome; tel. (06) 3609640; telex 610234; Ambassador: Rayko Nikolov.

Burma: Via Bellini 20, Rome; tel. (06) 859374; Ambassador: U Tin Tun.

Cameroon: Corso Vittorio Emanuele 282, 00186 Rome; tel. (06) 6545406; telex 611558; Ambassador: Félix Sabal Lecco.

Canada: Via G. B. de Rossi 27, 00161 Rome; tel. 855341; telex 610056; Ambassador: Claude Charland.

Chile: Via Nazionale 54, 2nd Floor, 00184 Rome; tel. (06) 4742258; telex 611420; Chargé d'affaires a.i.: Carlos Ferreira Cannobio.

China, People's Republic: Via Bruxelles 56, 00198 Rome; tel. (06) 8448186; telex 680159; Ambassador: Godu Gong.

Colombia: Via Giuseppe Pisanelli 4, 00197 Rome; tel. (06) 3602704; telex 611266; Ambassador: Gen. Luis Carlos Camacho Leyva.

Congo: Via Barberini 29, 00100 Rome; tel. (06) 4746163; telex 626645; Ambassador: Jean Nitoud.

Costa Rica: Piazza della Torretta 26, 00100 Rome; tel. (06) 6785995; Ambassador: Francisco Antonio Pacheco Fernández.

Cuba: Via Licinia 7, 00153 Rome; tel. (06) 5133850; telex 610677; Ambassador: Prof. Roberto Mulet del Valle.

Cyprus: Via Michele Mercati 51, Rome; tel. (06) 879837; telex 621033; Ambassador: Kypros Kyprianou.

Czechoslovakia: Via Colli della Farnesina 144, 00194 Rome; tel. (06) 3278742; telex 610306; Ambassador: Norbert Žídek.

Denmark: Via dei Monti Parioli 50, 00197 Rome; tel. (06) 3600441; telex 624696; Ambassador: Niels Boel.

Dominican Republic: Via Domenico Chelini 9, 00197 Rome; tel. (06) 874665; Ambassador: Elena Annunziata Campagna de Read.

Ecuador: Via Guido d'Arezzo 14, 00198 Rome; tel. (06) 851784; telex 613256; Ambassador: Alfredo Luna Tobar.

Egypt: 119 Roma Villa Savoia, Via Salaria 267, 00199 Rome; tel. (06) 856193; telex 610044; Ambassador: Muhammad Sidky Hamed.

El Salvador: Piazza delle Belle Arti 1, 00196 Rome; tel. (06) 3601853; Ambassador: Dr Ivo P. Alvarenga.

Ethiopia: Via Nicolò Tartaglia 11, 00197 Rome; tel. (06) 803057; telex 614414; Ambassador: Geremew Debele.

Finland: Viale G. Rossini 18, 00198 Rome; tel. (06) 858329; telex 611160; Ambassador: Eeva-Kristiina Forsman.

France: Piazza Farnese 67, 00186 Rome; tel. (06) 6565241; telex 610093; Ambassador: Jacques Andréani.

Gabon: Via Cosenza 7, 00161 Rome; tel. (06) 865620; telex 612264; Ambassador: Edouard Teale.

German Democratic Republic: Via di Trasone 56–58, 00199 Rome; tel. (06) 8390045; telex 610353; Ambassador: Dr Wolfgang Kiesewetter.

Germany, Federal Republic: Via Po 25c, 00198 Rome; tel. (06) 860341; telex 610179; Ambassador: Dr Lothar Lahn.

Ghana: Via Ostrina 4, 00199 Rome; tel. (06) 836074; telex 610270; Ambassador: Prof. Eugene Bortei-Doku.

Greece: Via Mercadente 36, 00198 Rome; tel. (06) 859630; telex 621378; Ambassador: Cristos Stremmenos.

Guatemala: Via Archimede 35, 00197 Rome; tel. (06) 803936; Ambassador: Gen. Héctor Mario López Fuentes.

Guinea: Via Adelaide Ristori 9/13, 00197 Rome; tel. (06) 878989; telex 611487; Ambassador: Moumourou Toure.

Haiti: Via Ruggero Fauro 59, 00197 Rome; tel. (06) 872777; Ambassador: William Cambronne.

Holy See: Via Po 27–29, 00198 Rome; tel. (06) 862092; Apostolic Nuncio: Mgr Romolo Carboni.

Honduras: Via Antonio Baiamonti 4/19, 00195 Rome; tel. (06) 3581453; telex 622014; Ambassador: Edgardo Dumas Rodríguez.

Hungary: Via dei Villini 14, 00161 Rome; tel. (06) 860241; Ambassador: György Misur.

India: Via XX Settembre 5, 00187 Rome; tel. (06) 464642; telex 611274; Ambassador: Akbar Mirza Khaleeli.

Indonesia: Via Campania 55, 00187 Rome; tel. (06) 4759251; telex 610317; Ambassador: Jacob Piay.

Iraq: Via della Camilluccia 355, 00135 Rome; tel. (06) 346357; telex 622678; Ambassador: Muhammad Ali Karim Aref.

Ireland: Via del Pozzetto 105, 00187 Rome; tel. (06) 6782541; telex 626030; Ambassador: Eamon Kennedy.

Israel: Via M. Mercati 12, 00197 Rome; tel. (06) 874541; telex 610412; Ambassador: Eytan Ronn.

Ivory Coast: Via Lazzaro Spallanzani 4–6, 00161 Rome; tel. (06) 868040; telex 610396; Ambassador: Souleimane Sako.

Japan: Via Quintino Sella 58, 00187 Rome; tel. (06) 4757151; telex 610063; Ambassador: Shinsuke Hori.

Jordan: Via Guido d'Arezzo 5, 00198 Rome; tel. (06) 857396; telex 612573; Ambassador: Taissir Tougan.

Korea, Republic: Via Barnaba Oriani 30, 00197 Rome; tel. (06) 805292; telex 610182; Ambassador: Youn Tai-Chi.

Kuwait: Piazza Monte Grappa 4, 00195 Rome; tel. (06) 3603841; telex 620426; Ambassador: Abd al-Aziz al-Khudur.

Lebanon: Via Luigi Settembrini 38, 00195 Rome; tel. (06) 3595937; telex 611411; Chargé d'affaires a.i.: Adnan Al-Kadi.

Lesotho: Via del Corso 4, 00186 Rome; tel. (06) 3606905; telex 610053; Chargé d'affaires a.i.: Teboho Kitleli.

Liberia: Viale Bruno Buozzi 64, 00197 Rome; tel. (06) 805810; telex 612569; Chargé d'affaires: S. Prince Porte.

Libya: Via Nomentana 365, 00162 Rome; tel. (06) 835942; telex 611114; Ambassador: (vacant).

Luxembourg: Via Guerrieri 3, 00153 Rome; tel. (06) 5780456; telex 680401; Ambassador: Paul Mertz.

Madagascar: Via Riccardo Zandonai 84a, 00194 Rome; tel. (06) 3277797; telex 680297; Ambassador: Apolinaire Andriatsiafajato.

Malaysia: Via Lazzaro Spallanzani 8, 00161 Rome; tel. (06) 855764; telex 611035; Ambassador: Raja Mansur bin Raja Razman.

Malta: Lungotevere Marzio 12, 00186 Rome; tel. (06) 659947; telex 611205; Ambassador: Leslie Agius.

Mexico: Via Lazzaro Spallanzani 16, 00161 Rome; tel. (06) 854093; telex 625279; Ambassador: Dr Luis Weckmann Muñoz.

Monaco: Via Bertoloni 36, 00197 Rome: tel. (06) 803361; Ambassador: René Novella.

Morocco: Via Lazzaro Spallanzani 8, 00196 Rome; tel. (06) 8448653; telex 620854; Ambassador: M. M. Yahia Benslimane.

Netherlands: Via Michele Mercati 8, 00197 Rome; tel. (06) 873141; telex 610138; Ambassador: Baron W. Van Pallandt.

New Zealand: Via Zara 28, 00198 Rome; tel. (06) 851225; telex 626615; Ambassador: Gordon Noel Parkinson.

Nicaragua: Via Panama 12, 00198 Rome; tel. (06) 865476; telex 616295; Ambassador: Dr Ernesto Fonseca Pasos.

Nigeria: Via Orazio 14–18, 00198 Rome; tel. (06) 380841; telex 610666; Ambassador: Albert Ajanaku.

Norway: Via delle Terme Deciane 7, 00153 Rome; tel. (06) 5755833; telex 610585; Ambassador: Torbjørn Christiansen.

Oman: Via Enrico Petrella 4, 00198 Rome; tel. (06) 8448038; telex 612524; Ambassador: Muhammad bin Taher Aideed.

Pakistan: Lungotevere delle Armi 22, 00195 Rome; tel. (06) 311470; telex 622083; Ambassador: Abdul Waheed.

Panama: Via Po 10, 20 Piso, 00198 Rome; tel. (06) 8445589; telex 622670; Ambassador: Nelva Torrijos Herrera.

Paraguay: Via Emilio de Cavalieri 12, 00198 Rome; tel. (06) 8448236; Ambassador: Dr Roque J. Yódice Codas.

Peru: Via Po 22, 00198 Rome; tel. (06) 856556; telex 625589; Ambassador: (vacant).

Philippines: Via San Valentino 12-14, 00197 Rome; tel. (06) 803530; telex 610104; Ambassador: Jacobo C. Clave.

Poland: Via Paolo Rubens 20, Monti Panoli, 00197 Rome; tel. (06) 3609455; telex 610325; Ambassador: Józef Wiejacz.

Portugal: Via Giacinta Pezzana 9, 00197 Rome; tel. (06) 878016; telex 612304; Ambassador: Tomas Andresen.

Romania: Via Nicolò Tartaglia 36, 00197 Rome; tel. (06) 804567; Ambassador: Constantin Tudor.

San Marino: Via Eleonora Duse 35, 00197 Rome; tel. (06) 804567; Ambassador: Remy Giacomini.

Saudi Arabia: Via G. B. Pergolesi 9, 00198 Rome; tel. (06) 868161; telex 613115; Ambassador: Khaled an-Nasser at-Turki.

Senegal: Via Bartolomeo Eustacchio 12, 00161 Rome; tel. (06) 859497; telex 612522; Ambassador: Henri Pierre Arphang Senghor.

ITALY   Directory

Somalia: Via dei Villini 9–11, 00161 Rome; tel. (06) 853740; telex 613123; Ambassador: MUHAMMAD MUHAMOUD ABDULLAH.
South Africa: Piazza Monte Grappa 4, 00195 Rome; tel. (06) 3608441; telex 611221; Ambassador: VERNON R. W. STEWARD.
Spain: Palazzo Borghese, Largo Fontenella Borghese 19, 00186 Rome; tel. (06) 6798506; telex 612435; Ambassador: JORGE DE ESTEBAN ALONSO.
Sri Lanka: Via Giuseppe Cuboni 68, 00197 Rome; tel. (06) 805362; telex 612602; Ambassador: M. A. PIYASEKERA.
Sudan: Via di Porta Ardeatina 1, 00184 Rome; tel. (06) 7573344; telex 610302; Ambassador: ABD AL-A'AS-SINADA.
Sweden: Piazza Rio de Janeiro 3, 00161 Rome; tel. (06) 860441; telex 610264; Ambassador: ERIC VIRGIN.
Switzerland: Via Barnaba Oriani 61; 00197 Rome; tel. (06) 803641; telex 610304; Ambassador: GASPARD BODMER.
Syria: Piazza Araecoli 1, 00186 Rome; tel. (06) 6797791; telex 613083; Ambassador: BURHAN KAIAL.
Tanzania: Via G.B. Vico 9, 00196 Rome; tel. (06) 3610901; telex 612286; Ambassador: ABBAS KLEIST SYKES.
Thailand: Via Nomentana 132, 00162 Rome; tel. (06) 837073; telex 616297; Ambassador: SOMPUNG SUCHARITKUL.
Tunisia: Via Asmara 7, 00199 Rome; tel. (06) 8390748; telex 610190; Ambassador: AHMAD BENNOUR.
Turkey: Via Palestro 28, 00185 Rome; tel. (06) 4751549; telex 611223; Ambassador: FAHIR ALAÇAM.
USSR: Via Gaeta 5, 00185 Rome; tel. (06) 4743989; telex 611286; Ambassador: NIKOLAI LUNKOV.
United Arab Emirates: Via S. Crescenziano 25, 00199 Rome; tel. (06) 8394839; telex 622671; Ambassador: NASSER SALMAN AL-ABOODI.
United Kingdom: Via XX Settembre 80A, 00187 Rome; tel. (06) 4755441; telex 610049; Ambassador: Lord BRIDGES.
USA: Via Vittorio Veneto 119A, 00187 Rome; tel. (06) 4674; telex 610450; Ambassador: MAXWELL RABB.
Uruguay: Via Vittorio Veneto 183, 00187 Rome; tel. (06) 492796; telex 611201; Ambassador: MATEO MÁRQUEZ SERÉ.
Venezuela: Viale Bruno Buozzi 109, Apto 6, 00197 Rome; tel. (06) 872552; telex 610361; Ambassador: LUIS MANUEL PEÑALVER.
Viet-Nam: Piazza Barberini 12, 00187 Rome; tel. (06) 4754098; telex 610121; Ambassador: PHAN THI MINH.
Yemen Arab Republic: Via Verona 3, 00161 Rome; tel. (06) 4270811; telex 621447; Ambassador: ABDULLAH ADH-DHABBI.
Yugoslavia: Via dei Monti Parioli 20, 00197 Rome; tel. (06) 3600796; telex 616303; Ambassador: ANTE SKATARETIKO.
Zaire: Via Mecenate 24–30, 00184 Rome; tel. (06) 730695; telex 611104; Ambassador: TUMAWAKU BAZICA.
Zambia: Via Ennio Quirino Visconti 8, 00193 Rome; tel. (06) 310307; telex 611421; Ambassador: HARRY NZUNGA.

Judicial System

The Constitutional Court was established in 1956 and is an autonomous constitutional body, standing apart from the judicial system. Its most important function is to pronounce on the constitutionality of legislation both subsequent and prior to the present Constitution of 1948. It also judges accusations brought against the President of the Republic or ministers.

At the base of the system of penal jurisdiction are the Preture (District Courts), where offences carrying a sentence of up to three years' imprisonment are tried. Above the Preture are the Tribunali (Tribunals) and the Corti di Assise presso i Tribunali (Assize Courts attached to the Tribunals), where graver offences are dealt with. From these courts appeal lies to the Corti d'Appello (Courts of Appeal) and the parallel Corti di Assise d'Appello (Assize Courts of Appeal). Final appeal may be made, on juridical grounds only, to the Corte Suprema di Cassazione.

Civil cases may be taken in the first instance to the Giudici Conciliatori (Justices of the Peace), Preture or Tribunali, according to the economic value of the case. Appeal from the Giudici Conciliatori lies to the Preture, from the Preture to the Tribunali, from the Tribunali to the Corti d'Appello, and finally, as in penal justice, to the Corte Suprema di Cassazione on juridical grounds only.

Special divisions for cases concerning labour relations or young persons are attached to civil courts. Cases concerned with the public service and its employees are tried by Tribunali Amministrativi Regionali and the Consiglio di Stato.

Consiglio Superiore della Magistratura (CSM): Piazza dell' Indipendenza 6, 00185 Rome; f. 1958; tel. (06) 497981; supervisory body of judicial system; 33 mems.
President: FRANCESCO COSSIGA.
Vice-President: GIANCARLO DE CAROLIS.

CONSTITUTIONAL COURT
Corte Costituzionale: Palazzo della Consulta, Piazza del Quirinale 41, 00187 Rome; tel. (06) 46981; consists of 15 judges, one-third appointed by the President of the Republic, one-third elected by Parliament in joint session, one-third by the ordinary and administrative supreme courts.
President: LIVIO PALADIN.
Vice-President: GUGLIELMO ROHERSSEN.

ADMINISTRATIVE COURTS
Consiglio di Stato: Palazzo Spada, Piazza Capo di Ferro 13, 00186 Rome; tel. (06) 650801; established in accordance with Article 10 of the Constitution; has both consultative and judicial functions.
President: GABRIELE PESCATORE.

Corte dei Conti: Via Baiamonti 25, Rome, and Via Barberini 38, Rome; functions as the court of public auditors for the state.
President: SILVIO PIRRAMI TRAVERSARI.

SUPREME COURT OF APPEAL
Corte Suprema di Cassazione: Palazzo di Giustizia, 00100 Rome; tel. (06) 6568941; supreme court of civil and criminal appeal.
First President: GIUSEPPE TAMBURRINO.
Vice-President: MARIO BARBA.

Religion

More than 90% of the population of Italy are adherents of the Roman Catholic Church.

Under the terms of the Concordat signed in 1929, Roman Catholicism was recognized as the official religion of Italy. However, a new Concordat was signed in February 1984 between the Prime Minister and Cardinal Agostino Casaroli, the Papal Secretary of State, to replace the earlier agreement. Following approval by both chambers of the Italian Parliament, the new Concordat was formally ratified in June 1985. The Concordat stated that Roman Catholicism would no longer be the state religion, abolished compulsory religious instruction in schools and reduced state financial contributions. The Vatican City's sovereign rights as an independent state, under the terms of the Lateran Treaty of 1929, were not affected.

CHRISTIANITY
The Roman Catholic Church

For ecclesiastical purposes, Italy comprises the Papal See of Rome, the Patriarchate of Venice, 58 archdioceses (including nine directly responsible to the Holy See), 216 dioceses (including seven within the jurisdiction of the Pope, as Archbishop of the Roman Province, and 36 directly responsible to the Holy See), four territorial prelatures (including two directly responsible to the Holy See) and seven territorial abbacies (including five directly responsible to the Holy See). Almost all adherents follow the Latin rite, but there are two dioceses and one abbacy (all directly responsible to the Holy See) for Catholics of the Italo-Albanian (Byzantine) rite.

Bishops' Conference: Conferenza Episcopale Italiana, Circonvallazione Aurelia 50, 00165 Rome; tel. (06) 6237141; f. 1985; Pres. HE Cardinal UGO POLETTI, Vicar-General of Rome.

Primate of Italy, Archbishop and Metropolitan of the Roman Province and Bishop of Rome: His Holiness Pope JOHN PAUL II.

Patriarch of Venice: HE Cardinal MARCO CÈ.

Archbishops:
Acerenza: Most Rev. FRANCESCO CUCCARESE.
Amalfi: Most Rev. FERDINANDO PALATUCCI.
Ancona: Most Rev. CARLO MACCARI.
Bari: Most Rev. MARIANO MAGRASSI.
Benevento: Most Rev. CARLO MINCHIATTI.
Bologna: HE Cardinal GIACOMO BIFFI.
Brindisi: Most Rev. SETTIMIO TODISCO.
Cagliari: Most Rev. GIOVANNI CANESTRI.
Camerino: Most Rev. BRUNO FRATTEGIANI.
Campobasso-Boiano: Most Rev. PIETRO SANTORO.

ITALY

Capua: Most Rev. LUIGI DILIGENZA.
Catania: Most Rev. DOMENICO PICCHINENNA.
Catanzaro: Most Rev. ANTONIO CANTISANI.
Chieti: Most Rev. ANTONIO VALENTINI.
Conza: Most Rev. ANTONIO NUZZI.
Cosenza: Most Rev. DINO TRABALZINI.
Fermo: Most Rev. CLETO BELLUCCI.
Ferrara: Most Rev. LUIGI MAVERNA.
Florence: HE Cardinal SILVANO PIOVANELLI.
Foggia: Most Rev. SALVATORE DE GIORGI.
Gaeta: Most Rev. LUIGI CARLI.
Genoa: HE Cardinal GIUSEPPE SIRI.
Gorizia and Gradisca: Most Rev. ANTONIO VITALE BOMMARCO.
Lanciano: Most Rev. ENZIO D'ANTONIO.
L'Aquila: Most Rev. MARIO PERESSIN.
Lecce: Most Rev. MICHELE MINCUZZI.
Lucca: Most Rev. GIULIANO AGRESTI.
Manfredonia: Most Rev. VALENTINO VAILATI.
Matera: Most Rev. MICHELE GIORDANO.
Messina: Most Rev. IGNAZIO CANNAVÓ.
Milan: HE Cardinal CARLO MARIA MARTINI.
Modena: Most Rev. SANTO BARTOLOMEO QUADRI.
Monreale: Most Rev. SALVATORE CASSISA.
Naples: HE Cardinal CORRADO URSI.
Oristano: Most Rev. PIER LUIGI TIDDIA.
Otranto: Most Rev. VINCENZO FRANCO.
Palermo: HE Cardinal SALVATORE PAPPALARDO.
Perugia: Most Rev. CESARE PAGANI.
Pescara-Penne: Most Rev. ANTONIO JANNUCCI.
Pisa: Most Rev. BENVENUTO MATTEUCCI.
Potenza: Most Rev. GIUSEPPE VAIRO.
Ravenna: Most Rev. ERSILIO TONINI.
Reggio Calabria: Most Rev. AURELIO SORRENTINO.
Rossano: Most Rev. SERAFINO SPROVIERI.
Salerno: Most Rev. GUERINO GRIMALDI.
Santa Severina: Most Rev. GIUSEPPE AGOSTINO.
Sassari: Most Rev. SALVATORE ISGRÒ.
Siena: Most Rev. ISMAELE MARIO CASTELLANO.
Sorrento: Most Rev. ANTONIO ZAMA.
Spoleto: Most Rev. OTTORINO PIETRO ALBERTI.
Syracuse: Most Rev. CALOGERO LAURICELLA.
Taranto: Most Rev. GUGLIELMO MOTOLESE.
Trani and Barletta: Most Rev. GIUSEPPE CARATA.
Trento: Most Rev. ALESSANDRO MARIA GOTTARDI.
Turin: HE Cardinal ANASTASIO ALBERTO BALLESTRERO.
Udine: Most Rev. ALFREDO BATTISTI.
Urbino: Most Rev. DONATO UGO BIANCHI.
Vercelli: Most Rev. ALBINO MENSA.

In addition, the Most Rev. VITO ROBERTI, the Bishop of Caserti, has been granted the personal title of Archbishop.

Azione Cattolica Italiana (ACI) (Catholic Action): Via della Conciliazione 1, 00193 Rome; tel. (06) 6568751; most of the nation-wide lay Catholic organizations in Italy are affiliated to Catholic Action, which has a total membership of one and a half million and is organized in the following divisions: Settore Adulti (Adult Section), Settore Giovani (Youth Section), Azione Cattolica Ragazzi (Children's Catholic Action), Federazione Universitaria Cattolica Italiana—FUCI (University Federation), Movimento Laureati (Graduates' Movement), Movimento Maestri (Teachers' Movement), Movimento Lavoratori (Workers' Movement) and Movimento Studenti (Students' Movement). The Presidency-National is the supreme executive body and co-ordinator of the different branches of Catholic Action. Pres. Avv. RAFFAELE CANANZI; Chaplain Mgr FIORINO TAGLIAFERRI; Sec.-Gen. Dott. IDA BOZZINI.

Protestant Churches

Federation of the Protestant Churches in Italy: Via Firenze 38, 00184 Rome; tel. (06) 4755120; the Federation was formed in 1967; total mems approx 50,000; Pres. Pastor AURELIO SBAFFI; includes the following organizations:

Chiesa Luterana (Lutheran Church): Via Toscana 7, 00187 Rome; tel. (06) 4757519; Via Palestrina 14, 20124 Milan; Dean JOACHIM MIETZ; 20,100 mems.

Chiesa Evangelica Metodista d'Italia (Evangelical Methodist Church of Italy): Via Firenze 38, 00184 Rome; tel. (06) 4743695; f. 1861; Pres. Pastor PAOLO SBAFFI; 4,000 mems.

Tavola Valdese (Waldensian Church): Via Firenze 38, 00184 Rome; tel. (06) 475537; Moderator Pastor GIORGIO BOUCHARD; Sec.-Treas. Pastor ROBERTO COMBA; 25,050 mems (1977).

Unione Cristiana Evangelica Battista d'Italia (Italian Baptist Union): Piazza in Lucina 35, 00186 Rome; tel. (06) 6876124; f. 1873; Pres. Pastor PAOLO SPANU; Admin. Sec. DOMENICO DENTICO; 5,000 mems.

Associated Organizations

Salvation Army (Esercito della Salvezza): Via degli Apuli 40, 00185 Rome; tel. (06) 492614; Officer Commanding for Italy Lt-Col BRAMWELL BOOTH; 16 regional centres.

Seventh-day Adventists: Lungotevere Michelangelo 7, 00192 Rome; tel. (06) 315936; represents 87 communities in Italy; Supt ENRICO LONG; Sec. SALVATORE DALFINO.

JUDAISM

Union of Italian Jewish Communities: Lungotevere Sanzio 9, 00153 Rome; tel. (06) 5803670; f. 1930; represents 21 Jewish communities in Italy; Pres. TULLIA ZEVI; Chief Rabbi of Rome Dr ELIO TOAFF.

Rabbinical Council: Chief Rabbi Dott. ELIO R. TOAFF (Via Catalana 1A, Rome), Rabbi Dott. GIUSEPPE LARAS (Via Guastalla 19, Milan), Rabbi Dott. SERGIO SIERRA (Via San Pio V 12, Turin).

BAHÁ'Í FAITH

Assemblea Spirituale Nazionale: Via Antonio Stoppani 10, 00197 Rome; tel. (06) 879647; mems resident in 270 localities.

The Press

In view of Italy's population the number of daily newspapers is rather small (79 titles), with the bulk of them appearing in the industrial north. Between 1944 and 1967 no fewer than 161 newspapers ceased publication. The average total daily circulation in 1985 was about 8.4m., while sales totalled about 6.1m. copies per day; sales in the north and centre of the country accounted for 81% of this figure, in the south for 19%. Between 1980 and 1985, sales of daily newspapers increased by approximately 21%, and they were expected to reach 6.3m., on a daily average, at the end of 1986.

Rome and Milan are the main press centres. The most important national dailies are *Corriere della Sera* in Milan and Rome and *Il Giorno* in Milan, followed by *La Repubblica* in Rome and Turin's *La Stampa* circulating in the north and centre. The other large dailies circulate in and reflect their own region; e.g. *La Nazione* serves Florence and its region, *Il Messaggero* and *Il Tempo* Rome and the centre, *Il Secolo XIX*, based in Genova, extends throughout the Italian riviera, *Il Mattino* serves the Naples region and *La Sicilia* and *Giornale di Sicilia* serve Sicily. Although there are comparatively few small dailies, weekly papers are numerous.

The daily press has experienced economic difficulties for many years, but since 1973 rises in labour costs and the price of raw materials have created a critical situation. The dailies have become entirely dependent on financial support from large industrial companies, political parties or other social groups with substantial capital who are prepared to stand a financial loss in return for a measure of control over an important information medium. The Montedison chemical company has effective financial control of important dailies such as *Il Messaggero*. Fiat or other Agnelli concerns control *La Stampa, Stampa Sera, Corriere dello Sport* and a number of magazines and regional newspapers. Other important papers backed by industry include *Il Resto del Carlino* and *La Nazione*, associated with Eridaina, *Il Giorno* owned by ENI, and *Il Sole/24 Ore* controlled by Confindustria. Financial institutions also have interests in the press. The Banco di Napoli, for example, has a large holding in *La Gazzetta del Mezzogiorno* and *Il Mattino*. In 1984 ownership of the *Corriere della Sera*, Italy's leading daily newspaper, passed to a consortium of leading industrialists and financiers. The paper's previous ownership by the Rizzoli publishing group, which had extensive connections with the secret masonic lodge, P-2, and the Banco Ambrosiano (see Recent History), illustrated the extent to which control of the press exerted an appeal for interested groups.

All the political parties represented in parliament have a daily or weekly paper as party organ. The most important are the Communist *L'Unità*, the Socialist *Avanti!* and the Christian Democrat *Il Popolo*. In addition, political parties own or have a holding in papers which are not run as party organs. The Christian Democrats, for example, control seven provincial dailies. Catholic organizations have a controlling interest in several papers and *Avvenire* is owned totally by the Church.

The most important dailies in terms of circulation are: Milan's *Corriere della Sera* (633,000), Turin's *La Stampa* (556,000), Rome's

ITALY

La Repubblica (504,000) and *Il Messaggero* (313,000), *L'Unità* (Milan edition 296,000; Rome edition 300,000), Milan's *Il Giorno* (294,000), Florence's *La Nazione* (288,000), Bologna's *Il Resto del Carlino* (312,000), and the sports newspapers, Milan's *Gazzetta dello Sport* (576,000) and Rome's *Corriere dello Sport* (518,000). The five dailies accorded most prestige for the standard of their articles and news coverage are *Corriere della Sera, Il Giorno, Il Giornale, La Stampa* and *La Repubblica*. The leading financial paper is Milan's *Il Sole/24 Ore*. Italy's first 'popular' daily, *L'Occhio*, was launched in 1979, but failed to find a wide readership. In November 1986 a new financial tabloid, *Italia Oggi*, was founded.

There are some 430 non-daily newspapers and over 7,000 periodicals. The illustrated weekly papers and magazines frequently have higher sales than the average daily. Ten of the largest appear in Milan, five in Rome and one in Turin. Many tend towards sensationalism, particularly the popular *Domenica del Corriere*, which has a circulation of 201,000, and the right wing *Oggi* and *Gente*. Other weekly illustrated periodicals with a large circulation include *Epoca, L'Europeo* and, largest of all, the Catholic *La Famiglia Cristiana*. Among the serious and influential magazines should be mentioned *Panorama, L'Espresso, L'Europeo, Epoca, Il Tempo*, the financial *Mondo Economico*, the small circulating political and cultural *Il Ponte*, the Communist *Rinascita* and the right-wing *Il Borghese*.

DAILIES

Ancona
Corriere Adriatico: Via Berti 20, 60126 Ancona; tel. (071) 42985; f. 1971; Dir Dott. DARIO BENI; circ. 29,000.

Bari
La Gazzetta del Mezzogiorno: Viale Scipione l'Africano 264, 70124 Bari; tel. (080) 270310; telex 810844; f. 1887; independent; Pres. STEFANO ROMANAZZI; Man. Dir GIUSEPPE GORJUX; Dir GIUSEPPE GIACOVAZZO; circ. 104,000.

Bergamo
Bergamo-Oggi: Via Don Luigi Palazzolo 89, 24100 Bergamo; tel. (035) 247196; f. 1981; Dir SERGIO MILANI; Editor AURELIO LOCATI; circ. 12,000.

L'Eco di Bergamo: Viale Papa Giovanni XXIII 118, 24100 Bergamo; tel. (035) 212344; f. 1880; Catholic; Dir and Editor Mgr ANDREA SPADA; circ 45,491.

Bologna
Il Resto del Carlino: Via E. Mattei 106, 40138 Bologna; tel. (051) 536111; f. 1885; independent; Dir FRANCO CANGINI; circ. 312,000.

Bolzano
Alto Adige: Lungotalvera S. Quirino 26, 39100 Bolzano; tel. (0471) 46666; f. 1945; independent; Dir LUCIANO CESCHIA; circ. 47,435.

Dolomiten: Via del Vigneto 7, 39100 Bolzano; tel. (0471) 932000; telex 400161; f. 1923; independent; German language; Editor Dr JOSEF RAMPOLD; circ. 35,000.

Brescia
Bresciaoggi Nuovo: Via Malta 4, 25121 Brescia; tel. (030) 22941; telex 300838; f. 1974; Man. SERGIO MILANI; circ. 15,826.

Il Giornale di Brescia: Via Aurelio Saffi 13, 25100 Brescia; tel. (030) 50491; f. 1945; Dir GIAN BATTISTA LANZANI; circ. 48,375.

Cagliari
L'Unione Sarda: Viale Regina Elena 12, 09100 Cagliari; tel. (070) 6013; f. 1889; independent; Dir GIANNI FILIPPINI; circ. 87,741.

Catania
Espresso Sera: Catania; Dir GIUSEPPE SIMILI; circ. 4,145.

La Sicilia: Viale Odorico da Pordenone 50, 95126 Catania; tel. (095) 330544; telex 911321; f. 1945; independent; Dir Dott. MARIO CIANCIO SANFILIPPO; circ. 74,961.

Como
L'Ordine: Via Giovio 1, 22070 Grandate; tel. (031) 450858; f. 1879; Catholic; Dir EGIDIO MAGGIONI; circ. 8,752.

La Provincia: Via Anzani 52, 22100 Como; tel. (031) 261282; f. 1892; independent; Dir SERGIO CARLESI; circ. 30,000.

Cremona
La Provincia: Via delle Industrie 2, 26100 Cremona; tel. (0372) 21392; f. 1947; independent; Pres. ANGELO DUCHI; Man. Editor LUCIANO DACQUATI; circ. 19,341.

Florence
La Città: Via Campo di Marte 13/15, 50137 Florence; tel. (055) 663663; f. 1980; Man. Dir ELVIO BERTUCCELLI; circ. 15,144.

La Nazione: Via Ferdinando Paolieri 2, 50121 Florence; tel. (055) 24851; f. 1859; independent; Dir TINO NEIROTTI; circ. 288,000.

Foggia
Qui Foggia: Via Salomone 75, 71100 Foggia; tel. (0881) 25262; Dir MATTEO TATARELLA.

Genova
L'Avvisatore Marittimo: Via San Vincenzo 42, 16121 Genova; tel. (010) 562929; telex 213155; f. 1919; shipping and financial; Editor CARLO BELLIO; circ. 4,765.

Corriere Mercantile: Via Archimede 169, 16142 Genova; tel. (010) 517851; f. 1824; political and financial; independent; Dir MIMMO ANGELI; circ. 33,650.

Il Lavoro: Salita di Negro 7, 16123 Genova, tel. (010) 540184; f. 1903; socialist; Editor CESARE LANZA; circ. 32,245.

Il Secolo XIX: Via Varese 2, 16122 Genova; tel. (010) 593211; f. 1887; independent; Dir TOMMASO GIGLIO; circ. 177,684.

Lecce
Quotidiano di Lecce/Brindisi/Taranto: Viale degli Studenti (Palazzo Casto), 73100 Lecce; f. 1979; Man. Editor VITTORIO BRUNO STAMMERRA; circ. 21,788.

Livorno
Il Tirreno: Viale Alfieri 9, 57100 Livorno; tel. (0586) 401141; f. 1877; independent; Editor LUIGI BIANCHI; circ. 80,170.

Mantova
Gazzetta di Mantova: Via Fratelli Bandiera 32, 46100 Mantova; tel. (0376) 32341; f. 1964; independent; Man. Editor RINO BULBARELLI; circ. 28,088.

Messina
Gazzetta del Sud: Via Taormina 15, 98100 Messina; tel. (090) 21801; f. 1952; independent; Dir NINO CALARCO; circ. 69,232.

Milan
Avvenire: Via Mauro Macchi 61, 20124 Milan; tel. (02) 69661; telex 325096; f. 1968; Catholic; Dir GUIDO FOLLONI; circ. 117,254.

Corriere della Sera: Via Solferino 28, 20121 Milan; tel. (02) 6353; telex 310031; f. 1876; independent; Dir MICHELE KAMENETZKY; circ. 633,000.

La Gazzetta dello Sport: Via Solferino 36, 20121 Milan; tel. (02) 6353; telex 321697; f. 1896; sport; Dir CANDIDO CANNAVÒ; circ. 214,973 (daily), 361,047 (Monday edition).

Il Giornale: Via Gaetano Negri 4, 20123 Milan; tel. (02) 85661; telex 333279; f. 1974; independent, controlled by staff; Man. Editor INDRO MONTANELLI; circ. 274,000.

Il Giorno: Via Angelo Fava 20, 20125 Milan; tel. (02) 69901; Rome office: Largo Goldoni 44; tel. (06) 6780304; f. 1965; independent; Editor LINO RIZZI; circ. 294,000.

La Notte: Piazza Cavour 2, 20121 Milan; tel. (02) 7739; f. 1952; evening; independent; Editor PIERO GIORGIANNI; circ. 153,888.

Il Sole/24 Ore: Via Paolo Lomazzo 52, 20154 Milan; tel. (02) 31031; f. 1965; financial, political, economic; Dir GIANNI LOCATELLI; Editor FABIO CAVAZZA ROSSI; circ. 263,000.

Modena
Nuova Gazzetta di Modena: Via Emilia Est 36, 41100 Modena; tel. (059) 236180; Dir CARLO ACCORSI; circ. 10,820.

Naples
Il Mattino: Via Chiatamone 65, 80121 Naples; tel. (081) 7947111; f. 1892, reformed 1950; independent; Dir FRANCO ANGRISANI; circ. 178,971.

Napoli-Notte: Naples; tel. (081) 417011; Dir GINO GRASSI.

Padova
Il Mattino di Padova: Via Pelizzo 15, 35100 Padova; f. 1978; Dir FABIO BARBIERI; circ. 34,739.

Palermo
Giornale di Sicilia: Via Lincoln 21, 90133 Palermo; tel. (091) 6165355; telex 911088; f. 1860; independent; Dir ANTONIO ARDIZZONE; circ. 69,520.

ITALY

L'Ora: Via Stabile, 90141 Palermo; tel. (091) 581733; f. 1900; independent; Dir PAOLO BRUNO CARBONE; circ. 21,613.

Parma
Gazzetta di Parma: Via Emilio Casa 5, 43100 Parma; tel. (0521) 30003; f. 1735; Pres. GIUSEPPE ZANARDI; Dir N. H. BALDASSARRE MOLOSSI; circ. 47,949.

Pavia
La Provincia Pavese: Via Tasso 47, 27100 Pavia; tel. (0382) 472101; f. 1870; independent; Editor GAETANO RIZZUTO; circ. 22,005.

Piacenza
Libertà: Via Benedettine 68, 29100 Piacenza; tel. (0523) 21718; f. 1883; Dir ERNESTO PRATI; circ. 34,356.

Reggio Emilia
Gazzetta di Reggio: Via Farini 8, 42100 Reggio Emilia; tel. (0552) 31830; Dir UMBERTO BONAFINI; circ. 13,865.

Rome
Avanti!: Via Tomacelli 146, 00186 Rome, tel. (06) 497891; f. 1896; organ of Socialist Party; Dir UGO INTINI; circ. 54,000.

Corriere dello Sport-Stadio: Piazza Indipendenza 11b, 00185 Rome, tel. (06) 4992; telex 614472; f. 1924; 13 regional editions; Editor GIORGIO TOSATTI; circ. 518,000.

Il Fiorino: Via Parigi 11, 00185 Rome, tel. (06) 461073; f. 1969; business; Editor L. D'AMATO; circ. 29,546.

Il Giornale d'Italia: Via Parigi 11, 00185 Rome; tel. (06) 47490; Dir LUIGI D'AMATO; Editor FRANCO SIMEONI; circ. 123,678.

International Daily News: Via Barberini 3, 00187 Rome; tel. (06) 4740673; telex 614495; f. 1976; English; Editor G. CARLO RIPOSIO.

Il Manifesto: Via Tomacelli 146, 00186 Rome; tel. (06) 6790151; f. 1971; splinter communist; Man. Editor VALENTINO PARLATO; circ. 58,602.

Il Messaggero: Via del Tritone 152, 00187 Rome; tel. (06) 47201; telex 680173; f. 1897; independent; Editor (vacant); circ. 313,658.

Ore 12: Via Paisiello 6, 00198 Rome; tel. (06) 8442680; financial; independent; Dir ENZO CARETTI; circ. 35,000.

Paese Sera: Via del Tritone 61/62, 00187 Rome; tel. (06) 672151; f. 1949; left wing; Dir CLAUDIO FRACASSI; circ. 62,261.

Il Popolo: Corso Rinascimento 113, 00186 Rome; tel. (06) 65151; telex 613276; f. 1944; organ of Christian Democrat Party, Editor MARCELLO GILMOZZI; circ. 43,000.

Puglia: Via due Marelli 23, 00187 Rome; tel. (06) 6787751; Dir MARIO GISMONDI; circ. 6,777.

La Repubblica: Piazza Indipendenza 11b, 00185 Rome; tel. (06) 49821; telex 620660; f. 1976; left-wing; Editor EUGENIO SCALFARI; circ. 504,000.

Il Tempo: Piazza Colonna 366, 00187 Rome; tel. (06) 65041; telex 614087; f. 1944; right-wing; Editor GIANNI LETTA; circ. 216,000.

L'Umanità: Via S. Maria in Via 12, 00187 Rome; tel. (06) 6727222; f. 1947; organ of the Social Democrat Party; Dir Prof. RUGGERO PULETTI; circ. 16,000.

L'Unità: Via dei Taurini 19, 00185 Rome; tel. (06) 4950351; telex 613461; f. 1924; organ of the Communist Party; Dir EMANUELE MACALUSO; circ. 300,000 (weekday), 800,000 (Sunday).

La Voce Repubblicana: Piazza dei Caprettari 70, 00186 Rome; tel. (06) 6875297; organ of the Republican Party; circ. 12,000.

Sassari
La Nuova Sardegna: Via Porcellana 9, 07100 Sassari; tel. (079) 279299; f. 1891; independent; Editor ALBERTO STATERA; circ. 58,345.

Taranto
Corriere del Giorno: Piazza Dante 5, Zona 'Bestat', 74100 Taranto; tel. (099) 3203; f. 1947; Editor LORENZO GAGLIARDI; circ. 10,151.

Trento
L'Adige: Via Rosmini 35, 38100 Trento; tel. (0461) 985111; f. 1945; Christian Democrat; Editor-in-Chief AMEDEO TRENTINI; circ. 16,759.

Treviso
La Tribuna de Treviso: Piazza Ancilotto 8, 31100 Treviso; tel. (0422) 50801; Dir PAOLO OJETTI; circ. 21,071.

Trieste
Il Piccolo (Giornale di Trieste): Via Silvio Pellico 8, 34122 Trieste; tel. (040) 778161; f. 1881; independent; Dir ALBERTO MARCOLIN; circ. 65,716.

Primorski dnevnik: Via dei Montecchi 6, 34137 Trieste; tel. (040) 793808; telex 460270; f. 1945; Slovene; Man. Dir SAMSA BOGUMIL.

Turin
La Stampa and Stampa Sera: Via Marenco 32, 10126 Turin; tel. (011) 65681; telex 221121; f. 1867; independent; morning edition, La Stampa; evening edition, Stampa Sera; circ. 556,000 (morning), 31,000 (evening); Dirs GAETANO SCARDOCCHIA (morning), MICHELE TORRE (evening).

Tuttosport: Via Villar 2, 10147 Turin; tel. (011) 26121; telex 224230; f. 1945; sport; Dir PIERO DARDANELLO.

Udine
Messaggero Veneto: Viale Palmanova 290, 33100 Udine; tel. (0432) 600312; telex 450449; f. 1946; Editor VITTORINO MELONI; circ. 57,517.

Varese
La Prealpina: Viale Tamagno 13, 21100 Varese; tel. (0332) 286177; f. 1888; Dir MARIO LODI; circ. 26,219.

Venice
Il Gazzettino: Via Torino 110, 30172 Venezia-Mestre; tel. (041) 665111; f. 1887; independent; Dir GIORGIO LAGO; circ. 138,495.

La Nuova Venezia: Salizzada S. Lio 5620, 30122 Venice; tel. (041) 710300; Dir PAOLO OJETTI.

Verona
L'Arena: Viale del Lavoro 11, 37036 S. Martino Buon Albergo, Verona; tel. (045) 990077; telex 481815; f. 1866; independent; Dir GIUSEPPE BRUGNOLI; circ. 51,755.

Vicenza
Il Giornale di Vicenza: Viale S. Lazzaro 89, 36100 Vicenza; tel. (0444) 564533; f. 1945; Editor MINO ALLIONE; circ. 36,759.

SELECTED PERIODICALS
Fine Arts

Casabella: Via Marconi 17, 20090 Segrate, Milan; tel. (02) 2131851; f. 1928; 11 a year; architecture and interior design; Editor VITTORIO GREGOTTI; circ. 54,000.

Domus: Via A. Grandi 5/7, 20089 Rozzano, Milan; tel. (02) 824721; telex 313589; f. 1928; monthly; architecture, interior design and art; Editor MARIO BELLINI; circ. 60,000.

Il Dramma: Piazza Campo Marzio 5, 00186 Rome; tel. (06) 657307; f. 1924; monthly; theatre; Dir DIEGO FABBRI.

Flash Art/Heute Kunst: Via Donatello 36, 20131 Milan; tel. (02) 2364133; bi-monthly; Dir GIANCARLO POLITI.

Il Fotografo: Via Rivoltana 8, 20090 Segrate, Milan; tel. (02) 75421; monthly; photography; Dir GIORGIO COPPIN.

Graphicus: Viale Mattioli 39 (Castello del Valentino), 10125 Turin; tel. (011) 6509659; f. 1911; monthly; graphic arts; Dir STEFANO AJANI; Editor LUCIANO LOVERA; circ. 4,600/5,500.

L'Illustrazione Italiana: Via Gen. Biancardi 1 bis, 21052 Busto Arsizio (VA); f. 1873; quarterly; fine arts.

Interni: Via Trentacoste 7, 20134 Milan; tel. (02) 215631; telex 350523; monthly; interior decoration and design; Editor DOROTHEA BALLUFF; circ. 92,000.

Lotus: Via Trentacoste 7, 20134 Milan; tel. (02) 23693293; telex 313123; quarterly; architecture, town-planning; Editor PIERLUIGI NICOLIN.

Rivista Italiana di Musicologia: Leo S. Olschki, Viuzzo del Pozzetto, 50126 Florence; tel. (055) 687444; f. 1966; every 6 months; music; Editors F. A. GALLO, R. DI BENEDETTO, A. POMPILIO, G. PESTELLI, P. FABBRI.

Storia dell'Arte: Via Ernesto Codignola, 50018 Casellina di Scandicci; tel. (055) 2798; telex 573690; quarterly; art history; Dir GIULIO CARLO ARGAN.

General, Literary and Political

Archivio Storico Italiano: Leo S. Olschki, Viuzzo del Pozzetto, 50126 Florence; tel. (055) 687444; f. 1842; quarterly; history; Editor E. SESTAN.

ITALY

Belfagor: POB 66, 50100 Florence; tel. (055) 687444; f. 1946; every 2 months; historical and literary criticism; Editor CARLO FERDINANDO RUSSO; circ. 5,000.

La Bibliofilia: Leo S. Olschki, Viuzzo del Pozzetto, 50126 Florence; tel. (055) 687444; f. 1899; every 4 months; bibliography; Editor L. BALSAMO.

Il Borghese: Viale Regina Margherita 7, 20122 Milan; tel. (02) 592966; f. 1950; weekly; extreme right-wing, political and cultural; Editor MARIO TEDESCHI.

Civitas: Via Tirso 92, 00198 Rome; tel. (06) 865651; f. 1919; monthly; magazine of political studies; Dir PAOLO EMILIO TAVIANI.

Comunità: Via Manzoni 12, 20121 Milan; tel. (02) 790957; f. 1945; quarterly; culture; Editor RENZO ZORZI; circ. 9,000.

Critica Letteraria: Via Stazio 15, 80123 Napoli; f. 1973; quarterly; literary criticism; Editor P. GIANNANTONIO; circ. 3,000.

Critica Marxista: Via dei Polacchi 41, 00186 Rome; tel. (06) 6789680; f. 1962; 6 a year; Dir ALDO ZANARDO.

Critica Sociale: Foro Buonaparte 24, 20121 Milan; tel. (02) 806319; f. 1891; monthly; Socialist; Dir CARLO TOGNOLI; circ. 25,000.

La Discussione: Piazzale L. Sturzo 31, 00144 Rome; tel. (06) 5901353; f. 1953; weekly; Christian Democrat; Dir PIERLUIGI MAGNASCHI; circ. 50,000.

Domenica del Corriere: Via Solferino 28, 20121 Milan; tel. (02) 6339; telex 310031; f. 1899; illustrated weekly review; Dir ANTONIO TERZI; circ. 201,000.

Epoca: Arnoldo Mondadori SpA, Via Marconi 27, 20090 Segrate, Milan; tel. (02) 7542; telex 310119; f. 1950; illustrated; topical weekly; Dir CARLO ROGNONI; circ. 94,000.

L'Espresso: Via Po 12, 00198 Rome; tel. (06) 84781; telex 610629; weekly; independent left; political; illustrated; Editor GIOVANNI VALENTINI; circ. 311,000.

L'Europeo: Via Angelo Rizzoli 2, 20132 Milan; tel. (02) 2588; f. 1945; weekly; Liberal; political and news; Dir SALVATORE GIANNELLA; circ. 125,000.

La Famiglia Cristiana: Via Giotto 36, 20145 Milan; tel. (02) 467071; telex 332232; f. 1931; weekly; Catholic; illustrated; Dir LEONARDO ZEGA; circ. 1,106,000.

Gazzetta del Lunedì: Via Archimede 169R, Genova; tel. (010) 517851; f. 1952; weekly; political; Dir MIMMO ANGELI; circ. 150,000.

Gente: Via Vitruvio 43, Milan; tel. (02) 472871; f. 1956; weekly; illustrated political, cultural and current events; Editor A. TERZI; circ. 722,000.

Giornale della Libreria: Viale Vittorio Veneto 24, 20124 Milan; tel. (02) 6597950; f. 1888; monthly; organ of the Associazione Italiana Editori; bibliographical; Editor CARLO ENRICO RIVOLTA.

Il Giornale del Mezzogiorno: Via Messina 31, 00198 Rome; tel. (06) 8443151; telex 621401; f. 1946; weekly; politics, economics; Dir VITO BLANCO.

Giorni: Via Zuretti 34, 20125 Milan; tel. (02) 6883151; left-wing weekly; Dir DAVIDE LAJOLO; circ. 180,000.

The International Spectator: Viale Mazzini 88, 00195 Rome; tel. (06) 319806; quarterly; English journal of the Istituto Affari Internazionale; Editor GIANNI BONVICINI.

Lettere Italiane: Leo S. Olschki, POB 66, 50100 Florence; tel. (055) 687444; f. 1949; quarterly; literary; Dirs V. BRANCA, G. GETTO.

Mondo Economico: Via P. Lomazzo 47, 20154 Milan; tel. (02) 3492451; f. 1948; weekly; economics; business, finance; Editor GIANNI LOCATELLI; circ. 50,000.

Il Mulino: Strada Maggiore 37, 40125 Bologna; tel. (051) 226080; f. 1951; every 2 months; culture and politics; Editor NICOLA MATTEUCCI.

Nuovi Argomenti: Via Sicilia 136, 00187 Rome; tel. (06) 47497376; f. 1953; quarterly; Liberal; Editors ALBERTO MORAVIA, LEONARDO SCIASCIA, ENZO SICILIANO.

Oggi: Via Angelo Rizzoli 2, 20132 Milan; tel. (02) 2588; f. 1945; weekly; topical, literary; illustrated; Dir WILLY MOLCO; circ. 599,000.

Panorama: Segrate, 20090 Milan; tel. (02) 7542; f. 1962; weekly; current affairs; Editor CLAUDIO RINALDI; circ. 359,000.

Il Pensiero Politico: Leo S. Olschki, Viuzzo del Pozzetto, 50126 Florence; tel. (055) 687444; f. 1968; every 4 months; political and social history; Editor S. MASTELLONE.

Il Ponte: Via B. Varchi 47, 50132 Florence; tel. (055) 2798; f. 1945; monthly; politics and literature; Publr Sansoni Editore Nuova SpA; Editor ENZO ENRIQUES AGNOLETTI.

Rinascita: Via dei Taurini 19, 00185 Rome; tel. (06) 4951251; f. 1944; weekly; Communist; Dir GIUSEPPE CHIARANTE; Editor LUCIANO BARCA; circ. 80,000.

Rivista Critica di Storia della Filosofia: Viale Monza 106, 20127 Milan; f. 1946; quarterly; philosophy; Publr Franco Angel Editore Srl; Editor Prof. MARIO DAL PRA.

Scuola e Didattica: Via L. Cadorna 11, 25186 Brescia; tel. (030) 29931; telex 300836; fortnightly; education.

Selezione dal Reader's Digest: Via Alserio 10, 20159 Milan; tel. (02) 69871; telex 311286; monthly; Dir B. BRANDOLINI D'ADDA.

Il Settimanale: Via Bissolati 76, 00187 Rome; tel. (06) 465588; weekly; political, economic, cultural and current events.

Storia Illustrata: Via Marconi 27, 20090 Segrate, Milan; tel. (02) 75421; f. 1957; monthly; history; circ. 105,701.

Tempo: Via S. Valeria 5, 20100 Milan; f. 1938; topical illustrated weekly; Dir CARLO GREGORETTI; circ. 230,000.

Volksbote: Via Museo 42, 39100 Bolzano; organ of the Südtiroler Volkspartei; German language.

Religion

Città di Vita: Piazza Santa Croce 16, 50122 Florence; tel. (055) 242783; f. 1946; every 2 months; cultural review of religious research in theology, art and science; Dir P. M. GIUSEPPE ROSITO; circ. 2,000.

La Civiltà Cattolica: Via di Porta Pinciana 1, 00187 Rome; tel. (06) 6798351; f. 1850; fortnightly; Catholic; Editor GIAN PAOLO SALVINI.

Il Fuoco: Via Giacinto Carini 28, 00152 Rome; tel. (06) 5810969; every 2 months; art, literature, science, philosophy, psychology, theology; Dir PASQUALE MAGNI.

Humanitas: Via G. Rosa 71, 25100 Brescia; tel. (030) 46451; f. 1946; every 2 months; religion, philosophy, science, politics, history, sociology, literature, etc.; Dir STEFANO MINELLI.

Protestantesimo: Via Pietro Cossa 42, 00193 Rome; tel. (06) 631585; f. 1946; quarterly; theology and current problems, book reviews; Prof. Dr VITTORIO SUBILIA.

La Rivista del Clero Italiano: Largo Gemelli 1, 20123 Milan; tel. (02) 8856; telex 321033; f. 1920; monthly; Dir FRANCO BROVELLI.

Rivista di Storia della Chiesa in Italia: c/o Herder Editrice e Libreria, Piazza Montecitorio 117–120, 00186 Rome; f. 1947; 2 a year.

Rivista di Storia e Letteratura Religiosa: Biblioteca Erik Peterson, Università di Torino, Via S. Ottavio 20, 10124 Turin; tel. (011) 830556; f. 1965; every 4 months; religious history and literature; Dir FRANCO BOLGIANI.

Science and Technology

L'Automobile: Viale Regina Margherita 290, 00198 Rome; tel. (06) 866156; f. 1945; monthly; motor mechanics, tourism; Dir DARIO BALDI; circ. 1,500,000.

Fonderia: Via Roncaglia 14, 20146 Milan; tel. (02) 436006; telex 332547; f. 1952; every 2 months; foundry techniques; Dir CARLO ARCARI; circ. 4,500.

Gazzetta Medica Italiana-Archivio per le Scienze Mediche: Corso Bramante 83–85, 10126 Turin; tel. (011) 678282; monthly; medical science; Dir TOMASO OLIARO.

Il Giornale dell' Officina: Via Roncaglia 14, 20146 Milan; tel. (02) 436006; telex 332547; f. 1964; every 2 months; contains supplement entitled *Tranciatura e Stampaggio*, about metal shearing and pressing techniques; Dir GABRIELE FAPPIANO; circ. 4,500.

L'Italia Agricola: Via Nazionale 89/A, 00184 Rome; tel. (06) 463651; f. 1864; quarterly; agriculture; Dir BORIS FISCHETTI; circ. 20,000.

Macchine: Via Roncaglia 14, 20146 Milan; tel. (02) 436006; telex 332547; f. 1946; monthly; mechanical engineering in industry; Dir CARLO ARCARI; circ. 10,000.

Meccanica: Piazza Leonardo da Vinci 32, 20133 Milan; tel. (02) 23994209; telex 333467; quarterly; Journal of Italian Association of Theoretical and Applied Mechanics; Dir Prof. CARLO CERCIGNANI.

Il Medico d'Italia: Piazza Cola di Rienzo 80A, 00192 Rome; medical science; Editor D. POGGIOLINI.

Minerva Medica: Corso Bramante 83–85, 10126 Turin; tel. (011) 678282; 2 a week, medical science; Dir TOMASO OLIARO.

Monti e Boschi: Via Emilia Levante 31/2, 40139 Bologna; tel. (051) 492211; telex 510336; f. 1949; bi-monthly; ecology and forestry; Publisher EDAGRICOLE; Editor UMBERTO BAGNARESI; circ. 15,600.

Motor: Piazzale Belle Arti 6, 00196 Rome; tel. (06) 3606754; f. 1942; monthly; motor mechanics; Dir SERGIO FAVIA DEL CORE; circ. 120,000.

ITALY   Directory

Officina: Via Roncaglia 14, 20146 Milan; tel. (02) 436006; telex 332547; f. 1956; monthly; organization and management in mechanical engineering; Dir CARLO ARCARI; circ. 16,000.

Physis: Leo S. Olschki, Viuzzo del Pozzetto, 50126 Florence; tel. (055) 687444; f. 1959; quarterly; history of science; Editor V. CAPPELLETTI.

La Rivista dei Combustibili: Viale De Gasperi 3, 20097 S. Donato Milanese; tel. (02) 510031; telex 321622; f. 1947; monthly; fuels review; Dir Prof. ALBERTO GIRELLI; circ. 2,000.

Rivista Geografica Italiana: Via Curtatone 1, 50123 Florence; f. 1894; quarterly geographical review; Editor PIERO INNOCENTI.

Utensil: Via Roncaglia 14, 20146 Milan; tel. (02) 436006; telex 332547; f. 1979; 9 a year; technology and marketing in the tool industry; Dir CARLO ARCARI; circ. 12,000.

Women's Publications

Amica: Via Scarsellini 17, 20161 Milan; tel. (02) 6339; telex 310031; weekly; Editor P. PIETRONI; circ. 211,000.

Annabella: RCS Rizzoli Periodici SpA, Via A. Rizzoli 2, 20132 Milan; tel. (02) 25843213; telex 312119; weekly; Editor M. VENTURI; circ. 270,000.

Confidenze: Arnoldo Mondadori Editore SpA, Via Marconi 27, 19587 Segrate, Milan; tel. (02) 75421; telex 320457; weekly; Dir ALDO GUSTAVO CIMARELLI; circ. 380,000.

Gioia: Via Vitruvio 43, 20124 Milan; weekly; Editor S. GIACOBINI; circ. 351,000.

Grazia: Arnoldo Mondadori Editore SpA, Via Marconi 27, Segrate, 20090 Milan; f. 1938; weekly; Dir ANDREINA VANNI; circ. 344,000.

Intimità: Via Borgogna 5, 20122 Milan; tel. (02) 781051; weekly; published by Cino del Duca; Dir G. GALLUZZO; circ. 468,000.

Mille Idee per la Donna: Rizzoli Editore SpA, Via Angelo Rizzoli 2, 20132 Milan; tel. (02) 2588; monthly; Dir MARA SANTINI; circ. 362,800.

Vogue Italia: Piazza Castello 27, 20121 Milan; tel. (02) 8561; telex 313454; monthly; Editor F. SARTORI.

Miscellaneous

Annali della Scuola Normale Superiore di Pisa: Scuola Normale Superiore, Pisa; tel. (050) 597111; telex 590548; f. 1873; quarterly; mathematics, philosophy, philology, history, literature; Editor (Mathematics) Prof. EDOARDO VESENTINI; Editor (literature and philosophy) Prof. GIUSEPPE NENCI; circ. 1,300.

Atlante: Via Mosè Bianchi 6, 20149 Milan; tel. (02) 4694451; telex 333183; published by Istituto Geografico de Agostini (Novara); travel, art, geography, ethnology, archaeology; Dir Dott. GUIDO RE.

Comunità Mediterranea: Lungotevere Flaminio 34, 00196 Rome; quarterly; legal; Editor ENRICO NOUNÈ.

Cooperazione Educativa: La Nuova Italia, Via dei Piceni 16, 00185 Rome; tel. (06) 4940228; f. 1952; monthly; education; Dir GIORGIO TESTA.

Israel: Largo Don Morosini 1, 00195 Rome; f. 1916; weekly; cultural; Jewish; Editor C. A. VITERBO.

Il Maestro: Clivo Monte del Gallo 50, 00165 Rome; f. 1945; fortnightly; Catholic teachers' magazine; Dir RITA LUDOVICO; circ. 40,000.

Quattroruote: Via A. Grandi 5/7, 20089 Rozzano, Milan; telex 313589; f. 1956; motoring; monthly; Editor RAFFAELE MASTROSTEFANO; circ. 600,000.

Qui Touring: Touring Club Italiano, Corso Italia 10, 20122 Milan; tel. (02) 85261; telex 321160; f. 1971; monthly; travel, art, geography; Man. Dir PIERO CHIARA; Editor MARIO ORIANI; circ. 510,000.

Radiocorriere TV: Via Arsenale 41, 10121 Turin; tel. (011) 5710; weekly; RAI official guide to radio and television programmes; Dir GINO NEBIOLO.

NEWS AGENCIES

Agenzia Giornalistica Italia (AGI): Via Nomentana 92, 00161 Rome; tel. (06) 841181; telex 610512; Man. BRUNO NOBILI.

Agenzia Nazionale Stampa Associata (ANSA): Via della Dataria 94, 00187 Rome; tel. (06) 67741; telex 612220; f. 1945; 18 regional offices in Italy and 89 branches all over the world; service in Italian, Spanish, French, English; Pres. GIOVANNI GIOVANNINI; Man. Dir and Gen. Man. PAOLO DE PALMA; Chief Editor SERGIO LEPRI.

Inter Press Service: Via Panisperna 207, 00184 Rome; tel. (06) 4742973; telex 610574; Editor-in-Chief PABLO PIACENTINI.

Foreign Bureaux

Agencia EFE (Spain): Via dei Canestrari 5, 00186 Rome; tel. (06) 6548802; telex 622323; Bureau Chief JORGE DEL CORRAL Y DIEZ DEL CORRAL.

Agence France-Presse (AFP): Piazza Santi-Apostoli 66, 00187 Rome; tel. (06) 6793623; Bureau Chief FRANCIS LARA.

Allgemeiner Deutscher Nachrichtendienst (ADN) (German Democratic Republic): Via Prato della Signora 22, 00141 Rome; Bureau Chief Dr HEINZ SIMON.

Associated Press (AP) (USA): Piazza Grazioli 5, 00186 Rome; tel. (06) 6798382; telex 610196; Bureau Chief DENNIS F. REDMONT.

Československá tisková kancelář (ČTK) (Czechoslovakia): Via Bevagna 1147, 00191 Rome; tel. (06) 3270777; telex 610135.

Deutsche Presse-Agentur (dpa) (Federal Republic of Germany): Via della Mercede 55, Int. 15, 00187 Rome; tel. (06) 6789810; telex 610046; Correspondent FRANK RAFALSKI.

Kyodo Tsushin (Japan): Via Panama 110, 00198 Rome, tel. (06) 8440709; telex 680840; Bureau Chief KATSUO UEDA.

Magyar Távirati Iroda (MTI) (Hungary): Via Topino 29, 00199 Rome; Correspondent ERNŐ KIRÁLY.

Reuters (UK): Via della Cordonata 7, 00187 Rome; tel. (06) 6782560; telex 620602.

Telegrafnoye Agentstvo Sovetskovo Soyuza (TASS) (USSR): Viale dell'Umanesimo 172, 00144 Rome; tel. (06) 5915883; telex 610034; Correspondent YEVGENIY BABENKO.

United Press International (UPI) (USA): Via della Dataria 94, 00187 Rome; tel. (06) 6795747; telex 610046; Manager for Italy PEGGY POLK.

Xinhua (New China) News Agency (People's Republic of China): Via Bruxelles 59, 00198 Rome; tel. (06) 865028; telex 612208; Bureau Chief FENG BIN.

The following are also represented: CNA (Taiwan) and Jiji Tsushin-Sha (Japan).

PRESS ASSOCIATIONS

Associazione della Stampa Estera in Italia: Via della Mercede 55, 00187 Rome; tel. (06) 6786005; foreign correspondents' asscn; Pres. DENNIS REDMONT; Sec. SANTIAGO FERNÁNDEZ ARDANAZ.

Federazione Italiana Editori Giornali (FIEG): Via Piemonte 64, 00187 Rome; tel. (06) 461683; f. 1950; association of newspaper proprietors; Pres. GIOVANNI GIOVANNINI; Dir-Gen. SEBASTIANO SORTINO; 276 mems.

Federazione Nazionale della Stampa Italiana: Corso Vittorio Emanuele 349, 00186 Rome; tel. (06) 6547741; f. 1877; 17 affiliated unions; Pres. GUIDO GUIDI; Nat. Sec. GIULIANA DEL BUFALO; 16,000 mems.

Unione Stampa Periodica Italiana (USPI): Via Nazionale 163, 00184 Rome; tel. (06) 6783117; Pres. Dott. ERNESTO REDAELLI; Sec.-Gen. GIAN DOMENICO ZUCCALÀ; 4,000 mems.

Publishers

There are over 300 major publishing houses and many smaller ones.

Bologna

Edizioni Calderini: Via Emilia Levante 31, 40139 Bologna; tel. (051) 492211; telex 214821; f. 1952; art, sport, electronics, mechanics, university and school textbooks, travel guides, nursing, architecture; Man. Dir SERGIO PERDISA.

Capitol Editrice Dischi CEB: Via Minghetti 17/19, 40057 Cadriano di Granarolo Emilia, Bologna; tel. (051) 766612; telex 511039; f. 1956; children's fiction, textbooks, reference, medicine, art, biography, educational films and records; Man. Dir MAURIZIO MALIPIERO.

Cappelli Licinio Nuova SpA: Via Marsili 9, 40124 Bologna; tel. (051) 330411; f. 1851; medical science, history, politics, literature, textbooks; Man. Dir MARIO MUSSO; Editor PAOLO PULLEGA.

Edagricole: Via Emilia Levante 31, 40139 Bologna; tel. (51) 492211; telex 510336; f. 1936; agriculture, veterinary science, gardening, biology, textbooks, directories; Man. Dir SERGIO PERDISA; Editor LUISA MANZONI.

Malipiero SpA: Via Liguria 12–14, CP 788, 40064 Ozzano Emilia, Bologna; tel. (051) 799264; telex 510260; f. 1969; albums and books for children and young people, dictionaries, pocket dictionaries, stamp albums, etc.; Editorial Dir DONATA MALIPIERO.

ITALY

Società Editrice Il Mulino: Via S. Stefano 6, 40125 Bologna; tel. (051) 233415; f. 1954; politics, history, philosophy, social sciences, linguistics, literary criticism, law, music, theatre, psychology, economics, journals; Gen. Man. GIOVANNI EVANGELISTI.

Nicola Zanichelli: Via Irnerio 34, 40126 Bologna; tel. (051) 293111; telex 214885; f. 1859; educational, history, literature, philosophy, science, technical books, law, psychology, architecture, earth sciences, linguistics, medicine and economics; Chair. GIOVANNI ENRIQUES; Man. Dir FEDERICO ENRIQUES.

Brescia

Editrice La Scuola SpA: Via Cadorna 11, Brescia; tel. (030) 29931; telex 300836; f. 1904; educational magazines, educational text books, audiovisual aids and toys; Chair. PAOLO PERONI; Man. Dir ADOLFO LOMBARDI; Gen. Man. GIUSTO MARCHESE.

Busto Arsizio

Bramante Editrice: Via G. Biancardi 1 bis, 21052 Busto Arsizio; tel. (0331) 620324; f. 1958; art, history, encyclopaedias, natural sciences, interior decoration, arms and armour, music; Man. Dir Dr GUIDO CERIOTTI.

Casale Monferrato

Casa Editrice Marietti SpA CEM: Via Adam 19, 15033 Casale Monferrato; tel. (0142) 76311; telex 212458; f. 1820; liturgy, theology, fiction, history, politics, literature, philosophy, art, children's books, textbooks; Editor ANTONIO BALLETTO.

Florence

Bonechi: Via dei Cairoli 18B, 50131 Florence; tel. (055) 576841; telex 571323; art, travel, reference, Man. Dir GIAMPAOLO BONECHI; Editor GIOVANNA MAGI.

Edizioni Cremonese: Borgo Santa Croce 17, 50122 Florence; tel. (055) 2476371; f. 1930; history, reference, engineering, science, textbooks, architecture, mathematics, aviation; Man. Dir ALBERTO STIANTI.

Giunti Barbera Editore; Via Vincenzo Gioberti 34, 50121 Florence; tel. (055) 670451; telex 571438; f. 1854; art, psychology, literature, science, law; Dir Dott. SERGIO GIUNTI.

Le Monnier: Via A. Meucci 2, 50015 Grassina, Florence; tel. (055) 6813801; f. 1836; academic and cultural books, textbooks, dictionaries; Man. Dirs Dott. MARCO PAOLETTI, Dott. VANNI PAOLETTI, Dott. ENRICO PAOLETTI.

La Nuova Italia Editrice: Via Antonio Giacomini 8, 50132 Florence; tel. (055) 572798; f. 1926; biography, psychology, philosophy, philology, education, history, politics, belles-lettres, art, music and science; Pres. MARIO CASALINI; Man. Dirs FEDERICO CODIGNOLA, MARIO ERMINI, SERGIO PICCIONI.

Nuovo Vallecchi Editore SpA: Via Gino Capponi 26, 50121 Florence; tel. (055) 587141; f. 1975; art, fiction, classics; Man. Dir LODOVICO BEVILACQUA.

Casa Editrice Leo S. Olschki: POB 66, 50100 Florence; tel. (055) 687444; f. 1886; reference, periodicals, textbooks, humanities; Man. ALESSANDRO OLSCHKI.

Adriano Salani SpA: Via Cittadella 7, 50144 Florence; tel. (055) 472968; f. 1862; art, classics, history, children's books; Gen. Man. MAURO FINARDI.

Edizioni Remo Sandron: Via L.C. Farini 10, 50121 Florence; f. 1839; textbooks; Pres. E. MULINACCI.

Casa Editrice G. C. Sansoni SpA: Via Benedetto Varchi 47, 50132 Florence; tel. (055) 243334; telex 57466; f. 1873; art, archaeology, literature, philology, philosophy, essays, science, social sciences, natural sciences, history, law, teach-yourself books, magazines; Man. Dir VALERIO LEVI.

Valmartina: Viale Gramsci 42, 50132 Florence; tel. (055) 242958; foreign languages, guide books.

Genova

Libreria degli Studi (formerly LUPA): Via Balbi 42, Genova; f. 1943; textbooks, fine arts; Dir MARIO BOZZI.

Milan

Adelphi Edizioni SpA: Via S. Giovanni sul Muro 14, 20121 Milan; tel. (02) 871266; f. 1962; classics, philosophy, biography, music, art, psychology, religion and fiction; Man. Dir LUCIANO FOÀ; Editor ROBERTO CALASSO.

Editrice Àncora: Via G. B. Niccolini 8, 20154 Milan; tel. (02) 3189941; f. 1935; religious, educational; Dir SEVERINO MEDICI.

Franco Angeli Editore: Viale Monza 106, CP 17130, 20127, Milan; tel. (02) 2827651; f. 1956; general; Man. Dir FRANCO ANGELI.

Carisch SpA: Via General Fara 39, 20124 Milan; tel. (02) 6702741; telex 326397; f. 1884; music and musicology; records; Pres. PIETRO MERAVIGLIA MANTEGAZZA.

Casa Editrice Ciancimino: Via Fontana 16, Milan; f. 1936; encyclopaedias and technical books for mechanical, electrical and radio industries; Dir MICHELE CIANCIMINO.

Edizioni di Comunità SpA: Via Manzoni 12, 20121 Milan; tel. (02) 790957; f. 1946; philosophy, psychology, architecture, town planning, social sciences; Dir Dr VITTORIO DI GIURO.

Gruppo Editoriale Fabbri SpA: Via Mecenate 91, 20138 Milan; tel. (02) 50951; telex 311321; f. 1946; juveniles, education, textbooks, reference, literature, maps and encyclopaedia series, art books; Man. Dir ROBERTO D'ALESSANDRO.

Bompiani: Via Mecenate 91, 20138 Milan; tel. (02) 50951; telex 311321; f. 1929; modern literature, biographies, theatre, science, art, history, classics, dictionaries, pocket books; Dir VITTORIO DI GIURO.

Sonzogno: Via Mecenate 91, 20138 Milan; tel (02) 50951; telex 311321; f. 1861; fiction, non-fiction, illustrated, guides; Dir MARIO ANDREOSE.

Giangiacomo Feltrinelli SpA: Via Andegari 6, 20121 Milan; tel. (02) 808346; f. 1954; fiction, juvenile, science, technology, textbooks, poetry, art, music, history, literature, political science, philosophy, reprint editions of periodicals.

Garzanti Editore: Via Senato 25, 20121 Milan; tel. (02) 7787; telex 325218; f. 1861; literature, poetry, science, art, history, politics, encyclopaedias, dictionaries, scholastic and children's books; Publisher Dr LIVIO GARZANTI; Editor PIERO GELLI.

Antonio Vallardi: Via Senato 25, 20121 Milan; tel. (02) 7787; telex 325218; f. 1822; art, literature, travel, reference, dictionaries, children's books, teach-yourself books; Editor VANNA MASSAROTTI.

Ghisetti e Corvi Editori: Corso Concordia 7, 20129 Milan; tel. (02) 706232; f. 1937; educational textbooks.

Ulrico Hoepli: Via Ulrico Hoepli 5, 20121 Milan; tel. (02) 865446; telex 313395; f. 1870; grammars, art, technical, scientific and school books, encyclopaedias; Dirs ULRICO HOEPLI, GIANNI HOEPLI, U. C. HOEPLI.

Edizioni Labor: Viale Beatrice d'Este 34, 20122 Milan; f. 1934; encyclopaedias, art, history, children's books, religion; Gen. Mans ERCOLE ERCOLI, Dott. GIANCARLO AGAZZI.

Longanesi e C.: Via T. Salvini 3, 20122 Milan; tel. (02) 782551; telex 34208; f. 1946; religion, music, art, history, philosophy, fiction; Pres. S. PASSIGLI; Man. Dir M. SPAGNOL.

Editrice Massimo: Corso di Porta Romana 122, 20122 Milan; tel. (02) 5454104; f. 1951; fiction, biography, history, social science, philosophy, pedagogy, theology, school texts; Man. Dir CESARE CRESPI.

Arnoldo Mondadori Editore: Via Marconi 27, 20090 Segrate, Milan; tel. (02) 75421; telex 34457; f. 1912; literature, fiction, politics, science, music, art, religion, philosophy, children's books, magazines; Man. Dir SERGIO POLILLO.

Ugo Mursia Editore SpA: Via Tadino 29, 20124 Milan; tel. (02) 209341; telex 325294; f. 1922; general fiction and non-fiction, textbooks, reference, art, history, philosophy, biography, children's books; Gen. Man. Dott. GIANCARLA MURSIA.

Nuova Accademia Editrice: Via Cavalcabò 9, 20146 Milan; tel. (02) 464884; f. 1946; books on general culture; Pres. LUIGI PINELLI.

Editore dall'Oglio: Via Santa Croce 20/2, 20122 Milan; tel. (02) 8351575; f. 1925; general literature, biography, history, fiction; Gen. Man. BRUNO ROMANO.

Edizioni Paoline: Piazza Soncino 5, 20092 Cinisello Balsamo—Milan; tel. (02) 6128732; telex 325183; f. 1914; religious; Gen. Man. ANTONIO TARZIA.

Etas Periodici SpA: Via Mecenate 86/7, 20138 Milan; tel. (02) 5075; telex 331342; technical periodicals; Man. Dir Dott. EUGENIO DE ROSA.

Editrice Piccoli SpA: Via S. Sofia 10, 20122 Milan; tel. (02) 861847; f. 1943; children's books; Man. Dir EMANUELA COLLINI.

Riccardo Ricciardi Editore SpA: Via Alessandro Manzoni 10, 20121 Milan; f. 1907; classics, philology, history, literature; Gen. Man. Dott. MAURIZIO MATTIOLI.

G. and C. Ricordi SpA: Via Berchet 2, 20121 Milan; tel. (02) 8881; telex 310177; f. 1808; academic, art, music; Pres. GIANNI BABINI; Vice-Pres. EUGENIO CLAUSETTI; Man. Dir and Gen. Man. GUIDO RIGNANO.

ITALY

Editore Rizzoli SpA: Via Angelo Rizzoli 2, 20132 Milan; f. 1929; newspapers, magazines and books; Chair. ANTONIO COPPI.

Rusconi Libri SpA: Via Livraghi 1B, 20126 Milan; tel. (02) 2574141; telex 312233; books; Pres. EDILIO RUSCONI; Gen. Man. UGO BRAGA.

Edizioni di Vanni Scheiwiller: Via Melzi d'Eril 6, Milan; f. 1925; art, literature.

L'Editrice Scientifica: Via Ariberto 20, 20123 Milan; tel. (02) 8390274; f. 1949; university publications in chemistry and medicine; Dirs Dotts. LEONARDA and GUIDO GUADAGNI.

Edizioni Scolastiche Bruno Mondadori: Via Archimede 23, 20129 Milan; tel. (02) 5456036; f. 1946; textbooks and educational books; Chair. and Man. Dir ROBERTA MONDADORI; Man. Dir ROBERTO GULLI; Gen. Man. MARIO CANDIANI.

Selezione dal Reader's Digest SpA: Via Alserio 10, 20159 Milan; tel. (02) 69871; telex 330378; f. 1948; educational, reference, general interest; Man. Dir EDOARDO LUCHESCHI.

Carlo Signorelli SpA: Via Siusi 7, 20132 Milan; children's and text books, dictionaries.

La Sorgente: Via Garofalo 44, 20133 Milan; tel. (02) 230720; f. 1935; children's books; Man. Dir Dr GIORGIO VIGNATI.

Sugarco Edizioni: Viale Tunisia 41, 20124 Milan; tel. (02) 652192; f. 1956; fiction, biography, history, philosophy, guidebooks; Dir MASSIMO PINI.

Casa Editrice Luigi Trevisini: Via Tito Livio 12, Milan; tel. (02) 5450704; f. 1849; school textbooks; Dirs ENRICO TREVISINI, LUIGI TREVISINI.

Il Vaglio Cultura Arte: Via Vitruvio 39, 20124 Milan; tel. (02) 2846903; f. 1985; art and architecture; *Arte Lombarda nuova serie* (4 a year); Man. Prof. MARIA LUISA GATTI PERER.

Vita e Pensiero: Largo A. Gemelli 1, 20123 Milan; tel. (02) 8856; telex 321033; f. 1918; publisher to the Catholic University of the Sacred Heart; cultural, scientific books and magazines.

Naples

Casa Editrice Libraria Idelson: Via Alcide De Gasperi 55, 80133 Naples; tel. (081) 324733; f. 1911; medicine, biology; CEO GUIDO GNOCCHI.

Liguori Editore: Via Mezzocannone 19, 80134 Naples; tel. (081) 206077; f. 1949; linguistics, mathematics, engineering, economics, law, history, philosophy, sociology; Man. Dir Dott. ROLANDO LIGUORI.

Gaetano Macchiaroli Editore: Via Carducci 55–59, Naples; tel. (081) 206602; archaeology, classical studies, history, philosophy, political science.

Società Editrice Napoletana: Corso Umberto I 34, 80138 Naples; tel. (081) 206602; f. 1973; art, poetry, literature, history; Dir A. DE DOMINICIS.

Novara

Instituto Geografico De Agostini: Via G. da Verrazano 15, 28100 Novara; tel. (0321) 4241; telex 200290; geography, maps, encyclopaedias, dictionaries, art, literature, textbooks, science.

Padova

CEDAM—Casa Editrice Dr A. Milani: Via Jappelli 5/6, 35121 Padova; tel. (049) 757677; f. 1902; law, economics, political and social sciences, engineering, science, medicine, literature, philosophy, textbooks; Dirs ANTONIO MILANI, CARLO PORTA.

Libreria Editrice Gregoriana: Via Roma 37, 35100 Padova; tel. (049) 36133; f. 1684; *Lexicon Totius Latinitatis*, religion, philosophy, social studies; Dir Prof. MARIO MORELLATO.

Libreria Editrice Internazionale Zannoni e Figlio: Corso Garibaldi 14, 35122 Padova; tel. (049) 44170; f. 1919; medicine, technical books, scholastic books, miscellaneous; Dir GIULIANA ZANNONI.

Piccin Nuova Libraria SpA: Via Altinate 107, 35100 Padova; tel. (049) 655566; f. 1980; scientific textbooks and journals; Man. Dir Dr MASSIMO PICCIN.

Rome

Armando Armando Editore Srl: Piazza Sidney Sonnino 13, 00153 Rome; tel. (06) 5806420; philosophy, psychology, social sciences, languages; Man. Dir ENRICO JACOMETTI.

Edizioni Borla: Via delle Fornaci 50, 00165 Rome; tel. (06) 6381618; f. 1863; religion, philosophy, psychoanalysis, ethnology, literature, novels for teenagers; Man. Dir VINCENZO D'AGOSTINO.

Edizioni d'Arte di Carlo E. Bestetti & C. Sas: Via di S. Giacomo 18, 00187 Rome; tel. (06) 6790174; f. 1978; art and de luxe editions.

Editoriale Arte e Storia: Via Pietro Cossa 3, 00193 Rome; f. 1943; philosophy, law, actuarial mathematics, narrative, cinema, school textbooks; Chair. LUIGI DE POMPEIS; Man. Dir VERA ZAMPA.

Ausonia: Viale dei Primati Sportivi 27, EUR, 00144 Rome; tel. (06) 595959; f. 1919; textbooks; Pres. E. LUCCHINI; Gen. Man. G. LUCCHINI.

AVE (Anonima Veritas Editrice): Via Aurelia 481, 00165 Rome; tel. (06) 6233041; f. 1935; theology, sociology, pedagogy, psychology, essays, learned journals, religious textbooks; Man. Dir ANTONIO SANTANGELO.

Vito Bianco Editore: Via Messina 31, 00198 Rome; tel. (06) 8443151; telex 621401; various, especially marine publications; Chair. Dott. VITO BIANCO.

Bulzoni Editore—Le edizioni universitarie d'Italia: Via dei Liburni 14, 00185 Rome; tel. (06) 4955207; f. 1969; science, arts, fiction, textbooks; Man. Dir MARIO BULZONI.

E. Calzono: Via del Collegio Romano 9, Rome; f. 1872; art, archaeology, philosophy, science, religion, economics; Dir Dr RICCARDO GAMBERINI MONGENET.

Editrice Ciranna: Via Gioberti 7, 04100 Latina, Rome; tel. (06) 631217; f. 1940; school textbooks; Man. Dir LIDIA FABIANO.

Armando Curcio Editore SpA: Via Arno 64, 00198 Rome; tel. (0773) 481601; telex 614666; f. 1928; encyclopaedias, classics, history, science, reference, geography, art; Chair. Dr ALFREDO CURCIO; Man. Dir SILVIO ROTUNNO.

Editrice Dante Alighieri (Albrighi, Segati & C.): Via Timavo 3, 00195 Rome; tel. (06) 383491; f. 1895; school textbooks, science and general culture; Pres. SALVATORE SPINELLI.

Edizioni Europa: Via G.B. Martini 6, 00198 Rome; tel. (06) 8449124; f. 1944; essays, literature, art, history, politics, music, economics; Chair. Prof. PIER FAUSTO PALUMBO.

Hermes Edizioni: Via Flaminia 158, 00196 Rome; tel. (06) 3601656; f. 1979; alternative medicine, astrology, nature, dietetics; Gen. Man. GIOVANNI CANONICO.

Laterza, Giuseppe e Figli SpA: Via di Villa Sacchetti 17, 00197 Rome; tel. (06) 803693; f. 1889; belles lettres, biography, reference, religion, art, classics, history, economics, philosophy, social science; Dir VITO LATERZA.

Le Edizioni del Lavoro: Via G. B. Martini 6, 00198 Rome; tel. (06) 8449124; f. 1945; history, politics, economics, philology, sociology, periodicals; Chair. Prof. PIER FAUSTO PALUMBO.

Guida Monaci SpA: Via Francesco Crispi 10, 00187 Rome; tel. (06) 483401; telex 613462; f. 1870; commercial and industrial, financial, administrative and medical directories; publishes *Annuario Generale Italiano, Annuario Administrativo Italiano, Chi Sono Nelle Attività Italiane, Annuario Sanitario, Agenda* (yearly); Dir ALBERTO ZAPPONINI.

Fratelli Palombi: Via dei Gracchi 181, 00195 Rome; tel. (06) 350606; f. 1904; history, art, etc. of Rome; Man. Dir MARIO PALOMBI.

Jandi Sapi Editori: Via Crescenzio 62, 00193 Rome; tel. (06) 6545515; f. 1941; industrial and legal publications; Dir Dr FRANCO VOLPINI.

Angelo Signorelli Editore: Via Paola Falconieri 84, 00152 Rome; tel. (06) 539954; f. 1911; science, general literature, textbooks; Chair. OLIVIERO ALPA.

Edizioni Studium: Via Cassiodoro 14, 00193 Rome; tel. (06) 6565846; f. 1927; philosophy, literature, sociology, pedagogy, religion, economics, law, science, history, psychology; periodical *Studium*.

Stresa

Libraria Editoriale Sodalitas: Centro Internazionale Studi Rosminiani, Corso Umberto 1°, 15, 28049 Stresa; tel. (0323) 31623; f. 1906; philosophy, theology, *Rivista Rosminiana* (quarterly); Dir Prof. PIER PAOLO OTTONELLO.

Trento

G.B. Monauni: Via Manci 141, 38100 Trento; tel. (0461) 21445; f. 1725; art, archaeology, ethnology, folklore, science, history; Man. Dir Dott. G. B. MONAUNI.

Turin

Editrice L'Artist Modern: Via Garibaldi 59, 10121 Turin; tel. (011) 541371; f. 1901; art; Dir. F. NELVA.

ITALY Directory

Editore Boringhieri SpA: Corso Vittorio Emanuele 86, 10100 Turin; f. 1957; psychology and sciences; Man. Dir PAOLO BORINGHIERI.

Giulio Einaudi Editore; Via Umberto Biancamano 1, CP 245, 10121 Turin; tel. (011) 533653; telex 220344; f. 1933; fiction, classics, general; Gen. Man. GIULIO EINAUDI.

Giorgio Giappichelli Editore: Via Po 21, 10124 Turin; tel. (011) 8397019; f. 1921; University publications on literature, law, economics, politics and sociology.

Lattes S. e C. Editori: Via Confienza 6, 10121 Turin; f. 1893; technical, textbooks; Pres. MARIO LATTES.

Levrotto & Bella, Libreria Editrice Universitaria: Corso Vittorio Emanuele II 26, 10123 Turin; tel. (011) 832535; f. 1914; university textbooks; Dir GUALINI TERENZIO.

Loescher Editore: Via Vittorio Amedeo 18, 10121 Turin; tel. (011) 549333; f. 1861; school textbooks, general literature, academic books; Man. Dir MAURIZIO PAVIA.

Edizioni Minerva Medica: Corso Bramante 83–85, 10126 Turin; tel. (011) 678282; medical books and journals; Dir Prof. TOMASO OLIARO.

Edizioni Paoline: Corso Regina Margherita 1, 10124 Turin; f. 1914; religion, history, psychology, science, fiction, children's books, encyclopaedias, dictionaries.

Petrini Editore SpA: Corso Trapani 48, Turin; tel. (011) 3358641; f. 1872; school textbooks; Dir VITTORIO GALLEA.

Pozzo Gros Monti SpA: Via Brofferio 3, 10121 Turin; tel. (011) 540833; f. 1868; *Orario Generale delle Ferrovie dello Stato* (railway timetable), and other official publications; Dir Conte LUIGI FERRARI ARDICINI.

Rosenberg & Sellier: Via Andrea Doria 14, 10123 Turin; tel. (011) 532150; telex 224202; f. 1883; philology, social sciences, literature, philosophy; Man. Dirs KATIE ROGGERO, UGO GIANNI ROSENBERG.

Società Editrice Internazionale pA (SEI): Corso Regina Margherita 176, 10152 Turin; tel. (011) 5211441; telex 216216; f. 1908; textbooks, fiction, art, literature, philosophy, children's books, etc.; Man. Dir Dr GIAN NICOLA PIVANO.

Unione Tipografico-Editrice Torinese (UTET): Corso Raffaello 28, 10125 Turin; tel. (011) 6502184; f. 1795; university and specialized editions on history, geography, art, literature, economics, law, sciences, encyclopaedias, dictionaries, etc.; Pres. Dott. GIANNI MERLINI.

Venice

Alfieri-Edizioni d'Arte: Cannaregio 6099, 30124 Venice; tel. (041) 23323; f. 1939; modern art, Venetian art, architecture, periodicals; Dirs GIORGIO FANTONI, MASSIMO VITTA.

Marsilio Editori: S. Croce 518A, Fondamenta S. Chiara, 30125 Venice; tel. (041) 707188; f. 1961; literature, arts, fiction, history, music, cinema, philosophy, social sciences; Man. Dirs Dott. EMANUELA BASSETTI, Dott. PAOLO LENARDA, Dott. MARIA CONCETIA FOZZER.

Verona

Bertani Editore: Via S. Salvatore Corte Regia 4, 37121 Verona; tel. (045) 32686; f. 1973; politics, literature, anthropology, sociology, theatre, cinema, geography, humanities, history of Verona, psychology, cultural journals; Editorial Dir GIORGIO BERTANI.

Arnoldo Mondadori Editore: Via Zeviani 2, 37131 Verona; tel. (045) 934532; telex 480071; f. 1946; juvenile books; Dir-Gen. LEONARDO MONDADORI; Man. Dir ALESSANDRO DALAI; Man. Ed. MARGHERITA FORESTAN.

Vicenza

Neri Pozza Editore: Contrà Oratorio dei Servi 19–21, 36100 Vicenza; tel. (0444) 27228; f. 1946; art, fiction, history, politics; Man. Dir NERI POZZA.

Government Publishing House

Istituto Poligrafico dello Stato: Piazza Verdi 10, 00100 Rome; tel. (06) 8508; f. 1928; State publishing house (Italian State Stationery Office); art books and reproductions; Dir Dr DANIEL TOZZI.

PUBLISHERS' ASSOCIATION

Associazione Italiana Editori: Via Delle Erbe 2, 20121 Milan; tel. (02) 8059244; Via Crescenzio 19, 00193 Rome; tel. (06) 6540298; Pres. CARLO ENRICO RIVOLTA; Sec.-Gen. ACHILLE ORMEZZANO.

Radio and Television

In 1985 there were an estimated 14,015,000 radio receivers and 13,900,000 television receivers in use.

In April 1975 a law was passed designed to guarantee the political independence of the RAI and the objectivity of its news coverage. Notably, the new law sought to increase the autonomy of the two existing television channels and to reinforce parliamentary supervision of programme planning. Since the state monopoly on broadcasting was abolished in 1976, approximately 450 local private commercial television stations have been set up all over Italy. Although electronically-transmitted national networks in competition to RAI are technically illegal, three stations in particular (Canale-5, Italia Uno and Rete Quattro) are national networks with an audience equal to that of RAI. A thousand private local radio stations have also begun broadcasting since a court case in 1975 established the right of every citizen to free local information.

Radiotelevisione Italiana (RAI-TV): Viale Mazzini 14, 00195 Rome; tel. (06) 3878; telex 61142; f. 1924; a public share capital company; a permanent parliamentary commission of senators and deputies from all political groups formulates and oversees general guidelines for programmes; the board of directors nominates the President and Vice-President from within its members and appoints the Director-General; Pres. SERGIO ZAVOLI; Vice-Pres. Prof. GIAM-PIERO ORSELLO; Dir-Gen. Dr BIAGIO AGNES.

RADIO

Programmes comprise the National Programme (general), Second Programme (recreational), Third Programme (educational); there are also regional programmes in Italian and in the languages of ethnic minorities. The Foreign and Overseas Service (Radio Roma) broadcasts in 27 languages to Africa, the Americas, Australia, Europe, Japan, the Near East and South Asia.

TELEVISION

There are three RAI television channels, the National Programme, the Second Programme and the Third Programme. Between them the former carry some 200 hours of advertising annually. There are local programmes in Italian and also in German for the Alto Adige.

Canale 5: Palazzo dei Cigni, Milano 2, 20090 Segrate, Milan; tel. (02) 21622508; telex 316197; f. 1979.

Italia Uno: Via Paleocapa 8, 200090 Milan.

Rete Quattro: Via Rivoltana 8, 20090 Segrate, Milan.

Finance

(cap. = capital; p.u. = paid up; res = reserves; dep. = deposits; m. = million; brs = branches; amounts in lire)

There are more than 1,000 banks in Italy, with a total of over 13,000 branches. Many of them are state controlled, including the majority of the large banks. There are more than 100 private banks, and a large number of co-operative and savings banks (*banche populari, casse di risparmio, casse rurali*) of widely varying size and importance. In addition, there are 90 specialized credit institutions which provide medium- and long-term finance, and other services outside the scope of the banks. In early 1987 reforms giving the Central Bank the right to authorize commercial banks to establish merchant banking subsidiaries were announced.

BANKING
Central Bank

Banca d'Italia: Via Nazionale 91, 00184 Rome; tel. (06) 47921; telex 610021; f. 1893; cap. 300m., res 2,083,225m. (Dec. 1984); since 1926 the Bank has had the sole right to issue notes in Italy; Gov. Dott. CARLO AZEGLIO CIAMPI; Gen. Man. LAMBERTO DINI; 97 brs.

Major Commercial Banks

Banca Agricola Mantovana: Corso Vittorio Emanuele 30, 46100 Mantova; tel. (0376) 3311; telex 304265; f. 1870; cap. 2,824m., res 552,383m., dep. 2,831,450m. (Dec. 1985); Pres. PIERMARIA PACCHIONI; Gen. Man. MARCELLO MELANI; 86 brs.

Banca Agricola Milanese SpA: Via Mazzini 9–11, 20123 Milan; tel. (02) 88091; telex 310608; f. 1874; cap. 27,600m., res 281,109m., dep. 2,654,420m. (Dec. 1984); Pres. Dott. CARLO VITTADINI; Gen. Man. Dott. AMBROGIO MONTI; 45 brs.

ITALY

Banca d'America e d'Italia: Via Borgogna 8, 20122 Milan; tel. (02) 77951; telex 311350; f. 1917; cap. 46,246m., res 336,722m. (1985); Chair. VINCENZO POLLI; Man. Dir MANLIO SESENNA; 98 brs.

Banca Antoniana di Padova e Trieste: Via 8 Febbraio 5, 35100 Padova; tel. (049) 839111; telex 430081; f. 1893; cap. 3,843m., res 348,976m., dep. 3,704,136m. (Dec. 1985); Pres. Dr GUSTAVO PROTTI; Gen. Man. ANICETO VITTORIO RANIERI; 42 brs.

Banca Cattolica del Veneto SpA: Via S. Corona, 25, 36100 Vicenza; tel. (0444) 519111; telex 480082; f. 1892; cap. and res 284,774m., dep. 5,854,635m. (Dec. 1985); Chair. FELICIANO BENVENUTI; Man. Dir GINO TROMBI; Gen. Man. DOMENICO SPEDALE; 200 brs.

Banca Commerciale Italiana SpA: Piazza della Scala 6, 20121 Milan; tel. (02) 88501; telex 310080; f. 1894; cap. 420,000m., res 124,000m., dep. 61,044,235m. (Dec. 1985); Chair. Dott. ANTONIO MONTI; Man. Dirs Dott. FRANCESCO CINGANO, ENRICO BRAGGIOTTI; 461 brs, including many overseas brs.

Banca Credito Agrario Bresciano SpA: Via Trieste 8, 25175 Brescia; tel. (030) 22931; telex 301558; f. 1883; cap. 75,000m., res 232,564m., dep. 2,954,892m. (Dec. 1983); Chair. Dott. MARIO AMBROSIONE; Gen. Man. Dott. LUIGI OROMBELLI; 72 brs.

Banca del Friuli SpA: Via Vittorio Veneto 20, 33100 Udine; tel. (0432) 4921; telex 450152; f. 1872; cap. 24,000m.; res 315,026m.; dep. 3,270,548m. (Dec. 1985); Pres. Dott. PAOLO MALIGNANI; Gen. Man. LORENZO SCARPIS; 89 brs.

Banca Nazionale dell'Agricoltura SpA: Via Salaria 231, 00198 Rome; tel. (06) 85881; telex 612121; f. 1921; cap. 81,000m., res 1,087,808m., dep. 23,079,494m. (Dec. 1984); Chair. Count GIOVANNI AULETTA ARMENISE; Man. Dirs FREDERICO PEPE, ULPIANO QUARANTA; 209 brs including brs abroad.

Banca Nazionale delle Comunicazioni: Via S. Martino della Battaglia 4, 00185 Rome; tel. (06) 46761; telex 625593; f. 1927; cap. 9,481m., res 131,688m., dep. 2,334,865m. (Dec. 1984); Pres. Dr GIUSEPPE CADARIO; Gen. Man. Dr VINCENZO MARIANI; 39 brs.

Banca Nazionale del Lavoro: Via Vittorio Veneto 119, 00187 Rome; tel. (06) 47021; telex 610116; f. 1913; cap. 1,176,250m., res 3,164,644m., dep. 79,114,809m. (1985); Chair. of the Board Dott. NERIO NESI; Man. Dir and Chief Gen. Man. Prof. FRANCESCO BIGNARDI; 414 brs incl. 11 overseas brs.

Banca Popolare Commercio e Industria: Via della Moscova 33, 20121 Milan; tel. (02) 62751; telex 310276; f. 1888; cap. 8,340m., res 257,927m., dep. 2,586,614m. (Dec. 1984); Chair. ENRICO GIANZINI; Gen. Man. GIUSEPPE VIGORELLI; 20 brs.

Banca Popolare dell' Emilia: Via San Carlo 820, 41100 Modena; tel. (059) 222223; telex 511392; f. 1867; cap. 1,990m., res 452,795m., dep. 3,173,672m. (Dec. 1984); Chair. PIER LUIGI COLIZZI; Gen. Man. Avv. FAUSTO BATTINI; 64 brs.

Banca Popolare di Bergamo: Piazza Vittorio Veneto 8, 24100 Bergamo; tel. (035) 392111; telex 300410; f. 1869; co-operative bank; cap. 21,316m., res 936,336m., dep. 7,056,444m. (Dec. 1984); Chair. LORENZO SUARDI; Gen. Man. GIUSEPPE A. BANFI; 119 brs.

Banca Popolare di Cremona: Via Cesare Battisti 14, 26100 Cremona; tel. (0372) 4041; telex 321099; f. 1865; cap. 3,722m., res 87,163m. (April 1985); Pres. FRANCESCO FROSI; Gen. Man. Dott. FRANCO CARNIGLIA; 28 brs.

Banca Popolare di Lecco SpA: Piazza Garibaldi 12, 22053 Lecco; tel. (0341) 480111; telex 380003; f. 1872; cap. 16,111m., res 246,724m., dep. 3,238,287m. (Dec. 1985); Pres. Dott. GIANCARLO BELLEMO; Gen. Man. ROBERTO POLVERINI; 59 brs.

Banca Popolare di Milano: Piazza F. Meda 4, 20121 Milan; tel. (02) 77001; telex 310202; f. 1865; cap. 34,038m., res 1,167,104m., dep. 14,314,858m. (Dec. 1984); Pres. PIERO SCHLESINGER; Gen. Man. ALDO COVA; 18 brs.

Banca Popolare di Novara: Via Carlo Negroni 12, 28100 Novara; tel. (0321) 4451; telex 200371; f. 1871; co-operative bank; cap. 47,119m., res 1,792,228m., dep. 15,661,701m. (Dec. 1984); Chair. ROBERTO DI TIERI; Man. Dirs PIERO BONGIANINO, CARLO PIANTANIDA; 376 brs.

Banca Popolare di Padova Treviso Rovigo: Piazza Salvemini 18, 35100 Padova; tel. (049) 843111; telex 430866; f. 1866; cap. 12,521m., res 249,579m., dep. 2,695,519m. (Dec. 1984); Chair. Dott. GIORGIO DE BENEDETTI; Gen. Man. Dott. ANTONIO CEOLA; 61 brs.

Banca Popolare di Verona: Piazza Nogara 2, 37100 Verona; tel. (045) 930111; telex 480009; f. 1867; cap. 6,332m., res 671,291m., dep. 3,872,249m. (Dec. 1984); Pres. Prof. GIORGIO ZANOTTO; Gen. Man. GIANFRANCO DEL NERO; 75 brs.

Banca Popolare di Vicenza: Contrà Porti 12, 36100 Vicenza; tel. (0444) 991111; telex 480092; cap. 3,992m., res 195,643m., dep. 1,369,353m. (Dec. 1985); Pres. GIUSEPPE NARDINI; Gen. Man. CARLO PAVESI.

Banca Provinciale Lombarda: Via Gennaro Sora 4, 24100 Bergamo; tel. (035) 394111; telex 300140; f. 1932; cap. 72,000m., res 360,452m., dep. 6,361,358m. (Dec. 1985); Chair. SILVIO GOLZIO; Man. Dir CORRADO FAISSOLA; 118 brs.

Banca San Paolo-Brescia SpA: Corso Martiri della Libertà 13, 25100 Brescia; tel. (030) 29921; telex 300010; f. 1888; cap. 70,000m., res 283,100m., dep. 4,480,225m. (Dec. 1984); Pres. Dott. Ing. ADOLFO LOMBARDI; Gen. Man. Dott. FLORIO GRADI; 73 brs.

Banca Toscana SpA: Corso 6, 50122 Florence; tel. (055) 43911; telex 570507; f. 1904; cap. and res 1,100,000m., dep. 9,067,000m. (Dec. 1985); Pres. GIUSEPPE BARTOLOMEI; Man. Dir. FABIO TAITI; 182 brs.

Banco Lariano SpA: Piazza Cavour 15, 22100 Como; tel. (031) 271356; telex 380018; f. 1908; cap. 150,000m., res 542,337m., dep. 6,643,184m. (Dec. 1984); Chair. Dr CARLO GAY; Gen. Man. ANTONIO ROMANO; 123 brs.

Banco di Napoli: Via Toledo 17718, 80132 Naples; tel. (081) 7911111; telex 710570; f. 1539; chartered public institution with no shareholders; cap. and res 622,000m., dep. 43,895,000m. (Dec. 1985); Chair. Prof. LUIGI COCCIOLI; Gen. Man. Prof. FERDINANDO VENTRIGLIA; 500 brs.

Banco di Roma SpA: Vialell. Tupini 180, Rome; tel. (06) 54451; telex 616184; f. 1880; cap. 280,000m., res 1,523,929m. dep. 42,252,231m. (Dec. 1984); Chair. Dott. ROMANO DELLA CHIESA; Man. Dirs Dott. ERCOLE CECCATELLI, Dott. MARCELLO TACCI; 333 brs including agencies and overseas brs.

Banco San Geminiano e San Prospero SpA: Via Mondatora 14, 41100 Modena; tel. (059) 236301; telex 511198; f. 1897; cap. 24,000m., res 426,351m., dep. 3,390,002m. (Dec. 1984); Chair. GUSTAVO VIGNOCCHI; Gen. Man. FRANCO FRANCESCHINI; 77 brs.

Banco di Santo Spirito SpA: Largo A. Fochetti 16, 00154 Rome; tel. (06) 51721; telex 610162; f. 1605; cap. 870,700m., dep. 19,433,500m. (Dec. 1985); Chair. RODOLFO RINALDI; Man. Dir GIOSUÉ CIAPPARELLI; 236 brs.

Banco di Sardegna: Viale Umberto 36, 07100 Sassari; tel. (079) 279111; telex 791106; f. 1953; public credit institution; cap. and res 505,209m., dep. 3,592,716m. (1984); Pres. and Chair. Dr ANGELO SOLINAS; Gen. Man. Dr ANGELO GIAGU DE MARTINI; 80 brs.

Banco di Sicilia: Via Mariano Stabile 182, 90141 Palermo; tel. (091) 587933; telex 910050; f. 1860; public credit institution; cap. and res 1,227,615m., dep. 25,179,933m. (Dec. 1985); Chair. Prof. GIANNINO PARRAVICINI; Gen. Man. and CEO Dr OTTAVIO SALAMONE; 347 brs.

Cassa di Risparmi e Depositi di Prato: Via degli Alberti 2, 50047 Prato; tel. (0574) 4921; telex 572382; f. 1830; savings bank; cap. 8,188m., res 231,611m., dep. 2,175,765m. (Dec. 1985); Pres. Avv. JOSEF BRANDSTÄTTER; Gen. Man. Dott. FRANZ OBERMAIR; 45 brs.

Cassa di Risparmio di Firenze: Via Bufalini 4/6, 50122 Florence; tel. (055) 27801; telex 572391; f. 1829; commercial bank; cap. 167,441m., dep. 4,441,584m. (Dec. 1983); Chair. and Pres. LAPO MAZZEI; Gen. Man. LUIGI TINTI; 170 brs.

Cassa di Risparmio di Genova e Imperia: Via Cassa di Risparmio 15, 16123 Genova; tel. (010) 20911; telex 270089; f. 1846; cap. and res 286,500m., dep. 4,428,000m. (Dec. 1983); Pres. Avv. GIOVANNI DAGNINO; Gen. Man. Dott. GIOVAN BATTISTA VILLA; 123 brs.

Cassa di Risparmio della Provincia di Bolzano—Südtiroler Landessparkasse: Via Cassa di Risparmio 12B, 39100 Bolzano; tel. (0471) 901111; telex 400090; f. 1854; cap. and res 156,955m., dep. 1,760,211m. (Dec. 1983); Pres. JOSEF BRANDSTÄTTER; Gen. Man. FRANZ OBERMAIR; 47 brs.

Cassa di Risparmio delle Provincie Lombarde (CARIPLO): Via Monte di Pietà 8, 20100 Milan; tel. (02) 88661; telex 310268; f. 1823; savings bank; cap. and res 2,617,000m., dep. 23,543,000m. (Dec. 1983); Chair. ANTONIO CONFALONIERI; Man. Dir ERNESTO UGOLINI; 464 brs.

Cassa di Risparmio di Roma: Via del Corso 320, 00186 Rome; tel. (06) 67071; telex 613540; f. 1836; savings bank; cap. 229,999m., res 1,872,715m., dep. 9,242,433m. (Dec. 1984); Chair. Prof. REMO CACCIAFESTA; Gen. Man. CESARE GERONZI; 157 brs.

Cassa di Risparmio di Torino: Via XX Settembre 31, 10121 Turin; tel. (011) 57661; telex 212278; f. 1827; savings bank; cap. 640,928m., dep. 9,510,436m. (Dec. 1983); Chair. Prof. ENRICO FILIPPI; Man. Dirs ALESSANDRO CONFORTI, GIANFRANCO PENONE; 221 brs.

ITALY

Cassa di Risparmio di Venezia: San Marco 4216, 30124 Venice; tel. (041) 707644; telex 410049; cap. and res 292,624m., dep. 2,221,414m. (Dec. 1983); Pres. Prof. ALFREDO GUARINI; Gen. Man. Dott. ERNESTO DE BEI; 55 brs.

Cassa di Risparmio di Verona, Vicenza e Belluno: Via Garibaldi 1, 37100 Verona; tel. (045) 936111; telex 480056; f. 1825; res 452,403m., dep. 6,598,115m. (Dec. 1984); Pres. Dott. GINO BARBIERI; Gen. Man. Dott. ERNESTO FRANCO COLOMBINI; 147 brs.

Cassa di Risparmio VE per le Province Siciliane: Piazza Cassa di Risparmio 4, 90133 Palermo; tel. (091) 273111; telex 910024; f. 1861; savings bank; cap. and res 320,161m., dep. 4,787,365m. (Dec. 1985); Pres. Dott. GIOVANNI FERRARO; Gen. Man. Dott. AGOSTINO MULÈ; 230 brs.

Credito Commerciale, SpA: Via Armorari 4, 20123 Milan; tel. (02) 88241; telex 321573; f. 1907; subsidiary of Monte dei Paschi de Siena; cap. and res 140,426m. (Dec. 1984); Pres. CESARE PANIZZA; Gen. Man. GIOVANNI DELLA ROSA; 85 brs.

Credito Emiliano: Via Emilia S. Pietro 4, 42100 Reggio-Emilia; tel. (0522) 4651; telex 530305; f. 1910; cap. 27.9m., res 124.672m., dep. 2,044,766m. (Dec. 1985); Pres. GIORGIO FERRARI; Gen. Man. FRANCO BIZZOCHI; 52 brs.

Credito Italiano SpA: Piazza Cordusio 2, 20123 Milan; tel. (02) 88621; telex 312401; f. 1870; cap. and res 2,026,806m. (April 1986), dep. 50,081,731m. (Dec. 1985); Chair. ALBERTO BOYER; Man. Dirs LUCIO RONDELLI, P. C. MARENGO; 477 brs including five overseas.

Credito Romagnolo: Via Zamboni 20, 40126 Bologna; tel. (051) 338111; telex 510131; f. 1896; cap. and res 985,000m., dep. 10,749,000m. (Dec. 1985); Pres. Prof. Avv. GERARDO SANTINI; Gen. Man. MARIO FANTINI; 186 brs.

Credito Varesino SpA: Via Vittorio Veneto 2, 21100 Varese; tel. (0332) 253111; telex 326695; f. 1898; cap. 30,000m., res 248,078m., dep. 3,901,628m. (Dec. 1985); Chair. RINALDO OSSOLA; Chief Gen. Man. PIERO FORTI; 64 brs.

Istituto Bancario Italiano SpA (IBI): Via Manzoni 3, 20121 Milan; tel. (02) 88901; telex 321434; f. 1918; cap. 100,000m., res 112,200m., dep. 8,368,300m. (Dec. 1984); Chair. GIAMPIERO CANTONI; Gen. Man. CARLO GILTRI; 54 brs.

Istituto Bancario San Paolo di Torino: Piazza San Carlo 156, 10121 Turin; tel. (011) 57701; telex 212040; Public Law Bank; f. 1563; cap. and res 2,636,526m., dep. 55,825,957m. (Dec. 1985); Chair. Prof. GIANNI ZANDANO; Chief Gen. Man. Prof. ZEFFERINO FRANCO; 367 brs including overseas brs.

Monte dei Paschi di Siena: Piazza Salimbeni 3, 53100 Siena; tel. (0577) 294111; telex 570079; f. 1472; public law credit institution; cap. and res 2,430,900m., dep. 36,228,600m. (Dec. 1982); Chair. GIOVANNI CODA NUNZIANTE; CEO and Gen. Man. Dr GIOVANNI CRESTI; Chief Man. (international) GIORGIO MAURETTI; 671 brs in Italy; rep. offices in London, Frankfurt, New York, São Paulo and Singapore.

Nuovo Banco Ambrosiano SpA: Piazza Paolo Ferrari 10, 20121 Milan; tel. (02) 85941; telex 335687; f. 1982 (formerly Banco Ambrosiano, f. 1896); 65% owned by a consortium of 10 banks and 35% owned by 70,000 private shareholders; total assets 9,087,145m. (June 1986); Chair. GIOVANNI BAZOLI; CEO and Gen. Man. PIER DOMENICO GALLO; 112 brs.

FINANCIAL INSTITUTIONS

Centrobanca Banca Centrale di Credito Popolare SpA: Corso Europa 20, 20122 Milan; tel. (02) 77811; telex 320387; f. 1946; cap. 125,000m., res 360,618m., dep. 5,391,749m. (Dec. 1984); central organization for medium- and long-term operations of Banche Popolari (co-operative banks) throughout Italy; Chair. LINO VENINI; Gen. Man. MARCELLO GENTILE; 234 brs.

Consorzio di Credito per le Opere Pubbliche (CREDIOP): Via Quintino Sella 2, 00187 Rome; tel. (06) 47711; telex 611020; f. 1919; cap. and res 1,045,275m.; provides loans to industrial, commercial and service companies, medium- and long-term loans to public authorities and their agencies, and export credits; Pres. and Chair. Ing. PAOLO BARATTA; Gen. Man. Dr GIORGIO CIGLIANA.

INTERBANCA (Banca per Finanziamenti a Medio e Lungo Termine SpA): Corso Venezia 56, 20121 Milan; tel. (02) 77311; telex 312649; cap. 45,644m., res 112,806m. (May 1985); Pres. GIORGIO CAPPON; Gen. Man. GASTONE TESTA.

Istituto Mobiliare Italiano (IMI): Viale dell'Arte 25, 00144 Rome; tel. (06) 54501; telex 610256; f. 1931; public-law credit institute; specializes in medium- and long-term finance for industry and public utilities, merchant banking, personal financial services and asset management. These facilities are also available to foreign concerns willing to make productive investment in Italy or to import Italian-made capital goods; cap. p.u. 1,650,000m.; legal res 1,445,000m.; outstanding loans 25,166,000m. (March 1986); Pres. Dr LUIGI ARCUTI; Gen. Man. Dr GIUSEPPE SARACINI; 10 regional offices in Italy.

Istituto per l'Assistenza allo Sviluppo del Mezzogiorno (IASM) (Institute for assistance in the development of southern Italy): Viale Pilsudski 124, 00197 Rome; tel. (06) 84721; telex 680232; f. 1962; aids investment to promote economic development in the South; Pres. Dr NINO NOVACCO.

Istituto Regionale per il Finanziamento alle Industrie in Sicilia (IRFIS): Via Giovanni Bonanno 47, 90143 Palermo; tel. (091) 266200; telex 910332; f. 1950; provides credit facilities for business ventures in Sicily, credit for domestic and export trade and for developing tourist facilities; Pres. Prof. ANTONIO MUCCIOLI; Dir-Gen. GIUSEPPE BIONDO.

Istituto per lo Sviluppo Economico dell'Italia Meridionale (ISVEIMER): Via A. De Gasperi 71, 80133 Naples; tel. (081) 7853111; telex 711020; public credit institution granting medium-term loans in mainland southern Italy; cap. and res 457,800m.; Pres. GIUSEPPE DI VAGNO; Dir-Gen. Dott. ANTONIO MERCUSA; 8 brs.

Mediobanca SpA, Banca di Credito Finanziario: Via Filodrammatici 10, 20121 Milan; tel. (02) 88291; telex 311093; f. 1946; deals in all medium- and long-term credit transactions; accepts medium-term time deposits either direct or through all the branches (approx. 1,100) of Banca Commerciale Italiana, Credito Italiano and Banco di Roma, and their subsidiaries. It grants advances of any type, provided they have a duration of from one to 20 years. It also promotes and manages syndicates to underwrite and/or place bond issues and syndicates to underwrite capital increases; cap. 170,000m. listed on the Italian Stock Exchanges; total res 751,924m. (June 1985); Chair. ANTONIO MACCANICO; Gen. Man. SILVIO SALTERI.

BANKERS' ORGANIZATIONS

Associazione Bancaria Italiana: Piazza del Gesú 49, 00186 Rome; tel. (06) 67671; telex 622107; Via della Posta 3, 20123 Milan; tel. (02) 806689; telex 324195; f. 1919; Pres. GIANNINO PARRAVICINI; Gen. Man. Dr FELICE GIANANI; membership (1,098 mems) is comprised of the following institutions: public credit institutions; banks of national interest (big commercial banks); private banks and bankers; co-operative banks; saving banks; rural banks; agricultural credit institutions; mortgage banks; industrial credit institutions; leasing and factoring; finance houses.

Associazione fra le Casse di Risparmio Italiane: Viale di Villa Grazioli 23, 00198 Rome; tel. (06) 866253; telex 680204; f. 1912; Pres. CAMILLO FERRARI; Man. Dott. RENATO DE MATTIA.

Associazione Nazionale Aziende Ordinarie di Credito (ASSBANK): Via Brennero 1, 20123 Milan; tel. (02) 4988235; telex 334355; Piazza di Spagna 20, Rome; Pres. Dott. Prof. TANCREDI BIANCHI; Dir-Gen. Dott. GIOVANNI LA SCALA.

Associazione Nazionale fra gli Istituti de Credito Agrario (ANICA): Via Bertoloni 3, 00197 Rome; tel. (06) 877506; telex 620311; Pres. Prof. GIUSEPPE GUERRIERI; Sec.-Gen. Dr ERNESTO DE MEDIO.

Associazione Nazionale L. Luzzatti fra le Banche Popolari: Via Montevideo 18, 00198 Rome; tel. (06) 852051; Pres. Prof. FRANCESCO PARRILLO; Dir-Gen. Prof. GIUSEPPE MURÈ.

Associazione Sindacale fra le Aziende del Credito (ASSICREDITO): Via G. Paisiello 5, 00198 Rome; tel. (06) 858041; Via della Posta 7, 20123 Milan; Pres. Dott. VITTORIO CORNA; Dir Dott. PERUSINO PERUSINI.

Associazione Tecnica delle Banche Popolari Italiane: Via Nazionale 230, 00184 Rome; tel. (06) 4742214; Pres. LINO VENINI; Dir-Gen. Dott. ARTURO FANTECHI.

THE STOCK EXCHANGE

Commissione nazionale per le Società e la borsa (CONSOB) (Commission for companies and the Stock Exchange): Via Isonzo 19, 00198 Rome; tel. (06) 8440451; telex 612434; f. 1974 to have regulatory control over companies quoted on stock exchanges, convertible bonds, unlisted securities, insider trading. A law passed in April 1983 extended its powers to all forms of public saving except bank deposits and mutual funds; Chair. FRANCO PIGA; Governors BRUNO PAZZI, ALDO POLINETTI, GIANNI PASINI, VINCENZO MATTURI. There are 10 stock exchanges, of which the following are the most important:

Genova: Borsa Valori, Via G. Boccardo 1; tel. (010) 589451; Pres. Dott. E. RAMELLA.

ITALY

Milan: Borsa Valori, Piazza Affari 6; tel. (02) 85341; telex 321430: Foreign Relations Dept, tel. (02) 8057674; Pres. Dott. ETTORE FUMAGALLI.

Naples: Borsa Valori, Palazzo Borsa, Piazza Bovio; tel. (081) 323232; Pres. GIORGIO FOCAS.

Rome: Borsa Valori, Via dei Burro 147, 00186; tel. (06) 6794541; f. 1821; Pres. Dott. FRANCO BALLARINI.

Turin: Borsa Valori, Via San Francesco da Paola 28; tel. (011) 547743; telex 220614; Pres. Dr FRANCO ILOTTE.

INSURANCE

L'Abeille, SpA: Via Leopardi 15, 20123 Milan; tel. (02) 85891; telex 316029; f. 1956; cap. 7,527m. (March 1986); Chair. Dott. MICHEL MARCHAL; Vice-Chair. J. MARJOULET; Man. Dir Dott. PIERRE BAUER.

Agricoltura Assicurazioni, SpA: Via R. Montecuccoli 20, 20147 Milan; tel. (02) 41441; f. 1947; cap. 5,000m. (March 1986); Chair. Avv. EMILIO DUSI; Vice-Chair. Dott. ANGELO COLNAGHI; Man. Dir AUGUSTO TRAINA.

Alleanza Assicurazioni: Viale Luigi Sturzo 37, 20154 Milan; tel. (02) 62961; telex 331303; f. 1898; cap. 120,000m. (March 1986); Chair. Prof. LIBERO LENTI; Vice-Chair. Avv. ENRICO RANDONE; Gen. Mans Dott. ALBERTO GIORGETTI, Dott. DANTE LAMPERTI.

Assicuratrice Edile: Via A. De Togni 2, 20123 Milan; tel. (02) 809681; telex 334697; f. 1960; cap. 5,000m. (March 1986); Chair. GIAN CARLO BORINI; Vice-Pres. Avv. EMILIO DUSI; Man. Dir GIAMPIERO SVEVO.

Assicurazioni Generali SpA: Central Head Office: Piazza Duca degli Abruzzi 2, 34132 Trieste; tel. (040) 6711; telex 460190; Head offices: Piazza San Marco 105, 30124 Venice; Via Tiziano 32, 20145 Milan; f. 1831; cap. 350,000m. (January 1986); Chair. and Man. Dir Avv. ENRICO RANDONE; Vice-Chair. Dott. CAMILLO DE BENEDETTI, Dott. MARIO LUZZATTO, ANDRÉ ROSA; Man. Dirs Dott. EUGENIO COPPOLA DI CANZANO, Dott. ALFONSO DESIATA.

Le Assicurazioni d'Italia (ASSITALIA): Corso d'Italia 33, 00198 Rome; tel. (06) 84831; telex 611051; f. 1923; cap. 100,000m. (March 1986); Pres. Dott. GIOVANNI PIERACCINI; Dir-Gen. Dott. Ing. IGNAZIO MORGANTI.

Ausonia Assicurazioni: Palazzo Ausonia, Milanofiori, 20089 Rozzano, Milan; tel. (02) 824731; telex 321225; f. 1907; cap. 18,000m. (March 1986); Chair. and Man. Dir LAMBERTO MAZZA.

Compagnia Assicuratrice Unipol: Via Stalingrado 45, 40128 Bologna; tel. (051) 507111; telex 510674; f. 1961; cap. 44,448m. (March 1986); Chair. Dott. ENEA MAZZOLI; Vice-Chair. and Man. Dir CINZIO ZAMBELLI; Man. Dir VITALIANO NERI.

Compagnia Italiana di Assicurazioni (COMITAS): Via Martin Piaggio 13/A, 16122 Genova; tel. (010) 814374; telex 270543; f. 1947; cap. 6,000m. (March 1986); Chair. Ing. EMANUELE RAVANO; Man. Dir Dott. FERDINANDO MENCONI.

Compagnia Latina di Assicurazioni: Viale Regina Giovanna 27, 20129 Milan; tel. (02) 20571; telex 310083; f. 1958; cap. 10,000m. (March 1986); Pres. ALDO MANETTI; Vice-Chair. Prof. Avv. ALBERTO CALTABIANO; Dir-Gen. SILLA GIULIO GRAZIOLI.

Compagnia Tirrena: Via Massimi 158, 00136 Rome; tel. (06) 33071; telex 621394; f. 1945; cap. 25,000m. (March 1986); Chair. and Gen. Man. Avv. MARIO AMABILE.

Compagnie Riunite di Assicurazione (CRA): Via Consolata 3, 10122 Turin; tel. (011) 57741; telex 212597; f. 1935; cap. 20,000m. (March 1986); Chair. GIUSEPPE BIANCO; Pres. JEAN LAMSON.

L'Edera: Piazzale de Matthaeis 41, 03100 Frosinone; tel. (0775) 872579; telex 613448; f. 1959; cap. 1,000m. (March 1986); Pres. Avv. GIUSEPPE TODINI; Man. Dir LUCIANO ZEPPIERI.

FATA (Fondo Assicurativo Tra Agricoltori) SpA: Via Urbana 169/A, 00184 Rome; tel. (06) 47651; telex 620838; f. 1927; cap. 12,757m. (March 1986); Chair. ARCANGELO LOBIANCO; Man. Dir LUIGI SCOTTI; Gen. Man. FRANCO RIZZI.

La Fiduciaria: Via A. Finelli 8, 40126 Bologna; tel. (051) 240901; telex 511491; f. 1969; cap. 3,993m. (March 1986); Chair. Dott. LEONARDO DI DONNA; Vice-Chair. Prof. MICHELE TOSSANI; Gen. Man. Ing. GIAN FRANCO POGGI.

Firs Italiana di Assicurazioni: Viale Sacco e Vanzetti, 00155 Rome; tel. (06) 43651; telex 620185; f. 1959; cap. 7,000m. (March 1986); Chair. (vacant); Man. Dir Dott. ANDREA GOTTI LEGA.

La Fondiaria: Via Lorenzo il Magnifico 1, 50129 Florence; tel. (055) 47941; telex 570430; cap. 43,500m. (March 1986); Pres. Avv. MICHELE CASTELNUOVO-TEDESCO; Dir Gen. ALFONSO SCARPA.

Intercontinentale Assicurazioni SpA: Via di Priscilla 101, 00199 Rome; tel. (06) 8300; telex 611155; f. 1955; cap. 20,000m. (March 1986); Pres. GUIDO NOÈ; Gen. Man. Dott. DOMENICO RIZZO.

Istituto Nazionale delle Assicurazioni (INA): Via Sallustiana 51, 00187 Rome; tel. (06) 47221; telex 610336; f. 1912; National Insurance Institute; a state institute with an autonomous management; Chair. Prof. ANTONIO LONGO; Dir-Gen. Dott. MARIO FORNARI.

Italia Assicurazioni, SpA: Via Fieschi 9, 16121 Genova; tel. (010) 53801; telex 270136; f. 1872; cap. 30,000m. (March 1986); Chair. Avv. MICHELE CASTELNUOVO-TEDESCO; Vice-Chair. ALFONSO SCARPA; Man. Dir Dott. CARLO GALEAZZI.

ITAS, Istituto Trentino-Alto Adige per Assicurazioni: Via Mantova 67, 38100 Trento; tel. (0461) 982112; telex 400884; f. 1821; cap. 13,000m. (March 1986); Chair. Dott. EDO BENEDETTI; Man. Dir Dott. ALDO MATASSONI.

Latina Renana Assicurazioni SpA: Via Nazario Sauro 26, 40121 Bologna; tel. (051) 266567; telex 214661; f. 1959; cap. 11,000m. (March 1986); Pres. Prof. Avv. ALBERTO CALTABIANO; Vice-Chair. ALDO MANETTI; Dir-Gen. SILLA GIULIO GRAZIOLI.

Lavoro e Sicurtà: Piazza Erculea 13–15, 20122 Milan; tel. (02) 8575; telex 320038; f. 1962; cap. 3,250m. (March 1986); Chair. FRANCESCO GETTULI; Vice-Pres. and Man. Dir ENZO ZENI.

Lloyd Adriatico SpA: Via Lazzaretto Vecchio 8–11, 34123 Trieste; tel. (040) 7353; telex 460350; f. 1936; cap. 24,000m. (March 1986); Chair. Avv. GIORGIO IRNERI; Dir-Gen. Dott. ANTONIO SODARO.

Lloyd Internazionale, SpA: Via Massimi 158, 00136 Rome; tel. (06) 33071; telex 621394; f. 1957; cap. 10,000m. (March 1986); Pres. Prof. ROBERTO TANA; Dir-Gen. Dott. LUIGI APUZZO.

Lloyd Italico (Divisione dell'Italia Assicurazioni): Via Martin Piaggio 1, 16122 Genova; tel. (010) 20961; telex 270555; f. 1917; cap. 8,400m.; Pres. ANDREA CROCE; Dir-Gen. GIOVANNI BATTISTA CAMBIASO.

MAA Assicurazioni Auto e Rischi Diversi SpA: Via Tonale 26, 20125 Milan; tel. (02) 69791; telex 334397; f. 1952; cap. 15,000m. (March 1986); Pres. Dott. Ing. ENRICO BONZANO; Vice-Chair. GIANCARLO GORRINI; Dir-Gen. CARLO GIUSSANI.

MILL. Ri.: Via Assarotti 5/4, 16122 Genova; tel. (010) 870293; telex 271297; cap. 30,000m. (March 1986); Pres. Dr GIORGIO CALVINI BENEDETTI; Man. Dir GIOVANNI BATTISTA CAMBIASO; Gen. Man. EDOARDO DANTI.

La Minerva: Via Milano 2, 20090 Segrate, Milan; tel. (02) 216081; telex 321284; f. 1942; cap. 8,000m. (March 1986); Chair. Avv. CHARLES WYNIGER; Man. Dott. SERGIO GUSELLA.

La Nationale: Piazza del Porto di Ripetta 1, 00186 Rome; tel. (06) 67701; telex 611032; f. 1962; cap. 12,600m. (March 1986); Chair. Dott. SERGIO BORLENGHI; Dir-Gen. Dott. GUIDO GUANTI.

Norditalia Assicurazioni: Viale Certosa 222, 20156 Milan; tel. (02) 30761; telex 331345; f. 1963; cap. 55,250m. (March 1986); Chair. Prof. Avv. ENRICO ZANELLI; Gen. Man. CESARE CANAVESIO.

La Pace, Assicurazioni e Riassicurazioni SpA: Piazza Cavour 5, 20121 Milan; tel. (02) 62421; telex 311636; f. 1919; cap. 3,000m.; Pres. Conte LEO SPAUR DI FLAVON E VALER; Dir Gen. H. G. KLAU.

La Peninsulare: Via G. Marcora 7, 20121 Milan; tel. (02) 630601; f. 1969; cap. 4,000m.; Chair. ELIO CAPPELLARI; Dir-Gen. AMBROGIO GUERRINI.

La Previdente Assicurazioni SpA: Via Copernico 36/38, 20125 Milan; tel. (02) 69561; telex 330488; f. 1917; cap. 25,000m. (March 1986); Pres. Avv. MICHELE CASTELNUOVO-TEDESCO; Admin. Del. ROBERTO PONTREMOLI.

Riunione Adriatica di Sicurtà (RAS): Corso Italia 23, 20122 Milan; tel. (02) 88441; telex 320065; and Piazza della Repubblica 1, 34122 Trieste; tel. (040) 7692; telex 460006; f. 1838; cap. 87,500m., res 551,900m. (Dec. 1985); Chair. and Man. Dir Dott. Umberto ZANNI.

SAI—Società Assicuratrice Industriale: Corso Galileo Galilei 12, 10126 Turin; tel. (011) 65621; telex 212080; f. 1921; cap. 40,800m. (March 1986); Chair. Avv. CARMELO CARUSO; Dir-Gen. Dott. ENRICO PIANTÀ.

SAPA (Security and Property Assurance) SpA: Via Riva Villasanta 3, 20145 Milan; tel. (02) 38841; telex 312061; f. 1963; cap. 10,000m. (March 1986); Pres. and Man. Dir Dott. JEAN PAUL FESTEAU.

SARA Assicurazioni SpA: Via Po 20, 00198 Rome; tel. (06) 84751; telex 614526; f. 1924; official insurer for Automobile Club d'Italia; cap. 18,000m. (March 1986); Chair. FILIPPO CARPI DE RESMINI; Gen. Man. ENZO BOIANI.

Savoia: Via S. Vigilio 1, 20142 Milan; tel. (02) 84421; telex 311270; cap. 9,000m. (March 1986); Pres. GIOVANNI BONELLI; Dir.-Gen. Dr FERDINANDO MENCONI.

Società Cattolica di Assicurazione: Lungadige Cangrande 16, 37126 Verona; tel. (045) 938711; telex 480482; f. 1896; cap. 6,766m. (March 1986); Chair. Dott. ALFREDO BERZANTI; Dir-Gen. Ing. GIULIO BISOFFI.

Società Italiana di Assicurazioni, SpA (SIDA): Via Massimi 158, 00136 Rome; tel. (06) 33071; telex 621394; f. 1914; cap. 6,000m.; Pres. ALBERTO PUGLIESE; Gen. Man. MARIO AMABILE.

Società Italiana Assicurazioni Trasporti (SIAT): Via Bosco 15, 16121 Genova; tel. (010) 593231; telex 270307; f. 1966; cap. 5,700m.; Chair. Dr ENRICO PIANTÀ; Dir-Gen. GIORGIO MITOLO.

Società Italiana Cauzioni (SIC): Via Crescenzio 12, 00193 Rome; tel. (06) 6530848; telex 611050; f. 1948; cap. 10,000m. (March 1986); Chair. CARLO D'AMELIO; Man. Dir GIANLUIGI BOCCIA.

Società Reale Mutua di Assicurazioni: Via Corte d'Appello 11, 10122 Turin; tel. (011) 55961; telex 215105; f. 1828; res 745,742m. (1985); Chair. PIER CARLO ROMAGNOLI; Gen. Mans ITI MIHALICH and GIUSEPPE SOLINAS.

Toro Assicurazioni: Via Arcivescovado 16, 10121 Turin; tel. (011) 57331; telex 221567; f. 1833; cap. 55,000m. (March 1986); Chair. Dott. UMBERTO AGNELLI; Deputy Chair. and Man. Dir Dott. CARLO ACUTIS; Gen. Man. Dott. GIUSEPPE DE CHIARA.

Trans-Atlantica: Via Arno 36, 80121 Naples; tel. (081) 640233; telex 710305; f. 1972; cap. 8,000m. (March 1986); Pres. and Man. Dir Ing. ANTONIO NORMALE; Dir-Gen. MICHELE D'IMPERIO.

Unica Assicurazioni SpA: Via R. Bertieri 4, 20146 Milan; tel. (02) 478861; telex 313249; f. 1973; cap. 3,000m.; Pres. GIUSEPPE AZZARITI; Dir-Gen. SANDRO RAMORINO.

Unione Italiana di Riassicurazione SpA: Via dei Giuochi Istmici 40, 00194 Rome; tel. (06) 365931; telex 610348; f. 1922; cap. 70,000m. (March 1986); Chair. Dott. MARIO LUZZATTO; Man. Dir Prof. A. LONGO.

Unione Subalpina di Assicurazioni: Via Alfieri 22, 10121 Turin; tel. (011) 514646; telex 221201; ; f. 1912; cap. 5,250m. (March 1986); Chair. Avv. VITTORIO BADINI CONFALONIERI; Man. Dir ROBERTO GAVAZZI.

Universo Assicurazioni SpA: Strada Maggiore 53, 40125 Bologna; tel. (051) 587511; telex 511170; f. 1971; cap. 10,000m. (March 1986); Chair. and Man. Dir SERGIO GETICI; Dir-Gen. Dott. GIORGIO DI GIANSANTE.

Veneta Assicurazioni: Via Enrico degli Scrovegni, 35131 Padova; tel. (049) 848111; telex 430482; f. 1960; cap. 6,000m. (March 1986); Pres. Conte NICOLÒ DONA DALLE ROSE; Man. Dir and Gen. Man. Dott. JEAN PAUL FESTEAU.

Vittoria Assicurazioni SpA: Piazza San Babila 3, 20122 Milan; tel. (02) 7790; telex 331030; cap. 2,500m. (March 1986); Pres. Prof. LUIGI GUATRI; Dir-Gen. EDOARDO RICCIO.

INSURANCE ASSOCIATIONS

Associazione Nazionale fra le Imprese Assicuratrici (ANIA): Head Office: Piazza S. Babila 1, 20122 Milan; tel. (02) 77641; telex 333288; Deputation: Via della Frezza 70, 00186 Rome; tel. (06) 6782941; telex 613621; f. 1944; Chair. EMILIO DUSI; Cons. Del. Dott. ENRICO TONELLI; 166 mems.

Trade and Industry

CHAMBERS OF COMMERCE

Unione Italiana delle Camere di Commercio, Industria, Artigianato e Agricoltura (Italian Union of Chambers of Commerce, Industry, Crafts and Agriculture): Piazza Sallustio 21, 00187 Rome; tel. (06) 47041; telex 622327; f. 1954 to promote the development of chambers of commerce, industry, trade and agriculture; Pres. PIERO BASSETTI; Sec.-Gen. Dott. GIUSEPPE CERRONI; 765 mems.

EXPORT INSTITUTE

Istituto Nazionale per il Commercio Estero (ICE) (National Institute for Foreign Trade): Via Liszt 21, EUR, 00100 Rome; tel. (06) 59921; telex 610160; f. 1919; government agency for the promotion of foreign trade; Pres. Dott. GIUSEPPE RATTI; Dir-Gen. Dott. MASSIMO MANCINI.

EMPLOYERS' ASSOCIATION

Confederazione Generale dell'Industria Italiana (CONFINDUSTRIA) (General Confederation of Italian Industry): Viale dell'Astronomia 30, EUR, 00144 Rome; tel. (06) 59031; telex 611393; f. 1919, re-established 1944; mems: 106 territorial asscns and 98 branch asscns, totalling 100,000 firms and 3,000,000 employers; office in Brussels; Pres. Dott. LUIGI LUCCHINI; Dir-Gen. Dott. PAOLO ANNIBALDI.

Principal Affiliated Industrial Organizations

Associazione degli Industriali della Birra e del Malto (Brewers): Via Savoia 29, 00198 Rome; tel. (06) 865161; telex 614486; Pres. Ing. ALDO BASSETTI; Pres. Del. CESARE MARTIN.

Associazione Industrie Aerospaziali (AIA) (Aerospace Industry): Via Nazionale 200, 00184 Rome; tel. (06) 460247; telex 680440; f. 1946; Pres. FAUSTO CERETI; Sec.-Gen. Dott. SERGIO LIBERI.

Associazione Industrie Siderurgiche Italiane (ASSIDER) (Iron and Steel Industries): Via XX Settembre 3, 20122 Milan; tel. (02) 860351; telex 311438; Via XX Settembre 1, 00187 Rome; tel. (06) 463867; f. 1946; Pres. Ing. ADAMO ADAMI; Dir Gen. Dr GIANCARLO LONGHI; 140 mems.

Associazione Italiana degli Industriali dell' Abbigliamento (Clothing Manufacturers): Foro Buonaparte 70, 20121 Milan; tel. (02) 809016; telex 333594; f. 1945; Pres. CESARE GAMBIRASI; Sec.-Gen. Dott. ARMANDO BRANCHINI; 650 mems.

Associazione Italiana Industriali Prodotti Alimentari (AIIPA) (Food Manufacturers): Via Pietro Verri 8, 20121 Milan; tel. (02) 708660; telex 330881; Viale Umberto Tupini 103, 00144 Rome; tel. (06) 5924449; f. 1946; Pres. Dott. DEMETRIO CORNO; Dir Dott. GIOVANNI FRANCO CRIPPA; 300 mems.

Associazione Italiana Tecnico Economica del Cemento (AITEC) (Cement): Via di S. Teresa 23, 00198 Rome; tel. (06) 864714; Via Borgonuovo 12, 20121 Milan; tel. (02) 6571861; f. 1959; Pres. Dott. Ing. MARIO FEDERICI; Dir Dott. ANTONIO TRIFOGLI.

Associazione Mineraria Italiana (Mining): Via Cola di Rienzo 297, 00192 Rome; tel. (06) 352261; telex 622264; f. 1144; Pres. VITO GUARRASI; Dir Dott. FRANCESCO SAVERIO GUIDI; 150 mems.

Associazione Nazionale Calzaturifici Italiani (ANCI) (Footwear Manufacturers): Via Dogana 1, 20123 Milan; tel. (02) 809721; telex 34018; f. 1945; Pres. LUIGINO ROSSI; Dir LEONARDO SOANA.

Associazione Nazionale Costruttori Edili (ANCE) (Builders): Via Guattani 16, 00161 Rome; tel. (06) 84881; telex 626846; f. 1946; Pres. FRANCESCO PERRI; Man. Dir CARLO FERRONI; mems: 19,000 firms in 99 provincial and 20 regional asscns.

Associazione Nazionale delle Fonderie (ASSOFOND) (Foundries): Via F. Rismondo 78, 27100 Pavia; tel. (0382) 308403; telex 326344; f. 1948; Pres. Dott. Ing. GIAMPIERO BECCARIA; Dir Dott. GIUSEPPE MAZZONE.

Associazione Nazionale dell'Industria Farmaceutica (FARMINDUSTRIA) (Pharmaceutical Industry): Piazza di Pietra 34, 00196 Rome; tel. (06) 650981; telex 614281; f. 1978; Pres. Dott. ALBERTO ALEOTTI; Dir Dott. DOMENICO MUSCOLO; 265 mem. firms.

Associazione Nazionale fra Industrie Automobilistiche (ANFIA) (Motor Vehicle Industries): Corso Galileo Ferraris 61, 10128 Turin; tel. (011) 5761; telex 221334; f. 1912; Pres. Dott. Ing. CARLO RIGHINI; Dir-Gen. Dott. ALBERTO BERSANI; 220 mems.

Associazione Nazionale Industria Meccanica Varia ed Affine (ANIMA) (Engineering and Allied Industries): Piazza Diaz 2, 20123 Milan; tel. (02) 809006; telex 310392; f. 1945; Pres. LUIGI CAZZANIGA; Sec.-Gen. Dott. Ing. ENRICO MALCOVATI; 1,100 mems.

Associazione Nazionale Industrie Elettrotecniche ed Elettroniche (ANIE) (Electrotechnic and Electronic Industries): Via Algardi 2, 20148 Milan; tel. (02) 32641; telex 321616; Pres. ALESSANDRO SIGNORINI; Sec.-Gen. Dott. LORENZO TRINGALI-CASANUOVA.

Associazione Nazionale Italiana Industrie Grafiche, Cartotecniche e Trasformatrici (Printing, Paper-Making and Processing Industries): Piazza Conciliazione 1, 20123 Milan; tel. (02) 4981051; telex 331674; f. 1946; Pres. Dott. PIERFRANCO GIUNCAIOLI; Sec.-Gen. Dott. FELICE SCIOMACHEN; 1,052 mems.

Federazione Italiana delle Industrie delle Acque Minerali, delle Terme e delle Bevande Analcooliche (Mineral Water and Non-Alcoholic Beverage Industries): Via Sicilia 186, 00187 Rome; tel. (06) 4557251; telex 626063; f. 1919; Pres. Dr CARLO VIOLATI; Dir Dr CARMELO CALLIPO.

Federazione Italiana Industriali Produttori Esportatori ed Importatori di Vini, Acquaviti, Liquori, Sciroppi, Aceti ed Affini (FEDERVINI) (Producers, Importers and Exporters of Wines, Liqueurs and Allied Products): Via Mentana 2B, 00185 Rome; tel. (06) 4740700; telex 612506; f. 1921; Pres. Conte ALBERTO MARONE CINZANO; Dir FRANCESCO ARTALE.

ITALY

Federazione Nazionale dell'Industria Chimica (FEDERCHIMICA) (Chemical Industry): Via Fatebenefratelli 10, 20121 Milan; tel. (02) 63621; telex 332488; Via Tomacelli 132, 00186 Rome; tel. (06) 6794954; telex 612504; f. 1945; Pres. GIANNI VARASI; Dir-Gen. Dott. GIANLUIGI VENTURA.

Unione Industriali Pastai Italiani (UNIPI) (Pasta Manufacturers): Via Po 102, 00198 Rome; tel. (06) 853291; telex 611540; Pres. Ing. GIANFRANCO CARLONE; Dir Dr GIUSEPPE MENCONI.

Unione Nazionale Cantieri e Industrie Nautiche ed Affini (UCINA) (Shipyard and Nautical Industries): Via G. Giardino 4, 20123 Milan; Via Vincenzo Renieri 23, 00143 Rome; tel. (06) 5919744; telex 611585; Pres. GIORGIO ADREANI.

Unione Petrolifera (Petroleum Industries): Viale Civiltà del Lavoro 38, 00144 Rome; tel. (06) 5914841; telex 611455; f. 1948; Pres. Dott. ACHILLE ALBONETTI; Dir-Gen. Ing. BRUNO DATTILO; 40 mems.

Other Employers' and Industrial Organizations

Associazione Nazionale Comuni Italiani (ANCI): Via dei Prefetti 46, 00186 Rome; tel. (06) 6793601; Pres. Sen. RICCARDO TRIGLIA; Sec.-Gen. GIOVANNI SANTO.

Associazione Nazionale Esattori e Ricevitori delle Imposte Dirette e dei Tesorieri degli Enti Locali (ANERT) (Local Government Tax Administrators): Via Parigi 11, 00185 Rome; tel. (06) 485764; Pres. Prof. ANGELO SENIN; Sec.-Gen. RAFFAELE FORNARIO.

Associazione Sindacale Intersind: Via Cristoforo Colombo 98, 00147 Rome; tel. (06) 51751; f. 1960; represents state-controlled firms; Pres. Dr AGOSTINO PACI; Dir-Gen. Dr GIUSEPPE CAPO.

Associazione Sindacale per le Aziende Petrochimiche e Collegate a Partecipazione Statale (State-controlled Petrochemical Companies): Via Due Macelli 66, 00187 Rome; tel. (06) 67341; Pres. Dott. BENEDETTO DE CESARIS.

Associazione fra le Società Italiane per Azioni (ASSONIME) (Limited Companies): Piazza Venezia 11, 00187 Rome; tel. (06) 6784413; telex 613381; f. 1936; Pres. Dott. EMANUELE DUBINI; Dir-Gen. ALFONSO DE TOMMASI.

Confederazione Generale della Agricoltura Italiana (General Agricultural): Corso Vittorio Emanuele 101, 00186 Rome; tel. (06) 65121; telex 612533; f. 1945; Pres. STEFANO WALLNER; Dir-Gen. RINALDO CHIDICHIMO.

Confederazione Generale Italiana del Commercio e del Turismo (CONFCOMMERCIO) (Commerce and Tourism): Piazza G.G. Belli 2, 00153 Rome; tel. (06) 58661; f. 1946; Pres. GIUSEPPE ORLANDO; Sec.-Gen. FILIPPO CAGETTI; 93 national and 97 territorial asscns affiliated.

Confederazione Italiana della Piccola e Media Industria (CONFAPI) (Small and Medium Industry): Via Colonna Antonina 52, 00186 Rome; tel. (06) 6782441; f. 1947; Pres. Dr GIUSEPPE SPINELLA; Sec.-Gen. CARLO BAGNI; 20,000 mems.

Confederazione Italiana della Proprietà Edilizia (CONFEDILIZIA) (Property and Building): Via Pisanelli 25, 00196 Rome; tel. (06) 3606764; Pres. Dott. Ing. ATTILIO VIZIANO; Man. Dir Dott. Ing. ADRIANO PASTA.

Delegazione Sindacale Industriale Autonoma della Valle d'Aosta (Autonomous Industrial Delegation of the Valle d'Aosta): Via G. Elter 6, 11100 Aosta; Pres. Dr ETTORE FORTUNA; Sec. Dr ROBERTO ANSALDO.

Federazione Associazioni Industriali (Industrial Asscns): Via Petitti 16, 20149 Milan; tel. (02) 324846; telex 331098; Pres. GIAMPAOLO BERTA; Dir Dott. UMBERTO MALTAGLIATI.

Federazione delle Associazioni Italiane Alberghi e Turismo (FAIAT) (Hotels and Tourism): Via Toscana 1, 00187 Rome; tel. (06) 4741151; telex 613116; f. 1950; Pres. ANGELO BETTOJA; Gen. Man. BONAVENTURA VACCARELLA; 20,000 mems.

Federazione Italiana della Pubblicità (FIP) (Advertisers): Via Maurizio Gonzaga 4, 20123 Milan; tel. (02) 865262; Pres. GIANFRANCO MAI; Sec.-Gen. MARIO CORNELIO.

Federazione Nazionale Imprese Trasporti (FENIT) (Transport Undertakings): Via Parigi 11, 00185 Rome; tel. (06) 4741043; f. 1946; Pres. ANGELO MARIA SANZA; Gen. Man. Dr CARLO GIZZI; 234 mems.

Unione Nazionale Aziende Autoproduttrici e Consumatrici di Energia Elettrica (UNAPACE) (Concerns producing and consuming their own Electrical Power): Via Paraguay 2, 00198 Rome; tel. (06) 864602; telex 616387; f. 1946; Pres. Dr Ing. LODOVICO PRIORI; Dir Dr Ing. ALDO BUSCAGLIONE.

TRADE UNIONS

There are three main federations of Italian trade unions, CGIL, CISL and UIL, all of which have close ties with political parties. The CGIL is dominated by the Communists, the CISL has links with the Christian Democrats and the UIL is associated with the Socialists. In 1972 all the confederations formally agreed that union leadership and holding party political office were not compatible with independence from party line and a united front between the confederations was seen as crucial to the success of the unions.

National Federations

Confederazione Autonomi Sindacati Artigiani (CASA): V. A. Bargoni 8, 00153 Rome; tel. (06) 5892275; f. 1958; federation of artisans' unions and regional and provincial associations; Pres. GIUSEPPE GUARINO; Sec.-Gen. GIACOMO BASSO.

Confederazione Generale Italiana dell' Artigianato (Artisans): Piazza Venezia 11, 00187 Rome; telex 616261; f. 1945; independent; 157 mem. unions; 600,000 associate enterprises; Pres. MANLIO GERMOZZI.

Confederazione Generale Italiana dei Professionisti e Artisti (CIPA) (Artists and Professional People): Via S. Nicola da Tolentino 21, 00187 Rome; tel. (06) 461849; federation of 19 unions; Pres. Prof. Ing. G. B. ORMEA.

Confederazione Generale Italiana del Lavoro (CGIL) (General Union of Italian Workers): Corso d'Italia 25, 00198 Rome; tel. (06) 84761; telex 623063; f. 1944; Communist and Socialist; federation of 17 unions; Gen. Sec. ANTONIO PIZZINATO; 4,556,000 mems.

Confederazione Italiana Dirigenti di Azienda (CIDA): Via Nazionale 75, 00184 Rome; tel. (06) 4758551; federation of six managers' unions; Pres. Dott. FAUSTO D'ELIA; Sec.-Gen. RAFFAELE CIABATTINI.

Confederazione Italiana dei Sindacati Autonomi Lavoratori (CISAL): Via Cavour 310, 00184 Rome; tel. (06) 6785402; f. 1957; no international affiliations; federation of 67 unions; Gen. Sec. Dr GUSSONI GERMANO; 1,423,000 mems.

Confederazione Italiana dei Sindacati Lavoratori (CISL): Via Po 21, 00198 Rome; tel. (06) 84731; telex 614045; f. 1950; affiliated to the International Confederation of Free Trade Unions and the European Trade Union Confederation; federation of 17 unions; Sec.-Gen. FRANCO MARINI; Dep. Secs-Gen. ERALDO CREA, MARIO COLOMBO; 2,953,000 mems.

Confederazione Italiana Sindacati Nazionali dei Lavoratori (CISNAL): Via P. Amedeo 42, 00185 Rome; tel. (06) 4757919; f. 1950; upholds traditions of national syndicalism; federation of 64 unions, 90 provincial unions; Gen. Sec. IVO LAGHI; 1,969,635 mems.

Confederazione Nazionale dell' Artigianato (CNA): Via di S. Prassede 24, 00187 Rome; tel. (06) 4757441; telex 622543; provincial associations; Pres. BRUNO MARIANI; Gen. Sec. Dr MAURO TOGNONI.

Federazione fra le Associazioni e i Sindacati Nazionali dei Quadri Direttivi dell'amministrazione dello Stato (DIRSTAT): Via Plinio 21 00193 Rome; tel. (06) 381516; f. 1948; federation of 33 unions and associations of civil service executives and officers; Sec.-Gen. Prof. FRANCESCO SAVERIO VESTRI; Treas. Dr V. DONATO.

Unione Italiana del Lavoro (UIL): Via Lucullo 6, 00187 Rome; tel. (06) 49731; telex 29115; f. 1950; Socialist, Social Democrat and Republican; affiliated to the International Confederation of Free Trade Unions and European Trade Union Confederation; 35 national trade union federations and 95 provincial union councils; Gen. Sec. GIORGIO BENVENUTO; 1,351,398 mems.

Principal Unions

Banking and Insurance

Federazione Autonoma Bancari Italiana (FABI) (Bank Workers): Via Tevere 46, Rome; tel. (06) 855751; f. 1948; independent; Sec. LUIGI MARMIROLI; 55,000 mems.

Federazione Autonoma Lavoratori Casse di Risparmio Italiane (FALCRI) (Savings Banks Workers): Via Mercato 5, Milan; Via Carducci 4, Rome.

Federazione Italiana Bancari e Assicuratori (FIBA): Via Modena 5, 00184 Rome; tel. (06) 4741245; affiliated to the CISL; Gen. Sec. SERGIO AMMANNATI; 58,980 mems.

Federazione Italiana Sindacale Lavoratori Assicurazioni Credito (Employees of Credit Institutions): Via Vicenza 5A, 00184 Rome; tel. (06) 4958261; affiliated to the CGIL; Sec. TEBALDO ZIRULIA; 60,000 mems.

ITALY

Federazione Nazionale Assicuratori (FISAC) (Insurance Workers): Via Vincenzo Monti 25, Milan; Via Val d'Ossola 100, Rome; independent; Pres. GIUSEPPE PAGANI; Sec.-Gen. EZIO MARTONE.

Unione Italiana Lavoratori Assicurazioni (UILAS) (Assurance Co Workers): Via Piemonte 39/A, Rome; affiliated to the UIL; National Sec. GUGLIELMO BRONZI; 13,000 mems.

Building and Building Materials

Federazione Autonoma Italiana Lavoratori Cemento, Legno, Edilizia ed Affini (FAILCLEA) (Workers in Cement, Wood, Construction and related industries): Piazza E. Duse 3, Milan; affiliated to the CISAL; Sec. ENZO BOZZI.

Federazione Lavoratori delle Costruzioni (FLC): includes the following three organizations:

Federazione Italiana Lavoratori delle Costruzioni a Affini (FILCA) (Building Industries' Workers): Via dei Mille 23, Rome; tel. (06) 497801; f. 1955; affiliated to the CISL; Sec.-Gen. CARLO MITRA; 194,493 mems.

Federazione Nazionale Lavoratori Edili Affini e del Legno (FeNEAL) (Builders and Woodworkers): Via dei Mille 23, Rome; affiliated to the UIL and the FLC; Sec.-Gen. GIANCARLO SERAFINI; 135,000 mems.

Federazione Italiana Lavoratori del Legno, Edili ed Affini (FILLEA) (Wood-workers, Construction Workers and Allied Trades): Via dei Mille 23, 00184 Rome; tel. (06) 497801; affiliated to the CGIL; Sec. ANNIO BRESCHI; 434,154 mems.

Chemical, Mining and Allied Industries

Federazione Unitaria Lavoratori Chimici (FULC) (Chemical and Allied Workers): Via Bolzano 16, Rome; affiliated to the CGIL, CISL and UIL; Secs.-Gen. FAUSTO VIGEVANI, DANILO BERETTA, ERNESTO CORNELLI; 450,000 mems.

Unione Italiana Lavoratori Miniere e Cave (Mine Workers): Rome; independent; National Sec. BACCI LUCIANO; 16,000 mems.

Clothing and Textiles

Federazione Italiana Lavoratori Tessili Abbigliamento, Calzaturieri (FILTEA) (Textile and Clothing Workers and Shoe Manufacturers): Via Leopoldo Serra 31, 00153 Rome; tel. (06) 55431; affiliated to the CGIL; Gen. Sec. ALDO AMORETTI; 250,000 mems.

Federazione Italiana dei Lavoratori Tessili e Abbigliamento (FILTA-CISL): Via Goito 39, 00185 Rome; tel. (06) 421921; affiliated to the CISL; Gen. Sec. RINO CAVIGLIOLI; 125,084 mems.

Engineering and Metallurgy

Confederazione Italiana dei Sindacati Ingegneri e Architetti (CONFISIA) (Engineers and Architects): Piazza Sallustio 24, Rome; independent; Pres. On. Ing. CORRADO TERRANOVA; Sec.-Gen. Ing. PIETRO ARMOCIDA.

Federazione Impiegati Operai Metallurgici (FIOM—CGIL) (Metalworkers): Corso Trieste 36, 00198 Rome; tel. (06) 8471; f. 1902; affiliated to the CGIL; Sec. SERGIO GARAVINI; 450,000 mems.

Federazione Italiana Metalmeccanici (FIM) (Metal Mechanic Workers): Corso Trieste 36, 00198 Rome; tel. (06) 8471; affiliated to the CISL; Sec. Gen. RAFFAELE MORESE; 277,789 mems.

Unione Italiana Lavoratori Metallurgici (UILM) (Metalworkers): Corso Trieste 36, 00198 Rome; tel. (06) 8442757; f. 1950; affiliated to the UIL; Sec. FRANCO LOTITO; 139,000 mems.

Food and Agriculture

Confederazione Italiana Coltivatori (Farmers): Via Mariano Fortuny 20, 00196 Rome; tel. (06) 3969931; independent; Pres. GIUSEPPE AVOLIO; Vice-Pres. MASSIMO BELLOTTI.

Confederazione Nazionale Coltivatori Diretti (CONA-COLTIVATORI) (Small-holders): Via XXIV Maggio 43, 00187 Rome; tel. (06) 46821; independent; Pres. On. ARCANGELO LOBIANCO; Sec.-Gen. PIETRO GNISCI.

Federazione Italiana Lavoratori Zuccherieri Industrie Alimentari Tabacchine (Food Industries, Sugar and Tobacco Workers): Via del Viminale 43, 00184 Rome; tel. (06) 465125; f. 1944; affiliated to the CGIL; Sec.-Gen. ANDREA AMARO; 108,000 mems.

Federazione Italiana Salariati Braccianti Agricoli e Maestranze Specializzate (FISBA) (Permanent Unskilled and Skilled Agricultural Workers): Via Tevere 20, 00198 Rome; tel. (06) 855455; f. 1950; Sec. CARLO BIFFI; 347,265 mems.

Federazione Nazionale Braccianti, Salariati, Tecnici, (FEDERBRACCIANTI) (Agricultural Workers): Via Boncompagni 19, 00187 Rome; tel. (06) 461760; affiliated to the CGIL; Sec. ANDREA GIANFAGNA; 600,000 mems.

Federazione Unitaria Lavoratori Prodotti Industrie Alimentari (Workers in the Manufactured Food Industry): Via Romagna 17, Rome; affiliated to the CISL and the IUF; Sec. Dr E. CREA; 40,000 mems.

Unione Coltivatori Italiana (UCI) (Farmers): Via in Lucina 10, 00186 Rome.

Unione Generale Coltivatori (UGC): Via Tevere 20, 00198 Rome; tel. (06) 862857; affiliated to the CISL; Pres. SANTE RICCI; 131,562 mems.

Unione Italiana Lavoratori Industrie Alimentari Saccariferi (UILIAS) (Food Workers): Via del Viminale 43, 00184 Rome; tel. (06) 463486; affiliated to the UIL; Sec. LIVIO CAUDURO.

Unione Italiana Mezzadri e Coltivatori Diretti (UIMEC) (Land Workers): Via XX Settembre 118, 00187 Rome; tel. (06) 4750911; affiliated to the UIL; Sec. FURIO VENARUCCI; 100,000 mems.

Medical

Federazione Italiana Sindacati Ospedalieri (FISOS) (Hospital Workers' Unions): Via Salaria 89, 00198 Rome; tel. (06) 854815; affiliated to the CISL; Sec. Gen. MORENO GORI; 150,501 mems.

Sindacato Nazionale Medici (SNM) (Doctors): Via S. Nicola da Tolentino 21, 00184 Rome; affiliated to the CISNAL; Sec. VINCENZO AGAMENNONE.

Papermaking, Printing and Publishing

Federazione Italiana Lavoratori del Libro (FEDERLIBRO): Via Fabio Massimo 57, 00192 Rome; tel. (06) 318202; affiliated to the CISL; Gen. Sec. GIUSEPPE SURRENTI; 35,000 mems.

Federazione Italiana Lavoratori Poligrafici e Cartai (Printing Workers and Papermakers): Via Piemonte 39, 00186 Rome; affiliated to the CGIL; Sec.-Gen. GIORGIO COLZI; 80,000 mems.

Public Services

Federazione Autonoma Italiana Lavoratori Elettrici (FAILE) (Electrical Workers): Via Cavour 310, Rome; affiliated to CISAL; Sec. ANGELO ISERNIA.

Federazione della Funzione Pubblica (FP): Via Rovereto 11, 00198 Rome; tel. (06) 869578; affiliated to the CISL; Sec. Gen. DARIO PAPPUCIA; 244,835 mems.

Federazione Italiana Dipendenti Aziende Elettriche (FIDAE) (Electrical Undertakings): Via Piemonte 32, Rome; affiliated to the CGIL; f. 1920; Gen. Sec. GIORGIO BUCCI; 57,000 mems.

Federazione Italiana Dipendenti Enti Locali (Local Government Employees): Via XX Settembre 40, Rome; tel. (06) 4759295; f. 1951; affiliated to the CISL; Sec. CRISTOFORO MELINELLI; 150,000 mems.

Federazione Italiana Lavoratori Esattoriali (Tax Collectors): Via A. Poliziano 80, 00184 Rome; tel. (06) 732246; affiliated to the UIL; Sec. LUCIANO PARODI.

Federazione Italiana Lavoratori Statali (State Employees): Via Livenza 7, 00198 Rome; affiliated to the CISL; Gen. Sec. MARZIO BASTIANONI; 60,605 mems.

Federazione Lavoratori Aziende Elettriche Italiane (FLAEI) (Workers in Italian Electrical Undertakings): Via Salaria 83, 00198 Rome; tel. (06) 862352; f. 1948; affiliated to the CISL; Sec. FRANCO ALVERINO; 43,440 mems.

Federazione Nazionale Dipendenti Enti Locali (Employers of Local Authorities): Via Principe Amadeo 42, 00185 Rome; tel. (06) 4750202; affiliated to the CISNAL; Sec. Dott. ARMANDO LA ROCCA.

Federazione Nazionale Dipendenti Enti Pubblici (UIL-DEP) (Public Employees): Via Lucullo 6, Rome; f. 1962; affiliated to the UIL; Gen. Sec. GIAMPIETRO SESTINI; 30,000 mems.

Federazione Nazionale Lavoratori Funzione Pubblica: Via Leopoldo Serra 31, 00153 Rome; tel. (06) 55431; affiliated to the CGIL and Public Services International; Sec.-Gen. ALDO GIUNTI.

Federazione Nazionale Lavoratori Energia (Employees of Gas Undertakings): Via Piemonte 32, 00187 Rome; tel. (06) 484526; affiliated to the CGIL; Sec. GIORGIO BUCCI; 72,000 mems (gas, water and electricity workers).

ITALY

Unione Italiana Lavoratori Pubblico Impiego (UIIPI) (Public Office Workers): Via Lucullo 6, 00187 Rome; affiliated to the UIL; Sec. BRUNO BUGLI; 238,000 mems.

Unione Italiana Lavoratori Servizi Pubblici (Public Services Workers): Via Nizza 33, 00198 Rome; tel. (06) 865303; f. 1958; affiliated to the UIL; Sec. GIUSEPPE AUGIERI; 15,500 mems.

Unione Nazionale Dipendenti Enti Locali (UNDEL) (Local Authority Employees): Via Po 162, 00198 Rome; tel. (06) 852340; affiliated to the UIL; Gen. Sec. FABRIZIO LUCARINI; 85,000 mems.

Teachers

Federazione Italiana Scuola Università e Ricerca (University Teachers): Via S. Croce in Gerusalemme 107, 00185 Rome; tel. (06) 757941; affiliated to the CISL; Gen. Secs GIORGIO ALESSANDRINI, PIETRO TALAMO; 184,235 mems.

Sindacato Nazionale Autonomo Lavoratori della Scuola (SNALS): Via Leopoldo Serra 5, 00153 Rome; tel. (06) 5898741; f. 1976; grouping of all independent teachers' unions; National Sec. NINO GALLOTTA.

Sindacato Nazionale Scuola Elementare (Elementary School Teachers): Via Santa Croce in Gerusalemme 91, 00185 Rome; tel. (06) 7574856; f. 1944; affiliated to the CISL; Sec.-Gen. LUIGI PICCINATO; 124,000 mems.

Tourism and Entertainments

Federazione Informazione Spettacolo (FIS): Via Fabio Massimo 57, 00192 Rome; tel. (06) 318573; affiliated to the CISL; Gen. Sec. GIUSEPPE SURRENTI; 43,388 mems.

Federazione Italiana Lavoratori Commercio Albergo Mensa e Servizi (FILCAMS) (Hotel and Catering Workers): Via Boncompagni 19, 00187 Rome; tel. (06) 4750300; f. 1960; affiliated to the CGIL; Sec.-Gen. GILBERTO PASCUCCI; 189,000 mems.

Federazione Italiana Lavoratori Informazione Spettacolo (FILIS) (Theatre Workers): Via E. Manfredi 10A, 00197 Rome; tel. (06) 877532; affiliated to the CGIL; Gen. Sec. GUGLIELMO EPIFANI.

Federazione Italiana Personale Aviazione Civile (Aviation Employees): Via Ostiense 224, Rome; affiliated to the CGIL; Sec. PIERRO TORINO.

Federazione Italiana Sindacati Addetti Servizi Commerciali Affini e del Turismo (Commercial and Tourist Unions): Via Livenza 7, 00198 Rome; tel. (06) 851042; affiliated to the CISL; Sec.-Gen. RENATO DI MARCO; 99,860 mems.

Unione Italiana Lavoratori Turismo Commercio e Servizi (UILTuCS): Via Nizza 59, 00198 Rome; tel. (06) 8444947; f. 1977; affiliated to the UIL; Gen. Sec. RAFFAELE VANNI; 140,000 mems.

Transport and Telecommunications

Federazione Italiana Dipendenti Aziende Telecomunicazioni (FIDAT) (Employees of Telecommunications Undertakings): Via Po 102, 00198 Rome; tel. (06) 855651; affiliated to the CGIL; Sec. GIANFRANCO TESTI; 12,000 mems.

Federazione Italiana Lavoratori Trasporti e Ausiliari del Traffici (FILTAT) (Transport and Associated Workers): Via Nizza 45, Rome; tel. (06) 8448640; affiliated to the CISL; Sec. PIETRO LOMBARDI; 60,000 mems.

Federazione Italiana dei Postelegrafonici (Postal, Telegraph and Telephone Workers): Via Cavour 185, 00187 Rome; tel. (06) 461321; affiliated to the CGIL; Sec. GIUSEPPE MASTRACCHI; 35,000 mems.

Federazione Italiana Trasporti Settore Marittimi (Italian Maritime): Viale Angelico 35, 00195 Rome; tel. (06) 386356; telex 622005; affiliated to the International Transport Workers' Federation; Nat. Sec. MARIO GUIDI.

Federazione Nazionale Autoferrotranvieri Internavigatori (FNAI) (Bus, Railway and Tram Workers): Via Cavour 171, 00184 Rome; tel. (06) 483783; affiliated to the UIL; Sec. BRUNO MONOSILIO.

Federazione Italiana Sindacati dei Trasporti (FILT): Via G. B. Morgagni 27, 00198 Rome; tel. (06) 89961; affiliated to the CGIL; Sec. LUCIO DE CARLINI.

Federazione Italiana Trasporti (FIT): Via Livenza 7, 00198 Rome; tel. (06) 866742; affiliated to the CISL; Sec.-Gen. GAETANO ARCONTI; 152,085 mems.

Federazione Nazionale Lavoratori Auto-Ferrotramvieri e Internavigatori (FENLAI): Via Isonzo 20, Rome; affiliated to the CISL; Gen. Sec. LAURO MORRA; 28,091 mems.

Federazione Poste e Telecomunicazioni (FPT): Via dell'Esquilino 38, 00185 Rome; tel. (06) 476981; affiliated to the CISL; Sec.-Gen. GIOVANNI MARIA NIEDDU; 133,696 mems.

Federazione dei Sindacati Dipendenti Aziende di Navigazione (FEDERSINDAN): Via Tevere 48, Rome; independent; Sec.-Gen. Dott. GIUSEPPE AURICCHIO.

Sindacato Autonomo Unificato Ferrovieri Italiani (Railway Workers): Via Anamari 20, 00185 Rome; tel. (06) 4955251; f. 1950; affiliated to the CISL; National Sec. SILVIO SATURNO; 40,000 mems.

Sindacato Italiano Lavoratori Uffici Locali ed Agenzie Postelegrafoniche (Post and Telegraph Workers): Via Esquilino 38, 00185 Rome; affiliated to the CISL; Gen. Sec. GIOVANNI MARIA NIEDDU; 62,268 mems.

UILTRASPORTI: Via Gaeta 15, 00185 Rome; tel. (06) 479911; affiliated to the UIL; Sec. RAFFAELE LIGUORI.

Unione Italiana Lavoratori Trasporti Ausiliari Traffico e Portuali (UILTATEP) (Transport and Associated Workers): Via Palestro 78, 00185 Rome; tel. (06) 4950698; f. 1950; affiliated to the UIL; Sec.-Gen. RAFFAELE LIGOURI; 134,280 mems.

Unione Italiana Marittimi (UIM) (Seamen): Viale Ippocrate 15, 00161 Rome; tel. (06) 422800; affiliated to the UIL; National Sec. GIORGIO MARANGONI; 12,500 mems.

Miscellaneous

Federazione Italiana Agenti Rappresentanti Viaggiatori-Piazzisti 'Fiarvep' (Commercial Travellers and Representatives): Corso Porta Vittoria 43, Milan; affiliated to the CGIL; Sec. LIONELLO GIANNINI.

Federazione Nazionale Pensionati (FNP) (Pensioners): Via Alessandria 26, 00198 Rome; tel. (06) 861218; f. 1952; affiliated to the CISL; Sec. GIANFRANCO CHIAPELLA; 800,000 mems.

Sindacato Nazionale Musicisti (Musicians): Via Palestro 56, 00185 Rome; tel. (06) 490467; independent; National Sec. Maestro SALVATORE ALLEGRA.

Sindacato Pensionati Italiani: Via Morgagni 27, Rome; affiliated to the CGIL; Gen. Sec. ARVEDO FORNI; 1,800,000 mems.

Co-operative Unions

Confederazione Cooperative Italiane (CONFCOOPERATIVE): Borgo S. Spirito 78, 00193 Rome; tel. (06) 6565605; telex 622465; f. 1945; federation of co-operative unions; Pres. DARIO MENGOZZI; Sec.-Gen. VINCENZO MANNINO.

Associazione Generale delle Cooperative Italiane (AGCI): Viale Somalia 164, 00199 Rome; tel. (06) 8313753; telex 622285; f. 1952; Pres. RENATO ASCARI RACCAGNI; Sec.-Gen. GINO MARINONI.

Federazione Italiana dei Consorzi Agari (FEDERCONCORZI) (Landowners' Consortia): Via Curtatone 3, 00185 Rome; tel. (06) 46641; telex 610010; Pres. FERNANDINO TRUZZI; Dir-Gen. LUIGI SCOTTI.

Federazione Nazionale della Cooperazione Agricola (Agricultural Co-operatives): Via Nazionale 69, 00184 Rome; tel. (06) 483824; Pres. CARLO FORCELLA; Dir Dr SANRO ROSSI.

Lega Nazionale delle Cooperative e Mutue (National League of Co-operative and Friendly Societies): Via Guattani 9, 00161 Rome; tel. (06) 841371; telex 611346; 10 affiliated unions; Pres. ONELIO PRANDINI.

STATE HOLDINGS AND NATIONALIZED BODIES

Ente Nazionale Idrocarburi (ENI): 1 Piazzale Enrico Mattei, 00144 Rome; tel. (06) 59001; state-owned energy corporation with subsidiaries including AGIP, AGIP Petroli, SNAM and AGIP Carbone operating in the energy sector; Enichem in chemicals; SAMIM in mining and metallurgy; SNAMPROGETTI and SAIPEM in engineering and services; Nuovo Pignone in mechanical sector; Lanerossi in textiles; SOFID and Hydrocarbons International Holding SA in the financial sector; Chair. FRANCO REVIGLIO.

Ente Nazionale per l'Energia Elettrica (ENEL): Via Giovanni Battista Martini 3, 00198 Rome; tel. (06) 85091; f. 1962 to generate and distribute electrical power throughout various areas of the country and to work in conjunction with the Ministry of Industry and Trade; Chair. FRANCESCO CORBELLINI.

Ente Partecipazioni e Finanziamento Industria Manifatturiera (EFIM): Via XXIV Maggio 43/45, 00187 Rome; tel. (06) 47101; telex 621381; f. 1962 as a state law agency, managing four holding companies and more than 100 companies. Its main fields of activity are on-land transports, aeronautics, armaments and defence systems, glass, aluminium and food processing; Pres. STEFANO SANDRI.

ITALY

Istituto per la Ricostruzione Industriale (IRI): Via Vittorio Veneto 89, 00187 Rome; tel. (06) 47271; f. 1933 as an autonomous agency controlling banking and industrial undertakings, IRI is responsible for many of the companies in which the State participates, including the national airline Alitalia, the road company ANAS, the RAI television service, the SIP telephone network, the three main commercial banks, the iron and steel producer Finsider, the shipping company Italmare, the Alfa Romeo car company and the holding company SPA; Chair. Prof. ROMANO PRODI.

Società Italiana per l'esercizio telefonico pA (SIP): Via San Dalmazzo 15, 10122 Turin; tel. (011) 5771; telex 610467; cap. 880,000m. (1980); operates, under government licence, the telephone system over the entire country except for intertoll system; 21.7m. telephones (1983).

Transport

Direzione Generale della Motorizzazione Civile e del Trasporti in Concessione: Viale del Policlinico 2, 00100 Rome; tel. (06) 859271; telex 616041; controls road transport and traffic, and public transport services (railways operated by private companies, motor-buses, trolley-buses, funicular railways and inland waterways); Dir-Gen. Ing. GAETANO DANESE.

RAILWAYS

The majority of Italian lines are in the hands of the State. The first railway line (Naples–Portici) was opened in 1839. The present-day Italian State Railways comprise an amalgamation, begun in 1905 and completed in 1907, of three private companies. In 1984 the total length was 16,105 km, of which 8,811 km were electrified. Apart from the state railway system there are 27 local and municipal railway companies, many of whose lines are narrow gauge. There are metro systems in Rome, Milan and Turin.

Ferrovie dello Stato: Piazza della Croce Rossa, 00161 Rome; tel. (06) 865198; telex 610089; an autonomous body which administers the State Railways; it is controlled by the Minister of Transport, who is assisted by an Administrative Board; Pres. C. SIGNORILE; Vice-Pres. Dott. LUIGI MISITI.

ROADS

In 1984 there were 301,307 km of road in Italy, including 45,618 km of major roads, 108,082 km of secondary roads and 5,941 km of motorway. All the *autostrade* (motorways) are toll roads except for the one between Salerno and Reggio Calabria and motorways in Sicily. By law ANAS is responsible for the planning, construction and management of the motorway network. The 13-km Mount Frejus highway tunnel, linking Italy and France through the Alps, opened in 1980.

Azienda Nazionale Autonoma delle Strade Statali (ANAS) (National Autonomous Road Corporation): Via Monzambano 10, 00185 Rome; tel. (06) 4957641; f. 1928, reorganized 1946; responsible for the administration of state roads and their improvement and extension; the president is the Minister of Public Works.

SHIPPING

In 1984 the merchant fleet had a displacement of 9.1m. gross tons.

Genova

Costa Armatori SpA (Linea C): Via Gabriele D'Annunzio 2, 16100 Genova; tel. (010) 54831; telex 270068; passenger and cargo service; Mediterranean–North, Central and South America; Caribbean cruises; Chair. NICOLA COSTA.

'Garibaldi' Società Cooperativa di Navigazione Srl: Piazza Dante 8, 16121 Genova; tel. (010) 581635; telex 270548; f. 1918; tanker and cargo services; Pres. GIAN FRANCO VIALE; Man. Dir MARIO DI LELLA.

Industria Armamento SpA: POB 607, Via Martin Piaggio 13A, 16122 Genova; f. 1923; Pres. PIETRO RAVANO DI ALBERTO.

Industriale Marittima SpA: Via Porta d'Archi 10/21, 16121 Genova; tramp; Man. Dir A. PORTA FIGARI.

'Italia di Navigazione' SpA: Piazza de Ferrari 1, 16121 Genova; tel. (010) 20921; telex 270032; f. 1932; freight services to Mediterranean, North, South and Central America and South Pacific; Pres. PAOLO MAININI; Chair. R. COLONNELLO; Dir-Gen. Dott. GIULIANO ROSSI.

Messina, Ignazio and C. SpA: Via G. d'Annunzio 91, 16162 Genova; tel. (010) 53961; tel. 270450; services to Arabian Gulf, Nigeria, East and West Africa, Libya and Near East, Red Sea, Malta, Europe; Chair. I. MESSINA; Man. Dirs GINAFRANCO MESSINA, GIORGIO MESSINA, P. MESSINA.

Navigazione Alta Italia, SpA: Via Corsica 19, 16128 Genova; tel. (010) 56331; telex 270181; f. 1906; worldwide dry and bulk cargo; Chair. and Man. Dir PAOLO MANTOVANI; Gen. Man. GIUSEPPE CARCASSI.

Sidermar di Navigazione SpA: Via XX Settembre 41, Genova; tel. (010) 56341; telex 270412; f. 1956; cargo; Chair. Dott. DARIO DEL BUONO; Man. Dir Dott. CARLO CIONI.

Naples

Garolla Fratelli SpA: Pontile Falvio Giola 45, 80133 Naples; tel. (081) 260233; telex 710256; Chair. R. GAROLLA; Dirs F. GAROLLA, C. GAROLLA.

Fratelli Grimaldi Armatori: Via M. Campodisola 13, 80133 Naples; tel. (081) 205466; telex 710058; passenger, cargo, containers and tramp to Europe, Middle East, South, Central and North America; Dirs M. GRIMALDI, G. GRIMALDI, A. GRIMALDI, U. GRIMALDI.

Tirrenia di Navigazione SpA: Head Office: Palazzo Sirignano, Rione Sirignano 2, 80121 Naples; tel. (081) 7201111; telex 710028; Pres. GUIDO DE VITA; Dir Gen. PIETRO FERRIGNO.

Palermo

D'Amico Società di Navigazione SpA: Via Siracusa 27, 90141 Palermo; tel. (091) 298737; telex 610157; tramp and liner; Mans CIRO D'AMICO, ANTONIO D'AMICO.

Sicilia Regionale Marittima SpA (SIREMAR): Via Francesco Crispi 120, 90139 Palermo; tel. (091) 582688; telex 910135; ferry services; Pres. DOMENICO CANGIALOSI; Man. Dir LUIGI FIORENTINO.

Sicula Oceanicas SA (SIOSA): Via Mariano Stabile 179, 90139 Palermo; tel. (091) 217939; telex 910098; f. 1941; cruises, passenger and cargo; Italy to North Europe, South, Central, North America; Dir G. GRIMALDI.

Rome

D'Amico Fratelli, Armatori, SpA: Via Liguria 36, 00187 Rome; tel. (06) 4671; telex 614545; dry cargo, tankers and fruit transport; Dirs GIUSEPPE D'AMICO, VITTORIO D'AMICO.

Linee Marittime dell'Adriatico SpA: Via del Nuoto 11, 00194 Rome; tel. (06) 3272312; telex 611034.

Trieste

Fratelli Cosulich, SpA: Piazza S. Antonio 4, 34122 Trieste; tel. (040) 61583; telex 460018; f. 1854; shipowners and shipping agents; cargo to Near East, Red Sea, Far East and South America; brs in Catania, Genoa, Hong Kong, Livorno, Messina, Naples, Palermo, Salerno, Turin, Zürich; Chair. and Man. Dir GEROLIMICH COSULICH.

Lloyd Triestino di Navigazione SpA: Palazzo del Lloyd Triestino, Piazza Unità d'Italia 1, 34121 Trieste; tel. (040) 7364; telex 460321; f. 1836; cargo services by container, roll on/roll off and conventional vessels to Africa, Australasia and Far East; Pres. Dott. Ing. VITTORIO FANFANI; Gen. Dir SERGIO VIEZZOLI.

Other Towns

Adriatica di Navigazione SpA: Zattere 1411, CP 705, 30123 Venice; tel. (041) 781611; telex 410045; f. 1937; passenger and freight services from Italy to Eastern Mediterranean, Egypt, Greece, Yugoslavia; Pres. Dott. ROBERTO FIORENTINI; Man. Dir CLAUDIO BONICIOLLI.

Snam SpA: Piazza Vanoni 1, San Donato Milanese, POB 12060, 20097 Milan; tel. (02) 5201; telex 310246; f. 1941; purchase, transport and sale of natural gas, transport of crude oil and petroleum products by means of pipeline and tanker fleet; Pres. Ing. PIO PIGORINI; Vice-Pres. and Man. Dir Ing. LUIGI MEANTI; Vice-Pres. GIULIO SACCHI; Man. Dir Ing. LUIGI CROCE.

SHIPPING ASSOCIATIONS

Associazione Italiana dell' Armamento di Linea (FEDARLINEA): Via Ferdinando di Savoia 8, 00196 Rome; tel. (06) 3603447; f. 1967; Pres. Dr MARIO BONACCHI; Dir Dr GIUSEPPE RAVERA.

Confederazione Italiana degli Armatori Liberi (CONFITARMA): Via dei Sabini 7, 00187 Rome; tel. (06) 6787541; telex 626135; f. 1901; Pres. EGIDIO ORTONA; Dir GIUSEPPE PERASSO; 300 mems.

ITALY

CIVIL AVIATION

National Airline

Alitalia (Linee Aeree Italiane): Palazzo Alitalia, Piazzale Giulio Pastore, 00144 Rome; tel. (06) 54441; telex 610036; f. 1946; state-owned airline; international services throughout Europe and to Africa, North and South America, the Middle East, the Far East and Australia; Chair. UMBERTO NORDIO; Dep. Chair. VITTORIO VACCARI; Man. Dirs MAURIZIO MASPES, LUCIANO SARTORETTI, FRANCO CARRARO; fleet of 4 Boeing 747-200B Combi, 6 Boeing 747-200B, one Boeing 747-200F, 8 Airbus A300B4, 23 MD-80, 44 DC-9-30, 2 Fokker F.27, 2 Piaggio P166-DL3 and 4 SIAI Marchetti SF-260.

Other Airlines

Aero Trasporti Italiani SpA (ATI): Aeroporto Capodichino, 80144 Naples; tel. (081) 7091111; telex 711005; f. 1963; subsidiary of Alitalia; operates scheduled domestic services and services and charter flights to the Middle East, North Africa and Canary Islands and within Europe; Chair. Prof. CARLO BERNINI; Man. Dir and Gen. Man. TOMMASCO RICCI; fleet of 28 Douglas DC-9-30, 4 Fokker F-27-600, one Fokker F-27-200, 2 MD-80.

Alisarda SpA: 193 Corso Umberto, 07026 Olbia, 07026 Sardinia; tel. (0789) 69400; telex 790043; f. 1963; scheduled services between Olbia and Milan, Turin, Rome, Pisa, Bologna, Venice, Catania, Genova, Verona and Cagliari, seasonal services between Olbia, Nice, Paris, Geneva, Zürich, Frankfurt, Munich and Dusseldorf; Pres. PAOLO RICCARDI; Gen. Man. FRANCO TRIVI; Commercial Man. SEBASTIANO BARRERA; fleet of 3 DC-9-50 and 2 MD-80.

Tourism

Each of the 91 Provinces has a Board of Tourism; there are also about 300 Aziende Autonome di Cura, Soggiorno e Turismo, with information about tourist accommodation and health treatment, and about 2,000 Pro Loco Associations concerned with local amenities.

Ministero del Turismo e dello Spettacolo: Via della Ferratella in Laterano 51, 00100 Rome; tel. (06) 7732; the government department for tourism; Dirs-Gen. Dott. ROCCO MOCCIA (tourism), Dott. MARIO DE PAULIS (Entertainment).

Ente Nazionale Italiano per il Turismo (ENIT) (National Tourist Board): Via Marghera 2, 00185 Rome; tel. (06) 49711; telex 621314; f. 1919; Pres. Avv. GABRIELLO MORETTI; Dir Gen. GIAMPIERO GALLIAN.

Atomic Energy

Italy has only four completed nuclear power stations and the industry operates at under half its full capacity. However, plans have been made to build three more plants in Piedmont, Lombardy and Puglia. Each plant will consist of two 1,000 MW pressurized water reactors. Work is continuing on the 2,000 MW plant at Montalto di Castro. Nuclear power was expected to provide about 12% of electricity requirements by 1995. In 1984 it provided 3.8% of electricity production. A national conference on the future of nuclear energy in Italy was planned to be held in January 1987, following the accident at the Chernobyl nuclear power station, in the USSR, in April 1986.

ENEA—Comitato Nazionale per la Ricerca e per lo Sviluppo dell'Energia Nucleare e delle Energie Alternative: Via Regina Margherita 125, 00198 Rome; tel. (06) 85281; telex 610183; f. 1960; supervises pure and applied research into nuclear power plants, provides technical and economic evaluations and supervision of health and environmental protection; promotes energy saving and the use of renewable energy sources; Chair. UMBERTO COLOMBO; Vice-Pres. Prof. LUIGI NOÈ; Dir-Gen. Dr FABIO PISTELLA.

Ente Nazionale per l'Energia Elettrica (ENEL): Via G.B. Martini 3 (Piazza Verdi), 00198 Rome; tel. (06) 85091; state electricity authority; has nuclear power stations in operation in the following areas: Caorso: a 860 MWe plant; Latina: a 210 MWe (MAGNOX) plant; Garigliano: a 160 MWe (BWR) plant; Trino Vercellese: a 256 MWe (PWR) plant; Pres. Dr FRANCESCO CORBELLINI; Dir-Gen. Dr GIOVANNI MASSINI.

THE IVORY COAST

Introductory Survey

Location, Climate, Language, Religion, Flag, Capital

The Republic of the Ivory Coast (known in French as la Côte d'Ivoire) lies on the west coast of Africa, between Ghana to the east and Liberia to the west, with Guinea, Mali and Burkina Faso to the north. The climate is hot and wet, with temperatures varying from 14°C to 39°C (57°F to 103°F). The official language is French, and a large number of African languages are also spoken. Most of the inhabitants follow traditional beliefs, while about 12% are Christians, mainly Roman Catholics, and 23% Muslims. The national flag (proportions 3 by 2) has three equal vertical stripes, of orange, white and green. The process of transferring the capital from Abidjan to Yamoussoukro (the President's birthplace), about 220 km (135 miles) north-west of Abidjan, was begun in March 1983.

Recent History

Formerly a province of French West Africa, the Ivory Coast achieved self-government, within the French Community, in December 1958. Félix Houphouët-Boigny, leader of the Parti démocratique de la Côte d'Ivoire (PDCI), became Prime Minister in 1959. The country became fully independent on 7 August 1960.

A new constitution was adopted in October 1960, and Houphouët-Boigny became President in November. The ruling PDCI has been the country's only organized political party since it was founded in 1946. The Ivory Coast has retained close links with France, and the country's foreign policy is generally pro-Western. A high rate of economic growth, particularly during the 1970s, and strong support from the French have contributed to the stability of the regime. Political unrest has occurred sporadically, though without strong leadership. Two plots were uncovered in 1963, apparently representing a youthful radical element and northerners who resented southern domination in the Government. The army was reduced in size to reduce the risk of military intervention. The Government responded to criticism by implementing a policy of regional development and increased Ivorian management of commercial enterprises.

In 1977 Houphouët-Boigny replaced the Ministers of Finance, Economic Planning and Foreign Affairs, and legislation was enacted against corrupt trading and speculation in commodities. In May 1978 a significant step towards the relaxation of the PDCI's political dominance was taken when it was decided that, with the exception of Abidjan and Bouaké, the capitals of all the Departments would be administered by elected mayors, rather than by party appointees. Elections to the National Assembly were held in November 1980 and, for the first time, more than one candidate was permitted to contest each seat.

A series of strikes and demonstrations took place in the period from late 1980 to mid-1983, mainly involving students and professional groups. The longest strike, lasting from mid-April to early May of 1983, was staged by teachers protesting against the withdrawal of free housing rights, and was supported by members of the medical profession. The strike was terminated by a presidential decree ordering a return to work, and two education ministers were subsequently dismissed from the Government. In 1984 the Government implemented anti-corruption measures, including the imprisonment of several former government officials in the state housing sector, accused of malpractice. In 1985 a much-publicized court case, concerning debts of US $58m., was brought by the National Bank for Agricultural Development (BNDA) against COGEXIM, a private cocoa- and coffee-exporting company whose chairman was the mayor of Abidjan, Emmanuel Dioulo. The ensuing scandal prompted Dioulo to flee to Belgium in March; he was, however, granted amnesty in December, and returned to the Ivory Coast in February 1986.

A government reshuffle in November 1983 reduced the number of ministers from 35 to 28, in an attempt to cut administrative costs. The eighth ordinary congress of the PDCI, held in Abidjan in October 1985, approved the adoption of a constitutional amendment suppressing the post of Vice-President of the Republic and allowing for the president of the National Assembly to succeed the President of the Republic, on an interim basis, in the event of a vacancy. Later that month, Houphouët-Boigny was re-elected President for a sixth five-year term. Municipal and legislative elections were held in November, and in January 1986 Henri Konan-Bédié was re-elected to the presidency of the National Assembly. In July the Council of Ministers was reshuffled, and its membership increased to 40, in response to the easing of the country's economic crisis.

The presence in the Ivory Coast of large numbers of Europeans and Levantines has led to sporadic clashes between Ivorians and immigrant groups. In 1981 more than 1m. foreigners were resident in the country; the Ivory Coast's French community, numbering some 35,000, is the largest in Africa. Increasing unemployment among university leavers, a concern for 'Ivorianization' and the need for reductions in public spending, however, led to the Government's decision to reduce the level of foreign assistance in the country; in 1985 there were still 3,200 French 'coopérants' employed by the Government. Following riots after a football match in September 1985, members of the resident Ghanaian population in Abidjan were attacked, and many fled the country, leading to a strain in relations between the two neighbouring countries.

In February 1986 the Ivory Coast re-established formal diplomatic relations with Israel, following a 13-year suspension as a result of the Arab–Israeli war in 1973. Diplomatic links with the Soviet Union and several Eastern bloc states were also renewed in 1986. In April it was announced that the country wished to be known internationally by its French name of Côte d'Ivoire, rather than by translations of it. The request was subsequently endorsed by the UN. However, translations of the name were still in widespread use in early 1987. President Houphouët-Boigny is committed to a policy of dialogue between Black Africa and white-ruled South Africa, for which he has been strongly criticized by other African leaders. He spent nearly five months abroad during 1983, paying official visits to the USA, Canada, France and the United Kingdom.

Government

Executive power is vested in the President, who is elected for a five-year term by direct universal suffrage. The Council of Ministers is appointed by, and directly responsible to, the President. In 1980 provision was made for the appointment of a Vice-President, but in 1985 this was rescinded, and a constitutional amendment was adopted to provide for the president of the National Assembly to carry out the functions of the Head of State, in case of the latter's death or incapacitation, until a presidential election can be held. Legislative power is vested in the unicameral National Assembly, which is directly elected (using two ballots if necessary) for five years. The Assembly was expanded from 147 to 175 members following the 1985 elections. The ruling Parti démocratique de la Côte d'Ivoire is the only political party. It has an executive committee of 13 members, a political bureau of 35 and a guiding committee of 100. The country is divided into 26 Departments, each with its own elected Council.

Defence

Defence matters are the concern of the Regional Defence Council of the Conseil de l'Entente, through which agreements with France have been negotiated. France supplies equipment and training, and maintains a force of 500 men. In July 1986 the Ivory Coast had 6,100 men in the army, 930 in the air force and 690 in the navy. In addition, there are paramilitary forces of approximately 7,800 men. Estimated defence expenditure in 1985 was US $71.7m.

Economic Affairs

For most of its first 20 years of independence, the Ivory Coast achieved rapid economic growth, led by expansion in the agricultural sector, particularly the cultivation of plantation crops for export. In 1980 the country's gross national product (GNP) per head was estimated at US $1,150, one of the highest levels in Black Africa. However, the subsequent collapse of world prices for cocoa, coffee and timber (the country's three main exports) led to a period of severe recession, and by 1984, according to estimates by the World Bank, the Ivory Coast's GNP per head had declined to $610 (at average 1982–84 prices). Average annual growth in GNP per head between 1965 and 1984 was only 0.2% in real terms.

Following independence, the Ivory Coast successfully developed its economy from a largely agricultural base, and 65% of the labour force still worked in the agricultural sector in 1980. From 1965 to 1973 the country's gross domestic product (GDP) grew at an average annual rate of 7.1%. Between 1973 and 1984, however, the average fell to 3.7%, with real GDP declining by 2.9% in 1982, by 4.1% in 1983, and by 3.6% in 1984. During this period, several development projects were postponed, and widespread reforms of state corporations were implemented, in an effort to curb public expenditure. Real GDP growth subsequently resumed, totalling around 5% per year in both 1985 and 1986.

In the 1977/78 season the Ivory Coast overtook Ghana as the world's largest producer of cocoa beans. The cocoa crop reached 456,000 metric tons in 1981/82, but dropped to 355,000 tons in the following year, after drought and bush fires caused extensive damage to plantations. Production recovered to 405,000 tons in 1983/84, rising to 552,000 tons in 1984/85, and was estimated at a record 580,000 tons in 1985/86. The Ivory Coast is the world's third largest producer of coffee, its output being surpassed only by that of Brazil and Colombia. Production of green coffee reached a record 367,000 tons in 1980/81, but fell to only 85,000 tons in 1983/84, owing to drought. Production recovered strongly the following year, to total an estimated 300,000 tons, before declining slightly, to 259,800 tons, in 1985/86. Proposals were announced in 1986 for the extension of the cultivation area to increase annual production potential to over 330,000 tons.

Exports of cocoa, coffee and timber together accounted for more than one-half of total export earnings in 1985. Crop diversification has been increasingly encouraged, however, and the Ivory Coast has become one of the world's largest producers of palm oil and palm-kernel oil, with an estimated output of 190,000 metric tons in 1985/86. Production of seed (unginned) cotton reached a record 215,700 tons in 1984/85. Rice production fell slightly from 292,400 tons in 1981/82 to 278,000 tons in the following year, and in 1984 the Government imposed restrictions on rice imports in an attempt to increase production levels. In 1983/84, following the return of rain, the rice crop increased to 490,000 tons. An ambitious sugar development plan was launched in the 1970s, but unsuitable climatic conditions and the slump in world sugar prices led to severe financial losses, and in 1984 the Government was forced to convert two of the country's six sugar complexes to rice and seed cultivation. Production of raw sugar totalled an estimated 138,000 tons in 1985/86. In 1986 it was announced that a new restructuring scheme was to be implemented, aiming to increase annual output to 185,000 tons by 1990/91. The rubber industry has shown considerable success, and annual production is expected to rise to 80,000 tons by 1990. An estimated 48,000 tons of natural rubber were produced in 1986, and plantations are being increased. Timber resources have been severely depleted in recent years: since 1960 the country has lost around 70% of its forest reserves. An extensive reafforestation programme was announced in 1984, at an estimated cost of 22,900m. francs CFA. In 1983 420,000 cu m of timber products were exported.

In 1977 the Ivory Coast's first significant petroleum deposits were discovered off the coast. The Belier field, 15 km south of Grand Bassam, began production in 1980, and was yielding an estimated 20,000 barrels per day (b/d) by late 1982. In early 1980 the Espoir field was discovered off shore, with reserves estimated at 500m. metric tons. However, offshore oil production has increased much more slowly than was originally hoped, reaching only 1.2m. tons in 1983, compared with projected output of 1.5m. tons. The target of 3m. tons per year by 1985 was soon abandoned, and total petroleum production in 1986 was estimated at just under 1m. tons. Reserves of offshore natural gas are estimated at 50,000m. cu m, but have not yet been exploited, owing to the high cost of initial investment. There are large quantities of high-quality iron ore at Bangolo. Reserves of copper, nickel, molybdenum, cobalt, bauxite and uranium have also been discovered. Small-scale diamond mining is carried out by private companies.

The share of agriculture in GDP declined from 36% in 1965 to 28% in 1984, but industry increased its share from 17% in 1965 to 26% in 1984. Industrial development has been based on the processing of primary commodities before export. Most exported palm oil is now refined, and large quantities of fruit (particularly pineapple) are tinned or preserved. Industrial output declined sharply in 1983, as the prolonged drought caused widespread interruptions in the electric power supply. Four of the Ivory Coast's five hydroelectric plants, which provide 92% of the country's electricity, were brought to a halt as a result of the drought. The Soubre hydroelectric project was indefinitely postponed in 1984, owing to the economic recession and doubts about increased dependence on hydroelectric power. The 1981–85 development plan aimed at a large increase in food production and also provided for cultural and social development. In 1984 the Government announced a new investment code, including measures to encourage decentralization and the creation of small and medium-sized enterprises.

After 1977 the Ivory Coast's trade surplus dwindled, as commodity prices weakened, initially for coffee and, in 1980, for cocoa, while import prices, especially for petroleum, increased. In 1985, however, exports totalled an estimated 1,419,390m. francs CFA, while imports totalled only 772,990m. francs CFA. Meanwhile, substantial borrowing, to finance the ambitious capital investment programmes of the 1970s, had increased the debt service ratio from 6.8% of the country's annual export earnings in 1970 to 32% in 1985. According to World Bank estimates, the total external public debt was US $4,835m. at the end of 1984. Short-term debt reschedulings were organized in 1984–85 by both the 'Paris Club' of official creditors and the 'London Club' of commercial creditors, and during 1986 both institutions granted the Ivory Coast multiannual rescheduling agreements, thus helping to free resources for the promotion of economic recovery. It was the first time that an African country had succeeded in obtaining such an accord from the 'Paris Club'. In June 1986, prior to the reschedulings, the IMF approved a stand-by credit of $116m., and the World Bank a structural adjustment loan of $250m. Under the 1987 budget proposals, planned public investment, which had been severely curtailed during the 1981–85 development plan period, was increased by 26%, to 145,879m. francs CFA. Total recurrent expenditure was projected at 480,980m. francs CFA.

Social Welfare

Medical services are organized by the State. In 1980 the country had 8,799 hospital beds and 518 physicians. There is a minimum wage for workers in industry and commerce. Projects to increase the social and health services to regional centres and villages are being carried out.

Education

In 1985, according to UNESCO estimates, adult illiteracy averaged 57.3% (males 46.9%; females 68.9%). Education at all levels is free. Primary education, which is officially compulsory, begins at seven years of age and lasts for six years. Enrolment at primary schools in 1982 was equivalent to 79% of all children between six and 11 years of age (93% of boys; 64% of girls). In the towns, however, average attendance is more than 90%. Secondary education, beginning at the age of 13, lasts for up to seven years. In 1982 the total enrolment at secondary schools was equivalent to 19% of children aged 12 to 18 (27% of boys; 11% of girls). The National University at Abidjan has five faculties, and in 1984/85 had 12,755 students. In addition, many students attend French universities. In 1981–85 five technical training institutes were to be built, and the University was to be decentralized.

Tourism

The game reserves, forests, lagoons, rich tribal folklore and the lively city of Abidjan, the former capital, are all of interest to tourists. There were 194,869 visitors in 1984. The 10-km coastal strip along the Lagune Ebrié, to the west of Abidjan, is being developed as a tourist riviera. In 1983 there were 7,000 hotel rooms in the Ivory Coast.

Public Holidays

1987: 1 January (New Year), 17 April (Good Friday), 20 April (Easter Monday), 1 May (Labour Day), 28 May (Ascension Day), 30 May (Id al-Fitr, end of Ramadan), 8 June (Whit Monday), 6 August (Id al-Adha, feast of the Sacrifice), 15 August (Assumption), 1 November (All Saints' Day), 7 December (Independence Day), 25 December (Christmas).

1988: 1 January (New Year), 1 April (Good Friday), 4 April (Easter Monday), 1 May (Labour Day), 12 May (Ascension Day), 18 May (Id al-Fitr, end of Ramadan), 23 May (Whit Monday), 25 July (Id al-Adha, feast of the Sacrifice), 15 August (Assumption), 1 November (All Saints' Day), 7 December (Independence Day), 25 December (Christmas).

Weights and Measures

The metric system is in force.

Currency and Exchange Rates

100 centimes = 1 franc de la Communauté financière africaine (CFA).

Exchange rates (30 September 1986):
  1 franc CFA = 2 French centimes;
  £1 sterling = 480.625 francs CFA;
  US $1 = 332.125 francs CFA.

THE IVORY COAST — *Statistical Survey*

Statistical Survey

Source (unless otherwise stated): Direction de la Statistique, Ministère de l'Economie et des Finances, 01 BP V55, Abidjan 01; tel. 32-15-38.

Area and Population

AREA, POPULATION AND DENSITY

Area (sq km)	322,462*
Population (census of 30 April 1975)†	
Males	3,474,750
Females	3,234,850
Total	6,709,600
Population (official estimates at mid-year)	
1980	8,262,300
1983	9,334,800‡
1984	9,742,900‡
Density (per sq km) at mid-1984	30.2

* 124,503 sq miles. † Provisional result. Revised total is 6,702,866.
‡ Provisional. Figures for 1981–82 are not available.

PRINCIPAL TOWNS (population in 1976)
Abidjan (capital) 951,216; Bouaké 175,264; Daloa 60,837.

BIRTHS AND DEATHS
Average annual birth rate 44.5 per 1,000 in 1970–75, 45.9 per 1,000 in 1975–80; death rate 21.0 per 1,000 in 1970–75, 19.5 per 1,000 in 1975–80 (UN estimates).

ECONOMICALLY ACTIVE POPULATION
(ILO estimates, '000 persons at mid-1980)

	Males	Females	Total
Agriculture, etc.	1,385	928	2,314
Industry	231	62	293
Services	693	248	940
Total	2,309	1,238	3,547

Source: ILO, *Economically Active Population Estimates and Projections, 1950–2025.*

PROVINCES

	Area (sq km)	Population (1975 census)
Abengourou	6,900	177,692
Abidjan*	14,200	1,389,141
Aboisso	6,250	148,823
Adzopé	5,230	162,837
Agboville	3,850	141,970
Biankouma	4,950	75,711
Bondoukou	16,530	296,551
Bouaflé	8,500	263,609
Bouaké*	23,670	808,048
Bouna	21,470	84,290
Boundiali	10,095	132,278
Dabakala	9,670	56,230
Daloa	15,200	369,610
Danané	4,600	170,249
Dimbokro	14,100	475,023
Divo	10,650	278,526
Ferkessedougou	17,728	90,423
Gagnoa	6,900	259,504
Guiglo	14,150	137,672
Katiola	9,420	77,875
Korhogo	12,500	276,816
Man	7,050	278,659
Odienné	20,600	124,010
Sassandra	25,800	191,994
Séguéla	21,900	157,539
Touba	8,720	77,786
Total	320,633†	6,702,866

* Including commune.
† Other sources give the total area as 322,462 sq km.
Source: *La Côte d'Ivoire en Chiffres*, 1979.

THE IVORY COAST

Statistical Survey

Agriculture

PRINCIPAL CROPS ('000 metric tons)

	1983	1984	1985
Maize	435	468	530†
Millet	25	30	40*
Sorghum	17	20	25*
Rice (paddy)	360	490	570†
Potatoes*	24	24	24
Sweet potatoes	12	12	12*
Cassava (Manioc)	1,210	1,230	1,500†
Yams	2,450	2,600	2,900
Taro (Coco yam)	195	202	235†
Pulses*	8	8	8
Tree nuts*	5	5	4
Sugar cane*	2,000	1,400	1,300
Palm kernels	39	33	45
Groundnuts (in shell)	80	98†	80*
Cottonseed	87	79	120†
Coconuts*	260	290	300
Copra*	38	43	44
Tomatoes*	29	31	32
Aubergines (Eggplants)*	19	19	19
Chillies, peppers*	21	21	22
Other vegetables*	315	336	394
Oranges*	25	26	27
Other citrus fruit*	40	40	40
Bananas*	130	140	140
Plantains*	1,150	1,440	1,400*
Pineapples*	207	229	210*
Other fruit*	28	30	31
Coffee (green)	271	85	300†
Cocoa beans	411	550	500*
Tobacco (leaves)*	2	3	3
Cotton (lint)	66	58	85†
Natural rubber (dry weight)	29	35	39

* FAO estimates.   † Unofficial figures.
Source: FAO, *Production Yearbook*.

LIVESTOCK
(FAO estimates, '000 head, year ending September)

	1983	1984	1985
Cattle	780	820	843
Pigs	400	410	430
Sheep	1,380	1,400	1,450
Goats	1,380	1,400	1,450

Poultry (FAO estimates, million): 17 in 1983; 16 in 1984; 16 in 1985.
Source: FAO, *Production Yearbook*.

LIVESTOCK PRODUCTS (FAO estimates, '000 metric tons)

	1983	1984	1985
Total meat production	125	124	127
Beef and veal	42	42	42
Mutton and lamb	6	6	6
Goats' meat	6	6	6
Pig meat	16	16	17
Poultry meat	27	25	27
Cows' milk	14	15	16
Hen eggs	11.7	12.2	10.1
Cattle hides	5.5	5.5	5.6
Sheepskins	1.5	1.5	1.6
Goatskins	1.6	1.6	1.6

Source: FAO, *Production Yearbook*.

Forestry

ROUNDWOOD REMOVALS ('000 cubic metres)

	1982	1983	1984
Sawlogs, veneer logs and logs for sleepers	4,106	4,088	3,895
Other industrial wood*	559	578	598
Fuel wood*	7,198	7,445	7,697
Total	11,863	12,111	12,190

* FAO estimates.
Source: FAO, *Yearbook of Forest Products*.

SAWNWOOD PRODUCTION ('000 cubic metres)

	1982	1983	1984
Total (incl. boxboards)	748	718	646

Source: FAO, *Yearbook of Forest Products*.

Fishing

('000 metric tons, live weight)

	1982	1983	1984
Inland waters	15.0	14.7	18.0
Atlantic Ocean	77.5	79.3	65.7
Total catch	92.5	94.0	83.7

Source: FAO, *Yearbook of Fishery Statistics*.

Mining

	1981	1982	1983
Crude petroleum ('000 metric tons)	389*	757	1,158*

* UN estimate.
Source: UN, *Industrial Statistics Yearbook*.

Industry

SELECTED PRODUCTS

		1981	1982	1983
Palm and palm-kernel oil	'000 metric tons	155	177	200
Wheat flour	'000 metric tons	140	145	129
Biscuits	'000 metric tons	4.5	4.6	4.0
Pineapple juice (unconcentrated)	'000 metric tons	27.8	2.4	9.1
Salted, dried or smoked fish*	'000 metric tons	15.0	15.0	15.0
Cocoa butter (exports)	'000 metric tons	13.6	15.5	16.3
Raw sugar	'000 metric tons	147†	170	150
Beer	'000 hectolitres	1,348	1,285	1,400
Soft drinks	'000 hectolitres	748	426	564
Cigarettes	million	3,700	3,500	3,640
Synthetic textile materials	million metres	1.7†	1.7†	2.3
Plywood	'000 cubic metres	25	24	33
Motor spirit (Petrol)	'000 metric tons	233	240	250
Jet fuel	'000 metric tons	95	95	97
Distillate fuel oils	'000 metric tons	516	510	612
Chemical fertilizers*	'000 metric tons	6	2	5
Cement	'000 metric tons	1,317	988	636
Electric energy	million kWh	1,903	1,929	1,932

* FAO estimates. † UN estimates.

Source: UN, *Industrial Statistics Yearbook*.

Finance

CURRENCY AND EXCHANGE RATES

Monetary Units
100 centimes = 1 franc de la Communauté financière africaine (CFA).

Denominations
Coins: 1, 5, 10, 25, 50 and 100 francs CFA.
Notes: 500, 1,000, 5,000 and 10,000 francs CFA.

French Franc, Sterling and Dollar Equivalents
(30 September 1986)
1 French franc = 50 francs CFA;
£1 sterling = 480.625 francs CFA;
US $1 = 332.125 francs CFA;
1,000 francs CFA = £2.081 = $3.011.

Average Exchange Rate (francs CFA per US $)
1983 381.06
1984 436.96
1985 449.26

GENERAL BUDGET ESTIMATES (million francs CFA)

Revenue	1982	1983	1984
Direct taxes	96,325	104,015	109,065
Indirect taxes	306,375	331,665	299,885
Registration	11,800	13,365	13,925
Land, services	2,700	2,655	2,475
Other revenue	3,500	3,550	3,500
Total	420,700	435,250	428,850

Expenditure	1982	1983	1984
Public debt	2,575	2,575	2,602
Public authority	6,632	7,257	6,391
Services	239,486	258,505	235,115
Expenses of communes	79,454	74,401	79,668
Transfers and interventions	92,229	92,512	105,074
Total (incl. others)	420,700	435,250	428,850

1985 (million francs CFA): Recurrent budget 418,130; Special Investment budget 102,000.

1986 (million francs CFA): Recurrent budget 458,850; Special Investment budget 153,465.

1987 (proposals, million francs CFA): Recurrent budget 480,980; Special Investment budget 145,879.

THE IVORY COAST

SPECIAL INVESTMENT BUDGET (BSIE)
(million francs CFA)

Revenue	1982	1983	1984
Internal sources	52,724	57,612	48,752
Treasury	34,930	39,800	39,500
Stabilization fund (CSSPPA)	17,812	9,252	6,603
External sources	239,283	191,596	193,006
International organizations	58,103	38,208	33,159
Governments	14,346	24,728	20,045
Private bodies	111,501	66,724	79,754
Credits from suppliers	55,333	25,465	1,810
Total	292,025	240,648	239,109

Expenditure	1982	1983	1984
Agriculture	94,801	64,259	62,141
Towns and the environment	47,279	42,199	42,747
Transport	67,150	56,358	64,004
Training	37,645	23,944	29,237
Defence	17,042	3,731	2,912
Administration	19,696	22,947	20,334
Energy	5,085	10,030	6,700
Mining and industry	3,327	875	2,256
Total	292,025	240,648	239,109

CENTRAL BANK RESERVES (US $ million at 31 December)

	1983	1984	1985
Gold*	17.2	14.8	14.4
IMF special drawing rights	16.2	0.2	0.1
Foreign exchange	3.5	5.2	4.7
Total	36.9	20.2	19.2

* Valued at market-related prices.

Source: IMF, *International Financial Statistics*.

MONEY SUPPLY ('000 million francs CFA at 31 December)

	1983	1984	1985
Currency outside banks	232.0	278.7	307.1
Demand deposits at deposit money banks*	253.1	290.6	311.2

* Excluding the deposits of public establishments of an administrative or social nature.

Source: IMF, *International Financial Statistics*.

COST OF LIVING
(Consumer Price Index for Africans in Abidjan. Base: 1980 = 100)

	1983	1984	1985
Food	114.4	120.1	122.0
Fuel, light, water and soap	112.1	121.8	125.9
Clothing	187.5	203.0	207.3
Rent	149.8	150.9	152.6
All items (incl. others)	123.4	128.8	131.1

Source: ILO, *Year Book of Labour Statistics*.

NATIONAL ACCOUNTS
('000 million francs CFA at current prices)
Expenditure on the Gross Domestic Product

	1981	1982	1983
Government final consumption expenditure	450.6	493.4	527.3
Private final consumption expenditure	1,428.4	1,564.1	1,665.2
Increase in stocks	30.2	−33.6	10.6
Gross fixed capital formation	560.0	577.4	541.5
Total domestic expenditure	2,469.2	2,601.3	2,744.6
Exports of goods and services	800.9	941.9	1,019.5
Less Imports of goods and services	955.1	1,059.2	1,266.4
GDP in purchasers' values	2,315.0	2,484.0	2,497.7

Source: IMF, *International Financial Statistics*.

BALANCE OF PAYMENTS (US $ million)

	1983	1984	1985
Merchandise exports f.o.b.	2,066.3	2,645.6	2,882.5
Merchandise imports f.o.b.	−1,635.2	−1,343.4	−1,400.1
Trade balance	431.2	1,302.2	1,482.4
Export of services	489.9	423.4	438.5
Import of services	−1,538.6	−1,567.7	−1,567.0
Balance on goods and services	−617.5	157.8	353.9
Private unrequited transfers (net)	−319.6	−274.6	−264.9
Government unrequited transfers (net)	28.5	9.6	11.3
Current balance	−908.6	−107.2	100.3
Long-term capital (net)	398.1	−98.2	−72.5
Short-term capital (net)	−11.3		
Net errors and omissions	6.8	166.7	
Total (net monetary movements)	−515.0	−38.6	27.8
Valuation changes (net)	26.8	39.4	−63.2
Exceptional financing (net)	368.8	12.2	4.3
Official financing (net)	−1.6	1.8	—
Changes in reserves	−121.0	14.8	−31.1

Source: IMF, *International Financial Statistics*.

THE IVORY COAST

Statistical Survey

External Trade

PRINCIPAL COMMODITIES
(million francs CFA, excluding gold)

Imports c.i.f.	1981	1982	1983
Machinery	62,363	27,710	34,572
Road vehicles	n.a.	41,806	43,812
Petroleum and products	143,932	154,211	130,691
Crude petroleum	118,851	125,636	93,517
Iron and steel	38,250	34,992	34,982
Electrical equipment	27,853	25,441	29,674
Cereals	47,602	45,333	51,073
Rice	35,139	34,270	36,633
Wheat	10,885	10,547	14,128
Paper and paperboard	21,615	28,003	28,260
Construction materials	n.a.	22,883	20,096
Clinker	11,275	13,121	11,293
Pharmaceutical products	15,415	18,379	21,405
Fish	21,780	25,298	25,343
Fresh vegetables and fruit	3,976	10,692	5,044
Metal products	n.a.	27,708	27,359
Total (incl. others)	653,320	718,593.2	714,827.5

1984 (million francs CFA): Crude petroleum 82,670; Total (incl. others) 658,570.
1985 (million francs CFA): Crude petroleum 133,400; Total (incl. others) 772,990.
Source: IMF, *International Financial Statistics*.

Exports f.o.b.	1981	1982	1983
Coffee (green)	69,143	152,172	159,474
Cocoa beans	199,701	163,220	162,731
Wood	94,187	94,366	107,249
Refined petroleum products	40,188	65,672	68,435
Cocoa butter	19,810	20,371	18,034
Pineapples	20,134	16,000	13,350
Cotton fabrics	13,102	13,166	13,105
Conserved fish	12,498	14,780	20,022
Raw cotton	18,006	18,038	31,922
Rubber	6,267	7,011	10,897
Soluble coffee	10,822	13,463	14,698
Total (incl. others)	689,298	747,452	796,774

1984 (million francs CFA): Coffee 183,380; Cocoa beans 396,610; Wood 78,860; Total (incl. others) 1,184,340.
1985 (million francs CFA): Coffee 277,670; Cocoa beans 398,410; Wood 58,030; Total (incl. others) 1,419,390.
Source: IMF, *International Financial Statistics*.

PRINCIPAL TRADING PARTNERS (million francs CFA)

Imports	1981	1982	1983
Belgium/Luxembourg	15,723	12,800	13,033
France	203,066	227,100	248,154
Gabon	108	245	15,987
Germany, Fed. Republic	28,232	28,100	37,783
Italy	23,008	22,500	24,136
Japan	31,936	48,500	31,606
Nigeria	24,961	29,583	37,639
Senegal	13,442	13,267	12,512
Spain	13,602	14,800	26,368
United Kingdom	16,826	16,300	13,662
USA	47,356	36,861	28,026
Total (incl. others)	653,320	718,593.2	714,827.5

Exports	1981	1982	1983
Algeria	9,105	7,872	2,326
Belgium/Luxembourg	13,210	14,866	17,557
Burkina Faso	26,024	34,278	31,787
France	128,326	146,871	151,779
Germany, Fed. Republic	45,582	33,971	31,458
Italy	54,696	64,706	70,232
Japan	13,186	15,155	20,760
Mali	24,197	26,596	33,180
Netherlands	90,808	91,095	92,647
Niger	8,632	10,309	7,536
Portugal	9,901	10,334	10,410
Senegal	8,384	9,461	12,169
Spain	20,284	21,752	22,501
USSR	26,693	17,201	21,312
United Kingdom	26,821	26,524	35,531
USA	79,077	104,934	99,160
Total (incl. others)	689,298	747,452	796,774

Transport

RAILWAYS (including Burkina Faso traffic)

	1982	1983	1984
Passengers ('000)	3,171.8	2,941.0	2,574.9
Passenger-km (million)	892.6	971.8	857.8
Freight ('000 metric tons)	731	601	702
Freight (million net ton-km)	610.6	468.7	530.2

ROAD TRAFFIC (motor vehicles in use at 31 December)

	1981	1982	1984[†]
Passenger cars	157,076	166,920	182,956
Buses and coaches	10,608	11,417	12,944
Goods vehicles*	66,795	69,467	30,057

* Including vans. † Figures for 1983 are not available.
Source: International Road Federation, *World Road Statistics*.

INTERNATIONAL SEA-BORNE SHIPPING
(freight traffic, '000 metric tons)

	1982	1983	1984
Goods loaded	4,660	4,590	4,830
Goods unloaded	4,350	4,310	5,310

CIVIL AVIATION (traffic on scheduled services*)

	1980	1981	1982
Kilometres flown ('000)	2,800	4,700	4,500
Passengers carried	151,000	379,000	385,000
Passenger-km ('000)	215,000	298,000	316,000
Freight ton-km ('000)	18,200	21,400	21,600
Mail ton-km ('000)	700	900	900

* Including an apportionment of the traffic of Air Afrique.
Source: UN, *Statistical Yearbook*.

Communications Media

	1981	1982	1983
Radio receivers ('000 in use)	1,050	1,100	1,200
Television receivers ('000 in use)	330	350	370
Book production:			
Titles	n.a.	n.a.	46*
Copies ('000)	n.a.	n.a.	3,766*
Daily newspapers:			
Number	n.a.	2	n.a.
Average circulation ('000 copies)	n.a.	85	n.a.
Non-daily newspapers:			
Number	n.a.	6	n.a.
Average circulation ('000 copies)	n.a.	145	n.a.
Other periodicals:			
Number	n.a.	12	n.a.
Average circulation ('000 copies)	n.a.	325	n.a.

* Excluding pamphlets.
Source: UNESCO, *Statistical Yearbook*.
Telephones (1980): 88,000 in use (Source: UN, *Statistical Yearbook*).

Tourism

	1980	1981	1982
Tourist arrivals	194,101	194,869	200,005*

* Estimate.
Source: Ministère du Tourisme, Abidjan.

Education

PUPILS ENROLLED

	1982/83	1983/84	1984/85
Primary	1,134,915	1,159,824	1,179,456
Public	1,001,647	1,029,628	1,046,790
Private	133,268	130,196	132,666
Secondary	217,824	230,128	245,342
National University	12,363	12,862	12,755

Teachers: Primary 31,297 in 1982; Secondary (General) 4,601 in 1979 (public education only); Secondary (Vocational) 1,947 in 1981; Higher education 1,204 in 1981 (Source: UNESCO, *Statistical Yearbook*).

Directory

The Constitution

The Constitution was promulgated on 31 October 1960. It was amended in June 1971, October 1975, August 1980, November 1980, October 1985 and January 1986.

PREAMBLE

The Republic of the Ivory Coast is one and indivisible. It is secular, democratic and social. Sovereignty belongs to the people who exercise it through their representatives or through referenda. There is universal, equal and secret suffrage. French is the official language.

HEAD OF STATE

The President is elected for a five-year term by direct universal suffrage and is eligible for re-election. He is Head of the Administration and the Armed Forces and has power to ask the National Assembly to reconsider a Bill, which must then be passed by two-thirds of the members of the Assembly; he may also have a Bill submitted to a referendum. In case of the death or incapacitation of the President, the functions of the Head of State are carried out by the president of the National Assembly, until a presidential election has been held, within 45–60 days.

EXECUTIVE POWER

Executive power is vested in the President. He appoints a Council of Ministers, who are responsible only to him. Any member of the National Assembly appointed minister must renounce his seat in the Assembly, but may regain it on leaving the Government.

LEGISLATIVE POWER

Legislative power is vested in a National Assembly of 175 members, elected for a five-year term of office. Legislation may be introduced either by the President or by a member of the National Assembly.

JUDICIAL POWER

The independence of the judiciary is guaranteed by the President, assisted by a High Council of Judiciary.

ECONOMIC AND SOCIAL COUNCIL

This is an advisory commission of 120 members, appointed by the President because of their specialist knowledge or experience.

The Government

HEAD OF STATE

President: Dr Félix Houphouët-Boigny (took office November 1960, re-elected for sixth term of office October 1985).

COUNCIL OF MINISTERS
(January 1987)

President of the Republic: Dr Félix Houphouët-Boigny.
Minister of State: Auguste Denise.
Minister of State: Mathieu Ekra.
Minister of State: Camille Alliali.
Minister of State: Maurice Séri Gnoléba.
Minister of State: Emile Kéï Boguinard.
Minister of State: Lazéni N. P. Coulibaly.
Minister of State: Amadou Thiam.
Minister of State: Paul Gui Dibo.
Minister of State: Lamine Diabaté.
Minister of the Economy and Finance: Abdoulaye Koné.
Minister of Justice and Keeper of the Seals: Noël Némin.
Minister of Defence: Jean Konan Banny.
Minister of the Interior: Léon Konan Koffi.
Minister of Foreign Affairs: Siméon Aké.
Minister of Industry: Bernard Ehui Koutoua.
Minister of Public Health and Population: Alphonse Djédjé Madi.
Minister of Water and Forestry Resources: Vincent Pierre Lokrou.
Minister of National Education responsible for Secondary and Higher Education: Dr Balla Kéita.
Minister of Social Affairs: Yaya Ouattara.
Minister of Trade: Nicolas Kouandi Angba.
Minister of Public Works and Transport: Aoussou Koffi.
Minister of Construction and Town Planning: Vammoussa Bamba.
Minister of Posts and Telecommunications: Vincent Tieko Djédjé.
Minister of Labour: Albert Vanié Bi Tra.
Minister of Information, Cultural Affairs, Youth and Sport: Laurent Dona-Fologo.
Minister of Mining: Yed Esaïe Angoran.
Minister of Internal Security: Gen. Oumar N'Daw.
Minister of Maritime Affairs: Lamine Fadika.
Minister of the Civil Service: Jean-Jacques Bechio.
Minister of Tourism: Duon Sadia.
Minister in charge of Relations with the National Assembly: Emile Brou.
Minister of Rural Development and Civil Defence: Gilles Laubhouet Vally.
Minister of Agriculture: Denis Bra Kanon.
Minister of Women's Promotion: Mme Hortense Aka Anghui.
Minister of Scientific Research: Alhassane Salif N'Diaye.
Minister of the Budget: Moïse Koumoué Koffi.
Minister of Primary Education: Mme Odette Kouamé N'Guessan.
Minister of Animal Husbandry: Christopher Gobowo.
Minister of Technical Education and Professional Training: Ange-François Barry-Battesti.
Minister of Planning: Oumar Diarra.

MINISTRIES

Ministry of Agriculture, Water and Forestry Resources: BP V82, Abidjan; telex 23612.
Ministry of Cultural Affairs: BP V39, Abidjan.
Ministry of Defence: BP V11, Abidjan.
Ministry of the Economy and Finance: Immeuble SCIAM, ave Marchand, BP V163, Abidjan; tel. 32-05-66; telex 23747.
Ministry of Foreign Affairs: BP V109, Abidjan; telex 23752.
Ministry of Industry: BP V65, Abidjan.
Ministry of Information: BP V138, Abidjan; telex 23781.
Ministry of the Interior: BP V241, Abidjan.
Ministry of Internal Security: BP V241, Abidjan; telex 23873.
Ministry of Justice: BP V107, Abidjan.
Ministry of Labour: BP V119, Abidjan.
Ministry of Maritime Affairs: BP V57, Abidjan; telex 23399.
Ministry of Mining: BP V50, Abidjan; telex 22262.
Ministry of National Education and Scientific Research: BP V120, Abidjan; telex 23377.
Ministry of Public Health and Population: BP V4, Abidjan; telex 42213.
Ministry of Public Works, Transport, Construction, Posts and Telecommunications: ave Jean Paul II, BP V6, Abidjan; tel. 29-13-67; telex 22108.
Ministry of Rural Development: BP V185, Abidjan.
Ministry of Social Affairs: BP V124, Abidjan; telex 23480.
Ministry of Tourism: BP V184, Abidjan; telex 23438.
Ministry of Trade: BP V142, Abidjan; telex 23704.

Legislature

ASSEMBLÉE NATIONALE

At elections in November 1985, a total of 546 candidates contested the 175 seats in the National Assembly, all of which were won by the Parti démocratique de la Côte d'Ivoire.

President: Henri Konan-Bédié.
Vice-Presidents: Gladys Anoma, Marie-Bernard Koissy, Clément Anet Bilé, Gon Coulibaly, Maurice Oulaté, Benoît Toussagnon.

Political Organization

Parti démocratique de la Côte d'Ivoire (PDCI): Maison du Parti, Abidjan; f. 1946 as the local section of the Rassemblement démocratique africain; headed by an executive cttee of 13 mems, a political bureau of 35 and a guiding cttee of 100; Chair. Dr Félix Houphouët-Boigny.

Diplomatic Representation

EMBASSIES IN THE IVORY COAST

Algeria: 53 blvd Clozel, 01 BP 1015, Abidjan 01; tel. 32-23-40; telex 23243; Ambassador: Ahmed Amrani.
Argentina: 08 BP 860, Abidjan 08; tel. 44-41-78; telex 22112; Ambassador: Héctor Sains Ballestros.
Austria: 70 bis, ave Jean-Mermoz, Cocody, 01 BP 1837, Abidjan 01; tel. 44-03-02; telex 22182; Ambassador: Dr Wolfgang Kriechbaum.
Belgium: Immeuble Alliance, ave Terrasson de Fougères, 01 BP 1800, Abidjan 01; tel. 32-20-88; telex 23633; Ambassador: Paul Duque.
Benin: rue des Jardins, 09 BP 238, Abidjan 09; tel. 41-44-14; telex 23922; Ambassador: Nicholas Benon.
Brazil: Immeuble Alpha 2000, 01 BP 3820, Abidjan 01; tel. 22-23-41; telex 23443; Ambassador: Ernesto Ferreira de Carvalho.
Burkina Faso: 2 ave Terrasson de Fougères, 01 BP 908, Abidjan 01; tel. 32-13-13; telex 23453; Ambassador: Frédéric Assomption Korsaga.
Cameroon: 01 BP 2886, Abidjan 01; Ambassador: Fidèle Moïse Bonny Eboubou.
Canada: Immeuble Trade Centre, 01 BP 4104, Abidjan 01; tel. 32-20-09; telex 23593; Ambassador: John P. Bell.
Central African Republic: rue des Combattants, 01 BP 3387, Abidjan 01; tel. 32-36-46; telex 22102; Ambassador: (vacant).
Chile: Immeuble Le Jeceda, 52F, 08 BP 1367, Abidjan 08; tel. 32-92-37; telex 22173; Ambassador: Luis Winter Igualt.
China, People's Republic: 01 BP 3691, Abidjan 01; tel. 41-32-48; telex 22104; Ambassador: Zhu Chengcai.
Colombia: 01 BP 3874, Abidjan 01; tel. 33-12-44; telex 22576; Ambassador: Octavio Gallón Restrepo.

THE IVORY COAST
Directory

Denmark: Immeuble Le Mans, blvd Boitreau Roussel, angle ave Noguès, Plateau, 01 BP 4569, Abidjan 01; tel. 33-17-65; telex 23871; Chargé d'affaires: MOGENS HOLM PEDERSEN.

Egypt: Immeuble El Nasr, ave du Général de Gaulle, 01 BP 2104, Abidjan 01; tel. 32-79-25; telex 23537; Ambassador: AHMADEIN KHALIL.

Ethiopia: Immeuble Nour Al-Hayat, 01 BP 3712, Abidjan 01; tel. 32-33-65; telex 23848; Ambassador: MAHMOUD SEYOUM.

France: rue Lecoeur, quartier du Plateau, 17 BP 175, Abidjan 17; tel. 32-67-49; telex 23699; Ambassador: MICHEL DUPUCH.

Gabon: Immeuble Shell, 46 ave Lamblin, 01 BP 3765, Abidjan 01; tel. 22-86-12; telex 23561; Ambassador: ABOUBAKAR BOKOKO.

Germany, Federal Republic: Immeuble Le Mans, blvd Boitreau Roussel, 01 BP 1900, Abidjan 01; tel. 32-47-27; telex 23642; Ambassador: Dr MICHAEL SCHMIDT.

Ghana: résidence de la Corniche, blvd du Général de Gaulle, 01 BP 1871, Abidjan 01; tel. 33-11-24; Ambassador: ATE ALLOTEY.

Guinea: Immeuble Crosson Duplessis, 08 BP 2280, Abidjan 08; tel. 32-86-00; Ambassador: SEKOU PHILO CAMARA.

Holy See: 08 BP 1347, Abidjan 08; tel. 44-38-35; telex 26182; Apostolic Nuncio: Mgr ANTONIO MATTIAZZO.

India: 10 rue du Belier, 06 BP 318, Abidjan 06; tel. 44-52-31; Ambassador: PRITHVI RAJ SOOD.

Iran: 08 BP 2279, Abidjan 08; telex 23172; Chargé d'affaires: ABOL MOHSEN SHARIF MOHAMMADI.

Israel: Immeuble Nour Al-Hayat, 01 BP 1877, Abidjan 01; Chargé d'affaires: SHIMON AGOUR.

Italy: 16 rue de la Canebière, Cocody, 01 BP 1905, Abidjan 01; tel. 44-61-70; telex 26123; Ambassador: CARLO CALIA.

Japan: Immeuble Alpha 2000, 01 BP 1329, Abidjan 01; tel. 33-28-63; telex 23400; Ambassador: KATSUHIRO ICHIKA.

Korea, Republic: Immeuble Le Général, 01 BP 3950, Abidjan 01; tel. 32-22-90; telex 23638; Ambassador: BONG-RHEUM CHOI.

Lebanon: 01 BP 2227, Abidjan 01; tel. 33-28-24; Ambassador: MICHEL SALAMEH.

Liberia: Immeuble La Symphonie, 30 ave du Général de Gaulle, Abidjan; tel. 22-23-59; telex 23535; Ambassador: HAROLD TARR.

Mali: Maison du Mali, rue du Commerce, 01 BP 2746, Abidjan 01; tel. 32-31-47; telex 23429; Ambassador: MODIBO DIARRA.

Mauritania: 01 BP 2275, Abidjan 01; tel. 35-20-68; telex 22371; Ambassador: BA MAHMOUD.

Morocco: 24 rue de la Canebière, Cocody, 01 BP 146, Abidjan 01; tel. 44-58-78; telex 26147; Ambassador: CHAWKI KERDOUDI KOLALI.

Netherlands: Immeuble Les Harmonies, blvd Carde, 01 BP 1086, Abidjan 01; tel. 22-77-12; telex 23694; Ambassador: GUY WESTEROUEN VAN MEETEREN.

Niger: 01 BP 2743, Abidjan 01; tel. 35-50-98; Ambassador: MAGAGI GOUROUZA.

Nigeria: 35 blvd de la République, 01 BP 1906, Abidjan 01; tel. 32-19-82; telex 23532; Ambassador: Dr LAWRENCE B. EKPEBU.

Norway: Immeuble N' Zarama, blvd du Général de Gaulle, 01 BP 607, Abidjan 01; tel. 22-25-34; telex 23355; Ambassador: LEIF EDWARDSEN.

Poland: 04 BP 308, Abidjan 04; tel. 44-12-25; telex 22403; Ambassador: STANISŁAW SMYSLO.

Rwanda: 01 BP 3905, Abidjan 01; tel. 41-38-31; Ambassador: CALLIXTE HATUNGIMANA.

Senegal: Résidence Nabil, blvd du Général de Gaulle, 08 BP 2165, Abidjan 08; tel. 33-28-76; telex 23897; Ambassador: MATAR NDIAYE.

Spain: 01 BP 2589, Abidjan 01; tel. 33-25-37; telex 23632; Ambassador: MARIANO URIARTE Y LLODRÁ.

Sweden: rue Gourgas, 04 BP 992, Abidjan 04; tel. 33-24-10; telex 23293; Ambassador: BENGT BORGLUND.

Switzerland: Immeuble Alpha 2000, 01 BP 1914, Abidjan 01; tel. 32-17-21; telex 23492; Ambassador: CLAUDIO CARATSCH.

Tunisia: Immeuble Shell, 48 ave Lamblin, 01 BP 3906, Abidjan 01; tel. 32-23-04; telex 23709; Ambassador: ALI JERAD.

USSR: Abidjan; Ambassador: BORIS MINAKOV.

United Kingdom: Immeuble Les Harmonies, 01 BP 2581, Abidjan 01; tel. 22-68-50; telex 23706; Ambassador: J. M. WILLSON.

USA: 5 rue Jesse Owens, 01 BP 1712, Abidjan 01; tel. 32-09-79; telex 23660; Ambassador: DENNIS KUX.

Zaire: 29 blvd Clozel, 01 BP 3961, Abidjan 01; tel. 22-20-80; telex 23795; Ambassador: LOUYA LONDOALE.

Judicial System

Since 1964 all civil, criminal, commercial and administrative cases have come under the jurisdiction of the Tribunaux de première instance (Magistrates' courts), the assize courts and the Court of Appeal, with the Supreme Court as supreme court of appeal.

The Supreme Court: rue Gourgas, BP V30, Abidjan; has four chambers: constitutional, judicial, administrative and auditing; Pres. ALPHONSE BONI.

Courts of Appeal: Abidjan and Bouaké; hear appeals from the Courts of First Instance; Abidjan, First Pres. CAMILLE HOGUIE, Attorney-General LOUIS FOLQUET; Bouaké, First Pres. AHIOUA MOULARE, Attorney-General ANOMAN OGUIE.

The High Court of Justice: composed of Deputies elected from and by the National Assembly. It is competent to impeach the President or other member of the government; Pres. HENRI KONAN-BÉDIÉ.

State Security Court: composed of a president and six regular judges, all appointed for five years; deals with all offences against the security of the State; Pres. ALPHONSE BONI.

Courts of First Instance: Abidjan, Pres. ROBERT COULOUD NATCHA; Bouaké, Pres. KABLAN AKA ÉDOUKOU; Daloa, Pres. WOUNE BLEKA; there are a further 25 courts in the principal centres.

Religion

It is estimated that 65% of the population follow traditional animist beliefs, while 23% are Muslims and 12% are Christians, mainly Roman Catholics.

CHRISTIANITY
The Roman Catholic Church

The Ivory Coast comprises one archdiocese and nine dioceses. At 31 December 1984 there were an estimated 995,000 adherents in the country.

Bishops' Conference: Conférence Episcopale de la Côte d'Ivoire, 01 BP 1287, Abidjan 01; tel. 33-22-56; f. 1973; Pres. Cardinal BERNARD YAGO, Archbishop of Abidjan.

Archbishop of Abidjan: Cardinal BERNARD YAGO, Archevêché, 01 BP 1287, Abidjan 01; tel. 33-22-56.

Protestant Churches

Christian and Missionary Alliance: BP 585, Bouaké 01; tel. 63-23-12; f. 1929; 13 mission stations; Supt Rev. DAVID ARNOLD.

Conservative Baptist Foreign Mission Society: BP 109, Korhogo; tel. 86-00-33; f. 1947; active in Abidjan and in the northern area in evangelism, teaching and medical work.

Eglise Protestante Méthodiste: 41 blvd de la République, 01 BP 1282, Abidjan 01; c. 120,000 mems; Pres. Pastor EMMANUEL YANDO.

Mission Évangélique de l'Afrique Occidentale: 08 BP 653, Abidjan 08; tel. 44-02-68; f. 1934; 11 mission stations; Field Dir WOLFGANG LIPSCHÜTZ; affiliated church: Alliance des Eglises Evangéliques de Côte d'Ivoire; 75 churches, 52 missionaries; Pres. TEHI TIECOURA EMMANUEL.

Union des Eglises Évangéliques du Sud-Ouest de la Côte d'Ivoire and **Mission Biblique:** BP 8020, Abidjan; f. 1927; c. 250 places of worship.

BAHÁ'Í FAITH

Assemblée Spirituelle Nationale des Bahá'ís de Côte d'Ivoire et Mali: 04 BP 770, Abidjan 04; tel. 44-06-79; mems resident in 235 localities.

The Press

Abidjan 7 Jours: 01 BP 1965, Abidjan 01; tel. 35-39-39; telex 24317; f. 1964; weekly local information; circ. 10,000.

Afrique-Sports: Abidjan; weekly.

Bulletin mensuel de Statistiques: Direction de la Statistique, BP V55, Abidjan.

Djeliba—le journal des jeunes Chrétiens: 01 BP 1287, Abidjan 01; f. 1974; 5 a year; Editor PIERRE TRICHET; circ. 5,500.

Eburnea: Ministry of Information, BP VI38, Abidjan; telex 23781; monthly.

THE IVORY COAST

Entente Africaine: BP 20991, Abidjan; publ. by Inter Afrique Presse; illustrated; quarterly in French and English; Editor Justin Vieyra.

Fraternité-Hebdo: 01 BP 1212, Abidjan 01; tel. 22-25-05; organ of the PDCI; weekly; Political Dir Dr Félix Houphouët-Boigny; Man. Editor Auguste Miremont.

Fraternité-Matin: blvd du Général de Gaulle, 01 BP 1807, Abidjan 01; tel. 33-27-27; telex 23718; f. 1964; organ of the PDCI; daily; Man. Dir Amadou Thiam; Editor Marcellin Abougnan; circ. 80,000.

Gazette du Centre: Abidjan; weekly.

Ivoire-Dimanche: 01 BP 1807, Abidjan 01; f. 1971; weekly; circ. 75,000.

Journal des Amis du Progrès de l'Afrique Noire: BP 694, Abidjan; 5 a week.

Journal Officiel de la Côte d'Ivoire: Ministry of the Interior, BP V241, Abidjan; weekly.

Le Messager: BP 1776, Abidjan; 6 a year; Editor André Leroux.

La Semaine d'Abidjan: BP 20991, Abidjan; tel. 32-64-78; weekly; local information; Editor Justin Vieyra.

Revue Ivoirienne de Droit: BP 3811, Abidjan; f. 1969; publ. by the Centre ivoirien de recherches et d'études juridiques (CIREJ); circ. 1,500.

Télé-Miroir: Abidjan; monthly.

NEWS AGENCIES

Agence Ivoirienne de Presse (AIP): 11 ave Bir-Hakeim, BP 4312, Abidjan; telex 23476; f. 1961; Dir Denis Oussou Essui.

Foreign Bureaux

Agence France-Presse (AFP): Les deux plateaux de Cocody, Lot 478, 01 BP 726, Abidjan 01; tel. 41-41-57; telex 27129; Dir Bernard Aubert.

Agenzia Nazionale Stampa Associata (ANSA) (Italy): 16 rue de la Canebière, Cocody, 01 BP 1905, Abidjan 01; Agent Silvia de Angeli.

Associated Press (AP) (USA): 01 BP 5843, Abidjan 01; tel. 41-38-95; telex 28129; Correspondent Robert Weller.

Reuters (UK): Résidence Les Acacias, 20 blvd Clozel, 01 BP 2338, Abidjan 01; tel. 33-27-01; Chief Correspondent C. Regin.

Xinhua (New China) News Agency (People's Republic of China): Cocody Danga Nord Lot 46, 08 BP 1212, Abidjan 08; tel. 44-01-24; Chief Correspondent Xiong Shanwu.

Central News Agency (Taiwan) also has an office in Abidjan.

Publishers

Centre d'Édition et de Diffusion Africaines (CEDA): 04 BP 541, Abidjan 04; tel. 22-20-55; telex 22451; f. 1961; general non-fiction; Man. Dir Venace Kacou.

Centre de Publications Évangéliques: 08 BP 900, Abidjan 08; tel. 44-48-05; f. 1970; religious; Dir Robert Bryan.

Inter Afrique Presse: Abidjan; telex 23861.

Université Nationale de Côte d'Ivoire: 01 BP V34, Abidjan; tel. 43-90-00; f. 1964; general non-fiction; Sec.-Gen. Mrs Dehail-Michèle.

Government Publishing House

Imprimerie Nationale: BP V87, Abidjan; telex 23868.

Radio and Television

In 1983 there were an estimated 1,200,000 radio receivers and 370,000 television receivers in use.

Radiodiffusion Ivoirienne: BP V191, Abidjan 01; tel. 32-41-52; govt radio station broadcasting in French, English and local languages; MW station at Abidjan, relay at Bouaké; VHF transmitters at Abidjan, Bouaflé, Man and Koun-Abbrosso; Dir Koné Ibrahim.

Télévision Ivoirienne: 08 BP 883, Abidjan 08; tel. 43-90-39; telex 22293; f. 1963; 40 hours a week French broadcasts; colour transmissions since 1973; stations at Abobo-gare, Bouaflé, Man, Koun, Niangbo, Tiémé, Dimbokro, Bouaké, Digo, San Pedro; Man. Mamadou Soumahoro.

Finance

(br. = branch; cap. = capital; res = reserves; dep. = deposits; m. = million; amounts in francs CFA)

BANKING

Central Bank

Banque Centrale des Etats de l'Afrique de l'Ouest (BCEAO): ave Terrasson de Fougères, 01 BP 1769, Abidjan 01; tel. 32-04-66; telex 23474; Headquarters in Dakar, Senegal; bank of issue and central bank for the seven states of the Union monétaire ouest africaine (UMOA), comprising Benin, Burkina Faso, the Ivory Coast, Mali, Niger, Senegal and Togo; f. 1955; cap. 32,564m. (Sept. 1985); Gov. Abdoulaye Fadiga; Ivory Coast Dir Charles Konan Banny; 5 brs.

Other Banks

Banque Atlantique-Côte d'Ivoire: ave du Général de Gaulle, 04 BP 1036, Abidjan 04; tel. 32-82-18; telex 23834; f. 1978; cap. 1,000m.; Chair. Casimir Kra Kouadio; Man. Dir Jean-Luc de la Serre.

Banque Internationale pour l'Afrique Occidentale-Côte d'Ivoire (BIAO-CI): 810 ave Joseph Anoma, 01 BP 1274, Abidjan 01; tel. 32-07-22; telex 23641; f. 1980; cap. 5,000m.; 35% state-owned, 65% BIAO (France); Chair. Auguste Daubrey; Dir-Gen. Arnaud de Montigny; 37 brs in Ivory Coast.

Banque Internationale pour le Commerce et l'Industrie de la Côte d'Ivoire SA (BICICI): ave Franchet d'Espérey, 01 BP 1298, Abidjan 01; tel. 32-03-79; telex 23651; f. 1962; cap. 4,000m., res 6,929m., dep. 257.2m. (Sept. 1984); 23.5% state-owned, 21% by Banque Nationale de Paris (BNP), 28% by Société Financière pour les Pays d'Outre-Mer (comprises BNP, Banque Bruxelles Lambert and Dresdner Bank); Chair. Lambert Konan; Gen. Man. Joachim Richmond; 46 brs.

Banque Ivoirienne de Construction et de Travaux Publics (BICT): Maison du Mali, ave du Général de Gaulle, 01 BP 3729, Abidjan 01; tel. 32-71-14; telex 23841; f. 1979; cap. 2,000m.; Chair. Martin Kouadio Kouakou; Man. Dir Denis Kouadio M'bra (acting).

Banque Ivoirienne de Développement Industriel (BIDI): 13 ave Joseph Anoma, 04 BP 470, Abidjan 04; tel. 32-01-11; telex 23484; f. 1964; cap. 2,100m.; 21% state-owned, 11% by Caisse Centrale de Coopération Economique (France); Man. Soungalo Traoré (acting).

Banque Nationale pour le Développement Agricole (BNDA): 11 ave Joseph Anoma, 01 BP 2508, Abidjan 01; tel. 32-07-57; telex 22298; f. 1968; cap. 3,000m.; 61% state-owned, 17% by BCEAO; Chair. Lamine Diabaté; Man. Dir Patrice Kouame; 32 brs.

Banque Nationale pour l'Epargne et le Crédit (BNEC): 25 ave Joseph Anoma, 09 BP 257, Abidjan 09; tel. 32-20-06; telex 22285; f. 1975 as national savings bank; privatized 1980; cap. 1,100m.; 51% owned by BICT; Chair. and Man. Dir Patrice Yao Konan.

Banque Paribas Côte d'Ivoire (France): Immeuble Alliance, ave Terrasson de Fougères, 17 BP 09, Abidjan 17; tel. 32-86-86; telex 22870; f. 1984; cap. 1,000m.; Chair. Philippe Drillet; Man. Dir Roger Gibert.

Banque Real de Côte d'Ivoire SA: ave Joseph Anoma, 04 BP 411, Abidjan 04; tel. 32-84-52; telex 22430; f. 1976; cap. 1,000m.; wholly-owned subsidiary of Banco Real SA (Brazil); Chair. Juarez Soares; Man. Dir Ronaldo Bastos Tavares.

Caisse Autonome d'Amortissement: Immeuble SCIAM, ave Marchand, 01 BP 610, Abidjan 01; tel. 32-06-11; telex 23798; f. 1959; Man. Dir Léon Naka; Sec.-Gen. Mathieu N'Goran.

Compagnie Financière de la Côte d'Ivoire (COFINCI): rue Gourgas, 01 BP 1566, Abidjan 01; tel. 32-27-32; telex 22228; f. 1974; cap. 1,100m.; 19% state-owned, 51% by BICICI; Chair. Joachim Richmond; Man. Dir Yves Fofana.

Crédit de la Côte d'Ivoire (CCI): 22 ave Joseph Anoma, 01 BP 1720, Abidjan 01; tel. 32-03-57; telex 22106; f. 1955; cap. 4,800m.; 58% state-owned, 33% by BCEAO; Man. Soungalo Traoré (acting); 5 brs.

Société Générale de Banques en Côte d'Ivoire SA (SGBCI): 5/7 ave Joseph Anoma, 01 BP 1355, Abidjan 01; tel. 32-03-33; telex 23437; f. 1962; cap. 6,000m. (1984); 8.5% state-owned, 37.2% by Société Générale (France); Chair. and Man. Dir Tiemoko Coulibaly; 48 brs.

THE IVORY COAST																																						Directory

Société Générale de Financement et de Participations en Côte d'Ivoire (SOGEFINANCE): 7 ave Joseph Anoma, 01 BP 3904, Abidjan 01; tel. 32-03-33; telex 23502; f. 1978; cap. 1,000m. (Sept. 1984); 15% state-owned, 58% by SGBCI, 12% by Société Générale; Chair. TIEMOKO COULIBALY; Dir JACQUES DE MALEVILLE.

Société Ivoirienne de Banque (SIB): 34 blvd de la République, 01 BP 1300, Abidjan 01; tel. 32-00-00; telex 23751; f. 1962; cap. 6,000m.; 41% state-owned, 41% by Crédit Lyonnais (France); Chair. ABOU DOUMBIA; Man. Dir ROBERT PLISSON; 37 brs.

Union de Banques en Côte d'Ivoire (BANAFRIQUE): Résidence Nabil, ave du Général de Gaulle, 01 BP 4132, Abidjan 01; tel. 33-15-36; telex 22513; f. 1980; cap. 1,000m.; 37% owned by Banque du Liban et d'Outremer (Lebanon); Chair. NAAMAN AZHARI; Gen. Man. DANIEL PIERRE; 2 brs.

Bankers' Association

Association Professionnelle des Banques et Etablissements Financiers de Côte d'Ivoire: 01 BP 3810, Abidjan 01; Pres. TIEMOKO COULIBALY.

INSURANCE

Assurances Générales de Côte d'Ivoire (AGCI): 01 BP 4092, Abidjan 01; tel. 33-99-32; telex 22502; f. 1979; cap. 630m.; Chair. JOACHIM RICHMOND.

Assurmafer: 11 ave Joseph Anoma, 01 BP 62, Abidjan 01; tel. 32-10-52; telex 23231; f. 1941; cap. 700m.; Dir GILBERT HIS.

Compagnie des Assurances Colina SA: 01 BP 3832, Abidjan 01; tel. 32-37-17; telex 20983; f. 1980; cap. 300m.; Chair. MICHEL POUPARD; Dir E. MALARTRE.

Compagnie Nationale d'Assurances (CNA): 30 ave du Général de Gaulle, 01 BP 1333, Abidjan 01; tel. 32-63-63; telex 22176; f. 1972; cap. 400m.; insurance and reinsurance; Chair. and Man. Dir LÉON AMON.

Mutuelle Universelle de Garantie (UNIWARRANT): 01 BP 301, Abidjan 01; tel. 32-41-18; f. 1970; cap. 208m.; Chair. and Man. Dir FATIMA SYLLA.

La Sécurité Ivoirienne: Immeuble La Pyramide, 01 BP 569, Abidjan 01; tel. 33-14-99; telex 23817; f. 1971; cap. 300m.; general; Chair. DIA HOUPHOUËT-BOIGNY; Man. Dir JEAN-BAPTISTE BABO ZOBO.

Société Africaine d'Assurances et de Réassurances en République de Côte d'Ivoire (SAFFARRIV): 22 rue Gourgas, 01 BP 1741, Abidjan 01; tel. 32-11-57; f. 1975; cap. 500m.; Dir JEAN-MARIE COMBES.

Société Nouvelle d'Assurances de Côte d'Ivoire (SNACI): 9 ave Houdaille, 01 BP 1014, Abidjan 01; tel. 32-10-11; telex 22225; cap. 1,008m.; subsidiary of Axa International; Chair. L. BROSSIER.

Société Tropicale d'Assurances Mutuelles Vie (STAM-VIE): Maison de la Mutualité, 15 ave Barthe, 01 BP 1337, Abidjan 01; tel. 33-20-24; telex 23774; f. 1969; cap. 150m.; life; Chair. JEAN-BAPTISTE AMETHIER; Dir ALBERT AFFOUE-FAUSTE.

SOGERCO-SAFRACI: 43 ave du Général de Gaulle, 01 BP 1539, Abidjan 01; tel. 32-77-00; telex 22414; f. 1972; cap. 108m.; general; Chair. A. JUSTET.

Union Africaine: 01 BP 378, Abidjan 01; tel. 32-73-81; telex 23568; f. 1980; cap. 1,000m.; insurance and reinsurance; Chair. ERNEST AMOS AJORO; Dir JEAN-KALOU DIAGOU.

Union Africaine Vie: 01 BP 2016, Abidjan 01; f. 1985; cap. 300m., life; Chair. ERNEST AMOS AJORO; Dir JEAN-KALOU DIAGOU.

Trade and Industry

DEVELOPMENT ORGANIZATION

Conseil Economique et Social: 04 BP 301, Abidjan; tel. 32-20-60; govt body with overall responsibility for economic development; Pres. PHILIPPE YACÉ; Vice-Pres. F. KONIAN KODJO, B. BEDA YAO, Mme J. CHAPMAN.

STATE COMPANIES

Caisse de Stabilisation et de Soutien des Prix des Productions Agricoles (CSSPPA): BP V132, Abidjan; tel. 32-08-33; telex 23612; f. 1964; cap. 4,000m. francs CFA; controls price, quality and export of agricultural products; offices in Paris, London and New York; Man. Dir RENÉ AMANI.

Palmindustrie: 01 BP V239, Abidjan 01; tel. 36-93-88; telex 43100; f. 1969; cap. 3,365m. francs CFA; development of palm, coconut and copra products; Man. Dir DOSSONGUI KONE.

Société d'Assistance Technique pour la Modernisation Agricole de la Côte d'Ivoire (SATMACI): ave Barthe, 01 BP 1565, Abidjan; tel. 32-62-76; telex 23774; f. 1958; cap. 150m. francs CFA; agricultural development and advisory service; rice plantations; Man. Dir JOSEPH NIAMKE.

Société Nationale de Conditionnement (SONACO): 01 BP 1119, Abidjan; tel. 33-16-45; telex 22288; f. 1975; cap. 300m. francs CFA; distribution and packaging of Ivory Coast banana production; Chair. CLÉMENT ANET-BILE; Man. Dir JOSEPH EMISSAH KOUAO.

Société Nationale d'Opérations Pétrolières de la Côte d'Ivoire (PETROCI): BP V194, Abidjan 12; tel. 32-40-58; telex 22135; f. 1975; cap. 2,000m. francs CFA; all aspects of petroleum development; Pres. Minister of Mining; Man. Dir PAUL AHUI.

Société pour le Développement Minier de la Côte d'Ivoire (SODEMI): 31 blvd André Latrille, 01 BP 2816, Abidjan 01; tel. 44-29-94; telex 26162; f. 1962; cap. 65.3m. francs CFA; mineral research; Man. Dir JOSEPH N'ZI.

Société pour le Développement de l'Exploitation du Palmier à Huile (SODEPALM): 01 BP 2049, Abidjan; tel. 32-00-79; telex 23347; f. 1963; cap. 400m. francs CFA; national development organization for palm oil; Man. Dir LAZARE KOFFI KROU.

Société pour le Développement de la Motorisation de l'Agriculture (MOTORAGRI): Km 5, route d'Abobo, 01 BP 3745, Abidjan; tel. 37-46-17; f. 1966; cap. 230m. francs CFA; state organization for rationalizing machinery use for agricultural development; Chair. Minister of Agriculture; Man. Dir EMMANUEL AMANY YAO.

Société pour le Développement des Plantations de Canne à Sucre, l'Industrialisation et la Commercialisation du Sucre (SODESUCRE): 16 ave du Docteur Crozet, 01 BP 2164, Abidjan 01; tel. 32-04-79; telex 23451; f. 1977; cap. 67,000m. francs CFA; development of sugar plantations and refinery; Chair. J. A. KACOU AOULOU; Man. Dir JOSEPH KOUAMÉ KRA.

Société pour le Développement des Productions Animales (SODEPRA): 01 BP 1249, Abidjan 01; tel. 32-13-10; telex 22123; f. 1970; cap. 404m. francs CFA; state development organization for animal husbandry; Chair. CHARLES DONWAHI; Man. Dir PAUL LAMIZANA.

Société pour le Développement de la Production des Fruits et Légumes (SODEFEL): 11 ave Barthe, 01 BP 3032, Abidjan 01; tel. 32-63-40; telex 22100; f. 1968; cap. 120m. francs CFA; state organization for fruit and vegetable production and marketing; Chair. FÉLICIEN KONAN KODJO; Man. Dir BOA BOADOU.

CHAMBERS OF COMMERCE

Chambre d'Agriculture de la Côte d'Ivoire: 11 ave Lamblin, 01 BP 1291, Abidjan 01; tel. 32-16-11; Pres. AUGUSTE BASTIDE; Sec.-Gen. M. MAEDER.

Chambre de Commerce de la Côte d'Ivoire: ave Louis Barthe, 01 BP 1399, Abidjan 01; tel. 32-46-79; telex 23224; Pres. F. MASSIEYE; Sec.-Gen. MAURICE DELAFOSSE.

Chambre d'Industrie de la Côte d'Ivoire: 11 ave Lamblin, 01 BP 1758, Abidjan 01; tel. 22-55-04; telex 22291; Pres. LAMBERT KONAN; Sec.-Gen. MAXIME EKRA.

EMPLOYERS' ASSOCIATIONS

Fédération Maritime de la Côte d'Ivoire (FEDERMAR): 01 BP 1546, Abidjan; Sec.-Gen. VACABA TOURÉ.

Groupement Interprofessionnel de l'Automobile (GIPA): 01 BP 1340, Abidjan; tel. 35-71-42; f. 1953; 30 mems; Pres. D. DUBOIS; Sec.-Gen. P. MEYER.

Syndicat des Commerçants Importateurs, Exportateurs et Distributeurs de la Côte d'Ivoire (SCIMPEX): 01 BP 3792, Abidjan 01; tel. 32-54-27; Pres. JACQUES ROSSIGNOL; Sec.-Gen. PIERRE DE LA MOTTE.

Syndicat des Employeurs Agricoles (SYNDAGRI): 01 BP 2300, Abidjan 01; tel. 32-26-42; Pres. JEAN-BAPTISTE AMETHIER.

Syndicat des Entrepreneurs et des Industriels de la Côte d'Ivoire (SEICI): 18 ave Joseph Anoma, 01 BP 464, Abidjan 01; tel. 32-11-18; f. 1937; Pres. SEKOU DIAKITÉ.

Syndicat des Entrepreneurs de Manutention du Port d'Abidjan (SEMPA): 01 BP 172, Abidjan 01; tel. 32-18-82; Vice-Pres. P. SOMICOA.

THE IVORY COAST

Syndicat des Exportateurs et Négociants en Bois de la Côte d'Ivoire: 01 BP 1979, Abidjan 01; tel. 32-12-39; Pres. CLAUDE PAINPARAY.

Syndicat des Industriels de la Côte d'Ivoire: 01 BP 1340, Abidjan 01; tel. 35-71-42; Pres. RÉMY LAUBER; Sec.-Gen. PHILIPPE MEYER.

Syndicat des Producteurs Industriels du Bois: 1 ave Noguès, 01 BP 318, Abidjan 01; tel. 32-12-39; f. 1973; Pres. ISIDORO BIANCHI.

Union des Employeurs Agricoles et Forestiers: ave Noguès, 01 BP 2300, Abidjan 01; tel. 32-26-42; f. 1952; Pres. JEAN-BAPTISTE AMETHIER.

Union Patronale de Côte d'Ivoire (UPACI): 01 BP 1340, Abidjan 01; tel. 35-71-42; telex 43280; fmrly Association Interprofessionnelle des Employeurs de la Côte d'Ivoire (AICI); Pres. J. AKA ANGHUI; Sec.-Gen. P. MEYER.

TRADE UNION

Union Générale des Travailleurs de Côte d'Ivoire (UGTCI): 05 BP 1203, Abidjan 05; f. 1962; 100,000 individual mems; 190 affiliated unions; Sec.-Gen. ADIKO NIAMKEY.

Transport

RAILWAYS

Régie des Chemins de Fer Abidjan-Niger (RAN): 01 BP 1394, Abidjan 01; tel. 32-02-45; telex 23564; f. 1904; 1,156 km of track linking Abidjan to Ouagadougou, in Burkina Faso, and also carrying traffic for Mali and Niger; work on a 375-km extension to Tambao was begun in 1985; Chair. D. BONI; Man. Dir L. KONATÉ.

ROADS

In 1984 there were 53,736 km of roads, of which 6,330 km were main or national roads and 128 km motorways.

Société Ivoirienne de Transports Publics: 01 BP 2949, Abidjan 01; tel. 35-33-68; telex 23685; f. 1964; road transport; Chair. JOSEPH ALLOU BRIGHT; Dir BASILE ABRE.

SHIPPING

There are two major ports, Abidjan and San Pedro. Abidjan is the largest port in West Africa, and has a rapidly growing container traffic (over 9m. metric tons in 1980). It has 5,485 m of quays and a depth of 15 m in the Vridi channel. Work began in 1980 on special quays at Locodjoro, Abidjan. The port at San Pedro is also being extended.

Port Autonome d'Abidjan: BP V85, Abidjan; tel. 32-01-66; telex 22778; f. 1950; public undertaking supervised by the navy; Man. Dir JEAN-MICHEL MOULOD.

Port Autonome de San Pedro: BP 339, San Pedro; tel. 71-14-79; f. 1971; Man. Dir KOFFI KOUASSI.

Compagnie Maritime Africaine-Côte d'Ivoire (COMAF-CI): 08 BP 867, Abidjan 08; tel. 32-40-77; f. 1973; navigational equipment and management of ships; Dirs FRANCO BERNARDINI, FRANCESCO GUARDIONE.

Société Agence Maritime de l'Ouest Africain Côte d'Ivoire (SAMOA-CI): rue des Gallions, 01 BP 1611, Abidjan 01; tel. 33-29-65; telex 23765; f. 1955; agents for Gold Star Line, Lloyd Triestino, Seven Star Line; Man. Dir C. PERDRIAUD.

Société Ivoirienne de Navigation Maritime (SIVOMAR): 01 BP 1395, Abidjan 01; tel. 32-73-23; telex 22226; f. 1977; services to Mediterranean and Far East; Dir SIMPLICE ZINSOU.

Société Ivoirienne de Transport Maritime (SITRAM): ave Lamblin, 01 BP 1546, Abidjan 01; tel. 36-92-00; telex 22132; f. 1967, nationalized 1976; services between Europe and West Africa; owns 9 cargo, passenger/cargo and reefer ships; Chair B. PEGAWAGNABA; Dir MATHIAS AHIBE.

Société Ouest-Africaine d'Entreprises Maritimes et de Transit en Côte d'Ivoire (SOAEM-CI TRANSIT): 01 BP 1477, Abidjan 01; tel. 32-59-69; telex 23654; f. 1978; merchandise handling, transit and storage; Dir MICHEL FIEMEYER.

SOCOPAO Côte d'Ivoire: 01 BP 1297, Abidjan; tel. 32-02-11; telex 23745; agents for Italian West Africa Line, K Line, Palm Line, Splošna Plovba; air and sea freight transport; Dir J. GUY VIOULES.

Transcap-CI-Shipping: 01 BP 358, Abidjan 01; tel. 32-69-16; telex 23648; f. 1960; agents for Elder Dempster Lines, Barber Line, Guinea Gulf Line, Mitsui-OSK Line, Palm Line, Nautilus Line, Nigerian National Lines, Black Star Lines, Naviera García Minaur (Madrid), Krag Shipping (Denmark), Nigerian Green Lines; Dir C. VASSEROT.

CIVIL AVIATION

There is an international airport at Abidjan–Port-Bouët. There are regional airports at Berebi, Bouaké, Daloa, Korhogo, Man, Odienne, San Pedro, Sassandra, Tabou and Yamoussoukro. Contracts have been awarded by the Government for the construction of a new international airport at Abidjan, and design proposals are being studied.

Air Afrique (Société Aérienne Africaine Multinationale): 3 ave Joseph Anoma, 01 BP 3927, Abidjan 01; tel. 32-09-00; telex 23785; f. 1961; services between 22 African countries and to Canary Islands, France, Italy, Switzerland and the USA; Chair. and Gen. Man. (vacant); fleet of 1 DC-8-63F, 3 DC-8-50, 1 DC-8-50F, 3 DC-10-30, 1 Boeing 747-200F, 3 Airbus A-300 Super B-4, 2 727-200.

Air Afrique was established by an agreement between SODETRAF (Société pour le Développement du Transport Aérien en Afrique) and 11 states, members of the Organisation Commune Africaine et Mauricienne (OCAM), who each had a 6% share; Togo joined later, Cameroon withdrew in 1971 and Gabon in 1976. SODETRAF has a 28% share and the following states each has a 7.2% holding: Benin, Burkina Faso, the Central African Republic, Chad, the Congo, the Ivory Coast, Mauritania, Niger, Senegal, Togo.

Air Ivoire: 13 ave Barthe, 01 BP 1027, Abidjan 01; tel. 32-34-29; telex 23727; f. 1960, government-owned since January 1976; internal flights and services to Bamako (Mali) and Ouagadougou (Burkina Faso); Man. Dir Col ABDOULAYE COULIBALY; fleet of 2 Fokker F28-4000, 2 F28-1000, 2 F27-600, 1 F27-400; 1 Beech Super King Air 200.

Tourism

Direction de la Promotion Touristique et de l'Artisanat d'Art: BP V184, Abidjan; tel. 32-07-33; telex 23438; Dir PIERRE POOULOU.

JAMAICA

Introductory Survey

Location, Climate, Language, Religion, Flag, Capital

Jamaica is the third largest island in the Caribbean Sea, lying 145 km (90 miles) to the south of Cuba and 160 km (100 miles) to the south-west of Haiti. The climate varies with altitude, being tropical at sea-level and temperate in the mountain areas. The average annual temperature is 27°C (80°F) and mean annual rainfall is 198 cm (78 inches). The official language is English, although a local patois is widely spoken. The majority of the population belong to Christian churches, of which the Anglican Communion is the strongest. There is also a large community of Rastafarians. The national flag (proportions 2 by 1) consists of a diagonal gold cross on a background of black (left and right) and green (above and below). The capital is Kingston.

Recent History

A British colony from 1655, the island consisted mainly of large plantations, worked by African slaves, with absentee landlords. Wars and unrest in the 18th century ended with the abolition of slavery in 1834 and the declaration of complete freedom for slaves in 1838. Business flourished and the island became prosperous. An earthquake in 1907, crop disease, and the slump of the 1930s led to a period of economic instability which culminated in riots in 1938, the beginnings of rival political parties and a great increase in trade union activity. Plans for independence were made in the 1940s. Internal self-government was achieved in 1959 and full independence, within the Commonwealth, on 6 August 1962. In 1958 Jamaica joined with Trinidad, Barbados, the Leeward Islands and the Windward Islands to form the West Indies Federation. Jamaica seceded in 1961, following a referendum, and the Federation broke up.

The two dominant political figures after the Second World War were the late Sir Alexander Bustamante, leader of the Jamaica Labour Party (JLP), who retired as Prime Minister in 1967, and Norman Manley, a former Premier and leader of the People's National Party (PNP), who died in 1969. The JLP won the elections of 1962 and 1967 but, under the premiership of Hugh Shearer, it lost the elections of February 1972 to the PNP, led by Michael Manley, the son of Norman Manley. Michael Manley was an advocate of democratic socialism and his government put great emphasis on social reform and economic independence.

The early 1970s were marked by escalating street violence and crime, with gang warfare rife in the slum areas of Kingston. Between January and June 1976 162 people were killed, and in June the Government declared a state of public emergency. Despite the unrest, high unemployment and severe economic stagnation, the PNP was returned to power in December 1976 with an increased majority. The state of emergency was lifted in June 1977. By January 1979, however, there was again widespread political unrest, and violent demonstrations signalled growing discontent with the Manley Government.

In February 1980, with a worsening economic crisis, Manley rejected the IMF's conditions for further loans to Jamaica and called a general election to seek support for his economic policies and his decision to end dependence on the IMF. The electoral campaign was one of the most violent in Jamaica's history, although the level of violence dropped after a joint plea by Manley and Edward Seaga, leader of the opposition JLP, to their supporters for an end to the bloodshed. In the October election, in contrast to the close result predicted, the JLP had a decisive victory, receiving about 57% of the total votes and winning 51 of the 60 seats in the House of Representatives. Seaga was thus given a convincing mandate to implement his policies for a return to close political and economic links with the USA and the promotion of free enterprise. Diplomatic relations with Cuba were severed in October 1981, and Jamaica was seen to be moving nearer to the USA, with whose financial support the Seaga administration was giving a credible economic performance. The PNP, wishing to regain support, dissociated itself from the communist Workers' Party of Jamaica (WPJ) in an attempt to win back its more moderate voters. Electoral reforms were also called for, and a new electoral roll was to be completed before the next general election, due in 1985.

In November 1983, when only 70% of this work was complete, the JLP called an early election, to be held on 15 December. Only four days were allowed for the nomination of candidates. The PNP, unable to put up candidates at such short notice, refused to take part and declared the elections void. The JLP, opposed by minor independent candidates in only six constituencies, won all 60 seats in the House of Representatives and formed a one-party legislature. The PNP claimed that the JLP had broken an agreement not to use the old electoral lists, which, they stated, were inaccurate and disenfranchised many voters. Manley announced that the PNP would undertake extraparliamentary opposition to the JLP Government. At the inauguration of the new Parliament in January 1984, there were violent demonstrations by about 7,000 PNP supporters, led by Michael Manley.

Devaluations of the Jamaican dollar, and the withdrawal of food subsidies, provoked demonstrations and sporadic violence as the prices of foodstuffs and energy increased by between 50% and 100%. In order to offset the effects of economic austerity measures, imposed at the instigation of the IMF, the Government extended its programme of food stamps to cover more than one-half of the population. Unemployment, and the consequences of illicit trading in drugs, contributed to a rise in the incidence of crime and violence, especially in Kingston. The Government increased its powers to combat political and violent crime, although the measures were criticized as autocratic by the PNP. The PNP warned of social instability as a result of Seaga's economic policies, and argued for the need to hold fresh elections after the completion of the new electoral roll, while opinion polls highlighted the unpopularity of the Seaga administration. In January 1985 violent demonstrations erupted again in Kingston after a further rise in the price of petrol. Widespread opposition by government employees to redundancies, price rises and wage restraint led to a virtual general strike in June, organized by six major trade unions. Seaga remained unmoved and stressed the necessity for further austerity.

In May 1986, however, Seaga defied recommendations by the IMF, the World Bank and the US Agency for International Development for a continuation of restrictive policies, and, instead, introduced an expansionary budget for 1986/87, in an attempt to stimulate economic growth (see Economic Affairs). This move, however, was criticized by opposition parties. Municipal elections, originally scheduled for June 1984, were held in July 1986, having been postponed three times. The PNP obtained control of 11 of the 13 municipalities in which polling took place, winning 57% of the total votes. In the light of these results, Manley appealed again for an early general election (constitutionally due by October 1988) but this demand was ignored by Seaga. Further criticisms of government economic policies were expressed when large debt arrears to the IMF led to the suspension, in September, of the Fund's loan agreement. In October Seaga announced his decision to resign as Prime Minister in August 1987 but, following a unanimous vote by the JLP not to accept his resignation, the decision was withdrawn.

In October 1983 Jamaica contributed troops to the US-led invasion of Grenada and led the Caribbean force which remained, after the removal of the majority of the American forces, to keep the peace and to assist in training the new Grenadian police force.

Government

The Head of State is the British monarch, who is represented locally by a Governor-General, appointed on the recommendation of the Prime Minister. The Governor-General acts, in almost all matters, on the advice of the Cabinet.

Legislative power is vested in the bicameral Parliament: a Senate, with 21 appointed members, and a House of Representatives, with 60 elected members. Thirteen members of the Senate are appointed by the Governor-General on the advice of the Prime Minister and eight on the advice of the Leader of the Opposition. Members of the House are elected by universal adult suffrage for five years (subject to dissolution). Executive power lies with the Cabinet. The Governor-General appoints the Prime Minister and, on the latter's recommendation, other Ministers. The Cabinet is responsible to Parliament.

Defence

In July 1986 Jamaica had a total defence force of 3,130 men, including an army of 1,780, a navy of 150, an air force of 170 men and reserves of 1,030. There is also a mobile paramilitary reserve of 1,000 men (forming part of the police force). Defence expenditure in 1985/86 was estimated to be US $5.0m.

Economic Affairs

The economy is based mainly on sugar, bauxite and tourism. In 1984, according to estimates by the World Bank, Jamaica's gross national product (GNP) per head, measured at average 1982–84 prices, was US $1,150. In the period 1965–84 GNP per head was estimated to have fallen, in real terms, by an average of 0.4% per year.

The traditional major crops of the agricultural sector are sugar cane, bananas, coffee and cocoa. A wide range of citrus and tropical fruits and vegetables are also grown. In 1983 agricultural production accounted for 7.8% of Jamaica's gross domestic product (GDP), and the sector employed 33.3% of the population. Sugar production has been affected by the low international prices and by poor crops. Jamaica's annual output of raw sugar declined from 290,000 metric tons in 1978 to 197,000 tons in 1982, and in 1984 the crop yielded only 190,000 tons. In 1985, however, production rose by 12.2%, to 206,707 tons, and export earnings increased from J$ 226.2m. in 1984 to J$ 273.2m. The Government has closed all but two of the state-run sugar factories, in an attempt to restructure the industry, and in June 1986 announced plans for a six-year scheme to improve efficiency. This was to include the rehabilitation of two factories, the improvement of irrigation systems and an increase in research. The scheme aimed to achieve production of 220,000 tons of raw sugar per year, to cover EEC and US quotas and domestic demands.

Jamaica's banana plantations were damaged by Hurricane Allen in 1980, and the country's annual exports fell from the usual level of 70,000 tons to 19,000 tons in 1981, rising to only 23,000 tons in 1983, as output continued to be depressed by poor prices and high production costs. Exports fell to 14,000 tons in 1984, but soared in 1985 to 40,000 tons. Cocoa production in 1983 reached 2,782 tons, the highest yield for 20 years. Coffee is being developed with aid from Japan, the principal market for Jamaica's Blue Mountain coffee. In 1983 3,231 tons were produced. Local rice production is being increased in order to reduce Jamaica's imports (up to 53,000 tons per year) by more than one-half. Production in 1985 reached 13,500 tons, an increase of 237% on the 1984 total. Since 1980 the Government has encouraged the diversification of crops, the improvement of techniques and the cultivation of under-used land, in order to reduce the country's growing demand for imported food. During 1986, however, several government agricultural projects experienced difficulties. The most significant of these was a US $30m. joint venture with Israeli investors, which was begun in 1982 and was designed to demonstrate the island's potential for the production of vegetables, fruit and fish, using the latest technology. The collapse of this project was announced in August 1986. Severe flooding during June was estimated to have caused agricultural losses of J$ 124m. In November the Inter-American Development Bank (IDB) approved a US$ 16.2m. loan to help finance an agricultural credit programme, designed to stimulate farm production.

Jamaica is one of the world's largest producers of bauxite and alumina, and production levies make the industry an important source of government revenue. Exports of bauxite and alumina contribute, in normal years, 75% of total foreign exchange earnings. However, the slump in the international aluminium market has led to reduced demand and total bauxite production has fallen substantially, from 12m. tons in 1980 to an estimated 7.5m. tons in 1983. In 1984 output rose to 8.6m. tons, owing to purchases by the USA and USSR for their respective strategic mineral stockpiles, although net earnings fell by 12%, to US $220m. Production of alumina fell to 1.69m. tons in 1984, and a number of the country's refineries were operating below full capacity. In March Reynolds Metals declared its intention to cease mining operations in Jamaica because of the poor international market for bauxite. In February 1985 the Aluminium Company of America (Alcoa) announced its intention to close its alumina refinery. After negotiations with the Government, it was agreed to reopen the plant under state ownership and managed by Alcoa. In August the alumina refinery owned by Alumina Partners of Jamaica (Alpart) ceased production, owing to the falling international price of alumina. However, it was hoped that the refinery would be reopened in early 1987. A reduction in mining activity during 1985 led to a fall in bauxite output to 6.14m. tons in that year, with export earnings of only US $145m. Production of alumina also continued to decline, with exports falling to 730,707 tons, from 815,823 tons in 1984. In March 1986 the Government announced its intention to reopen any mines or refineries that had been abandoned by multinational companies, and in September it agreed to a reduction in the production levy on bauxite. During 1986 total bauxite production was estimated to have increased by 11.4%, to 6.95m. tons.

Tourism is a major earner of foreign exchange. An influx of tourists in 1978 was followed by a record figure in 1979, but in 1980 the industry was again suffering the effects of political unrest in the capital. By 1981 it was showing some recovery, and in 1982, owing partly to a US $12m. foreign advertising campaign, arrivals soared by 60% to 650,000. Tourist arrivals increased by a further 21% in 1983, and also rose during 1984 to reach 843,775. There was an increase of 13.2% in the number of cruiseship passenger arrivals during 1985, but the number of stop-over visitors fell by 5.3% and tourist arrivals totalled 833,221. Gross earnings from tourism rose to US $435m. in 1984, from $399m. in 1983, but fell to $394m. in 1985.

Manufacturing is an expanding sector, and includes cement, textiles, tobacco and a number of consumer goods. 'Free zones' were set up at Kingston and Montego Bay, and a wide range of manufacturing and assembly industries were encouraged by the Government. Plans for a third 'free zone', at Spanish Town, were announced in 1986. Although by 1985 250 new companies had started production since 1980, average investment has been small, and the promised benefits of the US Government's Caribbean Basin Initiative (CBI) have proved disappointing. It was hoped, however, that exports of garments to the USA would increase significantly during 1987, following the signing of a bilateral agreement in May 1986. Trade is chiefly with the USA, Canada and the United Kingdom. A joint consortium of US and Italian companies failed to find commercially exploitable offshore deposits of petroleum to ease Jamaica's high import bill for petroleum. Further explorations off-shore were to continue, financed by Canada.

The cultivation of hemp (marijuana), and the use of Jamaica as a transit centre for the movement of illegal drugs, has posed a serious problem for the Government. It has been estimated that marijuana worth US $750m. is exported to the USA annually, making it unofficially the country's largest export earner. In 1984 1,091 acres (442 ha) of cultivated marijuana were destroyed by the authorities, 450,000 lb (204 metric tons) of cured marijuana were seized, and 4,451 people were arrested for drug-related offences.

The decline in production of Jamaica's traditional export crops and industries, and low international prices, has been compounded by the rising level of imports. As a result, the current deficit on the balance of payments grew from US $42.1m. in 1977 to $408.5m. in 1982. The dramatic devaluations of the Jamaica dollar in 1983 and 1984 (see below), while assisting the competitiveness of Jamaican export industries, increased the cost of imports, especially of petroleum and foodstuffs, which comprise about 50% of total imports. The price of staple foods, such as rice and chicken, rose sharply in 1984. Petrol prices increased by 50% in January 1984, and by a further 21% in 1985. However, the merchandise trade deficit was reduced from US $441.5m. in 1982 to $334.7m. in 1984. Although imports were reduced in 1985, a fall of 20% in the value of exports increased the trade deficit to US $430.2m. A fall in the world price of crude petroleum during 1986 enabled the Government to reduce the cost of oil purchases by 45%. In the 1986/87 budget, price reductions on basic commodities were announced, as a result of these savings. The Government also announced a 4% reduction in the statutory 20% interest rate payable on savings by commercial banks. This was reduced to 15% in July. High interest rates, and other financial problems caused by the devaluation of the currency, have resulted in curbs on manufacturing output and development, and threatened this success.

The Jamaican economy suffered from a prolonged recession during the 1970s, and by 1980 was in a state of crisis. The Government's budget balance had moved from a current surplus of J $11.8m. in 1976 to a deficit of J $180.6m. in 1978, and Jamaica was forced to borrow heavily from the international community. Unemployment had risen to 27.8% of the workforce by 1978, and the rate of inflation was estimated at about 30%. The JLP Government, on coming to power in 1980, prepared a three-year economic recovery plan which called for a considerable injection of foreign investment into the private sector. In 1980 the PNP Government had rejected the terms of an IMF support package, but the JLP Government reopened negotiations and secured a three-year agreement worth US $650m. The restoration of Jamaica's credit with the IMF encouraged aid from Western countries: US aid in 1982 totalled US $144m., the highest in Central and Latin America. The full potential of foreign investment in export manufacturing industries, however, was not realized, and in September 1983 the economy failed to meet the IMF's conditions for further payments, achieving average growth rates of only 1.5% per year, and failing to produce the promised current surplus on the balance of payments. An IMF stand-by agreement for US $143m. was finalized in April. The conditions for the agreement included a reduction of the budget deficit by half, from an equivalent of 15.4% of GDP, within a year. The Government therefore introduced a package of public spending cuts, increases in taxes, and the removal of subsidies on food. Although the Jamaican economy failed to meet all the IMF requirements in the September test period, the Fund granted a technical waiver to allow further payments to be made. Another agreement was reached for facilities of US $115m. over a 22-month period, commencing in July 1985, subject to continued restraints on government spending. Although the Jamaican economy failed the quarterly performance test in September 1985 and payments were temporarily suspended, a waiver of the IMF-imposed conditions was granted. The economy passed the December test, postponed until January 1986, satisfying the condition that a positive balance of payments of US $60m. should be shown for 1985. In addition, the budget deficit was reduced to 5.7% of GDP. Despite recommendations by officials of the IMF, the World Bank and the US Agency for International Development (USAID) for continued economic austerity, the 1986/87 budget proposals, presented in May 1986, introduced an increase in capital expenditure, a cut in interest rates and reductions in commodity prices. The Government claimed that these expansionary measures could produce an annual growth rate of 5% in real GDP. By September, however, Jamaica had incurred debt arrears of US $70m. in its payments to the IMF, making the withdrawal of new payments and the servicing of external debts virtually impossible, although an agreement was signed in October for US $60m. to be paid in two loans by the World Bank. Jamaica's gross external debt in 1982 reached US $2,300m. By 1985 it was estimated to have risen to $3,200m., causing a heavy burden of servicing payments, equivalent to about 34% of export earnings for the financial year 1985/86.

The overvaluation of the Jamaican dollar, in relation to the US dollar, led to the creation in January 1983 of a 'parallel market' in exchange rates in order to attract foreign exchange earnings back into Jamaica's banks. By November, however, the exchange rate had not stabilized and, to comply with IMF requirements, the official and 'parallel' exchange rates were unified. As a result, the Jamaican dollar was effectively devalued by 43%. Further smaller devaluations continued during 1984 and 1985, reducing the exchange rate for one US dollar from J $1.78 in November 1983 to J $5.76 by July 1985. After a rapid decline in the Jamaican dollar's value in October, the Government intervened to stabilize the exchange rate at US $1 = J $5.50, which it pledged to maintain during the financial year 1986/87. Negotiations with the IMF in October 1986, to discuss the renewal of the suspended loan agreement, reached deadlock when the Government refused to comply with the IMF's demand for an immediate currency devaluation of 9.2%, although it was willing to devalue in the financial year 1987/88. The Government argued, instead, in favour of a wage 'freeze' and the removal of price controls. In January 1987, however, a new 15-month agreement with the IMF was announced, giving access to credits of US $132.8m. Although no devaluation of the Jamaican dollar was imposed, it was stipulated that the annual rate of inflation should be kept below 7% in 1987, by means of price controls and limits on pay increases. In addition, import duties and corporate taxes were to be reduced. Inflation, which had been running at 30% in 1980, had fallen to 6.5% in 1982. However, the depreciation of the currency, and the rise in prices, caused increases in the rate of inflation, which rose to 16.5% in 1983, and to an average of 31.2% in 1984. In 1985, however, inflation fell to an average of 23%. In spite of government incentives to create jobs, unemployment affected 25.6% of the labour force by the end of 1985. GDP, measured in constant prices, contracted by 5.4% in 1980, but grew by 1.5% in 1981, and by 0.5% in 1982. After growth of 2.0% in 1983, GDP contracted by 0.4% during 1984 and by 3.7% in 1985, owing to the recession in the bauxite industry.

Jamaica is a member of the Organization of American States (see p. 189), the Caribbean Common Market (CARICOM, p. 108) and the International Bauxite Association (p. 222).

Social Welfare

Social welfare is undertaken by the Government. The Social Development Commission arranges and co-ordinates social welfare in the villages. Contributory national insurance and housing trust schemes are run by the Government. In 1979 Jamaica had 30 government-controlled hospitals, with a total of 7,648 beds, and there were 759 physicians working in the country.

Education

Primary education is compulsory in certain districts, and free education is ensured. The education system consists of a primary cycle of six years, followed by two secondary cycles of three and four years respectively. In 1980 an estimated 93% of children between six and 11 years of age were enrolled at primary schools, while 56% of those aged 12 to 18 attended secondary schools. In 1981 only 2% of the adult population had received no schooling. Higher education is provided by technical colleges and by the University of the West Indies, which has five faculties situated at its Mona campus in Kingston. Expenditure on education in 1980 was J $303.8m., or 13.1% of total government spending. In 1986 the Government announced that students were to be charged higher education fees, covering up to 30% of tuition costs. The new fees were to be introduced progressively, over two years at the technical colleges and over three years at the University.

Tourism

Jamaica attracts many tourists, mainly from the USA, to its beaches, mountains and historic buildings. In 1985 the island received 833,221 foreign visitors, including cruise passengers. Revenue from tourism in 1985 was US $394m. Hotel proprietors receive tax concessions to encourage development. During 1986 the Government announced several tourism development plans, including proposals to construct a J $100m. tourist complex at Montego Bay.

Public Holidays

1987: 1 January (New Year's Day), 4 March (Ash Wednesday), 17–20 April (Easter), 23 May (Labour Day), 3 August (for Independence Day), 19 October (National Heroes' Day), 25–26 December (Christmas).

JAMAICA

1988: 1 January (New Year's Day), 17 February (Ash Wednesday), 1–4 April (Easter), 23 May (Labour Day), 8 August (for Independence Day), 17 October (for National Heroes' Day), 25–26 December (Christmas).

Weights and Measures
Both the imperial and the metric systems are in use.

Currency and Exchange Rates
100 cents = 1 Jamaican dollar (J $).

Exchange rates (30 September 1986):
  £1 sterling = J $7.915;
  US $1 = J $5.470.

JAMAICA

Statistical Survey

Source (unless otherwise stated): Department of Statistics, 9 Swallowfield Rd, Kingston, Jamaica; tel. 926-2175.

Area and Population

AREA, POPULATION AND DENSITY

Area (sq km)	10,991*
Population (census results)	
7 April 1970	1,848,512
8 June 1982	2,095,878
Population (official estimates at 31 December)	
1984	2,190,000
Density (per sq km) at 31 December 1984	199.3

* 4,243.6 sq miles.

PARISHES

	Area (sq miles)	Population (31 Dec. 1977)
Kingston	8.406	643,809
St Andrew	186.308	
St Thomas	286.800	78,050
Portland	314.347	74,781
St Mary	235.745	108,913
St Ann	468.213	134,314
Trelawny	337.651	67,562
St James	229.728	122,794
Hanover	173.855	64,219
Westmorland	311.604	121,585
St Elizabeth	468.085	138,952
Manchester	320.482	142,551
Clarendon	461.864	193,850
St Catherine	460.396	217,903
Total	4,263.484*	2,109,283

* Other sources give the total area of the country as 4,243.6 square miles.
Capital: Kingston (population 111,879 at 1970 census).
Other towns: Montego Bay (42,800); Spanish Town (41,600).

BIRTHS, MARRIAGES AND DEATHS*

	Registered live births		Registered marriages		Registered deaths	
	Number	Rate (per 1,000)	Number	Rate (per 1,000)	Number	Rate (per 1,000)
1974	61,506	30.8	9,021	4.5	14,374	7.2
1975	61,462	30.3	10,188	5.0	14,004	6.9
1976	60,658	29.3	9,168	4.4	14,671	7.1
1977	60,500	28.9	8,820	4.2	14,200	6.8
1978	58,189	27.4	9,523	4.5	12,484	5.9
1979	58,257	26.9	8,949	4.1	13,297	6.2
1980	58,589	27.0	7,781	3.6	12,706	5.8
1981	58,955	26.8	7,020	3.2	13,453	6.1

1984: Live births 53,752; Deaths 12,305.

* Data are tabulated by year of registration rather than by year of occurrence.

CIVILIAN LABOUR FORCE (at October)*

	1980	1981	1982
Agriculture, forestry and fishing	288,800	285,000	278,100
Mining, quarrying and refining	9,400	9,300	8,500
Manufacturing	103,800	106,500	109,300
Construction and installation	38,100	41,600	45,600
Transport, communications and public utilities	39,900	39,400	40,900
Commerce	111,200	119,100	124,400
Public administration	139,800	139,000	133,700
Other services	165,600	169,700	178,900
Activities not adequately defined	4,000	6,600	6,400
Total	900,600	916,200	925,800

* Figures exclude persons seeking work for the first time (106,300 in 1980; 106,700 in 1981; 122,800 in 1982), but include other unemployed persons (164,500 in 1980; 154,800 in 1981).

Agriculture

PRINCIPAL CROPS ('000 metric tons)

	1983	1984	1985
Sweet potatoes	24	36	30*
Cassava	17	20	19*
Other roots and tubers	164	192	182*
Coconuts*	112	120*	120*
Vegetables and melons	117	147	136
Sugar cane	2,350	2,350†	2,350†
Oranges	32	32*	33*
Lemons and limes*	23	23	24
Grapefruit and pomelo	19	21*	22*
Bananas*	160	160	160
Coffee (green)	2	2†	2†

* FAO estimates.   † Unofficial figures.
Source: FAO, *Production Yearbook*.

LIVESTOCK
(FAO estimates, '000 head, year ending September)

	1983	1984	1985
Horses	4	4	4
Mules	10	10	10
Asses	24	24	23
Cattle	310	320	321
Pigs	230	235	238
Sheep	3	3	3
Goats	410	420	430
Poultry	5,000	5,000	5,000

Source: FAO, *Production Yearbook*.

LIVESTOCK PRODUCTS ('000 metric tons)

	1983	1984	1985
Beef and veal	14	16	16*
Goats' meat*	2	2	2
Pig meat	7	7	7*
Poultry meat	33	34	35*
Cows' milk	49	49*	50*
Hen eggs*	17.0	17.4	17.5

* FAO estimates.
Source: FAO, *Production Yearbook*.

Forestry

ROUNDWOOD REMOVALS ('000 cubic metres, excl. bark)

	1982	1983	1984
Total	43	102	117

Source: FAO, *Yearbook of Forest Products*.

Fishing

('000 metric tons, live weight)

	1982	1983	1984
Total catch	7.9	8.7	9.6

Source: FAO, *Yearbook of Fishery Statistics*.

Mining

('000 metric tons)

	1982	1983	1984
Bauxite*	8,334	7,531	8,605

* Dried equivalent of crude ore.
Source: UN, *Monthly Bulletin of Statistics*.

Industry

SELECTED PRODUCTS

		1981	1982	1983
Margarine and lard	'000 metric tons	6.7	8.3	8.4
Crude vegetable oil	'000 kilolitres	13	11	13
Wheat flour	'000 metric tons	45	55	62
Other flour	'000 metric tons	22	21	n.a.
Raw sugar	'000 metric tons	204	198	202
Animal foodstuffs	'000 metric tons	190	184	217
Rum and gin	'000 hectolitres	222	173	147
Beer	'000 hectolitres	552	581	604
Soft drinks	'000 hectolitres	385	373	393
Cigars	million	11	21	19
Cigarettes	million	1,246	1,340	1,359
Woven cotton fabrics	'000 metres	4	4	4
Footwear	'000 pairs	890	592	600*
Jet fuels	'000 metric tons	50	40	50
Motor gasoline (Petrol)	'000 metric tons	160	150	150
Kerosene	'000 metric tons	80	75	80
Distillate fuel oils	'000 metric tons	200	190	200
Residual fuel oils	'000 metric tons	375	355	370
Lubricating oils	'000 metric tons	28	25	25
Bitumen (Asphalt)	'000 metric tons	14	15	18
Liquefied petroleum gas	'000 metric tons	20*	20*	20*
Rubber tyres	'000	232	215	195
Quicklime	'000 metric tons	132	114	109*
Cement	'000 metric tons	168	236	277
Electric energy	million kWh	2,225	2,250	2,350

* Estimates.
Source: UN, *Industrial Statistics Yearbook*.

JAMAICA   *Statistical Survey*

Finance

CURRENCY AND EXCHANGE RATES

Monetary Units
100 cents = 1 Jamaican dollar (J $).

Denominations
Coins: 1, 5, 10, 20, 25 and 50 cents.
Notes: 50 cents; 1, 2, 5, 10, 20 and 100 dollars.

Sterling and US Dollar Equivalents (30 September 1986)
£1 sterling = J $7.915;
US $1 = J $5.470;
J $100 = £12.63 = US $18.28.

Average Exchange Rate (J $ per US $)
1983   1.9322
1984   3.9428
1985   5.5586

Note: Since November 1983, when the previous official and 'parallel' market rates were unified, the exchange rate has been determined by the commercial banks in an auction market.

COST OF LIVING (Consumer Price Index; end of December. Base: January 1975 = 100)

	1981	1982	1983
Food and drink	353.0	379.5	445.1
Fuel and household supplies	400.6	427.1	519.7
Housing	230.2	252.1	272.1
Household furnishings and furniture	417.3	434.3	508.7
Personal clothing and accessories	327.1	337.4	384.7
Personal expenses	327.2	346.7	424.6
Transport	287.8	326.2	383.5
Miscellaneous expenses	274.8	286.3	313.6
All items	332.7	356.0	415.3

BUDGET (J $ million, year ending 31 March)

Revenue	1980/81
Recurrent Revenue:	
Customs	42.5
Excise duties	16.9
Income tax	471.1
Land and property tax	25.0
Stamp duties	37.3
Motor vehicle licences	14.8
Consumption duty	271.0
Entertainment tax	17.1
Retail sales tax	12.6
Other taxes and duties	15.4
Sub-total	923.6
Non-tax receipts	41.2
Transfer from Capital Development Fund	230.6
Capital Revenue	108.4
Total	1,303.8

Expenditure	1980/81
Recurrent Expenditure:	
Interest on public debt	414.6
General administration	383.7
Public order and safety	201.9
Agriculture	43.8
Education and social welfare	337.0
Public health	175.2
Trade and industry	15.2
Communications	39.4
Housing	40.1
Other	27.0
Sub-total	1,677.9
Capital Expenditure:	
General administration	132.3
Agriculture	82.3
Education and social welfare	18.3
Housing	92.1
Health	7.6
Communications	19.5
Financing of public enterprises	42.4
Public debt	227.1
Sub-total	687.7
Total	2,365.6

NATIONAL ACCOUNTS (J $ million at current prices)

	1982	1983	1984
Government final consumption expenditure	1,288.0	1,421.1	1,577.8
Private final consumption expenditure	4,019.2	4,832.7	6,103.8
Increase in stocks	45.9	69.7	143.7
Gross fixed capital formation	1,167.8	1,417.4	1,962.5
Total domestic expenditure	6,520.9	7,740.9	9,787.8
Exports of goods and services	2,239.9	2,621.1	5,154.9
Less Imports of goods and services	2,918.9	3,465.0	5,574.9
Gross domestic product	5,841.9	6,897.0	9,367.8
Net factor income from abroad	−322.4	−299.4	−1,193.4
Gross national product	5,519.5	6,597.6	8,174.4

Source: IMF, *International Financial Statistics*.

JAMAICA

Statistical Survey

BALANCE OF PAYMENTS (US $ million)

	1983	1984	1985
Merchandise exports f.o.b.	685.7	702.3	568.6
Merchandise imports f.o.b.	−1,124.2	−1,037.0	−998.8
Trade balance	**−438.5**	**−334.7**	**−430.2**
Exports of services	646.5	632.9	521.8
Imports of services	−664.6	−750.9	−282.6
Balance on goods and services	**−456.6**	**−452.7**	**−191.0**
Private unrequited transfers (net)	94.7	80.4	92.0
Government unrequited transfers (net)	3.2	37.1	77.5
Current balance	**−358.7**	**−335.3**	**−21.5**
Direct capital investment (net)	−18.7	12.2	⎱ −273.5
Other long-term capital (net)	89.5	377.8	⎰
Short-term capital (net)	−73.1	160.5	31.5
Net errors and omissions	−0.9	−64.0	204.4
Total (net monetary movements)	**−361.9**	**151.2**	**−59.1**
Valuation changes (net)	15.9	52.5	−33.5
Exceptional financing	253.5	−131.1	100.7
Official financing (net)	−24.8	1.5	−13.4
Changes in reserves	**−117.4**	**74.1**	**−5.2**

Source: IMF, *International Financial Statistics*.

External Trade

COMMODITY GROUPS (J $'000)

Imports	1981	1982	1983
Food and live animals	408,234	390,793	392,226
Beverages and tobacco	14,999	17,392	19,342
Crude materials (inedible) except fuels	76,610	76,680	96,561
Mineral fuels, lubricants, etc.	886,096	759,243	857,400
Animal and vegetable oils and fats	28,673	24,696	31,496
Chemicals	324,151	275,728	291,366
Basic manufactures	388,860	363,622	460,710
Machinery and transport equipment	389,065	421,814	521,772
Miscellaneous manufactured articles	88,911	98,606	118,423
Other commodities and transactions	17,769	31,735	46,423
Total	**2,623,368**	**2,460,309**	**2,840,991**

Exports	1981	1982	1983
Food and live animals	165,229	175,673	234,555
Beverages and tobacco	58,515	57,948	75,587
Crude materials (inedible) except fuels	1,362,761	924,371	837,624
Mineral fuels, lubricants, etc.	30,299	38,937	54,754
Animal and vegetable oils and fats	118	115	56
Chemicals	28,547	39,932	47,823
Basic manufactures	26,390	24,122	33,341
Machinery and transport equipment	23,443	46,337	33,588
Miscellaneous manufactured articles	39,685	59,558	74,397
Other commodities and transactions	76	4	25
Total	**1,735,064**	**1,366,997**	**1,392,050**

PRINCIPAL TRADING PARTNERS (J $'000)

Imports	1982	1983
Canada	107,885	121,268
Japan	99,130	109,373
Netherlands	29,055	18,324
Netherlands Antilles	324,187	307,994
Trinidad and Tobago	103,535	63,721
United Kingdom	191,842	190,484
USA	868,860	1,111,374
Venezuela	353,345	313,769
Total (incl. others)	**2,460,309**	**2,840,991**

Exports*	1982	1983
Barbados	19,319	27,551
Canada	159,139	166,475
Ghana	51,584	13,843
Germany, Federal Republic	6,659	7,195
Norway	108,489	113,345
Trinidad and Tobago	96,320	127,001
United Kingdom	250,536	272,503
USA	441,720	455,518
Venezuela	18,743	11,188
Total (incl. others)	**1,328,108**	**1,363,671**

* Excluding re-exports.

Transport

RAILWAYS
(1977): 1.2m. passengers carried; 83m. net passenger-km; 186m. net freight ton-km.

ROAD TRAFFIC
(vehicles in use at 31 December 1984)

Passenger Cars	40,271
Buses and coaches	
Goods vehicles	29,709
Tractors (non-agricultural)	
Motocycles and scooters	4,554

Source: IRF, *World Road Statistics*.

SHIPPING
International Sea-borne Freight Traffic
(estimates, '000 metric tons)

	1981	1982	1983
Goods loaded	9,190	6,965	6,905
Goods unloaded	4,024	4,169	3,468

Source: UN, *Monthly Bulletin of Statistics*.

CIVIL AVIATION (traffic on scheduled services)

	1982	1983	1984
Kilometres flown (million)	14.5	9.8	10.4
Passengers carried ('000)	873	716	747
Passenger-km (million)	1,230	1,079	1,303
Freight ton-km (million)	11.6	16.6	19.5

Source: UN, *Statistical Yearbook*.

Tourism

Total number of visitors (1985): 833,221.

Communications Media

RADIO RECEIVERS
(1983): 856,960 in use.

TELEVISION RECEIVERS
(1983): 160,000 in use.

TELEPHONES
(1980): 119,000 in use.

DAILY NEWSPAPERS
(1982): 3 (estimated daily circulation 104,000).
Source: UNESCO, *Statistical Yearbook*.

Education

(1980)

	Institutions	Teachers	Students
Basic schools	1,190	n.a.	119,508
Primary	894	8,676	359,488
Secondary	n.a.	7,525	248,001
Tertiary	11	n.a.	9,451
University	1	397	4,548

Directory

The Constitution

The Constitution came into force at the independence of Jamaica on 6 August 1962.

HEAD OF STATE

The Head of State is the British monarch, who is locally represented by a Governor-General, appointed on the recommendation of the Jamaican Prime Minister.

THE LEGISLATURE

The Senate or Upper House consists of 21 Senators of whom 13 will be appointed by the Governor-General on the advice of the Prime Minister and eight by the Governor-General on the advice of the Leader of the Opposition.

The House of Representatives consists of 60 elected members called Members of Parliament.

A person is qualified for appointment to the Senate or for election to the House of Representatives if he or she is a citizen of Jamaica or other Commonwealth country, of the age of 21 or more and has been ordinarily resident in Jamaica for the immediately preceding 12 months.

THE PRIVY COUNCIL

The Privy Council consists of six members appointed by the Governor-General after consultation with the Prime Minister, of whom at least two are persons who hold or who have held public office. The functions of the Council are to advise the Governor-General on the exercise of the Royal Prerogative of Mercy and on appeals on disciplinary matters from the three Service Commissions.

THE EXECUTIVE

The Prime Minister is appointed from the House of Representatives by the Governor-General as the person who, in the Governor-General's judgement, is best able to command the support of the majority of the members of that House.

The Leader of the Opposition is appointed by the Governor-General as the member of the House of Representatives who, in the Governor-General's judgement, is best able to command the support of the majority of those members of the House who do not support the Government.

The Cabinet consists of the Prime Minister and not fewer than 11 other Ministers appointed by the Governor-General on the advice of the Prime Minister.

THE JUDICATURE

The Judicature consists of a Supreme Court, a Court of Appeal and minor courts. Judicial matters, notably advice to the Governor-General on appointments, are considered by a Judicial Service Commission, the Chairman of which is the Chief Justice, members being the President of the Court of Appeal, the Chairman of the Public Service Commission and three others.

CITIZENSHIP

All persons born in Jamaica after independence automatically acquire Jamaican citizenship and there is also provision for the acquisition of citizenship by persons born outside Jamaica of Jamaican parents. Persons born in Jamaica (or persons born outside

JAMAICA

Jamaica of Jamaican parents) before independence who immediately prior to independence were citizens of the United Kingdom and colonies also automatically become citizens of Jamaica.

Appropriate provision is made which permits persons who do not automatically become citizens of Jamaica to be registered as such.

FUNDAMENTAL RIGHTS AND FREEDOMS

The Constitution includes provisions safeguarding the fundamental freedoms of the individual, irrespective of race, place of origin, political opinions, colour, creed or sex, subject only to respect for the rights and freedoms of others and for the public interest. The fundamental freedoms include the rights of life, liberty, security of the person and protection from arbitrary arrest or restriction of movement, the enjoyment of property and the protection of the law, freedom of conscience, of expression and of peaceful assembly and association, and respect for private and family life.

The Government

Head of State: HM Queen ELIZABETH II.

Governor-General: Sir FLORIZEL AUGUSTUS GLASSPOLE (took office 27 June 1973).

PRIVY COUNCIL OF JAMAICA

C. H. BROWNE, L. E. ASHENHEIM, Dr VERNON LINDO, EWART FORREST, QC, G. OWEN, W. H. SWABY.

THE CABINET
(February 1987)

Prime Minister, Minister of Finance and Planning, Information and Culture: EDWARD P. G. SEAGA.
Deputy Prime Minister and Minister of Foreign Affairs and Industry: HUGH L. SHEARER.
Minister of Construction (with responsibility for electoral matters): BRUCE GOLDING.
Minister of Public Service: CLIFTON STONE.
Minister of Labour: J. A. G. SMITH.
Minister of Education: NEVILLE GALLIMORE.
Minister of Community, Social Security and Consumer Affairs: MAVIS GILMOUR.
Minister of Health: KENNETH BAUGH.
Minister of Local Government: NEVILLE LEWIS.
Minister of Youth, Sports and Community Development: EDMUND BARTLETT.
Minister of Agriculture, Environment, Science and Technology: PERCIVAL BRODERICK.
Minister of Mining, Energy and Tourism: HUGH HART.
Minister of National Security: ERROL ANDERSON.
Minister of Justice and Attorney General: OSWALD HARDING.
Minister of Public Utilities and Transport: PEARNEL CHARLES.

MINISTRIES

Office of the Prime Minister: 1 Devon Rd, Kingston 10; tel. 927-9941; telex 2398.
Ministry of Agriculture: Hope Gardens, Kingston 6; tel. 927-9831.
Ministry of Community, Social Security and Consumer Affairs: National Heroes Circle, Kingston; tel. 922-8000.
Ministry of Construction: 2 Hagley Park Rd, Kingston 10; tel. 926-1590.
Ministry of Education: 2 National Heroes Circle, Kingston 4; tel. 922-1400.
Ministry of Finance and Planning: 30 National Heroes Circle, Kingston 4; tel. 922-8600; telex 2447.
Ministry of Foreign Affairs and Industry: 85 Knutsford Blvd, Kingston 5; tel. 926-4220; telex 2114.
Ministry of Health: 10 Caledonia Ave, Kingston 5; tel. 926-9220.
Ministry of Justice: 12 Ocean Blvd, Kingston; tel. 922-0080.
Ministry of Labour: 100 East St, Kingston; tel. 922-8750.
Ministry of Local Government: Ocean Blvd, Kingston; tel. 922-1670.
Ministry of Mining and Energy: 2 St Lucia Ave, Kingston 5; tel. 926-9170.

Directory

Ministry of National Security: 12 Ocean Blvd, Kingston; tel. 922-0080.
Ministry of Public Service: Citibank Bldg, 63 Knutsford Blvd, Kingston 5; tel. 926-3235.
Ministry of Public Utilities and Transport: 2 St Lucia Ave, Kingston 5; tel. 926-8130.
Ministry of Tourism: 85 Knutsford Blvd, Kingston 5; tel. 926-4220.
Ministry of Youth, Sports and Community Development: 12 Ocean Blvd, Kingston; tel. 922-1710.

Legislature

PARLIAMENT

Senate

President: JEANETTE GRANT-WOODHAM.

The Senate has 21 members, all of whom were nominated by the Prime Minister following the December 1983 elections, as there was no Leader of the Opposition.

House of Representatives

Speaker: ALVA ROSS.

Election, December 1983

	Seats
Jamaica Labour Party (JLP)	60*

* During 1986 two members of the House of Representatives resigned from the JLP. They continue to sit in the House as independent members.

Political Organizations

Jamaica American Party: Kingston; f. 1986; advocates US statehood for Jamaica; Leader JAMES CHISHOLM.
Jamaica Labour Party (JLP): 20 Belmont Rd, Kingston 5; f. 1943 by Sir Alexander Bustamante as political wing of the Bustamante Industrial Trade Union; supports free enterprise in a mixed economy and close co-operation with the USA; Leader EDWARD SEAGA; Chair. BRUCE GOLDING; Gen. Sec. RYAN PERALTO.
People's National Party (PNP): 89 Old Hope Rd, Kingston 5; f. 1938 by Norman Manley on socialist principles, with national independence as its goal; advocates social and economic change and nationalization of public utilities; foreign policy of non-alignment, although acknowledging a special relationship with third world countries; affiliated with the National Workers' Union; Pres. MICHAEL MANLEY; Chair. P. J. PATTERSON; Gen. Sec. Dr PAUL ROBERTSON.
Workers' Party of Jamaica (WPJ): f. 1978 out of the Workers Liberation League; pro-Soviet Communist party; Gen. Sec. Dr TREVOR MONROE.

Diplomatic Representation

EMBASSIES AND HIGH COMMISSIONS IN JAMAICA

Argentina: Dyoll Bldg, Knutsford Blvd, Kingston 5; tel. 926-5588; telex 2107; Ambassador: IGNACIO E. PICO ESTRADA.
Australia: National Life Bldg, 64 Knutsford Blvd, Kingston 5; tel. 926-3550; telex 2355; High Commissioner: MICHAEL LANDALE.
Belgium: Oxford House, 6 Oxford Rd, Kingston 5; tel. 926-4295; telex 2430; Ambassador: JAN BOUSSE.
Brazil: First Life Bldg, 64 Knutsford Blvd, Kingston 5; tel. 929-8607; telex 2221; Ambassador: OVÍDIO DE ANDRADE MELO.
Canada: Royal Bank Bldg, 30–36 Knutsford Blvd, POB 1500, Kingston 5; tel. 926-1500; telex 2130; High Commissioner: R. G. WOOLHAM.
China, People's Republic: 8 Seaview Ave, Kingston 10; tel. 927-0850; telex 2202; Ambassador: WU JIAXUAN.
Colombia: 53 Knutsford Blvd, Kingston 5; tel. 929-1701; telex 2200; Ambassador: Dr VÍCTOR ALCIDES RAMÍREZ PERDOMO.
Costa Rica: 34 Beverly Drive, Kingston 6; tel. 927-3410; Ambassador: GERADO GONZÁLES.

JAMAICA

France: 13 Hillcrest Ave, Kingston 6; tel. 927-9811; telex 2367; Ambassador: MICHEL REUILLARD.
Germany, Federal Republic: 10 Waterloo Rd, Kingston 10; tel. 926-6728; telex 2146; Ambassador: RICHARD WAGNER.
Guyana: 27 Seymour Ave, Kingston 6; tel. 927-5666; telex 2261; High Commissioner: Sir JOHN CARTER.
India: 4 Retreat Ave, POB 446, Kingston 6; tel. 927-0486; High Commissioner: RAM LAL.
Israel: Imperial Life Bldg, 60 Knutsford Blvd, Kingston 5; tel. 926-8768; telex 2466; Ambassador: YEHOSHUA HAKOHEN.
Japan: 'The Atrium', 3rd Floor, 32 Trafalgar Rd, Kingston 5; tel. 929-3338; telex 2304; Chargé d'affaires a.i.: TATSUO NOGUCHI.
Korea, Democratic People's Republic: 3 Upper Carmel Ave, Kingston 8; telex 2491; Ambassador: YU YONG-GUK.
Korea, Republic: 25 Seymour Ave, Kingston 6; tel. 927-7474; telex 2491; Ambassador: SANG JIN CHOI.
Mexico: Xerox Bldg (2nd Floor), 53 Knutsford Blvd, Kingston 5; tel. 926-6891; telex 2255; Ambassador: GUSTAVO IRUEGAS EVARISTO.
Netherlands: Xerox Bldg, 53 Knutsford Blvd, Kingston 5; tel. 926-2026; telex 2177; Chargé d'affaires a.i.: HANS VAN DEN DOOL.
Nigeria: 5 Waterloo Rd, Kingston 10; tel. 926-6400; telex 2443; High Commissioner: E. A. OGUOKON.
Panama: 64 Knutsford Blvd, Kingston 5; tel. 929-5467; Ambassador: VÍCTOR M. BOCANEGRA.
Peru: 10 Haining Rd, Kingston 5; tel. 926-5522; Ambassador: MIGUEL BARANDIARAN.
Spain: Xerox Bldg (3rd Floor), 53 Knutsford Blvd, Kingston 5; tel. 929-6710; telex 2364; Ambassador: JUAN LUGO ROIG.
Trinidad and Tobago: 60 Knutsford Blvd, Kingston 5; tel. 926-5730; telex 2387; High Commissioner: (vacant).
USSR: 22 Norbrook Drive, Kingston 8; tel. 924-1048; telex 2216; Ambassador: DMITRI PETROVICH MOUSSINE.
United Kingdom: Trafalgar Rd, POB 575, Kingston 10; tel. 926-9050; telex 2110; High Commissioner: MARTIN REID.
USA: Mutual Life Centre, 2 Oxford Rd, Kingston 5; tel. 929-4850; Ambassador: MICHAEL SOTIRHOS.
Venezuela: Royal Bank Bldg (5th Floor), 30–36 Knutsford Blvd, Kingston 5; tel. 926-5510; telex 2179; Ambassador: PEDRO LUIS ECHEVERRÍA.

Judicial System

The Judicial System is based on English common law and practice. Final appeal is to the Judicial Committee of the Privy Council in the United Kingdom.

Justice is administered by the Supreme Court, Court of Appeal, Resident Magistrates' Court, Revenue Court, Gun Court, Family Court and Traffic Court. There are also Courts of Petty Sessions.

THE SUPREME COURT
POB 491, Kingston.
Chief Justice: Hon. EDWARD ZACCA.
Senior Puisne Judge: MARTIN L. WRIGHT.
Puisne Judges: O. D. MARSH, C. F. B. ORR, W. D. MARSH, V. O. MALCOLM, Miss M. E. MORGAN, D. O. BINGHAM, U. D. GORDON, C. A. PATTERSON, T. N. THEOBALDS, Miss A. E. MCKAIN, L. H. WOLFE, H. E. DOWNER, C. W. WALKER, L. B. ELLIS, R. E. ALEXANDER, P. T. HARRISON.
Master: A. J. LAMBERT.
Registrar: H. E. HARRIS.
Deputy Registrars: Mrs C. MORGAN-GREAVES, Mrs D. B. MAYNE.

COURT OF APPEAL
President: I. D. ROWE.
Judges: J. S. KERR, H. D. CARBERRY, B. H. CAREY, R. O. C. WHITE, C. A. B. ROSS, U. V. CAMPBELL.
Registrar: Mrs N. MCKINTOSH.

JUDICIAL SERVICE COMMISSION
Chairman: Chief Justice.
Members: President of the Court of Appeal, Chairman of the Public Service Commission and three others.

Religion

There are over 100 Christian denominations. The Anglican Church is the largest religious body, and had 317,600 adherents according to a 1970 estimate. Presbyterians number about 92,000. Other religious bodies include the Methodist, Baptist and Congregational Churches, The Society of Friends and the Seventh-day Adventist Church. Rastafarianism is growing in importance.

CHRISTIANITY
The Anglican Communion
Anglicans in Jamaica are adherents of the Church in the Province of the West Indies. The Archbishop of the Province is the Bishop of Antigua and the Windward Islands. The Bishop of Jamaica is assisted by two suffragan Bishops (of Mandeville and Montego Bay).
Bishop of Jamaica: NEVILLE DESOUZA, Church Offices, 2 Caledonia Ave, Kingston 5; tel. 926-6609.

The Roman Catholic Church
Jamaica comprises the archdiocese of Kingston in Jamaica (also including the Cayman Islands) and the diocese of Montego Bay. At 31 December 1984 the estimated total of adherents in Jamaica and the Cayman Islands was 151,000, representing about 7% of the total population.
Bishops' Conference: Antilles Episcopal Conference, 21 Hopefield Ave, POB 43, Kingston 6; tel. 927-9915; f. 1975; 17 mems from the Caribbean region and Bermuda; Pres. Most Rev. SAMUEL EMMANUEL CARTER, Archbishop of Kingston in Jamaica.
Archbishop of Kingston in Jamaica: Most Rev. SAMUEL EMMANUEL CARTER, Archbishop's Residence, 21 Hopefield Ave, POB 43, Kingston 6; tel. 927-9915.

Other Christian Churches
Assembly of God: Evangel Temple, 3 Friendship Park Rd, Kingston 3; tel. 928-2728; 191,200 mems; Pastor C. M. DARELL-HUCKERBY.
Baptist Union: 6 Hope Rd, Kingston 10; tel. 926-1395; Pres. Rev. N. G. CALLAM; Gen. Sec. Rev. CAWLEY BOLT (acting); Pastor Rev. BURCHELL TAYLOR.
First Church of Christ, Scientist: 17 National Heroes Circle, Kingston.
Methodist: 143 Constant Spring Rd, POB 892, Kingston 8; tel. 924-2597; f. 1789; 18,819 mems; Chair. Rev. C. EVANS BAILEY; Synod Sec. Rev. GILBERT G. BOWEN.
Moravian: 3 Hector St, Kingston 5; tel. 928-1861; Bishop S. U. HASTINGS.
Seventh-day Adventist: 56 James St, Kingston; tel. 922-7440; f. 1901; 6,125 mems; Pastor Rev. P. N. HOSTEN.
United Church of Jamaica and Grand Cayman: 12 Carlton Cres, Kingston 10; tel. 926-8734; 15,000 mems; Gen. Sec. Rev. SAM H. SMELLIE.

BAHÁ'Í FAITH
National Spiritual Assembly: 208 Mountain View Ave, Kingston 6; tel. 927-7051; 6,300 mems resident in 320 localities.

JUDAISM
United Congregation of Israelites: 92 Duke St, Kingston; tel. 922-5931; f. 1655; c. 250 mems; Spiritual Leader and Sec. ERNEST H. DE SOUZA; Pres. SOLOMON DE SOUZA.

The Press
DAILIES
Daily Gleaner: 7 North St, POB 40, Kingston; tel. 922-3400; telex 2319; f. 1834; morning; independent; Chair. and Man. Dir OLIVER CLARKE; Editor J. C. PROUTE (acting); circ. 42,228.
Star: 7 North St, POB 40, Kingston; tel. 922-3400; evening; Editor D. C. STOKES; circ. 42,103.

PERIODICALS
Beacon: 1 Church Lane, POB 1258, Montego Bay, Kingston; 2 a week.
Caribbean Challenge: 55 Church St, POB 186, Kingston; f. 1957; 11 a year; circ. 22,000.
Caribbean Shipping: Creative Communications Inc, POB 105, Kingston 10; 6 a year.

JAMAICA

Catholic Opinion: 11 Duke St, Kingston; weekly; religious.

Children's Own: 7 North St, POB 40, Kingston; weekly; distributed during term time; circ. 78,622.

Government Gazette: POB 487, Kingston; f. 1868; Government Printer R. HINES; circ. 4,817.

Jamaica Chamber of Commerce Journal: 7–8 East Parade, Kingston; monthly.

Jamaica Churchman: 2 Caledonia Ave, Kingston 5; monthly; Editor Rev. LAURENCE SMALL; circ. 6,000.

Jamaican Housewife: Kingston; weekly.

Jamaica Journal: 12–16 East St, Kingston; tel. 922-0620; f. 1967; quarterly; literary, historical and cultural review.

Jamaica Manufacturer: 85A Duke St, Kingston; quarterly; circ. 3,000.

Jamaica Weekly Gleaner: 7 North St, POB 40, Kingston; tel. 922-3400; weekly; overseas; Chair. and Man. Dir OLIVER CLARKE; circ. 13,599.

Public Opinion: 2 Torrington Rd, Kingston; weekly.

Sports Life: 18 East St, Kingston; weekly.

Sunday Gleaner: 7 North St, POB 40, Kingston; tel. 922-3400; weekly; circ. 81,605.

Swing: 102 East St, Kingston; f. 1968; monthly; entertainment and culture; Editor ANDELL FORGIE; circ. 12,000.

The Visitor Vacation Guide: POB 1258, Westgate Plaza, Montego Bay; f. 1980; weekly; Editor LLOYD B. SMITH; circ. 8,000.

The Western Mirror: POB 1258, Westgate Plaza, Montego Bay; tel. 952-5253; f. 1980; 2 a week; Editor LLOYD B. SMITH; circ. 10,000.

Weekend Star: 7 North St, POB 40, Kingston; tel. 922-3400; weekly; Editor D. C. STOKES; circ. 86,128.

West Indian Medical Journal: Faculty of Medical Sciences, University of the West Indies, Kingston 7; tel. 927-1214; f. 1951; quarterly; Editor Dr VASIL PERSAUD; Asst Editor BRIDGET WILLIAMS; circ. 2,000.

West Indian Sportsman: 75 Church St, Kingston; quarterly; circ. 7,000.

PRESS ASSOCIATION

Press Association of Jamaica (PAJ): 10 Surbiton Rd, Kingston 10; tel. 926-8810; f. 1943; 220 mems; Pres. CLIFTON SEGREE; Sec. CLAIRE FORRESTER.

NEWS AGENCIES

Jampress: 3 Chelsea Ave, Kingston 10; tel. 926-3740; telex 3552; f. 1984; government news agency; Editor-in-Chief GLORIA MARAGH (acting).

Foreign Bureaux

Agencia EFE (Spain): Apt 23, 2 Leighton Rd, Kingston 5; Rep. FRAGANO LEDGISTER LÓPEZ.

Inter Press Service (IPS) (Italy): 2 Balmoral Ave, Kingston 10; tel. 929-2973; Correspondent FITZROY NATION.

Associated Press (USA), CANA (Caribbean News Agency) and Reuters (UK) are also represented in Jamaica.

Publishers

Caribbean Publishing Company Ltd: 18 East Kings House Rd, Kingston 6; tel. 927-0810.

Caribbean Universities Press Jamaica Ltd: POB 83, Kingston 7; tel. 926-2628; academic; Man. Dir CARMEN LATTY.

Hallmark Publishers Ltd: 10 Hagley Park Plaza, Kingston 10; tel. 929-4823.

Jamaica Publishing House Ltd: 97 Church St, Kingston; tel. 922-2038; f. 1969; wholly-owned subsidiary of Jamaica Teachers' Asscn; educational, English language and literature, mathematics, history, geography, social sciences, music; Chair. FAY E. SAUNDERS; Man. LEO A. OAKLEY.

Kingston Publishers Ltd: 1A Norwood Ave, Kingston 5; tel. 926-0091; telex 2293; f. 1970; educational textbooks, general, travel, atlases; Chair. MICHAEL HENRY.

Unique Publications Ltd: 18 East Kings House Rd, Kingston 6; tel. 927-0810.

Government Publishing House

Government Printing Office: 77 Duke St, Kingston; tel. 922-5950; law; Government Printer R. HINES.

Radio and Television

In 1984 there were an estimated 856,960 radio receivers and 200,500 TV sets in use.

Jamaica Broadcasting Corporation (JBC): 5 South Odeon Ave, POB 100, Kingston 10; tel. 926-5620; telex 2218; f. 1959; a publicly-owned statutory corporation; semi-commercial radio and television; 2 radio stations; Chair. FRANK PHIPPS; Gen. Man. B. C. BAROVIER (acting).

Educational Broadcasting Service: Ministry of Education, Multi-Media Centre, 1–3 Caenwood Rd, Kingston 5; f. 1964; radio and television broadcasts during school term; Pres. OUIDA HYLTON-TOMLINSON.

Radio Jamaica Ltd (RJR): Broadcasting House, 32 Lyndhurst Rd, POB 23, Kingston 5; tel. 926-1100; f. 1950; island-wide commercial and public service AM and FM radio broadcasting 24 hrs a day; Man. Dir J. A. LESTER SPAULDING; Programme Dir DOROTHY LACROIX.

Finance

(cap. = capital; p.u. = paid up; res = reserves; dep. = deposits; m. = million; amounts in Jamaican dollars; brs = branches)

BANKING

Central Bank

Bank of Jamaica: Nethersole Place, POB 621, Kingston; tel. 922-0750; telex 2165; f. 1960; cap. p.u. 4m., res 4.9m., dep. 1,896.6m. (Dec. 1984); Gov. Dr HEADLEY BROWN.

Commercial Banks

Bank of Commerce Jamaica Ltd: 121 Harbour St, Kingston; tel. 922-2485; telex 2169; cap. p.u. 4.3m., res 7.5m. dep. 325.7m. (Aug. 1985); Man. Dir G. I. MCGREGOR.

The Bank of Nova Scotia Jamaica Ltd: Scotiabank Centre Bldg, Duke and Port Royal Sts, POB 709, Kingston; tel. 922-1000; telex 2433; f. 1967; cap. p.u. 40.7m., res 37.5m., dep. 1,667.0m. (Oct. 1985); Gen. Man. J. M. A. TIEMENS; 46 brs.

First National Bank of Chicago (Jamaica) Ltd: 1 King St, POB 219, Kingston; tel. 922-0110; telex 2149; cap. p.u. 2m., dep. 21m. (Dec. 1977); Man. Dir MANLIO BLASETI; 6 brs.

Jamaica Citizens Bank Ltd: 4 King St, POB 483, Kingston 1; tel. 922-5850; telex 2129; f. 1976; cap. and res 7m., dep. 132m. (March 1982); Gen. Man. ELON BECKFORD.

National Commercial Bank Jamaica Ltd: 'The Atrium', 32 Trafalgar Rd, POB 88, Kingston; tel. 929-9053; telex 2139; f. 1977; cap. 10m., dep. 1,880m. (Sept. 1985); Chair. C. D. R. BOVELL; Man. Dir D. A. BANKS; 40 brs and agencies.

Royal Bank Jamaica Ltd: 30–36 Knutsford Blvd, POB 612, Kingston 5; tel. 929-8950; telex 2306; f. 1971; cap. 5.6m., dep. 413.4m. (Sept. 1983); Chair. RICHARD ASENHEIM; Man. Dir JAMES HAGEL; 16 brs.

Workers Savings and Loan Bank: 134 Tower St, POB 270, Kingston; tel. 922-8650; telex 2226; f. 1973; cap. p.u. 7.4m., dep. 507.4m. (Sept. 1985); Gen. Man. WINSTON DWYER; 10 brs.

Development Banks

Jamaica Development Bank: 15 Oxford Rd, Kingston 5; tel. 929-4000; telex 2381; f. 1969; replaced Development Finance Corporation, f. 1959; cap. 40m.; Chair. Dr MARSHALL HALL; Man. Dir ROY A. JONES.

Jamaica Mortgage Bank: 33 Tobago Ave, POB 950, Kingston 5; tel. 929-6350; f. 1971; became a statutory organization wholly owned by the Government in June 1973; established by the Government and the United States Agency for International Development to function primarily as a secondary market facility for home mortgages and to mobilize long-term funds for housing developments in Jamaica; also insures home mortgage loans made by approved financial institutions, thus transferring risk of default on a loan to the Government.

STOCK EXCHANGE

Jamaica Stock Exchange Ltd: POB 621, Bank of Jamaica Tower, Nethersole Place, Kingston; tel. 922-0806; f. 1968; Chair. LOUIS BYLES; Gen. Man. JOYCE WOODHAM.

INSURANCE

Government Supervisory Authority: Office of the Superintendent of Insurance, 51 St Lucia Ave, POB 800, Kingston 5; tel. 926-1790; Superintendent E. W. TAYLOR.

Jamaica Insurance Advisory Council: 9 King St, Kingston; tel. 922-8710; Man. DENISE Y. COLE.

British Caribbean Insurance Co Ltd: 36 Duke St, POB 170, Kingston; tel. 922-1260.

Dyoll Insurance Co Ltd: 40-46 Knutsford Blvd, POB 313, Kingston 5; tel. 926-4711; telex 2208.

Globe Insurance Co of the West Indies Ltd: 60 Knutsford Blvd, Kingston 10; tel. 926-3720; telex 2150.

Home Insurance Co: 21 Constant Spring Rd, Kingston 10; tel. 929-4690.

Insurance Co of the West Indies Ltd (ICWI): ICWI Building, 2 St Lucia Ave, POB 306, Kingston 5; tel. 926-9182; telex 2246.

Jamaica Export Credit Insurance Corporation: 10th floor, Bank of Jamaica Bldg, Nethersole Place, POB 3, Kingston; tel. 922-9690; telex 2165; provides export credit financing, loans, insurance.

Jamaica General Insurance Co Ltd: 9 Duke St, Kingston; tel. 922-6420.

Jamaica Mutual Life Assurance Society: 2 Oxford Rd, POB 430, Kingston 5; tel. 926-9024; f. 1844; Pres. A. TENNYSON PALMER.

Life of Jamaica Ltd: 17 Dominica Drive, Kingston 5; tel. 929-8920; f. 1970; Pres. ADRIAN B. FOREMAN; Exec. Vice-Pres. H. A. HALL.

National Employers' Mutual General Insurance Association Ltd: 9 King St, Kingston; tel. 922-1460.

Trade and Industry

CHAMBER OF COMMERCE

Jamaica Chamber of Commerce: 7-8 East Parade, POB 172, Kingston; tel. 922-0150; f. 1779; 8 associated Chambers of Commerce on island; 400 mems; Pres. SAMEER YOUNIS.

ASSOCIATIONS

All-Island Banana Growers' Association Ltd: Banana Industry Bldg, 10 South Ave, Kingston 4; tel. 922-5492; f. 1946; 5,089 mems (1986); Chair. A. A. POTTINGER; Sec. I. CHANG.

All-Island Jamaica Cane Farmers' Association: 4 North Ave, Kingston 4; tel. 922-7076; f. 1941; registered cane farmers; 23,000 mems; Chair. T. G. MIGNOTT; Man. D. D. MCCALLA.

Banana Export Company (BECO): 10 South Ave, Kingston 4; tel. 922-5490; telex 2148; f. 1985 to replace Banana Co of Jamaica; oversees the development of the banana industry.

Citrus Growers' Association Ltd: 1A North Ave, Kingston Gdns, POB 159, Kingston 4; tel. 922-8230; telex 2315; f. 1944; 18,000 mems; Chair. IVAN H. TOMLINSON.

Jamaica Banana Producers' Association Ltd: 6 Oxford Rd, POB 237, Kingston 5; tel. 926-3503; telex 2278; f. 1927; Chair. G. W. N. DOWNER; Man. Dir Dr MARSHALL HALL.

Jamaica Exporters' Association (JEA): 13 Dominica Drive, POB 9, Kingston 5; tel. 929-1292; telex 2421; Pres. PRAKESH VASWANI.

Jamaica Livestock Association: Newport East, POB 36, Kingston; f. 1941; tel. 922-7130; telex 2382; 7,268 mems; Chair. Brig. DAVID SMITH; Man. Dir HENRY J. RAINFORD.

Jamaica Manufacturers' Association Ltd: 85A Duke St, Kingston; tel. 922-8880; f. 1947; 640 mems; Pres. PAUL THOMAS.

Jamaican Association of Sugar Technologists: c/o Sugar Industry Research Institute, Mandeville; tel. 962-2241; f. 1936; 299 mems; Pres. K. E. NEWMAN; Hon. Sec. T. FALLOON.

Private Sector Organization of Jamaica (PSOJ): 39 Hope Rd, Kingston 10; tel. 927-6238; telex 2412; federative body of private business individuals, companies and associations; Pres. SAM MAHFOOD.

Sugar Manufacturing Corporation of Jamaica Ltd: 5 Trevennion Park Rd, Kingston 5; tel. 926-5930; 8 mems; established to represent the sugar manufacturers in Jamaica; deals with all aspects of the sugar industry and its by-products; provides liaison between the Government, the Sugar Industry Authority and the All-Island Jamaica Cane Farmers' Asscn; Chair. DAVID BICKNELL; Man. Dir Lt Col DELROY C. M. ORMSBY.

GOVERNMENT ORGANIZATIONS

Agricultural Development Corporation: 46 Trinidad Terrace, Kingston; tel. 926-9160; f. 1952; Chair. Dr C. L. BENT; Sec. D. FORRESTER.

Cocoa Industry Board: Marcus Garvey Drive, POB 68, Kingston 15; tel. 923-6411; f. 1957; has wide statutory powers to regulate and develop the industry; owns and operates four central fermentaries; Chair. L. O. MINOTT; Man. FITZ SHAW.

Coconut Industry Board: 18 Waterloo Rd, Half Way Tree, Kingston 10; tel. 926-1770; 9 mems; Chair. P. D. MCCONNELL; Gen. Man. R. A. WILLIAMS.

Coffee Industry Board: Marcus Garvey Drive, POB 508, Kingston; tel. 923-7211; f. 1950; 7 mems; has wide statutory powers to regulate and develop the industry; is the sole exporter of coffee; Chair. DONALD BANKS; Man. J. PICKERSGILL.

Coffee Industry Development Company: Kingston; f. 1981; to implement a coffee expansion programme financed by the Commonwealth Development Corporation.

Jamaica Bauxite Institute: Hope Gdns, POB 355, Kingston 6; tel. 927-2073; telex 2309; f. 1975; adviser to the Government in the negotiation of agreements, consultancy services to clients in the bauxite/alumina and related industries, laboratory services for mineral and soil-related services, Pilot Plant services for materials and equipment testing, research and development; Exec. Dir Dr CARLTON DAVIS.

Jamaica Commodity Trading Co Ltd: 8 Ocean Blvd, POB 1021, Kingston; tel. 922-0971; telex 2318; f. 1981 as successor to State Trading Corpn; oversees all importing on behalf of state; Chair. DAVID HENRIQUES; Man. Dir PAUL S. ELLIS.

Jamaica Industrial Development Corporation (JIDC): 76 Marcus Garvey Drive, POB 505, Kingston; tel. 923-5700; telex 2193; f. 1984; responsible for improving the performance of export industries, implementing government industrial plans and providing consultancy and training services for Jamaican industry; Chair. LASCELLES CHIN; Man. Dir WARREN WOODHAM.

Jamaica National Export Corporation: 8 Waterloo Rd, POB 645, Kingston 10; tel. 926-1200; telex 2124; f. 1970; responsible to Ministry of Foreign Affairs for facilitating and encouraging the development of Jamaica's export trade; Chair. S. C. ALEXANDER; Exec. Dir PETER KING.

Jamaica National Investment Promotion Ltd: 15 Oxford Rd, Kingston 5; tel. 929-7190; telex 2222; f. 1981; economic development agency responsible for promoting all private investments; Man. Dir CORINNE MCLARTY.

National Development Agency Ltd: 12 Ocean Blvd, Kingston; tel. 922-5445; telex 2444.

Petroleum Corporation of Jamaica (PCJ): 12 Ocean Blvd, Kingston; tel. 922-9670; telex 2356; state oil company; owns and operates petroleum refinery; holds exploration and exploitation rights to local petroleum and gas reserves; Chair. BILL SAUNDERS.

Sugar Industry Authority: 5 Trevennion Park Rd, Kingston 5; tel. 926-5930; telex 2113; Chair. F. G. DOWNIE.

Urban Development Corporation: 12 Ocean Blvd, 8th Floor, Kingston; tel. 922-8310; telex 2281; f. 1968; responsibility for urban renewal and development within designated areas; Chair. ARTHUR ZAIDIE; Gen. Man. GLORIA KNIGHT.

TRADE UNIONS

Bustamante Industrial Trade Union (BITU): 98 Duke St, Kingston; tel. 922-2443; f. 1938; Pres. HUGH SHEARER; Gen. Sec. Miss EDITH NELSON; 100,459 mems.

National Workers' Union of Jamaica (NWU): 130-132 East St, Kingston 16; tel. 922-1150; f. 1952; affiliated to ICFTU, ORIT, etc.; Pres. MICHAEL MANLEY; Gen. Sec. LLOYD GOODLEIGH; 102,000 mems.

Trades Union Congress of Jamaica: POB 19, 25 Sutton St, Kingston; tel. 922-5313; affiliated to CCL and ICFTU; Pres. EDWARD SMITH; Gen. Sec. HOPETON CAVEN; 20,000 mems.

Principal Independent Unions

Dockers' and Marine Workers' Union: 48 East St, Kingston; tel. 922-6067; Pres. MILTON A. SCOTT.

Independent Portworkers' Union: Kingston.

Industrial Trade Union Action Council: 2 Wildman St, Kingston; Pres. RODERICK FRANCIS.

JAMAICA

Jamaica Federation of Musicians' Union and Affiliated Artistes: POB 24, Kingston 3; f. 1958; Pres. Cecil V. Bradshaw; Sec. Myrna Hague; 1,300 mems.

Jamaica Local Government Officers' Union: c/o Public Service Commission, Knutsford Blvd, Kingston; Pres. E. Lloyd Taylor.

Jamaica Teachers' Association: 97 Church St, Kingston; tel. 922-1385; Chair. Noel Monteith.

Master Printers' Association of Jamaica: POB 24, Kingston 11; f. 1943; 44 mems; Pres. Hermon Spoerri; Sec. Ralph Gordon.

National Union of Democratic Teachers (NUDT): 69 Church St, Kingston; tel. 922-3092; f. 1978; Pres. Paulette Chevannes; Gen. Sec. John Haughton.

Union of School and Agricultural Workers: 2 Wildman St, Kingston; Pres. Douglas Jones.

United Portworkers' and Seamen's Union: Kingston.

University and Allied Workers' Union (UAWU): Students' Union, University of West Indies, Mona; affiliated to the WPJ; Pres. Dr Trevor Munroe.

There are also 17 employers' associations registered as trade unions.

CO-OPERATIVES

The Jamaica Social Welfare Commission promotes Co-operative Societies in the following categories: Consumer, Co-operative Farming, Credit, Credit and Marketing, Fishermen's Irrigation, Land Lease, Land Purchase, Marketing, Supplies Co-ops, Thrift, Transport and Tillage.

Transport

RAILWAYS

There are 294 km (182 miles) of standard-gauge railway operated by the Jamaica Railway Corporation. The main lines are from Kingston to Montego Bay and Spanish Town to Port Antonio. The railway is subsidized by the Government. There are also two railways for the transport of bauxite.

Jamaica Railway Corporation (JRC): POB 489, Kingston; tel. 922-6621; telex 2190; f. 1845 as earliest British colonial railway; transferred to JRC in 1960; autonomous; govt-owned; Chair. G. Martin; Gen. Man. K. Foster.

Alpart Railway: Spur Tree; industrial; Gen. Man. F. J. Heydel.

Kaiser Jamaica Bauxite Co Railway: Discovery Bay; industrial.

ROADS

Jamaica has a good network of tar-surfaced and metalled motoring roads. At the end of 1984 there were 16,638 km (10,332 miles) of roads, of which about 4,991 km (3,099 miles) were paved. This included 786 km (488 miles) of main roads and 689 km (428 miles) of secondary roads.

SHIPPING

The principal ports are Kingston and Montego Bay. The port at Kingston has four container berths, and is a major transhipment terminal for the Caribbean area. Jamaica has interests in two multi-national shipping lines: NAMUCAR (Naviera Multinacional del Caribe) and WISCO (West Indies Shipping Corporation). Services are also provided by a number of foreign lines.

Jamaica Freight and Shipping Co Ltd (JFS): 80–82 Second St, Port Bustamante, POB 167, Kingston 13; tel. 923-9271; telex 2260; express cargo services to and from Miami, Port-of-Spain and Bridgetown; Chair. E. M. Johnston; Man. Dir C. H. Johnston.

Jamaica Merchant Marine (JMM): 7th floor, Dyoll Bldg, 40/46 Knutsford Blvd, Kingston 5; tel. 929-1982; telex 2483; f. 1975; carries bauxite, grain, bananas and produce to/from USA and UK; Chair. Noel Aylton.

Port Authority of Jamaica: 15–17 Duke St, Kingston; tel. 922-0290; telex 2386; Gen. Man. Lucien Rattray.

Shipping Association of Jamaica: 5–7 King St, Kingston 15; tel. 922-8220; telex 2431; f. 1939; 29 mems; Chair. R. Smith; Gen. Man. Alister Cooke.

CIVIL AVIATION

There are two international airports linking Jamaica with North America, Europe, and other Caribbean islands. The Norman Manley International Airport is situated 22.5 km (14 miles) outside Kingston. The Donald Sangster International Airport is 5 km (3 miles) from Montego Bay.

Air Jamaica Ltd: 72–76 Harbour St, Kingston; tel. 922-3460; telex 2389; f. 1968; government-owned; services to Canada, the Cayman Islands, Haiti, Puerto Rico and the USA; Chair. Tony Hart; Pres./Man. Dir Noel A. Hylton; fleet of 2 Airbus A300B4, 4 Boeing 727-200.

Trans-Jamaican Airlines: POB 218, Montego Bay; tel. 952-5401; internal services to Kingston, Mandeville, Negril, Ocho Rios and Port Antonio; government corporation; Chair. Lotse Harvey; Admin. Dir B. G. Osborne.

Tourism

Jamaica Tourist Board (JTB): 21 Dominica Drive, POB 360, Kingston 5; tel. 929-9200; telex 2140; f. 1955; a statutory body set up by the Government to implement the policies of Ministry of Tourism; Chair. John Issa; Dir of Tourism Carrole Guntley; in 1985 846,716 tourists visited Jamaica.

Jamaica Hotel and Tourist Association: 2 Ardenne Rd, Kingston 10; tel. 926-3635; telex 2426; Pres. Butch Stewart; Gen. Man. Camille Needham.

JAPAN

Introductory Survey

Location, Climate, Language, Religion, Flag, Capital

Japan lies in eastern Asia and comprises a curved chain of more than 3,000 islands. Four large islands, named (from north to south) Hokkaido, Honshu, Shikoku and Kyushu, account for about 98% of the land area. Hokkaido lies just to the south of Sakhalin, a large Soviet island, and about 1,300 km (800 miles) east of the USSR's mainland port of Vladivostok. Southern Japan is about 150 km (93 miles) east of Korea. Although summers are temperate everywhere, the climate in winter varies sharply from cold in the north to mild in the south. Temperatures in Tokyo are generally between −6°C (21°F) and 30°C (86°F). Typhoons and heavy rains are common in summer. The language is Japanese. The major religions are Shintoism and Buddhism, and there is a minority of Christians. The national flag (proportions usually 3 by 2) is white, with a red disc (a sun without rays) in the centre. The capital is Tokyo.

Recent History

Following Japan's defeat in the Second World War, Japanese forces surrendered in August 1945. Japan signed an armistice in September 1945, agreeing to give up many of its outer islands, and the country was placed under US military occupation. A new democratic constitution, which was promulgated in November 1946 and took effect from May 1947, renounced war and abandoned the doctrine of the Emperor's divinity. Following the peace treaty of September 1951, Japan regained its sovereignty on 28 April 1952. The Tokara Archipelago and the Amami Islands (parts of the Ryukyu group) were restored to Japanese sovereignty in December 1951 and December 1953 respectively. Rival conservative political groups merged in November 1955 to form the Liberal-Democratic Party (LDP), which has held power ever since. The Bonin Islands and the remainder of the Ryukyu Islands (including Okinawa), administered by the USA from 1945, were returned to Japan in June 1968 and May 1972 respectively.

Nobusuke Kishi became Prime Minister in February 1957 and held office until July 1960, when he was succeeded by Hayato Ikeda. In November 1964 Ikeda resigned, owing to ill health, and was replaced by Eisaku Sato, who was to become the longest-serving Prime Minister in Japanese history. Sato remained in office until July 1972, when he was succeeded by Kakuei Tanaka, hitherto the Minister of International Trade and Industry. Tanaka visited Beijing in September 1972, when he agreed to Japan's recognition of the People's Republic of China and a consequent severance of Japanese diplomatic (though not commercial) relations with Taiwan. At a general election to the House of Representatives (the Lower House of the Diet) in December, the LDP won 271 of the 491 seats, giving the party a reduced majority. After elections for one-half of the seats in the House of Councillors (the Upper House of the Diet) in July 1974, the LDP's majority in that chamber was reduced from 26 to seven seats. Following this setback, Tanaka resigned as Prime Minister in December 1974. He was succeeded by Takeo Miki, a former Deputy Prime Minister.

During his premiership, Tanaka allegedly accepted bribes, totalling 500m. yen, from the Marubeni Corporation, a representative in Japan of the Lockheed Aircraft Corporation (a leading US aerospace company), in return for using his influence to promote the purchase of Lockheed TriStar airliners by All Nippon Airways, Japan's principal domestic airline. In July 1976 Tanaka was arrested, on charges of accepting bribes, and resigned from the LDP. In December a general election for the House of Representatives resulted in a major setback for the LDP, which lost its overall majority for the first time. The party held 265 of the 491 seats when the House was dissolved, but in the election it won only 249 of the 511 seats in an enlarged chamber. The decline in support for the LDP was partly attributed to the voters' disapproval of the party's alleged involvement in corruption, particularly the Lockheed scandal. Following the election, Miki resigned as Prime Minister, and was succeeded by Takeo Fukuda, who had resigned in November as Deputy Prime Minister.

The LDP suffered another setback in July 1977, at elections for one-half of the seats in the House of Councillors, and in November Fukuda carried out a major reshuffle of the Cabinet, giving ministerial office to some economic experts. In the LDP presidential election of November 1978 Fukuda was unexpectedly defeated by Masayoshi Ohira, the LDP Secretary-General. Ohira became Prime Minister in December, and a new Cabinet was formed. Lacking an overall majority in the Lower House and facing increasing opposition to proposed tax increases, the Government's legislative programme was seriously hindered.

At elections to the Lower House in October 1979 the LDP again failed to win an overall majority, and significant gains were made by the Communists. Ohira survived a challenge to his leadership of the LDP, but in May 1980 the Government was defeated in a motion of 'no confidence', proposed by the Japan Socialist Party, and Ohira dissolved the Lower House. Ohira died before the elections in June, when the LDP won 284 of the 511 seats, although obtaining only a minority of the votes cast. In July Zenko Suzuki, a relatively unknown compromise candidate, was elected President of the LDP and subsequently appointed Prime Minister. He faced a series of crises during 1981, including a setback in relations with the USA and criticism from the opposition over Japan's defence policy. Economic tensions with the USA and the EEC heightened, owing to the continued growth of Japanese exports, which were partly curbed by voluntary restraints. In November 1981 Suzuki reshuffled the Cabinet, distributing major posts among the five feuding LDP factions. The growing factionalism of the LDP and the worsening economic crisis (with the yen falling dramatically to its lowest level against the US dollar for five years) led to the resignation of Suzuki as Prime Minister and LDP President in October 1982.

Suzuki's successor was Yasuhiro Nakasone, who was supported by the Suzuki and Tanaka factions of the LDP. In his former post, as Minister of State and Director-General of the Administrative Management Agency, Nakasone had been responsible for implementing the Suzuki Government's expenditure cuts. At elections in June 1983 for one-half of the seats in the Upper House, a new electoral system was used. Of the 126 contested seats, 50 were filled on the basis of proportional representation. As a result, two small parties entered the House for the first time. Nevertheless, the LDP increased its strength from 134 to 137 members in the 252-seat chamber. This result was seen as an endorsement of Nakasone's policies of increased spending on defence, closer ties with the USA and greater Japanese involvement in international affairs.

In October 1983, after judicial proceedings lasting nearly seven years, a Tokyo court found Kakuei Tanaka, the former Prime Minister, guilty of accepting bribes. In September 1985 he began appeal proceedings against the conviction and the sentence (a heavy fine and four years' imprisonment), and he continued to be an 'independent' member of the Diet. Despite resigning from the LDP, Tanaka remained a major influence on the party, and members of the Tanaka faction held important positions in Nakasone's Cabinet. Tanaka's refusal to resign his legislative seat led to a boycott of the Diet by the opposition, which forced Nakasone to dissolve the House of Representatives in preparation for a premature general election in December 1983. The election campaign was dominated by the issues of political ethics and Nakasone's forthright style of leadership. The LDP suffered the worst defeat in its history, losing 36 seats (and its majority) in the Lower House. Its previous strength in the Lower House, however, had been inflated by a sympathy vote following the death of Ohira during the 1980 election campaign. In 1983 the LDP won 45.8% of the total votes (on a 67% turn-out), compared with 47.9% in 1980. Nakasone came second (behind Takeo Fukuda) in his district, whereas Tanaka was returned with an overwhelming majority. The Komeito, Democratic Socialist and Socialist Parties gained seats, while the Communists and the New Liberal Club (NLC) lost seats. A coalition was formed between the LDP and the NLC (which had split from the LDP over the Tanaka affair in 1976) and several independents, and Nakasone remained as President of the LDP by promising to reduce Tanaka's influence. Six members of Tanaka's faction held posts in Nakasone's new Cabinet, including that of Minister of Finance.

Following the trial of Tanaka, a series of reforms was introduced, whereby Cabinet members were required to disclose the extent of their personal assets. Owing to the many opportunities for evasion, however, these reforms were regarded by some as superficial. Nakasone's domestic policy was based on the 'Three Reforms': administrative reforms, particularly of government-run enterprises such as the railways; fiscal reforms, to enable the Government to balance its budget after many years of persistent deficit; and educational reforms, to liberalize the rigid examination-dominated system. In March 1984 Nakasone introduced Japan's most austere budget since 1955, based on a target economic growth rate of 4.1% for the coming year.

In November 1984 Nakasone was re-elected as President of the LDP, guaranteeing him two further years in office as Prime Minister, the first to serve a second term since Eisaku Sato (1964–72). The unexpected late challenge to his leadership by part of the Tanaka faction (headed by Susumu Nikaido, Vice-President of the LDP) was indicative of the widespread disaffection with Nakasone's assertive style of leadership. The continued importance of the Tanaka faction was emphasized when six members were awarded portfolios in the new Cabinet. However, the future extent of Tanaka's personal influence was uncertain after he suffered a cerebral haemorrhage in February 1985. (Tanaka was too ill to contest the general election in July 1986.)

In December 1985 Nakasone reshuffled his Cabinet but retained the three senior ministers from rival factions within the ruling party. He preserved a balance in the Cabinet among the five major factions. In March 1986 plans to denationalize the Japanese National Railways in 1987 were approved by the Cabinet but strongly opposed by the Japanese Socialist Party and, initially, by the railway workers' union, Kokuro.

In May 1986 the problem of over-representation of Japan's rural voters in the House of Representatives and serious under-representation of voters in urban areas was alleviated by an agreement on redistribution, involving the elimination of seven rural seats and the creation of eight seats in urban areas. In June Nakasone secured approval for the dissolution of the Diet in spite of objections from the opposition parties, which boycotted a special session of the Diet. This enabled the Prime Minister to announce the holding of a premature general election for the House of Representatives (18 months ahead of schedule) to coincide with the triennial election for one-half of the seats in the House of Councillors on 6 July. The Government hoped to benefit from the higher level of participation expected to arise from the holding of both polls on the same day. The polling resulted in an overwhelming victory for the LDP in the election to the House of Representatives. The increased LDP majority was achieved largely at the expense of the Japan Socialist Party and the Democratic Socialist Party. Of the main opposition parties, only the Communists maintained their strength in the House of Representatives. The LDP, therefore, was able to dispense with its coalition partner, the NLC (which disbanded in August and rejoined the LDP). The new Cabinet was composed entirely of LDP members. In September the leaders of the LDP agreed to alter bylaws to allow party presidents one-year extensions beyond the normal limit of two terms of two years each, and then applied this provision to Nakasone. Nakasone could thus retain the posts of president of the LDP and Prime Minister of Japan until October 1987. In September 1986 the Minister of Education, Masayuki Fujio, was dismissed by Nakasone for his remarks about Japan's past actions in China and Korea.

Nakasone was committed to raising Japan's international status by fostering friendly relations with other world leaders. He made successful tours to the USA, Australia and South-East Asia in 1984, and to Europe in 1985, to promote political and social links. Further tours were undertaken by Nakasone and the Minister of Foreign Affairs, Shintaro Abe, to the USA, Canada and Europe in 1986. During a meeting with the US President Ronald Reagan, in Washington in April 1986, Nakasone stressed his 'commitment' to changing the structure of Japan's economy, so that domestic consumption, rather than exports, would be increasingly important in the promotion of growth. However, there is continued concern in the EEC over trade protectionism in Japan, and in the USA over the imbalance of bilateral trade. Partial deregulation of the financial markets has been introduced in an attempt to alleviate the problem, and in July 1985 the Government announced a three-year programme to encourage imports, amid continued criticism that it did not include any significant new proposals. Further measures to stimulate imports were introduced in 1986.

Japan continues to receive military support from the USA. Since 1982 Japan has been under continued pressure from the USA to increase its defence spending (which was equivalent to about 0.9% of the country's gross national product in 1983–85) and to assume greater responsibility for security in the Western Pacific area. In 1986 the Japanese Government decided to exceed the self-imposed limit on defence expenditure of 1% of the gross national product (GNP), set in 1976. The Government proposed defence spending equivalent to 1.004% of the forecast GNP in 1987/88, and also announced that it would maintain defence expenditure at around this level until 1991. This increase was welcomed by the USA but Yasuhiro Nakasone stressed that Japan would not become a major military power. In February 1987 Japan agreed to contribute technical personnel to UN peace-keeping operations for the first time. The Japan Socialist Party (since September 1986 chaired by Takako Doi, the first woman to lead a major political party in Japan) accused the Nakasone Government of seeking to revive the nationalism of the pre-1945 militarist era.

Stability in South-East Asia is a vital consideration in Japanese foreign policy, since Japan depends on Asia for about one-third of its foreign trade, including imports of vital raw materials. In 1978 a treaty of peace and friendship was signed with the People's Republic of China. A meeting between Chinese and Japanese leaders, held in Beijing in June 1986, ended with a pledge by both sides to reduce China's large trade deficit with Japan. This pledge was reiterated when the Japanese Prime Minister visited China in November.

Japan has demanded from the USSR the return of four small islands (the 'Northern Territories') lying a few kilometres from Hokkaido, which were annexed in 1945 by the USSR. Japan claims sovereignty over the islands under the provisions of an 1855 treaty between Japan and Russia. The Soviet claims are based on possession and on the 1945 Yalta agreement, in which the USA and the United Kingdom agreed that the Kurile Islands would be occupied by the USSR. Japan, supported since the early 1950s by the USA, argues that the islands are not part of the Kuriles. There has been no progress in the matter since 1956, when Japan and the USSR resumed diplomatic relations. Consequently, the two countries have still not signed a peace treaty formally ending the Second World War. In 1986, however, the USSR allowed about 50 Japanese to visit ancestral tombs on the disputed islands.

There was a noticeable improvement in relations between Japan and the USSR in 1986. In January the Soviet Minister of Foreign Affairs, Eduard Shevardnadze, visited Japan (the first visit of a Soviet Foreign Minister to Japan for 10 years). The two countries agreed to improve economic and trade relations, and to resume regular ministerial consultations. Japan and the USSR signed a new cultural agreement in June, when the Japanese Foreign Minister, Shintaro Abe, visited Moscow. In December, however, the USSR refused Japan's invitation to the Soviet leader, Mikhail Gorbachev, to visit Tokyo. In January 1987 the new Japanese Foreign Minister, Tadashi Kuranari, went on a tour of Oceania, ostensibly to counter the allegedly growing Soviet influence in the South Pacific. In the same month, Nakasone embarked on a tour of Eastern Europe, the first such tour by a Japanese Prime Minister.

Government

Under the Constitution of 1946, the Emperor is Head of State but has no governing power. Legislative power is vested in the bicameral Diet, consisting of the House of Representatives or

JAPAN

Lower House (512 seats), whose members are elected for a four-year term, and the House of Councillors or Upper House (252 seats), members of which are elected for six years, one-half being elected every three years. At the Upper House election of June 1983, an element of proportional representation was introduced, when 50 national seats were determined according to the number of votes for each party. There is universal suffrage for all adults from 20 years of age. Executive power is vested in the Cabinet. The Prime Minister is appointed by the Emperor (on designation by the Diet) and himself appoints the other Ministers. The Cabinet is responsible to the Diet.

Japan has 47 prefectures, each administered by an elected Governor.

Defence

Although the Constitution renounces war and the use of force, the right of self-defence is not excluded. Japan maintains ground, maritime and air self-defence forces. Military service is voluntary. The USA provides equipment and training staff and also maintains bases. The total strength of the self-defence forces in July 1986 was 243,000, comprising: army 155,000, navy 44,000 and air force 44,000. Proposed expenditure on defence for 1986/87 was 3,344,000m. yen.

Economic Affairs

Japan is not well endowed with natural resources, and more than 67% of the total land area is forested. The country is self-sufficient in rice but has to import about 50% of its requirements of other cereals and fodder crops. Mineral resources are meagre, except for limestone and sulphur, and Japanese industry is heavily dependent on imported raw materials and fuels. In 1986 the Japanese Government decided that nearly 40% of Japanese coal production was to cease by 1991 (closing about one-half of its 11 coal-mines). Apart from its high cost, the coal industry has suffered from the rising importance of nuclear power. In 1986 Japan was the world's third largest consumer of petroleum, and, because the country produces virtually none of its own, petroleum accounted for 27% of Japan's import costs in 1985. The Government has authorized the construction of three nuclear and eight coal-fired power stations as part of a programme to reduce the country's dependence on imported petroleum. Nuclear energy accounted for 26.3% of Japan's electricity output in 1986 compared with 25% contributed by petroleum-fired power stations. Petroleum was previously the largest source of electricity in Japan. Japan relies on imports for 88% of its total energy requirements. Since 1969 concessions have been granted for offshore petroleum exploration in the Korean Straits, the Sea of Japan and off Hokkaido Island. Drilling began in 1971. The Japan National Oil Company (JNOC) was established in 1978.

Based on the promotion of manufacturing industries for the export market, Japan achieved and maintained a very high rate of economic growth after 1945. Gross national product (GNP) grew at an average annual rate of 10.3% between 1962 and 1972, and in 1971 Japan's GNP became the second largest in the world, ranking behind only the USA (Soviet bloc countries excluded). In 1985 Japan's GNP per head was US $11,040, a level comparable to that of industrialized countries in Western Europe. Between 1965 and 1984 the average annual increase in Japan's GNP per head was 4.7% in real terms, the highest national growth rate among non-communist industrial countries. Overall, Japan's gross domestic product (GDP), measured in constant prices, increased at an average rate of 9.8% per year in 1965–73, but the rise slowed to 4.3% per year in 1973–83. Real GDP per head, which had increased by more than 9% annually in the early 1970s, rose by 4.2% per year over the period 1975–80. Its growth eased to 3.5% in 1981, and to 2.3% in 1982. In the financial year ending 31 March 1984 the growth rate of GNP in real terms was 5.3% (compared with 3.3% in 1982/83), showing the underlying strength of the Japanese economy in a worldwide recession. Growth increased to 5.7% in 1984/85, but fell to 4.3% in 1985/86, and was likely to be as low as 2% in 1986/87 because of the expected effect on exports of the recent large increase in the value of the yen in relation to the US dollar. Increased consumer spending accounted for a large part of the recent growth in the economy.

The 1982/83 budget represented the lowest rate of expansion for 26 years. Proposed spending in the 1984/85 budget increased by only 1.9% over 1982/83 figures, while the 1985/86 budget projected total expenditure of 52,500,000m. yen, which represented a 3.6% increase over 1984/85. The cost of servicing government bonds became the largest item of expenditure for the first time. A five-year 'freeze' on general expenditure was introduced, to enable the Government to cease issuing deficit-financing bonds to make up the 30% of government spending not covered by tax revenues. The Nakasone Government was unable to introduce tax reforms because of almost universal opposition, and the proportion of government spending that is covered by tax revenue is far lower than in any other advanced nation. In December 1986, however, the tax committee of the ruling Liberal-Democratic Party issued proposals for a new programme of tax reforms, including the introduction of value-added tax (VAT) and the abolition of tax-free savings schemes. These proposals were certain to form the basis of the new tax system that the Government was to introduce gradually from 1987.

For the fifth consecutive year, the main aim of the budget proposals for 1986/87 was to reduce the government deficit. The proposals envisaged total expenditure of 54,089,000m. yen (representing a 3.0% increase over the level of spending in the 1985/86 budget), to be funded by increases in tax revenue. The single largest expenditure increase was for the payment of interest on the national debt, followed by foreign aid, which was to rise by 7% to 621,700m. yen, and defence spending, which was to increase by 6.58%, to 3,344,000m. yen, in order to remain marginally below the upper limit of 1% of GNP that had been imposed in 1976. In September 1986 the Japanese Cabinet, reacting to pressure from US and domestic business leaders, proposed a supplementary budget (involving additional spending of US $23,500m.) in an attempt to stimulate domestic growth. Priority was given to public works and new housing construction, which were allocated $20,000m. The budget proposals for 1987/88 projected the smallest increase in spending for 32 years. The proposals envisaged total expenditure of 54,101,000m. yen, representing an increase of only 0.02% over the corresponding total in the 1986/87 budget. Only spending on defence (increased by 5.2%) and overseas development aid (up by 5.3%) were allowed to rise significantly. An important development was the decision by the Government to exceed the self-imposed limit of 1% of GNP on defence expenditure. The proposed spending on defence for 1987/88 was 3,517,400m. yen, which was equivalent to 1.004% of the forecast GNP in that financial year. In 1986 Japan was one of the world's three biggest donors of development aid, and planned to double its aid budget by 1992. In December 1986 Japan and the World Bank held talks on the establishment of a special fund to channel some of Japan's huge trade surpluses to developing countries.

In 1986 the level of unemployment began to cause concern in Japan, as the high value of the yen forced manufacturers to transfer production overseas. The unemployment rate rose to 2.9% of the labour force in 1985, the highest level since records began in 1953, and remained at a similar level throughout 1986. In 1983 consumer prices rose by only 1.9% over the previous year, the lowest annual rise in 24 years. In 1984 consumer prices increased by 2.4%, and in 1985 they rose by 2.1%. By December 1986 inflation had been eliminated, with the consumer price index at the same level as 12 months previously.

Japan's economy was adversely affected by the large increase in petroleum prices in 1979. After achieving massive trade surpluses in 1977 and 1978, a deficit of US $13,451m. was recorded in 1979/80. In 1980/81, however, there were signs of recovery and the deficit narrowed to $10,720.7m. There was a surplus of $8,740.5m. in 1981/82, and this fell to $6,900m. in 1982/83, with exports declining by 8.7% and imports by 7.9%. The 1983/84 trade surplus, however, soared to $20,534m., with exports increasing by 13.9% and imports declining by 4.3%. In 1984/85 the trade surplus increased to $33,611m., with exports increasing by 19.7% and imports by 7%. The trade surplus for 1985/86 increased to a massive $61,640m., with exports increasing by 7.5% and imports 'declining' by 2.4% (despite the huge appreciation of the yen against the US dollar). In 1986 imports were expected to increase as the strength of the yen lowered import prices and the Government's 'Action Programme' (including reductions in tariffs and the simplification of import procedures) promoted imports of manufactured goods. Since

1984 there has been continual criticism from the USA concerning the strength and extent of trade protectionism in Japan. In 1986, as exports from Japan to Europe continued to rise, a further dispute between Japan and the EEC appeared likely. EEC officials claimed that Japanese exporters were actively transferring sales to Europe, where the appreciation of the yen in relation to local currencies had not been as marked as its appreciation against the US dollar. In 1984/85 the People's Republic of China became Japan's second largest export market (after the USA), while exports to the Federal Republic of Germany, Saudi Arabia, the Republic of Korea, Taiwan and Hong Kong were also considerable. The current surplus on the balance of payments reached a record $46,169m. in 1985. The strength of the yen was not expected immediately to reduce Japan's trade surplus, because the adverse affect on exports was being offset by the fall in petroleum prices and reductions in the cost of raw materials and other imports. The increase in the value of the yen was widely expected to lead to a shift in the emphasis of the Japanese economy from exports to expansion of domestic demand. Industrial production rose by 7.0% in 1980, and by 3.7% in 1981, but in 1982 it fell by 0.6% because of increased resistance by other states to Japanese exports. Industrial production went up by 3.6% in 1983, and by 11.2% in 1984, the largest annual increase for 11 years. In 1985 Japan became the world's largest exporter of manufactured goods, surpassing the USA and the Federal Republic of Germany. Industrial production was projected to rise by 4.1% in 1985/86 and by 3.6% in 1986/87. In 1986, however, the combined output of mining and manufacturing declined for the first time since 1975.

Farming in Japan is labour-intensive, but the proportion of the working population employed in agriculture, forestry and fishing fell from 19% in 1970 to 8.8% in 1985. Japan's agricultural labour force totalled 4.6m. in 1985. Japan produces about 70% of its total food requirements. The principal crops are rice (which contributed 34% to total agricultural output in 1984), wheat, barley and potatoes. Japan is a leading fishing nation, both in coastal and deep-sea waters. Since 1976, however, the fishing industry has been seriously affected by the establishment of exclusive fishing zones by many countries. In 1986, yielding to US pressure, Japan agreed to end all commercial whaling in 1988.

Industrial activity (mining, manufacturing and construction) employed 34% of the labour force in 1985, compared with 44% in 1970. Heavy industries predominate in the manufacturing sector, particularly motor vehicles, steel, machinery, electrical equipment and chemicals. In 1983 Japan was the world's largest producer of ships and passenger cars, and the second largest producer of synthetic fibres, cement, synthetic resins and steel. By 1985 the shipbuilding market had contracted sharply, and the world's largest operator of oil tankers, Sanko Steamship, became the biggest company in Japan ever to file for bankruptcy. As a whole, Japan ranks second in the world (after the USA) in industrial production. Japan's estimated investment in technology in 1984/85 was $28,800m., which was surpassed only by the USA.

Japan has been under pressure to revalue its currency in view of the favourable conditions of Japanese exports on the world market. The yen was revalued in December 1971 and floated in February 1973, and remained steady until 1977 when, until early 1979, it appreciated greatly against the US dollar and other currencies. The impact of increases in the price of petroleum abruptly reversed this trend, and during 1979 the yen fell by approximately 30% against the US dollar, despite continued intervention by the Bank of Japan and a restrictive monetary policy, which included a 4% increase in bank rate to 6.25%. At the beginning of 1980 the yen depreciated against the US dollar, reflecting an increase in Japan's current account deficit. However, monetary measures, introduced to attract foreign investment, allowed the yen to appreciate, a trend which did not, as expected, continue into 1981. The yen reached a five-year low in November 1982, largely as a result of the high level of US interest rates, but it quickly recovered. By February 1985, however, the yen had fallen against the US dollar to its lowest level since November 1982. In September 1985, following the agreement of the Group of Five (comprising the USA, Japan, the Federal Republic of Germany, the United Kingdom and France) to curb the continued increase in the value of the US dollar, the yen appreciated in value. The exchange rate was US $1 = 152 yen in September 1986, compared with $1 = 240 yen in September 1985. This rapid appreciation of the yen resulted in trading difficulties for Japan's export industries. In October 1986 Japan and the USA agreed on the desirability of maintaining the exchange rate at around $1 = 160 yen. In January 1987, however, the rate stood at $1 = 151 yen: the US dollar's lowest level in relation to the Japanese currency since the Second World War.

As part of a major privatization scheme, Japanese National Railways were to be denationalized in 1987. The Japanese Government also planned to sell all or part of its shares in Nippon Telegraph and Telephone, Japan Tobacco and Japan Air Lines by 1990.

Social Welfare

Almost all of the population are insured under the various schemes covering health, welfare annuities, unemployment and industrial accidents. Workers normally retire at the age of 55, the average pension being about 40% of salary. In 1982 Japan had 9,403 hospital establishments, with a total of 1,401,999 beds, equivalent to one for every 84 inhabitants, and there were 161,260 physicians working in the country.

Education

A kindergarten system provides education for children aged between three and five years of age, although the majority of kindergartens are privately controlled. At the age of six, children are required to attend elementary schools (shogakko), from which they proceed, after six years, to lower secondary schools (chugakko) for a further three years. Education is compulsory to the age of 15, and there are plans to increase the age limit to 18. In 1982 all children aged six to 11 were enrolled at primary schools, while 94% of those aged 12 to 17 received secondary education. Upper secondary schools provide a three-year course in general topics or a vocational course in subjects such as agriculture, commerce, fine art and technical studies. Higher education is divided into three types of institution. Universities (daigaku) offer a four-year degree course, as well as post-graduate courses. Japan has more than 400 universities, both public and private. Junior colleges (tanki-daigaku) provide less specialized two- to three-year courses. Both universities and junior colleges provide facilities for teacher-training. Technical colleges (tokushu-kyoiku-gakko) offer a five-year specialized training for technicians in many fields of engineering.

Tourism

The ancient capital of Kyoto, pagodas and temples, forests and mountains, traditional festivals and the classical Kabuki theatre are some of the many tourist attractions of Japan. In 1985 there were 2,327,047 foreign visitors to Japan, and receipts from tourism totalled US $1,137m.

Public Holidays

1987: 1 January (New Year's Day), 15 January (Adults' Day), 11 February (National Foundation Day), 21 March (Vernal Equinox Day), 29 April (Emperor's Birthday), 3 May (Constitution Memorial Day), 5 May (Children's Day), 15 September (Respect for the Aged Day), 23 September (Autumnal Equinox), 10 October (Sports Day), 3 November (Culture Day), 23 November (Labour Thanksgiving Day).

1988: 1 January (New Year's Day), 15 January (Adults' Day), 11 February (National Foundation Day), 21 March (Vernal Equinox Day), 29 April (Emperor's Birthday), 3 May (Constitution Memorial Day), 5 May (Children's Day), 15 September (Respect for the Aged Day), 23 September (Autumnal Equinox), 10 October (Sports Day), 3 November (Culture Day), 23 November (Labour Thanksgiving Day).

Weights and Measures

The metric system is in force.

Currency and Exchange Rates

1,000 rin = 100 sen = 1 yen.
Exchange rates (30 September 1986):
  £1 sterling = 223.35 yen;
  US $1 = 154.35 yen

JAPAN

Statistical Survey

Source (unless otherwise stated): Statistics Bureau, Management and Co-ordination Agency, 19-1 Wakamatsucho, Shinjuku-ku, Tokyo 162, tel. (3) 202-1111, *Monthly Statistics of Japan, Japan Statistical Yearbook*.

Area and Population

AREA, POPULATION AND DENSITY

Area (sq km)	377,800*
Population (census results)†	
1 October 1980	117,060,396
1 October 1985‡	
Males	59,496,000
Females	61,551,000
Total	121,047,196
Population (official estimates at 1 October)†	
1982	118,693,000
1983	119,483,000
1984	120,235,000
Density (per sq km) at 1 October 1985	320.4

* 145,869 sq miles.
† Excluding foreign military and diplomatic personnel and their dependants.
‡ Figures are provisional. The totals for males and females are rounded.

BIRTHS, MARRIAGES AND DEATHS*

	Registered live births		Registered marriages†		Registered deaths	
	Number	Rate (per '000)	Number	Rate (per '000)	Number	Rate (per '000)
1978	1,708,643	14.9	793,257	6.9	695,821	6.1
1979	1,642,580	14.2	788,505	6.8	689,664	6.0
1980	1,576,889	13.6	774,702	6.7	722,801	6.2
1981	1,529,455	13.0	776,531	6.6	720,262	6.1
1982	1,515,392	12.8	781,252	6.6	711,883	6.0
1983	1,508,687	12.7	762,552	6.4	740,038	6.2
1984	1,489,786	12.5	739,993	6.2	740,255	6.2
1985	1,431,577	11.9	735,852	6.1	752,259	6.3

* Figures relate only to Japanese nationals in Japan.
† Data are tabulated by year of registration rather than by year of occurrence.

PRINCIPAL CITIES* (population at 1 October 1985)

Tokyo (capital)†	8,353,674	Oita	390,105
Yokohama	2,992,644	Takatsuki	384,783
Osaka	2,636,260	Hirakata	382,257
Nagoya	2,116,350	Urawa	377,233
Sapporo	1,542,979	Omiya	373,015
Kyoto	1,479,125	Asahikawa	363,630
Kobe	1,410,843	Fukuyama	360,264
Fukuoka	1,160,402	Iwaki	350,566
Kawasaki	1,088,611	Suita	348,946
Kitakyushu	1,056,400	Nagano	336,967
Hiroshima	1,044,129	Fujisawa	328,387
Sakai	818,368	Nara	327,702
Chiba	788,920	Takamatsu	327,001
Sendai	700,248	Toyohashi	322,142
Okayama	572,423	Machida	321,182
Kumamoto	555,722	Hakodate	319,190
Kagoshima	530,496	Toyama	314,111
Higashiosaka	522,798	Kochi	312,253
Hamamatsu	514,118	Toyoda	308,106
Amagasaki	509,115	Naha	303,680
Funabashi	506,967	Koriyama	301,672
Sagamihara	482,778	Akita	296,381
Niigata	475,633	Aomori	294,050
Shizuoka	468,362	Kawagoe	285,435
Himeji	452,916	Okazaki	284,996
Nagasaki	449,382	Miyazaki	279,118
Kanazawa	430,480	Maebashi	277,319
Matsudo	427,479	Yao	276,397
Yokosuka	427,087	Fukushima	270,252
Hachioji	426,650	Shimonoseki	269,167
Matsuyama	426,646	Akashi	263,365
Nishinomiya	421,267	Yokkaichi	263,003
Kurashiki	413,644	Kashiwa	261,331‡
Toyonaka	413,219	Neyagawa	258,230
Gifu	411,740	Tokushima	257,886
Utsunomiya	405,384	Ichinomiya	257,392
Kawaguchi	403,012	Tokorozawa	257,033‡
Wakayama	401,357	Sasebo	250,635
Ichikawa	397,806	Kasugai	249,122‡

* Except for Tokyo, the data for each city refer to an urban county (*shi*), an administrative division which may include some scattered or rural population as well as an urban centre.
† The figure refers to the 23 wards (*ku*) of Tokyo. The population of Tokyo-to (Tokyo Prefecture) was 11,828,262.
‡ Estimated population at 1 October 1983.

ECONOMICALLY ACTIVE POPULATION*
(annual averages, '000 persons aged 15 and over)

	1983	1984	1985
Agriculture and forestry	4,850	4,680	4,640
Fishing and aquatic culture	460	440	450
Mining and quarrying	100	80	90
Manufacturing	14,060	14,380	14,530
Electricity, gas and water	360	350	330
Construction	5,410	5,270	5,300
Trade and restaurants	13,130	13,190	13,180
Transport, storage and communications	3,500	3,410	3,430
Financing, insurance and real estate	2,130	2,160	2,170

	1983	1984	1985
Government services	1,950	1,950	1,990
Other services	11,220	11,540	11,730
Activities not adequately defined	150	210	230
Total employed	57,330	57,660	58,070
Unemployed	1,560	1,610	1,560
Total labour force	58,890	59,270	59,630
Males	35,640	35,800	35,960
Females	23,240	23,470	23,670

* All figures are rounded, so totals may not always be the sum of their component parts.

Agriculture

PRINCIPAL CROPS ('000 metric tons)*

	1983	1984	1985
Rice (brown)†	10,366	11,878	11,662
Barley	340	353	340
Wheat	695	741	874
Potatoes	3,480	3,621	3,649
Sweet potatoes	1,379	1,400	1,527
Silk cocoons	61	50	47
Soybeans (Soya beans)	217	238	228
Tobacco (leaves)	137	136	116

* Data at harvest time.
† To obtain the equivalent in paddy rice, the conversion factor is 150 kg of brown rice equals 186.6 kg of paddy.

LIVESTOCK ('000 head)

	1984	1985	1986
Cattle	4,682	4,698	4,742
Sheep	22	24	26
Goats	54	51	48
Horses	24	23	23
Pigs	10,423	10,718	11,061
Chickens	309,205	n.a.	n.a.

LIVESTOCK PRODUCTS (metric tons)

	1983	1984	1985
Beef and veal	494,934	536,057	555,379
Pig meat	1,428,824	1,424,204	1,531,727
Poultry meat	1,584,092	1,685,153	1,763,205
Cows' milk	7,042,300	7,137,500	7,380,400
Butter*	74,259	77,604	88,933
Cheese*	67,800	69,326	68,367
Hen eggs	2,085,641	2,129,948	2,140,727
Raw silk	12,457	10,780	9,592

* Industrial production only (i.e. butter and cheese manufactured at milk plants), excluding farm production.

Forestry

INDUSTRIAL ROUNDWOOD ('000 cu m)

	1982	1983	1984
Sawn timber	19,953	19,392	18,946
Pulp	1,820	1,894	1,748
Veneer sheets and plywood	443	442	457
Others	9,688	10,262	11,360
Total	31,904	31,990	32,511

Source: Ministry of Agriculture, Forestry and Fisheries, *Report on Demand and Supply of Lumber*.

Fishing

('000 metric tons, live weight)

	1982	1983	1984*
Freshwater fishes	100.2	93.5	90.3
Chum salmon (Keta or Dog salmon)	111.8	133.5	136.4
Flounders, halibuts, soles, etc.	278.3	258.1	260.7
Pacific cod	95.9	104.1	114.0
Alaska pollack	1,570.4	1,434.4	1,604.9
Pacific sandlance	126.7	120.2	164.4
Atka mackerel	103.0	55.5	65.7
Pacific saury (Skipper)	207.0	239.7	210.0
Japanese jack mackerel	108.8	134.5	139.4
Japanese scad	69.1	44.0	98.2
Japanese amberjack	146.3	155.9	152.5
Japanese pilchard (sardine)	3,290.0	3,745.1	4,179.4
Japanese anchovy	197.5	207.6	224.1
Skipjack tuna (Oceanic skipjack)	303.0	352.7	446.2
Yellowfin tuna	117.4	116.0	119.4
Bigeye tuna	139.1	132.0	127.9
Chub mackerel	717.6	804.8	813.5
Other fishes (incl. unspecified)	1,562.5	1,463.6	1,443.1
Total fish	9,244.4	9,595.3	10,390.0
Marine crabs	90.3	100.9	98.7
Other crustaceans	102.2	113.4	117.8
Pacific cupped oyster	250.3	253.2	257.1
Japanese scallop	176.4	213.2	209.2
Japanese (Manila) clam	139.4	160.4	128.3
Other marine clams	100.7	80.9	98.1
Japanese flying squid	181.7	192.1	173.7
Other squids and cuttlefishes	369.0	346.5	352.2
Other molluscs	94.4	89.0	83.3
Other sea creatures†	78.0	110.1	112.8
Total catch†	10,826.7	11,255.1	12,021.2
Inland waters	221.4	209.8	202.7
Atlantic Ocean	168.1	118.2	206.0
Indian Ocean	61.0	82.3	54.3
Pacific Ocean	10,376.2	10,844.8	11,558.2

* Provisional.
† Excluding aquatic mammals (including whales, see below).

Source: FAO, *Yearbook of Fishery Statistics*.

WHALING*

	1982	1983	1984
Number of whales caught	5,294	4,605	4,356

* Figures include whales caught during the Antarctic summer season beginning in the year prior to the year stated.

Aquatic plants ('000 metric tons): 630.8 in 1982; 711.4 in 1983; 762.5 in 1984.

Source: FAO, *Yearbook of Fishery Statistics*.

Mining

	1983	1984	1985
Coal ('000 metric tons)	17,062	16,645	16,383
Zinc ore ('000 metric tons)	255	253	253
Iron ('000 metric tons)	298	324	338
Manganese ('000 metric tons)	77	62	21
Silica stone ('000 metric tons)	13,773	13,973	14,357
Limestone ('000 metric tons)	169,780	169,821	164,156
Chromite (metric tons)	8,396	7,420	11,920
Copper ore (metric tons)	46,045	43,309	43,208
Lead (metric tons)	46,888	48,735	49,951
Gold ore (kg)	3,139	3,220	5,309
Crude petroleum (million litres)	492	476	623
Natural gas ('000 cu m)	2,085,392	2,132,069	2,224,640

Source: Ministry of International Trade and Industry.

Industry

SELECTED PRODUCTS

		1983	1984	1985
Wheat flour[1]	'000 metric tons	4,356	4,445	n.a.
Sugar*	'000 metric tons	2,041.1	2,147.2	2,079.2
Distilled alcoholic beverages	'000 hectolitres	8,349	9,008	4,425
Beer[1]	'000 hectolitres	50,534	45,978	48,522
Cigarettes[1]	million	306,320	306,867	308,500
Cotton yarn (pure)	metric tons	399,833	390,709	392,526
Cotton yarn (mixed)	metric tons	37,865	46,031	44,505
Woven cotton fabrics (pure and mixed)	million sq m	2,078.6	2,089.8	206,087
Flax, ramie and hemp yarn	metric tons	5,224	6,404	6,293
Jute yarn	metric tons	9,485	8,794	6,577
Linen fabrics	'000 sq m	20,473	24,786	25,247
Jute fabrics	'000 sq m	3,080	612	481
Woven silk fabrics (pure and mixed)	'000 sq m	121,794	115,116	114,538
Wool yarn (pure and mixed)	metric tons	110,000	120,930	123,427
Woven woollen fabrics (pure and mixed)[2]	'000 sq m	301,823	327,134	325,601
Rayon continuous filaments	metric tons	84,683	79,714	76,381
Acetate continuous filaments	metric tons	32,124	31,107	28,213
Rayon discontinuous fibres	metric tons	271,020	266,562	244,910
Acetate discontinuous fibres[3]	metric tons	36,807	41,140	38,427
Woven rayon fabrics (pure and mixed)[2]	million sq m	650.0	632.2	656.3
Woven acetate fabrics (pure and mixed)[2]	million sq m	58.6	64.6	63.0
Non-cellulosic continuous filaments	metric tons	611,255	648,114	653,638
Non-cellulosic discontinuous fibres	metric tons	749,979	767,037	792,287
Woven synthetic fabrics[2,4]	million sq m	3,218.7	3,296.8	3,067.6
Leather footwear[5]	'000 pairs	48,408	55,708	53,387
Mechanical wood pulp Chemical wood pulp[6]	'000 metric tons '000 metric tons	8,860.2	9,127.3	9,278.9
Newsprint	'000 metric tons	2,561.6	2,553.4	2,592.1
Other printing and writing paper	'000 metric tons	4,319.2	4,551.1	4,746.4
Other paper	'000 metric tons	4,051.3	4,324.7	4,451.5
Paperboard	'000 metric tons	7,509.9	7,915.4	8,678.9
Synthetic rubber	'000 metric tons	1,002.5	1,160.5	1,158.0
Motor vehicle tyres	'000	135,754	143,311	149,513
Rubber footwear	'000 pairs	64,992	64,998	62,367
Ethylene (Ethene)	'000 metric tons	3,687.7	4,385.7	4,226.9
Propylene (Propene)	'000 metric tons	2,657.5	2,980.7	3,057.1
Benzene (Benzol)	'000 metric tons	1,938.0	2,217.6	n.a.
Toluene (Toluol)	'000 metric tons	856.2	811.2	829.3
Xylenes (Xylol)	'000 metric tons	1,270.4	1,400.9	1,523.5
Methyl alcohol (Methanol)	'000 metric tons	373.2	280.1	254.3
Ethyl alcohol (95%)	kilolitres	163,423	167,627	179,197
Sulphuric acid (100%)	'000 metric tons	6,661.8	6,451.4	6,580.0
Caustic soda (Sodium hydroxide)	'000 metric tons	2,863.3	3,085.3	3,074.1

continued overleaf

JAPAN

Statistical Survey

continued

		1983	1984	1985
Soda ash (Sodium carbonate)	'000 metric tons	1,103.4	1,036.2	1,057.1
Ammonium sulphate	'000 metric tons	1,719.6	1,829.4	1,837.0
Nitrogenous fertilizers (a)[7]	'000 metric tons	1,126	1,075	1,210
Phosphate fertilizers (b)[7]	'000 metric tons	623	647	641
Liquefied petroleum gas	'000 metric tons	7,933	8,139	8,354
Naphtha	million litres	11,528	11,672	10,348
Motor spirit (Gasoline)[8]	million litres	35,713	36,383	36,453
Kerosene	million litres	22,431	26,841	24,248
Jet fuel	million litres	4,441	3,737	4,327
Gas oil	million litres	23,047	24,782	25,468
Heavy fuel oil	million litres	77,287	76,441	65,117
Lubricating oil	million litres	2,110	2,228	2,256
Petroleum bitumen (Asphalt)	'000 metric tons	4,965	5,137	5,001
Coke-oven coke	'000 metric tons	46,674	51,275	51,742
Gas coke	'000 metric tons	3,098	n.a.	n.a.
Cement	'000 metric tons	80,892	78,851	72,847
Pig-iron	'000 metric tons	73,936	80,403	80,569
Ferro-alloys[9]	'000 metric tons	1,258	1,418	1,389
Crude steel	'000 metric tons	97,169	105,588	105,279
Aluminium (unwrought):				
primary	'000 metric tons	255.9	286.7	226.5
secondary[10]	'000 metric tons	837.7	840	n.a.
Electrolytic copper	'000 metric tons	1,091.9	935.1	936.0
Refined lead (unwrought)	metric tons	241,304	278,494	285,372
Electrolytic, distilled and rectified zinc (unwrought)	metric tons	701,291	754,445	739,624
Calculating machines	'000	66,547	83,713	86,031
Radio receivers	'000	13,339	13,589	12,995
Television receivers	'000	13,276	15,512	17,727
Merchant vessels launched	'000 g.r.t.	6,831	9,435	9,101
Passenger motor cars	'000	7,151.9	7,073.2	7,646.8
Lorries and trucks	'000	3,903.8	4,319.5	4,544.7
Motorcycles, scooters and mopeds	'000	4,807.4	4,026.3	4,536.3
Cameras:				
photographic	'000	14,184	15,337	16,995
cinematographic	'000	110.4	79.1	51.1
Watches and clocks	'000	173,545	221,907	257,354
Construction: new dwellings started[11]	'000	1,136.8	1,187.2	1,236.1
Electric energy[1]	million kWh	618,100	648.572	671,952
Town gas	teracalories	110,903	121,840	124,515

* Twelve months ending September.
[1] Twelve months beginning 1 April of the year stated. [2] Including finished fabrics.
[3] Including cigarette filtration tow. [4] Including blankets made of synthetic fibres.
[5] Sales. [6] Including pulp prepared by semi-chemical processes.
[7] Figures refer to the 12 months ending 30 June of the year stated and are in terms of (a) nitrogen, 100%, and (b) phosphoric acid, 100%.
[8] Including aviation gasoline. [9] Including silico-chromium.
[10] Including alloys. [11] Including buildings and dwelling units created by conversion.

Sources: Ministry of Agriculture, Forestry and Fisheries, Ministry of International Trade and Industry, Ministry of Finance and Ministry of Construction.

Finance

CURRENCY AND EXCHANGE RATES

Monetary Units

1,000 rin = 100 sen = 1 yen.

Denominations

Coins: 1, 5, 10, 50 and 100 yen.
Notes: 500, 1,000, 5,000 and 10,000 yen.

Sterling and Dollar Equivalents (30 September 1986)
£1 sterling = 223.35 yen;
US $1 = 154.35 yen;
1,000 yen = £4.477 = $6.479.

Average Exchange Rate (yen per US $)
1983   237.51
1984   237.52
1985   238.54

INTERNATIONAL RESERVES
(US $ million at 31 December)

	1983	1984	1985
Gold*	888	831	931
IMF special drawing rights	1,935	1,927	2,116
Reserve position in IMF	2,303	2,219	2,275
Foreign exchange	20,364	22,283	22,328
Total	25,490	27,260	27,650

* Valued at 35 SDRs per troy ounce.

Source: IMF, *International Financial Statistics*.

JAPAN

GENERAL BUDGET ESTIMATES
('000 million yen, year ending 31 March)

Revenue	1984/85	1985/86	1986/87
Taxes and stamps	34,596	38,550	40,560
Public bonds	12,680	11,680	10,946
Others	3,351	2,270	2,583
Total	50,627	52,500	54,089

Expenditure	1984/85	1985/86	1986/87
Social security	9,321	9,574	9,835
Education and science	4,832	4,841	4,845
Government bond servicing	9,155	10,224	11,320
Defence	2,935	3,137	3,344
Public works	6,520	6,369	6,223
Local finance	9,069	9,690	10,185
Pensions	1,886	1,864	1,850
Total (incl. others)	50,627	52,500	54,089

MONEY SUPPLY ('000 million yen at 31 December)

	1983	1984	1985
Currency outside banks	20,575.1	22,113.6	23,406.8
Demand deposits at deposit money banks	60,226.7	64,260.7	65,572.7
Total money	80,801.8	86,374.3	88,979.5

COST OF LIVING (Consumer Price Index; average of monthly figures. Base: 1980 = 100)

	1983	1984	1985
Food (incl. beverages)	109.4	112.5	114.4
Housing	110.3	113.2	116.2
Rent	113.3	117.1	120.8
Fuel and light	111.2	111.0	110.6
Clothing	109.5	112.3	116.1
Miscellaneous	110.5	113.0	114.5
All items	109.7	112.1	114.4

NATIONAL ACCOUNTS ('000 million yen at current prices)

	1983	1984	1985
Government final consumption expenditure	27,996.2	29,448.8	30,748.1
Private final consumption expenditure	167,809.3	175,984.3	184,427.2
Increase in stocks	217.3	1,137.8	2,540.0
Gross fixed capital formation	79,217.3	83,176.0	87,623.5
Total domestic expenditure	275,240.2	289,746.9	305,339.0
Exports of goods and services	39,274.5	45,066.0	46,307.2
Less Imports of goods and services	34,258.2	36,865.5	35,531.6
Gross domestic product	280,256.5	297,947.5	316,114.5
Factor income received from abroad	4,211.5	4,953.4	5,768.4
Less Factor income paid abroad	3,900.4	4,448.2	4,631.1
Gross national product	280,567.6	298,452.7	317,251.8
Less Consumption of fixed capital	38,393.8	40,715.4	43,581.6
Statistical discrepancy	−1,087.5	−1,278.8	−1,461.8
National income in market prices	241,086.3	256,458.7	272,208.3

Gross Domestic Product by Economic Activity

	1983	1984	1985
Agriculture, forestry and fishing	9,264.3	9,625.6	9,949.0
Mining and quarrying	1,220.6	1,207.6	1,225.7
Manufacturing	81,415.6	88,845.0	94,257.3
Electricity, gas and water	8,875.7	9,658.1	10,549.1
Construction	22,097.3	22,437.0	23,128.9
Wholesale and retail trade	41,773.5	42,288.6	43,313.3
Transport, storage and communications	17,300.0	18,716.3	19,652.4
Finance and insurance	15,886.7	16,540.5	17,782.2
Real estate	27,360.7	29,204.8	30,996.6
Public administration	13,121.7	13,765.3	14,358.1
Other services	52,675.8	56,853.5	62,882.4
Sub-total	290,992.0	309,142.3	328,094.9
Import duties	1,187.1	1,337.3	1,268.1
Less Imputed bank service charge	13,010.0	13,810.9	14,710.2
Total	279,169.0	296,668.7	314,652.7
Statistical discrepancy	1,087.5	1,278.7	1,461.8
Gross domestic product	280,256.5	297,947.5	316,114.5

JAPAN

Statistical Survey

BALANCE OF PAYMENTS (US $ million)

	1984 Credit	1984 Debit	1984 Balance	1985 Credit	1985 Debit	1985 Balance
Goods and services:						
Merchandise f.o.b.	168,290	124,033	44,257	174,015	118,029	55,986
Freight	7,359	3,812	3,547	7,371	3,680	3,691
Insurance on merchandise	290	385	−95	261	364	−103
Non-merchandise insurance	−196	277	−473	−248	178	−426
Other transportation	5,237	11,720	−6,483	4,812	11,049	−6,237
Tourists	670	2,385	−1,715	1,137	4,814	−3,677
Other travel	300	2,222	−1,922			
Investment income	18,768	14,537	4,231	22,107	15,267	6,840
Military transactions	1,491	—	1,491	1,629	—	1,629
Other government services	970	331	639	1,038	392	646
Other private services	7,265	14,231	−6,966	7,404	14,932	−7,528
Total	210,444	173,934	36,510	219,526	168,705	50,821
Unrequited transfers:						
Private transfer payments	478	613	−135	347	624	−277
Reparations	—	—	—	—	—	—
Other government transfers	87	1,459	−1,372	77	1,452	−1,375
Total	565	2,072	−1,507	424	2,076	−1,652
Total current account	211,009	176,006	35,003	219,950	170,781	49,169
Capital flows:						
Long-term capital:						
Direct investments	−10	5,965	−5,975	642	6,452	−5,810
Trade credits (net)	3	4,937	−4,934	29	2,817	−2,788
Loans (net)	−77	11,922	−11,999	−75	10,427	−10,502
Securities (net)	−156	30,795	−30,951	3,851	59,773	−55,922
External bonds	12,269	4,919	7,350	16,619	3,729	12,890
Others (net)	14	3,156	−3,142	−64	2,346	−2,410
Balance	12,043	61,694	−49,651	21,002	85,544	−64,542
Short-term capital:						
Trade credits (net)	—	2,110	−2,110	—	1,367	−1,367
Others (net)	—	2,185	−2,185	431	—	431
Balance on capital account	12,043	65,989	−53,941	21,433	86,911	−65,478
Net errors and omissions	3,743	—	3,743	3,991	—	3,991
Overall balance (net monetary movements)			−15,200			−12,318
of which:						
Gold and foreign exchange reserves			1,817			197
Others			−17,017			−12,515
of which: commercial banks			−17,560			−10,848

Source: Bank of Japan, *Balance of Payments, Monthly*.

JAPANESE DEVELOPMENT ASSISTANCE (US $ '000)

	1983	1984	1985
Official:			
Bilateral grants:			
Donations	993,000	1,064,000	1,185,000
Reparations	535,000	543,000	636,000
Technical assistance	458,000	521,000	549,000
Direct loans	1,432,000	1,363,000	1,372,000
Total	2,425,000	2,427,000	2,557,000
Capital subscriptions or grants to international agencies	1,336,000	1,891,000	1,240,000
Total	3,761,000	4,319,000	3,797,000
Other Government capital:			
Export credits	472,000	493,000	−152,000
Direct investment capital	1,442,000	380,000	−1,000
Loans to international agencies	41,000	−130,000	−148,000
Total	1,954,000	743,000	−302,000
Total official	5,715,000	5,062,000	3,495,000
Private:			
Export credits	−2,069,000	−655,000	−994,000
Direct investments	433,000	1,489,000	1,046,000
Other bilateral security investments	4,840,000	6,828,000	6,705,000
Loans to international agencies	1,574,000	2,306,000	2,575,000
Donations to non-profit organizations	30,000	41,000	101,000
Total	4,809,000	10,009,000	9,433,000
Grand total	10,523,000	15,071,000	12,928,000

External Trade

PRINCIPAL COMMODITIES (US $ million)

Imports c.i.f.	1983	1984	1985
Food and live animals	14,051.0	15,190.8	14,787.4
Meat and meat preparations	1,771.6	1,897.0	1,926.6
Fresh, chilled or frozen meat	1,701.4	1,807.1	n.a.
Fish and fish preparations*	3,884.3	4,096.2	4,610.0
Crustacea and molluscs (fresh and simply preserved)	2,027.8	2,099.3	n.a.
Cereals and cereal preparations	4,200.0	4,743.3	3,950.7
Wheat and meslin (unmilled)	1,126.3	1,113.9	973.8
Maize (unmilled) for feeding	1,571.6	1,668.9	1,362.7
Fruit and vegetables	1,612.8	1,827.9	1,828.1
Sugar, sugar preparations and honey	541.9	449.4	344.2
Sugar and honey	523.9	433.5	n.a.
Raw sugar	392.9	294.5	209.6
Coffee, tea, cocoa and spices	972.2	1,128.0	1,138.7
Beverages and tobacco	844.9	835.8	760.0
Crude materials (inedible) except fuels	17,943.4	19,152.9	17,715.0
Oil-seeds, oil nuts and oil kernels	1,952.3	2,209.6	1,875.2
Soya beans (excl. flour)	1,375.4	1,447.2	1,206.1
Wood, lumber and cork	3,902.8	2,209.6	3,720.4
Rough or roughly squared wood	3,045.1	3,931.8	3,699.6
Coniferous sawlogs and veneer logs	1,437.6	1,381.1	n.a.
Non-coniferous sawlogs and veneer logs	1,565.1	1,675.2	n.a.
Textile fibres and waste	2,076.6	2,483.8	2,155.1
Cotton	1,145.0	1,342.4	1,048.7
Raw cotton (excl. linters)	1,120.8	1,308.4	1,021.3
Metalliferous ores and metal scrap	6,513.0	6,572.1	6,232.1
Iron ore and concentrates	3,146.6	3,199.1	3,044.9
Non-ferrous ores and concentrates	2,403.4	2,334.2	2,229.0
Copper ores and concentrates (excl. matte)	1,475.3	1,254.7	1,209.3
Mineral fuels, lubricants, etc.	58,924.6	60,337.1	55,799.2
Coal, coke and briquettes	4,888.6	5,321.5	5,209.3
Coal (excl. briquettes)	4,877.4	5,310.9	5,196.5
Petroleum and petroleum products	45,704.5	45,486.2	40,574.9
Crude and partly refined petroleum	40,062.6	39,379.0	34,599.4
Crude petroleum	39,662.2	38,999.9	n.a.
Petroleum products	5,641.8	6,107.2	5,975.5
Residual fuel oils	1,807.2	2,129.7	2,019.5
Gas (natural and manufactured)	8,331.6	9,529.3	10,006.1
Animal and vegetable oils and fats	268.1	372.3	328.9
Chemicals	7,207.4	8,346.4	8,072.7
Chemical elements and compounds	3,553.5	4,370.4	4,142.4
Organic chemicals	2,111.8	2,432.4	2,410.6
Inorganic chemicals	525.8	677.3	742.1
Medicinal and pharmaceutical products	1,214.5	1,258.5	1,291.9
Basic manufactures	10,146.8	11,932.2	10,885.5
Textile yarn, fabrics, etc.	1,436.8	1,925.5	1,891.1
Non-metallic mineral manufactures	1,101.2	1,201.4	1,264.3
Iron and steel	1,348.7	1,911.7	1,479.5
Non-ferrous metals	4,126.6	4,699.6	4,041.5
Aluminium and aluminium alloys	2,164.7	2,076.0	1,861.3
Unwrought aluminium and alloys	2,088.4	1,978.3	n.a.
Machinery and transport equipment	9,384.5	10,808.9	11,106.3
Non-electric machinery	3,664.7	4,494.6	4,727.9
Electrical machinery, apparatus, etc.	3,220.5	3,989.0	3,795.2
Transport equipment	2,499.4	2,325.3	2,583.1
Aircraft and parts†	1,472.2	928.4	1,483.6
Miscellaneous manufactured articles	5,204.4	6,087.5	6,349.2
Clothing (excl. footwear)	1,500.6	1,949.1	1,995.1
Other commodities and transactions	2,417.8	3,439.4	3,743.5
Re-imports	943.6	1,045.3	1,568.9
Non-monetary gold	1,376.2	2,245.7	2,026.7
Total	126,393.1	136,503.0	129,538.7

* Including crustacea and molluscs.
† Excluding tyres, engines and electrical parts.

Exports f.o.b.	1983	1984	1985
Food and live animals	1,245.6	1,289.9	1,202.0
Beverages and tobacco	143.6	149.7	113.7
Crude materials (inedible) except fuels	1,193.6	1,249.6	1,240.2
Mineral fuels, lubricants, etc.	432.3	504.9	589.9
Animal and vegetable oils and fats	118.2	148.2	111.4
Chemicals	6,982.8	7,625.7	7,697.7
Chemical elements and compounds	2,945.0	3,121.1	3,242.9
Organic chemicals	2,177.3	2,370.6	2,511.8
Plastic materials, etc.	2,038.6	2,350.8	2,260.6
Basic manufactures	28,935.4	30,137.0	28,835.8
Rubber manufactures	1,823.3	1,972.5	1,894.7
Rubber tyres and tubes	1,516.6	1,633.9	1,544.6
Textile yarn, fabrics, etc.	5,310.6	5,317.7	4,900.1
Woven textile fabrics (excl. narrow or special fabrics)	3,625.5	3,545.6	3,360.6
Fabrics of synthetic (excl. regenerated) fibres	2,417.8	2,248.3	2,033.5
Non-metallic mineral manufactures	2,150.4	2,272.1	2,147.5
Iron and steel	12,843.2	13,852.1	13,565.8
Ingots and other primary forms	969.5	1,031.8	n.a.
Coils for re-rolling	933.8	992.6	n.a.
Bars, rods, angles, shapes, etc.	1,815.9	1,715.4	1,777.4
Universals, plates and sheets	5,338.8	5,706.3	5,209.2
Thin plates and sheets (uncoated)	2,590.2	2,609.9	2,420.9
Tubes, pipes and fittings	3,370.4	3,741.7	3,659.5
Seamless tubes and pipes	1,587.7*	2,019.0*	n.a.
Welded (excl. cast iron) tubes and pipes	1,351.0*	1,352.2*	n.a.
Non-ferrous metals	1,587.9	1,501.4	1,466.9
Other metal manufactures	3,941.2	3,812.0	3,458.4
Machinery and transport equipment	85,132.5	102,680.0	108,387.4
Non-electric machinery	23,103.4	27,879.4	29,537.2
Power generating machinery	2,992.0	3,834.8	3,788.9
Internal combustion engines (non-aircraft)	2,239.9	2,800.0	2,884.7
Office machines	5,139.0	7,554.3	7,785.2
Metalworking machinery	1,489.2	2,020.8	2,599.2
Heating and cooling eqipment	2,142.4	1,887.0	1,588.0
Electrical machinery, apparatus, etc.	22,886.0	29,245.0	29,700.9
Electric power machinery	1,873.0	2,136.6	2,057.8
Telecommunications apparatus	8,866.8	11,076.7	12,242.1
Television receivers	1,472.0	1,904.7	2,624.8
Radio receivers	2,439.9	2,819.8	2,654.4
Thermionic valves, tubes, etc.	3,730.5	5,816.1	4,953.4
Transport equipment	39,143.0	45,555.6	49,149.4
Road motor vehicles and parts†	32,213.1	34,334.3	n.a.
Passenger cars (excl. buses)	19,535.3	21,898.7	25,402.2
Lorries and trucks (incl. ambulances)	5,174.9	6,372.0	7,396.0
Parts for cars, buses, etc.†	3,423.4	3,518.7	5,227.7
Motor cycles and parts	2,667.0	2,597.8	2,625.9
Motor cycles	2,082.9	2,043.7	2,092.4
Ships and boats	5,995.8	7,352.6	5,929.4
Miscellaneous manufactured articles	21,197.9	24,654.5	25,751.9
Scientific instruments, watches, etc.	8,212.8	9,268.4	10,046.1
Scientific instruments and photographic equipment	5,438.9	6,160.0	6,830.9
Watches, clocks and parts	1,549.8	1,747.0	1,730.2
Musical instruments, sound recorders, etc.	9,377.4	9,222.1	14,537.4
Sound recorders, phonographs and parts	7,438.9	n.a.	9,230.4
Sound recorders and phonographs	6,975.3	8,665.9	n.a.
Other commodities and transactions	1,545.6	1,674.4	1,758.6
Re-exports	1,419.4	1,595.6	1,712.6
Total	146,927.5	170,113.9	175,637.8

* Provisional.   † Excluding tyres, engines and electrical parts.

JAPAN

PRINCIPAL TRADING PARTNERS* (US $ million)

Imports c.i.f.	1983	1984	1985
Australia	6,641.5	7,296.4	7,452.2
Brazil	1,669.0	1,990.8	1,840.2
Brunei	2,366.7	2,202.5	1,892.2
Canada	4,429.7	4,945.1	4,772.9
China, People's Republic	5,087.4	5,957.6	6,482.7
France	1,302.0	1,236.0	1,323.7
Germany, Federal Republic	2,413.7	2,684.4	2,928.0
India	1,130.8	1,132.4	1,188.6
Indonesia	10,432.3	11,175.5	10,119.0
Iran	4,231.4	2,868.8	2,505.8
Italy	980.5	1,048.9	1,049.8
Korea, Republic	3,365.0	4,212.7	4,091.9
Kuwait	1,387.4	1,588.5	1,162.3
Malaysia	3,130.7	4,412.1	4,330.1
Mexico	1,889.0	2,259.8	1,869.9
Oman	2,012.2	2,419.7	3,065.9
Philippines	1,306.5	1,418.6	1,243.1
Qatar	1,700.8	2,593.6	2,185.1
Saudi Arabia	15,530.0	14,734.1	10,244.7
Singapore	1,467.5	1,775.4	1,593.9
South Africa	1,587.3	1,610.8	1,843.9
Switzerland	1,412.3	1,964.9	1,758.1
Taiwan	2,622.3	3,203.9	3,385.5
Thailand	1,018.7	1,039.6	1,026.9
USSR	1,456.0	1,394.0	1,429.3
United Arab Emirates	7,793.0	7,720.3	8,916.3
United Kingdom	1,940.0	2,266.6	1,816.8
USA	24,179.2	26,862.0	25,093.0
Total (incl. others)	126,393.1	136,503.0	129,538.7

Exports f.o.b.	1983	1984	1985
Australia	4,279.9	5,184.3	5,379.0
Belgium and Luxembourg	1,335.0	1,349.5	1,492.9
Canada	3,624.9	4,297.8	4,520.2
China, People's Republic	4,912.3	7,216.7	12,477.4
France	2,009.5	1,935.4	2,083.1
Germany, Federal Republic	5,877.4	6,621.6	6,937.8
Hong Kong	5,288.8	6,559.1	6,509.2
India	1,430.7	1,167.8	1,596.4
Indonesia	3,552.1	3,073.1	2,172.5
Iran	2,819.9	1,692.1	1,347.7
Iraq	631.6	806.0	1,305.6
Italy	874.5	1,032.1	n.a.
Korea, Republic	6,003.8	7,226.8	7,097.2
Kuwait	1,762.6	1,431.9	1,536.1
Malaysia	2,770.8	2,874.8	2,168.2
Mexico	578.9	887.9	994.0
Netherlands	1,726.4	1,815.5	2,071.1
New Zealand	962.4	1,162.9	1,072.4
Panama	2,169.3	3,444.0	3,326.1
Philippines	1,743.6	1,079.9	936.6
Saudi Arabia	6,686.6	5,634.1	3,890.0
Singapore	4,448.2	4,610.2	3,860.5
South Africa	1,738.0	1,839.9	1,019.9
Sweden	797.6	1,009.4	n.a.
Switzerland	1,143.5	1,089.4	1,160.8
Taiwan	5,086.0	5,986.2	5,025.5
Thailand	2,506.5	2,424.6	2,030.4
USSR	2,821.2	2,518.3	2,750.6
United Arab Emirates	1,356.7	1,126.3	1,164.4
United Kingdom	4,982.5	4,675.0	4,722.8
USA	42,828.8	59,937.3	65,277.6
Total (incl. others)	146,927.5	170,113.9	175,637.8

* Imports by country of production; exports by country of last consignment.

Source: Ministry of Finance, *The Summary Report, Trade of Japan*.

Transport

RAILWAYS (traffic—million)

	1982/83	1983/84	1984/85
National railways			
Passengers	6,742	6,797	6,884
Freight ton-km	30,246	27,086	22,721
Private railways			
Passengers	11,527	11,741	11,869
Freight ton-km	636	560	513

ROAD TRAFFIC
('000 licensed vehicles, year ending 31 March)

	1982/83	1983/84	1984/85
Cars	24,283	25,028	25,848
Buses	230	230	231
Lorries	8,462	8,382	8,306
Special purpose vehicles	880	912	944
Total	33,854	34,551	35,328

Source: Ministry of Transport.

SHIPPING
Merchant Fleet (registered at 30 June)

	1983	1984	1985
Vessels	10,593	10,425	10,288
Displacement ('000 gt)	40,752	40,358	39,940

Source: *Lloyd's Register of Shipping*.

International Sea-borne Traffic

	1983	1984	1985
Vessels entered:			
Number	37,740	38,980	39,856
Displacement ('000 net tons)	332,147	347,907	352,589
Goods ('000 metric tons):			
Loaded	91,052	94,320	93,821
Unloaded	552,445	602,776	603,277

Source: Ministry of Finance.

CIVIL AVIATION (domestic and international services)

	1983	1984	1985
Passengers carried ('000)	46,544	51,018	50,337
Passenger/km (million)	58,449	64,601	65,529
Freight ton/km* ('000)	2,506,080	2,699,260	3,089,530

* Including excess baggage.
Original Source: Ministry of Transport.

Tourism

	1983	1984	1985
Foreign visitors	1,968,461	2,110,346	2,327,047
Money received (US $ million)	825	970	1,137

Communications Media

('000)

	1983	1984	1985
Television subscribers*	30,799	31,062	31,509
Daily newspaper circulation†	47,041	48,232	48,232

* At 31 March.   † In October.

Education

(1985)

	Institutions	Teachers	Students
Primary schools	25,040	464,193	11,095,372
Secondary schools	11,131	298,799	5,990,183
High schools	5,453	316,536	5,177,681
Technological colleges	62	5,909	48,288
Junior colleges	543	44,953	371,095
Graduate schools and universities	460	189,016	1,848,698

Directory

The Constitution

The Constitution of Japan was promulgated on 3 November 1946 and came into force on 3 May 1947. The following is a summary of its major provisions:

THE EMPEROR

Articles 1–8. The Emperor derives his position from the will of the people. In the performance of any state act as defined in the Constitution, he must seek the advice and approval of the Cabinet though he may delegate the exercise of his functions, which include: (i) the appointment of the Prime Minister and the Chief Justice of the Supreme Court; (ii) promulgation of laws, cabinet orders, treaties and constitutional amendments; (iii) the convocation of the Diet, dissolution of the House of Representatives and proclamation of elections to the Diet; (iv) the appointment and dismissal of Ministers of State and as well as the granting of amnesties, reprieves and pardons and the ratification of treaties, conventions or protocols; (v) the awarding of honours and performance of ceremonial functions.

RENUNCIATION OF WAR

Article 9. Japan renounces for ever the use of war as a means of settling international disputes.
Articles 10–40 refer to the legal and human rights of individuals guaranteed by the Constitution.

THE DIET

Articles 41–64. The Diet is convened once a year, is the highest organ of state power and has exclusive legislative authority. It comprises the House of Representatives (511 seats) and the House of Councillors (252 seats). The members of the former are elected for four years whilst those of the latter are elected for six years and election for half the members takes place every three years. If the House of Representatives is dissolved, a general election must take place within 40 days and the Diet must be convoked within 30 days of the date of the election. Extraordinary sessions of the Diet may be convened by the Cabinet when one quarter or more of the members of either House request it. Emergency sessions of the House of Councillors may also be held. A quorum of at least one third of the Diet members is needed to carry on Parliamentary business. Any decision arising therefrom must be passed by a majority vote of those present. A bill becomes law having passed both Houses except as provided by the Constitution. If the House of Councillors either vetoes or fails to take action within 60 days upon a bill already passed by the House of Representatives, the bill becomes law when passed a second time by the House of Representatives, by at least a two-thirds majority of those members present.

The Budget must first be submitted to the House of Representatives. If, when it is approved by the House of Representatives, the House of Councillors votes against it or fails to take action on it within 30 days, or failing agreement being reached by a joint committee of both Houses, a decision of the House of Representatives shall be the decision of the Diet. The above procedure also applies in respect of the conclusion of treaties.

THE EXECUTIVE

Articles 65–75. Executive power is vested in the cabinet consisting of a Prime Minister and such other Ministers as may be appointed. The Cabinet is collectively responsible to the Diet. The Prime

JAPAN

Minister is designated from among members of the Diet by a resolution thereof.

If the House of Representatives and the House of Councillors disagree on the designation of the Prime Minister, and if no agreement can be reached even through a joint committee of both Houses, provided for by law, or if the House of Councillors fails to make designation within 10 days, exclusive of the period of recess, after the House of Representatives has made designation, the decision of the House of Representatives shall be the decision of the Diet.

The Prime Minister appoints and may remove other Ministers, a majority of whom must be from the Diet. If the House of Representatives passes a no-confidence motion or rejects a confidence motion, the whole Cabinet resigns unless the House of Representatives is dissolved within 10 days. When there is a vacancy in the post of Prime Minister, or upon the first convocation of the Diet after a general election of members of the House of Representatives, the whole Cabinet resigns.

The Prime Minister submits bills, reports on national affairs and foreign relations to the Diet. He exercises control and supervision over various administrative branches of the Government. The Cabinet's primary functions (in addition to administrative ones) are to: (a) administer the law faithfully; (b) conduct State affairs; (c) conclude treaties subject to prior (or subsequent) Diet approval; (d) administer the civil service in accordance with law; (e) prepare and present the budget to the Diet; (f) enact Cabinet orders in order to make effective legal and constitutional provisions; (g) decide on amnesties, reprieves or pardons. All laws and Cabinet orders are signed by the competent Minister of State and countersigned by the Prime Minister. The Ministers of State, during their tenure of office, are not subject to legal action without the consent of the Prime Minister. However, the right to take that action is not impaired.

Articles 76–95. Relate to the Judiciary, Finance and Local Government.

AMENDMENTS

Article 96. Amendments to the Constitution are initiated by the Diet, through a concurring vote of two-thirds or more of all the members of each House and are submitted to the people for ratification, which requires the affirmative vote of a majority of all votes cast at a special referendum or at such election as the Diet may specify.

Amendments when so ratified must immediately be promulgated by the Emperor in the name of the people, as an integral part of the Constitution.

Articles 97–99 outline the Supreme Law, while Articles 100–103 consist of Supplementary Provisions.

The Government

HEAD OF STATE

His Imperial Majesty HIROHITO, Emperor of Japan (succeeded to the throne 25 December 1926).

THE CABINET
(February 1987)

Prime Minister: YASUHIRO NAKASONE.
Deputy Prime Minister and Minister without Portfolio: SHIN KANEMARU.
Minister of Justice: KANAME ENDO.
Minister of Foreign Affairs: TADASHI KURANARI.
Minister of Finance: KEIICHI MIYAZAWA.
Minister of Education: MASAJURO SHIOKAWA.
Minister of Health and Welfare: JURO SAITO.
Minister of Agriculture, Forestry and Fisheries: MUTSUKI KATO.
Minister of International Trade and Industry: HAJUME TAMURA.
Minister of Transport: RYUTARO HASHIMOTO.
Minister of Posts and Telecommunications: SHUNJIRO KARASAWA.
Minister of Labour: TAKUSHI HIRAI.
Minister of Construction: KOSEI AMANO.
Minister of Home Affairs and Chairman of the Public Safety Commission: NOBUYUKI HANASHI.
Minister of State and Chief Cabinet Secretary: MASAHARU GOTODA.
Minister of State and Director-General of the Management and Co-ordination Agency: TAKUO YAMASHITA.
Minister of State and Director-General of the National Land, Hokkaido Development and Okinawa Development Agencies: TAMISUKE WATANUKI.
Minister of State and Director-General of the Defence Agency: YUKO KURIHARA.
Minister of State and Director-General of the Economic Planning Agency: TETSUO KONDO.
Minister of State, Director-General of the Science and Technology Agency and Chairman of the Atomic Energy Commission: YATARO MITSUBAYASHI.
Minister of State and Director-General of the Environment Agency: TOSHIYUKI INAMURA.
Director of the Cabinet Legislative Bureau: OSAMU MIMURA.

MINISTRIES

Imperial Household Agency: 1-1, Chiyoda, Chiyoda-ku, Tokyo; tel. (3) 213-1111.
Prime Minister's Office: 1-6, Nagata-cho, Chiyoda-ku, Tokyo; tel. (3) 581-2361.
Ministry of Agriculture, Forestry and Fisheries: 1-2, Kasumigaseki, Chiyoda-ku, Tokyo; tel.(3) 502-8111.
Ministry of Construction: 2-1, Kasumigaseki, Chiyoda-ku, Tokyo; tel. (3) 580-4311.
Ministry of Education: 3-2, Kasumigaseki, Chiyoda-ku, Tokyo; tel. (3) 581-4211.
Ministry of Finance: 3-1-1, Kasumigaseki, Chiyoda-ku, Tokyo; tel. (3) 581-4111; telex 24980.
Ministry of Foreign Affairs: 2-2, Kasumigaseki, Chiyoda-ku, Tokyo; tel. (3) 580-3311; telex 22350.
Ministry of Health and Welfare: 1-2, Kasumigaseki, Chiyoda-ku, Tokyo 100; tel. (3) 503-1711.
Ministry of Home Affairs: 2-1, Kasumigaseki, Chiyoda-ku, Tokyo; tel. (3) 581-5311.
Ministry of International Trade and Industry: 1-3, Kasumigaseki, Chiyoda-ku, Tokyo; tel. (3) 501-1511; telex 22916.
Ministry of Justice: 1-1-1, Kasumigaseki, Chiyoda-ku, Tokyo 100; tel. (3) 580-4111.
Ministry of Labour: 2-2, Kasumigaseki, 1-chome, Chiyoda-ku, Tokyo; tel. (3) 593-1211.
Ministry of Posts and Telecommunications: 1-3, Kasumigaseki, Chiyoda-ku, Tokyo; tel. (3) 504-4798.
Ministry of Transport: 2-1, Kasumigaseki, Chiyoda-ku, Tokyo; tel. (3) 580-3111.
Cabinet Legislation Bureau: 3-1, Kasumigaseki, Chiyoda-ku, Tokyo; tel. (3) 581-7271.
Cabinet Secretariat: 2-3, Nagato-cho, Chiyoda-ku, Tokyo; tel. (3) 581-0101.
Defence Agency: 9-7, Akasaka, Minato-ku, Tokyo; tel. (3) 408-5211.
Economic Planning Agency: 3-1, Kasumigaseki, Chiyoda-ku, Tokyo; tel. (3) 581-0261.
Environment Agency: 1-2-2, Kasumigaseki, Chiyoda-ku, Tokyo; tel. (3) 581-3351; telex 33855.
Management and Co-ordination Agency: 3-1-1, Kasumigaseki, Chiyoda-ku, Tokyo; tel. (3) 581-6361.
National Land Agency and Hokkaido Development Agency: 1-6, Azabudai, Minato-ku, Tokyo; tel. (3) 583-831.
Okinawa Development Agency: 1-6, Nagata-cho, Chiyoda-ku, Tokyo; tel. (3) 581-2361.
Science and Technology Agency: 2-2, Kasumigaseki, Chiyoda-ku, Tokyo; tel. (3) 581-5271.

Legislature

KOKKAI
(Diet)

The Diet consists of two Chambers: the House of Councillors (Upper House) and the House of Representatives. The 512 members of the House of Representatives are elected for a period of four

JAPAN

years (subject to dissolution). For the House of Councillors, which has 252 members, the term of office is six years, with one-half of the members elected every three years.

House of Councillors

Speaker: MASAAKI FUJITA.

Party	Seats after elections* 26 June 1983	6 July 1986
Liberal-Democratic Party	137	142
Japan Socialist Party	44	41
Komeito	26	25
Japanese Communist Party	14	16
Democratic Socialist Party	11	12
New Liberal Club	2	2
Second Chamber Club	2	3
Salaried Workers' Party	—	3
Tax Party	—	2
Social Democratic Federation	—	1
Independents	—	4
Others	13	—
Vacant	3	1

* One-half of the 252 seats are renewable every three years. At each election, 50 of the 126 seats were allocated on the basis of proportional representation.

House of Representatives

Speaker: KENZABURO HARA.

General Election, 6 July 1986

Party	Votes	% of votes	Seats
Liberal-Democratic Party	29,875,496	49.42	304
Japan Socialist Party	10,412,583	17.23	86
Komeito	5,701,277	9.43	57
Japanese Communist Party	5,313,246	8.79	27
Democratic Socialist Party	3,895,927	6.45	26
New Liberal Club	1,114,800	1.84	6
Social Democratic Federation	499,670	0.83	4
Other parties	120,627	0.20	—
Independents	3,515,042	5.81	2
Total	60,448,668	100.00	512

Political Organizations

The Political Funds Regulation Law provides that any organization which wishes to support a candidate for an elective public office must be registered as a political party. There are over 10,000 registered parties in the country, mostly of local or regional significance. The conservative Liberal-Democratic Party has the support of big business and the rural population and is also by far the richest of the political parties. The proportion of votes for the two socialist parties increased slowly at each election after 1952. The split between the two parties reflects a long-standing division between supporters of a mass popular party (now represented by the DSP) and those seeking a class party on Socialist lines. The Communist Party of Japan split in 1964, the official party being independent and supporting neither the USSR nor the People's Republic of China.

Democratic Socialist Party—DSP (Minshato): 19–12 Shiba Sakuragawa-cho 1, Minato-ku, Tokyo; tel. (3) 501-1411; f. 1960 by a right-wing faction of the Socialist Party of Japan; advocates an independent foreign policy; 72,000 mems (1983); Chair. RYOSAKU SASAKI; Sec.-Gen. SABURO TSUKAMOTO.

Japan Socialist Party—JSP (Nippon Shakaito): 1–8–1 Nagata-cho, Chiyoda-ku, Tokyo; tel. (3) 580-1171; f. 1945; seeks the establishment of collective non-agression and a mutual security system, including Japan, the USA, the USSR and the People's Republic of China; 55,000 mems (1983); Chair. TAKAKO DOI; Sec.-Gen. MAKOTO TANABE.

Japanese Commmunist Party—JCP: Sendagaya 4–26–7, Shibuya-ku, Tokyo; tel. (3) 403-6111; f. 1922; 470,000 mems (1982); Chair. Cen. Cttee KENJI MIYAMOTO; Chair. Presidium TETSUZO FUWA; Chief Sec. MITSUHIRO KANEKO.

Komeito (Clean Government Party): 17 Minamimoto-machi, Shinjuku-ku, Tokyo; tel. (3) 353-0111; f. 1964; advocates political moderation, humanitarian socialism, and policies respecting 'dignity of human life'; 183,000 mems (1985); Founder DAISAKU IKEDA; Chair. JUNYA YANO.

Liberal-Democratic Party—LDP (Jiyu-Minshuto): 1-11-23, Nagata-cho, Chiyoda-ku, Tokyo 100; tel. (3) 581-0111; f. 1955; advocates the establishment of a welfare state, the build-up of industrial development, the levelling up of educational and cultural systems and the revision of the Constitution where necessary; follows a foreign policy of alignment with the USA; 3.6m. mems (1985); Pres. YASUHIRO NAKASONE; Vice-Pres. SUSUMU NIKAIDO; Sec.-Gen. NOBORU TAKESHITA; Chair. of Executive Council SHINTARO ABE.

New Liberal Club—NLC (Shin Jiyu Club): 1–11–28, Nagato-cho, Chiyoda-ku, Tokyo; tel. (3) 581-9911; f. 1976 by splinter group of LDP; rejoined LDP Aug. 1986; Leader YOHEI KONO; Sec.-Gen. TOSHIO YAMAGUCHI; other mems formed Progressive Party (Leader SEIICHI TAGAWA) Jan. 1987.

Salaried Workers' Party (Salaryman Shinto): c/o House of Councillors, 1–7–1 Nagata-cho, Chiyoda-ku, Tokyo; advocates reform of the tax system; Leader Prof. SHIGERU AOKI.

Second Chamber Club (Ni-In Club): c/o House of Councillors, 1–7–1 Nagata-cho, Chiyoda-ku, Tokyo; successor to the Green Wind Club (Ryukufukai), which originated in the House of Councillors in 1946–47; Sec. ISAMU YAMADA.

Social Democratic Federation—SDF (Shaminren): Yotsuya Bldg, Yotsuya 2–1, Tokyo; f. 1977 as the Socialist Citizens' League; Leader HIDEO DEN.

Tax Party (Zeikinto): c/o House of Councillors, 1–7–1 Nagatacho, Chiyoda-ku, Tokyo.

Welfare Party (Fukushi-to): c/o House of Councillors, 1–7–1 Nagata-cho, Chiyoda-ku, Tokyo; Leader EITA YASHIRO.

Diplomatic Representation

EMBASSIES IN JAPAN

Algeria: 10–67, Mita 2-chome, Meguro-ku, Tokyo; tel. (3) 711-2661; telex 23260; Ambassador: NACEREDDINE HAFFAD.

Argentina: Chiyoda House, 17–8, Nagata-cho 2-chome, Chiyoda-ku, Tokyo 100; tel. (3) 592-0321; telex 22489; Ambassador: ENRIQUE J. ROS.

Australia: 1–14, Mita 2-chome, Minato-ku, Tokyo 108; tel. (3) 453-0251; telex 22298; Ambassador: GEOFFREY MILLER.

Austria: 1–20, Moto Azabu 1-chome, Minato-ku, Tokyo; tel. (3) 451-8281; telex 26361; Ambassador: Dr GEORG HENNIG.

Bangladesh: 7–45, Shirogane 2-chome, Minato-ku, Tokyo 108; tel. (3) 442-1501; telex 28826; Ambassador: A. K. N. AHMED.

Belgium: 5, Niban-cho, Chiyoda-ku, Tokyo 102; tel. (3) 262-0191; telex 24974; Ambassador: MARCEL DEPASSE.

Bolivia: Kowa Bldg, No. 38, Room 804, 12-24, Nishi-Azabu 4-chome, Minato-ku, Tokyo 106; tel. (3) 499-5441; telex 32177; Ambassador: ARNOLD HOFMAN-BANG SOLETO.

Brazil: 11–12, Kita Aoyama 2-chome, Minato-ku, Tokyo; tel. (3) 404-5211; telex 22590; Ambassador: LUIZ PAULO LINDENBERG SETTE.

Bulgaria: 36–3, Yoyogi 5-chome, Shibuya-ku, Tokyo; tel. (3) 465-1021; Ambassador: ANGEL ANGELOV.

Burma: 8–26, Kita-Shinagawa 4-chome, Shinagawa-ku, Tokyo; tel. (3) 441-9291; Ambassador: U THEIN AUNG.

Cameroon: Tokyo; Ambassador: ETIENNE NTSAMA.

Canada: 3–38, Akasaka 7-chome, Minato-ku, Tokyo; tel. (3) 408-2101; telex 22218; Ambassador: BARRY CONNELL STEERS.

Central African Republic: 4–11–19, Seta, Setagaya-ku, Tokyo 158; tel. (3) 707-5061; telex 24793; Ambassador: JOSÉ-MARIA PEHOUA.

Chile: Nihon Seimei Akabanebashi Bldg, 8th Floor, 3-1-14 Shiba, Minato-ku, Tokyo 105; tel. (3) 452-7561; telex 24585; Ambassador: EDUARDO BRAVO WOODHOUSE.

China, People's Republic: 4–5–30, Minami Azabu, Minato-ku, Tokyo; tel. (3) 403-3380; telex 28705; Ambassador: ZHANG SHU.

Colombia: 12-24 Nishi Azabu, 4-chome, Minato-ku, Tokyo; tel. (3) 440-6491; Ambassador: JOSÉ MARÍA VILLARREAL.

Costa Rica: 12-24 Nishi Azabu, 4-chome, Minato-ku, Tokyo; tel. (3) 486-1812; Chargé d'affaires (a.i.): ANA LUCÍA NASSAR SOTO.

JAPAN

Cuba: 2-51 Minami-Azabu 4-chome, Minato-ku, Tokyo; tel. (3) 449-7511; telex 22369; Ambassador: AMADEO BLANCO VALDÉS-FAUY.

Czechoslovakia: 16-14, Hiroo 2-chome, Shibuya-ku, Tokyo; tel. (3) 400-8122; Ambassador: GUSTAV ŠMÍD.

Denmark: 29-6, Sarugaku-cho, Shibuya-ku, Tokyo 150; tel.(3) 496-3001; telex 24417; Ambassador: BENNY KIMBERG.

Dominican Republic: Kowa Bldg, No. 38, Room 904, 12-24, Nishi-Azabu 4-chome, Minato-ku, Tokyo 106; tel. (3) 499-6020; Ambassador: ALBERTO E. DESPRADEL.

Ecuador: Kowa Bldg, No. 38, Room 806, 12-24, Nishi Azabu 4-chome, Minato-ku, Tokyo; tel. (3) 499-2800; telex 25880; Ambassador: NELSON THURDEKOOS.

Egypt: 5-4, Aobadai 1-chome, Meguro-ku, Tokyo; tel. (3) 463-4565; Ambassador: ABDELFATTAH M. SHABANA.

El Salvador: Kowa Bldg, No. 38, 8th Floor, 12-24, Nishi Azabu 4-chome, Minato-ku, Tokyo; tel. (3) 499-4461; telex 25829; Ambassador: GUILLERMO PAZ LARIN.

Ethiopia: Roppongi Hilltop House, B-1, 4-25, Roppongi 3-chome, Minato-ku, Tokyo; tel. (3) 585-3151; telex 28402; Ambassador: Brig.-Gen. AFEWORK ATLABACHEW.

Fiji: Noa Bldg, 10th Floor, 3-5 Azabudai 2-chome, Minato-ku, Tokyo 106; tel. (3) 582-0110; Ambassador: JOSEPH DAVID GIBSON.

Finland: 3-5-39 Minami-Azabu, Minato-ku, Tokyo 106; tel. (3) 442-2231; telex 26277; Ambassador: PAULI OPAS.

France: 11-44, Minami-Azabu 4-chome, Minato-ku, Tokyo; tel. (3) 473-0171; Ambassador: GILBERT PÉROL.

Gabon: 16-2, Hiroo 2-chome, Shibuya-ku, Tokyo; tel. (3) 409-5119; telex 24812; Ambassador: MARTIN NZUE-NKOGHE.

German Democratic Republic: Akasaka Mansion, 5-16 Akasaka 7-chome, Minato-ku, Tokyo 107; tel. (3) 585-5404; telex 28283; Ambassador: DIETER JAEGER.

Germany, Federal Republic: 5-10, Minami-Azabu 4-chome, Minato-ku, Tokyo; tel. (3) 473-0151; telex 22292; Ambassador: Dr HANS-JOACHIM HALLIER.

Ghana: Mori Bldg, 11th Floor, 16-13, Nishi-Azabu 4-chome, Minato-ku, Tokyo; tel. (3) 409-3861; telex 22487; Ambassador: JAMES LESLIE MAYNE AMISSAH.

Greece: 4th Floor, Green Fantasia Bldg, 11-11, Jingumae 1-chome, Shibuya-ku, Tokyo; tel. (3) 403-0871; Ambassador: CONSTANTINOS LYBEROPOULOS.

Guatemala: 38 Kowa Bldg, 4-12-24, Nishi Azabu 4-chome, Minato-ku, Tokyo 106; tel. (3) 400-1830; Ambassador: JOSÉ ALBERTO SANDÓVAL COJULUN.

Haiti: Room 906, No. 38, Kowa Bldg, 12-24, Nishi Azabu 4-chome, Minato-ku, Tokyo 106; tel. (3) 486-7070; telex 29601; Chargé d'affaires a.i.: FRITZNEL LAFONTANT.

Holy See: Apostolic Nunciature, 9-2, Sanban-cho, Chiyoda-ku, Tokyo 102; tel. (3) 263-6851; Apostolic Pro-Nuncio: Archbishop WILLIAM AQUIN CAREW.

Honduras: Kowa Bldg, No. 38, 12-24, Nishi Azabu 4-chome, Minato-ku, Tokyo 106; tel. (3) 409-1150; telex 28591; Ambassador: JORGE ELÍAS FLEFIL LARACH.

Hungary: 3-1, Aobadai 2-chome, Meguro-ku, Tokyo; tel. (3) 476-6061; Ambassador: KÁROLY SZARKA.

India: 2-11, Kudan-Minami 2-chome, Chiyoda-ku, Tokyo; tel. (3) 262-2391; Ambassador: ANANTHANARAYANA MADHAVAN.

Indonesia: 2-9, Higashi Gotanda 5-chome, Shinagawa-ku, Tokyo 141; tel. (3) 441-4201; telex 22920; Ambassador: Lt-Gen. (retd) WIYOGO ATMODARMINTO.

Iran: 10-32, Minami-Azabu 3-chome, Minato-ku, Tokyo; tel. (3) 446-8011; telex 22753; Ambassador: ABDOLRAHIM GAVAHI.

Iraq: Rooms 1 and 5, Greenleaves Hill, 17-12, Sarugaku-cho, Shibuya-ku, Tokyo; tel. (3) 464-2031; telex 28825; Ambassador: MOHAMMED AMEEEN AL-JAFF.

Ireland: Kowa Bldg, No. 25, 8-7, Sanban-cho, Chiyoda-ku, Tokyo; tel. (3) 263-0695; telex 23926; Ambassador: SEÁN G. RONAN.

Israel: 3, Niban-cho, Chiyoda-ku, Tokyo; tel. (3) 264-0911; telex 22636; Ambassador: Dr YAACOV COHEN.

Italy: 5-4, Mita 2-chome, Minato-ku, Tokyo; tel. (3) 453-5291; telex 22433; Ambassador: BARTOLOMEO ATTOLICO.

Ivory Coast: Kowa Bldg, No. 38, 7F, 12-24, Nishi-Azabu 4-chome, Minato-ku, Tokyo 106; tel. (3) 499-7021; Ambassador: PIERRE NELSON COFFI.

Jordan: 4A, B, Chiyoda House, 17-8, Nagatacho 2-chome, Chiyoda-ku, Tokyo; tel. (3) 580-5856; telex 23708; Ambassador: SAAD M. BATAINAH.

Kenya: 24-20, Nishi-Azabu 3-chome, Minato-ku, Tokyo 106; tel. (3) 479-4006; telex 2422378; Ambassador: P. G. GITONGA.

Korea, Republic: 2-5, Minami-Azabu 1-chome, Minato-ku, Tokyo; tel. (3) 452-7611; telex 22045; Ambassador: RHEE KYU-HO.

Kuwait: 13-12, Mita 4-chome, Minato-ku, Tokyo 106; tel. (3) 455-0361; telex 25501; Ambassador: AHMAD GAITH ABDULLAH.

Laos: 3-3-21, Nishi-Azabu, Minato-ku, Tokyo 106; tel. (3) 408-1166; Ambassador: SOUPHANTHAHEUANGSI SISALEUMSAK.

Lebanon: 5th Floor, Chiyoda House, 17-8, Nagata-cho 2-chome, Chiyoda-ku, Tokyo; tel. (3) 580-1227; telex 25356; Ambassador: SAMIR EL-KHOURY.

Liberia: Odakyu Minami Aoyama Bldg, 6th Floor, 8-1, Minami Aoyama 7-chome, Minato-ku, Tokyo 107; tel. (3) 499-2451; Ambassador: STEPHEN J. KOFFA, Sr.

Libya: 6-1, Akasaka 4-chome, Minato-ku, Tokyo 107; tel. (3) 586-1886; Secretary of the People's Bureau: Dr ALI AHMED S. ELHOUDERI.

Madagascar: 3-23, Moto-Azabu 2-chome, Minato-ku, Tokyo 106; tel. (3) 446-7252; telex 25941; Ambassador: ARMAND RAZAFINDRABE.

Malaysia: 20-16, Nanpeidaimachi, Shibuya-ku, Tokyo 150; tel. (3) 463-0241; Ambassador: Dato' AHMAD KAMIL JAAFAR.

Mexico: 15-1, Nagata-cho 2-chome, Chiyoda-ku, Tokyo 100; tel. (3) 581-1131; telex 26875; Ambassador: SERGIO GONZÁLEZ GÁLVEZ.

Mongolia: Pine Crest Mansion, 21-4 Shoto, Kamiyama-cho, Shibuya-ku, Tokyo 150; tel. (3) 469-2088; Ambassador: BUYANTYN DASHTSEREN.

Morocco: 5th and 6th Floors, Silver Kingdom Mansion, 16-3, Sendagaya 3-chome, Shibuya-ku, Tokyo 151; tel. (3) 478-3271; Ambassador: ABDELSAM TADLAOUI.

Nepal: 3-16-23, Higashi Gotanda, Shinagawa-ku, Tokyo 141; tel. (3) 444-7303; telex 23936; Ambassador: NARAYAN PRASAD ARJAL.

Netherlands: 6-3, Shibakoen 3-chome, Minato-ku, Tokyo 105; tel. (3) 431-5126; telex 22855; Ambassador: HERMAN POSTHUMUS MEYES.

New Zealand: 20-40, Kamiyama-cho, Shibuya-ku, Tokyo 150; tel. (3) 467-2271; telex 22462; Ambassador: GRAHAM KEITH ANSELL.

Nicaragua: Kowa Bldg, No. 38, Nishi-Azabu 4-chome, Minato-ku, Tokyo; tel. (3) 499-0400; Ambassador: JORGE HUEZO CASTRILLO.

Nigeria: 2-19-7 Uehara, Shibuya-ku, Tokyo 151; tel. (3) 468-5531; telex 24397; Ambassador: YUSUF WAKILI SADA.

Norway: 12-2, Minami-Azabu 5-chome, Minato-ku, Tokyo 106; tel. (3) 440-2611; telex 26440; Ambassador: H. W. FREIHOW.

Oman: Tokyo; tel. (3) 402-0877; telex 29544; Ambassador: MARHOON A. AL-MARHOON.

Pakistan: 14-9, 2-chome, Moto-Azabu, Minato-ku, Tokyo 106; tel. (3) 454-4861; Ambassador: NAJMUL SAQIB KHAN.

Panama: No. 38, Kowa Bldg, Room 202, 12-24, Nishi-Azabu, 4-chome, Minato-ku, Tokyo 106; tel. (3) 499-3741; telex 22157; Ambassador: ALBERTO A. CALVO PONCE.

Papua New Guinea: Mita Kokusai Bldg, Room 313, 3rd Floor, 1-4-28 Mita, Minato-ku, Tokyo 108; tel. (3) 454-7801; telex 25488; Ambassador: JOSEPH KAAL NOMBRI.

Paraguay: Asahi Kamiosaki Bldg, 5th Floor, 5-8 Kamiosaki 3-chome, Shinagawa-ku, Tokyo 141; tel. (3) 447-7496; telex 27496; Ambassador: JUAN CARLOS A. HRASE VON BARGEN.

Peru: Higashi 4-4-27, Shibuya-ku, Tokyo 150; tel. (3) 406-4240; telex 26435; Ambassador: LUIS MACCHIAVELLO.

Philippines: 11-24, Nampeidai-cho, Shibuya-ku, Tokyo 150; tel. (3) 496-2731; telex 22694; Ambassador: RAMON V. DEL ROSARIO.

Poland: 13-5, Mita 2-chome, Meguro-ku, Tokyo 153; tel. (3) 711-5224; Ambassador: RYSZARD FRACKIEWICZ.

Portugal: Olympia Annex, Apt 306, 31-21, Jingumae 6-chome, Shibuya-ku, Tokyo 150; tel. (3) 400-7907; Ambassador: FRANCISCO MANUEL BALTAZAR MOITA.

Qatar: 16-22, Shirogane 6-chome, Minato-ku, Tokyo 108; tel. (3) 446-7561; telex 24877; Ambassador: MOHAMED ALI AL-ANSARI.

Romania: 16-19, Nishi Azabu 3-chome, Minato-ku, Tokyo 106; tel. (3) 479-0311; telex 22664; Ambassador: Prof. Dr CONSTANTIN VLAD.

Rwanda: Tokyo; tel. (3) 486-7800; telex 27701; Ambassador: ALOYS UWIMANA.

Saudi Arabia: 6-2, Hiroo 2-chome, Shibuya-ku, Tokyo 150; tel. (3) 409-8291; telex 25731; Ambassador: FAWZI BIN ABDUL MAJEED SHOBOKSHI.

JAPAN

Senegal: 3–4 Aobadai 1-chome, Meguro-ku, Tokyo 153; tel. (3) 464-8451; telex 25493; Ambassador: Kéba Birane Cissé.

Singapore: 12–3 Roppongi 5-chome, Minato-ku, Tokyo 106; tel. (3) 586-9111; telex 22404; Ambassador: Lee Khoon Choy.

Somalia: 9–10, Shiroganedai 5-chome, Minato-ku, Tokyo 108; tel. (3) 442-7138; Ambassador: Mohamed Ismail Kahin.

Spain: 3–29, Roppongi 1-chome, Minato-ku, Tokyo 106; tel. (3) 583-8531; telex 22471; Ambassador: Camilo Barcia García-Villamil.

Sri Lanka: 14–1, Akasaka 1-chome, Minato-ku, Tokyo 107; tel. (3) 585-7431; telex 24524; Ambassador: Arthur Basnayake.

Sudan: Yada Mansion, 6–20, Minami-Aoyama 6-chome, Minato-ku, Tokyo 107; tel. (3) 406-0811; Ambassador: Saeed Saad Mahgoub Saad.

Sweden: 10–3, Roppongi 1-chome, Minato-ku, Tokyo 106; tel. (3) 582-6981; telex 24586; Ambassador: Ove Fredrik Heyman.

Switzerland: 9–12, Minami-Azabu 5-chome, Minato-ku, Tokyo 106; tel. (3) 473-0121; telex 24282; Ambassador: Dr Dieter Chenaux-Repond.

Syria: 12–6, Roppongi 5-chome, Minato-ku, Tokyo 106; tel. (3) 586-8977; Ambassador: Abdul Wadoud Atassi.

Tanzania: 21–9, Kamiyoga 4-chome, Setagaya-ku, Tokyo 158; tel. (3) 425-4531; telex 22121; Ambassador: Raphael Haji Lukindo.

Thailand: 14–6, Kami-Osaki 3-chome, Shinagawa-ku, Tokyo 141; tel. (3) 441-7352; Ambassador: Wichian Watanakun.

Tunisia: 18–8, 1-chome, Wakaba-cho, Shinjuku-ku, Tokyo 160; tel. (3) 353-4111; telex 27146; Ambassador: Moncef Jaafar.

Turkey: 33–6, Jingumae 2-chome, Shibuya-ku, Tokyo 150; tel. (3) 470-5131; Ambassador: Nurver Nures.

Uganda: 2–2, Shoto 2-chome, Shibuya-ku, Tokyo 150; tel. (3) 469-3641; telex 23937; Ambassador: Obitre-Gama.

USSR: 2-1-1 Azabudai, Minato-ku, Tokyo 106; tel. (3) 583-4224; Ambassador: Nikolai Nikolayevich Solovev.

United Arab Emirates: Kotsu Anzen Kyoiku Centre Bldg, 24–20, Nishi Azabu 3-chome, Minato-ku, Tokyo 106; tel. (3) 478-0650; telex 23552; Ambassador: Mohammed Darweesh Benkaram.

United Kingdom: 1 Ichiban-cho, Chiyoda-ku, Tokyo 102; tel. (3) 265-5511; telex 22755; Ambassador: Sir John Whitehead.

USA: 10–5, Akasaka 1-chome, Minato-ku, Tokyo 107; tel. (3) 583-7141; telex 22118; Ambassador: Michael J. Mansfield.

Uruguay: Room 908, No. 38, Kowa Bldg, 12–24, Nishi-Azabu 4-chome, Minato-ku, Tokyo 106; tel. (3) 486-1888; telex 25622; Ambassador: Aureliano Aguirre.

Venezuela: 7th Floor No. 38 Kowa Bldg, 12–24, Nishi-Azabu 4-chome, Minato-ku, Tokyo 106; tel. (3) 409-1501; telex 25255; Ambassador: Dr Jesús María Ponce.

Viet-Nam: 50–11, Moto Yoyogi-Cho, Shibuya-ku, Tokyo 151; tel. (3) 466-3311; Ambassador: Nguyen Tien.

Yemen Arab Republic: Tokyo; tel. (3) 499-7151; telex 32431; Ambassador: Muhammad Abdel Qaddous.

Yugoslavia: 7–24, Kitashinagawa 4-chome, Shinagawa-ku, Tokyo 140; tel. (3) 447-3571; telex 22360; Ambassador: Tarik Ajanović.

Zaire: Harajuku Green Heights 701, 53–17 Sendagaya 3-chome, Shibuya-ku, Tokyo; tel. (3) 423-3981; telex 24211; Ambassador: Mitima Kaneno Murairi.

Zambia: 3-9-19, Ebisu, Shibuya-ku, Tokyo 150; tel. (3) 445-1043; telex 25210; Ambassador: Axson Chibeka Chalikulima.

Zimbabwe: Tokyo; tel. (3) 473-0266; telex 32975; Ambassador: Nyamayaro Herbert Katedza.

Judicial System

The basic principles of the legal system are set forth in the Constitution, which lays down that the whole judicial power is vested in a Supreme Court and in such inferior courts as are established by law, and enunciates the principle that no organ or agency of the Executive shall be given final judicial power. Judges are to be independent in the exercise of their conscience, and may not be removed except by public impeachment, unless judicially declared mentally or physically incompetent to perform official duties. The justices of the Supreme Court are appointed by the Cabinet, the sole exception being the Chief Justice, who is appointed by the Emperor after designation by the Cabinet.

The Court Organization Law, which came into force on 3 May 1947, decreed the constitution of the Supreme Court and the establishment of four types of inferior court—High, District, Family (established 1 January 1949), and Summary Courts. The constitution and functions of the courts are as follows:

THE SUPREME COURT

This court is the highest legal authority in the land, and consists of a Chief Justice and 14 associate justices. It has jurisdiction over Jokoku (appeals) and Kokoku (complaints), prescribed specially in codes of procedure. It conducts its hearings and renders decisions through a Grand Bench or three Petty Benches. Both are collegiate bodies, the former consisting of all justices of the Court, and the latter of five justices. A Supreme Court Rule prescribes which cases are to be handled by the respective Benches. It is, however, laid down by law that the Petty Bench cannot make decisions as to the constitutionality of a statute, ordinance, regulation, or disposition, or as to cases in which an opinion concerning the interpretation and application of the Constitution or of any laws or ordinances is at variance with a previous decision of the Supreme Court.

Chief Justice: Koichi Yaguchi.

INFERIOR COURTS

High Court

A High Court conducts its hearings and renders decisions through a collegiate body, consisting of three judges, though for cases of insurrection the number of judges must be five. The Court has jurisdiction over the following matters:

Koso appeals from judgments in the first instance rendered by District Courts, from judgments rendered by Family Courts, and from judgments concerning criminal cases rendered by Summary Courts.

Kokoku complaints against rulings and orders rendered by District Courts and Family Courts, and against rulings and orders concerning criminal cases rendered by Summary Courts, except those coming within the jurisdiction of the Supreme Court.

Jokoku appeals from judgments in the second instance rendered by District Courts and from judgments rendered by Summary Courts, except those concerning criminal cases.

Actions in the first instance relating to cases of insurrection.

District Court

A District Court conducts hearings and renders decisions through a single judge or, for certain types of cases, through a collegiate body of three judges. It has jurisdiction over the following matters:

Actions in the first instance, except offences relating to insurrection, claims where the subject matter of the action does not exceed 900,000 yen, and offences liable to a fine or lesser penalty.

Koso appeals from judgments rendered by Summary Courts, except those concerning criminal cases.

Kokoku complaints against rulings and orders rendered by Summary Courts, except those coming within the jurisdiction of the Supreme Court and High Courts.

Family Court

A Family Court handles cases through a single judge in case of rendering judgments or decisions. However, in accordance with the provisions of other statutes it conducts its hearings and renders decisions through a collegiate body of three judges. A conciliation is effected through a collegiate body consisting of a judge and two or more members of the conciliation committee selected from among citizens.

It has jurisdiction over the following matters:

Judgment and conciliation with regard to cases relating to family as provided for by the Law for Adjustment of Domestic Relations.

Judgment with regard to the matters of protection of juveniles as provided for by the Juvenile Law.

Actions in the first instance relating to adult criminal cases of violation of the Labour Standard Law, the Law for Prohibiting Liquors to Minors, or other laws especially enacted for protection of juveniles.

Summary Court

A Summary Court handles cases through a single judge, and has jurisdiction in the first instance over the following matters:

Claims where the value of the subject matter does not exceed 900,000 yen (excluding claims for cancellation or change of administrative dispositions).

Actions which relate to offences liable to fine or lesser penalty, offences liable to a fine as an optional penalty, and certain specified offences such as habitual gambling and larceny.

A Summary Court cannot impose imprisonment or a graver penalty. When it deems proper the imposition of a sentence of imprisonment or a graver penalty, it must transfer such cases to a District Court, but it can impose imprisonment with hard labour not exceeding three years for certain specified offences.

A Procurator's Office, with its complement of procurators, is established for each of these courts. The procurators conduct searches, institute prosecutions and supervise the execution of judgments in criminal cases, and act as representatives of the public interests in civil cases of public concern.

Religion

The traditional religions of Japan are Shintoism and Buddhism. Neither is exclusive, and many Japanese subscribe at least nominally to both. Since 1945 a number of new religions (Shinko Shukyo) have evolved, based on a fusion of Shinto, Buddhist, Daoist, Confucian and Christian beliefs.

SHINTOISM

Shintoism is an indigenous cult of nature and ancestor worship. It is divided into two cults: national Shintoism, which is represented by the shrines; and sectarian Shintoism, which developed towards the end of the Tokugawa Shogunate. In 1868, Shinto was designated a national religion, and all Shinto shrines acquired the privileged status of a national institution. After the adoption of the present constitution in 1947, however, complete freedom of religion was introduced, and state support of Shinto was banned. There are an estimated 81,000 shrines, 101,000 priests and c. 90m. adherents.

BUDDHISM

World Buddhist Fellowship: Rev. Fuji Nakayama, Hozenji Buddhist Temple, 3-24-2 Akabane-dai, Kita-ku, Tokyo.

CHRISTIANITY

In 1982 the number of Christians in Japan was estimated at 1,266,402.

The Anglican Communion

Nippon Sei Ko Kai (Holy Catholic Church in Japan): 4-21, Higashi 1-chome, Shibuya-ku, Tokyo 150; tel. (3) 400-2314; f. 1887; 11 dioceses; Bishop of Osaka and Primate of Japan Rt Rev. Christopher Ichiro Kikawada; 56,516 mems (1985).

The Orthodox Church

Japanese Orthodox Church: Holy Resurrection Cathedral (Nicolai-Do), 1-3, 4-chome, Surugadai, Kanda, Chiyoda-ku, Tokyo 101; Archbishop of Tokyo, Primate and Metropolitan of All Japan Most Rev. Theodosius; 24,783 mems.

Protestant Church

United Church of Christ in Japan: Japan Christian Center, Room 31, 3-18, Nishi Waseda 2-chome, Shinjuku-ku, Tokyo 160; tel. (3) 202-0541; f. 1941; union of 34 Congregational, Methodist, Presbyterian, Reformed and other Protestant denominations; Moderator Rev. Toshio Ushiroku; Gen. Sec Rev. John M. Nakajima; 198,269 mems (1985).

The Roman Catholic Church

Japan comprises three archdioceses and 13 dioceses. There were 421,090 adherents in 1983.

Roman Catholic Bishops' Conference of Japan (Chuo Kyogikai): 10-1, Rokubancho, Chiyoda-ku, Tokyo 102; tel. (3) 262-3691; telex 32624; f. 1973; Pres. Mgr Peter Seichi Shirayanagi, Archbishop of Tokyo.

Archbishop of Nagasaki: Cardinal Joseph Asajiro Satowaki, Catholic Center, 5-3, Minami Yamate-cho, Nagasaki-shi 850; tel. (958) 23-2934.

Archbishop of Osaka: Mgr Paul Hisao Yasuda, 1-15, Nishiyamacho, Koyoen, Nishinomiya-shi, Hyogo-ken, 662; tel. (798) 73-0921.

Archbishop of Tokyo: Mgr Peter Seiichi Shirayanagi, Archbishop's House, 16-15 Sekiguchi, 3-chome, Bunkyo-ku, Tokyo 112; tel. (3) 943-2301.

OTHER COMMUNITIES

The various other religious groups have about 1,200 shrines and temples and 15,000 priests.

The New Religions

Many new cults have grown up in Japan since the end of the Second World War. Collectively these are known as the New Religions (Shinko Shukyo), of which the following are the most important:

Rissho Kosei-kai: 2-11-1, Wada Suginami-ku, Tokyo 166; f. 1938; Buddhist lay organization based on the teaching of the Lotus Sutra; Pres. Rev. Nikkyo Niwano; 5.7m. mems worldwide (1986).

Soka Gakkai: 32 Shinano-machi, Shinjuku-ku, Tokyo; tel. (3) 353-0616; telex 33145; f. 1930; the lay society of Nichiren Shoshu (Orthodox Nichiren Buddhism); membership of 7.95m. households (1984); Buddhist groups promoting education, international cultural exchange and world peace; Hon. Pres. Daisaku Ikeda; Pres. Einosuke Akiya.

Bahá'í Faith

The National Spiritual Assembly of the Bahá'ís of Japan: 2-13, 7-chome, Shinjuku Shinjuku-ku, Tokyo 160; tel. (3) 209-7521.

The Press

The average circulation of Japanese dailies is the highest in the world after the USSR and the USA, and the circulation per head of population is highest at about 565 copies per 1,000 inhabitants (1984). The large number of weekly news journals is a notable feature of the Japanese press. In 1984 a total of 2,700 magazines were published by 1,200 magazine publishing companies. Technically the Japanese press is highly advanced, and the major newspapers are issued in simultaneous editions in the main centres.

The two newspapers with the largest circulations are the *Asahi Shimbun* and *Yomiuri Shimbun*. Other influential papers include *Mainichi Shimbun, Nihon Keizai Shimbun, Chunichi Shimbun* and *Sankei Shimbun*.

PRINCIPAL DAILIES

Tokyo

Asahi Evening News: 8-5, Tsukiji 7-chome, Chuo-ku, Tokyo 104; tel. (3) 543-3321; f. 1954; evening; English; Editor-in-Chief Shigeo Omori; circ. 26,838.

Asahi Shimbun: 3-2, Tsukiji 5-chome, Chuo-ku, Tokyo 104; tel. (3) 545-0131; telex 22226; f. 1879; Exec. Dir (Editorial Affairs) M. Itoh; circ. morning 7.6m., evening 4.6m.

Daily Sports: 1-1-17, Higashi-Shimbashi, Minato-ku, Tokyo 105; tel. (3) 571-6681; f. 1948; morning; Man. Editor Takashi Kondo; circ. 410,000.

The Daily Yomiuri: 7-1, 1-chome, Otemachi, Chiyoda-ku, Tokyo 100; tel. (3) 242-1111; f. 1955; morning; English; Editor Tatsu Okuyama; circ. 38,000.

Dempa Shimbun: 11-15, Higashi Gotanda 1-chome, Shinagawa-ku, Tokyo 141; tel. (3) 445-6111; telex 02424461; f. 1950; morning; Man. Editor Hajime Ninomiya; circ. 285,000.

Hochi Shimbun: 1-1, 2-chome, Hirakawa-cho, Chiyoda-ku, Tokyo 102; tel. (3) 265-2311; f. 1872; morning; Man. Editor Tokutei Endo; circ. 654,000.

The Japan Times: 5-4, 4-chome, Shibaura, Minato-ku, Tokyo 108; tel. (3) 453-5311; telex 02422319; f. 1897; morning; English; Chair. Toshiaki Ogasawara; Pres. J. Suzuki; circ. 49,983.

Komei Shimbun: 17 Minami-motomachi, Shinjuku-ku, Tokyo; tel. (3) 353-0111; organ of the Komeito political party; circ. 800,000, Sunday edn 1.4m.

The Mainichi Daily News: 1-1-1 Hitotsubashi, Chiyoda-ku, Tokyo 100; tel. (3) 212-0321; f. 1922; morning; English; also publ. from Osaka; Man. Editor Takaharu Yoshizawa; circ. 40,000.

Mainichi Shimbun: 1-1, 1-chome, Hitotsubashi, Chiyoda-ku, Toyko 100; tel. (3) 212-0321; telex 22324; f. 1872; Man. Editor J. Watanabe; circ. morning 4.2m., evening 2.2m.

Naigai Times: 14-14, 7-chome, Ginza, Chuo-ku, Tokyo 104; tel. (3) 543-1061; f. 1949; evening; Editor-in-Chief Kenichi Touya; circ. 296,000.

Nihon Keizai Shimbun: 9-5, 1-chome, Otemachi, Chiyoda-ku, Tokyo 100; tel. (3) 270-0251; telex 22308; f. 1876; morning, evening and weekly (English edn: The Japan Economic Journal); economic news; Man. Editor T. Ohta; circ. morning 1.37m., evening 1.36m.

Nihon Kogyo Shimbun: 7-2, 1-chome, Otemachi, Chiyoda-ku, Tokyo 100; tel. (3) 231-7111; f. 1933; morning; business and financial; Pres. Terumi Nagata; Man. Editor Hiroshi Kondo; circ. 409,000.

JAPAN — Directory

Nihon Nogyo Shimbun (Agriculture): 2–3 Akihabara, Taito-ku, Tokyo 110; tel. (3) 255-5211; f. 1928; morning; Man. Editor Masao Oku; circ. 502,766.

Nikkan Kogyo Shimbun (Industrial Daily News): 8–10, 1-chome, Kudan-kita, Chiyoda-ku, Tokyo 102; tel. (3) 263-2311; f. 1917; morning; Man. Editor Nagaru Shibuya; circ. 545,000.

Nikkan Sports: 5–10, 3-chome, Tsukiji, Chuo-ku, Tokyo 104; tel. (3) 542-2111; f. 1946; morning; Editor Fumiki Okazaki; circ. 728,000.

Nikkan Suisan Keizai Shimbun (Fisheries): 6–8–19, Roppongi, Minato-ku, Tokyo 106; tel. (3) 404-6531; f. 1948; morning; Man. Editor Shoichi Sakane; circ. 57,000.

Sankei Shimbun: 7–2, 1-chome, Otemachi, Chiyoda-ku, Tokyo 100; tel. (3) 231-7111; f. 1950; Man. Editor Y. Hosoya; circ. morning 801,839, evening 354,624.

Sankei Sports: 7–2, 1-chome, Otemachi, Chiyoda-ku, Tokyo 100; tel. (3) 231-7111; f. 1963; morning; Man. Editor Shunichiro Kondo; circ. 649,000.

Seikyo Shimbun: 18 Shinano-machi, Shinjuku-ku, Tokyo 160; tel. (3) 353-0616; telex 33145; f. 1951; organ of Soka Gakkai Buddhist movement; Prin. Officer Einosuke Akiya; circ. 4.5m.

Shipping and Trade News: Tokyo News Service Ltd, Tsukiji Hamarikyu Bldg, 3–3 Tsukiji 5-chome, Chuo-ku, Tokyo 104; tel. (3) 542-6511; telex 252-3285; f. 1949; English; Man. Editor S. Yasuda; circ. 15,000.

Sports Nippon: Palace Side Bldg, 1–1, 1-chome, Hitotsubashi, Chiyoda-ku, Tokyo 100; tel. (3) 213-3351; f. 1949; morning; Man. Editor Jansuke Eguma; circ. 784,917.

Tokyo Shimbun: 3–13, 2-chome, Konan, Minato-ku, Tokyo 108; tel. (3) 471-2211; f. 1942; Man. Editor Katsumi Matsumoto; circ. morning 803,181, evening 589,741.

Tokyo Sports: 5–10, 3-chome, Tsukiji, Chuo-ku, Tokyo 104; tel. (3) 543-6760; f. 1959; evening; Man. Editor Masaaki Wakita; circ. 872,000.

Tokyo Times: 1–16, 1-chome, Higashi-Shimbashi, Minato-ku, Tokyo 105; tel. (3) 571-4831; f. 1946; morning; Man. Editor Yoshiharu Takeuchi; circ. 199,000.

Yomiuri Shimbun: 7–1, 1-chome, Otemachi Chiyoda-ku, Tokyo 100; tel. (3) 242-1111; f. 1874; Man. Editor Kenya Mizukami; circ. morning 5,429,933, evening 3,115,701m.

Yukan Fuji: 7–2, 1-chome, Otemachi, Chiyoda-ku, Tokyo 100; tel. (3) 231-7111; f. 1969; evening; Editor T. Mamizuka; circ. 1.2m.

Osaka District

Asahi Shimbun: 2–4, 3-chome, Nakano-shima, Kita-ku, Osaka 530; tel. (6) 231-0131; f. 1879; Man. Editor T. Shibata; circ. morning 2,180,060, evening 1,365,437.

Daily Sports: 1–18–11, Edobori, Nishi-ku, Osaka 550; tel. (6) 443-0421; f. 1948; morning; Editor Saburo Nakazato; circ. 585,000.

Hochi Shimbun: 2–22–17, Honjo-Nishi, Oyodo-ku, Osaka 531; tel. (6) 374-2311; f. 1964; morning; Man. Editor S. Suzuki; circ. 336,000.

Kansai Shimbun: 1–9–3 Hirano-cho, Higashi-ku, Osaka; tel. (6) 941-6001; f. 1950; evening; Man. Editor T. Kimura; circ. 151,000.

The Mainichi Daily News: 1–6–20, Dojima, Kita-ku, Osaka; tel. (6) 343-1121; f. 1922; morning; English; Man. Editor Yoshio Hidachi; circ. 30,000.

Mainichi Shimbun: 1–6–20, Dojima, Kita-ku, Osaka 530; tel. (6) 343-1121; f. 1882; Man. Editor Futoshi Sakota; circ. morning 1,611,061, evening 932,000.

Nihon Keizai Shimbun: 1–1, Kyobashi-maeno-cho, Higashi-ku, Osaka 540; tel. (6) 943-7111; f. 1950; Man. Editor Keiji Samejima; circ. morning 596,404, evening 387,343.

Nikkan Sports: 92–1, 5-chome, Hattori-kotubuki-cho, Toyonaka City 561; tel. (6) 862-1011; f. 1950; morning; Editor Youji Kugai; circ. 452,000.

Osaka Nichi-nichi Shimbun: 1–5–13, Kitadori, Edobori, Nishi-ku, Osaka 550; tel. (6) 441-5551; f. 1946; evening; Man. Editor Mitsuke Kishimoto; circ. 89,000.

Osaka Shimbun: 2–4–9 Umeda, Kita-ku, Osaka 530; tel. (6) 343-1221; f. 1922; evening; Man. Editor Terukazu Higashiyama; circ. 163,000.

Osaka Sports: 4th Floor, Osaka-ekimae Daiichi Bldg, 1–3–1–400, Umeda, Kita-ku, Osaka 530; tel. (6) 345-7657; f. 1968; evening; Editor Sen Asano; circ. 510,000.

Sankei Shimbun: 2–4–9 Umeda, Kita-ku, Osaka 530; tel. (6) 343-1221; f. 1933; Man. Editor A. Sawa; circ. morning 1,185,739, evening 708,261.

Sankei Sports: 2–4–9 Umeda, Kita-ku, Osaka 530; tel. (6) 343-1221; f. 1955; morning; Editor Hirokazu Takeda; circ. 490,000.

Shin Osaka: 1–10–1, Minami-horie, Nishi-ku, Osaka 550; tel. (6) 534-1251; f. 1946; evening; Man. Editor Yoshiyuki Enoki; circ. 29,000.

Sports Nippon: 3–2–25, Oyodo-minami, Oyodo-ku, Osaka 531; tel. (6) 458-5981; f. 1949; morning; Man. Editor Jiro Tanaka; circ. 555,000.

Yomiuri Shimbun: 8–10, Nozaki-cho, Kita-ku, Osaka 530; tel. (6) 361-1111; f. 1952; Pres. G. Sakata; Man. Editor Koutaro Furusawa; circ. morning 2,210,443, evening 1,400,945.

Kanto District

Chiba Nippo (Chiba Daily News): 4–14–10 Chuo, Chiba City 280; tel. (472) 22-9211; f. 1957; morning; Man. Editor Masaki Ishibashi; circ. 129,000.

Ibaraki: 2–15 Kitami-machi, Mito City 310; tel. (292) 21-3121; f. 1891; morning; Man. Editor Isamu Murofushi; circ. 122,483.

Jyomo Shimbun: 1–50–21 Furuichi-machi, Maebashi City 371; tel. (272) 51-4341; f. 1887; morning; Man. Editor Toshio Higuchi; circ. 199,437.

Kanagawa Shimbun: 23, 2-chome, Otomachi, Naka-ku, Yokohama City 231; tel. (45) 201-0831; f. 1942; morning; Man. Editor Rikuo Uchiyama; circ. 210,557.

Shimotsuke Shimbun: 1–8–11, Showa, Utsunomiya City 320; tel. (286) 25-1111; f. 1884; morning; Man. Editor Michiyoshi Yasunaga; circ. 234,870.

Tochigi Shimbun: 45, Shimo-tomatsuri 1-chome, Utsunomiya City 320; tel. (286) 22-5291; f. 1950; morning; Man. Editor Tadashi Toyosaka; circ. 75,590.

Tohoku District
(North-east Honshu)

Akita Sakigake Shimpo: 2–6, 1-chome, O-machi, Akita 010; tel. (188) 62-1231; f. 1874; Man. Editor Saburo Washio; circ. morning and evening each 231,017.

Daily Tohoku: 1-3-12, Jyoka, Hachinohe 031; tel. (178) 44-5111; f. 1945; morning; Editor Hiroaki Niiyama; circ. 83,878.

Fukushima Mimpo: 13–17, Ohta-machi, Fukushima City 960; tel. (245) 31-4111; f. 1892; Man. Editor Shigeo Takahashi; circ. morning 247,900, evening 11,995.

Fukushima Minyu: 9–9, Naka-Machi, Fukushima City 960; tel. (245) 23-1191; f. 1895; Man. Editor Teruo Abe; circ. morning 167,590, evening 8,776.

Iwate Nippo: 3–2, Uchimaru, Morioka City 020; tel. (196) 53-4111; f. 1938; Man. Editor Gen-ichiro Murata; circ. morning and evening each 210,093.

Kahoku Shimpo: 2–28, 1-chome, Itsutsubashi, Sendai City 980, tel. (222) 22-6121; f. 1897; Man. Editor T. Suzuki; circ. morning 450,000, evening 175,000.

Too Nippoh: 2–11, 2-chome, Shin-machi, Aomori City 030; tel. (177) 73-1111; f. 1888; Man. Editor Kouji Yamada; circ. morning 241,059, evening 236,432.

Yamagata Shimbun: 5–12, 2-chome Hatago-cho, Yamagata City 990; tel. (236) 22-5271; f. 1876; Man. Editor Kenichi Sohma; circ. morning and evening each 216,098.

Chubu District
(Central Honshu)

Asahi Shimbun: 3–3, 1-chome, Sakae, Naka-ku, Nagoya City 460; tel. (52) 231-8131; telex 22226; f. 1935; Editor Youichi Hosokawa; circ. morning 485,194, evening 246,789.

Chubu Keizai Shimbun: 4–4–12, Meieki, Nakamura-ku, Nagoya City 450; tel. (52) 561-5211; f. 1946; morning; Man. Editor Tadanori Kato; circ. 96,074.

Chukyo Sports: Chukei Bldg, 4–4–12, Meieki, Nakamura-ku, Nagoya City 450; tel. (52) 582-4076; f. 1968; evening; Man. Editor Ryotaro Motoyama; circ. 299,000.

Chunichi Shimbun: 6–1, 1-chome Sannomaru, Naka-ku, Nagoya City 460; tel. (52) 201-8811; f. 1942; Man. Editor Tadashi Yamaguchi; circ. morning 1,979,959, evening 829,961.

Chunichi Sports: 6–1, 1-chome, Sannomaru, Naka-ku, Nagoya City 460; tel. (52) 201-8811; f. 1954; evening; Dir Yasuo Mizutani; circ. 579,000.

Gifu Nichi-nichi Shimbun: 9 Imakomachi, Gifu City 500; tel. (582) 64-1151; f. 1879; Pres. Mikio Sugiyama; Man. Editor Kiminori Muto; circ. morning 123,188, evening 30,598.

JAPAN

Mainichi Shimbun: 4–7–35, Meieki, Nakamura-ku, Nagoya City 450; tel. (52) 561-2211; f. 1935; Man. Editor AKIRA HORIKOSHI; circ. morning 220,749, evening 101,467.

Nagoya Times: 3–10, 1-chome, Marunouchi, Naka-ku, Nagoya City 460; tel. (52) 231-1331; f. 1946; evening; Man. Editor ISAO KIMI; circ. 143,449.

Shinano Mainichi Shimbun: 657 Minamiagata-cho, Nagano City 380; tel. (262) 34-4151; f. 1873; Man. Editor NOBUYUKI SHINOHARA; circ. morning 222,169, evening 39,068.

Shizuoka Shimbun: 3–1–1, Toro, Shizuoka City 422; tel. (542) 82-1111; f. 1941; Man. Editor KAKUJI OISHI; circ. morning 621,351, evening 621,349.

Yamanashi Nichi-Nichi Shimbun: 6–10, 2-chome, Kitaguchi, Kofu City 400, tel. (552) 31-3000; f. 1872; morning; Man. Editor TAKEHISA NAKAGOMI; circ. 158,233.

Hokuriku District
(North Coastal Honshu)

Fukui Shimbun: 1–14, 1-chome, Haruyama, Fukui City 910; tel. (776) 23-5111; f. 1899; morning; Man. Editor MAKOTO TSUCHIDA; circ. 150,092.

Hokkoku Shimbun: 5–1, 2-chome, Korinbo, Kanazawa City 920; tel. (762) 63-2111; f. 1893; Man. Editor S. ARAI; circ. morning 244,000, evening 84,000.

Hokuriku Chunichi Shimbun: 7–15, 2-chome, Korinbo, Kanazawa City 920; f. 1960; Editor K. OYAIZU; circ. morning 120,000, evening 20,000.

Kita Nihon Shimbun: 2–14 Yasuzumi-cho, Toyama City 930; tel. (763) 32-1111; f. 1940; Man. Editor RUUZO UENO; circ. morning 197,049, evening 31,644.

Niigata Nippo: 274-1, Niban-cho, Higashinaka-dori, Niigata City 951; tel. (252) 29-2211; f. 1942; Man. Editor SACHIO IGARASHI; circ. morning 418,382, evening 97,601.

Yomiuri Shimbun: 4–5 Shimonoseki-machi, Takaoka City 933; tel. (766) 23-1234; f. 1961; Editor M. NAGAHARA; circ. morning 146,000, evening 11,000.

Kinki District
(West Central Honshu)

Ise Shimbun: 34–6, Hon-cho, Tsu City 514; tel. (592) 24-0003; f. 1878; morning; Man. Editor MASAO KOBAYASHI; circ. 97,000.

Kobe Shimbun: 1–1, 7-chome, Kumoidori, Chuo-ku, Kobe City 651; tel. (78) 221-4121; f. 1898; Man. Editor TADAO TANAKA; circ. morning 472,875, evening 276,748.

Kyoto Shimbun: 239 Shoshoi-machi Ebisugawa-kitairu, Karasuma-dori, Nakakyo-ku, Kyoto 604; tel. (75) 222-2111; f. 1879; Man. Editor T. ADACHI; circ. morning 466,880, evening 354,826.

Nara Shimbun: 606 Sanjo-machi, Nara City 630; tel. (742) 26-1331; f. 1946; morning; Man. Editor YOSHIKATA HIROSHIBA; circ. 87,480.

Chugoku District
(Western Honshu)

Chugoku Shimbun: 7–1 Dobashi-cho, Naka-ku, Hiroshima City 733; tel. (82) 291-2111; f. 1892; Pres. AKIRA YAMAMOTO; Man. Editor YUKIO OGATA; circ. morning 622,489, evening 112,503.

Oka-Nichi: 6–30, Hon-cho, Okayama 700; tel. (862) 31-4211; f. 1946; evening; Man. Editor KEIJI FUKUHARA; circ. 39,641.

San-In Chuo Shimpo: 383 Tomo-machi, Matsue 690; tel. (852) 21-4491; f. 1942; morning; Man. Editor TADASHI SUGITANI; circ. 150,638.

Sanyo Shimbun: 1–23, 2-chome, Yanagi-cho, Okayama 700; tel. (862) 31-2211; f. 1879; Man. Editor HITOSHI KAWAI; circ. morning 396,424, evening 83,001.

Yamaguchi Shimbun: 1–1–7, Higashi-Yamato-cho, Shimonoseki 750; tel. (832) 66-3211; f. 1946; morning; Pres. KAZUYUGI OGAWA; Editor ATSUMU YOSHIKURA; circ. 58,000.

Shikoku Island

Ehime Shimbun: 12–1, 1-chome, Otemachi, Matsuyama, 790; tel. (899) 41-8111; f. 1941; Man. Editor AKIRA YAMADA; circ. morning 212,683, evening 23,680.

Kochi Shimbun: 2–15, 3-chome, Honcho, Kochi City 780; tel. (888) 22-2111; f. 1904; Man. Editor SHOROKU HASHII; circ. morning 211,548, evening 127,405.

Shikoku Shimbun: 15–1, Nakano-machi, Takamatsu 760; tel. (878) 33-1111; f. 1889; Man. Editor TASUO MURAI; circ. morning 178,640, evening 20,000.

Directory

Tokushima Shimbun: 6, 1-chome, Saiwai-cho, Tokushima 770; tel. (886) 23-2121; f. 1941; Editor-in-Chief YOSHIMI IBATA; circ. morning 212,198, evening 39,168.

Hokkaido Island

Asahi Shimbun: 1–1, 1-chome, Nishi, Kita Nijo, Chuo-ku, Sapporo 060; tel. (11) 281-2131; f. 1959; Editor A. ISHIZUKA; circ. morning 177,699, evening 116,866.

Hokkai Times: 6, 10-chome, Nishi Minami-Ichijo, Chuo-ku, Sapporo 060; tel. (011) 231-0131; f. 1946; Man. Editor KIICHI SHIOGUCHI; circ. morning 167,301, evening 40,096.

Hokkaido Shimbun: 6, 3-chome, Odori-Nishi, Chuo-ku, Sapporo 060; tel. (11) 221-2111; f. 1942; Editor TOSHIRO OTA; circ. morning 1,079,413, evening 799,155.

Mainichi Shimbun: 1, Nishi 6, Kita-yojo, Chuo-ku, Sapporo 060; tel. (11) 221-4141; f. 1959; Rep. ISAO MIYASIMA; circ. morning 101,156, evening 47,450.

Nikkan Sports: Times Bldg, 10–6, Nishi, Minami-Ichijo, Chuo-ku, Sapporo 060; tel. (11) 231-5110; f. 1962; morning; Man. Editor AKIRA ABE; circ. 148,000.

Yomiuri Shimbun: 1, 4-chome, Kita-yojo, Chuo-ku, Sapporo 060; tel. (11) 231-7611; f. 1959; Editor A. SHIDARA; circ. morning 259,651, evening 132,784.

Kyushu Island

Asahi Shimbun: 12–1, 1-chome, Sunatsu, Kokura Kita-ku, Kita-Kyushu City 802; tel. (93) 531-1131; f. 1935; Man. Editor TOMOHIRO NISHIMURA; circ. morning 821,377, evening 225,813.

Fukunichi: 2–1, 1-chome, Imaizumi, Chuo-ku, Fukuoka 810; tel. (92) 711-2520; f. 1946; morning; Man. Editor TAKAAKI SATANI; circ. 135,000.

Kagoshima Shimpo: 7–28 Jonan-cho, Kagoshima 892; tel. (992) 26-2100; f. 1959; morning; Man. Editor MOTOYOSH HAGIWARA; circ. 56,577.

Kumamoto Nichi-nichi Shimbun: 2–33, Kamidori-machi, Kumamoto 860; tel. (96) 326-1111; f. 1942; Editor KEISUKE HISANO; circ. morning 331,967, evening 106,932.

Kyushu Sports: Fukuoka Tenjin Centre Bldg, 2–14–8, Tenjin-cho, Chuo-ku, Fukuoka 810; tel. (92) 781-7452; f. 1966; morning; Man. Editor T. OKAMIYA; circ. 262,000.

Mainichi Shimbun: 13–1, Konya-machi, Kokura Kita-ku, Kitakyushu 802; tel. (93) 541-3131; f. 1935; Man. Editor HARUJI SHINOHARA; circ. morning 651,625, evening 166,208.

Minami Nihon Shinbun: 1–2 Yasui-cho, Kagoshima-shi, Kagoshima 892; tel. (992) 26-4111; f. 1881; Man. Editor SHINOBU FUKUISHI; circ. morning 343,937, evening 33,602.

Miyazaki Nichi-nichi Shimbun: 1–33, 1-chome Takachihodori, Miyazaki 880; tel. (985) 25-2371; f. 1940; Man. Editor RYOJI TANAKA; morning; circ. 200,406.

Nagasaki Shimbun: 3–1, Mori-machi, Nagasaki 852; tel. (958) 44-2111; f. 1889; Man. Editor HISASHI IWANAGA; circ. morning 166,860; evening 53,531.

The Nihon Keizai Shimbun: 3–1, 2-chome, Sumiyoshi, Hakata-ku, Fukuoka City; tel. (92) 281-4931; f. 1964; Editor TAKESHI INOUE; circ. morning 157,010, evening 62,186.

Nishi Nippon Shimbun: 4–1, 1-chome, Tenjin, Chuo-ku, Fukuoka 810; tel. (92) 711-5555; f. 1877; Man. Editor TSUNEO TAKIGUCHI; circ. morning 771,018, evening 217,337.

Oita Godo Shimbun: 9–15, 3-chome, Fudai-cho, Oita 870; tel. (975) 36-2121; f. 1886; Man. Editor MOTOO ASAKUNO; circ. morning 202,332, evening 202,383.

Okinawa Times: 2–2–2, Kumoji, Naha City, 900; tel. (988) 67-3111; f. 1948; Man. Editor TAKAO MIYAGI; circ. morning 244,606, evening 244,071.

Ryukyu Shimpo: 1–10–3, Izumisaki, Naha City 900; tel. (988) 67-1131; f. 1893; Man. Editor AKIYA MIYASATO; circ. morning 249,152, evening 248,077.

Saga Shimbun: 3–18, 1-chome, Matsubara, Saga City 840; tel. (952) 22-1411; f. 1884; morning; Man. Editor SHIGEO INADA; circ. 114,205.

Sports Nippon: 4–1, 1-chome, Kiyotaki, Moji-ku, Kita-kyushu 801; tel. (93) 321-4001; f. 1955; morning; Man. Editor T. DOI; circ. 230,000.

Yomiuri Shimbun: 1–11 Meiwa-machi, Kokurakita-ku, Kitakyushu 802; tel. (93) 531-5131; f. 1964; Man. Editor MAKOTO WATARAI; circ. morning 886,733, evening 155,773.

JAPAN

WEEKLIES

Asahi Graphic: Asahi Shimbun Publishing Co, 5-3-2 Tsukiji, Chuo-ku, Tokyo 104; tel. (3) 545-0131; telex 22226; f. 1923; pictorial review; Editor Toshiaki Fujii; circ. 200,000.

Asahi Journal: Asahi Shimbun Publications Dept, 5-3-2 Tsukiji, Chuo-ku, Tokyo 104; tel. (3) 545-0131; telex 22226; f. 1959; review; Editor Tetsuya Tsukushi.

Asiaweek: 7F Anzai Bldg, 2-5-5 Kudan-Minami, Chiyoda-ku, Tokyo; tel. (3) 221-7141; telex 23942; f. 1975; Asian news; Publr Robert B. Klaverkamp; Editor for Japan (vacant); circ. 65,000.

Economist: Mainichi Newspapers Publishing Dept, 1-1-1, Hitotsubashi, Chiyoda-ku, Tokyo; tel. (3) 212-0321; telex 24851; f. 1923; Editorial Chief Eisuke Toda; circ. 117,000.

Shukan Asahi: Asahi Shimbun Publishing Co, 5-3-2 Tsukiji, Chuo-ku, Tokyo 104; tel. (3) 545-0131; telex 22226; f. 1922; general interest; Editor Hideo Kinoshita; circ. 600,000.

Shukan Bunshun: Bungei-Shunju Ltd., 3-23 Kioicho, Chiyoda-ku, Tokyo 102; tel. (3) 265-1211; f. 1959; general interest; Editor Masaru Shiraishi; circ. 491,288.

Shukan Daiyamondo: Diamond Inc, 1-4-2, Kasumi-gaseki, Chiyoda-ku, Tokyo; tel. (3) 504-6517; telex 02424461; f. 1913; economics; Editor Masato Oguma.

Shukan Gendai: Kodansha Co Ltd, 2-12-21, Otowa, Bunkyo-ku, Tokyo; tel. (3) 945-1111; f. 1959; general; Editor Akiya Sugimoto.

Shukan Post: Shogakukan Publishing Co Ltd, 2-3-1, Hitotsubashi, Chiyoda-ku, Tokyo; tel. (3) 230-5211; telex 0232-2192; f. 1969; general; Editor Susumu Sekine.

Shukan Sankei: Sankei Publishing Ltd, 6-1-25, Kojimanchi, Chiyoda-ku, Tokyo; tel. (3) 234-0301; f. 1952; general interest; Editor Osamu Sasaki.

Shukan Shincho: Shinchosha, 71 Yarai-cho, Shinjuku-ku, Tokyo; tel. (3) 266-5381; f. 1956; general interest; Editor Hikoya Yamada; circ. 587,287.

Shukan Toyo Keizai: Tokyo Keizai Shinpo Sha, 1-4 Hongoku-cho, Nihonbashi, Chuo-ku, Tokyo; tel. (3) 246-5401; f. 1895; business and economics; Editor Hisayoshi Katsumata; circ. 60,000.

Shukan Yomiuri: Yomiuri Shimbun Publications Dept, 1-7-1 Otemachi, Chiyoda-ku, Tokyo 100; tel. (3) 242-1111; telex 22228; f. 1938; general interest; Editor Hiroshi Kanda.

Student Times: Japan Times Inc, 4-5-4 Shibaura, Minato-ku, Tokyo; tel. (3) 453-5311; f. 1951; English and Japanese; Editor Yukio Kakuchi.

Sunday Mainichi: Mainichi Newspapers Publications Dept, 1-1-1 Hitotsubashi, Chiyoda-ku, Tokyo; tel. (3) 212-0321; telex 22324; f. 1922; general interest; Editor Iwami Takao; circ. 321,827.

Tenji Mainichi: Mainichi Newspapers Publications Dept, 1-1-1 Hitotsubashi, Chiyoda-ku, Tokyo; tel. (3) 212-0321; telex 22324; f. 1922; in Japanese braille; Editor Michitoshi Zenimoto; circ. 12,000.

PERIODICALS

Airview: Kantosha Co Ltd, 601 Kojun Bldg, 6-8-7 Ginza, Chuo-ku, Tokyo; tel. (3) 572-3421; f. 1951; monthly; aviation engineering; Editor T. Aoki; circ. 50,000.

All Yomimono: Bungei-Shunju Ltd, 3-23 Kioicho, Chiyoda-ku, Tokyo 102; tel. (3) 265-1211; f. 1930; monthly; popular fiction; Editor Shoji Tadokoro.

Asahi Camera: Asahi Shimbun Publications Dept, 5-3-2, Tsukiji, Chuo-ku, Tokyo 104; tel. (3) 545-0131; telex 22226; f. 1926; monthly; photography; Editor Yuzo Fujita; circ. 150,000.

Bijutsu Techô: Bijutsu Shuppan-sha, Inaoka Bldg, 2-36 Kanda, Jinbo-cho, Chiyoda-ku, Tokyo; tel. (3) 234-2151; f. 1948; monthly; fine arts; Editor Norio Ohashi.

Bungaku (Literature): Iwanami Shoten, 2-5-5, Hitotsubashi, Chiyoda-ku, Tokyo; tel. (3) 265-4111; telex 29495; f. 1933; monthly; Editor Koichiro Hoshino.

Bungei-Shunju: Bungei-Shunju Ltd, 3-23 Kioi-cho, Chiyoda-ku, Tokyo; tel. (3) 265-1211; f. 1923; monthly; general; Editor Takashi Tsutsumi.

Business JAPAN: Nihon Kogyo Shimbun Co, Sankei Bldg, 1-7-2, Otemachi, Chiyoda-ku, Tokyo; tel. (3) 231-7111; f. 1955; monthly; Pres. T. Nagata; Editor Hokaji Mino; circ. 63,000.

Chuo Koron: Chuskoron-Sha Inc, 2-8-7, Kyobashi, Chuo-ku, Tokyo; tel. (3) 563-1261; f. 1887; monthly; general interest; Chief Editor Shigetake Mochizuki.

Directory

Fujin Koron: Chuo Koron Sha Inc 2-8-7, Kyobashi, Chuo-ku, Tokyo 104; tel. (3) 563-1261; f. 1966; women's literary monthly; Editor Keiichi Yokoyama; circ. 263,017.

Fujin-Seikatsu: Fujin Seikatsu-Sha, 2-19-5, Yasima, Bunkyo-ku, Tokyo; tel. (3) 815-7161; f. 1947; monthly; women's; Editor Takashi Kimura.

Gakujin (Alpinist): Tokyo Shimbun Publications Dept, 2-3-13, Konan, Minato-ku, Tokyo 108; f. 1947; monthly; Editor T. Nishiyama; circ. 100,000.

Geijutsu Shincho: Shinchosha, 71 Yarai-cho, Shinjuku-ku, Tokyo; tel. (3) 266-5381; telex 27433; f. 1950; monthly; fine arts, music, architecture, drama and design; Editor-in-Chief Midori Yamakawa.

Gendai: Kodansha Co Ltd, 2-12-21, Otowa, Bunkyo-ku, Tokyo; tel. (3) 945-1111; telex 0272-2570; f. 1966; monthly; cultural and political; Editor Tadayuki Tashiro.

Gengo-Seikatsu: Chikuma-shobo, 2-8 Kandaogawacho, Chiyoda-ku, Tokyo; tel. (3) 291-7651; f. 1951; language and life monthly; Editor Mineo Nakajima; circ. 20,000.

Gunzo: Kodansha Ltd, 2-12-21, Otowa, Bunkyo-ku, Tokyo 112; tel. (3) 945-1111; telex 345509; f. 1946; literary monthly; Editor Keiko Amano.

Horitsu Jiho: Nippon Hyoron Sha Co Ltd, 14 Sugamachi, Shinjuku-ku, Tokyo 160; tel. (3) 341-6161; f. 1929; monthly; law journal; Editor Akira Tokunaga.

Ie-no-Hikari (Light of Home): Ie-no-Hikari Asscn, 11 Ichigaya, Funagawara-cho, Shinjuku-ku, Tokyo 160; tel. (3) 260-3151; telex 02322367; f. 1925; monthly; rural and general interest; Pres. Mitsugu Horiuchi; Editor Kenji Yokoyama; circ. 1.2m.

Iwa-To-Yuki (Rock and Snow): Yama-kei Publrs Co, 1-1-33, Shiba Daimon, Minato-ku, Tokyo 105; tel. (3) 436-4021; every 2 months; mountaineering; Editor Tsunemichi Ikeda.

Japan Company Handbook: Toyo Keiza Shinpo-Sha, 1-4, Hongoku-cho Nihonbashi, Chuo-ku, Tokyo 103; tel. (3) 246-5655; f. 1974; 2 a year; English, publ. by *Toyo Keizai Shinposha*; Editor Masaharu Kumano.

Japan Quarterly: Asahi Shimbun, 5-3-2 Tsukiji, Chuo-ku, Tokyo 104; tel. (3) 545-0131; f. 1954; English; political, economic and cultural; Exec. Editor Aoki Toshio.

Jitsugyo No Nihon: Jitsugyo No Nihon Sha Ltd, 1-3-9, Ginza, Chuo-ku, Tokyo 104; tel. (3) 562-1021; f. 1897; every 2 months; economics and business; Editor Nobuyoshi Yoshida; circ. 100,000.

Journal of Electronic Engineering: Dempa Publications Inc, 1-11-15, Higashi Gotanda, Shinagawa-ku, Tokyo 141; tel. (3) 445-6111; telex 02424461; f. 1950; monthly; Editor Ryoji Minagawa; circ. 51,000.

Journal of the Electronics Industry: Dempa Publications Inc, 1-11-15, Higashi Gotanda, Shingawa-ku, Tokyo 141; tel. (3) 445-6111; telex 024-24461; f. 1954; monthly; Editor Mas Hasegawa; circ. 110,000.

Kagaku (Science): Iwanami Shoten Publishers, 2-5-5, Hitotsubashi, Chiyoda-ku, Tokyo 101; tel. (3) 265-4111; telex 29495; f. 1931; Editor Shigeki Kobayashi.

Kagaku Asahi: Asahi Shimbun Publications Dept, 5-3-2, Tsukiji, Chuo-ku, Tokyo 104; tel. (3) 545-0131; telex 22226; f. 1941; monthly; scientific; Editor Akeo Mori.

Kagakushi-Kenkyu: (History of Science Society of Japan), Iwanami Shoten, 2-5-5 Hitotsubashi, Chiyoda-ku, Tokyo; tel. (3) 265-4111; telex 29495; f. 1941; quarterly journal; Editor Ichiro Yabe.

Kaisha Shikiho: Toyo Keizai Shinpo Sha, 1-4, Hongoku-cho, Nihonbashi, Chuo-ku, Tokyo 103; tel. (3) 246-5518; f. 1936; quarterly; economics; Editor Norio Imai; circ. 1,000,000.

Keizai Hyoron: Nippon Hyoron Sha Co Ltd, 14 Sugamachi, Shinjuku, Tokyo 160; tel. (3) 341-6161; f. 1946; monthly; economic review; Editor Isao Kaneda.

Keizaijin: Kansai Economic Federation, Nakanoshima Center Bldg, 6-2-27, Nakanoshima, Kita-ku, Osaka 530; tel. (6) 441-0101; monthly; economics; Editor I. Moriguchi.

Kokka: Asahi Shimbun Publications Dept, 5-3-2, Tsukiji, Chuo-ku, Tokyo 104; tel. (3) 542-6722; telex 22226; f. 1889; monthly; Far Eastern art; Chief Editor Yoshiho Yonezawa.

Mizue: Bijutsu Shuppan-sha, Inaoka Bldg, 2-36 Kanda, Jimbo-cho, Chiyoda-ku, Tokyo 101; tel. (3) 234-2155; f. 1905; quarterly; fine arts; Editor Ryohei Kumono.

Ongaku No Tomo (Friends of Music): Ongaku No Tomo Sha Corpn, 6-30 Kagurazaka, Shinjuku-ku, Tokyo 162; tel. (3) 235-2111;

JAPAN

telex 23718; monthly; classical music; Editor MIYAKO HORIUCHI; circ. 120,000.

Sekai: Iwanami Shoten, 2-5-5, Hitotsubashi, Tokyo 101; tel. (3) 265-4111; telex 29495; f. 1946; monthly; review of world and domestic affairs; Editor RYOSUKE YASUE; circ. 100,000.

Sincho: Shinchosha, 71, Yarai-cho, Shinjuku-ku, Tokyo; tel. (3) 266-5371; f. 1904; monthly; literary; Editor TADAO SAKAMOTO; circ. 20,000.

Shinkenchiku: 2-31-2, Yushima, Bunkyo-ku, Tokyo 113; f. 1924; monthly; architecture; Editor SHOZO BABA; circ. 48,000.

Shiso (Thought): Iwanami Shoten, 2-5-5, Hitotsubashi, Chiyoda-ku, Tokyo 101; tel. (3) 265-4111; telex 29495; f. 1921; monthly; philosophy, social sciences and humanities; Editor ATSUSHI AIBA.

Shosetsu Shincho: Shincho-Sha Publishing Co, 71 Yarai-cho, Shinjuku-ku, Tokyo 162; tel. (3) 266-5381; f. 1945; monthly; literature; Chief Editor REIKO KAWANO.

Shukan FM: Ongaku No Tomo Sha Corpn, 6-30, Kagurazaka, Shinjuku-ku, Tokyo 162; tel. (3) 235-2111; telex 0235-2129; fortnightly; guide to music broadcasts; Editor HIDIO SAGA; circ. 200,000.

So-en: Bunka Publishing Bureau, 3-1-22, Yoyogi, Shibuya-ku, Tokyo 151; tel. (3) 370-3111; telex 0232475; fashion monthly; Editor SUMIKO AKIMOTO; circ. 400,000.

Statistics Monthly: Toyo Keizai Shinpo Sha, 1-4, Hongoku-cho, Nihonbashi, Chuo-ku, Tokyo 103; tel. (3) 246-5574; f. 1939; monthly; Editor RYUICHI NAGANO.

Stereo: Ongaku No Tomo Sha Corpn, 6-30, Kagurazaka, Shinjuku-ku, Tokyo 162; tel. (3) 235-2111; telex 235-2129; monthly; records and audio; Editor SEIZABURO MOGAMI; circ. 140,000.

Sûgaku (Mathematics): Mathematical Society of Japan, 25-9-203, Hongo 4 chome, Bunkyo-ku, Tokyo 113; tel. (3) 265-4111; telex 29495; f. 1947; quarterly.

Tokyo Business Today: Toyo Keizai Shinposha, 1-4 Nihonbashi Hongokucho, Chuo-ku, Tokyo 103; tel. (3) 246-5655; f. 1982; 2 a year; English; business and finance; publ. by *Toyo Keizai Shinposha*; Editor MASAHARU KUMANO.

The-Yama-To-Keikoku (Mountain and Valley): Yama-Kei Publishing Co, 1-1-33, Shiba-Daimon, Minato-ku, Tokyo 105; tel. (3) 436-4021; monthly; mountaineering; Editor FUMIHIRO ITO.

NEWS AGENCIES

Jiji Tsushin-Sha (Jiji Press): Shisei Kaikan, 1-3 Hibiya Park, Chiyoda-ku, Tokyo 100; tel. (3) 591-1111; f. 1945; Pres. KAZUO HARANO.

Kyodo Tsushin (Kyodo News Service): 2-2-5 Toranomon, Minato-ku, Tokyo 105; tel. (3) 584-4111; telex 22207; f. 1945; Pres. SHINJI SAKAI; Man. Dir TOSHIO HARA; Man. Editor KAZUMI FUKASE.

Radiopress Inc.: Fuji TV Bldg, 3-1 Kawada-cho, Shinjuku-ku, Tokyo 162; tel. (3) 353-1621; f. 1945; provides news from China, the USSR, Democratic People's Repub. of Korea, Viet-Nam and elsewhere to the press and govt offices; Pres. JIRO INAGAWA.

Sun Telephoto: Palaceside Bldg, 1-1, 1-chome, Hitotsubashi, Chiyoda-ku, Tokyo 100; tel. (3) 213-6771; f. 1952; Pres. KEN-ICHIRO MATSUOKA; Man. Editor YU YAMAMOTO.

Foreign Bureaux

Agence France-Presse (AFP): Asahi Shimbun Bldg, 11th Floor, 5-3-2 Tsukiji, Chuo-ku, Tokyo 104; tel. (3) 545-3061; telex 22368; Bureau Chief RENÉ FLIPO.

Agencia EFE (Spain): Kyodo Tsushin Kaikan, 9th Floor, 2-2-5 Toranomon, Minato-ku, Tokyo 105; tel. (3) 585-8940; telex 34502; Correspondent DAVID CORRAL.

Agentstvo Pechati Novosti (APN) (USSR): 3-9-13, Higashigotanda, Shinagawa-ku, Tokyo 141; tel. (3) 441-9241; Bureau Chief ALEXEI K. PANTELEYEV.

Agenzia Nazionale Stampa Associata (ANSA) (Italy): Kyodo Tsushin Kaikan, 2-2-5 Toranomon, Minato-ku, Tokyo 105; tel. (3) 584-6667; telex 0072-28286; Correspondent ALFONSO MAFFETTONE.

Allgemeiner Deutscher Nachrichtendienst (ADN) (German Democratic Republic): 4-9-9, Jingumae, Shibuya-ku, Tokyo 150; tel. (3) 478-3842; Correspondent JÜRGEN SIEMUND.

Antara (Indonesia): Kyodo Tsushin Bldg, 9th Floor, 2-2-5 Toranomon, Minato-ku, Tokyo 107; tel. (3) 584-4234; Correspondent PIDWAN SURYANTHO.

Associated Press (AP) (USA): Asahi Shimbun Bldg, 11th Floor, 5-3-2, Tsukiji, Chuo-ku, Tokyo 104; tel. (3) 545-5901; telex 22260; Bureau Chief ROY K. ESSOYAN.

Directory

Bulgarian Telegraph Agency (BTA): Daiichi Aoyama Mansion, Room 802, 1-10, 5-chome, Minami Aoyama, Minato-ku, Tokyo 107; tel. (3) 407-6926; Correspondent IVAN A. GAYTANDJIEV.

Central News Agency Inc. (Taiwan): Kyowa Bldg, Room 503, 1-5-6 Iidabashi, Chiyoda-ku, Tokyo; tel. (3) 264-4717; Bureau Chief CHIEM CHAO HUNG.

Deutsche Presse-Agentur (dpa) (Federal Republic of Germany): CPOB 1512, Shisei Kaikan, Room 202, 1-3 Hibiya Park, Chiyoda-ku, Tokyo 100; tel. (3) 580-6629; telex 22-533; Bureau Chief HELMUT RÄTHER.

Keystone Press Agency (UK): Kaneda Bldg, 3-17-2 Shibuya, Shibuya-ku, Tokyo 150; tel. (3) 407-0375; Pres. JUNZO SUZUKI.

Magyar Távirati Iroda (MTI) (Hungary): 22-1 Minami-Aoyama, 4-chome, Minato-ku, Tokyo; tel. (3) 410-4049; Bureau Chief: LAJOS PIETSCH.

Prensa Latina (Cuba): 36-6, 3-chome, Nozawa Setagoya-ku, Tokyo; tel. (3) 421-9455; telex 29962; Correspondent JOSÉ AGUILAR.

Reuters (UK): Shuwa Kamiyacho Bldg, 4-3-13 Toranomon, Minato-ku, Tokyo 105; tel. (3) 432 2389; telex 22349; Man. Dir MICHAEL SALAMAN.

Tanjug News Agency (Yugoslavia): 5-8-15, Kitashinagawa, Shinagawa-ku, Tokyo 141; tel. (3) 443-7366; Correspondent ŽARKO MODRIĆ.

Telegrafnoye Agentstvo Sovetskovo Soyuza (TASS) (USSR): 5-1, 1-chome, Hon-cho, Shibuya-ku, Tokyo 151; tel. (3) 377-0380; Correspondent VIKTOR ZATSEPIN.

United Press International (UPI) (USA): Palaceside Bldg, 1-1, Hitotsubashi 1-chome, Chiyoda-ku, Tokyo 100; tel. (3) 212-7911; Bureau Man. J. L. BATTENFELD.

Xinhua (New China) News Agency (People's Republic of China): 3-35-23, Ebisu, Shibuya-ku, Tokyo 150; tel. (3) 441-3766; Correspondent LIU WENYU.

Yonhap (United) News Agency (Republic of Korea): Kyodo Tsushin Bldg, 2-2-5 Toranomon, Minato-ku, Tokyo 105; tel. (3) 584-4681; f. 1945; Bureau Chief LEE SANG-KWON.

PRESS ASSOCIATIONS

Foreign Press Center: 6th Floor, Nippon Press Centre Bldg, 2-2-1 Uchisaiwai-cho, Chiyoda-ku, Tokyo 100; tel. (3) 501-3401; f. 1976; est. by Japan Newspaper Publishers' and Editors' Asscn and the Japan Fed. of Economic Organizations; provides services to the foreign press; Pres. KINJI KAWAMURA; Man. Dir MASANAO NISHIKATA.

Foreign Press in Japan: 20F Yurakucho Denki Bldg, 1-7-1 Yurakucho, Chiyoda-ku, Tokyo; tel. (3) 211-3161; f. 1960; 140 companies; Pres. WILLIAM HORSLEY; Man. HAJIME HORIKAWA.

Nihon Shinbun Kyokai (Japan Newspaper Publishers' and Editors' Asscn): Nippon Press Center Bldg, 2-1, Uchisaiwai-cho 2-chome, Chiyoda-ku, Tokyo 100; tel. (3) 591-4401; telex 27504; f. 1946; mems include 164 companies, including 114 daily newspapers, 4 news agencies and 46 radio and TV companies; Pres. YOSAJI KOBAYASHI; Man. Dir and Sec.-Gen. TOSHIE YAMADA.

Nihon Zasshi Kyokai (Japan Magazine Publishers' Association): 7, 1-chome, Kanda Surugadai, Chiyoda-ku, Tokyo; tel. (3) 291-0775; f. 1956; 68 mems; Pres. GENZO CHIBA; Sec. JUN TANAKA.

Publishers

In 1985 there were 4,183 publishing companies in Japan.

Akane Shobo Co Ltd: 3-2-1, Nishikanda, Chiyoda-ku, Tokyo; tel. (3) 363-0641; f. 1949; juvenile; Pres. MASAHARU OKAMOTO.

Akita Publishing Shoten Co Ltd: 2-10-8, Iidabashi, Chiyoda-ku, Tokyo 102; tel. (3) 264-7011; f. 1948; social science, history, juvenile; Chair. TEIO AKITA; Man. Dir SADAMI AKITA.

Asahi Shimbun Publications Dept: 5-3-2 Tsukiji, Chuo-ku, Tokyo; tel. (3) 545-0131; telex 22226; f. 1879; general; Pres. TOICHIRO HITOTSUYANAGI; Man. Dir TADASHI KOJIMA.

Baifukan Co Ltd: 3-12, Kudan Minami 4-chome, Chiyoda-ku, Tokyo 102; tel. (3) 262-5256; f. 1924; engineering, natural and social sciences, psychology; Pres. ITARU YAMAMOTO.

Bijutsu Shuppan-Sha: 6th Floor, Inaoka Bldg, 2-36, Kanda Jimbo-cho, Chiyoda-ku, Tokyo 101; tel. (3) 234-2151; f. 1905; art and architecture; Pres. ATSUSHI OSHITA.

Chikuma Shobo Publishing Co Ltd: 2-8, Kanda Ogawamachi, Chiyoda-ku, Tokyo 101-91; tel. (3) 294-6711; f. 1940; general fiction and non-fiction; Rep. KAKUZAEMON NUNOKAWA.

Chuokoron-Sha Inc: 2-8-7, Kyobashi, Chuo-ku, Tokyo; tel. (3) 563-1261; telex 32505; f. 1887; philosophy, history, economic, political and natural science, literature, fine arts; Pres. HOJI SHIMANAKA; Man. Dir SHIGERU TAKANASHI.

Froebel-Kan Co Ltd: 3-1, Kanda Ogawa-machi, Chiyoda-ku, Tokyo 101; tel. (3) 292-7786; telex 24907; f. 1907; juvenile, educational, music; Pres. YUUJI OKAYASU; Dir HARRY IDICHI.

Fukuinkan Shoten: 6-6-3, Honkomagome, Bunkyo-ku, Tokyo 113; tel. (3) 942-0032; telex 33597; f. 1950; juvenile; Pres. KATSUMI SATO; Man. Dir TADASHI MATSUI.

Gakken Co Ltd: 4-40-5, Kamiikedai, Ohta-ku, Tokyo 145; tel. (3) 726-8131; telex 26389; f. 1946; fiction, juvenile, educational, art, history, reference, encyclopaedias, dictionaries, languages; Pres. HIROSHI FURUOKA; Chair. HIDETO FURUOKA.

Hakusui-Sha: 3-24, Kanda Ogawa-machi, Chiyoda-ku, Tokyo; tel. (3) 291-7811; f. 1915; general literature, science and languages; Chair. SUEO NAKAMORI.

Heibonsha Ltd Publishers: 5, Sanbancho, Chiyoda-ku, Tokyo 102; tel. (3) 265-0451; f. 1914; encyclopaedias, art, history, geography, Japanese and Chinese literature; Pres. NAOYA SHIMONAKA.

Hirokawa Publishing Co: 3-27-14, Hongo, Bunkyo-ku, Tokyo; tel. (3) 815-3651; f. 1926; natural sciences, medicine, textbooks; Pres. SETSUO HIROKAWA.

The Hokuseido Press: 12, Kanda Nishikicho 3-chome, Chiyoda-ku, Tokyo 101; tel. (3) 294-3301; f. 1914; regional non-fiction, textbooks; Pres. MASAZO YAMAMOTO.

Ie-No-Hikari Association: 11 Funagawara-cho, Ichigaya, Shinjuku-ku, Tokyo 162; tel. (3) 260-3151; telex 02322367; f. 1925; social science, industry; Pres. YASUO OGUSHI; Man. Dir AKIRA SUZUKI.

Iwanami Shoten Publishers: 2-5-5 Hitotsubashi, Chiyoda-ku, Tokyo 101; tel. (3) 265-4111; telex 29495; f. 1913; natural and social sciences, literature, history, geography; Chair. YUJIRO IWANAMI; Pres. TORU MIDORIKAWA.

Jimbun Shoin: Takakura-Nishi-iru, Bukkoji-dori, Shimogyo-ku, Kyoto; tel. 75-351-3343; f. 1922; literary, philosophy, history, fine arts; Pres. MUTSUHISA WATANABE.

Kanehara & Co Ltd: 31-14, Yushima 2-chome, Bunkyo-ku, Tokyo; tel. (3) 811-7161; f. 1875; medical, agricultural, engineering and scientific; Pres. HIDEO KANEHARA.

Kodansha Ltd: 12-21, Otowa 2-chome, Bunkyo-ku, Tokyo 112; tel. (3) 945-1111; telex 34509; f. 1909; art, educational, illustrated children's, fiction, cookery, encyclopaedias, natural science, paperbacks, magazines; Pres. KOREMICHI NOMA; Chair. TOSHIYUKI HATTORI.

Kyoritsu Shuppan Co Ltd: 4-6-19, Kobinata 4-chome, Bunkyo-ku, Tokyo 112; tel. (3) 947-2511; f. 1926; scientific and technical; Pres. MASAO NANJO; Gen. Man. Publishing Division HIROSHI WAKAI.

Maruzen Co Ltd: 3-10, Nihonbashi 2-chome, Chuo-ku, Tokyo 103; tel. (3) 272-7211; telex 26516; f. 1869; general; Pres. KUMAO EBIHARA; Chair. SHINGO IIZUMI.

Minerva Shobo Co Ltd: 1 Tsutsumidani-cho, Hinooka, Yamashina-ku, Kyoto 607; tel. 75-581-5191; f. 1948; general non-fiction and reference; Pres. NOBUO SUGITA.

Misuzu Shobo Publishing Co: 3-17-15, Hongo, Bunkyo-ku, Tokyo; tel. (3) 815-9181; f. 1947; general, philosophy, history, literature, science, art; Pres. TAMIO KITANO; Man. Dir TOSHITO OBI.

Nanzando Co Ltd: 4-1-11, Yushima, Bunkyo-ku, Tokyo; tel. (3) 814-3681; medical reference, paperbacks; Man. Dir KIMIO SUZUKI.

Obunsha Co Ltd: 55 Yokodera-cho, Shinjuku-ku, Tokyo; tel. (3) 266-6000; f. 1931; textbooks, reference, general science and fiction, magazines, encyclopaedias; audio-visual aids; Pres. KAZUO AKAO.

Ohmsha Ltd: 1-3, Kanda Nishiki-cho, Chiyoda-ku, Tokyo 101; tel. (3) 233-0641; telex 02223125; f. 1914; engineering, technical and scientific; Pres. N. TANEDA; Exec. Dir S. SATO.

Ongaku No Tomo Sha Corpn (ONT): 6-30, Kagurazaka, Shinjuku-ku, Tokyo; tel. (3) 235-2111; telex 23718; f. 1941; folios, concert hall, music magazines; Pres. SUNAO ASAKA.

Risosha: 46 Akagishita-machi, Shinjuku-ku, Tokyo 162; tel. (3) 268-1306; f. 1927; philosophy, religion, social sciences; Pres. YUKIHO KAWABE.

Sankei Shimbun Shuppankyoku Co: 3-15, Otemachi, Chiyoda-ku, Tokyo; tel. (3) 231-7111; f. 1950; history, social sciences, politics, juvenile; Man. Dir SHINYA UEDA.

Sanseido Co Ltd: 2-22-14, Misakicho, Chiyoda-ku, Tokyo 101; tel. (3) 230-9411; f. 1881; dictionaries, educational, languages, social and natural science; Chair. HISANORI UENO; Man. Dir MASEAKI MORIYA.

Seibundo-Shinkosha Publishing Co Ltd: 1-5-5, Kanda Nishiki-cho, Chiyoda-ku, Tokyo; tel. (3) 292-1211; f. 1912; technical, scientific, general non-fiction; Pres. and Man. Dir SHIGEO OGAWA.

Shinkenchiku-Sha Ltd: 31-2, Yushima 2-chome, Bunkyo-ku, Tokyo; tel. (3) 811-7101; f. 1925; architecture; Editor SHOZO BABA; Publr YOSHIO YOSHIDA.

Shogakukan Inc.: 2-3-1, Hitotsubashi, Chiyoda-ku, Tokyo 101; tel. (3) 230-5655; telex 02322192; f. 1922; juvenile, education, geography, history, encyclopaedias, dictionaries; Pres. TETSUO OHGA.

Shokokusha Publishing Co Ltd: 25 Saka-machi, Shinjuku-ku, Tokyo 160; tel. (3) 359-3231; f. 1932; architectural, technical and fine arts; Chair. and Pres. TAISHIRO YAMAMOTO.

Shufunotomo Co Ltd: 9, Kanda Surugadai 2-chome, Chiyoda-ku, Tokyo 101; tel. (3) 294-1118; telex 26925; f. 1916; domestic science, fine arts, gardening, handicraft, cookery and magazines; Pres. HARUHIKO ISHIKAWA.

Shunju-Sha Co Ltd: 2-18-6, Soto-kanda, Chiyoda-ku, Tokyo; tel. (3) 255-9611; f. 1918; philosophy, religion, literary, economics, music; Pres. AKIRA KANDA; Man. Dir OSAMU KANDA.

Taishukan Shoten: 3-24, Kanda Nishiki-cho, Chiyoda-ku, Tokyo 101; tel. (3) 294-2221; f. 1918; reference, Japanese and foreign languages, sports, dictionaries, audio-visual aids; Man. Dir TOSHIO SUZUKI.

Tokyo News Service Ltd: Tsukiji Hamarikyu Bldg, 10th Floor, 3-3, Tsukiji 5-chome, Chuo-ku, Tokyo 104; tel. (3) 542-6511; telex 252-3285; f. 1947; shipping and shipbuilding; Pres. T. OKUYAMA.

University of Tokyo Press: 7-3-1 Hongo, Bunkyo-ku, Tokyo 113; tel. (3) 811-0964; f. 1951; natural and social sciences, humanities; Japanese and English; Man. Dir KAZUO ISHII.

Yama-kei Publishing Co Ltd: 1-1-33, Shiba-Daimon, Minato-ku, Tokyo 105; tel. (3) 436-4021; f. 1930; natural science, geography, mountaineering; Pres. YOSHIMITSU KAWASAKI.

Yuhikaku Publishing Co Ltd: 2-17, Kanda Jimbo-cho, Chiyoda-ku, Tokyo; tel. (3) 264-1311; f. 1877; social sciences, law, economics; Pres. TADATAKA EGUSA; Chair. SHIRO EGUSA.

Zoshindo Juken Kenkyusha: 2-19-15, Shinmachi, Nishi-ku, Osaka 550; tel. (6) 532-1581; f. 1890; educational, juvenile; Pres. SHIGETOSHI OKAMOTO.

Government Publishing House

Government Publications' Service Centre: 2-1, 1-chome, Kasumigaseki, Chiyoda-ku, Tokyo 100; tel. (3) 504-3885.

PUBLISHERS' ASSOCIATIONS

Japan Book Publishers' Association: 6 Fukuro-machi, Shinjuku-ku, Tokyo 162; tel. (3) 268-1301; Pres. TOSHIYUKI HATTORI; Exec. Dir SADAYA MURAYAMA.

Publishers Association for Cultural Exchange: 2-1, Sarugaku-cho 1-chome, Chiyoda-ku, Tokyo 101; tel. (3) 291-5685; f. 1953; 135 mems; Pres. TOSHIYUKI HATTORI; Dir SHOICHI NAKAJIMA.

Radio and Television

There were an estimated 94.5m. radio receivers and 31.5m. television licences in 1986. Japan's first operational communications satellite, designed to improve links between Honshu and outlying islands, was launched in 1983.

Nippon Hoso Kyokai, NHK (Japan Broadcasting Corporation): Broadcasting Centre, NHK Hoso Centre, 2-2-1, Jinnan, Shibuya-ku, Tokyo 150; tel. (3) 465-1234; telex 34778; f. 1925; non-commercial public corpn; operates five (two TV and three radio) networks and 2 DBS TV services; TV channels equally divided between general and educational networks; central stations at Tokyo, Osaka, Nagoya, Hiroshima, Kumamoto, Sendai, Sapporo and Matsuyama, besides 46 local stations; overseas service broadcasts in 21 languages; Chair. Board of Govs KOTARO TAKEDA; Pres. MASATO KAWAHARA.

National Association of Commercial Broadcasters in Japan (MINPOREN): Bungei Shunju Bldg, 3, Kioi-cho, Chiyoda-ku, Tokyo 102; tel. (3) 265-7481; telex 29889; Pres. SUNAO NAKAGAWA; Exec. Dir. NAGATO IZUMI; Sec.-Gen. SEIGO NAGATAKE; asscn of 137 companies (103 TV companies, 34 radio companies). Among the TV companies, 36 operate radio and TV, with 307 radio stations and 6,284 TV stations. These include:

Asahi Hoso—Asahi Broadcasting Corpn: 2-2-48, Oyodo-Minami, Oyodo-ku, Osaka 531; tel. (6) 458-5321; Chair. TSUNEJIRO HIRAI; Pres. KIYOSHI HARA.

Bunka Hoso—Nippon Cultural Broadcasting, Inc: 1-5, Wakabo, Shinjuku-ku, Tokyo 160; f. 1952; Chair. YOSHIO AKAO; Pres. MASATOSHI IWAMOTO.

Nippon Hoso—Nippon Broadcasting System, Inc: 1-9-3, Yuraku-cho, Chiyoda-ku, Tokyo 100; tel. (3) 287-1111; f. 1954; Chair. N. SHIKANAI; Pres. S. HIRAYAMA.

Nihon Tampa Hoso—Nihon Short-Wave Broadcasting Co: 9-15, Akasaka 1-chome, Minato-ku, Tokyo 107; tel. (3) 583-8151; f. 1954; Pres. SHIGERU ANDO.

Okinawa Televi Hoso—Okinawa Television Broadcasting Co Ltd: 2-32-1, Kume, Naha 900, Okinawa; f. 1959; Pres. Y. YAMASHIRO.

Ryukyu Hoso—Ryukyu Broadcasting Corpn Ltd: 2-3-1, Kumoji, Naha 900, Okinawa; f. 1954; Pres. KUNIO OROKU.

Tokyo Hoso—Tokyo Broadcasting System, Inc: 5-3-6, Akasaka, Minato-ku, Tokyo 107; tel. (3) 584-3111; telex 24883; f. 1951; Chair. HIROSHI SUWA; Pres. YOSHIYUKI YAMANISHI.

There are also 92 commercial television stations operated by Asahi Broadcasting Co, Nippon TV Network Co, Fuji Telecasting Co and others, including:

Televi Asahi—Asahi National Broadcasting Co Ltd: 4-10, Roppongi 6-chome, Minato-ku, Tokyo 106; tel. (3) 405-3211; f. 1959; Chair. YOSHIO AKAO; Pres. KIKUO TASHIRO.

Yomiuri Televi Hoso—Yomiuri Telecasting Corporation: 1-8-11, Higashi-Tenma, Kita-ku, Osaka 530; tel. (6) 356-3500; f. 1958; 20 hrs colour broadcasting daily; Chair. MITSUO MUTAI; Pres. IKUO AOYAMA.

Television News Agencies

Asahi Video Projects Ltd: 6-4-10 Roppongi, Minato-ku, Tokyo; tel. (3) 405-3211; f. 1958; Pres. K. SAMEJIMA.

Kyodo Television Ltd: 28 Sanbancho, Chiyoda-ku, Tokyo 102; tel. (3) 263-4161; telex (232) 2906; f. 1958; Pres. TOSHIKANE BOJO.

Finance

(cap. = capital; p.u. = paid up; res = reserves; dep. = deposits; m. = million; amounts in yen)

BANKING

Japan's central bank and bank of issue is the Bank of Japan, founded in 1882. More than half the credit business of the country is handled by 77 commercial banks (13 city banks and 64 regional banks), 16 trust banks and three long-term credit banks, collectively designated 'All Banks'.

Of the latter category, the most important are the city banks, some of which have a long and distinguished history, originating in the time of the *zaibatsu*, the private entrepreneurial organizations on which Japan's capital wealth was built up before the Second World War. Although the *zaibatsu* were abolished as integral industrial and commercial enterprises during the Allied Occupation, the several businesses and industries which bear the former *zaibatsu* names, such as Mitsubishi, Mitsui and Sumitomo, continue to flourish and to give each other mutual assistance through their respective banks and trust corporations.

Among the commercial banks, one, the Bank of Tokyo, specializes in foreign exchange business, while the Industrial Bank of Japan provides a large proportion of the finance for capital investment by industry. The Long-Term Credit Bank of Japan and Nippon Credit Bank Ltd also specialize in industrial finance; the work of these three privately-owned banks is supplemented by the government-controlled Japan Development Bank.

The government has established a number of other specialized organs to supply essential services not performed by the private banks. Thus the Japan Export-Import Bank advances credits for exports of heavy industrial products and imports of raw materials in bulk. A Housing Loan Corporation assists firms building housing for their employees, while the Agriculture, Forestry and Fisheries Finance Corporation gives loans to the named industries for equipment purchases. Similar services are provided for small businesses by the Small Business Finance Corporation.

An important financial role is played by co-operatives and by the many small enterprise institutions. Each prefecture has its own federation of co-operatives, with the Central Co-operative Bank of Agriculture and Forestry as the common central financial institution. This Central Co-operative Bank also serves as an agent for the Government's Agriculture, Forestry and Fisheries Finance Corporation.

There are also three types of private financial institutions for small business. The 69 Sogo Banks (Mutual Loan and Savings Banks) are now similar to commercial banks. There are 446 Credit Associations and 455 Shinkin Banks (Credit Associations), which loan only to members. The latter also receive deposits.

The commonest form of savings is through the government-operated Postal Savings System, which collects petty savings from the public by means of the post office network. Total deposits stood at 1,029,979,000m. yen in March 1986. The funds thus made available are used as loan funds by the Government financial institutions, through the Ministry of Finance's Trust Fund Bureau.

Clearing houses operate in each major city of Japan, and total 184 institutions. The largest are those of Tokyo and Osaka.

Central Bank

Nippon Ginko (Bank of Japan): 2-2-1 Hongoku-cho, Chuo-ku, Tokyo 103; tel. (3) 279-1111; telex 22763; f. 1882; cap. 100m., res 1,045,391.8m., dep. 1,303,942.1m. (March 1986); Gov. M. SATOSHI SUMITA.

Principal Commercial Banks

Bank of Tokyo Ltd: 6-3, Nihonbashi Hongokucho 1-chome, Chuo-ku, Tokyo 103; tel. (3) 245-1111; telex 22220; f. 1946; specializes in foreign exchange business; cap. p.u. 106,500m., dep. 11,224,988m. (March 1986); Chair. YUSUKE KASHIWAGI; Pres. MINORU INOUE; 283 brs.

Bank of Yokohama Ltd: 47, Honcho 5-chome, Naka-ku, Yokohama 231; tel. (45) 201-4991; telex 24945; f. 1920; cap. p.u. 39,100m., dep. 6,112,482m. (March 1986); Pres. MASATAKA OKURA; 197 brs.

Dai-Ichi Kangyo Bank Ltd: 1-5, Uchisaiwai-cho 1-chome, Chiyoda-ku, Tokyo 100; tel. (3) 596-1111; telex 22315; f. 1971; cap. p.u. 137,277m., dep. 26,630,479m. (March 1986); Chair. TETSUO FUJIMORI; Pres. NOBUYA HAGURA; 363 brs.

Daiwa Bank Ltd: 21, Bingomachi 2-chome, Higashi-ku, Osaka 541; tel. (6) 271-1221; telex 63977; f. 1918; cap. 60,000m., dep. 12,744,142m. (March 1986); Chair. SUSUMU FURUKAWA; Pres. SUMIO ABEKAWA; 196 brs.

Fuji Bank Ltd: 5-5, Otemachi 1-chome, Chiyoda-ku, Tokyo 100; tel. (3) 216-2211; telex 22367; f. 1880; cap. 127,548m., dep. 23,074,599m. (March 1986); Chair. TAKUJI MATSUZAWA; Pres. YOSHIRO ARAKI; 282 brs.

Hokkaido Takushoku Bank Ltd: 7 Nishi 3-chome, Odori, Chuo-ku, Sapporo 060; tel. (11) 271-2111; telex 932533; f. 1900; cap. 39,200m., dep. 6,331,769m. (March 1986); Chair. AKIRA GOMI; Pres. SHIGERU SUZUKI; 202 brs.

Kyowa Bank Ltd: 1-2, Otemachi 1-chome, Chiyoda-ku, Tokyo 100; tel. (3) 287-2111; telex 24278; f. 1948; cap. 52,500m., dep. 8,626,488m. (March 1986); Pres. TETSUO YAMANAKA; Chair. KOSUKE YOKOTE; 239 brs.

Mitsubishi Bank Ltd: 7-1 Marunouchi, 2-chome, Chiyoda-ku, Tokyo 100; tel. (3) 240-1111; telex 22358; f. 1919; cap. 126,547m., dep. 21,736,437m. (March 1986); Chair. HAJIME YAMADA; Pres. KAZUO IBUKI; 261 brs.

Mitsui Bank Ltd: 1-2, Yuraku-cho 1-chome, Chiyoda-ku, Tokyo 100; tel. (3) 501-1111; telex 22378; f. 1876; cap. p.u. 92,000m., dep. 15,148,029m. (March 1986); Chair. TOSHIRO KUSABA; Pres. KENICHI KAMIYA; Dir GORO KOYAMA; 227 brs.

Saitama Bank Ltd: 4-1, Tokiwa 7-chome, Urawa City, Saitama Prefecture 336; tel. (488) 24-2411; telex 22811; f. 1943; cap. 50,000m., dep. 7,762,976m. (March 1986); Chair. TSUNESHIRO OHKI; Pres. SHIGETAKE IJICHI; 198 brs.

Sanwa Bank Ltd: 4-10, Fushimimachi, Higashi-ku, Osaka 541; tel. (6) 202-2281; telex 63234; f. 1933; cap. 125,563m., dep. 21,355,499m. (March 1986); Chair. KENJI KAWAKATSU; 277 brs.

Sumitomo Bank Ltd: 22, Kitahama 5-chome, Higashi-ku, Osaka 541; tel. (6) 227-2111; telex 63266; f. 1895; cap. 118,621m., dep. 22,508,594m. (March 1986); Chair. ICHIRO ISODA; Pres. KOH KOMATSU; 261 brs.

Taiyo Kobe Bank Ltd: 56 Naniwa-cho, Chuo-ku, Kobe 650; tel. (78) 331-8101; telex 78823; f. 1973; cap. p.u. 88,306m., dep. 13,635,927m. (March 1986); Chair. TADAO SHIOTANI; Pres. TERUYUKI OKUMURA; 363 brs.

Tokai Bank Ltd: 21-24 Nishiki, 3-chome, Naka-ku, Nagoya 460; tel. (52) 211-1111; telex 59612; f. 1941; cap. p.u. 90,750m., dep. 16,051,817m. (March 1985); Chair. SHIGEMITSU MIYAKE; Pres. RYUICHI KATO; 240 brs.

JAPAN

Principal Trust Banks

Chuo Trust and Banking Co Ltd: 7-1 Kyobashi, 1-chome, Chuo-ku, Tokyo 104; tel. (3) 567-1451; telex 33368; f. 1962; cap. 10,100m., dep. 6,105,986m. (March 1986); Chair. ISAMU KUMAZAKI; Pres. TAKESHI SEKIGUCHI; 52 brs.

Mitsubishi Trust and Banking Corporation: 4-5 Marunouchi, 1-chome, Chiyoda-ku, Tokyo 100; tel. (3) 212-1211; telex 24259; f. 1927; cap. 50,054m., dep. 15,823,044m. (March 1986); Pres. TAKUJI SHIDACHI; 61 brs.

Mitsui Trust and Banking Co Ltd: 1-1 Nihonbashi Muromachi, 2-chome, Chuo-ku, Tokyo 103; tel. (3) 270-9511; telex 26397; f. 1924; cap. 50,054m., total assets 16,567,283m. (March 1986); Pres. SEIICHI KAWASAKI; 55 brs in Japan, 11 brs overseas.

Sumitomo Trust and Banking Co Ltd: 15, Kitahama 5-chome, Higashi-ku, Osaka; tel. 220-2121; telex 63775; f. 1925; cap. 50,054m., dep. 15,384,696m. (March 1986); Chair. TAKESHI TASHIRO; Pres. OSAMU SAKURAI; 54 brs.

Toyo Trust and Banking Co Ltd: 4-3, Marunouchi 1-chome, Chiyoda-ku, Tokyo 100; tel. (3) 287-2211; telex 22123; f. 1959; cap. p.u. 32,766m., dep. 10,215,029m. (March 1986); Chair. CHIGAZO MORITA; Pres. HIROSHI MATSUSHITA; 62 brs.

Yasuda Trust and Banking Co Ltd: 2-1 Yaesu, 1-chome, Chuo-ku, Tokyo 103; tel. (3) 278-8111; telex 23720; f. 1925; cap. 45,337m., dep. 11,933,920m. (March 1986); Pres. YOSHIO YAMAGUCHI; 60 brs.

Long-Term Credit Banks

The Long-Term Credit Bank of Japan Ltd: 2-4 Otemachi 1-chome, Chiyoda-ku, Tokyo 100; tel. (3) 211-5111; telex 24308; f. 1952; cap. 100,000m., dep. and debentures 15,000,865m. (March 1986); Chair. BINSUKE SUGIURA; Pres. MAMORU SAKAI; 27 brs.

Nippon Credit Bank Ltd: 13-10 Kudan-Kita 1-chome, Chiyoda-ku, Tokyo 102; tel. (3) 263-1111; telex 26921; f. 1957; cap. 78,500m., dep. and debentures 9,857,674m. (March 1986); Chair. TATSUO SHODA; Pres. SHIRO EGAWA; 23 brs.

Nippon Kogyo Ginko (The Industrial Bank of Japan, Ltd): 3-3, Marunouchi 1-chome, Chiyoda-ku, Tokyo 100; tel. (3) 214-1111; telex 22325; f. 1902; medium- and long-term financing; cap. p.u. 103,680m., dep. and debentures 19,296,187m., loans and discounts 13,747,706m. (March 1986); Chair. KISABURO IKEURA; Pres. KANEO NAKAMURA; 30 brs.

Principal Government Credit Institutions

Agriculture, Forestry and Fisheries Finance Corporation: Koko Bldg, 9-3, Otemachi 1-chome, Chiyoda-ku, Tokyo 100; tel. (3) 270-2261; f. 1953; finances plant and equipment investment; cap. 168,233m. (March 1986); Pres. SAKUE MATSUMOTO; Vice-Pres. YASUTAKA MIYAMOTO.

The Export-Import Bank of Japan: 4-1, Otemachi 1-chome, Chiyoda-ku, Tokyo 100; tel. (3) 287-1221; telex 2223728; f. 1950 to supplement and encourage the financing of exports, imports and overseas investment by ordinary financial institutions; cap. p.u. 967,300m. (March 1986); Pres. TAKASHI TANAKA; 1 br.

Housing Loan Corporation: 4-10, Koraku 1-chome, Bunkyoku, Tokyo 112; tel. (3) 812-1111; f. 1950 to provide long-term capital for the construction of housing at low interest rates; cap. 97,200m. (March 1986); Pres. SHOZO KONO; Vice-Pres. RYOICHI FUKUSHIMA.

The Japan Development Bank: 9-1, Otemachi 1-chome, Chiyoda-ku, Tokyo 100; tel. (3) 270-3211; telex 24343; f. 1951; provides long-term loans; subscribes for corporate bonds; guarantees corporate obligations; invests in specific projects; borrows funds from govt and abroad; issues external bonds and notes; cap. 233,971m.; loans outstanding 7,679,729m. (March 1986); Gov. SHIGEYA YOSHISE; Deputy Gov. AKIRA OKA; 7 brs.

National Finance Corporation: Koko Bldg, 9-3, Otemachi 1-chome, Chiyoda-ku, Tokyo 100; tel. (3) 270-1361; f. 1949 to supply business funds particularly to very small enterprises unable to obtain loans from banks and other private financial institutions; cap. 26,000m. (March 1986); Gov. HIROSHI YOSHIMOT; Deputy Gov. TETSUEI TOKUGOUA.

Norinchukin Bank (Central Co-operative Bank for Agriculture, Forestry and Fisheries): 8-3, Otemachi 1-chome, Chiyoda-ku, Tokyo 100; tel. (3) 279-0111; telex 23918; f. 1923; main banker to agricultural, forestry and fisheries co-operatives; receives deposits from individual co-operatives, federations and agricultural enterprises; extends loans to these and to local govt authorities and public corpns; adjusts excess and shortage of funds within co-operative system; issues debentures, invests funds and engages in other regular banking business; cap. 45,000m., dep. and debentures 21,798,414m. (March 1986); Pres. OSAMU MORIMOTO; Vice-Pres. SEIGO URANO; 40 brs.

The Overseas Economic Co-operation Fund: Takebashi Godo Bldg, 4-1, Otemachi 1-chome, Chiyoda-ku, Tokyo 100; tel. (3) 215-1311; telex 28790; f. 1961 to provide long-term loans or investments for projects in developing countries; cap. 1,412,244m. (1984); Pres. TAKASHI HOSOMI; Deputy Pres. SHINZO AOKI.

Shoko Chukin Bank (Central Co-operative Bank for Commerce and Industry): 10-17 2-chome, Yaesu, Chuo-ku, Tokyo 104; tel. (3) 272-6111; telex 25388; f. 1936 to provide general banking services to facilitate finance for smaller enterprise co-operatives and other organizations formed mainly by small- and medium-sized enterprises; issues debentures; cap. 195,600m.; dep. and debentures 9,164,039m. (March 1986); Pres. SATOSHI SASAKI; Deputy Pres. HIROSHI YONESATO; 98 brs.

Small Business Finance Corporation: Koko Bldg, 9-3, Otemachi 1-chome, Chiyoda-ku, Tokyo 100; tel. (3) 270-1261; f. 1953 to lend plant and equipment funds and long-term operating funds to small businesses (capital not more than 100m., or not more than 300 employees) which are not easily secured from other financial institutions; cap. p.u. 31,210m. (March 1986) wholly subscribed by govt; Gov. KIYOSHI SHŌ; Vice-Gov. TŌRU HARA.

Social Welfare and Medical Service Project Corporation: 4-3-13, Toranomon, Minato-ku, Tokyo; tel. (3) 438-0211; f. 1985; provides long-term low-interest loans and management advice to social welfare facilities, hospitals and clinics; cap. 1,050m. (March 1986); Pres. HAJIME KAMIMURA; 1 br.

Principal Foreign Banks

Algemene Bank Nederland NV (Netherlands): Fuji Bldg, 2-3, Marunouchi 3-chome, Chiyoda-ku, Tokyo 100, CPOB 374; tel. (3) 211-1760; brs in Kobe, Osaka, Fukuoka; Man. W. A. J. KORTEKAAS.

American Express International Banking Corpn (USA): Toranomon Mitsui Bldg, 8-1, Kasumigaseki, 3-chome Chiyoda-ku, Tokyo 100; tel. (3) 504-3341; brs in Naha, Okinawa; Vice-Pres. and Gen. Man. RYUSUKE FUKUDA.

Amro Bank (Netherlands): Yurakucho Denki Bldg, 7-1, Yuraku-cho 1-chome, Chiyoda-ku, Tokyo 105; tel. (3) 284-0701.

Bangkok Bank Ltd (Thailand): Bangkok Bank Bldg, 8-10, Nishishinbashi, 2-chome, Minato-ku, Tokyo 105; tel. (3) 503-3333; 1 br.

Bank of America NT & SA: Ark Mori Bldg, 12-32, Akasaka 1-chome, Minato-ku, Tokyo 107; tel. (3) 587-3111; brs in Yokohama, Osaka and Kobe; Exec. Vice-Pres. V. C. GIBB.

Bank of India: Mitsubishi Denki Bldg, 2-3, Marunouchi 2-chome, Chiyoda-ku, Tokyo 100; tel. (3) 212-0911; Chief Man. P. K. MUKERJI; br. in Osaka.

Bank Indonesia: Hibiya Park Bldg, 8-1, Yuraku-cho 1-chome, Chiyoda-ku, Tokyo 100; tel. (3) 271-3415.

Bank Negara Indonesia 1946: Kokusai Bldg, 1-1, Marunouchi 3-chome, Chiyoda-ku, Tokyo 100; tel. (3) 214-5621; Gen. Man. KOESNANDAR.

Bankers Trust Co (USA): Kishimoto Bldg, 2-1, Marunouchi 2-chome, Chiyoda-ku, Tokyo 100; tel. (3) 214-7171; Vice-Pres. and Gen. Man. ROY W. ALLEN.

Banque Indosuez (France): Banque Indosuez Bldg, 1-2, Akasaka 1-chome, Minato-ku, Tokyo 107; tel. (3) 582-0271; telex 24309; Gen. Man. BERNARD DELAGE; br. in Osaka and Nagoya.

Banque Nationale de Paris (France): Yusen Bldg, 3-2, Marunouchi 2-chome, Chiyoda-ku, Tokyo 100; tel. (3) 214-2881; telex 24825; Gen. Man. ANDRÉ JULLIEN.

Banque Paribas (France): Yurakucho Denki Bldg, 7-1, Yuraku-cho 1-chome, Chiyoda-ku, Tokyo 100; tel. (3) 214-5881; Gen. Man. DENIS ANTOINE.

Barclays Bank (UK): Mitsubishi Bldg, 5-2, Marunouchi 2-chome, Chiyoda-ku, Tokyo 100; (CPOB 466); tel. (3) 214-3611; telex 24968; Gen. Man. MICHAEL H. TOMALIN.

Bayerische Vereinsbank (Federal Republic of Germany): Togin Bldg, 4-2, Marunouchi 1-chome, Chiyoda-ku, Tokyo 100; tel. (3) 284-1341; telex 26351; Gen. Man. Dr KAI WERHAHN-MEES.

Chase Manhattan Bank, NA (USA): AIU Bldg, 1-3, Marunouchi 1-chome, Chiyoda-ku, Tokyo 100; tel. (3) 287-4000; Sr Vice-Pres. ROBERT H. BINNEY; br. in Osaka.

Chemical Bank (USA): Mitsubishi Shoji Bldg, Annex, 3-1, Marunouchi 2-chome, Chiyoda-ku, Tokyo 100; tel. (3) 214-1351; Vice-Pres. and Gen. Man. DON H. WILSON, III.

JAPAN   Directory

Citibank NA (USA): 2–1, Otemachi 2-chome, Chiyoda-ku, Tokyo 100; tel. (3) 279-5411; brs in Kobe, Osaka, Yokohama, Nagoya; Division Exec. JAMES J. COLLINS.

Commerzbank AG (Federal Republic of Germany): Nippon Press Center Bldg, 2–1, Uchisaiwai-cho 2-chome, Chiyoda-ku, Tokyo 100; tel. (3) 502-4371; Gen. Mans RAINER H. WEDEL, DIETER BRAMMER.

Continental Illinois National Bank and Trust Company of Chicago (USA): Mitsui Seimei Bldge, 2–3, Otemachi 1-chome, Chiyoda-ku, Tokyo 100; tel. (3) 216-1661; telex 0222-2265; Vice-Pres. and Gen. Man. DENNIS J. ZIENGS; 1 br.

Deutsche Bank AG (Federal Republic of Germany): Ark Mori Bldg, 12–32, Akasaka 1-chome, Minato-ku, Tokyo 107; tel. (3) 588-1971; telex 24814; Gen. Mans Dr H. J. BECK, P. G. BARTHEL.

Dresdner Bank AG (Federal Republic of Germany): Tokyo branch: Mitsubishi Bldg, 5–2, Marunouchi 2-chome, Chiyoda-ku, Tokyo 100; tel. (3) 214-5961; telex 0222-5295; Chief Gen. Man. Dr PETER-JÖRG KLEIN; Gen. Mans KARL GRUTSCHNIG, HIROSHI MATSUURA.

First National Bank of Chicago (USA): Hibiya Central Bldg, 7th Floor, 2–9, Nishishimbashi 1-chome, Minato-ku, Tokyo 105; tel. (3) 502-4961; telex 2224977; Vice-Pres. and Gen. Man. THOMAS H. HODGES.

Hongkong and Shanghai Banking Corpn (Hong Kong): CPOB 336, 1–2, Marunouchi 2-chome, Chiyoda-ku, Tokyo 100; tel. (3) 211-6461; telex 22372; Chief Exec. J. H. MASON; 4 brs.

International Commercial Bank of China (Taiwan): Togin Bldg, 4–2, Marunouchi 1-chome, Chiyoda-ku, Tokyo 100; tel. (3) 211-2501; Sr Vice-Pres. and Man. THEODORE S. S. CHENG; 2 brs.

Korea Exchange Bank (Republic of Korea): Shin Kokusai Bldg, 4–1, Marunouchi 3-chome, Chiyoda-ku, Tokyo 100; tel. (3) 216-3561; telex 24243; f. 1967; Gen. Man. NAM-JIK LEE; 3 brs.

Lloyds Bank International Ltd (UK): Ote Center Bldg, 5th Floor, 1–3 Otemachi 1-chome, Chiyoda-ku, Tokyo 100 (CPOB 464); tel. (3) 214-6771; telex 22343; Man. K. J. HIGLEY.

Manufacturers Hanover Trust Co (USA): 21st Floor, Asahi Tokai Bldg, 6–1, Otemachi 2-chome, Chiyoda-ku, Tokyo 100; tel. (3) 242-6511; telex 22687; Sr Vice-Pres. KEITH K. KANEKO; Vice-Pres. and Gen. Man. JAMES R. BOARDMAN.

Marine Midland Bank NA (USA): Kokusai Bldg, 1–1, Marunouchi 3-chome, Chiyoda-ku, Tokyo 100; tel. (3) 216-0531; telex 28510; Vice-Pres. and Gen. Man. JOHN W. BROWN III.

Midland Bank PLC (UK): AIU Bldg, 1–3, Marunouchi 1-chome, Chiyoda-ku, Tokyo 100; tel. (3) 284-1861; telex 26137; Country Man. RAY SOUDAH; Chief Man. WALTER HULATT.

Morgan Guaranty Trust Co (USA): Shin Yurakucho Bldg, 12–1, Yurakucho 1-chome, Chiyoda-ku, Tokyo 100; tel. (3) 282-0230; Sr Vice-Pres. and Gen. Man. WILLIAM R. BARRETT, Jr.

National Bank of Pakistan: 20 Mori Bldg, 7–4, Nishi Shinbashi 2-chome, Minato-ku, Tokyo 105; tel. (3) 502-0331; f. 1949; Man. HAFIZ M. IQBAL.

National Westminster Bank PLC (UK): Mitsubishi Bldg, 5–2, Marunouchi 2-chome, Chiyoda-ku, Tokyo 100; tel. (3) 216-5301; telex 28292; Chief Man. (Japan) A. G. W. HODGE.

Oversea-Chinese Banking Corpn (Singapore): 128 Shin Tokyo Bldg, 3–1, Marunouchi 3-chome, Chiyoda-ku, Tokyo 100; tel. (3) 214-2841; telex 26186; Man. CHONG KONG WONG.

Security Pacific National Bank (USA): POB 524, Ark Mori Bldg, 12–32 Akasaka 1-chome, Minato-ku, Tokyo 107; tel. (3) 587-4800; telex 24981; First Vice-Pres. and Gen. Man. GORDON A. NEBEKER.

Société Générale (France): Hibiya Central Bldg, 1–2–9, Nishi-Shinbashi, Minato-ku, Tokyo 105; tel. (3) 503-9781; telex 28611; Gen. Man. GILBERT W. GREY; Man. KAZUHIDE KITANOSONO.

Standard Chartered Bank (UK): Fuji Bldg, 2–3, Marunouchi 3-chome, Tokyo 100; tel. (3) 213-6541; telex 22484; brs in Kobe and Osaka; Man. D. G. GRANT.

State Bank of India: South Tower 352, Yurakucho Denki Bldg, 1–7–1 Yurakucho, Chiyoda-ku, Tokyo 100; tel. (3) 284-0085; telex 27377; Chief Man. A. K. SEN.

Swiss Bank Corpn: Furukawa Sogo Bldg, 6–1, Marunouchi 2-chome, Chiyoda-ku, Tokyo 100; tel. (3) 214-1731; Sr Vice-Pres. and Man. ERIC TSCHIRREN.

Union Bank of Switzerland: Yurakucho Bldg, 10–1, Yurakucho 1-chome, Chiyoda-ku, Tokyo 100; tel. (3) 214-7471; Man. RALPH ZIEGLER.

Union de Banques Arabes et Françaises (UBAF) (France): Fukoku Seimei Bldg, 10F, 2–2–2 Uchisaiwai-cho, Chiyoda-ku, Tokyo 100; tel. (3) 595-0801; Man. MAXIME ROCHE.

Westdeutsche Landesbank Girozentrale (Federal Republic of Germany): Kokusai Bldg, 1–1, Marunouchi 3-chome, Chiyoda-ku, Tokyo 100; tel. (3) 216-0581; telex 23859; Gen. Mans KLAUS R. PESCH, ULRICH ZIERKE.

Bankers' Associations

Federation of Bankers' Associations of Japan: 3–1, Marunouchi 1-chome, Chiyoda-ku, Tokyo 100; tel. (3) 216-3761; telex 26830; f. 1945; 72 mem. asscns; Chair. YOSHIRA ARAKI; Vice-Chairs SUMIO ABEKAWA, CHIAKI KURAHARA; Man. Dir MICHITSURA KITAHARA.

   Tokyo Bankers' Association Inc: 3–1, Marunouchi 1-chome, Chiyoda-ku, Tokyo 100; tel. (3) 216-3761; telex 26830; f. 1945; 87 mem. banks; conducts the above Federation's routine business; Chair. YOSHIRO ARAKI; Vice-Chairs MAMORU SAKAI, CHIAKI KURAHARA.

Regional Banks Association of Japan: 3–1–2 Uchikanda, Chiyoda-ku, Tokyo 101; tel. (3) 252-5171; f. 1936; 64 member banks; Chair. TARO OGATA.

STOCK EXCHANGES

Fukuoka Stock Exchange: 2–14–12, Tenjin, Chuo-ku, Fukuoka 810.

Hiroshima Stock Exchange: 14–18, Kanayama-cho, Hiroshima; f. 1949; 16 mems; Prin. Officer FUBITO SHIMOMURA.

Nagoya Stock Exchange: 3–17, Sakae-Sanchome, Naka-ku, Nagoya 460; f. 1949; tel. (52) 241-1521; Pres. JUNICHIRO KUMADA; Man. Dir ICHIRO KAWAI.

Osaka Securities Exchange: 2–1, Kitahama, Higashi-ku, Osaka 541; tel. (6) 229-8643; telex 5222215; f. 1949; 58 regular mems and one Nakadachi mem.; Pres. HIROSHI YAMANOUCHI; Chair. GORO TATSUMI.

Sapporo Stock Exchange: 5–14–1, Nishi, Minami Ichijo, Chuo-ku, Sapporo.

Tokyo Stock Exchange: 2–1–1 Nihonbashi-Kayaba-cho, Chuo-ku, Tokyo; f. 1949; 93 mems (including 6 foreign mems and 4 Nakodachi mems); Pres. MICHIO TAKEUCHI.

There are also Stock Exchanges at Kyoto and Niigata.

INSURANCE
Principal Life Companies

Asahi Mutual Life Insurance Co: 7–3, Nishishinjuku 1-chome, Shinjuku-ku, Tokyo 163; tel. (3) 342-3111; telex 02323229; f. 1888; Pres. YASUYUKI WAKAHARA.

Chiyoda Mutual Life Insurance Co: 19–18, 2-chome, Kamimeguro Meguro, Tokyo 153; tel. (3) 719-5111; telex 02466725; f. 1904; Pres. YASUTARO KANZAKI.

Daido Mutual Life Insurance Co: 1–23–101, Esaka, Suitashi, Osaka 564; tel. (6) 385-1131; telex 05233311; f. 1902; Chair. TAKESHI MASUMURA; Pres. EIJI FUKUMOTO.

Daihyaku Mutual Life Insurance Co: 34–1, Kokuryocho 4-chome, Chofsu-shi, Tokyo 182; tel. (3) 0424-85-8111; telex 2423063; f. 1914; Pres. MINORU KAWASAKI.

Dai-ichi Mutual Life Insurance Co: 13–1, Yurakucho 1-chome, Chiyoda-ku, Tokyo 100; tel. (3) 216-1211; f. 1902; Chair. RYOICHI TSUKAMOTO; Pres. SHIN-ICHI NISHIO.

Equitable Life Insurance Co Ltd: Togin Kurita Bldg, 3–26 Kanda Nishiki-cho, Chiyoda-ku, Tokyo 101; tel. (3) 233-3911; f. 1986; Chair. and CEO DONALD J. MOONEY.

Fukoku Mutual Life Insurance Co: 2–2, Uchisaiwaicho 2-chome, Chiyoda-ku, Tokyo 100; tel. (3) 508-1101; f. 1923; Pres. TETSUO FURUYA.

Heiwa Life Insurance Co Ltd: 2–16, Ginza 3-chome, Chuo-ku, Tokyo 104; tel. (3) 562-0351; f. 1907; Pres. TADAYOSHI TAKEMOTO.

INA Life Insurance Co Ltd: Shinjuku Center Bldg, 48F, 1–25–1 Nishi-Shinjuku, Shinjuku-ku, Tokyo 163; tel. (3) 348-7011; telex 32471; f. 1981; Pres. NOBORU OKA; 5 brs.

Kyoei Life Insurance Co Ltd: 4–2 Hongokucho, Nihonbashi, Chuoku, Tokyo 103; tel. (3) 270-8511; telex 02226826; f. 1947; Hon. Chair. and Dir of Board SABURO KAWAI; Chair. MASAYUKI KITOKU; Pres. YOSHIO TAYAMA.

Meiji Mutual Life Insurance Co: 1–1, Marunouchi 2-chome, Chiyoda-ku, Tokyo 100; tel. (3) 283-8111; telex 02224861; f. 1881; Chair. HIROSHI YAMANAKA; Pres. TERUMICHI TSUCHIDA.

Mitsui Mutual Life Insurance Co: 2–3, Otemachi 1-chome, Chiyoda-ku, Tokyo 100; tel. (3) 211-6111; telex 02223261; f. 1927; Chair. TAKAHIRO TAJIMA; Pres. MASAMI ONIZAWA.

JAPAN — Directory

Nippon Dantai Life Insurance Co Ltd: 1-2-19, Higashi, Shibuy-ku, Tokyo 150; tel. (3) 407-6211; telex 2423342; f. 1934; Chair. SAKAE SAWABE; Pres. HAJIME ODAKA.

Nippon Life Insurance Co (Nissei): 7, Imabashi 4-chome, Higashi-ku, Osaka 541; tel. (6) 209-4500; telex 5228783; f. 1889; Chair. Gen. HIROSE; Pres. GENTARO KAWASE.

Nissan Mutual Life Insurance Co: 6-30, Aobadai 3-chome, Meguro-ku, Tokyo 153; tel. (3) 463-1101; f. 1909; Pres. YASUNORI YAZAKI.

Seibu Allstate Insurance Co Ltd: Sunshine Sixty Bldg, 37th–39th Floors, 1-1, Higashi Ikebukuro 3-chome, Toshima-ku, Tokyo 170; tel. (3) 983-6666; f. 1975; Chair. SEIJI TSUTSUMI; Pres. SHIGEO IKUNO.

Sony Prudential Life Insurance Co Ltd: 1-1, Minami-Aoyama 1-chome, Minato-ku, Tokyo 107; tel. (3) 475-8811; Chair. TATSUAKI HIRAI; Pres. KIYOFUMI SAKAGUCHI.

Sumitomo Life Insurance Co: 2-5, Nakanoshima 2-chome, Kita-ku, Osaka 530; tel. (6) 231-8401; telex 0522-2584; f. 1926; Chair. KENJI CHISHIRO; Pres. YASUHIKO UEYAMA.

Taisho Life Insurance Co Ltd: 9-1, Yurakucho 1-chome, Chiyoda-ku, Tokyo 100; tel. (3) 281-7651; f. 1913; Pres. TOSHIYUKI KOYAMA.

Taiyo Mutual Life Insurance Co: 11-2, Nihonbashi 2-chome, Chuo-ku, Tokyo 103; tel. (3) 272-6211; Chair. MAGODAYU DAIBU; Pres. KYOJIRO NISHIWAKI; Vice-Chair. TAKUO KOIZUMI.

Toho Mutual Life Insurance Co: 15-1, Shibuya 2-chome, Shibuya-ku, Tokyo 150; tel. (3) 499-1111; telex 0242-8069; f. 1898; Chair. MAKOTO YASUI; Pres. and Chief Exec. Officer SEIZO OTA.

Tokyo Mutual Life Insurance Co: 5-2, Uchisaiwaicho 1-chome, Chiyoda-ku, Tokyo 100; tel. (3) 504-2211; telex 2228517; f. 1895; Pres. MASAKAZU YOGAI.

Yamato Mutual Life Insurance Co: 1-7, Uchisaiwaicho 1-chome, Chiyoda-ku, Tokyo 100; tel. (3) 508-3111; f. 1911; Pres. YOSHIO KOHARA.

Yasuda Mutual Life Insurance Co: 9-1 Nishi-shinjuku 1-chome, Shinjuku-ku, Tokyo 160; tel. (3) 342-7111; telex 232-2887; f. 1880; Chair. HAJIME YASUDA; Pres. NORIKAZU OKAMOTO.

Principal Non-Life Companies

Allstate Automobile and Fire Insurance Co Ltd: Sunshine 60 Bldg, 1-1, Higashi-Ikebukuro 3-chome, Toshima-ku, Tokyo; tel. (3) 988-2711; telex 2722056; Pres. TERU KHONO.

Asahi Fire and Marine Insurance Co Ltd: 6-2, Kajicho 2-chome, Chiyoda-ku, Tokyo; tel. (3) 254-2211; f. 1951; Pres. MICHINOSUKE TANAKA.

Chiyoda Fire and Marine Insurance Co Ltd: Kyobashi Chiyoda Bldg, 1-9, Kyobashi 2-chome, Chuo-ku, Tokyo 104; tel. (3) 281-3311; telex 24975; f. 1897; Chair. HIROYASU ONO; Pres. TADAO KAWAMURA.

Daido Fire and Marine Insurance Co Ltd: 12-1, 1-chome, Kumoji, Naha-shi, Okinawa; tel. 67-1161; f. 1971; Pres. YUSHO UEZU.

Dai-ichi Mutual Fire and Marine Insurance Co: 5-1, Niban-cho, Chiyoda-ku, Tokyo; tel. (3) 239-0011; telex 26554; f. 1949; Chair. NAOKADO NISHIHARA; Pres. SABURO KANEKO.

Dai-Tokyo Fire and Marine Insurance Co Ltd: 1-6, Nihonbashi 3-chome, Chuo-ku, Tokyo; tel. (3) 272-8811; telex 26968; f. 1918; Chair. SEIICHI SORIMACHI; Pres. YOSHIHIKO SHIOKAWA.

Dowa Fire and Marine Insurance Co Ltd: 5-15, Nihonbashi 3-chome, Chuo-ku, Tokyo; tel. (3) 274-5511; telex 22852; f. 1944; Pres. MASAO OKAZAKI.

Fuji Fire and Marine Insurance Co Ltd: 18-9, 1-chome, Minamisenba, Minami-ku, Osaka; tel. (3) 271-2741; telex 05332326; f. 1918; Chair. ISAMU WATANABE; Pres. HIROSHI KUZUHARA.

Japan Earthquake Reinsurance Co Ltd: 6-5, 3-chome, Kanda Surugadai, Chiyoda-ku, Tokyo; tel. (3) 253-3171; f. 1966; Pres. KENJI ATSUMI.

Koa Fire and Marine Insurance Co Ltd: 7-3, 3-chome, Kasumigaseki, Chiyoda-ku, Tokyo; tel. (3) 593-3111; telex 23524; f. 1944; Pres. MINORU HOKARI; Chair. KAISUKE AKAGI.

Kyoei Mutual Fire and Marine Insurance Co: 18-6, 1-chome, Shimbashi, Minato-ku, Tokyo; tel. (3) 504-0131; telex 22977; f. 1942; Chair. HIDEYUKI TAKAGI; Pres. KATSUMI GYOTOKU.

Nichido Fire and Marine Insurance Co Ltd: 3-16, 5-chome, Ginza, Chuo-ku, Tokyo; tel. (3) 571-5141; f. 1914; Chair. TORAJIRO KUBO; Pres. YOSHIKAZU SATO.

Nippon Fire and Marine Insurance Co Ltd: 2-10, Nihonbashi 2-chome, Chuo-ku, Tokyo 103; tel. (3) 272-8111; telex 24214; f. 1892; Chair. SHICHISABURO KAWASAKI; Pres. MASAJI SHINAGAWA.

Nissan Fire and Marine Insurance Co Ltd: 9-5, 2-chome, Kita-Aoyama, Minato-ku, Tokyo; tel. (3) 404-4111; f. 1911; Pres. SEIICHI HONDA.

Nisshin Fire and Marine Insurance Co Ltd: 5-1, 1-chome, Otemachi, Chiyoda-ku, Tokyo; tel. (3) 211-1311; f. 1908; Pres. TATSUO FUJISAWA; Chair. MICHIYOSHI SHIROISHI.

Sumitomo Marine and Fire Insurance Co Ltd: 3-5, Yaesu 1-chome, Chuo-ku, Tokyo; tel. (3) 272-3211; telex 0222-3051; f. 1944; Pres. SUMAO TOKUMASU.

Taisei Fire and Marine Insurance Co Ltd: 2-1, 4-chome, Kudankita, Chiyoda-ku, Tokyo; tel. (3) 234-3111; telex 28351; f. 1950; Pres. FUMIO SATO; Chair. YUTAKA SHIBAIKE.

Taisho Marine and Fire Insurance Co Ltd: 9, Kanda Surugadai 3-chome, Chiyoda-ku, Tokyo; tel. (3) 259-3111; telex 24670; f. 1918; Pres. TAKERU ISHIKAWA; Chair. AKIO HIRATA.

Taiyo Fire and Marine Insurance Co Ltd: 18, Kanda Nishikicho 3-chome, Chiyoda-ku, Tokyo 101; tel. (3) 293-6511; telex 0222-5379; f. 1951; Chair. TAMOTSU YOKOTA; Pres. KIYOSHI ENDO.

Toa Fire and Marine Reinsurance Co Ltd: 6-5, 3-chome, Kanda Surugadai, Chiyoda-ku, Tokyo; tel. (3) 253-3171; f. 1940; Pres. MOKUJI KASHIWAGI.

Tokio Marine and Fire Insurance Co Ltd (Tokio Kaijo): 2-1, Marunouchi 1-chome, Chiyoda-ku, Tokyo 100; tel. (3) 212-6211; telex 24858; f. 1879; Chair. FUMIO WATANABE; Pres. HARUO TAKEDA.

Toyo Fire and Marine Insurance Co Ltd: 4-7, 1-chome, Nihonbashi-Honcho, Chuo-ku, Tokyo 103; tel. (3) 245-1411; telex 02226334; f. 1950; Chair. TSUNEKAZU SAKANO; Pres. EIZO TAKAO.

The Yasuda Fire and Marine Insurance Co Ltd: 26-1, Nishi-shinjuku, 1-chome, Shinjuku-ku, Tokyo; tel. (3) 349-3111; telex 0232-2790; f. 1887; Pres. YASUO GOTO.

In addition to the commercial companies, the Post Office operates life insurance and annuity schemes.

Insurance Associations

Fire and Marine Insurance Rating Association of Japan: Non-Life Insurance Bldg, 9, Kanda Awajicho 2-chome, Chiyoda-ku, Tokyo 101; tel. (3) 255-1211; f. 1948; Pres. YOSHIKAZU SATO; Exec. Dir KENJIRO YAMAZAKI.

Life Insurance Association of Japan (Seimei Hoken Kyokai): New Kokusai Bldg, 4-1, Marunouchi 3-chome, Chiyoda-ku, Tokyo 100; tel. (3) 286-2734; f. 1908; 23 mem. cos; Chair. GENTARO KAWASE; Vice-Chair. MASANORI YAMANOUCHI; Exec. Dir YOSHIKATA NAKAOJI; Man. Dirs TEIJIRO NAKAHARA, TERUO SAYAMA.

Marine and Fire Insurance Association of Japan Inc: Non-Life Insurance Bldg, 9, Kanda Awajicho 2-chome, Chiyoda-ku, Tokyo; tel. (3) 255-1211; telex 02224829; f. 1917; 23 mems; Pres. HARUO TAKEDA; Vice-Pres YASUO GOTO, YOSHIHIKO SHIOKAWA, SEIICHI HONDA.

Trade and Industry

CHAMBERS OF COMMERCE AND INDUSTRY

The Japan Chamber of Commerce and Industry (Nippon Shoko Kaigi-sho): 2-2, 3-chome, Marunouchi, Chiyoda-ku, Tokyo; tel. (3) 283-7852; f. 1922; mems 485 local chambers of commerce and industry; the cen. org. of all chambers of commerce and industry in Japan; Chair. NOBORU GOTOH.

Principal chambers include:

Kobe Chamber of Commerce and Industry: Kobe CIT Center Bldg, 1-14, Hamabe-dori 5-chome, Chuo-ku, Kobe 651; tel. (78) 251-1001; f. 1878; 10,000 mems; Pres. SHINICHI ISHINO; Sr Man. Dir SHOICHI YAMADA.

Kyoto Chamber of Commerce and Industry: 240, Shoshoicho, Ebisugawa-agaru, Karasumadori, Nakakyo-ku, Kyoto 604; f. 1882; 7,877 mems; Pres. KOICHI TSUKAMOTO; Man. Dir KUNIO SHIMADZU.

Nagoya Chamber of Commerce and Industry: 10-19, Sakae 2-chome, Naka-ku, Nagoya, Aichi 460; tel. (52) 221-7211; telex 0442-4836; f. 1881; 10,235 mems; Pres. KOTARO TAKEDA; Sr Man. YOSHIHISA HARADA.

Naha Chamber of Commerce and Industry: 2-2-4, Kume Naha, Okinawa; tel. 68-3758; f. 1950; 2,856 mems; Pres. KOTARO KOKUBA.

Osaka Chamber of Commerce and Industry: 58-7, Uchihonmachi Hashizume-cho, Higashi-ku, Osaka; tel. 944-6215; f. 1878; 25,850 mems; Pres. Susumu Furukawa; Sr Man. Dir Hironari Masago.

Tokyo Chamber of Commerce and Industry: 2-2, Marunouchi 3-chome, Chiyoda-ku, Tokyo; tel. (3) 283-7500; telex 222-4920; f. 1878; 48,000 mems; Pres. Noboru Gotoh; Man. Dir Hiroshi Ikawa.

Yokohama Chamber of Commerce and Industry: 2, Yamashita-cho, Naka-ku, Yokohama; tel. 671-7400; f. 1880; 12,000 mems; Pres. Yutaka Uyeno; Sr Man. Dir Hirochika Kobayashi.

FOREIGN TRADE ORGANIZATIONS

The Association for the Promotion of International Trade, Japan: Nippon Bldg, 5th Floor, No. 2-6-2, Otemachi, Chiyoda-ku, Tokyo; tel. (3) 245-1561; telex 222-8471; for the promotion of private trade with the People's Republic of China, handles 100% of Sino-Japanese trade; Pres. Y. Sakurauchi; Chair. Takamaru Morita.

Council of All-Japan Exporters' Association: Kikai Shinko Kaikan Bldg, 5-8, Shibakoen 3-chome, Minato-ku, Tokyo; tel. (3) 431-9507.

Japan External Trade Organization (JETRO): 2-5, Toranomon 2-chome, Minato-ku, Tokyo 105; tel. (3) 582-5511; f. 1958; information for foreign firms, investigation of foreign markets, exhbns of Japanese commodities abroad, import promotion, etc.; Chair. Shoichi Akazawa; Pres. Shiro Miyamoto.

Nihon Boeki-Kai (Japan Foreign Trade Council, Inc.): 6th Floor, World Trade Center Bldg, 4-1, 2-chome, Hamamatsu-cho, Minato-ku, Tokyo 105; tel. (3) 435-5952; f. 1947; 318 mems; Pres. Yohei Mimura; Exec. Man. Dir Masao Saito; Man. Dirs Kikuo Kunugi, Takekuni Ebihara.

TRADE ASSOCIATIONS

Fertilizer Traders' Association: Daiichi Saegusa Bldg 10-5, Ginza 5-chome, Chuo-ku, Tokyo; tel. (3) 573-6758.

Japan Agricultural Products Exporters' Association: Ikeden Bldg, 12-5, 2-chome, Shimbashi, Minato-ku, Tokyo; tel. (3) 591-9325.

Japan Canned Foods Exporters' Association: New Kokusai Bldg, 4-1, Marunouchi 3-chome, Chiyoda-ku, Tokyo; tel. (3) 281-5341.

Japan Cement Exporters' Association: Hattori Bldg, 10-3, Kyobashi 1-chome, Chuo-ku, Tokyo; tel. (3) 561-8631; telex 252-2439.

Japan General Merchandise Exporters' Association: 4-1, Hamamatsu-cho 2-chome, Minato-ku, Tokyo; tel. (3) 435-3471; f. 1953; 320 mems; Pres. Hiroshi Toyama.

Japan Hardwood Exporters' Association: Matsuda Bldg 9-1, 1-chome, Ironai, Otaru, Hokkaido 047; tel. 23-8411; telex 952701.

Japan Iron and Steel Exporters' Association: 3-2-10, Nihonbashi-Kayabacho, Chuo-ku, Tokyo; tel. (3) 669-4811.

Japan Lumber Importers' Association: Yushi Kogyo Bldg, 13-11, Nihonbashi 3-chome, Chuo-ku, Tokyo 103; tel. (3) 271-0926; f. 1950; 118 mems; Pres. S. Otsubo.

Japan Machinery Exporters' Association: Kikai Shinko Kaikan Bldg, 5-8, Shiba Koen 3-chome, Minato-ku, Tokyo 105; tel. (3) 431-9507; telex 24744; Pres. Taiichiro Matsuo.

Japan Machinery Importers' Association: Koyo Bldg, 2-11, Toranomon 1-chome, Minato-ku, Tokyo; tel. (3) 503-9736; f. 1985; 113 mems; Pres. Taiichiro Matsuo.

Japan Paper Exporters' Association: Kami Parupu Kaikan Bldg, 9-11, Ginza 3-chome, Chuo-ku, Tokyo; tel. (3) 541-8108; f. 1959; 68 mems; Chair. Shinzo Fuse.

Japan Paper Importers' Association: Kami Parupu Kaikan Bldg, 9-11, Ginza 3-chome, Chuo-ku, Tokyo; tel. (3) 541-8109; f. 1981; 56 mems; Chair. Takaharu Matsui.

Japan Pearl Exporters' Association: 122 Higashi-machi, Chuo-ku, Kobe; Tokyo branch: 6-15, 3-chome, Kyobashi, Chuo-ku; tel. (3) 561-7807; f. 1954; Pres. Hiro Otsuki.

Japan Pharmaceutical, Medical and Dental Supply Exporters' Association: 3-6, Nihonbashi-Honcho 4-chome, Chuo-ku, Tokyo 103; tel. (3) 241-2106; f. 1953; 180 mem. firms; Pres. Kimio Uyeno; Man. Dir Mitsuo Sasaki.

Japan Ship Exporters' Association: Senpaku-Shinko Bldg, 1-15-16, Toranomon, Minato-ku, Tokyo 105; tel. (3) 502-2094; telex 26421.

Japan Sugar Import and Export Council: Ginza Gas-Hall, 9-15, 7-chome, Ginza, Chuo-ku, Tokyo; tel. (3) 571-2362.

Japan Tea Exporters' Association: 81-1, Kitaban-cho, Shinzuoka, Shinzuoka Prefecture; tel. 71-3428.

TRADE FAIR

Tokyo International Trade Fair Commission: 7-24, Harumi 4-chome, Chuo-ku, Tokyo 104; CPOB 1201; tel. (3) 531-3371; telex 02523935.

PRINCIPAL INDUSTRIAL ORGANIZATIONS

General

Industry Club of Japan: 4-6, Marunouchi, 1-chome, Chiyoda-ku, Tokyo; tel. (3) 281-1711; f. 1917 to develop closer relations between industrialists at home and abroad and promote expansion of Japanese business activities; c. 1,600 mems; Pres. Toshio Doko; Exec. Dir Takashi Dai.

Japan Commercial Arbitration Association: Tokyo Chamber of Commerce and Industry Bldg, 2-2, 3-chome, Marunouchi, Chiyoda-ku, Tokyo 100; tel. (3) 214-0641; f. 1950; 1,141 mems; provides facilities for mediation, conciliation and arbitration in international trade disputes; Pres. Noboru Gotoh.

Japan Committee for Economic Development (Keizai Doyukai): Nippon Kogyo Club Bldg, 1-4-6, Marunouchi, Chiyoda-ku, Tokyo; tel. (3) 211-1271; f. 1946; mems: business groups concerned with national and international economic and social policies; Chair. Takashi Ishihara.

Japan Federation of Economic Organizations (KEIDANREN) (Keizaidantai Rengo-Kai): 9-4, Otemachi 1-chome, Chiyoda-ku, Tokyo, 100; tel. (3) 279-1411; telex 02223188; f. 1946; private non-profit asscn to study domestic and international economic problems; mems 121 industrial orgs, 877 corpns (1986); Chair. Eishiro Saito; Pres. Nihachiro Hanamura.

Japan Federation of Smaller Enterprise Organizations (JFSEO): 2-8-4 Nihonbashi, Kayabacho, Chuo-ku, Tokyo 103; tel. (3) 668-2481; f. 1948; 18 mems and about 1,000 co-operative socs; Pres. Masataka Toyoda.

Japan Productivity Centre (Nihon Seisansei Honbu): 3-1-1 Shibuya, Shibuya-ku, Tokyo; tel. (3) 409-1111; telex 23296; f. 1955; 10,000 mems; concerned with management problems; Chair. Tomitaro Hirata; Pres. Jinnosuke Miyai.

Nihon Keieisha Dantai Renmei (NIKKEIREN) (Japan Federation of Employers' Asscns): 4-6, Marunouchi 1-chome, Chiyoda-ku, Tokyo 100; tel. (3) 213-4463; telex 02223244; f. 1948; 102 mem. asscns; Dir-Gen. Yoshinobu Matsuzaki; Sec.-Gen. Hiroshi Kitamura.

Chemicals

Federation of Pharmaceutical Manufacturers' Associations of Japan: 9, 2-chome, Nihonbashi Hon-chu, Chuo-ku, Tokyo; tel. (3) 270-0581.

Japan Perfumery and Flavouring Association: Nitta Bldg, 2-1, 8-chome, Ginza, Chuo-ku, Tokyo; tel. (3) 571-3855.

Japan Chemical Industry Association: Tokyo Club Bldg, 2-6, 3-chome, Kasumigaseki, Chiyoda-ku, Tokyo 104; tel. (3) 580-0751; telex 23557; f. 1948; 239 mems; Pres. Yasunobu Kishimoto.

Japan Cosmetic Industry Association: Hatsumei Bldg, 9-14, Toranomon 2-chome, Minato-ku, Tokyo; tel. (3) 502-0576; f. 1959; 450 mem. cos; Rep. Dirs Kamenosuke Sawada, Hikoji Nishimura; Man. Dir Kaoru Miyazawa.

The Japan Gas Association: 15-12, Toranomon 1-chome, Minato-ku, Tokyo 105; tel. (3) 502-0111; telex 2222374; f. 1912; Chair. Masafumi Ohnishi; Vice-Chair. Yoshimitsu Shibasaki.

Japan Inorganic Chemical Industry Association: Sanko Bldg, 1-13-1, Ginza Chuo-ku, Tokyo; tel. (3) 563-1326; f. 1948; Pres. Kan-ichi Tanahashi.

Japan Urea and Ammonium Sulphate Industry Association: Tokyo Takugin Bldg, 3-13, 1-chome, Nihonbashi, Chuo-ku, Tokyo; tel. (3) 281-4331.

The Photo-Sensitized Materials Manufacturers' Association: Kyodo Bldg, No. 2, 2-chome, Kanda Nishikicho, Chiyoda-ku, Tokyo; tel. (3) 291-6626.

Fishing and Pearl Cultivation

Japan Fisheries Association (Dai-nippon Suisan Kai): Sankaido Bldg, 9-13, Akasaka 1, Minato-ku, Tokyo; tel. (3) 582-7451; Pres. Tomoyoshi Kamenaga.

JAPAN

Japan Pearl Export and Processing Co-operative Association: 7, 3-chome, Kyobashi, Chuo-ko, Tokyo; f. 1951; 130 mems.

National Federation of Medium Trawlers: Toranomon Chuo Bldg, 1–16 Toranomon 1, Minato-ku, Tokyo; tel. (3) 508-0361; telex 02225404; f. 1948.

Paper and Printing

The Japan Federation of Printing Industries: 1–16–8, Shintomi, Chuo-ku, Tokyo; tel. (3) 553-6051; Pres. YOSHITOSHI KITAJIMA; Exec. Dir OSAMU NAKAMURA.

Japan Paper Association: Kami-Parupu Kaikan Bldg, Ginza 3-chome, 9–11 Chuo-ku, Tokyo; tel. (3) 543-2411; telex 02522907; f. 1946; 75 mems; Chair. F. TANAKA; Pres. T. HASHIMOTO.

Japan Paper Products Manufacturers' Association: 2–6, Kotobuki 4-chome, Taito-ku, Tokyo; tel. (3) 543-2411; f. 1949; Exec. Dir KIYOSHI SATOH.

Mining and Petroleum

Asbestos Cement Products Association: Takahashi Bldg, 10–8, 7-chome, Ginza, Chuo-ku, Tokyo; tel. (3) 571-1359; f. 1937; Chair. KOSHIRO SHIMIZU.

Cement Association of Japan: Hattori Bldg, 10–3, Kyobashi 1-chome, Chuo-ku, Tokyo 104; tel. (3) 561-8631; f. 1948; 22 mem. cos; Chair. H. KOBAYASHI; Exec. Man. Dir H. KUROSAWA.

Japan Coal Association: Hibiya Park Bldg, 1–8, Yuraku-cho 1-chome, Chiyoda-ku, Tokyo; tel. (3) 271-3484.

Japan Mining Industry Association: Shin-hibiya Bldg, 3–6, Uchisaiwai-cho 1-chome, Chiyoda-ku, Tokyo 100; tel. (3) 502-7451; f. 1948; 74 mem. cos; Pres. J. NISHIKAWA; Vice-Pres. J. SATO.

Japan Petroleum Development Association: Keidanren Kaikan, 9–4, 1-chome, Otemachi, Chiyoda-ku, Tokyo; tel. (3) 279-5841; telex 29400; f. 1961; Chair. JUN'NOSUKE HIDAKA.

Metals

Japan Brass Makers' Association: 12–22, 1-chome, Tsukiji, Chuo-ku, Tokyo; f. 1948; 30 mems; Pres. K. TAKAHASHI; Man. Dir K. ABE.

Japan Iron and Steel Federation: Keidanren Kaikan, 1–9–4, Otemachi, Chiyoda-ku, Tokyo; tel. (3) 279-3611; telex 0222-4210; f. 1948; Chair. Y. TAKEDA.

Japan Light Metal Association: Nihonbashi Asahiseimei Bldg, 1–3, Nihonbashi 2-chome, Chuo-ku, Tokyo 103; tel. (3) 273-3041; f. 1947; 176 mems.

Japan Stainless Steel Association: Tekko Kaikan Bldg, 2–10, Nihonbashi Kayaba-cho 3-chome, Chuo-ku, Tokyo 103; tel. (3) 669-4431; Pres. TATSUO SAEKI; Exec. Dir KENICHIRO AOKI.

The Kozai Club: c/o Tekko Kaikan, 3-2-10, Nihonbashi Kayabacho, Chuo-ku, Tokyo; tel. (3) 669-4811; telex 0252-3607; f. 1947; mems 34 mfrs, 86 dealers; Chair. EISHIRO SAITO.

Steel Castings and Forgings Association of Japan (JSCFA): Tekko Bldg, 8–2, 1-chome, Marunouchi, Chiyoda-ku, Tokyo 100; f. 1972; mems 71 cos, 82 plants; Exec. Dir ATSUO NAKAJIMA.

Machinery and Precision Equipment

Electronic Industries Association of Japan: Tosho Bldg, 2–2, 3-chome, Marunouchi, Chiyoda-ku, Tokyo; tel. (3) 211-2765; f. 1948; mems 580 firms; Pres. SADAKAZU SHINDOH.

Japan Camera Industry Association: Mori Bldg, 2–2, Atago 1-chome, Minato-ku, Tokyo 105; tel. (3) 434-2631; f. 1954; Pres. TOHRU MATSUMOTO.

Japan Clock and Watch Association: Nomura Bldg, 2-1-1, Otemachi, Chiyoda-ku, Tokyo.

Japan Electric Association: 1-7-1, Yurakucho, Chiyoda-ku, Tokyo 100; tel. (3) 216-0551; f. 1921; 4,385 mems; Pres. SEIZO YOSHIMURA.

Japan Electric Measuring Instruments Manufacturers' Association: 1-9-10, Toranomon Minato-ku, Tokyo; tel. (3) 502-0601.

Japan Electrical Manufacturers' Association: 4–15, 2-chome, Nagata-cho, Chiyoda-ku, Tokyo 100; tel. (3) 581-4844; telex 0222-2619; f. 1948; mems 238 firms; Pres. H. ABE; Chair. KATSUSHIGE MITA.

The Japan Machinery Federation: Kikai Shinko Bldg, 5-8-3, Shiba-Koen, Minato-ku, Tokyo 105; tel. (3) 434-5381; f. 1952; Exec. Vice-Pres. (vacant).

Japan Machine Tool Builders' Association: Kikai Shinko Bldg, 3–5–8, Shiba-Koen, Minato-ku, Tokyo 105; tel. (3) 434-3961; telex 22943; f. 1951; 113 mems; Exec. Dir S. ABE.

Japan Microscope Manufacturers' Association: c/o Olympus Optical Co Ltd, 43–2, Hatagaya, 2-chome, Shibuya-ku, Tokyo; tel. (3) 377-2111; f. 1954; mems 25 firms; Chair. S. KITAMURA.

Japan Motion Picture Equipment Industrial Association: Kikai-Shinko Bldg, 5–8, Shiba-Koen 3-chome, Minato-ku, Tokyo 105; tel. (3) 434-3911.

Japan Optical Industry Association: Kikai-Shinko Bldg, 3–5–8, Shiba-Koen, Minato-ku, Tokyo 105; tel. (3) 431-7073; f. 1946; 200 mems; Exec. Dir M. SUZUKI.

Japan Power Association: Uchisaiwai Bldg, 1–4–2, Uchisaiwai-cho, Chiyoda-ku, Tokyo; tel. (3) 501-3988; telex 24137; f. 1954; 66 mems; Pres. TOMICHIRO SHIRASAWA; Sec. FUJIO SAKAGAMI.

Japan Society of Industrial Machinery Manufacturers: Kikai-Shinko Kaikan, 3-5-8, Shiba-Koen, Minato-ku, Tokyo; tel. (3) 434-6821; f. 1948; 307 mems; Chair. GAKUJI MORIYA.

The Japan Textile Machinery Manufacturers' Association: Kikai Shinko Kaikan, Room 310, 3-5-8 Shiba-Koen, Minato-ku, Tokyo; tel. (3) 434-3821; f. 1951; Pres. YOSHITOSHI TOYODA.

Textiles

Central Raw Silk Association of Japan: 7, 1-chome, Yuraku-cho, Chiyoda-ku, Tokyo.

Japan Chemical Fibres Association: 3–3, Nihonbashi-Muromachi, Chuo-ku, Tokyo 103; tel. (3) 241-2311; telex 02222304; f. 1948; 57 mems, 19 assoc. mems; Pres. YUTAKA HIRATA; Dir-Gen. RYOHEI SUZUKI.

Japan Cotton and Staple Fibre Weavers' Association: 8–7, Nishi-Azabu 1-chome, Minato-ku, Tokyo; tel. (3) 403-9671.

Japan Knitting Industry Association: Tokyo; tel. (3) 662-4701.

Japan Silk Association, Inc: Tokyo; tel. (3) 362-6711; f. 1959; 11 mem. assocns; Pres. TADASHI ARITA.

Japan Silk and Rayon Weavers' Association: 15–12, Kudankita 1-chome, Chiyoda-ku, Tokyo; tel. (3) 262-4101.

Japan Silk Spinners' Association: Mengyo Kaikan Bldg, 8, 3-chome, Bingo Machi, Higashi-ku, Osaka; tel. 6-232-3886; f. 1948; 95 mem. firms; Chair. ICHIJI OHTANI.

Japan Textile Council: Sen-i-Kaikan Bldg, 9, 3-chome, Nihonbashi Honcho, Chuo-ku, Tokyo; tel. (3) 241-7801; f. 1948; 24 mem. asscns.

Japan Wool Spinners' Association: Sen-i-Kaikan 9, 3-chome, Nihonbashi Honcho, Chuo-ku, Tokyo; tel. (3) 279-3371; f. 1948; Chair. S. HASEGAWA.

Japan Worsted and Woollen Weavers' Association: Sen-i-Kaikan 9, 3-chome, Nihonbashi Honcho, Chuo-ku, Tokyo; f. 1948; Chair. S. OGAWA; Man. Dir K. OHTANI.

Transport Machinery

Japan Association of Rolling Stock Industries: Daiichi Tekko Bldg, 8–2, Marunouchi 1-chome, Chiyoda-ku, Tokyo; tel. (3) 201-1911.

Japan Auto Parts Industries Association: 1-16-15, Takanawa, Minato-ku, Tokyo 108; tel. (3) 445-4211; telex 0242-2829; f. 1948; 390 mem. firms; Chair. Y. NOBUMOTO; Exec. Dir Y. NAKAMURA.

Japan Automobile Manufacturers Association, Inc: Otemachi Bldg, 6-1, Otemachi 1-chome, Chiyoda-ku, Tokyo; tel. (3) 216-5771; telex 02223410; f. 1967; 13 mem. firms; Pres. S. TOYODA; Exec. Man. Dir T. NAKAMURA.

Japan Bicycle Manufacturers' Association: 9–3, Akasaka 1-chome, Minato-ku, Tokyo 107; tel. (3) 583-3123; f. 1955.

Japanese Shipowners' Association: Kaiun Bldg, 6–4, Hirakawa-cho 2-chome, Chiyoda-ku, Tokyo; tel. (3) 264-7171; telex 2322148.

Shipbuilders' Association of Japan: Senpaku Shinko Bldg, 1–15–16, Toranomon, Minato-ku, Tokyo 105; tel. (3) 502-2011; telex 2227056; f. 1947; 50 mems; Pres. TSUNESABURO NISHIMURA; Chair. Dr KAZUO MAEDA; Exec. Man. Dir TAKASHI NAKASO.

The Ship-Machinery Manufacturers' Association of Japan: Senpaku-Shinko Bldg, 1–15–16, Toranomon, Minato-ku, Tokyo; tel. (3) 502-2041; f. 1956; 269 mems; Pres. TOMIO NOJIMA.

The Society of Japanese Aerospace Companies Inc (SJAC): Hibiya Park Bldg, Suite 518, 8–1, Yurakucho 1-chome, Chiyoda-ku, Tokyo 100; tel. (3) 211-5678; f. 1952; reorg. 1974; 127 mems, 27 assoc. mems; Chair. YOTARO IIDA; Exec. Dir YASUICHI ARAO.

JAPAN
Directory

Miscellaneous

Communications Industry Association of Japan (CIA-J): Sankei Bldg (annex), 1-7-2, Otemachi, Chiyoda-ku, Tokyo 100; tel. (3) 231-3156; f. 1948; non-profit org. of telecommunications equipment mfrs; Pres. HARUO OZAWA; Chair. NAMIO HASHIMOTO; 205 mems.

Japan Canners' Association: Marunouchi Bldg, 4-1, Marunouchi 2-chome, Chiyoda-ku, Tokyo; tel. (3) 213-4751.

Japan Construction Materials Association: Tokyo; tel. (3) 561-7260; f. 1947; Pres. KENTARO ITO.

Japan Fur Association: Ginza-Toshin Bldg, 3-11-15, Ginza, Chuo-ku, Tokyo; tel. (3) 541-6987; f. 1950; Chair. KIYOJI NAKAMURA; Sec. NORIHIDE SATOH.

Japan Plastics Industry Association: Tokyo Club Bldg, 2-6, Kasumigaseki 3-chome, Chiyoda-ku, Tokyo; tel. (3) 580-0771.

Japan Plywood Manufacturers' Association: Meisan Bldg, 18-17, 1-chome, Nishishinbashi, Minato-ku, Tokyo; tel. (3) 591-9246; f. 1965; 149 mems; Pres. AKIO FUJINAKA.

Japan Pottery Manufacturers' Federation: Toto Bldg, 1-28, Toranomon 1-chome, Minato-ku, Tokyo; tel. (3) 503-6761.

Japan Rubber Manufacturers' Association: Tobu Bldg, 1-5-26, Moto Akasaka, Minato-ku, Tokyo; tel. (3) 408-7101; f. 1950; 165 mems; Pres. KANICHIRO ISHIBASHI.

Japan Spirits and Liquors Makers' Association: Koura Dai-ichi Bldg, 7th Floor, 1-6, Nihombashi-Kayabacho 1-chome, Chuo-ku, Tokyo 103; tel. (3) 668-4621.

Japan Sugar Refiners' Association: 5-7, Sanbancho, Chiyoda-ku, Tokyo; tel. (3) 262-0176; f. 1949; 18 mems; Man. Dir SACHIO AIGA.

Motion Picture Producers Association of Japan: Sankei Bldg, 7-2, 1-chome, Otemachi, Chiyoda-ku, Tokyo 100; tel. (3) 231-6417; Pres. SHIGERU OKADA.

Tokyo Toy Manufacturers' Association: 4-16-3, Higashi-Komagata Sumida-ku, Tokyo 130; tel. (3) 624-0461.

TRADE UNIONS

A feature of Japan's trade union movement is that the unions are in general based on single enterprises, embracing workers of different occupations in that enterprise. In 1986 union membership stood at 12.4m. workers (28.9% of the total labour force).

Principal Federations

Nihon Rodo Kumiai Sohyogikai (SOHYO) (General Council of Trade Unions of Japan): Sohyo Kaikan Bldg, 2-2, Kanda Surugadai 3-chome, Chiyoda-ku, Tokyo; tel. (3) 251-0311; f. 1950; c. 4.6m. mems; Pres. MOTOFUMI MAKIEDA; Sec.-Gen. MITSUO TOMIZUKA.

Major affiliated unions:

Federation of Telecommunications Electronic Information and Allied Workers (Dentsuroren): Zendentsu Kaikan Bldg, 6, Kanda Surugadai 3-chome, Chiyoda-ku, Tokyo; tel. (3) 253-3214; 331,897 mems; Pres. K. OIKAWA.

General Federation of Private Railway and Bus Workers' Unions (Shitetsusoren): Shitetsu Kaikan Bldg, 3-5, Takanawa 4-chome, Minato-ku, Tokyo; tel. (3) 473-0166; 200,000 mems; Pres. TAKESHI KUROKAWA.

Japan Federation of National Public Service Employees' Unions (Kokkororen): Tsukasa Bldg, 6-2, Nishishinbashi 3-chome, Minato-ku, Tokyo; tel. (3) 436-1261; 91,661 mems; Pres. S. UTSUNOMIYA.

Japan Postal Workers' Union (Zentei): Zentei Kaikan Bldg, 2-7, Koraku 1-chome, Bunkyo-ku, Tokyo; tel. (3) 812-4261; 186,170 mems; Pres. K. OOTA.

Japan Teachers' Union (Nikkyoso): Kyoiku Kaikan Bldg, 6-2, Hitotsubashi 2-chome, Chiyoda-ku, Tokyo; tel. (3) 262-8901; 677,300 mems; Pres. M. MAKIEDA.

Japanese Federation of Steel Workers' Unions (Tekko Roren): 1-23-4, Shinkawa, Chuo-ku, Tokyo 104; tel. (3) 555-0401; 211,886 mems; Pres. K. NIINUMA.

National Council of Local and Municipal Government Workers' Unions (Jichiro): Jichiro Kaikan Bldg, 1 Rokuban-cho, Chiyoda-ku, Tokyo; tel. (3) 263-0261; 1,273,261 mems; Pres. Y. MARUYAMA.

National Federation of Chemical and Synthetic Chemical Industry Workers' Unions (Gokaroren): Senbai Bldg, 26-30 Shiba 5-chome, Minato-ku, Tokyo; tel. (3) 452-5591; 125,292 mems; Pres. G. TACHIBANA.

National Metal and Engineering Workers Union (Zenkoku Kinzoku): 15-11, Sakuragaoka, Shibuya-ku, Tokyo; tel. (3) 463-4231; f. 1950; 157,159 mems; Pres. YOSHIO HASHIMURA.

National Railway Workers' Union (Kokuro): Kokuro Kaikan Bldg, 11-4, Marunouchi 1-chome, Chiyoda-ku, Tokyo; tel. (3) 212-0480; 245,505 mems; Pres. M. MORIKAGE.

National Union of General Workers, Sohyo (Zenkoku Ippan): 5-6, Misakicho 3-chome, Chiyoda-ku, Tokyo; tel. (3) 230-4071; 123,000 mems; Pres. S. MORISHITA.

Zen Nihon Rodo Sodomei (DOMEI) (Japanese Confederation of Labour): 20-12, Shiba 2-chome, Minato-ku, Tokyo; tel. (3) 453-5371; telex 25908; f. 1964; c. 2.2m. mems; affiliated to ICFTU; Pres. TADANOBU USAMI; Gen. Sec. YOSHIKAZU TANAKA.

Major affiliated unions:

All-Japan Postal Labour Union (Zenyusei): 20-6, Sandagaya 1-chome, Shibuya-ku, Tokyo 151; tel. (3) 478-7101; 60,962 mems; Pres. HIDEMASA FUKUI; Gen. Sec. KENJI HACHISU.

All-Japan Seamen's Union (Kaiin Kumiai): 15-26, Roppongi 7-chome, Minato-ku, Tokyo; tel. (3) 403-6261; telex 02425112; 142,733 mems; Pres. KAZUKIYO DOI.

Federation of Electric Workers' Unions of Japan (Denryokuroren): 7-15, Mita 2-chome, Minato-ku, Tokyo 108; tel. (3) 454-0231; 136,704 mems; Pres. OSAMU SUZUKI; Gen. Sec. SEIJI NODA.

Federation of Japan Automobile Workers' Unions (Jidosharoren): 4-26, Kaigan 1-chome, Minato-ku, Tokyo 105; tel. (3) 434-4721; telex 242-2385; 220,000 mems; Pres. HARUKI SHIMIZU; Gen. Sec. AKIHISA TERASAKI.

Japan Confederation of Shipbuilding and Engineering Workers' Unions (Zosenjukiroren): 2-20-12 Shiba, Minato-ku, Tokyo 105; tel. (3) 451-6783; 155,154 mems; Pres. TOSHINORI ARIMURA; Gen. Sec. SUKESADA ITOH.

Japan Federation of Transport Workers' Unions (Kotsuroren): 2-20-12 Shiba, Minato-ku, Tokyo 105; tel. (3) 451-7243; 101,388 mems; Pres. HIROO MITSUOKA; Gen. Sec. BUNICHI TAMURA.

Japan Railway Workers' Union (Tetsuro): 2-20-12 Shiba, Minato-ku, Tokyo; tel. (3) 453-9081; 46,247 mems; Pres. SHIGEYUKI TSUJIMOTO; Gen. Sec. YOSHITATSU SHIMA.

Japanese Federation of Chemical and General Trade Unions (Zenkadomei): 2-20-12 Shiba, Minato-ku, Tokyo 105; tel.(3) 453-3801; f. 1951; 115,000 mems; Pres. HIROICHI HONDA; Gen. Sec. YOSHIKAZU UENO.

Japanese Federation of Textile, Garment, Chemical, Mercantile and Allied Industry Workers' Unions (Zensen): 8-16, Kudan Minami 4-chome, Chiyoda-ku, Tokyo 102; tel. (3) 265-7521; f. 1946; 1,497 affiliates; 515,029 mems; Pres. USAMI TADANOBU; Gen. Sec. JINNOSUKE ASHIDA.

Japanese Metal Industrial Workers' Union (Zenkin Domei): 2-20-12 Shiba, Minato-ku, Tokyo 105; tel. (3) 451-2141; f. 1951; 300,000 mems; Pres. IWAO FUJIWARA; Gen. Sec. AKIRA IMAIZUMI.

National Federation of General Workers' Unions (Ippan Domei): 2-20-12 Shiba, Minato-ku, Tokyo 105; tel. (3) 453-5869; 110,938 mems; Pres. KAZUO MAEKAWA; Gen. Sec. TSUTAE SATOH.

Churitsu Rodo Kumiai Renraku Kaigil (CHURITSUROREN) (Federation of Independent Unions of Japan): 3rd Floor, Denkiroren Kaikan Bldg, 10-3, 1-chome, Mita, Minato-ku, Tokyo; tel. (3) 455-6801; f. 1956; 1,512,352 mems; Pres. MITSUHARU WARASHINA; Gen. Sec. MANABU TAGUCHI.

Major affiliated unions:

Japanese Federation of Electrical Machine Workers' Unions (Denki Roren): Denkiroren Kaikan Bldg, 10-3, 1-chome, Mita, Minato-ku, Tokyo; tel. (3) 455-6911; f. 1953; 609,197 mems; Pres. MITSHARU WARASHINA.

Japanese Federation of Food and Allied Workers' Unions (Shokuhin Roren): Hiroo Office Bldg, 3-18, Hiroo 1-chome, Shibuya-ku, Tokyo; tel. (3) 446-2082; f. 1965; 68,979 mems; Pres. KENICHI TAMURA; Gen. Sec. EIJI TAKADA.

National Federation of Construction Workers' Unions (Zenkensoren): 7-15, Takadanobaba 2-chome, Shinjuku-ku, Tokyo; tel. (3) 200-6221; f. 1960; 338,255 mems; Pres. RISAKU EGUCHI.

National Federation of Life Insurance Workers' Unions (Seiho Roren): Hiroo Office Bldg, 3-18, Hiroo 1-chome, Shibuya-ku, Tokyo; tel.(3) 446-2031; 359,440 mems; Pres. SHIRO YAMANOBE.

JAPAN   Directory

Zenkoku Sangyobetsu Rodo Kumiai Rengo (SHINSAM-BETSU) (National Federation of Industrial Organizations): Takahashi Bldg, 9-7, Nishi Shinbashi 3-chome, Minato-ku, Tokyo; tel. (3) 433-3461; 63,997 mems; Pres. TETSUZO OGATA.

Major affiliated unions:

Kyoto-Shiga-block Workers' Federation (Keijichiren): Kyoto Rodosha Sogokaikan Bldg, 30-2, Mibusennen-cho, Nakagyo-ku, Kyoto-shi, Tokyo; 10,615 mems; Pres. MEIWA IKEDA.

National Machinery and Metal Workers' Union (Zenkikin): Takahashi Bldg, 9-7, Nishi Shinbashi 3-chome, Minato-ku, Tokyo; tel. (3) 434-3084; 33,935 mems; Pres. TETSUZO OGATA.

National Organization of All Chemical Workers (Shinkagaku): 9-7, Nishi Shinbashi 3-chome, Minato-ku, Tokyo; tel. (3) 433-6486; 11,430 mems; Pres. AKIHIRO KAWAI.

Major Non-Affiliated Unions

All-Japan Federation of Transport Workers' Unions (Unyu Roren): 3-3-3 Kasumigaseki, Chiyoda-ku, Tokyo; 124,481 mems; Pres. JIRO TAI.

Confederation of Japan Automobile Workers' Unions (JAW—Jidoshasoren): Kokuryu Shibakoen Bldg, 6-15, Shiba-Koen 2-chome, Minato-ku, Tokyo; tel. (3) 434-7641; f. 1972; 680,000 mems; Pres. TERUHITO TOKUMOTO.

Federation of City Bank Employees' Unions (Shiginren): Ida Bldg, 3-8, Yaesu 1-chome, Chuo-ku, Tokyo; tel. (3) 274-5611; 174,135 mems; Pres. Y. OKUMOTO.

Japan Council of Construction Industry Employees' Unions (Nikkenkyo): Dai-7 Daikyo Bldg, 30-8, Sendagaya 1-chome, Shibuya-ku, Tokyo; tel. (3) 403-7976; f. 1954; 65,479 mems; Pres. MASANORI OKAMURA.

Japan Federation of Commercial Workers' Unions (Shogyororen): 2-23-1, Yoyogi, Shibuya-ku, Tokyo; tel. (3) 370-4121; telex 29575; 140,000 mems; Pres. KENSHO SUZUKI.

National Federation of Agricultural Mutual Aid Societies Employees' Unions (Zennokyororen): Shinkuku Nokyo Kaikan Bldg, 5-5, Yoyogi 2-chome, Shibuya-ku, Tokyo; tel. (3) 370-8327; 93,382 mems; Pres. HIDEO GOTO.

National Councils

Co-ordinating bodies for unions whose members are in the same industry or have the same employer.

All-Japan Council of Traffic and Transport Workers' Unions (Zen Nippon Kotsu Unyu Rodo Kumiai Kyogikai—Zenkoun): c/o Kokutetsu Rodo Kaikan, 11-4, Marunouchi 1-chome, Chiyoda-ku, Tokyo; tel. (3) 215-0681; f. 1947; 842,813 mems; Pres. K. YOSHIOKA; Gen. Sec. ICHIZO SAKAI.

Council of Public Corporations and National Enterprise Workers' Unions (Korokyo): Sohyo Kaikan, 2-11, Kanda Surugadai 3-chome, Chiyoda-ku, Tokyo; tel. (3) 251-7471; 852,632 mems; Gen. Sec. A. YAMAGISHI.

Council of SOHYO-affiliated Federations in the Private Sector (Sohyo Minkan Tansan Kaigi): Sohyo Kaikan, 2-11, Kanda Surugadai 3-chome, Chiyoda-ku, Tokyo; tel. (3) 251-0311; 1,479,942 mems; Gen. Sec. SIZUO MISHIMA.

FIET Japanese Liaison Council (FIET-JLC) (Nihon Kameisoshiki Renraku Kyogikai): 2-23-1 Yoyogi, Shibuya-ku, Tokyo 151; tel. (3) 370-4121; f. 1981; 301,100 mems; Sec. Gen. KATSUICHI YAMAMOTO.

Japan Council of Metalworkers' Unions (Zen Nihon Kinzoku Sangyo Rodokumiai Kyogikai): Santoku Yaesu Bldg, 6-21, Yaesu 2-chome, Chuo-ku, Tokyo 104; tel. (3) 274-2461; telex 0222-2534; f. 1964; 2,041,000 mems; Chair. TAKUHIKO NAKAMURA; Gen. Sec. ICHIRO SETO.

Japan Council of Public Service Workers' Unions (Nihon Komuin Rodo Kumiai Kyoto Kaigi): Sohyo Kaikan, 2-11, Kanda Surugadai 3-chome, Chiyoda-ku, Tokyo; tel. (3) 251-6263; 2,303,107 mems; Gen. Sec. YASUO MARUYAMA.

National Council of Dockworkers' Unions (Zenkokukowan): Shimokawa Bldg, 6-24-14, Minami 001, Shinagawaka, Tokyo; tel. (3) 768-1350; f. 1972; 65,000 mems; Chair. TOKUJI YOSHIOKA.

Trade Union Council for Policy Promotion (Seisaku Suishin Roso Kaigi): c/o Denryokuroren, 7-15, Mita 2-chome, Minato-ku, Tokyo 108; 5m. mems; Gen. Secs KOICHIRO HASHIMOTO, TOSHIFUMI TATEYAMA.

Trade Union Council for Multinational Companies (Takokuseki-Kigyo Taisaku Rodo Kumiai Kaiji): c/o IMF-JC, Santoku Yaesu Bldg, 6-21, Yaesu 2-chome, Chuo-ku, Tokyo 104; tel. (3) 274-2461; telex 02222534; 2.92m. mems; Chair. TAKUHIKO NAKAMURA.

CO-OPERATIVE ORGANIZATION

National Federation of Agricultural Co-operative Associations (ZEN-NOH): 8-3, Otemachi 1-chome, Chiyoda-ku, Tokyo; tel. (3) 245-0746; telex 0222-3686; purchasers of agricultural materials and marketers of agricultural products.

Transport

RAILWAYS

Japanese National Railways (JNR): 1-6-5, Marunouchi, Chiyoda-ku, Tokyo; tel. 3-212-3587; telex 24873; f. 1949; state-controlled (to be transferred to eight semi-state corpns in April 1987); very high-speed Tokaido-Sanyo Shinkansen line (1,069 km) links Tokyo with Shin-Yokohama, Nagoya, Kyoto, Shin-Osaka, Okayama, Hiroshima and Hakata. Tohoku Shinkansen (493 km) links Ueno in Tokyo with Omiya, Fukushima, Sendai and Morioka. Joetsu Shinkansen (297 km) links Ueno (Tokyo) with Omiya and Niigata. A section between Ueno (Tokyo) and Omiya (31 km) was opened in March 1985. In 1985 the total railway route length was 20,789 km, of which 9,109 km was electrified. Work began in 1971 on a new 'super express' railway network, linking all the major cities. To be completed by the end of the century, it will total 7,000 km in length. Pres. and Chair. TAKAYA SUGIURA; Exec. Vice-Pres. MASASHI HASHIMOTO; Exec. Vice-Pres. (Engineering) KOICHI SAKATA.

Principal Private Companies

Hankyu Corporation: 8-8, Kakuta-cho, Kita-ku, Osaka 530; tel. (6) 373-5092; f. 1907; links Osaka, Kyoto, Kobe and Takarazuka; Pres. SADAO SHIBATANI.

Hanshin Electric Railway Co Ltd: 3-19, Umeda 2-chome, Kita-ku, Osaka 530; tel. (6) 347-6035; f. 1899; Pres. SHUNJIRO KUMA.

Keihan Electric Railway Co Ltd: 47-5, 1-chome, Kyobashi, Higashi-ku, Osaka; tel. (6) 944-2521; f. 1906; Chair. SEITARO AOKI; Pres. HIROSHI SUMITA.

Keihin Electric Express Railway Co Ltd: 20-20, Takanawa 2-chome, Minato-ku, Tokyo 140; tel. (3) 443-5111; Pres. MICHIO IIDA.

Keio Teito Electric Railway Co Ltd: 3-1-24, Shinjuku, Shinjuku-ku, Tokyo 160; tel. (3) 356-3111; Pres. MADOKA MINOWA.

Keisei Electric Railway Co Ltd: 10-3, 1-chome, Oshiage, Sumida-ku, Tokyo 131; tel. (3) 621-2231; f. 1909; Pres. M. SATO.

Kinki Nippon Railway Co Ltd: 1-55, 6-chome, Uehommachi, Tennoji-ku, Osaka 543; tel. (6) 771-3331; f. 1910; Pres. YOSHINORI UEYAMA.

Nagoya Railroad Co Ltd: 2-4, 1-chome, Meieki, Nakamura-ku, Nagoya-shi 450; tel. (571) 2111; Chair. KENICHI KAJII; Pres. KENICHI KAJII.

Nankai Electric Railway Co Ltd: 1-60, Nanba 5-chome, Minami-ku, Osaka 542; tel. (6) 631-1151; Pres. S. YOSHIMURA; Vice-Pres. K. KUBO.

Nishi-Nippon Railroad Co Ltd: 1-11-17 Tenjin-cho, Chuo-ku, Fukuoka; tel. (092) 761-6631; serves northern Kyushu; Pres. GENKEI KIMOTO; Chair. H. YOSHIMOTO.

Odakyu Electric Railway Co Ltd: 8-3, 1-chome, Nishi Shinjuku, Shinjuku-ku, Tokyo 160; tel. (3) 349-2301; f. 1948; Pres. TATSUZO TOSHIMITSU; Chair. S. HIROTA.

Seibu Railway Co Ltd: 16-15, 1-chome, Minami-Ikebukuro, Toshima-ku, Tokyo 171; tel. (3) 989-2035; f. 1912; Pres. YOSHIAKI TSUTSUMI.

Tobu Railway Co Ltd: 1-2, 1-chome, Oshiage, Sumida-ku, Tokyo 131; tel. (3) 621-5057; Pres. KAICHIRO NEZU.

Tokyu Corporation: 26-20, Sakuragaoka, Shibuya-ku, Tokyo; tel. (3) 477-6076; telex 02423395; f. 1922; Chair. and Pres. NOBORU GOTOH.

Subways, Monorails and Tunnels

Subway service is available in Tokyo, Osaka, Kobe, Nagoya, Sapporo, Yokohama, Kyoto and Fukuoka with a combined network of about 420 km. Most new subway lines are directly linked with existing JNR or private railway terminals which connect the cities with suburban areas.

Japan started its first monorail system on a commercial scale in 1964 with straddle-type cars between central Tokyo and Tokyo

International Airport, a distance of 13 km. In 1984 the total length of monorail was 22.2 km.

In 1985 the 54-km Seikan Tunnel (the world's longest undersea tunnel), linking the islands of Honshu and Hokkaido, was completed at an estimated cost of 690,000m. yen. Electric rail services through the tunnel were expected to be in operation by 1987 or 1988.

Kobe Municipal Rapid Transit: 6-5-1, Kanocho Chuoku, Kobe; Dir TOSHIRO YAMANAKA; 10 km open; 13.2 km under construction.

Nagoya Underground Railway: Nagoya Municipal Transportation Bureau, City Hall Annexe, 1-1, Sannomaru 3-chome, Naka-ku, Nagoya; tel. (52) 961-1111; 60.2 km open (1986); Gen. Man. THOMATSU KOSUKE.

Osaka Underground Railway: Osaka Municipal Transportation Bureau, 11-53, 1-chome, Kujo Minami-dori, Nishi-ku, Osaka; tel. (6) 582-1101; f. 1903; 94.1 km open in 1984 and the 6.6 km computer-controlled 'New Tram' service began between Suminoekoen and Nakafuto; Gen. Man. SHICHIRO TERAMOTO.

Sapporo Rapid Transit: Municipal Transportation Bureau, Sapporo, Hokkaido; 31.6 km open; 9.1 km under construction; Dir M. OGUNI.

Tokyo Underground Railway: Teito Rapid Transit Authority, 19-6, Higashi Ueno, 3-chome, Taito-ku, Tokyo; tel. (3) 832-2111; f. 1941; Pres. SHIRO NAKAMURA; 142.1 km open; and Transportation Bureau of Tokyo Metropolitan Govt, 2-10-1 Yuraku-cho, Chiyoda-ku, Tokyo; f. 1960; tel. (3) 216-1411; Dir-Gen. TSUNEHARU OCHI; 61.5 km open; combined length of underground system 203.6 km (1986).

Yokohama Rapid Transit: Municipal Transportation Bureau, 231 Minato-machi, Naka-ku, Yokohama; 2 lines of 11.5 km; Dir-Gen. M. OGURA.

ROADS

In April 1985 Japan's road network extended to 1,127,501 km, including 3,551 km of motorways. Plans have been made to cover the country with a trunk automobile highway network with a total length of 7,600 km, of which 4,330 km were expected to be completed by 1989. In April 1986 work was started on what is to be the world's longest suspension bridge, a 3.9-km structure spanning the southwestern Akashi Strait between Kobe and the island of Awaiicho.

There is a national omnibus service, 60 publicly operated services and 298 privately operated services.

SHIPPING

Shipping in Japan is not nationalized but is supervised by the Ministry of Transport. At 30 June 1985 the Japanese merchant fleet had a total displacement of 39,940,000 gross tons. The main ports are Yokohama, Nagoya and Kobe.

Principal Companies

Daiichi Chuo Kisen Kaisha: Dowa Bldg, 5-15, Nihonbashi 3-chome, Chuo-ku, Tokyo 103; tel. (3) 278-6800; telex 0222-24322; f. 1960; fleet of 13 vessels; liner and tramp services; Chair. K. YAMADA; Pres. K. MORITA.

Iino Kaiun Kasha Ltd: 1-1, 2-chome, Uchisaiwai-cho, Chiyoda-ku, Tokyo 100; tel. (3) 506-3066; telex 0222-2032; f. 1918; fleet of 12 vessels; cargo and tanker services; Chair. T. CHIBA.

Japan Line Ltd: Kokusai Bldg, 1-1, Marunouchi 3-chome, Chiyoda-ku, Tokyo 100; tel. (3) 286-6599; telex 0222-2888; f. 1964; fleet of 17 vessels; container ship, tanker, liner, tramp and specialized carrier services; Chair. (vacant); Pres. SEISHIRO KATAOKA.

Kansai Kisen Kaisha: 7-15, Benten 6-chome, Minato-ku, Osaka; tel. 574-9131; telex 0222-2874; f. 1942; fleet of 19 vessels; domestic passenger services; Pres. M. OKI.

Kawasaki Kisen Kaisha Ltd (K Line): 8 Kaigan-dori, Chuo-ku, Kobe; tel. 391-8151; telex 0562-2120; f. 1919; fleet of 48 vessels; cargo, tankers and bulk ore-carrying services worldwide; Pres. K. ITOH; Dir and Chair. K. KUMAGAI.

Mitsui OSK Lines Ltd: Shosen Mitsui Bldg, 2-1-1, Toranomon, Minato-ku, Tokyo 105-91; tel. (3) 584-5111; telex 22266; f. 1942; 72 vessels; world-wide container, liner, tramp and specialized carrier and tanker services; Pres. KIICHIRO AIURA.

Nippon Yusen Kabushiki Kaisha: 3-2, Marunouchi 2-chome, Chiyoda-ku, Tokyo 100; tel. (3) 284-5151; telex 22236; f. 1885; 115 vessels; world-wide container, cargo, tanker and bulk carrying services; Chair. SUSUMU ONO; Pres. KIMIO MIYAOKA.

Nissho Shipping Co Ltd: 33 Mori Bldg, 8-21, Toranomon 3-chome, Minato-ku, Tokyo 105; tel. (3) 438-3511; telex 22573; f. 1943; fleet of 11 vessels; Pres. MINORU IKEDA.

Ryukyu Kaiun Kaisha: 24-11, 1-chome Nishi, Naha City, Okinawa; tel. 0988 688161; telex 0795217; fleet of 6 vessels; cargo and passenger services on domestic routes; Pres. CHICHIO IJI; Man. THUTOMU OSHIRO.

Sankyo Kaiun Kabushiki Kaisha: Miki Bldg, No. 12-1, 3-chome, Nihonbashi, Chuo-ku, Tokyo 103; tel. (3) 273-1811; telex 2222109; f. 1959; fleet of 22 vessels; liner and tramp services; Pres. K. IKEMURA; Vice-Pres. T. KIKUOKA; Dir G. KUNISHIGE.

Shinwa Kaiun Kaisha Ltd: Fukokuseimei Bldg, 2-2, 2-chome, Uchiwaiwai-cho, Chiyoda-ku, Tokyo 100; tel. (3) 597-6076; telex 22348; f. 1950; fleet of 17 vessels; ore carriers, dry cargo and tankers; Pres. MICHIO HAKKAKU.

Showa Line Ltd: 2-3, 2-chome, Uchisaiwai-cho, Chiyoda-ku, Tokyo 100; tel. (3) 595-2211; telex 22310; f. 1944; fleet of 34 vessels; cargo, tanker, tramping and container services world-wide; Chair. SOHTARO YAMADA; Pres. DAIJIRO ISHII.

Taiheiyo Kaiun Co Ltd. (The Pacific Transportation Co Ltd): Marunouchi Bldg, 4-1, 2-chome, Chiyoda-ku, Tokyo 100; tel. (3) 2012166; telex 2223434; f. 1951; fleet of 7 vessels; cargo and tanker services; Pres. SANPEI YAMAJI.

Yamashita-Shinnihon Steamship Co Ltd: 1-1, Hitotsu-bashi, 1-chome, Chiyoda-ku, Tokyo 101; tel. (3) 282-7500; telex 22345; f. 1917; fleet of 20 vessels; liner, tramp and tanker services worldwide; Pres. T. KAIJI.

CIVIL AVIATION

There are international airports at Tokyo, Osaka and Narita. In July 1986 construction of the world's first offshore international airport (to be called New Kansai International Airport) began in Osaka Bay.

All Nippon Airways Co Ltd: 2-5, Kasumigaseki 3-chome, Chiyoda-ku, Tokyo 100; tel. (3) 580-4711; telex 33670; f. 1952; operates domestic passenger and freight services; scheduled international services to Guam, Los Angeles and Washington; charter services to Hong Kong, the People's Republic of China, Singapore, Thailand, Guam and Saipan (Northern Mariana Islands); Pres. TAIZO NAKAMURA; fleet of 18 Boeing 727, 14 Boeing 737, 17 Boeing 747, 7 Boeing 767, 17 TriStar, 19 YS-11, 3 Jet Ranger, 2 Aerospacial AS350.

Japan Air Lines—JAL (Nihon Koku Kabushiki Kaisha): 7-3, 2-chome, Marunouchi, Chiyoda-ku, Tokyo 100; tel. (3) 284-2081; telex 32653; f. 1951; 34.5% govt-owned; domestic and international services, from Tokyo to Australia, Bahrain, Brazil, Canada, People's Republic of China, Denmark, Egypt, Fiji, France, Federal Republic of Germany, Greece, Hong Kong, India, Indonesia, Italy, the Republic of Korea, Kuwait, Malaysia, Mexico, Netherlands, New Zealand, Pakistan, the Philippines, Saudi Arabia, Singapore, Spain, Switzerland, Thailand, USSR, United Arab Emirates, the UK and the USA; Pres. SUSUMU YAMAJI; Chair. JUNJI ITOH; fleet of 2 Boeing 727, 48 Boeing 747, 3 Boeing 767, 10 DC-8, 20 DC-10.

Japan Asia Airways Co: Yurakucho Denki Bldg, 7-1, Yurakucho 1-chome, Chiyoda-ku, Tokyo 100; tel. (3) 284-2957; f. 1975; wholly-owned subsidiary of JAL; international services to Hong Kong and Taiwan; Pres. TAKESHI TSUNOGAE; fleet of 2 Boeing 747, 6 DC-8.

Nihon Kinkyori Airways Co (Nihon Kinkyori Koku KK): Dai-2, Akiyama Bldg, 3-6-2 Toranomon, Minato-ku, Tokyo 105; telex 02422124; f. 1974; domestic services; Pres. KANICHI MARUI; fleet of 8 YS-11, 1 Boeing 737.

Southwest Air Lines Co Ltd (Nansei Koku KK): 3-1, Yamashita-cho, Naha City, Okinawa 900; telex 0795477; f. 1967; subsidiary of JAL; inter-island service in Okinawa; Pres. MICHIHISA IHARA; fleet of 6 YS-11, 4 Twin Otter, 5 Boeing 737.

Toa Domestic Airlines Co: 18 Mori Bldg, 3-13, 2-chome Toranomon, Minato-ku, Tokyo 105; tel. (3) 507-8030; telex 02225182; f. 1971; domestic services to 39 cities; Pres. ISAMU TANAKA; Sr Vice-Pres. TOSHIHIKO KUBOTA; Man. Dir SHOGO UCHIYAMA; fleet of 7 Airbus A-300, 8 DC-9-80, 14 DC-9-41, 40 YS-11A, 4 Bell 214B, 4 Bell 47G, 3 Bell 204B, 5 Hughes 500.

Tourism

Department of Tourism: 2-1-3 Kasumigaseki, Chiyoda-ku, Tokyo 100; f. 1946; a dept of the Ministry of Transport; Dir-Gen. HIROKUNI TSUJI.

Japan National Tourist Organization: Tokyo Kotsu Kaikan Bldg, 2-10-1 Yuraku-cho, Chiyoda-ku, Tokyo; tel. (3) 216-1901;

telex 24132; Pres. Shunichi Sumita; Exec. Dirs Masaya Tashiro, Kiyoshi Nakajima, Michitaro Yamaoka, Hideo Nagaoka, Kaoru Sakurada.

Japan Travel Bureau Inc: 1–13–1, Nihombashi, Chuo-ku, Tokyo 103; tel. (3) 276-7811; telex 24418; f. 1912; c. 11,000 mems; Chair. T. Nagase; Pres. H. Ishida; Man. Shunichi Oyama.

Atomic Energy

Thirty-three nuclear power stations were in operation by July 1986 and 6 more are expected to become operational by 1990, with a combined capacity of 31,480 MW. Projected generating capacity: 48,000 MW by 1995.

Atomic Energy Bureau (AEB): Science and Technology Agency, 2–2–1 Kasumigaseki, Chiyoda-ku, Tokyo; tel. (3) 581-5271; f. 1956; administers and controls research and development; Dir Moritaka Nakamura.

Japan Atomic Energy Commission (JAEC): 2–2–1 Kasumigaseki, Chiyoda-ku, Tokyo; tel. (3) 581-5271; f. 1955; policy board for research, development and peaceful uses of atomic energy; Chair. Yataro Mitsubayashi.

Japan Atomic Energy Research Institute (JAERI): Fukokuseimei Bldg, 2–2–2 Uchisaiwaicho, Chiyoda-ku, Tokyo; tel. (3) 503-6111; telex 24596; f. 1956; all aspects of nuclear research: water reactor safety, fusion, HTR and utilization of radiation; Pres. Tsuneo Fujinami.

Japan Atomic Industrial Forum Inc (JAIF): Toshin Bldg, 1–13 Shimbashi 1-chome, Minato-ku, Tokyo 105; tel. (3) 508-2411; telex 0222-6623; f. 1956; non-profit org. representing c. 820 orgs involved in atomic energy development in Japan; also c. 120 overseas mems; aims to promote the peaceful use of atomic energy and the acceptance of nuclear power among the public; carries out related field surveys; Chair. Hiromi Arisawa; Exec. Man. Dir Kazuhisa Mori.

Japan Nuclear Safety Commission (JNSC): 2–2–1 Kasumigaseki, Chiyoda-ku, Tokyo; tel. (3) 581-1880; f. 1978; responsible for all matters relating to safety regulations; Chair. Keisuke Misono.

Japan Nuclear Ship Research and Development (JNSRDA): 1–15–16 Toranomon, Minato-ku, Tokyo; tel. (3) 501-4970; f. 1963; research and development of nuclear ship; 145 mems; Pres. Keijiro Inoue.

Nuclear Safety Bureau (NSB): Science and Technology Agency, 2–2–1 Kasumigaseki, Chiyoda-ku, Tokyo; tel. (3) 581-5271; telex 0222-6720; f. 1976; admin. agency for nuclear safety and regulatory matters; Dir Eiichi Tsuji.

Power Reactor and Nuclear Fuel Development Corporation (PNC): 1–9–13 Akasaka, Minato-ku, Tokyo; tel. (3) 586-3311; telex 26462; f. 1967; research and development of FBR, ATR and fuel cycle technologies; Pres. Minoru Yoshida.

JORDAN

Introductory Survey

Location, Climate, Language, Religion, Flag, Capital

The Hashemite Kingdom of Jordan is an almost land-locked state in western Asia. It is bordered by Israel to the west, by Syria to the north, by Iraq to the east and by Saudi Arabia to the south. The port of Aqaba, in the far south, gives Jordan a narrow outlet to the Red Sea. The climate is hot and dry. The average annual temperature is about 15°C (60°F) but there are wide diurnal variations. Temperatures in Amman are generally between −1°C (30°F) and 32°C (90°F). More extreme conditions are found in the valley of the River Jordan and on the shores of the Dead Sea (a lake on the Israeli-Jordanian frontier), where the temperature may exceed 50°C (122°F) in summer. The official language is Arabic. More than 90% of the population are Sunni Muslims, while there are small communities of Christians and Shi'i Muslims. The national flag (proportions 2 by 1) has three equal horizontal stripes, of black, white and green, with a red triangle, containing a seven-pointed white star, at the hoist. The capital is Amman.

Recent History

Palestine (including the present-day West Bank of Jordan) and Transjordan (the East Bank) were formerly parts of Turkey's Ottoman Empire. During the First World War (1914–18), when Turkey was allied with Germany, the Arabs under Ottoman rule rebelled. British forces, with Arab support, occupied Palestine and Transjordan in 1917–18, when the Turks withdrew.

British occupation continued after the war, when the Ottoman Empire was dissolved. In 1920 Palestine and Transjordan were formally placed under British administration by a League of Nations mandate. In 1921 Abdullah ibn Hussein, a member of the Hashimi (Hashemite) dynasty of Arabia, was proclaimed Amir (Emir) of Transjordan. In the same year, his brother, Faisal, became King of neighbouring Iraq (also administered by the United Kingdom (UK) under a League of Nations mandate). The two new monarchs were sons of Hussein ibn Ali, the Sharif of Mecca, who had proclaimed himself King of the Hidjaz (now part of Saudi Arabia) in 1916. The British decision to nominate Hashemite princes to be rulers of Iraq and Transjordan was a reward for Hussein's co-operation in the wartime campaign against Turkey.

During the period of the British mandate, Transjordan (formally separated from Palestine in 1923) gained increasing autonomy. In 1928 the UK acknowledged the nominal independence of Transjordan, although retaining certain financial and military powers. Amir Abdullah followed a generally pro-British policy and supported the Allied cause in the Second World War (1939–45). The mandate was terminated on 22 March 1946, when Transjordan attained full independence. On 25 May Abdullah was proclaimed King, and a new constitution took effect.

When the British Government terminated its mandate in Palestine in May 1948, Jewish leaders in the area proclaimed the State of Israel, but Palestinian Arabs, supported by the armies of Arab states, opposed Israeli claims and hostilities continued until July. Transjordan's forces occupied about 5,900 sq km of Palestine, including East Jerusalem, and this was confirmed by the armistice with Israel in April 1949. In June 1949 the country was renamed Jordan, and in April 1950, following a referendum, King Abdullah formally annexed the West Bank territory, which contained many Arab refugees from Israeli-held areas.

In July 1951 King Abdullah was assassinated in Jerusalem by a Palestinian Arab belonging to an extremist Islamic organization. The murdered king was succeeded by his eldest son, Talal ibn Abdullah, hitherto Crown Prince. At the time of the assassination, Talal was abroad, receiving medical treatment for a nervous disorder. He returned to Jordan in September 1951. A new constitution was adopted in November 1951, and approved by King Talal in January 1952. Because of Talal's mental illness, however, a joint session of the National Assembly proclaimed him unfit to reign, and declared him deposed, in August 1952. The crown passed to his son, Hussein ibn Talal, then 16 years of age. King Hussein formally took power in May 1953.

In March 1956, responding to Arab nationalist sentiment, King Hussein dismissed Lieut-Gen. John Glubb ('Glubb Pasha'), the British army officer who had been Chief of Staff of the Arab Legion (the Jordanian armed forces) since 1939. The Legion, with about 20,000 men, had been created in 1920 by the UK and was financed and equipped by the British Government. However, Jordan's treaty relationship with the UK was ended in March 1957. British troops completed their withdrawal from Jordan in July.

In February 1958 Jordan and Iraq formed an Arab Federation, with King Faisal II of Iraq (a second cousin of King Hussein) as Head of State. In July, however, the Federation was ended when a revolution overthrew the Iraqi monarchy, and King Faisal was killed.

The refugee camps in the West Bank became centres of Palestinian Arab nationalism, with the aim of recovering the homeland from which Arabs had been dispossessed (about 400,000 Arab residents of Palestine evacuated their homes prior to May 1948, when the British mandate ended and Israel was established, and a further 400,000 fled subsequently). In the 1950s there were numerous attacks on Israeli territory by groups of Palestinian *fedayeen* ('martyrs'), which developed into guerrilla movements. The principal Palestinian guerrilla organization was the Palestine National Liberation Movement, known as Al-Fatah ('Conquest'), originally based in the Gaza Strip (then under Egyptian administration). In September 1963 the creation of a unified 'Palestinian entity' was approved by the Council of the League of Arab States (the Arab League, see p. 171), despite opposition from the Jordanian Government, which regarded the proposal as a threat to Jordan's sovereignty over the West Bank. The first congress of Palestinian Arab groups was held in the Jordanian sector of Jerusalem in May–June 1964, when the participants unanimously agreed to form the Palestine Liberation Organization (PLO) as 'the only legitimate spokesman for all matters concerning the Palestinian people'. The PLO was to be financed by the Arab League and was to recruit military units, from among refugees, to constitute a Palestine Liberation Army (PLA). From the outset, King Hussein refused to allow the PLA to train forces in Jordan or the PLO to levy taxes from Palestinian refugees in his country.

During the turbulent reign of Hussein, Jordan has had a succession of Prime Ministers, but the King himself holds executive power and has remained the central figure in the country's political life. Despite political upheavals in Jordan and elsewhere in the Middle East, King Hussein has vigorously maintained his personal rule and has survived attempted assassination and revolt. In April 1965 Hussein nominated his brother, Hassan ibn Talal, to be Crown Prince, so excluding the King's own children from succession to the throne.

Jordan and Israel each have a small strip of coastline on the Gulf of Aqaba, providing access to the Red Sea. In May 1967 the United Arab Republic (Egypt) barred Israeli shipping from entering the Red Sea. In retaliation, Israel launched attacks on its Arab neighbours in June 1967, quickly overcoming opposition and making substantial territorial gains. The Six-Day War, as it is known, left Israel in possession of all Jordanian territory on the West Bank. The Old City of Jerusalem was incorporated into Israel, while the remainder of the conquered area has the status of an Israeli 'administered territory'. Many refugees are still housed in camps on the East Bank. Jordan was formerly a base for several Palestinian Arab guerrilla groups, mainly forces of the PLO, which made armed raids on the administered territories. The strength of these organizations frequently constituted a challenge to the Jordanian Government and, after a civil war lasting from September 1970 to July 1971, King Hussein expelled the guerrilla groups. Since then, Hussein has not allowed guerrilla activity from Jordan, but by 1979 he was again on good terms with the PLO.

In September 1971 King Hussein announced the formation of the Jordanian National Union, to be the country's sole permitted political organization. In March 1972 it was renamed the Arab National Union (ANU), but in April 1974 Hussein dissolved its executive committee. The ANU was abolished in February 1976, and since then Jordan has had no formal political parties.

In March 1972 King Hussein presented a plan for a United Arab Kingdom in which a Palestinian region (capital Jerusalem) would be federated with the Jordanian region, whose capital, Amman, would be the federal capital. Israel, the PLO and Egypt reacted unfavourably, and Egypt broke off diplomatic relations, which were not restored until September 1973, when King Hussein became reconciled with President Sadat of Egypt and President Assad of Syria.

In October 1973 another Arab–Israeli war broke out when Egypt and Syria launched simultaneous attacks on Israeli-held territory. Units of the Jordanian army were sent to support the Syrian offensive on the Golan Heights. Aid to Jordan from Kuwait and other wealthy Arab states, which had been suspended following the Jordanian action against Palestinian commandos, was restored after the 1973 war.

During early 1974 King Hussein became increasingly estranged from the governments of other Arab states when it became clear that they considered the PLO, rather than Jordan, to be the legitimate representative of the Palestinian Arabs. At an Arab summit meeting in Rabat, Morocco, in October 1974, King Hussein acknowledged this view, and supported a unanimous resolution which gave the PLO the right to establish an independent national authority on any piece of Palestinian land to be liberated.

The summit meeting at Rabat adopted a resolution which recognized the PLO as 'the sole legitimate representative of the Palestinian people'. In November 1974, as a response to this resolution, both chambers of the Jordanian National Assembly (which had equal representation for the East and West Banks) approved constitutional amendments which empowered the King to dissolve the Assembly and to postpone elections for up to 12 months. The Assembly was dissolved later that month, although it was briefly reconvened in February 1976, when it approved a constitutional amendment which gave the King power to postpone elections indefinitely and to convene the Assembly as required. A royal decree of April 1978 provided for the creation of a National Consultative Council, with 60 members appointed for a two-year term by the King, on the Prime Minister's recommendation, to debate proposed legislation. The Council was dissolved, and the National Assembly reconvened, in January 1984 (see below).

During the late 1970s Jordan and Syria co-operated closely, but in late 1980 mediation by Saudi Arabia was necessary to prevent military build-ups on both sides of the Jordanian-Syrian border from escalating into war. In the Gulf War between Iran and Iraq, which began in September 1980, Syria supports Iran and disapproves of Jordan's support for Iraq. Syria also suspects Jordan of being sympathetic towards the Camp David agreements of September 1978, which brought about peace between Egypt and Israel, though King Hussein has publicly condemned the accords.

After the Israeli invasion of Lebanon in June 1982, Hussein found himself with a key role in a plan for peace in the Middle East, proposed by President Ronald Reagan of the USA. The plan involved the creation of an autonomous Palestinian authority on the West Bank, in association with Jordan. However, following talks with Hussein, Yasser Arafat, the Chairman of the PLO, rejected the plan. Jordan subsequently gave diplomatic support to Arafat when a Syrian-backed revolt erupted in May 1983 against his leadership of Al-Fatah, the major guerrilla group within the PLO. During the last three months of the year, Jordanian diplomats in several European countries, and targets in Amman, came under attack from terrorists who were thought to be members of a radical Arab group, based in Syria, which was angered by Jordan's backing for Arafat, by its call for Egypt to be readmitted to the community of Arab states and by the possibility of a revival of the Reagan plan.

With a view to recovering something from the West Bank before Jewish settlement there produces a *de facto* extension of Israel, Hussein dissolved the National Consultative Council in January 1984 and recalled the National Assembly for its first session since 1967. He thereby created the kind of Palestinian forum (60% of Jordan's population of 2.4m. are Palestinian and there are 1.3m. Palestinians living on the West Bank) which was called for in the Reagan plan, and effectively infringed the Rabat resolution of 1974, which recognized the PLO as the sole representative of the Palestinian people. Israel allowed the surviving West Bank deputies to attend the Assembly, which approved constitutional amendments enabling elections to be held on the East Bank alone, and West Bank deputies to be chosen by the Assembly itself. Also in January, the Jordanian Council of Ministers resigned, and a new one, containing a higher proportion of Palestinians, took office. King Hussein embarked on a series of talks with Yasser Arafat in January 1984. There was strong opposition to the Reagan plan among Jordanian Palestinians, while Hussein and Arafat stood by the resolution which had been adopted at the Arab summit meeting of 1974, recognizing the PLO as 'the sole legitimate representative of the Palestinian people'.

These developments revealed a split in the Arab world between a moderate body of opinion (formed by the alliance of Jordan, Egypt and Arafat's wing of the PLO) on one side, and a more radical group, including Syria, Libya and the rebel wing of the PLO, on the other. In February 1984 the Jordanian Embassy in Tripoli, Libya, was burnt down during a demonstration, and Jordan responded by severing diplomatic relations with Libya. Attacks by militant Arab groups on Jordanian diplomats around the world took place throughout 1984 and during 1985.

At the beginning of 1984 the US Government renewed its efforts to gain Congressional approval for a $220m. plan to supply Jordan with arms and equipment for an 8,000-strong Jordanian strike force. The US envisaged this force responding to requests for military assistance from Arab governments within a 2,400-km (1,500-mile) radius of Jordan. King Hussein tried to distance Jordan from any interest or involvement in the creation of such a force. Then, in March, the planned sale to Jordan of 1,613 Stinger anti-aircraft missiles was cancelled by President Reagan, partly owing to pro-Israeli opposition to the plan in the US Congress, but also owing to King Hussein's recent harsh criticism of US policy in the Middle East. In June the Reagan administration abandoned its plans for a Jordanian strike force. Jordan consequently purchased an air defence system from the USSR in January 1985, having already made an agreement to buy French anti-aircraft missiles in September 1984.

In 1985 US President Reagan advocated the sale of arms worth $500m.–$570m. to Jordan, but there was considerable opposition to the proposal. Instead, in June, King Hussein was offered extra economic aid of $250m., to be spread over 1985 and 1986. Jordan received US aid of $136m. in 1984, and the level of aid in 1985 and 1986 had originally been set at $111.7m. and $117m. respectively. The US Senate authorized the aid but ordered it to be spread over 27 months, rather than the 15-month period that had been requested by the Reagan administration. In February 1986 the administration indefinitely postponed a proposed sale to Jordan of military equipment worth $1,500m., when it became clear that the proposal would not be approved by the Senate.

In September 1984 Jordan re-established diplomatic relations with Egypt, which had been broken off in protest at the Egypt-Israel peace treaty of 1979. President Mubarak of Egypt has since given his support to King Hussein's proposals for peace negotiations between the Arabs and the Israelis. Hussein rejected the Israeli offer of direct negotiations, excluding the PLO, in October, calling instead for a conference of all the concerned parties in the Middle East, including the PLO, on an equal footing. He requires Israel to accept the principle of 'land for peace', i.e. negotiations leading to the restoration of occupied territories (including East Jerusalem) to Jordan, in return for a comprehensive Arab-Israeli peace treaty.

The Palestine National Council (PNC), which finally met in Amman in November 1984, replied non-committally to King Hussein's offer of a joint Jordanian-Palestinian peace initiative, with UN Security Council Resolution 242 as the basis for negotiations, referring the proposal to the PLO Executive Committee. Resolution 242 has consistently been an impediment to progress towards peace. The PLO has refused to recognize the resolution as it makes mention only of a Palestinian 'refugee problem' and not of the right of Palestinians to self-determination.

In February 1985 King Hussein and Yasser Arafat announced the terms of a joint Jordanian-Palestinian agreement on the framework for a peace settlement in the Middle East. It held that peace talks should take the form of an international conference including the five permanent members of the UN Security Council and all parties to the conflict, including the PLO, representing the Palestinian people in a joint Jordanian-Palestinian delegation. The Palestinian people would in future exercise their right to self-determination in the context of a proposed confederated state of Jordan and Palestine. The text of the agreement stated that one of its principles was 'the solution of the Palestinian refugee problem in accordance with United Nations resolutions', but the PLO Executive Committee, in approving the accord, stressed that it stemmed from the rejection of the Camp David agreements, the Reagan plan and Resolution 242.

In May King Hussein put forward a quadripartite plan in Washington. The first stage of the plan was to involve preliminary talks between the USA and a Jordanian-Palestinian delegation not including members of the PLO. In the second stage the Jordanian-Palestinian delegation would be joined by representatives of the PLO. The third stage would then take the form of an international conference under UN auspices leading to direct negotiations between Israel and a Jordanian-Palestinian delegation. Although Israel supported the involvement of the five permanent members of the UN Security Council in the peace process, it rejected the reiterated proposal of an international peace conference and the suggestion of preliminary talks between the USA and a Jordanian-Palestinian delegation containing members of the PLO. Israel remained committed to direct talks with a delegation containing only 'authentic Palestinian representatives' from the Occupied Territories, while the USA has refused to talk to members of the PLO or its nominees until it recognizes Israel's right to exist, renounces terrorism and, in essence, accepts UN Security Council Resolution 242.

In July Israel independently rejected a list of seven Palestinians, five of whom were members of the PLO or had links with the PNC, whom King Hussein had presented to the USA as candidates for a joint Jordanian-Palestinian delegation to preliminary peace talks.

An extraordinary meeting of the Arab states in August (which was boycotted by Syria, Libya, Lebanon, the PDRY and Algeria) neither condemned nor endorsed the Hussein/Arafat peace initiative but reaffirmed Arab allegiance to the Fez plan of September 1982.

In September the UK offered to receive a joint Jordanian-Palestinian delegation including two members of the Executive Committee of the PNC, Bishop Ilya Khuri and Muhammad Milhem. The meeting in London in October was cancelled, however, when Muhammad Milhem refused to sign a statement, the terms of which, it was thought, had previously been agreed by all parties, specifically recognizing Israel's right to exist within its 1967 borders and rejecting terrorism as a solution to the Palestine question.

Richard Murphy, the US Assistant Secretary of State, refused to meet a Jordanian-Palestinian delegation, while on a tour of the Middle East in September 1985. Further progress was then hampered by a series of terrorist incidents in which the PLO was implicated. (For details, see chapter on Israel, p. 1469.)

These incidents gave Israel further cause to reject the PLO as a credible partner in peace negotiations. King Hussein was under increasing pressure to advance the peace process, if necessary without the participation of the PLO. In September President Reagan revived the plan to sell arms worth $1,900m. to Jordan. The proposal was approved by Congress on the condition that Jordan enter into direct talks with Israel before 1 March 1986. However, a *rapprochement* developed between Jordan and Syria. Both countries support a Middle East peace settlement through an international conference, and at talks in Riyadh in October 1985 they rejected 'partial and unilateral' solutions and affirmed their adherence to the Fez plan omitting any mention of the Jordanian-Palestinian initiative. Through a reconciliation with Syria, which is opposed to Yasser Arafat's leadership of the PLO, King Hussein may have hoped to exert pressure on Arafat to take the initiative in the peace process and signal PLO acceptance of Resolution 242. In November, in Cairo, Arafat renounced the use of terrorism by the PLO outside Israeli-occupied territories but in December the PLO Executive Committee reiterated its opposition to Resolution 242.

Although he remained opposed to the concept of preliminary negotiations, Peres intimated, in a speech at the UN in October 1985, that he would not rule out the possibility of an international conference. Rumours of secret meetings between the two leaders were followed, at the end of October, by the unofficial disclosure to the Israeli press of a document drawn up by the Israeli Prime Minister's office, which purported to summarize the state of negotiations between Israel and Jordan, listing points of agreement and dispute in peace proposals, should formal talks commence. The document suggested the establishment of an interim Israeli-Jordanian condominium of the West Bank, granting a form of Palestinian autonomy, and recorded mutual agreement on the desirability of an international forum for peace talks, with Israel consenting to the participation of the USSR (provided it re-establishes diplomatic relations with Israel) and Syria but not of the PLO, on whose involvement King Hussein still insisted.

The Jordanian Prime Minister, Ahmad Ubeidat, resigned in April 1985. A new Cabinet, only four of whose 23 members were retained from the previous Government, was sworn in under the premiership of Zaid ar-Rifai, who had been Prime Minister during the 1970s. The Cabinet was subsequently reshuffled in April and October 1986.

Frustrated by the lack of co-operation from Yasser Arafat in advancing the aims of the Jordanian-PLO peace initiative, King Hussein publicly severed political links with the PLO on 19 February 1986. In January, according to King Hussein, the USA had undertaken to invite the PLO to an international peace conference (whereas, before, it had agreed only to consider talks with the PLO) if it would officially acknowledge UN Security Council Resolutions 242 and 338 as the basis for negotiations. Arafat refused to make such a commitment without prior acknowledgement by the USA of the Palestinian right to self-determination.

Following King Hussein's announcement, Arafat was ordered to close his main PLO offices in Jordan by 1 April. The activities of the PLO were henceforth to be restricted to an even greater extent than before, and a number of Fatah officers loyal to Arafat were expelled. King Hussein urged the PLO either to change its policies or its leadership. In July Jordan closed all 25 Fatah offices in Amman, so that only 12 belonging to the PLO remained.

Since the termination of political co-ordination with the PLO, Jordan has continued to reject Israeli requests for direct peace talks which exclude a form of PLO representation. However, Jordan's subsequent efforts to strengthen its influence in Israeli-occupied territories and to foster a Palestinian constituency there, independent of Arafat's PLO, have coincided with Israeli measures to grant a limited autonomy to the Palestinian community in the West Bank (for example, by appointing Arab mayors in three towns in place of Israeli military governors). In March 1986 the Jordanian House of Representatives approved a draft law increasing the number of seats in the House from 60 to 142 (71 seats each for the East and West Banks), thereby providing for greater representation for West Bank Palestinians in the National Assembly. Then, in August, a five-year development plan for the West Bank and the Gaza Strip, involving projected expenditure of US $1,300m., was announced in Amman; and in November, by mutual agreement with Israel, a branch of the Jordan-based Cairo-Amman Bank was opened at Nablus, in the West Bank region, to provide financial services to the Palestinian community.

Government

Jordan is a constitutional monarchy. Legislative power is vested in a bicameral National Assembly. The Senate (House of Notables) has 30 members, appointed by the King for eight years (one-half of the members retiring every four years), while the House of Representatives (House of Deputies) has 60 members, including 50 Muslims and 10 Christians, elected by universal adult suffrage for four years (subject to dissolution). In each House there is equal representation for the East Bank and the (occupied) West Bank. In March 1986 the House of Representatives approved a draft law to increase its membership from 60 to 142. Executive power is vested in the King, who governs with the assistance of an appointed Council of Ministers, responsible to the Assembly.

There are eight administrative provinces, of which three have been occupied by Israel since June 1967.

Defence

The total strength of the Jordanian armed forces in July 1986 was 70,200. The army had 62,750 men, the air force 7,200 and the navy 250. Reserves number 35,000 (30,000 in the army). There are paramilitary forces of 6,000 men: a Civil Militia of 2,500 and a Public Security Force of 3,500. Military service is voluntary. The Government plans to set up a 200,000-strong force to defend the border with Israel. The defence budget in 1987 was an estimated 252.5m. dinars (US $781.5m.).

Economic Affairs

At the end of the 1970s approximately 18% of the labour force was employed in agriculture, but during the early 1980s numbers fell, so that agriculture now accounts for a little over 10% of the work-force. Israeli occupation of the West Bank in 1967 resulted in the loss of 80% of the fruit-growing area and 45% of the area under vegetables, and had a serious effect on cereal production. Only about 6% of Jordan's land is arable. The principal crops are wheat, barley, lentils, citrus fruits, tomatoes and watermelons. The Jordan Valley Authority has made great progress with irrigation schemes in the valley of the River Jordan.

Jordan, its economy underpinned by foreign aid and by remittances from Jordanian workers abroad (some 310,000 in 1983), has enjoyed sustained economic growth since the mid-1970s. Between 1974 and 1980, the East Bank region's gross domestic product (GDP) expanded, in real terms, at an average annual rate of more than 8%. Real GDP increased by 17.6% in 1980, but thereafter the growth rate slowed: it was 9.8% in 1981, 5.6% in 1982, 2.5% in 1983 and only 0.8% in 1984. Growth recovered to an estimated 3% in 1985. The current deficit on the balance of payments declined from US $390.7m. in 1983 to $260.5m. in 1985. Transfer payments (including receipts of workers' remittances) partly offset the chronic deficit on merchandise trade. The trade deficit was more than $2,400m. in each of the three years 1981–83, but eased to $2,032m. in 1984, when export earnings reached $752m. (compared with $579m. in 1983). The value of imports fell by 2.5% in 1985, exports rose by the same percentage, and the trade deficit narrowed to an estimated JD 856m. Recurring deficits have led the Government to seek new loans. In 1984 it obtained a $200.8m. Euroloan and in 1985 one of $215m. both with eight years' credit. The targets of the 1981–85 Development Plan were not met, and, owing to lack of funds, expenditure on development in the 1984 budget was reduced by 16.4%. to $533m., anticipating a budget deficit of $28.7m., and causing many large projects to be delayed. The 1985 budget proposals envisaged a 5% rise in public spending, presupposing a lower rate of economic growth than in the late 1970s, and the budget for 1986 proposed total expenditure of JD 923.7m. ($2,858m.), 14% higher than the figure proposed for 1985 (JD 811m.) and 5% higher than the revised total. Imports declined by 18.5% in 1986, and exports by 13.5%, as the balance of trade continued its gradual improvement. The budget for 1987 proposed total expenditure of JD 1,018.7m. ($3,150m.) (an increase of 10% compared with 1986), incorporating development spending of JD 433.6m. ($1,342m.), compared with JD 359.9m. ($1,113.9m.) in 1986, an increase of 20.5%. The budget deficit was projected at JD 39.6m. ($122.6m.), an increase of 5% compared with the 1986 figure of JD 37.7m. ($117.6m.).

There are a number of reasons for the relative decline in Jordan's economy. The bulk of Jordan's foreign aid comes from oil-rich Arab states and, as a 'front-line state' in the Arab–Israeli conflict, the country was pledged annual aid of $1,250m. for 10 years by the Arab League at its 1978 summit meeting in Baghdad. This figure has never been achieved, and the shortfall in anticipated aid widened from $500m. in 1982 to $669m. in 1983, and to $738m. in 1984. Jordan's stance on the split within the PLO, relations with Egypt and the search for a settlement of the Palestinian question is, undoubtedly, largely responsible for the failure of certain Arab countries to fulfil their aid obligations. Total Arab aid under the Baghdad agreement fell to $322m. in 1984, when Qatar and the UAE failed to pay and Kuwait reduced its payments by 40%. Only Saudi Arabia, of the seven original Arab donor countries, made its payments in full. In August 1985 Kuwait suspended its payments and put all future aid on a discretionary basis.

The amount of aid which Jordan receives is also dependent on the condition of the Middle East's petroleum industry. The falling price of petroleum has meant that less money has been available for the oil-based economies to give in aid. For similar reasons, there are fewer jobs and lower wages for expatriate Jordanian workers, 85% of whom work in the Gulf states, reducing the remittances which Jordan receives from them. Between 10,000 and 18,000 Jordanian workers returned to Jordan from the Gulf in 1984 and 1985, adding to an unemployment rate which was estimated at 6% of the working population in 1985. Workers' remittances are Jordan's principal source of foreign exchange, and their amount rose by 30% between 1980 and 1981. In real terms the income from remittances fell in 1982 but rose by 5% to JD 402m. ($1,040m.) in 1983. In 1984 remittances from the 320,000 Jordanians working abroad were worth JD 475m. ($1,228m.). The value of remittances declined to JD 403m. ($1,174m.) in 1985, but recovered to JD 435m. ($1,268m.) in 1986.

A further blow to Jordan's economy has been the loss of its major export market in Iraq, which is reduced to buying only goods that are essential to its war effort. Sales to Iraq fell from $174.2m. in 1982 to $67.6m. in 1983. The total recovered to $176.8m. in 1984, after the Jordanian Government proposed a barter system whereby Iraq undertook to pay for Jordanian goods in oil. Iraq originally replaced Syria, which had itself succeeded Egypt as Jordan's main trading partner after the severing of links with Egypt, which followed its peace treaty with Israel in 1979. Jordan's trade with Egypt is now developing again in tandem with the recently improved diplomatic relations between the two countries. Trade protocols with Egypt set bilateral trade at $150m. in 1985 and $250m. in 1986. Under the 1986–90 Five-Year Development Plan, expenditure has been set at JD 3,115m. ($9,727m.), 33% of which will be provided by foreign borrowing. The Plan aims for real growth in GDP of 5% per year, and, with 39% of total investment to be allocated to the services sector (compared with less than 30% in the previous Plan), it is hoped that as many as 100,000 jobs will be created during its term. The phosphate and potash industries and other important export industries are to be developed with a view to increasing the value of exports by an annual rate of 8.3%. It is also planned to restrict the annual growth of imports to 2.8% for goods and to 3.6% for services. These measures are intended to reduce the deficit on the current account—one of the Plan's key objectives.

In a country which is short of natural resources, phosphates predominate; they are Jordan's largest export commodity, accounting for 40% of sales ($160m.) in 1983. Returns have been affected by the low world price for phosphates, and Jordan is seeking to arrange part-payment of foreign contracts in phosphates. The Ruseifa mine closed in July 1985 because of falling world demand for low-grade phosphate. Production totalled an estimated 7m. tons in 1985 (compared with 6.26m. tons in 1984), but sales fell by 1.8%, to 4.61m. tons. Development plans centre on the Jordan Phosphate Mines Company's (JPMC's) three existing sites. In the longer term, however, the industry will probably focus on a major new mine at Shidiyah, in the south-east, which has proven phosphate reserves of 1,000m. tons and is expected to start producing at an annual rate of 800,000 tons in 1988, rising to 3m. tons by 1990 and to 7m. tons by the year 2000. Allied industries form an important part of Jordan's industrial development programme. A $450m. potash project on the Dead Sea began production in September 1982, and a $400m. phosphate fertilizer complex opened at Aqaba in December. The increased economic activity of Amman, owing to the disturbances in Beirut, and of Aqaba, because the Gulf War has closed Basra to the Iraqis, have benefited the economy.

Jordan possesses 45,000m. tons of oil-bearing shale, but the exploitation of this resource is in its infancy and the country is almost wholly dependent on imported petroleum for its energy needs. The imported crude petroleum is refined at Jordan's only refinery, at Zarqa. The annual capacity of the refinery was increased to about 4.5m. tons in 1984, and output rose to 2.6m. tons in 1985. Of this total, 1.8m. tons came from Saudi Arabia, 698,600 tons from Iraq, and 2,800 tons from Jordan's Hamzah oilfield. The country's oil import bill was $8m. in 1974, but higher prices for oil and greater domestic consumption caused the figure to rise to $540m. in 1983, and to $610m. in 1984. In December 1984 the Government announced a plan to double investment in oil exploration, following promising discoveries in Azraq, and to reduce oil consumption by cutting oil subsidies and by increasing the prices of electricity and petroleum-based products. The aim was to reduce the annual increase in oil consumption to zero in 1986. The level of oil subsidies was reduced from $92m. in 1984 to $70m. (JD 25m.) in 1985, and to $14m. (JD 5m.) in 1986. Overall energy consumption grew by only 3–4% in 1984, compared with the previous annual average of 17%. The cost of imported oil rose to $650m. in 1985, but fell to $600m. in 1986, or the equivalent of 90% of the value of export earnings. A Ministry of Energy and Mineral Wealth was created in November 1984. The delay in the proposed pipeline from Iraq to Aqaba was one reason for the renewal of an agreement to receive Saudi Arabian crude oil, via the Trans-Arabian Pipeline (Tapline), at the Zarqa refinery. Tapline had been due to close in November 1983 and, again, in 1985. Transit dues have trebled, however, and the total annual cost of the deal to Jordan is calculated at $26m.

Jordan's banking sector has grown with the economy, but the recent downturn has enforced a new caution. New rules for foreign banks were introduced by the Central Bank in the autumn of 1983, requiring 51% of their equity to be owned by Jordanians within three (later extended to five) years, to bring banks into line with all other foreign commercial establishments operating in Jordan since 1967, except insurance companies. However, in April 1985, the new Government of Zaid ar-Rifai abandoned the regulation, although this did not affect the requirement for all banks to raise their capital from JD 3m. to JD 5m. in common with local commercial banks. In July Said Nabulsi resigned as Governor of the Central Bank, as a result, it was thought, of the rejection of his measures to 'Jordanize' foreign banks. A moratorium on the issuing of licences for new banks is now operating. The number of institutions grew nearly three-fold to 36 in the decade from 1973.

Social Welfare

There is no comprehensive welfare scheme but the Government runs medical and health services. In 1985 the East Bank region had 44 hospital establishments, with 3,578 beds, and 2,576 physicians. A new Social Security Law, providing security for both employers and employees, was put into effect in 1978 and extended in 1981. In June 1986 there were 822,624 refugees registered with UNRWA in Jordan and a further 365,315 on the West Bank.

Education

Primary education is free and, where possible, compulsory. It starts at the age of five years and eight months and lasts for six years. A further three-year period, known as the preparatory cycle, is also compulsory. The preparatory cycle is followed by the three-year secondary cycle. UNRWA provides schooling for Palestinian Arab refugees. In 1983/84 there were 2,895 primary and secondary schools, of which more than 2,000 were state-run, with 820,113 pupils and 31,003 teachers. In 1981 an estimated 92% of East Bank children aged six to 11 attended primary schools. In 1979 about 70% of those aged 12 to 17 received secondary education. There are three universities, at Amman, Irbid and Mo'ata. In 1985 education accounted for JD 65.3m., or 8% of the total budget.

Tourism

The ancient cities of Jerash and Petra, and Jordan's proximity to biblical sites, have encouraged tourism. In 1984 there were 1,588,195 visitors to Jordan.

Public Holidays

1987: 15 January (Arbor Day), 22 March (Arab League Day), 28 March (Leilat al-Meiraj, Ascension of the Prophet), 25 May (Independence Day), 30 May (Id al-Fitr, end of Ramadan), 6 August (Id al-Adha), 11 August (King Hussein's Accession), 26 August (Islamic New Year), 4 November (Mouloud, Birth of the Prophet), 14 November (King Hussein's Birthday).

1988: 15 January (Arbor Day), 16 March (Leilat al-Meiraj), 22 March (Arab League Day), 18 May (Id al-Fitr, end of Ramadan), 25 May (Independence Day), 25 July (Id al-Adha), 11 August (King Hussein's Accession), 14 August (Islamic New Year), 23 October (Mouloud), 14 November (King Hussein's Birthday).

Weights and Measures

The metric system is in force. In Jordan the dunum is 1,000 sq m (0.247 acre).

Currency and Exchange Rates

1,000 fils = 1 Jordanian dinar (JD).
Exchange rates (30 September 1986):
 £1 sterling = 494.9 fils;
 US $1 = 342.0 fils.

JORDAN

Statistical Survey

Source: Department of Statistics, Jabal Amman, 1st Circle, POB 2015, Amman; tel. 24313.

Area and Population

AREA, POPULATION AND DENSITY
(East and West Banks)

Area (sq km)	97,740*
Population (UN estimates at mid-year)	
1984	3,380,000
1985	3,515,000
Density (per sq km) at mid-1985	36.0

* 37,738 sq miles.

East Bank: Area 89,206 sq km; population 2,132,997 at census of 10 November 1979; estimated population 2,693,700 at the end of 1985.

PRINCIPAL TOWNS
Population in December 1983: Amman (capital) 744,000; Zarqa 255,500; Irbid 131,200.

BIRTHS, MARRIAGES AND DEATHS (East Bank only)*

	Live Births	Marriages	Deaths
1980	89,635	15,597	6,771
1981	95,628	15,325	7,162
1982	97,974	17,488	7,741
1983	98,398	17,055	7,860
1984	102,521	18,189	8,303
1985	104,893	20,152	8,961

* Data are tabulated by year of registration rather than by year of occurrence. Figures exclude foreigners, but include registered Palestinian refugees.

Agriculture

PRINCIPAL CROPS (East Bank only; '000 metric tons)

	1983	1984	1985
Barley	28.2	11.9	19.7
Wheat	130.7	49.7	62.8
Lentils	8.4	n.a.	4.1
Citrus fruits	50.2	48.3	n.a.
Bananas	6.9	n.a.	n.a.
Olives	50.0	49.9	22.6
Tomatoes	212.3	208.7	293.5
Eggplants (Aubergines)	47.8	51.1	67.7
Onions and Garlic	7.2	n.a.	9.1
Cauliflowers and Cabbages	11.0	n.a.	25.3
Watermelons and Melons	48.4	n.a.	24.6
Potatoes	8.5	n.a.	16.6
Broadbeans (green)	3.6	n.a.	5.9
Cucumbers	53.7	n.a.	179.1

LIVESTOCK
(East Bank only; '000 head, year ending September)

	1983	1984	1985*
Horses	5	3	3
Mules	7	4	4
Asses	19	19	19
Cattle	35	35	35
Camels	17	16	15
Sheep	980	980	990
Goats	442	450	500
Poultry	30,000*	30,000	30,000

* FAO estimates.   † Unofficial figure.
Source: FAO, *Production Yearbook*.

Forestry

ROUNDWOOD REMOVALS ('000 cubic metres)*

	1982	1983	1984
Industrial wood	4	4	4
Fuel wood	5	5	5
Total	9	9	9

* FAO estimates.
Source: FAO, *Yearbook of Forest Products*.

Fishing

(East Bank only)

	1982	1983	1984
Quantity of fish landed at Aqaba and on Jordan and Yarmuk rivers (tons)	19.4	17.0	1.5

Mining and Industry

(East Bank only)

	1983	1984	1985
Phosphates ('000 metric tons)	4,745.9	6,119.6	6,067.1
Petroleum products ('000 metric tons)	2,231.5	2,272.3	2,182.6
Cement ('000 metric tons)	1,268.8	1,994.1	2,023.0
Iron ('000 metric tons)	148.2	112.5	136.3
Alcohol ('000 litres)	635.8	995.2	272.4
Beer ('000 litres)	6,279.3	5,021.6	4,639.0
Cigarettes (metric tons)	4,534.4	5,027.1	3,904.6
Electricity (million kWh)	1,918.2	2,265.0	2,496.0

1985: Potash 908,560 metric tons; Crude petroleum 1,882 metric tons.

Finance

CURRENCY AND EXCHANGE RATES

Monetary Units
1,000 fils = 1 Jordanian dinar (JD).

Denominations
Coins: 1, 5, 10, 20, 25, 50, 100 and 250 fils.
Notes: 500 fils; 1, 5, 10 and 20 dinars.

Sterling and Dollar Equivalents (30 September 1986)
£1 sterling = 494.9 fils;
US $1 = 342.0 fils;
100 JD = £202.07 = $292.40.

Average Exchange Rates (US $ per JD)
1983   2.7550
1984   2.6036
1985   2.5379

Note: Since 1975 the value of the Jordanian dinar has been linked to the IMF's special drawing right, with a mid-point exchange rate of JD 1 = SDR 2.579.

DEVELOPMENT EXPENDITURE ESTIMATES
(Five-Year Plan, 1981–85; US $ million)

Industry and mining	1,993
Transport	1,527
Water and irrigation	1,115
Housing	1,115
Education, culture and information	709
Agriculture	706
Electrical power	537
Municipal and rural affairs	475
Communications	306
Health	224
Tourism	178
Labour and social development	138
Trade	108
Royal Scientific Society and Dept of Statistics	33
Religious endowments	19
Other	49
Total	**9,233**

Source: National Planning Council.

BUDGET ESTIMATES (East Bank only; JD '000)*

Revenue	1984	1985
Direct taxes	49,000	55,000
Indirect taxes	200,700	230,000
Fees	65,870	81,600
Other internal receipts	122,150	113,300
Sub-total	437,720	479,900
Grants and loans	226,125	314,587
Total	663,845	794,487

Expenditure	1984	1985
Education	61,632	65,300
Health and social welfare	22,040	25,130
Defence and police	194,490	203,500
Other current expenditure	208,622	193,617
Development expenditure	259,367	323,675
Total	746,151	811,222

* Total expenditure comprises regular, military and development budgets.

1986: Revenue JD 886.0m.; Expenditure JD 923.7m.
1987: Revenue JD 979.1m.; Expenditure JD 1,018.7m.

CENTRAL BANK RESERVES
(US $ million at 31 December)

	1983	1984	1985
Gold*	199.5	172.2	189.8
IMF special drawing rights	18.2	15.5	24.1
Reserve position in IMF	7.6	—	—
Foreign exchange	798.4	499.5	398.7
Total	1,023.7	687.2	612.6

* National valuation.
Source: IMF, *International Financial Statistics*.

JORDAN

MONEY SUPPLY
(JD million at 31 December)

	1983	1984	1985
Currency outside banks	516.05	530.52	531.79
Demand deposits at commercial banks	338.68	336.87	308.45

Source: IMF, *International Financial Statistics*.

COST OF LIVING
(Consumer Price Index; base: 1980 = 100).

	1983	1984	1985
Food	116.1	118.4	121.0
Fuel and light	123.6	123.9	128.5
Clothing	138.0	138.7	138.5
Rent	123.2	130.4	138.1
All items (incl. others)	121.5	126.2	130.0

Source: ILO, *Year Book of Labour Statistics*.

NATIONAL ACCOUNTS (East Bank only; JD million at current prices)
Expenditure on the Gross Domestic Product

	1983	1984	1985
Government final consumption expenditure	348.3	376.9	405.9
Private final consumption expenditure	1,347.1	1,364.9	1,379.4
Increase in stocks	7.3	485.6	485.6
Gross fixed capital formation	502.8		
Total domestic expenditure	2,205.5	2,227.4	2,270.9
Exports of goods and services	638.2	744.1	779.1
Less Imports of goods and services	1,421.0	1,481.5	1,469.0
GDP in purchasers' values	1,422.7	1,490.0	1,581.0
GDP at constant 1980 prices	1,171.0	1,180.7	1,216.2

Source: IMF, *International Financial Statistics*.

BALANCE OF PAYMENTS (US $ million)

	1983	1984	1985
Merchandise exports f.o.b.	580.0	751.9	788.9
Merchanidse imports	−2,700.1	−2,472.6	−2,426.7
Trade balance	−2,120.1	−1,720.7	−1,637.9
Exports of services	1,297.5	1,231.7	1,268.2
Imports of services	−1,287.4	−1,491.6	−1,476.6
Balance on goods and services	−2,110.0	−1,980.6	−1,846.3
Private unrequited transfers (net)	923.9	1,028.1	846.2
Government unrequited transfers (net)	795.4	687.8	739.6
Current balance	−390.7	−264.7	−260.5
Direct capital investment (net)	30.1	74.8	25.7
Other long-term capital (net)	402.5	89.3	332.8
Short-term capital (net)	127.7	172.5	57.5
Net errors and omissions	−40.0	−48.2	−85.0
Total (net monetary movements)	129.6	23.6	70.5
Monetization of gold (net)	14.4	−11.7	0.3
Valuation changes (net)	−94.2	−319.2	29.1
Changes in reserves	49.8	−307.3	99.9

Source: IMF, *International Financial Statistics*.

External Trade

PRINCIPAL COMMODITIES (JD '000)

Imports	1983	1984	1985
Food and live animals	180,366	184,317	174,932
Beverages and tobacco	8,800	7,683	4,000
Crude materials (inedible) except fuels	31,403	29,890	33,044
Mineral fuels, lubricants, etc.	212,720	213,551	223,270
Animal and vegetable oils and fats	4,105	10,479	10,152
Chemicals	57,783	79,895	67,138
Basic manufactures	198,015	166,435	169,156
Machinery and transport equipment	262,035	215,853	205,579
Miscellaneous manufactured articles	92,333	95,927	103,529
Other commodities and transactions	55,750	67,310	75,925
Total	1,103,310	1,071,340	1,066,725

Exports	1983	1984	1985
Phosphates	51,611	69,613	66,084
Chemicals	36,791	67,629	50,959
Cement	17,981	33,777	39,718
Tomatoes	6,466	6,752	6,078
Other vegetables, fruit and nuts	32,928	35,900	32,524
Cigarettes	3,528	4,004	1,716
Machinery and transport equipment	1,996	1.972	2,104
Miscellaneous manufactured articles	9,227	33,416	18,513
Total (incl. others)	160,085	261,085	255,346

PRINCIPAL TRADING PARTNERS (JD '000)

Imports	1983	1984	1985
Belgium	19,188	21,075	21,621
France	42,320	48,370	33,938
Germany, Fed. Republic	87,743	67,033	65,638
Italy	60,233	62,661	73,427
Japan	102,889	79,064	67,814
Netherlands	24,391	26,708	26,006
Romania	16,350	16,004	14,668
Saudi Arabia	210,963	208,774	159,058
Spain	15,577	15,369	15,926
Switzerland	15,638	46,272	58,889
Taiwan	23,750	20,991	20,856
Turkey	30,614	34,854	28,583
USSR	13,936	11,093	6,262
United Kingdom	65,610	72,346	63,276
USA	131,048	119,263	128,045

Exports	1983	1984	1985
Australia	494	2,814	387
China, People's Republic	3,274	8,848	2,278
France	2,106	2,984	5,252
India	13,745	34,109	45,310
Indonesia	3,935	7,163	9,081
Iraq	26,011	67,755	65,850
Italy	4,927	5,761	3,654
Kuwait	10,454	10,393	7,734
Pakistan	5,976	11,218	5,941
Saudi Arabia	35,213	38,659	39,084
Syria	3,567	2,912	3,901
Taiwan	5,135	3,859	3,414
United Arab Emirates	4,764	3,450	3,612
Yugoslavia	2,605	5,979	3,069

Transport

RAILWAYS (East Bank only)

	1983	1984	1985
Passengers carried	33,438	30,196	34,247
Freight carried (tons)	2,595,279	3,152,663	2,582,702

ROAD TRAFFIC (motor vehicles registered, East Bank only)

	1983	1984	1985
Cars (private)	110,389	118,497	121,502
Taxis	12,308	12,439	12,699
Buses	3,050	3,346	3,513
Motorcycles	6,316	6,377	6,439
Others*	65,720	70,998	77,301
Total	197,783	211,657	221,454

* Trucks, vans, tankers, agricultural, construction and government vehicles.

SHIPPING (East Bank only; Aqaba port)

	1983	1984	1985
Number of vessels calling	2,454	2,329	2,671
Freight loaded ('000 tons)	5,059.1	7,158.1	8,177.6
Freight unloaded ('000 tons)	6,098.8	6,448.3	6,370.1

CIVIL AVIATION (East Bank only)

	1983	1984	1985
Passengers (number)	1,581,500	1,346,800	1,290,300
Freight (tons)	40,096	37,879	43,095

Tourism

(East Bank only)

	1983	1984	1985
Visitors to Jordan	2,424,900	2,271,600	2,677,021

Communications Media

(East Bank only)

	1983	1984	1985
Telephones in use	95,048	113,663	144,972

Radio receivers (1983): 620,000 in use.
Television receivers (1983): 220,000 in use.

Education

(East Bank)

	Schools	Teachers	Pupils
1982/83	2,840	30,115	795,877
1983/84	3,000	31,476	856,262
1984/85	3,065	34,119	863,892

Directory

The Constitution

The revised Constitution was approved by King Talal I on 1 January 1952.

The Hashemite Kingdom of Jordan is an independent, indivisible sovereign state. Its official religion is Islam; its official language Arabic.

RIGHTS OF THE INDIVIDUAL

There is to be no discrimination between Jordanians on account of race, religion or language. Work, education and equal opportunities shall be afforded to all as far as is possible. The freedom of the individual is guaranteed, as are his dwelling and property. No Jordanian shall be exiled. Labour shall be made compulsory only in a national emergency, or as a result of a conviction; conditions, hours worked and allowances are under the protection of the State.

The Press, and all opinions, are free, except under martial law. Societies can be formed, within the law. Schools may be established freely, but they must follow a recognized curriculum and educational policy. Elementary education is free and compulsory. All religions are tolerated. Every Jordanian is eligible for public office, and choices are to be made by merit only. Power belongs to the people.

THE LEGISLATIVE POWER

Is vested in the National Assembly and the King. The National Assembly consists of two houses: the Senate and the House of Representatives.

THE SENATE

The number of Senators is one-half of the number of members of the House of Representatives. Senators must be unrelated to the King, over 40, and are chosen from present and past Prime Ministers and Ministers, past Ambassadors or Ministers Plenipotentiary, past Presidents of the House of Representatives, past Presidents and members of the Court of Cassation and of the Civil and Sharia Courts of Appeal, retired officers of the rank of General and above, former members of the House of Representatives who have been elected twice to that House, etc. ... They may not hold public office. Senators are appointed for four years. They may be reappointed. The President of the Senate is appointed for two years.

THE HOUSE OF REPRESENTATIVES

The members of the House of Representatives are elected by secret ballot in a general direct election and retain their mandate for four years. General elections take place during the four months preceding the end of the term. The President of the House is elected by secret ballot each year by the Representatives. Representatives must be Jordanians of over 30, they must have a clean record, no active business interests, and are debarred from public office. Close relatives of the King are not eligible. If the House of Representatives is dissolved, the new House shall assemble in extraordinary session not more than four months after the date of dissolution. The new House cannot be dissolved for the same reason as the last. (The House was dissolved by Royal Decree in November 1974, and a National Consultative Council was formed in April 1978.)

GENERAL PROVISIONS FOR THE NATIONAL ASSEMBLY

The King summons the National Assembly to its ordinary session on 1 November each year. This date can be postponed by the King for two months, or he can dissolve the Assembly before the end of its three months' session. Alternatively, he can extend the session up to a total period of six months. Each session is opened by a speech from the throne.

Decisions in the House of Representatives and the Senate are made by a majority vote. The quorum is two-thirds of the total number of members in each House. When the voting concerns the Constitution, or confidence in the Council of Ministers, 'the votes shall be taken by calling the members by name in a loud voice'. Sessions are public, though secret sessions can be held at the request of the Government or of five members. Complete freedom of speech, within the rules of either House, is allowed.

The Prime Minister places proposals before the House of Representatives; if accepted there, they are referred to the Senate and finally sent to the King for confirmation. If one house rejects a law while the other accepts it, a joint session of the House of Representatives and the Senate is called, and a decision made by a two-thirds majority. If the King withholds his approval from a law, he returns it to the Assembly within six months with the reasons for his dissent; a joint session of the Houses then makes a decision, and if the law is accepted by this decision it is promulgated. The Budget is submitted to the National Assembly one month before the beginning of the financial year.

THE KING

The throne of the Hashemite Kingdom devolves by male descent in the dynasty of King Abdullah Ibn al Hussein. The King attains his majority on his eighteenth lunar year; if the throne is inherited by a minor, the powers of the King are exercised by a Regent or a Council of Regency. If the King, through illness or absence, cannot perform his duties, his powers are given to a Deputy, or to a Council of the Throne. This Deputy, or Council, may be appointed by

Iradas (decrees) by the King, or, if he is incapable, by the Council of Ministers.

On his accession, the King takes the oath to respect and observe the provisions of the Constitution and to be loyal to the nation. As head of the State he is immune from all liability or responsibility. He approves laws and promulgates them. He declares war, concludes peace and signs treaties; treaties, however, must be approved by the National Assembly. The King is Commander-in-Chief of the Navy, the Army and the Air Force. He orders the holding of elections; convenes, inaugurates, adjourns and prorogues the House of Representatives. The Prime Minister is appointed by him, as are the President and members of the Senate. Military and civil ranks are also granted, or withdrawn, by the King. No death sentence is carried out until he has confirmed it.

MINISTERS

The Council of Ministers consists of the Prime Minister, President of the Council, and of his Ministers. Ministers are forbidden to become members of any company, to receive a salary from any company, or to participate in any financial act of trade. The Council of Ministers is entrusted with the conduct of all affairs of State, internal and external.

The Council of Ministers is responsible to the House of Representatives for matters of general policy. Ministers may speak in either House, and, if they are members of one House, they may also vote in that House. Votes of confidence in the Council are cast in the House of Representatives, and decided by a two-thirds majority. If a vote of 'no confidence' is returned, the Ministers are bound to resign. Every newly-formed Council of Ministers must present its programme to the House of Representatives and ask for a vote of confidence. The House of Representatives can impeach Ministers, as it impeaches its own members.

AMENDMENTS

Two amendments were passed in November 1974 giving the King the right to dissolve the Senate or to take away membership from any of its members, and to postpone general elections for a period not to exceed a year, if there are circumstances in which the Council of Ministers feels that it is impossible to hold elections. A further amendment in February 1976 enabled the King to postpone elections indefinitely. In January 1984 two amendments were passed, allowing elections 'in any part of the country where it is possible to hold them' (effectively, only the East Bank) and empowering the National Assembly to elect deputies from the Israeli-held West Bank.

The Government

HEAD OF STATE

King HUSSEIN IBN TALAL (proclaimed King on 11 August 1952; crowned on 2 May 1953).
Chief of Royal Court: MARWAN AL-KASIM.
Minister to the Royal Court: ADNAN ABU AWDAH.

CABINET
(February 1987)

Prime Minister and Minister of Defence: ZAID AR-RIFAI.
Deputy Prime Minister and Minister of State for Prime Ministerial Affairs: ABDAL-WAHHAB AL-MAJALI.
Minister of Finance and Customs: Dr HANNA AWDAH.
Minister of Information, Culture, Tourism and Antiquities: MUHAMMAD AL-KHATIB.
Minister of Youth: EID AD-DAHAYYAT.
Minister of Justice: RIYADH ASH-SHAKAA.
Minister of Agriculture: MARWAN AL-HAMOUD.
Minister of Energy and Mineral Resources: Dr HISHAM AL-KHATIB.
Minister of Communications: MOHIEDDIN AL-HUSSAINI.
Minister of Occupied Territories Affairs: MARWAN DOUDIN.
Minister of Waqfs and Religious Affairs: ABDAL-AZIZ AL-KHAYAT.
Minister of Foreign Affairs: TAHER AL-MASRI.
Minister of Trade and Industry, and of Supply: Dr RAJAI AL-MUASHER.
Minister of Transport: AHMAD DAHQAN.
Minister of Education: DHOUQAN AL-HINDAWI.
Minister of Higher Education: NASR AD-DIN AL-ASAD.
Minister of Health: ZAID HAMZEH.
Minister of Labour and Social Development: KHALED AL-HAJ HASSAN.
Minister of the Interior: RAJAI AD-DAJANI.
Minister of Planning: ABDULLAH AL-MUSOUR.
Minister of Public Works: MAHMOUD HAWAMDEH.
Minister of Municipal, Rural and Environmental Affairs: YOUSEF HAMDAN.
Minister of State for Parliamentary Affairs: SAMI JOUDEH.

MINISTRIES

Office of the Prime Minister: POB 80, 35216, Amman; tel. 641211; telex 21444.
Ministry of Agriculture: POB 2099, Amman; tel. 636152.
Ministry of Communications: POB 71, Amman; tel. 624301; telex 21666.
Ministry of Culture and Information: POB 1794, Amman; tel. 661147; telex 21749.
Ministry of Defence: POB 1577, Amman; tel. 644361; telex 21200.
Ministry of Education: POB 1646, Amman; tel. 638781; telex 21396.
Ministry of Finance: POB 85, Amman; tel. 636321; telex 21424.
Ministry of Foreign Affairs: POB 1577, Amman; tel. 644361; telex 21255.
Ministry of Health: POB 86, Amman; tel. 665131; telex 21595.
Ministry of the Interior: POB 100, Amman; tel. 663111; telex 23162.
Ministry of Justice: POB 6040, Amman; tel. 663101.
Ministry of Labour: POB 9052, Amman; tel. 630343.
Ministry of Municipal, Rural and Environmental Affairs: POB 1799, Amman; tel. 641393.
Ministry of Occupied Territories Affairs: POB 2469, Amman; tel. 666172.
Ministry of Public Works: POB 1220, Amman; tel. 624191; telex 21944.
Ministry of Social Development: POB 6720, Amman; tel. 643838.
Ministry of Supply: POB 830, Amman; tel. 630371; telex 21278.
Ministry of Tourism and Antiquities: POB 224, Amman; tel. 642311; telex 21741.
Ministry of Trade and Industry: POB 2019, Amman; tel. 663191; telex 21163.
Ministry of Transport: POB 1929, Amman; tel. 641461; telex 21541.
Ministry of Waqfs and Religious Affairs: POB 659, Amman; tel. 666141; telex 21559.

Legislature

MAJLIS AL-UMMA
(National Assembly)

Senate

The Senate (House of Notables) consists of 30 members, appointed by the King. A new Senate was appointed by the King on 12 January 1984.
President: AHMAD AL-LOUZI.

House of Representatives

Elections to the then 60-seat House of Representatives (30 from both the East and West Banks) took place in April 1967. There were no political parties. The House was dissolved by Royal Decree on 23 November 1974, but reconvened briefly on 15 February 1976. Elections were postponed indefinitely.

In April 1978 a National Consultative Council was formed by Royal Decree. It consisted of 60 members appointed by the King, and served terms of two years. The third term began on 20 April 1982. The King, by his constitutional right, dissolved the Council on 7 January 1984 and reconvened the House of Representatives. Eight members from the East Bank had died since the House was last convened and by-elections to fill their seats took place on 12 March 1984. The seven vacant seats of members from the Israeli-

JORDAN

occupied West Bank, where elections could not take place, were filled by a vote of the members of the House in accordance with a constitutional amendment unanimously approved on 9 January 1984.

In March 1986 the House of Representatives approved a draft electoral law increasing the number of seats in the House from 60 to 142 (71 from the East Bank and 71 from the West Bank, including 11 from the refugee camps in the East Bank).

Speaker: AKEF AL-FAYEZ.

Political Organizations

Political parties were banned before the elections of July 1963. In September 1971 King Hussein announced the formation of a Jordanian National Union. This was the only political organization allowed. Communists, Marxists and 'other advocates of imported ideologies' were ineligible for membership. In March 1972 the organization was renamed the Arab National Union. In April 1974 King Hussein dissolved the executive committee of the Arab National Union, and accepted the resignation of the Secretary-General. In February 1976 the Cabinet approved a law abolishing the Union. Membership was estimated at about 100,000.

Diplomatic Representation

EMBASSIES IN JORDAN

Algeria: 3rd Circle, Jabal Amman; tel. 641271; Ambassador: ABDERRAHMAN SHRAYYET.
Australia: 4th Circle, Jabal Amman; tel. 673246; telex 21743; Ambassador: RICHARD GATE.
Austria: POB 815368, Amman; tel. 644635; telex 22484; Ambassador: Dr ARNOLD MOEBIUS.
Bahrain: Amman; tel. 664148; Ambassador: IBRAHIM ALI IBRAHIM.
Belgium: Amman; tel. 675683; telex 22340; Ambassador: GUIDO VANSINA.
Brazil: POB 5497, Amman; tel. 642183; telex 23827; Ambassador: FELIX BAPTISTA DE FARIA.
Bulgaria: POB 950578, Um Uzaina al-Janoubi, Amman; tel. 818151; telex 22247; Ambassador: YANTCHO DEMIREV.
Canada: POB 815403, Pearl of Shmeisani Bldg, Shmeisani, Amman; tel. 666124; telex 23080; Ambassador: GARY R. HARMAN.
Chile: Shmeisani, Amman; tel. 661336; telex 21696; Chargé d'affaires a.i.: ALBERTO YOACHAM.
China, People's Republic: Shmeisani, Amman; tel. 666139; telex 21770; Ambassador: ZHANG ZHEN.
Czechoslovakia: POB 2213, Amman; tel. 665105; Ambassador: KAREL FISER.
Egypt: POB 35178, Zahran St, 3rd Circle, Jabal Amman; tel. 641375; Ambassador: IHAB SEID WAHBA.
France: POB 374, Jabal Amman; tel. 641273; telex 21219; Ambassador: PATRICK LECLERCQ.
Germany, Federal Republic: Al-Afghani St, POB 183, Jabal Amman; tel. 641351; telex 1235; Ambassador: Dr HERWIG BARTELS.
Greece: POB 35069, Jabal Amman; tel. 672331; telex 21566; Ambassador: HANNIBAL VELLIADIS.
Hungary: POB 3441, Amman; tel. 674916; telex 21815; Ambassador: ZOLTÁN SZEPHELYI.
India: POB 2168, 1st Circle, Jabal Amman; tel. 637262; telex 21068; Ambassador: GURCHARAN SINGH.
Iran: POB 173, Jabal Amman; tel. 641281 telex 21218.
Iraq: POB 2025, 1st Circle, Jabal Amman; tel. 639331; telex 21277; Ambassador: (vacant).
Italy: POB 9800, Jabal Luweibdeh, Amman; tel. 638185; telex 21113; Ambassador: LUIGI AMADUZZI.
Japan: Jabal Amman; tel. 672486; telex 21518; Ambassador: AKIRA NAKAYAMA.
Korea, Democratic People's Republic: Amman; tel. 666349; Chargé d'affaires: KIM YONG HO.
Korea, Republic: 3rd Circle, Jabal Amman, Abu Tamman St, POB 3060, Amman; tel. 642268; telex 29457; Ambassador: DONG-SOON PARK.

Directory

Kuwait: POB 2107, Jabal Amman; tel. 641235; telex 21377; Ambassador: IBRAHIM AL-BAHO.
Lebanon: 2nd Circle, Jabal Amman; tel. 641381; Ambassador: PIERRE ZIADÉ.
Morocco: Jabal Amman; tel. 641451; telex 21661; Chargé d'affaires: SALEM FANKHAR ASH-SHANFARI.
Oman: Amman; tel. 661131; telex 21550; Ambassador: KHAMIS BIN HAMAD AL-BATASHI.
Pakistan: Amman; tel. 622787; Ambassador: Prof. EHSAN RASHID.
Philippines: Shmeisani, Amman; tel. 661642; telex 23321; Ambassador: CESAR PASTORES.
Poland: 1st Circle, Jabal Amman; tel. 637153; telex 21119; Ambassador: LUDWIK JANCZYSZYN.
Qatar: Amman; tel. 644331; telex 21248; Ambassador: Sheikh HAMAD BIN MUHAMMAD BIN JABER ATH-THANI.
Romania: Amman; tel. 663161; Ambassador: TEODOR COMAN.
Saudi Arabia: POB 2133, 5th Circle, Jabal Amman; tel. 644154; Ambassador: Sheikh IBRAHIM MUHAMMAD AS-SULTAN.
Spain: Jabal Amman; tel. 622140; telex 21224; Ambassador: EMILIO MENÉNDEZ DEL VALLE.
Sudan: Jabal Amman; tel. 624145; telex 21778; Ambassador: AHMAD DIAB.
Sweden: Shmeisani, Amman; tel. 669177; Ambassador: INGEMAR STJERNBERG.
Switzerland: Jabal Amman; tel. 644416; telex 21237; Ambassador: HARALD BORNER.
Syria: POB 1377, 4th Circle, Jabal Amman; tel. 641935; Chargé d'affaires: MAJID ABOU SALEH.
Tunisia: Jabal Amman; tel. 674307; telex 21849; Ambassador: SAID BEN MUSTAPHA.
Turkey: POB 2062, Queen Zain ash-Sharaf St, 2nd Circle, Jabal Amman; tel. 641251; telex 21237; Ambassador: SEMIH BELEN.
USSR: Amman; tel. 641158; Ambassador: ALEKSANDR IVANOVICH ZINCHUK.
United Arab Emirates: Jabal Amman; tel. 644369; telex 21832; Ambassador: ABDULLAH ALI ASH-SHURAFA.
United Kingdom: POB 87, 3rd Circle, Jabal Amman, Amman; tel. 641261; telex 22209; Ambassador: A. J. COLES.
USA: POB 354, Jabal Amman; tel. 644371; telex 21510; Ambassador: PAUL BOEKER.
Yemen Arab Republic: Amman; tel. 642381; telex 23526; Ambassador: ALI ABDULLAH ABU LUHOUM.
Yugoslavia: POB 5227, Amman; tel. 665107; telex 21505; Ambassador: TODOR BOJADZIJEVSKI.

Judicial System

With the exception of matters of purely personal nature concerning members of non-Muslim communities, the law of Jordan was based on Islamic Law for both civil and criminal matters. During the days of the Ottoman Empire, certain aspects of Continental law, especially French commercial law and civil and criminal procedure, were introduced. Due to British occupation of Palestine and Transjordan from 1917 to 1948, the Palestine territory has adopted, either by statute or case law, much of the English common law. Since the annexation of the non-occupied part of Palestine and the formation of the Hashemite Kingdom of Jordan, there has been a continuous effort to unify the law.

Court of Cassation. The Court of Cassation consists of seven judges, who sit in full panel for exceptionally important cases. In most appeals, however, only five members sit to hear the case. All cases involving amounts of more than JD100 may be reviewed by this Court, as well as cases involving lesser amounts and cases which cannot be monetarily valued. However, for the latter types of cases, review is available only by leave of the Court of Appeal, or, upon refusal by the Court of Appeal, by leave of the President of the Court of Cassation. In addition to these functions as final and Supreme Court of Appeal, the Court of Cassation also sits as High Court of Justice to hear applications in the nature of habeas corpus, mandamus and certiorari dealing with complaints of a citizen against abuse of governmental authority.

Courts of Appeal. There are two Courts of Appeal, each of which is composed of three judges, whether for hearing of appeals or for

JORDAN

dealing with Magistrates Courts' judgments in chambers. Jurisdiction of the two Courts is geographical, with the Court for the Western Region sitting in Jerusalem (which has not sat since June 1967) and the Court for the Eastern Region sitting in Amman. The regions are separated by the River Jordan. Appellate review of the Courts of Appeal extends to judgments rendered in the Courts of First Instance, the Magistrates' Courts, and Religious Courts.

Courts of First Instance. The Courts of First Instance are courts of general jurisdiction in all matters civil and criminal except those specifically allocated to the Magistrates' Courts. Three judges sit in all felony trials, while only two judges sit for misdemeanour and civil cases. Each of the seven Courts of First Instance also exercises appellate jurisdiction in cases involving judgments of less than JD20 and fines of less than JD10, rendered by the Magistrates' Courts.

Magistrates' Courts. There are 14 Magistrates' Courts, which exercise jurisdiction in civil cases involving no more than JD250 and in criminal cases involving maximum fines of JD100 or maximum imprisonment of one year.

Religious Courts. There are two types of religious court: The Shari'ah Courts (Muslims): and the Ecclesiastical Courts (Eastern Orthodox, Greek Melkite, Roman Catholic and Protestant). Jurisdiction extends to personal (family) matters, such as marriage, divorce, alimony, inheritance, guardianship, wills, interdiction and, for the Muslim community, the constitution of Waqfs (Religious Endowments). When a dispute involves persons of different religious communities, the Civil Courts have jurisdiction in the matter unless the parties agree to submit to the jurisdiction of one or the other of the Religious Courts involved.

Each Shari'ah (Muslim) Court consists of one judge (Qadi), while most of the Ecclesiastical (Christian) Courts are normally composed of three judges, who are usually clerics. Shari'ah Courts apply the doctrines of Islamic Law, based on the Koran and the Hadith (Precepts of Muhammad), while the Ecclesiastical Courts base their law on various aspects of Canon Law. In the event of conflict between any two Religious Courts or between a Religious Court and a Civil Court, a Special Tribunal of three judges is appointed by the President of the Court of Cassation, to decide which court shall have jurisdiction. Upon the advice of experts on the law of the various communities, this Special Tribunal decides on the venue for the case at hand.

Religion

Over 80% of the population are Sunni Muslims, and the King can trace unbroken descent from the Prophet Muhammad. There is a Christian minority, living mainly in the towns, and there are smaller numbers of non-Sunni Muslims.

ISLAM

Chief Justice and President of the Supreme Muslim Secular Council: Sheikh MUHAMMAD MHELAN.

Director of Shari'ah Courts: Sheikh SUBHI AL-MUWQQAT.

Mufti of the Hashemite Kingdom of Jordan: Sheikh MUHAMMAD ABDO HASHEM.

CHRISTIANITY
The Roman Catholic Church

Latin Rite

Jordan forms part of the Patriarchate of Jerusalem (see chapter on Israel).

Vicar-General for Transjordan: Mgr SELIM SAYEGH (Titular Bishop of Aquae in Proconsulari), Latin Vicariate, POB 1317, Amman.

Melkite Rite

The Greek-Melkite archdiocese of Petra (Wadi Musa) and Philadelphia (Amman) contained an estimated 18,506 adherents at 31 December 1984.

Archbishop of Petra and Philadelphia: Most Rev. SABA YOUAKIM, Archevêché Grec-Melkite Catholique, POB 2434, Jabal Amman; tel. 624757.

Syrian Rite

The Patriarch of Antioch is resident in Beirut, Lebanon.

Patriarchal Vicariate of Jerusalem: Mont Achrafieh, Rue Barto, POB 10041, Amman; Vicar Patriarchal Mgr PIERRE ABDAL-AHAD.

The Press
DAILIES

Al-Akhbar (News): POB 62420, Amman; f. 1976; Arabic; publ. by the Arab Press Co; Editor RACAN EL-MAJALI; circ. 15,000.

Ad-Dustour (The Constitution): POB 591, Amman; tel. 664153; telex 21392; f. 1967; Arabic; publ. by the Jordan Press and Publishing Co; owns commercial printing facilities; Chair. OSAMA M. ASH-SHERIF; Gen. Man. KAMEL ASH-SHERIF; circ. 85,000.

Ar-Rai (Opinion): POB 6710, Amman; tel. 667161; telex 1497; f. 1971; Arabic; independent; published by Jordan Press Foundation; Gen. Man. JUMA'A HAMMAD; Editor-in-Chief MAHMOUD KAYED; circ. 80,000.

The Jordan Times: POB 6710, Amman; tel. 667171; telex 1497; f. 1975; English; published by Jordan Press Foundation; Responsible Editor MUHAMMAD AMAD; Editor GEORGE S. HAWATMEH; circ. 15,000.

Sawt ash-Shaab (Voice of the People): Amman; f. 1983.

PERIODICALS

Akhbar al-Usbou (News of the Week): POB 605, Amman; tel. 677881; telex 21644; f. 1959; weekly; Arabic; economic, social, political; Chief Editor and Publr ABDUL-HAFIZ MUHAMMAD; circ. 100,000.

Al-Aqsa (The Ultimate): POB 1957, Amman; weekly; armed forces magazines.

Al-Fajr al-Iqtisadi (Economic Dawn): Amman; f. 1982; weekly; economic; owned by Al-Fajr for Press, Publication and Distribution; Dir-Gen. and Editor-in-Chief YOUSSEF ABU-LAIL.

Huda El-Islam (The Right Way of Islam): POB 659, Amman; tel. 666141; telex 21559; f. 1956; monthly; Islamic; scientific and literary; published by the Ministry of Waqfs and Religious Affairs; Editor Dr AHMAD MUHAMMAD HULAYYEL.

The Jerusalem Star: POB 591, Amman; tel. 664153; telex 21392; f. 1982; weekly; English; publ. by Jordan Press and Publishing Co; Dir SAIF ASH-SHARIF; Editor-in-Chief OSAMA M. ASH-SHERIF; circ. 15,000.

Jordan: POB 224, Amman; f. 1969; published quarterly by Jordan Information Bureau, Washington; circ. 100,000.

Al-Liwa (The Standard): Amman; f. 1972; weekly; Arabic; Chief Editor HASSAN ATTEL.

Military Magazine: Army Headquarters, Amman; f. 1955; quarterly; dealing with military and literary subjects; published by Armed Forces.

Shari'ah: POB 585, Amman; f. 1959; fortnightly; Islamic affairs; published by Shari'ah College; circ. 5,000.

Shehan: Al-Karak; Editor REYAD AL-HROUB.

NEWS AGENCIES

Jordan News Agency (PETRA): POB 6845, Amman; f. 1965; government-controlled; Dir-Gen. JAWAD MARAQA.

Foreign News Bureaux

Agence France-Presse (AFP): POB 3340, Amman; Bureau Man. FOUAD NAIM.

Agenzia Nazionale Stampa Associata (ANSA) (Italy): POB 35111, Amman; tel. 642936; telex 00493; Correspondent JOHN HALABI.

Deutsche Presse Agentur (dpa) (Federal Republic of Germany): POB 35111, Amman; tel. 623907; telex 21207; Correspondent JOHN HALABI.

Reuters (UK): POB 667, Amman; tel. 623776; telex 21414.

Telegrafnoye Agentstvo Sovetskovo Soyuza (TASS) (USSR): Jabal Amman, Nabich Faris St, Block 111/83 124, Amman; Correspondent NIKOLAI LEBEDINSKY.

AP (USA), Central News Agency (Taiwan), Iraqi News Agency, Middle East News Agency (Egypt), Qatar News Agency, Saudi Press Agency and UPI (USA) also maintain bureaux in Amman.

Publishers

Jordan Press and Publishing Co Ltd: Amman; tel. 664153; telex 21392; f. 1967 by *Al-Manar* and *Falastin* dailies; publishes *Ad-Dustour* (daily), and *The Jerusalem Star* (English weekly);

Chair. Osama M. ash-Sharif; Gen. Man. Kamel ash-Sharif; Editor-in-Chief Abd as-Salam Tarawneh.

Other publishers in Amman include: Dairat al-Ihsaat al-Amman, George N. Kawar, Al-Matbaat al-Hashmiya and The National Press.

Radio and Television

Number of radio receivers, an estimated 700,000; number of TV receivers 240,000 (East Bank only).

Jordan Radio and Television Corporation: POB 1041, Amman; tel. 773111; telex 21285; f. 1968; government station broadcasting for 90 hours weekly in Arabic and English; in colour; advertising accepted; Dir-Gen. Nasouh Majali; Dir (Television) Dr Marwan Khair; Dir (Eng.) Radi Alkhas.

Finance

(cap.=capital; p.u.=paid up; dep.=deposits; m.=million; res=reserves; brs=branches; JD=Jordanian dinars)

BANKING

Central Bank

Central Bank of Jordan: POB 37, King Hussein St, Amman; tel. 630301; telex 21250; f. 1966; cap. p.u. JD6m., dep. JD158.6m., res JD12m. (Dec. 1984); Gov. Hussain al-Kasim.

National Banks

Arab Bank Ltd: POB 950545, King Faisal St, Amman; tel. 660131; telex 23091; f. 1930; cap. p.u. JD22m., dep. JD2,902.8m., total assets JD3,079.8m. (Dec. 1985); 23 brs in Jordan, more than 80 brs and affiliates abroad; Chair. Abd al-Majid Shoman.

Bank of Jordan Ltd: POB 2140, 3rd Circle, Jabal Amman, Amman; tel. 644327; telex 22033; f. 1960; cap. p.u. JD3m., dep. JD73m., total assets 95.6m. (Dec. 1985); 23 brs; Chair. Tawfik Shaker Fakhouri; Gen. Man. Michael Marto.

Cairo Amman Bank: POB 715, Shabsough St, Amman; tel. 639321; telex 21240; f. 1960; cap. p.u. JD5m., (Dec. 1985); 12 brs; Chair. and Gen. Man. Jawdat Shasha'a; associated with Banque du Caire, Cairo, which has a 12% share in the bank, and succeeded their Amman Branch; remaining 88% is owned by local interests.

Jordan-Gulf Bank SA: POB 9989, Shmeissani, Al-Burj Area, Amman; tel. 603931; telex 21959; f. 1977; cap. p.u. JD6m., dep. JD96.2m., total assets JD117.1m. (June 1985); 60% Jordanian-owned and 40% by Gulf businessmen; 22 brs; Chair. HE Muhammad Nazzal al-Armouti; Gen. Man. Adnan Darwaza.

Jordan Islamic Bank for Finance and Investment: POB 926225, Amman; tel. 677377; telex 21125; f. 1978; cap. p.u. JD6m., dep. JD115.9m., total assets JD297.4m. (June 1986); 12 brs; Chair. Sheikh Saleh Kamel; Gen. Man. Musa A. Shihadeh.

Jordan Kuwait Bank: POB 9776, Amman; tel. 662125; telex 21994; f. 1976; cap. p.u. JD5m., dep. JD108m. (Dec. 1985); Chair. Sheikh Nasser Al-Sabah; Deputy Chair. and Gen. Man. Sufian Ibrahim Yassin Sartawi; 14 brs.

Jordan National Bank SA: POB 1578, Amman; tel. 642391; telex 21820; f. 1956; cap. p.u. JD9.2m., dep. JD111m., res JD12.8m. (Dec. 1985); 30 brs in Jordan, 5 brs in Lebanon, 1 br. in Cyprus; Chair. HE Abd al-Kader Tash; Deputy Chair. Yousif I. Mou'asher.

Petra Bank: POB 6854, Seil St, Amman; tel. 630396; telex 21868; f. 1977; cap. p.u. JD5m. (Dec. 1985); 60% owned by Jordanians and 40% by other Arab interests; 23 brs in Jordan; Chair. and Gen. Man. Dr Ahmad Chalabi.

Syrian Jordanian Bank: POB 926636, King Hussein St, Amman; tel. 661138; telex 22102; f. 1979; cap. p.u. JD1m. total assets 11.5m. (1985); Chair. Management Cttee Dr Maher G. Shukri.

Foreign Banks

The British Bank of the Middle East (Hong Kong): POB 925286, Amman; tel. 669121; telex 22338; f. 1889; cap. p.u. JD5m., dep. JD53.2m., total assets JD61.2m. (Dec. 1985); 5 brs; Chair. M. G. R. Sandberg; Area Man. C. R. Morgan.

Grindlays Bank (United Kingdom): POB 9997, Shmeissani, Amman; tel. 660301; telex 21980; cap. p.u. JD5m., dep. JD42m. (Dec. 1986); brs in Amman (8 brs), Aqaba, Irbid (sub-branch in Northern Shouneh), Zerka and Kerak; Gen. Man. in Jordan D. F. McKenzie.

Rafidain Bank (Iraq): POB 1194, Amman; tel. 624365; telex 1334; f. 1941; 4 brs; cap. p.u. JD3m., res JD548,263, dep. JD10.2m. (Dec. 1983); Gen. Man. Adnan al-Azawi.

Other foreign banks with branches in Amman are Arab Land Bank, Bank Al-Mashrek, Bank of Credit and Commerce International and Citibank.

Specialized Credit Institutions

Agricultural Credit Corporation: POB 77, Amman; tel. 661105; f. 1959; cap. p.u. JD12m., total assets JD27m. (Dec. 1985); Chair. Dr Sami Suna'a; 18 brs.

The Arab Jordan Investment Bank: POB 8797, Amman; tel. 664126; telex 21719; f. 1978; cap. p.u. JD84.9m., total assets JD100m. (Dec. 1985); Chair. and Gen. Man. Abd al-Kader al-Qadi.

Cities and Villages Development Bank: POB 1572, Amman; tel. 668151; telex 22476; f. 1979; cap. p.u. JD11.3m., dep. JD9.7m., total assets JD4.9m. (Dec. 1984); Gen. Man. Muhammad Saleh Hourani.

Housing Bank: Police College St, Abdali, POB 7693, Amman; tel. 667126; telex 21693; f. 1973; cap. p.u. JD12m. (Dec. 1983), total assets JD382m. (Dec. 1985); Chair. and Dir-Gen. Zuhair Khouri; 65 brs.

Industrial Development Bank: POB 1982, Jabal Amman, Zahran St, Amman; tel. 642216; telex 21349; f. 1965; cap. p.u. JD5.69m., total assets JD55.86m. (1985); Chair. Rouhi el-Khateeb; Gen. Man. Ziyad Annab.

Jordan Co-operative Organization: POB 1343, Amman; tel. 665171; telex 21835; f. 1968; cap. p.u. JD2.4m., dep JD2.3m., total assets JD32m. (Dec. 1983); Pres. and Dir-Gen. Hassan S. Nabulsi.

Jordan Islamic Bank for Finance and Investment: POB 926225, Shmeissani, Amman; tel. 666325; telex 21125; f. 1978; cap. p.u. JD4m., dep. JD59.1m., res JD359,283, total assets JD79.9m (Dec. 1983); Gen. Man. Musa A. Shihadeh; 8 brs.

Jordan Securities Corporation: POB 926691, Amman; tel. 664183; telex 22258; f. 1979; cap. p.u. JD4m., res JD1.9m., dep. JD17.6m., total assets JD30.9m. (Dec. 1985); Chair. Zuhair Khouri; Gen. Mans Salem Masa'deh, Abdel Kadir Dweek.

Social Security Corporation: POB 926031, Amman; telex 22287; f. 1978; Dir-Gen. Dr M. Mahdi el-Farhan.

STOCK EXCHANGE

Amman Financial Market: POB 8802, Amman; tel. 663170; telex 21711; f. 1978; Gen. Man. Dr Hashim Sabagh.

INSURANCE

Al-Ahlia Insurance Co (Jordan) Ltd: POB 2938, UTG. Bldg, Shmeisani, opposite Syndicates Bldg, Sharif Abdel Hamid Sharaf St, Amman; tel. 677689; telex 23503; merged with the National Insurance Co Dec. 1985.

Jordan Insurance Co Ltd: POB 279, King Hussein St, Amman; tel. 622186; telex 21486; f. 1951; cap. p.u. JD1,100,000m.; Chair. and Man. Dir Jawdat Shasha'a; 9 brs (4 in Saudi Arabia, 4 in the United Arab Emirates, 1 in Kuwait).

Middle East Insurance Co Ltd: POB 1802, King Hussein St, Amman; tel. 621245; telex 21420; f. 1963; cap. p.u. JD1m.; Chair. Samir F. Kawar; Gen. Man. S. I. Gammoh.

United Insurance Co Ltd: POB 7521, United Bldg, King Hussein St, Amman; tel. 625161; telex 21323; f. 1972; merged with the Arab Belgium Insurance Co Jan. 1986; all types of insurance; Chair. Raouf Sa'ad Abujaber.

A new regulation of December 1984, affecting nine of the local insurance companies, required companies to raise their capital to JD600,000 by the end of 1986 or to merge with other companies. Three mergers had taken place by August 1986, reducing the number of local companies to 18. There are also 11 foreign insurance companies operating in Jordan. The first reinsurance company in the country was registered on 1 January 1987.

Trade and Industry

CHAMBERS OF COMMERCE AND INDUSTRY

Amman Chamber of Commerce: POB 287, Amman; tel. 666151; telex 21543; f. 1923; Pres. Muhammad Ali Bdeir; Dr Rajeh Amin.

Amman Chamber of Industry: POB 1800, Amman; tel. 641648; telex 22079; f. 1962; Pres. Isam Bdeir; Exec. Dir Muhammad S. Jaber.

JORDAN   Directory

PUBLIC CORPORATION

Jordan Valley Authority: POB 2769, Amman; tel. 642472; telex 21692; Stage I development projects now complete, and addition of 9,300 ha to the irrigated land has been accomplished. Infrastructure projects also completed include 1,100 km of roads, 2,100 housing units, 100 schools, 15 health centres, 14 administration buildings, 4 marketing centres, 2 community centres, 2 vocational training centres. Electricity is now provided to all the towns and villages in the valley from the national network and domestic water is supplied to them from tube wells. Contributions to the cost of development came through loans from Kuwait Fund, Abu Dhabi Fund, Saudi Fund, Arab Fund, USAID, Fed. Germany, World Bank, EEC, Italy, Netherlands, UK, Japan and OPEC Special Fund. Many of the Stage II irrigation projects are now completed or under implementation. Projects under way include the construction of the Wadi al-Arab Dam, the raising of the King Talal Dam and the 14.5-km extension of the 98-km East Ghor Main Canal. Stage II will include the irrigation of 4,700 ha in the southern Ghors. The target for the programme is to irrigate 43,000 ha of land in the Jordan Valley. Future development in irrigation will include the construction of the Maqarin Dam and the Wadi Malaha Storage Dam.

PHOSPHATES

Jordan Phosphate Mines Co Ltd (JPMC): POB 30, Amman; tel. 660141; telex 21223; engaged in production and export of rock phosphate; Chair. ALI KHRAIS; Dir-Gen. WASEF AZAR; Marketing and Sales Man. MAKRAM ZOREKAT; production (1984) 6.26m. tons.

TRADE UNIONS

The General Federation of Jordanian Trade Unions: Wadi as-Sir Rd, POB 1065, Amman; f. 1954; 33,000 mems; member of Arab Trade Unions Confederation; Chair. SAMI HASSAN MANSOUR; Gen. Sec. ABDAR-RAZZAQ HAMAD.

There are also a number of independent unions, including:

Drivers' Union: POB 846, Amman; Sec.-Gen. SAMI HASSAN MANSOUR.

Union of Petroleum Workers and Employees: POB 1346, Amman; Sec.-Gen. BRAHIM HADI.

Transport

RAILWAYS

Aqaba Railway Corporation: POB 50, Ma'an; tel. 332234; telex 62225; f. 1979; length of track 292 km (1,050-mm gauge); Dir-Gen. M. QATAMIN.

Formerly a division of the Hedjaz Jordan Railway; it retains close links with the Hedjaz but there is no regular through traffic between Aqaba and Amman. It comprises the Hedjaz line south of Menzil and the 115-km extension to Aqaba, opened in October 1975, which serves phosphate mines at El-Hasa and Wadi El-Abyad. A development programme is being implemented to increase the transport capacity of the line to 4m. tons of phosphate per year. Plans for connecting the new phosphate mine at Shidiya to the railway system by 1990/91 are under consideration.

Hedjaz Jordan Railway (administered by the Ministry of Transport): POB 582, Amman; tel. 655413; telex 1236; f. 1902; length of track 326 km (1,050-mm gauge); Chair. and Dir-Gen. A. H. AD-DJAZI.

This was formerly a section of the Hedjaz railway (Damascus to Medina) for Muslim pilgrims to Medina and Mecca. It crosses the Syrian border and enters Jordanian territory south of Dera'a, and runs for approximately 366 km to Naqb Ishtar, passing through Zarka, Amman, Qatrana and Ma'an. Some 844 km of the line, from Ma'an to Medina in Saudi Arabia, have been abandoned for over sixty years. Reconstruction of the Medina line, begun in 1965, was scheduled to be completed in 1971 at a cost of £15m., divided equally between Jordan, Saudi Arabia and Syria. However, the reconstruction work has been suspended at the request of the Arab States concerned, pending further studies on costs. The line between Ma'an and Saudi Arabia (114 km) is now completed, as well as 15 km in Saudi Arabia as far as Halet Ammar Station. A new 115-km extension to Aqaba was opened in 1975 (see Aqaba Railway Corpn above). On 27 January 1980 an agreement was signed between the Supreme Commission of the Hedjaz Railway and Dorsch Consult (Federal Republic of Germany) for a feasibility study for construction of the Hedjaz Railway to high international specifications to connect Saudi Arabia, Jordan and Syria. The feasibility study was still awaiting a decision in 1986.

ROADS

Amman is linked by road with all parts of the kingdom and with neighbouring countries. All cities and most towns are connected by a two-lane paved road system. In addition, several thousand km of tracks make all villages accessible to motor transport. In 1981, the latest inventory showed the East Bank of Jordan to have 2,000 km of main roads, 820 km of secondary roads (both types asphalted) and 2,404 km of paved village roads. There are also 1,950 km of unsurfaced roads. In 1985 the Government announced that there was a total of more than 7,000 km of roads in the Kingdom. Road building schemes valued at JD108m. are to be carried out in the 1986–90 Five-Year Plan. In November 1985 Jordan, Egypt and Iraq signed an agreement providing for the operation of an overland route between Cairo, Amman and Baghdad.

SHIPPING

The port of Aqaba is Jordan's only outlet to the sea and has two general berths of 340 m and 215 m, with seven main transit sheds, covered storage area of 4,150 sq m, an open area of 50,600 sq m and a phosphate berth 210 m long and 10 m deep. Ten new berths and storage facilities are being built, and a separate potash berth, a container terminal, an oil terminal and a fertilizer jetty are planned. A ferry link between Aqaba and the Egyptian port of Nuweibeh was opened in April 1985 and is expected to increase tourism and trade between the two countries.

Arab Bridge Maritime Navigation Co: Amman; f. 1986; joint venture by Egypt, Iraq and Jordan to improve economic co-operation.

T. Gargour & Fils: POB 419, Amman; tel. 622307; telex 21213; f. 1928; shipping agents and owners; Chair. JOHN GARGOUR.

Jordan Maritime Navigation Co: Amman; privately owned.

Jordan National Shipping Lines Ltd: Shmeisani, POB 5406, Amman; tel. 666214; telex 21730; POB 657 Aqaba; tel. 315342; telex 62276; owned 75% by the government; service from Antwerp, Zeebrugge, Bremen and Sheerness to Aqaba; daily passenger ferry service from Aqaba to Nuweibeh (Egypt); land transportation to destinations in Iraq and elsewhere in the region; two bulk carriers, one general cargo ship; Chair. WASIF AZAR; Gen. Man. Y. ET-TAL.

Jordanian Shipping Transport Co: Amman; f. 1984; two cargo vessels.

Kawar, Amin & Sons: POB 222, Amman; tel. 22324; telex 21212; operates four general cargo ships; Chair. T. KAWAR; Gen. Man. G. KAWAR.

PIPELINES

Two oil pipelines cross Jordan. The former Iraq Petroleum Company pipeline, carrying petroleum from the oilfields in Iraq to Haifa, has not operated since 1967. The 1,717-km (1,067-mile) pipeline, known as the Trans-Arabian Pipeline (Tapline), carries petroleum from the oilfields of Dhahran in Saudi Arabia to Sidon on the Mediterranean seaboard in Lebanon. Tapline traverses Jordan for a distance of 177 km (110 miles) and has frequently been cut by hostile action. Tapline stopped pumping to Syria and Lebanon at the end of 1983, when it was first due to close. It was later scheduled to close in 1985, but in September 1984 Jordan renewed an agreement to receive Saudi Arabian crude oil through Tapline. The agreement can be cancelled by either party at two years' notice. Plans for a pipeline of about 1,600 km (1,000 miles) from Kirkuk, in Iraq, to the port of Aqaba, on the Red Sea, in Jordan were suspended in 1985.

CIVIL AVIATION

There are international airports at Amman and Aqaba. The new Queen Alia International Airport at Zizya, 40 km south of Amman, was opened in May 1983.

Alia (The Royal Jordanian Airline): Head Office: Housing Bank Commercial Centre, Shmeisani, POB 302, Amman; tel. 672872; telex 21501; f. 1963; government-owned; services to Middle East, North Africa, Europe, USA and Far East; fleet of two Boeing 747-200B, three Boeing 707-320C, four Boeing 727-200A, eight Lockheed L-1011-500; Pres. MAHMOUD JAMAL BALQEZ; Chair. ALI GHANDOUR.

Arab Wings Co Ltd: POB 341018, Amman; tel. 891994; telex 21608; f. 1975; subsidiary of Alia; executive jet charter service, air ambulances, priority cargo; Pres. MAHMOUD JAMAL BALQAZ; Chair. ALI GHANDOUR; Man. Dir HE SHARIF GHAZI RAKAN NASSER.

Arab Air Cargo: 5th Circle, POB 811824, Jabal Amman; tel. 674191; telex 22559; f. 1981; joint venture of Iraqi and Jordanian govts; fleet of two Boeing 707-320C; Chair. MUHAMMAD FATHI AMIN; Dir-Gen. GHASSAN ALI.

Tourism

Ministry of Tourism and Antiquities: Tourism Authority, POB 224, Amman; tel. 642311; telex 21741; f. 1952; Minister MUHAMMAD AL-KHATIB; Dir-Gen. Jordan Tourism Authority NASRI ATALLAH (acting).

INDEX OF INTERNATIONAL ORGANIZATIONS

(Main reference only)

A

AAAID, 216
ABEDA, 95
Academy of Arab Music, 172
— — Diplomacy and International Affairs, 257
ACP Institutions, 149
Acuerdo de Cartagena, 92
Administrative Telegraph and Telephone Conference (ITU), 77
Advisory Group for Aerospace Research and Development (NATO), 180
Aerospace Medical Association, 239
AFESD, 97
Africa Reinsurance Corporation—Africa-Re, 91
African Adult Education Association, 225
— Airlines Association, 273
— Association for Literacy and Adult Education, 225
— — — Public Administration and Management, 229
— — of Cartography, 265
— Caribbean and Pacific States—ACP States, 149
— Centre for Applied Research and Training in Social Development, 30
— — — Monetary Studies, 223
— Civil Aviation Commission—AFCAC, 188
— Commission on Agricultural Statistics (FAO), 57
— Development Bank—ADB, 90
— — Fund—ADF, 90
— Forestry Commission (FAO), 57
— Groundnut Council, 221
— Monetary Fund, 30
— Posts and Telecommunications Union, 244
— Regional Centre for Technology, 30
— — Federation of Chambers of Commerce, 30
— — Organization for Standardization, 268
— Timber Organization, 213
— Training and Research Centre for Women, 28
— — — — — in Administration for Development—CAFRAD, 216
Afro-Asian Housing Organization, 216
— People's Solidarity Organization, 229
— Rural Reconstruction Organization, 216
AFROLIT Society (for the Promotion of Adult Literacy in Africa), 225
Agence de coopération culturelle et technique, 216
Agency for the Prohibition of Nuclear Weapons in Latin America, 229
AGFUND, 217
Agudath Israel World Organisation, 246
Aid to Displaced Persons and its European Villages, 258
ALADI, 170
ALECSO, 172
All Africa Conference of Churches, 246
Alliance Graphique Internationale, 232
— Internationale de Tourisme, 267
— Israélite Universelle, 246
Allied Communications Security Agency (NATO), 180
— Data Systems Interoperability Agency (NATO), 180
— Long Lines Agency (NATO), 180
— Naval Communications Agency (NATO), 180
— Radio Frequency Agency (NATO), 180
— Tactical Communications Agency (NATO), 180
Al-Quds Committee (OIC), 193
Amnesty International, 259
Andean Development Corporation, 92
— Group, 92
— Judicial Tribunal, 92
— Parliament, 92
— Reserve Fund, 92
Anti-Slavery Society for the Protection of Human Rights, 259
ANZUS, 94
Arab Academy of Maritime Transport, 172
— Air Carriers' Organization, 273
— Authority for Agricultural Investment and Development, 216
— Bank for Economic Development in Africa—BADEA, 95
— Bankers Association, 224
— Bureau for Narcotics, 172

— — — Prevention of Crime, 172
— — of Criminal Police, 172
— Centre for the Study of Arid Zones and Dry Lands, 172
— Civil Aviation Council, 172
— Common Market, 128
— Company for Drug Industries and Medical Appliances, 128
— — — Industrial Investment, 128
— — — Livestock Development, 128
— Drilling and Workover Company, 192
— Engineering Company (OAPEC), 192
— Federation for Cement and Building Materials, 128
— — of Chemical Fertilizers Producers, 128
— — — Engineering Industries, 128
— — — Leather Industries, 128
— — — Paper Industries, 128
— — — Petroleum, Mining and Chemicals Workers, 233
— — — Shipping Industries, 128
— — — Textile Industries, 129
— Fund for Economic and Social Development—AFESD, 97
— — — Technical Assistance to African and Arab Countries, 172
— Gulf Programme for the United Nations Development Organizations—AGFUND, 217
— Industrial Development Organization, 172
— Iron and Steel Union, 268
— Labour Organization, 172
— League, 171
— — Educational, Cultural and Scientific Organization—ALECSO, 172
— Logging Company, 192
— Maritime Petroleum Transport Company, 192
— Mining Company, 128
— Monetary Fund, 98
— Organization for Agricultural Development, 172
— — — Social Defence against Crime, 172
— — — Standardization and Metrology, 172
— — of Administrative Sciences, 172
— Petroleum Investments Corporation—APICORP, 192
— — Services Company, 192
— — Training Institute, 192
— Postal Union, 172
— Satellite Communication Organization, 172
— Seaports Federation, 129
— Shipbuilding and Repair Yard Company, 192
— Sports Confederation, 262
— States Broadcasting Union, 172
— Sugar Federation, 129
— Telecommunications Union, 172
— Tourism Union, 268
— Towns Organization, 256
— Union of Fish Producers, 129
— — — Food Industries, 129
— — — Land Transport, 129
— — — Railways, 273
ASEAN, 103
— Finance Corporation, 104
Asia and Pacific Commission on Agricultural Statistics (FAO), 57
— — — Plant Protection Commission (FAO), 57
— Pacific Academy of Ophthalmology, 238
ASIAFEDOP, 208
Asian and Pacific Centre for Transfer of Technology, 25
— — — Coconut Community, 25
— — — Development Centre (ESCAP), 25
— — — Clearing Union—ACU, 25
— — Development Bank—ADB, 100
— — Fund—ADF, 101
— — Free Trade Zone, 25
— — Highway Network Project, 26
— — Productivity Organization, 268
— — Reinsurance Corporation, 25
— — Students' Association, 275
— — Vegetable Research and Development Center, 213
Asia-Pacific Broadcasting Union, 244
— Forestry Commission (FAO), 57
— Telecommunity, 26
Asian-African Legal Consultative Committee, 234

INDEX

Asian-Pacific Dental Federation, 239
— Postal Union, 244
Asistencia Recíproca Petrolera Estatal Latinoamericana, 223
Asociación de Empresas Estatales de Telecomunicaciones, 93
— del Congreso Panamericano de Ferrocarriles, 275
— Interamericana de Bibliotecarios y Documentalistas Agrícolas, 214
— Latinoamericana de Instituciones Financieros de Desarrollo, 218
— — — Integración—ALADI, 170
— Médica Panamericana, 243
Associated Country Women of the World, 259
Association des universités partiellement ou entièrement de langue française, 226
— for Childhood Education International, 225
— — Paediatric Education in Europe, 238
— — Systems Management, 233
— — the Advancement of Agricultural Science in Africa, 213
— — — Promotion of the International Circulation of the Press, 244
— — — Study of the World Refugee Problem, 256
— — — Taxonomic Study of the Flora of Tropical Africa, 250
— of African Central Banks, 224
— — — Development Finance Institutions, 91
— — — Geological Surveys, 250
— — — Tax Administrators, 224
— — — Trade Promotion Organizations, 268
— — Universities, 225
— — Arab Universities, 225
— — Caribbean Universities and Research Institutes, 225
— — Commonwealth Universities, 118
— — Development Financing Institutions in Asia and the Pacific, 217
— — Environmental Institutions of the Pacific, 200
— — European Airlines, 273
— — — Atomic Forums—FORATOM, 250
— — — Chambers of Commerce, 269
— — — Institutes of Economic Research, 224
— — — Journalists, 244
— — — Jute Industries, 221
— — French-Language Television Services, 244
— — Geoscientists for International Development, 250
— — Institutes for European Studies, 226
— — International Bond Dealers, 224
— — Iron Ore Exporting Countries, 221
— — National European and Mediterranean Societies of Gastro-enterology, 239
— — Natural Rubber Producing Countries, 221
— — Partially or Wholly French-Language Universities, 226
— — Secretaries General of Parliaments, 229
— — Social Work Education in Africa, 259
— — South Pacific Airlines, 203
— — South-east Asian Institutions of Higher Learning, 226
— — — — Nations—ASEAN, 103
Assofoto (CMEA), 127
Atlantic Institute for International Affairs, 229
— Treaty Association, 229
Autorité du bassin du Niger, 218
Aviation sans frontières, 259

B

BADEA, 95
Bahá'í International Community, 246
Balkan Medical Union, 239
Baltic and International Maritime Council, 273
BAM International, 217
Banco Centroamericano de Integración Económica—BCIE, 110
Bangkok Declaration (ASEAN), 103
Bank for International Settlements—BIS, 106
Banque arabe pour le Développement économique en Afrique—BADEA, 95
— centrale des états de l'Afrique de l'ouest—BCEAO, 155
— de développement des états de l'Afrique centrale, 155
— des Etats de l'Afrique centrale, 155
— ouest-africaine de développement—BOAD, 155
Baptist World Alliance, 246
Benelux Economic Union, 224
Berne Union, 86
Biometric Society, 250
BIS, 106
British Commonwealth Ex-services League, 119
Broadcasting Organizations of Non-aligned Countries, 244

International Organizations

Bureau international de la récupération, 265
Business Co-operation Centre (EEC), 146

C

CAB International, 116
— — Institute of Entomology, 117
— — — — Parasitology, 117
— — — Mycological Institute, 117
CACM, 110
Cadmium Association, 221
CAFRAD, 216
Caisse centrale de coopération économique (Franc Zone), 156
Caribbean Agricultural Research and Development Institute, 109
— Community and Common Market—CARICOM, 108
— Congress of Labour, 233
— Development and Co-operation Committee (ECLAC), 27
— — Bank, 109
— Examinations Council, 109
— Food and Nutrition Institute, 213
— Free Trade Association, 108
— Meteorological Institute, 109
— Plant Protection Commission (FAO), 57
— Tourism Association, 268
CARICOM, 108
CARIFTA, 108
Caritas Internationalis, 217
Cartagena Agreement (Andean Group), 92
Catholic International Education Office, 226
— — Federation for Physical and Sports Education, 226
— — Union for Social Service, 259
CEAO, 121
CEEAC, 217
Celtic League, 229
Central American Air Navigation Service Corporation, 111
— — Bank for Economic Integration, 110
— — Common Market—CACM, 110
— — Economic Co-operation Committee (ECLAC), 27
— — Institute for Business Administration, 111
— — — of Public Administration, 111
— — Monetary Council, 111
— — — Union, 110
— — Research Institute for Industry, 111
— — University Confederation, 111
— Commission for the Navigation of the Rhine, 273
— Control Administration of the United Power Grids of European CMEA Members, 127
— Office for International Carriage by Rail, 273
Centre africain de formation et de recherches administratives pour le développement—CAFRAD, 216
— de Recherches sur les Méningites et les Schistosomiases (OCCGE), 243
— for Educational Research and Innovation (OECD), 182
— — Latin American Monetary Studies, 224
— — Research and Documentation on International Language Problems, 226
— Muraz (OCCGE), 243
Centro de Estudios Monetarios Latinoamericanos, 224
— Interamericano de Investigación y Documentación sobre Formación Profesional, 226
— Internacional de Agricultura Tropical, 214
— Latinoamericano de Demografía, 27
— Regional de Educación de Adultos y Alfabetización Funcional para América Latina, 228
CERN, 251
CFA franc (Franc Zone), 156
Charles Darwin Foundation for the Galapagos Isles, 250
Chicago Convention (ICAO), 68
Christian Conference of Asia, 246
— Democratic World Union, 230
— Medical Commission (WCC), 209
— Peace Conference, 246
CILSS, 216
CIOMS, 236
CLASEP, 208
CLTC, 208
Club of Dakar, 217
CMEA, 126
Cocoa Producers' Alliance, 221
Codex Alimentarius Commission (FAO/WHO), 58
Collaborative International Pesticides Analytical Council Ltd, 213
Colombo Plan for Co-operative Economic and Social Development in Asia and the Pacific, 112

INDEX

COMECON, 126
Comisión Técnica de las Telecomunicaciones de Centroamerica—COMTELCA, 111
Commission for Inland Fisheries of Latin America (FO), 57
— of the European Communities, 140
— on African Animal Trypanosomiasis (FAO), 57
— — Fertilizers (FAO), 57
— — Plant Genetic Resources (FAO), 57
Commissions for Controlling the Desert Locust (FAO), 57
Committee for Co-ordination of Investigations of the Lower Mekong Basin, 25
— — — — Joint Prospecting for Mineral Resources in Asian Offshore Areas—CCOP/East Asia (ESCAP), 25
— — — — — for Mineral Resources in the South Pacific Area—CCOP/SOPAC (ESCAP), 26
— — European Construction Equipment, 269
— of European Foundry Associations, 269
Common Organization for the Control of Desert Locust and Bird Pests, 213
Commonwealth, 114
— Advisory Aeronautical Research Council, 119
— Agricultural Bureaux, 116
— Air Transport Council, 118
— Association of Architects, 119
— — — Science, Technology and Mathematics Educators—CASTME, 118
— Broadcasting Association, 118
— Bureau of Agricultural Economics, 117
— — — Animal Breeding and Genetics, 117
— — — Dairy Science and Technology, 117
— — — Horticulture and Plantation Crops, 117
— — — Nutrition, 117
— — — Pastures and Field Crops, 117
— — — Plant Breeding and Genetics, 117
— — — Soils, 117
— Council for Educational Administration, 118
— Countries League, 119
— Declaration of Principles, 120
— Engineers Council, 119
— Forestry Association, 117
— — Bureau, 117
— Foundation, 119
— Fund for Technical Co-operation, 116
— Games Federation, 119
— Geological Surveys Consultative Group, 119
— Institute, London, 118
— — (Scotland), Edinburgh, 118
— — of Biological Control, 117
— Journalists' Association, 118
— Lawyers' Association, 118
— Legal Advisory Service, 118
— — Education Association, 119
— Magistrates' Association, 119
— Medical Association, 118
— Parliamentary Association, 119
— Pharmaceutical Association, 118
— Press Union, 118
— Secretariat, 115
— Society for the Deaf, 118
— Telecommunications Organisation, 118
— War Graves Commission, 119
— Youth Exchange Council, 119
Communauté des radios publiques de langue française, 244
— — télévisions francophones, 244
— économique de l'Afrique de l'Ouest—CEAO, 121
— des Etats de l'Afrique Centrale, 217
— — — pays des Grands Lacs, 224
— — du bétail et de la viande du Conseil de l'Entente, 123
Community of French-Language Radio Broadcasters, 244
Comparative Education Society in Europe, 226
Computers (CMEA), 127
Confederación Interamericana de Educación Católica, 226
— Latinoamericana de Asociaciones Cristianas de Jóvenes, 276
— Universitaria Centroamericana, 111
Confederation of ASEAN Journalists, 244
— — Asia-Pacific Chambers of Commerce and Industry, 269
— — European Soft Drinks Associations, 269
— — International Contractors Associations, 269
— — Socialist Parties of the European Community, 230
Conference of European Churches, 247
— — — Statisticians, 23
— — International Catholic Organizations, 247
— — Local and Regional Authorities in Europe, 132

International Organizations

— — Ministers of African Least-Developed Countries, 29
— — Regions in North-West Europe, 217
Conférence permanente des Recteurs, Présidents et Vice-chanceliers des Universités européennes, 229
Conseil de l'Entente, 123
— international des radios-télévisions d'expression française, 245
Consejo de Fundaciones Americanas de Desarrollo, 217
— Interamericano de Música, 219
— Monetario Centroamericano, 111
Consultative Committee of the Bars and Law Societies of the European Community, 234
— Council for Postal Studies (UPU), 83
— — of Jewish Organizations, 247
— Group for International Agricultural Research—CGIAR (IBRD), 63
Contadora Group, 230
Convention on International Trade in Endangered Species, 42
Co-operation Council for the Arab States of the Gulf, 124
Co-ordinating Committee for International Voluntary Service, 259
— — — the Liberation Movements of Africa (OAU), 187
Corporación Andina de Fomento, 92
— Centroamericana de Servicios de Navegación Aérea, 111
Council for International Organisations of Medical Sciences, 236
— — Mutual Economic Assistance—CMEA (COMECON), 126
— — the Development of Economic and Social Research in Africa, 256
— — — International Congresses of Entomology, 250
— of American Development Foundations, 217
— — Arab Economic Unity, 128
— — Europe, 130
— — European National Youth Committees, 276
— — the Professional Photographers of Europe, 233
— — World Organizations Interested in the Handicapped, 259
— on International Educational Exchange, 276
Court of Auditors of the European Communities, 143
— — Justice of the European Communities, 142
Customs Co-operation Council, 269

D

Dairy Society International, 213
Danube Commission, 274
Desert Locust Control Organization for Eastern Africa, 213
Duke of Edinburgh's Award Scheme, 119

E

East Asia Travel Association, 268
Eastern and Southern African Management Institute, 31
— — — — Mineral Resources Development Centre, 30
— Regional Organization for Planning and Housing, 256
— — — — Public Administration, 230
ECA, 28
ECLAC, 27
Ecobank, 134
Econometric Society, 224
Economic and Social Commission for Asia and the Pacific—ESCAP (UN), 24
— Commission for Africa—ECA (UN), 28
— — — Europe—ECE (UN), 23
— — — Latin America and the Caribbean—ECLAC (UN), 27
— Community of Central African States, 217
— — — the Great Lakes Countries, 224
— — — West African States—ECOWAS, 133
— Co-operation Organization—ECO, 217
— Development Institute (IBRD), 63
— Research Committee of the Gas Industry, 269
ECOSOC, 13, 19
Ecosystem Conservation Group, 43
ECOWAS, 133
ECSC, 146
EEC, 135
EFTA, 153
EIB, 143
EIRENE—International Christian Service for Peace, 259
English-speaking Union of the Commonwealth, 256
Entente Council, 123
ESCAP, 24
ESCAP/WMO Typhoon Committee, 26
ESCWA, 32
Euratom, 145
EUROCONTROL, 274
EUROFEDOP, 208

INDEX — *International Organizations*

Eurofinas, 224
EUROGROUP, 230
Euronet DIANE, 145
Europa Nostra, 219
European Agricultural Guidance and Guarantee Fund, 152
— Air Navigation Planning Group (ICAO), 68
— Aluminium Association, 221
— and Mediterranean Plant Protection Organization, 213
— Alliance of Press Agencies, 244
— Association for Animal Production, 213
— — — Cancer Research, 239
— — — Personnel Management, 233
— — — Population Studies, 256
— — — Research on Plant Breeding, 213
— — — the Exchange of Technical Literature in the Field of Metallurgy, 250
— — — — Study of Diabetes, 239
— — — — Trade in Jute Products, 221
— — of Advertising Agencies, 269
— — — Conservatoires, Music Academies and Music High Schools, 219
— — — Exploration Geophysicists, 250
— — — Internal Medicine, 239
— — — Manufacturers of Radiators, 269
— — — Music Festivals, 220
— — — National Productivity Centres, 269
— — — Programmes in Health Services Studies, 239
— — — Radiology, 239
— — — Social Medicine, 239
— — — Teachers, 226
— — — Veterinary Anatomists, 250
— Atomic Energy Community—Euratom, 145
— — — Society, 251
— Baptist Federation, 247
— Brain and Behaviour Society, 239
— Brewery Convention, 269
— Broadcasting Union, 244
— Builders of Internal Combustion Engines and Electric Locomotives, 265
— Bureau of Adult Education, 226
— Ceramic Association, 269
— Civil Aviation Conference, 274
— — Service Federation, 233
— Coal and Steel Community—ECSC, 146
— Commission for the Control of Foot-and-Mouth Disease (FAO), 58
— — of Human Rights, 130
— — on Agriculture (FAO), 58
— Committee for Standardization, 269
— — — the Conservation of Nature and Natural Resources, 132
— — — — Protection of the Population against the Hazards of Chronic Toxicity, 239
— — of Associations of Manufacturers of Agricultural Machinery, 269
— — — Manufacturers of Domestic Heating and Cooking Appliances, 269
— — — Paint, Printing Ink and Artists' Colours Manufacturers' Associations, 269
— — — Sugar Manufacturers, 221
— — — Textile Machinery Manufacturers, 269
— — on Crime Problems, 131
— — — Legal Co-operation, 131
— Communities, 135
— — Commission, 140
— — Council of Ministers, 141
— — Court of Auditors, 143
— — — Justice, 142
— — Economic and Social Committee, 144
— — Joint Research Centre, 145
— Computer Manufacturers Association, 265
— Confederation of Agriculture, 213
— — — Iron and Steel Industries, 269
— — — Woodworking Industries, 270
— Conference of Ministers of Transport, 274
— — — Postal and Telecommunications Administrations, 244
— Convention for Constructional Steelwork, 265
— — the Protection of Human Rights, 130
— — on Social Security, 131
— Co-ordination Centre for Research and Documentation in Social Sciences, 256
— Council, 141
— — for Education by Correspondence, 226
— — of Chemical Manufacturers' Federations, 270
— Court of Human Rights, 130
— Cultural Centre, 219
— — Foundation, 226
— Currency Unit, 151
— Dehydrators Association, 270
— Development Fund, 152
— Dialysis and Transplant Association, 239
— Economic Community—EEC, 135
— Federation for Catholic Adult Education, 226
— — — the Welfare of the Elderly, 259
— — of Associations of Engineers and Heads of Industrial Safety Services, 270
— — — — — Insulation Enterprises, 270
— — — — Chemical Engineering, 265
— — — — Christian Miners' Unions, 208
— — — — Conference Towns, 233
— — — — Corrosion, 265
— — — — Fibreboard Manufacturers, 270
— — — — Financial Analysts' Societies, 224
— — — — Handling Industries, 270
— — — — Management Consultants' Associations, 270
— — — — National Associations of Engineers, 265
— — — — Particle Board Manufacturers, 270
— — — — Plywood Industry, 270
— — — — Productivity Services, 270
— — — — Tile and Brick Manufacturers, 270
— — — — Trade Unions of Non-Manual Workers, 208
— — — — Unions of Joinery Manufacturers, 270
— Financial Marketing Association, 224
— Forestry Commission (FAO), 58
— Foundation for Management Development, 226
— Free Trade Association—EFTA, 153
— Furniture Manufacturers Federation, 270
— General Galvanizers Association, 270
— Glass Container Manufacturers' Committee, 270
— Grassland Federation, 213
— Industrial Research Management Association, 233
— Inland Fisheries Advisory Commission (FAO), 58
— Insurance Committee, 224
— Investment Bank, 143
— League Against Rheumatism, 239
— Livestock and Meat Trade Union, 213
— Molecular Biology Organization, 251
— Monetary Co-operation Fund, 152
— — Fund, 152
— — System, 147
— Motel Federation, 268
— Movement, 230
— Organisation for the Safety of Air Navigation, 274
— Organization for Caries Research, 239
— — — Civil Aviation Electronics, 265
— — — Nuclear Research, 251
— — — Quality Control, 270
— Orthodontic Society, 239
— Packaging Federation, 270
— Parliament, 142
— Passenger Time-Table Conference, 274
— Patent Office, 270
— Railway Wagon Pool, 274
— Regional Development Fund, 152
— Social Charter, 131
— — Fund, 152
— Society for Comparative Endocrinology, 239
— — — Opinion and Marketing Research, 270
— — — Rural Sociology, 257
— — of Cardiology, 239
— — — Culture, 219
— Space Agency, 251
— Strategic Research Programme in Information Technology—ESPRIT, 145
— Trade Union Confederation, 233
— Travel Commission, 268
— Union of Arabic and Islamic Scholars, 226
— — — Coachbuilders, 271
— — — Medical Specialists, 239
— — — Veterinary Surgeons, 233
— — — Women, 230
— Unit of Account, 151
— University Institute, 147
— Young Christian Democrats, 230
— Youth Centre, 132
— — Foundation, 132
European-Mediterranean Seismological Centre, 251

INDEX

Eurospace, 265
Eurotransplant Foundation, 239
Eurovision, 245
Evangelical Alliance, 247
Experiment in International Living, 257

F

FAO, 56
Federación Campesina Latinoamericana, 234
— de Cámaras de Comercio del Istmo Centroamericano, 111
— — — y Asociaciones Industriales Centroamericanas, 111
— Latinoamericana de Bancos, 225
— Odontológica de Centro America y Panamá, 243
Federation of Arab Scientific Research Councils, 251
— — Asian Scientific Academies and Societies, 251
— — — Women's Associations, 259
— — Central American Chambers of Commerce, 111
— — European Biochemical Societies, 251
— — — Industrial Editors' Associations, 245
— — French-Language Obstetricians and Gynaecologists, 240
— — Industrial Chambers and Associations in Central America, 111
— — International Civil Servants' Associations, 233
— — — Music Competitions, 220
— — the European Dental Industry, 240
— — World Health Foundations, 240
Fédération Aéronautique Internationale, 262
— des gynécologues et obstétriciens de langue française, 240
FEOGA, 152
Fondo Andino de Reservas, 92
Fonds d'aide et de coopération (Franc Zone), 156
— d'Entraide et de Garantie des Emprunts (Conseil de l'Entente), 123
Food Aid Committee, 217
— and Agriculture Organization—FAO, 56
Foundation for International Scientific Co-ordination, 251
— — the Peoples of the South Pacific, 217
Franc Zone, 155
Frères des Hommes, 217
Friends (Quakers) World Committee for Consultation, 247
Fund for Co-operation, Compensation and Development (ECOWAS), 133

G

Gambia River Basin Development Organization, 217
General Agreement on Tariffs and Trade—GATT, 59
— Anthroposophical Society, 247
— Association of International Sports Federations, 262
— — — Municipal Health and Technical Experts, 240
— Fisheries Council for the Mediterranean—GFCM (FAO), 58
— Union of Chambers of Commerce, Industry and Agriculture for Arab Countries, 271
Generalized System of Preferences, 40
Geneva Conventions (Red Cross), 166
Graduate Institute of International Studies, 226
Graphical International Federation, 208
Group of Latin American and Caribbean Sugar Exporting Countries, 221
Grupo Andino, 92
Gulf Co-operation Council, 124
— Investment Corporation, 125
— Organization for Industrial Consulting, 271

H

Habitat, 37
Hague Conference on Private International Law, 234
Halden Project, 185
Hansard Society for Parliamentary Government, 230

I

IAEA, 33
IATA, 274
IBEC, 159
IBRD, 60
ICAO, 68
ICC, 160
ICCROM, 219
ICFTU, 162
ICPHS, 255
ICSU, 249
IDA, 66
IDB, 157
IFAD, 69
IFC, 66
ILO, 70
IMCO, 72
IMF, 73
— Institute, 75
IMO, 72
Inca-Fiej Research Association, 245
Indian Ocean Commission, 217
— — Fishery Commission (FAO), 58
Indo-Pacific Fishery Commission (FAO), 58
Industrial Development Fund for Portugal (EFTA), 153
INMARSAT, 244
Institut atlantique des affaires internationales, 229
— d'émission des départements d'outre-mer (Franc Zone), 155
— de formation et de recherche démographique, 29
— — Recherches sur les Trypanosomiases et l'Onchocercose (OCCGE), 243
— d'Ophtalmologie tropicale africaine (OCCGE), 243
— Marchoux de Léprologie (OCCGE), 243
— universitaire de hautes études internationales, 226
Institute for International Sociological Research, 256
— — Latin American Integration, 158
— of Air Transport, 274
— — Commonwealth Studies, London, 118
— — Economic Growth, Asian Research Centre, 217
— — International Business Law and Practice (ICC), 161
— — — Law, 234
— — Nutrition of Central America and Panama, 111
Instituto Centroamericano de Administración de Empresas, 111
— — — — Pública, 111
— — — Estudios Sociales, 208
— — — Investigación y Tecnología Industrial, 111
— de Nutrición de Centro América y Panamá, 111
— del Cono Sur, 208
— Latinoamericano de Planificación Económica y Social, 27
— Latino Americano de Estudios Sociales, 208
— para la Integración de América Latina—INTAL, 158
Integrated Programme for Commodities (UNCTAD), 39
INTELSAT, 244
Inter-African Bureau for Animal Resources, Nairobi, 188
— — — Soils, 188
— — of Languages (OAU), 188
— Coffee Organization, 222
— Committee for Hydraulic Studies, 265
— Phytosanitary Commission, 188
— Socialist Organization, 230
Inter-American Association of Agricultural Librarians and Documentalists, 214
— — — Sanitary and Environmental Engineering, 240
— Bar Association, 234
— Centre for Research and Documentation on Vocational Training, 226
— Children's Institute, 190
— Commercial Arbitration Commission, 271
— Commission of Women, 190
— — on Human Rights, 189
— Confederation for Catholic Education, 226
— Conference on Social Security, 259
— Council for Education, Science and Culture, 189
— Court of Human Rights, 189
— Defense Board, 191
— Development Bank—IDB, 157
— Economic and Social Council, 189
— Indian Institute, 190
— Institute for Co-operation on Agriculture, 191
— — of Capital Markets, 224
— Investment Corporation, 157
— Juridical Committee, 189
— Music Council, 219
— Nuclear Energy Commission, 191
— Planning Society, 217
— Press Association, 245
— Regional Organization of Workers—ORIT, 162
— Society of Cardiology, 240
— Statistical Institute, 191
— Tropical Tuna Commission, 214
Inter-Arab Investment Guarantee Corporation, 172
Interatomenergo (CMEA), 127
Interatominstrument (CMEA), 127

INDEX *International Organizations*

Interchim (CMEA), 127
Interchimvolokno (CMEA), 127
Inter-Church Aid, Refugee and World Service (WCC), 209
Interelektro (CMEA), 127
Interetalonpribor (CMEA), 127
Interfilm, 219
Intergovernmental Authority on Drought and
  Development—IGADD, 217
— Bureau for Informatics, 265
— Committee for Migration, 259
— — — Physical Education and Sport, 81
— Copyright Committee, 234
— Council of Copper Exporting Countries, 222
— Maritime Consultative Organization—IMCO, 72
— Oceanographic Commission, 251
— Programme for the Development of Communication
  (UNESCO), 81
Interkosmos (CMEA), 127
Intermediate Technology Development Group, 217
Intermetall (CMEA), 127
International Abolitionist Federation, 259
— Academic Union, 256
— Academy of Astronautics, 251
— — — Aviation and Space Medicine, 240
— — — Cytology, 240
— — — Legal and Social Medicine, 237
— — — Social and Moral Sciences, Arts and Letters, 257
— — — Tourism, 268
— Accounting Standards Committee, 224
— Advertising Association Inc., 271
— Aeronautical Federation, 262
— African Institute, 257
— — Migratory Locust Organization, 214
— Agency for Research on Cancer, 85
— — — the Prevention of Blindness, 237
— Air Transport Association, 274
— Alliance of Distribution by Cable, 245
— — — Women, 230
— Amateur Athletic Federation, 262
— — Boxing Association, 262
— — Radio Union, 262
— — Swimming Federation, 263
— — Wrestling Federation, 263
— Anatomical Congress, 240
— Association against Noise, 259
— — for Bridge and Structural Engineering, 265
— — — Business Research and Corporate Development, 271
— — — Cereal Science and Technology, 214
— — — Child and Adolescent Psychiatry and Allied Professions,
      240
— — — Children's International Summer Villages, 259
— — — Cybernetics, 265
— — — Dental Research, 240
— — — Earthquake Engineering, 251
— — — Ecology, 251
— — — Education to a Life without Drugs, 260
— — — Educational and Vocational Guidance, 227
— — — — — Information, 227
— — — Hydraulic Research, 264
— — — Mass Communication Research, 257
— — — Mathematical Geology, 251
— — — Mathematics and Computers in Simulation, 251
— — — Mutual Benefit Societies, 259
— — — Plant Physiology, 252
— — — — Taxonomy, 252
— — — Religious Freedom, 247
— — — Research in Income and Wealth, 224
— — — Suicide Prevention, 259
— — — the Development of Documentation, Libraries and
      Archives in Africa, 227
— — — — Exchange of Students for Technical Experience, 276
— — — — History of Religions, 256
— — — — Physical Sciences of the Ocean, 251
— — — — Protection of Industrial Property, 234
— — — — Rhine Vessels Register, 274
— — — — Study of the Liver, 237
— — — — Vegetation Science, 214
— — of Agricultural Economists, 214
— — — Librarians and Documentalists, 214
— — — — Medicine and Rural Health, 240
— — — — Allergology and Clinical Immunology, 237
— — — — Applied Linguistics, 257
— — — — Psychology, 240
— — — — Art Critics, 219
— — — — (Painting-Sculpture-Graphic Art), 219
— — — Asthmology, 240
— — — Bibliophiles, 219
— — — Bicycle and Motorcycle Trading and Repair, 271
— — — Biological Standardization, 252
— — — Botanic Gardens, 252
— — — Broadcasting, 245
— — — Buddhist Studies, 247
— — — Chain Stores, 271
— — — Colleges of Physical Education, 227
— — — Conference Interpreters, 233
— — — — Translators, 233
— — — Congress Centres, 271
— — — Crafts and Small and Medium-Sized Enterprises, 233
— — — Democratic Lawyers, 235
— — — Dental Students, 276
— — — Department Stores, 271
— — — Documentalists and Information Officers, 257
— — — Educators for World Peace, 230
— — — Electrical Contractors, 271
— — — Geodesy, 252
— — — Geomagnetism and Aeronomy, 252
— — — Gerontology, 237
— — — Group Psychotherapy, 240
— — — Horticultural Producers, 214
— — — Hydatid Disease, 238
— — — Hydrological Sciences, 252
— — — Islamic Banks, 224
— — — Juvenile and Family Court Magistrates, 235
— — — Law Libraries, 235
— — — Legal Sciences, 235
— — — Lighthouse Authorities, 264
— — — Logopedics and Phoniatrics, 240
— — — Medical Laboratory Technologists, 233
— — — Medicine and Biology of the Environment, 238
— — — Meteorology and Atmospheric Physics, 252
— — — Metropolitan City Libraries, 257
— — — Museums of Arms and Military History, 219
— — — Music Libraries, Archives and Documentation Centres,
      220
— — — Mutual Insurance Companies, 233
— — — Oral and Maxillofacial Surgeons, 240
— — — Papyrologists, 227
— — — Photobiology, 252
— — — Ports and Harbors, 274
— — — Rolling Stock Builders, 265
— — — Scholarly Publishers, 271
— — — Schools of Social Work, 260
— — — Scientific Experts in Tourism, 268
— — — Sedimentologists, 252
— — — Sound Archives, 245
— — — Students in Economics and Business Management, 276
— — — Technological University Libraries, 257
— — — Textile Dyers and Printers, 271
— — — Theoretical and Applied Limnology, 252
— — — Universities, 227
— — — University Professors and Lecturers, 227
— — — Volcanology and Chemistry of the Earth's Interior, 252
— — — Wood Anatomists, 252
— — — Workers for Maladjusted Children, 260
— — on Water Pollution Research and Control, 252
— Astronautical Federation, 252
— Astronomical Union, 249
— Atomic Energy Agency—IAEA, 33
— Automobile Federation, 274
— Baccalaureate Office, 227
— Bank for Economic Co-operation—IBEC, 159
— — — Reconstruction and Development—IBRD (World Bank),
      60
— Bar Association, 235
— Bauxite Association, 222
— Bee Research Association, 214
— Bible Reading Association, 247
— Board on Books for Young People, 219
— Booksellers Federation, 271
— Botanical Congress, 252
— Brain Research Organization, 240
— Bridge, Tunnel and Turnpike Association, 264
— Broncoesophagological Society, 240
— Bureau for Epilepsy, 240
— — the Standardization of Man-Made Fibres, 271
— — of Chambers of Commerce (ICC), 161

INDEX — *International Organizations*

— — — Education—IBE, 81
— — — Fiscal Documentation, 224
— — — Insurance and Reinsurance Producers, 271
— — — Weights and Measures, 252
— Cargo Handling Co-ordination Association, 265
— Cartographic Association, 253
— Catholic Confederation of Hospitals, 240
— — Migration Commission, 260
— — Union of the Press, 245
— Cell Research Organization, 240
— Cello Centre, 219
— Center of Information on Antibiotics, 241
— Centre for Advanced Mediterranean Agronomic Studies, 214
— — — — Technical and Vocational Training (ILO), 71
— — — Agricultural Education, 214
— — — Genetic Engineering and Biotechnology, 82
— — — Local Credit, 224
— — — Scientific and Technological Information (CMEA), 127
— — — Settlement of Investment Disputes (IBRD), 63
— — — Technical Expertise (ICC), 160
— — — the Study of the Preservation and Restoration of Cultural Property—ICCROM, 219
— — — Theoretical Physics (IAEA), 34
— — — Tropical Agriculture, 214
— — of Films for Children and Young People, 219
— — — Insect Physiology and Ecology, 253
— Chamber of Commerce—ICC, 160
— — — Shipping, 274
— Children's Centre, 260
— Chiropractors Association, 241
— Christian Federation for the Prevention of Alcoholism and Drug Addiction, 260
— — Service for Peace, 259
— Civil Airports Association, 274
— — Aviation Organization—ICAO, 68
— — Defence Organization, 260
— — Service Commission, 18
— Cocoa Organization, 222
— Coffee Organization, 222
— College of Surgeons, 237
— Colour Association, 265
— Commission for Agricultural and Food Industries, 214
— — — Bee Botany, 253
— — — Optics, 241
— — — Physics Education, 253
— — — the Conservation of Atlantic Tunas, 214
— — — — History of Representative and Parliamentary Institutions, 230
— — — — Islamic Heritage, 194
— — — — Prevention of Alcoholism and Drug Dependence, 260
— — — — Protection of the Rhine against Pollution, 260
— — — — Scientific Exploration of the Mediterranean Sea, 253
— — — — Southeast Atlantic Fisheries, 214
— — of Agricultural Engineering, 264
— — — Jurists, 235
— — — Sugar Technology, 214
— — on Civil Status, 235
— — — Glass, 253
— — — Illumination, 265
— — — Irrigation and Drainage, 264
— — — Large Dams, 264
— — — Occupational Health, 241
— — — Radiation Units and Measurements, 253
— — — Radiological Protection, 241
— — — Zoological Nomenclature, 253
— Committee for Historical Sciences, 256
— — — Recording the Productivity of Milk Animals, 214
— — — Social Sciences Information and Documentation, 257
— — — the Diffusion of Arts and Literature through the Cinema, 219
— — of Aesthetics and Cosmetology, 241
— — — Catholic Nurses, 241
— — — Foundry Technical Associations, 264
— — — Military Medicine and Pharmacy, 238
— — — the Red Cross—ICRC, 166
— — on Aeronautical Fatigue, 266
— — — the History of Art, 256
— — — Veterinary Gross Anatomical Nomenclature, 214
— Comparative Literature Association, 220
— Confederation for Printing and Allied Industries, 271
— — of Art Dealers, 271
— — — European Sugar Beet Growers, 222
— — — Executive and Professional Staffs, 233

— — — Free Trade Unions—ICFTU, 162
— — — Professional and Intellectual Workers, 233
— — — Societies of Authors and Composers, 220
— — — the Butchers' and Delicatessen Trade, 271
— Conference on Assistance to Refugees in Africa, 46
— — — Large High-Voltage Electric Systems, 266
— Congress and Convention Association, 268
— — of Africanists, 227
— — on Fracture, 264
— — — Tropical Medicine and Malaria, 238
— Container Bureau, 274
— Co-operation for Socio-Economic Development, 218
— Co-operative Alliance, 271
— Copper Research Association, Inc., 266
— Copyright Society, 235
— Cotton Advisory Committee, 222
— Council for Adult Education, 227
— — — Bird Preservation, 253
— — — Building Research, Studies and Documentation, 266
— — — Laboratory Animal Science, 238
— — — Philosophy and Humanistic Studies—ICPHS, 255
— — — Physical Fitness Research, 241
— — — the Exploration of the Sea, 253
— — — Traditional Music, 220
— — of Environmental Law, 235
— — — French-speaking Radio and Television Organizations, 245
— — — Jewish Women, 247
— — — Museums, 220
— — — Nurses, 241
— — — Psychologists, 253
— — — Scientific Unions, 249
— — — Shopping Centres, 271
— — — Societies of Industrial Design, 271
— — — Tanners, 272
— — — the Aeronautical Sciences, 253
— — — Voluntary Agencies, 260
— — — Women, 260
— — on Alcohol and Addictions, 260
— — — Archives, 257
— — — Health, Physical Education and Recreation, 263
— — — Jewish Social and Welfare Services, 260
— — — Marketing Practice (ICC), 161
— — — Monuments and Sites, 220
— — — Social Welfare, 260
— Court of Justice, 15, 21
— Cricket Conference, 263
— Criminal Police Organization, 235
— Crops Research Institute for the Semi-Arid Tropics, 214
— Customs Tariffs Bureau, 235
— Cycling Union, 263
— Cystic Fibrosis Association, 241
— Dachau Committee, 260
— Dairy Federation, 214
— Dental Federation, 237
— Development Association—IDA, 66
— — Law Institute, 235
— Diabetes Federation, 237
— Economic Association, 225
— Electrotechnical Commission, 266
— Emergency Food Reserve, 52
— Energy Agency (OECD), 184
— Epidemiological Association, 237
— Ergonomics Association, 257
— European Construction Federation, 233
— Exhibitions Bureau, 272
— Falcon Movement, 232
— Federation for Documentation, 266
— — — European Law, 235
— — — Household Maintenance Products, 272
— — — Housing and Planning, 257
— — — Hygiene, Preventive Medicine and Social Medicine, 241
— — — Information Processing, 266
— — — Medical and Biological Engineering, 241
— — — — Psychotherapy, 241
— — — Parent Education, 227
— — — the Theory of Machines and Mechanisms, 264
— — — Theatre Research, 220
— — of Accountants, 225
— — — Actors, 233
— — — Agricultural Producers, 215
— — — Air Line Pilots' Associations, 234
— — — Airworthiness, 266

1609

INDEX *International Organizations*

— — — Association Football, 263
— — — Associations of Textile Chemists and Colourists, 272
— — — Automatic Control, 264
— — — Automobile Engineers' Associations, 266
— — — Beekeepers' Associations, 215
— — — Blue Cross Societies, 260
— — — Building and Woodworkers, 162
— — — Business and Professional Women, 234
— — — Buying Societies, 272
— — — Catholic Universities, 227
— — — Cell Biology, 253
— — — Chemical, Energy and General Workers' Unions, 162
— — — Clinical Chemistry, 239
— — — Commercial, Clerical, Professional and Technical Employees—FIET, 163
— — — Consulting Engineers, 266
— — — Disabled Workers and Civilian Handicapped, 261
— — — 'Ecole Moderne' Movements, 227
— — — Educative Communities, 260
— — — Fertility Societies, 241
— — — Film Archives, 220
— — — — Producers' Associations, 220
— — — Free Teachers' Unions, 163
— — — Freight Forwarders' Associations, 274
— — — Grocers' Associations, 272
— — — Gynecology and Obstetrics, 241
— — — Hospital Engineering, 266
— — — Industrial Energy Consumers, 264
— — — Institutes for Socio-religious Research, 257
— — — 'Jeunesses Musicales', 220
— — — Journalists, 163
— — — Library Associations and Institutions, 227
— — — Medical Students Associations, 276
— — — Modern Languages and Literatures, 256
— — — Multiple Sclerosis Societies, 241
— — — Musicians, 220
— — — Newspaper Publishers, 245
— — — Operational Research Societies, 253
— — — Ophthalmological Societies, 241
— — — Organisations for School Correspondence and Exchange, 227
— — — Oto-Rhino-Laryngological Societies, 237
— — — Park and Recreation Administration, 263
— — — Pharmaceutical Manufacturers Associations, 241
— — — Philosophical Societies, 256
— — — Phonogram and Videogram Producers, 272
— — — Physical Education, 227
— — — — Medicine and Rehabilitation, 237
— — — Plantation, Agricultural and Allied Workers, 163
— — — Popular Travel Organizations, 268
— — — Press Cutting Agencies, 245
— — — Resistance Movements, 230
— — — Secondary Teachers, 227
— — — Senior Police Officers, 235
— — — Social Science Organizations, 257
— — — — Workers, 261
— — — Societies for Electroencephalography and Clinical Neurophysiology, 237
— — — — — Electron Microscopy, 253
— — — — — of Classical Studies, 256
— — — Stock Exchanges, 225
— — — Surgical Colleges, 241
— — — Teachers' Associations, 227
— — — — of Modern Languages, 227
— — — Textile and Clothing Workers, 208
— — — the Cinematographic Press, 245
— — — — Periodical Press, 245
— — — — Socialist and Democratic Press, 245
— — — Thermalism and Climatism, 241
— — — Tourist Centres, 268
— — — Trade Unions of Employees in Public Service, 208
— — — — — — Transport Workers, 208
— — — University Women, 227
— — — Vexillological Associations, 257
— — — Workers' Educational Associations, 228
— Fellowship of Former Scouts and Guides, 261
— — — Reconciliation, 247
— Fertilizer Industry Association, 264
— Film and Television Council, 245
— Finance Corporation—IFC, 67
— Fiscal Association, 225
— Food Information Service, 253
— Foundation of the High-Altitude Research Stations Jungfraujoch and Gornergrat, 253
— Fragrance Association, 272
— Frequency Registration Board (ITU), 78
— Fund for Agricultural Development—IFAD, 69
— Fur Trade Federation, 272
— Gas Union, 264
— Geographical Union, 249
— Glaciological Society, 253
— Graphical Federation, 163
— Group of National Associations of Agrochemical Manufacturers, 272
— — — Scientific, Technical and Medical Publishers, 253
— — — Users of Information Systems, 272
— Guild of Dispensing Opticians, 241
— Gymnastic Federation, 263
— Hibernation Society, 254
— Ho-Re-Ca, 268
— Hockey Federation, 263
— Hop Growers' Convention, 215
— Hospital Federation, 242
— Hotel Association, 268
— Humanist and Ethical Union, 247
— Hydrographic Organization, 254
— Industrial Relations Association, 234
— Information Management Congress, 266
— Institute for Adult Literacy Methods, 228
— — — Children's Literature and Reading Research, 220
— — — Comparative Music Studies and Documentation, 220
— — — Conservation of Historic and Artistic Works, 220
— — — Cotton, 222
— — — Educational Planning (UNESCO), 81
— — — Labour Studies (ILO), 71
— — — Ligurian Studies, 257
— — — Peace, 230
— — — Strategic Studies, 230
— — — Sugar Beet Research, 215
— — — the Unification of Private Law, 235
— — of Administrative Sciences, 257
— — — Banking Studies, 225
— — — Communications, 245
— — — Iberoamerican Literature, 220
— — — Philosophy, 228
— — — Public Administration, 228
— — — — Finance, 225
— — — Refrigeration, 254
— — — Seismology and Earthquake Engineering, 266
— — — Sociology, 258
— — — Space Law, 235
— — — Tropical Agriculture, 215
— — — Welding, 264
— Institution for Production Engineering Research, 264
— Interchurch Film Centre, 219
— Investment Bank, 164
— Iron and Steel Institute, 266
— Islamic Law Commission, 194
— — News Agency, 194
— Jazz Federation, 221
— Judo Federation, 263
— Juridical Institute, 235
— Jute Organization, 222
— Laboratory for Research on Animal Diseases, 215
— — of Marine Radioactivity, 33
— Labour Conference (ILO), 70
— — Office (ILO), 71
— — Organisation—ILO, 70
— Law Association, 236
— — Commission, 18
— Lead and Zinc Study Group, 222
— League against Epilepsy, 242
— — — Rheumatism, 237
— — for Human Rights, 231
— — of Societies for Persons with Mental Handicap, 261
— Leprosy Association, 237
— Liaison Centre for Cinema and Television Schools, 220
— Lifeboat Conference, 261
— Livestock Centre for Africa, 215
— Maize and Wheat Improvement Center, 215
— Maritime Arbitration Organization (ICC), 161
— — Bureau (ICC), 160
— — Committee, 236
— — Organization—IMO, 72
— — Radio Committee, 245

INDEX — *International Organizations*

— — Satellite Organization, 244
— Master Printers' Association, 272
— Mathematical Union, 249
— Measurement Confederation, 264
— Medical Association for the Study of Living Conditions and Health, 242
— — Society of Paraplegia, 239
— Metalworkers' Federation, 163
— Mineralogical Association, 254
— Monetary Fund—IMF, 73
— Montessori Association, 228
— Movement of Catholic Students, 248
— Music Centre, 221
— — Council, 220
— Narcotics Control Board, 242
— Natural Rubber Organization, 222
— North Pacific Fisheries Commission, 215
— Nuclear Information System—INIS, 34
— — Law Association, 236
— — Safety Advisory Group, 33
— Office of Cocoa, Chocolate and Confectionery, 222
— Olive Federation, 222
— — Oil Council, 222
— Olympic Committee, 165
— Optometric and Optical League, 242
— Organisation of Legal Metrology, 254
— Organization for Biological Control of Noxious Animals and Plants, 215
— — — Medical Physics, 242
— — — Motor Trades and Repairs, 272
— — — Standardization, 266
— — — the Study of the Old Testament, 247
— — of Citrus Virologists, 215
— — — Consumers' Unions, 270
— — — Employers, 234
— — — Experts, 234
— — — Journalists, 245
— — — Motor Manufacturers, 272
— — — the Flavour Industry, 272
— Palaeontological Association, 254
— Patent Documentation Centre, 86
— Peace Academy, 258
— — Bureau, 231
— — Research Association, 258
— Peat Society, 254
— Pediatric Association, 237
— PEN, 221
— Penal and Penitentiary Foundation, 236
— — Law Association, 236
— Pepper Community, 25
— Pharmaceutical Federation, 242
— — Students' Federation, 276
— Phenomenological Society, 258
— Philatelic Federation, 263
— Phonetic Association, 254
— Phycological Society, 254
— Planned Parenthood Federation, 261
— Polar Motion Service, 254
— Police Association, 236
— Political Science Association, 231
— Poplar Commission (FAO), 58
— Press Institute, 246
— — Telecommunications Council, 246
— Primatological Society, 254
— Prisoners' Aid Association, 261
— Psycho-Analytical Association, 242
— Public Relations Association, 234
— Publishers' Association, 272
— Radiation Protection Association, 254
— Radio and Television Organization, 246
— — Consultative Committee (ITU), 78
— Rail Transport Committee, 274
— Railway Congress Association, 275
— Rayon and Synthetic Fibres Committee, 272
— Reading Association, 228
— Red Cross, 166
— — Locust Control Organization for Central and Southern Africa, 215
— Regional Organization of Plant Protection and Animal Health, 215
— Register of Potentially Toxic Chemicals, 43
— Rehabilitation Medicine Association, 242
— Research Group on Wood Preservation, 267

— Rhinologic Society, 237
— Rice Commission (FAO), 58
— — Research Institute, 215
— Road Federation, 275
— — Safety, 275
— — Transport Union, 275
— Rowing Federation, 263
— Rubber Research and Development Board, 267
— — Study Group, 222
— Savings Banks Institute, 225
— Schools Association, 228
— Scientific Council for Trypanosomiasis Research and Control, 242
— — Film Library, 254
— Sea-Bed Authority, 35
— Secretariat for Arts, Mass Media and Entertainment Trade Unions, 163
— Seed Testing Association, 215
— Sericultural Commission, 215
— Service for National Agricultural Research, 215
— Shipowners' Association (CMEA), 127
— Shipping Federation Ltd, 275
— Shooting Union, 263
— Shopfitting Organisation, 272
— Silk Association, 222
— Skating Union, 263
— Ski Federation, 263
— Social Science Council, 258
— — Security Association, 261
— — Service, 261
— Society and Federation of Cardiology, 237
— — for Business Education, 228
— — — Cardiovascular Surgery, 242
— — — Clinical and Experimental Hypnosis, 242
— — — Contemporary Music, 221
— — — Education through Art, 228
— — — Ethnology and Folklore, 258
— — — General Semantics, 254
— — — Horticultural Science, 216
— — — Human and Animal Mycology, 254
— — — Labour Law and Social Security, 236
— — — Mental Imagery Techniques, 242
— — — Music Education, 228
— — — Photogrammetry and Remote Sensing, 267
— — — Research on Civilization Diseases and Environment, 242
— — — Rock Mechanics, 254
— — — Soil Mechanics and Foundation Engineering, 264
— — — Soilless Culture, 216
— — — Stereology, 254
— — — the Study of Medieval Philosophy, 228
— — — Tropical Ecology, 254
— — of Art and Psychopathology, 242
— — — Audiology, 237
— — — Biometeorology, 254
— — — Blood Transfusion, 242
— — — City and Regional Planners, 234
— — — Criminology, 237
— — — Cybernetic Medicine, 242
— — — Dermatology: Tropical, Geographic and Ecologic, 243
— — — Developmental Biologists, 242
— — — Electrochemistry, 255
— — — Geographical Pathology, 237
— — — Internal Medicine, 237
— — — Lymphology, 242
— — — Neuropathology, 239
— — — Orthopaedic Surgery and Traumatology, 243
— — — Psychosomatic Obstetrics and Gynaecology, 237
— — — Radiology, 243
— — — Social Defence, 258
— — — Soil Science, 216
— — — the History of Medicine, 237
— — — Urology, 243
— Sociological Association, 258
— Solar Energy Society, 267
— Solid Wastes and Public Cleansing Association, 264
— Special Committee on Radio Interference, 266
— Statistical Institute, 258
— Sugar Organization, 222
— Table Tennis Federation, 263
— Tea Committee, 223
— — Promotion Organization, 223
— Telecommunication Union—ITU, 77
— Telecommunications Satellite Organization, 244

INDEX *International Organizations*

— Telegraph and Telephone Consultative Committee (ITU), 78
— Tennis Federation, 263
— Textile Care and Rental Association, 272
— — Garment and Leather Workers' Federation, 163
— — Manufacturers Federation, 272
— Theatre Institute, 221
— Time Bureau, 255
— Tin Council, 223
— — Research Council, 267
— Trade Centre (GATT/UNCTAD), 59
— Translations Centre, 255
— Transport Workers' Federation, 163
— Tropical Timber Organization, 223
— Typographic Association, 221
— Union against Cancer, 238
— — — Tuberculosis, 238
— — — for Conservation of Nature and Natural Resources, 255
— — — Electro-heat, 264
— — — Health Education, 238
— — — Inland Navigation, 275
— — — Land-Value Taxation and Free Trade, 225
— — — Moral and Social Action, 261
— — — Oriental and Asian Studies, 256
— — — Pure and Applied Biophysics, 249
— — — Quaternary Research, 255
— — — the Protection of Industrial Property (Paris Convention), 86
— — — — — Literary and Artistic Works (Berne Union), 86
— — — — Scientific Study of Population, 258
— — — — Study of Social Insects, 255
— — — Vacuum Science, Technique and Applications, 267
— — of Air Pollution Prevention Associations, 264
— — — Angiology, 238
— — — Anthropological and Ethnological Sciences, 256
— — — Architects, 234
— — — Biochemistry, 249
— — — Biological Sciences, 249
— — — Building Societies and Savings Associations, 225
— — — Crystallography, 249
— — — Family Organisations, 261
— — — Food and Allied Workers' Associations, 163
— — — — Science and Technology, 255
— — — Forestry Research Organizations, 216
— — — Geodesy and Geophysics, 249
— — — Geological Sciences, 249
— — — Heat Distributors, 267
— — — Immunological Societies, 249
— — — Latin Notaries, 236
— — — Lawyers, 236
— — — Local Authorities, 231
— — — Long-Distance Lorry-Drivers, 234
— — — Marine Insurance, 273
— — — Metal, 267
— — — Microbiological Societies, 249
— — — Nutritional Sciences, 249
— — — Pharmacology, 250
— — — Physiological Sciences, 250
— — — Prehistoric and Protohistoric Sciences, 256
— — — Producers and Distributors of Electrical Energy, 264
— — — Psychological Science, 250
— — — Public Transport, 275
— — — Pure and Applied Chemistry, 250
— — — — — — Physics, 250
— — — Radio Science, 250
— — — Railways, 275
— — — Socialist Youth, 232
— — — Societies for the Aid of Mental Health, 261
— — — Students, 276
— — — Tenants, 261
— — — Testing and Research Laboratories for Materials and Structures, 264
— — — the History and Philosophy of Science, 250
— — — Theoretical and Applied Mechanics, 250
— — — Therapeutics, 238
— — — Young Christian Democrats, 231
— Veterinary Association of Animal Production, 216
— Vine and Wine Office, 223
— Water Resources Association, 267
— — Supply Association, 267
— Waterfowl Research Bureau, 255
— Weed Science Society, 255
— Weightlifting Federation, 263
— Whaling Commission, 273

— Wheat Council, 223
— Wool Secretariat, 223
— — Study Group, 223
— — Textile Organisation, 273
— Workers' Aid, 261
— Wrought Copper Council, 273
— Yacht Racing Union, 263
— Young Christian Workers, 276
— Youth and Student Movement for the United Nations, 276
— — Hostel Federation, 276
— — Library, 228
Inter-Parliamentary Union, 230
INTERPOL, 235
Interport (CMEA), 127
Interrobot (CMEA), 127
Intertextilmash (CMEA), 127
Inter-University European Institute on Social Welfare, 261
Inuit Circumpolar Conference, 231
Islamic Capitals Organization, 194
— Centre for Technical and Vocational Training and Research, 194
— — — the Development of Trade, 194
— Chamber of Commerce, Industry and Commodity Exchange, 194
— Civil Aviation Council, 194
— Commission for Economic, Cultural and Social Affairs (OIC), 193
— — the International Crescent, 193
— Conference, 193
— Council of Europe, 247
— Court of Justice, 194
— Development Bank, 168
— Educational, Scientific and Cultural Organization, 194
— Foundation for Science, Technology and Development, 194
— Jurisprudence Academy, 194
— Research and Training Institute, 168
— Shipowners' Association, 194
— Solidarity Fund, 194
— States Broadcasting Organization, 194
ITU, 77

J

Jaycees International, 276
Jewish Agency for Israel, 231
Joint Commonwealth Societies' Council, 119
— Conference of African Planners, Statisticians and Demographers (ECA), 29
— European Torus—JET, 146
— Institute for Nuclear Research, 255

K

Kagera River Basin Organization, 218

L

LAFTA, 170
Lagos Plan of Action, 29
LAIA, 170
Lake Chad Basin Commission, 218
Latin American Association of Development Financing Institutions, 218
— — — — National Academies of Medicine, 238
— — Banking Federation, 225
— — Catholic Press Union, 246
— — Confederation of Tourist Organizations, 268
— — — — Trade Unions (WCL), 208
— — — — Young Men's Christian Associations, 276
— — Demographic Centre, 27
— — Economic System—SELA, 218
— — Energy Organization—OLADE, 267
— — Episcopal Council, 247
— — Farmworkers Federation, 234
— — Forestry Commission (FAO), 58
— — Free Trade Association—LAFTA, 170
— — Institute for Economic and Social Planning, 27
— — Integration Association—ALADI, 170
— — Iron and Steel Institute, 267
— — Parliament, 231
Law Association for Asia and the Pacific, 236
— of the Sea Convention, 35

INDEX *International Organizations*

Lead Development Association, 223
League Against Trachoma, 243
— for the Exchange of Commonwealth Teachers, 118
— of Arab States, 171
— — European Research Libraries, 228
— — Red Cross and Red Crescent Societies—LRCS, 167
Liaison Organization of the European Engineering Industries, 273
Liberal International, 231
Lima Declaration and Plan of Action on Industrial Development and Co-operation, 82
Lions Clubs International, 261
Liptako-Gourma Integrated Development Authority, 218
Lomé Convention, 149
Lutheran World Federation, 247

M

Malacological Union, 255
Mano River Union, 218
Marine Environment Protection Committee (IMO), 72
Maritime Safety Committee (IMO), 72
Médecins sans frontières, 262
Medical Women's International Association, 238
Mensa International, 258
Mercado Común Centroamericano, 110
Middle East Neurosurgical Society, 243
Military Agency for Standardization (NATO), 180
Miners' International Federation, 163
Multi-fibre Arrangement, 60
Multilateral Investment Guarantee Agency, 62
Muslim World League, 247
Mutual Aid and Loan Guarantee Fund (Conseil de l'Entente), 123
— Assistance of the Latin-American Government Oil Companies, 223

N

NATO, 179
Near East Forestry Commission (FAO), 58
— — Regional Commission on Agriculture (FAO), 58
— — — Economic and Social Policy Commission (FAO), 58
New World Information and Communication Order—NWICO, 81
Niger Basin Authority, 218
Nigeria Trust Fund (ADB), 91
Non-aligned Movement, 231
NORDEL, 177
Nordic Council, 176
— — of Ministers, 177
— Cultural Fund, 178
— Economic Research Council, 177
— Federation of Factory Workers' Unions, 234
— Industrial Fund, 177
— — Theoretical Atomic Physics—NORDITA, 255
— Investment Bank, 177
— Society for Cell Biology, 255
Nordisk Neurokirurgisk Forening, 243
NORDITA, 255
NORDTEST, 177
North American Forestry Commission (FAO), 58
— Atlantic Assembly, 231
— — Council, 179
— — Treaty Organisation—NATO, 179
— Pacific Fur Seal Commission, 216
Northern Shipowners' Defence Club, 275
Northwest Atlantic Fisheries Organization, 216
Nuclear Energy Agency (OECD), 184

O

OAPEC, 192
OAS, 189
OAU, 186
OCAM, 225
Oceanographic Institute, 255
ODECA, 231
Odontological Federation of Central America and Panama, 243
OECD, 182
OECS, 109
Office de Recherches sur l'Alimentation et la Nutrition africaine (OCCGE), 243
— of the United Nations Disaster Relief Co-ordinator—UNDRO, 36

OIC, 193
OMVG, 217
OPEC, 195
— Fund for International Development, 198
— News Agency, 195
Open Door International, 231
Opus Dei, 247
OPW (CMEA), 127
Organisation commune africaine et mauricienne—OCAM, 225
— de mise en valeur du fleuve Gambie—OMVG, 217
— for Economic Co-operation and Development—OECD, 182
— — the Collaboration of Railways, 275
— of Eastern Caribbean States—OECS, 109
— pour la Mise en Valeur du Fleuve Sénégal—OMVS, 218
— — l'aménagement et le développement du bassin de la rivière Kagera, 218
Organismo Internacional Regional de Sanidad Agropecuaria, 215
— para la Proscripción de las Armas Nucleares en la América Latina, 229
Organización de Estados Centroamericanas—ODECA, 231
— — — Iberoamericanos para la Educación, la Ciencia y la Cultura, 228
— — las cooperativas de América, 231
— — Universidades Católicas de América Latina, 228
— Latinoamericana de Energía, 267
— Regional Interamericana de Trabajadores—ORIT, 162
Organization for Co-operation in the Roller-Bearings Industry (CMEA), 127
— — Co-ordination and Co-operation in the Fight against Endemic Diseases, 243
— — — in the Fight against Endemic Diseases in Central Africa, 243
— — Museums, Monuments and Sites in Africa, 228
— — the Development of the Senegal River, 218
— — — Management and Development of the Kagera River Basin, 218
— of African Unity—OAU, 186
— — — Trade Union Unity—OATUU, 188
— — American States—OAS, 189
— — Arab Petroleum Exporting Countries—OAPEC, 192
— — Asia-Pacific News Agencies, 246
— — Central American States, 231
— — Ibero-American States for Education, Science and Culture, 228
— — Solidarity of the Peoples of Africa, Asia and Latin America, 231
— — the Catholic Universities of Latin America, 228
— — — Co-operatives of America, 231
— — — Islamic Conference, 193
— — — Petroleum Exporting Countries—OPEC, 195
— — Trade Unions of West Africa, 134
Orient Airlines Association, 275
ORIT, 162

P

Pacific Asia Travel Association, 268
— Basin Economic Council, 218
— Forum Line, 203
— Science Association, 255
— Telecommunications Council, 244
Pan-African Documentation and Information Service, 30
— Institute for Development, 218
— News Agency, 188
— Postal Union, 188
— Telecommunications Union, 188
— Youth Movement, 276
Pan American Development Foundation, 218
— — Health Organization, 191
— — Railway Congress Association, 275
Pan-American Association of Ophthalmology, 243
— Institute of Geography and History, 191
— Medical Association, 243
Pan-European Union, 231
Pan-Pacific and South East Asia Women's Association, 262
— Surgical Association, 243
Paris Convention, 86
Parlamento Andino, 92
— Latinoamericano, 231
Parliamentary Association for Euro-Arab Co-operation, 231
Pax Romana International Catholic Movement for Intellectual and Cultural Affairs, 248
Permanent Court of Arbitration, 236

1613

— International Association of Navigation Congresses, 264
— — — — Road Congresses, 265
— — — Committee of Linguists, 256
— Inter-State Committee on Drought Control in the Sahel, 216
Population Council, 218
— Information Network for Africa, 29
Postal, Telegraph and Telephone International, 163
— Union of the Americas and Spain, 244
Preferential Trade Area for Eastern and Southern African States, 218
Press Foundation of Asia, 246
Primary Tungsten Association, 223
Public Services International, 163
Pugwash Conferences on Science and World Affairs, 255

R

Rabitat al-Alam al-Islami, 247
Red Cross, 166
Regional Animal Production and Health Commission for Asia, the Far East and the South-West Pacific (FAO), 58
— Centre for Consulting Engineering and Management (ECA), 30
— — — Engineering Design and Manufacturing (ECA), 30
— — — Adult Education and Functional Literacy in Latin America, 228
— — — Services in Surveying, Mapping and Remote Sensing, 267
— — — Solar Energy Research and Development, 30
— — — Training in Aerial Surveys, 267
— Commission on Farm Management for Asia and the Far East (FAO), 58
— — — Food Security for Asia and the Pacific (FAO), 58
— — — Land and Water Use in the Near East (FAO), 58
— Co-ordination Centre for Research and Development of Coarse Grains, Pulses, Roots and Tuber Crops (ESCAP), 25
— Energy Development Programme (ESCAP), 26
— Fisheries Advisory Commission for the Southwest Atlantic (FAO), 58
— Food and Nutrition Commission for Africa (FAO/WHO/OAU), 58
— Institute for Population Studies (ECA), 29
— Mineral Resources Development Centre (ESCAP), 26
— Network for Agricultural Machinery (ESCAP), 25
Rehabilitation International, 243
Research Centre for Islamic History, Art and Culture, 194
Revolving Fund for Natural Resources Exploration (UNDP), 41
Rotary International, 262
Royal Asiatic Society of Great Britain and Ireland, 221
— Commonwealth Society, 119
— — — for the Blind, 118
— Over-Seas League, 119

S

SAARC, 218
SADCC, 204
Salvation Army, 248
Scandinavian Council for Applied Research—NORDFORSK, 177
— Neurosurgical Society, 243
Scientific, Technical and Research Commission (OAU), 188
SELA, 218
Service Civil International, 262
Shelter-Afrique, 91
Ship-chartering Co-ordination Bureau (CMEA), 127
SIFIDA, 91
Sistema Económica Latinoamericano—SELA, 218
Socialist Educational International, 232
— International, 232
— — Women, 232
Sociedad Interamericana de Cardiología, 240
— — — Planificación, 217
— — — Prensa, 245
Société de neuro-chirurgie de langue française, 243
— internationale financière pour les investissements et le développement en Afrique (ADB), 91
Society for International Development, 218
— of African Culture, 221
— — Comparative Legislation, 236
— — French-Speaking Neuro-Surgeons, 243
— — Saint Vincent de Paul, 262
— — Ski Traumatology, 243
SOLIDARIOS, 217
Soroptimist International, 248

South Asian Association for Regional Co-operation—SAARC, 218
— Pacific Bureau for Economic Cooperation—SPEC, 202
— — Commission, 200
— — Conference, 200
— — Forum, 202
— — — Fisheries Agency, 203
— — Regional Environment Programme, 200
— — Trade Commission, 203
South-east Asia Tin Research and Development Centre, 26
— Asian Ministers of Education Organization, 228
Southern African Development Co-ordination Conference—SADCC, 204
— — Transport and Communications Commission (SADCC), 204
SPEC, 202
Special Arab Assistance Fund for Africa (BADEA), 95
— Bureau for Boycotting Israel (Arab League), 172
Standing Committee on Commonwealth Forestry, 117
— Conference of Rectors and Vice-Chancellors of the European Universities, 229
Statistical, Economic and Social Research and Training Centre for the Islamic Countries, 194
— Institute for Asia and the Pacific, 26
Stockholm International Peace Research Institute, 232
Sugar Association of the Caribbean, Inc., 223
Supreme Council for Sports in Africa, 188

T

Technical Commission for Telecommunications in Central America, 111
Theosophical Society, 248
Toc H, 248
Trade Unions International of Agricultural, Forestry and Plantation Workers, 210
— — — — Chemical, Oil and Allied Workers, 210
— — — — Food, Tobacco, Hotel and Allied Industries Workers, 210
— — — — Metal and Engineering Workers, 210
— — — — Public and Allied Employees, 210
— — — — Textile, Clothing, Leather and Fur Workers, 210
— — — — Transport Workers, 210
— — — — Workers in Commerce, 210
— — — — — Energy, 210
— — — — of the Building, Wood and Building Materials Industries, 210
Transnational Association of Acupuncture and Taoist Medicine, 243
Transplantation Society, 239
Trans-Sahara Liaison Committee, 275
Treaty for the Prohibition of Nuclear Weapons in Latin America (Tlatelolco Treaty), 34
— of Brussels (WEU), 207
— — Helsinki (Nordic Council of Ministers), 177
— — Lagos (ECOWAS), 133
— — Montevideo (ALADI), 170
— — Rome (EEC), 137
— on the Non-Proliferation of Nuclear Weapons—NPT, 34
Trilateral Commission, 232
Trusteeship Council (United Nations), 14, 20

U

UATI, 264
UDEAC, 155
UMOA, 155
UNCHS, 37
UNCTAD, 39
UNDOF, 48
UNDP, 40
UNDRO, 36
UNEP, 42
UNESCO, 79
UNFICYP, 49
UNFPA, 44
UNHCR, 45
UNICEF, 38
UNIDO, 82
UNIFIL, 48
Union douanière et économique de l'Afrique centrale—UDEAC, 155
— mondiale des voix françaises, 221
— monétaire ouest-africaine—UMOA, 155

INDEX — *International Organizations*

— of African News Agencies, 246
— — — Railways, 188
— — Arab Jurists, 236
— — Banana Exporting Countries, 223
— — European Federalists, 232
— — — Railway Industries, 275
— — — — Road Services, 275
— — Industries of the European Community, 273
— — International Associations, 236
— — — Fairs, 273
— — — Technical Associations, 264
— — Latin American Universities, 229
— — National Radio and Television Organizations of Africa, 246
Unión de Universidades de América Latina, 229
— Internacional del Notariado Latino, 236
— Postal de las Américas y España, 244
UNITAR, 47
Unitas Malacologica, 255
United Bible Societies, 248
— Lodge of Theosophists, 248
— Methodist Committee on Relief, 219
— Nations, 3
— — Budget, 8
— — Capital Development Fund, 41
— — Centre for Human Settlements—UNCHS (Habitat), 37
— — Charter, 9
— — Children's Fund—UNICEF, 38
— — Commission on Human Settlements, 19, 37
— — Conference on the Law of the Sea—UNCLOS, 35
— — — — Trade and Development—UNCTAD, 39
— — Conferences, 17
— — Department of Technical Co-operation for Development, 40
— — Development Fund for Women, 41
— — — Programme—UNDP, 40
— — Disaster Relief Co-ordinator's Office—UNDRO, 36
— — Disengagement Observer Force—UNDOF, 48
— — Economic and Social Commission for Asia and the Pacific—ESCAP, 24
— — — — — — — Western Asia—ESCWA, 32
— — — — — Council—ECOSOC, 13, 19
— — — — — Commission for Africa—ECA, 28
— — — — — — Europe—ECE, 23
— — — — — — Latin America and the Caribbean—ECLAC, 27
— — Educational, Scientific and Cultural Organization—UNESCO, 79
— — Environment Programme—UNEP, 42
— — Financing System for Science and Technology for Development, 41
— — Fund for Population Activities—UNFPA, 44
— — General Assembly, 9, 18
— — High Commissioner for Refugees—UNHCR, 45
— — Industrial Development Fund, 82
— — — Organization—UNIDO, 82
— — Information Centres, 6
— — Institute for Training and Research—UNITAR, 47
— — Interim Force in Lebanon—UNIFIL, 48
— — Observer Mission and Peace-Keeping Forces in the Middle East, 48
— — Observers, 6
— — Peace-Keeping Force in Cyprus—UNFICYP, 49
— — Relief and Works Agency for Palestine Refugees in the Near East—UNRWA, 49
— — Research Institute for Social Development —UNRISD, 51
— — Revolving Fund for Natural Resources Exploration, 41
— — Secretariat, 15, 17
— — Security Council, 10, 19
— — Sudano-Sahelian Office, 41
— — Transport and Communications Decade in Africa, 29
— — Truce Supervision Organization—UNTSO, 48
— — Trusteeship Council, 14, 20
— — University, 81
— — Volunteers, 42
— Schools International, 229
— Towns Organization, 221
Universal Alliance of Diamond Workers, 163
— Esperanto Association, 229
— Federation of Travel Agents' Associations, 268
— Postal Union—UPU, 83
Universidad de Trabajadores de América Latina, 208
UNRISD, 51
UNRWA, 49
UNTSO, 48
UPU, 83

V
Victoria League for Commonwealth Friendship, 119
Vienna Institute for Development, 219

W
War Resisters' International, 232
Warsaw Treaty of Friendship, Co-operation and Mutual Assistance—Warsaw Pact, 206
Watch Tower Bible and Tract Society, 248
WCC, 209
WCL, 208
West Africa Women's Association, 134
— African Clearing House, 225
— — Development Bank, 155
— — Economic Community—CEAO, 121
— — Monetary Union, 155
— — Rice Development Association, 223
— — Universities' Association, 134
— — Youth Association, 134
— Indian Sea Island Cotton Association Inc., 223
Western Central Atlantic Fishery Commission (FAO), 58
— European Union—WEU, 207
WFC, 51
WFP, 52
WFTU, 210
WHO, 84
WIPO, 86
WMO, 87
WMO/ESCAP Panel on Tropical Cyclones, 26
Women's International Democratic Federation, 232
— — Zionist Organization, 262
World Administrative Radio Conference (ITU), 78
— Airlines Clubs Association, 275
— Alliance of Reformed Churches (Presbyterian and Congregational), 248
— — — Young Men's Christian Associations, 276
— Assembly for Moral Rearmament, 248
— Association for Animal Production, 216
— — — Christian Communication, 246
— — — Educational Research, 229
— — — Public Opinion Research, 258
— — of Girl Guides and Girl Scouts, 276
— — — Industrial and Technological Research Organizations, 267
— — — Judges, 236
— — — Law Professors, 236
— — — Lawyers, 236
— — — Societies of (Anatomic and Clinical) Pathology, 238
— — — Travel Agencies, 268
— — — Veterinary Food-Hygienists, 216
— — — — Microbiologists, Immunologists and Specialists in Infectious Diseases, 216
— — — World Federalists, 232
— Bank—IBRD, 60
— Blind Union, 262
— Bridge Federation, 263
— Bureau of Metal Statistics, 267
— Chess Federation, 263
— Confederation for Physical Therapy, 243
— — of Jewish Community Centres, 248
— — — Labour—WCL, 208
— — — Organizations of the Teaching Profession, 229
— — — Teachers, 208
— Conference on Religion and Peace, 248
— Congress of Authors and Composers, 220
— — — Faiths, 248
— Council of Churches, 209
— — — Credit Unions, 225
— — — Indigenous Peoples, 232
— — — Management, 273
— — — Young Men's Service Clubs, 277
— Disarmament Campaign, 232
— Education Fellowship, 229
— Employment Programme, 71
— Energy Conference, 265
— Federalist Youth, 277
— Federation for Cancer Care, 243
— — — Mental Health, 243
— — of Advertisers, 273
— — — Agriculture and Food Workers, 208

1615

— — — Associations of Clinical Toxicology Centres and Poison Control Centres, 238
— — — — — Paediatric Surgeons, 238
— — — Building and Woodworkers Unions, 208
— — — Catholic Youth, 277
— — — Christian Life Communities, 248
— — — Democratic Youth, 277
— — — Diamond Bourses, 223
— — — Engineering Organizations, 267
— — — Neurology, 238
— — — Neurosurgical Societies, 244
— — — Occupational Therapists, 244
— — — Public Health Associations, 244
— — — Scientific Workers, 234
— — — Societies of Anaesthesiologists, 238
— — — Teachers' Unions, 210
— — — the Deaf, 262
— — — Trade Unions—WFTU, 210
— — — — — for Energy, Chemical and Miscellaneous Industries, 208
— — — United Nations Associations, 232
— Fellowship of Buddhists, 248
— Food Council, 51
— — Programme—WFP, 52
— Health Organization—WHO, 84
— Intellectual Property Organization—WIPO, 86
— Jewish Congress, 248
— Medical Association, 238
— Meteorological Organization—WMO, 87
— Methodist Council, 248
— Movement of Christian Workers, 234
— Organization of Gastroenterology, 238
— — — General Systems and Cybernetics, 255
— — — the Scout Movement, 277

— ORT Union, 262
— Packaging Organisation, 273
— Peace Council, 232
— — through Law Center, 236
— Petroleum Congresses, 267
— Ploughing Organization, 216
— Poultry Science Association, 216
— Psychiatric Association, 238
— Sephardi Federation, 248
— Society for the Protection of Animals, 262
— — of Ekistics, 258
— Student Christian Federation, 248
— Tourism Organization, 268
— Trade Centers Association, 273
— — Union Congress, 210
— Underwater Federation, 264
— Union for Progressive Judaism, 248
— — of Catholic Philosophical Societies, 258
— — — — Teachers, 229
— — — — Women's Organisations, 249
— — — French Speakers, 221
— — — Jewish Students, 277
— University Service, 219
— Veterans Federation, 262
— Veterinary Association, 216
— Wildlife Fund, 255
— Young Women's Christian Association, 277

Z

Zinc Development Association, 223
Zone Franc, 155
Zonta International, 262